Peterson's College Money Handbook

2006

THOMSON

PETERSON'S™

Australia • Canada • Mexico • Singapore • Spain • United Kingdom • United States

About Thomson Peterson's

Thomson Peterson's (www.petersons.com) is a leading provider of education information and advice, with books and online resources focusing on education search, test preparation, and financial aid. Its Web site offers searchable databases and interactive tools for contacting educational institutions, online practice tests and instruction, and planning tools for securing financial aid. Thomson Peterson's serves 110 million education consumers annually.

For more information, contact Thomson Peterson's, 2000 Lenox Drive, Lawrenceville, NJ 08648; 800-338-3282; or find us on the World Wide Web at www.petersons.com/about.

Editor: Joe Krasowski; Production Editor: Bret Bollmann; Copy Editor: Valerie Bolus Vaughan; Research Project Manager: Dan Margolin; Research Associate: Marianne Hurley; Programmer: Phyllis Johnson; Manufacturing Manager: Ray Golaszewski; Composition Managers: Michele Able and Linda M. Williams.

ISSN 1089-831X
ISBN 0-7689-1937-1   MAR 30 06

Printed in the United States of America

10 9 8 7 6 5 4 3 2 1   07 06 05

Twenty-third Edition

Contents

Other Recommended Titles

Peterson's Scholarships, Grants & Prizes
Peterson's Sports Scholarships & College Athletic Programs

A Note from the Peterson's Editors

The news media seem to constantly remind us that a college education is expensive. It certainly appears to be beyond the means of many Americans. The sticker price for four years at state-supported colleges can be more than $40,000, and private colleges and universities could cost more than $100,000. And these numbers continue to rise.

But there is good news. The system operates to provide the needed money so that most families and students are able to afford a college education while making only a reasonable financial sacrifice. However, because the college financial aid system is complex, finding the money is often easier said than done. That is why the process demands study, planning, calculation, flexibility, filling out forms, and meeting deadlines. Fortunately, for most people it can produce positive results.

For more than thirty-five years, Thomson Peterson's has given students and parents the most comprehensive, up-to-date information on how to get their fair share of the financial aid pie. *Peterson's College Money Handbook* is both a quick reference and a comprehensive resource that puts valuable information about college costs and financial aid opportunities at your fingertips.

- **The ABC's of Paying for College** provides insight into federal financial aid programs that are available, offers an overview of the financial aid landscape, walks you through the process of filing for aid, and provides proven tips on how to successfully navigate the financial aid process to obtain the federal, state, and institutional aid you deserve.
- The **Quick-Reference Chart** offers a snapshot comparison of the financial aid programs available at more than 2,100 four-year institutions across the country.
- The **Profiles of College Financial Aid Programs** provide unbiased financial aid data for each of the more than 2,100 four-year institutions listed.
- The **Appendix** lists the state scholarship and grant programs offered by all fifty states and the District of Columbia.

- The six **Indexes** included in the back of the book allow you to search for specific award programs based on a variety of criteria, including merit-based awards, athletic grants, ROTC programs, and much more.

The challenge of paying for college requires forethought, organization, and resourcefulness. However, there are many ways to manage college costs and many channels through which you can receive help. If typical financial aid packages are taken into consideration, the actual cost of four years of college is likely to be less than what most families spend on a new car and, unlike a car, the value of a college education will increase as time goes on. Be sure to take full advantage of the many real opportunities that have been opened up to students and their families by the many organizations, foundations, and businesses that have organized to help you with the burden of college expenses.

The editors at Peterson's wish you the best of luck during the financial aid process!

The ABCs of Paying for College

A Guide to Financing Your Child's College Education

Don Betterton
Director of Undergraduate Financial Aid
Princeton University

Given the lifelong benefit of a college degree (college graduates are projected to earn in a lifetime $1 million more than those with only a high school diploma), higher education is a worthwhile investment. However, it is also an expensive one made even harder to manage by cost increases that have outpaced both inflation and gains in family income. This reality of higher education economics means that parental concern about how to pay for a child's college education is a dilemma that shows no sign of getting easier.

Because of the high cost involved (even the most inexpensive four-year education at a public institution costs about $10,000 a year), good information about college budgets and strategies for reducing the "sticker price" is essential. You have made a good start by taking the time to read *Peterson's College Money Handbook*. In the pages that follow, you will find valuable information about the four main sources of aid—federal, state, institutional, and private. Before you learn about the various programs, however, it will be helpful if you have an overview of how the college financial aid system operates and what long-range financing strategies are available.

Financial Aid

Financial aid refers to money that is awarded to a student, usually in a "package" that consists of gift aid (commonly called a scholarship or grant), a student loan, and a campus job.

College Costs

The starting point for organizing a plan to pay for your college education is to make a good estimate of the yearly cost of attendance. You can use the "College Cost Worksheet" on the next page to do this.

To estimate your college costs for 2006-07, refer to the tuition and fees and room and board figures shown in the "College Costs At-a-Glance" chart on page 36, and inflate 2004-05 costs by 10 percent. If 2003-04 costs are listed, inflate those numbers by 18 percent. If you will commute from your home, use $2500 instead of the college's room and board charges and $900 for transportation. We have used $800 for books and $1300 for personal expenses. Finally, estimate the cost of two round trips if your home is more than a few hundred miles from the college. Add the items to calculate the total budget. You should now have a reasonably good estimate of college costs for 2006-07. (To determine the costs for later years, adding 5 percent per year will probably give you a fairly accurate estimate.)

Do You Qualify for Need-Based Aid?

The next step is to evaluate whether or not you are likely to qualify for financial aid based on need. This step is critical, since more than 90 percent of the yearly total of $122 billion in student aid is awarded only after a determination is made that the family lacks sufficient financial resources to pay the full cost of college on its own. To judge your chance of receiving need-based aid, it is necessary to estimate an Expected Family Contribution (EFC) according to a government formula known as the Federal Methodology (FM). You can do so by referring to the "Approximate Expected Family Contribution Chart" for 2006-07 on page 6.

Applying for Need-Based Aid

Because the federal government provides about 67 percent of all aid awarded, the application and need evaluation process is controlled by Congress and the U.S. Department of Education. The application is the Free Application for Federal Student Aid, or FAFSA. In addition, nearly every state that offers student assistance uses the federal government's system to award its own aid. Furthermore, many colleges, besides arranging

College Cost Worksheet

	College 1	College 2	College 3	Commuter College
Tuition and Fees				
Room and Board				$2,000
Books	$ 800	$ 800	$ 800	$ 750
Personal Expenses	$1,300	$1,300	$1,300	$1,300
Travel				$ 900
Total Budget				

for the payment of federal and state aid, use the FAFSA to award their own funds to needy students. (Note: In addition to the FAFSA, some colleges also ask the family to complete the CSS/PROFILE® application.)

The FAFSA is your "passport" to receiving your share of the billions of dollars awarded annually in need-based aid. Even if you're uncertain as to whether or not you qualify for need-based aid, everyone who might need assistance in financing an education should pick up a FAFSA from the high school guidance office after mid-November 2005. This form will ask for 2005 financial data, and it should be filed after January 1, 2006, in time to meet the earliest college or state scholarship deadline. Within two to four weeks after you submit the form, you will receive a summary of the FAFSA information, called the Student Aid Report, or SAR. The SAR will give you the EFC and also allow you to make corrections to the data you submitted.

You can also apply for federal student aid over the Internet using FAFSA on the Web. FAFSA on the Web can be accessed at www.fafsa.ed.gov. Both the student and at least one parent should apply for a federal PIN number at www.pin.ed.gov. The PIN number serves as your electronic signature when applying for aid on the Web. (Note: Many colleges provide the option to apply for early decision or early action admission. If you apply for this before January 1, 2006, which is prior to when the FAFSA can be used, follow the college's instructions. Many colleges use either PROFILE or their own application form for early admission candidates.)

Awarding Aid

About the same time you receive the SAR, the colleges you list will receive your FAFSA information so they can calculate a financial aid award in a package that typically includes aid from at least one of the major sources—federal, state, college, or private. In addition, the award will probably consist of a combination of a scholarship or a grant, a loan, and a campus job. These last two pieces—loan and job—are called self-help aid because they require effort on your part (that is, the aid must be either earned through work or paid back later). Scholarships or grants are outright gifts that have no such obligation.

It is important that you understand each part of the package. You'll want to know, for example, how much is gift aid, the interest rate and repayment terms of the student loan, and how many hours per week the campus job requires. There should be an enclosure with the award letter that answers these questions. If not, make a list of your questions and call or visit the financial aid office.

Once you understand the terms of each item in the award letter, you should turn your attention to the "bottom line"—how much you will have to pay at each college where you were admitted. In addition to understanding the aid award, this means having a good estimate of the college budget so you can accurately calculate how much you and your family will have to contribute (often, an aid package does

How Need Is Calculated and Aid Is Awarded

	College X	College Y
Total Cost of Attendance	$10,000	$ 24,000
−Expected Family Contribution	− 5,500	− 5,500
= Financial Need	$ 4,500	$ 18,500
− Grant Aid Awarded	− 675	−14,575
− Campus Job (Work-Study) Awarded	− 1,400	− 1,300
− Student Loan Awarded	− 2,425	− 2,625
= Unmet Need	0	0

Note: Sometimes an institution is unable to meet all need. The amount of unmet need is called "the gap."

Approximate Expected Family Contribution Chart

Income Before Taxes

ASSETS	Family Size	$20,000	30,000	40,000	50,000	60,000	70,000	80,000	90,000	100,000
$20,000										
	3	$ 0	1,180	2,850	5,000	8,100	10,000	13,350	16,700	20,300
	4	0	300	1,950	3,750	6,300	8,100	11,500	14,800	18,400
	5	0	0	1,100	2,750	4,900	6,400	9,600	13,000	16,600
	6	0	0	150	1,800	3,600	4,800	7,600	11,000	14,600
$30,000										
	3	$ 0	1,180	2,850	5,000	8,100	10,000	13,350	16,700	20,300
	4	0	300	1,950	3,750	6,300	8,100	11,500	14,800	18,400
	5	0	0	1,100	2,750	4,900	6,400	9,600	13,000	16,600
	6	0	0	150	1,800	3,600	4,800	7,600	11,000	14,600
$40,000										
	3	$ 0	1,180	2,850	5,000	8,600	10,500	13,850	17,200	20,800
	4	0	300	1,950	3,750	6,800	8,500	1,200	15,300	18,900
	5	0	0	1,100	2,750	5,400	6,900	10,100	13,500	17,100
	6	0	0	150	1,800	4,100	5,300	8,100	11,500	15,100
$50,000										
	3	$ 0	1,180	3,200	5,000	9,100	11,000	14,350	17,700	21,300
	4	0	300	2,260	3,750	7,300	9,100	12,500	15,800	19,400
	5	0	0	1,400	2,750	5,900	7,400	10,600	14,000	17,600
	6	0	0	480	1,800	4,600	5,800	8,600	12,000	15,600
$60,000										
	3	$ 0	1,180	3,500	6,500	9,600	11,500	14,850	18,200	21,800
	4	0	300	2,500	5,250	7,800	9,600	13,000	15,300	19,900
	5	0	0	1,700	4,250	6,400	7,900	11,100	14,500	18,100
	6	0	0	750	3,300	5,100	6,300	9,200	12,500	16,100
$80,000										
	3	$ 0	1,180	4,200	7,500	10,600	12,500	15,850	19,200	22,800
	4	0	300	3,100	6,250	8,800	10,600	14,000	17,300	20,900
	5	0	0	2,200	5,250	7,400	8,900	12,100	15,500	19,100
	6	0	0	1,250	4,300	6,100	7,300	10,200	13,500	17,100
$100,000										
	3	$ 0	1,180	5,000	8,500	11,600	13,500	16,850	20,200	23,800
	4	0	300	3,700	7,250	9,800	11,600	15,000	18,300	21,900
	5	0	0	2,700	6,250	8,400	9,900	13,100	16,500	20,100
	6	0	0	1,800	5,300	7,100	8,300	11,200	14,500	18,100
$120,000										
	3	$ 0	1,180	5,850	9,500	12,600	14,500	17,850	21,200	24,800
	4	0	300	4,400	8,250	10,800	12,600	16,000	19,300	22,900
	5	0	0	3,350	7,250	9,400	10,900	14,100	17,500	21,100
	6	0	0	2,300	6,300	8,100	9,300	12,200	15,500	19,100
$140,000										
	3	$ 0	1,180	6,800	10,500	13,600	15,500	18,850	22,200	24,800
	4	0	300	5,200	9,250	11,800	13,600	17,000	20,300	23,900
	5	0	0	4,000	8,250	10,400	11,900	15,100	18,500	22,100
	6	0	0	2,875	7,300	9,100	10,300	13,200	16,500	20,100

This chart makes the following assumptions:

- Two-parent family where age of older parent is 45
- Lower income families will file the 1040A or 1040EZ tax form
- Student income is less than $2300
- There are no student assets
- There is only one family member in college

All figures are estimates and may vary when the complete FAFSA or CSS/PROFILE® application is submitted.

Comparing Financial Aid Awards and Family Contribution Worksheet

	College 1	College 2	College 3
Cost of Attendance			
Aid Awarded			
Grant/Scholarship			
Loan			
Job			
Total Aid			
Expected Family Contribution			
Student Contribution			
Parent Contribution			

the type of financing that families use when purchasing a home or automobile. A tuition payment plan is essentially a short-term loan and allows you to pay the costs over ten to twelve months. It is an option for families who have the resources available but need help with managing their cash flow. See the section, Financing Your Child's College Education for more information.

Non-Need-Based Aid

Regardless of whether or not you might qualify for a need-based award, it is always worthwhile to look into merit, or non-need, scholarships from sources such as foundations, agencies, religious groups, and service organizations. For a family that isn't eligible for need-based aid, merit scholarships are the only form of gift aid available. If you later qualify for a need-based award, a merit scholarship can be quite helpful in providing additional resources if the aid does not fully cover the costs. Even if the college meets 100 percent of need, a merit scholarship can benefit you by reducing the self-help (loan and job) portion of an award.

In searching for merit-based scholarships, keep in mind that there are relatively few awards (compared to those that are need-based), and most of them are highly competitive. Use the following checklist when investigating merit scholarships.

■ Take advantage of any scholarships for which you are automatically eligible based on parents' employer benefits, military service, association or church membership, other affiliations, or student or parent attributes (ethnic background, nationality, etc.). Company or union tuition remissions are the most common examples of these awards.

■ Look for other awards for which you might be eligible based on the characteristics and affiliations indi-

not cover the entire need). Colleges follow different practices in how much detail they include in their award notifications. Many colleges provide full information—types and amounts of aid, yearly costs, and the EFC divided into the parent and student shares. If these important items are missing or incomplete, you can do the work on your own. (See the Comparing Financial Aid Awards and Family Contribution Worksheet on this page.) For example, if only the college's direct charges for tuition, room, and board are shown on the award letter, make your own estimate of indirect costs like books, personal expenses, and travel. Then subtract the total aid awarded from the yearly cost to get the EFC. A portion of that amount may be your contribution (35 percent of your assets and 50 percent of your earnings over $2440), and the remainder is the parental share. If you can afford this amount at your first-choice college, the financial aid system has worked well for you, and your college attendance plans can go forward.

But if you think your EFC is too high, you should contact the college's financial aid office and ask whether additional aid is available. Many colleges, private high-cost colleges in particular, are enrollment-oriented—they are willing to work with families to help make attendance at their institutions possible. Most colleges also allow applicants to appeal their financial aid awards, the budget used for you, or any of the elements used to determine the family contribution, especially if there are extenuating circumstances or if the information has changed since the application was submitted. Some colleges may also reconsider an award based on a "competitive appeal," the submission of a more favorable award letter from another college.

If your appeal is unsuccessful and there is still a gap between the expected family contribution and what you feel you can pay from income and savings, you are left with two choices. One option is to attend a college where paying your share of the bill will not be a problem. (This assumes that an affordable option was included on your original list of colleges, a wise admission application strategy.) The second is to look into alternate methods of financing. At this stage, parental loans and tuition payment plans are the best financing options. A parental loan can bring the yearly cost down to a manageable level by spreading payments over a number of years. This is

What Is CSS/PROFILE®?

There are many complexities in the financial aid process: knowing which aid is merit-based and which aid is need-based; understanding the difference between grants, loans, and work-study; and determining whether funds are from federal, state, institutional, or private sources.

In addition, the aid application process itself can be confusing. It can involve more than the Free Application for Federal Student Aid (FAFSA) and the Federal Methodology (FM). Among the approximately 2,100 four-year colleges, about 400 are private institutions with more than $2 billion of their own scholarship money. Many of these colleges feel that the federal aid system (FAFSA and FM) does not collect or evaluate information thoroughly enough for them to award their institutional funds. These colleges have made an arrangement with the College Scholarship Service, a branch of the College Board, to establish a separate application system.

The application is called the CSS/PROFILE®, and the need analysis formula is referred to as the Institutional Methodology (IM). If you apply for financial aid at one of the colleges that use PROFILE, the admission material will state that PROFILE is required in addition to the FAFSA. You should read the information carefully and file PROFILE to meet the earliest college deadline. Before you can receive PROFILE, however, you must register, either by phone or through the Web (http://www.collegeboard.org/finaid/fastud/html/proform.html), providing enough basic information so the PROFILE package can be designed specifically for you. The FAFSA is free, but there is a charge for PROFILE. As with the FAFSA, PROFILE can be submitted via the Internet.

In addition to the requirement by certain colleges that you submit both the FAFSA and PROFILE (when used, PROFILE is always in addition to the FAFSA; it does not replace it), you should understand that each system has its own method for analyzing a family's ability to pay for college. The main differences between PROFILE's Institutional Methodology and the FAFSA's Federal Methodology are:

- PROFILE includes equity in the family home as an asset; the FAFSA doesn't.

- PROFILE takes a broader look at assets not included on the FAFSA.

- PROFILE expects a minimum student contribution, usually in the form of summer earnings; the FAFSA has no such minimum.

- PROFILE may collect information on the noncustodial parent; the FAFSA does not.

- PROFILE allows for more professional judgment than the FAFSA. Medical expenses, private secondary school costs, and a variety of special circumstances are considered under PROFILE, subject to the discretion of the aid counselor on campus.

- PROFILE collects information on the noncustodial parent; the FAFSA doesn't.

- PROFILE includes information on assets not reported on the FAFSA, including life insurance, annuities, retirement plans, etc.

To summarize: PROFILE's Institutional Methodology tends to be both more complete in its data collection and more rigorous in its analysis than the FAFSA's Federal Methodology. When IM results are compared to FM results for thousands of applicants, IM will usually come up with a somewhat higher expected parental contribution than FM.

cated above, but where there is a selection process and an application is required. Free computerized searches are available on the Internet (you should not pay a fee for a scholarship search). Peterson's free scholarship search can be accessed by logging on to www.petersons. com/finaid. Scholarship directories, such as *Peterson's Scholarships, Grants & Prizes*, which details more than 3,800 scholarship pro-

Creditworthiness

If you will be borrowing to pay for your college education, making sure you qualify for a loan is critical. For the most part, that means your credit record must be free of default or delinquency. You can check your credit history with one or more of the following three major credit bureaus and clean up any adverse information that appears. The numbers below will offer specific information on what you need to provide to obtain a report. All of the credit bureaus accept credit report requests over their Web sites. You will usually be asked to provide your full name, phone number, social security number, birth date, and addresses for the last five years.

Equifax
P.O. Box 740241
Atlanta, GA 30374
800-685-5000
http://www.equifax.com

Trans Union^SM
P.O. Box 2000
Chester, PA 19022
800-888-4213
http://www.tuc.com

Experian National
 Consumer
 Assistance Center
475 Anton Boulevard
Costa Mesa, CA 92626
888-397-3742
800-972-0322
(TTY/TDD)
http://www.experian.com

Note

A point of clarification about whether to put college savings in the parents' or your name: If you are certain that you will not be a candidate for need-based aid, there may be a tax advantage to accumulating money in your name. However, when it comes to maximizing aid eligibility, it is important to understand that student assets are assessed at a 35 percent rate and parental assets at about 5 percent. Therefore, if your college savings are in your name, it may be wise to reestablish title to these funds before applying for financial aid. You should contact your financial planner or accountant before making any modifications to your asset structure.

grams, are useful resources and can be found in bookstores, high school guidance offices, or public libraries.

- See if your state has a merit scholarship program.

- Look into national scholarship competitions. High school guidance counselors usually know about these scholarships. Examples of these awards are the National Merit Scholarship, the Coca-Cola Scholarship, Aid Association for Lutherans, Gates Millennium Scholars, Intel Science Talent Search, and the U.S. Senate Youth Program.

- ROTC (Reserve Officers' Training Corps) scholarships are offered by the Army, Navy, Air Force, and Marine Corps. A full ROTC scholarship covers tuition, fees, textbook costs and, in some cases, a stipened. Acceptance of an ROTC scholarship entails a commitment to take military science courses and to serve for a specific number of years

as an officer in the sponsoring branch of the service. Competition is heavy, and preference may be given to students in certain fields of study, such as engineering, languages, science, and health professions. Application procedures vary by service. Contact an armed services recruiter or high school guidance counselor for further information.

- Investigate community scholarships. High school guidance counselors usually have a list of these awards, and announcements are published in local newspapers. Most common are awards given by service organizations like the American Legion, Rotary International, and the local women's club.

If you are strong academically (for example, a National Merit Commended Scholar or better) or are very talented in fields such as athletics or performing/ creative arts, you may want to consider

colleges that offer their own merit awards to gifted students they wish to enroll. Refer to the *Non-Need Scholarships for Undergraduates Index* for lists of colleges that award non-need scholarships.

In addition to merit scholarships, there are loan and job opportunities for students who do not qualify for need-based aid. Federal loan programs include the unsubsidized Federal Stafford and Direct Loans. See "Federal Financial Aid Programs" for more information. Some of the organizations that sponsor scholarships—for example, the Air Force Aid Society—also provide loans.

Work opportunities during the academic year are another type of assistance that is not restricted to aid recipients. Many colleges will, after assigning jobs to students on aid, open campus positions to all students looking for work. In addition, there are usually off-campus employment opportunities available to everyone.

Financing Your Child's College Education

In this section, "financing" means putting together resources to pay the balance due the college over and above payments from the primary sources of aid—grants, scholarships, student loans, and jobs. Financing strategies are important because the high cost of a college education today often requires a family, whether or not it receives aid, to think about stretching its college payment beyond the four-year period of enrollment. For high-cost colleges, it is not unreasonable to think about a 10-4-10 plan: ten years of saving; four years of paying college bills out of current income, savings, and borrowing; and ten years to repay a parental loan.

Savings

Although saving for college is always a good idea, many families are unclear about its advantages. Some families do not save because after normal living expenses have been covered, they do not have much money to set aside. An affordable but regular savings plan through a payroll deduction is usually the answer to the problem of spending your entire paycheck every month.

The second reason why saving for college is not a high priority is the belief that the financial aid system penalizes a family by lowering aid eligibility. The Federal Methodology of need determination is very kind to savers. In fact, savings are ignored completely for most families that earn less than $50,000. Savings in the form of home equity, retirement plans, and most annuities are excluded from the calculation. And even when savings are counted, a maximum of 5 percent of the total is expected each year. In other words, if a family has $40,000 in savings after an asset protection allowance is considered, the contribution is no greater than $2000. Given the impact of compound interest it is easy to see that a long-term savings plan can make paying for college much easier.

A sensible savings plan is important because of the financial advantage of saving compared to borrowing. The amount of money students borrow for college is now greater than the amount they receive in grants and scholarships. With loans becoming so widespread, savings should be carefully considered as an alternative to borrowing. Your incentive for saving is that a dollor saved is a dollar not borrowed.

Borrowing

Once you've calculated your "bottom-line" parental contribution and determined that the amount is not affordable out of your current income and assets, the most likely alternative is borrowing. First determine if you are eligible for a larger subsidized Federal Stafford or Direct Loan. Because no interest is due while you attend college, these are the most favorable loans. If this is not possible, look into the unsubsidized Stafford or Direct Loan, which is not based on need but where the interest accures each year. The freshman year limit (either subsidized or unsubsidized) is $2625.

After you have taken out the maximum amount of student loans, the next step is to look into parental loans. The federal government's parent loan program is called PLUS and is the standard against which other loans should be judged. A local bank that participates in the PLUS program can give you a schedule of monthly repayments per $1000 borrowed. Use this repayment figure to compare other parental loans available from commercial lenders (including home equity loans), state programs, or colleges themselves. Choose the one that offers the best terms after all up-front costs, tax advantages, and the amount of monthly payments are considered. Be sure to check with your financial aid office before making a final decision. Often, the financial aid office will have reviewed the various programs that are available and can help direct you to the best choice.

Make Financial Aid Work for You

This overview is intended to provide you with a road map to help you think about financing strategies and navigate through the complexities of the financial aid process. Much of the information you will need to help you determine your plan to pay for your education can be found within the pages of this publication. First use the parental contribution tables in conjunction with the College Cost Worksheet to estimate need eligibility. If there is a chance you will need financial assistance, complete the FAFSA (and PROFILE, if required). At the same time, look into merit scholarships. Once you are accepted at a school, use the Comparing Financial Aid Awards Worksheet and family contribution chart to figure out your parents' obligation. If you can't afford the payment, present your arguments to the institution's financial aid office before checking out the terms of PLUS and other parental loan options. And finally, if there are younger children at home, think about starting a college savings fund to get a head start on their future education costs.

If you are like millions of families that benefit from financial aid, it is likely that your college plans can go forward without undue worry about the costs involved. The key is to understand the financial aid system and to follow the best path for your family. The result of good information and good planning should be that you will receive your fair share of the billions of dollars available each year and that the cost of college will not prevent you from attending.

Middle-Income Families: Making the Financial Aid Process Work

Richard Woodland
Director of Financial Aid
Rutgers University–Camden

A recent report from the U.S. Department of Education's National Center for Education Statistics (August 2001) researched how middle-income families finance a college education. The report, *Middle Income Undergraduates: Where They Enroll and How They Pay for Their Education*, was one of the first detailed studies of these families. Although 31 percent of middle-income families have the entire cost of college covered by financial aid, there is widespread angst among these families that, while they earn too much to qualify for grant assistance, they are too financially strapped to pay the spiraling cost of higher education.

First, we have to agree on what constitutes a "middle-income" family. For the purposes of the federal study, middle-income families are defined as those families with incomes between $35,000 and $70,000. The good news is that 52 percent of these families received grants, while the balance received loans. Other sources of aid, including work-study, also helped close the gap.

So how do these families do it? Is there a key that will open the door to significant amounts of grants and scholarships?

The report found some interesting trends. One way families make college more affordable is by choosing a more affordable school. In fact, in this income group, 29 percent of middle-income students choose to enroll in low- to moderate-cost schools. These include schools where the total cost is less than $8500 per year, including community colleges and lower-priced state colleges and universities. But almost half of these middle-income families choose higher-priced schools, with costs between $8500 and $16,000. The remaining 23 percent enroll at the highest-priced schools, with costs above $16,000. Clearly cost is a factor, but middle-income families are not limiting their choices based on cost alone.

The report shows that families pay these higher costs through a combination of family assets, current income, and long-term borrowing. This is often referred to as the "past-present-future" model of financing. In fact, just by looking at the Expected Family Contribution, it is clear that there is a significant gap in what families need and what the financial aid process can provide. However, families are closing this gap by making the necessary financial sacrifices to pay the current price of higher-cost schools, especially if they think their

child is academically strong. The report concludes that parents are more likely to pay for a higher-priced education if their child scores above 2000 on the SATs.

The best place for middle-income families to start financing their children's education is through their high school guidance office. Here they can find valuable information on financial aid and leads on local scholarships. Most guidance counselors report that there are far fewer applicants for these locally based scholarships than one would expect. So read the information they send home, and be sure to follow up during the application process. Remember, a few of those $500 to $1000 scholarships can add up.

Second, be sure to attend a financial aid awareness program. If your school does not offer one, contact your local college financial aid office and see when and where one is available. These programs offer a lot of inside information on how the financial aid process works.

Next, be sure to file the correct applications for aid. Remember, each school can have a different set of requirements. For example, many higher-cost private colleges require that the CSS/PROFILE® application be filed. Other schools have their own institutional aid applications. All schools require the

Free Application for Federal Student Aid. Watch the deadlines! It is important that you meet the school's published application deadline. Generally, schools are not very flexible about this, so be sure to double-check the due date of your application.

Finally, become a smart educational consumer. Peterson's has a wide range of resources available to help you understand the process. Be sure to check your local library, bookstore, and of course, the Internet. Two great Web sites to check out are www.petersons.com and www.finaid.org.

Once you are admitted to the colleges and universities of your choice, you will receive an award notice outlining the aid you are eligible to receive. If you feel the offer is not sufficient, or if you have some unique financial problems, call the college or university's financial aid office to see if you can have your case reviewed. The financial aid office is the best source for putting the pieces together to help you finance your college education.

The financial aid office will help you determine what the "net price" is. This is the actual out-of-pocket costs that you will need to pay. Through a combination of student and parent loans, most families are able to cover these expenses.

Furthermore, many students help close the gap by working throughout their college career. While this works for many students, research shows that too many hours spent away from one's studies will negatively impact one's academic success. Most experts feel that working 10 to 15 hours a week is optimal.

An overlooked source of aid is the recent tax credits given to middle-income families. Rather than extending eligibility for traditional sources of grant assistance to middle-income families, Congress and the President have built a number of significant tax credits for middle-income families into the federal tax system. While it may take seven or eight months

before you see the tax credit, families in this income group can safely count on this benefit, usually about $1500 to $2000 per student. This is real money in your pocket and you do not need to itemize your deductions to qualify for this tax credit. Another option for upper-middle-income families not qualifying for the Hope/Lifetime tax credit is a tuition and fee duduction of up to $4000.

A tool to help you get a handle on the ever-rising costs of college is to assume you can pay a third of "net charges" from savings, another third from available (non-retiremnet) assets, and the rest from parent borrowing. If any one of these is not available, shift to one of the other resources. But if it looks like you will be financing most or all of the costs from future income (borrowing), it may be wise to consider a lower-cost college.

Millions of middle-income families send their children to colleges and universities every year. Only 8 percent attend the lowest-priced schools. By using the concept of past-present-future financing, institutional assistance, meaningful targeted tax relief, and student earnings, you can afford even the highest-priced schools.

Alternative Financing Options

For many families, traditional financial aid programs come up short in meeting the tuition bill each semester. Rather than exhausting their savings, many families are turning to private or alternative loans to help defray the cost. Today the private/alternative loan financing market is the fastest growing source of financial aid. Organizations such as *Citibank*, *Sallie Mae*, *American Education Services*, and *Key Education Resources,* offer a number of money-saving options in alternative loan financing. Consult their microsite content

centers at www.petersons.com/finaid for more information on the types of financing plans available.

The most common source of alternative funding is the federal Parent Loans for Undergraduate Students (PLUS). These are federally insured loans that offer creditworthy borrowers significant funding at reasonable interest rates. To qualify, you need to pass a credit check. A good idea is to check your credit report annually. This can be done for free at freecreditreport.com. Contact the college financial aid office; some schools are in the Direct Loan program and will process the application from the financial aid office. Other schools will recommend a bank or other financial institution where you can begin the PLUS loan process. In general, you can borrow the full cost of tuition less any other aid received. This can run into the thousands of dollars.

Remember, though, that PLUS loans are not always the best deal. Many states have alternative loan programs that offer far better terms than PLUS loans. For example, New Jersey and Pennsylvania offer programs backed by state bond issues that generally are more attractive than the federal PLUS loans. Check with your state's Higher Education Office or with a school in your area for more information. In most cases, these loans are portable, meaning they can be used at any school across the country. By doing some research you can save hundreds of dollars in interest charges.

Many schools have arranged special financing plans with private lenders. When you are working with the financial aid office to put your total aid package together, be sure to check for any special programs that may be available. There are many lenders available to help families finance higher education. Every day, new and better products are brought into the market.

Middle-Income Families: Making the Financial Aid Process Work

The world of private/alternative educational loans can be confusing. There are varying interest rates, loan fees, up-front costs, and capitalization dates. Unlike home mortgages, there is no single place to go and search for the best deal. But trust the financial aid counselors. They do this work every day and can point you in the right direction.

Common Questions Answered

Q *Are a student's chances of being admitted to a college reduced if the student applies for financial aid?*

A Generally not. Nearly all colleges have a policy of "need-blind" admissions, which means that a student's financial need is not taken into account in the admission decision. There are a few selective colleges, however, that do consider ability to pay before deciding whether or not to admit a student. Some colleges will mention this in their literature; others may not. The best advice is to apply for financial aid if the student needs assistance to attend college.

Q *Are parents penalized for saving money for college?*

A No. As a matter of fact, families that have made a concerted effort to save money for college are in a much better position than those that have not. For example, a student from a family that has saved money may not have to borrow as much. Furthermore, the "taxing rate" on savings is quite low—only about 5 percent of the parents' assets are assessed and neither the home equity nor retirement savings are included. For example, a single 40-year-old parent who saved $40,000 for college expenses will have about $1900 counted as part of the parental contribution. Two parents, if the older one is 40 years old (a parent's age factors into the formulation), would have about $300 counted. (Note: The "taxing rate" for student assets is much higher—35 percent—compared to 5 percent for parents.)

Q *How does the financial aid system work in cases of divorce or separation? How are stepparents treated?*

A In cases of divorce or separation, the financial aid application(s) should be completed by the parent with whom the student lived for the longest period of time in the past twelve months. If the custodial parent has remarried, the stepparent is considered a family member and must complete the application along with the natural parent. If your family has any special circumstances, you should discuss these directly with the financial aid office. (Note: Colleges that award their own aid may ask the noncustodial natural parent to complete a separate aid application and a contribution will be calculated.)

Q *When are students considered independent of parental support in applying for financial aid?*

A The student must be at least 24 years of age in order to be considered independent. If younger than 24, the student must be married, be a graduate or professional student, have legal dependents other than a spouse, be an orphan or ward of the court, or be a veteran of the armed forces. However, in very unusual situations, students who can clearly document estrangement from their parents can appeal to the financial aid office for additional consideration.

Q *What can a family do if a job loss occurs?*

A Financial aid eligibility is based on the previous year's income. So the family's 2005 income would be reported to determine eligibility for the 2006-07 academic year. In that way, the family's income can be verified with an income tax return. But the previous year's income may not accurately reflect the current financial situation, particularly if a parent lost a job or retired. In these instances, the projected income for the coming year can be used instead. Families should discuss the situation directly with the financial aid office and be prepared to provide appropriate documentation.

Q *When my daughter first went to college, we applied for financial aid and were denied because our expected family contribution was too high. Now, my son is a high school senior, and we will soon have two in college. Will we get the same results?*

A The results will definitely be different. Both your son and your daughter should apply. As we described earlier, need-based financial aid is based on your expected family contribution, or EFC. When you have two children in college, this amount is divided in half for each child.

Q *I've heard about the "middle-income squeeze" in regard to financial aid. What is it?*

A The so-called "middle-income squeeze" is the idea that low-income families qualify for aid, high-income families have adequate resources to pay for education, and those in the middle are caught in between, not eligible for aid but without the ability to pay full college costs. There is no provision in the Federal Methodology that treats middle-income students differently than others (such as an income cutoff for eligibility). The Expected Family Contribution rises proportionately as income and assets increase. If a middle-income family does not qualify for aid, it is because the need analysis formula yields a contribution

Common Questions Answered

that exceeds college costs. But keep in mind that if a $60,000-income family does not qualify for aid at a public university with a $10,000 cost, the same family will likely be eligible for aid at a private college with a cost of $25,000 or more. Also, there are now loan programs available to parents and students that are not based on need. Middle-income families should realize, however, that many of the grant programs funded by federal and state governments are directed at lower-income families. It is therefore likely that a larger share of an aid package for a middle-income student will consist of loans rather than grants.

Q *Given our financial condition, my daughter will be receiving financial aid. We will help out as much as we can, and, in fact, we ourselves will be borrowing. But I am concerned that she will have to take on a lot of loans in order to go to the college of her choice. Does she have any options?*

A She does. If offered a loan, she can decline all or part of it. One option is for her to ask in the financial aid office to have some of the loan changed to a work-study job. If this is not possible, she can find her own part-time work. Often there is an employment office on campus that can help her locate a job. In most cases, the more she works, the less she has to borrow. It is important to remember that the educational loans offered to students have very attractive terms and conditions, with flexible repayment options. Students should look upon these loans as a long-term investment that will reap significant rewards.

Q *Is it possible to change your financial aid package?*

A Yes. Most colleges have an appeal process. A request to change a need-based loan to a work-study job is usually approved if funds are available. A request to consider special financial circumstances may also be granted. At most colleges, a request for more grant money is rarely approved unless it is based on a change in the

information reported. Applicants should speak with the financial aid office if they have reasons for a concern about their financial appeal. Some colleges may even respond to a competitive appeal, that is, a request to match another college's offer.

Q *My son was awarded a Federal Stafford Loan as part of his financial aid package. His award letter also indicated that we could take out a PLUS loan. How do we go about choosing our lender? Do we go to our local bank?*

A Read the material that came with the financial aid award letter. It is likely that the college has an "approved lender" list for Stafford and PLUS Loans. Although you can borrow from any bank, your loan application will be processed more quickly if you use a lender recommended by the college.

Q *The cost of attending college seems to be going up so much faster than the Consumer Price Index. Why is that, and how can I plan for my child's four years?*

A The cost of higher education cannot be compared to the Consumer Price Index (CPI). The CPI does not take into account most of the costs faced by colleges. For example, the dollars that universities spend on grants and scholarships have risen rapidly. Many universities have increased enrollment of students from less affluent families, further increasing the need for institutional financial aid. Second, colleges are expected to be on the cutting edge of technology, not only in research but also in the classroom and in the library. Last, during the high-inflation years of the 1970s, most colleges deferred needed maintenance and repairs that can no longer be put off. In general, you can expect that college costs will rise about 2 to 3 percent faster than inflation.

Q *I'm struggling with the idea that all students should apply to the college of their choice, regardless of cost, because financial aid will level the playing field. I feel I will be penalized because I have saved for college. My son has been required to save half of his allowance since age six for his college education. Will that count against him when he applies for financial aid? It's difficult to explain to him that his college choices may be limited because of the responsible choices and sacrifices we have made as a family. What can we do to make the most of our situation?*

A In general, it is always better to have planned ahead for college by saving. Families that have put away sufficient funds to pay for college will quickly realize that they have made the burden easier for themselves and their children. In today's college financing world, schools assume that paying for the cost of attendance is a 10-year commitment, similar to a 30-year mortgage on a home, or a 5-year loan for a car. So by saving when your child is young, you reap significant advantages from compound interest on the assets and reduce the need to borrow as much while in school. This should reduce the number of years after college that you will be burdened with student and parent loans. We advise families to spend the student's assets first, since the financial aid formulas count these more heavily than parental assets. Then, after the first year, you can explain to the college how you spent these assets, and why you might now need assistance. When looking at parental information, the income of the family is by far the most important component. Contrary to popular belief, parental assets play a very minor role in the calculations of need. With this strategy, you have done the right thing, and in the long run, it should prove to be a wise financial plan.

Picking the right college also involves other factors. Students should select the colleges they are going to apply to in two ways. First and most important is to look at colleges that meet your son's academic and life style interests. Most experts will tell him to pick a few "reach" schools (i.e., schools where he is not sure he has the grades and scores required) and at least one or two academically "safe" schools. He should also select one or two financially "safe" schools that you are sure you can afford with either moderate or little financial aid. Most students do not get into all of their first choice schools and not everyone can afford the schools they are admitted to. By working closely with the guidance office in high school and the admissions and financial aid offices at the college, you can maximize your options.

Q *My son was awarded a $2500 scholarship. This can be split and used for two years. When filling out the FAFSA, do we have to claim the full amount, or just the $1250 he plans to use the first year?*

A Congratulations to your son on the scholarship. Nowhere on the FAFSA should you report this scholarship. It is not considered income or an asset. However, once you choose a school to attend, you must notify the financial aid office for its advice on how to take the funds. But remember, do NOT report it on the FAFSA.

Q *I will be receiving a scholarship from my local high school. How will this scholarship be treated in my financial aid award?*

A Federal student aid regulations specify that all forms of aid must be included within the defined level of need. This means that additional aid, such as outside scholarships, must be combined with any need-based aid you receive; it may not be kept separate and used to reduce your family's contribution. If the college has not filled 100 percent of your need, it will usually allow outside scholarships to close the gap. Once your total need has been met, however, the

college must reduce other aid and replace it with the outside award. Most colleges will allow you to use some, if not all, of an outside scholarship to replace self-help aid (loans and Federal Work-Study) rather than grant aid.

Q *I know we're supposed to apply for financial aid as soon as possible after January 1. What if I don't have my W-2s yet and my tax return isn't done?*

A The first financial aid application deadlines usually fall in early February, and many are much later. Chances are you'll have your W-2 forms by then, but you won't have a completed tax return. If that is the case, complete the financial aid application using your best estimates. Then, when you receive the Student Aid Report (SAR), you can use your tax return to make corrections.

Q *Is there enough aid available to make it worthwhile for me to consider colleges that are more expensive than I can afford?*

A Definitely. More than $84 billion in aid is awarded to undergraduates every year. With more than half of all enrolled students qualifying for some type of assistance, this totals more than $5500 per student. You should view financial aid as a large, national system of tuition discounts, some given according to a student's ability and talent, others based on what a student's family can afford to pay. If you qualify for need-based financial aid, you will essentially pay only your calculated family contribution, regardless of the cost of the college. You will not pay the "sticker price" (the cost of attendance listed in the college catalog) but a lower rate that is reduced by the amount of aid you receive. No college should be ruled out until after financial aid is considered. In addition, when deciding which college

to attend, consider that the short-term cost of a college education is only one criterion. If the college meets your educational needs and you are convinced it can launch you on an exciting career, a significant up-front investment may turn out to be a bargain over the long run.

Q *If I don't qualify for need-based aid, what options are available?*

A You should try to put together your own aid package to help reduce your parents' share. There are three sources to look into. First, search for merit scholarships. Second, seek employment, during both the summer and the academic year. The student employment office should be able to help you find a campus job. Third, look into borrowing. Even if you don't qualify for the need-based loan programs, the unsubsidized Federal Stafford and Direct Loans are available to all students. The terms and conditions are the same as the subsidized loan programs except that interest accrues while you are in college.

After you have contributed what you can through scholarships, employment, and loans, your parents will be faced with their share of the college bill. Many colleges have monthly payment plans that allow families to spread their payments over the academic year. If these monthly payments turn out to be more than your parents can afford, they can take out a parent loan. By borrowing from the college itself, from a commercial agency or lender, or through PLUS, your parents can extend their college payments over a ten-year period or longer. Borrowing reduces the monthly obligation to its lowest level, but the total amount paid will be the highest due to principal and interest payments. Before making a decision on where to borrow parental loan funds, be sure to first check with the financial aid office to determine what is the best source of alternative funds.

Federal Financial Aid Programs

There are a number of sources of financial aid available to students: federal and state governments, private agencies, and the colleges themselves. In addition, as discussed earlier, there are three different forms of aid: grants, earnings, and loans.

The federal government is the single largest source of financial aid for students. In the 2003-04 academic year, the U.S. Department of Education's student financial aid programs provided approximately $81 billion in aid to about 11 million people. At the present time, there are two federal grant programs—the Federal Pell Grant and the Federal Supplemental Educational Opportunity Grant (FSEOG). There are three federal loan programs: the Federal Perkins Loan, the Federal Direct Loan, and the Federal Stafford Loan. The federal government also has a job program, Federal Work-Study, or FWS, that helps colleges provide employment for stu-

dents. In addition to the student aid programs, there are also tuition tax credits. They are the HOPE Scholarship for freshmen and sophomores and the Lifetime Learning Tax Credit for undergraduate students after their second year and for graduate students. Both programs work the same way. The federal tax bill is reduced by the amount of tuition paid up to specified limits.

Ninety-two percent of federal higher education loans are either Direct or Stafford. The difference between these loans is the lending source, but for the borrower, the terms and conditions are essentially the same. Both Direct and Stafford programs make available two kinds of loans: loans to students and loans to parents. These loans are either subsidized or unsubsidized. Subsidized loans are made on the basis of demonstrated student need and have the interest paid by the government during the time you are in

school. For the non-need-based loans, unsubsidized loans and PLUS Loans, interest begins to accrue as soon as the money is received.

To qualify for the Pell and FSEOG programs, Federal Work-Study, the Perkins Loan, and the subsidized Stafford Loan, you must demonstrate financial need.

Pell Grant

The Federal Pell Grant is the largest grant program; more than 5 million students receive Pell Grants annually. This grant is intended to be the starting point of assistance for lower-income families. Eligibility for a Federal Pell Grant depends on the Expected Family Contribution. The amount you receive will depend on your EFC and the cost of education at the college you will attend. The highest award depends on how

Table Used to Estimate Federal Pell Grants for 2005–2006

Adjusted Gross Income	Family Assets							
	$50,000	$55,000	$60,000	$65,000	$70,000	$75,000	$80,000	$85,000
$ 5,000	$ 4,050	$ 4,050	$ 4,050	$ 4,050	$ 4,050	$ 4,050	$ 4,050	$ 4,050
$ 10,000	4,050	4,050	4,050	4,050	4,050	4,050	4,050	4,050
$ 15,000	4,050	4,050	4,050	4,050	4,050	4,050	4,050	4,050
$ 20,000	4,000	4,050	4,050	4,050	4,050	4,050	3,850	3,650
$ 25,000	3,850	3,650	3,450	3,350	2,850	2,650	2,450	2,250
$ 30,000	3,050	2,950	2,850	2,750	2,650	2,450	2,250	2,150
$ 35,000	2,050	1,950	1,850	1,750	1,650	1,550	1,450	1,350

Note: Based on family of four, one child enrolled in college, oldest parent age 41.
This chart should only be used as an estimate since the formula to determine EFC takes into account a number of variables.

Federal Financial Aid Programs

Program	Maximum Award Per Year
Federal Pell Grant	$4050 (undergraduate only)
Federal Supplemental Educational Opportunity Grant (FSEOG)	$4000 (undergraduate only)
Federal Perkins Loan	$4000 (undergraduate) $6000 (graduate)
Federal Stafford/Direct Loan (subsidized)	$2625 (first year) $3500 (second year) $5500 (third and fourth years) $8500 (graduate)
Federal Stafford/DirectLoan (unsubsidized) These amounts are inclusive of subsidized loans.	$2625 (first year) $3500 (second year) $5500 (third and fourth years) $6625 (independent first year students) $7500 (independent second year students) $10,500 (independent third and fourth year students) $18,500 (graduate)
Federal PLUS Loan	Up to cost of attendance (for parents only) (Less other financial aid received)
Federal Work-Study	No maximum

much funding the program receives from the government. The maximum for 2005-06 is $4050.

To give you some idea of your possible eligibility for a Pell Grant, the table in this section may be helpful. The amounts shown are based on a family of four, with one student in college, no emergency expenses, no contribution from student income or assets, and college costs of at least $4050 per year.

Federal Supplemental Educational Opportunity Grant (FSEOG)

As its name implies, the Federal Supplemental Educational Opportunity Grant provides additional need-based federal grant money to supplement the Federal

Pell Grant. Each participating college is given funds to award to especially needy students. The maximum award is $4000 per year, but the amount you receive depends on the college's policy, the availability of FSEOG funds, the total cost of education, and the amount of other aid awarded.

Federal Work-Study (FWS)

This program provides jobs for students who demonstrate need. Salaries are paid by funds from the federal government as well as the college. You work on an hourly basis on or off campus and must be paid at least the federal minimum wage. You may earn only up to the amount awarded in the financial aid package.

Federal Perkins Loan

This is a low-interest (5 percent) loan for students with exceptional financial need. Federal Perkins Loans are made through the college's financial aid office with the college as the lender. You can borrow a maximum of $4000 per year for up to five years of undergraduate study. Borrowers may take up to ten years to repay the loan, beginning nine months after they graduate, leave school, or drop below half-time status. No interest accrues while they are in school, and, under certain conditions (e.g., they teach in low-income areas, work in law enforcement, are full-time nurses or medical technicians, serve as Peace Corps or VISTA volunteers, etc.), some or all of the loan can be cancelled. In addition, payments can be deferred under certain conditions such as unemployment.

Federal Stafford and Direct Loans

Stafford and Direct Loans have the same interest rates, loan maximums, deferments, and cancellation benefits. A Stafford Loan may be borrowed from a commercial lender, such as a bank or credit union. A Direct Loan is borrowed directly from the U.S. Department of Education through the college's financial aid office.

The interest rate varies annually (there is a maximum of 8.25 percent), and the interest rates is currently at 5.3 percent. If you qualify for a need-based subsidized Stafford Loan, the interest is paid by the federal government while you are enrolled in college. There is also an unsubsidized Stafford Loan that is not based on need for which you are eligible regardless of your family income.

The maximum amount dependent students may borrow in any one year is $2625 for freshmen, $3500 for sophomores, and $5500 for juniors and seniors, with a maximum of $23,000 for the total undergraduate program. The maximum amount independent students can borrow is $6625 for freshmen (of which no more than $2625 can be subsidized), $7500 for sophomores (of which no more than $3500 can be subsidized), and $10,500 for juniors and seniors (of which no more than $5500 can be subsidized). Borrowers may be charged an origination fee that cannot exceed 3 percent of the amount of the loan. Some lenders offer reduced or zero-fee loans.

To apply for a Stafford Loan, you must first complete a FAFSA to determine eligibility for a subsidized loan and then complete a separate loan application that is submitted to a lender. The financial aid office can help in selecting a lender. The lender will send a master promissory note

by which you agree to repay the loan. The proceeds of the loan, less the origination fee, will be sent to the college to be either credited to your account or released to you directly.

If the school you are attending participates in the federal Direct Loan program, the application process is easier. To apply for a federal Direct Loan, simply complete the FAFSA. The school serves as a lender, and all loan processing is handled by the financial aid officer.

Once the repayment period starts, borrowers of both subsidized and unsubsidized Stafford or Direct Loans will have to pay a combination of interest and principal monthly for up to a ten-year period. There are a number of repayment options, as well as opportunities to consolidate your federal loans. There are also provisions for deferments and repayment forberance.

Federal PLUS Loans

PLUS is for parents of dependent students to help families who may not have cash readily available to pay the educational costs not covered by the financial aid programs. There is no needs test to qualify. The loan has a variable interest rate that cannot exceed 9 percent (the current interest rate is 6.1 percent). There is no yearly limit; you can borrow up to the cost of your education, less other financial aid received. Repayment begins sixty days after the money is advanced. A 3 or 4 percent fee may be subtracted from the proceeds. Parent borrowers must generally have a good credit record to qualify. PLUS Loans may be processed under either the Direct or Stafford Loan system, depending on the type of loan program for which the college has contracted.

Tuition Tax Credits

Tuition tax credits allow families to reduce their tax bill by the amount of out-of-pocket college tuition expense. Unlike a tax deduction, which is modified according to your tax bracket, a tax credit is a dollar-for-dollar reduction in taxes paid.

There are two programs: the HOPE Scholarship and the Lifetime Learning Tax Credit. As is true of many federal programs, there are numerous rules and restrictions that apply. You should check with your tax preparer or financial adviser for information about your own particular situation.

HOPE Scholarship
The HOPE Scholarship offsets some of the expense for the first two years of college or vocational school. Students or the parents of dependent students can claim an annual income tax credit of up to $1500—100 percent of the first $1000 of tuition and required fees and 50 percent of the second $1000. Grants, scholarships, and other tax-free educational assistance must be deducted from the total tuition and fee payments.

This credit can be claimed for students who are in their first two years of college and who are enrolled on at least a half-time basis in a degree or certificate program for any portion of the year. This credit phases out for joint filers who have an income between $85,000 and $105,000 and for single filers who have between $42,000 and $52,000 of income. Parents may claim credits for more than one qualifying student. (The income figures are subject to change.)

Lifetime Learning Tax Credit
The Lifetime Learning Tax Credit is the counterpart of the HOPE Scholarship; it is for college juniors, seniors, graduate students, and part-time students pursuing

lifelong learning to improve or upgrade their job skills. The qualifying taxpayer can claim an annual tax credit of up to $2000—20 percent of the first $10,000 of tuition. The credit is available for net tuition and fees, less grant aid. The total credit available is limited to $2000 per year per taxpayer (or joint-filing couple), and is phased out at the same income levels as the HOPE Scholarship. (The income figures are subject to change.)

AmeriCorps

AmeriCorps is a national umbrella group of service programs for students. Participants work in a public or private nonprofit agency and provide service to the community in one of four priority areas: education, human services, the environment, and public safety. In exchange, you earn a stipend (for living expenses) of between $7400 and $14,800 a year, health insurance coverage, and $4725 per year for up to two years to apply toward college expenses. Many student-loan lenders will postpone the repayment of student loans during service in AmeriCorps, and AmeriCorps will pay the interest that is accrued on qualified student loans for members who complete the service program. You can work before, during, or after you go to college and can use the funds to either pay current educational expenses or repay federal student loans. For more information, please visit www.americorps.org.

Online Filing of FAFSA and CSS/PROFILE® Applications

Richard Woodland
Director of Financial Aid
Rutgers University–Camden

Over the past few years, there have been major advancements in the way students apply both for admission to college and for financial aid. The two primary financial aid applications, the Free Application for Federal Student Aid (FAFSA) and the CSS/PROFILE® application from the College Scholarship Service now offer direct, online applications. FAFSA on the Web and PROFILE are available in both English and Spanish.

Why File Online?

There are two reasons why it is a good idea to file online. First, the online environment prevents you from making many mistakes. For example, if there is a question that is required of all applicants, you cannot inadvertently skip it. If the application software thinks your answer may not be accurate, it will prompt you to check it before proceeding. The financial aid process can be complicated, and applying online greatly reduces the chance for error. The second reason is turnaround time. The online applications are processed in a matter of days, not weeks. Since time is an important factor when applying for financial aid, it is prudent to have your application processed as quickly as possible.

Some Common Concerns about Online Filing

Both the FASFA and PROFILE online applications have become much more user-friendly. You do not have to be a computer expert to use these programs. Both applications allow you to save your completed data and return later if you are interrupted or need to gather some additional information. Both systems use secure encryption technology to protect your privacy. FASFA information is shared only with other federal agencies as are required as part of the application process, online or paper. The information on the application is highly personal, and every precaution is taken to safeguard your privacy

Now, let's discuss some specific issues related to each application.

The FAFSA

The FAFSA is the universal application for all federal financial aid programs. It is the primary application used for most state and college financial aid programs. Before using the FAFSA online application, you need to secure an electronic signature, or Personal Identification Number (PIN). This is similar to the access codes used at ATM machines, online banking, etc. It is easy to obtain a PIN number. Simply go to www.pin.ed.gov and apply online. You will receive a reply via e-mail in about 48 hours. If you are under 24 years of age, you and one parent will need a PIN number. If there is more than one child in college, a parent only needs one PIN number. However, each college applicant will need to have his or her own PIN.

The FASFA online application is not presented in the same format as the paper FAFSA. Although all of the questions are exactly the same, the order of some of the items on the online application has been rearranged to make it easier to complete and allow for some built-in skip-logic. You can easily obtain a copy of the electronic FAFSA by logging on to www.fafsa.ed.gov. Just click-on "Pre-Application Worksheet." Completing this first will make the online entry that much easier. There are a number of other worksheets available that can also make the process easier. You should print them out and decide which are applicable to your situation. Everyone should review Worksheets A, B, and C. If you have not completed your federal tax return, the "Income Estimator" worksheets are easy to use and can reduce much of the guesswork.

After completing the online FASFA, be sure to print a copy of the pages at the end of the process that give you a copy of your answers and the confirmation number. Although lost applications are extremely rare, having this information will give you peace of mind. You can go online as often as you wish to check the status of your application.

The CSS/PROFILE®

The CSS/PROFILE® is a more comprehensive financial aid application that is used primarily at private, higher-cost colleges and universities to award nonfederal student aid funds. Many private scholarship programs also use the PROFILE. A complete list of colleges and programs that use the PROFILE can be found at www.collegeboard.com.

The PROFILE application charges a $5 registration fee and an additional $18 for each school or program you select to receive your information. You must have a credit card, debit card, or checking account to use this service.

Note: A limited number of fee waivers are available for families with incomes below the poverty line.

See your high school guidance officer for more information on the fee waiver program.

Complete information on the online PROFILE application is available at www.collegeboard.com/profile. Although the customized PROFILE application is processed in about one week, you should allow for enough processing time (usually 2 to 3 weeks) to meet the earliest deadline established by the school or program.

What Happens Next?

Both the FAFSA and CSS/PROFILE® processors want more applicants to use the online environment. Not only is the process easier for them, but it is faster and more accurate. Once you decide to apply online, the processors will only respond to you electronically. You will not receive any paper acknowledgments—all confirmations will be sent via e-mail. When it is time to reapply for aid in subsequent years, all reminders will be sent to the e-mail address that is on file,

so it is important to report any changes of your e-mail address. It is an easy process since much of the data is carried over from the previous application. (In general, the PROFILE is a one-time application, filed well before tax season. Any updates are usually done directly through the schools.)

It is easy to update the FAFSA following your initial application. For example, if you used estimated income information and now you have your federal tax return completed, you can simply return to www.fafsa.ed.gov and change your income figures. But be sure to go through the entire process and print out the updated confirmation page.

Both processors offer helpful information, both in print and online. Check with your high school guidance office or local college financial aid office for additional assistance. If you need to call the FAFSA processor, the phone number is 800-4-FED-AID (toll-free). You can contact the College Scholarship Service via e-mail at help@cssprofile.org or by phone at 305-829-9793.

Searching for Scholarships Online

Today's students need all the help they can get when looking for ways to pay for their college education. Skyrocketing tuition costs, state budget cuts, and diminished personal savings have combined to make financing a college education perhaps the number one concern for parents. College sticker shock is driving many families away from college. No wonder. The "purchasing power" of all aid programs from federal, state, and institutional sources has declined over the past two decades. State education budgets have been slashed. Tuition at public institutions has increased at an average annual rate of 10.5 percent; private tuition by 6 percent. And it's not only lower-income families who are affected. Some families fear they make *too much* money to qualify for financial aid. Regardless of their situation, most families struggle to make sense of the college financial aid process and to decide which aid package is the right one for them.

Despite the confusion, students and parents can and should continue to research as many sources as they can to find the money they need. The Internet can be a great source of information. There are many worthwhile sites that are ready to help you search and apply for your fair share of awards, including Thomson Peterson's comprehensive financial aid site at www.petersons.com/finaid.

Thomson Peterson's Scholarship Search

Need money to pay for college? Simply fill out an online application and gain access to Thomson Peterson's *free* Scholarship Search that will connect you to over 1.7 million scholarships, grants, and prizes worth more than $8 billion.

Once you register, you can access the Thomson Peterson's scholarship database as often as you like simply by logging in with your username and password. Access to Thomson Peterson's scholarship search will enable you to complete your very own student profile by providing information about your academic background, your preferred majors, the type of institution in which you are interested, and your career goals.

In addition to the abundant award opportunities available, www.petersons. com/finaid provides information on the basics of financial aid, including:

- Financial Aid Overview
- Financial Aid: Terms Defined
- Financial Aid: Discover Your Financial Aid Literacy
- Family Financial Situations
- Federal Student Aid
- Estimated Expected Family Contribution (EFC)

Thomson Peterson's has also partnered with many of today's leading providers of federal and private student aid. You can access these providers and apply for loans immediately by logging on to www. petersons.com/finaid.

Find Your Best College Deal

Thomson Peterson's financial aid site is also home to the Internet's first online financial aid resource to provide truly personalized assistance.

For a fee, Thomson Peterson's BestCollegeDeals® (www.BestCollegeDeals. com) allows participating families to assess the reality of their situation *before* they submit their paperwork to colleges for review. BestCollegeDeals has collected information on more than 2,000 scholarships, grants, and other awards (both need- and non-need-based) that are generally not well publicized. No matter what their income, parents will discover what each college expects them to pay for freshman through senior years and find out the latest information on scholarships, tuition discounts, and other financial packages to help minimize out-of-pocket costs.

Through extensive secondary research, Thomson Peterson's has compiled the latest information on exceptional college deals— financial award packages, including the average grant award, offered by more than 1,800 accredited undergraduate institutions all over the country. Surprisingly, many institutions offer "free money" deals in the form of no-strings grants or scholarships, regardless of an applicant's income. In fact, there are more than 2,000 of these "free money" deals in Peterson's database, which are available to students for performing community service, for being valedictorians, or for being the sibling of a current college student.

Use the Tools to Your Advantage

Searching and applying for financial aid is an involved and complicated process.

The tools available to you on www.petersons.com/finaid and www.BestCollegeDeals.com can help you get your fair share of the financial aid pie.

So, what are you waiting for? Fire up the computer; free money for college is just a mouse click away.

How to Use This Guide

Quick-Reference Chart

The amount of aid available at colleges can vary greatly. College Costs At-a-Glance lists the percent of freshmen who applied for and received need-based gift aid and the percent of those whose need was fully met. Also listed are the average freshman financial aid package, the average cost after aid, and the average graduate indebtedness.

Profiles of College Financial Aid Programs

After the federal government, colleges provide the largest amount of financial aid to students. In addition, they control most of the money channeled to students from the federal government. The amount and makeup of your financial aid package will depend on the institution's particular circumstances and its decisions concerning your application. The main section of this book shows you the pattern and extent of each college's current awards. The profiles present detailed factual and statistical data for each school in a uniform format to make easy, quick references and comparisons. Items that could not be collected in time for publication are designated as *N/A*. Items for which the specific figures could not be gathered in time are given as *available*. Colleges that supplied no data are listed by name and address only so that you do not overlook them in your search for colleges.

There is much anecdotal evidence that students and their families fail to apply for financial aid under the misapprehension that student aid goes only to poor families. Financial need in the context of college expenses is not the same as being needy in the broad social context. Middle-class families typically qualify for need-based financial aid; at expensive schools, even upper-middle-income families can qualify for need-based financial aid. Thomson Peterson's encourages you to apply for financial aid whether or not you think that you will qualify.

To help you understand the definition and significance of each item, the following outline of the profile format explains what is covered in each section. The term college or colleges is frequently used below to refer to any institution of higher education, regardless of its official definition.

The College

The name of the college is the official name as it appears on the institution's charter. The city and state listed are the official location of the school. The subhead line shows tuition and required fees, as they were charged to the majority of full-time undergraduate students in the 2004-05 academic year. Any exceptions to the 2004-05 academic year figures are so noted. For a public institution, the tuition and fees shown are for state residents, and this is noted. If a college's annual expenses are expressed as a comprehensive fee (including full-time tuition, mandatory fees, and college room and board), this is noted, as are any unusual definitions, such as tuition only. The average undergraduate aid package is the average total package of grant, loan, and work-study aid that was awarded to defray the officially defined financial need of full-time undergraduates enrolled in fall 2004 (or fall 2003) who applied for

financial aid, were determined to have need, and then actually received financial aid. This information appears in more detail below in each profile.

About the Institution

This paragraph gives the reader a brief introduction to a college. It contains the following elements:

Institutional Control

Private institutions are designated as *independent* (nonprofit), *independent/religious* (sponsored by or affiliated with a religious group or having a nondenominational or interdenominational religious orientation), or *proprietary* (profit-making). Public institutions are designated by their primary source of support, such as *federal*, *state*, *commonwealth* (Puerto Rico), *territory* (U.S. territories), *county, district* (an administrative unit of public education, often having boundaries different from those of units of local government), *state- and locally-supported* ("locally" refers to county, district, or city), *state-supported* (funded by the state), or *state-related* (funded primarily by the state but administered autonomously).

Type of Student Body

The categories are *men* (100 percent of student body), *coed-primarily men*, *women* (100 percent of student body), *coed-primarily women*, and *coed*.

Degrees Awarded

Associate, bachelor's (baccalaureate), *master's, doctoral* (doctorate), and *first professional* (in such fields as law and medicine). There are no institutions in this book that award the associate degree only. Many award the bachelor's as their highest degree. You will need to talk to your family and your guidance counselor to decide whether you want to attend a college that concentrates on undergraduate education or an institution with professional schools and research activities.

Number of Undergraduate Majors

This shows the number of academic fields in which the institution offers associate and/or bachelor's degrees. The purpose of this is to give you an indication of the range of subjects available.

Enrollment

These figures are based on the actual number of full-time and part-time students enrolled in degree programs as of fall 2004. In most instances, they are designated as *total enrollment* (for the specific college or university) and *freshmen*. If the institution is a university and its total enrollment figure includes graduate students, a separate figure for *undergraduates* may be provided. If the profiled institution is a subunit of a university, the figures may be designated *total university enrollment* for the entire university and *total unit enrollment* for the specific subunit.

Methodology Used for Determining Need

Private colleges usually have larger financial aid programs, but public colleges usually have lower sticker prices, especially for in-state or local students. At a public college, your financial need will be less, and you will receive a smaller financial aid package. The note on whether a college uses federal (FAFSA) or institutional methodology (usually PRO-FILE) will let you know whether you will have to complete one or two kinds of financial aid application forms. Federal Methodology is the needs-analysis formula used by the U.S. Department of Education to determine the Expected Family Contribution (EFC), which, when subtracted from the cost of attendance at an institution, determines the financial

need of a student. There is no relative advantage or disadvantage to using one methodology over the other.

Undergraduate Expenses

If provided by the institution, the one-time application fee is listed. Costs are given for the 2005-06 academic year (or estimated for the 2005-06 academic year) or for the 2004-05 academic year if 2005-06 figures were not yet available. Annual expenses may be expressed as a comprehensive fee (including full-time tuition, mandatory fees, and college room and board) or may be given as separate figures for full-time tuition, fees, room and board, or room only. For public institutions where tuition differs according to state residence, separate figures are given for area or state residents and for nonresidents. Part-time tuition is expressed in terms of a per-unit rate (per credit, per semester hour, etc.), as specified by the institution.

The tuition structure at some institutions is complex. Freshmen and sophomores may be charged a different rate from the rate charged to juniors and seniors, a professional or vocational division may have a different fee structure from the liberal arts division of the same institution, or part-time tuition may be prorated on a sliding scale according to the number of credit hours taken. Tuition and fees may vary according to academic program, campus/location, class time (day, evening, weekend), course/credit load, course level, degree level, reciprocity agreements, and student level. If tuition and fees differ for international students, the rate charged is listed.

Room and board charges are reported as an average for one academic year and may vary according to board plan selected, campus/location, gender, type of housing facility, or student level. If no college-owned or -operated housing facilities are offered, the phrase *college housing not available* will appear.

If a college offers a *guaranteed tuition* plan, it promises that the tuition rate of an entering student will not increase for the entire term of enrollment, from entrance to graduation. Other payment plans might include *tuition prepayment*, which allows an entering student to lock in the current tuition rate for the entire term of enrollment by paying the full amount in advance rather than year by year, and *installment* and *deferred payment* plans, which allow students to delay the payment of the full tuition.

Guaranteed tuition and tuition prepayment help you to plan the total cost of your education and can save you from the financial distress sometimes caused by tuition hikes. Colleges that offer such plans may also help you to arrange financing, which in the long run can cost less than the total of four years of increasing tuition rates. Deferred payment or installment payments may better fit your personal financial situation, especially if you do not qualify for financial aid and, due to other financial commitments, find that obtaining the entire amount due is burdensome. Carefully investigate these plans, however, to see what premium you may pay at the end to allow you to defer immediate payment.

Freshman Financial Aid

Usually, these are actual figures for the 2004-05 term, beginning in fall 2004; figures may also be estimated for that term, or they could be 2003-04 figures. The particular term for which these data apply is indicated. The figures are for degree-seeking full-time freshman students. The first figure is the number of freshmen who applied for any kind of financial aid. The next figure is the percentage of those freshmen financial aid applicants who were determined to have financial need—that is, through the formal needs-assessment process, had a calculated expected family contribution that was less than the total college cost. The next figure is the percentage of this group of eligible freshmen who received any financial aid. The next figure is the percentage of this preceding group of eligible aid recipients whose need was fully met by financial aid. The *Average percent of need met* is the average percentage of financial need met for freshmen who received any need-based aid. The *Average financial aid package* is the average dollar amount awarded (need-based or non-need-based) to freshmen who applied for aid, were deemed eligible, and received any aid; awards used to reduce the expected family contribution are excluded from this average. The final line in most profiles is the percentage of freshmen who had no financial need but who received non-need-based aid other than athletic scholarships or special-group tuition benefits.

What do these data mean to you? If financial aid is important in your comparison of colleges, the relative percentage of students who received any aid, whose need was fully met, and the average percentage of need met have the most weight. These figures reflect the relative abundance of student aid available to the average eligible applicant. The average dollar amount of the aid package has real meaning, but only in relation to the college's expense; you will be especially interested in the difference between this figure and the costs figure, which is what the average student (in any given statistical group, there actually may be no average individual) will have to pay. Of course, if the financial aid package is largely loans rather than grants, you will have to pay this amount eventually. Relative differences in the figures of the number of students who apply for aid and who are deemed eligible can hinge on any number of factors: the relative sticker price of the college, the relative level of wealth of the students' families, the proportion of only children in college and students with siblings in college (families with two or more children in college are more likely to apply for aid and be considered eligible), or the relative sophistication in financial aid matters (or quality of college counseling they may have received) of the students and their families. While these may be interesting, they will not mean too much to most students and families. If you are among the unlucky (or, perhaps, lucky) students who do not qualify for need-based financial aid, the final sentence of this paragraph in the profile will be of interest because it reveals the relative policies that the college has in distributing merit-based aid to students who cannot demonstrate need.

Undergraduate Financial Aid

This is the parallel paragraph to the Freshman Financial Aid paragraph (see above). The same definitions apply, except that the group being considered is degree-seeking full-time undergraduate students (including freshmen).

There are cases of students who chose a particular college because they received a really generous financial aid package in their freshman year and then had to scramble to pay the tuition bill in their later years. If a financial aid package is a key factor in your decision to attend a particular college, you want to be certain that the package offered to all undergraduates is not too far from that offered to freshmen. The key figures are those for the percentage of students who received any aid, the percentage of financial aid recipients whose need was fully met, the average percentage of need met, and the dollar figure of the average financial aid package. Generally, colleges assume that after the freshman year, students develop study habits and time-management skills that will allow them to take on part-time and summer employment without hurting their academic performance. So, the proportion of self-help aid (work-study and student loans) in the financial aid package tends to increase after the freshman year. This pattern, which is true of most colleges, can be verified below, in the freshman-undergraduate figures in the paragraph on Gift Aid (Need-Based).

Gift Aid (Need-Based)

Total amount is the total dollar figure in 2004-05 (actual or estimated) or 2003-04 (actual) of need-based scholarships and grant (gift) aid awarded to degree-seeking full-time and part-time students that was used to meet financial need. The percentages of this aid from federal, state, institutional (college or university), and external (e.g., foundations, civic organizations, etc.) sources are shown. *Receiving aid* shows the percentages (and number, in parentheses) of freshmen and of all undergraduates who applied for aid, were considered eligible, and received any need-based gift aid. *Scholarships, grants, and awards by category* cites major categories of need-based gift aid provided by the college; these include Federal Pell Grants, Federal Supplemental Educational Opportunity Grants (FSEOG), state scholarships, private scholarships, college/university gift aid from institutional funds, United Negro College Fund aid, Federal Nursing Scholarships, and others.

Scholarships and grants are gifts awarded to students that do not need to be repaid. These are preferable to loans, which have to be repaid, or work-study wages, which may take time away from studies and personal pursuits. The total amount of need-based gift aid has to be placed into the context of the total number of undergraduate students (shown above, in the About the Institution paragraph) and the relative expense of the institution. Filing the FAFSA automatically puts you in line to receive any available federal grants for which you may qualify. However, if the college that you are considering has a higher than usual proportion of gift aid coming from state, institutional, or external sources, be sure to check with the financial aid office to find out what these sources may be and how to apply for them. For almost all colleges, the percentage of freshmen receiving need-based gift aid will be higher than the percentage of all undergraduates receiving need-based gift aid. However, if you are dependent on need-based gift aid, and the particular college you are considering shows a sharper drop from the freshman to undergraduate years than other colleges of a similar type, you might want to think about how this change will affect your ability to pay for later years at this college.

Gift Aid (Non-Need-Based)

Total amount is the total dollar figure in 2004-05 (actual or estimated) or 2003-04 (actual) of non-need-based scholarships and grant (gift) aid awarded to degree-seeking full-time and part-time students. Non-need-based aid that was used to meet financial need is not included in this total. The percentages of this aid from federal, state, institutional (college or university), and external (e.g., National Merit Scholarships, civic, religious, fraternal organizations, etc.) sources are shown. *Receiving aid* shows the percentages (and number, in parentheses) of freshmen and of all undergraduates who did not receive need-based aid but who received non-need-based gift aid. *Average award* is the average dollar amount of awards to the students in this immediately preceding group. *Scholarships, grants, and awards by category* cites the major categories in which non-need-based awards are available and the number of awards made in that category (in parentheses, the total dollar value of these awards). The categories listed are *Academic Interests/ Achievement*, which includes agriculture, business, communication, computer science, education, engineering/technologies, English, foreign languages, general academic interests/achievements, health fields, home economics, mathematics, military science, physical sciences, and social sciences; *Creative Arts/Performance*, which includes applied art and

design, art/fine arts, creative writing, dance, debating, music, and theater/ drama; *Special Achievements/Activities*, which includes general special achievements/activities, community service, leadership, religious involvement, and rodeo; and *Special Characteristics*, which includes adult students, children and siblings of alumni, disabilities, ethnic background, first-generation college students, international students, parents of current students, and veterans. *Tuition waivers* indicate special categories of students (minority students, children of alumni, college employees or children of employees, adult students, and senior citizens) who may qualify for a full or partial waiver of tuition. *ROTC* indicates Army, Navy, and Air Force ROTC programs that are offered on campus; a program offered by arrangement on another campus is indicated by the word *cooperative*.

This section covers college-administered scholarships awarded to undergraduates on the basis of merit or personal attributes without regard to need. If you do not qualify for financial aid but nevertheless lack the resources to pay for college, non-need-based awards will be of special interest to you. Some personal characteristics are completely beyond an individual's control, and talents and achievements take a number of years to develop or attain. However, certain criteria for these awards, such as religious involvement, community service, and special academic interests can be attained in a relatively brief period of time. ROTC programs offer such benefits as tuition, the cost of textbooks, and living allowances. In return, you must fulfill a service obligation after graduating from college. Because they can be a significant help in paying for college, these programs have become quite competitive. Certain subject areas, such as nursing, health care, or the technical fields, are in stronger demand than others. Among the obligations to consider about ROTC are that you must

spend a regular portion of your available time in military training programs and that ROTC entails a multiyear commitment after your graduation to serve as an officer in the armed services branch sponsoring the program.

Loans

The figures here represent loans that are part of the financial aid award package. These are typically offered at rates lower than can be found in the normal loan marketplace. *Student loans* represents the total dollar amount of loans from all sources to full-time and part-time degree-seeking undergraduates or their parents. The percentage of these loans that goes to meet financial need and the percentage that goes to pay the non-need portion (the expected family contribution) are indicated. The percentage of the last graduating class who borrowed through any loan program (except parent loans) while enrolled at the college is shown, as is the average dollar figure per-borrower of cumulative undergraduate indebtedness (this does not include loans from other institutions). *Parent loans* shows the total amount borrowed through parent loan programs as well as the percentages that were applied to the need-based and non-need-based portions of financial need. *Programs* indicates the major loan programs available to undergraduates. These include Direct and Stafford Loans (subsidized and unsubsidized and PLUS), Perkins Loans, Federal Nursing Loans, state loans, college/university loans, and other types.

Loans are forms of aid that must be repaid with interest. Most people will borrow money to pay college costs. The loans available through financial aid programs are offered at very favorable interest rates. Student loans are preferable to parent loans because the payoff is deferred. In comparing colleges, the dollar amount of total indebtedness of the last class is a factor to be considered. Typically, this amount would increase

How to Use This Guide

proportionate to the tuition. However, if it does not, this could mean that the college provides relatively generous grant or work-study aid rather than loans in its financial aid package.

Work-Study

The total dollar amounts, number, and average dollar amount of *Federal Work-Study* (FWS) jobs appears first. The total dollar figure of *State or other work-study/employment*, if available, is shown, as is the percentage of those dollars that go to meet financial need. The number of part-time jobs available on campus to undergraduates, other than work-study, is shown last.

FWS is a federally funded program that enables students with demonstrated need to earn money by working on or off campus, usually in a nonprofit organization. FWS jobs are a special category of jobs that are open to students only through the financial aid office. Other kinds of part-time jobs are routinely available at most colleges and may vary widely. In comparing colleges, you may find characteristic differences in how the "self-help" portions (loans and work-study) are proportioned. Families and students will differ as to how they ideally would proportion this self-help component. This preference may change as you mature and progress in class standing and your own ability to manage academic work and job responsibilities.

Athletic Awards

The total dollar amount of athletic scholarships given by the college to undergraduate students, whether or not it goes to meet financial need, is indicated.

If you are a serious student-athlete candidate, this may provide a broad context, but actual awards will depend upon your specific talents and the college's athletic needs at the particular time you want to attend. If you are a good athlete but not of starter caliber in a marquee sport, you might be able to secure a partial scholarship, depending on talent and the college's needs. In this case, the number of students receiving athletic awards in relation to the number of total undergraduates may be important.

Applying for Financial Aid

Required financial aid forms include the FAFSA (Free Application for Federal Student Aid), the institution's own form, CSS/PROFILE®, a state aid form, a noncustodial (divorced/separated) parent's statement, a business/farm supplement, and others. The college's financial aid application deadline is noted as the *Financial aid deadline* and is shown in one of three ways: as a specific date if it is an absolute deadline; noted as *Continuous*, which means processing goes on without a deadline or until all available aid has been awarded; or as a date with the note *(priority)*, meaning that you are encouraged to apply before that date in order to have the best chance of obtaining aid. *Notification date* is listed as either a specific date or *Continuous*. The date by which you must reply to the college with your decision to accept or decline its financial aid package is listed as either a specific date or as a number of weeks from the date of notification.

Be prepared to check early with the colleges you are interested in as to exactly which forms will be required from you. All colleges require the FAFSA for students applying for federal aid. In most cases, colleges have a limited amount of funds set aside to use as financial aid. It is only natural that the first eligible students will get a larger share of what is available. The sooner you apply, the more likely it is that your financial need will be fully met and that a higher proportion of your financial aid package will consist of gift aid.

Contact

The name, title, address, telephone and fax numbers, and e-mail address of the person to contact for further information (student financial aid contact, chief financial aid officer, or office of financial aid) are given at the end of the profile. You should feel free to write or call for any materials you need or if you have questions.

Appendix

This section lists more than 400 state-specific grants and loans. Eligibility requirements, award amounts, and contact information are given for all programs.

Indexes

Six indexes in the back of the book allow you to search for particular award programs based on the following criteria:

Non-Need Scholarships for Undergraduates

This index lists the colleges that report that they offer scholarships to freshmen based on academic interests, abilities, achievements, or personal characteristics other than financial need. Specific categories appear in alphabetical order under the following broad groups:

- Academic Interests/Achievements (e.g., Agriculture, Health Fields, Mathematics)
- Creative Arts/Performance (e.g., Applied Art and Design, Dance, Theater/Drama)
- Special Achievements/Activities (e.g., Cheerleading/Drum Major, Hobbies/Interests, Rodeo)
- Special Characteristics (e.g., Adult Students, Local/State Students, Veterans)

Athletic Grants for Undergraduates

This index lists the colleges that report offering scholarships for freshmen on the basis of their athletic achievements or abilities.

Co-Op Programs

This index lists colleges that report offering cooperative education programs. These are formal arrangements with off-campus employers that are designed to allow students to combine study and work, often in a position related to the student's field of study. Salaries typically are set at regular marketplace levels, and academic credit is often given.

ROTC Programs

This index lists colleges that offer Reserve Officers' Training Corps programs. The index is arranged by the branch of service that sponsors the program.

Tuition Waivers

This index lists colleges that report offering full or partial tuition waivers for certain categories of students. A majority of colleges offer tuition waivers to employees or children of employees. Because this benefit is so common and the affected employees usually are aware of it, no separate index of schools offering this option is provided. However, this information is included in the individual college profiles.

Tuition Payment Alternatives

This index lists colleges that report offering tuition payment alternatives. These payment alternatives include deferred payment plans, guaranteed tuition plans, installment payment plans, and prepayment plans.

Data Collection Procedures

The data contained in the college chart, profiles, and indexes were collected in fall and winter 2004 and spring 2005 through *Thomson Peterson's Annual Sur-*vey of Undergraduate Financial Aid and the *Thomson Peterson's Annual Survey of Undergraduate Institutions*. Questionnaires were sent to the more than 2,100 institutions of higher education that are accredited in the U.S. and U.S. territories and offer full four- or five-year baccalaureate degrees via full-time on-campus programs of study. Officials at the colleges—usually the financial aid or admission officers but sometimes the registrars or institutional research staff members—completed and returned the forms. Thomson Peterson's attempts to verify all data that is collected. Because of the comprehensive editorial review that takes place Thomson Peterson's has every reason to believe that the data presented in this book is accurate. However, students should always confirm costs and other facts with a specific school at the time of application, since colleges can and do change policies and fees whenever necessary.

The state aid data presented in *Peterson's College Money Handbook* was submitted by state officials (usually the director of the state scholarship commission) to Thomson Peterson's in spring 2005. Because regulations for any government-sponsored program may be changed at any time, you should request written descriptive materials from the office administering a program in which you are interested.

Criteria for Inclusion in This Book

Peterson's College Money Handbook covers accredited baccalaureate-degree-granting institutions in the United States and U.S. territories. Institutions have full accreditation or candidate-for-accreditation (preaccreditation) status granted by an institutional or specialized accrediting body recognized by the U.S. Department of Education or Council for Higher Education Accreditation. Recognized institutional accrediting bodies, which consider each institution as a whole, are the six regional associations of schools and colleges (Middle States, New England, North Central, Northwest, Southern, and Western), each of which is responsible for a specified portion of the United States and its territories; the Accrediting Association of Bible Colleges (AABC); the Accrediting Council for Independent Colleges and Schools (ACICS); the Accrediting Commission for Career Schools and Colleges of Technology (ACCSCT); the Distance Education and Training Council (DETC); the American Academy for Liberal Education; the Council on Occupational Education; and the Transnational Association of Christian Colleges and Schools (TRACS). Program registration by the New York State Board of Regents is considered to be the equivalent of institutional accreditation, since the Board requires that all programs offered by an institution meet its standards before recognition is granted. There are recognized specialized accrediting bodies in more than forty different fields, each of which is authorized to accredit specific programs in its particular field. This can serve as the equivalent of institutional accreditation for specialized institutions that offer programs in one field only (schools of art, music, optometry, theology, etc.).

Quick-Reference Chart

College Costs At-a-Glance

Michael Steidel
Director of Admissions
Carnegie Mellon University

To help shed some light on the typical patterns of financial aid offered by colleges, we have prepared the following chart. This chart can help you to better understand financial aid practices in general, form realistic expectations about the amounts of aid that might be provided by specific colleges or universities, and prepare for meaningful discussions with the financial aid officers at colleges you are considering. The data appearing in the chart have been supplied by the schools themselves and are also shown in the individual college profiles.

Tuition and fees are based on the total of full-time tuition and mandatory fees for the 2005-06 academic year (or estimated 2005-06) or for the 2004-05 academic year if 2005-06 figures are not available. More information about these costs, as well as the costs of room and board and the year for which they are current, can be found in the individual college profiles. For institutions that have two or more tuition rates for different categories of students or types of programs, the lowest rate is used in figuring the cost.

The colleges are listed alphabetically by state. An "NR" in any individual column indicates that the applicable data element was "Not Reported."

The chart is divided into seven columns of information for each college:

A. Institutional Control

Whether the school is independent (ind.), including independent, independent–religious, and proprietary, or public, including federal, state, commonwealth, territory, county, district, city, state, local, and state-related.

B. Tuition and Fees

Based on the total of full-time tuition and mandatory fees. An asterisk indicates that the school includes room and board in their mandatory fees.

C. Room and Board

The costs of room and board. If a school has room and board costs that vary according to the type of accommodation and meal plan, either the lowest figures are represented or the figures are for the most common room arrangement and a full meal plan. If a school has only housing arrangements, a dagger appears to the right of the number. An "NA" will appear in this column if no college-owned or -operated housing facilities are offered at all.

D. Percent of Eligible Freshmen Receiving Need-Based Gift Awards

Calculated by dividing the number of freshman students determined to have need who received need-based gift aid by the number of full-time freshmen.

E. Percent of Freshmen Whose Need Was Fully Met

Calculated by dividing the number of freshman students whose financial need was fully met by the number of full-time freshmen.

F. Average Financial Aid Package for Freshmen

The average dollar amount from all sources, including *gift aid* (scholarships and grants) and *self-help* (jobs and loans), awarded to aided freshmen. Note that this aid package may exceed tuition and fees if the average aid package included coverage of room and board expenses.

G. Average Net Cost After Aid

Average aid package subtracted from published costs (tuition, fees, room, and board) to produce what the average student will have to pay.

H. 2004 Graduate's Average Indebtedness

Average per-student indebtedness of graduating seniors.

Because personal situations vary widely, it is very important to note that an individual's aid package can be quite different from the averages. Moreover, the data shown for each school can fluctuate widely from year to year, depending on the number of applicants, the amount of need to be met, and the financial resources and policies of the college. Our intent in presenting this chart is to provide you with useful facts and figures that can serve as general guidelines in your pursuit of financial aid. We caution you to use the data only as a jumping-off point for further investigation and analysis, not as a means to rank or select colleges.

After you have narrowed down the colleges in which you are interested based on academic and personal criteria, we recommend that you carefully study this chart. From it, you can develop a list of questions for financial aid officers at the colleges you are seriously considering attending. Here are just a few questions you might want to ask:

- What are the specific types and sources of aid provided to freshmen at this school?

- What factors does this college consider in determining whether a financial aid applicant is qualified for its need-based aid programs?

- How does the college determine the combination of types of aid that make up an individual's package?

- How are non-need-based awards treated: as a part of the aid package or as a part of the parental/family contribution?

- Does this school "guarantee" financial aid and, if so, how is its policy implemented? Guaranteed aid means that by policy, 100 percent of need is met for all students judged to have need. Implementation determines *how* need is met and varies widely from school to school. For example, grade point average may determine the proportioning of scholarship, loan, and work-study aid. Rules for freshmen may be different from those for upperclass students.

- To what degree is the admission process "need-blind"? Need-blindness means that admission decisions are made without regard to the student's need for financial aid.

- What are the norms and practices for upperclass students? Our chart presents information on *freshman* financial aid only; however, the financial aid office should be able and willing to provide you with comparable figures for upperclass students. A college might offer a wonderful package for the freshman year, then leave you mostly on your own to fund the remaining three years. Or the school may provide a higher proportion of scholarship money for freshmen, then rebalance its aid packages to contain more self-help aid (loans and work-study) in upper-class years. There is an assumption that, all other factors being equal, students who have settled into the pattern of college time management can handle more work-study hours than freshmen. Grade point average, tuition increases, changes in parental financial circumstances, and other factors may also affect the redistribution.

College Costs At-a-Glance

College Costs At-a-Glance	Institutional Control ind.=independent; pub.=public	Tuition and Fees	Room and Board	Percent of Eligible Freshmen Receiving Need-Based Gift Awards	Percent of Freshmen Whose Need Was Fully Met	Average Financial Aid Package for Freshmen	Average Net Cost After Aid	2004 Graduate's Average Indebtedness
Alabama								
Athens State University	pub.	$ 3870	$ 900†	NR	NR	NR	NR	$ 8137
Auburn University	pub.	$ 4828	$6686	81%	20%	$ 7,127	$ 4,387	$19,419
Auburn University Montgomery	pub.	$ 4460	$5780	70%	10%	$ 6,025	$ 4,215	$15,000
Faulkner University	ind.	$10,425	$5200	74%	10%	$ 4,600	$11,025	$18,600
Heritage Christian University	ind.	$ 8264	$1500†	NR	NR	$ 2,174	$ 7,590	$23,236
Jacksonville State University	pub.	$ 4040	$3312	8%	50%	$ 3,400	$ 3,952	$17,125
Judson College	ind.	$ 9950	$6100	100%	17%	$10,763	$ 5,287	$16,502
Samford University	ind.	$13,944	$5506	94%	25%	$10,272	$ 9,178	$15,959
Southeastern Bible College	ind.	$ 6770	$4000	100%	NR	$ 5,125	$ 5,645	$20,000
Southern Christian University	ind.	$10,040	NA	NR	NR	NR	NR	$18,000
South University	ind.	$11,085	NA	93%	NR	$ 5,600	$ 5,485	$ 9600
Spring Hill College	ind.	$19,950	$7192	99%	21%	$19,016	$ 8,126	$12,041
Talladega College	ind.	$ 7128	$4420	100%	100%	$ 4,586	$ 6,962	$12,790
Troy University	pub.	$ 4162	$4812	71%	100%	$ 2,970	$ 6,004	$14,564
Troy University Dothan	pub.	$ 4162	NA	36%	100%	NR	NR	$ 6038
Troy University Montgomery	pub.	$ 3920	NA	71%	NR	$ 3,213	$ 707	NR
Tuskegee University	ind.	$11,590	$5940	85%	70%	$13,824	$ 3,706	$30,000
The University of Alabama	pub.	$ 4630	$4734	60%	31%	$ 7,414	$ 1,950	$18,989
The University of Alabama at Birmingham	pub.	$ 4662	$3060†	62%	13%	$10,410	—	$17,594
The University of Alabama in Huntsville	pub.	$ 4516	$5200	52%	17%	$ 5,508	$ 4,208	$17,242
University of North Alabama	pub.	$ 4096	$4140	67%	21%	$ 3,516	$ 4,720	$15,835
Alaska								
Alaska Pacific University	ind.	$18,342	$6960	62%	NR	$ 8,226	$17,076	$23,791
University of Alaska Anchorage	pub.	$ 3465	$7810	72%	29%	$ 8,007	$ 3,268	$15,621
University of Alaska Fairbanks	pub.	$ 4762	$5580	74%	30%	$ 8,098	$ 2,244	$12,403
University of Alaska Southeast	pub.	$ 3342	$5370	78%	22%	$ 5,901	$ 2,811	$18,249
Arizona								
Arizona State University	pub.	$ 4064	$6574	91%	13%	$ 6,883	$ 3,755	$17,509
Arizona State University East	pub.	$ 4015	$5155	NR	NR	NR	NR	NR
Arizona State University West	pub.	$ 4064	$4455†	92%	100%	$ 5,952	$ 2,567	NR
Embry-Riddle Aeronautical University	ind.	$23,490	$6516	99%	NR	$ 6,596	$23,410	$43,425
Midwestern University, Glendale Campus	ind.	$15,556	$8785	NR	NR	NR	NR	$52,677
Northern Arizona University	pub.	$ 4073	$5785	58%	24%	$ 6,597	$ 3,261	$17,901
Prescott College	ind.	$17,450	NA	50%	NR	$ 3,795	$13,655	$14,255
Southwestern College	ind.	$11,570	$4360	83%	NR	$ 3,800	$12,130	$17,125
The University of Arizona	pub.	$ 4093	$7108	NR	NR	$ 8,878	$ 2,323	$16,881
University of Phoenix Online Campus	ind.	$13,200	NA	95%	NR	$ 2,910	$10,290	NR
University of Phoenix–Phoenix Campus	ind.	$ 9090	NA	84%	NR	$ 5,072	$ 4,018	NR
University of Phoenix–Southern Arizona Campus	ind.	$ 8910	NA	83%	NR	$ 4,208	$ 4,702	NR
Arkansas								
Arkansas State University	pub.	$ 5155	$4000	85%	37%	$ 3,275	$ 5,880	$15,700
Arkansas Tech University	pub.	$ 4468	$3841	77%	32%	$ 3,716	$ 4,593	$16,330

NA = not applicable; NR = not reported; * = includes room and board; † = room only; — = not available.

College Costs At-a-Glance

	Institutional Control ind.=independent; pub.=public	Tuition and Fees	Room and Board	Percent of Eligible Freshmen Receiving Need-Based Gift Awards	Percent of Freshmen Whose Need Was Fully Met	Average Financial Aid Package for Freshmen	Average Net Cost After Aid	2004 Graduate's Average Indebtedness
Arkansas—continued								
Harding University	ind.	$10,780	$ 5182	100%	24%	$ 8,687	$ 7,275	$21,183
Hendrix College	ind.	$21,636	$ 6010	100%	47%	$14,422	$13,224	$15,234
John Brown University	ind.	$14,434	$ 5324	92%	8%	$ 8,713	$11,045	$17,400
Lyon College	ind.	$13,905	$ 6085	100%	29%	$13,809	$ 6,181	$13,423
Ouachita Baptist University	ind.	$15,920	$ 5000	79%	39%	$11,306	$ 9,614	$11,131
Southern Arkansas University–Magnolia	pub.	$ 3858	$ 3600	87%	100%	$ 5,711	$ 1,747	$22,124
University of Arkansas at Fort Smith	pub.	$ 2280	NA	86%	11%	$ 5,372	—	$ 7339
University of Arkansas at Monticello	pub.	$ 3765	$ 3150	NR	NR	NR	NR	$13,599
University of Arkansas at Pine Bluff	pub.	$ 4044	$ 5436	100%	73%	$ 2,823	$ 6,657	NR
University of Arkansas for Medical Sciences	pub.	$ 3672	NR	NR	NR	NR	NR	$ 7000
University of the Ozarks	ind.	$13,312	$ 4880	100%	12%	$12,787	$ 5,405	$12,160
Williams Baptist College	ind.	$ 8600	$ 4000	91%	NR	$ 9,893	$ 2,707	$14,880
California								
Academy of Art University	ind.	$13,280	$12,000	53%	NR	$ 4,985	$20,295	$32,000
Alliant International University	ind.	$19,360	$ 7430	100%	38%	$21,250	$ 5,540	$17,125
Art Center College of Design	ind.	$25,044	NA	93%	NR	$11,619	$13,425	$60,000
Azusa Pacific University	ind.	$20,666	$ 6132	98%	69%	$17,672	$ 9,126	NR
Biola University	ind.	$22,702	$ 7100	84%	11%	$16,857	$12,945	$27,285
California Baptist University	ind.	$15,940	$ 6310	98%	18%	$ 8,300	$13,950	$19,700
California College of the Arts	ind.	$24,640	$ 8230	100%	9%	$16,271	$16,599	$31,295
California Institute of Technology	ind.	$25,551	$ 8013	100%	100%	$24,813	$ 8,751	$ 7400
California Institute of the Arts	ind.	$27,260	$ 7697	98%	9%	$22,935	$12,022	$30,674
California Lutheran University	ind.	$22,285	$ 7570	100%	18%	$17,020	$12,835	$17,568
California State University, Bakersfield	pub.	$ 2959	$ 5946	92%	11%	$ 6,672	$ 2,233	$ 4045
California State University, Chico	pub.	$ 3154	$ 7493	63%	10%	$ 6,032	$ 4,615	NR
California State University, Dominguez Hills	pub.	$ 2478	$ 5022†	94%	8%	$ 7,080	$ 420	$15,112
California State University, East Bay	pub.	$ 2706	$ 3705†	91%	9%	$ 7,412	—	$12,584
California State University, Fresno	pub.	$ 2704	$ 7073	71%	30%	$ 4,197	$ 5,580	$11,457
California State University, Fullerton	pub.	$ 2804	$ 4356†	85%	4%	$ 6,289	$ 871	$13,089
California State University, Sacramento	pub.	$ 3010	$ 6574	85%	4%	$ 8,191	$ 1,393	$17,305
California State University, San Bernardino	pub.	$ 3398	$ 5886	90%	9%	$ 6,614	$ 2,670	NR
California State University, San Marcos	pub.	$ 2786	$ 7470†	100%	NR	$ 5,481	$ 4,775	$12,850
California State University, Stanislaus	pub.	$ 2807	$ 6522	80%	3%	$ 7,036	$ 2,293	$14,500
Chapman University	ind.	$26,150	$10,000	75%	100%	$20,045	$16,105	$18,583
Christian Heritage College	ind.	$14,840	$ 5990	100%	72%	$12,356	$ 8,474	$16,000
Claremont McKenna College	ind.	$29,210	$ 9780	100%	100%	$25,761	$13,229	$10,769
Columbia College Hollywood	ind.	$12,500	$ 5850	62%	NR	$ 2,338	$16,012	$35,125
Concordia University	ind.	$19,930	$ 7050	99%	21%	$18,818	$ 8,162	$23,709
Dominican University of California	ind.	$24,454	$10,270	100%	18%	$19,393	$15,331	$ 7395
Fresno Pacific University	ind.	$18,728	$ 5600	100%	29%	$16,527	$ 7,801	$14,436
Harvey Mudd College	ind.	$30,237	$ 9845	97%	100%	$24,049	$16,033	$16,940
Holy Names University	ind.	$21,640	$ 7800	83%	10%	$18,995	$10,445	$16,652

NA = not applicable; NR = not reported; * = includes room and board; † = room only; — = not available.

College Costs At-a-Glance	Institutional Control ind.=independent; pub.=public	Tuition and Fees	Room and Board	Percent of Eligible Freshmen Receiving Need-Based Gift Awards	Percent of Freshmen Whose Need Was Fully Met	Average Financial Aid Package for Freshmen	Average Net Cost After Aid	2004 Graduate's Average Indebtedness
California—*continued*								
Humboldt State University	pub.	$ 2866	$ 7281	87%	30%	$ 8,550	$ 1,597	NR
Humphreys College	ind.	$ 7560	NR	4%	99%	$ 7,422	$ 138	$30,000
John F. Kennedy University	ind.	$14,436	NA	NR	NR	NR	NR	$23,000
Laguna College of Art & Design	ind.	$16,600	NA	86%	NR	$ 8,000	$ 8,600	$35,125
La Sierra University	ind.	$19,083	$ 5244	100%	22%	$16,480	$ 7,847	$25,277
Life Pacific College	ind.	$10,100	$ 5000	81%	2%	$ 2,997	$12,103	$17,125
Loyola Marymount University	ind.	$25,756	$ 9456	83%	22%	$19,138	$16,074	$21,164
Menlo College	ind.	$24,450	$ 9600	100%	12%	$18,055	$15,995	$20,598
Otis College of Art and Design	ind.	$25,100	NR	100%	NR	$12,517	$12,583	$32,156
Pacific Union College	ind.	$18,054	$ 5136	100%	38%	$14,503	$ 8,687	$14,000
Pepperdine University	ind.	$28,720	$ 8640	92%	44%	$27,105	$10,255	$29,148
Pitzer College	ind.	$31,438	$ 8222	97%	100%	$28,203	$11,457	$20,900
Pomona College	ind.	$28,370	$10,380	100%	100%	$26,700	$12,050	$15,600
Saint Mary's College of California	ind.	$25,150	$ 9530	97%	12%	$20,850	$13,830	$19,510
San Francisco State University	pub.	$ 3066	$ 8870	76%	21%	$ 8,377	$ 3,559	$16,088
Scripps College	ind.	$29,000	$ 9000	99%	100%	$26,411	$11,589	$12,076
Simpson University	ind.	$17,000	$ 5900	100%	64%	$10,998	$11,902	$17,600
Sonoma State University	pub.	$ 3408	$ 8805	59%	79%	$ 9,062	$ 3,151	$ 8775
Southern California Institute of Architecture	ind.	$18,446	NA	100%	NR	$ 8,867	$ 9,579	$33,000
Stanford University	ind.	$29,847	$ 9500	99%	95%	$26,893	$12,454	$15,590
Thomas Aquinas College	ind.	$18,600	$ 5800	91%	100%	$15,164	$ 9,236	$14,000
University of California, Berkeley	pub.	$ 6730	$11,630	94%	44%	$15,425	$ 2,935	$13,277
University of California, Davis	pub.	$ 6936	$10,234	96%	15%	$12,171	$ 4,999	$12,231
University of California, Irvine	pub.	$ 6313	$ 9176	86%	35%	$11,999	$ 3,490	$13,226
University of California, Los Angeles	pub.	$ 6576	$11,187	97%	48%	$14,143	$ 3,620	$13,894
University of California, Riverside	pub.	$ 6685	$ 9800	86%	52%	$13,876	$ 2,609	$14,119
University of California, San Diego	pub.	$ 6224	$ 8996	93%	27%	$13,310	$ 1,910	$14,535
University of California, Santa Barbara	pub.	$ 6495	$ 9897	95%	39%	$11,572	$ 4,820	NR
University of California, Santa Cruz	pub.	$ 7023	$10,947	87%	33%	$12,633	$ 5,337	$13,419
University of La Verne	ind.	$22,800	$ 9110	96%	15%	$21,985	$ 9,925	NR
University of Phoenix–Northern California Campus	ind.	$12,630	NA	100%	NR	$ 2,727	$ 9,903	NR
University of Phoenix–Sacramento Campus	ind.	$11,850	NA	89%	NR	$ 6,164	$ 5,686	NR
University of Phoenix–San Diego Campus	ind.	$11,370	NA	89%	NR	$ 5,761	$ 5,609	NR
University of Phoenix–Southern California Campus	ind.	$12,360	NA	88%	NR	$ 4,576	$ 7,784	NR
University of Redlands	ind.	$25,524	$ 8696	99%	47%	$23,508	$10,712	$23,946
University of San Diego	ind.	$26,856	$10,190	97%	58%	$20,708	$16,338	$26,665
University of San Francisco	ind.	$26,840	$10,240	82%	14%	$19,459	$17,621	$24,718
University of Southern California	ind.	$30,512	$ 8988	88%	95%	$27,377	$12,123	$18,968
University of the Pacific	ind.	$24,750	$ 7858	98%	31%	$20,347	$12,261	NR
Vanguard University of Southern California	ind.	$20,330	$ 6756	100%	62%	$ 9,700	$17,386	$21,244
Westmont College	ind.	$26,240	$ 8610	97%	11%	$16,706	$18,144	$19,969
Whittier College	ind.	$26,138	$ 7928	76%	50%	$26,518	$ 7,548	$22,104
Woodbury University	ind.	$21,314	$ 7702	99%	2%	$17,208	$11,808	NR

NA = not applicable; NR = not reported; * = includes room and board; † = room only; — = not available.

College Costs At-a-Glance	Institutional Control ind.=independent; pub.=public	Tuition and Fees	Room and Board	Percent of Eligible Freshmen Receiving Need-Based Gift Awards	Percent of Freshmen Whose Need Was Fully Met	Average Financial Aid Package for Freshmen	Average Net Cost After Aid	2004 Graduate's Average Indebtedness
Colorado								
The Art Institute of Colorado	ind.	$ 23,040	$ 5985†	NR	NR	NR	NR	$30,000
Colorado Christian University	ind.	$ 16,060	$ 6500	94%	11%	$ 9,981	$12,579	$18,633
The Colorado College	ind.	$ 28,644	$ 7216	99%	78%	$27,330	$ 8,530	$16,401
Colorado School of Mines	pub.	$ 7224	$ 6600	84%	78%	$13,300	$ 524	$17,500
Colorado State University	pub.	$ 3790	$ 5766	82%	39%	$ 6,485	$ 3,071	$16,312
Colorado State University-Pueblo	pub.	$ 3220	$ 5912	83%	6%	$ 5,385	$ 3,747	$17,149
Fort Lewis College	pub.	$ 3060	$ 5894	55%	19%	$ 6,206	$ 2,748	$14,100
Jones International University	ind.	$ 9407	NA	NR	NR	NR	NR	NR
Mesa State College	pub.	$ 2724	$ 6501	73%	19%	$ 5,739	$ 3,486	$16,522
Metropolitan State College of Denver	pub.	$ 2859	NA	78%	NR	$ 4,838	—	$10,366
Naropa University	ind.	$ 16,548	$ 7236	92%	12%	$15,239	$ 8,545	$20,768
Nazarene Bible College	ind.	$ 7340	NA	70%	NR	NR	NR	$19,141
Regis University	ind.	$ 22,400	$ 7870	99%	30%	$21,750	$ 8,520	$22,000
Rocky Mountain College of Art & Design	ind.	$ 16,490	$ 4200†	75%	36%	$ 3,694	$16,996	NR
University of Colorado at Boulder	pub.	$ 4341	$ 7564	58%	51%	$ 7,187	$ 4,718	$16,348
University of Colorado at Colorado Springs	pub.	$ 4106	$ 6729	77%	10%	$ 5,574	$ 5,261	$12,694
University of Colorado at Denver and Health Sciences Center—Downtown Denver Campus	pub.	$ 4457	NA	80%	13%	$ 5,318	—	$16,315
University of Colorado at Denver and Health Sciences Center—Health Sciences Program	pub.	$ 6560	NA	NR	NR	NR	NR	$21,592
University of Denver	ind.	$ 26,610	$ 8363	98%	15%	$19,204	$15,769	$20,551
University of Northern Colorado	pub.	$ 3370	$ 5954	44%	46%	$ 7,079	$ 2,245	NR
University of Phoenix–Denver Campus	ind.	$ 9000	NA	100%	NR	$ 7,815	$ 1,185	NR
University of Phoenix–Southern Colorado Campus	ind.	$ 9000	NA	100%	NR	$ 5,593	$ 3,407	NR
Western State College of Colorado	pub.	$ 2761	$ 6705	60%	15%	$ 6,625	$ 2,841	$15,000
Connecticut								
Central Connecticut State University	pub.	$ 5902	$ 7036	73%	6%	$ 6,537	$ 6,401	$10,500
Connecticut College	ind.	$39,975*	NR	92%	100%	$26,077	$13,898	$21,012
Fairfield University	ind.	$ 28,415	$ 9270	88%	24%	$15,823	$21,862	$24,251
Lyme Academy College of Fine Arts	ind.	$ 16,916	NA	NR	NR	$ 8,400	$ 8,516	NR
Mitchell College	ind.	$ 20,705	$ 9330	100%	NR	$13,783	$16,252	NR
Post University	ind.	$ 18,800	$ 7950	100%	NR	$11,405	$15,345	$17,500
Quinnipiac University	ind.	$ 24,340	$10,300	98%	11%	$13,019	$21,621	$20,269
Saint Joseph College	ind.	$ 21,970	$ 9225	100%	27%	$18,123	$13,072	$14,859
Southern Connecticut State University	pub.	$ 5814	$ 7698	79%	25%	$ 7,318	$ 6,194	NR
Trinity College	ind.	$ 31,940	$ 8260	93%	100%	$23,890	$16,310	$16,100
University of Bridgeport	ind.	$ 20,595	$ 9000	98%	NR	$20,204	$ 9,391	NR
University of Connecticut	pub.	$ 7912	$ 7848	73%	25%	$ 8,604	$ 7,156	$18,045
University of Hartford	ind.	$ 23,480	$ 8996	83%	26%	$17,211	$15,265	$24,878
University of New Haven	ind.	$ 22,982	$ 9550	96%	29%	$16,794	$15,738	$29,200
Wesleyan University	ind.	$ 31,670	$ 8474	95%	100%	$27,948	$12,196	$21,320
Western Connecticut State University	pub.	$ 5661	$ 6582	76%	33%	$ 6,517	$ 5,726	$ 6005
Yale University	ind.	$ 29,820	$ 9030	99%	100%	$26,995	$11,855	$16,911

NA = not applicable; NR = not reported; * = includes room and board; † = room only; — = not available.

College Costs At-a-Glance

	Institutional Control ind.=independent; pub.=public	Tuition and Fees	Room and Board	Percent of Eligible Freshmen Receiving Need-Based Gift Awards	Percent of Freshmen Whose Need Was Fully Met	Average Financial Aid Package for Freshmen	Average Net Cost After Aid	2004 Graduate's Average Indebtedness
Delaware								
Delaware State University	pub.	$ 4976	$ 6816	67%	32%	$ 6,368	$ 5,424	NR
Goldey-Beacom College	ind.	$13,736	$ 4240†	NR	NR	NR	NR	NR
University of Delaware	pub.	$ 6954	$ 6458	81%	45%	$ 9,800	$ 3,612	$14,639
Wesley College	ind.	$15,379	$ 6960	78%	NR	$14,000	$ 8,339	$11,500
Wilmington College	ind.	$ 7340	NA	72%	NR	$ 4,409	$ 2,931	$17,486
District of Columbia								
American University	ind.	$26,307	$10,260	77%	49%	$25,029	$11,538	$19,796
The Catholic University of America	ind.	$26,000	$ 9838	48%	38%	$15,073	$20,765	NR
Corcoran College of Art and Design	ind.	$21,300	$ 9800	69%	1%	$11,322	$19,778	$28,247
Gallaudet University	ind.	$11,255	$ 8420	99%	40%	$14,561	$ 5,114	$10,210
Georgetown University	ind.	$30,163	$10,554	95%	100%	$22,939	$17,778	$22,906
The George Washington University	ind.	$34,030	$10,210	97%	82%	$28,229	$16,011	$25,943
Howard University	ind.	$11,645	$ 5870	56%	67%	$16,042	$ 1,473	$11,288
Trinity (Washington) University	ind.	$17,360	$ 7574	100%	12%	$15,793	$ 9,141	$29,875
University of the District of Columbia	pub.	$ 2070	NA	46%	35%	$ 4,821	—	$16,270
Florida								
The Baptist College of Florida	ind.	$ 6660	$ 3348	90%	7%	$ 4,495	$ 5,513	$12,824
Barry University	ind.	$22,430	$ 7620	90%	9%	$18,727	$11,323	$23,322
Bethune-Cookman College	ind.	$10,610	$ 6374	79%	29%	$10,740	$ 6,244	$25,880
Clearwater Christian College	ind.	$10,850	$ 4820	49%	1%	$ 6,320	$ 9,350	$ 8500
Eckerd College	ind.	$24,362	$ 6326	100%	27%	$19,716	$10,972	$ 9448
Embry-Riddle Aeronautical University	ind.	$23,500	$ 6936	95%	NR	$ 7,276	$23,160	$43,053
Embry-Riddle Aeronautical University, Extended Campus	ind.	$ 4224	NR	63%	NR	$ 1,769	$ 2,455	$14,108
Flagler College	ind.	$ 8600	$ 5190	50%	19%	$10,122	$ 3,668	$15,012
Florida Atlantic University	pub.	$ 3092	$ 7100	92%	17%	$ 6,657	$ 3,535	NR
Florida College	ind.	$10,310	$ 5240	74%	4%	$ 6,078	$ 9,472	$ 3259
Florida Gulf Coast University	pub.	$ 3151	$ 8500	62%	16%	$ 6,038	$ 5,613	$13,472
Florida Institute of Technology	ind.	$23,730	$ 6220	86%	31%	$20,438	$ 9,512	$26,764
Florida Metropolitan University–Pinellas Campus	ind.	$11,430	NA	100%	NR	$ 6,675	$ 4,755	$26,000
Florida Metropolitan University–Tampa Campus	ind.	$ 9900	NA	96%	71%	$ 5,000	$ 4,900	$12,000
Florida Southern College	ind.	$18,240	$ 6410	93%	43%	$17,056	$ 7,594	$16,703
Florida State University	pub.	$ 3038	$ 7208	72%	23%	$ 6,884	$ 3,362	$16,647
International College	ind.	$ 9020	NA	93%	10%	$ 6,500	$ 2,520	$19,500
Lynn University	ind.	$25,850	$ 9100	97%	36%	$19,301	$15,649	$21,852
New College of Florida	pub.	$ 3483	$ 5965	100%	57%	$10,983	—	$15,045
Northwood University, Florida Campus	ind.	$15,183	$ 7257	85%	18%	$12,200	$10,240	$19,968
Nova Southeastern University	ind.	$15,820	$ 8126	98%	6%	$15,923	$ 8,023	$26,658
Palm Beach Atlantic University	ind.	$17,342	$ 6306	55%	26%	$11,322	$12,326	$18,627
Ringling School of Art and Design	ind.	$20,195	$ 8811	79%	6%	$ 8,038	$20,968	$26,099
Rollins College	ind.	$27,700	$ 8570	96%	40%	$23,737	$12,533	$14,018
Saint Leo University	ind.	$14,080	$ 7260	100%	33%	$14,259	$ 7,081	$15,714
St. Thomas University	ind.	$17,010	$10,720	86%	NR	$13,670	$14,060	$12,000

NA = not applicable; NR = not reported; * = includes room and board; † = room only; — = not available.

College Costs At-a-Glance

	Institutional Control ind.=independent; pub.=public	Tuition and Fees	Room and Board	Percent of Eligible Freshmen Receiving Need-Based Gift Awards	Percent of Freshmen Whose Need Was Fully Met	Average Financial Aid Package for Freshmen	Average Net Cost After Aid	2004 Graduate's Average Indebtedness
Florida—*continued*								
Southeastern College of the Assemblies of God	ind.	$10,140	$5470	91%	9%	$ 6,212	$ 9,398	$18,480
Stetson University	ind.	$24,135	$7060	100%	36%	$21,857	$ 9,338	$21,500
Trinity College of Florida	ind.	$ 7860	$4670	91%	50%	$ 6,900	$ 5,630	NR
University of Central Florida	pub.	$ 3180	$7232	32%	54%	$ 4,642	$ 5,770	$12,780
University of Florida	pub.	$ 2955	$6040	59%	34%	$ 8,995	—	NR
University of Miami	ind.	$27,840	$8602	98%	31%	$22,858	$13,584	$31,723
University of North Florida	pub.	$ 3101	$6278	40%	19%	$ 2,006	$ 7,373	$12,698
University of Phoenix–Fort Lauderdale Campus	ind.	$10,170	NA	80%	NR	$ 3,351	$ 6,819	NR
University of Phoenix–Jacksonville Campus	ind.	$10,170	NA	100%	NR	$ 5,123	$ 5,047	NR
University of Phoenix–Orlando Campus	ind.	$10,170	NA	100%	NR	$ 1,739	$ 8,431	NR
University of Phoenix–Tampa Campus	ind.	$10,170	NA	100%	NR	$ 4,966	$ 5,204	NR
University of South Florida	pub.	$ 3164	$6730	57%	7%	$ 7,268	$ 2,626	$17,304
The University of Tampa	ind.	$18,172	$6666	97%	36%	$15,008	$ 9,830	$24,402
University of West Florida	pub.	$ 3039	$6294	NR	NR	NR	NR	NR
Warner Southern College	ind.	$11,990	$5160	71%	NR	$19,722	—	$ 6846
Webber International University	ind.	$12,900	$4510	100%	19%	$10,851	$ 6,559	$16,051
Georgia								
Agnes Scott College	ind.	$22,210	$8200	98%	75%	$23,731	$ 6,679	$22,314
Armstrong Atlantic State University	pub.	$ 2734	$4500†	54%	90%	$ 5,787	$ 1,447	$11,000
Atlanta College of Art	ind.	$17,500	$5100†	98%	8%	$11,887	$10,713	$24,256
Augusta State University	pub.	$ 2702	NA	74%	2%	$ 783	$ 1,919	NR
Berry College	ind.	$16,240	$6450	100%	28%	$14,516	$ 8,174	$12,000
Beulah Heights Bible College	ind.	$ 4520	$2000†	89%	NR	$ 5,596	$ 924	$25,000
Brenau University	ind.	$14,710	$8060	100%	31%	$16,937	$ 5,833	$17,590
Brewton-Parker College	ind.	$12,600	$5200	100%	13%	$ 8,479	$ 9,321	$19,230
Clark Atlanta University	ind.	$13,486	$6816	68%	47%	$14,103	$ 6,199	$17,751
Clayton College & State University	pub.	$ 2802	NA	63%	9%	$ 2,372	$ 430	$16,156
Columbus State University	pub.	$ 2808	$5550	100%	63%	$ 3,891	$ 4,467	NR
Emory University	ind.	$29,322	$9650	92%	100%	$25,210	$13,762	$19,437
Georgia College & State University	pub.	$ 3862	$6482	33%	NR	NR	NR	$15,286
Georgia Institute of Technology	pub.	$ 4278	$6526	58%	53%	$ 8,830	$ 1,974	$16,154
Georgia Southern University	pub.	$ 3062	$6000	96%	26%	$ 6,267	$ 2,795	$17,536
Georgia State University	pub.	$ 4464	$7368	99%	21%	$ 6,788	$ 5,044	$15,419
Kennesaw State University	pub.	$ 2758	$5376†	48%	11%	$ 7,892	$ 242	$13,898
LaGrange College	ind.	$15,206	$6318	99%	36%	$13,962	$ 7,562	$15,499
Life University	ind.	$ 5496	NR	61%	29%	$ 6,500	—	$13,000
Luther Rice Bible College and Seminary	ind.	$ 3964	NA	90%	100%	$ 7,220	—	$12,551
Medical College of Georgia	pub.	$ 3954	$2334†	NR	NR	NR	NR	$20,453
Mercer University	ind.	$22,050	$7060	99%	57%	$22,387	$ 6,723	$13,974
Morehouse College	ind.	$15,740	$8748	42%	2%	$11,054	$13,434	$18,000
Oglethorpe University	ind.	$22,300	$8000	100%	66%	$23,190	$ 7,110	$16,273
Piedmont College	ind.	$13,500	$4700	88%	61%	$10,446	$ 7,754	$15,537

NA = not applicable; NR = not reported; * = includes room and board; † = room only; — = not available.

College Costs At-a-Glance

	Institutional Control ind.=independent; pub.=public	Tuition and Fees	Room and Board	Percent of Eligible Freshmen Receiving Need-Based Gift Awards	Percent of Freshmen Whose Need Was Fully Met	Average Financial Aid Package for Freshmen	Average Net Cost After Aid	2004 Graduate's Average Indebtedness
Georgia—*continued*								
Reinhardt College	ind.	$12,200	$5762	NR	NR	NR	NR	NR
Savannah College of Art and Design	ind.	$22,100	$8700	28%	41%	$ 7,900	$22,900	$20,000
Shorter College	ind.	$12,770	$5900	100%	26%	$10,104	$ 8,566	$10,516
Southern Polytechnic State University	pub.	$ 2892	$4946	60%	22%	$ 2,209	$ 5,629	$ 4063
South University	ind.	$11,085	NA	81%	47%	NR	NR	NR
Spelman College	ind.	$15,945	$8455	66%	5%	$ 5,663	$18,737	$16,700
Thomas University	ind.	$10,720	$2400†	55%	25%	$ 4,823	$ 8,297	$12,000
Toccoa Falls College	ind.	$12,050	$4600	77%	16%	$ 8,967	$ 7,683	$17,145
University of Georgia	pub.	$ 4628	$6376	95%	40%	$ 6,628	$ 4,376	$13,209
University of Phoenix–Atlanta Campus	ind.	$10,830	NA	100%	NR	$ 2,834	$ 7,996	NR
University of West Georgia	pub.	$ 2906	$4550	94%	28%	$ 6,868	$ 588	$12,249
Valdosta State University	pub.	$ 2992	$5208	56%	84%	$ 7,932	$ 268	$17,595
Hawaii								
Brigham Young University–Hawaii	ind.	$ 2660	$4800	85%	71%	$ 2,400	$ 5,060	$ 8400
Chaminade University of Honolulu	ind.	$14,330	$8870	99%	13%	$11,862	$11,338	$29,770
Hawai'i Pacific University	ind.	$11,002	$9020	51%	18%	$10,015	$10,007	$18,786
University of Hawaii at Hilo	pub.	$ 2604	$5374	61%	16%	$ 4,373	$ 3,605	$11,210
University of Hawaii at Manoa	pub.	$ 3504	$5942	81%	26%	$ 5,099	$ 4,347	$ 5379
University of Phoenix–Hawaii Campus	ind.	$10,650	NA	100%	NR	$ 6,297	$ 4,353	NR
Idaho								
Albertson College of Idaho	ind.	$15,890	$6475	71%	16%	$13,407	$ 8,958	$26,340
Boise State University	pub.	$ 3520	$5384	69%	18%	$ 7,029	$ 1,875	$17,200
Idaho State University	pub.	$ 3700	$4850	67%	12%	$ 4,653	$ 3,897	$29,467
Lewis-Clark State College	pub.	$ 3392	$3995	72%	8%	$ 3,900	$ 3,487	NR
Northwest Nazarene University	ind.	$17,730	$4860	73%	21%	$13,238	$ 9,352	$20,923
University of Idaho	pub.	$ 3632	$5034	67%	32%	$ 7,983	$ 683	$20,112
University of Phoenix–Idaho Campus	ind.	$ 9450	NA	NR	NR	NR	NR	NR
Illinois								
Aurora University	ind.	$15,600	$6840	66%	37%	$16,476	$ 5,964	$17,805
Benedictine University	ind.	$18,310	$6290	55%	43%	$11,385	$13,215	$ 6727
Blessing-Rieman College of Nursing	ind.	$14,250	$5775	NR	NR	NR	NR	$11,000
Bradley University	ind.	$17,730	$6150	99%	48%	$14,062	$ 9,818	$15,941
Columbia College Chicago	ind.	$15,998	$9300	NR	NR	NR	NR	NR
DePaul University	ind.	$19,765	$9307	83%	17%	$16,537	$12,535	$17,500
Dominican University	ind.	$19,000	$5890	100%	44%	$13,549	$11,341	$16,453
Eastern Illinois University	pub.	$ 5782	$7150	43%	75%	$ 8,527	$ 4,405	$14,836
Elmhurst College	ind.	$20,090	$6304	91%	22%	$18,159	$ 8,235	$15,986
Eureka College	ind.	$13,400	$5880	97%	54%	$12,214	$ 7,066	$13,227
Greenville College	ind.	$16,824	$5760	100%	10%	$14,519	$ 8,065	$17,896
Illinois College	ind.	$14,600	$6200	87%	28%	$14,224	$ 6,576	$12,038
Illinois State University	pub.	$ 6328	$5576	66%	41%	$ 7,684	$ 4,220	$14,620
Illinois Wesleyan University	ind.	$27,624	$6426	99%	49%	$18,812	$15,238	$22,603

NA = not applicable; NR = not reported; * = includes room and board; † = room only; — = not available.

College Costs At-a-Glance	Institutional Control ind.=independent; pub.=public	Tuition and Fees	Room and Board	Percent of Eligible Freshmen Receiving Need-Based Gift Awards	Percent of Freshmen Whose Need Was Fully Met	Average Financial Aid Package for Freshmen	Average Net Cost After Aid	2004 Graduate's Average Indebtedness
Illinois—continued								
Knox College	ind.	$25,236	$6102	100%	44%	$20,904	$10,434	$20,975
Lake Forest College	ind.	$25,828	$6222	100%	100%	$22,093	$ 9,957	$16,741
Lexington College	ind.	$15,337	NA	10%	NR	$13,507	$ 1,830	$ 3500
Lincoln Christian College	ind.	$10,000	$4750	NR	NR	$ 7,500	$ 7,250	$16,333
Loyola University Chicago	ind.	$23,836	$9060	91%	6%	$15,997	$16,899	$18,575
MacMurray College	ind.	$14,600	$5620	100%	11%	$11,539	$ 8,681	$17,477
McKendree College	ind.	$16,600	$6360	100%	26%	$15,024	$ 7,936	$16,240
North Central College	ind.	$20,400	$6747	100%	52%	$20,112	$ 7,035	$13,527
Northeastern Illinois University	pub.	$ 4235	NA	92%	6%	$ 5,324	—	$10,941
Northern Illinois University	pub.	$ 5760	$5740	66%	42%	$ 8,636	$ 2,864	$15,052
Northwestern University	ind.	$31,789	$9873	96%	100%	$24,897	$16,765	$15,136
Olivet Nazarene University	ind.	$16,490	$6100	100%	31%	$12,054	$10,536	$19,189
Principia College	ind.	$20,415	$7350	86%	59%	$18,251	$ 9,514	$11,936
Quincy University	ind.	$18,330	$6590	100%	30%	$15,162	$ 9,758	$16,837
Robert Morris College	ind.	$14,250	$6390	98%	3%	$10,085	$10,555	$16,666
St. Augustine College	ind.	$ 7128	NA	99%	NR	NR	NR	NR
Saint Francis Medical Center College of Nursing	ind.	$10,778	$1880†	NR	NR	NR	NR	$12,363
St. John's College	ind.	$ 9786	NA	NR	NR	NR	NR	NR
Saint Xavier University	ind.	$17,330	$6724	100%	21%	$16,522	$ 7,532	$19,134
School of the Art Institute of Chicago	ind.	$27,150	$8200†	93%	NR	$17,877	$17,473	$26,011
Shimer College	ind.	$17,645	$2900	NR	NR	NR	NR	NR
Southern Illinois University Carbondale	pub.	$ 6341	$5200	80%	78%	$ 7,363	$ 4,178	$13,712
Southern Illinois University Edwardsville	pub.	$ 5179	$5819	76%	23%	$ 7,418	$ 3,580	$16,606
Trinity International University	ind.	$18,150	$6080	67%	7%	$14,291	$ 9,939	$16,500
University of Illinois at Chicago	pub.	$ 8502	$7160	80%	54%	$11,550	$ 4,112	$17,000
University of Illinois at Springfield	pub.	$ 4962	$2878†	35%	66%	$ 7,123	$ 717	$11,049
University of Illinois at Urbana–Champaign	pub.	$ 8553	$6710	61%	54%	$16,848	—	$15,100
University of Phoenix–Chicago Campus	ind.	$10,350	NA	100%	NR	$ 2,113	$ 8,237	NR
University of St. Francis	ind.	$17,670	$6180	100%	87%	$14,891	$ 8,959	$15,199
VanderCook College of Music	ind.	$16,610	$7200	NR	NR	NR	NR	$18,500
Western Illinois University	pub.	$ 6183	$5768	68%	32%	$ 6,168	$ 5,783	$13,900
Wheaton College	ind.	$20,000	$6466	79%	20%	$18,243	$ 8,223	$17,382
Indiana								
Anderson University	ind.	$18,900	$6150	100%	44%	$18,071	$ 6,979	$21,500
Ball State University	pub.	$ 6260	$6228	69%	29%	$ 6,924	$ 5,564	$17,156
Butler University	ind.	$22,484	$7780	99%	19%	$17,954	$12,310	NR
DePauw University	ind.	$25,500	$7300	100%	86%	$24,120	$ 8,680	$17,486
Franklin College	ind.	$18,275	$5500	100%	23%	$12,549	$11,226	$26,094
Goshen College	ind.	$19,300	$6450	100%	66%	$17,302	$ 8,448	$17,126
Grace College	ind.	$15,030	$6150	99%	24%	$12,376	$ 8,804	$25,338
Hanover College	ind.	$20,600	$6200	100%	46%	$15,126	$11,674	$14,932
Huntington University	ind.	$18,490	$6340	95%	21%	$14,817	$10,013	$16,489

NA = not applicable; NR = not reported; * = includes room and board; † = room only; — = not available.

College Costs At-a-Glance	Institutional Control ind.=independent; pub.=public	Tuition and Fees	Room and Board	Percent of Eligible Freshmen Receiving Need-Based Gift Awards	Percent of Freshmen Whose Need Was Fully Met	Average Financial Aid Package for Freshmen	Average Net Cost After Aid	2004 Graduate's Average Indebtedness
Indiana—*continued*								
Indiana State University	pub.	$ 5640	$5615	59%	13%	$ 5,906	$ 5,349	$19,317
Indiana University Bloomington	pub.	$ 6777	$6006	33%	4%	$ 5,804	$ 6,979	$18,806
Indiana University East	pub.	$ 4601	NA	71%	3%	$ 4,918	—	$24,722
Indiana University Kokomo	pub.	$ 4632	NA	61%	2%	$ 4,105	$ 527	$14,607
Indiana University Northwest	pub.	$ 4707	NA	69%	16%	$ 5,997	—	$18,338
Indiana University–Purdue University Fort Wayne	pub.	$ 5312	NA	68%	5%	$ 5,176	$ 136	$15,867
Indiana University–Purdue University Indianapolis	pub.	$ 5930	$2656†	50%	3%	$ 5,970	$ 2,616	$24,556
Indiana University South Bend	pub.	$ 4755	NA	66%	4%	$ 4,544	$ 211	$20,227
Indiana University Southeast	pub.	$ 4673	NA	57%	5%	$ 4,472	$ 201	$16,597
Manchester College	ind.	$19,360	$6910	100%	48%	$17,874	$ 8,396	$14,180
Martin University	ind.	$11,420	NA	95%	10%	$ 7,346	$ 4,074	$27,193
Oakland City University	ind.	$13,560	$5030	NR	NR	NR	NR	NR
Purdue University	pub.	$ 6335	$7406	35%	31%	$ 9,990	$ 3,751	$17,510
Purdue University Calumet	pub.	$ 4662	$3990†	76%	1%	$ 3,211	$ 5,441	$18,940
Rose-Hulman Institute of Technology	ind.	$26,136	$7065	99%	12%	$17,842	$15,359	$27,745
Saint Joseph's College	ind.	$19,160	$6300	80%	40%	$13,400	$12,060	$18,500
Taylor University	ind.	$20,746	$5630	97%	23%	$14,337	$12,039	$16,014
Taylor University Fort Wayne	ind.	$17,714	$4960	99%	35%	$15,432	$ 7,242	$13,562
Tri-State University	ind.	$20,200	$6000	58%	89%	$18,596	$ 7,604	$15,240
University of Evansville	ind.	$20,515	$6010	97%	28%	$18,883	$ 7,642	$21,512
University of Indianapolis	ind.	$17,200	$6150	87%	27%	$14,673	$ 8,677	$21,200
University of Notre Dame	ind.	$29,512	$7418	97%	84%	$24,700	$12,230	$25,986
University of Saint Francis	ind.	$16,460	$5450	100%	30%	$12,856	$ 9,054	$20,005
University of Southern Indiana	pub.	$ 4077	$5480	77%	12%	$ 5,093	$ 4,464	$14,552
Valparaiso University	ind.	$21,700	$5840	100%	65%	$19,777	$ 7,763	$21,798
Wabash College	ind.	$22,274	$7050	99%	100%	$21,453	$ 7,871	$16,004
Iowa								
Allen College	ind.	$11,276	$5164	92%	NR	$ 1,850	$14,590	$18,030
Buena Vista University	ind.	$20,854	$5822	100%	20%	$19,482	$ 7,194	$24,705
Central College	ind.	$18,892	$6486	100%	45%	$15,675	$ 9,703	$26,257
Clarke College	ind.	$17,960	$6289	100%	23%	$16,917	$ 7,332	$18,641
Coe College	ind.	$22,650	$5950	99%	24%	$20,392	$ 8,208	$23,159
Cornell College	ind.	$22,650	$6240	100%	55%	$19,045	$ 9,845	$17,270
Dordt College	ind.	$16,670	$4650	100%	13%	$15,772	$ 5,548	$16,010
Drake University	ind.	$20,550	$5920	98%	36%	$17,695	$ 8,775	$24,400
Emmaus Bible College	ind.	$ 7812	$3580	100%	NR	$ 3,500	$ 7,892	$15,890
Faith Baptist Bible College and Theological Seminary	ind.	$10,930	$4210	73%	9%	$ 6,031	$ 9,109	$13,050
Graceland University	ind.	$16,150	$5400	100%	34%	$15,972	$ 5,578	$21,766
Grand View College	ind.	$15,392	$5436	100%	15%	$12,883	$ 7,945	$21,245
Grinnell College	ind.	$25,820	$6870	96%	100%	$22,639	$10,051	$16,496
Iowa State University of Science and Technology	pub.	$ 5426	$5958	83%	56%	$ 7,444	$ 3,940	$27,324
Iowa Wesleyan College	ind.	$16,070	$4920	96%	6%	$12,478	$ 8,512	$14,428

NA = not applicable; NR = not reported; * = includes room and board; † = room only; — = not available.

College Costs At-a-Glance	Institutional Control ind.=independent; pub.=public	Tuition and Fees	Room and Board	Percent of Eligible Freshmen Receiving Need-Based Gift Awards	Percent of Freshmen Whose Need Was Fully Met	Average Financial Aid Package for Freshmen	Average Net Cost After Aid	2004 Graduate's Average Indebtedness
Iowa—*continued*								
Loras College	ind.	$19,678	$5845	84%	32%	$17,631	$ 7,892	$21,913
Luther College	ind.	$23,070	$4170	100%	68%	$18,496	$ 8,744	$17,209
Maharishi University of Management	ind.	$24,430	$6000	100%	29%	NR	NR	$22,133
Mercy College of Health Sciences	ind.	$11,300	NR	68%	NR	$ 7,615	$ 3,685	$17,567
Morningside College	ind.	$17,170	$5400	87%	56%	$17,655	$ 4,915	$25,677
Mount Mercy College	ind.	$18,840	$5680	100%	46%	$15,046	$ 9,474	$19,930
Northwestern College	ind.	$16,360	$4656	84%	49%	$14,798	$ 6,218	$19,523
Palmer College of Chiropractic	ind.	$ 5895	NA	86%	48%	$15,420	—	$14,013
St. Ambrose University	ind.	$17,565	$6635	58%	29%	$14,468	$ 9,732	$28,075
Simpson College	ind.	$19,635	$5561	100%	21%	$18,739	$ 6,457	$23,558
University of Dubuque	ind.	$16,845	$5700	97%	54%	$17,697	$ 4,848	$26,500
University of Northern Iowa	pub.	$ 5387	$5261	63%	20%	$ 5,953	$ 4,695	$18,397
Waldorf College	ind.	$14,200	$4400	100%	19%	$12,597	$ 6,003	$15,873
Wartburg College	ind.	$19,700	$5515	100%	69%	$18,541	$ 6,674	$28,129
William Penn University	ind.	$14,604	$4746	NR	NR	NR	NR	$19,875
Kansas								
Baker University	ind.	$15,550	$5450	NR	NR	NR	NR	$18,958
Benedictine College	ind.	$15,126	$6128	85%	16%	$14,780	$ 6,474	$21,329
Bethany College	ind.	$15,460	$5200	89%	31%	$15,277	$ 5,383	$15,167
Bethel College	ind.	$15,450	$6100	77%	33%	$15,152	$ 6,398	$17,482
Central Christian College of Kansas	ind.	$13,600	$4500	68%	NR	$10,631	$ 7,469	$20,000
Emporia State University	pub.	$ 3036	$4474	71%	32%	$ 4,352	$ 3,158	$13,217
Fort Hays State University	pub.	$ 3217	$5061	93%	29%	$ 5,180	$ 3,098	$15,061
Friends University	ind.	$14,600	NR	92%	13%	$ 8,788	$ 5,812	$16,204
Kansas State University	pub.	$ 4665	$5738	72%	11%	$ 5,562	$ 4,841	$18,000
Manhattan Christian College	ind.	$ 9638	$5590	100%	17%	$ 9,334	$ 5,894	$12,046
McPherson College	ind.	$15,160	$5850	92%	28%	$16,230	$ 4,780	$16,015
MidAmerica Nazarene University	ind.	$14,780	$5790	97%	7%	$10,216	$10,354	$17,421
Pittsburg State University	pub.	$ 3294	$4234	88%	13%	$ 5,988	$ 1,540	$10,348
Southwestern College	ind.	$16,118	$2334†	100%	25%	$15,344	$ 3,108	$17,907
Sterling College	ind.	$13,907	$5789	97%	39%	$15,803	$ 3,893	$ 9647
Tabor College	ind.	$15,060	$5410	96%	15%	$14,608	$ 5,862	$20,077
University of Kansas	pub.	$ 4737	$5216	85%	23%	$ 5,523	$ 4,430	$16,945
Wichita State University	pub.	$ 3908	$4900	50%	6%	$ 6,305	$ 2,503	$18,510
Kentucky								
Alice Lloyd College	ind.	$ 1090	$3600	100%	29%	$ 8,433	—	$ 6034
Asbury College	ind.	$17,808	$4498	100%	27%	$13,644	$ 8,662	$18,972
Berea College	ind.	$ 516	$4748	100%	41%	$25,658	—	$ 6436
Campbellsville University	ind.	$13,952	$5440	100%	22%	$12,225	$ 7,167	$ 5300
Centre College	ind.	$21,800	$7300	99%	49%	$18,696	$10,404	$14,300
Clear Creek Baptist Bible College	ind.	$ 4520	$3310	100%	NR	$ 6,052	$ 1,778	NR
Georgetown College	ind.	$19,170	$5780	91%	42%	$16,354	$ 8,596	$16,272

NA = not applicable; NR = not reported; * = includes room and board; † = room only; — = not available.

College Costs At-a-Glance	Institutional Control ind.=independent; pub.=public	Tuition and Fees	Room and Board	Percent of Eligible Freshmen Receiving Need-Based Gift Awards	Percent of Freshmen Whose Need Was Fully Met	Average Financial Aid Package for Freshmen	Average Net Cost After Aid	2004 Graduate's Average Indebtedness
Kentucky—*continued*								
Kentucky Christian University	ind.	$ 10,640	$4355	73%	17%	$10,113	$ 4,882	$23,580
Kentucky Mountain Bible College	ind.	$ 5260	$3200	89%	NR	$ 2,000	$ 6,460	$ 2000
Kentucky Wesleyan College	ind.	$ 12,990	$5600	100%	25%	$11,171	$ 7,419	$17,929
Mid-Continent University	ind.	$ 9350	$5485	92%	17%	$ 5,496	$ 9,339	$ 6738
Midway College	ind.	$ 12,750	$5800	96%	31%	$10,789	$ 7,761	$15,026
Morehead State University	pub.	$ 3840	$4410	75%	35%	$ 6,464	$ 1,786	$14,972
Murray State University	pub.	$ 3984	$4510	75%	94%	$ 4,591	$ 3,903	$14,488
Northern Kentucky University	pub.	$ 4368	$4660	60%	NR	$ 5,624	$ 3,404	$18,758
Pikeville College	ind.	$ 10,500	$5000	91%	70%	$13,107	$ 2,393	$14,012
Thomas More College	ind.	$ 18,320	$6100	93%	100%	$16,376	$ 8,044	$23,318
Transylvania University	ind.	$ 19,650	$6590	100%	23%	$16,510	$ 9,730	$15,874
Union College	ind.	$ 13,750	$4400	99%	23%	$10,993	$ 7,157	$11,253
University of Louisville	pub.	$ 5532	$6036	95%	17%	$ 8,235	$ 3,333	$14,721
University of the Cumberlands	ind.	$ 12,658	$5526	73%	54%	$13,864	$ 4,320	$14,455
Western Kentucky University	pub.	$ 5391	$4778	62%	31%	$ 6,308	$ 3,861	$12,250
Louisiana								
Centenary College of Louisiana	ind.	$ 17,360	$6070	100%	43%	$13,863	$ 9,567	$17,360
Dillard University	ind.	$ 11,550	$6840	58%	100%	$13,771	$ 4,619	$26,000
Grambling State University	pub.	$ 3506	$4034	85%	4%	$ 5,900	$ 1,640	$30,000
Louisiana State University and Agricultural and Mechanical College	pub.	$ 4226	$5882	96%	18%	$ 5,389	$ 4,719	$18,352
Louisiana Tech University	pub.	$ 4375	$4035	91%	18%	$ 5,225	$ 3,185	$16,641
Loyola University New Orleans	ind.	$ 25,246	$8312	100%	43%	$19,284	$14,274	$18,543
Nicholls State University	pub.	$ 3240	$3534	86%	16%	$ 4,911	$ 1,863	NR
Northwestern State University of Louisiana	pub.	$ 3241	$3426	86%	NR	$ 4,536	$ 2,131	$13,606
Our Lady of the Lake College	ind.	$ 7280	NA	NR	NR	NR	NR	$30,000
Southeastern Louisiana University	pub.	$ 3191	$4290	55%	NR	$ 4,005	$ 3,476	$12,527
Southern University and Agricultural and Mechanical College	pub.	$ 3440	$4310	90%	9%	$ 6,792	$ 958	$23,000
University of New Orleans	pub.	$ 3492	$4122†	66%	11%	$ 5,331	$ 2,283	$22,272
University of Phoenix–Louisiana Campus	ind.	$ 9330	NA	100%	NR	$ 6,279	$ 3,051	NR
Xavier University of Louisiana	ind.	$ 12,200	$7100	NR	1%	$ 3,921	$15,379	$20,083
Maine								
Bates College	ind.	$39,900*	NR	99%	96%	$25,317	$14,583	$13,986
Bowdoin College	ind.	$ 31,626	$8054	100%	100%	$27,769	$11,911	$14,474
Colby College	ind.	$39,800*	NR	96%	100%	$25,210	$14,590	$18,627
College of the Atlantic	ind.	$ 25,245	$6732	97%	97%	$24,776	$ 7,201	$16,710
Husson College	ind.	$ 11,050	$5850	96%	31%	$ 7,317	$ 9,583	$17,125
Maine College of Art	ind.	$ 22,443	$8406	100%	7%	$13,856	$16,993	$25,743
Maine Maritime Academy	pub.	$ 7045	$6400	90%	10%	$10,287	$ 3,158	$25,866
New England School of Communications	ind.	$ 10,045	$5850	59%	35%	$ 4,023	$11,872	$21,000
Saint Joseph's College of Maine	ind.	$ 19,615	$8160	100%	27%	$16,616	$11,159	$24,301
Unity College	ind.	$ 17,680	$6630	100%	26%	$13,214	$11,096	NR
University of Maine	pub.	$ 6328	$6412	84%	22%	$ 9,306	$ 3,434	$19,795

NA = not applicable; NR = not reported; * = includes room and board; † = room only; — = not available.

College Costs At-a-Glance

	Institutional Control ind.=independent; pub.=public	Tuition and Fees	Room and Board	Percent of Eligible Freshmen Receiving Need-Based Gift Awards	Percent of Freshmen Whose Need Was Fully Met	Average Financial Aid Package for Freshmen	Average Net Cost After Aid	2004 Graduate's Average Indebtedness
Maine—*continued*								
The University of Maine at Augusta	pub.	$ 4695	NA	89%	12%	$ 5,866	—	$12,911
University of Maine at Farmington	pub.	$ 5240	$ 5700	90%	23%	$ 7,956	$ 2,984	$15,841
University of Maine at Fort Kent	pub.	$ 4514	$ 5600	90%	18%	$ 3,648	$ 6,466	$10,483
University of Maine at Presque Isle	pub.	$ 4460	$ 5114	91%	31%	$ 5,932	$ 3,642	$11,254
University of New England	ind.	$20,915	$ 8155	100%	12%	$18,604	$10,466	$34,371
University of Southern Maine	pub.	$ 5510	$ 6908	78%	12%	$ 7,306	$ 5,112	$21,912
Maryland								
Bowie State University	pub.	$ 6846	$ 8674	75%	36%	$ 9,499	$ 6,021	$10,842
Capitol College	ind.	$17,688	$ 3869†	93%	38%	$10,195	$11,362	$25,605
College of Notre Dame of Maryland	ind.	$21,600	$ 8000	79%	38%	$17,424	$12,176	$17,125
Coppin State University	pub.	$ 4879	$ 6239	85%	12%	$ 6,416	$ 4,702	$17,843
Frostburg State University	pub.	$ 6230	$ 6148	71%	20%	$ 6,183	$ 6,195	$15,319
Goucher College	ind.	$26,150	$ 8575	95%	38%	$19,849	$14,876	$16,062
The Johns Hopkins University	ind.	$30,140	$ 9516	87%	100%	$27,319	$12,337	$14,000
Loyola College in Maryland	ind.	$28,170	$ 8959	72%	96%	$18,945	$18,184	$15,030
McDaniel College	ind.	$24,800	$ 5600	98%	30%	$19,795	$10,605	$19,996
Mount St. Mary's University	ind.	$22,900	$ 8030	100%	26%	$15,428	$15,502	$16,213
Peabody Conservatory of Music of The Johns Hopkins University	ind.	$28,515	$ 9225	78%	4%	$11,012	$26,728	$19,196
St. Mary's College of Maryland	pub.	$ 9680	$ 7400	43%	NR	$ 7,495	$ 9,585	$17,125
Salisbury University	pub.	$ 5976	$ 7050	58%	11%	$ 5,036	$ 7,990	$16,557
Towson University	pub.	$ 6672	$ 6468	52%	18%	$ 5,930	$ 7,210	$15,575
University of Maryland, Baltimore County	pub.	$ 8020	$ 7620	51%	72%	$ 7,090	$ 8,550	$14,500
University of Maryland, College Park	pub.	$ 7410	$ 7931	64%	31%	$11,800	$ 3,541	$14,076
University of Maryland Eastern Shore	pub.	$ 5558	$ 5880	100%	22%	$11,180	$ 258	$ 8500
University of Maryland University College	pub.	$ 5424	NA	73%	NR	$ 3,252	$ 2,172	$ 1977
University of Phoenix–Maryland Campus	ind.	$10,800	NA	100%	NR	$ 1,674	$ 9,126	NR
Villa Julie College	ind.	$14,653	$ 6600†	90%	24%	$ 9,361	$11,892	$15,679
Washington Bible College	ind.	$14,880	$ 5250	48%	NR	$ 2,000	$18,130	$ 8000
Washington College	ind.	$26,550	$ 6000	99%	75%	$16,300	$16,250	$19,434
Massachusetts								
American International College	ind.	$18,000	$ 8500	52%	47%	$20,069	$ 6,431	$17,125
Amherst College	ind.	$31,364	$ 8160	94%	100%	$26,976	$12,548	$10,170
Anna Maria College	ind.	$20,135	$ 7415	98%	12%	$13,995	$13,555	$17,828
Assumption College	ind.	$22,655	$ 5395	98%	17%	$14,485	$13,565	$24,064
Atlantic Union College	ind.	$12,780	$ 3780	98%	15%	$ 9,016	$ 7,544	$25,000
Babson College	ind.	$28,832	$10,376	91%	91%	$24,615	$14,593	$23,500
Bay Path College	ind.	$19,440	$ 8260	100%	12%	$13,373	$14,327	$18,200
Becker College	ind.	$17,590	$ 8000	96%	11%	$ 8,027	$17,563	$21,938
Bentley College	ind.	$27,244	$ 9860	94%	25%	$22,405	$14,699	$27,523
Berklee College of Music	ind.	$26,307	$11,690	34%	NR	$15,593	$22,404	NR
Boston Architectural Center	ind.	$ 8630	NA	22%	NR	$ 3,055	$ 5,575	$25,387
Boston College	ind.	$29,396	$ 9620	90%	100%	$22,698	$16,318	$15,723

NA = not applicable; NR = not reported; * = includes room and board; † = room only; — = not available.

College Costs At-a-Glance	Institutional Control ind.=independent; pub.=public	Tuition and Fees	Room and Board	Percent of Eligible Freshmen Receiving Need-Based Gift Awards	Percent of Freshmen Whose Need Was Fully Met	Average Financial Aid Package for Freshmen	Average Net Cost After Aid	2004 Graduate's Average Indebtedness
Massachusetts—*continued*								
The Boston Conservatory	ind.	$24,520	$11,600	29%	5%	$15,580	$20,540	$15,000
Boston University	ind.	$30,402	$ 9680	93%	58%	$26,139	$13,943	$17,186
Brandeis University	ind.	$31,072	$ 8656	97%	29%	$21,201	$18,527	NR
Bridgewater State College	pub.	$ 5296	$ 6512	93%	42%	$ 6,842	$ 4,966	$ 8688
Clark University	ind.	$28,265	$ 5400	99%	66%	$22,413	$11,252	$19,385
College of the Holy Cross	ind.	$29,686	$ 8860	84%	84%	$24,786	$13,760	$19,380
Curry College	ind.	$21,670	$ 8180	96%	2%	$15,036	$14,814	$22,159
Emerson College	ind.	$24,064	$10,920	85%	79%	$11,209	$23,775	$19,647
Emmanuel College	ind.	$20,500	$ 9000	84%	29%	$15,624	$13,876	$15,523
Endicott College	ind.	$19,432	$ 9300	79%	11%	$11,677	$17,055	$17,125
Framingham State College	pub.	$ 4740	$ 5539	83%	18%	$ 6,670	$ 3,609	$11,000
Gordon College	ind.	$21,448	$ 6092	97%	20%	$14,132	$13,408	$ 9182
Hampshire College	ind.	$30,978	$ 8113	99%	59%	$24,510	$14,581	$17,825
Harvard University	ind.	$30,620	$ 9260	100%	100%	$26,946	$12,934	$ 9640
Lasell College	ind.	$19,700	$ 8800	99%	9%	$14,300	$14,200	$20,500
Lesley University	ind.	$22,750	$ 9950	100%	20%	$15,984	$16,716	$13,605
Massachusetts College of Art	pub.	$ 6400	$ 9737	54%	NR	$ 6,503	$ 9,634	$18,337
Massachusetts College of Pharmacy and Health Sciences	ind.	$20,220	$10,570	98%	9%	$15,733	$15,057	NR
Massachusetts Institute of Technology	ind.	$30,800	$ 9100	99%	100%	$24,460	$15,440	$20,079
Massachusetts Maritime Academy	pub.	$ 4963	$ 6157	38%	24%	$ 7,177	$ 3,943	$12,125
Merrimack College	ind.	$22,100	$ 9200	100%	88%	$15,125	$16,175	$25,000
Mount Holyoke College	ind.	$30,938	$ 9060	98%	100%	$26,119	$13,879	$20,039
Mount Ida College	ind.	$19,096	$ 9830	97%	7%	$10,362	$18,564	$31,105
New England Conservatory of Music	ind.	$27,500	$10,950	80%	16%	$14,468	$23,982	$23,869
Nichols College	ind.	$20,810	$ 8052	98%	25%	$15,722	$13,140	$26,626
Northeastern University	ind.	$27,080	$10,180	97%	14%	$17,725	$19,535	NR
Pine Manor College	ind.	$14,794	$ 9000	100%	15%	$14,673	$ 9,121	$14,312
Regis College	ind.	$20,500	$ 9360	89%	11%	$20,193	$ 9,667	$20,174
Salem State College	pub.	$ 5284	$ 7350	81%	3%	$ 6,084	$ 6,550	NR
School of the Museum of Fine Arts, Boston	ind.	$24,290	$10,600†	88%	7%	$18,420	$16,470	$20,554
Simmons College	ind.	$25,440	$10,200	91%	6%	$15,314	$20,326	$26,300
Simon's Rock College of Bard	ind.	$31,187	$ 8088	70%	17%	$19,644	$19,631	$14,000
Stonehill College	ind.	$23,008	$10,206	95%	27%	$17,171	$16,043	$16,615
Suffolk University	ind.	$19,870	$11,411	88%	8%	$10,960	$20,321	$19,376
Tufts University	ind.	$31,248	$ 9030	93%	100%	$22,304	$17,974	$14,683
University of Massachusetts Amherst	pub.	$ 9008	$ 6189	96%	12%	$ 9,173	$ 6,024	$12,677
University of Massachusetts Boston	pub.	$ 8034	NA	80%	40%	$ 8,087	—	$14,805
University of Massachusetts Dartmouth	pub.	$ 7802	$ 7471	74%	56%	$ 6,931	$ 8,342	$14,943
University of Massachusetts Lowell	pub.	$ 7891	$ 6011	87%	83%	$ 8,026	$ 5,876	$15,167
Wellesley College	ind.	$29,796	$ 9202	97%	100%	$26,118	$12,880	$11,621
Wentworth Institute of Technology	ind.	$18,500	$ 9000	34%	4%	$ 8,443	$19,057	$20,928
Western New England College	ind.	$21,986	$ 8524	99%	10%	$13,884	$16,626	NR
Westfield State College	pub.	$ 4857	$ 5742	74%	20%	$ 5,244	$ 5,355	$12,731

NA = not applicable; NR = not reported; * = includes room and board; † = room only; — = not available.

College Costs At-a-Glance

	Institutional Control ind.=independent; pub.=public	Tuition and Fees	Room and Board	Percent of Eligible Freshmen Receiving Need-Based Gift Awards	Percent of Freshmen Whose Need Was Fully Met	Average Financial Aid Package for Freshmen	Average Net Cost After Aid	2004 Graduate's Average Indebtedness
Massachusetts—*continued*								
Wheaton College	ind.	$30,580	$7580	97%	48%	$22,631	$15,529	$22,052
Williams College	ind.	$29,990	$8110	99%	100%	$28,988	$ 9,112	$10,753
Worcester Polytechnic Institute	ind.	$30,130	$9164	98%	42%	$20,839	$18,455	$30,016
Worcester State College	pub.	$ 4579	$6896	85%	45%	$ 5,494	$ 5,981	$11,843
Michigan								
Adrian College	ind.	$17,600	$5770	100%	93%	$17,687	$ 5,683	$16,870
Albion College	ind.	$22,918	$6536	100%	73%	$19,622	$ 9,832	$19,951
Alma College	ind.	$19,986	$7032	100%	26%	$18,109	$ 8,909	$19,437
Andrews University	ind.	$16,506	$5280	59%	46%	$17,283	$ 4,503	$21,063
Calvin College	ind.	$17,770	$6185	100%	29%	$13,056	$10,899	$18,805
Central Michigan University	pub.	$ 5365	$6160	93%	66%	$ 8,346	$ 3,179	$16,312
Cleary University	ind.	$11,760	NA	84%	5%	$11,108	$ 652	$13,304
College for Creative Studies	ind.	$23,116	$3900†	NR	NR	NR	NR	$26,482
Concordia University	ind.	$17,765	$6745	99%	37%	$15,628	$ 8,882	$28,045
Cornerstone University	ind.	$14,700	$5520	100%	25%	$13,287	$ 6,933	$21,209
Eastern Michigan University	pub.	$ 5762	$6082	57%	1%	$ 6,271	$ 5,573	$21,930
Ferris State University	pub.	$ 6332	$6522	63%	10%	$ 7,100	$ 5,754	$15,000
Finlandia University	ind.	$14,700	$5064	81%	3%	$14,000	$ 5,764	$17,500
Grace Bible College	ind.	$10,420	$6490	100%	NR	$ 8,350	$ 8,560	$13,919
Grand Valley State University	pub.	$ 5782	$6160	86%	100%	$ 7,095	$ 4,847	$16,200
Hillsdale College	ind.	$16,900	$6600	100%	44%	$11,800	$11,700	$15,800
Hope College	ind.	$20,420	$6318	84%	32%	$17,754	$ 8,984	$19,288
Kalamazoo College	ind.	$24,351	$6609	100%	83%	$18,900	$12,060	$23,890
Kettering University	ind.	$23,360	NR	74%	10%	$14,404	$ 8,956	$37,997
Lake Superior State University	pub.	$ 6372	$6165	61%	NR	$ 8,262	$ 4,275	$17,458
Lawrence Technological University	ind.	$17,210	$7035	97%	32%	$11,874	$12,371	$24,495
Michigan State University	pub.	$ 7000	$5458	61%	30%	$ 8,044	$ 4,414	$21,037
Michigan Technological University	pub.	$ 7610	$6096	89%	36%	$ 9,010	$ 4,696	$17,000
Northern Michigan University	pub.	$ 5434	$6182	80%	6%	$ 7,505	$ 4,111	$15,776
Northwood University	ind.	$15,183	$6696	90%	27%	$13,794	$ 8,085	$13,782
Oakland University	pub.	$ 5354	$5820	75%	38%	$ 5,564	$ 5,610	$15,513
Olivet College	ind.	$16,464	$5480	100%	11%	$12,733	$ 9,211	$23,258
Reformed Bible College	ind.	$10,920	$5500	88%	20%	$ 8,969	$ 7,451	$11,065
Rochester College	ind.	$11,456	$6316	49%	NR	$ 2,556	$15,216	NR
Spring Arbor University	ind.	$16,096	$5610	98%	69%	$16,141	$ 5,565	$11,634
University of Detroit Mercy	ind.	$22,470	$7328	86%	30%	$22,914	$ 6,884	NR
University of Michigan	pub.	$ 8201	$7030	47%	90%	$ 8,479	$ 6,752	$21,326
University of Michigan–Dearborn	pub.	$ 6112	NA	70%	2%	$ 8,370	—	$13,086
University of Michigan–Flint	pub.	$ 6018	NA	62%	7%	$ 5,608	$ 410	$20,010
University of Phoenix–Metro Detroit Campus	ind.	$11,790	NA	100%	NR	$ 3,538	$ 8,252	NR
University of Phoenix–West Michigan Campus	ind.	$11,520	NA	100%	NR	$ 3,772	$ 7,748	NR
Walsh College of Accountancy and Business Administration	ind.	$ 7550	NA	NR	NR	NR	NR	$ 8908

NA = not applicable; NR = not reported; * = includes room and board; † = room only; — = not available.

College Costs At-a-Glance	Institutional Control ind.=independent; pub.=public	Tuition and Fees	Room and Board	Percent of Eligible Freshmen Receiving Need-Based Gift Awards	Percent of Freshmen Whose Need Was Fully Met	Average Financial Aid Package for Freshmen	Average Net Cost After Aid	2004 Graduate's Average Indebtedness
Michigan—*continued*								
Wayne State University	pub.	$ 5399	$6700	73%	8%	$ 6,609	$ 5,490	$19,563
Minnesota								
Argosy University/Twin Cities (Eagan)	ind.	$12,220	NA	NR	NR	NR	NR	NR
Augsburg College	ind.	$20,758	$6080	99%	23%	$14,866	$11,972	$25,750
Bemidji State University	pub.	$ 6404	$5012	71%	38%	$ 6,944	$ 4,472	$16,045
Bethany Lutheran College	ind.	$15,716	$4982	100%	31%	$12,907	$ 7,791	$19,112
Bethel University	ind.	$21,300	$6800	100%	16%	$15,969	$12,131	$23,777
College of Saint Benedict	ind.	$22,148	$6208	99%	86%	$18,159	$10,197	$24,627
The College of St. Scholastica	ind.	$20,760	$5916	90%	83%	$17,299	$ 9,377	$27,245
College of Visual Arts	ind.	$18,040	NA	98%	2%	$ 5,546	$12,494	$31,691
Concordia College	ind.	$17,920	$4690	99%	62%	$13,386	$ 9,224	$20,323
Concordia University, St. Paul	ind.	$21,312	$6464	100%	22%	$14,593	$13,183	$15,900
Crown College	ind.	$15,646	$6572	78%	11%	$13,607	$ 8,611	$25,084
Gustavus Adolphus College	ind.	$22,955	$5810	100%	NR	$16,047	$12,718	$18,500
Hamline University	ind.	$22,070	$6536	85%	26%	$23,210	$ 5,396	$21,325
Macalester College	ind.	$28,810	$7858	100%	100%	$24,037	$12,631	NR
Minnesota State University Mankato	pub.	$ 5088	$4716	61%	41%	$ 6,278	$ 3,526	$16,500
Minnesota State University Moorhead	pub.	$ 4894	$4530	57%	NR	$ 3,748	$ 5,676	$19,209
North Central University	ind.	$11,284	$4350	NR	NR	NR	NR	$21,965
Northwestern College	ind.	$18,370	$6020	99%	8%	$13,197	$11,193	$19,238
St. Cloud State University	pub.	$ 5176	$4088	76%	58%	$10,431	—	$19,588
Saint John's University	ind.	$22,148	$6118	99%	57%	$18,607	$ 9,659	$23,924
Saint Mary's University of Minnesota	ind.	$17,925	$5450	100%	70%	$16,252	$ 7,123	$22,530
St. Olaf College	ind.	$26,500	$6300	100%	100%	$20,529	$12,271	$18,855
Southwest Minnesota State University	pub.	$ 5294	$4806	70%	22%	$ 6,139	$ 3,961	$17,038
University of Minnesota, Morris	pub.	$ 9056	$5250	93%	47%	$11,970	$ 2,336	$15,490
University of Minnesota, Twin Cities Campus	pub.	$ 8030	$6458	77%	45%	$ 9,377	$ 5,111	NR
University of St. Thomas	ind.	$21,828	$6542	99%	29%	$17,086	$11,284	$23,839
Winona State University	pub.	$ 6420	$4960	54%	11%	$ 4,589	$ 6,791	$14,987
Mississippi								
Alcorn State University	pub.	$ 4465	$4012	100%	70%	$ 7,800	$ 677	$10,000
Belhaven College	ind.	$14,050	$5430	92%	16%	$10,408	$ 9,072	$18,126
Blue Mountain College	ind.	$ 7320	$3766	66%	46%	NR	NR	$11,784
Magnolia Bible College	ind.	$ 6090	$1520†	100%	NR	$ 6,086	$ 1,524	NR
Millsaps College	ind.	$20,690	$7566	100%	37%	$18,452	$ 9,804	$22,535
Mississippi College	ind.	$12,058	$5694	65%	42%	$13,187	$ 4,565	$18,182
Mississippi State University	pub.	$ 4106	$5994	91%	33%	$ 6,470	$ 3,630	$17,910
Mississippi University for Women	pub.	$ 3495	$3778	32%	52%	$ 7,512	—	$20,704
Rust College	ind.	$ 6060	$2600	100%	59%	$ 6,985	$ 1,675	$ 9314
University of Mississippi	pub.	$ 4110	$5610	60%	20%	$ 6,938	$ 2,782	NR
University of Southern Mississippi	pub.	$ 4106	$5010	71%	17%	$ 6,095	$ 3,021	$12,073
Wesley College	ind.	$ 5100	$2960	NR	NR	NR	NR	NR

NA = not applicable; NR = not reported; * = includes room and board; † = room only; — = not available.

College Costs At-a-Glance

	Institutional Control ind.=independent; pub.=public	Tuition and Fees	Room and Board	Percent of Eligible Freshmen Receiving Need-Based Gift Awards	Percent of Freshmen Whose Need Was Fully Met	Average Financial Aid Package for Freshmen	Average Net Cost After Aid	2004 Graduate's Average Indebtedness
Mississippi—*continued*								
William Carey College	ind.	$ 8415	$ 3465	NR	NR	NR	NR	$15,000
Missouri								
Calvary Bible College and Theological Seminary	ind.	$ 6612	$ 3700	83%	6%	$ 6,356	$ 3,956	$ 4088
Central Bible College	ind.	$ 8722	$ 4560	88%	6%	$ 5,505	$ 7,777	$19,686
Central Methodist University	ind.	$15,200	$ 5360	100%	3%	$14,433	$ 6,127	$19,247
Central Missouri State University	pub.	$ 5970	$ 5180	60%	25%	$ 5,670	$ 5,480	$ 9960
College of the Ozarks	ind.	$ 280	$ 3850	100%	32%	$11,271	—	$ 6060
Columbia College	ind.	$11,995	$ 5011	89%	24%	$ 9,448	$ 7,558	$12,707
Culver-Stockton College	ind.	$13,390	$ 5775	100%	20%	$11,865	$ 7,300	$17,749
Evangel University	ind.	$12,750	$ 4620	90%	12%	$ 8,701	$ 8,669	$21,409
Hannibal-LaGrange College	ind.	$10,876	$ 4050	54%	NR	$ 7,264	$ 7,662	$17,916
Kansas City Art Institute	ind.	$21,326	$ 6800	100%	16%	$14,820	$13,306	$17,125
Lincoln University	pub.	$ 4952	$ 3790	68%	36%	$ 6,000	$ 2,742	$17,000
Lindenwood University	ind.	$11,720	$ 5600	NR	NR	NR	NR	NR
Maryville University of Saint Louis	ind.	$16,300	$ 7000	100%	15%	$12,787	$10,513	$11,167
Messenger College	ind.	$ 5410	$ 3500	79%	NR	$ 6,642	$ 2,268	$17,348
Missouri Baptist University	ind.	$13,030	$ 5800	NR	NR	NR	NR	$18,728
Missouri Southern State University	pub.	$ 3976	$ 4770	99%	NR	$ 5,591	$ 3,155	$16,137
Missouri State University	pub.	$ 5128	$ 4660	75%	22%	$ 5,342	$ 4,446	$13,381
Missouri Valley College	ind.	$13,500	$ 5200	100%	NR	$11,402	$ 7,298	$13,400
Park University	ind.	$ 6048	$ 5180	71%	24%	$ 4,180	$ 7,048	$12,800
Research College of Nursing	ind.	$19,540	$ 6100	NR	NR	NR	NR	$12,740
Rockhurst University	ind.	$18,560	$ 5500	68%	4%	$19,108	$ 4,952	$25,823
St. Louis Christian College	ind.	$ 7730	$ 5180	94%	39%	$ 8,245	$ 4,665	$13,977
Saint Louis University	ind.	$23,558	$ 7780	97%	10%	$18,204	$13,134	$22,534
Southeast Missouri State University	pub.	$ 4875	$ 5317	82%	17%	$ 5,713	$ 4,479	$14,492
Southwest Baptist University	ind.	$13,250	$ 3950	48%	24%	$10,652	$ 6,548	$11,159
Stephens College	ind.	$19,300	$ 7630	71%	29%	$16,481	$10,449	$ 6073
Truman State University	pub.	$ 5812	$ 5380	44%	57%	$ 6,454	$ 4,738	$16,208
University of Missouri–Columbia	pub.	$ 7100	$ 6220	90%	22%	$11,154	$ 2,166	$16,704
University of Missouri–Kansas City	pub.	$ 7250	$ 7505	70%	64%	$11,914	$ 2,841	$15,704
University of Missouri–St. Louis	pub.	$ 7378	$ 6194	76%	7%	$ 7,901	$ 5,671	$16,048
University of Phoenix–Kansas City Campus	ind.	$10,350	NA	NR	NR	NR	NR	NR
University of Phoenix–St. Louis Campus	ind.	$12,060	NA	100%	NR	$ 5,757	$ 6,303	NR
Washington University in St. Louis	ind.	$32,042	$10,064	97%	100%	$25,095	$17,011	NR
Webster University	ind.	$16,250	$ 6610	89%	NR	$17,293	$ 5,567	$17,502
Westminster College	ind.	$14,170	$ 5870	100%	63%	$13,217	$ 6,823	$15,843
William Jewell College	ind.	$17,500	$ 5100	99%	NR	$15,111	$ 7,489	$15,225
William Woods University	ind.	$14,720	$ 5700	61%	29%	$13,382	$ 7,038	$13,873
Montana								
Carroll College	ind.	$16,978	$ 6246	89%	23%	$14,718	$ 8,506	$23,067
Montana State University	pub.	$ 4577	$ 5500	82%	13%	$ 7,039	$ 3,038	$17,193

NA = not applicable; NR = not reported; * = includes room and board; † = room only; — = not available.

College Costs At-a-Glance

College Costs At-a-Glance	Institutional Control (ind.=independent; pub.=public)	Tuition and Fees	Room and Board	Percent of Eligible Freshmen Receiving Need-Based Gift Awards	Percent of Freshmen Whose Need Was Fully Met	Average Financial Aid Package for Freshmen	Average Net Cost After Aid	2004 Graduate's Average Indebtedness
Montana—*continued*								
Montana State University–Billings	pub.	$ 4550	$4500	78%	16%	$ 6,149	$ 2,901	$14,220
University of Great Falls	ind.	$14,000	$5950	77%	12%	$10,320	$ 9,630	$27,315
The University of Montana–Western	pub.	$ 3530	$4740	85%	2%	$ 2,263	$ 6,007	$20,703
Nebraska								
Bellevue University	ind.	$ 4740	NA	63%	NR	$ 2,692	$ 2,048	NR
Chadron State College	pub.	$ 3495	$3986	NR	NR	$ 2,406	$ 5,075	$11,000
College of Saint Mary	ind.	$17,000	$5700	97%	18%	$10,414	$12,286	$13,500
Concordia University	ind.	$16,880	$4580	74%	69%	$14,377	$ 7,083	$13,232
Creighton University	ind.	$21,118	$7200	100%	84%	$20,278	$ 8,040	$23,818
Doane College	ind.	$15,970	$4720	100%	89%	$14,404	$ 6,286	$12,670
Grace University	ind.	$11,980	$5400	91%	7%	$ 6,550	$10,830	$12,758
Hastings College	ind.	$16,290	$4760	100%	32%	$12,216	$ 8,834	$17,634
Midland Lutheran College	ind.	$17,210	$4560	100%	32%	$15,059	$ 6,711	$19,698
Nebraska Christian College	ind.	$ 6380	$3750	78%	NR	NR	NR	$11,593
Nebraska Wesleyan University	ind.	$17,390	$4630	100%	15%	$12,068	$ 9,952	$16,790
Peru State College	pub.	$ 3534	$4486	NR	NR	NR	NR	NR
University of Nebraska at Kearney	pub.	$ 4260	$4990	60%	41%	$ 6,543	$ 2,707	$14,930
University of Nebraska at Omaha	pub.	$ 4533	$5960	63%	NR	NR	NR	$22,000
University of Nebraska–Lincoln	pub.	$ 5268	$6008	84%	25%	$ 7,921	$ 3,355	$16,703
University of Nebraska Medical Center	pub.	$ 6657	NA	NR	NR	NR	NR	NR
Wayne State College	pub.	$ 3672	$4120	77%	30%	$ 3,470	$ 4,322	NR
York College	ind.	$11,930	$3800	NR	NR	NR	NR	$19,556
Nevada								
Sierra Nevada College	ind.	$19,650	$7450	100%	NR	$14,000	$13,100	$18,000
University of Nevada, Las Vegas	pub.	$ 3532	$8326	47%	59%	$ 5,681	$ 6,177	$12,900
University of Nevada, Reno	pub.	$ 3010	$7385	50%	21%	$ 6,228	$ 4,167	$16,273
University of Phoenix–Nevada Campus	ind.	$ 9300	NA	100%	NR	$ 4,708	$ 4,592	NR
New Hampshire								
Chester College of New England	ind.	$14,430	$7400	40%	NR	$ 6,772	$15,058	$32,632
Colby-Sawyer College	ind.	$24,700	$9490	93%	3%	$16,430	$17,760	$18,050
Daniel Webster College	ind.	$21,630	$8170	90%	NR	$16,717	$13,083	NR
Dartmouth College	ind.	$30,575	$9124	97%	100%	$28,113	$11,586	$18,095
Franklin Pierce College	ind.	$23,710	$7990	100%	8%	$15,790	$15,910	$21,357
Keene State College	pub.	$ 6900	$5966	66%	22%	$ 6,728	$ 6,138	$18,585
Magdalen College	ind.	$ 9000	$6000	100%	74%	$ 9,208	$ 5,792	$11,215
New England College	ind.	$23,010	$8456	95%	37%	$15,738	$15,728	$35,748
Plymouth State University	pub.	$ 6618	$6322	63%	5%	$ 6,831	$ 6,109	$22,916
Saint Anselm College	ind.	$24,660	$9070	100%	19%	$18,025	$15,705	$23,437
Southern New Hampshire University	ind.	$19,314	$7866	77%	12%	$14,536	$12,644	$22,200
Thomas More College of Liberal Arts	ind.	$10,650	$8000	100%	8%	$10,782	$ 7,868	$19,363
University of New Hampshire	pub.	$ 9226	$6612	69%	23%	$15,380	$ 458	$22,354
University of New Hampshire at Manchester	pub.	$ 6593	NA	34%	16%	$ 7,264	—	$14,728

NA = not applicable; NR = not reported; * = includes room and board; † = room only; — = not available.

College Costs At-a-Glance

	Institutional Control ind.=independent; pub.=public	Tuition and Fees	Room and Board	Percent of Eligible Freshmen Receiving Need-Based Gift Awards	Percent of Freshmen Whose Need Was Fully Met	Average Financial Aid Package for Freshmen	Average Net Cost After Aid	2004 Graduate's Average Indebtedness
New Jersey								
Bloomfield College	ind.	$15,100	$ 7400	98%	32%	$13,025	$ 9,475	NR
Caldwell College	ind.	$18,950	$ 7500	8%	79%	$10,800	$15,650	$16,000
Centenary College	ind.	$19,360	$ 7500	97%	14%	$13,555	$13,305	$18,986
The College of New Jersey	pub.	$ 8988	$ 8093	51%	42%	$ 9,545	$ 7,536	$18,524
Drew University	ind.	$29,546	$ 8018	100%	36%	$20,208	$17,356	$16,818
Fairleigh Dickinson University, College at Florham	ind.	$23,386	$ 8608	94%	NR	$18,044	$13,950	NR
Fairleigh Dickinson University, Metropolitan Campus	ind.	$21,734	$ 9056	96%	NR	$18,548	$12,242	NR
Georgian Court University	ind.	$17,924	$ 7200	91%	18%	$11,998	$13,126	$16,938
Kean University	pub.	$ 7151	$ 8093	76%	12%	$ 7,072	$ 8,172	$10,619
Monmouth University	ind.	$19,704	$ 7911	42%	16%	$11,462	$16,153	$27,600
Montclair State University	pub.	$ 7026	$ 8212	66%	42%	$ 9,082	$ 6,156	$16,694
New Jersey City University	pub.	$ 6550	$ 6958	80%	92%	$ 7,983	$ 5,525	NR
New Jersey Institute of Technology	pub.	$ 9180	$ 8242	78%	19%	$13,149	$ 4,273	$15,000
Princeton University	ind.	$29,910	$ 8387	100%	100%	$25,752	$12,545	$ 8050
Ramapo College of New Jersey	pub.	$ 8081	$ 8208	52%	17%	$10,501	$ 5,788	$15,666
The Richard Stockton College of New Jersey	pub.	$ 7203	$ 7252	51%	69%	$11,367	$ 3,088	$15,835
Rider University	ind.	$23,470	$ 8840	98%	20%	$18,235	$14,075	$27,113
Rowan University	pub.	$ 7970	$ 7642	64%	35%	$ 6,017	$ 9,595	$ 9575
Rutgers, The State University of New Jersey, Camden	pub.	$ 8389	$ 7862	72%	36%	$ 9,682	$ 6,569	$16,203
Rutgers, The State University of New Jersey, Newark	pub.	$ 8209	$ 8570	80%	27%	$ 9,856	$ 6,923	$15,495
Rutgers, The State University of New Jersey, New Brunswick/Piscataway	pub.	$ 8564	$ 8357	65%	36%	$10,709	$ 6,212	$15,863
Seton Hall University	ind.	$23,460	$10,162	64%	20%	$15,530	$18,092	$29,108
Stevens Institute of Technology	ind.	$29,760	$ 8926	76%	24%	$24,557	$14,129	$14,113
William Paterson University of New Jersey	pub.	$ 7952	$ 8340	59%	21%	$ 9,641	$ 6,651	$10,868
New Mexico								
College of Santa Fe	ind.	$20,840	$ 6250	93%	21%	$19,610	$ 7,480	$15,916
New Mexico Highlands University	pub.	$ 2300	$ 4274	99%	24%	$ 6,260	$ 314	$12,147
New Mexico Institute of Mining and Technology	pub.	$ 3280	$ 4670	58%	55%	$ 7,921	$ 29	$ 8788
New Mexico State University	pub.	$ 3666	$ 5046	96%	19%	$ 7,924	$ 788	NR
University of Phoenix–New Mexico Campus	ind.	$ 8940	NA	100%	NR	$ 4,544	$ 4,396	NR
New York								
Adelphi University	ind.	$18,700	$ 8500	85%	1%	$13,450	$13,750	$22,248
Alfred University	ind.	$20,060	$ 9374	100%	85%	$19,396	$10,038	$19,125
Bard College	ind.	$30,742	$ 9418	94%	61%	$23,753	$16,407	$15,921
Bernard M. Baruch College of the City University of New York	pub.	$ 4300	NA	77%	10%	$ 5,380	—	$10,100
Canisius College	ind.	$21,811	$ 8395	100%	32%	$19,369	$10,837	$21,892
Cazenovia College	ind.	$18,940	$ 7590	100%	13%	$14,600	$11,930	$15,843
City College of the City University of New York	pub.	$ 4339	NA	NR	NR	NR	NR	$16,800
Clarkson University	ind.	$25,585	$ 9345	80%	NR	$16,971	$17,959	$18,148
Colgate University	ind.	$31,440	$ 7620	100%	100%	$29,338	$ 9,722	$11,104
College of Mount Saint Vincent	ind.	$19,900	$ 8250	NR	NR	$16,000	$12,150	$17,000
The College of New Rochelle	ind.	$20,596	$ 7880	91%	100%	$21,529	$ 6,947	$33,000

NA = not applicable; NR = not reported; * = includes room and board; † = room only; — = not available.

College Costs At-a-Glance	Institutional Control ind.=independent; pub.=public	Tuition and Fees	Room and Board	Percent of Eligible Freshmen Receiving Need-Based Gift Awards	Percent of Freshmen Whose Need Was Fully Met	Average Financial Aid Package for Freshmen	Average Net Cost After Aid	2004 Graduate's Average Indebtedness
New York—*continued*								
The College of Saint Rose	ind.	$16,780	$ 7472	95%	4%	$ 7,675	$16,577	NR
College of Staten Island of the City University of New York	pub.	$ 4308	NA	99%	84%	$ 5,291	—	NR
Columbia College	ind.	$31,472	$ 9066	83%	100%	$27,464	$13,074	$16,080
Columbia University, The Fu Foundation School of Engineering and Applied Science	ind.	$31,472	$ 9066	86%	100%	$25,850	$14,688	$15,391
Cornell University	ind.	$30,167	$ 9882	94%	100%	$31,000	$ 9,049	$22,200
The Culinary Institute of America	ind.	$18,795	$ 6510	NR	NR	NR	NR	$18,000
Daemen College	ind.	$16,020	$ 7370	92%	26%	$14,621	$ 8,769	$13,024
Dominican College	ind.	$17,250	$ 8470	100%	12%	$13,324	$12,396	$17,358
Dowling College	ind.	$16,050	$ 5512†	100%	7%	$12,290	$ 9,272	$21,411
D'Youville College	ind.	$14,890	$ 7340	100%	43%	$15,754	$ 6,476	NR
Elmira College	ind.	$27,030	$ 8330	100%	17%	$22,012	$13,348	$22,636
Fashion Institute of Technology	pub.	$ 4720	$ 7066	73%	24%	$ 6,287	$ 5,499	$10,972
Five Towns College	ind.	$14,100	$10,250	81%	15%	$ 6,050	$18,300	$15,100
Fordham University	ind.	$27,047	$10,248	95%	23%	$19,464	$17,831	$16,590
Hamilton College	ind.	$31,700	$ 7825	96%	100%	$24,370	$15,155	$16,894
Hilbert College	ind.	$14,300	$ 5380	99%	23%	$ 8,963	$10,717	$19,129
Hobart and William Smith Colleges	ind.	$30,643	$ 7987	100%	78%	$23,426	$15,204	$21,859
Hofstra University	ind.	$20,012	$ 9000	100%	28%	$12,300	$16,712	$19,876
Houghton College	ind.	$18,660	$ 6320	100%	16%	$14,325	$10,655	$20,173
Iona College	ind.	$19,530	$ 9698	33%	23%	$13,531	$15,697	$23,551
Ithaca College	ind.	$23,690	$ 9704	93%	45%	$20,950	$12,444	NR
John Jay College of Criminal Justice of the City University of New York	pub.	$ 4259	NA	NR	NR	$ 5,100	—	$10,000
Keuka College	ind.	$17,080	$ 7790	100%	32%	$16,910	$ 7,960	$18,645
Laboratory Institute of Merchandising	ind.	$17,050	$11,000†	84%	NR	$ 7,350	$20,700	NR
Lehman College of the City University of New York	pub.	$ 4270	NA	95%	2%	$ 3,593	$ 677	$11,000
Le Moyne College	ind.	$20,150	$ 7890	100%	50%	$19,457	$ 8,583	$18,688
Long Island University, Brooklyn Campus	ind.	$21,922	$ 7350	90%	58%	$14,214	$15,058	$23,998
Manhattan College	ind.	$20,600	$ 9025	87%	7%	$13,099	$16,526	$15,715
Manhattan School of Music	ind.	$28,285	$12,500	94%	9%	$15,423	$25,362	$14,100
Manhattanville College	ind.	$24,570	$10,130	96%	11%	$22,413	$12,287	$22,966
Marist College	ind.	$21,015	$ 9218	100%	22%	$13,750	$16,483	$27,013
Marymount College of Fordham University	ind.	$19,702	$ 9760	99%	14%	$16,003	$13,459	$11,006
Marymount Manhattan College	ind.	$17,352	$12,366	95%	95%	NR	NR	$21,000
Medgar Evers College of the City University of New York	pub.	$ 4230	NA	99%	NR	NR	NR	NR
Mercy College	ind.	$11,374	$ 8426	NR	NR	NR	NR	NR
Molloy College	ind.	$15,850	NA	93%	20%	$ 9,221	$ 6,629	NR
Mount Saint Mary College	ind.	$15,690	$ 7640	90%	23%	$10,694	$12,636	$20,000
Nazareth College of Rochester	ind.	$18,776	$ 7840	100%	NR	$14,219	$12,397	$23,316
New York Institute of Technology	ind.	$18,190	$ 7780	86%	NR	$11,471	$14,499	$17,125
New York School of Interior Design	ind.	$19,050	NA	75%	NR	$ 6,500	$12,550	$13,250
New York University	ind.	$30,094	$11,390	94%	NR	$19,543	$21,941	$27,639

NA = not applicable; NR = not reported; * = includes room and board; † = room only; — = not available.

College Costs At-a-Glance

	Institutional Control ind.=independent; pub.=public	Tuition and Fees	Room and Board	Percent of Eligible Freshmen Receiving Need-Based Gift Awards	Percent of Freshmen Whose Need Was Fully Met	Average Financial Aid Package for Freshmen	Average Net Cost After Aid	2004 Graduate's Average Indebtedness
New York—*continued*								
Niagara University	ind.	$ 18,420	$ 8050	94%	45%	$17,257	$ 9,213	$16,621
Nyack College	ind.	$ 15,550	$ 7600	100%	17%	$12,709	$10,441	$20,915
Paul Smith's College of Arts and Sciences	ind.	$ 17,110	$ 7060	100%	3%	$ 6,500	$17,670	$ 6625
Polytechnic University, Brooklyn Campus	ind.	$ 27,170	$ 8000	96%	77%	$21,685	$13,485	$21,304
Rensselaer Polytechnic Institute	ind.	$ 29,786	$ 9083	100%	66%	$26,221	$12,648	$25,000
Roberts Wesleyan College	ind.	$ 19,324	$ 5028	100%	14%	$15,150	$ 9,202	NR
Rochester Institute of Technology	ind.	$ 22,413	$ 8136	95%	84%	$16,800	$13,749	NR
Russell Sage College	ind.	$ 22,270	$ 7050	99%	NR	NR	NR	$19,200
Sage College of Albany	ind.	$ 16,020	$ 7150	50%	NR	NR	NR	$ 8600
St. Bonaventure University	ind.	$ 19,485	$ 6910	100%	28%	$16,294	$10,101	$17,500
St. Francis College	ind.	$ 11,785	$ 8000	82%	72%	$ 9,680	$10,105	NR
St. John Fisher College	ind.	$ 18,450	$ 7900	100%	9%	$16,098	$10,252	$22,747
St. John's University	ind.	$ 23,280	$11,000	92%	18%	$18,485	$15,795	$18,196
St. Joseph's College, New York	ind.	$ 11,430	NA	100%	71%	$13,000	—	$16,681
St. Joseph's College, Suffolk Campus	ind.	$ 11,954	NA	100%	51%	$ 8,302	$ 3,652	$16,047
St. Lawrence University	ind.	$ 30,480	$ 7755	98%	39%	$26,725	$11,510	$23,091
Sarah Lawrence College	ind.	$ 32,416	$11,438	90%	75%	$25,919	$17,935	$15,121
School of Visual Arts	ind.	$ 19,620	$11,250	67%	3%	$11,803	$19,067	$30,600
Skidmore College	ind.	$ 31,108	$ 8710	100%	94%	$25,406	$14,412	$15,942
State University of New York at Binghamton	pub.	$ 5756	$ 7710	89%	78%	$10,531	$ 2,935	$14,656
State University of New York at New Paltz	pub.	$ 5220	$ 6860	87%	24%	$ 2,090	$ 9,990	$18,900
State University of New York at Oswego	pub.	$ 5238	$ 7890	95%	28%	$ 7,779	$ 5,349	$18,094
State University of New York at Plattsburgh	pub.	$ 5268	$ 6712	94%	28%	$ 8,156	$ 3,824	$16,956
State University of New York College at Brockport	pub.	$ 5263	$ 7226	92%	50%	$ 7,053	$ 5,436	$17,918
State University of New York College at Geneseo	pub.	$ 5435	$ 6820	90%	75%	$ 8,552	$ 3,703	$15,800
State University of New York College at Old Westbury	pub.	$ 5072	$ 7914	98%	17%	$ 7,784	$ 5,202	$14,064
State University of New York College at Oneonta	pub.	$ 5347	$ 7230	91%	14%	$ 7,844	$ 4,733	$16,904
State University of New York College at Potsdam	pub.	$ 5250	$ 7270	97%	79%	$11,810	$ 710	$17,019
State University of New York College of Agriculture and Technology at Cobleskill	pub.	$ 5345	$ 7270	15%	13%	$ 5,640	$ 6,975	NR
State University of New York College of Environmental Science and Forestry	pub.	$ 4991	$ 9790	100%	100%	$ 8,300	$ 6,481	$19,000
State University of New York, Fredonia	pub.	$ 5391	$ 6940	46%	80%	$ 4,830	$ 7,501	$12,288
State University of New York Institute of Technology	pub.	$ 5244	$ 7160	99%	30%	$ 6,131	$ 6,273	$14,189
State University of New York Upstate Medical University	pub.	$ 9166	$ 3586†	NR	NR	NR	NR	$ 9680
Stony Brook University, State University of New York	pub.	$ 5389	$ 7730	93%	15%	$ 8,394	$ 4,725	$13,912
Syracuse University	ind.	$ 26,734	$ 9970	89%	65%	$19,900	$16,804	$19,200
Union College	ind.	$38,703*	NR	100%	100%	$25,751	$12,952	$16,705
University at Albany, State University of New York	pub.	$ 5810	$ 7540	94%	26%	$ 8,632	$ 4,718	$16,033
University at Buffalo, The State University of New York	pub.	$ 5966	$ 7226	66%	65%	$ 5,926	$ 7,266	$17,657
University of Rochester	ind.	$ 28,982	$ 9565	100%	100%	$22,572	$15,975	$19,782
Utica College	ind.	$ 21,270	$ 8600	100%	17%	NR	NR	NR
Vassar College	ind.	$ 31,350	$ 7680	100%	100%	$24,075	$14,955	$18,729

NA = not applicable; NR = not reported; * = includes room and board; † = room only; — = not available.

College Costs At-a-Glance	Institutional Control ind.=independent; pub.=public	Tuition and Fees	Room and Board	Percent of Eligible Freshmen Receiving Need-Based Gift Awards	Percent of Freshmen Whose Need Was Fully Met	Average Financial Aid Package for Freshmen	Average Net Cost After Aid	2004 Graduate's Average Indebtedness
New York—continued								
Wells College	ind.	$14,900	$7000	100%	26%	$16,594	$ 5,306	$17,125
North Carolina								
Appalachian State University	pub.	$ 3351	$5270	86%	33%	$ 5,533	$ 3,088	$14,482
Barton College	ind.	$16,670	$5800	66%	19%	$13,944	$ 8,526	$16,703
Belmont Abbey College	ind.	$16,724	$8586	99%	15%	$13,198	$12,112	$15,500
Brevard College	ind.	$14,740	$5560	98%	16%	$12,725	$ 7,575	$17,800
Campbell University	ind.	$14,386	$5100	68%	100%	$16,616	$ 2,870	$12,009
Catawba College	ind.	$17,600	$5900	68%	33%	$14,843	$ 8,657	$19,000
Chowan College	ind.	$14,100	$6100	98%	13%	$10,053	$10,147	$22,580
Davidson College	ind.	$27,171	$7732	95%	100%	$16,178	$18,725	$21,901
Duke University	ind.	$30,720	$8520	96%	100%	$26,335	$12,905	$25,182
East Carolina University	pub.	$ 3454	$6640	71%	100%	$ 7,409	$ 2,685	$19,512
Elon University	ind.	$17,555	$6010	90%	NR	$11,456	$12,109	$18,601
Guilford College	ind.	$21,640	$6530	100%	20%	$18,329	$ 9,841	$16,208
Johnson C. Smith University	ind.	$13,712	$5298	92%	2%	$ 7,625	$11,385	$25,000
John Wesley College	ind.	$ 8220	$1990†	100%	NR	$ 7,400	$ 2,810	$15,000
Lenoir-Rhyne College	ind.	$18,920	$6680	100%	19%	$13,438	$12,162	$24,397
Mars Hill College	ind.	$16,598	$6136	100%	16%	$11,843	$10,891	$ 9518
Meredith College	ind.	$19,950	$5600	100%	16%	$13,995	$11,555	$18,133
Methodist College	ind.	$17,850	$6770	94%	7%	$13,050	$11,570	$18,656
Montreat College	ind.	$15,560	$5008	99%	12%	$11,143	$ 9,425	$18,512
Mount Olive College	ind.	$11,800	$4800	99%	17%	$ 7,067	$ 9,533	$ 8818
North Carolina Agricultural and Technical State University	pub.	$ 3066	$5070	81%	3%	$ 5,026	$ 3,110	$16,044
North Carolina School of the Arts	pub.	$ 4306	$5700	99%	8%	$ 9,792	$ 214	$19,384
North Carolina State University	pub.	$ 4667	$6851	97%	38%	$ 8,137	$ 3,381	$17,291
Peace College	ind.	$16,881	$6526	100%	18%	$12,469	$10,938	$ 9250
Pfeiffer University	ind.	$14,570	$5830	100%	30%	$11,813	$ 8,587	$16,700
Roanoke Bible College	ind.	$ 8225	$4760	100%	18%	$ 6,228	$ 6,757	$16,111
St. Andrews Presbyterian College	ind.	$15,725	$5630	99%	20%	$12,205	$ 9,150	$13,581
Shaw University	ind.	$ 9438	$6050	94%	NR	$ 8,613	$ 6,875	$17,125
The University of North Carolina at Asheville	pub.	$ 3392	$5212	90%	24%	$ 5,944	$ 2,660	$14,698
The University of North Carolina at Chapel Hill	pub.	$ 4451	$6245	99%	78%	$ 9,100	$ 1,596	$11,519
The University of North Carolina at Charlotte	pub.	$ 3473	$5304	86%	25%	$ 7,190	$ 1,587	$17,730
The University of North Carolina at Greensboro	pub.	$ 3435	$5000	89%	13%	$ 5,860	$ 2,575	$16,905
The University of North Carolina at Pembroke	pub.	$ 2832	$4560	91%	14%	$ 6,136	$ 1,256	$12,844
The University of North Carolina at Wilmington	pub.	$ 3626	$5800	72%	66%	$ 5,552	$ 3,874	$15,046
Wake Forest University	ind.	$30,210	$8500	96%	33%	$22,566	$16,144	$26,151
Warren Wilson College	ind.	$19,160	$5460	91%	17%	$13,074	$11,546	$15,041
Western Carolina University	pub.	$ 3449	$4028	99%	71%	$ 6,331	$ 1,146	$15,964
Wingate University	ind.	$16,000	$6200	75%	1%	$12,008	$10,192	$24,000
Winston-Salem State University	pub.	$ 2734	$5135	77%	3%	$ 3,471	$ 4,398	$10,800

NA = not applicable; NR = not reported; * = includes room and board; † = room only; — = not available.

College Costs At-a-Glance

	Institutional Control ind.=independent; pub.=public	Tuition and Fees	Room and Board	Percent of Eligible Freshmen Receiving Need-Based Gift Awards	Percent of Freshmen Whose Need Was Fully Met	Average Financial Aid Package for Freshmen	Average Net Cost After Aid	2004 Graduate's Average Indebtedness
North Dakota								
Dickinson State University	pub.	$ 4559	NR	NR	NR	NR	NR	NR
Jamestown College	ind.	$10,000	$4130	100%	21%	$ 8,102	$ 6,028	$17,488
Medcenter One College of Nursing	ind.	$ 8620	$1800†	NR	NR	NR	NR	$10,993
Minot State University	pub.	$ 3712	$3592	79%	100%	$ 5,190	$ 2,114	$15,575
North Dakota State University	pub.	$ 4775	$4727	80%	31%	$ 5,603	$ 3,899	$22,675
University of Mary	ind.	$10,817	$4110	100%	19%	NR	NR	NR
University of North Dakota	pub.	$ 4828	$4455	39%	39%	$ 7,432	$ 1,851	$26,225
Valley City State University	pub.	$ 3130	$4074	51%	27%	$ 5,920	$ 1,284	$15,750
Ohio								
Antioch College	ind.	$24,902	$6413	100%	78%	$25,424	$ 5,891	$17,125
Antioch University McGregor	ind.	$11,808	NA	NR	NR	NR	NR	$28,500
Art Academy of Cincinnati	ind.	$18,850	NA	97%	21%	$11,159	$ 7,691	$25,030
Ashland University	ind.	$19,778	$7314	100%	NR	$16,481	$10,611	$18,250
Baldwin-Wallace College	ind.	$19,494	$6418	100%	84%	$16,338	$ 9,574	$15,993
Bluffton University	ind.	$18,350	$6304	100%	66%	$17,726	$ 6,928	$22,982
Bowling Green State University	pub.	$ 8072	$6588	42%	15%	$ 5,014	$ 9,646	$20,010
Case Western Reserve University	ind.	$27,062	$8202	99%	93%	$25,426	$ 9,838	$27,780
Cedarville University	ind.	$16,032	$5010	39%	52%	$14,056	$ 6,986	$17,862
Cincinnati Christian University	ind.	$ 9690	$5390	97%	21%	$ 7,611	$ 7,469	$16,000
The Cleveland Institute of Art	ind.	$24,741	$8252	100%	5%	$13,044	$19,949	$29,700
Cleveland Institute of Music	ind.	$25,101	$8660	100%	25%	$17,177	$16,584	$24,070
Cleveland State University	pub.	$ 6792	$6610	79%	9%	$ 6,650	$ 6,752	NR
College of Mount St. Joseph	ind.	$18,790	$6070	91%	42%	$17,000	$ 7,860	$13,400
The College of Wooster	ind.	$28,230	$7060	100%	86%	$21,347	$13,943	$21,709
Columbus College of Art & Design	ind.	$19,330	$6400	100%	16%	$13,070	$12,660	$19,693
David N. Myers University	ind.	$11,170	NA	100%	NR	$10,759	$ 411	$19,300
Defiance College	ind.	$18,230	$5590	NR	NR	$11,914	$11,906	$15,871
Denison University	ind.	$27,310	$7670	99%	54%	$23,289	$11,691	$14,342
Heidelberg College	ind.	$14,900	$6710	100%	22%	$14,978	$ 6,632	$26,498
Kent State University	pub.	$ 7504	$6410	78%	11%	$ 6,751	$ 7,163	$21,489
Kenyon College	ind.	$32,170	$5270	97%	55%	$23,097	$14,343	$18,120
Lake Erie College	ind.	$18,590	$6014	NR	NR	NR	NR	$17,125
Laura and Alvin Siegal College of Judaic Studies	ind.	$15,025	NA	NR	NR	NR	NR	NR
Lourdes College	ind.	$12,270	NA	89%	NR	$12,480	—	NR
Malone College	ind.	$15,880	$6120	100%	18%	$12,626	$ 9,374	$16,262
Marietta College	ind.	$21,730	$6186	84%	32%	$19,622	$ 8,294	$17,643
Miami University	pub.	$ 9642	$7010	32%	32%	$15,101	$ 1,551	$19,718
Mount Union College	ind.	$18,810	$5630	100%	20%	$14,736	$ 9,704	$15,944
Mount Vernon Nazarene University	ind.	$14,976	$4734†	100%	28%	$10,969	$ 8,741	$17,796
Muskingum College	ind.	$15,630	$6200	100%	29%	$14,331	$ 7,499	$17,027
Oberlin College	ind.	$31,163	$7643	88%	100%	$22,771	$16,035	$17,800
Ohio Northern University	ind.	$25,815	$6360	61%	34%	$22,912	$ 9,263	$29,874

NA = not applicable; NR = not reported; * = includes room and board; † = room only; — = not available.

College Costs At-a-Glance	Institutional Control ind.=independent; pub.=public	Tuition and Fees	Room and Board	Percent of Eligible Freshmen Receiving Need-Based Gift Awards	Percent of Freshmen Whose Need Was Fully Met	Average Financial Aid Package for Freshmen	Average Net Cost After Aid	2004 Graduate's Average Indebtedness
Ohio—*continued*								
The Ohio State University	pub.	$ 7479	$6909	94%	28%	$ 8,939	$ 5,449	$15,963
Ohio University	pub.	$ 7770	$7539	46%	9%	$ 6,321	$ 8,988	$17,192
Ohio University–Southern Campus	pub.	$ 4026	NA	84%	6%	$ 6,317	—	NR
Ohio University–Zanesville	pub.	$ 4263	NA	64%	23%	$ 5,638	—	NR
Ohio Wesleyan University	ind.	$26,820	$7330	100%	35%	$23,697	$10,453	$21,841
Pontifical College Josephinum	ind.	$14,635	$7000	40%	40%	$14,125	$ 7,510	$13,698
Shawnee State University	pub.	$ 5202	$6510	91%	100%	$ 3,881	$ 7,831	$10,944
Tiffin University	ind.	$14,280	$6150	97%	7%	$10,945	$ 9,485	$17,125
The University of Akron	pub.	$ 7510	$6660	57%	6%	$ 5,263	$ 8,907	$15,036
University of Cincinnati	pub.	$ 8379	$8004	70%	13%	$ 7,182	$ 9,201	$22,425
University of Dayton	ind.	$20,250	$6300	99%	57%	$13,246	$13,304	$21,273
The University of Findlay	ind.	$20,914	$7274	100%	20%	$15,500	$12,688	$17,000
University of Phoenix–Cleveland Campus	ind.	$10,740	NA	100%	NR	$ 1,406	$ 9,334	NR
University of Rio Grande	ind.	$12,345	$6024	96%	51%	$ 7,343	$11,026	$13,750
The University of Toledo	pub.	$ 7054	$7488	70%	7%	$ 5,925	$ 8,617	$25,871
Urbana University	ind.	$14,220	$5680	51%	67%	$11,856	$ 8,044	$19,281
Ursuline College	ind.	$18,150	$5896	93%	19%	$16,371	$ 7,675	$21,680
Wilmington College	ind.	$18,728	$6718	100%	51%	$17,400	$ 8,046	$21,932
Wittenberg University	ind.	$26,196	$6686	100%	NR	$20,994	$11,888	$21,799
Xavier University	ind.	$20,400	$8250	99%	32%	$13,488	$15,162	$19,750
Youngstown State University	pub.	$ 5884	$6100	NR	NR	NR	NR	NR
Oklahoma								
Cameron University	pub.	$ 3000	$3126	NR	NR	NR	NR	$ 6300
East Central University	pub.	$ 3952	$2910	75%	36%	$ 7,292	—	$13,199
Northeastern State University	pub.	$ 3000	$3080	78%	14%	$ 6,477	—	$16,047
Northwestern Oklahoma State University	pub.	$ 3000	$2920	88%	46%	$ 4,732	$ 1,188	$ 9456
Oklahoma Baptist University	ind.	$13,162	$3800	87%	62%	$10,630	$ 6,332	$14,510
Oklahoma City University	ind.	$16,040	$5950	97%	25%	$12,581	$ 9,409	$20,584
Oklahoma Panhandle State University	pub.	$ 2720	$2810	NR	NR	NR	NR	NR
Oklahoma State University	pub.	$ 4071	$5602	72%	18%	$ 7,873	$ 1,800	$17,067
Oklahoma Wesleyan University	ind.	$13,750	$5200	60%	13%	$ 7,113	$11,837	$15,123
Oral Roberts University	ind.	$15,880	$6530	96%	53%	$13,969	$ 8,441	$27,956
St. Gregory's University	ind.	$11,076	$4888	47%	15%	$ 8,015	$ 7,949	$ 9845
Southeastern Oklahoma State University	pub.	$ 3123	$3470	60%	44%	$ 1,043	$ 5,550	$ 6579
University of Oklahoma	pub.	$ 4140	$5814	20%	47%	$ 7,639	$ 2,315	$17,723
University of Phoenix–Oklahoma City Campus	ind.	$ 8910	NA	100%	NR	$ 3,622	$ 5,288	NR
University of Phoenix–Tulsa Campus	ind.	$ 8910	NA	80%	NR	$ 4,280	$ 4,630	NR
University of Science and Arts of Oklahoma	pub.	$ 3180	$3990	99%	19%	$ 6,452	$ 718	$11,940
University of Tulsa	ind.	$17,630	$5926	49%	76%	$19,568	$ 3,988	$22,330
Oregon								
The Art Institute of Portland	ind.	$16,610	$5355	40%	1%	$ 4,723	$17,242	$23,500
Concordia University	ind.	$18,390	$5780	100%	65%	$13,000	$11,170	$15,000

NA = not applicable; NR = not reported; * = includes room and board; † = room only; — = not available.

College Costs At-a-Glance

	Institutional Control ind.=independent; pub.=public	Tuition and Fees	Room and Board	Percent of Eligible Freshmen Receiving Need-Based Gift Awards	Percent of Freshmen Whose Need Was Fully Met	Average Financial Aid Package for Freshmen	Average Net Cost After Aid	2004 Graduate's Average Indebtedness
Oregon—*continued*								
Corban College	ind.	$17,035	$ 6065	100%	24%	$14,038	$ 9,062	$21,800
Eastern Oregon University	pub.	$ 5517	$ 6099	83%	52%	$10,841	$ 775	$15,447
Eugene Bible College	ind.	$ 7851	$ 4200	54%	31%	$ 6,080	$ 5,971	$10,550
Lewis & Clark College	ind.	$27,710	$ 7648	100%	31%	$23,877	$11,481	$19,124
Linfield College	ind.	$22,022	$ 6370	73%	46%	$15,491	$12,901	$25,894
Marylhurst University	ind.	$14,220	NR	100%	14%	$ 7,380	$ 6,840	$17,906
Multnomah Bible College and Biblical Seminary	ind.	$11,090	$ 4890	97%	11%	$ 6,272	$ 9,708	$19,783
Oregon Health & Science University	pub.	$ 9369	NR	NR	NR	NR	NR	$25,960
Oregon State University	pub.	$ 5319	$ 6786	78%	25%	$ 8,191	$ 3,914	NR
Pacific Northwest College of Art	ind.	$16,080	NA	100%	18%	$15,764	$ 316	$18,917
Pacific University	ind.	$20,664	$ 5764	100%	35%	$17,781	$ 8,647	$21,003
Portland State University	pub.	$ 4311	$ 8310	58%	11%	$ 5,739	$ 6,882	$17,278
Reed College	ind.	$30,900	$ 8070	97%	95%	$29,224	$ 9,746	$15,879
Southern Oregon University	pub.	$ 4863	$ 7560	84%	7%	$ 6,516	$ 5,907	$19,375
University of Oregon	pub.	$ 5550	$ 7331	48%	23%	$ 7,265	$ 5,616	$17,802
University of Phoenix–Oregon Campus	ind.	$ 9960	NA	100%	NR	$ 2,786	$ 7,174	NR
University of Portland	ind.	$24,900	$ 7400	100%	31%	$19,726	$12,574	$18,972
Warner Pacific College	ind.	$18,020	$ 5100	96%	10%	$12,558	$10,562	$20,787
Western Oregon University	pub.	$ 4332	$ 6276	81%	12%	$ 6,155	$ 4,453	$ 1791
Pennsylvania								
Albright College	ind.	$24,580	$ 7510	100%	15%	$19,187	$12,903	$25,198
Allegheny College	ind.	$26,950	$ 6550	100%	48%	$21,065	$12,435	$23,846
Alvernia College	ind.	$17,675	$ 7330	100%	NR	$15,420	$ 9,585	$ 3495
Arcadia University	ind.	$24,270	$ 9300	100%	20%	$17,115	$16,455	$33,828
Bloomsburg University of Pennsylvania	pub.	$ 6089	$ 5200	89%	90%	$11,679	—	$16,022
Bryn Mawr College	ind.	$28,630	$ 9700	100%	99%	$26,446	$11,884	$15,194
Bucknell University	ind.	$32,788	$ 6872	96%	100%	$21,825	$17,835	$16,800
Carnegie Mellon University	ind.	$31,036	$ 8244	96%	33%	$21,646	$17,634	$22,902
Cedar Crest College	ind.	$23,012	$ 7953	99%	17%	$16,308	$14,657	$21,199
Central Pennsylvania College	ind.	$11,010	$ 6150	NR	NR	NR	NR	NR
Chatham College	ind.	$21,996	$ 7050	100%	NR	$24,350	$ 4,696	$18,655
Chestnut Hill College	ind.	$20,380	$ 7500	92%	NR	$15,550	$12,330	$16,745
Clarion University of Pennsylvania	pub.	$ 4810	$ 4816	86%	15%	$ 5,626	$ 4,000	NR
College Misericordia	ind.	$18,800	$ 7850	99%	13%	$13,364	$13,286	$19,582
The Curtis Institute of Music	ind.	$ 1650	NA	67%	22%	$ 9,162	—	$13,202
Delaware Valley College	ind.	$20,888	$ 7742	100%	46%	$15,645	$12,985	$17,327
DeSales University	ind.	$19,390	$ 7590	100%	21%	$13,056	$13,924	$13,977
Dickinson College	ind.	$32,120	$ 8050	92%	85%	$24,294	$15,876	$19,358
Drexel University	ind.	$22,020	$10,050	37%	14%	$14,873	$17,197	$21,504
Duquesne University	ind.	$20,360	$ 7820	98%	48%	$16,069	$12,111	$17,953
East Stroudsburg University of Pennsylvania	pub.	$ 6224	$ 4506	64%	69%	$ 4,043	$ 6,687	$20,265
Edinboro University of Pennsylvania	pub.	$ 6089	$ 5338	100%	7%	$ 5,736	$ 5,691	$16,748

NA = not applicable; NR = not reported; * = includes room and board; † = room only; — = not available.

College Costs At-a-Glance	Institutional Control ind.=independent; pub.=public	Tuition and Fees	Room and Board	Percent of Eligible Freshmen Receiving Need-Based Gift Awards	Percent of Freshmen Whose Need Was Fully Met	Average Financial Aid Package for Freshmen	Average Net Cost After Aid	2004 Graduate's Average Indebtedness
Pennsylvania—continued								
Elizabethtown College	ind.	$23,710	$6600	100%	33%	$17,970	$12,340	$24,545
Franklin and Marshall College	ind.	$30,440	$7540	97%	99%	$22,282	$15,698	$18,625
Gannon University	ind.	$17,500	$6990	99%	19%	$14,545	$ 9,945	$22,624
Geneva College	ind.	$16,590	$6600	100%	18%	$13,585	$ 9,605	$21,120
Gettysburg College	ind.	$30,240	$7354	98%	100%	$24,818	$12,776	$20,193
Grove City College	ind.	$10,107	$5092	100%	12%	$ 4,887	$10,312	$22,035
Gwynedd-Mercy College	ind.	$17,400	$7500	97%	82%	$14,255	$10,645	$17,860
Haverford College	ind.	$30,270	$9420	92%	100%	$25,441	$14,249	$17,553
Indiana University of Pennsylvania	pub.	$ 6085	$4868	77%	17%	$ 7,662	$ 3,291	$17,550
Juniata College	ind.	$25,890	$7240	100%	21%	$19,441	$13,689	$21,063
King's College	ind.	$20,110	$8250	80%	16%	$15,107	$13,253	$16,417
Kutztown University of Pennsylvania	pub.	$ 6256	$5274	75%	46%	$ 5,549	$ 5,981	$15,015
Lafayette College	ind.	$29,982	$9285	90%	100%	$22,492	$16,775	$17,995
Lancaster Bible College	ind.	$12,360	$5520	64%	11%	$ 8,353	$ 9,527	$14,621
La Roche College	ind.	$16,582	$6862	73%	22%	$15,668	$ 7,776	$18,000
La Salle University	ind.	$26,190	$9410	100%	23%	$17,725	$17,875	$24,345
Lebanon Valley College	ind.	$23,600	$6590	99%	34%	$17,363	$12,827	$22,166
Lehigh University	ind.	$29,340	$8230	93%	37%	$24,148	$13,422	$18,635
Lincoln University	pub.	$ 7268	$6560	81%	29%	$14,000	—	$25,000
Lock Haven University of Pennsylvania	pub.	$ 6100	$5516	66%	55%	$ 5,540	$ 6,076	$17,021
Lycoming College	ind.	$22,886	$6242	100%	16%	$17,436	$11,692	$23,364
Mercyhurst College	ind.	$19,113	$7074	99%	80%	$12,403	$13,784	$22,000
Messiah College	ind.	$20,790	$6560	84%	26%	$13,648	$13,702	$23,287
Millersville University of Pennsylvania	pub.	$ 6081	$5642	79%	21%	$ 6,067	$ 5,656	$14,969
Moore College of Art & Design	ind.	$22,091	$8654	100%	6%	$10,964	$19,781	$25,000
Moravian College	ind.	$23,574	$7310	99%	18%	$16,116	$14,768	NR
Mount Aloysius College	ind.	$14,530	$5960	93%	NR	$ 9,500	$10,990	$17,313
Neumann College	ind.	$17,190	$7740	88%	62%	$17,000	$ 7,930	$18,000
Peirce College	ind.	$12,310	NA	67%	100%	$ 4,000	$ 8,310	$13,000
Pennsylvania College of Technology	pub.	$ 9480	$5132	NR	NR	NR	NR	NR
The Pennsylvania State University Abington College	pub.	$ 9614	NA	84%	3%	$ 8,371	$ 1,243	$18,200
The Pennsylvania State University Altoona College	pub.	$10,026	$6230	72%	5%	$10,905	$ 5,351	$18,200
The Pennsylvania State University at Erie, The Behrend College	pub.	$10,026	$6230	70%	7%	$11,240	$ 5,016	$18,600
The Pennsylvania State University Berks Campus of the Berks–Lehigh Valley College	pub.	$10,026	$6810	69%	7%	$ 9,668	$ 7,168	$18,600
The Pennsylvania State University Harrisburg Campus of the Capital College	pub.	$10,016	$7650	65%	16%	$ 9,559	$ 8,107	$18,600
The Pennsylvania State University, Lehigh Valley Campus of the Berks-Lehigh Valley College	pub.	$ 9624	NA	86%	4%	$ 7,962	$ 1,662	$18,600
The Pennsylvania State University Schuylkill Campus of the Capital College	pub.	$ 9604	$3996†	85%	4%	$10,846	$ 2,754	$18,600
The Pennsylvania State University University Park Campus	pub.	$10,856	$6230	57%	9%	$12,630	$ 4,456	$18,600
Philadelphia Biblical University	ind.	$14,500	$6100	93%	17%	$10,346	$10,254	$13,700
Philadelphia University	ind.	$21,010	$7782	99%	11%	$16,063	$12,729	$24,422

NA = not applicable; NR = not reported; * = includes room and board; † = room only; — = not available.

College Costs At-a-Glance

College Costs At-a-Glance	Institutional Control ind.=independent; pub.=public	Tuition and Fees	Room and Board	Percent of Eligible Freshmen Receiving Need-Based Gift Awards	Percent of Freshmen Whose Need Was Fully Met	Average Financial Aid Package for Freshmen	Average Net Cost After Aid	2004 Graduate's Average Indebtedness
Pennsylvania—*continued*								
Point Park University	ind.	$15,960	$ 7000	98%	24%	$12,843	$10,117	$20,551
Robert Morris University	ind.	$14,226	$ 7286	99%	25%	$12,345	$ 9,167	NR
Rosemont College	ind.	$19,365	$ 8400	100%	28%	$18,345	$ 9,420	$20,506
Saint Vincent College	ind.	$20,822	$ 6424	100%	18%	$14,065	$13,181	NR
Seton Hill University	ind.	$20,630	$ 6420	100%	16%	$16,039	$11,011	$25,787
Shippensburg University of Pennsylvania	pub.	$ 5986	$ 5274	80%	13%	$ 5,364	$ 5,896	$16,819
Slippery Rock University of Pennsylvania	pub.	$ 6096	$ 4714	79%	41%	$ 6,352	$ 4,458	$20,041
Susquehanna University	ind.	$24,810	$ 6840	100%	26%	$17,336	$14,314	$18,119
Swarthmore College	ind.	$30,094	$ 9314	100%	100%	$27,396	$12,012	$13,134
Temple University	pub.	$ 9102	$ 7522	100%	30%	$12,488	$ 4,136	$23,772
Thiel College	ind.	$16,390	$ 6584	100%	16%	$14,675	$ 8,299	$19,559
Thomas Jefferson University	ind.	$20,914	$ 7983	67%	4%	NR	NR	$24,703
University of Pennsylvania	ind.	$30,716	$ 8918	93%	100%	$26,256	$13,378	$19,579
University of Phoenix–Philadelphia Campus	ind.	$12,000	NA	100%	NR	$ 1,334	$10,666	NR
University of Phoenix–Pittsburgh Campus	ind.	$12,000	NA	100%	NR	$ 5,355	$ 6,645	NR
University of Pittsburgh at Bradford	pub.	$ 9980	$ 6344	73%	18%	$11,495	$ 4,829	$19,733
University of Pittsburgh at Johnstown	pub.	$ 9972	$ 5930	82%	10%	$ 8,530	$ 7,372	$18,601
The University of Scranton	ind.	$22,474	$ 9524	96%	11%	$15,825	$16,173	$15,800
Ursinus College	ind.	$31,450	$ 7350	91%	60%	$22,606	$16,194	$18,000
Valley Forge Christian College	ind.	$10,982	$ 5460	94%	7%	$ 6,538	$ 9,904	$26,691
Villanova University	ind.	$27,850	$ 9067	91%	19%	$22,208	$14,709	$29,675
Washington & Jefferson College	ind.	$24,620	$ 6710	100%	29%	$17,146	$14,184	$16,384
Waynesburg College	ind.	$14,540	$ 5800	98%	26%	$11,587	$ 8,753	$20,000
Westminster College	ind.	$22,680	$ 6700	99%	22%	$18,644	$10,736	$17,930
Wilkes University	ind.	$20,408	$ 8924	100%	17%	$16,751	$12,581	$20,711
Wilson College	ind.	$18,408	$ 7308	100%	11%	$14,736	$10,980	$22,208
York College of Pennsylvania	ind.	$ 9184	$ 6250	80%	22%	$ 6,442	$ 8,992	$17,818
Puerto Rico								
American University of Puerto Rico	ind.	$ 4590	NA	92%	NR	$ 5,280	—	$ 7000
Inter American University of Puerto Rico, San Germán Campus	ind.	$ 4616	$ 2400	94%	1%	$ 364	$ 6,652	NR
Polytechnic University of Puerto Rico	ind.	$ 5550	NA	71%	NR	$ 3,982	$ 1,568	NR
Pontifical Catholic University of Puerto Rico	ind.	$ 4778	$ 3140	91%	8%	$ 6,550	$ 1,368	$ 3500
University of Phoenix–Puerto Rico Campus	ind.	$ 5910	NA	100%	NR	$ 8,777	—	NR
Rhode Island								
Bryant University	ind.	$24,762	$ 9568	93%	15%	$14,889	$19,441	$24,536
Johnson & Wales University	ind.	$20,100	$ 7545	86%	4%	$12,848	$14,797	$20,268
Providence College	ind.	$25,310	$ 9270	94%	20%	$15,625	$18,955	$23,000
Rhode Island School of Design	ind.	$27,975	$ 7722	62%	13%	$11,450	$24,247	$21,700
Roger Williams University	ind.	$22,866	$10,237	90%	53%	$15,043	$18,060	$17,125
Salve Regina University	ind.	$22,200	$ 9000	96%	17%	$16,647	$14,553	$25,485
University of Rhode Island	pub.	$ 6752	$ 7810	99%	77%	$ 9,949	$ 4,613	$14,000

NA = not applicable; NR = not reported; * = includes room and board; † = room only; — = not available.

College Costs At-a-Glance

	Institutional Control ind.=independent; pub.=public	Tuition and Fees	Room and Board	Percent of Eligible Freshmen Receiving Need-Based Gift Awards	Percent of Freshmen Whose Need Was Fully Met	Average Financial Aid Package for Freshmen	Average Net Cost After Aid	2004 Graduate's Average Indebtedness
South Carolina								
Anderson College	ind.	$15,200	$6050	100%	33%	$14,419	$ 6,831	$13,874
Clemson University	pub.	$ 8074	$5292	31%	30%	$ 9,147	$ 4,219	$15,260
Coastal Carolina University	pub.	$ 6100	$5970	32%	41%	$ 6,847	$ 5,223	$19,932
College of Charleston	pub.	$ 6202	$6506	71%	30%	$ 8,358	$ 4,350	$15,461
Columbia College	ind.	$18,040	$5620	100%	55%	$21,050	$ 2,610	$25,333
Columbia International University	ind.	$12,845	$5380	100%	9%	$ 7,896	$10,329	$15,300
Converse College	ind.	$19,960	$6110	100%	41%	$18,808	$ 7,262	$17,127
Erskine College	ind.	$18,128	$6026	95%	29%	$17,428	$ 6,726	$17,380
Francis Marion University	pub.	$ 5540	$4656	NR	NR	NR	NR	$22,311
Furman University	ind.	$24,408	$6272	99%	49%	$20,319	$10,361	$21,194
Limestone College	ind.	$14,040	$5800	97%	17%	$ 8,710	$11,130	$13,398
Medical University of South Carolina	pub.	$ 9446	NA	56%	14%	$ 9,398	$ 48	$32,486
Morris College	ind.	$ 7985	$3724	93%	9%	$12,100	—	$17,125
North Greenville College	ind.	$10,350	$5950	100%	40%	$ 8,100	$ 8,200	$10,000
South Carolina State University	pub.	$ 6355	$5776	NR	NR	NR	NR	$17,000
Southern Methodist College	ind.	$ 5200	$4200	100%	NR	$ 2,025	$ 7,375	$12,600
Southern Wesleyan University	ind.	$14,750	$5200	98%	25%	$12,845	$ 7,105	$22,648
University of South Carolina	pub.	$ 5778	$5590	47%	36%	$ 9,017	$ 2,351	$17,828
University of South Carolina Upstate	pub.	$ 6186	$5140	67%	21%	$ 7,613	$ 3,713	$ 9760
Voorhees College	ind.	$ 7276	$4572	96%	7%	$ 7,569	$ 4,279	$13,383
Winthrop University	pub.	$ 7836	$4992	97%	18%	$ 8,318	$ 4,510	$17,800
Wofford College	ind.	$22,300	$6440	100%	47%	$21,489	$ 7,251	$12,281
South Dakota								
Augustana College	ind.	$18,860	$5334	100%	16%	$15,693	$ 8,501	$18,385
Black Hills State University	pub.	$ 4820	$3449	NR	NR	NR	NR	$21,218
Dakota State University	pub.	$ 4614	$3192	54%	29%	$ 5,373	$ 2,433	$22,352
Mount Marty College	ind.	$14,936	$4764	100%	19%	$12,776	$ 6,924	$21,134
Northern State University	pub.	$ 4448	$3733	85%	100%	$ 5,642	$ 2,539	$19,330
Presentation College	ind.	$10,400	$4550	84%	1%	$ 6,069	$ 8,881	$25,978
South Dakota School of Mines and Technology	pub.	$ 4534	$3684	65%	21%	$ 5,434	$ 2,784	$12,975
South Dakota State University	pub.	$ 4732	$4769	54%	67%	$ 6,121	$ 3,380	$18,333
University of Sioux Falls	ind.	$14,900	$4350	NR	NR	NR	NR	NR
The University of South Dakota	pub.	$ 4749	$3741	52%	84%	$ 5,451	$ 3,039	$18,810
Tennessee								
American Baptist College of American Baptist Theological Seminary	ind.	$ 3143	$1600†	75%	NR	$ 2,025	$ 2,718	NR
Aquinas College	ind.	$10,768	NR	58%	53%	$ 7,850	$ 2,918	$ 8500
Austin Peay State University	pub.	$ 4224	$4296	62%	NR	$ 4,552	$ 3,968	NR
Belmont University	ind.	$16,220	$6156	70%	22%	$ 2,982	$19,394	$ 8651
Bethel College	ind.	$ 9630	$5384	52%	NR	$11,018	$ 3,996	NR
Bryan College	ind.	$14,800	$4470	56%	NR	$12,804	$ 6,466	$17,660
Carson-Newman College	ind.	$14,420	$4930	100%	33%	$13,567	$ 5,783	$14,245
Christian Brothers University	ind.	$18,230	$5300	52%	28%	$16,395	$ 7,135	$17,400

NA = not applicable; NR = not reported; * = includes room and board; † = room only; — = not available.

College Costs At-a-Glance

	Institutional Control ind.=independent; pub.=public	Tuition and Fees	Room and Board	Percent of Eligible Freshmen Receiving Need-Based Gift Awards	Percent of Freshmen Whose Need Was Fully Met	Average Financial Aid Package for Freshmen	Average Net Cost After Aid	2004 Graduate's Average Indebtedness
Tennessee—*continued*								
East Tennessee State University	pub.	$ 4059	$4858	63%	27%	$ 5,666	$ 3,251	$17,966
Freed-Hardeman University	ind.	$12,440	$6200	96%	21%	$10,471	$ 8,169	$22,792
Free Will Baptist Bible College	ind.	$ 7560	$4470	NR	NR	NR	NR	$14,509
Johnson Bible College	ind.	$ 6490	$4090	99%	NR	$ 3,037	$ 7,543	$14,776
King College	ind.	$17,680	$5720	100%	27%	$15,998	$ 7,402	$15,300
Lambuth University	ind.	$12,490	$5436	79%	34%	$14,132	$ 3,794	$11,000
Lee University	ind.	$ 9075	$4560	88%	23%	$ 6,729	$ 6,906	$23,174
LeMoyne-Owen College	ind.	$14,085	$4620	96%	7%	$ 7,992	$10,713	$15,682
Lincoln Memorial University	ind.	$12,600	$4910	69%	86%	$10,750	$ 6,760	$11,500
Lipscomb University	ind.	$13,486	$6090	50%	30%	$ 9,361	$10,215	$18,000
Martin Methodist College	ind.	$13,650	$4800	100%	57%	$ 6,750	$11,700	$14,200
Maryville College	ind.	$21,065	$6500	100%	20%	$21,071	$ 6,494	NR
Memphis College of Art	ind.	$15,860	$7400	21%	81%	$ 6,500	$16,760	$20,000
Middle Tennessee State University	pub.	$ 4230	$4814	52%	56%	$ 6,801	$ 2,243	$19,574
Milligan College	ind.	$16,360	$4600	100%	23%	$15,122	$ 5,838	$23,794
Southern Adventist University	ind.	$14,020	$4480	87%	12%	$ 8,500	$10,000	$15,500
Tennessee Technological University	pub.	$ 3998	$5270	65%	21%	$ 5,443	$ 3,825	$13,747
Tennessee Wesleyan College	ind.	$13,550	$5100	100%	18%	$10,846	$ 7,804	$18,159
Trevecca Nazarene University	ind.	$12,792	$5868	100%	33%	$10,578	$ 8,082	$ 6544
Tusculum College	ind.	$15,110	$5950	89%	24%	$12,929	$ 8,131	$14,633
Union University	ind.	$15,370	$4970	71%	NR	$10,402	$ 9,938	$15,328
The University of Memphis	pub.	$ 4480	$4920	60%	9%	$ 5,175	$ 4,225	$21,454
The University of Tennessee at Chattanooga	pub.	$ 4928	$5808	81%	43%	$ 8,875	$ 1,861	$14,750
The University of Tennessee at Martin	pub.	$ 4134	$4100	66%	37%	$ 8,107	$ 127	$14,458
University of the South	ind.	$25,580	$7120	99%	100%	$21,185	$11,515	$13,244
Vanderbilt University	ind.	$29,990	$9736	86%	100%	$30,404	$ 9,322	$24,044
Texas								
Abilene Christian University	ind.	$14,200	$5270	100%	46%	$10,325	$ 9,145	$25,086
Angelo State University	pub.	$ 3126	$4696	92%	82%	$ 4,309	$ 3,513	NR
Arlington Baptist College	ind.	$ 5040	$3660	NR	100%	$ 5,025	$ 3,675	$ 7800
Austin College	ind.	$20,495	$7376	100%	95%	$20,016	$ 7,855	$23,214
Austin Graduate School of Theology	ind.	$ 4200	NA	NR	NR	NR	NR	$ 9350
Baylor University	ind.	$21,070	$6485	100%	18%	$16,553	$11,002	NR
Dallas Baptist University	ind.	$11,610	$4644	68%	57%	$10,051	$ 6,203	$ 8268
Dallas Christian College	ind.	$ 7937	$5100	75%	NR	$ 6,973	$ 6,064	$15,000
East Texas Baptist University	ind.	$12,000	$3873	87%	17%	$11,005	$ 4,868	$15,005
Houston Baptist University	ind.	$12,915	$4566	98%	18%	$ 9,687	$ 7,794	$17,212
Howard Payne University	ind.	$12,000	$4242	98%	22%	$ 9,494	$ 6,748	$18,960
Lamar University	pub.	$ 3156	$5706	NR	NR	$ 1,953	$ 6,909	$ 7100
LeTourneau University	ind.	$15,890	$6286	100%	21%	$12,599	$ 9,577	$20,055
Lubbock Christian University	ind.	$11,994	$4130	100%	14%	$10,866	$ 5,258	$20,244
McMurry University	ind.	$14,350	$5500	98%	7%	$13,062	$ 6,788	$28,368

NA = not applicable; NR = not reported; * = includes room and board; † = room only; — = not available.

College Costs At-a-Glance

	Institutional Control ind.=independent; pub.=public	Tuition and Fees	Room and Board	Percent of Eligible Freshmen Receiving Need-Based Gift Awards	Percent of Freshmen Whose Need Was Fully Met	Average Financial Aid Package for Freshmen	Average Net Cost After Aid	2004 Graduate's Average Indebtedness
Texas—*continued*								
Midwestern State University	pub.	$ 3740	$4844	70%	2%	$ 3,504	$ 5,080	$12,000
Northwood University, Texas Campus	ind.	$15,183	$6849	81%	28%	$13,650	$ 8,382	$19,157
Rice University	ind.	$21,206	$8380	99%	100%	$19,565	$10,021	$13,452
St. Edward's University	ind.	$17,320	NR	96%	15%	$12,797	$ 4,523	$23,476
St. Mary's University of San Antonio	ind.	$17,756	$6498	87%	30%	$15,462	$ 8,792	$23,447
Sam Houston State University	pub.	$ 4260	$4336	71%	16%	$13,407	—	$26,340
Schreiner University	ind.	$14,443	$6880	98%	12%	$11,999	$ 9,324	$19,132
Southern Methodist University	ind.	$26,880	$9208	77%	71%	$22,731	$13,357	$16,906
Southwestern University	ind.	$20,220	$6359	100%	67%	$17,612	$ 8,967	$18,393
Stephen F. Austin State University	pub.	$ 4298	$5012	76%	31%	$ 4,481	$ 4,829	$16,624
Tarleton State University	pub.	$ 3835	$5900	48%	59%	$ 7,874	$ 1,861	$16,776
Texas A&M University	pub.	$ 5955	$6887	99%	97%	$10,049	$ 2,793	$15,927
Texas A&M University at Galveston	pub.	$ 4682	$4870	58%	35%	$ 9,335	$ 217	$10,857
Texas A&M University–Commerce	pub.	$ 4178	$5246	97%	20%	$ 6,570	$ 2,854	$16,236
Texas A&M University–Texarkana	pub.	$ 2340	NA	NR	NR	NR	NR	NR
Texas Christian University	ind.	$19,740	$5880	93%	52%	$13,314	$12,306	NR
Texas Lutheran University	ind.	$16,600	$5030	84%	27%	$12,643	$ 8,987	$25,050
Texas State University-San Marcos	pub.	$ 4680	$5456	49%	12%	$ 8,229	$ 1,907	$16,161
Texas Tech University	pub.	$ 5848	$6421	67%	NR	$ 5,875	$ 6,394	$19,972
Texas Wesleyan University	ind.	$13,000	$5400	94%	NR	NR	NR	NR
Trinity University	ind.	$20,010	$8205	95%	65%	$16,046	$12,169	NR
University of Dallas	ind.	$20,411	$7026	98%	25%	$15,167	$12,270	$21,700
University of Houston–Downtown	pub.	$ 3934	NA	93%	7%	$ 4,225	—	$10,372
University of Houston–Victoria	pub.	$ 4290	NA	NR	NR	NR	NR	$20,694
University of Mary Hardin-Baylor	ind.	$12,380	$4000	93%	15%	$ 9,741	$ 6,639	$15,819
University of North Texas	pub.	$ 5561	$5124	82%	22%	$ 6,782	$ 3,903	$18,175
University of Phoenix–Dallas Campus	ind.	$11,010	NA	100%	NR	$ 1,273	$ 9,737	NR
University of Phoenix–Houston Campus	ind.	$11,010	NA	100%	NR	$ 5,516	$ 5,494	NR
University of St. Thomas	ind.	$16,312	$7300	97%	7%	$12,523	$11,089	$20,491
The University of Texas at Arlington	pub.	$ 5300	$5212	71%	18%	$ 7,554	$ 2,958	$13,319
The University of Texas at Austin	pub.	$ 5735	$6184	87%	93%	$ 9,150	$ 2,769	$16,200
The University of Texas at Brownsville	pub.	$ 2805	$2300†	95%	NR	$ 2,615	$ 2,490	NR
The University of Texas at Dallas	pub.	$ 6363	$6244	74%	42%	$10,291	$ 2,316	NR
The University of Texas at El Paso	pub.	$ 5064	$4095†	95%	16%	$ 6,897	$ 2,262	$ 6041
The University of Texas at San Antonio	pub.	$ 5272	$5306	81%	10%	$ 5,761	$ 4,817	$17,000
The University of Texas at Tyler	pub.	$ 4046	$5373	93%	36%	$ 6,597	$ 2,822	$14,967
The University of Texas Health Science Center at Houston	pub.	$ 5602	NR	NR	NR	NR	NR	$17,505
The University of Texas Medical Branch	pub.	$ 3210	$2160†	NR	NR	NR	NR	NR
The University of Texas–Pan American	pub.	$ 3152	$4233	99%	4%	$ 5,572	$ 1,813	$12,080
The University of Texas Southwestern Medical Center at Dallas	pub.	$ 2820	NA	NR	NR	NR	NR	$34,946
University of the Incarnate Word	ind.	$17,072	$6234	99%	59%	$11,798	$11,508	$24,476
Wayland Baptist University	ind.	$ 9250	$3420	99%	23%	$ 8,453	$ 4,217	NR
West Texas A&M University	pub.	$ 3472	$4592	88%	93%	$ 5,639	$ 2,425	$11,875

NA = not applicable; NR = not reported; * = includes room and board; † = room only; — = not available.

College Costs At-a-Glance

	Institutional Control ind.=independent; pub.=public	Tuition and Fees	Room and Board	Percent of Eligible Freshmen Receiving Need-Based Gift Awards	Percent of Freshmen Whose Need Was Fully Met	Average Financial Aid Package for Freshmen	Average Net Cost After Aid	2004 Graduate's Average Indebtedness
Utah								
Brigham Young University	ind.	$ 4920	$5570	60%	NR	$ 2,383	$ 8,107	$12,478
Southern Utah University	pub.	$ 3054	$5400	61%	25%	$ 3,299	$ 5,155	$11,359
University of Phoenix–Utah Campus	ind.	$ 9540	NA	100%	NR	$ 3,612	$ 5,928	NR
University of Utah	pub.	$ 4000	$5726	79%	13%	$ 6,560	$ 3,166	$11,496
Utah State University	pub.	$ 3374	$4230	62%	13%	$ 3,300	$ 4,304	$12,430
Utah Valley State College	pub.	$ 2788	NA	43%	7%	$ 5,307	—	$ 6273
Westminster College	ind.	$ 18,476	$5636	100%	85%	$15,920	$ 8,192	$16,100
Vermont								
Bennington College	ind.	$ 31,070	$7710	98%	5%	$23,287	$15,493	$18,460
Burlington College	ind.	$ 14,170	$6000†	73%	NR	$ 9,371	$10,799	$19,210
Castleton State College	pub.	$ 6484	$6674	NR	NR	NR	NR	NR
Champlain College	ind.	$ 14,910	$9695	76%	19%	$ 8,667	$15,938	NR
College of St. Joseph	ind.	$ 13,200	$6600	100%	10%	$14,062	$ 5,738	$19,355
Goddard College	ind.	$ 9846	NA	45%	NR	$ 5,030	$ 4,816	$21,039
Green Mountain College	ind.	$ 21,214	$6990	99%	31%	$18,788	$ 9,416	$19,873
Marlboro College	ind.	$ 27,790	$8190	98%	83%	$20,907	$15,073	$18,212
Middlebury College	ind.	$40,400*	NR	100%	100%	$28,752	$11,648	$19,012
Saint Michael's College	ind.	$ 25,535	$6250	96%	25%	$18,366	$13,419	$19,437
Southern Vermont College	ind.	$ 14,373	$6944	94%	21%	$11,905	$ 9,412	$18,778
Sterling College	ind.	$ 16,434	$6082	100%	NR	$13,979	$ 8,537	$13,200
University of Vermont	pub.	$ 10,226	$7016	92%	82%	$16,231	$ 1,011	$23,114
Vermont Technical College	pub.	$ 7502	$6454	79%	15%	$ 8,666	$ 5,290	$12,000
Virgin Islands								
University of the Virgin Islands	pub.	$ 3796	$7740	92%	2%	$ 4,400	$ 7,136	$ 4400
Virginia								
Averett University	ind.	$ 18,430	$6330	100%	11%	$13,280	$11,480	$15,924
Bridgewater College	ind.	$ 18,990	$8800	100%	28%	$16,933	$10,857	$22,809
Christendom College	ind.	$ 15,818	$5776	100%	100%	$10,875	$10,719	$11,240
Christopher Newport University	pub.	$ 5314	$7200	72%	20%	$ 4,795	$ 7,719	$ 8510
The College of William and Mary	pub.	$ 7096	$6066	84%	23%	$ 9,254	$ 3,908	$13,688
Eastern Mennonite University	ind.	$ 19,500	$5950	66%	30%	$16,515	$ 8,935	$18,208
Emory & Henry College	ind.	$ 16,690	$6250	100%	27%	$14,251	$ 8,689	$15,482
Ferrum College	ind.	$ 16,870	$5700	100%	12%	$12,931	$ 9,639	$16,300
George Mason University	pub.	$ 5448	$6240	74%	57%	$ 7,099	$ 4,589	$15,015
Hampden-Sydney College	ind.	$ 22,946	$7370	100%	38%	$15,780	$14,536	$15,247
Hampton University	ind.	$ 14,996	$6424	28%	79%	$ 3,780	$17,640	$ 6980
Hollins University	ind.	$ 21,675	$7700	100%	17%	$18,593	$10,782	$19,305
James Madison University	pub.	$ 5476	$6116	51%	58%	$ 7,875	$ 3,717	$12,303
Liberty University	ind.	$ 14,550	$5400	53%	20%	$11,107	$ 8,843	$18,078
Longwood University	pub.	$ 6441	$5424	91%	16%	$ 6,295	$ 5,570	$14,326
Lynchburg College	ind.	$ 22,885	$5000	100%	26%	$17,808	$10,077	$18,932
Mary Baldwin College	ind.	$ 19,991	$5689	100%	45%	$20,796	$ 4,884	$21,242

NA = not applicable; NR = not reported; * = includes room and board; † = room only; — = not available.

College Costs At-a-Glance	Institutional Control ind.=independent; pub.=public	Tuition and Fees	Room and Board	Percent of Eligible Freshmen Receiving Need-Based Gift Awards	Percent of Freshmen Whose Need Was Fully Met	Average Financial Aid Package for Freshmen	Average Net Cost After Aid	2004 Graduate's Average Indebtedness
Virginia—*continued*								
Marymount University	ind.	$17,090	$7520	77%	23%	$13,774	$10,836	$21,981
Norfolk State University	pub.	$ 4295	$6236	90%	3%	$ 8,474	$ 2,057	$15,467
Old Dominion University	pub.	$ 5268	$5802	54%	51%	$ 6,039	$ 5,031	$16,775
Radford University	pub.	$ 4762	$5886	69%	64%	$ 6,421	$ 4,227	$14,908
Randolph-Macon College	ind.	$22,625	$6510	100%	39%	$17,305	$11,830	$18,031
Randolph-Macon Woman's College	ind.	$21,740	$8230	100%	35%	$21,385	$ 8,585	$22,869
Roanoke College	ind.	$22,109	$6912	84%	23%	$18,596	$10,425	$17,803
Saint Paul's College	ind.	$ 9420	$5290	80%	2%	$ 9,959	$ 4,751	$10,783
Shenandoah University	ind.	$19,240	$7090	52%	20%	$13,596	$12,734	$19,518
Southern Virginia University	ind.	$14,640	$5300	97%	14%	$10,371	$ 9,569	$13,152
Sweet Briar College	ind.	$22,430	$9030	75%	79%	$14,279	$17,181	$17,101
University of Mary Washington	pub.	$ 5128	$5744	90%	9%	$ 4,450	$ 6,422	$12,665
University of Richmond	ind.	$27,850	$5660	97%	81%	$20,250	$13,260	$16,900
University of Virginia	pub.	$ 6790	$5960	89%	65%	$13,115	—	$14,065
The University of Virginia's College at Wise	pub.	$ 5081	$6200	90%	95%	$ 5,574	$ 5,707	$ 8385
Virginia Commonwealth University	pub.	$ 5385	$7042	83%	5%	$ 6,529	$ 5,898	$19,337
Virginia Intermont College	ind.	$15,200	$5650	47%	3%	$15,466	$ 5,384	$15,065
Virginia Military Institute	pub.	$ 6529	$5474	94%	63%	$10,551	$ 1,452	$14,456
Virginia Polytechnic Institute and State University	pub.	$ 5836	$4288	77%	3%	$ 7,593	$ 2,531	$18,281
Virginia Union University	ind.	$12,260	$5436	72%	30%	$ 6,983	$10,713	$17,568
Virginia Wesleyan College	ind.	$20,448	$6600	41%	5%	$14,083	$12,965	NR
Washington and Lee University	ind.	$28,635	$7225	73%	85%	$22,468	$13,392	$17,374
Washington								
Antioch University Seattle	ind.	$13,815	NA	NR	NR	NR	NR	$15,999
Bastyr University	ind.	$14,400	$4500†	NR	NR	NR	NR	$21,000
Central Washington University	pub.	$ 4647	$6402	90%	35%	$ 4,347	$ 6,702	$15,686
City University	ind.	$ 9440	NA	36%	NR	$ 4,081	$ 5,359	$16,369
Cornish College of the Arts	ind.	$21,200	NA	96%	3%	$ 8,638	$12,562	$23,000
Eastern Washington University	pub.	$ 4056	$5460	77%	25%	$ 9,882	—	$17,516
The Evergreen State College	pub.	$ 4056	$5784	56%	30%	$ 9,824	$ 16	$10,486
Gonzaga University	ind.	$22,118	$6650	100%	21%	$13,737	$15,031	$21,546
Heritage University	ind.	$ 7120	NA	100%	2%	$ 8,475	—	$11,909
Northwest College of Art	ind.	$14,400	NA	NR	NR	NR	NR	NR
Northwest University	ind.	$15,944	$6450	100%	19%	$10,991	$11,403	$20,138
Pacific Lutheran University	ind.	$20,790	$6410	80%	37%	$18,299	$ 8,901	$24,244
Saint Martin's College	ind.	$19,980	$6200	100%	34%	$19,697	$ 6,483	$24,715
Seattle Pacific University	ind.	$20,466	$7368	98%	22%	$16,260	$11,574	$21,805
Trinity Lutheran College	ind.	$11,334	$5620	NR	NR	NR	NR	NR
University of Phoenix–Washington Campus	ind.	$10,290	NA	50%	NR	$ 4,669	$ 5,621	NR
University of Puget Sound	ind.	$26,880	$6730	99%	35%	$20,408	$13,202	$24,387
University of Washington	pub.	$ 5286	$7017	79%	53%	$ 9,000	$ 3,303	$15,210
Walla Walla College	ind.	$17,829	$3684	83%	20%	$15,588	$ 5,925	$22,235

NA = not applicable; NR = not reported; * = includes room and board; † = room only; — = not available.

College Costs At-a-Glance	Institutional Control ind.=independent; pub.=public	Tuition and Fees	Room and Board	Percent of Eligible Freshmen Receiving Need-Based Gift Awards	Percent of Freshmen Whose Need Was Fully Met	Average Financial Aid Package for Freshmen	Average Net Cost After Aid	2004 Graduate's Average Indebtedness
Washington—*continued*								
Washington State University	pub.	$ 5358	$6450	57%	33%	$ 8,728	$ 3,080	$20,216
Western Washington University	pub.	$ 4452	$6242	85%	27%	$ 8,304	$ 2,390	$15,139
Whitman College	ind.	$27,106	$7180	98%	77%	$19,385	$14,901	$17,927
Whitworth College	ind.	$22,678	$6760	100%	29%	$18,357	$11,081	$17,014
West Virginia								
Alderson-Broaddus College	ind.	$17,966	$5808	96%	3%	$18,525	$ 5,249	$22,125
Appalachian Bible College	ind.	$ 8408	$4400	100%	NR	$ 2,800	$10,008	$22,100
Bethany College	ind.	$15,440	$7200	96%	67%	$12,000	$10,640	$18,500
Bluefield State College	pub.	$ 3114	NA	100%	24%	$ 5,000	—	$10,200
Davis & Elkins College	ind.	$15,666	$5986	74%	46%	$16,512	$ 5,140	$15,500
Fairmont State University	pub.	$ 4112	$6052	76%	11%	$ 4,955	$ 5,209	$17,500
Glenville State College	pub.	$ 3276	$5060	78%	25%	$ 7,892	$ 444	$14,567
Marshall University	pub.	$ 4296	$6060	63%	33%	$ 6,841	$ 3,515	$15,258
Mountain State University	ind.	$ 5400	$5440	91%	NR	$ 5,281	$ 5,559	$24,870
Ohio Valley University	ind.	$12,012	$5380	93%	14%	$ 8,368	$ 9,024	$17,119
Shepherd University	pub.	$ 3654	$5574	54%	24%	$ 6,341	$ 2,887	$13,695
University of Charleston	ind.	$20,200	$7400	88%	40%	$18,750	$ 8,850	$19,825
West Liberty State College	pub.	$ 3380	$5006	82%	59%	$ 4,917	$ 3,469	$13,800
West Virginia University	pub.	$ 3938	$6084	49%	45%	$ 6,156	$ 3,866	$21,100
West Virginia Wesleyan College	ind.	$21,250	$5500	100%	33%	$20,276	$ 6,474	NR
Wheeling Jesuit University	ind.	$21,350	$6450	82%	42%	$18,884	$ 8,916	$15,001
Wisconsin								
Alverno College	ind.	$14,410	$5400	NR	NR	NR	NR	NR
Bellin College of Nursing	ind.	$13,830	NA	NR	NR	NR	NR	$18,256
Beloit College	ind.	$25,736	$5696	100%	100%	$18,316	$13,116	$20,339
Carroll College	ind.	$19,050	$5810	100%	80%	$15,912	$ 8,948	$16,462
Concordia University Wisconsin	ind.	$16,430	$6230	98%	33%	$16,300	$ 6,360	$17,500
Edgewood College	ind.	$16,050	$5691	98%	21%	$12,378	$ 9,363	$19,845
Lakeland College	ind.	$15,770	$5635	99%	23%	$12,437	$ 8,968	$12,253
Lawrence University	ind.	$27,924	$5900	100%	100%	$21,251	$12,573	$18,718
Maranatha Baptist Bible College	ind.	$ 8120	$4700	63%	1%	$ 6,455	$ 6,365	$13,587
Marian College of Fond du Lac	ind.	$15,825	$5240	100%	29%	$13,981	$ 7,084	$20,000
Milwaukee Institute of Art and Design	ind.	$22,510	$6800	99%	22%	$17,135	$12,175	$18,492
Milwaukee School of Engineering	ind.	$23,955	$5892	100%	11%	$14,759	$15,088	$31,253
Mount Mary College	ind.	$16,155	$5350	100%	18%	$11,881	$ 9,624	$21,345
Northland College	ind.	$19,715	$5610	98%	15%	$16,085	$ 9,240	$20,164
Ripon College	ind.	$20,730	$5360	100%	35%	$18,306	$ 7,784	$19,067
St. Norbert College	ind.	$21,510	$5980	100%	36%	$16,937	$10,553	$20,770
Silver Lake College	ind.	$16,000	$4250†	100%	4%	$13,107	$ 7,143	$16,708
University of Wisconsin–Eau Claire	pub.	$ 4864	$4310	61%	81%	$ 6,182	$ 2,992	$16,237
University of Wisconsin–Green Bay	pub.	$ 5154	$4716	66%	35%	$ 6,975	$ 2,895	$ 9238
University of Wisconsin–La Crosse	pub.	$ 4895	$4570	46%	78%	$ 4,316	$ 5,149	$14,481

NA = not applicable; NR = not reported; * = includes room and board; † = room only; — = not available.

College Costs At-a-Glance	Institutional Control ind.=independent; pub.=public	Tuition and Fees	Room and Board	Percent of Eligible Freshmen Receiving Need-Based Gift Awards	Percent of Freshmen Whose Need Was Fully Met	Average Financial Aid Package for Freshmen	Average Net Cost After Aid	2004 Graduate's Average Indebtedness
Wisconsin—*continued*								
University of Wisconsin–Madison	pub.	$5860	$6250	33%	35%	$10,502	$1,608	$17,528
University of Wisconsin–Milwaukee	pub.	$5835	$4505	43%	27%	$ 4,584	$5,756	$16,159
University of Wisconsin–Oshkosh	pub.	$4616	$4630	100%	50%	$ 2,500	$6,746	$14,000
University of Wisconsin–Parkside	pub.	$4652	$5415	48%	45%	$ 5,175	$4,892	$12,500
University of Wisconsin–Stevens Point	pub.	$4704	$4094	52%	51%	$ 5,120	$3,678	$13,935
University of Wisconsin–Stout	pub.	$6262	$4334	47%	55%	$ 6,867	$3,729	$18,172
University of Wisconsin–Superior	pub.	$4808	$4342	57%	31%	$ 6,035	$3,115	NR
University of Wisconsin–Whitewater	pub.	$5080	$4210	48%	41%	$ 5,360	$3,930	NR
Wyoming								
University of Wyoming	pub.	$3243	$5953	32%	55%	$ 7,834	$1,362	$15,352

NA = not applicable; NR = not reported; * = includes room and board; † = room only; — = not available.

Profiles of College Financial Aid Programs

ABILENE CHRISTIAN UNIVERSITY
Abilene, TX

Tuition & fees: $14,200 | **Average undergraduate aid package: $10,751**

ABOUT THE INSTITUTION Independent religious, coed. Awards: associate, bachelor's, master's, doctoral, and first professional degrees and post-bachelor's and post-master's certificates. 80 undergraduate majors. Total enrollment: 4,761. Undergraduates: 4,209. Freshmen: 1,020. Federal methodology is used as a basis for awarding need-based institutional aid.

UNDERGRADUATE EXPENSES for 2004–05 *Application fee:* $25. *Comprehensive fee:* $19,470 includes full-time tuition ($13,650), mandatory fees ($550), and room and board ($5270). *College room only:* $2240. Full-time tuition and fees vary according to course load. Room and board charges vary according to board plan and housing facility. *Part-time tuition:* $455 per semester hour. *Part-time fees:* $26.50 per semester hour; $10. Part-time tuition and fees vary according to course load. *Payment plans:* Tuition prepayment, installment.

FRESHMAN FINANCIAL AID (Fall 2003) 941 applied for aid; of those 61% were deemed to have need. 100% of freshmen with need received aid; of those 46% had need fully met. *Average percent of need met:* 73% (excluding resources awarded to replace EFC). *Average financial aid package:* $10,325 (excluding resources awarded to replace EFC). 31% of all full-time freshmen had no need and received non-need-based gift aid.

UNDERGRADUATE FINANCIAL AID (Fall 2003) 3,770 applied for aid; of those 62% were deemed to have need. 100% of undergraduates with need received aid; of those 51% had need fully met. *Average percent of need met:* 74% (excluding resources awarded to replace EFC). *Average financial aid package:* $10,751 (excluding resources awarded to replace EFC). 26% of all full-time undergraduates had no need and received non-need-based gift aid.

GIFT AID (NEED-BASED) *Total amount:* $16,079,748 (19% federal, 34% state, 40% institutional, 7% external sources). *Receiving aid:* Freshmen: 60% (570); All full-time undergraduates: 59% (2,294). *Average award:* Freshmen: $8057; Undergraduates: $7406. *Scholarships, grants, and awards:* Federal Pell, FSEOG, state, private, college/university gift aid from institutional funds, United Negro College Fund.

GIFT AID (NON-NEED-BASED) *Total amount:* $7,504,907 (1% state, 87% institutional, 12% external sources). *Receiving aid:* Freshmen: 56% (529); Undergraduates: 47% (1,827). *Average Award:* Freshmen: $5010; Undergraduates: $5084. *Scholarships, grants, and awards by category: Academic Interests/Achievement:* 2,582 awards ($7,993,049 total): agriculture, biological sciences, business, communication, education, English, foreign languages, general academic interests/achievements, home economics, mathematics, physical sciences, religion/biblical studies, social sciences. *Creative Arts/Performance:* 84 awards ($135,386 total): art/fine arts, debating, journalism/publications, music, theater/drama. *Special Achievements/Activities:* 137 awards ($125,670 total): cheerleading/drum major, leadership. *Special Characteristics:* 873 awards ($2,762,377 total): children of faculty/staff, ethnic background, first-generation college students, local/state students, members of minority groups, out-of-state students, previous college experience, relatives of clergy, religious affiliation. *Tuition waivers:* Full or partial for employees or children of employees.

LOANS *Student loans:* $22,249,482 (84% need-based, 16% non-need-based). 70% of past graduating class borrowed through all loan programs. *Average indebtedness per student:* $25,086. *Average need-based loan:* Freshmen: $2830; Undergraduates: $4034. *Parent loans:* $4,436,145 (61% need-based, 39% non-need-based). *Programs:* FFEL (Subsidized and Unsubsidized Stafford, PLUS), Perkins, state, college/university.

WORK-STUDY *Federal work-study:* Total amount: $642,690; 440 jobs averaging $1454. *State or other work-study/employment:* Total amount: $1,531,008 (10% need-based, 90% non-need-based). Part-time jobs available.

ATHLETIC AWARDS *Total amount:* $2,099,347 (36% need-based, 64% non-need-based).

APPLYING FOR FINANCIAL AID *Required financial aid forms:* FAFSA, institution's own form. *Financial aid deadline (priority):* 3/1. *Notification date:* Continuous beginning 4/1. Students must reply within 3 weeks of notification.

CONTACT Mr. Gary West, Director of Student Financial Services, Abilene Christian University, ACU Box 29007, Abilene, TX 79699-9007, 325-674-2643 or toll-free 800-460-6228. *E-mail:* westg@acu.edu.

ACADEMY OF ART UNIVERSITY
San Francisco, CA

Tuition & fees: $13,280 | **Average undergraduate aid package: $5952**

ABOUT THE INSTITUTION Proprietary, coed. Awards: associate, bachelor's, and master's degrees. 27 undergraduate majors. Total enrollment: 6,706. Undergraduates: 5,325. Freshmen: 1,742. Federal methodology is used as a basis for awarding need-based institutional aid.

UNDERGRADUATE EXPENSES for 2005–06 *Application fee:* $100. *Comprehensive fee:* $25,280 includes full-time tuition ($13,200), mandatory fees ($80), and room and board ($12,000). *College room only:* $8400. Full-time tuition and fees vary according to course load. Room and board charges vary according to housing facility. *Part-time tuition:* $550 per unit. *Part-time fees:* $40 per term. Part-time tuition and fees vary according to course load. *Payment plan:* Installment.

FRESHMAN FINANCIAL AID (Fall 2003) 300 applied for aid; of those 89% were deemed to have need. 84% of freshmen with need received aid. *Average percent of need met:* 26% (excluding resources awarded to replace EFC). *Average financial aid package:* $4985 (excluding resources awarded to replace EFC).

UNDERGRADUATE FINANCIAL AID (Fall 2003) 2,127 applied for aid; of those 90% were deemed to have need. 78% of undergraduates with need received aid. *Average percent of need met:* 40% (excluding resources awarded to replace EFC). *Average financial aid package:* $5952 (excluding resources awarded to replace EFC).

GIFT AID (NEED-BASED) *Total amount:* $6,394,057 (71% federal, 29% state). *Receiving aid:* Freshmen: 26% (120); All full-time undergraduates: 20% (764). *Average award:* Freshmen: $4163; Undergraduates: $5045. *Scholarships, grants, and awards:* Federal Pell, FSEOG, state, private.

GIFT AID (NON-NEED-BASED) *Total amount:* $30,000 (100% external sources). *Receiving aid:* Freshmen: 6% (28); Undergraduates: 2% (58).

LOANS *Student loans:* $22,053,166 (54% need-based, 46% non-need-based). 51% of past graduating class borrowed through all loan programs. *Average indebtedness per student:* $32,000. *Average need-based loan:* Freshmen: $2560; Undergraduates: $3406. *Parent loans:* $14,480,760 (100% non-need-based). *Programs:* Federal Direct (Subsidized and Unsubsidized Stafford, PLUS), alternative loans.

WORK-STUDY *Federal work-study:* Total amount: $244,421; 71 jobs averaging $3442.

APPLYING FOR FINANCIAL AID *Required financial aid forms:* FAFSA, institution's own form. *Financial aid deadline (priority):* 3/2. *Notification date:* Continuous beginning 7/1. Students must reply within 3 weeks of notification.

CONTACT Mr. Joe Vollaro, Executive Vice President of Financial Aid and Compliance, Academy of Art University, 79 New Montgomery Street, San Francisco, CA 94105-3410, 415-274-8688 or toll-free 800-544-ARTS. *Fax:* 415-296-2098. *E-mail:* jvollaro@academyart.edu.

ADAMS STATE COLLEGE
Alamosa, CO

ABOUT THE INSTITUTION State-supported, coed. Awards: associate, bachelor's, and master's degrees. 30 undergraduate majors. Total enrollment: 6,111. Undergraduates: 2,376. Freshmen: 406.

GIFT AID (NEED-BASED) *Scholarships, grants, and awards:* Federal Pell, FSEOG, state, private, college/university gift aid from institutional funds.

GIFT AID (NON-NEED-BASED) *Scholarships, grants, and awards by category: Academic Interests/Achievement:* biological sciences, business, communication, computer science, education, engineering/technologies, English, foreign languages, general academic interests/achievements, health fields, humanities, mathematics, premedicine, social sciences. *Creative Arts/Performance:* art/fine arts, music, performing arts, theater/drama. *Special Achievements/Activities:* community service, leadership, memberships. *Special Characteristics:* out-of-state students.

LOANS *Programs:* Federal Direct (Subsidized and Unsubsidized Stafford, PLUS), FFEL (Subsidized and Unsubsidized Stafford, PLUS), Perkins, college/university.

APPLYING FOR FINANCIAL AID *Required financial aid form:* FAFSA.

CONTACT Phil Schroeder, Student Financial Aid Director, Adams State College, 208 Edgemont Boulevard, Alamosa, CO 81102, 719-587-7306 or toll-free 800-824-6494. *Fax:* 719-587-7366.

ADELPHI UNIVERSITY
Garden City, NY

| Tuition & fees: $18,700 | Average undergraduate aid package: $13,450 |

ABOUT THE INSTITUTION Independent, coed. Awards: associate, bachelor's, master's, and doctoral degrees and post-bachelor's and post-master's certificates. 44 undergraduate majors. Total enrollment: 7,592. Undergraduates: 4,425. Freshmen: 815. Federal methodology is used as a basis for awarding need-based institutional aid.

UNDERGRADUATE EXPENSES for 2004–05 *Application fee:* $35. *Comprehensive fee:* $27,200 includes full-time tuition ($17,700), mandatory fees ($1000), and room and board ($8500). Full-time tuition and fees vary according to course level, location, and program. Room and board charges vary according to board plan and housing facility. *Part-time tuition:* $570 per credit. *Part-time fees:* $520 per year. Part-time tuition and fees vary according to course level, location, and program. *Payment plans:* Tuition prepayment, installment, deferred payment.

FRESHMAN FINANCIAL AID (Fall 2004, est.) 692 applied for aid; of those 85% were deemed to have need. 100% of freshmen with need received aid; of those 1% had need fully met. *Average percent of need met:* 30% (excluding resources awarded to replace EFC). *Average financial aid package:* $13,450 (excluding resources awarded to replace EFC). 18% of all full-time freshmen had no need and received non-need-based gift aid.

UNDERGRADUATE FINANCIAL AID (Fall 2004, est.) 2,976 applied for aid; of those 87% were deemed to have need. 100% of undergraduates with need received aid; of those 1% had need fully met. *Average percent of need met:* 30% (excluding resources awarded to replace EFC). *Average financial aid package:* $13,450 (excluding resources awarded to replace EFC). 22% of all full-time undergraduates had no need and received non-need-based gift aid.

GIFT AID (NEED-BASED) *Total amount:* $18,993,830 (23% federal, 22% state, 55% institutional). *Receiving aid:* Freshmen: 63% (502); All full-time undergraduates: 57% (2,136). *Average award:* Freshmen: $5149; Undergraduates: $3889. *Scholarships, grants, and awards:* Federal Pell, FSEOG, state, private, college/university gift aid from institutional funds, United Negro College Fund, endowed-donor scholarships.

GIFT AID (NON-NEED-BASED) *Total amount:* $6,784,765 (89% institutional, 11% external sources). *Receiving aid:* Freshmen: 49% (394); Undergraduates: 41% (1,530). *Average Award:* Freshmen: $9002; Undergraduates: $7379. *Scholarships, grants, and awards by category:* Academic Interests/Achievement: 2,172 awards ($14,189,517 total): communication, foreign languages, general academic interests/achievements. Creative Arts/Performance: 154 awards ($856,500 total): art/fine arts, dance, music, performing arts, theater/drama. Special Achievements/Activities: 246 awards ($212,100 total): community service, general special achievements/activities, memberships. Special Characteristics: 277 awards ($1,385,905 total): children and siblings of alumni, children of faculty/staff. *Tuition waivers:* Full or partial for employees or children of employees. *ROTC:* Army cooperative, Air Force cooperative.

LOANS *Student loans:* $15,098,132 (61% need-based, 39% non-need-based). 79% of past graduating class borrowed through all loan programs. *Average indebtedness per student:* $22,248. *Average need-based loan:* Freshmen: $3276; Undergraduates: $4121. *Parent loans:* $30,190,219 (80% need-based, 20% non-need-based). *Programs:* FFEL (Subsidized and Unsubsidized Stafford, PLUS), Perkins, Federal Nursing, alternative loans.

WORK-STUDY *Federal work-study:* Total amount: $1,498,800; 558 jobs averaging $2686. *State or other work-study/employment:* Total amount: $1,097,781 (100% non-need-based). 729 part-time jobs averaging $1506.

ATHLETIC AWARDS *Total amount:* $1,702,490 (51% need-based, 49% non-need-based).

APPLYING FOR FINANCIAL AID *Required financial aid forms:* FAFSA, state aid form. *Financial aid deadline (priority):* 3/1. *Notification date:* Continuous.

CONTACT Ms. Sheryl Mihopulos, Director of Student Financial Services, Adelphi University, 1 South Avenue, Garden City, NY 11530, 516-877-3080 or toll-free 800-ADELPHI. *Fax:* 516-877-3380.

ADRIAN COLLEGE
Adrian, MI

| Tuition & fees: $17,600 | Average undergraduate aid package: $16,697 |

ABOUT THE INSTITUTION Independent religious, coed. Awards: associate and bachelor's degrees. 44 undergraduate majors. Total enrollment: 1,013.

Undergraduates: 1,013. Freshmen: 293. Both federal and institutional methodology are used as a basis for awarding need-based institutional aid.

UNDERGRADUATE EXPENSES for 2004–05 *Application fee:* $20. *Comprehensive fee:* $23,370 includes full-time tuition ($17,500), mandatory fees ($100), and room and board ($5770). *College room only:* $2620. Room and board charges vary according to board plan. *Payment plan:* Installment.

FRESHMAN FINANCIAL AID (Fall 2004, est.) 291 applied for aid; of those 83% were deemed to have need. 100% of freshmen with need received aid; of those 93% had need fully met. *Average percent of need met:* 99% (excluding resources awarded to replace EFC). *Average financial aid package:* $17,687 (excluding resources awarded to replace EFC). 16% of all full-time freshmen had no need and received non-need-based gift aid.

UNDERGRADUATE FINANCIAL AID (Fall 2004, est.) 937 applied for aid; of those 80% were deemed to have need. 100% of undergraduates with need received aid; of those 76% had need fully met. *Average percent of need met:* 98% (excluding resources awarded to replace EFC). *Average financial aid package:* $16,697 (excluding resources awarded to replace EFC). 17% of all full-time undergraduates had no need and received non-need-based gift aid.

GIFT AID (NEED-BASED) *Total amount:* $7,076,541 (12% federal, 15% state, 67% institutional, 6% external sources). *Receiving aid:* Freshmen: 82% (241); All full-time undergraduates: 74% (744). *Average award:* Freshmen: $10,709; Undergraduates: $9470. *Scholarships, grants, and awards:* Federal Pell, FSEOG, state, private, college/university gift aid from institutional funds.

GIFT AID (NON-NEED-BASED) *Total amount:* $2,643,182 (1% state, 95% institutional, 4% external sources). *Receiving aid:* Freshmen: 29% (84); Undergraduates: 29% (297). *Average Award:* Freshmen: $7639; Undergraduates: $7276. *Scholarships, grants, and awards by category:* Academic Interests/Achievement: 657 awards ($3,932,433 total): business, general academic interests/achievements. Creative Arts/Performance: 234 awards ($438,543 total): art/fine arts, music, theater/drama. Special Achievements/Activities: 33 awards ($31,000 total): religious involvement. Special Characteristics: 115 awards ($143,642 total): children and siblings of alumni, children of faculty/staff, children of union members/company employees, international students, religious affiliation. *Tuition waivers:* Full or partial for children of alumni, employees or children of employees.

LOANS *Student loans:* $4,581,319 (72% need-based, 28% non-need-based). 78% of past graduating class borrowed through all loan programs. *Average indebtedness per student:* $16,870. *Average need-based loan:* Freshmen: $3845; Undergraduates: $4701. *Parent loans:* $7,975,794 (4% need-based, 96% non-need-based). *Programs:* FFEL (Subsidized and Unsubsidized Stafford, PLUS), Perkins.

WORK-STUDY *Federal work-study:* Total amount: $875,957; 654 jobs averaging $988.

APPLYING FOR FINANCIAL AID *Required financial aid form:* FAFSA. *Financial aid deadline (priority):* 3/1. *Notification date:* Continuous beginning 3/15. Students must reply by 5/1 or within 2 weeks of notification.

CONTACT Mr. Michael Hague, Associate Vice President for Student Financial Services, Adrian College, 110 South Madison Street, Adrian, MI 49221-2575, 517-265-5161 Ext. 4523 or toll-free 800-877-2246. *E-mail:* mhague@adrian.edu.

AGNES SCOTT COLLEGE
Decatur, GA

| Tuition & fees: $22,210 | Average undergraduate aid package: $23,111 |

ABOUT THE INSTITUTION Independent religious, women only. Awards: bachelor's and master's degrees and post-bachelor's certificates. 27 undergraduate majors. Total enrollment: 1,002. Undergraduates: 973. Freshmen: 256. Both federal and institutional methodology are used as a basis for awarding need-based institutional aid.

UNDERGRADUATE EXPENSES for 2004–05 *Application fee:* $35. *Comprehensive fee:* $30,410 includes full-time tuition ($22,050), mandatory fees ($160), and room and board ($8200). Room and board charges vary according to board plan and housing facility. *Part-time tuition:* $920 per credit hour. *Part-time fees:* $160 per year. Part-time tuition and fees vary according to course load. *Payment plan:* Installment.

FRESHMAN FINANCIAL AID (Fall 2004, est.) 227 applied for aid; of those 84% were deemed to have need. 100% of freshmen with need received aid; of those 75% had need fully met. *Average percent of need met:* 96% (excluding resources awarded to replace EFC). *Average financial aid package:* $23,731 (excluding resources awarded to replace EFC). 25% of all full-time freshmen had no need and received non-need-based gift aid.

UNDERGRADUATE FINANCIAL AID (Fall 2004, est.) 672 applied for aid; of those 86% were deemed to have need. 100% of undergraduates with need received aid; of those 71% had need fully met. *Average percent of need met:* 96% (excluding resources awarded to replace EFC). *Average financial aid package:* $23,111 (excluding resources awarded to replace EFC). 24% of all full-time undergraduates had no need and received non-need-based gift aid.
GIFT AID (NEED-BASED) *Total amount:* $10,352,042 (9% federal, 7% state, 83% institutional, 1% external sources). *Receiving aid:* Freshmen: 73% (188); All full-time undergraduates: 63% (567). *Average award:* Freshmen: $18,195; Undergraduates: $16,769. *Scholarships, grants, and awards:* Federal Pell, FSEOG, state, private, college/university gift aid from institutional funds.
GIFT AID (NON-NEED-BASED) *Total amount:* $3,554,698 (17% state, 78% institutional, 5% external sources). *Receiving aid:* Freshmen: 35% (89); Undergraduates: 24% (211). *Average Award: Freshmen:* $12,277; *Undergraduates:* $10,476. *Scholarships, grants, and awards by category: Academic Interests/Achievement:* 541 awards ($5,629,951 total): general academic interests/achievements. *Creative Arts/Performance:* 17 awards ($34,500 total): music. *Special Achievements/Activities:* 37 awards ($205,000 total): community service, leadership. *Special Characteristics:* 111 awards ($474,400 total): adult students, children of educators, children of faculty/staff, international students, local/state students. *Tuition waivers:* Full or partial for employees or children of employees. *ROTC:* Air Force cooperative.
LOANS *Student loans:* $3,205,446 (62% need-based, 38% non-need-based). 64% of past graduating class borrowed through all loan programs. *Average indebtedness per student:* $22,314. *Average need-based loan:* Freshmen: $2560; Undergraduates: $3873. *Parent loans:* $1,337,182 (6% need-based, 94% non-need-based). *Programs:* FFEL (Subsidized and Unsubsidized Stafford, PLUS), college/university.
WORK-STUDY *Federal work-study:* Total amount: $886,925; 461 jobs averaging $1924. *State or other work-study/employment:* Total amount: $254,600 (41% need-based, 59% non-need-based). 132 part-time jobs averaging $1928.
APPLYING FOR FINANCIAL AID *Required financial aid forms:* FAFSA, institution's own form, CSS Financial Aid PROFILE, 2004 tax forms. *Financial aid deadline:* 5/1 (priority: 2/15). *Notification date:* Continuous beginning 3/1. Students must reply within 2 weeks of notification.
CONTACT Karen Smith, Director of Financial Aid, Agnes Scott College, 141 East College Avenue, Decatur, GA 30030-3797, 404-471-6395 or toll-free 800-868-8602. *Fax:* 404-471-6159. *E-mail:* finaid@agnesscott.edu.

ALABAMA AGRICULTURAL AND MECHANICAL UNIVERSITY
Huntsville, AL

CONTACT Financial Aid Officer, Alabama Agricultural and Mechanical University, 4900 Meridian Street, Normal, AL 35762, 256-851-5400 or toll-free 800-553-0816. *Fax:* 256-851-5407.

ALABAMA STATE UNIVERSITY
Montgomery, AL

ABOUT THE INSTITUTION State-supported, coed. Awards: associate, bachelor's, master's, and doctoral degrees and post-master's certificates. 49 undergraduate majors. Total enrollment: 5,653. Undergraduates: 4,689. Freshmen: 1,163.
GIFT AID (NEED-BASED) *Scholarships, grants, and awards:* Federal Pell, FSEOG, state, college/university gift aid from institutional funds.
GIFT AID (NON-NEED-BASED) *Scholarships, grants, and awards by category: Academic Interests/Achievement:* biological sciences, business, education, general academic interests/achievements, health fields, mathematics. *Creative Arts/Performance:* art/fine arts, music, performing arts, theater/drama. *Special Achievements/Activities:* cheerleading/drum major, general special achievements/activities, leadership. *Special Characteristics:* children of union members/company employees, ethnic background, general special characteristics, handicapped students, local/state students, members of minority groups, out-of-state students, religious affiliation, veterans, veterans' children.
LOANS *Programs:* FFEL (Subsidized and Unsubsidized Stafford, PLUS), Perkins, state, college/university.
APPLYING FOR FINANCIAL AID *Required financial aid form:* FAFSA.
CONTACT Mrs. Dorenda A. Adams, Director of Financial Aid, Alabama State University, PO Box 271, Montgomery, AL 36101-0271, 334-229-4323 or toll-free 800-253-5037. *Fax:* 334-299-4924. *E-mail:* dadams@asunet.alasu.edu.

ALASKA BIBLE COLLEGE
Glennallen, AK

ABOUT THE INSTITUTION Independent nondenominational, coed. Awards: associate and bachelor's degrees. 2 undergraduate majors. Total enrollment: 61. Undergraduates: 61. Freshmen: 6.
GIFT AID (NEED-BASED) *Scholarships, grants, and awards:* private, college/university gift aid from institutional funds.
GIFT AID (NON-NEED-BASED) *Scholarships, grants, and awards by category: Academic Interests/Achievement:* general academic interests/achievements, religion/biblical studies. *Creative Arts/Performance:* music. *Special Achievements/Activities:* religious involvement. *Special Characteristics:* children of faculty/staff, local/state students, religious affiliation, spouses of current students.
LOANS *Programs:* state.
WORK-STUDY *State or other work-study/employment:* Total amount: $21,000 (100% need-based). 16 part-time jobs averaging $1800.
APPLYING FOR FINANCIAL AID *Required financial aid form:* institution's own form.
CONTACT Kevin Newman, Financial Aid Officer, Alaska Bible College, PO Box 289, Glennallen, AK 99588-0289, 907-822-3201 Ext. 253 or toll-free 800-478-7884. *Fax:* 907-822-5027. *E-mail:* knewman@akbible.edu.

ALASKA PACIFIC UNIVERSITY
Anchorage, AK

Tuition & fees: $18,342	Average undergraduate aid package: $10,113

ABOUT THE INSTITUTION Independent, coed. Awards: associate, bachelor's, and master's degrees. 10 undergraduate majors. Total enrollment: 785. Undergraduates: 568. Freshmen: 51. Both federal and institutional methodology are used as a basis for awarding need-based institutional aid.
UNDERGRADUATE EXPENSES for 2005–06 *Application fee:* $25. *Comprehensive fee:* $25,302 includes full-time tuition ($18,232), mandatory fees ($110), and room and board ($6960). *College room only:* $3450. Full-time tuition and fees vary according to class time, location, and program. Room and board charges vary according to board plan and housing facility. *Part-time tuition:* $760 per semester hour. *Part-time fees:* $55 per term. Part-time tuition and fees vary according to class time, location, and program. *Payment plans:* Guaranteed tuition, installment, deferred payment.
GIFT AID (NEED-BASED) *Total amount:* $619,305 (57% federal, 43% institutional). *Receiving aid:* Freshmen: 42% (10); All full-time undergraduates: 32% (65). *Average award:* Freshmen: $4840; Undergraduates: $4443. *Scholarships, grants, and awards:* Federal Pell, FSEOG, state, private, college/university gift aid from institutional funds, Bureau of Indian Affairs Grants.
GIFT AID (NON-NEED-BASED) *Total amount:* $1,178,036 (57% institutional, 43% external sources). *Receiving aid:* Freshmen: 67% (16); Undergraduates: 33% (68). *Average Award: Freshmen:* $15,786; *Undergraduates:* $6701. *Scholarships, grants, and awards by category: Academic Interests/Achievement:* 88 awards ($378,966 total): biological sciences, business, education, general academic interests/achievements, humanities, physical sciences, social sciences. *Special Achievements/Activities:* general special achievements/activities, leadership, religious involvement. *Special Characteristics:* children and siblings of alumni, children of faculty/staff, ethnic background, international students, local/state students, members of minority groups, out-of-state students, religious affiliation. *Tuition waivers:* Full or partial for employees or children of employees, adult students, senior citizens.
LOANS *Student loans:* $2,793,488 (30% need-based, 70% non-need-based). 68% of past graduating class borrowed through all loan programs. *Average indebtedness per student:* $23,791. *Average need-based loan:* Freshmen: $2625; Undergraduates: $4340. *Parent loans:* $333,412 (100% non-need-based). *Programs:* FFEL (Subsidized and Unsubsidized Stafford, PLUS), state.
ATHLETIC AWARDS *Total amount:* $5000 (100% non-need-based).
APPLYING FOR FINANCIAL AID *Required financial aid form:* FAFSA. *Financial aid deadline (priority):* 4/15. *Notification date:* Continuous. Students must reply within 4 weeks of notification.
CONTACT Peter Miller, Director of Financial Aid, Alaska Pacific University, 4101 University Drive, Grant Hall, Room 200-B, Anchorage, AK 99508-4672, 907-564-8341 or toll-free 800-252-7528. *Fax:* 907-564-8372. *E-mail:* financialaid@alaskapacific.edu.

ALBANY COLLEGE OF PHARMACY OF UNION UNIVERSITY
Albany, NY

CONTACT Tiffany M. Gutierrez, Director of Financial Aid, Albany College of Pharmacy of Union University, 106 New Scotland Avenue, Albany, NY 12208-3425, 518-445-7256 or toll-free 888-203-8010. *Fax:* 518-445-7322. *E-mail:* gutierrt@mail.acp.edu.

ALBANY STATE UNIVERSITY
Albany, GA

ABOUT THE INSTITUTION State-supported, coed. Awards: associate, bachelor's, and master's degrees and post-bachelor's certificates. 29 undergraduate majors. Total enrollment: 3,668. Undergraduates: 3,212. Freshmen: 603.

GIFT AID (NEED-BASED) *Scholarships, grants, and awards:* Federal Pell, FSEOG, state, private, college/university gift aid from institutional funds, Federal Nursing, Thurgood Marshall Scholarship Fund.

GIFT AID (NON-NEED-BASED) *Scholarships, grants, and awards by category: Academic Interests/Achievement:* biological sciences, computer science, education, general academic interests/achievements, health fields, mathematics, social sciences. *Creative Arts/Performance:* music.

LOANS *Programs:* Federal Direct (Subsidized and Unsubsidized Stafford, PLUS), Perkins, state.

WORK-STUDY *Federal work-study:* Total amount: $308,428; 440 jobs averaging $1050. *State or other work-study/employment:* Total amount: $182,425 (100% non-need-based). 178 part-time jobs averaging $1655.

APPLYING FOR FINANCIAL AID *Required financial aid form:* FAFSA.

CONTACT Ms. Kathleen J. Caldwell, Director of Financial Aid, Albany State University, 504 College Drive, Albany, GA 31705-2717, 912-430-4650 or toll-free 800-822-RAMS (in-state). *Fax:* 912-430-3936. *E-mail:* finaid@asurams.edu.

ALBERTSON COLLEGE OF IDAHO
Caldwell, ID

Tuition & fees: $15,890	Average undergraduate aid package: $14,534

ABOUT THE INSTITUTION Independent, coed. Awards: bachelor's and master's degrees. 27 undergraduate majors. Total enrollment: 807. Undergraduates: 789. Freshmen: 191. Federal methodology is used as a basis for awarding need-based institutional aid.

UNDERGRADUATE EXPENSES for 2005–06 *Application fee:* $50. *Comprehensive fee:* $22,365 includes full-time tuition ($15,200), mandatory fees ($690), and room and board ($6475). *College room only:* $3575. Room and board charges vary according to board plan and housing facility. *Part-time tuition:* $625 per credit. Part-time tuition and fees vary according to course load. *Payment plan:* Guaranteed tuition.

FRESHMAN FINANCIAL AID (Fall 2004, est.) 134 applied for aid; of those 100% were deemed to have need. 100% of freshmen with need received aid; of those 16% had need fully met. *Average percent of need met:* 85% (excluding resources awarded to replace EFC). *Average financial aid package:* $13,407 (excluding resources awarded to replace EFC). 31% of all full-time freshmen had no need and received non-need-based gift aid.

UNDERGRADUATE FINANCIAL AID (Fall 2004, est.) 493 applied for aid; of those 100% were deemed to have need. 99% of undergraduates with need received aid; of those 17% had need fully met. *Average percent of need met:* 83% (excluding resources awarded to replace EFC). *Average financial aid package:* $14,534 (excluding resources awarded to replace EFC). 55% of all full-time undergraduates had no need and received non-need-based gift aid.

GIFT AID (NEED-BASED) *Total amount:* $1,565,671 (47% federal, 1% state, 52% institutional). *Receiving aid:* Freshmen: 50% (95); All full-time undergraduates: 38% (285). *Average award:* Freshmen: $3672; Undergraduates: $4016. *Scholarships, grants, and awards:* Federal Pell, FSEOG, state, private, college/university gift aid from institutional funds.

GIFT AID (NON-NEED-BASED) *Total amount:* $4,457,909 (4% state, 86% institutional, 10% external sources). *Receiving aid:* Freshmen: 68% (130); Undergraduates: 62% (468). *Average Award:* Freshmen: $5818; Undergraduates: $6297. *Scholarships, grants, and awards by category: Academic Interests/ Achievement:* $4,513,871 total: biological sciences, education, general academic interests/achievements. *Creative Arts/Performance:* $365,829 total: art/fine arts,

debating, music, theater/drama. *Special Achievements/Activities:* $5500 total: junior miss. *Special Characteristics:* $903,822 total: children and siblings of alumni, children of faculty/staff, ethnic background, handicapped students, international students, local/state students, members of minority groups, religious affiliation, siblings of current students. *Tuition waivers:* Full or partial for children of alumni, employees or children of employees, adult students, senior citizens. *ROTC:* Army cooperative.

LOANS *Student loans:* $3,502,794 (48% need-based, 52% non-need-based). 94% of past graduating class borrowed through all loan programs. *Average indebtedness per student:* $26,340. *Average need-based loan:* Freshmen: $3512; Undergraduates: $4552. *Parent loans:* $831,132 (100% non-need-based). *Programs:* FFEL (Subsidized and Unsubsidized Stafford, PLUS), Perkins, alternative loans.

WORK-STUDY *Federal work-study:* Total amount: $162,935; 205 jobs averaging $795. *State or other work-study/employment:* Total amount: $69,596 (26% need-based, 74% non-need-based). 85 part-time jobs averaging $214.

ATHLETIC AWARDS *Total amount:* $895,006 (100% non-need-based).

APPLYING FOR FINANCIAL AID *Required financial aid forms:* FAFSA, institution's own form. *Financial aid deadline (priority):* 2/15. *Notification date:* Continuous beginning 12/1. Students must reply within 3 weeks of notification.

CONTACT Juanitta M. Pearson, Director, Office of Student Financial Services, Albertson College of Idaho, 2112 Cleveland Boulevard, Campus Box 39, Caldwell, ID 83605-4432, 208-459-5307 or toll-free 800-244-3246. *Fax:* 208-459-5844. *E-mail:* jpearson@albertson.edu.

ALBERTUS MAGNUS COLLEGE
New Haven, CT

ABOUT THE INSTITUTION Independent Roman Catholic, coed. Awards: associate, bachelor's, and master's degrees. 57 undergraduate majors. Total enrollment: 2,361. Undergraduates: 1,906. Freshmen: 199.

GIFT AID (NEED-BASED) *Scholarships, grants, and awards:* Federal Pell, FSEOG, state, college/university gift aid from institutional funds.

GIFT AID (NON-NEED-BASED) *Scholarships, grants, and awards by category: Academic Interests/Achievement:* biological sciences, business, communication, computer science, education, English, foreign languages, general academic interests/achievements, humanities, international studies, mathematics, physical sciences, premedicine, religion/biblical studies, social sciences. *Creative Arts/Performance:* art/fine arts, performing arts, theater/drama. *Special Achievements/Activities:* community service, leadership. *Special Characteristics:* religious affiliation.

LOANS *Programs:* FFEL (Subsidized and Unsubsidized Stafford, PLUS), Perkins.

WORK-STUDY *Federal work-study:* Total amount: $121,041; 83 jobs averaging $1310. *State or other work-study/employment:* Total amount: $110,350 (100% need-based). 46 part-time jobs averaging $2660.

APPLYING FOR FINANCIAL AID *Required financial aid forms:* FAFSA, institution's own form.

CONTACT Gladysa Ramos, Director of Financial Assistance, Albertus Magnus College, 700 Prospect Street, New Haven, CT 06511-1189, 203-773-8508 or toll-free 800-578-9160. *Fax:* 203-773-8972. *E-mail:* financial_aid@albertus.edu.

ALBION COLLEGE
Albion, MI

Tuition & fees: $22,918	Average undergraduate aid package: $19,544

ABOUT THE INSTITUTION Independent Methodist, coed. Awards: bachelor's degrees. 37 undergraduate majors. Total enrollment: 1,867. Undergraduates: 1,867. Freshmen: 559. Federal methodology is used as a basis for awarding need-based institutional aid.

UNDERGRADUATE EXPENSES for 2004–05 *Application fee:* $20. *Comprehensive fee:* $29,454 includes full-time tuition ($22,650), mandatory fees ($268), and room and board ($6536). *College room only:* $3196. Room and board charges vary according to housing facility. *Part-time tuition:* $962 per quarter hour. *Payment plan:* Installment.

FRESHMAN FINANCIAL AID (Fall 2003) 442 applied for aid; of those 80% were deemed to have need. 100% of freshmen with need received aid; of those 73% had need fully met. *Average percent of need met:* 97% (excluding resources awarded to replace EFC). *Average financial aid package:* $19,622 (excluding resources awarded to replace EFC). 34% of all full-time freshmen had no need and received non-need-based gift aid.

UNDERGRADUATE FINANCIAL AID (Fall 2003) 1,338 applied for aid; of those 87% were deemed to have need. 100% of undergraduates with need received aid; of those 61% had need fully met. *Average percent of need met:* 95% (excluding resources awarded to replace EFC). *Average financial aid package:* $19,544 (excluding resources awarded to replace EFC). 34% of all full-time undergraduates had no need and received non-need-based gift aid.

GIFT AID (NEED-BASED) *Total amount:* $18,885,353 (6% federal, 12% state, 79% institutional, 3% external sources). *Receiving aid:* Freshmen: 64% (355); All full-time undergraduates: 63% (1,166). *Average award:* Freshmen: $16,890; Undergraduates: $15,512. *Scholarships, grants, and awards:* Federal Pell, FSEOG, state, private, college/university gift aid from institutional funds.

GIFT AID (NON-NEED-BASED) *Total amount:* $7,224,841 (5% state, 92% institutional, 3% external sources). *Receiving aid:* Freshmen: 62% (346); Undergraduates: 57% (1,057). *Average Award:* Freshmen: $11,474; *Undergraduates:* $10,462. *Scholarships, grants, and awards by category:* Academic Interests/Achievement: 1,584 awards ($15,766,928 total): business, communication, education, general academic interests/achievements, mathematics, premedicine. *Creative Arts/Performance:* 202 awards ($262,475 total): art/fine arts, music, performing arts, theater/drama. *Special Characteristics:* 311 awards ($608,688 total): children and siblings of alumni, ethnic background, out-of-state students, relatives of clergy. *Tuition waivers:* Full or partial for children of alumni, employees or children of employees.

LOANS *Student loans:* $7,783,647 (51% need-based, 49% non-need-based). 60% of past graduating class borrowed through all loan programs. *Average indebtedness per student:* $19,951. *Average need-based loan:* Freshmen: $3297; Undergraduates: $4462. *Parent loans:* $1,709,746 (100% non-need-based). *Programs:* FFEL (Subsidized and Unsubsidized Stafford, PLUS), Perkins, state.

WORK-STUDY *Federal work-study:* Total amount: $685,606; 542 jobs averaging $1265.

APPLYING FOR FINANCIAL AID *Required financial aid form:* FAFSA. *Financial aid deadline (priority):* 2/15. *Notification date:* Continuous beginning 3/15.

CONTACT Kristi Maze, Director of Financial Aid, Albion College, Kellogg Center Box 4670, Albion, MI 49224-1831, 517-629-0440 or toll-free 800-858-6770. *Fax:* 517-629-0581. *E-mail:* kmaze@albion.edu.

ALBRIGHT COLLEGE
Reading, PA

Tuition & fees: $24,580	Average undergraduate aid package: $17,126

ABOUT THE INSTITUTION Independent religious, coed. Awards: bachelor's and master's degrees. 45 undergraduate majors. Total enrollment: 2,243. Undergraduates: 2,165. Freshmen: 506. Federal methodology is used as a basis for awarding need-based institutional aid.

UNDERGRADUATE EXPENSES for 2004–05 *Application fee:* $25. *Comprehensive fee:* $32,090 includes full-time tuition ($24,030), mandatory fees ($550), and room and board ($7510). *College room only:* $4275. Full-time tuition and fees vary according to program. Room and board charges vary according to board plan and housing facility. *Part-time tuition:* $3004 per course. Part-time tuition and fees vary according to class time. *Payment plan:* Installment.

FRESHMAN FINANCIAL AID (Fall 2004, est.) 470 applied for aid; of those 91% were deemed to have need. 100% of freshmen with need received aid; of those 15% had need fully met. *Average percent of need met:* 78% (excluding resources awarded to replace EFC). *Average financial aid package:* $19,187 (excluding resources awarded to replace EFC). 14% of all full-time freshmen had no need and received non-need-based gift aid.

UNDERGRADUATE FINANCIAL AID (Fall 2004, est.) 1,690 applied for aid; of those 90% were deemed to have need. 100% of undergraduates with need received aid; of those 16% had need fully met. *Average percent of need met:* 76% (excluding resources awarded to replace EFC). *Average financial aid package:* $17,126 (excluding resources awarded to replace EFC). 13% of all full-time undergraduates had no need and received non-need-based gift aid.

GIFT AID (NEED-BASED) *Total amount:* $19,809,648 (10% federal, 11% state, 72% institutional, 7% external sources). *Receiving aid:* Freshmen: 85% (428); All full-time undergraduates: 70% (1,476). *Average award:* Freshmen: $15,139; Undergraduates: $13,319. *Scholarships, grants, and awards:* Federal Pell, FSEOG, state, private, college/university gift aid from institutional funds.

GIFT AID (NON-NEED-BASED) *Total amount:* $2,874,474 (1% state, 79% institutional, 20% external sources). *Receiving aid:* Freshmen: 8% (43); Undergraduates: 7% (154). *Average Award:* Freshmen: $13,468; *Undergraduates:* $11,921. *Scholarships, grants, and awards by category:* Academic Interests/Achievement: 53 awards ($46,750 total): general academic interests/achievements. *Creative Arts/Performance:* 60 awards ($70,000 total): art/fine

arts, music, theater/drama. *Special Achievements/Activities:* 44 awards ($26,250 total): junior miss, memberships. *Special Characteristics:* 205 awards ($424,800 total): children and siblings of alumni, international students, members of minority groups, siblings of current students. *Tuition waivers:* Full or partial for children of alumni, employees or children of employees, senior citizens.

LOANS *Student loans:* $12,387,756 (71% need-based, 29% non-need-based). 43% of past graduating class borrowed through all loan programs. *Average indebtedness per student:* $25,198. *Average need-based loan:* Freshmen: $3889; Undergraduates: $4153. *Parent loans:* $3,559,542 (42% need-based, 58% non-need-based). *Programs:* FFEL (Subsidized and Unsubsidized Stafford, PLUS), Perkins, private educational loans.

WORK-STUDY *Federal work-study:* Total amount: $723,433; 750 jobs averaging $1390. *State or other work-study/employment:* Total amount: $597,835 (6% need-based, 94% non-need-based). 300 part-time jobs averaging $1300.

APPLYING FOR FINANCIAL AID *Required financial aid form:* FAFSA. *Financial aid deadline (priority):* 3/1. *Notification date:* Continuous beginning 2/8. Students must reply within 2 weeks of notification.

CONTACT Mary Ellen Duffy, Director of Financial Aid, Albright College, PO Box 15234, Reading, PA 19612-5234, 610-921-7515 or toll-free 800-252-1856. *Fax:* 610-921-7729. *E-mail:* finaid@alb.edu.

ALCORN STATE UNIVERSITY
Alcorn State, MS

Tuition & fees (MS res): $4465	Average undergraduate aid package: $10,500

ABOUT THE INSTITUTION State-supported, coed. Awards: associate, bachelor's, and master's degrees and post-master's certificates. 37 undergraduate majors. Total enrollment: 3,443. Undergraduates: 2,834. Freshmen: 565. Federal methodology is used as a basis for awarding need-based institutional aid.

UNDERGRADUATE EXPENSES for 2004–05 *Tuition, state resident:* full-time $3732; part-time $156 per hour. *Tuition, nonresident:* full-time $8463; part-time $353 per hour. *College room and board:* $4012; *room only:* $2272.

GIFT AID (NEED-BASED) *Total amount:* $6,933,935 (100% federal). *Receiving aid:* Freshmen: 92% (380); All full-time undergraduates: 81% (1,805). *Average award:* Freshmen: $4200; Undergraduates: $4500. *Scholarships, grants, and awards:* Federal Pell, FSEOG, state, private, college/university gift aid from institutional funds.

GIFT AID (NON-NEED-BASED) *Total amount:* $3,126,544 (19% state, 81% institutional). *Receiving aid:* Freshmen: 73% (301); Undergraduates: 80% (1,787). *Average Award:* Freshmen: $2500; Undergraduates: $4900. *Scholarships, grants, and awards by category:* Academic Interests/Achievement: 352 awards ($1,437,625 total): general academic interests/achievements. *Creative Arts/Performance:* 208 awards ($1,033,169 total): music. *Special Characteristics:* 477 awards ($484,169 total): children of faculty/staff, local/state students, members of minority groups. *Tuition waivers:* Full or partial for employees or children of employees. *ROTC:* Army.

LOANS *Student loans:* $14,315,020 (68% need-based, 32% non-need-based). 67% of past graduating class borrowed through all loan programs. *Average indebtedness per student:* $10,000. *Average need-based loan:* Freshmen: $2625; Undergraduates: $5500. *Parent loans:* $1,240,321 (100% non-need-based). *Programs:* Federal Direct (Subsidized and Unsubsidized Stafford, PLUS).

ATHLETIC AWARDS *Total amount:* $1,752,144 (100% non-need-based).

APPLYING FOR FINANCIAL AID *Required financial aid forms:* FAFSA, institution's own form. *Financial aid deadline (priority):* 4/1. *Notification date:* Continuous. Students must reply within 4 weeks of notification.

CONTACT Juanita M. Russell, Director of Financial Aid, Alcorn State University, 1000 ASU Drive #28, Alcorn State, MS 39096-7500, 601-877-6190 or toll-free 800-222-6790. *Fax:* 601-877-6110. *E-mail:* juanita@lorman.alcorn.edu.

ALDERSON-BROADDUS COLLEGE
Philippi, WV

Tuition & fees: $17,966	Average undergraduate aid package: $19,900

ABOUT THE INSTITUTION Independent religious, coed. Awards: associate, bachelor's, and master's degrees. 47 undergraduate majors. Total enrollment: 789. Undergraduates: 689. Freshmen: 150. Federal methodology is used as a basis for awarding need-based institutional aid.

UNDERGRADUATE EXPENSES for 2005–06 *Application fee:* $10. *Comprehensive fee:* $23,774 includes full-time tuition ($17,800), mandatory fees ($166), and room and board ($5808). Full-time tuition and fees vary according to degree level. Room and board charges vary according to housing facility. *Part-time tuition:* $592 per credit hour. *Part-time fees:* $41.50 per term. Part-time tuition and fees vary according to degree level. *Payment plan:* Installment.

FRESHMAN FINANCIAL AID (Fall 2004, est.) 150 applied for aid; of those 97% were deemed to have need. 100% of freshmen with need received aid; of those 3% had need fully met. *Average percent of need met:* 91% (excluding resources awarded to replace EFC). *Average financial aid package:* $18,525 (excluding resources awarded to replace EFC). 3% of all full-time freshmen had no need and received non-need-based gift aid.

UNDERGRADUATE FINANCIAL AID (Fall 2004, est.) 602 applied for aid; of those 91% were deemed to have need. 100% of undergraduates with need received aid; of those 5% had need fully met. *Average financial aid package:* $19,900 (excluding resources awarded to replace EFC). 4% of all full-time undergraduates had no need and received non-need-based gift aid.

GIFT AID (NEED-BASED) *Total amount:* $2,466,214 (51% federal, 19% state, 30% institutional). *Receiving aid:* Freshmen: 93% (139); All full-time undergraduates: 83% (503). *Average award:* Freshmen: $12,089; Undergraduates: $9800. *Scholarships, grants, and awards:* Federal Pell, FSEOG, state, private, college/ university gift aid from institutional funds, Federal Nursing, National Health Service Corp.

GIFT AID (NON-NEED-BASED) *Total amount:* $3,906,623 (2% federal, 8% state, 83% institutional, 7% external sources). *Receiving aid:* Freshmen: 12% (18); Undergraduates: 13% (78). *Average Award:* Freshmen: $17,868; Undergraduates: $12,263. *Scholarships, grants, and awards by category: Academic Interests/Achievement:* 569 awards ($2,737,500 total): biological sciences, business, communication, computer science, education, general academic interests/ achievements, health fields, humanities, mathematics, physical sciences, premedicine, religion/biblical studies, social sciences. *Creative Arts/Performance:* 66 awards ($508,673 total): art/fine arts, creative writing, debating, journalism/ publications, music, performing arts, theater/drama. *Special Achievements/ Activities:* general special achievements/activities, leadership. *Special Characteristics:* 45 awards ($412,729 total): children of faculty/staff, ethnic background, general special characteristics, international students, religious affiliation. *Tuition waivers:* Full or partial for employees or children of employees.

LOANS *Student loans:* $6,394,608 (51% need-based, 49% non-need-based). 80% of past graduating class borrowed through all loan programs. *Average indebtedness per student:* $22,125. *Average need-based loan:* Freshmen: $4125; Undergraduates: $5200. *Parent loans:* $541,466 (100% non-need-based). *Programs:* Federal Direct (Subsidized and Unsubsidized Stafford, PLUS), Perkins, Federal Nursing.

WORK-STUDY *Federal work-study:* Total amount: $348,620; 294 jobs averaging $1400. *State or other work-study/employment:* Total amount: $223,991 (100% non-need-based). 107 part-time jobs averaging $1400.

ATHLETIC AWARDS *Total amount:* $763,198 (100% non-need-based).

APPLYING FOR FINANCIAL AID *Required financial aid form:* FAFSA. *Financial aid deadline (priority):* 3/1. *Notification date:* Continuous beginning 2/15. Students must reply within 2 weeks of notification.

CONTACT Brian Weingart, Director of Financial Aid, Alderson-Broaddus College, College Hill Road, Philippi, WV 26416, 304-457-6354 or toll-free 800-263-1549. *Fax:* 304-457-6239.

ALFRED UNIVERSITY
Alfred, NY

Tuition & fees: $20,060	Average undergraduate aid package: $19,364

ABOUT THE INSTITUTION Independent, coed. Awards: bachelor's, master's, and doctoral degrees and post-master's certificates. 47 undergraduate majors. Total enrollment: 2,355. Undergraduates: 2,057. Freshmen: 506. Both federal and institutional methodology are used as a basis for awarding need-based institutional aid.

UNDERGRADUATE EXPENSES for 2004–05 *Application fee:* $40. *Comprehensive fee:* $29,434 includes full-time tuition ($19,250), mandatory fees ($810), and room and board ($9374). *College room only:* $4884. Full-time tuition and fees vary according to program and student level. Room and board charges vary according to board plan and housing facility. *Part-time tuition:* $630 per credit hour. Part-time tuition and fees vary according to course load and program. *Payment plans:* Tuition prepayment, installment, deferred payment.

FRESHMAN FINANCIAL AID (Fall 2004, est.) 452 applied for aid; of those 90% were deemed to have need. 100% of freshmen with need received aid; of those 85% had need fully met. *Average percent of need met:* 94% (excluding resources awarded to replace EFC). *Average financial aid package:* $19,396 (excluding resources awarded to replace EFC).

UNDERGRADUATE FINANCIAL AID (Fall 2004, est.) 1,731 applied for aid; of those 92% were deemed to have need. 100% of undergraduates with need received aid; of those 75% had need fully met. *Average percent of need met:* 90% (excluding resources awarded to replace EFC). *Average financial aid package:* $19,364 (excluding resources awarded to replace EFC). 13% of all full-time undergraduates had no need and received non-need-based gift aid.

GIFT AID (NEED-BASED) *Total amount:* $20,829,000 (12% federal, 13% state, 75% institutional). *Receiving aid:* Freshmen: 405; All full-time undergraduates: 80% (1,559). *Average award:* Freshmen: $14,574; Undergraduates: $14,364. *Scholarships, grants, and awards:* Federal Pell, FSEOG, state, private, college/ university gift aid from institutional funds.

GIFT AID (NON-NEED-BASED) *Total amount:* $2,876,000 (3% federal, 2% state, 78% institutional, 17% external sources). *Receiving aid:* Freshmen: 235; Undergraduates: 41% (801). *Average Award:* Freshmen: $7136; Undergraduates: $6680. *Scholarships, grants, and awards by category: Academic Interests/ Achievement:* biological sciences, business, communication, computer science, education, engineering/technologies, English, foreign languages, general academic interests/achievements, humanities, international studies, mathematics, military science, physical sciences, premedicine, social sciences. *Creative Arts/ Performance:* art/fine arts, general creative arts/performance, performing arts. *Special Achievements/Activities:* leadership. *Special Characteristics:* children of educators, children of faculty/staff, international students. *Tuition waivers:* Full or partial for employees or children of employees. *ROTC:* Army cooperative.

LOANS *Student loans:* $10,063,000 (65% need-based, 35% non-need-based). 89% of past graduating class borrowed through all loan programs. *Average indebtedness per student:* $19,125. *Average need-based loan:* Freshmen: $4146; Undergraduates: $4904. *Parent loans:* $2,633,000 (100% non-need-based). *Programs:* FFEL (Subsidized and Unsubsidized Stafford, PLUS), Perkins, college/ university, alternative loans.

WORK-STUDY *Federal work-study:* Total amount: $1,447,000; 1,064 jobs averaging $1328. *State or other work-study/employment:* Total amount: $20,000 (100% non-need-based). Part-time jobs available.

APPLYING FOR FINANCIAL AID *Required financial aid forms:* FAFSA, institution's own form, state aid form, noncustodial (divorced/separated) parent's statement, business/farm supplement. *Financial aid deadline:* Continuous. *Notification date:* Continuous beginning 2/15. Students must reply by 5/1 or within 2 weeks of notification.

CONTACT Mr. Earl Pierce, Director of Financial Aid, Alfred University, Alumni Hall, One Saxon Drive, Alfred, NY 14802-1205, 607-871-2159 or toll-free 800-541-9229. *Fax:* 607-871-2252. *E-mail:* pierce@alfred.edu.

ALICE LLOYD COLLEGE
Pippa Passes, KY

Tuition & fees: $1090	Average undergraduate aid package: $8581

ABOUT THE INSTITUTION Independent, coed. Awards: bachelor's degrees. 14 undergraduate majors. Total enrollment: 596. Undergraduates: 596. Freshmen: 175. Federal methodology is used as a basis for awarding need-based institutional aid.

UNDERGRADUATE EXPENSES for 2005–06 includes mandatory fees ($1090) and room and board ($3600). *College room only:* $1650. *Part-time tuition:* $212 per credit hour. Full-time students in the 108-county service area are granted guaranteed tuition. *Payment plan:* Deferred payment.

FRESHMAN FINANCIAL AID (Fall 2003) 175 applied for aid; of those 78% were deemed to have need. 100% of freshmen with need received aid; of those 29% had need fully met. *Average percent of need met:* 78% (excluding resources awarded to replace EFC). *Average financial aid package:* $8433 (excluding resources awarded to replace EFC). 22% of all full-time freshmen had no need and received non-need-based gift aid.

UNDERGRADUATE FINANCIAL AID (Fall 2003) 559 applied for aid; of those 86% were deemed to have need. 100% of undergraduates with need received aid; of those 22% had need fully met. *Average percent of need met:* 76% (excluding resources awarded to replace EFC). *Average financial aid package:* $8581 (excluding resources awarded to replace EFC). 17% of all full-time undergraduates had no need and received non-need-based gift aid.

GIFT AID (NEED-BASED) *Total amount:* $2,456,607 (37% federal, 39% state, 24% institutional). *Receiving aid:* Freshmen: 78% (136); All full-time undergraduates: 82% (474). *Average award:* Freshmen: $7053; Undergraduates: $7025. *Scholarships, grants, and awards:* Federal Pell, FSEOG, state, private, college/ university gift aid from institutional funds.

GIFT AID (NON-NEED-BASED) *Total amount:* $1,213,090 (41% state, 58% institutional, 1% external sources). *Receiving aid:* Freshmen: 15% (26);

Alice Lloyd College

Undergraduates: 10% (56). *Average Award:* Freshmen: $7795; *Undergraduates:* $6679. *Scholarships, grants, and awards by category: Special Achievements/ Activities:* 33 awards ($196,482 total): general special achievements/activities. *Special Characteristics:* 5 awards ($13,248 total): members of minority groups. *Tuition waivers:* Full or partial for minority students, employees or children of employees.

LOANS *Student loans:* $295,000 (53% need-based, 47% non-need-based). 44% of past graduating class borrowed through all loan programs. *Average indebtedness per student:* $6034. *Average need-based loan:* Freshmen: $228; Undergraduates: $380. *Parent loans:* $10,000 (100% need-based). *Programs:* FFEL (Subsidized and Unsubsidized Stafford, PLUS), Perkins, college/university, Bagby Loans (for freshmen).

WORK-STUDY *Federal work-study:* Total amount: $783,964; 438 jobs averaging $1751. *State or other work-study/employment:* Total amount: $300,000 (100% non-need-based). 157 part-time jobs averaging $1910.

ATHLETIC AWARDS *Total amount:* $196,482 (100% non-need-based).

APPLYING FOR FINANCIAL AID *Required financial aid form:* FAFSA. *Financial aid deadline (priority):* 3/15. *Notification date:* Continuous beginning 4/15.

CONTACT Ms. Nancy M. Melton, Director of Financial Aid, Alice Lloyd College, 100 Purpose Road, Pippa Passes, KY 41844, 606-368-6059. *E-mail:* nancymelton@ alc.edu.

ALLEGHENY COLLEGE
Meadville, PA

Tuition & fees: $26,950	Average undergraduate aid package: $20,370

ABOUT THE INSTITUTION Independent, coed. Awards: bachelor's degrees. 47 undergraduate majors. Total enrollment: 1,955. Undergraduates: 1,955. Freshmen: 651. Federal methodology is used as a basis for awarding need-based institutional aid.

UNDERGRADUATE EXPENSES for 2005–06 *Application fee:* $35. *Comprehensive fee:* $33,500 includes full-time tuition ($26,650), mandatory fees ($300), and room and board ($6550). *College room only:* $3340. Room and board charges vary according to board plan and housing facility. *Part-time tuition:* $1100 per credit hour. *Part-time fees:* $150 per term. Part-time tuition and fees vary according to course load. *Payment plans:* Tuition prepayment, installment.

GIFT AID (NEED-BASED) *Total amount:* $19,045,961 (7% federal, 10% state, 79% institutional, 4% external sources). *Receiving aid:* Freshmen: 72% (470); All full-time undergraduates: 72% (1,370). *Average award:* Freshmen: $15,293; Undergraduates: $14,293. *Scholarships, grants, and awards:* Federal Pell, FSEOG, state, private, college/university gift aid from institutional funds.

GIFT AID (NON-NEED-BASED) *Total amount:* $5,900,295 (93% institutional, 7% external sources). *Receiving aid:* Freshmen: 17% (111); Undergraduates: 14% (258). *Average Award:* Freshmen: $11,490; Undergraduates: $9941. *Scholarships, grants, and awards by category: Academic Interests/Achievement:* 1,416 awards ($15,172,915 total): general academic interests/achievements. *Special Characteristics:* 73 awards ($1,342,856 total): adult students, children of educators, children of faculty/staff, international students. *Tuition waivers:* Full or partial for employees or children of employees.

LOANS *Student loans:* $12,142,278 (41% need-based, 59% non-need-based). 78% of past graduating class borrowed through all loan programs. *Average indebtedness per student:* $23,846. *Average need-based loan:* Freshmen: $4235; Undergraduates: $4579. *Parent loans:* $2,128,587 (100% non-need-based). *Programs:* FFEL (Subsidized and Unsubsidized Stafford, PLUS), Perkins, state, private loans from commercial lenders.

APPLYING FOR FINANCIAL AID *Required financial aid form:* FAFSA. *Financial aid deadline (priority):* 2/15. *Notification date:* Continuous beginning 3/1. Students must reply by 5/1 or within 4 weeks of notification.

CONTACT Ms. Sheryle Proper, Director of Financial Aid, Allegheny College, 520 North Main Street, Meadville, PA 16335, 814-332-2701 or toll-free 800-521-5293. *Fax:* 814-337-0431. *E-mail:* fao@allegheny.edu.

ALLEGHENY WESLEYAN COLLEGE
Salem, OH

CONTACT Financial Aid Office, Allegheny Wesleyan College, 2161 Woodsdale Road, Salem, OH 44460, 330-337-6403 or toll-free 800-292-3153.

ALLEN COLLEGE
Waterloo, IA

Tuition & fees: $11,276	Average undergraduate aid package: $7580

ABOUT THE INSTITUTION Independent, coed, primarily women. Awards: associate, bachelor's, and master's degrees (liberal arts and general education courses offered at either University of North Iowa or Wartburg College). 2 undergraduate majors. Total enrollment: 364. Undergraduates: 333. Freshmen: 33. Federal methodology is used as a basis for awarding need-based institutional aid.

UNDERGRADUATE EXPENSES for 2004–05 *Application fee:* $50. *Comprehensive fee:* $16,440 includes full-time tuition ($9901), mandatory fees ($1375), and room and board ($5164). *College room only:* $2582. Full-time tuition and fees vary according to course load, location, program, and student level. Room and board charges vary according to board plan and housing facility. *Part-time tuition:* $380 per credit hour. *Part-time fees:* $35 per credit hour; $205 per term. Part-time tuition and fees vary according to program. *Payment plan:* Installment.

FRESHMAN FINANCIAL AID (Fall 2003) 33 applied for aid; of those 73% were deemed to have need. 100% of freshmen with need received aid. *Average percent of need met:* 58% (excluding resources awarded to replace EFC). *Average financial aid package:* $1850 (excluding resources awarded to replace EFC). 18% of all full-time freshmen had no need and received non-need-based gift aid.

UNDERGRADUATE FINANCIAL AID (Fall 2003) 221 applied for aid; of those 99% were deemed to have need. 100% of undergraduates with need received aid; of those 11% had need fully met. *Average percent of need met:* 65% (excluding resources awarded to replace EFC). *Average financial aid package:* $7580 (excluding resources awarded to replace EFC). 11% of all full-time undergraduates had no need and received non-need-based gift aid.

GIFT AID (NEED-BASED) *Total amount:* $757,372 (33% federal, 57% state, 10% institutional). *Receiving aid:* Freshmen: 67% (22); All full-time undergraduates: 57% (157). *Average award:* Freshmen: $3113; Undergraduates: $4528. *Scholarships, grants, and awards:* Federal Pell, FSEOG, state, private, college/ university gift aid from institutional funds, Federal Nursing, Federal Scholarships for Disadvantaged Students.

GIFT AID (NON-NEED-BASED) *Total amount:* $17,877 (52% institutional, 48% external sources). *Average Award:* Freshmen: $397; Undergraduates: $1153. *Scholarships, grants, and awards by category: Academic Interests/Achievement:* 20 awards ($12,101 total): health fields. *Special Achievements/Activities:* community service, general special achievements/activities, leadership. *Special Characteristics:* local/state students, members of minority groups, out-of-state students. *ROTC:* Army cooperative.

LOANS *Student loans:* $1,766,240 (57% need-based, 43% non-need-based). 82% of past graduating class borrowed through all loan programs. *Average indebtedness per student:* $18,030. *Average need-based loan:* Freshmen: $1849; Undergraduates: $3491. *Parent loans:* $455,835 (29% need-based, 71% non-need-based). *Programs:* Federal Direct (Subsidized and Unsubsidized Stafford, PLUS), Perkins, Federal Nursing, state, college/university.

WORK-STUDY *Federal work-study:* Total amount: $18,583; 18 jobs averaging $2000. *State or other work-study/employment:* Part-time jobs available.

APPLYING FOR FINANCIAL AID *Required financial aid forms:* FAFSA, institution's own form. *Financial aid deadline:* Continuous. *Notification date:* Continuous beginning 4/1.

CONTACT Kathie S. Walters, Financial Aid Director, Allen College, Barrett Forum, 1825 Logan Avenue, Waterloo, IA 50703, 319-226-2003. *Fax:* 319-226-2051. *E-mail:* walterks@ihs.org.

ALLEN UNIVERSITY
Columbia, SC

ABOUT THE INSTITUTION Independent African Methodist Episcopal, coed. Awards: bachelor's degrees. 11 undergraduate majors. Total enrollment: 565. Undergraduates: 565. Freshmen: 145.

GIFT AID (NEED-BASED) *Scholarships, grants, and awards:* Federal Pell, FSEOG, state, private.

GIFT AID (NON-NEED-BASED) *Scholarships, grants, and awards by category: Academic Interests/Achievement:* general academic interests/achievements.

LOANS *Programs:* FFEL (Subsidized and Unsubsidized Stafford, PLUS).

WORK-STUDY *Federal work-study:* Total amount: $189,180; 160 jobs averaging $1000.

APPLYING FOR FINANCIAL AID *Required financial aid form:* FAFSA.

CONTACT Ms. Donna Foster, Director of Financial Aid, Allen University, 1530 Harden Street, Columbia, SC 29204-1085, 803-376-5736 or toll-free 877-625-5368 (in-state). *E-mail:* donnaf@allenuniversity.edu.

ALLIANT INTERNATIONAL UNIVERSITY
San Diego, CA

Tuition & fees: $19,360	Average undergraduate aid package: $21,250

ABOUT THE INSTITUTION Independent, coed. Awards: bachelor's, master's, and doctoral degrees and post-bachelor's certificates. 10 undergraduate majors. Total enrollment: 3,556. Undergraduates: 346. Freshmen: 77. Federal methodology is used as a basis for awarding need-based institutional aid.
UNDERGRADUATE EXPENSES for 2004–05 *Application fee:* $40. *Comprehensive fee:* $26,790 includes full-time tuition ($18,990), mandatory fees ($370), and room and board ($7430). Full-time tuition and fees vary according to course load. Room and board charges vary according to board plan. *Part-time tuition:* $695 per unit. Part-time tuition and fees vary according to course load. *Payment plan:* Installment.
FRESHMAN FINANCIAL AID (Fall 2004, est.) 57 applied for aid; of those 70% were deemed to have need. 100% of freshmen with need received aid; of those 38% had need fully met. *Average percent of need met:* 100% (excluding resources awarded to replace EFC). *Average financial aid package:* $21,250 (excluding resources awarded to replace EFC). 34% of all full-time freshmen had no need and received non-need-based gift aid.
UNDERGRADUATE FINANCIAL AID (Fall 2004, est.) 304 applied for aid; of those 60% were deemed to have need. 100% of undergraduates with need received aid; of those 28% had need fully met. *Average percent of need met:* 100% (excluding resources awarded to replace EFC). *Average financial aid package:* $21,250 (excluding resources awarded to replace EFC). 17% of all full-time undergraduates had no need and received non-need-based gift aid.
GIFT AID (NEED-BASED) *Total amount:* $1,044,952 (51% federal, 49% state). *Receiving aid:* Freshmen: 66% (40); All full-time undergraduates: 54% (183). *Average award:* Freshmen: $6000; Undergraduates: $6000. *Scholarships, grants, and awards:* Federal Pell, FSEOG, state, private, college/university gift aid from institutional funds.
GIFT AID (NON-NEED-BASED) *Total amount:* $1,269,041 (97% institutional, 3% external sources). *Receiving aid:* Freshmen: 66% (40); Undergraduates: 54% (183). *Average Award:* Freshmen: $2000; Undergraduates: $2000. *Scholarships, grants, and awards by category: Academic Interests/Achievement:* business, communication, computer science, education, English, foreign languages, general academic interests/achievements, humanities, international studies, social sciences. *Special Achievements/Activities:* community service, general special achievements/activities, leadership. *Special Characteristics:* children and siblings of alumni, children of current students, children of faculty/staff, ethnic background, international students, local/state students, members of minority groups. *Tuition waivers:* Full or partial for children of alumni, employees or children of employees. *ROTC:* Army cooperative.
LOANS *Student loans:* $955,048 (68% need-based, 32% non-need-based). 67% of past graduating class borrowed through all loan programs. *Average indebtedness per student:* $17,125. *Average need-based loan:* Freshmen: $6625; Undergraduates: $7500. *Parent loans:* $748,454 (100% non-need-based). *Programs:* FFEL (Subsidized and Unsubsidized Stafford, PLUS), Perkins, alternative loans.
WORK-STUDY *Federal work-study:* Total amount: $216,506; 55 jobs averaging $4100. *State or other work-study/employment:* Total amount: $85,250 (100% need-based). 30 part-time jobs averaging $4207.
ATHLETIC AWARDS *Total amount:* $586,333 (100% non-need-based).
APPLYING FOR FINANCIAL AID *Required financial aid form:* FAFSA. *Financial aid deadline (priority):* 3/2. *Notification date:* Continuous beginning 4/1. Students must reply within 3 weeks of notification.
CONTACT Deborah Spindler, Director of Financial Aid, Alliant International University, 10455 Pomerado Road, San Diego, CA 92131-1799, 858-635-4559 Ext. 4700 or toll-free 866-825-5426. *Fax:* 858-635-4848.

ALMA COLLEGE
Alma, MI

Tuition & fees: $19,986	Average undergraduate aid package: $17,188

ABOUT THE INSTITUTION Independent Presbyterian, coed. Awards: bachelor's degrees. 69 undergraduate majors. Total enrollment: 1,268. Undergraduates: 1,268. Freshmen: 323. Federal methodology is used as a basis for awarding need-based institutional aid.
UNDERGRADUATE EXPENSES for 2004–05 *Application fee:* $25. *Comprehensive fee:* $27,018 includes full-time tuition ($19,786), mandatory fees ($200), and room and board ($7032). *College room only:* $3482. Room and board charges vary according to board plan and housing facility. *Part-time tuition:* $767 per credit. Part-time tuition and fees vary according to course load. *Payment plans:* Installment, deferred payment.
FRESHMAN FINANCIAL AID (Fall 2004, est.) 315 applied for aid; of those 78% were deemed to have need. 100% of freshmen with need received aid; of those 26% had need fully met. *Average percent of need met:* 86% (excluding resources awarded to replace EFC). *Average financial aid package:* $18,109 (excluding resources awarded to replace EFC). 21% of all full-time freshmen had no need and received non-need-based gift aid.
UNDERGRADUATE FINANCIAL AID (Fall 2004, est.) 1,203 applied for aid; of those 78% were deemed to have need. 100% of undergraduates with need received aid; of those 26% had need fully met. *Average percent of need met:* 84% (excluding resources awarded to replace EFC). *Average financial aid package:* $17,188 (excluding resources awarded to replace EFC). 21% of all full-time undergraduates had no need and received non-need-based gift aid.
GIFT AID (NEED-BASED) *Total amount:* $11,702,828 (9% federal, 14% state, 74% institutional, 3% external sources). *Receiving aid:* Freshmen: 78% (246); All full-time undergraduates: 76% (927). *Average award:* Freshmen: $14,907; Undergraduates: $12,929. *Scholarships, grants, and awards:* Federal Pell, FSEOG, state, private, college/university gift aid from institutional funds.
GIFT AID (NON-NEED-BASED) *Total amount:* $2,956,298 (7% state, 84% institutional, 9% external sources). *Receiving aid:* Freshmen: 13% (41); Undergraduates: 10% (118). *Average Award:* Freshmen: $15,142; Undergraduates: $11,822. *Scholarships, grants, and awards by category: Academic Interests/Achievement:* 845 awards ($5,857,871 total): general academic interests/achievements. *Creative Arts/Performance:* 294 awards ($606,594 total): art/fine arts, dance, music, theater/drama. *Special Achievements/Activities:* 6 awards ($19,500 total): leadership. *Special Characteristics:* 260 awards ($919,956 total): children and siblings of alumni, children of faculty/staff, previous college experience. *Tuition waivers:* Full or partial for employees or children of employees. *ROTC:* Army cooperative.
LOANS *Student loans:* $5,961,058 (70% need-based, 30% non-need-based). 86% of past graduating class borrowed through all loan programs. *Average indebtedness per student:* $19,437. *Average need-based loan:* Freshmen: $4124; Undergraduates: $5330. *Parent loans:* $1,947,946 (29% need-based, 71% non-need-based). *Programs:* Federal Direct (Subsidized and Unsubsidized Stafford, PLUS), Perkins, state, college/university, alternative loans.
WORK-STUDY *Federal work-study:* Total amount: $173,000; 140 jobs averaging $950. *State or other work-study/employment:* Total amount: $21,000 (100% need-based). 30 part-time jobs averaging $700.
APPLYING FOR FINANCIAL AID *Required financial aid form:* FAFSA. *Financial aid deadline (priority):* 3/1. *Notification date:* Continuous beginning 3/1. Students must reply within 3 weeks of notification.
CONTACT Mr. Christopher A. Brown, Director of Financial Aid, Alma College, 614 West Superior Street, Alma, MI 48801-1599, 989-463-7347 or toll-free 800-321-ALMA. *Fax:* 989-463-7993. *E-mail:* cabrown@alma.edu.

ALVERNIA COLLEGE
Reading, PA

Tuition & fees: $17,675	Average undergraduate aid package: $17,907

ABOUT THE INSTITUTION Independent Roman Catholic, coed. Awards: associate, bachelor's, and master's degrees and post-bachelor's and post-master's certificates. 40 undergraduate majors. Total enrollment: 2,380. Undergraduates: 1,848. Freshmen: 292. Federal methodology is used as a basis for awarding need-based institutional aid.
UNDERGRADUATE EXPENSES for 2004–05 *Application fee:* $25. *Comprehensive fee:* $25,005 includes full-time tuition ($17,500), mandatory fees ($175), and room and board ($7330). *College room only:* $3690. Full-time tuition and fees vary according to class time and reciprocity agreements. Room and board charges vary according to board plan and housing facility. *Part-time tuition:* $515 per credit. Part-time tuition and fees vary according to class time and course load. *Payment plan:* Installment.
GIFT AID (NEED-BASED) *Total amount:* $10,844,818 (16% federal, 14% state, 69% institutional, 1% external sources). *Receiving aid:* Freshmen: 77% (256);

All full-time undergraduates: 93% (1,163). *Average award:* Freshmen: $10,428; Undergraduates: $9245. *Scholarships, grants, and awards:* Federal Pell, FSEOG, state, private, college/university gift aid from institutional funds.

GIFT AID (NON-NEED-BASED) *Total amount:* $915,357 (2% state, 98% institutional). *Receiving aid:* Freshmen: 1; Undergraduates: 10% (127). *Average Award:* Freshmen: $13,421; Undergraduates: $15,489. *Scholarships, grants, and awards by category: Academic Interests/Achievement:* 20 awards ($120,000 total): general academic interests/achievements. *Special Achievements/Activities:* 20 awards ($60,000 total): community service, junior miss, leadership, religious involvement. *Special Characteristics:* children and siblings of alumni, children of faculty/staff, international students, local/state students, out-of-state students, previous college experience, religious affiliation, siblings of current students. *Tuition waivers:* Full or partial for employees or children of employees, senior citizens. *ROTC:* Army cooperative.

LOANS *Student loans:* $9,218,608 (80% need-based, 20% non-need-based). 92% of past graduating class borrowed through all loan programs. *Average indebtedness per student:* $3495. *Average need-based loan:* Freshmen: $2405; Undergraduates: $3552. *Parent loans:* $1,261,445 (100% need-based). *Programs:* FFEL (Subsidized and Unsubsidized Stafford, PLUS), Perkins, college/university, Health Professions Loans.

APPLYING FOR FINANCIAL AID *Required financial aid forms:* FAFSA, state aid form, noncustodial (divorced/separated) parent's statement. *Financial aid deadline:* Continuous. *Notification date:* Continuous beginning 1/1. Students must reply within 2 weeks of notification.

CONTACT Lora Myers, Director of Financial Aid, Alvernia College, 400 St. Bernardine Street, Reading, PA 19607-1799, 610-796-8200 Ext. 1473 or toll-free 888-ALVERNIA (in-state). *Fax:* 610-796-8336. *E-mail:* bra.myers@alvernia.edu.

ALVERNO COLLEGE
Milwaukee, WI

Tuition & fees: $14,410	Average undergraduate aid package: N/A

ABOUT THE INSTITUTION Independent Roman Catholic, women only. Awards: associate, bachelor's, and master's degrees (also offers weekend program with significant enrollment not reflected in profile). 43 undergraduate majors. Total enrollment: 2,241. Undergraduates: 2,053. Freshmen: 302. Federal methodology is used as a basis for awarding need-based institutional aid.

UNDERGRADUATE EXPENSES for 2004–05 *Application fee:* $20. *Comprehensive fee:* $19,810 includes full-time tuition ($14,160), mandatory fees ($250), and room and board ($5400). *College room only:* $2000. Full-time tuition and fees vary according to class time and program. Room and board charges vary according to board plan and housing facility. *Part-time tuition:* $590 per credit hour. *Part-time fees:* $125 per term. Part-time tuition and fees vary according to class time and program. *Payment plans:* Installment, deferred payment.

GIFT AID (NEED-BASED) *Total amount:* $9,260,812 (32% federal, 24% state, 43% institutional, 1% external sources). *Scholarships, grants, and awards:* Federal Pell, FSEOG, state, private, college/university gift aid from institutional funds, transfer student scholarships.

GIFT AID (NON-NEED-BASED) *Total amount:* $215,348 (100% external sources). *Scholarships, grants, and awards by category: Academic Interests/Achievement:* general academic interests/achievements. *Creative Arts/Performance:* art/fine arts, music. *Special Achievements/Activities:* community service. *Special Characteristics:* children and siblings of alumni. *Tuition waivers:* Full or partial for employees or children of employees. *ROTC:* Army cooperative, Air Force cooperative.

LOANS *Student loans:* $10,856,061 (54% need-based, 46% non-need-based). *Parent loans:* $249,776 (100% non-need-based). *Programs:* FFEL (Subsidized and Unsubsidized Stafford, PLUS), Perkins.

WORK-STUDY *Federal work-study:* Total amount: $236,296; 164 jobs averaging $2560.

APPLYING FOR FINANCIAL AID *Required financial aid forms:* FAFSA, institution's own form, business/farm supplement, income tax forms. *Financial aid deadline (priority):* 4/1. *Notification date:* Continuous beginning 4/15. Students must reply within 2 weeks of notification.

CONTACT Mark Levine, Director of Financial Aid, Alverno College, 3400 South 43rd Street, PO Box 343922, Milwaukee, WI 53234-3922, 414-382-6046 or toll-free 800-933-3401. *Fax:* 414-382-6354. *E-mail:* mark.levine@alverno.edu.

AMERICAN ACADEMY OF ART
Chicago, IL

CONTACT Ms. Ione Fitzgerald, Director of Financial Aid, American Academy of Art, 332 South Michigan Avenue, Suite 300, Chicago, IL 60604, 312-461-0600. *Fax:* 312-294-9570.

AMERICAN BAPTIST COLLEGE OF AMERICAN BAPTIST THEOLOGICAL SEMINARY
Nashville, TN

Tuition & fees: $3143	Average undergraduate aid package: $2025

ABOUT THE INSTITUTION Independent Baptist, coed. Awards: associate and bachelor's degrees. 2 undergraduate majors. Total enrollment: 103. Undergraduates: 103. Freshmen: 6. Federal methodology is used as a basis for awarding need-based institutional aid.

UNDERGRADUATE EXPENSES for 2004–05 *Application fee:* $20. *Tuition:* full-time $3003; part-time $143 per credit hour. *Required fees:* full-time $140; $140 per year part-time. Full-time tuition and fees vary according to course load. Part-time tuition and fees vary according to course load. Room and board charges vary according to housing facility. *Payment plan:* Deferred payment.

GIFT AID (NEED-BASED) *Total amount:* $264,163 (60% federal, 14% state, 26% external sources). *Receiving aid:* Freshmen: 75% (12); All full-time undergraduates: 21% (12). *Average award:* Freshmen: $1161; Undergraduates: $1161. *Scholarships, grants, and awards:* Federal Pell, FSEOG, state.

GIFT AID (NON-NEED-BASED) *Scholarships, grants, and awards by category: Special Characteristics:* religious affiliation.

APPLYING FOR FINANCIAL AID *Required financial aid form:* FAFSA. *Financial aid deadline:* 7/23 (priority: 1/1). *Notification date:* Continuous beginning 7/30. Students must reply by 8/1 or within 2 weeks of notification.

CONTACT Marcella Lockhart, Executive Assistant for Administrator, American Baptist College of American Baptist Theological Seminary, 1800 Baptist World Center Drive, Nashville, TN 37207, 615-256-1463 Ext. 2227. *Fax:* 615-226-7855. *E-mail:* mlockhart@abcnash.edu.

AMERICAN INDIAN COLLEGE OF THE ASSEMBLIES OF GOD, INC.
Phoenix, AZ

CONTACT Office of Student Financial Aid, American Indian College of the Assemblies of God, Inc., 10020 North Fifteenth Avenue, Phoenix, AZ 85021-2199, 800-933-3828.

AMERICAN INTERCONTINENTAL UNIVERSITY
Los Angeles, CA

CONTACT Mr. Joe Johnson, Director of Financial Aid, American InterContinental University, 12655 West Jefferson Boulevard, Los Angeles, CA 90066, 310-302-2000 Ext. 2447 or toll-free 800-333-2652 (out-of-state). *Fax:* 310-302-2002.

AMERICAN INTERCONTINENTAL UNIVERSITY
Weston, FL

CONTACT Financial Aid Office, American InterContinental University, 2250 North Commerce Parkway, Suite 100, Weston, FL 33326, 954-446-6100 or toll-free 866-248-4723 (out-of-state).

AMERICAN INTERCONTINENTAL UNIVERSITY
Atlanta, GA

CONTACT Sherry Rizzi, Financial Aid Director, American InterContinental University, 3330 Peachtree Road NE, Atlanta, GA 30326, 404-965-5796 or toll-free 888-999-4248 (out-of-state). *Fax:* 404-965-5704.

AMERICAN INTERCONTINENTAL UNIVERSITY
Atlanta, GA

CONTACT Financial Aid Office, American InterContinental University, 6600 Peachtree-Dunwoody Road, 500 Embassy Row, Atlanta, GA 30328, 404-965-6500 or toll-free 800-255-6839.

AMERICAN INTERCONTINENTAL UNIVERSITY
Houston, TX

CONTACT Financial Aid Office, American InterContinental University, 9999 Richmond Avenue, Houston, TX 77042, 832-242-5788.

AMERICAN INTERCONTINENTAL UNIVERSITY ONLINE
Hoffman Estates, IL

CONTACT Financial Aid Office, American InterContinental University Online, 5550 Prairie Stone Parkway, Suite 400, Hoffman Estates, IL 60192, 847-851-5000 or toll-free 877-701-3800.

AMERICAN INTERNATIONAL COLLEGE
Springfield, MA

Tuition & fees: $18,000	Average undergraduate aid package: $17,839

ABOUT THE INSTITUTION Independent, coed. Awards: associate, bachelor's, master's, and doctoral degrees and post-bachelor's and post-master's certificates. 45 undergraduate majors. Total enrollment: 1,625. Undergraduates: 1,227. Freshmen: 299. Federal methodology is used as a basis for awarding need-based institutional aid.

UNDERGRADUATE EXPENSES for 2004–05 *Application fee:* $20. *Comprehensive fee:* $26,500 includes full-time tuition ($18,000) and room and board ($8500). *College room only:* $4232. Full-time tuition and fees vary according to program. Room and board charges vary according to board plan. *Part-time tuition:* $405 per credit. *Payment plans:* Tuition prepayment, installment, deferred payment.

FRESHMAN FINANCIAL AID (Fall 2004, est.) 299 applied for aid; of those 99% were deemed to have need. 100% of freshmen with need received aid; of those 47% had need fully met. *Average percent of need met:* 84% (excluding resources awarded to replace EFC). *Average financial aid package:* $20,069 (excluding resources awarded to replace EFC). 7% of all full-time freshmen had no need and received non-need-based gift aid.

UNDERGRADUATE FINANCIAL AID (Fall 2004, est.) 1,040 applied for aid; of those 93% were deemed to have need. 95% of undergraduates with need received aid; of those 51% had need fully met. *Average percent of need met:* 79% (excluding resources awarded to replace EFC). *Average financial aid package:* $17,839 (excluding resources awarded to replace EFC). 5% of all full-time undergraduates had no need and received non-need-based gift aid.

GIFT AID (NEED-BASED) *Total amount:* $8,518,147 (21% federal, 6% state, 71% institutional, 2% external sources). *Receiving aid:* Freshmen: 51% (152); All full-time undergraduates: 75% (788). *Average award:* Freshmen: $10,914; Undergraduates: $9730. *Scholarships, grants, and awards:* Federal Pell, FSEOG, state, private, college/university gift aid from institutional funds.

GIFT AID (NON-NEED-BASED) *Receiving aid:* Freshmen: 70% (209); Undergraduates: 57% (595). *Average Award:* Freshmen: $7339; Undergraduates: $6027. *Scholarships, grants, and awards by category:* Academic Interests/Achievement: 418 awards ($2,121,774 total): general academic interests/achievements. *Special Achievements/Activities:* 9 awards ($58,450 total): general special achievements/activities. *Tuition waivers:* Full or partial for employees or children of employees, senior citizens. *ROTC:* Army cooperative, Air Force cooperative.

LOANS *Student loans:* $7,351,688 (47% need-based, 53% non-need-based). 85% of past graduating class borrowed through all loan programs. *Average indebtedness per student:* $17,125. *Average need-based loan:* Freshmen: $3677; Undergraduates: $4404. *Parent loans:* $1,419,470 (100% need-based). *Programs:* FFEL (Subsidized and Unsubsidized Stafford, PLUS), Perkins, state, college/university, alternative loans.

WORK-STUDY *Federal work-study:* Total amount: $724,950; 200 jobs averaging $2400. *State or other work-study/employment:* Total amount: $295,000 (100% non-need-based). 200 part-time jobs averaging $2400.

ATHLETIC AWARDS *Total amount:* $2,048,117 (100% need-based).

APPLYING FOR FINANCIAL AID *Required financial aid form:* FAFSA. *Financial aid deadline (priority):* 5/1. *Notification date:* Continuous beginning 3/15. Students must reply within 2 weeks of notification.

CONTACT Ms. Irene D. Martin, Director of Financial Aid, American International College, 1000 State Street, Springfield, MA 01109-3189, 413-205-3259. *Fax:* 413-205-3912. *E-mail:* finaid@aic.edu.

AMERICAN UNIVERSITY
Washington, DC

Tuition & fees: $26,307	Average undergraduate aid package: $25,846

ABOUT THE INSTITUTION Independent Methodist, coed. Awards: associate, bachelor's, master's, doctoral, and first professional degrees and post-bachelor's certificates. 71 undergraduate majors. Total enrollment: 11,185. Undergraduates: 5,811. Freshmen: 1,209. Both federal and institutional methodology are used as a basis for awarding need-based institutional aid.

UNDERGRADUATE EXPENSES for 2004–05 *Application fee:* $45. *Comprehensive fee:* $36,567 includes full-time tuition ($25,920), mandatory fees ($387), and room and board ($10,260). Room and board charges vary according to board plan and housing facility. *Part-time tuition:* $864 per semester hour. *Part-time fees:* $130 per year. *Payment plan:* Installment.

FRESHMAN FINANCIAL AID (Fall 2004, est.) 890 applied for aid; of those 70% were deemed to have need. 99% of freshmen with need received aid; of those 49% had need fully met. *Average percent of need met:* 74% (excluding resources awarded to replace EFC). *Average financial aid package:* $25,029 (excluding resources awarded to replace EFC). 21% of all full-time freshmen had no need and received non-need-based gift aid.

UNDERGRADUATE FINANCIAL AID (Fall 2004, est.) 3,433 applied for aid; of those 79% were deemed to have need. 99% of undergraduates with need received aid; of those 50% had need fully met. *Average percent of need met:* 78% (excluding resources awarded to replace EFC). *Average financial aid package:* $25,846 (excluding resources awarded to replace EFC). 13% of all full-time undergraduates had no need and received non-need-based gift aid.

GIFT AID (NEED-BASED) *Total amount:* $30,609,207 (7% federal, 1% state, 87% institutional, 5% external sources). *Receiving aid:* Freshmen: 39% (476); All full-time undergraduates: 37% (2,175). *Average award:* Freshmen: $13,791; Undergraduates: $13,304. *Scholarships, grants, and awards:* Federal Pell, FSEOG, state, private, college/university gift aid from institutional funds.

GIFT AID (NON-NEED-BASED) *Total amount:* $17,875,490 (100% institutional). *Receiving aid:* Freshmen: 16% (192); Undergraduates: 10% (596). *Average Award:* Freshmen: $15,813; Undergraduates: $14,153. *Scholarships, grants, and awards by category:* Academic Interests/Achievement: general academic interests/achievements. Creative Arts/Performance: general creative arts/performance. Special Achievements/Activities: general special achievements/activities, leadership, memberships. Special Characteristics: adult students, children and siblings of alumni, children of faculty/staff, ethnic background, first-generation college students, local/state students, members of minority groups, previous college experience, relatives of clergy, spouses of current students. *Tuition waivers:* Full or partial for employees or children of employees. *ROTC:* Army cooperative, Air Force cooperative.

LOANS *Student loans:* $32,976,388 (61% need-based, 39% non-need-based). 50% of past graduating class borrowed through all loan programs. *Average indebtedness per student:* $19,796. *Average need-based loan:* Freshmen: $5722; Undergraduates: $7592. *Parent loans:* $10,019,344 (100% non-need-based). *Programs:* Federal Direct (Subsidized and Unsubsidized Stafford, PLUS), FFEL (PLUS), Perkins, college/university.

WORK-STUDY *Federal work-study:* Total amount: $4,373,649; 2,169 jobs averaging $2016.

ATHLETIC AWARDS *Total amount:* $3,012,268 (100% non-need-based).

APPLYING FOR FINANCIAL AID *Required financial aid forms:* FAFSA, institution's own form. *Financial aid deadline:* 2/15. *Notification date:* 4/1. Students must reply by 5/1 or within 4 weeks of notification.

CONTACT Brian Lee Sang, Office of Enrollment, American University, 4400 Massachusetts Avenue, NW, Washington, DC 20016-8001, 202-885-6100. *Fax:* 202-885-1025. *E-mail:* financialaid@american.edu.

AMERICAN UNIVERSITY OF PUERTO RICO
Bayamón, PR

Tuition & fees: $4590	Average undergraduate aid package: $5280

ABOUT THE INSTITUTION Independent, coed. Awards: associate and bachelor's degrees. 9 undergraduate majors. Total enrollment: 3,691. Undergraduates: 3,691. Federal methodology is used as a basis for awarding need-based institutional aid.

UNDERGRADUATE EXPENSES for 2004–05 *Application fee:* $25. *Tuition:* full-time $4350; part-time $2175 per term. *Required fees:* full-time $240; $160 per term part-time.

FRESHMAN FINANCIAL AID (Fall 2004, est.) 400 applied for aid; of those 95% were deemed to have need. 100% of freshmen with need received aid. *Average percent of need met:* 45% (excluding resources awarded to replace EFC). *Average financial aid package:* $5280 (excluding resources awarded to replace EFC).

UNDERGRADUATE FINANCIAL AID (Fall 2004, est.) 2,800 applied for aid; of those 99% were deemed to have need. 100% of undergraduates with need received aid. *Average percent of need met:* 45% (excluding resources awarded to replace EFC). *Average financial aid package:* $5280 (excluding resources awarded to replace EFC).

GIFT AID (NEED-BASED) *Total amount:* $12,142,278 (95% federal, 5% state). *Receiving aid:* Freshmen: 88% (350); All full-time undergraduates: 93% (2,600). *Average award:* Freshmen: $5; Undergraduates: $5. *Scholarships, grants, and awards:* Federal Pell, FSEOG, state, college/university gift aid from institutional funds.

GIFT AID (NON-NEED-BASED) *ROTC:* Army cooperative.

LOANS *Student loans:* $1,104,302 (100% need-based). 10% of past graduating class borrowed through all loan programs. *Average indebtedness per student:* $7000. *Average need-based loan:* Freshmen: $30; Undergraduates: $30. *Parent loans:* $29,117 (100% need-based). *Programs:* Federal Direct (Subsidized and Unsubsidized Stafford, PLUS).

WORK-STUDY *Federal work-study:* Total amount: $352,896; jobs available.

ATHLETIC AWARDS *Total amount:* $380,000 (100% need-based).

APPLYING FOR FINANCIAL AID *Required financial aid forms:* FAFSA, institution's own form. *Financial aid deadline:* 5/30 (priority: 4/15). *Notification date:* Continuous beginning 6/30. Students must reply within 2 weeks of notification.

CONTACT Mr. Yahaira Melendez, Financial Aid Director, American University of Puerto Rico, PO Box 2037, Bayamón, PR 00960-2037, 787-620-2040 Ext. 2031. *Fax:* 787-785-7377. *E-mail:* melendezy@aupr.edu.

AMHERST COLLEGE
Amherst, MA

Tuition & fees: $31,364	Average undergraduate aid package: $27,288

ABOUT THE INSTITUTION Independent, coed. Awards: bachelor's degrees. 36 undergraduate majors. Total enrollment: 1,638. Undergraduates: 1,638. Freshmen: 427. Institutional methodology is used as a basis for awarding need-based institutional aid.

UNDERGRADUATE EXPENSES for 2004–05 *Application fee:* $55. *Comprehensive fee:* $39,524 includes full-time tuition ($30,780), mandatory fees ($584), and room and board ($8160). *College room only:* $4380. *Payment plans:* Installment, deferred payment.

FRESHMAN FINANCIAL AID (Fall 2004, est.) 250 applied for aid; of those 80% were deemed to have need. 100% of freshmen with need received aid; of those 100% had need fully met. *Average percent of need met:* 100% (excluding resources awarded to replace EFC). *Average financial aid package:* $26,976 (excluding resources awarded to replace EFC).

UNDERGRADUATE FINANCIAL AID (Fall 2004, est.) 858 applied for aid; of those 89% were deemed to have need. 100% of undergraduates with need received aid; of those 100% had need fully met. *Average percent of need met:* 100% (excluding resources awarded to replace EFC). *Average financial aid package:* $27,288 (excluding resources awarded to replace EFC).

GIFT AID (NEED-BASED) *Total amount:* $20,318,807 (5% federal, 93% institutional, 2% external sources). *Receiving aid:* Freshmen: 44% (189); All full-time undergraduates: 44% (719). *Average award:* Freshmen: $25,727; Undergraduates: $25,662. *Scholarships, grants, and awards:* Federal Pell, FSEOG, state, private, college/university gift aid from institutional funds, United Negro College Fund.

GIFT AID (NON-NEED-BASED) *Total amount:* $1,266,176 (4% federal, 2% state, 94% external sources).

LOANS *Student loans:* $2,536,394 (70% need-based, 30% non-need-based). 50% of past graduating class borrowed through all loan programs. *Average indebtedness per student:* $10,170. *Average need-based loan:* Freshmen: $1839; Undergraduates: $2263. *Parent loans:* $3,168,465 (100% non-need-based). *Programs:* Federal Direct (Subsidized and Unsubsidized Stafford, PLUS, Perkins, college/university.

WORK-STUDY *Federal work-study:* Total amount: $708,059; jobs available. *State or other work-study/employment:* Total amount: $155,724 (100% need-based). Part-time jobs available.

APPLYING FOR FINANCIAL AID *Required financial aid forms:* FAFSA, CSS Financial Aid PROFILE, noncustodial (divorced/separated) parent's statement, income tax form(s), W-2 forms. *Financial aid deadline (priority):* 2/15. *Notification date:* 4/1. Students must reply by 5/1.

CONTACT Joe Paul Case, Dean/Director of Financial Aid, Amherst College, 202 Converse Hall, PO Box 5000, Amherst, MA 01002-5000, 413-542-2296. *Fax:* 413-542-2628. *E-mail:* finaid@amherst.edu.

ANDERSON COLLEGE
Anderson, SC

Tuition & fees: $15,200	Average undergraduate aid package: $13,714

ABOUT THE INSTITUTION Independent Baptist, coed. Awards: bachelor's degrees. 41 undergraduate majors. Total enrollment: 1,666. Undergraduates: 1,666. Freshmen: 327. Federal methodology is used as a basis for awarding need-based institutional aid.

UNDERGRADUATE EXPENSES for 2005–06 *Application fee:* $40. *Comprehensive fee:* $21,250 includes full-time tuition ($14,100), mandatory fees ($1100), and room and board ($6050). *College room only:* $3050. Full-time tuition and fees vary according to program. Room and board charges vary according to board plan and housing facility. *Part-time tuition:* $390 per credit hour. Part-time tuition and fees vary according to program. *Payment plan:* Installment.

FRESHMAN FINANCIAL AID (Fall 2004, est.) 317 applied for aid; of those 87% were deemed to have need. 100% of freshmen with need received aid; of those 33% had need fully met. *Average percent of need met:* 77% (excluding resources awarded to replace EFC). *Average financial aid package:* $14,419 (excluding resources awarded to replace EFC). 11% of all full-time freshmen had no need and received non-need-based gift aid.

UNDERGRADUATE FINANCIAL AID (Fall 2004, est.) 1,214 applied for aid; of those 88% were deemed to have need. 100% of undergraduates with need received aid; of those 32% had need fully met. *Average percent of need met:* 79% (excluding resources awarded to replace EFC). *Average financial aid package:* $13,714 (excluding resources awarded to replace EFC). 7% of all full-time undergraduates had no need and received non-need-based gift aid.

GIFT AID (NEED-BASED) *Total amount:* $7,824,681 (18% federal, 21% state, 61% institutional). *Receiving aid:* Freshmen: 86% (276); All full-time undergraduates: 83% (1,042). *Average award:* Freshmen: $7232; Undergraduates: $6809. *Scholarships, grants, and awards:* Federal Pell, FSEOG, state, college/university gift aid from institutional funds.

GIFT AID (NON-NEED-BASED) *Total amount:* $4,316,606 (66% state, 34% institutional). *Receiving aid:* Freshmen: 79% (254); Undergraduates: 60% (760). *Average Award:* Freshmen: $5464; Undergraduates: $5724. *Tuition waivers:* Full or partial for employees or children of employees, adult students, senior citizens. *ROTC:* Army cooperative, Air Force cooperative.

LOANS *Student loans:* $3,255,831 (91% need-based, 9% non-need-based). 75% of past graduating class borrowed through all loan programs. *Average indebtedness per student:* $13,874. *Average need-based loan:* Freshmen: $3073; Undergraduates: $4079. *Parent loans:* $3,030,441 (100% non-need-based). *Programs:* FFEL (Subsidized and Unsubsidized Stafford, PLUS), Perkins.

WORK-STUDY *Federal work-study:* Total amount: $181,095; 106 jobs averaging $1708. *State or other work-study/employment:* Total amount: $1547 (100% non-need-based). 1 part-time job averaging $1547.

ATHLETIC AWARDS *Total amount:* $790,640 (100% non-need-based).

APPLYING FOR FINANCIAL AID *Required financial aid form:* FAFSA. *Financial aid deadline:* 7/30 (priority: 3/1). *Notification date:* Continuous beginning 3/15. Students must reply within 2 weeks of notification.

CONTACT Jeff Holliday, Director of Financial Aid, Anderson College, 316 Boulevard, Anderson, SC 29621-4035, 864-231-2070 or toll-free 800-542-3594. *Fax:* 864-231-2008. *E-mail:* jholliday@ac.edu.

ANDERSON UNIVERSITY
Anderson, IN

Tuition & fees: $18,900	Average undergraduate aid package: $18,408

ABOUT THE INSTITUTION Independent religious, coed. Awards: associate, bachelor's, master's, doctoral, and first professional degrees. 61 undergraduate majors. Total enrollment: 2,677. Undergraduates: 2,270. Freshmen: 592. Federal methodology is used as a basis for awarding need-based institutional aid.

UNDERGRADUATE EXPENSES for 2005–06 *Application fee:* $20. *Comprehensive fee:* $25,050 includes full-time tuition ($18,900) and room and board ($6150). *College room only:* $3730. Room and board charges vary according to board plan. *Part-time tuition:* $788 per semester hour. Part-time tuition and fees vary according to course load. *Payment plan:* Installment.

FRESHMAN FINANCIAL AID (Fall 2004, est.) 500 applied for aid; of those 88% were deemed to have need. 100% of freshmen with need received aid; of those 44% had need fully met. *Average percent of need met:* 97% (excluding resources awarded to replace EFC). *Average financial aid package:* $18,071 (excluding resources awarded to replace EFC). 21% of all full-time freshmen had no need and received non-need-based gift aid.

UNDERGRADUATE FINANCIAL AID (Fall 2004, est.) 1,620 applied for aid; of those 89% were deemed to have need. 100% of undergraduates with need received aid; of those 46% had need fully met. *Average percent of need met:* 91% (excluding resources awarded to replace EFC). *Average financial aid package:* $18,408 (excluding resources awarded to replace EFC). 24% of all full-time undergraduates had no need and received non-need-based gift aid.

GIFT AID (NEED-BASED) *Total amount:* $15,752,500 (12% federal, 18% state, 62% institutional, 8% external sources). *Receiving aid:* Freshmen: 79% (438); All full-time undergraduates: 76% (1,441). *Average award:* Freshmen: $12,279; Undergraduates: $16,372. *Scholarships, grants, and awards:* Federal Pell, FSEOG, state, private, college/university gift aid from institutional funds.

GIFT AID (NON-NEED-BASED) *Total amount:* $3,850,025 (1% state, 81% institutional, 18% external sources). *Receiving aid:* Freshmen: 11% (63); Undergraduates: 8% (145). *Average Award:* Freshmen: $11,761; Undergraduates: $11,216. *Scholarships, grants, and awards by category: Academic Interests/Achievement:* 1,824 awards ($8,380,000 total): general academic interests/achievements. *Creative Arts/Performance:* 60 awards ($70,000 total): art/fine arts, music. *Special Achievements/Activities:* 30 awards ($74,000 total): leadership. *Special Characteristics:* 373 awards ($2,200,000 total): adult students, children of faculty/staff, international students, relatives of clergy. *Tuition waivers:* Full or partial for employees or children of employees, adult students.

LOANS *Student loans:* $11,971,310 (88% need-based, 12% non-need-based). 77% of past graduating class borrowed through all loan programs. *Average indebtedness per student:* $21,500. *Average need-based loan:* Freshmen: $4895; Undergraduates: $6161. *Parent loans:* $2,322,988 (67% need-based, 33% non-need-based). *Programs:* FFEL (Subsidized and Unsubsidized Stafford, PLUS), Perkins, GATE Loans.

WORK-STUDY *Federal work-study:* Total amount: $2,314,444; 1,048 jobs averaging $2208. *State or other work-study/employment:* Part-time jobs available.

APPLYING FOR FINANCIAL AID *Required financial aid form:* FAFSA. *Financial aid deadline (priority):* 3/1. *Notification date:* Continuous beginning 3/1.

CONTACT Mr. Kenneth Nieman, Director of Student Financial Services, Anderson University, 1100 East Fifth Street, Anderson, IN 46012-3495, 765-641-4180 or toll-free 800-421-3014 (in-state), 800-428-6414 (out-of-state). *Fax:* 765-641-3831. *E-mail:* kfnieman@anderson.edu.

ANDREWS UNIVERSITY
Berrien Springs, MI

Tuition & fees: $16,506	Average undergraduate aid package: $19,431

ABOUT THE INSTITUTION Independent Seventh-day Adventist, coed. Awards: associate, bachelor's, master's, doctoral, and first professional degrees and post-master's certificates. 85 undergraduate majors. Total enrollment: 3,017. Undergraduates: 1,730. Freshmen: 307. Federal methodology is used as a basis for awarding need-based institutional aid.

UNDERGRADUATE EXPENSES for 2005–06 *Application fee:* $30. *Comprehensive fee:* $21,786 includes full-time tuition ($16,030), mandatory fees ($476), and room and board ($5280). *College room only:* $2850. Full-time tuition and fees vary according to course load. Room and board charges vary according to

board plan and housing facility. *Part-time tuition:* $670 per credit hour. Part-time tuition and fees vary according to course load. *Payment plans:* Tuition prepayment, installment.

FRESHMAN FINANCIAL AID (Fall 2003) 323 applied for aid; of those 66% were deemed to have need. 100% of freshmen with need received aid; of those 46% had need fully met. *Average percent of need met:* 99% (excluding resources awarded to replace EFC). *Average financial aid package:* $17,283 (excluding resources awarded to replace EFC). 33% of all full-time freshmen had no need and received non-need-based gift aid.

UNDERGRADUATE FINANCIAL AID (Fall 2003) 1,501 applied for aid; of those 67% were deemed to have need. 100% of undergraduates with need received aid; of those 49% had need fully met. *Average percent of need met:* 98% (excluding resources awarded to replace EFC). *Average financial aid package:* $19,431 (excluding resources awarded to replace EFC). 31% of all full-time undergraduates had no need and received non-need-based gift aid.

GIFT AID (NEED-BASED) *Total amount:* $4,764,595 (42% federal, 8% state, 50% institutional). *Receiving aid:* Freshmen: 39% (127); All full-time undergraduates: 48% (731). *Average award:* Freshmen: $6291; Undergraduates: $6357. *Scholarships, grants, and awards:* Federal Pell, FSEOG, state, private, college/university gift aid from institutional funds.

GIFT AID (NON-NEED-BASED) *Total amount:* $6,977,733 (4% state, 70% institutional, 26% external sources). *Receiving aid:* Freshmen: 66% (214); Undergraduates: 60% (905). *Average Award:* Freshmen: $4973; Undergraduates: $4775. *Scholarships, grants, and awards by category: Academic Interests/Achievement:* 1,868 awards ($4,579,106 total): general academic interests/achievements. *Creative Arts/Performance:* 85 awards ($74,762 total): music. *Special Achievements/Activities:* 265 awards ($246,624 total): leadership, religious involvement. *Special Characteristics:* 209 awards ($1,119,247 total): children of faculty/staff, general special characteristics, international students. *Tuition waivers:* Full or partial for employees or children of employees, senior citizens.

LOANS *Student loans:* $9,504,782 (39% need-based, 61% non-need-based). 60% of past graduating class borrowed through all loan programs. *Average indebtedness per student:* $21,063. *Average need-based loan:* Freshmen: $2553; Undergraduates: $4705. *Parent loans:* $2,062,665 (100% non-need-based). *Programs:* Federal Direct (Subsidized and Unsubsidized Stafford, PLUS), Perkins.

WORK-STUDY *Federal work-study:* Total amount: $718,982; 502 jobs averaging $1432. *State or other work-study/employment:* Total amount: $287,294 (100% need-based). 255 part-time jobs averaging $1127.

APPLYING FOR FINANCIAL AID *Required financial aid forms:* FAFSA, institution's own form. *Financial aid deadline:* Continuous. *Notification date:* Continuous beginning 3/1.

CONTACT Ellen Murdick, Assistant Director of Student Financial Services, Andrews University, Student Financial Services Administration Building, Berrien Springs, MI 49104, 269-471-3221 or toll-free 800-253-2874. *Fax:* 269-471-3228.

ANGELO STATE UNIVERSITY
San Angelo, TX

Tuition & fees (TX res): $3126	Average undergraduate aid package: $4299

ABOUT THE INSTITUTION State-supported, coed. Awards: associate, bachelor's, and master's degrees. 41 undergraduate majors. Total enrollment: 6,137. Undergraduates: 5,712. Freshmen: 1,239. Federal methodology is used as a basis for awarding need-based institutional aid.

UNDERGRADUATE EXPENSES for 2004–05 *Application fee:* $20. *Tuition, state resident:* full-time $2208; part-time $92 per credit. *Tuition, nonresident:* full-time $8400; part-time $350 per credit. *Required fees:* full-time $918; $35 per credit or $93 per term part-time. Full-time tuition and fees vary according to course load. Part-time tuition and fees vary according to course load. *College room and board:* $4696; *room only:* $3024. Room and board charges vary according to board plan and housing facility. *Payment plan:* Installment.

GIFT AID (NEED-BASED) *Total amount:* $8,848,335 (65% federal, 34% state, 1% institutional). *Receiving aid:* Freshmen: 51% (592); All full-time undergraduates: 51% (2,844). *Average award:* Freshmen: $2490; Undergraduates: $2193. *Scholarships, grants, and awards:* Federal Pell, FSEOG, state, private, college/university gift aid from institutional funds.

GIFT AID (NON-NEED-BASED) *Total amount:* $4,953,344 (71% institutional, 29% external sources). *Receiving aid:* Freshmen: 49% (562); Undergraduates: 32% (1,773). *Average Award:* Freshmen: $2023; *Undergraduates:* $1872. *Scholarships, grants, and awards by category: Academic Interests/Achievement:* agriculture, biological sciences, business, communication, computer science, education, English, foreign languages, general academic interests/achievements, international studies, mathematics, military science, physical sciences, premedicine,

Angelo State University

social sciences. *Creative Arts/Performance:* art/fine arts, dance, journalism/publications, music, performing arts, theater/drama. *Special Achievements/Activities:* cheerleading/drum major, general special achievements/activities, hobbies/interests, leadership, memberships, rodeo. *ROTC:* Air Force.

LOANS *Student loans:* $11,254,082 (52% need-based, 48% non-need-based). *Average need-based loan:* Freshmen: $1973; Undergraduates: $2500. *Parent loans:* $585,770 (100% non-need-based). *Programs:* FFEL (Subsidized and Unsubsidized Stafford, PLUS), Perkins, state, college/university, alternative loans.

ATHLETIC AWARDS *Total amount:* $681,389 (100% non-need-based).

APPLYING FOR FINANCIAL AID *Required financial aid forms:* FAFSA, institution's own form. *Financial aid deadline (priority):* 5/1. *Notification date:* Continuous.

CONTACT Ms. Lyn Wheeler, Director of Financial Aid, Angelo State University, ASU Station #11015, San Angelo, TX 76909-1015, 325-942-2246 or toll-free 800-946-8627 (in-state). *Fax:* 325-942-2082. *E-mail:* lyn.wheeler@angelo.edu.

ANNA MARIA COLLEGE
Paxton, MA

Tuition & fees: $20,135	Average undergraduate aid package: $14,182

ABOUT THE INSTITUTION Independent Roman Catholic, coed. Awards: associate, bachelor's, and master's degrees and post-bachelor's and post-master's certificates. 28 undergraduate majors. Total enrollment: 1,108. Undergraduates: 744. Freshmen: 199. Federal methodology is used as a basis for awarding need-based institutional aid.

UNDERGRADUATE EXPENSES for 2004–05 *Application fee:* $40. *Comprehensive fee:* $27,550 includes full-time tuition ($18,545), mandatory fees ($1590), and room and board ($7415). Room and board charges vary according to board plan. *Part-time tuition:* $1,855 per course. *Payment plan:* Installment.

FRESHMAN FINANCIAL AID (Fall 2004, est.) 187 applied for aid; of those 93% were deemed to have need. 100% of freshmen with need received aid; of those 12% had need fully met. *Average percent of need met:* 69% (excluding resources awarded to replace EFC). *Average financial aid package:* $13,995 (excluding resources awarded to replace EFC). 8% of all full-time freshmen had no need and received non-need-based gift aid.

UNDERGRADUATE FINANCIAL AID (Fall 2004, est.) 520 applied for aid; of those 92% were deemed to have need. 100% of undergraduates with need received aid; of those 17% had need fully met. *Average percent of need met:* 71% (excluding resources awarded to replace EFC). *Average financial aid package:* $14,182 (excluding resources awarded to replace EFC). 13% of all full-time undergraduates had no need and received non-need-based gift aid.

GIFT AID (NEED-BASED) *Total amount:* $4,660,614 (11% federal, 7% state, 81% institutional, 1% external sources). *Receiving aid:* Freshmen: 90% (170); All full-time undergraduates: 85% (467). *Average award:* Freshmen: $10,640; Undergraduates: $10,229. *Scholarships, grants, and awards:* Federal Pell, FSEOG, state, private, college/university gift aid from institutional funds.

GIFT AID (NON-NEED-BASED) *Total amount:* $569,454 (93% institutional, 7% external sources). *Receiving aid:* Freshmen: 7% (13); Undergraduates: 8% (42). *Average Award:* Freshmen: $10,770; Undergraduates: $11,454. *Scholarships, grants, and awards by category: Academic Interests/Achievement:* 318 awards ($1,998,725 total): general academic interests/achievements. *Creative Arts/Performance:* 9 awards ($16,375 total): music. *Special Achievements/Activities:* 87 awards ($98,250 total): religious involvement. *Special Characteristics:* 165 awards ($467,736 total): children and siblings of alumni, children of faculty/staff, children with a deceased or disabled parent, general special characteristics, local/state students, siblings of current students. *Tuition waivers:* Full or partial for children of alumni, employees or children of employees, senior citizens. *ROTC:* Air Force cooperative.

LOANS *Student loans:* $3,951,226 (70% need-based, 30% non-need-based). 84% of past graduating class borrowed through all loan programs. *Average indebtedness per student:* $17,828. *Average need-based loan:* Freshmen: $3569; Undergraduates: $4392. *Parent loans:* $962,869 (54% need-based, 46% non-need-based). *Programs:* FFEL (Subsidized and Unsubsidized Stafford, PLUS), Perkins, state, college/university.

WORK-STUDY *Federal work-study:* Total amount: $104,884; 113 jobs averaging $1028.

APPLYING FOR FINANCIAL AID *Required financial aid form:* FAFSA. *Financial aid deadline:* Continuous. *Notification date:* Continuous beginning 3/15. Students must reply within 4 weeks of notification.

CONTACT Nicole Brennan, Director of Financial Aid and Admission, Anna Maria College, 50 Sunset Lane, Paxton, MA 01612-1198, 508-849-3367 or toll-free 800-344-4586 Ext. 360. *Fax:* 508-849-3362. *E-mail:* nbrennan@annamaria.edu.

ANTIOCH COLLEGE
Yellow Springs, OH

Tuition & fees: $24,902	Average undergraduate aid package: $27,424

ABOUT THE INSTITUTION Independent, coed. Awards: bachelor's degrees. 56 undergraduate majors. Total enrollment: 599. Undergraduates: 591. Freshmen: 93. Both federal and institutional methodology are used as a basis for awarding need-based institutional aid.

UNDERGRADUATE EXPENSES for 2004–05 *Application fee:* $35. *Comprehensive fee:* $31,315 includes full-time tuition ($24,260), mandatory fees ($642), and room and board ($6413). *College room only:* $3137. Room and board charges vary according to board plan. *Part-time tuition:* $428 per credit hour. *Payment plan:* Installment.

FRESHMAN FINANCIAL AID (Fall 2003) 119 applied for aid; of those 67% were deemed to have need. 100% of freshmen with need received aid; of those 78% had need fully met. *Average percent of need met:* 100% (excluding resources awarded to replace EFC). *Average financial aid package:* $25,424 (excluding resources awarded to replace EFC).

UNDERGRADUATE FINANCIAL AID (Fall 2003) 100% of undergraduates with need received aid; of those 78% had need fully met. *Average percent of need met:* 100% (excluding resources awarded to replace EFC). *Average financial aid package:* $27,424 (excluding resources awarded to replace EFC).

GIFT AID (NEED-BASED) *Total amount:* $4,527,317 (28% federal, 4% state, 64% institutional, 4% external sources). *Receiving aid:* Freshmen: 80; All full-time undergraduates: 431. *Average award:* Freshmen: $5132; Undergraduates: $6750. *Scholarships, grants, and awards:* Federal Pell, FSEOG, state, private, college/university gift aid from institutional funds.

GIFT AID (NON-NEED-BASED) *Receiving aid:* Freshmen: 62; Undergraduates: 336. *Average Award:* Freshmen: $7717; Undergraduates: $6374. *Scholarships, grants, and awards by category: Academic Interests/Achievement:* 23 awards ($156,214 total): biological sciences, education, general academic interests/achievements, humanities, international studies, mathematics, physical sciences, social sciences. *Special Achievements/Activities:* 414 awards ($2,653,321 total): community service. *Special Characteristics:* 207 awards ($336,467 total): local/state students. *Tuition waivers:* Full or partial for employees or children of employees.

LOANS *Student loans:* $1,578,271 (86% need-based, 14% non-need-based). 97% of past graduating class borrowed through all loan programs. *Average indebtedness per student:* $17,125. *Average need-based loan:* Freshmen: $2625; Undergraduates: $2939. *Parent loans:* $870,015 (100% non-need-based). *Programs:* FFEL (Subsidized and Unsubsidized Stafford, PLUS), Perkins.

WORK-STUDY *Federal work-study:* Total amount: $781,992; 373 jobs averaging $1970.

APPLYING FOR FINANCIAL AID *Required financial aid forms:* FAFSA, institution's own form. *Financial aid deadline (priority):* 4/1. *Notification date:* Continuous beginning 4/1.

CONTACT Mr. Larry Brickman, Financial Aid Director, Antioch College, 795 Livermore Street, Yellow Springs, OH 45387-1697, 937-769-1120 or toll-free 800-543-9436. *Fax:* 937-769-1133. *E-mail:* lbobo@antioch-college.edu.

ANTIOCH UNIVERSITY MCGREGOR
Yellow Springs, OH

Tuition & fees: $11,808	Average undergraduate aid package: $10,500

ABOUT THE INSTITUTION Independent, coed. Awards: bachelor's and master's degrees and post-master's certificates. 6 undergraduate majors. Total enrollment: 715. Undergraduates: 171. Both federal and institutional methodology are used as a basis for awarding need-based institutional aid.

UNDERGRADUATE EXPENSES for 2004–05 *Application fee:* $45. *Tuition:* full-time $11,808; part-time $246 per credit hour. *Required fees:* $75 per term part-time. *Payment plan:* Installment.

UNDERGRADUATE FINANCIAL AID (Fall 2003) 114 applied for aid; of those 100% were deemed to have need. 100% of undergraduates with need received aid. *Average percent of need met:* 40% (excluding resources awarded to replace EFC). *Average financial aid package:* $10,500 (excluding resources awarded to replace EFC). 1% of all full-time undergraduates had no need and received non-need-based gift aid.

GIFT AID (NEED-BASED) *Total amount:* $264,647 (73% federal, 27% state). *Receiving aid:* All full-time undergraduates: 44% (71). *Average award:* Undergraduates: $1500. *Scholarships, grants, and awards:* Federal Pell, FSEOG, state, college/university gift aid from institutional funds.

GIFT AID (NON-NEED-BASED) *Total amount:* $50,434 (100% state). *Average Award: Undergraduates:* $10,500.

LOANS *Student loans:* $1,183,853 (57% need-based, 43% non-need-based). 63% of past graduating class borrowed through all loan programs. *Average indebtedness per student:* $28,500. *Average need-based loan:* Undergraduates: $5000. *Programs:* FFEL (Subsidized and Unsubsidized Stafford, PLUS), Perkins.

WORK-STUDY *Federal work-study:* Total amount: $5750; 2 jobs available.

APPLYING FOR FINANCIAL AID *Required financial aid forms:* FAFSA, institution's own form. *Financial aid deadline:* Continuous. *Notification date:* Continuous beginning 3/1.

CONTACT Kathy John, Director of Financial Aid, Antioch University McGregor, 800 Livermore Street, Yellow Springs, OH 45387-1609, 937-769-1840 or toll-free 937-769-1818. *Fax:* 937-769-1804. *E-mail:* kjohn@mcgregor.edu.

ANTIOCH UNIVERSITY SANTA BARBARA
Santa Barbara, CA

ABOUT THE INSTITUTION Independent, coed. Awards: bachelor's and master's degrees. 1 undergraduate major. Total enrollment: 289. Undergraduates: 103.

GIFT AID (NEED-BASED) *Scholarships, grants, and awards:* Federal Pell, FSEOG, state, college/university gift aid from institutional funds.

LOANS *Programs:* FFEL (Subsidized and Unsubsidized Stafford, PLUS), Perkins.

WORK-STUDY *Federal work-study:* 23 jobs averaging $2120.

APPLYING FOR FINANCIAL AID *Required financial aid forms:* FAFSA, institution's own form, income tax forms.

CONTACT Cecilia Schneider, Financial Aid Director, Antioch University Santa Barbara, 801 Garden Street, Santa Barbara, CA 93101-1580, 805-962-8179 Ext. 108. *Fax:* 805-962-4786.

ANTIOCH UNIVERSITY SEATTLE
Seattle, WA

Tuition & fees: $13,815	Average undergraduate aid package: $6681

ABOUT THE INSTITUTION Independent, coed. Awards: bachelor's, master's, and doctoral degrees. 1 undergraduate major. Total enrollment: 950. Undergraduates: 209. Federal methodology is used as a basis for awarding need-based institutional aid.

UNDERGRADUATE EXPENSES for 2004–05 *Application fee:* $50. *Tuition:* full-time $13,680; part-time $380 per credit. *Required fees:* full-time $135; $25 per term part-time. Full-time tuition and fees vary according to course load and program. Part-time tuition and fees vary according to course load and program. *Payment plan:* Installment.

UNDERGRADUATE FINANCIAL AID (Fall 2004, est.) 201 applied for aid; of those 100% were deemed to have need. 100% of undergraduates with need received aid; of those 75% had need fully met. *Average percent of need met:* 75% (excluding resources awarded to replace EFC). *Average financial aid package:* $6681 (excluding resources awarded to replace EFC).

GIFT AID (NEED-BASED) *Total amount:* $806,439 (38% federal, 51% state, 2% institutional, 9% external sources). *Receiving aid:* All full-time undergraduates: 24% (93). *Average award:* Undergraduates: $4000. *Scholarships, grants, and awards:* Federal Pell, FSEOG, state, college/university gift aid from institutional funds.

GIFT AID (NON-NEED-BASED) *Receiving aid:* Undergraduates: 4% (15). *Tuition waivers:* Full or partial for employees or children of employees.

LOANS *Student loans:* $1,706,553 (53% need-based, 47% non-need-based). 85% of past graduating class borrowed through all loan programs. *Average indebtedness per student:* $15,999. *Average need-based loan:* Undergraduates: $5500. *Parent loans:* $40,623 (100% non-need-based). *Programs:* FFEL (Subsidized and Unsubsidized Stafford, PLUS), Perkins.

WORK-STUDY *Federal work-study:* Total amount: $105,000; 18 jobs averaging $6000. *State or other work-study/employment:* Total amount: $10,000 (100% need-based). 2 part-time jobs averaging $5000.

APPLYING FOR FINANCIAL AID *Required financial aid forms:* FAFSA, institution's own form. *Financial aid deadline (priority):* 4/15. *Notification date:* Continuous beginning 5/1. Students must reply within 2 weeks of notification.

CONTACT Katy Gilroy, Director of Financial Aid, Antioch University Seattle, 2326 Sixth Avenue, Seattle, WA 98121-1814, 206-268-4004. *Fax:* 206-268-4242. *E-mail:* kgilroy@antiochsea.edu.

APEX SCHOOL OF THEOLOGY
Durham, NC

CONTACT Financial Aid Office, Apex School of Theology, 5104 Revere Road, Durham, NC 27713, 919-572-1625.

APPALACHIAN BIBLE COLLEGE
Bradley, WV

Tuition & fees: $8408	Average undergraduate aid package: $3750

ABOUT THE INSTITUTION Independent nondenominational, coed. Awards: associate and bachelor's degrees. 2 undergraduate majors. Total enrollment: 304. Undergraduates: 304. Freshmen: 54. Both federal and institutional methodology are used as a basis for awarding need-based institutional aid.

UNDERGRADUATE EXPENSES for 2005–06 *Application fee:* $10. *Comprehensive fee:* $12,808 includes full-time tuition ($7140), mandatory fees ($1268), and room and board ($4400). *Part-time tuition:* $297 per credit hour. *Part-time fees:* $32 per credit hour. *Payment plan:* Installment.

FRESHMAN FINANCIAL AID (Fall 2003) 61 applied for aid; of those 100% were deemed to have need. 100% of freshmen with need received aid. *Average percent of need met:* 85% (excluding resources awarded to replace EFC). *Average financial aid package:* $2800 (excluding resources awarded to replace EFC).

UNDERGRADUATE FINANCIAL AID (Fall 2003) 264 applied for aid; of those 100% were deemed to have need. 100% of undergraduates with need received aid. *Average percent of need met:* 90% (excluding resources awarded to replace EFC). *Average financial aid package:* $3750 (excluding resources awarded to replace EFC).

GIFT AID (NEED-BASED) *Total amount:* $1,035,586 (44% federal, 15% state, 29% institutional, 12% external sources). *Receiving aid:* Freshmen: 100% (61); All full-time undergraduates: 89% (264). *Average award:* Freshmen: $3250; Undergraduates: $3750. *Scholarships, grants, and awards:* Federal Pell, FSEOG, state, private, college/university gift aid from institutional funds.

GIFT AID (NON-NEED-BASED) *Scholarships, grants, and awards by category: Academic Interests/Achievement:* 27 awards ($27,000 total): general academic interests/achievements, religion/biblical studies. *Special Achievements/Activities:* 31 awards ($27,500 total): general special achievements/activities, religious involvement. *Special Characteristics:* 206 awards ($193,727 total): children and siblings of alumni, children of educators, children of faculty/staff, general special characteristics, international students, married students, relatives of clergy, religious affiliation, spouses of current students, veterans. *Tuition waivers:* Full or partial for employees or children of employees, senior citizens.

LOANS *Student loans:* $461,525 (100% need-based). 43% of past graduating class borrowed through all loan programs. *Average indebtedness per student:* $22,100. *Average need-based loan:* Freshmen: $2625; Undergraduates: $4525. *Parent loans:* $96,350 (100% need-based). *Programs:* FFEL (Subsidized and Unsubsidized Stafford, PLUS).

WORK-STUDY *Federal work-study:* Total amount: $25,583; 34 jobs averaging $750.

APPLYING FOR FINANCIAL AID *Required financial aid forms:* FAFSA, institution's own form. *Financial aid deadline:* 6/15 (priority: 3/1). *Notification date:* Continuous. Students must reply by 7/30 or within 4 weeks of notification.

CONTACT Mrs. Shirley Carfrey, Director of Financial Aid, Appalachian Bible College, PO Box ABC, Sandbranch Road, Bradley, WV 25818, 304-877-6428 Ext. 3244 or toll-free 800-678-9ABC Ext. 3213. *Fax:* 304-877-5082. *E-mail:* scarfrey@abc.edu.

APPALACHIAN STATE UNIVERSITY
Boone, NC

Tuition & fees (NC res): $3351	Average undergraduate aid package: $6091

ABOUT THE INSTITUTION State-supported, coed. Awards: bachelor's, master's, and doctoral degrees and post-master's certificates. 84 undergraduate majors. Total enrollment: 14,653. Undergraduates: 13,146. Freshmen: 2,516. Federal methodology is used as a basis for awarding need-based institutional aid.

Appalachian State University

UNDERGRADUATE EXPENSES for 2004–05 *Application fee:* $45. *Tuition, state resident:* full-time $1821. *Tuition, nonresident:* full-time $11,188. Part-time tuition and fees vary according to course load. *College room and board:* $5270; *room only:* $2770. Room and board charges vary according to board plan and housing facility. *Payment plan:* Installment.

FRESHMAN FINANCIAL AID (Fall 2004, est.) 1552 applied for aid; of those 52% were deemed to have need. 94% of freshmen with need received aid; of those 33% had need fully met. *Average percent of need met:* 76% (excluding resources awarded to replace EFC). *Average financial aid package:* $5533 (excluding resources awarded to replace EFC). 9% of all full-time freshmen had no need and received non-need-based gift aid.

UNDERGRADUATE FINANCIAL AID (Fall 2004, est.) 7,165 applied for aid; of those 61% were deemed to have need. 92% of undergraduates with need received aid; of those 39% had need fully met. *Average percent of need met:* 78% (excluding resources awarded to replace EFC). *Average financial aid package:* $6091 (excluding resources awarded to replace EFC). 6% of all full-time undergraduates had no need and received non-need-based gift aid.

GIFT AID (NEED-BASED) *Total amount:* $12,965,948 (48% federal, 35% state, 10% institutional, 7% external sources). *Receiving aid:* Freshmen: 26% (653); All full-time undergraduates: 29% (3,408). *Average award:* Freshmen: $4165; Undergraduates: $3893. *Scholarships, grants, and awards:* Federal Pell, FSEOG, state, private, college/university gift aid from institutional funds.

GIFT AID (NON-NEED-BASED) *Total amount:* $4,450,657 (18% federal, 41% state, 21% institutional, 20% external sources). *Receiving aid:* Freshmen: 11% (272); Undergraduates: 7% (837). *Average Award:* Freshmen: $2289; *Undergraduates:* $3036. *Scholarships, grants, and awards by category: Academic Interests/ Achievement:* 3,578 awards ($2,283,576 total): general academic interests/ achievements. *Creative Arts/Performance:* general creative arts/performance. *Special Achievements/Activities:* general special achievements/activities. *Special Characteristics:* 452 awards ($1,711,885 total): first-generation college students, general special characteristics, handicapped students, members of minority groups, out-of-state students, veterans, veterans' children. *Tuition waivers:* Full or partial for employees or children of employees. *ROTC:* Army.

LOANS *Student loans:* $24,169,523 (72% need-based, 28% non-need-based). 48% of past graduating class borrowed through all loan programs. *Average indebtedness per student:* $14,482. *Average need-based loan:* Freshmen: $2533; Undergraduates: $3381. *Parent loans:* $13,150,120 (53% need-based, 47% non-need-based). *Programs:* FFEL (Subsidized and Unsubsidized Stafford, PLUS), Perkins, college/university.

WORK-STUDY *Federal work-study:* Total amount: $711,900; 431 jobs averaging $1800. *State or other work-study/employment:* Total amount: $1,135,509 (100% non-need-based). 1,687 part-time jobs averaging $673.

ATHLETIC AWARDS *Total amount:* $2,037,130 (36% need-based, 64% non-need-based).

APPLYING FOR FINANCIAL AID *Required financial aid form:* FAFSA. *Financial aid deadline (priority):* 3/15. *Notification date:* Continuous beginning 4/1. Students must reply within 3 weeks of notification.

CONTACT Kay Stroud, Associate Director of Student Financial Aid, Appalachian State University, Office of Student Financial Aid, ASU Box 32059, Boone, NC 28608-2059, 828-262-8687. *Fax:* 828-262-2585. *E-mail:* stroudkn@appstate. edu.

AQUINAS COLLEGE
Grand Rapids, MI

ABOUT THE INSTITUTION Independent Roman Catholic, coed. Awards: associate, bachelor's, and master's degrees. 60 undergraduate majors. Total enrollment: 2,235. Undergraduates: 1,813. Freshmen: 316.

GIFT AID (NEED-BASED) *Scholarships, grants, and awards:* Federal Pell, FSEOG, state, private, college/university gift aid from institutional funds.

GIFT AID (NON-NEED-BASED) *Scholarships, grants, and awards by category: Special Characteristics:* children and siblings of alumni, children of faculty/staff.

LOANS *Programs:* FFEL (Subsidized and Unsubsidized Stafford, PLUS), Perkins.

WORK-STUDY *Federal work-study:* Total amount: $165,000; 134 jobs averaging $700. *State or other work-study/employment:* Total amount: $450,000 (44% need-based, 56% non-need-based). Part-time jobs available.

APPLYING FOR FINANCIAL AID *Required financial aid form:* FAFSA.

CONTACT David J. Steffee, Director Financial Aid, Aquinas College, 1607 Robinson Road, Grand Rapids, MI 49506-1799, 616-459-8281 Ext. 5127 or toll-free 800-678-9593. *Fax:* 616-732-4547. *E-mail:* steffdav@aquinas.edu.

AQUINAS COLLEGE
Nashville, TN

Tuition & fees: $10,768	Average undergraduate aid package: $7050

ABOUT THE INSTITUTION Independent Roman Catholic, coed. Awards: associate and bachelor's degrees and post-bachelor's certificates. 3 undergraduate majors. Total enrollment: 870. Undergraduates: 870. Freshmen: 43. Federal methodology is used as a basis for awarding need-based institutional aid.

UNDERGRADUATE EXPENSES for 2005–06 *Application fee:* $25. *Tuition:* full-time $10,368; part-time $432 per credit hour. *Payment plan:* Installment.

FRESHMAN FINANCIAL AID (Fall 2003) 43 applied for aid; of those 84% were deemed to have need. 100% of freshmen with need received aid; of those 53% had need fully met. *Average percent of need met:* 85% (excluding resources awarded to replace EFC). *Average financial aid package:* $7850 (excluding resources awarded to replace EFC).

UNDERGRADUATE FINANCIAL AID (Fall 2003) 154 applied for aid; of those 80% were deemed to have need. 100% of undergraduates with need received aid; of those 68% had need fully met. *Average percent of need met:* 76% (excluding resources awarded to replace EFC). *Average financial aid package:* $7050 (excluding resources awarded to replace EFC).

GIFT AID (NEED-BASED) *Total amount:* $847,167 (63% federal, 25% state, 12% institutional). *Receiving aid:* Freshmen: 49% (21); All full-time undergraduates: 60% (93). *Average award:* Freshmen: $2000; Undergraduates: $2550. *Scholarships, grants, and awards:* Federal Pell, FSEOG, state, private, college/ university gift aid from institutional funds.

GIFT AID (NON-NEED-BASED) *Total amount:* $298,324 (36% institutional, 64% external sources). *Scholarships, grants, and awards by category: Academic Interests/Achievement:* 59 awards ($76,500 total): business, education, general academic interests/achievements, health fields. *Special Achievements/Activities:* 3 awards ($3500 total): leadership. *Special Characteristics:* 25 awards ($40,000 total): general special characteristics. *Tuition waivers:* Full or partial for employees or children of employees. *ROTC:* Army cooperative, Air Force cooperative.

LOANS *Student loans:* $2,353,900 (40% need-based, 60% non-need-based). 75% of past graduating class borrowed through all loan programs. *Average indebtedness per student:* $8500. *Average need-based loan:* Freshmen: $2600; Undergraduates: $3150. *Parent loans:* $1,149,272 (100% non-need-based). *Programs:* FFEL (Subsidized and Unsubsidized Stafford, PLUS), alternative loans.

WORK-STUDY *Federal work-study:* Total amount: $84,683; 52 jobs averaging $1200.

APPLYING FOR FINANCIAL AID *Required financial aid form:* institution's own form. *Financial aid deadline (priority):* 3/15. *Notification date:* Continuous. Students must reply within 2 weeks of notification.

CONTACT Zelena O'Sullivan, Director of Financial Aid, Aquinas College, 4210 Harding Road, Nashville, TN 37205-2005, 615-297-7545 Ext. 431 or toll-free 800-649-9956. *Fax:* 615-279-3891. *E-mail:* osullivanz@aquinas-tn.edu.

ARCADIA UNIVERSITY
Glenside, PA

Tuition & fees: $24,270	Average undergraduate aid package: $16,465

ABOUT THE INSTITUTION Independent religious, coed. Awards: bachelor's, master's, and doctoral degrees. 50 undergraduate majors. Total enrollment: 3,391. Undergraduates: 1,929. Freshmen: 487. Federal methodology is used as a basis for awarding need-based institutional aid.

UNDERGRADUATE EXPENSES for 2005–06 *Application fee:* $30. *Comprehensive fee:* $33,570 includes full-time tuition ($23,990), mandatory fees ($280), and room and board ($9300). Full-time tuition and fees vary according to course load, degree level, and program. Room and board charges vary according to board plan. *Part-time tuition:* $420 per credit. *Payment plans:* Installment, deferred payment.

FRESHMAN FINANCIAL AID (Fall 2004, est.) 474 applied for aid; of those 89% were deemed to have need. 99% of freshmen with need received aid; of those 20% had need fully met. *Average percent of need met:* 77% (excluding resources awarded to replace EFC). *Average financial aid package:* $17,115 (excluding resources awarded to replace EFC). 10% of all full-time freshmen had no need and received non-need-based gift aid.

UNDERGRADUATE FINANCIAL AID (Fall 2004, est.) 1,702 applied for aid; of those 90% were deemed to have need. 97% of undergraduates with need

received aid; of those 23% had need fully met. *Average percent of need met:* 79% (excluding resources awarded to replace EFC). *Average financial aid package:* $16,465 (excluding resources awarded to replace EFC). 8% of all full-time undergraduates had no need and received non-need-based gift aid.
GIFT AID (NEED-BASED) *Total amount:* $9,747,049 (15% federal, 19% state, 55% institutional, 11% external sources). *Receiving aid:* Freshmen: 87% (418); All full-time undergraduates: 87% (1,482). *Average award:* Freshmen: $12,623; Undergraduates: $11,566. *Scholarships, grants, and awards:* Federal Pell, FSEOG, state, private, college/university gift aid from institutional funds.
GIFT AID (NON-NEED-BASED) *Total amount:* $10,296,299 (99% institutional, 1% external sources). *Receiving aid:* Freshmen: 81% (388); Undergraduates: 79% (1,356). *Average Award:* Freshmen: $8759; Undergraduates: $7142. *Scholarships, grants, and awards by category: Academic Interests/Achievement:* 994 awards ($8,027,219 total): general academic interests/achievements. *Creative Arts/Performance:* 62 awards ($101,550 total): applied art and design, art/fine arts, theater/drama. *Special Achievements/Activities:* 631 awards ($1,711,250 total): community service, general special achievements/activities, leadership, memberships. *Special Characteristics:* 29 awards ($81,005 total): children and siblings of alumni, relatives of clergy, religious affiliation. *Tuition waivers:* Full or partial for employees or children of employees. *ROTC:* Army cooperative.
LOANS *Student loans:* $17,791,495 (61% need-based, 39% non-need-based). 79% of past graduating class borrowed through all loan programs. *Average indebtedness per student:* $33,828. *Average need-based loan:* Freshmen: $4269; Undergraduates: $5120. *Parent loans:* $3,408,018 (91% need-based, 9% non-need-based). *Programs:* FFEL (Subsidized and Unsubsidized Stafford, PLUS), Perkins, college/university.
WORK-STUDY *Federal work-study:* Total amount: $1,193,635; 914 jobs averaging $1294. *State or other work-study/employment:* Total amount: $220,110 (100% non-need-based). 224 part-time jobs averaging $870.
APPLYING FOR FINANCIAL AID *Required financial aid forms:* FAFSA, institution's own form. *Financial aid deadline (priority):* 3/1. *Notification date:* Continuous. Students must reply by 5/1.
CONTACT Elizabeth Rihl Lewinsky, Director of Financial Aid, Arcadia University, 450 South Easton Road, Glenside, PA 19038, 215-572-2980 or toll-free 877-ARCADIA. *Fax:* 215-572-4049. *E-mail:* finaid@arcadia.edu.

ARGOSY UNIVERSITY/ATLANTA
Atlanta, GA

ABOUT THE INSTITUTION Proprietary, coed. Awards: bachelor's, master's, and doctoral degrees and post-master's certificates. Total enrollment: 13. Undergraduates: 13.
GIFT AID (NEED-BASED) *Scholarships, grants, and awards:* Federal Pell, FSEOG, state, college/university gift aid from institutional funds.
GIFT AID (NON-NEED-BASED) *Scholarships, grants, and awards by category: Academic Interests/Achievement:* general academic interests/achievements. *Special Achievements/Activities:* community service, general special achievements/activities, leadership. *Special Characteristics:* adult students, general special characteristics.
LOANS *Programs:* FFEL (Subsidized and Unsubsidized Stafford, PLUS), Perkins.
WORK-STUDY *Federal work-study:* Total amount: $441; 1 job averaging $441.
APPLYING FOR FINANCIAL AID *Required financial aid forms:* FAFSA, institution's own form.
CONTACT Ashley Manker, Financial Aid Office, Argosy University/Atlanta, One Lakeside Commons, Building One, 990 Hammond Drive, 11th Floor, Atlanta, GA 30328, 770-671-1200 Ext. 1036 or toll-free 888-671-4777. *Fax:* 770-407-1110. *E-mail:* amanker@argosyu.edu.

ARGOSY UNIVERSITY/CHICAGO
Chicago, IL

ABOUT THE INSTITUTION Proprietary, coed. Awards: bachelor's, master's, and doctoral degrees. 2 undergraduate majors. Total enrollment: 890. Undergraduates: 37.
GIFT AID (NEED-BASED) *Scholarships, grants, and awards:* Federal Pell, FSEOG, state, college/university gift aid from institutional funds.
GIFT AID (NON-NEED-BASED) *Scholarships, grants, and awards by category: Academic Interests/Achievement:* general academic interests/achievements. *Special Achievements/Activities:* community service, general special achievements/activities, leadership. *Special Characteristics:* adult students, general special characteristics.
LOANS *Programs:* FFEL (Subsidized and Unsubsidized Stafford, PLUS), Perkins.

WORK-STUDY *Federal work-study:* Total amount: $1363; 1 job averaging $1363.
APPLYING FOR FINANCIAL AID *Required financial aid forms:* FAFSA, institution's own form.
CONTACT Ardie Elgersma, Financial Aid Office, Argosy University/Chicago, Two First National Plaza, 20 South Clark Street, Third Floor, Chicago, IL 60603, 312-201-0200 Ext. 3909 or toll-free 800-626-4123 (in-state). *Fax:* 312-201-1907. *E-mail:* aelgersma@argosyu.edu.

ARGOSY UNIVERSITY/DALLAS
Dallas, TX

ABOUT THE INSTITUTION Proprietary, coed. Awards: bachelor's, master's, and doctoral degrees. 1 undergraduate major. Total enrollment: 330. Undergraduates: 30.
GIFT AID (NEED-BASED) *Scholarships, grants, and awards:* Federal Pell, FSEOG, college/university gift aid from institutional funds.
GIFT AID (NON-NEED-BASED) *Scholarships, grants, and awards by category: Academic Interests/Achievement:* general academic interests/achievements. *Special Achievements/Activities:* community service, general special achievements/activities, leadership. *Special Characteristics:* adult students, general special characteristics.
LOANS *Programs:* FFEL (Subsidized and Unsubsidized Stafford, PLUS), Perkins.
WORK-STUDY *Federal work-study:* Total amount: $805; jobs available (averaging $805).
APPLYING FOR FINANCIAL AID *Required financial aid forms:* FAFSA, institution's own form.
CONTACT Beth Kirkman, Financial Aid Office, Argosy University/Dallas, One North Park, Suite 315, 8950 North Central Expressway, Dallas, TX 75231, 214-459-2204 or toll-free 866-954-9900. *Fax:* 214-696-3900. *E-mail:* bkirkman@argosyu.edu.

ARGOSY UNIVERSITY/HONOLULU
Honolulu, HI

ABOUT THE INSTITUTION Proprietary, coed.
GIFT AID (NEED-BASED) *Scholarships, grants, and awards:* Federal Pell, FSEOG, college/university gift aid from institutional funds.
GIFT AID (NON-NEED-BASED) *Scholarships, grants, and awards by category: Academic Interests/Achievement:* general academic interests/achievements. *Special Achievements/Activities:* community service, general special achievements/activities, leadership. *Special Characteristics:* adult students, general special characteristics.
LOANS *Programs:* FFEL (Subsidized and Unsubsidized Stafford, PLUS), Perkins.
WORK-STUDY Federal work-study jobs available.
APPLYING FOR FINANCIAL AID *Required financial aid forms:* FAFSA, institution's own form.
CONTACT Mary Vee Cheung, Financial Aid Office, Argosy University/Honolulu, 400 Pacific Tower, 1001 Bishop Street, Honolulu, HI 96813, 808-536-5555 Ext. 204 or toll-free 888-323-2777 (in-state). *Fax:* 808-536-5505. *E-mail:* mvee@argosyu.edu.

ARGOSY UNIVERSITY/NASHVILLE
Franklin, TN

CONTACT Financial Aid Office, Argosy University/Nashville, 341 Cool Springs Boulevard, Suite 210, Franklin, TN 37067-7226, 615-369-0616.

ARGOSY UNIVERSITY/ORANGE COUNTY
Santa Ana, CA

ABOUT THE INSTITUTION Proprietary, coed. Awards: bachelor's, master's, and doctoral degrees. Total enrollment: 646. Undergraduates: 81.
GIFT AID (NEED-BASED) *Scholarships, grants, and awards:* Federal Pell, FSEOG, state, college/university gift aid from institutional funds.
GIFT AID (NON-NEED-BASED) *Scholarships, grants, and awards by category: Academic Interests/Achievement:* general academic interests/achievements. *Special Achievements/Activities:* general special achievements/activities. *Special Characteristics:* adult students, general special characteristics.
LOANS *Programs:* FFEL (Subsidized and Unsubsidized Stafford, PLUS), Perkins.

Argosy University/Orange County

WORK-STUDY *Federal work-study:* Total amount: $13,981; 3 jobs averaging $4660.
CONTACT Thomas Cameron, Financial Aid Officer, Argosy University/Orange County, 3745 West Chapman Avenue, Suite 100, Orange, CA 92868, 714-450-4826 or toll-free 800-716-9598 Ext. 4819. *Fax:* 714-450-0776. *E-mail:* tcameron@argosyu.edu.

ARGOSY UNIVERSITY/PHOENIX
Phoenix, AZ

ABOUT THE INSTITUTION Proprietary, coed. Awards: bachelor's, master's, and doctoral degrees. 1 undergraduate major. Total enrollment: 394. Undergraduates: 36.
GIFT AID (NEED-BASED) *Scholarships, grants, and awards:* Federal Pell, FSEOG, college/university gift aid from institutional funds.
GIFT AID (NON-NEED-BASED) *Scholarships, grants, and awards by category: Academic Interests/Achievement:* general academic interests/achievements. *Special Achievements/Activities:* community service, general special achievements/activities, leadership. *Special Characteristics:* adult students, general special characteristics.
LOANS *Programs:* FFEL (Subsidized and Unsubsidized Stafford, PLUS), Perkins.
WORK-STUDY Federal work-study jobs available.
APPLYING FOR FINANCIAL AID *Required financial aid forms:* FAFSA, institution's own form.
CONTACT Amy Vincent, Financial Aid Office, Argosy University/Phoenix, 2301 West Dunlap, Suite 211, Phoenix, AZ 85021, 602-216-2600 or toll-free 866-216-2777. *Fax:* 602-216-2601. *E-mail:* avincent@argosyu.edu.

ARGOSY UNIVERSITY/SAN FRANCISCO BAY AREA
Point Richmond, CA

ABOUT THE INSTITUTION Proprietary, coed. Awards: bachelor's, master's, and doctoral degrees. Total enrollment: 45. Undergraduates: 45.
GIFT AID (NEED-BASED) *Scholarships, grants, and awards:* Federal Pell, FSEOG, state, college/university gift aid from institutional funds.
GIFT AID (NON-NEED-BASED) *Scholarships, grants, and awards by category: Academic Interests/Achievement:* general academic interests/achievements. *Special Achievements/Activities:* community service, general special achievements/activities, leadership. *Special Characteristics:* adult students, general special characteristics.
LOANS *Programs:* FFEL (Subsidized and Unsubsidized Stafford, PLUS), Perkins.
WORK-STUDY Federal work-study jobs available.
APPLYING FOR FINANCIAL AID *Required financial aid forms:* FAFSA, institution's own form.
CONTACT Adrian Ramos, Financial Aid Office, Argosy University/San Francisco Bay Area, 999 Canal Boulevard, Point Richmond, CA 94804, 510-215-0277 Ext. 217 or toll-free 866-215-2777 Ext. 205 (in-state), 866-215-2777 (out-of-state). *Fax:* 510-215-0299. *E-mail:* aramos@argosyu.edu.

ARGOSY UNIVERSITY/SARASOTA
Sarasota, FL

ABOUT THE INSTITUTION Proprietary, coed. Awards: bachelor's, master's, and doctoral degrees. 6 undergraduate majors. Total enrollment: 40. Undergraduates: 40.
GIFT AID (NEED-BASED) *Scholarships, grants, and awards:* Federal Pell, FSEOG, state, college/university gift aid from institutional funds.
GIFT AID (NON-NEED-BASED) *Scholarships, grants, and awards by category: Academic Interests/Achievement:* general academic interests/achievements. *Special Achievements/Activities:* community service, leadership. *Special Characteristics:* adult students.
LOANS *Programs:* FFEL (Subsidized and Unsubsidized Stafford, PLUS), Perkins.
WORK-STUDY Federal work-study jobs available.
APPLYING FOR FINANCIAL AID *Required financial aid forms:* FAFSA, institution's own form.
CONTACT Deborah Kerris, Financial Aid Office, Argosy University/Sarasota, 5250 17th Street, Sarasota, FL 34235, 800-331-5995 Ext. 244 or toll-free 800-331-5995. *Fax:* 941-371-8910. *E-mail:* dkerris@argosyu.edu.

ARGOSY UNIVERSITY/SCHAUMBURG
Schaumburg, IL

ABOUT THE INSTITUTION Proprietary, coed. Awards: bachelor's, master's, and doctoral degrees and post-master's certificates. 2 undergraduate majors.
GIFT AID (NEED-BASED) *Scholarships, grants, and awards:* Federal Pell, FSEOG, state, college/university gift aid from institutional funds.
GIFT AID (NON-NEED-BASED) *Scholarships, grants, and awards by category: Academic Interests/Achievement:* general academic interests/achievements. *Special Achievements/Activities:* community service, general special achievements/activities, leadership. *Special Characteristics:* adult students, general special characteristics.
LOANS *Programs:* FFEL (Subsidized and Unsubsidized Stafford, PLUS), Perkins.
WORK-STUDY Federal work-study jobs available.
APPLYING FOR FINANCIAL AID *Required financial aid forms:* FAFSA, institution's own form.
CONTACT Virginia Carlin, Financial Aid Office, Argosy University/Schaumburg, One Continental Towers, 1701 Golf Road, Suite 101, Rolling Meadows, IL 60008, 847-290-7400 or toll-free 866-290-2777. *Fax:* 847-290-8432. *E-mail:* vcarlin@argosyu.edu.

ARGOSY UNIVERSITY/SEATTLE
Seattle, WA

ABOUT THE INSTITUTION Proprietary, coed. Awards: bachelor's, master's, and doctoral degrees. 2 undergraduate majors. Total enrollment: 293. Undergraduates: 41.
GIFT AID (NEED-BASED) *Scholarships, grants, and awards:* Federal Pell, FSEOG, college/university gift aid from institutional funds.
GIFT AID (NON-NEED-BASED) *Scholarships, grants, and awards by category: Academic Interests/Achievement:* general academic interests/achievements. *Special Achievements/Activities:* community service, leadership. *Special Characteristics:* adult students.
LOANS *Programs:* FFEL (Subsidized and Unsubsidized Stafford, PLUS), Perkins.
WORK-STUDY *Federal work-study:* Total amount: $452; 1 job averaging $452.
APPLYING FOR FINANCIAL AID *Required financial aid forms:* FAFSA, institution's own form.
CONTACT Eun-Ju Lee, Assistant Director of Student Services, Argosy University/Seattle, 1019 Eighth Avenue North, Seattle, WA 98109, 206-283-4500 Ext. 235 or toll-free 866-283-2777 (out-of-state). *Fax:* 206-283-5777. *E-mail:* elee@argosyu.edu.

ARGOSY UNIVERSITY/TAMPA
Tampa, FL

ABOUT THE INSTITUTION Proprietary, coed. Awards: bachelor's and master's degrees. 3 undergraduate majors. Total enrollment: 409. Undergraduates: 49.
GIFT AID (NEED-BASED) *Scholarships, grants, and awards:* Federal Pell, FSEOG, state, college/university gift aid from institutional funds.
GIFT AID (NON-NEED-BASED) *Scholarships, grants, and awards by category: Academic Interests/Achievement:* general academic interests/achievements. *Special Achievements/Activities:* community service, general special achievements/activities, leadership. *Special Characteristics:* adult students, general special characteristics.
LOANS *Programs:* FFEL (Subsidized and Unsubsidized Stafford, PLUS), Perkins.
WORK-STUDY Federal work-study jobs available.
APPLYING FOR FINANCIAL AID *Required financial aid forms:* FAFSA, institution's own form.
CONTACT Donna Page, Financial Aid Office, Argosy University/Tampa, 4401 North Hines Avenue, Tampa, FL 33614, 813-393-5290 or toll-free 800-850-6488 Ext. 5260 (in-state), 800-850-6488 (out-of-state). *Fax:* 813-874-1989. *E-mail:* dpage@edmc.edu.

ARGOSY UNIVERSITY/TWIN CITIES
Eagan, MN

| Tuition & fees: $12,220 | Average undergraduate aid package: N/A |

ABOUT THE INSTITUTION Proprietary, coed. Awards: associate, bachelor's, master's, and doctoral degrees and post-master's and first professional

86 *www.petersons.com*   *Peterson's College Money Handbook 2006*

certificates. 9 undergraduate majors. Total enrollment: 1,580. Undergraduates: 1,105. Federal methodology is used as a basis for awarding need-based institutional aid.

UNDERGRADUATE EXPENSES for 2005–06 *Application fee:* $50. *Tuition:* full-time $11,970; part-time $400 per credit hour. *Payment plan:* Installment.

GIFT AID (NEED-BASED) *Total amount:* $1,394,671 (63% federal, 37% state). *Scholarships, grants, and awards:* Federal Pell, FSEOG, state, private, college/university gift aid from institutional funds.

GIFT AID (NON-NEED-BASED) *Total amount:* $41,423 (100% institutional). *Tuition waivers:* Full or partial for employees or children of employees.

LOANS *Student loans:* $8,718,201 (37% need-based, 63% non-need-based). *Parent loans:* $293,159 (100% non-need-based). *Programs:* FFEL (Subsidized and Unsubsidized Stafford, PLUS), state, alternative loans.

WORK-STUDY *Federal work-study:* Total amount: $47,882; 20 jobs averaging $3000. *State or other work-study/employment:* Total amount: $22,740 (100% need-based). 20 part-time jobs averaging $1500.

APPLYING FOR FINANCIAL AID *Required financial aid forms:* FAFSA, institution's own form. *Financial aid deadline:* Continuous. *Notification date:* Continuous.

CONTACT Office of Student Finance, Argosy University/Twin Cities, 1515 Central Parkway, Eagan, MN 55121-1756, 651-846-3384 or toll-free 651-846-3300 (in-state), 888-844-2004 (out-of-state). *Fax:* 651-994-0170. *E-mail:* financialaidautc@argosyu.edu.

ARGOSY UNIVERSITY/TWIN CITIES
Eagan, MN

ABOUT THE INSTITUTION Proprietary, coed, primarily women. Awards: bachelor's, master's, and doctoral degrees and post-master's certificates. 10 undergraduate majors. Total enrollment: 1,334. Undergraduates: 919.

GIFT AID (NEED-BASED) *Scholarships, grants, and awards:* Federal Pell, FSEOG, state, college/university gift aid from institutional funds.

GIFT AID (NON-NEED-BASED) *Scholarships, grants, and awards by category: Academic Interests/Achievement:* general academic interests/achievements. *Special Achievements/Activities:* general special achievements/activities. *Special Characteristics:* general special characteristics.

LOANS *Programs:* FFEL (Subsidized and Unsubsidized Stafford, PLUS), Perkins, state, Minnesota SELF Loans.

WORK-STUDY *Federal work-study:* Total amount: $17,755; 8 jobs averaging $2219.

APPLYING FOR FINANCIAL AID *Required financial aid forms:* FAFSA, institution's own form.

CONTACT Financial Aid Office, Argosy University/Twin Cities, 1515 Central Parkway, Eagan, MN 55121, 651-846-3384 or toll-free 888-844-2004 (out-of-state). *Fax:* 651-994-0170.

ARGOSY UNIVERSITY/WASHINGTON D.C.
Arlington, VA

ABOUT THE INSTITUTION Proprietary, coed. Awards: bachelor's, master's, and doctoral degrees. 1 undergraduate major. Total enrollment: 13. Undergraduates: 13.

GIFT AID (NEED-BASED) *Scholarships, grants, and awards:* Federal Pell, FSEOG, college/university gift aid from institutional funds.

GIFT AID (NON-NEED-BASED) *Scholarships, grants, and awards by category: Academic Interests/Achievement:* general academic interests/achievements. *Special Achievements/Activities:* general special achievements/activities. *Special Characteristics:* general special characteristics.

LOANS *Programs:* FFEL (Subsidized and Unsubsidized Stafford, PLUS), Perkins.

APPLYING FOR FINANCIAL AID *Required financial aid forms:* FAFSA, institution's own form.

CONTACT Financial Aid Office, Argosy University/Washington D.C., 1550 Wilson Boulevard, Suite 600, Arlington, VA 22209, 703-526-5800 or toll-free 866-703-2777 Ext. 5833.

ARIZONA STATE UNIVERSITY
Tempe, AZ

Tuition & fees (AZ res): $4064	Average undergraduate aid package: $7810

ABOUT THE INSTITUTION State-supported, coed. Awards: bachelor's, master's, doctoral, and first professional degrees and post-bachelor's and post-master's

certificates. 93 undergraduate majors. Total enrollment: 49,171. Undergraduates: 39,377. Freshmen: 7,147. Federal methodology is used as a basis for awarding need-based institutional aid.

UNDERGRADUATE EXPENSES for 2004–05 *Application fee:* $25; $50 for nonresidents. *Tuition, state resident:* full-time $3973; part-time $207 per credit. *Tuition, nonresident:* full-time $12,828; part-time $535 per credit. *Required fees:* full-time $91; $23 per term part-time. Full-time tuition and fees vary according to program. Part-time tuition and fees vary according to program. *College room and board:* $6574; *room only:* $4178. Room and board charges vary according to board plan and housing facility. *Payment plan:* Installment.

FRESHMAN FINANCIAL AID (Fall 2003) 3997 applied for aid; of those 71% were deemed to have need. 100% of freshmen with need received aid; of those 13% had need fully met. *Average percent of need met:* 60% (excluding resources awarded to replace EFC). *Average financial aid package:* $6883 (excluding resources awarded to replace EFC). 18% of all full-time freshmen had no need and received non-need-based gift aid.

UNDERGRADUATE FINANCIAL AID (Fall 2003) 16,788 applied for aid; of those 79% were deemed to have need. 100% of undergraduates with need received aid; of those 9% had need fully met. *Average percent of need met:* 61% (excluding resources awarded to replace EFC). *Average financial aid package:* $7810 (excluding resources awarded to replace EFC). 11% of all full-time undergraduates had no need and received non-need-based gift aid.

GIFT AID (NEED-BASED) *Total amount:* $59,959,557 (42% federal, 1% state, 45% institutional, 12% external sources). *Receiving aid:* Freshmen: 37% (2,570); All full-time undergraduates: 36% (11,030). *Average award:* Freshmen: $5147; Undergraduates: $4956. *Scholarships, grants, and awards:* Federal Pell, FSEOG, state, private, college/university gift aid from institutional funds, Federal Nursing.

GIFT AID (NON-NEED-BASED) *Total amount:* $24,527,696 (76% institutional, 24% external sources). *Receiving aid:* Freshmen: 4% (283); Undergraduates: 2% (653). *Average Award:* Freshmen: $5209; Undergraduates: $4993. *Scholarships, grants, and awards by category: Academic Interests/Achievement:* architecture, area/ethnic studies, biological sciences, business, communication, computer science, education, engineering/technologies, English, foreign languages, general academic interests/achievements, health fields, home economics, humanities, mathematics, military science, physical sciences, premedicine, social sciences. *Creative Arts/Performance:* applied art and design, art/fine arts, cinema/film/broadcasting, creative writing, dance, debating, general creative arts/performance, journalism/publications, music, performing arts, theater/drama. *Special Achievements/Activities:* general special achievements/activities. *Tuition waivers:* Full or partial for employees or children of employees. *ROTC:* Army, Air Force.

LOANS *Student loans:* $85,095,291 (76% need-based, 24% non-need-based). 45% of past graduating class borrowed through all loan programs. *Average indebtedness per student:* $17,509. *Average need-based loan:* Freshmen: $2474; Undergraduates: $3912. *Parent loans:* $28,390,918 (32% need-based, 68% non-need-based). *Programs:* Federal Direct (Subsidized and Unsubsidized Stafford, PLUS), FFEL (PLUS), Perkins.

WORK-STUDY *Federal work-study:* Total amount: $1,370,104; 615 jobs averaging $2228. *State or other work-study/employment:* Total amount: $12,993,658 (23% need-based, 77% non-need-based). 4,493 part-time jobs averaging $2892.

ATHLETIC AWARDS *Total amount:* $5,364,276 (24% need-based, 76% non-need-based).

APPLYING FOR FINANCIAL AID *Required financial aid form:* FAFSA. *Financial aid deadline (priority):* 2/15. *Notification date:* Continuous beginning 3/15. Students must reply within 4 weeks of notification.

CONTACT Craig Fennell, Director of Student Financial Assistance, Arizona State University, Box 870412, Tempe, AZ 85287-0412, 480-965-3355. *Fax:* 480-965-9484. *E-mail:* financialaid@asu.edu.

ARIZONA STATE UNIVERSITY EAST
Mesa, AZ

Tuition & fees (AZ res): $4015	Average undergraduate aid package: $7420

ABOUT THE INSTITUTION State-supported, coed. Awards: bachelor's and master's degrees. 18 undergraduate majors. Total enrollment: 3,983. Undergraduates: 3,312. Freshmen: 150. Federal methodology is used as a basis for awarding need-based institutional aid.

UNDERGRADUATE EXPENSES for 2004–05 *Application fee:* $50. *Tuition, state resident:* full-time $3974; part-time $207 per semester hour. *Tuition, nonresident:* full-time $12,828; part-time $535 per semester hour. Full-time tuition and fees vary according to degree level, location, and program. Part-time tuition and fees vary according to course load, degree level, location, and program. *College*

room and board: $5155; **room only:** $2655. Room and board charges vary according to board plan and housing facility. **Payment plan:** Installment.

FRESHMAN FINANCIAL AID (Fall 2003) 4 applied for aid; of those 25% were deemed to have need. 100% of freshmen with need received aid. 40% of all full-time freshmen had no need and received non-need-based gift aid.

UNDERGRADUATE FINANCIAL AID (Fall 2003) 696 applied for aid; of those 77% were deemed to have need. 100% of undergraduates with need received aid; of those 3% had need fully met. **Average percent of need met:** 57% (excluding resources awarded to replace EFC). **Average financial aid package:** $7420 (excluding resources awarded to replace EFC). 4% of all full-time undergraduates had no need and received non-need-based gift aid.

GIFT AID (NEED-BASED) Total amount: $3,577,521 (47% federal, 1% state, 42% institutional, 10% external sources). **Receiving aid:** All full-time undergraduates: 40% (422). **Average award:** Undergraduates: $4392. **Scholarships, grants, and awards:** Federal Pell, FSEOG, state, private, college/university gift aid from institutional funds.

GIFT AID (NON-NEED-BASED) Total amount: $390,709 (54% institutional, 46% external sources). **Receiving aid:** Undergraduates: 1% (6). **Average Award:** Freshmen: $2879; Undergraduates: $3701. **Scholarships, grants, and awards by category:** Academic Interests/Achievement: general academic interests/achievements. Creative Arts/Performance: general creative arts/performance. Special Achievements/Activities: general special achievements/activities. Special Characteristics: general special characteristics. **Tuition waivers:** Full or partial for employees or children of employees. **ROTC:** Army cooperative, Air Force cooperative.

LOANS Student loans: $7,145,227 (80% need-based, 20% non-need-based). **Average need-based loan:** Undergraduates: $4508. **Parent loans:** $1,285,687 (32% need-based, 68% non-need-based). **Programs:** Federal Direct (Subsidized and Unsubsidized Stafford, PLUS), FFEL (PLUS), Perkins.

WORK-STUDY Federal work-study: Total amount: $49,732; 17 jobs averaging $2925. **State or other work-study/employment:** Total amount: $452,214 (23% need-based, 77% non-need-based). 167 part-time jobs averaging $2708.

ATHLETIC AWARDS Total amount: $9907 (100% non-need-based).

APPLYING FOR FINANCIAL AID Required financial aid form: FAFSA. **Financial aid deadline (priority):** 3/1. **Notification date:** Continuous beginning 4/15. Students must reply within 4 weeks of notification.

CONTACT Heather Klotz, Financial Aid Counselor, Arizona State University East, 7001 East Williams Field Road, Building 370, Mesa, AZ 85212, 480-727-1042. Fax: 480-727-1008. E-mail: heather.klotz@asu.edu.

ARIZONA STATE UNIVERSITY WEST
Phoenix, AZ

Tuition & fees (AZ res): $4064	Average undergraduate aid package: $7479

ABOUT THE INSTITUTION State-supported, coed. Awards: bachelor's and master's degrees and post-bachelor's certificates. 22 undergraduate majors. Total enrollment: 7,348. Undergraduates: 6,137. Freshmen: 396. Federal methodology is used as a basis for awarding need-based institutional aid.

UNDERGRADUATE EXPENSES for 2004–05 Application fee: $50. **Tuition, state resident:** full-time $3973; part-time $207 per credit hour. **Tuition, nonresident:** full-time $12,828; part-time $535 per credit hour. **Required fees:** full-time $91; $21 per term part-time. Part-time tuition and fees vary according to course load. **College room and board: room only:** $4455. **Payment plan:** Installment.

FRESHMAN FINANCIAL AID (Fall 2003) 216 applied for aid; of those 75% were deemed to have need. 100% of freshmen with need received aid; of those 100% had need fully met. **Average percent of need met:** 100% (excluding resources awarded to replace EFC). **Average financial aid package:** $5952 (excluding resources awarded to replace EFC). 27% of all full-time freshmen had no need and received non-need-based gift aid.

UNDERGRADUATE FINANCIAL AID (Fall 2003) 2,000 applied for aid; of those 85% were deemed to have need. 100% of undergraduates with need received aid; of those 100% had need fully met. **Average percent of need met:** 100% (excluding resources awarded to replace EFC). **Average financial aid package:** $7479 (excluding resources awarded to replace EFC). 16% of all full-time undergraduates had no need and received non-need-based gift aid.

GIFT AID (NEED-BASED) Total amount: $8,703,411 (50% federal, 41% institutional, 9% external sources). **Receiving aid:** Freshmen: 44% (149); All full-time undergraduates: 45% (1,438). **Average award:** Freshmen: $4872; Undergraduates: $4739. **Scholarships, grants, and awards:** Federal Pell, FSEOG, state, private, college/university gift aid from institutional funds.

GIFT AID (NON-NEED-BASED) Total amount: $1,106,184 (66% institutional, 34% external sources). **Receiving aid:** Freshmen: 5% (17); Undergraduates: 1% (42). **Average Award:** Freshmen: $3226; Undergraduates: $4432. **Scholarships, grants, and awards by category:** Academic Interests/Achievement: general academic interests/achievements. **Tuition waivers:** Full or partial for employees or children of employees.

LOANS Student loans: $15,246,737 (81% need-based, 19% non-need-based). **Average need-based loan:** Freshmen: $2179; Undergraduates: $4033. **Parent loans:** $753,867 (31% need-based, 69% non-need-based). **Programs:** Federal Direct (Subsidized and Unsubsidized Stafford), FFEL (PLUS), Perkins, college/university.

WORK-STUDY Federal work-study: Total amount: $254,624; 99 jobs averaging $2572. **State or other work-study/employment:** Total amount: $615,829 (29% need-based, 71% non-need-based). 213 part-time jobs averaging $2891.

APPLYING FOR FINANCIAL AID Required financial aid form: FAFSA. **Financial aid deadline (priority):** 3/1. **Notification date:** Continuous beginning 3/15. Students must reply within 4 weeks of notification.

CONTACT Leah Samudio, Financial Aid Manager, Arizona State University West, 4701 West Thunderbird Road, PO Box 37100, Phoenix, AZ 85069-7100, 602-543-8178.

ARKANSAS BAPTIST COLLEGE
Little Rock, AR

CONTACT Director of Financial Aid, Arkansas Baptist College, 1600 Bishop Street, Little Rock, AR 72202-6067, 501-374-7856.

ARKANSAS STATE UNIVERSITY
Jonesboro, AR

Tuition & fees (AR res): $5155	Average undergraduate aid package: $3900

ABOUT THE INSTITUTION State-supported, coed. Awards: associate, bachelor's, master's, and doctoral degrees and post-bachelor's and post-master's certificates. 77 undergraduate majors. Total enrollment: 10,508. Undergraduates: 9,262. Freshmen: 1,378. Federal methodology is used as a basis for awarding need-based institutional aid.

UNDERGRADUATE EXPENSES for 2004–05 Application fee: $15. **Tuition, state resident:** full-time $4035; part-time $134.50 per credit hour. **Tuition, nonresident:** full-time $10,395; part-time $346.50 per credit hour. **Required fees:** full-time $1120; $35 per credit hour or $25 per term part-time. Full-time tuition and fees vary according to course load, location, and program. Part-time tuition and fees vary according to course load, location, and program. **College room and board:** $4000. Room and board charges vary according to board plan and housing facility. **Payment plan:** Installment.

FRESHMAN FINANCIAL AID (Fall 2003) 989 applied for aid; of those 74% were deemed to have need. 98% of freshmen with need received aid; of those 37% had need fully met. **Average percent of need met:** 60% (excluding resources awarded to replace EFC). **Average financial aid package:** $3275 (excluding resources awarded to replace EFC). 44% of all full-time freshmen had no need and received non-need-based gift aid.

UNDERGRADUATE FINANCIAL AID (Fall 2003) 4,763 applied for aid; of those 87% were deemed to have need. 97% of undergraduates with need received aid; of those 46% had need fully met. **Average percent of need met:** 55% (excluding resources awarded to replace EFC). **Average financial aid package:** $3900 (excluding resources awarded to replace EFC). 26% of all full-time undergraduates had no need and received non-need-based gift aid.

GIFT AID (NEED-BASED) Total amount: $25,386,982 (49% federal, 12% state, 36% institutional, 3% external sources). **Receiving aid:** Freshmen: 46% (605); All full-time undergraduates: 43% (3,128). **Average award:** Freshmen: $2200; Undergraduates: $2600. **Scholarships, grants, and awards:** Federal Pell, FSEOG, state, private, college/university gift aid from institutional funds.

GIFT AID (NON-NEED-BASED) Receiving aid: Freshmen: 52% (677); Undergraduates: 35% (2,531). **Average Award:** Freshmen: $1900; Undergraduates: $2600. **Scholarships, grants, and awards by category:** Academic Interests/Achievement: 3,162 awards ($7,650,750 total): agriculture, biological sciences, business, communication, computer science, education, engineering/technologies, English, general academic interests/achievements, health fields, humanities, library science, mathematics, military science, physical sciences, premedicine, social sciences. Creative Arts/Performance: 256 awards ($408,040 total): art/fine arts, cinema/film/broadcasting, debating, journalism/publications, music, performing arts, theater/drama. Special Achievements/Activities: 164 awards ($127,513

total): cheerleading/drum major, community service, general special achievements/ activities. *Special Characteristics:* 41 awards ($153,015 total): adult students, children and siblings of alumni, children of current students, children of union members/company employees, children of workers in trades, children with a deceased or disabled parent, ethnic background, first-generation college students, general special characteristics, handicapped students, out-of-state students, veterans, veterans' children. *Tuition waivers:* Full or partial for children of alumni, employees or children of employees, senior citizens. *ROTC:* Army.
LOANS *Student loans:* $37,373,486 (59% need-based, 41% non-need-based). 65% of past graduating class borrowed through all loan programs. *Average indebtedness per student:* $15,700. *Average need-based loan:* Freshmen: $1400; Undergraduates: $2100. *Programs:* FFEL (Subsidized and Unsubsidized Stafford, PLUS), Perkins.
WORK-STUDY *Federal work-study:* Total amount: $547,187; 344 jobs averaging $1591. *State or other work-study/employment:* Total amount: $3,142,092 (100% non-need-based). Part-time jobs available.
ATHLETIC AWARDS *Total amount:* $1,859,000 (100% non-need-based).
APPLYING FOR FINANCIAL AID *Required financial aid forms:* FAFSA, institution's own form. *Financial aid deadline:* 7/1 (priority: 2/15). *Notification date:* Continuous beginning 6/1. Students must reply within 2 weeks of notification.
CONTACT Mr. Gregory Thornburg, Director of Financial Aid, Arkansas State University, PO Box 1620, State University, AR 72467, 870-972-2310 or toll-free 800-382-3030 (in-state). *Fax:* 870-972-2794. *E-mail:* gthorn@astate.edu.

ARKANSAS TECH UNIVERSITY
Russellville, AR

Tuition & fees (AR res): $4468	Average undergraduate aid package: $4840

ABOUT THE INSTITUTION State-supported, coed. Awards: associate, bachelor's, and master's degrees. 53 undergraduate majors. Total enrollment: 6,483. Undergraduates: 6,091. Freshmen: 1,460. Federal methodology is used as a basis for awarding need-based institutional aid.
UNDERGRADUATE EXPENSES for 2004–05 *Tuition, state resident:* full-time $4158; part-time $154 per hour. *Tuition, nonresident:* full-time $8316; part-time $308 per hour. *Required fees:* full-time $310; $4 per hour or $70 per term part-time. Full-time tuition and fees vary according to course load and location. Part-time tuition and fees vary according to course load and location. *College room and board:* $3841; *room only:* $2078. Room and board charges vary according to board plan and housing facility. *Payment plans:* Installment, deferred payment.
FRESHMAN FINANCIAL AID (Fall 2003) 1095 applied for aid; of those 82% were deemed to have need. 99% of freshmen with need received aid; of those 32% had need fully met. *Average percent of need met:* 43% (excluding resources awarded to replace EFC). *Average financial aid package:* $3716 (excluding resources awarded to replace EFC). 28% of all full-time freshmen had no need and received non-need-based gift aid.
UNDERGRADUATE FINANCIAL AID (Fall 2003) 3,618 applied for aid; of those 87% were deemed to have need. 99% of undergraduates with need received aid; of those 28% had need fully met. *Average percent of need met:* 47% (excluding resources awarded to replace EFC). *Average financial aid package:* $4840 (excluding resources awarded to replace EFC). 20% of all full-time undergraduates had no need and received non-need-based gift aid.
GIFT AID (NEED-BASED) *Total amount:* $8,913,679 (78% federal, 22% state). *Receiving aid:* Freshmen: 47% (681); All full-time undergraduates: 47% (2,405). *Average award:* Freshmen: $2477; Undergraduates: $2535. *Scholarships, grants, and awards:* Federal Pell, FSEOG, state, private, college/university gift aid from institutional funds.
GIFT AID (NON-NEED-BASED) *Total amount:* $8,070,456 (1% federal, 7% state, 82% institutional, 10% external sources). *Receiving aid:* Freshmen: 34% (493); Undergraduates: 22% (1,109). *Average Award:* Freshmen: $5014; Undergraduates: $4858. *Scholarships, grants, and awards by category:* Academic Interests/Achievement: 1,194 awards ($5,225,907 total): agriculture, general academic interests/achievements. Creative Arts/Performance: 311 awards ($665,246 total): creative writing, general creative arts/performance, music. Special Achievements/Activities: 47 awards ($39,583 total): general special achievements/activities, leadership. Special Characteristics: 560 awards ($759,210 total): adult students, children of faculty/staff, ethnic background, general special characteristics, international students, out-of-state students, public servants. *Tuition waivers:* Full or partial for employees or children of employees, senior citizens. *ROTC:* Army cooperative.
LOANS *Student loans:* $14,964,597 (57% need-based, 43% non-need-based). 53% of past graduating class borrowed through all loan programs. *Average

indebtedness per student:* $16,330. *Average need-based loan:* Freshmen: $1193; Undergraduates: $2217. *Parent loans:* $551,736 (100% non-need-based). *Programs:* FFEL (Subsidized and Unsubsidized Stafford, PLUS), Perkins.
WORK-STUDY *Federal work-study:* Total amount: $291,145; 235 jobs averaging $1239. *State or other work-study/employment:* Total amount: $488,593 (100% non-need-based). 415 part-time jobs averaging $1177.
ATHLETIC AWARDS *Total amount:* $615,865 (100% non-need-based).
APPLYING FOR FINANCIAL AID *Required financial aid form:* FAFSA. *Financial aid deadline (priority):* 4/15. *Notification date:* Continuous beginning 5/1. Students must reply within 2 weeks of notification.
CONTACT Niki Harrison, Financial Aid Officer, Arkansas Tech University, Bryan Student Services Building, Room 117, Russellville, AR 72801-2222, 479-968-0399 or toll-free 800-582-6953. *Fax:* 479-964-0857. *E-mail:* niki.harrison@mail.atu.edu.

ARLINGTON BAPTIST COLLEGE
Arlington, TX

Tuition & fees: $5040	Average undergraduate aid package: $5025

ABOUT THE INSTITUTION Independent Baptist, coed. Awards: bachelor's degrees. 10 undergraduate majors. Total enrollment: 201. Undergraduates: 201. Freshmen: 44. Federal methodology is used as a basis for awarding need-based institutional aid.
UNDERGRADUATE EXPENSES for 2004–05 *Application fee:* $15. *Comprehensive fee:* $8700 includes full-time tuition ($4500), mandatory fees ($540), and room and board ($3660). *Part-time tuition:* $150 per semester hour. *Part-time fees:* $270 per term. *Payment plan:* Installment.
FRESHMAN FINANCIAL AID (Fall 2003) 39 applied for aid; of those 97% were deemed to have need. 100% of freshmen with need received aid; of those 100% had need fully met. *Average financial aid package:* $5025 (excluding resources awarded to replace EFC).
UNDERGRADUATE FINANCIAL AID (Fall 2003) 166 applied for aid; of those 95% were deemed to have need. 100% of undergraduates with need received aid; of those 100% had need fully met. *Average financial aid package:* $5025 (excluding resources awarded to replace EFC).
GIFT AID (NEED-BASED) *Total amount:* $350,978 (53% federal, 47% institutional). *Scholarships, grants, and awards:* Federal Pell, private, college/university gift aid from institutional funds.
GIFT AID (NON-NEED-BASED) *Scholarships, grants, and awards by category:* Special Characteristics: children of faculty/staff, spouses of current students. *Tuition waivers:* Full or partial for employees or children of employees.
LOANS *Student loans:* $523,137 (100% need-based). 65% of past graduating class borrowed through all loan programs. *Average indebtedness per student:* $7800. *Programs:* FFEL (Subsidized and Unsubsidized Stafford, PLUS).
WORK-STUDY Federal work-study jobs available.
APPLYING FOR FINANCIAL AID *Required financial aid form:* FAFSA. *Financial aid deadline (priority):* 8/1. *Notification date:* Continuous beginning 9/1.
CONTACT Mr. David B. Clogston Jr., Business Manager, Arlington Baptist College, 3001 West Division Street, Arlington, TX 76012-3425, 817-461-8741 Ext. 110. *Fax:* 817-274-1138.

ARMSTRONG ATLANTIC STATE UNIVERSITY
Savannah, GA

Tuition & fees (GA res): $2734	Average undergraduate aid package: $6847

ABOUT THE INSTITUTION State-supported, coed. Awards: associate, bachelor's, and master's degrees. 34 undergraduate majors. Total enrollment: 6,653. Undergraduates: 5,743. Freshmen: 847. Federal methodology is used as a basis for awarding need-based institutional aid.
UNDERGRADUATE EXPENSES for 2004–05 *Application fee:* $20. *Tuition, state resident:* full-time $2322; part-time $97 per hour. *Tuition, nonresident:* full-time $9250; part-time $388 per hour. Full-time tuition and fees vary according to program. Part-time tuition and fees vary according to course load and program. *College room and board: room only:* $4500.
FRESHMAN FINANCIAL AID (Fall 2003) 625 applied for aid; of those 58% were deemed to have need. 100% of freshmen with need received aid; of those 90% had need fully met. *Average percent of need met:* 90% (excluding resources

awarded to replace EFC). *Average financial aid package:* $5787 (excluding resources awarded to replace EFC). 38% of all full-time freshmen had no need and received non-need-based gift aid.

UNDERGRADUATE FINANCIAL AID (Fall 2003) 2,979 applied for aid; of those 60% were deemed to have need. 100% of undergraduates with need received aid; of those 89% had need fully met. *Average percent of need met:* 90% (excluding resources awarded to replace EFC). *Average financial aid package:* $6847 (excluding resources awarded to replace EFC). 19% of all full-time undergraduates had no need and received non-need-based gift aid.

GIFT AID (NEED-BASED) *Total amount:* $4,436,734 (98% federal, 1% state, 1% external sources). *Receiving aid:* Freshmen: 27% (197); All full-time undergraduates: 35% (1,145). *Average award:* Freshmen: $2669; Undergraduates: $2795. *Scholarships, grants, and awards:* Federal Pell, FSEOG, state, private, college/university gift aid from institutional funds, Federal Nursing.

GIFT AID (NON-NEED-BASED) *Total amount:* $4,496,562 (91% state, 3% institutional, 6% external sources). *Receiving aid:* Freshmen: 40% (287); Undergraduates: 22% (718). *Average Award:* Freshmen: $3016; Undergraduates: $2735. *Scholarships, grants, and awards by category:* Academic Interests/Achievement: 367 awards ($405,223 total): biological sciences, computer science, education, engineering/technologies, English, general academic interests/achievements, health fields, humanities, international studies, mathematics, military science, physical sciences. *Creative Arts/Performance:* 87 awards ($51,811 total): art/fine arts, music. *Special Achievements/Activities:* 1 award ($750 total): community service. *Special Characteristics:* 15 awards ($37,614 total): international students, religious affiliation. *Tuition waivers:* Full or partial for senior citizens. *ROTC:* Army, Naval cooperative.

LOANS *Student loans:* $10,666,154 (57% need-based, 43% non-need-based). 55% of past graduating class borrowed through all loan programs. *Average indebtedness per student:* $11,000. *Average need-based loan:* Freshmen: $2184; Undergraduates: $3305. *Parent loans:* $249,406 (100% non-need-based). *Programs:* FFEL (Subsidized and Unsubsidized Stafford, PLUS), state, college/university, alternative loans.

WORK-STUDY *Federal work-study:* Total amount: $453,742; 114 jobs averaging $4000. *State or other work-study/employment:* Part-time jobs available.

ATHLETIC AWARDS *Total amount:* $502,131 (100% non-need-based).

APPLYING FOR FINANCIAL AID *Required financial aid form:* FAFSA. *Financial aid deadline (priority):* 3/15. *Notification date:* Continuous beginning 4/1. Students must reply within 2 weeks of notification.

CONTACT Lee Ann Kirkland, Director of Financial Aid, Armstrong Atlantic State University, 11935 Abercorn Street, Savannah, GA 31419-1997, 912-921-5990 or toll-free 800-633-2349. *Fax:* 912-921-7357. *E-mail:* finaid@mail.armstrong.edu.

ART ACADEMY OF CINCINNATI
Cincinnati, OH

Tuition & fees: $18,850	Average undergraduate aid package: $12,020

ABOUT THE INSTITUTION Independent, coed. Awards: associate, bachelor's, and master's degrees. 11 undergraduate majors. Total enrollment: 222. Undergraduates: 218. Freshmen: 58. Federal methodology is used as a basis for awarding need-based institutional aid.

UNDERGRADUATE EXPENSES for 2005–06 *Application fee:* $25. *Tuition:* full-time $18,500; part-time $775 per credit hour. *Required fees:* full-time $350; $175 per term part-time. Part-time tuition and fees vary according to course load. *Payment plan:* Installment.

FRESHMAN FINANCIAL AID (Fall 2003) 37 applied for aid; of those 89% were deemed to have need. 100% of freshmen with need received aid; of those 21% had need fully met. *Average percent of need met:* 66% (excluding resources awarded to replace EFC). *Average financial aid package:* $11,159 (excluding resources awarded to replace EFC). 23% of all full-time freshmen had no need and received non-need-based gift aid.

UNDERGRADUATE FINANCIAL AID (Fall 2003) 145 applied for aid; of those 87% were deemed to have need. 99% of undergraduates with need received aid; of those 22% had need fully met. *Average percent of need met:* 69% (excluding resources awarded to replace EFC). *Average financial aid package:* $12,020 (excluding resources awarded to replace EFC). 26% of all full-time undergraduates had no need and received non-need-based gift aid.

GIFT AID (NEED-BASED) *Total amount:* $949,627 (20% federal, 22% state, 49% institutional, 9% external sources). *Receiving aid:* Freshmen: 73% (32); All full-time undergraduates: 69% (121). *Average award:* Freshmen: $6943;

Undergraduates: $7439. *Scholarships, grants, and awards:* Federal Pell, FSEOG, state, private, college/university gift aid from institutional funds.

GIFT AID (NON-NEED-BASED) *Total amount:* $278,461 (12% state, 82% institutional, 6% external sources). *Receiving aid:* Freshmen: 5% (2); Undergraduates: 7% (12). *Average Award:* Freshmen: $7460; Undergraduates: $7762. *Scholarships, grants, and awards by category:* Creative Arts/Performance: 104 awards ($455,350 total): applied art and design, art/fine arts. *Tuition waivers:* Full or partial for employees or children of employees.

LOANS *Student loans:* $1,017,348 (78% need-based, 22% non-need-based). 64% of past graduating class borrowed through all loan programs. *Average indebtedness per student:* $25,030. *Average need-based loan:* Freshmen: $4682; Undergraduates: $5322. *Parent loans:* $475,853 (42% need-based, 58% non-need-based). *Programs:* FFEL (Subsidized and Unsubsidized Stafford, PLUS), college/university, alternative loans.

WORK-STUDY *Federal work-study:* Total amount: $32,454; 47 jobs available. *State or other work-study/employment:* Part-time jobs available.

APPLYING FOR FINANCIAL AID *Required financial aid form:* FAFSA. *Financial aid deadline:* Continuous. *Notification date:* Continuous beginning 2/1. Students must reply within 2 weeks of notification.

CONTACT Ms. Karen Geiger, Director of Financial Aid, Art Academy of Cincinnati, 1125 Saint Gregory Street, Cincinnati, OH 45202-1700, 513-562-8773 or toll-free 800-323-5692 (in-state). *Fax:* 513-562-8778. *E-mail:* financialaid@artacademy.edu.

ART CENTER COLLEGE OF DESIGN
Pasadena, CA

Tuition & fees: $25,044	Average undergraduate aid package: $14,146

ABOUT THE INSTITUTION Independent, coed. Awards: bachelor's and master's degrees. 19 undergraduate majors. Total enrollment: 1,519. Undergraduates: 1,394. Freshmen: 42. Federal methodology is used as a basis for awarding need-based institutional aid.

UNDERGRADUATE EXPENSES for 2004–05 *Application fee:* $45. *Tuition:* full-time $24,844. *Payment plan:* Installment.

FRESHMAN FINANCIAL AID (Fall 2004, est.) 219 applied for aid; of those 93% were deemed to have need. 100% of freshmen with need received aid. *Average percent of need met:* 56% (excluding resources awarded to replace EFC). *Average financial aid package:* $11,619 (excluding resources awarded to replace EFC). 1% of all full-time freshmen had no need and received non-need-based gift aid.

UNDERGRADUATE FINANCIAL AID (Fall 2004, est.) 1,150 applied for aid; of those 95% were deemed to have need. 96% of undergraduates with need received aid. *Average percent of need met:* 62% (excluding resources awarded to replace EFC). *Average financial aid package:* $14,146 (excluding resources awarded to replace EFC). 1% of all full-time undergraduates had no need and received non-need-based gift aid.

GIFT AID (NEED-BASED) *Total amount:* $4,776,925 (30% federal, 21% state, 48% institutional, 1% external sources). *Receiving aid:* Freshmen: 68% (190); All full-time undergraduates: 55% (773). *Average award:* Freshmen: $6039; Undergraduates: $7246. *Scholarships, grants, and awards:* Federal Pell, FSEOG, state, private, college/university gift aid from institutional funds.

GIFT AID (NON-NEED-BASED) *Scholarships, grants, and awards by category:* Creative Arts/Performance: art/fine arts. *Tuition waivers:* Full or partial for employees or children of employees.

LOANS *Student loans:* $10,625,031 (36% need-based, 64% non-need-based). 70% of past graduating class borrowed through all loan programs. *Average indebtedness per student:* $60,000. *Average need-based loan:* Freshmen: $4579; Undergraduates: $5867. *Parent loans:* $1,770,421 (100% non-need-based). *Programs:* FFEL (Subsidized and Unsubsidized Stafford, PLUS), college/university, alternative loans.

WORK-STUDY *Federal work-study:* Total amount: $375,000; 187 jobs averaging $2000. *State or other work-study/employment:* Part-time jobs available.

APPLYING FOR FINANCIAL AID *Required financial aid form:* FAFSA. *Financial aid deadline (priority):* 3/1. *Notification date:* Continuous beginning 5/15. Students must reply within 4 weeks of notification.

CONTACT Clema McKenzie, Director of Financial Aid, Art Center College of Design, 1700 Lida Street, Pasadena, CA 91103-1999, 626-396-2215. *Fax:* 626-683-8684.

THE ART CENTER DESIGN COLLEGE
Tucson, AZ

CONTACT Ms. Margarita Carey, Education Finance Director, The Art Center Design College, 2525 North Country Club Road, Tucson, AZ 85716-2505, 520-325-0123 or toll-free 800-825-8753. *Fax:* 520-325-5535.

THE ART INSTITUTE OF ATLANTA
Atlanta, GA

ABOUT THE INSTITUTION Proprietary, coed. Awards: associate and bachelor's degrees. 10 undergraduate majors. Total enrollment: 2,651. Undergraduates: 2,651. Freshmen: 359.

GIFT AID (NEED-BASED) *Scholarships, grants, and awards:* Federal Pell, FSEOG, state, private, college/university gift aid from institutional funds.

GIFT AID (NON-NEED-BASED) *Scholarships, grants, and awards by category: Academic Interests/Achievement:* general academic interests/achievements. *Creative Arts/Performance:* applied art and design, general creative arts/performance.

LOANS *Programs:* Federal Direct (Subsidized and Unsubsidized Stafford, PLUS), FFEL (Subsidized and Unsubsidized Stafford, PLUS), Perkins, Sallie Mae Loans.

WORK-STUDY *Federal work-study:* Total amount: $45,617; jobs available. *State or other work-study/employment:* Total amount: $2925 (100% non-need-based).

APPLYING FOR FINANCIAL AID *Required financial aid forms:* FAFSA, state aid form.

CONTACT Rena Marroquin, Financial Aid Office, The Art Institute of Atlanta, 6600 Peachtree Dunwoody Road, 100 Embassy Road, Atlanta, GA 30326, 770-394-8300 or toll-free 800-275-4242.

THE ART INSTITUTE OF BOSTON AT LESLEY UNIVERSITY
Boston, MA

ABOUT THE INSTITUTION Independent, coed. Awards: bachelor's and master's degrees and post-bachelor's certificates. 4 undergraduate majors. Total enrollment: 6,521. Undergraduates: 1,042. Freshmen: 233.

GIFT AID (NEED-BASED) *Scholarships, grants, and awards:* Federal Pell, FSEOG, state, private, college/university gift aid from institutional funds.

GIFT AID (NON-NEED-BASED) *Scholarships, grants, and awards by category: Academic Interests/Achievement:* general academic interests/achievements. *Creative Arts/Performance:* applied art and design, art/fine arts. *Special Achievements/Activities:* community service, general special achievements/activities, memberships. *Special Characteristics:* ethnic background, local/state students, members of minority groups.

LOANS *Programs:* FFEL (Subsidized and Unsubsidized Stafford, PLUS), state.

WORK-STUDY *Federal work-study:* Total amount: $181,551; 142 jobs averaging $1278. *State or other work-study/employment:* Total amount: $153,889 (100% non-need-based). 132 part-time jobs averaging $1177.

APPLYING FOR FINANCIAL AID *Required financial aid forms:* FAFSA, institution's own form, parent and student federal income tax forms.

CONTACT Financial Aid Officer, The Art Institute of Boston at Lesley University, 700 Beacon Street, Boston, MA 02215-2598, 617-349-8714 or toll-free 800-773-0494 (in-state). *Fax:* 617-437-1226.

THE ART INSTITUTE OF CALIFORNIA–LOS ANGELES
Santa Monica, CA

CONTACT Financial Aid Office, The Art Institute of California–Los Angeles, 2900 31st Street, Santa Monica, CA 90405-3035, 310-752-4700 or toll-free 888-646-4610.

THE ART INSTITUTE OF CALIFORNIA–ORANGE COUNTY
Santa Ana, CA

CONTACT Financial Aid Office, The Art Institute of California–Orange County, 3601 West Sunflower Avenue, Santa Ana, CA 92704-9888, 714-830-0200 or toll-free 888-549-3055.

THE ART INSTITUTE OF CALIFORNIA–SAN DIEGO
San Diego, CA

CONTACT Monica McCormick, Financial Aid Administrator, The Art Institute of California–San Diego, 10025 Mesa Rim Road, San Diego, CA 92121, 619-546-0602 or toll-free 800-591-2422 Ext. 3117 (in-state).

THE ART INSTITUTE OF CALIFORNIA–SAN FRANCISCO
San Francisco, CA

CONTACT Director of Student Financial Services, The Art Institute of California–San Francisco, 1170 Market Street, San Francisco, CA 94102-4908, 415-865-0198 or toll-free 888-493-3261. *Fax:* 415-863-5831.

THE ART INSTITUTE OF COLORADO
Denver, CO

Tuition & fees: $23,040	Average undergraduate aid package: N/A

ABOUT THE INSTITUTION Proprietary, coed. Awards: associate and bachelor's degrees. 10 undergraduate majors. Total enrollment: 2,226. Undergraduates: 2,226. Freshmen: 674. Federal methodology is used as a basis for awarding need-based institutional aid.

UNDERGRADUATE EXPENSES for 2004–05 *Tuition:* full-time $23,040; part-time $369 per credit. Full-time tuition and fees vary according to course load. Part-time tuition and fees vary according to course load. *Payment plans:* Guaranteed tuition, installment.

UNDERGRADUATE FINANCIAL AID (Fall 2004, est.) 1,621 applied for aid; of those 100% were deemed to have need. 100% of undergraduates with need received aid. 3% of all full-time undergraduates had no need and received non-need-based gift aid.

GIFT AID (NEED-BASED) *Total amount:* $2,174,888 (62% federal, 15% state, 23% institutional). *Receiving aid:* All full-time undergraduates: 30% (591). *Scholarships, grants, and awards:* Federal Pell, FSEOG, state, private, college/university gift aid from institutional funds.

GIFT AID (NON-NEED-BASED) *Total amount:* $1,131,209 (8% state, 29% institutional, 63% external sources). *Receiving aid:* Undergraduates: 3% (65). *Scholarships, grants, and awards by category: Academic Interests/Achievement:* general academic interests/achievements. *Creative Arts/Performance:* applied art and design, art/fine arts, cinema/film/broadcasting, general creative arts/performance. *Special Achievements/Activities:* general special achievements/activities, junior miss. *Tuition waivers:* Full or partial for employees or children of employees.

LOANS *Student loans:* $10,683,917 (55% need-based, 45% non-need-based). 70% of past graduating class borrowed through all loan programs. *Average indebtedness per student:* $30,000. *Parent loans:* $3,626,966 (100% need-based). *Programs:* FFEL (Subsidized and Unsubsidized Stafford, PLUS), Perkins, state.

WORK-STUDY *Federal work-study:* Total amount: $88,142; jobs available. *State or other work-study/employment:* Total amount: $208,110 (100% need-based). 34 part-time jobs available.

APPLYING FOR FINANCIAL AID *Required financial aid forms:* FAFSA, institution's own form. *Financial aid deadline:* Continuous. *Notification date:* Continuous beginning 2/1. Students must reply within 2 weeks of notification.

CONTACT Shannon May, Director of Student Financial Services, The Art Institute of Colorado, 1200 Lincoln Street, Denver, CO 80203-2903, 303-837-0825 Ext. 4747 or toll-free 800-275-2420. *Fax:* 303-860-8520. *E-mail:* mays@aii.edu.

THE ART INSTITUTE OF DALLAS
Dallas, TX

CONTACT Maria A. Maldonado, Director of Accounting and Financial Services / Vice President, The Art Institute of Dallas, 2 Northpark, 8080 Park Lane, Suite 100, Dallas, TX 75231, 214-692-8080 Ext. 680 or toll-free 800-275-4243. *Fax:* 214-692-6541. *E-mail:* maldonam@aii.edu.

THE ART INSTITUTE OF FORT LAUDERDALE
Fort Lauderdale, FL

CONTACT Office of Student Financial Services, The Art Institute of Fort Lauderdale, 1799 Southeast 17th Street Causeway, Fort Lauderdale, FL 33316-3000, 954-527-1799 or toll-free 800-275-7603.

THE ART INSTITUTE OF HOUSTON
Houston, TX

CONTACT Sara Benson, Director of Accounting and Financial Services, The Art Institute of Houston, 1900 Yorktown, Houston, TX 77056, 713-623-2040 Ext. 780 or toll-free 800-275-4244. *Fax:* 713-966-2700. *E-mail:* bensons@aii.edu.

THE ART INSTITUTE OF LAS VEGAS
Henderson, NV

CONTACT Financial Aid Office, The Art Institute of Las Vegas, 2350 Corporate Circle Drive, Henderson, NV 89074, 702-369-9944.

THE ART INSTITUTE OF PHOENIX
Phoenix, AZ

CONTACT Paula Cady, Director of Student Financial Services, The Art Institute of Phoenix, 2233 West Dunlap Avenue, Phoenix, AZ 85021, 602-678-4300 Ext. 109 or toll-free 800-474-2479. *Fax:* 602-997-0191. *E-mail:* cadyp@aii.edu.

THE ART INSTITUTE OF PITTSBURGH
Pittsburgh, PA

ABOUT THE INSTITUTION Proprietary, coed. Awards: associate and bachelor's degrees. 36 undergraduate majors. Total enrollment: 4,872. Undergraduates: 4,872. Freshmen: 1,270.
GIFT AID (NEED-BASED) *Scholarships, grants, and awards:* Federal Pell, FSEOG, state, private, college/university gift aid from institutional funds.
LOANS *Programs:* FFEL (Subsidized and Unsubsidized Stafford, PLUS), Perkins, alternative loans.
APPLYING FOR FINANCIAL AID *Required financial aid form:* FAFSA.
CONTACT Ms. Gayle J. Knight, Student Financial Services Director, The Art Institute of Pittsburgh, 526 Penn Avenue, Pittsburgh, PA 15222-3269, 412-263-6600 or toll-free 800-275-2470.

THE ART INSTITUTE OF PORTLAND
Portland, OR

Tuition & fees: $16,610	Average undergraduate aid package: $7643

ABOUT THE INSTITUTION Proprietary, coed. Awards: associate and bachelor's degrees. 7 undergraduate majors. Total enrollment: 1,543. Undergraduates: 1,543. Freshmen: 196. Federal methodology is used as a basis for awarding need-based institutional aid.
UNDERGRADUATE EXPENSES for 2005–06 *Application fee:* $50. *Comprehensive fee:* $21,965 includes full-time tuition ($16,560), mandatory fees ($50), and room and board ($5355). Full-time tuition and fees vary according to course load. Room and board charges vary according to housing facility. *Part-time tuition:* $368 per credit. Part-time tuition and fees vary according to course load. *Payment plans:* Guaranteed tuition, installment.
FRESHMAN FINANCIAL AID (Fall 2004, est.) 220 applied for aid; of those 97% were deemed to have need. 100% of freshmen with need received aid; of those 1% had need fully met. *Average percent of need met:* 1% (excluding resources awarded to replace EFC). *Average financial aid package:* $4723 (excluding resources awarded to replace EFC). 10% of all full-time freshmen had no need and received non-need-based gift aid.
UNDERGRADUATE FINANCIAL AID (Fall 2004, est.) 1,046 applied for aid; of those 89% were deemed to have need. 98% of undergraduates with need received aid; of those .4% had need fully met. *Average percent of need met:* 1% (excluding resources awarded to replace EFC). *Average financial aid package:* $7643 (excluding resources awarded to replace EFC). 7% of all full-time undergraduates had no need and received non-need-based gift aid.
GIFT AID (NEED-BASED) *Total amount:* $2,249,197 (86% federal, 12% institutional, 2% external sources). *Receiving aid:* Freshmen: 37% (86); All full-time undergraduates: 49% (552). *Average award:* Freshmen: $1611; Undergraduates: $1642. *Scholarships, grants, and awards:* Federal Pell, FSEOG, private, college/university gift aid from institutional funds, Bureau of Indian Affairs Grants.
GIFT AID (NON-NEED-BASED) *Total amount:* $976,439 (38% federal, 10% state, 44% institutional, 8% external sources). *Receiving aid:* Freshmen: 33% (77); Undergraduates: 9% (97). *Average Award:* Freshmen: $1063; Undergraduates: $4240. *Scholarships, grants, and awards by category:* Creative Arts/Performance: applied art and design, general creative arts/performance. *Special Characteristics:* 16 awards ($170,042 total): children of faculty/staff. *Tuition waivers:* Full or partial for employees or children of employees.
LOANS *Student loans:* $12,727,827 (41% need-based, 59% non-need-based). 87% of past graduating class borrowed through all loan programs. *Average indebtedness per student:* $23,500. *Average need-based loan:* Freshmen: $2625; Undergraduates: $4469. *Parent loans:* $5,286,942 (100% non-need-based). *Programs:* FFEL (Subsidized and Unsubsidized Stafford, PLUS), state, alternative loans.
WORK-STUDY *Federal work-study:* Total amount: $73,701; 30 jobs averaging $2457.
APPLYING FOR FINANCIAL AID *Required financial aid forms:* FAFSA, financial aid transcript (for transfers). *Financial aid deadline (priority):* 3/1. *Notification date:* Continuous beginning 1/1. Students must reply within 2 weeks of notification.
CONTACT Mr. Mickey Jacobson, Director of Student Financial Services, The Art Institute of Portland, 1122 Northwest Davis Street, Portland, OR 97209-2911, 503-228-6528 Ext. 4728 or toll-free 888-228-6528. *Fax:* 503-228-4227. *E-mail:* mjacobson@aii.edu.

THE ART INSTITUTE OF SEATTLE
Seattle, WA

CONTACT Shelly DuBois, Vice President/Director of Administrative and Financial Services, The Art Institute of Seattle, 2323 Elliott Avenue, Seattle, WA 98121, 206-448-0900 or toll-free 800-275-2471. *Fax:* 206-448-2501.

THE ART INSTITUTE OF TAMPA
Tampa, FL

CONTACT Financial Aid Office, The Art Institute of Tampa, 4401 North Himes Avenue, Suite 150, Tampa, FL 33614, 866-703-3277.

THE ART INSTITUTE OF WASHINGTON
Arlington, VA

CONTACT Director of Student Financial Services, The Art Institute of Washington, 1820 North Fort Myer Drive, Arlington, VA 22209, 703-247-6849 or toll-free 877-303-3771. *Fax:* 703-247-6829.

THE ART INSTITUTES INTERNATIONAL MINNESOTA
Minneapolis, MN

CONTACT Tiffany Robb, Student Financial Planner, The Art Institutes International Minnesota, 825 2nd Avenue South, Minneapolis, MN 55402, 612-332-3361 Ext. 110 or toll-free 800-777-3643. *Fax:* 612-332-3934. *E-mail:* robbt@aii.edu.

ASBURY COLLEGE
Wilmore, KY

Tuition & fees: $17,808	Average undergraduate aid package: $13,104

ABOUT THE INSTITUTION Independent nondenominational, coed. Awards: bachelor's and master's degrees. 37 undergraduate majors. Total enrollment: 1,278. Undergraduates: 1,218. Freshmen: 302. Federal methodology is used as a basis for awarding need-based institutional aid.

UNDERGRADUATE EXPENSES for 2004–05 *Application fee:* $30. *Comprehensive fee:* $22,306 includes full-time tuition ($17,660), mandatory fees ($148), and room and board ($4498). *College room only:* $2560. Full-time tuition and fees vary according to course load. Room and board charges vary according to board plan, housing facility, and location. *Part-time tuition:* $679 per semester hour. Part-time tuition and fees vary according to course load. *Payment plans:* Installment, deferred payment.

FRESHMAN FINANCIAL AID (Fall 2004, est.) 263 applied for aid; of those 83% were deemed to have need. 100% of freshmen with need received aid; of those 27% had need fully met. *Average percent of need met:* 82% (excluding resources awarded to replace EFC). *Average financial aid package:* $13,644 (excluding resources awarded to replace EFC). 12% of all full-time freshmen had no need and received non-need-based gift aid.

UNDERGRADUATE FINANCIAL AID (Fall 2004, est.) 940 applied for aid; of those 87% were deemed to have need. 100% of undergraduates with need received aid; of those 25% had need fully met. *Average percent of need met:* 80% (excluding resources awarded to replace EFC). *Average financial aid package:* $13,104 (excluding resources awarded to replace EFC). 8% of all full-time undergraduates had no need and received non-need-based gift aid.

GIFT AID (NEED-BASED) *Total amount:* $7,844,775 (13% federal, 10% state, 70% institutional, 7% external sources). *Receiving aid:* Freshmen: 72% (217); All full-time undergraduates: 70% (809). *Average award:* Freshmen: $7937; Undergraduates: $7786. *Scholarships, grants, and awards:* Federal Pell, FSEOG, state, private, college/university gift aid from institutional funds.

GIFT AID (NON-NEED-BASED) *Total amount:* $1,340,511 (9% state, 82% institutional, 9% external sources). *Receiving aid:* Freshmen: 31% (93); Undergraduates: 21% (239). *Average Award: Freshmen:* $10,856; *Undergraduates:* $10,655. *Scholarships, grants, and awards by category: Academic Interests/Achievement:* general academic interests/achievements. *Creative Arts/Performance:* music. *Special Achievements/Activities:* leadership. *Special Characteristics:* children and siblings of alumni, children of faculty/staff, ethnic background, international students, siblings of current students. *Tuition waivers:* Full or partial for employees or children of employees, senior citizens. *ROTC:* Army cooperative, Air Force cooperative.

LOANS *Student loans:* $4,704,706 (91% need-based, 9% non-need-based). 70% of past graduating class borrowed through all loan programs. *Average indebtedness per student:* $18,972. *Average need-based loan:* Freshmen: $3176; Undergraduates: $4041. *Parent loans:* $1,114,541 (85% need-based, 15% non-need-based). *Programs:* FFEL (Subsidized and Unsubsidized Stafford, PLUS), Perkins, state, college/university, alternative loans.

WORK-STUDY *Federal work-study:* Total amount: $429,723; jobs available. *State or other work-study/employment:* Total amount: $306,241 (100% need-based). Part-time jobs available.

ATHLETIC AWARDS *Total amount:* $66,255 (85% need-based, 15% non-need-based).

APPLYING FOR FINANCIAL AID *Required financial aid forms:* FAFSA, institution's own form. *Financial aid deadline (priority):* 3/1. *Notification date:* Continuous beginning 2/15. Students must reply within 4 weeks of notification.

CONTACT Ronald Anderson, Director of Financial Aid, Asbury College, 1 Macklem Drive, Wilmore, KY 40390-1198, 859-858-3511 Ext. 2195 or toll-free 800-888-1818. *Fax:* 859-858-3921.

ASHLAND UNIVERSITY
Ashland, OH

Tuition & fees: $19,778	Average undergraduate aid package: $16,698

ABOUT THE INSTITUTION Independent religious, coed. Awards: associate, bachelor's, master's, doctoral, and first professional degrees. 70 undergraduate majors. Total enrollment: 6,922. Undergraduates: 2,859. Freshmen: 575.

UNDERGRADUATE EXPENSES for 2005–06 *Application fee:* $25. *Comprehensive fee:* $27,092 includes full-time tuition ($19,314), mandatory fees ($464), and room and board ($7314). *College room only:* $3928. Full-time tuition and fees vary according to location and reciprocity agreements. Room and board charges vary according to board plan and housing facility. *Part-time tuition:* $593 per credit hour. Part-time tuition and fees vary according to course load, location, and program. *Payment plan:* Installment.

FRESHMAN FINANCIAL AID (Fall 2004, est.) 572 applied for aid; of those 85% were deemed to have need. 99% of freshmen with need received aid. *Average percent of need met:* 90% (excluding resources awarded to replace EFC). *Average financial aid package:* $16,481 (excluding resources awarded to replace EFC). 12% of all full-time freshmen had no need and received non-need-based gift aid.

UNDERGRADUATE FINANCIAL AID (Fall 2004, est.) 2,111 applied for aid; of those 85% were deemed to have need. 100% of undergraduates with need received aid. *Average percent of need met:* 90% (excluding resources awarded to replace EFC). *Average financial aid package:* $16,698 (excluding resources awarded to replace EFC). 14% of all full-time undergraduates had no need and received non-need-based gift aid.

GIFT AID (NEED-BASED) *Total amount:* $17,098,660 (13% federal, 18% state, 67% institutional, 2% external sources). *Receiving aid:* Freshmen: 83% (478); All full-time undergraduates: 79% (1,790). *Average award:* Freshmen: $12,031; Undergraduates: $11,313. *Scholarships, grants, and awards:* Federal Pell, FSEOG, state, private, college/university gift aid from institutional funds.

GIFT AID (NON-NEED-BASED) *Total amount:* $2,192,248 (19% state, 78% institutional, 3% external sources). *Average Award: Freshmen:* $5829; *Undergraduates:* $5871. *Scholarships, grants, and awards by category: Academic Interests/Achievement:* 1,377 awards ($6,295,000 total): general academic interests/achievements, mathematics, physical sciences, social sciences. *Creative Arts/Performance:* 162 awards ($340,000 total): art/fine arts, music, theater/drama. *Special Characteristics:* 400 awards ($2,392,000 total): children and siblings of alumni, children of faculty/staff, international students, relatives of clergy, religious affiliation. *Tuition waivers:* Full or partial for children of alumni, employees or children of employees, senior citizens.

LOANS *Student loans:* $12,021,756 (75% need-based, 25% non-need-based). 75% of past graduating class borrowed through all loan programs. *Average indebtedness per student:* $18,250. *Average need-based loan:* Freshmen: $3201; Undergraduates: $4120. *Parent loans:* $3,719,860 (78% need-based, 22% non-need-based). *Programs:* Federal Direct (Subsidized and Unsubsidized Stafford, PLUS), Perkins, college/university.

WORK-STUDY *Federal work-study:* Total amount: $2,030,720; 1,107 jobs averaging $1834.

ATHLETIC AWARDS *Total amount:* $3,117,226 (71% need-based, 29% non-need-based).

APPLYING FOR FINANCIAL AID *Required financial aid forms:* FAFSA, institution's own form. *Financial aid deadline:* Continuous. *Notification date:* Continuous.

CONTACT Mr. Stephen C. Howell, Director of Financial Aid, Ashland University, 401 College Avenue, Room 310, Ashland, OH 44805-3702, 419-289-5944 or toll-free 800-882-1548. *Fax:* 419-289-5976. *E-mail:* showell@ashland.edu.

ASPEN UNIVERSITY
Denver, CO

CONTACT Financial Aid Office, Aspen University, 501 South Cherry Street, Suite 350, Denver, CO 80246, 303-333-4224 or toll-free 800-441-4746 Ext. 177 (in-state).

ASSUMPTION COLLEGE
Worcester, MA

Tuition & fees: $22,655	Average undergraduate aid package: $14,941

ABOUT THE INSTITUTION Independent Roman Catholic, coed. Awards: bachelor's and master's degrees and post-master's certificates. 33 undergraduate majors. Total enrollment: 2,452. Undergraduates: 2,184. Freshmen: 633. Federal methodology is used as a basis for awarding need-based institutional aid.

UNDERGRADUATE EXPENSES for 2004–05 *Application fee:* $50. *Comprehensive fee:* $28,050 includes full-time tuition ($22,260), mandatory fees ($395), and room and board ($5395). *College room only:* $3245. Full-time tuition and fees vary according to course load and reciprocity agreements. Room and board charges vary according to board plan and housing facility. *Part-time tuition:* $742 per credit hour. *Part-time fees:* $165 per year. Part-time tuition and fees vary according to course load. *Payment plan:* Installment.

FRESHMAN FINANCIAL AID (Fall 2003) 545 applied for aid; of those 85% were deemed to have need. 100% of freshmen with need received aid; of those 17%

had need fully met. *Average percent of need met:* 70% (excluding resources awarded to replace EFC). *Average financial aid package:* $14,485 (excluding resources awarded to replace EFC). 20% of all full-time freshmen had no need and received non-need-based gift aid.

UNDERGRADUATE FINANCIAL AID (Fall 2003) 1,789 applied for aid; of those 88% were deemed to have need. 100% of undergraduates with need received aid; of those 18% had need fully met. *Average percent of need met:* 72% (excluding resources awarded to replace EFC). *Average financial aid package:* $14,941 (excluding resources awarded to replace EFC). 21% of all full-time undergraduates had no need and received non-need-based gift aid.

GIFT AID (NEED-BASED) *Total amount:* $16,304,447 (5% federal, 5% state, 87% institutional, 3% external sources). *Receiving aid:* Freshmen: 72% (457); All full-time undergraduates: 71% (1,534). *Average award:* Freshmen: $11,485; Undergraduates: $10,894. *Scholarships, grants, and awards:* Federal Pell, FSEOG, state, private, college/university gift aid from institutional funds.

GIFT AID (NON-NEED-BASED) *Total amount:* $3,643,245 (95% institutional, 5% external sources). *Receiving aid:* Freshmen: 8% (50); Undergraduates: 7% (143). *Average Award: Freshmen:* $12,243; *Undergraduates:* $12,000. *Scholarships, grants, and awards by category: Academic Interests/Achievement:* 1,151 awards ($9,641,875 total): general academic interests/achievements. *Tuition waivers:* Full or partial for minority students, employees or children of employees. *ROTC:* Army cooperative, Air Force cooperative.

LOANS *Student loans:* $11,458,452 (71% need-based, 29% non-need-based). 92% of past graduating class borrowed through all loan programs. *Average indebtedness per student:* $24,064. *Average need-based loan:* Freshmen: $3277; Undergraduates: $4477. *Parent loans:* $6,203,434 (34% need-based, 66% non-need-based). *Programs:* FFEL (Subsidized and Unsubsidized Stafford, PLUS), Perkins, state, college/university.

WORK-STUDY *Federal work-study:* Total amount: $495,799; 519 jobs averaging $1436.

ATHLETIC AWARDS *Total amount:* $488,802 (12% need-based, 88% non-need-based).

APPLYING FOR FINANCIAL AID *Required financial aid form:* FAFSA. *Financial aid deadline (priority):* 2/1. *Notification date:* Continuous beginning 2/15. Students must reply by 4/30.

CONTACT Karen Puntillo, Director of Financial Aid, Assumption College, 500 Salisbury Street, Worcester, MA 01609-1296, 508-767-7157 or toll-free 888-882-7786. *Fax:* 508-767-7376. *E-mail:* fa@assumption.edu.

ATHENS STATE UNIVERSITY
Athens, AL

Tuition & fees (AL res): $3870	Average undergraduate aid package: N/A

ABOUT THE INSTITUTION State-supported, coed. Awards: bachelor's degrees. 29 undergraduate majors. Total enrollment: 2,577. Undergraduates: 2,577. Federal methodology is used as a basis for awarding need-based institutional aid.

UNDERGRADUATE EXPENSES for 2004–05 *Application fee:* $30. *Tuition, state resident:* full-time $3330; part-time $111 per semester hour. *Tuition, nonresident:* full-time $6660; part-time $222 per semester hour. *Required fees:* full-time $540; $18 per semester hour. *College room and board: room only:* $900.

UNDERGRADUATE FINANCIAL AID (Fall 2003) 1,293 applied for aid; of those 100% were deemed to have need. 97% of undergraduates with need received aid.

GIFT AID (NEED-BASED) *Total amount:* $2,345,970 (99% federal, 1% state). *Receiving aid:* All full-time undergraduates: 37% (937). *Scholarships, grants, and awards:* Federal Pell, FSEOG, state, private, college/university gift aid from institutional funds.

GIFT AID (NON-NEED-BASED) *Total amount:* $837,106 (49% state, 30% institutional, 21% external sources). *Scholarships, grants, and awards by category: Academic Interests/Achievement:* 40 awards ($167,987 total): biological sciences, business, computer science, education, English, general academic interests/achievements, humanities, international studies, mathematics, physical sciences, religion/biblical studies, social sciences. *Creative Arts/Performance:* art/fine arts, journalism/publications. *Special Achievements/Activities:* cheerleading/drum major, general special achievements/activities, leadership. *Special Characteristics:* children and siblings of alumni, children of faculty/staff. *Tuition waivers:* Full or partial for employees or children of employees, senior citizens.

LOANS *Student loans:* $8,024,243 (56% need-based, 44% non-need-based). 49% of past graduating class borrowed through all loan programs. *Average indebtedness per student:* $8137. *Programs:* Federal Direct (Subsidized and Unsubsidized Stafford).

WORK-STUDY *Federal work-study:* Total amount: $82,341; 57 jobs averaging $2587. *State or other work-study/employment:* Total amount: $117,588 (100% non-need-based). Part-time jobs available.

ATHLETIC AWARDS *Total amount:* $131,276 (100% non-need-based).

APPLYING FOR FINANCIAL AID *Required financial aid form:* FAFSA. *Financial aid deadline:* Continuous. *Notification date:* Continuous beginning 5/1. Students must reply within 2 weeks of notification.

CONTACT Renee Stanford, Financial Aid Officer, Athens State University, 300 North Beaty Street, Athens, AL 35611, 256-233-8122 or toll-free 800-522-0272. *Fax:* 256-233-8178. *E-mail:* dobbsar@athens.edu.

ATLANTA CHRISTIAN COLLEGE
East Point, GA

CONTACT Blair Walker, Director of Financial Aid, Atlanta Christian College, 2605 Ben Hill Road, East Point, GA 30344, 404-761-8861 or toll-free 800-776-1ACC. *Fax:* 404-669-2024. *E-mail:* blairw@acc.edu.

ATLANTA COLLEGE OF ART
Atlanta, GA

Tuition & fees: $17,500	Average undergraduate aid package: $11,981

ABOUT THE INSTITUTION Independent, coed. Awards: bachelor's degrees. 12 undergraduate majors. Total enrollment: 330. Undergraduates: 330. Freshmen: 72. Federal methodology is used as a basis for awarding need-based institutional aid.

UNDERGRADUATE EXPENSES for 2004–05 *Application fee:* $30. *Tuition:* full-time $16,900; part-time $705 per semester hour. *Required fees:* full-time $600; $80 per year part-time. Full-time tuition and fees vary according to course load. Part-time tuition and fees vary according to course load. *Payment plan:* Installment.

FRESHMAN FINANCIAL AID (Fall 2004, est.) 70 applied for aid; of those 90% were deemed to have need. 100% of freshmen with need received aid; of those 8% had need fully met. *Average percent of need met:* 62% (excluding resources awarded to replace EFC). *Average financial aid package:* $11,887 (excluding resources awarded to replace EFC). 10% of all full-time freshmen had no need and received non-need-based gift aid.

UNDERGRADUATE FINANCIAL AID (Fall 2004, est.) 241 applied for aid; of those 93% were deemed to have need. 100% of undergraduates with need received aid; of those 9% had need fully met. *Average percent of need met:* 61% (excluding resources awarded to replace EFC). *Average financial aid package:* $11,981 (excluding resources awarded to replace EFC). 6% of all full-time undergraduates had no need and received non-need-based gift aid.

GIFT AID (NEED-BASED) *Total amount:* $2,006,198 (19% federal, 15% state, 58% institutional, 8% external sources). *Receiving aid:* Freshmen: 86% (62); All full-time undergraduates: 74% (219). *Average award:* Freshmen: $9455; Undergraduates: $8610. *Scholarships, grants, and awards:* Federal Pell, FSEOG, state, private, college/university gift aid from institutional funds.

GIFT AID (NON-NEED-BASED) *Total amount:* $136,229 (33% state, 58% institutional, 9% external sources). *Receiving aid:* Freshmen: 7% (5); Undergraduates: 4% (11). *Average Award: Freshmen:* $9012; *Undergraduates:* $12,944. *Scholarships, grants, and awards by category: Academic Interests/ Achievement:* 27 awards ($132,775 total): general academic interests/ achievements. *Creative Arts/Performance:* 80 awards ($224,070 total): art/fine arts. *Tuition waivers:* Full or partial for employees or children of employees.

LOANS *Student loans:* $1,556,506 (87% need-based, 13% non-need-based). 75% of past graduating class borrowed through all loan programs. *Average indebtedness per student:* $24,256. *Average need-based loan:* Freshmen: $2525; Undergraduates: $3437. *Parent loans:* $1,097,548 (47% need-based, 53% non-need-based). *Programs:* FFEL (Subsidized and Unsubsidized Stafford, PLUS), college/university.

WORK-STUDY *Federal work-study:* Total amount: $69,843; 65 jobs averaging $1898. *State or other work-study/employment:* 32 part-time jobs averaging $1898.

APPLYING FOR FINANCIAL AID *Required financial aid forms:* FAFSA, institution's own form, need-based aid application form. *Financial aid deadline (priority):* 3/15. *Notification date:* 4/1. Students must reply within 3 weeks of notification.

CONTACT Ms. Teresa Tantillo, Director of Financial Aid, Atlanta College of Art, 1280 Peachtree Street, NE, Atlanta, GA 30309-3582, 404-733-5111 or toll-free 800-832-2104. *Fax:* 404-733-5107.

ATLANTIC COLLEGE
Guaynabo, PR

Tuition & fees: N/R	Average undergraduate aid package: N/A

ABOUT THE INSTITUTION Independent. Awards: associate and bachelor's degrees. Total enrollment: 370. Undergraduates: 370. Freshmen: 132. Federal methodology is used as a basis for awarding need-based institutional aid.

GIFT AID (NEED-BASED) *Total amount:* $2,110,797 (92% federal, 8% state). *Scholarships, grants, and awards:* Federal Pell, FSEOG, state.

LOANS *Student loans:* $92,802 (100% need-based). 12% of past graduating class borrowed through all loan programs. *Parent loans:* $31,334 (100% non-need-based). *Programs:* FFEL (Subsidized and Unsubsidized Stafford, PLUS).

APPLYING FOR FINANCIAL AID *Required financial aid forms:* FAFSA, institution's own form, commonwealth aid form. *Financial aid deadline:* Continuous. *Notification date:* Continuous. Students must reply within 2 weeks of notification.

CONTACT Mrs. Velma Aponte, Financial Aid Coordinator, Atlantic College, Calle Colton #9, Guaynabo, PR 00970, 787-720-1092. *E-mail:* atlaneco@coqui.net.

ATLANTIC UNION COLLEGE
South Lancaster, MA

Tuition & fees: $12,780	Average undergraduate aid package: $10,291

ABOUT THE INSTITUTION Independent Seventh-day Adventist, coed. Awards: associate, bachelor's, and master's degrees. 45 undergraduate majors. Total enrollment: 473. Undergraduates: 398. Federal methodology is used as a basis for awarding need-based institutional aid.

UNDERGRADUATE EXPENSES for 2004–05 *Application fee:* $25. *Comprehensive fee:* $16,560 includes full-time tuition ($12,000), mandatory fees ($780), and room and board ($3780). *College room only:* $2180. Full-time tuition and fees vary according to course load and program. Room and board charges vary according to board plan and housing facility. *Part-time tuition:* $500 per credit hour. Part-time tuition and fees vary according to class time, course load, and program.

FRESHMAN FINANCIAL AID (Fall 2004, est.) 58 applied for aid; of those 95% were deemed to have need. 98% of freshmen with need received aid; of those 15% had need fully met. *Average percent of need met:* 65% (excluding resources awarded to replace EFC). *Average financial aid package:* $9016 (excluding resources awarded to replace EFC). 40% of all full-time freshmen had no need and received non-need-based gift aid.

UNDERGRADUATE FINANCIAL AID (Fall 2004, est.) 317 applied for aid; of those 96% were deemed to have need. 98% of undergraduates with need received aid; of those 13% had need fully met. *Average percent of need met:* 69% (excluding resources awarded to replace EFC). *Average financial aid package:* $10,291 (excluding resources awarded to replace EFC). 22% of all full-time undergraduates had no need and received non-need-based gift aid.

GIFT AID (NEED-BASED) *Total amount:* $1,760,839 (46% federal, 5% state, 43% institutional, 6% external sources). *Receiving aid:* Freshmen: 55% (53); All full-time undergraduates: 70% (280). *Average award:* Freshmen: $5281; Undergraduates: $5913. *Scholarships, grants, and awards:* Federal Pell, FSEOG, state, private, college/university gift aid from institutional funds, Federal Nursing.

GIFT AID (NON-NEED-BASED) *Total amount:* $411,154 (81% institutional, 19% external sources). *Receiving aid:* Freshmen: 1% (1); Undergraduates: 2% (7). *Average Award:* Freshmen: $3470; Undergraduates: $5580. *Scholarships, grants, and awards by category: Academic Interests/Achievement:* 18 awards ($4500 total): general academic interests/achievements. *Creative Arts/Performance:* 78 awards ($343,656 total): music. *Special Achievements/Activities:* 83 awards ($139,401 total): leadership. *Special Characteristics:* 92 awards ($262,997 total): children of current students, children of faculty/staff, international students, siblings of current students. *Tuition waivers:* Full or partial for employees or children of employees, senior citizens.

LOANS *Student loans:* $2,564,289 (80% need-based, 20% non-need-based). 91% of past graduating class borrowed through all loan programs. *Average indebtedness per student:* $25,000. *Average need-based loan:* Freshmen: $3382; Undergraduates: $4289. *Parent loans:* $255,189 (61% need-based, 39% non-need-based). *Programs:* FFEL (Subsidized and Unsubsidized Stafford, PLUS), Perkins, Federal Nursing, state, college/university, TERI Loans, Signature Loans, Campus Door.

WORK-STUDY *Federal work-study:* Total amount: $208,290; 130 jobs averaging $1602. *State or other work-study/employment:* Total amount: $122,357 (21% need-based, 79% non-need-based). 45 part-time jobs averaging $576.

APPLYING FOR FINANCIAL AID *Required financial aid form:* FAFSA. *Financial aid deadline (priority):* 4/15. *Notification date:* Continuous beginning 4/16. Students must reply within 2 weeks of notification.

CONTACT Sandra Boucher, Acting Director of Student Financial Services, Atlantic Union College, PO Box 1000, South Lancaster, MA 01561-1000, 978-368-2275 or toll-free 800-282-2030. *Fax:* 978-368-2283. *E-mail:* sboucher@atlanticuc.edu.

AUBURN UNIVERSITY
Auburn University, AL

Tuition & fees (AL res): $4828	Average undergraduate aid package: $7626

ABOUT THE INSTITUTION State-supported, coed. Awards: bachelor's, master's, doctoral, and first professional degrees and post-master's certificates. 136 undergraduate majors. Total enrollment: 22,928. Undergraduates: 18,896. Freshmen: 3,594. Federal methodology is used as a basis for awarding need-based institutional aid.

UNDERGRADUATE EXPENSES for 2004–05 *Application fee:* $25. *Tuition, state resident:* full-time $4610; part-time $191 per credit hour. *Tuition, nonresident:* full-time $13,830; part-time $573 per credit hour. Full-time tuition and fees vary according to course load and program. Part-time tuition and fees vary according to course load and program. *College room and board:* $6686; *room only:* $2648. Room and board charges vary according to housing facility. *Payment plan:* Installment.

FRESHMAN FINANCIAL AID (Fall 2003) 1826 applied for aid; of those 65% were deemed to have need. 96% of freshmen with need received aid; of those 20% had need fully met. *Average percent of need met:* 50% (excluding resources awarded to replace EFC). *Average financial aid package:* $7127 (excluding resources awarded to replace EFC). 9% of all full-time freshmen had no need and received non-need-based gift aid.

UNDERGRADUATE FINANCIAL AID (Fall 2003) 8,164 applied for aid; of those 77% were deemed to have need. 97% of undergraduates with need received aid; of those 15% had need fully met. *Average percent of need met:* 51% (excluding resources awarded to replace EFC). *Average financial aid package:* $7626 (excluding resources awarded to replace EFC). 5% of all full-time undergraduates had no need and received non-need-based gift aid.

GIFT AID (NEED-BASED) *Total amount:* $17,466,031 (48% federal, 6% state, 28% institutional, 18% external sources). *Receiving aid:* Freshmen: 25% (919); All full-time undergraduates: 24% (4,176). *Average award:* Freshmen: $3983; Undergraduates: $3949. *Scholarships, grants, and awards:* Federal Pell, FSEOG, state, private, college/university gift aid from institutional funds.

GIFT AID (NON-NEED-BASED) *Total amount:* $4,949,310 (8% state, 2% institutional, 90% external sources). *Receiving aid:* Freshmen: 3% (104); Undergraduates: 2% (348). *Average Award: Freshmen:* $2709; *Undergraduates:* $3343. *Scholarships, grants, and awards by category: Academic Interests/Achievement:* agriculture, architecture, biological sciences, business, communication, computer science, education, engineering/technologies, English, foreign languages, general academic interests/achievements, health fields, home economics, humanities, international studies, mathematics, physical sciences, premedicine, social sciences. *Creative Arts/Performance:* applied art and design, art/fine arts, cinema/film/broadcasting, creative writing, journalism/publications, music, performing arts, theater/drama. *Special Achievements/Activities:* cheerleading/drum major, leadership, memberships. *Special Characteristics:* children and siblings of alumni, children of faculty/staff, children of union members/company employees, ethnic background, local/state students, married students, out-of-state students. *Tuition waivers:* Full or partial for employees or children of employees. *ROTC:* Army, Naval, Air Force.

LOANS *Student loans:* $41,800,962 (72% need-based, 28% non-need-based). 64% of past graduating class borrowed through all loan programs. *Average indebtedness per student:* $19,419. *Average need-based loan:* Freshmen: $2937; Undergraduates: $3985. *Parent loans:* $14,950,191 (29% need-based, 71% non-need-based). *Programs:* FFEL (Subsidized and Unsubsidized Stafford, PLUS), Perkins, college/university.

WORK-STUDY *Federal work-study:* Total amount: $1,550,022; 564 jobs averaging $2748.

Auburn University

ATHLETIC AWARDS *Total amount:* $5,945,298 (28% need-based, 72% non-need-based).

APPLYING FOR FINANCIAL AID *Required financial aid forms:* FAFSA, institution's own form. *Financial aid deadline (priority):* 3/1. *Notification date:* Continuous. Students must reply within 2 weeks of notification.

CONTACT Mr. Mike Reynolds, Director of Financial Aid, Auburn University, 203 Mary Martin Hall, Auburn University, AL 36849, 334-844-4367 or toll-free 800-AUBURN9 (in-state). *Fax:* 334-844-6085. *E-mail:* finaid7@auburn.edu.

AUBURN UNIVERSITY MONTGOMERY
Montgomery, AL

Tuition & fees (AL res): $4460	Average undergraduate aid package: $7850

ABOUT THE INSTITUTION State-supported, coed. Awards: bachelor's, master's, and doctoral degrees and post-master's certificates. 24 undergraduate majors. Total enrollment: 5,123. Undergraduates: 4,340. Freshmen: 760. Federal methodology is used as a basis for awarding need-based institutional aid.

UNDERGRADUATE EXPENSES for 2004–05 *Application fee:* $25. *Tuition, state resident:* full-time $4230; part-time $141 per semester hour. *Tuition, nonresident:* full-time $12,690; part-time $423 per semester hour. *Required fees:* full-time $230; $5 per semester hour or $40 per term part-time. Full-time tuition and fees vary according to course load. *College room and board:* $5780; *room only:* $2560. Room and board charges vary according to housing facility. *Payment plan:* Deferred payment.

FRESHMAN FINANCIAL AID (Fall 2003) 391 applied for aid; of those 84% were deemed to have need. 100% of freshmen with need received aid; of those 10% had need fully met. *Average percent of need met:* 75% (excluding resources awarded to replace EFC). *Average financial aid package:* $6025 (excluding resources awarded to replace EFC). 3% of all full-time freshmen had no need and received non-need-based gift aid.

UNDERGRADUATE FINANCIAL AID (Fall 2003) 1,919 applied for aid; of those 80% were deemed to have need. 99% of undergraduates with need received aid; of those 25% had need fully met. *Average percent of need met:* 65% (excluding resources awarded to replace EFC). *Average financial aid package:* $7850 (excluding resources awarded to replace EFC). 1% of all full-time undergraduates had no need and received non-need-based gift aid.

GIFT AID (NEED-BASED) *Total amount:* $5,519,986 (88% federal, 1% state, 11% institutional). *Receiving aid:* Freshmen: 34% (229); All full-time undergraduates: 26% (743). *Average award:* Freshmen: $3400; Undergraduates: $3000. *Scholarships, grants, and awards:* Federal Pell, FSEOG, state, college/university gift aid from institutional funds.

GIFT AID (NON-NEED-BASED) *Total amount:* $118,058 (24% institutional, 76% external sources). *Receiving aid:* Freshmen: 13% (84); Undergraduates: 46% (1,316). *Average Award:* Freshmen: $4200; Undergraduates: $4200. *Scholarships, grants, and awards by category: Academic Interests/Achievement:* 392 awards ($1,100,000 total): general academic interests/achievements. *Tuition waivers:* Full or partial for employees or children of employees. *ROTC:* Army, Air Force cooperative.

LOANS *Student loans:* $14,573,917 (99% need-based, 1% non-need-based). 45% of past graduating class borrowed through all loan programs. *Average indebtedness per student:* $15,000. *Average need-based loan:* Freshmen: $2625; Undergraduates: $4855. *Parent loans:* $395,428 (100% need-based). *Programs:* FFEL (Subsidized and Unsubsidized Stafford, PLUS), Perkins.

WORK-STUDY *Federal work-study:* Total amount: $262,509; 55 jobs averaging $4200.

ATHLETIC AWARDS *Total amount:* $497,541 (46% need-based, 54% non-need-based).

APPLYING FOR FINANCIAL AID *Required financial aid forms:* FAFSA, institution's own form. *Financial aid deadline (priority):* 3/1. *Notification date:* 5/15. Students must reply within 3 weeks of notification.

CONTACT Dan Miller, Director of Financial Aid, Auburn University Montgomery, PO Box 244023, Montgomery, AL 36124-4023, 334-244-3570 or toll-free 800-227-2649 (in-state). *Fax:* 334-244-3913. *E-mail:* dmiller7@mail.aum.edu.

AUGSBURG COLLEGE
Minneapolis, MN

Tuition & fees: $20,758	Average undergraduate aid package: $12,467

ABOUT THE INSTITUTION Independent Lutheran, coed. Awards: bachelor's and master's degrees and post-bachelor's and post-master's certificates. 64 undergraduate majors. Total enrollment: 3,375. Undergraduates: 2,916. Freshmen: 361. Federal methodology is used as a basis for awarding need-based institutional aid.

UNDERGRADUATE EXPENSES for 2004–05 *Application fee:* $25. *Comprehensive fee:* $26,838 includes full-time tuition ($20,260), mandatory fees ($498), and room and board ($6080). *College room only:* $3100. Full-time tuition and fees vary according to location. Room and board charges vary according to board plan and housing facility. *Part-time tuition:* $2460 per course. *Part-time fees:* $48.75 per course. Part-time tuition and fees vary according to course load and location. *Payment plans:* Installment, deferred payment.

FRESHMAN FINANCIAL AID (Fall 2003) 282 applied for aid; of those 84% were deemed to have need. 100% of freshmen with need received aid; of those 23% had need fully met. *Average percent of need met:* 81% (excluding resources awarded to replace EFC). *Average financial aid package:* $14,866 (excluding resources awarded to replace EFC). 17% of all full-time freshmen had no need and received non-need-based gift aid.

UNDERGRADUATE FINANCIAL AID (Fall 2003) 1,688 applied for aid; of those 86% were deemed to have need. 99% of undergraduates with need received aid; of those 20% had need fully met. *Average percent of need met:* 67% (excluding resources awarded to replace EFC). *Average financial aid package:* $12,467 (excluding resources awarded to replace EFC). 13% of all full-time undergraduates had no need and received non-need-based gift aid.

GIFT AID (NEED-BASED) *Total amount:* $13,729,158 (17% federal, 15% state, 58% institutional, 10% external sources). *Receiving aid:* Freshmen: 65% (235); All full-time undergraduates: 56% (1,294). *Average award:* Freshmen: $11,926; Undergraduates: $9431. *Scholarships, grants, and awards:* Federal Pell, FSEOG, state, private, college/university gift aid from institutional funds, Federal Nursing.

GIFT AID (NON-NEED-BASED) *Total amount:* $2,367,354 (1% state, 86% institutional, 13% external sources). *Receiving aid:* Freshmen: 10% (37); Undergraduates: 6% (151). *Average Award:* Freshmen: $12,153; *Undergraduates:* $12,158. *Scholarships, grants, and awards by category: Academic Interests/Achievement:* biological sciences, business, communication, computer science, education, English, foreign languages, general academic interests/achievements, health fields, international studies, mathematics, physical sciences, religion/biblical studies, social sciences. *Creative Arts/Performance:* music, performing arts, theater/drama. *Special Achievements/Activities:* community service, general special achievements/activities, junior miss, leadership, religious involvement. *Special Characteristics:* children and siblings of alumni, international students, members of minority groups, relatives of clergy, siblings of current students. *Tuition waivers:* Full or partial for children of alumni, employees or children of employees, senior citizens. *ROTC:* Army cooperative, Naval cooperative, Air Force cooperative.

LOANS *Student loans:* $17,401,023 (68% need-based, 32% non-need-based). 74% of past graduating class borrowed through all loan programs. *Average indebtedness per student:* $25,750. *Average need-based loan:* Freshmen: $3624; Undergraduates: $4255. *Parent loans:* $1,290,060 (19% need-based, 81% non-need-based). *Programs:* FFEL (Subsidized and Unsubsidized Stafford, PLUS), Perkins, Federal Nursing, state.

WORK-STUDY *Federal work-study:* Total amount: $253,620; 213 jobs averaging $1534. *State or other work-study/employment:* Total amount: $203,519 (100% need-based). 263 part-time jobs averaging $2144.

APPLYING FOR FINANCIAL AID *Required financial aid forms:* FAFSA, institution's own form. *Financial aid deadline:* 4/15. *Notification date:* Continuous. Students must reply within 3 weeks of notification.

CONTACT Mr. Paul L. Terrio, Director of Financial Aid, Augsburg College, 2211 Riverside Avenue, Minneapolis, MN 55454-1351, 612-330-1049 or toll-free 800-788-5678. *Fax:* 612-330-1308. *E-mail:* terriop@augsburg.edu.

AUGUSTANA COLLEGE
Rock Island, IL

ABOUT THE INSTITUTION Independent religious, coed. Awards: bachelor's degrees. 67 undergraduate majors. Total enrollment: 2,309. Undergraduates: 2,309. Freshmen: 614.

GIFT AID (NEED-BASED) *Scholarships, grants, and awards:* Federal Pell, FSEOG, state, private, college/university gift aid from institutional funds.

GIFT AID (NON-NEED-BASED) *Scholarships, grants, and awards by category: Academic Interests/Achievement:* biological sciences, business, communication, education, general academic interests/achievements, mathematics, physical sciences, religion/biblical studies, social sciences. *Creative Arts/Performance:* art/fine arts, creative writing, debating, music, theater/drama. *Special Characteristics:* children and siblings of alumni, children of faculty/staff, international students, members of minority groups, religious affiliation, siblings of current students.

LOANS *Programs:* FFEL (Subsidized and Unsubsidized Stafford, PLUS), Perkins.
WORK-STUDY *Federal work-study:* Total amount: $1,311,958; 1,007 jobs averaging $1303.
APPLYING FOR FINANCIAL AID *Required financial aid forms:* FAFSA, institution's own form.
CONTACT Sue Standley, Director of Financial Aid, Augustana College, 639 38th Street, Rock Island, IL 61201-2296, 309-794-7207 or toll-free 800-798-8100. *Fax:* 309-794-7174. *E-mail:* afass@augustana.edu.

AUGUSTANA COLLEGE
Sioux Falls, SD

Tuition & fees: $18,860	Average undergraduate aid package: $14,679

ABOUT THE INSTITUTION Independent religious, coed. Awards: bachelor's and master's degrees. 51 undergraduate majors. Total enrollment: 1,799. Undergraduates: 1,770. Freshmen: 411. Federal methodology is used as a basis for awarding need-based institutional aid.
UNDERGRADUATE EXPENSES for 2005–06 *Comprehensive fee:* $24,194 includes full-time tuition ($18,634), mandatory fees ($226), and room and board ($5334). *College room only:* $2678. Room and board charges vary according to board plan and housing facility. *Part-time tuition:* $273 per credit. Part-time tuition and fees vary according to course load. *Payment plan:* Installment.
FRESHMAN FINANCIAL AID (Fall 2004, est.) 346 applied for aid; of those 79% were deemed to have need. 100% of freshmen with need received aid; of those 16% had need fully met. *Average percent of need met:* 94% (excluding resources awarded to replace EFC). *Average financial aid package:* $15,693 (excluding resources awarded to replace EFC). 29% of all full-time freshmen had no need and received non-need-based gift aid.
UNDERGRADUATE FINANCIAL AID (Fall 2004, est.) 1,345 applied for aid; of those 84% were deemed to have need. 100% of undergraduates with need received aid; of those 14% had need fully met. *Average percent of need met:* 88% (excluding resources awarded to replace EFC). *Average financial aid package:* $14,679 (excluding resources awarded to replace EFC). 30% of all full-time undergraduates had no need and received non-need-based gift aid.
GIFT AID (NEED-BASED) *Total amount:* $9,474,318 (17% federal, 77% institutional, 6% external sources). *Receiving aid:* Freshmen: 69% (274); All full-time undergraduates: 68% (1,123). *Average award:* Freshmen: $11,504; Undergraduates: $10,221. *Scholarships, grants, and awards:* Federal Pell, FSEOG, state, private, college/university gift aid from institutional funds, need-linked special talent scholarships and minority scholarships.
GIFT AID (NON-NEED-BASED) *Total amount:* $3,991,829 (2% state, 86% institutional, 12% external sources). *Receiving aid:* Freshmen: 69% (274); Undergraduates: 66% (1,099). *Average Award:* Freshmen: $7890; Undergraduates: $6830. *Scholarships, grants, and awards by category: Academic Interests/Achievement:* biological sciences, business, communication, computer science, education, English, foreign languages, general academic interests/achievements, health fields, humanities, international studies, mathematics, physical sciences, premedicine, religion/biblical studies, social sciences. *Creative Arts/Performance:* art/fine arts, music, theater/drama. *Special Achievements/Activities:* general special achievements/activities, leadership. *Special Characteristics:* children and siblings of alumni, children of current students, children of faculty/staff, ethnic background, international students, members of minority groups, religious affiliation, siblings of current students, spouses of current students, veterans. *Tuition waivers:* Full or partial for employees or children of employees, adult students, senior citizens.
LOANS *Student loans:* $8,654,070 (64% need-based, 36% non-need-based). 76% of past graduating class borrowed through all loan programs. *Average indebtedness per student:* $18,385. *Average need-based loan:* Freshmen: $4645; Undergraduates: $4864. *Parent loans:* $1,361,985 (18% need-based, 82% non-need-based). *Programs:* FFEL (Subsidized and Unsubsidized Stafford, PLUS), Perkins, Federal Nursing, college/university, Minnesota SELF Loans, alternative loans.
WORK-STUDY *Federal work-study:* Total amount: $591,599; 435 jobs averaging $1360. *State or other work-study/employment:* Total amount: $65,462 (100% non-need-based). 104 part-time jobs averaging $629.
ATHLETIC AWARDS *Total amount:* $1,856,013 (47% need-based, 53% non-need-based).
APPLYING FOR FINANCIAL AID *Required financial aid form:* FAFSA. *Financial aid deadline (priority):* 3/1. *Notification date:* Continuous beginning 4/1. Students must reply by 5/1 or within 3 weeks of notification.

CONTACT Ms. Brenda L. Murtha, Director of Financial Aid, Augustana College, 2001 South Summit Avenue, Sioux Falls, SD 57197, 605-274-5216 or toll-free 800-727-2844 Ext. 5516 (in-state), 800-727-2844 (out-of-state). *Fax:* 605-274-5295. *E-mail:* brenda_murtha@augie.edu.

AUGUSTA STATE UNIVERSITY
Augusta, GA

Tuition & fees (GA res): $2702	Average undergraduate aid package: $1013

ABOUT THE INSTITUTION State-supported, coed. Awards: associate, bachelor's, and master's degrees and post-master's certificates. 32 undergraduate majors. Total enrollment: 6,353. Undergraduates: 5,502. Freshmen: 963. Federal methodology is used as a basis for awarding need-based institutional aid.
UNDERGRADUATE EXPENSES for 2004–05 *Application fee:* $20. *Tuition, state resident:* full-time $2322; part-time $97 per hour. *Tuition, nonresident:* full-time $9290; part-time $388 per hour. *Required fees:* full-time $380; $190 per term part-time.
GIFT AID (NEED-BASED) *Total amount:* $7,819,411 (100% federal). *Receiving aid:* Freshmen: 32% (274); All full-time undergraduates: 38% (1,383). *Average award:* Freshmen: $1482; Undergraduates: $1440. *Scholarships, grants, and awards:* Federal Pell, FSEOG, state, private, college/university gift aid from institutional funds.
GIFT AID (NON-NEED-BASED) *Total amount:* $5,906,959 (87% state, 7% institutional, 6% external sources). *Receiving aid:* Freshmen: 29% (246); Undergraduates: 18% (652). *Average Award: Freshmen:* $501; *Undergraduates:* $505. *Scholarships, grants, and awards by category: Academic Interests/Achievement:* 69 awards ($90,123 total): biological sciences, business, communication, education, English, general academic interests/achievements, health fields, mathematics, military science, physical sciences, social sciences. *Creative Arts/Performance:* 59 awards ($37,293 total): art/fine arts, creative writing, general creative arts/performance, music, performing arts, theater/drama. *Special Achievements/Activities:* 3 awards ($3994 total): community service, general special achievements/activities, hobbies/interests. *Special Characteristics:* 2,068 awards ($4,518,028 total): general special characteristics, handicapped students, local/state students. *Tuition waivers:* Full or partial for employees or children of employees, senior citizens. *ROTC:* Army.
LOANS *Student loans:* $12,054,315 (58% need-based, 42% non-need-based). *Average need-based loan:* Freshmen: $1076; Undergraduates: $1573. *Parent loans:* $100,076 (100% non-need-based). *Programs:* FFEL (Subsidized and Unsubsidized Stafford, PLUS), Perkins, state, college/university, alternative loans.
ATHLETIC AWARDS *Total amount:* $465,111 (100% non-need-based).
APPLYING FOR FINANCIAL AID *Required financial aid form:* FAFSA. *Financial aid deadline:* 5/1 (priority: 4/15). *Notification date:* Continuous.
CONTACT Ms. Roxanne Padgett, Assistant Director of Financial Aid, Augusta State University, 2500 Walton Way, Augusta, GA 30904-2200, 706-737-1431 or toll-free 800-341-4373. *Fax:* 706-737-1777. *E-mail:* bpadgett@aug.edu.

AURORA UNIVERSITY
Aurora, IL

Tuition & fees: $15,600	Average undergraduate aid package: $16,498

ABOUT THE INSTITUTION Independent, coed. Awards: bachelor's, master's, and doctoral degrees and post-bachelor's and post-master's certificates. 32 undergraduate majors. Total enrollment: 3,326. Undergraduates: 1,719. Freshmen: 295. Federal methodology is used as a basis for awarding need-based institutional aid.
UNDERGRADUATE EXPENSES for 2005–06 *Application fee:* $25. *Comprehensive fee:* $22,440 includes full-time tuition ($15,500), mandatory fees ($100), and room and board ($6840). *College room only:* $3020. Full-time tuition and fees vary according to course load, location, and program. Room and board charges vary according to board plan and housing facility. *Part-time tuition:* $475 per semester hour. Part-time tuition and fees vary according to location and program. *Payment plans:* Installment, deferred payment.
FRESHMAN FINANCIAL AID (Fall 2004, est.) 294 applied for aid; of those 79% were deemed to have need. 100% of freshmen with need received aid; of those 37% had need fully met. *Average percent of need met:* 88% (excluding resources awarded to replace EFC). *Average financial aid package:* $16,476 (excluding resources awarded to replace EFC). 19% of all full-time freshmen had no need and received non-need-based gift aid.

UNDERGRADUATE FINANCIAL AID (Fall 2004, est.) 1,471 applied for aid; of those 78% were deemed to have need. 100% of undergraduates with need received aid; of those 40% had need fully met. *Average percent of need met:* 88% (excluding resources awarded to replace EFC). *Average financial aid package:* $16,498 (excluding resources awarded to replace EFC). 20% of all full-time undergraduates had no need and received non-need-based gift aid.
GIFT AID (NEED-BASED) *Total amount:* $4,940,136 (32% federal, 57% state, 11% institutional). *Receiving aid:* Freshmen: 52% (153); All full-time undergraduates: 57% (846). *Average award:* Freshmen: $5818; Undergraduates: $5635. *Scholarships, grants, and awards:* Federal Pell, FSEOG, state, private, college/university gift aid from institutional funds.
GIFT AID (NON-NEED-BASED) *Total amount:* $8,417,856 (96% institutional, 4% external sources). *Receiving aid:* Freshmen: 79% (232); Undergraduates: 73% (1,094). *Average Award:* Freshmen: $8691; Undergraduates: $8328. *Scholarships, grants, and awards by category: Academic Interests/Achievement:* 1,590 awards ($7,946,171 total): education, general academic interests/achievements, mathematics. *Special Achievements/Activities:* 147 awards ($326,906 total): general special achievements/activities. *Special Characteristics:* 200 awards ($384,402 total): children and siblings of alumni, children of educators, children of faculty/staff, out-of-state students, parents of current students, siblings of current students, spouses of current students. *Tuition waivers:* Full or partial for employees or children of employees, senior citizens.
LOANS *Student loans:* $7,006,784 (51% need-based, 49% non-need-based). 73% of past graduating class borrowed through all loan programs. *Average indebtedness per student:* $17,805. *Average need-based loan:* Freshmen: $2422; Undergraduates: $3832. *Parent loans:* $1,154,861 (100% non-need-based). *Programs:* FFEL (Subsidized and Unsubsidized Stafford, PLUS), Perkins, college/university.
WORK-STUDY *Federal work-study:* Total amount: $763,502; 507 jobs averaging $1506.
APPLYING FOR FINANCIAL AID *Required financial aid form:* FAFSA. *Financial aid deadline (priority):* 4/15. *Notification date:* Continuous. Students must reply by 5/1 or within 3 weeks of notification.
CONTACT Heather Gutierrez, Dean of Student Financial Services, Aurora University, 347 South Gladstone Avenue, Aurora, IL 60506-4892, 630-844-5533 or toll-free 800-742-5281. *Fax:* 630-844-5535. *E-mail:* finaid@aurora.edu.

AUSTIN COLLEGE
Sherman, TX

Tuition & fees: $20,495	Average undergraduate aid package: $20,391

ABOUT THE INSTITUTION Independent Presbyterian, coed. Awards: bachelor's and master's degrees. 29 undergraduate majors. Total enrollment: 1,323. Undergraduates: 1,288. Freshmen: 370. Federal methodology is used as a basis for awarding need-based institutional aid.
UNDERGRADUATE EXPENSES for 2005–06 *Application fee:* $35. *Comprehensive fee:* $27,871 includes full-time tuition ($20,310), mandatory fees ($185), and room and board ($7376). *College room only:* $3385. Room and board charges vary according to board plan. *Part-time tuition:* $2945 per course. *Payment plan:* Installment.
FRESHMAN FINANCIAL AID (Fall 2004, est.) 282 applied for aid; of those 79% were deemed to have need. 100% of freshmen with need received aid; of those 95% had need fully met. *Average percent of need met:* 100% (excluding resources awarded to replace EFC). *Average financial aid package:* $20,016 (excluding resources awarded to replace EFC). 38% of all full-time freshmen had no need and received non-need-based gift aid.
UNDERGRADUATE FINANCIAL AID (Fall 2004, est.) 948 applied for aid; of those 80% were deemed to have need. 100% of undergraduates with need received aid; of those 93% had need fully met. *Average percent of need met:* 99% (excluding resources awarded to replace EFC). *Average financial aid package:* $20,391 (excluding resources awarded to replace EFC). 38% of all full-time undergraduates had no need and received non-need-based gift aid.
GIFT AID (NEED-BASED) *Total amount:* $9,418,477 (11% federal, 18% state, 69% institutional, 2% external sources). *Receiving aid:* Freshmen: 61% (224); All full-time undergraduates: 59% (757). *Average award:* Freshmen: $13,227; Undergraduates: $12,756. *Scholarships, grants, and awards:* Federal Pell, FSEOG, state, private, college/university gift aid from institutional funds.
GIFT AID (NON-NEED-BASED) *Total amount:* $4,823,538 (94% institutional, 6% external sources). *Receiving aid:* Freshmen: 21% (76); Undergraduates: 13% (165). *Average Award:* Freshmen: $8356; Undergraduates: $8021. *Scholarships, grants, and awards by category: Academic Interests/Achievement:* biological sciences, business, communication, education, engineering/technologies,

English, foreign languages, general academic interests/achievements, health fields, humanities, international studies, physical sciences, premedicine, religion/biblical studies, social sciences. *Creative Arts/Performance:* art/fine arts, music, theater/drama. *Special Achievements/Activities:* general special achievements/activities, leadership, religious involvement. *Special Characteristics:* children of faculty/staff, ethnic background, first-generation college students, handicapped students, international students, local/state students, relatives of clergy. *Tuition waivers:* Full or partial for employees or children of employees.
LOANS *Student loans:* $7,433,914 (55% need-based, 45% non-need-based). 73% of past graduating class borrowed through all loan programs. *Average indebtedness per student:* $23,214. *Average need-based loan:* Freshmen: $5093; Undergraduates: $5355. *Parent loans:* $6,725,078 (4% need-based, 96% non-need-based). *Programs:* FFEL (Subsidized and Unsubsidized Stafford, PLUS), Perkins, state, college/university.
WORK-STUDY *Federal work-study:* Total amount: $529,950; 292 jobs averaging $1450. *State or other work-study/employment:* Total amount: $251,750 (6% need-based, 94% non-need-based). 215 part-time jobs averaging $1258.
APPLYING FOR FINANCIAL AID *Required financial aid forms:* FAFSA, institution's own form. *Financial aid deadline (priority):* 4/1. *Notification date:* Continuous beginning 3/1. Students must reply by 5/1.
CONTACT Mrs. Laurie Coulter, Director of Financial Aid, Austin College, 900 North Grand Avenue, Sherman, TX 75090, 903-813-2900 or toll-free 800-442-5363. *E-mail:* finaid@austincollege.edu.

AUSTIN GRADUATE SCHOOL OF THEOLOGY
Austin, TX

Tuition & fees: $4200	Average undergraduate aid package: $2270

ABOUT THE INSTITUTION Independent religious, coed. Awards: bachelor's and master's degrees. 1 undergraduate major. Total enrollment: 67. Undergraduates: 31. Federal methodology is used as a basis for awarding need-based institutional aid.
UNDERGRADUATE EXPENSES for 2004–05 *Tuition:* full-time $4200; part-time $525 per course. Full-time tuition and fees vary according to course load. Part-time tuition and fees vary according to course load. *Payment plan:* Installment.
UNDERGRADUATE FINANCIAL AID (Fall 2003) 4 applied for aid; of those 100% were deemed to have need. 100% of undergraduates with need received aid. *Average financial aid package:* $2270 (excluding resources awarded to replace EFC).
GIFT AID (NEED-BASED) *Total amount:* $32,696 (70% federal, 30% institutional). *Receiving aid:* All full-time undergraduates: 100% (4). *Average award:* Undergraduates: $764. *Scholarships, grants, and awards:* Federal Pell, FSEOG, college/university gift aid from institutional funds.
GIFT AID (NON-NEED-BASED) *Receiving aid:* Undergraduates: 50% (2). *Scholarships, grants, and awards by category: Academic Interests/Achievement:* religion/biblical studies. *Tuition waivers:* Full or partial for employees or children of employees.
LOANS *Student loans:* $59,136 (100% need-based). 44% of past graduating class borrowed through all loan programs. *Average indebtedness per student:* $9350. *Average need-based loan:* Undergraduates: $1750. *Programs:* FFEL (Subsidized and Unsubsidized Stafford, PLUS), college/university.
WORK-STUDY Federal work-study jobs available.
APPLYING FOR FINANCIAL AID *Required financial aid forms:* FAFSA, institution's own form. *Financial aid deadline:* Continuous.
CONTACT David Arthur, Financial Aid Officer, Austin Graduate School of Theology, 1909 University Avenue, Austin, TX 78705-5610, 512-476-2772 Ext. 204 or toll-free 866-AUS-GRAD. *Fax:* 512-476-3919. *E-mail:* darthur@austingrad.edu.

AUSTIN PEAY STATE UNIVERSITY
Clarksville, TN

Tuition & fees (TN res): $4224	Average undergraduate aid package: $5620

ABOUT THE INSTITUTION State-supported, coed. Awards: associate, bachelor's, and master's degrees and post-bachelor's and post-master's certificates. 34

undergraduate majors. Total enrollment: 8,650. Undergraduates: 8,108. Freshmen: 1,606. Federal methodology is used as a basis for awarding need-based institutional aid.

UNDERGRADUATE EXPENSES for 2004–05 *Application fee:* $15. *Tuition, state resident:* full-time $3352; part-time $147 per credit hour. *Tuition, nonresident:* full-time $11,840; part-time $515 per credit hour. *Required fees:* full-time $872; $41 per credit hour or $4. Part-time tuition and fees vary according to location. *College room and board:* $4296; *room only:* $1696. Room and board charges vary according to board plan and housing facility. *Payment plans:* Installment, deferred payment.

FRESHMAN FINANCIAL AID (Fall 2003) 732 applied for aid; of those 88% were deemed to have need. 98% of freshmen with need received aid. *Average financial aid package:* $4552 (excluding resources awarded to replace EFC). 3% of all full-time freshmen had no need and received non-need-based gift aid.

UNDERGRADUATE FINANCIAL AID (Fall 2003) 3,774 applied for aid; of those 90% were deemed to have need. 98% of undergraduates with need received aid. *Average financial aid package:* $5620 (excluding resources awarded to replace EFC). 2% of all full-time undergraduates had no need and received non-need-based gift aid.

GIFT AID (NEED-BASED) *Total amount:* $8,855,132 (84% federal, 16% state). *Receiving aid:* Freshmen: 40% (390); All full-time undergraduates: 42% (2,207). *Average award:* Freshmen: $3392; Undergraduates: $3596. *Scholarships, grants, and awards:* Federal Pell, FSEOG, state, private, college/university gift aid from institutional funds, corporate.

GIFT AID (NON-NEED-BASED) *Total amount:* $4,199,250 (3% state, 40% institutional, 57% external sources). *Receiving aid:* Freshmen: 27% (257); Undergraduates: 19% (1,001). *Average Award:* Freshmen: $2182; Undergraduates:* $2882. *Scholarships, grants, and awards by category: Academic Interests/ Achievement:* 671 awards ($801,634 total): general academic interests/ achievements. *Creative Arts/Performance:* $371,250 total: art/fine arts, creative writing, debating, music, theater/drama. *Special Achievements/Activities:* 19 awards ($20,300 total): cheerleading/drum major. *Special Characteristics:* 716 awards ($1,200,417 total): children of educators, children of faculty/staff, veterans. *Tuition waivers:* Full or partial for employees or children of employees, senior citizens. *ROTC:* Army.

LOANS *Student loans:* $17,493,088 (56% need-based, 44% non-need-based). *Parent loans:* $997,009 (100% non-need-based). *Programs:* FFEL (Subsidized and Unsubsidized Stafford, PLUS), Perkins.

WORK-STUDY *Federal work-study:* Total amount: $284,694; 452 jobs averaging $2000. *State or other work-study/employment:* Total amount: $396 (100% non-need-based). 373 part-time jobs averaging $1300.

ATHLETIC AWARDS *Total amount:* $1,077,635 (100% non-need-based).

APPLYING FOR FINANCIAL AID *Required financial aid form:* FAFSA. *Financial aid deadline (priority):* 4/1. *Notification date:* Continuous beginning 5/1. Students must reply within 2 weeks of notification.

CONTACT Greg Ross, Associate Director of Student Financial Aid, Austin Peay State University, PO Box 4546, Clarksville, TN 37044-0001, 931-221-7907 or toll-free 800-844-2778 (out-of-state). *Fax:* 931-221-6329. *E-mail:* rossg@apsu.edu.

AVE MARIA COLLEGE
Ypsilanti, MI

CONTACT Mr. Bob Hickey, Director of Financial Aid, Ave Maria College, 300 West Forest Avenue, Ypsilanti, MI 48197, 734-337-4504 or toll-free 866-866-3030. *Fax:* 734-337-4140. *E-mail:* bhickey@avemaria.edu.

AVE MARIA UNIVERSITY
Naples, FL

CONTACT Financial Aid Office, Ave Maria University, 1025 Commons Circle, Naples, FL 34119, 239-280-2554 or toll-free 877-AVE-UNIV.

AVERETT UNIVERSITY
Danville, VA

Tuition & fees: $18,430	Average undergraduate aid package: $10,305

ABOUT THE INSTITUTION Independent religious, coed. Awards: associate, bachelor's, and master's degrees. 65 undergraduate majors. Total enrollment: 2,719. Undergraduates: 2,071. Freshmen: 216. Federal methodology is used as a basis for awarding need-based institutional aid.

UNDERGRADUATE EXPENSES for 2004–05 *Comprehensive fee:* $24,760 includes full-time tuition ($17,430), mandatory fees ($1000), and room and board ($6330). *College room only:* $4690. Full-time tuition and fees vary according to location and program. Room and board charges vary according to board plan and housing facility. *Part-time tuition:* $295 per credit. Part-time tuition and fees vary according to course load, location, and program. *Payment plan:* Installment.

FRESHMAN FINANCIAL AID (Fall 2003) 205 applied for aid; of those 93% were deemed to have need. 100% of freshmen with need received aid; of those 11% had need fully met. *Average percent of need met:* 71% (excluding resources awarded to replace EFC). *Average financial aid package:* $13,280 (excluding resources awarded to replace EFC). 17% of all full-time freshmen had no need and received non-need-based gift aid.

UNDERGRADUATE FINANCIAL AID (Fall 2003) 1,240 applied for aid; of those 93% were deemed to have need. 100% of undergraduates with need received aid; of those 13% had need fully met. *Average percent of need met:* 62% (excluding resources awarded to replace EFC). *Average financial aid package:* $10,305 (excluding resources awarded to replace EFC). 14% of all full-time undergraduates had no need and received non-need-based gift aid.

GIFT AID (NEED-BASED) *Total amount:* $8,251,450 (19% federal, 19% state, 45% institutional, 17% external sources). *Receiving aid:* Freshmen: 82% (190); All full-time undergraduates: 74% (990). *Average award:* Freshmen: $10,101; Undergraduates: $7897. *Scholarships, grants, and awards:* Federal Pell, FSEOG, state, private, college/university gift aid from institutional funds.

GIFT AID (NON-NEED-BASED) *Total amount:* $1,453,568 (24% state, 54% institutional, 22% external sources). *Receiving aid:* Freshmen: 6% (15); Undergraduates: 6% (79). *Average Award:* Freshmen: $11,709; *Undergraduates:* $9715. *Scholarships, grants, and awards by category: Academic Interests/ Achievement:* 117 awards ($178,659 total): biological sciences, business, education, engineering/technologies, English, foreign languages, general academic interests/achievements, health fields, home economics, humanities, mathematics, physical sciences, premedicine, religion/biblical studies. *Creative Arts/ Performance:* 11 awards ($8306 total): art/fine arts, journalism/publications, music, theater/drama. *Special Achievements/Activities:* 8 awards ($10,617 total): general special achievements/activities, religious involvement. *Special Characteristics:* 224 awards ($195,508 total): adult students, children and siblings of alumni, children of union members/company employees, first-generation college students, general special characteristics, international students, local/state students, out-of-state students, relatives of clergy, religious affiliation. *Tuition waivers:* Full or partial for employees or children of employees, senior citizens.

LOANS *Student loans:* $8,778,231 (79% need-based, 21% non-need-based). 34% of past graduating class borrowed through all loan programs. *Average indebtedness per student:* $15,924. *Average need-based loan:* Freshmen: $3384; Undergraduates: $3826. *Parent loans:* $1,269,951 (38% need-based, 62% non-need-based). *Programs:* FFEL (Subsidized and Unsubsidized Stafford, PLUS), Perkins, alternative loans.

WORK-STUDY *Federal work-study:* Total amount: $125,668; 166 jobs averaging $757.

APPLYING FOR FINANCIAL AID *Required financial aid forms:* FAFSA, state aid form. *Financial aid deadline:* Continuous. *Notification date:* Continuous beginning 2/1. Students must reply within 2 weeks of notification.

CONTACT Carl Bradsher, Dean of Financial Assistance, Averett University, 420 West Main Street, Danville, VA 24541-3692, 434-791-5646 or toll-free 800-AVERETT. *Fax:* 434-791-5647. *E-mail:* carl.bradsher@averett.edu.

AVILA UNIVERSITY
Kansas City, MO

ABOUT THE INSTITUTION Independent Roman Catholic, coed. Awards: bachelor's and master's degrees. 32 undergraduate majors. Total enrollment: 2,104. Undergraduates: 1,579. Freshmen: 132.

GIFT AID (NEED-BASED) *Scholarships, grants, and awards:* Federal Pell, FSEOG, state, private, college/university gift aid from institutional funds.

GIFT AID (NON-NEED-BASED) *Scholarships, grants, and awards by category: Academic Interests/Achievement:* biological sciences, communication, general academic interests/achievements, humanities, premedicine. *Creative Arts/ Performance:* art/fine arts, music, performing arts, theater/drama. *Special Characteristics:* children and siblings of alumni, children of current students, children of faculty/staff, religious affiliation, siblings of current students, spouses of current students.

LOANS *Programs:* FFEL (Subsidized and Unsubsidized Stafford, PLUS), Perkins.

WORK-STUDY *Federal work-study:* Total amount: $104,679; jobs available. *State or other work-study/employment:* Total amount: $46,138 (100% non-need-based). Part-time jobs available.

APPLYING FOR FINANCIAL AID *Required financial aid form:* FAFSA.

CONTACT Angie Comstock, Director of Financial Aid, Avila University, 11901 Wornall Road, Kansas City, MO 64145, 816-501-3600 or toll-free 800-GO-AVILA. *Fax:* 816-501-2462.

AZUSA PACIFIC UNIVERSITY
Azusa, CA

Tuition & fees: $20,666	Average undergraduate aid package: $15,844

ABOUT THE INSTITUTION Independent nondenominational, coed. Awards: bachelor's, master's, doctoral, and first professional degrees. 38 undergraduate majors. Total enrollment: 8,162. Undergraduates: 4,441. Freshmen: 903. Federal methodology is used as a basis for awarding need-based institutional aid.

UNDERGRADUATE EXPENSES for 2004–05 *Application fee:* $45. *Comprehensive fee:* $26,798 includes full-time tuition ($20,006), mandatory fees ($660), and room and board ($6132). *College room only:* $3340. Room and board charges vary according to board plan, housing facility, and student level. *Part-time tuition:* $835 per unit. Part-time tuition and fees vary according to course load. *Payment plan:* Installment.

FRESHMAN FINANCIAL AID (Fall 2003) 903 applied for aid; of those 39% were deemed to have need. 100% of freshmen with need received aid; of those 69% had need fully met. *Average percent of need met:* 88% (excluding resources awarded to replace EFC). *Average financial aid package:* $17,672 (excluding resources awarded to replace EFC). 17% of all full-time freshmen had no need and received non-need-based gift aid.

UNDERGRADUATE FINANCIAL AID (Fall 2003) 2,733 applied for aid; of those 100% were deemed to have need. 100% of undergraduates with need received aid; of those 68% had need fully met. *Average percent of need met:* 86% (excluding resources awarded to replace EFC). *Average financial aid package:* $15,844 (excluding resources awarded to replace EFC). 22% of all full-time undergraduates had no need and received non-need-based gift aid.

GIFT AID (NEED-BASED) *Total amount:* $22,657,338 (14% federal, 35% state, 44% institutional, 7% external sources). *Receiving aid:* Freshmen: 38% (345); All full-time undergraduates: 54% (2,374). *Average award:* Freshmen: $11,145; Undergraduates: $9450. *Scholarships, grants, and awards:* Federal Pell, FSEOG, state, private, college/university gift aid from institutional funds, Federal Nursing.

GIFT AID (NON-NEED-BASED) *Total amount:* $2,633,846 (1% state, 79% institutional, 20% external sources). *Receiving aid:* Freshmen: 17% (149); Undergraduates: 22% (976). *Average Award:* Freshmen: $7534; Undergraduates: $8569. *Scholarships, grants, and awards by category: Academic Interests/Achievement:* 6,938 awards ($8,950,326 total): biological sciences, computer science, general academic interests/achievements, health fields, religion/biblical studies. *Creative Arts/Performance:* 1,283 awards ($1,288,343 total): debating, music, theater/drama. *Special Achievements/Activities:* 859 awards ($376,076 total): cheerleading/drum major, leadership, religious involvement. *Special Characteristics:* 975 awards ($2,032,927 total): children of faculty/staff, ethnic background, international students, relatives of clergy, religious affiliation, siblings of current students. *Tuition waivers:* Full or partial for employees or children of employees. *ROTC:* Army cooperative.

LOANS *Student loans:* $15,837,257 (87% need-based, 13% non-need-based). *Average need-based loan:* Freshmen: $10,323; Undergraduates: $10,162. *Parent loans:* $14,325,091 (52% need-based, 48% non-need-based). *Programs:* FFEL (Subsidized and Unsubsidized Stafford, PLUS), Perkins, Federal Nursing.

WORK-STUDY *Federal work-study:* Total amount: $662,195; 463 jobs averaging $1430.

ATHLETIC AWARDS *Total amount:* $1,591,005 (100% need-based).

APPLYING FOR FINANCIAL AID *Required financial aid forms:* FAFSA, institution's own form. *Financial aid deadline:* 7/1 (priority: 3/2). *Notification date:* Continuous. Students must reply within 3 weeks of notification.

CONTACT Todd Ross, Interim Director, Student Financial Services, Azusa Pacific University, 901 East Alosta Avenue, PO Box 7000, Azusa, CA 91702-7000, 626-812-3009 or toll-free 800-TALK-APU. *E-mail:* tross@apu.edu.

BABSON COLLEGE
Wellesley, MA

Tuition & fees: $28,832	Average undergraduate aid package: $23,500

ABOUT THE INSTITUTION Independent, coed. Awards: bachelor's and master's degrees and post-master's certificates. 24 undergraduate majors. Total enrollment: 3,288. Undergraduates: 1,697. Freshmen: 426. Both federal and institutional methodology are used as a basis for awarding need-based institutional aid.

UNDERGRADUATE EXPENSES for 2004–05 *Application fee:* $60. *Comprehensive fee:* $39,208 includes full-time tuition ($28,832) and room and board ($10,376). *College room only:* $6696. Room and board charges vary according to board plan and housing facility. *Payment plan:* Installment.

FRESHMAN FINANCIAL AID (Fall 2004, est.) 237 applied for aid; of those 82% were deemed to have need. 100% of freshmen with need received aid; of those 91% had need fully met. *Average percent of need met:* 98% (excluding resources awarded to replace EFC). *Average financial aid package:* $24,615 (excluding resources awarded to replace EFC). 9% of all full-time freshmen had no need and received non-need-based gift aid.

UNDERGRADUATE FINANCIAL AID (Fall 2004, est.) 806 applied for aid; of those 94% were deemed to have need. 100% of undergraduates with need received aid; of those 91% had need fully met. *Average percent of need met:* 98% (excluding resources awarded to replace EFC). *Average financial aid package:* $23,500 (excluding resources awarded to replace EFC). 7% of all full-time undergraduates had no need and received non-need-based gift aid.

GIFT AID (NEED-BASED) *Total amount:* $13,957,000 (6% federal, 3% state, 91% institutional). *Receiving aid:* Freshmen: 42% (177); All full-time undergraduates: 40% (680). *Average award:* Freshmen: $20,589; Undergraduates: $18,500. *Scholarships, grants, and awards:* Federal Pell, FSEOG, state, college/university gift aid from institutional funds.

GIFT AID (NON-NEED-BASED) *Total amount:* $1,776,000 (84% institutional, 16% external sources). *Receiving aid:* Freshmen: 11% (46); Undergraduates: 8% (130). *Average Award:* Freshmen: $16,800; Undergraduates: $12,200. *Scholarships, grants, and awards by category: Academic Interests/Achievement:* 140 awards ($1,600,000 total): general academic interests/achievements. *Special Achievements/Activities:* 140 awards ($2,000,000 total): leadership. *Tuition waivers:* Full or partial for employees or children of employees. *ROTC:* Army cooperative, Naval cooperative, Air Force cooperative.

LOANS *Student loans:* $6,120,000 (47% need-based, 53% non-need-based). 48% of past graduating class borrowed through all loan programs. *Average indebtedness per student:* $23,500. *Average need-based loan:* Freshmen: $2686; Undergraduates: $3825. *Parent loans:* $3,655,000 (100% non-need-based). *Programs:* FFEL (Subsidized and Unsubsidized Stafford, PLUS), Perkins, state.

WORK-STUDY *Federal work-study:* Total amount: $418,000; 290 jobs averaging $1440. *State or other work-study/employment:* Total amount: $1,160,000 (100% non-need-based). 476 part-time jobs averaging $2430.

APPLYING FOR FINANCIAL AID *Required financial aid forms:* FAFSA, CSS Financial Aid PROFILE, noncustodial (divorced/separated) parent's statement, business/farm supplement, federal income tax form(s), W-2 forms, verification worksheet. *Financial aid deadline:* 2/15 (priority: 2/15). *Notification date:* 4/1. Students must reply by 5/1.

CONTACT Ms. Melissa Shaak, Director of Financial Aid, Babson College, Hollister Hall, 3rd Floor, Babson Park, MA 02457-0310, 781-239-4219 or toll-free 800-488-3696. *Fax:* 781-239-5510. *E-mail:* shaak@babson.edu.

BACONE COLLEGE
Muskogee, OK

ABOUT THE INSTITUTION Independent religious, coed. Awards: associate and bachelor's degrees. 31 undergraduate majors. Total enrollment: 914. Undergraduates: 914. Freshmen: 231.

GIFT AID (NEED-BASED) *Scholarships, grants, and awards:* Federal Pell, FSEOG, state, private, college/university gift aid from institutional funds.

LOANS *Programs:* FFEL (Subsidized and Unsubsidized Stafford, PLUS).

APPLYING FOR FINANCIAL AID *Required financial aid forms:* FAFSA, institution's own form.

CONTACT Office of Financial Aid, Bacone College, 2299 Old Bacone Road, Muskogee, OK 74403-1597, 918-683-4581 Ext. 7298 or toll-free 888-682-5514 Ext. 7340. *Fax:* 918-682-5514. *E-mail:* financialaid@bacone.edu.

BAKER UNIVERSITY
Baldwin City, KS

Tuition & fees: $15,550	Average undergraduate aid package: N/A

ABOUT THE INSTITUTION Independent United Methodist, coed. Awards: bachelor's and master's degrees. 35 undergraduate majors. Total enrollment: 856. Undergraduates: 856. Freshmen: 203. Federal methodology is used as a basis for awarding need-based institutional aid.

UNDERGRADUATE EXPENSES for 2004–05 *One-time required fee:* $80. *Comprehensive fee:* $21,000 includes full-time tuition ($15,200), mandatory fees ($350), and room and board ($5450). *College room only:* $2500. Full-time tuition and fees vary according to location and program. Room and board charges vary according to board plan and housing facility. *Part-time tuition:* $470 per credit hour. Part-time tuition and fees vary according to course load. *Payment plan:* Installment.

GIFT AID (NEED-BASED) *Total amount:* $2,105,431 (34% federal, 45% state, 21% institutional). *Scholarships, grants, and awards:* Federal Pell, FSEOG, state, private, college/university gift aid from institutional funds.

GIFT AID (NON-NEED-BASED) *Total amount:* $3,593,433 (88% institutional, 12% external sources). *Scholarships, grants, and awards by category:* Academic Interests/Achievement: general academic interests/achievements. Creative Arts/Performance: art/fine arts, cinema/film/broadcasting, dance, debating, journalism/publications, music, theater/drama. Special Achievements/Activities: cheerleading/drum major, leadership, religious involvement. Special Characteristics: children and siblings of alumni, children of faculty/staff, ethnic background, international students, members of minority groups, out-of-state students, relatives of clergy. *Tuition waivers:* Full or partial for employees or children of employees, senior citizens. *ROTC:* Army cooperative, Air Force cooperative.

LOANS *Student loans:* $4,461,664 (91% need-based, 9% non-need-based). 68% of past graduating class borrowed through all loan programs. *Average indebtedness per student:* $18,958. *Parent loans:* $1,443,711 (100% non-need-based). *Programs:* FFEL (Subsidized and Unsubsidized Stafford, PLUS), Perkins, college/university, alternative loans.

WORK-STUDY *Federal work-study:* Total amount: $252,828; jobs available. *State or other work-study/employment:* Total amount: $182,055 (100% non-need-based). Part-time jobs available.

ATHLETIC AWARDS *Total amount:* $1,126,535 (100% non-need-based).

APPLYING FOR FINANCIAL AID *Required financial aid forms:* FAFSA, institution's own form. *Financial aid deadline (priority):* 3/1. *Notification date:* Continuous. Students must reply by 5/1 or within 6 weeks of notification.

CONTACT Mrs. Jeanne Mott, Financial Aid Director, Baker University, Box 65, Baldwin City, KS 66006-0065, 785-594-4595 or toll-free 800-873-4282. *Fax:* 785-594-8358.

BALDWIN-WALLACE COLLEGE
Berea, OH

Tuition & fees: $19,494	Average undergraduate aid package: $14,915

ABOUT THE INSTITUTION Independent Methodist, coed. Awards: bachelor's and master's degrees. 69 undergraduate majors. Total enrollment: 4,600. Undergraduates: 3,771. Freshmen: 712. Federal methodology is used as a basis for awarding need-based institutional aid.

UNDERGRADUATE EXPENSES for 2004–05 *Application fee:* $25. *Comprehensive fee:* $25,912 includes full-time tuition ($19,494) and room and board ($6418). *College room only:* $3134. *Part-time tuition:* $620 per semester hour. Part-time tuition and fees vary according to class time. *Payment plans:* Installment, deferred payment.

FRESHMAN FINANCIAL AID (Fall 2004, est.) 682 applied for aid; of those 85% were deemed to have need. 100% of freshmen with need received aid; of those 84% had need fully met. *Average percent of need met:* 94% (excluding resources awarded to replace EFC). *Average financial aid package:* $16,338 (excluding resources awarded to replace EFC). 15% of all full-time freshmen had no need and received non-need-based gift aid.

UNDERGRADUATE FINANCIAL AID (Fall 2004, est.) 2,906 applied for aid; of those 90% were deemed to have need. 100% of undergraduates with need received aid; of those 76% had need fully met. *Average percent of need met:* 94% (excluding resources awarded to replace EFC). *Average financial aid package:* $14,915 (excluding resources awarded to replace EFC). 11% of all full-time undergraduates had no need and received non-need-based gift aid.

GIFT AID (NEED-BASED) *Total amount:* $21,329,000 (12% federal, 15% state, 71% institutional, 2% external sources). *Receiving aid:* Freshmen: 81% (577); All full-time undergraduates: 86% (2,613). *Average award:* Freshmen: $12,242; Undergraduates: $10,135. *Scholarships, grants, and awards:* Federal Pell, FSEOG, state, private, college/university gift aid from institutional funds.

GIFT AID (NON-NEED-BASED) *Total amount:* $7,823,000 (12% state, 79% institutional, 9% external sources). *Receiving aid:* Freshmen: 31% (223); Undergraduates: 37% (1,112). *Average Award:* Freshmen: $5595; Undergraduates: $5931. *Scholarships, grants, and awards by category:* Academic Interests/Achievement: 2,055 awards ($13,326,099 total): general academic interests/achievements. Creative Arts/Performance: 90 awards ($199,233 total): music. Special Achievements/Activities: 107 awards ($379,500 total): leadership. Special Characteristics: 299 awards ($740,958 total): children and siblings of alumni, members of minority groups, religious affiliation. *Tuition waivers:* Full or partial for children of alumni, employees or children of employees. *ROTC:* Air Force cooperative.

LOANS *Student loans:* $16,197,000 (66% need-based, 34% non-need-based). 95% of past graduating class borrowed through all loan programs. *Average indebtedness per student:* $15,993. *Average need-based loan:* Freshmen: $4066; Undergraduates: $4417. *Parent loans:* $3,533,000 (15% need-based, 85% non-need-based). *Programs:* FFEL (Subsidized and Unsubsidized Stafford, PLUS), Perkins, private, educational loans.

WORK-STUDY *Federal work-study:* Total amount: $466,000; 756 jobs averaging $609. *State or other work-study/employment:* Total amount: $972,000 (17% need-based, 83% non-need-based). 756 part-time jobs averaging $1285.

APPLYING FOR FINANCIAL AID *Required financial aid form:* FAFSA. *Financial aid deadline:* 9/1 (priority: 4/1). *Notification date:* Continuous beginning 2/14.

CONTACT Dr. George L. Rolleston, Director of Financial Aid, Baldwin-Wallace College, 275 Eastland Road, Berea, OH 44017-2088, 440-826-2108 or toll-free 877-BWAPPLY (in-state). *E-mail:* grollest@bw.edu.

BALL STATE UNIVERSITY
Muncie, IN

Tuition & fees (IN res): $6260	Average undergraduate aid package: $7263

ABOUT THE INSTITUTION State-supported, coed. Awards: associate, bachelor's, master's, and doctoral degrees and post-bachelor's and post-master's certificates. 124 undergraduate majors. Total enrollment: 20,544. Undergraduates: 17,535. Freshmen: 3,687. Federal methodology is used as a basis for awarding need-based institutional aid.

UNDERGRADUATE EXPENSES for 2004–05 *Application fee:* $25. *Tuition, state resident:* full-time $5752. *Tuition, nonresident:* full-time $14,928. Part-time tuition and fees vary according to course load. *College room and board:* $6228. Room and board charges vary according to board plan and housing facility. *Payment plan:* Installment.

FRESHMAN FINANCIAL AID (Fall 2004, est.) 3101 applied for aid; of those 71% were deemed to have need. 99% of freshmen with need received aid; of those 29% had need fully met. *Average percent of need met:* 62% (excluding resources awarded to replace EFC). *Average financial aid package:* $6924 (excluding resources awarded to replace EFC). 5% of all full-time freshmen had no need and received non-need-based gift aid.

UNDERGRADUATE FINANCIAL AID (Fall 2004, est.) 12,131 applied for aid; of those 75% were deemed to have need. 99% of undergraduates with need received aid; of those 35% had need fully met. *Average percent of need met:* 68% (excluding resources awarded to replace EFC). *Average financial aid package:* $7263 (excluding resources awarded to replace EFC). 3% of all full-time undergraduates had no need and received non-need-based gift aid.

GIFT AID (NEED-BASED) *Total amount:* $28,344,060 (38% federal, 55% state, 7% institutional). *Receiving aid:* Freshmen: 41% (1,512); All full-time undergraduates: 36% (5,863). *Average award:* Freshmen: $4154; Undergraduates: $4355. *Scholarships, grants, and awards:* Federal Pell, FSEOG, state, private, college/university gift aid from institutional funds.

GIFT AID (NON-NEED-BASED) *Total amount:* $18,025,067 (6% federal, 20% state, 52% institutional, 22% external sources). *Receiving aid:* Freshmen: 27% (1,004); Undergraduates: 18% (2,932). *Average Award:* Freshmen: $3538; Undergraduates: $3695. *Scholarships, grants, and awards by category:* Academic Interests/Achievement: 1,810 awards ($6,351,969 total): architecture, biological sciences, business, communication, education, English, foreign languages, general academic interests/achievements, health fields, mathematics, social sciences. Creative Arts/Performance: 233 awards ($236,783 total): art/fine arts, dance, general creative arts/performance, journalism/publications, music, theater/drama. Special Achievements/Activities: 39 awards ($114,464 total): leadership. Special Characteristics: 234 awards ($743,239 total): children of faculty/staff. *Tuition waivers:* Full or partial for employees or children of employees. *ROTC:* Army.

LOANS *Student loans:* $54,136,405 (50% need-based, 50% non-need-based). 61% of past graduating class borrowed through all loan programs. *Average*

indebtedness per student: $17,156. *Average need-based loan:* Freshmen: $2793; Undergraduates: $3526. *Parent loans:* $74,345,117 (100% non-need-based). *Programs:* Federal Direct (Subsidized and Unsubsidized Stafford, PLUS), Perkins. **WORK-STUDY** *Federal work-study:* Total amount: $2,890,601; 1,268 jobs averaging $2280. *State or other work-study/employment:* Total amount: $6,491,798 (10% need-based, 90% non-need-based). 4,141 part-time jobs averaging $1568. **ATHLETIC AWARDS** *Total amount:* $3,873,291 (100% non-need-based). **APPLYING FOR FINANCIAL AID** *Required financial aid form:* FAFSA. *Financial aid deadline (priority):* 3/1. *Notification date:* Continuous beginning 4/1. **CONTACT** Robert Zellers, Director of Scholarships and Financial Aid, Ball State University, Lucina Hall, Room 202, Muncie, IN 47306-1099, 765-285-8898 or toll-free 800-482-4BSU. *Fax:* 765-285-2173. *E-mail:* finaid@bsu.edu.

BALTIMORE HEBREW UNIVERSITY
Baltimore, MD

CONTACT Ms. Yelena Feldman, Financial Aid Counselor, Baltimore Hebrew University, 5800 Park Heights Avenue, Baltimore, MD 21215-3996, 410-578-6913 or toll-free 888-248-7420 (out-of-state). *Fax:* 410-578-6940.

BAPTIST BIBLE COLLEGE
Springfield, MO

CONTACT Ms. Shirley Cutburth, Director of Financial Aid, Baptist Bible College, 628 East Kearney, Springfield, MO 65803-3498, 417-268-6034. *Fax:* 417-268-6694.

BAPTIST BIBLE COLLEGE OF PENNSYLVANIA
Clarks Summit, PA

CONTACT Mr. Thomas Pollock, Director of Student Financial Services, Baptist Bible College of Pennsylvania, 538 Venard Road, Clarks Summit, PA 18411, 570-586-2400 Ext. 9205 or toll-free 800-451-7664. *Fax:* 570-586-1753. *E-mail:* tpollock@bbc.edu.

THE BAPTIST COLLEGE OF FLORIDA
Graceville, FL

Tuition & fees: $6660	Average undergraduate aid package: $5939

ABOUT THE INSTITUTION Independent Southern Baptist, coed. Awards: associate and bachelor's degrees. 9 undergraduate majors. Total enrollment: 652. Undergraduates: 652. Freshmen: 48. Federal methodology is used as a basis for awarding need-based institutional aid.
UNDERGRADUATE EXPENSES for 2004–05 *Application fee:* $20. *Comprehensive fee:* $10,008 includes full-time tuition ($6450), mandatory fees ($210), and room and board ($3348). Full-time tuition and fees vary according to course load. Room and board charges vary according to board plan and housing facility. *Part-time tuition:* $210 per semester hour. *Part-time fees:* $100 per term. Part-time tuition and fees vary according to course load. *Payment plan:* Installment.
FRESHMAN FINANCIAL AID (Fall 2003) 51 applied for aid; of those 82% were deemed to have need. 100% of freshmen with need received aid; of those 7% had need fully met. *Average percent of need met:* 50% (excluding resources awarded to replace EFC). *Average financial aid package:* $4495 (excluding resources awarded to replace EFC). 32% of all full-time freshmen had no need and received non-need-based gift aid.
UNDERGRADUATE FINANCIAL AID (Fall 2003) 307 applied for aid; of those 89% were deemed to have need. 100% of undergraduates with need received aid; of those 5% had need fully met. *Average percent of need met:* 55% (excluding resources awarded to replace EFC). *Average financial aid package:* $5939 (excluding resources awarded to replace EFC). 21% of all full-time undergraduates had no need and received non-need-based gift aid.
GIFT AID (NEED-BASED) *Total amount:* $951,300 (84% federal, 16% state). *Receiving aid:* Freshmen: 61% (38); All full-time undergraduates: 74% (257). *Scholarships, grants, and awards:* Federal Pell, FSEOG, state, private, college/university gift aid from institutional funds.
GIFT AID (NON-NEED-BASED) *Total amount:* $783,833 (27% state, 62% institutional, 11% external sources). *Receiving aid:* Freshmen: 5% (3); Undergraduates: 3% (10). *Average Award:* Freshmen: $600; Undergraduates:

$600. *Scholarships, grants, and awards by category:* Academic Interests/Achievement: 307 awards ($321,200 total): education, religion/biblical studies. Creative Arts/Performance: 13 awards ($52,688 total): music. Special Characteristics: 313 awards ($325,386 total): children with a deceased or disabled parent, religious affiliation, spouses of current students. *Tuition waivers:* Full or partial for employees or children of employees.
LOANS *Student loans:* $1,232,259 (69% need-based, 31% non-need-based). 55% of past graduating class borrowed through all loan programs. *Average indebtedness per student:* $12,824. *Average need-based loan:* Freshmen: $1551; Undergraduates: $2803. *Parent loans:* $64,276 (44% need-based, 56% non-need-based). *Programs:* FFEL (Subsidized and Unsubsidized Stafford, PLUS), college/university.
WORK-STUDY *Federal work-study:* Total amount: $50,111; 33 jobs averaging $1518.
APPLYING FOR FINANCIAL AID *Required financial aid forms:* FAFSA, institution's own form, state aid form, business/farm supplement. *Financial aid deadline:* 4/15 (priority: 3/1). *Notification date:* Continuous beginning 6/15. Students must reply within 4 weeks of notification.
CONTACT Angela Rathel, Director of Financial Aid, The Baptist College of Florida, 5400 College Drive, Graceville, FL 32440-3306, 850-263-3261 Ext. 461 or toll-free 800-328-2660 Ext. 460. *Fax:* 850-263-7506. *E-mail:* finaid@baptistcollege.edu.

BAPTIST COLLEGE OF HEALTH SCIENCES
Memphis, TN

CONTACT Ms. Janet Bonney-Baker, Financial Aid Officer, Baptist College of Health Sciences, 1003 Monroe Avenue, Memphis, TN 38104, 901-227-6805 or toll-free 866-575-2247. *Fax:* 901-227-4311. *E-mail:* janet.bonney@bchs.edu.

BAPTIST MISSIONARY ASSOCIATION THEOLOGICAL SEMINARY
Jacksonville, TX

CONTACT Dr. Philip Attebery, Dean/Registrar, Baptist Missionary Association Theological Seminary, 1530 East Pine Street, Jacksonville, TX 75766-5407, 903-586-2501. *Fax:* 903-586-0378. *E-mail:* bmatsem@bmats.edu.

BAPTIST UNIVERSITY OF THE AMERICAS
San Antonio, TX

CONTACT Financial Aid Office, Baptist University of the Americas, 8019 South Pan Am Expressway, San Antonio, TX 78224-2701, 210-924-4338 or toll-free 800-721-1396.

BARBER-SCOTIA COLLEGE
Concord, NC

CONTACT Financial Aid Counselor, Barber-Scotia College, 145 Cabarrus Avenue, Concord, NC 28025-5187, 704-789-2908 or toll-free 800-610-0778. *Fax:* 704-789-2911.

BARCLAY COLLEGE
Haviland, KS

ABOUT THE INSTITUTION Independent religious, coed. Awards: associate and bachelor's degrees. 8 undergraduate majors. Total enrollment: 183. Undergraduates: 183. Freshmen: 28.
GIFT AID (NEED-BASED) *Scholarships, grants, and awards:* Federal Pell, FSEOG, state, private, college/university gift aid from institutional funds.
GIFT AID (NON-NEED-BASED) *Scholarships, grants, and awards by category:* Academic Interests/Achievement: general academic interests/achievements. Creative Arts/Performance: art/fine arts, music. Special Achievements/Activities: general special achievements/activities, leadership. Special Characteristics: children and siblings of alumni, children of current students, children of faculty/staff, international students, local/state students, married students, parents of current students, relatives of clergy, religious affiliation, siblings of current students, spouses of current students.
LOANS *Programs:* FFEL (Subsidized and Unsubsidized Stafford, PLUS).

WORK-STUDY *Federal work-study:* Total amount: $40,000; 33 jobs averaging $1200. *State or other work-study/employment:* Total amount: $60,000 (67% need-based, 33% non-need-based). 67 part-time jobs averaging $600.
APPLYING FOR FINANCIAL AID *Required financial aid form:* FAFSA.
CONTACT Christina Foster, Financial Aid Coordinator, Barclay College, 607 North Kingman, Haviland, KS 67059, 800-862-0226. *Fax:* 620-862-5403. *E-mail:* financialaid@barclaycollege.edu.

BARD COLLEGE
Annandale-on-Hudson, NY

Tuition & fees: $30,742	Average undergraduate aid package: $23,991

ABOUT THE INSTITUTION Independent, coed. Awards: associate, bachelor's, master's, and doctoral degrees. 88 undergraduate majors. Total enrollment: 1,726. Undergraduates: 1,484. Freshmen: 398. Both federal and institutional methodology are used as a basis for awarding need-based institutional aid.
UNDERGRADUATE EXPENSES for 2004–05 *Application fee:* $50. *One-time required fee:* $510. *Comprehensive fee:* $40,160 includes full-time tuition ($29,910), mandatory fees ($832), and room and board ($9418). *College room only:* $4464. *Part-time tuition:* $935 per credit. *Part-time fees:* $200 per term. *Payment plans:* Tuition prepayment, installment.
FRESHMAN FINANCIAL AID (Fall 2004, est.) 266 applied for aid; of those 84% were deemed to have need. 100% of freshmen with need received aid; of those 61% had need fully met. *Average percent of need met:* 85% (excluding resources awarded to replace EFC). *Average financial aid package:* $23,753 (excluding resources awarded to replace EFC). 2% of all full-time freshmen had no need and received non-need-based gift aid.
UNDERGRADUATE FINANCIAL AID (Fall 2004, est.) 899 applied for aid; of those 98% were deemed to have need. 100% of undergraduates with need received aid; of those 49% had need fully met. *Average percent of need met:* 88% (excluding resources awarded to replace EFC). *Average financial aid package:* $23,991 (excluding resources awarded to replace EFC). 3% of all full-time undergraduates had no need and received non-need-based gift aid.
GIFT AID (NEED-BASED) *Total amount:* $15,226,944 (8% federal, 5% state, 85% institutional, 2% external sources). *Receiving aid:* Freshmen: 53% (210); All full-time undergraduates: 62% (825). *Average award:* Freshmen: $21,464; Undergraduates: $18,869. *Scholarships, grants, and awards:* Federal Pell, FSEOG, state, private, college/university gift aid from institutional funds.
GIFT AID (NON-NEED-BASED) *Total amount:* $621,739 (3% state, 95% institutional, 2% external sources). *Average Award: Freshmen:* $7778; *Undergraduates:* $14,460. *Scholarships, grants, and awards by category: Academic Interests/Achievement:* 13 awards ($491,962 total): biological sciences, general academic interests/achievements, physical sciences. *Special Achievements/Activities:* 13 awards ($28,900 total): leadership. *Special Characteristics:* 16 awards ($390,451 total): children of educators, children of faculty/staff. *Tuition waivers:* Full or partial for employees or children of employees.
LOANS *Student loans:* $4,851,776 (92% need-based, 8% non-need-based). 63% of past graduating class borrowed through all loan programs. *Average indebtedness per student:* $15,921. *Average need-based loan:* Freshmen: $3434; Undergraduates: $4435. *Parent loans:* $3,436,513 (75% need-based, 25% non-need-based). *Programs:* FFEL (Subsidized and Unsubsidized Stafford, PLUS), Perkins, college/university loans from institutional funds (for international students only).
WORK-STUDY *Federal work-study:* Total amount: $890,993; 586 jobs averaging $1520. *State or other work-study/employment:* Total amount: $244,206 (97% need-based, 3% non-need-based). 59 part-time jobs averaging $1637.
APPLYING FOR FINANCIAL AID *Required financial aid forms:* FAFSA, CSS Financial Aid PROFILE, state aid form, noncustodial (divorced/separated) parent's statement, business/farm supplement. *Financial aid deadline:* 2/15 (priority: 2/1). *Notification date:* 4/1. Students must reply by 5/1 or within 2 weeks of notification.
CONTACT Denise Ann Ackerman, Director of Financial Aid, Bard College, Annandale Road, Annandale-on-Hudson, NY 12504, 845-758-7525. *Fax:* 845-758-7336. *E-mail:* ackerman@bard.edu.

BARNARD COLLEGE
New York, NY

ABOUT THE INSTITUTION Independent, women only. Awards: bachelor's degrees. 66 undergraduate majors. Total enrollment: 2,287. Undergraduates: 2,287. Freshmen: 553.

GIFT AID (NEED-BASED) *Scholarships, grants, and awards:* Federal Pell, FSEOG, state, private, college/university gift aid from institutional funds.
LOANS *Programs:* FFEL (Subsidized and Unsubsidized Stafford, PLUS), Perkins, state, college/university, alternative loans.
WORK-STUDY *Federal work-study:* Total amount: $722,824; 449 jobs averaging $1610. *State or other work-study/employment:* Total amount: $873,036 (58% need-based, 42% non-need-based). 586 part-time jobs averaging $1490.
APPLYING FOR FINANCIAL AID *Required financial aid forms:* FAFSA, institution's own form, CSS Financial Aid PROFILE, state aid form, noncustodial (divorced/separated) parent's statement, business/farm supplement, federal income tax form(s).
CONTACT Ms. SuzanneClair Guard, Director of Financial Aid, Barnard College, 3009 Broadway, New York, NY 10027-6598, 212-854-2154. *Fax:* 212-531-1058. *E-mail:* sguard@barnard.edu.

BARNES-JEWISH COLLEGE OF NURSING AND ALLIED HEALTH
St. Louis, MO

ABOUT THE INSTITUTION Independent, coed, primarily women. Awards: associate, bachelor's, and master's degrees and post-bachelor's and post-master's certificates. 3 undergraduate majors. Total enrollment: 781. Undergraduates: 686. Freshmen: 42.
GIFT AID (NEED-BASED) *Scholarships, grants, and awards:* Federal Pell, FSEOG, state, private, college/university gift aid from institutional funds.
GIFT AID (NON-NEED-BASED) *Scholarships, grants, and awards by category: Academic Interests/Achievement:* general academic interests/achievements.
LOANS *Programs:* FFEL (Subsidized and Unsubsidized Stafford, PLUS), state, college/university.
WORK-STUDY *Federal work-study:* Total amount: $32,000; 10 jobs averaging $3300.
APPLYING FOR FINANCIAL AID *Required financial aid forms:* FAFSA, institution's own form.
CONTACT Regina Blackshear, Chief Financial Aid Officer, Barnes-Jewish College of Nursing and Allied Health, 306 South Kingshighway, St. Louis, MO 63110-1091, 314-454-7770 or toll-free 800-832-9009 (in-state).

BARRY UNIVERSITY
Miami Shores, FL

Tuition & fees: $22,430	Average undergraduate aid package: $14,855

ABOUT THE INSTITUTION Independent Roman Catholic, coed. Awards: bachelor's, master's, doctoral, and first professional degrees and post-bachelor's certificates. 58 undergraduate majors. Total enrollment: 9,207. Undergraduates: 5,942. Freshmen: 553. Federal methodology is used as a basis for awarding need-based institutional aid.
UNDERGRADUATE EXPENSES for 2005–06 *Application fee:* $30. *Comprehensive fee:* $30,050 includes full-time tuition ($22,430) and room and board ($7620). Room and board charges vary according to board plan. Part-time tuition and fees vary according to course load. *Payment plans:* Tuition prepayment, installment, deferred payment.
FRESHMAN FINANCIAL AID (Fall 2004, est.) 482 applied for aid; of those 90% were deemed to have need. 100% of freshmen with need received aid; of those 9% had need fully met. *Average percent of need met:* 73% (excluding resources awarded to replace EFC). *Average financial aid package:* $18,727 (excluding resources awarded to replace EFC). 14% of all full-time freshmen had no need and received non-need-based gift aid.
UNDERGRADUATE FINANCIAL AID (Fall 2004, est.) 3,661 applied for aid; of those 93% were deemed to have need. 100% of undergraduates with need received aid; of those 8% had need fully met. *Average percent of need met:* 65% (excluding resources awarded to replace EFC). *Average financial aid package:* $14,855 (excluding resources awarded to replace EFC). 8% of all full-time undergraduates had no need and received non-need-based gift aid.
GIFT AID (NEED-BASED) *Total amount:* $15,946,123 (41% federal, 11% state, 48% institutional). *Receiving aid:* Freshmen: 71% (390); All full-time undergraduates: 58% (2,574). *Average award:* Freshmen: $9866; Undergraduates: $6514. *Scholarships, grants, and awards:* Federal Pell, FSEOG, state, private, college/university gift aid from institutional funds, Federal Nursing.
GIFT AID (NON-NEED-BASED) *Total amount:* $22,339,526 (1% federal, 32% state, 66% institutional, 1% external sources). *Receiving aid:* Freshmen: 78%

(428); Undergraduates: 73% (3,252). *Average Award: Freshmen:* $5340; *Undergraduates:* $5623. *Scholarships, grants, and awards by category: Academic Interests/Achievement:* general academic interests/achievements. *Creative Arts/Performance:* applied art and design, art/fine arts, theater/drama. *Special Achievements/Activities:* community service, general special achievements/ activities, leadership, memberships, religious involvement. *ROTC:* Air Force cooperative.

LOANS *Student loans:* $31,144,886 (45% need-based, 55% non-need-based). 70% of past graduating class borrowed through all loan programs. *Average indebtedness per student:* $23,322. *Average need-based loan:* Freshmen: $2629; Undergraduates: $4418. *Parent loans:* $4,369,866 (100% non-need-based). *Programs:* FFEL (Subsidized and Unsubsidized Stafford, PLUS), Perkins, Federal Nursing, college/university, alternative loans.

WORK-STUDY *Federal work-study:* Total amount: $977,516; 598 jobs averaging $2432. *State or other work-study/employment:* Total amount: $226,595 (100% non-need-based). Part-time jobs available.

ATHLETIC AWARDS *Total amount:* $1,983,606 (100% non-need-based).

APPLYING FOR FINANCIAL AID *Required financial aid form:* FAFSA. *Financial aid deadline:* Continuous. *Notification date:* Continuous beginning 1/25.

CONTACT Mr. Dart Humeston, Assistant Dean of Enrollment Services/Director of Financial Aid, Barry University, 11300 Northeast Second Avenue, Miami Shores, FL 33161-6695, 305-899-3673 or toll-free 800-695-2279. *E-mail:* finaid@ mail.barry.edu.

BARTON COLLEGE
Wilson, NC

Tuition & fees: $16,670	Average undergraduate aid package: $14,074

ABOUT THE INSTITUTION Independent religious, coed. Awards: bachelor's degrees and post-bachelor's certificates. 32 undergraduate majors. Total enrollment: 1,231. Undergraduates: 1,231. Freshmen: 262. Federal methodology is used as a basis for awarding need-based institutional aid.

UNDERGRADUATE EXPENSES for 2005–06 *Application fee:* $25. *Comprehensive fee:* $22,470 includes full-time tuition ($15,390), mandatory fees ($1280), and room and board ($5800). *College room only:* $2774. Full-time tuition and fees vary according to course load and program. Room and board charges vary according to housing facility. *Part-time tuition:* $654 per credit hour. Part-time tuition and fees vary according to course load and program. *Payment plan:* Installment.

FRESHMAN FINANCIAL AID (Fall 2004, est.) 222 applied for aid; of those 92% were deemed to have need. 100% of freshmen with need received aid; of those 19% had need fully met. *Average percent of need met:* 77% (excluding resources awarded to replace EFC). *Average financial aid package:* $13,944 (excluding resources awarded to replace EFC). 15% of all full-time freshmen had no need and received non-need-based gift aid.

UNDERGRADUATE FINANCIAL AID (Fall 2004, est.) 764 applied for aid; of those 92% were deemed to have need. 100% of undergraduates with need received aid; of those 18% had need fully met. *Average percent of need met:* 73% (excluding resources awarded to replace EFC). *Average financial aid package:* $14,074 (excluding resources awarded to replace EFC). 20% of all full-time undergraduates had no need and received non-need-based gift aid.

GIFT AID (NEED-BASED) *Total amount:* $2,421,369 (56% federal, 39% state, 1% institutional, 4% external sources). *Receiving aid:* Freshmen: 52% (135); All full-time undergraduates: 51% (494). *Average award:* Freshmen: $4290; Undergraduates: $4672. *Scholarships, grants, and awards:* Federal Pell, FSEOG, state, private, college/university gift aid from institutional funds, Federal Nursing.

GIFT AID (NON-NEED-BASED) *Total amount:* $2,836,504 (49% state, 45% institutional, 6% external sources). *Receiving aid:* Freshmen: 74% (191); Undergraduates: 66% (643). *Average Award:* Freshmen: $2954; Undergraduates: $3012. *Scholarships, grants, and awards by category: Academic Interests/ Achievement:* 1,243 awards ($2,326,841 total): biological sciences, business, communication, computer science, education, English, general academic interests/ achievements, health fields, humanities, mathematics, physical sciences, religion/ biblical studies, social sciences. *Creative Arts/Performance:* 11 awards ($6600 total): art/fine arts, music, theater/drama. *Special Achievements/Activities:* 21 awards ($31,500 total): general special achievements/activities, leadership, religious involvement. *Special Characteristics:* 145 awards ($478,000 total): adult students, children and siblings of alumni, children of faculty/staff, international students, local/state students, relatives of clergy, religious affiliation, siblings of current students, veterans. *Tuition waivers:* Full or partial for children of alumni, employees or children of employees, adult students, senior citizens.

LOANS *Student loans:* $4,851,086 (53% need-based, 47% non-need-based). 69% of past graduating class borrowed through all loan programs. *Average indebtedness per student:* $16,703. *Average need-based loan:* Freshmen: $2976; Undergraduates: $4243. *Parent loans:* $1,274,426 (100% non-need-based). *Programs:* FFEL (Subsidized and Unsubsidized Stafford, PLUS), Perkins, alternative loans.

WORK-STUDY *Federal work-study:* Total amount: $525,100; 468 jobs averaging $1038.

ATHLETIC AWARDS *Total amount:* $742,893 (100% non-need-based).

APPLYING FOR FINANCIAL AID *Required financial aid form:* FAFSA. *Financial aid deadline (priority):* 4/1. *Notification date:* Continuous. Students must reply by 5/1 or within 2 weeks of notification.

CONTACT Ms. Bettie Westbrook, Director of Financial Aid, Barton College, Box 5000, Wilson, NC 27893, 252-399-6316 or toll-free 800-345-4973. *Fax:* 252-399-6572. *E-mail:* aid@barton.edu.

BASTYR UNIVERSITY
Kenmore, WA

Tuition & fees: $14,400	Average undergraduate aid package: $16,050

ABOUT THE INSTITUTION Independent, coed. Awards: bachelor's, master's, and first professional degrees and post-bachelor's, post-master's, and first professional certificates. 6 undergraduate majors. Total enrollment: 996. Undergraduates: 246. Entering class: . Federal methodology is used as a basis for awarding need-based institutional aid.

UNDERGRADUATE EXPENSES for 2004–05 *Application fee:* $60. *Tuition:* full-time $13,140; part-time $269 per credit. Full-time tuition and fees vary according to course load and program. Part-time tuition and fees vary according to course load and program. Room and board charges vary according to board plan and housing facility.

UNDERGRADUATE FINANCIAL AID (Fall 2003) 200 applied for aid; of those 100% were deemed to have need. 100% of undergraduates with need received aid. *Average percent of need met:* 50% (excluding resources awarded to replace EFC). *Average financial aid package:* $16,050 (excluding resources awarded to replace EFC).

GIFT AID (NEED-BASED) *Total amount:* $709,709 (55% federal, 32% state, 10% institutional, 3% external sources). *Receiving aid:* All full-time undergraduates: 89% (192). *Average award:* Undergraduates: $8005. *Scholarships, grants, and awards:* Federal Pell, FSEOG, state, private, college/university gift aid from institutional funds.

GIFT AID (NON-NEED-BASED) *Scholarships, grants, and awards by category: Academic Interests/Achievement:* health fields. *Tuition waivers:* Full or partial for employees or children of employees.

LOANS *Student loans:* $2,660,686 (100% need-based). 80% of past graduating class borrowed through all loan programs. *Average indebtedness per student:* $21,000. *Average need-based loan:* Undergraduates: $5500. *Parent loans:* $12,000 (100% need-based). *Programs:* FFEL (Subsidized and Unsubsidized Stafford, PLUS), Perkins.

WORK-STUDY *Federal work-study:* Total amount: $82,636; 40 jobs averaging $3000. *State or other work-study/employment:* Total amount: $10,365 (100% need-based). 31 part-time jobs averaging $3000.

APPLYING FOR FINANCIAL AID *Required financial aid forms:* FAFSA, institution's own form. *Financial aid deadline (priority):* 5/1. *Notification date:* Continuous beginning 5/15. Students must reply within 3 weeks of notification.

CONTACT Maria Rebecchi, Assistant Director of Financial Aid, Bastyr University, 14500 Juanita Drive NE, Kenmore, WA 98028-4966, 425-602-3081. *Fax:* 425-602-3090. *E-mail:* finaid@bastyr.edu.

BATES COLLEGE
Lewiston, ME

Comprehensive fee: $39,900	Average undergraduate aid package: $25,836

ABOUT THE INSTITUTION Independent, coed. Awards: bachelor's degrees. 34 undergraduate majors. Total enrollment: 1,743. Undergraduates: 1,743. Freshmen: 467. Both federal and institutional methodology are used as a basis for awarding need-based institutional aid.

UNDERGRADUATE EXPENSES for 2004–05 *Application fee:* $60. *Comprehensive fee:* $39,900. *Payment plans:* Tuition prepayment, installment.

FRESHMAN FINANCIAL AID (Fall 2004, est.) 245 applied for aid; of those 82% were deemed to have need. 93% of freshmen with need received aid; of those 96% had need fully met. *Average percent of need met:* 100% (excluding resources awarded to replace EFC). *Average financial aid package:* $25,317 (excluding resources awarded to replace EFC).

UNDERGRADUATE FINANCIAL AID (Fall 2004, est.) 830 applied for aid; of those 92% were deemed to have need. 92% of undergraduates with need received aid; of those 96% had need fully met. *Average percent of need met:* 100% (excluding resources awarded to replace EFC). *Average financial aid package:* $25,836 (excluding resources awarded to replace EFC).

GIFT AID (NEED-BASED) *Total amount:* $15,216,609 (4% federal, 93% institutional, 3% external sources). *Receiving aid:* Freshmen: 40% (185); All full-time undergraduates: 40% (690). *Average award:* Freshmen: $21,983; Undergraduates: $22,053. *Scholarships, grants, and awards:* Federal Pell, FSEOG, state, private, college/university gift aid from institutional funds.

GIFT AID (NON-NEED-BASED) *Total amount:* $53,364 (100% external sources). *Tuition waivers:* Full or partial for employees or children of employees.

LOANS *Student loans:* $3,015,294 (61% need-based, 39% non-need-based). 41% of past graduating class borrowed through all loan programs. *Average indebtedness per student:* $13,986. *Average need-based loan:* Freshmen: $3230; Undergraduates: $3683. *Parent loans:* $1,696,782 (100% non-need-based). *Programs:* FFEL (Subsidized and Unsubsidized Stafford, PLUS), Perkins, state.

WORK-STUDY *Federal work-study:* Total amount: $894,715; 557 jobs averaging $1606. *State or other work-study/employment:* Total amount: $135,900 (100% need-based). 78 part-time jobs averaging $1742.

APPLYING FOR FINANCIAL AID *Required financial aid forms:* FAFSA, CSS Financial Aid PROFILE, business/farm supplement. *Financial aid deadline:* 2/1. *Notification date:* 4/2. Students must reply by 5/1.

CONTACT Meredith Braz, Registrar/Director of Student Financial Services, Bates College, 44 Mountain Avenue, Lewiston, ME 04240, 207-786-6096. *Fax:* 207-786-8350. *E-mail:* mbraz@bates.edu.

BAYAMÓN CENTRAL UNIVERSITY
Bayamón, PR

CONTACT Financial Aid Director, Bayamón Central University, PO Box 1725, Bayamón, PR 00960-1725, 787-786-3030 Ext. 2115. *Fax:* 787-785-4365.

BAYLOR UNIVERSITY
Waco, TX

Tuition & fees: $21,070	Average undergraduate aid package: $14,153

ABOUT THE INSTITUTION Independent Baptist, coed. Awards: bachelor's, master's, doctoral, and first professional degrees and post-master's certificates. 131 undergraduate majors. Total enrollment: 13,799. Undergraduates: 11,580. Freshmen: 2,785. Federal methodology is used as a basis for awarding need-based institutional aid.

UNDERGRADUATE EXPENSES for 2005–06 *Application fee:* $35. *Comprehensive fee:* $27,555 includes full-time tuition ($19,050), mandatory fees ($2020), and room and board ($6485). *College room only:* $3346. Room and board charges vary according to board plan and housing facility. *Part-time tuition:* $794 per semester hour. *Part-time fees:* $78 per semester hour. *Payment plan:* Installment.

FRESHMAN FINANCIAL AID (Fall 2004, est.) 1974 applied for aid; of those 79% were deemed to have need. 100% of freshmen with need received aid; of those 18% had need fully met. *Average percent of need met:* 75% (excluding resources awarded to replace EFC). *Average financial aid package:* $16,553 (excluding resources awarded to replace EFC). 35% of all full-time freshmen had no need and received non-need-based gift aid.

UNDERGRADUATE FINANCIAL AID (Fall 2004, est.) 6,796 applied for aid; of those 81% were deemed to have need. 99% of undergraduates with need received aid; of those 19% had need fully met. *Average percent of need met:* 68% (excluding resources awarded to replace EFC). *Average financial aid package:* $14,153 (excluding resources awarded to replace EFC). 29% of all full-time undergraduates had no need and received non-need-based gift aid.

GIFT AID (NEED-BASED) *Total amount:* $48,137,546 (13% federal, 22% state, 59% institutional, 6% external sources). *Receiving aid:* Freshmen: 56% (1,544); All full-time undergraduates: 46% (5,075). *Average award:* Freshmen: $11,850; Undergraduates: $9743. *Scholarships, grants, and awards:* Federal Pell, FSEOG, state, private, college/university gift aid from institutional funds.

GIFT AID (NON-NEED-BASED) *Total amount:* $22,612,916 (85% institutional, 15% external sources). *Receiving aid:* Freshmen: 43% (1,189); Undergradu-

ates: 32% (3,509). *Average Award:* Freshmen: $6767; Undergraduates: $6412. *Scholarships, grants, and awards by category:* Academic Interests/Achievement: 7,470 awards ($32,426,392 total): business, communication, computer science, education, engineering/technologies, English, foreign languages, general academic interests/achievements, health fields, home economics, humanities, international studies, mathematics, military science, physical sciences, premedicine, religion/biblical studies, social sciences. *Creative Arts/Performance:* 526 awards ($1,573,128 total): art/fine arts, cinema/film/broadcasting, debating, journalism/publications, music, theater/drama. *Special Achievements/Activities:* 595 awards ($1,156,127 total): community service, leadership, religious involvement. *Special Characteristics:* 288 awards ($4,154,933 total): children of faculty/staff. *Tuition waivers:* Full or partial for employees or children of employees. *ROTC:* Air Force.

LOANS *Student loans:* $49,152,586 (68% need-based, 32% non-need-based). *Average need-based loan:* Freshmen: $2382; Undergraduates: $2494. *Parent loans:* $18,197,501 (24% need-based, 76% non-need-based). *Programs:* FFEL (Subsidized and Unsubsidized Stafford, PLUS), Perkins, Federal Nursing, state, college/university.

WORK-STUDY *Federal work-study:* Total amount: $7,600,968; 2,998 jobs averaging $2535. *State or other work-study/employment:* Part-time jobs available.

ATHLETIC AWARDS *Total amount:* $5,606,950 (27% need-based, 73% non-need-based).

APPLYING FOR FINANCIAL AID *Required financial aid form:* FAFSA. *Financial aid deadline (priority):* 3/1. *Notification date:* Continuous. Students must reply by 5/1 or within 2 weeks of notification.

CONTACT Office of Admission Services, Baylor University, PO Box 97056, Waco, TX 76798-7056, 254-710-3435 or toll-free 800-BAYLOR U. *Fax:* 254-710-3436. *E-mail:* admissions@baylor.edu.

BAY PATH COLLEGE
Longmeadow, MA

Tuition & fees: $19,440	Average undergraduate aid package: $11,453

ABOUT THE INSTITUTION Independent, women only. Awards: associate, bachelor's, and master's degrees and post-bachelor's certificates. 13 undergraduate majors. Total enrollment: 1,417. Undergraduates: 1,347. Freshmen: 256. Federal methodology is used as a basis for awarding need-based institutional aid.

UNDERGRADUATE EXPENSES for 2004–05 *Application fee:* $25. *Comprehensive fee:* $27,700 includes full-time tuition ($19,440) and room and board ($8260). Room and board charges vary according to board plan. *Part-time tuition:* $440 per credit. *Payment plans:* Installment, deferred payment.

FRESHMAN FINANCIAL AID (Fall 2004, est.) 196 applied for aid; of those 92% were deemed to have need. 100% of freshmen with need received aid; of those 12% had need fully met. *Average percent of need met:* 71% (excluding resources awarded to replace EFC). *Average financial aid package:* $13,373 (excluding resources awarded to replace EFC). 10% of all full-time freshmen had no need and received non-need-based gift aid.

UNDERGRADUATE FINANCIAL AID (Fall 2004, est.) 858 applied for aid; of those 91% were deemed to have need. 100% of undergraduates with need received aid; of those 10% had need fully met. *Average percent of need met:* 66% (excluding resources awarded to replace EFC). *Average financial aid package:* $11,453 (excluding resources awarded to replace EFC). 13% of all full-time undergraduates had no need and received non-need-based gift aid.

GIFT AID (NEED-BASED) *Total amount:* $6,558,242 (23% federal, 6% state, 68% institutional, 3% external sources). *Receiving aid:* Freshmen: 90% (181); All full-time undergraduates: 87% (781). *Average award:* Freshmen: $9215; Undergraduates: $7465. *Scholarships, grants, and awards:* Federal Pell, FSEOG, state, private, college/university gift aid from institutional funds.

GIFT AID (NON-NEED-BASED) *Total amount:* $715,201 (95% institutional, 5% external sources). *Receiving aid:* Freshmen: 5% (10); Undergraduates: 5% (45). *Average Award:* Freshmen: $10,651; Undergraduates: $10,982. *Scholarships, grants, and awards by category:* Academic Interests/Achievement: 298 awards ($2,469,899 total): general academic interests/achievements. *Creative Arts/Performance:* dance, performing arts, theater/drama. *Special Achievements/Activities:* general special achievements/activities, memberships. *Special Characteristics:* 1 award ($16,890 total): adult students, children of faculty/staff, children of public servants, children with a deceased or disabled parent, general special characteristics, international students, out-of-state students, siblings of current students, twins. *Tuition waivers:* Full or partial for employees or children of employees. *ROTC:* Army cooperative, Air Force cooperative.

Bay Path College

LOANS *Student loans:* $8,534,062 (72% need-based, 28% non-need-based). 67% of past graduating class borrowed through all loan programs. *Average indebtedness per student:* $18,200. *Average need-based loan:* Freshmen: $3996; Undergraduates: $4045. *Parent loans:* $988,935 (41% need-based, 59% non-need-based). *Programs:* Federal Direct (Subsidized and Unsubsidized Stafford, PLUS), FFEL (Subsidized and Unsubsidized Stafford, PLUS), Perkins, state.

WORK-STUDY *Federal work-study:* Total amount: $161,481; 146 jobs averaging $2000.

APPLYING FOR FINANCIAL AID *Required financial aid forms:* FAFSA, institution's own form. *Financial aid deadline (priority):* 3/15. *Notification date:* Continuous. Students must reply within 2 weeks of notification.

CONTACT Phyllis Brand, Financial Aid Assistant, Bay Path College, 588 Longmeadow Street, Longmeadow, MA 01106-2292, 413-565-1261 or toll-free 800-782-7284 Ext. 331. *Fax:* 413-565-1101. *E-mail:* pbrand@baypath.edu.

BEACON COLLEGE
Leesburg, FL

CONTACT Financial Aid Office, Beacon College, 105 East Main Street, Leesburg, FL 34748, 352-787-7660.

BEACON COLLEGE AND GRADUATE SCHOOL
Columbus, GA

ABOUT THE INSTITUTION Independent religious, coed. Awards: associate, bachelor's, master's, and doctoral degrees. 3 undergraduate majors. Total enrollment: 141. Undergraduates: 107.

GIFT AID (NEED-BASED) *Scholarships, grants, and awards:* Federal Pell.

GIFT AID (NON-NEED-BASED) *Scholarships, grants, and awards by category: Academic Interests/Achievement:* business, religion/biblical studies, social sciences.

LOANS *Programs:* FFEL (Subsidized and Unsubsidized Stafford, PLUS).

APPLYING FOR FINANCIAL AID *Required financial aid form:* FAFSA.

CONTACT Mrs. Rita Roberts, Director of Student Financial Affairs, Beacon College and Graduate School, 6003 Veterans Parkway, Columbus, GA 31909-4663, 706-323-5364 Ext. 254. *Fax:* 706-323-3236. *E-mail:* rita.roberts@beacon.edu.

BECKER COLLEGE
Worcester, MA

Tuition & fees: $17,590	Average undergraduate aid package: $8871

ABOUT THE INSTITUTION Independent, coed. Awards: associate and bachelor's degrees (also includes Leicester, MA small town campus). 38 undergraduate majors. Total enrollment: 1,660. Undergraduates: 1,660. Freshmen: 496. Federal methodology is used as a basis for awarding need-based institutional aid.

UNDERGRADUATE EXPENSES for 2004–05 *Application fee:* $30. *Comprehensive fee:* $25,590 includes full-time tuition ($17,200), mandatory fees ($390), and room and board ($8000). *Part-time tuition:* $575 per credit. Part-time tuition and fees vary according to program. *Payment plan:* Installment.

FRESHMAN FINANCIAL AID (Fall 2003) 246 applied for aid; of those 92% were deemed to have need. 100% of freshmen with need received aid; of those 11% had need fully met. *Average percent of need met:* 49% (excluding resources awarded to replace EFC). *Average financial aid package:* $8027 (excluding resources awarded to replace EFC). 9% of all full-time freshmen had no need and received non-need-based gift aid.

UNDERGRADUATE FINANCIAL AID (Fall 2003) 720 applied for aid; of those 92% were deemed to have need. 100% of undergraduates with need received aid; of those 10% had need fully met. *Average percent of need met:* 51% (excluding resources awarded to replace EFC). *Average financial aid package:* $8871 (excluding resources awarded to replace EFC). 9% of all full-time undergraduates had no need and received non-need-based gift aid.

GIFT AID (NEED-BASED) *Total amount:* $3,686,876 (28% federal, 8% state, 60% institutional, 4% external sources). *Receiving aid:* Freshmen: 87% (218); All full-time undergraduates: 86% (634). *Average award:* Freshmen: $5318; Undergraduates: $5493. *Scholarships, grants, and awards:* Federal Pell, FSEOG, state, private, college/university gift aid from institutional funds.

GIFT AID (NON-NEED-BASED) *Total amount:* $45,474 (1% federal, 8% state, 69% institutional, 22% external sources). *Receiving aid:* Freshmen: 1% (2);

Undergraduates: 2% (13). *Average Award:* Freshmen: $11,278; Undergraduates: $10,957. *Scholarships, grants, and awards by category: Academic Interests/Achievement:* 16 awards ($33,500 total): general academic interests/achievements. *Special Achievements/Activities:* 12 awards ($23,500 total): general special achievements/activities, leadership. *Special Characteristics:* 19 awards ($110,290 total): children of faculty/staff, siblings of current students, twins. *Tuition waivers:* Full or partial for employees or children of employees, senior citizens. *ROTC:* Army cooperative, Naval cooperative, Air Force cooperative.

LOANS *Student loans:* $6,983,366 (71% need-based, 29% non-need-based). 97% of past graduating class borrowed through all loan programs. *Average indebtedness per student:* $21,938. *Average need-based loan:* Freshmen: $2298; Undergraduates: $2770. *Parent loans:* $1,519,603 (55% need-based, 45% non-need-based). *Programs:* FFEL (Subsidized and Unsubsidized Stafford, PLUS), state, alternative loans.

WORK-STUDY *Federal work-study:* Total amount: $451,573; 321 jobs averaging $1090.

APPLYING FOR FINANCIAL AID *Required financial aid form:* FAFSA. *Financial aid deadline (priority):* 3/1. *Notification date:* Continuous. Students must reply within 2 weeks of notification.

CONTACT Denise Lawrie, Director of Financial Aid, Becker College, 61 Sever Street, PO Box 15071, Worcester, MA 01615-0071, 508-791-9241 Ext. 242 or toll-free 877-5BECKER Ext. 245. *Fax:* 508-890-1511. *E-mail:* lawrie@beckercollege.edu.

BEIS MEDRASH HEICHAL DOVID
Far Rockaway, NY

CONTACT Financial Aid Office, Beis Medrash Heichal Dovid, 257 Beach 17th Street, Far Rockaway, NY 11691, 718-868-2300.

BELHAVEN COLLEGE
Jackson, MS

Tuition & fees: $14,050	Average undergraduate aid package: $9376

ABOUT THE INSTITUTION Independent Presbyterian, coed. Awards: associate, bachelor's, and master's degrees. 22 undergraduate majors. Total enrollment: 2,505. Undergraduates: 2,164. Freshmen: 181. Federal methodology is used as a basis for awarding need-based institutional aid.

UNDERGRADUATE EXPENSES for 2005–06 *Application fee:* $25. *Comprehensive fee:* $19,480 includes full-time tuition ($13,400), mandatory fees ($650), and room and board ($5430). Room and board charges vary according to housing facility. *Part-time tuition:* $375 per semester hour. *Part-time fees:* $70 per term. Part-time tuition and fees vary according to course load. *Payment plan:* Installment.

FRESHMAN FINANCIAL AID (Fall 2004, est.) 146 applied for aid; of those 73% were deemed to have need. 100% of freshmen with need received aid; of those 16% had need fully met. *Average percent of need met:* 54% (excluding resources awarded to replace EFC). *Average financial aid package:* $10,408 (excluding resources awarded to replace EFC). 24% of all full-time freshmen had no need and received non-need-based gift aid.

UNDERGRADUATE FINANCIAL AID (Fall 2004, est.) 2,092 applied for aid; of those 65% were deemed to have need. 100% of undergraduates with need received aid; of those 6% had need fully met. *Average percent of need met:* 52% (excluding resources awarded to replace EFC). *Average financial aid package:* $9376 (excluding resources awarded to replace EFC). 7% of all full-time undergraduates had no need and received non-need-based gift aid.

GIFT AID (NEED-BASED) *Total amount:* $2,748,478 (97% federal, 3% state). *Receiving aid:* Freshmen: 54% (98); All full-time undergraduates: 56% (1,251). *Average award:* Freshmen: $7582; Undergraduates: $5325. *Scholarships, grants, and awards:* Federal Pell, FSEOG, state, private, college/university gift aid from institutional funds.

GIFT AID (NON-NEED-BASED) *Total amount:* $3,643,095 (13% state, 81% institutional, 6% external sources). *Receiving aid:* Freshmen: 59% (107); Undergraduates: 50% (1,104). *Average Award:* Freshmen: $7867; Undergraduates: $5583. *Scholarships, grants, and awards by category: Academic Interests/Achievement:* 732 awards ($2,135,171 total): biological sciences, business, communication, computer science, education, English, foreign languages, general academic interests/achievements, humanities, mathematics, premedicine, religion/biblical studies, social sciences. *Creative Arts/Performance:* 166 awards ($275,667 total): applied art and design, art/fine arts, dance, music, performing arts, theater/drama. *Special Achievements/Activities:* 441 awards ($183,225 total):

cheerleading/drum major, general special achievements/activities, junior miss, leadership. *Special Characteristics:* 176 awards ($231,800 total): children of faculty/staff, general special characteristics, international students, local/state students, relatives of clergy, religious affiliation. *Tuition waivers:* Full or partial for employees or children of employees.
LOANS *Student loans:* $13,107,891 (50% need-based, 50% non-need-based). 87% of past graduating class borrowed through all loan programs. *Average indebtedness per student:* $18,126. *Average need-based loan:* Freshmen: $3000; Undergraduates: $4310. *Parent loans:* $694,469 (100% non-need-based). *Programs:* FFEL (Subsidized and Unsubsidized Stafford, PLUS), Perkins.
WORK-STUDY *Federal work-study:* Total amount: $291,549; 124 jobs averaging $1600. *State or other work-study/employment:* Total amount: $3299 (100% need-based).
ATHLETIC AWARDS *Total amount:* $995,721 (100% non-need-based).
APPLYING FOR FINANCIAL AID *Required financial aid forms:* FAFSA, state aid form. *Financial aid deadline (priority):* 3/1. *Notification date:* Continuous beginning 3/1. Students must reply within 4 weeks of notification.
CONTACT Ms. Linda Phillips, Director of Student Financial Planning, Belhaven College, 1500 Peachtree Street, Jackson, MS 39202-1789, 601-968-5934 or toll-free 800-960-5940. *Fax:* 601-353-0701. *E-mail:* lphillips@belhaven.edu.

BELLARMINE UNIVERSITY
Louisville, KY

CONTACT Associate Director of Financial Aid, Bellarmine University, 2001 Newburg Road, Louisville, KY 40205-0671, 502-452-8124 or toll-free 800-274-4723 Ext. 8131. *Fax:* 502-452-8002.

BELLEVUE UNIVERSITY
Bellevue, NE

Tuition & fees: $4740 | **Average undergraduate aid package: $4107**

ABOUT THE INSTITUTION Independent, coed. Awards: bachelor's and master's degrees. 14 undergraduate majors. Total enrollment: 5,524. Undergraduates: 4,293. Freshmen: 175. Federal methodology is used as a basis for awarding need-based institutional aid.
UNDERGRADUATE EXPENSES for 2004–05 *Application fee:* $25. *Tuition:* full-time $4650; part-time $155 per credit hour. *Required fees:* full-time $90; $45 per term part-time. Full-time tuition and fees vary according to program. Part-time tuition and fees vary according to program. *Payment plans:* Installment, deferred payment.
FRESHMAN FINANCIAL AID (Fall 2003) 83 applied for aid; of those 100% were deemed to have need. 100% of freshmen with need received aid. *Average financial aid package:* $2692 (excluding resources awarded to replace EFC). 34% of all full-time freshmen had no need and received non-need-based gift aid.
UNDERGRADUATE FINANCIAL AID (Fall 2003) 2,477 applied for aid; of those 100% were deemed to have need. 100% of undergraduates with need received aid. *Average financial aid package:* $4107 (excluding resources awarded to replace EFC). 32% of all full-time undergraduates had no need and received non-need-based gift aid.
GIFT AID (NEED-BASED) *Total amount:* $2,732,566 (91% federal, 9% state). *Receiving aid:* Freshmen: 43% (52); All full-time undergraduates: 38% (1,071). *Average award:* Freshmen: $2160; Undergraduates: $2325. *Scholarships, grants, and awards:* Federal Pell, FSEOG, state.
GIFT AID (NON-NEED-BASED) *Total amount:* $1,058,757 (93% institutional, 7% external sources). *Average Award:* Freshmen: $1525; Undergraduates: $1134. *Scholarships, grants, and awards by category: Academic Interests/Achievement:* 937 awards ($1,058,757 total): business, general academic interests/achievements, humanities, mathematics, social sciences. *Tuition waivers:* Full or partial for employees or children of employees. *ROTC:* Army cooperative, Air Force cooperative.
LOANS *Student loans:* $16,806,782 (100% need-based). *Average need-based loan:* Freshmen: $1916; Undergraduates: $3326. *Parent loans:* $519,212 (100% need-based). *Programs:* FFEL (Subsidized and Unsubsidized Stafford, PLUS).
WORK-STUDY *Federal work-study:* Total amount: $78,901; 44 jobs averaging $1793.
ATHLETIC AWARDS *Total amount:* $175,240 (100% non-need-based).
APPLYING FOR FINANCIAL AID *Required financial aid forms:* FAFSA, institution's own form. *Financial aid deadline:* Continuous. *Notification date:* Continuous beginning 4/1. Students must reply within 2 weeks of notification.

CONTACT Mr. Jon Dotterer, Director of Financial Aid, Bellevue University, 1000 Galvin Road South, Bellevue, NE 68005, 402-293-3762 or toll-free 800-756-7920. *Fax:* 402-293-2062.

BELLIN COLLEGE OF NURSING
Green Bay, WI

Tuition & fees: $13,830 | **Average undergraduate aid package: $13,157**

ABOUT THE INSTITUTION Independent, coed, primarily women. Awards: bachelor's and master's degrees. 1 undergraduate major. Total enrollment: 239. Undergraduates: 216. Freshmen: 32. Federal methodology is used as a basis for awarding need-based institutional aid.
UNDERGRADUATE EXPENSES for 2004–05 *Application fee:* $30. *Tuition:* full-time $13,559; part-time $646 per credit. *Required fees:* full-time $271; $271 per year part-time. Full-time tuition and fees vary according to course level and student level. Part-time tuition and fees vary according to course load. *Payment plan:* Installment.
UNDERGRADUATE FINANCIAL AID (Fall 2003) 78 applied for aid; of those 92% were deemed to have need. 100% of undergraduates with need received aid; of those 15% had need fully met. *Average percent of need met:* 89% (excluding resources awarded to replace EFC). *Average financial aid package:* $13,157 (excluding resources awarded to replace EFC).
GIFT AID (NEED-BASED) *Total amount:* $516,710 (17% federal, 16% state, 47% institutional, 20% external sources). *Receiving aid:* All full-time undergraduates: 41% (69). *Average award:* Undergraduates: $6059. *Scholarships, grants, and awards:* Federal Pell, FSEOG, state, private, college/university gift aid from institutional funds.
GIFT AID (NON-NEED-BASED) *Total amount:* $6188 (12% institutional, 88% external sources). *Receiving aid:* Undergraduates: 1% (1). *Scholarships, grants, and awards by category: Academic Interests/Achievement:* 40 awards ($58,400 total): general academic interests/achievements. *ROTC:* Army cooperative.
LOANS *Student loans:* $891,276 (78% need-based, 22% non-need-based). 87% of past graduating class borrowed through all loan programs. *Average indebtedness per student:* $18,256. *Average need-based loan:* Undergraduates: $4655. *Parent loans:* $177,870 (38% need-based, 62% non-need-based). *Programs:* FFEL (Subsidized and Unsubsidized Stafford, PLUS), state, college/university.
WORK-STUDY *Federal work-study:* Total amount: $9800; 7 jobs averaging $1400.
APPLYING FOR FINANCIAL AID *Required financial aid form:* FAFSA. *Financial aid deadline (priority):* 3/1. *Notification date:* 4/1. Students must reply within 2 weeks of notification.
CONTACT Ms. Lena C. Terry, Director of Financial Aid, Bellin College of Nursing, 725 South Webster Avenue, PO Box 23400, Green Bay, WI 54305-3400, 920-433-5801 or toll-free 800-236-8707. *Fax:* 920-433-7416. *E-mail:* lcterry@bcon.edu.

BELMONT ABBEY COLLEGE
Belmont, NC

Tuition & fees: $16,724 | **Average undergraduate aid package: $12,003**

ABOUT THE INSTITUTION Independent Roman Catholic, coed. Awards: bachelor's degrees. 23 undergraduate majors. Total enrollment: 800. Undergraduates: 800. Freshmen: 174. Federal methodology is used as a basis for awarding need-based institutional aid.
UNDERGRADUATE EXPENSES for 2005–06 *Application fee:* $35. *One-time required fee:* $672. *Comprehensive fee:* $25,310 includes full-time tuition ($15,910), mandatory fees ($814), and room and board ($8586). *College room only:* $4829. Full-time tuition and fees vary according to class time, course level, course load, location, program, reciprocity agreements, and student level. Room and board charges vary according to board plan, housing facility, location, and student level. *Part-time tuition:* $499 per credit. *Part-time fees:* $201 per hour. Part-time tuition and fees vary according to class time, course level, course load, location, reciprocity agreements, and student level. *Payment plans:* Installment, deferred payment.
FRESHMAN FINANCIAL AID (Fall 2004, est.) 151 applied for aid; of those 84% were deemed to have need. 100% of freshmen with need received aid; of those 15% had need fully met. *Average percent of need met:* 64% (excluding resources

awarded to replace EFC). *Average financial aid package:* $13,198 (excluding resources awarded to replace EFC). 28% of all full-time freshmen had no need and received non-need-based gift aid.

UNDERGRADUATE FINANCIAL AID (Fall 2004, est.) 582 applied for aid; of those 89% were deemed to have need. 99% of undergraduates with need received aid; of those 15% had need fully met. *Average percent of need met:* 59% (excluding resources awarded to replace EFC). *Average financial aid package:* $12,003 (excluding resources awarded to replace EFC). 26% of all full-time undergraduates had no need and received non-need-based gift aid.

GIFT AID (NEED-BASED) *Total amount:* $3,982,908 (20% federal, 21% state, 47% institutional, 12% external sources). *Receiving aid:* Freshmen: 56% (126); All full-time undergraduates: 57% (447). *Average award:* Freshmen: $10,830; Undergraduates: $8708. *Scholarships, grants, and awards:* Federal Pell, FSEOG, state, private, college/university gift aid from institutional funds.

GIFT AID (NON-NEED-BASED) *Total amount:* $1,412,170 (12% state, 74% institutional, 14% external sources). *Receiving aid:* Freshmen: 8% (17); Undergraduates: 7% (51). *Average Award: Freshmen:* $13,499; *Undergraduates:* $10,597. *Scholarships, grants, and awards by category: Academic Interests/Achievement:* 405 awards ($2,215,206 total): general academic interests/achievements. *Special Achievements/Activities:* 38 awards ($68,082 total): general special achievements/activities, leadership, religious involvement. *Special Characteristics:* 55 awards ($170,793 total): children of faculty/staff, religious affiliation. *Tuition waivers:* Full or partial for employees or children of employees, senior citizens. *ROTC:* Army cooperative, Air Force cooperative.

LOANS *Student loans:* $2,313,824 (79% need-based, 21% non-need-based). 65% of past graduating class borrowed through all loan programs. *Average indebtedness per student:* $15,500. *Average need-based loan:* Freshmen: $2232; Undergraduates: $3605. *Parent loans:* $3,502,430 (40% need-based, 60% non-need-based). *Programs:* Federal Direct (Subsidized and Unsubsidized Stafford, PLUS), Perkins.

WORK-STUDY *Federal work-study:* Total amount: $167,763; 174 jobs averaging $951.

ATHLETIC AWARDS *Total amount:* $733,561 (51% need-based, 49% non-need-based).

APPLYING FOR FINANCIAL AID *Required financial aid form:* FAFSA. *Financial aid deadline (priority):* 4/1. *Notification date:* Continuous beginning 3/1. Students must reply within 2 weeks of notification.

CONTACT Ms. Julie Hodge, Associate Director of Financial Aid, Belmont Abbey College, 100 Belmont Mt. Holly Road, Belmont, NC 28012-1802, 704-825-6718 or toll-free 888-BAC-0110. *Fax:* 704-825-6882. *E-mail:* juliehodge@bac.edu.

BELMONT UNIVERSITY
Nashville, TN

Tuition & fees: $16,220	Average undergraduate aid package: $3527

ABOUT THE INSTITUTION Independent Baptist, coed. Awards: bachelor's, master's, and doctoral degrees and post-bachelor's certificates. 73 undergraduate majors. Total enrollment: 3,941. Undergraduates: 3,317. Freshmen: 731. Federal methodology is used as a basis for awarding need-based institutional aid.

UNDERGRADUATE EXPENSES for 2004–05 *Application fee:* $35. *Comprehensive fee:* $22,376 includes full-time tuition ($15,360), mandatory fees ($860), and room and board ($6156). *College room only:* $2950. Full-time tuition and fees vary according to class time and course load. Room and board charges vary according to board plan, housing facility, and location. *Part-time tuition:* $585 per credit hour. *Part-time fees:* $290 per term. Part-time tuition and fees vary according to course load. *Payment plans:* Installment, deferred payment.

FRESHMAN FINANCIAL AID (Fall 2003) 510 applied for aid; of those 60% were deemed to have need. 94% of freshmen with need received aid; of those 22% had need fully met. *Average percent of need met:* 35% (excluding resources awarded to replace EFC). *Average financial aid package:* $2982 (excluding resources awarded to replace EFC). 23% of all full-time freshmen had no need and received non-need-based gift aid.

UNDERGRADUATE FINANCIAL AID (Fall 2003) 2,229 applied for aid; of those 64% were deemed to have need. 96% of undergraduates with need received aid; of those 19% had need fully met. *Average percent of need met:* 37% (excluding resources awarded to replace EFC). *Average financial aid package:* $3527 (excluding resources awarded to replace EFC). 19% of all full-time undergraduates had no need and received non-need-based gift aid.

GIFT AID (NEED-BASED) *Total amount:* $4,685,793 (31% federal, 8% state, 50% institutional, 11% external sources). *Receiving aid:* Freshmen: 34% (202); All full-time undergraduates: 35% (936). *Average award:* Freshmen: $2338; Undergraduates: $2463. *Scholarships, grants, and awards:* Federal Pell, FSEOG, state, private, college/university gift aid from institutional funds.

GIFT AID (NON-NEED-BASED) *Total amount:* $4,249,759 (100% institutional). *Receiving aid:* Freshmen: 27% (163); Undergraduates: 21% (552). *Average Award: Freshmen:* $6954; *Undergraduates:* $6503. *Scholarships, grants, and awards by category: Academic Interests/Achievement:* 713 awards ($2,558,350 total): general academic interests/achievements, religion/biblical studies. *Creative Arts/Performance:* 187 awards ($217,195 total): music. *Special Characteristics:* 46 awards ($491,214 total): children of faculty/staff. *Tuition waivers:* Full or partial for employees or children of employees, senior citizens. *ROTC:* Army cooperative, Naval cooperative.

LOANS *Student loans:* $10,618,497 (100% need-based). 56% of past graduating class borrowed through all loan programs. *Average indebtedness per student:* $8651. *Average need-based loan:* Freshmen: $2280; Undergraduates: $3765. *Parent loans:* $6,419,412 (100% non-need-based). *Programs:* FFEL (Subsidized and Unsubsidized Stafford, PLUS), Perkins, college/university.

WORK-STUDY *Federal work-study:* Total amount: $272,352; 197 jobs averaging $1382.

ATHLETIC AWARDS *Total amount:* $2,006,255 (100% non-need-based).

APPLYING FOR FINANCIAL AID *Required financial aid form:* FAFSA. *Financial aid deadline (priority):* 3/1. *Notification date:* Continuous beginning 3/15. Students must reply by 5/1 or within 2 weeks of notification.

CONTACT Mrs. Paula A. Gill, Director, Student Financial Services, Belmont University, 1900 Belmont Boulevard, Nashville, TN 37212-3757, 615-460-6403 or toll-free 800-56E-NROL. *E-mail:* gillp@mail.belmont.edu.

BELOIT COLLEGE
Beloit, WI

Tuition & fees: $25,736	Average undergraduate aid package: $18,737

ABOUT THE INSTITUTION Independent, coed. Awards: bachelor's degrees. 56 undergraduate majors. Total enrollment: 1,389. Undergraduates: 1,389. Freshmen: 325. Both federal and institutional methodology are used as a basis for awarding need-based institutional aid.

UNDERGRADUATE EXPENSES for 2004–05 *Application fee:* $30. *Comprehensive fee:* $31,432 includes full-time tuition ($25,516), mandatory fees ($220), and room and board ($5696). *College room only:* $2778. Room and board charges vary according to board plan. *Part-time tuition:* $3190 per course. *Payment plan:* Installment.

FRESHMAN FINANCIAL AID (Fall 2004, est.) 324 applied for aid; of those 90% were deemed to have need. 100% of freshmen with need received aid; of those 100% had need fully met. *Average percent of need met:* 100% (excluding resources awarded to replace EFC). *Average financial aid package:* $18,316 (excluding resources awarded to replace EFC). 10% of all full-time freshmen had no need and received non-need-based gift aid.

UNDERGRADUATE FINANCIAL AID (Fall 2004, est.) 982 applied for aid; of those 92% were deemed to have need. 100% of undergraduates with need received aid; of those 100% had need fully met. *Average percent of need met:* 100% (excluding resources awarded to replace EFC). *Average financial aid package:* $18,737 (excluding resources awarded to replace EFC). 13% of all full-time undergraduates had no need and received non-need-based gift aid.

GIFT AID (NEED-BASED) *Total amount:* $13,241,427 (6% federal, 3% state, 89% institutional, 2% external sources). *Receiving aid:* Freshmen: 89% (290); All full-time undergraduates: 70% (900). *Average award:* Freshmen: $14,929; Undergraduates: $13,543. *Scholarships, grants, and awards:* Federal Pell, FSEOG, state, private, college/university gift aid from institutional funds.

GIFT AID (NON-NEED-BASED) *Total amount:* $2,700,324 (96% institutional, 4% external sources). *Receiving aid:* Freshmen: 53% (171); Undergraduates: 39% (508). *Average Award: Freshmen:* $12,990; *Undergraduates:* $11,791. *Scholarships, grants, and awards by category: Academic Interests/Achievement:* 176 awards ($2,082,013 total): general academic interests/achievements. *Creative Arts/Performance:* 30 awards ($75,000 total): music. *Special Achievements/Activities:* 47 awards ($153,000 total): community service, general special achievements/activities. *Special Characteristics:* 26 awards ($144,500 total): members of minority groups, siblings of current students. *Tuition waivers:* Full or partial for employees or children of employees.

LOANS *Student loans:* $5,095,247 (55% need-based, 45% non-need-based). 59% of past graduating class borrowed through all loan programs. *Average indebtedness per student:* $20,339. *Average need-based loan:* Freshmen: $4405;

Undergraduates: $5916. *Parent loans:* $2,105,837 (100% non-need-based). *Programs:* FFEL (Subsidized and Unsubsidized Stafford, PLUS), Perkins, college/university.
WORK-STUDY *Federal work-study:* Total amount: $795,620; 546 jobs averaging $1436. *State or other work-study/employment:* Total amount: $491,781 (65% need-based, 35% non-need-based). 431 part-time jobs averaging $1157.
APPLYING FOR FINANCIAL AID *Required financial aid forms:* FAFSA, institution's own form, state aid form. *Financial aid deadline (priority):* 3/1. *Notification date:* Continuous beginning 4/1. Students must reply by 5/1 or within 2 weeks of notification.
CONTACT Mr. Jon Urish, Director of Freshman Financial Aid, Beloit College, 700 College Street, Beloit, WI 53511-5596, 800-356-0751 or toll-free 800-9-BELOIT. *Fax:* 608-363-2179.

BEMIDJI STATE UNIVERSITY
Bemidji, MN

Tuition & fees (MN res): $6404   Average undergraduate aid package: $7709

ABOUT THE INSTITUTION State-supported, coed. Awards: associate, bachelor's, and master's degrees. 71 undergraduate majors. Total enrollment: 4,971. Undergraduates: 4,554. Freshmen: 600. Federal methodology is used as a basis for awarding need-based institutional aid.
UNDERGRADUATE EXPENSES for 2004–05 *Application fee:* $20. *Tuition, state resident:* full-time $5653; part-time $187 per credit. *Tuition, nonresident:* full-time $12,421; part-time $347 per credit. *Required fees:* full-time $751; $80 per credit. Part-time tuition and fees vary according to course load. *College room and board:* $5012. Room and board charges vary according to board plan and housing facility. *Payment plan:* Installment.
GIFT AID (NEED-BASED) *Total amount:* $6,697,998 (60% federal, 36% state, 1% institutional, 3% external sources). *Receiving aid:* Freshmen: 41% (244); All full-time undergraduates: 44% (1,534). *Average award:* Freshmen: $4157; Undergraduates: $4116. *Scholarships, grants, and awards:* Federal Pell, FSEOG, state, private, college/university gift aid from institutional funds.
GIFT AID (NON-NEED-BASED) *Total amount:* $4,882,219 (15% federal, 10% state, 62% institutional, 13% external sources). *Receiving aid:* Freshmen: 33% (195); Undergraduates: 36% (1,275). *Average Award:* *Freshmen:* $5199; *Undergraduates:* $6228. *Scholarships, grants, and awards by category:* Academic Interests/Achievement: 431 awards ($525,247 total): general academic interests/achievements. Creative Arts/Performance: 31 awards ($55,301 total). Special Characteristics: 365 awards ($1,118,445 total): children and siblings of alumni, children of faculty/staff, international students, out-of-state students. *Tuition waivers:* Full or partial for employees or children of employees, senior citizens.
LOANS *Student loans:* $15,377,891 (46% need-based, 54% non-need-based). 69% of past graduating class borrowed through all loan programs. *Average indebtedness per student:* $16,045. *Average need-based loan:* Freshmen: $2688; Undergraduates: $3452. *Parent loans:* $390,642 (100% non-need-based). *Programs:* Federal Direct (Subsidized and Unsubsidized Stafford, PLUS), Perkins, state, Alaska Loans, Canada Student Loans, Norwest Collegiate Loans, CitiAssist Loans and other alternative loans.
ATHLETIC AWARDS *Total amount:* $735,427 (100% non-need-based).
APPLYING FOR FINANCIAL AID *Required financial aid forms:* FAFSA, institution's own form. *Financial aid deadline (priority):* 5/15. *Notification date:* Continuous beginning 5/15.
CONTACT Financial Aid Office, Bemidji State University, 1500 Birchmont Drive, NE, Bemidji, MN 56601-2699, 218-755-2034 or toll-free 800-475-2001 (in-state), 800-652-9747 (out-of-state). *Fax:* 218-755-4361.

BENEDICT COLLEGE
Columbia, SC

CONTACT Assistant Director of Financial Aid, Benedict College, 1600 Harden Street, Columbia, SC 29204, 803-253-5105 or toll-free 800-868-6598 (in-state).

BENEDICTINE COLLEGE
Atchison, KS

Tuition & fees: $15,126   Average undergraduate aid package: $15,508

ABOUT THE INSTITUTION Independent Roman Catholic, coed. Awards: associate, bachelor's, and master's degrees. 33 undergraduate majors. Total enrollment: 1,441. Undergraduates: 1,394. Freshmen: 313. Federal methodology is used as a basis for awarding need-based institutional aid.
UNDERGRADUATE EXPENSES for 2004–05 *Application fee:* $25. *Comprehensive fee:* $21,254 includes full-time tuition ($14,576), mandatory fees ($550), and room and board ($6128). *College room only:* $2650. Full-time tuition and fees vary according to course load and degree level. Room and board charges vary according to board plan and housing facility. *Part-time tuition:* $300 per credit hour. Part-time tuition and fees vary according to course load and degree level. *Payment plan:* Installment.
FRESHMAN FINANCIAL AID (Fall 2004, est.) 313 applied for aid; of those 78% were deemed to have need. 100% of freshmen with need received aid; of those 16% had need fully met. *Average percent of need met:* 74% (excluding resources awarded to replace EFC). *Average financial aid package:* $14,780 (excluding resources awarded to replace EFC). 7% of all full-time freshmen had no need and received non-need-based gift aid.
UNDERGRADUATE FINANCIAL AID (Fall 2004, est.) 1,070 applied for aid; of those 79% were deemed to have need. 100% of undergraduates with need received aid; of those 16% had need fully met. *Average percent of need met:* 74% (excluding resources awarded to replace EFC). *Average financial aid package:* $15,508 (excluding resources awarded to replace EFC). 5% of all full-time undergraduates had no need and received non-need-based gift aid.
GIFT AID (NEED-BASED) *Total amount:* $6,327,396 (22% federal, 13% state, 62% institutional, 3% external sources). *Receiving aid:* Freshmen: 66% (207); All full-time undergraduates: 75% (799). *Average award:* Freshmen: $8883; Undergraduates: $9497. *Scholarships, grants, and awards:* Federal Pell, FSEOG, state, private, college/university gift aid from institutional funds.
GIFT AID (NON-NEED-BASED) *Total amount:* $356,160 (1% federal, 3% state, 95% institutional, 1% external sources). *Average Award:* Freshmen: $6777; *Undergraduates:* $6288. *Scholarships, grants, and awards by category:* Academic Interests/Achievement: 755 awards ($4,216,774 total): general academic interests/achievements. Creative Arts/Performance: 85 awards ($103,250 total): music, theater/drama. Special Achievements/Activities: 200 awards ($413,225 total): general special achievements/activities. Special Characteristics: 50 awards ($138,351 total): children of educators, ethnic background, general special characteristics, international students, local/state students, members of minority groups, out-of-state students, religious affiliation, veterans' children. *Tuition waivers:* Full or partial for employees or children of employees, senior citizens. *ROTC:* Army.
LOANS *Student loans:* $4,041,140 (94% need-based, 6% non-need-based). 80% of past graduating class borrowed through all loan programs. *Average indebtedness per student:* $21,329. *Average need-based loan:* Freshmen: $3855; Undergraduates: $4883. *Parent loans:* $1,341,631 (100% non-need-based). *Programs:* FFEL (Subsidized and Unsubsidized Stafford, PLUS), Perkins, alternative loans.
WORK-STUDY *Federal work-study:* Total amount: $330,701; 323 jobs averaging $1024. *State or other work-study/employment:* Total amount: $72,350 (93% need-based, 7% non-need-based). 101 part-time jobs averaging $716.
ATHLETIC AWARDS *Total amount:* $1,389,849 (96% need-based, 4% non-need-based).
APPLYING FOR FINANCIAL AID *Required financial aid form:* FAFSA. *Financial aid deadline (priority):* 3/15. *Notification date:* Continuous beginning 2/1. Students must reply within 2 weeks of notification.
CONTACT Mr. Keith Jaloma, Assistant Dean of Enrollment Management/Director of Financial Aid, Benedictine College, 1020 North Second Street, Atchison, KS 66002-1499, 913-360-7484 or toll-free 800-467-5340. *Fax:* 913-367-5462. *E-mail:* kjaloma@benedictine.edu.

BENEDICTINE UNIVERSITY
Lisle, IL

Tuition & fees: $18,310   Average undergraduate aid package: $11,209

ABOUT THE INSTITUTION Independent Roman Catholic, coed. Awards: associate, bachelor's, master's, and doctoral degrees and post-bachelor's certificates. 50 undergraduate majors. Total enrollment: 3,232. Undergraduates: 2,148. Freshmen: 302. Federal methodology is used as a basis for awarding need-based institutional aid.
UNDERGRADUATE EXPENSES for 2004–05 *Application fee:* $40. *Comprehensive fee:* $24,600 includes full-time tuition ($17,800), mandatory fees ($510), and room and board ($6290). Full-time tuition and fees vary according to class time and degree level. Room and board charges vary according to board plan and

Benedictine University

housing facility. *Part-time tuition:* $600 per credit hour. *Part-time fees:* $15 per credit hour. Part-time tuition and fees vary according to class time and degree level. *Payment plan:* Installment.

FRESHMAN FINANCIAL AID (Fall 2004, est.) 235 applied for aid; of those 100% were deemed to have need. 99% of freshmen with need received aid; of those 43% had need fully met. *Average percent of need met:* 86% (excluding resources awarded to replace EFC). *Average financial aid package:* $11,385 (excluding resources awarded to replace EFC). 21% of all full-time freshmen had no need and received non-need-based gift aid.

UNDERGRADUATE FINANCIAL AID (Fall 2004, est.) 1,098 applied for aid; of those 100% were deemed to have need. 99% of undergraduates with need received aid; of those 46% had need fully met. *Average percent of need met:* 86% (excluding resources awarded to replace EFC). *Average financial aid package:* $11,209 (excluding resources awarded to replace EFC). 19% of all full-time undergraduates had no need and received non-need-based gift aid.

GIFT AID (NEED-BASED) *Total amount:* $7,849,827 (19% federal, 32% state, 49% institutional). *Receiving aid:* Freshmen: 42% (127); All full-time undergraduates: 42% (621). *Average award:* Freshmen: $6118; Undergraduates: $6120. *Scholarships, grants, and awards:* Federal Pell, FSEOG, state, private, college/university gift aid from institutional funds.

GIFT AID (NON-NEED-BASED) *Total amount:* $3,547,380 (1% state, 96% institutional, 3% external sources). *Receiving aid:* Freshmen: 75% (225); Undergraduates: 63% (940). *Average Award: Freshmen:* $5365; *Undergraduates:* $6491. *Scholarships, grants, and awards by category: Academic Interests/Achievement:* biological sciences, business, education, general academic interests/achievements, humanities, mathematics, physical sciences. *Creative Arts/Performance:* music. *Special Characteristics:* children and siblings of alumni, out-of-state students, previous college experience, siblings of current students. *Tuition waivers:* Full or partial for minority students, children of alumni, employees or children of employees. *ROTC:* Army cooperative.

LOANS *Student loans:* $7,126,269 (48% need-based, 52% non-need-based). 50% of past graduating class borrowed through all loan programs. *Average indebtedness per student:* $6727. *Average need-based loan:* Freshmen: $3617; Undergraduates: $4453. *Parent loans:* $2,063,754 (100% non-need-based). *Programs:* FFEL (Subsidized and Unsubsidized Stafford, PLUS), Perkins, alternative loans.

WORK-STUDY *Federal work-study:* Total amount: $105,000; jobs available.

APPLYING FOR FINANCIAL AID *Required financial aid forms:* FAFSA, institution's own form. *Financial aid deadline:* Continuous. *Notification date:* Continuous beginning 2/1. Students must reply within 2 weeks of notification.

CONTACT Diane Battistella, Director, Benedictine Central, Benedictine University, 5700 College Road, Lisle, IL 60532, 630-829-6415 or toll-free 888-829-6363 (out-of-state). *Fax:* 630-829-6456. *E-mail:* dbattistella@ben.edu.

BENNETT COLLEGE
Greensboro, NC

ABOUT THE INSTITUTION Independent United Methodist, women only. Awards: bachelor's degrees. 25 undergraduate majors. Total enrollment: 506. Undergraduates: 506. Freshmen: 172.

GIFT AID (NEED-BASED) *Scholarships, grants, and awards:* Federal Pell, FSEOG, state, private, college/university gift aid from institutional funds, United Negro College Fund, United Methodist Church Scholarships.

GIFT AID (NON-NEED-BASED) *Scholarships, grants, and awards by category: Academic Interests/Achievement:* general academic interests/achievements. *Special Characteristics:* children of faculty/staff, relatives of clergy, religious affiliation.

LOANS *Programs:* Federal Direct (Subsidized and Unsubsidized Stafford, PLUS), Perkins.

WORK-STUDY *Federal work-study:* Total amount: $97,348; jobs available.

APPLYING FOR FINANCIAL AID *Required financial aid forms:* FAFSA, institution's own form, state aid form.

CONTACT Monty K. Hickman, Financial Aid Director, Bennett College, 900 East Washington Street, Greensboro, NC 27401, 336-370-8677. *Fax:* 336-517-2204. *E-mail:* mhickman@bennett.edu.

BENNINGTON COLLEGE
Bennington, VT

Tuition & fees: $31,070	Average undergraduate aid package: $24,063

ABOUT THE INSTITUTION Independent, coed. Awards: bachelor's and master's degrees and post-bachelor's certificates. 56 undergraduate majors. Total enrollment: 820. Undergraduates: 671. Freshmen: 201. Federal methodology is used as a basis for awarding need-based institutional aid.

UNDERGRADUATE EXPENSES for 2004–05 *Application fee:* $50. *Comprehensive fee:* $38,780 includes full-time tuition ($30,270), mandatory fees ($800), and room and board ($7710). *College room only:* $4130. *Part-time tuition:* $946 per credit. *Payment plan:* Installment.

FRESHMAN FINANCIAL AID (Fall 2004, est.) 141 applied for aid; of those 92% were deemed to have need. 100% of freshmen with need received aid; of those 5% had need fully met. *Average percent of need met:* 76% (excluding resources awarded to replace EFC). *Average financial aid package:* $23,287 (excluding resources awarded to replace EFC). 1% of all full-time freshmen had no need and received non-need-based gift aid.

UNDERGRADUATE FINANCIAL AID (Fall 2004, est.) 438 applied for aid; of those 92% were deemed to have need. 100% of undergraduates with need received aid; of those 5% had need fully met. *Average percent of need met:* 75% (excluding resources awarded to replace EFC). *Average financial aid package:* $24,063 (excluding resources awarded to replace EFC). 11% of all full-time undergraduates had no need and received non-need-based gift aid.

GIFT AID (NEED-BASED) *Total amount:* $7,825,580 (8% federal, 1% state, 88% institutional, 3% external sources). *Receiving aid:* Freshmen: 64% (128); All full-time undergraduates: 65% (398). *Average award:* Freshmen: $20,481; Undergraduates: $19,704. *Scholarships, grants, and awards:* Federal Pell, FSEOG, state, private, college/university gift aid from institutional funds.

GIFT AID (NON-NEED-BASED) *Total amount:* $359,184 (81% institutional, 19% external sources). *Receiving aid:* Freshmen: 1% (2); Undergraduates: 2% (10). *Average Award: Freshmen:* $6167; *Undergraduates:* $4309. *Scholarships, grants, and awards by category: Academic Interests/Achievement:* general academic interests/achievements. *Creative Arts/Performance:* general creative arts/performance. *Special Achievements/Activities:* general special achievements/activities. *Special Characteristics:* children of educators, children of faculty/staff, general special characteristics. *Tuition waivers:* Full or partial for employees or children of employees.

LOANS *Student loans:* $2,446,607 (81% need-based, 19% non-need-based). 72% of past graduating class borrowed through all loan programs. *Average indebtedness per student:* $18,460. *Average need-based loan:* Freshmen: $2334; Undergraduates: $3793. *Parent loans:* $2,306,834 (43% need-based, 57% non-need-based). *Programs:* FFEL (Subsidized and Unsubsidized Stafford, PLUS), college/university.

WORK-STUDY *Federal work-study:* Total amount: $368,922; 330 jobs averaging $1600. *State or other work-study/employment:* Total amount: $38,600 (100% need-based). 50 part-time jobs averaging $1600.

APPLYING FOR FINANCIAL AID *Required financial aid forms:* FAFSA, institution's own form, CSS Financial Aid PROFILE, noncustodial (divorced/separated) parent's statement, federal income tax form(s), W-2 forms. *Financial aid deadline (priority):* 3/1. *Notification date:* 4/1. Students must reply by 5/1 or within 2 weeks of notification.

CONTACT Meg Woolmington, Financial Aid Director, Bennington College, One College Drive, Bennington, VT 05201-9993, 802-440-4325 or toll-free 800-833-6845. *Fax:* 802-440-4350. *E-mail:* finaid@bennington.edu.

BENTLEY COLLEGE
Waltham, MA

Tuition & fees: $27,244	Average undergraduate aid package: $23,198

ABOUT THE INSTITUTION Independent, coed. Awards: associate, bachelor's, and master's degrees and post-bachelor's and post-master's certificates. 17 undergraduate majors. Total enrollment: 5,601. Undergraduates: 4,304. Freshmen: 939. Both federal and institutional methodology are used as a basis for awarding need-based institutional aid.

UNDERGRADUATE EXPENSES for 2004–05 *Application fee:* $50. *Comprehensive fee:* $37,104 includes full-time tuition ($27,030), mandatory fees ($214), and room and board ($9860). *College room only:* $5850. Full-time tuition and fees vary according to student level. Room and board charges vary according to board plan and housing facility. *Part-time tuition:* $1302 per course. *Part-time fees:* $10 per term. Part-time tuition and fees vary according to class time. *Payment plan:* Installment.

FRESHMAN FINANCIAL AID (Fall 2004, est.) 694 applied for aid; of those 78% were deemed to have need. 97% of freshmen with need received aid; of those 25% had need fully met. *Average percent of need met:* 90% (excluding resources

awarded to replace EFC). *Average financial aid package:* $22,405 (excluding resources awarded to replace EFC). 9% of all full-time freshmen had no need and received non-need-based gift aid.

UNDERGRADUATE FINANCIAL AID (Fall 2004, est.) 2,516 applied for aid; of those 85% were deemed to have need. 98% of undergraduates with need received aid; of those 36% had need fully met. *Average percent of need met:* 90% (excluding resources awarded to replace EFC). *Average financial aid package:* $23,198 (excluding resources awarded to replace EFC). 8% of all full-time undergraduates had no need and received non-need-based gift aid.

GIFT AID (NEED-BASED) *Total amount:* $31,001,412 (6% federal, 2% state, 92% institutional). *Receiving aid:* Freshmen: 53% (495); All full-time undergraduates: 49% (1,907). *Average award:* Freshmen: $16,436; Undergraduates: $14,679. *Scholarships, grants, and awards:* Federal Pell, FSEOG, state, private, college/ university gift aid from institutional funds.

GIFT AID (NON-NEED-BASED) *Total amount:* $5,280,508 (1% federal, 98% institutional, 1% external sources). *Receiving aid:* Freshmen: 5% (47); Undergraduates: 4% (147). *Average Award:* Freshmen: $11,843; Undergraduates: $11,371. *Scholarships, grants, and awards by category: Academic Interests/Achievement:* 758 awards ($8,014,078 total): general academic interests/ achievements. *Special Achievements/Activities:* 17 awards ($85,000 total): community service. *Special Characteristics:* 38 awards ($810,935 total): members of minority groups. *Tuition waivers:* Full or partial for employees or children of employees. *ROTC:* Army cooperative.

LOANS *Student loans:* $16,455,343 (62% need-based, 38% non-need-based). 66% of past graduating class borrowed through all loan programs. *Average indebtedness per student:* $27,523. *Average need-based loan:* Freshmen: $3123; Undergraduates: $4745. *Parent loans:* $8,658,624 (17% need-based, 83% non-need-based). *Programs:* FFEL (Subsidized and Unsubsidized Stafford, PLUS), Perkins, state, college/university.

WORK-STUDY *Federal work-study:* Total amount: $2,282,974; 1,290 jobs averaging $1788. *State or other work-study/employment:* Total amount: $1,603,008 (30% need-based, 70% non-need-based). 444 part-time jobs averaging $1985.

APPLYING FOR FINANCIAL AID *Required financial aid forms:* FAFSA, CSS Financial Aid PROFILE, noncustodial (divorced/separated) parent's statement, business/farm supplement. *Financial aid deadline:* 2/1. *Notification date:* Continuous beginning 3/25.

CONTACT Ms. Donna Kendall, Director of Financial Assistance, Bentley College, 175 Forest Street, Waltham, MA 02452-4705, 781-891-3441 or toll-free 800-523-2354.

BEREA COLLEGE
Berea, KY

Tuition & fees: $516	Average undergraduate aid package: $26,373

ABOUT THE INSTITUTION Independent, coed. Awards: bachelor's degrees. 52 undergraduate majors. Total enrollment: 1,556. Undergraduates: 1,556. Freshmen: 400. Federal methodology is used as a basis for awarding need-based institutional aid.

UNDERGRADUATE EXPENSES for 2004–05 includes mandatory fees ($516) and room and board ($4748). Financial aid is provided to all students for tuition costs.

FRESHMAN FINANCIAL AID (Fall 2004, est.) 400 applied for aid; of those 100% were deemed to have need. 100% of freshmen with need received aid; of those 41% had need fully met. *Average percent of need met:* 90% (excluding resources awarded to replace EFC). *Average financial aid package:* $25,658 (excluding resources awarded to replace EFC).

UNDERGRADUATE FINANCIAL AID (Fall 2004, est.) 1,522 applied for aid; of those 100% were deemed to have need. 100% of undergraduates with need received aid; of those 22% had need fully met. *Average percent of need met:* 92% (excluding resources awarded to replace EFC). *Average financial aid package:* $26,373 (excluding resources awarded to replace EFC).

GIFT AID (NEED-BASED) *Total amount:* $40,405,407 (10% federal, 6% state, 84% institutional). *Receiving aid:* Freshmen: 100% (400); All full-time undergraduates: 100% (1,522). *Average award:* Freshmen: $24,464; Undergraduates: $24,526. *Scholarships, grants, and awards:* Federal Pell, FSEOG, state, private, college/university gift aid from institutional funds.

LOANS *Student loans:* $1,385,061 (53% need-based, 47% non-need-based). 79% of past graduating class borrowed through all loan programs. *Average indebtedness per student:* $6436. *Average need-based loan:* Freshmen: $920; Undergraduates: $1617. *Parent loans:* $1400 (100% need-based). *Programs:* FFEL (Subsidized and Unsubsidized Stafford, PLUS), Perkins, college/university.

WORK-STUDY *Federal work-study:* Total amount: $1,979,596; 1,365 jobs averaging $1450. *State or other work-study/employment:* Total amount: $442,103 (100% need-based). 235 part-time jobs averaging $1881.

APPLYING FOR FINANCIAL AID *Required financial aid form:* FAFSA. *Financial aid deadline:* 8/1 (priority: 4/15). *Notification date:* Continuous beginning 4/19.

CONTACT Student Financial Aid Services, Berea College, CPO 2172, Berea, KY 40404, 859-985-3310 or toll-free 800-326-5948.

BERKLEE COLLEGE OF MUSIC
Boston, MA

Tuition & fees: $26,307	Average undergraduate aid package: $18,195

ABOUT THE INSTITUTION Independent, coed. Awards: bachelor's degrees. 12 undergraduate majors. Total enrollment: 3,882. Undergraduates: 3,882. Federal methodology is used as a basis for awarding need-based institutional aid.

UNDERGRADUATE EXPENSES for 2005–06 *Application fee:* $100. *Comprehensive fee:* $37,997 includes full-time tuition ($21,790), mandatory fees ($4517), and room and board ($11,690). *Payment plans:* Tuition prepayment, installment.

FRESHMAN FINANCIAL AID (Fall 2004, est.) 607 applied for aid; of those 66% were deemed to have need. 100% of freshmen with need received aid. *Average percent of need met:* 57% (excluding resources awarded to replace EFC). *Average financial aid package:* $15,593 (excluding resources awarded to replace EFC). 14% of all full-time freshmen had no need and received non-need-based gift aid.

UNDERGRADUATE FINANCIAL AID (Fall 2004, est.) 2,789 applied for aid; of those 61% were deemed to have need. 100% of undergraduates with need received aid. *Average percent of need met:* 60% (excluding resources awarded to replace EFC). *Average financial aid package:* $18,195 (excluding resources awarded to replace EFC). 17% of all full-time undergraduates had no need and received non-need-based gift aid.

GIFT AID (NEED-BASED) *Total amount:* $3,266,428 (90% federal, 10% state). *Receiving aid:* Freshmen: 16% (134); All full-time undergraduates: 16% (630). *Average award:* Freshmen: $5677; Undergraduates: $5291. *Scholarships, grants, and awards:* Federal Pell, FSEOG, state, private, college/university gift aid from institutional funds.

GIFT AID (NON-NEED-BASED) *Total amount:* $11,614,218 (83% institutional, 17% external sources). *Receiving aid:* Freshmen: 23% (189); Undergraduates: 16% (634). *Average Award:* Freshmen: $7559; Undergraduates: $8918. *Scholarships, grants, and awards by category: Creative Arts/Performance:* 1,900 awards ($9,500,000 total): music. *Tuition waivers:* Full or partial for employees or children of employees.

LOANS *Student loans:* $32,673,681 (100% need-based). *Average need-based loan:* Freshmen: $3021; Undergraduates: $4361. *Parent loans:* $12,780,316 (100% non-need-based). *Programs:* Federal Direct (Subsidized and Unsubsidized Stafford, PLUS), Perkins, state.

WORK-STUDY *Federal work-study:* Total amount: $285,925; 269 jobs averaging $1063. *State or other work-study/employment:* Total amount: $277,301 (100% non-need-based). Part-time jobs available.

APPLYING FOR FINANCIAL AID *Required financial aid form:* FAFSA. *Financial aid deadline (priority):* 3/1. *Notification date:* Continuous beginning 4/1. Students must reply within 3 weeks of notification.

CONTACT Julie Poorman, Director of Financial Aid, Berklee College of Music, 1140 Boylston Street, Boston, MA 02215-3693, 617-747-2274 or toll-free 800-BERKLEE. *Fax:* 617-747-2073. *E-mail:* jpoorman@berklee.edu.

BERNARD M. BARUCH COLLEGE OF THE CITY UNIVERSITY OF NEW YORK
New York, NY

Tuition & fees (NY res): $4300	Average undergraduate aid package: $4930

ABOUT THE INSTITUTION State and locally supported, coed. Awards: bachelor's, master's, and doctoral degrees and post-master's certificates. 33 undergraduate majors. Total enrollment: 15,537. Undergraduates: 12,734. Freshmen: 1,718. Federal methodology is used as a basis for awarding need-based institutional aid.

UNDERGRADUATE EXPENSES for 2005–06 *Application fee:* $70. *Tuition, state resident:* full-time $4000; part-time $170 per credit. *Tuition, nonresident:*

Bernard M. Baruch College of the City University of New York

full-time $8640; part-time $360 per credit. *Required fees:* full-time $300; $150 per term or $75 per term part-time. Full-time tuition and fees vary according to class time and course load. Part-time tuition and fees vary according to class time and course load. *Payment plans:* Installment, deferred payment.

FRESHMAN FINANCIAL AID (Fall 2004, est.) 1541 applied for aid; of those 93% were deemed to have need. 95% of freshmen with need received aid; of those 10% had need fully met. *Average percent of need met:* 67% (excluding resources awarded to replace EFC). *Average financial aid package:* $5380 (excluding resources awarded to replace EFC). 2% of all full-time freshmen had no need and received non-need-based gift aid.

UNDERGRADUATE FINANCIAL AID (Fall 2004, est.) 8,145 applied for aid; of those 94% were deemed to have need. 91% of undergraduates with need received aid; of those 23% had need fully met. *Average percent of need met:* 63% (excluding resources awarded to replace EFC). *Average financial aid package:* $4930 (excluding resources awarded to replace EFC). 7% of all full-time undergraduates had no need and received non-need-based gift aid.

GIFT AID (NEED-BASED) *Total amount:* $34,006,519 (49% federal, 49% state, 2% institutional). *Receiving aid:* Freshmen: 61% (1,044); All full-time undergraduates: 70% (6,440). *Average award:* Freshmen: $4800; Undergraduates: $4300. *Scholarships, grants, and awards:* Federal Pell, FSEOG, state, college/university gift aid from institutional funds.

GIFT AID (NON-NEED-BASED) *Total amount:* $4,065,785 (67% institutional, 33% external sources). *Receiving aid:* Freshmen: 72% (1,245); Undergraduates: 26% (2,416). *Average Award:* Freshmen: $1600; Undergraduates: $1800. *Scholarships, grants, and awards by category:* Academic Interests/Achievement: general academic interests/achievements. *Tuition waivers:* Full or partial for senior citizens.

LOANS *Student loans:* $11,050,320 (57% need-based, 43% non-need-based). 19% of past graduating class borrowed through all loan programs. *Average indebtedness per student:* $10,100. *Average need-based loan:* Freshmen: $2350; Undergraduates: $2910. *Parent loans:* $128,000 (100% non-need-based). *Programs:* Federal Direct (Subsidized and Unsubsidized Stafford, PLUS), Perkins.

WORK-STUDY *Federal work-study:* Total amount: $340,000; 520 jobs available. *State or other work-study/employment:* Total amount: $500,000 (100% non-need-based). Part-time jobs available.

APPLYING FOR FINANCIAL AID *Required financial aid forms:* FAFSA, state aid form. *Financial aid deadline:* 4/30 (priority: 3/15). *Notification date:* Continuous. Students must reply by 6/1 or within 6 weeks of notification.

CONTACT Financial Aid Office, Bernard M. Baruch College of the City University of New York, 151 East 25th Street, Room 720, New York, NY 10010-5585, 646-312-1360. *Fax:* 646-312-1363. *E-mail:* financial_aid@baruch.cuny.edu.

BERRY COLLEGE
Mount Berry, GA

Tuition & fees: $16,240	Average undergraduate aid package: $14,480

ABOUT THE INSTITUTION Independent interdenominational, coed. Awards: bachelor's and master's degrees and post-master's certificates. 36 undergraduate majors. Total enrollment: 2,008. Undergraduates: 1,878. Freshmen: 514. Federal methodology is used as a basis for awarding need-based institutional aid.

UNDERGRADUATE EXPENSES for 2004–05 *Application fee:* $50. *Comprehensive fee:* $22,690 includes full-time tuition ($16,240) and room and board ($6450). *College room only:* $3650. Room and board charges vary according to board plan and housing facility. *Part-time tuition:* $540 per credit hour. *Payment plan:* Installment.

FRESHMAN FINANCIAL AID (Fall 2004, est.) 422 applied for aid; of those 75% were deemed to have need. 100% of freshmen with need received aid; of those 28% had need fully met. *Average percent of need met:* 88% (excluding resources awarded to replace EFC). *Average financial aid package:* $14,516 (excluding resources awarded to replace EFC). 39% of all full-time freshmen had no need and received non-need-based gift aid.

UNDERGRADUATE FINANCIAL AID (Fall 2004, est.) 1,355 applied for aid; of those 80% were deemed to have need. 99% of undergraduates with need received aid; of those 22% had need fully met. *Average percent of need met:* 86% (excluding resources awarded to replace EFC). *Average financial aid package:* $14,480 (excluding resources awarded to replace EFC). 41% of all full-time undergraduates had no need and received non-need-based gift aid.

GIFT AID (NEED-BASED) *Total amount:* $11,219,960 (12% federal, 22% state, 62% institutional, 4% external sources). *Receiving aid:* Freshmen: 61% (315); All full-time undergraduates: 58% (1,064). *Average award:* Freshmen: $11,997;

Undergraduates: $10,907. *Scholarships, grants, and awards:* Federal Pell, FSEOG, state, private, college/university gift aid from institutional funds.

GIFT AID (NON-NEED-BASED) *Total amount:* $6,199,504 (39% state, 53% institutional, 8% external sources). *Receiving aid:* Freshmen: 15% (77); Undergraduates: 10% (188). *Average Award:* Freshmen: $12,871; Undergraduates: $11,836. *Scholarships, grants, and awards by category:* Academic Interests/Achievement: 850 awards ($4,200,000 total): agriculture, communication, education, English, general academic interests/achievements, humanities, religion/biblical studies. Creative Arts/Performance: 150 awards ($350,000 total): art/fine arts, debating, journalism/publications, music, theater/drama. Special Achievements/Activities: 90 awards ($165,000 total): community service, religious involvement. Special Characteristics: 250 awards ($800,000 total): adult students, children of faculty/staff, ethnic background, local/state students, members of minority groups. *Tuition waivers:* Full or partial for employees or children of employees, senior citizens.

LOANS *Student loans:* $3,999,417 (71% need-based, 29% non-need-based). 52% of past graduating class borrowed through all loan programs. *Average indebtedness per student:* $12,000. *Average need-based loan:* Freshmen: $2564; Undergraduates: $3271. *Parent loans:* $3,457,473 (18% need-based, 82% non-need-based). *Programs:* FFEL (Subsidized and Unsubsidized Stafford, PLUS), Perkins, college/university.

WORK-STUDY *Federal work-study:* Total amount: $500,000; 400 jobs averaging $1800. *State or other work-study/employment:* Total amount: $2,600,000 (23% need-based, 77% non-need-based). 1,200 part-time jobs averaging $1800.

ATHLETIC AWARDS *Total amount:* $1,489,394 (26% need-based, 74% non-need-based).

APPLYING FOR FINANCIAL AID *Required financial aid forms:* FAFSA, institution's own form, state aid form. *Financial aid deadline (priority):* 4/1. *Notification date:* Continuous. Students must reply by 5/1.

CONTACT Mr. William G. Fron, Director of Financial Aid, Berry College, 2277 Martha Berry Highway, NW, Mount Berry, GA 30149-5007, 706-236-2276 or toll-free 800-237-7942. *Fax:* 706-290-2160. *E-mail:* wfron@berry.edu.

BETHANY COLLEGE
Lindsborg, KS

Tuition & fees: $15,460	Average undergraduate aid package: $15,310

ABOUT THE INSTITUTION Independent Lutheran, coed. Awards: bachelor's degrees. 39 undergraduate majors. Total enrollment: 585. Undergraduates: 585. Freshmen: 154. Federal methodology is used as a basis for awarding need-based institutional aid.

UNDERGRADUATE EXPENSES for 2005–06 *Application fee:* $20. *Comprehensive fee:* $20,660 includes full-time tuition ($15,250), mandatory fees ($210), and room and board ($5200). *College room only:* $2850. Room and board charges vary according to board plan. Part-time tuition and fees vary according to course load. *Payment plan:* Installment.

FRESHMAN FINANCIAL AID (Fall 2003) 166 applied for aid; of those 83% were deemed to have need. 100% of freshmen with need received aid; of those 31% had need fully met. *Average percent of need met:* 94% (excluding resources awarded to replace EFC). *Average financial aid package:* $15,277 (excluding resources awarded to replace EFC). 5% of all full-time freshmen had no need and received non-need-based gift aid.

UNDERGRADUATE FINANCIAL AID (Fall 2003) 551 applied for aid; of those 86% were deemed to have need. 100% of undergraduates with need received aid; of those 36% had need fully met. *Average percent of need met:* 93% (excluding resources awarded to replace EFC). *Average financial aid package:* $15,310 (excluding resources awarded to replace EFC). 6% of all full-time undergraduates had no need and received non-need-based gift aid.

GIFT AID (NEED-BASED) *Total amount:* $1,957,722 (43% federal, 29% state, 28% institutional). *Receiving aid:* Freshmen: 71% (122); All full-time undergraduates: 71% (412). *Average award:* Freshmen: $4640; Undergraduates: $4881. *Scholarships, grants, and awards:* Federal Pell, FSEOG, state, private, college/university gift aid from institutional funds.

GIFT AID (NON-NEED-BASED) *Total amount:* $436,055 (70% institutional, 30% external sources). *Receiving aid:* Freshmen: 17% (29); Undergraduates: 17% (100). *Average Award:* Freshmen: $2333; Undergraduates: $4086. *Scholarships, grants, and awards by category:* Academic Interests/Achievement: 409 awards ($1,390,670 total): general academic interests/achievements. Creative Arts/Performance: 140 awards ($309,770 total): art/fine arts, music, theater/drama. Special Achievements/Activities: 8 awards ($2391 total): cheerleading/

drum major. *Special Characteristics:* 9 awards ($6595 total): international students, relatives of clergy. *Tuition waivers:* Full or partial for employees or children of employees.

LOANS *Student loans:* $2,790,766 (71% need-based, 29% non-need-based). 83% of past graduating class borrowed through all loan programs. *Average indebtedness per student:* $15,167. *Average need-based loan:* Freshmen: $4376; Undergraduates: $5012. *Parent loans:* $440,600 (100% non-need-based). *Programs:* FFEL (Subsidized and Unsubsidized Stafford, PLUS), Perkins, college/university.

WORK-STUDY *Federal work-study:* Total amount: $173,000; 211 jobs averaging $650. *State or other work-study/employment:* Total amount: $100,000 (100% non-need-based). 154 part-time jobs averaging $650.

ATHLETIC AWARDS *Total amount:* $810,898 (83% need-based, 17% non-need-based).

APPLYING FOR FINANCIAL AID *Required financial aid form:* FAFSA. *Financial aid deadline:* Continuous. *Notification date:* Continuous beginning 2/1. Students must reply within 3 weeks of notification.

CONTACT Ms. Brenda Meagher, Director of Financial Aid, Bethany College, 421 North First Street, Lindsborg, KS 67456-1897, 785-227-3311 Ext. 8248 or toll-free 800-826-2281. *Fax:* 785-227-2004. *E-mail:* meagherb@bethanylb.edu.

BETHANY COLLEGE
Bethany, WV

Tuition & fees: $15,440	Average undergraduate aid package: $14,600

ABOUT THE INSTITUTION Independent religious, coed. Awards: bachelor's degrees. 34 undergraduate majors. Total enrollment: 900. Undergraduates: 900. Freshmen: 271. Both federal and institutional methodology are used as a basis for awarding need-based institutional aid.

UNDERGRADUATE EXPENSES for 2005–06 *Application fee:* $25. *Comprehensive fee:* $22,640 includes full-time tuition ($14,370), mandatory fees ($1070), and room and board ($7200). *College room only:* $3630. Room and board charges vary according to housing facility. *Payment plan:* Installment.

FRESHMAN FINANCIAL AID (Fall 2004, est.) 230 applied for aid; of those 88% were deemed to have need. 100% of freshmen with need received aid; of those 67% had need fully met. *Average percent of need met:* 85% (excluding resources awarded to replace EFC). *Average financial aid package:* $12,000 (excluding resources awarded to replace EFC). 19% of all full-time freshmen had no need and received non-need-based gift aid.

UNDERGRADUATE FINANCIAL AID (Fall 2004, est.) 807 applied for aid; of those 96% were deemed to have need. 100% of undergraduates with need received aid; of those 54% had need fully met. *Average percent of need met:* 88% (excluding resources awarded to replace EFC). *Average financial aid package:* $14,600 (excluding resources awarded to replace EFC). 7% of all full-time undergraduates had no need and received non-need-based gift aid.

GIFT AID (NEED-BASED) *Total amount:* $5,445,000 (22% federal, 3% state, 72% institutional, 3% external sources). *Receiving aid:* Freshmen: 81% (194); All full-time undergraduates: 83% (711). *Scholarships, grants, and awards:* Federal Pell, FSEOG, state, private, college/university gift aid from institutional funds.

GIFT AID (NON-NEED-BASED) *Total amount:* $3,250,000 (9% state, 89% institutional, 2% external sources). *Receiving aid:* Freshmen: 78% (187); Undergraduates: 82% (697). *Scholarships, grants, and awards by category:* Academic Interests/Achievement: 411 awards ($2,900,000 total): general academic interests/achievements. Creative Arts/Performance: 5 awards ($7500 total): music. Special Achievements/Activities: 36 awards ($120,000 total): leadership, religious involvement. Special Characteristics: 207 awards ($1,150,000 total): children and siblings of alumni, children of faculty/staff, ethnic background, international students, local/state students, relatives of clergy, religious affiliation. *Tuition waivers:* Full or partial for children of alumni, employees or children of employees.

LOANS *Student loans:* $3,600,000 (83% need-based, 17% non-need-based). 82% of past graduating class borrowed through all loan programs. *Average indebtedness per student:* $18,500. *Average need-based loan:* Freshmen: $3125; Undergraduates: $4300. *Parent loans:* $1,200,000 (100% non-need-based). *Programs:* Federal Direct (Subsidized and Unsubsidized Stafford, PLUS), Perkins, alternative loans.

WORK-STUDY *Federal work-study:* Total amount: $650,000; 423 jobs averaging $1100. *State or other work-study/employment:* Total amount: $115,000 (100% non-need-based). 310 part-time jobs averaging $290.

APPLYING FOR FINANCIAL AID *Required financial aid forms:* FAFSA, institution's own form. *Financial aid deadline (priority):* 3/1. *Notification date:* Continuous. Students must reply within 3 weeks of notification.

CONTACT Financial Aid Office, Bethany College, Main Street, Bethany, WV 26032, 304-829-7141 or toll-free 800-922-7611 (out-of-state).

BETHANY COLLEGE OF THE ASSEMBLIES OF GOD
Scotts Valley, CA

ABOUT THE INSTITUTION Independent Assemblies of God, coed. Awards: associate, bachelor's, and master's degrees. 18 undergraduate majors. Total enrollment: 602. Undergraduates: 538. Freshmen: 87.

GIFT AID (NEED-BASED) *Scholarships, grants, and awards:* Federal Pell, FSEOG, state, private, college/university gift aid from institutional funds.

GIFT AID (NON-NEED-BASED) *Scholarships, grants, and awards by category:* Academic Interests/Achievement: general academic interests/achievements. Creative Arts/Performance: music, theater/drama. Special Achievements/Activities: leadership. Special Characteristics: children of faculty/staff, relatives of clergy.

LOANS *Programs:* FFEL (Subsidized and Unsubsidized Stafford, PLUS), Perkins, alternative loans.

WORK-STUDY *Federal work-study:* Total amount: $76,413; 38 jobs averaging $2011.

APPLYING FOR FINANCIAL AID *Required financial aid forms:* FAFSA, institution's own form.

CONTACT Deborah Snow, Financial Aid Director, Bethany College of the Assemblies of God, 800 Bethany Drive, Scotts Valley, CA 95066-2820, 831-438-3800 Ext. 1477 or toll-free 800-843-9410. *Fax:* 831-461-1533.

BETHANY LUTHERAN COLLEGE
Mankato, MN

Tuition & fees: $15,716	Average undergraduate aid package: $12,659

ABOUT THE INSTITUTION Independent Lutheran, coed. Awards: associate and bachelor's degrees. 15 undergraduate majors. Total enrollment: 568. Undergraduates: 568. Freshmen: 217. Federal methodology is used as a basis for awarding need-based institutional aid.

UNDERGRADUATE EXPENSES for 2005–06 *Application fee:* $20. *Comprehensive fee:* $20,698 includes full-time tuition ($15,456), mandatory fees ($260), and room and board ($4982). *College room only:* $1852. Room and board charges vary according to board plan. *Part-time tuition:* $660 per credit. *Part-time fees:* $130 per term. *Payment plan:* Installment.

FRESHMAN FINANCIAL AID (Fall 2003) 167 applied for aid; of those 92% were deemed to have need. 100% of freshmen with need received aid; of those 31% had need fully met. *Average percent of need met:* 89% (excluding resources awarded to replace EFC). *Average financial aid package:* $12,907 (excluding resources awarded to replace EFC). 25% of all full-time freshmen had no need and received non-need-based gift aid.

UNDERGRADUATE FINANCIAL AID (Fall 2003) 436 applied for aid; of those 92% were deemed to have need. 100% of undergraduates with need received aid; of those 34% had need fully met. *Average percent of need met:* 89% (excluding resources awarded to replace EFC). *Average financial aid package:* $12,659 (excluding resources awarded to replace EFC). 15% of all full-time undergraduates had no need and received non-need-based gift aid.

GIFT AID (NEED-BASED) *Total amount:* $3,180,086 (18% federal, 21% state, 58% institutional, 3% external sources). *Receiving aid:* Freshmen: 70% (154); All full-time undergraduates: 82% (402). *Average award:* Freshmen: $9723; Undergraduates: $9253. *Scholarships, grants, and awards:* Federal Pell, FSEOG, state, private, college/university gift aid from institutional funds.

GIFT AID (NON-NEED-BASED) *Total amount:* $246,878 (3% state, 85% institutional, 12% external sources). *Receiving aid:* Freshmen: 9% (20); Undergraduates: 9% (45). *Average Award:* Freshmen: $4569; Undergraduates: $5537. *Scholarships, grants, and awards by category:* Creative Arts/Performance: 103 awards ($169,312 total): art/fine arts, debating, journalism/publications, music, theater/drama. Special Characteristics: 38 awards ($400,471 total): children of faculty/staff. *Tuition waivers:* Full or partial for employees or children of employees. *ROTC:* Army cooperative.

LOANS *Student loans:* $2,090,598 (66% need-based, 34% non-need-based). 81% of past graduating class borrowed through all loan programs. *Average indebtedness per student:* $19,112. *Average need-based loan:* Freshmen: $3522;

Undergraduates: $3821. *Parent loans:* $270,220 (24% need-based, 76% non-need-based). *Programs:* FFEL (Subsidized and Unsubsidized Stafford, PLUS), Perkins, state, alternative loans.

WORK-STUDY *Federal work-study:* Total amount: $36,807; 43 jobs averaging $856. *State or other work-study/employment:* Total amount: $136,189 (48% need-based, 52% non-need-based). 209 part-time jobs averaging $653.

ATHLETIC AWARDS *Total amount:* $161,535 (78% need-based, 22% non-need-based).

APPLYING FOR FINANCIAL AID *Required financial aid forms:* FAFSA, institution's own form, business/farm supplement, federal income tax form(s), W-2 forms. *Financial aid deadline (priority):* 4/15. *Notification date:* Continuous. Students must reply within 3 weeks of notification.

CONTACT Financial Aid Office, Bethany Lutheran College, 700 Luther Drive, Mankato, MN 56001-6163, 507-344-7328 or toll-free 800-944-3066 Ext. 331. *Fax:* 507-344-7376.

BETH BENJAMIN ACADEMY OF CONNECTICUT
Stamford, CT

CONTACT Financial Aid Office, Beth Benjamin Academy of Connecticut, 132 Prospect Street, Stamford, CT 06901-1202, 203-325-4351.

BETHEL COLLEGE
Mishawaka, IN

ABOUT THE INSTITUTION Independent religious, coed. Awards: associate, bachelor's, and master's degrees. 72 undergraduate majors. Total enrollment: 1,847. Undergraduates: 1,740. Freshmen: 306.

GIFT AID (NEED-BASED) *Scholarships, grants, and awards:* Federal Pell, FSEOG, state, private, college/university gift aid from institutional funds, Federal Nursing.

GIFT AID (NON-NEED-BASED) *Scholarships, grants, and awards by category: Academic Interests/Achievement:* biological sciences, business, communication, computer science, education, English, general academic interests/achievements, health fields, mathematics, physical sciences, religion/biblical studies, social sciences. *Creative Arts/Performance:* art/fine arts, journalism/publications, music, theater/drama. *Special Achievements/Activities:* cheerleading/drum major, general special achievements/activities, leadership, religious involvement. *Special Characteristics:* adult students, children of faculty/staff, international students, members of minority groups, relatives of clergy, religious affiliation, siblings of current students, spouses of current students.

LOANS *Programs:* FFEL (Subsidized and Unsubsidized Stafford, PLUS), Perkins, college/university, GATE Loans.

WORK-STUDY *Federal work-study:* Total amount: $206,865; jobs available (averaging $2000). *State or other work-study/employment:* Total amount: $292,894 (100% non-need-based). Part-time jobs available (averaging $2000).

APPLYING FOR FINANCIAL AID *Required financial aid forms:* FAFSA, institution's own form.

CONTACT Mr. Guy A. Fisher, Director of Financial Aid, Bethel College, 1001 West McKinley Avenue, Mishawaka, IN 46545-5591, 574-257-3316 or toll-free 800-422-4101. *Fax:* 574-257-3326. *E-mail:* fisherg@bethelcollege.edu.

BETHEL COLLEGE
North Newton, KS

Tuition & fees: $15,450	Average undergraduate aid package: $15,881

ABOUT THE INSTITUTION Independent religious, coed. Awards: bachelor's degrees. 29 undergraduate majors. Total enrollment: 509. Undergraduates: 509. Freshmen: 119. Federal methodology is used as a basis for awarding need-based institutional aid.

UNDERGRADUATE EXPENSES for 2005–06 *Application fee:* $20. *Comprehensive fee:* $21,550 includes full-time tuition ($15,450) and room and board ($6100). *College room only:* $3200. Full-time tuition and fees vary according to course load. Room and board charges vary according to board plan and housing facility. *Part-time tuition:* $550 per credit hour. Part-time tuition and fees vary according to course load. *Payment plans:* Installment, deferred payment.

FRESHMAN FINANCIAL AID (Fall 2003) 84 applied for aid; of those 100% were deemed to have need. 100% of freshmen with need received aid; of those 33% had need fully met. *Average percent of need met:* 89% (excluding resources

awarded to replace EFC). *Average financial aid package:* $15,152 (excluding resources awarded to replace EFC). 11% of all full-time freshmen had no need and received non-need-based gift aid.

UNDERGRADUATE FINANCIAL AID (Fall 2003) 377 applied for aid; of those 99% were deemed to have need. 100% of undergraduates with need received aid; of those 35% had need fully met. *Average percent of need met:* 90% (excluding resources awarded to replace EFC). *Average financial aid package:* $15,881 (excluding resources awarded to replace EFC). 11% of all full-time undergraduates had no need and received non-need-based gift aid.

GIFT AID (NEED-BASED) *Total amount:* $1,142,436 (55% federal, 34% state, 11% institutional). *Receiving aid:* Freshmen: 68% (65); All full-time undergraduates: 66% (286). *Average award:* Freshmen: $4474; Undergraduates: $4571. *Scholarships, grants, and awards:* Federal Pell, FSEOG, state, college/university gift aid from institutional funds.

GIFT AID (NON-NEED-BASED) *Total amount:* $1,825,282 (87% institutional, 13% external sources). *Receiving aid:* Freshmen: 85% (81); Undergraduates: 72% (309). *Average Award:* Freshmen: $5480; Undergraduates: $5814. *Scholarships, grants, and awards by category: Academic Interests/Achievement:* 279 awards ($1,033,864 total): general academic interests/achievements. *Creative Arts/Performance:* 101 awards ($169,774 total): art/fine arts, debating, music, theater/drama. *Special Characteristics:* 354 awards ($598,217 total): children and siblings of alumni, children of faculty/staff, international students, previous college experience, relatives of clergy, religious affiliation. *Tuition waivers:* Full or partial for children of alumni, employees or children of employees, senior citizens.

LOANS *Student loans:* $2,514,186 (75% need-based, 25% non-need-based). 84% of past graduating class borrowed through all loan programs. *Average indebtedness per student:* $17,482. *Average need-based loan:* Freshmen: $4075; Undergraduates: $5896. *Parent loans:* $448,475 (100% non-need-based). *Programs:* FFEL (Subsidized and Unsubsidized Stafford, PLUS), Perkins.

WORK-STUDY *Federal work-study:* Total amount: $329,245; 234 jobs averaging $1407. *State or other work-study/employment:* Total amount: $15,750 (100% need-based). 11 part-time jobs averaging $1432.

ATHLETIC AWARDS *Total amount:* $331,087 (100% non-need-based).

APPLYING FOR FINANCIAL AID *Required financial aid form:* FAFSA. *Financial aid deadline (priority):* 3/15. *Notification date:* Continuous. Students must reply by 5/1 or within 2 weeks of notification.

CONTACT Mr. Tony Graber, Financial Aid Director, Bethel College, 300 East 27th Street, North Newton, KS 67117, 316-284-5232 or toll-free 800-522-1887 Ext. 230. *Fax:* 316-284-5286. *E-mail:* tgraber@bethelks.edu.

BETHEL COLLEGE
McKenzie, TN

Tuition & fees: $9630	Average undergraduate aid package: N/A

ABOUT THE INSTITUTION Independent Cumberland Presbyterian, coed. Awards: bachelor's, master's, and first professional degrees. 24 undergraduate majors. Total enrollment: 1,297. Undergraduates: 1,134. Freshmen: 260. Both federal and institutional methodology are used as a basis for awarding need-based institutional aid.

UNDERGRADUATE EXPENSES for 2004–05 *Application fee:* $30. *Comprehensive fee:* $15,014 includes full-time tuition ($9360), mandatory fees ($270), and room and board ($5384). *Part-time tuition:* $290 per credit hour. *Part-time fees:* $10 per credit hour. Part-time tuition and fees vary according to course load. *Payment plan:* Installment.

FRESHMAN FINANCIAL AID (Fall 2003) *Average percent of need met:* 79% (excluding resources awarded to replace EFC). *Average financial aid package:* $11,018 (excluding resources awarded to replace EFC).

GIFT AID (NEED-BASED) *Total amount:* $2,403,661 (72% federal, 28% state). *Receiving aid:* Freshmen: 71. *Average award:* Freshmen: $2976. *Scholarships, grants, and awards:* college/university gift aid from institutional funds.

GIFT AID (NON-NEED-BASED) *Total amount:* $1,414,170 (6% federal, 7% state, 84% institutional, 3% external sources). *Receiving aid:* Freshmen: 134. *Scholarships, grants, and awards by category: Academic Interests/Achievement:* general academic interests/achievements, religion/biblical studies. *Creative Arts/Performance:* music. *Special Characteristics:* children of faculty/staff, local/state students, religious affiliation. *Tuition waivers:* Full or partial for employees or children of employees.

LOANS *Student loans:* $6,895,964 (52% need-based, 48% non-need-based). 99% of past graduating class borrowed through all loan programs. *Parent* *loans:* $110,818 (100% non-need-based). *Programs:* FFEL (Subsidized and Unsubsidized Stafford, PLUS), Perkins, alternative loans.

WORK-STUDY *Federal work-study:* Total amount: $124,758; jobs available. *State or other work-study/employment:* Part-time jobs available.

ATHLETIC AWARDS *Total amount:* $1,746,210 (100% non-need-based).

APPLYING FOR FINANCIAL AID *Required financial aid forms:* FAFSA, institution's own form. *Financial aid deadline (priority):* 3/1. *Notification date:* Continuous.

CONTACT Laura Bateman, Office of Financial Aid, Bethel College, 325 Cherry Avenue, McKenzie, TN 38201, 901-352-4007. *Fax:* 901-352-4069.

BETHEL UNIVERSITY
St. Paul, MN

Tuition & fees: $21,300	Average undergraduate aid package: $15,225

ABOUT THE INSTITUTION Independent religious, coed. Awards: associate, bachelor's, and master's degrees and post-bachelor's and post-master's certificates. 55 undergraduate majors. Total enrollment: 3,605. Undergraduates: 3,051. Freshmen: 638. Federal methodology is used as a basis for awarding need-based institutional aid.

UNDERGRADUATE EXPENSES for 2005–06 *Application fee:* $25. *Comprehensive fee:* $28,100 includes full-time tuition ($21,190), mandatory fees ($110), and room and board ($6800). *College room only:* $4020. Room and board charges vary according to board plan. *Part-time tuition:* $810 per credit. Part-time tuition and fees vary according to course load. *Payment plan:* Installment.

FRESHMAN FINANCIAL AID (Fall 2004, est.) 548 applied for aid; of those 82% were deemed to have need. 100% of freshmen with need received aid; of those 16% had need fully met. *Average percent of need met:* 82% (excluding resources awarded to replace EFC). *Average financial aid package:* $15,969 (excluding resources awarded to replace EFC). 26% of all full-time freshmen had no need and received non-need-based gift aid.

UNDERGRADUATE FINANCIAL AID (Fall 2004, est.) 2,112 applied for aid; of those 86% were deemed to have need. 100% of undergraduates with need received aid; of those 23% had need fully met. *Average percent of need met:* 81% (excluding resources awarded to replace EFC). *Average financial aid package:* $15,225 (excluding resources awarded to replace EFC). 23% of all full-time undergraduates had no need and received non-need-based gift aid.

GIFT AID (NEED-BASED) *Total amount:* $15,620,000 (11% federal, 16% state, 66% institutional, 7% external sources). *Receiving aid:* Freshmen: 67% (451); All full-time undergraduates: 68% (1,816). *Average award:* Freshmen: $10,294; Undergraduates: $9146. *Scholarships, grants, and awards:* Federal Pell, FSEOG, state, private, college/university gift aid from institutional funds.

GIFT AID (NON-NEED-BASED) *Total amount:* $2,410,000 (89% institutional, 11% external sources). *Receiving aid:* Freshmen: 6% (37); Undergraduates: 5% (131). *Average Award:* Freshmen: $3359; Undergraduates: $3226. *Scholarships, grants, and awards by category: Academic Interests/Achievement:* 1,420 awards ($4,000,000 total): general academic interests/achievements. *Creative Arts/Performance:* 90 awards ($135,000 total): art/fine arts, debating, music, theater/drama. *Special Achievements/Activities:* 2,000 awards ($2,100,000 total): community service, junior miss, leadership, religious involvement. *Special Characteristics:* 1,200 awards ($3,475,000 total): children and siblings of alumni, children of faculty/staff, ethnic background, international students, members of minority groups, out-of-state students, relatives of clergy, religious affiliation. *Tuition waivers:* Full or partial for employees or children of employees, senior citizens. *ROTC:* Army cooperative, Air Force cooperative.

LOANS *Student loans:* $10,000,000 (100% need-based). 78% of past graduating class borrowed through all loan programs. *Average indebtedness per student:* $23,777. *Average need-based loan:* Freshmen: $3905; Undergraduates: $4392. *Programs:* FFEL (Subsidized and Unsubsidized Stafford, PLUS), Perkins, state, alternative loans.

WORK-STUDY *Federal work-study:* Total amount: $850,000; 550 jobs averaging $1550. *State or other work-study/employment:* Total amount: $1,800,000 (100% need-based). 1,125 part-time jobs averaging $1600.

APPLYING FOR FINANCIAL AID *Required financial aid forms:* FAFSA, institution's own form. *Financial aid deadline (priority):* 4/15. *Notification date:* Continuous. Students must reply by 5/1 or within 3 weeks of notification.

CONTACT Mr. Daniel C. Nelson, Assistant to the President for Financial Aid, Enrollment, Institutional Research and Planning, Bethel University, 3900 Bethel Drive, St. Paul, MN 55112-6999, 651-638-6241 or toll-free 800-255-8706 Ext. 6242. *Fax:* 651-635-1491. *E-mail:* dc-nelson@bethel.edu.

BETHESDA CHRISTIAN UNIVERSITY
Anaheim, CA

ABOUT THE INSTITUTION Independent religious, coed. Awards: bachelor's, master's, and first professional degrees. 14 undergraduate majors. Total enrollment: 206. Undergraduates: 164. Freshmen: 32.

GIFT AID (NEED-BASED) *Scholarships, grants, and awards:* Federal Pell, college/university gift aid from institutional funds.

GIFT AID (NON-NEED-BASED) *Scholarships, grants, and awards by category: Creative Arts/Performance:* music.

LOANS *Programs:* FFEL (Subsidized and Unsubsidized Stafford).

APPLYING FOR FINANCIAL AID *Required financial aid form:* FAFSA.

CONTACT Myongha Prince, Financial Aid Administrator, Bethesda Christian University, 730 North Euclid Street, Anaheim, CA 92801, 714-517-1945 Ext. 130. *Fax:* 714-517-1948. *E-mail:* financialaid@bcu.edu.

BETH HAMEDRASH SHAAREI YOSHER INSTITUTE
Brooklyn, NY

CONTACT Financial Aid Office, Beth HaMedrash Shaarei Yosher Institute, 4102-10 16th Avenue, Brooklyn, NY 11204, 718-854-2290.

BETH HATALMUD RABBINICAL COLLEGE
Brooklyn, NY

CONTACT Financial Aid Office, Beth Hatalmud Rabbinical College, 2127 82nd Street, Brooklyn, NY 11204, 718-259-2525.

BETH MEDRASH GOVOHA
Lakewood, NJ

CONTACT Financial Aid Office, Beth Medrash Govoha, 617 Sixth Street, Lakewood, NJ 08701-2797, 732-367-1060.

BETHUNE-COOKMAN COLLEGE
Daytona Beach, FL

Tuition & fees: $10,610	Average undergraduate aid package: $11,555

ABOUT THE INSTITUTION Independent Methodist, coed. Awards: bachelor's degrees. 37 undergraduate majors. Total enrollment: 2,895. Undergraduates: 2,895. Freshmen: 841. Federal methodology is used as a basis for awarding need-based institutional aid.

UNDERGRADUATE EXPENSES for 2004–05 *Application fee:* $25. *Comprehensive fee:* $16,984 includes full-time tuition ($10,610) and room and board ($6374). *Part-time tuition:* $442 per credit hour.

FRESHMAN FINANCIAL AID (Fall 2004, est.) 813 applied for aid; of those 99% were deemed to have need. 99% of freshmen with need received aid; of those 29% had need fully met. *Average percent of need met:* 63% (excluding resources awarded to replace EFC). *Average financial aid package:* $10,740 (excluding resources awarded to replace EFC). 2% of all full-time freshmen had no need and received non-need-based gift aid.

UNDERGRADUATE FINANCIAL AID (Fall 2004, est.) 2,655 applied for aid; of those 90% were deemed to have need. 98% of undergraduates with need received aid; of those 21% had need fully met. *Average percent of need met:* 63% (excluding resources awarded to replace EFC). *Average financial aid package:* $11,555 (excluding resources awarded to replace EFC). 3% of all full-time undergraduates had no need and received non-need-based gift aid.

GIFT AID (NEED-BASED) *Total amount:* $12,945,963 (58% federal, 11% state, 28% institutional, 3% external sources). *Receiving aid:* Freshmen: 77% (628); All full-time undergraduates: 71% (1,895). *Average award:* Freshmen: $6265; Undergraduates: $6635. *Scholarships, grants, and awards:* Federal Pell, FSEOG, state, private, college/university gift aid from institutional funds, United Negro College Fund, Federal Nursing.

GIFT AID (NON-NEED-BASED) *Total amount:* $4,347,132 (72% state, 28% institutional). *Receiving aid:* Freshmen: 11% (94); Undergraduates: 12% (308). *Average Award:* Freshmen: $7225; Undergraduates: $7893. *Scholarships, grants, and awards by category: Academic Interests/Achievement:* 128 awards

($1,235,867 total): general academic interests/achievements. *Tuition waivers:* Full or partial for employees or children of employees. *ROTC:* Army cooperative, Air Force cooperative.

LOANS *Student loans:* $14,456,847 (51% need-based, 49% non-need-based). 79% of past graduating class borrowed through all loan programs. *Average indebtedness per student:* $25,880. *Average need-based loan:* Freshmen: $2628; Undergraduates: $3430. *Parent loans:* $4,064,655 (100% non-need-based). *Programs:* Federal Direct (Subsidized and Unsubsidized Stafford, PLUS), FFEL (PLUS).

WORK-STUDY *Federal work-study:* Total amount: $569,068; 300 jobs averaging $1660. *State or other work-study/employment:* Total amount: $203,008 (100% non-need-based). 125 part-time jobs averaging $1660.

ATHLETIC AWARDS *Total amount:* $3,166,643 (100% non-need-based).

APPLYING FOR FINANCIAL AID *Required financial aid form:* FAFSA. *Financial aid deadline (priority):* 4/1. *Notification date:* Continuous. Students must reply within 3 weeks of notification.

CONTACT Mr. Joseph Coleman, Director of Financial Aid, Bethune-Cookman College, 640 Mary McLeod Bethune Boulevard, Daytona Beach, FL 32114-3099, 386-481-2626 or toll-free 800-448-0228. *Fax:* 386-481-2621. *E-mail:* colemanj@cookman.edu.

BEULAH HEIGHTS BIBLE COLLEGE
Atlanta, GA

Tuition & fees: $4520	Average undergraduate aid package: $7202

ABOUT THE INSTITUTION Independent Pentecostal, coed. Awards: associate and bachelor's degrees. 2 undergraduate majors. Total enrollment: 620. Undergraduates: 620. Freshmen: 155. Federal methodology is used as a basis for awarding need-based institutional aid.

UNDERGRADUATE EXPENSES for 2004–05 *Application fee:* $20. *Tuition:* full-time $4320; part-time $180 per semester hour. *Required fees:* full-time $200; $100 per term part-time. Full-time tuition and fees vary according to course load. *Payment plans:* Installment, deferred payment.

GIFT AID (NEED-BASED) *Total amount:* $1,147,258 (90% federal, 8% institutional, 2% external sources). *Receiving aid:* Freshmen: 89% (41); All full-time undergraduates: 96% (184). *Average award:* Freshmen: $2645; Undergraduates: $2500. *Scholarships, grants, and awards:* Federal Pell, FSEOG, private.

GIFT AID (NON-NEED-BASED) *Total amount:* $4320 (100% institutional). *Receiving aid:* Undergraduates: 4% (7). *Scholarships, grants, and awards by category: Academic Interests/Achievement:* 2 awards ($2800 total): religion/biblical studies. *Special Characteristics:* 31 awards ($100,833 total): children of faculty/staff, general special characteristics, international students, married students, religious affiliation, spouses of current students. *Tuition waivers:* Full or partial for employees or children of employees.

LOANS *Student loans:* $2,984,328 (47% need-based, 53% non-need-based). 44% of past graduating class borrowed through all loan programs. *Average indebtedness per student:* $25,000. *Average need-based loan:* Freshmen: $1778; Undergraduates: $3334. *Parent loans:* $4000 (100% non-need-based). *Programs:* FFEL (Subsidized and Unsubsidized Stafford, PLUS).

APPLYING FOR FINANCIAL AID *Required financial aid forms:* FAFSA, institution's own form. *Financial aid deadline (priority):* 5/15. *Notification date:* 7/30. Students must reply within 2 weeks of notification.

CONTACT Ms. Patricia Banks, Financial Aid Director, Beulah Heights Bible College, 892 Berne Street, SE, Atlanta, GA 30316, 404-627-2681 or toll-free 888-777-BHBC. *Fax:* 404-627-0702. *E-mail:* pat.banks@beulah.org.

BIOLA UNIVERSITY
La Mirada, CA

Tuition & fees: $22,702	Average undergraduate aid package: $16,977

ABOUT THE INSTITUTION Independent interdenominational, coed. Awards: bachelor's, master's, doctoral, and first professional degrees. 40 undergraduate majors. Total enrollment: 5,370. Undergraduates: 3,595. Freshmen: 702. Federal methodology is used as a basis for awarding need-based institutional aid.

UNDERGRADUATE EXPENSES for 2005–06 *Application fee:* $45. *Comprehensive fee:* $29,802 includes full-time tuition ($22,602), mandatory fees ($100), and room and board ($7100). *College room only:* $3900. Room and board charges

vary according to board plan and housing facility. *Part-time tuition:* $942 per unit. Part-time tuition and fees vary according to course load. *Payment plan:* Installment.

FRESHMAN FINANCIAL AID (Fall 2004, est.) 602 applied for aid; of those 83% were deemed to have need. 100% of freshmen with need received aid; of those 11% had need fully met. *Average percent of need met:* 73% (excluding resources awarded to replace EFC). *Average financial aid package:* $16,857 (excluding resources awarded to replace EFC). 15% of all full-time freshmen had no need and received non-need-based gift aid.

UNDERGRADUATE FINANCIAL AID (Fall 2004, est.) 2,394 applied for aid; of those 86% were deemed to have need. 100% of undergraduates with need received aid; of those 14% had need fully met. *Average percent of need met:* 73% (excluding resources awarded to replace EFC). *Average financial aid package:* $16,977 (excluding resources awarded to replace EFC). 10% of all full-time undergraduates had no need and received non-need-based gift aid.

GIFT AID (NEED-BASED) *Total amount:* $19,857,677 (12% federal, 33% state, 50% institutional, 5% external sources). *Receiving aid:* Freshmen: 57% (419); All full-time undergraduates: 56% (1,747). *Average award:* Freshmen: $10,425; Undergraduates: $10,045. *Scholarships, grants, and awards:* Federal Pell, FSEOG, state, private, college/university gift aid from institutional funds.

GIFT AID (NON-NEED-BASED) *Total amount:* $1,213,211 (1% state, 81% institutional, 18% external sources). *Receiving aid:* Freshmen: 55% (402); Undergraduates: 48% (1,520). *Average Award:* Freshmen: $8956; Undergraduates: $11,005. *Scholarships, grants, and awards by category: Academic Interests/Achievement:* 1,082 awards ($4,249,886 total): communication, general academic interests/achievements, health fields. *Creative Arts/Performance:* 163 awards ($494,560 total): art/fine arts, debating, journalism/publications, music, performing arts, theater/drama. *Special Achievements/Activities:* 67 awards ($178,000 total): community service. *Special Characteristics:* 256 awards ($1,980,056 total): adult students, children of faculty/staff, ethnic background, international students, relatives of clergy. *Tuition waivers:* Full or partial for employees or children of employees. *ROTC:* Army cooperative, Air Force cooperative.

LOANS *Student loans:* $14,830,882 (82% need-based, 18% non-need-based). 74% of past graduating class borrowed through all loan programs. *Average indebtedness per student:* $27,285. *Average need-based loan:* Freshmen: $2722; Undergraduates: $2918. *Parent loans:* $6,204,754 (100% need-based). *Programs:* FFEL (Subsidized and Unsubsidized Stafford, PLUS), Perkins, Federal Nursing, college/university, alternative loans.

WORK-STUDY *Federal work-study:* Total amount: $241,576; 117 jobs averaging $2064.

ATHLETIC AWARDS *Total amount:* $1,121,945 (100% need-based).

APPLYING FOR FINANCIAL AID *Required financial aid forms:* FAFSA, state aid form. *Financial aid deadline:* Continuous. *Notification date:* Continuous beginning 5/1.

CONTACT Financial Aid Office, Biola University, 13800 Biola Avenue, La Mirada, CA 90639-0001, 562-903-4742 or toll-free 800-652-4652. *Fax:* 562-906-4541. *E-mail:* finaid@biola.edu.

BIRMINGHAM-SOUTHERN COLLEGE
Birmingham, AL

ABOUT THE INSTITUTION Independent Methodist, coed. Awards: bachelor's and master's degrees. 44 undergraduate majors. Total enrollment: 1,453. Undergraduates: 1,356. Freshmen: 367.

GIFT AID (NEED-BASED) *Scholarships, grants, and awards:* Federal Pell, FSEOG, state, private, college/university gift aid from institutional funds.

GIFT AID (NON-NEED-BASED) *Scholarships, grants, and awards by category: Academic Interests/Achievement:* business, computer science, education, general academic interests/achievements, health fields, premedicine. *Creative Arts/Performance:* art/fine arts, dance, music, performing arts, theater/drama. *Special Achievements/Activities:* junior miss, memberships, religious involvement. *Special Characteristics:* children and siblings of alumni, children of faculty/staff, relatives of clergy, religious affiliation.

LOANS *Programs:* FFEL (Subsidized and Unsubsidized Stafford, PLUS), Perkins, college/university.

WORK-STUDY *Federal work-study:* Total amount: $223,694; 142 jobs averaging $1818. *State or other work-study/employment:* Total amount: $110,330 (100% need-based). 157 part-time jobs averaging $1371.

APPLYING FOR FINANCIAL AID *Required financial aid forms:* FAFSA, state aid form.

CONTACT Financial Aid Office, Birmingham-Southern College, 900 Arkadelphia Road, Box 549016, Birmingham, AL 35254, 205-226-4688 or toll-free 800-523-5793. *Fax:* 205-226-3082. *E-mail:* finaid@bsc.edu.

BIRTHINGWAY COLLEGE OF MIDWIFERY
Portland, OR

CONTACT Financial Aid Office, Birthingway College of Midwifery, 12113 SE Foster Road, Portland, OR 97299, 503-760-3131.

BLACKBURN COLLEGE
Carlinville, IL

ABOUT THE INSTITUTION Independent Presbyterian, coed. Awards: bachelor's degrees. 34 undergraduate majors. Total enrollment: 590. Undergraduates: 590. Freshmen: 178.

GIFT AID (NEED-BASED) *Scholarships, grants, and awards:* Federal Pell, FSEOG, state, private, college/university gift aid from institutional funds.

GIFT AID (NON-NEED-BASED) *Scholarships, grants, and awards by category:* *Academic Interests/Achievement:* general academic interests/achievements. *Special Achievements/Activities:* general special achievements/activities.

LOANS *Programs:* FFEL (Subsidized and Unsubsidized Stafford, PLUS), Perkins, college/university.

WORK-STUDY Federal work-study jobs available. *State or other work-study/ employment:* Part-time jobs available.

APPLYING FOR FINANCIAL AID *Required financial aid form:* FAFSA.

CONTACT Mrs. Jane Kelsey, Financial Aid Administrator, Blackburn College, 700 College Avenue, Carlinville, IL 62626-1498, 217-854-3231 Ext. 4227 or toll-free 800-233-3550. *Fax:* 217-854-3731.

BLACK HILLS STATE UNIVERSITY
Spearfish, SD

Tuition & fees (SD res): $4820	Average undergraduate aid package: $4638

ABOUT THE INSTITUTION State-supported, coed. Awards: associate, bachelor's, and master's degrees and post-bachelor's and post-master's certificates. 47 undergraduate majors. Total enrollment: 3,846. Undergraduates: 3,653. Freshmen: 657. Federal methodology is used as a basis for awarding need-based institutional aid.

UNDERGRADUATE EXPENSES for 2004–05 *Application fee:* $20. *Tuition, state resident:* full-time $2372; part-time $150.60 per credit. *Tuition, nonresident:* full-time $7538; part-time $312.05 per credit. *Required fees:* full-time $2448; $76.50 per credit. Full-time tuition and fees vary according to course load and reciprocity agreements. Part-time tuition and fees vary according to course load and reciprocity agreements. *College room and board:* $3449; *room only:* $1903. Room and board charges vary according to board plan and housing facility.

UNDERGRADUATE FINANCIAL AID (Fall 2003) *Average financial aid package:* $4638 (excluding resources awarded to replace EFC).

GIFT AID (NEED-BASED) *Total amount:* $4,002,408 (92% federal, 8% external sources). *Scholarships, grants, and awards:* Federal Pell, FSEOG, state, private, college/university gift aid from institutional funds.

GIFT AID (NON-NEED-BASED) *Total amount:* $794,029 (50% institutional, 50% external sources). *Scholarships, grants, and awards by category:* *Academic Interests/Achievement:* biological sciences, business, communication, computer science, education, English, foreign languages, general academic interests/ achievements, health fields, humanities, mathematics, military science, physical sciences, social sciences. *Creative Arts/Performance:* art/fine arts, music, theater/ drama. *Tuition waivers:* Full or partial for employees or children of employees, senior citizens. *ROTC:* Army.

LOANS *Student loans:* $13,440,817 (51% need-based, 49% non-need-based). 81% of past graduating class borrowed through all loan programs. *Average indebtedness per student:* $21,218. *Parent loans:* $341,285 (100% non-need-based). *Programs:* FFEL (Subsidized and Unsubsidized Stafford, PLUS), Perkins.

WORK-STUDY *Federal work-study:* Total amount: $348,077; 267 jobs averaging $1304. *State or other work-study/employment:* Total amount: $611,382 (100% non-need-based). 383 part-time jobs averaging $1596.

ATHLETIC AWARDS *Total amount:* $274,681 (100% non-need-based).

APPLYING FOR FINANCIAL AID *Required financial aid form:* FAFSA. *Financial aid deadline (priority):* 3/1. *Notification date:* Continuous beginning 5/1. Students must reply within 3 weeks of notification.

CONTACT Ms. Deb Henriksen, Director of Financial Aid, Black Hills State University, 1200 University Street, Box 9670, Spearfish, SD 57799-9670, 605-642-6581 or toll-free 800-255-2478. *Fax:* 605-642-6254. *E-mail:* debhenriksen@bhsu.edu.

BLESSING-RIEMAN COLLEGE OF NURSING
Quincy, IL

Tuition & fees: $14,250	Average undergraduate aid package: N/A

ABOUT THE INSTITUTION Independent, coed, primarily women. Awards: bachelor's degrees. 1 undergraduate major. Total enrollment: 228. Undergraduates: 228. Freshmen: 36. Federal methodology is used as a basis for awarding need-based institutional aid.

UNDERGRADUATE EXPENSES for 2005–06 *Comprehensive fee:* $20,025 includes full-time tuition ($13,900), mandatory fees ($350), and room and board ($5775). Full-time tuition and fees vary according to course load, location, and student level. Room and board charges vary according to location. Part-time tuition and fees vary according to course load, location, and student level. *Payment plan:* Installment.

UNDERGRADUATE FINANCIAL AID (Fall 2003) 87 applied for aid; of those 100% were deemed to have need. 100% of undergraduates with need received aid. *Average percent of need met:* 75% (excluding resources awarded to replace EFC).

GIFT AID (NEED-BASED) *Total amount:* $390,175 (24% federal, 25% state, 45% institutional, 6% external sources). *Receiving aid:* All full-time undergraduates: 94% (87). *Scholarships, grants, and awards:* Federal Pell, state, private, college/university gift aid from institutional funds.

GIFT AID (NON-NEED-BASED) *Tuition waivers:* Full or partial for employees or children of employees.

LOANS *Student loans:* $327,205 (100% need-based). 70% of past graduating class borrowed through all loan programs. *Average indebtedness per student:* $11,000. *Parent loans:* $15,769 (100% need-based). *Programs:* FFEL (Subsidized and Unsubsidized Stafford, PLUS), Federal Nursing, college/university.

APPLYING FOR FINANCIAL AID *Required financial aid form:* FAFSA. *Financial aid deadline:* Continuous.

CONTACT Ms. Sara Brehm, Financial Aid Officer, Blessing-Rieman College of Nursing, Broadway at 11th Street, Quincy, IL 62301, 217-223-8400 Ext. 6993 or toll-free 800-877-9140 Ext. 6964. *Fax:* 217-223-1781. *E-mail:* sbrehm@ blessinghospital.org.

BLOOMFIELD COLLEGE
Bloomfield, NJ

Tuition & fees: $15,100	Average undergraduate aid package: $12,405

ABOUT THE INSTITUTION Independent religious, coed. Awards: bachelor's degrees. 49 undergraduate majors. Total enrollment: 2,166. Undergraduates: 2,166. Freshmen: 424. Federal methodology is used as a basis for awarding need-based institutional aid.

UNDERGRADUATE EXPENSES for 2005–06 *Application fee:* $35. *Comprehensive fee:* $22,500 includes full-time tuition ($14,850), mandatory fees ($250), and room and board ($7400). *College room only:* $3700. *Part-time tuition:* $1495 per course. *Part-time fees:* $25 per term. Part-time tuition and fees vary according to course load. *Payment plans:* Installment, deferred payment.

FRESHMAN FINANCIAL AID (Fall 2003) 379 applied for aid; of those 59% were deemed to have need. 100% of freshmen with need received aid; of those 32% had need fully met. *Average percent of need met:* 91% (excluding resources awarded to replace EFC). *Average financial aid package:* $13,025 (excluding resources awarded to replace EFC). 10% of all full-time freshmen had no need and received non-need-based gift aid.

UNDERGRADUATE FINANCIAL AID (Fall 2003) 1,388 applied for aid; of those 63% were deemed to have need. 100% of undergraduates with need received aid; of those 44% had need fully met. *Average percent of need met:* 99% (excluding resources awarded to replace EFC). *Average financial aid package:* $12,405 (excluding resources awarded to replace EFC). 6% of all full-time undergraduates had no need and received non-need-based gift aid.

GIFT AID (NEED-BASED) *Total amount:* $12,781,916 (30% federal, 48% state, 22% institutional). *Receiving aid:* Freshmen: 57% (219); All full-time undergradu-

---

Bloomfield College

ates: 60% (855). *Average award:* Freshmen: $11,016; Undergraduates: $9859. *Scholarships, grants, and awards:* Federal Pell, FSEOG, state, private, college/university gift aid from institutional funds.

GIFT AID (NON-NEED-BASED) *Total amount:* $877,206 (2% state, 76% institutional, 22% external sources). *Receiving aid:* Freshmen: 13% (50); Undergraduates: 10% (137). *Average Award: Freshmen:* $3818; *Undergraduates:* $4212. *Scholarships, grants, and awards by category: Academic Interests/Achievement:* 227 awards ($276,572 total): general academic interests/achievements. *Special Characteristics:* 17 awards ($40,173 total): children and siblings of alumni. *Tuition waivers:* Full or partial for employees or children of employees, senior citizens. *ROTC:* Army cooperative.

LOANS *Student loans:* $6,148,216 (100% need-based). *Average need-based loan:* Freshmen: $2491; Undergraduates: $3472. *Parent loans:* $451,475 (100% need-based). *Programs:* FFEL (Subsidized and Unsubsidized Stafford, PLUS), state.

WORK-STUDY *Federal work-study:* Total amount: $419,337; 367 jobs averaging $1415. *State or other work-study/employment:* Part-time jobs available.

ATHLETIC AWARDS *Total amount:* $600,483 (100% non-need-based).

APPLYING FOR FINANCIAL AID *Required financial aid form:* FAFSA. *Financial aid deadline:* 6/1 (priority: 3/15). *Notification date:* Continuous beginning 3/15. Students must reply by 3/15 or within 2 weeks of notification.

CONTACT Mr. Luis Gonzalez, Director of Financial Aid, Bloomfield College, Bloomfield College, 467 Franklin Street, Bloomfield, NJ 07003-9981, 973-748-9000 Ext. 212 or toll-free 800-848-4555 Ext. 230. *Fax:* 973-748-9735. *E-mail:* l_gonzalez@bloomfield.edu.

BLOOMSBURG UNIVERSITY OF PENNSYLVANIA
Bloomsburg, PA

Tuition & fees (PA res): $6089	Average undergraduate aid package: $10,465

ABOUT THE INSTITUTION State-supported, coed. Awards: associate, bachelor's, master's, and doctoral degrees and post-bachelor's certificates. 53 undergraduate majors. Total enrollment: 8,304. Undergraduates: 7,524. Freshmen: 1,542. Federal methodology is used as a basis for awarding need-based institutional aid.

UNDERGRADUATE EXPENSES for 2004–05 *Application fee:* $30. *Tuition, state resident:* full-time $4810; part-time $200 per credit. *Tuition, nonresident:* full-time $12,026; part-time $501 per credit. Full-time tuition and fees vary according to course load. Part-time tuition and fees vary according to course load. *College room and board:* $5200; *room only:* $3012. Room and board charges vary according to board plan and housing facility.

FRESHMAN FINANCIAL AID (Fall 2004, est.) 1336 applied for aid; of those 80% were deemed to have need. 95% of freshmen with need received aid; of those 90% had need fully met. *Average percent of need met:* 65% (excluding resources awarded to replace EFC). *Average financial aid package:* $11,679 (excluding resources awarded to replace EFC).

UNDERGRADUATE FINANCIAL AID (Fall 2004, est.) 5,623 applied for aid; of those 80% were deemed to have need. 95% of undergraduates with need received aid; of those 90% had need fully met. *Average percent of need met:* 65% (excluding resources awarded to replace EFC). *Average financial aid package:* $10,465 (excluding resources awarded to replace EFC).

GIFT AID (NEED-BASED) *Total amount:* $12,204,908 (46% federal, 49% state, 2% institutional, 3% external sources). *Receiving aid:* Freshmen: 59% (906); All full-time undergraduates: 45% (3,132). *Average award:* Freshmen: $4147; Undergraduates: $3897. *Scholarships, grants, and awards:* Federal Pell, FSEOG, state, private, college/university gift aid from institutional funds.

GIFT AID (NON-NEED-BASED) *Total amount:* $2,414,273 (4% federal, 20% state, 26% institutional, 50% external sources). *Receiving aid:* Freshmen: 32% (487); Undergraduates: 16% (1,117). *Scholarships, grants, and awards by category: Academic Interests/Achievement:* 299 awards ($248,522 total): biological sciences, business, communication, computer science, education, English, foreign languages, general academic interests/achievements, health fields, humanities, international studies, mathematics, physical sciences, religion/biblical studies, social sciences. *Special Characteristics:* 197 awards ($807,668 total): children of faculty/staff, international students. *Tuition waivers:* Full or partial for minority students, employees or children of employees, senior citizens. *ROTC:* Army, Air Force cooperative.

LOANS *Student loans:* $24,389,774 (53% need-based, 47% non-need-based). 73% of past graduating class borrowed through all loan programs. *Average indebtedness per student:* $16,022. *Average need-based loan:* Freshmen: $2699;

Undergraduates: $3541. *Parent loans:* $6,033,615 (100% non-need-based). *Programs:* FFEL (Subsidized and Unsubsidized Stafford, PLUS), Perkins, state, alternative loans.

WORK-STUDY *Federal work-study:* Total amount: $2,913,220; 1,141 jobs averaging $2553. *State or other work-study/employment:* Total amount: $2,799,962 (100% non-need-based). 1,073 part-time jobs averaging $2609.

ATHLETIC AWARDS *Total amount:* $477,660 (100% non-need-based).

APPLYING FOR FINANCIAL AID *Required financial aid forms:* FAFSA, state aid form. *Financial aid deadline (priority):* 3/15. *Notification date:* Continuous beginning 4/1.

CONTACT Mr. Thomas M. Lyons, Director of Financial Aid, Bloomsburg University of Pennsylvania, 119 Student Services Center, 400 East 2nd Street, Bloomsburg, PA 17815-1301, 570-389-4279. *Fax:* 570-389-4795. *E-mail:* tlyons@bloomu.edu.

BLUEFIELD COLLEGE
Bluefield, VA

ABOUT THE INSTITUTION Independent Southern Baptist, coed. Awards: bachelor's degrees. 43 undergraduate majors. Total enrollment: 814. Undergraduates: 814. Freshmen: 123.

GIFT AID (NEED-BASED) *Scholarships, grants, and awards:* Federal Pell, FSEOG, state, college/university gift aid from institutional funds.

GIFT AID (NON-NEED-BASED) *Scholarships, grants, and awards by category: Academic Interests/Achievement:* biological sciences, business, education, English, general academic interests/achievements, mathematics, premedicine, religion/biblical studies. *Creative Arts/Performance:* art/fine arts, music, performing arts, theater/drama. *Special Achievements/Activities:* community service, general special achievements/activities, leadership, religious involvement. *Special Characteristics:* children of educators, children of faculty/staff, ethnic background, first-generation college students, general special characteristics, international students, local/state students, members of minority groups, out-of-state students, relatives of clergy, religious affiliation, spouses of current students, veterans.

LOANS *Programs:* FFEL (Subsidized and Unsubsidized Stafford, PLUS), alternative loans.

WORK-STUDY *Federal work-study:* Total amount: $74,498; 98 jobs averaging $800. *State or other work-study/employment:* Total amount: $15,750 (49% need-based, 51% non-need-based). Part-time jobs available.

APPLYING FOR FINANCIAL AID *Required financial aid forms:* FAFSA, institution's own form, state aid form.

CONTACT Mrs. Debbie Checchio, Director of Financial Aid, Bluefield College, 3000 College Drive, Bluefield, VA 24605, 276-326-4215 or toll-free 800-872-0175. *Fax:* 276-326-4356. *E-mail:* dchecchio@bluefield.edu.

BLUEFIELD STATE COLLEGE
Bluefield, WV

Tuition & fees (WV res): $3114	Average undergraduate aid package: $5000

ABOUT THE INSTITUTION State-supported, coed. Awards: associate and bachelor's degrees. 28 undergraduate majors. Total enrollment: 3,506. Undergraduates: 3,506. Freshmen: 588. Federal methodology is used as a basis for awarding need-based institutional aid.

UNDERGRADUATE EXPENSES for 2004–05 *Tuition, state resident:* full-time $3114; part-time $130 per credit. *Tuition, nonresident:* full-time $6894; part-time $289 per credit. Full-time tuition and fees vary according to degree level, program, and reciprocity agreements. Part-time tuition and fees vary according to course load, program, and reciprocity agreements. *Payment plan:* Deferred payment.

FRESHMAN FINANCIAL AID (Fall 2004, est.) 450 applied for aid; of those 83% were deemed to have need. 100% of freshmen with need received aid; of those 24% had need fully met. *Average percent of need met:* 70% (excluding resources awarded to replace EFC). *Average financial aid package:* $5000 (excluding resources awarded to replace EFC). 13% of all full-time freshmen had no need and received non-need-based gift aid.

UNDERGRADUATE FINANCIAL AID (Fall 2004, est.) 1,600 applied for aid; of those 56% were deemed to have need. 100% of undergraduates with need received aid; of those 18% had need fully met. *Average percent of need met:* 70% (excluding resources awarded to replace EFC). *Average financial aid package:* $5000 (excluding resources awarded to replace EFC). 13% of all full-time undergraduates had no need and received non-need-based gift aid.

GIFT AID (NEED-BASED) *Total amount:* $7,270,000 (83% federal, 17% state). *Receiving aid:* Freshmen: 66% (375); All full-time undergraduates: 38% (900). *Average award:* Freshmen: $3000; Undergraduates: $3060. *Scholarships, grants, and awards:* Federal Pell, FSEOG, state, private, college/university gift aid from institutional funds.

GIFT AID (NON-NEED-BASED) *Total amount:* $2,225,000 (16% state, 17% institutional, 67% external sources). *Receiving aid:* Freshmen: 11% (60); Undergraduates: 7% (160). *Average Award:* Freshmen: $1400; *Undergraduates:* $1400. *Scholarships, grants, and awards by category: Academic Interests/ Achievement:* 400 awards ($200,000 total): engineering/technologies, general academic interests/achievements. *Special Achievements/Activities:* 11 awards ($5100 total): cheerleading/drum major, general special achievements/activities, junior miss, leadership. *Special Characteristics:* 1 award ($500 total): general special characteristics. *Tuition waivers:* Full or partial for senior citizens.

LOANS *Student loans:* $8,200,000 (59% need-based, 41% non-need-based). 50% of past graduating class borrowed through all loan programs. *Average indebtedness per student:* $10,200. *Average need-based loan:* Freshmen: $3000; Undergraduates: $3000. *Parent loans:* $80,000 (100% non-need-based). *Programs:* Federal Direct (Subsidized and Unsubsidized Stafford, PLUS), Perkins.

WORK-STUDY *Federal work-study:* Total amount: $170,000; 125 jobs averaging $1400. *State or other work-study/employment:* Total amount: $300,000 (100% non-need-based). 150 part-time jobs averaging $1650.

ATHLETIC AWARDS *Total amount:* $65,000 (100% non-need-based).

APPLYING FOR FINANCIAL AID *Required financial aid forms:* FAFSA, institution's own form. *Financial aid deadline (priority):* 3/1. *Notification date:* 6/1.

CONTACT Mr. Tom Ilse, Director of Financial Aid, Bluefield State College, 219 Rock Street, Bluefield, WV 24701-2198, 304-327-4020 or toll-free 800-344-8892 Ext. 4065 (in-state), 800-654-7798 Ext. 4065 (out-of-state). *Fax:* 304-325-7747. *E-mail:* tilse@bluefieldstate.edu.

BLUE MOUNTAIN COLLEGE
Blue Mountain, MS

Tuition & fees: $7320	Average undergraduate aid package: N/A

ABOUT THE INSTITUTION Independent Southern Baptist, women only. Awards: bachelor's degrees (also offers a coordinate academic program for men preparing for church-related vocations). 35 undergraduate majors. Total enrollment: 388. Undergraduates: 388. Freshmen: 53. Federal methodology is used as a basis for awarding need-based institutional aid.

UNDERGRADUATE EXPENSES for 2005–06 *Application fee:* $10. *Comprehensive fee:* $11,086 includes full-time tuition ($6780), mandatory fees ($540), and room and board ($3766). *College room only:* $1400. Full-time tuition and fees vary according to course load. Room and board charges vary according to board plan and gender. *Part-time tuition:* $230 per hour. *Part-time fees:* $80 per term. Part-time tuition and fees vary according to course load. *Payment plan:* Installment.

FRESHMAN FINANCIAL AID (Fall 2004, est.) 43 applied for aid; of those 95% were deemed to have need. 100% of freshmen with need received aid; of those 46% had need fully met. *Average percent of need met:* 42% (excluding resources awarded to replace EFC). 4% of all full-time freshmen had no need and received non-need-based gift aid.

UNDERGRADUATE FINANCIAL AID (Fall 2004, est.) 265 applied for aid; of those 89% were deemed to have need. 100% of undergraduates with need received aid; of those 30% had need fully met. *Average percent of need met:* 29% (excluding resources awarded to replace EFC). 16% of all full-time undergraduates had no need and received non-need-based gift aid.

GIFT AID (NEED-BASED) *Total amount:* $587,221 (99% federal, 1% state). *Receiving aid:* Freshmen: 56% (27); All full-time undergraduates: 55% (162). *Average award:* Freshmen: $1725; Undergraduates: $2166. *Scholarships, grants, and awards:* Federal Pell, FSEOG, state, private, college/university gift aid from institutional funds.

GIFT AID (NON-NEED-BASED) *Total amount:* $669,301 (36% state, 58% institutional, 6% external sources). *Receiving aid:* Freshmen: 81% (39); Undergraduates: 75% (223). *Average Award:* Freshmen: $3288; *Undergraduates:* $1849. *Scholarships, grants, and awards by category: Academic Interests/ Achievement:* biological sciences, business, education, English, general academic interests/achievements, mathematics, premedicine, religion/biblical studies, social sciences. *Creative Arts/Performance:* music, theater/drama. *Special Achievements/ Activities:* leadership, memberships, religious involvement. *Special Characteristics:* children and siblings of alumni, children of current students, general special

characteristics, parents of current students, religious affiliation, siblings of current students, spouses of current students. *Tuition waivers:* Full or partial for employees or children of employees.

LOANS *Student loans:* $1,030,326 (92% need-based, 8% non-need-based). 74% of past graduating class borrowed through all loan programs. *Average indebtedness per student:* $11,784. *Average need-based loan:* Freshmen: $2728; Undergraduates: $3567. *Parent loans:* $78,565 (100% non-need-based). *Programs:* FFEL (Subsidized and Unsubsidized Stafford, PLUS), Perkins.

WORK-STUDY *Federal work-study:* Total amount: $67,534; 52 jobs averaging $1400. *State or other work-study/employment:* Total amount: $62,161 (100% non-need-based). 46 part-time jobs averaging $1400.

ATHLETIC AWARDS *Total amount:* $137,783 (100% non-need-based).

APPLYING FOR FINANCIAL AID *Required financial aid forms:* FAFSA, institution's own form. *Financial aid deadline (priority):* 3/1. *Notification date:* Continuous. Students must reply within 2 weeks of notification.

CONTACT Angie Gossett, Director of Financial Aid, Blue Mountain College, PO Box 160, Blue Mountain, MS 38610-0160, 662-685-4771 Ext. 141 or toll-free 800-235-0136. *Fax:* 662-685-4776. *E-mail:* agossett@bmc.edu.

BLUFFTON UNIVERSITY
Bluffton, OH

Tuition & fees: $18,350	Average undergraduate aid package: $17,369

ABOUT THE INSTITUTION Independent Mennonite, coed. Awards: bachelor's and master's degrees. 39 undergraduate majors. Total enrollment: 1,191. Undergraduates: 1,103. Freshmen: 266. Both federal and institutional methodology are used as a basis for awarding need-based institutional aid.

UNDERGRADUATE EXPENSES for 2004–05 *Application fee:* $20. *Comprehensive fee:* $24,654 includes full-time tuition ($17,950), mandatory fees ($400), and room and board ($6304). *College room only:* $2902. Full-time tuition and fees vary according to course load and program. Room and board charges vary according to board plan and housing facility. *Part-time tuition:* $748 per credit hour. Part-time tuition and fees vary according to course load and program. *Payment plan:* Installment.

FRESHMAN FINANCIAL AID (Fall 2004, est.) 252 applied for aid; of those 90% were deemed to have need. 100% of freshmen with need received aid; of those 66% had need fully met. *Average percent of need met:* 95% (excluding resources awarded to replace EFC). *Average financial aid package:* $17,726 (excluding resources awarded to replace EFC). 12% of all full-time freshmen had no need and received non-need-based gift aid.

UNDERGRADUATE FINANCIAL AID (Fall 2004, est.) 802 applied for aid; of those 94% were deemed to have need. 100% of undergraduates with need received aid; of those 50% had need fully met. *Average percent of need met:* 92% (excluding resources awarded to replace EFC). *Average financial aid package:* $17,369 (excluding resources awarded to replace EFC). 11% of all full-time undergraduates had no need and received non-need-based gift aid.

GIFT AID (NEED-BASED) *Total amount:* $8,643,440 (11% federal, 15% state, 66% institutional, 8% external sources). *Receiving aid:* Freshmen: 85% (226); All full-time undergraduates: 73% (751). *Average award:* Freshmen: $12,869; Undergraduates: $11,428. *Scholarships, grants, and awards:* Federal Pell, FSEOG, state, private, college/university gift aid from institutional funds.

GIFT AID (NON-NEED-BASED) *Total amount:* $1,386,037 (10% state, 65% institutional, 25% external sources). *Receiving aid:* Freshmen: 7% (18); Undergraduates: 7% (68). *Average Award:* Freshmen: $7893; *Undergraduates:* $8216. *Scholarships, grants, and awards by category: Academic Interests/ Achievement:* 505 awards ($3,454,316 total): general academic interests/ achievements. *Creative Arts/Performance:* 23 awards ($21,800 total): art/fine arts, music. *Special Achievements/Activities:* 79 awards ($226,780 total): leadership. *Special Characteristics:* 436 awards ($1,186,476 total): children of faculty/staff, international students, members of minority groups, out-of-state students, relatives of clergy, religious affiliation. *Tuition waivers:* Full or partial for employees or children of employees.

LOANS *Student loans:* $5,777,464 (95% need-based, 5% non-need-based). 78% of past graduating class borrowed through all loan programs. *Average indebtedness per student:* $22,982. *Average need-based loan:* Freshmen: $3775; Undergraduates: $4803. *Parent loans:* $961,646 (75% need-based, 25% non-need-based). *Programs:* FFEL (Subsidized and Unsubsidized Stafford, PLUS), Perkins, college/university, alternative loans.

WORK-STUDY *Federal work-study:* Total amount: $905,330; 593 jobs averaging $1536. *State or other work-study/employment:* Total amount: $525,308 (58% need-based, 42% non-need-based). 337 part-time jobs averaging $1570.

APPLYING FOR FINANCIAL AID *Required financial aid form:* FAFSA. *Financial aid deadline:* 10/1 (priority: 5/1). *Notification date:* Continuous beginning 3/1. Students must reply within 3 weeks of notification.

CONTACT Lawrence Matthews, Director of Financial Aid, Bluffton University, 1 University Drive, Bluffton, OH 45817-2104, 419-358-3266 or toll-free 800-488-3257. *Fax:* 419-358-3073. *E-mail:* matthewsl@bluffton.edu.

BOB JONES UNIVERSITY
Greenville, SC

CONTACT Mr. Chris Baker, Director of Financial Aid, Bob Jones University, 1700 Wade Hampton Boulevard, Greenville, SC 29614, 803-242-5100 Ext. 3037.

BOISE BIBLE COLLEGE
Boise, ID

ABOUT THE INSTITUTION Independent nondenominational, coed. Awards: associate and bachelor's degrees. 7 undergraduate majors. Total enrollment: 134. Undergraduates: 134.

GIFT AID (NEED-BASED) *Scholarships, grants, and awards:* Federal Pell, FSEOG, private, college/university gift aid from institutional funds.

GIFT AID (NON-NEED-BASED) *Scholarships, grants, and awards by category: Academic Interests/Achievement:* religion/biblical studies. *Creative Arts/Performance:* music. *Special Achievements/Activities:* leadership. *Special Characteristics:* children of faculty/staff, relatives of clergy, spouses of current students.

LOANS *Programs:* FFEL (Subsidized and Unsubsidized Stafford, PLUS), alternative loans.

WORK-STUDY *Federal work-study:* Total amount: $10,250; 7 jobs averaging $1464.

APPLYING FOR FINANCIAL AID *Required financial aid forms:* FAFSA, institution's own form.

CONTACT Beth Turner, Financial Aid Counselor, Boise Bible College, 8695 West Marigold Street, Boise, ID 83714-1220, 208-376-7731 Ext. 12 or toll-free 800-893-7755. *Fax:* 208-376-7743. *E-mail:* bethht@boisebible.edu.

BOISE STATE UNIVERSITY
Boise, ID

Tuition & fees (ID res): $3520	Average undergraduate aid package: $8703

ABOUT THE INSTITUTION State-supported, coed. Awards: associate, bachelor's, master's, and doctoral degrees. 97 undergraduate majors. Total enrollment: 18,332. Undergraduates: 16,719. Freshmen: 2,143. Federal methodology is used as a basis for awarding need-based institutional aid.

UNDERGRADUATE EXPENSES for 2004–05 *Application fee:* $30. *Tuition, state resident:* full-time $3520; part-time $177 per credit. *Tuition, nonresident:* full-time $10,567; part-time $177 per credit. Part-time tuition and fees vary according to course load. *College room and board:* $5384. Room and board charges vary according to board plan and housing facility. *Payment plan:* Deferred payment.

FRESHMAN FINANCIAL AID (Fall 2004, est.) 1315 applied for aid; of those 81% were deemed to have need. 89% of freshmen with need received aid; of those 18% had need fully met. *Average percent of need met:* 65% (excluding resources awarded to replace EFC). *Average financial aid package:* $7029 (excluding resources awarded to replace EFC). 22% of all full-time freshmen had no need and received non-need-based gift aid.

UNDERGRADUATE FINANCIAL AID (Fall 2004, est.) 7,527 applied for aid; of those 91% were deemed to have need. 76% of undergraduates with need received aid; of those 18% had need fully met. *Average percent of need met:* 75% (excluding resources awarded to replace EFC). *Average financial aid package:* $8703 (excluding resources awarded to replace EFC). 9% of all full-time undergraduates had no need and received non-need-based gift aid.

GIFT AID (NEED-BASED) *Total amount:* $18,458,333 (77% federal, 7% state, 10% institutional, 6% external sources). *Receiving aid:* Freshmen: 37% (652); All full-time undergraduates: 35% (3,744). *Average award:* Freshmen: $3107; Undergraduates: $3037. *Scholarships, grants, and awards:* Federal Pell, FSEOG, state, private, college/university gift aid from institutional funds, Leveraged Educational Assistance Program (LEAP).

GIFT AID (NON-NEED-BASED) *Total amount:* $1,789,884 (26% state, 47% institutional, 27% external sources). *Receiving aid:* Freshmen: 40% (693);

Undergraduates: 23% (2,486). *Average Award:* Freshmen: $1113; Undergraduates: $1437. *Scholarships, grants, and awards by category: Academic Interests/Achievement:* biological sciences, business, communication, computer science, education, engineering/technologies, English, foreign languages, general academic interests/achievements, health fields, humanities, international studies, mathematics, military science, physical sciences, premedicine, social sciences. *Creative Arts/Performance:* art/fine arts, dance, debating, general creative arts/performance, journalism/publications, music, performing arts, theater/drama. *Special Achievements/Activities:* cheerleading/drum major, community service, leadership, rodeo. *Special Characteristics:* ethnic background, first-generation college students, general special characteristics, handicapped students, international students, local/state students, members of minority groups, out-of-state students, previous college experience, spouses of current students, veterans, veterans' children. *Tuition waivers:* Full or partial for employees or children of employees, senior citizens. *ROTC:* Army.

LOANS *Student loans:* $40,470,783 (56% need-based, 44% non-need-based). 60% of past graduating class borrowed through all loan programs. *Average indebtedness per student:* $17,200. *Average need-based loan:* Freshmen: $2733; Undergraduates: $4027. *Parent loans:* $827,776 (79% need-based, 21% non-need-based). *Programs:* Federal Direct (Subsidized and Unsubsidized Stafford, PLUS), Perkins, state, college/university, Alaska Loans.

WORK-STUDY *Federal work-study:* Total amount: $700,000; jobs available (averaging $4000). *State or other work-study/employment:* Total amount: $560,000 (96% need-based, 4% non-need-based). Part-time jobs available (averaging $4000).

ATHLETIC AWARDS *Total amount:* $2,960,748 (100% non-need-based).

APPLYING FOR FINANCIAL AID *Required financial aid form:* FAFSA. *Financial aid deadline:* 6/1 (priority: 2/15). *Notification date:* Continuous beginning 3/5. Students must reply by 6/1 or within 4 weeks of notification.

CONTACT Office of Financial Aid and Scholarships, Boise State University, Administration Building, Room 123, 1910 University Drive, Boise, ID 83725-1315, 208-426-1664 or toll-free 800-632-6586 (in-state), 800-824-7017 (out-of-state). *Fax:* 208-426-1305. *E-mail:* faquest@boisestate.edu.

BORICUA COLLEGE
New York, NY

CONTACT Ms. Rosalia Cruz, Financial Aid Administrator, Boricua College, 3755 Broadway, New York, NY 10032-1560, 212-694-1000 Ext. 611.

BOSTON ARCHITECTURAL CENTER
Boston, MA

Tuition & fees: $8630	Average undergraduate aid package: $3525

ABOUT THE INSTITUTION Independent, coed. Awards: bachelor's and master's degrees. 2 undergraduate majors. Total enrollment: 910. Undergraduates: 507. Freshmen: 72. Federal methodology is used as a basis for awarding need-based institutional aid.

UNDERGRADUATE EXPENSES for 2005–06 *Application fee:* $50. *Tuition:* full-time $8610; part-time $717 per credit. *Required fees:* full-time $20; $150. Full-time tuition and fees vary according to course load, degree level, program, and reciprocity agreements. Part-time tuition and fees vary according to course load, degree level, program, and reciprocity agreements. *Payment plan:* Installment.

FRESHMAN FINANCIAL AID (Fall 2003) 40 applied for aid; of those 100% were deemed to have need. 100% of freshmen with need received aid. *Average percent of need met:* 12% (excluding resources awarded to replace EFC). *Average financial aid package:* $3055 (excluding resources awarded to replace EFC).

UNDERGRADUATE FINANCIAL AID (Fall 2003) 176 applied for aid; of those 92% were deemed to have need. 100% of undergraduates with need received aid. *Average percent of need met:* 17% (excluding resources awarded to replace EFC). *Average financial aid package:* $3525 (excluding resources awarded to replace EFC).

GIFT AID (NEED-BASED) *Total amount:* $227,487 (63% federal, 9% state, 20% institutional, 8% external sources). *Receiving aid:* Freshmen: 22% (9); All full-time undergraduates: 44% (93). *Average award:* Freshmen: $2786; Undergraduates: $1657. *Scholarships, grants, and awards:* Federal Pell, state, college/university gift aid from institutional funds.

GIFT AID (NON-NEED-BASED) *Total amount:* $36,866 (19% institutional, 81% external sources). *Scholarships, grants, and awards by category: Academic*

Interests/Achievement: 30 awards ($40,200 total): architecture. **Tuition waivers:** Full or partial for employees or children of employees.
LOANS Student loans: $1,964,012 (84% need-based, 16% non-need-based). 69% of past graduating class borrowed through all loan programs. *Average indebtedness per student:* $25,387. **Average need-based loan:** Freshmen: $2066; Undergraduates: $2958. **Parent loans:** $310,643 (69% need-based, 31% non-need-based). **Programs:** FFEL (Subsidized and Unsubsidized Stafford, PLUS).
APPLYING FOR FINANCIAL AID Required financial aid form: FAFSA. **Financial aid deadline (priority):** 4/15. **Notification date:** Continuous. Students must reply within 2 weeks of notification.
CONTACT Maureen Samways, Director of Financial Aid, Boston Architectural Center, 320 Newbury Street, Boston, MA 02115, 617-585-0125 or toll-free 877-585-0100. *Fax:* 617-585-0131. *E-mail:* maureen.samways@the-bac.edu.

BOSTON BAPTIST COLLEGE
Boston, MA

CONTACT Curt A. Wiedenroth, Financial Aid Director, Boston Baptist College, 950 Metropolitan Avenue, Boston, MA 02136, 617-364-3510 or toll-free 888-235-2014 (out-of-state). *Fax:* 617-364-0723. *E-mail:* cw9083@aol.com.

BOSTON COLLEGE
Chestnut Hill, MA

Tuition & fees: $29,396	Average undergraduate aid package: $23,215

ABOUT THE INSTITUTION Independent Roman Catholic (Jesuit), coed. Awards: bachelor's, master's, doctoral, and first professional degrees and post-master's certificates (also offers continuing education program with significant enrollment not reflected in profile). 45 undergraduate majors. Total enrollment: 13,814. Undergraduates: 9,059. Freshmen: 2,309. Institutional methodology is used as a basis for awarding need-based institutional aid.
UNDERGRADUATE EXPENSES for 2004–05 Application fee: $60. **Comprehensive fee:** $39,016 includes full-time tuition ($28,940), mandatory fees ($456), and room and board ($9620). **College room only:** $5970. Room and board charges vary according to housing facility. **Payment plans:** Tuition prepayment, installment.
FRESHMAN FINANCIAL AID (Fall 2003) 1082 applied for aid; of those 81% were deemed to have need. 100% of freshmen with need received aid; of those 100% had need fully met. *Average percent of need met:* 100% (excluding resources awarded to replace EFC). *Average financial aid package:* $22,698 (excluding resources awarded to replace EFC). 3% of all full-time freshmen had no need and received non-need-based gift aid.
UNDERGRADUATE FINANCIAL AID (Fall 2003) 4,700 applied for aid; of those 78% were deemed to have need. 100% of undergraduates with need received aid; of those 100% had need fully met. *Average percent of need met:* 100% (excluding resources awarded to replace EFC). *Average financial aid package:* $23,215 (excluding resources awarded to replace EFC). 3% of all full-time undergraduates had no need and received non-need-based gift aid.
GIFT AID (NEED-BASED) Total amount: $59,060,787 (7% federal, 2% state, 87% institutional, 4% external sources). **Receiving aid:** Freshmen: 36% (788); All full-time undergraduates: 37% (3,282). **Average award:** Freshmen: $17,638; Undergraduates: $17,698. **Scholarships, grants, and awards:** Federal Pell, FSEOG, state, private, college/university gift aid from institutional funds.
GIFT AID (NON-NEED-BASED) Total amount: $2,236,685 (99% institutional, 1% external sources). **Receiving aid:** Freshmen: 4% (98); Undergraduates: 7% (579). **Average Award:** *Freshmen:* $4769; *Undergraduates:* $7305. **Scholarships, grants, and awards by category:** *Academic Interests/Achievement:* general academic interests/achievements. **Tuition waivers:** Full or partial for employees or children of employees. **ROTC:** Army cooperative, Air Force cooperative.
LOANS Student loans: $19,144,254 (83% need-based, 17% non-need-based). 48% of past graduating class borrowed through all loan programs. *Average indebtedness per student:* $15,723. **Average need-based loan:** Freshmen: $4104; Undergraduates: $4521. **Parent loans:** $24,184,598 (100% non-need-based). **Programs:** FFEL (Subsidized and Unsubsidized Stafford, PLUS), Perkins, Federal Nursing, state.
WORK-STUDY Federal work-study: Total amount: $4,906,547; 2,764 jobs averaging $1775.
ATHLETIC AWARDS Total amount: $8,518,357 (100% non-need-based).
APPLYING FOR FINANCIAL AID Required financial aid forms: FAFSA, CSS Financial Aid PROFILE, noncustodial (divorced/separated) parent's statement, business/farm supplement, federal income tax form(s), W-2 forms. **Financial aid deadline (priority):** 2/1. **Notification date:** 4/1. Students must reply by 5/1.

CONTACT Office of Financial Services, Boston College, Lyons Hall, Chestnut Hill, MA 02467, 800-294-0294 or toll-free 800-360-2522. *Fax:* 617-552-4889. *E-mail:* studentservices@bc.edu.

THE BOSTON CONSERVATORY
Boston, MA

Tuition & fees: $24,520	Average undergraduate aid package: $15,931

ABOUT THE INSTITUTION Independent, coed. Awards: bachelor's and master's degrees and post-bachelor's and post-master's certificates. 9 undergraduate majors. Total enrollment: 537. Undergraduates: 407. Freshmen: 122. Institutional methodology is used as a basis for awarding need-based institutional aid.
UNDERGRADUATE EXPENSES for 2004–05 Application fee: $100. **Comprehensive fee:** $36,120 includes full-time tuition ($23,300), mandatory fees ($1220), and room and board ($11,600). Full-time tuition and fees vary according to course load, degree level, and program. **Part-time tuition:** $960 per credit. Part-time tuition and fees vary according to course load, degree level, and program.
FRESHMAN FINANCIAL AID (Fall 2004, est.) 120 applied for aid; of those 62% were deemed to have need. 74% of freshmen with need received aid; of those 5% had need fully met. *Average percent of need met:* 50% (excluding resources awarded to replace EFC). *Average financial aid package:* $15,580 (excluding resources awarded to replace EFC). 10% of all full-time freshmen had no need and received non-need-based gift aid.
UNDERGRADUATE FINANCIAL AID (Fall 2004, est.) 396 applied for aid; of those 59% were deemed to have need. 95% of undergraduates with need received aid; of those 22% had need fully met. *Average percent of need met:* 50% (excluding resources awarded to replace EFC). *Average financial aid package:* $15,931 (excluding resources awarded to replace EFC). 13% of all full-time undergraduates had no need and received non-need-based gift aid.
GIFT AID (NEED-BASED) Total amount: $231,107 (95% federal, 5% state). **Receiving aid:** Freshmen: 13% (16); All full-time undergraduates: 13% (53). **Average award:** Freshmen: $3841; Undergraduates: $4163. **Scholarships, grants, and awards:** Federal Pell, FSEOG, state, private, college/university gift aid from institutional funds.
GIFT AID (NON-NEED-BASED) Total amount: $1,933,892 (94% institutional, 6% external sources). **Receiving aid:** Freshmen: 26% (32); Undergraduates: 42% (169). **Average Award:** Freshmen: $12,708; Undergraduates: $11,031. **Scholarships, grants, and awards by category:** Creative Arts/Performance: 262 awards ($2,499,923 total): dance, music, theater/drama.
LOANS Student loans: $805,597 (100% need-based). 68% of past graduating class borrowed through all loan programs. *Average indebtedness per student:* $15,000. **Average need-based loan:** Freshmen: $2629; Undergraduates: $4331. **Parent loans:** $4,228,309 (100% non-need-based). **Programs:** FFEL (Subsidized and Unsubsidized Stafford, PLUS), college/university, alternative loans.
WORK-STUDY Federal work-study: Total amount: $127,000; 90 jobs averaging $1025. **State or other work-study/employment:** Total amount: $40,000 (100% need-based). 30 part-time jobs averaging $1335.
APPLYING FOR FINANCIAL AID Required financial aid forms: FAFSA, institution's own form. **Financial aid deadline:** 2/1. **Notification date:** 4/1. Students must reply by 5/1.
CONTACT James T. Bynum, Director of Financial Aid, The Boston Conservatory, 8 The Fenway, Boston, MA 02215, 617-912-9120. *Fax:* 617-536-1496. *E-mail:* jbynum@bostonconservatory.edu.

BOSTON UNIVERSITY
Boston, MA

Tuition & fees: $30,402	Average undergraduate aid package: $26,687

ABOUT THE INSTITUTION Independent, coed. Awards: bachelor's, master's, doctoral, and first professional degrees and post-bachelor's, post-master's, and first professional certificates. 121 undergraduate majors. Total enrollment: 29,596. Undergraduates: 17,740. Freshmen: 4,352. Both federal and institutional methodology are used as a basis for awarding need-based institutional aid.
UNDERGRADUATE EXPENSES for 2004–05 Application fee: $70. **Comprehensive fee:** $40,082 includes full-time tuition ($29,988), mandatory fees ($414), and room and board ($9680). **College room only:** $6180. Full-time tuition and fees vary according to class time and degree level. Room and board charges vary according to board plan and housing facility. **Part-time tuition:** $937 per credit.

Boston University

Part-time fees: $40 per term. Part-time tuition and fees vary according to class time, course load, and degree level. **Payment plans:** Tuition prepayment, installment.

FRESHMAN FINANCIAL AID (Fall 2003) 2748 applied for aid; of those 81% were deemed to have need. 100% of freshmen with need received aid; of those 58% had need fully met. *Average percent of need met:* 91% (excluding resources awarded to replace EFC). *Average financial aid package:* $26,139 (excluding resources awarded to replace EFC). 8% of all full-time freshmen had no need and received non-need-based gift aid.

UNDERGRADUATE FINANCIAL AID (Fall 2003) 7,945 applied for aid; of those 91% were deemed to have need. 100% of undergraduates with need received aid; of those 51% had need fully met. *Average percent of need met:* 90% (excluding resources awarded to replace EFC). *Average financial aid package:* $26,687 (excluding resources awarded to replace EFC). 8% of all full-time undergraduates had no need and received non-need-based gift aid.

GIFT AID (NEED-BASED) *Total amount:* $137,268,541 (8% federal, 2% state, 86% institutional, 4% external sources). *Receiving aid:* Freshmen: 47% (2,054); All full-time undergraduates: 43% (6,761). *Average award:* Freshmen: $18,112; Undergraduates: $17,748. *Scholarships, grants, and awards:* Federal Pell, FSEOG, state, private, college/university gift aid from institutional funds.

GIFT AID (NON-NEED-BASED) *Total amount:* $27,513,549 (9% federal, 73% institutional, 18% external sources). *Receiving aid:* Freshmen: 22% (956); Undergraduates: 14% (2,113). *Average Award: Freshmen:* $12,569; *Undergraduates:* $13,403. *Scholarships, grants, and awards by category:* Academic Interests/Achievement: 2,293 awards ($30,506,920 total): education, engineering/technologies, foreign languages, general academic interests/achievements. Creative Arts/Performance: 192 awards ($1,245,838 total): art/fine arts, music, theater/drama. Special Achievements/Activities: 81 awards ($967,454 total): general special achievements/activities, leadership, memberships. Special Characteristics: 692 awards ($7,991,009 total): children and siblings of alumni, local/state students, relatives of clergy, religious affiliation. *Tuition waivers:* Full or partial for employees or children of employees, senior citizens. *ROTC:* Army, Naval, Air Force.

LOANS *Student loans:* $57,196,076 (69% need-based, 31% non-need-based). 59% of past graduating class borrowed through all loan programs. *Average indebtedness per student:* $17,186. *Average need-based loan:* Freshmen: $3630; Undergraduates: $4937. *Parent loans:* $44,011,711 (30% need-based, 70% non-need-based). *Programs:* Federal Direct (Subsidized and Unsubsidized Stafford, PLUS), Perkins, state, alternative loans.

WORK-STUDY *Federal work-study:* Total amount: $6,548,040; 3,043 jobs averaging $2152. *State or other work-study/employment:* Total amount: $2,302,498 (37% need-based, 63% non-need-based). 179 part-time jobs averaging $12,863.

ATHLETIC AWARDS *Total amount:* $7,978,185 (17% need-based, 83% non-need-based).

APPLYING FOR FINANCIAL AID *Required financial aid forms:* FAFSA, CSS Financial Aid PROFILE. *Financial aid deadline (priority):* 2/15. *Notification date:* Continuous beginning 2/15. Students must reply by 5/1 or within 2 weeks of notification.

CONTACT Christine McGuire, Director of Financial Assistance, Boston University, 881 Commonwealth Avenue, 5th Floor, Boston, MA 02215, 617-353-4176. *Fax:* 617-353-8200. *E-mail:* finaid@bu.edu.

BOWDOIN COLLEGE
Brunswick, ME

Tuition & fees: $31,626	Average undergraduate aid package: $27,447

ABOUT THE INSTITUTION Independent, coed. Awards: bachelor's degrees. 43 undergraduate majors. Total enrollment: 1,677. Undergraduates: 1,677. Freshmen: 470. Institutional methodology is used as a basis for awarding need-based institutional aid.

UNDERGRADUATE EXPENSES for 2004–05 *Application fee:* $60. *Comprehensive fee:* $39,680 includes full-time tuition ($30,944), mandatory fees ($682), and room and board ($8054). *College room only:* $3623. Room and board charges vary according to board plan. *Payment plans:* Installment, deferred payment.

FRESHMAN FINANCIAL AID (Fall 2004, est.) 259 applied for aid; of those 76% were deemed to have need. 100% of freshmen with need received aid; of those 100% had need fully met. *Average percent of need met:* 100% (excluding resources awarded to replace EFC). *Average financial aid package:* $27,769 (excluding resources awarded to replace EFC). 3% of all full-time freshmen had no need and received non-need-based gift aid.

UNDERGRADUATE FINANCIAL AID (Fall 2004, est.) 906 applied for aid; of those 84% were deemed to have need. 100% of undergraduates with need received aid; of those 100% had need fully met. *Average percent of need met:* 100% (excluding resources awarded to replace EFC). *Average financial aid package:* $27,447 (excluding resources awarded to replace EFC). 3% of all full-time undergraduates had no need and received non-need-based gift aid.

GIFT AID (NEED-BASED) *Total amount:* $16,975,758 (5% federal, 1% state, 90% institutional, 4% external sources). *Receiving aid:* Freshmen: 42% (198); All full-time undergraduates: 46% (759). *Average award:* Freshmen: $24,041; Undergraduates: $23,266. *Scholarships, grants, and awards:* Federal Pell, FSEOG, state, private, college/university gift aid from institutional funds.

GIFT AID (NON-NEED-BASED) *Total amount:* $404,110 (38% institutional, 62% external sources). *Receiving aid:* Freshmen: 1% (5); Undergraduates: 3% (45). *Average Award: Freshmen:* $1000; *Undergraduates:* $1000. *Scholarships, grants, and awards by category:* Academic Interests/Achievement: 49 awards ($49,000 total): general academic interests/achievements. Special Achievements/Activities: leadership. Special Characteristics: children of faculty/staff. *Tuition waivers:* Full or partial for employees or children of employees.

LOANS *Student loans:* $2,734,203 (80% need-based, 20% non-need-based). 50% of past class borrowed through all loan programs. *Average indebtedness per student:* $14,474. *Average need-based loan:* Freshmen: $3275; Undergraduates: $3646. *Parent loans:* $3,303,320 (100% non-need-based). *Programs:* FFEL (Subsidized and Unsubsidized Stafford, PLUS), Perkins, state, college/university.

WORK-STUDY *Federal work-study:* Total amount: $480,000; 331 jobs averaging $1450. *State or other work-study/employment:* Total amount: $571,336 (99% need-based, 1% non-need-based). 379 part-time jobs averaging $1500.

APPLYING FOR FINANCIAL AID *Required financial aid forms:* FAFSA, institution's own form, CSS Financial Aid PROFILE, noncustodial (divorced/separated) parent's statement, business/farm supplement. *Financial aid deadline:* 2/15. *Notification date:* 4/5. Students must reply by 5/1 or within 1 week of notification.

CONTACT Mr. Stephen H. Joyce, Director of Student Aid, Bowdoin College, 5300 College Station, Brunswick, ME 04011-8444, 207-725-3273. *Fax:* 207-725-3864. *E-mail:* sjoyce@bowdoin.edu.

BOWIE STATE UNIVERSITY
Bowie, MD

Tuition & fees (MD res): $6846	Average undergraduate aid package: $9311

ABOUT THE INSTITUTION State-supported, coed. Awards: bachelor's, master's, and doctoral degrees and post-bachelor's certificates. 29 undergraduate majors. Total enrollment: 5,415. Undergraduates: 4,027. Freshmen: 649. Both federal and institutional methodology are used as a basis for awarding need-based institutional aid.

UNDERGRADUATE EXPENSES for 2005–06 *Application fee:* $40. *Tuition, state resident:* full-time $5096. *Tuition, nonresident:* full-time $13,088. *College room and board:* $8674; *room only:* $6513.

GIFT AID (NEED-BASED) *Total amount:* $5,927,662 (69% federal, 31% state). *Receiving aid:* Freshmen: 46% (345); All full-time undergraduates: 40% (1,366). *Average award:* Freshmen: $6974; Undergraduates: $5601. *Scholarships, grants, and awards:* Federal Pell, FSEOG, state, private, college/university gift aid from institutional funds.

GIFT AID (NON-NEED-BASED) *Total amount:* $4,388,512 (16% federal, 12% state, 63% institutional, 9% external sources). *Receiving aid:* Freshmen: 32% (245); Undergraduates: 30% (1,039). *Average Award: Freshmen:* $4097; *Undergraduates:* $3305. *Scholarships, grants, and awards by category:* Academic Interests/Achievement: 1,319 awards ($7,368,969 total): biological sciences, business, communication, computer science, engineering/technologies, mathematics, military science. Creative Arts/Performance: 135 awards ($635,973 total): applied art and design, art/fine arts, general creative arts/performance, music. Special Characteristics: 1,205 awards ($6,332,635 total): first-generation college students. *ROTC:* Army.

LOANS *Student loans:* $10,225,842 (58% need-based, 42% non-need-based). 34% of past graduating class borrowed through all loan programs. *Average indebtedness per student:* $10,842. *Average need-based loan:* Freshmen: $2456; Undergraduates: $357. *Parent loans:* $2,694,531 (100% non-need-based). *Programs:* Federal Direct (Subsidized and Unsubsidized Stafford, PLUS), Perkins.

ATHLETIC AWARDS *Total amount:* $511,818 (100% non-need-based).

APPLYING FOR FINANCIAL AID *Required financial aid form:* FAFSA. *Financial aid deadline (priority):* 3/1. *Notification date:* Continuous beginning 4/15. Students must reply within 1 week of notification.

CONTACT Veronica Pickett, Financial Aid Director, Bowie State University, 14000 Jericho Park Road, Bowie, MD 20715, 301-860-3543 or toll-free 877-772-6943. *Fax:* 301-860-3549. *E-mail:* vpickett@bowiestate.edu.

BOWLING GREEN STATE UNIVERSITY
Bowling Green, OH

Tuition & fees (OH res): $8072   **Average undergraduate aid package: $6717**

ABOUT THE INSTITUTION State-supported, coed. Awards: bachelor's, master's, and doctoral degrees and post-master's certificates. 139 undergraduate majors. Total enrollment: 18,989. Undergraduates: 15,909. Freshmen: 3,879. Federal methodology is used as a basis for awarding need-based institutional aid.

UNDERGRADUATE EXPENSES for 2004–05 *Application fee:* $35. *Tuition, state resident:* full-time $6818; part-time $321 per credit hour. *Tuition, nonresident:* full-time $14,126; part-time $670 per credit hour. *Required fees:* full-time $1254; $62 per credit hour. Part-time tuition and fees vary according to course load. *College room and board:* $6588; *room only:* $3996. Room and board charges vary according to board plan and housing facility. *Payment plan:* Installment.

GIFT AID (NEED-BASED) *Total amount:* $13,422,023 (76% federal, 20% state, 4% institutional). *Receiving aid:* Freshmen: 27% (940); All full-time undergraduates: 24% (3,656). *Average award:* Freshmen: $3279; Undergraduates: $3464. *Scholarships, grants, and awards:* Federal Pell, FSEOG, state, private, college/university gift aid from institutional funds.

GIFT AID (NON-NEED-BASED) *Total amount:* $23,631,430 (5% federal, 19% state, 63% institutional, 13% external sources). *Receiving aid:* Freshmen: 30% (1,074); Undergraduates: 20% (3,024). *Average Award:* Freshmen: $4289; *Undergraduates:* $4925. *Scholarships, grants, and awards by category:* *Academic Interests/Achievement:* biological sciences, business, communication, computer science, education, engineering/technologies, English, foreign languages, general academic interests/achievements, health fields, home economics, humanities, international studies, mathematics, military science, physical sciences, social sciences. *Creative Arts/Performance:* art/fine arts, cinema/film/broadcasting, creative writing, dance, debating, journalism/publications, music, performing arts, theater/drama. *Special Achievements/Activities:* general special achievements/activities, leadership. *Special Characteristics:* children and siblings of alumni, children of faculty/staff, general special characteristics, international students, members of minority groups. *Tuition waivers:* Full or partial for employees or children of employees, senior citizens. *ROTC:* Army, Air Force.

LOANS *Student loans:* $65,158,835 (45% need-based, 55% non-need-based). 68% of past graduating class borrowed through all loan programs. *Average indebtedness per student:* $20,010. *Average need-based loan:* Freshmen: $2655; Undergraduates: $3469. *Parent loans:* $1,331,949 (100% non-need-based). *Programs:* Federal Direct (Subsidized and Unsubsidized Stafford, PLUS), Perkins, Federal Nursing, state, college/university.

ATHLETIC AWARDS *Total amount:* $4,199,998 (100% non-need-based).

APPLYING FOR FINANCIAL AID *Required financial aid form:* FAFSA. *Financial aid deadline:* Continuous. *Notification date:* Continuous beginning 4/15. Students must reply within 3 weeks of notification.

CONTACT Tina Coulter, Assistant Director, Office of Student Financial Aid, Bowling Green State University, 231 Administration Building, Bowling Green, OH 43403, 419-372-2651. *Fax:* 419-372-0404.

BRADLEY UNIVERSITY
Peoria, IL

Tuition & fees: $17,730   **Average undergraduate aid package: $13,805**

ABOUT THE INSTITUTION Independent, coed. Awards: bachelor's and master's degrees. 73 undergraduate majors. Total enrollment: 6,069. Undergraduates: 5,315. Freshmen: 1,014. Federal methodology is used as a basis for awarding need-based institutional aid.

UNDERGRADUATE EXPENSES for 2004–05 *Application fee:* $35. *Comprehensive fee:* $23,880 includes full-time tuition ($17,600), mandatory fees ($130), and room and board ($6150). *College room only:* $3500. Full-time tuition and fees vary according to program. Room and board charges vary according to board plan. *Part-time tuition:* $480 per credit. Part-time tuition and fees vary according to course load. *Payment plans:* Installment, deferred payment.

FRESHMAN FINANCIAL AID (Fall 2003) 1035 applied for aid; of those 80% were deemed to have need. 100% of freshmen with need received aid; of those 48% had need fully met. *Average percent of need met:* 84% (excluding resources

awarded to replace EFC). *Average financial aid package:* $14,062 (excluding resources awarded to replace EFC). 20% of all full-time freshmen had no need and received non-need-based gift aid.

UNDERGRADUATE FINANCIAL AID (Fall 2003) 4,271 applied for aid; of those 84% were deemed to have need. 100% of undergraduates with need received aid; of those 63% had need fully met. *Average percent of need met:* 85% (excluding resources awarded to replace EFC). *Average financial aid package:* $13,805 (excluding resources awarded to replace EFC). 23% of all full-time undergraduates had no need and received non-need-based gift aid.

GIFT AID (NEED-BASED) *Total amount:* $30,121,371 (11% federal, 22% state, 63% institutional, 4% external sources). *Receiving aid:* Freshmen: 74% (820); All full-time undergraduates: 70% (3,441). *Average award:* Freshmen: $10,612; Undergraduates: $8664. *Scholarships, grants, and awards:* Federal Pell, FSEOG, state, private, college/university gift aid from institutional funds.

GIFT AID (NON-NEED-BASED) *Total amount:* $6,635,097 (91% institutional, 9% external sources). *Receiving aid:* Freshmen: 10% (109); Undergraduates: 8% (415). *Average Award:* Freshmen: $9781; *Undergraduates:* $8939. *Scholarships, grants, and awards by category:* *Academic Interests/Achievement:* 2,727 awards ($18,003,050 total): general academic interests/achievements. *Creative Arts/Performance:* 197 awards ($229,555 total): art/fine arts, music, theater/drama. *Special Achievements/Activities:* 53 awards ($51,401 total): community service, leadership. *Special Characteristics:* 894 awards ($3,300,778 total): children and siblings of alumni, children of faculty/staff, members of minority groups. *Tuition waivers:* Full or partial for employees or children of employees, senior citizens. *ROTC:* Army.

LOANS *Student loans:* $18,026,368 (77% need-based, 23% non-need-based). 74% of past graduating class borrowed through all loan programs. *Average indebtedness per student:* $15,941. *Average need-based loan:* Freshmen: $3115; Undergraduates: $4523. *Parent loans:* $6,008,236 (26% need-based, 74% non-need-based). *Programs:* Federal Direct (Subsidized and Unsubsidized Stafford, PLUS), FFEL (PLUS), Perkins, Federal Nursing.

WORK-STUDY *Federal work-study:* Total amount: $1,846,676; 1,217 jobs averaging $1496.

ATHLETIC AWARDS *Total amount:* $1,736,999 (42% need-based, 58% non-need-based).

APPLYING FOR FINANCIAL AID *Required financial aid form:* FAFSA. *Financial aid deadline (priority):* 3/1. *Notification date:* Continuous. Students must reply within 3 weeks of notification.

CONTACT Mr. David L. Pardieck, Director of Financial Assistance, Bradley University, 1501 West Bradley Avenue, Peoria, IL 61625-0002, 309-677-3089 or toll-free 800-447-6460. *E-mail:* dlp@bradley.edu.

BRANDEIS UNIVERSITY
Waltham, MA

Tuition & fees: $31,072   **Average undergraduate aid package: $22,809**

ABOUT THE INSTITUTION Independent, coed. Awards: bachelor's, master's, and doctoral degrees and post-bachelor's certificates. 43 undergraduate majors. Total enrollment: 5,072. Undergraduates: 3,200. Freshmen: 762. Both federal and institutional methodology are used as a basis for awarding need-based institutional aid.

UNDERGRADUATE EXPENSES for 2004–05 *Application fee:* $55. *Comprehensive fee:* $39,728 includes full-time tuition ($30,160), mandatory fees ($912), and room and board ($8656). *College room only:* $4862. Room and board charges vary according to board plan and housing facility. *Part-time tuition:* $3770 per course. Part-time tuition and fees vary according to course load. *Payment plan:* Installment.

FRESHMAN FINANCIAL AID (Fall 2004, est.) 574 applied for aid; of those 76% were deemed to have need. 100% of freshmen with need received aid; of those 29% had need fully met. *Average percent of need met:* 84% (excluding resources awarded to replace EFC). *Average financial aid package:* $21,201 (excluding resources awarded to replace EFC). 63% of all full-time freshmen had no need and received non-need-based gift aid.

UNDERGRADUATE FINANCIAL AID (Fall 2004, est.) 1,819 applied for aid; of those 84% were deemed to have need. 100% of undergraduates with need received aid; of those 23% had need fully met. *Average percent of need met:* 82% (excluding resources awarded to replace EFC). *Average financial aid package:* $22,809 (excluding resources awarded to replace EFC). 22% of all full-time undergraduates had no need and received non-need-based gift aid.

GIFT AID (NEED-BASED) *Total amount:* $26,075,494 (7% federal, 2% state, 88% institutional, 3% external sources). *Receiving aid:* Freshmen: 56% (424);

Brandeis University

All full-time undergraduates: 46% (1,459). *Average award:* Freshmen: $18,002; Undergraduates: $17,872. *Scholarships, grants, and awards:* Federal Pell, FSEOG, state, college/university gift aid from institutional funds.

GIFT AID (NON-NEED-BASED) *Total amount:* $9,431,558 (92% institutional, 8% external sources). *Receiving aid:* Freshmen: 9% (72); Undergraduates: 5% (144). *Average Award:* Freshmen: $16,317; Undergraduates: $17,454. *Scholarships, grants, and awards by category: Academic Interests/Achievement:* 618 awards ($8,896,000 total): general academic interests/achievements. *Tuition waivers:* Full or partial for employees or children of employees. *ROTC:* Army cooperative, Air Force cooperative.

LOANS *Student loans:* $11,298,818 (65% need-based, 35% non-need-based). *Average need-based loan:* Freshmen: $3855; Undergraduates: $5529. *Parent loans:* $5,625,433 (31% need-based, 69% non-need-based). *Programs:* Federal Direct (Subsidized and Unsubsidized Stafford, PLUS), Perkins, state, college/university.

WORK-STUDY *Federal work-study:* Total amount: $1,361,546; 884 jobs averaging $1561. *State or other work-study/employment:* Total amount: $473,000 (26% need-based, 74% non-need-based). 148 part-time jobs averaging $2804.

APPLYING FOR FINANCIAL AID *Required financial aid forms:* FAFSA, CSS Financial Aid PROFILE, noncustodial (divorced/separated) parent's statement, business/farm supplement. *Financial aid deadline (priority):* 1/31. *Notification date:* 4/1. Students must reply by 5/1.

CONTACT Peter Giumette, Director of Financial Aid, Brandeis University, 415 South Street, Kutz Hall 121, MS 027, Waltham, MA 02454-9110, 781-736-3700 or toll-free 800-622-0622 (out-of-state). *Fax:* 781-736-3719. *E-mail:* finaid@brandeis.edu.

BRENAU UNIVERSITY
Gainesville, GA

Tuition & fees: $14,710	Average undergraduate aid package: $15,452

ABOUT THE INSTITUTION Independent, women only. Awards: bachelor's and master's degrees (also offers coed evening and weekend programs with significant enrollment not reflected in profile). 35 undergraduate majors. Total enrollment: 696. Undergraduates: 680. Freshmen: 196. Federal methodology is used as a basis for awarding need-based institutional aid.

UNDERGRADUATE EXPENSES for 2004–05 *Application fee:* $35. *Comprehensive fee:* $22,770 includes full-time tuition ($14,610), mandatory fees ($100), and room and board ($8060). Full-time tuition and fees vary according to class time, location, and program. Room and board charges vary according to board plan and housing facility. *Part-time tuition:* $487 per semester hour. *Part-time fees:* $50 per term. Part-time tuition and fees vary according to class time, location, and program. *Payment plan:* Installment.

FRESHMAN FINANCIAL AID (Fall 2004, est.) 168 applied for aid; of those 91% were deemed to have need. 100% of freshmen with need received aid; of those 31% had need fully met. *Average percent of need met:* 85% (excluding resources awarded to replace EFC). *Average financial aid package:* $16,937 (excluding resources awarded to replace EFC). 17% of all full-time freshmen had no need and received non-need-based gift aid.

UNDERGRADUATE FINANCIAL AID (Fall 2004, est.) 523 applied for aid; of those 90% were deemed to have need. 100% of undergraduates with need received aid; of those 33% had need fully met. *Average percent of need met:* 81% (excluding resources awarded to replace EFC). *Average financial aid package:* $15,452 (excluding resources awarded to replace EFC). 21% of all full-time undergraduates had no need and received non-need-based gift aid.

GIFT AID (NEED-BASED) *Total amount:* $6,108,957 (12% federal, 19% state, 67% institutional, 2% external sources). *Receiving aid:* Freshmen: 78% (153); All full-time undergraduates: 75% (472). *Average award:* Freshmen: $14,625; Undergraduates: $12,114. *Scholarships, grants, and awards:* Federal Pell, FSEOG, state, private, college/university gift aid from institutional funds.

GIFT AID (NON-NEED-BASED) *Total amount:* $1,112,938 (29% state, 69% institutional, 2% external sources). *Receiving aid:* Freshmen: 15% (29); Undergraduates: 11% (70). *Average Award: Freshmen:* $6826; *Undergraduates:* $8127. *Scholarships, grants, and awards by category: Academic Interests/Achievement:* 417 awards ($2,367,645 total): biological sciences, business, communication, education, general academic interests/achievements, health fields, humanities. *Creative Arts/Performance:* 110 awards ($258,225 total): applied art and design, art/fine arts, cinema/film/broadcasting, creative writing, dance, journalism/publications, music, theater/drama. *Special Achievements/Activities:* 65 awards ($390,989 total): general special achievements/activities, leadership. *Special Characteristics:* 12 awards ($112,855 total): children of

faculty/staff, first-generation college students, general special characteristics, international students. *Tuition waivers:* Full or partial for employees or children of employees.

LOANS *Student loans:* $1,823,479 (55% need-based, 45% non-need-based). 66% of past graduating class borrowed through all loan programs. *Average indebtedness per student:* $17,590. *Average need-based loan:* Freshmen: $2424; Undergraduates: $3482. *Parent loans:* $252,848 (100% non-need-based). *Programs:* FFEL (Subsidized and Unsubsidized Stafford, PLUS), Perkins, state.

WORK-STUDY *Federal work-study:* Total amount: $208,257; 162 jobs averaging $1286. *State or other work-study/employment:* Total amount: $13,755 (100% non-need-based). 6 part-time jobs averaging $2293.

ATHLETIC AWARDS *Total amount:* $198,590 (44% need-based, 56% non-need-based).

APPLYING FOR FINANCIAL AID *Required financial aid forms:* FAFSA, state aid form. *Financial aid deadline (priority):* 4/1. *Notification date:* Continuous beginning 3/1.

CONTACT Pam Barrett, Director of Scholarships and Financial Assistance, Brenau University, 500 Washington Street, SE, Gainesville, GA 30501-3697, 770-534-6152 or toll-free 800-252-5119. *Fax:* 770-538-4306. *E-mail:* pbarrett@lib.brenau.edu.

.

BRESCIA UNIVERSITY
Owensboro, KY

CONTACT Martie Ruxer-Boyken, Director of Financial Aid, Brescia University, 717 Frederica Street, Owensboro, KY 42301-3023, 270-686-4290 or toll-free 877-273-7242. *Fax:* 270-686-4266. *E-mail:* martieb@brescia.edu.

BREVARD COLLEGE
Brevard, NC

Tuition & fees: $14,740	Average undergraduate aid package: $13,785

ABOUT THE INSTITUTION Independent United Methodist, coed. Awards: bachelor's degrees. 20 undergraduate majors. Total enrollment: 584. Undergraduates: 584. Freshmen: 157. Federal methodology is used as a basis for awarding need-based institutional aid.

UNDERGRADUATE EXPENSES for 2004–05 *Application fee:* $30. *Comprehensive fee:* $20,300 includes full-time tuition ($14,450), mandatory fees ($290), and room and board ($5560). Full-time tuition and fees vary according to course load. Room and board charges vary according to board plan and housing facility. *Part-time tuition:* $580 per semester hour. *Part-time fees:* $25 per term. Part-time tuition and fees vary according to course load. *Payment plan:* Installment.

FRESHMAN FINANCIAL AID (Fall 2004, est.) 124 applied for aid; of those 74% were deemed to have need. 100% of freshmen with need received aid; of those 16% had need fully met. *Average percent of need met:* 74% (excluding resources awarded to replace EFC). *Average financial aid package:* $12,725 (excluding resources awarded to replace EFC). 35% of all full-time freshmen had no need and received non-need-based gift aid.

UNDERGRADUATE FINANCIAL AID (Fall 2004, est.) 446 applied for aid; of those 85% were deemed to have need. 100% of undergraduates with need received aid; of those 18% had need fully met. *Average percent of need met:* 78% (excluding resources awarded to replace EFC). *Average financial aid package:* $13,785 (excluding resources awarded to replace EFC). 23% of all full-time undergraduates had no need and received non-need-based gift aid.

GIFT AID (NEED-BASED) *Total amount:* $2,823,800 (23% federal, 10% state, 62% institutional, 5% external sources). *Receiving aid:* Freshmen: 59% (90); All full-time undergraduates: 68% (371). *Average award:* Freshmen: $9650; Undergraduates: $9855. *Scholarships, grants, and awards:* Federal Pell, FSEOG, state, private, college/university gift aid from institutional funds.

GIFT AID (NON-NEED-BASED) *Total amount:* $816,870 (53% state, 43% institutional, 4% external sources). *Receiving aid:* Freshmen: 2% (3); Undergraduates: 5% (27). *Average Award: Freshmen:* $4045; *Undergraduates:* $4215. *Scholarships, grants, and awards by category: Academic Interests/Achievement:* 220 awards ($531,350 total): biological sciences, business, English, general academic interests/achievements, health fields, mathematics, physical sciences, premedicine, social sciences. *Creative Arts/Performance:* 95 awards ($190,840 total): art/fine arts, journalism/publications, music, theater/drama. *Special Achievements/Activities:* 140 awards ($103,365 total): cheerleading/drum major, community service, general special achievements/activities, hobbies/interests, leadership. *Special Characteristics:* 400 awards ($720,850 total):

children of faculty/staff, local/state students, previous college experience, relatives of clergy, religious affiliation, veterans' children. *Tuition waivers:* Full or partial for employees or children of employees, senior citizens.
LOANS *Student loans:* $2,009,810 (79% need-based, 21% non-need-based). 68% of past graduating class borrowed through all loan programs. *Average indebtedness per student:* $17,800. *Average need-based loan:* Freshmen: $3115; Undergraduates: $3925. *Parent loans:* $844,990 (39% need-based, 61% non-need-based). *Programs:* FFEL (Subsidized and Unsubsidized Stafford, PLUS), Perkins.
WORK-STUDY *Federal work-study:* Total amount: $64,020; 82 jobs averaging $1075. *State or other work-study/employment:* Total amount: $33,250 (100% non-need-based). 30 part-time jobs averaging $1110.
ATHLETIC AWARDS *Total amount:* $593,850 (87% need-based, 13% non-need-based).
APPLYING FOR FINANCIAL AID *Required financial aid forms:* FAFSA, state aid form. *Financial aid deadline (priority):* 4/15. *Notification date:* Continuous. Students must reply within 4 weeks of notification.
CONTACT Ms. Lisanne J. Masterson, Director of Financial Aid, Brevard College, 400 North Broad Street, Brevard, NC 28712, 828-884-8287 or toll-free 800-527-9090. *Fax:* 828-884-3790. *E-mail:* finaid@brevard.edu.

BREWTON-PARKER COLLEGE
Mt. Vernon, GA

Tuition & fees: $12,600	Average undergraduate aid package: $9399

ABOUT THE INSTITUTION Independent Southern Baptist, coed. Awards: associate and bachelor's degrees. 31 undergraduate majors. Total enrollment: 1,136. Undergraduates: 1,136. Freshmen: 251. Federal methodology is used as a basis for awarding need-based institutional aid.
UNDERGRADUATE EXPENSES for 2005–06 *Application fee:* $25. *Comprehensive fee:* $17,800 includes full-time tuition ($11,500), mandatory fees ($1100), and room and board ($5200). *College room only:* $2150. Room and board charges vary according to board plan and housing facility. *Part-time tuition:* $362 per credit hour. *Payment plan:* Installment.
FRESHMAN FINANCIAL AID (Fall 2003) 248 applied for aid; of those 86% were deemed to have need. 100% of freshmen with need received aid; of those 13% had need fully met. *Average percent of need met:* 62% (excluding resources awarded to replace EFC). *Average financial aid package:* $8479 (excluding resources awarded to replace EFC). 16% of all full-time freshmen had no need and received non-need-based gift aid.
UNDERGRADUATE FINANCIAL AID (Fall 2003) 822 applied for aid; of those 91% were deemed to have need. 99% of undergraduates with need received aid; of those 11% had need fully met. *Average percent of need met:* 59% (excluding resources awarded to replace EFC). *Average financial aid package:* $9399 (excluding resources awarded to replace EFC). 12% of all full-time undergraduates had no need and received non-need-based gift aid.
GIFT AID (NEED-BASED) *Total amount:* $6,193,632 (30% federal, 27% state, 35% institutional, 8% external sources). *Receiving aid:* Freshmen: 83% (214); All full-time undergraduates: 87% (741). *Average award:* Freshmen: $6851; Undergraduates: $6813. *Scholarships, grants, and awards:* Federal Pell, FSEOG, state, private, college/university gift aid from institutional funds, Georgia Baptist Funds; Ministerial Grants.
GIFT AID (NON-NEED-BASED) *Total amount:* $802,423 (36% state, 49% institutional, 15% external sources). *Receiving aid:* Freshmen: 9% (22); Undergraduates: 8% (64). *Average Award:* Freshmen: $6399; Undergraduates: $6470. *Scholarships, grants, and awards by category: Academic Interests/Achievement:* 593 awards ($886,368 total): biological sciences, business, communication, education, general academic interests/achievements, mathematics, religion/biblical studies. *Creative Arts/Performance:* 51 awards ($88,650 total): art/fine arts, journalism/publications, music, theater/drama. *Special Achievements/Activities:* 41 awards ($36,647 total): cheerleading/drum major, general special achievements/activities, leadership. *Special Characteristics:* 1,394 awards ($2,322,844 total): children of faculty/staff, first-generation college students, general special characteristics, international students, local/state students, out-of-state students, relatives of clergy, religious affiliation. *Tuition waivers:* Full or partial for employees or children of employees, senior citizens.
LOANS *Student loans:* $5,314,526 (89% need-based, 11% non-need-based). 83% of past graduating class borrowed through all loan programs. *Average indebtedness per student:* $19,230. *Average need-based loan:* Freshmen: $2250; Undergraduates: $3187. *Parent loans:* $263,661 (54% need-based, 46% non-need-based). *Programs:* FFEL (Subsidized and Unsubsidized Stafford, PLUS), Perkins.

WORK-STUDY *Federal work-study:* Total amount: $177,273; 238 jobs averaging $745. *State or other work-study/employment:* Total amount: $41,783 (11% need-based, 89% non-need-based). 32 part-time jobs averaging $1306.
ATHLETIC AWARDS *Total amount:* $573,817 (53% need-based, 47% non-need-based).
APPLYING FOR FINANCIAL AID *Required financial aid forms:* FAFSA, state aid form, certification statement. *Financial aid deadline (priority):* 4/1. *Notification date:* Continuous beginning 2/27.
CONTACT Ms. Rachel Jones, Assistant Director of Financial Aid, Brewton-Parker College, Highway 280, PO Box 2018, Mt. Vernon, GA 30445-0197, 800-342-1087 Ext. 215 or toll-free 800-342-1087. *Fax:* 912-583-3598. *E-mail:* finaid@bpc.edu.

BRIARCLIFFE COLLEGE
Bethpage, NY

ABOUT THE INSTITUTION Proprietary, coed. Awards: associate and bachelor's degrees. 11 undergraduate majors. Total enrollment: 3,227. Undergraduates: 3,227. Freshmen: 843.
GIFT AID (NEED-BASED) *Scholarships, grants, and awards:* Federal Pell, FSEOG, state.
LOANS *Programs:* FFEL (Subsidized and Unsubsidized Stafford, PLUS), state.
APPLYING FOR FINANCIAL AID *Required financial aid form:* FAFSA.
CONTACT Johanna Kelly, Financial Aid Director, Briarcliffe College, 1055 Stewart Avenue, Bethpage, NY 11714, 516-918-3600 or toll-free 888-333-1150 (in-state).

BRIAR CLIFF UNIVERSITY
Sioux City, IA

ABOUT THE INSTITUTION Independent Roman Catholic, coed. Awards: associate, bachelor's, and master's degrees. 50 undergraduate majors. Total enrollment: 1,116. Undergraduates: 1,084. Freshmen: 254.
GIFT AID (NEED-BASED) *Scholarships, grants, and awards:* Federal Pell, FSEOG, state, private, college/university gift aid from institutional funds.
GIFT AID (NON-NEED-BASED) *Scholarships, grants, and awards by category: Academic Interests/Achievement:* biological sciences, business, communication, computer science, education, English, foreign languages, general academic interests/achievements, health fields, humanities, mathematics, physical sciences, religion/biblical studies, social sciences. *Creative Arts/Performance:* art/fine arts, music, theater/drama. *Special Achievements/Activities:* leadership, religious involvement. *Special Characteristics:* children and siblings of alumni, international students, members of minority groups.
LOANS *Programs:* FFEL (Subsidized and Unsubsidized Stafford, PLUS), Perkins, alternative loans, partnership loans, Minnesota SELF Loans.
APPLYING FOR FINANCIAL AID *Required financial aid forms:* FAFSA, income tax form(s).
CONTACT Financial Aid Office, Briar Cliff University, 3303 Rebecca Street, PO Box 2100, Sioux City, IA 51104-2100, 712-279-5200 or toll-free 800-662-3303 Ext. 5200. *Fax:* 712-279-5410.

BRIDGEWATER COLLEGE
Bridgewater, VA

Tuition & fees: $18,990	Average undergraduate aid package: $16,700

ABOUT THE INSTITUTION Independent religious, coed. Awards: bachelor's degrees. 58 undergraduate majors. Total enrollment: 1,532. Undergraduates: 1,532. Freshmen: 539. Federal methodology is used as a basis for awarding need-based institutional aid.
UNDERGRADUATE EXPENSES for 2005–06 *Application fee:* $30. *Comprehensive fee:* $27,790 includes full-time tuition ($18,990) and room and board ($8800). *College room only:* $4465. Room and board charges vary according to board plan and housing facility. *Part-time tuition:* $620 per credit hour. *Payment plan:* Installment.
FRESHMAN FINANCIAL AID (Fall 2004, est.) 480 applied for aid; of those 83% were deemed to have need. 100% of freshmen with need received aid; of those 28% had need fully met. *Average percent of need met:* 89% (excluding resources awarded to replace EFC). *Average financial aid package:* $16,933 (excluding resources awarded to replace EFC). 26% of all full-time freshmen had no need and received non-need-based gift aid.

UNDERGRADUATE FINANCIAL AID (Fall 2004, est.) 1,245 applied for aid; of those 87% were deemed to have need. 100% of undergraduates with need received aid; of those 28% had need fully met. *Average percent of need met:* 87% (excluding resources awarded to replace EFC). *Average financial aid package:* $16,700 (excluding resources awarded to replace EFC). 29% of all full-time undergraduates had no need and received non-need-based gift aid.
GIFT AID (NEED-BASED) *Total amount:* $13,546,346 (8% federal, 16% state, 73% institutional, 3% external sources). *Receiving aid:* Freshmen: 74% (397); All full-time undergraduates: 71% (1,077). *Average award:* Freshmen: $13,740; Undergraduates: $12,768. *Scholarships, grants, and awards:* Federal Pell, FSEOG, state, private, college/university gift aid from institutional funds.
GIFT AID (NON-NEED-BASED) *Total amount:* $4,017,448 (21% state, 77% institutional, 2% external sources). *Receiving aid:* Freshmen: 73% (395); Undergraduates: 57% (868). *Average Award:* Freshmen: $7672; Undergraduates: $7157. *Scholarships, grants, and awards by category: Academic Interests/ Achievement:* 937 awards ($7,474,098 total): general academic interests/ achievements. *Creative Arts/Performance:* 30 awards ($21,390 total): music. *Special Characteristics:* 561 awards ($1,336,976 total): ethnic background, international students, out-of-state students, religious affiliation, siblings of current students. *Tuition waivers:* Full or partial for minority students, employees or children of employees, senior citizens.
LOANS *Student loans:* $7,467,850 (91% need-based, 9% non-need-based). 77% of past graduating class borrowed through all loan programs. *Average indebtedness per student:* $22,809. *Average need-based loan:* Freshmen: $3481; Undergraduates: $4612. *Parent loans:* $2,933,919 (77% need-based, 23% non-need-based). *Programs:* FFEL (Subsidized and Unsubsidized Stafford, PLUS), Perkins, GATE Loans.
WORK-STUDY *Federal work-study:* Total amount: $500,126; 432 jobs averaging $1158. *State or other work-study/employment:* Total amount: $74,946 (30% need-based, 70% non-need-based). 58 part-time jobs averaging $908.
APPLYING FOR FINANCIAL AID *Required financial aid forms:* FAFSA, state aid form. *Financial aid deadline (priority):* 3/1. *Notification date:* Continuous beginning 3/15. Students must reply within 2 weeks of notification.
CONTACT Mr. J. Vern Fairchilds, Director of Financial Aid, Bridgewater College, College Box 27, Bridgewater, VA 22812-1599, 540-828-5376 or toll-free 800-759-8328. *Fax:* 540-828-5671. *E-mail:* vfairchi@bridgewater.edu.

BRIDGEWATER STATE COLLEGE
Bridgewater, MA

Tuition & fees (MA res): $5296	Average undergraduate aid package: $7777

ABOUT THE INSTITUTION State-supported, coed. Awards: bachelor's and master's degrees and post-bachelor's and post-master's certificates. 70 undergraduate majors. Total enrollment: 9,626. Undergraduates: 7,597. Freshmen: 1,304. Federal methodology is used as a basis for awarding need-based institutional aid.
UNDERGRADUATE EXPENSES for 2004–05 *Application fee:* $25. *Tuition, state resident:* full-time $910; part-time $38 per credit hour. *Tuition, nonresident:* full-time $7050; part-time $294 per credit hour. *Required fees:* full-time $4386; $181 per credit hour. *College room and board:* $6512; *room only:* $4048. Room and board charges vary according to board plan and housing facility. *Payment plan:* Installment.
FRESHMAN FINANCIAL AID (Fall 2003) 956 applied for aid; of those 63% were deemed to have need. 97% of freshmen with need received aid; of those 42% had need fully met. *Average percent of need met:* 72% (excluding resources awarded to replace EFC). *Average financial aid package:* $6842 (excluding resources awarded to replace EFC). 20% of all full-time freshmen had no need and received non-need-based gift aid.
UNDERGRADUATE FINANCIAL AID (Fall 2003) 2,942 applied for aid; of those 73% were deemed to have need. 98% of undergraduates with need received aid; of those 47% had need fully met. *Average percent of need met:* 72% (excluding resources awarded to replace EFC). *Average financial aid package:* $7777 (excluding resources awarded to replace EFC). 14% of all full-time undergraduates had no need and received non-need-based gift aid.
GIFT AID (NEED-BASED) *Total amount:* $9,054,264 (40% federal, 50% state, 10% institutional). *Receiving aid:* Freshmen: 45% (545); All full-time undergraduates: 38% (1,774). *Average award:* Freshmen: $3094; Undergraduates: $3336. *Scholarships, grants, and awards:* Federal Pell, FSEOG, state, private, college/university gift aid from institutional funds.
GIFT AID (NON-NEED-BASED) *Total amount:* $760,386 (13% state, 37% institutional, 50% external sources). *Receiving aid:* Freshmen: 20% (236); Undergraduates: 14% (658). *Average Award:* Freshmen: $4201; Undergraduates: $5453. *Scholarships, grants, and awards by category: Academic Interests/*

Achievement: 55 awards ($253,040 total): general academic interests/ achievements. *Tuition waivers:* Full or partial for employees or children of employees. *ROTC:* Army cooperative, Air Force cooperative.
LOANS *Student loans:* $16,671,457 (45% need-based, 55% non-need-based). 42% of past graduating class borrowed through all loan programs. *Average indebtedness per student:* $8688. *Average need-based loan:* Freshmen: $2486; Undergraduates: $3438. *Parent loans:* $2,179,256 (100% non-need-based). *Programs:* Federal Direct (Subsidized and Unsubsidized Stafford, PLUS), Perkins, state.
WORK-STUDY *Federal work-study:* Total amount: $646,091; 517 jobs averaging $1250.
APPLYING FOR FINANCIAL AID *Required financial aid form:* FAFSA. *Financial aid deadline (priority):* 3/1. *Notification date:* 3/15.
CONTACT Office of Financial Aid, Bridgewater State College, Tillinghast Hall, Bridgewater, MA 02325-0001, 508-531-1341. *Fax:* 508-531-1728.

BRIGHAM YOUNG UNIVERSITY
Provo, UT

Tuition & fees: $4920	Average undergraduate aid package: $4168

ABOUT THE INSTITUTION Independent religious, coed. Awards: bachelor's, master's, doctoral, and first professional degrees. 201 undergraduate majors. Total enrollment: 34,609. Undergraduates: 30,847. Freshmen: 4,633. Both federal and institutional methodology are used as a basis for awarding need-based institutional aid.
UNDERGRADUATE EXPENSES for 2004–05 *Application fee:* $30. *Comprehensive fee:* $10,490 includes full-time tuition ($4920) and room and board ($5570). Full-time tuition and fees vary according to reciprocity agreements. Room and board charges vary according to board plan and housing facility. *Part-time tuition:* $252 per credit hour. Part-time tuition and fees vary according to course load and reciprocity agreements. Latter Day Saints full-time student $3280 per year; part-time student $168 per credit hour. *Payment plan:* Deferred payment.
FRESHMAN FINANCIAL AID (Fall 2003) 5257 applied for aid; of those 23% were deemed to have need. 86% of freshmen with need received aid. *Average percent of need met:* 28% (excluding resources awarded to replace EFC). *Average financial aid package:* $2383 (excluding resources awarded to replace EFC). 38% of all full-time freshmen had no need and received non-need-based gift aid.
UNDERGRADUATE FINANCIAL AID (Fall 2003) 27,617 applied for aid; of those 45% were deemed to have need. 93% of undergraduates with need received aid. *Average percent of need met:* 42% (excluding resources awarded to replace EFC). *Average financial aid package:* $4168 (excluding resources awarded to replace EFC). 30% of all full-time undergraduates had no need and received non-need-based gift aid.
GIFT AID (NEED-BASED) *Total amount:* $32,490,000 (95% federal, 1% state, 4% institutional). *Receiving aid:* Freshmen: 12% (629); All full-time undergraduates: 28% (9,235). *Average award:* Freshmen: $1670; Undergraduates: $2431. *Scholarships, grants, and awards:* Federal Pell, state, private, college/university gift aid from institutional funds.
GIFT AID (NON-NEED-BASED) *Total amount:* $32,798,498 (81% institutional, 19% external sources). *Receiving aid:* Freshmen: 11% (563); Undergraduates: 15% (4,850). *Average Award:* Freshmen: $2702; Undergraduates: $2882. *Scholarships, grants, and awards by category: Academic Interests/Achievement:* 12,300 awards ($25,066,000 total): agriculture, area/ethnic studies, biological sciences, business, communication, computer science, education, engineering/ technologies, English, foreign languages, general academic interests/ achievements, health fields, home economics, humanities, international studies, mathematics, military science, physical sciences, premedicine, religion/biblical studies, social sciences. *Creative Arts/Performance:* 380 awards ($318,000 total): applied art and design, art/fine arts, cinema/film/broadcasting, creative writing, dance, journalism/publications, music, performing arts, theater/drama. *Special Achievements/Activities:* cheerleading/drum major, community service, general special achievements/activities, leadership, memberships. *Special Characteristics:* 1,837 awards ($4,034,000 total): adult students, ethnic background, general special characteristics, handicapped students, international students, local/state students, members of minority groups, out-of-state students, religious affiliation. *Tuition waivers:* Full or partial for employees or children of employees. *ROTC:* Army, Air Force.
LOANS *Student loans:* $30,239,198 (72% need-based, 28% non-need-based). 34% of past graduating class borrowed through all loan programs. *Average indebtedness per student:* $12,478. *Average need-based loan:* Freshmen: $713;

Undergraduates: $1737. *Parent loans:* $2,777,953 (100% non-need-based). *Programs:* FFEL (Subsidized and Unsubsidized Stafford, PLUS), college/university.
WORK-STUDY *State or other work-study/employment:* Total amount: $266,482 (100% need-based). 234 part-time jobs averaging $636.
ATHLETIC AWARDS *Total amount:* $2,878,881 (100% non-need-based).
APPLYING FOR FINANCIAL AID *Required financial aid form:* FAFSA. *Financial aid deadline (priority):* 4/15. *Notification date:* Continuous beginning 4/1.
CONTACT Paul R. Conrad, Director of Financial Aid, Brigham Young University, A-41 Abraham Smoot Building, Provo, UT 84602-1009, 801-378-4104. *Fax:* 801-422-0234. *E-mail:* financial_aid@byu.edu.

BRIGHAM YOUNG UNIVERSITY–HAWAII
Laie, HI

Tuition & fees: $2660	Average undergraduate aid package: $2850

ABOUT THE INSTITUTION Independent Latter-day Saints, coed. Awards: associate and bachelor's degrees and post-bachelor's certificates. 51 undergraduate majors. Total enrollment: 2,486. Undergraduates: 2,486. Freshmen: 206. Both federal and institutional methodology are used as a basis for awarding need-based institutional aid.
UNDERGRADUATE EXPENSES for 2004–05 *Application fee:* $30. *Comprehensive fee:* $7460 includes full-time tuition ($2660) and room and board ($4800). *College room only:* $2164. Full-time tuition and fees vary according to program. Room and board charges vary according to board plan and housing facility. *Part-time tuition:* $181 per credit. Part-time tuition and fees vary according to program. *Payment plan:* Installment.
FRESHMAN FINANCIAL AID (Fall 2003) 180 applied for aid; of those 78% were deemed to have need. 100% of freshmen with need received aid; of those 71% had need fully met. *Average percent of need met:* 80% (excluding resources awarded to replace EFC). *Average financial aid package:* $2400 (excluding resources awarded to replace EFC). 29% of all full-time freshmen had no need and received non-need-based gift aid.
UNDERGRADUATE FINANCIAL AID (Fall 2003) 2,200 applied for aid; of those 91% were deemed to have need. 96% of undergraduates with need received aid; of those 68% had need fully met. *Average percent of need met:* 80% (excluding resources awarded to replace EFC). *Average financial aid package:* $2850 (excluding resources awarded to replace EFC). 20% of all full-time undergraduates had no need and received non-need-based gift aid.
GIFT AID (NEED-BASED) *Total amount:* $2,916,000 (71% federal, 2% state, 12% institutional, 15% external sources). *Receiving aid:* Freshmen: 59% (120); All full-time undergraduates: 71% (1,800). *Average award:* Freshmen: $3000; Undergraduates: $3000. *Scholarships, grants, and awards:* Federal Pell, private, college/university gift aid from institutional funds.
GIFT AID (NON-NEED-BASED) *Total amount:* $1,700,000 (94% institutional, 6% external sources). *Receiving aid:* Freshmen: 15% (30); Undergraduates: 12% (300). *Average Award:* Freshmen: $1300; Undergraduates: $1300. *Scholarships, grants, and awards by category: Academic Interests/Achievement:* 600 awards ($600,000 total): area/ethnic studies, biological sciences, business, communication, computer science, education, English, foreign languages, general academic interests/achievements, humanities, international studies, library science, mathematics, physical sciences, religion/biblical studies, social sciences. *Creative Arts/Performance:* 120 awards ($70,000 total): art/fine arts, creative writing, journalism/publications, music, theater/drama. *Special Achievements/Activities:* 100 awards ($75,000 total): cheerleading/drum major, community service, general special achievements/activities, junior miss, leadership, religious involvement. *Special Characteristics:* 80 awards ($80,000 total): children and siblings of alumni, children of educators, children of faculty/staff, ethnic background, international students, local/state students, married students, members of minority groups, religious affiliation, veterans. *Tuition waivers:* Full or partial for employees or children of employees. *ROTC:* Army cooperative, Naval cooperative, Air Force cooperative.
LOANS *Student loans:* $2,507,000 (45% need-based, 55% non-need-based). 23% of past graduating class borrowed through all loan programs. *Average indebtedness per student:* $8400. *Average need-based loan:* Freshmen: $1410; Undergraduates: $1410. *Parent loans:* $96,440 (100% non-need-based). *Programs:* FFEL (Subsidized and Unsubsidized Stafford, PLUS), college/university.
WORK-STUDY *State or other work-study/employment:* Total amount: $8,605,000 (58% need-based, 42% non-need-based). 600 part-time jobs averaging $4500.
ATHLETIC AWARDS *Total amount:* $406,000 (100% non-need-based).

APPLYING FOR FINANCIAL AID *Required financial aid forms:* FAFSA, institution's own form. *Financial aid deadline (priority):* 4/30. *Notification date:* 6/1. Students must reply by 8/31.
CONTACT Wes Duke, Director of Financial Aid, Brigham Young University–Hawaii, BYUH #1980, 55-220 Kulanui Street, Laie, HI 96762, 808-293-3530. *Fax:* 808-293-3349. *E-mail:* dukew@byuh.edu.

BROOKLYN COLLEGE OF THE CITY UNIVERSITY OF NEW YORK
Brooklyn, NY

ABOUT THE INSTITUTION State and locally supported, coed. Awards: bachelor's and master's degrees and post-bachelor's and post-master's certificates. 76 undergraduate majors. Total enrollment: 15,384. Undergraduates: 11,172. Freshmen: 1,215.
GIFT AID (NEED-BASED) *Scholarships, grants, and awards:* Federal Pell, FSEOG, state, private, college/university gift aid from institutional funds.
GIFT AID (NON-NEED-BASED) *Scholarships, grants, and awards by category: Academic Interests/Achievement:* general academic interests/achievements. *Creative Arts/Performance:* general creative arts/performance. *Special Achievements/Activities:* general special achievements/activities. *Special Characteristics:* general special characteristics.
LOANS *Programs:* Federal Direct (Subsidized and Unsubsidized Stafford, PLUS), Perkins.
WORK-STUDY *Federal work-study:* Total amount: $837,440; 1,100 jobs averaging $1200.
APPLYING FOR FINANCIAL AID *Required financial aid form:* FAFSA.
CONTACT Sherwood Johnson, Director of Financial Aid, Brooklyn College of the City University of New York, 2900 Bedford Avenue, Brooklyn, NY 11210-2889, 718-951-5045. *Fax:* 718-951-4778. *E-mail:* sjohnson@brooklyn.cuny.edu.

BROOKS INSTITUTE OF PHOTOGRAPHY
Santa Barbara, CA

CONTACT Debra Johnson, Financial Aid Officer, Brooks Institute of Photography, 801 Alston Road, Santa Barbara, CA 93108, 805-966-3888 Ext. 3032 or toll-free 888-304-3456 (out-of-state). *Fax:* 805-966-2909.

BROWN UNIVERSITY
Providence, RI

ABOUT THE INSTITUTION Independent, coed. Awards: bachelor's, master's, doctoral, and first professional degrees. 77 undergraduate majors. Total enrollment: 8,004. Undergraduates: 6,014. Freshmen: 1,429.
GIFT AID (NEED-BASED) *Scholarships, grants, and awards:* Federal Pell, FSEOG, state, private, college/university gift aid from institutional funds.
LOANS *Programs:* Federal Direct (Subsidized and Unsubsidized Stafford, PLUS), Perkins, state, college/university.
WORK-STUDY *Federal work-study:* Total amount: $2,688,856; 1,372 jobs averaging $1960. *State or other work-study/employment:* Total amount: $143,257 (100% need-based). 71 part-time jobs averaging $2018.
APPLYING FOR FINANCIAL AID *Required financial aid forms:* FAFSA, CSS Financial Aid PROFILE, noncustodial (divorced/separated) parent's statement, business/farm supplement.
CONTACT Michael Bartini, Director of Financial Aid, Brown University, Box 1827, Providence, RI 02912, 401-863-2721. *Fax:* 401-863-7575. *E-mail:* financial_aid@brown.edu.

BRYAN COLLEGE
Dayton, TN

Tuition & fees: $14,800	Average undergraduate aid package: $10,039

ABOUT THE INSTITUTION Independent interdenominational, coed. Awards: associate and bachelor's degrees. 27 undergraduate majors. Total enrollment: 615. Undergraduates: 557. Both federal and institutional methodology are used as a basis for awarding need-based institutional aid.
UNDERGRADUATE EXPENSES for 2005–06 *Application fee:* $30. *Comprehensive fee:* $19,270 includes full-time tuition ($14,800) and room and board ($4470). *Part-time tuition:* $600 per credit hour. *Payment plan:* Installment.

FRESHMAN FINANCIAL AID (Fall 2004, est.) 130 applied for aid; of those 92% were deemed to have need. 100% of freshmen with need received aid. *Average financial aid package:* $12,804 (excluding resources awarded to replace EFC). 32% of all full-time freshmen had no need and received non-need-based gift aid.

UNDERGRADUATE FINANCIAL AID (Fall 2004, est.) 561 applied for aid; of those 84% were deemed to have need. 100% of undergraduates with need received aid. *Average financial aid package:* $10,039 (excluding resources awarded to replace EFC). 23% of all full-time undergraduates had no need and received non-need-based gift aid.

GIFT AID (NEED-BASED) *Total amount:* $1,046,442 (57% federal, 27% state, 16% institutional). *Receiving aid:* Freshmen: 50% (67); All full-time undergraduates: 44% (276). *Average award:* Freshmen: $3507; Undergraduates: $4409. *Scholarships, grants, and awards:* Federal Pell, FSEOG, state, private, college/university gift aid from institutional funds.

GIFT AID (NON-NEED-BASED) *Total amount:* $1,782,009 (10% state, 80% institutional, 10% external sources). *Receiving aid:* Freshmen: 90% (120); Undergraduates: 75% (472). *Average Award: Freshmen:* $4766; *Undergraduates:* $4417. *Scholarships, grants, and awards by category: Academic Interests/Achievement:* 332 awards ($926,750 total): biological sciences, business, communication, computer science, education, English, foreign languages, general academic interests/achievements, humanities, mathematics, physical sciences, premedicine, religion/biblical studies, social sciences. *Creative Arts/Performance:* 41 awards ($37,950 total): art/fine arts, journalism/publications, music, performing arts, theater/drama. *Special Achievements/Activities:* 63 awards ($51,551 total): cheerleading/drum major, community service, general special achievements/activities, leadership, religious involvement. *Special Characteristics:* 144 awards ($797,789 total): children and siblings of alumni, children of current students, children of educators, children of faculty/staff, general special characteristics, handicapped students, international students, local/state students, relatives of clergy, religious affiliation, spouses of current students. *Tuition waivers:* Full or partial for children of alumni, employees or children of employees.

LOANS *Student loans:* $2,430,719 (70% need-based, 30% non-need-based). 66% of past graduating class borrowed through all loan programs. *Average indebtedness per student:* $17,660. *Average need-based loan:* Freshmen: $3945; Undergraduates: $4140. *Parent loans:* $897,137 (100% non-need-based). *Programs:* FFEL (Subsidized and Unsubsidized Stafford, PLUS), Perkins, state, college/university.

WORK-STUDY *Federal work-study:* Total amount: $208,000; 183 jobs averaging $1500.

ATHLETIC AWARDS *Total amount:* $505,765 (100% non-need-based).

APPLYING FOR FINANCIAL AID *Required financial aid forms:* FAFSA, institution's own form. *Financial aid deadline (priority):* 5/1. *Notification date:* Continuous. Students must reply within 2 weeks of notification.

CONTACT Michael Sapienza, Director of Financial Aid, Bryan College, PO Box 7000, Dayton, TN 37321-7000, 423-775-7339 or toll-free 800-277-9522. *Fax:* 423-775-7300. *E-mail:* finaid@bryan.edu.

BRYANT AND STRATTON COLLEGE
Cleveland, OH

CONTACT Bill Davenport, Financial Aid Supervisor, Bryant and Stratton College, 1700 East 13th Street, Cleveland, OH 44114-3203, 216-771-1700. *Fax:* 216-771-7787.

BRYANT UNIVERSITY
Smithfield, RI

Tuition & fees: $24,762	Average undergraduate aid package: $12,628

ABOUT THE INSTITUTION Independent, coed. Awards: bachelor's and master's degrees and post-master's certificates. 15 undergraduate majors. Total enrollment: 3,518. Undergraduates: 3,047. Freshmen: 761. Federal methodology is used as a basis for awarding need-based institutional aid.

UNDERGRADUATE EXPENSES for 2005–06 *Application fee:* $50. *Comprehensive fee:* $34,330 includes full-time tuition ($24,762) and room and board ($9568). *College room only:* $5550. Full-time tuition and fees vary according to course load. Room and board charges vary according to board plan and housing facility. *Part-time tuition:* $891 per course. Part-time tuition and fees vary according to course load. Full-time tuition includes cost of personal laptop computer. *Payment plan:* Installment.

FRESHMAN FINANCIAL AID (Fall 2003) 531 applied for aid; of those 87% were deemed to have need. 100% of freshmen with need received aid; of those 15% had need fully met. *Average percent of need met:* 77% (excluding resources awarded to replace EFC). *Average financial aid package:* $14,889 (excluding resources awarded to replace EFC). 8% of all full-time freshmen had no need and received non-need-based gift aid.

UNDERGRADUATE FINANCIAL AID (Fall 2003) 1,904 applied for aid; of those 89% were deemed to have need. 100% of undergraduates with need received aid; of those 13% had need fully met. *Average percent of need met:* 74% (excluding resources awarded to replace EFC). *Average financial aid package:* $12,628 (excluding resources awarded to replace EFC). 16% of all full-time undergraduates had no need and received non-need-based gift aid.

GIFT AID (NEED-BASED) *Total amount:* $14,985,764 (8% federal, 2% state, 87% institutional, 3% external sources). *Receiving aid:* Freshmen: 57% (430); All full-time undergraduates: 48% (1,344). *Average award:* Freshmen: $10,040; Undergraduates: $8688. *Scholarships, grants, and awards:* Federal Pell, FSEOG, state, private, college/university gift aid from institutional funds.

GIFT AID (NON-NEED-BASED) *Total amount:* $5,897,705 (94% institutional, 6% external sources). *Receiving aid:* Freshmen: 30% (226); Undergraduates: 37% (1,040). *Average Award:* Freshmen: $8500; *Undergraduates:* $7482. *Scholarships, grants, and awards by category: Academic Interests/Achievement:* 1,113 awards ($5,811,305 total): general academic interests/achievements. *Special Characteristics:* 162 awards ($1,593,246 total): children and siblings of alumni, members of minority groups, siblings of current students. *Tuition waivers:* Full or partial for employees or children of employees. *ROTC:* Army.

LOANS *Student loans:* $15,146,088 (35% need-based, 65% non-need-based). 68% of past graduating class borrowed through all loan programs. *Average indebtedness per student:* $24,536. *Average need-based loan:* Freshmen: $4390; Undergraduates: $4850. *Parent loans:* $6,011,067 (10% need-based, 90% non-need-based). *Programs:* Federal Direct (Subsidized and Unsubsidized Stafford), FFEL (PLUS), Perkins, alternative loans.

WORK-STUDY *Federal work-study:* Total amount: $348,445; 286 jobs averaging $1120. *State or other work-study/employment:* Total amount: $1,767,724 (100% need-based). 1,011 part-time jobs averaging $1494.

ATHLETIC AWARDS *Total amount:* $1,700,878 (46% need-based, 54% non-need-based).

APPLYING FOR FINANCIAL AID *Required financial aid form:* FAFSA. *Financial aid deadline (priority):* 2/15. *Notification date:* 3/24. Students must reply by 5/1.

CONTACT Mr. John B. Canning, Director of Financial Aid, Bryant University, Office of Financial Aid, 1150 Douglas Pike, Smithfield, RI 02917-1284, 401-232-6020 or toll-free 800-622-7001. *Fax:* 401-232-6293. *E-mail:* jcanning@bryant.edu.

BRYN ATHYN COLLEGE OF THE NEW CHURCH
Bryn Athyn, PA

ABOUT THE INSTITUTION Independent Swedenborgian, coed. Awards: associate, bachelor's, master's, and first professional degrees and first professional certificates. 7 undergraduate majors. Total enrollment: 155. Undergraduates: 134. Freshmen: 40.

GIFT AID (NEED-BASED) *Scholarships, grants, and awards:* private, college/university gift aid from institutional funds.

GIFT AID (NON-NEED-BASED) *Scholarships, grants, and awards by category: Academic Interests/Achievement:* general academic interests/achievements.

LOANS *Programs:* college/university.

APPLYING FOR FINANCIAL AID *Required financial aid forms:* FAFSA, institution's own form, income tax form(s).

CONTACT Les Alden, Business Manager, Bryn Athyn College of the New Church, Box 711, Bryn Athyn, PA 19009, 215-938-2635. *Fax:* 215-938-2616. *E-mail:* wlalden@newchurch.edu.

BRYN MAWR COLLEGE
Bryn Mawr, PA

Tuition & fees: $28,630	Average undergraduate aid package: $26,624

ABOUT THE INSTITUTION Independent, women only. Awards: bachelor's, master's, and doctoral degrees and post-bachelor's certificates. 31 undergraduate majors. Total enrollment: 1,772. Undergraduates: 1,327. Freshmen: 358. Both federal and institutional methodology are used as a basis for awarding need-based institutional aid.

UNDERGRADUATE EXPENSES for 2004–05 *Application fee:* $50. *Comprehensive fee:* $38,330 includes full-time tuition ($27,900), mandatory fees ($730), and room and board ($9700). *College room only:* $5570. Room and board charges vary according to board plan. *Part-time tuition:* $3490 per course. Part-time tuition and fees vary according to course load. *Payment plans:* Tuition prepayment, installment.

FRESHMAN FINANCIAL AID (Fall 2004, est.) 234 applied for aid; of those 79% were deemed to have need. 100% of freshmen with need received aid; of those 99% had need fully met. *Average percent of need met:* 100% (excluding resources awarded to replace EFC). *Average financial aid package:* $26,446 (excluding resources awarded to replace EFC). 6% of all full-time freshmen had no need and received non-need-based gift aid.

UNDERGRADUATE FINANCIAL AID (Fall 2004, est.) 775 applied for aid; of those 90% were deemed to have need. 100% of undergraduates with need received aid; of those 99% had need fully met. *Average percent of need met:* 99% (excluding resources awarded to replace EFC). *Average financial aid package:* $26,624 (excluding resources awarded to replace EFC). 2% of all full-time undergraduates had no need and received non-need-based gift aid.

GIFT AID (NEED-BASED) *Total amount:* $14,971,031 (5% federal, 2% state, 91% institutional, 2% external sources). *Receiving aid:* Freshmen: 52% (185); All full-time undergraduates: 53% (685). *Average award:* Freshmen: $22,406; Undergraduates: $21,881. *Scholarships, grants, and awards:* Federal Pell, FSEOG, state, private, college/university gift aid from institutional funds.

GIFT AID (NON-NEED-BASED) *Total amount:* $452,729 (3% federal, 79% institutional, 18% external sources). *Receiving aid:* Freshmen: 3% (9); Undergraduates: 1% (14). *Average Award:* Freshmen: $8995; Undergraduates: $11,185. *Tuition waivers:* Full or partial for employees or children of employees, senior citizens. *ROTC:* Air Force cooperative.

LOANS *Student loans:* $3,628,203 (74% need-based, 26% non-need-based). 58% of past graduating class borrowed through all loan programs. *Average indebtedness per student:* $15,194. *Average need-based loan:* Freshmen: $3472; Undergraduates: $4701. *Parent loans:* $2,685,021 (100% non-need-based). *Programs:* FFEL (Subsidized and Unsubsidized Stafford, PLUS), Perkins.

WORK-STUDY *Federal work-study:* Total amount: $918,269; 502 jobs averaging $1727. *State or other work-study/employment:* Total amount: $200,470 (100% need-based). 103 part-time jobs averaging $1706.

APPLYING FOR FINANCIAL AID *Required financial aid forms:* FAFSA, CSS Financial Aid PROFILE, noncustodial (divorced/separated) parent's statement, business/farm supplement, income tax form(s) student and parent tax returns. *Financial aid deadline:* 2/2. *Notification date:* 3/20. Students must reply by 5/1.

CONTACT Ethel M. Desmarais, Director of Financial Aid, Bryn Mawr College, 101 North Merion Avenue, Bryn Mawr, PA 19010-2899, 610-526-7922 or toll-free 800-BMC-1885 (out-of-state). *Fax:* 610-526-5249. *E-mail:* edesmara@brynmawr.edu.

BUCKNELL UNIVERSITY
Lewisburg, PA

Tuition & fees: $32,788	Average undergraduate aid package: $20,000

ABOUT THE INSTITUTION Independent, coed. Awards: bachelor's and master's degrees. 54 undergraduate majors. Total enrollment: 3,609. Undergraduates: 3,454. Freshmen: 907. Both federal and institutional methodology are used as a basis for awarding need-based institutional aid.

UNDERGRADUATE EXPENSES for 2005–06 *Application fee:* $60. *Comprehensive fee:* $39,660 includes full-time tuition ($32,592), mandatory fees ($196), and room and board ($6872). *College room only:* $3670. Room and board charges vary according to board plan and housing facility. *Part-time tuition:* $3725 per course. *Payment plan:* Installment.

FRESHMAN FINANCIAL AID (Fall 2004, est.) 560 applied for aid; of those 77% were deemed to have need. 100% of freshmen with need received aid; of those 100% had need fully met. *Average percent of need met:* 100% (excluding resources awarded to replace EFC). *Average financial aid package:* $21,825 (excluding resources awarded to replace EFC). 1% of all full-time freshmen had no need and received non-need-based gift aid.

UNDERGRADUATE FINANCIAL AID (Fall 2004, est.) 1,860 applied for aid; of those 93% were deemed to have need. 100% of undergraduates with need received aid; of those 100% had need fully met. *Average percent of need met:*

100% (excluding resources awarded to replace EFC). *Average financial aid package:* $20,000 (excluding resources awarded to replace EFC). 1% of all full-time undergraduates had no need and received non-need-based gift aid.

GIFT AID (NEED-BASED) *Total amount:* $29,139,245 (5% federal, 4% state, 88% institutional, 3% external sources). *Receiving aid:* Freshmen: 46% (415); All full-time undergraduates: 45% (1,532). *Average award:* Freshmen: $17,300; Undergraduates: $16,800. *Scholarships, grants, and awards:* Federal Pell, FSEOG, state, private, college/university gift aid from institutional funds.

GIFT AID (NON-NEED-BASED) *Total amount:* $202,000 (100% institutional). *Receiving aid:* Freshmen: 1% (12); Undergraduates: 1% (21). *Average Award:* Freshmen: $9571; Undergraduates: $10,222. *Scholarships, grants and awards by category: Academic Interests/Achievement:* 9 awards ($94,500 total): business, engineering/technologies, general academic interests/achievements, physical sciences. *Creative Arts/Performance:* 6 awards ($50,400 total): art/fine arts, music, performing arts. *Tuition waivers:* Full or partial for employees or children of employees. *ROTC:* Army.

LOANS *Student loans:* $12,000,000 (100% need-based). 62% of past graduating class borrowed through all loan programs. *Average indebtedness per student:* $16,800. *Average need-based loan:* Freshmen: $4000; Undergraduates: $5200. *Parent loans:* $5,517,734 (100% non-need-based). *Programs:* FFEL (Subsidized and Unsubsidized Stafford, PLUS), Perkins.

WORK-STUDY *Federal work-study:* Total amount: $1,131,700; 1,000 jobs averaging $1132. *State or other work-study/employment:* Total amount: $80,000 (100% need-based). 53 part-time jobs averaging $1509.

ATHLETIC AWARDS *Total amount:* $110,000 (100% non-need-based).

APPLYING FOR FINANCIAL AID *Required financial aid forms:* FAFSA, CSS Financial Aid PROFILE, noncustodial (divorced/separated) parent's statement. *Financial aid deadline:* 1/1. *Notification date:* 4/1. Students must reply by 5/1.

CONTACT Andrea Leithner, Director of Financial Aid, Bucknell University, Office of Financial Aid, Lewisburg, PA 17837, 570-577-1331. *Fax:* 570-577-1481.

BUENA VISTA UNIVERSITY
Storm Lake, IA

Tuition & fees: $20,854	Average undergraduate aid package: $19,522

ABOUT THE INSTITUTION Independent religious, coed. Awards: bachelor's and master's degrees. 58 undergraduate majors. Total enrollment: 1,316. Undergraduates: 1,276. Freshmen: 331. Federal methodology is used as a basis for awarding need-based institutional aid.

UNDERGRADUATE EXPENSES for 2004–05 *Comprehensive fee:* $26,676 includes full-time tuition ($20,854) and room and board ($5822). *Part-time tuition:* $701 per semester hour.

FRESHMAN FINANCIAL AID (Fall 2004, est.) 328 applied for aid; of those 94% were deemed to have need. 100% of freshmen with need received aid; of those 20% had need fully met. *Average percent of need met:* 91% (excluding resources awarded to replace EFC). *Average financial aid package:* $19,482 (excluding resources awarded to replace EFC). 2% of all full-time freshmen had no need and received non-need-based gift aid.

UNDERGRADUATE FINANCIAL AID (Fall 2004, est.) 1,209 applied for aid; of those 95% were deemed to have need. 100% of undergraduates with need received aid; of those 24% had need fully met. *Average percent of need met:* 90% (excluding resources awarded to replace EFC). *Average financial aid package:* $19,522 (excluding resources awarded to replace EFC). 2% of all full-time undergraduates had no need and received non-need-based gift aid.

GIFT AID (NEED-BASED) *Total amount:* $14,898,791 (11% federal, 17% state, 72% institutional). *Receiving aid:* Freshmen: 93% (308); All full-time undergraduates: 92% (1,137). *Average award:* Freshmen: $12,774; Undergraduates: $12,248. *Scholarships, grants, and awards:* Federal Pell, FSEOG, state, private, college/university gift aid from institutional funds.

GIFT AID (NON-NEED-BASED) *Total amount:* $2,062,282 (2% state, 80% institutional, 18% external sources). *Receiving aid:* Freshmen: 76% (253); Undergraduates: 57% (711). *Average Award:* Freshmen: $11,472; Undergraduates: $13,033. *Scholarships, grants, and awards by category: Academic Interests/Achievement:* 1,188 awards ($6,960,706 total): biological sciences, business, computer science, education, general academic interests/achievements, humanities, mathematics. *Creative Arts/Performance:* 123 awards ($159,635 total): art/fine arts, music, theater/drama. *Special Achievements/Activities:* general special achievements/activities, leadership. *Special Characteristics:* 315 awards ($866,929 total): children of faculty/staff, international students, out-of-state students, religious affiliation, siblings of current students. *Tuition waivers:* Full or partial for employees or children of employees.

Buena Vista University

LOANS *Student loans:* $5,633,385 (85% need-based, 15% non-need-based). 91% of past graduating class borrowed through all loan programs. *Average indebtedness per student:* $24,705. *Average need-based loan:* Freshmen: $4037; Undergraduates: $4715. *Programs:* FFEL (Subsidized and Unsubsidized Stafford, PLUS), Perkins, college/university.

WORK-STUDY *Federal work-study:* Total amount: $656,675; 613 jobs averaging $1070. *State or other work-study/employment:* Total amount: $149,100 (100% non-need-based). 148 part-time jobs averaging $1007.

APPLYING FOR FINANCIAL AID *Required financial aid form:* FAFSA. *Financial aid deadline (priority):* 6/1. *Notification date:* Continuous beginning 3/5. Students must reply by 5/1 or within 2 weeks of notification.

CONTACT Mrs. Leanne Valentine, Director of Financial Assistance, Buena Vista University, 610 West Fourth Street, Storm Lake, IA 50588, 712-749-2164 or toll-free 800-383-9600. *Fax:* 712-749-1451. *E-mail:* valentinel@bvu.edu.

BUFFALO STATE COLLEGE, STATE UNIVERSITY OF NEW YORK
Buffalo, NY

ABOUT THE INSTITUTION State-supported, coed. Awards: bachelor's and master's degrees and post-master's certificates. 79 undergraduate majors. Total enrollment: 11,072. Undergraduates: 9,008. Freshmen: 1,333.

GIFT AID (NEED-BASED) *Scholarships, grants, and awards:* Federal Pell, FSEOG, state, private, college/university gift aid from institutional funds.

GIFT AID (NON-NEED-BASED) *Scholarships, grants, and awards by category: Academic Interests/Achievement:* general academic interests/achievements. *Creative Arts/Performance:* general creative arts/performance. *Special Achievements/ Activities:* general special achievements/activities.

LOANS *Programs:* FFEL (Subsidized and Unsubsidized Stafford, PLUS), Perkins.

WORK-STUDY *Federal work-study:* Total amount: $469,319; jobs available. *State or other work-study/employment:* Part-time jobs available.

APPLYING FOR FINANCIAL AID *Required financial aid form:* FAFSA.

CONTACT Mr. Kent McGowan, Director of Financial Aid, Buffalo State College, State University of New York, 1300 Elmwood Avenue, Buffalo, NY 14222-1095, 716-878-4902. *Fax:* 716-878-4903.

BURLINGTON COLLEGE
Burlington, VT

Tuition & fees: $14,170	Average undergraduate aid package: $9796

ABOUT THE INSTITUTION Independent, coed. Awards: associate and bachelor's degrees. 20 undergraduate majors. Total enrollment: 241. Undergraduates: 241. Freshmen: 17. Federal methodology is used as a basis for awarding need-based institutional aid.

UNDERGRADUATE EXPENSES for 2004–05 *Application fee:* $35. *Tuition:* full-time $14,170; part-time $470 per credit hour. Full-time tuition and fees vary according to course load. Part-time tuition and fees vary according to course load. Room and board charges vary according to housing facility. *Payment plan:* Installment.

FRESHMAN FINANCIAL AID (Fall 2004, est.) 18 applied for aid; of those 72% were deemed to have need. 85% of freshmen with need received aid. *Average percent of need met:* 54% (excluding resources awarded to replace EFC). *Average financial aid package:* $9371 (excluding resources awarded to replace EFC).

UNDERGRADUATE FINANCIAL AID (Fall 2004, est.) 91 applied for aid; of those 89% were deemed to have need. 94% of undergraduates with need received aid; of those 1% had need fully met. *Average percent of need met:* 57% (excluding resources awarded to replace EFC). *Average financial aid package:* $9796 (excluding resources awarded to replace EFC).

GIFT AID (NEED-BASED) *Total amount:* $426,145 (55% federal, 40% state, 2% institutional, 3% external sources). *Receiving aid:* Freshmen: 42% (8); All full-time undergraduates: 41% (54). *Average award:* Freshmen: $5208; Undergraduates: $4820. *Scholarships, grants, and awards:* Federal Pell, FSEOG, state, private, college/university gift aid from institutional funds.

GIFT AID (NON-NEED-BASED) *Scholarships, grants, and awards by category: Special Achievements/Activities:* general special achievements/activities. *Tuition waivers:* Full or partial for employees or children of employees.

LOANS *Student loans:* $1,209,388 (88% need-based, 12% non-need-based). 65% of past graduating class borrowed through all loan programs. *Average indebtedness per student:* $19,210. *Average need-based loan:* Freshmen: $4900;

Undergraduates: $6058. *Parent loans:* $152,229 (60% need-based, 40% non-need-based). *Programs:* FFEL (Subsidized and Unsubsidized Stafford, PLUS), Perkins.

WORK-STUDY *Federal work-study:* Total amount: $58,942; 41 jobs averaging $1432.

APPLYING FOR FINANCIAL AID *Required financial aid form:* FAFSA. *Financial aid deadline:* Continuous. *Notification date:* Continuous beginning 4/1. Students must reply within 4 weeks of notification.

CONTACT Ms. Yvonne Whitaker, Assistant Director of Financial Aid Services, Burlington College, PO Box 2000, Winooski, VT 05404, 877-685-7787 or toll-free 800-862-9616. *Fax:* 802-654-3765. *E-mail:* bc@vsac.org.

BUTLER UNIVERSITY
Indianapolis, IN

Tuition & fees: $22,484	Average undergraduate aid package: $17,165

ABOUT THE INSTITUTION Independent, coed. Awards: associate, bachelor's, master's, and first professional degrees and post-bachelor's certificates. 52 undergraduate majors. Total enrollment: 4,415. Undergraduates: 3,722. Freshmen: 927. Federal methodology is used as a basis for awarding need-based institutional aid.

UNDERGRADUATE EXPENSES for 2004–05 *Application fee:* $35. *Comprehensive fee:* $30,264 includes full-time tuition ($22,250), mandatory fees ($234), and room and board ($7780). *College room only:* $3400. Full-time tuition and fees vary according to program. Room and board charges vary according to housing facility. *Part-time tuition:* $930 per credit. Part-time tuition and fees vary according to program. *Payment plan:* Installment.

FRESHMAN FINANCIAL AID (Fall 2004, est.) 837 applied for aid; of those 69% were deemed to have need. 100% of freshmen with need received aid; of those 19% had need fully met. *Average financial aid package:* $17,954 (excluding resources awarded to replace EFC). 24% of all full-time freshmen had no need and received non-need-based gift aid.

UNDERGRADUATE FINANCIAL AID (Fall 2004, est.) 3,454 applied for aid; of those 67% were deemed to have need. 100% of undergraduates with need received aid; of those 20% had need fully met. *Average financial aid package:* $17,165 (excluding resources awarded to replace EFC). 26% of all full-time undergraduates had no need and received non-need-based gift aid.

GIFT AID (NEED-BASED) *Total amount:* $26,801,922 (6% federal, 11% state, 73% institutional, 10% external sources). *Receiving aid:* Freshmen: 62% (572); All full-time undergraduates: 58% (2,224). *Average award:* Freshmen: $13,530; Undergraduates: $12,380. *Scholarships, grants, and awards:* Federal Pell, FSEOG, state, private, college/university gift aid from institutional funds.

GIFT AID (NON-NEED-BASED) *Total amount:* $86,417,411 (97% institutional, 3% external sources). *Receiving aid:* Freshmen: 13% (125); Undergraduates: 10% (376). *Average Award:* Freshmen: $8670; Undergraduates: $9080. *Scholarships, grants, and awards by category: Academic Interests/Achievement:* biological sciences, business, communication, computer science, education, engineering/technologies, English, foreign languages, general academic interests/achievements, humanities, international studies, mathematics, physical sciences, social sciences. *Creative Arts/Performance:* art/fine arts, cinema/film/broadcasting, dance, music, theater/drama. *Tuition waivers:* Full or partial for employees or children of employees. *ROTC:* Army, Air Force cooperative.

LOANS *Student loans:* $20,897,760 (67% need-based, 33% non-need-based). 62% of past graduating class borrowed through all loan programs. *Average need-based loan:* Freshmen: $3980; Undergraduates: $5320. *Parent loans:* $5,182,040 (20% need-based, 80% non-need-based). *Programs:* FFEL (Subsidized and Unsubsidized Stafford, PLUS), Perkins.

WORK-STUDY *Federal work-study:* Total amount: $280,000; jobs available. *State or other work-study/employment:* Part-time jobs available.

ATHLETIC AWARDS *Total amount:* $2,777,910 (32% need-based, 68% non-need-based).

APPLYING FOR FINANCIAL AID *Required financial aid form:* FAFSA. *Financial aid deadline (priority):* 3/1. *Notification date:* 3/15. Students must reply within 3 weeks of notification.

CONTACT Ms. Kristine Butz, Associate Director of Financial Aid, Butler University, 4600 Sunset Avenue, Indianapolis, IN 46208-3485, 317-940-8200 or toll-free 888-940-8100. *Fax:* 317-940-8250. *E-mail:* kbutz@butler.edu.

CABARRUS COLLEGE OF HEALTH SCIENCES
Concord, NC

ABOUT THE INSTITUTION Independent, coed, primarily women. Awards: associate and bachelor's degrees. 6 undergraduate majors. Total enrollment: 365. Undergraduates: 306. Freshmen: 34.

GIFT AID (NEED-BASED) *Scholarships, grants, and awards:* Federal Pell, FSEOG, state, private, college/university gift aid from institutional funds.

LOANS *Programs:* FFEL (Subsidized and Unsubsidized Stafford, PLUS), state.

APPLYING FOR FINANCIAL AID *Required financial aid form:* FAFSA.

CONTACT Joanne Yurchison, Business Officer, Cabarrus College of Health Sciences, 431 Copperfield Boulevard NE, Concord, NC 28025, 704-783-1754. *Fax:* 704-783-1764. *E-mail:* jyurch@northeastmedical.org.

CABRINI COLLEGE
Radnor, PA

ABOUT THE INSTITUTION Independent Roman Catholic, coed. Awards: bachelor's and master's degrees and post-bachelor's certificates. 38 undergraduate majors. Total enrollment: 2,176. Undergraduates: 1,649. Freshmen: 391.

GIFT AID (NEED-BASED) *Scholarships, grants, and awards:* Federal Pell, FSEOG, state, private, college/university gift aid from institutional funds.

GIFT AID (NON-NEED-BASED) *Scholarships, grants, and awards by category: Academic Interests/Achievement:* general academic interests/achievements. *Special Characteristics:* children and siblings of alumni, children of faculty/staff, ethnic background, siblings of current students.

LOANS *Programs:* FFEL (Subsidized and Unsubsidized Stafford, PLUS), Perkins, alternative loans.

WORK-STUDY *Federal work-study:* Total amount: $155,455; 203 jobs averaging $765.

APPLYING FOR FINANCIAL AID *Required financial aid form:* FAFSA.

CONTACT Mike Colahan, Director of Financial Aid, Cabrini College, 610 King of Prussia Road, Grace Hall, Radnor, PA 19087-3698, 610-902-8420 or toll-free 800-848-1003. *Fax:* 610-902-8426.

CALDWELL COLLEGE
Caldwell, NJ

Tuition & fees: $18,950	Average undergraduate aid package: $9700

ABOUT THE INSTITUTION Independent Roman Catholic, coed. Awards: bachelor's and master's degrees and post-bachelor's and post-master's certificates. 26 undergraduate majors. Total enrollment: 2,175. Undergraduates: 1,709. Freshmen: 321. Both federal and institutional methodology are used as a basis for awarding need-based institutional aid.

UNDERGRADUATE EXPENSES for 2005–06 *Application fee:* $40. *Comprehensive fee:* $26,450 includes full-time tuition ($18,700), mandatory fees ($250), and room and board ($7500). Room and board charges vary according to board plan and housing facility. *Part-time tuition:* $450 per credit. Part-time tuition and fees vary according to course load. *Payment plans:* Installment, deferred payment.

FRESHMAN FINANCIAL AID (Fall 2004, est.) 275 applied for aid; of those 98% were deemed to have need. 100% of freshmen with need received aid; of those 79% had need fully met. *Average percent of need met:* 75% (excluding resources awarded to replace EFC). *Average financial aid package:* $10,800 (excluding resources awarded to replace EFC). 28% of all full-time freshmen had no need and received non-need-based gift aid.

UNDERGRADUATE FINANCIAL AID (Fall 2004, est.) 1,000 applied for aid; of those 99% were deemed to have need. 100% of undergraduates with need received aid; of those 50% had need fully met. *Average percent of need met:* 72% (excluding resources awarded to replace EFC). *Average financial aid package:* $9700 (excluding resources awarded to replace EFC). 32% of all full-time undergraduates had no need and received non-need-based gift aid.

GIFT AID (NEED-BASED) *Total amount:* $8,665,000 (16% federal, 27% state, 57% institutional). *Receiving aid:* Freshmen: 7% (21); All full-time undergraduates: 62% (652). *Average award:* Freshmen: $7300; Undergraduates: $7800. *Scholarships, grants, and awards:* Federal Pell, FSEOG, state, private, college/university gift aid from institutional funds.

GIFT AID (NON-NEED-BASED) *Total amount:* $137,000 (9% state, 91% external sources). *Receiving aid:* Freshmen: 28% (90); Undergraduates: 32% (342). *Average Award:* Freshmen: $3500; *Undergraduates:* $3200. *Scholarships, grants, and awards by category: Academic Interests/Achievement:* 372 awards ($3,297,000 total): general academic interests/achievements. *Tuition waivers:* Full or partial for children of alumni, employees or children of employees, senior citizens. *ROTC:* Army cooperative.

LOANS *Student loans:* $5,800,000 (66% need-based, 34% non-need-based). 70% of past graduating class borrowed through all loan programs. *Average indebtedness per student:* $16,000. *Average need-based loan:* Freshmen: $3800; Undergraduates: $4200. *Programs:* Federal Direct (Subsidized and Unsubsidized Stafford, PLUS), FFEL (Subsidized and Unsubsidized Stafford, PLUS), college/university.

WORK-STUDY *Federal work-study:* Total amount: $38,000; 159 jobs averaging $1500. *State or other work-study/employment:* Total amount: $10,000 (100% need-based).

ATHLETIC AWARDS *Total amount:* $477,000 (100% need-based).

APPLYING FOR FINANCIAL AID *Required financial aid forms:* FAFSA, state aid form. *Financial aid deadline:* Continuous. *Notification date:* Continuous beginning 2/15. Students must reply within 4 weeks of notification.

CONTACT Ms. Lissa B. Anderson, Executive Director of Financial Aid, Caldwell College, Caldwell College, 9 Ryerson Avenue, Caldwell, NJ 07006, 973-618-3221 or toll-free 888-864-9516 (out-of-state). *E-mail:* landerson@caldwell.edu.

CALIFORNIA BAPTIST UNIVERSITY
Riverside, CA

Tuition & fees: $15,940	Average undergraduate aid package: $10,400

ABOUT THE INSTITUTION Independent Southern Baptist, coed. Awards: bachelor's and master's degrees. 30 undergraduate majors. Total enrollment: 2,905. Undergraduates: 2,243. Freshmen: 311. Federal methodology is used as a basis for awarding need-based institutional aid.

UNDERGRADUATE EXPENSES for 2004–05 *Application fee:* $45. *Comprehensive fee:* $22,250 includes full-time tuition ($14,950), mandatory fees ($990), and room and board ($6310). *College room only:* $2640. Full-time tuition and fees vary according to course load and program. Room and board charges vary according to board plan and housing facility. *Part-time tuition:* $575 per semester hour. Part-time tuition and fees vary according to course load and program. *Payment plans:* Installment, deferred payment.

FRESHMAN FINANCIAL AID (Fall 2003) 296 applied for aid; of those 95% were deemed to have need. 100% of freshmen with need received aid; of those 18% had need fully met. *Average percent of need met:* 71% (excluding resources awarded to replace EFC). *Average financial aid package:* $8300 (excluding resources awarded to replace EFC). 5% of all full-time freshmen had no need and received non-need-based gift aid.

UNDERGRADUATE FINANCIAL AID (Fall 2003) 1,778 applied for aid; of those 98% were deemed to have need. 100% of undergraduates with need received aid; of those 18% had need fully met. *Average percent of need met:* 63% (excluding resources awarded to replace EFC). *Average financial aid package:* $10,400 (excluding resources awarded to replace EFC). 1% of all full-time undergraduates had no need and received non-need-based gift aid.

GIFT AID (NEED-BASED) *Total amount:* $9,837,449 (21% federal, 44% state, 31% institutional, 4% external sources). *Receiving aid:* Freshmen: 89% (277); All full-time undergraduates: 96% (1,735). *Average award:* Freshmen: $6800; Undergraduates: $8300. *Scholarships, grants, and awards:* Federal Pell, FSEOG, state, private, college/university gift aid from institutional funds.

GIFT AID (NON-NEED-BASED) *Total amount:* $768,964 (81% institutional, 19% external sources). *Receiving aid:* Freshmen: 70% (218); Undergraduates: 94% (1,709). *Average Award:* Freshmen: $4500; Undergraduates: $4200. *Scholarships, grants, and awards by category: Academic Interests/Achievement:* 326 awards ($849,817 total): general academic interests/achievements, religion/biblical studies. *Creative Arts/Performance:* 262 awards ($666,175 total): art/fine arts, music, theater/drama. *Special Characteristics:* 379 awards ($953,287 total): adult students, children and siblings of alumni, children of faculty/staff, relatives of clergy, siblings of current students. *Tuition waivers:* Full or partial for employees or children of employees. *ROTC:* Army cooperative, Air Force cooperative.

LOANS *Student loans:* $22,725,254 (87% need-based, 13% non-need-based). 89% of past graduating class borrowed through all loan programs. *Average indebtedness per student:* $19,700. *Average need-based loan:* Freshmen: $2700;

Undergraduates: $4900. *Parent loans:* $1,343,478 (70% need-based, 30% non-need-based). *Programs:* FFEL (Subsidized and Unsubsidized Stafford, PLUS), Perkins, alternative loans.

WORK-STUDY *Federal work-study:* Total amount: $83,606; 105 jobs averaging $796.

ATHLETIC AWARDS *Total amount:* $1,546,972 (70% need-based, 30% non-need-based).

APPLYING FOR FINANCIAL AID *Required financial aid forms:* FAFSA, state aid form. *Financial aid deadline (priority):* 3/2. *Notification date:* Continuous. Students must reply by 4/1 or within 3 weeks of notification.

CONTACT Mrs. Eileen Terry, Director of Financial Aid, California Baptist University, 8432 Magnolia Avenue, Riverside, CA 92504-3297, 951-343-4368 or toll-free 877-228-8866. *Fax:* 951-343-4518. *E-mail:* eterry@calbaptist.edu.

CALIFORNIA CHRISTIAN COLLEGE
Fresno, CA

ABOUT THE INSTITUTION Independent religious, coed. Awards: associate and bachelor's degrees. 2 undergraduate majors. Total enrollment: 52. Undergraduates: 52. Freshmen: 5.

GIFT AID (NEED-BASED) *Scholarships, grants, and awards:* Federal Pell, FSEOG, state, private.

LOANS *Programs:* FFEL (Subsidized and Unsubsidized Stafford, PLUS), SELF Loans.

WORK-STUDY *Federal work-study:* Total amount: $7700; 8 jobs averaging $963.

APPLYING FOR FINANCIAL AID *Required financial aid forms:* FAFSA, institution's own form, GPA verification form (for CA residents).

CONTACT Mindy Scroggins, Financial Aid Coordinator, California Christian College, 4881 East University, Fresno, CA 93703, 559-455-5580. *Fax:* 559-251-4231. *E-mail:* cccfadir@aol.com.

CALIFORNIA COLLEGE FOR HEALTH SCIENCES
Salt Lake City, UT

CONTACT Financial Aid Director, California College for Health Sciences, 2423 Hoover Avenue, National City, CA 91950-6605, 619-477-4800 or toll-free 800-791-7353. *Fax:* 619-477-5202.

CALIFORNIA COLLEGE OF THE ARTS
San Francisco, CA

Tuition & fees: $24,640	Average undergraduate aid package: $16,923

ABOUT THE INSTITUTION Independent, coed. Awards: bachelor's and master's degrees. 17 undergraduate majors. Total enrollment: 1,587. Undergraduates: 1,319. Freshmen: 171. Federal methodology is used as a basis for awarding need-based institutional aid.

UNDERGRADUATE EXPENSES for 2004–05 *Application fee:* $50. *Comprehensive fee:* $32,870 includes full-time tuition ($24,350), mandatory fees ($290), and room and board ($8230). *College room only:* $5800. Full-time tuition and fees vary according to course load. Room and board charges vary according to housing facility. *Part-time tuition:* $1015 per unit. Part-time tuition and fees vary according to course load. *Payment plans:* Installment, deferred payment.

FRESHMAN FINANCIAL AID (Fall 2004, est.) 134 applied for aid; of those 88% were deemed to have need. 100% of freshmen with need received aid; of those 9% had need fully met. *Average percent of need met:* 62% (excluding resources awarded to replace EFC). *Average financial aid package:* $16,271 (excluding resources awarded to replace EFC). 9% of all full-time freshmen had no need and received non-need-based gift aid.

UNDERGRADUATE FINANCIAL AID (Fall 2004, est.) 912 applied for aid; of those 93% were deemed to have need. 100% of undergraduates with need received aid; of those 4% had need fully met. *Average percent of need met:* 56% (excluding resources awarded to replace EFC). *Average financial aid package:* $16,923 (excluding resources awarded to replace EFC). 4% of all full-time undergraduates had no need and received non-need-based gift aid.

GIFT AID (NEED-BASED) *Total amount:* $9,655,511 (14% federal, 10% state, 74% institutional, 2% external sources). *Receiving aid:* Freshmen: 69% (118); All full-time undergraduates: 72% (852). *Average award:* Freshmen: $10,745;

Undergraduates: $10,736. *Scholarships, grants, and awards:* Federal Pell, FSEOG, state, private, college/university gift aid from institutional funds.

GIFT AID (NON-NEED-BASED) *Total amount:* $526,300 (100% institutional). *Receiving aid:* Freshmen: 53% (90); Undergraduates: 30% (349). *Average Award:* Freshmen: $6172; Undergraduates: $5136. *Scholarships, grants, and awards by category:* Academic Interests/Achievement: architecture, general academic interests/achievements. Creative Arts/Performance: applied art and design, art/fine arts, creative writing, general creative arts/performance. *Tuition waivers:* Full or partial for employees or children of employees.

LOANS *Student loans:* $6,417,205 (63% need-based, 37% non-need-based). 79% of past graduating class borrowed through all loan programs. *Average indebtedness per student:* $31,295. *Average need-based loan:* Freshmen: $2892; Undergraduates: $4674. *Parent loans:* $3,163,659 (100% non-need-based). *Programs:* FFEL (Subsidized and Unsubsidized Stafford, PLUS), Perkins, private education loans.

WORK-STUDY *Federal work-study:* Total amount: $366,784; 321 jobs averaging $1534. *State or other work-study/employment:* Total amount: $157,029 (100% non-need-based). 81 part-time jobs averaging $1938.

APPLYING FOR FINANCIAL AID *Required financial aid form:* FAFSA. *Financial aid deadline (priority):* 3/1. *Notification date:* Continuous beginning 4/1. Students must reply by 5/1 or within 3 weeks of notification.

CONTACT Financial Aid Office, California College of the Arts, 1111 Eighth Street, San Francisco, CA 94107, 415-703-9528 or toll-free 800-447-1ART. *Fax:* 415-551-9261. *E-mail:* finaid@ccac.edu.

CALIFORNIA DESIGN COLLEGE
Los Angeles, CA

CONTACT Mr. Jason F. Li, Director of Financial Aid, California Design College, 3440 Wilshire Boulevard, Seventh Floor, Los Angeles, CA 90010, 213-251-3636 Ext. 209 or toll-free 213-251-3636 (in-state), 877-468-6232 (out-of-state). *Fax:* 213-385-3545. *E-mail:* jason@cdc.edu.

CALIFORNIA INSTITUTE OF INTEGRAL STUDIES
San Francisco, CA

CONTACT Financial Aid Office, California Institute of Integral Studies, 1453 Mission Street, San Francisco, CA 94103, 415-575-6122. *Fax:* 415-575-1268. *E-mail:* finaid@ciis.edu.

CALIFORNIA INSTITUTE OF TECHNOLOGY
Pasadena, CA

Tuition & fees: $25,551	Average undergraduate aid package: $26,877

ABOUT THE INSTITUTION Independent, coed. Awards: bachelor's, master's, and doctoral degrees. 32 undergraduate majors. Total enrollment: 2,172. Undergraduates: 891. Freshmen: 191. Both federal and institutional methodology are used as a basis for awarding need-based institutional aid.

UNDERGRADUATE EXPENSES for 2004–05 *Application fee:* $50. *Comprehensive fee:* $33,564 includes full-time tuition ($25,335), mandatory fees ($216), and room and board ($8013). *Payment plans:* Installment, deferred payment.

FRESHMAN FINANCIAL AID (Fall 2004, est.) 153 applied for aid; of those 76% were deemed to have need. 100% of freshmen with need received aid; of those 100% had need fully met. *Average percent of need met:* 100% (excluding resources awarded to replace EFC). *Average financial aid package:* $24,813 (excluding resources awarded to replace EFC). 4% of all full-time freshmen had no need and received non-need-based gift aid.

UNDERGRADUATE FINANCIAL AID (Fall 2004, est.) 615 applied for aid; of those 83% were deemed to have need. 100% of undergraduates with need received aid; of those 100% had need fully met. *Average percent of need met:* 100% (excluding resources awarded to replace EFC). *Average financial aid package:* $26,877 (excluding resources awarded to replace EFC). 8% of all full-time undergraduates had no need and received non-need-based gift aid.

GIFT AID (NEED-BASED) *Total amount:* $12,940,288 (7% federal, 6% state, 84% institutional, 3% external sources). *Receiving aid:* Freshmen: 56% (116); All full-time undergraduates: 58% (513). *Average award:* Freshmen: $23,455; Undergraduates: $25,225. *Scholarships, grants, and awards:* Federal Pell, FSEOG, state, private, college/university gift aid from institutional funds.

GIFT AID (NON-NEED-BASED) *Total amount:* $2,483,381 (3% state, 80% institutional, 17% external sources). *Receiving aid:* Freshmen: 2% (4); Undergraduates: 2% (17). *Average Award: Freshmen:* $29,395; *Undergraduates:* $27,896. *Scholarships, grants, and awards by category: Academic Interests/Achievement:* 71 awards ($1,980,593 total): general academic interests/ achievements. *Tuition waivers:* Full or partial for employees or children of employees. *ROTC:* Army cooperative, Air Force cooperative.

LOANS *Student loans:* $431,737 (60% need-based, 40% non-need-based). 46% of past graduating class borrowed through all loan programs. *Average indebtedness per student:* $7400. *Average need-based loan:* Freshmen: $1798; Undergraduates: $1318. *Parent loans:* $661,616 (100% non-need-based). *Programs:* Federal Direct (Subsidized and Unsubsidized Stafford, PLUS), Perkins, college/university.

WORK-STUDY *Federal work-study:* Total amount: $459,481; jobs available. *State or other work-study/employment:* Total amount: $79,403 (100% need-based). Part-time jobs available.

APPLYING FOR FINANCIAL AID *Required financial aid forms:* FAFSA, CSS Financial Aid PROFILE, state aid form, noncustodial (divorced/separated) parent's statement, business/farm supplement. *Financial aid deadline (priority):* 1/15. *Notification date:* 4/15. Students must reply by 5/1 or within 4 weeks of notification.

CONTACT David Levy, Director of Financial Aid, California Institute of Technology, Financial Aid Office, MC 110-87, Pasadena, CA 91125-0001, 626-395-6280. *Fax:* 626-564-8136. *E-mail:* davidlevy@finaid.caltech.edu.

CALIFORNIA INSTITUTE OF THE ARTS
Valencia, CA

Tuition & fees: $27,260	Average undergraduate aid package: $24,214

ABOUT THE INSTITUTION Independent, coed. Awards: bachelor's and master's degrees and post-bachelor's certificates. 23 undergraduate majors. Total enrollment: 1,325. Undergraduates: 812. Freshmen: 157. Federal methodology is used as a basis for awarding need-based institutional aid.

UNDERGRADUATE EXPENSES for 2005–06 *Application fee:* $60. *Comprehensive fee:* $34,957 includes full-time tuition ($27,260) and room and board ($7697). *College room only:* $4095. Full-time tuition and fees vary according to course load. Room and board charges vary according to board plan, housing facility, and location. *Payment plan:* Deferred payment.

FRESHMAN FINANCIAL AID (Fall 2004, est.) 124 applied for aid; of those 76% were deemed to have need. 99% of freshmen with need received aid; of those 9% had need fully met. *Average percent of need met:* 86% (excluding resources awarded to replace EFC). *Average financial aid package:* $22,935 (excluding resources awarded to replace EFC). 15% of all full-time freshmen had no need and received non-need-based gift aid.

UNDERGRADUATE FINANCIAL AID (Fall 2004, est.) 661 applied for aid; of those 85% were deemed to have need. 99% of undergraduates with need received aid; of those 10% had need fully met. *Average percent of need met:* 84% (excluding resources awarded to replace EFC). *Average financial aid package:* $24,214 (excluding resources awarded to replace EFC). 9% of all full-time undergraduates had no need and received non-need-based gift aid.

GIFT AID (NEED-BASED) *Total amount:* $6,207,487 (18% federal, 15% state, 65% institutional, 2% external sources). *Receiving aid:* Freshmen: 58% (91); All full-time undergraduates: 68% (543). *Average award:* Freshmen: $9630; Undergraduates: $11,348. *Scholarships, grants, and awards:* Federal Pell, FSEOG, state, private, college/university gift aid from institutional funds.

GIFT AID (NON-NEED-BASED) *Total amount:* $383,092 (89% institutional, 11% external sources). *Average Award: Freshmen:* $3818; *Undergraduates:* $5177. *Scholarships, grants, and awards by category: Creative Arts/Performance:* 74 awards ($383,098 total): applied art and design, art/fine arts, cinema/film/ broadcasting, creative writing, dance, music, performing arts, theater/drama. *Tuition waivers:* Full or partial for employees or children of employees.

LOANS *Student loans:* $5,616,910 (94% need-based, 6% non-need-based). 66% of past graduating class borrowed through all loan programs. *Average indebtedness per student:* $30,674. *Average need-based loan:* Freshmen: $4163; Undergraduates: $5626. *Parent loans:* $2,251,908 (74% need-based, 26% non-need-based). *Programs:* FFEL (Subsidized and Unsubsidized Stafford, PLUS), Perkins, college/university.

WORK-STUDY *Federal work-study:* Total amount: $544,557; 231 jobs averaging $2357. *State or other work-study/employment:* Total amount: $9958 (100% need-based). 6 part-time jobs averaging $1660.

APPLYING FOR FINANCIAL AID *Required financial aid form:* FAFSA. *Financial aid deadline (priority):* 3/2. *Notification date:* Continuous beginning 4/1. Students must reply by 5/1 or within 3 weeks of notification.

CONTACT Ms. Bobbi Heuer, Director of Financial Aid, California Institute of the Arts, 24700 McBean Parkway, Valencia, CA 91355-2340, 661-253-7869 or toll-free 800-545-2787. *Fax:* 661-287-3816.

CALIFORNIA LUTHERAN UNIVERSITY
Thousand Oaks, CA

Tuition & fees: $22,285	Average undergraduate aid package: $16,970

ABOUT THE INSTITUTION Independent Lutheran, coed. Awards: bachelor's, master's, and doctoral degrees and post-bachelor's and post-master's certificates. 51 undergraduate majors. Total enrollment: 3,019. Undergraduates: 1,972. Freshmen: 402. Federal methodology is used as a basis for awarding need-based institutional aid.

UNDERGRADUATE EXPENSES for 2005–06 *Application fee:* $45. *Comprehensive fee:* $29,855 includes full-time tuition ($21,820), mandatory fees ($465), and room and board ($7570). *College room only:* $3770. Room and board charges vary according to board plan. *Part-time tuition:* $715 per unit. *Part-time fees:* $465 per year. *Payment plan:* Installment.

FRESHMAN FINANCIAL AID (Fall 2003) 297 applied for aid; of those 80% were deemed to have need. 100% of freshmen with need received aid; of those 18% had need fully met. *Average percent of need met:* 80% (excluding resources awarded to replace EFC). *Average financial aid package:* $17,020 (excluding resources awarded to replace EFC). 24% of all full-time freshmen had no need and received non-need-based gift aid.

UNDERGRADUATE FINANCIAL AID (Fall 2003) 1,081 applied for aid; of those 82% were deemed to have need. 100% of undergraduates with need received aid; of those 22% had need fully met. *Average percent of need met:* 81% (excluding resources awarded to replace EFC). *Average financial aid package:* $16,970 (excluding resources awarded to replace EFC). 24% of all full-time undergraduates had no need and received non-need-based gift aid.

GIFT AID (NEED-BASED) *Total amount:* $12,909,505 (7% federal, 19% state, 71% institutional, 3% external sources). *Receiving aid:* Freshmen: 72% (238); All full-time undergraduates: 65% (883). *Average award:* Freshmen: $13,470; Undergraduates: $12,660. *Scholarships, grants, and awards:* Federal Pell, FSEOG, state, private, college/university gift aid from institutional funds.

GIFT AID (NON-NEED-BASED) *Total amount:* $3,014,447 (96% institutional, 4% external sources). *Receiving aid:* Freshmen: 29% (97); Undergraduates: 24% (321). *Average Award: Freshmen:* $8166; *Undergraduates:* $8075. *Scholarships, grants, and awards by category: Academic Interests/Achievement:* 476 awards ($3,332,000 total): biological sciences, business, communication, computer science, education, English, foreign languages, general academic interests/achievements, humanities, mathematics, physical sciences, religion/ biblical studies, social sciences. *Creative Arts/Performance:* 67 awards ($1,139,000 total): art/fine arts, creative writing, journalism/publications, music, performing arts, theater/drama. *Special Achievements/Activities:* 18 awards ($22,000 total): community service, general special achievements/activities, leadership, religious involvement. *Special Characteristics:* 127 awards ($190,500 total): adult students, children and siblings of alumni, children of faculty/staff, ethnic background, first-generation college students, international students, relatives of clergy, religious affiliation. *Tuition waivers:* Full or partial for employees or children of employees. *ROTC:* Army cooperative, Air Force cooperative.

LOANS *Student loans:* $6,372,236 (89% need-based, 11% non-need-based). 71% of past graduating class borrowed through all loan programs. *Average indebtedness per student:* $17,568. *Average need-based loan:* Freshmen: $3000; Undergraduates: $4400. *Parent loans:* $3,088,884 (80% need-based, 20% non-need-based). *Programs:* FFEL (Subsidized and Unsubsidized Stafford, PLUS), Perkins, college/university.

WORK-STUDY *Federal work-study:* Total amount: $375,207; 557 jobs averaging $2000. *State or other work-study/employment:* Total amount: $137,825 (64% need-based, 36% non-need-based). 200 part-time jobs averaging $2000.

APPLYING FOR FINANCIAL AID *Required financial aid forms:* FAFSA, loan application. *Financial aid deadline (priority):* 3/1. *Notification date:* 3/15. Students must reply by 5/1 or within 2 weeks of notification.

CONTACT Brett Schraeder, Director of Financial Aid, California Lutheran University, 60 West Olsen Road, Thousand Oaks, CA 91360-2787, 805-493-3115 or toll-free 877-258-3678. *Fax:* 805-493-3114.

CALIFORNIA MARITIME ACADEMY
Vallejo, CA

ABOUT THE INSTITUTION State-supported, coed. Awards: bachelor's degrees. 4 undergraduate majors. Total enrollment: 702. Undergraduates: 702.

GIFT AID (NEED-BASED) *Scholarships, grants, and awards:* Federal Pell, FSEOG, state, private, college/university gift aid from institutional funds.

GIFT AID (NON-NEED-BASED) *Scholarships, grants, and awards by category: Academic Interests/Achievement:* general academic interests/achievements. *Special Achievements/Activities:* community service, leadership. *Special Characteristics:* first-generation college students, general special characteristics, local/state students, out-of-state students.

LOANS *Programs:* FFEL (Subsidized and Unsubsidized Stafford, PLUS), Perkins.

WORK-STUDY Federal work-study jobs available.

APPLYING FOR FINANCIAL AID *Required financial aid form:* FAFSA.

CONTACT Financial Aid Manager, California Maritime Academy, 200 Maritime Academy Drive, Vallejo, CA 94590-0644, 707-654-1275 or toll-free 800-561-1945. *Fax:* 707-654-1007.

CALIFORNIA POLYTECHNIC STATE UNIVERSITY, SAN LUIS OBISPO
San Luis Obispo, CA

ABOUT THE INSTITUTION State-supported, coed. Awards: bachelor's and master's degrees. 61 undergraduate majors. Total enrollment: 17,582. Undergraduates: 16,639. Freshmen: 2,933.

GIFT AID (NEED-BASED) *Scholarships, grants, and awards:* Federal Pell, FSEOG, state, private, college/university gift aid from institutional funds.

GIFT AID (NON-NEED-BASED) *Scholarships, grants, and awards by category: Academic Interests/Achievement:* agriculture, architecture, biological sciences, business, communication, computer science, education, engineering/technologies, English, foreign languages, general academic interests/achievements, health fields, home economics, humanities, international studies, library science, mathematics, military science, physical sciences, social sciences. *Creative Arts/Performance:* applied art and design, art/fine arts, cinema/film/broadcasting, creative writing, dance, debating, general creative arts/performance, journalism/publications, music, performing arts, theater/drama. *Special Achievements/Activities:* community service, general special achievements/activities, leadership, rodeo. *Special Characteristics:* general special characteristics.

LOANS *Programs:* FFEL (Subsidized and Unsubsidized Stafford, PLUS), Perkins, college/university, alternative loans.

WORK-STUDY *Federal work-study:* Total amount: $851,704; jobs available.

APPLYING FOR FINANCIAL AID *Required financial aid forms:* FAFSA, institution's own form.

CONTACT Mary E. Spady, Associate Director of Financial Aid, California Polytechnic State University, San Luis Obispo, 1 Grand Avenue, San Luis Obispo, CA 93407, 805-756-5886. *Fax:* 805-756-7243. *E-mail:* mspady@calpoly.edu.

CALIFORNIA STATE POLYTECHNIC UNIVERSITY, POMONA
Pomona, CA

ABOUT THE INSTITUTION State-supported, coed. Awards: bachelor's and master's degrees. 88 undergraduate majors. Total enrollment: 19,002. Undergraduates: 16,955. Freshmen: 1,950.

GIFT AID (NEED-BASED) *Scholarships, grants, and awards:* Federal Pell, FSEOG, state, private, college/university gift aid from institutional funds.

GIFT AID (NON-NEED-BASED) *Scholarships, grants, and awards by category: Academic Interests/Achievement:* agriculture, architecture, biological sciences, business, computer science, education, engineering/technologies, general academic interests/achievements, humanities, mathematics, physical sciences, social sciences. *Special Achievements/Activities:* hobbies/interests, leadership. *Special Characteristics:* children and siblings of alumni, children of current students, members of minority groups.

LOANS *Programs:* FFEL (Subsidized and Unsubsidized Stafford, PLUS), Perkins, college/university, alternative loans.

WORK-STUDY *Federal work-study:* Total amount: $1,849,258; 660 jobs averaging $2800.

APPLYING FOR FINANCIAL AID *Required financial aid form:* FAFSA.

CONTACT Diana Minor, Associate Director of Financial Aid, California State Polytechnic University, Pomona, 3801 West Temple Avenue, Pomona, CA 91768-2557, 909-869-3704. *Fax:* 909-869-4757. *E-mail:* dyminor@csupomona.edu.

CALIFORNIA STATE UNIVERSITY, BAKERSFIELD
Bakersfield, CA

Tuition & fees (CA res): $2959	Average undergraduate aid package: $6791

ABOUT THE INSTITUTION State-supported, coed. Awards: bachelor's and master's degrees. 30 undergraduate majors. Total enrollment: 7,924. Undergraduates: 5,882. Federal methodology is used as a basis for awarding need-based institutional aid.

UNDERGRADUATE EXPENSES for 2005–06 *Application fee:* $55. *Tuition, state resident:* full-time $0. *Tuition, nonresident:* full-time $6780; part-time $226 per unit. *Required fees:* full-time $2959; $579 per term part-time. *College room and board:* $5946.

FRESHMAN FINANCIAL AID (Fall 2003) 574 applied for aid; of those 82% were deemed to have need. 96% of freshmen with need received aid; of those 11% had need fully met. *Average percent of need met:* 82% (excluding resources awarded to replace EFC). *Average financial aid package:* $6672 (excluding resources awarded to replace EFC). 10% of all full-time freshmen had no need and received non-need-based gift aid.

UNDERGRADUATE FINANCIAL AID (Fall 2003) 3,893 applied for aid; of those 88% were deemed to have need. 96% of undergraduates with need received aid; of those 15% had need fully met. *Average percent of need met:* 84% (excluding resources awarded to replace EFC). *Average financial aid package:* $6791 (excluding resources awarded to replace EFC). 3% of all full-time undergraduates had no need and received non-need-based gift aid.

GIFT AID (NEED-BASED) *Total amount:* $14,726,170 (51% federal, 49% state). *Receiving aid:* Freshmen: 55% (413); All full-time undergraduates: 53% (2,893). *Average award:* Freshmen: $5840; Undergraduates: $4921. *Scholarships, grants, and awards:* Federal Pell, FSEOG, state, private, college/university gift aid from institutional funds, Federal Nursing.

GIFT AID (NON-NEED-BASED) *Total amount:* $870,866 (51% institutional, 49% external sources). *Receiving aid:* Freshmen: 16% (119); Undergraduates: 7% (382). *Average Award:* Freshmen: $1791; Undergraduates: $1855. *Scholarships, grants, and awards by category: Academic Interests/Achievement:* 569 awards ($827,324 total): architecture, biological sciences, business, communication, education, general academic interests/achievements, health fields, mathematics, physical sciences, social sciences. *Creative Arts/Performance:* 71 awards ($32,910 total): art/fine arts, dance, music, theater/drama. *Special Achievements/Activities:* 29 awards ($34,112 total): community service, general special achievements/activities. *Special Characteristics:* 178 awards ($236,519 total): adult students, children of faculty/staff, first-generation college students, general special characteristics, handicapped students.

LOANS *Student loans:* $8,884,278 (77% need-based, 23% non-need-based). 11% of past graduating class borrowed through all loan programs. *Average indebtedness per student:* $4045. *Average need-based loan:* Freshmen: $2124; Undergraduates: $3459. *Parent loans:* $87,645 (100% non-need-based). *Programs:* Federal Direct (Subsidized and Unsubsidized Stafford, PLUS), Perkins, Federal Nursing, college/university.

WORK-STUDY *Federal work-study:* Total amount: $309,904; 179 jobs averaging $1861.

ATHLETIC AWARDS *Total amount:* $597,058 (100% non-need-based).

APPLYING FOR FINANCIAL AID *Required financial aid form:* FAFSA. *Financial aid deadline (priority):* 3/2. *Notification date:* 5/1. Students must reply within 3 weeks of notification.

CONTACT Mr. John Casdorph, Associate Director of Financial Aid, California State University, Bakersfield, 9001 Stockdale Highway, Bakersfield, CA 93311-1099, 661-664-3016 or toll-free 800-788-2782 (in-state). *Fax:* 661-665-6800.

CALIFORNIA STATE UNIVERSITY, CHICO
Chico, CA

Tuition & fees (CA res): $3154	Average undergraduate aid package: $7875

ABOUT THE INSTITUTION State-supported, coed. Awards: bachelor's and master's degrees and post-bachelor's and post-master's certificates. 121 undergraduate majors. Total enrollment: 15,734. Undergraduates: 14,279. Freshmen: 2,234. Federal methodology is used as a basis for awarding need-based institutional aid.

UNDERGRADUATE EXPENSES for 2004–05 *Application fee:* $55. *Tuition, state resident:* full-time $0. *Tuition, nonresident:* full-time $12,504; part-time $339 per unit. Part-time tuition and fees vary according to course load. *College room and board:* $7493; *room only:* $5114. Room and board charges vary according to board plan and housing facility. *Payment plans:* Installment, deferred payment.

FRESHMAN FINANCIAL AID (Fall 2003) 1337 applied for aid; of those 95% were deemed to have need. 83% of freshmen with need received aid; of those 10% had need fully met. *Average percent of need met:* 65% (excluding resources awarded to replace EFC). *Average financial aid package:* $6032 (excluding resources awarded to replace EFC).

UNDERGRADUATE FINANCIAL AID (Fall 2003) 7,361 applied for aid; of those 97% were deemed to have need. 93% of undergraduates with need received aid; of those 13% had need fully met. *Average percent of need met:* 78% (excluding resources awarded to replace EFC). *Average financial aid package:* $7875 (excluding resources awarded to replace EFC).

GIFT AID (NEED-BASED) *Total amount:* $29,006,633 (52% federal, 48% state). *Receiving aid:* Freshmen: 30% (665); All full-time undergraduates: 35% (4,476). *Average award:* Freshmen: $5345; Undergraduates: $5400. *Scholarships, grants, and awards:* Federal Pell, FSEOG, state, private, college/university gift aid from institutional funds, United Negro College Fund.

GIFT AID (NON-NEED-BASED) *Total amount:* $2,433,466 (1% federal, 2% state, 48% institutional, 49% external sources). *Receiving aid:* Freshmen: 12% (256); Undergraduates: 19% (2,480). *Scholarships, grants, and awards by category: Academic Interests/Achievement:* agriculture, area/ethnic studies, biological sciences, business, communication, computer science, education, engineering/technologies, English, foreign languages, general academic interests/achievements, health fields, humanities, international studies, mathematics, physical sciences, social sciences. *Creative Arts/Performance:* applied art and design, art/fine arts, cinema/film/broadcasting, creative writing, dance, debating, general creative arts/performance, journalism/publications, music, performing arts, theater/drama. *Special Achievements/Activities:* community service, general special achievements/activities, hobbies/interests, leadership, memberships. *Special Characteristics:* adult students, children of faculty/staff, ethnic background, first-generation college students, handicapped students, international students, local/state students, married students, members of minority groups, out-of-state students. *Tuition waivers:* Full or partial for employees or children of employees, senior citizens.

LOANS *Student loans:* $36,048,793 (71% need-based, 29% non-need-based). *Average need-based loan:* Freshmen: $2796; Undergraduates: $4155. *Parent loans:* $3,199,393 (100% non-need-based). *Programs:* Federal Direct (Subsidized and Unsubsidized Stafford, PLUS), Perkins, college/university.

WORK-STUDY *Federal work-study:* Total amount: $5,821,558; 750 jobs averaging $2500.

ATHLETIC AWARDS *Total amount:* $362,362 (70% need-based, 30% non-need-based).

APPLYING FOR FINANCIAL AID *Required financial aid forms:* FAFSA, scholarship application form. *Financial aid deadline:* Continuous. *Notification date:* Continuous beginning 2/15.

CONTACT Yvonne Lydon, Administrative Support Coordinator, California State University, Chico, Financial Aid Office, Chico, CA 95929-0705, 530-898-6451 or toll-free 800-542-4426. *Fax:* 530-898-6883. *E-mail:* ylydon@csuchico.edu.

CALIFORNIA STATE UNIVERSITY, DOMINGUEZ HILLS
Carson, CA

Tuition & fees (CA res): $2478   **Average undergraduate aid package: $7625**

ABOUT THE INSTITUTION State-supported, coed. Awards: bachelor's and master's degrees. 70 undergraduate majors. Total enrollment: 12,613. Undergraduates: 8,698. Freshmen: 733. Federal methodology is used as a basis for awarding need-based institutional aid.

UNDERGRADUATE EXPENSES for 2004–05 *Application fee:* $55. *Tuition, state resident:* full-time $0. *Tuition, nonresident:* full-time $8460; part-time $282 per unit. *Required fees:* full-time $2478; $216 per term part-time. Part-time tuition and fees vary according to course load. *College room and board: room only:* $5022. Room and board charges vary according to housing facility. *Payment plan:* Installment.

FRESHMAN FINANCIAL AID (Fall 2003) 503 applied for aid; of those 98% were deemed to have need. 99% of freshmen with need received aid; of those 8% had need fully met. *Average percent of need met:* 74% (excluding resources awarded to replace EFC). *Average financial aid package:* $7080 (excluding resources awarded to replace EFC). 1% of all full-time freshmen had no need and received non-need-based gift aid.

UNDERGRADUATE FINANCIAL AID (Fall 2003) 3,831 applied for aid; of those 99% were deemed to have need. 98% of undergraduates with need received aid; of those 9% had need fully met. *Average percent of need met:* 68% (excluding resources awarded to replace EFC). *Average financial aid package:* $7625 (excluding resources awarded to replace EFC). 1% of all full-time undergraduates had no need and received non-need-based gift aid.

GIFT AID (NEED-BASED) *Total amount:* $21,606,600 (54% federal, 44% state, 2% external sources). *Receiving aid:* Freshmen: 66% (460); All full-time undergraduates: 64% (3,522). *Average award:* Freshmen: $5692; Undergraduates: $4679. *Scholarships, grants, and awards:* Federal Pell, FSEOG, state, private, college/university gift aid from institutional funds.

GIFT AID (NON-NEED-BASED) *Total amount:* $27,172 (1% federal, 4% state, 19% institutional, 76% external sources). *Receiving aid:* Freshmen: 16% (110); Undergraduates: 6% (312). *Average Award:* Freshmen: $2274; Undergraduates:* $3337. *Scholarships, grants, and awards by category: Academic Interests/Achievement:* 329 awards ($239,511 total): general academic interests/achievements. *Special Characteristics:* 50 awards ($51,458 total): ethnic background, members of minority groups. *Tuition waivers:* Full or partial for employees or children of employees. *ROTC:* Army cooperative, Air Force cooperative.

LOANS *Student loans:* $14,834,155 (94% need-based, 6% non-need-based). 55% of past graduating class borrowed through all loan programs. *Average indebtedness per student:* $15,112. *Average need-based loan:* Freshmen: $2340; Undergraduates: $4316. *Parent loans:* $113,067 (68% need-based, 32% non-need-based). *Programs:* Federal Direct (Subsidized and Unsubsidized Stafford), FFEL (PLUS), Perkins.

WORK-STUDY *Federal work-study:* Total amount: $678,047; 241 jobs averaging $2671.

ATHLETIC AWARDS *Total amount:* $207,103 (84% need-based, 16% non-need-based).

APPLYING FOR FINANCIAL AID *Required financial aid forms:* FAFSA, institution's own form, state aid form. *Financial aid deadline:* 4/15 (priority: 3/2). *Notification date:* Continuous. Students must reply within 4 weeks of notification.

CONTACT Mrs. Delores S. Lee, Director of Financial Aid, California State University, Dominguez Hills, 1000 East Victoria Street, Carson, CA 90747-0001, 310-243-3691. *E-mail:* dslee@csudh.edu.

CALIFORNIA STATE UNIVERSITY, EAST BAY
Hayward, CA

Tuition & fees (CA res): $2706   **Average undergraduate aid package: $7614**

ABOUT THE INSTITUTION State-supported, coed. Awards: bachelor's and master's degrees and post-bachelor's certificates. 91 undergraduate majors. Total enrollment: 13,061. Undergraduates: 9,402. Federal methodology is used as a basis for awarding need-based institutional aid.

UNDERGRADUATE EXPENSES for 2004–05 *Application fee:* $55. *Tuition, state resident:* full-time $0. *Tuition, nonresident:* full-time $10,170; part-time $226 per unit. *Required fees:* full-time $2706; $576 per term part-time. *College room and board: room only:* $3705.

FRESHMAN FINANCIAL AID (Fall 2004, est.) 360 applied for aid; of those 89% were deemed to have need. 96% of freshmen with need received aid; of those 9% had need fully met. *Average percent of need met:* 69% (excluding resources awarded to replace EFC). *Average financial aid package:* $7412 (excluding resources awarded to replace EFC).

UNDERGRADUATE FINANCIAL AID (Fall 2004, est.) 3,544 applied for aid; of those 93% were deemed to have need. 99% of undergraduates with need received aid; of those 9% had need fully met. *Average percent of need met:* 62% (excluding resources awarded to replace EFC). *Average financial aid package:* $7614 (excluding resources awarded to replace EFC).

GIFT AID (NEED-BASED) *Receiving aid:* Freshmen: 33% (281); All full-time undergraduates: 36% (2,654). *Average award:* Freshmen: $7036; Undergraduates: $6081. *Scholarships, grants, and awards:* Federal Pell, FSEOG, state, private, college/university gift aid from institutional funds.

GIFT AID (NON-NEED-BASED) *Scholarships, grants, and awards by category:* *Academic Interests/Achievement:* general academic interests/achievements. *Creative Arts/Performance:* 5 awards ($4100 total): music.
LOANS *Student loans:* $13,907,885 (82% need-based, 18% non-need-based). 35% of past graduating class borrowed through all loan programs. *Average indebtedness per student:* $12,584. *Average need-based loan:* Freshmen: $2624; Undergraduates: $5656. *Parent loans:* $688,455 (24% need-based, 76% non-need-based). *Programs:* FFEL (Subsidized and Unsubsidized Stafford, PLUS), Perkins, college/university.
WORK-STUDY *Federal work-study:* Total amount: $536,849; jobs available.
APPLYING FOR FINANCIAL AID *Required financial aid form:* FAFSA. *Financial aid deadline (priority):* 3/2. *Notification date:* Continuous beginning 5/31. Students must reply within 3 weeks of notification.
CONTACT Office of Financial Aid, California State University, East Bay, 25800 Carlos Bee Boulevard, Hayward, CA 94542-3028, 510-885-2784. *Fax:* 510-885-2161. *E-mail:* finaid@csuhayward.edu.

CALIFORNIA STATE UNIVERSITY, FRESNO
Fresno, CA

Tuition & fees (CA res): $2704	Average undergraduate aid package: $5084

ABOUT THE INSTITUTION State-supported, coed. Awards: bachelor's, master's, and doctoral degrees. 87 undergraduate majors. Total enrollment: 19,781. Undergraduates: 16,650. Freshmen: 2,302. Federal methodology is used as a basis for awarding need-based institutional aid.
UNDERGRADUATE EXPENSES for 2004–05 *Application fee:* $55. *Tuition, state resident:* full-time $0. *Tuition, nonresident:* full-time $11,164; part-time $282 per unit. *Required fees:* full-time $2704; $863 per term part-time. *College room and board:* $7073. Room and board charges vary according to board plan.
FRESHMAN FINANCIAL AID (Fall 2004, est.) 1952 applied for aid; of those 84% were deemed to have need. 62% of freshmen with need received aid; of those 30% had need fully met. *Average percent of need met:* 29% (excluding resources awarded to replace EFC). *Average financial aid package:* $4197 (excluding resources awarded to replace EFC). 2% of all full-time freshmen had no need and received non-need-based gift aid.
UNDERGRADUATE FINANCIAL AID (Fall 2004, est.) 12,494 applied for aid; of those 75% were deemed to have need. 92% of undergraduates with need received aid; of those 45% had need fully met. *Average percent of need met:* 44% (excluding resources awarded to replace EFC). *Average financial aid package:* $5084 (excluding resources awarded to replace EFC). 1% of all full-time undergraduates had no need and received non-need-based gift aid.
GIFT AID (NEED-BASED) *Total amount:* $44,066,884 (50% federal, 50% state). *Receiving aid:* Freshmen: 32% (717); All full-time undergraduates: 45% (7,011). *Average award:* Freshmen: $4334; Undergraduates: $3640. *Scholarships, grants, and awards:* Federal Pell, FSEOG, state, private, college/university gift aid from institutional funds.
GIFT AID (NON-NEED-BASED) *Total amount:* $4,338,704 (53% institutional, 47% external sources). *Receiving aid:* Freshmen: 10% (225); Undergraduates: 10% (1,560). *Average Award:* Freshmen: $1431; Undergraduates: $2021. *Scholarships, grants, and awards by category:* Academic Interests/Achievement: 1,306 awards ($2,215,940 total): agriculture, area/ethnic studies, biological sciences, business, communication, education, engineering/technologies, English, foreign languages, general academic interests/achievements, health fields, humanities, mathematics, social sciences. *Creative Arts/Performance:* 236 awards ($183,814 total): art/fine arts, journalism/publications, music, theater/drama. *Special Achievements/Activities:* 23 awards ($27,600 total): community service. *Special Characteristics:* 10 awards ($8860 total): handicapped students, local/state students. *ROTC:* Army, Air Force.
LOANS *Student loans:* $24,862,528 (67% need-based, 33% non-need-based). 39% of past graduating class borrowed through all loan programs. *Average indebtedness per student:* $11,457. *Average need-based loan:* Freshmen: $2302; Undergraduates: $3405. *Parent loans:* $1,322,899 (100% non-need-based). *Programs:* FFEL (Subsidized and Unsubsidized Stafford, PLUS), Perkins, Federal Nursing, college/university.
WORK-STUDY *Federal work-study:* Total amount: $997,229; 333 jobs averaging $3012.
ATHLETIC AWARDS *Total amount:* $3,017,753 (100% non-need-based).
APPLYING FOR FINANCIAL AID *Required financial aid form:* FAFSA. *Financial aid deadline (priority):* 3/1. *Notification date:* Continuous beginning 4/1. Students must reply within 3 weeks of notification.

CONTACT Financial Aid Office, California State University, Fresno, 5150 North Maple Avenue, Mail Stop JA 64, Fresno, CA 93740, 559-278-2182. *Fax:* 559-278-4833.

CALIFORNIA STATE UNIVERSITY, FULLERTON
Fullerton, CA

Tuition & fees (CA res): $2804	Average undergraduate aid package: $6689

ABOUT THE INSTITUTION State-supported, coed. Awards: bachelor's and master's degrees. 88 undergraduate majors. Total enrollment: 32,744. Undergraduates: 27,228. Freshmen: 3,627. Federal methodology is used as a basis for awarding need-based institutional aid.
UNDERGRADUATE EXPENSES for 2004–05 *Application fee:* $55. *Tuition, state resident:* full-time $0. *Tuition, nonresident:* full-time $10,170; part-time $339 per unit. *Required fees:* full-time $2804; $913 per term. Full-time tuition and fees vary according to course load. Part-time tuition and fees vary according to course load. *College room and board: room only:* $4356. *Payment plans:* Installment, deferred payment.
FRESHMAN FINANCIAL AID (Fall 2004, est.) 2486 applied for aid; of those 69% were deemed to have need. 73% of freshmen with need received aid; of those 4% had need fully met. *Average percent of need met:* 62% (excluding resources awarded to replace EFC). *Average financial aid package:* $6289 (excluding resources awarded to replace EFC). 11% of all full-time freshmen had no need and received non-need-based gift aid.
UNDERGRADUATE FINANCIAL AID (Fall 2004, est.) 11,080 applied for aid; of those 81% were deemed to have need. 80% of undergraduates with need received aid; of those 3% had need fully met. *Average percent of need met:* 61% (excluding resources awarded to replace EFC). *Average financial aid package:* $6689 (excluding resources awarded to replace EFC). 7% of all full-time undergraduates had no need and received non-need-based gift aid.
GIFT AID (NEED-BASED) *Total amount:* $38,810,090 (51% federal, 49% state). *Receiving aid:* Freshmen: 30% (1,076); All full-time undergraduates: 29% (5,671). *Average award:* Freshmen: $6122; Undergraduates: $5648. *Scholarships, grants, and awards:* Federal Pell, FSEOG, state, private, college/university gift aid from institutional funds.
GIFT AID (NON-NEED-BASED) *Total amount:* $876,346 (29% institutional, 71% external sources). *Average Award:* Freshmen: $3197; Undergraduates: $4087. *Scholarships, grants, and awards by category:* Academic Interests/Achievement: 1,936 awards ($3,757,129 total): business, communication, engineering/technologies, general academic interests/achievements, humanities, mathematics, military science, social sciences. *Creative Arts/Performance:* 19 awards ($59,684 total): art/fine arts, music. *Special Achievements/Activities:* 5 awards ($14,716 total): general special achievements/activities, leadership. *Special Characteristics:* 40 awards ($168,471 total): general special characteristics. *Tuition waivers:* Full or partial for employees or children of employees, senior citizens. *ROTC:* Army.
LOANS *Student loans:* $35,815,144 (63% need-based, 37% non-need-based). 42% of past graduating class borrowed through all loan programs. *Average indebtedness per student:* $13,089. *Average need-based loan:* Freshmen: $2528; Undergraduates: $4082. *Parent loans:* $1,701,151 (100% non-need-based). *Programs:* FFEL (Subsidized and Unsubsidized Stafford, PLUS), Perkins, college/university.
WORK-STUDY *Federal work-study:* Total amount: $1,263,066; 1,424 jobs averaging $2940.
ATHLETIC AWARDS *Total amount:* $1,280,042 (100% non-need-based).
APPLYING FOR FINANCIAL AID *Required financial aid form:* FAFSA. *Financial aid deadline (priority):* 3/2. *Notification date:* Continuous beginning 4/2. Students must reply within 3 weeks of notification.
CONTACT Ms. Deborah S. McCracken, Director of Financial Aid, California State University, Fullerton, 800 North State College Boulevard, Fullerton, CA 92831-3599, 714-278-3128. *Fax:* 714-278-1328. *E-mail:* dmccracken@fullerton.edu.

CALIFORNIA STATE UNIVERSITY, HAYWARD
Hayward, CA

See California State University, East Bay.

CALIFORNIA STATE UNIVERSITY, LONG BEACH
Long Beach, CA

ABOUT THE INSTITUTION State-supported, coed. Awards: bachelor's and master's degrees and post-bachelor's certificates. 150 undergraduate majors. Total enrollment: 33,479. Undergraduates: 27,180. Freshmen: 3,408.

GIFT AID (NEED-BASED) *Scholarships, grants, and awards:* Federal Pell, FSEOG, state, private, college/university gift aid from institutional funds.

GIFT AID (NON-NEED-BASED) *Scholarships, grants, and awards by category: Academic Interests/Achievement:* general academic interests/achievements. *Creative Arts/Performance:* applied art and design, cinema/film/broadcasting, dance, music, performing arts, theater/drama.

LOANS *Programs:* FFEL (Subsidized and Unsubsidized Stafford, PLUS), Perkins.

WORK-STUDY *Federal work-study:* Total amount: $1,600,000; 850 jobs averaging $1882.

APPLYING FOR FINANCIAL AID *Required financial aid form:* FAFSA.

CONTACT Office of Financial Aid, California State University, Long Beach, 1250 Bellflower Boulevard, Long Beach, CA 90840, 562-985-8403.

CALIFORNIA STATE UNIVERSITY, LOS ANGELES
Los Angeles, CA

ABOUT THE INSTITUTION State-supported, coed. Awards: bachelor's, master's, and doctoral degrees. 65 undergraduate majors. Total enrollment: 20,637. Undergraduates: 14,421.

GIFT AID (NEED-BASED) *Scholarships, grants, and awards:* Federal Pell, FSEOG, state, private, college/university gift aid from institutional funds.

GIFT AID (NON-NEED-BASED) *Scholarships, grants, and awards by category: Academic Interests/Achievement:* biological sciences, business, communication, computer science, education, engineering/technologies, English, foreign languages, general academic interests/achievements, health fields, mathematics, physical sciences, social sciences. *Creative Arts/Performance:* art/fine arts, general creative arts/performance, journalism/publications, music, theater/drama. *Special Achievements/Activities:* community service, general special achievements/activities. *Special Characteristics:* general special characteristics.

LOANS *Programs:* Federal Direct (Subsidized and Unsubsidized Stafford), FFEL (PLUS), Perkins, Federal Nursing.

WORK-STUDY *Federal work-study:* Total amount: $1,215,089; 276 jobs averaging $4402.

APPLYING FOR FINANCIAL AID *Required financial aid form:* FAFSA.

CONTACT Lindy W. Fong, Director, Center for Student Financial Aid, California State University, Los Angeles, 5151 State University Drive, Los Angeles, CA 90032, 323-343-3247. *Fax:* 323-343-3166. *E-mail:* lfong@cslanet.calstatela.edu.

CALIFORNIA STATE UNIVERSITY, MONTEREY BAY
Seaside, CA

ABOUT THE INSTITUTION State-supported, coed. Awards: bachelor's and master's degrees and post-bachelor's certificates. 16 undergraduate majors. Total enrollment: 3,020. Undergraduates: 2,753. Freshmen: 565.

GIFT AID (NEED-BASED) *Scholarships, grants, and awards:* Federal Pell, FSEOG, state, college/university gift aid from institutional funds.

GIFT AID (NON-NEED-BASED) *Scholarships, grants, and awards by category: Academic Interests/Achievement:* business. *Special Characteristics:* general special characteristics, local/state students.

LOANS *Programs:* FFEL (Subsidized and Unsubsidized Stafford, PLUS), Perkins.

APPLYING FOR FINANCIAL AID *Required financial aid forms:* FAFSA, state aid form.

CONTACT Campus Service Center, California State University, Monterey Bay, 100 Campus Center, Seaside, CA 93955-8001, 831-582-4074. *Fax:* 831-582-3782.

CALIFORNIA STATE UNIVERSITY, NORTHRIDGE
Northridge, CA

ABOUT THE INSTITUTION State-supported, coed. Awards: bachelor's and master's degrees. 132 undergraduate majors. Total enrollment: 31,448. Undergraduates: 24,462. Freshmen: 3,298.

GIFT AID (NEED-BASED) *Scholarships, grants, and awards:* Federal Pell, FSEOG, state, private, college/university gift aid from institutional funds.

GIFT AID (NON-NEED-BASED) *Scholarships, grants, and awards by category: Academic Interests/Achievement:* business, communication, computer science, education, engineering/technologies, English, general academic interests/achievements, mathematics, social sciences. *Creative Arts/Performance:* journalism/publications, music. *Special Achievements/Activities:* leadership.

LOANS *Programs:* FFEL (Subsidized and Unsubsidized Stafford, PLUS), Perkins, college/university.

WORK-STUDY *Federal work-study:* Total amount: $1,748,076; 859 jobs averaging $1823.

APPLYING FOR FINANCIAL AID *Required financial aid forms:* FAFSA, state aid form.

CONTACT Kathryn J. Anderson, Director of Financial Aid and Scholarships, California State University, Northridge, 18111 Nordhoff Street, Northridge, CA 91330-8307, 818-677-3827. *Fax:* 818-677-6787. *E-mail:* kathryn.anderson@csun.edu.

CALIFORNIA STATE UNIVERSITY, SACRAMENTO
Sacramento, CA

Tuition & fees (CA res): $3010   **Average undergraduate aid package: $8273**

ABOUT THE INSTITUTION State-supported, coed. Awards: bachelor's, master's, and doctoral degrees. 84 undergraduate majors. Total enrollment: 27,972. Undergraduates: 22,555. Freshmen: 2,340. Federal methodology is used as a basis for awarding need-based institutional aid.

UNDERGRADUATE EXPENSES for 2004–05 *Application fee:* $55. *Tuition, state resident:* full-time $0. *Tuition, nonresident:* full-time $12,690; part-time $339 per unit. *Required fees:* full-time $3010; $245 per term part-time. *College room and board:* $6574; *room only:* $4338. Room and board charges vary according to board plan. *Payment plan:* Installment.

FRESHMAN FINANCIAL AID (Fall 2003) 1489 applied for aid; of those 77% were deemed to have need. 91% of freshmen with need received aid; of those 4% had need fully met. *Average percent of need met:* 67% (excluding resources awarded to replace EFC). *Average financial aid package:* $8191 (excluding resources awarded to replace EFC). 5% of all full-time freshmen had no need and received non-need-based gift aid.

UNDERGRADUATE FINANCIAL AID (Fall 2003) 10,401 applied for aid; of those 86% were deemed to have need. 93% of undergraduates with need received aid; of those 7% had need fully met. *Average percent of need met:* 66% (excluding resources awarded to replace EFC). *Average financial aid package:* $8273 (excluding resources awarded to replace EFC). 5% of all full-time undergraduates had no need and received non-need-based gift aid.

GIFT AID (NEED-BASED) *Total amount:* $39,980,767 (50% federal, 46% state, 1% institutional, 3% external sources). *Receiving aid:* Freshmen: 39% (879); All full-time undergraduates: 38% (6,551). *Average award:* Freshmen: $2125; Undergraduates: $2154. *Scholarships, grants, and awards:* Federal Pell, FSEOG, state, private, college/university gift aid from institutional funds, Federal Nursing.

GIFT AID (NON-NEED-BASED) *Total amount:* $5562 (50% institutional, 50% external sources). *Receiving aid:* Freshmen: 1; Undergraduates: 6. *Average Award:* Freshmen: $5633; Undergraduates: $5731. *Scholarships, grants, and awards by category: Academic Interests/Achievement:* general academic interests/achievements. *Creative Arts/Performance:* general creative arts/performance. *Special Achievements/Activities:* general special achievements/activities. *Special Characteristics:* general special characteristics. *Tuition waivers:* Full or partial for employees or children of employees, senior citizens. *ROTC:* Army cooperative, Air Force.

LOANS *Student loans:* $40,139,987 (62% need-based, 38% non-need-based). 36% of past graduating class borrowed through all loan programs. *Average indebtedness per student:* $17,305. *Average need-based loan:* Freshmen: $2498;

California State University, Sacramento

Undergraduates: $4037. *Parent loans:* $8,445,289 (100% non-need-based). *Programs:* Federal Direct (Subsidized and Unsubsidized Stafford), FFEL (PLUS), Perkins, Federal Nursing, state, college/university.

WORK-STUDY *Federal work-study:* Total amount: $1,491,507; 587 jobs averaging $2540. *State or other work-study/employment:* Total amount: $61,531 (100% need-based). 26 part-time jobs averaging $2350.

ATHLETIC AWARDS *Total amount:* $2,117,149 (100% need-based).

APPLYING FOR FINANCIAL AID *Required financial aid form:* FAFSA. *Financial aid deadline (priority):* 3/2. *Notification date:* 4/1. Students must reply within 2 weeks of notification.

CONTACT Linda Joy Clemons, Financial Aid Director, California State University, Sacramento, 6000 J Street, Sacramento, CA 95819-6044, 916-278-6554. *Fax:* 916-278-6082. *E-mail:* ljclemons@csus.edu.

CALIFORNIA STATE UNIVERSITY, SAN BERNARDINO
San Bernardino, CA

Tuition & fees (CA res): $3398	Average undergraduate aid package: $8810

ABOUT THE INSTITUTION State-supported, coed. Awards: bachelor's and master's degrees. 55 undergraduate majors. Total enrollment: 16,195. Undergraduates: 12,109. Freshmen: 1,629. Federal methodology is used as a basis for awarding need-based institutional aid.

UNDERGRADUATE EXPENSES for 2005–06 *Application fee:* $55. *Tuition, state resident:* full-time $0. *Tuition, nonresident:* full-time $8136; part-time $226 per unit. Part-time tuition and fees vary according to course load. *College room and board:* $5886; *room only:* $4376. Room and board charges vary according to board plan and housing facility.

FRESHMAN FINANCIAL AID (Fall 2003) 999 applied for aid; of those 91% were deemed to have need. 100% of freshmen with need received aid; of those 9% had need fully met. *Average percent of need met:* 68% (excluding resources awarded to replace EFC). *Average financial aid package:* $6614 (excluding resources awarded to replace EFC). 1% of all full-time freshmen had no need and received non-need-based gift aid.

UNDERGRADUATE FINANCIAL AID (Fall 2003) 7,935 applied for aid; of those 92% were deemed to have need. 100% of undergraduates with need received aid; of those 14% had need fully met. *Average percent of need met:* 41% (excluding resources awarded to replace EFC). *Average financial aid package:* $8810 (excluding resources awarded to replace EFC). 1% of all full-time undergraduates had no need and received non-need-based gift aid.

GIFT AID (NEED-BASED) *Total amount:* $34,958,264 (53% federal, 46% state, 1% external sources). *Receiving aid:* Freshmen: 51% (824); All full-time undergraduates: 51% (6,232). *Average award:* Freshmen: $5772; Undergraduates: $5153. *Scholarships, grants, and awards:* Federal Pell, FSEOG, state, college/university gift aid from institutional funds.

GIFT AID (NON-NEED-BASED) *Total amount:* $2,345,442 (64% federal, 3% state, 13% institutional, 20% external sources). *Receiving aid:* Freshmen: 9% (154); Undergraduates: 2% (284). *Average Award:* Freshmen: $791; Undergraduates: $936. *Scholarships, grants, and awards by category: Academic Interests/Achievement:* 127 awards ($305,350 total): biological sciences, business, computer science, education, foreign languages, general academic interests/achievements, health fields. *Creative Arts/Performance:* 25 awards ($23,410 total): art/fine arts, music, theater/drama. *Special Achievements/Activities:* 36 awards ($36,000 total): community service, general special achievements/activities, hobbies/interests. *Special Characteristics:* 6 awards ($14,800 total): children of public servants, children with a deceased or disabled parent, ethnic background, first-generation college students, handicapped students. *Tuition waivers:* Full or partial for employees or children of employees. *ROTC:* Army, Air Force.

LOANS *Student loans:* $51,069,962 (54% need-based, 46% non-need-based). *Average need-based loan:* Freshmen: $2032; Undergraduates: $3616. *Parent loans:* $508,246 (100% non-need-based). *Programs:* Federal Direct (Subsidized and Unsubsidized Stafford), FFEL (PLUS), Perkins.

WORK-STUDY *Federal work-study:* Total amount: $1,220,115; 414 jobs averaging $2947. *State or other work-study/employment:* Part-time jobs available.

ATHLETIC AWARDS *Total amount:* $409,063 (100% non-need-based).

APPLYING FOR FINANCIAL AID *Required financial aid forms:* FAFSA, state aid form. *Financial aid deadline (priority):* 3/2. *Notification date:* Continuous beginning 4/1.

CONTACT Lois E. Madsen, Director of Financial Aid, California State University, San Bernardino, 5500 University Parkway, San Bernardino, CA 92407-2397, 909-880-5223. *Fax:* 909-880-7024. *E-mail:* lemadsen@csusb.edu.

CALIFORNIA STATE UNIVERSITY, SAN MARCOS
San Marcos, CA

Tuition & fees (CA res): $2786	Average undergraduate aid package: $6904

ABOUT THE INSTITUTION State-supported, coed. Awards: bachelor's and master's degrees. 23 undergraduate majors. Total enrollment: 6,728. Undergraduates: 6,194. Freshmen: 722. Federal methodology is used as a basis for awarding need-based institutional aid.

UNDERGRADUATE EXPENSES for 2004–05 *Application fee:* $55. *Tuition, state resident:* full-time $0. *Tuition, nonresident:* full-time $8136; part-time $339 per credit hour. Part-time tuition and fees vary according to course load. *College room and board: room only:* $7470. Room and board charges vary according to housing facility.

FRESHMAN FINANCIAL AID (Fall 2003) 428 applied for aid; of those 65% were deemed to have need. 92% of freshmen with need received aid. *Average financial aid package:* $5481 (excluding resources awarded to replace EFC).

UNDERGRADUATE FINANCIAL AID (Fall 2003) 2,219 applied for aid; of those 82% were deemed to have need. 94% of undergraduates with need received aid. *Average financial aid package:* $6904 (excluding resources awarded to replace EFC).

GIFT AID (NEED-BASED) *Total amount:* $9,621,783 (55% federal, 37% state, 7% institutional, 1% external sources). *Receiving aid:* Freshmen: 39% (256); All full-time undergraduates: 42% (1,698). *Average award:* Undergraduates: $3588. *Scholarships, grants, and awards:* Federal Pell, FSEOG, state, private, college/university gift aid from institutional funds.

GIFT AID (NON-NEED-BASED) *Receiving aid:* Freshmen: 1% (4); Undergraduates: 17. *Scholarships, grants, and awards by category: Academic Interests/Achievement:* general academic interests/achievements, mathematics. *Tuition waivers:* Full or partial for employees or children of employees, senior citizens. *ROTC:* Army cooperative, Naval cooperative, Air Force cooperative.

LOANS *Student loans:* $8,160,629 (61% need-based, 39% non-need-based). 44% of past graduating class borrowed through all loan programs. *Average indebtedness per student:* $12,850. *Average need-based loan:* Undergraduates: $4026. *Parent loans:* $372,799 (100% non-need-based). *Programs:* Federal Direct (Subsidized and Unsubsidized Stafford, PLUS), Perkins, college/university.

WORK-STUDY *Federal work-study:* Total amount: $411,652; 193 jobs averaging $2035. *State or other work-study/employment:* Total amount: $10,887 (100% need-based). 18 part-time jobs averaging $821.

ATHLETIC AWARDS *Total amount:* $115,573 (100% non-need-based).

APPLYING FOR FINANCIAL AID *Required financial aid form:* FAFSA. *Financial aid deadline (priority):* 3/2. *Notification date:* 4/15.

CONTACT Addalou Davis, Director of Financial Aid, California State University, San Marcos, 333 South Twin Oaks Valley Road, San Marcos, CA 92096-0001, 760-750-4852. *Fax:* 760-750-3047. *E-mail:* finaid@csusm.edu.

CALIFORNIA STATE UNIVERSITY, STANISLAUS
Turlock, CA

Tuition & fees (CA res): $2807	Average undergraduate aid package: $7353

ABOUT THE INSTITUTION State-supported, coed. Awards: bachelor's and master's degrees. 35 undergraduate majors. Total enrollment: 7,858. Undergraduates: 6,192. Freshmen: 747. Federal methodology is used as a basis for awarding need-based institutional aid.

UNDERGRADUATE EXPENSES for 2004–05 *Application fee:* $55. *Tuition, state resident:* full-time $0. *Tuition, nonresident:* full-time $10,170; part-time $339 per unit. *Required fees:* full-time $2807; $756 per term part-time. *College room and board:* $6522; *room only:* $3622. Room and board charges vary according to board plan and housing facility. *Payment plans:* Installment, deferred payment.

FRESHMAN FINANCIAL AID (Fall 2004, est.) 585 applied for aid; of those 74% were deemed to have need. 96% of freshmen with need received aid; of those 3% had need fully met. *Average percent of need met:* 69% (excluding resources

awarded to replace EFC). *Average financial aid package:* $7036 (excluding resources awarded to replace EFC). 11% of all full-time freshmen had no need and received non-need-based gift aid.

UNDERGRADUATE FINANCIAL AID (Fall 2004, est.) 3,746 applied for aid; of those 77% were deemed to have need. 97% of undergraduates with need received aid; of those 7% had need fully met. *Average percent of need met:* 64% (excluding resources awarded to replace EFC). *Average financial aid package:* $7353 (excluding resources awarded to replace EFC). 3% of all full-time undergraduates had no need and received non-need-based gift aid.

GIFT AID (NEED-BASED) *Total amount:* $14,678,673 (55% federal, 44% state, 1% institutional). *Receiving aid:* Freshmen: 51% (331); All full-time undergraduates: 60% (2,559). *Average award:* Freshmen: $5275; Undergraduates: $5147. *Scholarships, grants, and awards:* Federal Pell, FSEOG, state, private, college/university gift aid from institutional funds.

GIFT AID (NON-NEED-BASED) *Total amount:* $837,844 (39% institutional, 61% external sources). *Receiving aid:* Freshmen: 4% (29); Undergraduates: 2% (102). *Average Award:* *Freshmen:* $1601; *Undergraduates:* $1541. *Scholarships, grants, and awards by category: Academic Interests/Achievement:* 92 awards ($153,600 total): agriculture, area/ethnic studies, biological sciences, business, communication, computer science, education, English, foreign languages, general academic interests/achievements, health fields, humanities, mathematics, physical sciences, premedicine, social sciences. *Creative Arts/Performance:* 45 awards ($37,160 total): art/fine arts, music. *Special Achievements/Activities:* 141 awards ($255,750 total): community service, general special achievements/activities, leadership, memberships. *Special Characteristics:* 70 awards ($204,840 total): children of faculty/staff, ethnic background, first-generation college students, general special characteristics, local/state students, members of minority groups. *Tuition waivers:* Full or partial for employees or children of employees, adult students, senior citizens.

LOANS *Student loans:* $12,612,300 (100% need-based). 23% of past graduating class borrowed through all loan programs. *Average indebtedness per student:* $14,500. *Average need-based loan:* Freshmen: $2613; Undergraduates: $3935. *Parent loans:* $533,362 (100% non-need-based). *Programs:* FFEL (Subsidized and Unsubsidized Stafford, PLUS), Perkins, college/university.

WORK-STUDY *Federal work-study:* Total amount: $489,882; 172 jobs averaging $2848. *State or other work-study/employment:* Part-time jobs available.

ATHLETIC AWARDS *Total amount:* $252,177 (100% non-need-based).

APPLYING FOR FINANCIAL AID *Required financial aid forms:* FAFSA, state aid form. *Financial aid deadline (priority):* 3/2. *Notification date:* Continuous beginning 3/15. Students must reply within 3 weeks of notification.

CONTACT Mr. David Gomes, Interim Director of Financial Aid, California State University, Stanislaus, 801 West Monte Vista Avenue, Turlock, CA 95382, 209-667-3336 or toll-free 800-300-7420 (in-state). *Fax:* 209-664-7064. *E-mail:* dgomes@stan.csustan.edu.

CALIFORNIA UNIVERSITY OF PENNSYLVANIA
California, PA

CONTACT Financial Aid Office, California University of Pennsylvania, 250 University Avenue, California, PA 15419-1394, 724-938-4415.

CALUMET COLLEGE OF SAINT JOSEPH
Whiting, IN

ABOUT THE INSTITUTION Independent Roman Catholic, coed. Awards: associate, bachelor's, and master's degrees and post-bachelor's certificates. 28 undergraduate majors. Total enrollment: 1,327. Undergraduates: 1,249. Freshmen: 104.

GIFT AID (NEED-BASED) *Scholarships, grants, and awards:* Federal Pell, FSEOG, state, private, college/university gift aid from institutional funds.

LOANS *Programs:* FFEL (Subsidized and Unsubsidized Stafford, PLUS).

WORK-STUDY *Federal work-study:* Total amount: $65,000; 27 jobs averaging $2708. *State or other work-study/employment:* Total amount: $18,000 (100% need-based). 8 part-time jobs averaging $2250.

APPLYING FOR FINANCIAL AID *Required financial aid form:* FAFSA.

CONTACT Alexandra Victor, Vice President for Student Affairs, Calumet College of Saint Joseph, 2400 New York Avenue, Whiting, IN 46394-2195, 219-473-4219 or toll-free 877-700-9100. *E-mail:* avictor@ccsj.edu.

CALVARY BIBLE COLLEGE AND THEOLOGICAL SEMINARY
Kansas City, MO

Tuition & fees: $6612	Average undergraduate aid package: $6093

ABOUT THE INSTITUTION Independent nondenominational, coed. Awards: associate, bachelor's, master's, and first professional degrees. 18 undergraduate majors. Total enrollment: 320. Undergraduates: 262. Freshmen: 37. Federal methodology is used as a basis for awarding need-based institutional aid.

UNDERGRADUATE EXPENSES for 2004–05 *Application fee:* $25. *Comprehensive fee:* $10,312 includes full-time tuition ($6180), mandatory fees ($432), and room and board ($3700). Full-time tuition and fees vary according to course load. Room and board charges vary according to housing facility. *Part-time tuition:* $230 per credit. *Part-time fees:* $18 per credit. Part-time tuition and fees vary according to course load. *Payment plan:* Installment.

GIFT AID (NEED-BASED) *Total amount:* $356,910 (78% federal, 22% institutional). *Receiving aid:* Freshmen: 50% (15); All full-time undergraduates: 56% (105). *Average award:* Freshmen: $2278; Undergraduates: $2330. *Scholarships, grants, and awards:* Federal Pell, FSEOG, private, college/university gift aid from institutional funds.

GIFT AID (NON-NEED-BASED) *Total amount:* $48,788 (22% institutional, 78% external sources). *Receiving aid:* Freshmen: 27% (8); Undergraduates: 18% (34). *Scholarships, grants, and awards by category: Academic Interests/Achievement:* general academic interests/achievements. *Special Achievements/Activities:* general special achievements/activities, religious involvement. *Special Characteristics:* children and siblings of alumni, children of educators, relatives of clergy. *Tuition waivers:* Full or partial for employees or children of employees.

LOANS *Student loans:* $779,856 (67% need-based, 33% non-need-based). 42% of past graduating class borrowed through all loan programs. *Average indebtedness per student:* $4088. *Average need-based loan:* Freshmen: $849; Undergraduates: $1636. *Parent loans:* $47,442 (100% need-based). *Programs:* FFEL (Subsidized and Unsubsidized Stafford, PLUS), alternative loans.

APPLYING FOR FINANCIAL AID *Required financial aid forms:* FAFSA, institution's own form. *Financial aid deadline:* 4/1 (priority: 3/1). *Notification date:* Continuous beginning 5/15.

CONTACT Bonnie Baker, Financial Aid Administrator, Calvary Bible College and Theological Seminary, 15800 Calvary Road, Kansas City, MO 64147-1341, 816-322-5152 Ext. 1323 or toll-free 800-326-3960. *Fax:* 816-331-4474. *E-mail:* finaid@calvary.edu.

CALVIN COLLEGE
Grand Rapids, MI

Tuition & fees: $17,770	Average undergraduate aid package: $12,963

ABOUT THE INSTITUTION Independent religious, coed. Awards: bachelor's and master's degrees and post-bachelor's certificates. 82 undergraduate majors. Total enrollment: 4,180. Undergraduates: 4,127. Freshmen: 902. Both federal and institutional methodology are used as a basis for awarding need-based institutional aid.

UNDERGRADUATE EXPENSES for 2004–05 *Application fee:* $35. *Comprehensive fee:* $23,955 includes full-time tuition ($17,770) and room and board ($6185). *College room only:* $3360. Full-time tuition and fees vary according to program. Room and board charges vary according to board plan. *Part-time tuition:* $430 per credit hour. Part-time tuition and fees vary according to course load. *Payment plans:* Tuition prepayment, installment.

FRESHMAN FINANCIAL AID (Fall 2003) 853 applied for aid; of those 84% were deemed to have need. 100% of freshmen with need received aid; of those 29% had need fully met. *Average percent of need met:* 86% (excluding resources awarded to replace EFC). *Average financial aid package:* $13,056 (excluding resources awarded to replace EFC). 27% of all full-time freshmen had no need and received non-need-based gift aid.

UNDERGRADUATE FINANCIAL AID (Fall 2003) 3,093 applied for aid; of those 88% were deemed to have need. 100% of undergraduates with need received aid; of those 31% had need fully met. *Average percent of need met:* 84% (excluding resources awarded to replace EFC). *Average financial aid package:* $12,963 (excluding resources awarded to replace EFC). 26% of all full-time undergraduates had no need and received non-need-based gift aid.

GIFT AID (NEED-BASED) *Total amount:* $20,328,112 (11% federal, 13% state, 72% institutional, 4% external sources). *Receiving aid:* Freshmen: 68% (711);

Calvin College

All full-time undergraduates: 65% (2,668). *Average award:* Freshmen: $8304; Undergraduates: $7500. *Scholarships, grants, and awards:* Federal Pell, FSEOG, state, private, college/university gift aid from institutional funds.

GIFT AID (NON-NEED-BASED) *Total amount:* $4,422,747 (1% federal, 6% state, 86% institutional, 7% external sources). *Receiving aid:* Freshmen: 9% (94); Undergraduates: 7% (300). *Average Award:* Freshmen: $3617; Undergraduates: $3304. *Scholarships, grants, and awards by category: Academic Interests/ Achievement:* 3,330 awards ($8,350,000 total): biological sciences, business, communication, computer science, education, engineering/technologies, English, foreign languages, general academic interests/achievements, health fields, humanities, international studies, mathematics, physical sciences, premedicine, religion/ biblical studies, social sciences. *Creative Arts/Performance:* 65 awards ($72,000 total): art/fine arts, music, performing arts, theater/drama. *Special Achievements/ Activities:* 98 awards ($66,000 total): community service, religious involvement. *Special Characteristics:* 3,000 awards ($4,000,000 total): children and siblings of alumni, children of faculty/staff, children of union members/company employees, ethnic background, handicapped students, international students, members of minority groups, religious affiliation. *Tuition waivers:* Full or partial for employees or children of employees. *ROTC:* Army cooperative.

LOANS *Student loans:* $17,918,924 (72% need-based, 28% non-need-based). 68% of past graduating class borrowed through all loan programs. *Average indebtedness per student:* $18,805. *Average need-based loan:* Freshmen: $4335; Undergraduates: $6283. *Parent loans:* $1,038,927 (25% need-based, 75% non-need-based). *Programs:* Federal Direct (Subsidized and Unsubsidized Stafford, PLUS), Perkins, state, college/university, alternative loans.

WORK-STUDY *Federal work-study:* Total amount: $1,637,197; 660 jobs averaging $1140. *State or other work-study/employment:* Total amount: $1,610,106 (38% need-based, 62% non-need-based). 1,250 part-time jobs averaging $1150.

APPLYING FOR FINANCIAL AID *Required financial aid forms:* FAFSA, institution's own form. *Financial aid deadline (priority):* 2/15. *Notification date:* Continuous beginning 3/15.

CONTACT Mr. Dave Brummel, Financial Aid Counselor, Calvin College, Spoelhof Center 356, 3201 Burton Street, SE, Grand Rapids, MI 49546-4388, 616-526-6134 or toll-free 800-688-0122. *Fax:* 616-526-6883. *E-mail:* dlbrum@calvin. edu.

CAMBRIDGE COLLEGE
Cambridge, MA

ABOUT THE INSTITUTION Independent, coed. Awards: bachelor's and master's degrees and post-master's certificates. 4 undergraduate majors. Total enrollment: 3,795. Undergraduates: 793. Freshmen: 186.

GIFT AID (NEED-BASED) *Scholarships, grants, and awards:* Federal Pell, FSEOG, state, private, college/university gift aid from institutional funds.

GIFT AID (NON-NEED-BASED) *Scholarships, grants, and awards by category: Academic Interests/Achievement:* education.

LOANS *Programs:* FFEL (Subsidized and Unsubsidized Stafford, PLUS), Perkins, state.

APPLYING FOR FINANCIAL AID *Required financial aid forms:* FAFSA, institution's own form.

CONTACT Dr. Gerri Major, Director of Financial Aid, Cambridge College, 1000 Massachusetts Avenue, Cambridge, MA 02138, 617-868-1000 Ext. 137 or toll-free 800-877-4723. *Fax:* 617-349-3561. *E-mail:* gmajor@idea.cambridge. edu.

CAMERON UNIVERSITY
Lawton, OK

Tuition & fees (OK res): $3000	Average undergraduate aid package: N/A

ABOUT THE INSTITUTION State-supported, coed. Awards: bachelor's and master's degrees. 34 undergraduate majors. Total enrollment: 5,933. Undergraduates: 5,482. Freshmen: 1,084. Federal methodology is used as a basis for awarding need-based institutional aid.

UNDERGRADUATE EXPENSES for 2004–05 *Application fee:* $15. *Tuition, state resident:* full-time $3000; part-time $100 per semester hour. *Tuition, nonresident:* full-time $7260; part-time $242 per semester hour. Full-time tuition and fees vary according to course level, course load, degree level, and student level. Part-time tuition and fees vary according to course level, course load, degree level, and student level. *College room and board:* $3126. Room and board charges vary according to board plan. *Payment plan:* Installment.

GIFT AID (NEED-BASED) *Total amount:* $6,549,500 (82% federal, 8% state, 1% institutional, 9% external sources). *Scholarships, grants, and awards:* Federal Pell, FSEOG, state, private, college/university gift aid from institutional funds.

GIFT AID (NON-NEED-BASED) *Total amount:* $1,794,888 (10% institutional, 90% external sources). *Scholarships, grants, and awards by category: Academic Interests/Achievement:* agriculture, biological sciences, business, communication, computer science, education, engineering/technologies, English, foreign languages, general academic interests/achievements, mathematics, military science, social sciences. *Creative Arts/Performance:* art/fine arts, creative writing, debating, journalism/publications, music, theater/drama. *Special Achievements/ Activities:* 77 awards ($196,372 total): leadership. *Special Characteristics:* members of minority groups. *Tuition waivers:* Full or partial for employees or children of employees, senior citizens. *ROTC:* Army.

LOANS *Student loans:* $6,811,110 (66% need-based, 34% non-need-based). 35% of past graduating class borrowed through all loan programs. *Average indebtedness per student:* $6300. *Parent loans:* $30,127 (100% non-need-based). *Programs:* FFEL (Subsidized and Unsubsidized Stafford, PLUS).

WORK-STUDY *Federal work-study:* Total amount: $182,303; 150 jobs averaging $1215. *State or other work-study/employment:* Total amount: $440,955 (100% non-need-based). 286 part-time jobs averaging $1542.

ATHLETIC AWARDS *Total amount:* $341,315 (100% non-need-based).

APPLYING FOR FINANCIAL AID *Required financial aid form:* FAFSA. *Financial aid deadline:* Continuous. *Notification date:* Continuous beginning 7/1.

CONTACT Caryn Pacheco, Financial Aid Director, Cameron University, 2800 West Gore Boulevard, Lawton, OK 73505-6377, 580-581-2293 or toll-free 888-454-7600. *Fax:* 580-581-2556.

CAMPBELLSVILLE UNIVERSITY
Campbellsville, KY

Tuition & fees: $13,952	Average undergraduate aid package: $11,272

ABOUT THE INSTITUTION Independent religious, coed. Awards: associate, bachelor's, and master's degrees and post-bachelor's certificates. 54 undergraduate majors. Total enrollment: 2,187. Undergraduates: 1,814. Freshmen: 394. Federal methodology is used as a basis for awarding need-based institutional aid.

UNDERGRADUATE EXPENSES for 2004–05 *Application fee:* $20. *Comprehensive fee:* $19,392 includes full-time tuition ($13,632), mandatory fees ($320), and room and board ($5440). *College room only:* $2500. Room and board charges vary according to board plan and housing facility. *Part-time tuition:* $568 per credit. *Part-time fees:* $50 per term. *Payment plan:* Installment.

FRESHMAN FINANCIAL AID (Fall 2003) 345 applied for aid; of those 91% were deemed to have need. 100% of freshmen with need received aid; of those 22% had need fully met. *Average percent of need met:* 77% (excluding resources awarded to replace EFC). *Average financial aid package:* $12,225 (excluding resources awarded to replace EFC). 12% of all full-time freshmen had no need and received non-need-based gift aid.

UNDERGRADUATE FINANCIAL AID (Fall 2003) 1,041 applied for aid; of those 93% were deemed to have need. 99% of undergraduates with need received aid; of those 15% had need fully met. *Average percent of need met:* 69% (excluding resources awarded to replace EFC). *Average financial aid package:* $11,272 (excluding resources awarded to replace EFC). 7% of all full-time undergraduates had no need and received non-need-based gift aid.

GIFT AID (NEED-BASED) *Total amount:* $8,873,515 (21% federal, 35% state, 37% institutional, 7% external sources). *Receiving aid:* Freshmen: 86% (313); All full-time undergraduates: 82% (951). *Average award:* Freshmen: $9103; Undergraduates: $8310. *Scholarships, grants, and awards:* Federal Pell, FSEOG, state, college/university gift aid from institutional funds.

GIFT AID (NON-NEED-BASED) *Total amount:* $902,035 (23% state, 64% institutional, 13% external sources). *Receiving aid:* Freshmen: 10% (38); Undergraduates: 7% (80). *Average Award:* Freshmen: $6639; Undergraduates: $8280. *Scholarships, grants, and awards by category: Academic Interests/ Achievement:* 372 awards ($1,643,188 total): biological sciences, education, general academic interests/achievements, religion/biblical studies. *Creative Arts/ Performance:* 120 awards ($234,430 total): art/fine arts, journalism/publications, music, theater/drama. *Special Achievements/Activities:* 150 awards ($266,478 total): cheerleading/drum major, junior miss, leadership, religious involvement. *Special Characteristics:* 221 awards ($409,911 total): adult students, children of educators, international students, relatives of clergy, religious affiliation. *Tuition waivers:* Full or partial for employees or children of employees, senior citizens.

LOANS *Student loans:* $4,393,523 (84% need-based, 16% non-need-based). 51% of past graduating class borrowed through all loan programs. *Average indebtedness per student:* $5300. *Average need-based loan:* Freshmen: $2891; Undergraduates: $3267. *Parent loans:* $563,878 (43% need-based, 57% non-need-based). *Programs:* FFEL (Subsidized and Unsubsidized Stafford, PLUS), Perkins, college/university.

WORK-STUDY *Federal work-study:* Total amount: $529,866; 325 jobs averaging $1630. *State or other work-study/employment:* Total amount: $147,848 (69% need-based, 31% non-need-based). 76 part-time jobs averaging $1945.

ATHLETIC AWARDS *Total amount:* $1,193,997 (72% need-based, 28% non-need-based).

APPLYING FOR FINANCIAL AID *Required financial aid form:* FAFSA. *Financial aid deadline (priority):* 3/1. *Notification date:* Continuous beginning 3/15. Students must reply within 3 weeks of notification.

CONTACT Mr. Aaron Gabehart, Financial Aid Counselor, Campbellsville University, 1 University Drive, Campbellsville, KY 42718, 270-789-5305 or toll-free 800-264-6014. *Fax:* 270-789-5050. *E-mail:* finaid@campbellsville.edu.

CAMPBELL UNIVERSITY
Buies Creek, NC

Tuition & fees: $14,386	Average undergraduate aid package: $18,979

ABOUT THE INSTITUTION Independent religious, coed. Awards: associate, bachelor's, master's, doctoral, and first professional degrees. 98 undergraduate majors. Total enrollment: 4,256. Undergraduates: 2,694. Freshmen: 739. Federal methodology is used as a basis for awarding need-based institutional aid.

UNDERGRADUATE EXPENSES for 2004–05 *Application fee:* $25. *Comprehensive fee:* $19,486 includes full-time tuition ($14,200), mandatory fees ($186), and room and board ($5100). Full-time tuition and fees vary according to course load, location, and program. Room and board charges vary according to board plan and housing facility. *Part-time tuition:* $230 per semester hour. Part-time tuition and fees vary according to course load, location, and program. *Payment plan:* Installment.

FRESHMAN FINANCIAL AID (Fall 2004, est.) 672 applied for aid; of those 85% were deemed to have need. 100% of freshmen with need received aid; of those 100% had need fully met. *Average percent of need met:* 100% (excluding resources awarded to replace EFC). *Average financial aid package:* $16,616 (excluding resources awarded to replace EFC). 17% of all full-time freshmen had no need and received non-need-based gift aid.

UNDERGRADUATE FINANCIAL AID (Fall 2004, est.) 2,568 applied for aid; of those 87% were deemed to have need. 99% of undergraduates with need received aid; of those 100% had need fully met. *Average percent of need met:* 100% (excluding resources awarded to replace EFC). *Average financial aid package:* $18,979 (excluding resources awarded to replace EFC). 17% of all full-time undergraduates had no need and received non-need-based gift aid.

GIFT AID (NEED-BASED) *Total amount:* $17,602,910 (21% federal, 27% state, 48% institutional, 4% external sources). *Receiving aid:* Freshmen: 51% (388); All full-time undergraduates: 44% (1,481). *Average award:* Freshmen: $4117; Undergraduates: $4221. *Scholarships, grants, and awards:* Federal Pell, FSEOG, state, private, college/university gift aid from institutional funds.

GIFT AID (NON-NEED-BASED) *Total amount:* $6,468,795 (12% federal, 59% state, 27% institutional, 2% external sources). *Receiving aid:* Freshmen: 70% (534); Undergraduates: 58% (1,958). *Average Award:* Freshmen: $14,954; Undergraduates: $12,426. *Scholarships, grants, and awards by category:* Academic Interests/Achievement: 1,565 awards ($8,076,333 total): general academic interests/achievements. Creative Arts/Performance: 32 awards ($27,200 total): art/fine arts, creative writing, journalism/publications, music, theater/drama. Special Achievements/Activities: 88 awards ($95,100 total): cheerleading/drum major, junior miss, religious involvement. Special Characteristics: 68 awards ($538,553 total): children of faculty/staff. *Tuition waivers:* Full or partial for employees or children of employees. *ROTC:* Army.

LOANS *Student loans:* $20,536,307 (83% need-based, 17% non-need-based). 60% of past graduating class borrowed through all loan programs. *Average indebtedness per student:* $12,009. *Average need-based loan:* Freshmen: $2401; Undergraduates: $3899. *Parent loans:* $10,528,303 (83% need-based, 17% non-need-based). *Programs:* FFEL (Subsidized and Unsubsidized Stafford, PLUS), Perkins, state.

WORK-STUDY *Federal work-study:* Total amount: $729,233; 998 jobs averaging $731. *State or other work-study/employment:* Total amount: $580,000 (100% non-need-based). 580 part-time jobs averaging $1000.

ATHLETIC AWARDS *Total amount:* $2,164,283 (83% need-based, 17% non-need-based).

APPLYING FOR FINANCIAL AID *Required financial aid form:* FAFSA. *Financial aid deadline (priority):* 3/15. *Notification date:* Continuous beginning 3/1. Students must reply within 2 weeks of notification.

CONTACT Office of Financial Aid, Campbell University, PO Box 36, Buies Creek, NC 27506, 910-893-1310 or toll-free 800-334-4111.

CANISIUS COLLEGE
Buffalo, NY

Tuition & fees: $21,811	Average undergraduate aid package: $17,869

ABOUT THE INSTITUTION Independent Roman Catholic (Jesuit), coed. Awards: bachelor's and master's degrees and post-master's certificates. 45 undergraduate majors. Total enrollment: 5,018. Undergraduates: 3,519. Freshmen: 886. Both federal and institutional methodology are used as a basis for awarding need-based institutional aid.

UNDERGRADUATE EXPENSES for 2004–05 *Application fee:* $25. *Comprehensive fee:* $30,206 includes full-time tuition ($20,910), mandatory fees ($901), and room and board ($8395). *College room only:* $4860. Room and board charges vary according to board plan and housing facility. *Part-time tuition:* $596 per credit. *Part-time fees:* $20.50 per credit; $18 per term. *Payment plans:* Tuition prepayment, installment, deferred payment.

FRESHMAN FINANCIAL AID (Fall 2004, est.) 805 applied for aid; of those 92% were deemed to have need. 100% of freshmen with need received aid; of those 32% had need fully met. *Average percent of need met:* 86% (excluding resources awarded to replace EFC). *Average financial aid package:* $19,369 (excluding resources awarded to replace EFC). 14% of all full-time freshmen had no need and received non-need-based gift aid.

UNDERGRADUATE FINANCIAL AID (Fall 2004, est.) 2,710 applied for aid; of those 91% were deemed to have need. 99% of undergraduates with need received aid; of those 26% had need fully met. *Average percent of need met:* 79% (excluding resources awarded to replace EFC). *Average financial aid package:* $17,869 (excluding resources awarded to replace EFC). 18% of all full-time undergraduates had no need and received non-need-based gift aid.

GIFT AID (NEED-BASED) *Total amount:* $28,821,392 (10% federal, 15% state, 74% institutional, 1% external sources). *Receiving aid:* Freshmen: 83% (737); All full-time undergraduates: 75% (2,437). *Average award:* Freshmen: $13,181; Undergraduates: $12,253. *Scholarships, grants, and awards:* Federal Pell, FSEOG, state, private, college/university gift aid from institutional funds.

GIFT AID (NON-NEED-BASED) *Total amount:* $3,662,519 (2% federal, 2% state, 95% institutional, 1% external sources). *Receiving aid:* Freshmen: 21% (182); Undergraduates: 18% (575). *Average Award:* Freshmen: $9176; Undergraduates: $9425. *Scholarships, grants, and awards by category:* Academic Interests/Achievement: 1,878 awards ($14,337,851 total): general academic interests/achievements. Creative Arts/Performance: 54 awards ($110,500 total): art/fine arts, music. Special Achievements/Activities: 149 awards ($281,125 total): community service, leadership, religious involvement. Special Characteristics: 567 awards ($1,768,872 total): children and siblings of alumni, children of educators, children of faculty/staff, international students, religious affiliation, siblings of current students, spouses of current students. *Tuition waivers:* Full or partial for employees or children of employees. *ROTC:* Army.

LOANS *Student loans:* $15,754,749 (70% need-based, 30% non-need-based). 74% of past graduating class borrowed through all loan programs. *Average indebtedness per student:* $21,892. *Average need-based loan:* Freshmen: $3169; Undergraduates: $4134. *Programs:* FFEL (Subsidized and Unsubsidized Stafford, PLUS), Perkins, college/university.

WORK-STUDY *Federal work-study:* Total amount: $815,713; 584 jobs averaging $1396. *State or other work-study/employment:* Total amount: $87,239 (39% need-based, 61% non-need-based). Part-time jobs available.

ATHLETIC AWARDS *Total amount:* $671,889 (54% need-based, 46% non-need-based).

APPLYING FOR FINANCIAL AID *Required financial aid forms:* FAFSA, institution's own form, state aid form. *Financial aid deadline (priority):* 2/15. *Notification date:* Continuous beginning 3/1. Students must reply by 5/1.

CONTACT Mr. Curtis Gaume, Director of Student Financial Aid, Canisius College, 2001 Main Street, Buffalo, NY 14208-1098, 716-888-2300 or toll-free 800-843-1517. *Fax:* 716-888-2377. *E-mail:* gaume@canisius.edu.

CAPELLA UNIVERSITY
Minneapolis, MN

CONTACT University Services, Capella University, 222 South Ninth Street, Minneapolis, MN 55402, 888-227-3552 or toll-free 888-CAPELLA.

CAPITAL UNIVERSITY
Columbus, OH

ABOUT THE INSTITUTION Independent religious, coed. Awards: bachelor's, master's, and first professional degrees. 90 undergraduate majors. Total enrollment: 3,894. Undergraduates: 2,796. Freshmen: 522.

GIFT AID (NEED-BASED) *Scholarships, grants, and awards:* Federal Pell, FSEOG, state, private, college/university gift aid from institutional funds.

GIFT AID (NON-NEED-BASED) *Scholarships, grants, and awards by category: Academic Interests/Achievement:* general academic interests/achievements. *Creative Arts/Performance:* music. *Special Achievements/Activities:* hobbies/interests, leadership, religious involvement. *Special Characteristics:* children and siblings of alumni, children of faculty/staff, ethnic background, international students, members of minority groups, relatives of clergy, religious affiliation, siblings of current students.

LOANS *Programs:* FFEL (Subsidized and Unsubsidized Stafford, PLUS), Perkins, Federal Nursing, state, college/university.

WORK-STUDY *Federal work-study:* Total amount: $2,162,106; jobs available. *State or other work-study/employment:* Part-time jobs available.

APPLYING FOR FINANCIAL AID *Required financial aid form:* FAFSA.

CONTACT Office of Financial Aid, Capital University, 2199 East Main Street, Columbus, OH 43209-2394, 614-236-6511 or toll-free 800-289-6289. *Fax:* 614-236-6926. *E-mail:* finaid@capital.edu.

CAPITOL COLLEGE
Laurel, MD

Tuition & fees: $17,688	Average undergraduate aid package: $9746

ABOUT THE INSTITUTION Independent, coed. Awards: associate, bachelor's, and master's degrees and post-bachelor's certificates. 7 undergraduate majors. Total enrollment: 801. Undergraduates: 630. Freshmen: 61. Federal methodology is used as a basis for awarding need-based institutional aid.

UNDERGRADUATE EXPENSES for 2005–06 *Application fee:* $25. *Tuition:* full-time $17,688. Room and board charges vary according to housing facility. *Payment plans:* Installment, deferred payment.

GIFT AID (NEED-BASED) *Total amount:* $1,379,656 (29% federal, 14% state, 42% institutional, 15% external sources). *Receiving aid:* Freshmen: 66% (27); All full-time undergraduates: 55% (113). *Average award:* Freshmen: $6383; Undergraduates: $6357. *Scholarships, grants, and awards:* Federal Pell, FSEOG, state, private, college/university gift aid from institutional funds.

GIFT AID (NON-NEED-BASED) *Total amount:* $279,184 (2% federal, 11% state, 67% institutional, 20% external sources). *Receiving aid:* Freshmen: 44% (18); Undergraduates: 16% (34). *Average Award:* Freshmen: $7363; *Undergraduates:* $8534. *Tuition waivers:* Full or partial for employees or children of employees. *ROTC:* Army cooperative.

LOANS *Student loans:* $1,739,014 (83% need-based, 17% non-need-based). 66% of past graduating class borrowed through all loan programs. *Average indebtedness per student:* $25,605. *Average need-based loan:* Freshmen: $4909; Undergraduates: $4667. *Parent loans:* $744,734 (64% need-based, 36% non-need-based). *Programs:* FFEL (Subsidized and Unsubsidized Stafford, PLUS), Perkins.

APPLYING FOR FINANCIAL AID *Required financial aid forms:* FAFSA, institution's own form. *Financial aid deadline:* Continuous. *Notification date:* Continuous. Students must reply within 3 weeks of notification.

CONTACT Suzanne Thompson, Director of Financial Aid, Capitol College, 11301 Springfield Road, Laurel, MD 20708-9759, 301-369-2800 Ext. 3037 or toll-free 800-950-1992. *Fax:* 301-369-2328. *E-mail:* sthompson@capitol-college.edu.

CARDINAL STRITCH UNIVERSITY
Milwaukee, WI

ABOUT THE INSTITUTION Independent Roman Catholic, coed. Awards: associate, bachelor's, master's, and doctoral degrees and post-bachelor's certificates. 42 undergraduate majors. Total enrollment: 6,785. Undergraduates: 3,251. Freshmen: 241.

GIFT AID (NEED-BASED) *Scholarships, grants, and awards:* Federal Pell, FSEOG, state, private, college/university gift aid from institutional funds.

GIFT AID (NON-NEED-BASED) *Scholarships, grants, and awards by category: Academic Interests/Achievement:* general academic interests/achievements. *Creative Arts/Performance:* art/fine arts, music, theater/drama. *Special Achievements/Activities:* leadership.

LOANS *Programs:* FFEL (Subsidized and Unsubsidized Stafford, PLUS), Perkins, state.

APPLYING FOR FINANCIAL AID *Required financial aid forms:* FAFSA, institution's own form.

CONTACT Financial Aid Director, Cardinal Stritch University, 6801 North Yates Road, Milwaukee, WI 53217-3985, 414-410-4000 or toll-free 800-347-8822 Ext. 4040.

CARIBBEAN UNIVERSITY
Bayamón, PR

CONTACT Financial Aid Office, Caribbean University, Box 493, Bayamón, PR 00960-0493, 787-780-0070.

CARLETON COLLEGE
Northfield, MN

ABOUT THE INSTITUTION Independent, coed. Awards: bachelor's degrees. 35 undergraduate majors. Total enrollment: 1,951. Undergraduates: 1,951. Freshmen: 487.

GIFT AID (NEED-BASED) *Scholarships, grants, and awards:* Federal Pell, FSEOG, state, private, college/university gift aid from institutional funds.

GIFT AID (NON-NEED-BASED) *Scholarships, grants, and awards by category: Academic Interests/Achievement:* general academic interests/achievements. *Creative Arts/Performance:* music.

LOANS *Programs:* FFEL (Subsidized and Unsubsidized Stafford, PLUS), Perkins, state, college/university.

APPLYING FOR FINANCIAL AID *Required financial aid forms:* FAFSA, CSS Financial Aid PROFILE, noncustodial (divorced/separated) parent's statement, business/farm supplement.

CONTACT Mr. Rodney M. Oto, Director of Student Financial Services, Carleton College, One North College Street, Northfield, MN 55057-4001, 507-646-4138 or toll-free 800-995-2275. *Fax:* 507-646-4269.

CARLOS ALBIZU UNIVERSITY
San Juan, PR

CONTACT Financial Aid Office, Carlos Albizu University, PO Box 9023711, San Juan, PR 00902-3711, 787-725-6500.

CARLOS ALBIZU UNIVERSITY, MIAMI CAMPUS
Miami, FL

ABOUT THE INSTITUTION Independent, coed, primarily women. Awards: bachelor's, master's, and doctoral degrees. 4 undergraduate majors. Total enrollment: 1,007. Undergraduates: 427. Freshmen: 36.

GIFT AID (NEED-BASED) *Scholarships, grants, and awards:* Federal Pell, FSEOG, state, college/university gift aid from institutional funds.

GIFT AID (NON-NEED-BASED) *Scholarships, grants, and awards by category: Academic Interests/Achievement:* general academic interests/achievements. *Special Characteristics:* children of faculty/staff.

LOANS *Programs:* FFEL (Subsidized and Unsubsidized Stafford, PLUS), college/university.

WORK-STUDY *Federal work-study:* Total amount: $82,600; 27 jobs averaging $3059.

APPLYING FOR FINANCIAL AID *Required financial aid forms:* FAFSA, institution's own form.

CONTACT Maria V. Chavez, Senior Financial Aid Officer, Carlos Albizu University, Miami Campus, 2173 Northwest 99th Avenue, Miami, FL 33172, 305-593-1223 Ext. 153 or toll-free 800-672-3246. *Fax:* 305-593-8902. *E-mail:* mchavez@albizu.edu.

CARLOW UNIVERSITY
Pittsburgh, PA

ABOUT THE INSTITUTION Independent Roman Catholic, coed, primarily women. Awards: bachelor's and master's degrees and post-master's certificates. 33 undergraduate majors. Total enrollment: 2,088. Undergraduates: 1,645. Freshmen: 238.

GIFT AID (NEED-BASED) *Scholarships, grants, and awards:* Federal Pell, FSEOG, state, private, college/university gift aid from institutional funds, Federal Nursing.

GIFT AID (NON-NEED-BASED) *Scholarships, grants, and awards by category: Academic Interests/Achievement:* biological sciences, business, communication, computer science, education, English, general academic interests/achievements, humanities, mathematics, social sciences. *Special Achievements/Activities:* leadership, religious involvement. *Special Characteristics:* children and siblings of alumni, children of educators, children of faculty/staff, international students, religious affiliation, siblings of current students.

LOANS *Programs:* FFEL (Subsidized and Unsubsidized Stafford, PLUS), Perkins, Federal Nursing.

WORK-STUDY *Federal work-study:* Total amount: $334,567; 431 jobs averaging $776.

APPLYING FOR FINANCIAL AID *Required financial aid form:* FAFSA.

CONTACT Ms. Natalie Wilson, Director of Financial Aid, Carlow University, 3333 Fifth Avenue, Pittsburgh, PA 15213-3165, 412-578-6171 or toll-free 800-333-CARLOW.

CARNEGIE MELLON UNIVERSITY
Pittsburgh, PA

Tuition & fees: $31,036 | Average undergraduate aid package: $21,476

ABOUT THE INSTITUTION Independent, coed. Awards: bachelor's, master's, and doctoral degrees and post-master's certificates. 59 undergraduate majors. Total enrollment: 9,803. Undergraduates: 5,529. Freshmen: 1,367. Federal methodology is used as a basis for awarding need-based institutional aid.

UNDERGRADUATE EXPENSES for 2004–05 *Application fee:* $60. *Comprehensive fee:* $39,280 includes full-time tuition ($30,650), mandatory fees ($386), and room and board ($8244). *College room only:* $4964. Room and board charges vary according to board plan, housing facility, and student level. *Part-time tuition:* $426 per unit. *Part-time fees:* $193 per term. *Payment plan:* Installment.

GIFT AID (NEED-BASED) *Total amount:* $40,982,436 (10% federal, 2% state, 84% institutional, 4% external sources). *Receiving aid:* Freshmen: 52% (707); All full-time undergraduates: 48% (2,548). *Average award:* Freshmen: $17,064; Undergraduates: $15,986. *Scholarships, grants, and awards:* Federal Pell, FSEOG, state, private, college/university gift aid from institutional funds.

GIFT AID (NON-NEED-BASED) *Total amount:* $12,393,831 (86% institutional, 14% external sources). *Receiving aid:* Freshmen: 23% (315); Undergraduates: 24% (1,238). *Average Award:* Freshmen: $9932; Undergraduates: $11,721. *Scholarships, grants, and awards by category: Academic Interests/Achievement:* 1,121 awards ($8,675,813 total): general academic interests/achievements. *Creative Arts/Performance:* art/fine arts, music, theater/drama. *Tuition waivers:* Full or partial for employees or children of employees. *ROTC:* Army, Naval, Air Force.

LOANS *Student loans:* $18,276,291 (91% need-based, 9% non-need-based). 49% of past graduating class borrowed through all loan programs. *Average indebtedness per student:* $22,902. *Average need-based loan:* Freshmen: $3506; Undergraduates: $4664. *Parent loans:* $8,583,439 (16% need-based, 84% non-need-based). *Programs:* FFEL (Subsidized and Unsubsidized Stafford, PLUS), Perkins, GATE Loans.

APPLYING FOR FINANCIAL AID *Required financial aid forms:* FAFSA, institution's own form, parent and student federal income tax returns, parents' W-2 forms. *Financial aid deadline:* 5/1 (priority: 2/15). *Notification date:* 3/15.

CONTACT Linda M. Anderson, Director, Enrollment Services, Carnegie Mellon University, 5000 Forbes Avenue, Pittsburgh, PA 15213-3890, 412-268-8186. *Fax:* 412-268-8084. *E-mail:* thehub@andrew.cmu.edu.

CARROLL COLLEGE
Helena, MT

Tuition & fees: $16,978 | Average undergraduate aid package: $14,376

ABOUT THE INSTITUTION Independent Roman Catholic, coed. Awards: associate and bachelor's degrees. 56 undergraduate majors. Total enrollment: 1,461. Undergraduates: 1,461. Freshmen: 361. Federal methodology is used as a basis for awarding need-based institutional aid.

UNDERGRADUATE EXPENSES for 2005–06 *Application fee:* $35. *Comprehensive fee:* $23,224 includes full-time tuition ($16,778), mandatory fees ($200), and room and board ($6246). *College room only:* $3000. Full-time tuition and fees vary according to course load. Room and board charges vary according to board plan and housing facility. Part-time tuition and fees vary according to course load. *Payment plan:* Installment.

FRESHMAN FINANCIAL AID (Fall 2004, est.) 356 applied for aid; of those 67% were deemed to have need. 100% of freshmen with need received aid; of those 23% had need fully met. *Average percent of need met:* 85% (excluding resources awarded to replace EFC). *Average financial aid package:* $14,718 (excluding resources awarded to replace EFC). 28% of all full-time freshmen had no need and received non-need-based gift aid.

UNDERGRADUATE FINANCIAL AID (Fall 2004, est.) 1,229 applied for aid; of those 69% were deemed to have need. 100% of undergraduates with need received aid; of those 18% had need fully met. *Average percent of need met:* 80% (excluding resources awarded to replace EFC). *Average financial aid package:* $14,376 (excluding resources awarded to replace EFC). 30% of all full-time undergraduates had no need and received non-need-based gift aid.

GIFT AID (NEED-BASED) *Total amount:* $6,771,445 (16% federal, 1% state, 79% institutional, 4% external sources). *Receiving aid:* Freshmen: 60% (214); All full-time undergraduates: 64% (782). *Average award:* Freshmen: $8974; Undergraduates: $8310. *Scholarships, grants, and awards:* Federal Pell, FSEOG, state, private, college/university gift aid from institutional funds.

GIFT AID (NON-NEED-BASED) *Total amount:* $2,943,219 (4% federal, 84% institutional, 12% external sources). *Receiving aid:* Freshmen: 10% (35); Undergraduates: 7% (83). *Average Award:* Freshmen: $6575; Undergraduates: $6123. *Scholarships, grants, and awards by category: Academic Interests/Achievement:* 1,165 awards ($6,300,015 total): general academic interests/achievements. *Creative Arts/Performance:* 21 awards ($33,000 total): debating, theater/drama. *Special Achievements/Activities:* 169 awards ($1,198,094 total): general special achievements/activities, religious involvement. *Special Characteristics:* 94 awards ($822,360 total): children of faculty/staff, children of union members/company employees, international students, siblings of current students, spouses of current students, veterans. *Tuition waivers:* Full or partial for employees or children of employees, senior citizens. *ROTC:* Army.

LOANS *Student loans:* $6,408,546 (50% need-based, 50% non-need-based). 78% of past graduating class borrowed through all loan programs. *Average indebtedness per student:* $23,067. *Average need-based loan:* Freshmen: $4418; Undergraduates: $4680. *Parent loans:* $834,204 (6% need-based, 94% non-need-based). *Programs:* FFEL (Subsidized and Unsubsidized Stafford, PLUS), Perkins.

WORK-STUDY *Federal work-study:* Total amount: $733,125; 457 jobs averaging $2207. *State or other work-study/employment:* Total amount: $21,702 (63% need-based, 37% non-need-based). 9 part-time jobs averaging $2411.

ATHLETIC AWARDS *Total amount:* $1,202,094 (45% need-based, 55% non-need-based).

APPLYING FOR FINANCIAL AID *Required financial aid form:* FAFSA. *Financial aid deadline:* Continuous. *Notification date:* Continuous beginning 3/1. Students must reply within 4 weeks of notification.

CONTACT Ms. Janet Riis, Director of Financial Aid, Carroll College, 1601 North Benton Avenue, Helena, MT 59625-0002, 406-447-5423 or toll-free 800-992-3648. *Fax:* 406-447-4533. *E-mail:* jriis@carroll.edu.

CARROLL COLLEGE
Waukesha, WI

Tuition & fees: $19,050 | Average undergraduate aid package: $14,718

ABOUT THE INSTITUTION Independent Presbyterian, coed. Awards: bachelor's and master's degrees. 79 undergraduate majors. Total enrollment: 3,014. Undergraduates: 2,763. Freshmen: 628. Both federal and institutional methodology are used as a basis for awarding need-based institutional aid.

UNDERGRADUATE EXPENSES for 2005–06 *Comprehensive fee:* $24,860 includes full-time tuition ($18,650), mandatory fees ($400), and room and board ($5810). *College room only:* $3150. Full-time tuition and fees vary according to program. Room and board charges vary according to board plan and housing facility. *Part-time tuition:* $230 per credit. Part-time tuition and fees vary according to course load and program. *Payment plan:* Installment.

FRESHMAN FINANCIAL AID (Fall 2003) 528 applied for aid; of those 84% were deemed to have need. 100% of freshmen with need received aid; of those 80% had need fully met. *Average percent of need met:* 100% (excluding resources awarded to replace EFC). *Average financial aid package:* $15,912 (excluding resources awarded to replace EFC). 16% of all full-time freshmen had no need and received non-need-based gift aid.

UNDERGRADUATE FINANCIAL AID (Fall 2003) 2,051 applied for aid; of those 83% were deemed to have need. 100% of undergraduates with need received aid; of those 80% had need fully met. *Average percent of need met:* 100% (excluding resources awarded to replace EFC). *Average financial aid package:* $14,718 (excluding resources awarded to replace EFC). 18% of all full-time undergraduates had no need and received non-need-based gift aid.

GIFT AID (NEED-BASED) *Total amount:* $15,587,286 (10% federal, 11% state, 76% institutional, 3% external sources). *Receiving aid:* Freshmen: 83% (441); All full-time undergraduates: 82% (1,693). *Average award:* Freshmen: $11,836; Undergraduates: $10,220. *Scholarships, grants, and awards:* Federal Pell, FSEOG, state, private, college/university gift aid from institutional funds.

GIFT AID (NON-NEED-BASED) *Total amount:* $4,191,035 (1% federal, 1% state, 94% institutional, 4% external sources). *Receiving aid:* Freshmen: 16% (87); Undergraduates: 18% (369). *Average Award:* Freshmen: $7345; Undergraduates:* $7084. *Scholarships, grants, and awards by category: Academic Interests/Achievement:* 1,862 awards ($8,370,171 total): biological sciences, business, computer science, education, general academic interests/achievements, health fields, humanities, international studies, mathematics, physical sciences, premedicine, social sciences. *Creative Arts/Performance:* 140 awards ($216,250 total): art/fine arts, journalism/publications, music, performing arts, theater/drama. *Special Achievements/Activities:* 133 awards ($199,449 total): general special achievements/activities, junior miss, leadership, memberships, religious involvement. *Special Characteristics:* 832 awards ($1,251,765 total): adult students, children and siblings of alumni, children of current students, children of faculty/staff, general special characteristics, international students, siblings of current students, spouses of current students. *Tuition waivers:* Full or partial for employees or children of employees. *ROTC:* Air Force cooperative.

LOANS *Student loans:* $10,713,435 (54% need-based, 46% non-need-based). 79% of past graduating class borrowed through all loan programs. *Average indebtedness per student:* $16,462. *Average need-based loan:* Freshmen: $2779; Undergraduates: $3980. *Parent loans:* $1,493,940 (75% need-based, 25% non-need-based). *Programs:* FFEL (Subsidized and Unsubsidized Stafford, PLUS), Perkins, college/university.

WORK-STUDY *Federal work-study:* Total amount: $889,535; 533 jobs averaging $1669. *State or other work-study/employment:* Total amount: $1,078,215 (100% non-need-based). 677 part-time jobs averaging $1593.

APPLYING FOR FINANCIAL AID *Required financial aid form:* FAFSA. *Financial aid deadline:* Continuous. *Notification date:* Continuous beginning 2/15. Students must reply by 5/1 or within 2 weeks of notification.

CONTACT Dawn Scott, Director of Financial Aid, Carroll College, 100 North East Avenue, Waukesha, WI 53186-5593, 262-524-7297 or toll-free 800-CARROLL. *Fax:* 262-951-3037. *E-mail:* dthomas@cc.edu.

CARSON-NEWMAN COLLEGE
Jefferson City, TN

Tuition & fees: $14,420	Average undergraduate aid package: $12,525

ABOUT THE INSTITUTION Independent Southern Baptist, coed. Awards: associate, bachelor's, and master's degrees. 68 undergraduate majors. Total enrollment: 2,053. Undergraduates: 1,889. Freshmen: 451. Federal methodology is used as a basis for awarding need-based institutional aid.

UNDERGRADUATE EXPENSES for 2004–05 *Application fee:* $25. *Comprehensive fee:* $19,350 includes full-time tuition ($13,700), mandatory fees ($720), and room and board ($4930). *College room only:* $1850. Full-time tuition and fees vary according to class time. Room and board charges vary according to board plan. *Part-time tuition:* $565 per semester hour. *Part-time fees:* $220 per term. Part-time tuition and fees vary according to class time. *Payment plan:* Installment.

FRESHMAN FINANCIAL AID (Fall 2003) 318 applied for aid; of those 86% were deemed to have need. 100% of freshmen with need received aid; of those 14% had need fully met. *Average percent of need met:* 73% (excluding resources awarded to replace EFC). *Average financial aid package:* $12,542 (excluding resources awarded to replace EFC). 19% of all full-time freshmen had no need and received non-need-based gift aid.

UNDERGRADUATE FINANCIAL AID (Fall 2003) 1,476 applied for aid; of those 88% were deemed to have need. 100% of undergraduates with need received aid; of those 14% had need fully met. *Average percent of need met:* 72% (excluding resources awarded to replace EFC). *Average financial aid package:* $12,525 (excluding resources awarded to replace EFC). 21% of all full-time undergraduates had no need and received non-need-based gift aid.

GIFT AID (NEED-BASED) *Total amount:* $9,721,013 (27% federal, 11% state, 59% institutional, 3% external sources). *Receiving aid:* Freshmen: 68% (246); All full-time undergraduates: 67% (1,185). *Average award:* Freshmen: $8721; Undergraduates: $8095. *Scholarships, grants, and awards:* Federal Pell, FSEOG, state, private, college/university gift aid from institutional funds.

GIFT AID (NON-NEED-BASED) *Total amount:* $2,980,774 (8% federal, 1% state, 84% institutional, 7% external sources). *Receiving aid:* Freshmen: 6% (23); Undergraduates: 6% (100). *Average Award:* Freshmen: $4730; Undergraduates:* $4585. *Scholarships, grants, and awards by category: Academic Interests/Achievement:* biological sciences, business, education, general academic interests/achievements, home economics, mathematics, military science, religion/biblical studies. *Creative Arts/Performance:* art/fine arts, debating, journalism/publications, music. *Special Achievements/Activities:* leadership, memberships. *Special Characteristics:* children and siblings of alumni, members of minority groups, relatives of clergy, siblings of current students. *Tuition waivers:* Full or partial for employees or children of employees, senior citizens. *ROTC:* Army, Air Force cooperative.

LOANS *Student loans:* $5,955,363 (73% need-based, 27% non-need-based). 70% of past graduating class borrowed through all loan programs. *Average indebtedness per student:* $11,957. *Average need-based loan:* Freshmen: $3112; Undergraduates: $3752. *Parent loans:* $1,629,260 (15% need-based, 85% non-need-based). *Programs:* FFEL (Subsidized and Unsubsidized Stafford, PLUS), Perkins, state, college/university, alternative loans.

WORK-STUDY *Federal work-study:* Total amount: $688,450; 399 jobs averaging $1725. *State or other work-study/employment:* Total amount: $437,983 (27% need-based, 73% non-need-based). 296 part-time jobs averaging $1587.

ATHLETIC AWARDS *Total amount:* $1,309,105 (53% need-based, 47% non-need-based).

APPLYING FOR FINANCIAL AID *Required financial aid forms:* FAFSA, institution's own form. *Financial aid deadline (priority):* 4/1. *Notification date:* Continuous. Students must reply within 2 weeks of notification.

CONTACT Parker Leake, Director of Financial Aid, Carson-Newman College, 1646 Russell Avenue, Jefferson City, TN 37760, 800-478-9061 or toll-free 800-678-9061. *Fax:* 865-471-3502. *E-mail:* delia@cn.edu.

CARTHAGE COLLEGE
Kenosha, WI

ABOUT THE INSTITUTION Independent religious, coed. Awards: bachelor's and master's degrees. 51 undergraduate majors. Total enrollment: 2,679. Undergraduates: 2,560. Freshmen: 585.

GIFT AID (NEED-BASED) *Scholarships, grants, and awards:* Federal Pell, FSEOG, state, private, college/university gift aid from institutional funds.

GIFT AID (NON-NEED-BASED) *Scholarships, grants, and awards by category: Academic Interests/Achievement:* biological sciences, computer science, engineering/technologies, foreign languages, general academic interests/achievements, health fields, mathematics, physical sciences, premedicine. *Creative Arts/Performance:* applied art and design, art/fine arts, music, theater/drama. *Special Achievements/Activities:* general special achievements/activities, leadership, religious involvement. *Special Characteristics:* children and siblings of alumni, children of educators, children of faculty/staff, children of public servants, local/state students, members of minority groups, previous college experience, relatives of clergy, religious affiliation, siblings of current students.

LOANS *Programs:* FFEL (Subsidized and Unsubsidized Stafford, PLUS), Perkins, state, college/university.

APPLYING FOR FINANCIAL AID *Required financial aid form:* FAFSA.

CONTACT William Henderson, Director of Student Financial Planning, Carthage College, 2001 Alford Park Drive, Kenosha, WI 53140-1994, 262-551-6001 or toll-free 800-351-4058. *Fax:* 262-551-5762. *E-mail:* whenderson@carthage.edu.

CASCADE COLLEGE
Portland, OR

ABOUT THE INSTITUTION Independent religious, coed. Awards: bachelor's degrees. 9 undergraduate majors. Total enrollment: 283. Undergraduates: 283. Freshmen: 44.

GIFT AID (NEED-BASED) *Scholarships, grants, and awards:* Federal Pell, FSEOG, private, college/university gift aid from institutional funds.

GIFT AID (NON-NEED-BASED) *Scholarships, grants, and awards by category:* *Academic Interests/Achievement:* business, education, English, general academic interests/achievements, international studies, religion/biblical studies. *Creative Arts/Performance:* music, theater/drama. *Special Achievements/Activities:* cheerleading/drum major, general special achievements/activities, leadership, memberships. *Special Characteristics:* children and siblings of alumni, children of current students, children of faculty/staff, general special characteristics, international students, out-of-state students, parents of current students, siblings of current students, spouses of current students.

LOANS *Programs:* FFEL (Subsidized and Unsubsidized Stafford, PLUS), alternative loans.

WORK-STUDY *Federal work-study:* Total amount: $45,000; 35 jobs averaging $1256. *State or other work-study/employment:* Total amount: $66,000 (100% non-need-based). 52 part-time jobs averaging $1269.

APPLYING FOR FINANCIAL AID *Required financial aid forms:* FAFSA, institution's own form.

CONTACT Jim Murphy, Director of Financial Services, Cascade College, 9101 East Burnside Street, Portland, OR 97216-1515, 503-257-1218 or toll-free 800-550-7678. *Fax:* 503-257-1222. *E-mail:* jmurphy@cascade.edu.

CASE WESTERN RESERVE UNIVERSITY
Cleveland, OH

Tuition & fees: $27,062	Average undergraduate aid package: $25,758

ABOUT THE INSTITUTION Independent, coed. Awards: bachelor's, master's, doctoral, and first professional degrees. 63 undergraduate majors. Total enrollment: 9,095. Undergraduates: 3,516. Freshmen: 784. Both federal and institutional methodology are used as a basis for awarding need-based institutional aid.

UNDERGRADUATE EXPENSES for 2004–05 *Application fee:* $35. *Comprehensive fee:* $35,264 includes full-time tuition ($26,500), mandatory fees ($562), and room and board ($8202). *College room only:* $5110. Room and board charges vary according to board plan, housing facility, and student level. *Part-time tuition:* $1104 per credit hour. Part-time tuition and fees vary according to course load. *Payment plan:* Installment.

GIFT AID (NEED-BASED) *Total amount:* $33,148,299 (9% federal, 7% state, 80% institutional, 4% external sources). *Receiving aid:* Freshmen: 71% (558); All full-time undergraduates: 57% (1,852). *Average award:* Freshmen: $18,052; Undergraduates: $17,506. *Scholarships, grants, and awards:* Federal Pell, FSEOG, state, private, college/university gift aid from institutional funds.

GIFT AID (NON-NEED-BASED) *Total amount:* $12,554,379 (1% federal, 6% state, 90% institutional, 3% external sources). *Receiving aid:* Freshmen: 61% (475); Undergraduates: 49% (1,588). *Average Award:* Freshmen: $8823; *Undergraduates:* $12,650. *Scholarships, grants, and awards by category:* *Academic Interests/Achievement:* 1,017 awards ($12,598,243 total): biological sciences, engineering/technologies, general academic interests/achievements. *Creative Arts/Performance:* 21 awards ($116,500 total): art/fine arts, creative writing, dance, general creative arts/performance, music, theater/drama. *Special Achievements/Activities:* 83 awards ($250,850 total): leadership. *Special Characteristics:* 192 awards ($4,579,818 total): children of faculty/staff. *Tuition waivers:* Full or partial for employees or children of employees. *ROTC:* Army cooperative, Air Force cooperative.

LOANS *Student loans:* $18,398,715 (44% need-based, 56% non-need-based). 54% of past graduating class borrowed through all loan programs. *Average indebtedness per student:* $27,780. *Average need-based loan:* Freshmen: $3506; Undergraduates: $3445. *Parent loans:* $2,139,777 (43% need-based, 57% non-need-based). *Programs:* FFEL (Subsidized and Unsubsidized Stafford, PLUS), Perkins, Federal Nursing, college/university, alternative loans-Custom Signature.

APPLYING FOR FINANCIAL AID *Required financial aid forms:* FAFSA, noncustodial (divorced/separated) parent's statement, business/farm supplement, income tax form(s), W-2 forms. *Financial aid deadline (priority):* 2/15. *Notification date:* Continuous beginning 3/15. Students must reply by 5/1 or within 2 weeks of notification.

CONTACT Ms. Nancy Issa, Associate Director of University Financial Aid, Case Western Reserve University, 10900 Euclid Avenue, Cleveland, OH 44106-7049, 216-368-4530. *Fax:* 216-368-5054. *E-mail:* nxi@po.cwru.edu.

CASTLETON STATE COLLEGE
Castleton, VT

Tuition & fees (VT res): $6484	Average undergraduate aid package: N/A

ABOUT THE INSTITUTION State-supported, coed. Awards: associate, bachelor's, and master's degrees and post-master's certificates. 42 undergraduate majors. Total enrollment: 1,971. Undergraduates: 1,796. Freshmen: 435. Federal methodology is used as a basis for awarding need-based institutional aid.

UNDERGRADUATE EXPENSES for 2005–06 *Application fee:* $34. *One-time required fee:* $170. *Tuition, state resident:* full-time $6312; part-time $263 per credit. *Tuition, nonresident:* full-time $13,632; part-time $568 per credit. Part-time tuition and fees vary according to course load. *College room and board:* $6674. Room and board charges vary according to board plan. *Payment plan:* Installment.

GIFT AID (NEED-BASED) *Scholarships, grants, and awards:* Federal Pell, FSEOG, state, private, college/university gift aid from institutional funds.

GIFT AID (NON-NEED-BASED) *Scholarships, grants, and awards by category:* *Academic Interests/Achievement:* foreign languages, general academic interests/ achievements. *Creative Arts/Performance:* applied art and design, art/fine arts, music. *Tuition waivers:* Full or partial for employees or children of employees, senior citizens. *ROTC:* Army cooperative.

LOANS *Programs:* FFEL (Subsidized and Unsubsidized Stafford, PLUS), Perkins, Federal Nursing, state.

APPLYING FOR FINANCIAL AID *Required financial aid forms:* FAFSA, state aid form. *Financial aid deadline (priority):* 3/31. *Notification date:* Continuous beginning 1/15. Students must reply by 5/1 or within 2 weeks of notification.

CONTACT Audrey Reed, Director of Financial Aid, Castleton State College, Castleton, VT 05735, 802-468-1286 or toll-free 800-639-8521. *Fax:* 802-468-6470. *E-mail:* audrey.reed@castleton.edu.

CATAWBA COLLEGE
Salisbury, NC

Tuition & fees: $17,600	Average undergraduate aid package: $12,311

ABOUT THE INSTITUTION Independent religious, coed. Awards: bachelor's and master's degrees. 42 undergraduate majors. Total enrollment: 1,395. Undergraduates: 1,375. Freshmen: 260. Federal methodology is used as a basis for awarding need-based institutional aid.

UNDERGRADUATE EXPENSES for 2004–05 *Application fee:* $25. *Comprehensive fee:* $23,500 includes full-time tuition ($17,600) and room and board ($5900). Full-time tuition and fees vary according to class time. *Part-time tuition:* $475 per semester hour. Part-time tuition and fees vary according to class time, course load, and degree level. *Payment plan:* Installment.

FRESHMAN FINANCIAL AID (Fall 2003) 212 applied for aid; of those 83% were deemed to have need. 100% of freshmen with need received aid; of those 33% had need fully met. *Average percent of need met:* 90% (excluding resources awarded to replace EFC). *Average financial aid package:* $14,843 (excluding resources awarded to replace EFC). 13% of all full-time freshmen had no need and received non-need-based gift aid.

UNDERGRADUATE FINANCIAL AID (Fall 2003) 1,110 applied for aid; of those 87% were deemed to have need. 100% of undergraduates with need received aid; of those 32% had need fully met. *Average percent of need met:* 67% (excluding resources awarded to replace EFC). *Average financial aid package:* $12,311 (excluding resources awarded to replace EFC). 7% of all full-time undergraduates had no need and received non-need-based gift aid.

GIFT AID (NEED-BASED) *Total amount:* $2,460,427 (55% federal, 45% state). *Receiving aid:* Freshmen: 48% (121); All full-time undergraduates: 43% (602). *Average award:* Freshmen: $3977; Undergraduates: $4062. *Scholarships, grants, and awards:* Federal Pell, FSEOG, state, private, college/university gift aid from institutional funds.

GIFT AID (NON-NEED-BASED) *Total amount:* $6,710,048 (24% state, 73% institutional, 3% external sources). *Receiving aid:* Freshmen: 70% (177); Undergraduates: 69% (957). *Average Award:* Freshmen: $6905; *Undergraduates:* $5896. *Scholarships, grants, and awards by category:* *Academic Interests/ Achievement:* 900 awards ($4,724,524 total): education, general academic interests/achievements. *Creative Arts/Performance:* 87 awards ($138,875 total):

Catawba College

music, theater/drama. *Special Characteristics:* 12 awards ($107,925 total): children of faculty/staff. *Tuition waivers:* Full or partial for employees or children of employees. *ROTC:* Army cooperative.
LOANS *Student loans:* $5,606,680 (57% need-based, 43% non-need-based). 71% of past graduating class borrowed through all loan programs. *Average indebtedness per student:* $19,000. *Average need-based loan:* Freshmen: $4141; Undergraduates: $4179. *Parent loans:* $1,509,487 (100% non-need-based). *Programs:* FFEL (Subsidized and Unsubsidized Stafford, PLUS), Perkins, college/university, TERI Loans, Nellie Mae Loans, Advantage Loans, alternative loans, Citiassist Loans, "Extra" loans.
WORK-STUDY *Federal work-study:* Total amount: $261,244; 214 jobs averaging $1221. *State or other work-study/employment:* Total amount: $220,268 (100% non-need-based). 179 part-time jobs averaging $1231.
ATHLETIC AWARDS *Total amount:* $1,592,893 (100% non-need-based).
APPLYING FOR FINANCIAL AID *Required financial aid forms:* FAFSA, state aid form. *Financial aid deadline (priority):* 3/1. *Notification date:* Continuous. Students must reply within 2 weeks of notification.
CONTACT Melanie McCulloh, Director of Scholarships and Financial Aid, Catawba College, 2300 West Innes Street, Salisbury, NC 28144-2488, 704-637-4416 or toll-free 800-CATAWBA. *Fax:* 704-637-4252. *E-mail:* mcmccull@catawba.edu.

THE CATHOLIC UNIVERSITY OF AMERICA
Washington, DC

Tuition & fees: $26,000	Average undergraduate aid package: $14,995

ABOUT THE INSTITUTION Independent religious, coed. Awards: bachelor's, master's, doctoral, and first professional degrees and post-master's certificates. 77 undergraduate majors. Total enrollment: 5,981. Undergraduates: 2,910. Freshmen: 719. Federal methodology is used as a basis for awarding need-based institutional aid.
UNDERGRADUATE EXPENSES for 2005–06 *Application fee:* $55. *One-time required fee:* $365. *Comprehensive fee:* $35,838 includes full-time tuition ($24,800), mandatory fees ($1200), and room and board ($9838). *College room only:* $5646. Full-time tuition and fees vary according to program. Room and board charges vary according to board plan and housing facility. *Part-time tuition:* $940 per credit. *Part-time fees:* $605 per year. Part-time tuition and fees vary according to course load. *Payment plans:* Tuition prepayment, installment.
FRESHMAN FINANCIAL AID (Fall 2004, est.) 719 applied for aid; of those 85% were deemed to have need. 98% of freshmen with need received aid; of those 38% had need fully met. *Average percent of need met:* 57% (excluding resources awarded to replace EFC). *Average financial aid package:* $15,073 (excluding resources awarded to replace EFC). 15% of all full-time freshmen had no need and received non-need-based gift aid.
UNDERGRADUATE FINANCIAL AID (Fall 2004, est.) 2,630 applied for aid; of those 90% were deemed to have need. 94% of undergraduates with need received aid; of those 34% had need fully met. *Average percent of need met:* 54% (excluding resources awarded to replace EFC). *Average financial aid package:* $14,995 (excluding resources awarded to replace EFC). 10% of all full-time undergraduates had no need and received non-need-based gift aid.
GIFT AID (NEED-BASED) *Total amount:* $22,652,373 (4% federal, 1% state, 92% institutional, 3% external sources). *Receiving aid:* Freshmen: 40% (285); All full-time undergraduates: 25% (658). *Average award:* Freshmen: $4160; Undergraduates: $4391. *Scholarships, grants, and awards:* Federal Pell, FSEOG, state, private, college/university gift aid from institutional funds, Federal Nursing.
GIFT AID (NON-NEED-BASED) *Total amount:* $2,222,138 (1% state, 96% institutional, 3% external sources). *Receiving aid:* Freshmen: 80% (573); Undergraduates: 78% (2,070). *Average Award:* Freshmen: $8471; Undergraduates: $8475. *Scholarships, grants, and awards by category:* Academic Interests/Achievement: general academic interests/achievements. *Creative Arts/Performance:* music, theater/drama. *Special Achievements/Activities:* general special achievements/activities. *Special Characteristics:* adult students, children of faculty/staff, ethnic background, first-generation college students, handicapped students, local/state students, religious affiliation, siblings of current students, twins. *Tuition waivers:* Full or partial for employees or children of employees. *ROTC:* Army cooperative, Naval cooperative, Air Force cooperative.
LOANS *Student loans:* $11,977,288 (90% need-based, 10% non-need-based). *Average need-based loan:* Freshmen: $3616; Undergraduates: $4765. *Parent loans:* $9,522,820 (83% need-based, 17% non-need-based). *Programs:* FFEL (Subsidized and Unsubsidized Stafford, PLUS), Perkins, Federal Nursing.
WORK-STUDY *Federal work-study:* Total amount: $967,339; jobs available.

APPLYING FOR FINANCIAL AID *Required financial aid form:* FAFSA. *Financial aid deadline:* 4/15 (priority: 2/1). *Notification date:* Continuous beginning 4/1. Students must reply by 5/1 or within 2 weeks of notification.
CONTACT Ms. Doris Torosian, Director of Financial Aid, The Catholic University of America, 620 Michigan Avenue, NE, 6 McMahon Hall, Washington, DC 20064, 202-319-5307 or toll-free 202-319-5305 (in-state), 800-673-2772 (out-of-state). *Fax:* 202-319-5573. *E-mail:* torosian@cua.edu.

CAZENOVIA COLLEGE
Cazenovia, NY

Tuition & fees: $18,940	Average undergraduate aid package: $14,800

ABOUT THE INSTITUTION Independent, coed. Awards: associate and bachelor's degrees. 23 undergraduate majors. Total enrollment: 1,180. Undergraduates: 1,180. Freshmen: 226. Federal methodology is used as a basis for awarding need-based institutional aid.
UNDERGRADUATE EXPENSES for 2005–06 *Application fee:* $25. *Comprehensive fee:* $26,530 includes full-time tuition ($18,940) and room and board ($7590). *College room only:* $4080. Full-time tuition and fees vary according to course load. Room and board charges vary according to board plan. *Part-time tuition:* $400 per credit. Part-time tuition and fees vary according to class time and course load. *Payment plan:* Installment.
FRESHMAN FINANCIAL AID (Fall 2004, est.) 214 applied for aid; of those 92% were deemed to have need. 100% of freshmen with need received aid; of those 13% had need fully met. *Average percent of need met:* 80% (excluding resources awarded to replace EFC). *Average financial aid package:* $14,600 (excluding resources awarded to replace EFC). 9% of all full-time freshmen had no need and received non-need-based gift aid.
UNDERGRADUATE FINANCIAL AID (Fall 2004, est.) 732 applied for aid; of those 86% were deemed to have need. 100% of undergraduates with need received aid; of those 23% had need fully met. *Average percent of need met:* 80% (excluding resources awarded to replace EFC). *Average financial aid package:* $14,800 (excluding resources awarded to replace EFC). 9% of all full-time undergraduates had no need and received non-need-based gift aid.
GIFT AID (NEED-BASED) *Total amount:* $7,054,101 (16% federal, 21% state, 60% institutional, 3% external sources). *Receiving aid:* Freshmen: 86% (197); All full-time undergraduates: 77% (618). *Average award:* Freshmen: $12,000; Undergraduates: $10,000. *Scholarships, grants, and awards:* Federal Pell, FSEOG, state, private, college/university gift aid from institutional funds.
GIFT AID (NON-NEED-BASED) *Total amount:* $781,859 (1% state, 92% institutional, 7% external sources). *Receiving aid:* Freshmen: 40% (91); Undergraduates: 37% (295). *Average Award:* Freshmen: $3700; Undergraduates: $4600. *Scholarships, grants, and awards by category:* Academic Interests/Achievement: 400 awards ($2,708,969 total): general academic interests/achievements. *Tuition waivers:* Full or partial for employees or children of employees. *ROTC:* Army cooperative, Air Force cooperative.
LOANS *Student loans:* $2,834,413 (77% need-based, 23% non-need-based). 84% of past graduating class borrowed through all loan programs. *Average indebtedness per student:* $15,843. *Average need-based loan:* Freshmen: $2554; Undergraduates: $3750. *Parent loans:* $1,448,654 (71% need-based, 29% non-need-based). *Programs:* Federal Direct (Subsidized and Unsubsidized Stafford, PLUS).
WORK-STUDY *Federal work-study:* Total amount: $220,249; 200 jobs averaging $1000.
APPLYING FOR FINANCIAL AID *Required financial aid forms:* FAFSA, state aid form. *Financial aid deadline (priority):* 3/15. *Notification date:* Continuous beginning 3/1. Students must reply within 3 weeks of notification.
CONTACT Ms. Christine L. Mandel, Director of Financial Aid, Cazenovia College, 22 Sullivan Street, Cazenovia, NY 13035, 315-655-7250 or toll-free 800-654-3210. *Fax:* 315-655-7219. *E-mail:* cmandel@cazenovia.edu.

CEDAR CREST COLLEGE
Allentown, PA

Tuition & fees: $23,012	Average undergraduate aid package: $15,583

ABOUT THE INSTITUTION Independent religious, women only. Awards: associate, bachelor's, and master's degrees and post-bachelor's certificates. 53 undergraduate majors. Total enrollment: 1,856. Undergraduates: 1,784. Freshmen: 320. Federal methodology is used as a basis for awarding need-based institutional aid.

UNDERGRADUATE EXPENSES for 2005–06 *Application fee:* $30. *Comprehensive fee:* $30,965 includes full-time tuition ($22,712), mandatory fees ($300), and room and board ($7953). Full-time tuition and fees vary according to course load. Room and board charges vary according to board plan. Part-time tuition and fees vary according to class time. *Payment plan:* Installment.

FRESHMAN FINANCIAL AID (Fall 2004, est.) 246 applied for aid; of those 89% were deemed to have need. 100% of freshmen with need received aid; of those 17% had need fully met. *Average percent of need met:* 76% (excluding resources awarded to replace EFC). *Average financial aid package:* $16,308 (excluding resources awarded to replace EFC). 12% of all full-time freshmen had no need and received non-need-based gift aid.

UNDERGRADUATE FINANCIAL AID (Fall 2004, est.) 844 applied for aid; of those 91% were deemed to have need. 100% of undergraduates with need received aid; of those 16% had need fully met. *Average percent of need met:* 76% (excluding resources awarded to replace EFC). *Average financial aid package:* $15,583 (excluding resources awarded to replace EFC). 12% of all full-time undergraduates had no need and received non-need-based gift aid.

GIFT AID (NEED-BASED) *Total amount:* $9,588,126 (15% federal, 14% state, 66% institutional, 5% external sources). *Receiving aid:* Freshmen: 86% (217); All full-time undergraduates: 85% (742). *Average award:* Freshmen: $12,954; Undergraduates: $11,908. *Scholarships, grants, and awards:* Federal Pell, FSEOG, state, private, college/university gift aid from institutional funds.

GIFT AID (NON-NEED-BASED) *Total amount:* $1,103,128 (2% state, 78% institutional, 20% external sources). *Receiving aid:* Freshmen: 12% (30); Undergraduates: 9% (77). *Average Award:* Freshmen: $8374; *Undergraduates:* $11,466. *Scholarships, grants, and awards by category: Academic Interests/ Achievement:* 327 awards ($2,557,767 total): general academic interests/ achievements. *Creative Arts/Performance:* 130 awards ($191,311 total): art/fine arts, dance, performing arts, theater/drama. *Special Achievements/Activities:* 79 awards ($99,401 total): community service, general special achievements/ activities, junior miss, leadership, memberships, religious involvement. *Special Characteristics:* 69 awards ($222,000 total): adult students, children and siblings of alumni, general special characteristics, previous college experience, relatives of clergy, religious affiliation, siblings of current students. *Tuition waivers:* Full or partial for children of alumni, employees or children of employees. *ROTC:* Army cooperative.

LOANS *Student loans:* $8,801,291 (74% need-based, 26% non-need-based). 96% of past graduating class borrowed through all loan programs. *Average indebtedness per student:* $21,199. *Average need-based loan:* Freshmen: $3228; Undergraduates: $3934. *Parent loans:* $1,713,204 (38% need-based, 62% non-need-based). *Programs:* FFEL (Subsidized and Unsubsidized Stafford, PLUS), Perkins, Federal Nursing, college/university.

WORK-STUDY *Federal work-study:* Total amount: $143,275; 95 jobs averaging $1500. *State or other work-study/employment:* Total amount: $558,800 (59% need-based, 41% non-need-based). 328 part-time jobs averaging $1700.

APPLYING FOR FINANCIAL AID *Required financial aid forms:* FAFSA, institution's own form. *Financial aid deadline:* Continuous. *Notification date:* Continuous. Students must reply by 5/1.

CONTACT Ms. Lori Williams, Director of Financial Aid, Cedar Crest College, 100 College Drive, Allentown, PA 18104-6196, 610-740-3785 or toll-free 800-360-1222. *Fax:* 610-606-4653. *E-mail:* finaid@cedarcrest.edu.

CEDARVILLE UNIVERSITY
Cedarville, OH

Tuition & fees: $16,032	Average undergraduate aid package: $14,401

ABOUT THE INSTITUTION Independent Baptist, coed. Awards: bachelor's and master's degrees. 71 undergraduate majors. Total enrollment: 3,070. Undergraduates: 3,070. Freshmen: 762. Federal methodology is used as a basis for awarding need-based institutional aid.

UNDERGRADUATE EXPENSES for 2004–05 *Application fee:* $30. *Comprehensive fee:* $21,042 includes full-time tuition ($16,032) and room and board ($5010). *College room only:* $2684. Room and board charges vary according to board plan. *Part-time tuition:* $501 per credit hour. Part-time tuition and fees vary according to course load. *Payment plan:* Installment.

FRESHMAN FINANCIAL AID (Fall 2003) 705 applied for aid; of those 82% were deemed to have need. 99% of freshmen with need received aid; of those 52% had need fully met. *Average percent of need met:* 25% (excluding resources awarded to replace EFC). *Average financial aid package:* $14,056 (excluding resources awarded to replace EFC). 28% of all full-time freshmen had no need and received non-need-based gift aid.

UNDERGRADUATE FINANCIAL AID (Fall 2003) 2,042 applied for aid; of those 86% were deemed to have need. 99% of undergraduates with need received aid; of those 50% had need fully met. *Average percent of need met:* 43% (excluding resources awarded to replace EFC). *Average financial aid package:* $14,401 (excluding resources awarded to replace EFC). 22% of all full-time undergraduates had no need and received non-need-based gift aid.

GIFT AID (NEED-BASED) *Total amount:* $3,090,038 (45% federal, 9% state, 31% institutional, 15% external sources). *Receiving aid:* Freshmen: 25% (223); All full-time undergraduates: 31% (889). *Average award:* Freshmen: $1173; Undergraduates: $1654. *Scholarships, grants, and awards:* Federal Pell, FSEOG, state, private, college/university gift aid from institutional funds.

GIFT AID (NON-NEED-BASED) *Total amount:* $8,459,157 (13% state, 57% institutional, 30% external sources). *Receiving aid:* Freshmen: 55% (497); Undergraduates: 43% (1,208). *Average Award:* Freshmen: $7012; *Undergraduates:* $7422. *Scholarships, grants, and awards by category: Academic Interests/ Achievement:* 767 awards ($1,380,367 total): general academic interests/ achievements. *Creative Arts/Performance:* 59 awards ($81,375 total): debating, music. *Special Achievements/Activities:* 417 awards ($616,456 total): leadership. *Special Characteristics:* 229 awards ($1,702,323 total): children and siblings of alumni, children of faculty/staff, ethnic background, general special characteristics, religious affiliation, veterans. *Tuition waivers:* Full or partial for employees or children of employees, senior citizens. *ROTC:* Army cooperative, Air Force cooperative.

LOANS *Student loans:* $8,718,305 (68% need-based, 32% non-need-based). 65% of past graduating class borrowed through all loan programs. *Average indebtedness per student:* $17,862. *Average need-based loan:* Freshmen: $2712; Undergraduates: $4058. *Parent loans:* $10,103,520 (100% non-need-based). *Programs:* FFEL (Subsidized and Unsubsidized Stafford, PLUS), Perkins, Federal Nursing, college/university.

WORK-STUDY *Federal work-study:* Total amount: $338,509; 566 jobs averaging $894. *State or other work-study/employment:* Total amount: $1,159,626 (100% non-need-based). 1,310 part-time jobs averaging $885.

ATHLETIC AWARDS *Total amount:* $560,037 (100% non-need-based).

APPLYING FOR FINANCIAL AID *Required financial aid form:* FAFSA. *Financial aid deadline (priority):* 3/1. *Notification date:* Continuous. Students must reply within 4 weeks of notification.

CONTACT Mr. Fred Merritt, Director of Financial Aid, Cedarville University, 251 North Main Street, Cedarville, OH 45314-0601, 937-766-7866 or toll-free 800-CEDARVILLE. *E-mail:* merrittf@cedarville.edu.

CENTENARY COLLEGE
Hackettstown, NJ

Tuition & fees: $19,360	Average undergraduate aid package: $12,579

ABOUT THE INSTITUTION Independent religious, coed. Awards: associate, bachelor's, and master's degrees and post-bachelor's certificates. 24 undergraduate majors. Total enrollment: 2,600. Undergraduates: 2,010. Freshmen: 312. Federal methodology is used as a basis for awarding need-based institutional aid.

UNDERGRADUATE EXPENSES for 2004–05 *Application fee:* $30. *Comprehensive fee:* $26,860 includes full-time tuition ($18,450), mandatory fees ($910), and room and board ($7500). Full-time tuition and fees vary according to location and program. *Part-time tuition:* $385 per credit. *Part-time fees:* $20 per term. Part-time tuition and fees vary according to location and program. *Payment plan:* Installment.

FRESHMAN FINANCIAL AID (Fall 2004, est.) 228 applied for aid; of those 86% were deemed to have need. 100% of freshmen with need received aid; of those 14% had need fully met. *Average percent of need met:* 68% (excluding resources awarded to replace EFC). *Average financial aid package:* $13,555 (excluding resources awarded to replace EFC). 12% of all full-time freshmen had no need and received non-need-based gift aid.

UNDERGRADUATE FINANCIAL AID (Fall 2004, est.) 975 applied for aid; of those 86% were deemed to have need. 99% of undergraduates with need received aid; of those 16% had need fully met. *Average percent of need met:* 65% (excluding resources awarded to replace EFC). *Average financial aid package:* $12,579 (excluding resources awarded to replace EFC). 7% of all full-time undergraduates had no need and received non-need-based gift aid.

GIFT AID (NEED-BASED) *Total amount:* $7,412,309 (15% federal, 29% state, 49% institutional, 7% external sources). *Receiving aid:* Freshmen: 74% (190); All full-time undergraduates: 44% (752). *Average award:* Freshmen: $10,831; Undergraduates: $9759. *Scholarships, grants, and awards:* Federal Pell, FSEOG, state, private, college/university gift aid from institutional funds.

GIFT AID (NON-NEED-BASED) *Total amount:* $577,690 (80% institutional, 20% external sources). *Receiving aid:* Freshmen: 7% (17); Undergraduates: 4% (65). *Average Award:* Freshmen: $12,944; Undergraduates: $11,668. *Scholarships, grants, and awards by category: Academic Interests/Achievement:* 128 awards ($310,586 total): general academic interests/achievements. *Special Achievements/Activities:* 132 awards ($413,425 total): leadership. *Special Characteristics:* 346 awards ($1,044,532 total): children and siblings of alumni, ethnic background, general special characteristics, local/state students, out-of-state students, previous college experience, religious affiliation, siblings of current students. *Tuition waivers:* Full or partial for children of alumni, employees or children of employees, senior citizens.

LOANS *Student loans:* $6,734,953 (73% need-based, 27% non-need-based). 100% of past graduating class borrowed through all loan programs. *Average indebtedness per student:* $18,986. *Average need-based loan:* Freshmen: $3067; Undergraduates: $4042. *Parent loans:* $2,332,925 (42% need-based, 58% non-need-based). *Programs:* FFEL (Subsidized and Unsubsidized Stafford, PLUS), Perkins, state, NJ Class Loans.

WORK-STUDY *Federal work-study:* Total amount: $164,054; 268 jobs averaging $614. *State or other work-study/employment:* Total amount: $127,407 (36% need-based, 64% non-need-based). 235 part-time jobs averaging $544.

APPLYING FOR FINANCIAL AID *Required financial aid form:* FAFSA. *Financial aid deadline (priority):* 4/15. *Notification date:* Continuous. Students must reply within 2 weeks of notification.

CONTACT Michael Corso, Director of Financial Aid, Centenary College, 400 Jefferson Street, Hackettstown, NJ 07840-2100, 908-852-1400 Ext. 2207 or toll-free 800-236-8679. *Fax:* 908-813-2632.

CENTENARY COLLEGE OF LOUISIANA
Shreveport, LA

Tuition & fees: $17,360	Average undergraduate aid package: $13,197

ABOUT THE INSTITUTION Independent United Methodist, coed. Awards: bachelor's and master's degrees. 73 undergraduate majors. Total enrollment: 1,040. Undergraduates: 905. Freshmen: 282. Federal methodology is used as a basis for awarding need-based institutional aid.

UNDERGRADUATE EXPENSES for 2004–05 *Comprehensive fee:* $23,430 includes full-time tuition ($16,750), mandatory fees ($610), and room and board ($6070). *College room only:* $3000. Full-time tuition and fees vary according to course load. Room and board charges vary according to board plan and housing facility. *Part-time tuition:* $560 per semester hour. *Part-time fees:* $50 per term. *Payment plans:* Installment, deferred payment.

FRESHMAN FINANCIAL AID (Fall 2004, est.) 258 applied for aid; of those 74% were deemed to have need. 100% of freshmen with need received aid; of those 43% had need fully met. *Average percent of need met:* 84% (excluding resources awarded to replace EFC). *Average financial aid package:* $13,863 (excluding resources awarded to replace EFC). 25% of all full-time freshmen had no need and received non-need-based gift aid.

UNDERGRADUATE FINANCIAL AID (Fall 2004, est.) 739 applied for aid; of those 77% were deemed to have need. 97% of undergraduates with need received aid; of those 39% had need fully met. *Average percent of need met:* 76% (excluding resources awarded to replace EFC). *Average financial aid package:* $13,197 (excluding resources awarded to replace EFC). 26% of all full-time undergraduates had no need and received non-need-based gift aid.

GIFT AID (NEED-BASED) *Total amount:* $6,008,116 (10% federal, 15% state, 73% institutional, 2% external sources). *Receiving aid:* Freshmen: 67% (191); All full-time undergraduates: 63% (551). *Average award:* Freshmen: $11,988; Undergraduates: $10,862. *Scholarships, grants, and awards:* Federal Pell, FSEOG, state, private, college/university gift aid from institutional funds.

GIFT AID (NON-NEED-BASED) *Total amount:* $3,771,987 (11% state, 88% institutional, 1% external sources). *Receiving aid:* Freshmen: 22% (63); Undergraduates: 19% (169). *Average award:* Freshmen: $9371; Undergraduates: $9808. *Scholarships, grants, and awards by category: Academic Interests/Achievement:* 655 awards ($5,516,331 total): biological sciences, business, communication, education, engineering/technologies, English, foreign languages, general academic interests/achievements, humanities, mathematics, physical sciences, premedicine, religion/biblical studies, social sciences. *Creative Arts/Performance:* 198 awards ($637,259 total): art/fine arts, dance, general creative arts/performance, music, performing arts, theater/drama. *Special Achievements/Activities:* 199 awards ($460,626 total): community service, general special achievements/activities, leadership, religious involvement. *Special Characteristics:* 130 awards ($516,031 total): children of educators, children of faculty/staff, ethnic background, general special characteristics, international students, local/

state students, members of minority groups, out-of-state students, relatives of clergy, religious affiliation. *Tuition waivers:* Full or partial for employees or children of employees.

LOANS *Student loans:* $1,981,822 (53% need-based, 47% non-need-based). 56% of past graduating class borrowed through all loan programs. *Average indebtedness per student:* $17,360. *Average need-based loan:* Freshmen: $2768; Undergraduates: $3886. *Parent loans:* $859,810 (100% non-need-based). *Programs:* FFEL (Subsidized and Unsubsidized Stafford, PLUS), Perkins.

WORK-STUDY *Federal work-study:* Total amount: $272,541; 186 jobs averaging $1493. *State or other work-study/employment:* Total amount: $61,750 (100% non-need-based). 59 part-time jobs averaging $1055.

ATHLETIC AWARDS *Total amount:* $2,139,448 (40% need-based, 60% non-need-based).

APPLYING FOR FINANCIAL AID *Required financial aid forms:* FAFSA, institution's own form. *Financial aid deadline (priority):* 2/15. *Notification date:* 3/15. Students must reply by 5/1.

CONTACT Ms. Mary Sue Rix, Director of Financial Aid, Centenary College of Louisiana, PO Box 41188, Shreveport, LA 71134-1188, 318-869-5137 or toll-free 800-234-4448. *Fax:* 318-841-7266. *E-mail:* msrix@centenary.edu.

CENTRAL BAPTIST COLLEGE
Conway, AR

CONTACT Christi Bell, Financial Aid Director, Central Baptist College, 1501 College Avenue, Conway, AR 72032-6470, 800-205-6872 Ext. 185 or toll-free 800-205-6872. *Fax:* 501-329-2941. *E-mail:* financialaid@cbc.edu.

CENTRAL BIBLE COLLEGE
Springfield, MO

Tuition & fees: $8722	Average undergraduate aid package: $7028

ABOUT THE INSTITUTION Independent Assemblies of God, coed. Awards: associate and bachelor's degrees. 7 undergraduate majors. Total enrollment: 817. Undergraduates: 817. Freshmen: 189. Federal methodology is used as a basis for awarding need-based institutional aid.

UNDERGRADUATE EXPENSES for 2004–05 *Application fee:* $25. *Comprehensive fee:* $13,282 includes full-time tuition ($8034), mandatory fees ($688), and room and board ($4560). Room and board charges vary according to board plan. *Part-time tuition:* $311 per credit hour. *Part-time fees:* $114 per term.

FRESHMAN FINANCIAL AID (Fall 2004, est.) 147 applied for aid; of those 88% were deemed to have need. 98% of freshmen with need received aid; of those 6% had need fully met. *Average percent of need met:* 38% (excluding resources awarded to replace EFC). *Average financial aid package:* $5505 (excluding resources awarded to replace EFC). 9% of all full-time freshmen had no need and received non-need-based gift aid.

UNDERGRADUATE FINANCIAL AID (Fall 2004, est.) 608 applied for aid; of those 94% were deemed to have need. 99% of undergraduates with need received aid; of those 3% had need fully met. *Average percent of need met:* 42% (excluding resources awarded to replace EFC). *Average financial aid package:* $7028 (excluding resources awarded to replace EFC). 4% of all full-time undergraduates had no need and received non-need-based gift aid.

GIFT AID (NEED-BASED) *Total amount:* $1,526,316 (74% federal, 17% institutional, 9% external sources). *Receiving aid:* Freshmen: 62% (112); All full-time undergraduates: 59% (489). *Average award:* Freshmen: $3172; Undergraduates: $3424. *Scholarships, grants, and awards:* Federal Pell, FSEOG, college/university gift aid from institutional funds.

GIFT AID (NON-NEED-BASED) *Total amount:* $107,343 (84% institutional, 16% external sources). *Receiving aid:* Freshmen: 1% (2); Undergraduates: 1% (5). *Average Award:* Freshmen: $10,553; Undergraduates: $11,613. *Scholarships, grants, and awards by category: Academic Interests/Achievement:* 46 awards ($28,750 total): general academic interests/achievements. *Creative Arts/Performance:* 55 awards ($73,745 total): art/fine arts, music, theater/drama. *Special Achievements/Activities:* community service, religious involvement. *Special Characteristics:* 56 awards ($74,691 total): children of faculty/staff, ethnic background, relatives of clergy, religious affiliation, siblings of current students, spouses of current students. *Tuition waivers:* Full or partial for employees or children of employees.

LOANS *Student loans:* $4,366,418 (55% need-based, 45% non-need-based). 73% of past graduating class borrowed through all loan programs. *Average indebtedness per student:* $19,686. *Average need-based loan:* Freshmen: $2820;

Undergraduates: $4072. *Parent loans:* $1,264,080 (51% need-based, 49% non-need-based). *Programs:* FFEL (Subsidized and Unsubsidized Stafford, PLUS), Perkins, college/university.

WORK-STUDY *Federal work-study:* Total amount: $164,635; 125 jobs averaging $1317.

APPLYING FOR FINANCIAL AID *Required financial aid form:* FAFSA. *Financial aid deadline (priority):* 3/1. *Notification date:* Continuous. Students must reply within 3 weeks of notification.

CONTACT Rick Woolverton, Director of Financial Aid, Central Bible College, 3000 North Grant, Springfield, MO 65803-1096, 417-833-2551 or toll-free 800-831-4222 Ext. 1184. *Fax:* 417-833-2168.

CENTRAL CHRISTIAN COLLEGE OF KANSAS
McPherson, KS

Tuition & fees: $13,600	Average undergraduate aid package: $10,705

ABOUT THE INSTITUTION Independent Free Methodist, coed. Awards: associate and bachelor's degrees. 122 undergraduate majors. Total enrollment: 324. Undergraduates: 324. Federal methodology is used as a basis for awarding need-based institutional aid.

UNDERGRADUATE EXPENSES for 2005–06 *Application fee:* $20. *Comprehensive fee:* $18,100 includes full-time tuition ($13,100), mandatory fees ($500), and room and board ($4500). *College room only:* $2100. Full-time tuition and fees vary according to course load. Room and board charges vary according to board plan and gender. *Part-time tuition:* $380 per credit hour. Part-time tuition and fees vary according to course load. *Payment plan:* Installment.

FRESHMAN FINANCIAL AID (Fall 2004, est.) 86 applied for aid; of those 88% were deemed to have need. 100% of freshmen with need received aid. *Average percent of need met:* 50% (excluding resources awarded to replace EFC). *Average financial aid package:* $10,631 (excluding resources awarded to replace EFC). 15% of all full-time freshmen had no need and received non-need-based gift aid.

UNDERGRADUATE FINANCIAL AID (Fall 2004, est.) 282 applied for aid; of those 90% were deemed to have need. 100% of undergraduates with need received aid. *Average percent of need met:* 50% (excluding resources awarded to replace EFC). *Average financial aid package:* $10,705 (excluding resources awarded to replace EFC). 11% of all full-time undergraduates had no need and received non-need-based gift aid.

GIFT AID (NEED-BASED) *Total amount:* $627,730 (84% federal, 16% state). *Receiving aid:* Freshmen: 56% (52); All full-time undergraduates: 58% (176). *Average award:* Freshmen: $3332; Undergraduates: $3420. *Scholarships, grants, and awards:* Federal Pell, FSEOG, state, private.

GIFT AID (NON-NEED-BASED) *Total amount:* $1,318,500 (93% institutional, 7% external sources). *Receiving aid:* Freshmen: 80% (74); Undergraduates: 78% (237). *Average Award:* Freshmen: $4030; Undergraduates: $4329. *Scholarships, grants, and awards by category:* Academic Interests/Achievement: 265 awards ($853,099 total): general academic interests/achievements, religion/biblical studies. Creative Arts/Performance: 23 awards ($16,300 total): music, theater/drama. Special Achievements/Activities: 166 awards ($201,232 total): cheerleading/drum major, general special achievements/activities, leadership, religious involvement. Special Characteristics: 26 awards ($86,415 total): children of faculty/staff, relatives of clergy. *Tuition waivers:* Full or partial for children of alumni, employees or children of employees.

LOANS *Student loans:* $1,770,801 (57% need-based, 43% non-need-based). 73% of past graduating class borrowed through all loan programs. *Average indebtedness per student:* $20,000. *Average need-based loan:* Freshmen: $4380; Undergraduates: $4700. *Parent loans:* $240,000 (100% non-need-based). *Programs:* FFEL (Subsidized and Unsubsidized Stafford, PLUS), Perkins.

WORK-STUDY *Federal work-study:* Total amount: $58,725; 58 jobs averaging $1000.

ATHLETIC AWARDS *Total amount:* $160,000 (100% non-need-based).

APPLYING FOR FINANCIAL AID *Required financial aid form:* FAFSA. *Financial aid deadline (priority):* 3/1. *Notification date:* Continuous beginning 3/1. Students must reply within 4 weeks of notification.

CONTACT Mike Reimer, Financial Aid Director, Central Christian College of Kansas, 1200 South Main, PO Box 1403, McPherson, KS 67460, 620-241-0723 Ext. 333 or toll-free 800-835-0078 Ext. 337. *Fax:* 620-241-6032. *E-mail:* miker@centralchristian.edu.

CENTRAL CHRISTIAN COLLEGE OF THE BIBLE
Moberly, MO

ABOUT THE INSTITUTION Independent religious, coed. Awards: associate and bachelor's degrees. 8 undergraduate majors. Total enrollment: 461. Undergraduates: 461. Freshmen: 174.

GIFT AID (NEED-BASED) *Scholarships, grants, and awards:* Federal Pell, FSEOG, private, college/university gift aid from institutional funds.

GIFT AID (NON-NEED-BASED) *Scholarships, grants, and awards by category:* Academic Interests/Achievement: religion/biblical studies.

LOANS *Programs:* FFEL (Subsidized and Unsubsidized Stafford, PLUS).

WORK-STUDY *Federal work-study:* Total amount: $11,000; 10 jobs averaging $1100.

APPLYING FOR FINANCIAL AID *Required financial aid form:* institution's own form.

CONTACT Rhonda J. Dunham, Financial Aid Director, Central Christian College of the Bible, 911 East Urbandale Drive, Moberly, MO 65270-1997, 660-263-3900 Ext. 21 or toll-free 888-263-3900 (in-state). *Fax:* 660-263-3936. *E-mail:* rdunham@cccb.edu.

CENTRAL COLLEGE
Pella, IA

Tuition & fees: $18,892	Average undergraduate aid package: $15,553

ABOUT THE INSTITUTION Independent religious, coed. Awards: bachelor's degrees. 36 undergraduate majors. Total enrollment: 1,750. Undergraduates: 1,750. Freshmen: 442. Federal methodology is used as a basis for awarding need-based institutional aid.

UNDERGRADUATE EXPENSES for 2004–05 *Application fee:* $25. *Comprehensive fee:* $25,378 includes full-time tuition ($18,648), mandatory fees ($244), and room and board ($6486). *College room only:* $3180. Room and board charges vary according to board plan. *Part-time tuition:* $647 per credit hour. Part-time tuition and fees vary according to course load. *Payment plan:* Installment.

FRESHMAN FINANCIAL AID (Fall 2004, est.) 411 applied for aid; of those 91% were deemed to have need. 100% of freshmen with need received aid; of those 45% had need fully met. *Average percent of need met:* 81% (excluding resources awarded to replace EFC). *Average financial aid package:* $15,675 (excluding resources awarded to replace EFC). 15% of all full-time freshmen had no need and received non-need-based gift aid.

UNDERGRADUATE FINANCIAL AID (Fall 2004, est.) 1,408 applied for aid; of those 93% were deemed to have need. 100% of undergraduates with need received aid; of those 27% had need fully met. *Average percent of need met:* 80% (excluding resources awarded to replace EFC). *Average financial aid package:* $15,553 (excluding resources awarded to replace EFC). 18% of all full-time undergraduates had no need and received non-need-based gift aid.

GIFT AID (NEED-BASED) *Total amount:* $14,746,076 (9% federal, 19% state, 69% institutional, 3% external sources). *Receiving aid:* Freshmen: 85% (374); All full-time undergraduates: 81% (1,300). *Average award:* Freshmen: $12,529; Undergraduates: $11,655. *Scholarships, grants, and awards:* Federal Pell, FSEOG, state, private, college/university gift aid from institutional funds.

GIFT AID (NON-NEED-BASED) *Total amount:* $2,600,037 (96% institutional, 4% external sources). *Receiving aid:* Freshmen: 11% (48); Undergraduates: 8% (130). *Average Award:* Freshmen: $7915; Undergraduates: $7550. *Scholarships, grants, and awards by category:* Academic Interests/Achievement: 1,516 awards ($8,590,316 total): biological sciences, business, communication, computer science, education, foreign languages, general academic interests/achievements, health fields, humanities, international studies, mathematics, physical sciences, religion/biblical studies. Creative Arts/Performance: 227 awards ($466,110 total): art/fine arts, music, theater/drama. Special Achievements/Activities: 7 awards ($40,750 total): religious involvement. Special Characteristics: 732 awards ($1,014,494 total): children and siblings of alumni, children of current students, children of faculty/staff, general special characteristics, handicapped students, international students, members of minority groups, out-of-state students, previous college experience, religious affiliation, siblings of current students. *Tuition waivers:* Full or partial for employees or children of employees.

LOANS *Student loans:* $9,989,548 (68% need-based, 32% non-need-based). 84% of past graduating class borrowed through all loan programs. *Average indebtedness per student:* $26,257. *Average need-based loan:* Freshmen: $3745;

Undergraduates: $4582. *Parent loans:* $1,626,130 (24% need-based, 76% non-need-based). *Programs:* Federal Direct (Subsidized and Unsubsidized Stafford, PLUS), Perkins, college/university, alternative loans.

WORK-STUDY *Federal work-study:* Total amount: $1,033,369; 926 jobs averaging $1116. *State or other work-study/employment:* Total amount: $555,551 (27% need-based, 73% non-need-based). 520 part-time jobs averaging $1068.

APPLYING FOR FINANCIAL AID *Required financial aid form:* FAFSA. *Financial aid deadline (priority):* 3/15. *Notification date:* Continuous beginning 3/15. Students must reply by 5/1 or within 2 weeks of notification.

CONTACT Ms. Jean Vander Wert, Director of Financial Aid, Central College, 812 University Street, Box 5800, Pella, IA 50219-1999, 641-628-5336 or toll-free 877-462-3687 (in-state), 877-462-3689 (out-of-state). *Fax:* 641-628-7199. *E-mail:* vanderwertj@central.edu.

CENTRAL CONNECTICUT STATE UNIVERSITY
New Britain, CT

Tuition & fees (CT res): $5902	Average undergraduate aid package: $6731

ABOUT THE INSTITUTION State-supported, coed. Awards: bachelor's, master's, and doctoral degrees and post-bachelor's and post-master's certificates. 53 undergraduate majors. Total enrollment: 12,320. Undergraduates: 9,604. Freshmen: 1,295. Federal methodology is used as a basis for awarding need-based institutional aid.

UNDERGRADUATE EXPENSES for 2004–05 *Application fee:* $50. *One-time required fee:* $50. *Tuition, state resident:* full-time $2862; part-time $276 per credit. *Tuition, nonresident:* full-time $10,379; part-time $276 per credit. *Required fees:* full-time $3040; $55 per term part-time. Full-time tuition and fees vary according to class time, course level, and reciprocity agreements. Part-time tuition and fees vary according to class time and course level. *College room and board:* $7036; *room only:* $4012. Room and board charges vary according to board plan. *Payment plans:* Installment, deferred payment.

FRESHMAN FINANCIAL AID (Fall 2004, est.) 967 applied for aid; of those 68% were deemed to have need. 96% of freshmen with need received aid; of those 6% had need fully met. *Average percent of need met:* 76% (excluding resources awarded to replace EFC). *Average financial aid package:* $6537 (excluding resources awarded to replace EFC). 9% of all full-time freshmen had no need and received non-need-based gift aid.

UNDERGRADUATE FINANCIAL AID (Fall 2004, est.) 4,931 applied for aid; of those 77% were deemed to have need. 96% of undergraduates with need received aid; of those 3% had need fully met. *Average percent of need met:* 72% (excluding resources awarded to replace EFC). *Average financial aid package:* $6731 (excluding resources awarded to replace EFC). 2% of all full-time undergraduates had no need and received non-need-based gift aid.

GIFT AID (NEED-BASED) *Total amount:* $10,070,487 (44% federal, 24% state, 32% institutional). *Receiving aid:* Freshmen: 39% (459); All full-time undergraduates: 34% (2,289). *Average award:* Freshmen: $5306; Undergraduates: $4738. *Scholarships, grants, and awards:* Federal Pell, FSEOG, state, private, college/university gift aid from institutional funds.

GIFT AID (NON-NEED-BASED) *Total amount:* $1,611,204 (64% institutional, 36% external sources). *Receiving aid:* Freshmen: 5% (58); Undergraduates: 6% (404). *Average Award:* Freshmen: $2081; Undergraduates: $2272. *Scholarships, grants, and awards by category: Academic Interests/Achievement:* general academic interests/achievements. *Special Characteristics:* members of minority groups. *Tuition waivers:* Full or partial for employees or children of employees, senior citizens. *ROTC:* Army cooperative, Air Force cooperative.

LOANS *Student loans:* $26,243,309 (59% need-based, 41% non-need-based). 38% of past graduating class borrowed through all loan programs. *Average indebtedness per student:* $10,500. *Average need-based loan:* Freshmen: $2814; Undergraduates: $3704. *Parent loans:* $2,901,491 (100% non-need-based). *Programs:* Federal Direct (Subsidized and Unsubsidized Stafford, PLUS), FFEL (Subsidized and Unsubsidized Stafford, PLUS), Perkins.

WORK-STUDY *Federal work-study:* Total amount: $352,254; 289 jobs averaging $1990. *State or other work-study/employment:* 110 part-time jobs averaging $544.

ATHLETIC AWARDS *Total amount:* $1,635,897 (100% non-need-based).

APPLYING FOR FINANCIAL AID *Required financial aid forms:* FAFSA, institution's own form. *Financial aid deadline (priority):* 3/1. *Notification date:* Continuous. Students must reply within 3 weeks of notification.

CONTACT Ms. Keri Lupachino, Assistant Director of Financial Aid, Central Connecticut State University, Memorial Hall, Room 103, 1615 Stanley Street, New Britain, CT 06050-4010, 860-832-2200 or toll-free 800-755-2278 (in-state). *Fax:* 860-832-1105. *E-mail:* lupachinok@ccsu.edu.

CENTRAL METHODIST UNIVERSITY
Fayette, MO

Tuition & fees: $15,200	Average undergraduate aid package: $14,229

ABOUT THE INSTITUTION Independent Methodist, coed. Awards: associate, bachelor's, and master's degrees. 47 undergraduate majors. Total enrollment: 781. Undergraduates: 781. Freshmen: 193. Federal methodology is used as a basis for awarding need-based institutional aid.

UNDERGRADUATE EXPENSES for 2005–06 *Application fee:* $20. *Comprehensive fee:* $20,560 includes full-time tuition ($14,490), mandatory fees ($710), and room and board ($5360). *College room only:* $2640. Room and board charges vary according to board plan and housing facility. *Part-time tuition:* $140 per credit hour. Part-time tuition and fees vary according to course load. *Payment plan:* Installment.

FRESHMAN FINANCIAL AID (Fall 2003) 171 applied for aid; of those 85% were deemed to have need. 100% of freshmen with need received aid; of those 3% had need fully met. *Average percent of need met:* 72% (excluding resources awarded to replace EFC). *Average financial aid package:* $14,433 (excluding resources awarded to replace EFC). 3% of all full-time freshmen had no need and received non-need-based gift aid.

UNDERGRADUATE FINANCIAL AID (Fall 2003) 601 applied for aid; of those 100% were deemed to have need. 100% of undergraduates with need received aid; of those 4% had need fully met. *Average percent of need met:* 71% (excluding resources awarded to replace EFC). *Average financial aid package:* $14,229 (excluding resources awarded to replace EFC). 4% of all full-time undergraduates had no need and received non-need-based gift aid.

GIFT AID (NEED-BASED) *Total amount:* $1,768,091 (59% federal, 35% state, 6% institutional). *Receiving aid:* Freshmen: 76% (146); All full-time undergraduates: 80% (601). *Average award:* Freshmen: $4662; Undergraduates: $5326. *Scholarships, grants, and awards:* Federal Pell, FSEOG, state, private, college/university gift aid from institutional funds.

GIFT AID (NON-NEED-BASED) *Total amount:* $3,187,202 (1% state, 94% institutional, 5% external sources). *Receiving aid:* Freshmen: 76% (146); Undergraduates: 66% (498). *Average Award:* Freshmen: $6600; Undergraduates:* $6931. *Scholarships, grants, and awards by category: Academic Interests/Achievement:* 532 awards ($1,773,465 total): biological sciences, business, communication, computer science, education, English, foreign languages, general academic interests/achievements, health fields, humanities, mathematics, physical sciences, premedicine, religion/biblical studies, social sciences. *Creative Arts/Performance:* 68 awards ($311,350 total): music, theater/drama. *Special Achievements/Activities:* 44 awards ($100,440 total): cheerleading/drum major, leadership, religious involvement. *Special Characteristics:* 295 awards ($500,886 total): children and siblings of alumni, children of faculty/staff, general special characteristics, international students, relatives of clergy, religious affiliation, siblings of current students, spouses of current students. *Tuition waivers:* Full or partial for employees or children of employees. *ROTC:* Army cooperative, Air Force cooperative.

LOANS *Student loans:* $3,316,072 (52% need-based, 48% non-need-based). 88% of past graduating class borrowed through all loan programs. *Average indebtedness per student:* $19,247. *Average need-based loan:* Freshmen: $2625; Undergraduates: $3789. *Parent loans:* $1,284,068 (100% non-need-based). *Programs:* FFEL (Subsidized and Unsubsidized Stafford, PLUS), college/university.

WORK-STUDY *Federal work-study:* Total amount: $178,197; 145 jobs averaging $1000. *State or other work-study/employment:* Total amount: $117,007 (100% non-need-based). 90 part-time jobs averaging $1619.

ATHLETIC AWARDS *Total amount:* $2,415,465 (100% non-need-based).

APPLYING FOR FINANCIAL AID *Required financial aid form:* FAFSA. *Financial aid deadline (priority):* 3/15. *Notification date:* Continuous beginning 1/30. Students must reply within 2 weeks of notification.

CONTACT Linda Mackey, Director of Financial Assistance, Central Methodist University, 411 CMC Square, Fayette, MO 65248-1198, 660-248-6244 or toll-free 888-CMU-1854 (in-state). *Fax:* 660-248-6288. *E-mail:* lmackey@cmc.edu.

CENTRAL MICHIGAN UNIVERSITY
Mount Pleasant, MI

Tuition & fees (MI res): $5365 **Average undergraduate aid package: $8404**

ABOUT THE INSTITUTION State-supported, coed. Awards: bachelor's, master's, and doctoral degrees and post-bachelor's and post-master's certificates. 117 undergraduate majors. Total enrollment: 27,683. Undergraduates: 19,916. Freshmen: 3,755. Federal methodology is used as a basis for awarding need-based institutional aid.

UNDERGRADUATE EXPENSES for 2004–05 *Application fee:* $35. *Tuition, state resident:* full-time $4610; part-time $153.65 per credit. *Tuition, nonresident:* full-time $11,712; part-time $390.40 per credit. *Required fees:* full-time $755; $212.50 per term part-time. *College room and board:* $6160; *room only:* $3080. Room and board charges vary according to board plan, housing facility, and location. *Payment plan:* Installment.

FRESHMAN FINANCIAL AID (Fall 2004, est.) 2824 applied for aid; of those 69% were deemed to have need. 100% of freshmen with need received aid; of those 66% had need fully met. *Average percent of need met:* 94% (excluding resources awarded to replace EFC). *Average financial aid package:* $8346 (excluding resources awarded to replace EFC). 15% of all full-time freshmen had no need and received non-need-based gift aid.

UNDERGRADUATE FINANCIAL AID (Fall 2004, est.) 11,990 applied for aid; of those 76% were deemed to have need. 100% of undergraduates with need received aid; of those 61% had need fully met. *Average percent of need met:* 90% (excluding resources awarded to replace EFC). *Average financial aid package:* $8404 (excluding resources awarded to replace EFC). 11% of all full-time undergraduates had no need and received non-need-based gift aid.

GIFT AID (NEED-BASED) *Total amount:* $26,971,207 (53% federal, 20% state, 23% institutional, 4% external sources). *Receiving aid:* Freshmen: 49% (1,813); All full-time undergraduates: 42% (7,254). *Average award:* Freshmen: $4154; Undergraduates: $3097. *Scholarships, grants, and awards:* Federal Pell, FSEOG, state, private, college/university gift aid from institutional funds.

GIFT AID (NON-NEED-BASED) *Total amount:* $10,845,051 (7% federal, 30% state, 50% institutional, 13% external sources). *Receiving aid:* Freshmen: 6% (236); Undergraduates: 4% (620). *Average Award:* Freshmen: $2486; *Undergraduates:* $2620. *Scholarships, grants, and awards by category: Academic Interests/Achievement:* 8,736 awards ($12,628,566 total): biological sciences, business, communication, computer science, education, engineering/technologies, English, foreign languages, general academic interests/achievements, health fields, humanities, mathematics, military science, physical sciences, social sciences. *Creative Arts/Performance:* 201 awards ($202,438 total): applied art and design, art/fine arts, cinema/film/broadcasting, creative writing, dance, journalism/publications, music, performing arts, theater/drama. *Special Achievements/Activities:* 371 awards ($1,065,796 total): leadership. *Special Characteristics:* 875 awards ($2,446,022 total): children and siblings of alumni, children of faculty/staff, children of union members/company employees, ethnic background, first-generation college students, international students, local/state students, members of minority groups, out-of-state students, veterans, veterans' children. *Tuition waivers:* Full or partial for children of alumni, employees or children of employees, senior citizens. *ROTC:* Army.

LOANS *Student loans:* $69,251,867 (61% need-based, 39% non-need-based). 61% of past graduating class borrowed through all loan programs. *Average indebtedness per student:* $16,312. *Average need-based loan:* Freshmen: $3193; Undergraduates: $4520. *Parent loans:* $8,991,214 (21% need-based, 79% non-need-based). *Programs:* Federal Direct (Subsidized and Unsubsidized Stafford, PLUS), Perkins, state, alternative loans.

WORK-STUDY *Federal work-study:* Total amount: $1,729,465; 939 jobs averaging $1841. *State or other work-study/employment:* Total amount: $6,778,313 (31% need-based, 69% non-need-based). 3,659 part-time jobs averaging $1854.

ATHLETIC AWARDS *Total amount:* $3,052,863 (36% need-based, 64% non-need-based).

APPLYING FOR FINANCIAL AID *Required financial aid form:* FAFSA. *Financial aid deadline (priority):* 3/1. *Notification date:* Continuous beginning 4/1.

CONTACT Mr. Michael Owens, Director of Scholarships and Financial Aid, Central Michigan University, WA 202, Mount Pleasant, MI 48859, 989-774-7428 or toll-free 888-292-5366. *Fax:* 989-774-3634. *E-mail:* viau1tb@cmich.edu.

CENTRAL MISSOURI STATE UNIVERSITY
Warrensburg, MO

Tuition & fees (MO res): $5970 **Average undergraduate aid package: $6797**

ABOUT THE INSTITUTION State-supported, coed. Awards: associate, bachelor's, and master's degrees and post-bachelor's and post-master's certificates. 96 undergraduate majors. Total enrollment: 10,051. Undergraduates: 8,303. Freshmen: 1,508. Federal methodology is used as a basis for awarding need-based institutional aid.

UNDERGRADUATE EXPENSES for 2005–06 *Application fee:* $30. *Tuition, state resident:* full-time $5550; part-time $185 per credit. *Tuition, nonresident:* full-time $10,680; part-time $356 per credit. *Required fees:* full-time $420; $14 per credit. Full-time tuition and fees vary according to course load and location. *College room and board:* $5180; *room only:* $4444. Room and board charges vary according to board plan and housing facility. *Payment plans:* Installment, deferred payment.

FRESHMAN FINANCIAL AID (Fall 2003) 1123 applied for aid; of those 74% were deemed to have need. 98% of freshmen with need received aid; of those 25% had need fully met. *Average percent of need met:* 72% (excluding resources awarded to replace EFC). *Average financial aid package:* $5670 (excluding resources awarded to replace EFC). 39% of all full-time freshmen had no need and received non-need-based gift aid.

UNDERGRADUATE FINANCIAL AID (Fall 2003) 5,883 applied for aid; of those 79% were deemed to have need. 98% of undergraduates with need received aid; of those 38% had need fully met. *Average percent of need met:* 90% (excluding resources awarded to replace EFC). *Average financial aid package:* $6797 (excluding resources awarded to replace EFC). 30% of all full-time undergraduates had no need and received non-need-based gift aid.

GIFT AID (NEED-BASED) *Total amount:* $8,662,692 (96% federal, 4% state). *Receiving aid:* Freshmen: 35% (489); All full-time undergraduates: 39% (2,779). *Average award:* Freshmen: $3313; Undergraduates: $3293. *Scholarships, grants, and awards:* Federal Pell, FSEOG, state, private, college/university gift aid from institutional funds.

GIFT AID (NON-NEED-BASED) *Total amount:* $8,186,903 (5% federal, 11% state, 62% institutional, 22% external sources). *Receiving aid:* Freshmen: 40% (554); Undergraduates: 33% (2,342). *Average Award:* Freshmen: $2438; *Undergraduates:* $2253. *Scholarships, grants, and awards by category: Academic Interests/Achievement:* 451 awards ($182,425 total): agriculture, biological sciences, business, communication, computer science, education, engineering/technologies, English, foreign languages, general academic interests/achievements, health fields, home economics, humanities, mathematics, military science, physical sciences, premedicine, social sciences. *Creative Arts/Performance:* 699 awards ($227,550 total): applied art and design, art/fine arts, cinema/film/broadcasting, creative writing, debating, journalism/publications, music, performing arts, theater/drama. *Special Achievements/Activities:* 52 awards ($37,960 total): cheerleading/drum major, leadership. *Special Characteristics:* 541 awards ($527,850 total): adult students, children and siblings of alumni, children of faculty/staff, ethnic background, members of minority groups, out-of-state students, previous college experience. *Tuition waivers:* Full or partial for children of alumni, employees or children of employees, senior citizens. *ROTC:* Army, Air Force cooperative.

LOANS *Student loans:* $24,977,525 (58% need-based, 42% non-need-based). 66% of past graduating class borrowed through all loan programs. *Average indebtedness per student:* $9960. *Average need-based loan:* Freshmen: $2412; Undergraduates: $4018. *Parent loans:* $6,581,049 (100% non-need-based). *Programs:* Federal Direct (Subsidized and Unsubsidized Stafford, PLUS), Perkins, state.

WORK-STUDY *Federal work-study:* Total amount: $199,921; 400 jobs averaging $999. *State or other work-study/employment:* Total amount: $752,762 (100% non-need-based). 1,391 part-time jobs averaging $1187.

ATHLETIC AWARDS *Total amount:* $1,484,031 (100% non-need-based).

APPLYING FOR FINANCIAL AID *Required financial aid form:* FAFSA. *Financial aid deadline (priority):* 3/1. *Notification date:* Continuous beginning 3/1. Students must reply within 2 weeks of notification.

CONTACT Mr. Phil Shreves, Director of Student Financial Assistance, Central Missouri State University, Office of Financial Aid, Administration Building 104, Warrensburg, MO 64093, 660-543-4040 or toll-free 800-729-2678 (in-state). *Fax:* 660-543-8080. *E-mail:* fedaid@cmsuvmb.cmsu.edu.

CENTRAL PENNSYLVANIA COLLEGE
Summerdale, PA

Tuition & fees: $11,010	Average undergraduate aid package: N/A

ABOUT THE INSTITUTION Proprietary, coed. Awards: associate and bachelor's degrees. 22 undergraduate majors. Total enrollment: 866. Undergraduates: 866. Freshmen: 237. Federal methodology is used as a basis for awarding need-based institutional aid.

UNDERGRADUATE EXPENSES for 2004–05 *Comprehensive fee:* $17,160 includes full-time tuition ($10,440), mandatory fees ($570), and room and board ($6150). *College room only:* $4500. Full-time tuition and fees vary according to course load and program. Room and board charges vary according to board plan and housing facility. *Part-time tuition:* $290 per credit hour. *Part-time fees:* $190 per term. Part-time tuition and fees vary according to course load and program. *Payment plan:* Deferred payment.

GIFT AID (NEED-BASED) *Scholarships, grants, and awards:* Federal Pell, FSEOG, state, private, college/university gift aid from institutional funds.

GIFT AID (NON-NEED-BASED) *Scholarships, grants, and awards by category: Academic Interests/Achievement:* 5 awards ($37,500 total): general academic interests/achievements. *Special Achievements/Activities:* 60 awards ($50,000 total): leadership, memberships. *Special Characteristics:* 315 awards ($335,000 total): general special characteristics, out-of-state students. *Tuition waivers:* Full or partial for employees or children of employees.

LOANS *Student loans:* $4,233,950 (51% need-based, 49% non-need-based). *Parent loans:* $1,536,818 (100% need-based). *Programs:* FFEL (Subsidized and Unsubsidized Stafford, PLUS).

WORK-STUDY *Federal work-study:* Total amount: $84,427; 50 jobs averaging $1500.

APPLYING FOR FINANCIAL AID *Required financial aid forms:* FAFSA, institution's own form, state aid form, Federal Stafford Loan. *Financial aid deadline:* 5/1 (priority: 3/15). *Notification date:* Continuous beginning 1/1. Students must reply by 3/15 or within 2 weeks of notification.

CONTACT Kathy Shepard, Financial Aid Director, Central Pennsylvania College, College Hill Road, Summerdale, PA 17093, 717-728-2261 or toll-free 800-759-2727 Ext. 2201. *Fax:* 717-728-2300. *E-mail:* financial-aid@centralpenn.edu.

CENTRAL STATE UNIVERSITY
Wilberforce, OH

ABOUT THE INSTITUTION State-supported, coed. Awards: bachelor's and master's degrees and post-bachelor's certificates. 37 undergraduate majors. Total enrollment: 1,621. Undergraduates: 1,611. Freshmen: 550.

GIFT AID (NEED-BASED) *Scholarships, grants, and awards:* Federal Pell, FSEOG, state, private, college/university gift aid from institutional funds.

GIFT AID (NON-NEED-BASED) *Scholarships, grants, and awards by category: Academic Interests/Achievement:* business, computer science, education, engineering/technologies, general academic interests/achievements, physical sciences. *Creative Arts/Performance:* music. *Special Characteristics:* children of faculty/staff, veterans, veterans' children.

LOANS *Programs:* FFEL (Subsidized and Unsubsidized Stafford, PLUS).

WORK-STUDY Federal work-study jobs available.

APPLYING FOR FINANCIAL AID *Required financial aid form:* FAFSA.

CONTACT Veronica J. Leech, Director of Student Financial Aid, Central State University, PO Box 1004, Wilberforce, OH 45384, 937-376-6579 or toll-free 800-388-CSU1 (in-state).

CENTRAL WASHINGTON UNIVERSITY
Ellensburg, WA

Tuition & fees (WA res): $4647	Average undergraduate aid package: $4575

ABOUT THE INSTITUTION State-supported, coed. Awards: bachelor's and master's degrees and post-bachelor's certificates. 72 undergraduate majors. Total enrollment: 9,985. Undergraduates: 9,395. Freshmen: 1,388. Federal methodology is used as a basis for awarding need-based institutional aid.

UNDERGRADUATE EXPENSES for 2004–05 *Application fee:* $35. *Tuition, state resident:* full-time $4278; part-time $130.60 per credit. *Tuition, nonresident:* full-time $11,799; part-time $381.60 per credit. Full-time tuition and fees vary according to location. Part-time tuition and fees vary according to course load and location. *College room and board:* $6402. Room and board charges vary according to board plan and housing facility.

FRESHMAN FINANCIAL AID (Fall 2003) 976 applied for aid; of those 68% were deemed to have need. 98% of freshmen with need received aid; of those 35% had need fully met. *Average percent of need met:* 78% (excluding resources awarded to replace EFC). *Average financial aid package:* $4347 (excluding resources awarded to replace EFC). 11% of all full-time freshmen had no need and received non-need-based gift aid.

UNDERGRADUATE FINANCIAL AID (Fall 2003) 5,561 applied for aid; of those 75% were deemed to have need. 97% of undergraduates with need received aid; of those 11% had need fully met. *Average percent of need met:* 78% (excluding resources awarded to replace EFC). *Average financial aid package:* $4575 (excluding resources awarded to replace EFC). 5% of all full-time undergraduates had no need and received non-need-based gift aid.

GIFT AID (NEED-BASED) *Total amount:* $17,644,759 (37% federal, 38% state, 6% institutional, 19% external sources). *Receiving aid:* Freshmen: 44% (583); All full-time undergraduates: 43% (3,366). *Average award:* Freshmen: $5081; Undergraduates: $5037. *Scholarships, grants, and awards:* Federal Pell, FSEOG, state, private, college/university gift aid from institutional funds, Title III grants, McNair scholarships, WA Regional Achievers Awards.

GIFT AID (NON-NEED-BASED) *Average Award:* Freshmen: $2911; Undergraduates: $2647. *Scholarships, grants, and awards by category: Academic Interests/Achievement:* 963 awards ($2,930,702 total): business, communication, computer science, education, engineering/technologies, English, foreign languages, general academic interests/achievements, health fields, international studies, mathematics, military science, physical sciences, premedicine. *Creative Arts/Performance:* 90 awards ($260,000 total): applied art and design, art/fine arts, journalism/publications, music, performing arts, theater/drama. *Special Achievements/Activities:* 30 awards ($80,000 total): community service, general special achievements/activities, hobbies/interests, leadership, memberships. *Special Characteristics:* adult students, children and siblings of alumni, general special characteristics, handicapped students, local/state students, previous college experience. *Tuition waivers:* Full or partial for employees or children of employees, senior citizens. *ROTC:* Army, Air Force.

LOANS *Student loans:* $34,965,593 (52% need-based, 48% non-need-based). 63% of past graduating class borrowed through all loan programs. *Average indebtedness per student:* $15,686. *Average need-based loan:* Freshmen: $2314; Undergraduates: $2397. *Parent loans:* $11,313,281 (100% non-need-based). *Programs:* Federal Direct (Subsidized and Unsubsidized Stafford, PLUS), FFEL (Subsidized and Unsubsidized Stafford, PLUS), Perkins, state, college/university.

WORK-STUDY *Federal work-study:* Total amount: $428,009; 242 jobs averaging $2027. *State or other work-study/employment:* Total amount: $6,503,535 (100% need-based). 234 part-time jobs averaging $2484.

ATHLETIC AWARDS *Total amount:* $188,672 (100% non-need-based).

APPLYING FOR FINANCIAL AID *Required financial aid form:* FAFSA. *Financial aid deadline (priority):* 3/1. *Notification date:* Continuous beginning 4/15. Students must reply within 4 weeks of notification.

CONTACT Ms. Agnes Canedo, Director of Financial Aid, Central Washington University, 400 East University Way, Ellensburg, WA 98926-7495, 509-963-3049 or toll-free 866-298-4968. *Fax:* 509-963-1788. *E-mail:* canedoa@cwu.edu.

CENTRAL YESHIVA TOMCHEI TMIMIM-LUBAVITCH
Brooklyn, NY

CONTACT Rabbi Moshe M. Gluckowsky, Director of Financial Aid, Central Yeshiva Tomchei Tmimim-Lubavitch, 841-853 Ocean Parkway, Brooklyn, NY 11230, 718-859-2277.

CENTRE COLLEGE
Danville, KY

Tuition & fees: $21,800	Average undergraduate aid package: $18,053

ABOUT THE INSTITUTION Independent religious, coed. Awards: bachelor's degrees. 28 undergraduate majors. Total enrollment: 1,069. Undergraduates: 1,069. Freshmen: 297. Both federal and institutional methodology are used as a basis for awarding need-based institutional aid.

UNDERGRADUATE EXPENSES for 2004–05 *Application fee:* $40. *Comprehensive fee:* $29,100 includes full-time tuition ($21,800) and room and board ($7300).

College room only: $3700. Room and board charges vary according to board plan. **Part-time tuition:** $785 per credit hour. Part-time tuition and fees vary according to course load. **Payment plan:** Installment.

FRESHMAN FINANCIAL AID (Fall 2004, est.) 251 applied for aid; of those 74% were deemed to have need. 100% of freshmen with need received aid; of those 49% had need fully met. *Average percent of need met:* 91% (excluding resources awarded to replace EFC). *Average financial aid package:* $18,696 (excluding resources awarded to replace EFC). 36% of all full-time freshmen had no need and received non-need-based gift aid.

UNDERGRADUATE FINANCIAL AID (Fall 2004, est.) 794 applied for aid; of those 83% were deemed to have need. 100% of undergraduates with need received aid; of those 37% had need fully met. *Average percent of need met:* 88% (excluding resources awarded to replace EFC). *Average financial aid package:* $18,053 (excluding resources awarded to replace EFC). 31% of all full-time undergraduates had no need and received non-need-based gift aid.

GIFT AID (NEED-BASED) Total amount: $10,018,031 (6% federal, 21% state, 70% institutional, 3% external sources). *Receiving aid:* Freshmen: 62% (185); All full-time undergraduates: 62% (658). *Average award:* Freshmen: $16,993; Undergraduates: $15,187. *Scholarships, grants, and awards:* Federal Pell, FSEOG, state, private, college/university gift aid from institutional funds.

GIFT AID (NON-NEED-BASED) Total amount: $3,336,385 (13% state, 83% institutional, 4% external sources). *Average Award: Freshmen:* $18,281; *Undergraduates:* $9929. *Scholarships, grants, and awards by category: Academic Interests/Achievement:* 688 awards ($5,034,325 total): general academic interests/achievements. *Creative Arts/Performance:* 79 awards ($269,750 total): music, theater/drama. *Special Characteristics:* 111 awards ($771,020 total): children and siblings of alumni, children of faculty/staff, members of minority groups. *Tuition waivers:* Full or partial for children of alumni, employees or children of employees. *ROTC:* Army cooperative, Air Force cooperative.

LOANS Student loans: $2,627,988 (72% need-based, 28% non-need-based). 60% of past graduating class borrowed through all loan programs. *Average indebtedness per student:* $14,300. *Average need-based loan:* Freshmen: $2582; Undergraduates: $4134. *Parent loans:* $1,406,544 (100% need-based). *Programs:* FFEL (Subsidized and Unsubsidized Stafford, PLUS), Perkins, college/university.

WORK-STUDY Federal work-study: Total amount: $378,300; 283 jobs averaging $1336. *State or other work-study/employment:* Total amount: $45,190 (32% need-based, 68% non-need-based). 26 part-time jobs averaging $1738.

APPLYING FOR FINANCIAL AID Required financial aid forms: FAFSA, institution's own form. *Financial aid deadline:* 3/1. *Notification date:* 4/1. Students must reply by 5/1.

CONTACT Ms. Elaine Larson, Director of Student Financial Planning, Centre College, 600 West Walnut Street, Danville, KY 40422-1394, 859-238-5365 or toll-free 800-423-6236. *Fax:* 859-238-5373. *E-mail:* finaid@centre.edu.

CHADRON STATE COLLEGE
Chadron, NE

| Tuition & fees (NE res): $3495 | Average undergraduate aid package: $2615 |

ABOUT THE INSTITUTION State-supported, coed. Awards: bachelor's and master's degrees. 46 undergraduate majors. Total enrollment: 2,569. Undergraduates: 2,230. Freshmen: 370. Federal methodology is used as a basis for awarding need-based institutional aid.

UNDERGRADUATE EXPENSES for 2004–05 Application fee: $15. **Tuition, area resident:** part-time $95 per credit. **Tuition, state resident:** full-time $2850; part-time $95 per credit. **Tuition, nonresident:** full-time $5700; part-time $190 per credit. **Required fees:** full-time $645; $34.45 per credit. Full-time tuition and fees vary according to course load and location. Part-time tuition and fees vary according to course load and location. **College room and board:** $3986; **room only:** $1850. Room and board charges vary according to board plan and housing facility.

FRESHMAN FINANCIAL AID (Fall 2004, est.) *Average financial aid package:* $2406 (excluding resources awarded to replace EFC).

UNDERGRADUATE FINANCIAL AID (Fall 2004, est.) *Average financial aid package:* $2615 (excluding resources awarded to replace EFC).

GIFT AID (NEED-BASED) Total amount: $4,411,503 (68% federal, 21% state, 8% institutional, 3% external sources). *Average award:* Freshmen: $1842; Undergraduates: $1934. *Scholarships, grants, and awards:* Federal Pell, FSEOG, state, college/university gift aid from institutional funds.

GIFT AID (NON-NEED-BASED) Total amount: $76,996 (100% federal). **Tuition waivers:** Full or partial for employees or children of employees, senior citizens.

LOANS Student loans: $2,820,155 (67% need-based, 33% non-need-based). 50% of past graduating class borrowed through all loan programs. *Average indebtedness per student:* $11,000. *Average need-based loan:* Freshmen: $909; Undergraduates: $1273. *Parent loans:* $1,316,080 (32% need-based, 68% non-need-based). *Programs:* Federal Direct (Subsidized and Unsubsidized Stafford, PLUS), FFEL (Subsidized and Unsubsidized Stafford, PLUS), Perkins.

WORK-STUDY Federal work-study: Total amount: $440,904; jobs available.

ATHLETIC AWARDS *Total amount:* $407,392 (100% need-based).

APPLYING FOR FINANCIAL AID Required financial aid forms: FAFSA, institution's own form. *Financial aid deadline (priority):* 6/1. *Notification date:* Continuous. Students must reply within 2 weeks of notification.

CONTACT Ms. Sherry Douglas, Director of Financial Aid, Chadron State College, 1000 Main Street, Chadron, NE 69337, 308-432-6230 or toll-free 800-242-3766 (in-state). *Fax:* 308-432-6229. *E-mail:* finaid@csc.edu.

CHAMINADE UNIVERSITY OF HONOLULU
Honolulu, HI

| Tuition & fees: $14,330 | Average undergraduate aid package: $12,846 |

ABOUT THE INSTITUTION Independent Roman Catholic, coed. Awards: associate, bachelor's, and master's degrees and post-bachelor's certificates. 23 undergraduate majors. Total enrollment: 1,783. Undergraduates: 1,079. Freshmen: 248. Federal methodology is used as a basis for awarding need-based institutional aid.

UNDERGRADUATE EXPENSES for 2005–06 Application fee: $50. **Comprehensive fee:** $23,200 includes full-time tuition ($14,330) and room and board ($8870). **College room only:** $4680. Full-time tuition and fees vary according to course load. Room and board charges vary according to board plan. **Part-time tuition:** $478 per credit. Part-time tuition and fees vary according to course load. **Payment plan:** Installment.

FRESHMAN FINANCIAL AID (Fall 2004, est.) 202 applied for aid; of those 83% were deemed to have need. 100% of freshmen with need received aid; of those 13% had need fully met. *Average percent of need met:* 65% (excluding resources awarded to replace EFC). *Average financial aid package:* $11,862 (excluding resources awarded to replace EFC). 14% of all full-time freshmen had no need and received non-need-based gift aid.

UNDERGRADUATE FINANCIAL AID (Fall 2004, est.) 852 applied for aid; of those 89% were deemed to have need. 100% of undergraduates with need received aid; of those 14% had need fully met. *Average percent of need met:* 65% (excluding resources awarded to replace EFC). *Average financial aid package:* $12,846 (excluding resources awarded to replace EFC). 17% of all full-time undergraduates had no need and received non-need-based gift aid.

GIFT AID (NEED-BASED) Total amount: $6,682,275 (25% federal, 60% institutional, 15% external sources). *Receiving aid:* Freshmen: 67% (166); All full-time undergraduates: 73% (757). *Average award:* Freshmen: $8258; Undergraduates: $8257. *Scholarships, grants, and awards:* Federal Pell, FSEOG, state, private, college/university gift aid from institutional funds.

GIFT AID (NON-NEED-BASED) Total amount: $1,087,935 (86% institutional, 14% external sources). *Receiving aid:* Freshmen: 7% (18); Undergraduates: 7% (77). *Average Award:* Freshmen: $4994; *Undergraduates:* $4565. *Scholarships, grants, and awards by category: Academic Interests/Achievement:* 992 awards ($4,434,024 total): general academic interests/achievements. *Tuition waivers:* Full or partial for employees or children of employees. *ROTC:* Army cooperative, Air Force cooperative.

LOANS Student loans: $5,614,698 (77% need-based, 23% non-need-based). 65% of past graduating class borrowed through all loan programs. *Average indebtedness per student:* $29,770. *Average need-based loan:* Freshmen: $2879; Undergraduates: $4156. *Parent loans:* $3,640,772 (38% need-based, 62% non-need-based). *Programs:* FFEL (Subsidized and Unsubsidized Stafford, PLUS), Perkins, alternative loans.

WORK-STUDY Federal work-study: Total amount: $175,000; 120 jobs averaging $1500.

ATHLETIC AWARDS *Total amount:* $491,358 (72% need-based, 28% non-need-based).

APPLYING FOR FINANCIAL AID Required financial aid form: FAFSA. *Financial aid deadline (priority):* 3/1. *Notification date:* Continuous. Students must reply within 4 weeks of notification.

CONTACT Mr. Eric Nemoto, Associate Dean of Enrollment Management, Chaminade University of Honolulu, 3140 Waialae Avenue, Honolulu, HI 96816-1578, 808-735-4780 or toll-free 800-735-3733 (out-of-state). *Fax:* 808-739-8362. *E-mail:* enemoto@chaminade.edu.

CHAMPLAIN COLLEGE
Burlington, VT

Tuition & fees: $14,910   **Average undergraduate aid package:** $9229

ABOUT THE INSTITUTION Independent, coed. Awards: associate, bachelor's, and master's degrees and post-bachelor's certificates (baccalaureate programs are part of the 2+2 curriculum). 57 undergraduate majors. Total enrollment: 2,555. Undergraduates: 2,491. Freshmen: 402. Both federal and institutional methodology are used as a basis for awarding need-based institutional aid.

UNDERGRADUATE EXPENSES for 2005–06 *Application fee:* $40. *Comprehensive fee:* $24,605 includes full-time tuition ($14,660), mandatory fees ($250), and room and board ($9695). *College room only:* $5855. Full-time tuition and fees vary according to course load. Room and board charges vary according to board plan and housing facility. *Part-time tuition:* $420 per credit hour. Part-time tuition and fees vary according to course load. *Payment plan:* Installment.

FRESHMAN FINANCIAL AID (Fall 2004, est.) 360 applied for aid; of those 74% were deemed to have need. 97% of freshmen with need received aid; of those 19% had need fully met. *Average percent of need met:* 58% (excluding resources awarded to replace EFC). *Average financial aid package:* $8667 (excluding resources awarded to replace EFC). 2% of all full-time freshmen had no need and received non-need-based gift aid.

UNDERGRADUATE FINANCIAL AID (Fall 2004, est.) 1,332 applied for aid; of those 78% were deemed to have need. 97% of undergraduates with need received aid; of those 20% had need fully met. *Average percent of need met:* 64% (excluding resources awarded to replace EFC). *Average financial aid package:* $9229 (excluding resources awarded to replace EFC). 1% of all full-time undergraduates had no need and received non-need-based gift aid.

GIFT AID (NEED-BASED) *Total amount:* $4,451,852 (34% federal, 36% state, 21% institutional, 9% external sources). *Receiving aid:* Freshmen: 49% (196); All full-time undergraduates: 44% (771). *Average award:* Freshmen: $4847; Undergraduates: $5195. *Scholarships, grants, and awards:* Federal Pell, FSEOG, state, private, college/university gift aid from institutional funds.

GIFT AID (NON-NEED-BASED) *Total amount:* $191,941 (72% institutional, 28% external sources). *Receiving aid:* Freshmen: 1% (5); Undergraduates: 1% (19). *Average Award:* Freshmen: $27,000; Undergraduates: $46,000. *Scholarships, grants, and awards by category:* Academic Interests/Achievement: 9 awards ($7200 total): business, health fields. *Tuition waivers:* Full or partial for employees or children of employees, senior citizens. *ROTC:* Army cooperative.

LOANS *Student loans:* $10,438,291 (66% need-based, 34% non-need-based). *Average need-based loan:* Freshmen: $4826; Undergraduates: $5201. *Parent loans:* $5,845,309 (35% need-based, 65% non-need-based). *Programs:* FFEL (Subsidized and Unsubsidized Stafford, PLUS), Perkins, state.

WORK-STUDY *Federal work-study:* Total amount: $503,637; 228 jobs averaging $2200.

APPLYING FOR FINANCIAL AID *Required financial aid forms:* FAFSA, institution's own form, state aid form, noncustodial (divorced/separated) parent's statement. *Financial aid deadline (priority):* 5/1. *Notification date:* Continuous beginning 3/1. Students must reply within 2 weeks of notification.

CONTACT David B. Myette, Director of Financial Aid, Champlain College, 163 South Willard Street, Burlington, VT 05401, 802-860-2730 or toll-free 800-570-5858. *Fax:* 802-860-2775. *E-mail:* myette@champlain.edu.

CHAPMAN UNIVERSITY
Orange, CA

Tuition & fees: $26,150   **Average undergraduate aid package:** $18,900

ABOUT THE INSTITUTION Independent religious, coed. Awards: bachelor's, master's, and first professional degrees and post-bachelor's certificates. 59 undergraduate majors. Total enrollment: 5,565. Undergraduates: 3,733. Freshmen: 830. Both federal and institutional methodology are used as a basis for awarding need-based institutional aid.

UNDERGRADUATE EXPENSES for 2004–05 *Application fee:* $50. *Comprehensive fee:* $36,150 includes full-time tuition ($25,500), mandatory fees ($650), and room and board ($10,000). Room and board charges vary according to board plan and housing facility. *Part-time tuition:* $795 per credit. Part-time tuition and fees vary according to course load. *Payment plans:* Tuition prepayment, installment, deferred payment.

FRESHMAN FINANCIAL AID (Fall 2003) 764 applied for aid; of those 71% were deemed to have need. 100% of freshmen with need received aid; of those 100% had need fully met. *Average percent of need met:* 100% (excluding resources

awarded to replace EFC). *Average financial aid package:* $20,045 (excluding resources awarded to replace EFC). 23% of all full-time freshmen had no need and received non-need-based gift aid.

UNDERGRADUATE FINANCIAL AID (Fall 2003) 2,928 applied for aid; of those 71% were deemed to have need. 99% of undergraduates with need received aid; of those 100% had need fully met. *Average percent of need met:* 100% (excluding resources awarded to replace EFC). *Average financial aid package:* $18,900 (excluding resources awarded to replace EFC). 22% of all full-time undergraduates had no need and received non-need-based gift aid.

GIFT AID (NEED-BASED) *Total amount:* $30,796,643 (9% federal, 14% state, 74% institutional, 3% external sources). *Receiving aid:* Freshmen: 48% (409); All full-time undergraduates: 50% (1,656). *Average award:* Freshmen: $17,153; Undergraduates: $15,412. *Scholarships, grants, and awards:* Federal Pell, FSEOG, state, private, college/university gift aid from institutional funds, United Negro College Fund.

GIFT AID (NON-NEED-BASED) *Total amount:* $7,109,475 (98% institutional, 2% external sources). *Average Award:* Freshmen: $14,694; Undergraduates: $13,364. *Scholarships, grants, and awards by category:* Academic Interests/Achievement: 47 awards ($92,250 total): biological sciences, physical sciences. Creative Arts/Performance: 267 awards ($1,626,777 total): art/fine arts, cinema/film/broadcasting, creative writing, dance, music, performing arts, theater/drama. Special Characteristics: 35 awards ($34,500 total): children and siblings of alumni. *Tuition waivers:* Full or partial for children of alumni, employees or children of employees. *ROTC:* Army cooperative, Air Force cooperative.

LOANS *Student loans:* $11,518,104 (92% need-based, 8% non-need-based). 66% of past graduating class borrowed through all loan programs. *Average indebtedness per student:* $18,583. *Average need-based loan:* Freshmen: $2095; Undergraduates: $2768. *Parent loans:* $7,047,466 (76% need-based, 24% non-need-based). *Programs:* FFEL (Subsidized and Unsubsidized Stafford, PLUS), Perkins, college/university.

WORK-STUDY *Federal work-study:* Total amount: $1,202,503; 750 jobs averaging $1744.

APPLYING FOR FINANCIAL AID *Required financial aid forms:* FAFSA, state aid form. *Financial aid deadline (priority):* 3/2. *Notification date:* Continuous beginning 3/15. Students must reply within 3 weeks of notification.

CONTACT Gregory L. Ball, Director of Financial Aid, Chapman University, One University Drive, Orange, CA 92866, 714-997-6741 or toll-free 888-CUAPPLY. *Fax:* 714-997-6743. *E-mail:* gball@chapman.edu.

CHARLES R. DREW UNIVERSITY OF MEDICINE AND SCIENCE
Los Angeles, CA

CONTACT Financial Aid Office, Charles R. Drew University of Medicine and Science, 1731 East 120th Street, Los Angeles, CA 90059, 323-563-4824. *Fax:* 323-569-0597.

CHARLESTON SOUTHERN UNIVERSITY
Charleston, SC

ABOUT THE INSTITUTION Independent Baptist, coed. Awards: associate, bachelor's, and master's degrees. 73 undergraduate majors. Total enrollment: 2,875. Undergraduates: 2,482. Freshmen: 518.

GIFT AID (NEED-BASED) *Scholarships, grants, and awards:* Federal Pell, FSEOG, state, private, college/university gift aid from institutional funds.

GIFT AID (NON-NEED-BASED) *Scholarships, grants, and awards by category:* Academic Interests/Achievement: business, education, general academic interests/achievements. Creative Arts/Performance: art/fine arts, music, performing arts. Special Achievements/Activities: religious involvement. Special Characteristics: adult students, children of faculty/staff, out-of-state students, relatives of clergy, religious affiliation.

LOANS *Programs:* FFEL (Subsidized and Unsubsidized Stafford, PLUS), Perkins, state, college/university.

APPLYING FOR FINANCIAL AID *Required financial aid form:* FAFSA.

CONTACT Director of Financial Aid, Charleston Southern University, PO Box 118087, 9200 University Boulevard, Charleston, SC 29423-8087, 843-863-7050 or toll-free 800-947-7474. *Fax:* 843-863-7070.

CHARTER OAK STATE COLLEGE
New Britain, CT

Tuition & fees: N/R **Average undergraduate aid package: $4464**

ABOUT THE INSTITUTION State-supported, coed. Awards: associate and bachelor's degrees (offers only external degree programs). 1 undergraduate major. Total enrollment: 1,495. Undergraduates: 1,495. Federal methodology is used as a basis for awarding need-based institutional aid.

UNDERGRADUATE EXPENSES for 2005–06 *Application fee:* $50. *Tuition, state resident:* part-time $160 per credit. *Tuition, nonresident:* part-time $227 per credit. *Payment plan:* Installment.

UNDERGRADUATE FINANCIAL AID (Fall 2003) 355 applied for aid; of those 64% were deemed to have need. 93% of undergraduates with need received aid; of those 12% had need fully met. *Average percent of need met:* 75% (excluding resources awarded to replace EFC). *Average financial aid package:* $4464 (excluding resources awarded to replace EFC).

GIFT AID (NEED-BASED) *Total amount:* $550,053 (85% federal, 4% state, 11% institutional). *Receiving aid:* All full-time undergraduates: 9% (133). *Scholarships, grants, and awards:* Federal Pell, state, college/university gift aid from institutional funds, foundation grants.

GIFT AID (NON-NEED-BASED) *Total amount:* $387,235 (100% federal). *Scholarships, grants, and awards by category: Academic Interests/Achievement:* general academic interests/achievements. *Tuition waivers:* Full or partial for adult students.

LOANS *Student loans:* $665,313 (42% need-based, 58% non-need-based). *Average need-based loan:* Undergraduates: $1800. *Programs:* FFEL (Subsidized and Unsubsidized Stafford, PLUS), alternative loans.

WORK-STUDY *State or other work-study/employment:* Part-time jobs available.

APPLYING FOR FINANCIAL AID *Required financial aid forms:* FAFSA, institution's own form. *Financial aid deadline (priority):* 7/1. *Notification date:* Continuous beginning 8/1.

CONTACT Velma Walters, Director, Financial Aid, Charter Oak State College, 55 Paul J. Manafort Drive, New Britain, CT 06053-2142, 860-832-3872. *Fax:* 860-832-3999. *E-mail:* sfa@charteroak.edu.

CHATHAM COLLEGE
Pittsburgh, PA

Tuition & fees: $21,996 **Average undergraduate aid package: $22,273**

ABOUT THE INSTITUTION Independent, women only. Awards: bachelor's, master's, and doctoral degrees and post-bachelor's and post-master's certificates. 46 undergraduate majors. Total enrollment: 1,249. Undergraduates: 665. Freshmen: 91. Both federal and institutional methodology are used as a basis for awarding need-based institutional aid.

UNDERGRADUATE EXPENSES for 2004–05 *Application fee:* $35. *Comprehensive fee:* $29,046 includes full-time tuition ($21,780), mandatory fees ($216), and room and board ($7050). *College room only:* $3690. Room and board charges vary according to board plan and housing facility. *Part-time tuition:* $530 per credit. *Part-time fees:* $9 per credit. Part-time tuition and fees vary according to course load. *Payment plan:* Installment.

FRESHMAN FINANCIAL AID (Fall 2004, est.) 87 applied for aid; of those 79% were deemed to have need. 100% of freshmen with need received aid. *Average percent of need met:* 70% (excluding resources awarded to replace EFC). *Average financial aid package:* $24,350 (excluding resources awarded to replace EFC). 11% of all full-time freshmen had no need and received non-need-based gift aid.

UNDERGRADUATE FINANCIAL AID (Fall 2004, est.) 381 applied for aid; of those 94% were deemed to have need. 100% of undergraduates with need received aid. *Average percent of need met:* 72% (excluding resources awarded to replace EFC). *Average financial aid package:* $22,273 (excluding resources awarded to replace EFC). 11% of all full-time undergraduates had no need and received non-need-based gift aid.

GIFT AID (NEED-BASED) *Total amount:* $2,678,478 (24% federal, 17% state, 58% institutional, 1% external sources). *Receiving aid:* Freshmen: 77% (69); All full-time undergraduates: 89% (349). *Average award:* Freshmen: $9354; Undergraduates: $6429. *Scholarships, grants, and awards:* Federal Pell, FSEOG, state, private, college/university gift aid from institutional funds.

GIFT AID (NON-NEED-BASED) *Total amount:* $3,339,867 (99% institutional, 1% external sources). *Average Award:* Freshmen: $6915; Undergraduates:

$5180. *Scholarships, grants, and awards by category: Academic Interests/Achievement:* 322 awards ($3,336,867 total): biological sciences, business, communication, education, English, general academic interests/achievements, international studies, mathematics, physical sciences, premedicine, social sciences. *Creative Arts/Performance:* 1 award ($1000 total): theater/drama. *Special Characteristics:* 23 awards ($41,000 total): children and siblings of alumni, children of faculty/staff, siblings of current students. *Tuition waivers:* Full or partial for employees or children of employees. *ROTC:* Army cooperative, Air Force cooperative.

LOANS *Student loans:* $1,819,833 (66% need-based, 34% non-need-based). 97% of past graduating class borrowed through all loan programs. *Average indebtedness per student:* $18,655. *Average need-based loan:* Freshmen: $4625; Undergraduates: $4275. *Parent loans:* $410,330 (68% need-based, 32% non-need-based). *Programs:* FFEL (Subsidized and Unsubsidized Stafford, PLUS), Perkins, alternative loans.

WORK-STUDY *Federal work-study:* Total amount: $370,151; 180 jobs averaging $2200. *State or other work-study/employment:* Total amount: $34,700 (100% non-need-based). 25 part-time jobs averaging $1500.

APPLYING FOR FINANCIAL AID *Required financial aid form:* FAFSA. *Financial aid deadline (priority):* 5/1. *Notification date:* Continuous beginning 2/15. Students must reply by 5/1 or within 2 weeks of notification.

CONTACT Jennifer Burns, Director of Financial Aid, Chatham College, Woodland Road, Pittsburgh, PA 15232-2826, 800-837-1610 or toll-free 800-837-1290. *Fax:* 412-365-1643. *E-mail:* jburns@chatham.edu.

CHESTER COLLEGE OF NEW ENGLAND
Chester, NH

Tuition & fees: $14,430 **Average undergraduate aid package: $7678**

ABOUT THE INSTITUTION Independent, coed. Awards: associate and bachelor's degrees. 7 undergraduate majors. Total enrollment: 203. Undergraduates: 203. Freshmen: 47. Federal methodology is used as a basis for awarding need-based institutional aid.

UNDERGRADUATE EXPENSES for 2005–06 *Application fee:* $35. *Comprehensive fee:* $21,830 includes full-time tuition ($13,900), mandatory fees ($530), and room and board ($7400). Full-time tuition and fees vary according to course load and program. *Part-time tuition:* $465 per credit. *Part-time fees:* $530 per year. Part-time tuition and fees vary according to course load and program. *Payment plan:* Installment.

FRESHMAN FINANCIAL AID (Fall 2004, est.) 73 applied for aid; of those 100% were deemed to have need. 100% of freshmen with need received aid. *Average percent of need met:* 38% (excluding resources awarded to replace EFC). *Average financial aid package:* $6772 (excluding resources awarded to replace EFC). 11% of all full-time freshmen had no need and received non-need-based gift aid.

UNDERGRADUATE FINANCIAL AID (Fall 2004, est.) 157 applied for aid; of those 97% were deemed to have need. 97% of undergraduates with need received aid. *Average percent of need met:* 38% (excluding resources awarded to replace EFC). *Average financial aid package:* $7678 (excluding resources awarded to replace EFC). 7% of all full-time undergraduates had no need and received non-need-based gift aid.

GIFT AID (NEED-BASED) *Total amount:* $173,919 (87% federal, 13% state). *Receiving aid:* Freshmen: 36% (29); All full-time undergraduates: 32% (59). *Average award:* Freshmen: $1681; Undergraduates: $1909. *Scholarships, grants, and awards:* Federal Pell, FSEOG, state, private, college/university gift aid from institutional funds.

GIFT AID (NON-NEED-BASED) *Total amount:* $353,261 (94% institutional, 6% external sources). *Average Award:* Freshmen: $3569; Undergraduates: $3384. *Scholarships, grants, and awards by category: Academic Interests/Achievement:* 98 awards ($332,025 total): general academic interests/achievements. *Creative Arts/Performance:* 90 awards ($308,920 total): applied art and design, art/fine arts, creative writing. *Tuition waivers:* Full or partial for employees or children of employees.

LOANS *Student loans:* $1,366,018 (36% need-based, 64% non-need-based). 88% of past graduating class borrowed through all loan programs. *Average indebtedness per student:* $32,632. *Average need-based loan:* Freshmen: $2545; Undergraduates: $3299. *Parent loans:* $302,232 (100% non-need-based). *Programs:* FFEL (Subsidized and Unsubsidized Stafford, PLUS), alternative loans.

WORK-STUDY *Federal work-study:* Total amount: $10,476; 22 jobs averaging $800.

Chester College of New England

APPLYING FOR FINANCIAL AID *Required financial aid form:* FAFSA. *Financial aid deadline (priority):* 3/15. *Notification date:* Continuous beginning 4/1. Students must reply within 2 weeks of notification.

CONTACT Jay Walker, Director of Financial Aid, Chester College of New England, 40 Chester Street, Chester, NH 03036-4331, 603-887-4401 Ext. 7404 or toll-free 800-974-6372. *Fax:* 603-887-1777. *E-mail:* financialaid@chestercollege.edu.

CHESTNUT HILL COLLEGE
Philadelphia, PA

Tuition & fees: $20,380	Average undergraduate aid package: $16,785

ABOUT THE INSTITUTION Independent Roman Catholic, coed, primarily women. Awards: associate, bachelor's, master's, and doctoral degrees and post-bachelor's and post-master's certificates (profile includes figures from both traditional and accelerated (part-time) programs. 35 undergraduate majors. Total enrollment: 1,679. Undergraduates: 1,002. Freshmen: 204. Federal methodology is used as a basis for awarding need-based institutional aid.

UNDERGRADUATE EXPENSES for 2004–05 *Application fee:* $35. *Comprehensive fee:* $27,880 includes full-time tuition ($19,660), mandatory fees ($720), and room and board ($7500). Full-time tuition and fees vary according to course load. Room and board charges vary according to housing facility. *Part-time tuition:* $450 per credit. *Part-time fees:* $37.50 per term. *Payment plans:* Installment, deferred payment.

FRESHMAN FINANCIAL AID (Fall 2004, est.) 185 applied for aid; of those 82% were deemed to have need. 100% of freshmen with need received aid. *Average percent of need met:* 59% (excluding resources awarded to replace EFC). *Average financial aid package:* $15,550 (excluding resources awarded to replace EFC). 14% of all full-time freshmen had no need and received non-need-based gift aid.

UNDERGRADUATE FINANCIAL AID (Fall 2004, est.) 635 applied for aid; of those 88% were deemed to have need. 100% of undergraduates with need received aid. *Average percent of need met:* 63% (excluding resources awarded to replace EFC). *Average financial aid package:* $16,785 (excluding resources awarded to replace EFC). 9% of all full-time undergraduates had no need and received non-need-based gift aid.

GIFT AID (NEED-BASED) *Total amount:* $5,641,474 (17% federal, 17% state, 64% institutional, 2% external sources). *Receiving aid:* Freshmen: 71% (140); All full-time undergraduates: 69% (498). *Average award:* Freshmen: $8525; Undergraduates: $9500. *Scholarships, grants, and awards:* Federal Pell, FSEOG, state, private, college/university gift aid from institutional funds.

GIFT AID (NON-NEED-BASED) *Total amount:* $425,075 (100% institutional). *Receiving aid:* Freshmen: 58% (115); Undergraduates: 45% (326). *Average Award:* Freshmen: $7150; Undergraduates: $7225. *Scholarships, grants, and awards by category:* Special Characteristics: children and siblings of alumni, religious affiliation. *Tuition waivers:* Full or partial for employees or children of employees, senior citizens.

LOANS *Student loans:* $12,056,323 (67% need-based, 33% non-need-based). 90% of past graduating class borrowed through all loan programs. *Average indebtedness per student:* $16,745. *Average need-based loan:* Freshmen: $2625; Undergraduates: $5500. *Parent loans:* $2,040,828 (59% need-based, 41% non-need-based). *Programs:* FFEL (Subsidized and Unsubsidized Stafford, PLUS), Perkins.

WORK-STUDY *Federal work-study:* Total amount: $154,808; 214 jobs averaging $1500.

APPLYING FOR FINANCIAL AID *Required financial aid form:* FAFSA. *Financial aid deadline:* 4/15. *Notification date:* Continuous beginning 1/31. Students must reply by 5/1 or within 3 weeks of notification.

CONTACT Jeanne Cavalieri-Grover, Director of Financial Aid, Chestnut Hill College, Chestnut Hill College, 9601 Germantown Avenue, Philadelphia, PA 19118-2693, 215-248-7182 or toll-free 800-248-0052 (out-of-state). *Fax:* 215-242-7217. *E-mail:* finaid@chc.edu.

CHEYNEY UNIVERSITY OF PENNSYLVANIA
Cheyney, PA

ABOUT THE INSTITUTION State-supported, coed. Awards: bachelor's and master's degrees. 31 undergraduate majors. Total enrollment: 1,545. Undergraduates: 1,376. Freshmen: 423.

GIFT AID (NEED-BASED) *Scholarships, grants, and awards:* Federal Pell, FSEOG, state, private, college/university gift aid from institutional funds.

GIFT AID (NON-NEED-BASED) *Scholarships, grants, and awards by category:* Academic Interests/Achievement: biological sciences, computer science, education, general academic interests/achievements, mathematics, premedicine. *Special Characteristics:* children of faculty/staff, ethnic background.

LOANS *Programs:* FFEL (Subsidized and Unsubsidized Stafford, PLUS), Perkins.

WORK-STUDY *Federal work-study:* Total amount: $279,500; 215 jobs averaging $1300. *State or other work-study/employment:* Total amount: $80,000 (100% need-based). 133 part-time jobs averaging $600.

APPLYING FOR FINANCIAL AID *Required financial aid form:* FAFSA.

CONTACT Mr. James Brown, Director of Financial Aid, Cheyney University of Pennsylvania, 1837 University Circle, Cheyney, PA 19319, 610-399-2302 or toll-free 800-CHEYNEY. *Fax:* 610-399-2411. *E-mail:* jbrown@cheyney.edu.

CHICAGO STATE UNIVERSITY
Chicago, IL

ABOUT THE INSTITUTION State-supported, coed. Awards: bachelor's and master's degrees. 63 undergraduate majors. Total enrollment: 6,835. Undergraduates: 4,867. Freshmen: 622.

GIFT AID (NEED-BASED) *Scholarships, grants, and awards:* Federal Pell, FSEOG, state, private, college/university gift aid from institutional funds, United Negro College Fund.

GIFT AID (NON-NEED-BASED) *Scholarships, grants, and awards by category:* Academic Interests/Achievement: general academic interests/achievements, physical sciences. *Creative Arts/Performance:* art/fine arts, journalism/publications, music. *Special Achievements/Activities:* leadership.

LOANS *Programs:* FFEL (Subsidized and Unsubsidized Stafford, PLUS), state, college/university.

APPLYING FOR FINANCIAL AID *Required financial aid form:* FAFSA.

CONTACT Director of Student Financial Aid, Chicago State University, 9501 South Martin Luther King Drive, Chicago, IL 60628, 773-995-2304.

CHOWAN COLLEGE
Murfreesboro, NC

Tuition & fees: $14,100	Average undergraduate aid package: $10,300

ABOUT THE INSTITUTION Independent Baptist, coed. Awards: associate and bachelor's degrees. 33 undergraduate majors. Total enrollment: 687. Undergraduates: 687. Freshmen: 208. Federal methodology is used as a basis for awarding need-based institutional aid.

UNDERGRADUATE EXPENSES for 2004–05 *Application fee:* $20. *Comprehensive fee:* $20,200 includes full-time tuition ($14,000), mandatory fees ($100), and room and board ($6100). *College room only:* $2900. Room and board charges vary according to board plan. *Part-time tuition:* $210 per hour. Part-time tuition and fees vary according to course load. *Payment plans:* Installment, deferred payment.

FRESHMAN FINANCIAL AID (Fall 2003) 227 applied for aid; of those 91% were deemed to have need. 100% of freshmen with need received aid; of those 13% had need fully met. *Average percent of need met:* 71% (excluding resources awarded to replace EFC). *Average financial aid package:* $10,053 (excluding resources awarded to replace EFC). 14% of all full-time freshmen had no need and received non-need-based gift aid.

UNDERGRADUATE FINANCIAL AID (Fall 2003) 663 applied for aid; of those 92% were deemed to have need. 100% of undergraduates with need received aid; of those 14% had need fully met. *Average percent of need met:* 71% (excluding resources awarded to replace EFC). *Average financial aid package:* $10,300 (excluding resources awarded to replace EFC). 13% of all full-time undergraduates had no need and received non-need-based gift aid.

GIFT AID (NEED-BASED) *Total amount:* $4,933,511 (25% federal, 11% state, 50% institutional, 14% external sources). *Receiving aid:* Freshmen: 84% (202); All full-time undergraduates: 85% (604). *Average award:* Freshmen: $7684; Undergraduates: $7195. *Scholarships, grants, and awards:* Federal Pell, FSEOG, state, private, college/university gift aid from institutional funds.

GIFT AID (NON-NEED-BASED) *Total amount:* $684,189 (14% state, 69% institutional, 17% external sources). *Receiving aid:* Freshmen: 8% (19); Undergraduates: 8% (54). *Average Award:* Freshmen: $11,373; Undergraduates: $10,846. *Scholarships, grants, and awards by category:* Academic Interests/Achievement: 537 awards ($2,554,475 total): general academic interests/achievements. *Creative Arts/Performance:* 39 awards ($76,850 total): music. *Special Achievements/Activities:* 19 awards ($114,650 total): leadership. *Special Characteristics:* 371 awards ($555,957 total): children of faculty/staff, first-generation college students, international students, local/state students, relatives of clergy, religious affiliation. *Tuition waivers:* Full or partial for employees or children of employees, senior citizens.

LOANS *Student loans:* $3,998,195 (81% need-based, 19% non-need-based). 93% of past graduating class borrowed through all loan programs. *Average indebtedness per student:* $22,580. *Average need-based loan:* Freshmen: $2641; Undergraduates: $3504. *Parent loans:* $1,774,204 (32% need-based, 68% non-need-based). *Programs:* FFEL (Subsidized and Unsubsidized Stafford, PLUS), Perkins, state, alternative loans.

WORK-STUDY *Federal work-study:* Total amount: $157,834; 206 jobs averaging $766. *State or other work-study/employment:* Total amount: $148,813 (100% non-need-based). 148 part-time jobs averaging $1005.

APPLYING FOR FINANCIAL AID *Required financial aid form:* FAFSA. *Financial aid deadline (priority):* 5/1. *Notification date:* Continuous. Students must reply within 2 weeks of notification.

CONTACT Mrs. Stephanie W. Harrell, Director of Financial Aid, Chowan College, 200 Jones Drive, Murfreesboro, NC 27855, 252-398-1229 or toll-free 800-488-4101. *Fax:* 252-398-6513. *E-mail:* harres@chowan.edu.

CHRISTENDOM COLLEGE
Front Royal, VA

Tuition & fees: $15,818	Average undergraduate aid package: $10,865

ABOUT THE INSTITUTION Independent Roman Catholic, coed. Awards: associate, bachelor's, and master's degrees. 8 undergraduate majors. Total enrollment: 438. Undergraduates: 371. Freshmen: 104. Institutional methodology is used as a basis for awarding need-based institutional aid.

UNDERGRADUATE EXPENSES for 2005–06 *Application fee:* $25. *Comprehensive fee:* $21,594 includes full-time tuition ($15,368), mandatory fees ($450), and room and board ($5776). *Payment plans:* Tuition prepayment, installment.

GIFT AID (NEED-BASED) *Total amount:* $967,644 (100% institutional). *Receiving aid:* Freshmen: 43% (41); All full-time undergraduates: 47% (173). *Average award:* Freshmen: $5450; Undergraduates: $5590. *Scholarships, grants, and awards:* private, college/university gift aid from institutional funds.

GIFT AID (NON-NEED-BASED) *Total amount:* $394,653 (88% institutional, 12% external sources). *Average Award:* Freshmen: $5400; Undergraduates: $4549. *Scholarships, grants, and awards by category: Academic Interests/Achievement:* 130 awards ($543,638 total): general academic interests/achievements. *Tuition waivers:* Full or partial for employees or children of employees.

LOANS *Student loans:* $688,704 (100% need-based). 56% of past graduating class borrowed through all loan programs. *Average indebtedness per student:* $11,240. *Average need-based loan:* Freshmen: $4280; Undergraduates: $4103. *Programs:* college/university.

APPLYING FOR FINANCIAL AID *Required financial aid form:* institution's own form. *Financial aid deadline (priority):* 4/1. *Notification date:* Continuous beginning 2/1. Students must reply within 4 weeks of notification.

CONTACT Mrs. Alisa Polk, Financial Aid Officer, Christendom College, 134 Christendom Drive, Front Royal, VA 22630-5103, 800-877-5456 Ext. 214 or toll-free 800-877-5456 Ext. 290. *Fax:* 540-636-1655. *E-mail:* finaid@christendom.edu.

CHRISTIAN BROTHERS UNIVERSITY
Memphis, TN

Tuition & fees: $18,230	Average undergraduate aid package: $13,967

ABOUT THE INSTITUTION Independent Roman Catholic, coed. Awards: bachelor's and master's degrees. 40 undergraduate majors. Total enrollment: 1,907. Undergraduates: 1,572. Freshmen: 249. Both federal and institutional methodology are used as a basis for awarding need-based institutional aid.

UNDERGRADUATE EXPENSES for 2004–05 *Application fee:* $25. *Comprehensive fee:* $23,530 includes full-time tuition ($17,710), mandatory fees ($520), and room and board ($5300). *College room only:* $2390. Full-time tuition and fees vary according to class time. Room and board charges vary according to board plan and housing facility. *Part-time tuition:* $555 per credit hour. Part-time tuition and fees vary according to class time. *Payment plans:* Installment, deferred payment.

FRESHMAN FINANCIAL AID (Fall 2004, est.) 244 applied for aid; of those 83% were deemed to have need. 100% of freshmen with need received aid; of those 28% had need fully met. *Average percent of need met:* 99% (excluding resources

awarded to replace EFC). *Average financial aid package:* $16,395 (excluding resources awarded to replace EFC). 20% of all full-time freshmen had no need and received non-need-based gift aid.

UNDERGRADUATE FINANCIAL AID (Fall 2004, est.) 970 applied for aid; of those 84% were deemed to have need. 100% of undergraduates with need received aid; of those 20% had need fully met. *Average percent of need met:* 75% (excluding resources awarded to replace EFC). *Average financial aid package:* $13,967 (excluding resources awarded to replace EFC). 27% of all full-time undergraduates had no need and received non-need-based gift aid.

GIFT AID (NEED-BASED) *Total amount:* $2,900,810 (63% federal, 37% state). *Receiving aid:* Freshmen: 41% (106); All full-time undergraduates: 35% (431). *Average award:* Freshmen: $5622; Undergraduates: $5832. *Scholarships, grants, and awards:* Federal Pell, FSEOG, state, private, college/university gift aid from institutional funds.

GIFT AID (NON-NEED-BASED) *Total amount:* $8,064,169 (10% state, 86% institutional, 4% external sources). *Receiving aid:* Freshmen: 74% (190); Undergraduates: 53% (649). *Average Award:* Freshmen: $10,358; Undergraduates: $9410. *Scholarships, grants, and awards by category: Academic Interests/Achievement:* 798 awards ($4,941,000 total): general academic interests/achievements. *Creative Arts/Performance:* 64 awards ($230,000 total): general creative arts/performance. *Special Characteristics:* children and siblings of alumni, children of faculty/staff, general special characteristics, religious affiliation. *Tuition waivers:* Full or partial for children of alumni, employees or children of employees. *ROTC:* Army cooperative, Naval cooperative, Air Force cooperative.

LOANS *Student loans:* $6,748,830 (45% need-based, 55% non-need-based). 73% of past graduating class borrowed through all loan programs. *Average indebtedness per student:* $17,400. *Average need-based loan:* Freshmen: $3338; Undergraduates: $4195. *Parent loans:* $788,324 (100% non-need-based). *Programs:* FFEL (Subsidized and Unsubsidized Stafford, PLUS), Perkins, college/university, alternative loans.

WORK-STUDY *Federal work-study:* Total amount: $267,500; 289 jobs averaging $1050. *State or other work-study/employment:* Total amount: $282,000 (100% non-need-based). 313 part-time jobs averaging $1000.

ATHLETIC AWARDS *Total amount:* $881,615 (100% non-need-based).

APPLYING FOR FINANCIAL AID *Required financial aid form:* FAFSA. *Financial aid deadline (priority):* 2/15. *Notification date:* Continuous beginning 2/28. Students must reply by 5/1 or within 2 weeks of notification.

CONTACT Mr. Jim Shannon, Student Financial Resources Director, Christian Brothers University, 650 East Parkway South, Memphis, TN 38104, 901-321-3305 or toll-free 800-288-7576. *E-mail:* jshannon@cbu.edu.

CHRISTIAN HERITAGE COLLEGE
El Cajon, CA

Tuition & fees: $14,840	Average undergraduate aid package: $13,596

ABOUT THE INSTITUTION Independent nondenominational, coed. Awards: bachelor's degrees and post-bachelor's certificates. 29 undergraduate majors. Total enrollment: 549. Undergraduates: 518. Freshmen: 85. Both federal and institutional methodology are used as a basis for awarding need-based institutional aid.

UNDERGRADUATE EXPENSES for 2004–05 *Application fee:* $25. *Comprehensive fee:* $20,830 includes full-time tuition ($14,840) and room and board ($5990). Full-time tuition and fees vary according to class time, course load, and program. Room and board charges vary according to housing facility. *Part-time tuition:* $498 per credit. Part-time tuition and fees vary according to class time, course load, and program. *Payment plan:* Installment.

FRESHMAN FINANCIAL AID (Fall 2003) 147 applied for aid; of those 59% were deemed to have need. 100% of freshmen with need received aid; of those 72% had need fully met. *Average percent of need met:* 85% (excluding resources awarded to replace EFC). *Average financial aid package:* $12,356 (excluding resources awarded to replace EFC). 16% of all full-time freshmen had no need and received non-need-based gift aid.

UNDERGRADUATE FINANCIAL AID (Fall 2003) 483 applied for aid; of those 82% were deemed to have need. 100% of undergraduates with need received aid; of those 71% had need fully met. *Average percent of need met:* 80% (excluding resources awarded to replace EFC). *Average financial aid package:* $13,596 (excluding resources awarded to replace EFC). 25% of all full-time undergraduates had no need and received non-need-based gift aid.

GIFT AID (NEED-BASED) *Total amount:* $1,770,454 (29% federal, 56% state, 15% institutional). *Receiving aid:* Freshmen: 57% (86); All full-time undergradu-

ates: 73% (394). *Average award:* Freshmen: $4000; Undergraduates: $3500. *Scholarships, grants, and awards:* Federal Pell, FSEOG, state, private, college/university gift aid from institutional funds.
GIFT AID (NON-NEED-BASED) *Total amount:* $1,195,208 (93% institutional, 7% external sources). *Receiving aid:* Freshmen: 57% (86); Undergraduates: 56% (306). *Average Award:* Freshmen: $5200; Undergraduates: $4150. *Scholarships, grants, and awards by category: Academic Interests/Achievement:* 240 awards ($534,578 total): general academic interests/achievements. *Creative Arts/Performance:* 14 awards ($45,800 total): music, theater/drama. *Special Achievements/Activities:* 66 awards ($140,648 total): leadership, memberships, religious involvement. *Special Characteristics:* 82 awards ($226,956 total): children of faculty/staff, international students, out-of-state students, relatives of clergy. *Tuition waivers:* Full or partial for employees or children of employees. *ROTC:* Army cooperative, Air Force cooperative.
LOANS *Student loans:* $2,199,129 (47% need-based, 53% non-need-based). 86% of past graduating class borrowed through all loan programs. *Average indebtedness per student:* $16,000. *Average need-based loan:* Freshmen: $2625; Undergraduates: $3850. *Parent loans:* $419,988 (100% non-need-based). *Programs:* FFEL (Subsidized and Unsubsidized Stafford, PLUS), Perkins.
WORK-STUDY *Federal work-study:* Total amount: $54,812; 35 jobs averaging $1566. *State or other work-study/employment:* Total amount: $25,664 (100% need-based). 19 part-time jobs averaging $1351.
ATHLETIC AWARDS *Total amount:* $405,096 (100% non-need-based).
APPLYING FOR FINANCIAL AID *Required financial aid forms:* FAFSA, institution's own form, state aid form. *Financial aid deadline (priority):* 3/2. *Notification date:* Continuous. Students must reply by 9/1 or within 4 weeks of notification.
CONTACT Nancy DeMars, Director of Financial Aid, Christian Heritage College, 2100 Greenfield Drive, El Cajon, CA 92019, 619-590-1786 Ext. 1187 or toll-free 800-676-2242. *Fax:* 619-590-1708. *E-mail:* ndemars@christianheritage.edu.

CHRISTIAN LIFE COLLEGE
Mount Prospect, IL

ABOUT THE INSTITUTION Independent religious, coed. Awards: associate and bachelor's degrees. Total enrollment: 80. Undergraduates: 80. Freshmen: 8.
GIFT AID (NEED-BASED) *Scholarships, grants, and awards:* Federal Pell, FSEOG.
GIFT AID (NON-NEED-BASED) *Scholarships, grants, and awards by category: Special Characteristics:* children of faculty/staff, general special characteristics, relatives of clergy, religious affiliation.
LOANS *Programs:* Federal Direct (Subsidized and Unsubsidized Stafford, PLUS).
APPLYING FOR FINANCIAL AID *Required financial aid form:* FAFSA.
CONTACT Jeanna Wilson, Office of Financial Aid, Christian Life College, 400 East Gregory Street, Mt. Prospect, IL 60056, 847-259-1840. *Fax:* 847-259-3888.

CHRISTOPHER NEWPORT UNIVERSITY
Newport News, VA

Tuition & fees (VA res): $5314	Average undergraduate aid package: $5684

ABOUT THE INSTITUTION State-supported, coed. Awards: bachelor's and master's degrees. 43 undergraduate majors. Total enrollment: 4,681. Undergraduates: 4,540. Freshmen: 1,176. Federal methodology is used as a basis for awarding need-based institutional aid.
UNDERGRADUATE EXPENSES for 2004–05 *Application fee:* $35. *Tuition, state resident:* full-time $3152; part-time $221 per credit hour. *Tuition, nonresident:* full-time $10,464; part-time $528 per credit hour. *Required fees:* full-time $2162; $90 per credit hour. Full-time tuition and fees vary according to course load. Part-time tuition and fees vary according to course load. *College room and board:* $7200; *room only:* $4700. Room and board charges vary according to housing facility. *Payment plan:* Installment.
FRESHMAN FINANCIAL AID (Fall 2003) 916 applied for aid; of those 56% were deemed to have need. 99% of freshmen with need received aid; of those 20% had need fully met. *Average percent of need met:* 72% (excluding resources awarded to replace EFC). *Average financial aid package:* $4795 (excluding resources awarded to replace EFC). 9% of all full-time freshmen had no need and received non-need-based gift aid.
UNDERGRADUATE FINANCIAL AID (Fall 2003) 2,737 applied for aid; of those 67% were deemed to have need. 98% of undergraduates with need received aid; of those 26% had need fully met. *Average percent of need met:* 74% (excluding resources awarded to replace EFC). *Average financial aid package:*

$5684 (excluding resources awarded to replace EFC). 7% of all full-time undergraduates had no need and received non-need-based gift aid.
GIFT AID (NEED-BASED) *Total amount:* $4,578,309 (44% federal, 54% state, 2% institutional). *Receiving aid:* Freshmen: 32% (369); All full-time undergraduates: 32% (1,301). *Average award:* Freshmen: $3461; Undergraduates: $3442. *Scholarships, grants, and awards:* Federal Pell, FSEOG, state, private, college/university gift aid from institutional funds.
GIFT AID (NON-NEED-BASED) *Total amount:* $971,528 (41% institutional, 59% external sources). *Receiving aid:* Freshmen: 12% (141); Undergraduates: 7% (294). *Average Award:* Freshmen: $1242; Undergraduates: $1351. *Scholarships, grants, and awards by category: Academic Interests/Achievement:* 59 awards ($81,076 total): education, general academic interests/achievements, humanities, mathematics, military science. *Creative Arts/Performance:* 28 awards ($26,750 total): art/fine arts, music, theater/drama. *Special Achievements/Activities:* 244 awards ($285,700 total): general special achievements/activities, leadership. *Tuition waivers:* Full or partial for employees or children of employees, senior citizens. *ROTC:* Army.
LOANS *Student loans:* $9,782,462 (49% need-based, 51% non-need-based). 71% of past graduating class borrowed through all loan programs. *Average indebtedness per student:* $8510. *Average need-based loan:* Freshmen: $1983; Undergraduates: $2829. *Parent loans:* $2,623,872 (100% non-need-based). *Programs:* FFEL (Subsidized and Unsubsidized Stafford, PLUS), state, college/university, alternative loans.
WORK-STUDY *Federal work-study:* Total amount: $208,588; 227 jobs averaging $914. *State or other work-study/employment:* Total amount: $1,398,141 (100% non-need-based). 553 part-time jobs averaging $2528.
APPLYING FOR FINANCIAL AID *Required financial aid form:* FAFSA. *Financial aid deadline (priority):* 3/1. *Notification date:* Continuous. Students must reply within 2 weeks of notification.
CONTACT Mary L. Wigginton, Director of Financial Aid, Christopher Newport University, 1 University Place, Newport News, VA 23606, 757-594-7278 or toll-free 800-333-4268. *Fax:* 757-594-7113.

CINCINNATI CHRISTIAN UNIVERSITY
Cincinnati, OH

Tuition & fees: $9690	Average undergraduate aid package: $7702

ABOUT THE INSTITUTION Independent religious, coed. Awards: associate, bachelor's, master's, and first professional degrees. 12 undergraduate majors. Total enrollment: 922. Undergraduates: 626. Freshmen: 135. Federal methodology is used as a basis for awarding need-based institutional aid.
UNDERGRADUATE EXPENSES for 2005–06 *Application fee:* $35. *Comprehensive fee:* $15,080 includes full-time tuition ($9120), mandatory fees ($570), and room and board ($5390). *Part-time tuition:* $285 per credit hour. *Part-time fees:* $75 per term.
FRESHMAN FINANCIAL AID (Fall 2003) 79 applied for aid; of those 89% were deemed to have need. 100% of freshmen with need received aid; of those 21% had need fully met. *Average percent of need met:* 68% (excluding resources awarded to replace EFC). *Average financial aid package:* $7611 (excluding resources awarded to replace EFC). 18% of all full-time freshmen had no need and received non-need-based gift aid.
UNDERGRADUATE FINANCIAL AID (Fall 2003) 421 applied for aid; of those 76% were deemed to have need. 100% of undergraduates with need received aid; of those 15% had need fully met. *Average percent of need met:* 60% (excluding resources awarded to replace EFC). *Average financial aid package:* $7702 (excluding resources awarded to replace EFC). 19% of all full-time undergraduates had no need and received non-need-based gift aid.
GIFT AID (NEED-BASED) *Total amount:* $979,569 (49% federal, 20% state, 13% institutional, 18% external sources). *Receiving aid:* Freshmen: 61% (68); All full-time undergraduates: 60% (305). *Average award:* Freshmen: $5020; Undergraduates: $4360. *Scholarships, grants, and awards:* Federal Pell, FSEOG, state, college/university gift aid from institutional funds.
GIFT AID (NON-NEED-BASED) *Total amount:* $1,134,488 (28% state, 51% institutional, 21% external sources). *Receiving aid:* Freshmen: 9% (10); Undergraduates: 5% (25). *Average Award:* Freshmen: $9265; Undergraduates: $8005. *Scholarships, grants, and awards by category: Creative Arts/Performance:* 8 awards ($5400 total): music. *Special Characteristics:* 62 awards ($209,620 total): children of current students, children of faculty/staff, international students, married students, parents of current students, siblings of current students, spouses of current students, twins.

LOANS *Student loans:* $1,909,760 (62% need-based, 38% non-need-based). 68% of past graduating class borrowed through all loan programs. *Average indebtedness per student:* $16,000. *Average need-based loan:* Freshmen: $2633; Undergraduates: $3454. *Parent loans:* $628,436 (100% non-need-based). *Programs:* FFEL (Subsidized and Unsubsidized Stafford, PLUS), alternative loans.

WORK-STUDY *Federal work-study:* Total amount: $80,398; 128 jobs averaging $628.

APPLYING FOR FINANCIAL AID *Required financial aid forms:* FAFSA, institution's own form, state aid form. *Financial aid deadline (priority):* 3/15. *Notification date:* Continuous beginning 4/1. Students must reply within 2 weeks of notification.

CONTACT Robbin D. Moore, Financial Aid Coordinator, Cincinnati Christian University, 2700 Glenway Avenue, Cincinnati, OH 45204-1799, 513-244-8450 or toll-free 800-949-4CBC. *Fax:* 513-244-8140. *E-mail:* financialaid@cincybible. edu.

CIRCLEVILLE BIBLE COLLEGE
Circleville, OH

ABOUT THE INSTITUTION Independent religious, coed. Awards: associate and bachelor's degrees. 12 undergraduate majors. Total enrollment: 317. Undergraduates: 317. Freshmen: 45.

GIFT AID (NEED-BASED) *Scholarships, grants, and awards:* Federal Pell, FSEOG, state, private, college/university gift aid from institutional funds.

GIFT AID (NON-NEED-BASED) *Scholarships, grants, and awards by category: Academic Interests/Achievement:* business, education, general academic interests/ achievements, health fields, religion/biblical studies. *Creative Arts/Performance:* music. *Special Achievements/Activities:* leadership. *Special Characteristics:* children of faculty/staff, international students, out-of-state students, relatives of clergy, religious affiliation, siblings of current students, veterans, veterans' children.

LOANS *Programs:* FFEL (Subsidized and Unsubsidized Stafford, PLUS), Perkins, college/university, state nursing loans.

WORK-STUDY *Federal work-study:* Total amount: $66,000; 60 jobs averaging $1100. *State or other work-study/employment:* Total amount: $5000 (100% need-based). Part-time jobs available.

APPLYING FOR FINANCIAL AID *Required financial aid form:* FAFSA.

CONTACT Financial Aid Officer, Circleville Bible College, 1476 Lancaster Pike, PO Box 458, Circleville, OH 43113-9487, 740-477-7774 or toll-free 800-701-0222. *Fax:* 740-477-7755.

THE CITADEL, THE MILITARY COLLEGE OF SOUTH CAROLINA
Charleston, SC

ABOUT THE INSTITUTION State-supported, coed, primarily men. Awards: bachelor's and master's degrees and post-master's certificates. 23 undergraduate majors. Total enrollment: 3,351. Undergraduates: 2,177. Freshmen: 569.

GIFT AID (NEED-BASED) *Scholarships, grants, and awards:* Federal Pell, FSEOG, state, private, college/university gift aid from institutional funds.

GIFT AID (NON-NEED-BASED) *Scholarships, grants, and awards by category: Academic Interests/Achievement:* biological sciences, business, engineering/ technologies, general academic interests/achievements, humanities, military science, religion/biblical studies. *Creative Arts/Performance:* journalism/ publications, music. *Special Achievements/Activities:* community service, leadership, religious involvement. *Special Characteristics:* children and siblings of alumni, children with a deceased or disabled parent, local/state students, out-of-state students.

LOANS *Programs:* Federal Direct (Subsidized and Unsubsidized Stafford, PLUS), Perkins, state, college/university.

APPLYING FOR FINANCIAL AID *Required financial aid form:* FAFSA.

CONTACT Lt. Col. Hank M. Fuller, Director of Financial Aid and Scholarships, The Citadel, The Military College of South Carolina, 171 Moultrie Street, Charleston, SC 29409, 843-953-5187 or toll-free 800-868-1842. *Fax:* 843-953-6759. *E-mail:* fullerh@citadel.edu.

CITY COLLEGE OF THE CITY UNIVERSITY OF NEW YORK
New York, NY

Tuition & fees (NY res): $4339	Average undergraduate aid package: $5771

ABOUT THE INSTITUTION State and locally supported, coed. Awards: bachelor's, master's, and first professional degrees and post-master's certificates. 67 undergraduate majors. Total enrollment: 12,108. Undergraduates: 9,117. Freshmen: 1,213. Federal methodology is used as a basis for awarding need-based institutional aid.

UNDERGRADUATE EXPENSES for 2004–05 *Application fee:* $65. *Tuition, state resident:* full-time $4080; part-time $170 per credit. *Tuition, nonresident:* full-time $8640; part-time $360 per credit. Full-time tuition and fees vary according to class time and program. Part-time tuition and fees vary according to class time, course load, and program. *Payment plan:* Deferred payment.

FRESHMAN FINANCIAL AID (Fall 2004, est.) *Average percent of need met:* 68% (excluding resources awarded to replace EFC). 8% of all full-time freshmen had no need and received non-need-based gift aid.

UNDERGRADUATE FINANCIAL AID (Fall 2004, est.) 5,375 applied for aid; of those 85% were deemed to have need. 89% of undergraduates with need received aid; of those 17% had need fully met. *Average percent of need met:* 68% (excluding resources awarded to replace EFC). *Average financial aid package:* $5771 (excluding resources awarded to replace EFC). 6% of all full-time undergraduates had no need and received non-need-based gift aid.

GIFT AID (NEED-BASED) *Total amount:* $26,003,000 (50% federal, 47% state, 2% institutional, 1% external sources). *Receiving aid:* All full-time undergraduates: 61% (3,862). *Average award:* Undergraduates: $5005. *Scholarships, grants, and awards:* Federal Pell, FSEOG, state, private, college/university gift aid from institutional funds.

GIFT AID (NON-NEED-BASED) *Total amount:* $1,311,000 (20% state, 46% institutional, 34% external sources). *Receiving aid:* Undergraduates: 16% (1,042). *Average Award:* Undergraduates: $3000. *Scholarships, grants, and awards by category: Academic Interests/Achievement:* architecture, area/ethnic studies, biological sciences, communication, computer science, education, engineering/ technologies, English, foreign languages, general academic interests/ achievements, humanities, international studies, mathematics, premedicine, social sciences. *Creative Arts/Performance:* applied art and design, art/fine arts, cinema/ film/broadcasting, creative writing, general creative arts/performance, music, performing arts. *Special Achievements/Activities:* community service, general special achievements/activities, leadership. *ROTC:* Army cooperative, Air Force cooperative.

LOANS *Student loans:* $11,243,000 (97% need-based, 3% non-need-based). *Average indebtedness per student:* $16,800. *Average need-based loan:* Undergraduates: $2234. *Parent loans:* $135,000 (100% non-need-based). *Programs:* Federal Direct (Subsidized and Unsubsidized Stafford, PLUS), Perkins.

WORK-STUDY *Federal work-study:* Total amount: $2,289,000; 1,704 jobs averaging $1343.

APPLYING FOR FINANCIAL AID *Required financial aid forms:* FAFSA, state aid form. *Financial aid deadline (priority):* 4/1. *Notification date:* Continuous beginning 4/15.

CONTACT Thelma Mason, Director of Financial Aid, City College of the City University of New York, 138th Street and Convent Avenue, Administration Building, Room 104, New York, NY 10031, 212-650-5819. *Fax:* 212-650-5829. *E-mail:* thelma@finance.ccny.cuny.edu.

CITY UNIVERSITY
Bellevue, WA

Tuition & fees: $9440	Average undergraduate aid package: $4943

ABOUT THE INSTITUTION Independent, coed. Awards: associate, bachelor's, and master's degrees and post-bachelor's certificates. 12 undergraduate majors. Total enrollment: 9,847. Undergraduates: 3,857. Freshmen: 207. Federal methodology is used as a basis for awarding need-based institutional aid.

UNDERGRADUATE EXPENSES for 2005–06 *Application fee:* $80. *Tuition:* full-time $9320; part-time $233 per credit hour. *Required fees:* full-time $120; $30 per term part-time.

FRESHMAN FINANCIAL AID (Fall 2003) 17 applied for aid; of those 65% were deemed to have need. 100% of freshmen with need received aid. *Average percent of need met:* 3% (excluding resources awarded to replace EFC). *Aver-*

City University

age financial aid package: $4081 (excluding resources awarded to replace EFC). 2% of all full-time freshmen had no need and received non-need-based gift aid.

UNDERGRADUATE FINANCIAL AID (Fall 2003) 824 applied for aid; of those 88% were deemed to have need. 100% of undergraduates with need received aid. *Average percent of need met:* 15% (excluding resources awarded to replace EFC). *Average financial aid package:* $4943 (excluding resources awarded to replace EFC). 1% of all full-time undergraduates had no need and received non-need-based gift aid.

GIFT AID (NEED-BASED) *Total amount:* $767,716 (89% federal, 9% institutional, 2% external sources). *Receiving aid:* Freshmen: 6% (4); All full-time undergraduates: 11% (319). *Average award:* Freshmen: $1303; Undergraduates: $2344. *Scholarships, grants, and awards:* Federal Pell, FSEOG, private, college/university gift aid from institutional funds.

GIFT AID (NON-NEED-BASED) *Total amount:* $201,500 (97% state, 3% institutional). *Receiving aid:* Undergraduates: 1. *Average Award:* Freshmen: $2259; Undergraduates: $3738. *Scholarships, grants, and awards by category:* Academic Interests/Achievement: 4 awards ($5757 total): general academic interests/achievements.

LOANS *Student loans:* $6,236,881 (98% need-based, 2% non-need-based). 23% of past graduating class borrowed through all loan programs. *Average indebtedness per student:* $16,369. *Average need-based loan:* Freshmen: $3607; Undergraduates: $4353. *Programs:* FFEL (Subsidized and Unsubsidized Stafford, PLUS).

WORK-STUDY *Federal work-study:* Total amount: $1300; 1 job averaging $1300.

APPLYING FOR FINANCIAL AID *Required financial aid forms:* FAFSA, institution's own form. *Financial aid deadline:* Continuous. *Notification date:* Continuous beginning 7/1.

CONTACT Ms. Jean L. Roberts, Director of Student Financial Services, City University, 11900 Northeast 1st Street, Bellevue, WA 98005, 425-709-5251 or toll-free 888-42-CITYU. *Fax:* 425-709-5263. *E-mail:* jroberts@cityu.edu.

CLAFLIN UNIVERSITY
Orangeburg, SC

CONTACT Director of Student Financial Aid, Claflin University, Tingly Hall, Suite 12, 400 Magnolia Street, Orangeburg, SC 29115, 803-535-5720 or toll-free 800-922-1276 (in-state).

CLAREMONT MCKENNA COLLEGE
Claremont, CA

Tuition & fees: $29,210	Average undergraduate aid package: $25,138

ABOUT THE INSTITUTION Independent, coed. Awards: bachelor's degrees. 84 undergraduate majors. Total enrollment: 1,066. Undergraduates: 1,066. Freshmen: 280. Both federal and institutional methodology are used as a basis for awarding need-based institutional aid.

UNDERGRADUATE EXPENSES for 2004–05 *Application fee:* $50. *Comprehensive fee:* $38,990 includes full-time tuition ($29,010), mandatory fees ($200), and room and board ($9780). *College room only:* $4870. Full-time tuition and fees vary according to location and reciprocity agreements. Room and board charges vary according to board plan and housing facility. *Payment plans:* Tuition prepayment, installment.

FRESHMAN FINANCIAL AID (Fall 2004, est.) 178 applied for aid; of those 78% were deemed to have need. 100% of freshmen with need received aid; of those 100% had need fully met. *Average percent of need met:* 100% (excluding resources awarded to replace EFC). *Average financial aid package:* $25,761 (excluding resources awarded to replace EFC). 6% of all full-time freshmen had no need and received non-need-based gift aid.

UNDERGRADUATE FINANCIAL AID (Fall 2004, est.) 689 applied for aid; of those 86% were deemed to have need. 100% of undergraduates with need received aid; of those 100% had need fully met. *Average percent of need met:* 100% (excluding resources awarded to replace EFC). *Average financial aid package:* $25,138 (excluding resources awarded to replace EFC). 6% of all full-time undergraduates had no need and received non-need-based gift aid.

GIFT AID (NEED-BASED) *Total amount:* $12,910,786 (6% federal, 6% state, 84% institutional, 4% external sources). *Receiving aid:* Freshmen: 49% (138); All full-time undergraduates: 52% (590). *Average award:* Freshmen: $23,283; Undergraduates: $21,755. *Scholarships, grants, and awards:* Federal Pell, FSEOG, state, private, college/university gift aid from institutional funds.

GIFT AID (NON-NEED-BASED) *Total amount:* $705,938 (64% institutional, 36% external sources). *Receiving aid:* Freshmen: 30% (84); Undergraduates: 21% (234). *Average Award:* Freshmen: $4294; Undergraduates: $6656. *Scholarships, grants, and awards by category:* Academic Interests/Achievement: 159 awards ($595,500 total): general academic interests/achievements. *Special Characteristics:* 33 awards ($162,500 total): ethnic background. *Tuition waivers:* Full or partial for employees or children of employees. *ROTC:* Army, Air Force cooperative.

LOANS *Student loans:* $3,093,343 (41% need-based, 59% non-need-based). 52% of past graduating class borrowed through all loan programs. *Average indebtedness per student:* $10,769. *Average need-based loan:* Freshmen: $2728; Undergraduates: $3441. *Parent loans:* $1,421,984 (100% non-need-based). *Programs:* FFEL (Subsidized and Unsubsidized Stafford, PLUS), Perkins, college/university, alternative loans.

WORK-STUDY *Federal work-study:* Total amount: $250,000; 404 jobs averaging $1536. *State or other work-study/employment:* Total amount: $950,000 (11% need-based, 89% non-need-based). 162 part-time jobs averaging $1445.

APPLYING FOR FINANCIAL AID *Required financial aid forms:* FAFSA, CSS Financial Aid PROFILE. *Financial aid deadline:* 2/1. *Notification date:* 4/1. Students must reply by 5/1.

CONTACT Ms. Georgette R. DeVeres, Director of Financial Aid/Associate Dean of Admission, Claremont McKenna College, 890 Columbia Avenue, Claremont, CA 91711, 909-621-8356 or toll-free 909-621-8088. *Fax:* 909-621-8516. *E-mail:* gdeveres@claremontmckenna.edu.

CLARION UNIVERSITY OF PENNSYLVANIA
Clarion, PA

Tuition & fees (PA res): $4810	Average undergraduate aid package: $6654

ABOUT THE INSTITUTION State-supported, coed. Awards: associate, bachelor's, and master's degrees and post-master's certificates. 55 undergraduate majors. Total enrollment: 6,497. Undergraduates: 5,943. Freshmen: 1,315. Federal methodology is used as a basis for awarding need-based institutional aid.

UNDERGRADUATE EXPENSES for 2004–05 *Application fee:* $30. *Tuition, state resident:* full-time $4810; part-time $200 per credit hour. *Tuition, nonresident:* full-time $9620; part-time $401 per credit hour. *College room and board:* $4816; *room only:* $3194.

FRESHMAN FINANCIAL AID (Fall 2003) 1121 applied for aid; of those 81% were deemed to have need. 96% of freshmen with need received aid; of those 15% had need fully met. *Average percent of need met:* 76% (excluding resources awarded to replace EFC). *Average financial aid package:* $5626 (excluding resources awarded to replace EFC). 6% of all full-time freshmen had no need and received non-need-based gift aid.

UNDERGRADUATE FINANCIAL AID (Fall 2003) 4,448 applied for aid; of those 84% were deemed to have need. 97% of undergraduates with need received aid; of those 19% had need fully met. *Average percent of need met:* 93% (excluding resources awarded to replace EFC). *Average financial aid package:* $6654 (excluding resources awarded to replace EFC). 6% of all full-time undergraduates had no need and received non-need-based gift aid.

GIFT AID (NEED-BASED) *Total amount:* $12,673,678 (43% federal, 43% state, 8% institutional, 6% external sources). *Receiving aid:* Freshmen: 60% (743); All full-time undergraduates: 57% (2,977). *Average award:* Freshmen: $5592; Undergraduates: $6493. *Scholarships, grants, and awards:* Federal Pell, FSEOG, state, private, college/university gift aid from institutional funds, United Negro College Fund.

GIFT AID (NON-NEED-BASED) *Receiving aid:* Freshmen: 18% (225); Undergraduates: 19% (991). *Average Award:* Freshmen: $2212; Undergraduates: $2577. *Scholarships, grants, and awards by category:* Academic Interests/Achievement: biological sciences, business, communication, computer science, education, English, foreign languages, general academic interests/achievements, humanities, international studies, library science, mathematics, physical sciences, premedicine, social sciences. *Creative Arts/Performance:* art/fine arts, performing arts, theater/drama. *Special Achievements/Activities:* leadership. *Special Characteristics:* children of faculty/staff, ethnic background, local/state students, members of minority groups, veterans.

LOANS *Student loans:* $17,936,610 (62% need-based, 38% non-need-based). *Average need-based loan:* Freshmen: $2452; Undergraduates: $3401. *Parent loans:* $3,032,220 (100% non-need-based). *Programs:* FFEL (Subsidized and Unsubsidized Stafford, PLUS), Perkins.

WORK-STUDY *Federal work-study:* Total amount: $447,950; 300 jobs averaging $1540. *State or other work-study/employment:* Total amount: $1,268,824 (100% non-need-based). Part-time jobs available.

ATHLETIC AWARDS *Total amount:* $499,486 (100% need-based).
APPLYING FOR FINANCIAL AID *Required financial aid form:* FAFSA. *Financial aid deadline (priority):* 5/1. *Notification date:* Continuous.
CONTACT Ms. Mary Jo Phillips, Freshman Financial Aid Adviser, Clarion University of Pennsylvania, 890 Wood Street, Clarion, PA 16214, 814-393-2315 or toll-free 800-672-7171. *E-mail:* maphillips@clarion.edu.

CLARK ATLANTA UNIVERSITY
Atlanta, GA

Tuition & fees: $13,486	Average undergraduate aid package: $10,935

ABOUT THE INSTITUTION Independent United Methodist, coed. Awards: bachelor's, master's, and doctoral degrees and post-bachelor's and post-master's certificates. 47 undergraduate majors. Total enrollment: 4,598. Undergraduates: 3,701. Freshmen: 813. Federal methodology is used as a basis for awarding need-based institutional aid.
UNDERGRADUATE EXPENSES for 2004–05 *Application fee:* $35. *Comprehensive fee:* $20,302 includes full-time tuition ($12,936), mandatory fees ($550), and room and board ($6816). *College room only:* $4689. Room and board charges vary according to board plan and housing facility. *Part-time tuition:* $560 per credit. *Part-time fees:* $550 per year. *Payment plan:* Deferred payment.
GIFT AID (NEED-BASED) *Total amount:* $13,239,556 (59% federal, 41% institutional). *Receiving aid:* Freshmen: 62% (613); All full-time undergraduates: 64% (2,586). *Average award:* Freshmen: $5651; Undergraduates: $3818. *Scholarships, grants, and awards:* Federal Pell, FSEOG, state, private, college/university gift aid from institutional funds, United Negro College Fund.
GIFT AID (NON-NEED-BASED) *Total amount:* $5,836,610 (36% state, 64% external sources). *Receiving aid:* Freshmen: 28% (274); Undergraduates: 27% (1,112). *Scholarships, grants, and awards by category: Academic Interests/Achievement:* general academic interests/achievements. *Creative Arts/Performance:* music. *Special Achievements/Activities:* general special achievements/activities, leadership. *Special Characteristics:* general special characteristics. *Tuition waivers:* Full or partial for employees or children of employees. *ROTC:* Army, Air Force.
LOANS *Student loans:* $20,267,429 (60% need-based, 40% non-need-based). 10% of past graduating class borrowed through all loan programs. *Average indebtedness per student:* $17,751. *Average need-based loan:* Freshmen: $3534; Undergraduates: $4526. *Parent loans:* $14,924,466 (100% non-need-based). *Programs:* FFEL (Subsidized and Unsubsidized Stafford, PLUS), Perkins.
ATHLETIC AWARDS *Total amount:* $1,220,002 (100% non-need-based).
APPLYING FOR FINANCIAL AID *Required financial aid form:* FAFSA. *Financial aid deadline (priority):* 4/1. *Notification date:* Continuous beginning 2/15. Students must reply within 2 weeks of notification.
CONTACT Office of Financial Aid, Clark Atlanta University, 223 James P. Brawley Drive, Atlanta, GA 30314, 404-880-8992 or toll-free 800-688-3228. *Fax:* 404-880-8070. *E-mail:* studentfinancialaid@cau.edu.

CLARKE COLLEGE
Dubuque, IA

Tuition & fees: $17,960	Average undergraduate aid package: $15,305

ABOUT THE INSTITUTION Independent Roman Catholic, coed. Awards: associate, bachelor's, and master's degrees. 42 undergraduate majors. Total enrollment: 1,180. Undergraduates: 1,053. Freshmen: 206. Federal methodology is used as a basis for awarding need-based institutional aid.
UNDERGRADUATE EXPENSES for 2004–05 *Application fee:* $25. *Comprehensive fee:* $24,249 includes full-time tuition ($17,410), mandatory fees ($550), and room and board ($6289). *College room only:* $3059. Full-time tuition and fees vary according to class time. Room and board charges vary according to board plan and housing facility. *Part-time tuition:* $443 per credit. Part-time tuition and fees vary according to class time. *Payment plans:* Installment, deferred payment.
FRESHMAN FINANCIAL AID (Fall 2004, est.) 185 applied for aid; of those 89% were deemed to have need. 100% of freshmen with need received aid; of those 23% had need fully met. *Average percent of need met:* 100% (excluding resources awarded to replace EFC). *Average financial aid package:* $16,917 (excluding resources awarded to replace EFC). 16% of all full-time freshmen had no need and received non-need-based gift aid.
UNDERGRADUATE FINANCIAL AID (Fall 2004, est.) 761 applied for aid; of those 91% were deemed to have need. 100% of undergraduates with need

received aid; of those 25% had need fully met. *Average percent of need met:* 100% (excluding resources awarded to replace EFC). *Average financial aid package:* $15,305 (excluding resources awarded to replace EFC). 15% of all full-time undergraduates had no need and received non-need-based gift aid.
GIFT AID (NEED-BASED) *Total amount:* $7,695,935 (13% federal, 16% state, 70% institutional, 1% external sources). *Receiving aid:* Freshmen: 84% (164); All full-time undergraduates: 82% (681). *Average award:* Freshmen: $13,659; Undergraduates: $11,445. *Scholarships, grants, and awards:* Federal Pell, FSEOG, state, private, college/university gift aid from institutional funds.
GIFT AID (NON-NEED-BASED) *Total amount:* $692,331 (98% institutional, 2% external sources). *Receiving aid:* Freshmen: 82% (161); Undergraduates: 75% (624). *Average Award:* Freshmen: $10,859; Undergraduates: $10,118. *Scholarships, grants, and awards by category: Academic Interests/Achievement:* 658 awards ($3,097,794 total): computer science, foreign languages, general academic interests/achievements. *Creative Arts/Performance:* 69 awards ($145,955 total): art/fine arts, music, theater/drama. *Special Achievements/Activities:* 16 awards ($10,994 total): leadership. *Special Characteristics:* 817 awards ($1,385,912 total): children and siblings of alumni, children of faculty/staff, children with a deceased or disabled parent, general special characteristics, international students, local/state students, members of minority groups, relatives of clergy, religious affiliation, siblings of current students. *Tuition waivers:* Full or partial for children of alumni, employees or children of employees, adult students, senior citizens.
LOANS *Student loans:* $5,366,375 (52% need-based, 48% non-need-based). 74% of past graduating class borrowed through all loan programs. *Average indebtedness per student:* $18,641. *Average need-based loan:* Freshmen: $2965; Undergraduates: $4088. *Parent loans:* $545,667 (79% need-based, 21% non-need-based). *Programs:* FFEL (Subsidized and Unsubsidized Stafford, PLUS), Perkins, Federal Nursing, state, college/university, alternative loans.
WORK-STUDY *Federal work-study:* Total amount: $332,080; 246 jobs averaging $1349. *State or other work-study/employment:* Part-time jobs available.
APPLYING FOR FINANCIAL AID *Required financial aid form:* FAFSA. *Financial aid deadline (priority):* 4/15. *Notification date:* Continuous beginning 3/15. Students must reply by 5/1 or within 2 weeks of notification.
CONTACT Ann Heisler, Director of Financial Aid, Clarke College, 1550 Clarke Drive, Dubuque, IA 52001-3198, 563-588-6327 or toll-free 800-383-2345. *Fax:* 563-588-6789. *E-mail:* ann.heisler@clarke.edu.

CLARKSON COLLEGE
Omaha, NE

CONTACT Pam Shelton, Director of Financial Aid, Clarkson College, 101 South 42nd Street, Omaha, NE 68131-2739, 402-552-2749 or toll-free 800-647-5500. *Fax:* 402-552-6165. *E-mail:* shelton@clarksoncollege.edu.

CLARKSON UNIVERSITY
Potsdam, NY

Tuition & fees: $25,585	Average undergraduate aid package: $17,163

ABOUT THE INSTITUTION Independent, coed. Awards: bachelor's, master's, and doctoral degrees. 59 undergraduate majors. Total enrollment: 3,123. Undergraduates: 2,736. Freshmen: 659. Federal methodology is used as a basis for awarding need-based institutional aid.
UNDERGRADUATE EXPENSES for 2005–06 *Application fee:* $50. *Comprehensive fee:* $34,930 includes full-time tuition ($25,185), mandatory fees ($400), and room and board ($9345). *College room only:* $4896. Full-time tuition and fees vary according to course load. Room and board charges vary according to housing facility. *Part-time tuition:* $840 per credit. Part-time tuition and fees vary according to course load. *Payment plans:* Tuition prepayment, installment.
FRESHMAN FINANCIAL AID (Fall 2004, est.) 634 applied for aid; of those 89% were deemed to have need. 100% of freshmen with need received aid. *Average percent of need met:* 86% (excluding resources awarded to replace EFC). *Average financial aid package:* $16,971 (excluding resources awarded to replace EFC). 15% of all full-time freshmen had no need and received non-need-based gift aid.
UNDERGRADUATE FINANCIAL AID (Fall 2004, est.) 2,442 applied for aid; of those 90% were deemed to have need. 100% of undergraduates with need received aid. *Average percent of need met:* 87% (excluding resources awarded to replace EFC). *Average financial aid package:* $17,163 (excluding resources awarded to replace EFC). 8% of all full-time undergraduates had no need and received non-need-based gift aid.

Clarkson University

GIFT AID (NEED-BASED) *Total amount:* $25,050,896 (13% federal, 15% state, 71% institutional, 1% external sources). *Receiving aid:* Freshmen: 69% (453); All full-time undergraduates: 66% (1,795). *Average award:* Freshmen: $9511; Undergraduates: $11,709. *Scholarships, grants, and awards:* Federal Pell, FSEOG, state, private, college/university gift aid from institutional funds.

GIFT AID (NON-NEED-BASED) *Total amount:* $21,492,182 (1% state, 88% institutional, 11% external sources). *Receiving aid:* Freshmen: 63% (416); Undergraduates: 76% (2,053). *Average Award:* Freshmen: $7628; *Undergraduates:* $9748. *Scholarships, grants, and awards by category: Academic Interests/ Achievement:* 1,129 awards ($6,279,548 total): biological sciences, business, computer science, engineering/technologies, general academic interests/ achievements, humanities, mathematics, military science, physical sciences. *Special Achievements/Activities:* 549 awards ($4,363,500 total): general special achievements/activities, leadership. *Special Characteristics:* 509 awards ($2,738,919 total): children of faculty/staff, general special characteristics, international students, local/state students, members of minority groups. *Tuition waivers:* Full or partial for employees or children of employees. *ROTC:* Army, Air Force.

LOANS *Student loans:* $25,471,159 (86% need-based, 14% non-need-based). 83% of past graduating class borrowed through all loan programs. *Average indebtedness per student:* $18,148. *Average need-based loan:* Freshmen: $3618; Undergraduates: $7352. *Parent loans:* $4,843,262 (35% need-based, 65% non-need-based). *Programs:* Federal Direct (Subsidized and Unsubsidized Stafford, PLUS), Perkins, college/university, GATE Loans.

WORK-STUDY *Federal work-study:* Total amount: $518,438; 725 jobs averaging $1411. *State or other work-study/employment:* Total amount: $543,210 (24% need-based, 76% non-need-based). 126 part-time jobs averaging $965.

ATHLETIC AWARDS *Total amount:* $1,007,514 (100% non-need-based).

APPLYING FOR FINANCIAL AID *Required financial aid forms:* FAFSA, institution's own form, state aid form. *Financial aid deadline (priority):* 3/1. *Notification date:* 3/23. Students must reply by 5/1 or within 2 weeks of notification.

CONTACT April L. Grant, Associate Director of Financial Aid, Clarkson University, Box 5615, Cubley-Reynolds, Potsdam, NY 13699-5615, 315-268-6413 or toll-free 800-527-6577. *E-mail:* agrant@clarkson.edu.

CLARK UNIVERSITY
Worcester, MA

Tuition & fees: $28,265	Average undergraduate aid package: $22,413

ABOUT THE INSTITUTION Independent, coed. Awards: bachelor's, master's, and doctoral degrees and post-bachelor's and post-master's certificates. 51 undergraduate majors. Total enrollment: 3,115. Undergraduates: 2,204. Freshmen: 528. Institutional methodology is used as a basis for awarding need-based institutional aid.

UNDERGRADUATE EXPENSES for 2004–05 *Application fee:* $50. *Comprehensive fee:* $33,665 includes full-time tuition ($28,000), mandatory fees ($265), and room and board ($5400). *College room only:* $3300. Room and board charges vary according to board plan and housing facility. *Part-time tuition:* $875 per credit hour. *Payment plans:* Tuition prepayment, installment.

FRESHMAN FINANCIAL AID (Fall 2004, est.) 389 applied for aid; of those 80% were deemed to have need. 99% of freshmen with need received aid; of those 66% had need fully met. *Average percent of need met:* 95% (excluding resources awarded to replace EFC). *Average financial aid package:* $22,413 (excluding resources awarded to replace EFC). 19% of all full-time freshmen had no need and received non-need-based gift aid.

UNDERGRADUATE FINANCIAL AID (Fall 2004, est.) 1,504 applied for aid; of those 80% were deemed to have need. 99% of undergraduates with need received aid; of those 66% had need fully met. *Average percent of need met:* 95% (excluding resources awarded to replace EFC). *Average financial aid package:* $22,413 (excluding resources awarded to replace EFC). 19% of all full-time undergraduates had no need and received non-need-based gift aid.

GIFT AID (NEED-BASED) *Total amount:* $16,835,284 (11% federal, 4% state, 82% institutional, 3% external sources). *Receiving aid:* Freshmen: 58% (305); All full-time undergraduates: 58% (1,179). *Average award:* Freshmen: $17,630; Undergraduates: $17,630. *Scholarships, grants, and awards:* Federal Pell, FSEOG, state, college/university gift aid from institutional funds.

GIFT AID (NON-NEED-BASED) *Total amount:* $6,169,682 (100% institutional). *Receiving aid:* Freshmen: 32% (165); Undergraduates: 32% (638). *Average Award:* Freshmen: $11,740; Undergraduates: $11,740. *Scholarships, grants, and awards by category: Academic Interests/Achievement:* general academic interests/achievements. *Special Achievements/Activities:* community service,

general special achievements/activities. *Tuition waivers:* Full or partial for employees or children of employees. *ROTC:* Army cooperative, Naval cooperative, Air Force cooperative.

LOANS *Student loans:* $7,862,188 (70% need-based, 30% non-need-based). 87% of past graduating class borrowed through all loan programs. *Average indebtedness per student:* $19,385. *Average need-based loan:* Freshmen: $3633; Undergraduates: $3633. *Parent loans:* $3,353,789 (7% need-based, 93% non-need-based). *Programs:* FFEL (Subsidized and Unsubsidized Stafford, PLUS), Perkins, state, college/university.

WORK-STUDY *Federal work-study:* Total amount: $1,473,981; jobs available.

APPLYING FOR FINANCIAL AID *Required financial aid forms:* FAFSA, CSS Financial Aid PROFILE. *Financial aid deadline (priority):* 2/1. *Notification date:* 3/31. Students must reply by 5/1.

CONTACT Mary Ellen Severance, Director of Financial Aid, Clark University, 950 Main Street, Worcester, MA 01610-1477, 508-793-7478 or toll-free 800-GO-CLARK. *Fax:* 508-793-8802. *E-mail:* finaid@clarku.edu.

CLAYTON COLLEGE & STATE UNIVERSITY
Morrow, GA

Tuition & fees (GA res): $2802	Average undergraduate aid package: $3347

ABOUT THE INSTITUTION State-supported, coed. Awards: associate and bachelor's degrees. 93 undergraduate majors. Total enrollment: 5,954. Undergraduates: 5,954. Freshmen: 962. Federal methodology is used as a basis for awarding need-based institutional aid.

UNDERGRADUATE EXPENSES for 2004–05 *Application fee:* $40. *Tuition, state resident:* full-time $2322; part-time $97 per credit hour. *Tuition, nonresident:* full-time $9290; part-time $388 per credit hour. *Required fees:* full-time $480; $240 per term part-time.

FRESHMAN FINANCIAL AID (Fall 2004, est.) 476 applied for aid; of those 81% were deemed to have need. 96% of freshmen with need received aid; of those 9% had need fully met. *Average percent of need met:* 51% (excluding resources awarded to replace EFC). *Average financial aid package:* $2372 (excluding resources awarded to replace EFC). 4% of all full-time freshmen had no need and received non-need-based gift aid.

UNDERGRADUATE FINANCIAL AID (Fall 2004, est.) 2,211 applied for aid; of those 86% were deemed to have need. 96% of undergraduates with need received aid; of those 10% had need fully met. *Average percent of need met:* 59% (excluding resources awarded to replace EFC). *Average financial aid package:* $3347 (excluding resources awarded to replace EFC). 4% of all full-time undergraduates had no need and received non-need-based gift aid.

GIFT AID (NEED-BASED) *Total amount:* $2,442,518 (100% federal). *Receiving aid:* Freshmen: 38% (232); All full-time undergraduates: 37% (1,126). *Average award:* Freshmen: $2858; Undergraduates: $1569. *Scholarships, grants, and awards:* Federal Pell, FSEOG, state, college/university gift aid from institutional funds, Federal Nursing.

GIFT AID (NON-NEED-BASED) *Total amount:* $2,891,789 (2% federal, 93% state, 3% institutional, 2% external sources). *Receiving aid:* Freshmen: 46% (281); Undergraduates: 16% (481). *Average Award:* Freshmen: $966; *Undergraduates:* $743. *Scholarships, grants, and awards by category: Special Characteristics:* general special characteristics. *Tuition waivers:* Full or partial for employees or children of employees, senior citizens. *ROTC:* Army cooperative, Naval cooperative, Air Force cooperative.

LOANS *Student loans:* $7,367,704 (51% need-based, 49% non-need-based). 29% of past graduating class borrowed through all loan programs. *Average indebtedness per student:* $16,156. *Average need-based loan:* Freshmen: $1272; Undergraduates: $1816. *Parent loans:* $96,407 (100% non-need-based). *Programs:* FFEL (Subsidized and Unsubsidized Stafford, PLUS), Federal Nursing, state.

WORK-STUDY *Federal work-study:* Total amount: $67,988; jobs available.

ATHLETIC AWARDS *Total amount:* $103,950 (100% non-need-based).

APPLYING FOR FINANCIAL AID *Required financial aid forms:* FAFSA, institution's own form, state aid form. *Financial aid deadline (priority):* 7/8. *Notification date:* Continuous.

CONTACT Melody Hodge, Director of Financial Aid, Clayton College & State University, 5900 North Lee Street, Morrow, GA 30260, 770-961-3511. *Fax:* 770-960-4258. *E-mail:* financialaid@mail.clayton.edu.

CLEAR CREEK BAPTIST BIBLE COLLEGE
Pineville, KY

Tuition & fees: $4520	Average undergraduate aid package: $5134

ABOUT THE INSTITUTION Independent Southern Baptist, coed, primarily men. Awards: bachelor's degrees. 2 undergraduate majors. Total enrollment: 212. Undergraduates: 212. Both federal and institutional methodology are used as a basis for awarding need-based institutional aid.

UNDERGRADUATE EXPENSES for 2005–06 *Application fee:* $40. *Comprehensive fee:* $7830 includes full-time tuition ($4520) and room and board ($3310). *College room only:* $1870. *Part-time tuition:* $205 per semester hour.

FRESHMAN FINANCIAL AID (Fall 2003) 21 applied for aid; of those 62% were deemed to have need. 100% of freshmen with need received aid. *Average percent of need met:* 38% (excluding resources awarded to replace EFC). *Average financial aid package:* $6052 (excluding resources awarded to replace EFC). 23% of all full-time freshmen had no need and received non-need-based gift aid.

UNDERGRADUATE FINANCIAL AID (Fall 2003) 162 applied for aid; of those 78% were deemed to have need. 100% of undergraduates with need received aid. *Average percent of need met:* 35% (excluding resources awarded to replace EFC). *Average financial aid package:* $5134 (excluding resources awarded to replace EFC). 20% of all full-time undergraduates had no need and received non-need-based gift aid.

GIFT AID (NEED-BASED) *Total amount:* $739,704 (62% federal, 7% state, 22% institutional, 9% external sources). *Receiving aid:* Freshmen: 59% (13); All full-time undergraduates: 76% (127). *Scholarships, grants, and awards:* Federal Pell, FSEOG, state, private, college/university gift aid from institutional funds.

GIFT AID (NON-NEED-BASED) *Total amount:* $174,660 (36% federal, 64% institutional). *Receiving aid:* Freshmen: 18% (4); Undergraduates: 76% (127). *Average Award:* Freshmen: $680; Undergraduates: $887. *Scholarships, grants, and awards by category:* Academic Interests/Achievement: 8 awards ($1350 total): general academic interests/achievements. Creative Arts/Performance: 7 awards ($1400 total): music. Special Characteristics: 2 awards ($1344 total): handicapped students, international students.

WORK-STUDY *Federal work-study:* Total amount: $28,562; 29 jobs averaging $1313. *State or other work-study/employment:* Total amount: $9521 (100% need-based). Part-time jobs available.

APPLYING FOR FINANCIAL AID *Required financial aid forms:* FAFSA, institution's own form. *Financial aid deadline (priority):* 6/30. *Notification date:* 7/1.

CONTACT Mr. Sam Risner, Director of Financial Aid, Clear Creek Baptist Bible College, 300 Clear Creek Road, Pineville, KY 40977-9754, 606-337-3196 Ext. 142. *Fax:* 606-337-2372. *E-mail:* srisner@ccbbc.edu.

CLEARWATER CHRISTIAN COLLEGE
Clearwater, FL

Tuition & fees: $10,850	Average undergraduate aid package: $6585

ABOUT THE INSTITUTION Independent nondenominational, coed. Awards: associate and bachelor's degrees. 32 undergraduate majors. Total enrollment: 623. Undergraduates: 623. Freshmen: 178. Federal methodology is used as a basis for awarding need-based institutional aid.

UNDERGRADUATE EXPENSES for 2004–05 *Application fee:* $35. *Comprehensive fee:* $15,670 includes full-time tuition ($10,220), mandatory fees ($630), and room and board ($4820). Full-time tuition and fees vary according to course load and program. *Part-time tuition:* $400 per semester hour. *Part-time fees:* $150 per semester hour. Part-time tuition and fees vary according to course load and program. *Payment plan:* Installment.

FRESHMAN FINANCIAL AID (Fall 2004, est.) 176 applied for aid; of those 100% were deemed to have need. 85% of freshmen with need received aid; of those 1% had need fully met. *Average percent of need met:* 42% (excluding resources awarded to replace EFC). *Average financial aid package:* $6320 (excluding resources awarded to replace EFC).

UNDERGRADUATE FINANCIAL AID (Fall 2004, est.) 628 applied for aid; of those 100% were deemed to have need. 84% of undergraduates with need received aid; of those 3% had need fully met. *Average percent of need met:* 65% (excluding resources awarded to replace EFC). *Average financial aid package:* $6585 (excluding resources awarded to replace EFC).

GIFT AID (NEED-BASED) *Total amount:* $846,289 (75% federal, 18% state, 7% institutional). *Receiving aid:* Freshmen: 42% (74); All full-time undergraduates:

38% (237). *Average award:* Freshmen: $3381; Undergraduates: $3375. *Scholarships, grants, and awards:* Federal Pell, FSEOG, state, private, college/university gift aid from institutional funds.

GIFT AID (NON-NEED-BASED) *Total amount:* $1,831,756 (44% state, 47% institutional, 9% external sources). *Receiving aid:* Freshmen: 71% (125); Undergraduates: 66% (415). *Scholarships, grants, and awards by category:* Academic Interests/Achievement: 141 awards ($297,647 total): business, education, general academic interests/achievements, premedicine, religion/biblical studies. Creative Arts/Performance: 30 awards ($59,125 total): music. Special Characteristics: 12 awards ($20,250 total): children and siblings of alumni, religious affiliation. ROTC: Army cooperative, Air Force cooperative.

LOANS *Student loans:* $1,654,765 (52% need-based, 48% non-need-based). 60% of past graduating class borrowed through all loan programs. *Average indebtedness per student:* $8500. *Average need-based loan:* Freshmen: $2489; Undergraduates: $3665. *Parent loans:* $585,828 (100% non-need-based). *Programs:* FFEL (Subsidized and Unsubsidized Stafford, PLUS), state, alternative loans.

WORK-STUDY *Federal work-study:* Total amount: $58,000; 48 jobs averaging $615. *State or other work-study/employment:* Total amount: $17,000 (100% need-based). 14 part-time jobs averaging $394.

APPLYING FOR FINANCIAL AID *Required financial aid forms:* FAFSA, institution's own form, state aid form. *Financial aid deadline (priority):* 3/15. *Notification date:* Continuous. Students must reply within 2 weeks of notification.

CONTACT Mrs. Ruth Strum, Director of Financial Aid, Clearwater Christian College, 3400 Gulf-to-Bay Boulevard, Clearwater, FL 33759-4595, 727-726-1153 Ext. 214 or toll-free 800-348-4463. *Fax:* 727-791-1347. *E-mail:* ruthstrum@clearwater.edu.

CLEARY UNIVERSITY
Ann Arbor, MI

Tuition & fees: $11,760	Average undergraduate aid package: $10,636

ABOUT THE INSTITUTION Independent, coed. Awards: associate, bachelor's, and master's degrees. 8 undergraduate majors. Total enrollment: 895. Undergraduates: 831. Federal methodology is used as a basis for awarding need-based institutional aid.

UNDERGRADUATE EXPENSES for 2004–05 *Application fee:* $25. *Tuition:* full-time $11,760; part-time $245 per quarter hour. Full-time tuition and fees vary according to degree level. *Payment plans:* Guaranteed tuition, installment, deferred payment.

FRESHMAN FINANCIAL AID (Fall 2004, est.) 20 applied for aid; of those 95% were deemed to have need. 100% of freshmen with need received aid; of those 5% had need fully met. *Average percent of need met:* 30% (excluding resources awarded to replace EFC). *Average financial aid package:* $11,108 (excluding resources awarded to replace EFC). 16% of all full-time freshmen had no need and received non-need-based gift aid.

UNDERGRADUATE FINANCIAL AID (Fall 2004, est.) 253 applied for aid; of those 91% were deemed to have need. 100% of undergraduates with need received aid; of those 1% had need fully met. *Average percent of need met:* 26% (excluding resources awarded to replace EFC). *Average financial aid package:* $10,636 (excluding resources awarded to replace EFC). 9% of all full-time undergraduates had no need and received non-need-based gift aid.

GIFT AID (NEED-BASED) *Total amount:* $511,362 (56% federal, 41% state, 3% institutional). *Receiving aid:* Freshmen: 52% (16); All full-time undergraduates: 33% (161). *Average award:* Freshmen: $1165; Undergraduates: $1069. *Scholarships, grants, and awards:* Federal Pell, FSEOG, state, private, college/university gift aid from institutional funds.

GIFT AID (NON-NEED-BASED) *Total amount:* $18,579 (81% state, 19% institutional). *Receiving aid:* Freshmen: 16% (5); Undergraduates: 2% (10). *Average Award:* Freshmen: $2216; Undergraduates: $2609. *Scholarships, grants, and awards by category:* Academic Interests/Achievement: 46 awards ($5265 total): business, general academic interests/achievements. Special Achievements/Activities: 4 awards ($5500 total): community service, general special achievements/activities. Special Characteristics: $176,917 total: adult students, children of faculty/staff. *Tuition waivers:* Full or partial for employees or children of employees, senior citizens.

LOANS *Student loans:* $1,716,167 (43% need-based, 57% non-need-based). 36% of past graduating class borrowed through all loan programs. *Average indebtedness per student:* $13,304. *Average need-based loan:* Freshmen: $1321; Undergraduates: $1381. *Parent loans:* $84,687 (100% non-need-based). *Programs:* FFEL (Subsidized and Unsubsidized Stafford, PLUS).

Cleary University

WORK-STUDY *Federal work-study:* Total amount: $41,600; 13 jobs averaging $3124. *State or other work-study/employment:* Part-time jobs available.
APPLYING FOR FINANCIAL AID *Required financial aid forms:* FAFSA, institution's own form. *Financial aid deadline (priority):* 3/1. *Notification date:* Continuous beginning 5/1. Students must reply by 7/15 or within 2 weeks of notification.
CONTACT Vesta Smith-Campbell, Director of Financial Aid, Cleary University, 3750 Cleary Drive, Howell, MI 48843, 800-589-1979 Ext. 2234 or toll-free 888-5-CLEARY Ext. 2249. *Fax:* 517-552-8022. *E-mail:* vscampbell@cleary.edu.

CLEMSON UNIVERSITY
Clemson, SC

Tuition & fees (SC res): $8074 — **Average undergraduate aid package: $8707**

ABOUT THE INSTITUTION State-supported, coed. Awards: bachelor's, master's, and doctoral degrees. 76 undergraduate majors. Total enrollment: 17,110. Undergraduates: 13,936. Freshmen: 3,018. Federal methodology is used as a basis for awarding need-based institutional aid.
UNDERGRADUATE EXPENSES for 2004–05 *Application fee:* $50. *Tuition, state resident:* full-time $7840; part-time $324 per hour. *Tuition, nonresident:* full-time $16,404; part-time $676 per hour. *Required fees:* full-time $234; $6 per term part-time. *College room and board:* $5292; *room only:* $3094. Room and board charges vary according to board plan and housing facility. *Payment plan:* Installment.
FRESHMAN FINANCIAL AID (Fall 2004, est.) 1907 applied for aid; of those 68% were deemed to have need. 97% of freshmen with need received aid; of those 30% had need fully met. *Average percent of need met:* 34% (excluding resources awarded to replace EFC). *Average financial aid package:* $9147 (excluding resources awarded to replace EFC). 13% of all full-time freshmen had no need and received non-need-based gift aid.
UNDERGRADUATE FINANCIAL AID (Fall 2004, est.) 6,826 applied for aid; of those 76% were deemed to have need. 96% of undergraduates with need received aid; of those 27% had need fully met. *Average percent of need met:* 43% (excluding resources awarded to replace EFC). *Average financial aid package:* $8707 (excluding resources awarded to replace EFC). 13% of all full-time undergraduates had no need and received non-need-based gift aid.
GIFT AID (NEED-BASED) *Total amount:* $10,063,250 (57% federal, 20% state, 9% institutional, 14% external sources). *Receiving aid:* Freshmen: 13% (388); All full-time undergraduates: 18% (2,283). *Average award:* Freshmen: $3264; Undergraduates: $3308. *Scholarships, grants, and awards:* Federal Pell, FSEOG, state, private, college/university gift aid from institutional funds, Federal Nursing.
GIFT AID (NON-NEED-BASED) *Total amount:* $36,756,236 (76% state, 13% institutional, 11% external sources). *Receiving aid:* Freshmen: 36% (1,078); Undergraduates: 22% (2,873). *Average Award:* Freshmen: $3692; Undergraduates: $3720. *Scholarships, grants, and awards by category: Academic Interests/Achievement:* agriculture, architecture, biological sciences, business, communication, computer science, education, engineering/technologies, English, foreign languages, general academic interests/achievements, health fields, humanities, international studies, mathematics, military science, physical sciences, premedicine, social sciences. *Creative Arts/Performance:* applied art and design, art/fine arts, performing arts, theater/drama. *Special Achievements/Activities:* community service, general special achievements/activities, leadership. *Special Characteristics:* children of faculty/staff, ethnic background, local/state students, members of minority groups. *Tuition waivers:* Full or partial for senior citizens. *ROTC:* Army, Air Force.
LOANS *Student loans:* $35,039,651 (46% need-based, 54% non-need-based). 46% of past graduating class borrowed through all loan programs. *Average indebtedness per student:* $15,260. *Average need-based loan:* Freshmen: $3071; Undergraduates: $4161. *Parent loans:* $9,411,570 (100% non-need-based). *Programs:* FFEL (Subsidized and Unsubsidized Stafford, PLUS), Perkins, state, college/university.
WORK-STUDY *Federal work-study:* Total amount: $1,213,606; 563 jobs averaging $1790. *State or other work-study/employment:* Total amount: $7,810,000 (100% non-need-based). 3,152 part-time jobs averaging $2478.
ATHLETIC AWARDS *Total amount:* $3,861,683 (100% non-need-based).
APPLYING FOR FINANCIAL AID *Required financial aid form:* FAFSA. *Financial aid deadline (priority):* 4/1. *Notification date:* Continuous beginning 4/15. Students must reply within 3 weeks of notification.
CONTACT Mr. Marvin G. Carmichael, Director of Financial Aid, Clemson University, G01 Sikes Hall, Clemson, SC 29634-5123, 864-656-2280. *Fax:* 864-656-1831. *E-mail:* finaid@clemson.edu.

THE CLEVELAND INSTITUTE OF ART
Cleveland, OH

Tuition & fees: $24,741 — **Average undergraduate aid package: $13,097**

ABOUT THE INSTITUTION Independent, coed. Awards: bachelor's and master's degrees. 17 undergraduate majors. Total enrollment: 610. Undergraduates: 604. Freshmen: 123. Federal methodology is used as a basis for awarding need-based institutional aid.
UNDERGRADUATE EXPENSES for 2004–05 *Application fee:* $30. *Comprehensive fee:* $32,993 includes full-time tuition ($23,271), mandatory fees ($1470), and room and board ($8252). *College room only:* $5110. Room and board charges vary according to board plan and housing facility. *Part-time tuition:* $975 per credit. *Part-time fees:* $85 per credit. Part-time tuition and fees vary according to course load. *Payment plan:* Installment.
FRESHMAN FINANCIAL AID (Fall 2003) 84 applied for aid; of those 94% were deemed to have need. 97% of freshmen with need received aid; of those 5% had need fully met. *Average percent of need met:* 51% (excluding resources awarded to replace EFC). *Average financial aid package:* $13,044 (excluding resources awarded to replace EFC). 20% of all full-time freshmen had no need and received non-need-based gift aid.
UNDERGRADUATE FINANCIAL AID (Fall 2003) 503 applied for aid; of those 93% were deemed to have need. 100% of undergraduates with need received aid; of those 5% had need fully met. *Average percent of need met:* 52% (excluding resources awarded to replace EFC). *Average financial aid package:* $13,097 (excluding resources awarded to replace EFC). 21% of all full-time undergraduates had no need and received non-need-based gift aid.
GIFT AID (NEED-BASED) *Total amount:* $3,991,376 (15% federal, 18% state, 62% institutional, 5% external sources). *Receiving aid:* Freshmen: 76% (77); All full-time undergraduates: 77% (464). *Average award:* Freshmen: $9338; Undergraduates: $8561. *Scholarships, grants, and awards:* Federal Pell, FSEOG, state, private, college/university gift aid from institutional funds.
GIFT AID (NON-NEED-BASED) *Total amount:* $957,375 (7% state, 91% institutional, 2% external sources). *Receiving aid:* Freshmen: 3% (3); Undergraduates: 3% (18). *Average Award: Freshmen:* $9135; *Undergraduates:* $10,467. *Scholarships, grants, and awards by category: Creative Arts/Performance:* art/fine arts. *Tuition waivers:* Full or partial for employees or children of employees.
LOANS *Student loans:* $4,412,498 (81% need-based, 19% non-need-based). 95% of past graduating class borrowed through all loan programs. *Average indebtedness per student:* $29,700. *Average need-based loan:* Freshmen: $3704; Undergraduates: $4514. *Parent loans:* $957,105 (60% need-based, 40% non-need-based). *Programs:* FFEL (Subsidized and Unsubsidized Stafford, PLUS), Perkins.
WORK-STUDY *Federal work-study:* Total amount: $212,776; jobs available.
APPLYING FOR FINANCIAL AID *Required financial aid forms:* FAFSA, institution's own form. *Financial aid deadline (priority):* 3/15. *Notification date:* Continuous beginning 3/16. Students must reply within 4 weeks of notification.
CONTACT Delores Hall, Assistant Director of Financial Aid, The Cleveland Institute of Art, 11141 East Boulevard, Cleveland, OH 44106-1700, 216-421-7425 or toll-free 800-223-4700. *Fax:* 216-754-3634. *E-mail:* finaid@gate.cia.edu.

CLEVELAND INSTITUTE OF MUSIC
Cleveland, OH

Tuition & fees: $25,101 — **Average undergraduate aid package: $17,130**

ABOUT THE INSTITUTION Independent, coed. Awards: bachelor's, master's, and doctoral degrees and post-bachelor's certificates. 7 undergraduate majors. Total enrollment: 423. Undergraduates: 229. Freshmen: 40. Federal methodology is used as a basis for awarding need-based institutional aid.
UNDERGRADUATE EXPENSES for 2004–05 *Application fee:* $100. *Comprehensive fee:* $33,761 includes full-time tuition ($24,054), mandatory fees ($1047), and room and board ($8660). *College room only:* $4710. Room and board charges vary according to board plan. *Part-time tuition:* $1002 per credit hour. *Part-time fees:* $640 per term. *Payment plan:* Installment.
FRESHMAN FINANCIAL AID (Fall 2004, est.) 31 applied for aid; of those 77% were deemed to have need. 100% of freshmen with need received aid; of those 25% had need fully met. *Average percent of need met:* 77% (excluding resources awarded to replace EFC). *Average financial aid package:* $17,177 (excluding resources awarded to replace EFC). 23% of all full-time freshmen had no need and received non-need-based gift aid.

UNDERGRADUATE FINANCIAL AID (Fall 2004, est.) 198 applied for aid; of those 78% were deemed to have need. 100% of undergraduates with need received aid; of those 30% had need fully met. *Average percent of need met:* 77% (excluding resources awarded to replace EFC). *Average financial aid package:* $17,130 (excluding resources awarded to replace EFC). 21% of all full-time undergraduates had no need and received non-need-based gift aid.

GIFT AID (NEED-BASED) *Total amount:* $1,756,129 (8% federal, 4% state, 83% institutional, 5% external sources). *Receiving aid:* Freshmen: 77% (24); All full-time undergraduates: 78% (155). *Average award:* Freshmen: $12,429; Undergraduates: $11,254. *Scholarships, grants, and awards:* Federal Pell, FSEOG, state, private, college/university gift aid from institutional funds.

GIFT AID (NON-NEED-BASED) *Total amount:* $354,831 (3% state, 87% institutional, 10% external sources). *Receiving aid:* Freshmen: 13% (4); Undergraduates: 10% (19). *Average Award:* Freshmen: $11,699; *Undergraduates:* $9921. *Scholarships, grants, and awards by category:* Creative Arts/Performance: music. *Tuition waivers:* Full or partial for employees or children of employees. *ROTC:* Army cooperative, Air Force cooperative.

LOANS *Student loans:* $1,143,332 (71% need-based, 29% non-need-based). 80% of past graduating class borrowed through all loan programs. *Average indebtedness per student:* $24,070. *Average need-based loan:* Freshmen: $4847; Undergraduates: $5869. *Parent loans:* $508,432 (31% need-based, 69% non-need-based). *Programs:* Federal Direct (Subsidized and Unsubsidized Stafford, PLUS), Perkins, college/university.

WORK-STUDY *Federal work-study:* Total amount: $154,386; 100 jobs averaging $1552. *State or other work-study/employment:* Total amount: $27,750 (100% non-need-based). 29 part-time jobs averaging $957.

APPLYING FOR FINANCIAL AID *Required financial aid forms:* FAFSA, institution's own form. *Financial aid deadline:* 2/15. *Notification date:* 4/1. Students must reply by 5/1 or within 4 weeks of notification.

CONTACT Ms. Kristie Gripp, Director of Financial Aid, Cleveland Institute of Music, 11021 East Boulevard, Cleveland, OH 44106-1776, 216-791-5000 Ext. 262. *Fax:* 216-795-3141. *E-mail:* kxg26@cwru.edu.

CLEVELAND STATE UNIVERSITY
Cleveland, OH

Tuition & fees (OH res): $6792 **Average undergraduate aid package: $7070**

ABOUT THE INSTITUTION State-supported, coed. Awards: bachelor's, master's, doctoral, and first professional degrees and post-bachelor's, post-master's, and first professional certificates. 83 undergraduate majors. Total enrollment: 15,673. Undergraduates: 9,842. Freshmen: 986. Federal methodology is used as a basis for awarding need-based institutional aid.

UNDERGRADUATE EXPENSES for 2004–05 *Application fee:* $30. *Tuition, state resident:* full-time $6792; part-time $283 per semester hour. *Tuition, nonresident:* full-time $9216; part-time $384 per semester hour. Full-time tuition and fees vary according to program and student level. Part-time tuition and fees vary according to program and student level. *College room and board:* $6610; *room only:* $3972. Room and board charges vary according to board plan and housing facility. *Payment plan:* Installment.

FRESHMAN FINANCIAL AID (Fall 2004, est.) 830 applied for aid; of those 91% were deemed to have need. 99% of freshmen with need received aid; of those 9% had need fully met. *Average percent of need met:* 45% (excluding resources awarded to replace EFC). *Average financial aid package:* $6650 (excluding resources awarded to replace EFC). 12% of all full-time freshmen had no need and received non-need-based gift aid.

UNDERGRADUATE FINANCIAL AID (Fall 2004, est.) 5,289 applied for aid; of those 92% were deemed to have need. 98% of undergraduates with need received aid; of those 9% had need fully met. *Average percent of need met:* 51% (excluding resources awarded to replace EFC). *Average financial aid package:* $7070 (excluding resources awarded to replace EFC). 10% of all full-time undergraduates had no need and received non-need-based gift aid.

GIFT AID (NEED-BASED) *Total amount:* $17,215,168 (61% federal, 21% state, 11% institutional, 7% external sources). *Receiving aid:* Freshmen: 64% (586); All full-time undergraduates: 52% (3,400). *Average award:* Freshmen: $5240; Undergraduates: $4772. *Scholarships, grants, and awards:* Federal Pell, FSEOG, state, private, college/university gift aid from institutional funds.

GIFT AID (NON-NEED-BASED) *Total amount:* $1,187,729 (1% federal, 7% state, 67% institutional, 25% external sources). *Receiving aid:* Freshmen: 2% (19); Undergraduates: 1% (70). *Average Award:* Freshmen: $8600; *Undergraduates:* $7464. *Scholarships, grants, and awards by category:* Academic Interests/Achievement: engineering/technologies, general academic interests/achievements. Creative Arts/Performance: art/fine arts, creative writing, dance, music, theater/

drama. *Special Characteristics:* general special characteristics. *Tuition waivers:* Full or partial for employees or children of employees, senior citizens. *ROTC:* Army cooperative, Naval cooperative, Air Force cooperative.

LOANS *Student loans:* $35,873,167 (86% need-based, 14% non-need-based). *Average need-based loan:* Freshmen: $2795; Undergraduates: $3975. *Parent loans:* $5,802,087 (38% need-based, 62% non-need-based). *Programs:* FFEL (Subsidized and Unsubsidized Stafford, PLUS), Perkins, state, alternative loans.

WORK-STUDY *Federal work-study:* Total amount: $851,506; jobs available. *State or other work-study/employment:* Part-time jobs available.

ATHLETIC AWARDS *Total amount:* $1,778,844 (32% need-based, 68% non-need-based).

APPLYING FOR FINANCIAL AID *Required financial aid forms:* FAFSA, income tax form(s). *Financial aid deadline (priority):* 2/15. *Notification date:* Continuous beginning 3/15. Students must reply within 4 weeks of notification.

CONTACT Director of Financial Aid, Cleveland State University, 2121 Euclid Avenue, University Center, Room 560, Cleveland, OH 44115, 216-687-3764 or toll-free 888-CSU-OHIO.

COASTAL CAROLINA UNIVERSITY
Conway, SC

Tuition & fees (SC res): $6100 **Average undergraduate aid package: $7378**

ABOUT THE INSTITUTION State-supported, coed. Awards: bachelor's and master's degrees and post-bachelor's certificates. 28 undergraduate majors. Total enrollment: 7,021. Undergraduates: 6,020. Freshmen: 1,323. Federal methodology is used as a basis for awarding need-based institutional aid.

UNDERGRADUATE EXPENSES for 2004–05 *Application fee:* $35. *Tuition, state resident:* full-time $6020; part-time $250 per credit hour. *Tuition, nonresident:* full-time $14,120; part-time $595 per credit hour. Full-time tuition and fees vary according to course load. Part-time tuition and fees vary according to course load. *College room and board:* $5970; *room only:* $3820. Room and board charges vary according to board plan and housing facility. *Payment plans:* Installment, deferred payment.

FRESHMAN FINANCIAL AID (Fall 2003) 974 applied for aid; of those 81% were deemed to have need. 100% of freshmen with need received aid; of those 41% had need fully met. *Average percent of need met:* 61% (excluding resources awarded to replace EFC). *Average financial aid package:* $6847 (excluding resources awarded to replace EFC). 27% of all full-time freshmen had no need and received non-need-based gift aid.

UNDERGRADUATE FINANCIAL AID (Fall 2003) 3,735 applied for aid; of those 85% were deemed to have need. 100% of undergraduates with need received aid; of those 37% had need fully met. *Average percent of need met:* 60% (excluding resources awarded to replace EFC). *Average financial aid package:* $7378 (excluding resources awarded to replace EFC). 24% of all full-time undergraduates had no need and received non-need-based gift aid.

GIFT AID (NEED-BASED) *Total amount:* $4,405,728 (92% federal, 8% state). *Receiving aid:* Freshmen: 20% (252); All full-time undergraduates: 25% (1,243). *Average award:* Freshmen: $3333; Undergraduates: $3200. *Scholarships, grants, and awards:* Federal Pell, FSEOG, state, private, college/university gift aid from institutional funds.

GIFT AID (NON-NEED-BASED) *Total amount:* $6,382,949 (65% state, 13% institutional, 22% external sources). *Receiving aid:* Freshmen: 29% (362); Undergraduates: 15% (739). *Average Award:* Freshmen: $6904; *Undergraduates:* $6328. *Scholarships, grants, and awards by category:* Academic Interests/Achievement: 974 awards ($3,129,259 total): biological sciences, business, education, general academic interests/achievements, humanities, mathematics. Creative Arts/Performance: 34 awards ($25,750 total): art/fine arts, music, theater/drama. *Special Characteristics:* 604 awards ($3,558,099 total): general special characteristics, international students, local/state students, out-of-state students, veterans' children. *Tuition waivers:* Full or partial for employees or children of employees, senior citizens.

LOANS *Student loans:* $18,521,727 (44% need-based, 56% non-need-based). 60% of past graduating class borrowed through all loan programs. *Average indebtedness per student:* $19,932. *Average need-based loan:* Freshmen: $5554; Undergraduates: $6703. *Parent loans:* $6,240,828 (100% non-need-based). *Programs:* FFEL (Subsidized and Unsubsidized Stafford, PLUS), Perkins, state.

WORK-STUDY *Federal work-study:* Total amount: $230,488; 157 jobs averaging $1468. *State or other work-study/employment:* Total amount: $806,363 (100% non-need-based). 527 part-time jobs averaging $1530.

ATHLETIC AWARDS *Total amount:* $1,408,029 (100% non-need-based).

Coastal Carolina University

APPLYING FOR FINANCIAL AID *Required financial aid form:* FAFSA. *Financial aid deadline (priority):* 4/1. *Notification date:* Continuous beginning 3/1.

CONTACT Glenn Hanson, Director of Financial Aid, Coastal Carolina University, PO Box 261954, Conway, SC 29528-6054, 843-349-2325 or toll-free 800-277-7000. *Fax:* 843-349-2347. *E-mail:* glenn@coastal.edu.

COE COLLEGE
Cedar Rapids, IA

Tuition & fees: $22,650	Average undergraduate aid package: $20,076

ABOUT THE INSTITUTION Independent religious, coed. Awards: bachelor's and master's degrees. 64 undergraduate majors. Total enrollment: 1,354. Undergraduates: 1,336. Freshmen: 318. Both federal and institutional methodology are used as a basis for awarding need-based institutional aid.

UNDERGRADUATE EXPENSES for 2004–05 *Application fee:* $30. *Comprehensive fee:* $28,600 includes full-time tuition ($22,290), mandatory fees ($360), and room and board ($5950). *College room only:* $2800. Room and board charges vary according to board plan and housing facility. *Part-time tuition:* $1060 per course. *Payment plan:* Installment.

FRESHMAN FINANCIAL AID (Fall 2004, est.) 292 applied for aid; of those 90% were deemed to have need. 100% of freshmen with need received aid; of those 24% had need fully met. *Average percent of need met:* 93% (excluding resources awarded to replace EFC). *Average financial aid package:* $20,392 (excluding resources awarded to replace EFC). 16% of all full-time freshmen had no need and received non-need-based gift aid.

UNDERGRADUATE FINANCIAL AID (Fall 2004, est.) 1,062 applied for aid; of those 92% were deemed to have need. 100% of undergraduates with need received aid; of those 19% had need fully met. *Average percent of need met:* 92% (excluding resources awarded to replace EFC). *Average financial aid package:* $20,076 (excluding resources awarded to replace EFC). 18% of all full-time undergraduates had no need and received non-need-based gift aid.

GIFT AID (NEED-BASED) *Total amount:* $12,775,029 (10% federal, 13% state, 75% institutional, 2% external sources). *Receiving aid:* Freshmen: 84% (261); All full-time undergraduates: 80% (964). *Average award:* Freshmen: $14,421; Undergraduates: $13,218. *Scholarships, grants, and awards:* Federal Pell, FSEOG, state, private, college/university gift aid from institutional funds.

GIFT AID (NON-NEED-BASED) *Total amount:* $2,917,012 (97% institutional, 3% external sources). *Receiving aid:* Freshmen: 16% (50); Undergraduates: 11% (134). *Average Award:* Freshmen: $11,516; Undergraduates: $10,204. *Scholarships, grants, and awards by category:* Academic Interests/Achievement: 1,227 awards ($7,304,406 total): biological sciences, business, foreign languages, general academic interests/achievements, physical sciences, premedicine. *Creative Arts/Performance:* 382 awards ($1,196,375 total): art/fine arts, creative writing, music, performing arts, theater/drama. *Special Characteristics:* 290 awards ($906,328 total): adult students, children and siblings of alumni, children of faculty/staff, international students. *Tuition waivers:* Full or partial for children of alumni, employees or children of employees, adult students, senior citizens. *ROTC:* Army cooperative, Air Force cooperative.

LOANS *Student loans:* $7,472,854 (73% need-based, 27% non-need-based). 78% of past graduating class borrowed through all loan programs. *Average indebtedness per student:* $23,159. *Average need-based loan:* Freshmen: $4964; Undergraduates: $6328. *Parent loans:* $1,969,008 (28% need-based, 72% non-need-based). *Programs:* Federal Direct (Subsidized and Unsubsidized Stafford, PLUS), Perkins, college/university.

WORK-STUDY *Federal work-study:* Total amount: $199,848; jobs available (averaging $1200). *State or other work-study/employment:* Total amount: $510,689 (66% need-based, 34% non-need-based). Part-time jobs available (averaging $1200).

APPLYING FOR FINANCIAL AID *Required financial aid form:* FAFSA. *Financial aid deadline (priority):* 3/1. *Notification date:* Continuous beginning 3/15. Students must reply by 5/1 or within 2 weeks of notification.

CONTACT Ms. Barbara Hoffman, Director of Financial Aid, Coe College, 1220 1st Avenue, NE, Cedar Rapids, IA 52402-5070, 319-399-8540 or toll-free 877-225-5263. *Fax:* 319-399-8886.

COGSWELL POLYTECHNICAL COLLEGE
Sunnyvale, CA

ABOUT THE INSTITUTION Independent, coed, primarily men. Awards: bachelor's degrees. 7 undergraduate majors. Total enrollment: 376. Undergraduates: 376. Freshmen: 25.

GIFT AID (NEED-BASED) *Scholarships, grants, and awards:* Federal Pell, FSEOG, state, private, college/university gift aid from institutional funds.

GIFT AID (NON-NEED-BASED) *Scholarships, grants, and awards by category:* Academic Interests/Achievement: computer science, engineering/technologies.

LOANS *Programs:* FFEL (Subsidized and Unsubsidized Stafford, PLUS), Alaska Loans.

APPLYING FOR FINANCIAL AID *Required financial aid forms:* FAFSA, institution's own form.

CONTACT Guillermo S. Gaeta, Financial Aid Director, Cogswell Polytechnical College, 1175 Bordeaux Drive, Sunnyvale, CA 94089, 408-541-0100 Ext. 107 or toll-free 800-264-7955. *Fax:* 408-747-0766. *E-mail:* ggaeta@cogswell.edu.

COKER COLLEGE
Hartsville, SC

ABOUT THE INSTITUTION Independent, coed. Awards: bachelor's degrees (also offers evening program with significant enrollment not reflected in profile). 57 undergraduate majors. Total enrollment: 482. Undergraduates: 482. Freshmen: 148.

GIFT AID (NEED-BASED) *Scholarships, grants, and awards:* Federal Pell, FSEOG, state, private, college/university gift aid from institutional funds.

GIFT AID (NON-NEED-BASED) *Scholarships, grants, and awards by category:* Academic Interests/Achievement: general academic interests/achievements. *Creative Arts/Performance:* art/fine arts, creative writing, dance, general creative arts/performance, music, theater/drama. *Special Characteristics:* children and siblings of alumni, children of faculty/staff, international students, previous college experience.

LOANS *Programs:* FFEL (Subsidized and Unsubsidized Stafford, PLUS), Perkins.

WORK-STUDY *Federal work-study:* Total amount: $169,181; 157 jobs averaging $1078.

APPLYING FOR FINANCIAL AID *Required financial aid form:* FAFSA.

CONTACT Betty Williams, Director of Financial Aid, Coker College, 300 East College Avenue, Hartsville, SC 29550, 843-383-8055 or toll-free 800-950-1908. *Fax:* 843-383-8056. *E-mail:* bwilliams@coker.edu.

THE COLBURN SCHOOL CONSERVATORY OF MUSIC
Los Angeles, CA

CONTACT Financial Aid Office, The Colburn School Conservatory of Music, 200 South Grand Avenue, Los Angeles, CA 90012, 213-621-2200.

COLBY COLLEGE
Waterville, ME

Comprehensive fee: $39,800	Average undergraduate aid package: $26,265

ABOUT THE INSTITUTION Independent, coed. Awards: bachelor's degrees. 42 undergraduate majors. Total enrollment: 1,821. Undergraduates: 1,821. Freshmen: 507. Institutional methodology is used as a basis for awarding need-based institutional aid.

UNDERGRADUATE EXPENSES for 2004–05 *Application fee:* $55. *Comprehensive fee:* $39,800.

FRESHMAN FINANCIAL AID (Fall 2004, est.) 268 applied for aid; of those 74% were deemed to have need. 100% of freshmen with need received aid; of those 100% had need fully met. *Average percent of need met:* 100% (excluding resources awarded to replace EFC). *Average financial aid package:* $25,210 (excluding resources awarded to replace EFC).

UNDERGRADUATE FINANCIAL AID (Fall 2004, est.) 828 applied for aid; of those 85% were deemed to have need. 100% of undergraduates with need received aid; of those 100% had need fully met. *Average percent of need met:* 100% (excluding resources awarded to replace EFC). *Average financial aid package:* $26,265 (excluding resources awarded to replace EFC).

GIFT AID (NEED-BASED) *Total amount:* $16,269,365 (5% federal, 91% institutional, 4% external sources). *Receiving aid:* Freshmen: 38% (191); All full-time undergraduates: 37% (675). *Average award:* Freshmen: $23,348; Undergraduates: $24,103. *Scholarships, grants, and awards:* Federal Pell, FSEOG, state, private, college/university gift aid from institutional funds.

GIFT AID (NON-NEED-BASED) *ROTC:* Army cooperative.

LOANS *Student loans:* $3,519,949 (44% need-based, 56% non-need-based). 44% of past graduating class borrowed through all loan programs. *Average indebtedness per student:* $18,627. *Average need-based loan:* Freshmen: $2984; Undergraduates: $3343. *Parent loans:* $2,534,013 (100% non-need-based). *Programs:* Federal Direct (Subsidized and Unsubsidized Stafford, PLUS), FFEL (Subsidized and Unsubsidized Stafford, PLUS), Perkins, state, college/university, alternative loans.

WORK-STUDY *Federal work-study:* Total amount: $651,584; 442 jobs averaging $1474. *State or other work-study/employment:* Total amount: $110,574 (100% need-based). 85 part-time jobs averaging $1301.

APPLYING FOR FINANCIAL AID *Required financial aid forms:* FAFSA, either institution's own financial aid form or CSS/Financial Aid PROFILE and institutional supplement. *Financial aid deadline:* 2/1. *Notification date:* 4/1. Students must reply by 5/1.

CONTACT Ms. Lucia Whittelsey, Director of Financial Aid, Colby College, 4850 Mayflower Hill, Waterville, ME 04901-8848, 207-872-3168 or toll-free 800-723-3032. *Fax:* 207-872-3474. *E-mail:* finaid@colby.edu.

COLBY-SAWYER COLLEGE
New London, NH

Tuition & fees: $24,700	Average undergraduate aid package: $15,250

ABOUT THE INSTITUTION Independent, coed. Awards: associate and bachelor's degrees. 20 undergraduate majors. Total enrollment: 964. Undergraduates: 964. Freshmen: 266. Federal methodology is used as a basis for awarding need-based institutional aid.

UNDERGRADUATE EXPENSES for 2005–06 *Application fee:* $40. *Comprehensive fee:* $34,190 includes full-time tuition ($24,700) and room and board ($9490). *College room only:* $5280. *Part-time tuition:* $825 per credit hour. Part-time tuition and fees vary according to course load. *Payment plan:* Installment.

FRESHMAN FINANCIAL AID (Fall 2003) 231 applied for aid; of those 91% were deemed to have need. 100% of freshmen with need received aid; of those 3% had need fully met. *Average percent of need met:* 88% (excluding resources awarded to replace EFC). *Average financial aid package:* $16,430 (excluding resources awarded to replace EFC). 17% of all full-time freshmen had no need and received non-need-based gift aid.

UNDERGRADUATE FINANCIAL AID (Fall 2003) 816 applied for aid; of those 91% were deemed to have need. 100% of undergraduates with need received aid; of those 2% had need fully met. *Average percent of need met:* 86% (excluding resources awarded to replace EFC). *Average financial aid package:* $15,250 (excluding resources awarded to replace EFC). 14% of all full-time undergraduates had no need and received non-need-based gift aid.

GIFT AID (NEED-BASED) *Total amount:* $6,613,856 (12% federal, 3% state, 85% institutional). *Receiving aid:* Freshmen: 64% (196); All full-time undergraduates: 70% (637). *Average award:* Freshmen: $8500; Undergraduates: $7500. *Scholarships, grants, and awards:* Federal Pell, FSEOG, state, private, college/university gift aid from institutional funds.

GIFT AID (NON-NEED-BASED) *Total amount:* $2,165,165 (90% institutional, 10% external sources). *Receiving aid:* Freshmen: 44% (133); Undergraduates: 39% (354). *Average Award:* Freshmen: $4450; Undergraduates: $4155. *Scholarships, grants, and awards by category: Academic Interests/Achievement:* 389 awards ($1,311,898 total): general academic interests/achievements. *Creative Arts/Performance:* 118 awards ($282,200 total): art/fine arts, creative writing, music. *Special Achievements/Activities:* 239 awards ($467,000 total): community service, leadership. *Special Characteristics:* children of faculty/staff. *Tuition waivers:* Full or partial for employees or children of employees. *ROTC:* Army cooperative, Air Force cooperative.

LOANS *Student loans:* $4,498,321 (57% need-based, 43% non-need-based). 77% of past graduating class borrowed through all loan programs. *Average indebtedness per student:* $18,050. *Average need-based loan:* Freshmen: $2768; Undergraduates: $4098. *Parent loans:* $2,967,507 (100% non-need-based). *Programs:* FFEL (Subsidized and Unsubsidized Stafford, PLUS), Perkins, state, college/university.

WORK-STUDY *Federal work-study:* Total amount: $226,348; 298 jobs averaging $939. *State or other work-study/employment:* Total amount: $73,138 (100% non-need-based). 78 part-time jobs averaging $906.

APPLYING FOR FINANCIAL AID *Required financial aid forms:* FAFSA, institution's own form. *Financial aid deadline (priority):* 2/15. *Notification date:* Continuous beginning 3/1. Students must reply within 2 weeks of notification.

CONTACT Office of Financial Aid, Colby-Sawyer College, 541 Main Street, New London, NH 03257-7835, 603-526-3717 or toll-free 800-272-1015. *Fax:* 603-526-3452. *E-mail:* cscfinaid@colby-sawyer.edu.

COLEGIO BIBLICO PENTECOSTAL
St. Just, PR

CONTACT Mr. Eric Ayala, Director of Financial Aid, Colegio Biblico Pentecostal, PO Box 901, St. Just, PR 00978-0901, 787-761-0640.

COLEGIO PENTECOSTAL MIZPA
Río Piedras, PR

CONTACT Financial Aid Office, Colegio Pentecostal Mizpa, Km. 0 Hm. 2, Bo. Caimito, Apartado 20966, Río Piedras, PR 00928-0966, 787-720-4476.

COLEMAN COLLEGE
La Mesa, CA

CONTACT Financial Aid Office, Coleman College, 7380 Parkway Drive, La Mesa, CA 91942, 619-465-3990. *Fax:* 619-465-0162. *E-mail:* faoffice@coleman.edu.

COLGATE UNIVERSITY
Hamilton, NY

Tuition & fees: $31,440	Average undergraduate aid package: $26,923

ABOUT THE INSTITUTION Independent, coed. Awards: bachelor's and master's degrees. 52 undergraduate majors. Total enrollment: 2,830. Undergraduates: 2,823. Freshmen: 737. Both federal and institutional methodology are used as a basis for awarding need-based institutional aid.

UNDERGRADUATE EXPENSES for 2004–05 *Application fee:* $55. *Comprehensive fee:* $39,060 includes full-time tuition ($31,230), mandatory fees ($210), and room and board ($7620). *College room only:* $3680. Full-time tuition and fees vary according to course load. Room and board charges vary according to board plan and housing facility. *Part-time tuition:* $3903 per course. Part-time tuition and fees vary according to course load. *Payment plans:* Tuition prepayment, installment, deferred payment.

FRESHMAN FINANCIAL AID (Fall 2004, est.) 317 applied for aid; of those 83% were deemed to have need. 100% of freshmen with need received aid; of those 100% had need fully met. *Average percent of need met:* 100% (excluding resources awarded to replace EFC). *Average financial aid package:* $29,338 (excluding resources awarded to replace EFC).

UNDERGRADUATE FINANCIAL AID (Fall 2004, est.) 1,338 applied for aid; of those 92% were deemed to have need. 100% of undergraduates with need received aid; of those 100% had need fully met. *Average percent of need met:* 100% (excluding resources awarded to replace EFC). *Average financial aid package:* $26,923 (excluding resources awarded to replace EFC).

GIFT AID (NEED-BASED) *Total amount:* $28,688,285 (4% federal, 3% state, 90% institutional, 3% external sources). *Receiving aid:* Freshmen: 36% (262); All full-time undergraduates: 42% (1,161). *Average award:* Freshmen: $24,234; Undergraduates: $23,971. *Scholarships, grants, and awards:* Federal Pell, FSEOG, state, college/university gift aid from institutional funds.

GIFT AID (NON-NEED-BASED) *Receiving aid:* Freshmen: 4% (32); Undergraduates: 1% (33). *Tuition waivers:* Full or partial for employees or children of employees. *ROTC:* Army cooperative.

LOANS *Student loans:* $3,619,320 (83% need-based, 17% non-need-based). 43% of past graduating class borrowed through all loan programs. *Average indebtedness per student:* $11,104. *Average need-based loan:* Freshmen: $2296; Undergraduates: $4200. *Parent loans:* $4,325,589 (100% non-need-based). *Programs:* FFEL (Subsidized and Unsubsidized Stafford, PLUS), Perkins.

WORK-STUDY *Federal work-study:* Total amount: $1,107,498; 659 jobs averaging $1681. *State or other work-study/employment:* Total amount: $324,121 (100% need-based). 203 part-time jobs averaging $1597.

ATHLETIC AWARDS *Total amount:* $995,812 (100% non-need-based).

APPLYING FOR FINANCIAL AID *Required financial aid forms:* FAFSA, CSS Financial Aid PROFILE, noncustodial (divorced/separated) parent's statement, business/farm supplement. *Financial aid deadline:* 2/1. *Notification date:* 4/1. Students must reply by 5/1 or within 2 weeks of notification.

CONTACT Office of Financial Aid, Colgate University, 13 Oak Drive, Hamilton, NY 13346, 315-228-7431. *Fax:* 315-228-7050. *E-mail:* financialaid@mail.colgate. edu.

COLLEGE FOR CREATIVE STUDIES
Detroit, MI

Tuition & fees: $23,116	Average undergraduate aid package: N/A

ABOUT THE INSTITUTION Independent, coed. Awards: bachelor's degrees. 25 undergraduate majors. Total enrollment: 1,265. Undergraduates: 1,265. Freshmen: 180. Federal methodology is used as a basis for awarding need-based institutional aid.

UNDERGRADUATE EXPENSES for 2005–06 *Application fee:* $35. *Tuition:* full-time $21,990; part-time $733 per credit hour. *Required fees:* full-time $1126; $563 per term part-time.

GIFT AID (NEED-BASED) *Total amount:* $2,392,158 (38% federal, 41% state, 21% institutional). *Scholarships, grants, and awards:* Federal Pell, FSEOG, state, private, college/university gift aid from institutional funds.

GIFT AID (NON-NEED-BASED) *Total amount:* $4,107,105 (7% state, 84% institutional, 9% external sources). *Scholarships, grants, and awards by category:* Creative Arts/Performance: applied art and design, art/fine arts.

LOANS *Student loans:* $6,559,256 (100% need-based). 67% of past graduating class borrowed through all loan programs. *Average indebtedness per student:* $26,482. *Parent loans:* $1,326,237 (100% need-based). *Programs:* FFEL (Subsidized and Unsubsidized Stafford, PLUS), state, alternative loans.

WORK-STUDY *Federal work-study:* Total amount: $89,484; jobs available (averaging $1000). *State or other work-study/employment:* Total amount: $193,749 (100% need-based). Part-time jobs available (averaging $1000).

APPLYING FOR FINANCIAL AID *Required financial aid form:* FAFSA. *Financial aid deadline (priority):* 2/21. *Notification date:* Continuous beginning 3/21. Students must reply within 3 weeks of notification.

CONTACT Financial Aid Office, College for Creative Studies, 201 East Kirby, Detroit, MI 48202-4034, 313-664-7495 or toll-free 800-952-ARTS. *Fax:* 313-872-1521. *E-mail:* finaid@ccscad.edu.

COLLEGE MISERICORDIA
Dallas, PA

Tuition & fees: $18,800	Average undergraduate aid package: $13,740

ABOUT THE INSTITUTION Independent Roman Catholic, coed. Awards: bachelor's and master's degrees and post-bachelor's and post-master's certificates. 31 undergraduate majors. Total enrollment: 2,271. Undergraduates: 2,071. Freshmen: 321. Federal methodology is used as a basis for awarding need-based institutional aid.

UNDERGRADUATE EXPENSES for 2004–05 *Application fee:* $25. *Comprehensive fee:* $26,650 includes full-time tuition ($17,850), mandatory fees ($950), and room and board ($7850). *College room only:* $4500. Room and board charges vary according to board plan and housing facility. *Part-time tuition:* $395 per credit. *Payment plans:* Installment, deferred payment.

FRESHMAN FINANCIAL AID (Fall 2004, est.) 309 applied for aid; of those 89% were deemed to have need. 100% of freshmen with need received aid; of those 13% had need fully met. *Average percent of need met:* 73% (excluding resources awarded to replace EFC). *Average financial aid package:* $13,364 (excluding resources awarded to replace EFC). 10% of all full-time freshmen had no need and received non-need-based gift aid.

UNDERGRADUATE FINANCIAL AID (Fall 2004, est.) 1,315 applied for aid; of those 90% were deemed to have need. 100% of undergraduates with need received aid; of those 23% had need fully met. *Average percent of need met:* 76% (excluding resources awarded to replace EFC). *Average financial aid package:* $13,740 (excluding resources awarded to replace EFC). 9% of all full-time undergraduates had no need and received non-need-based gift aid.

GIFT AID (NEED-BASED) *Total amount:* $11,717,721 (13% federal, 19% state, 67% institutional, 1% external sources). *Receiving aid:* Freshmen: 86% (274); All full-time undergraduates: 83% (1,165). *Average award:* Freshmen: $9791; Undergraduates: $9635. *Scholarships, grants, and awards:* Federal Pell, FSEOG, state, private, college/university gift aid from institutional funds, Federal Nursing.

GIFT AID (NON-NEED-BASED) *Total amount:* $1,525,951 (96% institutional, 4% external sources). *Receiving aid:* Freshmen: 11% (35); Undergraduates: 18% (252). *Average Award:* Freshmen: $5629; Undergraduates: $5789. *Scholarships, grants, and awards by category:* Academic Interests/Achievement: 934

awards ($3,727,700 total): business, computer science, education, general academic interests/achievements, health fields, social sciences. *Special Achievements/Activities:* 868 awards ($2,186,470 total): community service, general special achievements/activities, leadership. *Special Characteristics:* 497 awards ($1,131,241 total): children and siblings of alumni, children of current students, children of faculty/staff, general special characteristics, out-of-state students, previous college experience, relatives of clergy, religious affiliation, siblings of current students. *Tuition waivers:* Full or partial for employees or children of employees. *ROTC:* Army cooperative, Air Force cooperative.

LOANS *Student loans:* $9,376,168 (86% need-based, 14% non-need-based). 80% of past graduating class borrowed through all loan programs. *Average indebtedness per student:* $19,582. *Average need-based loan:* Freshmen: $6454; Undergraduates: $6992. *Parent loans:* $2,647,288 (34% need-based, 66% non-need-based). *Programs:* FFEL (Subsidized and Unsubsidized Stafford, PLUS), Perkins, Federal Nursing, state.

WORK-STUDY *Federal work-study:* Total amount: $248,641; 245 jobs averaging $1000. *State or other work-study/employment:* Part-time jobs available.

APPLYING FOR FINANCIAL AID *Required financial aid forms:* FAFSA, institution's own form. *Financial aid deadline (priority):* 3/1. *Notification date:* 3/15. Students must reply within 2 weeks of notification.

CONTACT Margaret R. Charnick, Director of Financial Aid, College Misericordia, 301 Lake Street, Dallas, PA 18612-1098, 570-674-6313 or toll-free 866-262-6363 (in-state), 866-2626363 (out-of-state). *Fax:* 570-675-2441. *E-mail:* pcharnic@misericordia.edu.

COLLEGE OF AERONAUTICS
Flushing, NY

See Vaughn College of Aeronautics and Technology.

COLLEGE OF BIBLICAL STUDIES–HOUSTON
Houston, TX

CONTACT Financial Aid Office, College of Biblical Studies–Houston, 6000 Dale Carnegie Drive, Houston, TX 77036, 713-785-5995.

COLLEGE OF CHARLESTON
Charleston, SC

Tuition & fees (SC res): $6202	Average undergraduate aid package: $8820

ABOUT THE INSTITUTION State-supported, coed. Awards: bachelor's and master's degrees (also offers graduate degree programs through University of Charleston, South Carolina). 41 undergraduate majors. Total enrollment: 11,607. Undergraduates: 9,866. Freshmen: 1,944. Federal methodology is used as a basis for awarding need-based institutional aid.

UNDERGRADUATE EXPENSES for 2004–05 *Application fee:* $45. *Tuition, state resident:* full-time $6202; part-time $258 per semester hour. *Tuition, nonresident:* full-time $14,140; part-time $589 per semester hour. Part-time tuition and fees vary according to course load. *College room and board:* $6506; *room only:* $4446. Room and board charges vary according to board plan and housing facility. *Payment plan:* Installment.

FRESHMAN FINANCIAL AID (Fall 2004, est.) 1148 applied for aid; of those 64% were deemed to have need. 96% of freshmen with need received aid; of those 30% had need fully met. *Average percent of need met:* 63% (excluding resources awarded to replace EFC). *Average financial aid package:* $8358 (excluding resources awarded to replace EFC). 13% of all full-time freshmen had no need and received non-need-based gift aid.

UNDERGRADUATE FINANCIAL AID (Fall 2004, est.) 4,690 applied for aid; of those 76% were deemed to have need. 97% of undergraduates with need received aid; of those 26% had need fully met. *Average percent of need met:* 62% (excluding resources awarded to replace EFC). *Average financial aid package:* $8820 (excluding resources awarded to replace EFC). 9% of all full-time undergraduates had no need and received non-need-based gift aid.

GIFT AID (NEED-BASED) *Total amount:* $11,750,281 (39% federal, 44% state, 12% institutional, 5% external sources). *Receiving aid:* Freshmen: 26% (497); All full-time undergraduates: 24% (2,180). *Average award:* Freshmen: $3190; Undergraduates: $2877. *Scholarships, grants, and awards:* Federal Pell, FSEOG, state, private, college/university gift aid from institutional funds.

GIFT AID (NON-NEED-BASED) *Total amount:* $15,654,633 (64% state, 31% institutional, 5% external sources). *Receiving aid:* Freshmen: 26% (502);

Undergraduates: 15% (1,293). *Average Award: Freshmen:* $9427; *Undergraduates:* $10,003. *Scholarships, grants, and awards by category: Academic Interests/Achievement:* biological sciences, business, communication, computer science, education, engineering/technologies, English, foreign languages, general academic interests/achievements, health fields, humanities, mathematics, physical sciences, premedicine, social sciences. *Creative Arts/Performance:* art/fine arts, music, performing arts, theater/drama. *Special Characteristics:* general special characteristics. *Tuition waivers:* Full or partial for senior citizens. *ROTC:* Air Force cooperative.
LOANS *Student loans:* $22,018,179 (64% need-based, 36% non-need-based). 44% of past graduating class borrowed through all loan programs. *Average indebtedness per student:* $15,461. *Average need-based loan:* Freshmen: $2315; Undergraduates: $3527. *Parent loans:* $16,078,257 (49% need-based, 51% non-need-based). *Programs:* Federal Direct (Subsidized and Unsubsidized Stafford, PLUS), Perkins.
WORK-STUDY *Federal work-study:* Total amount: $332,970; jobs available. *State or other work-study/employment:* Total amount: $2,075,465 (100% non-need-based). Part-time jobs available.
ATHLETIC AWARDS *Total amount:* $2,067,127 (26% need-based, 74% non-need-based).
APPLYING FOR FINANCIAL AID *Required financial aid form:* FAFSA. *Financial aid deadline (priority):* 3/15. *Notification date:* Continuous beginning 4/10.
CONTACT Mr. Don Griggs, Financial Aid Director, College of Charleston, 66 George Street, Charleston, SC 29424, 843-953-5540 or toll-free 843-953-5670 (in-state). *Fax:* 843-953-7192.

COLLEGE OF MOUNT ST. JOSEPH
Cincinnati, OH

Tuition & fees: $18,790	Average undergraduate aid package: $16,473

ABOUT THE INSTITUTION Independent Roman Catholic, coed. Awards: associate, bachelor's, and master's degrees and post-bachelor's certificates. 43 undergraduate majors. Total enrollment: 2,158. Undergraduates: 1,858. Freshmen: 337. Federal methodology is used as a basis for awarding need-based institutional aid.
UNDERGRADUATE EXPENSES for 2005–06 *Application fee:* $25. *Comprehensive fee:* $24,860 includes full-time tuition ($18,400), mandatory fees ($390), and room and board ($6070). *College room only:* $3000. Full-time tuition and fees vary according to course load, program, and reciprocity agreements. Room and board charges vary according to board plan and housing facility. *Part-time tuition:* $430 per semester hour. *Part-time fees:* $65 per term. Part-time tuition and fees vary according to course load, location, program, and reciprocity agreements. *Payment plans:* Installment, deferred payment.
FRESHMAN FINANCIAL AID (Fall 2004, est.) 292 applied for aid; of those 92% were deemed to have need. 100% of freshmen with need received aid; of those 42% had need fully met. *Average percent of need met:* 89% (excluding resources awarded to replace EFC). *Average financial aid package:* $17,000 (excluding resources awarded to replace EFC). 13% of all full-time freshmen had no need and received non-need-based gift aid.
UNDERGRADUATE FINANCIAL AID (Fall 2004, est.) 1,167 applied for aid; of those 92% were deemed to have need. 100% of undergraduates with need received aid; of those 42% had need fully met. *Average percent of need met:* 89% (excluding resources awarded to replace EFC). *Average financial aid package:* $16,473 (excluding resources awarded to replace EFC). 14% of all full-time undergraduates had no need and received non-need-based gift aid.
GIFT AID (NEED-BASED) *Total amount:* $9,779,970 (16% federal, 19% state, 63% institutional, 2% external sources). *Receiving aid:* Freshmen: 76% (245); All full-time undergraduates: 75% (979). *Average award:* Freshmen: $9238; Undergraduates: $9000. *Scholarships, grants, and awards:* Federal Pell, FSEOG, state, private, college/university gift aid from institutional funds.
GIFT AID (NON-NEED-BASED) *Total amount:* $2,294,639 (10% federal, 26% state, 59% institutional, 5% external sources). *Receiving aid:* Freshmen: 12% (38); Undergraduates: 12% (151). *Average Award: Freshmen:* $7234; *Undergraduates:* $3800. *Scholarships, grants, and awards by category: Academic Interests/Achievement:* 690 awards ($3,087,731 total): general academic interests/achievements. *Creative Arts/Performance:* 92 awards ($101,775 total): art/fine arts, music. *Special Achievements/Activities:* 76 awards ($1,136,486 total): community service, leadership. *Special Characteristics:* 16 awards ($14,217 total): adult students, children and siblings of alumni, children of faculty/staff. *Tuition waivers:* Full or partial for employees or children of employees, senior citizens. *ROTC:* Army cooperative, Air Force cooperative.

LOANS *Student loans:* $9,470,597 (73% need-based, 27% non-need-based). 80% of past graduating class borrowed through all loan programs. *Average indebtedness per student:* $13,400. *Average need-based loan:* Freshmen: $3665; Undergraduates: $4156. *Parent loans:* $1,424,787 (20% need-based, 80% non-need-based). *Programs:* FFEL (Subsidized and Unsubsidized Stafford, PLUS), Perkins, Federal Nursing, state.
WORK-STUDY *Federal work-study:* Total amount: $172,654; 115 jobs averaging $1500. *State or other work-study/employment:* Total amount: $204,521 (80% need-based, 20% non-need-based). 109 part-time jobs averaging $1501.
APPLYING FOR FINANCIAL AID *Required financial aid form:* FAFSA. *Financial aid deadline (priority):* 3/1. *Notification date:* Continuous beginning 2/15. Students must reply by 5/1 or within 4 weeks of notification.
CONTACT Ms. Kathryn Kelly, Director of Student Administrative Services, College of Mount St. Joseph, 5701 Delhi Road, Cincinnati, OH 45233-1670, 513-244-4418 or toll-free 800-654-9314. *Fax:* 513-244-4201. *E-mail:* kathy_kelly@mail.msj.edu.

COLLEGE OF MOUNT SAINT VINCENT
Riverdale, NY

Tuition & fees: $19,900	Average undergraduate aid package: $15,000

ABOUT THE INSTITUTION Independent, coed. Awards: associate, bachelor's, and master's degrees and post-master's certificates. 38 undergraduate majors. Total enrollment: 1,685. Undergraduates: 1,393. Freshmen: 357. Federal methodology is used as a basis for awarding need-based institutional aid.
UNDERGRADUATE EXPENSES for 2005–06 *Application fee:* $35. *Comprehensive fee:* $28,150 includes full-time tuition ($19,900) and room and board ($8250). *Payment plan:* Installment.
GIFT AID (NEED-BASED) *Total amount:* $8,000,000 *Scholarships, grants, and awards:* Federal Pell, FSEOG, state, private, college/university gift aid from institutional funds.
GIFT AID (NON-NEED-BASED) *Scholarships, grants, and awards by category: Academic Interests/Achievement:* general academic interests/achievements. *Special Achievements/Activities:* leadership. *Special Characteristics:* children and siblings of alumni, children of faculty/staff, siblings of current students. *Tuition waivers:* Full or partial for employees or children of employees, senior citizens. *ROTC:* Army cooperative, Air Force cooperative.
LOANS *Student loans:* Average indebtedness per student: $17,000. *Programs:* FFEL (Subsidized and Unsubsidized Stafford, PLUS), Perkins, Federal Nursing.
APPLYING FOR FINANCIAL AID *Required financial aid form:* FAFSA. *Financial aid deadline (priority):* 2/15. *Notification date:* Continuous beginning 3/3. Students must reply by 5/1 or within 2 weeks of notification.
CONTACT Ms. Monica Simotas, Director of Financial Aid, College of Mount Saint Vincent, 6301 Riverdale Avenue, Riverdale, NY 10471, 718-405-3290 or toll-free 800-665-CMSV. *Fax:* 718-405-3490. *E-mail:* msimotas@mountsaintvincent.edu.

THE COLLEGE OF NEW JERSEY
Ewing, NJ

Tuition & fees (NJ res): $8988	Average undergraduate aid package: $8897

ABOUT THE INSTITUTION State-supported, coed. Awards: bachelor's and master's degrees and post-bachelor's and post-master's certificates. 54 undergraduate majors. Total enrollment: 6,812. Undergraduates: 5,918. Freshmen: 1,231. Federal methodology is used as a basis for awarding need-based institutional aid.
UNDERGRADUATE EXPENSES for 2004–05 *Application fee:* $50. *Tuition, state resident:* full-time $6621; part-time $234 per credit. *Tuition, nonresident:* full-time $11,562; part-time $409 per credit. *Required fees:* full-time $2367; $83 per credit. Part-time tuition and fees vary according to course load. *College room and board:* $8093. Room and board charges vary according to board plan. *Payment plan:* Installment.
FRESHMAN FINANCIAL AID (Fall 2004, est.) 1039 applied for aid; of those 55% were deemed to have need. 99% of freshmen with need received aid; of those 42% had need fully met. *Average percent of need met:* 76% (excluding resources awarded to replace EFC). *Average financial aid package:* $9545 (excluding resources awarded to replace EFC). 24% of all full-time freshmen had no need and received non-need-based gift aid.
UNDERGRADUATE FINANCIAL AID (Fall 2004, est.) 3,882 applied for aid; of those 64% were deemed to have need. 98% of undergraduates with need received aid; of those 33% had need fully met. *Average percent of need met:*

73% (excluding resources awarded to replace EFC). *Average financial aid package:* $8897 (excluding resources awarded to replace EFC). 20% of all full-time undergraduates had no need and received non-need-based gift aid.

GIFT AID (NEED-BASED) *Total amount:* $8,546,315 (27% federal, 55% state, 15% institutional, 3% external sources). *Receiving aid:* Freshmen: 23% (286); All full-time undergraduates: 21% (1,184). *Average award:* Freshmen: $9794; Undergraduates: $7157. *Scholarships, grants, and awards:* Federal Pell, FSEOG, state, private, college/university gift aid from institutional funds, Federal Nursing.

GIFT AID (NON-NEED-BASED) *Total amount:* $12,709,865 (37% state, 53% institutional, 10% external sources). *Receiving aid:* Freshmen: 26% (322); Undergraduates: 19% (1,063). *Average Award:* Freshmen: $3209; Undergraduates: $4124. *Scholarships, grants, and awards by category: Academic Interests/Achievement:* engineering/technologies, general academic interests/achievements, physical sciences. *Creative Arts/Performance:* music. *Special Characteristics:* children with a deceased or disabled parent, members of minority groups. *Tuition waivers:* Full or partial for employees or children of employees, senior citizens. *ROTC:* Army cooperative, Air Force cooperative.

LOANS *Student loans:* $18,358,841 (44% need-based, 56% non-need-based). 57% of past graduating class borrowed through all loan programs. *Average indebtedness per student:* $18,524. *Average need-based loan:* Freshmen: $3416; Undergraduates: $4595. *Parent loans:* $4,374,831 (3% need-based, 97% non-need-based). *Programs:* Federal Direct (Subsidized and Unsubsidized Stafford, PLUS), FFEL (Subsidized and Unsubsidized Stafford, PLUS), Perkins, Federal Nursing, state.

WORK-STUDY *Federal work-study:* Total amount: $575,297; 222 jobs averaging $1111. *State or other work-study/employment:* Part-time jobs available.

APPLYING FOR FINANCIAL AID *Required financial aid form:* FAFSA. *Financial aid deadline:* 10/1 (priority: 3/1). *Notification date:* Continuous beginning 7/15. Students must reply within 2 weeks of notification.

CONTACT Jamie Hightower, Acting Director of Financial Aid and Student Accounts, The College of New Jersey, PO Box 7718, Ewing, NJ 08628, 609-771-2211 or toll-free 800-624-0967. *Fax:* 609-637-5154. *E-mail:* hightowe@tcnj.edu.

THE COLLEGE OF NEW ROCHELLE
New Rochelle, NY

Tuition & fees: $20,596	Average undergraduate aid package: $18,052

ABOUT THE INSTITUTION Independent, coed, primarily women. Awards: bachelor's and master's degrees and post-bachelor's and post-master's certificates (also offers a non-traditional adult program with significant enrollment not reflected in profile). 36 undergraduate majors. Total enrollment: 2,564. Undergraduates: 1,080. Freshmen: 152. Federal methodology is used as a basis for awarding need-based institutional aid.

UNDERGRADUATE EXPENSES for 2005–06 *Application fee:* $20. *Comprehensive fee:* $28,476 includes full-time tuition ($20,246), mandatory fees ($350), and room and board ($7880). Full-time tuition and fees vary according to course load and program. Room and board charges vary according to housing facility. *Part-time tuition:* $682 per credit. *Part-time fees:* $60 per term. Part-time tuition and fees vary according to course load. *Payment plans:* Tuition prepayment, installment.

FRESHMAN FINANCIAL AID (Fall 2003) 99 applied for aid; of those 100% were deemed to have need. 100% of freshmen with need received aid; of those 100% had need fully met. *Average percent of need met:* 100% (excluding resources awarded to replace EFC). *Average financial aid package:* $21,529 (excluding resources awarded to replace EFC). 7% of all full-time freshmen had no need and received non-need-based gift aid.

UNDERGRADUATE FINANCIAL AID (Fall 2003) 601 applied for aid; of those 100% were deemed to have need. 100% of undergraduates with need received aid; of those 100% had need fully met. *Average percent of need met:* 100% (excluding resources awarded to replace EFC). *Average financial aid package:* $18,052 (excluding resources awarded to replace EFC). 5% of all full-time undergraduates had no need and received non-need-based gift aid.

GIFT AID (NEED-BASED) *Total amount:* $3,268,380 (32% federal, 37% state, 31% institutional). *Receiving aid:* Freshmen: 83% (90); All full-time undergraduates: 95% (581). *Average award:* Freshmen: $12,431; Undergraduates: $7715. *Scholarships, grants, and awards:* Federal Pell, FSEOG, state, private, college/university gift aid from institutional funds.

GIFT AID (NON-NEED-BASED) *Total amount:* $2,180,820 (92% institutional, 8% external sources). *Receiving aid:* Freshmen: 78% (85); Undergraduates: 56% (340). *Average Award:* Freshmen: $8878; Undergraduates: $5552. *Scholarships, grants, and awards by category: Academic Interests/Achievement:* 315 awards ($2,000,000 total): area/ethnic studies, biological sciences, business,

communication, education, English, foreign languages, general academic interests/achievements, health fields, humanities, mathematics, physical sciences, premedicine, religion/biblical studies, social sciences. *Creative Arts/Performance:* 85 awards ($500,000 total): applied art and design, art/fine arts, cinema/film/broadcasting, creative writing, dance, debating, general creative arts/performance, journalism/publications, music, performing arts, theater/drama. *Special Achievements/Activities:* 45 awards ($250,000 total): community service, general special achievements/activities, hobbies/interests, junior miss, leadership, memberships, religious involvement. *Special Characteristics:* 60 awards ($350,000 total): children of current students, children of faculty/staff, general special characteristics, out-of-state students, parents of current students, previous college experience, siblings of current students, spouses of current students. *Tuition waivers:* Full or partial for employees or children of employees, senior citizens.

LOANS *Student loans:* $3,109,350 (79% need-based, 21% non-need-based). 80% of past graduating class borrowed through all loan programs. *Average indebtedness per student:* $33,000. *Average need-based loan:* Freshmen: $7086; Undergraduates: $8325. *Parent loans:* $272,460 (100% non-need-based). *Programs:* Federal Direct (Subsidized and Unsubsidized Stafford), FFEL (PLUS), Perkins, Federal Nursing.

WORK-STUDY *Federal work-study:* Total amount: $1,174,800; 484 jobs averaging $2012. *State or other work-study/employment:* Total amount: $45,000 (100% non-need-based). 10 part-time jobs averaging $4500.

APPLYING FOR FINANCIAL AID *Required financial aid forms:* FAFSA, institution's own form, federal income tax form(s). *Financial aid deadline:* Continuous. *Notification date:* Continuous beginning 1/1. Students must reply within 2 weeks of notification.

CONTACT Anne Pelak, Director of Financial Aid, The College of New Rochelle, 29 Castle Place, New Rochelle, NY 10805-2339, 914-654-5551 or toll-free 800-933-5923. *Fax:* 914-654-5420. *E-mail:* apelak@cnr.edu.

COLLEGE OF NOTRE DAME OF MARYLAND
Baltimore, MD

Tuition & fees: $21,600	Average undergraduate aid package: $15,614

ABOUT THE INSTITUTION Independent Roman Catholic, women only. Awards: bachelor's, master's, and doctoral degrees and post-bachelor's certificates. 33 undergraduate majors. Total enrollment: 3,307. Undergraduates: 1,686. Freshmen: 201. Federal methodology is used as a basis for awarding need-based institutional aid.

UNDERGRADUATE EXPENSES for 2005–06 *Application fee:* $25. *Comprehensive fee:* $29,600 includes full-time tuition ($21,100), mandatory fees ($500), and room and board ($8000). *Part-time tuition:* $345 per credit. *Part-time fees:* $60 per term. *Payment plan:* Installment.

FRESHMAN FINANCIAL AID (Fall 2004, est.) 132 applied for aid; of those 92% were deemed to have need. 100% of freshmen with need received aid; of those 38% had need fully met. *Average percent of need met:* 85% (excluding resources awarded to replace EFC). *Average financial aid package:* $17,424 (excluding resources awarded to replace EFC). 7% of all full-time freshmen had no need and received non-need-based gift aid.

UNDERGRADUATE FINANCIAL AID (Fall 2004, est.) 515 applied for aid; of those 93% were deemed to have need. 99% of undergraduates with need received aid; of those 36% had need fully met. *Average percent of need met:* 73% (excluding resources awarded to replace EFC). *Average financial aid package:* $15,614 (excluding resources awarded to replace EFC). 4% of all full-time undergraduates had no need and received non-need-based gift aid.

GIFT AID (NEED-BASED) *Total amount:* $6,411,126 (13% federal, 16% state, 69% institutional, 2% external sources). *Receiving aid:* Freshmen: 64% (95); All full-time undergraduates: 64% (390). *Average award:* Freshmen: $9327; Undergraduates: $7752. *Scholarships, grants, and awards:* Federal Pell, FSEOG, state, private, college/university gift aid from institutional funds.

GIFT AID (NON-NEED-BASED) *Total amount:* $978,213 (12% state, 87% institutional, 1% external sources). *Receiving aid:* Freshmen: 66% (98); Undergraduates: 62% (376). *Average Award:* Freshmen: $8280; Undergraduates: $6822. *Scholarships, grants, and awards by category: Academic Interests/Achievement:* 264 awards ($1,583,836 total): general academic interests/achievements. *Creative Arts/Performance:* 88 awards ($266,500 total): art/fine arts, general creative arts/performance. *Special Achievements/Activities:* 399 awards ($1,367,928 total): community service, general special achievements/activities, leadership, memberships, religious involvement. *Special Characteristics:* 9 awards ($49,755 total): international students. *Tuition waivers:* Full or partial for employees or children of employees. *ROTC:* Army cooperative.

LOANS *Student loans:* $5,073,637 (88% need-based, 12% non-need-based). 80% of past graduating class borrowed through all loan programs. *Average indebtedness per student:* $17,125. *Average need-based loan:* Freshmen: $3898; Undergraduates: $4120. *Parent loans:* $777,684 (84% need-based, 16% non-need-based). *Programs:* FFEL (Subsidized and Unsubsidized Stafford, PLUS), Perkins.

WORK-STUDY *Federal work-study:* Total amount: $70,245; 58 jobs averaging $1211.

APPLYING FOR FINANCIAL AID *Required financial aid form:* FAFSA. *Financial aid deadline (priority):* 2/15. *Notification date:* Continuous beginning 3/1. Students must reply by 5/1.

CONTACT Zhanna Goltser, Director of Financial Aid, College of Notre Dame of Maryland, 4701 North Charles Street, Baltimore, MD 21210-2404, 410-532-5369 or toll-free 800-435-0200 (in-state), 800-435-0300 (out-of-state). *Fax:* 410-532-6287. *E-mail:* finaid@ndm.edu.

COLLEGE OF SAINT BENEDICT
Saint Joseph, MN

Tuition & fees: $22,148	Average undergraduate aid package: $17,898

ABOUT THE INSTITUTION Independent Roman Catholic, coed, primarily women. Awards: bachelor's degrees (coordinate with Saint John's University for men). 54 undergraduate majors. Total enrollment: 2,033. Undergraduates: 2,033. Freshmen: 483. Federal methodology is used as a basis for awarding need-based institutional aid.

UNDERGRADUATE EXPENSES for 2004–05 *Comprehensive fee:* $28,356 includes full-time tuition ($21,758), mandatory fees ($390), and room and board ($6208). *College room only:* $3292. Room and board charges vary according to board plan and housing facility. *Part-time tuition:* $907 per credit. *Part-time fees:* $195 per term. Part-time tuition and fees vary according to course load. *Payment plans:* Tuition prepayment, installment.

FRESHMAN FINANCIAL AID (Fall 2004, est.) 477 applied for aid; of those 70% were deemed to have need. 100% of freshmen with need received aid; of those 86% had need fully met. *Average percent of need met:* 92% (excluding resources awarded to replace EFC). *Average financial aid package:* $18,159 (excluding resources awarded to replace EFC). 29% of all full-time freshmen had no need and received non-need-based gift aid.

UNDERGRADUATE FINANCIAL AID (Fall 2004, est.) 1,937 applied for aid; of those 67% were deemed to have need. 100% of undergraduates with need received aid; of those 87% had need fully met. *Average percent of need met:* 87% (excluding resources awarded to replace EFC). *Average financial aid package:* $17,898 (excluding resources awarded to replace EFC). 29% of all full-time undergraduates had no need and received non-need-based gift aid.

GIFT AID (NEED-BASED) *Total amount:* $14,440,651 (9% federal, 13% state, 74% institutional, 4% external sources). *Receiving aid:* Freshmen: 69% (331); All full-time undergraduates: 65% (1,275). *Average award:* Freshmen: $12,229; Undergraduates: $11,293. *Scholarships, grants, and awards:* Federal Pell, FSEOG, state, private, college/university gift aid from institutional funds.

GIFT AID (NON-NEED-BASED) *Total amount:* $5,225,776 (2% federal, 96% institutional, 2% external sources). *Receiving aid:* Freshmen: 65% (312); Undergraduates: 60% (1,175). *Average Award:* Freshmen: $6224; Undergraduates: $5924. *Scholarships, grants, and awards by category: Academic Interests/Achievement:* general academic interests/achievements, military science. *Creative Arts/Performance:* art/fine arts, music, theater/drama. *Special Achievements/Activities:* junior miss, memberships. *Special Characteristics:* ethnic background, international students. *Tuition waivers:* Full or partial for employees or children of employees. *ROTC:* Army cooperative.

LOANS *Student loans:* $9,235,285 (91% need-based, 9% non-need-based). 73% of past graduating class borrowed through all loan programs. *Average indebtedness per student:* $24,627. *Average need-based loan:* Freshmen: $4904; Undergraduates: $5526. *Parent loans:* $1,872,923 (79% need-based, 21% non-need-based). *Programs:* FFEL (Subsidized and Unsubsidized Stafford, PLUS), Perkins, state, alternative loans.

WORK-STUDY *Federal work-study:* Total amount: $1,253,502; 600 jobs averaging $2000. *State or other work-study/employment:* Total amount: $1,145,746 (67% need-based, 33% non-need-based). 300 part-time jobs averaging $2000.

APPLYING FOR FINANCIAL AID *Required financial aid forms:* FAFSA, institution's own form. *Financial aid deadline (priority):* 3/15. *Notification date:* Continuous beginning 3/1. Students must reply by 5/1.

CONTACT Ms. Jane Haugen, Executive Director of Financial Aid, College of Saint Benedict, 37 South College Avenue, Saint Joseph, MN 56374-2099, 320-363-5388 or toll-free 800-544-1489. *Fax:* 320-363-6099. *E-mail:* jhaugen@csbsju.edu.

COLLEGE OF ST. CATHERINE
St. Paul, MN

ABOUT THE INSTITUTION Independent Roman Catholic, women only. Awards: associate, bachelor's, master's, and doctoral degrees and post-bachelor's and post-master's certificates. 76 undergraduate majors. Total enrollment: 4,809. Undergraduates: 3,582.

GIFT AID (NEED-BASED) *Scholarships, grants, and awards:* Federal Pell, FSEOG, state, private, college/university gift aid from institutional funds, Federal Nursing.

GIFT AID (NON-NEED-BASED) *Scholarships, grants, and awards by category: Academic Interests/Achievement:* business, education, English, foreign languages, general academic interests/achievements, health fields, home economics, humanities, mathematics, physical sciences, premedicine, social sciences. *Creative Arts/Performance:* art/fine arts, music. *Special Achievements/Activities:* community service, general special achievements/activities, leadership, memberships. *Special Characteristics:* adult students, children and siblings of alumni, children of educators, children of faculty/staff, ethnic background, general special characteristics, international students, local/state students, out-of-state students, religious affiliation, siblings of current students.

LOANS *Programs:* FFEL (Subsidized and Unsubsidized Stafford, PLUS), Perkins, Federal Nursing, state, college/university.

WORK-STUDY *Federal work-study:* Total amount: $1,118,000; 500 jobs available. *State or other work-study/employment:* Total amount: $275,000 (100% non-need-based). Part-time jobs available.

APPLYING FOR FINANCIAL AID *Required financial aid forms:* FAFSA, institution's own form.

CONTACT Sandy Sundstrom, Director of Financial Aid, College of St. Catherine, Mail #F-11, 2004 Randolph Avenue, St. Paul, MN 55105-1789, 651-690-6540 or toll-free 800-945-4599 (in-state). *Fax:* 651-690-6558.

COLLEGE OF ST. CATHERINE–MINNEAPOLIS
Minneapolis, MN

CONTACT Mr. Cal Mosley, Associate Dean/Director of Financial Aid, College of St. Catherine–Minneapolis, 601 25th Avenue South, Minneapolis, MN 55454, 651-690-8600 or toll-free 800-945-4599 Ext. 7800. *Fax:* 651-690-8119. *E-mail:* pajohnson@stkate.edu.

COLLEGE OF SAINT ELIZABETH
Morristown, NJ

ABOUT THE INSTITUTION Independent Roman Catholic, women only. Awards: bachelor's and master's degrees and post-bachelor's certificates (also offers coed adult undergraduate degree program and coed graduate programs). 32 undergraduate majors. Total enrollment: 1,976. Undergraduates: 1,327. Freshmen: 164.

GIFT AID (NEED-BASED) *Scholarships, grants, and awards:* Federal Pell, FSEOG, state, private, college/university gift aid from institutional funds.

GIFT AID (NON-NEED-BASED) *Scholarships, grants, and awards by category: Academic Interests/Achievement:* biological sciences, business, communication, education, English, foreign languages, general academic interests/achievements, health fields, home economics, premedicine, religion/biblical studies. *Creative Arts/Performance:* art/fine arts, creative writing. *Special Achievements/Activities:* general special achievements/activities, junior miss, leadership. *Special Characteristics:* adult students, children and siblings of alumni, children of faculty/staff, children with a deceased or disabled parent, ethnic background, handicapped students, international students, members of minority groups, relatives of clergy, religious affiliation, siblings of current students.

LOANS *Programs:* FFEL (Subsidized and Unsubsidized Stafford, PLUS), Perkins, state.

APPLYING FOR FINANCIAL AID *Required financial aid forms:* FAFSA, income tax form(s), federal verification worksheet.

College of Saint Elizabeth

CONTACT Vincent Tunstall, Director of Financial Aid, College of Saint Elizabeth, 2 Convent Road, Morristown, NJ 07960-6989, 973-290-4445 or toll-free 800-210-7900. *Fax:* 973-290-4421.

COLLEGE OF ST. JOSEPH
Rutland, VT

Tuition & fees: $13,200	Average undergraduate aid package: $11,856

ABOUT THE INSTITUTION Independent Roman Catholic, coed. Awards: associate, bachelor's, and master's degrees and post-bachelor's certificates. 20 undergraduate majors. Total enrollment: 486. Undergraduates: 266. Freshmen: 40. Federal methodology is used as a basis for awarding need-based institutional aid.

UNDERGRADUATE EXPENSES for 2004–05 *Application fee:* $25. *Comprehensive fee:* $19,800 includes full-time tuition ($13,000), mandatory fees ($200), and room and board ($6600). *College room only:* $3200. Full-time tuition and fees vary according to program. Room and board charges vary according to housing facility. *Part-time tuition:* $220 per credit. *Part-time fees:* $45 per term. Part-time tuition and fees vary according to program. *Payment plan:* Installment.

FRESHMAN FINANCIAL AID (Fall 2004, est.) 35 applied for aid; of those 83% were deemed to have need. 100% of freshmen with need received aid; of those 10% had need fully met. *Average percent of need met:* 71% (excluding resources awarded to replace EFC). *Average financial aid package:* $14,062 (excluding resources awarded to replace EFC). 16% of all full-time freshmen had no need and received non-need-based gift aid.

UNDERGRADUATE FINANCIAL AID (Fall 2004, est.) 151 applied for aid; of those 89% were deemed to have need. 100% of undergraduates with need received aid; of those 16% had need fully met. *Average percent of need met:* 66% (excluding resources awarded to replace EFC). *Average financial aid package:* $11,856 (excluding resources awarded to replace EFC). 10% of all full-time undergraduates had no need and received non-need-based gift aid.

GIFT AID (NEED-BASED) *Total amount:* $953,346 (30% federal, 20% state, 48% institutional, 2% external sources). *Receiving aid:* Freshmen: 78% (29); All full-time undergraduates: 77% (128). *Average award:* Freshmen: $9921; Undergraduates: $6727. *Scholarships, grants, and awards:* Federal Pell, FSEOG, state, private, college/university gift aid from institutional funds.

GIFT AID (NON-NEED-BASED) *Total amount:* $54,142 (97% institutional, 3% external sources). *Receiving aid:* Undergraduates: 2% (3). *Average Award:* Freshmen: $9293; *Undergraduates:* $8839. *Scholarships, grants, and awards by category:* Academic Interests/Achievement: 14 awards ($35,000 total): general academic interests/achievements. Special Achievements/Activities: 17 awards ($17,550 total): community service, leadership. Special Characteristics: 6 awards ($6450 total): local/state students, religious affiliation. *Tuition waivers:* Full or partial for employees or children of employees, senior citizens.

LOANS *Student loans:* $1,198,993 (78% need-based, 22% non-need-based). 67% of past graduating class borrowed through all loan programs. *Average indebtedness per student:* $19,355. *Average need-based loan:* Freshmen: $2625; Undergraduates: $4910. *Parent loans:* $159,770 (38% need-based, 62% non-need-based). *Programs:* FFEL (Subsidized and Unsubsidized Stafford, PLUS), Perkins.

WORK-STUDY *Federal work-study:* Total amount: $50,634; 53 jobs averaging $955. *State or other work-study/employment:* Total amount: $46,731 (100% need-based). 54 part-time jobs averaging $865.

APPLYING FOR FINANCIAL AID *Required financial aid forms:* FAFSA, institution's own form. *Financial aid deadline:* Continuous. *Notification date:* Continuous beginning 3/15. Students must reply within 2 weeks of notification.

CONTACT Yvonne Payrits, Financial Aid Coordinator, College of St. Joseph, 71 Clement Road, Rutland, VT 05701-3899, 802-773-5900 Ext. 3218 or toll-free 877-270-9998 (in-state). *Fax:* 802-773-5900. *E-mail:* finaid@csj.edu.

COLLEGE OF SAINT MARY
Omaha, NE

Tuition & fees: $17,000	Average undergraduate aid package: $10,609

ABOUT THE INSTITUTION Independent Roman Catholic, women only. Awards: associate, bachelor's, and master's degrees. 33 undergraduate majors. Total enrollment: 994. Undergraduates: 969. Freshmen: 101. Federal methodology is used as a basis for awarding need-based institutional aid.

UNDERGRADUATE EXPENSES for 2004–05 *Application fee:* $30. *Comprehensive fee:* $22,700 includes full-time tuition ($16,640), mandatory fees ($360), and room and board ($5700). Room and board charges vary according to housing facility. *Part-time tuition:* $480 per credit hour. *Part-time fees:* $12 per credit hour. Part-time tuition and fees vary according to class time. *Payment plans:* Installment, deferred payment.

FRESHMAN FINANCIAL AID (Fall 2004, est.) 127 applied for aid; of those 87% were deemed to have need. 93% of freshmen with need received aid; of those 18% had need fully met. *Average percent of need met:* 59% (excluding resources awarded to replace EFC). *Average financial aid package:* $10,414 (excluding resources awarded to replace EFC). 13% of all full-time freshmen had no need and received non-need-based gift aid.

UNDERGRADUATE FINANCIAL AID (Fall 2004, est.) 747 applied for aid; of those 89% were deemed to have need. 94% of undergraduates with need received aid; of those 13% had need fully met. *Average percent of need met:* 58% (excluding resources awarded to replace EFC). *Average financial aid package:* $10,609 (excluding resources awarded to replace EFC). 10% of all full-time undergraduates had no need and received non-need-based gift aid.

GIFT AID (NEED-BASED) *Total amount:* $4,452,492 (33% federal, 4% state, 57% institutional, 6% external sources). *Receiving aid:* Freshmen: 48% (99); All full-time undergraduates: 66% (579). *Average award:* Freshmen: $8275; Undergraduates: $7314. *Scholarships, grants, and awards:* Federal Pell, FSEOG, state, college/university gift aid from institutional funds.

GIFT AID (NON-NEED-BASED) *Total amount:* $534,555 (84% institutional, 16% external sources). *Receiving aid:* Freshmen: 7% (14); Undergraduates: 3% (29). *Average Award:* Freshmen: $7025; Undergraduates: $8996. *Scholarships, grants, and awards by category:* Academic Interests/Achievement: general academic interests/achievements. Creative Arts/Performance: music. Special Achievements/Activities: community service, leadership. *Tuition waivers:* Full or partial for employees or children of employees, senior citizens. *ROTC:* Army cooperative, Air Force cooperative.

LOANS *Student loans:* $5,902,597 (78% need-based, 22% non-need-based). 86% of past graduating class borrowed through all loan programs. *Average indebtedness per student:* $13,500. *Average need-based loan:* Freshmen: $3738; Undergraduates: $4455. *Parent loans:* $800,932 (51% need-based, 49% non-need-based). *Programs:* FFEL (Subsidized and Unsubsidized Stafford, PLUS), Perkins, Federal Nursing.

WORK-STUDY *Federal work-study:* Total amount: $111,356; 122 jobs averaging $1250. *State or other work-study/employment:* Total amount: $57,700 (36% need-based, 64% non-need-based). Part-time jobs available.

ATHLETIC AWARDS *Total amount:* $262,245 (60% need-based, 40% non-need-based).

APPLYING FOR FINANCIAL AID *Required financial aid form:* FAFSA. *Financial aid deadline (priority):* 3/1. *Notification date:* Continuous. Students must reply within 2 weeks of notification.

CONTACT Caprice E. Calamaio, Director/Express Center, College of Saint Mary, 1901 South 72nd Street, Omaha, NE 68124, 402-399-2415 or toll-free 800-926-5534. *Fax:* 402-399-2480. *E-mail:* ccalamaio@csm.edu.

THE COLLEGE OF SAINT ROSE
Albany, NY

Tuition & fees: $16,780	Average undergraduate aid package: $7095

ABOUT THE INSTITUTION Independent, coed. Awards: bachelor's and master's degrees and post-bachelor's and post-master's certificates. 42 undergraduate majors. Total enrollment: 4,971. Undergraduates: 2,958. Freshmen: 564. Federal methodology is used as a basis for awarding need-based institutional aid.

UNDERGRADUATE EXPENSES for 2004–05 *Application fee:* $35. *Comprehensive fee:* $24,252 includes full-time tuition ($16,230), mandatory fees ($550), and room and board ($7472). *College room only:* $3542. Full-time tuition and fees vary according to course load and program. Room and board charges vary according to board plan. *Part-time tuition:* $540 per credit hour. Part-time tuition and fees vary according to class time.

FRESHMAN FINANCIAL AID (Fall 2003) 510 applied for aid; of those 86% were deemed to have need. 100% of freshmen with need received aid; of those 4% had need fully met. *Average percent of need met:* 59% (excluding resources awarded to replace EFC). *Average financial aid package:* $7675 (excluding resources awarded to replace EFC). 11% of all full-time freshmen had no need and received non-need-based gift aid.

UNDERGRADUATE FINANCIAL AID (Fall 2003) 2,374 applied for aid; of those 88% were deemed to have need. 100% of undergraduates with need received aid; of those 3% had need fully met. *Average percent of need met:* 55% (excluding resources awarded to replace EFC). *Average financial aid package:*

$7095 (excluding resources awarded to replace EFC). 10% of all full-time undergraduates had no need and received non-need-based gift aid.

GIFT AID (NEED-BASED) *Total amount:* $16,356,353 (15% federal, 20% state, 43% institutional, 22% external sources). *Receiving aid:* Freshmen: 78% (419); All full-time undergraduates: 82% (1,992). *Average award:* Freshmen: $3520; Undergraduates: $3271. *Scholarships, grants, and awards:* Federal Pell, FSEOG, state, private, college/university gift aid from institutional funds.

GIFT AID (NON-NEED-BASED) *Total amount:* $1,237,480 (5% state, 63% institutional, 32% external sources). *Average Award:* Freshmen: $1878; Undergraduates: $1808. *Scholarships, grants, and awards by category: Academic Interests/Achievement:* 684 awards ($2,593,711 total): business, education, engineering/technologies, English, foreign languages, general academic interests/achievements, mathematics, premedicine, social sciences. *Creative Arts/Performance:* art/fine arts, music. *Special Achievements/Activities:* community service. *Special Characteristics:* adult students, children and siblings of alumni, children of union members/company employees, ethnic background, general special characteristics, members of minority groups, siblings of current students, twins. *Tuition waivers:* Full or partial for employees or children of employees.

LOANS *Student loans:* $12,072,580 (93% need-based, 7% non-need-based). *Average need-based loan:* Freshmen: $1278; Undergraduates: $1178. *Parent loans:* $3,716,172 (87% need-based, 13% non-need-based). *Programs:* FFEL (Subsidized and Unsubsidized Stafford, PLUS).

WORK-STUDY *Federal work-study:* Total amount: $697,778; 406 jobs averaging $815. *State or other work-study/employment:* Total amount: $287,775 (78% need-based, 22% non-need-based). 83 part-time jobs averaging $892.

ATHLETIC AWARDS *Total amount:* $1,260,602 (77% need-based, 23% non-need-based).

APPLYING FOR FINANCIAL AID *Required financial aid form:* FAFSA. *Financial aid deadline (priority):* 3/1. *Notification date:* Continuous beginning 3/15. Students must reply by 5/1 or within 2 weeks of notification.

CONTACT Steven Dwire, Director of Financial Aid, The College of Saint Rose, 432 Western Avenue, Albertus Hall, Room 206, Albany, NY 12203-1419, 518-458-4915 or toll-free 800-637-8556. *Fax:* 518-454-2802. *E-mail:* finaid@strose.edu.

THE COLLEGE OF ST. SCHOLASTICA
Duluth, MN

Tuition & fees: $20,760	Average undergraduate aid package: $16,496

ABOUT THE INSTITUTION Independent religious, coed. Awards: bachelor's, master's, and first professional degrees and post-bachelor's and post-master's certificates. 45 undergraduate majors. Total enrollment: 3,012. Undergraduates: 2,441. Freshmen: 446. Federal methodology is used as a basis for awarding need-based institutional aid.

UNDERGRADUATE EXPENSES for 2004–05 *Application fee:* $25. *Comprehensive fee:* $26,676 includes full-time tuition ($20,630), mandatory fees ($130), and room and board ($5916). *College room only:* $3356. Full-time tuition and fees vary according to class time. Room and board charges vary according to board plan and housing facility. *Part-time tuition:* $646 per credit hour. Part-time tuition and fees vary according to class time and course load. *Payment plan:* Installment.

FRESHMAN FINANCIAL AID (Fall 2004, est.) 399 applied for aid; of those 88% were deemed to have need. 99% of freshmen with need received aid; of those 83% had need fully met. *Average percent of need met:* 83% (excluding resources awarded to replace EFC). *Average financial aid package:* $17,299 (excluding resources awarded to replace EFC). 15% of all full-time freshmen had no need and received non-need-based gift aid.

UNDERGRADUATE FINANCIAL AID (Fall 2004, est.) 1,552 applied for aid; of those 91% were deemed to have need. 100% of undergraduates with need received aid; of those 86% had need fully met. *Average percent of need met:* 85% (excluding resources awarded to replace EFC). *Average financial aid package:* $16,496 (excluding resources awarded to replace EFC). 15% of all full-time undergraduates had no need and received non-need-based gift aid.

GIFT AID (NEED-BASED) *Total amount:* $8,026,745 (21% federal, 29% state, 50% institutional). *Receiving aid:* Freshmen: 72% (314); All full-time undergraduates: 72% (1,268). *Average award:* Freshmen: $5591; Undergraduates: $5796. *Scholarships, grants, and awards:* Federal Pell, FSEOG, state, private, college/university gift aid from institutional funds, Federal Nursing.

GIFT AID (NON-NEED-BASED) *Total amount:* $11,650,957 (3% federal, 90% institutional, 7% external sources). *Receiving aid:* Freshmen: 77% (338);

Undergraduates: 71% (1,254). *Average Award: Freshmen:* $8223; *Undergraduates:* $7366. *Scholarships, grants, and awards by category: Academic Interests/Achievement:* 1,494 awards ($10,363,352 total): general academic interests/achievements. *Creative Arts/Performance:* 14 awards: music. *Special Characteristics:* 707 awards ($1,902,850 total): children and siblings of alumni, children of faculty/staff, international students, members of minority groups, previous college experience, religious affiliation, siblings of current students. *Tuition waivers:* Full or partial for employees or children of employees. *ROTC:* Air Force cooperative.

LOANS *Student loans:* $11,317,054 (43% need-based, 57% non-need-based). 82% of past graduating class borrowed through all loan programs. *Average indebtedness per student:* $27,245. *Average need-based loan:* Freshmen: $3791; Undergraduates: $4750. *Parent loans:* $1,669,312 (100% non-need-based). *Programs:* FFEL (Subsidized and Unsubsidized Stafford, PLUS), Perkins, Federal Nursing, state, private supplemental loans.

WORK-STUDY *Federal work-study:* Total amount: $394,952; 221 jobs averaging $1787. *State or other work-study/employment:* Total amount: $394,699 (80% need-based, 20% non-need-based). 204 part-time jobs averaging $1934.

APPLYING FOR FINANCIAL AID *Required financial aid forms:* FAFSA, institution's own form. *Financial aid deadline (priority):* 3/15. *Notification date:* Continuous beginning 3/1. Students must reply by 5/1 or within 2 weeks of notification.

CONTACT Mr. Jon P. Erickson, Director of Financial Aid, The College of St. Scholastica, 1200 Kenwood Avenue, Duluth, MN 55811-4199, 218-723-6725 or toll-free 800-249-6412. *Fax:* 218-733-2229. *E-mail:* jerickso@css.edu.

THE COLLEGE OF SAINT THOMAS MORE
Fort Worth, TX

CONTACT Mrs. Sharon Kirk, Financial Aid Officer, The College of Saint Thomas More, 3013 Lubbock Avenue, Fort Worth, TX 76109-2323, 817-923-8459 or toll-free 800-583-6489 (out-of-state). *Fax:* 817-924-3206. *E-mail:* more-info@cstm.edu.

COLLEGE OF SANTA FE
Santa Fe, NM

Tuition & fees: $20,840	Average undergraduate aid package: $18,932

ABOUT THE INSTITUTION Independent, coed. Awards: associate, bachelor's, and master's degrees. 45 undergraduate majors. Total enrollment: 1,769. Undergraduates: 1,430. Freshmen: 173. Federal methodology is used as a basis for awarding need-based institutional aid.

UNDERGRADUATE EXPENSES for 2004–05 *Application fee:* $35. *Comprehensive fee:* $27,090 includes full-time tuition ($20,214), mandatory fees ($626), and room and board ($6250). *College room only:* $2980. Room and board charges vary according to board plan and housing facility. *Part-time tuition:* $674 per credit hour. *Part-time fees:* $10 per credit hour. *Payment plan:* Installment.

GIFT AID (NEED-BASED) *Total amount:* $5,132,619 (29% federal, 19% state, 52% institutional). *Receiving aid:* Freshmen: 63% (99); All full-time undergraduates: 65% (430). *Average award:* Freshmen: $10,838; Undergraduates: $9600. *Scholarships, grants, and awards:* Federal Pell, FSEOG, state, private, college/university gift aid from institutional funds.

GIFT AID (NON-NEED-BASED) *Total amount:* $1,993,834 (96% institutional, 4% external sources). *Receiving aid:* Freshmen: 52% (81); Undergraduates: 49% (327). *Average Award:* Freshmen: $5250; Undergraduates: $3939. *Tuition waivers:* Full or partial for employees or children of employees, senior citizens. *ROTC:* Air Force cooperative.

LOANS *Student loans:* $5,433,751 (55% need-based, 45% non-need-based). 51% of past graduating class borrowed through all loan programs. *Average indebtedness per student:* $15,916. *Average need-based loan:* Freshmen: $3404; Undergraduates: $4525. *Parent loans:* $1,497,161 (100% non-need-based). *Programs:* FFEL (Subsidized and Unsubsidized Stafford, PLUS), Perkins, state, college/university.

ATHLETIC AWARDS *Total amount:* $143,071 (100% non-need-based).

APPLYING FOR FINANCIAL AID *Required financial aid form:* FAFSA. *Financial aid deadline (priority):* 3/15. *Notification date:* Continuous beginning 3/1. Students must reply by 5/1 or within 2 weeks of notification.

CONTACT Financial Aid Counselor, College of Santa Fe, 1600 St. Michael's Drive, Santa Fe, NM 87505-7634, 505-473-6454 or toll-free 800-456-2673. *Fax:* 505-473-6464.

College of Staten Island of the City University of New York

COLLEGE OF STATEN ISLAND OF THE CITY UNIVERSITY OF NEW YORK
Staten Island, NY

Tuition & fees (NY res): $4308   **Average undergraduate aid package: $5132**

ABOUT THE INSTITUTION State and locally supported, coed. Awards: associate, bachelor's, and master's degrees and post-master's certificates. 37 undergraduate majors. Total enrollment: 12,442. Undergraduates: 11,130. Freshmen: 2,247. Federal methodology is used as a basis for awarding need-based institutional aid.

UNDERGRADUATE EXPENSES for 2004–05 *Application fee:* $60. *Tuition, state resident:* full-time $4000; part-time $170 per credit. *Tuition, nonresident:* full-time $8640; part-time $360 per credit. *Required fees:* full-time $308; $90.50 per term part-time. Full-time tuition and fees vary according to course load. Part-time tuition and fees vary according to course load. *Payment plan:* Installment.

FRESHMAN FINANCIAL AID (Fall 2004, est.) 1585 applied for aid; of those 75% were deemed to have need. 97% of freshmen with need received aid; of those 84% had need fully met. *Average percent of need met:* 54% (excluding resources awarded to replace EFC). *Average financial aid package:* $5291 (excluding resources awarded to replace EFC). 8% of all full-time freshmen had no need and received non-need-based gift aid.

UNDERGRADUATE FINANCIAL AID (Fall 2004, est.) 5,228 applied for aid; of those 79% were deemed to have need. 96% of undergraduates with need received aid; of those 5% had need fully met. *Average percent of need met:* 50% (excluding resources awarded to replace EFC). *Average financial aid package:* $5132 (excluding resources awarded to replace EFC). 4% of all full-time undergraduates had no need and received non-need-based gift aid.

GIFT AID (NEED-BASED) *Total amount:* $22,159,299 (50% federal, 47% state, 3% external sources). *Receiving aid:* Freshmen: 57% (1,140); All full-time undergraduates: 52% (3,845). *Average award:* Freshmen: $5204; Undergraduates: $4962. *Scholarships, grants, and awards:* Federal Pell, FSEOG, state, private, college/university gift aid from institutional funds, Federal Nursing.

GIFT AID (NON-NEED-BASED) *Total amount:* $1,171,075 (4% federal, 52% state, 44% external sources). *Receiving aid:* Freshmen: 12% (237); Undergraduates: 6% (425). *Average Award:* Freshmen: $1319; Undergraduates: $1773. *Scholarships, grants, and awards by category: Academic Interests/Achievement:* 162 awards ($239,200 total): biological sciences, business, computer science, education, engineering/technologies, general academic interests/achievements, health fields, international studies, mathematics, physical sciences, premedicine. *Creative Arts/Performance:* 4 awards ($4500 total): art/fine arts, music, theater/drama. *Special Achievements/Activities:* 5 awards ($5500 total): general special achievements/activities. *Special Characteristics:* 7 awards ($7500 total): children of public servants, children with a deceased or disabled parent, general special characteristics, international students, members of minority groups, public servants, spouses of deceased or disabled public servants. *Tuition waivers:* Full or partial for employees or children of employees, senior citizens.

LOANS *Student loans:* $6,402,785 (100% need-based). *Average need-based loan:* Freshmen: $2281; Undergraduates: $3438. *Programs:* Federal Direct (Subsidized and Unsubsidized Stafford, PLUS), Perkins.

WORK-STUDY *Federal work-study:* Total amount: $1,090,120; 332 jobs averaging $1256.

APPLYING FOR FINANCIAL AID *Required financial aid forms:* FAFSA, state aid form. *Financial aid deadline:* Continuous. *Notification date:* Continuous beginning 5/1.

CONTACT Sherman Whipkey, Director of Financial Aid, College of Staten Island of the City University of New York, 2800 Victory Boulevard, 2A-401A, Staten Island, NY 10314-6600, 718-982-2030. *Fax:* 718-982-2037. *E-mail:* whipkey@ mail.csi.cuny.edu.

COLLEGE OF THE ATLANTIC
Bar Harbor, ME

Tuition & fees: $25,245   **Average undergraduate aid package: $23,490**

ABOUT THE INSTITUTION Independent, coed. Awards: bachelor's and master's degrees. 37 undergraduate majors. Total enrollment: 283. Undergraduates: 272. Freshmen: 68. Both federal and institutional methodology are used as a basis for awarding need-based institutional aid.

UNDERGRADUATE EXPENSES for 2004–05 *Application fee:* $45. *Comprehensive fee:* $31,977 includes full-time tuition ($24,870), mandatory fees ($375), and room and board ($6732). *College room only:* $4161. Room and board charges vary according to board plan. *Part-time tuition:* $8290 per term. *Part-time fees:* $125 per term. *Payment plan:* Installment.

FRESHMAN FINANCIAL AID (Fall 2004, est.) 73 applied for aid; of those 92% were deemed to have need. 100% of freshmen with need received aid; of those 97% had need fully met. *Average percent of need met:* 98% (excluding resources awarded to replace EFC). *Average financial aid package:* $24,776 (excluding resources awarded to replace EFC). 6% of all full-time freshmen had no need and received non-need-based gift aid.

UNDERGRADUATE FINANCIAL AID (Fall 2004, est.) 239 applied for aid; of those 99% were deemed to have need. 100% of undergraduates with need received aid; of those 85% had need fully met. *Average percent of need met:* 91% (excluding resources awarded to replace EFC). *Average financial aid package:* $23,490 (excluding resources awarded to replace EFC). 3% of all full-time undergraduates had no need and received non-need-based gift aid.

GIFT AID (NEED-BASED) *Total amount:* $4,238,524 (6% federal, 1% state, 52% institutional, 41% external sources). *Receiving aid:* Freshmen: 84% (65); All full-time undergraduates: 81% (214). *Average award:* Freshmen: $20,844; Undergraduates: $19,478. *Scholarships, grants, and awards:* Federal Pell, FSEOG, state, private, college/university gift aid from institutional funds.

GIFT AID (NON-NEED-BASED) *Total amount:* $22,500 (100% institutional). *Receiving aid:* Freshmen: 9% (7); Undergraduates: 17% (46). *Average Award:* Freshmen: $4500; Undergraduates: $3656. *Scholarships, grants, and awards by category: Academic Interests/Achievement:* 32 awards ($171,825 total): general academic interests/achievements. *Special Achievements/Activities:* 47 awards ($294,000 total): community service, general special achievements/activities, leadership. *Tuition waivers:* Full or partial for employees or children of employees, adult students, senior citizens.

LOANS *Student loans:* $973,092 (71% need-based, 29% non-need-based). 50% of past graduating class borrowed through all loan programs. *Average indebtedness per student:* $16,710. *Average need-based loan:* Freshmen: $2942; Undergraduates: $4014. *Parent loans:* $268,386 (100% non-need-based). *Programs:* FFEL (Subsidized and Unsubsidized Stafford, PLUS), Perkins.

WORK-STUDY *Federal work-study:* Total amount: $265,017; 133 jobs averaging $2061. *State or other work-study/employment:* Total amount: $72,796 (100% need-based). 57 part-time jobs averaging $1200.

APPLYING FOR FINANCIAL AID *Required financial aid forms:* FAFSA, institution's own form, noncustodial (divorced/separated) parent's statement, financial aid transcript (for transfers). *Financial aid deadline (priority):* 2/15. *Notification date:* 4/1. Students must reply by 5/1 or within 2 weeks of notification.

CONTACT Bruce Hazam, Director of Financial Aid, College of the Atlantic, 105 Eden Street, Bar Harbor, ME 04609-1198, 207-288-5015 Ext. 232 or toll-free 800-528-0025. *Fax:* 207-288-4126. *E-mail:* bhazam@ecology.coa.edu.

COLLEGE OF THE HOLY CROSS
Worcester, MA

Tuition & fees: $29,686   **Average undergraduate aid package: $25,984**

ABOUT THE INSTITUTION Independent Roman Catholic (Jesuit), coed. Awards: bachelor's degrees. 41 undergraduate majors. Total enrollment: 2,745. Undergraduates: 2,745. Freshmen: 700. Both federal and institutional methodology are used as a basis for awarding need-based institutional aid.

UNDERGRADUATE EXPENSES for 2004–05 *Application fee:* $50. *Comprehensive fee:* $38,546 includes full-time tuition ($29,220), mandatory fees ($466), and room and board ($8860). *College room only:* $4430. Room and board charges vary according to board plan and housing facility. *Payment plan:* Installment.

GIFT AID (NEED-BASED) *Total amount:* $18,936,315 (7% federal, 3% state, 83% institutional, 7% external sources). *Receiving aid:* Freshmen: 46% (320); All full-time undergraduates: 43% (1,156). *Average award:* Freshmen: $17,379; Undergraduates: $17,257. *Scholarships, grants, and awards:* Federal Pell, FSEOG, state, private, college/university gift aid from institutional funds.

GIFT AID (NON-NEED-BASED) *Total amount:* $1,571,104 (100% institutional). *Receiving aid:* Freshmen: 2% (14); Undergraduates: 5% (133). *Average Award:* Freshmen: $29,220; Undergraduates: $16,071. *Scholarships, grants, and awards by category: Academic Interests/Achievement:* 188 awards ($1,768,350 total): general academic interests/achievements, humanities, military science. *Creative Arts/Performance:* 5 awards ($146,100 total): music. *Special Characteristics:* 26 awards ($584,400 total): children of faculty/staff. *Tuition waivers:* Full or partial for employees or children of employees. *ROTC:* Army cooperative, Naval, Air Force cooperative.

LOANS *Student loans:* $7,369,210 (67% need-based, 33% non-need-based). 58% of past graduating class borrowed through all loan programs. *Average indebtedness per student:* $19,380. *Average need-based loan:* Freshmen: $5117; Undergraduates: $6247. *Parent loans:* $8,913,613 (100% non-need-based). *Programs:* FFEL (Subsidized and Unsubsidized Stafford, PLUS), Perkins, MEFA Loans.

ATHLETIC AWARDS *Total amount:* $4,577,035 (80% need-based, 20% non-need-based).

APPLYING FOR FINANCIAL AID *Required financial aid forms:* FAFSA, CSS Financial Aid PROFILE, noncustodial (divorced/separated) parent's statement, business/farm supplement, federal income tax form(s). *Financial aid deadline:* 2/1. *Notification date:* 4/2. Students must reply by 5/1.

CONTACT Lynne Myers, Director of Financial Aid, College of the Holy Cross, One College Street, Worcester, MA 01610-2395, 508-793-2265 or toll-free 800-442-2421. *Fax:* 508-793-2527.

COLLEGE OF THE HUMANITIES AND SCIENCES
Tempe, AZ

CONTACT Financial Aid Office, College of the Humanities and Sciences, 1105 East Broadway, Tempe, AZ 85282, 480-317-5955 or toll-free 877-248-6724.

COLLEGE OF THE OZARKS
Point Lookout, MO

Tuition & fees: $280	Average undergraduate aid package: $11,775

ABOUT THE INSTITUTION Independent Presbyterian, coed. Awards: bachelor's degrees. 98 undergraduate majors. Total enrollment: 1,723. Undergraduates: 1,723. Freshmen: 268. Federal methodology is used as a basis for awarding need-based institutional aid.

UNDERGRADUATE EXPENSES for 2005–06 includes mandatory fees ($280) and room and board ($3850). *College room only:* $1850. *Part-time tuition:* $275 per credit. *Part-time fees:* $140 per term. Part-time tuition and fees vary according to course load. *Payment plan:* Installment.

FRESHMAN FINANCIAL AID (Fall 2004, est.) 373 applied for aid; of those 94% were deemed to have need. 100% of freshmen with need received aid; of those 32% had need fully met. *Average percent of need met:* 84% (excluding resources awarded to replace EFC). *Average financial aid package:* $11,271 (excluding resources awarded to replace EFC). 13% of all full-time freshmen had no need and received non-need-based gift aid.

UNDERGRADUATE FINANCIAL AID (Fall 2004, est.) 1,404 applied for aid; of those 93% were deemed to have need. 100% of undergraduates with need received aid; of those 36% had need fully met. *Average percent of need met:* 84% (excluding resources awarded to replace EFC). *Average financial aid package:* $11,775 (excluding resources awarded to replace EFC). 9% of all full-time undergraduates had no need and received non-need-based gift aid.

GIFT AID (NEED-BASED) *Total amount:* $13,065,440 (18% federal, 4% state, 76% institutional, 2% external sources). *Receiving aid:* Freshmen: 87% (349); All full-time undergraduates: 91% (1,300). *Average award:* Freshmen: $9135; Undergraduates: $9712. *Scholarships, grants, and awards:* Federal Pell, FSEOG, state, private, college/university gift aid from institutional funds.

GIFT AID (NON-NEED-BASED) *Total amount:* $2,201,293 (1% state, 97% institutional, 2% external sources). *Receiving aid:* Freshmen: 14% (56); Undergraduates: 18% (263). *Average Award: Freshmen:* $11,471; *Undergraduates:* $12,047. *Scholarships, grants, and awards by category: Academic Interests/Achievement:* general academic interests/achievements. *Tuition waivers:* Full or partial for employees or children of employees. *ROTC:* Army.

LOANS *Student loans:* 21% of past graduating class borrowed through all loan programs. *Average indebtedness per student:* $6060. *Programs:* alternative loans.

WORK-STUDY *Federal work-study:* 778 jobs averaging $2884. *State or other work-study/employment:* 700 part-time jobs averaging $2884.

ATHLETIC AWARDS *Total amount:* $164,000 (100% non-need-based).

APPLYING FOR FINANCIAL AID *Required financial aid forms:* FAFSA, federal income tax form(s). *Financial aid deadline (priority):* 3/15. *Notification date:* 7/1.

CONTACT Kyla R. McCarty, Director of Financial Aid, College of the Ozarks, PO Box 17, Point Lookout, MO 65726, 417-334-6411 Ext. 4290 or toll-free 800-222-0525. *Fax:* 417-334-6737.

COLLEGE OF THE SOUTHWEST
Hobbs, NM

ABOUT THE INSTITUTION Independent, coed. Awards: bachelor's and master's degrees. 22 undergraduate majors. Total enrollment: 741. Undergraduates: 608. Freshmen: 90.

GIFT AID (NEED-BASED) *Scholarships, grants, and awards:* Federal Pell, FSEOG, state, private, college/university gift aid from institutional funds.

GIFT AID (NON-NEED-BASED) *Scholarships, grants, and awards by category: Academic Interests/Achievement:* business, education, English, general academic interests/achievements, mathematics, social sciences. *Creative Arts/Performance:* music, theater/drama. *Special Achievements/Activities:* general special achievements/activities. *Special Characteristics:* children of faculty/staff, first-generation college students, relatives of clergy.

LOANS *Programs:* FFEL (Subsidized and Unsubsidized Stafford, PLUS), state.

WORK-STUDY *Federal work-study:* Total amount: $73,333; 43 jobs averaging $1395. *State or other work-study/employment:* Total amount: $72,892 (100% need-based). 50 part-time jobs averaging $1236.

APPLYING FOR FINANCIAL AID *Required financial aid form:* institution's own form.

CONTACT David Arnold, Vice President for Student Services, College of the Southwest, 6610 Lovington Highway, Hobbs, NM 88240-9129, 505-392-6561 Ext. 1006 or toll-free 800-530-4400. *Fax:* 505-392-6006. *E-mail:* darnold@csw. edu.

COLLEGE OF VISUAL ARTS
St. Paul, MN

Tuition & fees: $18,040	Average undergraduate aid package: $7055

ABOUT THE INSTITUTION Independent, coed. Awards: bachelor's degrees. 8 undergraduate majors. Total enrollment: 199. Undergraduates: 199. Freshmen: 60. Federal methodology is used as a basis for awarding need-based institutional aid.

UNDERGRADUATE EXPENSES for 2005–06 *Application fee:* $40. *Tuition:* full-time $17,510; part-time $875 per credit. *Required fees:* full-time $530; $53 per course. Full-time tuition and fees vary according to course load. Part-time tuition and fees vary according to course load. *Payment plan:* Installment.

FRESHMAN FINANCIAL AID (Fall 2004, est.) 40 applied for aid; of those 100% were deemed to have need. 100% of freshmen with need received aid; of those 2% had need fully met. *Average percent of need met:* 36% (excluding resources awarded to replace EFC). *Average financial aid package:* $5546 (excluding resources awarded to replace EFC). 12% of all full-time freshmen had no need and received non-need-based gift aid.

UNDERGRADUATE FINANCIAL AID (Fall 2004, est.) 145 applied for aid; of those 90% were deemed to have need. 100% of undergraduates with need received aid; of those 4% had need fully met. *Average percent of need met:* 41% (excluding resources awarded to replace EFC). *Average financial aid package:* $7055 (excluding resources awarded to replace EFC). 9% of all full-time undergraduates had no need and received non-need-based gift aid.

GIFT AID (NEED-BASED) *Total amount:* $491,900 (33% federal, 28% state, 38% institutional, 1% external sources). *Receiving aid:* Freshmen: 78% (39); All full-time undergraduates: 55% (121). *Average award:* Freshmen: $4766; Undergraduates: $3656. *Scholarships, grants, and awards:* Federal Pell, FSEOG, state, private, college/university gift aid from institutional funds.

GIFT AID (NON-NEED-BASED) *Total amount:* $60,150 (96% institutional, 4% external sources). *Receiving aid:* Freshmen: 32% (16); Undergraduates: 19% (41). *Average Award: Freshmen:* $1469; *Undergraduates:* $2554. *Scholarships, grants, and awards by category: Academic Interests/Achievement:* 36 awards ($45,101 total): general academic interests/achievements. *Creative Arts/Performance:* 39 awards ($66,881 total): art/fine arts. *Special Characteristics:* 1 award ($17,530 total): children of faculty/staff. *Tuition waivers:* Full or partial for children of alumni, employees or children of employees.

LOANS *Student loans:* $1,663,855 (77% need-based, 23% non-need-based). 93% of past graduating class borrowed through all loan programs. *Average indebtedness per student:* $31,691. *Average need-based loan:* Freshmen: $2113; Undergraduates: $3531. *Parent loans:* $187,015 (59% need-based, 41% non-need-based). *Programs:* FFEL (Subsidized and Unsubsidized Stafford, PLUS), state, alternative loans.

WORK-STUDY *Federal work-study:* Total amount: $33,870; 19 jobs averaging $2215. *State or other work-study/employment:* Total amount: $91,511 (64% need-based, 36% non-need-based). 34 part-time jobs averaging $2006.

APPLYING FOR FINANCIAL AID *Required financial aid forms:* FAFSA, institution's own form. *Financial aid deadline:* 6/1 (priority: 4/1). *Notification date:* Continuous beginning 1/1. Students must reply within 2 weeks of notification.
CONTACT Mrs. Bonnie Burgoyne, Director of Financial Aid, College of Visual Arts, 344 Summit Avenue, St. Paul, MN 55102-2124, 651-224-3416 or toll-free 800-224-1536. *Fax:* 651-224-8854. *E-mail:* bburgoyne@cva.edu.

THE COLLEGE OF WILLIAM AND MARY
Williamsburg, VA

Tuition & fees (VA res): $7096	Average undergraduate aid package: $9503

ABOUT THE INSTITUTION State-supported, coed. Awards: bachelor's, master's, doctoral, and first professional degrees and post-master's certificates. 44 undergraduate majors. Total enrollment: 7,575. Undergraduates: 5,642. Freshmen: 1,341. Federal methodology is used as a basis for awarding need-based institutional aid.
UNDERGRADUATE EXPENSES for 2004–05 *Application fee:* $60. *Tuition, state resident:* full-time $4330; part-time $170 per credit. *Tuition, nonresident:* full-time $19,030; part-time $675 per credit. Full-time tuition and fees vary according to program. Part-time tuition and fees vary according to program. *College room and board:* $6066; *room only:* $3630. Room and board charges vary according to board plan and housing facility. *Payment plan:* Installment.
GIFT AID (NEED-BASED) *Total amount:* $8,529,863 (19% federal, 22% state, 49% institutional, 10% external sources). *Receiving aid:* Freshmen: 23% (305); All full-time undergraduates: 23% (1,290). *Average award:* Freshmen: $9513; Undergraduates: $9975. *Scholarships, grants, and awards:* Federal Pell, FSEOG, state, private, college/university gift aid from institutional funds.
GIFT AID (NON-NEED-BASED) *Total amount:* $5,560,378 (4% federal, 27% state, 34% institutional, 35% external sources). *Receiving aid:* Freshmen: 15% (202); Undergraduates: 20% (1,139). *Average Award:* Freshmen: $6511; *Undergraduates:* $4794. *Scholarships, grants, and awards by category:* *Academic Interests/Achievement:* general academic interests/achievements. *Tuition waivers:* Full or partial for employees or children of employees, senior citizens. *ROTC:* Army.
LOANS *Student loans:* $9,282,492 (46% need-based, 54% non-need-based). 40% of past graduating class borrowed through all loan programs. *Average indebtedness per student:* $13,688. *Average need-based loan:* Freshmen: $2194; Undergraduates: $2817. *Parent loans:* $6,061,163 (100% non-need-based). *Programs:* FFEL (Subsidized and Unsubsidized Stafford, PLUS), Perkins.
ATHLETIC AWARDS *Total amount:* $3,543,251 (16% need-based, 84% non-need-based).
APPLYING FOR FINANCIAL AID *Required financial aid form:* FAFSA. *Financial aid deadline:* 3/15 (priority: 2/15). *Notification date:* 4/1. Students must reply by 5/1.
CONTACT Mr. Edward P. Irish, Director of Financial Aid, The College of William and Mary, PO Box 8795, Williamsburg, VA 23187-8795, 757-221-2425. *Fax:* 757-221-2515. *E-mail:* epiris@wm.edu.

THE COLLEGE OF WOOSTER
Wooster, OH

Tuition & fees: $28,230	Average undergraduate aid package: $21,570

ABOUT THE INSTITUTION Independent religious, coed. Awards: bachelor's degrees. 45 undergraduate majors. Total enrollment: 1,827. Undergraduates: 1,827. Freshmen: 477. Both federal and institutional methodology are used as a basis for awarding need-based institutional aid.
UNDERGRADUATE EXPENSES for 2005–06 *Application fee:* $40. *Comprehensive fee:* $35,290 includes full-time tuition ($28,230) and room and board ($7060). *College room only:* $3210. Full-time tuition and fees vary according to course load and reciprocity agreements. Part-time tuition and fees vary according to course load. *Payment plan:* Installment.
FRESHMAN FINANCIAL AID (Fall 2004, est.) 378 applied for aid; of those 88% were deemed to have need. 100% of freshmen with need received aid; of those 86% had need fully met. *Average percent of need met:* 97% (excluding resources awarded to replace EFC). *Average financial aid package:* $21,347 (excluding resources awarded to replace EFC). 28% of all full-time freshmen had no need and received non-need-based gift aid.
UNDERGRADUATE FINANCIAL AID (Fall 2004, est.) 1,243 applied for aid; of those 89% were deemed to have need. 100% of undergraduates with need received aid; of those 89% had need fully met. *Average percent of need met:* 98% (excluding resources awarded to replace EFC). *Average financial aid package:* $21,570 (excluding resources awarded to replace EFC). 36% of all full-time undergraduates had no need and received non-need-based gift aid.
GIFT AID (NEED-BASED) *Total amount:* $18,418,575 (5% federal, 5% state, 88% institutional, 2% external sources). *Receiving aid:* Freshmen: 69% (331); All full-time undergraduates: 63% (1,106). *Average award:* Freshmen: $16,830; Undergraduates: $16,980. *Scholarships, grants, and awards:* Federal Pell, FSEOG, state, private, college/university gift aid from institutional funds.
GIFT AID (NON-NEED-BASED) *Total amount:* $8,409,914 (5% state, 93% institutional, 2% external sources). *Receiving aid:* Freshmen: 9% (43); Undergraduates: 7% (129). *Average Award:* Freshmen: $10,950; Undergraduates: $11,200. *Scholarships, grants, and awards by category:* *Academic Interests/Achievement:* 1,241 awards ($13,585,000 total): biological sciences, general academic interests/achievements, mathematics, physical sciences, social sciences. *Creative Arts/Performance:* 55 awards ($220,000 total): dance, music, theater/drama. *Special Achievements/Activities:* 212 awards ($1,150,000 total): community service, leadership, religious involvement. *Special Characteristics:* 262 awards ($3,100,000 total): children of faculty/staff, international students, local/state students, members of minority groups. *Tuition waivers:* Full or partial for employees or children of employees.
LOANS *Student loans:* $7,004,427 (62% need-based, 38% non-need-based). 62% of past graduating class borrowed through all loan programs. *Average indebtedness per student:* $21,709. *Average need-based loan:* Freshmen: $4110; Undergraduates: $4620. *Parent loans:* $2,639,118 (11% need-based, 89% non-need-based). *Programs:* Federal Direct (Subsidized and Unsubsidized Stafford, PLUS), Perkins, college/university.
WORK-STUDY *Federal work-study:* Total amount: $917,834; 690 jobs averaging $1342. *State or other work-study/employment:* Total amount: $219,050 (93% need-based, 7% non-need-based). 118 part-time jobs averaging $1931.
APPLYING FOR FINANCIAL AID *Required financial aid forms:* FAFSA, institution's own form, CSS Financial Aid PROFILE. *Financial aid deadline (priority):* 2/15. *Notification date:* 4/1. Students must reply by 5/1.
CONTACT Office of Financial Aid, The College of Wooster, 1189 Beall Avenue, Wooster, OH 44691, 330-263-2317 or toll-free 800-877-9905. *Fax:* 330-263-2634. *E-mail:* financialaid@wooster.edu.

COLLINS COLLEGE: A SCHOOL OF DESIGN AND TECHNOLOGY
Tempe, AZ

ABOUT THE INSTITUTION Proprietary, coed. Awards: associate and bachelor's degrees. 4 undergraduate majors. Total enrollment: 2,142. Undergraduates: 2,142.
GIFT AID (NEED-BASED) *Scholarships, grants, and awards:* Federal Pell, FSEOG, private.
GIFT AID (NON-NEED-BASED) *Scholarships, grants, and awards by category:* *Creative Arts/Performance:* applied art and design.
LOANS *Programs:* FFEL (Subsidized and Unsubsidized Stafford, PLUS), college/university.
WORK-STUDY *Federal work-study:* Total amount: $196,935; 62 jobs averaging $2400.
APPLYING FOR FINANCIAL AID *Required financial aid forms:* FAFSA, institution's own form.
CONTACT Carol Clapp, Director of Financial Aid, Collins College: A School of Design and Technology, 1140 South Priest Drive, Tempe, AZ 85281, 480-966-3000 Ext. 127 or toll-free 800-876-7070 (out-of-state). *Fax:* 480-446-1172. *E-mail:* cclapp@collinscollege.edu.

COLORADO CHRISTIAN UNIVERSITY
Lakewood, CO

Tuition & fees: $16,060	Average undergraduate aid package: $8931

ABOUT THE INSTITUTION Independent interdenominational, coed. Awards: associate, bachelor's, and master's degrees. 26 undergraduate majors. Total enrollment: 1,583. Undergraduates: 1,462. Freshmen: 265. Federal methodology is used as a basis for awarding need-based institutional aid.
UNDERGRADUATE EXPENSES for 2004–05 *Application fee:* $40. *Comprehensive fee:* $22,560 includes full-time tuition ($15,950), mandatory fees ($110), and room and board ($6500). *College room only:* $3750. Full-time tuition and fees vary according to degree level, location, and program. Room and board charges

vary according to board plan and housing facility. **Part-time tuition:** $670 per credit hour. Part-time tuition and fees vary according to degree level, location, and program. **Payment plan:** Installment.

FRESHMAN FINANCIAL AID (Fall 2004, est.) 182 applied for aid; of those 81% were deemed to have need. 100% of freshmen with need received aid; of those 11% had need fully met. *Average percent of need met:* 59% (excluding resources awarded to replace EFC). *Average financial aid package:* $9981 (excluding resources awarded to replace EFC). 26% of all full-time freshmen had no need and received non-need-based gift aid.

UNDERGRADUATE FINANCIAL AID (Fall 2004, est.) 750 applied for aid; of those 82% were deemed to have need. 100% of undergraduates with need received aid; of those 9% had need fully met. *Average percent of need met:* 54% (excluding resources awarded to replace EFC). *Average financial aid package:* $8931 (excluding resources awarded to replace EFC). 27% of all full-time undergraduates had no need and received non-need-based gift aid.

GIFT AID (NEED-BASED) Total amount: $3,373,713 (31% federal, 59% institutional, 10% external sources). **Receiving aid:** Freshmen: 67% (138); All full-time undergraduates: 57% (521). **Average award:** Freshmen: $7603; Undergraduates: $6056. **Scholarships, grants, and awards:** Federal Pell, FSEOG, private, college/university gift aid from institutional funds.

GIFT AID (NON-NEED-BASED) Total amount: $1,066,941 (1% federal, 71% institutional, 28% external sources). **Receiving aid:** Freshmen: 5% (11); Undergraduates: 4% (35). **Average Award:** Freshmen: $15,133; Undergraduates: $12,655. **Scholarships, grants, and awards by category:** Academic Interests/Achievement: 552 awards ($1,749,891 total): general academic interests/achievements. Creative Arts/Performance: 52 awards ($59,900 total): music, theater/drama. Special Achievements/Activities: 164 awards ($125,478 total): community service, leadership, religious involvement. Special Characteristics: 41 awards ($519,367 total): children of faculty/staff, first-generation college students. **Tuition waivers:** Full or partial for minority students, employees or children of employees. **ROTC:** Army cooperative.

LOANS Student loans: $7,550,106 (75% need-based, 25% non-need-based). 88% of past graduating class borrowed through all loan programs. *Average indebtedness per student:* $18,633. **Average need-based loan:** Freshmen: $2946; Undergraduates: $3946. **Parent loans:** $6,356,095 (32% need-based, 68% non-need-based). **Programs:** FFEL (Subsidized and Unsubsidized Stafford, PLUS), Perkins.

WORK-STUDY Federal work-study: Total amount: $19,327; 16 jobs averaging $2000. **State or other work-study/employment:** Total amount: $74,175 (12% need-based, 88% non-need-based). Part-time jobs available.

ATHLETIC AWARDS Total amount: $300,923 (35% need-based, 65% non-need-based).

APPLYING FOR FINANCIAL AID Required financial aid form: FAFSA. **Financial aid deadline (priority):** 3/15. **Notification date:** Continuous beginning 4/1. Students must reply by 5/1 or within 4 weeks of notification.

CONTACT Steve Woodburn, Director of Financial Aid, Colorado Christian University, 180 South Garrison Street, Lakewood, CO 80226-7499, 303-963-3230 or toll-free 800-44-FAITH. *Fax:* 303-963-3231. *E-mail:* sfs@ccu.edu.

THE COLORADO COLLEGE
Colorado Springs, CO

Tuition & fees: $28,644	Average undergraduate aid package: $25,986

ABOUT THE INSTITUTION Independent, coed. Awards: bachelor's and master's degrees (master's degree in education only). 46 undergraduate majors. Total enrollment: 2,044. Undergraduates: 2,011. Freshmen: 581. Both federal and institutional methodology are used as a basis for awarding need-based institutional aid.

UNDERGRADUATE EXPENSES for 2004–05 Application fee: $50. **Comprehensive fee:** $35,860 includes full-time tuition ($28,644) and room and board ($7216). **College room only:** $3880. Room and board charges vary according to board plan. **Payment plan:** Installment.

FRESHMAN FINANCIAL AID (Fall 2003) 314 applied for aid; of those 86% were deemed to have need. 100% of freshmen with need received aid; of those 78% had need fully met. *Average percent of need met:* 97% (excluding resources awarded to replace EFC). *Average financial aid package:* $27,330 (excluding resources awarded to replace EFC). 6% of all full-time freshmen had no need and received non-need-based gift aid.

UNDERGRADUATE FINANCIAL AID (Fall 2003) 938 applied for aid; of those 91% were deemed to have need. 100% of undergraduates with need received aid; of those 56% had need fully met. *Average percent of need met:* 90%

(excluding resources awarded to replace EFC). *Average financial aid package:* $25,986 (excluding resources awarded to replace EFC). 6% of all full-time undergraduates had no need and received non-need-based gift aid.

GIFT AID (NEED-BASED) Total amount: $16,975,499 (6% federal, 2% state, 90% institutional, 2% external sources). **Receiving aid:** Freshmen: 45% (266); All full-time undergraduates: 40% (802). **Average award:** Freshmen: $23,951; Undergraduates: $22,323. **Scholarships, grants, and awards:** Federal Pell, FSEOG, state, private, college/university gift aid from institutional funds.

GIFT AID (NON-NEED-BASED) Total amount: $3,333,210 (73% institutional, 27% external sources). **Receiving aid:** Freshmen: 5% (32); Undergraduates: 4% (85). **Average Award:** Freshmen: $16,237; Undergraduates: $16,338. **Scholarships, grants, and awards by category:** Academic Interests/Achievement: 114 awards ($1,640,000 total): biological sciences, general academic interests/achievements, mathematics, physical sciences. Special Characteristics: 30 awards ($777,866 total): international students. **Tuition waivers:** Full or partial for employees or children of employees. **ROTC:** Army cooperative.

LOANS Student loans: $3,897,529 (67% need-based, 33% non-need-based). 48% of past graduating class borrowed through all loan programs. *Average indebtedness per student:* $16,401. **Average need-based loan:** Freshmen: $3704; Undergraduates: $4861. **Parent loans:** $3,621,789 (15% need-based, 85% non-need-based). **Programs:** FFEL (Subsidized and Unsubsidized Stafford, PLUS), Perkins.

WORK-STUDY Federal work-study: Total amount: $530,833. **State or other work-study/employment:** Total amount: $546,346 (47% need-based, 53% non-need-based).

ATHLETIC AWARDS Total amount: $1,075,613 (17% need-based, 83% non-need-based).

APPLYING FOR FINANCIAL AID Required financial aid forms: FAFSA, CSS Financial Aid PROFILE, noncustodial (divorced/separated) parent's statement, federal income tax form(s) for parents and student. **Financial aid deadline:** 2/15 (priority: 2/15). **Notification date:** 3/20. Students must reply by 5/1.

CONTACT Mr. James M. Swanson, Director of Financial Aid, The Colorado College, 14 East Cache La Poudre Street, Colorado Springs, CO 80903-3294, 719-389-6651 or toll-free 800-542-7214. *Fax:* 719-389-6173. *E-mail:* FinancialAid@ColoradoCollege.edu.

COLORADO SCHOOL OF MINES
Golden, CO

Tuition & fees (CO res): $7224	Average undergraduate aid package: $13,300

ABOUT THE INSTITUTION State-supported, coed. Awards: bachelor's, master's, doctoral, and first professional degrees. 16 undergraduate majors. Total enrollment: 3,666. Undergraduates: 2,873. Freshmen: 750. Federal methodology is used as a basis for awarding need-based institutional aid.

UNDERGRADUATE EXPENSES for 2005–06 Application fee: $45. **Tuition, state resident:** full-time $6464. **Tuition, nonresident:** full-time $19,624. Part-time tuition and fees vary according to course load. **College room and board:** $6600; **room only:** $3500. Room and board charges vary according to board plan and housing facility. **Payment plan:** Installment.

FRESHMAN FINANCIAL AID (Fall 2004, est.) 592 applied for aid; of those 92% were deemed to have need. 100% of freshmen with need received aid; of those 78% had need fully met. *Average percent of need met:* 93% (excluding resources awarded to replace EFC). *Average financial aid package:* $13,300 (excluding resources awarded to replace EFC). 10% of all full-time freshmen had no need and received non-need-based gift aid.

UNDERGRADUATE FINANCIAL AID (Fall 2004, est.) 2,032 applied for aid; of those 92% were deemed to have need. 100% of undergraduates with need received aid; of those 82% had need fully met. *Average percent of need met:* 93% (excluding resources awarded to replace EFC). *Average financial aid package:* $13,300 (excluding resources awarded to replace EFC). 9% of all full-time undergraduates had no need and received non-need-based gift aid.

GIFT AID (NEED-BASED) Total amount: $7,550,000 (18% federal, 13% state, 57% institutional, 12% external sources). **Receiving aid:** Freshmen: 60% (456); All full-time undergraduates: 59% (1,620). **Average award:** Freshmen: $6800; Undergraduates: $6800. **Scholarships, grants, and awards:** Federal Pell, FSEOG, state, private, college/university gift aid from institutional funds.

GIFT AID (NON-NEED-BASED) Total amount: $2,140,000 (7% state, 51% institutional, 42% external sources). **Receiving aid:** Freshmen: 23% (175); Undergraduates: 22% (610). **Average Award:** Freshmen: $4900; Undergraduates: $4900. **Scholarships, grants, and awards by category:** Academic Interests/Achievement: 350 awards ($1,100,000 total): business, computer science,

Colorado School of Mines

engineering/technologies, general academic interests/achievements, mathematics, military science, physical sciences. *Special Characteristics:* 10 awards ($10,000 total): children and siblings of alumni. *ROTC:* Army.

LOANS *Student loans:* $7,650,000 (64% need-based, 36% non-need-based). 69% of past graduating class borrowed through all loan programs. *Average indebtedness per student:* $17,500. *Average need-based loan:* Freshmen: $4000; Undergraduates: $4000. *Parent loans:* $2,700,000 (100% non-need-based). *Programs:* FFEL (Subsidized and Unsubsidized Stafford, PLUS), Perkins, college/university.

WORK-STUDY *Federal work-study:* Total amount: $230,000; 270 jobs averaging $850. *State or other work-study/employment:* Total amount: $690,000 (48% need-based, 52% non-need-based). 812 part-time jobs averaging $850.

ATHLETIC AWARDS *Total amount:* $960,000 (66% need-based, 34% non-need-based).

APPLYING FOR FINANCIAL AID *Required financial aid form:* FAFSA. *Financial aid deadline (priority):* 3/1. *Notification date:* 4/1. Students must reply by 5/1 or within 2 weeks of notification.

CONTACT Mr. Roger A. Koester, Director of Financial Aid, Colorado School of Mines, 1500 Illinois Street, Golden, CO 80401-1887, 303-273-3220 or toll-free 800-446-9488 Ext. 3220 (out-of-state). *Fax:* 303-384-2252. *E-mail:* rkoester@mines.edu.

COLORADO STATE UNIVERSITY
Fort Collins, CO

Tuition & fees (CO res): $3790	Average undergraduate aid package: $7948

ABOUT THE INSTITUTION State-supported, coed. Awards: bachelor's, master's, doctoral, and first professional degrees. 124 undergraduate majors. Total enrollment: 26,801. Undergraduates: 21,729. Freshmen: 4,078. Federal methodology is used as a basis for awarding need-based institutional aid.

UNDERGRADUATE EXPENSES for 2004–05 *Application fee:* $50. *Tuition, state resident:* full-time $2940; part-time $163 per credit. *Tuition, nonresident:* full-time $13,527; part-time $751 per credit. *Required fees:* full-time $850; $52 per term part-time. Part-time tuition and fees vary according to course load. *College room and board:* $5766. Room and board charges vary according to board plan and housing facility. *Payment plan:* Installment.

FRESHMAN FINANCIAL AID (Fall 2003) 2477 applied for aid; of those 62% were deemed to have need. 100% of freshmen with need received aid; of those 39% had need fully met. *Average percent of need met:* 87% (excluding resources awarded to replace EFC). *Average financial aid package:* $6485 (excluding resources awarded to replace EFC). 11% of all full-time freshmen had no need and received non-need-based gift aid.

UNDERGRADUATE FINANCIAL AID (Fall 2003) 10,416 applied for aid; of those 70% were deemed to have need. 99% of undergraduates with need received aid; of those 49% had need fully met. *Average percent of need met:* 82% (excluding resources awarded to replace EFC). *Average financial aid package:* $7948 (excluding resources awarded to replace EFC). 4% of all full-time undergraduates had no need and received non-need-based gift aid.

GIFT AID (NEED-BASED) *Total amount:* $22,433,645 (46% federal, 25% state, 20% institutional, 9% external sources). *Receiving aid:* Freshmen: 34% (1,262); All full-time undergraduates: 34% (6,330). *Average award:* Freshmen: $4618; Undergraduates: $4288. *Scholarships, grants, and awards:* Federal Pell, FSEOG, state, private, college/university gift aid from institutional funds.

GIFT AID (NON-NEED-BASED) *Total amount:* $4,813,836 (1% federal, 24% state, 41% institutional, 34% external sources). *Average Award:* Freshmen: $896; *Undergraduates:* $1402. *Scholarships, grants, and awards by category: Academic Interests/Achievement:* 4,359 awards ($7,020,007 total): general academic interests/achievements. *Creative Arts/Performance:* 165 awards ($150,000 total): art/fine arts, creative writing, dance, debating, music, theater/drama. *Special Achievements/Activities:* 287 awards ($685,290 total): general special achievements/activities. *Special Characteristics:* 497 awards ($953,448 total): children of faculty/staff, first-generation college students. *Tuition waivers:* Full or partial for employees or children of employees. *ROTC:* Army, Air Force.

LOANS *Student loans:* $46,655,319 (74% need-based, 26% non-need-based). 52% of past graduating class borrowed through all loan programs. *Average indebtedness per student:* $16,312. *Average need-based loan:* Freshmen: $3440; Undergraduates: $5312. *Parent loans:* $20,638,631 (53% need-based, 47% non-need-based). *Programs:* Federal Direct (Subsidized and Unsubsidized Stafford, PLUS), Perkins, college/university, alternative loans.

WORK-STUDY *Federal work-study:* Total amount: $1,078,452; 623 jobs averaging $1872. *State or other work-study/employment:* Total amount: $2,236,497 (74% need-based, 26% non-need-based). 1,156 part-time jobs averaging $1800.

ATHLETIC AWARDS *Total amount:* $3,173,206 (30% need-based, 70% non-need-based).

APPLYING FOR FINANCIAL AID *Required financial aid form:* FAFSA. *Financial aid deadline (priority):* 3/1. *Notification date:* Continuous.

CONTACT Office of Student Financial Services, Colorado State University, Room 103, Administration Annex Building, Fort Collins, CO 80523-8024, 970-491-6321. *E-mail:* sfs@colostate.edu.

COLORADO STATE UNIVERSITY-PUEBLO
Pueblo, CO

Tuition & fees (CO res): $3220	Average undergraduate aid package: $6780

ABOUT THE INSTITUTION State-supported, coed. Awards: bachelor's and master's degrees. 65 undergraduate majors. Total enrollment: 5,835. Undergraduates: 5,417. Freshmen: 709. Federal methodology is used as a basis for awarding need-based institutional aid.

UNDERGRADUATE EXPENSES for 2004–05 *Application fee:* $25. *Tuition, state resident:* full-time $2524; part-time $105.17 per credit. *Tuition, nonresident:* full-time $13,543; part-time $564.29 per credit. *Required fees:* full-time $696; $27.73 per credit. Full-time tuition and fees vary according to reciprocity agreements. Part-time tuition and fees vary according to reciprocity agreements. *College room and board:* $5912; *room only:* $2876. Room and board charges vary according to board plan and housing facility. *Payment plans:* Installment, deferred payment.

GIFT AID (NEED-BASED) *Total amount:* $9,031,105 (60% federal, 24% state, 11% institutional, 5% external sources). *Receiving aid:* Freshmen: 63% (360); All full-time undergraduates: 53% (1,345). *Average award:* Freshmen: $4140; Undergraduates: $4324. *Scholarships, grants, and awards:* Federal Pell, FSEOG, state, private, college/university gift aid from institutional funds.

GIFT AID (NON-NEED-BASED) *Total amount:* $878,107 (7% state, 64% institutional, 29% external sources). *Receiving aid:* Freshmen: 4% (25); Undergraduates: 1% (37). *Average Award:* Freshmen: $6738; Undergraduates: $5449. *Scholarships, grants, and awards by category: Academic Interests/Achievement:* 844 awards ($1,641,421 total): biological sciences, business, computer science, engineering/technologies, general academic interests/achievements, international studies, mathematics, premedicine, social sciences. *Creative Arts/Performance:* applied art and design, art/fine arts, cinema/film/broadcasting, journalism/publications, music, performing arts, theater/drama. *Special Achievements/Activities:* community service, general special achievements/activities, leadership. *Special Characteristics:* first-generation college students, general special characteristics. *Tuition waivers:* Full or partial for employees or children of employees, senior citizens. *ROTC:* Army.

LOANS *Student loans:* $13,955,852 (83% need-based, 17% non-need-based). 73% of past graduating class borrowed through all loan programs. *Average indebtedness per student:* $17,149. *Average need-based loan:* Freshmen: $1931; Undergraduates: $3142. *Parent loans:* $2,684,687 (35% need-based, 65% non-need-based). *Programs:* FFEL (Subsidized and Unsubsidized Stafford, PLUS), Perkins.

ATHLETIC AWARDS *Total amount:* $398,135 (41% need-based, 59% non-need-based).

APPLYING FOR FINANCIAL AID *Required financial aid form:* FAFSA. *Financial aid deadline (priority):* 3/1. *Notification date:* Continuous beginning 3/25. Students must reply within 3 weeks of notification.

CONTACT Ms. Ofelia Morales, Director of Student Financial Services, Colorado State University-Pueblo, 2200 Bonforte Boulevard, Pueblo, CO 81001-4901, 719-549-2913. *Fax:* 719-549-2088.

COLORADO TECHNICAL UNIVERSITY
Colorado Springs, CO

CONTACT Anne Marie Alba, Financial Aid Coordinator, Colorado Technical University, 4435 North Chestnut Street, Colorado Springs, CO 80907-3896, 719-598-0200. *Fax:* 719-598-3740.

COLORADO TECHNICAL UNIVERSITY DENVER CAMPUS
Greenwood Village, CO

CONTACT Ms. Natalie Dietsch, Financial Aid Manager, Colorado Technical University Denver Campus, 5775 Denver Tech Center Boulevard, Suite 100, Greenwood Village, CO 80111, 303-694-6600. *Fax:* 303-694-6673.

COLORADO TECHNICAL UNIVERSITY SIOUX FALLS CAMPUS
Sioux Falls, SD

CONTACT Vikki Van Hull, Financial Aid Officer, Colorado Technical University Sioux Falls Campus, 3901 West 59th Street, Sioux Falls, SD 57108, 605-361-0200 Ext. 140. *Fax:* 605-361-5954. *E-mail:* vvanhull@sf.coloradotech.edu.

COLUMBIA COLLEGE
Columbia, MO

Tuition & fees: $11,995	Average undergraduate aid package: $12,096

ABOUT THE INSTITUTION Independent religious, coed. Awards: associate, bachelor's, and master's degrees (offers continuing education program with significant enrollment not reflected in profile). 37 undergraduate majors. Total enrollment: 1,108. Undergraduates: 953. Freshmen: 184. Both federal and institutional methodology are used as a basis for awarding need-based institutional aid.

UNDERGRADUATE EXPENSES for 2004–05 *Application fee:* $25. *Comprehensive fee:* $17,006 includes full-time tuition ($11,995) and room and board ($5011). *College room only:* $3152. Full-time tuition and fees vary according to class time and course load. Room and board charges vary according to board plan. *Part-time tuition:* $248 per credit hour. Part-time tuition and fees vary according to class time, course load, and location. *Payment plan:* Deferred payment.

FRESHMAN FINANCIAL AID (Fall 2004, est.) 154 applied for aid; of those 72% were deemed to have need. 98% of freshmen with need received aid; of those 24% had need fully met. *Average percent of need met:* 67% (excluding resources awarded to replace EFC). *Average financial aid package:* $9448 (excluding resources awarded to replace EFC). 22% of all full-time freshmen had no need and received non-need-based gift aid.

UNDERGRADUATE FINANCIAL AID (Fall 2004, est.) 621 applied for aid; of those 72% were deemed to have need. 98% of undergraduates with need received aid; of those 29% had need fully met. *Average percent of need met:* 71% (excluding resources awarded to replace EFC). *Average financial aid package:* $12,096 (excluding resources awarded to replace EFC). 20% of all full-time undergraduates had no need and received non-need-based gift aid.

GIFT AID (NEED-BASED) *Total amount:* $1,301,037 (59% federal, 22% state, 17% institutional, 2% external sources). *Receiving aid:* Freshmen: 58% (97); All full-time undergraduates: 44% (327). *Average award:* Freshmen: $2739; Undergraduates: $3364. *Scholarships, grants, and awards:* Federal Pell, FSEOG, state, private, college/university gift aid from institutional funds, VA, vocational rehabilitation.

GIFT AID (NON-NEED-BASED) *Total amount:* $3,287,075 (3% state, 87% institutional, 10% external sources). *Receiving aid:* Freshmen: 66% (109); Undergraduates: 56% (411). *Average Award:* Freshmen: $6736; Undergraduates: $8759. *Scholarships, grants, and awards by category: Academic Interests/Achievement:* biological sciences, business, education, English, general academic interests/achievements, humanities, physical sciences, religion/biblical studies, social sciences. *Creative Arts/Performance:* applied art and design, art/fine arts, music. *Special Achievements/Activities:* leadership, memberships, religious involvement. *Special Characteristics:* children and siblings of alumni, children of current students, children of educators, children of faculty/staff, children of union members/company employees, children with a deceased or disabled parent, international students, local/state students, parents of current students, previous college experience, religious affiliation, siblings of current students, spouses of current students, veterans. *Tuition waivers:* Full or partial for children of alumni, employees or children of employees. *ROTC:* Army cooperative, Air Force cooperative.

LOANS *Student loans:* $3,367,352 (47% need-based, 53% non-need-based). 56% of past graduating class borrowed through all loan programs. *Average indebtedness per student:* $12,707. *Average need-based loan:* Freshmen: $2796;

Undergraduates: $4291. *Parent loans:* $907,875 (100% non-need-based). *Programs:* Federal Direct (Subsidized and Unsubsidized Stafford, PLUS), Perkins.

WORK-STUDY *Federal work-study:* Total amount: $51,063; 92 jobs averaging $555.

ATHLETIC AWARDS *Total amount:* $742,667 (100% non-need-based).

APPLYING FOR FINANCIAL AID *Required financial aid forms:* FAFSA, institution's own form. *Financial aid deadline (priority):* 3/1. *Notification date:* Continuous beginning 3/15. Students must reply within 2 weeks of notification.

CONTACT Sharon Abernathy, Director of Financial Aid, Columbia College, 1001 Rogers Street, Columbia, MO 65216-0002, 573-875-7360 or toll-free 800-231-2391 Ext. 7366. *E-mail:* saabernathy@ccis.edu.

COLUMBIA COLLEGE
New York, NY

Tuition & fees: $31,472	Average undergraduate aid package: $27,749

ABOUT THE INSTITUTION Independent, coed. Awards: bachelor's degrees. 64 undergraduate majors. Total enrollment: 4,115. Undergraduates: 4,115. Freshmen: 1,011. Both federal and institutional methodology are used as a basis for awarding need-based institutional aid.

UNDERGRADUATE EXPENSES for 2004–05 *Application fee:* $65. *Comprehensive fee:* $40,538 includes full-time tuition ($30,260), mandatory fees ($1212), and room and board ($9066). *College room only:* $5290. *Payment plans:* Tuition prepayment, installment.

FRESHMAN FINANCIAL AID (Fall 2004, est.) 557 applied for aid; of those 88% were deemed to have need. 100% of freshmen with need received aid; of those 100% had need fully met. *Average percent of need met:* 100% (excluding resources awarded to replace EFC). *Average financial aid package:* $27,464 (excluding resources awarded to replace EFC).

UNDERGRADUATE FINANCIAL AID (Fall 2004, est.) 2,116 applied for aid; of those 91% were deemed to have need. 100% of undergraduates with need received aid; of those 100% had need fully met. *Average percent of need met:* 100% (excluding resources awarded to replace EFC). *Average financial aid package:* $27,749 (excluding resources awarded to replace EFC).

GIFT AID (NEED-BASED) *Total amount:* $41,876,549 (7% federal, 3% state, 85% institutional, 5% external sources). *Receiving aid:* Freshmen: 40% (409); All full-time undergraduates: 41% (1,685). *Average award:* Freshmen: $24,726; Undergraduates: $22,782. *Scholarships, grants, and awards:* Federal Pell, FSEOG, state, private, college/university gift aid from institutional funds.

GIFT AID (NON-NEED-BASED) *ROTC:* Army cooperative, Naval cooperative, Air Force cooperative.

LOANS *Student loans:* $6,884,966 (100% need-based). 32% of past graduating class borrowed through all loan programs. *Average indebtedness per student:* $16,080. *Average need-based loan:* Freshmen: $3487; Undergraduates: $4889. *Parent loans:* $4,944,152 (100% need-based). *Programs:* FFEL (Subsidized and Unsubsidized Stafford, PLUS), Perkins, alternative loans.

WORK-STUDY *Federal work-study:* Total amount: $3,166,203; 1,347 jobs averaging $2350. *State or other work-study/employment:* Total amount: $347,910 (100% need-based). 130 part-time jobs averaging $2676.

APPLYING FOR FINANCIAL AID *Required financial aid forms:* FAFSA, institution's own form, CSS Financial Aid PROFILE, noncustodial (divorced/separated) parent's statement, parent and student income tax form(s). *Financial aid deadline:* 2/10. *Notification date:* 4/1. Students must reply by 5/1 or within 4 weeks of notification.

CONTACT Office of Financial Aid and Educational Financing, Columbia College, 407 Lerner Hall MC 2802, 1130 Amsterdam Avenue, New York, NY 10027, 212-854-3711. *Fax:* 212-854-8223. *E-mail:* ugrad-finaid@columbia.edu.

COLUMBIA COLLEGE
Caguas, PR

CONTACT Financial Aid Officer, Columbia College, Carr 183, Km 1.7, PO Box 8517, Caguas, PR 00726, 787-743-4041 Ext. 244 or toll-free 800-981-4877 Ext. 239 (in-state).

COLUMBIA COLLEGE
Columbia, SC

Tuition & fees: $18,040	Average undergraduate aid package: $19,176

ABOUT THE INSTITUTION Independent United Methodist, women only. Awards: bachelor's and master's degrees. 41 undergraduate majors. Total enrollment: 1,453. Undergraduates: 1,149. Freshmen: 268. Federal methodology is used as a basis for awarding need-based institutional aid.

UNDERGRADUATE EXPENSES for 2004–05 *Application fee:* $25. *Comprehensive fee:* $23,660 includes full-time tuition ($17,690), mandatory fees ($350), and room and board ($5620). *College room only:* $2930. Room and board charges vary according to board plan and housing facility. *Part-time tuition:* $475 per credit hour. Part-time tuition and fees vary according to course load. *Payment plans:* Tuition prepayment, installment.

FRESHMAN FINANCIAL AID (Fall 2003) 166 applied for aid; of those 95% were deemed to have need. 100% of freshmen with need received aid; of those 55% had need fully met. *Average percent of need met:* 81% (excluding resources awarded to replace EFC). *Average financial aid package:* $21,050 (excluding resources awarded to replace EFC). 7% of all full-time freshmen had no need and received non-need-based gift aid.

UNDERGRADUATE FINANCIAL AID (Fall 2003) 864 applied for aid; of those 92% were deemed to have need. 100% of undergraduates with need received aid; of those 33% had need fully met. *Average percent of need met:* 66% (excluding resources awarded to replace EFC). *Average financial aid package:* $19,176 (excluding resources awarded to replace EFC). 9% of all full-time undergraduates had no need and received non-need-based gift aid.

GIFT AID (NEED-BASED) *Total amount:* $5,108,868 (33% federal, 30% state, 37% institutional). *Receiving aid:* Freshmen: 88% (157); All full-time undergraduates: 83% (770). *Average award:* Freshmen: $10,899; Undergraduates: $8995. *Scholarships, grants, and awards:* Federal Pell, FSEOG, state, private, college/university gift aid from institutional funds.

GIFT AID (NON-NEED-BASED) *Total amount:* $5,281,211 (34% state, 60% institutional, 6% external sources). *Receiving aid:* Freshmen: 39% (70); Undergraduates: 20% (188). *Average Award: Freshmen:* $6574; *Undergraduates:* $6826. *Scholarships, grants, and awards by category: Academic Interests/Achievement:* 736 awards ($1,480,587 total): biological sciences, business, communication, education, English, foreign languages, general academic interests/achievements, humanities, mathematics, religion/biblical studies. *Creative Arts/Performance:* 108 awards ($257,500 total): applied art and design, art/fine arts, dance, music. *Special Achievements/Activities:* 199 awards ($469,719 total): leadership. *Special Characteristics:* 22 awards ($116,584 total): children of faculty/staff, relatives of clergy. *Tuition waivers:* Full or partial for employees or children of employees. *ROTC:* Army cooperative, Naval cooperative, Air Force cooperative.

LOANS *Student loans:* $9,107,012 (54% need-based, 46% non-need-based). 87% of past graduating class borrowed through all loan programs. *Average indebtedness per student:* $25,333. *Average need-based loan:* Freshmen: $3331; Undergraduates: $4094. *Parent loans:* $507,775 (100% non-need-based). *Programs:* FFEL (Subsidized and Unsubsidized Stafford, PLUS), Perkins, state, South Carolina Teacher Loans, United Methodist Student Loans.

WORK-STUDY *Federal work-study:* Total amount: $256,839; 200 jobs averaging $1000. *State or other work-study/employment:* Total amount: $54,241 (100% non-need-based). Part-time jobs available.

ATHLETIC AWARDS *Total amount:* $78,750 (100% non-need-based).

APPLYING FOR FINANCIAL AID *Required financial aid form:* FAFSA. *Financial aid deadline (priority):* 3/15. *Notification date:* Continuous beginning 4/1. Students must reply within 2 weeks of notification.

CONTACT Anita Kaminer Elliott, Director of Financial Aid, Columbia College, 1301 Columbia College Drive, Columbia, SC 29203-5998, 803-786-3612 or toll-free 800-277-1301. *Fax:* 803-786-3560.

COLUMBIA COLLEGE CHICAGO
Chicago, IL

Tuition & fees: $15,998	Average undergraduate aid package: N/A

ABOUT THE INSTITUTION Independent, coed. Awards: bachelor's and master's degrees and post-bachelor's certificates. 40 undergraduate majors. Total enrollment: 10,354. Undergraduates: 9,706. Freshmen: 1,772. Both federal and institutional methodology are used as a basis for awarding need-based institutional aid.

UNDERGRADUATE EXPENSES for 2005–06 *Application fee:* $35. *Comprehensive fee:* $25,298 includes full-time tuition ($15,588), mandatory fees ($410), and room and board ($9300). *College room only:* $7155. Room and board charges vary according to board plan and housing facility. *Part-time tuition:* $540 per semester hour. *Part-time fees:* $85 per term. *Payment plan:* Installment.

GIFT AID (NEED-BASED) *Total amount:* $20,966,697 (35% federal, 49% state, 9% institutional, 7% external sources). *Scholarships, grants, and awards:* Federal Pell, FSEOG, state, private, college/university gift aid from institutional funds.

GIFT AID (NON-NEED-BASED) *Total amount:* $53,132 (62% federal, 38% state). *Scholarships, grants, and awards by category: Academic Interests/Achievement:* business, communication, education, general academic interests/achievements. *Creative Arts/Performance:* applied art and design, art/fine arts, cinema/film/broadcasting, creative writing, dance, journalism/publications, music, performing arts, theater/drama. *Special Achievements/Activities:* leadership. *Special Characteristics:* children of faculty/staff, first-generation college students, handicapped students. *Tuition waivers:* Full or partial for employees or children of employees.

LOANS *Student loans:* $38,169,423 (100% need-based). *Programs:* Federal Direct (Subsidized and Unsubsidized Stafford, PLUS).

WORK-STUDY *Federal work-study:* Total amount: $540,430; jobs available. *State or other work-study/employment:* Total amount: $2,167,144 (100% need-based). Part-time jobs available.

APPLYING FOR FINANCIAL AID *Required financial aid forms:* FAFSA, institution's own form. *Financial aid deadline (priority):* 8/1. *Notification date:* Continuous.

CONTACT Mr. Timothy Bauhs, Executive Director of Student Financial Services, Columbia College Chicago, 600 South Michigan Avenue, Chicago, IL 60605-1996, 312-663-1600 Ext. 7054 or toll-free 312-663-1600 Ext. 7130 (in-state). *Fax:* 312-986-1091. *E-mail:* tbauhs@colum.edu.

COLUMBIA COLLEGE HOLLYWOOD
Tarzana, CA

Tuition & fees: $12,500	Average undergraduate aid package: $3827

ABOUT THE INSTITUTION Independent, coed. Awards: associate and bachelor's degrees. 5 undergraduate majors. Total enrollment: 177. Undergraduates: 177. Federal methodology is used as a basis for awarding need-based institutional aid.

UNDERGRADUATE EXPENSES for 2005–06 *Application fee:* $50. *Comprehensive fee:* $18,350 includes full-time tuition ($11,400), mandatory fees ($1100), and room and board ($5850). *Part-time tuition:* $325 per unit.

FRESHMAN FINANCIAL AID (Fall 2003) 24 applied for aid; of those 100% were deemed to have need. 100% of freshmen with need received aid. *Average financial aid package:* $2338 (excluding resources awarded to replace EFC).

UNDERGRADUATE FINANCIAL AID (Fall 2003) 103 applied for aid; of those 100% were deemed to have need. 100% of undergraduates with need received aid. *Average financial aid package:* $3827 (excluding resources awarded to replace EFC).

GIFT AID (NEED-BASED) *Total amount:* $302,030 (66% federal, 34% state). *Receiving aid:* Freshmen: 48% (15); All full-time undergraduates: 50% (76). *Average award:* Freshmen: $2900; Undergraduates: $3745. *Scholarships, grants, and awards:* Federal Pell, FSEOG, state, private.

LOANS *Student loans:* $838,646 (100% need-based). 95% of past graduating class borrowed through all loan programs. *Average indebtedness per student:* $35,125. *Parent loans:* $234,998 (100% need-based). *Programs:* FFEL (Subsidized and Unsubsidized Stafford, PLUS).

WORK-STUDY *Federal work-study:* Total amount: $11,100; 3 jobs averaging $2023.

APPLYING FOR FINANCIAL AID *Required financial aid forms:* FAFSA, institution's own form. *Financial aid deadline:* Continuous. *Notification date:* Continuous.

CONTACT Mr. Chris Freeman, Financial Aid Administrator, Columbia College Hollywood, 18618 Oxnard Street, Tarzana, CA 91356, 818-345-8414 Ext. 110 or toll-free 800-785-0585 (in-state). *Fax:* 818-345-9053. *E-mail:* finaid@columbiacollege.edu.

COLUMBIA INTERNATIONAL UNIVERSITY
Columbia, SC

Tuition & fees: $12,845	Average undergraduate aid package: $9106

ABOUT THE INSTITUTION Independent nondenominational, coed. Awards: associate, bachelor's, master's, doctoral, and first professional degrees and post-bachelor's certificates. 16 undergraduate majors. Total enrollment: 1,016. Undergraduates: 594. Freshmen: 91. Both federal and institutional methodology are used as a basis for awarding need-based institutional aid.

UNDERGRADUATE EXPENSES for 2004–05 *Application fee:* $35. *Comprehensive fee:* $18,225 includes full-time tuition ($12,400), mandatory fees ($445), and room and board ($5380). Full-time tuition and fees vary according to course load. Room and board charges vary according to board plan. *Part-time tuition:* $517 per semester hour. Part-time tuition and fees vary according to course load. *Payment plan:* Installment.

FRESHMAN FINANCIAL AID (Fall 2003) 134 applied for aid; of those 84% were deemed to have need. 100% of freshmen with need received aid; of those 9% had need fully met. *Average percent of need met:* 68% (excluding resources awarded to replace EFC). *Average financial aid package:* $7896 (excluding resources awarded to replace EFC).

UNDERGRADUATE FINANCIAL AID (Fall 2003) 499 applied for aid; of those 87% were deemed to have need. 100% of undergraduates with need received aid; of those 11% had need fully met. *Average percent of need met:* 69% (excluding resources awarded to replace EFC). *Average financial aid package:* $9106 (excluding resources awarded to replace EFC).

GIFT AID (NEED-BASED) *Total amount:* $1,288,205 (57% federal, 26% state, 15% institutional, 2% external sources). *Receiving aid:* Freshmen: 73% (113); All full-time undergraduates: 75% (433). *Average award:* Freshmen: $3665; Undergraduates: $3840. *Scholarships, grants, and awards:* Federal Pell, FSEOG, state, private, college/university gift aid from institutional funds.

GIFT AID (NON-NEED-BASED) *Total amount:* $1,133,155 (36% state, 54% institutional, 10% external sources). *Receiving aid:* Freshmen: 58% (90); Undergraduates: 49% (285). *Scholarships, grants, and awards by category: Academic Interests/Achievement:* 213 awards ($429,460 total): general academic interests/achievements, international studies, religion/biblical studies. *Creative Arts/Performance:* 9 awards ($5200 total): music, performing arts. *Special Achievements/Activities:* 187 awards ($525,690 total): general special achievements/activities, leadership, religious involvement. *Special Characteristics:* 159 awards ($186,768 total): children and siblings of alumni, ethnic background, first-generation college students, international students, married students, relatives of clergy, religious affiliation, spouses of current students, veterans, veterans' children. *Tuition waivers:* Full or partial for employees or children of employees.

LOANS *Student loans:* $2,602,760 (69% need-based, 31% non-need-based). 60% of past graduating class borrowed through all loan programs. *Average indebtedness per student:* $15,300. *Average need-based loan:* Freshmen: $2803; Undergraduates: $3961. *Parent loans:* $2,835,785 (100% non-need-based). *Programs:* FFEL (Subsidized and Unsubsidized Stafford, PLUS).

WORK-STUDY *Federal work-study:* Total amount: $1,124,215; 412 jobs averaging $2729.

APPLYING FOR FINANCIAL AID *Required financial aid forms:* FAFSA, institution's own form. *Financial aid deadline:* 3/15. *Notification date:* Continuous beginning 4/1.

CONTACT Mr. Robert Patton, Financial Aid Counselor, Columbia International University, PO Box 3122, Columbia, SC 29230-3122, 803-754-4100 Ext. 3036 or toll-free 800-777-2227 Ext. 3024. *Fax:* 803-691-0739. *E-mail:* yesciu@ciu.edu.

COLUMBIA UNION COLLEGE
Takoma Park, MD

ABOUT THE INSTITUTION Independent Seventh-day Adventist, coed. Awards: associate, bachelor's, and master's degrees. 36 undergraduate majors. Total enrollment: 1,115. Undergraduates: 1,086. Freshmen: 208.

GIFT AID (NEED-BASED) *Scholarships, grants, and awards:* Federal Pell, FSEOG, state, private, college/university gift aid from institutional funds, Livingston Memorial Fund Scholarships, Kramer Scholarships.

GIFT AID (NON-NEED-BASED) *Scholarships, grants, and awards by category: Academic Interests/Achievement:* general academic interests/achievements. *Creative Arts/Performance:* music. *Special Achievements/Activities:* community service, leadership, religious involvement. *Special Characteristics:* relatives of clergy.

LOANS *Programs:* FFEL (Subsidized and Unsubsidized Stafford, PLUS), Perkins, alternative loans.

APPLYING FOR FINANCIAL AID *Required financial aid form:* FAFSA.

CONTACT Elaine Oliver, Director, Financial Aid, Columbia Union College, 7600 Flower Avenue, Takoma Park, MD 20912, 301-891-4005 or toll-free 800-835-4212.

COLUMBIA UNIVERSITY, SCHOOL OF GENERAL STUDIES
New York, NY

ABOUT THE INSTITUTION Independent, coed. Awards: bachelor's degrees and post-bachelor's certificates. 40 undergraduate majors. Total enrollment: 1,571. Undergraduates: 1,142.

GIFT AID (NEED-BASED) *Scholarships, grants, and awards:* Federal Pell, FSEOG, state, private, college/university gift aid from institutional funds.

GIFT AID (NON-NEED-BASED) *Scholarships, grants, and awards by category: Academic Interests/Achievement:* general academic interests/achievements.

LOANS *Programs:* FFEL (Subsidized and Unsubsidized Stafford, PLUS), Perkins, college/university.

WORK-STUDY *Federal work-study:* Total amount: $590,863; 252 jobs averaging $2728.

APPLYING FOR FINANCIAL AID *Required financial aid forms:* FAFSA, institution's own form.

CONTACT Student Financial Planning, Columbia University, School of General Studies, 208 Kent Hall, New York, NY 10027, 212-854-7040 or toll-free 800-895-1169 (out-of-state).

COLUMBIA UNIVERSITY, THE FU FOUNDATION SCHOOL OF ENGINEERING AND APPLIED SCIENCE
New York, NY

Tuition & fees: $31,472	Average undergraduate aid package: $26,036

ABOUT THE INSTITUTION Independent, coed. Awards: bachelor's, master's, and doctoral degrees. 15 undergraduate majors. Total enrollment: 1,387. Undergraduates: 1,387. Freshmen: 320. Both federal and institutional methodology are used as a basis for awarding need-based institutional aid.

UNDERGRADUATE EXPENSES for 2004–05 *Application fee:* $65. *Comprehensive fee:* $40,538 includes full-time tuition ($30,260), mandatory fees ($1212), and room and board ($9066). *College room only:* $5290. Room and board charges vary according to board plan. *Payment plans:* Tuition prepayment, installment.

FRESHMAN FINANCIAL AID (Fall 2004, est.) 219 applied for aid; of those 89% were deemed to have need. 100% of freshmen with need received aid; of those 100% had need fully met. *Average percent of need met:* 100% (excluding resources awarded to replace EFC). *Average financial aid package:* $25,850 (excluding resources awarded to replace EFC).

UNDERGRADUATE FINANCIAL AID (Fall 2004, est.) 870 applied for aid; of those 90% were deemed to have need. 100% of undergraduates with need received aid; of those 100% had need fully met. *Average percent of need met:* 100% (excluding resources awarded to replace EFC). *Average financial aid package:* $26,036 (excluding resources awarded to replace EFC).

GIFT AID (NEED-BASED) *Total amount:* $15,227,657 (7% federal, 5% state, 84% institutional, 4% external sources). *Receiving aid:* Freshmen: 52% (166); All full-time undergraduates: 49% (680). *Average award:* Freshmen: $22,409; Undergraduates: $20,875. *Scholarships, grants, and awards:* Federal Pell, FSEOG, state, private, college/university gift aid from institutional funds.

GIFT AID (NON-NEED-BASED) *ROTC:* Army cooperative, Naval cooperative, Air Force cooperative.

LOANS *Student loans:* $3,082,492 (100% need-based). 44% of past graduating class borrowed through all loan programs. *Average indebtedness per student:* $15,391. *Average need-based loan:* Freshmen: $3416; Undergraduates: $5029. *Parent loans:* $1,915,185 (100% need-based). *Programs:* FFEL (Subsidized and Unsubsidized Stafford, PLUS), Perkins, alternative loans.

WORK-STUDY *Federal work-study:* Total amount: $1,368,051; 594 jobs averaging $2300. *State or other work-study/employment:* Total amount: $221,490 (100% need-based). 64 part-time jobs averaging $3460.

APPLYING FOR FINANCIAL AID *Required financial aid forms:* FAFSA, institution's own form, CSS Financial Aid PROFILE, noncustodial (divorced/separated) parent's statement, student and parent income tax form(s). *Financial aid deadline:* 2/10. *Notification date:* 4/1. Students must reply by 5/1 or within 4 weeks of notification.

CONTACT Office of Financial Aid and Educational Financing, Columbia University, The Fu Foundation School of Engineering and Applied Science, 407 Lerner Hall, 1130 Amsterdam Avenue, New York, NY 10027, 212-854-3711. *Fax:* 212-854-8223. *E-mail:* ugrad-finaid@columbia.edu.

Columbus College of Art & Design

COLUMBUS COLLEGE OF ART & DESIGN
Columbus, OH

Tuition & fees: $19,330	Average undergraduate aid package: $12,922

ABOUT THE INSTITUTION Independent, coed. Awards: bachelor's degrees. 7 undergraduate majors. Total enrollment: 1,562. Undergraduates: 1,562. Freshmen: 234. Federal methodology is used as a basis for awarding need-based institutional aid.

UNDERGRADUATE EXPENSES for 2004–05 *Application fee:* $25. *Comprehensive fee:* $25,730 includes full-time tuition ($18,780), mandatory fees ($550), and room and board ($6400). Room and board charges vary according to housing facility and student level. *Part-time tuition:* $782.50 per credit. *Part-time fees:* $275 per term. Part-time tuition and fees vary according to course load. *Payment plans:* Installment, deferred payment.

FRESHMAN FINANCIAL AID (Fall 2003) 288 applied for aid; of those 85% were deemed to have need. 98% of freshmen with need received aid; of those 16% had need fully met. *Average percent of need met:* 65% (excluding resources awarded to replace EFC). *Average financial aid package:* $13,070 (excluding resources awarded to replace EFC). 19% of all full-time freshmen had no need and received non-need-based gift aid.

UNDERGRADUATE FINANCIAL AID (Fall 2003) 1,241 applied for aid; of those 87% were deemed to have need. 99% of undergraduates with need received aid; of those 19% had need fully met. *Average percent of need met:* 65% (excluding resources awarded to replace EFC). *Average financial aid package:* $12,922 (excluding resources awarded to replace EFC). 16% of all full-time undergraduates had no need and received non-need-based gift aid.

GIFT AID (NEED-BASED) *Total amount:* $9,340,431 (15% federal, 16% state, 67% institutional, 2% external sources). *Receiving aid:* Freshmen: 76% (242); All full-time undergraduates: 81% (1,047). *Average award:* Freshmen: $9848; Undergraduates: $8568. *Scholarships, grants, and awards:* Federal Pell, FSEOG, state, private, college/university gift aid from institutional funds.

GIFT AID (NON-NEED-BASED) *Total amount:* $2,014,433 (7% state, 89% institutional, 4% external sources). *Receiving aid:* Freshmen: 6% (19); Undergraduates: 7% (88). *Average Award:* Freshmen: $8086; Undergraduates: $10,172. *Scholarships, grants, and awards by category:* Creative Arts/Performance: 1,172 awards ($7,313,048 total): art/fine arts. *Special Characteristics:* children of educators, children of faculty/staff, local/state students. *Tuition waivers:* Full or partial for employees or children of employees.

LOANS *Student loans:* $8,528,576 (73% need-based, 27% non-need-based). 99% of past graduating class borrowed through all loan programs. *Average indebtedness per student:* $19,693. *Average need-based loan:* Freshmen: $3817; Undergraduates: $5363. *Parent loans:* $3,566,045 (60% need-based, 40% non-need-based). *Programs:* FFEL (Subsidized and Unsubsidized Stafford, PLUS), Perkins, state.

WORK-STUDY *Federal work-study:* Total amount: $157,376; 115 jobs averaging $3250. *State or other work-study/employment:* 217 part-time jobs averaging $3000.

APPLYING FOR FINANCIAL AID *Required financial aid forms:* FAFSA, institution's own form, income tax forms, verification statement. *Financial aid deadline (priority):* 3/3. *Notification date:* 3/15. Students must reply within 2 weeks of notification.

CONTACT Mrs. Anna Schofield, Director of Financial Aid, Columbus College of Art & Design, 107 North Ninth Street, Columbus, OH 43215-1758, 614-224-9101 Ext. 3274 or toll-free 877-997-2223. *Fax:* 614-222-4034. *E-mail:* aschofield@ccad.edu.

COLUMBUS STATE UNIVERSITY
Columbus, GA

Tuition & fees (GA res): $2808	Average undergraduate aid package: $4015

ABOUT THE INSTITUTION State-supported, coed. Awards: associate, bachelor's, and master's degrees and post-master's certificates. 68 undergraduate majors. Total enrollment: 7,224. Undergraduates: 6,300. Freshmen: 1,058. Federal methodology is used as a basis for awarding need-based institutional aid.

UNDERGRADUATE EXPENSES for 2004–05 *Application fee:* $25. *Tuition, state resident:* full-time $2322; part-time $97 per semester hour. *Tuition, nonresident:* full-time $9290; part-time $388 per semester hour. *College room and board:* $5550; *room only:* $3510. Room and board charges vary according to board plan and location.

FRESHMAN FINANCIAL AID (Fall 2004, est.) 708 applied for aid; of those 51% were deemed to have need. 92% of freshmen with need received aid; of those 63% had need fully met. *Average percent of need met:* 56% (excluding resources awarded to replace EFC). *Average financial aid package:* $3891 (excluding resources awarded to replace EFC). 39% of all full-time freshmen had no need and received non-need-based gift aid.

UNDERGRADUATE FINANCIAL AID (Fall 2004, est.) 2,731 applied for aid; of those 56% were deemed to have need. 100% of undergraduates with need received aid; of those 84% had need fully met. *Average percent of need met:* 70% (excluding resources awarded to replace EFC). *Average financial aid package:* $4015 (excluding resources awarded to replace EFC). 28% of all full-time undergraduates had no need and received non-need-based gift aid.

GIFT AID (NEED-BASED) *Total amount:* $2,896,634 (97% federal, 1% state, 1% institutional, 1% external sources). *Receiving aid:* Freshmen: 36% (336); All full-time undergraduates: 36% (1,514). *Average award:* Freshmen: $2578; Undergraduates: $3324. *Scholarships, grants, and awards:* Federal Pell, FSEOG, state, private, college/university gift aid from institutional funds.

GIFT AID (NON-NEED-BASED) *Total amount:* $3,735,746 (76% state, 18% institutional, 6% external sources). *Receiving aid:* Freshmen: 29% (274); Undergraduates: 33% (1,377). *Average Award:* Freshmen: $1538; Undergraduates: $1749. *Scholarships, grants, and awards by category: Academic Interests/Achievement:* biological sciences, business, communication, computer science, education, English, general academic interests/achievements, health fields, humanities, international studies, military science, physical sciences. *Creative Arts/Performance:* art/fine arts, music, performing arts, theater/drama. *Special Achievements/Activities:* cheerleading/drum major, community service, general special achievements/activities, leadership. *Tuition waivers:* Full or partial for employees or children of employees, senior citizens. *ROTC:* Army.

LOANS *Student loans:* $18,017,794 (46% need-based, 54% non-need-based). 69% of past graduating class borrowed through all loan programs. *Average need-based loan:* Freshmen: $2614; Undergraduates: $3501. *Parent loans:* $509,215 (100% need-based). *Programs:* Federal Direct (Subsidized and Unsubsidized Stafford, PLUS), Perkins, state, college/university.

WORK-STUDY *Federal work-study:* Total amount: $140,000; jobs available.

ATHLETIC AWARDS *Total amount:* $323,350 (100% non-need-based).

APPLYING FOR FINANCIAL AID *Required financial aid forms:* FAFSA, W-2 forms, tax returns. *Financial aid deadline (priority):* 5/1. *Notification date:* 6/1.

CONTACT Ms. Janis Bowles, Director of Financial Aid, Columbus State University, 4225 University Avenue, Columbus, GA 31907-5645, 706-568-2036 or toll-free 866-264-2035. *Fax:* 706-568-2230. *E-mail:* bowles_janis@colstate.edu.

CONCEPTION SEMINARY COLLEGE
Conception, MO

ABOUT THE INSTITUTION Independent Roman Catholic, men only. Awards: bachelor's degrees. 1 undergraduate major. Total enrollment: 100. Undergraduates: 100. Freshmen: 10.

GIFT AID (NEED-BASED) *Scholarships, grants, and awards:* Federal Pell, FSEOG, college/university gift aid from institutional funds.

GIFT AID (NON-NEED-BASED) *Scholarships, grants, and awards by category: Academic Interests/Achievement:* general academic interests/achievements. *Special Characteristics:* religious affiliation.

LOANS *Programs:* FFEL (Subsidized and Unsubsidized Stafford), alternative loans.

WORK-STUDY *Federal work-study:* Total amount: $21,609; 16 jobs averaging $1350. *State or other work-study/employment:* Total amount: $34,330 (100% non-need-based). 30 part-time jobs averaging $1144.

APPLYING FOR FINANCIAL AID *Required financial aid form:* FAFSA.

CONTACT Br. Justin Hernandez, OSB, Director of Financial Aid, Conception Seminary College, PO Box 502, Conception, MO 64433-0502, 660-944-2851. *Fax:* 660-944-2829. *E-mail:* justin@conception.edu.

CONCORDIA COLLEGE
Selma, AL

CONTACT Financial Aid Office, Concordia College, 1804 Green Street, Selma, AL 36701, 334-874-5700. *Fax:* 334-874-3728.

CONCORDIA COLLEGE
Moorhead, MN

Tuition & fees: $17,920	Average undergraduate aid package: $13,243

ABOUT THE INSTITUTION Independent religious, coed. Awards: bachelor's and master's degrees. 81 undergraduate majors. Total enrollment: 2,814. Undergraduates: 2,812. Freshmen: 744. Federal methodology is used as a basis for awarding need-based institutional aid.

UNDERGRADUATE EXPENSES for 2004–05 *Application fee:* $20. *Comprehensive fee:* $22,610 includes full-time tuition ($17,770), mandatory fees ($150), and room and board ($4690). Room and board charges vary according to board plan and housing facility. *Part-time tuition:* $2770 per course. Part-time tuition and fees vary according to course load. *Payment plan:* Installment.

FRESHMAN FINANCIAL AID (Fall 2003) 674 applied for aid; of those 83% were deemed to have need. 100% of freshmen with need received aid; of those 62% had need fully met. *Average percent of need met:* 95% (excluding resources awarded to replace EFC). *Average financial aid package:* $13,386 (excluding resources awarded to replace EFC). 28% of all full-time freshmen had no need and received non-need-based gift aid.

UNDERGRADUATE FINANCIAL AID (Fall 2003) 2,236 applied for aid; of those 86% were deemed to have need. 99% of undergraduates with need received aid; of those 66% had need fully met. *Average percent of need met:* 95% (excluding resources awarded to replace EFC). *Average financial aid package:* $13,243 (excluding resources awarded to replace EFC). 26% of all full-time undergraduates had no need and received non-need-based gift aid.

GIFT AID (NEED-BASED) *Total amount:* $20,727,223 (11% federal, 14% state, 72% institutional, 3% external sources). *Receiving aid:* Freshmen: 69% (552); All full-time undergraduates: 67% (1,921). *Average award:* Freshmen: $8752; Undergraduates: $7863. *Scholarships, grants, and awards:* Federal Pell, FSEOG, state, private, college/university gift aid from institutional funds.

GIFT AID (NON-NEED-BASED) *Total amount:* $8,261,552 (92% institutional, 8% external sources). *Receiving aid:* Freshmen: 9% (70); Undergraduates: 12% (350). *Average Award:* Freshmen: $5853; Undergraduates: $5633. *Scholarships, grants, and awards by category:* Academic Interests/Achievement: 1,919 awards ($7,939,183 total): general academic interests/achievements. Creative Arts/Performance: 151 awards ($317,586 total): debating, music, theater/drama. Special Characteristics: 233 awards ($1,634,181 total): international students, members of minority groups. *Tuition waivers:* Full or partial for employees or children of employees. *ROTC:* Army cooperative, Air Force cooperative.

LOANS *Student loans:* $13,889,059 (55% need-based, 45% non-need-based). 71% of past graduating class borrowed through all loan programs. *Average indebtedness per student:* $20,323. *Average need-based loan:* Freshmen: $3524; Undergraduates: $4197. *Parent loans:* $1,474,888 (100% non-need-based). *Programs:* FFEL (Subsidized and Unsubsidized Stafford, PLUS), Perkins, state, college/university, alternative loans.

WORK-STUDY *Federal work-study:* Total amount: $180,976; 285 jobs averaging $635. *State or other work-study/employment:* Total amount: $2,360,296 (95% need-based, 5% non-need-based). 1,441 part-time jobs averaging $1638.

APPLYING FOR FINANCIAL AID *Required financial aid forms:* FAFSA, institution's own form. *Financial aid deadline:* Continuous. *Notification date:* Continuous beginning 2/15.

CONTACT Mr. Dale E. Thornton, Financial Aid Director, Concordia College, 901 South 8th Street, Moorhead, MN 56562, 218-299-3010 or toll-free 800-699-9897. *Fax:* 218-299-3025. *E-mail:* thornton@cord.edu.

CONCORDIA COLLEGE
Bronxville, NY

CONTACT Mr. Ken Fick, Director of Financial Aid, Concordia College, 171 White Plains Road, Bronxville, NY 10708, 914-337-9300 Ext. 2146 or toll-free 800-YES-COLLEGE. *Fax:* 914-395-4500. *E-mail:* financialaid@concordia-ny.edu.

CONCORDIA UNIVERSITY
Irvine, CA

Tuition & fees: $19,930	Average undergraduate aid package: $19,230

ABOUT THE INSTITUTION Independent religious, coed. Awards: bachelor's and master's degrees and post-bachelor's certificates (associate's degree for international students only). 20 undergraduate majors. Total enrollment: 1,834. Undergraduates: 1,399. Freshmen: 262. Federal methodology is used as a basis for awarding need-based institutional aid.

UNDERGRADUATE EXPENSES for 2005–06 *Application fee:* $50. *Comprehensive fee:* $26,980 includes full-time tuition ($19,930) and room and board ($7050). *College room only:* $4250. Room and board charges vary according to board plan. *Part-time tuition:* $565 per unit. Part-time tuition and fees vary according to course load. *Payment plan:* Installment.

FRESHMAN FINANCIAL AID (Fall 2004, est.) 252 applied for aid; of those 71% were deemed to have need. 99% of freshmen with need received aid; of those 21% had need fully met. *Average percent of need met:* 70% (excluding resources awarded to replace EFC). *Average financial aid package:* $18,818 (excluding resources awarded to replace EFC). 23% of all full-time freshmen had no need and received non-need-based gift aid.

UNDERGRADUATE FINANCIAL AID (Fall 2004, est.) 1,150 applied for aid; of those 74% were deemed to have need. 99% of undergraduates with need received aid; of those 28% had need fully met. *Average percent of need met:* 73% (excluding resources awarded to replace EFC). *Average financial aid package:* $19,230 (excluding resources awarded to replace EFC). 21% of all full-time undergraduates had no need and received non-need-based gift aid.

GIFT AID (NEED-BASED) *Total amount:* $8,213,614 (13% federal, 27% state, 59% institutional, 1% external sources). *Receiving aid:* Freshmen: 66% (176); All full-time undergraduates: 63% (778). *Average award:* Freshmen: $10,578; Undergraduates: $10,526. *Scholarships, grants, and awards:* Federal Pell, FSEOG, state, private, college/university gift aid from institutional funds.

GIFT AID (NON-NEED-BASED) *Total amount:* $2,074,310 (100% institutional). *Receiving aid:* Freshmen: 10% (26); Undergraduates: 10% (126). *Average Award:* Freshmen: $6112; Undergraduates: $5700. *Scholarships, grants, and awards by category:* Academic Interests/Achievement: 938 awards ($2,603,817 total): general academic interests/achievements, religion/biblical studies. Creative Arts/Performance: 143 awards ($190,400 total): applied art and design, debating, music, theater/drama. Special Achievements/Activities: 28 awards ($113,000 total): general special achievements/activities. Special Characteristics: 471 awards ($1,155,478 total): children of faculty/staff, ethnic background, religious affiliation, siblings of current students. *Tuition waivers:* Full or partial for employees or children of employees.

LOANS *Student loans:* $5,780,219 (41% need-based, 59% non-need-based). 67% of past graduating class borrowed through all loan programs. *Average indebtedness per student:* $23,709. *Average need-based loan:* Freshmen: $2559; Undergraduates: $3894. *Parent loans:* $1,751,074 (100% non-need-based). *Programs:* FFEL (Subsidized and Unsubsidized Stafford, PLUS), alternative loan.

WORK-STUDY *Federal work-study:* Total amount: $93,070; 63 jobs averaging $1668. *State or other work-study/employment:* Total amount: $370,282 (100% need-based). 238 part-time jobs averaging $1668.

ATHLETIC AWARDS *Total amount:* $1,064,255 (62% need-based, 38% non-need-based).

APPLYING FOR FINANCIAL AID *Required financial aid forms:* FAFSA, institution's own form. *Financial aid deadline:* 4/1 (priority: 3/2). *Notification date:* Continuous. Students must reply within 4 weeks of notification.

CONTACT Lori McDonald, Director of Financial Aid, Concordia University, 1530 Concordia West, Irvine, CA 92612-3299, 949-854-8002 Ext. 1170 or toll-free 800-229-1200. *Fax:* 949-854-6709. *E-mail:* lori.mcdonald@cui.edu.

CONCORDIA UNIVERSITY
River Forest, IL

ABOUT THE INSTITUTION Independent religious, coed. Awards: bachelor's, master's, and doctoral degrees and post-bachelor's and post-master's certificates. 54 undergraduate majors. Total enrollment: 2,056. Undergraduates: 1,134. Freshmen: 185.

GIFT AID (NEED-BASED) *Scholarships, grants, and awards:* Federal Pell, FSEOG, state, private, college/university gift aid from institutional funds.

GIFT AID (NON-NEED-BASED) *Scholarships, grants, and awards by category:* Academic Interests/Achievement: biological sciences, business, communication, computer science, education, English, foreign languages, general academic interests/achievements, mathematics, religion/biblical studies. Creative Arts/Performance: art/fine arts, music. Special Characteristics: children and siblings of alumni, children of faculty/staff, international students, religious affiliation.

LOANS *Programs:* FFEL (Subsidized and Unsubsidized Stafford, PLUS), Perkins.

WORK-STUDY *Federal work-study:* Total amount: $124,465; 350 jobs averaging $356. *State or other work-study/employment:* Part-time jobs available.

APPLYING FOR FINANCIAL AID *Required financial aid forms:* FAFSA, institution's own form.
CONTACT Assistant Director of Student Financial Planning, Concordia University, 7400 Augusta Street, River Forest, IL 60305-1499, 708-209-3113 or toll-free 800-285-2668.

CONCORDIA UNIVERSITY
Ann Arbor, MI

Tuition & fees: $17,765	Average undergraduate aid package: $13,474

ABOUT THE INSTITUTION Independent religious, coed. Awards: associate, bachelor's, and master's degrees. 32 undergraduate majors. Total enrollment: 557. Undergraduates: 530. Freshmen: 123. Federal methodology is used as a basis for awarding need-based institutional aid.
UNDERGRADUATE EXPENSES for 2004–05 *Application fee:* $25. *Comprehensive fee:* $24,510 includes full-time tuition ($17,595), mandatory fees ($170), and room and board ($6745). *College room only:* $4945. Full-time tuition and fees vary according to course load and program. *Part-time tuition:* $576 per credit hour. Part-time tuition and fees vary according to course load and program. *Payment plan:* Installment.
FRESHMAN FINANCIAL AID (Fall 2004, est.) 119 applied for aid; of those 91% were deemed to have need. 99% of freshmen with need received aid; of those 37% had need fully met. *Average percent of need met:* 87% (excluding resources awarded to replace EFC). *Average financial aid package:* $15,628 (excluding resources awarded to replace EFC). 15% of all full-time freshmen had no need and received non-need-based gift aid.
UNDERGRADUATE FINANCIAL AID (Fall 2004, est.) 444 applied for aid; of those 91% were deemed to have need. 100% of undergraduates with need received aid; of those 37% had need fully met. *Average percent of need met:* 83% (excluding resources awarded to replace EFC). *Average financial aid package:* $13,474 (excluding resources awarded to replace EFC). 12% of all full-time undergraduates had no need and received non-need-based gift aid.
GIFT AID (NEED-BASED) *Total amount:* $3,155,122 (17% federal, 17% state, 54% institutional, 12% external sources). *Receiving aid:* Freshmen: 83% (106); All full-time undergraduates: 84% (393). *Average award:* Freshmen: $11,767; Undergraduates: $9452. *Scholarships, grants, and awards:* Federal Pell, FSEOG, state, private, college/university gift aid from institutional funds.
GIFT AID (NON-NEED-BASED) *Total amount:* $424,735 (14% state, 54% institutional, 32% external sources). *Receiving aid:* Freshmen: 15% (19); Undergraduates: 13% (63). *Average Award: Freshmen:* $7522; *Undergraduates:* $8251. *Scholarships, grants, and awards by category: Academic Interests/Achievement:* general academic interests/achievements, religion/biblical studies. *Creative Arts/Performance:* art/fine arts, music, performing arts, theater/drama. *Special Achievements/Activities:* general special achievements/activities. *Special Characteristics:* children and siblings of alumni, children of faculty/staff, ethnic background, relatives of clergy, religious affiliation, siblings of current students. *Tuition waivers:* Full or partial for employees or children of employees. *ROTC:* Army cooperative, Air Force cooperative.
LOANS *Student loans:* $3,146,855 (66% need-based, 34% non-need-based). 68% of past graduating class borrowed through all loan programs. *Average indebtedness per student:* $28,045. *Average need-based loan:* Freshmen: $4625; Undergraduates: $4940. *Parent loans:* $402,733 (28% need-based, 72% non-need-based). *Programs:* FFEL (Subsidized and Unsubsidized Stafford, PLUS), Perkins.
WORK-STUDY *Federal work-study:* Total amount: $73,262; jobs available. *State or other work-study/employment:* Total amount: $25,556 (61% need-based, 39% non-need-based). Part-time jobs available.
ATHLETIC AWARDS *Total amount:* $777,849 (78% need-based, 22% non-need-based).
APPLYING FOR FINANCIAL AID *Required financial aid forms:* FAFSA, institution's own form. *Financial aid deadline (priority):* 3/1. *Notification date:* Continuous. Students must reply by 5/1 or within 4 weeks of notification.
CONTACT Sandy Tarbox, Financial Aid Office, Concordia University, 4090 Geddes Road, Ann Arbor, MI 48105-2797, 734-995-4622 or toll-free 800-253-0680. *Fax:* 734-995-4610. *E-mail:* sandy.tarbox@cuaa.edu.

CONCORDIA UNIVERSITY
Seward, NE

Tuition & fees: $16,880	Average undergraduate aid package: $14,252

ABOUT THE INSTITUTION Independent religious, coed. Awards: bachelor's and master's degrees. 73 undergraduate majors. Total enrollment: 1,317. Undergraduates: 1,202. Freshmen: 222. Federal methodology is used as a basis for awarding need-based institutional aid.
UNDERGRADUATE EXPENSES for 2004–05 *Application fee:* $25. *Comprehensive fee:* $21,460 includes full-time tuition ($16,880) and room and board ($4580). Room and board charges vary according to board plan. Part-time tuition and fees vary according to course load. *Payment plan:* Installment.
FRESHMAN FINANCIAL AID (Fall 2004, est.) 239 applied for aid; of those 100% were deemed to have need. 100% of freshmen with need received aid; of those 69% had need fully met. *Average percent of need met:* 93% (excluding resources awarded to replace EFC). *Average financial aid package:* $14,377 (excluding resources awarded to replace EFC). 14% of all full-time freshmen had no need and received non-need-based gift aid.
UNDERGRADUATE FINANCIAL AID (Fall 2004, est.) 1,010 applied for aid; of those 100% were deemed to have need. 100% of undergraduates with need received aid; of those 64% had need fully met. *Average percent of need met:* 92% (excluding resources awarded to replace EFC). *Average financial aid package:* $14,252 (excluding resources awarded to replace EFC). 9% of all full-time undergraduates had no need and received non-need-based gift aid.
GIFT AID (NEED-BASED) *Total amount:* $2,600,397 (37% federal, 5% state, 41% institutional, 17% external sources). *Receiving aid:* Freshmen: 63% (176); All full-time undergraduates: 63% (701). *Average award:* Freshmen: $3822; Undergraduates: $4827. *Scholarships, grants, and awards:* Federal Pell, FSEOG, state, private, college/university gift aid from institutional funds.
GIFT AID (NON-NEED-BASED) *Total amount:* $6,229,610 (85% institutional, 15% external sources). *Receiving aid:* Freshmen: 65% (182); Undergraduates: 90% (993). *Average Award:* Freshmen: $5859; *Undergraduates:* $5540. *Scholarships, grants, and awards by category: Academic Interests/Achievement:* 821 awards ($1,761,925 total): biological sciences, business, communication, computer science, education, English, general academic interests/achievements, health fields, humanities, mathematics, physical sciences, premedicine, religion/biblical studies, social sciences. *Creative Arts/Performance:* 142 awards ($231,500 total): art/fine arts, music, theater/drama. *Special Achievements/Activities:* 490 awards ($425,325 total): memberships, religious involvement. *Special Characteristics:* 261 awards ($329,673 total): children and siblings of alumni, children of educators, children of faculty/staff, international students, local/state students, members of minority groups. *Tuition waivers:* Full or partial for employees or children of employees. *ROTC:* Army cooperative, Air Force cooperative.
LOANS *Student loans:* $4,789,771 (57% need-based, 43% non-need-based). 67% of past graduating class borrowed through all loan programs. *Average indebtedness per student:* $13,232. *Average need-based loan:* Freshmen: $2408; Undergraduates: $3657. *Parent loans:* $2,062,082 (100% non-need-based). *Programs:* FFEL (Subsidized and Unsubsidized Stafford, PLUS), Perkins.
WORK-STUDY *Federal work-study:* Total amount: $101,788; 140 jobs averaging $727. *State or other work-study/employment:* Part-time jobs available.
ATHLETIC AWARDS *Total amount:* $1,073,563 (100% non-need-based).
APPLYING FOR FINANCIAL AID *Required financial aid forms:* FAFSA, institution's own form. *Financial aid deadline (priority):* 3/1. *Notification date:* Continuous beginning 3/31. Students must reply within 4 weeks of notification.
CONTACT Mrs. Gloria F. Hennig, Director of Student Financial Services, Concordia University, 800 North Columbia Avenue, Seward, NE 68434-1599, 402-643-7270 or toll-free 800-535-5494. *Fax:* 402-643-3519. *E-mail:* gloria.hennig@cune.edu.

CONCORDIA UNIVERSITY
Portland, OR

Tuition & fees: $18,390	Average undergraduate aid package: $15,000

ABOUT THE INSTITUTION Independent religious, coed. Awards: associate, bachelor's, and master's degrees and post-bachelor's certificates. 31 undergraduate majors. Total enrollment: 1,404. Undergraduates: 883. Freshmen: 124. Federal methodology is used as a basis for awarding need-based institutional aid.
UNDERGRADUATE EXPENSES for 2004–05 *Application fee:* $20. *Comprehensive fee:* $24,170 includes full-time tuition ($18,300), mandatory fees ($90), and room and board ($5780). *College room only:* $3200. Full-time tuition and fees vary according to program. Room and board charges vary according to board plan and housing facility. *Part-time tuition:* $565 per credit. *Part-time fees:* $20 per term. Part-time tuition and fees vary according to course load and program. *Payment plan:* Installment.

GIFT AID (NEED-BASED) *Total amount:* $5,279,149 (19% federal, 4% state, 77% institutional). *Receiving aid:* Freshmen: 85% (105); All full-time undergraduates: 67% (500). *Average award:* Freshmen: $10,000; Undergraduates: $9000. *Scholarships, grants, and awards:* Federal Pell, FSEOG, state, private, college/university gift aid from institutional funds.

GIFT AID (NON-NEED-BASED) *Total amount:* $621,211 (99% institutional, 1% external sources). *Receiving aid:* Freshmen: 44% (55); Undergraduates: 18% (137). *Average Award:* Freshmen: $6000; Undergraduates: $5000. *Scholarships, grants, and awards by category: Academic Interests/Achievement:* general academic interests/achievements, religion/biblical studies. *Creative Arts/Performance:* music. *Special Achievements/Activities:* leadership, religious involvement. *Special Characteristics:* children of faculty/staff, relatives of clergy, religious affiliation. *Tuition waivers:* Full or partial for employees or children of employees, senior citizens. *ROTC:* Air Force cooperative.

LOANS *Student loans:* $5,036,840 (55% need-based, 45% non-need-based). 85% of past graduating class borrowed through all loan programs. *Average indebtedness per student:* $15,000. *Average need-based loan:* Freshmen: $3000; Undergraduates: $5000. *Parent loans:* $1,118,406 (100% non-need-based). *Programs:* FFEL (Subsidized and Unsubsidized Stafford, PLUS), Perkins, alternative loans.

ATHLETIC AWARDS *Total amount:* $621,297 (100% non-need-based).

APPLYING FOR FINANCIAL AID *Required financial aid form:* FAFSA. *Financial aid deadline:* Continuous. *Notification date:* Continuous beginning 3/15. Students must reply by 5/1 or within 2 weeks of notification.

CONTACT Mr. James W. Cullen, Director of Financial Aid, Concordia University, 2811 Northeast Holman Street, Portland, OR 97211-6099, 503-493-6508 or toll-free 800-321-9371. *Fax:* 503-280-8661. *E-mail:* jcullen@cu-portland.edu.

CONCORDIA UNIVERSITY AT AUSTIN
Austin, TX

ABOUT THE INSTITUTION Independent religious, coed. Awards: associate, bachelor's, and master's degrees and post-bachelor's certificates. 21 undergraduate majors. Total enrollment: 1,155. Undergraduates: 1,031. Freshmen: 170.

GIFT AID (NEED-BASED) *Scholarships, grants, and awards:* Federal Pell, FSEOG, state, college/university gift aid from institutional funds.

GIFT AID (NON-NEED-BASED) *Scholarships, grants, and awards by category: Academic Interests/Achievement:* general academic interests/achievements. *Creative Arts/Performance:* general creative arts/performance. *Special Achievements/Activities:* general special achievements/activities. *Special Characteristics:* general special characteristics.

LOANS *Programs:* FFEL (Subsidized and Unsubsidized Stafford, PLUS), state.

APPLYING FOR FINANCIAL AID *Required financial aid forms:* FAFSA, institution's own form.

CONTACT Ms. Pat M. Jost, Director of Financial Assistance, Concordia University at Austin, 3400 Interstate 35 North, Austin, TX 78705-2799, 512-486-2000 or toll-free 800-285-4252.

CONCORDIA UNIVERSITY, ST. PAUL
St. Paul, MN

Tuition & fees: $21,312	Average undergraduate aid package: $11,469

ABOUT THE INSTITUTION Independent religious, coed. Awards: associate, bachelor's, and master's degrees and post-bachelor's certificates. 45 undergraduate majors. Total enrollment: 2,217. Undergraduates: 1,835. Freshmen: 176. Federal methodology is used as a basis for awarding need-based institutional aid.

UNDERGRADUATE EXPENSES for 2005–06 *Application fee:* $30. *Comprehensive fee:* $27,776 includes full-time tuition ($21,312) and room and board ($6464). Full-time tuition and fees vary according to program. Room and board charges vary according to board plan and housing facility. Part-time tuition and fees vary according to course load. *Payment plan:* Installment.

FRESHMAN FINANCIAL AID (Fall 2004, est.) 173 applied for aid; of those 92% were deemed to have need. 100% of freshmen with need received aid; of those 22% had need fully met. *Average percent of need met:* 75% (excluding resources awarded to replace EFC). *Average financial aid package:* $14,593 (excluding resources awarded to replace EFC). 7% of all full-time freshmen had no need and received non-need-based gift aid.

UNDERGRADUATE FINANCIAL AID (Fall 2004, est.) 1,212 applied for aid; of those 84% were deemed to have need. 100% of undergraduates with need received aid; of those 17% had need fully met. *Average percent of need met:*

64% (excluding resources awarded to replace EFC). *Average financial aid package:* $11,469 (excluding resources awarded to replace EFC). 6% of all full-time undergraduates had no need and received non-need-based gift aid.

GIFT AID (NEED-BASED) *Total amount:* $7,530,559 (18% federal, 18% state, 53% institutional, 11% external sources). *Receiving aid:* Freshmen: 91% (160); All full-time undergraduates: 52% (826). *Average award:* Freshmen: $11,377; Undergraduates: $9004. *Scholarships, grants, and awards:* Federal Pell, FSEOG, state, private, college/university gift aid from institutional funds.

GIFT AID (NON-NEED-BASED) *Total amount:* $784,288 (2% state, 68% institutional, 30% external sources). *Average Award:* Freshmen: $6997; Undergraduates: $5788. *Scholarships, grants, and awards by category: Academic Interests/Achievement:* 737 awards ($2,264,077 total): biological sciences, business, communication, English, general academic interests/achievements, mathematics, physical sciences, religion/biblical studies, social sciences. *Creative Arts/Performance:* 111 awards ($91,100 total): art/fine arts, journalism/publications, music, theater/drama. *Special Characteristics:* 140 awards ($303,587 total): children of faculty/staff, religious affiliation. *Tuition waivers:* Full or partial for employees or children of employees. *ROTC:* Army cooperative, Naval cooperative, Air Force cooperative.

LOANS *Student loans:* $8,399,042 (87% need-based, 13% non-need-based). 81% of past graduating class borrowed through all loan programs. *Average indebtedness per student:* $15,900. *Average need-based loan:* Freshmen: $3611; Undergraduates: $4422. *Parent loans:* $970,977 (86% need-based, 14% non-need-based). *Programs:* FFEL (Subsidized and Unsubsidized Stafford, PLUS), Perkins, state.

WORK-STUDY *Federal work-study:* Total amount: $213,578; 134 jobs averaging $1594. *State or other work-study/employment:* Total amount: $470,664 (100% need-based). 286 part-time jobs averaging $1646.

ATHLETIC AWARDS *Total amount:* $1,007,210 (82% need-based, 18% non-need-based).

APPLYING FOR FINANCIAL AID *Required financial aid forms:* FAFSA, institution's own form. *Financial aid deadline (priority):* 5/1. *Notification date:* Continuous. Students must reply within 3 weeks of notification.

CONTACT Brian Heinemann, Financial Aid Director, Concordia University, St. Paul, 275 North Syndicate Street, St. Paul, MN 55104-5494, 651-641-8209 or toll-free 800-333-4705. *Fax:* 651-641-8889. *E-mail:* heinemann@csp.edu.

CONCORDIA UNIVERSITY WISCONSIN
Mequon, WI

Tuition & fees: $16,430	Average undergraduate aid package: $15,774

ABOUT THE INSTITUTION Independent religious, coed. Awards: associate, bachelor's, master's, and doctoral degrees. 62 undergraduate majors. Total enrollment: 5,395. Undergraduates: 4,011. Freshmen: 373. Federal methodology is used as a basis for awarding need-based institutional aid.

UNDERGRADUATE EXPENSES for 2004–05 *Application fee:* $35. *Comprehensive fee:* $22,660 includes full-time tuition ($16,370), mandatory fees ($60), and room and board ($6230). Full-time tuition and fees vary according to program. Room and board charges vary according to board plan. *Part-time tuition:* $683 per credit hour. Part-time tuition and fees vary according to class time and program. *Payment plans:* Installment, deferred payment.

FRESHMAN FINANCIAL AID (Fall 2004, est.) 370 applied for aid; of those 82% were deemed to have need. 100% of freshmen with need received aid; of those 33% had need fully met. *Average percent of need met:* 55% (excluding resources awarded to replace EFC). *Average financial aid package:* $16,300 (excluding resources awarded to replace EFC). 16% of all full-time freshmen had no need and received non-need-based gift aid.

UNDERGRADUATE FINANCIAL AID (Fall 2004, est.) 1,290 applied for aid; of those 82% were deemed to have need. 100% of undergraduates with need received aid; of those 38% had need fully met. *Average percent of need met:* 57% (excluding resources awarded to replace EFC). *Average financial aid package:* $15,774 (excluding resources awarded to replace EFC). 18% of all full-time undergraduates had no need and received non-need-based gift aid.

GIFT AID (NEED-BASED) *Total amount:* $15,350,630 (15% federal, 10% state, 68% institutional, 7% external sources). *Receiving aid:* Freshmen: 79% (299); All full-time undergraduates: 76% (1,000). *Average award:* Freshmen: $16,300; Undergraduates: $17,774. *Scholarships, grants, and awards:* Federal Pell, FSEOG, state, private, college/university gift aid from institutional funds.

GIFT AID (NON-NEED-BASED) *Total amount:* $1,465,174 (4% state, 90% institutional, 6% external sources). *Receiving aid:* Freshmen: 42% (160); Undergraduates: 45% (585). *Average Award:* Freshmen: $7300; Undergradu-

ates: $7290. *Scholarships, grants, and awards by category: Academic Interests/ Achievement:* 652 awards ($2,891,434 total): general academic interests/ achievements. *Creative Arts/Performance:* 34 awards ($25,000 total): music, performing arts. *Special Achievements/Activities:* 86 awards ($153,164 total): leadership. *Special Characteristics:* 635 awards ($2,025,534 total): children of faculty/staff, out-of-state students, religious affiliation. *Tuition waivers:* Full or partial for employees or children of employees.

LOANS *Student loans:* $18,260,224 (97% need-based, 3% non-need-based). 59% of past graduating class borrowed through all loan programs. *Average indebtedness per student:* $17,500. *Average need-based loan:* Freshmen: $2600; Undergraduates: $3682. *Parent loans:* $2,053,516 (87% need-based, 13% non-need-based). *Programs:* Federal Direct (Subsidized and Unsubsidized Stafford, PLUS), state.

WORK-STUDY *Federal work-study:* Total amount: $100,000; 80 jobs averaging $1600. *State or other work-study/employment:* Total amount: $25,000 (100% non-need-based). 80 part-time jobs averaging $400.

APPLYING FOR FINANCIAL AID *Required financial aid forms:* FAFSA, institution's own form. *Financial aid deadline (priority):* 5/1. *Notification date:* Continuous beginning 3/1. Students must reply within 3 weeks of notification.

CONTACT Mr. Steven P. Taylor, Director of Financial Aid, Concordia University Wisconsin, 12800 North Lake Shore Drive, Mequon, WI 53097-2402, 262-243-4392 or toll-free 888-628-9472. *Fax:* 262-243-2636. *E-mail:* steve.taylor@cuw.edu.

CONCORD UNIVERSITY
Athens, WV

ABOUT THE INSTITUTION State-supported, coed. Awards: associate, bachelor's, and master's degrees. 36 undergraduate majors. Total enrollment: 2,937. Undergraduates: 2,869. Freshmen: 578.

GIFT AID (NEED-BASED) *Scholarships, grants, and awards:* Federal Pell, FSEOG, state, college/university gift aid from institutional funds.

GIFT AID (NON-NEED-BASED) *Scholarships, grants, and awards by category: Academic Interests/Achievement:* business, communication, education, English, general academic interests/achievements, social sciences. *Creative Arts/ Performance:* art/fine arts, journalism/publications, music, theater/drama. *Special Achievements/Activities:* community service, leadership.

LOANS *Programs:* FFEL (Subsidized and Unsubsidized Stafford, PLUS), Perkins.

WORK-STUDY *Federal work-study:* Total amount: $317,755; 188 jobs averaging $1690. *State or other work-study/employment:* Total amount: $406,644 (100% need-based). 245 part-time jobs averaging $1659.

APPLYING FOR FINANCIAL AID *Required financial aid forms:* FAFSA, institution's own form, verification worksheet.

CONTACT Patricia Harmon, Financial Aid Director, Concord University, PO Box 1000, Athens, WV 24712-1000, 304-384-6069 or toll-free 888-384-5249. *Fax:* 304-384-9044.

CONNECTICUT COLLEGE
New London, CT

Comprehensive fee: $39,975	Average undergraduate aid package: $25,206

ABOUT THE INSTITUTION Independent, coed. Awards: bachelor's and master's degrees. 68 undergraduate majors. Total enrollment: 1,905. Undergraduates: 1,894. Freshmen: 498. Both federal and institutional methodology are used as a basis for awarding need-based institutional aid.

UNDERGRADUATE EXPENSES for 2004–05 *Application fee:* $55. *Comprehensive fee:* $39,975. Full-time tuition and fees vary according to program. *Part-time tuition:* $3715 per course. Part-time tuition and fees vary according to program. *Payment plan:* Installment.

FRESHMAN FINANCIAL AID (Fall 2004, est.) 276 applied for aid; of those 82% were deemed to have need. 100% of freshmen with need received aid; of those 100% had need fully met. *Average percent of need met:* 100% (excluding resources awarded to replace EFC). *Average financial aid package:* $26,077 (excluding resources awarded to replace EFC).

UNDERGRADUATE FINANCIAL AID (Fall 2004, est.) 913 applied for aid; of those 88% were deemed to have need. 100% of undergraduates with need received aid; of those 100% had need fully met. *Average percent of need met:* 100% (excluding resources awarded to replace EFC). *Average financial aid package:* $25,206 (excluding resources awarded to replace EFC).

GIFT AID (NEED-BASED) *Total amount:* $16,661,678 (5% federal, 3% state, 90% institutional, 2% external sources). *Receiving aid:* Freshmen: 42% (209);

All full-time undergraduates: 39% (720). *Average award:* Freshmen: $24,009; Undergraduates: $23,141. *Scholarships, grants, and awards:* Federal Pell, FSEOG, state, college/university gift aid from institutional funds.

GIFT AID (NON-NEED-BASED) *Total amount:* $212,948 (100% external sources). *Tuition waivers:* Full or partial for employees or children of employees, senior citizens.

LOANS *Student loans:* $3,907,026 (67% need-based, 33% non-need-based). 45% of past graduating class borrowed through all loan programs. *Average indebtedness per student:* $21,012. *Average need-based loan:* Freshmen: $2861; Undergraduates: $4229. *Parent loans:* $4,746,775 (100% non-need-based). *Programs:* FFEL (Subsidized and Unsubsidized Stafford, PLUS), Perkins, college/university.

WORK-STUDY *Federal work-study:* Total amount: $871,370; 637 jobs averaging $1117. *State or other work-study/employment:* Total amount: $22,361 (100% need-based). 12 part-time jobs averaging $1175.

APPLYING FOR FINANCIAL AID *Required financial aid forms:* FAFSA, CSS Financial Aid PROFILE, noncustodial (divorced/separated) parent's statement, business/farm supplement. *Financial aid deadline:* 1/15. *Notification date:* 4/1. Students must reply by 5/1 or within 2 weeks of notification.

CONTACT Ms. Elaine Solinga, Director of Financial Aid Services, Connecticut College, 270 Mohegan Avenue, New London, CT 06320-4196, 860-439-2058. *Fax:* 860-439-5357. *E-mail:* finaid@conncoll.edu.

CONSERVATORY OF MUSIC OF PUERTO RICO
San Juan, PR

CONTACT Mr. Jorge Medina, Director of Financial Aid, Conservatory of Music of Puerto Rico, 350 Rafael Lamar Street at FDR Avenue, San Juan, PR 00918, 787-751-0160 Ext. 230. *Fax:* 787-758-8268. *E-mail:* jmedina@cmpr.gobierno.pr.

CONVERSE COLLEGE
Spartanburg, SC

Tuition & fees: $19,960	Average undergraduate aid package: $17,050

ABOUT THE INSTITUTION Independent, women only. Awards: bachelor's and master's degrees and post-master's certificates. 43 undergraduate majors. Total enrollment: 1,419. Undergraduates: 756. Freshmen: 197. Federal methodology is used as a basis for awarding need-based institutional aid.

UNDERGRADUATE EXPENSES for 2004–05 *Application fee:* $35. *Comprehensive fee:* $26,070 includes full-time tuition ($19,960) and room and board ($6110). Full-time tuition and fees vary according to program. Part-time tuition and fees vary according to program. *Payment plan:* Installment.

FRESHMAN FINANCIAL AID (Fall 2004, est.) 154 applied for aid; of those 88% were deemed to have need. 100% of freshmen with need received aid; of those 41% had need fully met. *Average percent of need met:* 92% (excluding resources awarded to replace EFC). *Average financial aid package:* $18,808 (excluding resources awarded to replace EFC). 31% of all full-time freshmen had no need and received non-need-based gift aid.

UNDERGRADUATE FINANCIAL AID (Fall 2004, est.) 487 applied for aid; of those 92% were deemed to have need. 100% of undergraduates with need received aid; of those 37% had need fully met. *Average percent of need met:* 86% (excluding resources awarded to replace EFC). *Average financial aid package:* $17,050 (excluding resources awarded to replace EFC). 25% of all full-time undergraduates had no need and received non-need-based gift aid.

GIFT AID (NEED-BASED) *Total amount:* $6,248,759 (11% federal, 20% state, 67% institutional, 2% external sources). *Receiving aid:* Freshmen: 69% (135); All full-time undergraduates: 70% (440). *Average award:* Freshmen: $16,639; Undergraduates: $14,296. *Scholarships, grants, and awards:* Federal Pell, FSEOG, state, private, college/university gift aid from institutional funds.

GIFT AID (NON-NEED-BASED) *Total amount:* $3,104,373 (27% state, 70% institutional, 3% external sources). *Receiving aid:* Freshmen: 24% (47); Undergraduates: 20% (124). *Average Award: Freshmen:* $17,872; *Undergraduates:* $17,244. *Scholarships, grants, and awards by category: Academic Interests/Achievement:* 356 awards ($3,984,742 total): general academic interests/ achievements. *Creative Arts/Performance:* 106 awards ($998,500 total): applied art and design, music, theater/drama. *Special Achievements/Activities:* 92 awards ($625,610 total): leadership. *Special Characteristics:* 80 awards ($159,010 total):

children and siblings of alumni, children of faculty/staff. *Tuition waivers:* Full or partial for employees or children of employees, adult students, senior citizens. *ROTC:* Army cooperative.

LOANS *Student loans:* $3,072,228 (75% need-based, 25% non-need-based). 56% of past graduating class borrowed through all loan programs. *Average indebtedness per student:* $17,127. *Average need-based loan:* Freshmen: $3018; Undergraduates: $4073. *Parent loans:* $1,299,188 (18% need-based, 82% non-need-based). *Programs:* FFEL (Subsidized and Unsubsidized Stafford, PLUS), Perkins, state.

WORK-STUDY *Federal work-study:* Total amount: $234,924; 159 jobs averaging $1501. *State or other work-study/employment:* 60 part-time jobs averaging $1000.

ATHLETIC AWARDS *Total amount:* $317,186 (43% need-based, 57% non-need-based).

APPLYING FOR FINANCIAL AID *Required financial aid form:* FAFSA. *Financial aid deadline (priority):* 3/1. *Notification date:* Continuous beginning 3/15. Students must reply by 5/1 or within 2 weeks of notification.

CONTACT Ms. Margaret P. Collins, Director of Financial Assistance, Converse College, 580 East Main Street, Spartanburg, SC 29302-0006, 864-596-9019 or toll-free 800-766-1125. *Fax:* 864-596-9749. *E-mail:* peggy.collins@converse.edu.

COOPER UNION FOR THE ADVANCEMENT OF SCIENCE AND ART
New York, NY

ABOUT THE INSTITUTION Independent, coed. Awards: bachelor's degrees (also offers master's program primarily made up of currently-enrolled students). 8 undergraduate majors. Total enrollment: 955. Undergraduates: 918. Freshmen: 207.

GIFT AID (NEED-BASED) *Scholarships, grants, and awards:* Federal Pell, FSEOG, state, private, college/university gift aid from institutional funds.

LOANS *Programs:* FFEL (Subsidized and Unsubsidized Stafford, PLUS), Perkins, college/university.

APPLYING FOR FINANCIAL AID *Required financial aid forms:* FAFSA, CSS Financial Aid PROFILE.

CONTACT Ms. Mary Ruokonen, Director of Financial Aid, Cooper Union for the Advancement of Science and Art, 30 Cooper Square, New York, NY 10003-7120, 212-353-4130. *Fax:* 212-353-4343. *E-mail:* ruokon@cooper.edu.

COPPIN STATE UNIVERSITY
Baltimore, MD

Tuition & fees (MD res): $4879   **Average undergraduate aid package: $7050**

ABOUT THE INSTITUTION State-supported, coed. Awards: bachelor's and master's degrees. 26 undergraduate majors. Total enrollment: 4,003. Undergraduates: 3,092. Federal methodology is used as a basis for awarding need-based institutional aid.

UNDERGRADUATE EXPENSES for 2005–06 *Application fee:* $35. *Tuition, state resident:* full-time $3527; part-time $151 per credit hour. *Tuition, nonresident:* full-time $10,048; part-time $347 per credit hour. *Required fees:* full-time $1352; $22 per credit hour or $150 per term part-time. *College room and board:* $6239; *room only:* $3881.

FRESHMAN FINANCIAL AID (Fall 2004, est.) 515 applied for aid; of those 97% were deemed to have need. 90% of freshmen with need received aid; of those 12% had need fully met. *Average percent of need met:* 62% (excluding resources awarded to replace EFC). *Average financial aid package:* $6416 (excluding resources awarded to replace EFC). 1% of all full-time freshmen had no need and received non-need-based gift aid.

UNDERGRADUATE FINANCIAL AID (Fall 2004, est.) 2,177 applied for aid; of those 97% were deemed to have need. 92% of undergraduates with need received aid; of those 17% had need fully met. *Average percent of need met:* 69% (excluding resources awarded to replace EFC). *Average financial aid package:* $7050 (excluding resources awarded to replace EFC). 1% of all full-time undergraduates had no need and received non-need-based gift aid.

GIFT AID (NEED-BASED) *Total amount:* $8,591,529 (75% federal, 24% state, 1% institutional). *Receiving aid:* Freshmen: 67% (383); All full-time undergraduates: 65% (1,634). *Average award:* Freshmen: $4450; Undergraduates: $5258. *Scholarships, grants, and awards:* Federal Pell, FSEOG, state, private, college/university gift aid from institutional funds, Federal Nursing.

GIFT AID (NON-NEED-BASED) *Total amount:* $1,217,365 (25% state, 50% institutional, 25% external sources). *Receiving aid:* Freshmen: 13% (73); Undergraduates: 12% (289). *Average Award:* Freshmen: $2675; Undergraduates: $3025. *Scholarships, grants, and awards by category:* Academic Interests/Achievement: general academic interests/achievements. *ROTC:* Army.

LOANS *Student loans:* $8,089,359 (60% need-based, 40% non-need-based). 90% of past graduating class borrowed through all loan programs. *Average indebtedness per student:* $17,843. *Average need-based loan:* Freshmen: $2765; Undergraduates: $3530. *Parent loans:* $436,329 (100% non-need-based). *Programs:* Federal Direct (Subsidized and Unsubsidized Stafford), FFEL (PLUS), Perkins, alternative loans from lenders.

WORK-STUDY *Federal work-study:* Total amount: $451,915; 126 jobs averaging $1687.

ATHLETIC AWARDS *Total amount:* $983,081 (100% non-need-based).

APPLYING FOR FINANCIAL AID *Required financial aid form:* FAFSA. *Financial aid deadline (priority):* 3/4. *Notification date:* Continuous beginning 4/15. Students must reply within 4 weeks of notification.

CONTACT Fay Tayree, Associate Director of Financial Aid, Coppin State University, 2500 West North Avenue, Baltimore, MD 21216-3698, 410-951-3645 or toll-free 800-635-3674. *Fax:* 410-951-3637. *E-mail:* ftayree@coppin.edu.

CORBAN COLLEGE
Salem, OR

Tuition & fees: $17,035   **Average undergraduate aid package: $13,795**

ABOUT THE INSTITUTION Independent religious, coed. Awards: associate and bachelor's degrees. 46 undergraduate majors. Total enrollment: 754. Undergraduates: 735. Freshmen: 165. Federal methodology is used as a basis for awarding need-based institutional aid.

UNDERGRADUATE EXPENSES for 2004–05 *Application fee:* $40. *Comprehensive fee:* $23,100 includes full-time tuition ($16,825), mandatory fees ($210), and room and board ($6065). Room and board charges vary according to board plan. *Part-time tuition:* $700 per credit. *Part-time fees:* $30 per term. Part-time tuition and fees vary according to course load. *Payment plan:* Installment.

FRESHMAN FINANCIAL AID (Fall 2004, est.) 155 applied for aid; of those 92% were deemed to have need. 99% of freshmen with need received aid; of those 24% had need fully met. *Average percent of need met:* 71% (excluding resources awarded to replace EFC). *Average financial aid package:* $14,038 (excluding resources awarded to replace EFC). 13% of all full-time freshmen had no need and received non-need-based gift aid.

UNDERGRADUATE FINANCIAL AID (Fall 2004, est.) 543 applied for aid; of those 92% were deemed to have need. 100% of undergraduates with need received aid; of those 26% had need fully met. *Average percent of need met:* 72% (excluding resources awarded to replace EFC). *Average financial aid package:* $13,795 (excluding resources awarded to replace EFC). 13% of all full-time undergraduates had no need and received non-need-based gift aid.

GIFT AID (NEED-BASED) *Total amount:* $3,646,101 (16% federal, 4% state, 69% institutional, 11% external sources). *Receiving aid:* Freshmen: 84% (141); All full-time undergraduates: 86% (499). *Average award:* Freshmen: $8981; Undergraduates: $8593. *Scholarships, grants, and awards:* Federal Pell, FSEOG, state, private, college/university gift aid from institutional funds.

GIFT AID (NON-NEED-BASED) *Total amount:* $333,872 (85% institutional, 15% external sources). *Receiving aid:* Freshmen: 4% (7); Undergraduates: 6% (34). *Average Award:* Freshmen: $7789; Undergraduates: $8341. *Scholarships, grants, and awards by category:* Academic Interests/Achievement: 356 awards ($1,281,750 total): general academic interests/achievements. Creative Arts/Performance: 24 awards ($24,875 total): music, performing arts. Special Achievements/Activities: 20 awards ($15,000 total): general special achievements/activities, hobbies/interests, leadership, memberships, religious involvement. Special Characteristics: 142 awards ($387,563 total): children and siblings of alumni, children of faculty/staff, international students, relatives of clergy, siblings of current students. *Tuition waivers:* Full or partial for employees or children of employees. *ROTC:* Army cooperative, Air Force cooperative.

LOANS *Student loans:* $3,794,633 (76% need-based, 24% non-need-based). 70% of past graduating class borrowed through all loan programs. *Average indebtedness per student:* $21,800. *Average need-based loan:* Freshmen: $5659; Undergraduates: $6140. *Parent loans:* $616,472 (55% need-based, 45% non-need-based). *Programs:* Federal Direct (Subsidized and Unsubsidized Stafford, PLUS), Perkins, state, alternative loans.

WORK-STUDY *Federal work-study:* Total amount: $68,141; 110 jobs averaging $1500.

ATHLETIC AWARDS *Total amount:* $652,100 (79% need-based, 21% non-need-based).

APPLYING FOR FINANCIAL AID *Required financial aid form:* FAFSA. *Financial aid deadline (priority):* 2/15. *Notification date:* Continuous beginning 3/1. Students must reply within 4 weeks of notification.

CONTACT Nathan Warthan, Director of Financial Aid, Corban College, 5000 Deer Park Drive, SE, Salem, OR 97301-9392, 503-375-7006 or toll-free 800-845-3005 (out-of-state). *Fax:* 503-585-4316. *E-mail:* nwarthan@wbc.edu.

CORCORAN COLLEGE OF ART AND DESIGN
Washington, DC

Tuition & fees: $21,300	Average undergraduate aid package: $10,905

ABOUT THE INSTITUTION Independent, coed. Awards: associate, bachelor's, and master's degrees. 11 undergraduate majors. Total enrollment: 508. Undergraduates: 481. Freshmen: 52. Federal methodology is used as a basis for awarding need-based institutional aid.

UNDERGRADUATE EXPENSES for 2004–05 *Application fee:* $40. *Comprehensive fee:* $31,100 includes full-time tuition ($21,200), mandatory fees ($100), and room and board ($9800). *College room only:* $7900. Full-time tuition and fees vary according to degree level. *Part-time tuition:* $610 per credit. *Part-time fees:* $100. Part-time tuition and fees vary according to degree level. *Payment plan:* Installment.

FRESHMAN FINANCIAL AID (Fall 2003) 108 applied for aid; of those 84% were deemed to have need. 100% of freshmen with need received aid; of those 1% had need fully met. *Average percent of need met:* 15% (excluding resources awarded to replace EFC). *Average financial aid package:* $11,322 (excluding resources awarded to replace EFC). 14% of all full-time freshmen had no need and received non-need-based gift aid.

UNDERGRADUATE FINANCIAL AID (Fall 2003) 320 applied for aid; of those 88% were deemed to have need. 100% of undergraduates with need received aid; of those 1% had need fully met. *Average percent of need met:* 13% (excluding resources awarded to replace EFC). *Average financial aid package:* $10,905 (excluding resources awarded to replace EFC). 27% of all full-time undergraduates had no need and received non-need-based gift aid.

GIFT AID (NEED-BASED) *Total amount:* $387,273 (94% federal, 6% state). *Receiving aid:* Freshmen: 58% (63); All full-time undergraduates: 69% (265). *Average award:* Freshmen: $3909; Undergraduates: $5348. *Scholarships, grants, and awards:* Federal Pell, FSEOG, state, college/university gift aid from institutional funds.

GIFT AID (NON-NEED-BASED) *Total amount:* $379,555 (100% institutional). *Receiving aid:* Freshmen: 82% (89); Undergraduates: 52% (201). *Average Award:* Freshmen: $3043; Undergraduates: $5160. *Scholarships, grants, and awards by category:* Academic Interests/Achievement: 282 awards ($605,325 total): general academic interests/achievements. Creative Arts/Performance: 53 awards ($365,455 total): applied art and design. *Tuition waivers:* Full or partial for employees or children of employees.

LOANS *Student loans:* $2,430,411 (43% need-based, 57% non-need-based). 75% of past graduating class borrowed through all loan programs. *Average indebtedness per student:* $28,247. *Average need-based loan:* Freshmen: $1651; Undergraduates: $4072. *Parent loans:* $1,255,360 (100% non-need-based). *Programs:* FFEL (Subsidized and Unsubsidized Stafford, PLUS), Perkins.

WORK-STUDY *Federal work-study:* Total amount: $98,129; 89 jobs averaging $1103.

APPLYING FOR FINANCIAL AID *Required financial aid forms:* FAFSA, institution's own form. *Financial aid deadline (priority):* 4/15. *Notification date:* Continuous. Students must reply within 2 weeks of notification.

CONTACT Diane Morris, Financial Aid Director, Corcoran College of Art and Design, 500 17th Street, NW, Washington, DC 20006-4804, 202-639-1816 or toll-free 888-CORCORAN (out-of-state). *Fax:* 202-737-6921. *E-mail:* dmorris@corcoran.org.

CORNELL COLLEGE
Mount Vernon, IA

Tuition & fees: $22,650	Average undergraduate aid package: $20,975

ABOUT THE INSTITUTION Independent Methodist, coed. Awards: bachelor's degrees. 45 undergraduate majors. Total enrollment: 1,155. Undergraduates: 1,155. Freshmen: 292. Federal methodology is used as a basis for awarding need-based institutional aid.

UNDERGRADUATE EXPENSES for 2004–05 *Application fee:* $40. *Comprehensive fee:* $28,890 includes full-time tuition ($22,490), mandatory fees ($160), and room and board ($6240). *College room only:* $2920. Full-time tuition and fees vary according to reciprocity agreements. Room and board charges vary according to board plan. *Part-time tuition:* $423 per credit hour. *Part-time fees:* $160 per year. Part-time tuition and fees vary according to course load. *Payment plan:* Installment.

FRESHMAN FINANCIAL AID (Fall 2003) 261 applied for aid; of those 90% were deemed to have need. 100% of freshmen with need received aid; of those 55% had need fully met. *Average percent of need met:* 99% (excluding resources awarded to replace EFC). *Average financial aid package:* $19,045 (excluding resources awarded to replace EFC). 27% of all full-time freshmen had no need and received non-need-based gift aid.

UNDERGRADUATE FINANCIAL AID (Fall 2003) 956 applied for aid; of those 87% were deemed to have need. 100% of undergraduates with need received aid; of those 50% had need fully met. *Average percent of need met:* 82% (excluding resources awarded to replace EFC). *Average financial aid package:* $20,975 (excluding resources awarded to replace EFC). 22% of all full-time undergraduates had no need and received non-need-based gift aid.

GIFT AID (NEED-BASED) *Total amount:* $13,370,454 (7% federal, 6% state, 85% institutional, 2% external sources). *Receiving aid:* Freshmen: 81% (236); All full-time undergraduates: 73% (836). *Average award:* Freshmen: $17,235; Undergraduates: $15,585. *Scholarships, grants, and awards:* Federal Pell, FSEOG, state, private, college/university gift aid from institutional funds.

GIFT AID (NON-NEED-BASED) *Total amount:* $3,448,033 (97% institutional, 3% external sources). *Receiving aid:* Freshmen: 18% (52); Undergraduates: 22% (253). *Average Award:* Freshmen: $13,735; Undergraduates: $12,440. *Scholarships, grants, and awards by category:* Academic Interests/Achievement: 422 awards ($5,824,664 total): general academic interests/achievements. Creative Arts/Performance: 128 awards ($923,721 total): art/fine arts, music, theater/drama. Special Achievements/Activities: 531 awards ($4,802,440 total): community service, religious involvement. Special Characteristics: 29 awards ($468,957 total): children of educators, children of faculty/staff. *Tuition waivers:* Full or partial for employees or children of employees, adult students, senior citizens.

LOANS *Student loans:* $4,225,449 (70% need-based, 30% non-need-based). 93% of past graduating class borrowed through all loan programs. *Average indebtedness per student:* $17,270. *Average need-based loan:* Freshmen: $3290; Undergraduates: $4210. *Parent loans:* $804,891 (100% non-need-based). *Programs:* FFEL (Subsidized and Unsubsidized Stafford, PLUS), Perkins, state, college/university, United Methodist Student Loans.

WORK-STUDY *Federal work-study:* Total amount: $498,143; 554 jobs averaging $1045. *State or other work-study/employment:* Total amount: $159,236 (100% non-need-based). 182 part-time jobs averaging $1000.

APPLYING FOR FINANCIAL AID *Required financial aid forms:* FAFSA, institution's own form, noncustodial (divorced/separated) parent's statement. *Financial aid deadline:* 3/1. *Notification date:* Continuous beginning 10/1. Students must reply by 5/1 or within 2 weeks of notification.

CONTACT Ms. Cindi P. Reints, Director of Financial Assistance, Cornell College, Wade House, 600 1st Street West, Mount Vernon, IA 52314-1098, 319-895-4216 or toll-free 800-747-1112. *Fax:* 319-895-4451. *E-mail:* creints@cornellcollege.edu.

CORNELL UNIVERSITY
Ithaca, NY

Tuition & fees: $30,167	Average undergraduate aid package: $25,400

ABOUT THE INSTITUTION Independent, coed. Awards: bachelor's, master's, doctoral, and first professional degrees. 233 undergraduate majors. Total enrollment: 19,518. Undergraduates: 13,625. Freshmen: 3,054. Institutional methodology is used as a basis for awarding need-based institutional aid.

UNDERGRADUATE EXPENSES for 2004–05 *Application fee:* $65. *Comprehensive fee:* $40,049 includes full-time tuition ($30,000), mandatory fees ($167), and room and board ($9882). *College room only:* $5875. Room and board charges vary according to board plan and housing facility. *Payment plan:* Installment.

FRESHMAN FINANCIAL AID (Fall 2004, est.) 1930 applied for aid; of those 77% were deemed to have need. 100% of freshmen with need received aid; of those 100% had need fully met. *Average percent of need met:* 100% (excluding resources awarded to replace EFC). *Average financial aid package:* $31,000 (excluding resources awarded to replace EFC).

UNDERGRADUATE FINANCIAL AID (Fall 2004, est.) 7,587 applied for aid; of those 88% were deemed to have need. 100% of undergraduates with need

received aid; of those 100% had need fully met. *Average percent of need met:* 100% (excluding resources awarded to replace EFC). *Average financial aid package:* $25,400 (excluding resources awarded to replace EFC).

GIFT AID (NEED-BASED) *Total amount:* $110,300,000 (11% federal, 6% state, 77% institutional, 6% external sources). *Receiving aid:* Freshmen: 46% (1,401); All full-time undergraduates: 46% (6,290). *Average award:* Freshmen: $21,257; Undergraduates: $17,500. *Scholarships, grants, and awards:* Federal Pell, FSEOG, state, private, college/university gift aid from institutional funds.

GIFT AID (NON-NEED-BASED) *Tuition waivers:* Full or partial for employees or children of employees. *ROTC:* Army, Air Force.

LOANS *Student loans:* $50,700,000 (100% need-based). 51% of past graduating class borrowed through all loan programs. *Average indebtedness per student:* $22,200. *Average need-based loan:* Freshmen: $10,400; Undergraduates: $7958. *Parent loans:* $13,900,000 (100% need-based). *Programs:* Federal Direct (Subsidized and Unsubsidized Stafford, PLUS), FFEL (Subsidized and Unsubsidized Stafford, PLUS), Perkins, college/university, Key Bank Alternative Loans.

WORK-STUDY *Federal work-study:* Total amount: $9,500,000; 5,262 jobs averaging $1881.

APPLYING FOR FINANCIAL AID *Required financial aid forms:* FAFSA, institution's own form, CSS Financial Aid PROFILE, noncustodial (divorced/separated) parent's statement, business/farm supplement, income tax form(s). *Financial aid deadline:* 2/11. *Notification date:* 4/1. Students must reply by 5/1 or within 2 weeks of notification.

CONTACT Mr. Thomas Keane, Director of Financial Aid and Student Employment, Cornell University, 410 Thurston Avenue, Ithaca, NY 14853-2488, 607-255-5147.

CORNERSTONE UNIVERSITY
Grand Rapids, MI

Tuition & fees: $14,700	Average undergraduate aid package: $13,066

ABOUT THE INSTITUTION Independent nondenominational, coed. Awards: associate, bachelor's, master's, and first professional degrees. 52 undergraduate majors. Total enrollment: 2,414. Undergraduates: 2,085. Freshmen: 369. Federal methodology is used as a basis for awarding need-based institutional aid.

UNDERGRADUATE EXPENSES for 2005–06 *Application fee:* $25. *Comprehensive fee:* $20,220 includes full-time tuition ($14,700) and room and board ($5520). *College room only:* $2520. Room and board charges vary according to board plan. *Part-time tuition:* $566 per hour. Part-time tuition and fees vary according to course load. *Payment plan:* Installment.

FRESHMAN FINANCIAL AID (Fall 2004, est.) 269 applied for aid; of those 82% were deemed to have need. 100% of freshmen with need received aid; of those 25% had need fully met. *Average percent of need met:* 83% (excluding resources awarded to replace EFC). *Average financial aid package:* $13,287 (excluding resources awarded to replace EFC). 17% of all full-time freshmen had no need and received non-need-based gift aid.

UNDERGRADUATE FINANCIAL AID (Fall 2004, est.) 1,106 applied for aid; of those 79% were deemed to have need. 100% of undergraduates with need received aid; of those 20% had need fully met. *Average percent of need met:* 86% (excluding resources awarded to replace EFC). *Average financial aid package:* $13,066 (excluding resources awarded to replace EFC). 16% of all full-time undergraduates had no need and received non-need-based gift aid.

GIFT AID (NEED-BASED) *Total amount:* $5,608,477 (21% federal, 23% state, 52% institutional, 4% external sources). *Receiving aid:* Freshmen: 81% (219); All full-time undergraduates: 76% (864). *Average award:* Freshmen: $3771; Undergraduates: $3699. *Scholarships, grants, and awards:* Federal Pell, FSEOG, state, private, college/university gift aid from institutional funds.

GIFT AID (NON-NEED-BASED) *Total amount:* $1,012,786 (1% federal, 28% state, 63% institutional, 8% external sources). *Receiving aid:* Freshmen: 78% (211); Undergraduates: 71% (805). *Average Award:* Freshmen: $4418; Undergraduates: $3374. *Scholarships, grants, and awards by category: Academic Interests/Achievement:* 1,032 awards ($1,975,883 total): business, education, general academic interests/achievements, religion/biblical studies. *Creative Arts/Performance:* 74 awards ($196,107 total): music. *Special Achievements/Activities:* 70 awards ($116,300 total): leadership, religious involvement. *Special Characteristics:* 337 awards ($668,989 total): children of faculty/staff, children of union members/company employees, ethnic background, general special characteristics, international students, members of minority groups, out-of-state students. *Tuition waivers:* Full or partial for employees or children of employees. *ROTC:* Army cooperative.

LOANS *Student loans:* $6,988,988 (75% need-based, 25% non-need-based). 74% of past graduating class borrowed through all loan programs. *Average indebtedness per student:* $21,209. *Average need-based loan:* Freshmen: $3176; Undergraduates: $4093. *Parent loans:* $688,260 (44% need-based, 56% non-need-based). *Programs:* FFEL (Subsidized and Unsubsidized Stafford, PLUS), Perkins, state, college/university.

WORK-STUDY *Federal work-study:* Total amount: $203,395; 110 jobs averaging $1605. *State or other work-study/employment:* Total amount: $48,841 (100% need-based). 26 part-time jobs averaging $1879.

ATHLETIC AWARDS *Total amount:* $690,023 (58% need-based, 42% non-need-based).

APPLYING FOR FINANCIAL AID *Required financial aid form:* FAFSA. *Financial aid deadline:* 3/1. *Notification date:* Continuous beginning 3/1. Students must reply within 2 weeks of notification.

CONTACT Mr. Geoff Marsh, Director of Student Financial Services, Cornerstone University, 1001 East Beltline Avenue, NE, Grand Rapids, MI 49525-5897, 616-222-1424 or toll-free 800-787-9778. *Fax:* 616-222-1400. *E-mail:* geoff_a_marsh@cornerstone.edu.

CORNISH COLLEGE OF THE ARTS
Seattle, WA

Tuition & fees: $21,200	Average undergraduate aid package: $10,240

ABOUT THE INSTITUTION Independent, coed. Awards: bachelor's degrees. 15 undergraduate majors. Total enrollment: 696. Undergraduates: 696. Freshmen: 128. Federal methodology is used as a basis for awarding need-based institutional aid.

UNDERGRADUATE EXPENSES for 2005–06 *Application fee:* $35. *Tuition:* full-time $20,900; part-time $875 per credit.

FRESHMAN FINANCIAL AID (Fall 2003) 120 applied for aid; of those 89% were deemed to have need. 100% of freshmen with need received aid; of those 3% had need fully met. *Average percent of need met:* 42% (excluding resources awarded to replace EFC). *Average financial aid package:* $8638 (excluding resources awarded to replace EFC). 5% of all full-time freshmen had no need and received non-need-based gift aid.

UNDERGRADUATE FINANCIAL AID (Fall 2003) 573 applied for aid; of those 85% were deemed to have need. 100% of undergraduates with need received aid; of those 5% had need fully met. *Average percent of need met:* 51% (excluding resources awarded to replace EFC). *Average financial aid package:* $10,240 (excluding resources awarded to replace EFC). 5% of all full-time undergraduates had no need and received non-need-based gift aid.

GIFT AID (NEED-BASED) *Total amount:* $2,329,456 (36% federal, 17% state, 42% institutional, 5% external sources). *Receiving aid:* Freshmen: 39% (103); All full-time undergraduates: 56% (449). *Average award:* Freshmen: $4957; Undergraduates: $5265. *Scholarships, grants, and awards:* Federal Pell, FSEOG, state, private, college/university gift aid from institutional funds.

GIFT AID (NON-NEED-BASED) *Total amount:* $259,898 (88% institutional, 12% external sources). *Receiving aid:* Freshmen: 1; Undergraduates: 1% (8). *Scholarships, grants, and awards by category: Academic Interests/Achievement:* general academic interests/achievements. *Creative Arts/Performance:* art/fine arts, dance, music, theater/drama.

LOANS *Student loans:* $2,925,681 (85% need-based, 15% non-need-based). 83% of past graduating class borrowed through all loan programs. *Average indebtedness per student:* $23,000. *Average need-based loan:* Freshmen: $3077; Undergraduates: $4005. *Parent loans:* $1,248,025 (49% need-based, 51% non-need-based). *Programs:* FFEL (Subsidized and Unsubsidized Stafford, PLUS), Perkins, college/university.

WORK-STUDY *Federal work-study:* Total amount: $1,096,500; jobs available (averaging $4000).

APPLYING FOR FINANCIAL AID *Required financial aid forms:* FAFSA, institution's own form. *Financial aid deadline (priority):* 2/15. *Notification date:* 4/15. Students must reply by 5/1 or within 2 weeks of notification.

CONTACT Sharron Starling, Office of Admissions, Cornish College of the Arts, 1000 Lenora Street, Seattle, WA 98121, 206-726-5017 or toll-free 800-726-ARTS. *Fax:* 206-720-1011. *E-mail:* admissions@cornish.edu.

COVENANT COLLEGE
Lookout Mountain, GA

CONTACT Mrs. Carolyn Hays, Assistant Director of Student Financial Planning, Covenant College, 14049 Scenic Highway, Lookout Mountain, GA 30750, 706-820-1560 Ext. 1150 or toll-free 888-451-2683. *Fax:* 706-820-2820. *E-mail:* hays@covenant.edu.

CREIGHTON UNIVERSITY
Omaha, NE

Tuition & fees: $21,118	Average undergraduate aid package: $19,462

ABOUT THE INSTITUTION Independent Roman Catholic (Jesuit), coed. Awards: associate, bachelor's, master's, doctoral, and first professional degrees. 47 undergraduate majors. Total enrollment: 6,723. Undergraduates: 3,888. Freshmen: 972. Federal methodology is used as a basis for awarding need-based institutional aid.

UNDERGRADUATE EXPENSES for 2004–05 *Application fee:* $40. *Comprehensive fee:* $28,318 includes full-time tuition ($20,354), mandatory fees ($764), and room and board ($7200). *College room only:* $4080. Room and board charges vary according to board plan and housing facility. *Part-time tuition:* $636 per semester hour. *Part-time fees:* $126. *Payment plan:* Installment.

FRESHMAN FINANCIAL AID (Fall 2004, est.) 721 applied for aid; of those 80% were deemed to have need. 100% of freshmen with need received aid; of those 84% had need fully met. *Average percent of need met:* 88% (excluding resources awarded to replace EFC). *Average financial aid package:* $20,278 (excluding resources awarded to replace EFC). 29% of all full-time freshmen had no need and received non-need-based gift aid.

UNDERGRADUATE FINANCIAL AID (Fall 2004, est.) 2,402 applied for aid; of those 84% were deemed to have need. 99% of undergraduates with need received aid; of those 73% had need fully met. *Average percent of need met:* 63% (excluding resources awarded to replace EFC). *Average financial aid package:* $19,462 (excluding resources awarded to replace EFC). 29% of all full-time undergraduates had no need and received non-need-based gift aid.

GIFT AID (NEED-BASED) *Total amount:* $21,283,999 (11% federal, 1% state, 78% institutional, 10% external sources). *Receiving aid:* Freshmen: 59% (574); All full-time undergraduates: 57% (2,005). *Average award:* Freshmen: $12,967; Undergraduates: $10,673. *Scholarships, grants, and awards:* Federal Pell, FSEOG, state, private, college/university gift aid from institutional funds, Federal Nursing.

GIFT AID (NON-NEED-BASED) *Total amount:* $8,876,929 (93% institutional, 7% external sources). *Receiving aid:* Freshmen: 41% (395); Undergraduates: 31% (1,084). *Average Award:* Freshmen: $9339; Undergraduates: $9552. *Scholarships, grants, and awards by category: Academic Interests/Achievement:* business, education, general academic interests/achievements, military science. *Creative Arts/Performance:* art/fine arts, creative writing, debating. *Special Characteristics:* children of faculty/staff, first-generation college students, handicapped students, local/state students, members of minority groups, religious affiliation, siblings of current students. *Tuition waivers:* Full or partial for employees or children of employees, adult students. *ROTC:* Army, Air Force cooperative.

LOANS *Student loans:* $14,310,203 (92% need-based, 8% non-need-based). 64% of past graduating class borrowed through all loan programs. *Average indebtedness per student:* $23,818. *Average need-based loan:* Freshmen: $5747; Undergraduates: $7272. *Parent loans:* $4,519,158 (100% non-need-based). *Programs:* FFEL (Subsidized and Unsubsidized Stafford, PLUS), Perkins, Federal Nursing, college/university.

WORK-STUDY *Federal work-study:* Total amount: $1,469,364; 657 jobs averaging $1815.

ATHLETIC AWARDS *Total amount:* $2,650,191 (36% need-based, 64% non-need-based).

APPLYING FOR FINANCIAL AID *Required financial aid forms:* FAFSA, institution's own form. *Financial aid deadline (priority):* 5/15. *Notification date:* Continuous. Students must reply within 4 weeks of notification.

CONTACT Sarah Sell, Assistant Director of Financial Aid, Creighton University, 2500 California Plaza, Omaha, NE 68178, 402-280-2731 or toll-free 800-282-5835. *Fax:* 402-280-2895. *E-mail:* sarahsell@creighton.edu.

CRICHTON COLLEGE
Memphis, TN

ABOUT THE INSTITUTION Independent, coed. Awards: bachelor's degrees and post-bachelor's certificates. 22 undergraduate majors. Total enrollment: 969. Undergraduates: 969. Freshmen: 52.

GIFT AID (NEED-BASED) *Scholarships, grants, and awards:* Federal Pell, FSEOG, state, private, college/university gift aid from institutional funds.

GIFT AID (NON-NEED-BASED) *Scholarships, grants, and awards by category: Academic Interests/Achievement:* biological sciences, business, education, English, general academic interests/achievements, humanities, physical sciences, religion/biblical studies, social sciences. *Creative Arts/Performance:* music, theater/drama. *Special Achievements/Activities:* general special achievements/activities, leadership. *Special Characteristics:* children and siblings of alumni, children of faculty/staff, general special characteristics, international students, relatives of clergy, religious affiliation.

LOANS *Programs:* Federal Direct (Subsidized and Unsubsidized Stafford, PLUS), Perkins, state, college/university.

APPLYING FOR FINANCIAL AID *Required financial aid forms:* FAFSA, institution's own form.

CONTACT Mrs. Dede Pirtle, Financial Aid Director, Crichton College, 255 North Highland, Memphis, TN 38111, 901-320-9700 Ext. 1030 or toll-free 800-960-9777. *Fax:* 901-320-9709. *E-mail:* dede@crichton.edu.

THE CRISWELL COLLEGE
Dallas, TX

ABOUT THE INSTITUTION Independent religious, coed. Awards: associate, bachelor's, master's, and first professional degrees. 5 undergraduate majors. Total enrollment: 451. Undergraduates: 336.

GIFT AID (NEED-BASED) *Scholarships, grants, and awards:* private, college/university gift aid from institutional funds.

GIFT AID (NON-NEED-BASED) *Scholarships, grants, and awards by category: Academic Interests/Achievement:* general academic interests/achievements. *Special Achievements/Activities:* religious involvement.

LOANS *Programs:* college/university.

APPLYING FOR FINANCIAL AID *Required financial aid form:* institution's own form.

CONTACT Kirk Spencer, Financial Aid Director, The Criswell College, 4010 Gaston Avenue, Dallas, TX 75246, 800-899-0012. *Fax:* 214-818-1310. *E-mail:* kspencer@criswell.edu.

CROSSROADS BIBLE COLLEGE
Indianapolis, IN

CONTACT Mrs. Phyllis Dodson, Director of Financial Aid, Crossroads Bible College, 601 North Shortridge Road, Indianapolis, IN 46219, 317-352-8736 Ext. 28 or toll-free 800-273-2224 Ext. 230. *Fax:* 317-352-9145.

CROSSROADS COLLEGE
Rochester, MN

ABOUT THE INSTITUTION Independent religious, coed. Awards: associate and bachelor's degrees. 9 undergraduate majors. Total enrollment: 149. Undergraduates: 149. Freshmen: 34.

GIFT AID (NEED-BASED) *Scholarships, grants, and awards:* Federal Pell, FSEOG, state, private, college/university gift aid from institutional funds.

GIFT AID (NON-NEED-BASED) *Scholarships, grants, and awards by category: Academic Interests/Achievement:* general academic interests/achievements, religion/biblical studies. *Special Achievements/Activities:* general special achievements/activities, religious involvement. *Special Characteristics:* children of faculty/staff, general special characteristics, international students, parents of current students, religious affiliation, siblings of current students, spouses of current students.

LOANS *Programs:* FFEL (Subsidized and Unsubsidized Stafford, PLUS), state, college/university.

APPLYING FOR FINANCIAL AID *Required financial aid forms:* FAFSA, institution's own form.

CONTACT Polly Kellogg-Bradley, Director of Financial Aid, Crossroads College, 920 Mayowood Road SW, Rochester, MN 55902-2275, 507-535-3308 or toll-free 800-456-7651. *Fax:* 507-288-9046. *E-mail:* pkellogbradley@crossroadscollege.edu.

CROWN COLLEGE
St. Bonifacius, MN

Tuition & fees: $15,646 | **Average undergraduate aid package: $11,008**

ABOUT THE INSTITUTION Independent religious, coed. Awards: associate, bachelor's, and master's degrees. 29 undergraduate majors. Total enrollment: 1,106. Undergraduates: 1,047. Freshmen: 140. Both federal and institutional methodology are used as a basis for awarding need-based institutional aid.
UNDERGRADUATE EXPENSES for 2005–06 *Application fee:* $35. *Comprehensive fee:* $22,218 includes full-time tuition ($15,646) and room and board ($6572). *College room only:* $3208. Room and board charges vary according to board plan. *Part-time tuition:* $654 per credit. Part-time tuition and fees vary according to course load. *Payment plan:* Installment.
FRESHMAN FINANCIAL AID (Fall 2004, est.) 118 applied for aid; of those 93% were deemed to have need. 98% of freshmen with need received aid; of those 11% had need fully met. *Average percent of need met:* 53% (excluding resources awarded to replace EFC). *Average financial aid package:* $13,607 (excluding resources awarded to replace EFC). 5% of all full-time freshmen had no need and received non-need-based gift aid.
UNDERGRADUATE FINANCIAL AID (Fall 2004, est.) 548 applied for aid; of those 92% were deemed to have need. 99% of undergraduates with need received aid; of those 7% had need fully met. *Average percent of need met:* 64% (excluding resources awarded to replace EFC). *Average financial aid package:* $11,008 (excluding resources awarded to replace EFC). 3% of all full-time undergraduates had no need and received non-need-based gift aid.
GIFT AID (NEED-BASED) *Total amount:* $2,243,848 (34% federal, 28% state, 38% institutional). *Receiving aid:* Freshmen: 71% (84); All full-time undergraduates: 50% (373). *Average award:* Freshmen: $4952; Undergraduates: $4483. *Scholarships, grants, and awards:* Federal Pell, FSEOG, state, private, college/university gift aid from institutional funds.
GIFT AID (NON-NEED-BASED) *Total amount:* $1,023,507 (82% institutional, 18% external sources). *Receiving aid:* Freshmen: 75% (89); Undergraduates: 54% (408). *Average Award:* Freshmen: $1679; Undergraduates: $1106. *Scholarships, grants, and awards by category:* Academic Interests/Achievement: general academic interests/achievements. Creative Arts/Performance: 10 awards ($11,230 total): music. Special Achievements/Activities: 38 awards ($150,624 total): leadership. Special Characteristics: 80 awards ($406,967 total): children of faculty/staff, international students, relatives of clergy. *Tuition waivers:* Full or partial for employees or children of employees.
LOANS *Student loans:* $3,951,459 (43% need-based, 57% non-need-based). 85% of past graduating class borrowed through all loan programs. *Average indebtedness per student:* $25,084. *Average need-based loan:* Freshmen: $2605; Undergraduates: $4130. *Parent loans:* $423,292 (100% non-need-based). *Programs:* FFEL (Subsidized and Unsubsidized Stafford, PLUS), Perkins, state, SELF Loans, CitiAssist Loans, Signature Loans, Bremer Education Loans, U.S. Bank No Fee Educational Loans.
WORK-STUDY *Federal work-study:* Total amount: $293,566; 145 jobs averaging $2025. *State or other work-study/employment:* Total amount: $27,310 (100% need-based). 12 part-time jobs averaging $2276.
APPLYING FOR FINANCIAL AID *Required financial aid forms:* FAFSA, institution's own form. *Financial aid deadline (priority):* 4/1. *Notification date:* Continuous beginning 4/2. Students must reply within 4 weeks of notification.
CONTACT Cheryl Fernandez, Director of Financial Aid, Crown College, 8700 College View Drive, St. Bonifacius, MN 55375-9001, 952-446-4177 or toll-free 800-68-CROWN. *Fax:* 952-446-4178. *E-mail:* finlaid@crown.edu.

THE CULINARY INSTITUTE OF AMERICA
Hyde Park, NY

Tuition & fees: $18,795 | **Average undergraduate aid package: $10,663**

ABOUT THE INSTITUTION Independent, coed. Awards: associate and bachelor's degrees. 3 undergraduate majors. Total enrollment: 2,409. Undergraduates: 2,409. Freshmen: 618. Federal methodology is used as a basis for awarding need-based institutional aid.

UNDERGRADUATE EXPENSES for 2004–05 *Application fee:* $30. *Comprehensive fee:* $25,305 includes full-time tuition ($18,620), mandatory fees ($175), and room and board ($6510). Full-time tuition and fees vary according to degree level. *Payment plan:* Installment.
UNDERGRADUATE FINANCIAL AID (Fall 2003) 2,100 applied for aid; of those 93% were deemed to have need. 100% of undergraduates with need received aid; of those 1% had need fully met. *Average percent of need met:* 50% (excluding resources awarded to replace EFC). *Average financial aid package:* $10,663 (excluding resources awarded to replace EFC). 4% of all full-time undergraduates had no need and received non-need-based gift aid.
GIFT AID (NEED-BASED) *Total amount:* $10,404,098 (28% federal, 7% state, 62% institutional, 3% external sources). *Receiving aid:* All full-time undergraduates: 41% (1,000). *Average award:* Undergraduates: $2000. *Scholarships, grants, and awards:* Federal Pell, FSEOG, state, private, college/university gift aid from institutional funds.
GIFT AID (NON-NEED-BASED) *Total amount:* $2,157,126 (6% federal, 1% state, 93% institutional). *Receiving aid:* Undergraduates: 41% (1,000). *Average Award:* Undergraduates: $3000. *Scholarships, grants, and awards by category:* Academic Interests/Achievement: 513 awards ($1,000,000 total): general academic interests/achievements. Creative Arts/Performance: 11 awards ($75,000 total): general creative arts/performance. Special Achievements/Activities: 10 awards ($50,000 total): general special achievements/activities. Special Characteristics: children and siblings of alumni, children of faculty/staff, general special characteristics, handicapped students, international students, members of minority groups. *Tuition waivers:* Full or partial for employees or children of employees.
LOANS *Student loans:* $27,041,669 (85% need-based, 15% non-need-based). 86% of past graduating class borrowed through all loan programs. *Average indebtedness per student:* $18,000. *Average need-based loan:* Undergraduates: $4563. *Parent loans:* $5,349,033 (100% non-need-based). *Programs:* FFEL (Subsidized and Unsubsidized Stafford, PLUS), Perkins, alternative loans.
WORK-STUDY *Federal work-study:* Total amount: $632,719; 829 jobs averaging $764.
APPLYING FOR FINANCIAL AID *Required financial aid form:* FAFSA. *Financial aid deadline:* 2/15. *Notification date:* Continuous beginning 4/15. Students must reply within 2 weeks of notification.
CONTACT Patricia A. Arcuri, Director of Financial Aid, The Culinary Institute of America, 1946 Campus Drive, Hyde Park, NY 12538-1499, 845-451-1243 or toll-free 800-CULINARY. *Fax:* 845-905-4030. *E-mail:* p_arcuri@culinary.edu.

CULVER-STOCKTON COLLEGE
Canton, MO

Tuition & fees: $13,390 | **Average undergraduate aid package: $12,408**

ABOUT THE INSTITUTION Independent religious, coed. Awards: bachelor's degrees. 32 undergraduate majors. Total enrollment: 855. Undergraduates: 855. Freshmen: 182. Federal methodology is used as a basis for awarding need-based institutional aid.
UNDERGRADUATE EXPENSES for 2004–05 *Application fee:* $25. *Comprehensive fee:* $19,165 includes full-time tuition ($13,200), mandatory fees ($190), and room and board ($5775). *College room only:* $2675. Room and board charges vary according to board plan. *Part-time tuition:* $360 per credit hour. *Part-time fees:* $8 per credit hour. *Payment plan:* Installment.
FRESHMAN FINANCIAL AID (Fall 2004, est.) 183 applied for aid; of those 88% were deemed to have need. 100% of freshmen with need received aid; of those 20% had need fully met. *Average percent of need met:* 74% (excluding resources awarded to replace EFC). *Average financial aid package:* $11,865 (excluding resources awarded to replace EFC). 12% of all full-time freshmen had no need and received non-need-based gift aid.
UNDERGRADUATE FINANCIAL AID (Fall 2004, est.) 732 applied for aid; of those 87% were deemed to have need. 100% of undergraduates with need received aid; of those 25% had need fully met. *Average percent of need met:* 77% (excluding resources awarded to replace EFC). *Average financial aid package:* $12,408 (excluding resources awarded to replace EFC). 12% of all full-time undergraduates had no need and received non-need-based gift aid.
GIFT AID (NEED-BASED) *Total amount:* $4,801,254 (20% federal, 7% state, 71% institutional, 2% external sources). *Receiving aid:* Freshmen: 88% (161); All full-time undergraduates: 87% (638). *Average award:* Freshmen: $9100; Undergraduates: $8822. *Scholarships, grants, and awards:* Federal Pell, FSEOG, state, private, college/university gift aid from institutional funds.

Culver-Stockton College

GIFT AID (NON-NEED-BASED) *Total amount:* $738,321 (2% state, 88% institutional, 10% external sources). *Receiving aid:* Freshmen: 15% (27); Undergraduates: 12% (85). *Average Award:* Freshmen: $12,135; *Undergraduates:* $10,998. *Scholarships, grants, and awards by category:* Academic *Interests/Achievement:* 443 awards ($2,105,542 total): business, general academic interests/achievements, international studies. *Creative Arts/Performance:* 218 awards ($316,780 total): art/fine arts, debating, music, theater/drama. *Special Achievements/Activities:* 26 awards ($13,500 total): cheerleading/drum major, leadership. *Special Characteristics:* 235 awards ($505,753 total): children and siblings of alumni, children of faculty/staff, international students, local/state students, relatives of clergy, religious affiliation. *Tuition waivers:* Full or partial for employees or children of employees, senior citizens.
LOANS *Student loans:* $4,113,343 (73% need-based, 27% non-need-based). 96% of past graduating class borrowed through all loan programs. *Average indebtedness per student:* $17,749. *Average need-based loan:* Freshmen: $3027; Undergraduates: $3841. *Parent loans:* $1,367,597 (39% need-based, 61% non-need-based). *Programs:* Federal Direct (Subsidized and Unsubsidized Stafford, PLUS), Perkins, Federal Nursing, state, college/university.
WORK-STUDY *Federal work-study:* Total amount: $110,956; 119 jobs averaging $932. *State or other work-study/employment:* Total amount: $204,738 (32% need-based, 68% non-need-based). 172 part-time jobs averaging $1190.
ATHLETIC AWARDS *Total amount:* $913,963 (78% need-based, 22% non-need-based).
APPLYING FOR FINANCIAL AID *Required financial aid form:* FAFSA. *Financial aid deadline:* 6/15. *Notification date:* Continuous beginning 2/15. Students must reply within 2 weeks of notification.
CONTACT Ms. Tina M. Wiseman, Director of Financial Aid, Culver-Stockton College, One College Hill, Canton, MO 63435, 573-288-6306 Ext. 6307 or toll-free 800-537-1883. *Fax:* 573-288-6618. *E-mail:* twiseman@culver.edu.

CUMBERLAND COLLEGE
Williamsburg, KY

See University of the Cumberlands.

CUMBERLAND UNIVERSITY
Lebanon, TN

CONTACT Mr. Larry Vaughan, Director of Financial Aid, Cumberland University, One Cumberland Square, Lebanon, TN 37087-3554, 615-444-2562 Ext. 1222 or toll-free 800-467-0562. *Fax:* 615-443-8424. *E-mail:* lvaughan@cumberland.edu.

CURRY COLLEGE
Milton, MA

Tuition & fees: $21,670	Average undergraduate aid package: $14,549

ABOUT THE INSTITUTION Independent, coed. Awards: bachelor's and master's degrees. 27 undergraduate majors. Total enrollment: 2,877. Undergraduates: 2,695. Freshmen: 534. Federal methodology is used as a basis for awarding need-based institutional aid.
UNDERGRADUATE EXPENSES for 2004–05 *Application fee:* $40. *Comprehensive fee:* $29,850 includes full-time tuition ($20,860), mandatory fees ($810), and room and board ($8180). *College room only:* $4620. Room and board charges vary according to board plan. *Part-time tuition:* $695 per credit. *Payment plan:* Installment.
FRESHMAN FINANCIAL AID (Fall 2004, est.) 392 applied for aid; of those 99% were deemed to have need. 100% of freshmen with need received aid; of those 2% had need fully met. *Average percent of need met:* 67% (excluding resources awarded to replace EFC). *Average financial aid package:* $15,036 (excluding resources awarded to replace EFC). 2% of all full-time freshmen had no need and received non-need-based gift aid.
UNDERGRADUATE FINANCIAL AID (Fall 2004, est.) 1,266 applied for aid; of those 99% were deemed to have need. 100% of undergraduates with need received aid; of those 6% had need fully met. *Average percent of need met:* 68% (excluding resources awarded to replace EFC). *Average financial aid package:* $14,549 (excluding resources awarded to replace EFC). 2% of all full-time undergraduates had no need and received non-need-based gift aid.
GIFT AID (NEED-BASED) *Total amount:* $12,105,079 (12% federal, 6% state, 80% institutional, 2% external sources). *Receiving aid:* Freshmen: 70% (374); All full-time undergraduates: 59% (1,104). *Average award:* Freshmen: $10,839;

Undergraduates: $9998. *Scholarships, grants, and awards:* Federal Pell, FSEOG, state, private, college/university gift aid from institutional funds.
GIFT AID (NON-NEED-BASED) *Total amount:* $668,467 (21% institutional, 79% external sources). *Receiving aid:* Freshmen: 1% (3); Undergraduates: 1% (17). *Average Award:* Freshmen: $3510; *Undergraduates:* $4231. *Scholarships, grants, and awards by category:* Academic Interests/Achievement: 122 awards ($562,800 total): general academic interests/achievements. *Tuition waivers:* Full or partial for children of alumni, employees or children of employees, senior citizens. *ROTC:* Army cooperative.
LOANS *Student loans:* $12,138,001 (41% need-based, 59% non-need-based). 52% of past graduating class borrowed through all loan programs. *Average indebtedness per student:* $22,159. *Average need-based loan:* Freshmen: $2668; Undergraduates: $3806. *Parent loans:* $5,786,804 (100% non-need-based). *Programs:* FFEL (Subsidized and Unsubsidized Stafford, PLUS), Perkins, state.
WORK-STUDY *Federal work-study:* Total amount: $926,869; 797 jobs averaging $1163. *State or other work-study/employment:* Total amount: $5000 (100% non-need-based). 4 part-time jobs averaging $1250.
APPLYING FOR FINANCIAL AID *Required financial aid form:* FAFSA. *Financial aid deadline (priority):* 3/1. *Notification date:* Continuous beginning 3/1. Students must reply by 5/1.
CONTACT Jamey Palmieri, Director of Financial Aid, Curry College, 1071 Blue Hill Avenue, Milton, MA 02186-2395, 617-333-2146 or toll-free 800-669-0686. *Fax:* 617-333-2915.

THE CURTIS INSTITUTE OF MUSIC
Philadelphia, PA

Tuition & fees: $1650	Average undergraduate aid package: $10,841

ABOUT THE INSTITUTION Independent, coed. Awards: bachelor's and master's degrees. 5 undergraduate majors. Total enrollment: 160. Undergraduates: 144. Both federal and institutional methodology are used as a basis for awarding need-based institutional aid.
UNDERGRADUATE EXPENSES for 2004–05 *Application fee:* $60. *Tuition:* full-time $0.
FRESHMAN FINANCIAL AID (Fall 2004, est.) 9 applied for aid; of those 100% were deemed to have need. 100% of freshmen with need received aid; of those 22% had need fully met. *Average percent of need met:* 79% (excluding resources awarded to replace EFC). *Average financial aid package:* $9162 (excluding resources awarded to replace EFC).
UNDERGRADUATE FINANCIAL AID (Fall 2004, est.) 70 applied for aid; of those 100% were deemed to have need. 100% of undergraduates with need received aid; of those 36% had need fully met. *Average percent of need met:* 91% (excluding resources awarded to replace EFC). *Average financial aid package:* $10,841 (excluding resources awarded to replace EFC).
GIFT AID (NEED-BASED) *Total amount:* $358,024 (8% federal, 88% institutional, 4% external sources). *Receiving aid:* Freshmen: 43% (6); All full-time undergraduates: 67% (51). *Average award:* Freshmen: $5435; Undergraduates: $6143. *Scholarships, grants, and awards:* Federal Pell, state, college/university gift aid from institutional funds.
GIFT AID (NON-NEED-BASED) *Scholarships, grants, and awards by category:* Creative Arts/Performance: music.
LOANS *Student loans:* $269,625 (100% need-based). 52% of past graduating class borrowed through all loan programs. *Average indebtedness per student:* $13,202. *Average need-based loan:* Freshmen: $2625; Undergraduates: $3852. *Parent loans:* $5578 (100% need-based). *Programs:* FFEL (Subsidized and Unsubsidized Stafford, PLUS), TERI Loans.
WORK-STUDY *State or other work-study/employment:* Total amount: $131,250 (100% need-based). 63 part-time jobs averaging $2083.
APPLYING FOR FINANCIAL AID *Required financial aid forms:* FAFSA, institution's own form, CSS Financial Aid PROFILE, bank statements, tax returns. *Financial aid deadline:* 3/1. *Notification date:* 4/1. Students must reply by 5/1.
CONTACT Janice Miller, Director of Student Financial Assistance, The Curtis Institute of Music, 1726 Locust Street, Philadelphia, PA 19103-6107, 215-893-5252. *E-mail:* janice.miller@curtis.edu.

DAEMEN COLLEGE
Amherst, NY

Tuition & fees: $16,020	Average undergraduate aid package: $13,742

ABOUT THE INSTITUTION Independent, coed. Awards: bachelor's, master's, and first professional degrees and post-bachelor's and post-master's certificates. 33 undergraduate majors. Total enrollment: 2,186. Undergraduates: 1,594. Freshmen: 265. Federal methodology is used as a basis for awarding need-based institutional aid.

UNDERGRADUATE EXPENSES for 2004–05 *Application fee:* $25. *Comprehensive fee:* $23,390 includes full-time tuition ($15,570), mandatory fees ($450), and room and board ($7370). Room and board charges vary according to board plan and housing facility. *Part-time tuition:* $520 per credit. *Part-time fees:* $4 per credit; $68 per term. Part-time tuition and fees vary according to course load. *Payment plans:* Installment, deferred payment.

FRESHMAN FINANCIAL AID (Fall 2003) 352 applied for aid; of those 94% were deemed to have need. 100% of freshmen with need received aid; of those 26% had need fully met. *Average percent of need met:* 93% (excluding resources awarded to replace EFC). *Average financial aid package:* $14,621 (excluding resources awarded to replace EFC). 5% of all full-time freshmen had no need and received non-need-based gift aid.

UNDERGRADUATE FINANCIAL AID (Fall 2003) 1,326 applied for aid; of those 92% were deemed to have need. 100% of undergraduates with need received aid; of those 27% had need fully met. *Average percent of need met:* 90% (excluding resources awarded to replace EFC). *Average financial aid package:* $13,742 (excluding resources awarded to replace EFC). 7% of all full-time undergraduates had no need and received non-need-based gift aid.

GIFT AID (NEED-BASED) *Total amount:* $7,384,025 (24% federal, 34% state, 42% institutional). *Receiving aid:* Freshmen: 86% (304); All full-time undergraduates: 79% (1,113). *Average award:* Freshmen: $7401; Undergraduates: $6414. *Scholarships, grants, and awards:* Federal Pell, FSEOG, state, private, college/university gift aid from institutional funds.

GIFT AID (NON-NEED-BASED) *Total amount:* $5,195,417 (1% state, 99% institutional). *Receiving aid:* Freshmen: 69% (245); Undergraduates: 65% (917). *Average Award:* *Freshmen:* $5555; *Undergraduates:* $5849. *Scholarships, grants, and awards by category:* Academic Interests/Achievement: 881 awards ($4,057,941 total): general academic interests/achievements. Creative Arts/Performance: 1 award ($5000 total): art/fine arts. Special Characteristics: 54 awards ($472,115 total): children and siblings of alumni, children of faculty/staff, general special characteristics, siblings of current students. *Tuition waivers:* Full or partial for employees or children of employees, senior citizens. *ROTC:* Army cooperative.

LOANS *Student loans:* $7,354,831 (94% need-based, 6% non-need-based). 74% of past graduating class borrowed through all loan programs. *Average indebtedness per student:* $13,024. *Average need-based loan:* Freshmen: $3288; Undergraduates: $4061. *Parent loans:* $974,236 (91% need-based, 9% non-need-based). *Programs:* FFEL (Subsidized and Unsubsidized Stafford, PLUS), Perkins, college/university, alternative loans.

WORK-STUDY *Federal work-study:* Total amount: $1,077,082; 304 jobs averaging $1013. *State or other work-study/employment:* Total amount: $30,700 (76% need-based, 24% non-need-based). 20 part-time jobs averaging $1235.

ATHLETIC AWARDS *Total amount:* $492,787 (80% need-based, 20% non-need-based).

APPLYING FOR FINANCIAL AID *Required financial aid forms:* FAFSA, state aid form. *Financial aid deadline (priority):* 2/15. *Notification date:* Continuous. Students must reply within 2 weeks of notification.

CONTACT Jeffrey Pagano, Director of Financial Aid, Daemen College, 4380 Main Street, Amherst, NY 14226-3592, 716-839-8254 or toll-free 800-462-7652. *Fax:* 716-839-8378. *E-mail:* jpagano@daemen.edu.

DAKOTA STATE UNIVERSITY
Madison, SD

Tuition & fees (SD res): $4614	Average undergraduate aid package: $6117

ABOUT THE INSTITUTION State-supported, coed. Awards: associate, bachelor's, and master's degrees. 35 undergraduate majors. Total enrollment: 2,282. Undergraduates: 2,065. Freshmen: 275. Federal methodology is used as a basis for awarding need-based institutional aid.

UNDERGRADUATE EXPENSES for 2004–05 *Application fee:* $20. *Tuition, state resident:* full-time $4614; part-time $154 per credit hour. *Tuition, nonresident:* full-time $9657; part-time $315 per credit hour. Full-time tuition and fees vary according to course load, location, and reciprocity agreements. Part-time tuition and fees vary according to course load, location, and reciprocity agreements. *College room and board:* $3,192. Room and board charges vary according to board plan. *Payment plans:* Installment, deferred payment.

FRESHMAN FINANCIAL AID (Fall 2003) 276 applied for aid; of those 80% were deemed to have need. 98% of freshmen with need received aid; of those 29% had need fully met. *Average percent of need met:* 78% (excluding resources awarded to replace EFC). *Average financial aid package:* $5373 (excluding resources awarded to replace EFC). 16% of all full-time freshmen had no need and received non-need-based gift aid.

UNDERGRADUATE FINANCIAL AID (Fall 2003) 1,131 applied for aid; of those 81% were deemed to have need. 99% of undergraduates with need received aid; of those 33% had need fully met. *Average percent of need met:* 82% (excluding resources awarded to replace EFC). *Average financial aid package:* $6117 (excluding resources awarded to replace EFC). 16% of all full-time undergraduates had no need and received non-need-based gift aid.

GIFT AID (NEED-BASED) *Total amount:* $1,899,687 (84% federal, 6% institutional, 10% external sources). *Receiving aid:* Freshmen: 39% (116); All full-time undergraduates: 38% (495). *Average award:* Freshmen: $2764; Undergraduates: $2890. *Scholarships, grants, and awards:* Federal Pell, FSEOG, state, private, college/university gift aid from institutional funds.

GIFT AID (NON-NEED-BASED) *Total amount:* $119,423 (38% institutional, 62% external sources). *Receiving aid:* Freshmen: 38% (111); Undergraduates: 24% (316). *Average Award:* Freshmen: $3663; Undergraduates: $5028. *Scholarships, grants, and awards by category:* Academic Interests/Achievement: business, communication, computer science, education, English, general academic interests/achievements, mathematics. Creative Arts/Performance: music. Special Achievements/Activities: general special achievements/activities. Special Characteristics: children and siblings of alumni, ethnic background, local/state students, members of minority groups. *ROTC:* Air Force cooperative.

LOANS *Student loans:* $6,375,228 (71% need-based, 29% non-need-based). 84% of past graduating class borrowed through all loan programs. *Average indebtedness per student:* $22,352. *Average need-based loan:* Freshmen: $2953; Undergraduates: $4602. *Parent loans:* $359,284 (71% need-based, 29% non-need-based). *Programs:* FFEL (Subsidized and Unsubsidized Stafford, PLUS), Perkins, alternative loans.

WORK-STUDY *Federal work-study:* Total amount: $340,453; 180 jobs averaging $1900. *State or other work-study/employment:* Total amount: $302,920 (100% non-need-based). 169 part-time jobs averaging $1733.

ATHLETIC AWARDS *Total amount:* $127,120 (71% need-based, 29% non-need-based).

APPLYING FOR FINANCIAL AID *Required financial aid form:* FAFSA. *Financial aid deadline (priority):* 3/1. *Notification date:* Continuous beginning 4/10. Students must reply within 2 weeks of notification.

CONTACT Ms. Rose M. Jamison, Financial Aid Director, Dakota State University, 103 Heston Hall, 820 North Washington Avenue, Madison, SD 57042-1799, 605-256-5158 or toll-free 888-DSU-9988. *Fax:* 605-256-5316. *E-mail:* dsuinfo@pluto.dsu.edu.

DAKOTA WESLEYAN UNIVERSITY
Mitchell, SD

ABOUT THE INSTITUTION Independent United Methodist, coed. Awards: associate, bachelor's, and master's degrees. 42 undergraduate majors. Total enrollment: 681. Undergraduates: 654. Freshmen: 136.

GIFT AID (NEED-BASED) *Scholarships, grants, and awards:* Federal Pell, FSEOG, private, college/university gift aid from institutional funds, Federal Nursing.

GIFT AID (NON-NEED-BASED) *Scholarships, grants, and awards by category:* Academic Interests/Achievement: biological sciences, business, communication, education, English, general academic interests/achievements, health fields, international studies, library science, religion/biblical studies. Creative Arts/Performance: art/fine arts, debating, journalism/publications, music, theater/drama. Special Achievements/Activities: cheerleading/drum major, leadership, memberships, religious involvement, rodeo. Special Characteristics: children and siblings of alumni, ethnic background, relatives of clergy, religious affiliation, siblings of current students.

LOANS *Programs:* FFEL (Subsidized and Unsubsidized Stafford, PLUS), Perkins, Methodist Loans (for members of Methodist Church), Alternative Loans.

WORK-STUDY *Federal work-study:* Total amount: $104,099; 80 jobs averaging $1307. *State or other work-study/employment:* Total amount: $293,816 (98% need-based, 2% non-need-based). 134 part-time jobs averaging $1307.

APPLYING FOR FINANCIAL AID *Required financial aid form:* FAFSA.

CONTACT Marci Farmer, Administrative Assistant for Academic Affairs, Dakota Wesleyan University, 1200 West University Avenue, Mitchell, SD 57301-4398, 605-995-2645 or toll-free 800-333-8506. *Fax:* 605-995-2643. *E-mail:* @dwu.edu.

DALLAS BAPTIST UNIVERSITY
Dallas, TX

Tuition & fees: $11,610	Average undergraduate aid package: $9725

ABOUT THE INSTITUTION Independent religious, coed. Awards: associate, bachelor's, and master's degrees and post-bachelor's certificates. 39 undergraduate majors. Total enrollment: 4,714. Undergraduates: 3,541. Freshmen: 325. Federal methodology is used as a basis for awarding need-based institutional aid.

UNDERGRADUATE EXPENSES for 2004–05 *Application fee:* $25. *Comprehensive fee:* $16,254 includes full-time tuition ($11,610) and room and board ($4644). *College room only:* $1830. Room and board charges vary according to board plan and housing facility. *Part-time tuition:* $387 per credit hour. *Payment plan:* Installment.

FRESHMAN FINANCIAL AID (Fall 2004, est.) 300 applied for aid; of those 69% were deemed to have need. 100% of freshmen with need received aid; of those 57% had need fully met. *Average percent of need met:* 79% (excluding resources awarded to replace EFC). *Average financial aid package:* $10,051 (excluding resources awarded to replace EFC). 26% of all full-time freshmen had no need and received non-need-based gift aid.

UNDERGRADUATE FINANCIAL AID (Fall 2004, est.) 1,651 applied for aid; of those 73% were deemed to have need. 99% of undergraduates with need received aid; of those 40% had need fully met. *Average percent of need met:* 75% (excluding resources awarded to replace EFC). *Average financial aid package:* $9725 (excluding resources awarded to replace EFC). 19% of all full-time undergraduates had no need and received non-need-based gift aid.

GIFT AID (NEED-BASED) *Total amount:* $3,998,776 (57% federal, 43% state). *Receiving aid:* Freshmen: 43% (139); All full-time undergraduates: 43% (854). *Average award:* Freshmen: $2226; Undergraduates: $2460. *Scholarships, grants, and awards:* Federal Pell, FSEOG, state, private, college/university gift aid from institutional funds.

GIFT AID (NON-NEED-BASED) *Total amount:* $5,806,741 (87% institutional, 13% external sources). *Receiving aid:* Freshmen: 58% (188); Undergraduates: 44% (886). *Average Award:* Freshmen: $9787; Undergraduates: $8589. *Scholarships, grants, and awards by category:* Academic Interests/Achievement: 1,147 awards ($2,322,035 total): business, communication, computer science, education, general academic interests/achievements, humanities, mathematics, premedicine, religion/biblical studies. Creative Arts/Performance: 69 awards ($183,175 total): music. Special Achievements/Activities: 998 awards ($2,051,550 total): community service, general special achievements/activities, leadership, memberships, religious involvement. Special Characteristics: 214 awards ($629,476 total): children of faculty/staff, general special characteristics, relatives of clergy, religious affiliation. *Tuition waivers:* Full or partial for employees or children of employees. *ROTC:* Army cooperative, Air Force cooperative.

LOANS *Student loans:* $12,920,882 (43% need-based, 57% non-need-based). 51% of past graduating class borrowed through all loan programs. *Average indebtedness per student:* $8268. *Average need-based loan:* Freshmen: $2293; Undergraduates: $3337. *Parent loans:* $1,917,939 (100% non-need-based). *Programs:* FFEL (Subsidized and Unsubsidized Stafford, PLUS), Perkins, state, college/university.

WORK-STUDY *Federal work-study:* Total amount: $294,531; 139 jobs averaging $2604. *State or other work-study/employment:* Total amount: $32,877 (100% need-based). 30 part-time jobs averaging $1095.

ATHLETIC AWARDS *Total amount:* $595,857 (100% non-need-based).

APPLYING FOR FINANCIAL AID *Required financial aid forms:* FAFSA, institution's own form. *Financial aid deadline:* 5/1 (priority: 3/15). *Notification date:* Continuous.

CONTACT Mr. Donald Zackary, Director of Financial Aid, Dallas Baptist University, 3000 Mountain Creek Parkway, Dallas, TX 75211-9299, 214-333-5363 or toll-free 800-460-1328. *Fax:* 214-333-5586. *E-mail:* donz@dbu.edu.

DALLAS CHRISTIAN COLLEGE
Dallas, TX

Tuition & fees: $7937	Average undergraduate aid package: $7396

ABOUT THE INSTITUTION Independent religious, coed. Awards: bachelor's degrees and post-bachelor's certificates. 3 undergraduate majors. Total enrollment: 366. Undergraduates: 366. Freshmen: 52. Federal methodology is used as a basis for awarding need-based institutional aid.

UNDERGRADUATE EXPENSES for 2004–05 *Application fee:* $30. *Comprehensive fee:* $13,037 includes full-time tuition ($7232), mandatory fees ($705), and room and board ($5100). *College room only:* $2900. Full-time tuition and fees vary according to course load. Room and board charges vary according to housing facility. *Part-time tuition:* $226 per credit hour. Part-time tuition and fees vary according to course load. *Payment plan:* Installment.

FRESHMAN FINANCIAL AID (Fall 2004, est.) 57 applied for aid; of those 70% were deemed to have need. 100% of freshmen with need received aid. *Average percent of need met:* 52% (excluding resources awarded to replace EFC). *Average financial aid package:* $6973 (excluding resources awarded to replace EFC). 25% of all full-time freshmen had no need and received non-need-based gift aid.

UNDERGRADUATE FINANCIAL AID (Fall 2004, est.) 242 applied for aid; of those 70% were deemed to have need. 100% of undergraduates with need received aid. *Average percent of need met:* 43% (excluding resources awarded to replace EFC). *Average financial aid package:* $7396 (excluding resources awarded to replace EFC). 17% of all full-time undergraduates had no need and received non-need-based gift aid.

GIFT AID (NEED-BASED) *Total amount:* $370,299 (86% federal, 14% institutional). *Receiving aid:* Freshmen: 43% (30); All full-time undergraduates: 40% (112). *Average award:* Freshmen: $3145; Undergraduates: $1554. *Scholarships, grants, and awards:* Federal Pell, FSEOG, private, college/university gift aid from institutional funds.

GIFT AID (NON-NEED-BASED) *Total amount:* $420,453 (68% institutional, 32% external sources). *Receiving aid:* Freshmen: 46% (32); Undergraduates: 34% (97). *Average Award:* Freshmen: $1212; Undergraduates: $2195. *Scholarships, grants, and awards by category:* Academic Interests/Achievement: 60 awards ($154,697 total): education, general academic interests/achievements, religion/biblical studies. Creative Arts/Performance: 20 awards ($8000 total): music. Special Achievements/Activities: 45 awards ($43,797 total): general special achievements/activities, leadership. Special Characteristics: 31 awards ($79,866 total): children of faculty/staff, general special characteristics, religious affiliation. *Tuition waivers:* Full or partial for employees or children of employees.

LOANS *Student loans:* $707,642 (53% need-based, 47% non-need-based). 74% of past graduating class borrowed through all loan programs. *Average indebtedness per student:* $15,000. *Average need-based loan:* Freshmen: $2542; Undergraduates: $3717. *Parent loans:* $97,543 (100% non-need-based). *Programs:* FFEL (Subsidized and Unsubsidized Stafford, PLUS).

WORK-STUDY *Federal work-study:* Total amount: $25,258; 39 jobs averaging $2000.

APPLYING FOR FINANCIAL AID *Required financial aid forms:* FAFSA, institution's own form. *Financial aid deadline:* Continuous. *Notification date:* Continuous beginning 5/10. Students must reply within 2 weeks of notification.

CONTACT Robin L. Walker, Director of Student Financial Aid, Dallas Christian College, 2700 Christian Parkway, Dallas, TX 75234-7299, 972-241-3371 Ext. 105. *Fax:* 972-241-8021. *E-mail:* finaid@dallas.edu.

DALTON STATE COLLEGE
Dalton, GA

ABOUT THE INSTITUTION State-supported, coed. Awards: associate and bachelor's degrees. 64 undergraduate majors. Total enrollment: 4,252. Undergraduates: 4,252.

GIFT AID (NEED-BASED) *Scholarships, grants, and awards:* Federal Pell, FSEOG, state, private, college/university gift aid from institutional funds.

GIFT AID (NON-NEED-BASED) *Scholarships, grants, and awards by category:* Academic Interests/Achievement: business, education, engineering/technologies, health fields, humanities. Special Achievements/Activities: hobbies/interests, memberships. Special Characteristics: adult students, children and siblings of alumni.

LOANS *Programs:* FFEL (Subsidized and Unsubsidized Stafford, PLUS), Federal Nursing, state.

WORK-STUDY *Federal work-study:* Total amount: $82,639; 91 jobs averaging $1433. *State or other work-study/employment:* Total amount: $566,979 (41% need-based, 59% non-need-based). 98 part-time jobs averaging $3665.

APPLYING FOR FINANCIAL AID *Required financial aid form:* FAFSA.

CONTACT Kevin Wellwood, Director of Student Financial Aid, Dalton State College, 213 North College Drive, Dalton, GA 30720, 706-272-4545 or toll-free 800-829-4436. *Fax:* 706-272-2458. *E-mail:* kwellwood@en.daltonstate.edu.

DANA COLLEGE
Blair, NE

ABOUT THE INSTITUTION Independent religious, coed. Awards: bachelor's degrees. 41 undergraduate majors. Total enrollment: 639. Undergraduates: 639. Freshmen: 205.

GIFT AID (NEED-BASED) *Scholarships, grants, and awards:* Federal Pell, FSEOG, state, private, college/university gift aid from institutional funds.

GIFT AID (NON-NEED-BASED) *Scholarships, grants, and awards by category: Academic Interests/Achievement:* biological sciences, business, communication, education, English, foreign languages, general academic interests/achievements, health fields, international studies, mathematics, military science, premedicine, religion/biblical studies, social sciences. *Creative Arts/Performance:* applied art and design, art/fine arts, music, theater/drama. *Special Achievements/Activities:* general special achievements/activities, leadership, religious involvement. *Special Characteristics:* ethnic background, international students, local/state students, members of minority groups, out-of-state students, religious affiliation.

LOANS *Programs:* FFEL (Subsidized and Unsubsidized Stafford, PLUS), Perkins.

WORK-STUDY *Federal work-study:* Total amount: $214,439; jobs available (averaging $1000). *State or other work-study/employment:* Part-time jobs available.

APPLYING FOR FINANCIAL AID *Required financial aid forms:* FAFSA, institution's own form.

CONTACT Kris Weigelt, Assistant Director, Financial Aid, Dana College, 2848 College Drive, Blair, NE 68008-1099, 402-426-7245 or toll-free 800-444-3262. *Fax:* 402-426-7225. *E-mail:* kweigelt@fs1.dana.edu.

DANIEL WEBSTER COLLEGE
Nashua, NH

Tuition & fees: $21,630 | **Average undergraduate aid package: $15,006**

ABOUT THE INSTITUTION Independent, coed. Awards: associate and bachelor's degrees. 16 undergraduate majors. Total enrollment: 1,109. Undergraduates: 1,050. Freshmen: 141. Federal methodology is used as a basis for awarding need-based institutional aid.

UNDERGRADUATE EXPENSES for 2004–05 *Application fee:* $35. *Comprehensive fee:* $29,800 includes full-time tuition ($20,880), mandatory fees ($750), and room and board ($8170). *College room only:* $4110. *Part-time tuition:* $775 per credit. *Payment plan:* Installment.

FRESHMAN FINANCIAL AID (Fall 2004, est.) 157 applied for aid; of those 92% were deemed to have need. 100% of freshmen with need received aid. *Average percent of need met:* 75% (excluding resources awarded to replace EFC). *Average financial aid package:* $16,717 (excluding resources awarded to replace EFC). 9% of all full-time freshmen had no need and received non-need-based gift aid.

UNDERGRADUATE FINANCIAL AID (Fall 2004, est.) 521 applied for aid; of those 96% were deemed to have need. 100% of undergraduates with need received aid. *Average percent of need met:* 72% (excluding resources awarded to replace EFC). *Average financial aid package:* $15,006 (excluding resources awarded to replace EFC). 4% of all full-time undergraduates had no need and received non-need-based gift aid.

GIFT AID (NEED-BASED) *Total amount:* $2,809,720 (18% federal, 2% state, 75% institutional, 5% external sources). *Receiving aid:* Freshmen: 81% (130); All full-time undergraduates: 83% (470). *Average award:* Freshmen: $8720; Undergraduates: $8236. *Scholarships, grants, and awards:* Federal Pell, FSEOG, state, private, college/university gift aid from institutional funds.

GIFT AID (NON-NEED-BASED) *Total amount:* $2,210,650 (100% institutional). *Receiving aid:* Freshmen: 86% (137); Undergraduates: 74% (417). *Average Award:* Freshmen: $5632; Undergraduates: $7500. *Scholarships, grants, and awards by category: Academic Interests/Achievement:* $2,062,000 total: business, computer science, engineering/technologies, general academic interests/achievements, social sciences. *Special Achievements/Activities:* 12 awards ($115,800 total): general special achievements/activities, leadership. *Tuition waivers:* Full or partial for employees or children of employees. *ROTC:* Army cooperative, Air Force cooperative.

LOANS *Student loans:* $2,158,979 (83% need-based, 17% non-need-based). *Average need-based loan:* Freshmen: $3051; Undergraduates: $4057. *Parent loans:* $3,968,549 (100% non-need-based). *Programs:* Federal Direct (Subsidized and Unsubsidized Stafford, PLUS), Perkins, Signature Loans.

WORK-STUDY *Federal work-study:* Total amount: $634,440; 340 jobs averaging $2000. *State or other work-study/employment:* Part-time jobs available.

APPLYING FOR FINANCIAL AID *Required financial aid forms:* FAFSA, institution's own form. *Financial aid deadline (priority):* 3/1. *Notification date:* Continuous beginning 4/1. Students must reply within 3 weeks of notification.

CONTACT Anne-Marie Caruso, Director of Financial Assistance, Daniel Webster College, 20 University Drive, Nashua, NH 03063-1300, 603-577-6590 or toll-free 800-325-6876. *Fax:* 603-577-6593. *E-mail:* caruso@dwc.edu.

DARKEI NOAM RABBINICAL COLLEGE
Brooklyn, NY

CONTACT Ms. Rivi Horowitz, Director of Financial Aid, Darkei Noam Rabbinical College, 2822 Avenue J, Brooklyn, NY 11219, 718-338-6464.

DARTMOUTH COLLEGE
Hanover, NH

Tuition & fees: $30,575 | **Average undergraduate aid package: $25,900**

ABOUT THE INSTITUTION Independent, coed. Awards: bachelor's, master's, doctoral, and first professional degrees. 60 undergraduate majors. Total enrollment: 5,704. Undergraduates: 4,079. Freshmen: 1,081. Both federal and institutional methodology are used as a basis for awarding need-based institutional aid.

UNDERGRADUATE EXPENSES for 2004–05 *Application fee:* $70. *Comprehensive fee:* $39,699 includes full-time tuition ($30,279), mandatory fees ($296), and room and board ($9124). *College room only:* $5400. Room and board charges vary according to board plan. *Payment plan:* Tuition prepayment.

FRESHMAN FINANCIAL AID (Fall 2003) 646 applied for aid; of those 81% were deemed to have need. 100% of freshmen with need received aid; of those 100% had need fully met. *Average percent of need met:* 100% (excluding resources awarded to replace EFC). *Average financial aid package:* $28,113 (excluding resources awarded to replace EFC). 1% of all full-time freshmen had no need and received non-need-based gift aid.

UNDERGRADUATE FINANCIAL AID (Fall 2003) 2,392 applied for aid; of those 85% were deemed to have need. 100% of undergraduates with need received aid; of those 100% had need fully met. *Average percent of need met:* 100% (excluding resources awarded to replace EFC). *Average financial aid package:* $25,900 (excluding resources awarded to replace EFC). 1% of all full-time undergraduates had no need and received non-need-based gift aid.

GIFT AID (NEED-BASED) *Total amount:* $40,934,017 (7% federal, 88% institutional, 5% external sources). *Receiving aid:* Freshmen: 47% (505); All full-time undergraduates: 47% (1,905). *Average award:* Freshmen: $24,375; Undergraduates: $21,487. *Scholarships, grants, and awards:* Federal Pell, FSEOG, state, college/university gift aid from institutional funds.

GIFT AID (NON-NEED-BASED) *Total amount:* $679,089 (21% federal, 79% external sources). *Average Award:* Freshmen: $300; Undergraduates: $310. *ROTC:* Army cooperative.

LOANS *Student loans:* $11,557,646 (72% need-based, 28% non-need-based). 49% of past graduating class borrowed through all loan programs. *Average indebtedness per student:* $18,095. *Average need-based loan:* Freshmen: $3759; Undergraduates: $4081. *Parent loans:* $6,678,471 (100% need-based). *Programs:* FFEL (Subsidized and Unsubsidized Stafford, PLUS), Perkins, college/university.

WORK-STUDY *Federal work-study:* Total amount: $3,045,573; 1,563 jobs averaging $1949. *State or other work-study/employment:* Total amount: $383,433 (95% need-based, 5% non-need-based). 227 part-time jobs averaging $1689.

APPLYING FOR FINANCIAL AID *Required financial aid forms:* FAFSA, CSS Financial Aid PROFILE, noncustodial (divorced/separated) parent's statement, business/farm supplement, W-2 forms, federal income tax form(s). *Financial aid deadline:* 2/1. *Notification date:* 4/2. Students must reply by 5/1.

CONTACT Ms. Virginia S. Hazen, Director of Financial Aid, Dartmouth College, 6024 McNutt Hall, Hanover, NH 03755, 603-646-2451 or toll-free 603-646-2875 (in-state). *Fax:* 603-646-1414. *E-mail:* virginia.s.hazen@dartmouth.edu.

DAVENPORT UNIVERSITY
Dearborn, MI

ABOUT THE INSTITUTION Independent, coed. Awards: associate, bachelor's, and master's degrees. 31 undergraduate majors. Total university enrollment: 13,124.

GIFT AID (NEED-BASED) *Scholarships, grants, and awards:* Federal Pell, FSEOG, state, private, college/university gift aid from institutional funds, State of MI Nursing Scholarships.

GIFT AID (NON-NEED-BASED) *Scholarships, grants, and awards by category: Academic Interests/Achievement:* business, computer science, general academic interests/achievements. *Special Characteristics:* adult students, children and siblings of alumni, children of faculty/staff, children of public servants, general special characteristics, local/state students.

LOANS *Programs:* FFEL (Subsidized and Unsubsidized Stafford, PLUS), state.

APPLYING FOR FINANCIAL AID *Required financial aid form:* FAFSA.

CONTACT Director of Financial Aid, Davenport University, 4801 Oakman Boulevard, Dearborn, MI 48126-3799, 313-581-4400 or toll-free 800-632-9569. *Fax:* 313-581-1853.

DAVENPORT UNIVERSITY
Flint, MI

CONTACT Ms. Rita Miller, Director of Financial Aid, Davenport University, 3488 North Jennings Road, Flint, MI 48504-1700, 810-789-2200 or toll-free 800-727-1443. *Fax:* 810-789-2266. *E-mail:* flrmiller@dcb.edu.

DAVENPORT UNIVERSITY
Gaylord, MI

CONTACT Office of Financial Aid, Davenport University, 80 Livingston Boulevard, Gaylord, MI 49735, 989-705-3720 or toll-free 800-632-9569. *Fax:* 989-705-3727.

DAVENPORT UNIVERSITY
Grand Rapids, MI

CONTACT Mary Kay Bethune, Vice President for Financial Aid, Davenport University, 415 East Fulton Street, Grand Rapids, MI 49503, 616-451-3511 or toll-free 800-632-9569. *E-mail:* marykay.bethune@davenport.edu.

DAVENPORT UNIVERSITY
Holland, MI

CONTACT Office of Financial Aid, Davenport University, 643 South Waverly Road, Holland, MI 49423, 616-395-4600 or toll-free 800-632-9569. *Fax:* 616-395-4698.

DAVENPORT UNIVERSITY
Kalamazoo, MI

CONTACT Ms. Linda Reischer, Director of Financial Aid, Davenport University, 4123 West Main Street, Kalamazoo, MI 49006-2791, 269-552-3320 or toll-free 800-632-9569. *Fax:* 269-552-3305. *E-mail:* linda.reischer@davenport.edu.

DAVENPORT UNIVERSITY
Lansing, MI

CONTACT Libby Jean, Acting Director of Financial Aid, Davenport University, 220 East Kalamazoo Street, Lansing, MI 48933-2197, 517-484-2600 Ext. 8226 or toll-free 800-632-9569. *Fax:* 517-484-1132. *E-mail:* libby.jean@davenport.edu.

DAVENPORT UNIVERSITY
Lapeer, MI

CONTACT Office of Financial Aid, Davenport University, 550 Lake Drive, Suite B, Lapeer, MI 48446, 810-664-9655 or toll-free 800-632-9569. *Fax:* 810-664-1912.

DAVENPORT UNIVERSITY
Traverse City, MI

CONTACT Office of Financial Aid, Davenport University, 2200 Dendrinos Drive, Suite 110, Traverse City, MI 49684, 231-995-1740 or toll-free 800-632-9569. *Fax:* 231-995-1743.

DAVENPORT UNIVERSITY
Warren, MI

CONTACT Ms. Carol Agee, Director of Financial Aid, Davenport University, 27500 Dequindre Road, Warren, MI 48092-5209, 586-558-8700 Ext. 230 or toll-free 800-632-9569. *Fax:* 586-558-7528. *E-mail:* carol.agee@davenport.edu.

DAVID N. MYERS UNIVERSITY
Cleveland, OH

Tuition & fees: $11,170	Average undergraduate aid package: $6990

ABOUT THE INSTITUTION Independent, coed. Awards: associate, bachelor's, and master's degrees. 14 undergraduate majors. Total enrollment: 1,177. Undergraduates: 1,096. Freshmen: 115. Federal methodology is used as a basis for awarding need-based institutional aid.

UNDERGRADUATE EXPENSES for 2004–05 *Application fee:* $25. *Tuition:* full-time $11,170; part-time $390 per credit.

FRESHMAN FINANCIAL AID (Fall 2003) 10 applied for aid; of those 100% were deemed to have need. 100% of freshmen with need received aid. *Average percent of need met:* 80% (excluding resources awarded to replace EFC). *Average financial aid package:* $10,759 (excluding resources awarded to replace EFC).

UNDERGRADUATE FINANCIAL AID (Fall 2003) 999 applied for aid; of those 86% were deemed to have need. 100% of undergraduates with need received aid; of those 5% had need fully met. *Average percent of need met:* 65% (excluding resources awarded to replace EFC). *Average financial aid package:* $6990 (excluding resources awarded to replace EFC). 1% of all full-time undergraduates had no need and received non-need-based gift aid.

GIFT AID (NEED-BASED) *Total amount:* $3,211,847 (49% federal, 31% state, 16% institutional, 4% external sources). *Receiving aid:* Freshmen: 91% (10); All full-time undergraduates: 57% (664). *Average award:* Freshmen: $6782; Undergraduates: $4298. *Scholarships, grants, and awards:* Federal Pell, FSEOG, state, private, college/university gift aid from institutional funds, United Negro College Fund.

GIFT AID (NON-NEED-BASED) *Total amount:* $136,598 (8% state, 89% institutional, 3% external sources). *Receiving aid:* Freshmen: 82% (9); Undergraduates: 18% (204). *Average Award:* Undergraduates: $1860. *Scholarships, grants, and awards by category: Academic Interests/Achievement:* 47 awards ($59,106 total): business, general academic interests/achievements. *Special Achievements/Activities:* 88 awards ($62,404 total): leadership.

LOANS *Student loans:* $6,031,664 (88% need-based, 12% non-need-based). 68% of past graduating class borrowed through all loan programs. *Average indebtedness per student:* $19,300. *Average need-based loan:* Freshmen: $2652; Undergraduates: $2950. *Parent loans:* $8695 (69% need-based, 31% non-need-based). *Programs:* FFEL (Subsidized and Unsubsidized Stafford, PLUS), Perkins.

WORK-STUDY *Federal work-study:* Total amount: $79,841; 53 jobs averaging $1506.

APPLYING FOR FINANCIAL AID *Required financial aid forms:* FAFSA, institution's own form. *Financial aid deadline (priority):* 3/15. *Notification date:* Continuous beginning 4/1. Students must reply within 3 weeks of notification.

CONTACT Miria Batig, Director of Financial Aid, David N. Myers University, 112 Prospect Avenue, Cleveland, OH 44115-1096, 216-696-9000 Ext. 818 or toll-free 800-424-3953. *Fax:* 216-523-3826.

DAVIDSON COLLEGE
Davidson, NC

Tuition & fees: $27,171	Average undergraduate aid package: $17,480

ABOUT THE INSTITUTION Independent Presbyterian, coed. Awards: bachelor's degrees. 21 undergraduate majors. Total enrollment: 1,714. Undergraduates: 1,714. Freshmen: 462. Both federal and institutional methodology are used as a basis for awarding need-based institutional aid.

UNDERGRADUATE EXPENSES for 2004–05 *Application fee:* $50. *Comprehensive fee:* $34,903 includes full-time tuition ($26,211), mandatory fees ($960), and room and board ($7732). *College room only:* $4083.

FRESHMAN FINANCIAL AID (Fall 2003) 251 applied for aid; of those 68% were deemed to have need. 100% of freshmen with need received aid; of those 100% had need fully met. *Average percent of need met:* 100% (excluding resources

awarded to replace EFC). *Average financial aid package:* $16,178 (excluding resources awarded to replace EFC). 12% of all full-time freshmen had no need and received non-need-based gift aid.

UNDERGRADUATE FINANCIAL AID (Fall 2003) 702 applied for aid; of those 83% were deemed to have need. 100% of undergraduates with need received aid; of those 100% had need fully met. *Average percent of need met:* 100% (excluding resources awarded to replace EFC). *Average financial aid package:* $17,480 (excluding resources awarded to replace EFC). 15% of all full-time undergraduates had no need and received non-need-based gift aid.

GIFT AID (NEED-BASED) *Total amount:* $9,916,015 (5% federal, 5% state, 90% institutional). *Receiving aid:* Freshmen: 33% (162); All full-time undergraduates: 32% (551). *Average award:* Freshmen: $14,651; Undergraduates: $14,862. *Scholarships, grants, and awards:* Federal Pell, FSEOG, state, private, college/university gift aid from institutional funds, need-linked special talent scholarships.

GIFT AID (NON-NEED-BASED) *Total amount:* $4,485,262 (13% federal, 8% state, 63% institutional, 16% external sources). *Receiving aid:* Freshmen: 6% (30); Undergraduates: 5% (93). *Average Award:* Freshmen: $9503; Undergraduates: $7709. *Scholarships, grants, and awards by category: Academic Interests/Achievement:* 231 awards ($1,974,331 total): biological sciences, education, foreign languages, general academic interests/achievements, mathematics, physical sciences, premedicine. *Creative Arts/Performance:* 28 awards ($154,625 total): art/fine arts, creative writing, music. *Special Achievements/Activities:* 46 awards ($585,529 total): community service, general special achievements/activities, leadership, religious involvement. *Special Characteristics:* 57 awards ($559,320 total): children of faculty/staff, general special characteristics, relatives of clergy. *ROTC:* Army, Air Force cooperative.

LOANS *Student loans:* $3,727,847 (36% need-based, 64% non-need-based). 30% of past graduating class borrowed through all loan programs. *Average indebtedness per student:* $21,901. *Average need-based loan:* Freshmen: $2651; Undergraduates: $3889. *Parent loans:* $2,240,226 (100% non-need-based). *Programs:* FFEL (Subsidized and Unsubsidized Stafford, PLUS), Perkins, alternative loans.

WORK-STUDY *Federal work-study:* Total amount: $452,667; 265 jobs averaging $1595. *State or other work-study/employment:* Total amount: $233,655 (68% need-based, 32% non-need-based). 142 part-time jobs averaging $1445.

ATHLETIC AWARDS *Total amount:* $1,980,341 (100% non-need-based).

APPLYING FOR FINANCIAL AID *Required financial aid forms:* FAFSA, CSS Financial Aid PROFILE, noncustodial (divorced/separated) parent's statement, business/farm supplement, parent and student tax returns and W-2 forms; coporate tax returns, if applicable. *Financial aid deadline (priority):* 2/15. *Notification date:* 4/1. Students must reply by 5/1.

CONTACT Kathleen Stevenson-McNeely, Senior Associate Dean of Admission and Financial Aid, Davidson College, 413 North Main Street, PO Box 7157, Davidson, NC 28035-7157, 704-894-2232 or toll-free 800-768-0380. *Fax:* 704-894-2845. *E-mail:* kastevensonmcneely@davidson.edu.

DAVIS & ELKINS COLLEGE
Elkins, WV

Tuition & fees: $15,666	Average undergraduate aid package: $15,769

ABOUT THE INSTITUTION Independent Presbyterian, coed. Awards: associate and bachelor's degrees. 53 undergraduate majors. Total enrollment: 625. Undergraduates: 625. Federal methodology is used as a basis for awarding need-based institutional aid.

UNDERGRADUATE EXPENSES for 2004–05 *Application fee:* $35. *Comprehensive fee:* $21,652 includes full-time tuition ($15,246), mandatory fees ($420), and room and board ($5986). Room and board charges vary according to board plan. *Part-time tuition:* $500 per credit hour. *Part-time fees:* $500 per credit hour. Part-time tuition and fees vary according to course load. *Payment plan:* Installment.

FRESHMAN FINANCIAL AID (Fall 2003) 93 applied for aid; of those 89% were deemed to have need. 99% of freshmen with need received aid; of those 46% had need fully met. *Average percent of need met:* 88% (excluding resources awarded to replace EFC). *Average financial aid package:* $16,512 (excluding resources awarded to replace EFC). 10% of all full-time freshmen had no need and received non-need-based gift aid.

UNDERGRADUATE FINANCIAL AID (Fall 2003) 480 applied for aid; of those 92% were deemed to have need. 100% of undergraduates with need received aid; of those 58% had need fully met. *Average percent of need met:* 89% (excluding resources awarded to replace EFC). *Average financial aid package:* $15,769 (excluding resources awarded to replace EFC). 7% of all full-time undergraduates had no need and received non-need-based gift aid.

GIFT AID (NEED-BASED) *Total amount:* $1,774,665 (58% federal, 29% state, 7% institutional, 6% external sources). *Receiving aid:* Freshmen: 59% (61); All full-time undergraduates: 62% (354). *Average award:* Freshmen: $2807; Undergraduates: $2999. *Scholarships, grants, and awards:* Federal Pell, FSEOG, state, private, college/university gift aid from institutional funds.

GIFT AID (NON-NEED-BASED) *Total amount:* $2,240,898 (4% state, 87% institutional, 9% external sources). *Receiving aid:* Freshmen: 79% (82); Undergraduates: 77% (438). *Average Award: Freshmen:* $10,949; *Undergraduates:* $13,136. *Scholarships, grants, and awards by category:* Academic *Interests/Achievement:* 799 awards ($1,807,887 total): biological sciences, business, computer science, education, engineering/technologies, general academic interests/achievements, health fields, physical sciences, religion/biblical studies. *Creative Arts/Performance:* 60 awards ($110,350 total): art/fine arts, music, performing arts, theater/drama. *Special Achievements/Activities:* 64 awards ($63,000 total): leadership, religious involvement. *Special Characteristics:* 318 awards ($485,542 total): children of faculty/staff, first-generation college students, local/state students, religious affiliation. *Tuition waivers:* Full or partial for employees or children of employees.

LOANS *Student loans:* $3,586,543 (40% need-based, 60% non-need-based). 95% of past graduating class borrowed through all loan programs. *Average indebtedness per student:* $15,500. *Average need-based loan:* Freshmen: $2587; Undergraduates: $3692. *Parent loans:* $326,105 (100% non-need-based). *Programs:* FFEL (Subsidized and Unsubsidized Stafford, PLUS), Perkins, college/university.

WORK-STUDY *Federal work-study:* Total amount: $130,033; 176 jobs averaging $739. *State or other work-study/employment:* Total amount: $63,642 (100% non-need-based). 61 part-time jobs averaging $1043.

ATHLETIC AWARDS *Total amount:* $439,100 (100% non-need-based).

APPLYING FOR FINANCIAL AID *Required financial aid form:* FAFSA. *Financial aid deadline:* Continuous. *Notification date:* Continuous. Students must reply within 2 weeks of notification.

CONTACT Susan M. George, Director of Financial Planning, Davis & Elkins College, 100 Campus Drive, Elkins, WV 26241-3996, 304-637-1373 or toll-free 800-624-3157 Ext. 1230. *Fax:* 304-637-1986. *E-mail:* ssw@davisandelkins.edu.

DAVIS COLLEGE
Johnson City, NY

ABOUT THE INSTITUTION Independent nondenominational, coed. Awards: associate and bachelor's degrees. 1 undergraduate major. Total enrollment: 293. Undergraduates: 293.

GIFT AID (NEED-BASED) *Scholarships, grants, and awards:* Federal Pell, FSEOG, state, private, college/university gift aid from institutional funds.

GIFT AID (NON-NEED-BASED) *Scholarships, grants, and awards by category: Academic Interests/Achievement:* general academic interests/achievements, religion/biblical studies. *Creative Arts/Performance:* music. *Special Achievements/Activities:* leadership. *Special Characteristics:* children and siblings of alumni, children of educators, children of faculty/staff, general special characteristics, international students, married students, relatives of clergy, siblings of current students, spouses of current students.

LOANS *Programs:* FFEL (Subsidized and Unsubsidized Stafford, PLUS), college/university.

APPLYING FOR FINANCIAL AID *Required financial aid forms:* FAFSA, institution's own form, state aid form.

CONTACT Mr. James P. Devine, Financial Aid Director, Davis College, PO Box 601, Bible School Park, NY 13737-0601, 607-729-1581 Ext. 401 or toll-free 800-331-4137 Ext. 406. *Fax:* 607-770-6886. *E-mail:* financialaid@practical.edu.

DEACONESS COLLEGE OF NURSING
St. Louis, MO

CONTACT Financial Aid Counselor, Deaconess College of Nursing, 6150 Oakland Avenue, St. Louis, MO 63139-3215, 314-768-5604 or toll-free 800-942-4310.

DEFIANCE COLLEGE
Defiance, OH

Tuition & fees: $18,230	Average undergraduate aid package: $12,344

Defiance College

ABOUT THE INSTITUTION Independent religious, coed. Awards: associate, bachelor's, and master's degrees. 44 undergraduate majors. Total enrollment: 1,035. Undergraduates: 943. Freshmen: 239. Federal methodology is used as a basis for awarding need-based institutional aid.

UNDERGRADUATE EXPENSES for 2004–05 *Application fee:* $25. *Comprehensive fee:* $23,820 includes full-time tuition ($17,780), mandatory fees ($450), and room and board ($5590). *College room only:* $2850. Full-time tuition and fees vary according to program. Room and board charges vary according to board plan and housing facility. *Part-time tuition:* $300 per credit hour. *Part-time fees:* $60 per term. Part-time tuition and fees vary according to class time. *Payment plan:* Installment.

FRESHMAN FINANCIAL AID (Fall 2004, est.) 238 applied for aid; of those 84% were deemed to have need. 100% of freshmen with need received aid. *Average percent of need met:* 86% (excluding resources awarded to replace EFC). *Average financial aid package:* $11,914 (excluding resources awarded to replace EFC). 3% of all full-time freshmen had no need and received non-need-based gift aid.

UNDERGRADUATE FINANCIAL AID (Fall 2004, est.) 769 applied for aid; of those 84% were deemed to have need. 100% of undergraduates with need received aid. *Average percent of need met:* 85% (excluding resources awarded to replace EFC). *Average financial aid package:* $12,344 (excluding resources awarded to replace EFC). 7% of all full-time undergraduates had no need and received non-need-based gift aid.

GIFT AID (NEED-BASED) *Total amount:* $1,418,756 (61% federal, 28% state, 11% institutional). *Scholarships, grants, and awards:* Federal Pell, FSEOG, state, private, college/university gift aid from institutional funds.

GIFT AID (NON-NEED-BASED) *Total amount:* $5,968,348 (10% state, 84% institutional, 6% external sources). *Average Award: Freshmen:* $7625; *Undergraduates:* $7282. *Scholarships, grants, and awards by category: Academic Interests/Achievement:* biological sciences, business, communication, computer science, education, general academic interests/achievements, humanities, mathematics, physical sciences, premedicine, religion/biblical studies, social sciences. *Special Achievements/Activities:* community service, general special achievements/activities, leadership, religious involvement. *Special Characteristics:* children of faculty/staff, children with a deceased or disabled parent, first-generation college students, general special characteristics, international students, local/state students, members of minority groups, out-of-state students, previous college experience, relatives of clergy, religious affiliation. *Tuition waivers:* Full or partial for employees or children of employees, senior citizens.

LOANS *Student loans:* $5,275,907 (46% need-based, 54% non-need-based). 78% of past graduating class borrowed through all loan programs. *Average indebtedness per student:* $15,871. *Parent loans:* $1,175,153 (100% non-need-based). *Programs:* FFEL (Subsidized and Unsubsidized Stafford, PLUS), Perkins, alternative loans.

WORK-STUDY *Federal work-study:* Total amount: $92,547; 155 jobs averaging $597. *State or other work-study/employment:* Total amount: $109,512 (100% non-need-based). 140 part-time jobs averaging $782.

APPLYING FOR FINANCIAL AID *Required financial aid form:* FAFSA. *Financial aid deadline (priority):* 3/1. *Notification date:* Continuous. Students must reply within 3 weeks of notification.

CONTACT Ms. Amy Francis, Director of Financial Aid, Defiance College, 701 North Clinton Street, Defiance, OH 43512-1610, 419-784-4010 Ext. 376 or toll-free 800-520-4632 Ext. 2359.

DELAWARE STATE UNIVERSITY
Dover, DE

Tuition & fees (DE res): $4976	Average undergraduate aid package: $8026

ABOUT THE INSTITUTION State-supported, coed. Awards: bachelor's, master's, and doctoral degrees. 85 undergraduate majors. Total enrollment: 3,178. Undergraduates: 2,992. Freshmen: 618. Federal methodology is used as a basis for awarding need-based institutional aid.

UNDERGRADUATE EXPENSES for 2004–05 *Application fee:* $15. *Tuition, state resident:* full-time $4646; part-time $194 per credit. *Tuition, nonresident:* full-time $10,303; part-time $429 per credit hour. *Required fees:* full-time $330; $95 per term part-time. *College room and board:* $6816; *room only:* $4406.

FRESHMAN FINANCIAL AID (Fall 2004, est.) 566 applied for aid; of those 90% were deemed to have need. 98% of freshmen with need received aid; of those 32% had need fully met. *Average percent of need met:* 61% (excluding resources

awarded to replace EFC). *Average financial aid package:* $6368 (excluding resources awarded to replace EFC). 14% of all full-time freshmen had no need and received non-need-based gift aid.

UNDERGRADUATE FINANCIAL AID (Fall 2004, est.) 2,315 applied for aid; of those 89% were deemed to have need. 99% of undergraduates with need received aid; of those 38% had need fully met. *Average percent of need met:* 73% (excluding resources awarded to replace EFC). *Average financial aid package:* $8026 (excluding resources awarded to replace EFC). 18% of all full-time undergraduates had no need and received non-need-based gift aid.

GIFT AID (NEED-BASED) *Total amount:* $9,697,591 (47% federal, 3% state, 27% institutional, 23% external sources). *Receiving aid:* Freshmen: 56% (334); All full-time undergraduates: 54% (1,373). *Average award:* Freshmen: $2526; Undergraduates: $2443. *Scholarships, grants, and awards:* Federal Pell, FSEOG, state, Federal Nursing.

GIFT AID (NON-NEED-BASED) *Receiving aid:* Freshmen: 25% (152); Undergraduates: 30% (769). *Average Award: Freshmen:* $6243; *Undergraduates:* $5223. *Scholarships, grants, and awards by category: Academic Interests/Achievement:* general academic interests/achievements. *Creative Arts/Performance:* music. *Special Achievements/Activities:* general special achievements/activities. *Special Characteristics:* out-of-state students. *ROTC:* Army, Air Force.

LOANS *Student loans:* $13,796,059 (100% need-based). *Average need-based loan:* Freshmen: $4057; Undergraduates: $4925. *Parent loans:* $5,387,804 (100% need-based). *Programs:* FFEL (Subsidized and Unsubsidized Stafford, PLUS), Perkins, Federal Nursing.

WORK-STUDY *Federal work-study:* Total amount: $234,423; jobs available. *State or other work-study/employment:* Total amount: $146,816 (100% non-need-based). Part-time jobs available.

ATHLETIC AWARDS *Total amount:* $1,402,508 (100% need-based).

APPLYING FOR FINANCIAL AID *Required financial aid form:* FAFSA.

CONTACT Associate Director of Financial Aid, Delaware State University, 1200 North DuPont Highway, Dover, DE 19901-2277, 302-857-6250 or toll-free 800-845-2544.

DELAWARE VALLEY COLLEGE
Doylestown, PA

Tuition & fees: $20,888	Average undergraduate aid package: $16,613

ABOUT THE INSTITUTION Independent, coed. Awards: associate, bachelor's, and master's degrees and post-bachelor's certificates. 28 undergraduate majors. Total enrollment: 1,965. Undergraduates: 1,897. Freshmen: 451. Federal methodology is used as a basis for awarding need-based institutional aid.

UNDERGRADUATE EXPENSES for 2004–05 *Application fee:* $35. *Comprehensive fee:* $28,630 includes full-time tuition ($19,588), mandatory fees ($1300), and room and board ($7742). *College room only:* $3510. Full-time tuition and fees vary according to program. Room and board charges vary according to board plan. *Part-time tuition:* $525 per credit. *Part-time fees:* $50 per term.

FRESHMAN FINANCIAL AID (Fall 2004, est.) 389 applied for aid; of those 91% were deemed to have need. 100% of freshmen with need received aid; of those 46% had need fully met. *Average percent of need met:* 70% (excluding resources awarded to replace EFC). *Average financial aid package:* $15,645 (excluding resources awarded to replace EFC). 17% of all full-time freshmen had no need and received non-need-based gift aid.

UNDERGRADUATE FINANCIAL AID (Fall 2004, est.) 1,340 applied for aid; of those 92% were deemed to have need. 99% of undergraduates with need received aid; of those 32% had need fully met. *Average percent of need met:* 85% (excluding resources awarded to replace EFC). *Average financial aid package:* $16,613 (excluding resources awarded to replace EFC). 18% of all full-time undergraduates had no need and received non-need-based gift aid.

GIFT AID (NEED-BASED) *Total amount:* $12,408,513 (10% federal, 11% state, 78% institutional, 1% external sources). *Receiving aid:* Freshmen: 79% (355); All full-time undergraduates: 69% (1,042). *Average award:* Freshmen: $11,925; Undergraduates: $11,908. *Scholarships, grants, and awards:* Federal Pell, FSEOG, state, private, college/university gift aid from institutional funds.

GIFT AID (NON-NEED-BASED) *Total amount:* $2,698,650 (3% state, 89% institutional, 8% external sources). *Receiving aid:* Freshmen: 12% (56); Undergraduates: 11% (166). *Average Award: Freshmen:* $8808; *Undergraduates:* $7384. *Scholarships, grants, and awards by category: Academic Interests/Achievement:* 326 awards ($2,406,800 total): general academic interests/achievements. *Creative Arts/Performance:* 38 awards ($17,750 total): music.

Special Achievements/Activities: 2 awards ($3500 total): memberships. Special Characteristics: 2 awards ($1000 total): handicapped students. **Tuition waivers:** Full or partial for employees or children of employees.

LOANS *Student loans:* $5,441,882 (70% need-based, 30% non-need-based). 66% of past graduating class borrowed through all loan programs. *Average indebtedness per student:* $17,327. **Average need-based loan:** Freshmen: $2911; Undergraduates: $3832. **Parent loans:** $5,076,523 (35% need-based, 65% non-need-based). **Programs:** FFEL (Subsidized and Unsubsidized Stafford, PLUS), Perkins, state, alternative loans.

WORK-STUDY *Federal work-study:* Total amount: $255,580; 167 jobs averaging $1257. *State or other work-study/employment:* Total amount: $405,000 (74% need-based, 26% non-need-based). 157 part-time jobs averaging $1942.

APPLYING FOR FINANCIAL AID *Required financial aid form:* FAFSA. **Financial aid deadline (priority):** 4/1. **Notification date:** Continuous. Students must reply by 5/1.

CONTACT Mr. Robert Sauer, Director of Student Financial Aid, Delaware Valley College, 700 East Butler Avenue, Doylestown, PA 18901-2697, 215-489-2272 or toll-free 800-2DELVAL (in-state). *E-mail:* finaid@devalcol.edu.

DELTA STATE UNIVERSITY
Cleveland, MS

ABOUT THE INSTITUTION State-supported, coed. Awards: bachelor's, master's, and doctoral degrees and post-master's certificates. 48 undergraduate majors. Total enrollment: 3,853. Undergraduates: 3,148. Freshmen: 383.

GIFT AID (NEED-BASED) *Scholarships, grants, and awards:* Federal Pell, FSEOG, state, private, college/university gift aid from institutional funds.

GIFT AID (NON-NEED-BASED) *Scholarships, grants, and awards by category:* Academic Interests/Achievement: biological sciences, general academic interests/achievements. Creative Arts/Performance: art/fine arts, journalism/publications, music, performing arts. Special Achievements/Activities: cheerleading/drum major, general special achievements/activities, leadership, memberships. Special Characteristics: children and siblings of alumni, children of faculty/staff, general special characteristics, out-of-state students.

LOANS *Programs:* FFEL (Subsidized and Unsubsidized Stafford, PLUS), Perkins, college/university.

WORK-STUDY *Federal work-study:* Total amount: $509,719; 318 jobs averaging $1650.

APPLYING FOR FINANCIAL AID *Required financial aid forms:* FAFSA, institution's own form.

CONTACT Ms. Ann Margaret Mullins, Director of Student Financial Assistance, Delta State University, PO Box 3154, Cleveland, MS 38733-0001, 662-846-4670 or toll-free 800-468-6378. *E-mail:* amullins@deltastate.edu.

DENISON UNIVERSITY
Granville, OH

Tuition & fees: $27,310	Average undergraduate aid package: $23,968

ABOUT THE INSTITUTION Independent, coed. Awards: bachelor's degrees. 39 undergraduate majors. Total enrollment: 2,229. Undergraduates: 2,229. Freshmen: 616. Federal methodology is used as a basis for awarding need-based institutional aid.

UNDERGRADUATE EXPENSES for 2004–05 *Application fee:* $40. **Comprehensive fee:** $34,980 includes full-time tuition ($26,600), mandatory fees ($710), and room and board ($7670). **College room only:** $4220. Room and board charges vary according to housing facility. **Part-time tuition:** $830 per semester hour. Part-time tuition and fees vary according to course load. **Payment plan:** Installment.

FRESHMAN FINANCIAL AID (Fall 2004, est.) 403 applied for aid; of those 75% were deemed to have need. 100% of freshmen with need received aid; of those 54% had need fully met. *Average percent of need met:* 97% (excluding resources awarded to replace EFC). *Average financial aid package:* $23,289 (excluding resources awarded to replace EFC). 48% of all full-time freshmen had no need and received non-need-based gift aid.

UNDERGRADUATE FINANCIAL AID (Fall 2004, est.) 1,224 applied for aid; of those 84% were deemed to have need. 100% of undergraduates with need received aid; of those 59% had need fully met. *Average percent of need met:* 96% (excluding resources awarded to replace EFC). *Average financial aid package:* $23,968 (excluding resources awarded to replace EFC). 52% of all full-time undergraduates had no need and received non-need-based gift aid.

DePaul University

GIFT AID (NEED-BASED) *Total amount:* $16,943,785 (5% federal, 2% state, 93% institutional). *Receiving aid:* Freshmen: 49% (300); All full-time undergraduates: 48% (1,013). *Average award:* Freshmen: $17,921; Undergraduates: $17,873. **Scholarships, grants, and awards:** Federal Pell, FSEOG, state, private, college/university gift aid from institutional funds.

GIFT AID (NON-NEED-BASED) *Total amount:* $15,386,769 (6% state, 89% institutional, 5% external sources). *Receiving aid:* Freshmen: 46% (281); Undergraduates: 45% (936). *Average Award:* Freshmen: $11,986; Undergraduates: $11,507. *Scholarships, grants, and awards by category:* Academic Interests/Achievement: 1,870 awards ($20,253,794 total): biological sciences, communication, English, foreign languages, general academic interests/achievements, humanities, physical sciences. Creative Arts/Performance: 110 awards ($284,321 total): art/fine arts, dance, music, theater/drama. Special Achievements/Activities: 4 awards ($79,550 total): leadership. Special Characteristics: 179 awards ($2,094,826 total): members of minority groups. **Tuition waivers:** Full or partial for employees or children of employees. **ROTC:** Army cooperative.

LOANS *Student loans:* $5,004,744 (67% need-based, 33% non-need-based). 51% of past graduating class borrowed through all loan programs. *Average indebtedness per student:* $14,342. **Average need-based loan:** Freshmen: $4037; Undergraduates: $4828. **Parent loans:** $2,436,716 (100% non-need-based). **Programs:** Federal Direct (Subsidized and Unsubsidized Stafford, PLUS), Perkins, college/university.

WORK-STUDY *Federal work-study:* Total amount: $1,014,731; 559 jobs averaging $1793. *State or other work-study/employment:* Total amount: $2,160,809 (100% non-need-based). 1,111 part-time jobs averaging $1979.

APPLYING FOR FINANCIAL AID *Required financial aid form:* FAFSA. **Financial aid deadline (priority):** 2/15. **Notification date:** 3/31. Students must reply by 5/1 or within 2 weeks of notification.

CONTACT Ms. Nancy Hoover, Director of Financial Aid, Denison University, PO Box M, Granville, OH 43023-0613, 740-587-6279 or toll-free 800-DENISON. *Fax:* 740-587-5706. *E-mail:* hoover@denison.edu.

DePAUL UNIVERSITY
Chicago, IL

Tuition & fees: $19,765	Average undergraduate aid package: $15,280

ABOUT THE INSTITUTION Independent Roman Catholic, coed. Awards: bachelor's, master's, doctoral, and first professional degrees and post-bachelor's and post-master's certificates. 100 undergraduate majors. Total enrollment: 23,531. Undergraduates: 14,678. Freshmen: 2,278. Federal methodology is used as a basis for awarding need-based institutional aid.

UNDERGRADUATE EXPENSES for 2004–05 *Application fee:* $40. *One-time required fee:* $100. *Comprehensive fee:* $29,072 includes full-time tuition ($19,700), mandatory fees ($65), and room and board ($9307). **College room only:** $6316. Full-time tuition and fees vary according to program. Room and board charges vary according to board plan, housing facility, and location. **Part-time tuition:** $369 per quarter hour. Part-time tuition and fees vary according to program. **Payment plans:** Installment, deferred payment.

FRESHMAN FINANCIAL AID (Fall 2003) 1780 applied for aid; of those 86% were deemed to have need. 98% of freshmen with need received aid; of those 17% had need fully met. *Average percent of need met:* 74% (excluding resources awarded to replace EFC). *Average financial aid package:* $16,537 (excluding resources awarded to replace EFC). 10% of all full-time freshmen had no need and received non-need-based gift aid.

UNDERGRADUATE FINANCIAL AID (Fall 2003) 7,872 applied for aid; of those 90% were deemed to have need. 98% of undergraduates with need received aid; of those 15% had need fully met. *Average percent of need met:* 70% (excluding resources awarded to replace EFC). *Average financial aid package:* $15,280 (excluding resources awarded to replace EFC). 6% of all full-time undergraduates had no need and received non-need-based gift aid.

GIFT AID (NEED-BASED) *Total amount:* $60,260,000 (23% federal, 22% state, 54% institutional, 1% external sources). *Receiving aid:* Freshmen: 54% (1,254); All full-time undergraduates: 52% (5,765). *Average award:* Freshmen: $11,302; Undergraduates: $10,085. **Scholarships, grants, and awards:** Federal Pell, FSEOG, state, private, college/university gift aid from institutional funds, United Negro College Fund.

GIFT AID (NON-NEED-BASED) *Total amount:* $18,850,000 (1% state, 91% institutional, 8% external sources). *Receiving aid:* Freshmen: 29% (660); Undergraduates: 20% (2,180). *Average Award:* Freshmen: $7020; Undergraduates: $7194. *Scholarships, grants, and awards by category:* Academic Interests/ Achievement: 1,650 awards ($7,000,000 total): biological sciences, business, computer science, education, general academic interests/achievements. *Creative*

Peterson's College Money Handbook 2006   *www.petersons.com*   **199**

DePaul University

Arts/Performance: 375 awards ($2,600,000 total): art/fine arts, debating, music, performing arts, theater/drama. *Special Achievements/Activities:* 30 awards ($150,000 total): community service. *Special Characteristics:* children of faculty/staff. *Tuition waivers:* Full or partial for employees or children of employees. *ROTC:* Army cooperative.

LOANS *Student loans:* $75,700,000 (70% need-based, 30% non-need-based). 62% of past graduating class borrowed through all loan programs. *Average indebtedness per student:* $17,500. *Average need-based loan:* Freshmen: $3312; Undergraduates: $4457. *Parent loans:* $24,000,000 (100% non-need-based). *Programs:* Federal Direct (Subsidized and Unsubsidized Stafford, PLUS), Perkins.

WORK-STUDY *Federal work-study:* Total amount: $2,150,000; 900 jobs averaging $2000. *State or other work-study/employment:* Total amount: $4,550,000 (28% need-based, 72% non-need-based). Part-time jobs available.

ATHLETIC AWARDS *Total amount:* $3,000,000 (100% non-need-based).

APPLYING FOR FINANCIAL AID *Required financial aid form:* FAFSA. *Financial aid deadline:* 4/1 (priority: 3/1). *Notification date:* Continuous. Students must reply by 5/1 or within 4 weeks of notification.

CONTACT Christopher Rone, Associate Director of Financial Aid, DePaul University, 1 East Jackson Boulevard, Suite 9000, Chicago, IL 60604-2287, 773-325-7815. *Fax:* 773-325-7746.

DePAUW UNIVERSITY
Greencastle, IN

Tuition & fees: $25,500	Average undergraduate aid package: $24,053

ABOUT THE INSTITUTION Independent religious, coed. Awards: bachelor's degrees. 45 undergraduate majors. Total enrollment: 2,391. Undergraduates: 2,391. Freshmen: 661. Both federal and institutional methodology are used as a basis for awarding need-based institutional aid.

UNDERGRADUATE EXPENSES for 2004–05 *Application fee:* $40. *Comprehensive fee:* $32,800 includes full-time tuition ($25,000), mandatory fees ($500), and room and board ($7300). *College room only:* $3800. Room and board charges vary according to board plan. *Part-time tuition:* $781.25 per semester hour. *Payment plans:* Tuition prepayment, installment, deferred payment.

FRESHMAN FINANCIAL AID (Fall 2004, est.) 463 applied for aid; of those 77% were deemed to have need. 100% of freshmen with need received aid; of those 86% had need fully met. *Average percent of need met:* 98% (excluding resources awarded to replace EFC). *Average financial aid package:* $24,120 (excluding resources awarded to replace EFC). 44% of all full-time freshmen had no need and received non-need-based gift aid.

UNDERGRADUATE FINANCIAL AID (Fall 2004, est.) 1,407 applied for aid; of those 83% were deemed to have need. 100% of undergraduates with need received aid; of those 95% had need fully met. *Average percent of need met:* 99% (excluding resources awarded to replace EFC). *Average financial aid package:* $24,053 (excluding resources awarded to replace EFC). 47% of all full-time undergraduates had no need and received non-need-based gift aid.

GIFT AID (NEED-BASED) *Total amount:* $19,859,249 (4% federal, 7% state, 83% institutional, 6% external sources). *Receiving aid:* Freshmen: 54% (355); All full-time undergraduates: 50% (1,172). *Average award:* Freshmen: $13,514; Undergraduates: $13,750. *Scholarships, grants, and awards:* Federal Pell, FSEOG, state, private, college/university gift aid from institutional funds.

GIFT AID (NON-NEED-BASED) *Total amount:* $17,201,227 (1% federal, 86% institutional, 13% external sources). *Receiving aid:* Freshmen: 36% (235); Undergraduates: 44% (1,028). *Average Award:* Freshmen: $11,051; Undergraduates: $12,024. *Scholarships, grants, and awards by category: Academic Interests/Achievement:* biological sciences, business, communication, computer science, foreign languages, general academic interests/achievements, humanities, international studies, mathematics, physical sciences. *Creative Arts/Performance:* art/fine arts, cinema/film/broadcasting, journalism/publications, music. *Special Achievements/Activities:* community service, leadership. *Special Characteristics:* children and siblings of alumni, children of faculty/staff, ethnic background, international students, members of minority groups, relatives of clergy, religious affiliation. *Tuition waivers:* Full or partial for employees or children of employees. *ROTC:* Army cooperative, Air Force cooperative.

LOANS *Student loans:* $5,286,733 (73% need-based, 27% non-need-based). 54% of past graduating class borrowed through all loan programs. *Average indebtedness per student:* $17,486. *Average need-based loan:* Freshmen: $3550; Undergraduates: $4425. *Parent loans:* $4,059,130 (44% need-based, 56% non-need-based). *Programs:* FFEL (Subsidized and Unsubsidized Stafford, PLUS), Perkins, college/university, alternative loans.

WORK-STUDY *Federal work-study:* Total amount: $1,058,267; 681 jobs averaging $1583. *State or other work-study/employment:* Total amount: $18,100 (22% need-based, 78% non-need-based). 15 part-time jobs averaging $480.

APPLYING FOR FINANCIAL AID *Required financial aid forms:* FAFSA, institution's own form. *Financial aid deadline:* 2/15. *Notification date:* 3/31. Students must reply by 5/1.

CONTACT Joanne L. Haymaker, Associate Director of Financial Aid, DePauw University, 313 South Locust Street, Greencastle, IN 46135-0037, 765-658-4030 or toll-free 800-447-2495. *Fax:* 765-658-4177. *E-mail:* jhaymaker@depauw.edu.

DeSALES UNIVERSITY
Center Valley, PA

Tuition & fees: $19,390	Average undergraduate aid package: $14,325

ABOUT THE INSTITUTION Independent Roman Catholic, coed. Awards: bachelor's and master's degrees and post-bachelor's and post-master's certificates (also offers adult program with significant enrollment not reflected in profile). 38 undergraduate majors. Total enrollment: 2,927. Undergraduates: 2,175. Freshmen: 364. Federal methodology is used as a basis for awarding need-based institutional aid.

UNDERGRADUATE EXPENSES for 2004–05 *Application fee:* $30. *Comprehensive fee:* $26,980 includes full-time tuition ($19,000), mandatory fees ($390), and room and board ($7590). Full-time tuition and fees vary according to class time and course load. Room and board charges vary according to board plan and housing facility. *Part-time tuition:* $790 per credit. Part-time tuition and fees vary according to class time and course load. *Payment plans:* Installment, deferred payment.

FRESHMAN FINANCIAL AID (Fall 2004, est.) 338 applied for aid; of those 78% were deemed to have need. 100% of freshmen with need received aid; of those 21% had need fully met. *Average percent of need met:* 69% (excluding resources awarded to replace EFC). *Average financial aid package:* $13,056 (excluding resources awarded to replace EFC). 27% of all full-time freshmen had no need and received non-need-based gift aid.

UNDERGRADUATE FINANCIAL AID (Fall 2004, est.) 1,233 applied for aid; of those 79% were deemed to have need. 100% of undergraduates with need received aid; of those 34% had need fully met. *Average percent of need met:* 76% (excluding resources awarded to replace EFC). *Average financial aid package:* $14,325 (excluding resources awarded to replace EFC). 17% of all full-time undergraduates had no need and received non-need-based gift aid.

GIFT AID (NEED-BASED) *Total amount:* $9,551,872 (9% federal, 15% state, 74% institutional, 2% external sources). *Receiving aid:* Freshmen: 72% (261); All full-time undergraduates: 54% (951). *Average award:* Freshmen: $9727; Undergraduates: $10,044. *Scholarships, grants, and awards:* Federal Pell, FSEOG, state, private, college/university gift aid from institutional funds.

GIFT AID (NON-NEED-BASED) *Total amount:* $1,579,419 (1% federal, 95% institutional, 4% external sources). *Receiving aid:* Freshmen: 42% (153); Undergraduates: 27% (479). *Average Award:* Freshmen: $5264; Undergraduates: $5097. *Scholarships, grants, and awards by category: Academic Interests/Achievement:* 309 awards ($358,000 total): biological sciences, business, communication, computer science, education, English, foreign languages, general academic interests/achievements, health fields, humanities, mathematics, military science, physical sciences, premedicine, religion/biblical studies, social sciences. *Creative Arts/Performance:* 123 awards ($209,500 total): cinema/film/broadcasting, creative writing, dance, general creative arts/performance, music, performing arts, theater/drama. *Special Achievements/Activities:* 504 awards ($3,218,200 total): general special achievements/activities, leadership. *Special Characteristics:* 76 awards ($890,149 total): children of educators, children of faculty/staff, relatives of clergy, religious affiliation, siblings of current students. *Tuition waivers:* Full or partial for employees or children of employees, senior citizens. *ROTC:* Army cooperative.

LOANS *Student loans:* $7,535,185 (89% need-based, 11% non-need-based). 64% of past graduating class borrowed through all loan programs. *Average indebtedness per student:* $13,977. *Average need-based loan:* Freshmen: $2482; Undergraduates: $4785. *Parent loans:* $3,727,023 (83% need-based, 17% non-need-based). *Programs:* FFEL (Subsidized and Unsubsidized Stafford, PLUS), Perkins, Federal Nursing, alternative loans.

WORK-STUDY *Federal work-study:* Total amount: $567,399; 324 jobs averaging $631. *State or other work-study/employment:* Total amount: $251,800 (47% need-based, 53% non-need-based). 234 part-time jobs averaging $631.

APPLYING FOR FINANCIAL AID *Required financial aid forms:* FAFSA, institution's own form, state aid form. *Financial aid deadline (priority):* 2/1. *Notification date:* Continuous beginning 2/15. Students must reply within 2 weeks of notification.
CONTACT Mr. Peter Rautzhan, Director of Admissions and Financial Aid, DeSales University, 2755 Station Avenue, Center Valley, PA 18034-9568, 610-282-1100 Ext. 1332 or toll-free 877-4DESALES (in-state), 800-228-5114 (out-of-state). *Fax:* 610-282-0131. *E-mail:* peter.rautzhan@desales.edu.

DESIGN INSTITUTE OF SAN DIEGO
San Diego, CA

CONTACT Financial Aid Office, Design Institute of San Diego, 8555 Commerce Avenue, San Diego, CA 92121, 858-566-1200 or toll-free 800-619-4337.

DeVRY INSTITUTE OF TECHNOLOGY
Long Island City, NY

ABOUT THE INSTITUTION Proprietary, coed. Awards: associate, bachelor's, and master's degrees and post-bachelor's certificates. 6 undergraduate majors. Total enrollment: 1,453. Undergraduates: 1,453.
GIFT AID (NEED-BASED) *Scholarships, grants, and awards:* Federal Pell, FSEOG, state, private, college/university gift aid from institutional funds.
GIFT AID (NON-NEED-BASED) *Scholarships, grants, and awards by category:* *Academic Interests/Achievement:* general academic interests/achievements.
LOANS *Programs:* FFEL (Subsidized and Unsubsidized Stafford, PLUS), Perkins, college/university.
WORK-STUDY *Federal work-study:* Total amount: $132,049; jobs available.
APPLYING FOR FINANCIAL AID *Required financial aid form:* FAFSA.
CONTACT Elvira Senese, Dean of Student Finance, DeVry Institute of Technology, 30-20 Thomson Avenue, Long Island City, NY 11101, 718-472-2728 or toll-free 888-71-Devry. *Fax:* 718-269-4284.

DeVRY UNIVERSITY
Mesa, AZ

CONTACT Financial Aid Office, DeVry University, 1201 South Alma School Road, Mesa, AZ 85210-2011, 480-827-1511.

DeVRY UNIVERSITY
Phoenix, AZ

ABOUT THE INSTITUTION Proprietary, coed. Awards: associate, bachelor's, and master's degrees and post-bachelor's certificates. 7 undergraduate majors. Total enrollment: 1,446. Undergraduates: 1,446.
GIFT AID (NEED-BASED) *Scholarships, grants, and awards:* Federal Pell, FSEOG, state, private, college/university gift aid from institutional funds.
GIFT AID (NON-NEED-BASED) *Scholarships, grants, and awards by category:* *Academic Interests/Achievement:* general academic interests/achievements.
LOANS *Programs:* FFEL (Subsidized and Unsubsidized Stafford, PLUS), Perkins, college/university.
APPLYING FOR FINANCIAL AID *Required financial aid form:* FAFSA.
CONTACT Kathy Wyse, Dean of Student Finance, DeVry University, 2149 West Dunlap Avenue, Phoenix, AZ 85021-2995, 602-870-9222 or toll-free 800-528-0250. *Fax:* 602-870-1209.

DeVRY UNIVERSITY
Elk Grove, CA

CONTACT Financial Aid Office, DeVry University, Sacramento Center, 2218 Kausen Drive, Elk Grove, CA 95758, 916-478-2847 or toll-free 866-573-3879.

DeVRY UNIVERSITY
Fremont, CA

ABOUT THE INSTITUTION Proprietary, coed. Awards: associate, bachelor's, and master's degrees and post-bachelor's certificates. 7 undergraduate majors. Total enrollment: 1,462. Undergraduates: 1,462.
GIFT AID (NEED-BASED) *Scholarships, grants, and awards:* Federal Pell, FSEOG, state, private, college/university gift aid from institutional funds.

GIFT AID (NON-NEED-BASED) *Scholarships, grants, and awards by category:* *Academic Interests/Achievement:* general academic interests/achievements.
LOANS *Programs:* FFEL (Subsidized and Unsubsidized Stafford, PLUS), Perkins, college/university.
APPLYING FOR FINANCIAL AID *Required financial aid form:* FAFSA.
CONTACT Kim Kane, Director of Student Finance, DeVry University, 6600 Dumbarton Circle, Fremont, CA 94555, 510-574-1100 or toll-free 888-201-9941. *Fax:* 510-742-0868.

DeVRY UNIVERSITY
Irvine, CA

CONTACT Financial Aid Office, DeVry University, 3333 Michelson Drive, Suite 420, Irvine, CA 92612-1682, 949-752-5631.

DeVRY UNIVERSITY
Long Beach, CA

ABOUT THE INSTITUTION Proprietary, coed. Awards: associate, bachelor's, and master's degrees and post-bachelor's certificates. 7 undergraduate majors. Total enrollment: 1,459. Undergraduates: 1,459.
GIFT AID (NEED-BASED) *Scholarships, grants, and awards:* Federal Pell, FSEOG, state, private, college/university gift aid from institutional funds.
GIFT AID (NON-NEED-BASED) *Scholarships, grants, and awards by category:* *Academic Interests/Achievement:* general academic interests/achievements.
LOANS *Programs:* FFEL (Subsidized and Unsubsidized Stafford, PLUS), Perkins, college/university.
WORK-STUDY *Federal work-study:* Total amount: $224,622; jobs available.
APPLYING FOR FINANCIAL AID *Required financial aid form:* FAFSA.
CONTACT Kathy Odom, Director of Financial Aid, DeVry University, 3880 Kilroy Airport Way, Long Beach, CA 90806, 562-427-0861 or toll-free 800-597-0444. *Fax:* 562-989-1578.

DeVRY UNIVERSITY
Pomona, CA

ABOUT THE INSTITUTION Proprietary, coed. Awards: associate, bachelor's, and master's degrees and post-bachelor's certificates. 7 undergraduate majors. Total enrollment: 2,118. Undergraduates: 2,118.
GIFT AID (NEED-BASED) *Scholarships, grants, and awards:* Federal Pell, FSEOG, state, private, college/university gift aid from institutional funds.
GIFT AID (NON-NEED-BASED) *Scholarships, grants, and awards by category:* *Academic Interests/Achievement:* general academic interests/achievements.
LOANS *Programs:* FFEL (Subsidized and Unsubsidized Stafford, PLUS), Perkins.
APPLYING FOR FINANCIAL AID *Required financial aid form:* FAFSA.
CONTACT Kathy Odom, Director of Financial Aid, DeVry University, 901 Corporate Center Drive, Pomona, CA 91768-2642, 909-622-8866 or toll-free 800-882-7536. *Fax:* 909-623-5666.

DeVRY UNIVERSITY
San Diego, CA

CONTACT Financial Aid Office, DeVry University, 2655 Camino Del Rio North, Suite 201, San Diego, CA 92108-1633, 619-683-2446.

DeVRY UNIVERSITY
San Francisco, CA

CONTACT Financial Aid Office, DeVry University, 455 Market Street, Suite 1650, San Francisco, CA 94105-2472, 415-243-8787.

DeVRY UNIVERSITY
West Hills, CA

ABOUT THE INSTITUTION Proprietary, coed. Awards: associate, bachelor's, and master's degrees and post-bachelor's certificates. 7 undergraduate majors. Total enrollment: 902. Undergraduates: 902.
GIFT AID (NEED-BASED) *Scholarships, grants, and awards:* Federal Pell, FSEOG, state, private, college/university gift aid from institutional funds.

DeVry University

GIFT AID (NON-NEED-BASED) *Scholarships, grants, and awards by category: Academic Interests/Achievement:* general academic interests/achievements.
LOANS *Programs:* FFEL (Subsidized and Unsubsidized Stafford, PLUS), Perkins, college/university.
APPLYING FOR FINANCIAL AID *Required financial aid form:* FAFSA.
CONTACT Ann Logan, Dean of Student Finance, DeVry University, 22801 Roscoe Boulevard, West Hills, CA 91304, 818-932-3001 or toll-free 888-610-0800. *Fax:* 818-932-3131.

DeVRY UNIVERSITY
Broomfield, CO

CONTACT Terry Bargas, Director of Financial Aid, DeVry University, 925 South Niagara Street, Denver, CO 80224, 303-329-3340. *Fax:* 303-321-3412.

DeVRY UNIVERSITY
Colorado Springs, CO

ABOUT THE INSTITUTION Proprietary, coed. Awards: associate, bachelor's, and master's degrees and post-bachelor's certificates. 5 undergraduate majors. Total enrollment: 267. Undergraduates: 267.
GIFT AID (NEED-BASED) *Scholarships, grants, and awards:* Federal Pell, FSEOG, state, private, college/university gift aid from institutional funds.
GIFT AID (NON-NEED-BASED) *Scholarships, grants, and awards by category: Academic Interests/Achievement:* general academic interests/achievements.
LOANS *Programs:* FFEL (Subsidized and Unsubsidized Stafford, PLUS), Perkins, college/university.
WORK-STUDY *Federal work-study:* Total amount: $69,808; jobs available.
APPLYING FOR FINANCIAL AID *Required financial aid form:* FAFSA.
CONTACT Carol Oppman, Director of Financial Aid, DeVry University, 225 South Union Boulevard, Colorado Springs, CO 80910, 719-632-3000. *Fax:* 719-632-1909.

DeVRY UNIVERSITY
Westminster, CO

ABOUT THE INSTITUTION Proprietary, coed. Awards: associate and bachelor's degrees and post-bachelor's certificates. 12 undergraduate majors. Total enrollment: 673. Undergraduates: 673. Freshmen: 255.
GIFT AID (NEED-BASED) *Scholarships, grants, and awards:* Federal Pell, FSEOG, state, private, college/university gift aid from institutional funds.
GIFT AID (NON-NEED-BASED) *Scholarships, grants, and awards by category: Academic Interests/Achievement:* general academic interests/achievements.
LOANS *Programs:* FFEL (Subsidized and Unsubsidized Stafford, PLUS), Perkins, college/university.
APPLYING FOR FINANCIAL AID *Required financial aid form:* FAFSA.
CONTACT Office of Financial Aid, DeVry University, 1870 West 122nd Avenue, Westminster, CO 80234-2010, 303-280-7400 or toll-free 888-212-1857.

DeVRY UNIVERSITY
Miami, FL

CONTACT Financial Aid Office, DeVry University, 200 South Biscayne Boulevard, Suite 500, Miami, FL 33131-5351, 786-425-1113.

DeVRY UNIVERSITY
Miramar, FL

ABOUT THE INSTITUTION Proprietary, coed. Awards: associate, bachelor's, and master's degrees and post-bachelor's certificates. Total enrollment: 1,024. Undergraduates: 1,024.
GIFT AID (NEED-BASED) *Scholarships, grants, and awards:* Federal Pell, FSEOG, state, private, college/university gift aid from institutional funds.
GIFT AID (NON-NEED-BASED) *Scholarships, grants, and awards by category: Academic Interests/Achievement:* general academic interests/achievements.
LOANS *Programs:* FFEL (Subsidized and Unsubsidized Stafford, PLUS), Perkins, college/university.
WORK-STUDY *Federal work-study:* Total amount: $190,725; jobs available.
APPLYING FOR FINANCIAL AID *Required financial aid form:* FAFSA.

CONTACT Office of Financial Aid, DeVry University, 2300 Southwest 145th Avenue, Miramar, FL 33027, 954-499-9700 or toll-free 866-793-3879.

DeVRY UNIVERSITY
Orlando, FL

ABOUT THE INSTITUTION Proprietary, coed. Awards: associate, bachelor's, and master's degrees and post-bachelor's certificates. 6 undergraduate majors. Total enrollment: 1,250. Undergraduates: 1,250.
GIFT AID (NEED-BASED) *Scholarships, grants, and awards:* Federal Pell, FSEOG, state, private, college/university gift aid from institutional funds.
GIFT AID (NON-NEED-BASED) *Scholarships, grants, and awards by category: Academic Interests/Achievement:* general academic interests/achievements.
LOANS *Programs:* FFEL (Subsidized and Unsubsidized Stafford, PLUS), Perkins, college/university.
APPLYING FOR FINANCIAL AID *Required financial aid form:* FAFSA.
CONTACT Estrella Velazquez-Domenech, Director of Student Finance, DeVry University, 4000 Millenia Boulevard, Orlando, FL 32839, 407-345-2816 or toll-free 866-353-3879. *Fax:* 407-355-4855.

DeVRY UNIVERSITY
Tampa, FL

CONTACT Financial Aid Office, DeVry University, 3030 North Rocky Point Drive West, Suite 100, Tampa, FL 33607-5901, 813-288-8994.

DeVRY UNIVERSITY
Alpharetta, GA

ABOUT THE INSTITUTION Proprietary, coed. Awards: associate, bachelor's, and master's degrees and post-bachelor's certificates. 7 undergraduate majors. Total enrollment: 815. Undergraduates: 815.
GIFT AID (NEED-BASED) *Scholarships, grants, and awards:* Federal Pell, FSEOG, state, private, college/university gift aid from institutional funds.
GIFT AID (NON-NEED-BASED) *Scholarships, grants, and awards by category: Academic Interests/Achievement:* general academic interests/achievements.
LOANS *Programs:* FFEL (Subsidized and Unsubsidized Stafford, PLUS), Perkins, college/university.
APPLYING FOR FINANCIAL AID *Required financial aid form:* FAFSA.
CONTACT David Pickett, Assistant Director of Financial Aid, DeVry University, 2555 Northwinds Parkway, Alpharetta, GA 30004, 770-521-4900 or toll-free 800-221-4771. *Fax:* 770-664-8024.

DeVRY UNIVERSITY
Atlanta, GA

CONTACT Financial Aid Office, DeVry University, Fifteen Piedmont Center, Plaza Level 100, Atlanta, GA 30305-1543, 404-296-7400.

DeVRY UNIVERSITY
Decatur, GA

ABOUT THE INSTITUTION Proprietary, coed. Awards: associate, bachelor's, and master's degrees and post-bachelor's certificates. 7 undergraduate majors. Total enrollment: 2,248. Undergraduates: 2,248.
GIFT AID (NEED-BASED) *Scholarships, grants, and awards:* Federal Pell, FSEOG, state, private, college/university gift aid from institutional funds.
GIFT AID (NON-NEED-BASED) *Scholarships, grants, and awards by category: Academic Interests/Achievement:* general academic interests/achievements.
LOANS *Programs:* FFEL (Subsidized and Unsubsidized Stafford, PLUS), Perkins, college/university.
APPLYING FOR FINANCIAL AID *Required financial aid form:* FAFSA.
CONTACT Robin Winston, Director of Financial Aid, DeVry University, 250 North Arcadia Avenue, Decatur, GA 30030-2198, 404-292-7900 or toll-free 800-221-4771. *Fax:* 404-292-2321.

DeVRY UNIVERSITY
Duluth, GA

CONTACT Financial Aid Office, DeVry University, 3505 Koger Boulevard, Suite 170, Duluth, GA 30096-7671, 678-380-9780.

DeVRY UNIVERSITY
Addison, IL

ABOUT THE INSTITUTION Proprietary, coed. Awards: associate and bachelor's degrees. 7 undergraduate majors. Total enrollment: 1,853. Undergraduates: 1,853.
GIFT AID (NEED-BASED) *Scholarships, grants, and awards:* Federal Pell, FSEOG, state, private, college/university gift aid from institutional funds.
GIFT AID (NON-NEED-BASED) *Scholarships, grants, and awards by category: Academic Interests/Achievement:* general academic interests/achievements.
LOANS *Programs:* FFEL (Subsidized and Unsubsidized Stafford, PLUS), Perkins, college/university.
APPLYING FOR FINANCIAL AID *Required financial aid form:* FAFSA.
CONTACT Sejal Amin, Director of Student Finance, DeVry University, 1221 North Swift Road, Addison, IL 60101-6106, 630-953-1300 or toll-free 800-346-5420.

DeVRY UNIVERSITY
Chicago, IL

ABOUT THE INSTITUTION Proprietary, coed. Awards: associate and bachelor's degrees. 7 undergraduate majors. Total enrollment: 2,477. Undergraduates: 2,477.
GIFT AID (NEED-BASED) *Scholarships, grants, and awards:* Federal Pell, FSEOG, state, private, college/university gift aid from institutional funds.
GIFT AID (NON-NEED-BASED) *Scholarships, grants, and awards by category: Academic Interests/Achievement:* general academic interests/achievements.
LOANS *Programs:* FFEL (Subsidized and Unsubsidized Stafford, PLUS), Perkins, college/university.
APPLYING FOR FINANCIAL AID *Required financial aid form:* FAFSA.
CONTACT Milena Dobrina, Director of Financial Aid, DeVry University, 3300 North Campbell Avenue, Chicago, IL 60618-5994, 773-929-8500 or toll-free 800-383-3879. *Fax:* 773-348-1780.

DeVRY UNIVERSITY
Elgin, IL

CONTACT Financial Aid Office, DeVry University, 385 Airport Road, Elgin, IL 60123-9341, 847-622-1135.

DeVRY UNIVERSITY
Gurnee, IL

CONTACT Financial Aid Office, DeVry University, 1075 Tri-State Parkway, Suite 800, Gurnee, IL 60031-9126, 847-855-2649 or toll-free 866-563-3879.

DeVRY UNIVERSITY
Naperville, IL

CONTACT Financial Aid Office, DeVry University, 2056 Westings Avenue, Suite 40, Naperville, IL 60563-2361, 630-428-9086.

DeVRY UNIVERSITY
Oakbrook Terrace, IL

CONTACT Financial Aid Office, DeVry University, One Tower Lane, Oakbrook Terrace, IL 60181, 630-574-1960.

DeVRY UNIVERSITY
Tinley Park, IL

ABOUT THE INSTITUTION Proprietary, coed. Awards: associate, bachelor's, and master's degrees and post-bachelor's certificates. 7 undergraduate majors. Total enrollment: 1,238. Undergraduates: 1,238.
GIFT AID (NEED-BASED) *Scholarships, grants, and awards:* Federal Pell, FSEOG, state, private, college/university gift aid from institutional funds.
GIFT AID (NON-NEED-BASED) *Scholarships, grants, and awards by category: Academic Interests/Achievement:* general academic interests/achievements.
LOANS *Programs:* FFEL (Subsidized and Unsubsidized Stafford, PLUS), Perkins.
APPLYING FOR FINANCIAL AID *Required financial aid form:* FAFSA.
CONTACT Director of Student Finance, DeVry University, 18624 West Creek Drive, Tinley Park, IL 60477, 708-342-3300 or toll-free 877-305-8184. *Fax:* 708-342-3120.

DeVRY UNIVERSITY
Indianapolis, IN

CONTACT Financial Aid Office, DeVry University, 9100 Keystone Crossing, Suite 350, Indianapolis, IN 46240-2158, 317-581-8854.

DeVRY UNIVERSITY
Merrillville, IN

CONTACT Financial Aid Office, DeVry University, Twin Towers, 1000 East 80th Place, Suite 222 Mall, Merrillville, IN 46410-5673, 219-736-7440.

DeVRY UNIVERSITY
Bethesda, MD

CONTACT Financial Aid Office, DeVry University, 4550 Montgomery Avenue. Suite 100 North, Bethesda, MD 20814-3304, 301-652-8477.

DeVRY UNIVERSITY
Kansas City, MO

ABOUT THE INSTITUTION Proprietary, coed. Awards: associate, bachelor's, and master's degrees and post-bachelor's certificates. 7 undergraduate majors. Total enrollment: 1,380. Undergraduates: 1,380.
GIFT AID (NEED-BASED) *Scholarships, grants, and awards:* Federal Pell, FSEOG, private, college/university gift aid from institutional funds.
GIFT AID (NON-NEED-BASED) *Scholarships, grants, and awards by category: Academic Interests/Achievement:* general academic interests/achievements.
LOANS *Programs:* FFEL (Subsidized and Unsubsidized Stafford, PLUS).
APPLYING FOR FINANCIAL AID *Required financial aid form:* FAFSA.
CONTACT Maureen Kelly, Senior Associate Director of Financial Aid, DeVry University, 11224 Holmes Street, Kansas City, MO 64131-3698, 816-941-0430 or toll-free 800-821-3766.

DeVRY UNIVERSITY
Kansas City, MO

CONTACT Financial Aid Office, DeVry University, City Center Square, 1100 Main Street, Suite 118, Kansas City, MO 64105-2112, 816-221-1300.

DeVRY UNIVERSITY
St. Louis, MO

CONTACT Financial Aid Office, DeVry University, 1801 Park 270 Drive, Suite 260, St. Louis, MO 63146-4020, 314-542-4222.

DeVRY UNIVERSITY
Henderson, NV

CONTACT Financial Aid Office, DeVry University, 2490 Paseo Verde Parkway, Suite 150, Henderson, NV 89074-7120, 702-933-9700 or toll-free 866-78DEVRY.

DeVRY UNIVERSITY
North Brunswick, NJ

ABOUT THE INSTITUTION Proprietary, coed. Awards: associate and bachelor's degrees. 4 undergraduate majors. Total enrollment: 1,886. Undergraduates: 1,886.
GIFT AID (NEED-BASED) *Scholarships, grants, and awards:* Federal Pell, FSEOG, state, private, college/university gift aid from institutional funds.
GIFT AID (NON-NEED-BASED) *Scholarships, grants, and awards by category:* *Academic Interests/Achievement:* general academic interests/achievements.
LOANS *Programs:* FFEL (Subsidized and Unsubsidized Stafford, PLUS), Perkins, college/university.
WORK-STUDY *Federal work-study:* Total amount: $175,529; jobs available.
APPLYING FOR FINANCIAL AID *Required financial aid form:* FAFSA.
CONTACT Albert Cama, Director of Financial Aid, DeVry University, 630 US Highway 1, North Brunswick, NJ 08902, 732-435-4880 or toll-free 800-333-3879. *Fax:* 732-435-4867.

DeVRY UNIVERSITY
Charlotte, NC

CONTACT Financial Aid Office, DeVry University, 4521 Sharon Road, Suite 145, Charlotte, NC 28211-3627, 704-362-2345.

DeVRY UNIVERSITY
Cleveland, OH

CONTACT Financial Aid Office, DeVry University, 200 Public Square, Suite 150, Cleveland, OH 44114-2301, 216-781-8000.

DeVRY UNIVERSITY
Columbus, OH

ABOUT THE INSTITUTION Proprietary, coed. Awards: associate, bachelor's, and master's degrees and post-bachelor's certificates. 6 undergraduate majors. Total enrollment: 2,778. Undergraduates: 2,778.
GIFT AID (NEED-BASED) *Scholarships, grants, and awards:* Federal Pell, FSEOG, state, private, college/university gift aid from institutional funds.
GIFT AID (NON-NEED-BASED) *Scholarships, grants, and awards by category:* *Academic Interests/Achievement:* general academic interests/achievements.
LOANS *Programs:* FFEL (Subsidized and Unsubsidized Stafford, PLUS), Perkins, college/university.
APPLYING FOR FINANCIAL AID *Required financial aid form:* FAFSA.
CONTACT Cynthia Price, Director of Financial Aid, DeVry University, 1350 Alum Creek Drive, Columbus, OH 43209-2705, 614-253-7291 or toll-free 800-426-2206. *Fax:* 614-252-4108.

DeVRY UNIVERSITY
Seven Hills, OH

CONTACT Financial Aid Office, DeVry University, The Genesis Building, 6000 Lombardo Center, Seven Hills, OH 44131-6907, 216-328-8754 or toll-free 866-453-3879.

DeVRY UNIVERSITY
Portland, OR

CONTACT Financial Aid Office, DeVry University, Peterkort Center II, 9755 SW Barnes Road, Suite 150, Portland, OR 97225-6651, 503-296-7468.

DeVRY UNIVERSITY
Chesterbrook, PA

CONTACT Financial Aid Office, DeVry University, 701 Lee Road, Suite 103, Chesterbrook, PA 19087-5612, 610-889-9980.

DeVRY UNIVERSITY
Fort Washington, PA

ABOUT THE INSTITUTION Proprietary, coed. Awards: associate, bachelor's, and master's degrees and post-bachelor's certificates. Total enrollment: 627. Undergraduates: 627.
GIFT AID (NEED-BASED) *Scholarships, grants, and awards:* Federal Pell, FSEOG, state, private, college/university gift aid from institutional funds.
GIFT AID (NON-NEED-BASED) *Scholarships, grants, and awards by category:* *Academic Interests/Achievement:* general academic interests/achievements.
LOANS *Programs:* FFEL (Subsidized and Unsubsidized Stafford, PLUS), Perkins, college/university.
APPLYING FOR FINANCIAL AID *Required financial aid form:* FAFSA.
CONTACT Financial Aid Office, DeVry University, 1140 Virginia Drive, Fort Washington, PA 19034, 215-591-5700 or toll-free 866-303-3879.

DeVRY UNIVERSITY
Pittsburgh, PA

CONTACT Financial Aid Office, DeVry University, FreeMarkets Center, 210 Sixth Avenue, Suite 200, Pittsburgh, PA 15222-9123, 412-642-9072 or toll-free 866-77DEVRY.

DeVRY UNIVERSITY
Houston, TX

CONTACT Financial Aid Office, DeVry University, 11125 Equity Drive, Houston, TX 77041, 713-850-0888 or toll-free 866-703-3879 (out-of-state).

DeVRY UNIVERSITY
Irving, TX

ABOUT THE INSTITUTION Proprietary, coed. Awards: associate, bachelor's, and master's degrees and post-bachelor's certificates. 7 undergraduate majors. Total enrollment: 1,928. Undergraduates: 1,928.
GIFT AID (NEED-BASED) *Scholarships, grants, and awards:* Federal Pell, FSEOG, private, college/university gift aid from institutional funds.
GIFT AID (NON-NEED-BASED) *Scholarships, grants, and awards by category:* *Academic Interests/Achievement:* general academic interests/achievements.
LOANS *Programs:* FFEL (Subsidized and Unsubsidized Stafford, PLUS), Perkins, college/university.
APPLYING FOR FINANCIAL AID *Required financial aid form:* FAFSA.
CONTACT Tommy Sims, Financial Aid Officer, DeVry University, 4800 Regent Boulevard, Irving, TX 75063-2440, 972-929-6777 or toll-free 800-633-3879.

DeVRY UNIVERSITY
Plano, TX

CONTACT Financial Aid Office, DeVry University, Plano Corporate Center II, 2301 West Plano Parkway, Suite 101, Plano, TX 75075-8435, 972-943-8041.

DeVRY UNIVERSITY
Arlington, VA

ABOUT THE INSTITUTION Proprietary, coed. Awards: associate, bachelor's, and master's degrees and post-bachelor's certificates. 6 undergraduate majors. Total enrollment: 578. Undergraduates: 578.
GIFT AID (NEED-BASED) *Scholarships, grants, and awards:* Federal Pell, FSEOG, private, college/university gift aid from institutional funds.
GIFT AID (NON-NEED-BASED) *Scholarships, grants, and awards by category:* *Academic Interests/Achievement:* general academic interests/achievements.
LOANS *Programs:* FFEL (Subsidized and Unsubsidized Stafford, PLUS), Perkins, college/university.
APPLYING FOR FINANCIAL AID *Required financial aid form:* FAFSA.
CONTACT Roberta McDevitt, Director of Student Finance, DeVry University, 2341 Jefferson Davis Highway, Arlington, VA 22202, 866-338-7932. *Fax:* 703-414-4040.

DeVRY UNIVERSITY
McLean, VA

CONTACT Financial Aid Office, DeVry University, 1751 Pinnacle Drive, Suite 250, McLean, VA 22102-3832, 703-556-9669.

DeVRY UNIVERSITY
Bellevue, WA

CONTACT Financial Aid Office, DeVry University, 500 108th Avenue NE, Suite 320, Bellevue, WA 98004-5519, 425-455-2242.

DeVRY UNIVERSITY
Federal Way, WA

ABOUT THE INSTITUTION Proprietary, coed. Awards: associate and bachelor's degrees and post-bachelor's certificates. 6 undergraduate majors. Total enrollment: 1,005. Undergraduates: 1,005.

GIFT AID (NEED-BASED) *Scholarships, grants, and awards:* Federal Pell, FSEOG, state, private, college/university gift aid from institutional funds.

GIFT AID (NON-NEED-BASED) *Scholarships, grants, and awards by category: Academic Interests/Achievement:* general academic interests/achievements.

LOANS *Programs:* FFEL (Subsidized and Unsubsidized Stafford, PLUS), Perkins, college/university.

APPLYING FOR FINANCIAL AID *Required financial aid form:* FAFSA.

CONTACT Diane Rooney, Assistant Director of Student Finance, DeVry University, 3600 South 344th Way, Federal Way, WA 98001, 253-943-2800 or toll-free 877-923-3879. *Fax:* 253-943-5503.

DeVRY UNIVERSITY
Milwaukee, WI

CONTACT Financial Aid Office, DeVry University, 100 East Wisconsin Avenue, Suite 2550, Milwaukee, WI 53202-4107, 414-278-7677.

DeVRY UNIVERSITY
Waukesha, WI

CONTACT Financial Aid Office, DeVry University, 20935 Swenson Drive, Suite 450, Waukesha, WI 53186-4047, 262-798-9889.

DICKINSON COLLEGE
Carlisle, PA

Tuition & fees: $32,120	Average undergraduate aid package: $24,015

ABOUT THE INSTITUTION Independent, coed. Awards: bachelor's degrees. 45 undergraduate majors. Total enrollment: 2,321. Undergraduates: 2,321. Freshmen: 606. Both federal and institutional methodology are used as a basis for awarding need-based institutional aid.

UNDERGRADUATE EXPENSES for 2005–06 *Application fee:* $50. *Comprehensive fee:* $40,170 includes full-time tuition ($31,800), mandatory fees ($320), and room and board ($8050). *College room only:* $4150. *Part-time tuition:* $3975 per course. *Part-time fees:* $40 per credit.

FRESHMAN FINANCIAL AID (Fall 2004, est.) 390 applied for aid; of those 81% were deemed to have need. 100% of freshmen with need received aid; of those 85% had need fully met. *Average percent of need met:* 98% (excluding resources awarded to replace EFC). *Average financial aid package:* $24,294 (excluding resources awarded to replace EFC). 9% of all full-time freshmen had no need and received non-need-based gift aid.

UNDERGRADUATE FINANCIAL AID (Fall 2004, est.) 1,374 applied for aid; of those 86% were deemed to have need. 100% of undergraduates with need received aid; of those 70% had need fully met. *Average percent of need met:* 96% (excluding resources awarded to replace EFC). *Average financial aid package:* $24,015 (excluding resources awarded to replace EFC). 11% of all full-time undergraduates had no need and received non-need-based gift aid.

GIFT AID (NEED-BASED) *Total amount:* $20,965,514 (5% federal, 4% state, 88% institutional, 3% external sources). *Receiving aid:* Freshmen: 48% (293); All full-time undergraduates: 49% (1,110). *Average award:* Freshmen: $20,968;

Undergraduates: $19,254. *Scholarships, grants, and awards:* Federal Pell, FSEOG, state, private, college/university gift aid from institutional funds.

GIFT AID (NON-NEED-BASED) *Total amount:* $4,014,691 (7% federal, 85% institutional, 8% external sources). *Receiving aid:* Freshmen: 7% (45); Undergraduates: 6% (127). *Average Award:* Freshmen: $12,135; Undergraduates: $11,887. *Scholarships, grants, and awards by category: Academic Interests/Achievement:* 528 awards ($6,080,343 total): general academic interests/achievements, military science. *Special Characteristics:* 36 awards ($734,500 total): children and siblings of alumni, children of faculty/staff. *ROTC:* Army.

LOANS *Student loans:* $7,050,637 (67% need-based, 33% non-need-based). 71% of past graduating class borrowed through all loan programs. *Average indebtedness per student:* $19,358. *Average need-based loan:* Freshmen: $3432; Undergraduates: $4558. *Parent loans:* $4,632,186 (16% need-based, 84% non-need-based). *Programs:* FFEL (Subsidized and Unsubsidized Stafford, PLUS), Perkins, college/university.

WORK-STUDY *Federal work-study:* Total amount: $1,340,821; 864 jobs averaging $1552. *State or other work-study/employment:* Total amount: $378,480 (79% need-based, 21% non-need-based). 113 part-time jobs averaging $3349.

APPLYING FOR FINANCIAL AID *Required financial aid forms:* FAFSA, CSS Financial Aid PROFILE, state aid form, noncustodial (divorced/separated) parent's statement, business/farm supplement. *Financial aid deadline:* 2/1 (priority: 11/15). *Notification date:* 3/20. Students must reply by 5/1 or within 2 weeks of notification.

CONTACT Judith B. Carter, Director of Financial Aid, Dickinson College, PO Box 1773, Carlisle, PA 17013-2896, 717-245-1308 or toll-free 800-644-1773. *Fax:* 717-245-1972. *E-mail:* finaid@dickinson.edu.

DICKINSON STATE UNIVERSITY
Dickinson, ND

Tuition & fees (ND res): $4559	Average undergraduate aid package: N/A

ABOUT THE INSTITUTION State-supported, coed. Awards: associate and bachelor's degrees. 43 undergraduate majors. Total enrollment: 2,479. Undergraduates: 2,479. Freshmen: 416. Federal methodology is used as a basis for awarding need-based institutional aid.

UNDERGRADUATE EXPENSES for 2004–05 *Application fee:* $35. *Tuition, state resident:* full-time $3800; part-time $127 per credit. *Tuition, nonresident:* full-time $8877; part-time $338 per credit. *Required fees:* full-time $759; $31 per credit. Full-time tuition and fees vary according to location, program, and reciprocity agreements. Part-time tuition and fees vary according to course load, location, program, and reciprocity agreements. Room and board charges vary according to board plan.

GIFT AID (NEED-BASED) *Total amount:* $2,595,425 (97% federal, 3% state). *Scholarships, grants, and awards:* Federal Pell, FSEOG, state, college/university gift aid from institutional funds, National Guard tuition waivers, staff waivers.

GIFT AID (NON-NEED-BASED) *Total amount:* $874,263 (76% institutional, 24% external sources). *Scholarships, grants, and awards by category: Academic Interests/Achievement:* 487 awards ($443,640 total): agriculture, biological sciences, business, communication, computer science, education, English, foreign languages, general academic interests/achievements, health fields, humanities, mathematics, physical sciences, premedicine, social sciences. *Creative Arts/Performance:* 234 awards ($180,250 total): art/fine arts, creative writing, journalism/publications, music, theater/drama. *Special Achievements/Activities:* 20 awards ($38,569 total): cheerleading/drum major, leadership, rodeo. *Special Characteristics:* 337 awards ($957,608 total): children of faculty/staff, general special characteristics, international students. *Tuition waivers:* Full or partial for minority students, employees or children of employees, senior citizens.

LOANS *Student loans:* $6,230,686 (63% need-based, 37% non-need-based). *Parent loans:* $206,542 (100% non-need-based). *Programs:* FFEL (Subsidized and Unsubsidized Stafford, PLUS), Perkins, Federal Nursing, state, college/university, Alaska Loans, alternative loans.

WORK-STUDY *Federal work-study:* Total amount: $196,410; 176 jobs averaging $1116. *State or other work-study/employment:* Total amount: $269,699 (100% non-need-based). 225 part-time jobs averaging $1199.

ATHLETIC AWARDS *Total amount:* $140,011 (100% non-need-based).

APPLYING FOR FINANCIAL AID *Required financial aid form:* FAFSA. *Financial aid deadline (priority):* 3/15. *Notification date:* 5/5. Students must reply within 2 weeks of notification.

CONTACT Ms. Sandy Klein, Director of Financial Aid, Dickinson State University, 291 Campus Drive, Dickinson, ND 58601-4896, 701-483-2371 or toll-free 800-279-4295. *Fax:* 701-483-2720. *E-mail:* sandy.klein@dsu.nodak.edu.

DILLARD UNIVERSITY
New Orleans, LA

Tuition & fees: $11,550	Average undergraduate aid package: $14,220

ABOUT THE INSTITUTION Independent interdenominational, coed. Awards: bachelor's degrees. 51 undergraduate majors. Total enrollment: 2,155. Undergraduates: 2,155. Freshmen: 501. Federal methodology is used as a basis for awarding need-based institutional aid.

UNDERGRADUATE EXPENSES for 2004–05 *Application fee:* $20. *Comprehensive fee:* $18,390 includes full-time tuition ($11,200), mandatory fees ($350), and room and board ($6840). Room and board charges vary according to board plan and housing facility. *Part-time tuition:* $467 per credit hour. *Part-time fees:* $175 per term. *Payment plan:* Installment.

GIFT AID (NEED-BASED) *Total amount:* $10,563,344 (43% federal, 46% institutional, 11% external sources). *Receiving aid:* Freshmen: 49% (283); All full-time undergraduates: 54% (1,195). *Average award:* Freshmen: $3834; Undergraduates: $3965. *Scholarships, grants, and awards:* Federal Pell, FSEOG, state, private, college/university gift aid from institutional funds, United Negro College Fund.

GIFT AID (NON-NEED-BASED) *Total amount:* $785,240 (100% state). *Receiving aid:* Freshmen: 55% (314); Undergraduates: 43% (946). *Average Award:* Freshmen: $4254; *Undergraduates:* $4120. *Scholarships, grants, and awards by category: Academic Interests/Achievement:* 1,063 awards ($4,434,308 total): general academic interests/achievements. *Creative Arts/Performance:* 36 awards ($62,068 total): art/fine arts, music, theater/drama. *Special Characteristics:* 39 awards ($285,648 total): children of faculty/staff, religious affiliation. *Tuition waivers:* Full or partial for employees or children of employees. *ROTC:* Army cooperative, Air Force cooperative.

LOANS *Student loans:* $11,299,594 (54% need-based, 46% non-need-based). 90% of past graduating class borrowed through all loan programs. *Average indebtedness per student:* $26,000. *Average need-based loan:* Freshmen: $2511; Undergraduates: $3370. *Parent loans:* $2,622,487 (100% non-need-based). *Programs:* FFEL (Subsidized and Unsubsidized Stafford, PLUS), Perkins, alternative loans.

ATHLETIC AWARDS *Total amount:* $461,438 (100% non-need-based).

APPLYING FOR FINANCIAL AID *Required financial aid forms:* FAFSA, institution's own form. *Financial aid deadline (priority):* 3/1. *Notification date:* Continuous beginning 3/15. Students must reply within 2 weeks of notification.

CONTACT Mrs. Cynthia Thornton, Director of Financial Aid, Dillard University, 2601 Gentilly Boulevard, New Orleans, LA 70122-3097, 504-816-4677 or toll-free 800-216-6637 (out-of-state). *Fax:* 504-816-4353. *E-mail:* cthornton@dillard.edu.

DOANE COLLEGE
Crete, NE

Tuition & fees: $15,970	Average undergraduate aid package: $13,899

ABOUT THE INSTITUTION Independent religious, coed. Awards: bachelor's and master's degrees (non-traditional undergraduate programs and graduate programs offered at Lincoln campus). 40 undergraduate majors. Total enrollment: 2,429. Undergraduates: 1,655. Freshmen: 306. Federal methodology is used as a basis for awarding need-based institutional aid.

UNDERGRADUATE EXPENSES for 2004–05 *Application fee:* $15. *Comprehensive fee:* $20,690 includes full-time tuition ($15,620), mandatory fees ($350), and room and board ($4720). *College room only:* $1800. Full-time tuition and fees vary according to location. Room and board charges vary according to board plan, housing facility, and location. *Part-time tuition:* $521 per credit hour. *Part-time fees:* $120 per year. Part-time tuition and fees vary according to course load and location. *Payment plan:* Installment.

FRESHMAN FINANCIAL AID (Fall 2004, est.) 295 applied for aid; of those 86% were deemed to have need. 100% of freshmen with need received aid; of those 89% had need fully met. *Average percent of need met:* 97% (excluding resources awarded to replace EFC). *Average financial aid package:* $14,404 (excluding resources awarded to replace EFC).

UNDERGRADUATE FINANCIAL AID (Fall 2004, est.) 916 applied for aid; of those 87% were deemed to have need. 100% of undergraduates with need received aid; of those 85% had need fully met. *Average percent of need met:* 95% (excluding resources awarded to replace EFC). *Average financial aid package:* $13,899 (excluding resources awarded to replace EFC).

GIFT AID (NEED-BASED) *Total amount:* $3,595,866 (34% federal, 7% state, 49% institutional, 10% external sources). *Receiving aid:* Freshmen: 83% (253); All full-time undergraduates: 80% (798). *Average award:* Freshmen: $10,211; Undergraduates: $8624. *Scholarships, grants, and awards:* Federal Pell, FSEOG, state, private, college/university gift aid from institutional funds.

GIFT AID (NON-NEED-BASED) *Total amount:* $3,759,024 (100% institutional). *Receiving aid:* Freshmen: 3% (9); Undergraduates: 4% (44). *Scholarships, grants, and awards by category: Creative Arts/Performance:* art/fine arts, debating, music, theater/drama. *Special Characteristics:* religious affiliation, siblings of current students. *Tuition waivers:* Full or partial for employees or children of employees, senior citizens. *ROTC:* Army cooperative, Air Force cooperative.

LOANS *Student loans:* $3,550,316 (74% need-based, 26% non-need-based). 82% of past graduating class borrowed through all loan programs. *Average indebtedness per student:* $12,670. *Average need-based loan:* Freshmen: $3000; Undergraduates: $4005. *Parent loans:* $3,070,415 (100% non-need-based). *Programs:* FFEL (Subsidized and Unsubsidized Stafford, PLUS), Perkins.

WORK-STUDY *Federal work-study:* Total amount: $165,081; jobs available. *State or other work-study/employment:* Total amount: $212,740 (70% need-based, 30% non-need-based). Part-time jobs available.

ATHLETIC AWARDS *Total amount:* $1,118,225 (85% need-based, 15% non-need-based).

APPLYING FOR FINANCIAL AID *Required financial aid form:* FAFSA. *Financial aid deadline (priority):* 3/1. *Notification date:* Continuous beginning 3/1. Students must reply within 2 weeks of notification.

CONTACT Ms. Janet Dodson, Director of Financial Aid, Doane College, 1014 Boswell Avenue, Crete, NE 68333-2430, 402-826-8260 or toll-free 800-333-6263. *Fax:* 402-826-8600. *E-mail:* janet.dodson@doane.edu.

DOMINICAN COLLEGE
Orangeburg, NY

Tuition & fees: $17,250	Average undergraduate aid package: $13,007

ABOUT THE INSTITUTION Independent, coed. Awards: associate, bachelor's, and master's degrees. 35 undergraduate majors. Total enrollment: 1,639. Undergraduates: 1,535. Freshmen: 236. Federal methodology is used as a basis for awarding need-based institutional aid.

UNDERGRADUATE EXPENSES for 2004–05 *Application fee:* $35. *Comprehensive fee:* $25,720 includes full-time tuition ($16,600), mandatory fees ($650), and room and board ($8470). *Part-time tuition:* $490 per credit. *Part-time fees:* $150 per term. *Payment plans:* Installment, deferred payment.

FRESHMAN FINANCIAL AID (Fall 2004, est.) 263 applied for aid; of those 92% were deemed to have need. 100% of freshmen with need received aid; of those 12% had need fully met. *Average percent of need met:* 76% (excluding resources awarded to replace EFC). *Average financial aid package:* $13,324 (excluding resources awarded to replace EFC). 11% of all full-time freshmen had no need and received non-need-based gift aid.

UNDERGRADUATE FINANCIAL AID (Fall 2004, est.) 777 applied for aid; of those 90% were deemed to have need. 100% of undergraduates with need received aid; of those 15% had need fully met. *Average percent of need met:* 66% (excluding resources awarded to replace EFC). *Average financial aid package:* $13,007 (excluding resources awarded to replace EFC). 14% of all full-time undergraduates had no need and received non-need-based gift aid.

GIFT AID (NEED-BASED) *Total amount:* $6,845,552 (21% federal, 18% state, 55% institutional, 6% external sources). *Receiving aid:* Freshmen: 73% (242); All full-time undergraduates: 79% (680). *Average award:* Freshmen: $10,584; Undergraduates: $9251. *Scholarships, grants, and awards:* Federal Pell, FSEOG, state, private, college/university gift aid from institutional funds.

GIFT AID (NON-NEED-BASED) *Total amount:* $1,155,301 (4% state, 87% institutional, 9% external sources). *Receiving aid:* Freshmen: 8% (27); Undergraduates: 9% (78). *Average Award: Freshmen:* $12,314; *Undergraduates:* $12,046. *Scholarships, grants, and awards by category: Academic Interests/Achievement:* 621 awards ($4,601,500 total): general academic interests/achievements. *Special Achievements/Activities:* 4 awards ($7659 total): community service, leadership, memberships. *Special Characteristics:* 37 awards ($488,158 total): children of faculty/staff, general special characteristics, relatives of clergy. *Tuition waivers:* Full or partial for employees or children of employees.

LOANS *Student loans:* $6,320,721 (85% need-based, 15% non-need-based). 90% of past graduating class borrowed through all loan programs. *Average indebtedness per student:* $17,358. *Average need-based loan:* Freshmen: $2766;

Undergraduates: $4000. *Parent loans:* $2,060,030 (30% need-based, 70% non-need-based). *Programs:* FFEL (Subsidized and Unsubsidized Stafford, PLUS), Perkins, Federal Nursing.

WORK-STUDY *Federal work-study:* Total amount: $254,817; 138 jobs averaging $1806. *State or other work-study/employment:* Total amount: $53,173 (73% need-based, 27% non-need-based). 25 part-time jobs averaging $2102.

ATHLETIC AWARDS *Total amount:* $986,000 (90% need-based, 10% non-need-based).

APPLYING FOR FINANCIAL AID *Required financial aid forms:* FAFSA, state aid form. *Financial aid deadline (priority):* 2/15. *Notification date:* Continuous.

CONTACT Ms. Eileen Felske, Director of Financial Aid, Dominican College, 470 Western Highway, Orangeburg, NY 10962-1210, 845-359-7800 Ext. 225 or toll-free 866-432-4636. *Fax:* 845-359-2313. *E-mail:* eileen.felske@dc.edu.

DOMINICAN UNIVERSITY
River Forest, IL

Tuition & fees: $19,000　　　**Average undergraduate aid package: $12,295**

ABOUT THE INSTITUTION Independent Roman Catholic, coed. Awards: bachelor's and master's degrees and post-master's certificates. 49 undergraduate majors. Total enrollment: 3,188. Undergraduates: 1,276. Freshmen: 272. Federal methodology is used as a basis for awarding need-based institutional aid.

UNDERGRADUATE EXPENSES for 2004–05 *Application fee:* $20. *One-time required fee:* $100. *Comprehensive fee:* $24,890 includes full-time tuition ($18,900), mandatory fees ($100), and room and board ($5890). Full-time tuition and fees vary according to program. Room and board charges vary according to board plan and housing facility. *Part-time tuition:* $630 per semester hour. *Part-time fees:* $10 per course. Part-time tuition and fees vary according to location and program. *Payment plan:* Installment.

FRESHMAN FINANCIAL AID (Fall 2003) 220 applied for aid; of those 90% were deemed to have need. 100% of freshmen with need received aid; of those 44% had need fully met. *Average percent of need met:* 90% (excluding resources awarded to replace EFC). *Average financial aid package:* $13,549 (excluding resources awarded to replace EFC). 17% of all full-time freshmen had no need and received non-need-based gift aid.

UNDERGRADUATE FINANCIAL AID (Fall 2003) 1,001 applied for aid; of those 82% were deemed to have need. 100% of undergraduates with need received aid; of those 26% had need fully met. *Average percent of need met:* 83% (excluding resources awarded to replace EFC). *Average financial aid package:* $12,295 (excluding resources awarded to replace EFC). 12% of all full-time undergraduates had no need and received non-need-based gift aid.

GIFT AID (NEED-BASED) *Total amount:* $5,279,898 (19% federal, 37% state, 41% institutional, 3% external sources). *Receiving aid:* Freshmen: 83% (199); All full-time undergraduates: 78% (818). *Average award:* Freshmen: $11,257; Undergraduates: $9144. *Scholarships, grants, and awards:* Federal Pell, FSEOG, state, private, college/university gift aid from institutional funds.

GIFT AID (NON-NEED-BASED) *Total amount:* $3,139,012 (1% state, 97% institutional, 2% external sources). *Receiving aid:* Freshmen: 31% (73); Undergraduates: 28% (294). *Average Award:* Freshmen: $9252; Undergraduates: $10,117. *Scholarships, grants, and awards by category:* Academic Interests/Achievement: 568 awards ($2,533,455 total): general academic interests/achievements, physical sciences. Creative Arts/Performance: 1 award ($3000 total): creative writing. Special Achievements/Activities: 87 awards ($50,249 total): religious involvement. Special Characteristics: 116 awards ($411,250 total): children and siblings of alumni, children of faculty/staff, international students, siblings of current students, twins. *Tuition waivers:* Full or partial for children of alumni, employees or children of employees.

LOANS *Student loans:* $3,693,661 (67% need-based, 33% non-need-based). 56% of past graduating class borrowed through all loan programs. *Average indebtedness per student:* $16,453. *Average need-based loan:* Freshmen: $2625; Undergraduates: $3467. *Parent loans:* $517,886 (100% non-need-based). *Programs:* FFEL (Subsidized and Unsubsidized Stafford, PLUS), Perkins.

WORK-STUDY *Federal work-study:* Total amount: $240,427; 221 jobs averaging $1800. *State or other work-study/employment:* Total amount: $175,999 (100% non-need-based). 147 part-time jobs averaging $1660.

APPLYING FOR FINANCIAL AID *Required financial aid form:* FAFSA. *Financial aid deadline (priority):* 6/1. *Notification date:* Continuous. Students must reply within 2 weeks of notification.

CONTACT Michael Shields, Director of Financial Aid, Dominican University, 7900 West Division Street, River Forest, IL 60305-1099, 708-524-6807 or toll-free 800-828-8475. *Fax:* 708-366-6478. *E-mail:* mshields@dom.edu.

DOMINICAN UNIVERSITY OF CALIFORNIA
San Rafael, CA

Tuition & fees: $24,454　　　**Average undergraduate aid package: $17,436**

ABOUT THE INSTITUTION Independent religious, coed. Awards: bachelor's and master's degrees and post-bachelor's certificates. 26 undergraduate majors. Total enrollment: 1,910. Undergraduates: 1,273. Freshmen: 226. Federal methodology is used as a basis for awarding need-based institutional aid.

UNDERGRADUATE EXPENSES for 2004–05 *Application fee:* $40. *Comprehensive fee:* $34,724 includes full-time tuition ($24,254), mandatory fees ($200), and room and board ($10,270). Full-time tuition and fees vary according to course load, degree level, location, and program. Room and board charges vary according to board plan. *Part-time tuition:* $1011 per unit. *Part-time fees:* $100 per term. Part-time tuition and fees vary according to degree level, location, and program. *Payment plan:* Installment.

FRESHMAN FINANCIAL AID (Fall 2004, est.) 239 applied for aid; of those 88% were deemed to have need. 100% of freshmen with need received aid; of those 18% had need fully met. *Average percent of need met:* 18% (excluding resources awarded to replace EFC). *Average financial aid package:* $19,393 (excluding resources awarded to replace EFC). 8% of all full-time freshmen had no need and received non-need-based gift aid.

UNDERGRADUATE FINANCIAL AID (Fall 2004, est.) 925 applied for aid; of those 92% were deemed to have need. 100% of undergraduates with need received aid; of those 13% had need fully met. *Average percent of need met:* 13% (excluding resources awarded to replace EFC). *Average financial aid package:* $17,436 (excluding resources awarded to replace EFC). 14% of all full-time undergraduates had no need and received non-need-based gift aid.

GIFT AID (NEED-BASED) *Total amount:* $11,874,441 (11% federal, 17% state, 72% institutional). *Receiving aid:* Freshmen: 76% (209); All full-time undergraduates: 80% (842). *Average award:* Freshmen: $15,539; Undergraduates: $13,356. *Scholarships, grants, and awards:* Federal Pell, FSEOG, state, private, college/university gift aid from institutional funds, Federal Nursing.

GIFT AID (NON-NEED-BASED) *Total amount:* $1,149,204 (100% institutional). *Receiving aid:* Freshmen: 1; Undergraduates: 5. *Average Award:* Freshmen: $8446; Undergraduates: $7504. *Scholarships, grants, and awards by category:* Academic Interests/Achievement: 301 awards ($3,093,861 total): general academic interests/achievements. Creative Arts/Performance: 11 awards ($20,500 total): music. Special Achievements/Activities: 3 awards ($2750 total): community service, general special achievements/activities. Special Characteristics: 410 awards ($1,597,684 total): adult students, children and siblings of alumni, children of faculty/staff, ethnic background, first-generation college students, international students, local/state students, members of minority groups, out-of-state students. *Tuition waivers:* Full or partial for employees or children of employees, senior citizens.

LOANS *Student loans:* $7,264,585 (98% need-based, 2% non-need-based). 52% of past graduating class borrowed through all loan programs. *Average indebtedness per student:* $7395. *Average need-based loan:* Freshmen: $3896; Undergraduates: $5639. *Parent loans:* $7,948,891 (99% need-based, 1% non-need-based). *Programs:* FFEL (Subsidized and Unsubsidized Stafford, PLUS), Perkins, Private loans.

WORK-STUDY *Federal work-study:* Total amount: $802,566; 335 jobs averaging $2562. *State or other work-study/employment:* Total amount: $169,407 (55% need-based, 45% non-need-based). 29 part-time jobs averaging $5876.

ATHLETIC AWARDS *Total amount:* $352,756 (78% need-based, 22% non-need-based).

APPLYING FOR FINANCIAL AID *Required financial aid forms:* FAFSA, institution's own form, state aid form. *Financial aid deadline (priority):* 3/2. *Notification date:* Continuous beginning 3/15. Students must reply within 2 weeks of notification.

CONTACT Audrey Tanne, Assistant Vice President for Financial Aid and Student Services, Dominican University of California, 50 Acacia Avenue, San Rafael, CA 94901-2298, 415-257-1321 or toll-free 888-323-6763. *Fax:* 415-485-3294. *E-mail:* atanne@dominican.edu.

DORDT COLLEGE
Sioux Center, IA

Tuition & fees: $16,670　　　**Average undergraduate aid package: $15,583**

ABOUT THE INSTITUTION Independent Christian Reformed, coed. Awards: associate, bachelor's, and master's degrees. 84 undergraduate majors. Total enrollment: 1,346. Undergraduates: 1,285. Freshmen: 348. Federal methodology is used as a basis for awarding need-based institutional aid.

UNDERGRADUATE EXPENSES for 2004–05 *Application fee:* $25. *Comprehensive fee:* $21,320 includes full-time tuition ($16,450), mandatory fees ($220), and room and board ($4650). *College room only:* $2440. Room and board charges vary according to board plan and housing facility. *Part-time tuition:* $650 per credit hour. *Part-time fees:* $110 per term. *Payment plan:* Installment.

FRESHMAN FINANCIAL AID (Fall 2004, est.) 308 applied for aid; of those 88% were deemed to have need. 100% of freshmen with need received aid; of those 13% had need fully met. *Average percent of need met:* 82% (excluding resources awarded to replace EFC). *Average financial aid package:* $15,772 (excluding resources awarded to replace EFC). 17% of all full-time freshmen had no need and received non-need-based gift aid.

UNDERGRADUATE FINANCIAL AID (Fall 2004, est.) 1,045 applied for aid; of those 90% were deemed to have need. 100% of undergraduates with need received aid; of those 12% had need fully met. *Average percent of need met:* 84% (excluding resources awarded to replace EFC). *Average financial aid package:* $15,583 (excluding resources awarded to replace EFC). 17% of all full-time undergraduates had no need and received non-need-based gift aid.

GIFT AID (NEED-BASED) *Total amount:* $8,556,043 (14% federal, 14% state, 65% institutional, 7% external sources). *Receiving aid:* Freshmen: 79% (272); All full-time undergraduates: 77% (937). *Average award:* Freshmen: $9324; Undergraduates: $8231. *Scholarships, grants, and awards:* Federal Pell, FSEOG, state, private, college/university gift aid from institutional funds.

GIFT AID (NON-NEED-BASED) *Total amount:* $1,063,574 (90% institutional, 10% external sources). *Average Award:* Freshmen: $8659; *Undergraduates:* $7987. *Scholarships, grants, and awards by category: Academic Interests/ Achievement:* agriculture, biological sciences, business, communication, computer science, education, engineering/technologies, English, foreign languages, general academic interests/achievements, humanities, mathematics, physical sciences, premedicine, religion/biblical studies, social sciences. *Creative Arts/Performance:* 212 awards ($358,000 total): journalism/publications, music, theater/drama. *Special Achievements/Activities:* general special achievements/activities, leadership. *Special Characteristics:* children and siblings of alumni, children of faculty/staff, general special characteristics, handicapped students, international students, local/state students, members of minority groups, out-of-state students, religious affiliation. *Tuition waivers:* Full or partial for employees or children of employees, senior citizens.

LOANS *Student loans:* $6,565,757 (93% need-based, 7% non-need-based). 78% of past graduating class borrowed through all loan programs. *Average indebtedness per student:* $16,010. *Average need-based loan:* Freshmen: $3955; Undergraduates: $4736. *Parent loans:* $1,508,161 (90% need-based, 10% non-need-based). *Programs:* FFEL (Subsidized and Unsubsidized Stafford, PLUS), Perkins, state, college/university, alternative loans.

WORK-STUDY *Federal work-study:* Total amount: $769,250; 591 jobs averaging $1300. *State or other work-study/employment:* Total amount: $728,738 (75% need-based, 25% non-need-based). 475 part-time jobs averaging $1300.

ATHLETIC AWARDS *Total amount:* $448,400 (75% need-based, 25% non-need-based).

APPLYING FOR FINANCIAL AID *Required financial aid forms:* FAFSA, institution's own form. *Financial aid deadline (priority):* 4/1. *Notification date:* Continuous beginning 3/5. Students must reply within 3 weeks of notification.

CONTACT Michael Epema, Director of Financial Aid, Dordt College, 498 4th Avenue NE, Sioux Center, IA 51250-1697, 712-722-6087 Ext. 6082 or toll-free 800-343-6738. *Fax:* 712-722-1967.

DOWLING COLLEGE
Oakdale, NY

Tuition & fees: $16,050	Average undergraduate aid package: $13,671

ABOUT THE INSTITUTION Independent, coed. Awards: bachelor's, master's, and doctoral degrees and post-bachelor's and post-master's certificates. 52 undergraduate majors. Total enrollment: 6,092. Undergraduates: 3,357. Freshmen: 486. Federal methodology is used as a basis for awarding need-based institutional aid.

UNDERGRADUATE EXPENSES for 2004–05 *Application fee:* $25. *Tuition:* full-time $15,210; part-time $507 per credit. *Required fees:* full-time $840; $275 per term part-time. Part-time tuition and fees vary according to course load and degree level. Room and board charges vary according to housing facility and location. *Payment plans:* Installment, deferred payment.

FRESHMAN FINANCIAL AID (Fall 2004, est.) 368 applied for aid; of those 83% were deemed to have need. 100% of freshmen with need received aid; of those 7% had need fully met. *Average percent of need met:* 92% (excluding resources awarded to replace EFC). *Average financial aid package:* $12,290 (excluding resources awarded to replace EFC). 22% of all full-time freshmen had no need and received non-need-based gift aid.

UNDERGRADUATE FINANCIAL AID (Fall 2004, est.) 1,747 applied for aid; of those 86% were deemed to have need. 100% of undergraduates with need received aid; of those 20% had need fully met. *Average percent of need met:* 90% (excluding resources awarded to replace EFC). *Average financial aid package:* $13,671 (excluding resources awarded to replace EFC). 14% of all full-time undergraduates had no need and received non-need-based gift aid.

GIFT AID (NEED-BASED) *Total amount:* $10,303,025 (28% federal, 32% state, 39% institutional, 1% external sources). *Receiving aid:* Freshmen: 67% (307); All full-time undergraduates: 67% (1,501). *Average award:* Freshmen: $2544; Undergraduates: $2671. *Scholarships, grants, and awards:* Federal Pell, FSEOG, state, private, college/university gift aid from institutional funds.

GIFT AID (NON-NEED-BASED) *Total amount:* $1,397,624 (99% institutional, 1% external sources). *Average Award:* Freshmen: $3950; *Undergraduates:* $5006. *Scholarships, grants, and awards by category: Academic Interests/ Achievement:* business, education, general academic interests/achievements. *Special Achievements/Activities:* general special achievements/activities. *Special Characteristics:* children and siblings of alumni, children of educators, children of faculty/staff, children of public servants, children of union members/ company employees, children of workers in trades, first-generation college students, general special characteristics, local/state students, public servants. *Tuition waivers:* Full or partial for minority students, children of alumni, employees or children of employees, adult students, senior citizens. *ROTC:* Air Force cooperative.

LOANS *Student loans:* $11,438,977 (88% need-based, 12% non-need-based). 73% of past graduating class borrowed through all loan programs. *Average indebtedness per student:* $21,411. *Average need-based loan:* Freshmen: $2362; Undergraduates: $3545. *Parent loans:* $2,012,426 (75% need-based, 25% non-need-based). *Programs:* Federal Direct (Subsidized and Unsubsidized Stafford, PLUS), FFEL (PLUS), Perkins, alternative loans.

WORK-STUDY *Federal work-study:* Total amount: $330,388; 256 jobs averaging $1300. *State or other work-study/employment:* Part-time jobs available.

ATHLETIC AWARDS *Total amount:* $1,429,395 (46% need-based, 54% non-need-based).

APPLYING FOR FINANCIAL AID *Required financial aid forms:* FAFSA, institution's own form, state aid form. *Financial aid deadline (priority):* 4/1. *Notification date:* Continuous beginning 2/1. Students must reply within 4 weeks of notification.

CONTACT Diane Beltrani, Director of Enrollment Services/Financial Aid, Dowling College, Idle Hour Boulevard, Oakdale, NY 11769-1999, 631-244-3385 or toll-free 800-DOWLING. *Fax:* 631-563-3827. *E-mail:* beltranb@dowling.edu.

DRAKE UNIVERSITY
Des Moines, IA

Tuition & fees: $20,550	Average undergraduate aid package: $17,734

ABOUT THE INSTITUTION Independent, coed. Awards: bachelor's, master's, doctoral, and first professional degrees and post-master's certificates. 68 undergraduate majors. Total enrollment: 5,221. Undergraduates: 3,164. Freshmen: 782. Federal methodology is used as a basis for awarding need-based institutional aid.

UNDERGRADUATE EXPENSES for 2004–05 *Application fee:* $25. *Comprehensive fee:* $26,470 includes full-time tuition ($20,200), mandatory fees ($350), and room and board ($5920). *College room only:* $2870. Full-time tuition and fees vary according to class time, course load, and student level. Room and board charges vary according to board plan. *Part-time tuition:* $410 per hour. *Part-time fees:* $8 per hour. Part-time tuition and fees vary according to class time. *Payment plan:* Installment.

FRESHMAN FINANCIAL AID (Fall 2004, est.) 648 applied for aid; of those 72% were deemed to have need. 100% of freshmen with need received aid; of those 36% had need fully met. *Average percent of need met:* 91% (excluding resources awarded to replace EFC). *Average financial aid package:* $17,695 (excluding resources awarded to replace EFC). 35% of all full-time freshmen had no need and received non-need-based gift aid.

UNDERGRADUATE FINANCIAL AID (Fall 2004, est.) 2,340 applied for aid; of those 81% were deemed to have need. 100% of undergraduates with need received aid; of those 32% had need fully met. *Average percent of need met:*

86% (excluding resources awarded to replace EFC). *Average financial aid package:* $17,734 (excluding resources awarded to replace EFC). 32% of all full-time undergraduates had no need and received non-need-based gift aid.

GIFT AID (NEED-BASED) *Total amount:* $20,220,460 (10% federal, 9% state, 78% institutional, 3% external sources). *Receiving aid:* Freshmen: 58% (457); All full-time undergraduates: 59% (1,870). *Average award:* Freshmen: $11,515; Undergraduates: $10,611. *Scholarships, grants, and awards:* Federal Pell, FSEOG, state, private, college/university gift aid from institutional funds.

GIFT AID (NON-NEED-BASED) *Total amount:* $10,721,083 (2% federal, 93% institutional, 5% external sources). *Receiving aid:* Freshmen: 16% (126); Undergraduates: 12% (384). *Average Award:* Freshmen: $8858; *Undergraduates:* $8155. *Scholarships, grants, and awards by category: Academic Interests/ Achievement:* 2,723 awards ($24,144,527 total): general academic interests/ achievements. *Creative Arts/Performance:* 269 awards ($705,270 total): art/fine arts, music, theater/drama. *Special Characteristics:* 429 awards ($771,595 total): children and siblings of alumni, ethnic background, international students, members of minority groups. *Tuition waivers:* Full or partial for children of alumni, employees or children of employees, senior citizens. *ROTC:* Army, Air Force cooperative.

LOANS *Student loans:* $26,137,567 (49% need-based, 51% non-need-based). 75% of past graduating class borrowed through all loan programs. *Average indebtedness per student:* $24,400. *Average need-based loan:* Freshmen: $4788; Undergraduates: $5935. *Parent loans:* $20,844,285 (11% need-based, 89% non-need-based). *Programs:* FFEL (Subsidized and Unsubsidized Stafford, PLUS), Perkins, college/university.

WORK-STUDY *Federal work-study:* Total amount: $2,057,234; 1,141 jobs averaging $1803. *State or other work-study/employment:* Total amount: $282,750 (54% need-based, 46% non-need-based). 34 part-time jobs averaging $4875.

ATHLETIC AWARDS *Total amount:* $2,551,977 (26% need-based, 74% non-need-based).

APPLYING FOR FINANCIAL AID *Required financial aid form:* FAFSA. *Financial aid deadline (priority):* 3/1. *Notification date:* Continuous beginning 3/1. Students must reply by 5/1 or within 3 weeks of notification.

CONTACT Office of Student Financial Planning, Drake University, 2507 University Avenue, Des Moines, IA 50311-4516, 800-44-DRAKE Ext. 2905 or toll-free 800-44DRAKE Ext. 3181. *Fax:* 515-271-4042.

DREW UNIVERSITY
Madison, NJ

Tuition & fees: $29,546	Average undergraduate aid package: $21,032

ABOUT THE INSTITUTION Independent religious, coed. Awards: bachelor's, master's, doctoral, and first professional degrees and post-bachelor's certificates. 27 undergraduate majors. Total enrollment: 2,675. Undergraduates: 1,629. Freshmen: 418. Institutional methodology is used as a basis for awarding need-based institutional aid.

UNDERGRADUATE EXPENSES for 2004-05 *Application fee:* $50. *Comprehensive fee:* $37,564 includes full-time tuition ($29,000), mandatory fees ($546), and room and board ($8018). *College room only:* $5130. Full-time tuition and fees vary according to course load. Room and board charges vary according to board plan and housing facility. *Part-time tuition:* $1208 per credit. *Part-time fees:* $22.75 per credit. Part-time tuition and fees vary according to course load. *Payment plans:* Tuition prepayment, installment, deferred payment.

FRESHMAN FINANCIAL AID (Fall 2003) 294 applied for aid; of those 73% were deemed to have need. 100% of freshmen with need received aid; of those 36% had need fully met. *Average percent of need met:* 84% (excluding resources awarded to replace EFC). *Average financial aid package:* $20,208 (excluding resources awarded to replace EFC). 28% of all full-time freshmen had no need and received non-need-based gift aid.

UNDERGRADUATE FINANCIAL AID (Fall 2003) 934 applied for aid; of those 81% were deemed to have need. 100% of undergraduates with need received aid; of those 35% had need fully met. *Average percent of need met:* 84% (excluding resources awarded to replace EFC). *Average financial aid package:* $21,032 (excluding resources awarded to replace EFC). 27% of all full-time undergraduates had no need and received non-need-based gift aid.

GIFT AID (NEED-BASED) *Total amount:* $11,868,739 (9% federal, 12% state, 76% institutional, 3% external sources). *Receiving aid:* Freshmen: 51% (215); All full-time undergraduates: 50% (756). *Average award:* Freshmen: $15,926; Undergraduates: $15,699. *Scholarships, grants, and awards:* Federal Pell, FSEOG, state, private, college/university gift aid from institutional funds.

GIFT AID (NON-NEED-BASED) *Total amount:* $5,597,992 (2% state, 96% institutional, 2% external sources). *Receiving aid:* Freshmen: 10% (41); Undergraduates: 16% (242). *Average Award:* Freshmen: $12,526; *Undergraduates:* $11,781. *Scholarships, grants, and awards by category: Academic Interests/Achievement:* 869 awards ($8,735,863 total): general academic interests/ achievements. *Creative Arts/Performance:* 22 awards ($20,500 total): general creative arts/performance. *Special Characteristics:* 33 awards ($177,780 total): general special characteristics. *Tuition waivers:* Full or partial for employees or children of employees, senior citizens. *ROTC:* Army cooperative, Air Force cooperative.

LOANS *Student loans:* $3,810,237 (76% need-based, 24% non-need-based). 53% of past graduating class borrowed through all loan programs. *Average indebtedness per student:* $16,818. *Average need-based loan:* Freshmen: $3651; Undergraduates: $4929. *Parent loans:* $5,563,064 (23% need-based, 77% non-need-based). *Programs:* FFEL (Subsidized and Unsubsidized Stafford, PLUS), Perkins, state.

WORK-STUDY *Federal work-study:* Total amount: $378,856; 324 jobs averaging $1169. *State or other work-study/employment:* Total amount: $238,000 (63% need-based, 37% non-need-based). 37 part-time jobs averaging $6432.

APPLYING FOR FINANCIAL AID *Required financial aid forms:* FAFSA, institution's own form, CSS Financial Aid PROFILE. *Financial aid deadline:* 2/15. *Notification date:* 3/30. Students must reply by 5/1.

CONTACT Norma Betz, Director of Financial Assistance, Drew University, 36 Madison Avenue, Madison, NJ 07940-1493, 973-408-3112. *Fax:* 973-408-3188.

DREXEL UNIVERSITY
Philadelphia, PA

Tuition & fees: $22,020	Average undergraduate aid package: $13,735

ABOUT THE INSTITUTION Independent, coed. Awards: associate, bachelor's, master's, doctoral, and first professional degrees and post-bachelor's, post-master's, and first professional certificates. 55 undergraduate majors. Total enrollment: 17,656. Undergraduates: 11,960. Freshmen: 2,209. Federal methodology is used as a basis for awarding need-based institutional aid.

UNDERGRADUATE EXPENSES for 2004-05 *Application fee:* $50. *Comprehensive fee:* $32,070 includes full-time tuition ($20,800), mandatory fees ($1220), and room and board ($10,050). *College room only:* $5970. Full-time tuition and fees vary according to course load, program, and student level. Room and board charges vary according to board plan and housing facility. *Part-time tuition:* $480 per credit. *Part-time fees:* $95 per term. Part-time tuition and fees vary according to course load and program.

FRESHMAN FINANCIAL AID (Fall 2004, est.) 2030 applied for aid; of those 73% were deemed to have need. 100% of freshmen with need received aid; of those 14% had need fully met. *Average percent of need met:* 65% (excluding resources awarded to replace EFC). *Average financial aid package:* $14,873 (excluding resources awarded to replace EFC). 21% of all full-time freshmen had no need and received non-need-based gift aid.

UNDERGRADUATE FINANCIAL AID (Fall 2004, est.) 8,519 applied for aid; of those 77% were deemed to have need. 99% of undergraduates with need received aid; of those 11% had need fully met. *Average percent of need met:* 58% (excluding resources awarded to replace EFC). *Average financial aid package:* $13,735 (excluding resources awarded to replace EFC). 15% of all full-time undergraduates had no need and received non-need-based gift aid.

GIFT AID (NEED-BASED) *Total amount:* $13,260,433 (51% federal, 47% state, 2% external sources). *Receiving aid:* Freshmen: 25% (555); All full-time undergraduates: 30% (2,960). *Average award:* Freshmen: $4451; Undergraduates: $4518. *Scholarships, grants, and awards:* Federal Pell, FSEOG, state, private, college/university gift aid from institutional funds, United Negro College Fund.

GIFT AID (NON-NEED-BASED) *Total amount:* $60,007,037 (1% state, 98% institutional, 1% external sources). *Receiving aid:* Freshmen: 65% (1,424); Undergraduates: 55% (5,435). *Average Award:* Freshmen: $8927; *Undergraduates:* $8347. *Scholarships, grants, and awards by category: Academic Interests/Achievement:* 2,910 awards ($16,131,000 total): general academic interests/ achievements. *Creative Arts/Performance:* 100 awards ($96,000 total): dance, music, performing arts, theater/drama. *Special Achievements/Activities:* 28 awards ($20,300 total): cheerleading/drum major. *Special Characteristics:* 806 awards ($1,183,000 total): children and siblings of alumni, siblings of current students, twins. *Tuition waivers:* Full or partial for employees or children of employees. *ROTC:* Army, Air Force cooperative.

LOANS *Student loans:* $72,448,446 (61% need-based, 39% non-need-based). 82% of past graduating class borrowed through all loan programs. *Average*

Drexel University

indebtedness per student: $21,504. *Average need-based loan:* Freshmen: $3078; Undergraduates: $4507. *Parent loans:* $24,935,772 (100% non-need-based). *Programs:* FFEL (Subsidized and Unsubsidized Stafford, PLUS), Perkins, college/university.

WORK-STUDY *Federal work-study:* Total amount: $2,587,665; jobs available.

ATHLETIC AWARDS *Total amount:* $3,559,793 (100% non-need-based).

APPLYING FOR FINANCIAL AID *Required financial aid form:* FAFSA. *Financial aid deadline:* 3/15. *Notification date:* Continuous beginning 3/15.

CONTACT Cynthia Delone, Director of Financial Aid, Drexel University, 3141 Chestnut Street, Main Building, Room 208, Philadelphia, PA 19104-2875, 215-991-8210 or toll-free 800-2-DREXEL. *Fax:* 215-843-5243.

DRURY UNIVERSITY
Springfield, MO

ABOUT THE INSTITUTION Independent, coed. Awards: bachelor's and master's degrees (also offers evening program with significant enrollment not reflected in profile). 47 undergraduate majors. Total enrollment: 1,894. Undergraduates: 1,562. Freshmen: 367.

GIFT AID (NEED-BASED) *Scholarships, grants, and awards:* Federal Pell, FSEOG, state, private, college/university gift aid from institutional funds.

GIFT AID (NON-NEED-BASED) *Scholarships, grants, and awards by category: Academic Interests/Achievement:* architecture, biological sciences, business, communication, education, English, general academic interests/achievements, health fields, humanities, mathematics, physical sciences, premedicine, social sciences. *Creative Arts/Performance:* art/fine arts, creative writing, music, theater/drama. *Special Achievements/Activities:* cheerleading/drum major, leadership, religious involvement. *Special Characteristics:* children and siblings of alumni, children of faculty/staff, relatives of clergy, religious affiliation.

LOANS *Programs:* FFEL (Subsidized and Unsubsidized Stafford, PLUS), Perkins.

WORK-STUDY *Federal work-study:* Total amount: $309,840; 421 jobs averaging $2500. *State or other work-study/employment:* Total amount: $164,829 (100% non-need-based). 106 part-time jobs averaging $1555.

APPLYING FOR FINANCIAL AID *Required financial aid forms:* FAFSA, institution's own form.

CONTACT Ms. Annette Avery, Director of Financial Aid, Drury University, 900 North Benton Avenue, Springfield, MO 65802-3791, 417-873-7312 or toll-free 800-922-2274. *Fax:* 417-873-6906. *E-mail:* aavery@lib.drury.edu.

DUKE UNIVERSITY
Durham, NC

Tuition & fees: $30,720	Average undergraduate aid package: $26,914

ABOUT THE INSTITUTION Independent religious, coed. Awards: bachelor's, master's, doctoral, and first professional degrees and post-bachelor's and post-master's certificates. 45 undergraduate majors. Total enrollment: 12,770. Undergraduates: 6,301. Freshmen: 1,640. Both federal and institutional methodology are used as a basis for awarding need-based institutional aid.

UNDERGRADUATE EXPENSES for 2004–05 *Application fee:* $70. *Comprehensive fee:* $39,240 includes full-time tuition ($29,770), mandatory fees ($950), and room and board ($8520). *College room only:* $4610. Full-time tuition and fees vary according to program. Room and board charges vary according to board plan and housing facility. *Part-time tuition:* $3720 per course. Part-time tuition and fees vary according to program. *Payment plans:* Installment, deferred payment.

FRESHMAN FINANCIAL AID (Fall 2004, est.) 833 applied for aid; of those 82% were deemed to have need. 100% of freshmen with need received aid; of those 100% had need fully met. *Average percent of need met:* 100% (excluding resources awarded to replace EFC). *Average financial aid package:* $26,335 (excluding resources awarded to replace EFC). 1% of all full-time freshmen had no need and received non-need-based gift aid.

UNDERGRADUATE FINANCIAL AID (Fall 2004, est.) 2,809 applied for aid; of those 90% were deemed to have need. 100% of undergraduates with need received aid; of those 100% had need fully met. *Average percent of need met:* 100% (excluding resources awarded to replace EFC). *Average financial aid package:* $26,914 (excluding resources awarded to replace EFC). 4% of all full-time undergraduates had no need and received non-need-based gift aid.

GIFT AID (NEED-BASED) *Total amount:* $53,064,746 (7% federal, 3% state, 83% institutional, 7% external sources). *Receiving aid:* Freshmen: 40% (658); All full-time undergraduates: 38% (2,397). *Average award:* Freshmen: $23,268;

Undergraduates: $22,592. *Scholarships, grants, and awards:* Federal Pell, FSEOG, state, private, college/university gift aid from institutional funds.

GIFT AID (NON-NEED-BASED) *Total amount:* $7,627,540 (10% state, 74% institutional, 16% external sources). *Receiving aid:* Freshmen: 4% (70); Undergraduates: 3% (204). *Average Award:* Freshmen: $28,453; *Undergraduates:* $22,277. *Scholarships, grants, and awards by category: Academic Interests/Achievement:* 117 awards ($3,449,625 total): general academic interests/achievements, mathematics. *Creative Arts/Performance:* creative writing. *Special Achievements/Activities:* 73 awards ($2,164,233 total): general special achievements/activities, leadership. *Special Characteristics:* 39 awards ($1,143,403 total): children and siblings of alumni, ethnic background, local/state students. *Tuition waivers:* Full or partial for employees or children of employees. *ROTC:* Army, Air Force.

LOANS *Student loans:* $10,674,243 (97% need-based, 3% non-need-based). 39% of past graduating class borrowed through all loan programs. *Average indebtedness per student:* $25,182. *Average need-based loan:* Freshmen: $3700; Undergraduates: $5009. *Parent loans:* $12,085,634 (58% need-based, 42% non-need-based). *Programs:* FFEL (Subsidized and Unsubsidized Stafford, PLUS), Perkins, college/university, alternative loans.

WORK-STUDY *Federal work-study:* Total amount: $3,656,929; 2,025 jobs averaging $1868. *State or other work-study/employment:* Total amount: $766,393 (40% need-based, 60% non-need-based). 507 part-time jobs averaging $1515.

ATHLETIC AWARDS *Total amount:* $8,550,482 (19% need-based, 81% non-need-based).

APPLYING FOR FINANCIAL AID *Required financial aid forms:* FAFSA, CSS Financial Aid PROFILE, noncustodial (divorced/separated) parent's statement, business/farm supplement, income tax form(s). *Financial aid deadline:* 2/1. *Notification date:* 4/1. Students must reply by 5/1.

CONTACT Kelly Kay, Financial Aid Officer, Duke University, 2122 Campus Drive, Durham, NC 27708-0397, 919-684-6225. *Fax:* 919-660-9811. *E-mail:* finaid@duke.edu.

DUQUESNE UNIVERSITY
Pittsburgh, PA

Tuition & fees: $20,360	Average undergraduate aid package: $15,179

ABOUT THE INSTITUTION Independent Roman Catholic, coed. Awards: bachelor's, master's, doctoral, and first professional degrees and post-bachelor's and post-master's certificates. 74 undergraduate majors. Total enrollment: 9,722. Undergraduates: 5,584. Freshmen: 1,214. Federal methodology is used as a basis for awarding need-based institutional aid.

UNDERGRADUATE EXPENSES for 2004–05 *Application fee:* $50. *Comprehensive fee:* $28,180 includes full-time tuition ($18,693), mandatory fees ($1667), and room and board ($7820). *College room only:* $4266. Full-time tuition and fees vary according to program. Room and board charges vary according to board plan and housing facility. *Part-time tuition:* $608 per credit. *Part-time fees:* $65 per credit. Part-time tuition and fees vary according to program. *Payment plans:* Installment, deferred payment.

FRESHMAN FINANCIAL AID (Fall 2003) 1281 applied for aid; of those 82% were deemed to have need. 100% of freshmen with need received aid; of those 48% had need fully met. *Average percent of need met:* 87% (excluding resources awarded to replace EFC). *Average financial aid package:* $16,069 (excluding resources awarded to replace EFC). 23% of all full-time freshmen had no need and received non-need-based gift aid.

UNDERGRADUATE FINANCIAL AID (Fall 2003) 4,160 applied for aid; of those 86% were deemed to have need. 100% of undergraduates with need received aid; of those 48% had need fully met. *Average percent of need met:* 83% (excluding resources awarded to replace EFC). *Average financial aid package:* $15,179 (excluding resources awarded to replace EFC). 19% of all full-time undergraduates had no need and received non-need-based gift aid.

GIFT AID (NEED-BASED) *Total amount:* $29,741,573 (11% federal, 19% state, 64% institutional, 6% external sources). *Receiving aid:* Freshmen: 69% (1,019); All full-time undergraduates: 63% (3,362). *Average award:* Freshmen: $13,142; Undergraduates: $10,303. *Scholarships, grants, and awards:* Federal Pell, FSEOG, state, private, college/university gift aid from institutional funds.

GIFT AID (NON-NEED-BASED) *Total amount:* $6,298,097 (1% federal, 2% state, 90% institutional, 7% external sources). *Receiving aid:* Freshmen: 65% (961); Undergraduates: 48% (2,599). *Average Award:* Freshmen: $7957; *Undergraduates:* $8113. *Scholarships, grants, and awards by category: Academic Interests/Achievement:* 3,234 awards ($21,198,002 total): general academic interests/achievements. *Creative Arts/Performance:* 196 awards ($1,346,983 total): dance, music. *Special Characteristics:* 683 awards ($6,139,843 total): children of faculty/staff, international students, members of minority groups, relatives of clergy, religious affiliation. *Tuition waivers:* Full or partial for employees or children of employees, senior citizens. *ROTC:* Army, Naval cooperative, Air Force cooperative.

LOANS *Student loans:* $31,780,860 (90% need-based, 10% non-need-based). 64% of past graduating class borrowed through all loan programs. *Average indebtedness per student:* $17,953. *Average need-based loan:* Freshmen: $3512; Undergraduates: $4478. *Parent loans:* $10,041,963 (82% need-based, 18% non-need-based). *Programs:* FFEL (Subsidized and Unsubsidized Stafford, PLUS), Perkins, Federal Nursing, college/university, Health Professions Loans.

WORK-STUDY *Federal work-study:* Total amount: $4,787,528; 1,773 jobs averaging $2448.

ATHLETIC AWARDS *Total amount:* $3,698,062 (54% need-based, 46% non-need-based).

APPLYING FOR FINANCIAL AID *Required financial aid forms:* FAFSA, institution's own form. *Financial aid deadline:* 5/1. *Notification date:* Continuous. Students must reply within 3 weeks of notification.

CONTACT Mr. Frank M. Dutkovich Jr., Director of Financial Aid, Duquesne University, 600 Forbes Avenue, Pittsburgh, PA 15282-0299, 412-396-6607 or toll-free 800-456-0590. *Fax:* 412-396-5284. *E-mail:* dutkovic@duq.edu.

D'YOUVILLE COLLEGE
Buffalo, NY

Tuition & fees: $14,890	Average undergraduate aid package: $11,605

ABOUT THE INSTITUTION Independent, coed. Awards: bachelor's, master's, doctoral, and first professional degrees and post-bachelor's and post-master's certificates. 33 undergraduate majors. Total enrollment: 2,729. Undergraduates: 1,225. Freshmen: 228. Federal methodology is used as a basis for awarding need-based institutional aid.

UNDERGRADUATE EXPENSES for 2004–05 *Application fee:* $25. *Comprehensive fee:* $22,230 includes full-time tuition ($14,690), mandatory fees ($200), and room and board ($7340). Full-time tuition and fees vary according to course level and program. Room and board charges vary according to board plan and housing facility. *Part-time tuition:* $420 per credit. *Part-time fees:* $100 per term. Part-time tuition and fees vary according to course load. *Payment plans:* Guaranteed tuition, installment, deferred payment.

GIFT AID (NEED-BASED) *Total amount:* $5,810,072 (24% federal, 23% state, 48% institutional, 5% external sources). *Receiving aid:* Freshmen: 93% (126); All full-time undergraduates: 93% (1,246). *Average award:* Freshmen: $6184; Undergraduates: $4043. *Scholarships, grants, and awards:* Federal Pell, FSEOG, state, private, college/university gift aid from institutional funds.

GIFT AID (NON-NEED-BASED) *Total amount:* $1,661,893 (2% state, 92% institutional, 6% external sources). *Receiving aid:* Freshmen: 65% (88); Undergraduates: 34% (452). *Average Award:* Freshmen: $7263; Undergraduates: $6874. *Scholarships, grants, and awards by category:* Academic Interests/Achievement: 345 awards ($755,120 total): biological sciences, business, education, English, general academic interests/achievements, health fields, humanities, international studies, premedicine, social sciences. *Special Characteristics:* 61 awards ($354,198 total): children and siblings of alumni, children of faculty/staff. *Tuition waivers:* Full or partial for minority students, children of alumni, employees or children of employees, adult students, senior citizens. *ROTC:* Army cooperative.

LOANS *Student loans:* $26,758,195 (19% need-based, 81% non-need-based). *Average need-based loan:* Freshmen: $4041; Undergraduates: $6299. *Parent loans:* $199,711 (23% need-based, 77% non-need-based). *Programs:* FFEL (Subsidized and Unsubsidized Stafford, PLUS), Perkins, Federal Nursing, college/university.

APPLYING FOR FINANCIAL AID *Required financial aid form:* FAFSA. *Financial aid deadline (priority):* 3/1. *Notification date:* Continuous beginning 4/15. Students must reply within 3 weeks of notification.

CONTACT Ms. Lorraine A. Metz, Director of Financial Aid, D'Youville College, 320 Porter Avenue, Buffalo, NY 14201-1084, 716-829-7500 or toll-free 800-777-3921. *Fax:* 716-829-7779. *E-mail:* metzla@dyc.edu.

EARLHAM COLLEGE
Richmond, IN

ABOUT THE INSTITUTION Independent religious, coed. Awards: bachelor's, master's, and first professional degrees. 33 undergraduate majors. Total enrollment: 1,275. Undergraduates: 1,191. Freshmen: 336.

GIFT AID (NEED-BASED) *Scholarships, grants, and awards:* Federal Pell, FSEOG, state, private, college/university gift aid from institutional funds.

GIFT AID (NON-NEED-BASED) *Scholarships, grants, and awards by category:* Academic Interests/Achievement: general academic interests/achievements, physical sciences. *Special Characteristics:* ethnic background, international students, religious affiliation.

LOANS *Programs:* Federal Direct (Subsidized and Unsubsidized Stafford, PLUS), Perkins, college/university.

WORK-STUDY *Federal work-study:* Total amount: $435,000; jobs available. *State or other work-study/employment:* Total amount: $125,000 (60% need-based, 40% non-need-based). Part-time jobs available.

APPLYING FOR FINANCIAL AID *Required financial aid forms:* FAFSA, institution's own form.

CONTACT Mr. Robert W. Arnold, Director of Financial Aid, Earlham College, National Road West, Richmond, IN 47374-4095, 765-983-1217 or toll-free 800-327-5426. *Fax:* 765-983-1299.

EAST CAROLINA UNIVERSITY
Greenville, NC

Tuition & fees (NC res): $3454	Average undergraduate aid package: $8043

ABOUT THE INSTITUTION State-supported, coed. Awards: bachelor's, master's, doctoral, and first professional degrees and post-master's certificates. 91 undergraduate majors. Total enrollment: 22,767. Undergraduates: 17,510. Freshmen: 3,512. Federal methodology is used as a basis for awarding need-based institutional aid.

UNDERGRADUATE EXPENSES for 2004–05 *Application fee:* $50. *Tuition, state resident:* full-time $2135. *Tuition, nonresident:* full-time $12,349. Part-time tuition and fees vary according to course load. *College room and board:* $6640; *room only:* $3690. Room and board charges vary according to board plan and housing facility. *Payment plans:* Installment, deferred payment.

GIFT AID (NEED-BASED) *Total amount:* $24,673,557 (66% federal, 24% state, 10% institutional). *Receiving aid:* Freshmen: 30% (1,047); All full-time undergraduates: 27% (4,169). *Average award:* Freshmen: $6549; Undergraduates: $7287. *Scholarships, grants, and awards:* Federal Pell, FSEOG, state, private, college/university gift aid from institutional funds.

GIFT AID (NON-NEED-BASED) *Total amount:* $6,323,034 (37% state, 27% institutional, 36% external sources). *Receiving aid:* Freshmen: 8% (280); Undergraduates: 6% (904). *Average Award:* Freshmen: $8486; Undergraduates: $9925. *Scholarships, grants, and awards by category:* Academic Interests/Achievement: biological sciences, business, education, general academic interests/achievements, health fields, home economics, humanities, military science. Creative Arts/Performance: applied art and design, art/fine arts, music. *Special Achievements/Activities:* leadership. *Special Characteristics:* adult students, children of faculty/staff, ethnic background, handicapped students, local/state students. *Tuition waivers:* Full or partial for employees or children of employees, senior citizens. *ROTC:* Army, Air Force.

LOANS *Student loans:* $53,080,610 (51% need-based, 49% non-need-based). 57% of past graduating class borrowed through all loan programs. *Average indebtedness per student:* $19,512. *Average need-based loan:* Freshmen: $5816; Undergraduates: $6963. *Parent loans:* $12,117,752 (100% non-need-based). *Programs:* FFEL (Subsidized and Unsubsidized Stafford, PLUS), Perkins, Federal Nursing.

ATHLETIC AWARDS *Total amount:* $3,466,838 (100% non-need-based).

APPLYING FOR FINANCIAL AID *Required financial aid form:* FAFSA. *Financial aid deadline (priority):* 4/15. *Notification date:* 3/15. Students must reply within 2 weeks of notification.

CONTACT Rose Mary Stelma, Director, Student Financial Aid, East Carolina University, Office of Financial Aid, East 5th Street, Greenville, NC 27858-4353, 252-328-6610. *Fax:* 252-328-4347. *E-mail:* pattersonba@mail.ecu.edu.

EAST CENTRAL UNIVERSITY
Ada, OK

Tuition & fees (OK res): $3952	Average undergraduate aid package: $8013

ABOUT THE INSTITUTION State-supported, coed. Awards: bachelor's and master's degrees. 81 undergraduate majors. Total enrollment: 4,691. Undergraduates: 3,870. Freshmen: 653. Federal methodology is used as a basis for awarding need-based institutional aid.

East Central University

UNDERGRADUATE EXPENSES for 2004–05 *Application fee:* $20. *Tuition, state resident:* full-time $2996; part-time $99.85 per semester hour. *Tuition, nonresident:* full-time $7169; part-time $238.95 per semester hour. *Required fees:* full-time $956; $30.30 per semester hour or $23.50 per term part-time. Full-time tuition and fees vary according to course load. Part-time tuition and fees vary according to course load. *College room and board:* $2910; *room only:* $1040. Room and board charges vary according to board plan and housing facility.

FRESHMAN FINANCIAL AID (Fall 2004, est.) 390 applied for aid; of those 85% were deemed to have need. 98% of freshmen with need received aid; of those 36% had need fully met. *Average percent of need met:* 60% (excluding resources awarded to replace EFC). *Average financial aid package:* $7292 (excluding resources awarded to replace EFC). 9% of all full-time freshmen had no need and received non-need-based gift aid.

UNDERGRADUATE FINANCIAL AID (Fall 2004, est.) 2,068 applied for aid; of those 89% were deemed to have need. 98% of undergraduates with need received aid; of those 37% had need fully met. *Average percent of need met:* 66% (excluding resources awarded to replace EFC). *Average financial aid package:* $8013 (excluding resources awarded to replace EFC). 8% of all full-time undergraduates had no need and received non-need-based gift aid.

GIFT AID (NEED-BASED) *Total amount:* $7,132,176 (77% federal, 23% state). *Receiving aid:* Freshmen: 35% (244); All full-time undergraduates: 39% (1,331). *Average award:* Freshmen: $4910; Undergraduates: $5359. *Scholarships, grants, and awards:* Federal Pell, FSEOG, state, private, college/university gift aid from institutional funds.

GIFT AID (NON-NEED-BASED) *Total amount:* $2,832,861 (23% institutional, 77% external sources). *Receiving aid:* Freshmen: 22% (153); Undergraduates: 23% (766). *Average Award:* Freshmen: $1852; Undergraduates: $3189. *Scholarships, grants, and awards by category: Academic Interests/Achievement:* 602 awards ($467,781 total): communication, general academic interests/ achievements. *Creative Arts/Performance:* 118 awards ($165,466 total): music. *Special Achievements/Activities:* 14 awards ($4520 total): cheerleading/drum major. *Special Characteristics:* 436 awards ($737,904 total): children of faculty/ staff, general special characteristics, members of minority groups, out-of-state students, previous college experience, veterans, veterans' children. *Tuition waivers:* Full or partial for employees or children of employees, senior citizens.

LOANS *Student loans:* $9,707,101 (71% need-based, 29% non-need-based). 56% of past graduating class borrowed through all loan programs. *Average indebtedness per student:* $13,199. *Average need-based loan:* Freshmen: $1669; Undergraduates: $3762. *Parent loans:* $220,702 (100% non-need-based). *Programs:* FFEL (Subsidized and Unsubsidized Stafford, PLUS), Perkins, college/ university.

WORK-STUDY *Federal work-study:* Total amount: $411,210; 181 jobs averaging $2272. *State or other work-study/employment:* Total amount: $2,461,503 (100% non-need-based). 401 part-time jobs averaging $6138.

ATHLETIC AWARDS *Total amount:* $784,790 (100% non-need-based).

APPLYING FOR FINANCIAL AID *Required financial aid form:* FAFSA. *Financial aid deadline (priority):* 3/1. *Notification date:* Continuous beginning 4/15. Students must reply within 2 weeks of notification.

CONTACT Marcia Carter, Director of Financial Aid, East Central University, 1100 East 14th, Ada, OK 74820-6899, 580-332-8000 Ext. 242. *Fax:* 580-436-5612.

EASTERN CONNECTICUT STATE UNIVERSITY
Willimantic, CT

CONTACT Assistant to the Director of Financial Aid, Eastern Connecticut State University, 83 Windham Street, Willimantic, CT 06226-2295, 860-465-4428 or toll-free 877-353-3278. *Fax:* 860-465-4440.

EASTERN ILLINOIS UNIVERSITY
Charleston, IL

Tuition & fees (IL res): $5782	Average undergraduate aid package: $9126

ABOUT THE INSTITUTION State-supported, coed. Awards: bachelor's and master's degrees and post-bachelor's and post-master's certificates. 45 undergraduate majors. Total enrollment: 11,651. Undergraduates: 9,928. Freshmen: 1,741. Federal methodology is used as a basis for awarding need-based institutional aid.

UNDERGRADUATE EXPENSES for 2004–05 *Application fee:* $30. *Tuition, state resident:* full-time $4133; part-time $138 per credit hour. *Tuition, nonresident:*

full-time $12,398; part-time $413 per credit hour. *Required fees:* full-time $1649; $53 per credit hour. Full-time tuition and fees vary according to course load and student level. Part-time tuition and fees vary according to course load and student level. *College room and board:* $7150. Room and board charges vary according to board plan and housing facility. *Payment plans:* Guaranteed tuition, installment.

GIFT AID (NEED-BASED) *Total amount:* $14,531,050 (36% federal, 48% state, 11% institutional, 5% external sources). *Receiving aid:* Freshmen: 22% (391); All full-time undergraduates: 24% (2,150). *Average award:* Freshmen: $2519; Undergraduates: $2693. *Scholarships, grants, and awards:* Federal Pell, FSEOG, state, college/university gift aid from institutional funds.

GIFT AID (NON-NEED-BASED) *Total amount:* $2,967,304 (2% federal, 19% state, 57% institutional, 22% external sources). *Receiving aid:* Freshmen: 25% (454); Undergraduates: 23% (2,033). *Average Award:* Freshmen: $6486; *Undergraduates:* $6712. *Tuition waivers:* Full or partial for employees or children of employees. *ROTC:* Army.

LOANS *Student loans:* $25,347,344 (77% need-based, 23% non-need-based). 61% of past graduating class borrowed through all loan programs. *Average indebtedness per student:* $14,836. *Average need-based loan:* Freshmen: $2374; Undergraduates: $3348. *Parent loans:* $2,535,835 (95% need-based, 5% non-need-based). *Programs:* Federal Direct (Subsidized and Unsubsidized Stafford, PLUS), Perkins.

ATHLETIC AWARDS *Total amount:* $2,176,736 (27% need-based, 73% non-need-based).

APPLYING FOR FINANCIAL AID *Required financial aid form:* FAFSA. *Financial aid deadline (priority):* 4/15. *Notification date:* Continuous beginning 5/1. Students must reply within 2 weeks of notification.

CONTACT Tracy L. Hall, Assistant Director of Financial Aid, Eastern Illinois University, 600 Lincoln Avenue, Charleston, IL 61920-3099, 217-581-7511 or toll-free 800-252-5711. *Fax:* 217-581-6422. *E-mail:* cstlh@eiu.edu.

EASTERN KENTUCKY UNIVERSITY
Richmond, KY

ABOUT THE INSTITUTION State-supported, coed. Awards: associate, bachelor's, and master's degrees and post-bachelor's and post-master's certificates. 135 undergraduate majors. Total enrollment: 16,183. Undergraduates: 13,837. Freshmen: 2,554.

GIFT AID (NEED-BASED) *Scholarships, grants, and awards:* Federal Pell, FSEOG, state, private, college/university gift aid from institutional funds, Federal Nursing.

GIFT AID (NON-NEED-BASED) *Scholarships, grants, and awards by category: Academic Interests/Achievement:* agriculture, business, education, general academic interests/achievements, library science, mathematics, physical sciences. *Creative Arts/Performance:* art/fine arts, music, theater/drama. *Special Achievements/ Activities:* cheerleading/drum major. *Special Characteristics:* children and siblings of alumni, children of faculty/staff, children with a deceased or disabled parent, international students, members of minority groups, veterans.

LOANS *Programs:* FFEL (Subsidized and Unsubsidized Stafford, PLUS), Perkins, state, college/university.

WORK-STUDY *Federal work-study:* Total amount: $2,693,356; 1,573 jobs averaging $1712. *State or other work-study/employment:* Total amount: $2,181,972 (100% non-need-based). 1,288 part-time jobs averaging $1749.

APPLYING FOR FINANCIAL AID *Required financial aid forms:* FAFSA, institution's own form.

CONTACT Ms. Shelley Park, Director of Student Financial Assistance, Eastern Kentucky University, 521 Lancaster Avenue, Student Services Building, CPO 59, Richmond, KY 40475-3102, 859-622-2361 or toll-free 800-465-9191 (in-state). *E-mail:* shelley.park@eku.edu.

EASTERN MENNONITE UNIVERSITY
Harrisonburg, VA

Tuition & fees: $19,500	Average undergraduate aid package: $15,530

ABOUT THE INSTITUTION Independent Mennonite, coed. Awards: associate, bachelor's, master's, and first professional degrees and post-bachelor's certificates. 58 undergraduate majors. Total enrollment: 1,297. Undergraduates: 1,029. Freshmen: 208. Federal methodology is used as a basis for awarding need-based institutional aid.

UNDERGRADUATE EXPENSES for 2005–06 *Application fee:* $25. *Comprehensive fee:* $25,450 includes full-time tuition ($19,442), mandatory fees ($58), and room and board ($5950). *College room only:* $3150. Full-time tuition and fees vary according to course load and program. Room and board charges vary according to board plan, housing facility, and student level. *Part-time tuition:* $813 per credit hour. Part-time tuition and fees vary according to course load and program. *Payment plan:* Installment.

FRESHMAN FINANCIAL AID (Fall 2003) 186 applied for aid; of those 89% were deemed to have need. 99% of freshmen with need received aid; of those 30% had need fully met. *Average percent of need met:* 90% (excluding resources awarded to replace EFC). *Average financial aid package:* $16,515 (excluding resources awarded to replace EFC). 10% of all full-time freshmen had no need and received non-need-based gift aid.

UNDERGRADUATE FINANCIAL AID (Fall 2003) 735 applied for aid; of those 89% were deemed to have need. 98% of undergraduates with need received aid; of those 38% had need fully met. *Average percent of need met:* 87% (excluding resources awarded to replace EFC). *Average financial aid package:* $15,530 (excluding resources awarded to replace EFC). 9% of all full-time undergraduates had no need and received non-need-based gift aid.

GIFT AID (NEED-BASED) *Total amount:* $5,344,229 (20% federal, 11% state, 58% institutional, 11% external sources). *Receiving aid:* Freshmen: 52% (108); All full-time undergraduates: 39% (348). *Average award:* Freshmen: $7108; Undergraduates: $5520. *Scholarships, grants, and awards:* Federal Pell, FSEOG, state, private, college/university gift aid from institutional funds.

GIFT AID (NON-NEED-BASED) *Total amount:* $2,020,185 (11% state, 74% institutional, 15% external sources). *Receiving aid:* Freshmen: 73% (151); Undergraduates: 68% (601). *Average Award:* Freshmen: $8743; Undergraduates: $7765. *Scholarships, grants, and awards by category: Academic Interests/Achievement:* 835 awards ($1,561,505 total): biological sciences, business, education, English, foreign languages, general academic interests/achievements, humanities, mathematics, physical sciences, premedicine, religion/biblical studies, social sciences. *Creative Arts/Performance:* 7 awards ($8000 total): art/fine arts, music. *Special Achievements/Activities:* 13 awards ($9250 total): general special achievements/activities, religious involvement. *Special Characteristics:* 671 awards ($780,492 total): children and siblings of alumni, children of faculty/staff, ethnic background, general special characteristics, international students, religious affiliation. *Tuition waivers:* Full or partial for employees or children of employees.

LOANS *Student loans:* $4,565,068 (68% need-based, 32% non-need-based). 95% of past graduating class borrowed through all loan programs. *Average indebtedness per student:* $18,208. *Average need-based loan:* Freshmen: $4623; Undergraduates: $5665. *Parent loans:* $1,622,807 (37% need-based, 63% non-need-based). *Programs:* FFEL (Subsidized and Unsubsidized Stafford, PLUS), Perkins, Federal Nursing.

WORK-STUDY *Federal work-study:* Total amount: $479,000; 326 jobs averaging $1787. *State or other work-study/employment:* Total amount: $172,000 (100% non-need-based). Part-time jobs available (averaging $1800).

APPLYING FOR FINANCIAL AID *Required financial aid forms:* FAFSA, state aid form. *Financial aid deadline (priority):* 4/15. *Notification date:* Continuous beginning 2/1. Students must reply within 4 weeks of notification.

CONTACT Ms. Renee Leap, Assistant Director of Financial Assistance, Eastern Mennonite University, 1200 Park Road, Harrisonburg, VA 22802-2462, 540-432-4138 or toll-free 800-368-2665. *Fax:* 540-432-4081. *E-mail:* leapr@emu.edu.

EASTERN MICHIGAN UNIVERSITY
Ypsilanti, MI

Tuition & fees (MI res): $5762	Average undergraduate aid package: $8207

ABOUT THE INSTITUTION State-supported, coed. Awards: bachelor's, master's, and doctoral degrees and post-bachelor's and post-master's certificates. 187 undergraduate majors. Total enrollment: 23,593. Undergraduates: 18,868. Freshmen: 2,354. Federal methodology is used as a basis for awarding need-based institutional aid.

UNDERGRADUATE EXPENSES for 2004–05 *Application fee:* $30. *Tuition, state resident:* full-time $4707; part-time $156.90 per credit hour. *Tuition, nonresident:* full-time $14,714; part-time $490.45 per credit hour. *Required fees:* full-time $1055; $32.50 per credit hour or $40 per term part-time. Full-time tuition and fees vary according to reciprocity agreements. Part-time tuition and fees vary according to reciprocity agreements. *College room and board:* $6082; *room only:* $2856. Room and board charges vary according to housing facility and location. *Payment plan:* Installment.

GIFT AID (NEED-BASED) *Total amount:* $14,997,425 (86% federal, 8% state, 6% institutional). *Receiving aid:* Freshmen: 33% (813); All full-time undergraduates: 28% (3,781). *Average award:* Freshmen: $3521; Undergraduates: $3314.

Scholarships, grants, and awards: Federal Pell, FSEOG, state, private, college/university gift aid from institutional funds, Nursing Disadvantaged Student Grant.

GIFT AID (NON-NEED-BASED) *Total amount:* $14,320,554 (14% state, 41% institutional, 45% external sources). *Receiving aid:* Freshmen: 31% (770); Undergraduates: 13% (1,761). *Average Award:* Freshmen: $2050; Undergraduates: $2050. *Scholarships, grants, and awards by category: Academic Interests/Achievement:* 3,130 awards ($7,212,558 total): agriculture, architecture, biological sciences, business, communication, computer science, education, engineering/technologies, English, foreign languages, general academic interests/achievements, health fields, home economics, humanities, mathematics, physical sciences, religion/biblical studies, social sciences. *Creative Arts/Performance:* 138 awards ($110,299 total): applied art and design, art/fine arts, cinema/film/broadcasting, creative writing, dance, debating, general creative arts/performance, music, performing arts, theater/drama. *Special Achievements/Activities:* 618 awards ($357,736 total): general special achievements/activities, leadership, memberships, religious involvement. *Special Characteristics:* 207 awards ($1,099,744 total): children and siblings of alumni, ethnic background, international students, members of minority groups, out-of-state students, previous college experience, religious affiliation. *Tuition waivers:* Full or partial for employees or children of employees. *ROTC:* Army, Naval cooperative, Air Force cooperative.

LOANS *Student loans:* $60,859,306 (47% need-based, 53% non-need-based). 61% of past graduating class borrowed through all loan programs. *Average indebtedness per student:* $21,930. *Average need-based loan:* Freshmen: $2566; Undergraduates: $3826. *Parent loans:* $7,864,676 (100% non-need-based). *Programs:* FFEL (Subsidized and Unsubsidized Stafford, PLUS), Perkins, college/university.

ATHLETIC AWARDS *Total amount:* $4,214,219 (100% non-need-based).

APPLYING FOR FINANCIAL AID *Required financial aid form:* FAFSA. *Financial aid deadline (priority):* 3/15. *Notification date:* Continuous beginning 3/15.

CONTACT Ms. Bernice A. Lindke, Assistant Vice President, Enrollment Services, Eastern Michigan University, 403 Pierce Hall, Ypsilanti, MI 48197, 734-487-1048 or toll-free 800-GO TO EMU. *Fax:* 734-487-4281. *E-mail:* bernice.lindke@emich.edu.

EASTERN NAZARENE COLLEGE
Quincy, MA

CONTACT Financial Aid Department, Eastern Nazarene College, 23 East Elm Avenue, Quincy, MA 02170, 617-745-3712 or toll-free 800-88-ENC88. *Fax:* 617-745-3929. *E-mail:* finaid@enc.edu.

EASTERN NEW MEXICO UNIVERSITY
Portales, NM

CONTACT Ms. Patricia Willis, Financial Aid Specialist, Eastern New Mexico University, Station 54, Portales, NM 88130, 505-562-2194 or toll-free 800-367-3668. *Fax:* 505-562-2198. *E-mail:* pat.willis@enmu.edu.

EASTERN OREGON UNIVERSITY
La Grande, OR

Tuition & fees (OR res): $5517	Average undergraduate aid package: $11,762

ABOUT THE INSTITUTION State-supported, coed. Awards: bachelor's and master's degrees. 32 undergraduate majors. Total enrollment: 3,338. Undergraduates: 3,069. Freshmen: 348. Federal methodology is used as a basis for awarding need-based institutional aid.

UNDERGRADUATE EXPENSES for 2004–05 *Application fee:* $50. *Tuition, state resident:* full-time $4257. *Tuition, nonresident:* full-time $4257. Full-time tuition and fees vary according to course load. Part-time tuition and fees vary according to course load. *College room and board:* $6099. Room and board charges vary according to board plan and housing facility.

FRESHMAN FINANCIAL AID (Fall 2004, est.) 280 applied for aid; of those 68% were deemed to have need. 99% of freshmen with need received aid; of those 52% had need fully met. *Average percent of need met:* 48% (excluding resources awarded to replace EFC). *Average financial aid package:* $10,841 (excluding resources awarded to replace EFC). 10% of all full-time freshmen had no need and received non-need-based gift aid.

UNDERGRADUATE FINANCIAL AID (Fall 2004, est.) 1,558 applied for aid; of those 81% were deemed to have need. 99% of undergraduates with need

received aid; of those 34% had need fully met. *Average percent of need met:* 59% (excluding resources awarded to replace EFC). *Average financial aid package:* $11,762 (excluding resources awarded to replace EFC). 2% of all full-time undergraduates had no need and received non-need-based gift aid.

GIFT AID (NEED-BASED) *Total amount:* $4,551,019 (83% federal, 12% state, 5% institutional). *Receiving aid:* Freshmen: 50% (156); All full-time undergraduates: 51% (936). *Average award:* Freshmen: $3058; Undergraduates: $3698. *Scholarships, grants, and awards:* Federal Pell, FSEOG, state, private, college/university gift aid from institutional funds.

GIFT AID (NON-NEED-BASED) *Total amount:* $791,446 (100% external sources). *Average Award:* Freshmen: $1223; Undergraduates: $1298. *Scholarships, grants, and awards by category: Academic Interests/Achievement:* agriculture, biological sciences, business, education, general academic interests/achievements, mathematics, physical sciences. *Creative Arts/Performance:* art/fine arts, music, theater/drama. *Special Achievements/Activities:* community service, leadership, rodeo. *Special Characteristics:* adult students, general special characteristics, international students, members of minority groups, out-of-state students. *ROTC:* Army.

LOANS *Student loans:* $10,269,974 (43% need-based, 57% non-need-based). 67% of past graduating class borrowed through all loan programs. *Average indebtedness per student:* $15,447. *Average need-based loan:* Freshmen: $2503; Undergraduates: $3751. *Parent loans:* $1,912,227 (100% non-need-based). *Programs:* Federal Direct (Subsidized and Unsubsidized Stafford, PLUS), FFEL (Subsidized and Unsubsidized Stafford, PLUS), Perkins.

WORK-STUDY *Federal work-study:* Total amount: $336,861; 245 jobs averaging $1553.

ATHLETIC AWARDS *Total amount:* $66,334 (100% non-need-based).

APPLYING FOR FINANCIAL AID *Required financial aid form:* FAFSA. *Financial aid deadline:* Continuous. *Notification date:* Continuous beginning 4/1. Students must reply within 4 weeks of notification.

CONTACT Mr. Eric Bucks, Director of Financial Aid, Eastern Oregon University, One University Boulevard, La Grande, OR 97850-2899, 541-962-3550 or toll-free 800-452-8639 (in-state), 800-452-3393 (out-of-state). *Fax:* 541-962-3661. *E-mail:* eric.bucks@eou.edu.

EASTERN UNIVERSITY
St. Davids, PA

ABOUT THE INSTITUTION Independent American Baptist Churches in the USA, coed. Awards: associate, bachelor's, and master's degrees. 36 undergraduate majors. Total enrollment: 3,253. Undergraduates: 2,200. Freshmen: 415.

GIFT AID (NEED-BASED) *Scholarships, grants, and awards:* Federal Pell, FSEOG, state, college/university gift aid from institutional funds, United Negro College Fund.

GIFT AID (NON-NEED-BASED) *Scholarships, grants, and awards by category: Academic Interests/Achievement:* general academic interests/achievements. *Creative Arts/Performance:* music. *Special Achievements/Activities:* community service, leadership.

LOANS *Programs:* FFEL (Subsidized and Unsubsidized Stafford, PLUS), Perkins, state, alternative loans.

APPLYING FOR FINANCIAL AID *Required financial aid forms:* FAFSA, institution's own form.

CONTACT Financial Aid Office, Eastern University, 1300 Eagle Road, St. Davids, PA 19087-3696, 610-341-5842 or toll-free 800-452-0996. *Fax:* 610-341-1492. *E-mail:* finaid@eastern.edu.

EASTERN WASHINGTON UNIVERSITY
Cheney, WA

Tuition & fees (WA res): $4056	Average undergraduate aid package: $10,485

ABOUT THE INSTITUTION State-supported, coed. Awards: bachelor's, master's, and doctoral degrees. 112 undergraduate majors. Total enrollment: 10,707. Undergraduates: 9,390. Freshmen: 1,426. Federal methodology is used as a basis for awarding need-based institutional aid.

UNDERGRADUATE EXPENSES for 2004–05 *Application fee:* $35. *Tuition, state resident:* full-time $3822; part-time $127 per credit. *Tuition, nonresident:* full-time $13,299; part-time $443 per credit. Full-time tuition and fees vary according to course load. Part-time tuition and fees vary according to course load. *College room and board:* $5460. Room and board charges vary according to board plan and housing facility. *Payment plan:* Installment.

FRESHMAN FINANCIAL AID (Fall 2003) 1374 applied for aid; of those 75% were deemed to have need. 97% of freshmen with need received aid; of those 25% had need fully met. *Average percent of need met:* 43% (excluding resources awarded to replace EFC). *Average financial aid package:* $9882 (excluding resources awarded to replace EFC). 2% of all full-time freshmen had no need and received non-need-based gift aid.

UNDERGRADUATE FINANCIAL AID (Fall 2003) 5,468 applied for aid; of those 83% were deemed to have need. 97% of undergraduates with need received aid; of those 21% had need fully met. *Average percent of need met:* 42% (excluding resources awarded to replace EFC). *Average financial aid package:* $10,485 (excluding resources awarded to replace EFC). 1% of all full-time undergraduates had no need and received non-need-based gift aid.

GIFT AID (NEED-BASED) *Total amount:* $20,206,700 (49% federal, 35% state, 9% institutional, 7% external sources). *Receiving aid:* Freshmen: 43% (774); All full-time undergraduates: 45% (3,269). *Average award:* Freshmen: $4468; Undergraduates: $4793. *Scholarships, grants, and awards:* Federal Pell, FSEOG, state, private, college/university gift aid from institutional funds.

GIFT AID (NON-NEED-BASED) *Total amount:* $220,087 (17% institutional, 83% external sources). *Receiving aid:* Freshmen: 17% (306); Undergraduates: 10% (706). *Average Award:* Freshmen: $3050; Undergraduates: $2480. *Scholarships, grants, and awards by category: Academic Interests/Achievement:* 488 awards ($547,000 total): biological sciences, business, computer science, education, engineering/technologies, English, foreign languages, general academic interests/achievements, health fields, mathematics, physical sciences, social sciences. *Creative Arts/Performance:* 57 awards ($61,000 total): art/fine arts, cinema/film/broadcasting, creative writing, journalism/publications, music, theater/drama. *Special Characteristics:* 250 awards ($450,000 total): children and siblings of alumni, children of union members/company employees, ethnic background, handicapped students, local/state students. *Tuition waivers:* Full or partial for employees or children of employees. *ROTC:* Army.

LOANS *Student loans:* $41,347,982 (90% need-based, 10% non-need-based). 68% of past graduating class borrowed through all loan programs. *Average indebtedness per student:* $17,516. *Average need-based loan:* Freshmen: $2335; Undergraduates: $3713. *Parent loans:* $6,032,781 (65% need-based, 35% non-need-based). *Programs:* FFEL (Subsidized and Unsubsidized Stafford, PLUS), Perkins.

WORK-STUDY *Federal work-study:* Total amount: $756,879; 360 jobs averaging $2100. *State or other work-study/employment:* Total amount: $1,037,099 (73% need-based, 27% non-need-based). 503 part-time jobs averaging $2061.

ATHLETIC AWARDS *Total amount:* $1,099,324 (41% need-based, 59% non-need-based).

APPLYING FOR FINANCIAL AID *Required financial aid form:* FAFSA. *Financial aid deadline (priority):* 2/15. *Notification date:* Continuous beginning 4/1. Students must reply within 4 weeks of notification.

CONTACT Bruce DeFrates, Financial Aid Director, Eastern Washington University, 102 Sutton Hall, Cheney, WA 99004-2447, 509-359-2314. *Fax:* 509-359-4330. *E-mail:* finaid@mail.ewu.edu.

EAST STROUDSBURG UNIVERSITY OF PENNSYLVANIA
East Stroudsburg, PA

Tuition & fees (PA res): $6224	Average undergraduate aid package: $5237

ABOUT THE INSTITUTION State-supported, coed. Awards: associate, bachelor's, and master's degrees. 50 undergraduate majors. Total enrollment: 6,553. Undergraduates: 5,409. Freshmen: 1,175. Federal methodology is used as a basis for awarding need-based institutional aid.

UNDERGRADUATE EXPENSES for 2004–05 *Application fee:* $35. *Tuition, state resident:* full-time $4810. *Tuition, nonresident:* full-time $12,026; part-time $501 per credit. *Required fees:* full-time $1414; $55 per credit. Part-time tuition and fees vary according to course load. *College room and board:* $4506; *room only:* $2864. Room and board charges vary according to board plan and housing facility. *Payment plan:* Installment.

FRESHMAN FINANCIAL AID (Fall 2003) 925 applied for aid; of those 70% were deemed to have need. 96% of freshmen with need received aid; of those 69% had need fully met. *Average percent of need met:* 80% (excluding resources awarded to replace EFC). *Average financial aid package:* $4043 (excluding resources awarded to replace EFC). 22% of all full-time freshmen had no need and received non-need-based gift aid.

UNDERGRADUATE FINANCIAL AID (Fall 2003) 3,713 applied for aid; of those 74% were deemed to have need. 97% of undergraduates with need received aid; of those 80% had need fully met. *Average percent of need met:* 87% (excluding resources awarded to replace EFC). *Average financial aid package:* $5237 (excluding resources awarded to replace EFC). 20% of all full-time undergraduates had no need and received non-need-based gift aid.

GIFT AID (NEED-BASED) *Total amount:* $7,005,963 (48% federal, 43% state, 9% institutional). *Receiving aid:* Freshmen: 40% (398); All full-time undergraduates: 40% (1,745). *Average award:* Freshmen: $3180; Undergraduates: $3332. *Scholarships, grants, and awards:* Federal Pell, FSEOG, state, private, college/university gift aid from institutional funds.

GIFT AID (NON-NEED-BASED) *Total amount:* $272,583 (100% external sources). *Receiving aid:* Freshmen: 2% (17); Undergraduates: 3% (113). *Average Award:* Freshmen: $6903; Undergraduates: $7025. *Scholarships, grants, and awards by category: Academic Interests/Achievement:* 299 awards ($365,792 total): biological sciences, business, communication, computer science, education, English, foreign languages, general academic interests/achievements, health fields, mathematics, physical sciences, social sciences. *Creative Arts/Performance:* 44 awards ($9250 total): applied art and design, music, theater/drama. *Special Achievements/Activities:* 43 awards ($9450 total): general special achievements/activities. *Special Characteristics:* 63 awards ($223,794 total): adult students, handicapped students, international students, members of minority groups. *Tuition waivers:* Full or partial for employees or children of employees, senior citizens. *ROTC:* Army cooperative, Air Force cooperative.

LOANS *Student loans:* $22,620,997 (45% need-based, 55% non-need-based). 68% of past graduating class borrowed through all loan programs. *Average indebtedness per student:* $20,265. *Average need-based loan:* Freshmen: $2422; Undergraduates: $3594. *Parent loans:* $3,312,328 (100% non-need-based). *Programs:* FFEL (Subsidized and Unsubsidized Stafford, PLUS), Perkins, alternative loans.

WORK-STUDY *Federal work-study:* Total amount: $402,203; 386 jobs averaging $1042. *State or other work-study/employment:* Total amount: $860,311 (100% non-need-based). 624 part-time jobs averaging $1379.

ATHLETIC AWARDS *Total amount:* $337,416 (100% non-need-based).

APPLYING FOR FINANCIAL AID *Required financial aid form:* FAFSA. *Financial aid deadline:* 3/1. *Notification date:* 4/1. Students must reply by 5/1.

CONTACT Georgia K. Prell, Director of Enrollment Services, East Stroudsburg University of Pennsylvania, 200 Prospect Street, East Stroudsburg, PA 18301-2999, 570-422-2820 or toll-free 877-230-5547. *Fax:* 570-422-2849.

EAST TENNESSEE STATE UNIVERSITY
Johnson City, TN

Tuition & fees (TN res): $4059	Average undergraduate aid package: $4895

ABOUT THE INSTITUTION State-supported, coed. Awards: associate, bachelor's, master's, doctoral, and first professional degrees and post-bachelor's and post-master's certificates. 38 undergraduate majors. Total enrollment: 11,869. Undergraduates: 9,672. Freshmen: 1,509. Federal methodology is used as a basis for awarding need-based institutional aid.

UNDERGRADUATE EXPENSES for 2004–05 *Application fee:* $15. *Tuition, state resident:* full-time $3352; part-time $147 per hour. *Tuition, nonresident:* full-time $11,840; part-time $515 per hour. *Required fees:* full-time $707; $45 per hour or $4 per term part-time. Full-time tuition and fees vary according to course load and program. *College room and board:* $4858; *room only:* $2200. Room and board charges vary according to board plan and housing facility. *Payment plans:* Tuition prepayment, installment, deferred payment.

FRESHMAN FINANCIAL AID (Fall 2003) 525 applied for aid; of those 75% were deemed to have need. 96% of freshmen with need received aid; of those 27% had need fully met. *Average percent of need met:* 84% (excluding resources awarded to replace EFC). *Average financial aid package:* $5666 (excluding resources awarded to replace EFC). 5% of all full-time freshmen had no need and received non-need-based gift aid.

UNDERGRADUATE FINANCIAL AID (Fall 2003) 5,277 applied for aid; of those 70% were deemed to have need. 97% of undergraduates with need received aid; of those 43% had need fully met. *Average percent of need met:* 82% (excluding resources awarded to replace EFC). *Average financial aid package:* $4895 (excluding resources awarded to replace EFC). 15% of all full-time undergraduates had no need and received non-need-based gift aid.

GIFT AID (NEED-BASED) *Total amount:* $14,449,459 (67% federal, 31% state, 1% institutional, 1% external sources). *Receiving aid:* Freshmen: 16% (238); All full-time undergraduates: 31% (2,327). *Average award:* Freshmen: $2212; Undergraduates: $3228. *Scholarships, grants, and awards:* Federal Pell, FSEOG, state, private, college/university gift aid from institutional funds, Federal Nursing.

GIFT AID (NON-NEED-BASED) *Total amount:* $7,220,096 (6% federal, 13% state, 57% institutional, 24% external sources). *Receiving aid:* Freshmen: 8% (114); Undergraduates: 13% (1,010). *Average Award:* Freshmen: $4451; Undergraduates: $3267. *Scholarships, grants, and awards by category: Academic Interests/Achievement:* biological sciences, business, computer science, education, engineering/technologies, English, general academic interests/achievements, health fields, mathematics, military science, social sciences. *Creative Arts/Performance:* art/fine arts, journalism/publications, music, theater/drama. *Special Achievements/Activities:* leadership, memberships. *Special Characteristics:* children of union members/company employees, members of minority groups. *Tuition waivers:* Full or partial for employees or children of employees, senior citizens. *ROTC:* Army.

LOANS *Student loans:* $29,244,480 (66% need-based, 34% non-need-based). 33% of past graduating class borrowed through all loan programs. *Average indebtedness per student:* $17,966. *Average need-based loan:* Freshmen: $985; Undergraduates: $3343. *Parent loans:* $3,273,836 (100% non-need-based). *Programs:* FFEL (Subsidized and Unsubsidized Stafford, PLUS), Perkins, college/university.

WORK-STUDY *Federal work-study:* Total amount: $911,504; 751 jobs averaging $1183. *State or other work-study/employment:* Total amount: $337,372 (100% non-need-based). 426 part-time jobs averaging $916.

ATHLETIC AWARDS *Total amount:* $2,007,612 (100% non-need-based).

APPLYING FOR FINANCIAL AID *Required financial aid form:* FAFSA. *Financial aid deadline (priority):* 4/15. *Notification date:* Continuous. Students must reply within 3 weeks of notification.

CONTACT Cindy A. Johnson, Assistant Director of Financial Aid, East Tennessee State University, PO Box 70722, Johnson City, TN 37614, 423-439-4300 or toll-free 800-462-3878.

EAST TEXAS BAPTIST UNIVERSITY
Marshall, TX

Tuition & fees: $12,000	Average undergraduate aid package: $12,572

ABOUT THE INSTITUTION Independent Baptist, coed. Awards: associate and bachelor's degrees. 45 undergraduate majors. Total enrollment: 1,412. Undergraduates: 1,412. Freshmen: 348. Federal methodology is used as a basis for awarding need-based institutional aid.

UNDERGRADUATE EXPENSES for 2004–05 *Application fee:* $25. *Comprehensive fee:* $15,873 includes full-time tuition ($12,000) and room and board ($3873). Room and board charges vary according to board plan and housing facility. *Part-time tuition:* $375 per semester hour. *Payment plans:* Guaranteed tuition, installment.

FRESHMAN FINANCIAL AID (Fall 2004, est.) 277 applied for aid; of those 89% were deemed to have need. 100% of freshmen with need received aid; of those 17% had need fully met. *Average percent of need met:* 83% (excluding resources awarded to replace EFC). *Average financial aid package:* $11,005 (excluding resources awarded to replace EFC). 16% of all full-time freshmen had no need and received non-need-based gift aid.

UNDERGRADUATE FINANCIAL AID (Fall 2004, est.) 1,067 applied for aid; of those 87% were deemed to have need. 100% of undergraduates with need received aid; of those 17% had need fully met. *Average percent of need met:* 81% (excluding resources awarded to replace EFC). *Average financial aid package:* $12,572 (excluding resources awarded to replace EFC). 17% of all full-time undergraduates had no need and received non-need-based gift aid.

GIFT AID (NEED-BASED) *Total amount:* $3,958,593 (48% federal, 52% state). *Receiving aid:* Freshmen: 61% (213); All full-time undergraduates: 64% (819). *Average award:* Freshmen: $4068; Undergraduates: $4205. *Scholarships, grants, and awards:* Federal Pell, FSEOG, state, private, college/university gift aid from institutional funds.

GIFT AID (NON-NEED-BASED) *Total amount:* $5,457,116 (1% state, 90% institutional, 9% external sources). *Receiving aid:* Freshmen: 59% (203); Undergraduates: 61% (784). *Average Award:* Freshmen: $4987; Undergraduates: $4473. *Scholarships, grants, and awards by category: Academic Interests/Achievement:* biological sciences, business, communication, computer science, education, English, foreign languages, general academic interests/achievements, health fields, mathematics, physical sciences, religion/biblical studies. *Creative Arts/Performance:* music, theater/drama. *Special Achievements/Activities:* cheerleading/drum major, general special achievements/activities, leadership, religious involvement. *Special Characteristics:* children and siblings of alumni, children of educators, children of faculty/staff, general special characteristics,

international students, local/state students, previous college experience, religious affiliation, siblings of current students, twins. *Tuition waivers:* Full or partial for employees or children of employees.

LOANS *Student loans:* $5,869,042 (49% need-based, 51% non-need-based). 74% of past graduating class borrowed through all loan programs. *Average indebtedness per student:* $15,005. *Average need-based loan:* Freshmen: $1973; Undergraduates: $3970. *Parent loans:* $825,165 (100% non-need-based). *Programs:* FFEL (Subsidized and Unsubsidized Stafford, PLUS), Perkins, state, college/university.

WORK-STUDY *Federal work-study:* Total amount: $161,916; 106 jobs averaging $1620. *State or other work-study/employment:* Total amount: $443,148 (4% need-based, 96% non-need-based). 251 part-time jobs averaging $1492.

APPLYING FOR FINANCIAL AID *Required financial aid forms:* FAFSA, institution's own form. *Financial aid deadline (priority):* 6/1. *Notification date:* Continuous. Students must reply within 3 weeks of notification.

CONTACT Katherine Evans, Director of Financial Aid, East Texas Baptist University, 1209 North Grove Street, Marshall, TX 75670-1498, 903-923-2137 or toll-free 800-804-ETBU. *Fax:* 903-934-8120.

EAST-WEST UNIVERSITY
Chicago, IL

ABOUT THE INSTITUTION Independent, coed. Awards: associate and bachelor's degrees. 17 undergraduate majors. Total enrollment: 1,040. Undergraduates: 1,040.

GIFT AID (NEED-BASED) *Scholarships, grants, and awards:* Federal Pell, FSEOG, state, college/university gift aid from institutional funds.

GIFT AID (NON-NEED-BASED) *Scholarships, grants, and awards by category:* Academic Interests/Achievement: general academic interests/achievements.

LOANS *Programs:* Federal Direct (Subsidized Stafford).

APPLYING FOR FINANCIAL AID *Required financial aid form:* FAFSA.

CONTACT Financial Aid Office, East-West University, 816 South Michigan Avenue, Chicago, IL 60605-2103, 312-939-0111 Ext. 1809.

ECKERD COLLEGE
St. Petersburg, FL

Tuition & fees: $24,362	Average undergraduate aid package: $18,961

ABOUT THE INSTITUTION Independent Presbyterian, coed. Awards: bachelor's degrees. 41 undergraduate majors. Total enrollment: 1,688. Undergraduates: 1,688. Freshmen: 472. Federal methodology is used as a basis for awarding need-based institutional aid.

UNDERGRADUATE EXPENSES for 2004–05 *Application fee:* $35. *Comprehensive fee:* $30,688 includes full-time tuition ($24,116), mandatory fees ($246), and room and board ($6326). *College room only:* $2980. Room and board charges vary according to board plan and housing facility. *Part-time tuition:* $2902 per course. *Payment plan:* Installment.

FRESHMAN FINANCIAL AID (Fall 2004, est.) 347 applied for aid; of those 79% were deemed to have need. 100% of freshmen with need received aid; of those 27% had need fully met. *Average percent of need met:* 87% (excluding resources awarded to replace EFC). *Average financial aid package:* $19,716 (excluding resources awarded to replace EFC). 20% of all full-time freshmen had no need and received non-need-based gift aid.

UNDERGRADUATE FINANCIAL AID (Fall 2004, est.) 1,103 applied for aid; of those 84% were deemed to have need. 100% of undergraduates with need received aid; of those 17% had need fully met. *Average percent of need met:* 79% (excluding resources awarded to replace EFC). *Average financial aid package:* $18,961 (excluding resources awarded to replace EFC). 35% of all full-time undergraduates had no need and received non-need-based gift aid.

GIFT AID (NEED-BASED) *Total amount:* $12,722,947 (8% federal, 9% state, 80% institutional, 3% external sources). *Receiving aid:* Freshmen: 58% (272); All full-time undergraduates: 56% (923). *Average award:* Freshmen: $17,956; Undergraduates: $14,307. *Scholarships, grants, and awards:* Federal Pell, FSEOG, state, private, college/university gift aid from institutional funds.

GIFT AID (NON-NEED-BASED) *Total amount:* $6,229,692 (11% state, 85% institutional, 4% external sources). *Average Award:* Freshmen: $9250; Undergraduates: $8617. *Scholarships, grants, and awards by category:* Academic Interests/Achievement: 500 awards ($4,000,000 total): general academic interests/achievements. Creative Arts/Performance: 40 awards ($200,000 total): art/fine arts, creative writing, music, theater/drama. Special Achievements/Activities: 100 awards ($500,000 total): community service, leadership. Special Characteristics:

233 awards ($1,116,402 total): children of faculty/staff, international students, local/state students, religious affiliation. *Tuition waivers:* Full or partial for employees or children of employees. *ROTC:* Army cooperative, Air Force cooperative.

LOANS *Student loans:* $6,717,582 (63% need-based, 37% non-need-based). 59% of past graduating class borrowed through all loan programs. *Average indebtedness per student:* $9448. *Average need-based loan:* Freshmen: $2204; Undergraduates: $4383. *Parent loans:* $2,572,336 (34% need-based, 66% non-need-based). *Programs:* FFEL (Subsidized and Unsubsidized Stafford, PLUS), Perkins, college/university.

WORK-STUDY *Federal work-study:* Total amount: $1,370,018; 661 jobs averaging $2000. *State or other work-study/employment:* Total amount: $141,755 (100% non-need-based). 75 part-time jobs averaging $1500.

ATHLETIC AWARDS *Total amount:* $452,438 (36% need-based, 64% non-need-based).

APPLYING FOR FINANCIAL AID *Required financial aid form:* FAFSA. *Financial aid deadline (priority):* 4/1. *Notification date:* Continuous. Students must reply by 5/1.

CONTACT Dr. Pat Garrett Watkins, Director of Financial Aid, Eckerd College, 4200 54th Avenue, South, St. Petersburg, FL 33711, 727-864-8334 or toll-free 800-456-9009. *Fax:* 727-866-2304. *E-mail:* watkinpe@eckerd.edu.

EDGEWOOD COLLEGE
Madison, WI

Tuition & fees: $16,050	Average undergraduate aid package: $11,776

ABOUT THE INSTITUTION Independent Roman Catholic, coed. Awards: associate, bachelor's, and master's degrees. 41 undergraduate majors. Total enrollment: 2,454. Undergraduates: 1,960. Freshmen: 304. Federal methodology is used as a basis for awarding need-based institutional aid.

UNDERGRADUATE EXPENSES for 2004–05 *Application fee:* $25. *Comprehensive fee:* $21,741 includes full-time tuition ($16,050) and room and board ($5691). *College room only:* $2753. Full-time tuition and fees vary according to program. Room and board charges vary according to housing facility and location. *Part-time tuition:* $494 per credit. Part-time tuition and fees vary according to course load and program.

FRESHMAN FINANCIAL AID (Fall 2003) 267 applied for aid; of those 86% were deemed to have need. 100% of freshmen with need received aid; of those 21% had need fully met. *Average percent of need met:* 81% (excluding resources awarded to replace EFC). *Average financial aid package:* $12,378 (excluding resources awarded to replace EFC). 21% of all full-time freshmen had no need and received non-need-based gift aid.

UNDERGRADUATE FINANCIAL AID (Fall 2003) 1,128 applied for aid; of those 87% were deemed to have need. 100% of undergraduates with need received aid; of those 16% had need fully met. *Average percent of need met:* 75% (excluding resources awarded to replace EFC). *Average financial aid package:* $11,776 (excluding resources awarded to replace EFC). 20% of all full-time undergraduates had no need and received non-need-based gift aid.

GIFT AID (NEED-BASED) *Total amount:* $7,090,768 (19% federal, 18% state, 55% institutional, 8% external sources). *Receiving aid:* Freshmen: 76% (226); All full-time undergraduates: 75% (918). *Average award:* Freshmen: $8832; Undergraduates: $7050. *Scholarships, grants, and awards:* Federal Pell, FSEOG, state, private, college/university gift aid from institutional funds.

GIFT AID (NON-NEED-BASED) *Total amount:* $1,097,103 (2% federal, 3% state, 68% institutional, 27% external sources). *Receiving aid:* Freshmen: 8% (25); Undergraduates: 4% (55). *Average Award:* Freshmen: $9409; Undergraduates: $8668. *Scholarships, grants, and awards by category:* Academic Interests/Achievement: foreign languages, general academic interests/achievements. Creative Arts/Performance: art/fine arts, creative writing, music, performing arts, theater/drama. Special Achievements/Activities: community service, hobbies/interests, leadership. Special Characteristics: first-generation college students, handicapped students, local/state students, members of minority groups, religious affiliation. *Tuition waivers:* Full or partial for employees or children of employees.

LOANS *Student loans:* $9,010,801 (73% need-based, 27% non-need-based). 67% of past graduating class borrowed through all loan programs. *Average indebtedness per student:* $19,845. *Average need-based loan:* Freshmen: $2927; Undergraduates: $4219. *Parent loans:* $1,325,532 (40% need-based, 60% non-need-based). *Programs:* FFEL (Subsidized and Unsubsidized Stafford, PLUS), Perkins, state, college/university.

WORK-STUDY *Federal work-study:* Total amount: $977,474; 347 jobs averaging $1441. *State or other work-study/employment:* Total amount: $1,203,730 (31% need-based, 69% non-need-based). 795 part-time jobs averaging $1884.

APPLYING FOR FINANCIAL AID *Required financial aid forms:* FAFSA, institution's own form. *Financial aid deadline (priority):* 3/15. *Notification date:* 3/30. Students must reply within 2 weeks of notification.

CONTACT Kari Gribble, Director for Financial Aid, Edgewood College, 1000 Edgewood College Drive, Madison, WI 53711-1997, 608-663-2206 or toll-free 800-444-4861 Ext. 2294.

EDINBORO UNIVERSITY OF PENNSYLVANIA
Edinboro, PA

Tuition & fees (PA res): $6089	Average undergraduate aid package: $6569

ABOUT THE INSTITUTION State-supported, coed. Awards: associate, bachelor's, and master's degrees and post-bachelor's and post-master's certificates. 53 undergraduate majors. Total enrollment: 7,773. Undergraduates: 6,735. Freshmen: 1,277. Federal methodology is used as a basis for awarding need-based institutional aid.

UNDERGRADUATE EXPENSES for 2005–06 *Application fee:* $25. *Tuition, area resident:* part-time $200 per credit. *Tuition, state resident:* full-time $4810. *Tuition, nonresident:* full-time $9620; part-time $401 per credit. *Required fees:* full-time $1279; $47 per credit or $25 per term part-time. Part-time tuition and fees vary according to course load. *College room and board:* $5338; *room only:* $3320. Room and board charges vary according to board plan. *Payment plan:* Installment.

FRESHMAN FINANCIAL AID (Fall 2003) 1367 applied for aid; of those 83% were deemed to have need. 97% of freshmen with need received aid; of those 7% had need fully met. *Average percent of need met:* 79% (excluding resources awarded to replace EFC). *Average financial aid package:* $5736 (excluding resources awarded to replace EFC). 7% of all full-time freshmen had no need and received non-need-based gift aid.

UNDERGRADUATE FINANCIAL AID (Fall 2003) 6,065 applied for aid; of those 84% were deemed to have need. 97% of undergraduates with need received aid; of those 10% had need fully met. *Average percent of need met:* 83% (excluding resources awarded to replace EFC). *Average financial aid package:* $6569 (excluding resources awarded to replace EFC). 10% of all full-time undergraduates had no need and received non-need-based gift aid.

GIFT AID (NEED-BASED) *Total amount:* $13,003,923 (56% federal, 44% state). *Receiving aid:* Freshmen: 76% (1,100); All full-time undergraduates: 75% (4,975). *Average award:* Freshmen: $2860; Undergraduates: $1867. *Scholarships, grants, and awards:* Federal Pell, FSEOG, state, private, college/university gift aid from institutional funds.

GIFT AID (NON-NEED-BASED) *Total amount:* $2,174,140 (1% federal, 2% state, 41% institutional, 56% external sources). *Receiving aid:* Freshmen: 24% (348); Undergraduates: 14% (919). *Average Award:* Freshmen: $2000; Undergraduates: $2120. *Scholarships, grants, and awards by category:* *Academic Interests/Achievement:* 257 awards ($284,550 total): biological sciences, business, communication, computer science, education, engineering/technologies, English, foreign languages, general academic interests/achievements, health fields, humanities, mathematics, military science, physical sciences, premedicine, religion/biblical studies, social sciences. *Creative Arts/Performance:* 31 awards ($14,500 total): art/fine arts, cinema/film/broadcasting, journalism/publications, music. *Special Achievements/Activities:* 5 awards ($3500 total): general special achievements/activities. *Special Characteristics:* 831 awards ($2,328,577 total): adult students, children and siblings of alumni, children of faculty/staff, children of union members/company employees, children with a deceased or disabled parent, first-generation college students, general special characteristics, handicapped students, international students, local/state students, members of minority groups, out-of-state students, religious affiliation, veterans, veterans' children. *Tuition waivers:* Full or partial for minority students, employees or children of employees. *ROTC:* Army.

LOANS *Student loans:* $24,021,304 (59% need-based, 41% non-need-based). 63% of past graduating class borrowed through all loan programs. *Average indebtedness per student:* $16,748. *Average need-based loan:* Freshmen: $2107; Undergraduates: $3227. *Parent loans:* $2,940,004 (100% need-based). *Programs:* FFEL (Subsidized and Unsubsidized Stafford, PLUS), Perkins, Federal Nursing, college/university.

WORK-STUDY *Federal work-study:* Total amount: $623,909; 556 jobs averaging $1122. *State or other work-study/employment:* Total amount: $1,242,227 (100% non-need-based). 815 part-time jobs averaging $1524.

ATHLETIC AWARDS *Total amount:* $619,364 (1% need-based, 99% non-need-based).

APPLYING FOR FINANCIAL AID *Required financial aid form:* FAFSA. *Financial aid deadline (priority):* 3/15. *Notification date:* 3/31. Students must reply within 2 weeks of notification.

CONTACT Ms. Dorothy Body, Assistant Vice President for Student Financial Support and Services, Edinboro University of Pennsylvania, Hamilton Hall, Edinboro, PA 16444, 814-732-5555 Ext. 266 or toll-free 888-846-2676 (in-state), 800-626-2203 (out-of-state). *Fax:* 814-732-2129. *E-mail:* dbody@edinboro. edu.

ELECTRONIC DATA PROCESSING COLLEGE OF PUERTO RICO
San Juan, PR

CONTACT Dean of Financial Aid, Electronic Data Processing College of Puerto Rico, PO Box 192303, San Juan, PR 00919-2303, 787-765-3560 Ext. 4713. *Fax:* 787-765-2650.

ELIZABETH CITY STATE UNIVERSITY
Elizabeth City, NC

ABOUT THE INSTITUTION State-supported, coed. Awards: bachelor's and master's degrees. 45 undergraduate majors. Total enrollment: 2,470. Undergraduates: 2,437. Freshmen: 560.

GIFT AID (NEED-BASED) *Scholarships, grants, and awards:* Federal Pell, FSEOG, state, private, college/university gift aid from institutional funds, United Negro College Fund.

GIFT AID (NON-NEED-BASED) *Scholarships, grants, and awards by category:* *Academic Interests/Achievement:* computer science, education, general academic interests/achievements, mathematics, military science. *Creative Arts/Performance:* music, performing arts. *Special Characteristics:* ethnic background, handicapped students, international students, members of minority groups, veterans, veterans' children.

LOANS *Programs:* Federal Direct (Subsidized and Unsubsidized Stafford, PLUS), FFEL (Subsidized and Unsubsidized Stafford, PLUS), Perkins.

WORK-STUDY *Federal work-study:* Total amount: $427,352; jobs available.

APPLYING FOR FINANCIAL AID *Required financial aid form:* FAFSA.

CONTACT Assistant Director of Financial Aid, Elizabeth City State University, 1704 Weeksville Road, Campus Box 914, Elizabeth City, NC 27909-7806, 252-335-3285 or toll-free 800-347-3278. *Fax:* 252-335-3716.

ELIZABETHTOWN COLLEGE
Elizabethtown, PA

Tuition & fees: $23,710	Average undergraduate aid package: $17,750

ABOUT THE INSTITUTION Independent religious, coed. Awards: associate, bachelor's, and master's degrees and post-bachelor's certificates. 50 undergraduate majors. Total enrollment: 2,136. Undergraduates: 1,859. Freshmen: 539. Both federal and institutional methodology are used as a basis for awarding need-based institutional aid.

UNDERGRADUATE EXPENSES for 2004–05 *Application fee:* $30. *Comprehensive fee:* $30,310 includes full-time tuition ($23,710) and room and board ($6600). *College room only:* $3300. Full-time tuition and fees vary according to course load. Room and board charges vary according to board plan and housing facility. *Part-time tuition:* $600 per credit hour. Part-time tuition and fees vary according to class time and course load. *Payment plan:* Installment.

FRESHMAN FINANCIAL AID (Fall 2004, est.) 459 applied for aid; of those 83% were deemed to have need. 100% of freshmen with need received aid; of those 33% had need fully met. *Average percent of need met:* 85% (excluding resources awarded to replace EFC). *Average financial aid package:* $17,970 (excluding resources awarded to replace EFC). 14% of all full-time freshmen had no need and received non-need-based gift aid.

UNDERGRADUATE FINANCIAL AID (Fall 2004, est.) 1,536 applied for aid; of those 88% were deemed to have need. 100% of undergraduates with need received aid; of those 30% had need fully met. *Average percent of need met:* 87% (excluding resources awarded to replace EFC). *Average financial aid*

Elizabethtown College

package: $17,750 (excluding resources awarded to replace EFC). 9% of all full-time undergraduates had no need and received non-need-based gift aid.

GIFT AID (NEED-BASED) *Total amount:* $20,892,060 (5% federal, 9% state, 78% institutional, 8% external sources). *Receiving aid:* Freshmen: 71% (381); All full-time undergraduates: 71% (1,345). *Average award:* Freshmen $14,844; Undergraduates: $13,750. *Scholarships, grants, and awards:* Federal Pell, FSEOG, state, private, college/university gift aid from institutional funds.

GIFT AID (NON-NEED-BASED) *Total amount:* $2,151,947 (83% institutional, 17% external sources). *Receiving aid:* Freshmen: 14% (77); Undergraduates: 9% (172). *Average Award:* Freshmen: $13,317; Undergraduates: $14,620. *Scholarships, grants, and awards by category: Academic Interests/Achievement:* biological sciences, business, communication, computer science, education, engineering/technologies, English, foreign languages, general academic interests/ achievements, health fields, humanities, international studies, mathematics, physical sciences, premedicine, religion/biblical studies, social sciences. *Creative Arts/Performance:* art/fine arts, music, performing arts, theater/drama. *Special Achievements/Activities:* religious involvement. *Special Characteristics:* children of faculty/staff, international students, local/state students, members of minority groups, religious affiliation, siblings of current students. *Tuition waivers:* Full or partial for employees or children of employees.

LOANS *Student loans:* $9,617,270 (61% need-based, 39% non-need-based). 78% of past graduating class borrowed through all loan programs. *Average indebtedness per student:* $24,545. *Average need-based loan:* Freshmen: $2864; Undergraduates: $3881. *Parent loans:* $3,665,239 (23% need-based, 77% non-need-based). *Programs:* FFEL (Subsidized and Unsubsidized Stafford, PLUS), Perkins, state, college/university.

WORK-STUDY *Federal work-study:* Total amount: $1,138,926; 893 jobs averaging $1268.

APPLYING FOR FINANCIAL AID *Required financial aid forms:* FAFSA, institution's own form, state aid form, federal income tax form(s), W-2 forms. *Financial aid deadline (priority):* 3/15. *Notification date:* Continuous beginning 3/1. Students must reply by 5/1 or within 2 weeks of notification.

CONTACT M. Clarke Paine, Director of Financial Aid, Elizabethtown College, 1 Alpha Drive, Elizabethtown, PA 17022-2298, 717-361-1514. *Fax:* 717-361-1485. *E-mail:* painemc@etown.edu.

ELMHURST COLLEGE
Elmhurst, IL

Tuition & fees: $20,090	Average undergraduate aid package: $18,079

ABOUT THE INSTITUTION Independent religious, coed. Awards: bachelor's and master's degrees. 67 undergraduate majors. Total enrollment: 2,670. Undergraduates: 2,484. Freshmen: 415. Federal methodology is used as a basis for awarding need-based institutional aid.

UNDERGRADUATE EXPENSES for 2004–05 *Application fee:* $25. *Comprehensive fee:* $26,394 includes full-time tuition ($20,090) and room and board ($6304). *College room only:* $3634. Room and board charges vary according to board plan and housing facility. *Part-time tuition:* $572 per credit hour. *Payment plan:* Installment.

FRESHMAN FINANCIAL AID (Fall 2004, est.) 347 applied for aid; of those 83% were deemed to have need. 100% of freshmen with need received aid; of those 22% had need fully met. *Average percent of need met:* 94% (excluding resources awarded to replace EFC). *Average financial aid package:* $18,159 (excluding resources awarded to replace EFC). 8% of all full-time freshmen had no need and received non-need-based gift aid.

UNDERGRADUATE FINANCIAL AID (Fall 2004, est.) 1,878 applied for aid; of those 89% were deemed to have need. 100% of undergraduates with need received aid; of those 19% had need fully met. *Average percent of need met:* 91% (excluding resources awarded to replace EFC). *Average financial aid package:* $18,079 (excluding resources awarded to replace EFC). 15% of all full-time undergraduates had no need and received non-need-based gift aid.

GIFT AID (NEED-BASED) *Total amount:* $11,693,716 (16% federal, 27% state, 56% institutional, 1% external sources). *Receiving aid:* Freshmen: 68% (262); All full-time undergraduates: 70% (1,483). *Average award:* Freshmen: $13,370; Undergraduates: $12,972. *Scholarships, grants, and awards:* Federal Pell, FSEOG, state, private, college/university gift aid from institutional funds.

GIFT AID (NON-NEED-BASED) *Total amount:* $15,638,821 (1% state, 99% institutional). *Receiving aid:* Freshmen: 37% (142); Undergraduates: 52% (1,092). *Average Award:* Freshmen: $7992; Undergraduates: $7727. *Scholarships, grants, and awards by category: Academic Interests/Achievement:* 917 awards ($7,692,946 total): biological sciences, business, communication, computer science, education, English, foreign languages, general academic

interests/achievements, health fields, humanities, mathematics, physical sciences, premedicine, religion/biblical studies. *Creative Arts/Performance:* 104 awards ($127,050 total): art/fine arts, music, theater/drama. *Special Characteristics:* 175 awards ($927,653 total): members of minority groups, religious affiliation. *Tuition waivers:* Full or partial for employees or children of employees, senior citizens. *ROTC:* Army cooperative, Air Force cooperative.

LOANS *Student loans:* $10,288,576 (52% need-based, 48% non-need-based). 80% of past graduating class borrowed through all loan programs. *Average indebtedness per student:* $15,986. *Average need-based loan:* Freshmen: $4366; Undergraduates: $6180. *Parent loans:* $4,273,315 (33% need-based, 67% non-need-based). *Programs:* Federal Direct (Subsidized and Unsubsidized Stafford, PLUS), Perkins, alternative loans.

WORK-STUDY *Federal work-study:* Total amount: $336,124; 316 jobs averaging $1065. *State or other work-study/employment:* Total amount: $498,451 (100% non-need-based). 214 part-time jobs averaging $2300.

APPLYING FOR FINANCIAL AID *Required financial aid forms:* FAFSA, institution's own form. *Financial aid deadline (priority):* 4/15. *Notification date:* Continuous. Students must reply within 3 weeks of notification.

CONTACT Ruth A. Pusich, Director of Financial Aid, Elmhurst College, Goebel Hall 106A, 190 Prospect Avenue, Elmhurst, IL 60126-3296, 630-617-3080 or toll-free 800-697-1871 (out-of-state). *Fax:* 630-617-5188. *E-mail:* ruthp@elmhurst.edu.

ELMIRA COLLEGE
Elmira, NY

Tuition & fees: $27,030	Average undergraduate aid package: $21,331

ABOUT THE INSTITUTION Independent, coed. Awards: bachelor's and master's degrees (also offers master's degree in education primarily for local students). 67 undergraduate majors. Total enrollment: 1,853. Undergraduates: 1,558. Freshmen: 351. Federal methodology is used as a basis for awarding need-based institutional aid.

UNDERGRADUATE EXPENSES for 2004–05 *Application fee:* $50. *Comprehensive fee:* $35,360 includes full-time tuition ($26,130), mandatory fees ($900), and room and board ($8330). *Part-time tuition:* $250 per credit. *Payment plans:* Tuition prepayment, installment.

FRESHMAN FINANCIAL AID (Fall 2004, est.) 282 applied for aid; of those 93% were deemed to have need. 100% of freshmen with need received aid; of those 17% had need fully met. *Average percent of need met:* 82% (excluding resources awarded to replace EFC). *Average financial aid package:* $22,012 (excluding resources awarded to replace EFC). 18% of all full-time freshmen had no need and received non-need-based gift aid.

UNDERGRADUATE FINANCIAL AID (Fall 2004, est.) 1,040 applied for aid; of those 93% were deemed to have need. 99% of undergraduates with need received aid; of those 16% had need fully met. *Average percent of need met:* 82% (excluding resources awarded to replace EFC). *Average financial aid package:* $21,331 (excluding resources awarded to replace EFC). 18% of all full-time undergraduates had no need and received non-need-based gift aid.

GIFT AID (NEED-BASED) *Total amount:* $14,929,683 (8% federal, 7% state, 83% institutional, 2% external sources). *Receiving aid:* Freshmen: 81% (263); All full-time undergraduates: 77% (958). *Average award:* Freshmen: $17,262; Undergraduates: $15,825. *Scholarships, grants, and awards:* Federal Pell, FSEOG, state, private, college/university gift aid from institutional funds.

GIFT AID (NON-NEED-BASED) *Total amount:* $3,292,135 (2% state, 94% institutional, 4% external sources). *Receiving aid:* Freshmen: 11% (36); Undergraduates: 9% (115). *Average Award:* Freshmen: $15,729; Undergraduates: $15,743. *Scholarships, grants, and awards by category: Academic Interests/Achievement:* 736 awards ($8,665,579 total): general academic interests/ achievements. *Special Achievements/Activities:* 120 awards ($502,800 total): leadership. *Special Characteristics:* 133 awards ($1,484,534 total): children of faculty/staff, international students, local/state students, previous college experience, siblings of current students. *Tuition waivers:* Full or partial for employees or children of employees. *ROTC:* Army, Air Force cooperative.

LOANS *Student loans:* $8,861,217 (73% need-based, 27% non-need-based). 67% of past graduating class borrowed through all loan programs. *Average indebtedness per student:* $22,636. *Average need-based loan:* Freshmen: $5244; Undergraduates: $6112. *Parent loans:* $2,237,011 (33% need-based, 67% non-need-based). *Programs:* FFEL (Subsidized and Unsubsidized Stafford, PLUS), Perkins, college/university, GATE Loans, alternative loans.

WORK-STUDY *Federal work-study:* Total amount: $387,779; 371 jobs averaging $1045. *State or other work-study/employment:* Total amount: $218,650 (42% need-based, 58% non-need-based). 188 part-time jobs averaging $1160.

APPLYING FOR FINANCIAL AID *Required financial aid forms:* FAFSA, state aid form. *Financial aid deadline (priority):* 2/1. *Notification date:* Continuous beginning 2/15. Students must reply by 5/1 or within 3 weeks of notification. **CONTACT** Kathleen L. Cohen, Dean of Financial Aid, Elmira College, Hamilton Hall, One Park Place, Elmira, NY 14901-2099, 607-735-1728 or toll-free 800-935-6472. *Fax:* 607-735-1718. *E-mail:* kcohen@elmira.edu.

ELMS COLLEGE
Chicopee, MA

ABOUT THE INSTITUTION Independent Roman Catholic, coed, primarily women. Awards: associate, bachelor's, and master's degrees and post-bachelor's certificates. 47 undergraduate majors. Total enrollment: 932. Undergraduates: 792. Freshmen: 122.

GIFT AID (NEED-BASED) *Scholarships, grants, and awards:* Federal Pell, FSEOG, state, private, college/university gift aid from institutional funds.

GIFT AID (NON-NEED-BASED) *Scholarships, grants, and awards by category: Academic Interests/Achievement:* general academic interests/achievements. *Special Characteristics:* children of faculty/staff, general special characteristics, religious affiliation.

LOANS *Programs:* FFEL (Subsidized and Unsubsidized Stafford, PLUS), Perkins, state, alternative loans, MEFA Loans, Key Alternative Loans, CitiAssist Loans, Signature Loans.

WORK-STUDY *Federal work-study:* Total amount: $144,536; 164 jobs averaging $1328.

APPLYING FOR FINANCIAL AID *Required financial aid forms:* FAFSA, institution's own form.

CONTACT Ms. April Burns, Assistant Director of Student Financial Aid Services, Elms College, 291 Springfield Street, Chicopee, MA 01013-2839, 413-594-2761 Ext. 303 or toll-free 800-255-ELMS. *Fax:* 413-594-2781. *E-mail:* burnsa@elms.edu.

ELON UNIVERSITY
Elon, NC

Tuition & fees: $17,555	Average undergraduate aid package: $11,364

ABOUT THE INSTITUTION Independent religious, coed. Awards: bachelor's, master's, doctoral, and first professional degrees. 50 undergraduate majors. Total enrollment: 4,796. Undergraduates: 4,622. Freshmen: 1,232. Institutional methodology is used as a basis for awarding need-based institutional aid.

UNDERGRADUATE EXPENSES for 2004–05 *Application fee:* $40. *Comprehensive fee:* $23,565 includes full-time tuition ($17,310), mandatory fees ($245), and room and board ($6010). *College room only:* $2936. Room and board charges vary according to board plan and housing facility. *Part-time tuition:* $544 per hour. *Part-time fees:* $122.50 per term. Part-time tuition and fees vary according to course load. *Payment plan:* Installment.

FRESHMAN FINANCIAL AID (Fall 2004, est.) 698 applied for aid; of those 67% were deemed to have need. 99% of freshmen with need received aid. *Average percent of need met:* 75% (excluding resources awarded to replace EFC). *Average financial aid package:* $11,456 (excluding resources awarded to replace EFC). 22% of all full-time freshmen had no need and received non-need-based gift aid.

UNDERGRADUATE FINANCIAL AID (Fall 2004, est.) 2,113 applied for aid; of those 74% were deemed to have need. 99% of undergraduates with need received aid. *Average percent of need met:* 71% (excluding resources awarded to replace EFC). *Average financial aid package:* $11,364 (excluding resources awarded to replace EFC). 20% of all full-time undergraduates had no need and received non-need-based gift aid.

GIFT AID (NEED-BASED) *Total amount:* $9,815,162 (13% federal, 28% state, 56% institutional, 3% external sources). *Receiving aid:* Freshmen: 34% (420); All full-time undergraduates: 32% (1,420). *Average award:* Freshmen: $7169; Undergraduates: $6351. *Scholarships, grants, and awards:* Federal Pell, FSEOG, state, private, college/university gift aid from institutional funds.

GIFT AID (NON-NEED-BASED) *Total amount:* $4,766,587 (27% state, 67% institutional, 6% external sources). *Receiving aid:* Freshmen: 4% (53); Undergraduates: 4% (175). *Average Award:* Freshmen: $3757; Undergraduates: $3713. *Scholarships, grants, and awards by category: Academic Interests/Achievement:* 1,363 awards ($4,999,273 total): biological sciences, business, communication, computer science, education, engineering/technologies, general academic interests/achievements, mathematics, military science, physical sciences, premedicine, religion/biblical studies, social sciences. *Creative Arts/*

Performance: 74 awards ($127,875 total): art/fine arts, journalism/publications, music, performing arts, theater/drama. *Special Achievements/Activities:* 15 awards ($14,344 total): leadership. *Special Characteristics:* 42 awards ($467,395 total): children of faculty/staff, relatives of clergy. *Tuition waivers:* Full or partial for employees or children of employees. *ROTC:* Army, Air Force cooperative.

LOANS *Student loans:* $8,673,054 (67% need-based, 33% non-need-based). 43% of past graduating class borrowed through all loan programs. *Average indebtedness per student:* $18,601. *Average need-based loan:* Freshmen: $2577; Undergraduates: $3614. *Parent loans:* $10,464,482 (35% need-based, 65% non-need-based). *Programs:* FFEL (Subsidized and Unsubsidized Stafford, PLUS), Perkins, state, college/university, alternative loans.

WORK-STUDY *Federal work-study:* Total amount: $1,932,316; 826 jobs averaging $2271.

ATHLETIC AWARDS *Total amount:* $3,567,538 (45% need-based, 55% non-need-based).

APPLYING FOR FINANCIAL AID *Required financial aid forms:* FAFSA, institution's own form, CSS Financial Aid PROFILE. *Financial aid deadline (priority):* 2/15. *Notification date:* Continuous beginning 3/30.

CONTACT Pat Murphy, Director of Financial Planning, Elon University, 2700 Campus Box, Elon, NC 27244, 336-278-7640 or toll-free 800-334-8448. *E-mail:* murphyp@elon.edu.

EMBRY-RIDDLE AERONAUTICAL UNIVERSITY
Prescott, AZ

Tuition & fees: $23,490	Average undergraduate aid package: $6312

ABOUT THE INSTITUTION Independent, coed, primarily men. Awards: bachelor's and master's degrees. 10 undergraduate majors. Total enrollment: 1,668. Undergraduates: 1,637. Freshmen: 370. Federal methodology is used as a basis for awarding need-based institutional aid.

UNDERGRADUATE EXPENSES for 2005–06 *Application fee:* $30. *Comprehensive fee:* $30,006 includes full-time tuition ($22,820), mandatory fees ($670), and room and board ($6516). *College room only:* $3580. *Part-time tuition:* $955 per credit hour.

FRESHMAN FINANCIAL AID (Fall 2004, est.) 321 applied for aid; of those 86% were deemed to have need. 100% of freshmen with need received aid. *Average financial aid package:* $6596 (excluding resources awarded to replace EFC). 28% of all full-time freshmen had no need and received non-need-based gift aid.

UNDERGRADUATE FINANCIAL AID (Fall 2004, est.) 1,110 applied for aid; of those 100% were deemed to have need. 100% of undergraduates with need received aid. *Average financial aid package:* $6312 (excluding resources awarded to replace EFC). 20% of all full-time undergraduates had no need and received non-need-based gift aid.

GIFT AID (NEED-BASED) *Total amount:* $11,272,616 (11% federal, 61% institutional, 28% external sources). *Receiving aid:* Freshmen: 74% (273); All full-time undergraduates: 69% (1,016). *Average award:* Freshmen: $5122; Undergraduates: $4925. *Scholarships, grants, and awards:* Federal Pell, FSEOG, state, private, college/university gift aid from institutional funds.

GIFT AID (NON-NEED-BASED) *Average Award:* Freshmen: $2887; Undergraduates: $3412. *Scholarships, grants, and awards by category: Academic Interests/Achievement:* 645 awards ($3,106,834 total): general academic interests/achievements. *Special Achievements/Activities:* 21 awards ($66,562 total): leadership. *Special Characteristics:* 59 awards ($546,321 total): children and siblings of alumni, children of faculty/staff. *ROTC:* Army, Air Force.

LOANS *Student loans:* $14,711,561 (100% need-based). 77% of past graduating class borrowed through all loan programs. *Average indebtedness per student:* $43,425. *Average need-based loan:* Freshmen: $1794; Undergraduates: $2259. *Parent loans:* $5,242,261 (100% need-based). *Programs:* FFEL (Subsidized and Unsubsidized Stafford, PLUS), Perkins, state, college/university.

WORK-STUDY *Federal work-study:* Total amount: $23,000; 79 jobs averaging $2917. *State or other work-study/employment:* Total amount: $693,270 (100% need-based). 496 part-time jobs averaging $1397.

ATHLETIC AWARDS *Total amount:* $579,800 (100% need-based).

APPLYING FOR FINANCIAL AID *Required financial aid form:* FAFSA. *Financial aid deadline:* Continuous. *Notification date:* Continuous beginning 3/1. Students must reply within 4 weeks of notification.

CONTACT Mr. Dan Lupin, Director of Financial Aid, Embry-Riddle Aeronautical University, 3700 Willow Creek Road, Prescott, AZ 86301-3720, 928-777-3765 or toll-free 800-888-3728. *E-mail:* lupind@erau.edu.

EMBRY-RIDDLE AERONAUTICAL UNIVERSITY
Daytona Beach, FL

Tuition & fees: $23,500 | **Average undergraduate aid package: $7570**

ABOUT THE INSTITUTION Independent, coed, primarily men. Awards: associate, bachelor's, and master's degrees. 19 undergraduate majors. Total enrollment: 4,788. Undergraduates: 4,407. Freshmen: 939. Federal methodology is used as a basis for awarding need-based institutional aid.

UNDERGRADUATE EXPENSES for 2005–06 *Application fee:* $30. *Comprehensive fee:* $30,436 includes full-time tuition ($22,820), mandatory fees ($680), and room and board ($6936). *College room only:* $2800. *Part-time tuition:* $855 per credit hour.

FRESHMAN FINANCIAL AID (Fall 2003) 779 applied for aid; of those 83% were deemed to have need. 100% of freshmen with need received aid. *Average financial aid package:* $7276 (excluding resources awarded to replace EFC). 15% of all full-time freshmen had no need and received non-need-based gift aid.

UNDERGRADUATE FINANCIAL AID (Fall 2003) 2,902 applied for aid; of those 88% were deemed to have need. 100% of undergraduates with need received aid. *Average financial aid package:* $7570 (excluding resources awarded to replace EFC). 16% of all full-time undergraduates had no need and received non-need-based gift aid.

GIFT AID (NEED-BASED) *Total amount:* $19,891,552 (19% federal, 15% state, 62% institutional, 4% external sources). *Receiving aid:* Freshmen: 65% (612); All full-time undergraduates: 55% (2,243). *Average award:* Freshmen: $5403; Undergraduates: $5472. *Scholarships, grants, and awards:* Federal Pell, FSEOG, state, private, college/university gift aid from institutional funds.

GIFT AID (NON-NEED-BASED) *Average Award:* Freshmen: $2133; Undergraduates: $2027. *Scholarships, grants, and awards by category:* Academic Interests/Achievement: 2,055 awards ($8,869,127 total): general academic interests/achievements. *Special Achievements/Activities:* 52 awards ($136,669 total): leadership. *Special Characteristics:* 86 awards ($1,243,726 total): children and siblings of alumni, children of faculty/staff. *ROTC:* Army, Naval, Air Force.

LOANS *Student loans:* $44,906,750 (100% need-based). 69% of past graduating class borrowed through all loan programs. *Average indebtedness per student:* $43,053. *Average need-based loan:* Freshmen: $2015; Undergraduates: $2876. *Parent loans:* $8,706,486 (100% need-based). *Programs:* FFEL (Subsidized and Unsubsidized Stafford, PLUS), Perkins, state, college/university.

WORK-STUDY *Federal work-study:* Total amount: $297,609; 366 jobs averaging $813. *State or other work-study/employment:* Total amount: $2,636,837 (100% need-based). 1,307 part-time jobs averaging $2017.

ATHLETIC AWARDS *Total amount:* $1,210,966 (100% need-based).

APPLYING FOR FINANCIAL AID *Required financial aid form:* FAFSA. *Financial aid deadline:* 6/30 (priority: 4/15). *Notification date:* Continuous beginning 3/1. Students must reply within 4 weeks of notification. **CONTACT** Maria A. Shaulis, Director of Financial Aid, Embry-Riddle Aeronautical University, 600 South Clyde Morris Boulevard, Daytona Beach, FL 32114-3900, 800-943-6279 or toll-free 800-862-2416. *Fax:* 386-226-6307. *E-mail:* maria.shaulis@erau.edu.

EMBRY-RIDDLE AERONAUTICAL UNIVERSITY, EXTENDED CAMPUS
Daytona Beach, FL

Tuition & fees: $4224 | **Average undergraduate aid package: $2368**

ABOUT THE INSTITUTION Independent, coed, primarily men. Awards: associate, bachelor's, and master's degrees (programs offered at 100 military bases worldwide). 5 undergraduate majors. Total enrollment: 11,004. Undergraduates: 8,268. Freshmen: 386. Federal methodology is used as a basis for awarding need-based institutional aid.

UNDERGRADUATE EXPENSES for 2005–06 *Application fee:* $50. *Tuition:* full-time $4224.

FRESHMAN FINANCIAL AID (Fall 2003) 152 applied for aid; of those 86% were deemed to have need. 82% of freshmen with need received aid. *Average financial aid package:* $1769 (excluding resources awarded to replace EFC).

UNDERGRADUATE FINANCIAL AID (Fall 2003) 631 applied for aid; of those 86% were deemed to have need. 95% of undergraduates with need received

aid. *Average financial aid package:* $2368 (excluding resources awarded to replace EFC). 1% of all full-time undergraduates had no need and received non-need-based gift aid.

GIFT AID (NEED-BASED) *Total amount:* $2,253,944 (69% federal, 31% state). *Receiving aid:* Freshmen: 36% (67); All full-time undergraduates: 9% (305). *Average award:* Freshmen: $1479; Undergraduates: $697. *Scholarships, grants, and awards:* Federal Pell, state, private, college/university gift aid from institutional funds.

GIFT AID (NON-NEED-BASED) *Average Award:* Undergraduates: $913. *Scholarships, grants, and awards by category:* Academic Interests/Achievement: 38 awards ($6451 total): general academic interests/achievements. *Special Achievements/Activities:* 57 awards ($7517 total): leadership. *Special Characteristics:* 12 awards ($19,146 total): children and siblings of alumni.

LOANS *Student loans:* $12,060,069 (100% need-based). 13% of past graduating class borrowed through all loan programs. *Average indebtedness per student:* $14,108. *Average need-based loan:* Freshmen: $664; Undergraduates: $985. *Parent loans:* $46,403 (100% need-based). *Programs:* FFEL (Subsidized and Unsubsidized Stafford, PLUS).

APPLYING FOR FINANCIAL AID *Required financial aid form:* FAFSA. *Financial aid deadline:* Continuous. *Notification date:* Continuous beginning 3/1. Students must reply within 4 weeks of notification. **CONTACT** Maria A. Shaulis, Director of Financial Aid, Embry-Riddle Aeronautical University, Extended Campus, 600 South Clyde Morris Boulevard, Daytona Beach, FL 32114-3900, 800-943-6279 or toll-free 800-522-6787. *Fax:* 386-226-6307. *E-mail:* maria.shaulis@erau.edu.

EMERSON COLLEGE
Boston, MA

Tuition & fees: N/R | **Average undergraduate aid package: $11,820**

ABOUT THE INSTITUTION Independent, coed. Awards: bachelor's, master's, and doctoral degrees. 29 undergraduate majors. Total enrollment: 4,398. Undergraduates: 3,418. Freshmen: 700. Both federal and institutional methodology are used as a basis for awarding need-based institutional aid.

UNDERGRADUATE EXPENSES for 2005–06 *Application fee:* $60. *Tuition:* part-time $718 per credit hour.

FRESHMAN FINANCIAL AID (Fall 2003) 521 applied for aid; of those 80% were deemed to have need. 100% of freshmen with need received aid; of those 79% had need fully met. *Average percent of need met:* 80% (excluding resources awarded to replace EFC). *Average financial aid package:* $11,209 (excluding resources awarded to replace EFC). 19% of all full-time freshmen had no need and received non-need-based gift aid.

UNDERGRADUATE FINANCIAL AID (Fall 2003) 1,867 applied for aid; of those 84% were deemed to have need. 100% of undergraduates with need received aid; of those 86% had need fully met. *Average percent of need met:* 80% (excluding resources awarded to replace EFC). *Average financial aid package:* $11,820 (excluding resources awarded to replace EFC). 15% of all full-time undergraduates had no need and received non-need-based gift aid.

GIFT AID (NEED-BASED) *Total amount:* $13,603,822 (11% federal, 3% state, 81% institutional, 5% external sources). *Receiving aid:* Freshmen: 50% (353); All full-time undergraduates: 42% (1,253). *Average award:* Freshmen: $11,492; Undergraduates: $10,497. *Scholarships, grants, and awards:* Federal Pell, FSEOG, state, private, college/university gift aid from institutional funds.

GIFT AID (NON-NEED-BASED) *Total amount:* $1,236,034 (1% state, 85% institutional, 14% external sources). *Receiving aid:* Freshmen: 13% (93); Undergraduates: 10% (303). *Average Award:* Freshmen: $11,152; Undergraduates: $12,958. *Scholarships, grants, and awards by category:* Academic Interests/Achievement: 348 awards ($2,774,335 total): general academic interests/achievements. *Creative Arts/Performance:* 32 awards ($133,600 total): performing arts.

LOANS *Student loans:* $18,221,330 (64% need-based, 36% non-need-based). 59% of past graduating class borrowed through all loan programs. *Average indebtedness per student:* $19,647. *Average need-based loan:* Freshmen: $3062; Undergraduates: $4208. *Parent loans:* $7,032,632 (38% need-based, 62% non-need-based). *Programs:* FFEL (Subsidized and Unsubsidized Stafford, PLUS), Perkins, state.

WORK-STUDY *Federal work-study:* Total amount: $980,000; 357 jobs averaging $2000. *State or other work-study/employment:* Total amount: $569,902 (71% need-based, 29% non-need-based). 40 part-time jobs averaging $10,156.

APPLYING FOR FINANCIAL AID *Required financial aid forms:* FAFSA, institution's own form, noncustodial (divorced/separated) parent's statement, business/farm

supplement, Income Tax Returns. *Financial aid deadline (priority):* 3/1. *Notification date:* 4/1. Students must reply by 5/1 or within 3 weeks of notification.
CONTACT Michelle Smith, Director, Office of Student Financial Services, Emerson College, 120 Boylston Street, Boston, MA 02116-4624, 617-824-8655. *Fax:* 617-824-8619. *E-mail:* finaid@emerson.edu.

EMMANUEL COLLEGE
Franklin Springs, GA

CONTACT Mary Beadles, Director of Financial Aid, Emmanuel College, PO Box 129, Franklin Springs, GA 30639-0129, 706-245-2844 or toll-free 800-860-8800 (in-state). *Fax:* 706-245-4424. *E-mail:* mbeadles@emmanuel-college.edu.

EMMANUEL COLLEGE
Boston, MA

Tuition & fees: $20,500	Average undergraduate aid package: $16,504

ABOUT THE INSTITUTION Independent Roman Catholic, coed. Awards: bachelor's and master's degrees and post-bachelor's and post-master's certificates. 33 undergraduate majors. Total enrollment: 2,165. Undergraduates: 1,947. Freshmen: 455. Federal methodology is used as a basis for awarding need-based institutional aid.
UNDERGRADUATE EXPENSES for 2004–05 *Application fee:* $40. *Comprehensive fee:* $29,500 includes full-time tuition ($20,100), mandatory fees ($400), and room and board ($9000). Full-time tuition and fees vary according to course load, degree level, and program. Room and board charges vary according to housing facility. *Part-time tuition:* $628 per credit. Part-time tuition and fees vary according to program. *Payment plan:* Installment.
FRESHMAN FINANCIAL AID (Fall 2004, est.) 448 applied for aid; of those 90% were deemed to have need. 100% of freshmen with need received aid; of those 29% had need fully met. *Average percent of need met:* 70% (excluding resources awarded to replace EFC). *Average financial aid package:* $15,624 (excluding resources awarded to replace EFC). 7% of all full-time freshmen had no need and received non-need-based gift aid.
UNDERGRADUATE FINANCIAL AID (Fall 2004, est.) 1,197 applied for aid; of those 91% were deemed to have need. 99% of undergraduates with need received aid; of those 22% had need fully met. *Average percent of need met:* 73% (excluding resources awarded to replace EFC). *Average financial aid package:* $16,504 (excluding resources awarded to replace EFC). 9% of all full-time undergraduates had no need and received non-need-based gift aid.
GIFT AID (NEED-BASED) *Total amount:* $11,501,253 (12% federal, 7% state, 78% institutional, 3% external sources). *Receiving aid:* Freshmen: 66% (341); All full-time undergraduates: 68% (907). *Average award:* Freshmen: $11,459; Undergraduates: $9103. *Scholarships, grants, and awards:* Federal Pell, FSEOG, state, private, college/university gift aid from institutional funds.
GIFT AID (NON-NEED-BASED) *Total amount:* $1,689,351 (99% institutional, 1% external sources). *Receiving aid:* Freshmen: 20% (104); Undergraduates: 35% (463). *Average Award:* Freshmen: $8022; Undergraduates: $10,600. *Scholarships, grants, and awards by category: Academic Interests/Achievement:* 483 awards ($4,264,287 total): biological sciences, education, engineering/technologies, foreign languages, general academic interests/achievements, health fields, humanities, mathematics, physical sciences, religion/biblical studies, social sciences. *Creative Arts/Performance:* 1 award ($3375 total): general creative arts/performance. *Special Achievements/Activities:* 31 awards ($77,500 total): community service. *Special Characteristics:* 176 awards ($627,531 total): children and siblings of alumni, children of educators, children of faculty/staff, children of union members/company employees, ethnic background, general special characteristics, handicapped students, international students, local/state students, religious affiliation, siblings of current students. *Tuition waivers:* Full or partial for employees or children of employees. *ROTC:* Army cooperative.
LOANS *Student loans:* $7,933,472 (49% need-based, 51% non-need-based). 71% of past graduating class borrowed through all loan programs. *Average indebtedness per student:* $15,523. *Average need-based loan:* Freshmen: $3299; Undergraduates: $4164. *Parent loans:* $3,492,702 (55% need-based, 45% non-need-based). *Programs:* FFEL (Subsidized and Unsubsidized Stafford, PLUS), Perkins, state, alternative loans.
WORK-STUDY *Federal work-study:* Total amount: $432,000; 497 jobs averaging $869. *State or other work-study/employment:* Total amount: $229,000 (100% non-need-based). 226 part-time jobs averaging $1011.

APPLYING FOR FINANCIAL AID *Required financial aid forms:* FAFSA, institution's own form. *Financial aid deadline (priority):* 4/1. *Notification date:* Continuous. Students must reply within 2 weeks of notification.
CONTACT Jennifer Porter, Director of Student Financial Services, Emmanuel College, 400 The Fenway, Boston, MA 02115, 617-735-9938. *Fax:* 617-735-9939. *E-mail:* porterj@emmanuel.edu.

EMMAUS BIBLE COLLEGE
Dubuque, IA

Tuition & fees: $7812	Average undergraduate aid package: $4000

ABOUT THE INSTITUTION Independent nondenominational, coed. Awards: associate and bachelor's degrees. 5 undergraduate majors. Total enrollment: 296. Undergraduates: 296. Freshmen: 59. Federal methodology is used as a basis for awarding need-based institutional aid.
UNDERGRADUATE EXPENSES for 2004–05 *Application fee:* $25. *Comprehensive fee:* $11,392 includes full-time tuition ($7330), mandatory fees ($482), and room and board ($3580). Full-time tuition and fees vary according to course load. *Part-time tuition:* $326 per credit hour. Part-time tuition and fees vary according to course load. *Payment plan:* Installment.
FRESHMAN FINANCIAL AID (Fall 2003) 101 applied for aid; of those 80% were deemed to have need. 90% of freshmen with need received aid. *Average percent of need met:* 49% (excluding resources awarded to replace EFC). *Average financial aid package:* $3500 (excluding resources awarded to replace EFC).
UNDERGRADUATE FINANCIAL AID (Fall 2003) 137 applied for aid; of those 85% were deemed to have need. 92% of undergraduates with need received aid. *Average percent of need met:* 66% (excluding resources awarded to replace EFC). *Average financial aid package:* $4000 (excluding resources awarded to replace EFC).
GIFT AID (NEED-BASED) *Total amount:* $588,963 (52% federal, 24% institutional, 24% external sources). *Receiving aid:* Freshmen: 61% (73); All full-time undergraduates: 66% (108). *Average award:* Freshmen: $500; Undergraduates: $500. *Scholarships, grants, and awards:* Federal Pell, FSEOG, private, college/university gift aid from institutional funds.
GIFT AID (NON-NEED-BASED) *Receiving aid:* Freshmen: 27% (32); Undergraduates: 63% (103). *Scholarships, grants, and awards by category: Academic Interests/Achievement:* 71 awards ($44,550 total): general academic interests/achievements. *Creative Arts/Performance:* $270 total: music. *Special Achievements/Activities:* 33 awards ($36,430 total): leadership, religious involvement. *Special Characteristics:* 8 awards ($46,982 total): children of faculty/staff. *Tuition waivers:* Full or partial for employees or children of employees.
LOANS *Student loans:* $679,561 (76% need-based, 24% non-need-based). 79% of past graduating class borrowed through all loan programs. *Average indebtedness per student:* $15,890. *Average need-based loan:* Freshmen: $2900; Undergraduates: $3900. *Parent loans:* $77,775 (100% need-based). *Programs:* FFEL (Subsidized and Unsubsidized Stafford, PLUS), alternative loans.
APPLYING FOR FINANCIAL AID *Required financial aid forms:* FAFSA, institution's own form. *Financial aid deadline:* 6/10. *Notification date:* Continuous.
CONTACT Joel Laos, Financial Aid Director, Emmaus Bible College, 2570 Asbury Road, Dubuque, IA 52001-3097, 563-588-8000 Ext. 1309 or toll-free 800-397-2425. *Fax:* 563-557-0573. *E-mail:* financialaid@emmaus.edu.

EMORY & HENRY COLLEGE
Emory, VA

Tuition & fees: $16,690	Average undergraduate aid package: $12,395

ABOUT THE INSTITUTION Independent United Methodist, coed. Awards: bachelor's and master's degrees. 37 undergraduate majors. Total enrollment: 1,028. Undergraduates: 930. Freshmen: 268. Federal methodology is used as a basis for awarding need-based institutional aid.
UNDERGRADUATE EXPENSES for 2004–05 *Application fee:* $30. *Comprehensive fee:* $22,940 includes full-time tuition ($16,490), mandatory fees ($200), and room and board ($6250). *College room only:* $3050. Full-time tuition and fees vary according to course load. Room and board charges vary according to board plan. *Part-time tuition:* $690 per hour. *Part-time fees:* $10 per hour. Part-time tuition and fees vary according to course load. *Payment plan:* Installment.
FRESHMAN FINANCIAL AID (Fall 2004, est.) 227 applied for aid; of those 86% were deemed to have need. 100% of freshmen with need received aid; of those 27% had need fully met. *Average percent of need met:* 82% (excluding resources

awarded to replace EFC). *Average financial aid package:* $14,251 (excluding resources awarded to replace EFC). 8% of all full-time freshmen had no need and received non-need-based gift aid.

UNDERGRADUATE FINANCIAL AID (Fall 2004, est.) 739 applied for aid; of those 93% were deemed to have need. 100% of undergraduates with need received aid; of those 32% had need fully met. *Average percent of need met:* 73% (excluding resources awarded to replace EFC). *Average financial aid package:* $12,395 (excluding resources awarded to replace EFC). 8% of all full-time undergraduates had no need and received non-need-based gift aid.

GIFT AID (NEED-BASED) *Total amount:* $7,482,394 (11% federal, 17% state, 65% institutional, 7% external sources). *Receiving aid:* Freshmen: 73% (195); All full-time undergraduates: 74% (685). *Average award:* Freshmen: $11,730; Undergraduates: $9017. *Scholarships, grants, and awards:* Federal Pell, FSEOG, state, private, college/university gift aid from institutional funds.

GIFT AID (NON-NEED-BASED) *Total amount:* $1,254,039 (26% state, 69% institutional, 5% external sources). *Receiving aid:* Freshmen: 34% (90); Undergraduates: 28% (257). *Average Award: Freshmen:* $8439; *Undergraduates:* $5487. *Scholarships, grants, and awards by category: Academic Interests/ Achievement:* 433 awards ($867,106 total): biological sciences, business, communication, computer science, education, English, general academic interests/ achievements, international studies, mathematics, physical sciences, premedicine, religion/biblical studies. *Creative Arts/Performance:* 56 awards ($88,750 total): art/fine arts, music, theater/drama. *Special Achievements/Activities:* 74 awards ($160,293 total): community service. *Special Characteristics:* 195 awards ($782,067 total): children of faculty/staff, ethnic background, out-of-state students, previous college experience, relatives of clergy, religious affiliation. *Tuition waivers:* Full or partial for employees or children of employees.

LOANS *Student loans:* $3,046,055 (90% need-based, 10% non-need-based). 68% of past graduating class borrowed through all loan programs. *Average indebtedness per student:* $15,482. *Average need-based loan:* Freshmen: $2782; Undergraduates: $3754. *Parent loans:* $3,161,018 (78% need-based, 22% non-need-based). *Programs:* Federal Direct (Subsidized and Unsubsidized Stafford, PLUS), Perkins, college/university.

WORK-STUDY *Federal work-study:* Total amount: $177,673; 110 jobs averaging $1396.

APPLYING FOR FINANCIAL AID *Required financial aid forms:* FAFSA, state aid form. *Financial aid deadline:* 8/1 (priority: 4/1). *Notification date:* Continuous beginning 2/1. Students must reply within 2 weeks of notification.

CONTACT Scarlett Cortner, Coordinator of Financial Aid, Emory & Henry College, PO Box 10, Emory, VA 24327-0010, 276-944-6115 or toll-free 800-848-5493. *Fax:* 276-944-6935. *E-mail:* scortner@ehc.edu.

EMORY UNIVERSITY
Atlanta, GA

Tuition & fees: $29,322	Average undergraduate aid package: $26,373

ABOUT THE INSTITUTION Independent Methodist, coed. Awards: associate, bachelor's, master's, doctoral, and first professional degrees (enrollment figures include Emory University, Oxford College; application data for main campus only). 54 undergraduate majors. Total enrollment: 11,781. Undergraduates: 6,346. Freshmen: 1,589. Institutional methodology is used as a basis for awarding need-based institutional aid.

UNDERGRADUATE EXPENSES for 2004–05 *Application fee:* $40. *Comprehensive fee:* $38,972 includes full-time tuition ($28,940), mandatory fees ($382), and room and board ($9650). *College room only:* $6110. Room and board charges vary according to board plan, housing facility, and student level. *Payment plans:* Tuition prepayment, installment.

FRESHMAN FINANCIAL AID (Fall 2004, est.) 747 applied for aid; of those 73% were deemed to have need. 100% of freshmen with need received aid; of those 100% had need fully met. *Average percent of need met:* 100% (excluding resources awarded to replace EFC). *Average financial aid package:* $25,210 (excluding resources awarded to replace EFC). 5% of all full-time freshmen had no need and received non-need-based gift aid.

UNDERGRADUATE FINANCIAL AID (Fall 2004, est.) 2,782 applied for aid; of those 84% were deemed to have need. 100% of undergraduates with need received aid; of those 100% had need fully met. *Average percent of need met:* 100% (excluding resources awarded to replace EFC). *Average financial aid package:* $26,373 (excluding resources awarded to replace EFC). 6% of all full-time undergraduates had no need and received non-need-based gift aid.

GIFT AID (NEED-BASED) *Total amount:* $40,080,493 (9% federal, 3% state, 86% institutional, 2% external sources). *Receiving aid:* Freshmen: 32% (504); All full-time undergraduates: 35% (2,173). *Average award:* Freshmen: $20,394;

Undergraduates: $20,244. *Scholarships, grants, and awards:* Federal Pell, FSEOG, state, private, college/university gift aid from institutional funds.

GIFT AID (NON-NEED-BASED) *Total amount:* $12,976,194 (20% state, 65% institutional, 15% external sources). *Receiving aid:* Freshmen: 15% (242); Undergraduates: 14% (895). *Average Award:* Freshmen: $14,937; *Undergraduates:* $18,056. *Scholarships, grants, and awards by category: Academic Interests/Achievement:* 669 awards ($10,876,045 total): general academic interests/achievements. *Creative Arts/Performance:* 6 awards ($156,171 total): debating, music, performing arts. *Special Characteristics:* 1,468 awards ($11,656,910 total): children of faculty/staff, local/state students, relatives of clergy, religious affiliation, veterans. *Tuition waivers:* Full or partial for employees or children of employees. *ROTC:* Air Force cooperative.

LOANS *Student loans:* $16,573,356 (61% need-based, 39% non-need-based). 42% of past graduating class borrowed through all loan programs. *Average indebtedness per student:* $19,437. *Average need-based loan:* Freshmen: $3129; Undergraduates: $4890. *Parent loans:* $11,348,051 (100% non-need-based). *Programs:* FFEL (Subsidized and Unsubsidized Stafford, PLUS), Perkins, Federal Nursing, state, college/university.

WORK-STUDY *Federal work-study:* Total amount: $2,979,345; 1,696 jobs averaging $1757. *State or other work-study/employment:* Total amount: $465,760 (15% need-based, 85% non-need-based). 52 part-time jobs averaging $6640.

APPLYING FOR FINANCIAL AID *Required financial aid forms:* FAFSA, CSS Financial Aid PROFILE. *Financial aid deadline:* 4/1 (priority: 2/15). *Notification date:* 4/15. Students must reply within 4 weeks of notification.

CONTACT Julia Perreault, Director of Financial Aid, Emory University, 300 Boisfeuillet Jones Center, Atlanta, GA 30322-1100, 404-727-6039 or toll-free 800-727-6036. *Fax:* 404-727-6709. *E-mail:* finaid@emory.edu.

EMPORIA STATE UNIVERSITY
Emporia, KS

Tuition & fees (KS res): $3036	Average undergraduate aid package: $5430

ABOUT THE INSTITUTION State-supported, coed. Awards: bachelor's, master's, and doctoral degrees and post-bachelor's and post-master's certificates. 33 undergraduate majors. Total enrollment: 6,194. Undergraduates: 4,370. Freshmen: 729. Federal methodology is used as a basis for awarding need-based institutional aid.

UNDERGRADUATE EXPENSES for 2004–05 *Application fee:* $30. *Tuition, state resident:* full-time $2410; part-time $80 per credit hour. *Tuition, nonresident:* full-time $9130; part-time $304 per credit hour. *Required fees:* full-time $626; $38 per credit hour. Full-time tuition and fees vary according to degree level. Part-time tuition and fees vary according to degree level. *College room and board:* $4474; *room only:* $2208. Room and board charges vary according to board plan and housing facility. *Payment plans:* Installment, deferred payment.

FRESHMAN FINANCIAL AID (Fall 2003) 743 applied for aid; of those 62% were deemed to have need. 100% of freshmen with need received aid; of those 32% had need fully met. *Average percent of need met:* 69% (excluding resources awarded to replace EFC). *Average financial aid package:* $4352 (excluding resources awarded to replace EFC). 18% of all full-time freshmen had no need and received non-need-based gift aid.

UNDERGRADUATE FINANCIAL AID (Fall 2003) 3,400 applied for aid; of those 70% were deemed to have need. 100% of undergraduates with need received aid; of those 28% had need fully met. *Average percent of need met:* 71% (excluding resources awarded to replace EFC). *Average financial aid package:* $5430 (excluding resources awarded to replace EFC). 10% of all full-time undergraduates had no need and received non-need-based gift aid.

GIFT AID (NEED-BASED) *Total amount:* $6,294,793 (69% federal, 8% state, 13% institutional, 10% external sources). *Receiving aid:* Freshmen: 41% (324); All full-time undergraduates: 41% (1,591). *Average award:* Freshmen: $1595; Undergraduates: $1735. *Scholarships, grants, and awards:* Federal Pell, FSEOG, state, private, college/university gift aid from institutional funds, Jones Foundation Grants.

GIFT AID (NON-NEED-BASED) *Total amount:* $1,229,955 (3% federal, 6% state, 62% institutional, 29% external sources). *Receiving aid:* Freshmen: 43% (341); Undergraduates: 29% (1,097). *Average Award: Freshmen:* $771; *Undergraduates:* $880. *Scholarships, grants, and awards by category: Academic Interests/Achievement:* 2,320 awards ($1,170,405 total): biological sciences, business, communication, computer science, education, engineering/technologies, English, foreign languages, general academic interests/achievements, health fields, humanities, library science, mathematics, physical sciences, premedicine, social sciences. *Creative Arts/Performance:* 425 awards ($158,699 total): art/ fine arts, creative writing, debating, music, theater/drama. *Special Achievements/*

Activities: 269 awards ($778,416 total): cheerleading/drum major, general special achievements/activities, memberships. *Special Characteristics:* 34 awards ($14,962 total): children and siblings of alumni, children of faculty/staff, children of union members/company employees, handicapped students, international students, members of minority groups, religious affiliation, veterans, veterans' children. *Tuition waivers:* Full or partial for employees or children of employees, senior citizens.

LOANS *Student loans:* $13,015,874 (65% need-based, 35% non-need-based). 63% of past graduating class borrowed through all loan programs. *Average indebtedness per student:* $13,217. *Average need-based loan:* Freshmen: $2216; Undergraduates: $2899. *Parent loans:* $513,816 (16% need-based, 84% non-need-based). *Programs:* FFEL (Subsidized and Unsubsidized Stafford, PLUS), Perkins, Alaska Loans, alternative loans.

WORK-STUDY *Federal work-study:* Total amount: $361,417; 282 jobs averaging $1282. *State or other work-study/employment:* Total amount: $38,808 (32% need-based, 68% non-need-based). 38 part-time jobs averaging $1021.

ATHLETIC AWARDS *Total amount:* $794,951 (47% need-based, 53% non-need-based).

APPLYING FOR FINANCIAL AID *Required financial aid forms:* FAFSA, state aid form. *Financial aid deadline (priority):* 3/15. *Notification date:* Continuous. Students must reply within 2 weeks of notification.

CONTACT Elaine Henrie, Director of Financial Aid, Emporia State University, 1200 Commercial Street, Campus Box 4038, Emporia, KS 66801-5087, 620-341-5457 or toll-free 877-GOTOESU (in-state), 877-468-6378 (out-of-state). *Fax:* 620-341-6088. *E-mail:* henrieel@emporia.edu.

ENDICOTT COLLEGE
Beverly, MA

Tuition & fees: $19,432	Average undergraduate aid package: $12,120

ABOUT THE INSTITUTION Independent, coed. Awards: associate, bachelor's, and master's degrees. 21 undergraduate majors. Total enrollment: 3,285. Undergraduates: 1,973. Freshmen: 423. Federal methodology is used as a basis for awarding need-based institutional aid.

UNDERGRADUATE EXPENSES for 2004–05 *Application fee:* $40. *Comprehensive fee:* $28,732 includes full-time tuition ($18,752), mandatory fees ($680), and room and board ($9300). *College room only:* $6520. Full-time tuition and fees vary according to program and student level. Room and board charges vary according to board plan and housing facility. *Part-time tuition:* $576 per credit. *Part-time fees:* $180 per term. Part-time tuition and fees vary according to program and student level. *Payment plan:* Installment.

FRESHMAN FINANCIAL AID (Fall 2004, est.) 323 applied for aid; of those 79% were deemed to have need. 100% of freshmen with need received aid; of those 11% had need fully met. *Average percent of need met:* 56% (excluding resources awarded to replace EFC). *Average financial aid package:* $11,677 (excluding resources awarded to replace EFC). 10% of all full-time freshmen had no need and received non-need-based gift aid.

UNDERGRADUATE FINANCIAL AID (Fall 2004, est.) 1,397 applied for aid; of those 77% were deemed to have need. 99% of undergraduates with need received aid; of those 15% had need fully met. *Average percent of need met:* 59% (excluding resources awarded to replace EFC). *Average financial aid package:* $12,120 (excluding resources awarded to replace EFC). 13% of all full-time undergraduates had no need and received non-need-based gift aid.

GIFT AID (NEED-BASED) *Total amount:* $6,879,660 (10% federal, 5% state, 85% institutional). *Receiving aid:* Freshmen: 47% (200); All full-time undergraduates: 50% (826). *Average award:* Freshmen: $5886; Undergraduates: $5363. *Scholarships, grants, and awards:* Federal Pell, FSEOG, state, private, college/university gift aid from institutional funds.

GIFT AID (NON-NEED-BASED) *Total amount:* $1,902,627 (88% institutional, 12% external sources). *Receiving aid:* Freshmen: 33% (143); Undergraduates: 34% (555). *Average Award:* Freshmen: $4846; Undergraduates: $4827. *Scholarships, grants, and awards by category: Academic Interests/Achievement:* 673 awards ($3,362,202 total): business, education, general academic interests/achievements, health fields. *Creative Arts/Performance:* 4 awards ($2000 total): art/fine arts. *Special Achievements/Activities:* 10 awards ($10,800 total): community service, general special achievements/activities, leadership, religious involvement. *Special Characteristics:* 131 awards ($679,574 total): children and siblings of alumni, children of educators, general special characteristics, international students, local/state students, religious affiliation. *Tuition waivers:* Full or partial for employees or children of employees. *ROTC:* Army cooperative.

LOANS *Student loans:* $5,352,317 (73% need-based, 27% non-need-based). 60% of past graduating class borrowed through all loan programs. *Average*

indebtedness per student: $17,125. *Average need-based loan:* Freshmen: $3056; Undergraduates: $4071. *Parent loans:* $8,205,849 (100% non-need-based). *Programs:* FFEL (Subsidized and Unsubsidized Stafford, PLUS), Perkins, state, college/university.

WORK-STUDY *Federal work-study:* Total amount: $250,000; 338 jobs averaging $1500.

APPLYING FOR FINANCIAL AID *Required financial aid forms:* FAFSA, institution's own form. *Financial aid deadline (priority):* 3/15. *Notification date:* Continuous. Students must reply within 2 weeks of notification.

CONTACT Ms. Marcia Toomey, Director of Financial Aid, Endicott College, 376 Hale Street, Beverly, MA 01915-2096, 978-232-2060 or toll-free 800-325-1114 (out-of-state). *Fax:* 978-232-2085. *E-mail:* mtoomey@endicott.edu.

ERSKINE COLLEGE
Due West, SC

Tuition & fees: $18,128	Average undergraduate aid package: $17,428

ABOUT THE INSTITUTION Independent religious, coed. Awards: bachelor's, master's, doctoral, and first professional degrees. 31 undergraduate majors. Total enrollment: 962. Undergraduates: 617. Freshmen: 179. Both federal and institutional methodology are used as a basis for awarding need-based institutional aid.

UNDERGRADUATE EXPENSES for 2004–05 *Application fee:* $25. *Comprehensive fee:* $24,154 includes full-time tuition ($16,948), mandatory fees ($1180), and room and board ($6026). Room and board charges vary according to board plan and housing facility. *Part-time tuition:* $380 per semester hour. *Payment plan:* Installment.

FRESHMAN FINANCIAL AID (Fall 2004, est.) 172 applied for aid; of those 80% were deemed to have need. 100% of freshmen with need received aid; of those 29% had need fully met. *Average percent of need met:* 83% (excluding resources awarded to replace EFC). *Average financial aid package:* $17,428 (excluding resources awarded to replace EFC). 28% of all full-time freshmen had no need and received non-need-based gift aid.

UNDERGRADUATE FINANCIAL AID (Fall 2004, est.) 572 applied for aid; of those 80% were deemed to have need. 100% of undergraduates with need received aid; of those 31% had need fully met. *Average percent of need met:* 83% (excluding resources awarded to replace EFC). *Average financial aid package:* $17,428 (excluding resources awarded to replace EFC). 18% of all full-time undergraduates had no need and received non-need-based gift aid.

GIFT AID (NEED-BASED) *Total amount:* $2,251,823 (23% federal, 57% state, 20% institutional). *Receiving aid:* Freshmen: 72% (130); All full-time undergraduates: 74% (448). *Average award:* Freshmen: $7950; Undergraduates: $8125. *Scholarships, grants, and awards:* Federal Pell, FSEOG, state, private, college/university gift aid from institutional funds.

GIFT AID (NON-NEED-BASED) *Total amount:* $6,183,548 (12% state, 81% institutional, 7% external sources). *Receiving aid:* Freshmen: 67% (122); Undergraduates: 70% (421). *Average Award:* Freshmen: $8850; Undergraduates: $8552. *Scholarships, grants, and awards by category: Academic Interests/Achievement:* biological sciences, business, education, English, foreign languages, general academic interests/achievements, mathematics, premedicine, religion/biblical studies, social sciences. *Creative Arts/Performance:* music, theater/drama. *Special Achievements/Activities:* general special achievements/activities, leadership, memberships. *Special Characteristics:* children and siblings of alumni, children of faculty/staff, children with a deceased or disabled parent, ethnic background, first-generation college students, members of minority groups, out-of-state students, relatives of clergy, religious affiliation, siblings of current students. *Tuition waivers:* Full or partial for children of alumni, employees or children of employees.

LOANS *Student loans:* $1,840,977 (61% need-based, 39% non-need-based). 66% of past graduating class borrowed through all loan programs. *Average indebtedness per student:* $17,380. *Average need-based loan:* Freshmen: $3260; Undergraduates: $5000. *Parent loans:* $314,068 (100% non-need-based). *Programs:* FFEL (Subsidized and Unsubsidized Stafford, PLUS), Perkins, college/university, teacher loans.

WORK-STUDY *Federal work-study:* Total amount: $98,592; jobs available. *State or other work-study/employment:* Total amount: $50,048 (100% non-need-based). Part-time jobs available.

ATHLETIC AWARDS *Total amount:* $685,721 (100% non-need-based).

APPLYING FOR FINANCIAL AID *Required financial aid forms:* FAFSA, institution's own form. *Financial aid deadline (priority):* 4/1. *Notification date:* Continuous beginning 12/15. Students must reply within 2 weeks of notification.

CONTACT Rebecca Pressley, Director of Financial Aid, Erskine College, PO Box 337, Due West, SC 29639, 864-379-8832 or toll-free 800-241-8721. *Fax:* 864-379-2172. *E-mail:* pressley@erskine.edu.

ESCUELA DE ARTES PLASTICAS DE PUERTO RICO
San Juan, PR

CONTACT Ms. Marion E. Muñoz, Financial Aid Administrator, Escuela de Artes Plasticas de Puerto Rico, PO Box 9021112, San Juan, PR 00902-1112, 787-725-8120 Ext. 231. *Fax:* 787-725-8111. *E-mail:* mmunoz@coqui.net.

EUGENE BIBLE COLLEGE
Eugene, OR

Tuition & fees: $7851	Average undergraduate aid package: $5500

ABOUT THE INSTITUTION Independent religious, coed. Awards: bachelor's degrees. 7 undergraduate majors. Total enrollment: 186. Undergraduates: 186. Freshmen: 60. Both federal and institutional methodology are used as a basis for awarding need-based institutional aid.

UNDERGRADUATE EXPENSES for 2004–05 *Application fee:* $30. *Comprehensive fee:* $12,051 includes full-time tuition ($7200), mandatory fees ($651), and room and board ($4200). Room and board charges vary according to housing facility. *Part-time tuition:* $200 per credit. *Part-time fees:* $138 per term. Part-time tuition and fees vary according to class time and course load. *Payment plan:* Tuition prepayment.

GIFT AID (NEED-BASED) *Total amount:* $237,444 (89% federal, 11% institutional). *Receiving aid:* Freshmen: 38% (26); All full-time undergraduates: 80% (133). *Average award:* Freshmen: $3200; Undergraduates: $2557. *Scholarships, grants, and awards:* Federal Pell, FSEOG, private, college/university gift aid from institutional funds.

GIFT AID (NON-NEED-BASED) *Total amount:* $51,835 (66% institutional, 34% external sources). *Receiving aid:* Freshmen: 51% (35); Undergraduates: 10% (17). *Average Award:* Freshmen: $100; Undergraduates: $100. *Scholarships, grants, and awards by category: Academic Interests/Achievement:* general academic interests/achievements, religion/biblical studies. *Creative Arts/Performance:* music. *Special Achievements/Activities:* 2 awards ($5500 total): community service, general special achievements/activities, hobbies/interests, leadership, religious involvement. *Special Characteristics:* 3 awards: general special characteristics, married students, relatives of clergy, spouses of current students. *Tuition waivers:* Full or partial for employees or children of employees.

LOANS *Student loans:* $665,851 (99% need-based, 1% non-need-based). 82% of past graduating class borrowed through all loan programs. *Average indebtedness per student:* $10,550. *Average need-based loan:* Freshmen: $2400; Undergraduates: $3395. *Parent loans:* $129,922 (100% need-based). *Programs:* FFEL (Subsidized and Unsubsidized Stafford, PLUS), college/university, Key Alternative Loans.

ATHLETIC AWARDS *Total amount:* $1500 (100% need-based).

APPLYING FOR FINANCIAL AID *Required financial aid forms:* FAFSA, institution's own form, CSS Financial Aid PROFILE. *Financial aid deadline:* 9/1 (priority: 3/1). *Notification date:* Continuous.

CONTACT Mrs. Rulena Mellor, Financial Aid Director, Eugene Bible College, 2155 Bailey Hill Road, Eugene, OR 97405-1194, 541-485-1780 Ext. 125 or toll-free 800-322-2638. *Fax:* 541-343-5801. *E-mail:* finaid@ebc.edu.

EUGENE LANG COLLEGE, NEW SCHOOL UNIVERSITY
New York, NY

ABOUT THE INSTITUTION Independent, coed. Awards: bachelor's degrees. 21 undergraduate majors. Total enrollment: 742. Undergraduates: 742. Freshmen: 188.

GIFT AID (NEED-BASED) *Scholarships, grants, and awards:* Federal Pell, FSEOG, state, private, college/university gift aid from institutional funds.

GIFT AID (NON-NEED-BASED) *Scholarships, grants, and awards by category: Academic Interests/Achievement:* general academic interests/achievements. *Special Achievements/Activities:* general special achievements/activities.

LOANS *Programs:* FFEL (Subsidized and Unsubsidized Stafford, PLUS), Perkins, college/university.

WORK-STUDY *Federal work-study:* Total amount: $179,400; jobs available. *State or other work-study/employment:* Part-time jobs available.

APPLYING FOR FINANCIAL AID *Required financial aid forms:* FAFSA, state aid form.

CONTACT Financial Aid Counselor, Eugene Lang College, New School University, 65 West 11th Street, New York, NY 10011, 212-229-5665 or toll-free 877-528-3321.

EUREKA COLLEGE
Eureka, IL

Tuition & fees: $13,400	Average undergraduate aid package: $14,374

ABOUT THE INSTITUTION Independent religious, coed. Awards: bachelor's degrees. 42 undergraduate majors. Total enrollment: 516. Undergraduates: 516. Freshmen: 138. Federal methodology is used as a basis for awarding need-based institutional aid.

UNDERGRADUATE EXPENSES for 2005–06 *Comprehensive fee:* $19,280 includes full-time tuition ($13,000), mandatory fees ($400), and room and board ($5880). *College room only:* $2820. Full-time tuition and fees vary according to course load and program. Room and board charges vary according to board plan and housing facility. *Part-time tuition:* $375 per semester hour. Part-time tuition and fees vary according to course load and program. *Payment plan:* Installment.

FRESHMAN FINANCIAL AID (Fall 2004, est.) 114 applied for aid; of those 89% were deemed to have need. 100% of freshmen with need received aid; of those 54% had need fully met. *Average percent of need met:* 81% (excluding resources awarded to replace EFC). *Average financial aid package:* $12,214 (excluding resources awarded to replace EFC). 1% of all full-time freshmen had no need and received non-need-based gift aid.

UNDERGRADUATE FINANCIAL AID (Fall 2004, est.) 451 applied for aid; of those 95% were deemed to have need. 100% of undergraduates with need received aid; of those 82% had need fully met. *Average percent of need met:* 84% (excluding resources awarded to replace EFC). *Average financial aid package:* $14,374 (excluding resources awarded to replace EFC). 1% of all full-time undergraduates had no need and received non-need-based gift aid.

GIFT AID (NEED-BASED) *Total amount:* $4,732,152 (15% federal, 24% state, 59% institutional, 2% external sources). *Receiving aid:* Freshmen: 82% (99); All full-time undergraduates: 85% (420). *Average award:* Freshmen: $11,734; Undergraduates: $11,267. *Scholarships, grants, and awards:* Federal Pell, FSEOG, state, private, college/university gift aid from institutional funds.

GIFT AID (NON-NEED-BASED) *Total amount:* $500,857 (1% state, 99% institutional). *Receiving aid:* Freshmen: 12% (14); Undergraduates: 8% (42). *Average Award:* Freshmen: $3500; Undergraduates: $6592. *Scholarships, grants, and awards by category: Academic Interests/Achievement:* 427 awards ($2,772,871 total): general academic interests/achievements. *Creative Arts/Performance:* 51 awards ($104,055 total): art/fine arts, performing arts. *Special Achievements/Activities:* 21 awards ($336,766 total): leadership. *Special Characteristics:* 42 awards ($300,481 total): children of faculty/staff, religious affiliation. *Tuition waivers:* Full or partial for children of alumni, employees or children of employees, senior citizens.

LOANS *Student loans:* $2,171,694 (65% need-based, 35% non-need-based). 90% of past graduating class borrowed through all loan programs. *Average indebtedness per student:* $13,227. *Average need-based loan:* Freshmen: $715; Undergraduates: $3651. *Parent loans:* $435,258 (100% non-need-based). *Programs:* FFEL (Subsidized and Unsubsidized Stafford, PLUS), Perkins, college/university, alternative loans.

WORK-STUDY *Federal work-study:* Total amount: $119,070; 132 jobs averaging $902. *State or other work-study/employment:* Total amount: $129,074 (100% non-need-based). 73 part-time jobs averaging $1768.

APPLYING FOR FINANCIAL AID *Required financial aid form:* FAFSA. *Financial aid deadline (priority):* 4/15. *Notification date:* 5/1. Students must reply within 2 weeks of notification.

CONTACT Ms. Ellen Rigsby, Director of Financial Aid, Eureka College, 300 East College Avenue, Eureka, IL 61530, 309-467-6311 or toll-free 888-4-EUREKA. *Fax:* 309-467-6576. *E-mail:* eraid@eureka.edu.

EVANGEL UNIVERSITY
Springfield, MO

Tuition & fees: $12,750	Average undergraduate aid package: $8955

ABOUT THE INSTITUTION Independent religious, coed. Awards: associate, bachelor's, and master's degrees. 56 undergraduate majors. Total enrollment: 1,801. Undergraduates: 1,721. Freshmen: 423. Federal methodology is used as a basis for awarding need-based institutional aid.

UNDERGRADUATE EXPENSES for 2005–06 *Application fee:* $25. *Comprehensive fee:* $17,370 includes full-time tuition ($12,040), mandatory fees ($710), and room and board ($4620). *College room only:* $2270. Full-time tuition and fees vary according to course load. Room and board charges vary according to board plan. *Part-time tuition:* $469 per credit hour. *Part-time fees:* $235 per term. *Payment plan:* Installment.

FRESHMAN FINANCIAL AID (Fall 2004, est.) 311 applied for aid; of those 85% were deemed to have need. 99% of freshmen with need received aid; of those 12% had need fully met. *Average percent of need met:* 18% (excluding resources awarded to replace EFC). *Average financial aid package:* $8701 (excluding resources awarded to replace EFC). 21% of all full-time freshmen had no need and received non-need-based gift aid.

UNDERGRADUATE FINANCIAL AID (Fall 2004, est.) 1,370 applied for aid; of those 88% were deemed to have need. 99% of undergraduates with need received aid; of those 9% had need fully met. *Average percent of need met:* 33% (excluding resources awarded to replace EFC). *Average financial aid package:* $8955 (excluding resources awarded to replace EFC). 19% of all full-time undergraduates had no need and received non-need-based gift aid.

GIFT AID (NEED-BASED) *Total amount:* $4,060,551 (50% federal, 1% state, 32% institutional, 17% external sources). *Receiving aid:* Freshmen: 59% (238); All full-time undergraduates: 62% (1,007). *Average award:* Freshmen: $5646; Undergraduates: $5222. *Scholarships, grants, and awards:* Federal Pell, FSEOG, state, college/university gift aid from institutional funds.

GIFT AID (NON-NEED-BASED) *Total amount:* $720,663 (66% institutional, 34% external sources). *Receiving aid:* Freshmen: 5% (19); Undergraduates: 3% (57). *Average Award:* Freshmen: $6084; Undergraduates: $7503. *Scholarships, grants, and awards by category: Academic Interests/Achievement:* 753 awards ($1,310,288 total): business, communication, computer science, education, engineering/technologies, English, foreign languages, general academic interests/achievements, humanities, mathematics, physical sciences, premedicine, religion/biblical studies, social sciences. *Creative Arts/Performance:* 133 awards ($216,245 total): art/fine arts, debating, music. *Special Achievements/Activities:* 275 awards ($133,829 total): cheerleading/drum major, general special achievements/activities, leadership, religious involvement. *Special Characteristics:* 191 awards ($1,239,220 total): children of faculty/staff, general special characteristics, religious affiliation. *Tuition waivers:* Full or partial for employees or children of employees. *ROTC:* Army.

LOANS *Student loans:* $9,933,879 (78% need-based, 22% non-need-based). 85% of past graduating class borrowed through all loan programs. *Average indebtedness per student:* $21,409. *Average need-based loan:* Freshmen: $3114; Undergraduates: $4230. *Parent loans:* $2,389,001 (40% need-based, 60% non-need-based). *Programs:* FFEL (Subsidized and Unsubsidized Stafford, PLUS), Perkins, college/university.

WORK-STUDY *Federal work-study:* Total amount: $397,760; 350 jobs averaging $1600. *State or other work-study/employment:* Total amount: $191,242 (56% need-based, 44% non-need-based). 131 part-time jobs averaging $1147.

ATHLETIC AWARDS *Total amount:* $1,194,529 (65% need-based, 35% non-need-based).

APPLYING FOR FINANCIAL AID *Required financial aid form:* FAFSA. *Financial aid deadline (priority):* 3/1. *Notification date:* Continuous beginning 4/1. Students must reply within 4 weeks of notification.

CONTACT Mrs. Kathy White, Director of Financial Aid, Evangel University, 1111 North Glenstone Avenue, Springfield, MO 65802-2191, 417-865-2811 Ext. 7264 or toll-free 800-382-6435 (in-state). *E-mail:* whitek@evangel.edu.

EVERGLADES UNIVERSITY
Boca Raton, FL

ABOUT THE INSTITUTION Proprietary, coed. Awards: bachelor's and master's degrees. 5 undergraduate majors. Total enrollment: 439. Undergraduates: 398.

GIFT AID (NEED-BASED) *Scholarships, grants, and awards:* Federal Pell, FSEOG, state, private, college/university gift aid from institutional funds.

LOANS *Programs:* Federal Direct (Subsidized and Unsubsidized Stafford, PLUS), FFEL (Subsidized and Unsubsidized Stafford, PLUS), Perkins.

APPLYING FOR FINANCIAL AID *Required financial aid forms:* FAFSA, institution's own form.

CONTACT Fred Pfeffer, Financial Aid Office, Everglades University, 1500 Northwest 49th Street, Fort Lauderdale, FL 33309, 888-772-6077. *Fax:* 954-772-2695. *E-mail:* fredp@evergladesuniversity.edu.

EVERGLADES UNIVERSITY
Sarasota, FL

CONTACT Financial Aid Office, Everglades University, 6151 Lake Osprey Drive, Sarasota, FL 34240, 941-907-2262 or toll-free 866-907-2262.

THE EVERGREEN STATE COLLEGE
Olympia, WA

Tuition & fees (WA res): $4056	Average undergraduate aid package: $10,547

ABOUT THE INSTITUTION State-supported, coed. Awards: bachelor's and master's degrees. 23 undergraduate majors. Total enrollment: 4,410. Undergraduates: 4,138. Freshmen: 480. Federal methodology is used as a basis for awarding need-based institutional aid.

UNDERGRADUATE EXPENSES for 2004–05 *Application fee:* $37. *Tuition, state resident:* full-time $3900; part-time $130 per quarter hour. *Tuition, nonresident:* full-time $14,514; part-time $483.80 per quarter hour. *Required fees:* full-time $156; $1 per credit hour or $40 per term part-time. Full-time tuition and fees vary according to course load and degree level. Part-time tuition and fees vary according to course load and degree level. *College room and board:* $5784; *room only:* $3405. Room and board charges vary according to board plan, housing facility, and student level. *Payment plan:* Installment.

FRESHMAN FINANCIAL AID (Fall 2003) 398 applied for aid; of those 60% were deemed to have need. 95% of freshmen with need received aid; of those 30% had need fully met. *Average percent of need met:* 73% (excluding resources awarded to replace EFC). *Average financial aid package:* $9824 (excluding resources awarded to replace EFC). 4% of all full-time freshmen had no need and received non-need-based gift aid.

UNDERGRADUATE FINANCIAL AID (Fall 2003) 2,734 applied for aid; of those 79% were deemed to have need. 95% of undergraduates with need received aid; of those 35% had need fully met. *Average percent of need met:* 81% (excluding resources awarded to replace EFC). *Average financial aid package:* $10,547 (excluding resources awarded to replace EFC). 1% of all full-time undergraduates had no need and received non-need-based gift aid.

GIFT AID (NEED-BASED) *Total amount:* $8,490,321 (54% federal, 37% state, 9% institutional). *Receiving aid:* Freshmen: 28% (127); All full-time undergraduates: 45% (1,591). *Average award:* Freshmen: $4635; Undergraduates: $5343. *Scholarships, grants, and awards:* Federal Pell, FSEOG, state, private, college/university gift aid from institutional funds.

GIFT AID (NON-NEED-BASED) *Total amount:* $1,273,027 (22% state, 10% institutional, 68% external sources). *Receiving aid:* Freshmen: 31% (139); Undergraduates: 10% (341). *Average Award:* Freshmen: $3590; Undergraduates:* $2897. *Scholarships, grants, and awards by category: Academic Interests/Achievement:* 377 awards ($391,981 total): general academic interests/achievements. *Creative Arts/Performance:* 25 awards ($57,126 total): applied art and design, art/fine arts, creative writing. *Special Achievements/Activities:* 14 awards ($31,991 total): community service, general special achievements/activities. *Special Characteristics:* 49 awards ($154,559 total): adult students, first-generation college students, members of minority groups. *Tuition waivers:* Full or partial for employees or children of employees.

LOANS *Student loans:* $10,798,521 (62% need-based, 38% non-need-based). 51% of past graduating class borrowed through all loan programs. *Average indebtedness per student:* $10,486. *Average need-based loan:* Freshmen: $2882; Undergraduates: $4039. *Parent loans:* $3,080,862 (50% need-based, 50% non-need-based). *Programs:* FFEL (Subsidized and Unsubsidized Stafford, PLUS), Perkins, college/university.

WORK-STUDY *Federal work-study:* Total amount: $369,395; 167 jobs averaging $2212. *State or other work-study/employment:* Total amount: $498,565 (100% need-based). 218 part-time jobs averaging $2292.

ATHLETIC AWARDS *Total amount:* $62,996 (100% need-based).

APPLYING FOR FINANCIAL AID *Required financial aid forms:* FAFSA, institution's own form. *Financial aid deadline (priority):* 3/15. *Notification date:* Continuous beginning 4/15. Students must reply within 4 weeks of notification.

CONTACT Financial Aid Office, The Evergreen State College, 2700 Evergreen Parkway NW, Olympia, WA 98505, 360-867-6205. *Fax:* 360-866-6576.

EXCELSIOR COLLEGE
Albany, NY

Tuition & fees: N/R	Average undergraduate aid package: N/A

ABOUT THE INSTITUTION Independent, coed. Awards: associate, bachelor's, and master's degrees and post-bachelor's certificates (offers only external degree programs). 39 undergraduate majors. Total enrollment: 26,395. Undergraduates: 26,022. Both federal and institutional methodology are used as a basis for awarding need-based institutional aid.

UNDERGRADUATE EXPENSES for 2004–05 *Application fee:* $50. *Tuition:* part-time $240 per credit. *Required fees:* full-time $995; $495 per year part-time. *Payment plan:* Installment.

GIFT AID (NEED-BASED) *Total amount:* $142,042 (30% state, 64% institutional, 6% external sources). *Scholarships, grants, and awards:* state, private, college/university gift aid from institutional funds.

GIFT AID (NON-NEED-BASED) *Total amount:* $232,453 (100% external sources). *Scholarships, grants, and awards by category: Academic Interests/Achievement:* general academic interests/achievements. *Special Characteristics:* veterans, veterans' children. *Tuition waivers:* Full or partial for employees or children of employees.

LOANS *Student loans:* $1,996,806 (100% non-need-based). 1% of past graduating class borrowed through all loan programs. *Average indebtedness per student:* $5276. *Programs:* alternative loans, PLATO Loans, Excel, Citi Assist, Key.

APPLYING FOR FINANCIAL AID *Required financial aid form:* institution's own form. *Financial aid deadline (priority):* 7/1. *Notification date:* Continuous.

CONTACT Donna L. Cooper, Director of Financial Aid, Excelsior College, 7 Columbia Circle, Albany, NY 12203-5159, 518-464-8500 or toll-free 888-647-2388. *Fax:* 518-464-8777.

FAIRFIELD UNIVERSITY
Fairfield, CT

Tuition & fees: $28,415	Average undergraduate aid package: $16,360

ABOUT THE INSTITUTION Independent Roman Catholic (Jesuit), coed. Awards: bachelor's and master's degrees and post-master's certificates. 35 undergraduate majors. Total enrollment: 5,060. Undergraduates: 3,942. Freshmen: 856. Federal methodology is used as a basis for awarding need-based institutional aid.

UNDERGRADUATE EXPENSES for 2004–05 *Application fee:* $55. *One-time required fee:* $150. *Comprehensive fee:* $37,685 includes full-time tuition ($27,930), mandatory fees ($485), and room and board ($9270). *College room only:* $5470. Full-time tuition and fees vary according to student level. Room and board charges vary according to board plan and housing facility. *Part-time tuition:* $375 per credit. *Part-time fees:* $60 per term. Part-time tuition and fees vary according to course load. *Payment plan:* Installment.

FRESHMAN FINANCIAL AID (Fall 2004, est.) 592 applied for aid; of those 77% were deemed to have need. 99% of freshmen with need received aid; of those 24% had need fully met. *Average percent of need met:* 62% (excluding resources awarded to replace EFC). *Average financial aid package:* $15,823 (excluding resources awarded to replace EFC). 9% of all full-time freshmen had no need and received non-need-based gift aid.

UNDERGRADUATE FINANCIAL AID (Fall 2004, est.) 1,982 applied for aid; of those 82% were deemed to have need. 99% of undergraduates with need received aid; of those 21% had need fully met. *Average percent of need met:* 64% (excluding resources awarded to replace EFC). *Average financial aid package:* $16,360 (excluding resources awarded to replace EFC). 7% of all full-time undergraduates had no need and received non-need-based gift aid.

GIFT AID (NEED-BASED) *Total amount:* $18,269,418 (10% federal, 8% state, 82% institutional). *Receiving aid:* Freshmen: 46% (398); All full-time undergraduates: 44% (1,442). *Average award:* Freshmen: $10,258; Undergraduates: $10,898. *Scholarships, grants, and awards:* Federal Pell, FSEOG, state, private, college/university gift aid from institutional funds.

GIFT AID (NON-NEED-BASED) *Total amount:* $6,264,235 (91% institutional, 9% external sources). *Receiving aid:* Freshmen: 16% (140); Undergraduates: 14% (476). *Average Award: Freshmen:* $12,026; *Undergraduates:* $10,207. *Scholarships, grants, and awards by category: Academic Interests/Achievement:* 562 awards ($6,322,702 total): biological sciences, business, education, engineering/technologies, foreign languages, general academic interests/achievements, physical sciences. *Creative Arts/Performance:* 11 awards ($137,990 total): art/fine arts, music, performing arts. *Special Achievements/Activities:* 4

awards ($40,120 total): religious involvement. *Special Characteristics:* 78 awards ($546,632 total): children and siblings of alumni, ethnic background, first-generation college students, members of minority groups, religious affiliation. *Tuition waivers:* Full or partial for employees or children of employees. *ROTC:* Army cooperative.

LOANS *Student loans:* $15,492,052 (43% need-based, 57% non-need-based). 63% of past graduating class borrowed through all loan programs. *Average indebtedness per student:* $24,251. *Average need-based loan:* Freshmen: $3520; Undergraduates: $4131. *Parent loans:* $6,546,426 (100% non-need-based). *Programs:* FFEL (Subsidized and Unsubsidized Stafford, PLUS), Perkins, Federal Nursing, state, alternative loans.

WORK-STUDY *Federal work-study:* Total amount: $804,571; 457 jobs averaging $1405.

ATHLETIC AWARDS *Total amount:* $2,724,458 (100% non-need-based).

APPLYING FOR FINANCIAL AID *Required financial aid forms:* FAFSA, CSS Financial Aid PROFILE. *Financial aid deadline (priority):* 2/15. *Notification date:* Continuous beginning 4/5. Students must reply by 5/1 or within 2 weeks of notification.

CONTACT Mr. Erin Chiaro, Director of Financial Aid, Fairfield University, 1073 North Benson Road, Fairfield, CT 06824-5195, 203-254-4125. *Fax:* 203-254-4008. *E-mail:* echiaro@mail.fairfield.edu.

FAIRLEIGH DICKINSON UNIVERSITY, COLLEGE AT FLORHAM
Madison, NJ

Tuition & fees: $23,386	Average undergraduate aid package: $15,806

ABOUT THE INSTITUTION Independent, coed. Awards: associate, bachelor's, and master's degrees and post-bachelor's and post-master's certificates. 30 undergraduate majors. Total enrollment: 3,684. Undergraduates: 2,633. Freshmen: 613. Federal methodology is used as a basis for awarding need-based institutional aid.

UNDERGRADUATE EXPENSES for 2004–05 *Application fee:* $40. *Comprehensive fee:* $31,994 includes full-time tuition ($22,876), mandatory fees ($510), and room and board ($8608). *College room only:* $5098. Room and board charges vary according to board plan and housing facility. *Part-time tuition:* $681 per credit. *Part-time fees:* $122 per term. Part-time tuition and fees vary according to course load. *Payment plans:* Installment, deferred payment.

FRESHMAN FINANCIAL AID (Fall 2003) 512 applied for aid; of those 87% were deemed to have need. 100% of freshmen with need received aid. *Average financial aid package:* $18,044 (excluding resources awarded to replace EFC). 23% of all full-time freshmen had no need and received non-need-based gift aid.

UNDERGRADUATE FINANCIAL AID (Fall 2003) 1,772 applied for aid; of those 88% were deemed to have need. 100% of undergraduates with need received aid. *Average financial aid package:* $15,806 (excluding resources awarded to replace EFC). 30% of all full-time undergraduates had no need and received non-need-based gift aid.

GIFT AID (NEED-BASED) *Total amount:* $12,472,871 (16% federal, 26% state, 58% institutional). *Receiving aid:* Freshmen: 70% (415); All full-time undergraduates: 60% (1,350). *Average award:* Freshmen: $10,169; Undergraduates: $8290. *Scholarships, grants, and awards:* Federal Pell, FSEOG, state, private, college/university gift aid from institutional funds, United Negro College Fund, Federal Nursing.

GIFT AID (NON-NEED-BASED) *Total amount:* $7,354,256 (95% institutional, 5% external sources). *Receiving aid:* Freshmen: 52% (312); Undergraduates: 42% (936). *Average Award:* Freshmen: $4665; *Undergraduates:* $6952. *Tuition waivers:* Full or partial for employees or children of employees, senior citizens. *ROTC:* Army cooperative.

LOANS *Student loans:* $11,846,292 (59% need-based, 41% non-need-based). *Average need-based loan:* Freshmen: $2760; Undergraduates: $3653. *Parent loans:* $2,277,379 (100% non-need-based). *Programs:* FFEL (Subsidized and Unsubsidized Stafford, PLUS), Perkins, Federal Nursing, state.

WORK-STUDY *Federal work-study:* Total amount: $200,000; jobs available.

APPLYING FOR FINANCIAL AID *Required financial aid form:* FAFSA. *Financial aid deadline:* Continuous. *Notification date:* Continuous beginning 4/1. Students must reply by 5/1 or within 2 weeks of notification.

CONTACT Financial Aid Office, Fairleigh Dickinson University, College at Florham, 285 Madison Avenue, Madison, NJ 07940-1099, 973-443-8700 or toll-free 800-338-8803.

FAIRLEIGH DICKINSON UNIVERSITY, METROPOLITAN CAMPUS
Teaneck, NJ

Tuition & fees: $21,734	Average undergraduate aid package: $16,556

ABOUT THE INSTITUTION Independent, coed. Awards: associate, bachelor's, master's, and doctoral degrees and post-bachelor's and post-master's certificates. 42 undergraduate majors. Total enrollment: 7,634. Undergraduates: 5,417. Freshmen: 571. Federal methodology is used as a basis for awarding need-based institutional aid.

UNDERGRADUATE EXPENSES for 2004–05 *Application fee:* $40. *Comprehensive fee:* $30,790 includes full-time tuition ($21,224), mandatory fees ($510), and room and board ($9056). *College room only:* $5546. Room and board charges vary according to board plan and housing facility. *Part-time tuition:* $681 per credit. *Part-time fees:* $122. Part-time tuition and fees vary according to course load. *Payment plans:* Installment, deferred payment.

FRESHMAN FINANCIAL AID (Fall 2003) 442 applied for aid; of those 96% were deemed to have need. 100% of freshmen with need received aid. *Average financial aid package:* $18,548 (excluding resources awarded to replace EFC). 10% of all full-time freshmen had no need and received non-need-based gift aid.

UNDERGRADUATE FINANCIAL AID (Fall 2003) 1,599 applied for aid; of those 94% were deemed to have need. 99% of undergraduates with need received aid. *Average financial aid package:* $16,556 (excluding resources awarded to replace EFC). 13% of all full-time undergraduates had no need and received non-need-based gift aid.

GIFT AID (NEED-BASED) *Total amount:* $14,394,510 (22% federal, 31% state, 47% institutional). *Receiving aid:* Freshmen: 69% (407); All full-time undergraduates: 63% (1,329). *Average award:* Freshmen: $9184; Undergraduates: $7279. *Scholarships, grants, and awards:* Federal Pell, FSEOG, state, private, college/university gift aid from institutional funds, United Negro College Fund, Federal Nursing.

GIFT AID (NON-NEED-BASED) *Total amount:* $5,760,079 (1% state, 91% institutional, 8% external sources). *Receiving aid:* Freshmen: 46% (272); Undergraduates: 39% (826). *Average Award:* Freshmen: $5715; Undergraduates: $3658. *Tuition waivers:* Full or partial for employees or children of employees, senior citizens. *ROTC:* Army cooperative.

LOANS *Student loans:* $10,054,060 (79% need-based, 21% non-need-based). *Average need-based loan:* Freshmen: $2704; Undergraduates: $3666. *Parent loans:* $1,487,944 (100% non-need-based). *Programs:* FFEL (Subsidized and Unsubsidized Stafford, PLUS), Perkins, Federal Nursing, state.

WORK-STUDY *Federal work-study:* Total amount: $250,000; jobs available.

ATHLETIC AWARDS *Total amount:* $2,297,802 (100% non-need-based).

APPLYING FOR FINANCIAL AID *Required financial aid form:* FAFSA. *Financial aid deadline:* Continuous. *Notification date:* Continuous beginning 4/1. Students must reply by 5/1 or within 2 weeks of notification.

CONTACT Financial Aid Office, Fairleigh Dickinson University, Metropolitan Campus, 100 River Road, Teaneck, NJ 07666-1914, 201-692-2363 or toll-free 800-338-8803.

FAIRMONT STATE UNIVERSITY
Fairmont, WV

Tuition & fees (WV res): $4112	Average undergraduate aid package: $5480

ABOUT THE INSTITUTION State-supported, coed. Awards: associate, bachelor's, and master's degrees. 60 undergraduate majors. Total enrollment: 7,519. Undergraduates: 7,375. Freshmen: 1,285. Federal methodology is used as a basis for awarding need-based institutional aid.

UNDERGRADUATE EXPENSES for 2005–06 *Tuition, state resident:* full-time $3918; part-time $155 per hour. *Tuition, nonresident:* full-time $8508; part-time $331 per hour. *Required fees:* full-time $194; $17 per credit hour. *College room and board:* $6052; *room only:* $3192.

GIFT AID (NEED-BASED) *Total amount:* $9,766,999 (83% federal, 11% state, 3% institutional, 3% external sources). *Receiving aid:* Freshmen: 52% (649); All full-time undergraduates: 47% (2,667). *Average award:* Freshmen: $6413; Undergraduates: $7322. *Scholarships, grants, and awards:* Federal Pell, FSEOG, state, private, college/university gift aid from institutional funds.

GIFT AID (NON-NEED-BASED) *Total amount:* $828,412 (59% state, 23% institutional, 18% external sources). *Receiving aid:* Freshmen: 10% (125);

Undergraduates: 5% (257). *Average Award:* Freshmen: $739; Undergraduates: $2809. *Scholarships, grants, and awards by category: Academic Interests/Achievement:* 400 awards ($350,000 total): business, education, engineering/technologies, foreign languages, general academic interests/achievements, health fields, humanities, mathematics, physical sciences, social sciences. *Creative Arts/Performance:* 60 awards ($50,000 total): art/fine arts, debating, music, theater/drama. *Special Achievements/Activities:* 10 awards ($10,000 total): cheerleading/drum major. *Special Characteristics:* 40 awards ($64,000 total): adult students, children and siblings of alumni, general special characteristics, international students, local/state students, members of minority groups, out-of-state students. *ROTC:* Army.

LOANS *Student loans:* $14,217,391 (58% need-based, 42% non-need-based). 94% of past graduating class borrowed through all loan programs. *Average indebtedness per student:* $17,500. *Average need-based loan:* Freshmen: $2192; Undergraduates: $2891. *Parent loans:* $737,151 (70% need-based, 30% non-need-based). *Programs:* Federal Direct (Subsidized and Unsubsidized Stafford, PLUS), Perkins.

ATHLETIC AWARDS *Total amount:* $491,391 (65% need-based, 35% non-need-based).

APPLYING FOR FINANCIAL AID *Required financial aid forms:* FAFSA, state aid form. *Financial aid deadline:* 2/1 (priority: 3/1). *Notification date:* Continuous beginning 4/15. Students must reply within 2 weeks of notification.

CONTACT Sandra K. Oerly-Bennett, Director of Financial Aid and Scholarships, Fairmont State University, 1201 Locust Avenue, Fairmont, WV 26554, 304-367-4213 or toll-free 800-641-5678. *Fax:* 304-367-4584. *E-mail:* financialaid@fairmontstate.edu.

FAITH BAPTIST BIBLE COLLEGE AND THEOLOGICAL SEMINARY
Ankeny, IA

Tuition & fees: $10,930	Average undergraduate aid package: $6493

ABOUT THE INSTITUTION Independent religious, coed. Awards: associate, bachelor's, master's, and first professional degrees. 10 undergraduate majors. Total enrollment: 506. Undergraduates: 358. Freshmen: 116. Federal methodology is used as a basis for awarding need-based institutional aid.

UNDERGRADUATE EXPENSES for 2004–05 *Application fee:* $25. *Comprehensive fee:* $15,140 includes full-time tuition ($10,540), mandatory fees ($390), and room and board ($4210). *College room only:* $1960. Full-time tuition and fees vary according to course load. *Part-time tuition:* $385 per semester hour. *Part-time fees:* $90 per term.

FRESHMAN FINANCIAL AID (Fall 2003) 102 applied for aid; of those 96% were deemed to have need. 100% of freshmen with need received aid; of those 9% had need fully met. *Average percent of need met:* 31% (excluding resources awarded to replace EFC). *Average financial aid package:* $6031 (excluding resources awarded to replace EFC). 13% of all full-time freshmen had no need and received non-need-based gift aid.

UNDERGRADUATE FINANCIAL AID (Fall 2003) 339 applied for aid; of those 93% were deemed to have need. 99% of undergraduates with need received aid; of those 9% had need fully met. *Average percent of need met:* 50% (excluding resources awarded to replace EFC). *Average financial aid package:* $6493 (excluding resources awarded to replace EFC). 10% of all full-time undergraduates had no need and received non-need-based gift aid.

GIFT AID (NEED-BASED) *Total amount:* $1,019,247 (36% federal, 43% state, 21% institutional). *Receiving aid:* Freshmen: 64% (72); All full-time undergraduates: 64% (231). *Average award:* Freshmen: $4151; Undergraduates: $4273. *Scholarships, grants, and awards:* Federal Pell, state, private, college/university gift aid from institutional funds.

GIFT AID (NON-NEED-BASED) *Total amount:* $342,197 (56% institutional, 44% external sources). *Receiving aid:* Freshmen: 74% (83); Undergraduates: 53% (192). *Average Award:* Freshmen: $1671; Undergraduates: $3429. *Scholarships, grants, and awards by category: Academic Interests/Achievement:* 145 awards ($113,341 total): general academic interests/achievements. *Creative Arts/Performance:* 17 awards ($20,391 total): music. *Special Achievements/Activities:* 1 award ($297 total): leadership. *Special Characteristics:* 92 awards ($158,222 total): children of faculty/staff, relatives of clergy, spouses of current students. *Tuition waivers:* Full or partial for employees or children of employees.

LOANS *Student loans:* $1,480,847 (77% need-based, 23% non-need-based). 68% of past graduating class borrowed through all loan programs. *Average indebtedness per student:* $13,050. *Average need-based loan:* Freshmen: $4153;

Faith Baptist Bible College and Theological Seminary

Undergraduates: $4854. *Parent loans:* $121,101 (90% need-based, 10% non-need-based). *Programs:* FFEL (Subsidized and Unsubsidized Stafford, PLUS).

APPLYING FOR FINANCIAL AID *Required financial aid form:* FAFSA. *Financial aid deadline (priority):* 3/1. *Notification date:* Continuous. Students must reply within 4 weeks of notification.

CONTACT Mr. Breck Appell, Director of Financial Assistance, Faith Baptist Bible College and Theological Seminary, 1900 Northwest 4th Street, Ankeny, IA 50021-2152, 515-964-0601 or toll-free 888-FAITH 4U. *Fax:* 515-964-1638.

FARMINGDALE STATE UNIVERSITY OF NEW YORK
Farmingdale, NY

CONTACT Dionne Walker-Belgrave, Assistant Director of Financial Aid, Farmingdale State University of New York, 2350 Broadhollow Road, Route 110, Farmingdale, NY 11735, 631-420-2328 or toll-free 877-4-FARMINGDALE. *Fax:* 631-420-3662.

FASHION INSTITUTE OF TECHNOLOGY
New York, NY

Tuition & fees (NY res): $4720	Average undergraduate aid package: $7288

ABOUT THE INSTITUTION State and locally supported, coed, primarily women. Awards: associate, bachelor's, and master's degrees. 14 undergraduate majors. Total enrollment: 10,513. Undergraduates: 10,378. Freshmen: 1,055. Federal methodology is used as a basis for awarding need-based institutional aid.

UNDERGRADUATE EXPENSES for 2004–05 *Application fee:* $40. *Tuition, state resident:* full-time $4350; part-time $181 per credit. *Tuition, nonresident:* full-time $10,300; part-time $429 per credit. *Required fees:* full-time $370; $5 per term part-time. Full-time tuition and fees vary according to degree level and program. Part-time tuition and fees vary according to degree level and program. *College room and board:* $7066; *room only:* $6870. Room and board charges vary according to board plan and housing facility. *Payment plan:* Installment.

FRESHMAN FINANCIAL AID (Fall 2004, est.) 762 applied for aid; of those 61% were deemed to have need. 99% of freshmen with need received aid; of those 24% had need fully met. *Average percent of need met:* 76% (excluding resources awarded to replace EFC). *Average financial aid package:* $6287 (excluding resources awarded to replace EFC). 4% of all full-time freshmen had no need and received non-need-based gift aid.

UNDERGRADUATE FINANCIAL AID (Fall 2004, est.) 4,249 applied for aid; of those 66% were deemed to have need. 98% of undergraduates with need received aid; of those 18% had need fully met. *Average percent of need met:* 72% (excluding resources awarded to replace EFC). *Average financial aid package:* $7288 (excluding resources awarded to replace EFC). 2% of all full-time undergraduates had no need and received non-need-based gift aid.

GIFT AID (NEED-BASED) *Total amount:* $9,984,977 (57% federal, 38% state, 5% institutional). *Receiving aid:* Freshmen: 31% (337); All full-time undergraduates: 31% (2,134). *Average award:* Freshmen: $3726; Undergraduates: $4002. *Scholarships, grants, and awards:* Federal Pell, FSEOG, state, private, college/university gift aid from institutional funds.

GIFT AID (NON-NEED-BASED) *Total amount:* $528,724 (14% institutional, 86% external sources). *Receiving aid:* Freshmen: 5% (53); Undergraduates: 2% (141). *Average Award:* Freshmen: $1358; Undergraduates: $1681. *Scholarships, grants, and awards by category:* Creative Arts/Performance: 154 awards ($74,750 total): applied art and design. *Tuition waivers:* Full or partial for employees or children of employees.

LOANS *Student loans:* $17,101,112 (45% need-based, 55% non-need-based). 36% of past graduating class borrowed through all loan programs. *Average indebtedness per student:* $10,972. *Average need-based loan:* Freshmen: $2668; Undergraduates: $3726. *Parent loans:* $3,105,960 (100% non-need-based). *Programs:* FFEL (Subsidized and Unsubsidized Stafford, PLUS), Perkins, alternative loans.

WORK-STUDY *Federal work-study:* Total amount: $908,082; 453 jobs averaging $2000.

APPLYING FOR FINANCIAL AID *Required financial aid forms:* FAFSA, state aid form. *Financial aid deadline (priority):* 2/15. *Notification date:* Continuous beginning 4/15. Students must reply within 2 weeks of notification.

CONTACT Financial Aid Office, Fashion Institute of Technology, Seventh Avenue at 27th Street, New York, NY 10001-5992, 212-217-7439 or toll-free 800-GOTOFIT (out-of-state).

FAULKNER UNIVERSITY
Montgomery, AL

Tuition & fees: $10,425	Average undergraduate aid package: $7100

ABOUT THE INSTITUTION Independent religious, coed. Awards: associate, bachelor's, master's, and first professional degrees. 49 undergraduate majors. Total enrollment: 2,583. Undergraduates: 2,225. Freshmen: 238. Federal methodology is used as a basis for awarding need-based institutional aid.

UNDERGRADUATE EXPENSES for 2005–06 *Application fee:* $10. *Comprehensive fee:* $15,625 includes full-time tuition ($10,400), mandatory fees ($25), and room and board ($5200). *College room only:* $2500. Room and board charges vary according to board plan and housing facility. *Part-time tuition:* $365 per semester hour. *Payment plans:* Installment, deferred payment.

FRESHMAN FINANCIAL AID (Fall 2004, est.) 170 applied for aid; of those 80% were deemed to have need. 100% of freshmen with need received aid; of those 10% had need fully met. *Average percent of need met:* 60% (excluding resources awarded to replace EFC). *Average financial aid package:* $4600 (excluding resources awarded to replace EFC). 5% of all full-time freshmen had no need and received non-need-based gift aid.

UNDERGRADUATE FINANCIAL AID (Fall 2004, est.) 1,470 applied for aid; of those 80% were deemed to have need. 100% of undergraduates with need received aid; of those 10% had need fully met. *Average percent of need met:* 59% (excluding resources awarded to replace EFC). *Average financial aid package:* $7100 (excluding resources awarded to replace EFC). 3% of all full-time undergraduates had no need and received non-need-based gift aid.

GIFT AID (NEED-BASED) *Total amount:* $4,478,770 (100% federal). *Receiving aid:* Freshmen: 55% (101); All full-time undergraduates: 55% (870). *Average award:* Freshmen: $2450; Undergraduates: $2700. *Scholarships, grants, and awards:* Federal Pell, FSEOG, state, private, college/university gift aid from institutional funds.

GIFT AID (NON-NEED-BASED) *Total amount:* $2,556,121 (13% state, 80% institutional, 7% external sources). *Receiving aid:* Freshmen: 45% (84); Undergraduates: 46% (729). *Average Award:* Freshmen: $1650; Undergraduates: $1850. *Scholarships, grants, and awards by category:* Academic Interests/Achievement: 369 awards ($1,084,047 total): general academic interests/achievements, religion/biblical studies. Creative Arts/Performance: 30 awards ($56,470 total): journalism/publications, music, theater/drama. Special Achievements/Activities: 340 awards ($257,140 total): cheerleading/drum major, leadership, religious involvement. Special Characteristics: 164 awards ($281,491 total): adult students, children and siblings of alumni, children of faculty/staff, relatives of clergy, siblings of current students. *Tuition waivers:* Full or partial for children of alumni, employees or children of employees. *ROTC:* Army cooperative, Air Force cooperative.

LOANS *Student loans:* $17,634,568 (51% need-based, 49% non-need-based). 80% of past graduating class borrowed through all loan programs. *Average indebtedness per student:* $18,600. *Average need-based loan:* Freshmen: $2625; Undergraduates: $4850. *Parent loans:* $556,988 (100% non-need-based). *Programs:* FFEL (Subsidized and Unsubsidized Stafford, PLUS), Perkins.

WORK-STUDY *Federal work-study:* Total amount: $215,000; 143 jobs averaging $1503. *State or other work-study/employment:* Total amount: $3100 (100% non-need-based). 4 part-time jobs averaging $775.

ATHLETIC AWARDS *Total amount:* $712,565 (100% non-need-based).

APPLYING FOR FINANCIAL AID *Required financial aid forms:* FAFSA, institution's own form, state aid form. *Financial aid deadline (priority):* 5/1.

CONTACT William G. Jackson II, Director of Financial Aid, Faulkner University, 5345 Atlanta Highway, Montgomery, AL 36109-3398, 334-386-7195 or toll-free 800-879-9816. *Fax:* 334-386-7201.

FAYETTEVILLE STATE UNIVERSITY
Fayetteville, NC

CONTACT Lois L. McKoy, Director of Financial Aid, Fayetteville State University, 1200 Murchison Road, Fayetteville, NC 28301-4298, 910-672-1325 or toll-free 800-222-2594. *Fax:* 910-672-1423. *E-mail:* lmckoy@uncfsu.edu.

FELICIAN COLLEGE
Lodi, NJ

ABOUT THE INSTITUTION Independent Roman Catholic, coed. Awards: associate, bachelor's, and master's degrees and post-bachelor's certificates. 40 undergraduate majors. Total enrollment: 1,665. Undergraduates: 1,451. Freshmen: 245.

GIFT AID (NEED-BASED) *Scholarships, grants, and awards:* Federal Pell, FSEOG, state, college/university gift aid from institutional funds, Federal Nursing.

GIFT AID (NON-NEED-BASED) *Scholarships, grants, and awards by category: Academic Interests/Achievement:* area/ethnic studies, biological sciences, business, computer science, education, English, general academic interests/achievements, health fields, mathematics, premedicine, religion/biblical studies, social sciences.

LOANS *Programs:* FFEL (Subsidized and Unsubsidized Stafford, PLUS), state, NJ Class Loans, alternative loans.

APPLYING FOR FINANCIAL AID *Required financial aid forms:* FAFSA, institution's own form.

CONTACT Norma Betz, Financial Aid Director, Felician College, 262 South Main Street, Lodi, NJ 07644, 201-559-6040. *Fax:* 201-559-6188. *E-mail:* betzn@inet.felician.edu.

FERRIS STATE UNIVERSITY
Big Rapids, MI

Tuition & fees (MI res): $6332	Average undergraduate aid package: $8000

ABOUT THE INSTITUTION State-supported, coed. Awards: associate, bachelor's, master's, and first professional degrees. 83 undergraduate majors. Total enrollment: 11,803. Undergraduates: 10,711. Freshmen: 1,958. Federal methodology is used as a basis for awarding need-based institutional aid.

UNDERGRADUATE EXPENSES for 2004–05 *Application fee:* $30. *Tuition, state resident:* full-time $6190; part-time $256 per credit hour. *Tuition, nonresident:* full-time $12,380; part-time $512 per credit hour. Full-time tuition and fees vary according to reciprocity agreements. *College room and board:* $6522; *room only:* $3312. Room and board charges vary according to board plan and housing facility. *Payment plans:* Installment, deferred payment.

FRESHMAN FINANCIAL AID (Fall 2004, est.) 1780 applied for aid; of those 88% were deemed to have need. 79% of freshmen with need received aid; of those 10% had need fully met. *Average percent of need met:* 75% (excluding resources awarded to replace EFC). *Average financial aid package:* $7100 (excluding resources awarded to replace EFC). 6% of all full-time freshmen had no need and received non-need-based gift aid.

UNDERGRADUATE FINANCIAL AID (Fall 2004, est.) 7,893 applied for aid; of those 85% were deemed to have need. 84% of undergraduates with need received aid; of those 10% had need fully met. *Average percent of need met:* 80% (excluding resources awarded to replace EFC). *Average financial aid package:* $8000 (excluding resources awarded to replace EFC). 3% of all full-time undergraduates had no need and received non-need-based gift aid.

GIFT AID (NEED-BASED) *Total amount:* $13,303,634 (71% federal, 18% state, 11% institutional). *Receiving aid:* Freshmen: 40% (775); All full-time undergraduates: 41% (3,483). *Average award:* Freshmen: $3000; Undergraduates: $3500. *Scholarships, grants, and awards:* Federal Pell, FSEOG, state, private, college/university gift aid from institutional funds.

GIFT AID (NON-NEED-BASED) *Total amount:* $7,904,281 (32% state, 49% institutional, 19% external sources). *Receiving aid:* Freshmen: 22% (423); Undergraduates: 14% (1,172). *Average Award:* Freshmen: $2000; Undergraduates: $2000. *Scholarships, grants, and awards by category: Academic Interests/Achievement:* 1,350 awards ($2,000,000 total): general academic interests/achievements. *Creative Arts/Performance:* 175 awards ($87,500 total): debating, general creative arts/performance, journalism/publications, music, theater/drama. *Special Characteristics:* 430 awards ($1,091,080 total): children of faculty/staff, general special characteristics. *Tuition waivers:* Full or partial for employees or children of employees. *ROTC:* Army cooperative.

LOANS *Student loans:* $47,024,296 (56% need-based, 44% non-need-based). 85% of past graduating class borrowed through all loan programs. *Average indebtedness per student:* $15,000. *Average need-based loan:* Freshmen: $1800; Undergraduates: $3400. *Parent loans:* $3,993,980 (100% non-need-based). *Programs:* Federal Direct (Subsidized and Unsubsidized Stafford, PLUS), Perkins, Federal Nursing, college/university, alternative loans.

WORK-STUDY *Federal work-study:* Total amount: $596,000; 581 jobs averaging $1026. *State or other work-study/employment:* Total amount: $228,000 (100% need-based). 126 part-time jobs averaging $1810.

ATHLETIC AWARDS *Total amount:* $1,315,012 (100% non-need-based).

APPLYING FOR FINANCIAL AID *Required financial aid form:* FAFSA. *Financial aid deadline (priority):* 3/1. *Notification date:* Continuous beginning 4/1. Students must reply within 2 weeks of notification.

CONTACT Carla Erlewine, Associate Director of Financial Aid, Ferris State University, 1201 South State Street, CSS 101, Big Rapids, MI 49307-2020, 231-591-2110 or toll-free 800-433-7747. *Fax:* 231-591-2950. *E-mail:* erlewinc@ferris.edu.

FERRUM COLLEGE
Ferrum, VA

Tuition & fees: $16,870	Average undergraduate aid package: $13,457

ABOUT THE INSTITUTION Independent United Methodist, coed. Awards: bachelor's degrees. 33 undergraduate majors. Total enrollment: 941. Undergraduates: 941. Freshmen: 296. Federal methodology is used as a basis for awarding need-based institutional aid.

UNDERGRADUATE EXPENSES for 2004–05 *Application fee:* $25. *Comprehensive fee:* $22,570 includes full-time tuition ($16,840), mandatory fees ($30), and room and board ($5700). Room and board charges vary according to housing facility. *Part-time tuition:* $340 per hour. Part-time tuition and fees vary according to course load. *Payment plan:* Installment.

FRESHMAN FINANCIAL AID (Fall 2004, est.) 259 applied for aid; of those 90% were deemed to have need. 100% of freshmen with need received aid; of those 12% had need fully met. *Average percent of need met:* 73% (excluding resources awarded to replace EFC). *Average financial aid package:* $12,931 (excluding resources awarded to replace EFC). 19% of all full-time freshmen had no need and received non-need-based gift aid.

UNDERGRADUATE FINANCIAL AID (Fall 2004, est.) 804 applied for aid; of those 91% were deemed to have need. 100% of undergraduates with need received aid; of those 11% had need fully met. *Average percent of need met:* 75% (excluding resources awarded to replace EFC). *Average financial aid package:* $13,457 (excluding resources awarded to replace EFC). 18% of all full-time undergraduates had no need and received non-need-based gift aid.

GIFT AID (NEED-BASED) *Total amount:* $7,041,795 (18% federal, 19% state, 59% institutional, 4% external sources). *Receiving aid:* Freshmen: 79% (233); All full-time undergraduates: 80% (733). *Average award:* Freshmen: $9580; Undergraduates: $9973. *Scholarships, grants, and awards:* Federal Pell, FSEOG, state, private, college/university gift aid from institutional funds.

GIFT AID (NON-NEED-BASED) *Total amount:* $1,031,109 (34% state, 63% institutional, 3% external sources). *Receiving aid:* Freshmen: 17% (49); Undergraduates: 19% (177). *Average Award:* Freshmen: $6112; Undergraduates: $6128. *Scholarships, grants, and awards by category: Academic Interests/Achievement:* 462 awards ($1,616,700 total): general academic interests/achievements. *Creative Arts/Performance:* 45 awards ($59,250 total): art/fine arts, performing arts, theater/drama. *Special Achievements/Activities:* 80 awards ($143,805 total): community service, general special achievements/activities, leadership, religious involvement. *Special Characteristics:* 265 awards ($785,547 total): adult students, children and siblings of alumni, children of educators, children of faculty/staff, international students, local/state students, out-of-state students, relatives of clergy, religious affiliation, siblings of current students. *Tuition waivers:* Full or partial for employees or children of employees, senior citizens.

LOANS *Student loans:* $3,718,169 (94% need-based, 6% non-need-based). 72% of past graduating class borrowed through all loan programs. *Average indebtedness per student:* $16,300. *Average need-based loan:* Freshmen: $2274; Undergraduates: $3524. *Parent loans:* $1,924,121 (86% need-based, 14% non-need-based). *Programs:* FFEL (Subsidized and Unsubsidized Stafford, PLUS), Perkins, alternative loans.

WORK-STUDY *Federal work-study:* Total amount: $252,363; 235 jobs averaging $1074. *State or other work-study/employment:* Total amount: $58,914 (96% need-based, 4% non-need-based). 85 part-time jobs averaging $693.

APPLYING FOR FINANCIAL AID *Required financial aid forms:* FAFSA, state aid form. *Financial aid deadline (priority):* 3/1. *Notification date:* Continuous beginning 3/15.

CONTACT Mrs. Sheila M. Nelson-Hensley, Director of Financial Aid, Ferrum College, PO Box 1000, Spilman-Daniel House, Ferrum, VA 24088-9001, 540-365-4282 or toll-free 800-868-9797. *Fax:* 540-365-4266.

FINLANDIA UNIVERSITY
Hancock, MI

Tuition & fees: $14,700   **Average undergraduate aid package: $13,000**

ABOUT THE INSTITUTION Independent religious, coed. Awards: associate and bachelor's degrees. 15 undergraduate majors. Total enrollment: 520. Undergraduates: 520. Freshmen: 121. Federal methodology is used as a basis for awarding need-based institutional aid.

UNDERGRADUATE EXPENSES for 2004–05 *Application fee:* $30. *One-time required fee:* $75. *Comprehensive fee:* $19,764 includes full-time tuition ($14,700) and room and board ($5064). Full-time tuition and fees vary according to degree level and program. Room and board charges vary according to housing facility. *Part-time tuition:* $495 per credit. Part-time tuition and fees vary according to course load, program, and reciprocity agreements. *Payment plan:* Installment.

GIFT AID (NEED-BASED) *Total amount:* $4,090,840 (35% federal, 18% state, 45% institutional, 2% external sources). *Receiving aid:* Freshmen: 60% (73); All full-time undergraduates: 93% (417). *Average award:* Freshmen: $5000; Undergraduates: $5000. *Scholarships, grants, and awards:* Federal Pell, FSEOG, state, private, college/university gift aid from institutional funds.

GIFT AID (NON-NEED-BASED) *Receiving aid:* Freshmen: 73% (88); Undergraduates: 96% (429). *Average Award:* Freshmen: $4000; Undergraduates: $4000. *Scholarships, grants, and awards by category: Academic Interests/Achievement:* 157 awards ($211,076 total). *Creative Arts/Performance:* art/fine arts, general creative arts/performance. *Special Achievements/Activities:* community service, general special achievements/activities, leadership, religious involvement. *Special Characteristics:* 137 awards ($167,195 total): children of current students, children of faculty/staff, first-generation college students, international students, religious affiliation, siblings of current students, spouses of current students, twins. *Tuition waivers:* Full or partial for employees or children of employees. *ROTC:* Army cooperative, Air Force cooperative.

LOANS *Student loans:* $2,773,401 (100% need-based). 90% of past graduating class borrowed through all loan programs. *Average indebtedness per student:* $17,500. *Average need-based loan:* Freshmen: $2625; Undergraduates: $3500. *Parent loans:* $86,591 (100% need-based). *Programs:* FFEL (Subsidized and Unsubsidized Stafford, PLUS), state, Private Loan Program.

APPLYING FOR FINANCIAL AID *Required financial aid forms:* FAFSA, institution's own form. *Financial aid deadline (priority):* 3/1. *Notification date:* 3/1. Students must reply within 3 weeks of notification.

CONTACT Sandy Turnquist, Director of Financial Aid, Finlandia University, 601 Quincy Street, Hancock, MI 49930, 906-487-7240 or toll-free 877-202-5491. *Fax:* 906-487-7509. *E-mail:* sandy.turnquist@finlandia.edu.

FISK UNIVERSITY
Nashville, TN

ABOUT THE INSTITUTION Independent religious, coed. Awards: bachelor's and master's degrees and post-bachelor's certificates. 25 undergraduate majors. Total enrollment: 880. Undergraduates: 850. Freshmen: 231.

GIFT AID (NEED-BASED) *Scholarships, grants, and awards:* Federal Pell, FSEOG, state, private, college/university gift aid from institutional funds, United Negro College Fund.

GIFT AID (NON-NEED-BASED) *Scholarships, grants, and awards by category: Academic Interests/Achievement:* general academic interests/achievements. *Special Characteristics:* children of faculty/staff.

LOANS *Programs:* Federal Direct (Subsidized and Unsubsidized Stafford, PLUS), Perkins.

WORK-STUDY *Federal work-study:* Total amount: $220,000; 167 jobs averaging $1323.

APPLYING FOR FINANCIAL AID *Required financial aid form:* FAFSA.

CONTACT Director of Financial Aid, Fisk University, 1000 17th Avenue North, Nashville, TN 37208-3051, 615-329-8585 or toll-free 800-443-FISK. *Fax:* 615-329-8774.

FITCHBURG STATE COLLEGE
Fitchburg, MA

ABOUT THE INSTITUTION State-supported, coed. Awards: bachelor's and master's degrees and post-bachelor's and post-master's certificates. 66 undergraduate majors. Total enrollment: 5,201. Undergraduates: 3,522. Freshmen: 721.

GIFT AID (NEED-BASED) *Scholarships, grants, and awards:* Federal Pell, FSEOG, state, private, college/university gift aid from institutional funds.

GIFT AID (NON-NEED-BASED) *Scholarships, grants, and awards by category: Academic Interests/Achievement:* biological sciences, business, communication, computer science, education, English, general academic interests/achievements, health fields, mathematics, social sciences. *Special Achievements/Activities:* general special achievements/activities, leadership. *Special Characteristics:* adult students, children and siblings of alumni.

LOANS *Programs:* Federal Direct (Subsidized and Unsubsidized Stafford, PLUS), Perkins, Federal Nursing, state.

WORK-STUDY *Federal work-study:* Total amount: $250,000; 225 jobs averaging $1200.

APPLYING FOR FINANCIAL AID *Required financial aid form:* FAFSA.

CONTACT Pamela McCafferty, Director of Financial Aid, Fitchburg State College, 160 Pearl Street, Fitchburg, MA 01420-2697, 978-665-3156 or toll-free 800-705-9692. *Fax:* 978-665-3559. *E-mail:* finaid@fsc.edu.

FIVE TOWNS COLLEGE
Dix Hills, NY

Tuition & fees: $14,100   **Average undergraduate aid package: $7400**

ABOUT THE INSTITUTION Independent, coed. Awards: associate, bachelor's, master's, and doctoral degrees. 19 undergraduate majors. Total enrollment: 1,162. Undergraduates: 1,105. Freshmen: 259. Federal methodology is used as a basis for awarding need-based institutional aid.

UNDERGRADUATE EXPENSES for 2005–06 *Application fee:* $25. *Comprehensive fee:* $24,350 includes full-time tuition ($14,100) and room and board ($10,250). Room and board charges vary according to board plan and location. *Part-time tuition:* $585 per credit. *Payment plan:* Installment.

FRESHMAN FINANCIAL AID (Fall 2004, est.) 331 applied for aid; of those 82% were deemed to have need. 100% of freshmen with need received aid; of those 15% had need fully met. *Average percent of need met:* 45% (excluding resources awarded to replace EFC). *Average financial aid package:* $6050 (excluding resources awarded to replace EFC). 4% of all full-time freshmen had no need and received non-need-based gift aid.

UNDERGRADUATE FINANCIAL AID (Fall 2004, est.) 916 applied for aid; of those 92% were deemed to have need. 100% of undergraduates with need received aid; of those 13% had need fully met. *Average percent of need met:* 45% (excluding resources awarded to replace EFC). *Average financial aid package:* $7400 (excluding resources awarded to replace EFC). 4% of all full-time undergraduates had no need and received non-need-based gift aid.

GIFT AID (NEED-BASED) *Total amount:* $3,627,305 (31% federal, 38% state, 29% institutional, 2% external sources). *Receiving aid:* Freshmen: 53% (219); All full-time undergraduates: 56% (685). *Average award:* Freshmen: $4000; Undergraduates: $3480. *Scholarships, grants, and awards:* Federal Pell, FSEOG, state, private, college/university gift aid from institutional funds.

GIFT AID (NON-NEED-BASED) *Receiving aid:* Freshmen: 29% (120); Undergraduates: 30% (360). *Average Award:* Freshmen: $3400; Undergraduates: $3400. *Scholarships, grants, and awards by category: Academic Interests/Achievement:* 400 awards ($1,004,708 total): business, education, general academic interests/achievements. *Creative Arts/Performance:* 25 awards ($53,550 total): cinema/film/broadcasting, music, theater/drama. *Tuition waivers:* Full or partial for employees or children of employees.

LOANS *Student loans:* $4,307,781 (46% need-based, 54% non-need-based). 77% of past graduating class borrowed through all loan programs. *Average indebtedness per student:* $15,100. *Average need-based loan:* Freshmen: $2500; Undergraduates: $2800. *Parent loans:* $3,079,110 (100% non-need-based). *Programs:* Federal Direct (Subsidized and Unsubsidized Stafford, PLUS).

WORK-STUDY *Federal work-study:* Total amount: $144,000; 115 jobs averaging $1250.

APPLYING FOR FINANCIAL AID *Required financial aid forms:* FAFSA, institution's own form, state aid form. *Financial aid deadline (priority):* 3/31. *Notification date:* Continuous beginning 5/1. Students must reply within 4 weeks of notification.

CONTACT Ms. Mary Venezia, Financial Aid/Director, Five Towns College, 305 North Service Road, Dix Hills, NY 11746-6055, 631-656-2113. *Fax:* 631-656-2191. *E-mail:* mvenezia@ftc.edu.

FLAGLER COLLEGE
St. Augustine, FL

Tuition & fees: $8600	Average undergraduate aid package: $7683

ABOUT THE INSTITUTION Independent, coed. Awards: bachelor's degrees. 28 undergraduate majors. Total enrollment: 2,106. Undergraduates: 2,106. Freshmen: 498. Federal methodology is used as a basis for awarding need-based institutional aid.

UNDERGRADUATE EXPENSES for 2005–06 *Application fee:* $30. *Comprehensive fee:* $13,790 includes full-time tuition ($8600) and room and board ($5190). *College room only:* $2130. *Part-time tuition:* $295 per credit hour.

FRESHMAN FINANCIAL AID (Fall 2004, est.) 371 applied for aid; of those 59% were deemed to have need. 100% of freshmen with need received aid; of those 19% had need fully met. *Average percent of need met:* 75% (excluding resources awarded to replace EFC). *Average financial aid package:* $10,122 (excluding resources awarded to replace EFC). 2% of all full-time freshmen had no need and received non-need-based gift aid.

UNDERGRADUATE FINANCIAL AID (Fall 2004, est.) 1,311 applied for aid; of those 65% were deemed to have need. 100% of undergraduates with need received aid; of those 21% had need fully met. *Average percent of need met:* 76% (excluding resources awarded to replace EFC). *Average financial aid package:* $7683 (excluding resources awarded to replace EFC). 3% of all full-time undergraduates had no need and received non-need-based gift aid.

GIFT AID (NEED-BASED) *Total amount:* $3,713,828 (27% federal, 65% state, 4% institutional, 4% external sources). *Receiving aid:* Freshmen: 22% (110); All full-time undergraduates: 22% (449). *Average award:* Freshmen: $2969; Undergraduates: $3021. *Scholarships, grants, and awards:* Federal Pell, FSEOG, state, private, college/university gift aid from institutional funds.

GIFT AID (NON-NEED-BASED) *Total amount:* $3,256,156 (89% state, 7% institutional, 4% external sources). *Receiving aid:* Freshmen: 32% (158); Undergraduates: 29% (598). *Average Award:* Freshmen: $4802; *Undergraduates:* $3244. *Scholarships, grants, and awards by category: Academic Interests/ Achievement:* 30 awards ($17,900 total): business, communication, education, English, foreign languages, general academic interests/achievements, religion/ biblical studies, social sciences. *Creative Arts/Performance:* 2 awards ($8800 total): applied art and design, art/fine arts, cinema/film/broadcasting, performing arts, theater/drama. *Special Achievements/Activities:* 75 awards ($272,037 total): general special achievements/activities, leadership, memberships, religious involvement. *Special Characteristics:* 49 awards ($138,310 total): children of faculty/staff, ethnic background, first-generation college students, general special characteristics, local/state students, members of minority groups, out-of-state students. *Tuition waivers:* Full or partial for employees or children of employees.

LOANS *Student loans:* $5,207,210 (69% need-based, 31% non-need-based). 55% of past graduating class borrowed through all loan programs. *Average indebtedness per student:* $15,012. *Average need-based loan:* Freshmen: $2483; Undergraduates: $3633. *Parent loans:* $1,207,338 (53% need-based, 47% non-need-based). *Programs:* Federal Direct (Subsidized and Unsubsidized Stafford, PLUS), Perkins.

WORK-STUDY *Federal work-study:* Total amount: $138,651; 188 jobs averaging $683. *State or other work-study/employment:* Total amount: $53,250 (19% need-based, 81% non-need-based). 65 part-time jobs averaging $631.

ATHLETIC AWARDS *Total amount:* $362,260 (36% need-based, 64% non-need-based).

APPLYING FOR FINANCIAL AID *Required financial aid forms:* FAFSA, institution's own form. *Financial aid deadline (priority):* 4/1. *Notification date:* Continuous. Students must reply within 2 weeks of notification.

CONTACT Ms. Sheia Pleasant, Assistant Director of Financial Aid, Flagler College, PO Box 1027, St. Augustine, FL 32085-1027, 904-819-6225 or toll-free 800-304-4208. *Fax:* 904-829-6838. *E-mail:* spleasant@flagler.edu.

FLORIDA AGRICULTURAL AND MECHANICAL UNIVERSITY
Tallahassee, FL

ABOUT THE INSTITUTION State-supported, coed. Awards: associate, bachelor's, master's, doctoral, and first professional degrees. 84 undergraduate majors. Total enrollment: 13,064. Undergraduates: 10,576. Freshmen: 2,001.

GIFT AID (NEED-BASED) *Scholarships, grants, and awards:* Federal Pell, FSEOG, state, private, college/university gift aid from institutional funds, United Negro College Fund, Federal Nursing.

GIFT AID (NON-NEED-BASED) *Scholarships, grants, and awards by category: Academic Interests/Achievement:* agriculture, business, engineering/technologies, general academic interests/achievements, health fields.

LOANS *Programs:* Federal Direct (Subsidized and Unsubsidized Stafford, PLUS), Perkins.

WORK-STUDY *Federal work-study:* Total amount: $642,028; 524 jobs averaging $1227.

APPLYING FOR FINANCIAL AID *Required financial aid form:* FAFSA.

CONTACT Bryan Terry, Director of Student Financial Aid, Florida Agricultural and Mechanical University, 101 Foote-Hilyer Administration Center, Tallahassee, FL 32307, 850-599-3730. *E-mail:* finaid@famu.edu.

FLORIDA ATLANTIC UNIVERSITY
Boca Raton, FL

Tuition & fees (FL res): $3092	Average undergraduate aid package: $6845

ABOUT THE INSTITUTION State-supported, coed. Awards: associate, bachelor's, master's, and doctoral degrees and post-master's certificates. 62 undergraduate majors. Total enrollment: 25,383. Undergraduates: 21,358. Freshmen: 2,778. Federal methodology is used as a basis for awarding need-based institutional aid.

UNDERGRADUATE EXPENSES for 2004–05 *Application fee:* $30. *Tuition, state resident:* full-time $3092; part-time $103.07 per credit hour. *Tuition, nonresident:* full-time $15,599; part-time $519.95 per credit hour. Full-time tuition and fees vary according to course load. Part-time tuition and fees vary according to course load. *College room and board:* $7100. Room and board charges vary according to board plan and housing facility. *Payment plans:* Tuition prepayment, installment, deferred payment.

FRESHMAN FINANCIAL AID (Fall 2004, est.) 1793 applied for aid; of those 56% were deemed to have need. 96% of freshmen with need received aid; of those 17% had need fully met. *Average percent of need met:* 82% (excluding resources awarded to replace EFC). *Average financial aid package:* $6657 (excluding resources awarded to replace EFC). 3% of all full-time freshmen had no need and received non-need-based gift aid.

UNDERGRADUATE FINANCIAL AID (Fall 2004, est.) 8,080 applied for aid; of those 68% were deemed to have need. 95% of undergraduates with need received aid; of those 15% had need fully met. *Average percent of need met:* 72% (excluding resources awarded to replace EFC). *Average financial aid package:* $6845 (excluding resources awarded to replace EFC). 3% of all full-time undergraduates had no need and received non-need-based gift aid.

GIFT AID (NEED-BASED) *Total amount:* $28,120,692 (47% federal, 40% state, 4% institutional, 9% external sources). *Receiving aid:* Freshmen: 40% (892); All full-time undergraduates: 39% (4,415). *Average award:* Freshmen: $5768; Undergraduates: $5086. *Scholarships, grants, and awards:* Federal Pell, FSEOG, state, private, college/university gift aid from institutional funds, Federal Nursing.

GIFT AID (NON-NEED-BASED) *Average Award:* Freshmen: $2028; *Undergraduates:* $2144. *Scholarships, grants, and awards by category: Academic Interests/ Achievement:* business, engineering/technologies, general academic interests/ achievements, physical sciences, social sciences. *Tuition waivers:* Full or partial for employees or children of employees, senior citizens. *ROTC:* Army cooperative, Air Force cooperative.

LOANS *Student loans:* $39,932,480 (52% need-based, 48% non-need-based). *Average need-based loan:* Freshmen: $2345; Undergraduates: $3687. *Parent loans:* $2,471,908 (100% non-need-based). *Programs:* FFEL (Subsidized and Unsubsidized Stafford, PLUS), Perkins, college/university.

WORK-STUDY *Federal work-study:* Total amount: $585,894; 173 jobs averaging $3387. *State or other work-study/employment:* Total amount: $35,722 (100% need-based). 8 part-time jobs averaging $4472.

ATHLETIC AWARDS *Total amount:* $2,727,722 (100% need-based).

APPLYING FOR FINANCIAL AID *Required financial aid form:* FAFSA. *Financial aid deadline (priority):* 3/1. *Notification date:* Continuous beginning 5/1. Students must reply within 3 weeks of notification.

CONTACT Carole Pfeilsticker, Director of Student Financial Aid, Florida Atlantic University, 777 Glades Road, Student Services Building, Room 227, Boca Raton, FL 33431-0991, 561-297-3528 or toll-free 800-299-4FAU. *E-mail:* pfeilsti@fau.edu.

Florida Christian College

FLORIDA CHRISTIAN COLLEGE
Kissimmee, FL

CONTACT Ms. Sandra Peppard, Director of Student Financial Aid, Florida Christian College, 1011 Bill Beck Boulevard, Kissimmee, FL 34744-5301, 407-847-8966 Ext. 365 or toll-free 888-GO-TO-FCC (in-state). *Fax:* 407-847-3925. *E-mail:* sandi.peppard@fcc.edu.

FLORIDA COLLEGE
Temple Terrace, FL

Tuition & fees: $10,310	Average undergraduate aid package: $6271

ABOUT THE INSTITUTION Independent, coed. Awards: associate and bachelor's degrees. 3 undergraduate majors. Total enrollment: 503. Undergraduates: 503. Freshmen: 233. Both federal and institutional methodology are used as a basis for awarding need-based institutional aid.

UNDERGRADUATE EXPENSES for 2004–05 *Application fee:* $25. *Comprehensive fee:* $15,550 includes full-time tuition ($10,010), mandatory fees ($300), and room and board ($5240). Room and board charges vary according to board plan and housing facility. *Part-time tuition:* $405 per semester hour. *Part-time fees:* $150 per term. *Payment plan:* Installment.

FRESHMAN FINANCIAL AID (Fall 2004, est.) 155 applied for aid; of those 100% were deemed to have need. 100% of freshmen with need received aid; of those 4% had need fully met. *Average percent of need met:* 36% (excluding resources awarded to replace EFC). *Average financial aid package:* $6078 (excluding resources awarded to replace EFC). 16% of all full-time freshmen had no need and received non-need-based gift aid.

UNDERGRADUATE FINANCIAL AID (Fall 2004, est.) 317 applied for aid; of those 100% were deemed to have need. 100% of undergraduates with need received aid; of those 6% had need fully met. *Average percent of need met:* 37% (excluding resources awarded to replace EFC). *Average financial aid package:* $6271 (excluding resources awarded to replace EFC). 21% of all full-time undergraduates had no need and received non-need-based gift aid.

GIFT AID (NEED-BASED) *Total amount:* $1,170,685 (26% federal, 2% state, 72% institutional). *Receiving aid:* Freshmen: 48% (115); All full-time undergraduates: 47% (231). *Average award:* Freshmen: $5121; Undergraduates: $3674. *Scholarships, grants, and awards:* Federal Pell, FSEOG, state, private, college/university gift aid from institutional funds.

GIFT AID (NON-NEED-BASED) *Total amount:* $1,052,134 (42% state, 46% institutional, 12% external sources). *Receiving aid:* Freshmen: 49% (117); Undergraduates: 48% (234). *Average Award:* Freshmen: $1754; Undergraduates: $2393. *Scholarships, grants, and awards by category:* Academic Interests/Achievement: 194 awards ($174,515 total): general academic interests/achievements. Creative Arts/Performance: 32 awards ($37,550 total): debating, journalism/publications, music, theater/drama. Special Characteristics: 41 awards ($235,563 total): children of educators, children of faculty/staff. *Tuition waivers:* Full or partial for employees or children of employees. *ROTC:* Army cooperative, Air Force cooperative.

LOANS *Student loans:* $1,230,271 (67% need-based, 33% non-need-based). 51% of past graduating class borrowed through all loan programs. *Average indebtedness per student:* $3259. *Average need-based loan:* Freshmen: $2675; Undergraduates: $3071. *Parent loans:* $1,121,485 (100% non-need-based). *Programs:* FFEL (Subsidized and Unsubsidized Stafford, PLUS), Perkins.

WORK-STUDY *Federal work-study:* Total amount: $19,404; 31 jobs averaging $451. *State or other work-study/employment:* Total amount: $76,417 (100% non-need-based). 50 part-time jobs averaging $290.

ATHLETIC AWARDS *Total amount:* $257,229 (100% non-need-based).

APPLYING FOR FINANCIAL AID *Required financial aid form:* FAFSA. *Financial aid deadline:* 8/1 (priority: 4/1). *Notification date:* Continuous. Students must reply within 2 weeks of notification.

CONTACT Peggy Sweeney, Financial Aid Office, Florida College, 119 North Glen Arven Avenue, Temple Terrace, FL 33617-5578, 813-849-6720 or toll-free 800-326-7655. *Fax:* 813-899-6772.

FLORIDA GULF COAST UNIVERSITY
Fort Myers, FL

Tuition & fees (FL res): $3151	Average undergraduate aid package: $7123

ABOUT THE INSTITUTION State-supported, coed. Awards: associate, bachelor's, and master's degrees. 23 undergraduate majors. Total enrollment: 5,955. Undergraduates: 4,959. Freshmen: 937. Federal methodology is used as a basis for awarding need-based institutional aid.

UNDERGRADUATE EXPENSES for 2004–05 *Application fee:* $30. *Tuition, state resident:* full-time $3056; part-time $102 per credit. *Tuition, nonresident:* full-time $15,152; part-time $505 per credit. *Required fees:* full-time $95; $95 per term part-time. Full-time tuition and fees vary according to course load. Part-time tuition and fees vary according to course load. *College room and board:* $8500; *room only:* $4420. Room and board charges vary according to board plan.

FRESHMAN FINANCIAL AID (Fall 2003) 699 applied for aid; of those 49% were deemed to have need. 100% of freshmen with need received aid; of those 16% had need fully met. *Average percent of need met:* 71% (excluding resources awarded to replace EFC). *Average financial aid package:* $6038 (excluding resources awarded to replace EFC). 40% of all full-time freshmen had no need and received non-need-based gift aid.

UNDERGRADUATE FINANCIAL AID (Fall 2003) 2,424 applied for aid; of those 56% were deemed to have need. 100% of undergraduates with need received aid; of those 20% had need fully met. *Average percent of need met:* 75% (excluding resources awarded to replace EFC). *Average financial aid package:* $7123 (excluding resources awarded to replace EFC). 27% of all full-time undergraduates had no need and received non-need-based gift aid.

GIFT AID (NEED-BASED) *Total amount:* $4,046,011 (70% federal, 13% state, 16% institutional, 1% external sources). *Receiving aid:* Freshmen: 26% (212); All full-time undergraduates: 28% (896). *Average award:* Freshmen: $3501; Undergraduates: $3648. *Scholarships, grants, and awards:* Federal Pell, FSEOG, state, private, college/university gift aid from institutional funds, Federal Work Study.

GIFT AID (NON-NEED-BASED) *Total amount:* $4,434,016 (70% state, 18% institutional, 12% external sources). *Receiving aid:* Freshmen: 33% (273); Undergraduates: 21% (681). *Average Award:* Freshmen: $2303; Undergraduates: $2267. *Scholarships, grants, and awards by category:* Academic Interests/Achievement: biological sciences, business, education, general academic interests/achievements, health fields, humanities, social sciences. *Tuition waivers:* Full or partial for employees or children of employees, senior citizens.

LOANS *Student loans:* $12,629,560 (57% need-based, 43% non-need-based). 43% of past graduating class borrowed through all loan programs. *Average indebtedness per student:* $13,472. *Average need-based loan:* Freshmen: $2448; Undergraduates: $4505. *Programs:* FFEL (Subsidized and Unsubsidized Stafford, PLUS), state.

WORK-STUDY *Federal work-study:* Total amount: $205,807; 123 jobs averaging $1673. *State or other work-study/employment:* Total amount: $1,292,046 (100% need-based). 334 part-time jobs averaging $3868.

ATHLETIC AWARDS *Total amount:* $391,625 (100% non-need-based).

APPLYING FOR FINANCIAL AID *Required financial aid forms:* FAFSA, state aid form. *Financial aid deadline:* 3/15 (priority: 2/1). *Notification date:* Continuous beginning 2/15. Students must reply within 4 weeks of notification.

CONTACT Ms. Lenore T. Benefield, Director of Student Financial Aid and Scholarships, Florida Gulf Coast University, 10501 FGCU Boulevard South, Fort Myers, FL 33965, 941-590-7048 or toll-free 888-889-1095. *Fax:* 941-590-7923. *E-mail:* lbenfie@fgcu.edu.

FLORIDA INSTITUTE OF TECHNOLOGY
Melbourne, FL

Tuition & fees: $23,730	Average undergraduate aid package: $20,548

ABOUT THE INSTITUTION Independent, coed. Awards: bachelor's, master's, and doctoral degrees and post-master's certificates. 48 undergraduate majors. Total enrollment: 4,683. Undergraduates: 2,319. Freshmen: 552. Federal methodology is used as a basis for awarding need-based institutional aid.

UNDERGRADUATE EXPENSES for 2004–05 *Application fee:* $50. *Comprehensive fee:* $29,950 includes full-time tuition ($23,730) and room and board ($6220). *College room only:* $3350. Full-time tuition and fees vary according to course load and program. Room and board charges vary according to board plan and housing facility. *Part-time tuition:* $730 per credit hour. Part-time tuition and fees vary according to course load and program. *Payment plan:* Installment.

FRESHMAN FINANCIAL AID (Fall 2004, est.) 540 applied for aid; of those 73% were deemed to have need. 100% of freshmen with need received aid; of those 31% had need fully met. *Average percent of need met:* 87% (excluding resources

awarded to replace EFC). *Average financial aid package:* $20,438 (excluding resources awarded to replace EFC). 26% of all full-time freshmen had no need and received non-need-based gift aid.

UNDERGRADUATE FINANCIAL AID (Fall 2004, est.) 1,984 applied for aid; of those 72% were deemed to have need. 100% of undergraduates with need received aid; of those 28% had need fully met. *Average percent of need met:* 84% (excluding resources awarded to replace EFC). *Average financial aid package:* $20,548 (excluding resources awarded to replace EFC). 23% of all full-time undergraduates had no need and received non-need-based gift aid.

GIFT AID (NEED-BASED) *Total amount:* $17,689,505 (14% federal, 14% state, 70% institutional, 2% external sources). *Receiving aid:* Freshmen: 62% (340); All full-time undergraduates: 56% (1,252). *Average award:* Freshmen: $15,260; Undergraduates: $13,837. *Scholarships, grants, and awards:* Federal Pell, FSEOG, state, private, college/university gift aid from institutional funds.

GIFT AID (NON-NEED-BASED) *Total amount:* $4,974,648 (13% federal, 10% state, 74% institutional, 3% external sources). *Receiving aid:* Freshmen: 69% (381); Undergraduates: 51% (1,130). *Average Award:* Freshmen: $6897; Undergraduates: $7059. *Scholarships, grants, and awards by category: Academic Interests/Achievement:* 1,417 awards ($9,351,253 total): general academic interests/achievements, military science. *Special Characteristics:* 256 awards ($1,482,932 total): children and siblings of alumni, children of faculty/staff, general special characteristics, previous college experience. *Tuition waivers:* Full or partial for employees or children of employees, senior citizens. *ROTC:* Army.

LOANS *Student loans:* $14,175,903 (89% need-based, 11% non-need-based). 57% of past graduating class borrowed through all loan programs. *Average indebtedness per student:* $26,764. *Average need-based loan:* Freshmen: $4245; Undergraduates: $4849. *Parent loans:* $2,622,384 (89% need-based, 11% non-need-based). *Programs:* FFEL (Subsidized and Unsubsidized Stafford, PLUS), Perkins, college/university, alternative loans.

WORK-STUDY *Federal work-study:* Total amount: $813,002; 553 jobs averaging $1470.

ATHLETIC AWARDS *Total amount:* $1,878,797 (61% need-based, 39% non-need-based).

APPLYING FOR FINANCIAL AID *Required financial aid forms:* FAFSA, state aid form. *Financial aid deadline (priority):* 3/15. *Notification date:* Continuous beginning 3/1. Students must reply by 5/1 or within 4 weeks of notification.

CONTACT Ann Munroe or Amanda Howell, Financial Aid Administrative Clerk, Florida Institute of Technology, 150 West University Boulevard, Melbourne, FL 32901-6975, 321-674-8070 or toll-free 800-888-4348. *Fax:* 321-724-2778. *E-mail:* dtouma@fit.edu.

FLORIDA INTERNATIONAL UNIVERSITY
Miami, FL

ABOUT THE INSTITUTION State-supported, coed. Awards: bachelor's, master's, doctoral, and first professional degrees. 91 undergraduate majors. Total enrollment: 34,865. Undergraduates: 28,865. Freshmen: 3,786.

GIFT AID (NEED-BASED) *Scholarships, grants, and awards:* Federal Pell, FSEOG, state, private, college/university gift aid from institutional funds.

GIFT AID (NON-NEED-BASED) *Scholarships, grants, and awards by category: Academic Interests/Achievement:* biological sciences, business, communication, computer science, education, engineering/technologies, English, foreign languages, general academic interests/achievements, health fields, humanities, mathematics, physical sciences, social sciences. *Creative Arts/Performance:* dance, journalism/publications, music, performing arts, theater/drama. *Special Characteristics:* children and siblings of alumni, members of minority groups.

LOANS *Programs:* FFEL (Subsidized and Unsubsidized Stafford, PLUS), Perkins, college/university.

APPLYING FOR FINANCIAL AID *Required financial aid form:* FAFSA.

CONTACT Maria A. Tolon, Associate Director, Financial Aid, Florida International University, University Park PC 125, Miami, FL 33199, 305-348-2340. *Fax:* 305-348-2346. *E-mail:* tolonm@fiu.edu.

FLORIDA MEMORIAL COLLEGE
Miami-Dade, FL

ABOUT THE INSTITUTION Independent religious, coed. Awards: bachelor's degrees. 22 undergraduate majors. Total enrollment: 2,161.

GIFT AID (NEED-BASED) *Scholarships, grants, and awards:* Federal Pell, FSEOG, state, private, college/university gift aid from institutional funds, United Negro College Fund.

GIFT AID (NON-NEED-BASED) *Scholarships, grants, and awards by category: Academic Interests/Achievement:* biological sciences, business, communication, computer science, education, engineering/technologies, English, mathematics, premedicine, social sciences. *Creative Arts/Performance:* music. *Special Achievements/Activities:* community service, leadership, religious involvement. *Special Characteristics:* children of faculty/staff.

LOANS *Programs:* Federal Direct (Subsidized and Unsubsidized Stafford, PLUS).

WORK-STUDY *Federal work-study:* Total amount: $327,061; 350 jobs averaging $1600. *State or other work-study/employment:* Total amount: $22,080 (100% non-need-based). Part-time jobs available (averaging $1200).

APPLYING FOR FINANCIAL AID *Required financial aid forms:* FAFSA, institution's own form, state aid form.

CONTACT Brian Phillip, Director of Financial Aid, Florida Memorial College, 15800 Northwest 42nd Avenue, Miami, FL 33054, 305-626-3745 or toll-free 800-822-1362. *Fax:* 305-626-3106.

FLORIDA METROPOLITAN UNIVERSITY–BRANDON CAMPUS
Tampa, FL

CONTACT Ms. Ginger Waymire, Director of Financial Aid, Florida Metropolitan University–Brandon Campus, 3924 Coconut Palm Drive, Tampa, FL 33619, 813-621-0041 Ext. 118 or toll-free 877-338-0068. *Fax:* 813-621-6283. *E-mail:* gwaymire@cci.edu.

FLORIDA METROPOLITAN UNIVERSITY–JACKSONVILLE CAMPUS
Jacksonville, FL

CONTACT Financial Aid Office, Florida Metropolitan University–Jacksonville Campus, 8226 Phillips Highway, Jacksonville, FL 32256, 904-731-4949 or toll-free 888-741-4271.

FLORIDA METROPOLITAN UNIVERSITY–LAKELAND CAMPUS
Lakeland, FL

CONTACT Brian Jones, Senior Finance Officer, Florida Metropolitan University–Lakeland Campus, Office of Financial Aid, 995 East Memorial Boulevard, Lakeland, FL 33801, 863-686-1444 Ext. 118 or toll-free 877-225-0014 (in-state). *Fax:* 863-682-1077.

FLORIDA METROPOLITAN UNIVERSITY–MELBOURNE CAMPUS
Melbourne, FL

CONTACT Ronda Nabb-Landolfi, Director of Student Financial Aid, Florida Metropolitan University–Melbourne Campus, 2401 North Harbor City Boulevard, Melbourne, FL 32935-6657, 321-253-2929 Ext. 19.

FLORIDA METROPOLITAN UNIVERSITY–NORTH ORLANDO CAMPUS
Orlando, FL

CONTACT Ms. Linda Kaisrlik, Director of Student Finance, Florida Metropolitan University–North Orlando Campus, 5421 Diplomat Circle, Orlando, FL 32810-5674, 407-628-5870 Ext. 118 or toll-free 800-628-5870.

FLORIDA METROPOLITAN UNIVERSITY–PINELLAS CAMPUS
Clearwater, FL

Tuition & fees: $11,430	Average undergraduate aid package: $7550

Florida Metropolitan University–Pinellas Campus

ABOUT THE INSTITUTION Proprietary, coed. Awards: associate, bachelor's, and master's degrees. 6 undergraduate majors. Total enrollment: 1,201. Undergraduates: 1,057. Federal methodology is used as a basis for awarding need-based institutional aid.

UNDERGRADUATE EXPENSES for 2004–05 *Application fee:* $25. *Tuition:* full-time $11,250.

FRESHMAN FINANCIAL AID (Fall 2004, est.) 432 applied for aid; of those 53% were deemed to have need. 100% of freshmen with need received aid. *Average percent of need met:* 85% (excluding resources awarded to replace EFC). *Average financial aid package:* $6675 (excluding resources awarded to replace EFC).

UNDERGRADUATE FINANCIAL AID (Fall 2004, est.) 981 applied for aid; of those 72% were deemed to have need. 100% of undergraduates with need received aid. *Average percent of need met:* 90% (excluding resources awarded to replace EFC). *Average financial aid package:* $7550 (excluding resources awarded to replace EFC).

GIFT AID (NEED-BASED) *Total amount:* $12,150 (33% federal, 5% state, 62% institutional). *Receiving aid:* Freshmen: 53% (227). *Average award:* Freshmen: $2700; Undergraduates: $2700. *Scholarships, grants, and awards:* Federal Pell, FSEOG, state, private, college/university gift aid from institutional funds.

GIFT AID (NON-NEED-BASED) *Total amount:* $7500 (100% institutional). *Receiving aid:* Freshmen: 53% (227); Undergraduates: 68% (704). *Scholarships, grants, and awards by category: Academic Interests/Achievement:* business, computer science, general academic interests/achievements, health fields.

LOANS *Student loans:* $11,369,000 (43% need-based, 57% non-need-based). 80% of past graduating class borrowed through all loan programs. *Average indebtedness per student:* $26,000. *Parent loans:* $35,000 (100% non-need-based). *Programs:* FFEL (Subsidized and Unsubsidized Stafford, PLUS), Signature Loans; career training; NLSC.

WORK-STUDY *Federal work-study:* Total amount: $60,000; 7 jobs averaging $8280.

APPLYING FOR FINANCIAL AID *Required financial aid form:* FAFSA. *Financial aid deadline:* Continuous. *Notification date:* Continuous.

CONTACT Ms. Rebeca Handsaker, Director of Student Finance, Florida Metropolitan University–Pinellas Campus, 2471 North McMullen Booth Road, Clearwater, FL 33759, 727-725-2688 Ext. 166 or toll-free 800-353-FMUS. *Fax:* 727-796-3406.

FLORIDA METROPOLITAN UNIVERSITY– POMPANO BEACH CAMPUS
Pompano Beach, FL

CONTACT Sharon Scheible, Director of Student Financial Aid, Florida Metropolitan University–Pompano Beach Campus, 1040 Bayview Drive, Fort Lauderdale, FL 33304-2522, 954-568-1600 Ext. 52 or toll-free 800-468-0168. *Fax:* 954-564-5283. *E-mail:* scheible@cci.edu.

FLORIDA METROPOLITAN UNIVERSITY– SOUTH ORLANDO CAMPUS
Orlando, FL

CONTACT Sherri Williams, Director of Financial Aid, Florida Metropolitan University–South Orlando Campus, 2411 Sand Lake Road, Orlando, FL 32809, 407-851-2525 or toll-free 407-851 Ext. 2525 (in-state), 866-508 Ext. 0007 (out-of-state).

FLORIDA METROPOLITAN UNIVERSITY– TAMPA CAMPUS
Tampa, FL

Tuition & fees: $9900	Average undergraduate aid package: $5000

ABOUT THE INSTITUTION Proprietary, coed. Awards: associate, bachelor's, and master's degrees. 10 undergraduate majors. Total enrollment: 1,390. Undergraduates: 1,281. Freshmen: 167. Federal methodology is used as a basis for awarding need-based institutional aid.

UNDERGRADUATE EXPENSES for 2005–06 *Application fee:* $25. *Tuition:* full-time $9720; part-time $270 per quarter hour. *Required fees:* full-time $180; $60 per term part-time. Full-time tuition and fees vary according to program. Part-time tuition and fees vary according to program. *Payment plan:* Installment.

FRESHMAN FINANCIAL AID (Fall 2004, est.) 315 applied for aid; of those 100% were deemed to have need. 100% of freshmen with need received aid; of those 71% had need fully met. *Average percent of need met:* 82% (excluding resources awarded to replace EFC). *Average financial aid package:* $5000 (excluding resources awarded to replace EFC).

UNDERGRADUATE FINANCIAL AID (Fall 2004, est.) 1,309 applied for aid; of those 100% were deemed to have need. 100% of undergraduates with need received aid; of those 73% had need fully met. *Average percent of need met:* 82% (excluding resources awarded to replace EFC). *Average financial aid package:* $5000 (excluding resources awarded to replace EFC).

GIFT AID (NEED-BASED) *Total amount:* $3,045,368 (97% federal, 3% state). *Receiving aid:* Freshmen: 78% (301); All full-time undergraduates: 82% (1,259). *Average award:* Freshmen: $1300; Undergraduates: $1500. *Scholarships, grants, and awards:* Federal Pell, FSEOG, state, private, college/university gift aid from institutional funds.

GIFT AID (NON-NEED-BASED) *Receiving aid:* Freshmen: 66% (255); Undergraduates: 70% (1,085). *Tuition waivers:* Full or partial for employees or children of employees.

LOANS *Student loans:* $8,790,164 (54% need-based, 46% non-need-based). 81% of past graduating class borrowed through all loan programs. *Average indebtedness per student:* $12,000. *Average need-based loan:* Freshmen: $2625; Undergraduates: $2625. *Parent loans:* $249,737 (100% non-need-based). *Programs:* FFEL (Subsidized and Unsubsidized Stafford, PLUS).

WORK-STUDY *Federal work-study:* Total amount: $76,000; 25 jobs averaging $4000.

APPLYING FOR FINANCIAL AID *Required financial aid form:* FAFSA. *Financial aid deadline:* Continuous. *Notification date:* Continuous.

CONTACT Mr. Rod Kirkwood, Financial Aid Director, Florida Metropolitan University–Tampa Campus, 3319 West Hillsborough Avenue, Tampa, FL 33614, 813-879-6000 Ext. 145. *Fax:* 813-871-2483. *E-mail:* rkirkwoo@cci.edu.

FLORIDA SOUTHERN COLLEGE
Lakeland, FL

Tuition & fees: $18,240	Average undergraduate aid package: $15,998

ABOUT THE INSTITUTION Independent religious, coed. Awards: bachelor's and master's degrees. 57 undergraduate majors. Total enrollment: 1,990. Undergraduates: 1,894. Freshmen: 572. Federal methodology is used as a basis for awarding need-based institutional aid.

UNDERGRADUATE EXPENSES for 2004–05 *Application fee:* $30. *Comprehensive fee:* $24,650 includes full-time tuition ($17,860), mandatory fees ($380), and room and board ($6410). *College room only:* $3550. Full-time tuition and fees vary according to student level. Room and board charges vary according to board plan and housing facility. *Part-time tuition:* $450 per credit hour. *Part-time fees:* $380 per year. *Payment plan:* Installment.

FRESHMAN FINANCIAL AID (Fall 2004, est.) 511 applied for aid; of those 80% were deemed to have need. 100% of freshmen with need received aid; of those 43% had need fully met. *Average percent of need met:* 73% (excluding resources awarded to replace EFC). *Average financial aid package:* $17,056 (excluding resources awarded to replace EFC). 18% of all full-time freshmen had no need and received non-need-based gift aid.

UNDERGRADUATE FINANCIAL AID (Fall 2004, est.) 1,602 applied for aid; of those 82% were deemed to have need. 99% of undergraduates with need received aid; of those 34% had need fully met. *Average percent of need met:* 66% (excluding resources awarded to replace EFC). *Average financial aid package:* $15,998 (excluding resources awarded to replace EFC). 15% of all full-time undergraduates had no need and received non-need-based gift aid.

GIFT AID (NEED-BASED) *Total amount:* $14,916,866 (11% federal, 31% state, 53% institutional, 5% external sources). *Receiving aid:* Freshmen: 67% (376); All full-time undergraduates: 66% (1,235). *Average award:* Freshmen: $13,385; Undergraduates: $11,885. *Scholarships, grants, and awards:* Federal Pell, FSEOG, state, private, college/university gift aid from institutional funds.

GIFT AID (NON-NEED-BASED) *Total amount:* $1,127,426 (12% state, 88% institutional). *Receiving aid:* Freshmen: 48% (270); Undergraduates: 37% (693). *Average Award:* Freshmen: $12,923; Undergraduates: $11,111. *Scholarships, grants, and awards by category: Academic Interests/Achievement:* 1,235 awards ($5,059,686 total): agriculture, biological sciences, business, communication, education, general academic interests/achievements, physical sciences, religion/biblical studies, social sciences. *Creative Arts/Performance:* 358 awards ($614,097 total): art/fine arts, music, theater/drama. *Special Achievements/Activities:* 1,065 awards ($2,076,204 total): community service, general special achievements/activities, leadership. *Special Characteristics:* 1,200 awards ($3,328,496 total): children and siblings of alumni, children of faculty/staff, general special characteristics, local/state students, out-of-state students, relatives of clergy, siblings of current students. *Tuition waivers:* Full or partial for children of alumni, employees or children of employees. *ROTC:* Army, Air Force cooperative.

LOANS *Student loans:* $5,036,917 (95% need-based, 5% non-need-based). 73% of past graduating class borrowed through all loan programs. *Average indebtedness per student:* $16,703. *Average need-based loan:* Freshmen: $4252; Undergraduates: $5032. *Programs:* Federal Direct (Subsidized and Unsubsidized Stafford, PLUS), FFEL (Subsidized Stafford), Perkins.

WORK-STUDY *Federal work-study:* Total amount: $472,034; 342 jobs averaging $1380. *State or other work-study/employment:* Total amount: $153,007 (73% need-based, 27% non-need-based). 69 part-time jobs averaging $1612.

ATHLETIC AWARDS *Total amount:* $1,423,613 (92% need-based, 8% non-need-based).

APPLYING FOR FINANCIAL AID *Required financial aid forms:* FAFSA, institution's own form. *Financial aid deadline:* 8/1 (priority: 4/1). *Notification date:* Continuous beginning 3/15.

CONTACT David M. Bodwell, Financial Aid Director, Florida Southern College, 111 Lake Hollingsworth Drive, Lakeland, FL 33801-5698, 863-680-4140 or toll-free 800-274-4131. *Fax:* 863-680-4567. *E-mail:* dbodwell@flsouthern.edu.

FLORIDA STATE UNIVERSITY
Tallahassee, FL

Tuition & fees (FL res): $3038	Average undergraduate aid package: $8269

ABOUT THE INSTITUTION State-supported, coed. Awards: associate, bachelor's, master's, doctoral, and first professional degrees and post-bachelor's and post-master's certificates. 170 undergraduate majors. Total enrollment: 38,431. Undergraduates: 30,373. Freshmen: 6,240. Federal methodology is used as a basis for awarding need-based institutional aid.

UNDERGRADUATE EXPENSES for 2004–05 *Application fee:* $30. *Tuition, state resident:* full-time $3038; part-time $101.25 per credit hour. *Tuition, nonresident:* full-time $15,544; part-time $518.13 per credit hour. Full-time tuition and fees vary according to location. Part-time tuition and fees vary according to location. *College room and board:* $7208; *room only:* $4170. Room and board charges vary according to board plan and housing facility. *Payment plans:* Tuition prepayment, installment.

FRESHMAN FINANCIAL AID (Fall 2004, est.) 4096 applied for aid; of those 61% were deemed to have need. 100% of freshmen with need received aid; of those 23% had need fully met. *Average percent of need met:* 75% (excluding resources awarded to replace EFC). *Average financial aid package:* $6884 (excluding resources awarded to replace EFC). 23% of all full-time freshmen had no need and received non-need-based gift aid.

UNDERGRADUATE FINANCIAL AID (Fall 2004, est.) 15,375 applied for aid; of those 72% were deemed to have need. 100% of undergraduates with need received aid; of those 31% had need fully met. *Average percent of need met:* 83% (excluding resources awarded to replace EFC). *Average financial aid package:* $8269 (excluding resources awarded to replace EFC). 13% of all full-time undergraduates had no need and received non-need-based gift aid.

GIFT AID (NEED-BASED) *Total amount:* $35,362,285 (58% federal, 11% state, 31% institutional). *Receiving aid:* Freshmen: 29% (1,821); All full-time undergraduates: 31% (8,325). *Average award:* Freshmen: $3749; Undergraduates: $3917. *Scholarships, grants, and awards:* Federal Pell, FSEOG, state, private, college/university gift aid from institutional funds.

GIFT AID (NON-NEED-BASED) *Total amount:* $33,176,704 (55% state, 32% institutional, 13% external sources). *Receiving aid:* Freshmen: 35% (2,179); Undergraduates: 26% (6,821). *Average Award:* Freshmen: $1941; Undergraduates: $2302. *Scholarships, grants, and awards by category: Academic Interests/Achievement:* general academic interests/achievements. *Creative Arts/Performance:* music. *Special Characteristics:* local/state students. *Tuition waivers:* Full or partial for employees or children of employees, senior citizens. *ROTC:* Army, Naval cooperative, Air Force.

LOANS *Student loans:* $69,845,459 (51% need-based, 49% non-need-based). 53% of past graduating class borrowed through all loan programs. *Average indebtedness per student:* $16,647. *Average need-based loan:* Freshmen: $2769; Undergraduates: $3939. *Parent loans:* $10,545,429 (100% non-need-based). *Programs:* FFEL (Subsidized and Unsubsidized Stafford, PLUS), Perkins, college/university.

WORK-STUDY *Federal work-study:* Total amount: $1,339,693; 710 jobs averaging $1887. *State or other work-study/employment:* Part-time jobs available.

ATHLETIC AWARDS *Total amount:* $4,199,846 (100% non-need-based).

APPLYING FOR FINANCIAL AID *Required financial aid form:* FAFSA. *Financial aid deadline (priority):* 2/15. *Notification date:* Continuous beginning 3/15. Students must reply within 2 weeks of notification.

CONTACT Darryl Marshall, Director of Financial Aid, Florida State University, University Center A4400, Tallahassee, FL 32306-2430, 850-644-5716. *Fax:* 850-644-6404. *E-mail:* ofacs@admin.fsu.edu.

FONTBONNE UNIVERSITY
St. Louis, MO

ABOUT THE INSTITUTION Independent Roman Catholic, coed. Awards: bachelor's and master's degrees and post-bachelor's certificates. 41 undergraduate majors. Total enrollment: 2,827. Undergraduates: 2,016. Freshmen: 200.

GIFT AID (NEED-BASED) *Scholarships, grants, and awards:* Federal Pell, FSEOG, state, private, college/university gift aid from institutional funds.

GIFT AID (NON-NEED-BASED) *Scholarships, grants, and awards by category: Academic Interests/Achievement:* computer science, English, general academic interests/achievements. *Creative Arts/Performance:* art/fine arts, creative writing, theater/drama. *Special Achievements/Activities:* community service, general special achievements/activities, leadership. *Special Characteristics:* religious affiliation, siblings of current students.

LOANS *Programs:* FFEL (Subsidized and Unsubsidized Stafford, PLUS), Perkins, CitiAssist Loans.

WORK-STUDY Federal work-study jobs available. *State or other work-study/employment:* Part-time jobs available.

APPLYING FOR FINANCIAL AID *Required financial aid forms:* FAFSA, institution's own form.

CONTACT Financial Aid Office, Fontbonne University, 6800 Wydown Boulevard, St. Louis, MO 63105-3098, 314-889-1414. *Fax:* 314-889-1451.

FORDHAM UNIVERSITY
New York, NY

Tuition & fees: $27,047	Average undergraduate aid package: $18,363

ABOUT THE INSTITUTION Independent Roman Catholic (Jesuit), coed. Awards: bachelor's, master's, doctoral, and first professional degrees and post-master's certificates (branch locations at Rose Hill and Lincoln Center). 94 undergraduate majors. Total enrollment: 14,861. Undergraduates: 7,394. Freshmen: 1,703. Both federal and institutional methodology are used as a basis for awarding need-based institutional aid.

UNDERGRADUATE EXPENSES for 2004–05 *Application fee:* $50. *Comprehensive fee:* $37,295 includes full-time tuition ($26,200), mandatory fees ($847), and room and board ($10,248). *College room only:* $6615. Room and board charges vary according to board plan, housing facility, and location. *Part-time tuition:* $875 per credit. *Part-time fees:* $40 per term. *Payment plans:* Tuition prepayment, installment.

FRESHMAN FINANCIAL AID (Fall 2003) 1352 applied for aid; of those 85% were deemed to have need. 99% of freshmen with need received aid; of those 23% had need fully met. *Average percent of need met:* 80% (excluding resources awarded to replace EFC). *Average financial aid package:* $19,464 (excluding resources awarded to replace EFC). 9% of all full-time freshmen had no need and received non-need-based gift aid.

UNDERGRADUATE FINANCIAL AID (Fall 2003) 4,969 applied for aid; of those 89% were deemed to have need. 99% of undergraduates with need received aid; of those 23% had need fully met. *Average percent of need met:* 76% (excluding resources awarded to replace EFC). *Average financial aid package:* $18,363 (excluding resources awarded to replace EFC). 8% of all full-time undergraduates had no need and received non-need-based gift aid.

GIFT AID (NEED-BASED) *Total amount:* $53,933,672 (11% federal, 12% state, 74% institutional, 3% external sources). *Receiving aid:* Freshmen: 63% (1,077); All full-time undergraduates: 62% (4,136). *Average award:* Freshmen: $16,052; Undergraduates: $13,771. *Scholarships, grants, and awards:* Federal Pell, FSEOG, state, private, college/university gift aid from institutional funds.

GIFT AID (NON-NEED-BASED) *Total amount:* $6,045,522 (1% state, 79% institutional, 20% external sources). *Receiving aid:* Freshmen: 4% (75); Undergraduates: 4% (277). *Average Award:* Freshmen: $6831; Undergraduates: $8276. *Scholarships, grants, and awards by category: Academic Interests/Achievement:* communication, foreign languages, general academic interests/

Fordham University

achievements. *Creative Arts/Performance:* music. *Special Achievements/Activities:* general special achievements/activities. *Special Characteristics:* children and siblings of alumni, children of faculty/staff, children of union members/company employees, children with a deceased or disabled parent, handicapped students, veterans, veterans' children. *ROTC:* Army, Naval cooperative, Air Force cooperative.

LOANS *Student loans:* $29,593,925 (68% need-based, 32% non-need-based). 66% of past graduating class borrowed through all loan programs. *Average indebtedness per student:* $16,590. *Average need-based loan:* Freshmen: $2792; Undergraduates: $4262. *Parent loans:* $13,896,187 (37% need-based, 63% non-need-based). *Programs:* FFEL (Subsidized and Unsubsidized Stafford, PLUS), Perkins.

WORK-STUDY *Federal work-study:* Total amount: $3,593,219; jobs available. *State or other work-study/employment:* Total amount: $858,861 (45% need-based, 55% non-need-based). Part-time jobs available.

ATHLETIC AWARDS *Total amount:* $4,944,969 (67% need-based, 33% non-need-based).

APPLYING FOR FINANCIAL AID *Required financial aid forms:* FAFSA, CSS Financial Aid PROFILE, noncustodial (divorced/separated) parent's statement, business/farm supplement. *Financial aid deadline (priority):* 2/1. *Notification date:* 4/1. Students must reply by 5/1 or within 2 weeks of notification.

CONTACT Calvin Brian Ghanoo, Senior Associate Director of Student Financial Services, Fordham University, 441 East Fordham Road, Thebaud Hall, New York, NY 10458, 718-817-3800 or toll-free 800-FORDHAM. *E-mail:* ghanoo@fordham.edu.

FORT HAYS STATE UNIVERSITY
Hays, KS

Tuition & fees (KS res): $3217	Average undergraduate aid package: $5542

ABOUT THE INSTITUTION State-supported, coed. Awards: associate, bachelor's, and master's degrees and post-master's certificates. 55 undergraduate majors. Total enrollment: 7,373. Undergraduates: 5,920. Freshmen: 904. Federal methodology is used as a basis for awarding need-based institutional aid.

UNDERGRADUATE EXPENSES for 2004–05 *Application fee:* $30. *Tuition, state resident:* full-time $2585; part-time $96.70 per credit hour. *Tuition, nonresident:* full-time $8709; part-time $300.85 per credit hour. Full-time tuition and fees vary according to course load, location, and reciprocity agreements. Part-time tuition and fees vary according to course load and location. *College room and board:* $5061; *room only:* $2572. Room and board charges vary according to board plan, housing facility, and student level. *Payment plan:* Installment.

FRESHMAN FINANCIAL AID (Fall 2003) 601 applied for aid; of those 78% were deemed to have need. 100% of freshmen with need received aid; of those 29% had need fully met. *Average percent of need met:* 73% (excluding resources awarded to replace EFC). *Average financial aid package:* $5180 (excluding resources awarded to replace EFC). 35% of all full-time freshmen had no need and received non-need-based gift aid.

UNDERGRADUATE FINANCIAL AID (Fall 2003) 2,902 applied for aid; of those 82% were deemed to have need. 100% of undergraduates with need received aid; of those 28% had need fully met. *Average percent of need met:* 72% (excluding resources awarded to replace EFC). *Average financial aid package:* $5542 (excluding resources awarded to replace EFC). 29% of all full-time undergraduates had no need and received non-need-based gift aid.

GIFT AID (NEED-BASED) *Total amount:* $6,350,146 (68% federal, 7% state, 7% institutional, 18% external sources). *Receiving aid:* Freshmen: 54% (439); All full-time undergraduates: 55% (1,994). *Average award:* Freshmen: $3361; Undergraduates: $3015. *Scholarships, grants, and awards:* Federal Pell, FSEOG, state, private, college/university gift aid from institutional funds.

GIFT AID (NON-NEED-BASED) *Total amount:* $1,169,484 (1% federal, 28% institutional, 71% external sources). *Receiving aid:* Freshmen: 5% (43); Undergraduates: 4% (137). *Average Award:* Freshmen: $2125; *Undergraduates:* $2749. *Scholarships, grants, and awards by category: Academic Interests/Achievement:* agriculture, biological sciences, business, communication, computer science, education, engineering/technologies, English, foreign languages, general academic interests/achievements, health fields, humanities, international studies, library science, mathematics, physical sciences, premedicine, social sciences. *Creative Arts/Performance:* applied art and design, art/fine arts, cinema/film/broadcasting, creative writing, debating, journalism/publications, music, performing arts, theater/drama. *Special Achievements/Activities:* cheerleading/drum major, rodeo. *Special Characteristics:* adult students, members of minority groups. *Tuition waivers:* Full or partial for senior citizens.

LOANS *Student loans:* $12,907,336 (72% need-based, 28% non-need-based). 46% of past graduating class borrowed through all loan programs. *Average indebtedness per student:* $15,061. *Average need-based loan:* Freshmen: $2201; Undergraduates: $3160. *Parent loans:* $204,010 (18% need-based, 82% non-need-based). *Programs:* FFEL (Subsidized and Unsubsidized Stafford, PLUS), Perkins, state, college/university.

WORK-STUDY *Federal work-study:* Total amount: $636,781; 400 jobs available. *State or other work-study/employment:* Total amount: $94,962 (27% need-based, 73% non-need-based). Part-time jobs available.

ATHLETIC AWARDS *Total amount:* $877,734 (47% need-based, 53% non-need-based).

APPLYING FOR FINANCIAL AID *Required financial aid forms:* FAFSA, state aid form. *Financial aid deadline (priority):* 3/15. *Notification date:* Continuous beginning 4/1. Students must reply within 2 weeks of notification.

CONTACT Craig Karlin, Director of Financial Assistance, Fort Hays State University, Custer Hall, Room 306, 600 Park Street, Hays, KS 67601, 785-628-4408 or toll-free 800-628-FHSU. *Fax:* 785-628-4014. *E-mail:* finaid@bigcat.fhsu.edu.

FORT LEWIS COLLEGE
Durango, CO

Tuition & fees (CO res): $3060	Average undergraduate aid package: $7956

ABOUT THE INSTITUTION State-supported, coed. Awards: bachelor's degrees. 54 undergraduate majors. Total enrollment: 4,190. Undergraduates: 4,190. Freshmen: 990. Federal methodology is used as a basis for awarding need-based institutional aid.

UNDERGRADUATE EXPENSES for 2004–05 *Application fee:* $30. *Tuition, state resident:* full-time $2270; part-time $113 per credit hour. *Tuition, nonresident:* full-time $11,862; part-time $593 per credit hour. *Required fees:* full-time $790; $43.50 per credit hour. Full-time tuition and fees vary according to reciprocity agreements. Part-time tuition and fees vary according to course load and reciprocity agreements. *College room and board:* $5894; *room only:* $3104. Room and board charges vary according to board plan and housing facility.

FRESHMAN FINANCIAL AID (Fall 2003) 575 applied for aid; of those 74% were deemed to have need. 97% of freshmen with need received aid; of those 19% had need fully met. *Average percent of need met:* 64% (excluding resources awarded to replace EFC). *Average financial aid package:* $6206 (excluding resources awarded to replace EFC). 5% of all full-time freshmen had no need and received non-need-based gift aid.

UNDERGRADUATE FINANCIAL AID (Fall 2003) 2,275 applied for aid; of those 81% were deemed to have need. 98% of undergraduates with need received aid; of those 18% had need fully met. *Average percent of need met:* 52% (excluding resources awarded to replace EFC). *Average financial aid package:* $7956 (excluding resources awarded to replace EFC). 4% of all full-time undergraduates had no need and received non-need-based gift aid.

GIFT AID (NEED-BASED) *Total amount:* $6,435,143 (55% federal, 15% state, 1% institutional, 29% external sources). *Receiving aid:* Freshmen: 25% (228); All full-time undergraduates: 30% (1,127). *Average award:* Freshmen: $3410; Undergraduates: $3906. *Scholarships, grants, and awards:* Federal Pell, FSEOG, state, private, college/university gift aid from institutional funds.

GIFT AID (NON-NEED-BASED) *Total amount:* $9,494,453 (11% federal, 73% state, 2% institutional, 14% external sources). *Receiving aid:* Freshmen: 17% (154); Undergraduates: 16% (597). *Average Award:* Freshmen: $1528; *Undergraduates:* $1534. *Scholarships, grants, and awards by category: Academic Interests/Achievement:* 286 awards ($368,362 total): agriculture, area/ethnic studies, biological sciences, business, communication, computer science, education, English, general academic interests/achievements, humanities, mathematics, physical sciences, social sciences. *Creative Arts/Performance:* 41 awards ($23,010 total): art/fine arts, music, performing arts, theater/drama. *Special Achievements/Activities:* 41 awards ($56,173 total): general special achievements/activities, leadership. *Special Characteristics:* 149 awards ($197,138 total): children of faculty/staff, ethnic background, first-generation college students, general special characteristics, international students, local/state students, out-of-state students, veterans' children. *Tuition waivers:* Full or partial for minority students, employees or children of employees.

LOANS *Student loans:* $12,693,126 (70% need-based, 30% non-need-based). 58% of past graduating class borrowed through all loan programs. *Average indebtedness per student:* $14,100. *Average need-based loan:* Freshmen: $3337; Undergraduates: $4273. *Parent loans:* $1,583,246 (62% need-based, 38% non-need-based). *Programs:* FFEL (Subsidized and Unsubsidized Stafford, PLUS), Perkins, college/university.

WORK-STUDY *Federal work-study:* Total amount: $280,641; 170 jobs averaging $2500. *State or other work-study/employment:* Total amount: $764,425 (31% need-based, 69% non-need-based). 174 part-time jobs averaging $2500.
ATHLETIC AWARDS *Total amount:* $249,006 (5% need-based, 95% non-need-based).
APPLYING FOR FINANCIAL AID *Required financial aid form:* FAFSA. *Financial aid deadline:* Continuous. *Notification date:* Continuous beginning 4/1. Students must reply within 2 weeks of notification.
CONTACT Ms. Elaine Redwine, Director of Financial Aid, Fort Lewis College, 1000 Rim Drive, Durango, CO 81301-3999, 970-247-7464. *Fax:* 970-247-7108. *E-mail:* redwine_e@fortlewis.edu.

FORT VALLEY STATE UNIVERSITY
Fort Valley, GA

CONTACT Financial Aid Director, Fort Valley State University, PO Box 4129, Fort Valley, GA 31030-3298, 478-825-6182 or toll-free 800-248-7343. *Fax:* 478-825-6976.

FRAMINGHAM STATE COLLEGE
Framingham, MA

Tuition & fees (MA res): $4740 **Average undergraduate aid package: $6345**

ABOUT THE INSTITUTION State-supported, coed. Awards: bachelor's and master's degrees and post-bachelor's certificates. 89 undergraduate majors. Total enrollment: 6,015. Undergraduates: 3,873. Freshmen: 654. Federal methodology is used as a basis for awarding need-based institutional aid.
UNDERGRADUATE EXPENSES for 2004–05 *Application fee:* $25. *Tuition, state resident:* full-time $970; part-time $210 per credit. *Tuition, nonresident:* full-time $7050; part-time $463 per credit. *Required fees:* full-time $3770; $156 per credit. Full-time tuition and fees vary according to class time. Part-time tuition and fees vary according to class time and course load. *College room and board:* $5539. Room and board charges vary according to board plan and housing facility. *Payment plan:* Installment.
FRESHMAN FINANCIAL AID (Fall 2004, est.) 591 applied for aid; of those 62% were deemed to have need. 99% of freshmen with need received aid; of those 18% had need fully met. *Average percent of need met:* 80% (excluding resources awarded to replace EFC). *Average financial aid package:* $6670 (excluding resources awarded to replace EFC). 45% of all full-time freshmen had no need and received non-need-based gift aid.
UNDERGRADUATE FINANCIAL AID (Fall 2004, est.) 2,069 applied for aid; of those 69% were deemed to have need. 98% of undergraduates with need received aid; of those 36% had need fully met. *Average percent of need met:* 82% (excluding resources awarded to replace EFC). *Average financial aid package:* $6345 (excluding resources awarded to replace EFC). 25% of all full-time undergraduates had no need and received non-need-based gift aid.
GIFT AID (NEED-BASED) *Total amount:* $4,040,000 (38% federal, 48% state, 9% institutional, 5% external sources). *Receiving aid:* Freshmen: 47% (304); All full-time undergraduates: 38% (1,140). *Average award:* Freshmen: $3527; Undergraduates: $3450. *Scholarships, grants, and awards:* Federal Pell, FSEOG, state, college/university gift aid from institutional funds, Federal Nursing.
GIFT AID (NON-NEED-BASED) *Total amount:* $447,000 (20% state, 46% institutional, 34% external sources). *Receiving aid:* Freshmen: 1% (5); Undergraduates: 1% (18). *Average Award:* Freshmen: $3553; Undergraduates: $4861. *Scholarships, grants, and awards by category: Academic Interests/Achievement:* biological sciences, education, general academic interests/achievements, home economics, physical sciences. *Special Characteristics:* children of faculty/staff, children of public servants, children of union members/company employees, local/state students, veterans. *Tuition waivers:* Full or partial for employees or children of employees, senior citizens. *ROTC:* Army.
LOANS *Student loans:* $9,500,000 (56% need-based, 44% non-need-based). 65% of past graduating class borrowed through all loan programs. *Average indebtedness per student:* $11,000. *Average need-based loan:* Freshmen: $3135; Undergraduates: $3420. *Parent loans:* $1,561,000 (18% need-based, 82% non-need-based). *Programs:* Federal Direct (Subsidized and Unsubsidized Stafford, PLUS), FFEL (Subsidized and Unsubsidized Stafford, PLUS), Perkins, Federal Nursing, state, college/university.
WORK-STUDY *Federal work-study:* Total amount: $340,000; jobs available.
APPLYING FOR FINANCIAL AID *Required financial aid form:* FAFSA. *Financial aid deadline (priority):* 3/1. *Notification date:* 4/15. Students must reply within 2 weeks of notification.

CONTACT Financial Aid Office, Framingham State College, 100 State Street, PO Box 9101, Framingham, MA 01701-9101, 508-626-4534. *Fax:* 508-626-4598.

FRANCISCAN UNIVERSITY OF STEUBENVILLE
Steubenville, OH

ABOUT THE INSTITUTION Independent Roman Catholic, coed. Awards: associate, bachelor's, and master's degrees. 32 undergraduate majors. Total enrollment: 2,374. Undergraduates: 1,913. Freshmen: 377.
GIFT AID (NEED-BASED) *Scholarships, grants, and awards:* Federal Pell, FSEOG, state, private, college/university gift aid from institutional funds.
GIFT AID (NON-NEED-BASED) *Scholarships, grants, and awards by category: Academic Interests/Achievement:* general academic interests/achievements. *Special Achievements/Activities:* religious involvement. *Special Characteristics:* children of faculty/staff, international students, local/state students, siblings of current students.
LOANS *Programs:* FFEL (Subsidized and Unsubsidized Stafford, PLUS), Perkins, alternative loans.
WORK-STUDY *Federal work-study:* Total amount: $148,694; 300 jobs averaging $795. *State or other work-study/employment:* Total amount: $933,998 (89% need-based, 11% non-need-based). 577 part-time jobs averaging $1729.
APPLYING FOR FINANCIAL AID *Required financial aid form:* FAFSA.
CONTACT John Herrmann, Director of Student Financial Services, Franciscan University of Steubenville, 1235 University Boulevard, Steubenville, OH 43952-1763, 740-283-6211 or toll-free 800-783-6220. *Fax:* 740-284-5469. *E-mail:* jherrmann@franciscan.edu.

THE FRANCISCAN UNIVERSITY OF THE PRAIRIES
Clinton, IA

ABOUT THE INSTITUTION Independent Roman Catholic, coed. Awards: bachelor's and master's degrees. 32 undergraduate majors. Total enrollment: 459. Undergraduates: 391. Freshmen: 52.
GIFT AID (NEED-BASED) *Scholarships, grants, and awards:* Federal Pell, FSEOG, state, private, college/university gift aid from institutional funds.
GIFT AID (NON-NEED-BASED) *Scholarships, grants, and awards by category: Academic Interests/Achievement:* biological sciences, business, communication, computer science, education, English, general academic interests/achievements, health fields, humanities, mathematics, physical sciences, premedicine, religion/biblical studies, social sciences. *Creative Arts/Performance:* art/fine arts, general creative arts/performance, music. *Special Achievements/Activities:* community service, leadership, religious involvement. *Special Characteristics:* children and siblings of alumni, children of current students, children of faculty/staff, international students, local/state students, parents of current students, relatives of clergy, siblings of current students, spouses of current students, twins.
LOANS *Programs:* FFEL (Subsidized and Unsubsidized Stafford, PLUS), Perkins, state.
WORK-STUDY *Federal work-study:* Total amount: $123,047; jobs available. *State or other work-study/employment:* Total amount: $18,230 (100% non-need-based). Part-time jobs available.
APPLYING FOR FINANCIAL AID *Required financial aid form:* FAFSA.
CONTACT Lisa Kramer, Director of Financial Aid, The Franciscan University of the Prairies, 400 North Bluff Boulevard, PO Box 2967, Clinton, IA 52733-2967, 563-242-4023 Ext. 1243 or toll-free 800-242-4153. *Fax:* 563-242-8684.

FRANCIS MARION UNIVERSITY
Florence, SC

Tuition & fees (SC res): $5540 **Average undergraduate aid package: N/A**

ABOUT THE INSTITUTION State-supported, coed. Awards: bachelor's and master's degrees. 29 undergraduate majors. Total enrollment: 3,698. Undergraduates: 3,227. Freshmen: 746. Federal methodology is used as a basis for awarding need-based institutional aid.
UNDERGRADUATE EXPENSES for 2004–05 *Application fee:* $30. *Tuition, state resident:* full-time $5405; part-time $270 per credit hour. *Tuition, nonresident:* full-time $10,810; part-time $540 per credit hour. *Required fees:* full-time

Francis Marion University

$135; $2 per credit hour. Part-time tuition and fees vary according to course load. *College room and board:* $4656; *room only:* $2500. Room and board charges vary according to board plan and housing facility. *Payment plan:* Installment.

FRESHMAN FINANCIAL AID (Fall 2003) 540 applied for aid.

UNDERGRADUATE FINANCIAL AID (Fall 2003) 1,848 applied for aid.

GIFT AID (NEED-BASED) *Total amount:* $4,240,945 (90% federal, 10% state). *Scholarships, grants, and awards:* Federal Pell, FSEOG, state, private.

GIFT AID (NON-NEED-BASED) *Total amount:* $5,751,063 (76% state, 13% institutional, 11% external sources). *Scholarships, grants, and awards by category:* Academic Interests/Achievement: biological sciences, business, education, English, general academic interests/achievements, health fields, humanities, mathematics, premedicine, social sciences. *Creative Arts/Performance:* art/fine arts, music, theater/drama. *Special Achievements/Activities:* cheerleading/drum major. *Special Characteristics:* adult students, children and siblings of alumni, children of faculty/staff, handicapped students, international students, out-of-state students, spouses of deceased or disabled public servants, veterans, veterans' children. *Tuition waivers:* Full or partial for employees or children of employees, senior citizens.

LOANS *Student loans:* $12,059,338 (53% need-based, 47% non-need-based). *Average indebtedness per student:* $22,311. *Parent loans:* $549,429 (100% non-need-based). *Programs:* FFEL (Subsidized and Unsubsidized Stafford, PLUS), Perkins, state.

WORK-STUDY *Federal work-study:* Total amount: $181,907; 131 jobs averaging $1388. *State or other work-study/employment:* Total amount: $528,894 (100% non-need-based). Part-time jobs available.

ATHLETIC AWARDS *Total amount:* $398,400 (100% non-need-based).

APPLYING FOR FINANCIAL AID *Required financial aid forms:* FAFSA, institution's own form. *Financial aid deadline (priority):* 3/1. *Notification date:* 4/1.

CONTACT Kim Ellisor, Director of Financial Assistance, Francis Marion University, PO Box 100547, Florence, SC 29501-0547, 843-661-1190 or toll-free 800-368-7551.

FRANKLIN AND MARSHALL COLLEGE
Lancaster, PA

Tuition & fees: $30,440	Average undergraduate aid package: $23,456

ABOUT THE INSTITUTION Independent, coed. Awards: bachelor's degrees. 38 undergraduate majors. Total enrollment: 1,972. Undergraduates: 1,972. Freshmen: 531. Both federal and institutional methodology are used as a basis for awarding need-based institutional aid.

UNDERGRADUATE EXPENSES for 2004–05 *Application fee:* $50. *Comprehensive fee:* $37,980 includes full-time tuition ($30,390), mandatory fees ($50), and room and board ($7540). *College room only:* $4910. Full-time tuition and fees vary according to reciprocity agreements. Room and board charges vary according to board plan and housing facility. *Part-time tuition:* $3800 per course. Part-time tuition and fees vary according to course load. *Payment plans:* Installment, deferred payment.

FRESHMAN FINANCIAL AID (Fall 2004, est.) 318 applied for aid; of those 70% were deemed to have need. 100% of freshmen with need received aid; of those 99% had need fully met. *Average percent of need met:* 100% (excluding resources awarded to replace EFC). *Average financial aid package:* $22,282 (excluding resources awarded to replace EFC). 24% of all full-time freshmen had no need and received non-need-based gift aid.

UNDERGRADUATE FINANCIAL AID (Fall 2004, est.) 1,450 applied for aid; of those 53% were deemed to have need. 100% of undergraduates with need received aid; of those 100% had need fully met. *Average percent of need met:* 100% (excluding resources awarded to replace EFC). *Average financial aid package:* $23,456 (excluding resources awarded to replace EFC). 22% of all full-time undergraduates had no need and received non-need-based gift aid.

GIFT AID (NEED-BASED) *Total amount:* $14,091,080 (5% federal, 4% state, 91% institutional). *Receiving aid:* Freshmen: 41% (216); All full-time undergraduates: 37% (724). *Average award:* Freshmen: $17,107; Undergraduates: $17,506. *Scholarships, grants, and awards:* Federal Pell, FSEOG, state, private, college/university gift aid from institutional funds.

GIFT AID (NON-NEED-BASED) *Total amount:* $4,217,831 (83% institutional, 17% external sources). *Receiving aid:* Freshmen: 22% (118); Undergraduates: 17% (327). *Average Award:* Freshmen: $9465; Undergraduates: $8891. *Scholarships, grants, and awards by category:* Academic Interests/Achievement: 640

awards ($5,637,500 total): general academic interests/achievements. *Creative Arts/Performance:* 8 awards ($20,000 total): music. *Tuition waivers:* Full or partial for employees or children of employees.

LOANS *Student loans:* $6,668,138 (47% need-based, 53% non-need-based). 40% of past graduating class borrowed through all loan programs. *Average indebtedness per student:* $18,625. *Average need-based loan:* Freshmen: $3625; Undergraduates: $4281. *Parent loans:* $4,800,000 (100% non-need-based). *Programs:* FFEL (Subsidized and Unsubsidized Stafford, PLUS), Perkins, college/university.

WORK-STUDY *Federal work-study:* Total amount: $350,000; jobs available (averaging $1400). *State or other work-study/employment:* Total amount: $800,000 (100% non-need-based). Part-time jobs available.

APPLYING FOR FINANCIAL AID *Required financial aid forms:* FAFSA, institution's own form, CSS Financial Aid PROFILE, noncustodial (divorced/separated) parent's statement, business/farm supplement, federal income tax form(s), W-2 forms. *Financial aid deadline:* 3/1 (priority: 2/1). *Notification date:* 4/1. Students must reply by 5/1.

CONTACT Mr. Christopher K. Hanlon, Director of Student Aid, Franklin and Marshall College, PO Box 3003, Lancaster, PA 17604-3003, 717-291-3991. *Fax:* 717-291-4389. *E-mail:* c_hanlon@admin.fandm.edu.

FRANKLIN COLLEGE
Franklin, IN

Tuition & fees: $18,275	Average undergraduate aid package: $12,933

ABOUT THE INSTITUTION Independent religious, coed. Awards: bachelor's degrees. 32 undergraduate majors. Total enrollment: 994. Undergraduates: 994. Freshmen: 276. Federal methodology is used as a basis for awarding need-based institutional aid.

UNDERGRADUATE EXPENSES for 2004–05 *Application fee:* $30. *Comprehensive fee:* $23,775 includes full-time tuition ($18,100), mandatory fees ($175), and room and board ($5500). *College room only:* $3210. Room and board charges vary according to board plan and housing facility. Part-time tuition and fees vary according to course load. *Payment plan:* Installment.

FRESHMAN FINANCIAL AID (Fall 2003) 275 applied for aid; of those 89% were deemed to have need. 100% of freshmen with need received aid; of those 23% had need fully met. *Average percent of need met:* 87% (excluding resources awarded to replace EFC). *Average financial aid package:* $12,549 (excluding resources awarded to replace EFC). 16% of all full-time freshmen had no need and received non-need-based gift aid.

UNDERGRADUATE FINANCIAL AID (Fall 2003) 929 applied for aid; of those 89% were deemed to have need. 100% of undergraduates with need received aid; of those 20% had need fully met. *Average percent of need met:* 85% (excluding resources awarded to replace EFC). *Average financial aid package:* $12,933 (excluding resources awarded to replace EFC). 17% of all full-time undergraduates had no need and received non-need-based gift aid.

GIFT AID (NEED-BASED) *Total amount:* $8,369,741 (10% federal, 25% state, 61% institutional, 4% external sources). *Receiving aid:* Freshmen: 84% (244); All full-time undergraduates: 82% (821). *Average award:* Freshmen: $9905; Undergraduates: $10,086. *Scholarships, grants, and awards:* Federal Pell, FSEOG, state, private, college/university gift aid from institutional funds.

GIFT AID (NON-NEED-BASED) *Total amount:* $1,850,630 (2% state, 84% institutional, 14% external sources). *Receiving aid:* Freshmen: 17% (51); Undergraduates: 15% (151). *Average Award:* Freshmen: $9607; Undergraduates: $10,717. *Scholarships, grants, and awards by category:* Academic Interests/Achievement: 698 awards ($3,661,511 total): general academic interests/achievements, mathematics. *Creative Arts/Performance:* 67 awards ($452,353 total): journalism/publications, music, performing arts, theater/drama. *Special Characteristics:* 268 awards ($593,737 total): children and siblings of alumni, children of faculty/staff, ethnic background, local/state students, religious affiliation. *Tuition waivers:* Full or partial for employees or children of employees, senior citizens. *ROTC:* Army cooperative.

LOANS *Student loans:* $4,478,708 (66% need-based, 34% non-need-based). 96% of past graduating class borrowed through all loan programs. *Average indebtedness per student:* $26,094. *Average need-based loan:* Freshmen: $3474; Undergraduates: $3645. *Parent loans:* $1,623,507 (15% need-based, 85% non-need-based). *Programs:* FFEL (Subsidized and Unsubsidized Stafford, PLUS), Perkins, college/university.

WORK-STUDY *Federal work-study:* Total amount: $86,035; 159 jobs averaging $754. *State or other work-study/employment:* Total amount: $92,822 (46% need-based, 54% non-need-based). 106 part-time jobs averaging $623.

APPLYING FOR FINANCIAL AID *Required financial aid forms:* FAFSA, institution's own form. *Financial aid deadline:* 3/1. *Notification date:* 4/1. Students must reply by 5/1 or within 4 weeks of notification.

CONTACT Richard A. Nash, Director of Financial Aid, Franklin College, 101 Branigin Boulevard, Franklin, IN 46131-2598, 317-738-8075 or toll-free 800-852-0232. *Fax:* 317-738-8072. *E-mail:* rnash@franklincollege.edu.

FRANKLIN PIERCE COLLEGE
Rindge, NH

Tuition & fees: $23,710	Average undergraduate aid package: $16,629

ABOUT THE INSTITUTION Independent, coed. Awards: bachelor's degrees (profile does not reflect significant enrollment at 6 continuing education sites; master's degree is only offered at these sites). 50 undergraduate majors. Total enrollment: 1,608. Undergraduates: 1,608. Freshmen: 568. Federal methodology is used as a basis for awarding need-based institutional aid.

UNDERGRADUATE EXPENSES for 2005–06 *Comprehensive fee:* $31,700 includes full-time tuition ($23,100), mandatory fees ($610), and room and board ($7990). *College room only:* $4480. *Part-time tuition:* $770 per credit.

FRESHMAN FINANCIAL AID (Fall 2003) 472 applied for aid; of those 91% were deemed to have need. 100% of freshmen with need received aid; of those 8% had need fully met. *Average percent of need met:* 66% (excluding resources awarded to replace EFC). *Average financial aid package:* $15,790 (excluding resources awarded to replace EFC). 21% of all full-time freshmen had no need and received non-need-based gift aid.

UNDERGRADUATE FINANCIAL AID (Fall 2003) 1,256 applied for aid; of those 92% were deemed to have need. 100% of undergraduates with need received aid; of those 10% had need fully met. *Average percent of need met:* 70% (excluding resources awarded to replace EFC). *Average financial aid package:* $16,629 (excluding resources awarded to replace EFC). 21% of all full-time undergraduates had no need and received non-need-based gift aid.

GIFT AID (NEED-BASED) *Total amount:* $12,904,631 (11% federal, 1% state, 87% institutional, 1% external sources). *Receiving aid:* Freshmen: 76% (429); All full-time undergraduates: 73% (1,145). *Average award:* Freshmen: $11,986; Undergraduates: $11,811. *Scholarships, grants, and awards:* Federal Pell, FSEOG, state, private, college/university gift aid from institutional funds, United Negro College Fund.

GIFT AID (NON-NEED-BASED) *Total amount:* $2,845,546 (97% institutional, 3% external sources). *Receiving aid:* Freshmen: 6% (33); Undergraduates: 6% (91). *Average Award:* Freshmen: $10,975; Undergraduates: $11,223. *Scholarships, grants, and awards by category:* Academic Interests/Achievement: 1,330 awards ($9,605,692 total): communication, general academic interests/achievements. Creative Arts/Performance: 19 awards ($37,000 total): performing arts, theater/drama. Special Characteristics: 218 awards ($1,405,711 total): adult students, children and siblings of alumni, children of current students, children of educators, children of faculty/staff, general special characteristics, international students, local/state students, married students, parents of current students, siblings of current students, spouses of current students. *ROTC:* Army cooperative, Air Force cooperative.

LOANS *Student loans:* $10,199,081 (78% need-based, 22% non-need-based). 76% of past graduating class borrowed through all loan programs. *Average indebtedness per student:* $21,357. *Average need-based loan:* Freshmen: $3429; Undergraduates: $4724. *Parent loans:* $5,028,755 (49% need-based, 51% non-need-based). *Programs:* FFEL (Subsidized and Unsubsidized Stafford, PLUS), Perkins, state.

WORK-STUDY *Federal work-study:* Total amount: $680,761; 758 jobs averaging $1467. *State or other work-study/employment:* Total amount: $304,018 (51% need-based, 49% non-need-based). 183 part-time jobs averaging $2128.

ATHLETIC AWARDS *Total amount:* $1,022,318 (30% need-based, 70% non-need-based).

APPLYING FOR FINANCIAL AID *Required financial aid form:* FAFSA. *Financial aid deadline (priority):* 3/1. *Notification date:* Continuous beginning 4/1. Students must reply within 4 weeks of notification.

CONTACT JoEllen Soucier, Director of Financial Aid, Franklin Pierce College, College Road, PO Box 60, Rindge, NH 03461-0060, 603-899-4180 or toll-free 800-437-0048. *Fax:* 603-899-4372. *E-mail:* soucierj@fpc.edu.

FRANKLIN UNIVERSITY
Columbus, OH

ABOUT THE INSTITUTION Independent, coed. Awards: associate, bachelor's, and master's degrees and post-master's certificates. 13 undergraduate majors. Total enrollment: 6,823. Undergraduates: 5,820. Freshmen: 124.

GIFT AID (NEED-BASED) *Scholarships, grants, and awards:* Federal Pell, FSEOG, state, private, college/university gift aid from institutional funds.

GIFT AID (NON-NEED-BASED) *Scholarships, grants, and awards by category:* Academic Interests/Achievement: general academic interests/achievements. Special Achievements/Activities: leadership. Special Characteristics: members of minority groups.

LOANS *Programs:* FFEL (Subsidized and Unsubsidized Stafford, PLUS), college/university.

WORK-STUDY *Federal work-study:* Total amount: $223,360; 29 jobs averaging $7702.

APPLYING FOR FINANCIAL AID *Required financial aid form:* FAFSA.

CONTACT Ms. Marlowe Collier, Financial Aid Assistant, Franklin University, 201 South Grant Avenue, Columbus, OH 43215-5399, 614-797-4700 or toll-free 877-341-6300. *Fax:* 614-220-8931. *E-mail:* finaid@franklin.edu.

FREED-HARDEMAN UNIVERSITY
Henderson, TN

Tuition & fees: $12,440	Average undergraduate aid package: $10,146

ABOUT THE INSTITUTION Independent religious, coed. Awards: bachelor's and master's degrees and post-master's certificates. 53 undergraduate majors. Total enrollment: 1,942. Undergraduates: 1,440. Freshmen: 373. Federal methodology is used as a basis for awarding need-based institutional aid.

UNDERGRADUATE EXPENSES for 2005–06 *Comprehensive fee:* $18,640 includes full-time tuition ($10,500), mandatory fees ($1940), and room and board ($6200). *College room only:* $3440. Full-time tuition and fees vary according to course load and degree level. Room and board charges vary according to board plan and housing facility. *Part-time tuition:* $350 per semester hour. *Part-time fees:* $72 per semester hour. Part-time tuition and fees vary according to course load and degree level. *Payment plans:* Tuition prepayment, installment.

FRESHMAN FINANCIAL AID (Fall 2004, est.) 335 applied for aid; of those 87% were deemed to have need. 100% of freshmen with need received aid; of those 21% had need fully met. *Average percent of need met:* 70% (excluding resources awarded to replace EFC). *Average financial aid package:* $10,471 (excluding resources awarded to replace EFC). 15% of all full-time freshmen had no need and received non-need-based gift aid.

UNDERGRADUATE FINANCIAL AID (Fall 2004, est.) 1,081 applied for aid; of those 87% were deemed to have need. 100% of undergraduates with need received aid; of those 13% had need fully met. *Average percent of need met:* 63% (excluding resources awarded to replace EFC). *Average financial aid package:* $10,146 (excluding resources awarded to replace EFC). 21% of all full-time undergraduates had no need and received non-need-based gift aid.

GIFT AID (NEED-BASED) *Total amount:* $6,721,829 (22% federal, 21% state, 55% institutional, 2% external sources). *Receiving aid:* Freshmen: 67% (281); All full-time undergraduates: 66% (839). *Average award:* Freshmen: $7545; Undergraduates: $6946. *Scholarships, grants, and awards:* Federal Pell, FSEOG, state, private, college/university gift aid from institutional funds.

GIFT AID (NON-NEED-BASED) *Total amount:* $2,361,230 (9% state, 88% institutional, 3% external sources). *Receiving aid:* Freshmen: 14% (57); Undergraduates: 8% (102). *Average Award:* Freshmen: $11,802; Undergraduates: $10,538. *Scholarships, grants, and awards by category:* Academic Interests/Achievement: biological sciences, business, computer science, education, engineering/technologies, English, general academic interests/achievements, humanities, mathematics, physical sciences, premedicine, religion/biblical studies. Creative Arts/Performance: art/fine arts, cinema/film/broadcasting, journalism/publications, music, performing arts, theater/drama. Special Achievements/Activities: leadership. Special Characteristics: adult students, children of faculty/staff. *Tuition waivers:* Full or partial for employees or children of employees, senior citizens.

LOANS *Student loans:* $9,357,368 (75% need-based, 25% non-need-based). 81% of past graduating class borrowed through all loan programs. *Average indebtedness per student:* $22,792. *Average need-based loan:* Freshmen: $3722;

Freed-Hardeman University

Undergraduates: $4144. *Parent loans:* $3,086,403 (37% need-based, 63% non-need-based). *Programs:* FFEL (Subsidized and Unsubsidized Stafford, PLUS), Perkins, alternative loans.

WORK-STUDY *Federal work-study:* Total amount: $494,518; jobs available. *State or other work-study/employment:* Total amount: $1080 (100% non-need-based). Part-time jobs available.

APPLYING FOR FINANCIAL AID *Required financial aid form:* FAFSA. *Financial aid deadline (priority):* 3/1. *Notification date:* Continuous beginning 3/1. Students must reply within 4 weeks of notification.

CONTACT Larry Cyr, Director of Financial Aid, Freed-Hardeman University, 158 East Main Street, Henderson, TN 38340-2399, 731-989-6662 or toll-free 800-630-3480. *Fax:* 731-989-6775. *E-mail:* lcyr@fhu.edu.

FREE WILL BAPTIST BIBLE COLLEGE
Nashville, TN

Tuition & fees: $7560	Average undergraduate aid package: N/A

ABOUT THE INSTITUTION Independent Free Will Baptist, coed. Awards: associate and bachelor's degrees. 13 undergraduate majors. Total enrollment: 358. Undergraduates: 358. Freshmen: 85. Federal methodology is used as a basis for awarding need-based institutional aid.

UNDERGRADUATE EXPENSES for 2004–05 *Application fee:* $35. *Comprehensive fee:* $12,030 includes full-time tuition ($6970), mandatory fees ($590), and room and board ($4470). Room and board charges vary according to board plan. *Part-time tuition:* $296 per semester hour. Part-time tuition and fees vary according to course load. *Payment plans:* Installment, deferred payment.

GIFT AID (NEED-BASED) *Total amount:* $742,187 (42% federal, 5% state, 37% institutional, 16% external sources). *Scholarships, grants, and awards:* Federal Pell, FSEOG, state, private, college/university gift aid from institutional funds.

GIFT AID (NON-NEED-BASED) *Total amount:* $75,325 (100% state). *Scholarships, grants, and awards by category:* Special Characteristics: 26 awards ($100,781 total): children of faculty/staff, international students, married students. *ROTC:* Army cooperative, Air Force cooperative.

LOANS *Student loans:* $1,047,058 (69% need-based, 31% non-need-based). 70% of past graduating class borrowed through all loan programs. *Average indebtedness per student:* $14,509. *Parent loans:* $387,665 (100% non-need-based). *Programs:* FFEL (Subsidized and Unsubsidized Stafford, PLUS), alternative loans.

WORK-STUDY *Federal work-study:* Total amount: $22,359; 15 jobs averaging $1491. *State or other work-study/employment:* Total amount: $145,000 (100% non-need-based). 80 part-time jobs averaging $1800.

APPLYING FOR FINANCIAL AID *Required financial aid forms:* FAFSA, institution's own form. *Financial aid deadline (priority):* 4/15. *Notification date:* Continuous beginning 7/1.

CONTACT Jeff Caudill, Director of Enrollment Services, Free Will Baptist Bible College, 3606 West End Avenue, Nashville, TN 37205, 615-844-5000 or toll-free 800-763-9222. *Fax:* 615-269-6028. *E-mail:* jcaudill@fwbbc.edu.

FRESNO PACIFIC UNIVERSITY
Fresno, CA

Tuition & fees: $18,728	Average undergraduate aid package: $16,690

ABOUT THE INSTITUTION Independent religious, coed. Awards: associate, bachelor's, and master's degrees. 42 undergraduate majors. Total enrollment: 2,255. Undergraduates: 1,417. Freshmen: 186. Federal methodology is used as a basis for awarding need-based institutional aid.

UNDERGRADUATE EXPENSES for 2004–05 *Application fee:* $40. *Comprehensive fee:* $24,328 includes full-time tuition ($18,500), mandatory fees ($228), and room and board ($5600). *College room only:* $2700. Full-time tuition and fees vary according to program. Room and board charges vary according to board plan and housing facility. *Part-time tuition:* $660 per unit. *Part-time fees:* $72 per term. Part-time tuition and fees vary according to program. *Payment plan:* Installment.

FRESHMAN FINANCIAL AID (Fall 2003) 176 applied for aid; of those 89% were deemed to have need. 100% of freshmen with need received aid; of those 29% had need fully met. *Average percent of need met:* 90% (excluding resources awarded to replace EFC). *Average financial aid package:* $16,527 (excluding resources awarded to replace EFC). 5% of all full-time freshmen had no need and received non-need-based gift aid.

UNDERGRADUATE FINANCIAL AID (Fall 2003) 848 applied for aid; of those 87% were deemed to have need. 100% of undergraduates with need received aid; of those 32% had need fully met. *Average percent of need met:* 87% (excluding resources awarded to replace EFC). *Average financial aid package:* $16,690 (excluding resources awarded to replace EFC). 5% of all full-time undergraduates had no need and received non-need-based gift aid.

GIFT AID (NEED-BASED) *Total amount:* $12,496,812 (14% federal, 38% state, 48% institutional). *Receiving aid:* Freshmen: 85% (156); All full-time undergraduates: 81% (736). *Average award:* Freshmen: $13,334; Undergraduates: $12,364. *Scholarships, grants, and awards:* Federal Pell, FSEOG, state, private, college/university gift aid from institutional funds.

GIFT AID (NON-NEED-BASED) *Total amount:* $805,845 (27% institutional, 73% external sources). *Receiving aid:* Freshmen: 53% (98); Undergraduates: 39% (352). *Average Award:* Freshmen: $1050; Undergraduates: $1397. *Scholarships, grants, and awards by category:* Academic Interests/Achievement: 522 awards ($1,655,077 total): general academic interests/achievements, humanities, religion/biblical studies, social sciences. Creative Arts/Performance: 131 awards ($149,400 total): art/fine arts, journalism/publications, music, theater/drama. Special Achievements/Activities: 375 awards ($440,195 total): general special achievements/activities, leadership, memberships, religious involvement. Special Characteristics: 338 awards ($543,553 total): children of faculty/staff, ethnic background, international students, members of minority groups, religious affiliation. *Tuition waivers:* Full or partial for employees or children of employees, senior citizens.

LOANS *Student loans:* $4,756,789 (100% need-based). 78% of past graduating class borrowed through all loan programs. *Average indebtedness per student:* $14,436. *Average need-based loan:* Freshmen: $2773; Undergraduates: $5359. *Parent loans:* $542,477 (100% need-based). *Programs:* FFEL (Subsidized and Unsubsidized Stafford, PLUS), Perkins, alternative loans.

WORK-STUDY *Federal work-study:* Total amount: $1,263,236; 481 jobs averaging $2626. *State or other work-study/employment:* Part-time jobs available.

ATHLETIC AWARDS *Total amount:* $882,825 (100% need-based).

APPLYING FOR FINANCIAL AID *Required financial aid forms:* FAFSA, institution's own form. *Financial aid deadline (priority):* 3/2. *Notification date:* Continuous beginning 2/21. Students must reply by 7/30 or within 3 weeks of notification.

CONTACT Amber Blodgett, Associate Director of Financial Aid, Fresno Pacific University, 1717 South Chestnut Avenue, #2004, Fresno, CA 93702, 559-453-7137 or toll-free 800-660-6089 (in-state). *Fax:* 559-453-5595. *E-mail:* finaid@fresno.edu.

FRIENDS UNIVERSITY
Wichita, KS

Tuition & fees: $14,600	Average undergraduate aid package: $7591

ABOUT THE INSTITUTION Independent, coed. Awards: associate, bachelor's, and master's degrees. 59 undergraduate majors. Total enrollment: 3,190. Undergraduates: 2,629. Federal methodology is used as a basis for awarding need-based institutional aid.

UNDERGRADUATE EXPENSES for 2004–05 *Application fee:* $15. *Tuition:* full-time $14,430; part-time $481 per credit hour.

FRESHMAN FINANCIAL AID (Fall 2003) 308 applied for aid; of those 91% were deemed to have need. 99% of freshmen with need received aid; of those 13% had need fully met. *Average percent of need met:* 62% (excluding resources awarded to replace EFC). *Average financial aid package:* $8788 (excluding resources awarded to replace EFC). 15% of all full-time freshmen had no need and received non-need-based gift aid.

UNDERGRADUATE FINANCIAL AID (Fall 2003) 1,894 applied for aid; of those 92% were deemed to have need. 100% of undergraduates with need received aid; of those 12% had need fully met. *Average percent of need met:* 56% (excluding resources awarded to replace EFC). *Average financial aid package:* $7591 (excluding resources awarded to replace EFC). 11% of all full-time undergraduates had no need and received non-need-based gift aid.

GIFT AID (NEED-BASED) *Total amount:* $6,789,921 (38% federal, 11% state, 34% institutional, 17% external sources). *Receiving aid:* Freshmen: 78% (256); All full-time undergraduates: 66% (1,294). *Average award:* Freshmen: $6510; Undergraduates: $5158. *Scholarships, grants, and awards:* Federal Pell, FSEOG, state, private, college/university gift aid from institutional funds.

GIFT AID (NON-NEED-BASED) *Total amount:* $852,153 (1% state, 75% institutional, 24% external sources). *Receiving aid:* Freshmen: 8% (25); Undergraduates: 4% (80). *Average Award:* Freshmen: $5738; Undergraduates: $7033. *Scholarships, grants, and awards by category:* Academic Interests/

Achievement: 808 awards ($2,265,872 total): biological sciences, business, communication, computer science, education, English, foreign languages, general academic interests/achievements, health fields, humanities, mathematics, physical sciences, premedicine, religion/biblical studies, social sciences. *Creative Arts/Performance:* 181 awards ($266,145 total): applied art and design, art/fine arts, dance, music, performing arts, theater/drama. *Special Achievements/ Activities:* 122 awards ($70,400 total): leadership. *Special Characteristics:* 52 awards ($43,875 total): children and siblings of alumni, international students, relatives of clergy, religious affiliation.
LOANS *Student loans:* $14,142,754 (84% need-based, 16% non-need-based). 99% of past graduating class borrowed through all loan programs. *Average indebtedness per student:* $16,204. *Average need-based loan:* Freshmen: $2898; Undergraduates: $3752. *Parent loans:* $676,849 (45% need-based, 55% non-need-based). *Programs:* FFEL (Subsidized and Unsubsidized Stafford, PLUS), Perkins, college/university.
WORK-STUDY *Federal work-study:* Total amount: $294,021; 233 jobs averaging $1416. *State or other work-study/employment:* Total amount: $352,499 (100% non-need-based). 240 part-time jobs averaging $1469.
ATHLETIC AWARDS *Total amount:* $713,385 (100% need-based).
APPLYING FOR FINANCIAL AID *Required financial aid forms:* FAFSA, institution's own form. *Financial aid deadline (priority):* 3/15. *Notification date:* Continuous beginning 3/1. Students must reply within 3 weeks of notification.
CONTACT Myra Pfannenstiel, Director of Financial Aid, Friends University, 2100 University Street, Wichita, KS 67213, 316-295-5590 or toll-free 800-577-2233. *Fax:* 316-295-5703. *E-mail:* pfannem@friends.edu.

FROSTBURG STATE UNIVERSITY
Frostburg, MD

Tuition & fees (MD res): $6230	Average undergraduate aid package: $6689

ABOUT THE INSTITUTION State-supported, coed. Awards: bachelor's and master's degrees and post-bachelor's and post-master's certificates. 48 undergraduate majors. Total enrollment: 5,327. Undergraduates: 4,522. Freshmen: 958. Both federal and institutional methodology are used as a basis for awarding need-based institutional aid.
UNDERGRADUATE EXPENSES for 2005–06 *Application fee:* $30. *Tuition, state resident:* full-time $5000; part-time $207 per credit hour. *Tuition, nonresident:* full-time $13,250; part-time $374 per credit hour. *Required fees:* full-time $1230; $59 per credit hour or $9 per term part-time. Full-time tuition and fees vary according to course load and program. Part-time tuition and fees vary according to course load and program. *College room and board:* $6148; *room only:* $3072. Room and board charges vary according to board plan and housing facility. *Payment plans:* Installment, deferred payment.
FRESHMAN FINANCIAL AID (Fall 2004, est.) 753 applied for aid; of those 67% were deemed to have need. 95% of freshmen with need received aid; of those 20% had need fully met. *Average percent of need met:* 65% (excluding resources awarded to replace EFC). *Average financial aid package:* $6183 (excluding resources awarded to replace EFC). 13% of all full-time freshmen had no need and received non-need-based gift aid.
UNDERGRADUATE FINANCIAL AID (Fall 2004, est.) 3,120 applied for aid; of those 73% were deemed to have need. 94% of undergraduates with need received aid; of those 26% had need fully met. *Average percent of need met:* 71% (excluding resources awarded to replace EFC). *Average financial aid package:* $6689 (excluding resources awarded to replace EFC). 9% of all full-time undergraduates had no need and received non-need-based gift aid.
GIFT AID (NEED-BASED) *Total amount:* $6,978,284 (46% federal, 39% state, 9% institutional, 6% external sources). *Receiving aid:* Freshmen: 35% (340); All full-time undergraduates: 35% (1,534). *Average award:* Freshmen: $4581; Undergraduates: $4229. *Scholarships, grants, and awards:* Federal Pell, FSEOG, state, private, college/university gift aid from institutional funds.
GIFT AID (NON-NEED-BASED) *Total amount:* $2,705,498 (42% state, 52% institutional, 6% external sources). *Receiving aid:* Freshmen: 15% (147); Undergraduates: 13% (574). *Average Award:* Freshmen: $2100; *Undergraduates:* $2788. *Scholarships, grants, and awards by category: Academic Interests/ Achievement:* 587 awards ($1,089,084 total): biological sciences, business, communication, computer science, education, engineering/technologies, English, foreign languages, general academic interests/achievements, health fields, humanities, international studies, mathematics, physical sciences, premedicine, social sciences. *Creative Arts/Performance:* 90 awards ($87,225 total): art/fine arts, creative writing, dance, journalism/publications, music, performing arts, theater/ drama. *Special Achievements/Activities:* 60 awards ($37,700 total): community service, leadership. *Special Characteristics:* adult students, children and siblings

of alumni, children of union members/company employees, international students, local/state students, out-of-state students, veterans, veterans' children. *Tuition waivers:* Full or partial for employees or children of employees, senior citizens.
LOANS *Student loans:* $11,838,293 (49% need-based, 51% non-need-based). 62% of past graduating class borrowed through all loan programs. *Average indebtedness per student:* $15,319. *Average need-based loan:* Freshmen: $2345; Undergraduates: $3271. *Parent loans:* $4,104,852 (100% non-need-based). *Programs:* FFEL (Subsidized and Unsubsidized Stafford, PLUS), Perkins.
WORK-STUDY *Federal work-study:* Total amount: $184,471; 196 jobs averaging $958. *State or other work-study/employment:* Total amount: $504,222 (100% non-need-based). 535 part-time jobs averaging $360.
APPLYING FOR FINANCIAL AID *Required financial aid form:* FAFSA. *Financial aid deadline (priority):* 3/1. *Notification date:* Continuous beginning 3/15. Students must reply within 3 weeks of notification.
CONTACT Mrs. Angela Hovatter, Director of Financial Aid, Frostburg State University, 101 Braddock Road, Frostburg, MD 21532-1099, 301-687-4301. *Fax:* 301-687-7074.

FURMAN UNIVERSITY
Greenville, SC

Tuition & fees: $24,408	Average undergraduate aid package: $20,417

ABOUT THE INSTITUTION Independent, coed. Awards: bachelor's and master's degrees and post-bachelor's certificates. 45 undergraduate majors. Total enrollment: 3,359. Undergraduates: 2,807. Freshmen: 736. Both federal and institutional methodology are used as a basis for awarding need-based institutional aid.
UNDERGRADUATE EXPENSES for 2004–05 *Application fee:* $40. *Comprehensive fee:* $30,680 includes full-time tuition ($23,968), mandatory fees ($440), and room and board ($6272). *College room only:* $3488. Room and board charges vary according to board plan and housing facility. *Part-time tuition:* $749 per credit hour. Part-time tuition and fees vary according to course load. *Payment plan:* Installment.
FRESHMAN FINANCIAL AID (Fall 2004, est.) 450 applied for aid; of those 69% were deemed to have need. 100% of freshmen with need received aid; of those 49% had need fully met. *Average percent of need met:* 89% (excluding resources awarded to replace EFC). *Average financial aid package:* $20,319 (excluding resources awarded to replace EFC). 34% of all full-time freshmen had no need and received non-need-based gift aid.
UNDERGRADUATE FINANCIAL AID (Fall 2004, est.) 1,448 applied for aid; of those 80% were deemed to have need. 100% of undergraduates with need received aid; of those 45% had need fully met. *Average percent of need met:* 87% (excluding resources awarded to replace EFC). *Average financial aid package:* $20,417 (excluding resources awarded to replace EFC). 27% of all full-time undergraduates had no need and received non-need-based gift aid.
GIFT AID (NEED-BASED) *Total amount:* $14,513,341 (7% federal, 9% state, 78% institutional, 6% external sources). *Receiving aid:* Freshmen: 43% (309); All full-time undergraduates: 42% (1,143). *Average award:* Freshmen: $18,304; Undergraduates: $16,617. *Scholarships, grants, and awards:* Federal Pell, FSEOG, state, private, college/university gift aid from institutional funds.
GIFT AID (NON-NEED-BASED) *Total amount:* $12,659,076 (28% state, 65% institutional, 7% external sources). *Receiving aid:* Freshmen: 39% (281); Undergraduates: 35% (934). *Average Award:* Freshmen: $8435; *Undergraduates:* $9952. *Scholarships, grants, and awards by category: Academic Interests/ Achievement:* 1,297 awards ($10,689,863 total): area/ethnic studies, biological sciences, business, communication, computer science, education, engineering/ technologies, English, foreign languages, general academic interests/ achievements, health fields, humanities, international studies, mathematics, military science, physical sciences, premedicine, religion/biblical studies, social sciences. *Creative Arts/Performance:* 303 awards ($964,864 total): art/fine arts, creative writing, music, theater/drama. *Special Achievements/Activities:* 21 awards ($91,600 total): community service, leadership, religious involvement. *Special Characteristics:* 721 awards ($5,171,609 total): children of faculty/staff, ethnic background, international students, local/state students, members of minority groups, relatives of clergy, religious affiliation, veterans. *Tuition waivers:* Full or partial for employees or children of employees. *ROTC:* Army.
LOANS *Student loans:* $7,924,554 (83% need-based, 17% non-need-based). 35% of past graduating class borrowed through all loan programs. *Average indebtedness per student:* $21,194. *Average need-based loan:* Freshmen: $2602; Undergraduates: $5026. *Parent loans:* $2,939,906 (58% need-based, 42% non-need-based). *Programs:* FFEL (Subsidized and Unsubsidized Stafford, PLUS), Perkins, state, alternative loans.

Furman University

WORK-STUDY *Federal work-study:* Total amount: $745,899; 483 jobs averaging $1530.
ATHLETIC AWARDS *Total amount:* $4,965,979 (33% need-based, 67% non-need-based).
APPLYING FOR FINANCIAL AID *Required financial aid forms:* FAFSA, institution's own form, state aid form. *Financial aid deadline:* 1/15. *Notification date:* 3/15. Students must reply by 5/1.
CONTACT Martin Carney, Director of Financial Aid, Furman University, 3300 Poinsett Highway, Greenville, SC 29613, 864-294-2204. *Fax:* 864-294-3127. *E-mail:* martin.carney@furman.edu.

GALLAUDET UNIVERSITY
Washington, DC

Tuition & fees: $11,255	Average undergraduate aid package: $13,935

ABOUT THE INSTITUTION Independent, coed. Awards: bachelor's, master's, and doctoral degrees and post-bachelor's certificates (undergraduate programs are open primarily to the hearing-impaired). 52 undergraduate majors. Total enrollment: 1,834. Undergraduates: 1,207. Freshmen: 227. Federal methodology is used as a basis for awarding need-based institutional aid.
UNDERGRADUATE EXPENSES for 2004–05 *Application fee:* $50. *Comprehensive fee:* $19,675 includes full-time tuition ($9630), mandatory fees ($1625), and room and board ($8420). *College room only:* $4720. Room and board charges vary according to board plan. *Part-time tuition:* $481.50 per credit. *Payment plan:* Installment.
FRESHMAN FINANCIAL AID (Fall 2004, est.) 178 applied for aid; of those 90% were deemed to have need. 97% of freshmen with need received aid; of those 40% had need fully met. *Average percent of need met:* 81% (excluding resources awarded to replace EFC). *Average financial aid package:* $14,561 (excluding resources awarded to replace EFC). 2% of all full-time freshmen had no need and received non-need-based gift aid.
UNDERGRADUATE FINANCIAL AID (Fall 2004, est.) 985 applied for aid; of those 92% were deemed to have need. 97% of undergraduates with need received aid; of those 36% had need fully met. *Average percent of need met:* 75% (excluding resources awarded to replace EFC). *Average financial aid package:* $13,935 (excluding resources awarded to replace EFC). 2% of all full-time undergraduates had no need and received non-need-based gift aid.
GIFT AID (NEED-BASED) *Total amount:* $10,509,745 (13% federal, 63% state, 22% institutional, 2% external sources). *Receiving aid:* Freshmen: 75% (155); All full-time undergraduates: 69% (881). *Average award:* Freshmen: $13,330; Undergraduates: $12,375. *Scholarships, grants, and awards:* Federal Pell, FSEOG, state, private, college/university gift aid from institutional funds.
GIFT AID (NON-NEED-BASED) *Total amount:* $1,430,978 (92% state, 8% institutional). *Receiving aid:* Freshmen: 25% (51); Undergraduates: 22% (277). *Average Award:* Freshmen: $9000; Undergraduates: $6622. *Scholarships, grants, and awards by category:* Academic Interests/Achievement: general academic interests/achievements. *Special Characteristics:* children of educators, children of faculty/staff, handicapped students, international students. *Tuition waivers:* Full or partial for employees or children of employees.
LOANS *Student loans:* $2,065,581 (96% need-based, 4% non-need-based). 50% of past graduating class borrowed through all loan programs. *Average indebtedness per student:* $10,210. *Average need-based loan:* Freshmen: $1949; Undergraduates: $2658. *Parent loans:* $243,736 (92% need-based, 8% non-need-based). *Programs:* FFEL (Subsidized and Unsubsidized Stafford, PLUS), Perkins.
WORK-STUDY *Federal work-study:* Total amount: $152,096; 250 jobs averaging $1800.
APPLYING FOR FINANCIAL AID *Required financial aid forms:* FAFSA, institution's own form. *Financial aid deadline (priority):* 7/1. *Notification date:* Continuous beginning 4/15. Students must reply within 4 weeks of notification.
CONTACT Mrs. Nancy C. Goodman, Director of Financial Aid, Gallaudet University, 800 Florida Avenue, NE, Washington, DC 20002-3695, 202-651-5290 or toll-free 800-995-0550 (out-of-state). *Fax:* 202-651-5740.

GANNON UNIVERSITY
Erie, PA

Tuition & fees: $17,500	Average undergraduate aid package: $14,573

ABOUT THE INSTITUTION Independent Roman Catholic, coed. Awards: associate, bachelor's, master's, and doctoral degrees and post-bachelor's and post-master's certificates. 54 undergraduate majors. Total enrollment: 3,441. Undergraduates: 2,430. Freshmen: 546. Federal methodology is used as a basis for awarding need-based institutional aid.
UNDERGRADUATE EXPENSES for 2004–05 *Application fee:* $25. *Comprehensive fee:* $24,490 includes full-time tuition ($17,030), mandatory fees ($470), and room and board ($6990). *College room only:* $3760. Full-time tuition and fees vary according to class time and program. Room and board charges vary according to board plan and housing facility. *Part-time tuition:* $530 per credit hour. *Part-time fees:* $15 per credit hour. Part-time tuition and fees vary according to class time and program. *Payment plans:* Installment, deferred payment.
FRESHMAN FINANCIAL AID (Fall 2004, est.) 501 applied for aid; of those 89% were deemed to have need. 100% of freshmen with need received aid; of those 19% had need fully met. *Average percent of need met:* 73% (excluding resources awarded to replace EFC). *Average financial aid package:* $14,545 (excluding resources awarded to replace EFC). 10% of all full-time freshmen had no need and received non-need-based gift aid.
UNDERGRADUATE FINANCIAL AID (Fall 2004, est.) 1,967 applied for aid; of those 93% were deemed to have need. 100% of undergraduates with need received aid; of those 18% had need fully met. *Average percent of need met:* 73% (excluding resources awarded to replace EFC). *Average financial aid package:* $14,573 (excluding resources awarded to replace EFC). 8% of all full-time undergraduates had no need and received non-need-based gift aid.
GIFT AID (NEED-BASED) *Total amount:* $17,937,065 (14% federal, 17% state, 64% institutional, 5% external sources). *Receiving aid:* Freshmen: 85% (443); All full-time undergraduates: 85% (1,801). *Average award:* Freshmen: $10,932; Undergraduates: $11,224. *Scholarships, grants, and awards:* Federal Pell, FSEOG, state.
GIFT AID (NON-NEED-BASED) *Total amount:* $1,324,905 (92% institutional, 8% external sources). *Receiving aid:* Freshmen: 13% (67); Undergraduates: 13% (264). *Average Award:* Freshmen: $6989; Undergraduates: $5797. *Scholarships, grants, and awards by category:* Academic Interests/Achievement: 1,319 awards ($4,531,230 total): biological sciences, business, education, engineering/technologies, English, foreign languages, general academic interests/achievements, international studies, mathematics, premedicine, religion/biblical studies. *Creative Arts/Performance:* 73 awards ($116,375 total): music, theater/drama. *Special Achievements/Activities:* 574 awards ($877,835 total): community service, leadership. *Special Characteristics:* 578 awards ($629,226 total): adult students, ethnic background, international students, members of minority groups, religious affiliation. *Tuition waivers:* Full or partial for employees or children of employees, senior citizens. *ROTC:* Army.
LOANS *Student loans:* $9,379,763 (68% need-based, 32% non-need-based). 80% of past graduating class borrowed through all loan programs. *Average indebtedness per student:* $22,624. *Average need-based loan:* Freshmen: $2505; Undergraduates: $3769. *Parent loans:* $2,085,019 (100% non-need-based). *Programs:* Federal Direct (Subsidized and Unsubsidized Stafford, PLUS), FFEL (Subsidized and Unsubsidized Stafford, PLUS), Perkins, Federal Nursing.
WORK-STUDY *Federal work-study:* Total amount: $577,583; 545 jobs averaging $1059. *State or other work-study/employment:* Total amount: $238,689 (100% non-need-based). 235 part-time jobs averaging $1016.
ATHLETIC AWARDS *Total amount:* $2,249,733 (74% need-based, 26% non-need-based).
APPLYING FOR FINANCIAL AID *Required financial aid forms:* FAFSA, institution's own form. *Financial aid deadline (priority):* 3/15. *Notification date:* Continuous beginning 11/1. Students must reply within 4 weeks of notification.
CONTACT Ms. Sharon Krahe, Director of Financial Aid, Gannon University, 109 University Square, Erie, PA 16541, 814-871-7670 or toll-free 800-GANNONU. *Fax:* 814-871-5826. *E-mail:* krahe001@gannon.edu.

GARDNER-WEBB UNIVERSITY
Boiling Springs, NC

CONTACT Ms. Cindy Wallace, Assistant Director of Financial Planning, Gardner-Webb University, PO Box 955, Boiling Springs, NC 28017, 704-406-4243 or toll-free 800-253-6472. *Fax:* 704-406-4102. *E-mail:* cwallace@gardner-webb.edu.

GENEVA COLLEGE
Beaver Falls, PA

Tuition & fees: $16,590	Average undergraduate aid package: $13,352

ABOUT THE INSTITUTION Independent religious, coed. Awards: associate, bachelor's, and master's degrees. 38 undergraduate majors. Total enrollment: 2,141. Undergraduates: 1,809. Both federal and institutional methodology are used as a basis for awarding need-based institutional aid.

UNDERGRADUATE EXPENSES for 2004–05 *Application fee:* $25. *Comprehensive fee:* $23,190 includes full-time tuition ($16,030), mandatory fees ($560), and room and board ($6600). *College room only:* $3440. Full-time tuition and fees vary according to course load. Room and board charges vary according to board plan and housing facility. *Part-time tuition:* $535 per credit. Part-time tuition and fees vary according to course load. *Payment plan:* Installment.

FRESHMAN FINANCIAL AID (Fall 2004, est.) 363 applied for aid; of those 93% were deemed to have need. 100% of freshmen with need received aid; of those 18% had need fully met. *Average percent of need met:* 76% (excluding resources awarded to replace EFC). *Average financial aid package:* $13,585 (excluding resources awarded to replace EFC). 7% of all full-time freshmen had no need and received non-need-based gift aid.

UNDERGRADUATE FINANCIAL AID (Fall 2004, est.) 1,210 applied for aid; of those 92% were deemed to have need. 100% of undergraduates with need received aid; of those 19% had need fully met. *Average percent of need met:* 76% (excluding resources awarded to replace EFC). *Average financial aid package:* $13,352 (excluding resources awarded to replace EFC). 13% of all full-time undergraduates had no need and received non-need-based gift aid.

GIFT AID (NEED-BASED) *Total amount:* $9,611,638 (16% federal, 20% state, 59% institutional, 5% external sources). *Receiving aid:* Freshmen: 92% (336); All full-time undergraduates: 83% (1,108). *Average award:* Freshmen: $9987; Undergraduates: $9448. *Scholarships, grants, and awards:* Federal Pell, FSEOG, state, private, college/university gift aid from institutional funds.

GIFT AID (NON-NEED-BASED) *Total amount:* $1,074,001 (6% state, 88% institutional, 6% external sources). *Receiving aid:* Freshmen: 8% (30); Undergraduates: 8% (101). *Average Award:* Freshmen: $8856; Undergraduates: $8100. *Scholarships, grants, and awards by category: Academic Interests/Achievement:* engineering/technologies, general academic interests/achievements, religion/biblical studies. *Creative Arts/Performance:* music. *Special Characteristics:* children of faculty/staff, relatives of clergy, religious affiliation. *Tuition waivers:* Full or partial for minority students, employees or children of employees. *ROTC:* Army cooperative.

LOANS *Student loans:* $7,987,833 (73% need-based, 27% non-need-based). 92% of past graduating class borrowed through all loan programs. *Average indebtedness per student:* $21,120. *Average need-based loan:* Freshmen: $3187; Undergraduates: $3686. *Parent loans:* $1,580,232 (37% need-based, 63% non-need-based). *Programs:* FFEL (Subsidized and Unsubsidized Stafford, PLUS), Perkins.

WORK-STUDY *Federal work-study:* Total amount: $776,796; jobs available (averaging $2000).

ATHLETIC AWARDS *Total amount:* $878,438 (80% need-based, 20% non-need-based).

APPLYING FOR FINANCIAL AID *Required financial aid form:* FAFSA. *Financial aid deadline (priority):* 3/15. *Notification date:* Continuous. Students must reply within 4 weeks of notification.

CONTACT Mr. Steve Bell, Director of Financial Aid, Geneva College, 3200 College Avenue, Beaver Falls, PA 15010-3599, 800-847-8255. *Fax:* 724-847-6776. *E-mail:* financialaid@geneva.edu.

GEORGE FOX UNIVERSITY
Newberg, OR

ABOUT THE INSTITUTION Independent Friends, coed. Awards: bachelor's, master's, doctoral, and first professional degrees. 45 undergraduate majors. Total enrollment: 2,981. Undergraduates: 1,713. Freshmen: 396.

GIFT AID (NEED-BASED) *Scholarships, grants, and awards:* Federal Pell, FSEOG, state, private, college/university gift aid from institutional funds.

GIFT AID (NON-NEED-BASED) *Scholarships, grants, and awards by category: Academic Interests/Achievement:* biological sciences, education, general academic interests/achievements, mathematics, physical sciences, religion/biblical studies. *Creative Arts/Performance:* art/fine arts, debating, music, theater/drama. *Special Achievements/Activities:* leadership, religious involvement. *Special Characteristics:* children and siblings of alumni, children of faculty/staff, ethnic background, international students, members of minority groups, out-of-state students, relatives of clergy, religious affiliation.

LOANS *Programs:* Federal Direct (Subsidized and Unsubsidized Stafford, PLUS), FFEL (Subsidized and Unsubsidized Stafford, PLUS), Perkins, Alaska Loans, alternative loans.

WORK-STUDY *Federal work-study:* 797 jobs averaging $1881. *State or other work-study/employment:* Total amount: $1,278,759 (100% need-based). Part-time jobs available.

APPLYING FOR FINANCIAL AID *Required financial aid form:* FAFSA.

CONTACT Associate Director of Financial Aid, George Fox University, 414 North Meridian, Newberg, OR 97132-2697, 503-554-2235 or toll-free 800-765-4369. *Fax:* 503-554-3880.

GEORGE MASON UNIVERSITY
Fairfax, VA

Tuition & fees (VA res): $5448	Average undergraduate aid package: $7221

ABOUT THE INSTITUTION State-supported, coed. Awards: bachelor's, master's, doctoral, and first professional degrees and post-bachelor's certificates. 47 undergraduate majors. Total enrollment: 28,874. Undergraduates: 17,408. Freshmen: 2,262. Federal methodology is used as a basis for awarding need-based institutional aid.

UNDERGRADUATE EXPENSES for 2004–05 *Application fee:* $40. *Tuition, state resident:* full-time $3942; part-time $164.25 per credit. *Tuition, nonresident:* full-time $14,310; part-time $596.25 per credit. *Required fees:* full-time $1506; $62.75 per credit. Full-time tuition and fees vary according to course load. Part-time tuition and fees vary according to course load. *College room and board:* $6240; *room only:* $3600. Room and board charges vary according to board plan and housing facility. *Payment plans:* Installment, deferred payment.

FRESHMAN FINANCIAL AID (Fall 2003) 1404 applied for aid; of those 60% were deemed to have need. 94% of freshmen with need received aid; of those 57% had need fully met. *Average percent of need met:* 68% (excluding resources awarded to replace EFC). *Average financial aid package:* $7099 (excluding resources awarded to replace EFC). 14% of all full-time freshmen had no need and received non-need-based gift aid.

UNDERGRADUATE FINANCIAL AID (Fall 2003) 7,654 applied for aid; of those 68% were deemed to have need. 94% of undergraduates with need received aid; of those 49% had need fully met. *Average percent of need met:* 71% (excluding resources awarded to replace EFC). *Average financial aid package:* $7221 (excluding resources awarded to replace EFC). 13% of all full-time undergraduates had no need and received non-need-based gift aid.

GIFT AID (NEED-BASED) *Total amount:* $17,628,639 (51% federal, 44% state, 5% institutional). *Receiving aid:* Freshmen: 26% (581); All full-time undergraduates: 28% (3,527). *Average award:* Freshmen: $5474; Undergraduates: $4310. *Scholarships, grants, and awards:* Federal Pell, FSEOG, state, private, college/university gift aid from institutional funds.

GIFT AID (NON-NEED-BASED) *Total amount:* $2,616,455 (52% institutional, 48% external sources). *Receiving aid:* Freshmen: 13% (299); Undergraduates: 7% (846). *Average Award:* Freshmen: $6056; Undergraduates: $7417. *Scholarships, grants, and awards by category: Academic Interests/Achievement:* 379 awards ($1,287,134 total): general academic interests/achievements. *Creative Arts/Performance:* general creative arts/performance. *Special Characteristics:* general special characteristics. *Tuition waivers:* Full or partial for employees or children of employees, senior citizens. *ROTC:* Army, Air Force cooperative.

LOANS *Student loans:* $33,826,761 (66% need-based, 34% non-need-based). 37% of past graduating class borrowed through all loan programs. *Average indebtedness per student:* $15,015. *Average need-based loan:* Freshmen: $2593; Undergraduates: $3773. *Parent loans:* $6,811,119 (17% need-based, 83% non-need-based). *Programs:* FFEL (Subsidized and Unsubsidized Stafford, PLUS), Perkins, Federal Nursing.

WORK-STUDY *Federal work-study:* Total amount: $1,037,310; 402 jobs averaging $2070.

ATHLETIC AWARDS *Total amount:* $2,617,447 (100% non-need-based).

APPLYING FOR FINANCIAL AID *Required financial aid form:* FAFSA. *Financial aid deadline (priority):* 3/1. *Notification date:* Continuous beginning 4/1. Students must reply within 3 weeks of notification.

CONTACT Office of Student Financial Aid, George Mason University, Mail Stop 3B5, Fairfax, VA 22030-4444, 703-993-2353. *Fax:* 703-993-2350. *E-mail:* finaid@gmu.edu.

GEORGE MEANY CENTER FOR LABOR STUDIES-THE NATIONAL LABOR COLLEGE
Silver Spring, MD

CONTACT Financial Aid Office, George Meany Center for Labor Studies-The National Labor College, 10000 New Hampshire Avenue, Silver Spring, MD 20903, 301-431-6400 or toll-free 800-GMC-4CDP.

GEORGETOWN COLLEGE
Georgetown, KY

Tuition & fees: $19,170	Average undergraduate aid package: $15,594

ABOUT THE INSTITUTION Independent religious, coed. Awards: bachelor's and master's degrees and post-master's certificates. 47 undergraduate majors. Total enrollment: 1,845. Undergraduates: 1,334. Freshmen: 356. Federal methodology is used as a basis for awarding need-based institutional aid.

UNDERGRADUATE EXPENSES for 2005–06 *Application fee:* $30. *Comprehensive fee:* $24,950 includes full-time tuition ($19,170) and room and board ($5780). *College room only:* $2790. *Part-time tuition:* $800 per hour.

FRESHMAN FINANCIAL AID (Fall 2004, est.) 311 applied for aid; of those 81% were deemed to have need. 100% of freshmen with need received aid; of those 42% had need fully met. *Average percent of need met:* 90% (excluding resources awarded to replace EFC). *Average financial aid package:* $16,354 (excluding resources awarded to replace EFC). 28% of all full-time freshmen had no need and received non-need-based gift aid.

UNDERGRADUATE FINANCIAL AID (Fall 2004, est.) 990 applied for aid; of those 87% were deemed to have need. 100% of undergraduates with need received aid; of those 41% had need fully met. *Average percent of need met:* 88% (excluding resources awarded to replace EFC). *Average financial aid package:* $15,594 (excluding resources awarded to replace EFC). 27% of all full-time undergraduates had no need and received non-need-based gift aid.

GIFT AID (NEED-BASED) *Total amount:* $9,086,892 (10% federal, 19% state, 68% institutional, 3% external sources). *Receiving aid:* Freshmen: 65% (229); All full-time undergraduates: 60% (752). *Average award:* Freshmen: $8253; Undergraduates: $7544. *Scholarships, grants, and awards:* Federal Pell, FSEOG, state, private, college/university gift aid from institutional funds.

GIFT AID (NON-NEED-BASED) *Total amount:* $4,345,410 (37% state, 61% institutional, 2% external sources). *Receiving aid:* Freshmen: 69% (246); Undergraduates: 60% (756). *Average Award:* Freshmen: $8109; Undergraduates: $8029. *Scholarships, grants, and awards by category:* Academic Interests/Achievement: 649 awards ($4,372,632 total): general academic interests/achievements. Creative Arts/Performance: 146 awards ($184,050 total): art/fine arts, music, performing arts, theater/drama. Special Achievements/Activities: 256 awards ($461,865 total): junior miss, leadership, religious involvement. Special Characteristics: 185 awards ($236,999 total): children of faculty/staff, local/state students, relatives of clergy, religious affiliation. *ROTC:* Army cooperative, Air Force cooperative.

LOANS *Student loans:* $2,846,126 (58% need-based, 42% non-need-based). 54% of past graduating class borrowed through all loan programs. *Average indebtedness per student:* $16,272. *Average need-based loan:* Freshmen: $3019; Undergraduates: $3916. *Parent loans:* $669,101 (100% non-need-based). *Programs:* FFEL (Subsidized and Unsubsidized Stafford, PLUS), Perkins, college/university.

WORK-STUDY *Federal work-study:* Total amount: $530,235; 472 jobs averaging $1117. *State or other work-study/employment:* Part-time jobs available.

ATHLETIC AWARDS *Total amount:* $867,381 (65% need-based, 35% non-need-based).

APPLYING FOR FINANCIAL AID *Required financial aid form:* FAFSA. *Financial aid deadline (priority):* 2/15. *Notification date:* Continuous beginning 3/15. Students must reply by 5/1.

CONTACT Rhyan Conyers, Director of Financial Planning, Georgetown College, 400 East College Street, Georgetown, KY 40324-1696, 502-863-8027 or toll-free 800-788-9985. *E-mail:* financialaid@georgetowncollege.edu.

GEORGETOWN UNIVERSITY
Washington, DC

Tuition & fees: $30,163	Average undergraduate aid package: $23,482

ABOUT THE INSTITUTION Independent Roman Catholic (Jesuit), coed. Awards: bachelor's, master's, doctoral, and first professional degrees. 41 undergraduate majors. Total enrollment: 13,233. Undergraduates: 6,522. Freshmen: 1,542. Both federal and institutional methodology are used as a basis for awarding need-based institutional aid.

UNDERGRADUATE EXPENSES for 2004–05 *Application fee:* $60. *Comprehensive fee:* $40,717 includes full-time tuition ($29,808), mandatory fees ($355), and room and board ($10,554). *College room only:* $6984. Room and board charges vary according to board plan and housing facility. *Part-time tuition:* $1242 per credit hour. Part-time tuition and fees vary according to course level. *Payment plans:* Installment, deferred payment.

FRESHMAN FINANCIAL AID (Fall 2004, est.) 888 applied for aid; of those 76% were deemed to have need. 100% of freshmen with need received aid; of those 100% had need fully met. *Average percent of need met:* 100% (excluding resources awarded to replace EFC). *Average financial aid package:* $22,939 (excluding resources awarded to replace EFC). 1% of all full-time freshmen had no need and received non-need-based gift aid.

UNDERGRADUATE FINANCIAL AID (Fall 2004, est.) 3,038 applied for aid; of those 86% were deemed to have need. 100% of undergraduates with need received aid; of those 100% had need fully met. *Average percent of need met:* 100% (excluding resources awarded to replace EFC). *Average financial aid package:* $23,482 (excluding resources awarded to replace EFC). 1% of all full-time undergraduates had no need and received non-need-based gift aid.

GIFT AID (NEED-BASED) *Total amount:* $45,702,000 (8% federal, 87% institutional, 5% external sources). *Receiving aid:* Freshmen: 42% (638); All full-time undergraduates: 37% (2,252). *Average award:* Freshmen: $18,464; Undergraduates: $17,123. *Scholarships, grants, and awards:* Federal Pell, FSEOG, state, private, college/university gift aid from institutional funds.

GIFT AID (NON-NEED-BASED) *Total amount:* $2,200,000 (55% federal, 45% external sources). *Receiving aid:* Freshmen: 1% (11); Undergraduates: 19. *Average Award:* Freshmen: $3500; Undergraduates: $3800. *Scholarships, grants, and awards by category:* Special Characteristics: children of faculty/staff. *Tuition waivers:* Full or partial for employees or children of employees. *ROTC:* Army, Naval cooperative, Air Force cooperative.

LOANS *Student loans:* $21,100,000 (53% need-based, 47% non-need-based). 43% of past graduating class borrowed through all loan programs. *Average indebtedness per student:* $22,906. *Average need-based loan:* Freshmen: $2010; Undergraduates: $3634. *Parent loans:* $15,500,000 (100% non-need-based). *Programs:* FFEL (Subsidized and Unsubsidized Stafford, PLUS), Perkins, Federal Nursing.

WORK-STUDY *Federal work-study:* Total amount: $6,000,000; 2,000 jobs averaging $3000.

ATHLETIC AWARDS *Total amount:* $3,700,000 (32% need-based, 68% non-need-based).

APPLYING FOR FINANCIAL AID *Required financial aid forms:* FAFSA, CSS Financial Aid PROFILE, noncustodial (divorced/separated) parent's statement, business/farm supplement. *Financial aid deadline:* 2/1. *Notification date:* 4/1. Students must reply by 5/1 or within 2 weeks of notification.

CONTACT Ms. Patricia A. McWade, Dean of Student Financial Services, Georgetown University, 37th and O Street, NW, Box 1252, Washington, DC 20057, 202-687-4547. *Fax:* 202-687-6542. *E-mail:* mcwadep@georgetown.edu.

THE GEORGE WASHINGTON UNIVERSITY
Washington, DC

Tuition & fees: $34,030	Average undergraduate aid package: $29,206

ABOUT THE INSTITUTION Independent, coed. Awards: associate, bachelor's, master's, doctoral, and first professional degrees and post-bachelor's and post-master's certificates. 79 undergraduate majors. Total enrollment: 23,092. Undergraduates: 10,967. Freshmen: 2,669. Both federal and institutional methodology are used as a basis for awarding need-based institutional aid.

UNDERGRADUATE EXPENSES for 2004–05 *Application fee:* $60. *Comprehensive fee:* $44,240 includes full-time tuition ($34,000), mandatory fees ($30), and room and board ($10,210). *College room only:* $7210. Full-time tuition and fees vary according to program and student level. Room and board charges vary according to board plan and housing facility. *Part-time tuition:* $964 per credit hour. *Part-time fees:* $1 per credit hour. Part-time tuition and fees vary according to program. *Payment plans:* Guaranteed tuition, installment, deferred payment.

FRESHMAN FINANCIAL AID (Fall 2003) 1404 applied for aid; of those 65% were deemed to have need. 99% of freshmen with need received aid; of those

82% had need fully met. *Average percent of need met:* 94% (excluding resources awarded to replace EFC). *Average financial aid package:* $28,229 (excluding resources awarded to replace EFC). 16% of all full-time freshmen had no need and received non-need-based gift aid.

UNDERGRADUATE FINANCIAL AID (Fall 2003) 4,826 applied for aid; of those 75% were deemed to have need. 99% of undergraduates with need received aid; of those 81% had need fully met. *Average percent of need met:* 94% (excluding resources awarded to replace EFC). *Average financial aid package:* $29,206 (excluding resources awarded to replace EFC). 20% of all full-time undergraduates had no need and received non-need-based gift aid.

GIFT AID (NEED-BASED) *Total amount:* $66,509,950 (7% federal, 93% institutional). *Receiving aid:* Freshmen: 39% (878); All full-time undergraduates: 38% (3,502). *Average award:* Freshmen: $15,823; Undergraduates: $16,744. *Scholarships, grants, and awards:* Federal Pell, FSEOG, state, college/university gift aid from institutional funds.

GIFT AID (NON-NEED-BASED) *Total amount:* $18,279,806 (100% institutional). *Receiving aid:* Freshmen: 12% (261); Undergraduates: 12% (1,154). *Average Award:* Freshmen: $13,757; Undergraduates: $12,291. *Scholarships, grants, and awards by category: Academic Interests/Achievement:* engineering/technologies, general academic interests/achievements, mathematics. *Creative Arts/Performance:* debating, music, performing arts, theater/drama. *Tuition waivers:* Full or partial for employees or children of employees. *ROTC:* Army cooperative, Naval, Air Force cooperative.

LOANS *Student loans:* $33,948,531 (99% need-based, 1% non-need-based). 51% of past graduating class borrowed through all loan programs. *Average indebtedness per student:* $25,943. *Average need-based loan:* Freshmen: $5417; Undergraduates: $7317. *Parent loans:* $23,411,761 (98% need-based, 2% non-need-based). *Programs:* FFEL (Subsidized and Unsubsidized Stafford, PLUS), Perkins.

WORK-STUDY *Federal work-study:* Total amount: $3,303,683; jobs available. *State or other work-study/employment:* Part-time jobs available.

ATHLETIC AWARDS *Total amount:* $4,217,691 (1% need-based, 99% non-need-based).

APPLYING FOR FINANCIAL AID *Required financial aid forms:* FAFSA, CSS Financial Aid PROFILE. *Financial aid deadline:* 2/1 (priority: 2/1). *Notification date:* Continuous beginning 3/24. Students must reply by 5/1.

CONTACT Dan Small, Director of Student Financial Assistance, The George Washington University, 2121 Eye Street, NW, Rice Hall, 3rd Floor, Washington, DC 20052, 202-994-6620 or toll-free 800-447-3765. *Fax:* 202-994-0906. *E-mail:* finaid@gwu.edu.

GEORGIA COLLEGE & STATE UNIVERSITY
Milledgeville, GA

Tuition & fees (GA res): $3862   **Average undergraduate aid package: N/A**

ABOUT THE INSTITUTION State-supported, coed. Awards: bachelor's and master's degrees and post-master's certificates. 38 undergraduate majors. Total enrollment: 5,531. Undergraduates: 4,575. Freshmen: 915. Federal methodology is used as a basis for awarding need-based institutional aid.

UNDERGRADUATE EXPENSES for 2004–05 *Application fee:* $25. *Tuition, state resident:* full-time $3152; part-time $132 per semester hour. *Tuition, nonresident:* full-time $12,608; part-time $526 per semester hour. *Required fees:* full-time $710; $355 per term part-time. Part-time tuition and fees vary according to course load. *College room and board:* $6482. Room and board charges vary according to board plan and housing facility.

FRESHMAN FINANCIAL AID (Fall 2003) 968 applied for aid; of those 60% were deemed to have need. 98% of freshmen with need received aid. 10% of all full-time freshmen had no need and received non-need-based gift aid.

UNDERGRADUATE FINANCIAL AID (Fall 2003) 3,631 applied for aid; of those 62% were deemed to have need. 96% of undergraduates with need received aid. 6% of all full-time undergraduates had no need and received non-need-based gift aid.

GIFT AID (NEED-BASED) *Total amount:* $2,993,323 (99% federal, 1% state). *Receiving aid:* Freshmen: 18% (185); All full-time undergraduates: 22% (869). *Scholarships, grants, and awards:* Federal Pell, FSEOG, state, college/university gift aid from institutional funds.

GIFT AID (NON-NEED-BASED) *Total amount:* $10,674,164 (91% state, 5% institutional, 4% external sources). *Receiving aid:* Freshmen: 56% (565); Undergraduates: 53% (2,111). *Scholarships, grants, and awards by category: Academic Interests/Achievement:* business, education, general academic interests/achievements, health fields, humanities, international studies, mathematics,

physical sciences, social sciences. *Creative Arts/Performance:* creative writing, debating, journalism/publications, music, theater/drama. *Special Achievements/Activities:* community service, general special achievements/activities, leadership. *Special Characteristics:* children of faculty/staff, children with a deceased or disabled parent, handicapped students, international students, local/state students, members of minority groups, out-of-state students, religious affiliation. *Tuition waivers:* Full or partial for employees or children of employees. *ROTC:* Army cooperative.

LOANS *Student loans:* $12,081,167 (57% need-based, 43% non-need-based). 44% of past graduating class borrowed through all loan programs. *Average indebtedness per student:* $15,286. *Parent loans:* $1,015,231 (100% non-need-based). *Programs:* Federal Direct (PLUS), FFEL (Subsidized and Unsubsidized Stafford, PLUS), Perkins, state, college/university.

WORK-STUDY *Federal work-study:* Total amount: $222,408; jobs available.

ATHLETIC AWARDS *Total amount:* $433,721 (100% non-need-based).

APPLYING FOR FINANCIAL AID *Required financial aid form:* FAFSA. *Financial aid deadline:* Continuous. *Notification date:* Continuous beginning 3/1. Students must reply within 2 weeks of notification.

CONTACT Mrs. Cathy Crawley, Associate Director of Financial Aid, Georgia College & State University, Campus Box 30, Milledgeville, GA 31061, 478-445-5149 or toll-free 800-342-0471 (in-state). *Fax:* 478-445-0729. *E-mail:* cathy.crawley@gcsu.edu.

GEORGIA INSTITUTE OF TECHNOLOGY
Atlanta, GA

Tuition & fees (GA res): $4278   **Average undergraduate aid package: $8566**

ABOUT THE INSTITUTION State-supported, coed. Awards: bachelor's, master's, and doctoral degrees. 37 undergraduate majors. Total enrollment: 16,841. Undergraduates: 11,546. Freshmen: 2,574. Federal methodology is used as a basis for awarding need-based institutional aid.

UNDERGRADUATE EXPENSES for 2004–05 *Application fee:* $50. *Tuition, state resident:* full-time $3368; part-time $141 per hour. *Tuition, nonresident:* full-time $16,648; part-time $694 per hour. *Required fees:* full-time $910; $455 per term part-time. Part-time tuition and fees vary according to course load. *College room and board:* $6526; *room only:* $3804. Room and board charges vary according to board plan and housing facility.

FRESHMAN FINANCIAL AID (Fall 2004, est.) 1752 applied for aid; of those 44% were deemed to have need. 98% of freshmen with need received aid; of those 53% had need fully met. *Average percent of need met:* 48% (excluding resources awarded to replace EFC). *Average financial aid package:* $8830 (excluding resources awarded to replace EFC). 9% of all full-time freshmen had no need and received non-need-based gift aid.

UNDERGRADUATE FINANCIAL AID (Fall 2004, est.) 5,330 applied for aid; of those 55% were deemed to have need. 97% of undergraduates with need received aid; of those 32% had need fully met. *Average percent of need met:* 53% (excluding resources awarded to replace EFC). *Average financial aid package:* $8566 (excluding resources awarded to replace EFC). 6% of all full-time undergraduates had no need and received non-need-based gift aid.

GIFT AID (NEED-BASED) *Total amount:* $17,655,387 (27% federal, 35% state, 31% institutional, 7% external sources). *Receiving aid:* Freshmen: 17% (437); All full-time undergraduates: 16% (1,664). *Average award:* Freshmen: $4758; Undergraduates: $4224. *Scholarships, grants, and awards:* Federal Pell, FSEOG, state, private, college/university gift aid from institutional funds.

GIFT AID (NON-NEED-BASED) *Total amount:* $19,458,113 (1% federal, 72% state, 13% institutional, 14% external sources). *Receiving aid:* Freshmen: 22% (555); Undergraduates: 15% (1,633). *Average Award:* Freshmen: $3249; Undergraduates: $3588. *Scholarships, grants, and awards by category: Academic Interests/Achievement:* 1,697 awards ($4,870,866 total): architecture, biological sciences, computer science, engineering/technologies, general academic interests/achievements, physical sciences. *Special Achievements/Activities:* 215 awards ($1,937,825 total): leadership. *Special Characteristics:* 154 awards ($467,507 total): children of faculty/staff, children of union members/company employees, ethnic background, general special characteristics, handicapped students, local/state students, members of minority groups, out-of-state students. *ROTC:* Army, Naval, Air Force.

LOANS *Student loans:* $23,521,527 (68% need-based, 32% non-need-based). 52% of past graduating class borrowed through all loan programs. *Average indebtedness per student:* $16,154. *Average need-based loan:* Freshmen: $2801; Undergraduates: $5018. *Parent loans:* $13,825,271 (51% need-based, 49% non-need-based). *Programs:* FFEL (Subsidized and Unsubsidized Stafford, PLUS), Perkins, college/university, CITIASSIST Alternative Loans.

Georgia Institute of Technology

WORK-STUDY *Federal work-study:* Total amount: $327,967; 235 jobs averaging $2150.

ATHLETIC AWARDS *Total amount:* $4,443,631 (64% need-based, 36% non-need-based).

APPLYING FOR FINANCIAL AID *Required financial aid forms:* FAFSA, institution's own form. *Financial aid deadline:* 3/1 (priority: 3/1). *Notification date:* 4/1. Students must reply by 5/1.

CONTACT Ms. Marie Mons, Director of Student Financial Planning and Services, Georgia Institute of Technology, 225 North Avenue, NW, Atlanta, GA 30332-0460, 404-894-4582. *Fax:* 404-894-7412. *E-mail:* marie.mons@finaid.gatech.edu.

GEORGIAN COURT UNIVERSITY
Lakewood, NJ

Tuition & fees: $17,924	Average undergraduate aid package: $11,350

ABOUT THE INSTITUTION Independent Roman Catholic, women only. Awards: bachelor's and master's degrees and post-bachelor's and post-master's certificates. 37 undergraduate majors. Total enrollment: 3,065. Undergraduates: 2,046. Freshmen: 187. Federal methodology is used as a basis for awarding need-based institutional aid.

UNDERGRADUATE EXPENSES for 2004–05 *Application fee:* $40. *Comprehensive fee:* $25,124 includes full-time tuition ($17,224), mandatory fees ($700), and room and board ($7200). Full-time tuition and fees vary according to program. Room and board charges vary according to board plan. *Part-time tuition:* $464 per credit. *Part-time fees:* $175 per term. Part-time tuition and fees vary according to course load and program. *Payment plans:* Installment, deferred payment.

FRESHMAN FINANCIAL AID (Fall 2003) 136 applied for aid; of those 85% were deemed to have need. 100% of freshmen with need received aid; of those 18% had need fully met. *Average percent of need met:* 64% (excluding resources awarded to replace EFC). *Average financial aid package:* $11,998 (excluding resources awarded to replace EFC). 13% of all full-time freshmen had no need and received non-need-based gift aid.

UNDERGRADUATE FINANCIAL AID (Fall 2003) 1,060 applied for aid; of those 96% were deemed to have need. 100% of undergraduates with need received aid; of those 18% had need fully met. *Average percent of need met:* 60% (excluding resources awarded to replace EFC). *Average financial aid package:* $11,350 (excluding resources awarded to replace EFC). 11% of all full-time undergraduates had no need and received non-need-based gift aid.

GIFT AID (NEED-BASED) *Total amount:* $7,994,217 (18% federal, 36% state, 43% institutional, 3% external sources). *Receiving aid:* Freshmen: 78% (106); All full-time undergraduates: 68% (853). *Average award:* Freshmen: $9825; Undergraduates: $8604. *Scholarships, grants, and awards:* Federal Pell, FSEOG, state, private, college/university gift aid from institutional funds.

GIFT AID (NON-NEED-BASED) *Total amount:* $981,951 (2% state, 91% institutional, 7% external sources). *Receiving aid:* Freshmen: 5% (7); Undergraduates: 7% (87). *Average Award:* Freshmen: $9850; Undergraduates: $10,761. *Scholarships, grants, and awards by category: Academic Interests/ Achievement:* biological sciences, business, English, foreign languages, general academic interests/achievements, mathematics, physical sciences. *Creative Arts/ Performance:* art/fine arts, creative writing, music. *Special Achievements/ Activities:* general special achievements/activities. *Special Characteristics:* children of faculty/staff, religious affiliation, spouses of current students, veterans. *Tuition waivers:* Full or partial for employees or children of employees, senior citizens.

LOANS *Student loans:* $8,970,276 (76% need-based, 24% non-need-based). 67% of past graduating class borrowed through all loan programs. *Average indebtedness per student:* $16,938. *Average need-based loan:* Freshmen: $3183; Undergraduates: $4537. *Parent loans:* $909,225 (42% need-based, 58% non-need-based). *Programs:* Federal Direct (Subsidized and Unsubsidized Stafford, PLUS), FFEL (Subsidized and Unsubsidized Stafford, PLUS), Perkins, state.

WORK-STUDY *Federal work-study:* Total amount: $133,333; 95 jobs averaging $813. *State or other work-study/employment:* Total amount: $196,792 (56% need-based, 44% non-need-based). 162 part-time jobs averaging $709.

ATHLETIC AWARDS *Total amount:* $5000 (100% need-based).

APPLYING FOR FINANCIAL AID *Required financial aid forms:* FAFSA, institution's own form. *Financial aid deadline:* Continuous. *Notification date:* Continuous beginning 2/1. Students must reply within 2 weeks of notification.

CONTACT Carol Straus, Director of Financial Aid, Georgian Court University, 900 Lakewood Avenue, Lakewood, NJ 08701-2697, 732-364-2200 Ext. 2258 or toll-free 800-458-8422. *Fax:* 732-987-2012. *E-mail:* financialaid@georgian.edu.

GEORGIA SOUTHERN UNIVERSITY
Statesboro, GA

Tuition & fees (GA res): $3062	Average undergraduate aid package: $6606

ABOUT THE INSTITUTION State-supported, coed. Awards: bachelor's, master's, and doctoral degrees and post-master's certificates. 79 undergraduate majors. Total enrollment: 16,100. Undergraduates: 14,092. Freshmen: 3,010. Federal methodology is used as a basis for awarding need-based institutional aid.

UNDERGRADUATE EXPENSES for 2004–05 *Application fee:* $20. *Tuition, state resident:* full-time $2232; part-time $97 per semester hour. *Tuition, nonresident:* full-time $9290; part-time $388 per semester hour. *Required fees:* full-time $830; $415 per term part-time. Full-time tuition and fees vary according to location. Part-time tuition and fees vary according to course load and location. *College room and board:* $6000; *room only:* $3734. Room and board charges vary according to board plan and housing facility.

FRESHMAN FINANCIAL AID (Fall 2003) 2587 applied for aid; of those 48% were deemed to have need. 99% of freshmen with need received aid; of those 26% had need fully met. *Average percent of need met:* 75% (excluding resources awarded to replace EFC). *Average financial aid package:* $6267 (excluding resources awarded to replace EFC). 4% of all full-time freshmen had no need and received non-need-based gift aid.

UNDERGRADUATE FINANCIAL AID (Fall 2003) 10,564 applied for aid; of those 59% were deemed to have need. 98% of undergraduates with need received aid; of those 22% had need fully met. *Average percent of need met:* 71% (excluding resources awarded to replace EFC). *Average financial aid package:* $6606 (excluding resources awarded to replace EFC). 3% of all full-time undergraduates had no need and received non-need-based gift aid.

GIFT AID (NEED-BASED) *Total amount:* $22,052,902 (53% federal, 44% state, 1% institutional, 2% external sources). *Receiving aid:* Freshmen: 43% (1,170); All full-time undergraduates: 42% (5,087). *Average award:* Freshmen: $5079; Undergraduates: $4294. *Scholarships, grants, and awards:* Federal Pell, FSEOG, state, private, college/university gift aid from institutional funds, Georgia HOPE Scholarships.

GIFT AID (NON-NEED-BASED) *Total amount:* $10,735,181 (92% state, 5% institutional, 3% external sources). *Receiving aid:* Freshmen: 6% (173); Undergraduates: 4% (486). *Average Award:* Freshmen: $1529; Undergraduates:* $1404. *Scholarships, grants, and awards by category: Academic Interests/ Achievement:* 591 awards ($727,280 total): biological sciences, business, communication, education, engineering/technologies, English, foreign languages, general academic interests/achievements, health fields, humanities, mathematics, military science, social sciences. *Creative Arts/Performance:* 68 awards ($62,550 total): art/fine arts, cinema/film/broadcasting, general creative arts/ performance, music, theater/drama. *Special Achievements/Activities:* 275 awards ($134,250 total): community service, junior miss, leadership, memberships. *Special Characteristics:* 15 awards ($32,954 total): children and siblings of alumni, children of public servants, first-generation college students, handicapped students, married students, members of minority groups. *Tuition waivers:* Full or partial for employees or children of employees, senior citizens. *ROTC:* Army.

LOANS *Student loans:* $33,995,157 (67% need-based, 33% non-need-based). 68% of past graduating class borrowed through all loan programs. *Average indebtedness per student:* $17,536. *Average need-based loan:* Freshmen: $2349; Undergraduates: $3737. *Parent loans:* $4,181,618 (54% need-based, 46% non-need-based). *Programs:* Federal Direct (Subsidized and Unsubsidized Stafford, PLUS), Perkins, Service-Cancelable State Direct Student Loans, alternative loans.

WORK-STUDY *Federal work-study:* Total amount: $435,038; 350 jobs averaging $1243.

ATHLETIC AWARDS *Total amount:* $1,657,426 (48% need-based, 52% non-need-based).

APPLYING FOR FINANCIAL AID *Required financial aid form:* FAFSA. *Financial aid deadline (priority):* 3/31. *Notification date:* 4/15.

CONTACT Ms. Elise Boyett, Associate Director of Financial Aid, Georgia Southern University, Box 8065, Statesboro, GA 30460-8065, 912-681-5413. *Fax:* 912-681-0573. *E-mail:* eboyett@georgiasouthern.edu.

GEORGIA SOUTHWESTERN STATE UNIVERSITY
Americus, GA

ABOUT THE INSTITUTION State-supported, coed. Awards: associate, bachelor's, and master's degrees and post-master's certificates. 57 undergraduate majors. Total enrollment: 2,323. Undergraduates: 2,102. Freshmen: 391.

GIFT AID (NEED-BASED) *Scholarships, grants, and awards:* Federal Pell, FSEOG, state, private, college/university gift aid from institutional funds.

GIFT AID (NON-NEED-BASED) *Scholarships, grants, and awards by category: Academic Interests/Achievement:* general academic interests/achievements. *Creative Arts/Performance:* art/fine arts, music. *Special Achievements/Activities:* leadership.

LOANS *Programs:* FFEL (Subsidized and Unsubsidized Stafford, PLUS), Perkins, state, college/university.

APPLYING FOR FINANCIAL AID *Required financial aid forms:* FAFSA, institution's own form.

CONTACT Ms. Freida Jones, Director of Financial Aid, Georgia Southwestern State University, 800 Wheatley Street, Americus, GA 31709-4693, 229-928-1378 or toll-free 800-338-0082. *Fax:* 229-931-2061.

GEORGIA STATE UNIVERSITY
Atlanta, GA

Tuition & fees (GA res): $4464	Average undergraduate aid package: $7780

ABOUT THE INSTITUTION State-supported, coed. Awards: bachelor's, master's, doctoral, and first professional degrees and post-bachelor's, post-master's, and first professional certificates. 49 undergraduate majors. Total enrollment: 27,267. Undergraduates: 19,894. Freshmen: 2,270. Federal methodology is used as a basis for awarding need-based institutional aid.

UNDERGRADUATE EXPENSES for 2005–06 *Application fee:* $50. *Tuition, state resident:* full-time $3638; part-time $152 per semester hour. *Tuition, nonresident:* full-time $14,552; part-time $607 per semester hour. *Required fees:* full-time $826; $413 per term part-time. Full-time tuition and fees vary according to course load, degree level, and program. Part-time tuition and fees vary according to course load, degree level, and program. *College room and board:* $7368; *room only:* $5380. Room and board charges vary according to board plan and housing facility.

FRESHMAN FINANCIAL AID (Fall 2003) 1497 applied for aid; of those 76% were deemed to have need. 99% of freshmen with need received aid; of those 21% had need fully met. *Average percent of need met:* 70% (excluding resources awarded to replace EFC). *Average financial aid package:* $6788 (excluding resources awarded to replace EFC). 19% of all full-time freshmen had no need and received non-need-based gift aid.

UNDERGRADUATE FINANCIAL AID (Fall 2003) 9,142 applied for aid; of those 81% were deemed to have need. 98% of undergraduates with need received aid; of those 18% had need fully met. *Average percent of need met:* 70% (excluding resources awarded to replace EFC). *Average financial aid package:* $7780 (excluding resources awarded to replace EFC). 14% of all full-time undergraduates had no need and received non-need-based gift aid.

GIFT AID (NEED-BASED) *Total amount:* $30,157,557 (55% federal, 42% state, 1% institutional, 2% external sources). *Receiving aid:* Freshmen: 42% (1,106); All full-time undergraduates: 63% (6,845). *Average award:* Freshmen: $5838; Undergraduates: $4538. *Scholarships, grants, and awards:* Federal Pell, FSEOG, state, private, college/university gift aid from institutional funds.

GIFT AID (NON-NEED-BASED) *Total amount:* $16,168,241 (94% state, 4% institutional, 2% external sources). *Receiving aid:* Freshmen: 10% (257); Undergraduates: 28% (3,091). *Average Award: Freshmen:* $4684; *Undergraduates:* $4024. *Scholarships, grants, and awards by category: Academic Interests/Achievement:* 440 awards ($702,834 total): general academic interests/achievements. *Creative Arts/Performance:* applied art and design, art/fine arts, journalism/publications, music, performing arts, theater/drama. *Special Achievements/Activities:* community service, leadership, memberships. *Tuition waivers:* Full or partial for employees or children of employees, senior citizens. *ROTC:* Army, Naval cooperative, Air Force cooperative.

LOANS *Student loans:* $79,686,966 (62% need-based, 38% non-need-based). 50% of past graduating class borrowed through all loan programs. *Average indebtedness per student:* $15,419. *Average need-based loan:* Freshmen: $2683;

Undergraduates: $5457. *Parent loans:* $2,644,798 (88% need-based, 12% non-need-based). *Programs:* Federal Direct (Subsidized and Unsubsidized Stafford, PLUS), Perkins, state, college/university.

WORK-STUDY *Federal work-study:* Total amount: $629,070; 292 jobs averaging $2154.

ATHLETIC AWARDS *Total amount:* $552,939 (50% need-based, 50% non-need-based).

APPLYING FOR FINANCIAL AID *Required financial aid forms:* FAFSA, Hope Alternate Application (for Hope Scholarships only). *Financial aid deadline:* 11/1 (priority: 4/1). *Notification date:* Continuous beginning 3/30. Students must reply within 2 weeks of notification.

CONTACT Financial Aid Office, Georgia State University, 102 Sparks Hall, Atlanta, GA 30303, 404-651-2227.

GETTYSBURG COLLEGE
Gettysburg, PA

Tuition & fees: $30,240	Average undergraduate aid package: $24,580

ABOUT THE INSTITUTION Independent religious, coed. Awards: bachelor's degrees. 83 undergraduate majors. Total enrollment: 2,471. Undergraduates: 2,471. Freshmen: 710. Both federal and institutional methodology are used as a basis for awarding need-based institutional aid.

UNDERGRADUATE EXPENSES for 2004–05 *Application fee:* $45. *Comprehensive fee:* $37,594 includes full-time tuition ($29,990), mandatory fees ($250), and room and board ($7354). *College room only:* $3900. Room and board charges vary according to board plan and housing facility. *Part-time tuition:* $3300 per course. *Payment plans:* Tuition prepayment, installment.

FRESHMAN FINANCIAL AID (Fall 2004, est.) 502 applied for aid; of those 82% were deemed to have need. 100% of freshmen with need received aid; of those 100% had need fully met. *Average percent of need met:* 100% (excluding resources awarded to replace EFC). *Average financial aid package:* $24,818 (excluding resources awarded to replace EFC). 8% of all full-time freshmen had no need and received non-need-based gift aid.

UNDERGRADUATE FINANCIAL AID (Fall 2004, est.) 1,673 applied for aid; of those 88% were deemed to have need. 100% of undergraduates with need received aid; of those 100% had need fully met. *Average percent of need met:* 100% (excluding resources awarded to replace EFC). *Average financial aid package:* $24,580 (excluding resources awarded to replace EFC). 8% of all full-time undergraduates had no need and received non-need-based gift aid.

GIFT AID (NEED-BASED) *Total amount:* $27,745,902 (4% federal, 3% state, 91% institutional, 2% external sources). *Receiving aid:* Freshmen: 57% (405); All full-time undergraduates: 57% (1,462). *Average award:* Freshmen: $19,800; Undergraduates: $18,860. *Scholarships, grants, and awards:* Federal Pell, FSEOG, state, private, college/university gift aid from institutional funds.

GIFT AID (NON-NEED-BASED) *Total amount:* $2,569,459 (80% institutional, 20% external sources). *Receiving aid:* Freshmen: 23% (160); Undergraduates: 17% (436). *Average Award: Freshmen:* $9210; *Undergraduates:* $9940. *Scholarships, grants, and awards by category: Academic Interests/Achievement:* 632 awards ($6,460,500 total): general academic interests/achievements. *Creative Arts/Performance:* 17 awards ($77,500 total): music. *Tuition waivers:* Full or partial for employees or children of employees. *ROTC:* Army cooperative.

LOANS *Student loans:* $10,021,628 (59% need-based, 41% non-need-based). 62% of past graduating class borrowed through all loan programs. *Average indebtedness per student:* $20,193. *Average need-based loan:* Freshmen: $3865; Undergraduates: $4828. *Parent loans:* $5,632,249 (100% non-need-based). *Programs:* FFEL (Subsidized and Unsubsidized Stafford, PLUS), Perkins, college/university.

WORK-STUDY *Federal work-study:* Total amount: $527,502; 569 jobs averaging $927. *State or other work-study/employment:* Total amount: $614,020 (15% need-based, 85% non-need-based). 586 part-time jobs averaging $1047.

APPLYING FOR FINANCIAL AID *Required financial aid forms:* FAFSA, CSS Financial Aid PROFILE, business/farm supplement, income tax form(s), verification worksheet. *Financial aid deadline:* 2/15. *Notification date:* 3/28. Students must reply by 5/1.

CONTACT Timothy A. Opgenorth, Director of Financial Aid, Gettysburg College, Campus Box 438, Gettysburg, PA 17325, 717-337-6611 or toll-free 800-431-0803. *Fax:* 717-337-8555. *E-mail:* finaid@gettysburg.edu.

GLENVILLE STATE COLLEGE
Glenville, WV

Tuition & fees (WV res): $3276   **Average undergraduate aid package:** $8135

ABOUT THE INSTITUTION State-supported, coed. Awards: associate and bachelor's degrees. 31 undergraduate majors. Total enrollment: 1,319. Undergraduates: 1,319. Freshmen: 292. Federal methodology is used as a basis for awarding need-based institutional aid.

UNDERGRADUATE EXPENSES for 2004–05 *Tuition, state resident:* full-time $3276; part-time $137 per credit hour. *Tuition, nonresident:* full-time $7854; part-time $327 per credit hour. *College room and board:* $5060; *room only:* $2500. Room and board charges vary according to housing facility. *Payment plan:* Installment.

FRESHMAN FINANCIAL AID (Fall 2004, est.) 273 applied for aid; of those 87% were deemed to have need. 97% of freshmen with need received aid; of those 25% had need fully met. *Average percent of need met:* 80% (excluding resources awarded to replace EFC). *Average financial aid package:* $7892 (excluding resources awarded to replace EFC). 10% of all full-time freshmen had no need and received non-need-based gift aid.

UNDERGRADUATE FINANCIAL AID (Fall 2004, est.) 1,000 applied for aid; of those 87% were deemed to have need. 98% of undergraduates with need received aid; of those 25% had need fully met. *Average percent of need met:* 81% (excluding resources awarded to replace EFC). *Average financial aid package:* $8135 (excluding resources awarded to replace EFC). 9% of all full-time undergraduates had no need and received non-need-based gift aid.

GIFT AID (NEED-BASED) *Total amount:* $2,940,459 (77% federal, 23% state). *Receiving aid:* Freshmen: 63% (182); All full-time undergraduates: 59% (674). *Average award:* Freshmen: $4102; Undergraduates: $4076. *Scholarships, grants, and awards:* Federal Pell, FSEOG, state, college/university gift aid from institutional funds.

GIFT AID (NON-NEED-BASED) *Total amount:* $982,947 (58% state, 24% institutional, 18% external sources). *Receiving aid:* Freshmen: 45% (132); Undergraduates: 31% (352). *Average Award:* Freshmen: $2644; Undergraduates:* $2192. *Scholarships, grants, and awards by category:* Academic Interests/Achievement: 166 awards ($247,732 total): biological sciences, education, general academic interests/achievements, mathematics. *Creative Arts/Performance:* 17 awards ($34,197 total): music. *Special Characteristics:* 2 awards ($2000 total): first-generation college students, veterans' children. *Tuition waivers:* Full or partial for senior citizens.

LOANS *Student loans:* $3,354,649 (68% need-based, 32% non-need-based). 71% of past graduating class borrowed through all loan programs. *Average indebtedness per student:* $14,567. *Average need-based loan:* Freshmen: $2327; Undergraduates: $3364. *Parent loans:* $391,806 (100% non-need-based). *Programs:* Federal Direct (Subsidized and Unsubsidized Stafford, PLUS).

WORK-STUDY *Federal work-study:* Total amount: $144,000; 109 jobs averaging $1321. *State or other work-study/employment:* Total amount: $240,000 (100% need-based). 250 part-time jobs averaging $936.

ATHLETIC AWARDS *Total amount:* $345,602 (100% non-need-based).

APPLYING FOR FINANCIAL AID *Required financial aid form:* FAFSA. *Financial aid deadline (priority):* 3/1. *Notification date:* Continuous beginning 4/1. Students must reply within 3 weeks of notification.

CONTACT Ms. Karen Lay, Financial Aid Administrator, Glenville State College, 200 High Street, Glenville, WV 26351-1200, 304-462-4103 Ext. 5 or toll-free 800-924-2010 (in-state). *Fax:* 304-462-4407.

GLOBE INSTITUTE OF TECHNOLOGY
New York, NY

CONTACT Office of Admissions, Globe Institute of Technology, 291 Broadway, 2nd Floor, New York, NY 10007, 212-349-4330 or toll-free 877-394-5623. *Fax:* 212-227-5920. *E-mail:* admission@globe.edu.

GODDARD COLLEGE
Plainfield, VT

Tuition & fees: $9846   **Average undergraduate aid package:** $6289

ABOUT THE INSTITUTION Independent, coed. Awards: bachelor's and master's degrees. 6 undergraduate majors. Total enrollment: 571. Undergraduates: 174. Freshmen: 10. Federal methodology is used as a basis for awarding need-based institutional aid.

UNDERGRADUATE EXPENSES for 2004–05 *Application fee:* $40. *Tuition:* full-time $9080. *Payment plan:* Installment.

FRESHMAN FINANCIAL AID (Fall 2004, est.) 13 applied for aid; of those 85% were deemed to have need. 100% of freshmen with need received aid. *Average percent of need met:* 33% (excluding resources awarded to replace EFC). *Average financial aid package:* $5030 (excluding resources awarded to replace EFC). 17% of all full-time freshmen had no need and received non-need-based gift aid.

UNDERGRADUATE FINANCIAL AID (Fall 2004, est.) 150 applied for aid; of those 97% were deemed to have need. 100% of undergraduates with need received aid; of those 5% had need fully met. *Average percent of need met:* 40% (excluding resources awarded to replace EFC). *Average financial aid package:* $6289 (excluding resources awarded to replace EFC). 3% of all full-time undergraduates had no need and received non-need-based gift aid.

GIFT AID (NEED-BASED) *Total amount:* $339,476 (72% federal, 7% state, 21% external sources). *Receiving aid:* Freshmen: 28% (5); All full-time undergraduates: 47% (101). *Average award:* Freshmen: $2545; Undergraduates: $3361. *Scholarships, grants, and awards:* Federal Pell, FSEOG, state, private, college/university gift aid from institutional funds.

GIFT AID (NON-NEED-BASED) *Total amount:* $28,475 (4% institutional, 96% external sources). *Average Award:* Freshmen: $4672; Undergraduates: $6156. *Tuition waivers:* Full or partial for employees or children of employees.

LOANS *Student loans:* $1,007,399 (92% need-based, 8% non-need-based). 81% of past graduating class borrowed through all loan programs. *Average indebtedness per student:* $21,039. *Average need-based loan:* Freshmen: $3873; Undergraduates: $4060. *Parent loans:* $82,611 (80% need-based, 20% non-need-based). *Programs:* FFEL (Subsidized and Unsubsidized Stafford, PLUS), Perkins, college/university.

APPLYING FOR FINANCIAL AID *Required financial aid form:* FAFSA. *Financial aid deadline (priority):* 3/1. *Notification date:* Continuous. Students must reply within 2 weeks of notification.

CONTACT Beverly Jene, Director of Financial Aid, Goddard College, 123 Pitkin Road, Plainfield, VT 05667, 802-454-8311 Ext. 324 or toll-free 800-906-8312 Ext. 243. *Fax:* 802-454-1029. *E-mail:* jeneb@goddard.edu.

GOD'S BIBLE SCHOOL AND COLLEGE
Cincinnati, OH

CONTACT Mrs. Lori Waggoner, Financial Aid Director, God's Bible School and College, 1810 Young Street, Cincinnati, OH 45202-6899, 513-721-7944 Ext. 205 or toll-free 800-486-4637. *Fax:* 513-721-1357. *E-mail:* lwaggoner@gbs.edu.

GOLDEN GATE UNIVERSITY
San Francisco, CA

ABOUT THE INSTITUTION Independent, coed. Awards: associate, bachelor's, master's, doctoral, and first professional degrees. 10 undergraduate majors. Total enrollment: 4,069. Undergraduates: 614.

GIFT AID (NEED-BASED) *Scholarships, grants, and awards:* Federal Pell, FSEOG, state, private, college/university gift aid from institutional funds.

GIFT AID (NON-NEED-BASED) *Scholarships, grants, and awards by category:* Academic Interests/Achievement: business, computer science, general academic interests/achievements. *Special Achievements/Activities:* leadership. *Special Characteristics:* adult students, general special characteristics, members of minority groups, previous college experience.

LOANS *Programs:* FFEL (Subsidized and Unsubsidized Stafford, PLUS), Perkins.

WORK-STUDY *Federal work-study:* Total amount: $10,000; 2 jobs averaging $5000.

APPLYING FOR FINANCIAL AID *Required financial aid forms:* FAFSA, institution's own form.

CONTACT Ken Walsh, Associate Director of Financial Services, Golden Gate University, 536 Mission Street, San Francisco, CA 94105-2968, 415-442-7262 or toll-free 800-448-4968. *Fax:* 415-442-7819. *E-mail:* kwalsh@ggu.edu.

Goshen College

GOLDEY-BEACOM COLLEGE
Wilmington, DE

Tuition & fees: $13,736 | **Average undergraduate aid package: N/A**

ABOUT THE INSTITUTION Independent, coed. Awards: associate, bachelor's, and master's degrees. 7 undergraduate majors. Total enrollment: 1,324. Undergraduates: 1,049. Federal methodology is used as a basis for awarding need-based institutional aid.

UNDERGRADUATE EXPENSES for 2005–06 *Application fee:* $30. *Tuition:* full-time $13,430.

GIFT AID (NEED-BASED) *Scholarships, grants, and awards:* Federal Pell, FSEOG, state, private, college/university gift aid from institutional funds.

GIFT AID (NON-NEED-BASED) *Scholarships, grants, and awards by category: Academic Interests/Achievement:* business.

LOANS *Programs:* FFEL (Subsidized and Unsubsidized Stafford, PLUS), Perkins.

APPLYING FOR FINANCIAL AID *Required financial aid form:* FAFSA. *Financial aid deadline (priority):* 4/1. *Notification date:* Continuous. Students must reply within 2 weeks of notification.

CONTACT Jane H. Lysle, Dean of Financial Aid and Advisement/Registrar, Goldey-Beacom College, 4701 Limestone Road, Wilmington, DE 19808-1999, 302-225-6274 or toll-free 800-833-4877. *Fax:* 302-998-8631. *E-mail:* lyslej@goldey.gbc.edu.

GONZAGA UNIVERSITY
Spokane, WA

Tuition & fees: $22,118 | **Average undergraduate aid package: $13,672**

ABOUT THE INSTITUTION Independent Roman Catholic, coed. Awards: bachelor's, master's, doctoral, and first professional degrees and post-master's certificates. 51 undergraduate majors. Total enrollment: 6,016. Undergraduates: 4,110. Freshmen: 972. Federal methodology is used as a basis for awarding need-based institutional aid.

UNDERGRADUATE EXPENSES for 2004–05 *Application fee:* $45. *Comprehensive fee:* $28,768 includes full-time tuition ($21,730), mandatory fees ($388), and room and board ($6650). *College room only:* $3240. Room and board charges vary according to board plan and housing facility. *Part-time tuition:* $630 per credit. *Part-time fees:* $35 per term. *Payment plans:* Installment, deferred payment.

FRESHMAN FINANCIAL AID (Fall 2003) 775 applied for aid; of those 74% were deemed to have need. 100% of freshmen with need received aid; of those 21% had need fully met. *Average percent of need met:* 84% (excluding resources awarded to replace EFC). *Average financial aid package:* $13,737 (excluding resources awarded to replace EFC). 33% of all full-time freshmen had no need and received non-need-based gift aid.

UNDERGRADUATE FINANCIAL AID (Fall 2003) 2,834 applied for aid; of those 85% were deemed to have need. 97% of undergraduates with need received aid; of those 30% had need fully met. *Average percent of need met:* 83% (excluding resources awarded to replace EFC). *Average financial aid package:* $13,672 (excluding resources awarded to replace EFC). 31% of all full-time undergraduates had no need and received non-need-based gift aid.

GIFT AID (NEED-BASED) *Total amount:* $23,046,560 (12% federal, 7% state, 76% institutional, 5% external sources). *Receiving aid:* Freshmen: 63% (575); All full-time undergraduates: 58% (2,107). *Average award:* Freshmen: $12,428; Undergraduates: $11,221. *Scholarships, grants, and awards:* Federal Pell, FSEOG, state, private, college/university gift aid from institutional funds, United Negro College Fund, Federal Nursing.

GIFT AID (NON-NEED-BASED) *Total amount:* $9,367,761 (83% institutional, 17% external sources). *Receiving aid:* Freshmen: 25% (228); Undergraduates: 24% (867). *Average Award:* Freshmen: $6379; Undergraduates: $6642. *Scholarships, grants, and awards by category: Academic Interests/Achievement:* 28 awards ($50,181 total): business, engineering/technologies. *Creative Arts/Performance:* 62 awards ($107,836 total): debating, music. *Special Achievements/Activities:* 98 awards ($282,000 total): leadership. *Special Characteristics:* 333 awards ($1,767,158 total): children and siblings of alumni, children of faculty/staff, members of minority groups, siblings of current students. *Tuition waivers:* Full or partial for employees or children of employees. *ROTC:* Army.

LOANS *Student loans:* $16,365,323 (73% need-based, 27% non-need-based). 68% of past graduating class borrowed through all loan programs. *Average indebtedness per student:* $21,546. *Average need-based loan:* Freshmen: $4633; Undergraduates: $5374. *Parent loans:* $5,017,118 (18% need-based, 82% non-need-based). *Programs:* FFEL (Subsidized and Unsubsidized Stafford, PLUS), Perkins, Federal Nursing, state, college/university.

WORK-STUDY *Federal work-study:* Total amount: $1,426,512; 445 jobs averaging $3206. *State or other work-study/employment:* Total amount: $1,769,123 (100% need-based). 388 part-time jobs averaging $4560.

ATHLETIC AWARDS *Total amount:* $1,985,841 (28% need-based, 72% non-need-based).

APPLYING FOR FINANCIAL AID *Required financial aid form:* FAFSA. *Financial aid deadline (priority):* 2/1. *Notification date:* Continuous beginning 3/1. Students must reply by 5/1 or within 3 weeks of notification.

CONTACT Darlene Hendrickson, Director of Operations for Financial Aid, Gonzaga University, 502 East Boone Avenue, Spokane, WA 99258-0072, 509-323-6568 or toll-free 800-322-2584 Ext. 6572. *Fax:* 509-323-5816. *E-mail:* hendrickson@gu.gonzaga.edu.

GORDON COLLEGE
Wenham, MA

Tuition & fees: $21,448 | **Average undergraduate aid package: $14,171**

ABOUT THE INSTITUTION Independent nondenominational, coed. Awards: bachelor's and master's degrees. 32 undergraduate majors. Total enrollment: 1,672. Undergraduates: 1,617. Freshmen: 402. Both federal and institutional methodology are used as a basis for awarding need-based institutional aid.

UNDERGRADUATE EXPENSES for 2004–05 *Application fee:* $40. *Comprehensive fee:* $27,540 includes full-time tuition ($20,494), mandatory fees ($954), and room and board ($6092). *College room only:* $4080. Room and board charges vary according to board plan and housing facility. Part-time tuition and fees vary according to course load. *Payment plan:* Installment.

GIFT AID (NEED-BASED) *Total amount:* $10,802,612 (9% federal, 4% state, 78% institutional, 9% external sources). *Receiving aid:* Freshmen: 60% (278); All full-time undergraduates: 68% (1,083). *Average award:* Freshmen: $10,979; Undergraduates: $9797. *Scholarships, grants, and awards:* Federal Pell, FSEOG, state, private, college/university gift aid from institutional funds.

GIFT AID (NON-NEED-BASED) *Total amount:* $4,072,224 (81% institutional, 19% external sources). *Receiving aid:* Freshmen: 8% (36); Undergraduates: 6% (97). *Average Award:* Freshmen: $11,423; Undergraduates: $11,654. *Scholarships, grants, and awards by category: Academic Interests/Achievement:* 940 awards ($5,727,560 total): general academic interests/achievements. *Creative Arts/Performance:* 46 awards ($140,250 total): music. *Special Achievements/Activities:* 84 awards ($922,500 total): leadership. *Special Characteristics:* 107 awards ($49,000 total): children and siblings of alumni, relatives of clergy. *Tuition waivers:* Full or partial for employees or children of employees. *ROTC:* Army cooperative, Air Force cooperative.

LOANS *Student loans:* $10,521,368 (66% need-based, 34% non-need-based). 51% of past graduating class borrowed through all loan programs. *Average indebtedness per student:* $9182. *Average need-based loan:* Freshmen: $3069; Undergraduates: $4395. *Parent loans:* $2,705,901 (46% need-based, 54% non-need-based). *Programs:* FFEL (Subsidized and Unsubsidized Stafford, PLUS), Perkins, state, college/university.

APPLYING FOR FINANCIAL AID *Required financial aid forms:* FAFSA, CSS Financial Aid PROFILE, state aid form, income tax form(s), W-2 forms. *Financial aid deadline (priority):* 3/1. *Notification date:* 4/15. Students must reply by 5/1 or within 2 weeks of notification.

CONTACT Barbara Ruth Layne, Associate Vice President and Student Services, Gordon College, 255 Grapevine Road, Wenham, MA 01984-1899, 978-867-4246 or toll-free 866-464-6736. *Fax:* 978-867-4657. *E-mail:* blayne@hope.gordon.edu.

GOSHEN COLLEGE
Goshen, IN

Tuition & fees: $19,300 | **Average undergraduate aid package: $17,181**

ABOUT THE INSTITUTION Independent Mennonite, coed. Awards: bachelor's degrees. 51 undergraduate majors. Total enrollment: 908. Undergraduates: 908. Freshmen: 169. Federal methodology is used as a basis for awarding need-based institutional aid.

UNDERGRADUATE EXPENSES for 2005–06 *Application fee:* $25. *Comprehensive fee:* $25,750 includes full-time tuition ($19,300) and room and board ($6450).

Goshen College

College room only: $3450. Room and board charges vary according to board plan and student level. Part-time tuition and fees vary according to course load. **Payment plan:** Installment.

FRESHMAN FINANCIAL AID (Fall 2003) 168 applied for aid; of those 83% were deemed to have need. 100% of freshmen with need received aid; of those 66% had need fully met. *Average percent of need met:* 88% (excluding resources awarded to replace EFC). *Average financial aid package:* $17,302 (excluding resources awarded to replace EFC). 10% of all full-time freshmen had no need and received non-need-based gift aid.

UNDERGRADUATE FINANCIAL AID (Fall 2003) 747 applied for aid; of those 79% were deemed to have need. 100% of undergraduates with need received aid; of those 32% had need fully met. *Average percent of need met:* 88% (excluding resources awarded to replace EFC). *Average financial aid package:* $17,181 (excluding resources awarded to replace EFC). 6% of all full-time undergraduates had no need and received non-need-based gift aid.

GIFT AID (NEED-BASED) *Total amount:* $6,310,255 (11% federal, 14% state, 65% institutional, 10% external sources). *Receiving aid:* Freshmen: 83% (139); All full-time undergraduates: 78% (587). *Average award:* Freshmen: $12,673; Undergraduates: $11,275. *Scholarships, grants, and awards:* Federal Pell, FSEOG, state, private, college/university gift aid from institutional funds.

GIFT AID (NON-NEED-BASED) *Total amount:* $1,298,632 (4% federal, 69% institutional, 27% external sources). *Receiving aid:* Freshmen: 77% (130); Undergraduates: 70% (525). *Average Award: Freshmen:* $8872; *Undergraduates:* $7503. *Scholarships, grants, and awards by category: Academic Interests/Achievement:* 475 awards ($2,150,321 total): business, communication, education, general academic interests/achievements. *Creative Arts/Performance:* 58 awards ($81,796 total): music. *Special Characteristics:* 66 awards ($760,890 total): international students. *Tuition waivers:* Full or partial for employees or children of employees.

LOANS *Student loans:* $3,066,694 (67% need-based, 33% non-need-based). 68% of past graduating class borrowed through all loan programs. *Average indebtedness per student:* $17,126. *Average need-based loan:* Freshmen: $3675; Undergraduates: $5296. *Parent loans:* $719,914 (100% need-based). *Programs:* Federal Direct (Subsidized and Unsubsidized Stafford, PLUS), Perkins, Federal Nursing, college/university.

WORK-STUDY *Federal work-study:* Total amount: $483,851; 633 jobs averaging $629. *State or other work-study/employment:* Total amount: $39,100 (77% need-based, 23% non-need-based). 20 part-time jobs averaging $865.

ATHLETIC AWARDS *Total amount:* $451,525 (85% need-based, 15% non-need-based).

APPLYING FOR FINANCIAL AID *Required financial aid forms:* FAFSA, institution's own form. *Financial aid deadline (priority):* 2/15. *Notification date:* Continuous beginning 3/1. Students must reply by 5/1 or within 2 weeks of notification.

CONTACT Galen L. Graber, Director of Student Financial Aid, Goshen College, 1700 South Main Street, Goshen, IN 46526-4794, 574-535-7525 or toll-free 800-348-7422. *Fax:* 574-535-7654.

GOUCHER COLLEGE
Baltimore, MD

Tuition & fees: $26,150	Average undergraduate aid package: $19,481

ABOUT THE INSTITUTION Independent, coed. Awards: bachelor's and master's degrees and post-bachelor's certificates. 30 undergraduate majors. Total enrollment: 2,349. Undergraduates: 1,366. Freshmen: 402. Both federal and institutional methodology are used as a basis for awarding need-based institutional aid.

UNDERGRADUATE EXPENSES for 2004–05 *Application fee:* $40. *Comprehensive fee:* $34,725 includes full-time tuition ($25,750), mandatory fees ($400), and room and board ($8575). *College room only:* $5525. Room and board charges vary according to board plan and housing facility. *Part-time tuition:* $900 per credit hour. *Payment plans:* Tuition prepayment, installment.

FRESHMAN FINANCIAL AID (Fall 2004, est.) 293 applied for aid; of those 78% were deemed to have need. 100% of freshmen with need received aid; of those 38% had need fully met. *Average percent of need met:* 81% (excluding resources awarded to replace EFC). *Average financial aid package:* $19,849 (excluding resources awarded to replace EFC). 27% of all full-time freshmen had no need and received non-need-based gift aid.

UNDERGRADUATE FINANCIAL AID (Fall 2004, est.) 878 applied for aid; of those 90% were deemed to have need. 100% of undergraduates with need received aid; of those 21% had need fully met. *Average percent of need met:* 68% (excluding resources awarded to replace EFC). *Average financial aid*

package: $19,481 (excluding resources awarded to replace EFC). 28% of all full-time undergraduates had no need and received non-need-based gift aid.

GIFT AID (NEED-BASED) *Total amount:* $10,812,747 (7% federal, 5% state, 86% institutional, 2% external sources). *Receiving aid:* Freshmen: 54% (218); All full-time undergraduates: 55% (746). *Average award:* Freshmen: $13,722; Undergraduates: $13,556. *Scholarships, grants, and awards:* Federal Pell, FSEOG, state, private, college/university gift aid from institutional funds.

GIFT AID (NON-NEED-BASED) *Total amount:* $3,802,851 (1% state, 97% institutional, 2% external sources). *Receiving aid:* Freshmen: 23% (92); Undergraduates: 12% (162). *Average Award: Freshmen:* $12,611; *Undergraduates:* $13,429. *Scholarships, grants, and awards by category: Creative Arts/Performance:* 11 awards ($55,000 total): fine arts, dance, music, theater/drama. *Tuition waivers:* Full or partial for employees or children of employees, adult students, senior citizens. *ROTC:* Army cooperative.

LOANS *Student loans:* $3,577,507 (94% need-based, 6% non-need-based). 68% of past graduating class borrowed through all loan programs. *Average indebtedness per student:* $16,062. *Average need-based loan:* Freshmen: $3607; Undergraduates: $3755. *Parent loans:* $2,161,672 (94% need-based, 6% non-need-based). *Programs:* Federal Direct (Subsidized and Unsubsidized Stafford), Perkins, college/university.

WORK-STUDY *Federal work-study:* Total amount: $364,133; 286 jobs averaging $1273. *State or other work-study/employment:* Total amount: $143,841 (100% non-need-based). 502 part-time jobs averaging $287.

APPLYING FOR FINANCIAL AID *Required financial aid forms:* FAFSA, CSS Financial Aid PROFILE. *Financial aid deadline (priority):* 2/15. *Notification date:* 4/1. Students must reply by 5/1 or within 2 weeks of notification.

CONTACT Sharon Hassan, Director of Student Financial Aid, Goucher College, 1021 Dulaney Valley Road, Baltimore, MD 21204-2794, 410-337-6141 or toll-free 800-468-2437. *Fax:* 410-337-6504.

GOVERNORS STATE UNIVERSITY
University Park, IL

CONTACT Financial Aid Office, Governors State University, One University Parkway, University Park, IL 60466-0975, 708-534-4480.

GRACE BIBLE COLLEGE
Grand Rapids, MI

Tuition & fees: $10,420	Average undergraduate aid package: $7307

ABOUT THE INSTITUTION Independent religious, coed. Awards: associate and bachelor's degrees. 22 undergraduate majors. Total enrollment: 172. Undergraduates: 172. Freshmen: 45. Federal methodology is used as a basis for awarding need-based institutional aid.

UNDERGRADUATE EXPENSES for 2004–05 *Comprehensive fee:* $16,910 includes full-time tuition ($9950), mandatory fees ($470), and room and board ($6490). Room and board charges vary according to housing facility. *Part-time tuition:* $425 per semester hour. Part-time tuition and fees vary according to course load. *Payment plan:* Installment.

FRESHMAN FINANCIAL AID (Fall 2003) 26 applied for aid; of those 88% were deemed to have need. 100% of freshmen with need received aid. *Average percent of need met:* 57% (excluding resources awarded to replace EFC). *Average financial aid package:* $8350 (excluding resources awarded to replace EFC). 10% of all full-time freshmen had no need and received non-need-based gift aid.

UNDERGRADUATE FINANCIAL AID (Fall 2003) 128 applied for aid; of those 92% were deemed to have need. 100% of undergraduates with need received aid; of those 4% had need fully met. *Average percent of need met:* 58% (excluding resources awarded to replace EFC). *Average financial aid package:* $7307 (excluding resources awarded to replace EFC). 7% of all full-time undergraduates had no need and received non-need-based gift aid.

GIFT AID (NEED-BASED) *Total amount:* $471,619 (39% federal, 30% state, 26% institutional, 5% external sources). *Receiving aid:* Freshmen: 74% (23); All full-time undergraduates: 79% (118). *Average award:* Freshmen: $6567; Undergraduates: $5245. *Scholarships, grants, and awards:* Federal Pell, FSEOG, state, private, college/university gift aid from institutional funds.

GIFT AID (NON-NEED-BASED) *Total amount:* $56,837 (14% state, 80% institutional, 6% external sources). *Receiving aid:* Undergraduates: 3% (5). *Average Award: Freshmen:* $1360; *Undergraduates:* $1247. *Scholarships, grants, and awards by category: Academic Interests/Achievement:* 35 awards ($45,687 total): general academic interests/achievements. *Creative Arts/Performance:* 24

awards ($23,000 total): music. *Special Characteristics:* 17 awards ($59,584 total): general special characteristics. *Tuition waivers:* Full or partial for employees or children of employees. *ROTC:* Army cooperative.

LOANS *Student loans:* $455,177 (74% need-based, 26% non-need-based). 68% of past graduating class borrowed through all loan programs. *Average indebtedness per student:* $13,919. *Average need-based loan:* Freshmen: $2412; Undergraduates: $3690. *Parent loans:* $35,685 (60% need-based, 40% non-need-based). *Programs:* FFEL (Subsidized and Unsubsidized Stafford, PLUS).

WORK-STUDY *Federal work-study:* Total amount: $29,833; 25 jobs averaging $1193. *State or other work-study/employment:* Total amount: $6843 (100% need-based). 12 part-time jobs averaging $570.

APPLYING FOR FINANCIAL AID *Required financial aid form:* FAFSA. *Financial aid deadline (priority):* 3/1. *Notification date:* Continuous beginning 5/15.

CONTACT Ms. Marlene DeVries, Director of Financial Aid, Grace Bible College, 1011 Aldon Street, SW, PO Box 910, Grand Rapids, MI 49509-1921, 616-538-2330 or toll-free 800-968-1887. *Fax:* 616-538-0599.

GRACE COLLEGE
Winona Lake, IN

Tuition & fees: $15,030	Average undergraduate aid package: $12,629

ABOUT THE INSTITUTION Independent religious, coed. Awards: associate, bachelor's, and master's degrees. 39 undergraduate majors. Total enrollment: 1,258. Undergraduates: 1,113. Freshmen: 180. Federal methodology is used as a basis for awarding need-based institutional aid.

UNDERGRADUATE EXPENSES for 2004–05 *Application fee:* $20. *Comprehensive fee:* $21,180 includes full-time tuition ($14,630), mandatory fees ($400), and room and board ($6150). *College room only:* $3070. Room and board charges vary according to board plan and housing facility. *Part-time tuition:* $275 per credit. *Part-time fees:* $280 per year. Part-time tuition and fees vary according to course load. *Payment plan:* Installment.

FRESHMAN FINANCIAL AID (Fall 2004, est.) 170 applied for aid; of those 89% were deemed to have need. 100% of freshmen with need received aid; of those 24% had need fully met. *Average percent of need met:* 80% (excluding resources awarded to replace EFC). *Average financial aid package:* $12,376 (excluding resources awarded to replace EFC). 16% of all full-time freshmen had no need and received non-need-based gift aid.

UNDERGRADUATE FINANCIAL AID (Fall 2004, est.) 677 applied for aid; of those 91% were deemed to have need. 100% of undergraduates with need received aid; of those 24% had need fully met. *Average percent of need met:* 83% (excluding resources awarded to replace EFC). *Average financial aid package:* $12,629 (excluding resources awarded to replace EFC). 18% of all full-time undergraduates had no need and received non-need-based gift aid.

GIFT AID (NEED-BASED) *Total amount:* $4,196,343 (17% federal, 29% state, 39% institutional, 15% external sources). *Receiving aid:* Freshmen: 68% (150); All full-time undergraduates: 77% (596). *Average award:* Freshmen: $8240; Undergraduates: $7626. *Scholarships, grants, and awards:* Federal Pell, FSEOG, state, college/university gift aid from institutional funds.

GIFT AID (NON-NEED-BASED) *Total amount:* $913,799 (1% state, 55% institutional, 44% external sources). *Receiving aid:* Freshmen: 8% (17); Undergraduates: 8% (62). *Average Award:* Freshmen: $7267; Undergraduates: $8544. *Scholarships, grants, and awards by category: Academic Interests/Achievement:* 490 awards ($1,273,316 total): general academic interests/achievements. *Creative Arts/Performance:* 44 awards ($44,765 total): art/fine arts, music, theater/drama. *Special Characteristics:* 168 awards ($607,485 total): children of faculty/staff, relatives of clergy. *Tuition waivers:* Full or partial for employees or children of employees.

LOANS *Student loans:* $4,771,102 (74% need-based, 26% non-need-based). 95% of past graduating class borrowed through all loan programs. *Average indebtedness per student:* $25,338. *Average need-based loan:* Freshmen: $4905; Undergraduates: $5964. *Parent loans:* $1,517,204 (32% need-based, 68% non-need-based). *Programs:* FFEL (Subsidized and Unsubsidized Stafford, PLUS), Perkins.

WORK-STUDY *Federal work-study:* Total amount: $150,156; jobs available (averaging $1300).

ATHLETIC AWARDS *Total amount:* $666,238 (64% need-based, 36% non-need-based).

APPLYING FOR FINANCIAL AID *Required financial aid form:* FAFSA. *Financial aid deadline (priority):* 3/1. *Notification date:* Continuous beginning 3/15.

CONTACT Office of Student Financial Aid Services, Grace College, 200 Seminary Drive, Winona Lake, IN 46590-1294, 800-544-7223 Ext. 6162 or toll-free 800-54-GRACE Ext. 6412 (in-state), 800-54 GRACE Ext. 6412 (out-of-state). *Fax:* 574-372-5144. *E-mail:* financialaid@grace.edu.

GRACELAND UNIVERSITY
Lamoni, IA

Tuition & fees: $16,150	Average undergraduate aid package: $14,695

ABOUT THE INSTITUTION Independent Community of Christ, coed. Awards: bachelor's and master's degrees and post-master's certificates. 54 undergraduate majors. Total enrollment: 2,351. Undergraduates: 1,945. Freshmen: 307. Federal methodology is used as a basis for awarding need-based institutional aid.

UNDERGRADUATE EXPENSES for 2005–06 *Application fee:* $50. *Comprehensive fee:* $21,550 includes full-time tuition ($16,000), mandatory fees ($150), and room and board ($5400). Full-time tuition and fees vary according to course load and location. Room and board charges vary according to board plan, housing facility, and location. *Part-time tuition:* $500 per semester hour. Part-time tuition and fees vary according to location. *Payment plan:* Installment.

FRESHMAN FINANCIAL AID (Fall 2004, est.) 266 applied for aid; of those 89% were deemed to have need. 99% of freshmen with need received aid; of those 34% had need fully met. *Average percent of need met:* 88% (excluding resources awarded to replace EFC). *Average financial aid package:* $15,972 (excluding resources awarded to replace EFC). 16% of all full-time freshmen had no need and received non-need-based gift aid.

UNDERGRADUATE FINANCIAL AID (Fall 2004, est.) 1,149 applied for aid; of those 87% were deemed to have need. 99% of undergraduates with need received aid; of those 28% had need fully met. *Average percent of need met:* 85% (excluding resources awarded to replace EFC). *Average financial aid package:* $14,695 (excluding resources awarded to replace EFC). 17% of all full-time undergraduates had no need and received non-need-based gift aid.

GIFT AID (NEED-BASED) *Total amount:* $7,830,849 (24% federal, 8% state, 61% institutional, 7% external sources). *Receiving aid:* Freshmen: 74% (233); All full-time undergraduates: 65% (935). *Average award:* Freshmen: $11,738; Undergraduates: $9980. *Scholarships, grants, and awards:* Federal Pell, FSEOG, state, private, college/university gift aid from institutional funds.

GIFT AID (NON-NEED-BASED) *Total amount:* $2,755,840 (2% federal, 82% institutional, 16% external sources). *Receiving aid:* Freshmen: 40% (125); Undergraduates: 30% (426). *Average Award:* Freshmen: $9444; Undergraduates: $9570. *Scholarships, grants, and awards by category: Academic Interests/Achievement:* 752 awards ($2,364,580 total): computer science, engineering/technologies, English, general academic interests/achievements, physical sciences. *Creative Arts/Performance:* 197 awards ($340,580 total): applied art and design, creative writing, music, theater/drama. *Special Achievements/Activities:* 165 awards ($282,701 total): cheerleading/drum major, general special achievements/activities, leadership, religious involvement. *Special Characteristics:* 1,370 awards ($4,533,971 total): children and siblings of alumni, children of faculty/staff, children of public servants, first-generation college students, general special characteristics, international students, local/state students, members of minority groups, religious affiliation. *Tuition waivers:* Full or partial for employees or children of employees, senior citizens.

LOANS *Student loans:* $7,915,556 (76% need-based, 24% non-need-based). 78% of past graduating class borrowed through all loan programs. *Average indebtedness per student:* $21,766. *Average need-based loan:* Freshmen: $4367; Undergraduates: $5561. *Parent loans:* $861,726 (27% need-based, 73% non-need-based). *Programs:* Federal Direct (Subsidized and Unsubsidized Stafford, PLUS), Perkins, state, college/university.

WORK-STUDY *Federal work-study:* Total amount: $680,234; 392 jobs averaging $1735. *State or other work-study/employment:* Total amount: $395,083 (25% need-based, 75% non-need-based). 262 part-time jobs averaging $1508.

ATHLETIC AWARDS *Total amount:* $1,728,616 (75% need-based, 25% non-need-based).

APPLYING FOR FINANCIAL AID *Required financial aid form:* FAFSA. *Financial aid deadline:* Continuous. *Notification date:* Continuous beginning 2/1. Students must reply within 2 weeks of notification.

CONTACT Mrs. Sherry Mesle-Morain, Director of Financial Aid, Graceland University, 1 University Place, Lamoni, IA 50140, 641-784-5140 or toll-free 866-GRACELAND. *Fax:* 641-784-5488. *E-mail:* smorain@graceland.edu.

LOANS *Student loans:* $6,813,427 (54% need-based, 46% non-need-based). 66% of past graduating class borrowed through all loan programs. *Average indebtedness per student:* $20,538. *Average need-based loan:* Freshmen: $1495; Undergraduates: $1306. *Parent loans:* $1,554,025 (100% non-need-based). *Programs:* FFEL (Subsidized and Unsubsidized Stafford, PLUS), Perkins, state, alternative loans.

WORK-STUDY *Federal work-study:* Total amount: $224,875; jobs available.

ATHLETIC AWARDS *Total amount:* $1,063,617 (100% non-need-based).

APPLYING FOR FINANCIAL AID *Required financial aid forms:* FAFSA, Different forms of aid. *Financial aid deadline:* Continuous.

CONTACT Director of Financial Aid, Grand Canyon University, 3300 West Camelback Road, PO Box 11097, Phoenix, AZ 85017-3030, 800-800-9776 Ext. 2885 or toll-free 800-800-9776 (in-state). *Fax:* 602-589-2044.

GRAND VALLEY STATE UNIVERSITY
Allendale, MI

Tuition & fees (MI res): $5782	Average undergraduate aid package: $7058

ABOUT THE INSTITUTION State-supported, coed. Awards: bachelor's and master's degrees and post-bachelor's and post-master's certificates. 122 undergraduate majors. Total enrollment: 22,063. Undergraduates: 18,393. Freshmen: 3,337. Federal methodology is used as a basis for awarding need-based institutional aid.

UNDERGRADUATE EXPENSES for 2004–05 *Application fee:* $30. *Tuition, state resident:* full-time $5782; part-time $252 per semester hour. *Tuition, nonresident:* full-time $12,510; part-time $532 per semester hour. Full-time tuition and fees vary according to course level, program, and student level. Part-time tuition and fees vary according to course level, course load, program, and student level. *College room and board:* $6160. Room and board charges vary according to board plan, housing facility, and location. *Payment plans:* Installment, deferred payment.

FRESHMAN FINANCIAL AID (Fall 2004, est.) 3031 applied for aid; of those 65% were deemed to have need. 100% of freshmen with need received aid; of those 100% had need fully met. *Average percent of need met:* 100% (excluding resources awarded to replace EFC). *Average financial aid package:* $7095 (excluding resources awarded to replace EFC). 37% of all full-time freshmen had no need and received non-need-based gift aid.

UNDERGRADUATE FINANCIAL AID (Fall 2004, est.) 12,560 applied for aid; of those 70% were deemed to have need. 100% of undergraduates with need received aid; of those 88% had need fully met. *Average percent of need met:* 88% (excluding resources awarded to replace EFC). *Average financial aid package:* $7058 (excluding resources awarded to replace EFC). 13% of all full-time undergraduates had no need and received non-need-based gift aid.

GIFT AID (NEED-BASED) *Total amount:* $24,534,447 (51% federal, 27% state, 22% institutional). *Receiving aid:* Freshmen: 51% (1,704); All full-time undergraduates: 34% (5,414). *Average award:* Freshmen: $4270; Undergraduates: $3020. *Scholarships, grants, and awards:* Federal Pell, FSEOG, state, private, college/university gift aid from institutional funds, Federal Nursing.

GIFT AID (NON-NEED-BASED) *Total amount:* $11,726,018 (33% state, 46% institutional, 21% external sources). *Receiving aid:* Freshmen: 53% (1,774); Undergraduates: 12% (1,894). *Average Award:* Freshmen: $2270; Undergraduates: $1988. *Scholarships, grants, and awards by category:* Academic Interests/ Achievement: 800 awards ($2,505,000 total): general academic interests/ achievements. Creative Arts/Performance: 190 awards ($210,000 total): art/fine arts, music, theater/drama. Special Characteristics: 1,150 awards ($4,300,000 total): children of faculty/staff, children of union members/company employees, handicapped students, local/state students, members of minority groups, out-of-state students. *Tuition waivers:* Full or partial for employees or children of employees.

LOANS *Student loans:* $62,507,000 (79% need-based, 21% non-need-based). 72% of past graduating class borrowed through all loan programs. *Average indebtedness per student:* $16,200. *Average need-based loan:* Freshmen: $2570; Undergraduates: $3414. *Parent loans:* $3,853,815 (100% non-need-based). *Programs:* Federal Direct (Subsidized and Unsubsidized Stafford, PLUS), Perkins, Federal Nursing, state.

WORK-STUDY *Federal work-study:* Total amount: $1,051,897; 865 jobs averaging $1200. *State or other work-study/employment:* Total amount: $6,590,353 (5% need-based, 95% non-need-based). 261 part-time jobs averaging $1340.

ATHLETIC AWARDS *Total amount:* $1,865,085 (100% non-need-based).

APPLYING FOR FINANCIAL AID *Required financial aid form:* FAFSA. *Financial aid deadline (priority):* 2/15. *Notification date:* 4/1. Students must reply within 3 weeks of notification.

CONTACT Mr. Ken Fridsma, Director of Financial Aid, Grand Valley State University, 100 Student Services Building, Allendale, MI 49401-9403, 616-331-3234 or toll-free 800-748-0246. *Fax:* 616-331-3180. *E-mail:* fridsmak@gvsu.edu.

GRAND VIEW COLLEGE
Des Moines, IA

Tuition & fees: $15,392	Average undergraduate aid package: $11,832

ABOUT THE INSTITUTION Independent religious, coed. Awards: associate and bachelor's degrees and post-bachelor's certificates. 30 undergraduate majors. Total enrollment: 1,759. Undergraduates: 1,759. Freshmen: 222. Federal methodology is used as a basis for awarding need-based institutional aid.

UNDERGRADUATE EXPENSES for 2004–05 *Application fee:* $35. *Comprehensive fee:* $20,828 includes full-time tuition ($15,052), mandatory fees ($340), and room and board ($5436). Full-time tuition and fees vary according to class time. Room and board charges vary according to board plan and housing facility. *Part-time tuition:* $425 per credit hour. Part-time tuition and fees vary according to class time. *Payment plan:* Installment.

FRESHMAN FINANCIAL AID (Fall 2004, est.) 211 applied for aid; of those 90% were deemed to have need. 100% of freshmen with need received aid; of those 15% had need fully met. *Average percent of need met:* 83% (excluding resources awarded to replace EFC). *Average financial aid package:* $12,883 (excluding resources awarded to replace EFC). 21% of all full-time freshmen had no need and received non-need-based gift aid.

UNDERGRADUATE FINANCIAL AID (Fall 2004, est.) 1,298 applied for aid; of those 91% were deemed to have need. 99% of undergraduates with need received aid; of those 16% had need fully met. *Average percent of need met:* 74% (excluding resources awarded to replace EFC). *Average financial aid package:* $11,832 (excluding resources awarded to replace EFC). 13% of all full-time undergraduates had no need and received non-need-based gift aid.

GIFT AID (NEED-BASED) *Total amount:* $9,275,569 (18% federal, 31% state, 47% institutional, 4% external sources). *Receiving aid:* Freshmen: 87% (189); All full-time undergraduates: 89% (1,166). *Average award:* Freshmen: $9753; Undergraduates: $8020. *Scholarships, grants, and awards:* Federal Pell, FSEOG, state, private, college/university gift aid from institutional funds.

GIFT AID (NON-NEED-BASED) *Total amount:* $1,062,579 (1% federal, 6% state, 83% institutional, 10% external sources). *Receiving aid:* Freshmen: 12% (27); Undergraduates: 8% (107). *Average Award:* Freshmen: $10,032; Undergraduates: $9980. *Scholarships, grants, and awards by category:* Academic Interests/ Achievement: 863 awards ($2,936,229 total): general academic interests/ achievements. Creative Arts/Performance: 56 awards ($58,750 total): art/fine arts, music, theater/drama. Special Characteristics: 111 awards ($451,115 total): children and siblings of alumni, children of educators, children of faculty/staff. *Tuition waivers:* Full or partial for employees or children of employees, senior citizens. *ROTC:* Army cooperative, Air Force cooperative.

LOANS *Student loans:* $11,343,355 (67% need-based, 33% non-need-based). 75% of past graduating class borrowed through all loan programs. *Average indebtedness per student:* $21,245. *Average need-based loan:* Freshmen: $3248; Undergraduates: $3989. *Parent loans:* $438,805 (28% need-based, 72% non-need-based). *Programs:* FFEL (Subsidized and Unsubsidized Stafford, PLUS), Perkins, Federal Nursing.

WORK-STUDY *Federal work-study:* Total amount: $400,222; jobs available (averaging $1500).

ATHLETIC AWARDS *Total amount:* $580,563 (59% need-based, 41% non-need-based).

APPLYING FOR FINANCIAL AID *Required financial aid form:* FAFSA. *Financial aid deadline (priority):* 3/1. *Notification date:* Continuous beginning 3/15. Students must reply by 5/1 or within 4 weeks of notification.

CONTACT Michele Dunne, Director of Financial Aid, Grand View College, 1200 Grandview Avenue, Des Moines, IA 50316-1599, 515-263-2820 or toll-free 800-444-6083 Ext. 2810. *Fax:* 515-263-6191. *E-mail:* mdunne@gvc.edu.

GRATZ COLLEGE
Melrose Park, PA

ABOUT THE INSTITUTION Independent Jewish, coed. Awards: bachelor's and master's degrees and post-master's certificates. 1 undergraduate major. Total enrollment: 696. Undergraduates: 16.

GIFT AID (NEED-BASED) *Scholarships, grants, and awards:* Federal Pell, state, private, college/university gift aid from institutional funds.
LOANS *Programs:* FFEL (Subsidized and Unsubsidized Stafford, PLUS).
APPLYING FOR FINANCIAL AID *Required financial aid forms:* FAFSA, institution's own form, income tax forms.
CONTACT Karen West, Student Financial Services Adviser, Gratz College, 7605 Old York Road, Melrose Park, PA 19027, 215-635-7300 Ext. 163 or toll-free 800-475-4635 Ext. 140 (out-of-state). *Fax:* 215-635-7320.

GREAT LAKES CHRISTIAN COLLEGE
Lansing, MI

CONTACT Financial Aid Officer, Great Lakes Christian College, 6211 West Willow Highway, Lansing, MI 48917-1299, 517-321-0242 or toll-free 800-YES-GLCC.

GREEN MOUNTAIN COLLEGE
Poultney, VT

Tuition & fees: $21,214	Average undergraduate aid package: $17,867

ABOUT THE INSTITUTION Independent religious, coed. Awards: bachelor's degrees. 24 undergraduate majors. Total enrollment: 639. Undergraduates: 639. Federal methodology is used as a basis for awarding need-based institutional aid.
UNDERGRADUATE EXPENSES for 2004–05 *Application fee:* $30. *Comprehensive fee:* $28,204 includes full-time tuition ($20,614), mandatory fees ($600), and room and board ($6990). *College room only:* $4350. Full-time tuition and fees vary according to course load. Room and board charges vary according to housing facility. *Part-time tuition:* $688 per credit. Part-time tuition and fees vary according to course load. *Payment plan:* Installment.
FRESHMAN FINANCIAL AID (Fall 2004, est.) 170 applied for aid; of those 85% were deemed to have need. 99% of freshmen with need received aid; of those 31% had need fully met. *Average percent of need met:* 81% (excluding resources awarded to replace EFC). *Average financial aid package:* $18,788 (excluding resources awarded to replace EFC). 25% of all full-time freshmen had no need and received non-need-based gift aid.
UNDERGRADUATE FINANCIAL AID (Fall 2004, est.) 533 applied for aid; of those 93% were deemed to have need. 88% of undergraduates with need received aid; of those 28% had need fully met. *Average percent of need met:* 76% (excluding resources awarded to replace EFC). *Average financial aid package:* $17,867 (excluding resources awarded to replace EFC). 13% of all full-time undergraduates had no need and received non-need-based gift aid.
GIFT AID (NEED-BASED) *Total amount:* $4,392,009 (24% federal, 5% state, 69% institutional, 2% external sources). *Receiving aid:* Freshmen: 74% (142); All full-time undergraduates: 71% (432). *Average award:* Freshmen: $11,928; Undergraduates: $10,643. *Scholarships, grants, and awards:* Federal Pell, FSEOG, state, private, college/university gift aid from institutional funds.
GIFT AID (NON-NEED-BASED) *Total amount:* $461,731 (95% institutional, 5% external sources). *Receiving aid:* Freshmen: 5% (9); Undergraduates: 4% (24). *Average Award:* Freshmen: $13,127; Undergraduates: $13,042. *Scholarships, grants, and awards by category: Creative Arts/Performance:* 16 awards ($28,900 total): art/fine arts, music, performing arts, theater/drama. *Special Achievements/ Activities:* 80 awards ($94,175 total): community service, leadership, religious involvement. *Special Characteristics:* 20 awards ($113,600 total): children and siblings of alumni, children of current students, international students, parents of current students, siblings of current students. *Tuition waivers:* Full or partial for employees or children of employees.
LOANS *Student loans:* $4,231,013 (76% need-based, 24% non-need-based). 95% of past graduating class borrowed through all loan programs. *Average indebtedness per student:* $19,873. *Average need-based loan:* Freshmen: $6408; Undergraduates: $7218. *Parent loans:* $1,208,227 (44% need-based, 56% non-need-based). *Programs:* FFEL (Subsidized and Unsubsidized Stafford, PLUS).
WORK-STUDY *Federal work-study:* Total amount: $94,420; 114 jobs averaging $1500. *State or other work-study/employment:* Total amount: $164,743 (99% need-based, 1% non-need-based). 233 part-time jobs averaging $1500.
ATHLETIC AWARDS *Total amount:* $67,000 (100% non-need-based).
APPLYING FOR FINANCIAL AID *Required financial aid forms:* FAFSA, CSS Financial Aid PROFILE, noncustodial (divorced/separated) parent's statement. *Financial aid deadline:* Continuous. *Notification date:* Continuous beginning 2/1. Students must reply by 5/1 or within 2 weeks of notification.

CONTACT Wendy J. Ellis, Director of Financial Aid, Green Mountain College, One College Circle, Poultney, VT 05764-1199, 800-776-6675 Ext. 8210 or toll-free 800-776-6675 (out-of-state). *Fax:* 802-287-8099. *E-mail:* ellisw@greenmtn.edu.

GREENSBORO COLLEGE
Greensboro, NC

ABOUT THE INSTITUTION Independent United Methodist, coed. Awards: bachelor's and master's degrees and post-bachelor's certificates. 48 undergraduate majors. Total enrollment: 1,226. Undergraduates: 1,165. Freshmen: 249.
GIFT AID (NEED-BASED) *Scholarships, grants, and awards:* Federal Pell, FSEOG, state, private, college/university gift aid from institutional funds.
GIFT AID (NON-NEED-BASED) *Scholarships, grants, and awards by category: Academic Interests/Achievement:* general academic interests/achievements. *Creative Arts/Performance:* art/fine arts, music, theater/drama. *Special Achievements/ Activities:* community service, leadership, religious involvement. *Special Characteristics:* adult students, children and siblings of alumni, children of faculty/staff, international students, relatives of clergy, religious affiliation, siblings of current students, veterans.
LOANS *Programs:* FFEL (Subsidized and Unsubsidized Stafford, PLUS), Perkins, college/university.
APPLYING FOR FINANCIAL AID *Required financial aid forms:* FAFSA, institution's own form, state aid form.
CONTACT Mr. Ron Elmore, Director of Financial Aid, Greensboro College, 815 West Market Street, Greensboro, NC 27401-1875, 336-272-7102 Ext. 339 or toll-free 800-346-8226. *Fax:* 336-271-6634. *E-mail:* relmore@gborocollege.edu.

GREENVILLE COLLEGE
Greenville, IL

Tuition & fees: $16,824	Average undergraduate aid package: $13,598

ABOUT THE INSTITUTION Independent Free Methodist, coed. Awards: bachelor's and master's degrees. 58 undergraduate majors. Total enrollment: 1,305. Undergraduates: 1,170. Freshmen: 239. Federal methodology is used as a basis for awarding need-based institutional aid.
UNDERGRADUATE EXPENSES for 2004–05 *Application fee:* $25. *Comprehensive fee:* $22,584 includes full-time tuition ($16,724), mandatory fees ($100), and room and board ($5760). *College room only:* $2726. Room and board charges vary according to housing facility. *Part-time tuition:* $352 per credit hour. Part-time tuition and fees vary according to course load.
GIFT AID (NEED-BASED) *Total amount:* $7,353,361 (15% federal, 20% state, 62% institutional, 3% external sources). *Receiving aid:* Freshmen: 84% (204); All full-time undergraduates: 85% (773). *Average award:* Freshmen: $10,483; Undergraduates: $9355. *Scholarships, grants, and awards:* Federal Pell, FSEOG, state, private, college/university gift aid from institutional funds.
GIFT AID (NON-NEED-BASED) *Total amount:* $735,864 (2% state, 93% institutional, 5% external sources). *Receiving aid:* Freshmen: 5% (11); Undergraduates: 4% (37). *Average Award:* Freshmen: $7021; Undergraduates: $7565. *Scholarships, grants, and awards by category: Academic Interests/ Achievement:* 425 awards ($1,545,379 total): biological sciences, business, education, engineering/technologies, general academic interests/achievements, mathematics, physical sciences, religion/biblical studies. *Creative Arts/ Performance:* 120 awards ($135,000 total): applied art and design, art/fine arts, music, performing arts. *Special Achievements/Activities:* 264 awards ($583,000 total): leadership, memberships, religious involvement. *Special Characteristics:* 626 awards ($1,361,418 total): children and siblings of alumni, children of faculty/staff, international students, local/state students, out-of-state students, relatives of clergy, religious affiliation, siblings of current students. *Tuition waivers:* Full or partial for employees or children of employees, senior citizens.
LOANS *Student loans:* $4,197,958 (84% need-based, 16% non-need-based). 86% of past graduating class borrowed through all loan programs. *Average indebtedness per student:* $17,896. *Average need-based loan:* Freshmen: $3385; Undergraduates: $3890. *Parent loans:* $1,746,156 (38% need-based, 62% non-need-based). *Programs:* Federal Direct (Subsidized and Unsubsidized Stafford, PLUS), Perkins, college/university.
APPLYING FOR FINANCIAL AID *Required financial aid form:* FAFSA. *Financial aid deadline:* Continuous. *Notification date:* Continuous beginning 3/15. Students must reply within 3 weeks of notification.
CONTACT Mr. Karl Somerville, Director of Financial Aid, Greenville College, 315 East College Avenue, Greenville, IL 62246-0159, 618-664-7110 or toll-free 800-345-4440. *Fax:* 618-664-9841. *E-mail:* karl.somerville@greenville.edu.

GRINNELL COLLEGE
Grinnell, IA

Tuition & fees: $25,820	Average undergraduate aid package: $22,426

ABOUT THE INSTITUTION Independent, coed. Awards: bachelor's degrees. 43 undergraduate majors. Total enrollment: 1,556. Undergraduates: 1,556. Freshmen: 434. Institutional methodology is used as a basis for awarding need-based institutional aid.

UNDERGRADUATE EXPENSES for 2004–05 *Application fee:* $30. *Comprehensive fee:* $32,690 includes full-time tuition ($25,200), mandatory fees ($620), and room and board ($6870). *College room only:* $3204. Room and board charges vary according to board plan and housing facility. *Part-time tuition:* $787 per credit hour. *Payment plans:* Guaranteed tuition, tuition prepayment, installment.

FRESHMAN FINANCIAL AID (Fall 2004, est.) 349 applied for aid; of those 72% were deemed to have need. 100% of freshmen with need received aid; of those 100% had need fully met. *Average percent of need met:* 100% (excluding resources awarded to replace EFC). *Average financial aid package:* $22,639 (excluding resources awarded to replace EFC). 33% of all full-time freshmen had no need and received non-need-based gift aid.

UNDERGRADUATE FINANCIAL AID (Fall 2004, est.) 911 applied for aid; of those 83% were deemed to have need. 100% of undergraduates with need received aid; of those 100% had need fully met. *Average percent of need met:* 100% (excluding resources awarded to replace EFC). *Average financial aid package:* $22,426 (excluding resources awarded to replace EFC). 32% of all full-time undergraduates had no need and received non-need-based gift aid.

GIFT AID (NEED-BASED) *Total amount:* $14,203,938 (5% federal, 2% state, 89% institutional, 4% external sources). *Receiving aid:* Freshmen: 56% (243); All full-time undergraduates: 49% (742). *Average award:* Freshmen: $16,922; Undergraduates: $16,192. *Scholarships, grants, and awards:* Federal Pell, FSEOG, state, private, college/university gift aid from institutional funds.

GIFT AID (NON-NEED-BASED) *Total amount:* $5,627,388 (89% institutional, 11% external sources). *Receiving aid:* Freshmen: 13% (55); Undergraduates: 6% (89). *Average Award:* Freshmen: $10,612; Undergraduates: $9708. *Scholarships, grants, and awards by category:* Academic Interests/Achievement: 719 awards ($7,232,620 total): general academic interests/achievements. *Tuition waivers:* Full or partial for employees or children of employees.

LOANS *Student loans:* $3,165,337 (100% need-based). 58% of past graduating class borrowed through all loan programs. *Average indebtedness per student:* $16,496. *Average need-based loan:* Freshmen: $4355; Undergraduates: $5150. *Programs:* FFEL (Subsidized and Unsubsidized Stafford, PLUS), Perkins, college/university.

WORK-STUDY *Federal work-study:* Total amount: $758,772; 469 jobs averaging $1618. *State or other work-study/employment:* Total amount: $458,111 (54% need-based, 46% non-need-based). 257 part-time jobs averaging $1783.

APPLYING FOR FINANCIAL AID *Required financial aid forms:* FAFSA, institution's own form, noncustodial (divorced/separated) parent's statement. *Financial aid deadline:* 2/1. *Notification date:* 4/1. Students must reply by 5/1.

CONTACT Mr. Arnold Woods, Director of Student Financial Aid, Grinnell College, 1121 Park Street, Grinnell, IA 50112-1690, 641-269-3250 or toll-free 800-247-0113. *Fax:* 641-269-4937. *E-mail:* woods@grinnell.edu.

GROVE CITY COLLEGE
Grove City, PA

Tuition & fees: $10,107	Average undergraduate aid package: $4441

ABOUT THE INSTITUTION Independent Presbyterian, coed. Awards: bachelor's degrees. 46 undergraduate majors. Total enrollment: 2,318. Undergraduates: 2,318. Freshmen: 605. Institutional methodology is used as a basis for awarding need-based institutional aid.

UNDERGRADUATE EXPENSES for 2004–05 *Application fee:* $50. *Comprehensive fee:* $15,199 includes full-time tuition ($9952), mandatory fees ($155), and room and board ($5092). Full-time tuition and fees vary according to course load. *Part-time tuition:* $318 per credit hour. *Payment plan:* Installment.

FRESHMAN FINANCIAL AID (Fall 2004, est.) 355 applied for aid; of those 72% were deemed to have need. 100% of freshmen with need received aid; of those 12% had need fully met. *Average percent of need met:* 57% (excluding resources awarded to replace EFC). *Average financial aid package:* $4887 (excluding resources awarded to replace EFC). 30% of all full-time freshmen had no need and received non-need-based gift aid.

UNDERGRADUATE FINANCIAL AID (Fall 2004, est.) 1,074 applied for aid; of those 83% were deemed to have need. 98% of undergraduates with need received aid; of those 9% had need fully met. *Average percent of need met:* 49% (excluding resources awarded to replace EFC). *Average financial aid package:* $4441 (excluding resources awarded to replace EFC). 32% of all full-time undergraduates had no need and received non-need-based gift aid.

GIFT AID (NEED-BASED) *Total amount:* $3,868,980 (26% state, 61% institutional, 13% external sources). *Receiving aid:* Freshmen: 42% (256); All full-time undergraduates: 36% (828). *Average award:* Freshmen: $4887; Undergraduates: $4672. *Scholarships, grants, and awards:* state, private, college/university gift aid from institutional funds.

GIFT AID (NON-NEED-BASED) *Total amount:* $1,616,489 (4% state, 59% institutional, 37% external sources). *Receiving aid:* Freshmen: 5% (32); Undergraduates: 3% (76). *Average Award:* Freshmen: $5273; Undergraduates: $6095. *Scholarships, grants, and awards by category:* Academic Interests/Achievement: 501 awards ($1,133,604 total): biological sciences, business, communication, education, engineering/technologies, English, foreign languages, general academic interests/achievements, physical sciences, religion/biblical studies, social sciences. Creative Arts/Performance: 6 awards ($5800 total): creative writing, music. Special Achievements/Activities: 28 awards ($43,700 total): general special achievements/activities, leadership, memberships, religious involvement. Special Characteristics: 10 awards ($43,300 total): ethnic background, general special characteristics, members of minority groups. *Tuition waivers:* Full or partial for employees or children of employees. *ROTC:* Army cooperative.

LOANS *Student loans:* $7,796,080 (100% non-need-based). 52% of past graduating class borrowed through all loan programs. *Average indebtedness per student:* $22,035. *Programs:* alternative loans.

WORK-STUDY *State or other work-study/employment:* Total amount: $10,925 (35% need-based, 65% non-need-based). 900 part-time jobs averaging $600.

APPLYING FOR FINANCIAL AID *Required financial aid forms:* institution's own form, state aid form. *Financial aid deadline:* 4/15. *Notification date:* Continuous beginning 3/15.

CONTACT Patty Peterson, Director of Financial Aid, Grove City College, 100 Campus Drive, Grove City, PA 16127-2104, 724-458-3300. *Fax:* 724-450-4040. *E-mail:* financialaid@gcc.edu.

GUILFORD COLLEGE
Greensboro, NC

Tuition & fees: $21,640	Average undergraduate aid package: $13,249

ABOUT THE INSTITUTION Independent religious, coed. Awards: bachelor's degrees. 37 undergraduate majors. Total enrollment: 2,511. Undergraduates: 2,511. Freshmen: 479. Federal methodology is used as a basis for awarding need-based institutional aid.

UNDERGRADUATE EXPENSES for 2005–06 *Application fee:* $25. *Comprehensive fee:* $28,170 includes full-time tuition ($21,310), mandatory fees ($330), and room and board ($6530). Room and board charges vary according to board plan, housing facility, and location. *Part-time tuition:* $655 per credit hour. *Part-time fees:* $330 per year. Part-time tuition and fees vary according to course load. *Payment plan:* Installment.

GIFT AID (NEED-BASED) *Total amount:* $12,725,827 (18% federal, 23% state, 56% institutional, 3% external sources). *Receiving aid:* Freshmen: 60% (264); All full-time undergraduates: 66% (1,347). *Average award:* Freshmen: $14,250; Undergraduates: $9100. *Scholarships, grants, and awards:* Federal Pell, FSEOG, state, private, college/university gift aid from institutional funds.

GIFT AID (NON-NEED-BASED) *Total amount:* $4,081,684 (10% state, 80% institutional, 10% external sources). *Receiving aid:* Freshmen: 40% (174); Undergraduates: 52% (1,049). *Average Award:* Freshmen: $7703; Undergraduates: $7191. *Scholarships, grants, and awards by category:* Academic Interests/Achievement: 1,145 awards ($4,551,172 total): biological sciences, general academic interests/achievements. Creative Arts/Performance: 32 awards ($40,980 total): music, theater/drama. Special Achievements/Activities: 28 awards ($79,425 total): religious involvement. Special Characteristics: 300 awards ($544,143 total): children of faculty/staff, first-generation college students, local/state students. *Tuition waivers:* Full or partial for employees or children of employees.

LOANS *Student loans:* $9,556,409 (93% need-based, 7% non-need-based). 61% of past graduating class borrowed through all loan programs. *Average indebtedness per student:* $16,208. *Average need-based loan:* Freshmen: $5096; Undergraduates: $4928. *Parent loans:* $1,775,946 (70% need-based, 30% non-need-based). *Programs:* FFEL (Subsidized and Unsubsidized Stafford, PLUS), Perkins, college/university.

APPLYING FOR FINANCIAL AID *Required financial aid forms:* FAFSA, noncustodial (divorced/separated) parent's statement, business/farm supplement. *Financial aid deadline (priority):* 3/1. *Notification date:* Continuous beginning 2/15. Students must reply by 5/1 or within 4 weeks of notification.

CONTACT Mr. Anthony E. Gurley, Associate Dean of Enrollment, Guilford College, 5800 West Friendly Avenue, Greensboro, NC 27410, 336-316-2142 or toll-free 800-992-7759. *Fax:* 336-316-2954. *E-mail:* agurley@guilford.edu.

GUSTAVUS ADOLPHUS COLLEGE
St. Peter, MN

Tuition & fees: $22,955	Average undergraduate aid package: $15,330

ABOUT THE INSTITUTION Independent religious, coed. Awards: bachelor's degrees. 64 undergraduate majors. Total enrollment: 2,577. Undergraduates: 2,577. Freshmen: 658. Both federal and institutional methodology are used as a basis for awarding need-based institutional aid.

UNDERGRADUATE EXPENSES for 2004–05 *Comprehensive fee:* $28,765 includes full-time tuition ($22,590), mandatory fees ($365), and room and board ($5810). *College room only:* $3410. Full-time tuition and fees vary according to student level. Room and board charges vary according to board plan, housing facility, and student level. *Part-time tuition:* $3000 per course. *Part-time fees:* $100. *Payment plans:* Guaranteed tuition, tuition prepayment, installment.

FRESHMAN FINANCIAL AID (Fall 2003) 580 applied for aid; of those 81% were deemed to have need. 100% of freshmen with need received aid. *Average percent of need met:* 87% (excluding resources awarded to replace EFC). *Average financial aid package:* $16,047 (excluding resources awarded to replace EFC). 31% of all full-time freshmen had no need and received non-need-based gift aid.

UNDERGRADUATE FINANCIAL AID (Fall 2003) 2,060 applied for aid; of those 84% were deemed to have need. 100% of undergraduates with need received aid. *Average percent of need met:* 88% (excluding resources awarded to replace EFC). *Average financial aid package:* $15,330 (excluding resources awarded to replace EFC). 26% of all full-time undergraduates had no need and received non-need-based gift aid.

GIFT AID (NEED-BASED) *Total amount:* $18,392,099 (7% federal, 13% state, 75% institutional, 5% external sources). *Receiving aid:* Freshmen: 71% (467); All full-time undergraduates: 66% (1,701). *Average award:* Freshmen: $12,484; Undergraduates: $11,267. *Scholarships, grants, and awards:* Federal Pell, FSEOG, state, private, college/university gift aid from institutional funds.

GIFT AID (NON-NEED-BASED) *Total amount:* $4,726,608 (89% institutional, 11% external sources). *Receiving aid:* Freshmen: 11% (70); Undergraduates: 7% (191). *Average Award:* Freshmen: $5436; Undergraduates: $5469. *Scholarships, grants, and awards by category:* Academic Interests/Achievement: 523 awards ($2,444,999 total): general academic interests/achievements. *Creative Arts/Performance:* 53 awards ($124,000 total): music, theater/drama. *Special Achievements/Activities:* 302 awards ($242,000 total): community service. *Special Characteristics:* 71 awards ($105,250 total): children and siblings of alumni. *Tuition waivers:* Full or partial for employees or children of employees. *ROTC:* Army cooperative.

LOANS *Student loans:* $12,236,263 (56% need-based, 44% non-need-based). 71% of past graduating class borrowed through all loan programs. *Average indebtedness per student:* $18,500. *Average need-based loan:* Freshmen: $3447; Undergraduates: $4203. *Parent loans:* $1,845,193 (12% need-based, 88% non-need-based). *Programs:* Federal Direct (Subsidized and Unsubsidized Stafford, PLUS), Perkins, state, private/alternative education loans from banks.

WORK-STUDY *Federal work-study:* Total amount: $914,193; 646 jobs averaging $1415. *State or other work-study/employment:* Total amount: $1,206,316 (73% need-based, 27% non-need-based). 841 part-time jobs averaging $1434.

APPLYING FOR FINANCIAL AID *Required financial aid forms:* FAFSA, institution's own form. *Financial aid deadline (priority):* 2/15. *Notification date:* Continuous beginning 3/1. Students must reply by 5/1 or within 2 weeks of notification.

CONTACT Mr. Kirk Carlson, Associate Director of Student Financial Assistance, Gustavus Adolphus College, 800 West College Avenue, St. Peter, MN 56082-1498, 507-933-7527 or toll-free 800-GUSTAVU(S). *Fax:* 507-933-7727. *E-mail:* kcarlson@gustavus.edu.

GUTENBERG COLLEGE
Eugene, OR

CONTACT Financial Aid Office, Gutenberg College, 1883 University Street, Eugene, OR 97403, 541-683-5141.

GWYNEDD-MERCY COLLEGE
Gwynedd Valley, PA

Tuition & fees: $17,400	Average undergraduate aid package: $14,448

ABOUT THE INSTITUTION Independent Roman Catholic, coed. Awards: associate, bachelor's, and master's degrees and post-bachelor's and post-master's certificates. 36 undergraduate majors. Total enrollment: 2,751. Undergraduates: 2,160. Freshmen: 216. Federal methodology is used as a basis for awarding need-based institutional aid.

UNDERGRADUATE EXPENSES for 2004–05 *Application fee:* $25. *Comprehensive fee:* $24,900 includes full-time tuition ($16,900), mandatory fees ($500), and room and board ($7500). Full-time tuition and fees vary according to program. Room and board charges vary according to board plan and housing facility. *Part-time tuition:* $340 per credit. *Part-time fees:* $10 per credit. Part-time tuition and fees vary according to program. *Payment plan:* Installment.

FRESHMAN FINANCIAL AID (Fall 2003) 309 applied for aid; of those 80% were deemed to have need. 97% of freshmen with need received aid; of those 82% had need fully met. *Average percent of need met:* 85% (excluding resources awarded to replace EFC). *Average financial aid package:* $14,255 (excluding resources awarded to replace EFC). 21% of all full-time freshmen had no need and received non-need-based gift aid.

UNDERGRADUATE FINANCIAL AID (Fall 2003) 1,067 applied for aid; of those 82% were deemed to have need. 98% of undergraduates with need received aid; of those 35% had need fully met. *Average percent of need met:* 82% (excluding resources awarded to replace EFC). *Average financial aid package:* $14,448 (excluding resources awarded to replace EFC). 17% of all full-time undergraduates had no need and received non-need-based gift aid.

GIFT AID (NEED-BASED) *Total amount:* $8,884,362 (12% federal, 22% state, 64% institutional, 2% external sources). *Receiving aid:* Freshmen: 69% (232); All full-time undergraduates: 63% (798). *Average award:* Freshmen: $10,785; Undergraduates: $11,224. *Scholarships, grants, and awards:* Federal Pell, FSEOG, state, private, college/university gift aid from institutional funds.

GIFT AID (NON-NEED-BASED) *Total amount:* $1,473,890 (97% institutional, 3% external sources). *Receiving aid:* Freshmen: 57% (192); Undergraduates: 54% (683). *Average Award:* Freshmen: $6585; Undergraduates: $6482. *Scholarships, grants, and awards by category:* Academic Interests/Achievement: 537 awards ($3,184,720 total): general academic interests/achievements. *Special Achievements/Activities:* 160 awards ($476,980 total): general special achievements/activities. *Special Characteristics:* 1 award ($1000 total): children and siblings of alumni. *Tuition waivers:* Full or partial for employees or children of employees.

LOANS *Student loans:* $8,393,361 (50% need-based, 50% non-need-based). 81% of past graduating class borrowed through all loan programs. *Average indebtedness per student:* $17,860. *Average need-based loan:* Freshmen: $3053; Undergraduates: $5076. *Parent loans:* $1,195,629 (10% need-based, 90% non-need-based). *Programs:* FFEL (Subsidized and Unsubsidized Stafford, PLUS), Perkins, Federal Nursing, alternative loans.

WORK-STUDY *Federal work-study:* Total amount: $473,647; 356 jobs averaging $1330. *State or other work-study/employment:* Total amount: $22,300 (100% need-based). 10 part-time jobs averaging $2230.

APPLYING FOR FINANCIAL AID *Required financial aid forms:* FAFSA, institution's own form, federal income tax form(s). *Financial aid deadline (priority):* 3/15. *Notification date:* Continuous. Students must reply by 5/1 or within 4 weeks of notification.

CONTACT Sr. Barbara A. Kaufmann, Director of Student Financial Aid, Gwynedd-Mercy College, PO Box 901, Gwynedd Valley, PA 19437-0901, 215-641-5570 or toll-free 800-DIAL-GMC (in-state). *Fax:* 215-641-5556.

HAMILTON COLLEGE
Clinton, NY

Tuition & fees: $31,700	Average undergraduate aid package: $24,032

ABOUT THE INSTITUTION
Independent, coed. Awards: bachelor's degrees. 47 undergraduate majors. Total enrollment: 1,792. Undergraduates: 1,792. Freshmen: 457. Both federal and institutional methodology are used as a basis for awarding need-based institutional aid.

UNDERGRADUATE EXPENSES for 2004–05 *Application fee:* $50. *Comprehensive fee:* $39,525 includes full-time tuition ($31,500), mandatory fees ($200), and room and board ($7825). *College room only:* $4125. Room and board charges vary according to board plan. *Part-time tuition:* $2900 per unit. *Payment plan:* Installment.

FRESHMAN FINANCIAL AID (Fall 2004, est.) 267 applied for aid; of those 89% were deemed to have need. 100% of freshmen with need received aid; of those 100% had need fully met. *Average percent of need met:* 99% (excluding resources awarded to replace EFC). *Average financial aid package:* $24,370 (excluding resources awarded to replace EFC). 2% of all full-time freshmen had no need and received non-need-based gift aid.

UNDERGRADUATE FINANCIAL AID (Fall 2004, est.) 1,124 applied for aid; of those 87% were deemed to have need. 100% of undergraduates with need received aid; of those 100% had need fully met. *Average percent of need met:* 99% (excluding resources awarded to replace EFC). *Average financial aid package:* $24,032 (excluding resources awarded to replace EFC). 4% of all full-time undergraduates had no need and received non-need-based gift aid.

GIFT AID (NEED-BASED) *Total amount:* $19,228,897 (3% federal, 4% state, 88% institutional, 5% external sources). *Receiving aid:* Freshmen: 50% (228); All full-time undergraduates: 54% (942). *Average award:* Freshmen: $21,038; Undergraduates: $20,413. *Scholarships, grants, and awards:* Federal Pell, FSEOG, state, private, college/university gift aid from institutional funds.

GIFT AID (NON-NEED-BASED) *Total amount:* $867,949 (1% state, 97% institutional, 2% external sources). *Receiving aid:* Undergraduates: 8. *Average Award:* Freshmen: $8777; *Undergraduates:* $11,861. *Scholarships, grants, and awards by category: Academic Interests/Achievement:* general academic interests/achievements. *Creative Arts/Performance:* general creative arts/performance. *Special Achievements/Activities:* general special achievements/activities. *Special Characteristics:* general special characteristics. *Tuition waivers:* Full or partial for employees or children of employees. *ROTC:* Army cooperative, Air Force cooperative.

LOANS *Student loans:* $2,612,294 (99% need-based, 1% non-need-based). 77% of past graduating class borrowed through all loan programs. *Average indebtedness per student:* $16,894. *Average need-based loan:* Freshmen: $3352; Undergraduates: $3921. *Programs:* FFEL (Subsidized and Unsubsidized Stafford, PLUS), Perkins, college/university.

WORK-STUDY *Federal work-study:* Total amount: $570,166; jobs available (averaging $1600).

APPLYING FOR FINANCIAL AID *Required financial aid forms:* FAFSA, institution's own form, CSS Financial Aid PROFILE, state aid form, noncustodial (divorced/separated) parent's statement, business/farm supplement. *Financial aid deadline:* 1/1 (priority: 1/1). *Notification date:* 4/1. Students must reply by 5/1.

CONTACT Mr. Kevin Michaelsen, Associate Director of Financial Aid, Hamilton College, 198 College Hill Road, Clinton, NY 13323, 315-859-4395 or toll-free 800-843-2655. *Fax:* 315-859-4457. *E-mail:* kmichael@hamilton.edu.

HAMILTON TECHNICAL COLLEGE
Davenport, IA

CONTACT Ms. Lisa Boyd, Executive Vice President/Director of Financial Aid, Hamilton Technical College, 1011 East 53rd Street, Davenport, IA 52807-2653, 563-386-3570 Ext. 33. *Fax:* 563-386-6756.

HAMLINE UNIVERSITY
St. Paul, MN

Tuition & fees: $22,070	Average undergraduate aid package: $23,164

ABOUT THE INSTITUTION
Independent religious, coed. Awards: bachelor's, master's, doctoral, and first professional degrees and post-bachelor's, post-master's, and first professional certificates. 61 undergraduate majors. Total enrollment: 4,490. Undergraduates: 1,993. Freshmen: 447. Federal methodology is used as a basis for awarding need-based institutional aid.

UNDERGRADUATE EXPENSES for 2004–05 *Comprehensive fee:* $28,606 includes full-time tuition ($21,820), mandatory fees ($250), and room and board ($6536). *College room only:* $3274. Full-time tuition and fees vary according to student level. Room and board charges vary according to board

plan and housing facility. *Part-time tuition:* $682 per credit hour. Part-time tuition and fees vary according to course load and student level. *Payment plan:* Installment.

FRESHMAN FINANCIAL AID (Fall 2004, est.) 430 applied for aid; of those 83% were deemed to have need. 100% of freshmen with need received aid; of those 26% had need fully met. *Average percent of need met:* 78% (excluding resources awarded to replace EFC). *Average financial aid package:* $23,210 (excluding resources awarded to replace EFC). 15% of all full-time freshmen had no need and received non-need-based gift aid.

UNDERGRADUATE FINANCIAL AID (Fall 2004, est.) 1,773 applied for aid; of those 79% were deemed to have need. 100% of undergraduates with need received aid; of those 27% had need fully met. *Average percent of need met:* 77% (excluding resources awarded to replace EFC). *Average financial aid package:* $23,164 (excluding resources awarded to replace EFC). 19% of all full-time undergraduates had no need and received non-need-based gift aid.

GIFT AID (NEED-BASED) *Total amount:* $10,059,669 (17% federal, 24% state, 57% institutional, 2% external sources). *Receiving aid:* Freshmen: 68% (302); All full-time undergraduates: 67% (1,251). *Average award:* Freshmen: $7498; Undergraduates: $6931. *Scholarships, grants, and awards:* Federal Pell, FSEOG, state, private, college/university gift aid from institutional funds.

GIFT AID (NON-NEED-BASED) *Total amount:* $9,032,451 (93% institutional, 7% external sources). *Receiving aid:* Freshmen: 63% (282); Undergraduates: 54% (996). *Average Award: Freshmen:* $11,230; *Undergraduates:* $11,730. *Scholarships, grants, and awards by category: Academic Interests/Achievement:* 1,220 awards ($8,042,858 total): area/ethnic studies, biological sciences, communication, education, English, foreign languages, general academic interests/achievements, health fields, humanities, international studies, mathematics, physical sciences, premedicine, religion/biblical studies, social sciences. *Creative Arts/Performance:* art/fine arts, creative writing, music, theater/drama. *Special Achievements/Activities:* religious involvement. *Special Characteristics:* children and siblings of alumni, children with a deceased or disabled parent, ethnic background, first-generation college students, general special characteristics, international students, local/state students, members of minority groups, religious affiliation. *Tuition waivers:* Full or partial for employees or children of employees. *ROTC:* Air Force cooperative.

LOANS *Student loans:* $7,495,912 (42% need-based, 58% non-need-based). 77% of past graduating class borrowed through all loan programs. *Average indebtedness per student:* $21,325. *Average need-based loan:* Freshmen: $1665; Undergraduates: $2193. *Parent loans:* $1,133,075 (100% non-need-based). *Programs:* Federal Direct (Subsidized and Unsubsidized Stafford, PLUS), FFEL (Subsidized and Unsubsidized Stafford, PLUS), Perkins, United Methodist Student Loans, SELF Loans.

WORK-STUDY *Federal work-study:* Total amount: $2,010,965; 875 jobs averaging $2298. *State or other work-study/employment:* Total amount: $1,559,730 (21% need-based, 79% non-need-based). 921 part-time jobs averaging $1694.

APPLYING FOR FINANCIAL AID *Required financial aid forms:* FAFSA, institution's own form, state aid form, noncustodial (divorced/separated) parent's statement. *Financial aid deadline (priority):* 3/1. *Notification date:* Continuous.

CONTACT Ms. Cheryl Anderson-Dooley, Associate Director, Financial Aid, Hamline University, 1536 Hewitt Avenue, MS C1915, St. Paul, MN 55104, 651-523-2280 or toll-free 800-753-9753. *Fax:* 651-523-2585. *E-mail:* cdooley@gw.hamline.edu.

HAMPDEN-SYDNEY COLLEGE
Hampden-Sydney, VA

Tuition & fees: $22,946	Average undergraduate aid package: $16,542

ABOUT THE INSTITUTION
Independent religious, men only. Awards: bachelor's degrees. 28 undergraduate majors. Total enrollment: 1,082. Undergraduates: 1,082. Freshmen: 321. Both federal and institutional methodology are used as a basis for awarding need-based institutional aid.

UNDERGRADUATE EXPENSES for 2005–06 *Application fee:* $30. *Comprehensive fee:* $30,316 includes full-time tuition ($21,878), mandatory fees ($1068), and room and board ($7370). *College room only:* $3116. Room and board charges vary according to board plan and housing facility. *Part-time tuition:* $704 per credit hour. *Payment plan:* Installment.

FRESHMAN FINANCIAL AID (Fall 2004, est.) 243 applied for aid; of those 71% were deemed to have need. 100% of freshmen with need received aid; of those 38% had need fully met. *Average percent of need met:* 84% (excluding resources awarded to replace EFC). *Average financial aid package:* $15,780 (excluding resources awarded to replace EFC). 46% of all full-time freshmen had no need and received non-need-based gift aid.

Hampden-Sydney College

UNDERGRADUATE FINANCIAL AID (Fall 2004, est.) 679 applied for aid; of those 79% were deemed to have need. 100% of undergraduates with need received aid; of those 33% had need fully met. *Average percent of need met:* 83% (excluding resources awarded to replace EFC). *Average financial aid package:* $16,542 (excluding resources awarded to replace EFC). 45% of all full-time undergraduates had no need and received non-need-based gift aid.

GIFT AID (NEED-BASED) *Total amount:* $6,799,011 (6% federal, 12% state, 79% institutional, 3% external sources). *Receiving aid:* Freshmen: 54% (172); All full-time undergraduates: 49% (528). *Average award:* Freshmen: $13,191; Undergraduates: $12,876. *Scholarships, grants, and awards:* Federal Pell, FSEOG, state, private, college/university gift aid from institutional funds.

GIFT AID (NON-NEED-BASED) *Total amount:* $4,429,227 (21% state, 71% institutional, 8% external sources). *Receiving aid:* Freshmen: 16% (51); Undergraduates: 11% (114). *Average Award: Freshmen:* $20,064; *Undergraduates:* $14,853. *Scholarships, grants, and awards by category: Academic Interests/Achievement:* 348 awards ($3,666,316 total): biological sciences, education, general academic interests/achievements, health fields, premedicine, religion/biblical studies. *Creative Arts/Performance:* 1 award ($5000 total): music. *Special Achievements/Activities:* 200 awards ($545,750 total): general special achievements/activities, leadership. *Special Characteristics:* 22 awards ($302,748 total): children of educators, children of faculty/staff, out-of-state students, religious affiliation. *Tuition waivers:* Full or partial for employees or children of employees. *ROTC:* Army cooperative.

LOANS *Student loans:* $4,412,486 (46% need-based, 54% non-need-based). 51% of past graduating class borrowed through all loan programs. *Average indebtedness per student:* $15,247. *Average need-based loan:* Freshmen: $2774; Undergraduates: $4113. *Parent loans:* $7,367,537 (17% need-based, 83% non-need-based). *Programs:* FFEL (Subsidized and Unsubsidized Stafford, PLUS), Perkins, college/university.

WORK-STUDY *Federal work-study:* Total amount: $315,203; 247 jobs averaging $1276.

APPLYING FOR FINANCIAL AID *Required financial aid forms:* FAFSA, CSS Financial Aid PROFILE. *Financial aid deadline (priority):* 3/1. *Notification date:* Continuous. Students must reply by 5/1 or within 2 weeks of notification.

CONTACT Mrs. Lynn Clements, Assistant Director of Financial Aid, Hampden-Sydney College, PO Box 726, Hampden-Sydney, VA 23943-0667, 434-223-6119 or toll-free 800-755-0733. *Fax:* 434-223-6075. *E-mail:* lclements@hsc.edu.

HAMPSHIRE COLLEGE
Amherst, MA

Tuition & fees: $30,978	Average undergraduate aid package: $25,660

ABOUT THE INSTITUTION Independent, coed. Awards: bachelor's degrees. 170 undergraduate majors. Total enrollment: 1,352. Undergraduates: 1,352. Freshmen: 370. Institutional methodology is used as a basis for awarding need-based institutional aid.

UNDERGRADUATE EXPENSES for 2004–05 *Application fee:* $55. *Comprehensive fee:* $39,091 includes full-time tuition ($30,418), mandatory fees ($560), and room and board ($8113). *College room only:* $5174. Room and board charges vary according to board plan. *Payment plan:* Installment.

FRESHMAN FINANCIAL AID (Fall 2004, est.) 240 applied for aid; of those 90% were deemed to have need. 100% of freshmen with need received aid; of those 59% had need fully met. *Average percent of need met:* 96% (excluding resources awarded to replace EFC). *Average financial aid package:* $24,510 (excluding resources awarded to replace EFC). 11% of all full-time freshmen had no need and received non-need-based gift aid.

UNDERGRADUATE FINANCIAL AID (Fall 2004, est.) 822 applied for aid; of those 91% were deemed to have need. 100% of undergraduates with need received aid; of those 83% had need fully met. *Average percent of need met:* 96% (excluding resources awarded to replace EFC). *Average financial aid package:* $25,660 (excluding resources awarded to replace EFC). 5% of all full-time undergraduates had no need and received non-need-based gift aid.

GIFT AID (NEED-BASED) *Total amount:* $14,581,075 (9% federal, 1% state, 89% institutional, 1% external sources). *Receiving aid:* Freshmen: 64% (214); All full-time undergraduates: 56% (750). *Average award:* Freshmen: $19,785; Undergraduates: $19,180. *Scholarships, grants, and awards:* Federal Pell, FSEOG, state, private, college/university gift aid from institutional funds.

GIFT AID (NON-NEED-BASED) *Total amount:* $330,460 (2% state, 83% institutional, 15% external sources). *Receiving aid:* Freshmen: 22% (74); Undergraduates: 13% (181). *Average Award: Freshmen:* $3700; *Undergraduates:* $3865. *Scholarships, grants, and awards by category: Academic Interests/Achievement:* 235 awards ($912,000 total): general academic interests/achievements, international studies, physical sciences, social sciences. *Creative Arts/Performance:* 1 award ($3500 total): creative writing. *Special Achievements/Activities:* 33 awards ($233,200 total): community service, leadership. *Special Characteristics:* 5 awards ($150,000 total): children of faculty/staff. *Tuition waivers:* Full or partial for employees or children of employees. *ROTC:* Army cooperative.

LOANS *Student loans:* $2,663,750 (92% need-based, 8% non-need-based). 54% of past graduating class borrowed through all loan programs. *Average indebtedness per student:* $17,825. *Average need-based loan:* Freshmen: $2625; Undergraduates: $4155. *Parent loans:* $4,720,474 (66% need-based, 34% non-need-based). *Programs:* Federal Direct (Subsidized and Unsubsidized Stafford), FFEL (PLUS), Perkins.

WORK-STUDY *Federal work-study:* Total amount: $1,251,825; 587 jobs averaging $2300. *State or other work-study/employment:* Total amount: $481,010 (65% need-based, 35% non-need-based). 250 part-time jobs averaging $2300.

APPLYING FOR FINANCIAL AID *Required financial aid forms:* FAFSA, institution's own form, CSS Financial Aid PROFILE. *Financial aid deadline (priority):* 2/1. *Notification date:* 4/1. Students must reply by 5/1 or within 2 weeks of notification.

CONTACT Ms. Kathleen Methot, Director of Financial Aid, Hampshire College, 893 West Street, Amherst, MA 01002, 413-559-5484 or toll-free 877-937-4267 (out-of-state). *Fax:* 413-559-5585. *E-mail:* sfs@hampshire.edu.

HAMPTON UNIVERSITY
Hampton, VA

Tuition & fees: $14,996	Average undergraduate aid package: $3266

ABOUT THE INSTITUTION Independent, coed. Awards: associate, bachelor's, master's, doctoral, and first professional degrees. 83 undergraduate majors. Total enrollment: 6,156. Undergraduates: 5,317. Freshmen: 1,349. Federal methodology is used as a basis for awarding need-based institutional aid.

UNDERGRADUATE EXPENSES for 2004–05 *Application fee:* $25. *Comprehensive fee:* $21,420 includes full-time tuition ($13,506), mandatory fees ($1490), and room and board ($6424). *College room only:* $3340. Room and board charges vary according to housing facility. *Part-time tuition:* $305 per credit. *Payment plan:* Deferred payment.

FRESHMAN FINANCIAL AID (Fall 2004, est.) 998 applied for aid; of those 72% were deemed to have need. 99% of freshmen with need received aid; of those 79% had need fully met. *Average percent of need met:* 54% (excluding resources awarded to replace EFC). *Average financial aid package:* $3780 (excluding resources awarded to replace EFC). 6% of all full-time freshmen had no need and received non-need-based gift aid.

UNDERGRADUATE FINANCIAL AID (Fall 2004, est.) 3,328 applied for aid; of those 74% were deemed to have need. 99% of undergraduates with need received aid; of those 69% had need fully met. *Average percent of need met:* 50% (excluding resources awarded to replace EFC). *Average financial aid package:* $3266 (excluding resources awarded to replace EFC). 5% of all full-time undergraduates had no need and received non-need-based gift aid.

GIFT AID (NEED-BASED) *Receiving aid:* Freshmen: 15% (201); All full-time undergraduates: 9% (444). *Average award:* Freshmen: $2700; Undergraduates: $3437. *Scholarships, grants, and awards:* Federal Pell, FSEOG, state, private, college/university gift aid from institutional funds, Federal Nursing.

GIFT AID (NON-NEED-BASED) *Receiving aid:* Freshmen: 6% (85); Undergraduates: 6% (279). *Average Award: Freshmen:* $7793; *Undergraduates:* $5767. *Scholarships, grants, and awards by category: Academic Interests/Achievement:* general academic interests/achievements. *Creative Arts/Performance:* music. *Special Characteristics:* international students, members of minority groups. *Tuition waivers:* Full or partial for employees or children of employees. *ROTC:* Army, Naval.

LOANS *Student loans:* $17,642,667 (92% need-based, 8% non-need-based). 67% of past graduating class borrowed through all loan programs. *Average indebtedness per student:* $6980. *Average need-based loan:* Freshmen: $3807; Undergraduates: $3265. *Parent loans:* $19,211,566 (81% need-based, 19% non-need-based). *Programs:* FFEL (Subsidized and Unsubsidized Stafford, PLUS), Perkins, Federal Nursing, college/university.

WORK-STUDY *Federal work-study:* Total amount: $615,513; 342 jobs averaging $1800.

ATHLETIC AWARDS *Total amount:* $2,611,557 (64% need-based, 36% non-need-based).

APPLYING FOR FINANCIAL AID *Required financial aid form:* FAFSA. *Financial aid deadline:* 3/1. *Notification date:* Continuous beginning 4/15. Students must reply within 2 weeks of notification.

CONTACT Marcia Boyd, Financial Aid Office, Hampton University, Hampton, VA 23668, 757-727-5332 or toll-free 800-624-3328. *Fax:* 757-727-5095. *E-mail:* marcia.boyd@hamptonu.edu.

HANNIBAL-LAGRANGE COLLEGE
Hannibal, MO

Tuition & fees: $10,876	Average undergraduate aid package: $11,289

ABOUT THE INSTITUTION Independent Southern Baptist, coed. Awards: associate and bachelor's degrees. 44 undergraduate majors. Total enrollment: 1,067. Undergraduates: 1,067. Freshmen: 173. Federal methodology is used as a basis for awarding need-based institutional aid.

UNDERGRADUATE EXPENSES for 2004–05 *Application fee:* $25. *One-time required fee:* $100. *Comprehensive fee:* $14,926 includes full-time tuition ($10,536), mandatory fees ($340), and room and board ($4050). Full-time tuition and fees vary according to course load. Room and board charges vary according to board plan and housing facility. *Part-time tuition:* $350 per hour. *Part-time fees:* $85 per term. Part-time tuition and fees vary according to course load. *Payment plan:* Installment.

FRESHMAN FINANCIAL AID (Fall 2004, est.) 93 applied for aid; of those 100% were deemed to have need. 98% of freshmen with need received aid. *Average financial aid package:* $7264 (excluding resources awarded to replace EFC).

UNDERGRADUATE FINANCIAL AID (Fall 2004, est.) 510 applied for aid; of those 100% were deemed to have need. 96% of undergraduates with need received aid. *Average financial aid package:* $11,289 (excluding resources awarded to replace EFC).

GIFT AID (NEED-BASED) *Total amount:* $943,837 (80% federal, 19% state, 1% institutional). *Receiving aid:* Freshmen: 34% (49); All full-time undergraduates: 39% (288). *Average award:* Freshmen: $1837; Undergraduates: $3251. *Scholarships, grants, and awards:* Federal Pell, FSEOG, state, private, college/university gift aid from institutional funds.

GIFT AID (NON-NEED-BASED) *Total amount:* $2,893,240 (1% state, 90% institutional, 9% external sources). *Scholarships, grants, and awards by category: Academic Interests/Achievement:* general academic interests/achievements, religion/biblical studies. *Creative Arts/Performance:* art/fine arts, journalism/publications, music, performing arts, theater/drama. *Special Characteristics:* children of faculty/staff, public servants, relatives of clergy, religious affiliation. *Tuition waivers:* Full or partial for employees or children of employees.

LOANS *Student loans:* $3,529,336 (57% need-based, 43% non-need-based). 73% of past graduating class borrowed through all loan programs. *Average indebtedness per student:* $17,916. *Average need-based loan:* Freshmen: $2788; Undergraduates: $6359. *Parent loans:* $979,302 (100% need-based). *Programs:* FFEL (Subsidized and Unsubsidized Stafford, PLUS), Perkins, state, college/university.

WORK-STUDY *Federal work-study:* Total amount: $6715; 57 jobs averaging $550.

ATHLETIC AWARDS *Total amount:* $526,729 (100% non-need-based).

APPLYING FOR FINANCIAL AID *Required financial aid forms:* FAFSA, institution's own form. *Financial aid deadline:* Continuous. *Notification date:* Continuous beginning 1/1.

CONTACT Amy Blackwell, Director of Financial Aid, Hannibal-LaGrange College, 2800 Palmyra Road, Hannibal, MO 63401-1940, 573-221-3675 Ext. 279 or toll-free 800-HLG-1119. *Fax:* 573-221-6594.

HANOVER COLLEGE
Hanover, IN

Tuition & fees: $20,600	Average undergraduate aid package: $14,751

ABOUT THE INSTITUTION Independent Presbyterian, coed. Awards: bachelor's degrees. 29 undergraduate majors. Total enrollment: 1,062. Undergraduates: 1,062. Freshmen: 380. Federal methodology is used as a basis for awarding need-based institutional aid.

UNDERGRADUATE EXPENSES for 2004–05 *Application fee:* $30. *Comprehensive fee:* $26,800 includes full-time tuition ($20,150), mandatory fees ($450), and room and board ($6200). *College room only:* $2950. Full-time tuition and fees

vary according to reciprocity agreements. Room and board charges vary according to housing facility. Part-time tuition and fees vary according to course load and reciprocity agreements. *Payment plan:* Installment.

FRESHMAN FINANCIAL AID (Fall 2003) 269 applied for aid; of those 84% were deemed to have need. 100% of freshmen with need received aid; of those 46% had need fully met. *Average percent of need met:* 81% (excluding resources awarded to replace EFC). *Average financial aid package:* $15,126 (excluding resources awarded to replace EFC). 21% of all full-time freshmen had no need and received non-need-based gift aid.

UNDERGRADUATE FINANCIAL AID (Fall 2003) 962 applied for aid; of those 89% were deemed to have need. 100% of undergraduates with need received aid; of those 38% had need fully met. *Average percent of need met:* 73% (excluding resources awarded to replace EFC). *Average financial aid package:* $14,751 (excluding resources awarded to replace EFC). 14% of all full-time undergraduates had no need and received non-need-based gift aid.

GIFT AID (NEED-BASED) *Total amount:* $10,619,943 (5% federal, 12% state, 75% institutional, 8% external sources). *Receiving aid:* Freshmen: 78% (226); All full-time undergraduates: 85% (855). *Average award:* Freshmen: $13,627; Undergraduates: $12,548. *Scholarships, grants, and awards:* Federal Pell, state, private, college/university gift aid from institutional funds.

GIFT AID (NON-NEED-BASED) *Total amount:* $1,883,449 (1% state, 83% institutional, 16% external sources). *Receiving aid:* Freshmen: 21% (61); Undergraduates: 14% (144). *Average Award:* Freshmen: $14,268; Undergraduates: $14,916. *Scholarships, grants, and awards by category: Academic Interests/Achievement:* general academic interests/achievements. *Creative Arts/Performance:* 31 awards ($55,250 total): music, theater/drama. *Special Characteristics:* 104 awards ($773,325 total): children of faculty/staff, international students, members of minority groups, religious affiliation. *Tuition waivers:* Full or partial for employees or children of employees, senior citizens.

LOANS *Student loans:* $2,707,296 (61% need-based, 39% non-need-based). 63% of past graduating class borrowed through all loan programs. *Average indebtedness per student:* $14,932. *Average need-based loan:* Freshmen: $2081; Undergraduates: $3064. *Parent loans:* $1,414,381 (17% need-based, 83% non-need-based). *Programs:* FFEL (Subsidized and Unsubsidized Stafford, PLUS), college/university.

APPLYING FOR FINANCIAL AID *Required financial aid form:* FAFSA. *Financial aid deadline (priority):* 3/10. *Notification date:* Continuous. Students must reply by 5/1.

CONTACT Jon Riester, Director of Financial Aid, Hanover College, PO Box 108, Hanover, IN 47243-0108, 800-213-2178. *Fax:* 812-866-7098.

HARDING UNIVERSITY
Searcy, AR

Tuition & fees: $10,780	Average undergraduate aid package: $8673

ABOUT THE INSTITUTION Independent religious, coed. Awards: bachelor's and master's degrees. 96 undergraduate majors. Total enrollment: 5,348. Undergraduates: 4,037. Freshmen: 968. Federal methodology is used as a basis for awarding need-based institutional aid.

UNDERGRADUATE EXPENSES for 2004–05 *Application fee:* $35. *Comprehensive fee:* $15,962 includes full-time tuition ($10,380), mandatory fees ($400), and room and board ($5182). *College room only:* $2572. Full-time tuition and fees vary according to course load. Room and board charges vary according to board plan and housing facility. *Part-time tuition:* $346 per semester hour. *Part-time fees:* $20 per semester hour. Part-time tuition and fees vary according to course load. *Payment plan:* Installment.

FRESHMAN FINANCIAL AID (Fall 2003) 913 applied for aid; of those 54% were deemed to have need. 100% of freshmen with need received aid; of those 24% had need fully met. *Average percent of need met:* 69% (excluding resources awarded to replace EFC). *Average financial aid package:* $8687 (excluding resources awarded to replace EFC). 39% of all full-time freshmen had no need and received non-need-based gift aid.

UNDERGRADUATE FINANCIAL AID (Fall 2003) 3,642 applied for aid; of those 54% were deemed to have need. 100% of undergraduates with need received aid; of those 10% had need fully met. *Average percent of need met:* 64% (excluding resources awarded to replace EFC). *Average financial aid package:* $8673 (excluding resources awarded to replace EFC). 38% of all full-time undergraduates had no need and received non-need-based gift aid.

GIFT AID (NEED-BASED) *Total amount:* $10,419,945 (39% federal, 6% state, 48% institutional, 7% external sources). *Receiving aid:* Freshmen: 51% (493); All full-time undergraduates: 51% (1,965). *Average award:* Freshmen: $5828;

Undergraduates: $5444. *Scholarships, grants, and awards:* Federal Pell, FSEOG, state, private, college/university gift aid from institutional funds.

GIFT AID (NON-NEED-BASED) *Total amount:* $5,860,102 (5% state, 90% institutional, 5% external sources). *Receiving aid:* Freshmen: 1% (8); Undergraduates: 2% (66). *Average Award: Freshmen:* $4118; *Undergraduates:* $7246. *Scholarships, grants, and awards by category: Academic Interests/ Achievement:* 2,109 awards ($4,513,969 total): general academic interests/ achievements. *Creative Arts/Performance:* 113 awards ($121,204 total): music. *Special Achievements/Activities:* 155 awards ($245,545 total): cheerleading/ drum major, religious involvement. *Special Characteristics:* 100 awards ($261,871 total): children with a deceased or disabled parent, international students, siblings of current students. *Tuition waivers:* Full or partial for employees or children of employees, senior citizens. *ROTC:* Army cooperative.

LOANS *Student loans:* $45,382,014 (39% need-based, 61% non-need-based). 67% of past graduating class borrowed through all loan programs. *Average indebtedness per student:* $21,183. *Average need-based loan: Freshmen:* $3892; Undergraduates: $4380. *Parent loans:* $5,117,277 (69% need-based, 31% non-need-based). *Programs:* FFEL (Subsidized and Unsubsidized Stafford, PLUS), Perkins, Federal Nursing, state, college/university.

WORK-STUDY *Federal work-study:* Total amount: $532,638; 2,034 jobs averaging $291. *State or other work-study/employment:* Total amount: $1,098,444 (50% need-based, 50% non-need-based). 1,629 part-time jobs averaging $512.

ATHLETIC AWARDS *Total amount:* $1,460,533 (45% need-based, 55% non-need-based).

APPLYING FOR FINANCIAL AID *Required financial aid form:* FAFSA. *Financial aid deadline:* Continuous. *Notification date:* Continuous beginning 2/15. Students must reply within 2 weeks of notification.

CONTACT Dr. Jonathan C. Roberts, Director of Student Financial Services, Harding University, Box 12282, Searcy, AR 72149-0001, 501-279-4257 or toll-free 800-477-4407. *Fax:* 501-279-4129. *E-mail:* jroberts@harding.edu.

HARDIN-SIMMONS UNIVERSITY
Abilene, TX

ABOUT THE INSTITUTION Independent Baptist, coed. Awards: bachelor's, master's, doctoral, and first professional degrees and post-bachelor's certificates. 80 undergraduate majors. Total enrollment: 2,392. Undergraduates: 1,942. Freshmen: 404.

GIFT AID (NEED-BASED) *Scholarships, grants, and awards:* Federal Pell, FSEOG, state, private, college/university gift aid from institutional funds.

GIFT AID (NON-NEED-BASED) *Scholarships, grants, and awards by category: Academic Interests/Achievement:* biological sciences, business, communication, education, English, foreign languages, general academic interests/ achievements, health fields, humanities, mathematics, physical sciences, premedicine, religion/biblical studies, social sciences. *Creative Arts/Performance:* art/fine arts, creative writing, journalism/publications, music, theater/drama. *Special Achievements/Activities:* general special achievements/activities, junior miss, leadership. *Special Characteristics:* children of faculty/staff, ethnic background, general special characteristics, local/state students, out-of-state students, public servants, relatives of clergy, religious affiliation, siblings of current students.

LOANS *Programs:* FFEL (Subsidized and Unsubsidized Stafford, PLUS), Perkins, state, college/university.

WORK-STUDY *Federal work-study:* Total amount: $296,856; 191 jobs averaging $1554. *State or other work-study/employment:* Total amount: $456,981 (6% need-based, 94% non-need-based). 381 part-time jobs averaging $1199.

APPLYING FOR FINANCIAL AID *Required financial aid form:* FAFSA.

CONTACT Rachel King, Director of Financial Aid, Hardin-Simmons University, PO Box 16050, Abilene, TX 79698-6050, 325-670-5891 or toll-free 877-464-7889. *Fax:* 325-671-2115. *E-mail:* rking@hsutx.edu.

HARRINGTON COLLEGE OF DESIGN
Chicago, IL

CONTACT Ms. Renee Darosky, Director of Financial Aid, Harrington College of Design, 410 South Michigan Avenue, Chicago, IL 60605-1496, 312-939-4975 or toll-free 877-939-4975. *Fax:* 312-697-8058. *E-mail:* financialaid@interiordesign.edu.

HARRIS-STOWE STATE COLLEGE
St. Louis, MO

ABOUT THE INSTITUTION State-supported, coed. Awards: bachelor's degrees and post-bachelor's certificates. 17 undergraduate majors. Total enrollment: 1,605. Undergraduates: 1,605. Freshmen: 259.

GIFT AID (NEED-BASED) *Scholarships, grants, and awards:* Federal Pell, FSEOG, state, private, college/university gift aid from institutional funds.

GIFT AID (NON-NEED-BASED) *Scholarships, grants, and awards by category: Academic Interests/Achievement:* general academic interests/achievements. *Creative Arts/Performance:* music, theater/drama.

LOANS *Programs:* FFEL (Subsidized and Unsubsidized Stafford, PLUS), Perkins, college/university.

APPLYING FOR FINANCIAL AID *Required financial aid forms:* FAFSA, institution's own form.

CONTACT Dave Wedemeyer, Director of Financial Aid, Harris-Stowe State College, 3026 Laclede Avenue, St. Louis, MO 63103-2136, 314-340-3502. *Fax:* 314-340-3503.

HARTWICK COLLEGE
Oneonta, NY

ABOUT THE INSTITUTION Independent, coed. Awards: bachelor's degrees. 32 undergraduate majors. Total enrollment: 1,479. Undergraduates: 1,479. Freshmen: 410.

GIFT AID (NEED-BASED) *Scholarships, grants, and awards:* Federal Pell, FSEOG, state, private, college/university gift aid from institutional funds.

GIFT AID (NON-NEED-BASED) *Scholarships, grants, and awards by category: Academic Interests/Achievement:* general academic interests/achievements. *Creative Arts/Performance:* art/fine arts, music. *Special Achievements/Activities:* general special achievements/activities. *Special Characteristics:* children and siblings of alumni, children of faculty/staff, siblings of current students.

LOANS *Programs:* FFEL (Subsidized and Unsubsidized Stafford, PLUS), Perkins, Federal Nursing, alternative loans.

APPLYING FOR FINANCIAL AID *Required financial aid forms:* FAFSA, institution's own form, state aid form.

CONTACT Kathleen Ryan-O'Neill, Director, Financial Aid Department, Hartwick College, One Hartwick Drive, Oneonta, NY 13820, 607-431-4158 or toll-free 888-HARTWICK (out-of-state). *Fax:* 607-431-4006. *E-mail:* oneillk@hartwick.edu.

HARVARD UNIVERSITY
Cambridge, MA

Tuition & fees: $30,620	Average undergraduate aid package: $26,773

ABOUT THE INSTITUTION Independent, coed. Awards: bachelor's, master's, doctoral, and first professional degrees. 141 undergraduate majors. Total enrollment: 20,130. Undergraduates: 6,635. Freshmen: 1,635. Both federal and institutional methodology are used as a basis for awarding need-based institutional aid.

UNDERGRADUATE EXPENSES for 2004–05 *Application fee:* $60. *Comprehensive fee:* $39,880 includes full-time tuition ($27,448), mandatory fees ($3172), and room and board ($9260). *College room only:* $4974.

FRESHMAN FINANCIAL AID (Fall 2003) 1057 applied for aid; of those 80% were deemed to have need. 100% of freshmen with need received aid; of those 100% had need fully met. *Average percent of need met:* 100% (excluding resources awarded to replace EFC). *Average financial aid package:* $26,946 (excluding resources awarded to replace EFC).

UNDERGRADUATE FINANCIAL AID (Fall 2003) 3,661 applied for aid; of those 90% were deemed to have need. 100% of undergraduates with need received aid; of those 100% had need fully met. *Average percent of need met:* 100% (excluding resources awarded to replace EFC). *Average financial aid package:* $26,773 (excluding resources awarded to replace EFC).

GIFT AID (NEED-BASED) *Total amount:* $79,025,367 (6% federal, 1% state, 87% institutional, 6% external sources). *Receiving aid:* Freshmen: 52% (846); All full-time undergraduates: 49% (3,264). *Average award:* Freshmen: $25,387; Undergraduates: $24,211. *Scholarships, grants, and awards:* Federal Pell, FSEOG, state, private, college/university gift aid from institutional funds.

GIFT AID (NON-NEED-BASED) *Total amount:* $7,222,438 (19% federal, 81% external sources). *ROTC:* Army cooperative, Air Force cooperative.

LOANS *Student loans:* $7,204,676 (76% need-based, 24% non-need-based). 44% of past graduating class borrowed through all loan programs. *Average indebtedness per student:* $9640. *Average need-based loan:* Freshmen: $2560; Undergraduates: $2706. *Parent loans:* $13,898,936 (100% non-need-based). *Programs:* Federal Direct (Subsidized and Unsubsidized Stafford, PLUS), Perkins, state, college/university.

WORK-STUDY *Federal work-study:* Total amount: $948,392; 734 jobs averaging $1292. *State or other work-study/employment:* Total amount: $4,479,947 (65% need-based, 35% non-need-based). 3,135 part-time jobs averaging $1429.

APPLYING FOR FINANCIAL AID *Required financial aid forms:* FAFSA, CSS Financial Aid PROFILE, income tax form(s). *Financial aid deadline (priority):* 2/1. *Notification date:* 4/1. Students must reply by 5/1 or within 2 weeks of notification.

CONTACT Financial Aid Office, Harvard University, 312 Byerly Hall, 8 Garden Street, Cambridge, MA 02138, 617-495-1581. *Fax:* 617-496-0256.

HARVEY MUDD COLLEGE
Claremont, CA

Tuition & fees: $30,237	Average undergraduate aid package: $24,732

ABOUT THE INSTITUTION Independent, coed. Awards: bachelor's and master's degrees. 6 undergraduate majors. Total enrollment: 704. Undergraduates: 704. Freshmen: 191. Both federal and institutional methodology are used as a basis for awarding need-based institutional aid.

UNDERGRADUATE EXPENSES for 2004–05 *Application fee:* $50. *Comprehensive fee:* $40,082 includes full-time tuition ($29,553), mandatory fees ($684), and room and board ($9845). *College room only:* $5030. Room and board charges vary according to board plan. *Payment plan:* Installment.

FRESHMAN FINANCIAL AID (Fall 2004, est.) 137 applied for aid; of those 84% were deemed to have need. 100% of freshmen with need received aid; of those 100% had need fully met. *Average percent of need met:* 100% (excluding resources awarded to replace EFC). *Average financial aid package:* $24,049 (excluding resources awarded to replace EFC). 20% of all full-time freshmen had no need and received non-need-based gift aid.

UNDERGRADUATE FINANCIAL AID (Fall 2004, est.) 452 applied for aid; of those 87% were deemed to have need. 100% of undergraduates with need received aid; of those 100% had need fully met. *Average percent of need met:* 100% (excluding resources awarded to replace EFC). *Average financial aid package:* $24,732 (excluding resources awarded to replace EFC). 20% of all full-time undergraduates had no need and received non-need-based gift aid.

GIFT AID (NEED-BASED) *Total amount:* $7,727,579 (5% federal, 9% state, 86% institutional). *Receiving aid:* Freshmen: 58% (111); All full-time undergraduates: 52% (374). *Average award:* Freshmen: $21,151; Undergraduates: $21,141. *Scholarships, grants, and awards:* Federal Pell, FSEOG, state, private, college/university gift aid from institutional funds.

GIFT AID (NON-NEED-BASED) *Total amount:* $1,642,499 (1% state, 40% institutional, 59% external sources). *Receiving aid:* Freshmen: 20% (38); Undergraduates: 20% (144). *Average Award: Freshmen:* $4438; *Undergraduates:* $7275. *Scholarships, grants, and awards by category: Academic Interests/ Achievement:* 249 awards ($1,381,469 total): general academic interests/ achievements. *Tuition waivers:* Full or partial for employees or children of employees. *ROTC:* Army cooperative, Air Force.

LOANS *Student loans:* $1,801,839 (58% need-based, 42% non-need-based). 61% of past graduating class borrowed through all loan programs. *Average indebtedness per student:* $16,940. *Average need-based loan:* Freshmen: $3554; Undergraduates: $3472. *Parent loans:* $1,958,005 (100% non-need-based). *Programs:* FFEL (Subsidized and Unsubsidized Stafford, PLUS), Perkins, college/ university, alternative loans.

WORK-STUDY *Federal work-study:* Total amount: $477,352; 251 jobs averaging $1902. *State or other work-study/employment:* Total amount: $24,550 (100% need-based). 12 part-time jobs averaging $2046.

APPLYING FOR FINANCIAL AID *Required financial aid forms:* FAFSA, CSS Financial Aid PROFILE, state aid form, business/farm supplement. *Financial aid deadline:* 2/1. *Notification date:* 4/1. Students must reply by 5/1 or within 2 weeks of notification.

CONTACT Office of Financial Aid, Harvey Mudd College, 301 Platt Boulevard, Claremont, CA 91711-5994, 909-621-8055. *Fax:* 909-607-7046. *E-mail:* financial_aid@hmc.edu.

HASKELL INDIAN NATIONS UNIVERSITY
Lawrence, KS

ABOUT THE INSTITUTION Federally supported, coed. Awards: associate and bachelor's degrees. 14 undergraduate majors. Total enrollment: 1,028. Undergraduates: 1,028. Freshmen: 350.

GIFT AID (NEED-BASED) *Scholarships, grants, and awards:* Federal Pell, FSEOG, college/university gift aid from institutional funds.

LOANS *Programs:* alternative loans.

WORK-STUDY *Federal work-study:* Total amount: $30,000; jobs available.

APPLYING FOR FINANCIAL AID *Required financial aid form:* FAFSA.

CONTACT Reta Beaver, Director of Financial Aid, Haskell Indian Nations University, 155 Indian Avenue, Box 5027, Lawrence, KS 66046-4800, 785-749-8468. *Fax:* 785-832-6617.

HASTINGS COLLEGE
Hastings, NE

Tuition & fees: $16,290	Average undergraduate aid package: $11,739

ABOUT THE INSTITUTION Independent Presbyterian, coed. Awards: bachelor's and master's degrees. 82 undergraduate majors. Total enrollment: 1,153. Undergraduates: 1,105. Freshmen: 289. Federal methodology is used as a basis for awarding need-based institutional aid.

UNDERGRADUATE EXPENSES for 2004–05 *Application fee:* $20. *Comprehensive fee:* $21,050 includes full-time tuition ($15,640), mandatory fees ($650), and room and board ($4760). *College room only:* $2034. Full-time tuition and fees vary according to degree level and program. Room and board charges vary according to board plan and housing facility. *Part-time tuition:* $647 per semester hour. *Part-time fees:* $171 per term. Part-time tuition and fees vary according to course load, degree level, and program. *Payment plans:* Installment, deferred payment.

FRESHMAN FINANCIAL AID (Fall 2004, est.) 258 applied for aid; of those 85% were deemed to have need. 100% of freshmen with need received aid; of those 32% had need fully met. *Average percent of need met:* 79% (excluding resources awarded to replace EFC). *Average financial aid package:* $12,216 (excluding resources awarded to replace EFC). 22% of all full-time freshmen had no need and received non-need-based gift aid.

UNDERGRADUATE FINANCIAL AID (Fall 2004, est.) 944 applied for aid; of those 88% were deemed to have need. 100% of undergraduates with need received aid; of those 29% had need fully met. *Average percent of need met:* 75% (excluding resources awarded to replace EFC). *Average financial aid package:* $11,739 (excluding resources awarded to replace EFC). 22% of all full-time undergraduates had no need and received non-need-based gift aid.

GIFT AID (NEED-BASED) *Total amount:* $5,377,931 (19% federal, 3% state, 69% institutional, 9% external sources). *Receiving aid:* Freshmen: 77% (220); All full-time undergraduates: 75% (825). *Average award:* Freshmen: $9885; Undergraduates: $8412. *Scholarships, grants, and awards:* Federal Pell, FSEOG, state, private, college/university gift aid from institutional funds.

GIFT AID (NON-NEED-BASED) *Total amount:* $2,056,390 (78% institutional, 22% external sources). *Receiving aid:* Freshmen: 17% (48); Undergraduates: 12% (136). *Average Award: Freshmen:* $9024; *Undergraduates:* $8577. *Scholarships, grants, and awards by category: Academic Interests/Achievement:* communication, general academic interests/achievements, religion/biblical studies. *Creative Arts/Performance:* art/fine arts, debating, music, performing arts, theater/ drama. *Special Characteristics:* adult students, children of educators, children of faculty/staff, relatives of clergy, religious affiliation, siblings of current students. *Tuition waivers:* Full or partial for employees or children of employees, adult students.

LOANS *Student loans:* $4,183,979 (73% need-based, 27% non-need-based). 90% of past graduating class borrowed through all loan programs. *Average indebtedness per student:* $17,634. *Average need-based loan:* Freshmen: $3074; Undergraduates: $4122. *Parent loans:* $2,047,844 (41% need-based, 59% non-need-based). *Programs:* FFEL (Subsidized and Unsubsidized Stafford, PLUS), Perkins, college/university.

WORK-STUDY *Federal work-study:* Total amount: $68,355; jobs available (averaging $600). *State or other work-study/employment:* Total amount: $116,277 (36% need-based, 64% non-need-based). Part-time jobs available.

ATHLETIC AWARDS *Total amount:* $2,174,810 (72% need-based, 28% non-need-based).

APPLYING FOR FINANCIAL AID *Required financial aid forms:* FAFSA, institution's own form. *Financial aid deadline:* 9/1 (priority: 5/1). *Notification date:* Continuous. Students must reply within 2 weeks of notification.

CONTACT Mr. Ian Roberts, Associate Vice President-Administration, Hastings College, 7th and Turner, Hastings, NE 68901, 402-461-7455 or toll-free 800-532-7642. *Fax:* 402-461-7714. *E-mail:* iroberts@hastings.edu.

HAVERFORD COLLEGE
Haverford, PA

Tuition & fees: $30,270	Average undergraduate aid package: $26,172

ABOUT THE INSTITUTION Independent, coed. Awards: bachelor's degrees. 44 undergraduate majors. Total enrollment: 1,172. Undergraduates: 1,172. Freshmen: 330. Institutional methodology is used as a basis for awarding need-based institutional aid.

UNDERGRADUATE EXPENSES for 2004–05 *Application fee:* $60. *Comprehensive fee:* $39,690 includes full-time tuition ($29,990), mandatory fees ($280), and room and board ($9420). *College room only:* $5290. Room and board charges vary according to board plan. *Payment plan:* Installment.

FRESHMAN FINANCIAL AID (Fall 2004, est.) 187 applied for aid; of those 76% were deemed to have need. 100% of freshmen with need received aid; of those 100% had need fully met. *Average percent of need met:* 100% (excluding resources awarded to replace EFC). *Average financial aid package:* $25,441 (excluding resources awarded to replace EFC).

UNDERGRADUATE FINANCIAL AID (Fall 2004, est.) 577 applied for aid; of those 87% were deemed to have need. 100% of undergraduates with need received aid; of those 100% had need fully met. *Average percent of need met:* 100% (excluding resources awarded to replace EFC). *Average financial aid package:* $26,172 (excluding resources awarded to replace EFC).

GIFT AID (NEED-BASED) *Total amount:* $10,660,450 (6% federal, 2% state, 89% institutional, 3% external sources). *Receiving aid:* Freshmen: 40% (132); All full-time undergraduates: 40% (467). *Average award:* Freshmen: $22,398; Undergraduates: $22,055. *Scholarships, grants, and awards:* Federal Pell, FSEOG, state, private, college/university gift aid from institutional funds.

GIFT AID (NON-NEED-BASED) *Tuition waivers:* Full or partial for employees or children of employees.

LOANS *Student loans:* $1,605,788 (76% need-based, 24% non-need-based). 39% of past graduating class borrowed through all loan programs. *Average indebtedness per student:* $17,553. *Average need-based loan:* Freshmen: $2674; Undergraduates: $3872. *Parent loans:* $2,448,488 (100% non-need-based). *Programs:* FFEL (Subsidized and Unsubsidized Stafford, PLUS), Perkins.

WORK-STUDY *Federal work-study:* Total amount: $314,045; jobs available. *State or other work-study/employment:* Total amount: $440,030 (50% need-based, 50% non-need-based). Part-time jobs available.

APPLYING FOR FINANCIAL AID *Required financial aid forms:* FAFSA, CSS Financial Aid PROFILE, state aid form, noncustodial (divorced/separated) parent's statement, business/farm supplement. *Financial aid deadline:* 1/31. *Notification date:* 4/15. Students must reply by 5/1.

CONTACT Mr. David J. Hoy, Director of Financial Aid Office, Haverford College, 370 Lancaster Avenue, Haverford, PA 19041-1392, 610-896-1350. *Fax:* 610-896-1338. *E-mail:* finaid@haverford.edu.

HAWAI'I PACIFIC UNIVERSITY
Honolulu, HI

Tuition & fees: $11,002	Average undergraduate aid package: $10,219

ABOUT THE INSTITUTION Independent, coed. Awards: associate, bachelor's, and master's degrees and post-bachelor's and post-master's certificates. 55 undergraduate majors. Total enrollment: 7,800. Undergraduates: 6,615. Freshmen: 671. Federal methodology is used as a basis for awarding need-based institutional aid.

UNDERGRADUATE EXPENSES for 2004–05 *Application fee:* $50. *Comprehensive fee:* $20,022 includes full-time tuition ($10,922), mandatory fees ($80), and room and board ($9020). Full-time tuition and fees vary according to program and student level. Room and board charges vary according to housing facility. *Part-time tuition:* $205 per credit. Part-time tuition and fees vary according to course load. *Payment plan:* Installment.

FRESHMAN FINANCIAL AID (Fall 2004, est.) 518 applied for aid; of those 58% were deemed to have need. 94% of freshmen with need received aid; of those 18% had need fully met. *Average percent of need met:* 80% (excluding resources

awarded to replace EFC). *Average financial aid package:* $10,015 (excluding resources awarded to replace EFC). 27% of all full-time freshmen had no need and received non-need-based gift aid.

UNDERGRADUATE FINANCIAL AID (Fall 2004, est.) 2,503 applied for aid; of those 60% were deemed to have need. 97% of undergraduates with need received aid; of those 23% had need fully met. *Average percent of need met:* 75% (excluding resources awarded to replace EFC). *Average financial aid package:* $10,219 (excluding resources awarded to replace EFC). 21% of all full-time undergraduates had no need and received non-need-based gift aid.

GIFT AID (NEED-BASED) *Total amount:* $3,646,117 (100% federal). *Receiving aid:* Freshmen: 22% (144); All full-time undergraduates: 21% (828). *Average award:* Freshmen: $4033; Undergraduates: $3826. *Scholarships, grants, and awards:* Federal Pell, FSEOG, state, private, college/university gift aid from institutional funds.

GIFT AID (NON-NEED-BASED) *Total amount:* $7,782,734 (69% institutional, 31% external sources). *Receiving aid:* Freshmen: 17% (113); Undergraduates: 12% (481). *Average Award:* Freshmen: $7618; Undergraduates: $6491. *Scholarships, grants, and awards by category: Academic Interests/Achievement:* 313 awards ($2,433,002 total): biological sciences, business, communication, general academic interests/achievements, health fields, social sciences. *Creative Arts/Performance:* 63 awards ($579,026 total): dance, journalism/publications, music. *Special Achievements/Activities:* 272 awards ($1,359,695 total): cheerleading/drum major, hobbies/interests, leadership, memberships, religious involvement. *Special Characteristics:* 179 awards ($488,426 total): ethnic background, international students, local/state students, out-of-state students, previous college experience, relatives of clergy, religious affiliation. *Tuition waivers:* Full or partial for employees or children of employees. *ROTC:* Army cooperative, Air Force cooperative.

LOANS *Student loans:* $12,933,165 (100% need-based). 37% of past graduating class borrowed through all loan programs. *Average indebtedness per student:* $18,786. *Average need-based loan:* Freshmen: $3109; Undergraduates: $4133. *Parent loans:* $6,507,782 (100% need-based). *Programs:* FFEL (Subsidized and Unsubsidized Stafford, PLUS), Perkins, Federal Nursing.

WORK-STUDY *Federal work-study:* Total amount: $1,141,376; 384 jobs averaging $2973.

ATHLETIC AWARDS *Total amount:* $1,103,984 (100% non-need-based).

APPLYING FOR FINANCIAL AID *Required financial aid form:* FAFSA. *Financial aid deadline (priority):* 3/1. *Notification date:* Continuous beginning 4/1. Students must reply within 2 weeks of notification.

CONTACT Catherine Ganung, Director of Financial Aid, Hawai'i Pacific University, 1164 Bishop Street, Honolulu, HI 96813-2785, 808-544-0253 or toll-free 866-225-5478 (out-of-state). *Fax:* 808-544-0884. *E-mail:* financialaid@hpu.edu.

HEBREW COLLEGE
Newton Centre, MA

CONTACT Ms. Norma Frankel, Registrar, Hebrew College, 160 Herrick Road, Newton Centre, MA 02459, 617-559-8612 or toll-free 800-866-4814 Ext. 8619. *Fax:* 617-559-8601.

HEBREW THEOLOGICAL COLLEGE
Skokie, IL

CONTACT Ms. Rhoda Morris, Financial Aid Administrator, Hebrew Theological College, 7135 Carpenter Road, Skokie, IL 60077-3263, 847-982-2500. *Fax:* 847-674-6381.

HEIDELBERG COLLEGE
Tiffin, OH

Tuition & fees: $14,900	Average undergraduate aid package: $15,836

ABOUT THE INSTITUTION Independent religious, coed. Awards: bachelor's and master's degrees. 46 undergraduate majors. Total enrollment: 1,398. Undergraduates: 1,189. Freshmen: 353. Federal methodology is used as a basis for awarding need-based institutional aid.

UNDERGRADUATE EXPENSES for 2004–05 *Application fee:* $25. *Comprehensive fee:* $21,610 includes full-time tuition ($14,575), mandatory fees ($325), and room and board ($6710). *College room only:* $3080. Full-time tuition and fees vary according to course load and location. Room and board charges vary according to board plan and housing facility. Part-time tuition and fees vary according to location. *Payment plans:* Installment, deferred payment.

GIFT AID (NEED-BASED) *Total amount:* $8,757,497 (14% federal, 17% state, 66% institutional, 3% external sources). *Receiving aid:* Freshmen: 85% (301); All full-time undergraduates: 83% (865). *Average award:* Freshmen: $9600; Undergraduates: $9800. *Scholarships, grants, and awards:* Federal Pell, FSEOG, state, private, college/university gift aid from institutional funds.
GIFT AID (NON-NEED-BASED) *Total amount:* $1,005,783 (16% state, 80% institutional, 4% external sources). *Receiving aid:* Freshmen: 85% (301); Undergraduates: 75% (776). *Average Award: Freshmen:* $7478; *Undergraduates:* $5316. *Scholarships, grants, and awards by category: Academic Interests/Achievement:* 402 awards ($1,582,512 total): general academic interests/achievements, mathematics, physical sciences. *Creative Arts/Performance:* 63 awards ($105,100 total): music. *Special Characteristics:* 131 awards ($571,990 total): children of faculty/staff, local/state students, out-of-state students, relatives of clergy, religious affiliation. *Tuition waivers:* Full or partial for children of alumni, employees or children of employees. *ROTC:* Army cooperative, Air Force cooperative.
LOANS *Student loans:* $2,647,723 (87% need-based, 13% non-need-based). 74% of past graduating class borrowed through all loan programs. *Average indebtedness per student:* $26,498. *Average need-based loan:* Freshmen: $3658; Undergraduates: $4280. *Parent loans:* $813,402 (91% need-based, 9% non-need-based). *Programs:* FFEL (Subsidized and Unsubsidized Stafford, PLUS), Perkins.
APPLYING FOR FINANCIAL AID *Required financial aid form:* FAFSA. *Financial aid deadline (priority):* 3/1. *Notification date:* Continuous beginning 3/15. Students must reply within 2 weeks of notification.
CONTACT Ms. Juli L. Weininger, Director of Financial Aid, Heidelberg College, 310 East Market Street, Tiffin, OH 44883-2462, 419-448-2293 or toll-free 800-434-3352. *Fax:* 419-448-2296.

HELLENIC COLLEGE
Brookline, MA

ABOUT THE INSTITUTION Independent Greek Orthodox, coed. Awards: bachelor's degrees (also offers graduate degree programs through Holy Cross Greek Orthodox School of Theology). 6 undergraduate majors. Total enrollment: 211. Undergraduates: 87. Freshmen: 22.
GIFT AID (NEED-BASED) *Scholarships, grants, and awards:* Federal Pell, FSEOG, state, private, college/university gift aid from institutional funds.
GIFT AID (NON-NEED-BASED) *Scholarships, grants, and awards by category: Academic Interests/Achievement:* general academic interests/achievements, religion/biblical studies. *Special Achievements/Activities:* leadership, religious involvement. *Special Characteristics:* children and siblings of alumni, children of faculty/staff, religious affiliation.
LOANS *Programs:* FFEL (Subsidized and Unsubsidized Stafford, PLUS), state.
WORK-STUDY *Federal work-study:* Total amount: $24,200; jobs available. *State or other work-study/employment:* Total amount: $6000 (100% need-based). Part-time jobs available.
APPLYING FOR FINANCIAL AID *Required financial aid forms:* FAFSA, institution's own form.
CONTACT George A. Georgenes, Director of Financial Aid, Hellenic College, 50 Goddard Avenue, Brookline, MA 02146-7496, 617-731-3500 or toll-free 866-424-2338. *Fax:* 617-850-1465 Ext. 1297. *E-mail:* ggeorgenes@hchc.edu.

HENDERSON STATE UNIVERSITY
Arkadelphia, AR

ABOUT THE INSTITUTION State-supported, coed. Awards: associate, bachelor's, and master's degrees. 43 undergraduate majors. Total enrollment: 3,461. Undergraduates: 3,036. Freshmen: 455.
GIFT AID (NEED-BASED) *Scholarships, grants, and awards:* Federal Pell, FSEOG, state, private, college/university gift aid from institutional funds.
GIFT AID (NON-NEED-BASED) *Scholarships, grants, and awards by category: Academic Interests/Achievement:* biological sciences, education, general academic interests/achievements, international studies, mathematics. *Creative Arts/Performance:* art/fine arts, cinema/film/broadcasting, dance, debating, journalism/publications, music, performing arts, theater/drama. *Special Achievements/Activities:* cheerleading/drum major, general special achievements/activities, leadership. *Special Characteristics:* children and siblings of alumni, children of faculty/staff, international students, out-of-state students.
LOANS *Programs:* FFEL (Subsidized and Unsubsidized Stafford, PLUS), Perkins.
APPLYING FOR FINANCIAL AID *Required financial aid form:* FAFSA.

CONTACT Ms. Jo Holland, Director of Financial Aid, Henderson State University, Box 7812, 1100 Henderson Street, Arkadelphia, AR 71999-0001, 870-230-5094 or toll-free 800-228-7333. *Fax:* 870-230-5144. *E-mail:* hollanj@hsu.edu.

HENDRIX COLLEGE
Conway, AR

Tuition & fees: $21,636	Average undergraduate aid package: $14,675

ABOUT THE INSTITUTION Independent United Methodist, coed. Awards: bachelor's and master's degrees. 26 undergraduate majors. Total enrollment: 1,049. Undergraduates: 1,042. Freshmen: 295. Federal methodology is used as a basis for awarding need-based institutional aid.
UNDERGRADUATE EXPENSES for 2005–06 *Application fee:* $40. *Comprehensive fee:* $27,646 includes full-time tuition ($21,336), mandatory fees ($300), and room and board ($6010). *College room only:* $2760. Full-time tuition and fees vary according to course load. Room and board charges vary according to board plan and housing facility. *Part-time tuition:* $562 per hour. *Part-time fees:* $40 per year. Part-time tuition and fees vary according to course load. *Payment plan:* Installment.
FRESHMAN FINANCIAL AID (Fall 2004, est.) 239 applied for aid; of those 74% were deemed to have need. 100% of freshmen with need received aid; of those 47% had need fully met. *Average percent of need met:* 91% (excluding resources awarded to replace EFC). *Average financial aid package:* $14,422 (excluding resources awarded to replace EFC). 38% of all full-time freshmen had no need and received non-need-based gift aid.
UNDERGRADUATE FINANCIAL AID (Fall 2004, est.) 706 applied for aid; of those 80% were deemed to have need. 100% of undergraduates with need received aid; of those 39% had need fully met. *Average percent of need met:* 86% (excluding resources awarded to replace EFC). *Average financial aid package:* $14,675 (excluding resources awarded to replace EFC). 40% of all full-time undergraduates had no need and received non-need-based gift aid.
GIFT AID (NEED-BASED) *Total amount:* $5,404,628 (14% federal, 8% state, 75% institutional, 3% external sources). *Receiving aid:* Freshmen: 60% (178); All full-time undergraduates: 55% (560). *Average award:* Freshmen: $10,539; Undergraduates: $10,383. *Scholarships, grants, and awards:* Federal Pell, FSEOG, state, private, college/university gift aid from institutional funds.
GIFT AID (NON-NEED-BASED) *Total amount:* $4,210,683 (18% state, 79% institutional, 3% external sources). *Receiving aid:* Freshmen: 15% (45); Undergraduates: 10% (104). *Average Award: Freshmen:* $13,854; *Undergraduates:* $13,403. *Scholarships, grants, and awards by category: Academic Interests/Achievement:* 749 awards ($4,463,916 total): general academic interests/achievements. *Creative Arts/Performance:* 106 awards ($118,250 total): art/fine arts, music, theater/drama. *Special Achievements/Activities:* 97 awards ($185,125 total): leadership, religious involvement. *Special Characteristics:* 76 awards ($572,604 total): children of faculty/staff, international students, previous college experience, relatives of clergy. *Tuition waivers:* Full or partial for employees or children of employees. *ROTC:* Army cooperative.
LOANS *Student loans:* $2,819,832 (73% need-based, 27% non-need-based). 45% of past graduating class borrowed through all loan programs. *Average indebtedness per student:* $15,234. *Average need-based loan:* Freshmen: $3883; Undergraduates: $4352. *Parent loans:* $3,196,371 (18% need-based, 82% non-need-based). *Programs:* FFEL (Subsidized and Unsubsidized Stafford, PLUS), Perkins, United Methodist Loan.
WORK-STUDY *Federal work-study:* Total amount: $395,488; 269 jobs averaging $1415. *State or other work-study/employment:* Total amount: $194,935 (100% non-need-based). 197 part-time jobs averaging $1068.
APPLYING FOR FINANCIAL AID *Required financial aid forms:* FAFSA, institution's own form, state aid form. *Financial aid deadline (priority):* 2/15. *Notification date:* Continuous beginning 3/1. Students must reply by 5/1 or within 2 weeks of notification.
CONTACT Clay Berry, Assistant Director of Financial Aid, Hendrix College, 1600 Washington Avenue, Conway, AR 72032, 501-450-1368 or toll-free 800-277-9017. *Fax:* 501-450-3871. *E-mail:* student_aid@hendrix.edu.

HENRY COGSWELL COLLEGE
Everett, WA

ABOUT THE INSTITUTION Independent, coed. Awards: bachelor's degrees. 5 undergraduate majors. Total enrollment: 229. Undergraduates: 229. Freshmen: 36.

Henry Cogswell College

GIFT AID (NEED-BASED) *Scholarships, grants, and awards:* Federal Pell, FSEOG, state, private, college/university gift aid from institutional funds.
GIFT AID (NON-NEED-BASED) *Scholarships, grants, and awards by category:* Academic Interests/Achievement: business, computer science, engineering/technologies, general academic interests/achievements.
LOANS *Programs:* FFEL (Subsidized and Unsubsidized Stafford, PLUS).
WORK-STUDY *Federal work-study:* Total amount: $16,692; 9 jobs averaging $903. *State or other work-study/employment:* Total amount: $22,100 (100% need-based). 9 part-time jobs averaging $684.
APPLYING FOR FINANCIAL AID *Required financial aid forms:* FAFSA, institution's own form.
CONTACT Financial Aid Director, Henry Cogswell College, 3002 Colby Avenue, Everett, WA 98201, 425-258-3351 Ext. 117 or toll-free 866-411-4221. *Fax:* 425-257-0405. *E-mail:* financialaid@henrycogswell.edu.

HERITAGE BIBLE COLLEGE
Dunn, NC

ABOUT THE INSTITUTION Independent Pentecostal Free Will Baptist, coed. Awards: associate and bachelor's degrees. 3 undergraduate majors. Total enrollment: 102. Undergraduates: 102. Freshmen: 22.
GIFT AID (NEED-BASED) *Scholarships, grants, and awards:* Federal Pell, FSEOG, private, college/university gift aid from institutional funds.
LOANS *Programs:* FFEL (Subsidized and Unsubsidized Stafford, PLUS).
WORK-STUDY *Federal work-study:* Total amount: $5616; 3 jobs available.
APPLYING FOR FINANCIAL AID *Required financial aid forms:* FAFSA, institution's own form, verification documents.
CONTACT Mrs. Vickie Williford, Director of Financial Aid, Heritage Bible College, Box 1628, Dunn, NC 28335, 800-297-6351 or toll-free 800-297-6351 Ext. 230. *Fax:* 910-892-1809. *E-mail:* vwilliford@heritagebiblecollege.org.

HERITAGE CHRISTIAN UNIVERSITY
Florence, AL

Tuition & fees: $8264	Average undergraduate aid package: $2174

ABOUT THE INSTITUTION Independent religious, coed, primarily men. Awards: associate, bachelor's, and master's degrees. 1 undergraduate major. Total enrollment: 123. Undergraduates: 109. Freshmen: 4. Federal methodology is used as a basis for awarding need-based institutional aid.
UNDERGRADUATE EXPENSES for 2005–06 *Application fee:* $25. *Tuition:* full-time $7784; part-time $278 per hour. *Required fees:* full-time $480; $20 per hour. *Payment plan:* Installment.
GIFT AID (NEED-BASED) *Scholarships, grants, and awards:* Federal Pell, FSEOG, college/university gift aid from institutional funds.
GIFT AID (NON-NEED-BASED) *Receiving aid:* Freshmen: 100% (4); Undergraduates: 67% (39). *Average Award:* Undergraduates: $250. *Scholarships, grants, and awards by category:* Academic Interests/Achievement: general academic interests/achievements. *Special Characteristics:* 6 awards ($11,744 total): children and siblings of alumni, children of educators, children of faculty/staff, spouses of current students. *Tuition waivers:* Full or partial for employees or children of employees.
LOANS *Student loans:* $404,096 (54% need-based, 46% non-need-based). 69% of past graduating class borrowed through all loan programs. *Average indebtedness per student:* $23,236. *Parent loans:* $5141 (100% need-based). *Programs:* FFEL (Subsidized and Unsubsidized Stafford, PLUS).
APPLYING FOR FINANCIAL AID *Required financial aid forms:* FAFSA, federal income tax form(s). *Financial aid deadline (priority):* 6/1. *Notification date:* Continuous beginning 7/15. Students must reply within 2 weeks of notification.
CONTACT Angie Horton, Financial Aid Counselor, Heritage Christian University, PO Box HCU, Florence, AL 35630, 800-367-3565 Ext. 24 or toll-free 800-367-3565. *Fax:* 256-766-9289. *E-mail:* ahorton@hcu.edu.

HERITAGE UNIVERSITY
Toppenish, WA

Tuition & fees: $7120	Average undergraduate aid package: $9516

ABOUT THE INSTITUTION Independent, coed. Awards: associate, bachelor's, and master's degrees and post-bachelor's certificates. 25 undergraduate majors.

Total enrollment: 1,355. Undergraduates: 810. Freshmen: 118. Federal methodology is used as a basis for awarding need-based institutional aid.
UNDERGRADUATE EXPENSES for 2004–05 *Tuition:* full-time $7080; part-time $295 per credit. Full-time tuition and fees vary according to course load. Part-time tuition and fees vary according to course load. *Payment plans:* Installment, deferred payment.
FRESHMAN FINANCIAL AID (Fall 2003) 94 applied for aid; of those 97% were deemed to have need. 90% of freshmen with need received aid; of those 2% had need fully met. *Average percent of need met:* 57% (excluding resources awarded to replace EFC). *Average financial aid package:* $8475 (excluding resources awarded to replace EFC).
UNDERGRADUATE FINANCIAL AID (Fall 2003) 342 applied for aid; of those 94% were deemed to have need. 90% of undergraduates with need received aid; of those 3% had need fully met. *Average percent of need met:* 61% (excluding resources awarded to replace EFC). *Average financial aid package:* $9516 (excluding resources awarded to replace EFC). 1% of all full-time undergraduates had no need and received non-need-based gift aid.
GIFT AID (NEED-BASED) *Total amount:* $4,285,994 (37% federal, 39% state, 16% institutional, 8% external sources). *Receiving aid:* Freshmen: 85% (82); All full-time undergraduates: 52% (277). *Average award:* Freshmen: $7033; Undergraduates: $7159. *Scholarships, grants, and awards:* Federal Pell, FSEOG, state, private, college/university gift aid from institutional funds.
GIFT AID (NON-NEED-BASED) *Total amount:* $56,865 (8% federal, 17% state, 54% institutional, 21% external sources). *Receiving aid:* Freshmen: 2% (2); Undergraduates: 1% (5). *Average Award:* Undergraduates: $6251. *Scholarships, grants, and awards by category:* Academic Interests/Achievement: 9 awards ($56,865 total): biological sciences, business, communication, computer science, education, general academic interests/achievements, physical sciences, social sciences. *Tuition waivers:* Full or partial for employees or children of employees.
LOANS *Student loans:* $3,100,227 (94% need-based, 6% non-need-based). 92% of past graduating class borrowed through all loan programs. *Average indebtedness per student:* $11,909. *Average need-based loan:* Freshmen: $1960; Undergraduates: $3175. *Parent loans:* $32,852 (66% need-based, 34% non-need-based). *Programs:* FFEL (Subsidized and Unsubsidized Stafford, PLUS), Perkins.
WORK-STUDY *Federal work-study:* Total amount: $131,336; 71 jobs averaging $1885. *State or other work-study/employment:* Total amount: $174,352 (99% need-based, 1% non-need-based). 91 part-time jobs averaging $1895.
APPLYING FOR FINANCIAL AID *Required financial aid forms:* FAFSA, institution's own form. *Financial aid deadline (priority):* 2/10. *Notification date:* Continuous. Students must reply within 2 weeks of notification.
CONTACT Mr. Norberto Espindola, Director of Enrollment Management Services, Heritage University, 3240 Fort Road, Toppenish, WA 98948-9599, 509-865-8500 or toll-free 888-272-6190 (in-state). *Fax:* 509-865-8659. *E-mail:* financial_aid@heritage.edu.

HIGH POINT UNIVERSITY
High Point, NC

ABOUT THE INSTITUTION Independent United Methodist, coed. Awards: bachelor's and master's degrees and post-bachelor's certificates. 49 undergraduate majors. Total enrollment: 2,842. Undergraduates: 2,619. Freshmen: 429.
GIFT AID (NEED-BASED) *Scholarships, grants, and awards:* Federal Pell, FSEOG, state, private, college/university gift aid from institutional funds.
GIFT AID (NON-NEED-BASED) *Scholarships, grants, and awards by category:* Academic Interests/Achievement: biological sciences, business, education, English, foreign languages, general academic interests/achievements, humanities, international studies, mathematics, physical sciences, premedicine, religion/biblical studies. *Creative Arts/Performance:* art/fine arts, music. *Special Achievements/Activities:* general special achievements/activities. *Special Characteristics:* relatives of clergy.
LOANS *Programs:* Federal Direct (Subsidized and Unsubsidized Stafford, PLUS), FFEL (Subsidized and Unsubsidized Stafford, PLUS), Perkins.
APPLYING FOR FINANCIAL AID *Required financial aid forms:* FAFSA, state aid form.
CONTACT Dana D. Kelly, Director of Financial Aid, High Point University, Box 3232, University Station, 833 Montlieu Avenue, High Point, NC 27262, 336-841-9128 or toll-free 800-345-6993. *Fax:* 336-884-0221. *E-mail:* dkelly@highpoint.edu.

HILBERT COLLEGE
Hamburg, NY

Tuition & fees: $14,300	Average undergraduate aid package: $9603

ABOUT THE INSTITUTION Independent, coed. Awards: associate and bachelor's degrees. 13 undergraduate majors. Total enrollment: 1,108. Undergraduates: 1,108. Freshmen: 161. Federal methodology is used as a basis for awarding need-based institutional aid.

UNDERGRADUATE EXPENSES for 2005–06 *Application fee:* $20. *Comprehensive fee:* $19,680 includes full-time tuition ($13,750), mandatory fees ($550), and room and board ($5380). *College room only:* $2350. Full-time tuition and fees vary according to course load. Room and board charges vary according to board plan and housing facility. *Part-time tuition:* $322 per credit hour. *Part-time fees:* $13 per credit hour; $30 per term. Part-time tuition and fees vary according to course load. *Payment plans:* Installment, deferred payment.

FRESHMAN FINANCIAL AID (Fall 2004, est.) 151 applied for aid; of those 96% were deemed to have need. 99% of freshmen with need received aid; of those 23% had need fully met. *Average percent of need met:* 73% (excluding resources awarded to replace EFC). *Average financial aid package:* $8963 (excluding resources awarded to replace EFC). 5% of all full-time freshmen had no need and received non-need-based gift aid.

UNDERGRADUATE FINANCIAL AID (Fall 2004, est.) 811 applied for aid; of those 90% were deemed to have need. 99% of undergraduates with need received aid; of those 30% had need fully met. *Average percent of need met:* 76% (excluding resources awarded to replace EFC). *Average financial aid package:* $9603 (excluding resources awarded to replace EFC). 10% of all full-time undergraduates had no need and received non-need-based gift aid.

GIFT AID (NEED-BASED) *Total amount:* $4,433,181 (25% federal, 30% state, 37% institutional, 8% external sources). *Receiving aid:* Freshmen: 94% (143); All full-time undergraduates: 85% (707). *Average award:* Freshmen: $6552; Undergraduates: $6012. *Scholarships, grants, and awards:* Federal Pell, FSEOG, state, private, college/university gift aid from institutional funds.

GIFT AID (NON-NEED-BASED) *Total amount:* $301,631 (17% state, 53% institutional, 30% external sources). *Receiving aid:* Freshmen: 8% (12); Undergraduates: 6% (50). *Average Award:* Freshmen: $10,981; Undergraduates:$8983. *Scholarships, grants, and awards by category: Academic Interests/Achievement:* 82 awards ($161,000 total): general academic interests/achievements. *Special Achievements/Activities:* 44 awards ($63,000 total): leadership. *Special Characteristics:* 37 awards ($37,750 total): children and siblings of alumni, members of minority groups, siblings of current students. *Tuition waivers:* Full or partial for children of alumni, employees or children of employees, senior citizens.

LOANS *Student loans:* $5,952,725 (67% need-based, 33% non-need-based). 87% of past graduating class borrowed through all loan programs. *Average indebtedness per student:* $19,129. *Average need-based loan:* Freshmen: $2859; Undergraduates: $4116. *Parent loans:* $629,065 (33% need-based, 67% non-need-based). *Programs:* FFEL (Subsidized and Unsubsidized Stafford, PLUS), Perkins, alternative loans.

WORK-STUDY *Federal work-study:* Total amount: $94,510; 55 jobs averaging $1718.

APPLYING FOR FINANCIAL AID *Required financial aid form:* FAFSA. *Financial aid deadline:* 5/1 (priority: 3/1). *Notification date:* Continuous beginning 3/15. Students must reply within 2 weeks of notification.

CONTACT Beverly Chudy, Director of Financial Aid, Hilbert College, 5200 South Park Avenue, Hamburg, NY 14075-1597, 716-649-7900 Ext. 207. *Fax:* 716-649-1152. *E-mail:* bchudy@hilbert.edu.

HILLSDALE COLLEGE
Hillsdale, MI

Tuition & fees: $16,900	Average undergraduate aid package: $12,700

ABOUT THE INSTITUTION Independent, coed. Awards: bachelor's degrees. 43 undergraduate majors. Total enrollment: 1,273. Undergraduates: 1,273. Freshmen: 350. Both federal and institutional methodology are used as a basis for awarding need-based institutional aid.

UNDERGRADUATE EXPENSES for 2004–05 *Application fee:* $15. *Comprehensive fee:* $23,500 includes full-time tuition ($16,500), mandatory fees ($400), and room and board ($6600). *College room only:* $3200. Room and board charges vary according to board plan. *Part-time tuition:* $650 per semester hour. *Payment plans:* Tuition prepayment, installment, deferred payment.

FRESHMAN FINANCIAL AID (Fall 2003) 360 applied for aid; of those 89% were deemed to have need. 100% of freshmen with need received aid; of those 44% had need fully met. *Average percent of need met:* 75% (excluding resources awarded to replace EFC). *Average financial aid package:* $11,800 (excluding resources awarded to replace EFC). 23% of all full-time freshmen had no need and received non-need-based gift aid.

UNDERGRADUATE FINANCIAL AID (Fall 2003) 1,126 applied for aid; of those 95% were deemed to have need. 100% of undergraduates with need received aid; of those 41% had need fully met. *Average percent of need met:* 78% (excluding resources awarded to replace EFC). *Average financial aid package:* $12,700 (excluding resources awarded to replace EFC). 25% of all full-time undergraduates had no need and received non-need-based gift aid.

GIFT AID (NEED-BASED) *Total amount:* $7,117,700 (6% state, 94% institutional). *Receiving aid:* Freshmen: 82% (320); All full-time undergraduates: 88% (1,070). *Average award:* Freshmen: $8500; Undergraduates: $10,600. *Scholarships, grants, and awards:* state, private, college/university gift aid from institutional funds.

GIFT AID (NON-NEED-BASED) *Total amount:* $1,880,800 (10% state, 68% institutional, 22% external sources). *Receiving aid:* Freshmen: 41% (160); Undergraduates: 51% (618). *Average Award:* Freshmen: $7500; Undergraduates: $8800. *Scholarships, grants, and awards by category: Academic Interests/Achievement:* 675 awards ($2,200,000 total): biological sciences, business, education, English, foreign languages, general academic interests/achievements, health fields, humanities, international studies, mathematics, physical sciences, premedicine, religion/biblical studies. *Creative Arts/Performance:* 60 awards ($100,000 total): art/fine arts, debating, journalism/publications, music, theater/drama. *Special Achievements/Activities:* 245 awards ($1,000,000 total): community service, general special achievements/activities, leadership. *Special Characteristics:* 40 awards ($330,000 total): children of faculty/staff, international students. *Tuition waivers:* Full or partial for children of alumni, employees or children of employees.

LOANS *Student loans:* $3,584,000 (45% need-based, 55% non-need-based). 65% of past graduating class borrowed through all loan programs. *Average indebtedness per student:* $15,800. *Average need-based loan:* Freshmen: $2500; Undergraduates: $4000. *Programs:* college/university, alternative loans.

ATHLETIC AWARDS *Total amount:* $1,579,700 (100% non-need-based).

APPLYING FOR FINANCIAL AID *Required financial aid forms:* institution's own form, FAFSA (for state aid only). *Financial aid deadline (priority):* 2/15. *Notification date:* Continuous beginning 2/15. Students must reply by 5/1 or within 3 weeks of notification.

CONTACT Mrs. Connie Bricker, Director of Student Financial Aid, Hillsdale College, 33 East College Street, Hillsdale, MI 49242-1298, 517-607-2550. *Fax:* 517-607-2298. *E-mail:* connie.bricker@hillsdale.edu.

HILLSDALE FREE WILL BAPTIST COLLEGE
Moore, OK

CONTACT Ms. Pamela Thompson, Director of Admissions and Financial Aid, Hillsdale Free Will Baptist College, PO Box 7208, Moore, OK 73153-1208, 405-912-9006. *Fax:* 405-912-9050. *E-mail:* pamthompson@hc.edu.

HIRAM COLLEGE
Hiram, OH

ABOUT THE INSTITUTION Independent religious, coed. Awards: bachelor's and master's degrees. 35 undergraduate majors. Total enrollment: 1,125. Undergraduates: 1,108. Freshmen: 218.

GIFT AID (NEED-BASED) *Scholarships, grants, and awards:* Federal Pell, FSEOG, state, private, college/university gift aid from institutional funds.

GIFT AID (NON-NEED-BASED) *Scholarships, grants, and awards by category: Academic Interests/Achievement:* general academic interests/achievements, humanities, physical sciences, religion/biblical studies, social sciences. *Creative Arts/Performance:* music. *Special Achievements/Activities:* memberships. *Special Characteristics:* children and siblings of alumni, general special characteristics, members of minority groups, relatives of clergy, religious affiliation.

LOANS *Programs:* FFEL (Subsidized and Unsubsidized Stafford, PLUS), Perkins.

APPLYING FOR FINANCIAL AID *Required financial aid form:* FAFSA.

CONTACT Ann Marie Gruber, Associate Director of Financial Aid, Hiram College, Box 67, Hiram, OH 44234-0067, 330-569-5107 or toll-free 800-362-5280. *Fax:* 330-569-5499.

HOBART AND WILLIAM SMITH COLLEGES
Geneva, NY

Tuition & fees: $30,643	Average undergraduate aid package: $23,371

ABOUT THE INSTITUTION Independent, coed. Awards: bachelor's degrees. 54 undergraduate majors. Total enrollment: 1,847. Undergraduates: 1,839. Freshmen: 482. Both federal and institutional methodology are used as a basis for awarding need-based institutional aid.

UNDERGRADUATE EXPENSES for 2004–05 *Application fee:* $45. *Comprehensive fee:* $38,630 includes full-time tuition ($30,076), mandatory fees ($567), and room and board ($7987). *College room only:* $4220. Room and board charges vary according to board plan. *Part-time tuition:* $3760 per course. *Payment plans:* Tuition prepayment, installment.

FRESHMAN FINANCIAL AID (Fall 2004, est.) 340 applied for aid; of those 85% were deemed to have need. 99% of freshmen with need received aid; of those 78% had need fully met. *Average percent of need met:* 92% (excluding resources awarded to replace EFC). *Average financial aid package:* $23,426 (excluding resources awarded to replace EFC). 19% of all full-time freshmen had no need and received non-need-based gift aid.

UNDERGRADUATE FINANCIAL AID (Fall 2004, est.) 1,311 applied for aid; of those 87% were deemed to have need. 99% of undergraduates with need received aid; of those 77% had need fully met. *Average percent of need met:* 90% (excluding resources awarded to replace EFC). *Average financial aid package:* $23,371 (excluding resources awarded to replace EFC). 15% of all full-time undergraduates had no need and received non-need-based gift aid.

GIFT AID (NEED-BASED) *Total amount:* $21,759,630 (8% federal, 7% state, 82% institutional, 3% external sources). *Receiving aid:* Freshmen: 59% (285); All full-time undergraduates: 61% (1,121). *Average award:* Freshmen: $20,989; Undergraduates: $19,402. *Scholarships, grants, and awards:* Federal Pell, FSEOG, state, private, college/university gift aid from institutional funds.

GIFT AID (NON-NEED-BASED) *Total amount:* $3,730,778 (2% state, 87% institutional, 11% external sources). *Receiving aid:* Freshmen: 11% (52); Undergraduates: 8% (138). *Average Award: Freshmen:* $9976; *Undergraduates:* $10,614. *Scholarships, grants, and awards by category:* Academic Interests/Achievement: 63 awards ($758,152 total): general academic interests/achievements. Creative Arts/Performance: 13 awards ($96,000 total): art/fine arts, creative writing, dance, music, performing arts. Special Achievements/Activities: 23 awards ($188,000 total): leadership. *Tuition waivers:* Full or partial for employees or children of employees.

LOANS *Student loans:* $7,126,367 (70% need-based, 30% non-need-based). 69% of past graduating class borrowed through all loan programs. *Average indebtedness per student:* $21,859. *Average need-based loan:* Freshmen: $2288; Undergraduates: $3773. *Parent loans:* $5,027,060 (24% need-based, 76% non-need-based). *Programs:* FFEL (Subsidized and Unsubsidized Stafford, PLUS), Perkins.

WORK-STUDY *Federal work-study:* Total amount: $1,388,058; 925 jobs averaging $1502. *State or other work-study/employment:* Total amount: $454,658 (21% need-based, 79% non-need-based). 177 part-time jobs averaging $1693.

APPLYING FOR FINANCIAL AID *Required financial aid forms:* FAFSA, CSS Financial Aid PROFILE, state aid form, noncustodial (divorced/separated) parent's statement, income tax form(s). *Financial aid deadline:* 3/15 (priority: 2/15). *Notification date:* 4/1. Students must reply by 5/1 or within 3 weeks of notification.

CONTACT Samantha Veeder, Director of Financial Aid, Hobart and William Smith Colleges, Geneva, NY 14456-3397, 315-781-3315 or toll-free 800-245-0100. *Fax:* 315-781-3655. *E-mail:* finaid@hws.edu.

HOBE SOUND BIBLE COLLEGE
Hobe Sound, FL

CONTACT Director of Financial Aid, Hobe Sound Bible College, PO Box 1065, Hobe Sound, FL 33475-1065, 561-546-5534 or toll-free 800-881-5534. *Fax:* 561-545-1422.

HOFSTRA UNIVERSITY
Hempstead, NY

Tuition & fees: $20,012	Average undergraduate aid package: $11,400

ABOUT THE INSTITUTION Independent, coed. Awards: bachelor's, master's, doctoral, and first professional degrees and post-bachelor's and post-master's certificates. 130 undergraduate majors. Total enrollment: 12,999. Undergraduates: 9,053. Freshmen: 1,743. Federal methodology is used as a basis for awarding need-based institutional aid.

UNDERGRADUATE EXPENSES for 2004–05 *Application fee:* $40. *Comprehensive fee:* $29,012 includes full-time tuition ($19,010), mandatory fees ($1002), and room and board ($9000). *College room only:* $5900. Full-time tuition and fees vary according to course load and program. Room and board charges vary according to board plan and housing facility. *Part-time tuition:* $615 per semester hour. *Part-time fees:* $155 per term. Part-time tuition and fees vary according to course load and program. *Payment plans:* Installment, deferred payment.

FRESHMAN FINANCIAL AID (Fall 2004, est.) 1390 applied for aid; of those 76% were deemed to have need. 100% of freshmen with need received aid; of those 28% had need fully met. *Average financial aid package:* $12,300 (excluding resources awarded to replace EFC). 20% of all full-time freshmen had no need and received non-need-based gift aid.

UNDERGRADUATE FINANCIAL AID (Fall 2004, est.) 5,816 applied for aid; of those 81% were deemed to have need. 99% of undergraduates with need received aid; of those 29% had need fully met. *Average financial aid package:* $11,400 (excluding resources awarded to replace EFC). 13% of all full-time undergraduates had no need and received non-need-based gift aid.

GIFT AID (NEED-BASED) *Total amount:* $32,531,080 (19% federal, 22% state, 56% institutional, 3% external sources). *Receiving aid:* Freshmen: 61% (1,056); All full-time undergraduates: 57% (4,594). *Average award:* Freshmen: $11,500; Undergraduates: $11,100. *Scholarships, grants, and awards:* Federal Pell, FSEOG, state, private, college/university gift aid from institutional funds.

GIFT AID (NON-NEED-BASED) *Total amount:* $9,441,170 (4% federal, 6% state, 80% institutional, 10% external sources). *Receiving aid:* Freshmen: 8% (133); Undergraduates: 5% (417). *Average Award: Freshmen:* $7900; *Undergraduates:* $6400. *Scholarships, grants, and awards by category:* Academic Interests/Achievement: 2,904 awards ($19,356,379 total): communication, general academic interests/achievements. Creative Arts/Performance: 172 awards ($292,432 total): art/fine arts, dance, music, theater/drama. Special Achievements/Activities: 152 awards ($318,550 total): general special achievements/activities, leadership. Special Characteristics: 30 awards ($134,612 total): general special characteristics. *Tuition waivers:* Full or partial for employees or children of employees, senior citizens. *ROTC:* Army.

LOANS *Student loans:* $49,046,400 (71% need-based, 29% non-need-based). 49% of past graduating class borrowed through all loan programs. *Average indebtedness per student:* $19,876. *Average need-based loan:* Freshmen: $4200; Undergraduates: $6600. *Parent loans:* $68,704,000 (17% need-based, 83% non-need-based). *Programs:* FFEL (Subsidized and Unsubsidized Stafford, PLUS), Perkins.

WORK-STUDY *Federal work-study:* Total amount: $1,002,000; 510 jobs averaging $1965. *State or other work-study/employment:* Total amount: $5,200,000 (100% non-need-based). 2,900 part-time jobs averaging $1800.

ATHLETIC AWARDS *Total amount:* $6,613,000 (46% need-based, 54% non-need-based).

APPLYING FOR FINANCIAL AID *Required financial aid forms:* FAFSA, state aid form. *Financial aid deadline (priority):* 2/15. *Notification date:* Continuous beginning 3/15. Students must reply within 2 weeks of notification.

CONTACT Amy Kahn, Senior Associate Director of Financial Aid, Hofstra University, 126 Hofstra University, Hempstead, NY 11549, 516-463-6680 or toll-free 800-HOFSTRA. *Fax:* 516-463-4936. *E-mail:* janice.m.contino@hofstra.edu.

HOLLINS UNIVERSITY
Roanoke, VA

Tuition & fees: $21,675	Average undergraduate aid package: $17,722

ABOUT THE INSTITUTION Independent, women only. Awards: bachelor's and master's degrees and post-master's certificates. 30 undergraduate majors. Total enrollment: 1,057. Undergraduates: 819. Freshmen: 184. Federal methodology is used as a basis for awarding need-based institutional aid.

UNDERGRADUATE EXPENSES for 2004–05 *Application fee:* $35. *Comprehensive fee:* $29,375 includes full-time tuition ($21,200), mandatory fees ($475), and room and board ($7700). *College room only:* $4600. *Part-time tuition:* $662 per credit. *Part-time fees:* $237.50 per year. *Payment plan:* Installment.

FRESHMAN FINANCIAL AID (Fall 2004, est.) 167 applied for aid; of those 79% were deemed to have need. 100% of freshmen with need received aid; of those

17% had need fully met. *Average percent of need met:* 84% (excluding resources awarded to replace EFC). *Average financial aid package:* $18,593 (excluding resources awarded to replace EFC). 24% of all full-time freshmen had no need and received non-need-based gift aid.

UNDERGRADUATE FINANCIAL AID (Fall 2004, est.) 628 applied for aid; of those 86% were deemed to have need. 100% of undergraduates with need received aid; of those 24% had need fully met. *Average percent of need met:* 75% (excluding resources awarded to replace EFC). *Average financial aid package:* $17,722 (excluding resources awarded to replace EFC). 21% of all full-time undergraduates had no need and received non-need-based gift aid.

GIFT AID (NEED-BASED) *Total amount:* $6,815,969 (13% federal, 10% state, 75% institutional, 2% external sources). *Receiving aid:* Freshmen: 72% (132); All full-time undergraduates: 70% (541). *Average award:* Freshmen: $13,791; Undergraduates: $12,824. *Scholarships, grants, and awards:* Federal Pell, FSEOG, state, private, college/university gift aid from institutional funds.

GIFT AID (NON-NEED-BASED) *Total amount:* $2,252,053 (11% state, 85% institutional, 4% external sources). *Receiving aid:* Freshmen: 49% (91); Undergraduates: 51% (392). *Average Award:* Freshmen: $8369; Undergraduates:* $8155. *Scholarships, grants, and awards by category: Academic Interests/ Achievement:* 325 awards ($2,909,290 total): general academic interests/ achievements. *Creative Arts/Performance:* 90 awards ($324,415 total): art/fine arts, creative writing, dance, music. *Special Achievements/Activities:* 52 awards ($55,095 total): community service, leadership. *Special Characteristics:* 376 awards ($1,954,926 total): adult students, children and siblings of alumni, international students, local/state students, out-of-state students, veterans. *Tuition waivers:* Full or partial for employees or children of employees.

LOANS *Student loans:* $3,126,848 (64% need-based, 36% non-need-based). 65% of past graduating class borrowed through all loan programs. *Average indebtedness per student:* $19,305. *Average need-based loan:* Freshmen: $4108; Undergraduates: $4643. *Parent loans:* $1,547,866 (80% need-based, 20% non-need-based). *Programs:* Federal Direct (Subsidized and Unsubsidized Stafford, PLUS), Perkins, Key Alternative Loans, PLATO Loans, CitiAssist Loans, GATE Loans, Sallie Mae Loans, OneChoice loans.

WORK-STUDY *Federal work-study:* Total amount: $568,428; 271 jobs averaging $2097. *State or other work-study/employment:* Total amount: $161,620 (100% non-need-based). 76 part-time jobs averaging $2126.

APPLYING FOR FINANCIAL AID *Required financial aid forms:* FAFSA, state aid form. *Financial aid deadline:* 2/15 (priority: 2/1). *Notification date:* Continuous beginning 3/1. Students must reply by 5/1.

CONTACT Mrs. Rebecca R. Eckstein, Director of Scholarships and Financial Assistance, Hollins University, PO Box 9718, Roanoke, VA 24020-1688, 540-362-6332 or toll-free 800-456-9595. *Fax:* 540-362-6093. *E-mail:* reckstein@ hollins.edu.

HOLY FAMILY UNIVERSITY
Philadelphia, PA

ABOUT THE INSTITUTION Independent Roman Catholic, coed. Awards: associate, bachelor's, and master's degrees and post-bachelor's certificates. 46 undergraduate majors. Total enrollment: 2,670. Undergraduates: 1,782. Freshmen: 230.

GIFT AID (NEED-BASED) *Scholarships, grants, and awards:* Federal Pell, FSEOG, state, private, college/university gift aid from institutional funds.

GIFT AID (NON-NEED-BASED) *Scholarships, grants, and awards by category: Academic Interests/Achievement:* general academic interests/achievements.

LOANS *Programs:* FFEL (Subsidized and Unsubsidized Stafford, PLUS), Perkins, Federal Nursing.

WORK-STUDY *Federal work-study:* Total amount: $351,504; 299 jobs averaging $1176. *State or other work-study/employment:* Part-time jobs available.

APPLYING FOR FINANCIAL AID *Required financial aid forms:* FAFSA, institution's own form.

CONTACT Financial Aid Office, Holy Family University, Grant and Frankford Avenues, Philadelphia, PA 19114-2094, 215-637-5538 or toll-free 800-637-1191. *Fax:* 215-599-1694. *E-mail:* hfcfinaid@holyfamily.edu.

HOLY NAMES UNIVERSITY
Oakland, CA

Tuition & fees: $21,640	Average undergraduate aid package: $16,743

ABOUT THE INSTITUTION Independent Roman Catholic, coed, primarily women. Awards: bachelor's and master's degrees and post-bachelor's certificates. 26

undergraduate majors. Total enrollment: 973. Undergraduates: 641. Freshmen: 109. Federal methodology is used as a basis for awarding need-based institutional aid.

UNDERGRADUATE EXPENSES for 2005–06 *Application fee:* $35. *Comprehensive fee:* $29,440 includes full-time tuition ($21,400), mandatory fees ($240), and room and board ($7800). *College room only:* $4000. Full-time tuition and fees vary according to course load. Room and board charges vary according to board plan. *Part-time tuition:* $710 per unit. *Part-time fees:* $120 per term. *Payment plan:* Installment.

FRESHMAN FINANCIAL AID (Fall 2004, est.) 91 applied for aid; of those 96% were deemed to have need. 100% of freshmen with need received aid; of those 10% had need fully met. *Average percent of need met:* 69% (excluding resources awarded to replace EFC). *Average financial aid package:* $18,995 (excluding resources awarded to replace EFC). 4% of all full-time freshmen had no need and received non-need-based gift aid.

UNDERGRADUATE FINANCIAL AID (Fall 2004, est.) 352 applied for aid; of those 95% were deemed to have need. 100% of undergraduates with need received aid; of those 8% had need fully met. *Average percent of need met:* 85% (excluding resources awarded to replace EFC). *Average financial aid package:* $16,743 (excluding resources awarded to replace EFC). 2% of all full-time undergraduates had no need and received non-need-based gift aid.

GIFT AID (NEED-BASED) *Total amount:* $2,420,198 (27% federal, 34% state, 39% institutional). *Receiving aid:* Freshmen: 67% (72); All full-time undergraduates: 55% (245). *Average award:* Freshmen: $8578; Undergraduates: $8844. *Scholarships, grants, and awards:* Federal Pell, FSEOG, state, private, college/ university gift aid from institutional funds.

GIFT AID (NON-NEED-BASED) *Total amount:* $1,313,270 (90% institutional, 10% external sources). *Receiving aid:* Freshmen: 71% (77); Undergraduates: 68% (305). *Average Award:* Freshmen: $13,925; Undergraduates: $12,088. *Scholarships, grants, and awards by category: Academic Interests/Achievement:* 88 awards ($432,628 total): general academic interests/achievements. *Creative Arts/Performance:* 10 awards ($36,897 total): music. *Special Achievements/ Activities:* 9 awards ($15,497 total): community service. *Special Characteristics:* 27 awards ($156,381 total): children and siblings of alumni, ethnic background, international students, religious affiliation. *Tuition waivers:* Full or partial for employees or children of employees. *ROTC:* Army cooperative, Air Force cooperative.

LOANS *Student loans:* $5,440,383 (47% need-based, 53% non-need-based). 57% of past graduating class borrowed through all loan programs. *Average indebtedness per student:* $16,652. *Average need-based loan:* Freshmen: $2685; Undergraduates: $3172. *Parent loans:* $761,086 (100% non-need-based). *Programs:* FFEL (Subsidized and Unsubsidized Stafford, PLUS), Perkins, alternative loans.

WORK-STUDY *Federal work-study:* Total amount: $96,399; 71 jobs averaging $1513.

ATHLETIC AWARDS *Total amount:* $811,230 (100% non-need-based).

APPLYING FOR FINANCIAL AID *Required financial aid forms:* FAFSA, institution's own form, state aid form. *Financial aid deadline (priority):* 3/2. *Notification date:* Continuous beginning 3/1. Students must reply by 5/1 or within 2 weeks of notification.

CONTACT Director of Financial Aid, Holy Names University, 3500 Mountain Boulevard, Oakland, CA 94619-1699, 510-436-1327 or toll-free 800-430-1321. *Fax:* 510-436-1199. *E-mail:* joseph@hnu.edu.

HOOD COLLEGE
Frederick, MD

ABOUT THE INSTITUTION Independent, coed. Awards: bachelor's and master's degrees and post-bachelor's certificates (also offers adult program with significant enrollment not reflected in profile). 29 undergraduate majors. Total enrollment: 1,948. Undergraduates: 1,027. Freshmen: 243.

GIFT AID (NEED-BASED) *Scholarships, grants, and awards:* Federal Pell, FSEOG, state, private, college/university gift aid from institutional funds.

GIFT AID (NON-NEED-BASED) *Scholarships, grants, and awards by category: Academic Interests/Achievement:* general academic interests/achievements. *Creative Arts/Performance:* creative writing. *Special Achievements/Activities:* community service, leadership, memberships. *Special Characteristics:* children and siblings of alumni, children of faculty/staff, ethnic background, international students, previous college experience, siblings of current students.

LOANS *Programs:* Federal Direct (Subsidized and Unsubsidized Stafford, PLUS), FFEL (Subsidized and Unsubsidized Stafford, PLUS), Perkins.

WORK-STUDY *Federal work-study:* Total amount: $220,908; 135 jobs averaging $1636. *State or other work-study/employment:* Total amount: $162,780 (19% need-based, 81% non-need-based). 100 part-time jobs averaging $1627.
APPLYING FOR FINANCIAL AID *Required financial aid form:* FAFSA.
CONTACT Director of Financial Aid, Hood College, 401 Rosemont Avenue, Frederick, MD 21701-8575, 301-696-3411 or toll-free 800-922-1599. *E-mail:* finaid@hood.edu.

HOPE COLLEGE
Holland, MI

Tuition & fees: $20,420	Average undergraduate aid package: $17,622

ABOUT THE INSTITUTION Independent religious, coed. Awards: bachelor's degrees. 63 undergraduate majors. Total enrollment: 3,112. Undergraduates: 3,112. Freshmen: 781. Federal methodology is used as a basis for awarding need-based institutional aid.
UNDERGRADUATE EXPENSES for 2004–05 *Application fee:* $35. *Comprehensive fee:* $26,738 includes full-time tuition ($20,300), mandatory fees ($120), and room and board ($6318). *College room only:* $2880. Full-time tuition and fees vary according to course load. Room and board charges vary according to board plan. *Payment plan:* Installment.
FRESHMAN FINANCIAL AID (Fall 2004, est.) 638 applied for aid; of those 75% were deemed to have need. 100% of freshmen with need received aid; of those 32% had need fully met. *Average percent of need met:* 86% (excluding resources awarded to replace EFC). *Average financial aid package:* $17,754 (excluding resources awarded to replace EFC). 32% of all full-time freshmen had no need and received non-need-based gift aid.
UNDERGRADUATE FINANCIAL AID (Fall 2004, est.) 2,061 applied for aid; of those 83% were deemed to have need. 100% of undergraduates with need received aid; of those 31% had need fully met. *Average percent of need met:* 87% (excluding resources awarded to replace EFC). *Average financial aid package:* $17,622 (excluding resources awarded to replace EFC). 28% of all full-time undergraduates had no need and received non-need-based gift aid.
GIFT AID (NEED-BASED) *Total amount:* $15,695,634 (8% federal, 14% state, 77% institutional, 1% external sources). *Receiving aid:* Freshmen: 51% (401); All full-time undergraduates: 52% (1,483). *Average award:* Freshmen: $13,344; Undergraduates: $11,867. *Scholarships, grants, and awards:* Federal Pell, FSEOG, state, private, college/university gift aid from institutional funds.
GIFT AID (NON-NEED-BASED) *Total amount:* $8,118,966 (15% state, 75% institutional, 10% external sources). *Receiving aid:* Freshmen: 53% (413); Undergraduates: 44% (1,258). *Average Award:* Freshmen: $7497; Undergraduates: $6999. *Scholarships, grants, and awards by category:* Academic Interests/Achievement: 1,948 awards ($11,160,254 total): general academic interests/achievements. Creative Arts/Performance: 142 awards ($354,230 total): art/fine arts, creative writing, dance, music, theater/drama. *Tuition waivers:* Full or partial for employees or children of employees. *ROTC:* Army cooperative.
LOANS *Student loans:* $10,363,491 (64% need-based, 36% non-need-based). 91% of past graduating class borrowed through all loan programs. *Average indebtedness per student:* $19,288. *Average need-based loan:* Freshmen: $3669; Undergraduates: $5079. *Programs:* Federal Direct (Subsidized and Unsubsidized Stafford, PLUS), Perkins, state, college/university.
WORK-STUDY *Federal work-study:* Total amount: $322,715; 249 jobs averaging $1296. *State or other work-study/employment:* Total amount: $1,610,727 (63% need-based, 37% non-need-based). 560 part-time jobs averaging $1804.
APPLYING FOR FINANCIAL AID *Required financial aid forms:* FAFSA, institution's own form. *Financial aid deadline (priority):* 3/1. *Notification date:* Continuous beginning 3/15. Students must reply by 5/1 or within 2 weeks of notification.
CONTACT Ms. Phyllis Hooyman, Director of Financial Aid, Hope College, 141 East 12th Street, PO Box 9000, Holland, MI 49422-9000, 616-395-7765 or toll-free 800-968-7850. *Fax:* 616-395-7160. *E-mail:* hooyman@hope.edu.

HOPE INTERNATIONAL UNIVERSITY
Fullerton, CA

ABOUT THE INSTITUTION Independent religious, coed. Awards: associate, bachelor's, and master's degrees. 19 undergraduate majors. Total enrollment: 1,275. Undergraduates: 1,009. Freshmen: 106.
GIFT AID (NEED-BASED) *Scholarships, grants, and awards:* Federal Pell, FSEOG, state, private, college/university gift aid from institutional funds.
GIFT AID (NON-NEED-BASED) *Scholarships, grants, and awards by category:* Academic Interests/Achievement: area/ethnic studies, business, communica-

tion, education, English, general academic interests/achievements, humanities, international studies, religion/biblical studies, social sciences. *Creative Arts/Performance:* music. *Special Achievements/Activities:* leadership, religious involvement. *Special Characteristics:* children and siblings of alumni, children of faculty/staff, international students, local/state students, relatives of clergy, siblings of current students, spouses of current students, veterans, veterans' children.
LOANS *Programs:* FFEL (Subsidized and Unsubsidized Stafford, PLUS), Perkins.
WORK-STUDY *Federal work-study:* Total amount: $163,187; 62 jobs averaging $2000.
APPLYING FOR FINANCIAL AID *Required financial aid forms:* FAFSA, institution's own form.
CONTACT Mr. Mai Bui, Director of Financial Aid, Hope International University, 2500 East Nutwood Avenue, Fullerton, CA 92831, 714-879-3901 or toll-free 800-762-1294. *Fax:* 714-526-0231. *E-mail:* mbui@hiu.edu.

HOUGHTON COLLEGE
Houghton, NY

Tuition & fees: $18,660	Average undergraduate aid package: $14,195

ABOUT THE INSTITUTION Independent Wesleyan, coed. Awards: associate, bachelor's, and master's degrees. 46 undergraduate majors. Total enrollment: 1,480. Undergraduates: 1,468. Freshmen: 326. Both federal and institutional methodology are used as a basis for awarding need-based institutional aid.
UNDERGRADUATE EXPENSES for 2004–05 *Application fee:* $40. *Comprehensive fee:* $24,980 includes full-time tuition ($18,660) and room and board ($6320). *College room only:* $3160. Full-time tuition and fees vary according to course load, program, and reciprocity agreements. Room and board charges vary according to board plan and housing facility. *Part-time tuition:* $780 per hour. *Payment plan:* Installment.
FRESHMAN FINANCIAL AID (Fall 2004, est.) 319 applied for aid; of those 94% were deemed to have need. 100% of freshmen with need received aid; of those 16% had need fully met. *Average percent of need met:* 75% (excluding resources awarded to replace EFC). *Average financial aid package:* $14,325 (excluding resources awarded to replace EFC). 8% of all full-time freshmen had no need and received non-need-based gift aid.
UNDERGRADUATE FINANCIAL AID (Fall 2004, est.) 1,003 applied for aid; of those 93% were deemed to have need. 100% of undergraduates with need received aid; of those 16% had need fully met. *Average percent of need met:* 76% (excluding resources awarded to replace EFC). *Average financial aid package:* $14,195 (excluding resources awarded to replace EFC). 14% of all full-time undergraduates had no need and received non-need-based gift aid.
GIFT AID (NEED-BASED) *Total amount:* $7,095,459 (17% federal, 17% state, 58% institutional, 8% external sources). *Receiving aid:* Freshmen: 92% (299); All full-time undergraduates: 67% (932). *Average award:* Freshmen: $11,337; Undergraduates: $10,318. *Scholarships, grants, and awards:* Federal Pell, FSEOG, state, private, college/university gift aid from institutional funds, United Negro College Fund.
GIFT AID (NON-NEED-BASED) *Total amount:* $1,092,175 (2% state, 86% institutional, 12% external sources). *Receiving aid:* Freshmen: 6% (19); Undergraduates: 4% (60). *Average Award:* Freshmen: $4869; Undergraduates: $4977. *Scholarships, grants, and awards by category:* Academic Interests/Achievement: 603 awards ($2,098,008 total): general academic interests/achievements. Creative Arts/Performance: 73 awards ($127,084 total): art/fine arts, music. Special Achievements/Activities: 153 awards ($333,395 total): religious involvement. Special Characteristics: 304 awards ($391,270 total): children and siblings of alumni, relatives of clergy, religious affiliation, siblings of current students. *Tuition waivers:* Full or partial for employees or children of employees, senior citizens. *ROTC:* Army cooperative.
LOANS *Student loans:* $6,713,325 (94% need-based, 6% non-need-based). 79% of past graduating class borrowed through all loan programs. *Average indebtedness per student:* $20,173. *Average need-based loan:* Freshmen: $3306; Undergraduates: $3890. *Parent loans:* $1,493,911 (87% need-based, 13% non-need-based). *Programs:* FFEL (Subsidized and Unsubsidized Stafford, PLUS), Perkins, college/university, alternative loans.
WORK-STUDY *Federal work-study:* Total amount: $389,000; 788 jobs averaging $1500. *State or other work-study/employment:* Total amount: $650,000 (100% non-need-based). 43 part-time jobs averaging $1500.
ATHLETIC AWARDS *Total amount:* $503,578 (75% need-based, 25% non-need-based).

APPLYING FOR FINANCIAL AID *Required financial aid forms:* FAFSA, state aid form. *Financial aid deadline (priority):* 3/1. *Notification date:* Continuous beginning 3/15. Students must reply within 4 weeks of notification.

CONTACT Mr. Troy Martin, Director of Financial Aid, Houghton College, One Willard Avenue, Houghton, NY 14744, 716-567-9328 or toll-free 800-777-2556. *Fax:* 716-567-9610. *E-mail:* troy.martin@houghton.edu.

HOUSTON BAPTIST UNIVERSITY
Houston, TX

Tuition & fees: $12,915	Average undergraduate aid package: $10,691

ABOUT THE INSTITUTION Independent Baptist, coed. Awards: associate, bachelor's, and master's degrees and post-bachelor's certificates. 65 undergraduate majors. Total enrollment: 2,227. Undergraduates: 1,818. Freshmen: 272. Federal methodology is used as a basis for awarding need-based institutional aid.

UNDERGRADUATE EXPENSES for 2004–05 *Application fee:* $25. *Comprehensive fee:* $17,481 includes full-time tuition ($11,850), mandatory fees ($1065), and room and board ($4566). Full-time tuition and fees vary according to course load and student level. Room and board charges vary according to board plan and housing facility. *Part-time tuition:* $395 per semester hour. Part-time tuition and fees vary according to course load and student level. *Payment plans:* Tuition prepayment, installment.

FRESHMAN FINANCIAL AID (Fall 2004, est.) 134 applied for aid; of those 80% were deemed to have need. 100% of freshmen with need received aid; of those 18% had need fully met. *Average percent of need met:* 63% (excluding resources awarded to replace EFC). *Average financial aid package:* $9687 (excluding resources awarded to replace EFC). 20% of all full-time freshmen had no need and received non-need-based gift aid.

UNDERGRADUATE FINANCIAL AID (Fall 2004, est.) 728 applied for aid; of those 88% were deemed to have need. 100% of undergraduates with need received aid; of those 13% had need fully met. *Average percent of need met:* 62% (excluding resources awarded to replace EFC). *Average financial aid package:* $10,691 (excluding resources awarded to replace EFC). 12% of all full-time undergraduates had no need and received non-need-based gift aid.

GIFT AID (NEED-BASED) *Total amount:* $6,949,105 (32% federal, 36% state, 23% institutional, 9% external sources). *Receiving aid:* Freshmen: 78% (105); All full-time undergraduates: 84% (612). *Average award:* Freshmen: $6944; Undergraduates: $7291. *Scholarships, grants, and awards:* Federal Pell, FSEOG, state, private, college/university gift aid from institutional funds.

GIFT AID (NON-NEED-BASED) *Total amount:* $574,940 (1% federal, 1% state, 77% institutional, 21% external sources). *Receiving aid:* Freshmen: 9% (12); Undergraduates: 6% (43). *Average Award:* Freshmen: $15,239; Undergraduates: $15,395. *Scholarships, grants, and awards by category:* Academic Interests/Achievement: 603 awards ($1,693,000 total): general academic interests/achievements, health fields, religion/biblical studies. *Creative Arts/Performance:* 121 awards ($243,000 total): art/fine arts, music. *Special Achievements/Activities:* 11 awards ($13,100 total): cheerleading/drum major, general special achievements/activities. *Special Characteristics:* 64 awards ($318,000 total): children of faculty/staff, general special characteristics, relatives of clergy. *Tuition waivers:* Full or partial for employees or children of employees, senior citizens. *ROTC:* Army cooperative.

LOANS *Student loans:* $7,930,216 (84% need-based, 16% non-need-based). 82% of past graduating class borrowed through all loan programs. *Average indebtedness per student:* $17,212. *Average need-based loan:* Freshmen: $2531; Undergraduates: $3461. *Parent loans:* $2,748,870 (31% need-based, 69% non-need-based). *Programs:* FFEL (Subsidized and Unsubsidized Stafford, PLUS), state, alternative loans.

WORK-STUDY *Federal work-study:* Total amount: $1,003,996; jobs available. *State or other work-study/employment:* Part-time jobs available.

ATHLETIC AWARDS *Total amount:* $588,128 (90% need-based, 10% non-need-based).

APPLYING FOR FINANCIAL AID *Required financial aid form:* FAFSA. *Financial aid deadline:* 4/15 (priority: 3/1). *Notification date:* Continuous.

CONTACT Sherry Byrd, Director of Student Aid Programs, Houston Baptist University, 109 Administration Building, 7502 Fondren Road, Houston, TX 77074-3298, 281-649-3471 or toll-free 800-696-3210. *Fax:* 281-649-3298.

HOWARD PAYNE UNIVERSITY
Brownwood, TX

Tuition & fees: $12,000	Average undergraduate aid package: $10,571

ABOUT THE INSTITUTION Independent religious, coed. Awards: associate and bachelor's degrees. 77 undergraduate majors. Total enrollment: 1,319. Undergraduates: 1,319. Freshmen: 302. Federal methodology is used as a basis for awarding need-based institutional aid.

UNDERGRADUATE EXPENSES for 2004–05 *Application fee:* $25. *Comprehensive fee:* $16,242 includes full-time tuition ($11,000), mandatory fees ($1000), and room and board ($4242). *College room only:* $1800. Room and board charges vary according to board plan, gender, and housing facility. *Part-time tuition:* $300 per credit hour. Part-time tuition and fees vary according to course load. *Payment plans:* Installment, deferred payment.

FRESHMAN FINANCIAL AID (Fall 2004, est.) 263 applied for aid; of those 87% were deemed to have need. 100% of freshmen with need received aid; of those 22% had need fully met. *Average percent of need met:* 74% (excluding resources awarded to replace EFC). *Average financial aid package:* $9494 (excluding resources awarded to replace EFC). 13% of all full-time freshmen had no need and received non-need-based gift aid.

UNDERGRADUATE FINANCIAL AID (Fall 2004, est.) 901 applied for aid; of those 88% were deemed to have need. 100% of undergraduates with need received aid; of those 29% had need fully met. *Average percent of need met:* 79% (excluding resources awarded to replace EFC). *Average financial aid package:* $10,571 (excluding resources awarded to replace EFC). 15% of all full-time undergraduates had no need and received non-need-based gift aid.

GIFT AID (NEED-BASED) *Total amount:* $4,811,387 (33% federal, 33% state, 29% institutional, 5% external sources). *Receiving aid:* Freshmen: 79% (224); All full-time undergraduates: 76% (770). *Average award:* Freshmen: $6981; Undergraduates: $6888. *Scholarships, grants, and awards:* Federal Pell, FSEOG, state, private, college/university gift aid from institutional funds.

GIFT AID (NON-NEED-BASED) *Total amount:* $1,681,173 (86% institutional, 14% external sources). *Receiving aid:* Freshmen: 8% (24); Undergraduates: 8% (81). *Average Award:* Freshmen: $4161; Undergraduates: $5155. *Scholarships, grants, and awards by category:* Academic Interests/Achievement: 400 awards ($1,217,159 total): biological sciences, business, communication, education, English, general academic interests/achievements, mathematics, physical sciences, premedicine, religion/biblical studies, social sciences. *Creative Arts/Performance:* 60 awards ($150,000 total): art/fine arts, music, theater/drama. *Special Achievements/Activities:* community service, leadership, religious involvement. *Special Characteristics:* children and siblings of alumni, children of faculty/staff, local/state students, relatives of clergy, religious affiliation. *Tuition waivers:* Full or partial for employees or children of employees, senior citizens. *LOANS Student loans:* $4,667,033 (65% need-based, 35% non-need-based). 69% of past graduating class borrowed through all loan programs. *Average indebtedness per student:* $18,960. *Average need-based loan:* Freshmen: $2263; Undergraduates: $3486. *Parent loans:* $1,087,852 (20% need-based, 80% non-need-based). *Programs:* FFEL (Subsidized and Unsubsidized Stafford, PLUS), Perkins, state.

WORK-STUDY *Federal work-study:* Total amount: $80,474; 118 jobs averaging $2000. *State or other work-study/employment:* Total amount: $15,000 (100% need-based). 9 part-time jobs averaging $2000.

APPLYING FOR FINANCIAL AID *Required financial aid forms:* FAFSA, institution's own form. *Financial aid deadline (priority):* 3/15. *Notification date:* Continuous beginning 3/1. Students must reply within 2 weeks of notification.

CONTACT Glenda Huff, Director of Financial Aid, Howard Payne University, 1000 Fisk Avenue, Brownwood, TX 76801, 325-649-8014 or toll-free 800-880-4478. *Fax:* 325-649-8901. *E-mail:* ghuff@hputx.edu.

HOWARD UNIVERSITY
Washington, DC

Tuition & fees: $11,645	Average undergraduate aid package: $15,717

ABOUT THE INSTITUTION Independent, coed. Awards: bachelor's, master's, doctoral, and first professional degrees and post-master's and first professional certificates. 64 undergraduate majors. Total enrollment: 10,623. Undergraduates: 7,112. Freshmen: 1,451. Federal methodology is used as a basis for awarding need-based institutional aid.

UNDERGRADUATE EXPENSES for 2004–05 *Application fee:* $45. *Comprehensive fee:* $17,515 includes full-time tuition ($10,840), mandatory fees ($805), and room and board ($5870). *College room only:* $3558. Room and board charges vary according to board plan and housing facility. *Part-time tuition:* $452 per credit hour. *Part-time fees:* $805 per year. *Payment plan:* Deferred payment.

FRESHMAN FINANCIAL AID (Fall 2003) 1214 applied for aid; of those 83% were deemed to have need. 96% of freshmen with need received aid; of those 67% had need fully met. *Average financial aid package:* $16,042 (excluding resources awarded to replace EFC). 11% of all full-time freshmen had no need and received non-need-based gift aid.

UNDERGRADUATE FINANCIAL AID (Fall 2003) 4,938 applied for aid; of those 86% were deemed to have need. 98% of undergraduates with need received aid; of those 60% had need fully met. *Average financial aid package:* $15,717 (excluding resources awarded to replace EFC). 11% of all full-time undergraduates had no need and received non-need-based gift aid.

GIFT AID (NEED-BASED) *Total amount:* $43,081,070 (19% federal, 69% institutional, 12% external sources). *Receiving aid:* Freshmen: 37% (541); All full-time undergraduates: 29% (2,379). *Average award:* Freshmen: $4340; Undergraduates: $4301. *Scholarships, grants, and awards:* Federal Pell, FSEOG, state, private, college/university gift aid from institutional funds, Federal Nursing.

GIFT AID (NON-NEED-BASED) *Receiving aid:* Freshmen: 63% (905); Undergraduates: 49% (4,003). *Average Award:* Freshmen: $12,989; Undergraduates: $10,147. *Scholarships, grants, and awards by category:* Creative Arts/Performance: art/fine arts, dance, music. *Tuition waivers:* Full or partial for employees or children of employees. *ROTC:* Army, Air Force.

LOANS *Student loans:* $74,986,625 (100% need-based). 90% of past graduating class borrowed through all loan programs. *Average indebtedness per student:* $11,288. *Average need-based loan:* Freshmen: $17,502; Undergraduates: $17,438. *Parent loans:* $23,314,589 (100% need-based). *Programs:* Federal Direct (Subsidized and Unsubsidized Stafford, PLUS), FFEL (Subsidized and Unsubsidized Stafford, PLUS), Perkins, Federal Nursing, district, college/university.

WORK-STUDY *Federal work-study:* Total amount: $1,591,361; 431 jobs averaging $3667. *State or other work-study/employment:* Total amount: $863,339 (100% need-based). 229 part-time jobs averaging $3590.

ATHLETIC AWARDS *Total amount:* $4,501,746 (100% need-based).

APPLYING FOR FINANCIAL AID *Required financial aid form:* FAFSA. *Financial aid deadline (priority):* 2/15. *Notification date:* Continuous beginning 4/1. Students must reply by 6/1 or within 2 weeks of notification.

CONTACT Mr. Steven G. Johnson, Director of Financial Aid and Scholarships, Howard University, 2400 Sixth Street, NW, Washington, DC 20059-0002, 202-806-2762 or toll-free 800-HOWARD-U.

HSI LAI UNIVERSITY
Rosemead, CA

See University of the West.

HUMBOLDT STATE UNIVERSITY
Arcata, CA

Tuition & fees (CA res): $2866	Average undergraduate aid package: $8050

ABOUT THE INSTITUTION State-supported, coed. Awards: bachelor's and master's degrees. 78 undergraduate majors. Total enrollment: 7,550. Undergraduates: 6,529. Freshmen: 760. Federal methodology is used as a basis for awarding need-based institutional aid.

UNDERGRADUATE EXPENSES for 2004–05 *Application fee:* $55. *Tuition, state resident:* full-time $0. *Tuition, nonresident:* full-time $11,002; part-time $339 per unit. *Required fees:* full-time $2866; $944 per term part-time. *College room and board:* $7281. Room and board charges vary according to board plan and housing facility. *Payment plan:* Installment.

FRESHMAN FINANCIAL AID (Fall 2003) 647 applied for aid; of those 68% were deemed to have need. 94% of freshmen with need received aid; of those 30% had need fully met. *Average percent of need met:* 85% (excluding resources awarded to replace EFC). *Average financial aid package:* $8550 (excluding resources awarded to replace EFC).

UNDERGRADUATE FINANCIAL AID (Fall 2003) *Average financial aid package:* $8050 (excluding resources awarded to replace EFC).

GIFT AID (NEED-BASED) *Total amount:* $18,544,610 (58% federal, 37% state, 2% institutional, 3% external sources). *Receiving aid:* Freshmen: 43% (361). *Average award:* Freshmen: $5100. *Scholarships, grants, and awards:* Federal Pell, FSEOG, state, private, college/university gift aid from institutional funds.

GIFT AID (NON-NEED-BASED) *Scholarships, grants, and awards by category:* Academic Interests/Achievement: general academic interests/achievements. *Tuition waivers:* Full or partial for employees or children of employees, senior citizens.

LOANS *Student loans:* $16,493,730 (100% need-based). *Average need-based loan:* Freshmen: $3200. *Parent loans:* $2,411,515 (100% need-based). *Programs:* Federal Direct (Subsidized and Unsubsidized Stafford, PLUS), Perkins.

WORK-STUDY *Federal work-study:* Total amount: $581,921; 350 jobs averaging $2000.

ATHLETIC AWARDS *Total amount:* $310,000 (100% need-based).

APPLYING FOR FINANCIAL AID *Required financial aid form:* FAFSA. *Financial aid deadline (priority):* 3/2. *Notification date:* Continuous beginning 4/1. Students must reply within 6 weeks of notification.

CONTACT Don Scheaffer, Director of Financial Aid, Humboldt State University, 1 Harpst Street, Arcata, CA 95521-8299, 707-826-4321. *E-mail:* des7001@humboldt.edu.

HUMPHREYS COLLEGE
Stockton, CA

Tuition & fees: $7560	Average undergraduate aid package: $9850

ABOUT THE INSTITUTION Independent, coed. Awards: associate, bachelor's, and first professional degrees. 13 undergraduate majors. Total enrollment: 721. Undergraduates: 597. Federal methodology is used as a basis for awarding need-based institutional aid.

UNDERGRADUATE EXPENSES for 2004–05 *Application fee:* $20. *Tuition:* full-time $7560; part-time $210 per quarter hour.

GIFT AID (NEED-BASED) *Total amount:* $22,290 (18% federal, 41% state, 41% institutional). *Receiving aid:* Freshmen: 3% (4); All full-time undergraduates: 2% (8). *Average award:* Freshmen: $4; Undergraduates: $8. *Scholarships, grants, and awards:* Federal Pell, FSEOG, state.

GIFT AID (NON-NEED-BASED) *Average Award:* Freshmen: $9600; Undergraduates: $9600. *Scholarships, grants, and awards by category:* Academic Interests/Achievement: business, computer science, general academic interests/achievements. *Special Achievements/Activities:* community service. *Special Characteristics:* ethnic background, members of minority groups.

LOANS *Student loans:* $21,000 (50% need-based, 50% non-need-based). 95% of past graduating class borrowed through all loan programs. *Average indebtedness per student:* $30,000. *Parent loans:* $18,000 (50% need-based, 50% non-need-based). *Programs:* FFEL (Subsidized and Unsubsidized Stafford, PLUS).

APPLYING FOR FINANCIAL AID *Required financial aid form:* FAFSA. *Financial aid deadline:* Continuous. *Notification date:* Continuous. Students must reply by 6/30.

CONTACT Judi LaFeber, Director of Financial Aid, Humphreys College, 6650 Inglewood Avenue, Stockton, CA 95207-3896, 209-478-0800. *Fax:* 209-478-8721.

HUNTER COLLEGE OF THE CITY UNIVERSITY OF NEW YORK
New York, NY

CONTACT Kevin McGowan, Director of Financial Aid, Hunter College of the City University of New York, 695 Park Avenue, New York, NY 10021-5085, 212-772-4820.

HUNTINGDON COLLEGE
Montgomery, AL

ABOUT THE INSTITUTION Independent United Methodist, coed. Awards: associate and bachelor's degrees. 50 undergraduate majors. Total enrollment: 731. Undergraduates: 731. Freshmen: 196.

GIFT AID (NEED-BASED) *Scholarships, grants, and awards:* Federal Pell, FSEOG, state, private, college/university gift aid from institutional funds.

GIFT AID (NON-NEED-BASED) *Scholarships, grants, and awards by category:* Academic Interests/Achievement: biological sciences, business, communication, computer science, education, English, general academic interests/achievements, premedicine. *Creative Arts/Performance:* applied art and design, art/fine arts, dance, music, performing arts, theater/drama. *Special Achievements/*

Activities: community service, junior miss, leadership. *Special Characteristics:* children and siblings of alumni, children of faculty/staff, international students, relatives of clergy, religious affiliation.

LOANS *Programs:* FFEL (Subsidized and Unsubsidized Stafford, PLUS), Perkins.

APPLYING FOR FINANCIAL AID *Required financial aid forms:* FAFSA, state aid form.

CONTACT Belinda Goris, Student Financial Aid Director, Huntingdon College, 1500 East Fairview Avenue, Montgomery, AL 36106-2148, 334-833-4519 or toll-free 800-763-0313. *E-mail:* bgoris@huntingdon.edu.

HUNTINGTON UNIVERSITY
Huntington, IN

Tuition & fees: $18,490	Average undergraduate aid package: $12,978

ABOUT THE INSTITUTION Independent religious, coed. Awards: associate, bachelor's, and master's degrees. 46 undergraduate majors. Total enrollment: 975. Undergraduates: 915. Freshmen: 204. Federal methodology is used as a basis for awarding need-based institutional aid.

UNDERGRADUATE EXPENSES for 2005–06 *Application fee:* $20. *Comprehensive fee:* $24,830 includes full-time tuition ($18,060), mandatory fees ($430), and room and board ($6340). Room and board charges vary according to board plan. *Part-time tuition:* $520 per semester hour. Part-time tuition and fees vary according to course load. *Payment plans:* Guaranteed tuition, installment.

FRESHMAN FINANCIAL AID (Fall 2004, est.) 186 applied for aid; of those 92% were deemed to have need. 100% of freshmen with need received aid; of those 21% had need fully met. *Average percent of need met:* 81% (excluding resources awarded to replace EFC). *Average financial aid package:* $14,817 (excluding resources awarded to replace EFC). 12% of all full-time freshmen had no need and received non-need-based gift aid.

UNDERGRADUATE FINANCIAL AID (Fall 2004, est.) 659 applied for aid; of those 91% were deemed to have need. 100% of undergraduates with need received aid; of those 14% had need fully met. *Average percent of need met:* 73% (excluding resources awarded to replace EFC). *Average financial aid package:* $12,978 (excluding resources awarded to replace EFC). 14% of all full-time undergraduates had no need and received non-need-based gift aid.

GIFT AID (NEED-BASED) *Total amount:* $5,058,591 (13% federal, 24% state, 55% institutional, 8% external sources). *Receiving aid:* Freshmen: 80% (162); All full-time undergraduates: 69% (547). *Average award:* Freshmen: $12,481; Undergraduates: $9791. *Scholarships, grants, and awards:* Federal Pell, FSEOG, state, private, college/university gift aid from institutional funds.

GIFT AID (NON-NEED-BASED) *Total amount:* $586,841 (74% institutional, 26% external sources). *Receiving aid:* Freshmen: 20% (41); Undergraduates: 14% (108). *Average Award:* Freshmen: $8706; Undergraduates: $6561. *Scholarships, grants, and awards by category: Academic Interests/Achievement:* 401 awards ($1,154,359 total): general academic interests/achievements. *Creative Arts/Performance:* 74 awards ($89,200 total): art/fine arts, journalism/publications, music, theater/drama. *Special Achievements/Activities:* 9 awards ($4225 total): cheerleading/drum major. *Special Characteristics:* 592 awards ($1,308,878 total): children and siblings of alumni, children of current students, children of faculty/staff, international students, parents of current students, relatives of clergy, religious affiliation, siblings of current students, spouses of current students. *Tuition waivers:* Full or partial for minority students, children of alumni, employees or children of employees, adult students, senior citizens.

LOANS *Student loans:* $3,988,841 (75% need-based, 25% non-need-based). 68% of past graduating class borrowed through all loan programs. *Average indebtedness per student:* $16,489. *Average need-based loan:* Freshmen: $3681; Undergraduates: $4543. *Parent loans:* $987,408 (39% need-based, 61% non-need-based). *Programs:* FFEL (Subsidized and Unsubsidized Stafford, PLUS), Perkins.

WORK-STUDY *Federal work-study:* Total amount: $313,050; 166 jobs averaging $1812.

ATHLETIC AWARDS *Total amount:* $594,389 (59% need-based, 41% non-need-based).

APPLYING FOR FINANCIAL AID *Required financial aid form:* FAFSA. *Financial aid deadline (priority):* 3/1. *Notification date:* Continuous beginning 3/1. Students must reply by 5/1 or within 2 weeks of notification.

CONTACT Mrs. Cindy Kreps, Financial Aid Secretary, Huntington University, 2303 College Avenue, Huntington, IN 46750-1299, 260-359-4015 or toll-free 800-642-6493. *Fax:* 260-358-3699. *E-mail:* ckreps@huntington.edu.

HUSSIAN SCHOOL OF ART
Philadelphia, PA

ABOUT THE INSTITUTION Proprietary, coed. Awards: associate degrees. 2 undergraduate majors. Total enrollment: 157. Undergraduates: 157. Freshmen: 57.

GIFT AID (NEED-BASED) *Scholarships, grants, and awards:* Federal Pell, FSEOG, state, private.

LOANS *Programs:* FFEL (Subsidized and Unsubsidized Stafford, PLUS).

APPLYING FOR FINANCIAL AID *Required financial aid forms:* FAFSA, institution's own form.

CONTACT Ms. Susan Cohen, Financial Aid and Placement Director, Hussian School of Art, 1118 Market Street, Philadelphia, PA 19107-3679, 215-981-0900.

HUSSON COLLEGE
Bangor, ME

Tuition & fees: $11,050	Average undergraduate aid package: $7630

ABOUT THE INSTITUTION Independent, coed. Awards: associate, bachelor's, and master's degrees and post-bachelor's and post-master's certificates. 28 undergraduate majors. Total enrollment: 2,039. Undergraduates: 1,778. Freshmen: 265. Federal methodology is used as a basis for awarding need-based institutional aid.

UNDERGRADUATE EXPENSES for 2004–05 *Application fee:* $25. *Comprehensive fee:* $16,900 includes full-time tuition ($10,800), mandatory fees ($250), and room and board ($5850). Full-time tuition and fees vary according to class time. *Part-time tuition:* $360 per credit hour. Part-time tuition and fees vary according to class time and course load. *Payment plans:* Tuition prepayment, installment.

FRESHMAN FINANCIAL AID (Fall 2004, est.) 818 applied for aid; of those 71% were deemed to have need. 93% of freshmen with need received aid; of those 31% had need fully met. *Average percent of need met:* 76% (excluding resources awarded to replace EFC). *Average financial aid package:* $7317 (excluding resources awarded to replace EFC). 21% of all full-time freshmen had no need and received non-need-based gift aid.

UNDERGRADUATE FINANCIAL AID (Fall 2004, est.) 1,892 applied for aid; of those 76% were deemed to have need. 93% of undergraduates with need received aid; of those 19% had need fully met. *Average percent of need met:* 71% (excluding resources awarded to replace EFC). *Average financial aid package:* $7630 (excluding resources awarded to replace EFC). 14% of all full-time undergraduates had no need and received non-need-based gift aid.

GIFT AID (NEED-BASED) *Total amount:* $7,057,899 (45% federal, 8% state, 40% institutional, 7% external sources). *Receiving aid:* Freshmen: 56% (522); All full-time undergraduates: 61% (1,222). *Average award:* Freshmen: $5787; Undergraduates: $5309. *Scholarships, grants, and awards:* Federal Pell, FSEOG, state, private, college/university gift aid from institutional funds.

GIFT AID (NON-NEED-BASED) *Total amount:* $762,295 (21% federal, 65% institutional, 14% external sources). *Receiving aid:* Freshmen: 15% (138); Undergraduates: 8% (168). *Average Award:* Freshmen: $4438; Undergraduates: $5339. *Scholarships, grants, and awards by category: Academic Interests/Achievement:* 152 awards ($15,897 total): business, computer science, education, general academic interests/achievements, health fields. *Special Achievements/Activities:* general special achievements/activities, leadership. *Special Characteristics:* children of union members/company employees. *Tuition waivers:* Full or partial for employees or children of employees, senior citizens. *ROTC:* Army cooperative, Naval cooperative.

LOANS *Student loans:* $8,665,213 (67% need-based, 33% non-need-based). 96% of past graduating class borrowed through all loan programs. *Average indebtedness per student:* $17,125. *Average need-based loan:* Freshmen: $2298; Undergraduates: $3302. *Parent loans:* $1,234,961 (42% need-based, 58% non-need-based). *Programs:* FFEL (Subsidized and Unsubsidized Stafford, PLUS), Perkins, alternative loans.

WORK-STUDY *Federal work-study:* Total amount: $543,413; 450 jobs averaging $1300.

APPLYING FOR FINANCIAL AID *Required financial aid forms:* FAFSA, state aid form. *Financial aid deadline (priority):* 4/15. *Notification date:* Continuous beginning 2/15. Students must reply by 5/1 or within 2 weeks of notification.

CONTACT Linda B. Conant, Director of Financial Aid, Husson College, One College Circle, Bangor, ME 04401, 207-941-7156 or toll-free 800-4-HUSSON. *Fax:* 207-973-1038. *E-mail:* conantl@husson.edu.

HUSTON-TILLOTSON COLLEGE
Austin, TX

CONTACT Anthony P. Barrientez, Director of Financial Aid, Huston-Tillotson College, 900 Chicon Street, Austin, TX 78702, 512-505-3031.

IDAHO STATE UNIVERSITY
Pocatello, ID

Tuition & fees (area res): $3700	Average undergraduate aid package: $8755

ABOUT THE INSTITUTION State-supported, coed. Awards: bachelor's, master's, doctoral, and first professional degrees and post-bachelor's, post-master's, and first professional certificates. 100 undergraduate majors. Total enrollment: 13,802. Undergraduates: 11,663. Freshmen: 1,764. Federal methodology is used as a basis for awarding need-based institutional aid.

UNDERGRADUATE EXPENSES for 2004–05 *Application fee:* $35. *One-time required fee:* $660. *Tuition, area resident:* full-time $0. *Tuition, state resident:* full-time $0; part-time $185 per credit hour. *Tuition, nonresident:* full-time $7080; part-time $287 per credit hour. Full-time tuition and fees vary according to reciprocity agreements. Part-time tuition and fees vary according to reciprocity agreements. *College room and board:* $4850; *room only:* $2060. Room and board charges vary according to board plan and housing facility. *Payment plan:* Deferred payment.

FRESHMAN FINANCIAL AID (Fall 2004, est.) 910 applied for aid; of those 77% were deemed to have need. 99% of freshmen with need received aid; of those 12% had need fully met. *Average percent of need met:* 59% (excluding resources awarded to replace EFC). *Average financial aid package:* $4653 (excluding resources awarded to replace EFC). 31% of all full-time freshmen had no need and received non-need-based gift aid.

UNDERGRADUATE FINANCIAL AID (Fall 2004, est.) 5,905 applied for aid; of those 90% were deemed to have need. 98% of undergraduates with need received aid; of those 30% had need fully met. *Average percent of need met:* 68% (excluding resources awarded to replace EFC). *Average financial aid package:* $8755 (excluding resources awarded to replace EFC). 16% of all full-time undergraduates had no need and received non-need-based gift aid.

GIFT AID (NEED-BASED) *Total amount:* $17,479,879 (99% federal, 1% state). *Receiving aid:* Freshmen: 41% (465); All full-time undergraduates: 55% (4,114). *Average award:* Freshmen: $2774; Undergraduates: $4391. *Scholarships, grants, and awards:* Federal Pell, FSEOG, state, private.

GIFT AID (NON-NEED-BASED) *Total amount:* $8,069,671 (3% federal, 2% state, 53% institutional, 42% external sources). *Receiving aid:* Freshmen: 44% (489); Undergraduates: 32% (2,393). *Average Award:* Freshmen: $5405; Undergraduates: $7893. *Scholarships, grants, and awards by category:* Academic Interests/Achievement: 2,687 awards ($2,884,386 total): biological sciences, business, communication, computer science, education, engineering/technologies, English, foreign languages, general academic interests/achievements, health fields, home economics, humanities, international studies, mathematics, military science, physical sciences, premedicine, religion/biblical studies, social sciences. Creative Arts/Performance: 288 awards ($165,765 total): art/fine arts, debating, music, performing arts, theater/drama. Special Achievements/Activities: 120 awards ($66,410 total): general special achievements/activities, junior miss, leadership, memberships, rodeo. Special Characteristics: 1,682 awards ($916,735 total): children and siblings of alumni, children of faculty/staff, first-generation college students, handicapped students, local/state students, members of minority groups, out-of-state students. *Tuition waivers:* Full or partial for employees or children of employees, senior citizens. *ROTC:* Army cooperative.

LOANS *Student loans:* $39,040,962 (57% need-based, 43% non-need-based). 69% of past graduating class borrowed through all loan programs. *Average indebtedness per student:* $29,467. *Average need-based loan:* Freshmen: $2283; Undergraduates: $5347. *Parent loans:* $448,209 (100% non-need-based). *Programs:* Federal Direct (Subsidized and Unsubsidized Stafford, PLUS), Perkins.

WORK-STUDY *Federal work-study:* Total amount: $950,554; 920 jobs averaging $1033. *State or other work-study/employment:* Total amount: $425,964 (100% need-based). 675 part-time jobs averaging $631.

ATHLETIC AWARDS *Total amount:* $2,211,331 (1% need-based, 99% non-need-based).

APPLYING FOR FINANCIAL AID *Required financial aid form:* FAFSA. *Financial aid deadline:* Continuous. *Notification date:* Continuous beginning 5/1.

CONTACT Mr. Doug Severs, Director of Financial Aid, Idaho State University, Campus Box 8077, Pocatello, ID 83209, 208-282-2981. *Fax:* 208-282-4755. *E-mail:* sevedoug@isu.edu.

ILLINOIS COLLEGE
Jacksonville, IL

Tuition & fees: $14,600	Average undergraduate aid package: $13,637

ABOUT THE INSTITUTION Independent interdenominational, coed. Awards: bachelor's degrees. 44 undergraduate majors. Total enrollment: 1,037. Undergraduates: 1,037. Freshmen: 258. Federal methodology is used as a basis for awarding need-based institutional aid.

UNDERGRADUATE EXPENSES for 2004–05 *Application fee:* $25. *Comprehensive fee:* $20,800 includes full-time tuition ($14,600) and room and board ($6200). *Part-time tuition:* $610 per credit hour. *Payment plans:* Installment, deferred payment.

FRESHMAN FINANCIAL AID (Fall 2004, est.) 241 applied for aid; of those 87% were deemed to have need. 100% of freshmen with need received aid; of those 28% had need fully met. *Average percent of need met:* 67% (excluding resources awarded to replace EFC). *Average financial aid package:* $14,224 (excluding resources awarded to replace EFC). 15% of all full-time freshmen had no need and received non-need-based gift aid.

UNDERGRADUATE FINANCIAL AID (Fall 2004, est.) 922 applied for aid; of those 85% were deemed to have need. 100% of undergraduates with need received aid; of those 28% had need fully met. *Average percent of need met:* 68% (excluding resources awarded to replace EFC). *Average financial aid package:* $13,637 (excluding resources awarded to replace EFC). 16% of all full-time undergraduates had no need and received non-need-based gift aid.

GIFT AID (NEED-BASED) *Total amount:* $4,634,247 (19% federal, 44% state, 34% institutional, 3% external sources). *Receiving aid:* Freshmen: 72% (182); All full-time undergraduates: 69% (692). *Average award:* Freshmen: $6730; Undergraduates: $6214. *Scholarships, grants, and awards:* Federal Pell, FSEOG, state, private, college/university gift aid from institutional funds.

GIFT AID (NON-NEED-BASED) *Total amount:* $3,796,674 (96% institutional, 4% external sources). *Receiving aid:* Freshmen: 72% (183); Undergraduates: 62% (620). *Average Award:* Freshmen: $6197; Undergraduates: $5432. *Scholarships, grants, and awards by category:* Academic Interests/Achievement: 629 awards ($3,219,055 total): general academic interests/achievements. Creative Arts/Performance: 53 awards ($33,000 total): art/fine arts, music. Special Characteristics: 110 awards ($294,105 total): members of minority groups, previous college experience, religious affiliation. *Tuition waivers:* Full or partial for employees or children of employees.

LOANS *Student loans:* $4,417,355 (66% need-based, 34% non-need-based). 80% of past graduating class borrowed through all loan programs. *Average indebtedness per student:* $12,038. *Average need-based loan:* Freshmen: $3721; Undergraduates: $4260. *Parent loans:* $1,182,901 (100% non-need-based). *Programs:* FFEL (Subsidized and Unsubsidized Stafford, PLUS), Perkins.

WORK-STUDY *Federal work-study:* Total amount: $876,091; 563 jobs averaging $1484. *State or other work-study/employment:* Total amount: $483,099 (100% non-need-based). 386 part-time jobs averaging $1252.

APPLYING FOR FINANCIAL AID *Required financial aid form:* FAFSA. *Financial aid deadline (priority):* 3/1. *Notification date:* Continuous. Students must reply within 2 weeks of notification.

CONTACT Kate Taylor, Director of Financial Aid, Illinois College, 1101 West College Avenue, Jacksonville, IL 62650-2299, 217-245-3035 or toll-free 866-464-5265. *Fax:* 217-245-3274. *E-mail:* finaid@hilltop.ic.edu.

THE ILLINOIS INSTITUTE OF ART
Chicago, IL

CONTACT Director of Student Financial Services, The Illinois Institute of Art, 350 North Orleans Street, Suite 136, Chicago, IL 60654-1593, 800-351-3450.

THE ILLINOIS INSTITUTE OF ART-SCHAUMBURG
Schaumburg, IL

ABOUT THE INSTITUTION Proprietary, coed. Awards: associate and bachelor's degrees. 6 undergraduate majors. Total enrollment: 1,187. Undergraduates: 1,187. Freshmen: 244.

GIFT AID (NEED-BASED) *Scholarships, grants, and awards:* Federal Pell, FSEOG, private, college/university gift aid from institutional funds.

GIFT AID (NON-NEED-BASED) *Scholarships, grants, and awards by category: Special Characteristics:* children of faculty/staff, siblings of current students.

LOANS *Programs:* FFEL (Subsidized and Unsubsidized Stafford, PLUS), Perkins, alternative loans.

APPLYING FOR FINANCIAL AID *Required financial aid form:* FAFSA.

CONTACT Financial Aid Office, The Illinois Institute of Art-Schaumburg, 1000 North Plaza Drive, Schaumburg, IL 60173, 800-314-3450.

ILLINOIS INSTITUTE OF TECHNOLOGY
Chicago, IL

ABOUT THE INSTITUTION Independent, coed. Awards: bachelor's, master's, doctoral, and first professional degrees and post-bachelor's certificates. 31 undergraduate majors. Total enrollment: 6,378. Undergraduates: 2,089. Freshmen: 464.

GIFT AID (NEED-BASED) *Scholarships, grants, and awards:* Federal Pell, FSEOG, state, private, college/university gift aid from institutional funds.

GIFT AID (NON-NEED-BASED) *Scholarships, grants, and awards by category: Academic Interests/Achievement:* architecture, biological sciences, communication, computer science, engineering/technologies, general academic interests/achievements, humanities, mathematics, military science, physical sciences, premedicine, social sciences. *Special Achievements/Activities:* general special achievements/activities, leadership. *Special Characteristics:* children and siblings of alumni, children of faculty/staff, ethnic background, general special characteristics, international students, local/state students, members of minority groups, out-of-state students, previous college experience, siblings of current students, spouses of current students.

LOANS *Programs:* FFEL (Subsidized and Unsubsidized Stafford, PLUS), Perkins, college/university.

APPLYING FOR FINANCIAL AID *Required financial aid form:* FAFSA.

CONTACT Virginia Foster, Director of Student Finances, Illinois Institute of Technology, 3300 South Federal Street, Chicago, IL 60616, 312-567-5725 or toll-free 800-448-2329 (out-of-state). *Fax:* 312-567-3982. *E-mail:* foster@iit. edu.

ILLINOIS STATE UNIVERSITY
Normal, IL

Tuition & fees (IL res): $6328	Average undergraduate aid package: $8717

ABOUT THE INSTITUTION State-supported, coed. Awards: bachelor's, master's, and doctoral degrees and post-bachelor's and post-master's certificates. 62 undergraduate majors. Total enrollment: 20,757. Undergraduates: 17,878. Freshmen: 2,834. Federal methodology is used as a basis for awarding need-based institutional aid.

UNDERGRADUATE EXPENSES for 2004–05 *Application fee:* $30. *Tuition, state resident:* full-time $4800; part-time $160 per credit hour. *Tuition, nonresident:* full-time $10,020; part-time $334 per credit hour. *Required fees:* full-time $1528; $43.20 per credit hour or $648 per term part-time. Full-time tuition and fees vary according to course load. Part-time tuition and fees vary according to course load. *College room and board:* $5576; *room only:* $2762. Room and board charges vary according to board plan. *Payment plans:* Guaranteed tuition, installment.

FRESHMAN FINANCIAL AID (Fall 2004, est.) 2088 applied for aid; of those 61% were deemed to have need. 96% of freshmen with need received aid; of those 41% had need fully met. *Average percent of need met:* 77% (excluding resources awarded to replace EFC). *Average financial aid package:* $7684 (excluding resources awarded to replace EFC). 2% of all full-time freshmen had no need and received non-need-based gift aid.

UNDERGRADUATE FINANCIAL AID (Fall 2004, est.) 10,714 applied for aid; of those 72% were deemed to have need. 97% of undergraduates with need received aid; of those 44% had need fully met. *Average percent of need met:* 81% (excluding resources awarded to replace EFC). *Average financial aid package:* $8717 (excluding resources awarded to replace EFC). 2% of all full-time undergraduates had no need and received non-need-based gift aid.

GIFT AID (NEED-BASED) *Total amount:* $31,756,919 (36% federal, 54% state, 7% institutional, 3% external sources). *Receiving aid:* Freshmen: 29% (809); All full-time undergraduates: 29% (4,838). *Average award:* Freshmen: $6091; Undergraduates: $6372. *Scholarships, grants, and awards:* Federal Pell, FSEOG, state, private, college/university gift aid from institutional funds, Federal Nursing.

GIFT AID (NON-NEED-BASED) *Total amount:* $6,592,422 (14% federal, 45% state, 27% institutional, 14% external sources). *Receiving aid:* Freshmen: 14% (386); Undergraduates: 9% (1,538). *Average Award:* Freshmen: $3907; Undergraduates: $4295. *Scholarships, grants, and awards by category: Academic Interests/Achievement:* 585 awards ($1,532,493 total): agriculture, biological sciences, business, communication, computer science, education, engineering/technologies, English, foreign languages, general academic interests/achievements, health fields, home economics, humanities, international studies, library science, mathematics, military science, physical sciences, premedicine, social sciences. *Creative Arts/Performance:* 164 awards ($167,808 total): applied art and design, art/fine arts, cinema/film/broadcasting, creative writing, debating, general creative arts/performance, music, performing arts, theater/drama. *Special Achievements/Activities:* 1 award ($1000 total): community service, leadership. *Special Characteristics:* 422 awards ($1,424,962 total): children of faculty/staff, children of union members/company employees, children with a deceased or disabled parent, first-generation college students, general special characteristics, members of minority groups, previous college experience. *Tuition waivers:* Full or partial for minority students, employees or children of employees, senior citizens. *ROTC:* Army.

LOANS *Student loans:* $51,274,516 (62% need-based, 38% non-need-based). 58% of past graduating class borrowed through all loan programs. *Average indebtedness per student:* $14,620. *Average need-based loan:* Freshmen: $3928; Undergraduates: $4988. *Parent loans:* $11,322,013 (23% need-based, 77% non-need-based). *Programs:* Federal Direct (Subsidized and Unsubsidized Stafford, PLUS), Perkins, Federal Nursing, alternative loans.

WORK-STUDY *Federal work-study:* Total amount: $1,050,488; 556 jobs averaging $1889. *State or other work-study/employment:* Total amount: $89,504 (20% need-based, 80% non-need-based). 39 part-time jobs averaging $2295.

ATHLETIC AWARDS *Total amount:* $2,535,272 (22% need-based, 78% non-need-based).

APPLYING FOR FINANCIAL AID *Required financial aid form:* FAFSA. *Financial aid deadline (priority):* 3/1. *Notification date:* Continuous beginning 4/1.

CONTACT Mr. David Krueger, Assistant Director of Financial Aid, Illinois State University, Campus Box 2320, Normal, IL 61790-2320, 309-438-2231 or toll-free 800-366-2478 (in-state). *E-mail:* askfao@ilstu.edu.

ILLINOIS WESLEYAN UNIVERSITY
Bloomington, IL

Tuition & fees: $27,624	Average undergraduate aid package: $18,393

ABOUT THE INSTITUTION Independent, coed. Awards: bachelor's degrees. 53 undergraduate majors. Total enrollment: 2,118. Undergraduates: 2,118. Freshmen: 549. Both federal and institutional methodology are used as a basis for awarding need-based institutional aid.

UNDERGRADUATE EXPENSES for 2005–06 *Comprehensive fee:* $34,050 includes full-time tuition ($27,474), mandatory fees ($150), and room and board ($6426). *College room only:* $3892. Room and board charges vary according to board plan and housing facility. *Part-time tuition:* $3434 per course. *Payment plan:* Installment.

FRESHMAN FINANCIAL AID (Fall 2003) 430 applied for aid; of those 77% were deemed to have need. 100% of freshmen with need received aid; of those 49% had need fully met. *Average percent of need met:* 93% (excluding resources awarded to replace EFC). *Average financial aid package:* $18,812 (excluding resources awarded to replace EFC). 31% of all full-time freshmen had no need and received non-need-based gift aid.

UNDERGRADUATE FINANCIAL AID (Fall 2003) 1,445 applied for aid; of those 85% were deemed to have need. 100% of undergraduates with need received aid; of those 49% had need fully met. *Average percent of need met:* 93% (excluding resources awarded to replace EFC). *Average financial aid package:* $18,393 (excluding resources awarded to replace EFC). 32% of all full-time undergraduates had no need and received non-need-based gift aid.

GIFT AID (NEED-BASED) *Total amount:* $15,154,340 (5% federal, 13% state, 80% institutional, 2% external sources). *Receiving aid:* Freshmen: 60% (327); All full-time undergraduates: 58% (1,214). *Average award:* Freshmen: $13,680; Undergraduates: $12,843. *Scholarships, grants, and awards:* Federal Pell, FSEOG, state, private, college/university gift aid from institutional funds.

GIFT AID (NON-NEED-BASED) *Total amount:* $6,548,449 (1% federal, 1% state, 95% institutional, 3% external sources). *Receiving aid:* Freshmen: 7% (40); Undergraduates: 5% (99). *Average Award:* Freshmen: $8987; Undergraduates: $8390. *Scholarships, grants, and awards by category: Academic Interests/Achievement:* 600 awards ($4,701,100 total): general academic interests/achievements. *Creative Arts/Performance:* 250 awards ($1,676,930 total): art/

fine arts, music, theater/drama. *Special Achievements/Activities:* community service, general special achievements/activities, hobbies/interests, leadership. *Special Characteristics:* 39 awards ($586,325 total): children of faculty/staff, international students. *Tuition waivers:* Full or partial for employees or children of employees. *ROTC:* Army cooperative.

LOANS *Student loans:* $6,037,415 (76% need-based, 24% non-need-based). 69% of past graduating class borrowed through all loan programs. *Average indebtedness per student:* $22,603. *Average need-based loan:* Freshmen: $3822; Undergraduates: $4830. *Parent loans:* $2,556,954 (100% non-need-based). *Programs:* FFEL (Subsidized and Unsubsidized Stafford, PLUS), Perkins, Federal Nursing, college/university.

WORK-STUDY *Federal work-study:* Total amount: $436,458; 295 jobs averaging $1429. *State or other work-study/employment:* Total amount: $1,454,623 (76% need-based, 24% non-need-based). 577 part-time jobs averaging $2521.

APPLYING FOR FINANCIAL AID *Required financial aid forms:* FAFSA, institution's own form, business/farm supplement. *Financial aid deadline:* 3/1 (priority: 3/1). *Notification date:* Continuous beginning 2/1. Students must reply by 5/1.

CONTACT Mr. Lynn Nichelson, Director of Financial Aid, Illinois Wesleyan University, 1312 North Park Street, PO Box 2900, Bloomington, IL 61702-2900, 309-556-3096 or toll-free 800-332-2498. *Fax:* 309-556-3833. *E-mail:* lnichels@ titan.iwu.edu.

IMMACULATA UNIVERSITY
Immaculata, PA

CONTACT Mr. Peter Lysionek, Director of Student Financial Aid, Immaculata University, 1145 King Road, Box 500, Immaculata, PA 19345, 610-647-4400 Ext. 3026 or toll-free 877-428-6328. *Fax:* 610-640-0836. *E-mail:* plysionek@ immaculata.edu.

INDIANA INSTITUTE OF TECHNOLOGY
Fort Wayne, IN

CONTACT Financial Aid Office, Indiana Institute of Technology, 1600 East Washington Boulevard, Fort Wayne, IN 46803-1297, 800-937-2448 or toll-free 888-666-TECH (out-of-state). *Fax:* 219-422-1578.

INDIANA STATE UNIVERSITY
Terre Haute, IN

Tuition & fees (IN res): $5640	Average undergraduate aid package: $6557

ABOUT THE INSTITUTION State-supported, coed. Awards: associate, bachelor's, master's, and doctoral degrees and post-bachelor's and post-master's certificates. 84 undergraduate majors. Total enrollment: 11,200. Undergraduates: 9,321. Freshmen: 1,851. Federal methodology is used as a basis for awarding need-based institutional aid.

UNDERGRADUATE EXPENSES for 2004–05 *Application fee:* $25. *Tuition, state resident:* full-time $5536; part-time $200 per credit. *Tuition, nonresident:* full-time $12,264; part-time $433 per credit. *Required fees:* full-time $104; $52 per term part-time. Full-time tuition and fees vary according to course load and student level. Part-time tuition and fees vary according to student level. *College room and board:* $5615; *room only:* $2972. Room and board charges vary according to board plan, housing facility, and student level. *Payment plans:* Installment, deferred payment.

GIFT AID (NEED-BASED) *Total amount:* $13,651,010 (56% federal, 40% state, 2% institutional, 2% external sources). *Receiving aid:* Freshmen: 36% (719); All full-time undergraduates: 36% (3,060). *Average award:* Freshmen: $4266; Undergraduates: $4294. *Scholarships, grants, and awards:* Federal Pell, FSEOG, state, private, college/university gift aid from institutional funds.

GIFT AID (NON-NEED-BASED) *Total amount:* $7,509,814 (30% state, 48% institutional, 22% external sources). *Receiving aid:* Freshmen: 28% (548); Undergraduates: 20% (1,681). *Average Award:* Freshmen $3335; *Undergraduates:* $2800. *Scholarships, grants, and awards by category: Academic Interests/Achievement:* 753 awards ($1,896,239 total): general academic interests/achievements. *Creative Arts/Performance:* 90 awards ($109,500 total): art/fine arts, performing arts. *Special Characteristics:* 209 awards ($401,558 total): children and siblings of alumni, children of faculty/staff, children with a deceased or disabled parent, members of minority groups, veterans' children. *Tuition waivers:* Full or partial for employees or children of employees. *ROTC:* Army, Air Force.

LOANS *Student loans:* $26,300,609 (50% need-based, 50% non-need-based). 59% of past graduating class borrowed through all loan programs. *Average indebtedness per student:* $19,317. *Average need-based loan:* Freshmen: $2637; Undergraduates: $3546. *Parent loans:* $5,680,858 (100% non-need-based). *Programs:* FFEL (Subsidized and Unsubsidized Stafford, PLUS), Perkins.

ATHLETIC AWARDS *Total amount:* $2,212,504 (100% non-need-based).

APPLYING FOR FINANCIAL AID *Required financial aid form:* FAFSA. *Financial aid deadline:* 3/1 (priority: 3/1). *Notification date:* Continuous beginning 4/15.

CONTACT Brenda Hall, Senior Associate Director, Indiana State University, Tirey Hall, Room 150, Terre Haute, IN 47809-1401, 812-237-2215 or toll-free 800-742-0891. *Fax:* 812-237-4330. *E-mail:* finaid@indstate.edu.

INDIANA UNIVERSITY BLOOMINGTON
Bloomington, IN

Tuition & fees (IN res): $6777	Average undergraduate aid package: $6171

ABOUT THE INSTITUTION State-supported, coed. Awards: associate, bachelor's, master's, doctoral, and first professional degrees and post-bachelor's and post-master's certificates. 141 undergraduate majors. Total enrollment: 37,821. Undergraduates: 29,549. Freshmen: 6,352. Federal methodology is used as a basis for awarding need-based institutional aid.

UNDERGRADUATE EXPENSES for 2004–05 *Application fee:* $50. *Tuition, state resident:* full-time $5986; part-time $186.90 per credit hour. *Tuition, nonresident:* full-time $17,799; part-time $556.25 per credit hour. Full-time tuition and fees vary according to location and program. Part-time tuition and fees vary according to course load, location, and program. *College room and board:* $6006; *room only:* $3616. Room and board charges vary according to board plan and housing facility. *Payment plan:* Deferred payment.

FRESHMAN FINANCIAL AID (Fall 2004, est.) 5176 applied for aid; of those 73% were deemed to have need. 96% of freshmen with need received aid; of those 4% had need fully met. *Average percent of need met:* 47% (excluding resources awarded to replace EFC). *Average financial aid package:* $5804 (excluding resources awarded to replace EFC). 10% of all full-time freshmen had no need and received non-need-based gift aid.

UNDERGRADUATE FINANCIAL AID (Fall 2004, est.) 16,121 applied for aid; of those 99% were deemed to have need. 94% of undergraduates with need received aid; of those 5% had need fully met. *Average percent of need met:* 54% (excluding resources awarded to replace EFC). *Average financial aid package:* $6171 (excluding resources awarded to replace EFC). 5% of all full-time undergraduates had no need and received non-need-based gift aid.

GIFT AID (NEED-BASED) *Total amount:* $27,747,656 (49% federal, 38% state, 13% institutional). *Receiving aid:* Freshmen: 19% (1,211); All full-time undergraduates: 20% (5,591). *Average award:* Freshmen: $5873; Undergraduates: $4835. *Scholarships, grants, and awards:* Federal Pell, FSEOG, state, private, college/university gift aid from institutional funds.

GIFT AID (NON-NEED-BASED) *Total amount:* $31,694,066 (3% federal, 6% state, 78% institutional, 13% external sources). *Receiving aid:* Freshmen: 33% (2,061); Undergraduates: 27% (7,444). *Average Award:* Freshmen: $3802; *Undergraduates:* $3679. *Scholarships, grants, and awards by category: Academic Interests/Achievement:* general academic interests/achievements. *Creative Arts/Performance:* general creative arts/performance. *Special Achievements/ Activities:* general special achievements/activities. *Special Characteristics:* general special characteristics. *Tuition waivers:* Full or partial for employees or children of employees. *ROTC:* Army, Air Force.

LOANS *Student loans:* $58,510,141 (61% need-based, 39% non-need-based). 42% of past graduating class borrowed through all loan programs. *Average indebtedness per student:* $18,806. *Average need-based loan:* Freshmen: $2816; Undergraduates: $3904. *Parent loans:* $35,302,063 (100% non-need-based). *Programs:* Federal Direct (Subsidized and Unsubsidized Stafford, PLUS), Perkins, Federal Nursing, college/university.

WORK-STUDY *Federal work-study:* Total amount: $1,451,386; 949 jobs averaging $1511.

ATHLETIC AWARDS *Total amount:* $4,671,604 (100% non-need-based).

APPLYING FOR FINANCIAL AID *Required financial aid form:* FAFSA. *Financial aid deadline:* Continuous. *Notification date:* Continuous beginning 4/1.

CONTACT Automated Client Inquiry System, Indiana University Bloomington, Franklin Hall, Room 208, Bloomington, IN 47405, 812-855-RSVP. *Fax:* 812-856-RSVP. *E-mail:* rsvposfa@indiana.edu.

INDIANA UNIVERSITY EAST
Richmond, IN

Tuition & fees (IN res): $4601   **Average undergraduate aid package: $6049**

ABOUT THE INSTITUTION State-supported, coed. Awards: associate and bachelor's degrees and post-bachelor's certificates. 21 undergraduate majors. Total enrollment: 2,516. Undergraduates: 2,449. Freshmen: 406. Federal methodology is used as a basis for awarding need-based institutional aid.

UNDERGRADUATE EXPENSES for 2004–05 *Application fee:* $25. *Tuition, state resident:* full-time $4283; part-time $142.75 per credit hour. *Tuition, nonresident:* full-time $10,673; part-time $355.75 per credit hour. Full-time tuition and fees vary according to course load and reciprocity agreements. Part-time tuition and fees vary according to course load and reciprocity agreements. *Payment plan:* Deferred payment.

FRESHMAN FINANCIAL AID (Fall 2004, est.) 240 applied for aid; of those 85% were deemed to have need. 93% of freshmen with need received aid; of those 3% had need fully met. *Average percent of need met:* 53% (excluding resources awarded to replace EFC). *Average financial aid package:* $4918 (excluding resources awarded to replace EFC). 3% of all full-time freshmen had no need and received non-need-based gift aid.

UNDERGRADUATE FINANCIAL AID (Fall 2004, est.) 1,128 applied for aid; of those 87% were deemed to have need. 95% of undergraduates with need received aid; of those 7% had need fully met. *Average percent of need met:* 59% (excluding resources awarded to replace EFC). *Average financial aid package:* $6049 (excluding resources awarded to replace EFC). 2% of all full-time undergraduates had no need and received non-need-based gift aid.

GIFT AID (NEED-BASED) *Total amount:* $3,797,265 (73% federal, 26% state, 1% institutional). *Receiving aid:* Freshmen: 50% (136); All full-time undergraduates: 54% (693). *Average award:* Freshmen: $4148; Undergraduates: $4361. *Scholarships, grants, and awards:* Federal Pell, FSEOG, state, private, college/university gift aid from institutional funds.

GIFT AID (NON-NEED-BASED) *Total amount:* $455,134 (24% federal, 26% state, 24% institutional, 26% external sources). *Receiving aid:* Freshmen: 16% (43); Undergraduates: 14% (173). *Average Award:* Freshmen: $2076; Undergraduates: $1723. *Scholarships, grants, and awards by category: Academic Interests/Achievement:* general academic interests/achievements. *Creative Arts/Performance:* general creative arts/performance. *Special Achievements/Activities:* general special achievements/activities. *Special Characteristics:* general special characteristics. *Tuition waivers:* Full or partial for employees or children of employees.

LOANS *Student loans:* $7,023,130 (48% need-based, 52% non-need-based). 59% of past graduating class borrowed through all loan programs. *Average indebtedness per student:* $24,722. *Average need-based loan:* Freshmen: $2506; Undergraduates: $3108. *Parent loans:* $69,499 (100% non-need-based). *Programs:* FFEL (Subsidized and Unsubsidized Stafford, PLUS), Perkins, Federal Nursing, college/university.

WORK-STUDY *Federal work-study:* Total amount: $147,521; 46 jobs averaging $3207.

APPLYING FOR FINANCIAL AID *Required financial aid forms:* FAFSA, institution's own form. *Financial aid deadline (priority):* 3/1. *Notification date:* Continuous beginning 5/1. Students must reply within 2 weeks of notification.

CONTACT James Bland, Financial Aid Director, Indiana University East, 2325 Chester Boulevard, Whitewater Hall, Richmond, IN 47374-1289, 765-973-8276 or toll-free 800-959-EAST. *Fax:* 765-973-8388. *E-mail:* jabland@indiana.edu.

INDIANA UNIVERSITY KOKOMO
Kokomo, IN

Tuition & fees (IN res): $4632   **Average undergraduate aid package: $5148**

ABOUT THE INSTITUTION State-supported, coed. Awards: associate, bachelor's, and master's degrees and post-bachelor's certificates. 17 undergraduate majors. Total enrollment: 2,903. Undergraduates: 2,732. Freshmen: 466. Federal methodology is used as a basis for awarding need-based institutional aid.

UNDERGRADUATE EXPENSES for 2004–05 *Application fee:* $30. *Tuition, state resident:* full-time $4283; part-time $142.75 per credit hour. *Tuition, nonresident:* full-time $10,673; part-time $355.75 per credit hour. Full-time tuition and fees vary according to course load. Part-time tuition and fees vary according to course load.

FRESHMAN FINANCIAL AID (Fall 2004, est.) 299 applied for aid; of those 68% were deemed to have need. 90% of freshmen with need received aid; of those

2% had need fully met. *Average percent of need met:* 52% (excluding resources awarded to replace EFC). *Average financial aid package:* $4105 (excluding resources awarded to replace EFC). 13% of all full-time freshmen had no need and received non-need-based gift aid.

UNDERGRADUATE FINANCIAL AID (Fall 2004, est.) 1,114 applied for aid; of those 75% were deemed to have need. 90% of undergraduates with need received aid; of those 8% had need fully met. *Average percent of need met:* 61% (excluding resources awarded to replace EFC). *Average financial aid package:* $5148 (excluding resources awarded to replace EFC). 6% of all full-time undergraduates had no need and received non-need-based gift aid.

GIFT AID (NEED-BASED) *Total amount:* $2,546,169 (68% federal, 30% state, 2% institutional). *Receiving aid:* Freshmen: 31% (112); All full-time undergraduates: 34% (480). *Average award:* Freshmen: $3751; Undergraduates: $4035. *Scholarships, grants, and awards:* Federal Pell, FSEOG, state, private, college/university gift aid from institutional funds.

GIFT AID (NON-NEED-BASED) *Total amount:* $848,455 (32% federal, 25% state, 21% institutional, 22% external sources). *Receiving aid:* Freshmen: 22% (79); Undergraduates: 15% (210). *Average Award:* Freshmen: $1208; Undergraduates: $1373. *Scholarships, grants, and awards by category: Academic Interests/Achievement:* general academic interests/achievements. *Special Characteristics:* general special characteristics. *Tuition waivers:* Full or partial for employees or children of employees. *ROTC:* Army cooperative.

LOANS *Student loans:* $5,045,194 (44% need-based, 56% non-need-based). 49% of past graduating class borrowed through all loan programs. *Average indebtedness per student:* $14,607. *Average need-based loan:* Freshmen: $2199; Undergraduates: $2893. *Parent loans:* $71,904 (100% non-need-based). *Programs:* FFEL (Subsidized and Unsubsidized Stafford, PLUS), Perkins, Federal Nursing, college/university.

WORK-STUDY *Federal work-study:* Total amount: $185,650; 106 jobs averaging $1751.

APPLYING FOR FINANCIAL AID *Required financial aid forms:* FAFSA, institution's own form. *Financial aid deadline (priority):* 3/1. *Notification date:* Continuous beginning 5/1.

CONTACT Jackie Kennedy-Fletcher, Director of Financial Aid, Indiana University Kokomo, 2300 South Washington Street, PO Box 9003, Kelley Student Center, Room 201H, Kokomo, IN 46904-9003, 765-455-9431 or toll-free 888-875-4485. *E-mail:* jacfletc@iuk.edu.

INDIANA UNIVERSITY NORTHWEST
Gary, IN

Tuition & fees (IN res): $4707   **Average undergraduate aid package: $6425**

ABOUT THE INSTITUTION State-supported, coed. Awards: associate, bachelor's, and master's degrees and post-bachelor's certificates. 44 undergraduate majors. Total enrollment: 5,138. Undergraduates: 4,536. Freshmen: 762. Federal methodology is used as a basis for awarding need-based institutional aid.

UNDERGRADUATE EXPENSES for 2004–05 *Application fee:* $35. *Tuition, state resident:* full-time $4283; part-time $142.75 per credit hour. *Tuition, nonresident:* full-time $10,673; part-time $355.75 per credit hour. Full-time tuition and fees vary according to course load. Part-time tuition and fees vary according to course load. *Payment plans:* Installment, deferred payment.

FRESHMAN FINANCIAL AID (Fall 2004, est.) 486 applied for aid; of those 81% were deemed to have need. 90% of freshmen with need received aid; of those 16% had need fully met. *Average percent of need met:* 66% (excluding resources awarded to replace EFC). *Average financial aid package:* $5997 (excluding resources awarded to replace EFC). 1% of all full-time freshmen had no need and received non-need-based gift aid.

UNDERGRADUATE FINANCIAL AID (Fall 2004, est.) 1,976 applied for aid; of those 83% were deemed to have need. 92% of undergraduates with need received aid; of those 17% had need fully met. *Average percent of need met:* 70% (excluding resources awarded to replace EFC). *Average financial aid package:* $6425 (excluding resources awarded to replace EFC). 2% of all full-time undergraduates had no need and received non-need-based gift aid.

GIFT AID (NEED-BASED) *Total amount:* $5,559,635 (70% federal, 30% state). *Receiving aid:* Freshmen: 40% (244); All full-time undergraduates: 39% (999). *Average award:* Freshmen: $4170; Undergraduates: $4485. *Scholarships, grants, and awards:* Federal Pell, FSEOG, state, private, college/university gift aid from institutional funds, Federal Nursing.

GIFT AID (NON-NEED-BASED) *Total amount:* $834,940 (1% federal, 16% state, 65% institutional, 18% external sources). *Receiving aid:* Freshmen: 9% (53); Undergraduates: 12% (314). *Average Award:* Freshmen: $1922; *Undergradu-*

ates: $1438. **Scholarships, grants, and awards by category:** *Academic Interests/Achievement:* general academic interests/achievements. *Creative Arts/Performance:* general creative arts/performance. *Special Achievements/Activities:* general special achievements/activities. *Special Characteristics:* general special characteristics. **Tuition waivers:** Full or partial for employees or children of employees, senior citizens. **ROTC:** Army.

LOANS *Student loans:* $11,052,796 (45% need-based, 55% non-need-based). 47% of past graduating class borrowed through all loan programs. *Average indebtedness per student:* $18,338. **Average need-based loan:** Freshmen: $2352; Undergraduates: $3157. **Parent loans:** $150,746 (100% non-need-based). **Programs:** FFEL (Subsidized and Unsubsidized Stafford, PLUS), Perkins, college/university.

WORK-STUDY *Federal work-study:* Total amount: $1,248,958; 494 jobs averaging $2528.

ATHLETIC AWARDS *Total amount:* $14,350 (100% non-need-based).

APPLYING FOR FINANCIAL AID *Required financial aid forms:* FAFSA, institution's own form. **Financial aid deadline (priority):** 3/1. **Notification date:** Continuous beginning 5/1. Students must reply within 2 weeks of notification.

CONTACT Dian Packard, Interim Director of Scholarships and Financial Aid, Indiana University Northwest, 3400 Broadway, Hawthorn Hall, Room 101, Gary, IN 46408-1197, 219-980-6767 or toll-free 800-968-7486. *Fax:* 219-981-4219.

INDIANA UNIVERSITY OF PENNSYLVANIA
Indiana, PA

Tuition & fees (PA res): $6085	Average undergraduate aid package: $7200

ABOUT THE INSTITUTION State-supported, coed. Awards: associate, bachelor's, master's, and doctoral degrees and post-bachelor's and post-master's certificates. 74 undergraduate majors. Total enrollment: 13,998. Undergraduates: 12,163. Freshmen: 2,678. Federal methodology is used as a basis for awarding need-based institutional aid.

UNDERGRADUATE EXPENSES for 2004–05 *Application fee:* $30. **Tuition, state resident:** full-time $4810; part-time $200 per credit hour. **Tuition, nonresident:** full-time $12,026; part-time $501 per credit hour. **Required fees:** full-time $1275; $20 per credit hour or $232.50 per term part-time. Full-time tuition and fees vary according to course load, location, and reciprocity agreements. Part-time tuition and fees vary according to course load, location, and reciprocity agreements. **College room and board:** $4868; **room only:** $2940. Room and board charges vary according to board plan, housing facility, and location. **Payment plans:** Installment, deferred payment.

FRESHMAN FINANCIAL AID (Fall 2003) 2495 applied for aid; of those 76% were deemed to have need. 100% of freshmen with need received aid; of those 17% had need fully met. *Average percent of need met:* 81% (excluding resources awarded to replace EFC). *Average financial aid package:* $7662 (excluding resources awarded to replace EFC). 3% of all full-time freshmen had no need and received non-need-based gift aid.

UNDERGRADUATE FINANCIAL AID (Fall 2003) 9,210 applied for aid; of those 80% were deemed to have need. 99% of undergraduates with need received aid; of those 21% had need fully met. *Average percent of need met:* 77% (excluding resources awarded to replace EFC). *Average financial aid package:* $7200 (excluding resources awarded to replace EFC). 3% of all full-time undergraduates had no need and received non-need-based gift aid.

GIFT AID (NEED-BASED) *Total amount:* $21,388,517 (52% federal, 48% state). *Receiving aid:* Freshmen: 51% (1,446); All full-time undergraduates: 50% (5,616). *Average award:* Freshmen: $3935; Undergraduates: $3645. **Scholarships, grants, and awards:** Federal Pell, FSEOG, state, private, college/university gift aid from institutional funds.

GIFT AID (NON-NEED-BASED) *Total amount:* $5,220,043 (1% state, 47% institutional, 52% external sources). *Receiving aid:* Freshmen: 19% (533); Undergraduates: 13% (1,421). *Average Award:* Freshmen: $1870; Undergraduates: $2458. **Scholarships, grants, and awards by category:** *Academic Interests/Achievement:* 1,086 awards ($1,887,348 total): area/ethnic studies, biological sciences, business, communication, computer science, education, engineering/technologies, English, foreign languages, general academic interests/achievements, health fields, home economics, humanities, international studies, mathematics, physical sciences, premedicine, social sciences. *Creative Arts/Performance:* applied art and design, art/fine arts, dance, general creative arts/performance, journalism/publications, music, performing arts, theater/drama. *Special Achievements/Activities:* community service, general special achievements/activities, hobbies/interests, leadership. *Special Characteristics:* 813 awards ($3,417,151 total): adult students, children of faculty/staff, ethnic

background, international students. **Tuition waivers:** Full or partial for minority students, employees or children of employees. **ROTC:** Army.

LOANS *Student loans:* $42,644,806 (54% need-based, 46% non-need-based). 76% of past graduating class borrowed through all loan programs. *Average indebtedness per student:* $17,550. **Average need-based loan:** Freshmen: $2896; Undergraduates: $3438. **Parent loans:** $6,166,531 (100% non-need-based). **Programs:** FFEL (Subsidized and Unsubsidized Stafford, PLUS), Perkins, alternative loans.

WORK-STUDY *Federal work-study:* Total amount: $5,440,690; 1,600 jobs averaging $1267. **State or other work-study/employment:** Total amount: $1,033,416 (100% non-need-based). 1,779 part-time jobs averaging $1161.

ATHLETIC AWARDS *Total amount:* $624,853 (100% non-need-based).

APPLYING FOR FINANCIAL AID *Required financial aid forms:* FAFSA, state aid form. **Financial aid deadline:** 4/15. **Notification date:** Continuous beginning 3/15.

CONTACT Ms. Christine A. Zuzack, Director of Financial Aid, Indiana University of Pennsylvania, 213 Clark Hall, Indiana, PA 15705, 724-357-2218 or toll-free 800-442-6830. *Fax:* 724-357-2094. *E-mail:* cazuzack@iup.edu.

INDIANA UNIVERSITY–PURDUE UNIVERSITY FORT WAYNE
Fort Wayne, IN

Tuition & fees (IN res): $5312	Average undergraduate aid package: $5976

ABOUT THE INSTITUTION State-supported, coed. Awards: associate, bachelor's, and master's degrees and post-master's certificates. 97 undergraduate majors. Total enrollment: 11,810. Undergraduates: 11,089. Freshmen: 1,910. Federal methodology is used as a basis for awarding need-based institutional aid.

UNDERGRADUATE EXPENSES for 2004–05 *Application fee:* $30. **Tuition, state resident:** full-time $4740; part-time $158 per semester hour. **Tuition, nonresident:** full-time $11,678; part-time $389.25 per semester hour. **Required fees:** full-time $572; $19.05 per semester hour. Full-time tuition and fees vary according to course load, location, and student level. Part-time tuition and fees vary according to course load, location, and student level. **Payment plans:** Installment, deferred payment.

GIFT AID (NEED-BASED) *Total amount:* $13,031,900 (58% federal, 36% state, 6% institutional). *Receiving aid:* Freshmen: 39% (533); All full-time undergraduates: 38% (2,397). *Average award:* Freshmen: $3786; Undergraduates: $4049. **Scholarships, grants, and awards:** Federal Pell, FSEOG, state, private, college/university gift aid from institutional funds.

GIFT AID (NON-NEED-BASED) *Total amount:* $2,956,127 (11% federal, 25% state, 18% institutional, 46% external sources). *Receiving aid:* Freshmen: 11% (147); Undergraduates: 8% (488). *Average Award:* Freshmen: $1701; Undergraduates: $1740. **Scholarships, grants, and awards by category:** *Academic Interests/Achievement:* 232 awards ($209,732 total): biological sciences, business, communication, computer science, education, engineering/technologies, English, foreign languages, general academic interests/achievements, health fields, humanities, mathematics, physical sciences, premedicine, social sciences. *Creative Arts/Performance:* 47 awards ($33,729 total): art/fine arts, music, theater/drama. *Special Characteristics:* 912 awards ($1,220,856 total): children and siblings of alumni, children of faculty/staff, children with a deceased or disabled parent, handicapped students, local/state students, spouses of deceased or disabled public servants. **Tuition waivers:** Full or partial for employees or children of employees.

LOANS *Student loans:* $27,610,841 (53% need-based, 47% non-need-based). 57% of past graduating class borrowed through all loan programs. *Average indebtedness per student:* $15,867. **Average need-based loan:** Freshmen: $2333; Undergraduates: $3028. **Parent loans:** $621,291 (100% non-need-based). **Programs:** FFEL (Subsidized and Unsubsidized Stafford, PLUS), Perkins.

ATHLETIC AWARDS *Total amount:* $983,651 (100% non-need-based).

APPLYING FOR FINANCIAL AID *Required financial aid form:* FAFSA. **Financial aid deadline (priority):** 3/10. **Notification date:** 4/30. Students must reply within 4 weeks of notification.

CONTACT Mr. Joel Wenger, Associate Director of Financial Aid, Indiana University–Purdue University Fort Wayne, 2101 East Coliseum Boulevard, Fort Wayne, IN 46805-1499, 260-481-6130 or toll-free 800-324-4739 (in-state). *E-mail:* wengerj@ipfw.edu.

INDIANA UNIVERSITY–PURDUE UNIVERSITY INDIANAPOLIS
Indianapolis, IN

Tuition & fees (IN res): $5930   **Average undergraduate aid package: $6811**

ABOUT THE INSTITUTION State-supported, coed. Awards: associate, bachelor's, master's, doctoral, and first professional degrees and post-bachelor's certificates. 77 undergraduate majors. Total enrollment: 29,953. Undergraduates: 21,172. Freshmen: 2,720. Federal methodology is used as a basis for awarding need-based institutional aid.

UNDERGRADUATE EXPENSES for 2004–05 *Application fee:* $50. *Tuition, state resident:* full-time $5357; part-time $178.55 per credit hour. *Tuition, nonresident:* full-time $15,194; part-time $506.45 per credit hour. Full-time tuition and fees vary according to course load and program. Part-time tuition and fees vary according to course load and program. *College room and board: room only:* $2656. Room and board charges vary according to board plan and housing facility. *Payment plans:* Installment, deferred payment.

FRESHMAN FINANCIAL AID (Fall 2004, est.) 1930 applied for aid; of those 83% were deemed to have need. 95% of freshmen with need received aid; of those 3% had need fully met. *Average percent of need met:* 53% (excluding resources awarded to replace EFC). *Average financial aid package:* $5970 (excluding resources awarded to replace EFC). 6% of all full-time freshmen had no need and received non-need-based gift aid.

UNDERGRADUATE FINANCIAL AID (Fall 2004, est.) 9,148 applied for aid; of those 99% were deemed to have need. 94% of undergraduates with need received aid; of those 4% had need fully met. *Average percent of need met:* 53% (excluding resources awarded to replace EFC). *Average financial aid package:* $6811 (excluding resources awarded to replace EFC). 3% of all full-time undergraduates had no need and received non-need-based gift aid.

GIFT AID (NEED-BASED) *Total amount:* $25,567,444 (61% federal, 38% state, 1% institutional). *Receiving aid:* Freshmen: 33% (753); All full-time undergraduates: 35% (4,736). *Average award:* Freshmen: $4673; Undergraduates: $4597. *Scholarships, grants, and awards:* Federal Pell, FSEOG, state, private, college/university gift aid from institutional funds.

GIFT AID (NON-NEED-BASED) *Total amount:* $8,426,556 (22% federal, 23% state, 40% institutional, 15% external sources). *Receiving aid:* Freshmen: 28% (650); Undergraduates: 17% (2,362). *Average Award:* Freshmen: $2811; Undergraduates: $2622. *Scholarships, grants, and awards by category:* Academic Interests/Achievement: general academic interests/achievements. Creative Arts/Performance: general creative arts/performance. Special Achievements/Activities: general special achievements/activities. Special Characteristics: general special characteristics. *Tuition waivers:* Full or partial for employees or children of employees. *ROTC:* Army, Naval cooperative, Air Force cooperative.

LOANS *Student loans:* $61,471,135 (58% need-based, 42% non-need-based). 53% of past graduating class borrowed through all loan programs. *Average indebtedness per student:* $24,556. *Average need-based loan:* Freshmen: $2545; Undergraduates: $3772. *Parent loans:* $2,661,365 (100% non-need-based). *Programs:* FFEL (Subsidized and Unsubsidized Stafford, PLUS), Perkins, Federal Nursing, college/university.

WORK-STUDY *Federal work-study:* Total amount: $3,483,363; 1,018 jobs averaging $3422.

ATHLETIC AWARDS *Total amount:* $1,146,937 (100% non-need-based).

APPLYING FOR FINANCIAL AID *Required financial aid form:* FAFSA. *Financial aid deadline (priority):* 3/1. *Notification date:* Continuous beginning 4/1.

CONTACT Rebecca Porter, Director of Financial Aid Services, Indiana University–Purdue University Indianapolis, 425 North University Boulevard, Cavanaugh Hall, Room 103, Indianapolis, IN 46202-5145, 317-278-FAST. *Fax:* 317-274-5930.

INDIANA UNIVERSITY SOUTH BEND
South Bend, IN

Tuition & fees (IN res): $4755   **Average undergraduate aid package: $5636**

ABOUT THE INSTITUTION State-supported, coed. Awards: associate, bachelor's, and master's degrees and post-bachelor's certificates. 53 undergraduate majors. Total enrollment: 7,501. Undergraduates: 6,322. Freshmen: 910. Federal methodology is used as a basis for awarding need-based institutional aid.

UNDERGRADUATE EXPENSES for 2004–05 *Application fee:* $42. *Tuition, state resident:* full-time $4349; part-time $144.95 per credit hour. *Tuition, nonresident:* full-time $11,420; part-time $380.65 per credit hour. Full-time tuition and fees vary according to course load. Part-time tuition and fees vary according to course load. *Payment plans:* Installment, deferred payment.

FRESHMAN FINANCIAL AID (Fall 2004, est.) 563 applied for aid; of those 82% were deemed to have need. 87% of freshmen with need received aid; of those 4% had need fully met. *Average percent of need met:* 48% (excluding resources awarded to replace EFC). *Average financial aid package:* $4544 (excluding resources awarded to replace EFC). 4% of all full-time freshmen had no need and received non-need-based gift aid.

UNDERGRADUATE FINANCIAL AID (Fall 2004, est.) 2,756 applied for aid; of those 83% were deemed to have need. 88% of undergraduates with need received aid; of those 8% had need fully met. *Average percent of need met:* 57% (excluding resources awarded to replace EFC). *Average financial aid package:* $5636 (excluding resources awarded to replace EFC). 2% of all full-time undergraduates had no need and received non-need-based gift aid.

GIFT AID (NEED-BASED) *Total amount:* $6,980,317 (68% federal, 32% state). *Receiving aid:* Freshmen: 38% (264); All full-time undergraduates: 39% (1,374). *Average award:* Freshmen: $3978; Undergraduates: $4013. *Scholarships, grants, and awards:* Federal Pell, FSEOG, state, private, college/university gift aid from institutional funds.

GIFT AID (NON-NEED-BASED) *Total amount:* $885,598 (6% federal, 34% state, 13% institutional, 47% external sources). *Receiving aid:* Freshmen: 16% (111); Undergraduates: 7% (260). *Average Award:* Freshmen: $1122; Undergraduates: $1170. *Scholarships, grants, and awards by category:* Academic Interests/Achievement: general academic interests/achievements. Creative Arts/Performance: general creative arts/performance. Special Achievements/Activities: general special achievements/activities. Special Characteristics: general special characteristics. *Tuition waivers:* Full or partial for employees or children of employees. *ROTC:* Army cooperative, Naval cooperative, Air Force cooperative.

LOANS *Student loans:* $12,101,276 (58% need-based, 42% non-need-based). 48% of past graduating class borrowed through all loan programs. *Average indebtedness per student:* $20,227. *Average need-based loan:* Freshmen: $2275; Undergraduates: $3318. *Parent loans:* $537,526 (100% non-need-based). *Programs:* Federal Direct (Subsidized and Unsubsidized Stafford, PLUS), Perkins, Federal Nursing, college/university.

WORK-STUDY *Federal work-study:* Total amount: $163,708; 70 jobs averaging $2339.

ATHLETIC AWARDS *Total amount:* $93,934 (100% non-need-based).

APPLYING FOR FINANCIAL AID *Required financial aid forms:* FAFSA, institution's own form. *Financial aid deadline (priority):* 3/1. *Notification date:* Continuous beginning 5/1. Students must reply within 2 weeks of notification.

CONTACT Bev Cooper, Financial Aid Director, Indiana University South Bend, 1700 Mishawaka Avenue, PO Box 7111, South Bend, IN 46634-7111, 219-237-4357 or toll-free 877-GO-2-IUSB. *E-mail:* beacoope@iusb.edu.

INDIANA UNIVERSITY SOUTHEAST
New Albany, IN

Tuition & fees (IN res): $4673   **Average undergraduate aid package: $5094**

ABOUT THE INSTITUTION State-supported, coed. Awards: associate, bachelor's, and master's degrees and post-bachelor's certificates. 37 undergraduate majors. Total enrollment: 6,238. Undergraduates: 5,419. Freshmen: 815. Federal methodology is used as a basis for awarding need-based institutional aid.

UNDERGRADUATE EXPENSES for 2004–05 *Application fee:* $30. *Tuition, state resident:* full-time $4283; part-time $142.75 per credit hour. *Tuition, nonresident:* full-time $10,673; part-time $355.75 per credit hour. Full-time tuition and fees vary according to course load and reciprocity agreements. Part-time tuition and fees vary according to course load and reciprocity agreements. *Payment plan:* Deferred payment.

FRESHMAN FINANCIAL AID (Fall 2004, est.) 586 applied for aid; of those 77% were deemed to have need. 94% of freshmen with need received aid; of those 5% had need fully met. *Average percent of need met:* 55% (excluding resources awarded to replace EFC). *Average financial aid package:* $4472 (excluding resources awarded to replace EFC). 8% of all full-time freshmen had no need and received non-need-based gift aid.

UNDERGRADUATE FINANCIAL AID (Fall 2004, est.) 2,409 applied for aid; of those 82% were deemed to have need. 93% of undergraduates with need received aid; of those 9% had need fully met. *Average percent of need met:* 59% (excluding resources awarded to replace EFC). *Average financial aid package:* $5094 (excluding resources awarded to replace EFC). 3% of all full-time undergraduates had no need and received non-need-based gift aid.

GIFT AID (NEED-BASED) *Total amount:* $4,982,789 (69% federal, 28% state, 3% institutional). *Receiving aid:* Freshmen: 34% (240); All full-time undergraduates: 34% (1,105). *Average award:* Freshmen: $3972; Undergraduates: $3755. *Scholarships, grants, and awards:* Federal Pell, FSEOG, state, private, college/university gift aid from institutional funds.
GIFT AID (NON-NEED-BASED) *Total amount:* $1,336,818 (24% state, 41% institutional, 35% external sources). *Receiving aid:* Freshmen: 21% (152); Undergraduates: 13% (432). *Average Award:* Freshmen: $1798; *Undergraduates:* $1833. *Scholarships, grants, and awards by category:* Academic Interests/Achievement: general academic interests/achievements. *Creative Arts/Performance:* general creative arts/performance. *Special Achievements/Activities:* general special achievements/activities. *Special Characteristics:* general special characteristics. *Tuition waivers:* Full or partial for employees or children of employees. *ROTC:* Army cooperative, Air Force cooperative.
LOANS *Student loans:* $10,345,835 (55% need-based, 45% non-need-based). 40% of past graduating class borrowed through all loan programs. *Average indebtedness per student:* $16,597. *Average need-based loan:* Freshmen: $2166; Undergraduates: $3249. *Parent loans:* $185,726 (100% non-need-based). *Programs:* FFEL (Subsidized and Unsubsidized Stafford, PLUS), Perkins, Federal Nursing, college/university.
WORK-STUDY *Federal work-study:* Total amount: $179,054; 99 jobs averaging $1809.
ATHLETIC AWARDS *Total amount:* $52,275 (100% non-need-based).
APPLYING FOR FINANCIAL AID *Required financial aid forms:* FAFSA, institution's own form. *Financial aid deadline (priority):* 3/1. *Notification date:* Continuous beginning 5/1.
CONTACT Mike Barlow, Director of Financial Aid, Indiana University Southeast, LB-002, New Albany, IN 47150, 812-941-2246 or toll-free 800-852-8835 (in-state). *E-mail:* mibarlow@ius.edu.

INDIANA WESLEYAN UNIVERSITY
Marion, IN

CONTACT Director of Financial Aid, Indiana Wesleyan University, 4201 South Washington Street, Marion, IN 46953-4999, 765-677-2116 or toll-free 800-332-6901. *Fax:* 765-677-2809.

INSTITUTE OF COMPUTER TECHNOLOGY
Los Angeles, CA

CONTACT Office of Financial Aid, Institute of Computer Technology, 3200 Wilshire Boulevard, Los Angeles, CA 90010, 213-381-3333 or toll-free 800-57 GO ICT (in-state). *Fax:* 213-383-9369.

INTER AMERICAN UNIVERSITY OF PUERTO RICO, AGUADILLA CAMPUS
Aguadilla, PR

CONTACT Mr. Juan Gonzalez, Director of Financial Aid, Inter American University of Puerto Rico, Aguadilla Campus, PO Box 20000, Aguadilla, PR 00605, 787-891-0925 Ext. 2108. *Fax:* 787-882-3020.

INTER AMERICAN UNIVERSITY OF PUERTO RICO, ARECIBO CAMPUS
Arecibo, PR

CONTACT Ramón O. de Jesús, Financial Aid Director, Inter American University of Puerto Rico, Arecibo Campus, PO Box 4050, Arecibo, PR 00614-4050, 787-878-5475 Ext. 2275. *Fax:* 787-880-1624.

INTER AMERICAN UNIVERSITY OF PUERTO RICO, BARRANQUITAS CAMPUS
Barranquitas, PR

CONTACT Mr. Eduardo Fontánez Colón, Financial Aid Officer, Inter American University of Puerto Rico, Barranquitas Campus, Box 517, Barranquitas, PR 00794, 787-857-3600 Ext. 2049. *Fax:* 787-857-2244.

INTER AMERICAN UNIVERSITY OF PUERTO RICO, BAYAMÓN CAMPUS
Bayamón, PR

CONTACT Financial Aid Office, Inter American University of Puerto Rico, Bayamón Campus, 500 Road 830, Bayamon, PR 00957, 787-279-1912 Ext. 2025.

INTER AMERICAN UNIVERSITY OF PUERTO RICO, FAJARDO CAMPUS
Fajardo, PR

CONTACT Financial Aid Director, Inter American University of Puerto Rico, Fajardo Campus, Call Box 700003, Fajardo, PR 00738-7003, 787-863-2390 Ext. 2208.

INTER AMERICAN UNIVERSITY OF PUERTO RICO, GUAYAMA CAMPUS
Guayama, PR

Tuition & fees: N/R	Average undergraduate aid package: $1609

ABOUT THE INSTITUTION Independent, coed. Awards: associate and bachelor's degrees. 15 undergraduate majors. Total enrollment: 1,246. Undergraduates: 866. Freshmen: 771. Federal methodology is used as a basis for awarding need-based institutional aid.
FRESHMAN FINANCIAL AID (Fall 2003) 467 applied for aid; of those 99% were deemed to have need. 78% of freshmen with need received aid; of those 1% had need fully met. *Average percent of need met:* 7% (excluding resources awarded to replace EFC). *Average financial aid package:* $350 (excluding resources awarded to replace EFC).
UNDERGRADUATE FINANCIAL AID (Fall 2003) 1,300 applied for aid; of those 99% were deemed to have need. 87% of undergraduates with need received aid; of those .1% had need fully met. *Average percent of need met:* 28% (excluding resources awarded to replace EFC). *Average financial aid package:* $1609 (excluding resources awarded to replace EFC).
GIFT AID (NEED-BASED) *Receiving aid:* Freshmen: 61% (285); All full-time undergraduates: 75% (993). *Average award:* Freshmen: $122; Undergraduates: $488. *Scholarships, grants, and awards:* Federal Pell, FSEOG, state, college/university gift aid from institutional funds, Federal Nursing.
GIFT AID (NON-NEED-BASED) *Total amount:* $875,733 (37% federal, 27% state, 36% institutional). *Receiving aid:* Undergraduates: 1% (10). *Tuition waivers:* Full or partial for employees or children of employees. *ROTC:* Army cooperative.
LOANS *Student loans:* $5,730,194 (48% need-based, 52% non-need-based). 80% of past graduating class borrowed through all loan programs. *Average need-based loan:* Freshmen: $376; Undergraduates: $1761. *Programs:* Federal Direct (Subsidized and Unsubsidized Stafford, PLUS), Perkins, Federal Nursing.
WORK-STUDY *Federal work-study:* Total amount: $394,135; 170 jobs averaging $1000. *State or other work-study/employment:* Part-time jobs available.
ATHLETIC AWARDS *Total amount:* $29,701 (53% need-based, 47% non-need-based).
APPLYING FOR FINANCIAL AID *Required financial aid form:* FAFSA. *Financial aid deadline:* Continuous. *Notification date:* Continuous beginning 7/1. Students must reply within 5 weeks of notification.
CONTACT Sr. Jose A. Vechini, Director of Financial Aid Office, Inter American University of Puerto Rico, Guayama Campus, Call Box 10004, Guyama, PR 00785, 787-864-2222 Ext. 2206 or toll-free 787-864-2222 Ext. 2243 (in-state). *Fax:* 787-864-8232. *E-mail:* javechi@inter.edu.

INTER AMERICAN UNIVERSITY OF PUERTO RICO, METROPOLITAN CAMPUS
San Juan, PR

CONTACT Mrs. Luz M. Medina, Acting Director of Financial Aid, Inter American University of Puerto Rico, Metropolitan Campus, PO Box 191293, San Juan, PR 00919-1293, 787-758-2891. *Fax:* 787-250-0782.

INTER AMERICAN UNIVERSITY OF PUERTO RICO, PONCE CAMPUS
Mercedita, PR

CONTACT Financial Aid Officer, Inter American University of Puerto Rico, Ponce Campus, Street #1, Km 123.2, Mercedita, PR 00715-2201, 787-284-1912 Ext. 2015.

INTER AMERICAN UNIVERSITY OF PUERTO RICO, SAN GERMÁN CAMPUS
San Germán, PR

Tuition & fees: $4616	Average undergraduate aid package: $1556

ABOUT THE INSTITUTION Independent, coed. Awards: associate, bachelor's, master's, and doctoral degrees and post-bachelor's certificates. 57 undergraduate majors. Total enrollment: 6,217. Undergraduates: 5,050. Freshmen: 833. Both federal and institutional methodology are used as a basis for awarding need-based institutional aid.

UNDERGRADUATE EXPENSES for 2005–06 *Comprehensive fee:* $7016 includes full-time tuition ($4200), mandatory fees ($416), and room and board ($2400). *College room only:* $900. Full-time tuition and fees vary according to degree level. Room and board charges vary according to board plan and housing facility. *Part-time tuition:* $140 per credit. *Part-time fees:* $208 per term. Part-time tuition and fees vary according to degree level. *Payment plan:* Deferred payment.

FRESHMAN FINANCIAL AID (Fall 2003) 1139 applied for aid; of those 96% were deemed to have need. 89% of freshmen with need received aid; of those 1% had need fully met. *Average percent of need met:* 1% (excluding resources awarded to replace EFC). *Average financial aid package:* $364 (excluding resources awarded to replace EFC).

UNDERGRADUATE FINANCIAL AID (Fall 2003) 3,011 applied for aid; of those 96% were deemed to have need. 90% of undergraduates with need received aid; of those 1% had need fully met. *Average percent of need met:* 33% (excluding resources awarded to replace EFC). *Average financial aid package:* $1556 (excluding resources awarded to replace EFC).

GIFT AID (NEED-BASED) *Total amount:* $16,683,761 (90% federal, 4% state, 6% institutional). *Receiving aid:* Freshmen: 76% (911); All full-time undergraduates: 74% (2,368). *Average award:* Freshmen: $180; Undergraduates: $567. *Scholarships, grants, and awards:* Federal Pell, FSEOG, state, college/university gift aid from institutional funds.

GIFT AID (NON-NEED-BASED) *Receiving aid:* Undergraduates: 2. *Scholarships, grants, and awards by category: Academic Interests/Achievement:* general academic interests/achievements. *Tuition waivers:* Full or partial for employees or children of employees. *ROTC:* Army cooperative, Naval cooperative, Air Force cooperative.

LOANS *Student loans:* $9,131,139 (100% need-based). *Average need-based loan:* Freshmen: $301; Undergraduates: $1756. *Parent loans:* $7760 (100% need-based). *Programs:* Federal Direct (Subsidized and Unsubsidized Stafford, PLUS), Perkins.

WORK-STUDY *Federal work-study:* Total amount: $416,554; jobs available.

ATHLETIC AWARDS *Total amount:* $786,320 (100% need-based).

APPLYING FOR FINANCIAL AID *Required financial aid forms:* FAFSA, institution's own form. *Financial aid deadline (priority):* 4/26. *Notification date:* Continuous beginning 6/15.

CONTACT Ms. María I. Lugo, Financial Aid Director, Inter American University of Puerto Rico, San Germán Campus, PO Box 5100, San Germán, PR 00683-5008, 787-264-1912 Ext. 7252. *Fax:* 787-892-6350.

INTERIOR DESIGNERS INSTITUTE
Newport Beach, CA

CONTACT Office of Financial Aid, Interior Designers Institute, 1061 Camelback Road, Newport Beach, CA 92660, 949-675-4451.

INTERNATIONAL ACADEMY OF DESIGN & TECHNOLOGY
Tampa, FL

CONTACT Financial Aid Office, International Academy of Design & Technology, 5225 Memorial Highway, Tampa, FL 33634-7350, 813-881-0007 or toll-free 800-ACADEMY. *Fax:* 813-881-3440.

INTERNATIONAL ACADEMY OF DESIGN & TECHNOLOGY
Chicago, IL

ABOUT THE INSTITUTION Proprietary, coed. Awards: associate and bachelor's degrees. 9 undergraduate majors. Total enrollment: 2,905. Undergraduates: 2,905. Freshmen: 815.

GIFT AID (NEED-BASED) *Scholarships, grants, and awards:* Federal Pell, FSEOG, private, college/university gift aid from institutional funds.

LOANS *Programs:* FFEL (Subsidized and Unsubsidized Stafford, PLUS), alternative loans.

APPLYING FOR FINANCIAL AID *Required financial aid forms:* FAFSA, institution's own form.

CONTACT Barbara Williams, Financial Aid Director, International Academy of Design & Technology, 1 North State Street, Suite 400, Chicago, IL 60602, 312-980-9200 or toll-free 877-ACADEMY (out-of-state). *Fax:* 312-541-3929.

INTERNATIONAL BAPTIST COLLEGE
Tempe, AZ

CONTACT Financial Aid Office, International Baptist College, 2150 East Southern Avenue, Tempe, AZ 85282, 480-838-7070 or toll-free 800-422-4858. *Fax:* 480-838-5432.

INTERNATIONAL COLLEGE
Naples, FL

Tuition & fees: $9020	Average undergraduate aid package: $7200

ABOUT THE INSTITUTION Independent, coed. Awards: associate, bachelor's, and master's degrees. 13 undergraduate majors. Total enrollment: 1,544. Undergraduates: 1,342. Freshmen: 138. Federal methodology is used as a basis for awarding need-based institutional aid.

UNDERGRADUATE EXPENSES for 2004–05 *Application fee:* $20. *Tuition:* full-time $8640; part-time $360 per credit. *Required fees:* full-time $380; $190 per term part-time. *Payment plan:* Installment.

GIFT AID (NEED-BASED) *Total amount:* $2,484,207 (92% federal, 5% state, 3% institutional). *Receiving aid:* Freshmen: 76% (75); All full-time undergraduates: 74% (989). *Average award:* Freshmen: $4300; Undergraduates: $4450. *Scholarships, grants, and awards:* Federal Pell, FSEOG, state, private, college/university gift aid from institutional funds.

GIFT AID (NON-NEED-BASED) *Total amount:* $2,209,793 (95% state, 3% institutional, 2% external sources). *Receiving aid:* Freshmen: 9% (9); Undergraduates: 3% (34). *Average Award:* Freshmen: $1200; Undergraduates: $1200. *Scholarships, grants, and awards by category: Special Achievements/Activities:* 114 awards ($143,000 total): general special achievements/activities. *Tuition waivers:* Full or partial for employees or children of employees.

LOANS *Student loans:* $12,237,048 (49% need-based, 51% non-need-based). 74% of past graduating class borrowed through all loan programs. *Average indebtedness per student:* $19,500. *Average need-based loan:* Freshmen: $1313; Undergraduates: $3100. *Parent loans:* $147,049 (100% non-need-based). *Programs:* FFEL (Subsidized and Unsubsidized Stafford, PLUS).

APPLYING FOR FINANCIAL AID *Required financial aid form:* FAFSA. *Financial aid deadline:* Continuous. *Notification date:* Continuous.

CONTACT Mr. Joe Gilchrist, Director of Financial Aid, International College, 2655 Northbrooke Drive, Naples, FL 34119, 239-513-1122 Ext. 116 or toll-free 800-466-8017. *Fax:* 239-513-9579. *E-mail:* jgilchrist@internationalcollege.edu.

INTERNATIONAL COLLEGE AND GRADUATE SCHOOL
Honolulu, HI

ABOUT THE INSTITUTION Independent interdenominational, coed. Awards: bachelor's, master's, and first professional degrees. 1 undergraduate major. Total enrollment: 58. Undergraduates: 22. Entering class: .

GIFT AID (NEED-BASED) *Scholarships, grants, and awards:* Federal Pell, FSEOG, private, college/university gift aid from institutional funds.

GIFT AID (NON-NEED-BASED) *Scholarships, grants, and awards by category: Academic Interests/Achievement:* religion/biblical studies. *Special Characteristics:* veterans.

APPLYING FOR FINANCIAL AID *Required financial aid forms:* FAFSA, institution's own form.

CONTACT Mr. Jon Rawlings, Executive Vice President, International College and Graduate School, 20 Dowsett Avenue, Honolulu, HI 96817, 808-595-4247. *Fax:* 808-595-4779. *E-mail:* icgs@hawaii.rr.com.

INTERNATIONAL IMPORT-EXPORT INSTITUTE
Phoenix, AZ

CONTACT Financial Aid Office, International Import-Export Institute, 2432 West Peoria Avenue, Suite 1026, Phoenix, AZ 85029, 602-648-5750 or toll-free 800-474-8013.

IONA COLLEGE
New Rochelle, NY

Tuition & fees: $19,530 — **Average undergraduate aid package: $13,197**

ABOUT THE INSTITUTION Independent religious, coed. Awards: bachelor's and master's degrees and post-bachelor's and post-master's certificates. 58 undergraduate majors. Total enrollment: 4,329. Undergraduates: 3,425. Freshmen: 897. Federal methodology is used as a basis for awarding need-based institutional aid.

UNDERGRADUATE EXPENSES for 2004–05 *Application fee:* $50. *Comprehensive fee:* $29,228 includes full-time tuition ($18,990), mandatory fees ($540), and room and board ($9698). Full-time tuition and fees vary according to class time. Room and board charges vary according to housing facility. *Part-time tuition:* $630 per credit. *Part-time fees:* $185 per term. Part-time tuition and fees vary according to class time and course load. *Payment plan:* Installment.

FRESHMAN FINANCIAL AID (Fall 2004, est.) 865 applied for aid; of those 82% were deemed to have need. 99% of freshmen with need received aid; of those 23% had need fully met. *Average percent of need met:* 18% (excluding resources awarded to replace EFC). *Average financial aid package:* $13,531 (excluding resources awarded to replace EFC). 17% of all full-time freshmen had no need and received non-need-based gift aid.

UNDERGRADUATE FINANCIAL AID (Fall 2004, est.) 2,934 applied for aid; of those 81% were deemed to have need. 99% of undergraduates with need received aid; of those 21% had need fully met. *Average percent of need met:* 24% (excluding resources awarded to replace EFC). *Average financial aid package:* $13,197 (excluding resources awarded to replace EFC). 17% of all full-time undergraduates had no need and received non-need-based gift aid.

GIFT AID (NEED-BASED) *Total amount:* $6,834,995 (38% federal, 57% state, 1% institutional, 4% external sources). *Receiving aid:* Freshmen: 26% (234); All full-time undergraduates: 29% (917). *Average award:* Freshmen: $3769; Undergraduates: $3160. *Scholarships, grants, and awards:* Federal Pell, FSEOG, state, private, college/university gift aid from institutional funds.

GIFT AID (NON-NEED-BASED) *Total amount:* $20,153,994 (99% institutional, 1% external sources). *Receiving aid:* Freshmen: 79% (705); Undergraduates: 73% (2,280). *Average Award:* Freshmen: $10,221; Undergraduates: $9704. *Scholarships, grants, and awards by category: Academic Interests/Achievement:* 2,641 awards ($18,485,739 total): general academic interests/achievements. *Creative Arts/Performance:* 24 awards ($95,700 total): music. *Special Characteristics:* 159 awards ($635,131 total): children and siblings of alumni, children of faculty/staff, religious affiliation, siblings of current students. *Tuition waivers:* Full or partial for employees or children of employees, senior citizens. *ROTC:* Army cooperative.

LOANS *Student loans:* $12,546,721 (44% need-based, 56% non-need-based). 90% of past graduating class borrowed through all loan programs. *Average indebtedness per student:* $23,551. *Average need-based loan:* Freshmen: $1570; Undergraduates: $2983. *Parent loans:* $5,540,542 (100% non-need-based). *Programs:* FFEL (Subsidized and Unsubsidized Stafford, PLUS), Perkins, alternative loans.

WORK-STUDY *Federal work-study:* Total amount: $576,682; 438 jobs averaging $1474. *State or other work-study/employment:* Total amount: $380,000 (100% non-need-based). 254 part-time jobs averaging $1373.

ATHLETIC AWARDS *Total amount:* $1,816,081 (100% non-need-based).

APPLYING FOR FINANCIAL AID *Required financial aid forms:* FAFSA, institution's own form, state aid form. *Financial aid deadline (priority):* 4/15. *Notification date:* Continuous. Students must reply by 5/1 or within 2 weeks of notification.

CONTACT Mary Grant, Associate Director of Student Financial Services, Iona College, 715 North Avenue, New Rochelle, NY 10801-1890, 914-633-2676 or toll-free 800-231-IONA (in-state). *Fax:* 914-633-2486.

IOWA STATE UNIVERSITY OF SCIENCE AND TECHNOLOGY
Ames, IA

Tuition & fees (IA res): $5426 — **Average undergraduate aid package: $7738**

ABOUT THE INSTITUTION State-supported, coed. Awards: bachelor's, master's, doctoral, and first professional degrees and post-master's certificates. 117 undergraduate majors. Total enrollment: 26,380. Undergraduates: 21,354. Freshmen: 3,729. Federal methodology is used as a basis for awarding need-based institutional aid.

UNDERGRADUATE EXPENSES for 2004–05 *Application fee:* $30. *Tuition, state resident:* full-time $4702; part-time $196 per semester hour. *Tuition, nonresident:* full-time $14,404; part-time $601 per semester hour. Full-time tuition and fees vary according to class time, degree level, and program. Part-time tuition and fees vary according to class time, course load, degree level, and program. *College room and board:* $5958; *room only:* $3168. Room and board charges vary according to board plan and housing facility. *Payment plans:* Installment, deferred payment.

FRESHMAN FINANCIAL AID (Fall 2004, est.) 3149 applied for aid; of those 64% were deemed to have need. 100% of freshmen with need received aid; of those 56% had need fully met. *Average percent of need met:* 83% (excluding resources awarded to replace EFC). *Average financial aid package:* $7444 (excluding resources awarded to replace EFC). 27% of all full-time freshmen had no need and received non-need-based gift aid.

UNDERGRADUATE FINANCIAL AID (Fall 2004, est.) 15,787 applied for aid; of those 72% were deemed to have need. 100% of undergraduates with need received aid; of those 53% had need fully met. *Average percent of need met:* 82% (excluding resources awarded to replace EFC). *Average financial aid package:* $7738 (excluding resources awarded to replace EFC). 17% of all full-time undergraduates had no need and received non-need-based gift aid.

GIFT AID (NEED-BASED) *Total amount:* $40,174,649 (37% federal, 4% state, 44% institutional, 15% external sources). *Receiving aid:* Freshmen: 45% (1,684); All full-time undergraduates: 43% (8,630). *Average award:* Freshmen: $3446; Undergraduates: $3148. *Scholarships, grants, and awards:* Federal Pell, FSEOG, state, college/university gift aid from institutional funds.

GIFT AID (NON-NEED-BASED) *Total amount:* $13,467,028 (8% federal, 2% state, 66% institutional, 24% external sources). *Receiving aid:* Freshmen: 30% (1,125); Undergraduates: 19% (3,794). *Average Award:* Freshmen: $3710; Undergraduates: $3480. *Scholarships, grants, and awards by category: Academic Interests/Achievement:* agriculture, architecture, area/ethnic studies, biological sciences, business, communication, computer science, education, engineering/technologies, English, foreign languages, general academic interests/achievements, health fields, home economics, humanities, international studies, library science, mathematics, military science, physical sciences, premedicine, social sciences. *Creative Arts/Performance:* applied art and design, art/fine arts, journalism/publications, music, theater/drama. *Special Achievements/Activities:* community service, general special achievements/activities, leadership, rodeo. *Special Characteristics:* adult students, children and siblings of alumni, ethnic background, first-generation college students, general special characteristics, international students, local/state students, members of minority groups, out-of-state students, religious affiliation. *ROTC:* Army, Naval, Air Force.

LOANS *Student loans:* $81,958,914 (57% need-based, 43% non-need-based). 68% of past graduating class borrowed through all loan programs. *Average indebtedness per student:* $27,324. *Average need-based loan:* Freshmen: $3070;

Undergraduates: $4489. *Parent loans:* $4,648,974 (26% need-based, 74% non-need-based). *Programs:* Federal Direct (Subsidized and Unsubsidized Stafford, PLUS), Perkins, state, college/university, private alternative loans.

WORK-STUDY *Federal work-study:* Total amount: $1,062,405; 779 jobs averaging $2168. *State or other work-study/employment:* 9,458 part-time jobs averaging $1779.

ATHLETIC AWARDS *Total amount:* $4,438,695 (39% need-based, 61% non-need-based).

APPLYING FOR FINANCIAL AID *Required financial aid form:* FAFSA. *Financial aid deadline (priority):* 3/1. *Notification date:* Continuous beginning 4/1. Students must reply by 5/1.

CONTACT Roberta Johnson, Director of Financial Aid, Iowa State University of Science and Technology, 0210 Beardshear Hall, Ames, IA 50011, 515-294-2223 or toll-free 800-262-3810. *Fax:* 515-294-3622. *E-mail:* rljohns@iastate.edu.

IOWA WESLEYAN COLLEGE
Mount Pleasant, IA

Tuition & fees: $16,070	Average undergraduate aid package: $10,775

ABOUT THE INSTITUTION Independent United Methodist, coed. Awards: bachelor's degrees. 37 undergraduate majors. Total enrollment: 776. Undergraduates: 776. Freshmen: 93. Federal methodology is used as a basis for awarding need-based institutional aid.

UNDERGRADUATE EXPENSES for 2004–05 *Comprehensive fee:* $20,990 includes full-time tuition ($16,070) and room and board ($4920). *College room only:* $2050. Room and board charges vary according to board plan and housing facility. *Part-time tuition:* $396 per credit hour. Part-time tuition and fees vary according to class time. *Payment plans:* Installment, deferred payment.

GIFT AID (NEED-BASED) *Total amount:* $3,573,707 (26% federal, 23% state, 50% institutional, 1% external sources). *Receiving aid:* Freshmen: 86% (91); All full-time undergraduates: 84% (408). *Average award:* Freshmen: $6180; Undergraduates: $6200. *Scholarships, grants, and awards:* Federal Pell, FSEOG, state, private, college/university gift aid from institutional funds.

GIFT AID (NON-NEED-BASED) *Total amount:* $280,905 (98% institutional, 2% external sources). *Receiving aid:* Freshmen: 14% (15); Undergraduates: 36% (176). *Average Award:* Freshmen: $3037; Undergraduates: $3021. *Scholarships, grants, and awards by category:* Academic Interests/Achievement: 119 awards ($266,304 total): general academic interests/achievements. Creative Arts/Performance: 25 awards ($33,750 total): art/fine arts, music. Special Achievements/Activities: cheerleading/drum major. Special Characteristics: 246 awards ($495,835 total): children of faculty/staff, international students, out-of-state students, relatives of clergy, religious affiliation. *Tuition waivers:* Full or partial for employees or children of employees.

LOANS *Student loans:* $3,305,992 (58% need-based, 42% non-need-based). 70% of past graduating class borrowed through all loan programs. *Average indebtedness per student:* $14,428. *Average need-based loan:* Freshmen: $2383; Undergraduates: $2746. *Parent loans:* $160,239 (85% need-based, 15% non-need-based). *Programs:* FFEL (Subsidized and Unsubsidized Stafford, PLUS), Perkins, alternative loans.

ATHLETIC AWARDS *Total amount:* $496,076 (84% need-based, 16% non-need-based).

APPLYING FOR FINANCIAL AID *Required financial aid form:* FAFSA. *Financial aid deadline (priority):* 4/1. *Notification date:* Continuous. Students must reply within 3 weeks of notification.

CONTACT Crystal Filer Ogden, Director of Financial Aid, Iowa Wesleyan College, 601 North Main Street, Mount Pleasant, IA 52641-1398, 319-385-6242 or toll-free 800-582-2383 Ext. 6231. *Fax:* 319-385-6219. *E-mail:* finaid@iwc.edu.

ITHACA COLLEGE
Ithaca, NY

Tuition & fees: $23,690	Average undergraduate aid package: $20,902

ABOUT THE INSTITUTION Independent, coed. Awards: bachelor's and master's degrees. 103 undergraduate majors. Total enrollment: 6,337. Undergraduates: 6,107. Freshmen: 1,461. Both federal and institutional methodology are used as a basis for awarding need-based institutional aid.

UNDERGRADUATE EXPENSES for 2004–05 *Application fee:* $55. *Comprehensive fee:* $33,394 includes full-time tuition ($23,690) and room and board ($9704).

College room only: $4946. Room and board charges vary according to board plan and housing facility. *Part-time tuition:* $790 per credit hour. *Payment plan:* Installment.

FRESHMAN FINANCIAL AID (Fall 2003) 1208 applied for aid; of those 87% were deemed to have need. 100% of freshmen with need received aid; of those 45% had need fully met. *Average percent of need met:* 89% (excluding resources awarded to replace EFC). *Average financial aid package:* $20,950 (excluding resources awarded to replace EFC). 9% of all full-time freshmen had no need and received non-need-based gift aid.

UNDERGRADUATE FINANCIAL AID (Fall 2003) 4,582 applied for aid; of those 90% were deemed to have need. 100% of undergraduates with need received aid; of those 42% had need fully met. *Average percent of need met:* 88% (excluding resources awarded to replace EFC). *Average financial aid package:* $20,902 (excluding resources awarded to replace EFC). 9% of all full-time undergraduates had no need and received non-need-based gift aid.

GIFT AID (NEED-BASED) *Total amount:* $53,638,826 (7% federal, 8% state, 83% institutional, 2% external sources). *Receiving aid:* Freshmen: 67% (978); All full-time undergraduates: 67% (3,955). *Average award:* Freshmen: $14,103; Undergraduates: $13,497. *Scholarships, grants, and awards:* Federal Pell, FSEOG, state, private, college/university gift aid from institutional funds.

GIFT AID (NON-NEED-BASED) *Total amount:* $8,251,666 (1% federal, 1% state, 91% institutional, 7% external sources). *Receiving aid:* Freshmen: 15% (220); Undergraduates: 13% (785). *Average Award:* Freshmen: $7812; Undergraduates: $8802. *Scholarships, grants, and awards by category:* Academic Interests/Achievement: 1,941 awards ($15,018,590 total): communication, general academic interests/achievements. Creative Arts/Performance: 25 awards ($289,690 total): dance, journalism/publications, music, performing arts, theater/drama. Special Achievements/Activities: 112 awards ($666,000 total): leadership. Special Characteristics: 246 awards ($247,000 total): children and siblings of alumni, siblings of current students. *Tuition waivers:* Full or partial for employees or children of employees. *ROTC:* Army cooperative, Air Force cooperative.

LOANS *Student loans:* $22,341,918 (87% need-based, 13% non-need-based). *Average need-based loan:* Freshmen: $5007; Undergraduates: $5407. *Parent loans:* $9,331,860 (23% need-based, 77% non-need-based). *Programs:* FFEL (Subsidized and Unsubsidized Stafford, PLUS), Perkins, college/university.

WORK-STUDY *Federal work-study:* Total amount: $1,300,000; jobs available. *State or other work-study/employment:* Total amount: $8,525,015 (57% need-based, 43% non-need-based). Part-time jobs available.

APPLYING FOR FINANCIAL AID *Required financial aid forms:* FAFSA, CSS/Financial Aid PROFILE (for Early Decision applicants only). *Financial aid deadline (priority):* 2/1. *Notification date:* Continuous beginning 2/15.

CONTACT Mr. Larry Chambers, Director of Financial Aid, Ithaca College, 350 Egbert Hall, Ithaca, NY 14850, 800-429-4275 or toll-free 800-429-4274. *Fax:* 607-274-1895. *E-mail:* finaid@ithaca.edu.

ITT TECHNICAL INSTITUTE
Tempe, AZ

CONTACT Financial Aid Office, ITT Technical Institute, 5005 S. Wendler Drive, Tempe, AZ 85282, 602-437-7500 or toll-free 800-879-4881.

JACKSON STATE UNIVERSITY
Jackson, MS

ABOUT THE INSTITUTION State-supported, coed. Awards: bachelor's, master's, and doctoral degrees and post-master's certificates. 62 undergraduate majors. Total enrollment: 8,351. Undergraduates: 6,605. Freshmen: 1,010.

GIFT AID (NEED-BASED) *Scholarships, grants, and awards:* Federal Pell, FSEOG, state, private, college/university gift aid from institutional funds.

GIFT AID (NON-NEED-BASED) *Scholarships, grants, and awards by category:* Academic Interests/Achievement: general academic interests/achievements. Creative Arts/Performance: music. Special Characteristics: children of faculty/staff, children of public servants.

LOANS *Programs:* Perkins, college/university.

WORK-STUDY Federal work-study jobs available.

APPLYING FOR FINANCIAL AID *Required financial aid forms:* FAFSA, institution's own form, state aid form.

CONTACT Director of Financial Aid, Jackson State University, 1400 J.R. Lynch Street, PO Box 17065, Jackson, MS 39217, 601-968-2227 or toll-free 800-682-5390 (in-state), 800-848-6817 (out-of-state).

JACKSONVILLE STATE UNIVERSITY
Jacksonville, AL

Tuition & fees (AL res): $4040   **Average undergraduate aid package: $5756**

ABOUT THE INSTITUTION State-supported, coed. Awards: bachelor's and master's degrees and post-master's certificates. 58 undergraduate majors. Total enrollment: 8,930. Undergraduates: 7,138. Freshmen: 1,057. Federal methodology is used as a basis for awarding need-based institutional aid.

UNDERGRADUATE EXPENSES for 2004–05 *Application fee:* $20. *Tuition, state resident:* full-time $4040; part-time $169 per credit hour. *Tuition, nonresident:* full-time $8080; part-time $338 per credit hour. *College room and board:* $3312; *room only:* $1700. Room and board charges vary according to board plan and housing facility.

FRESHMAN FINANCIAL AID (Fall 2004, est.) 803 applied for aid; of those 95% were deemed to have need. 100% of freshmen with need received aid; of those 50% had need fully met. *Average percent of need met:* 70% (excluding resources awarded to replace EFC). *Average financial aid package:* $3400 (excluding resources awarded to replace EFC). 15% of all full-time freshmen had no need and received non-need-based gift aid.

UNDERGRADUATE FINANCIAL AID (Fall 2004, est.) 4,692 applied for aid; of those 94% were deemed to have need. 100% of undergraduates with need received aid; of those 50% had need fully met. *Average percent of need met:* 80% (excluding resources awarded to replace EFC). *Average financial aid package:* $5756 (excluding resources awarded to replace EFC). 14% of all full-time undergraduates had no need and received non-need-based gift aid.

GIFT AID (NEED-BASED) *Total amount:* $17,065,790 (53% federal, 24% institutional, 23% external sources). *Receiving aid:* Freshmen: 6% (60); All full-time undergraduates: 6% (350). *Average award:* Freshmen: $1900; Undergraduates: $3124. *Scholarships, grants, and awards:* Federal Pell, FSEOG, state, private, college/university gift aid from institutional funds, Federal Nursing.

GIFT AID (NON-NEED-BASED) *Total amount:* $22,488 (100% external sources). *Receiving aid:* Freshmen: 35% (355); Undergraduates: 36% (2,075). *Average Award:* Freshmen: $1000; Undergraduates: $1000. *Scholarships, grants, and awards by category:* *Academic Interests/Achievement:* biological sciences, business, communication, computer science, education, English, health fields, home economics, humanities, mathematics, military science, physical sciences, social sciences. *Creative Arts/Performance:* art/fine arts, journalism/publications, music, theater/drama. *Special Achievements/Activities:* general special achievements/activities. *Tuition waivers:* Full or partial for employees or children of employees. *ROTC:* Army.

LOANS *Student loans:* $29,297,208 (58% need-based, 42% non-need-based). 46% of past graduating class borrowed through all loan programs. *Average indebtedness per student:* $17,125. *Average need-based loan:* Undergraduates: $4763. *Programs:* Federal Direct (Subsidized and Unsubsidized Stafford, PLUS), FFEL (Subsidized and Unsubsidized Stafford, PLUS), college/university.

WORK-STUDY *Federal work-study:* Total amount: $506,837; 337 jobs averaging $1504. *State or other work-study/employment:* Total amount: $1,480,884 (100% non-need-based). 624 part-time jobs averaging $2373.

ATHLETIC AWARDS *Total amount:* $1,567,852 (100% non-need-based).

APPLYING FOR FINANCIAL AID *Required financial aid forms:* FAFSA, institution's own form. *Financial aid deadline (priority):* 3/15. *Notification date:* Continuous beginning 5/15. Students must reply within 2 weeks of notification.

CONTACT Mrs. Vicki Adams, Director of Financial Aid, Jacksonville State University, 700 Pelham Road North, Jacksonville, AL 36265-9982, 256-782-5006 Ext. 8399 or toll-free 800-231-5291. *Fax:* 256-782-5476. *E-mail:* finaid@jsu.edu.

JACKSONVILLE UNIVERSITY
Jacksonville, FL

ABOUT THE INSTITUTION Independent, coed. Awards: bachelor's and master's degrees and first professional certificates. 58 undergraduate majors. Total enrollment: 2,948. Undergraduates: 2,561. Freshmen: 466.

GIFT AID (NEED-BASED) *Scholarships, grants, and awards:* Federal Pell, FSEOG, state, private, college/university gift aid from institutional funds.

GIFT AID (NON-NEED-BASED) *Scholarships, grants, and awards by category:* *Academic Interests/Achievement:* business, general academic interests/achievements. *Creative Arts/Performance:* general creative arts/performance. *Special Achievements/Activities:* community service, general special achievements/

activities, leadership. *Special Characteristics:* children and siblings of alumni, children of current students, children of faculty/staff, international students, siblings of current students, spouses of current students.

LOANS *Programs:* FFEL (Subsidized and Unsubsidized Stafford, PLUS), Perkins, college/university.

WORK-STUDY *Federal work-study:* Total amount: $321,285; 200 jobs averaging $2000.

APPLYING FOR FINANCIAL AID *Required financial aid forms:* FAFSA, institution's own form.

CONTACT Mrs. Catherine Huntress, Director of Student Financial Assistance, Jacksonville University, 2800 University Boulevard North, Jacksonville, FL 32211, 904-256-7060 or toll-free 800-225-2027. *Fax:* 904-256-7148. *E-mail:* chuntres@ju.edu.

JAMES MADISON UNIVERSITY
Harrisonburg, VA

Tuition & fees (VA res): $5476   **Average undergraduate aid package: $6342**

ABOUT THE INSTITUTION State-supported, coed. Awards: bachelor's, master's, and doctoral degrees and post-master's certificates (also offers specialist in education degree). 42 undergraduate majors. Total enrollment: 16,108. Undergraduates: 14,954. Freshmen: 3,285. Federal methodology is used as a basis for awarding need-based institutional aid.

UNDERGRADUATE EXPENSES for 2004–05 *Application fee:* $40. *Tuition, state resident:* full-time $5476. *Tuition, nonresident:* full-time $14,420. Part-time tuition and fees vary according to course load. *College room and board:* $6116; *room only:* $3166. Room and board charges vary according to board plan and housing facility. *Payment plan:* Installment.

FRESHMAN FINANCIAL AID (Fall 2004, est.) 2334 applied for aid; of those 53% were deemed to have need. 82% of freshmen with need received aid; of those 58% had need fully met. *Average percent of need met:* 34% (excluding resources awarded to replace EFC). *Average financial aid package:* $7875 (excluding resources awarded to replace EFC). 4% of all full-time freshmen had no need and received non-need-based gift aid.

UNDERGRADUATE FINANCIAL AID (Fall 2004, est.) 10,902 applied for aid; of those 63% were deemed to have need. 61% of undergraduates with need received aid; of those 45% had need fully met. *Average percent of need met:* 30% (excluding resources awarded to replace EFC). *Average financial aid package:* $6342 (excluding resources awarded to replace EFC). 2% of all full-time undergraduates had no need and received non-need-based gift aid.

GIFT AID (NEED-BASED) *Total amount:* $8,101,046 (43% federal, 42% state, 3% institutional, 12% external sources). *Receiving aid:* Freshmen: 16% (519); All full-time undergraduates: 13% (1,807). *Average award:* Freshmen: $4673; Undergraduates: $4029. *Scholarships, grants, and awards:* Federal Pell, FSEOG, state, private, college/university gift aid from institutional funds.

GIFT AID (NON-NEED-BASED) *Total amount:* $2,726,494 (3% state, 68% institutional, 29% external sources). *Receiving aid:* Freshmen: 11% (369); Undergraduates: 8% (1,084). *Average Award:* Freshmen: $1626; Undergraduates: $1525. *Scholarships, grants, and awards by category:* *Academic Interests/Achievement:* 382 awards ($572,445 total): architecture, biological sciences, business, computer science, education, engineering/technologies, English, general academic interests/achievements, health fields, humanities, international studies, mathematics, military science, physical sciences, premedicine, religion/biblical studies, social sciences. *Creative Arts/Performance:* 154 awards ($145,605 total): art/fine arts, cinema/film/broadcasting, dance, journalism/publications, music, theater/drama. *Special Achievements/Activities:* 97 awards ($51,645 total): cheerleading/drum major, general special achievements/activities, leadership. *Special Characteristics:* 143 awards ($524,578 total): children and siblings of alumni, children of faculty/staff, siblings of current students. *Tuition waivers:* Full or partial for employees or children of employees, senior citizens. *ROTC:* Army, Air Force cooperative.

LOANS *Student loans:* $29,854,502 (49% need-based, 51% non-need-based). 47% of past graduating class borrowed through all loan programs. *Average indebtedness per student:* $12,303. *Average need-based loan:* Freshmen: $2873; Undergraduates: $3670. *Parent loans:* $25,654,121 (100% non-need-based). *Programs:* FFEL (Subsidized and Unsubsidized Stafford, PLUS), Perkins.

WORK-STUDY *Federal work-study:* Total amount: $2,587,589; 2,022 jobs averaging $1280. *State or other work-study/employment:* Total amount: $2,861,061 (100% non-need-based). Part-time jobs available.

ATHLETIC AWARDS *Total amount:* $3,132,428 (100% non-need-based).

APPLYING FOR FINANCIAL AID *Required financial aid form:* FAFSA. *Financial aid deadline (priority):* 3/1. *Notification date:* Continuous beginning 4/1. Students must reply within 4 weeks of notification.

CONTACT Lisa L. Tumer, Director of Financial Aid and Scholarships, James Madison University, Warren Hall B504, MSC 3519, Harrisonburg, VA 22807, 540-568-7820.

JAMESTOWN COLLEGE
Jamestown, ND

Tuition & fees: $10,000	Average undergraduate aid package: $8002

ABOUT THE INSTITUTION Independent Presbyterian, coed. Awards: bachelor's degrees. 43 undergraduate majors. Total enrollment: 1,064. Undergraduates: 1,064. Freshmen: 241. Both federal and institutional methodology are used as a basis for awarding need-based institutional aid.

UNDERGRADUATE EXPENSES for 2005–06 *Application fee:* $20. *Comprehensive fee:* $14,130 includes full-time tuition ($10,000) and room and board ($4130). Room and board charges vary according to board plan. *Part-time tuition:* $280 per credit. Part-time tuition and fees vary according to course load. *Payment plan:* Installment.

FRESHMAN FINANCIAL AID (Fall 2004, est.) 208 applied for aid; of those 93% were deemed to have need. 100% of freshmen with need received aid; of those 21% had need fully met. *Average percent of need met:* 70% (excluding resources awarded to replace EFC). *Average financial aid package:* $8102 (excluding resources awarded to replace EFC). 16% of all full-time freshmen had no need and received non-need-based gift aid.

UNDERGRADUATE FINANCIAL AID (Fall 2004, est.) 864 applied for aid; of those 97% were deemed to have need. 100% of undergraduates with need received aid; of those 20% had need fully met. *Average percent of need met:* 66% (excluding resources awarded to replace EFC). *Average financial aid package:* $8002 (excluding resources awarded to replace EFC). 14% of all full-time undergraduates had no need and received non-need-based gift aid.

GIFT AID (NEED-BASED) *Total amount:* $3,245,549 (35% federal, 3% state, 54% institutional, 8% external sources). *Receiving aid:* Freshmen: 84% (193); All full-time undergraduates: 85% (831). *Average award:* Freshmen: $5361; Undergraduates: $4477. *Scholarships, grants, and awards:* Federal Pell, FSEOG, state, private, college/university gift aid from institutional funds, Federal Nursing.

GIFT AID (NON-NEED-BASED) *Total amount:* $531,139 (1% state, 88% institutional, 11% external sources). *Receiving aid:* Freshmen: 9% (21); Undergraduates: 7% (66). *Average Award:* Freshmen: $7043; Undergraduates: $7705. *Scholarships, grants, and awards by category: Academic Interests/Achievement:* 311 awards ($816,206 total): general academic interests/achievements, physical sciences. *Creative Arts/Performance:* 9 awards ($4500 total): art/fine arts. *Special Achievements/Activities:* 20 awards ($11,500 total): leadership. *Special Characteristics:* 26 awards ($106,250 total): children of faculty/staff, general special characteristics, international students, relatives of clergy. *Tuition waivers:* Full or partial for employees or children of employees.

LOANS *Student loans:* $5,124,861 (70% need-based, 30% non-need-based). 92% of past graduating class borrowed through all loan programs. *Average indebtedness per student:* $17,488. *Average need-based loan:* Freshmen: $3222; Undergraduates: $4008. *Parent loans:* $288,316 (37% need-based, 63% non-need-based). *Programs:* FFEL (Subsidized and Unsubsidized Stafford, PLUS), Perkins, college/university, alternative loans.

WORK-STUDY *Federal work-study:* Total amount: $219,358; 323 jobs averaging $679. *State or other work-study/employment:* Total amount: $41,250 (100% non-need-based). 54 part-time jobs averaging $764.

ATHLETIC AWARDS *Total amount:* $596,782 (74% need-based, 26% non-need-based).

APPLYING FOR FINANCIAL AID *Required financial aid form:* FAFSA. *Financial aid deadline (priority):* 3/15. *Notification date:* Continuous beginning 4/1. Students must reply within 6 weeks of notification.

CONTACT Margery Michael, Director of Financial Aid, Jamestown College, 6085 College Lane, Jamestown, ND 58405, 701-252-3467 Ext. 2556 or toll-free 800-336-2554. *Fax:* 701-253-4318. *E-mail:* mmichael@jc.edu.

JARVIS CHRISTIAN COLLEGE
Hawkins, TX

CONTACT Assistant Director of Financial Aid, Jarvis Christian College, PO Box 1470, Hawkins, TX 75765, 903-769-5743. *Fax:* 903-769-4842.

JEFFERSON COLLEGE OF HEALTH SCIENCES
Roanoke, VA

ABOUT THE INSTITUTION Independent, coed. Awards: associate and bachelor's degrees. 13 undergraduate majors. Total enrollment: 697. Undergraduates: 697. Freshmen: 77.

GIFT AID (NEED-BASED) *Scholarships, grants, and awards:* Federal Pell, FSEOG, state, private, college/university gift aid from institutional funds.

GIFT AID (NON-NEED-BASED) *Scholarships, grants, and awards by category: Academic Interests/Achievement:* biological sciences, health fields. *Special Characteristics:* local/state students.

LOANS *Programs:* FFEL (Subsidized and Unsubsidized Stafford, PLUS), alternative loans.

WORK-STUDY *Federal work-study:* Total amount: $77,476; jobs available.

APPLYING FOR FINANCIAL AID *Required financial aid forms:* FAFSA, state aid form.

CONTACT Debra A. Johnson, Director of Financial Aid, Jefferson College of Health Sciences, 920 South Jefferson Street, PO Box 13186, Roanoke, VA 24031-3186, 540-985-8492 or toll-free 888-985-8483. *Fax:* 540-224-6916. *E-mail:* djohnson@jchs.edu.

JEWISH HOSPITAL COLLEGE OF NURSING AND ALLIED HEALTH
St. Louis, MO

See Barnes-Jewish College of Nursing and Allied Health.

THE JEWISH THEOLOGICAL SEMINARY
New York, NY

CONTACT Linda Levine, Registrar/Director of Financial Aid, The Jewish Theological Seminary, 3080 Broadway, New York, NY 10027-4649, 212-678-8007. *Fax:* 212-678-8947. *E-mail:* financialaid@jtsa.edu.

JOHN BROWN UNIVERSITY
Siloam Springs, AR

Tuition & fees: $14,434	Average undergraduate aid package: $9149

ABOUT THE INSTITUTION Independent interdenominational, coed. Awards: bachelor's and master's degrees. 60 undergraduate majors. Total enrollment: 1,928. Undergraduates: 1,712. Freshmen: 295. Federal methodology is used as a basis for awarding need-based institutional aid.

UNDERGRADUATE EXPENSES for 2004–05 *Application fee:* $25. *Comprehensive fee:* $19,758 includes full-time tuition ($13,724), mandatory fees ($710), and room and board ($5324). Full-time tuition and fees vary according to program. Room and board charges vary according to board plan and housing facility. *Part-time tuition:* $572 per semester hour. Part-time tuition and fees vary according to course load and program. *Payment plan:* Installment.

FRESHMAN FINANCIAL AID (Fall 2004, est.) 224 applied for aid; of those 83% were deemed to have need. 99% of freshmen with need received aid; of those 8% had need fully met. *Average percent of need met:* 50% (excluding resources awarded to replace EFC). *Average financial aid package:* $8713 (excluding resources awarded to replace EFC). 30% of all full-time freshmen had no need and received non-need-based gift aid.

UNDERGRADUATE FINANCIAL AID (Fall 2004, est.) 1,162 applied for aid; of those 87% were deemed to have need. 100% of undergraduates with need received aid; of those 8% had need fully met. *Average percent of need met:* 50% (excluding resources awarded to replace EFC). *Average financial aid package:* $9149 (excluding resources awarded to replace EFC). 18% of all full-time undergraduates had no need and received non-need-based gift aid.

GIFT AID (NEED-BASED) *Total amount:* $5,187,856 (29% federal, 7% state, 64% institutional). *Receiving aid:* Freshmen: 57% (168); All full-time undergraduates: 48% (788). *Average award:* Freshmen: $4400; Undergraduates: $4016. *Scholarships, grants, and awards:* Federal Pell, FSEOG, state, private, college/university gift aid from institutional funds.

GIFT AID (NON-NEED-BASED) *Total amount:* $1,321,437 (9% state, 91% institutional). *Receiving aid:* Freshmen: 56% (167); Undergraduates: 39%

(633). *Average Award: Freshmen:* $4480; *Undergraduates:* $3763. *Scholarships, grants, and awards by category: Academic Interests/Achievement:* 782 awards ($2,189,089 total): general academic interests/achievements. *Creative Arts/Performance:* 72 awards ($98,705 total): journalism/publications, music. *Special Achievements/Activities:* 246 awards ($238,650 total): cheerleading/drum major, leadership. *Special Characteristics:* 359 awards ($847,555 total): children and siblings of alumni, children of educators, children of faculty/staff, ethnic background, international students, members of minority groups, relatives of clergy, siblings of current students. *Tuition waivers:* Full or partial for minority students, children of alumni, employees or children of employees, adult students, senior citizens. *ROTC:* Army cooperative, Air Force cooperative.
LOANS *Student loans:* $6,018,603 (97% need-based, 3% non-need-based). 60% of past graduating class borrowed through all loan programs. *Average indebtedness per student:* $17,400. *Average need-based loan:* Freshmen: $3756; Undergraduates: $4387. *Parent loans:* $1,488,266 (90% need-based, 10% non-need-based). *Programs:* FFEL (Subsidized and Unsubsidized Stafford, PLUS), Perkins, state.
WORK-STUDY *Federal work-study:* Total amount: $370,765; 267 jobs averaging $1397. *State or other work-study/employment:* Total amount: $319,775 (91% need-based, 9% non-need-based). 227 part-time jobs averaging $1339.
ATHLETIC AWARDS *Total amount:* $1,063,324 (95% need-based, 5% non-need-based).
APPLYING FOR FINANCIAL AID *Required financial aid forms:* FAFSA, institution's own form. *Financial aid deadline (priority):* 3/1. *Notification date:* Continuous. Students must reply within 4 weeks of notification.
CONTACT Mrs. Emily Nichols, Assistant Director of Student Financial Aid, John Brown University, 2000 West University Street, Siloam Springs, AR 72761-2121, 479-524-7115 or toll-free 877-JBU-INFO. *Fax:* 479-524-7405. *E-mail:* emnichols@jbu.edu.

JOHN CARROLL UNIVERSITY
University Heights, OH

CONTACT Financial Aid Counselor, John Carroll University, 20700 North Park Boulevard, University Heights, OH 44118-4581, 216-397-4248. *Fax:* 216-397-3098. *E-mail:* jcuofa@jcu.edu.

JOHN F. KENNEDY UNIVERSITY
Pleasant Hill, CA

Tuition & fees: $14,436   **Average undergraduate aid package: $7000**

ABOUT THE INSTITUTION Independent, coed. Awards: bachelor's, master's, doctoral, and first professional degrees and post-bachelor's certificates. 6 undergraduate majors. Total enrollment: 1,653. Undergraduates: 197. Federal methodology is used as a basis for awarding need-based institutional aid.
UNDERGRADUATE EXPENSES for 2004–05 *Application fee:* $50. *Tuition:* full-time $14,304; part-time $298 per quarter hour. *Required fees:* full-time $132; $44 per term part-time. Full-time tuition and fees vary according to course load and program. Part-time tuition and fees vary according to course load and program. *Payment plan:* Deferred payment.
UNDERGRADUATE FINANCIAL AID (Fall 2003) 11 applied for aid; of those 100% were deemed to have need. 100% of undergraduates with need received aid; of those 100% had need fully met. *Average percent of need met:* 60% (excluding resources awarded to replace EFC). *Average financial aid package:* $7000 (excluding resources awarded to replace EFC).
GIFT AID (NEED-BASED) *Total amount:* $190,276 (76% federal, 18% state, 6% institutional). *Receiving aid:* All full-time undergraduates: 16% (4). *Average award:* Undergraduates: $1000. *Scholarships, grants, and awards:* Federal Pell, FSEOG, state, private, college/university gift aid from institutional funds.
GIFT AID (NON-NEED-BASED) *Tuition waivers:* Full or partial for employees or children of employees.
LOANS *Student loans:* $5,000,000 (100% need-based). 51% of past graduating class borrowed through all loan programs. *Average indebtedness per student:* $23,000. *Average need-based loan:* Undergraduates: $6000. *Parent loans:* $50,000 (100% need-based). *Programs:* FFEL (Subsidized and Unsubsidized Stafford, PLUS), Perkins, college/university.
APPLYING FOR FINANCIAL AID *Required financial aid forms:* FAFSA, institution's own form. *Financial aid deadline (priority):* 3/2. *Notification date:* Continuous.
CONTACT Mindy Bergeron, Director of Financial Aid, John F. Kennedy University, 100 Ellinwood Way, Pleasant Hill, CA 94523, 925-969-3385 or toll-free 800-696-JFKU. *Fax:* 925-969-3390. *E-mail:* bergeron@jfku.edu.

JOHN JAY COLLEGE OF CRIMINAL JUSTICE OF THE CITY UNIVERSITY OF NEW YORK
New York, NY

Tuition & fees (NY res): $4259   **Average undergraduate aid package: $5100**

ABOUT THE INSTITUTION State and locally supported, coed. Awards: associate, bachelor's, master's, and doctoral degrees and post-bachelor's certificates. 16 undergraduate majors. Total enrollment: 12,984. Undergraduates: 11,515. Federal methodology is used as a basis for awarding need-based institutional aid.
UNDERGRADUATE EXPENSES for 2005–06 *Application fee:* $50. *Tuition, state resident:* full-time $4000; part-time $170 per credit. *Tuition, nonresident:* full-time $8640; part-time $360 per credit. *Required fees:* full-time $259; $82.35 per term part-time. Full-time tuition and fees vary according to course level and course load. Part-time tuition and fees vary according to course level and course load. *Payment plan:* Installment.
FRESHMAN FINANCIAL AID (Fall 2003) 2110 applied for aid; of those 100% were deemed to have need. 70% of freshmen with need received aid. *Average percent of need met:* 70% (excluding resources awarded to replace EFC). *Average financial aid package:* $5100 (excluding resources awarded to replace EFC). 1% of all full-time freshmen had no need and received non-need-based gift aid.
UNDERGRADUATE FINANCIAL AID (Fall 2003) 10,448 applied for aid; of those 100% were deemed to have need. 70% of undergraduates with need received aid. *Average percent of need met:* 70% (excluding resources awarded to replace EFC). *Average financial aid package:* $5100 (excluding resources awarded to replace EFC). 1% of all full-time undergraduates had no need and received non-need-based gift aid.
GIFT AID (NEED-BASED) *Total amount:* $36,657,549 (53% federal, 46% state, 1% institutional). *Scholarships, grants, and awards:* Federal Pell, FSEOG, state, college/university gift aid from institutional funds.
GIFT AID (NON-NEED-BASED) *Total amount:* $2,455,770 (45% federal, 31% state, 3% institutional, 21% external sources). *Average Award: Freshmen:* $500; *Undergraduates:* $500. *Scholarships, grants, and awards by category: Academic Interests/Achievement:* general academic interests/achievements. *ROTC:* Air Force cooperative.
LOANS *Student loans:* $16,517,739 (76% need-based, 24% non-need-based). 50% of past graduating class borrowed through all loan programs. *Average indebtedness per student:* $10,000. *Average need-based loan:* Freshmen: $2400; Undergraduates: $2400. *Parent loans:* $625,623 (70% need-based, 30% non-need-based). *Programs:* Federal Direct (Subsidized and Unsubsidized Stafford, PLUS), Perkins, alternative loans.
WORK-STUDY *Federal work-study:* Total amount: $523,879; 442 jobs averaging $1064. *State or other work-study/employment:* Part-time jobs available.
APPLYING FOR FINANCIAL AID *Required financial aid form:* FAFSA. *Financial aid deadline (priority):* 6/1. *Notification date:* Continuous. Students must reply within 2 weeks of notification.
CONTACT Mr. Arnold Osansky, Associate Director of Financial Aid, John Jay College of Criminal Justice of the City University of New York, 445 West 59th Street, New York, NY 10019-1093, 212-237-8158 or toll-free 877-JOHNJAY. *Fax:* 212-237-8936. *E-mail:* aosansky@jjay.cuny.edu.

THE JOHNS HOPKINS UNIVERSITY
Baltimore, MD

Tuition & fees: $30,140   **Average undergraduate aid package: $26,818**

ABOUT THE INSTITUTION Independent, coed. Awards: bachelor's, master's, doctoral, and first professional degrees and post-bachelor's and post-master's certificates. 64 undergraduate majors. Total enrollment: 5,898. Undergraduates: 4,273. Freshmen: 1,050. Both federal and institutional methodology are used as a basis for awarding need-based institutional aid.
UNDERGRADUATE EXPENSES for 2004–05 *Application fee:* $60. *One-time required fee:* $500. *Comprehensive fee:* $39,656 includes full-time tuition ($30,140) and room and board ($9516). *College room only:* $5456. Room and board charges vary according to board plan and housing facility. *Payment plan:* Installment.
FRESHMAN FINANCIAL AID (Fall 2004, est.) 755 applied for aid; of those 62% were deemed to have need. 100% of freshmen with need received aid; of those 100% had need fully met. *Average percent of need met:* 100% (excluding

resources awarded to replace EFC). *Average financial aid package:* $27,319 (excluding resources awarded to replace EFC). 5% of all full-time freshmen had no need and received non-need-based gift aid.

UNDERGRADUATE FINANCIAL AID (Fall 2004, est.) 3,617 applied for aid; of those 56% were deemed to have need. 87% of undergraduates with need received aid; of those 100% had need fully met. *Average percent of need met:* 95% (excluding resources awarded to replace EFC). *Average financial aid package:* $26,818 (excluding resources awarded to replace EFC). 6% of all full-time undergraduates had no need and received non-need-based gift aid.

GIFT AID (NEED-BASED) *Total amount:* $35,847,780 (5% federal, 1% state, 90% institutional, 4% external sources). *Receiving aid:* Freshmen: 39% (410); All full-time undergraduates: 38% (1,598). *Average award:* Freshmen $22,549; Undergraduates: $21,103. *Scholarships, grants, and awards:* Federal Pell, FSEOG, state, private, college/university gift aid from institutional funds.

GIFT AID (NON-NEED-BASED) *Total amount:* $4,458,548 (20% federal, 8% state, 65% institutional, 7% external sources). *Receiving aid:* Freshmen: 27% (285); Undergraduates: 23% (956). *Average Award:* Freshmen: $7722; Undergraduates: $13,016. *Scholarships, grants, and awards by category:* Academic Interests/Achievement: 20 awards ($400,000 total): engineering/technologies, general academic interests/achievements. Special Characteristics: 26 awards ($386,662 total): children of faculty/staff. *Tuition waivers:* Full or partial for employees or children of employees. *ROTC:* Army, Air Force cooperative.

LOANS *Student loans:* $7,222,009 (84% need-based, 16% non-need-based). 52% of past graduating class borrowed through all loan programs. *Average indebtedness per student:* $14,000. *Average need-based loan:* Freshmen: $2556; Undergraduates: $3959. *Parent loans:* $9,427,791 (100% non-need-based). *Programs:* Federal Direct (Subsidized and Unsubsidized Stafford), FFEL (PLUS), Perkins, college/university.

WORK-STUDY *Federal work-study:* Total amount: $3,230,614; 1,381 jobs averaging $1878. *State or other work-study/employment:* Part-time jobs available.

ATHLETIC AWARDS *Total amount:* $1,027,357 (100% non-need-based).

APPLYING FOR FINANCIAL AID *Required financial aid forms:* FAFSA, CSS Financial Aid PROFILE, noncustodial (divorced/separated) parent's statement, business/farm supplement, prior and current year federal income tax form(s). *Financial aid deadline:* 2/15 (priority: 2/1). *Notification date:* 4/1. Students must reply by 5/1 or within 2 weeks of notification.

CONTACT Dr. Ellen Frishberg, University Director of Student Financial Services, The Johns Hopkins University, 146 Garland Hall, Baltimore, MD 21218, 410-516-8028. *Fax:* 410-516-6015. *E-mail:* efrish@jhu.edu.

JOHNSON & WALES UNIVERSITY
Denver, CO

ABOUT THE INSTITUTION Independent, coed. Awards: associate and bachelor's degrees. 3 undergraduate majors. Total enrollment: 1,512. Undergraduates: 1,512.

GIFT AID (NEED-BASED) *Scholarships, grants, and awards:* Federal Pell, FSEOG, state, college/university gift aid from institutional funds.

GIFT AID (NON-NEED-BASED) *Scholarships, grants, and awards by category:* Academic Interests/Achievement: general academic interests/achievements. Special Achievements/Activities: leadership, memberships. Special Characteristics: children of current students, children of faculty/staff, siblings of current students, spouses of current students.

LOANS *Programs:* FFEL (Subsidized and Unsubsidized Stafford, PLUS), Perkins, college/university.

WORK-STUDY *Federal work-study:* Total amount: $589,350; jobs available.

APPLYING FOR FINANCIAL AID *Required financial aid form:* FAFSA.

CONTACT Ms. Lynn Robinson, Director of Financial Aid, Johnson & Wales University, 8 Abbott Park Place, Providence, RI 02903, 401-598-4648 or toll-free 877-598-3368. *Fax:* 401-598-1040. *E-mail:* fp@jwu.edu.

JOHNSON & WALES UNIVERSITY
North Miami, FL

ABOUT THE INSTITUTION Independent, coed. Awards: associate and bachelor's degrees. 11 undergraduate majors. Total enrollment: 2,389. Undergraduates: 2,389.

GIFT AID (NEED-BASED) *Scholarships, grants, and awards:* Federal Pell, FSEOG, state, college/university gift aid from institutional funds.

GIFT AID (NON-NEED-BASED) *Scholarships, grants, and awards by category:* Academic Interests/Achievement: general academic interests/achievements.

Special Achievements/Activities: leadership, memberships. Special Characteristics: children of current students, children of faculty/staff, siblings of current students, spouses of current students.

LOANS *Programs:* FFEL (Subsidized and Unsubsidized Stafford, PLUS), Perkins, college/university.

WORK-STUDY *Federal work-study:* Total amount: $1,076,301; jobs available. *State or other work-study/employment:* Part-time jobs available.

APPLYING FOR FINANCIAL AID *Required financial aid form:* FAFSA.

CONTACT Ms. Lynn Robinson, Director of Financial Aid, Johnson & Wales University, 8 Abbott Park Place, Providence, RI 02903, 401-598-4648 or toll-free 800-232-2433. *Fax:* 401-598-1040. *E-mail:* fp@jwu.edu.

JOHNSON & WALES UNIVERSITY
Charlotte, NC

CONTACT Financial Aid Office, Johnson & Wales University, 901 West Trade Street, Suite 175, Charlotte, NC 28202, 980-598-1000 or toll-free 866-598-2427.

JOHNSON & WALES UNIVERSITY
Providence, RI

Tuition & fees: $20,100   **Average undergraduate aid package: $11,459**

ABOUT THE INSTITUTION Independent, coed. Awards: associate, bachelor's, master's, and doctoral degrees (branch locations in Charleston, SC; Denver, CO; North Miami, FL; Norfolk, VA; Gothenberg, Sweden). 47 undergraduate majors. Total enrollment: 9,982. Undergraduates: 9,246. Federal methodology is used as a basis for awarding need-based institutional aid.

UNDERGRADUATE EXPENSES for 2005–06 *Comprehensive fee:* $27,645 includes full-time tuition ($19,200), mandatory fees ($900), and room and board ($7545). *Part-time tuition:* $355 per quarter hour. *Payment plans:* Installment, deferred payment.

FRESHMAN FINANCIAL AID (Fall 2003) 2070 applied for aid; of those 86% were deemed to have need. 99% of freshmen with need received aid; of those 4% had need fully met. *Average percent of need met:* 66% (excluding resources awarded to replace EFC). *Average financial aid package:* $12,848 (excluding resources awarded to replace EFC). 5% of all full-time freshmen had no need and received non-need-based gift aid.

UNDERGRADUATE FINANCIAL AID (Fall 2003) 6,934 applied for aid; of those 88% were deemed to have need. 96% of undergraduates with need received aid; of those 71% had need fully met. *Average percent of need met:* 69% (excluding resources awarded to replace EFC). *Average financial aid package:* $11,459 (excluding resources awarded to replace EFC). 4% of all full-time undergraduates had no need and received non-need-based gift aid.

GIFT AID (NEED-BASED) *Total amount:* $18,217,754 (46% federal, 5% state, 49% institutional). *Receiving aid:* Freshmen: 63% (1,527); All full-time undergraduates: 49% (4,472). *Average award:* Freshmen: $4560; Undergraduates: $4065. *Scholarships, grants, and awards:* Federal Pell, FSEOG, state, college/university gift aid from institutional funds.

GIFT AID (NON-NEED-BASED) *Total amount:* $14,215,272 (2% federal, 1% state, 77% institutional, 20% external sources). *Receiving aid:* Freshmen: 41% (1,002); Undergraduates: 38% (3,500). *Average Award:* Freshmen: $3633; Undergraduates: $3239. *Scholarships, grants, and awards by category:* Academic Interests/Achievement: general academic interests/achievements. Special Achievements/Activities: leadership, memberships. Special Characteristics: children of current students, children of faculty/staff, siblings of current students, spouses of current students.

LOANS *Student loans:* $52,921,045 (56% need-based, 44% non-need-based). 76% of past graduating class borrowed through all loan programs. *Average indebtedness per student:* $20,268. *Average need-based loan:* Freshmen: $5593; Undergraduates: $5250. *Parent loans:* $13,184,323 (100% non-need-based). *Programs:* FFEL (Subsidized and Unsubsidized Stafford, PLUS), Perkins, college/university.

WORK-STUDY *Federal work-study:* Total amount: $4,101,947; jobs available.

APPLYING FOR FINANCIAL AID *Required financial aid form:* FAFSA. *Financial aid deadline:* Continuous. *Notification date:* Continuous beginning 3/1. Students must reply within 2 weeks of notification.

CONTACT Ms. Lynn Robinson, Director of Financial Aid, Johnson & Wales University, 8 Abbott Park Place, Providence, RI 02903, 401-598-4648 or toll-free 800-598-1000 (in-state), 800-342-5598 (out-of-state). *Fax:* 401-598-1040.

JOHNSON BIBLE COLLEGE
Knoxville, TN

Tuition & fees: $6490	Average undergraduate aid package: $3231

ABOUT THE INSTITUTION Independent religious, coed. Awards: associate, bachelor's, and master's degrees. 6 undergraduate majors. Total enrollment: 889. Undergraduates: 756. Freshmen: 147. Federal methodology is used as a basis for awarding need-based institutional aid.

UNDERGRADUATE EXPENSES for 2005–06 *Application fee:* $35. *Comprehensive fee:* $10,580 includes full-time tuition ($5800), mandatory fees ($690), and room and board ($4090). *College room only:* $2595. Room and board charges vary according to board plan and housing facility. *Part-time tuition:* $242 per semester hour. *Part-time fees:* $20.42 per semester hour. Part-time tuition and fees vary according to course load. *Payment plan:* Installment.

FRESHMAN FINANCIAL AID (Fall 2004, est.) 147 applied for aid; of those 80% were deemed to have need. 100% of freshmen with need received aid. *Average percent of need met:* 41% (excluding resources awarded to replace EFC). *Average financial aid package:* $3037 (excluding resources awarded to replace EFC).

UNDERGRADUATE FINANCIAL AID (Fall 2004, est.) 693 applied for aid; of those 89% were deemed to have need. 100% of undergraduates with need received aid. *Average percent of need met:* 42% (excluding resources awarded to replace EFC). *Average financial aid package:* $3231 (excluding resources awarded to replace EFC).

GIFT AID (NEED-BASED) *Total amount:* $2,628,054 (13% federal, 3% state, 84% institutional). *Receiving aid:* Freshmen: 79% (117); All full-time undergraduates: 83% (599). *Average award:* Freshmen: $1526; Undergraduates: $1647. *Scholarships, grants, and awards:* Federal Pell, FSEOG, state, private, college/university gift aid from institutional funds.

GIFT AID (NON-NEED-BASED) *Total amount:* $399,803 (100% external sources). *Receiving aid:* Freshmen: 49% (72); Undergraduates: 41% (299). *Scholarships, grants, and awards by category: Academic Interests/Achievement:* 685 awards ($860,631 total): communication, education, general academic interests/achievements, religion/biblical studies. *Creative Arts/Performance:* 8 awards ($6250 total): art/fine arts, general creative arts/performance, music. *Special Achievements/Activities:* 54 awards ($71,830 total): community service, general special achievements/activities, leadership, religious involvement. *Special Characteristics:* 336 awards ($317,129 total): children of current students, children of educators, children of faculty/staff, ethnic background, general special characteristics, international students, married students, members of minority groups, parents of current students, relatives of clergy, religious affiliation, siblings of current students, spouses of current students. *Tuition waivers:* Full or partial for employees or children of employees.

LOANS *Student loans:* $912,663 (61% need-based, 39% non-need-based). 53% of past graduating class borrowed through all loan programs. *Average indebtedness per student:* $14,776. *Average need-based loan:* Freshmen: $1040; Undergraduates: $1614. *Parent loans:* $182,097 (100% non-need-based). *Programs:* FFEL (Subsidized and Unsubsidized Stafford, PLUS), college/university, alternative loans.

WORK-STUDY *Federal work-study:* Total amount: $65,772; 99 jobs averaging $664.

APPLYING FOR FINANCIAL AID *Required financial aid forms:* FAFSA, institution's own form. *Financial aid deadline (priority):* 5/1. *Notification date:* Continuous beginning 5/15. Students must reply within 2 weeks of notification.

CONTACT Mrs. Janette Overton, Financial Aid Director, Johnson Bible College, 7900 Johnson Drive, Knoxville, TN 37998, 865-251-2303 Ext. 2292 or toll-free 800-827-2122. *Fax:* 865-251-2337. *E-mail:* joverton@jbc.edu.

JOHNSON C. SMITH UNIVERSITY
Charlotte, NC

Tuition & fees: $13,712	Average undergraduate aid package: $9725

ABOUT THE INSTITUTION Independent, coed. Awards: bachelor's degrees. 37 undergraduate majors. Total enrollment: 1,415. Undergraduates: 1,415. Freshmen: 431. Federal methodology is used as a basis for awarding need-based institutional aid.

UNDERGRADUATE EXPENSES for 2004–05 *Application fee:* $25. *Comprehensive fee:* $19,010 includes full-time tuition ($11,542), mandatory fees ($2170), and room and board ($5298). *College room only:* $3049. Full-time tuition and fees vary according to course load. Room and board charges vary according to board plan and housing facility. *Part-time tuition:* $361 per credit hour. *Part-time fees:* $229. Part-time tuition and fees vary according to course load and program. *Payment plan:* Installment.

FRESHMAN FINANCIAL AID (Fall 2003) 445 applied for aid; of those 88% were deemed to have need. 100% of freshmen with need received aid; of those 2% had need fully met. *Average percent of need met:* 40% (excluding resources awarded to replace EFC). *Average financial aid package:* $7625 (excluding resources awarded to replace EFC).

UNDERGRADUATE FINANCIAL AID (Fall 2003) 1,246 applied for aid; of those 96% were deemed to have need. 88% of undergraduates with need received aid; of those 3% had need fully met. *Average percent of need met:* 59% (excluding resources awarded to replace EFC). *Average financial aid package:* $9725 (excluding resources awarded to replace EFC).

GIFT AID (NEED-BASED) *Total amount:* $5,833,979 (62% federal, 18% state, 13% institutional, 7% external sources). *Receiving aid:* Freshmen: 78% (359); All full-time undergraduates: 75% (1,056). *Average award:* Freshmen: $3000; Undergraduates: $3000. *Scholarships, grants, and awards:* Federal Pell, FSEOG, state, private, college/university gift aid from institutional funds, United Negro College Fund.

GIFT AID (NON-NEED-BASED) *Receiving aid:* Freshmen: 18% (84); Undergraduates: 9% (126). *Scholarships, grants, and awards by category: Academic Interests/Achievement:* computer science, general academic interests/achievements, mathematics. *Creative Arts/Performance:* music. *Special Achievements/Activities:* community service, general special achievements/activities, leadership. *Special Characteristics:* children of faculty/staff, ethnic background, siblings of current students. *Tuition waivers:* Full or partial for employees or children of employees. *ROTC:* Army, Air Force cooperative.

LOANS *Student loans:* $9,229,532 (100% need-based). 90% of past graduating class borrowed through all loan programs. *Average indebtedness per student:* $25,000. *Average need-based loan:* Freshmen: $2625; Undergraduates: $5500. *Parent loans:* $6,613,596 (100% need-based). *Programs:* Federal Direct (Subsidized and Unsubsidized Stafford, PLUS), FFEL (PLUS), Perkins, alternative loans.

WORK-STUDY *Federal work-study:* Total amount: $531,215; 460 jobs averaging $1200.

ATHLETIC AWARDS *Total amount:* $761,636 (100% need-based).

APPLYING FOR FINANCIAL AID *Required financial aid form:* FAFSA. *Financial aid deadline:* Continuous. *Notification date:* Continuous beginning 3/15. Students must reply within 2 weeks of notification.

CONTACT Ms. Cynthia Anderson, Director of Financial Aid, Johnson C. Smith University, 100 Beatties Ford Road, Charlotte, NC 28216, 704-378-1035 or toll-free 800-782-7303. *Fax:* 704-378-1292.

JOHNSON STATE COLLEGE
Johnson, VT

ABOUT THE INSTITUTION State-supported, coed. Awards: associate, bachelor's, and master's degrees. 57 undergraduate majors. Total enrollment: 1,759. Undergraduates: 1,532. Freshmen: 277.

GIFT AID (NEED-BASED) *Scholarships, grants, and awards:* Federal Pell, FSEOG, state, private, college/university gift aid from institutional funds.

GIFT AID (NON-NEED-BASED) *Scholarships, grants, and awards by category: Academic Interests/Achievement:* business, education, general academic interests/achievements, mathematics. *Creative Arts/Performance:* art/fine arts, dance, music, performing arts, theater/drama. *Special Achievements/Activities:* community service, general special achievements/activities, leadership, memberships. *Special Characteristics:* general special characteristics, international students, local/state students, members of minority groups.

LOANS *Programs:* Federal Direct (Subsidized and Unsubsidized Stafford, PLUS), Perkins.

WORK-STUDY Federal work-study jobs available.

APPLYING FOR FINANCIAL AID *Required financial aid form:* FAFSA.

CONTACT Ms. Kimberly Goodell, Financial Aid Officer, Johnson State College, 337 College Hill, Johnson, VT 05656-9405, 802-635-2356 or toll-free 800-635-2356. *Fax:* 802-635-1463. *E-mail:* goodellk@badger.jsc.vsc.edu.

JOHN WESLEY COLLEGE
High Point, NC

Tuition & fees: $8220	Average undergraduate aid package: $8600

ABOUT THE INSTITUTION Independent interdenominational, coed. Awards: associate and bachelor's degrees. 10 undergraduate majors. Total enrollment: 171. Undergraduates: 171. Freshmen: 11. Federal methodology is used as a basis for awarding need-based institutional aid.
UNDERGRADUATE EXPENSES for 2004–05 *Application fee:* $35. *Tuition:* full-time $7810; part-time $360 per semester hour. *Required fees:* full-time $410; $205 per term part-time. Full-time tuition and fees vary according to course load. Part-time tuition and fees vary according to course load. Room and board charges vary according to housing facility. *Payment plan:* Installment.
FRESHMAN FINANCIAL AID (Fall 2003) 14 applied for aid; of those 100% were deemed to have need. 100% of freshmen with need received aid. *Average percent of need met:* 42% (excluding resources awarded to replace EFC). *Average financial aid package:* $7400 (excluding resources awarded to replace EFC). 13% of all full-time freshmen had no need and received non-need-based gift aid.
UNDERGRADUATE FINANCIAL AID (Fall 2003) 151 applied for aid; of those 97% were deemed to have need. 91% of undergraduates with need received aid. *Average percent of need met:* 53% (excluding resources awarded to replace EFC). *Average financial aid package:* $8600 (excluding resources awarded to replace EFC). 1% of all full-time undergraduates had no need and received non-need-based gift aid.
GIFT AID (NEED-BASED) *Total amount:* $248,743 (83% federal, 1% state, 16% institutional). *Receiving aid:* Freshmen: 88% (14); All full-time undergraduates: 45% (76). *Average award:* Freshmen: $1500; Undergraduates: $2025. *Scholarships, grants, and awards:* Federal Pell, FSEOG, private, college/university gift aid from institutional funds.
GIFT AID (NON-NEED-BASED) *Total amount:* $41,449 (87% institutional, 13% external sources). *Receiving aid:* Freshmen: 44% (7); Undergraduates: 15% (26). *Average Award: Freshmen:* $1000; *Undergraduates:* $1000. *Scholarships, grants, and awards by category: Academic Interests/Achievement:* 19 awards ($19,200 total): education, general academic interests/achievements, religion/biblical studies. *Special Achievements/Activities:* religious involvement. *Special Characteristics:* 17 awards ($36,200 total): children of faculty/staff, general special characteristics, married students, spouses of current students. *Tuition waivers:* Full or partial for employees or children of employees.
LOANS *Student loans:* $606,977 (63% need-based, 37% non-need-based). 65% of past graduating class borrowed through all loan programs. *Average indebtedness per student:* $15,000. *Average need-based loan:* Freshmen: $2625; Undergraduates: $4500. *Parent loans:* $29,008 (100% non-need-based). *Programs:* FFEL (Subsidized and Unsubsidized Stafford, PLUS).
WORK-STUDY *Federal work-study:* Total amount: $17,156; 10 jobs averaging $2710.
APPLYING FOR FINANCIAL AID *Required financial aid forms:* FAFSA, institution's own form. *Financial aid deadline (priority):* 3/15. *Notification date:* 4/1. Students must reply within 2 weeks of notification.
CONTACT Mrs. Shirley Carter, Director of Financial Aid, John Wesley College, 2314 North Centennial Street, High Point, NC 27265-3197, 336-889-2262. *Fax:* 336-889-2261. *E-mail:* scarter@johnwesley.edu.

JONES COLLEGE
Jacksonville, FL

CONTACT Mrs. Becky Davis, Director of Financial Assistance, Jones College, 5353 Arlington Expressway, Jacksonville, FL 32211-5540, 904-743-1122. *Fax:* 904-743-4446.

JONES COLLEGE
Miami, FL

CONTACT Financial Aid Office, Jones College, 11430 North Kendall Drive, Suite 200, Miami, FL 33176, 305-275-9996.

JONES INTERNATIONAL UNIVERSITY
Centennial, CO

Tuition & fees: $9407	Average undergraduate aid package: N/A

ABOUT THE INSTITUTION Proprietary, coed. Awards: bachelor's and master's degrees (offers only online degree programs). 9 undergraduate majors. Total enrollment: 1,146. Undergraduates: 413. Federal methodology is used as a basis for awarding need-based institutional aid.

UNDERGRADUATE EXPENSES for 2005–06 *Application fee:* $100. *Tuition:* full-time $8927; part-time $1116 per course. *Required fees:* full-time $480; $60 per course. Full-time tuition and fees vary according to course load and degree level. Part-time tuition and fees vary according to course load. *Payment plans:* Tuition prepayment, deferred payment.
GIFT AID (NEED-BASED) *Scholarships, grants, and awards:* Federal Pell, private, Sallie Mae CASHE Scholarships.
GIFT AID (NON-NEED-BASED) *Tuition waivers:* Full or partial for employees or children of employees.
LOANS *Programs:* Federal Direct (Subsidized and Unsubsidized Stafford, PLUS), Sallie Mae Loans, PLATO Loans, alternative loans.
APPLYING FOR FINANCIAL AID *Required financial aid forms:* FAFSA, noncustodial (divorced/separated) parent's statement, Master Promissory Note. *Financial aid deadline:* Continuous. *Notification date:* Continuous.
CONTACT Steve Bidwell, Director of Financial And Accounting, Jones International University, 9697 East Mineral Avenue, Englewood, CO 80112, 303-784-8284 or toll-free 800-811-5663. *Fax:* 303-784-8524. *E-mail:* marketing@jonesknowledge.com.

JUDSON COLLEGE
Marion, AL

Tuition & fees: $9950	Average undergraduate aid package: $10,001

ABOUT THE INSTITUTION Independent Baptist, women only. Awards: bachelor's degrees. 24 undergraduate majors. Total enrollment: 360. Undergraduates: 360. Freshmen: 69. Both federal and institutional methodology are used as a basis for awarding need-based institutional aid.
UNDERGRADUATE EXPENSES for 2005–06 *Application fee:* $25. *Comprehensive fee:* $16,050 includes full-time tuition ($9350), mandatory fees ($600), and room and board ($6100). Full-time tuition and fees vary according to course load. *Part-time tuition:* $305 per semester hour. Part-time tuition and fees vary according to course load. *Payment plan:* Installment.
FRESHMAN FINANCIAL AID (Fall 2004, est.) 69 applied for aid; of those 91% were deemed to have need. 100% of freshmen with need received aid; of those 17% had need fully met. *Average percent of need met:* 79% (excluding resources awarded to replace EFC). *Average financial aid package:* $10,763 (excluding resources awarded to replace EFC). 11% of all full-time freshmen had no need and received non-need-based gift aid.
UNDERGRADUATE FINANCIAL AID (Fall 2004, est.) 236 applied for aid; of those 91% were deemed to have need. 100% of undergraduates with need received aid; of those 17% had need fully met. *Average percent of need met:* 71% (excluding resources awarded to replace EFC). *Average financial aid package:* $10,001 (excluding resources awarded to replace EFC). 14% of all full-time undergraduates had no need and received non-need-based gift aid.
GIFT AID (NEED-BASED) *Total amount:* $1,355,184 (29% federal, 3% state, 56% institutional, 12% external sources). *Receiving aid:* Freshmen: 89% (63); All full-time undergraduates: 74% (214). *Average award:* Freshmen: $7258; Undergraduates: $5926. *Scholarships, grants, and awards:* Federal Pell, FSEOG, state, private, college/university gift aid from institutional funds.
GIFT AID (NON-NEED-BASED) *Total amount:* $237,058 (5% state, 93% institutional, 2% external sources). *Receiving aid:* Freshmen: 11% (8); Undergraduates: 6% (16). *Average Award: Freshmen:* $2072; *Undergraduates:* $3092. *Scholarships, grants, and awards by category: Academic Interests/Achievement:* 14 awards ($52,000 total): general academic interests/achievements. *Creative Arts/Performance:* 22 awards ($18,150 total): art/fine arts, music. *Special Achievements/Activities:* 6 awards ($3500 total): general special achievements/activities, junior miss. *Special Characteristics:* 21 awards ($115,140 total): children of educators, children of faculty/staff, relatives of clergy, religious affiliation. *Tuition waivers:* Full or partial for employees or children of employees. *ROTC:* Army cooperative.
LOANS *Student loans:* $932,696 (93% need-based, 7% non-need-based). 68% of past graduating class borrowed through all loan programs. *Average indebtedness per student:* $16,502. *Average need-based loan:* Freshmen: $2601; Undergraduates: $3341. *Parent loans:* $245,281 (67% need-based, 33% non-need-based). *Programs:* FFEL (Subsidized and Unsubsidized Stafford, PLUS), Perkins, college/university.
WORK-STUDY *Federal work-study:* Total amount: $114,735; 83 jobs averaging $1382. *State or other work-study/employment:* Total amount: $58,175 (82% need-based, 18% non-need-based). 55 part-time jobs averaging $1057.
ATHLETIC AWARDS *Total amount:* $132,300 (90% need-based, 10% non-need-based).

APPLYING FOR FINANCIAL AID *Required financial aid forms:* FAFSA, institution's own form, state aid form. *Financial aid deadline (priority):* 3/1. *Notification date:* Continuous. Students must reply within 2 weeks of notification.

CONTACT Mrs. Doris A. Wilson, Director of Financial Aid, Judson College, PO Box 120, Marion, AL 36756, 334-683-5157 or toll-free 800-447-9472. *Fax:* 334-683-5282. *E-mail:* dwilson@judson.edu.

JUDSON COLLEGE
Elgin, IL

ABOUT THE INSTITUTION Independent Baptist, coed. Awards: bachelor's and master's degrees. 48 undergraduate majors. Total enrollment: 1,222. Undergraduates: 1,157. Freshmen: 153.

GIFT AID (NEED-BASED) *Scholarships, grants, and awards:* Federal Pell, FSEOG, state, private, college/university gift aid from institutional funds.

GIFT AID (NON-NEED-BASED) *Scholarships, grants, and awards by category:* *Academic Interests/Achievement:* general academic interests/achievements. *Creative Arts/Performance:* art/fine arts, journalism/publications, performing arts. *Special Achievements/Activities:* cheerleading/drum major, leadership.

LOANS *Programs:* Federal Direct (Subsidized and Unsubsidized Stafford, PLUS), Perkins.

APPLYING FOR FINANCIAL AID *Required financial aid form:* FAFSA.

CONTACT Amy Wemken, Financial Aid Counselor, Judson College, 1151 North State Street, Elgin, IL 60123-1498, 847-695-2534 or toll-free 800-879-5376. *E-mail:* awemken@judsoncollege.edu.

THE JUILLIARD SCHOOL
New York, NY

ABOUT THE INSTITUTION Independent, coed. Awards: bachelor's, master's, and doctoral degrees and post-bachelor's and post-master's certificates. 8 undergraduate majors. Total enrollment: 833. Undergraduates: 505. Freshmen: 118.

GIFT AID (NEED-BASED) *Scholarships, grants, and awards:* Federal Pell, FSEOG, state, private, college/university gift aid from institutional funds.

GIFT AID (NON-NEED-BASED) *Scholarships, grants, and awards by category:* *Academic Interests/Achievement:* general academic interests/achievements. *Creative Arts/Performance:* dance, music, performing arts, theater/drama.

LOANS *Programs:* Federal Direct (Subsidized and Unsubsidized Stafford, PLUS), Perkins, college/university.

WORK-STUDY *Federal work-study:* Total amount: $244,355; 204 jobs averaging $1936. *State or other work-study/employment:* Total amount: $380,458 (65% need-based, 35% non-need-based). 265 part-time jobs averaging $2147.

APPLYING FOR FINANCIAL AID *Required financial aid forms:* FAFSA, institution's own form, state aid form, income tax form(s).

CONTACT Mary K. Gray, Associate Dean for Admissions, The Juilliard School, 60 Lincoln Center Plaza, New York, NY 10023, 212-799-5000 Ext. 223. *Fax:* 212-769-6420.

JUNIATA COLLEGE
Huntingdon, PA

Tuition & fees: $25,890	Average undergraduate aid package: $19,213

ABOUT THE INSTITUTION Independent religious, coed. Awards: bachelor's degrees. 92 undergraduate majors. Total enrollment: 1,427. Undergraduates: 1,427. Freshmen: 390. Federal methodology is used as a basis for awarding need-based institutional aid.

UNDERGRADUATE EXPENSES for 2005–06 *Application fee:* $30. *Comprehensive fee:* $33,130 includes full-time tuition ($25,260), mandatory fees ($630), and room and board ($7240). *College room only:* $3800. *Part-time tuition:* $1055 per credit hour.

FRESHMAN FINANCIAL AID (Fall 2003) 343 applied for aid; of those 85% were deemed to have need. 100% of freshmen with need received aid; of those 21% had need fully met. *Average percent of need met:* 86% (excluding resources awarded to replace EFC). *Average financial aid package:* $19,441 (excluding resources awarded to replace EFC). 26% of all full-time freshmen had no need and received non-need-based gift aid.

UNDERGRADUATE FINANCIAL AID (Fall 2003) 1,214 applied for aid; of those 87% were deemed to have need. 100% of undergraduates with need received aid; of those 18% had need fully met. *Average percent of need met:* 83%

(excluding resources awarded to replace EFC). *Average financial aid package:* $19,213 (excluding resources awarded to replace EFC). 25% of all full-time undergraduates had no need and received non-need-based gift aid.

GIFT AID (NEED-BASED) *Total amount:* $4,737,935 (7% federal, 11% state, 78% institutional, 4% external sources). *Receiving aid:* Freshmen: 74% (289); All full-time undergraduates: 75% (1,032). *Average award:* Freshmen: $16,246; Undergraduates: $15,056. *Scholarships, grants, and awards:* Federal Pell, FSEOG, state, private, college/university gift aid from institutional funds.

GIFT AID (NON-NEED-BASED) *Total amount:* $1,078,057 (2% state, 95% institutional, 3% external sources). *Receiving aid:* Freshmen: 71% (277); Undergraduates: 69% (949). *Average Award:* Freshmen: $11,806; Undergraduates: $11,445. *Scholarships, grants, and awards by category:* *Academic Interests/Achievement:* business, general academic interests/achievements, premedicine. *Creative Arts/Performance:* general creative arts/performance. *Special Achievements/Activities:* community service, leadership. *Special Characteristics:* adult students, children and siblings of alumni, children of faculty/staff, ethnic background, international students, religious affiliation.

LOANS *Student loans:* $1,152,985 (68% need-based, 32% non-need-based). 78% of past graduating class borrowed through all loan programs. *Average indebtedness per student:* $21,063. *Average need-based loan:* Freshmen: $2600; Undergraduates: $3680. *Parent loans:* $1,052,247 (100% non-need-based). *Programs:* FFEL (Subsidized and Unsubsidized Stafford, PLUS), Perkins.

WORK-STUDY *Federal work-study:* Total amount: $232,820; 752 jobs averaging $629. *State or other work-study/employment:* Total amount: $179,400 (100% non-need-based). Part-time jobs available.

APPLYING FOR FINANCIAL AID *Required financial aid form:* FAFSA. *Financial aid deadline:* 5/1 (priority: 3/1). *Notification date:* Continuous beginning 2/1. Students must reply by 5/1 or within 2 weeks of notification.

CONTACT Mr. Randall S. Rennell, Director of Student Financial Planning, Juniata College, 1700 Moore Street, Huntingdon, PA 16652-2119, 814-641-3142 or toll-free 877-JUNIATA. *Fax:* 814-641-5311. *E-mail:* rennelr@juniata.edu.

KALAMAZOO COLLEGE
Kalamazoo, MI

Tuition & fees: $24,351	Average undergraduate aid package: N/A

ABOUT THE INSTITUTION Independent religious, coed. Awards: bachelor's degrees. 24 undergraduate majors. Total enrollment: 1,234. Undergraduates: 1,234. Freshmen: 310. Both federal and institutional methodology are used as a basis for awarding need-based institutional aid.

UNDERGRADUATE EXPENSES for 2004–05 *Application fee:* $35. *Comprehensive fee:* $30,960 includes full-time tuition ($24,351) and room and board ($6609). *College room only:* $3273. Room and board charges vary according to board plan. *Payment plan:* Installment.

FRESHMAN FINANCIAL AID (Fall 2004, est.) 237 applied for aid; of those 76% were deemed to have need. 100% of freshmen with need received aid; of those 83% had need fully met. *Average financial aid package:* $18,900 (excluding resources awarded to replace EFC). 42% of all full-time freshmen had no need and received non-need-based gift aid.

UNDERGRADUATE FINANCIAL AID (Fall 2004, est.) 766 applied for aid; of those 81% were deemed to have need. 100% of undergraduates with need received aid; of those 72% had need fully met. 40% of all full-time undergraduates had no need and received non-need-based gift aid.

GIFT AID (NEED-BASED) *Total amount:* $6,013,983 (9% federal, 11% state, 79% institutional, 1% external sources). *Receiving aid:* Freshmen: 58% (179); All full-time undergraduates: 51% (616). *Average award:* Freshmen: $15,100; Undergraduates: $13,930. *Scholarships, grants, and awards:* Federal Pell, FSEOG, state, private, college/university gift aid from institutional funds.

GIFT AID (NON-NEED-BASED) *Total amount:* $8,857,307 (6% state, 78% institutional, 16% external sources). *Receiving aid:* Freshmen: 56% (175); Undergraduates: 49% (587). *Average Award:* Freshmen: $9095; Undergraduates: $7840. *Scholarships, grants, and awards by category:* *Academic Interests/Achievement:* biological sciences, English, foreign languages, general academic interests/achievements, mathematics, physical sciences, social sciences. *Creative Arts/Performance:* art/fine arts, cinema/film/broadcasting, music, theater/drama. *Special Achievements/Activities:* general special achievements/activities. *Special Characteristics:* children of faculty/staff. *ROTC:* Army cooperative.

LOANS *Student loans:* $4,272,103 (55% need-based, 45% non-need-based). 54% of past graduating class borrowed through all loan programs. *Average indebtedness per student:* $23,890. *Average need-based loan:* Freshmen: $4100;

Undergraduates: $4786. **Parent loans:** $1,070,995 (100% non-need-based). **Programs:** Federal Direct (Subsidized and Unsubsidized Stafford, PLUS), Perkins, state.

WORK-STUDY Federal work-study: Total amount: $332,000; 440 jobs averaging $1500. **State or other work-study/employment:** Total amount: $10,000 (100% need-based). 12 part-time jobs averaging $834.

APPLYING FOR FINANCIAL AID Required financial aid forms: FAFSA, institution's own form. **Financial aid deadline (priority):** 2/15. **Notification date:** 3/21. Students must reply by 5/1.

CONTACT Judy Clark, Assistant Director of Financial Aid, Kalamazoo College, 1200 Academy Street, Kalamazoo, MI 49006-3295, 269-337-7192 or toll-free 800-253-3602. **Fax:** 269-337-7390.

KANSAS CITY ART INSTITUTE
Kansas City, MO

Tuition & fees: $21,326	Average undergraduate aid package: $14,581

ABOUT THE INSTITUTION Independent, coed. Awards: bachelor's degrees. 9 undergraduate majors. Total enrollment: 614. Undergraduates: 583. Freshmen: 139. Federal methodology is used as a basis for awarding need-based institutional aid.

UNDERGRADUATE EXPENSES for 2004–05 Application fee: $35. **Comprehensive fee:** $28,126 includes full-time tuition ($20,380), mandatory fees ($946), and room and board ($6800). Full-time tuition and fees vary according to program. Room and board charges vary according to board plan and housing facility. **Part-time tuition:** $850 per credit hour. **Part-time fees:** $46 per credit hour. Part-time tuition and fees vary according to program.

FRESHMAN FINANCIAL AID (Fall 2004, est.) 133 applied for aid; of those 84% were deemed to have need. 99% of freshmen with need received aid; of those 16% had need fully met. Average percent of need met: 66% (excluding resources awarded to replace EFC). Average financial aid package: $14,820 (excluding resources awarded to replace EFC). 22% of all full-time freshmen had no need and received non-need-based gift aid.

UNDERGRADUATE FINANCIAL AID (Fall 2004, est.) 515 applied for aid; of those 88% were deemed to have need. 100% of undergraduates with need received aid; of those 13% had need fully met. Average percent of need met: 60% (excluding resources awarded to replace EFC). Average financial aid package: $14,581 (excluding resources awarded to replace EFC). 21% of all full-time undergraduates had no need and received non-need-based gift aid.

GIFT AID (NEED-BASED) Total amount: $4,799,293 (14% federal, 4% state, 77% institutional, 5% external sources). **Receiving aid:** Freshmen: 76% (111); All full-time undergraduates: 78% (453). **Average award:** Freshmen: $11,094; Undergraduates: $9895. **Scholarships, grants, and awards:** Federal Pell, FSEOG, state, private, college/university gift aid from institutional funds.

GIFT AID (NON-NEED-BASED) Total amount: $929,332 (90% institutional, 10% external sources). **Receiving aid:** Freshmen: 7% (11); Undergraduates: 6% (37). **Average Award:** Freshmen: $10,865; Undergraduates: $10,853. **Scholarships, grants, and awards by category:** Creative Arts/Performance: 490 awards ($3,308,263 total): art/fine arts. **Tuition waivers:** Full or partial for employees or children of employees.

LOANS Student loans: $4,236,033 (85% need-based, 15% non-need-based). 85% of past graduating class borrowed through all loan programs. Average indebtedness per student: $17,125. **Average need-based loan:** Freshmen: $4159; Undergraduates: $4897. **Parent loans:** $2,443,827 (49% need-based, 51% non-need-based). **Programs:** FFEL (Subsidized and Unsubsidized Stafford, PLUS), Perkins, alternative loans.

WORK-STUDY Federal work-study: Total amount: $108,784; 100 jobs averaging $1088. **State or other work-study/employment:** Total amount: $35,647 (16% need-based, 84% non-need-based). 41 part-time jobs averaging $869.

APPLYING FOR FINANCIAL AID Required financial aid form: FAFSA. **Financial aid deadline (priority):** 3/15. **Notification date:** Continuous beginning 4/15. Students must reply within 2 weeks of notification.

CONTACT Ms. Christal D. Williams, Director of Financial Aid, Kansas City Art Institute, 4415 Warwick Boulevard, Kansas City, MO 64111-1874, 816-802-3448 or toll-free 800-522-5224. **Fax:** 816-802-3453. **E-mail:** cdwilliams@kcai.edu.

KANSAS CITY COLLEGE OF LEGAL STUDIES
Kansas City, MO

Tuition & fees: N/R	Average undergraduate aid package: N/A

ABOUT THE INSTITUTION Proprietary, coed. Awards: associate and bachelor's degrees. 2 undergraduate majors. Total enrollment: 123. Undergraduates: 123. Both federal and institutional methodology are used as a basis for awarding need-based institutional aid.

APPLYING FOR FINANCIAL AID Required financial aid forms: FAFSA, institution's own form, federal income tax form(s). **Financial aid deadline:** Continuous.

CONTACT Financial Aid Office, Kansas City College of Legal Studies, 17331 East Highway 40, Independence, MO 64055, 816-444-2232 or toll-free 877-582-3963 (out-of-state).

KANSAS STATE UNIVERSITY
Manhattan, KS

Tuition & fees (KS res): $4665	Average undergraduate aid package: $6198

ABOUT THE INSTITUTION State-supported, coed. Awards: associate, bachelor's, master's, doctoral, and first professional degrees. 88 undergraduate majors. Total enrollment: 23,151. Undergraduates: 19,098. Freshmen: 3,466. Federal methodology is used as a basis for awarding need-based institutional aid.

UNDERGRADUATE EXPENSES for 2004–05 Application fee: $30. **Tuition, state resident:** full-time $4110; part-time $137 per credit hour. **Tuition, nonresident:** full-time $12,870; part-time $429 per credit hour. **College room and board:** $5738. Room and board charges vary according to board plan. **Payment plans:** Installment, deferred payment.

FRESHMAN FINANCIAL AID (Fall 2003) 1645 applied for aid; of those 68% were deemed to have need. 97% of freshmen with need received aid; of those 11% had need fully met. Average percent of need met: 84% (excluding resources awarded to replace EFC). Average financial aid package: $5562 (excluding resources awarded to replace EFC). 10% of all full-time freshmen had no need and received non-need-based gift aid.

UNDERGRADUATE FINANCIAL AID (Fall 2003) 11,171 applied for aid; of those 74% were deemed to have need. 97% of undergraduates with need received aid; of those 20% had need fully met. Average percent of need met: 80% (excluding resources awarded to replace EFC). Average financial aid package: $6198 (excluding resources awarded to replace EFC). 5% of all full-time undergraduates had no need and received non-need-based gift aid.

GIFT AID (NEED-BASED) Total amount: $26,604,689 (50% federal, 8% state, 22% institutional, 20% external sources). **Receiving aid:** Freshmen: 34% (779); All full-time undergraduates: 47% (7,862). **Average award:** Freshmen: $1760; Undergraduates: $1891. **Scholarships, grants, and awards:** Federal Pell, FSEOG, state, college/university gift aid from institutional funds.

GIFT AID (NON-NEED-BASED) Total amount: $3,010,899 (56% institutional, 44% external sources). **Receiving aid:** Freshmen: 8% (178); Undergraduates: 12% (2,054). **Average Award:** Freshmen: $2156; Undergraduates: $1787. **Scholarships, grants, and awards by category:** Academic Interests/Achievement: agriculture, architecture, biological sciences, business, communication, computer science, education, engineering/technologies, English, foreign languages, general academic interests/achievements, health fields, home economics, humanities, mathematics, military science, physical sciences, premedicine, social sciences. Creative Arts/Performance: art/fine arts, debating, music, theater/drama. Special Achievements/Activities: general special achievements/activities, leadership. Special Characteristics: general special characteristics. **Tuition waivers:** Full or partial for employees or children of employees. **ROTC:** Army, Air Force.

LOANS Student loans: $70,316,799 (72% need-based, 27% non-need-based). 55% of past graduating class borrowed through all loan programs. Average indebtedness per student: $18,000. **Average need-based loan:** Freshmen: $2106; Undergraduates: $3111. **Programs:** FFEL (Subsidized and Unsubsidized Stafford, PLUS), Perkins, college/university.

WORK-STUDY Federal work-study: Total amount: $855,099; jobs available. **State or other work-study/employment:** Total amount: $13,300,000 (38% need-based, 62% non-need-based). Part-time jobs available.

ATHLETIC AWARDS Total amount: $3,630,389 (93% need-based, 7% non-need-based).

APPLYING FOR FINANCIAL AID *Required financial aid form:* FAFSA. *Financial aid deadline (priority):* 3/1. *Notification date:* Continuous beginning 3/15. Students must reply within 2 weeks of notification.

CONTACT Mr. Larry Moeder, Director of Admissions and Student Financial Assistance, Kansas State University, 104 Fairchild Hall, Manhattan, KS 66506, 785-532-6420 or toll-free 800-432-8270 (in-state). *E-mail:* larrym@ksu.edu.

KANSAS WESLEYAN UNIVERSITY
Salina, KS

CONTACT Mrs. Glenna Alexander, Director of Financial Assistance, Kansas Wesleyan University, 100 East Claflin, Salina, KS 67401-6196, 785-827-5541 Ext. 1130 or toll-free 800-874-1154 Ext. 1285. *Fax:* 785-827-0927. *E-mail:* kglennaa@acck.edu.

KEAN UNIVERSITY
Union, NJ

Tuition & fees (NJ res): $7151	Average undergraduate aid package: $7767

ABOUT THE INSTITUTION State-supported, coed. Awards: bachelor's and master's degrees and post-bachelor's and post-master's certificates. 48 undergraduate majors. Total enrollment: 12,897. Undergraduates: 9,947. Freshmen: 1,310. Federal methodology is used as a basis for awarding need-based institutional aid.

UNDERGRADUATE EXPENSES for 2004–05 *Application fee:* $50. *Tuition, state resident:* full-time $4665; part-time $155.50 per credit. *Tuition, nonresident:* full-time $7170; part-time $239 per credit. *Required fees:* full-time $2486; $83.60 per credit. Part-time tuition and fees vary according to course load. *College room and board:* $8093; *room only:* $5693. Room and board charges vary according to board plan and housing facility. *Payment plans:* Installment, deferred payment.

FRESHMAN FINANCIAL AID (Fall 2004, est.) 1011 applied for aid; of those 79% were deemed to have need. 95% of freshmen with need received aid; of those 12% had need fully met. *Average percent of need met:* 59% (excluding resources awarded to replace EFC). *Average financial aid package:* $7072 (excluding resources awarded to replace EFC). 3% of all full-time freshmen had no need and received non-need-based gift aid.

UNDERGRADUATE FINANCIAL AID (Fall 2004, est.) 5,120 applied for aid; of those 82% were deemed to have need. 94% of undergraduates with need received aid; of those 17% had need fully met. *Average percent of need met:* 53% (excluding resources awarded to replace EFC). *Average financial aid package:* $7767 (excluding resources awarded to replace EFC). 2% of all full-time undergraduates had no need and received non-need-based gift aid.

GIFT AID (NEED-BASED) *Total amount:* $15,899,695 (48% federal, 45% state, 6% institutional, 1% external sources). *Receiving aid:* Freshmen: 46% (578); All full-time undergraduates: 38% (2,801). *Average award:* Freshmen: $5589; Undergraduates: $5428. *Scholarships, grants, and awards:* Federal Pell, FSEOG, state, private, college/university gift aid from institutional funds.

GIFT AID (NON-NEED-BASED) *Total amount:* $79,000 (100% state). *Average Award:* Freshmen: $1806; Undergraduates: $1685. *Scholarships, grants, and awards by category: Academic Interests/Achievement:* business, education, general academic interests/achievements, health fields, humanities. *Special Achievements/Activities:* community service, leadership. *Special Characteristics:* children of faculty/staff. *Tuition waivers:* Full or partial for employees or children of employees, senior citizens. *ROTC:* Army cooperative, Air Force cooperative.

LOANS *Student loans:* $28,439,775 (51% need-based, 49% non-need-based). 30% of past graduating class borrowed through all loan programs. *Average indebtedness per student:* $10,619. *Average need-based loan:* Freshmen: $2641; Undergraduates: $3885. *Parent loans:* $3,350,539 (100% non-need-based). *Programs:* Federal Direct (Subsidized and Unsubsidized Stafford, PLUS), Perkins, state.

WORK-STUDY *Federal work-study:* Total amount: $405,405; 326 jobs averaging $1245.

APPLYING FOR FINANCIAL AID *Required financial aid form:* FAFSA. *Financial aid deadline (priority):* 3/15. *Notification date:* Continuous beginning 4/15. Students must reply within 2 weeks of notification.

CONTACT Sandra Bembry, Director of Financial Aid, Kean University, 1000 Morris Avenue, Union, NJ 07083, 908-737-3190. *Fax:* 908-737-3200.

KEENE STATE COLLEGE
Keene, NH

Tuition & fees (NH res): $6900	Average undergraduate aid package: $7258

ABOUT THE INSTITUTION State-supported, coed. Awards: bachelor's and master's degrees and post-bachelor's and post-master's certificates. 53 undergraduate majors. Total enrollment: 4,937. Undergraduates: 4,797. Freshmen: 1,078. Federal methodology is used as a basis for awarding need-based institutional aid.

UNDERGRADUATE EXPENSES for 2004–05 *Application fee:* $25. *Tuition, state resident:* full-time $5060; part-time $212 per credit. *Tuition, nonresident:* full-time $11,500; part-time $480 per credit. *Required fees:* full-time $1840; $74 per credit. Part-time tuition and fees vary according to course load. *College room and board:* $5966; *room only:* $4064. Room and board charges vary according to board plan and housing facility. *Payment plan:* Installment.

FRESHMAN FINANCIAL AID (Fall 2003) 819 applied for aid; of those 69% were deemed to have need. 98% of freshmen with need received aid; of those 22% had need fully met. *Average percent of need met:* 73% (excluding resources awarded to replace EFC). *Average financial aid package:* $6728 (excluding resources awarded to replace EFC). 6% of all full-time freshmen had no need and received non-need-based gift aid.

UNDERGRADUATE FINANCIAL AID (Fall 2003) 3,036 applied for aid; of those 73% were deemed to have need. 98% of undergraduates with need received aid; of those 28% had need fully met. *Average percent of need met:* 77% (excluding resources awarded to replace EFC). *Average financial aid package:* $7258 (excluding resources awarded to replace EFC). 8% of all full-time undergraduates had no need and received non-need-based gift aid.

GIFT AID (NEED-BASED) *Total amount:* $5,856,650 (41% federal, 9% state, 42% institutional, 8% external sources). *Receiving aid:* Freshmen: 36% (360); All full-time undergraduates: 33% (1,364). *Average award:* Freshmen: $4186; Undergraduates: $4031. *Scholarships, grants, and awards:* Federal Pell, FSEOG, state, private, college/university gift aid from institutional funds.

GIFT AID (NON-NEED-BASED) *Total amount:* $2,516,878 (77% institutional, 23% external sources). *Receiving aid:* Freshmen: 16% (159); Undergraduates: 13% (551). *Average Award: Freshmen:* $2158; *Undergraduates:* $2493. *Scholarships, grants, and awards by category: Academic Interests/Achievement:* 548 awards ($1,037,075 total): general academic interests/achievements. *Creative Arts/Performance:* 27 awards ($67,300 total): applied art and design, art/fine arts, cinema/film/broadcasting, dance, general creative arts/performance, music, theater/drama. *Special Achievements/Activities:* 7 awards ($19,800 total): general special achievements/activities. *Tuition waivers:* Full or partial for employees or children of employees. *ROTC:* Air Force cooperative.

LOANS *Student loans:* $17,842,088 (47% need-based, 53% non-need-based). 75% of past graduating class borrowed through all loan programs. *Average indebtedness per student:* $18,585. *Average need-based loan:* Freshmen: $2837; Undergraduates: $3784. *Parent loans:* $4,774,718 (100% non-need-based). *Programs:* FFEL (Subsidized and Unsubsidized Stafford, PLUS), Perkins, college/university.

WORK-STUDY *Federal work-study:* Total amount: $426,754; 559 jobs averaging $763. *State or other work-study/employment:* Total amount: $511,314 (100% non-need-based). 606 part-time jobs averaging $844.

APPLYING FOR FINANCIAL AID *Required financial aid form:* FAFSA. *Financial aid deadline:* 3/1. *Notification date:* Continuous. Students must reply within 4 weeks of notification.

CONTACT Ms. Patricia Blodgett, Director of Student Financial Management, Keene State College, 229 Main Street, Keene, NH 03435-2606, 603-358-2280 or toll-free 800-572-1909. *Fax:* 603-358-2794. *E-mail:* pblodget@keene.edu.

KEHILATH YAKOV RABBINICAL SEMINARY
Brooklyn, NY

CONTACT Financial Aid Office, Kehilath Yakov Rabbinical Seminary, 206 Wilson Street, Brooklyn, NY 11211-7207, 718-963-1212.

KENDALL COLLEGE
Chicago, IL

ABOUT THE INSTITUTION Independent United Methodist, coed. Awards: associate and bachelor's degrees. 24 undergraduate majors. Total enrollment: 669. Undergraduates: 669. Freshmen: 93.

GIFT AID (NEED-BASED) *Scholarships, grants, and awards:* Federal Pell, FSEOG, state, private, college/university gift aid from institutional funds.

GIFT AID (NON-NEED-BASED) *Scholarships, grants, and awards by category:* *Academic Interests/Achievement:* general academic interests/achievements. *Special Characteristics:* children of faculty/staff, international students, members of minority groups, out-of-state students, religious affiliation, veterans, veterans' children.

LOANS *Programs:* FFEL (Subsidized and Unsubsidized Stafford, PLUS), Perkins, Signature Loans, GATE Loans, CitiAssist Loans.

WORK-STUDY *Federal work-study:* Total amount: $44,550; 50 jobs averaging $1162. *State or other work-study/employment:* Part-time jobs available.

APPLYING FOR FINANCIAL AID *Required financial aid forms:* FAFSA, institution's own form.

CONTACT Cynthia Sabo, Director of Financial Aid, Kendall College, 2408 Orrington Avenue, Evanston, IL 60201, 847-448-2349 or toll-free 866-667-3344. *Fax:* 847-448-2403.

KENNESAW STATE UNIVERSITY
Kennesaw, GA

Tuition & fees (GA res): $2758	Average undergraduate aid package: $7892

ABOUT THE INSTITUTION State-supported, coed. Awards: bachelor's and master's degrees. 48 undergraduate majors. Total enrollment: 17,955. Undergraduates: 16,073. Freshmen: 1,862. Federal methodology is used as a basis for awarding need-based institutional aid.

UNDERGRADUATE EXPENSES for 2004–05 *Application fee:* $40. *Tuition, state resident:* full-time $2322; part-time $97 per credit hour. *Tuition, nonresident:* full-time $9290; part-time $388 per credit hour. *Required fees:* full-time $436; $218 per term part-time. *College room and board: room only:* $5376. Room and board charges vary according to housing facility. *Payment plan:* Deferred payment.

FRESHMAN FINANCIAL AID (Fall 2004, est.) 1571 applied for aid; of those 41% were deemed to have need. 98% of freshmen with need received aid; of those 11% had need fully met. *Average percent of need met:* 19% (excluding resources awarded to replace EFC). *Average financial aid package:* $7892 (excluding resources awarded to replace EFC). 54% of all full-time freshmen had no need and received non-need-based gift aid.

UNDERGRADUATE FINANCIAL AID (Fall 2004, est.) 7,902 applied for aid; of those 48% were deemed to have need. 100% of undergraduates with need received aid; of those 15% had need fully met. *Average percent of need met:* 20% (excluding resources awarded to replace EFC). *Average financial aid package:* $7892 (excluding resources awarded to replace EFC). 22% of all full-time undergraduates had no need and received non-need-based gift aid.

GIFT AID (NEED-BASED) *Total amount:* $10,063,938 (99% federal, 1% institutional). *Receiving aid:* Freshmen: 19% (303); All full-time undergraduates: 118% (1,256). *Average award:* Freshmen: $2676; Undergraduates: $2662. *Scholarships, grants, and awards:* Federal Pell, FSEOG, state, private, college/university gift aid from institutional funds.

GIFT AID (NON-NEED-BASED) *Total amount:* $1,893,084 (903% state, 2% external sources). *Receiving aid:* Freshmen: 34% (539); Undergraduates: 156% (1,661). *Average Award:* Freshmen: $1541; Undergraduates: $189. *Scholarships, grants, and awards by category:* Academic Interests/Achievement: 85 awards ($125,136 total): biological sciences, business, communication, computer science, education, English, foreign languages, general academic interests/achievements, health fields, humanities, international studies, mathematics, physical sciences, premedicine, social sciences. Creative Arts/Performance: 12 awards ($13,419 total): music, performing arts, theater/drama. Special Achievements/Activities: 4 awards ($4800 total): community service, leadership. Special Characteristics: 18 awards ($87,295 total): children and siblings of alumni, children of union members/company employees, children of workers in trades, general special characteristics, local/state students, members of minority groups, religious affiliation. *Tuition waivers:* Full or partial for senior citizens. *ROTC:* Army, Air Force.

LOANS *Student loans:* $20,639,532 (93% need-based, 7% non-need-based). 69% of past graduating class borrowed through all loan programs. *Average indebtedness per student:* $13,898. *Average need-based loan:* Freshmen: $2478; Undergraduates: $3318. *Parent loans:* $73,888 (100% non-need-based). *Programs:* FFEL (Subsidized and Unsubsidized Stafford, PLUS), Perkins, state, college/university.

WORK-STUDY *Federal work-study:* Total amount: $594,454; jobs available.

ATHLETIC AWARDS *Total amount:* $134,652 (100% non-need-based).

APPLYING FOR FINANCIAL AID *Required financial aid forms:* FAFSA, state aid form. *Financial aid deadline (priority):* 4/1. *Notification date:* Continuous beginning 5/1.

CONTACT Mr. Michael C. Roberts, Director of Student Financial Aid, Kennesaw State University, 1000 Chastain Road, Kennesaw, GA 30144-5591, 770-499-3240. *Fax:* 770-423-6708. *E-mail:* finaid@kennesaw.edu.

KENT STATE UNIVERSITY
Kent, OH

Tuition & fees (OH res): $7504	Average undergraduate aid package: $6943

ABOUT THE INSTITUTION State-supported, coed. Awards: associate, bachelor's, master's, and doctoral degrees and post-bachelor's and post-master's certificates. 148 undergraduate majors. Total enrollment: 24,347. Undergraduates: 19,060. Freshmen: 3,920. Federal methodology is used as a basis for awarding need-based institutional aid.

UNDERGRADUATE EXPENSES for 2004–05 *Application fee:* $30. *One-time required fee:* $100. *Tuition, state resident:* full-time $7504; part-time $343 per credit hour. *Tuition, nonresident:* full-time $14,516; part-time $663 per credit hour. Full-time tuition and fees vary according to course level, course load, degree level, location, program, reciprocity agreements, and student level. Part-time tuition and fees vary according to course level, course load, degree level, location, program, reciprocity agreements, and student level. *College room and board:* $6410; *room only:* $3890. Room and board charges vary according to board plan and housing facility. *Payment plans:* Tuition prepayment, installment, deferred payment.

FRESHMAN FINANCIAL AID (Fall 2004, est.) 2925 applied for aid; of those 82% were deemed to have need. 100% of freshmen with need received aid; of those 11% had need fully met. *Average percent of need met:* 55% (excluding resources awarded to replace EFC). *Average financial aid package:* $6751 (excluding resources awarded to replace EFC). 9% of all full-time freshmen had no need and received non-need-based gift aid.

UNDERGRADUATE FINANCIAL AID (Fall 2004, est.) 11,110 applied for aid; of those 86% were deemed to have need. 100% of undergraduates with need received aid; of those 13% had need fully met. *Average percent of need met:* 56% (excluding resources awarded to replace EFC). *Average financial aid package:* $6943 (excluding resources awarded to replace EFC). 7% of all full-time undergraduates had no need and received non-need-based gift aid.

GIFT AID (NEED-BASED) *Total amount:* $31,406,448 (48% federal, 19% state, 27% institutional, 6% external sources). *Receiving aid:* Freshmen: 48% (1,864); All full-time undergraduates: 36% (6,657). *Average award:* Freshmen: $4547; Undergraduates: $4439. *Scholarships, grants, and awards:* Federal Pell, FSEOG, state, private, college/university gift aid from institutional funds.

GIFT AID (NON-NEED-BASED) *Total amount:* $6,527,743 (1% federal, 19% state, 69% institutional, 11% external sources). *Receiving aid:* Freshmen: 7% (286); Undergraduates: 3% (599). *Average Award:* Freshmen: $3444; Undergraduates: $3588. *Scholarships, grants, and awards by category:* Academic Interests/Achievement: architecture, area/ethnic studies, biological sciences, business, communication, computer science, education, English, general academic interests/achievements, health fields, international studies, library science, mathematics, military science, physical sciences, social sciences. Creative Arts/Performance: art/fine arts, journalism/publications, music, theater/drama. Special Achievements/Activities: community service, general special achievements/activities, leadership. Special Characteristics: adult students, children and siblings of alumni, children of faculty/staff, children of union members/company employees, children with a deceased or disabled parent, ethnic background, handicapped students, international students, members of minority groups, out-of-state students. *Tuition waivers:* Full or partial for employees or children of employees. *ROTC:* Army, Air Force.

LOANS *Student loans:* $64,392,461 (87% need-based, 13% non-need-based). 63% of past graduating class borrowed through all loan programs. *Average indebtedness per student:* $21,489. *Average need-based loan:* Freshmen: $3411; Undergraduates: $3894. *Parent loans:* $28,345,567 (34% need-based, 66% non-need-based). *Programs:* Federal Direct (Subsidized and Unsubsidized Stafford, PLUS), Perkins, Federal Nursing, state, college/university, alternative loans.

WORK-STUDY *Federal work-study:* Total amount: $546,767; 1,042 jobs averaging $2316.

ATHLETIC AWARDS *Total amount:* $3,793,574 (49% need-based, 51% non-need-based).

APPLYING FOR FINANCIAL AID *Required financial aid forms:* FAFSA, University Scholarship Application form. *Financial aid deadline (priority):* 3/1. *Notification date:* 3/15. Students must reply within 2 weeks of notification.

CONTACT Constance Dubick, Associate Director of Student Financial Aid, Kent State University, 103 Michael Schwartz Center, PO Box 5190, Kent, OH 44242-0001, 330-672-2972 or toll-free 800-988-KENT. *Fax:* 330-672-4014. *E-mail:* cdubick@kent.edu.

KENTUCKY CHRISTIAN UNIVERSITY
Grayson, KY

Tuition & fees: $10,640	Average undergraduate aid package: $10,812

ABOUT THE INSTITUTION Independent religious, coed. Awards: associate, bachelor's, and master's degrees. 13 undergraduate majors. Total enrollment: 559. Undergraduates: 544. Freshmen: 127. Federal methodology is used as a basis for awarding need-based institutional aid.

UNDERGRADUATE EXPENSES for 2004–05 *Application fee:* $25. *Comprehensive fee:* $14,995 includes full-time tuition ($10,560), mandatory fees ($80), and room and board ($4355). Full-time tuition and fees vary according to course load. Room and board charges vary according to board plan and housing facility. *Part-time tuition:* $330 per credit hour. Part-time tuition and fees vary according to course load. *Payment plan:* Installment.

FRESHMAN FINANCIAL AID (Fall 2004, est.) 134 applied for aid; of those 93% were deemed to have need. 100% of freshmen with need received aid; of those 17% had need fully met. *Average percent of need met:* 68% (excluding resources awarded to replace EFC). *Average financial aid package:* $10,113 (excluding resources awarded to replace EFC). 16% of all full-time freshmen had no need and received non-need-based gift aid.

UNDERGRADUATE FINANCIAL AID (Fall 2004, est.) 522 applied for aid; of those 89% were deemed to have need. 100% of undergraduates with need received aid; of those 23% had need fully met. *Average percent of need met:* 72% (excluding resources awarded to replace EFC). *Average financial aid package:* $10,812 (excluding resources awarded to replace EFC). 16% of all full-time undergraduates had no need and received non-need-based gift aid.

GIFT AID (NEED-BASED) *Total amount:* $1,509,970 (47% federal, 29% state, 24% institutional). *Receiving aid:* Freshmen: 62% (91); All full-time undergraduates: 60% (335). *Average award:* Freshmen: $4774; Undergraduates: $4507. *Scholarships, grants, and awards:* Federal Pell, FSEOG, state, private, college/university gift aid from institutional funds.

GIFT AID (NON-NEED-BASED) *Total amount:* $2,166,015 (7% state, 67% institutional, 26% external sources). *Receiving aid:* Freshmen: 85% (124); Undergraduates: 81% (455). *Average Award:* Freshmen: $4029; Undergraduates: $4527. *Scholarships, grants, and awards by category:* Academic Interests/Achievement: 500 awards ($1,017,139 total): business, education, general academic interests/achievements, religion/biblical studies. Creative Arts/Performance: 33 awards ($180,056 total): debating, music, performing arts, theater/drama. Special Achievements/Activities: 2 awards ($1050 total): community service, general special achievements/activities, leadership, religious involvement. Special Characteristics: 78 awards ($248,667 total): children and siblings of alumni, children of faculty/staff, general special characteristics, international students, members of minority groups, religious affiliation. *Tuition waivers:* Full or partial for minority students, employees or children of employees.

LOANS *Student loans:* $2,514,704 (57% need-based, 43% non-need-based). 73% of past graduating class borrowed through all loan programs. *Average indebtedness per student:* $23,580. *Average need-based loan:* Freshmen: $2329; Undergraduates: $3616. *Parent loans:* $686,636 (100% non-need-based). *Programs:* FFEL (Subsidized and Unsubsidized Stafford, PLUS), Perkins.

WORK-STUDY *Federal work-study:* Total amount: $423,235; 249 jobs averaging $1700. *State or other work-study/employment:* Total amount: $104,175 (100% non-need-based). 56 part-time jobs averaging $1860.

APPLYING FOR FINANCIAL AID *Required financial aid form:* FAFSA. *Financial aid deadline (priority):* 4/1. *Notification date:* Continuous beginning 3/15. Students must reply within 2 weeks of notification.

CONTACT Mrs. Jennie M. Bender, Director of Financial Aid, Kentucky Christian University, 100 Academic Parkway, Grayson, KY 41143-2205, 606-474-3226 or toll-free 800-522-3181. *Fax:* 606-474-3155. *E-mail:* jbender@kcu.edu.

KENTUCKY MOUNTAIN BIBLE COLLEGE
Vancleve, KY

Tuition & fees: $5260	Average undergraduate aid package: $2000

ABOUT THE INSTITUTION Independent interdenominational, coed. Awards: associate and bachelor's degrees. 5 undergraduate majors. Total enrollment: 92. Undergraduates: 92. Freshmen: 19. Both federal and institutional methodology are used as a basis for awarding need-based institutional aid.

UNDERGRADUATE EXPENSES for 2005–06 *Application fee:* $25. *Comprehensive fee:* $8460 includes full-time tuition ($4800), mandatory fees ($460), and room and board ($3200). *College room only:* $1000. Full-time tuition and fees vary according to course load. Room and board charges vary according to housing facility. *Part-time tuition:* $160 per credit hour. *Part-time fees:* $160 per credit hour; $30 per term. Part-time tuition and fees vary according to course load. *Payment plans:* Installment, deferred payment.

FRESHMAN FINANCIAL AID (Fall 2003) 25 applied for aid; of those 76% were deemed to have need. 100% of freshmen with need received aid. *Average percent of need met:* 50% (excluding resources awarded to replace EFC). *Average financial aid package:* $2000 (excluding resources awarded to replace EFC).

UNDERGRADUATE FINANCIAL AID (Fall 2003) 55 applied for aid; of those 100% were deemed to have need. 100% of undergraduates with need received aid. *Average percent of need met:* 30% (excluding resources awarded to replace EFC). *Average financial aid package:* $2000 (excluding resources awarded to replace EFC). 2% of all full-time undergraduates had no need and received non-need-based gift aid.

GIFT AID (NEED-BASED) *Total amount:* $204,500 (86% federal, 12% institutional, 2% external sources). *Receiving aid:* Freshmen: 68% (17); All full-time undergraduates: 64% (53). *Average award:* Freshmen: $1500; Undergraduates: $1500. *Scholarships, grants, and awards:* Federal Pell, FSEOG, state, private, college/university gift aid from institutional funds.

GIFT AID (NON-NEED-BASED) *Total amount:* $30,400 (100% federal). *Average Award:* Undergraduates: $3800. *Scholarships, grants, and awards by category:* Academic Interests/Achievement: general academic interests/achievements. Creative Arts/Performance: 12 awards: music, theater/drama. Special Characteristics: 4 awards: children of faculty/staff. *Tuition waivers:* Full or partial for employees or children of employees.

LOANS *Student loans:* $30,000 (100% need-based). 2% of past graduating class borrowed through all loan programs. *Average indebtedness per student:* $2000. *Average need-based loan:* Freshmen: $2600; Undergraduates: $2600. *Programs:* FFEL (Subsidized and Unsubsidized Stafford, PLUS), college/university.

WORK-STUDY *Federal work-study:* Total amount: $19,212; 40 jobs averaging $480.

APPLYING FOR FINANCIAL AID *Required financial aid form:* FAFSA. *Financial aid deadline (priority):* 4/1. *Notification date:* Continuous.

CONTACT Mrs. Jewel MacGregor, Director of Financial Aid, Kentucky Mountain Bible College, PO Box 10, Vancleve, KY 41385-0010, 800-879-KMBC or toll-free 800-879-KMBC Ext. 130 (in-state), 800-879-KMBC Ext. 136 (out-of-state). *Fax:* 606-693-7744.

KENTUCKY STATE UNIVERSITY
Frankfort, KY

ABOUT THE INSTITUTION State-related, coed. Awards: associate, bachelor's, and master's degrees. 31 undergraduate majors. Total enrollment: 2,335. Undergraduates: 2,183. Freshmen: 352.

GIFT AID (NEED-BASED) *Scholarships, grants, and awards:* Federal Pell, FSEOG, state, private, college/university gift aid from institutional funds, Federal Nursing.

GIFT AID (NON-NEED-BASED) *Scholarships, grants, and awards by category:* Academic Interests/Achievement: general academic interests/achievements, mathematics. Creative Arts/Performance: art/fine arts, music. Special Characteristics: adult students, children with a deceased or disabled parent, handicapped students.

LOANS *Programs:* Federal Direct (Subsidized and Unsubsidized Stafford, PLUS), Perkins.

WORK-STUDY *Federal work-study:* Total amount: $400,000; 500 jobs available.

APPLYING FOR FINANCIAL AID *Required financial aid form:* FAFSA.

CONTACT Myrna C. Bryant, Office of Financial Aid, Kentucky State University, East Main Street, Frankfort, KY 40601, 502-597-5960 or toll-free 800-633-9415 (in-state), 800-325-1716 (out-of-state). *E-mail:* mbryant@gwmail.kysu.edu.

KENTUCKY WESLEYAN COLLEGE
Owensboro, KY

Tuition & fees: $12,990	Average undergraduate aid package: $11,110

ABOUT THE INSTITUTION Independent Methodist, coed. Awards: bachelor's degrees. 42 undergraduate majors. Total enrollment: 679. Undergraduates: 679. Freshmen: 211. Federal methodology is used as a basis for awarding need-based institutional aid.

UNDERGRADUATE EXPENSES for 2005–06 *Application fee:* $20. *Comprehensive fee:* $18,590 includes full-time tuition ($12,590), mandatory fees ($400), and room and board ($5600). *College room only:* $2550. Full-time tuition and fees vary according to course load. *Part-time tuition:* $390 per credit hour. *Part-time fees:* $25 per term. Part-time tuition and fees vary according to course load. *Payment plans:* Installment, deferred payment.

FRESHMAN FINANCIAL AID (Fall 2003) 178 applied for aid; of those 90% were deemed to have need. 100% of freshmen with need received aid; of those 25% had need fully met. *Average percent of need met:* 74% (excluding resources awarded to replace EFC). *Average financial aid package:* $11,171 (excluding resources awarded to replace EFC). 10% of all full-time freshmen had no need and received non-need-based gift aid.

UNDERGRADUATE FINANCIAL AID (Fall 2003) 587 applied for aid; of those 88% were deemed to have need. 100% of undergraduates with need received aid; of those 24% had need fully met. *Average percent of need met:* 73% (excluding resources awarded to replace EFC). *Average financial aid package:* $11,110 (excluding resources awarded to replace EFC). 12% of all full-time undergraduates had no need and received non-need-based gift aid.

GIFT AID (NEED-BASED) *Total amount:* $4,661,569 (15% federal, 26% state, 55% institutional, 4% external sources). *Receiving aid:* Freshmen: 90% (161); All full-time undergraduates: 88% (514). *Average award:* Freshmen: $9516; Undergraduates: $9013. *Scholarships, grants, and awards:* Federal Pell, FSEOG, state, private, college/university gift aid from institutional funds.

GIFT AID (NON-NEED-BASED) *Total amount:* $687,587 (18% state, 73% institutional, 9% external sources). *Receiving aid:* Freshmen: 13% (23); Undergraduates: 12% (73). *Average Award:* Freshmen: $9813; *Undergraduates:* $8375. *Scholarships, grants, and awards by category:* Academic Interests/ Achievement: 349 awards ($1,450,292 total): general academic interests/ achievements. Creative Arts/Performance: 40 awards ($47,540 total): art/fine arts, music, theater/drama. Special Achievements/Activities: 97 awards ($233,416 total): junior miss, leadership. Special Characteristics: 170 awards ($221,355 total): children and siblings of alumni, children of faculty/staff, children of union members/company employees, general special characteristics, out-of-state students, relatives of clergy, religious affiliation, siblings of current students. *Tuition waivers:* Full or partial for children of alumni, employees or children of employees, senior citizens.

LOANS *Student loans:* $1,559,437 (74% need-based, 26% non-need-based). 85% of past graduating class borrowed through all loan programs. *Average indebtedness per student:* $17,929. *Average need-based loan:* Freshmen: $2024; Undergraduates: $2891. *Parent loans:* $331,268 (47% need-based, 53% non-need-based). *Programs:* FFEL (Subsidized and Unsubsidized Stafford, PLUS), Perkins, alternative loans.

WORK-STUDY *Federal work-study:* Total amount: $119,795; 180 jobs averaging $1000.

ATHLETIC AWARDS *Total amount:* $725,510 (100% need-based).

APPLYING FOR FINANCIAL AID *Required financial aid form:* FAFSA. *Financial aid deadline (priority):* 3/15. *Notification date:* Continuous beginning 2/15. Students must reply within 2 weeks of notification.

CONTACT Mr. Kurt Osborne, Director of Financial Aid, Kentucky Wesleyan College, 3000 Frederica Street, Owensboro, KY 42302, 270-852-3130 or toll-free 800-999-0592 (in-state), 800-990-0592 (out-of-state). *Fax:* 270-926-3196. *E-mail:* kosborne@kwc.edu.

KENYON COLLEGE
Gambier, OH

Tuition & fees: $32,170	Average undergraduate aid package: $23,245

ABOUT THE INSTITUTION Independent, coed. Awards: bachelor's degrees. 54 undergraduate majors. Total enrollment: 1,634. Undergraduates: 1,634. Freshmen: 468. Both federal and institutional methodology are used as a basis for awarding need-based institutional aid.

UNDERGRADUATE EXPENSES for 2004–05 *Application fee:* $45. *Comprehensive fee:* $37,440 includes full-time tuition ($31,260), mandatory fees ($910), and room and board ($5270). *College room only:* $2480. Room and board charges vary according to housing facility. *Payment plan:* Installment.

FRESHMAN FINANCIAL AID (Fall 2004, est.) 267 applied for aid; of those 70% were deemed to have need. 100% of freshmen with need received aid; of those 55% had need fully met. *Average percent of need met:* 98% (excluding resources awarded to replace EFC). *Average financial aid package:* $23,097 (excluding resources awarded to replace EFC). 27% of all full-time freshmen had no need and received non-need-based gift aid.

UNDERGRADUATE FINANCIAL AID (Fall 2004, est.) 897 applied for aid; of those 83% were deemed to have need. 100% of undergraduates with need received aid; of those 50% had need fully met. *Average percent of need met:* 98% (excluding resources awarded to replace EFC). *Average financial aid package:* $23,245 (excluding resources awarded to replace EFC). 22% of all full-time undergraduates had no need and received non-need-based gift aid.

GIFT AID (NEED-BASED) *Total amount:* $14,478,639 (5% federal, 2% state, 89% institutional, 4% external sources). *Receiving aid:* Freshmen: 40% (182); All full-time undergraduates: 42% (722). *Average award:* Freshmen: $21,411; Undergraduates: $20,301. *Scholarships, grants, and awards:* Federal Pell, FSEOG, state, private, college/university gift aid from institutional funds.

GIFT AID (NON-NEED-BASED) *Total amount:* $3,291,649 (9% state, 80% institutional, 11% external sources). *Receiving aid:* Freshmen: 19% (88); Undergraduates: 16% (269). *Average Award:* Freshmen: $9998; *Undergraduates:* $11,221. *Scholarships, grants, and awards by category:* Academic Interests/Achievement: 369 awards ($3,234,250 total): general academic interests/ achievements. Special Characteristics: 46 awards ($649,000 total): ethnic background. *Tuition waivers:* Full or partial for employees or children of employees.

LOANS *Student loans:* $5,023,078 (51% need-based, 49% non-need-based). 63% of past graduating class borrowed through all loan programs. *Average indebtedness per student:* $18,120. *Average need-based loan:* Freshmen: $2371; Undergraduates: $3560. *Parent loans:* $3,110,750 (7% need-based, 93% non-need-based). *Programs:* FFEL (Subsidized and Unsubsidized Stafford, PLUS), Perkins, college/university.

WORK-STUDY *Federal work-study:* Total amount: $127,908; 316 jobs averaging $580. *State or other work-study/employment:* Total amount: $283,684 (61% need-based, 39% non-need-based). 176 part-time jobs averaging $560.

APPLYING FOR FINANCIAL AID *Required financial aid forms:* FAFSA, CSS Financial Aid PROFILE, noncustodial (divorced/separated) parent's statement, income tax form(s). *Financial aid deadline (priority):* 2/15. *Notification date:* 4/1. Students must reply by 5/1.

CONTACT Mr. Craig Daugherty, Director of Financial Aid, Kenyon College, Stephens Hall, Gambier, OH 43022-9623, 740-427-5430 or toll-free 800-848-2468. *Fax:* 740-427-5240. *E-mail:* daugherty@kenyon.edu.

KETTERING UNIVERSITY
Flint, MI

Tuition & fees: $23,360	Average undergraduate aid package: $12,851

ABOUT THE INSTITUTION Independent, coed. Awards: bachelor's and master's degrees. 21 undergraduate majors. Total enrollment: 2,992. Undergraduates: 2,512. Freshmen: 564. Federal methodology is used as a basis for awarding need-based institutional aid.

UNDERGRADUATE EXPENSES for 2005–06 *Application fee:* $35. *Tuition:* full-time $23,360; part-time $730 per credit. Room and board charges vary according to student level. *Payment plan:* Installment.

GIFT AID (NEED-BASED) *Total amount:* $11,986,805 (14% federal, 18% state, 63% institutional, 5% external sources). *Receiving aid:* Freshmen: 68% (384); All full-time undergraduates: 62% (1,314). *Average award:* Freshmen: $4178; Undergraduates: $3963. *Scholarships, grants, and awards:* Federal Pell, FSEOG, state, private, college/university gift aid from institutional funds.

GIFT AID (NON-NEED-BASED) *Total amount:* $2,920,006 (5% state, 86% institutional, 9% external sources). *Receiving aid:* Freshmen: 82% (462); Undergraduates: 67% (1,412). *Average Award:* Freshmen: $8470; *Undergraduates:* $5984. *Scholarships, grants, and awards by category:* Academic Interests/ Achievement: business, computer science, engineering/technologies, general academic interests/achievements, mathematics, physical sciences. *Special Achievements/Activities:* general special achievements/activities, memberships. *Tuition waivers:* Full or partial for employees or children of employees.

LOANS *Student loans:* $18,348,214 (81% need-based, 19% non-need-based). 56% of past graduating class borrowed through all loan programs. *Average indebtedness per student:* $37,997. *Average need-based loan:* Freshmen: $2577; Undergraduates: $3938. *Parent loans:* $1,486,008 (89% need-based, 11% non-need-based). *Programs:* FFEL (Subsidized and Unsubsidized Stafford, PLUS), state, alternative loans.

APPLYING FOR FINANCIAL AID *Required financial aid form:* FAFSA. *Financial aid deadline (priority):* 2/14. *Notification date:* Continuous beginning 2/15. Students must reply within 2 weeks of notification.

CONTACT Diane Bice, Director of Financial Aid, Kettering University, 1700 West Third Avenue, Flint, MI 48504-4898, 800-955-4464 Ext. 7859 or toll-free 800-955-4464 Ext. 7865 (in-state), 800-955-4464 (out-of-state). *Fax:* 810-762-9807. *E-mail:* finaid@kettering.edu.

KEUKA COLLEGE
Keuka Park, NY

Tuition & fees: $17,080	Average undergraduate aid package: $15,375

ABOUT THE INSTITUTION Independent religious, coed. Awards: bachelor's and master's degrees. 34 undergraduate majors. Total enrollment: 1,154. Undergraduates: 1,154. Freshmen: 252. Federal methodology is used as a basis for awarding need-based institutional aid.

UNDERGRADUATE EXPENSES for 2004–05 *Application fee:* $30. *Comprehensive fee:* $24,870 includes full-time tuition ($16,820), mandatory fees ($260), and room and board ($7790). *College room only:* $3700. Full-time tuition and fees vary according to program. Room and board charges vary according to board plan and housing facility. *Part-time tuition:* $525 per credit hour. Part-time tuition and fees vary according to program. *Payment plan:* Installment.

GIFT AID (NEED-BASED) *Total amount:* $8,836,580 (15% federal, 19% state, 64% institutional, 2% external sources). *Receiving aid:* Freshmen: 94% (234); All full-time undergraduates: 90% (916). *Average award:* Freshmen: $12,194; Undergraduates: $9975. *Scholarships, grants, and awards:* Federal Pell, FSEOG, state, private, college/university gift aid from institutional funds.

GIFT AID (NON-NEED-BASED) *Total amount:* $807,300 (8% state, 87% institutional, 5% external sources). *Receiving aid:* Freshmen: 14% (34); Undergraduates: 9% (96). *Average Award:* Freshmen: $10,913; Undergraduates: $12,033. *Scholarships, grants, and awards by category:* Academic Interests/Achievement: general academic interests/achievements, international studies. *Special Achievements/Activities:* community service, general special achievements/activities, leadership. *Special Characteristics:* children and siblings of alumni, children of faculty/staff, international students, siblings of current students. *Tuition waivers:* Full or partial for employees or children of employees.

LOANS *Student loans:* $8,226,813 (75% need-based, 25% non-need-based). 85% of past graduating class borrowed through all loan programs. *Average indebtedness per student:* $18,645. *Average need-based loan:* Freshmen: $4519; Undergraduates: $5808. *Parent loans:* $861,844 (47% need-based, 53% non-need-based). *Programs:* FFEL (Subsidized and Unsubsidized Stafford, PLUS), Perkins.

APPLYING FOR FINANCIAL AID *Required financial aid form:* FAFSA. *Financial aid deadline (priority):* 3/15. *Notification date:* Continuous. Students must reply within 2 weeks of notification.

CONTACT Jennifer Bates, Director of Financial Aid, Keuka College, Financial Aid Office, Keuka Park, NY 14478-0098, 315-279-5232 or toll-free 800-33-KEUKA. *Fax:* 315-536-5327. *E-mail:* jbates@mail.keuka.edu.

KING COLLEGE
Bristol, TN

Tuition & fees: $17,680	Average undergraduate aid package: $15,553

ABOUT THE INSTITUTION Independent religious, coed. Awards: bachelor's and master's degrees. 50 undergraduate majors. Total enrollment: 812. Undergraduates: 744. Freshmen: 172. Federal methodology is used as a basis for awarding need-based institutional aid.

UNDERGRADUATE EXPENSES for 2005–06 *Application fee:* $20. *Comprehensive fee:* $23,400 includes full-time tuition ($16,626), mandatory fees ($1054), and room and board ($5720). Full-time tuition and fees vary according to program.

Room and board charges vary according to board plan. *Part-time tuition:* $550 per credit hour. Part-time tuition and fees vary according to course load and program. *Payment plans:* Tuition prepayment, installment.

FRESHMAN FINANCIAL AID (Fall 2004, est.) 146 applied for aid; of those 88% were deemed to have need. 100% of freshmen with need received aid; of those 27% had need fully met. *Average percent of need met:* 81% (excluding resources awarded to replace EFC). *Average financial aid package:* $15,998 (excluding resources awarded to replace EFC). 12% of all full-time freshmen had no need and received non-need-based gift aid.

UNDERGRADUATE FINANCIAL AID (Fall 2004, est.) 515 applied for aid; of those 91% were deemed to have need. 100% of undergraduates with need received aid; of those 22% had need fully met. *Average percent of need met:* 79% (excluding resources awarded to replace EFC). *Average financial aid package:* $15,553 (excluding resources awarded to replace EFC). 8% of all full-time undergraduates had no need and received non-need-based gift aid.

GIFT AID (NEED-BASED) *Total amount:* $4,853,567 (15% federal, 13% state, 63% institutional, 9% external sources). *Receiving aid:* Freshmen: 75% (129); All full-time undergraduates: 70% (454). *Average award:* Freshmen: $14,254; Undergraduates: $12,526. *Scholarships, grants, and awards:* Federal Pell, FSEOG, state, private, college/university gift aid from institutional funds.

GIFT AID (NON-NEED-BASED) *Total amount:* $598,131 (24% state, 60% institutional, 16% external sources). *Receiving aid:* Freshmen: 19% (32); Undergraduates: 13% (83). *Average Award:* Freshmen: $8915; Undergraduates: $9338. *Scholarships, grants, and awards by category:* Academic Interests/Achievement: 340 awards ($2,344,596 total): general academic interests/achievements. *Creative Arts/Performance:* 27 awards ($28,533 total): music, performing arts, theater/drama. *Special Achievements/Activities:* 30 awards ($99,500 total): community service. *Special Characteristics:* 56 awards ($236,777 total): children of faculty/staff, members of minority groups, relatives of clergy. *Tuition waivers:* Full or partial for employees or children of employees.

LOANS *Student loans:* $2,479,178 (80% need-based, 20% non-need-based). 84% of past graduating class borrowed through all loan programs. *Average indebtedness per student:* $15,300. *Average need-based loan:* Freshmen: $2933; Undergraduates: $4442. *Parent loans:* $607,597 (39% need-based, 61% non-need-based). *Programs:* FFEL (Subsidized and Unsubsidized Stafford, PLUS), Perkins, college/university.

WORK-STUDY *Federal work-study:* Total amount: $57,204; 59 jobs averaging $970. *State or other work-study/employment:* Total amount: $107,532 (90% need-based, 10% non-need-based). 87 part-time jobs averaging $1236.

ATHLETIC AWARDS *Total amount:* $1,152,025 (75% need-based, 25% non-need-based).

APPLYING FOR FINANCIAL AID *Required financial aid form:* FAFSA. *Financial aid deadline (priority):* 3/1. *Notification date:* Continuous beginning 3/1. Students must reply within 2 weeks of notification.

CONTACT Brenda L. Clark, Director of Financial Aid, King College, 1350 King College Road, Bristol, TN 37620-2699, 423-652-4728 or toll-free 800-362-0014. *Fax:* 423-652-6039. *E-mail:* blclark@king.edu.

THE KING'S COLLEGE
New York, NY

CONTACT Financial Aid Office, The King's College, 350 Fifth Avenue, 15th Floor Empire State Building, New York, NY 10118, 212-659-7200 or toll-free 888-969-7200 Ext. 3610.

KING'S COLLEGE
Wilkes-Barre, PA

Tuition & fees: $20,110	Average undergraduate aid package: $16,637

ABOUT THE INSTITUTION Independent Roman Catholic, coed. Awards: associate, bachelor's, and master's degrees and post-bachelor's certificates. 41 undergraduate majors. Total enrollment: 2,223. Undergraduates: 2,060. Freshmen: 449. Federal methodology is used as a basis for awarding need-based institutional aid.

UNDERGRADUATE EXPENSES for 2004–05 *Application fee:* $30. *Comprehensive fee:* $28,360 includes full-time tuition ($19,260), mandatory fees ($850), and room and board ($8250). *College room only:* $3860. Room and board charges vary according to board plan and housing facility. *Part-time tuition:* $473 per credit hour. *Payment plans:* Installment, deferred payment.

FRESHMAN FINANCIAL AID (Fall 2004, est.) 426 applied for aid; of those 87% were deemed to have need. 100% of freshmen with need received aid; of those

16% had need fully met. *Average percent of need met:* 75% (excluding resources awarded to replace EFC). *Average financial aid package:* $15,107 (excluding resources awarded to replace EFC). 16% of all full-time freshmen had no need and received non-need-based gift aid.

UNDERGRADUATE FINANCIAL AID (Fall 2004, est.) 1,570 applied for aid; of those 90% were deemed to have need. 100% of undergraduates with need received aid; of those 14% had need fully met. *Average percent of need met:* 73% (excluding resources awarded to replace EFC). *Average financial aid package:* $16,637 (excluding resources awarded to replace EFC). 14% of all full-time undergraduates had no need and received non-need-based gift aid.

GIFT AID (NEED-BASED) *Total amount:* $15,358,776 (9% federal, 15% state, 74% institutional, 2% external sources). *Receiving aid:* Freshmen: 65% (294); All full-time undergraduates: 68% (1,202). *Average award:* Freshmen: $6483; Undergraduates: $6137. *Scholarships, grants, and awards:* Federal Pell, FSEOG, state, private, college/university gift aid from institutional funds.

GIFT AID (NON-NEED-BASED) *Total amount:* $2,541,045 (8% federal, 2% state, 89% institutional, 1% external sources). *Receiving aid:* Freshmen: 64% (289); Undergraduates: 54% (957). *Average Award:* Freshmen: $8368; Undergraduates: $8570. *Scholarships, grants, and awards by category: Academic Interests/Achievement:* 960 awards ($8,392,499 total): biological sciences, business, communication, computer science, education, English, foreign languages, general academic interests/achievements, health fields, humanities, mathematics, physical sciences, premedicine, religion/biblical studies, social sciences. *Creative Arts/Performance:* 27 awards ($96,299 total): debating, journalism/publications. *Special Achievements/Activities:* 169 awards ($855,098 total): community service, general special achievements/activities, leadership. *Special Characteristics:* 153 awards ($876,670 total): children of educators, children of faculty/staff, international students, members of minority groups, relatives of clergy, siblings of current students. *Tuition waivers:* Full or partial for employees or children of employees, senior citizens. *ROTC:* Army, Air Force.

LOANS *Student loans:* $9,864,612 (51% need-based, 49% non-need-based). 95% of past graduating class borrowed through all loan programs. *Average indebtedness per student:* $16,417. *Average need-based loan:* Freshmen: $3540; Undergraduates: $4238. *Parent loans:* $3,438,611 (87% need-based, 13% non-need-based). *Programs:* FFEL (Subsidized and Unsubsidized Stafford, PLUS), Perkins, alternative loans.

WORK-STUDY *Federal work-study:* Total amount: $280,000; 350 jobs averaging $800. *State or other work-study/employment:* Total amount: $267,135 (16% need-based, 84% non-need-based). 267 part-time jobs averaging $1000.

APPLYING FOR FINANCIAL AID *Required financial aid forms:* FAFSA, institution's own form. *Financial aid deadline (priority):* 2/15. *Notification date:* Continuous beginning 3/1. Students must reply by 5/1 or within 2 weeks of notification.

CONTACT Ellen E. McGuire, Director of Financial Aid, King's College, 133 North River Street, Wilkes-Barre, PA 18711-0801, 570-208-5868 or toll-free 888-KINGSPA. *Fax:* 570-208-6015. *E-mail:* finaid@kings.edu.

THE KING'S COLLEGE AND SEMINARY
Van Nuys, CA

CONTACT Financial Aid Office, The King's College and Seminary, 14800 Sherman Way, Van Nuys, CA 91405-8040, 818-779-8040 or toll-free 888-779-8040 (in-state).

KNOX COLLEGE
Galesburg, IL

Tuition & fees: $25,236	Average undergraduate aid package: $21,390

ABOUT THE INSTITUTION Independent, coed. Awards: bachelor's degrees. 34 undergraduate majors. Total enrollment: 1,205. Undergraduates: 1,205. Freshmen: 363. Both federal and institutional methodology are used as a basis for awarding need-based institutional aid.

UNDERGRADUATE EXPENSES for 2004–05 *Application fee:* $35. *Comprehensive fee:* $31,338 includes full-time tuition ($24,960), mandatory fees ($276), and room and board ($6102). *College room only:* $2703. Room and board charges vary according to board plan. *Part-time tuition:* $920 per credit. *Payment plan:* Installment.

FRESHMAN FINANCIAL AID (Fall 2004, est.) 304 applied for aid; of those 79% were deemed to have need. 100% of freshmen with need received aid; of those 44% had need fully met. *Average percent of need met:* 95% (excluding resources

awarded to replace EFC). *Average financial aid package:* $20,904 (excluding resources awarded to replace EFC). 32% of all full-time freshmen had no need and received non-need-based gift aid.

UNDERGRADUATE FINANCIAL AID (Fall 2004, est.) 936 applied for aid; of those 86% were deemed to have need. 100% of undergraduates with need received aid; of those 47% had need fully met. *Average percent of need met:* 95% (excluding resources awarded to replace EFC). *Average financial aid package:* $21,390 (excluding resources awarded to replace EFC). 26% of all full-time undergraduates had no need and received non-need-based gift aid.

GIFT AID (NEED-BASED) *Total amount:* $12,960,170 (8% federal, 9% state, 81% institutional, 2% external sources). *Receiving aid:* Freshmen: 66% (239); All full-time undergraduates: 69% (805). *Average award:* Freshmen: $16,434; Undergraduates: $16,059. *Scholarships, grants, and awards:* Federal Pell, FSEOG, state, private, college/university gift aid from institutional funds.

GIFT AID (NON-NEED-BASED) *Total amount:* $3,045,107 (98% institutional, 2% external sources). *Receiving aid:* Freshmen: 11% (40); Undergraduates: 8% (98). *Average Award:* Freshmen: $9942; Undergraduates: $9785. *Scholarships, grants, and awards by category: Academic Interests/Achievement:* general academic interests/achievements, mathematics. *Creative Arts/Performance:* art/fine arts, creative writing, dance, music, theater/drama. *Special Achievements/ Activities:* community service. *Tuition waivers:* Full or partial for employees or children of employees.

LOANS *Student loans:* $4,716,000 (68% need-based, 32% non-need-based). 71% of past graduating class borrowed through all loan programs. *Average indebtedness per student:* $20,975. *Average need-based loan:* Freshmen: $4578; Undergraduates: $5332. *Parent loans:* $1,776,106 (100% non-need-based). *Programs:* Federal Direct (Subsidized and Unsubsidized Stafford, PLUS), Perkins, college/university.

WORK-STUDY *Federal work-study:* Total amount: $968,216; 599 jobs averaging $1616. *State or other work-study/employment:* Total amount: $150,674 (90% need-based, 10% non-need-based). 99 part-time jobs averaging $1522.

APPLYING FOR FINANCIAL AID *Required financial aid forms:* FAFSA, institution's own form, income tax form(s). *Financial aid deadline (priority):* 3/1. *Notification date:* 4/15. Students must reply by 5/1 or within 2 weeks of notification.

CONTACT Ms. Teresa K. Jackson, Director of Financial Aid, Knox College, 2 East South Street, Galesburg, IL 61401, 309-341-7130 or toll-free 800-678-KNOX. *Fax:* 309-341-7070. *E-mail:* tjackson@knox.edu.

KOL YAAKOV TORAH CENTER
Monsey, NY

CONTACT Office of Financial Aid, Kol Yaakov Torah Center, 29 West Maple Avenue, Monsey, NY 10952-2954, 914-425-3863.

KUTZTOWN UNIVERSITY OF PENNSYLVANIA
Kutztown, PA

Tuition & fees (PA res): $6256	Average undergraduate aid package: $6204

ABOUT THE INSTITUTION State-supported, coed. Awards: bachelor's and master's degrees and post-bachelor's certificates. 64 undergraduate majors. Total enrollment: 9,584. Undergraduates: 8,527. Freshmen: 2,052. Federal methodology is used as a basis for awarding need-based institutional aid.

UNDERGRADUATE EXPENSES for 2004–05 *Application fee:* $35. *Tuition, state resident:* full-time $4810; part-time $200 per credit. *Tuition, nonresident:* full-time $12,026; part-time $501 per credit. *Required fees:* full-time $1446; $73.71 per credit. Part-time tuition and fees vary according to course load. *College room and board:* $5274; *room only:* $3792. Room and board charges vary according to board plan and housing facility. *Payment plans:* Tuition prepayment, installment, deferred payment.

GIFT AID (NEED-BASED) *Total amount:* $11,268,296 (43% federal, 48% state, 4% institutional, 5% external sources). *Receiving aid:* Freshmen: 47% (873); All full-time undergraduates: 42% (3,148). *Average award:* Freshmen: $4078; Undergraduates: $3773. *Scholarships, grants, and awards:* Federal Pell, FSEOG, state, private, college/university gift aid from institutional funds.

GIFT AID (NON-NEED-BASED) *Total amount:* $767,738 (22% federal, 22% state, 15% institutional, 41% external sources). *Receiving aid:* Freshmen: 2% (36); Undergraduates: 6% (444). *Average Award:* Freshmen: $1440; Undergraduates: $1817. *Scholarships, grants, and awards by category: Academic Interests/ Achievement:* 361 awards ($852,491 total): business, communication, computer science, education, English, foreign languages, general academic interests/

achievements, humanities, library science, mathematics, physical sciences. *Creative Arts/Performance:* 20 awards ($21,077 total): applied art and design, art/fine arts, dance, music, theater/drama. *Special Achievements/Activities:* 113 awards ($45,008 total): general special achievements/activities, leadership, religious involvement. *Special Characteristics:* 108 awards ($412,037 total): children of faculty/staff, children of union members/company employees, handicapped students. *Tuition waivers:* Full or partial for employees or children of employees, senior citizens. *ROTC:* Army cooperative, Air Force cooperative.

LOANS *Student loans:* $25,119,129 (63% need-based, 37% non-need-based). 77% of past graduating class borrowed through all loan programs. *Average indebtedness per student:* $15,015. *Average need-based loan:* Freshmen: $2555; Undergraduates: $3403. *Parent loans:* $4,222,413 (30% need-based, 70% non-need-based). *Programs:* FFEL (Subsidized and Unsubsidized Stafford, PLUS), Perkins.

ATHLETIC AWARDS *Total amount:* $385,576 (51% need-based, 49% non-need-based).

APPLYING FOR FINANCIAL AID *Required financial aid form:* FAFSA. *Financial aid deadline (priority):* 2/15. *Notification date:* Continuous beginning 3/30.

CONTACT Ms. Anita Faust, Director of Financial Aid, Kutztown University of Pennsylvania, 209A Stratton Administration Center, Kutztown, PA 19530-0730, 610-683-4077 or toll-free 877-628-1915. *Fax:* 610-683-1380. *E-mail:* faust@kutztown.edu.

LABORATORY INSTITUTE OF MERCHANDISING
New York, NY

Tuition & fees: $17,050 | **Average undergraduate aid package: $6754**

ABOUT THE INSTITUTION Proprietary, coed, primarily women. Awards: associate and bachelor's degrees. 2 undergraduate majors. Total enrollment: 608. Undergraduates: 608. Freshmen: 154. Federal methodology is used as a basis for awarding need-based institutional aid.

UNDERGRADUATE EXPENSES for 2005–06 *Application fee:* $40. *Tuition:* full-time $16,600; part-time $495 per credit. *Required fees:* full-time $450; $100 per term part-time. Room and board charges vary according to housing facility. *Payment plan:* Installment.

FRESHMAN FINANCIAL AID (Fall 2003) 95 applied for aid; of those 100% were deemed to have need. 100% of freshmen with need received aid. *Average financial aid package:* $7350 (excluding resources awarded to replace EFC). 8% of all full-time freshmen had no need and received non-need-based gift aid.

UNDERGRADUATE FINANCIAL AID (Fall 2003) 429 applied for aid; of those 100% were deemed to have need. 100% of undergraduates with need received aid. *Average financial aid package:* $6754 (excluding resources awarded to replace EFC). 5% of all full-time undergraduates had no need and received non-need-based gift aid.

GIFT AID (NEED-BASED) *Total amount:* $1,243,004 (37% federal, 35% state, 28% institutional). *Receiving aid:* Freshmen: 60% (80); All full-time undergraduates: 66% (298). *Average award:* Freshmen: $4659; Undergraduates: $4080. *Scholarships, grants, and awards:* Federal Pell, FSEOG, state, college/university gift aid from institutional funds.

GIFT AID (NON-NEED-BASED) *Receiving aid:* Freshmen: 22% (29); Undergraduates: 23% (106). *Average Award:* Freshmen: $2100; Undergraduates: $1583. *Scholarships, grants, and awards by category:* Academic Interests/Achievement: 105 awards ($212,250 total): general academic interests/achievements. *Special Achievements/Activities:* 1 award ($3725 total): memberships. *Special Characteristics:* local/state students. *Tuition waivers:* Full or partial for employees or children of employees.

LOANS *Student loans:* $2,187,590 (100% need-based). 75% of past graduating class borrowed through all loan programs. *Average need-based loan:* Freshmen: $2585; Undergraduates: $2593. *Parent loans:* $2,254,862 (100% need-based). *Programs:* Federal Direct (Subsidized and Unsubsidized Stafford, PLUS).

WORK-STUDY *Federal work-study:* Total amount: $35,226; 22 jobs averaging $1601.

APPLYING FOR FINANCIAL AID *Required financial aid forms:* FAFSA, institution's own form. *Financial aid deadline:* Continuous. *Notification date:* Continuous beginning 2/15. Students must reply within 2 weeks of notification.

CONTACT Mr. Christopher Barto, Director of Financial Aid, Laboratory Institute of Merchandising, 12 East 53rd Street, New York, NY 10022-5268, 212-752-1530 or toll-free 800-677-1323. *Fax:* 212-317-8602. *E-mail:* cbarto@limcollege.edu.

LAFAYETTE COLLEGE
Easton, PA

Tuition & fees: $29,982 | **Average undergraduate aid package: $22,888**

ABOUT THE INSTITUTION Independent religious, coed. Awards: bachelor's degrees. 34 undergraduate majors. Total enrollment: 2,303. Undergraduates: 2,303. Freshmen: 609. Institutional methodology is used as a basis for awarding need-based institutional aid.

UNDERGRADUATE EXPENSES for 2005–06 *Application fee:* $60. *Comprehensive fee:* $39,267 includes full-time tuition ($29,822), mandatory fees ($160), and room and board ($9285). *College room only:* $5345.

FRESHMAN FINANCIAL AID (Fall 2003) 422 applied for aid; of those 86% were deemed to have need. 99% of freshmen with need received aid; of those 100% had need fully met. *Average percent of need met:* 100% (excluding resources awarded to replace EFC). *Average financial aid package:* $22,492 (excluding resources awarded to replace EFC). 5% of all full-time freshmen had no need and received non-need-based gift aid.

UNDERGRADUATE FINANCIAL AID (Fall 2003) 1,374 applied for aid; of those 91% were deemed to have need. 99% of undergraduates with need received aid; of those 99% had need fully met. *Average percent of need met:* 99% (excluding resources awarded to replace EFC). *Average financial aid package:* $22,888 (excluding resources awarded to replace EFC). 7% of all full-time undergraduates had no need and received non-need-based gift aid.

GIFT AID (NEED-BASED) *Total amount:* $22,399,812 (3% federal, 3% state, 92% institutional, 2% external sources). *Receiving aid:* Freshmen: 53% (323); All full-time undergraduates: 50% (1,131). *Average award:* Freshmen: $21,499; Undergraduates: $20,754. *Scholarships, grants, and awards:* Federal Pell, FSEOG, state, private, college/university gift aid from institutional funds.

GIFT AID (NON-NEED-BASED) *Total amount:* $2,382,516 (78% institutional, 22% external sources). *Receiving aid:* Freshmen: 9% (56); Undergraduates: 6% (128). *Average Award:* Freshmen: $12,894; Undergraduates: $12,964. *Scholarships, grants, and awards by category:* Academic Interests/Achievement: 335 awards ($3,595,845 total): general academic interests/achievements. *ROTC:* Army cooperative.

LOANS *Student loans:* $5,881,325 (45% need-based, 55% non-need-based). 54% of past graduating class borrowed through all loan programs. *Average indebtedness per student:* $17,995. *Average need-based loan:* Freshmen: $3503; Undergraduates: $4313. *Parent loans:* $6,879,851 (2% need-based, 98% non-need-based). *Programs:* FFEL (Subsidized and Unsubsidized Stafford, PLUS), Perkins, state, college/university.

WORK-STUDY *Federal work-study:* Total amount: $204,353. *State or other work-study/employment:* Total amount: $597,338 (49% need-based, 51% non-need-based).

APPLYING FOR FINANCIAL AID *Required financial aid forms:* FAFSA, CSS Financial Aid PROFILE, business/farm supplement, CSS/Financial Aid non-custodial profile. *Financial aid deadline:* 3/15 (priority: 2/1). *Notification date:* 4/11. Students must reply by 5/1.

CONTACT Arlinda DeNardo, Director Financial Aid, Lafayette College, 107 Markle Hall, Easton, PA 18042-1777, 610-330-5055. *Fax:* 610-330-5758. *E-mail:* denardoa@lafayette.edu.

LAGRANGE COLLEGE
LaGrange, GA

Tuition & fees: $15,206 | **Average undergraduate aid package: $12,596**

ABOUT THE INSTITUTION Independent United Methodist, coed. Awards: associate, bachelor's, and master's degrees. 35 undergraduate majors. Total enrollment: 1,044. Undergraduates: 993. Freshmen: 220. Federal methodology is used as a basis for awarding need-based institutional aid.

UNDERGRADUATE EXPENSES for 2004–05 *Application fee:* $20. *Comprehensive fee:* $21,524 includes full-time tuition ($15,206) and room and board ($6318). Full-time tuition and fees vary according to class time, degree level, location, and program. Room and board charges vary according to housing facility. *Part-time tuition:* $627 per hour. Part-time tuition and fees vary according to class time, degree level, location, and program. *Payment plan:* Installment.

FRESHMAN FINANCIAL AID (Fall 2003) 184 applied for aid; of those 68% were deemed to have need. 100% of freshmen with need received aid; of those 36% had need fully met. *Average percent of need met:* 81% (excluding resources

awarded to replace EFC). *Average financial aid package:* $13,962 (excluding resources awarded to replace EFC). 31% of all full-time freshmen had no need and received non-need-based gift aid.

UNDERGRADUATE FINANCIAL AID (Fall 2003) 881 applied for aid; of those 72% were deemed to have need. 100% of undergraduates with need received aid; of those 33% had need fully met. *Average percent of need met:* 76% (excluding resources awarded to replace EFC). *Average financial aid package:* $12,596 (excluding resources awarded to replace EFC). 28% of all full-time undergraduates had no need and received non-need-based gift aid.

GIFT AID (NEED-BASED) *Total amount:* $5,622,666 (16% federal, 24% state, 55% institutional, 5% external sources). *Receiving aid:* Freshmen: 66% (125); All full-time undergraduates: 70% (623). *Average award:* Freshmen: $11,134; Undergraduates: $9169. *Scholarships, grants, and awards:* Federal Pell, FSEOG, state, private, college/university gift aid from institutional funds.

GIFT AID (NON-NEED-BASED) *Total amount:* $1,338,234 (36% state, 55% institutional, 9% external sources). *Receiving aid:* Freshmen: 14% (27); Undergraduates: 13% (117). *Average Award:* Freshmen: $8340; Undergraduates: $6556. *Scholarships, grants, and awards by category: Academic Interests/Achievement:* 483 awards ($1,965,131 total): biological sciences, business, computer science, education, English, general academic interests/achievements, health fields, physical sciences, religion/biblical studies, social sciences. *Creative Arts/Performance:* 25 awards ($56,539 total): applied art and design, art/fine arts, music, theater/drama. *Special Achievements/Activities:* 15 awards ($45,500 total): community service, leadership. *Special Characteristics:* 142 awards ($560,374 total): children of faculty/staff, ethnic background, first-generation college students, relatives of clergy, religious affiliation. *Tuition waivers:* Full or partial for employees or children of employees.

LOANS *Student loans:* $3,403,425 (91% need-based, 9% non-need-based). 63% of past graduating class borrowed through all loan programs. *Average indebtedness per student:* $15,499. *Average need-based loan:* Freshmen: $2228; Undergraduates: $3425. *Parent loans:* $860,889 (65% need-based, 35% non-need-based). *Programs:* FFEL (Subsidized and Unsubsidized Stafford, PLUS), Perkins.

WORK-STUDY *Federal work-study:* Total amount: $93,565; 99 jobs averaging $856. *State or other work-study/employment:* Total amount: $287,703 (67% need-based, 33% non-need-based). 282 part-time jobs averaging $935.

APPLYING FOR FINANCIAL AID *Required financial aid forms:* FAFSA, institution's own form, state aid form. *Financial aid deadline:* 3/1. *Notification date:* Continuous. Students must reply by 8/15 or within 2 weeks of notification.

CONTACT Sylvia Smith, Director of Financial Aid, LaGrange College, 601 Broad Street, LaGrange, GA 30240-2999, 706-880-8229 or toll-free 800-593-2885. *E-mail:* ssmith@lagrange.edu.

LAGUNA COLLEGE OF ART & DESIGN
Laguna Beach, CA

Tuition & fees: $16,600	Average undergraduate aid package: $8000

ABOUT THE INSTITUTION Independent, coed. Awards: bachelor's degrees. 12 undergraduate majors. Total enrollment: 310. Undergraduates: 310. Freshmen: 70. Federal methodology is used as a basis for awarding need-based institutional aid.

UNDERGRADUATE EXPENSES for 2004–05 *Application fee:* $45. *Tuition:* full-time $16,600; part-time $688 per unit. *Payment plan:* Installment.

GIFT AID (NEED-BASED) *Total amount:* $567,020 (53% federal, 47% state). *Receiving aid:* Freshmen: 80% (56); All full-time undergraduates: 85% (262). *Average award:* Freshmen: $2500; Undergraduates: $2500. *Scholarships, grants, and awards:* Federal Pell, FSEOG, state, private, college/university gift aid from institutional funds.

GIFT AID (NON-NEED-BASED) *Total amount:* $600,000 (100% institutional). *Receiving aid:* Freshmen: 93% (65); Undergraduates: 88% (274). *Average Award:* Freshmen: $2500; Undergraduates: $2500. *Scholarships, grants, and awards by category: Academic Interests/Achievement:* 278 awards ($544,000 total): general academic interests/achievements. *Creative Arts/Performance:* 278 awards ($544,000 total): applied art and design, art/fine arts. *Tuition waivers:* Full or partial for employees or children of employees.

LOANS *Student loans:* $1,057,500 (59% need-based, 41% non-need-based). 93% of past graduating class borrowed through all loan programs. *Average indebtedness per student:* $35,125. *Average need-based loan:* Freshmen: $3500; Undergraduates: $3500. *Parent loans:* $595,000 (100% need-based). *Programs:* FFEL (Subsidized and Unsubsidized Stafford, PLUS).

APPLYING FOR FINANCIAL AID *Required financial aid form:* FAFSA. *Financial aid deadline:* Continuous.

CONTACT Christopher Brown, Director of Student Services, Laguna College of Art & Design, 2222 Laguna Canyon Road, Laguna Beach, CA 92651-1136, 949-376-6000 or toll-free 800-255-0762. *Fax:* 949-497-5220. *E-mail:* cbrown@lagunacollege.edu.

LAKE ERIE COLLEGE
Painesville, OH

Tuition & fees: $18,590	Average undergraduate aid package: N/A

ABOUT THE INSTITUTION Independent, coed. Awards: bachelor's and master's degrees. 29 undergraduate majors. Total enrollment: 914. Undergraduates: 760. Freshmen: 141. Federal methodology is used as a basis for awarding need-based institutional aid.

UNDERGRADUATE EXPENSES for 2004–05 *Application fee:* $25. *Comprehensive fee:* $24,604 includes full-time tuition ($17,724), mandatory fees ($866), and room and board ($6014). Full-time tuition and fees vary according to course load and program. Room and board charges vary according to board plan. *Part-time tuition:* $483 per credit hour. *Part-time fees:* $25 per credit hour. Part-time tuition and fees vary according to course load. *Payment plans:* Guaranteed tuition, installment.

GIFT AID (NEED-BASED) *Total amount:* $2,145,234 (32% federal, 18% state, 50% institutional). *Scholarships, grants, and awards:* Federal Pell, FSEOG, state, private, college/university gift aid from institutional funds.

GIFT AID (NON-NEED-BASED) *Total amount:* $3,062,990 (12% state, 85% institutional, 3% external sources). *Scholarships, grants, and awards by category: Academic Interests/Achievement:* biological sciences, business, foreign languages, general academic interests/achievements, mathematics, physical sciences, social sciences. *Creative Arts/Performance:* art/fine arts, dance, general creative arts/performance, music, performing arts, theater/drama. *Special Achievements/Activities:* community service, general special achievements/activities, hobbies/interests. *Special Characteristics:* children of faculty/staff, twins. *Tuition waivers:* Full or partial for employees or children of employees, senior citizens.

LOANS *Student loans:* $3,649,069 (51% need-based, 49% non-need-based). *Average indebtedness per student:* $17,125. *Parent loans:* $876,860 (100% non-need-based). *Programs:* FFEL (Subsidized and Unsubsidized Stafford, PLUS), Perkins, college/university.

APPLYING FOR FINANCIAL AID *Required financial aid form:* FAFSA. *Financial aid deadline:* Continuous. *Notification date:* Continuous beginning 2/15. Students must reply by 5/1 or within 4 weeks of notification.

CONTACT Patricia Canfield, Director of Financial Aid, Lake Erie College, 391 West Washington Street, Painesville, OH 44077-3389, 440-375-7100 or toll-free 800-916-0904. *Fax:* 440-375-7005.

LAKE FOREST COLLEGE
Lake Forest, IL

Tuition & fees: $25,828	Average undergraduate aid package: $21,473

ABOUT THE INSTITUTION Independent, coed. Awards: bachelor's and master's degrees. 33 undergraduate majors. Total enrollment: 1,407. Undergraduates: 1,391. Freshmen: 405. Both federal and institutional methodology are used as a basis for awarding need-based institutional aid.

UNDERGRADUATE EXPENSES for 2004–05 *Application fee:* $40. *One-time required fee:* $200. *Comprehensive fee:* $32,050 includes full-time tuition ($25,518), mandatory fees ($310), and room and board ($6222). *College room only:* $3322. Room and board charges vary according to housing facility. *Part-time tuition:* $3190 per course. *Payment plan:* Installment.

FRESHMAN FINANCIAL AID (Fall 2004, est.) 337 applied for aid; of those 89% were deemed to have need. 100% of freshmen with need received aid; of those 100% had need fully met. *Average percent of need met:* 100% (excluding resources awarded to replace EFC). *Average financial aid package:* $22,093 (excluding resources awarded to replace EFC). 16% of all full-time freshmen had no need and received non-need-based gift aid.

UNDERGRADUATE FINANCIAL AID (Fall 2004, est.) 1,050 applied for aid; of those 92% were deemed to have need. 100% of undergraduates with need received aid; of those 100% had need fully met. *Average percent of need met:* 100% (excluding resources awarded to replace EFC). *Average financial aid*

package: $21,473 (excluding resources awarded to replace EFC). 19% of all full-time undergraduates had no need and received non-need-based gift aid.

GIFT AID (NEED-BASED) *Total amount:* $16,905,000 (9% federal, 7% state, 82% institutional, 2% external sources). *Receiving aid:* Freshmen: 74% (300); All full-time undergraduates: 71% (968). *Average award:* Freshmen: $18,611; Undergraduates: $17,464. *Scholarships, grants, and awards:* Federal Pell, FSEOG, state, private, college/university gift aid from institutional funds.

GIFT AID (NON-NEED-BASED) *Total amount:* $2,909,530 (97% institutional, 3% external sources). *Average Award:* Freshmen: $12,538; Undergraduates: $11,030. *Scholarships, grants, and awards by category: Academic Interests/ Achievement:* 795 awards ($7,048,972 total): biological sciences, foreign languages, general academic interests/achievements, physical sciences. *Creative Arts/Performance:* 229 awards ($845,950 total): art/fine arts, creative writing, music, theater/drama. *Special Achievements/Activities:* 130 awards ($500,750 total): leadership. *Special Characteristics:* 44 awards ($420,275 total): children and siblings of alumni, general special characteristics, previous college experience. *Tuition waivers:* Full or partial for employees or children of employees.

LOANS *Student loans:* $3,241,933 (94% need-based, 6% non-need-based). 58% of past graduating class borrowed through all loan programs. *Average indebtedness per student:* $16,741. *Average need-based loan:* Freshmen: $4097; Undergraduates: $5091. *Parent loans:* $1,713,235 (84% need-based, 16% non-need-based). *Programs:* FFEL (Subsidized and Unsubsidized Stafford, PLUS), Perkins, college/university, Alternative loans.

WORK-STUDY *Federal work-study:* Total amount: $829,749; 488 jobs averaging $1700.

APPLYING FOR FINANCIAL AID *Required financial aid forms:* FAFSA, federal income tax form(s). *Financial aid deadline (priority):* 2/25. *Notification date:* 3/15. Students must reply by 5/1.

CONTACT Mr. Jerry Cebrzynski, Director of Financial Aid, Lake Forest College, 555 North Sheridan Road, Lake Forest, IL 60045-2399, 847-735-5104 or toll-free 800-828-4751. *Fax:* 847-735-6271. *E-mail:* cebrzynski@lakeforest.edu.

LAKELAND COLLEGE
Sheboygan, WI

Tuition & fees: $15,770 **Average undergraduate aid package:** $10,302

ABOUT THE INSTITUTION Independent religious, coed. Awards: bachelor's and master's degrees. 29 undergraduate majors. Total enrollment: 4,013. Undergraduates: 3,443. Freshmen: 213. Federal methodology is used as a basis for awarding need-based institutional aid.

UNDERGRADUATE EXPENSES for 2005–06 *Application fee:* $20. *Comprehensive fee:* $21,405 includes full-time tuition ($15,100), mandatory fees ($670), and room and board ($5635). *College room only:* $2745. Full-time tuition and fees vary according to location. Room and board charges vary according to board plan and housing facility. *Part-time tuition:* $1515 per course. Part-time tuition and fees vary according to class time and location. *Payment plan:* Installment.

FRESHMAN FINANCIAL AID (Fall 2004, est.) 213 applied for aid; of those 91% were deemed to have need. 99% of freshmen with need received aid; of those 23% had need fully met. *Average percent of need met:* 84% (excluding resources awarded to replace EFC). *Average financial aid package:* $12,437 (excluding resources awarded to replace EFC). 27% of all full-time freshmen had no need and received non-need-based gift aid.

UNDERGRADUATE FINANCIAL AID (Fall 2004, est.) 1,034 applied for aid; of those 87% were deemed to have need. 100% of undergraduates with need received aid; of those 30% had need fully met. *Average percent of need met:* 83% (excluding resources awarded to replace EFC). *Average financial aid package:* $10,302 (excluding resources awarded to replace EFC). 24% of all full-time undergraduates had no need and received non-need-based gift aid.

GIFT AID (NEED-BASED) *Total amount:* $6,780,041 (26% federal, 12% state, 58% institutional, 4% external sources). *Receiving aid:* Freshmen: 69% (191); All full-time undergraduates: 68% (815). *Average award:* Freshmen: $9545; Undergraduates: $7645. *Scholarships, grants, and awards:* Federal Pell, FSEOG, state, private, college/university gift aid from institutional funds.

GIFT AID (NON-NEED-BASED) *Total amount:* $1,737,998 (1% federal, 89% institutional, 10% external sources). *Receiving aid:* Freshmen: 5% (14); Undergraduates: 7% (79). *Average Award:* Freshmen: $6707; Undergraduates: $7910. *Scholarships, grants, and awards by category: Academic Interests/ Achievement:* 463 awards ($2,711,374 total): business, engineering/technologies, English, general academic interests/achievements, religion/biblical studies. *Creative Arts/Performance:* 7 awards ($13,500 total): art/fine arts, creative writing, journalism/publications, music, performing arts. *Special Achievements/Activities:* 55 awards ($72,250 total): community service, leadership, religious involvement.

Special Characteristics: 127 awards ($380,940 total): children of faculty/staff, religious affiliation, siblings of current students. *Tuition waivers:* Full or partial for employees or children of employees.

LOANS *Student loans:* $9,343,226 (60% need-based, 40% non-need-based). 63% of past graduating class borrowed through all loan programs. *Average indebtedness per student:* $12,253. *Average need-based loan:* Freshmen: $2732; Undergraduates: $3574. *Parent loans:* $434,503 (30% need-based, 70% non-need-based). *Programs:* FFEL (Subsidized and Unsubsidized Stafford, PLUS), Perkins, alternative loans.

WORK-STUDY *Federal work-study:* Total amount: $227,535; 200 jobs averaging $1400. *State or other work-study/employment:* Total amount: $220,865 (3% need-based, 97% non-need-based). 75 part-time jobs averaging $1200.

APPLYING FOR FINANCIAL AID *Required financial aid forms:* FAFSA, institution's own form. *Financial aid deadline:* 7/1 (priority: 5/1). *Notification date:* Continuous beginning 3/1. Students must reply within 2 weeks of notification.

CONTACT Mr. Don Seymour, Director of Financial Aid, Lakeland College, PO Box 359, Sheboygan, WI 53082-0359, 920-565-1214 or toll-free 800-242-3347 (in-state). *Fax:* 920-565-1470.

LAKE SUPERIOR STATE UNIVERSITY
Sault Sainte Marie, MI

Tuition & fees (MI res): $6372 **Average undergraduate aid package:** $8594

ABOUT THE INSTITUTION State-supported, coed. Awards: associate, bachelor's, and master's degrees. 73 undergraduate majors. Total enrollment: 2,889. Undergraduates: 2,889. Freshmen: 554. Both federal and institutional methodology are used as a basis for awarding need-based institutional aid.

UNDERGRADUATE EXPENSES for 2004–05 *Application fee:* $20. *Tuition, state resident:* full-time $6054; part-time $225.75 per credit hour. *Tuition, nonresident:* full-time $11,472; part-time $451.50 per credit hour. Full-time tuition and fees vary according to reciprocity agreements. Part-time tuition and fees vary according to reciprocity agreements. *College room and board:* $6165; *room only:* $5494. Room and board charges vary according to board plan and housing facility. Residents of Ontario, Canada full-time tuition: $6,054, and Midwest Consortium students' tuition: $8,760. *Payment plans:* Installment, deferred payment.

FRESHMAN FINANCIAL AID (Fall 2004, est.) 537 applied for aid; of those 77% were deemed to have need. 100% of freshmen with need received aid. *Average percent of need met:* 78% (excluding resources awarded to replace EFC). *Average financial aid package:* $8262 (excluding resources awarded to replace EFC). 11% of all full-time freshmen had no need and received non-need-based gift aid.

UNDERGRADUATE FINANCIAL AID (Fall 2004, est.) 2,149 applied for aid; of those 74% were deemed to have need. 100% of undergraduates with need received aid. *Average percent of need met:* 81% (excluding resources awarded to replace EFC). *Average financial aid package:* $8594 (excluding resources awarded to replace EFC). 7% of all full-time undergraduates had no need and received non-need-based gift aid.

GIFT AID (NEED-BASED) *Total amount:* $3,375,962 (76% federal, 19% state, 5% institutional). *Receiving aid:* Freshmen: 44% (249); All full-time undergraduates: 39% (976). *Average award:* Freshmen: $3338; Undergraduates: $3160. *Scholarships, grants, and awards:* Federal Pell, FSEOG, state, private, college/university gift aid from institutional funds, Federal Nursing, third party payments.

GIFT AID (NON-NEED-BASED) *Total amount:* $3,305,628 (34% state, 48% institutional, 18% external sources). *Receiving aid:* Freshmen: 72% (407); Undergraduates: 50% (1,257). *Average Award:* Freshmen: $2359; Undergraduates: $2475. *Scholarships, grants, and awards by category: Academic Interests/ Achievement:* general academic interests/achievements. *Creative Arts/Performance:* general creative arts/performance. *Special Achievements/Activities:* general special achievements/activities. *Special Characteristics:* general special characteristics. *Tuition waivers:* Full or partial for minority students, children of alumni, employees or children of employees, senior citizens.

LOANS *Student loans:* $9,234,267 (100% need-based). 63% of past graduating class borrowed through all loan programs. *Average indebtedness per student:* $17,458. *Average need-based loan:* Freshmen: $3164; Undergraduates: $4528. *Parent loans:* $1,459,156 (100% need-based). *Programs:* Federal Direct (Subsidized and Unsubsidized Stafford, PLUS), Perkins, Federal Nursing, state.

WORK-STUDY *Federal work-study:* Total amount: $463,303; jobs available. *State or other work-study/employment:* Total amount: $279,195 (100% need-based). Part-time jobs available.

ATHLETIC AWARDS *Total amount:* $773,985 (100% non-need-based).

APPLYING FOR FINANCIAL AID *Required financial aid form:* FAFSA. *Financial aid deadline (priority):* 2/21. *Notification date:* Continuous. Students must reply within 3 weeks of notification.

CONTACT Ms. Deborah Rynberg, Director of Financial Aid, Lake Superior State University, 650 West Easterday Avenue, Sault Sainte Marie, MI 49783, 906-635-2678 or toll-free 888-800-LSSU Ext. 2231. *E-mail:* drynberg@lssu.edu.

LAKEVIEW COLLEGE OF NURSING
Danville, IL

CONTACT Director of Financial Aid, Lakeview College of Nursing, 903 North Logan Avenue, Danville, IL 61832, 217-443-5238 or toll-free 217-443-5238 Ext. 5454 (in-state).

LAMAR UNIVERSITY
Beaumont, TX

Tuition & fees (TX res): $3156	Average undergraduate aid package: $1855

ABOUT THE INSTITUTION State-supported, coed. Awards: associate, bachelor's, master's, and doctoral degrees. 102 undergraduate majors. Total enrollment: 10,804. Undergraduates: 9,620. Freshmen: 1,652. Federal methodology is used as a basis for awarding need-based institutional aid.

UNDERGRADUATE EXPENSES for 2004–05 *Tuition, area resident:* part-time $864 per term. *Tuition, state resident:* full-time $2304. *Tuition, nonresident:* full-time $9552; part-time $3582 per term. *Required fees:* full-time $852; $373.50 per term part-time. Part-time tuition and fees vary according to course load. *College room and board:* $5706; *room only:* $3225. Room and board charges vary according to board plan and housing facility. *Payment plan:* Installment.

FRESHMAN FINANCIAL AID (Fall 2004, est.) 1412 applied for aid; of those 90% were deemed to have need. 100% of freshmen with need received aid. *Average percent of need met:* 23% (excluding resources awarded to replace EFC). *Average financial aid package:* $1953 (excluding resources awarded to replace EFC). 46% of all full-time freshmen had no need and received non-need-based gift aid.

UNDERGRADUATE FINANCIAL AID (Fall 2004, est.) 4,353 applied for aid; of those 76% were deemed to have need. 100% of undergraduates with need received aid. *Average percent of need met:* 23% (excluding resources awarded to replace EFC). *Average financial aid package:* $1855 (excluding resources awarded to replace EFC). 22% of all full-time undergraduates had no need and received non-need-based gift aid.

GIFT AID (NEED-BASED) *Total amount:* $14,546,329 (67% federal, 32% state, 1% institutional). *Scholarships, grants, and awards:* Federal Pell, FSEOG, state, college/university gift aid from institutional funds.

GIFT AID (NON-NEED-BASED) *Total amount:* $3,481,889 (77% institutional, 23% external sources). *Receiving aid:* Freshmen: 2; Undergraduates: 9. *Average Award:* Freshmen: $1300; Undergraduates: $1300. *Scholarships, grants, and awards by category: Academic Interests/Achievement:* general academic interests/achievements. *Creative Arts/Performance:* general creative arts/performance. *Special Achievements/Activities:* general special achievements/activities.

LOANS *Student loans:* $18,352,064 (53% need-based, 47% non-need-based). 20% of past graduating class borrowed through all loan programs. *Average indebtedness per student:* $7100. *Parent loans:* $1,028,646 (100% need-based). *Programs:* FFEL (Subsidized and Unsubsidized Stafford, PLUS), Perkins, state, college/university.

WORK-STUDY *Federal work-study:* Total amount: $559,556; 94 jobs averaging $3000. *State or other work-study/employment:* Total amount: $55,286 (100% need-based). 21 part-time jobs averaging $3000.

ATHLETIC AWARDS *Total amount:* $1,264,112 (100% non-need-based).

APPLYING FOR FINANCIAL AID *Required financial aid forms:* FAFSA, institution's own form. *Financial aid deadline (priority):* 4/1. *Notification date:* Continuous beginning 5/1. Students must reply within 2 weeks of notification.

CONTACT Financial Aid Department, Lamar University, PO Box 10042, Beaumont, TX 77710, 409-880-8450. *Fax:* 409-880-8934. *E-mail:* finaid@hal.lamar.edu.

LAMBUTH UNIVERSITY
Jackson, TN

Tuition & fees: $12,490	Average undergraduate aid package: $13,230

ABOUT THE INSTITUTION Independent United Methodist, coed. Awards: bachelor's degrees. 68 undergraduate majors. Total enrollment: 806. Undergraduates: 806. Freshmen: 217. Federal methodology is used as a basis for awarding need-based institutional aid.

UNDERGRADUATE EXPENSES for 2004–05 *Application fee:* $25. *Comprehensive fee:* $17,926 includes full-time tuition ($12,190), mandatory fees ($300), and room and board ($5436). *College room only:* $2482. Room and board charges vary according to board plan and housing facility. *Part-time tuition:* $483 per credit hour. *Part-time fees:* $150 per term. Part-time tuition and fees vary according to class time and course load. *Payment plans:* Installment, deferred payment.

FRESHMAN FINANCIAL AID (Fall 2004, est.) 197 applied for aid; of those 80% were deemed to have need. 100% of freshmen with need received aid; of those 34% had need fully met. *Average percent of need met:* 97% (excluding resources awarded to replace EFC). *Average financial aid package:* $14,132 (excluding resources awarded to replace EFC). 27% of all full-time freshmen had no need and received non-need-based gift aid.

UNDERGRADUATE FINANCIAL AID (Fall 2004, est.) 795 applied for aid; of those 72% were deemed to have need. 100% of undergraduates with need received aid; of those 34% had need fully met. *Average percent of need met:* 97% (excluding resources awarded to replace EFC). *Average financial aid package:* $13,230 (excluding resources awarded to replace EFC). 21% of all full-time undergraduates had no need and received non-need-based gift aid.

GIFT AID (NEED-BASED) *Total amount:* $2,736,290 (31% federal, 22% state, 42% institutional, 5% external sources). *Receiving aid:* Freshmen: 57% (125); All full-time undergraduates: 64% (522). *Average award:* Freshmen: $7518; Undergraduates: $9125. *Scholarships, grants, and awards:* Federal Pell, FSEOG, state, private, college/university gift aid from institutional funds.

GIFT AID (NON-NEED-BASED) *Total amount:* $1,747,021 (39% state, 58% institutional, 3% external sources). *Receiving aid:* Freshmen: 5% (12); Undergraduates: 7% (55). *Average Award:* Freshmen: $6102; Undergraduates: $5563. *Scholarships, grants, and awards by category: Academic Interests/Achievement:* biological sciences, business, communication, computer science, education, English, foreign languages, general academic interests/achievements, home economics, humanities, international studies, mathematics, physical sciences, premedicine, religion/biblical studies, social sciences. *Creative Arts/Performance:* $20,000 total: dance, music, theater/drama. *Special Achievements/Activities:* cheerleading/drum major. *Special Characteristics:* 142 awards ($93,363 total): children and siblings of alumni, children of faculty/staff, relatives of clergy, religious affiliation. *Tuition waivers:* Full or partial for employees or children of employees, adult students, senior citizens.

LOANS *Student loans:* $2,662,987 (65% need-based, 35% non-need-based). 85% of past graduating class borrowed through all loan programs. *Average indebtedness per student:* $11,000. *Average need-based loan:* Freshmen: $4241; Undergraduates: $4519. *Parent loans:* $626,477 (100% non-need-based). *Programs:* FFEL (Subsidized and Unsubsidized Stafford, PLUS), Perkins, United Methodist Student Loans.

WORK-STUDY *Federal work-study:* Total amount: $184,580; 188 jobs averaging $982. *State or other work-study/employment:* Total amount: $48,999 (100% non-need-based). 42 part-time jobs averaging $1167.

ATHLETIC AWARDS *Total amount:* $1,640,798 (70% need-based, 30% non-need-based).

APPLYING FOR FINANCIAL AID *Required financial aid forms:* FAFSA, institution's own form. *Financial aid deadline (priority):* 2/15. *Notification date:* Continuous. Students must reply by 5/1 or within 2 weeks of notification.

CONTACT Ms. Lisa A. Warmath, Director of Scholarships and Financial Aid, Lambuth University, 705 Lambuth Boulevard, Jackson, TN 38301, 731-425-3331 or toll-free 800-526-2884. *Fax:* 731-425-3496. *E-mail:* warmath@lambuth.edu.

LANCASTER BIBLE COLLEGE
Lancaster, PA

Tuition & fees: $12,360	Average undergraduate aid package: $9111

ABOUT THE INSTITUTION Independent nondenominational, coed. Awards: associate, bachelor's, and master's degrees and post-bachelor's certificates. 17

undergraduate majors. Total enrollment: 973. Undergraduates: 810. Freshmen: 147. Federal methodology is used as a basis for awarding need-based institutional aid.

UNDERGRADUATE EXPENSES for 2004–05 *Application fee:* $25. *Comprehensive fee:* $17,880 includes full-time tuition ($11,850), mandatory fees ($510), and room and board ($5520). *College room only:* $2400. Full-time tuition and fees vary according to course load and program. Room and board charges vary according to board plan. *Part-time tuition:* $395 per credit. *Part-time fees:* $17 per credit. Part-time tuition and fees vary according to program. *Payment plan:* Installment.

FRESHMAN FINANCIAL AID (Fall 2004, est.) 133 applied for aid; of those 87% were deemed to have need. 100% of freshmen with need received aid; of those 11% had need fully met. *Average percent of need met:* 64% (excluding resources awarded to replace EFC). *Average financial aid package:* $8353 (excluding resources awarded to replace EFC). 14% of all full-time freshmen had no need and received non-need-based gift aid.

UNDERGRADUATE FINANCIAL AID (Fall 2004, est.) 487 applied for aid; of those 91% were deemed to have need. 100% of undergraduates with need received aid; of those 13% had need fully met. *Average percent of need met:* 64% (excluding resources awarded to replace EFC). *Average financial aid package:* $9111 (excluding resources awarded to replace EFC). 12% of all full-time undergraduates had no need and received non-need-based gift aid.

GIFT AID (NEED-BASED) *Total amount:* $2,509,600 (22% federal, 22% state, 50% institutional, 6% external sources). *Receiving aid:* Freshmen: 53% (74); All full-time undergraduates: 51% (286). *Average award:* Freshmen: $6524; Undergraduates: $6373. *Scholarships, grants, and awards:* Federal Pell, FSEOG, state, private, college/university gift aid from institutional funds, Office of Vocational Rehabilitation, Blindness and Visual Services Awards.

GIFT AID (NON-NEED-BASED) *Total amount:* $318,345 (91% institutional, 9% external sources). *Receiving aid:* Freshmen: 69% (97); Undergraduates: 58% (327). *Average Award:* Freshmen: $3331; Undergraduates: $3664. *Scholarships, grants, and awards by category:* Academic Interests/Achievement: 131 awards ($262,539 total): general academic interests/achievements. Creative Arts/Performance: 16 awards ($33,076 total): general creative arts/performance, music. Special Achievements/Activities: 97 awards ($89,809 total): leadership, religious involvement. Special Characteristics: 354 awards ($1,278,569 total): adult students, children and siblings of alumni, children of current students, children of faculty/staff, international students, married students, previous college experience, relatives of clergy, religious affiliation, siblings of current students, spouses of current students. *Tuition waivers:* Full or partial for children of alumni, employees or children of employees, adult students, senior citizens.

LOANS *Student loans:* $2,199,793 (83% need-based, 17% non-need-based). 64% of past graduating class borrowed through all loan programs. *Average indebtedness per student:* $14,621. *Average need-based loan:* Freshmen: $2457; Undergraduates: $3571. *Parent loans:* $693,911 (48% need-based, 52% non-need-based). *Programs:* FFEL (Subsidized and Unsubsidized Stafford, PLUS), Perkins, state, alternative loans.

WORK-STUDY *Federal work-study:* Total amount: $127,000; 85 jobs averaging $1500.

APPLYING FOR FINANCIAL AID *Required financial aid forms:* FAFSA, state aid form. *Financial aid deadline (priority):* 5/1. *Notification date:* Continuous. Students must reply within 3 weeks of notification.

CONTACT Karen Fox, Director of Financial Aid, Lancaster Bible College, PO Box 83403, Lancaster, PA 17608-3403, 717-560-8254 Ext. 5352 or toll-free 866-LBC4YOU. *Fax:* 717-560-8216. *E-mail:* kfox@lbc.edu.

LANDER UNIVERSITY
Greenwood, SC

ABOUT THE INSTITUTION State-supported, coed. Awards: bachelor's and master's degrees. 24 undergraduate majors. Total enrollment: 2,918. Undergraduates: 2,733. Freshmen: 655.

GIFT AID (NEED-BASED) *Scholarships, grants, and awards:* Federal Pell, FSEOG, state, private, college/university gift aid from institutional funds, Federal Nursing.

GIFT AID (NON-NEED-BASED) *Scholarships, grants, and awards by category:* Academic Interests/Achievement: biological sciences, business, computer science, education, engineering/technologies, English, foreign languages, general academic interests/achievements, health fields, humanities, mathematics, physical sciences. Creative Arts/Performance: art/fine arts, music, theater/drama. Special Achievements/Activities: leadership. Special Characteristics: members of minority groups, out-of-state students.

LOANS *Programs:* FFEL (Subsidized and Unsubsidized Stafford, PLUS), Perkins, state.

APPLYING FOR FINANCIAL AID *Required financial aid form:* FAFSA.

CONTACT Stephan L. Schnaiter, Director of Financial Aid, Lander University, 320 Stanley Avenue, Greenwood, SC 29649, 864-388-8340 or toll-free 888-452-6337. *Fax:* 864-388-8811. *E-mail:* sschnaiter@lander.edu.

LANE COLLEGE
Jackson, TN

ABOUT THE INSTITUTION Independent religious, coed. Awards: bachelor's degrees and post-bachelor's certificates. 17 undergraduate majors. Total enrollment: 1,045. Undergraduates: 1,045. Freshmen: 352.

GIFT AID (NEED-BASED) *Scholarships, grants, and awards:* Federal Pell, FSEOG, state, private, college/university gift aid from institutional funds, United Negro College Fund.

GIFT AID (NON-NEED-BASED) *Scholarships, grants, and awards by category:* Academic Interests/Achievement: general academic interests/achievements.

LOANS *Programs:* Federal Direct (Subsidized and Unsubsidized Stafford, PLUS).

WORK-STUDY *Federal work-study:* Total amount: $287,862; 378 jobs averaging $781.

APPLYING FOR FINANCIAL AID *Required financial aid form:* FAFSA.

CONTACT Ms. Ursula Singleton, Director of Financial Aid, Lane College, 545 Lane Avenue, Jackson, TN 38301, 731-426-7536 or toll-free 800-960-7533. *Fax:* 731-426-7652. *E-mail:* fao@lanecollege.edu.

LANGSTON UNIVERSITY
Langston, OK

Tuition & fees: N/R	Average undergraduate aid package: $8730

ABOUT THE INSTITUTION State-supported, coed. Awards: associate, bachelor's, and master's degrees. 56 undergraduate majors. Total enrollment: 3,008. Undergraduates: 2,896. Freshmen: 481. Federal methodology is used as a basis for awarding need-based institutional aid.

GIFT AID (NEED-BASED) *Total amount:* $7,260,064 (92% federal, 7% state, 1% external sources). *Receiving aid:* Freshmen: 13% (75); All full-time undergraduates: 18% (522). *Average award:* Freshmen: $941; Undergraduates: $1023. *Scholarships, grants, and awards:* Federal Pell, FSEOG, state.

GIFT AID (NON-NEED-BASED) *Total amount:* $2,123,872 (22% federal, 6% state, 58% institutional, 14% external sources). *Receiving aid:* Freshmen: 37% (209); Undergraduates: 31% (912). *Average Award:* Freshmen: $4129; Undergraduates: $2854. *Scholarships, grants, and awards by category:* Academic Interests/Achievement: 199 awards ($1,190,770 total): agriculture, business, education, engineering/technologies, general academic interests/achievements, health fields. Creative Arts/Performance: 66 awards ($47,000 total): music. Special Achievements/Activities: 9 awards ($11,500 total): cheerleading/drum major, leadership. Special Characteristics: 27 awards ($13,750 total): ethnic background. ROTC: Army cooperative.

LOANS *Student loans:* $15,148,776 (50% need-based, 50% non-need-based). 72% of past graduating class borrowed through all loan programs. *Average indebtedness per student:* $14,789. *Average need-based loan:* Freshmen: $2784; Undergraduates: $4102. *Parent loans:* $1,608,276 (100% need-based). *Programs:* Federal Direct (Subsidized and Unsubsidized Stafford, PLUS), FFEL (Subsidized and Unsubsidized Stafford, PLUS).

ATHLETIC AWARDS *Total amount:* $174,689 (100% non-need-based).

APPLYING FOR FINANCIAL AID *Required financial aid forms:* FAFSA, institution's own form. *Financial aid deadline (priority):* 3/15. *Notification date:* 6/30.

CONTACT Yvonne Maxwell, Director of Financial Aid, Langston University, Page Hall, Room 311, Langston, OK 73050, 405-466-3282 or toll-free 405-466-3428 (in-state). *Fax:* 405-466-2986. *E-mail:* ymaxwell@lunet.edu.

LA ROCHE COLLEGE
Pittsburgh, PA

Tuition & fees: $16,582	Average undergraduate aid package: $15,318

ABOUT THE INSTITUTION Independent religious, coed. Awards: associate, bachelor's, and master's degrees. 35 undergraduate majors. Total enrollment: 1,681. Undergraduates: 1,484. Freshmen: 217. Federal methodology is used as a basis for awarding need-based institutional aid.

UNDERGRADUATE EXPENSES for 2004–05 *Application fee:* $50. *Comprehensive fee:* $23,444 includes full-time tuition ($15,982), mandatory fees ($600), and room and board ($6862). *College room only:* $4250. Full-time tuition and fees vary according to program. *Part-time tuition:* $488 per credit. *Part-time fees:* $14 per credit; $50 per term. Part-time tuition and fees vary according to program. *Payment plan:* Installment.

FRESHMAN FINANCIAL AID (Fall 2004, est.) 194 applied for aid; of those 92% were deemed to have need. 100% of freshmen with need received aid; of those 22% had need fully met. *Average percent of need met:* 88% (excluding resources awarded to replace EFC). *Average financial aid package:* $15,668 (excluding resources awarded to replace EFC). 10% of all full-time freshmen had no need and received non-need-based gift aid.

UNDERGRADUATE FINANCIAL AID (Fall 2004, est.) 792 applied for aid; of those 91% were deemed to have need. 100% of undergraduates with need received aid; of those 25% had need fully met. *Average percent of need met:* 84% (excluding resources awarded to replace EFC). *Average financial aid package:* $15,318 (excluding resources awarded to replace EFC). 6% of all full-time undergraduates had no need and received non-need-based gift aid.

GIFT AID (NEED-BASED) *Total amount:* $3,736,979 (28% federal, 38% state, 30% institutional, 4% external sources). *Receiving aid:* Freshmen: 60% (130); All full-time undergraduates: 51% (559). *Average award:* Freshmen: $7193; Undergraduates: $4859. *Scholarships, grants, and awards:* Federal Pell, FSEOG, state, private, college/university gift aid from institutional funds.

GIFT AID (NON-NEED-BASED) *Total amount:* $3,488,335 (88% institutional, 12% external sources). *Receiving aid:* Freshmen: 74% (160); Undergraduates: 59% (649). *Average Award:* Freshmen: $4119; Undergraduates: $3879. *Scholarships, grants, and awards by category:* Creative Arts/Performance: 2 awards ($650 total): applied art and design. *Tuition waivers:* Full or partial for employees or children of employees, senior citizens. *ROTC:* Army cooperative, Air Force cooperative.

LOANS *Student loans:* $4,130,107 (64% need-based, 36% non-need-based). 80% of past graduating class borrowed through all loan programs. *Average indebtedness per student:* $18,000. *Average need-based loan:* Freshmen: $2886; Undergraduates: $3912. *Parent loans:* $1,136,242 (100% non-need-based). *Programs:* FFEL (Subsidized and Unsubsidized Stafford, PLUS), Perkins, state.

WORK-STUDY *Federal work-study:* Total amount: $815,367; jobs available (averaging $2000).

APPLYING FOR FINANCIAL AID *Required financial aid forms:* FAFSA, institution's own form, state aid form. *Financial aid deadline:* 3/1 (priority: 1/15). *Notification date:* Continuous beginning 3/15. Students must reply within 2 weeks of notification.

CONTACT Mr. John F. Matsko, Director of Financial Aid, La Roche College, 9000 Babcock Boulevard, Pittsburgh, PA 15237-5898, 412-536-1120 or toll-free 800-838-4LRC. *Fax:* 412-536-1072. *E-mail:* matskoj1@laroche.edu.

LA SALLE UNIVERSITY
Philadelphia, PA

Tuition & fees: $26,190	Average undergraduate aid package: $17,373

ABOUT THE INSTITUTION Independent Roman Catholic, coed. Awards: associate, bachelor's, master's, and doctoral degrees and post-bachelor's and post-master's certificates. 61 undergraduate majors. Total enrollment: 6,217. Undergraduates: 4,338. Freshmen: 876. Both federal and institutional methodology are used as a basis for awarding need-based institutional aid.

UNDERGRADUATE EXPENSES for 2005–06 *Application fee:* $35. *Comprehensive fee:* $35,600 includes full-time tuition ($25,880), mandatory fees ($310), and room and board ($9410). *College room only:* $4920. Full-time tuition and fees vary according to program. Room and board charges vary according to board plan, housing facility, and location. Part-time tuition and fees vary according to class time and course load. *Payment plans:* Installment, deferred payment.

GIFT AID (NEED-BASED) *Total amount:* $32,358,360 (11% federal, 10% state, 75% institutional, 4% external sources). *Receiving aid:* Freshmen: 77% (639); All full-time undergraduates: 73% (2,520). *Average award:* Freshmen: $14,875; Undergraduates: $13,462. *Scholarships, grants, and awards:* Federal Pell, FSEOG, state, private, college/university gift aid from institutional funds.

GIFT AID (NON-NEED-BASED) *Total amount:* $5,784,760 (96% institutional, 4% external sources). *Receiving aid:* Freshmen: 61% (510); Undergraduates: 56% (1,926). *Average Award:* Freshmen: $8863; Undergraduates: $9373. *Scholarships, grants, and awards by category:* Academic Interests/Achievement: general academic interests/achievements. *Special Achievements/Activities:* com-

---

munity service. *Special Characteristics:* children of faculty/staff. *Tuition waivers:* Full or partial for employees or children of employees. *ROTC:* Army cooperative, Air Force cooperative.

LOANS *Student loans:* $28,598,709 (88% need-based, 12% non-need-based). 74% of past graduating class borrowed through all loan programs. *Average indebtedness per student:* $24,345. *Average need-based loan:* Freshmen: $3336; Undergraduates: $4663. *Parent loans:* $5,807,104 (84% need-based, 16% non-need-based). *Programs:* FFEL (Subsidized and Unsubsidized Stafford, PLUS), Perkins.

ATHLETIC AWARDS *Total amount:* $3,161,286 (52% need-based, 48% non-need-based).

APPLYING FOR FINANCIAL AID *Required financial aid form:* FAFSA. *Financial aid deadline (priority):* 2/15. *Notification date:* Continuous beginning 3/15. Students must reply by 5/1 or within 2 weeks of notification.

CONTACT Robert G. Voss, Dean of Admission and Financial Aid, La Salle University, 1900 West Olney Avenue, Philadelphia, PA 19141-1199, 215-951-1500 or toll-free 800-328-1910.

LASELL COLLEGE
Newton, MA

Tuition & fees: $19,700	Average undergraduate aid package: $15,500

ABOUT THE INSTITUTION Independent, coed. Awards: bachelor's and master's degrees. 28 undergraduate majors. Total enrollment: 1,181. Undergraduates: 1,155. Freshmen: 387. Both federal and institutional methodology are used as a basis for awarding need-based institutional aid.

UNDERGRADUATE EXPENSES for 2005–06 *Application fee:* $40. *Comprehensive fee:* $28,500 includes full-time tuition ($18,700), mandatory fees ($1000), and room and board ($8800). Room and board charges vary according to housing facility. *Part-time tuition:* $620 per credit hour. *Part-time fees:* $250 per term.

GIFT AID (NEED-BASED) *Total amount:* $10,844,781 (12% federal, 4% state, 82% institutional, 2% external sources). *Receiving aid:* Freshmen: 81% (313); All full-time undergraduates: 81% (933). *Average award:* Freshmen: $11,500; Undergraduates: $11,500. *Scholarships, grants, and awards:* Federal Pell, FSEOG, state, private, college/university gift aid from institutional funds.

GIFT AID (NON-NEED-BASED) *Total amount:* $903,995 (93% institutional, 7% external sources). *Receiving aid:* Freshmen: 6% (22); Undergraduates: 10% (116). *Average Award:* Freshmen: $12,800; Undergraduates: $13,400. *Scholarships, grants, and awards by category:* Academic Interests/Achievement: 143 awards ($660,000 total): general academic interests/achievements. *Special Achievements/Activities:* 35 awards ($101,500 total): community service, general special achievements/activities. *Special Characteristics:* 19 awards ($37,605 total): children and siblings of alumni, children of faculty/staff, siblings of current students, twins.

LOANS *Student loans:* $7,248,445 (63% need-based, 37% non-need-based). 95% of past graduating class borrowed through all loan programs. *Average indebtedness per student:* $20,500. *Average need-based loan:* Freshmen: $2500; Undergraduates: $3500. *Parent loans:* $3,273,276 (41% need-based, 59% non-need-based). *Programs:* FFEL (Subsidized and Unsubsidized Stafford, PLUS), Perkins, state, alternative loans.

APPLYING FOR FINANCIAL AID *Required financial aid forms:* FAFSA, institution's own form. *Financial aid deadline (priority):* 3/1. *Notification date:* Continuous. Students must reply within 4 weeks of notification.

CONTACT Michele R. Kosboth, Director of Student Financial Planning, Lasell College, 1844 Commonwealth Avenue, Newton, MA 02466-2709, 617-243-2227 or toll-free 888-LASELL-4. *Fax:* 617-243-2326. *E-mail:* finaid@lasell.edu.

LA SIERRA UNIVERSITY
Riverside, CA

Tuition & fees: $19,083	Average undergraduate aid package: $16,253

ABOUT THE INSTITUTION Independent Seventh-day Adventist, coed. Awards: bachelor's, master's, and doctoral degrees and post-bachelor's and post-master's certificates. 38 undergraduate majors. Total enrollment: 1,924. Undergraduates: 1,585. Freshmen: 359. Federal methodology is used as a basis for awarding need-based institutional aid.

UNDERGRADUATE EXPENSES for 2005–06 *Application fee:* $30. *Comprehensive fee:* $24,327 includes full-time tuition ($18,432), mandatory fees ($651), and room and board ($5244). *Part-time tuition:* $512 per unit.

FRESHMAN FINANCIAL AID (Fall 2003) 314 applied for aid; of those 89% were deemed to have need. 100% of freshmen with need received aid; of those 22% had need fully met. *Average percent of need met:* 80% (excluding resources awarded to replace EFC). *Average financial aid package:* $16,480 (excluding resources awarded to replace EFC). 22% of all full-time freshmen had no need and received non-need-based gift aid.

UNDERGRADUATE FINANCIAL AID (Fall 2003) 1,016 applied for aid; of those 91% were deemed to have need. 100% of undergraduates with need received aid; of those 21% had need fully met. *Average percent of need met:* 77% (excluding resources awarded to replace EFC). *Average financial aid package:* $16,253 (excluding resources awarded to replace EFC). 26% of all full-time undergraduates had no need and received non-need-based gift aid.

GIFT AID (NEED-BASED) *Total amount:* $11,286,922 (20% federal, 28% state, 41% institutional, 11% external sources). *Receiving aid:* Freshmen: 77% (280); All full-time undergraduates: 72% (916). *Average award:* Freshmen: $13,210; Undergraduates: $11,345. *Scholarships, grants, and awards:* Federal Pell, FSEOG, state, private, college/university gift aid from institutional funds.

GIFT AID (NON-NEED-BASED) *Total amount:* $2,478,422 (81% institutional, 19% external sources). *Average Award: Freshmen:* $6650; *Undergraduates:* $5637. *Scholarships, grants, and awards by category: Academic Interests/Achievement:* general academic interests/achievements. *Creative Arts/Performance:* music, theater/drama. *Special Achievements/Activities:* leadership. *Special Characteristics:* adult students, children of faculty/staff, relatives of clergy, religious affiliation, siblings of current students.

LOANS *Student loans:* $6,644,999 (91% need-based, 9% non-need-based). 66% of past graduating class borrowed through all loan programs. *Average indebtedness per student:* $25,277. *Average need-based loan:* Freshmen: $3464; Undergraduates: $4942. *Parent loans:* $1,649,452 (76% need-based, 24% non-need-based). *Programs:* FFEL (Subsidized and Unsubsidized Stafford, PLUS), Perkins.

WORK-STUDY *Federal work-study:* Total amount: $678,043; 360 jobs averaging $1883.

APPLYING FOR FINANCIAL AID *Required financial aid forms:* FAFSA, state aid form. *Financial aid deadline (priority):* 3/2. *Notification date:* Continuous beginning 4/15. Students must reply by 9/1.

CONTACT Financial Aid Office, La Sierra University, 4500 Riverwalk Parkway, Riverside, CA 92515, 951-785-2175 or toll-free 800-874-5587. *Fax:* 951-785-2942.

LAURA AND ALVIN SIEGAL COLLEGE OF JUDAIC STUDIES
Beachwood, OH

Tuition & fees: $15,025	Average undergraduate aid package: $4800

ABOUT THE INSTITUTION Independent, coed. Awards: bachelor's and master's degrees. 7 undergraduate majors. Total enrollment: 146. Undergraduates: 11. Freshmen: 1. Institutional methodology is used as a basis for awarding need-based institutional aid.

UNDERGRADUATE EXPENSES for 2005–06 *Application fee:* $50. *Tuition:* full-time $15,000; part-time $500 per credit. Full-time tuition and fees vary according to course load. Part-time tuition and fees vary according to course load. *Payment plan:* Installment.

GIFT AID (NEED-BASED) *Total amount:* $85,000 (100% institutional). *Receiving aid:* All full-time undergraduates: 50% (1). *Average award:* Undergraduates: $700. *Scholarships, grants, and awards:* college/university gift aid from institutional funds.

GIFT AID (NON-NEED-BASED) *Scholarships, grants, and awards by category: Academic Interests/Achievement:* education, religion/biblical studies. *Tuition waivers:* Full or partial for employees or children of employees.

APPLYING FOR FINANCIAL AID *Required financial aid form:* institution's own form. *Financial aid deadline:* Continuous. *Notification date:* Continuous beginning 9/1. Students must reply within 2 weeks of notification.

CONTACT Ms. Linda Rosen, Director of Student Services, Laura and Alvin Siegal College of Judaic Studies, 26500 Shaker Boulevard, Beachwood, OH 44122-7116, 216-464-4050 Ext. 101 or toll-free 888-336-2257. *Fax:* 216-464-5827. *E-mail:* lrosen@siegalcollege.edu.

LAWRENCE TECHNOLOGICAL UNIVERSITY
Southfield, MI

Tuition & fees: $17,210	Average undergraduate aid package: $11,465

ABOUT THE INSTITUTION Independent, coed. Awards: associate, bachelor's, master's, and doctoral degrees. 31 undergraduate majors. Total enrollment: 4,148. Undergraduates: 2,906. Freshmen: 325. Federal methodology is used as a basis for awarding need-based institutional aid.

UNDERGRADUATE EXPENSES for 2004–05 *Application fee:* $30. *Comprehensive fee:* $24,245 includes full-time tuition ($16,960), mandatory fees ($250), and room and board ($7035). *College room only:* $5145. Full-time tuition and fees vary according to degree level, program, and student level. Room and board charges vary according to board plan and housing facility. *Part-time tuition:* $502 per hour. *Part-time fees:* $125 per term. Part-time tuition and fees vary according to degree level, program, and student level. *Payment plan:* Installment.

FRESHMAN FINANCIAL AID (Fall 2003) 336 applied for aid; of those 79% were deemed to have need. 100% of freshmen with need received aid; of those 32% had need fully met. *Average percent of need met:* 80% (excluding resources awarded to replace EFC). *Average financial aid package:* $11,874 (excluding resources awarded to replace EFC). 18% of all full-time freshmen had no need and received non-need-based gift aid.

UNDERGRADUATE FINANCIAL AID (Fall 2003) 1,164 applied for aid; of those 83% were deemed to have need. 99% of undergraduates with need received aid; of those 26% had need fully met. *Average percent of need met:* 76% (excluding resources awarded to replace EFC). *Average financial aid package:* $11,465 (excluding resources awarded to replace EFC). 20% of all full-time undergraduates had no need and received non-need-based gift aid.

GIFT AID (NEED-BASED) *Total amount:* $7,093,339 (23% federal, 33% state, 43% institutional, 1% external sources). *Receiving aid:* Freshmen: 66% (257); All full-time undergraduates: 55% (893). *Average award:* Freshmen: $7673; Undergraduates: $6581. *Scholarships, grants, and awards:* Federal Pell, FSEOG, state, private, college/university gift aid from institutional funds, Michigan National Guard and ROTC.

GIFT AID (NON-NEED-BASED) *Total amount:* $2,440,076 (1% federal, 7% state, 90% institutional, 2% external sources). *Receiving aid:* Freshmen: 54% (211); Undergraduates: 33% (546). *Average Award: Freshmen:* $4819; *Undergraduates:* $6113. *Scholarships, grants, and awards by category: Academic Interests/Achievement:* 1,226 awards ($5,297,004 total): architecture, business, computer science, education, engineering/technologies, general academic interests/achievements, humanities, international studies, mathematics, military science, physical sciences. *Special Achievements/Activities:* general special achievements/activities. *Special Characteristics:* 66 awards ($546,482 total): children of faculty/staff, members of minority groups. *Tuition waivers:* Full or partial for employees or children of employees. *ROTC:* Army cooperative, Air Force cooperative.

LOANS *Student loans:* $8,168,308 (90% need-based, 10% non-need-based). 50% of past graduating class borrowed through all loan programs. *Average indebtedness per student:* $24,495. *Average need-based loan:* Freshmen: $2693; Undergraduates: $3876. *Parent loans:* $3,069,046 (80% need-based, 20% non-need-based). *Programs:* FFEL (Subsidized and Unsubsidized Stafford, PLUS), Perkins, state, college/university, alternative loans.

WORK-STUDY *Federal work-study:* Total amount: $549,399; 137 jobs averaging $4000. *State or other work-study/employment:* Total amount: $31,530 (100% need-based). 16 part-time jobs averaging $2000.

APPLYING FOR FINANCIAL AID *Required financial aid form:* FAFSA. *Financial aid deadline (priority):* 4/1. *Notification date:* Continuous beginning 3/1. Students must reply within 2 weeks of notification.

CONTACT Mr. Mark Martin, Director of Financial Aid, Lawrence Technological University, 21000 West Ten Mile Road, Southfield, MI 48075-1058, 248-204-2126 or toll-free 800-225-5588. *Fax:* 248-204-2124. *E-mail:* m_martin@ltu.edu.

LAWRENCE UNIVERSITY
Appleton, WI

Tuition & fees: $27,924	Average undergraduate aid package: $21,753

ABOUT THE INSTITUTION Independent, coed. Awards: bachelor's degrees. 58 undergraduate majors. Total enrollment: 1,380. Undergraduates: 1,380. Freshmen: 352. Both federal and institutional methodology are used as a basis for awarding need-based institutional aid.

UNDERGRADUATE EXPENSES for 2005–06 *Application fee:* $40. *Comprehensive fee:* $33,824 includes full-time tuition ($27,714), mandatory fees ($210), and room and board ($5900). Room and board charges vary according to board plan and housing facility. *Payment plans:* Tuition prepayment, installment.

FRESHMAN FINANCIAL AID (Fall 2004, est.) 268 applied for aid; of those 74% were deemed to have need. 100% of freshmen with need received aid; of those 100% had need fully met. *Average percent of need met:* 100% (excluding resources awarded to replace EFC). *Average financial aid package:* $21,251 (excluding resources awarded to replace EFC). 35% of all full-time freshmen had no need and received non-need-based gift aid.

UNDERGRADUATE FINANCIAL AID (Fall 2004, est.) 964 applied for aid; of those 85% were deemed to have need. 100% of undergraduates with need received aid; of those 100% had need fully met. *Average percent of need met:* 100% (excluding resources awarded to replace EFC). *Average financial aid package:* $21,753 (excluding resources awarded to replace EFC). 30% of all full-time undergraduates had no need and received non-need-based gift aid.

GIFT AID (NEED-BASED) *Total amount:* $12,808,200 (7% federal, 5% state, 85% institutional, 3% external sources). *Receiving aid:* Freshmen: 56% (197); All full-time undergraduates: 61% (817). *Average award:* Freshmen: $15,746; Undergraduates: $16,177. *Scholarships, grants, and awards:* Federal Pell, FSEOG, state, private, college/university gift aid from institutional funds.

GIFT AID (NON-NEED-BASED) *Total amount:* $4,133,122 (1% federal, 95% institutional, 4% external sources). *Average Award:* Freshmen: $9557; Undergraduates: $9949. *Scholarships, grants, and awards by category:* Academic Interests/Achievement: 673 awards ($5,474,390 total): general academic interests/achievements. Creative Arts/Performance: 196 awards ($1,330,599 total): music. Special Characteristics: 97 awards ($438,041 total): children and siblings of alumni, local/state students, members of minority groups. *Tuition waivers:* Full or partial for employees or children of employees.

LOANS *Student loans:* $4,598,267 (86% need-based, 14% non-need-based). 57% of past graduating class borrowed through all loan programs. *Average indebtedness per student:* $18,718. *Average need-based loan:* Freshmen: $4609; Undergraduates: $5505. *Parent loans:* $2,511,270 (100% non-need-based). *Programs:* Federal Direct (Subsidized and Unsubsidized Stafford, PLUS), FFEL (PLUS), Perkins, college/university, alternative loans.

WORK-STUDY *Federal work-study:* Total amount: $1,161,251; 565 jobs averaging $2055. *State or other work-study/employment:* Total amount: $779,968 (29% need-based, 71% non-need-based). 333 part-time jobs averaging $2342.

APPLYING FOR FINANCIAL AID *Required financial aid forms:* FAFSA, institution's own form. *Financial aid deadline (priority):* 3/15. *Notification date:* Continuous. Students must reply by 5/1.

CONTACT Mrs. Sara Beth Holman, Director of Financial Aid, Lawrence University, PO Box 599, Appleton, WI 54912-0599, 920-832-6583 or toll-free 800-227-0982. *Fax:* 920-832-6582. *E-mail:* sara.b.holman@lawrence.edu.

LEBANON VALLEY COLLEGE
Annville, PA

Tuition & fees: $23,600	Average undergraduate aid package: $17,564

ABOUT THE INSTITUTION Independent United Methodist, coed. Awards: associate, bachelor's, master's, and first professional degrees and post-bachelor's certificates (offers master of business administration degree on a part-time basis only). 52 undergraduate majors. Total enrollment: 1,882. Undergraduates: 1,738. Freshmen: 416. Federal methodology is used as a basis for awarding need-based institutional aid.

UNDERGRADUATE EXPENSES for 2004–05 *Application fee:* $30. *Comprehensive fee:* $30,190 includes full-time tuition ($22,950), mandatory fees ($650), and room and board ($6590). *College room only:* $3220. Room and board charges vary according to board plan and housing facility. *Part-time tuition:* $430 per credit. Part-time tuition and fees vary according to class time and degree level. *Payment plans:* Tuition prepayment, installment.

FRESHMAN FINANCIAL AID (Fall 2004, est.) 380 applied for aid; of those 90% were deemed to have need. 100% of freshmen with need received aid; of those 34% had need fully met. *Average percent of need met:* 87% (excluding resources awarded to replace EFC). *Average financial aid package:* $17,363 (excluding resources awarded to replace EFC). 16% of all full-time freshmen had no need and received non-need-based gift aid.

UNDERGRADUATE FINANCIAL AID (Fall 2004, est.) 1,373 applied for aid; of those 88% were deemed to have need. 99% of undergraduates with need received aid; of those 32% had need fully met. *Average percent of need met:* 87% (excluding resources awarded to replace EFC). *Average financial aid*

package: $17,564 (excluding resources awarded to replace EFC). 17% of all full-time undergraduates had no need and received non-need-based gift aid.

GIFT AID (NEED-BASED) *Total amount:* $14,419,769 (6% federal, 13% state, 81% institutional). *Receiving aid:* Freshmen: 82% (340); All full-time undergraduates: 76% (1,178). *Average award:* Freshmen: $14,541; Undergraduates: $14,497. *Scholarships, grants, and awards:* Federal Pell, FSEOG, state, private, college/university gift aid from institutional funds.

GIFT AID (NON-NEED-BASED) *Total amount:* $3,772,579 (1% federal, 1% state, 83% institutional, 15% external sources). *Receiving aid:* Freshmen: 13% (56); Undergraduates: 9% (133). *Average Award:* Freshmen: $9274; Undergraduates: $9407. *Scholarships, grants, and awards by category:* Academic Interests/Achievement: 1,237 awards ($11,565,380 total): biological sciences, general academic interests/achievements. Creative Arts/Performance: 30 awards ($32,000 total): music. Special Achievements/Activities: 91 awards ($47,250 total): general special achievements/activities, junior miss. Special Characteristics: 149 awards ($783,775 total): children and siblings of alumni, children of faculty/staff, ethnic background, international students. *Tuition waivers:* Full or partial for employees or children of employees, senior citizens. *ROTC:* Army cooperative.

LOANS *Student loans:* $9,471,130 (44% need-based, 56% non-need-based). 73% of past graduating class borrowed through all loan programs. *Average indebtedness per student:* $22,166. *Average need-based loan:* Freshmen: $3598; Undergraduates: $4268. *Parent loans:* $3,818,862 (100% non-need-based). *Programs:* FFEL (Subsidized and Unsubsidized Stafford, PLUS), Perkins.

WORK-STUDY *Federal work-study:* Total amount: $946,716; 760 jobs averaging $1193.

APPLYING FOR FINANCIAL AID *Required financial aid forms:* FAFSA, institution's own form. *Financial aid deadline (priority):* 3/1. *Notification date:* Continuous beginning 3/1. Students must reply by 5/1 or within 2 weeks of notification.

CONTACT Kendra M. Feigert, Director of Financial Aid, Lebanon Valley College, 101 North College Avenue, Annville, PA 17003, 866-582-4236 or toll-free 866-LVC-4ADM. *Fax:* 717-867-6027. *E-mail:* feigert@lvc.edu.

LEES-MCRAE COLLEGE
Banner Elk, NC

ABOUT THE INSTITUTION Independent religious, coed. Awards: bachelor's degrees. 28 undergraduate majors. Total enrollment: 792. Undergraduates: 792. Freshmen: 199.

GIFT AID (NEED-BASED) *Scholarships, grants, and awards:* Federal Pell, FSEOG, state, private, college/university gift aid from institutional funds.

GIFT AID (NON-NEED-BASED) *Scholarships, grants, and awards by category:* Academic Interests/Achievement: biological sciences, education, general academic interests/achievements, mathematics. Creative Arts/Performance: dance, journalism/publications, performing arts, theater/drama. Special Achievements/Activities: cheerleading/drum major, general special achievements/activities, leadership. Special Characteristics: children of educators, children of faculty/staff, children with a deceased or disabled parent, international students, local/state students, previous college experience, relatives of clergy, religious affiliation, veterans.

LOANS *Programs:* FFEL (Subsidized and Unsubsidized Stafford, PLUS), Perkins, Federal Nursing.

APPLYING FOR FINANCIAL AID *Required financial aid forms:* FAFSA, state aid form.

CONTACT Lester McKenzie, Assistant Dean of Students for Financial Aid, Lees-McRae College, PO Box 128, Banner Elk, NC 28604-0128, 828-898-8793 or toll-free 800-280-4562. *Fax:* 828-898-8814. *E-mail:* mckenzie@lmc.edu.

LEE UNIVERSITY
Cleveland, TN

Tuition & fees: $9075	Average undergraduate aid package: $7157

ABOUT THE INSTITUTION Independent religious, coed. Awards: bachelor's and master's degrees. 35 undergraduate majors. Total enrollment: 3,849. Undergraduates: 3,571. Freshmen: 733. Federal methodology is used as a basis for awarding need-based institutional aid.

UNDERGRADUATE EXPENSES for 2004–05 *Application fee:* $25. *Comprehensive fee:* $13,635 includes full-time tuition ($8950), mandatory fees ($125), and room and board ($4560). *College room only:* $2350. Full-time tuition and fees vary according to program. Room and board charges vary according to board plan and housing facility. *Part-time tuition:* $373 per credit hour. *Part-time fees:* $25 per term. Part-time tuition and fees vary according to program. *Payment plan:* Deferred payment.

FRESHMAN FINANCIAL AID (Fall 2003) 612 applied for aid; of those 76% were deemed to have need. 98% of freshmen with need received aid; of those 23% had need fully met. *Average percent of need met:* 55% (excluding resources awarded to replace EFC). *Average financial aid package:* $6729 (excluding resources awarded to replace EFC). 50% of all full-time freshmen had no need and received non-need-based gift aid.

UNDERGRADUATE FINANCIAL AID (Fall 2003) 2,302 applied for aid; of those 85% were deemed to have need. 98% of undergraduates with need received aid; of those 13% had need fully met. *Average percent of need met:* 50% (excluding resources awarded to replace EFC). *Average financial aid package:* $7157 (excluding resources awarded to replace EFC). 21% of all full-time undergraduates had no need and received non-need-based gift aid.

GIFT AID (NEED-BASED) *Total amount:* $8,836,436 (42% federal, 14% state, 40% institutional, 4% external sources). *Receiving aid:* Freshmen: 56% (403); All full-time undergraduates: 49% (1,587). *Average award:* Freshmen: $5667; Undergraduates: $5021. *Scholarships, grants, and awards:* Federal Pell, FSEOG, state, private, college/university gift aid from institutional funds.

GIFT AID (NON-NEED-BASED) *Total amount:* $3,630,959 (13% state, 78% institutional, 9% external sources). *Receiving aid:* Freshmen: 12% (86); Undergraduates: 5% (170). *Average Award: Freshmen:* $6182; *Undergraduates:* $6422. *Scholarships, grants, and awards by category: Academic Interests/Achievement:* 1,062 awards ($5,014,811 total): biological sciences, business, communication, education, general academic interests/achievements, religion/biblical studies. *Creative Arts/Performance:* 197 awards ($172,685 total): music, theater/drama. *Special Achievements/Activities:* 36 awards ($64,600 total): cheerleading/drum major, leadership. *Special Characteristics:* 178 awards ($751,401 total): children of faculty/staff, spouses of current students. *Tuition waivers:* Full or partial for employees or children of employees.

LOANS *Student loans:* $15,683,737 (81% need-based, 19% non-need-based). 73% of past graduating class borrowed through all loan programs. *Average indebtedness per student:* $23,174. *Average need-based loan:* Freshmen: $2511; Undergraduates: $3706. *Parent loans:* $2,894,375 (44% need-based, 56% non-need-based). *Programs:* FFEL (Subsidized and Unsubsidized Stafford, PLUS), Perkins, college/university.

WORK-STUDY *Federal work-study:* Total amount: $252,199; 153 jobs averaging $1648. *State or other work-study/employment:* Total amount: $540,750 (100% non-need-based). 525 part-time jobs averaging $1030.

ATHLETIC AWARDS *Total amount:* $1,192,735 (31% need-based, 69% non-need-based).

APPLYING FOR FINANCIAL AID *Required financial aid forms:* FAFSA, institution's own form. *Financial aid deadline (priority):* 4/15. *Notification date:* Continuous beginning 2/1. Students must reply within 3 weeks of notification.

CONTACT Mr. Michael Ellis, Director of Student Financial Aid, Lee University, 1120 North Ocoee Street, Cleveland, TN 37320-3450, 423-614-8300 or toll-free 800-533-9930. *Fax:* 423-614-8308. *E-mail:* finaid@leeuniversity.edu.

LEHIGH UNIVERSITY
Bethlehem, PA

Tuition & fees: $29,340	Average undergraduate aid package: $24,251

ABOUT THE INSTITUTION Independent, coed. Awards: bachelor's, master's, and doctoral degrees and post-master's certificates. 71 undergraduate majors. Total enrollment: 6,641. Undergraduates: 4,577. Freshmen: 1,055. Institutional methodology is used as a basis for awarding need-based institutional aid.

UNDERGRADUATE EXPENSES for 2004–05 *Application fee:* $60. *Comprehensive fee:* $37,570 includes full-time tuition ($29,140), mandatory fees ($200), and room and board ($8230). *College room only:* $4700. Room and board charges vary according to board plan and student level. *Part-time tuition:* $1215 per credit. *Payment plans:* Tuition prepayment, installment.

FRESHMAN FINANCIAL AID (Fall 2004, est.) 686 applied for aid; of those 78% were deemed to have need. 100% of freshmen with need received aid; of those 37% had need fully met. *Average percent of need met:* 97% (excluding resources awarded to replace EFC). *Average financial aid package:* $24,148 (excluding resources awarded to replace EFC). 7% of all full-time freshmen had no need and received non-need-based gift aid.

UNDERGRADUATE FINANCIAL AID (Fall 2004, est.) 2,489 applied for aid; of those 87% were deemed to have need. 99% of undergraduates with need received aid; of those 52% had need fully met. *Average percent of need met:* 97% (excluding resources awarded to replace EFC). *Average financial aid package:* $24,251 (excluding resources awarded to replace EFC). 7% of all full-time undergraduates had no need and received non-need-based gift aid.

GIFT AID (NEED-BASED) *Total amount:* $35,756,538 (6% federal, 3% state, 91% institutional). *Receiving aid:* Freshmen: 48% (502); All full-time undergraduates: 43% (1,954). *Average award:* Freshmen: $19,980; Undergraduates: $18,986. *Scholarships, grants, and awards:* Federal Pell, FSEOG, state, private, college/university gift aid from institutional funds, United Negro College Fund.

GIFT AID (NON-NEED-BASED) *Total amount:* $5,661,319 (1% federal, 73% institutional, 26% external sources). *Receiving aid:* Freshmen: 3% (32); Undergraduates: 6% (257). *Average Award: Freshmen:* $10,800; *Undergraduates:* $13,027. *Scholarships, grants, and awards by category: Academic Interests/Achievement:* 372 awards ($3,697,590 total): communication, general academic interests/achievements, military science. *Creative Arts/Performance:* 34 awards ($48,750 total): general creative arts/performance, music, performing arts, theater/drama. *Special Achievements/Activities:* general special achievements/activities. *Tuition waivers:* Full or partial for employees or children of employees, senior citizens. *ROTC:* Army.

LOANS *Student loans:* $17,981,895 (50% need-based, 50% non-need-based). 54% of past graduating class borrowed through all loan programs. *Average indebtedness per student:* $18,635. *Average need-based loan:* Freshmen: $3214; Undergraduates: $4452. *Parent loans:* $6,764,913 (100% non-need-based). *Programs:* FFEL (Subsidized and Unsubsidized Stafford, PLUS), Perkins, college/university, alternative loans.

WORK-STUDY *Federal work-study:* Total amount: $2,297,692; 1,405 jobs averaging $1635. *State or other work-study/employment:* Total amount: $686,000 (12% need-based, 88% non-need-based). 204 part-time jobs averaging $3345.

ATHLETIC AWARDS *Total amount:* $2,546,493 (58% need-based, 42% non-need-based).

APPLYING FOR FINANCIAL AID *Required financial aid forms:* FAFSA, CSS Financial Aid PROFILE, noncustodial (divorced/separated) parent's statement, business/farm supplement. *Financial aid deadline:* 2/1. *Notification date:* 3/30. Students must reply by 5/1 or within 3 weeks of notification.

CONTACT Linda F. Bell, Director of Financial Aid, Lehigh University, 218 West Packer Avenue, Bethlehem, PA 18015-3094, 610-758-3181. *Fax:* 610-758-6211. *E-mail:* lfn0@lehigh.edu.

LEHMAN COLLEGE OF THE CITY UNIVERSITY OF NEW YORK
Bronx, NY

Tuition & fees (area res): $4270	Average undergraduate aid package: $3531

ABOUT THE INSTITUTION State and locally supported, coed. Awards: bachelor's and master's degrees and post-master's certificates. 53 undergraduate majors. Total enrollment: 10,281. Undergraduates: 8,108. Freshmen: 873. Federal methodology is used as a basis for awarding need-based institutional aid.

UNDERGRADUATE EXPENSES for 2005–06 *Application fee:* $50. *Tuition, area resident:* full-time $4000; part-time $170 per year. *Tuition, state resident:* part-time $170 per year. *Tuition, nonresident:* full-time $8640; part-time $360 per year. *Required fees:* full-time $270; $270 per year part-time. Full-time tuition and fees vary according to course load and program. Part-time tuition and fees vary according to course load and program. *Payment plan:* Installment.

FRESHMAN FINANCIAL AID (Fall 2003) 724 applied for aid; of those 99% were deemed to have need. 100% of freshmen with need received aid; of those 2% had need fully met. *Average percent of need met:* 70% (excluding resources awarded to replace EFC). *Average financial aid package:* $3593 (excluding resources awarded to replace EFC). 4% of all full-time freshmen had no need and received non-need-based gift aid.

UNDERGRADUATE FINANCIAL AID (Fall 2003) 3,852 applied for aid; of those 99% were deemed to have need. 100% of undergraduates with need received aid; of those 2% had need fully met. *Average percent of need met:* 65% (excluding resources awarded to replace EFC). *Average financial aid package:* $3531 (excluding resources awarded to replace EFC). 2% of all full-time undergraduates had no need and received non-need-based gift aid.

GIFT AID (NEED-BASED) *Total amount:* $24,138,078 (56% federal, 43% state, 1% institutional). *Receiving aid:* Freshmen: 86% (681); All full-time undergraduates: 78% (3,568). *Average award:* Freshmen: $1359; Undergraduates: $1313. *Scholarships, grants, and awards:* Federal Pell, FSEOG, state, college/university gift aid from institutional funds.

GIFT AID (NON-NEED-BASED) *Total amount:* $723,817 (7% state, 57% institutional, 36% external sources). *Receiving aid:* Freshmen: 25% (199); Undergraduates: 11% (480). *Average Award: Freshmen:* $966; *Undergraduates:* $1352. *Tuition waivers:* Full or partial for senior citizens. *ROTC:* Army cooperative.

LOANS *Student loans:* $4,754,224 (100% need-based). 17% of past graduating class borrowed through all loan programs. *Average indebtedness per student:* $11,000. *Average need-based loan:* Freshmen: $1128; Undergraduates: $1525. *Parent loans:* $367,618 (100% non-need-based). *Programs:* Federal Direct (Subsidized and Unsubsidized Stafford, PLUS), Perkins.

WORK-STUDY *Federal work-study:* Total amount: $1,518,828; 437 jobs averaging $975.

APPLYING FOR FINANCIAL AID *Required financial aid forms:* FAFSA, state aid form. *Financial aid deadline:* Continuous. *Notification date:* Continuous beginning 3/1.

CONTACT David Martinez, Director of Financial Aid, Lehman College of the City University of New York, 250 Bedford Park Boulevard West, Bronx, NY 10468-1589, 718-960-8545 or toll-free 877-Lehman1 (out-of-state). *Fax:* 718-960-8328. *E-mail:* aidlc@cunyvm.cuny.edu.

LE MOYNE COLLEGE
Syracuse, NY

Tuition & fees: $20,150	Average undergraduate aid package: $17,840

ABOUT THE INSTITUTION Independent Roman Catholic (Jesuit), coed. Awards: bachelor's and master's degrees and post-bachelor's certificates. 47 undergraduate majors. Total enrollment: 3,487. Undergraduates: 2,787. Freshmen: 473. Both federal and institutional methodology are used as a basis for awarding need-based institutional aid.

UNDERGRADUATE EXPENSES for 2004–05 *Application fee:* $35. *Comprehensive fee:* $28,040 includes full-time tuition ($19,640), mandatory fees ($510), and room and board ($7890). *College room only:* $4990. Room and board charges vary according to board plan and housing facility. *Part-time tuition:* $417 per credit hour. Part-time tuition and fees vary according to class time. *Payment plans:* Installment, deferred payment.

FRESHMAN FINANCIAL AID (Fall 2003) 464 applied for aid; of those 89% were deemed to have need. 100% of freshmen with need received aid; of those 50% had need fully met. *Average percent of need met:* 91% (excluding resources awarded to replace EFC). *Average financial aid package:* $19,457 (excluding resources awarded to replace EFC). 11% of all full-time freshmen had no need and received non-need-based gift aid.

UNDERGRADUATE FINANCIAL AID (Fall 2003) 2,040 applied for aid; of those 92% were deemed to have need. 100% of undergraduates with need received aid; of those 43% had need fully met. *Average percent of need met:* 85% (excluding resources awarded to replace EFC). *Average financial aid package:* $17,840 (excluding resources awarded to replace EFC). 9% of all full-time undergraduates had no need and received non-need-based gift aid.

GIFT AID (NEED-BASED) *Total amount:* $21,573,611 (12% federal, 16% state, 67% institutional, 5% external sources). *Receiving aid:* Freshmen: 82% (413); All full-time undergraduates: 80% (1,817). *Average award:* Freshmen: $16,115; Undergraduates: $13,980. *Scholarships, grants, and awards:* Federal Pell, FSEOG, state, private, college/university gift aid from institutional funds.

GIFT AID (NON-NEED-BASED) *Total amount:* $1,865,677 (5% state, 91% institutional, 4% external sources). *Receiving aid:* Freshmen: 46% (231); Undergraduates: 40% (907). *Average Award:* Freshmen: $8707; Undergraduates: $8411. *Scholarships, grants, and awards by category:* Academic Interests/Achievement: 278 awards ($3,033,250 total): general academic interests/achievements. Special Achievements/Activities: 507 awards ($2,761,550 total): leadership. Special Characteristics: 69 awards ($190,500 total): children and siblings of alumni, members of minority groups. *Tuition waivers:* Full or partial for employees or children of employees. *ROTC:* Army cooperative, Air Force cooperative.

LOANS *Student loans:* $9,176,181 (95% need-based, 5% non-need-based). 88% of past graduating class borrowed through all loan programs. *Average indebtedness per student:* $18,688. *Average need-based loan:* Freshmen: $3095; Undergraduates: $4358. *Parent loans:* $2,731,203 (90% need-based, 10% non-need-based). *Programs:* FFEL (Subsidized and Unsubsidized Stafford, PLUS), Perkins.

WORK-STUDY *Federal work-study:* Total amount: $388,526; 356 jobs averaging $1096.

ATHLETIC AWARDS *Total amount:* $1,143,613 (75% need-based, 25% non-need-based).

APPLYING FOR FINANCIAL AID *Required financial aid forms:* FAFSA, institution's own form, state aid form. *Financial aid deadline (priority):* 2/1. *Notification date:* 3/15. Students must reply by 5/1 or within 2 weeks of notification.

CONTACT Mr. William Cheetham, Director of Financial Aid, Le Moyne College, Financial Aid Office, Syracuse, NY 13214-1399, 315-445-4400 or toll-free 800-333-4733. *Fax:* 315-445-4182. *E-mail:* cheethwc@lemoyne.edu.

LEMOYNE-OWEN COLLEGE
Memphis, TN

Tuition & fees: $14,085	Average undergraduate aid package: $8915

ABOUT THE INSTITUTION Independent religious, coed. Awards: bachelor's degrees and post-bachelor's certificates. 20 undergraduate majors. Total enrollment: 852. Undergraduates: 852. Freshmen: 144. Federal methodology is used as a basis for awarding need-based institutional aid.

UNDERGRADUATE EXPENSES for 2004–05 *Application fee:* $25. *Comprehensive fee:* $18,705 includes full-time tuition ($13,885), mandatory fees ($200), and room and board ($4620). *College room only:* $2420. Room and board charges vary according to board plan. *Payment plan:* Installment.

FRESHMAN FINANCIAL AID (Fall 2003) 110 applied for aid; of those 95% were deemed to have need. 98% of freshmen with need received aid; of those 7% had need fully met. *Average percent of need met:* 56% (excluding resources awarded to replace EFC). *Average financial aid package:* $7992 (excluding resources awarded to replace EFC). 10% of all full-time freshmen had no need and received non-need-based gift aid.

UNDERGRADUATE FINANCIAL AID (Fall 2003) 493 applied for aid; of those 96% were deemed to have need. 98% of undergraduates with need received aid; of those 7% had need fully met. *Average percent of need met:* 58% (excluding resources awarded to replace EFC). *Average financial aid package:* $8915 (excluding resources awarded to replace EFC). 5% of all full-time undergraduates had no need and received non-need-based gift aid.

GIFT AID (NEED-BASED) *Total amount:* $3,830,006 (60% federal, 20% state, 17% institutional, 3% external sources). *Receiving aid:* Freshmen: 84% (98); All full-time undergraduates: 85% (428). *Average award:* Freshmen: $6024; Undergraduates: $6304. *Scholarships, grants, and awards:* Federal Pell, FSEOG, state, private, college/university gift aid from institutional funds, United Negro College Fund.

GIFT AID (NON-NEED-BASED) *Total amount:* $214,461 (93% institutional, 7% external sources). *Receiving aid:* Freshmen: 4% (5); Undergraduates: 4% (19). *Average Award:* Freshmen: $8117; Undergraduates: $8072. *Scholarships, grants, and awards by category:* Academic Interests/Achievement: 86 awards ($413,661 total): general academic interests/achievements. Creative Arts/Performance: 25 awards ($172,948 total): journalism/publications, music. Special Characteristics: 4 awards ($24,388 total): children of faculty/staff. *Tuition waivers:* Full or partial for employees or children of employees. *ROTC:* Army cooperative, Air Force cooperative.

LOANS *Student loans:* $3,377,696 (95% need-based, 5% non-need-based). 95% of past graduating class borrowed through all loan programs. *Average indebtedness per student:* $15,682. *Average need-based loan:* Freshmen: $2262; Undergraduates: $3121. *Parent loans:* $229,724 (58% need-based, 42% non-need-based). *Programs:* Federal Direct (Subsidized and Unsubsidized Stafford, PLUS).

WORK-STUDY *Federal work-study:* Total amount: $245,698; 317 jobs averaging $731.

ATHLETIC AWARDS *Total amount:* $277,744 (81% need-based, 19% non-need-based).

APPLYING FOR FINANCIAL AID *Required financial aid forms:* FAFSA, institution's own form. *Financial aid deadline (priority):* 4/1. *Notification date:* Continuous beginning 5/1. Students must reply within 2 weeks of notification.

CONTACT Phyllis Wilson, Director of Student Financial Services, LeMoyne-Owen College, 807 Walker Avenue, Memphis, TN 38126-6595, 901-942-7313. *Fax:* 901-942-6244. *E-mail:* phyllis_wilson@loc.edu.

LENOIR-RHYNE COLLEGE
Hickory, NC

Tuition & fees: $18,920	Average undergraduate aid package: $12,928

ABOUT THE INSTITUTION Independent Lutheran, coed. Awards: bachelor's and master's degrees. 54 undergraduate majors. Total enrollment: 1,579. Undergraduates: 1,407. Freshmen: 322. Both federal and institutional methodology are used as a basis for awarding need-based institutional aid.

UNDERGRADUATE EXPENSES for 2005–06 *Application fee:* $25. *One-time required fee:* $200. *Comprehensive fee:* $25,600 includes full-time tuition

Lenoir-Rhyne College

($18,150), mandatory fees ($770), and room and board ($6680). Room and board charges vary according to board plan and housing facility. *Part-time tuition:* $455 per credit. *Part-time fees:* $10 per term. Part-time tuition and fees vary according to class time. *Payment plans:* Installment, deferred payment.
FRESHMAN FINANCIAL AID (Fall 2004, est.) 301 applied for aid; of those 80% were deemed to have need. 100% of freshmen with need received aid; of those 19% had need fully met. *Average percent of need met:* 70% (excluding resources awarded to replace EFC). *Average financial aid package:* $13,438 (excluding resources awarded to replace EFC). 18% of all full-time freshmen had no need and received non-need-based gift aid.
UNDERGRADUATE FINANCIAL AID (Fall 2004, est.) 1,211 applied for aid; of those 85% were deemed to have need. 100% of undergraduates with need received aid; of those 13% had need fully met. *Average percent of need met:* 61% (excluding resources awarded to replace EFC). *Average financial aid package:* $12,928 (excluding resources awarded to replace EFC). 15% of all full-time undergraduates had no need and received non-need-based gift aid.
GIFT AID (NEED-BASED) *Total amount:* $10,292,528 (13% federal, 24% state, 62% institutional, 1% external sources). *Receiving aid:* Freshmen: 75% (242); All full-time undergraduates: 81% (1,030). *Average award:* Freshmen: $12,515; Undergraduates: $11,483. *Scholarships, grants, and awards:* Federal Pell, FSEOG, state, private, college/university gift aid from institutional funds, Federal Nursing.
GIFT AID (NON-NEED-BASED) *Total amount:* $1,394,622 (80% state, 80% institutional, 1% external sources). *Receiving aid:* Freshmen: 11% (37); Undergraduates: 10% (126). *Average Award:* Freshmen: $6430; Undergraduates: $6271. *Scholarships, grants, and awards by category: Academic Interests/Achievement:* 183 awards ($796,493 total): general academic interests/achievements. *Creative Arts/Performance:* 11 awards ($23,371 total): music. *Special Achievements/Activities:* 4 awards ($3500 total): cheerleading/drum major, community service, leadership. *Special Characteristics:* 36 awards ($72,820 total): children and siblings of alumni, children of faculty/staff, local/state students, relatives of clergy, religious affiliation, siblings of current students. *Tuition waivers:* Full or partial for employees or children of employees. *ROTC:* Army cooperative.
LOANS *Student loans:* $2,189,605 (95% need-based, 5% non-need-based). 91% of past graduating class borrowed through all loan programs. *Average indebtedness per student:* $24,397. *Average need-based loan:* Freshmen: $2348; Undergraduates: $2903. *Parent loans:* $851,781 (83% need-based, 17% non-need-based). *Programs:* FFEL (Subsidized and Unsubsidized Stafford, PLUS), Perkins, Federal Nursing, state.
WORK-STUDY *Federal work-study:* Total amount: $129,592; 168 jobs averaging $771. *State or other work-study/employment:* Total amount: $121,547 (100% need-based). 137 part-time jobs averaging $887.
ATHLETIC AWARDS *Total amount:* $1,393,721 (83% need-based, 17% non-need-based).
APPLYING FOR FINANCIAL AID *Required financial aid forms:* FAFSA, institution's own form. *Financial aid deadline (priority):* 3/1. *Notification date:* Continuous beginning 3/15. Students must reply by 5/1 or within 4 weeks of notification.
CONTACT Mrs. Rachel Nichols, Dean of Admissions and Financial Aid, Lenoir-Rhyne College, PO Box 7227, Hickory, NC 28603, 828-328-7300 or toll-free 800-277-5721. *Fax:* 828-328-7039. *E-mail:* admission@lrc.edu.

LESLEY UNIVERSITY
Cambridge, MA

Tuition & fees: $22,750	Average undergraduate aid package: $14,114

ABOUT THE INSTITUTION Independent, coed. Awards: associate, bachelor's, master's, and doctoral degrees and post-bachelor's and post-master's certificates. 21 undergraduate majors. Total enrollment: 6,526. Undergraduates: 1,047. Freshmen: 233. Institutional methodology is used as a basis for awarding need-based institutional aid.
UNDERGRADUATE EXPENSES for 2005–06 *Application fee:* $40. *Comprehensive fee:* $32,700 includes full-time tuition ($22,500), mandatory fees ($250), and room and board ($9950). *College room only:* $6100. Full-time tuition and fees vary according to program. Room and board charges vary according to housing facility. *Part-time tuition:* $665 per credit. *Payment plan:* Installment.
FRESHMAN FINANCIAL AID (Fall 2004, est.) 190 applied for aid; of those 91% were deemed to have need. 100% of freshmen with need received aid; of those 20% had need fully met. *Average percent of need met:* 70% (excluding resources awarded to replace EFC). *Average financial aid package:* $15,984 (excluding resources awarded to replace EFC). 6% of all full-time freshmen had no need and received non-need-based gift aid.

UNDERGRADUATE FINANCIAL AID (Fall 2004, est.) 730 applied for aid; of those 90% were deemed to have need. 100% of undergraduates with need received aid; of those 29% had need fully met. *Average percent of need met:* 70% (excluding resources awarded to replace EFC). *Average financial aid package:* $14,114 (excluding resources awarded to replace EFC). 5% of all full-time undergraduates had no need and received non-need-based gift aid.
GIFT AID (NEED-BASED) *Total amount:* $3,823,483 (20% federal, 10% state, 65% institutional, 5% external sources). *Receiving aid:* Freshmen: 78% (173); All full-time undergraduates: 69% (656). *Average award:* Freshmen: $11,412; Undergraduates: $10,683. *Scholarships, grants, and awards:* Federal Pell, FSEOG, state, private, college/university gift aid from institutional funds.
GIFT AID (NON-NEED-BASED) *Total amount:* $1,711,084 (100% institutional). *Receiving aid:* Freshmen: 12% (27); Undergraduates: 20% (187). *Average Award:* Freshmen: $6286; Undergraduates: $4033. *Scholarships, grants, and awards by category: Academic Interests/Achievement:* 4 awards ($80,410 total): general academic interests/achievements. *Creative Arts/Performance:* 9 awards ($10,500 total): art/fine arts. *Special Achievements/Activities:* 205 awards ($966,586 total): general special achievements/activities. *Special Characteristics:* 59 awards ($653,774 total): ethnic background, local/state students, members of minority groups. *Tuition waivers:* Full or partial for employees or children of employees.
LOANS *Student loans:* $4,532,958 (62% need-based, 38% non-need-based). 91% of past graduating class borrowed through all loan programs. *Average indebtedness per student:* $13,605. *Average need-based loan:* Freshmen: $2257; Undergraduates: $3899. *Parent loans:* $1,294,055 (100% non-need-based). *Programs:* FFEL (Subsidized and Unsubsidized Stafford, PLUS), Perkins, state.
WORK-STUDY *Federal work-study:* Total amount: $227,386; 232 jobs averaging $1270. *State or other work-study/employment:* 135 part-time jobs averaging $2016.
APPLYING FOR FINANCIAL AID *Required financial aid forms:* FAFSA, institution's own form, parent and student federal income tax returns. *Financial aid deadline (priority):* 3/12. *Notification date:* 4/1. Students must reply within 2 weeks of notification.
CONTACT Financial Aid Office, Lesley University, 29 Everett Street, Cambridge, MA 02138-2790, 617-349-8581 or toll-free 800-999-1959 Ext. 8800. *Fax:* 617-349-8667. *E-mail:* finaid@lesley.edu.

LESTER L. COX COLLEGE OF NURSING AND HEALTH SCIENCES
Springfield, MO

ABOUT THE INSTITUTION Independent, coed, primarily women. Awards: associate and bachelor's degrees. 1 undergraduate major. Total enrollment: 529. Undergraduates: 529. Freshmen: 53.
GIFT AID (NEED-BASED) *Scholarships, grants, and awards:* Federal Pell, FSEOG, state, private, college/university gift aid from institutional funds, United Negro College Fund, Federal Nursing.
GIFT AID (NON-NEED-BASED) *Scholarships, grants, and awards by category: Academic Interests/Achievement:* general academic interests/achievements.
LOANS *Programs:* FFEL (Subsidized and Unsubsidized Stafford, PLUS), Perkins, Federal Nursing, state, college/university.
APPLYING FOR FINANCIAL AID *Required financial aid form:* FAFSA.
CONTACT Brenda Smith, Financial Aid Coordinator, Lester L. Cox College of Nursing and Health Sciences, 1423 North Jefferson Avenue, Springfield, MO 65802, 417-269-3401 or toll-free 866-898-5355 (in-state). *Fax:* 417-269-3586. *E-mail:* bjsmit1@coxcollege.edu.

LETOURNEAU UNIVERSITY
Longview, TX

Tuition & fees: $15,890	Average undergraduate aid package: $12,078

ABOUT THE INSTITUTION Independent nondenominational, coed. Awards: associate, bachelor's, and master's degrees. 41 undergraduate majors. Total enrollment: 3,758. Undergraduates: 3,388. Freshmen: 328. Federal methodology is used as a basis for awarding need-based institutional aid.
UNDERGRADUATE EXPENSES for 2005–06 *Application fee:* $25. *Comprehensive fee:* $22,176 includes full-time tuition ($15,710), mandatory fees ($180), and room and board ($6286). Room and board charges vary according to board plan. *Part-time tuition:* $280 per hour. Part-time tuition and fees vary according to course load. *Payment plan:* Installment.

FRESHMAN FINANCIAL AID (Fall 2003) 302 applied for aid; of those 83% were deemed to have need. 100% of freshmen with need received aid; of those 21% had need fully met. *Average percent of need met:* 78% (excluding resources awarded to replace EFC). *Average financial aid package:* $12,599 (excluding resources awarded to replace EFC). 21% of all full-time freshmen had no need and received non-need-based gift aid.

UNDERGRADUATE FINANCIAL AID (Fall 2003) 1,007 applied for aid; of those 85% were deemed to have need. 100% of undergraduates with need received aid; of those 20% had need fully met. *Average percent of need met:* 74% (excluding resources awarded to replace EFC). *Average financial aid package:* $12,078 (excluding resources awarded to replace EFC). 18% of all full-time undergraduates had no need and received non-need-based gift aid.

GIFT AID (NEED-BASED) *Total amount:* $6,645,715 (41% federal, 19% state, 40% institutional). *Receiving aid:* Freshmen: 74% (252); All full-time undergraduates: 65% (817). *Average award:* Freshmen: $8864; Undergraduates: $7874. *Scholarships, grants, and awards:* Federal Pell, FSEOG, state, private, college/university gift aid from institutional funds.

GIFT AID (NON-NEED-BASED) *Total amount:* $1,986,729 (1% federal, 79% institutional, 20% external sources). *Receiving aid:* Freshmen: 52% (175); Undergraduates: 36% (445). *Average Award:* Freshmen: $1138; Undergraduates: $4002. *Scholarships, grants, and awards by category: Academic Interests/Achievement:* general academic interests/achievements. *Special Achievements/Activities:* general special achievements/activities. *Special Characteristics:* children of faculty/staff, international students, local/state students, relatives of clergy, spouses of current students. *Tuition waivers:* Full or partial for employees or children of employees.

LOANS *Student loans:* $19,336,926 (47% need-based, 53% non-need-based). 70% of past graduating class borrowed through all loan programs. *Average indebtedness per student:* $20,055. *Average need-based loan:* Freshmen: $3276; Undergraduates: $4199. *Parent loans:* $2,154,745 (100% non-need-based). *Programs:* FFEL (Subsidized and Unsubsidized Stafford, PLUS), Perkins.

WORK-STUDY *Federal work-study:* Total amount: $207,996; jobs available. *State or other work-study/employment:* Total amount: $30,656 (100% need-based). Part-time jobs available.

APPLYING FOR FINANCIAL AID *Required financial aid form:* FAFSA. *Financial aid deadline (priority):* 2/15. *Notification date:* Continuous beginning 3/1. Students must reply within 3 weeks of notification.

CONTACT Ms. Delinda Hall, Director of Financial Aid, LeTourneau University, 2100 South Mobberly Avenue, PO Box 7001, Longview, TX 75607, 903-233-3430 or toll-free 800-759-8811. *Fax:* 903-233-3411. *E-mail:* finaid@letu.edu.

LEWIS & CLARK COLLEGE
Portland, OR

Tuition & fees: $27,710	Average undergraduate aid package: $24,380

ABOUT THE INSTITUTION Independent, coed. Awards: bachelor's, master's, doctoral, and first professional degrees and post-master's and first professional certificates. 29 undergraduate majors. Total enrollment: 3,259. Undergraduates: 1,872. Freshmen: 537. Federal methodology is used as a basis for awarding need-based institutional aid.

UNDERGRADUATE EXPENSES for 2005–06 *Application fee:* $50. *Comprehensive fee:* $35,358 includes full-time tuition ($27,494), mandatory fees ($216), and room and board ($7648). *College room only:* $3974. Room and board charges vary according to board plan and housing facility. *Part-time tuition:* $1386 per credit hour. *Payment plan:* Installment.

FRESHMAN FINANCIAL AID (Fall 2003) 415 applied for aid; of those 84% were deemed to have need. 100% of freshmen with need received aid; of those 31% had need fully met. *Average percent of need met:* 89% (excluding resources awarded to replace EFC). *Average financial aid package:* $23,877 (excluding resources awarded to replace EFC). 15% of all full-time freshmen had no need and received non-need-based gift aid.

UNDERGRADUATE FINANCIAL AID (Fall 2003) 1,283 applied for aid; of those 89% were deemed to have need. 97% of undergraduates with need received aid; of those 34% had need fully met. *Average percent of need met:* 88% (excluding resources awarded to replace EFC). *Average financial aid package:* $24,380 (excluding resources awarded to replace EFC). 13% of all full-time undergraduates had no need and received non-need-based gift aid.

GIFT AID (NEED-BASED) *Total amount:* $18,030,861 (7% federal, 1% state, 89% institutional, 3% external sources). *Receiving aid:* Freshmen: 65% (347); All full-time undergraduates: 60% (1,099). *Average award:* Freshmen: $20,037; Undergraduates: $19,352. *Scholarships, grants, and awards:* Federal Pell, FSEOG, state, private, college/university gift aid from institutional funds.

GIFT AID (NON-NEED-BASED) *Total amount:* $1,978,197 (96% institutional, 4% external sources). *Receiving aid:* Freshmen: 3% (14); Undergraduates: 3% (46). *Average Award:* Freshmen: $7965; Undergraduates: $7876. *Scholarships, grants, and awards by category: Academic Interests/Achievement:* 557 awards ($4,073,018 total): general academic interests/achievements. *Creative Arts/Performance:* 51 awards ($193,429 total): debating, music. *Special Achievements/Activities:* 78 awards ($390,000 total): community service. *Tuition waivers:* Full or partial for employees or children of employees.

LOANS *Student loans:* $5,840,812 (93% need-based, 7% non-need-based). 58% of past graduating class borrowed through all loan programs. *Average indebtedness per student:* $19,124. *Average need-based loan:* Freshmen: $4319; Undergraduates: $5262. *Parent loans:* $2,163,842 (82% need-based, 18% non-need-based). *Programs:* FFEL (Subsidized and Unsubsidized Stafford, PLUS), Perkins.

WORK-STUDY *Federal work-study:* Total amount: $1,398,908; 734 jobs averaging $1832.

APPLYING FOR FINANCIAL AID *Required financial aid form:* FAFSA. *Financial aid deadline (priority):* 3/1. *Notification date:* Continuous beginning 3/1. Students must reply by 5/1.

CONTACT Glendi Gaddis, Director of Student Financial Services, Lewis & Clark College, Templeton Student Center, MS 56, Portland, OR 97219-7899, 503-768-7096 or toll-free 800-444-4111. *Fax:* 503-768-7074. *E-mail:* sfs@lclark.edu.

LEWIS-CLARK STATE COLLEGE
Lewiston, ID

Tuition & fees (ID res): $3392	Average undergraduate aid package: $6534

ABOUT THE INSTITUTION State-supported, coed. Awards: associate and bachelor's degrees. 50 undergraduate majors. Total enrollment: 3,325. Undergraduates: 3,325. Freshmen: 494. Federal methodology is used as a basis for awarding need-based institutional aid.

UNDERGRADUATE EXPENSES for 2004–05 *Application fee:* $35. *Tuition, state resident:* full-time $3392. *Tuition, nonresident:* full-time $6240. *Required fees:* $171 per credit. Full-time tuition and fees vary according to course load and reciprocity agreements. *College room and board:* $3995; *room only:* $1685. Room and board charges vary according to board plan and housing facility. *Payment plan:* Deferred payment.

FRESHMAN FINANCIAL AID (Fall 2003) 378 applied for aid; of those 86% were deemed to have need. 98% of freshmen with need received aid; of those 8% had need fully met. *Average percent of need met:* 8% (excluding resources awarded to replace EFC). *Average financial aid package:* $3900 (excluding resources awarded to replace EFC). 11% of all full-time freshmen had no need and received non-need-based gift aid.

UNDERGRADUATE FINANCIAL AID (Fall 2003) 1,532 applied for aid; of those 90% were deemed to have need. 99% of undergraduates with need received aid; of those 13% had need fully met. *Average percent of need met:* 13% (excluding resources awarded to replace EFC). *Average financial aid package:* $6534 (excluding resources awarded to replace EFC). 7% of all full-time undergraduates had no need and received non-need-based gift aid.

GIFT AID (NEED-BASED) *Total amount:* $5,396,239 (78% federal, 1% state, 13% institutional, 8% external sources). *Receiving aid:* Freshmen: 51% (230); All full-time undergraduates: 52% (1,027). *Average award:* Freshmen: $3065; Undergraduates: $3222. *Scholarships, grants, and awards:* Federal Pell, FSEOG, state, private, college/university gift aid from institutional funds.

GIFT AID (NON-NEED-BASED) *Total amount:* $387,185 (60% institutional, 40% external sources). *Receiving aid:* Freshmen: 30% (135); Undergraduates: 14% (272). *Average Award:* Freshmen: $1800; Undergraduates: $2883. *Scholarships, grants, and awards by category: Academic Interests/Achievement:* 144 awards ($158,525 total): education, general academic interests/achievements, health fields, humanities, mathematics, social sciences. *Creative Arts/Performance:* 20 awards ($48,551 total): art/fine arts, creative writing, music, theater/drama. *Special Achievements/Activities:* 23 awards ($5250 total): junior miss, leadership, rodeo. *Special Characteristics:* 202 awards ($567,132 total): ethnic background, first-generation college students, local/state students, members of minority groups, out-of-state students. *Tuition waivers:* Full or partial for employees or children of employees, senior citizens. *ROTC:* Army, Air Force cooperative.

LOANS *Student loans:* $8,037,788 (73% need-based, 27% non-need-based). 61% of past graduating class borrowed through all loan programs. *Average need-based loan:* Freshmen: $2022; Undergraduates: $3588. *Parent loans:* $189,073 (100% non-need-based). *Programs:* FFEL (Subsidized and Unsubsidized Stafford, PLUS), Perkins, Federal Nursing.

WORK-STUDY *Federal work-study:* Total amount: $125,359; 96 jobs averaging $1306. *State or other work-study/employment:* Total amount: $92,684 (87% need-based, 13% non-need-based). 78 part-time jobs averaging $1188.
ATHLETIC AWARDS *Total amount:* $795,225 (100% non-need-based).
APPLYING FOR FINANCIAL AID *Required financial aid form:* FAFSA. *Financial aid deadline (priority):* 3/1. *Notification date:* Continuous beginning 4/15. Students must reply within 2 weeks of notification.
CONTACT Ms. Laura Hughes, Director of Financial Aid, Lewis-Clark State College, 500 8th Avenue, Lewiston, ID 83501-2698, 208-792-2224 or toll-free 800-933-LCSC Ext. 2210. *Fax:* 208-792-2063. *E-mail:* lhughes@lcsc.edu.

LEWIS UNIVERSITY
Romeoville, IL

ABOUT THE INSTITUTION Independent religious, coed. Awards: associate, bachelor's, master's, and doctoral degrees and post-bachelor's certificates. 63 undergraduate majors. Total enrollment: 4,826. Undergraduates: 3,457. Freshmen: 510.
GIFT AID (NEED-BASED) *Scholarships, grants, and awards:* Federal Pell, FSEOG, state, private, college/university gift aid from institutional funds, Federal Nursing.
GIFT AID (NON-NEED-BASED) *Scholarships, grants, and awards by category: Academic Interests/Achievement:* general academic interests/achievements. *Creative Arts/Performance:* art/fine arts, music, theater/drama. *Special Achievements/ Activities:* community service, general special achievements/activities, memberships. *Special Characteristics:* children and siblings of alumni, children of faculty/staff, religious affiliation.
LOANS *Programs:* FFEL (Subsidized and Unsubsidized Stafford, PLUS), Perkins.
WORK-STUDY *Federal work-study:* Total amount: $281,551; 361 jobs averaging $2800. *State or other work-study/employment:* Total amount: $700,000 (100% non-need-based). 170 part-time jobs averaging $2800.
APPLYING FOR FINANCIAL AID *Required financial aid form:* FAFSA.
CONTACT Ms. Janeen Decharinte, Director of Financial Aid, Lewis University, One University Parkway, Romeoville, IL 60446, 815-836-5262 or toll-free 800-897-9000. *Fax:* 815-836-5135. *E-mail:* decharja@lewisu.edu.

LEXINGTON COLLEGE
Chicago, IL

Tuition & fees: $15,337	Average undergraduate aid package: $8400

ABOUT THE INSTITUTION Independent, women only. Awards: associate and bachelor's degrees. 12 undergraduate majors. Total enrollment: 49. Undergraduates: 49. Freshmen: 18. Federal methodology is used as a basis for awarding need-based institutional aid.
UNDERGRADUATE EXPENSES for 2004–05 *Application fee:* $30. *One-time required fee:* $50. *Tuition:* full-time $14,490; part-time $450 per credit hour. *Required fees:* full-time $847; $180 per term part-time. *Payment plan:* Installment.
FRESHMAN FINANCIAL AID (Fall 2003) 34 applied for aid; of those 71% were deemed to have need. 42% of freshmen with need received aid. *Average percent of need met:* 87% (excluding resources awarded to replace EFC). *Average financial aid package:* $13,507 (excluding resources awarded to replace EFC).
UNDERGRADUATE FINANCIAL AID (Fall 2003) 49 applied for aid; of those 80% were deemed to have need. 100% of undergraduates with need received aid. *Average percent of need met:* 92% (excluding resources awarded to replace EFC). *Average financial aid package:* $8400 (excluding resources awarded to replace EFC).
GIFT AID (NEED-BASED) *Total amount:* $254,664 (35% federal, 42% state, 17% institutional, 6% external sources). *Receiving aid:* Freshmen: 3% (1); All full-time undergraduates: 80% (39). *Average award:* Freshmen: $11,507; Undergraduates: $7900. *Scholarships, grants, and awards:* Federal Pell, FSEOG, state, private, college/university gift aid from institutional funds.
GIFT AID (NON-NEED-BASED) *Receiving aid:* Freshmen: 6% (2); Undergraduates: 59% (29). *Tuition waivers:* Full or partial for employees or children of employees.
LOANS *Student loans:* $159,181 (94% need-based, 6% non-need-based). 50% of past graduating class borrowed through all loan programs. *Average indebtedness per student:* $3500. *Average need-based loan:* Freshmen: $5251; Undergraduates: $1313. *Parent loans:* $17,800 (100% need-based). *Programs:* FFEL (Subsidized and Unsubsidized Stafford, PLUS), Sallie Mae Signature Student Loans, alternative loans.

WORK-STUDY *Federal work-study:* 5 jobs available.
APPLYING FOR FINANCIAL AID *Required financial aid form:* FAFSA. *Financial aid deadline:* 10/1 (priority: 5/15). *Notification date:* Continuous.
CONTACT Maria Lebron-Cardona, Director of Financial Aid, Lexington College, 310 South Peoria Street, Suite 512, Chicago, IL 60607, 312-226-6294 Ext. 227. *Fax:* 312-226-6405. *E-mail:* finaid@lexingtoncollege.edu.

LIBERTY UNIVERSITY
Lynchburg, VA

Tuition & fees: $14,550	Average undergraduate aid package: $10,538

ABOUT THE INSTITUTION Independent nondenominational, coed. Awards: associate, bachelor's, master's, doctoral, and first professional degrees and post-master's certificates (also offers external degree program with significant enrollment not reflected in profile). 73 undergraduate majors. Total enrollment: 13,464. Undergraduates: 10,642. Freshmen: 2,097. Federal methodology is used as a basis for awarding need-based institutional aid.
UNDERGRADUATE EXPENSES for 2005–06 *Application fee:* $35. *Comprehensive fee:* $19,950 includes full-time tuition ($13,700), mandatory fees ($850), and room and board ($5400). Full-time tuition and fees vary according to course load. Room and board charges vary according to housing facility. *Part-time tuition:* $465 per semester hour. *Part-time fees:* $850 per term. Part-time tuition and fees vary according to course load. *Payment plan:* Installment.
FRESHMAN FINANCIAL AID (Fall 2004, est.) 1979 applied for aid; of those 82% were deemed to have need. 100% of freshmen with need received aid; of those 20% had need fully met. *Average percent of need met:* 71% (excluding resources awarded to replace EFC). *Average financial aid package:* $11,107 (excluding resources awarded to replace EFC). 22% of all full-time freshmen had no need and received non-need-based gift aid.
UNDERGRADUATE FINANCIAL AID (Fall 2004, est.) 7,440 applied for aid; of those 84% were deemed to have need. 99% of undergraduates with need received aid; of those 16% had need fully met. *Average percent of need met:* 69% (excluding resources awarded to replace EFC). *Average financial aid package:* $10,538 (excluding resources awarded to replace EFC). 15% of all full-time undergraduates had no need and received non-need-based gift aid.
GIFT AID (NEED-BASED) *Total amount:* $12,134,279 (78% federal, 22% institutional). *Receiving aid:* Freshmen: 41% (863); All full-time undergraduates: 42% (3,391). *Average award:* Freshmen: $1612; Undergraduates: $1652. *Scholarships, grants, and awards:* Federal Pell, FSEOG, state, private, college/university gift aid from institutional funds.
GIFT AID (NON-NEED-BASED) *Total amount:* $50,453,247 (1% federal, 11% state, 85% institutional, 3% external sources). *Receiving aid:* Freshmen: 77% (1,616); Undergraduates: 66% (5,381). *Average Award: Freshmen:* $6743; *Undergraduates:* $5305. *Scholarships, grants, and awards by category: Academic Interests/Achievement:* 4,602 awards ($22,092,354 total): general academic interests/achievements. *Creative Arts/Performance:* 357 awards ($1,224,622 total): art/fine arts, debating, journalism/publications, music, performing arts. *Special Achievements/Activities:* 3,794 awards ($8,043,219 total): cheerleading/drum major, general special achievements/activities, leadership, religious involvement. *Special Characteristics:* 1,145 awards ($1,208,318 total): international students, religious affiliation. *Tuition waivers:* Full or partial for employees or children of employees. *ROTC:* Army, Air Force cooperative.
LOANS *Student loans:* $40,694,861 (46% need-based, 54% non-need-based). 56% of past graduating class borrowed through all loan programs. *Average indebtedness per student:* $18,078. *Average need-based loan:* Freshmen: $2433; Undergraduates: $4055. *Parent loans:* $22,301,044 (100% non-need-based). *Programs:* FFEL (Subsidized and Unsubsidized Stafford, PLUS).
WORK-STUDY *Federal work-study:* Total amount: $3,171,874; 2,712 jobs averaging $1170.
ATHLETIC AWARDS *Total amount:* $3,099,547 (100% non-need-based).
APPLYING FOR FINANCIAL AID *Required financial aid form:* FAFSA. *Financial aid deadline (priority):* 3/1. *Notification date:* Continuous. Students must reply within 2 weeks of notification.
CONTACT Rhonda Allbeck, Director, Financial Aid Office, Liberty University, 1971 University Boulevard, Lynchburg, VA 24502, 434-582-2288 or toll-free 800-543-5317. *Fax:* 434-582-2053. *E-mail:* rfallbeck@liberty.edu.

LIFE BIBLE COLLEGE EAST
Christiansburg, VA

CONTACT Financial Aid Office, LIFE Bible College East, 900 Life Drive, Christiansburg, VA 24073, 540-382-7100.

LIFE PACIFIC COLLEGE
San Dimas, CA

Tuition & fees: $10,100	Average undergraduate aid package: $6006

ABOUT THE INSTITUTION Independent religious, coed. Awards: associate and bachelor's degrees. 3 undergraduate majors. Total enrollment: 489. Undergraduates: 489. Freshmen: 52. Federal methodology is used as a basis for awarding need-based institutional aid.

UNDERGRADUATE EXPENSES for 2005–06 *Application fee:* $35. *Comprehensive fee:* $15,100 includes full-time tuition ($9750), mandatory fees ($350), and room and board ($5000). *Part-time tuition:* $325 per credit hour. Part-time tuition and fees vary according to course load. *Payment plan:* Installment.

FRESHMAN FINANCIAL AID (Fall 2003) 57 applied for aid; of those 81% were deemed to have need. 91% of freshmen with need received aid; of those 2% had need fully met. *Average percent of need met:* 31% (excluding resources awarded to replace EFC). *Average financial aid package:* $2997 (excluding resources awarded to replace EFC).

UNDERGRADUATE FINANCIAL AID (Fall 2003) 359 applied for aid; of those 85% were deemed to have need. 100% of undergraduates with need received aid; of those 5% had need fully met. *Average percent of need met:* 55% (excluding resources awarded to replace EFC). *Average financial aid package:* $6006 (excluding resources awarded to replace EFC). 2% of all full-time undergraduates had no need and received non-need-based gift aid.

GIFT AID (NEED-BASED) *Total amount:* $1,103,816 (47% federal, 23% state, 8% institutional, 22% external sources). *Receiving aid:* Freshmen: 49% (34); All full-time undergraduates: 54% (222). *Average award:* Freshmen: $2680; Undergraduates: $7053. *Scholarships, grants, and awards:* Federal Pell, FSEOG, state, private, college/university gift aid from institutional funds.

GIFT AID (NON-NEED-BASED) *Total amount:* $36,995 (42% institutional, 58% external sources). *Receiving aid:* Freshmen: 23% (16); Undergraduates: 8% (32). *Average Award:* Undergraduates: $1535. *Scholarships, grants, and awards by category: Academic Interests/Achievement:* 30 awards ($18,500 total): general academic interests/achievements. *Special Characteristics:* 62 awards ($95,230 total): children of faculty/staff, relatives of clergy. *Tuition waivers:* Full or partial for children of alumni, employees or children of employees.

LOANS *Student loans:* $2,007,117 (77% need-based, 23% non-need-based). 70% of past graduating class borrowed through all loan programs. *Average indebtedness per student:* $17,125. *Average need-based loan:* Freshmen: $2297; Undergraduates: $3252. *Parent loans:* $326,894 (56% need-based, 44% non-need-based). *Programs:* FFEL (Subsidized and Unsubsidized Stafford, PLUS).

WORK-STUDY *Federal work-study:* Total amount: $33,462; 24 jobs averaging $1394.

APPLYING FOR FINANCIAL AID *Required financial aid forms:* FAFSA, state aid form. *Financial aid deadline (priority):* 7/1. *Notification date:* Continuous. Students must reply by 8/15 or within 2 weeks of notification.

CONTACT Mrs. Becky Huyck, Director of Financial Aid, Life Pacific College, 1100 Covina Boulevard, San Dimas, CA 91773-3298, 909-599-5433 Ext. 319 or toll-free 877-886-5433 Ext. 314. *Fax:* 909-599-6690. *E-mail:* bhuyck@lifepacific.edu.

LIFE UNIVERSITY
Marietta, GA

Tuition & fees: $5496	Average undergraduate aid package: $7300

ABOUT THE INSTITUTION Independent, coed. Awards: associate, bachelor's, master's, and first professional degrees. 3 undergraduate majors. Total enrollment: 1,233. Undergraduates: 467. Freshmen: 28. Federal methodology is used as a basis for awarding need-based institutional aid.

UNDERGRADUATE EXPENSES for 2004–05 *Application fee:* $50. *Tuition:* full-time $5184; part-time $144 per hour. *Required fees:* full-time $312; $104 per term part-time. Full-time tuition and fees vary according to course load and program. Part-time tuition and fees vary according to course load and program.

FRESHMAN FINANCIAL AID (Fall 2004, est.) 75 applied for aid; of those 96% were deemed to have need. 100% of freshmen with need received aid; of those 29% had need fully met. *Average percent of need met:* 29% (excluding resources awarded to replace EFC). *Average financial aid package:* $6500 (excluding resources awarded to replace EFC). 2% of all full-time freshmen had no need and received non-need-based gift aid.

UNDERGRADUATE FINANCIAL AID (Fall 2004, est.) 292 applied for aid; of those 95% were deemed to have need. 99% of undergraduates with need received aid; of those 18% had need fully met. *Average percent of need met:* 18% (excluding resources awarded to replace EFC). *Average financial aid package:* $7300 (excluding resources awarded to replace EFC). 1% of all full-time undergraduates had no need and received non-need-based gift aid.

GIFT AID (NEED-BASED) *Total amount:* $668,200 (100% federal). *Receiving aid:* Freshmen: 39% (44); All full-time undergraduates: 38% (159). *Average award:* Freshmen: $2900; Undergraduates: $2000. *Scholarships, grants, and awards:* Federal Pell, FSEOG, state, private, college/university gift aid from institutional funds.

GIFT AID (NON-NEED-BASED) *Total amount:* $234,600 (78% state, 16% institutional, 6% external sources). *Receiving aid:* Freshmen: 49% (55); Undergraduates: 35% (143). *Average Award: Freshmen:* $3500; *Undergraduates:* $4200. *Scholarships, grants, and awards by category: Academic Interests/Achievement:* 5 awards ($24,000 total): general academic interests/achievements. *Tuition waivers:* Full or partial for employees or children of employees.

LOANS *Student loans:* $3,058,000 (69% need-based, 31% non-need-based). 78% of past graduating class borrowed through all loan programs. *Average indebtedness per student:* $13,000. *Average need-based loan:* Freshmen: $3500; Undergraduates: $3700. *Parent loans:* $124,000 (100% non-need-based). *Programs:* FFEL (Subsidized and Unsubsidized Stafford, PLUS), Perkins, college/university, alternative loans.

WORK-STUDY *Federal work-study:* Total amount: $202,500; 122 jobs averaging $1300.

ATHLETIC AWARDS *Total amount:* $19,000 (100% non-need-based).

APPLYING FOR FINANCIAL AID *Required financial aid forms:* FAFSA, institution's own form. *Financial aid deadline (priority):* 3/1. *Notification date:* Continuous beginning 5/1.

CONTACT Kay Freeland, Director of Financial Aid, Life University, 1269 Barclay Circle, Marietta, GA 30060, 770-426-2901 or toll-free 800-543-3202 (in-state). *Fax:* 770-426-2926. *E-mail:* finaid@life.edu.

LIMESTONE COLLEGE
Gaffney, SC

Tuition & fees: $14,040	Average undergraduate aid package: $9277

ABOUT THE INSTITUTION Independent, coed. Awards: associate and bachelor's degrees. 45 undergraduate majors. Total enrollment: 625. Undergraduates: 625. Freshmen: 190. Federal methodology is used as a basis for awarding need-based institutional aid.

UNDERGRADUATE EXPENSES for 2005–06 *Application fee:* $25. *Comprehensive fee:* $19,840 includes full-time tuition ($14,040) and room and board ($5800). Full-time tuition and fees vary according to course load and program. *Part-time tuition:* $585 per credit hour. Part-time tuition and fees vary according to program. *Payment plan:* Installment.

FRESHMAN FINANCIAL AID (Fall 2003) 166 applied for aid; of those 84% were deemed to have need. 100% of freshmen with need received aid; of those 17% had need fully met. *Average percent of need met:* 54% (excluding resources awarded to replace EFC). *Average financial aid package:* $8710 (excluding resources awarded to replace EFC). 19% of all full-time freshmen had no need and received non-need-based gift aid.

UNDERGRADUATE FINANCIAL AID (Fall 2003) 548 applied for aid; of those 87% were deemed to have need. 100% of undergraduates with need received aid; of those 18% had need fully met. *Average percent of need met:* 60% (excluding resources awarded to replace EFC). *Average financial aid package:* $9277 (excluding resources awarded to replace EFC). 14% of all full-time undergraduates had no need and received non-need-based gift aid.

GIFT AID (NEED-BASED) *Total amount:* $2,442,999 (35% federal, 27% state, 34% institutional, 4% external sources). *Receiving aid:* Freshmen: 78% (135); All full-time undergraduates: 83% (464). *Average award:* Freshmen: $6567; Undergraduates: $6403. *Scholarships, grants, and awards:* Federal Pell, FSEOG, state, private, college/university gift aid from institutional funds.

GIFT AID (NON-NEED-BASED) *Total amount:* $466,025 (39% state, 49% institutional, 12% external sources). *Receiving aid:* Freshmen: 13% (22);

Undergraduates: 13% (73). *Average Award: Freshmen:* $8280; *Undergraduates:* $8530. *Scholarships, grants, and awards by category: Academic Interests/ Achievement:* 298 awards ($395,743 total): biological sciences, business, communication, computer science, education, English, general academic interests/ achievements, humanities, mathematics, physical sciences, religion/biblical studies, social sciences. *Creative Arts/Performance:* 37 awards ($84,650 total): art/fine arts, music, performing arts, theater/drama. *Special Achievements/ Activities:* 213 awards ($207,100 total): cheerleading/drum major, leadership, religious involvement. *Special Characteristics:* 412 awards ($551,328 total): children and siblings of alumni, children of faculty/staff, first-generation college students, local/state leaders, out-of-state students, siblings of current students. *Tuition waivers:* Full or partial for employees or children of employees. *ROTC:* Army cooperative.

LOANS *Student loans:* $2,620,474 (80% need-based, 20% non-need-based). 86% of past graduating class borrowed through all loan programs. *Average indebtedness per student:* $13,398. *Average need-based loan:* Freshmen: $2542; Undergraduates: $3446. *Parent loans:* $519,417 (37% need-based, 63% non-need-based). *Programs:* FFEL (Subsidized and Unsubsidized Stafford, PLUS), Perkins.

WORK-STUDY *Federal work-study:* Total amount: $130,029; 85 jobs averaging $1512. *State or other work-study/employment:* Total amount: $45,784 (29% need-based, 71% non-need-based). 53 part-time jobs averaging $779.

ATHLETIC AWARDS *Total amount:* $692,841 (66% need-based, 34% non-need-based).

APPLYING FOR FINANCIAL AID *Required financial aid form:* FAFSA. *Financial aid deadline (priority):* 2/1. *Notification date:* Continuous beginning 1/15. Students must reply within 2 weeks of notification.

CONTACT Mrs. Summer Robertson, Director of Financial Aid, Limestone College, 1115 College Drive, Gaffney, SC 29340-3799, 864-488-4567 or toll-free 800-795-7151 Ext. 554. *Fax:* 864-487-8706. *E-mail:* srobertson@limestone.edu.

LINCOLN CHRISTIAN COLLEGE
Lincoln, IL

Tuition & fees: $10,000	Average undergraduate aid package: $8000

ABOUT THE INSTITUTION Independent religious, coed. Awards: associate and bachelor's degrees. 13 undergraduate majors. Total enrollment: 714. Undergraduates: 714. Freshmen: 160. Federal methodology is used as a basis for awarding need-based institutional aid.

UNDERGRADUATE EXPENSES for 2005–06 *Application fee:* $20. *Comprehensive fee:* $14,750 includes full-time tuition ($9750), mandatory fees ($250), and room and board ($4750). *Part-time tuition:* $325 per semester hour.

FRESHMAN FINANCIAL AID (Fall 2003) 102 applied for aid. *Average percent of need met:* 80% (excluding resources awarded to replace EFC). *Average financial aid package:* $7500 (excluding resources awarded to replace EFC). 12% of all full-time freshmen had no need and received non-need-based gift aid.

UNDERGRADUATE FINANCIAL AID (Fall 2003) 430 applied for aid. *Average percent of need met:* 80% (excluding resources awarded to replace EFC). *Average financial aid package:* $8000 (excluding resources awarded to replace EFC). 5% of all full-time undergraduates had no need and received non-need-based gift aid.

GIFT AID (NEED-BASED) *Total amount:* $1,728,421 (44% federal, 56% state). *Scholarships, grants, and awards:* Federal Pell, FSEOG, state.

GIFT AID (NON-NEED-BASED) *Total amount:* $916,334 (1% state, 47% institutional, 52% external sources). *Scholarships, grants, and awards by category: Academic Interests/Achievement:* 62 awards ($174,778 total): general academic interests/achievements. *Special Achievements/Activities:* 31 awards ($41,500 total): community service, leadership. *Special Characteristics:* 28 awards ($137,827 total): children of faculty/staff.

LOANS *Student loans:* $2,314,308 (62% need-based, 38% non-need-based). 61% of past graduating class borrowed through all loan programs. *Average indebtedness per student:* $16,333. *Parent loans:* $477,519 (100% non-need-based). *Programs:* FFEL (Subsidized and Unsubsidized Stafford, PLUS), Perkins, college/university.

WORK-STUDY *Federal work-study:* Total amount: $78,081; 100 jobs averaging $780. *State or other work-study/employment:* Total amount: $172,534 (23% need-based, 77% non-need-based). 109 part-time jobs averaging $1224.

APPLYING FOR FINANCIAL AID *Required financial aid form:* FAFSA. *Financial aid deadline:* Continuous. *Notification date:* Continuous beginning 3/1. Students must reply within 2 weeks of notification.

CONTACT Nancy Siddens, Co-Director of Financial Aid, Lincoln Christian College, 100 Campus View Drive, Lincoln, IL 62656, 217-732-3168 Ext. 2250 or toll-free 888-522-5228. *Fax:* 217-732-5914. *E-mail:* finaid@lccs.edu.

LINCOLN MEMORIAL UNIVERSITY
Harrogate, TN

Tuition & fees: $12,600	Average undergraduate aid package: $9800

ABOUT THE INSTITUTION Independent, coed. Awards: associate, bachelor's, and master's degrees and post-master's certificates. 46 undergraduate majors. Total enrollment: 2,442. Undergraduates: 1,117. Freshmen: 279. Federal methodology is used as a basis for awarding need-based institutional aid.

UNDERGRADUATE EXPENSES for 2004–05 *Application fee:* $25. *Comprehensive fee:* $17,510 includes full-time tuition ($12,600) and room and board ($4910). *College room only:* $2250. Room and board charges vary according to board plan and housing facility. *Part-time tuition:* $525 per semester hour. *Payment plans:* Installment, deferred payment.

GIFT AID (NEED-BASED) *Total amount:* $3,105,237 (49% federal, 27% state, 24% institutional). *Receiving aid:* Freshmen: 56% (128); All full-time undergraduates: 56% (496). *Average award:* Freshmen: $5410; Undergraduates: $5620. *Scholarships, grants, and awards:* Federal Pell, FSEOG, state, private, college/ university gift aid from institutional funds.

GIFT AID (NON-NEED-BASED) *Total amount:* $2,509,399 (80% institutional, 20% external sources). *Receiving aid:* Freshmen: 72% (164); Undergraduates: 37% (331). *Average Award: Freshmen:* $6550; *Undergraduates:* $5725. *Scholarships, grants, and awards by category: Academic Interests/Achievement:* 463 awards ($1,986,572 total): general academic interests/achievements. *Creative Arts/Performance:* 34 awards ($36,210 total): music. *Special Achievements/ Activities:* 10 awards ($8500 total): cheerleading/drum major. *Special Characteristics:* 13 awards ($106,400 total): children of faculty/staff. *Tuition waivers:* Full or partial for employees or children of employees, senior citizens.

LOANS *Student loans:* $7,098,252 (42% need-based, 58% non-need-based). 80% of past graduating class borrowed through all loan programs. *Average indebtedness per student:* $11,500. *Average need-based loan:* Freshmen: $2150; Undergraduates: $3000. *Parent loans:* $154,643 (100% non-need-based). *Programs:* FFEL (Subsidized and Unsubsidized Stafford, PLUS), Perkins.

ATHLETIC AWARDS *Total amount:* $1,225,562 (100% non-need-based).

APPLYING FOR FINANCIAL AID *Required financial aid form:* FAFSA. *Financial aid deadline (priority):* 4/1. *Notification date:* Continuous. Students must reply within 3 weeks of notification.

CONTACT Celena Rader-Lombdin, Director of Financial Aid, Lincoln Memorial University, Cumberland Gap Parkway, Harrogate, TN 37752-1901, 423-869-6465 or toll-free 800-325-0900. *Fax:* 423-869-6347. *E-mail:* clambdin@lmunet.edu.

LINCOLN UNIVERSITY
Jefferson City, MO

Tuition & fees (MO res): $4952	Average undergraduate aid package: $8000

ABOUT THE INSTITUTION State-supported, coed. Awards: associate, bachelor's, and master's degrees and first professional certificates. 40 undergraduate majors. Total enrollment: 3,275. Undergraduates: 3,041. Freshmen: 635. Both federal and institutional methodology are used as a basis for awarding need-based institutional aid.

UNDERGRADUATE EXPENSES for 2004–05 *Application fee:* $17. *Tuition, state resident:* full-time $4284; part-time $142.80 per credit hour. *Tuition, nonresident:* full-time $7824; part-time $260.80 per credit hour. *Required fees:* full-time $668; $5 per credit hour or $20 per term part-time. Full-time tuition and fees vary according to location. Part-time tuition and fees vary according to location. *College room and board:* $3790; *room only:* $1850. Room and board charges vary according to board plan and housing facility. *Payment plan:* Installment.

FRESHMAN FINANCIAL AID (Fall 2004, est.) 400 applied for aid; of those 98% were deemed to have need. 72% of freshmen with need received aid; of those 36% had need fully met. *Average percent of need met:* 30% (excluding resources awarded to replace EFC). *Average financial aid package:* $6000 (excluding resources awarded to replace EFC). 7% of all full-time freshmen had no need and received non-need-based gift aid.

UNDERGRADUATE FINANCIAL AID (Fall 2004, est.) 1,300 applied for aid; of those 93% were deemed to have need. 83% of undergraduates with need received aid; of those 2% had need fully met. *Average percent of need met:*

35% (excluding resources awarded to replace EFC). *Average financial aid package:* $8000 (excluding resources awarded to replace EFC). 9% of all full-time undergraduates had no need and received non-need-based gift aid.

GIFT AID (NEED-BASED) *Total amount:* $5,303,532 (65% federal, 2% state, 29% institutional, 4% external sources). *Receiving aid:* Freshmen: 32% (190); All full-time undergraduates: 29% (600). *Average award:* Freshmen: $3000; Undergraduates: $3000. *Scholarships, grants, and awards:* Federal Pell, FSEOG, state, private, college/university gift aid from institutional funds, Federal Nursing.
GIFT AID (NON-NEED-BASED) *Total amount:* $177,082 (96% federal, 1% state, 3% external sources). *Receiving aid:* Freshmen: 17% (100); Undergraduates: 3% (60). *Average Award:* Freshmen: $2000; Undergraduates: $3000. *Scholarships, grants, and awards by category:* Academic Interests/Achievement: 100 awards ($10,000 total): agriculture, education, general academic interests/achievements, military science. *Creative Arts/Performance:* 60 awards ($60,000 total): cinema/film/broadcasting, journalism/publications, music. *Tuition waivers:* Full or partial for employees or children of employees, senior citizens. *ROTC:* Army.
LOANS *Student loans:* $7,679,406 (100% need-based). 68% of past graduating class borrowed through all loan programs. *Average indebtedness per student:* $17,000. *Average need-based loan:* Freshmen: $2000; Undergraduates: $3500. *Parent loans:* $180,000 (100% non-need-based). *Programs:* Federal Direct (Subsidized and Unsubsidized Stafford, PLUS), FFEL (Subsidized and Unsubsidized Stafford, PLUS).
WORK-STUDY *Federal work-study:* Total amount: $190,000; 120 jobs averaging $1200. *State or other work-study/employment:* Total amount: $150,000 (100% non-need-based). 40 part-time jobs averaging $1000.
ATHLETIC AWARDS *Total amount:* $687,763 (100% non-need-based).
APPLYING FOR FINANCIAL AID *Required financial aid form:* FAFSA. *Financial aid deadline (priority):* 3/1. *Notification date:* Continuous. Students must reply within 2 weeks of notification.
CONTACT Mr. Alfred Robinson, Director of Financial Aid, Lincoln University, 820 Chestnut Street, Jefferson City, MO 65102-0029, 573-681-6156 or toll-free 800-521-5052. *Fax:* 573-681-5871.

LINCOLN UNIVERSITY
Lincoln University, PA

Tuition & fees (PA res): $7268	Average undergraduate aid package: $14,000

ABOUT THE INSTITUTION State-related, coed. Awards: bachelor's and master's degrees. 49 undergraduate majors. Total enrollment: 2,012. Undergraduates: 1,523. Freshmen: 470. Federal methodology is used as a basis for awarding need-based institutional aid.
UNDERGRADUATE EXPENSES for 2004–05 *Application fee:* $20. *Tuition, state resident:* full-time $5058; part-time $274 per credit hour. *Tuition, nonresident:* full-time $8610; part-time $442 per credit hour. Part-time tuition and fees vary according to course load. *College room and board:* $6560; *room only:* $3566. Room and board charges vary according to board plan. *Payment plans:* Installment, deferred payment.
FRESHMAN FINANCIAL AID (Fall 2004, est.) 430 applied for aid; of those 93% were deemed to have need. 100% of freshmen with need received aid; of those 29% had need fully met. *Average percent of need met:* 85% (excluding resources awarded to replace EFC). *Average financial aid package:* $14,000 (excluding resources awarded to replace EFC). 4% of all full-time freshmen had no need and received non-need-based gift aid.
UNDERGRADUATE FINANCIAL AID (Fall 2004, est.) 1,302 applied for aid; of those 94% were deemed to have need. 99% of undergraduates with need received aid; of those 33% had need fully met. *Average percent of need met:* 85% (excluding resources awarded to replace EFC). *Average financial aid package:* $14,000 (excluding resources awarded to replace EFC). 8% of all full-time undergraduates had no need and received non-need-based gift aid.
GIFT AID (NEED-BASED) *Total amount:* $5,081,354 (71% federal, 23% state, 1% institutional, 5% external sources). *Receiving aid:* Freshmen: 71% (325); All full-time undergraduates: 65% (955). *Average award:* Freshmen: $5300; Undergraduates: $5300. *Scholarships, grants, and awards:* Federal Pell, FSEOG, state, private, college/university gift aid from institutional funds.
GIFT AID (NON-NEED-BASED) *Total amount:* $3,096,548 (88% institutional, 12% external sources). *Receiving aid:* Freshmen: 35% (161); Undergraduates: 31% (455). *Average Award:* Freshmen: $5250; Undergraduates: $9000. *Scholarships, grants, and awards by category:* Academic Interests/Achievement: 56 awards ($189,457 total): biological sciences, business, communication, computer science, education, general academic interests/achievements, humanities,

mathematics, physical sciences, social sciences. *Creative Arts/Performance:* 49 awards ($38,050 total): music. *Special Achievements/Activities:* 2 awards ($6000 total): community service. *Special Characteristics:* 119 awards ($598,126 total): children and siblings of alumni, children of faculty/staff, international students. *Tuition waivers:* Full or partial for employees or children of employees. *ROTC:* Army cooperative, Air Force cooperative.
LOANS *Student loans:* $9,212,782 (88% need-based, 12% non-need-based). 80% of past graduating class borrowed through all loan programs. *Average indebtedness per student:* $25,000. *Average need-based loan:* Freshmen: $5210; Undergraduates: $5210. *Parent loans:* $2,447,591 (100% non-need-based). *Programs:* FFEL (Subsidized and Unsubsidized Stafford, PLUS), Perkins, alternative loans.
WORK-STUDY *Federal work-study:* Total amount: $260,167; 329 jobs averaging $791. *State or other work-study/employment:* Total amount: $21,577 (100% need-based). 25 part-time jobs averaging $863.
APPLYING FOR FINANCIAL AID *Required financial aid form:* FAFSA. *Financial aid deadline (priority):* 5/1. *Notification date:* Continuous. Students must reply within 2 weeks of notification.
CONTACT Thelma Ross, Director of Financial Aid, Lincoln University, PO Box 179, 1570 Baltimore Pike, Lincoln University, PA 19352, 610-932-8300 Ext. 3564 or toll-free 800-790-0191. *Fax:* 610-932-1298. *E-mail:* tross@lincoln.edu.

LINDENWOOD UNIVERSITY
St. Charles, MO

Tuition & fees: $11,720	Average undergraduate aid package: N/A

ABOUT THE INSTITUTION Independent Presbyterian, coed. Awards: bachelor's and master's degrees and post-master's certificates. 88 undergraduate majors. Total enrollment: 8,615. Undergraduates: 5,512. Freshmen: 917. Federal methodology is used as a basis for awarding need-based institutional aid.
UNDERGRADUATE EXPENSES for 2004–05 *Application fee:* $30. *Comprehensive fee:* $17,320 includes full-time tuition ($11,200), mandatory fees ($520), and room and board ($5600). *College room only:* $2800. *Part-time tuition:* $310 per credit hour. Part-time tuition and fees vary according to course load. *Payment plans:* Installment, deferred payment.
GIFT AID (NEED-BASED) *Total amount:* $17,586,322 (19% federal, 9% state, 72% institutional). *Scholarships, grants, and awards:* Federal Pell, FSEOG, state, private, college/university gift aid from institutional funds.
GIFT AID (NON-NEED-BASED) *Total amount:* $7,348,452 (2% state, 96% institutional, 2% external sources). *Scholarships, grants, and awards by category:* Academic Interests/Achievement: biological sciences, business, communication, computer science, education, engineering/technologies, English, foreign languages, general academic interests/achievements, health fields, humanities, international studies, library science, mathematics, military science, physical sciences, premedicine, social sciences. *Creative Arts/Performance:* applied art and design, art/fine arts, cinema/film/broadcasting, dance, general creative arts/performance, music, performing arts, theater/drama. *Special Achievements/Activities:* cheerleading/drum major, community service, general special achievements/activities, junior miss, leadership. *Tuition waivers:* Full or partial for senior citizens. *ROTC:* Army, Air Force cooperative.
LOANS *Student loans:* $14,025,399 (63% need-based, 37% non-need-based). *Parent loans:* $1,452,976 (100% non-need-based). *Programs:* FFEL (Subsidized and Unsubsidized Stafford, PLUS), Perkins.
WORK-STUDY *Federal work-study:* Total amount: $669,512; jobs available (averaging $1800). *State or other work-study/employment:* Total amount: $2,357,728 (64% need-based, 36% non-need-based). Part-time jobs available.
APPLYING FOR FINANCIAL AID *Required financial aid form:* FAFSA. *Financial aid deadline (priority):* 3/15. *Notification date:* Continuous. Students must reply within 1 week of notification.
CONTACT Lori Bode, Director of Financial Aid, Lindenwood University, 209 South Kingshighway, St. Charles, MO 63301-1695, 636-949-4925. *Fax:* 636-949-4924.

LINDSEY WILSON COLLEGE
Columbia, KY

CONTACT Ms. Marilyn D. Radford, Assistant Director of Student Financial Services, Lindsey Wilson College, 210 Lindsey Wilson Street, Columbia, KY 42728-1298, 270-384-8022 or toll-free 800-264-0138. *Fax:* 270-384-8591. *E-mail:* radfordm@lindsey.edu.

LINFIELD COLLEGE
McMinnville, OR

Tuition & fees: $22,022	Average undergraduate aid package: $15,614

ABOUT THE INSTITUTION Independent American Baptist Churches in the USA, coed. Awards: bachelor's degrees. 34 undergraduate majors. Total enrollment: 1,656. Undergraduates: 1,656. Freshmen: 433. Federal methodology is used as a basis for awarding need-based institutional aid.

UNDERGRADUATE EXPENSES for 2004–05 *Application fee:* $40. *Comprehensive fee:* $28,392 includes full-time tuition ($21,800), mandatory fees ($222), and room and board ($6370). *College room only:* $3360. Room and board charges vary according to board plan and housing facility. *Part-time tuition:* $680 per credit. *Part-time fees:* $65 per term. Part-time tuition and fees vary according to course load. *Payment plan:* Installment.

FRESHMAN FINANCIAL AID (Fall 2004, est.) 368 applied for aid; of those 100% were deemed to have need. 100% of freshmen with need received aid; of those 46% had need fully met. *Average percent of need met:* 84% (excluding resources awarded to replace EFC). *Average financial aid package:* $15,491 (excluding resources awarded to replace EFC). 7% of all full-time freshmen had no need and received non-need-based gift aid.

UNDERGRADUATE FINANCIAL AID (Fall 2004, est.) 1,324 applied for aid; of those 100% were deemed to have need. 100% of undergraduates with need received aid; of those 39% had need fully met. *Average percent of need met:* 83% (excluding resources awarded to replace EFC). *Average financial aid package:* $15,614 (excluding resources awarded to replace EFC). 7% of all full-time undergraduates had no need and received non-need-based gift aid.

GIFT AID (NEED-BASED) *Total amount:* $14,260,040 (8% federal, 2% state, 83% institutional, 7% external sources). *Receiving aid:* Freshmen: 62% (270); All full-time undergraduates: 53% (851). *Average award:* Freshmen: $6521; Undergraduates: $6157. *Scholarships, grants, and awards:* Federal Pell, FSEOG, state, private, college/university gift aid from institutional funds.

GIFT AID (NON-NEED-BASED) *Total amount:* $1,243,444 (85% institutional, 15% external sources). *Receiving aid:* Freshmen: 49% (214); Undergraduates: 52% (828). *Average Award:* Freshmen: $6850; Undergraduates: $8064. *Scholarships, grants, and awards by category: Academic Interests/Achievement:* 133 awards ($419,350 total): general academic interests/achievements. *Creative Arts/Performance:* 38 awards ($72,500 total): debating, music. *Special Achievements/Activities:* 32 awards ($61,000 total): leadership. *Special Characteristics:* 63 awards ($747,545 total): children of faculty/staff. *Tuition waivers:* Full or partial for employees or children of employees, senior citizens. *ROTC:* Air Force cooperative.

LOANS *Student loans:* $7,884,270 (99% need-based, 1% non-need-based). 75% of past graduating class borrowed through all loan programs. *Average indebtedness per student:* $25,894. *Average need-based loan:* Freshmen: $2218; Undergraduates: $4618. *Parent loans:* $87,460 (100% non-need-based). *Programs:* FFEL (Subsidized and Unsubsidized Stafford, PLUS), Perkins, college/university, alternative loans.

WORK-STUDY *Federal work-study:* Total amount: $1,429,992; 793 jobs averaging $1803. *State or other work-study/employment:* Total amount: $207,779 (100% non-need-based). 540 part-time jobs averaging $385.

APPLYING FOR FINANCIAL AID *Required financial aid form:* FAFSA. *Financial aid deadline (priority):* 2/1. *Notification date:* 4/1. Students must reply by 5/1.

CONTACT Crisanne Werner, Associate Director of Financial Aid, Linfield College, 900 Southeast Baker Street, McMinnville, OR 97128-6894, 503-883-2225 or toll-free 800-640-2287. *Fax:* 503-883-2486. *E-mail:* finaid@linfield.edu.

LIPSCOMB UNIVERSITY
Nashville, TN

Tuition & fees: $13,486	Average undergraduate aid package: $8909

ABOUT THE INSTITUTION Independent religious, coed. Awards: bachelor's, master's, and first professional degrees. 65 undergraduate majors. Total enrollment: 2,537. Undergraduates: 2,316. Federal methodology is used as a basis for awarding need-based institutional aid.

UNDERGRADUATE EXPENSES for 2004–05 *Application fee:* $50. *Comprehensive fee:* $19,576 includes full-time tuition ($13,022), mandatory fees ($464), and room and board ($6090). Full-time tuition and fees vary according to degree level and location. Room and board charges vary according to board plan,

housing facility, and location. *Part-time tuition:* $475 per hour. Part-time tuition and fees vary according to class time, degree level, and location. *Payment plan:* Installment.

FRESHMAN FINANCIAL AID (Fall 2003) 437 applied for aid; of those 76% were deemed to have need. 97% of freshmen with need received aid; of those 30% had need fully met. *Average percent of need met:* 83% (excluding resources awarded to replace EFC). *Average financial aid package:* $9361 (excluding resources awarded to replace EFC). 30% of all full-time freshmen had no need and received non-need-based gift aid.

UNDERGRADUATE FINANCIAL AID (Fall 2003) 1,801 applied for aid; of those 71% were deemed to have need. 92% of undergraduates with need received aid; of those 26% had need fully met. *Average percent of need met:* 79% (excluding resources awarded to replace EFC). *Average financial aid package:* $8909 (excluding resources awarded to replace EFC). 39% of all full-time undergraduates had no need and received non-need-based gift aid.

GIFT AID (NEED-BASED) *Total amount:* $7,756,207 (14% federal, 5% state, 75% institutional, 6% external sources). *Receiving aid:* Freshmen: 34% (161); All full-time undergraduates: 32% (664). *Average award:* Freshmen: $1559; Undergraduates: $1698. *Scholarships, grants, and awards:* Federal Pell, FSEOG, state, private, college/university gift aid from institutional funds.

GIFT AID (NON-NEED-BASED) *Total amount:* $4,601,557 (100% institutional). *Receiving aid:* Freshmen: 26% (125); Undergraduates: 43% (905). *Average Award:* Freshmen: $9305; Undergraduates: $5826. *Scholarships, grants, and awards by category: Academic Interests/Achievement:* general academic interests/ achievements, religion/biblical studies. *Creative Arts/Performance:* art/fine arts, journalism/publications, music, theater/drama. *Special Achievements/Activities:* cheerleading/drum major, leadership, religious involvement. *Special Characteristics:* adult students, children of educators, children of faculty/staff, children with a deceased or disabled parent, international students, members of minority groups, relatives of clergy. *Tuition waivers:* Full or partial for minority students, employees or children of employees. *ROTC:* Army cooperative, Air Force cooperative.

LOANS *Student loans:* $5,814,155 (100% need-based). 60% of past graduating class borrowed through all loan programs. *Average indebtedness per student:* $18,000. *Average need-based loan:* Freshmen: $3018; Undergraduates: $5755. *Parent loans:* $2,114,533 (100% non-need-based). *Programs:* FFEL (Subsidized and Unsubsidized Stafford, PLUS), Perkins, state.

WORK-STUDY *Federal work-study:* Total amount: $192,815; 124 jobs averaging $1545.

ATHLETIC AWARDS *Total amount:* $1,520,483 (100% non-need-based).

APPLYING FOR FINANCIAL AID *Required financial aid form:* FAFSA. *Financial aid deadline (priority):* 2/28. *Notification date:* Continuous beginning 3/15.

CONTACT Mrs. Karita McCaleb Waters, Director of Financial Aid, Lipscomb University, 3901 Granny White Pike, Nashville, TN 37204-3951, 615-269-1791 or toll-free 877-582-4766. *Fax:* 615-386-7640. *E-mail:* karita.waters@lipscomb.edu.

LIVINGSTONE COLLEGE
Salisbury, NC

CONTACT Mrs. Terry Jefferies, Financial Aid Director, Livingstone College, 701 West Monroe Street, Price Building, Salisbury, NC 28144-5298, 704-216-6069 or toll-free 800-835-3435. *Fax:* 704-216-6319. *E-mail:* tjefferies@livingstone.edu.

LOCK HAVEN UNIVERSITY OF PENNSYLVANIA
Lock Haven, PA

Tuition & fees (PA res): $6100	Average undergraduate aid package: $6120

ABOUT THE INSTITUTION State-supported, coed. Awards: associate, bachelor's, and master's degrees. 56 undergraduate majors. Total enrollment: 5,126. Undergraduates: 4,875. Freshmen: 1,025. Federal methodology is used as a basis for awarding need-based institutional aid.

UNDERGRADUATE EXPENSES for 2004–05 *Application fee:* $25. *Tuition, state resident:* full-time $4810; part-time $200 per credit. *Tuition, nonresident:* full-time $10,026; part-time $418 per credit. *Required fees:* full-time $1290; $63 per credit. Full-time tuition and fees vary according to course load and location. Part-time tuition and fees vary according to course load and location. *College room and board:* $5516; *room only:* $3140. Room and board charges vary according to board plan and housing facility. *Payment plans:* Installment, deferred payment.

FRESHMAN FINANCIAL AID (Fall 2003) 943 applied for aid; of those 78% were deemed to have need. 100% of freshmen with need received aid; of those 55% had need fully met. *Average percent of need met:* 73% (excluding resources awarded to replace EFC). *Average financial aid package:* $5540 (excluding resources awarded to replace EFC). 2% of all full-time freshmen had no need and received non-need-based gift aid.

UNDERGRADUATE FINANCIAL AID (Fall 2003) 3,966 applied for aid; of those 81% were deemed to have need. 100% of undergraduates with need received aid; of those 55% had need fully met. *Average percent of need met:* 77% (excluding resources awarded to replace EFC). *Average financial aid package:* $6120 (excluding resources awarded to replace EFC). 2% of all full-time undergraduates had no need and received non-need-based gift aid.

GIFT AID (NEED-BASED) *Total amount:* $8,396,117 (46% federal, 51% state, 3% institutional). *Receiving aid:* Freshmen: 49% (485); All full-time undergraduates: 51% (2,120). *Average award:* Freshmen: $3900; Undergraduates: $4568. *Scholarships, grants, and awards:* Federal Pell, FSEOG, state, private, college/university gift aid from institutional funds.

GIFT AID (NON-NEED-BASED) *Total amount:* $864,963 (13% state, 21% institutional, 66% external sources). *Receiving aid:* Freshmen: 5% (49); Undergraduates: 6% (271). *Average Award: Freshmen:* $1000; *Undergraduates:* $1575. *Scholarships, grants, and awards by category: Academic Interests/ Achievement:* 135 awards ($159,944 total): biological sciences, communication, education, English, foreign languages, general academic interests/ achievements, international studies, library science, mathematics, physical sciences, social sciences. *Creative Arts/Performance:* 15 awards ($24,635 total): art/fine arts, journalism/publications, music. *Special Achievements/Activities:* 12 awards ($12,500 total): leadership, memberships. *Special Characteristics:* 40 awards ($49,270 total): handicapped students, local/state students, members of minority groups, previous college experience. *Tuition waivers:* Full or partial for minority students, employees or children of employees, senior citizens. *ROTC:* Army.

LOANS *Student loans:* $19,832,432 (70% need-based, 30% non-need-based). 76% of past graduating class borrowed through all loan programs. *Average indebtedness per student:* $17,021. *Average need-based loan:* Freshmen: $2500; Undergraduates: $3767. *Parent loans:* $2,680,921 (100% non-need-based). *Programs:* FFEL (Subsidized and Unsubsidized Stafford, PLUS), Perkins.

WORK-STUDY *Federal work-study:* Total amount: $266,000; 253 jobs averaging $1174. *State or other work-study/employment:* Total amount: $648,099 (45% need-based, 55% non-need-based). 951 part-time jobs averaging $711.

ATHLETIC AWARDS *Total amount:* $344,541 (78% need-based, 22% non-need-based).

APPLYING FOR FINANCIAL AID *Required financial aid forms:* FAFSA, institution's own form. *Financial aid deadline (priority):* 3/15. *Notification date:* Continuous. Students must reply by 5/1 or within 2 weeks of notification.

CONTACT Dr. William A. Irwin, Director, Financial Aid Office, Lock Haven University of Pennsylvania, Russell Hall, Lock Haven, PA 17745-2390, 877-893-2344 or toll-free 800-332-8900 (in-state), 800-233-8978 (out-of-state). *Fax:* 570-893-2918. *E-mail:* finaid@lhup.edu.

LOGAN UNIVERSITY-COLLEGE OF CHIROPRACTIC
Chesterfield, MO

CONTACT Linda K. Haman, Director of Financial Aid, Logan University-College of Chiropractic, 1851 Schoettler Road, PO Box 1065, Chesterfield, MO 63006-1065, 636-227-2100 Ext. 141 or toll-free 800-533-9210.

LOMA LINDA UNIVERSITY
Loma Linda, CA

ABOUT THE INSTITUTION Independent Seventh-day Adventist, coed. Awards: associate, bachelor's, master's, doctoral, and first professional degrees and post-bachelor's certificates (associate degree and nursing students may enter at the sophomore level). 14 undergraduate majors. Total enrollment: 4,010. Undergraduates: 1,101.

GIFT AID (NEED-BASED) *Scholarships, grants, and awards:* Federal Pell, FSEOG, state, private, college/university gift aid from institutional funds, Federal Nursing.

LOANS *Programs:* FFEL (Subsidized and Unsubsidized Stafford, PLUS), Perkins, Federal Nursing, college/university.

APPLYING FOR FINANCIAL AID *Required financial aid forms:* FAFSA, institution's own form.

CONTACT Verdell Schaefer, Director of Financial Aid, Loma Linda University, 11139 Anderson Street, Loma Linda, CA 92350, 909-558-4509. *Fax:* 909-558-4879. *E-mail:* finaid@univ.llu.edu.

LONG ISLAND UNIVERSITY, BROOKLYN CAMPUS
Brooklyn, NY

Tuition & fees: $21,922	Average undergraduate aid package: $13,930

ABOUT THE INSTITUTION Independent, coed. Awards: associate, bachelor's, master's, doctoral, and first professional degrees and post-bachelor's, post-master's, and first professional certificates. 73 undergraduate majors. Total enrollment: 8,003. Undergraduates: 5,363. Freshmen: 994. Both federal and institutional methodology are used as a basis for awarding need-based institutional aid.

UNDERGRADUATE EXPENSES for 2004–05 *Application fee:* $30. *Comprehensive fee:* $29,272 includes full-time tuition ($20,832), mandatory fees ($1090), and room and board ($7350). *College room only:* $4420. Full-time tuition and fees vary according to program. Room and board charges vary according to board plan. *Part-time tuition:* $651 per credit. *Part-time fees:* $264 per term. Part-time tuition and fees vary according to course load and program. *Payment plan:* Deferred payment.

GIFT AID (NEED-BASED) *Total amount:* $29,876,850 (36% federal, 33% state, 29% institutional, 2% external sources). *Receiving aid:* Freshmen: 80% (744); All full-time undergraduates: 80% (4,270). *Average award:* Freshmen: $10,021; Undergraduates: $8874. *Scholarships, grants, and awards:* Federal Pell, FSEOG, state, private, college/university gift aid from institutional funds, Scholarships for Disadvantaged Students (Nursing and Pharmacy).

GIFT AID (NON-NEED-BASED) *Total amount:* $1,510,283 (96% institutional, 4% external sources). *Receiving aid:* Freshmen: 77% (720); Undergraduates: 77% (4,127). *Average Award:* Freshmen: $17,707; *Undergraduates:* $18,395. *Scholarships, grants, and awards by category: Academic Interests/Achievement:* 996 awards ($3,017,160 total): communication, education, general academic interests/achievements, health fields. *Creative Arts/Performance:* 50 awards ($146,250 total): art/fine arts, cinema/film/broadcasting, dance, music. *Special Achievements/Activities:* 38 awards ($136,740 total): cheerleading/drum major, general special achievements/activities, leadership. *Special Characteristics:* 3,113 awards ($4,943,242 total): children and siblings of alumni, children of faculty/staff, ethnic background, first-generation college students, general special characteristics, international students. *Tuition waivers:* Full or partial for employees or children of employees.

LOANS *Student loans:* $25,475,449 (84% need-based, 16% non-need-based). 87% of past graduating class borrowed through all loan programs. *Average indebtedness per student:* $23,998. *Average need-based loan:* Freshmen: $3267; Undergraduates: $4540. *Parent loans:* $14,117,979 (100% non-need-based). *Programs:* Federal Direct (Subsidized and Unsubsidized Stafford, PLUS), Perkins, Federal Health Professions Student Loans, alternative loans.

ATHLETIC AWARDS *Total amount:* $3,504,692 (92% need-based, 8% non-need-based).

APPLYING FOR FINANCIAL AID *Required financial aid form:* FAFSA. *Financial aid deadline:* Continuous. *Notification date:* Continuous beginning 4/1. Students must reply within 4 weeks of notification.

CONTACT Ms. Rose Iannicelli, Dean of Financial Aid, Long Island University, Brooklyn Campus, 1 University Plaza, Brooklyn, NY 11201-8423, 718-488-1037 or toll-free 800-LIU-PLAN.

LONG ISLAND UNIVERSITY, C.W. POST CAMPUS
Brookville, NY

ABOUT THE INSTITUTION Independent, coed. Awards: bachelor's, master's, and doctoral degrees and post-bachelor's and post-master's certificates. 96 undergraduate majors. Total enrollment: 8,421. Undergraduates: 4,897. Freshmen: 984.

GIFT AID (NEED-BASED) *Scholarships, grants, and awards:* Federal Pell, FSEOG, state, private, college/university gift aid from institutional funds.

GIFT AID (NON-NEED-BASED) *Scholarships, grants, and awards by category: Academic Interests/Achievement:* biological sciences, business, computer science, education, general academic interests/achievements, health fields, mathematics. *Creative Arts/Performance:* art/fine arts, cinema/film/broadcasting,

Long Island University, C.W. Post Campus

dance, music, theater/drama. *Special Characteristics:* adult students, children and siblings of alumni, children of faculty/staff, international students, siblings of current students.

LOANS *Programs:* Federal Direct (Subsidized and Unsubsidized Stafford, PLUS), Perkins.

APPLYING FOR FINANCIAL AID *Required financial aid forms:* FAFSA, CSS Financial Aid PROFILE.

CONTACT Office of Financial Assistance, Long Island University, C.W. Post Campus, 720 Northern Boulevard, Brookville, NY 11548-1300, 516-299-2338 or toll-free 800-LIU-PLAN. *Fax:* 516-299-3833. *E-mail:* finaid@cwpost.liu.edu.

LONGWOOD UNIVERSITY
Farmville, VA

Tuition & fees (VA res): $6441	Average undergraduate aid package: $7013

ABOUT THE INSTITUTION State-supported, coed. Awards: bachelor's and master's degrees. 74 undergraduate majors. Total enrollment: 4,289. Undergraduates: 3,739. Freshmen: 980. Federal methodology is used as a basis for awarding need-based institutional aid.

UNDERGRADUATE EXPENSES for 2004–05 *Application fee:* $40. *Tuition, state resident:* full-time $3320; part-time $139 per credit hour. *Tuition, nonresident:* full-time $9780; part-time $408 per credit hour. *College room and board:* $5424; *room only:* $3176. Room and board charges vary according to board plan. *Payment plan:* Installment.

FRESHMAN FINANCIAL AID (Fall 2003) 615 applied for aid; of those 62% were deemed to have need. 100% of freshmen with need received aid; of those 16% had need fully met. *Average percent of need met:* 66% (excluding resources awarded to replace EFC). *Average financial aid package:* $6295 (excluding resources awarded to replace EFC). 25% of all full-time freshmen had no need and received non-need-based gift aid.

UNDERGRADUATE FINANCIAL AID (Fall 2003) 2,307 applied for aid; of those 68% were deemed to have need. 100% of undergraduates with need received aid; of those 30% had need fully met. *Average percent of need met:* 77% (excluding resources awarded to replace EFC). *Average financial aid package:* $7013 (excluding resources awarded to replace EFC). 27% of all full-time undergraduates had no need and received non-need-based gift aid.

GIFT AID (NEED-BASED) *Total amount:* $5,522,237 (32% federal, 45% state, 16% institutional, 7% external sources). *Receiving aid:* Freshmen: 41% (348); All full-time undergraduates: 39% (1,397). *Average award:* Freshmen: $4053; Undergraduates: $3880. *Scholarships, grants, and awards:* Federal Pell, FSEOG, state, private, college/university gift aid from institutional funds.

GIFT AID (NON-NEED-BASED) *Total amount:* $2,524,526 (2% federal, 12% state, 33% institutional, 53% external sources). *Receiving aid:* Freshmen: 4% (32); Undergraduates: 5% (169). *Average Award:* Freshmen: $3430; Undergraduates: $4298. *Scholarships, grants, and awards by category:* Academic Interests/ Achievement: 185 awards ($192,140 total): biological sciences, business, computer science, education, English, general academic interests/achievements, humanities, mathematics, social sciences. Creative Arts/Performance: 30 awards ($21,984 total): art/fine arts, general creative arts/performance, music, theater/ drama. Special Achievements/Activities: 4 awards ($3844 total): memberships. Special Characteristics: 46 awards ($88,564 total): children and siblings of alumni, general special characteristics, local/state students. ROTC: Army.

LOANS *Student loans:* $10,322,063 (60% need-based, 40% non-need-based). 77% of past graduating class borrowed through all loan programs. *Average indebtedness per student:* $14,326. *Average need-based loan:* Freshmen: $3038; Undergraduates: $4102. *Parent loans:* $5,334,984 (16% need-based, 84% non-need-based). *Programs:* FFEL (Subsidized and Unsubsidized Stafford, PLUS), Perkins, college/university.

WORK-STUDY *Federal work-study:* Total amount: $287,870; 314 jobs averaging $916. *State or other work-study/employment:* Total amount: $335,729 (100% non-need-based). 435 part-time jobs averaging $771.

ATHLETIC AWARDS *Total amount:* $713,401 (32% need-based, 68% non-need-based).

APPLYING FOR FINANCIAL AID *Required financial aid form:* FAFSA. *Financial aid deadline (priority):* 3/1. *Notification date:* Continuous beginning 4/1. Students must reply within 2 weeks of notification.

CONTACT Michael Barree, Financial Aid Director, Longwood University, 201 High Street, Farmville, VA 23909, 434-395-2077 or toll-free 800-281-4677. *Fax:* 434-395-2829. *E-mail:* barreemw@longwood.edu.

LORAS COLLEGE
Dubuque, IA

Tuition & fees: $19,678	Average undergraduate aid package: $17,723

ABOUT THE INSTITUTION Independent Roman Catholic, coed. Awards: associate, bachelor's, and master's degrees. 54 undergraduate majors. Total enrollment: 1,743. Undergraduates: 1,618. Freshmen: 407. Federal methodology is used as a basis for awarding need-based institutional aid.

UNDERGRADUATE EXPENSES for 2004–05 *Application fee:* $25. *Comprehensive fee:* $25,523 includes full-time tuition ($18,670), mandatory fees ($1008), and room and board ($5845). *College room only:* $2950. Full-time tuition and fees vary according to course load and degree level. Room and board charges vary according to board plan and housing facility. *Part-time tuition:* $400 per credit. *Payment plan:* Installment.

FRESHMAN FINANCIAL AID (Fall 2004, est.) 379 applied for aid; of those 96% were deemed to have need. 100% of freshmen with need received aid; of those 32% had need fully met. *Average percent of need met:* 85% (excluding resources awarded to replace EFC). *Average financial aid package:* $17,631 (excluding resources awarded to replace EFC). 10% of all full-time freshmen had no need and received non-need-based gift aid.

UNDERGRADUATE FINANCIAL AID (Fall 2004, est.) 1,318 applied for aid; of those 90% were deemed to have need. 100% of undergraduates with need received aid; of those 33% had need fully met. *Average percent of need met:* 89% (excluding resources awarded to replace EFC). *Average financial aid package:* $17,723 (excluding resources awarded to replace EFC). 32% of all full-time undergraduates had no need and received non-need-based gift aid.

GIFT AID (NEED-BASED) *Total amount:* $11,177,319 (10% federal, 15% state, 75% institutional). *Receiving aid:* Freshmen: 76% (306); All full-time undergraduates: 68% (1,053). *Average award:* Freshmen: $6745; Undergraduates: $7203. *Scholarships, grants, and awards:* Federal Pell, FSEOG, state, college/university gift aid from institutional funds.

GIFT AID (NON-NEED-BASED) *Total amount:* $4,303,242 (1% state, 95% institutional, 4% external sources). *Receiving aid:* Freshmen: 88% (356); Undergraduates: 66% (1,028). *Average Award:* Freshmen: $7631; Undergraduates: $8641. *Scholarships, grants, and awards by category:* Academic Interests/ Achievement: 1,325 awards ($7,575,000 total): engineering/technologies, general academic interests/achievements, physical sciences. Creative Arts/Performance: 43 awards ($39,938 total): music. Special Achievements/Activities: memberships, religious involvement. Special Characteristics: 456 awards ($426,288 total): children and siblings of alumni, siblings of current students. Tuition waivers: Full or partial for employees or children of employees, senior citizens.

LOANS *Student loans:* $8,775,929 (54% need-based, 46% non-need-based). 87% of past graduating class borrowed through all loan programs. *Average indebtedness per student:* $21,913. *Average need-based loan:* Freshmen: $3467; Undergraduates: $4408. *Parent loans:* $751,096 (100% non-need-based). *Programs:* FFEL (Subsidized and Unsubsidized Stafford, PLUS), Perkins, college/ university.

WORK-STUDY *Federal work-study:* Total amount: $245,105; 280 jobs averaging $942. *State or other work-study/employment:* Total amount: $544,217 (100% non-need-based). 254 part-time jobs averaging $2581.

APPLYING FOR FINANCIAL AID *Required financial aid form:* FAFSA. *Financial aid deadline (priority):* 4/15. *Notification date:* Continuous. Students must reply within 3 weeks of notification.

CONTACT Ms. Julie A. Dunn, Director of Financial Planning, Loras College, 1450 Alta Vista Street, Dubuque, IA 52004-0178, 563-588-7136 or toll-free 800-245-6727. *Fax:* 563-588-7119. *E-mail:* Julie.Dunn@loras.edu.

LOUISIANA COLLEGE
Pineville, LA

ABOUT THE INSTITUTION Independent Southern Baptist, coed. Awards: bachelor's degrees. 56 undergraduate majors. Total enrollment: 1,085. Undergraduates: 1,085. Freshmen: 240.

GIFT AID (NEED-BASED) *Scholarships, grants, and awards:* Federal Pell, FSEOG, state, private, college/university gift aid from institutional funds, LEAP.

GIFT AID (NON-NEED-BASED) *Scholarships, grants, and awards by category:* Academic Interests/Achievement: business, general academic interests/ achievements, health fields, religion/biblical studies. Creative Arts/Performance: music, performing arts, theater/drama. Special Achievements/Activities: leadership. Special Characteristics: children of faculty/staff.

LOANS *Programs:* Federal Direct (Subsidized and Unsubsidized Stafford, PLUS), FFEL (Subsidized and Unsubsidized Stafford, PLUS), college/university.

WORK-STUDY *Federal work-study:* Total amount: $134,528; jobs available.

APPLYING FOR FINANCIAL AID *Required financial aid forms:* FAFSA, institution's own form.

CONTACT Shelley Jinks, Financial Aid Director, Louisiana College, 1140 College Drive, Pineville, LA 71359-0001, 318-487-7386 or toll-free 800-487-1906. *Fax:* 318-487-7449. *E-mail:* jinks@lacollege.edu.

LOUISIANA STATE UNIVERSITY AND AGRICULTURAL AND MECHANICAL COLLEGE
Baton Rouge, LA

Tuition & fees (LA res): $4226	Average undergraduate aid package: $6342

ABOUT THE INSTITUTION State-supported, coed. Awards: bachelor's, master's, doctoral, and first professional degrees and post-master's certificates. 70 undergraduate majors. Total enrollment: 32,241. Undergraduates: 26,387. Freshmen: 5,700. Federal methodology is used as a basis for awarding need-based institutional aid.

UNDERGRADUATE EXPENSES for 2004–05 *Application fee:* $40. *Tuition, state resident:* full-time $2855. *Tuition, nonresident:* full-time $9655. Part-time tuition and fees vary according to course load. *College room and board:* $5882; *room only:* $3540. Room and board charges vary according to board plan and housing facility. *Payment plan:* Deferred payment.

GIFT AID (NEED-BASED) *Total amount:* $35,670,444 (41% federal, 50% state, 7% institutional, 2% external sources). *Receiving aid:* Freshmen: 43% (2,329); All full-time undergraduates: 37% (8,869). *Average award:* Freshmen: $4460; Undergraduates: $4431. *Scholarships, grants, and awards:* Federal Pell, FSEOG, state, private, college/university gift aid from institutional funds, United Negro College Fund.

GIFT AID (NON-NEED-BASED) *Total amount:* $33,308,368 (1% federal, 76% state, 19% institutional, 4% external sources). *Receiving aid:* Freshmen: 1% (64); Undergraduates: 1% (195). *Average Award:* Freshmen: $3680; Undergraduates: $3765. *Scholarships, grants, and awards by category: Academic Interests/Achievement:* 594 awards ($861,577 total): agriculture, architecture, biological sciences, business, communication, computer science, education, engineering/technologies, English, foreign languages, general academic interests/achievements, home economics, humanities, mathematics, military science, physical sciences, premedicine. *Creative Arts/Performance:* 140 awards ($734,957 total): applied art and design, art/fine arts, journalism/publications, music, performing arts, theater/drama. *Special Achievements/Activities:* leadership. *Special Characteristics:* 246 awards ($809,252 total): children and siblings of alumni, children with a deceased or disabled parent, general special characteristics. *Tuition waivers:* Full or partial for children of alumni, employees or children of employees. *ROTC:* Army, Naval cooperative, Air Force.

LOANS *Student loans:* $44,510,945 (68% need-based, 32% non-need-based). 50% of past graduating class borrowed through all loan programs. *Average indebtedness per student:* $18,352. *Average need-based loan:* Freshmen: $2366; Undergraduates: $3862. *Parent loans:* $9,426,304 (25% need-based, 75% non-need-based). *Programs:* FFEL (Subsidized and Unsubsidized Stafford, PLUS), Perkins.

ATHLETIC AWARDS *Total amount:* $4,116,689 (38% need-based, 62% non-need-based).

APPLYING FOR FINANCIAL AID *Required financial aid forms:* FAFSA, institution's own form. *Financial aid deadline:* Continuous. *Notification date:* Continuous beginning 3/1. Students must reply within 3 weeks of notification.

CONTACT Mary G. Parker, Director of Student Aid and Scholarships, Louisiana State University and Agricultural and Mechanical College, LSU 208 Coates Hall, Baton Rouge, LA 70803-3103, 225-578-3113. *Fax:* 225-578-9460. *E-mail:* financialaid@lsu.edu.

LOUISIANA STATE UNIVERSITY HEALTH SCIENCES CENTER
New Orleans, LA

CONTACT Mr. Patrick Gorman, Director of Financial Aid, Louisiana State University Health Sciences Center, 433 Bolivar Street, New Orleans, LA 70112, 504-568-4821. *Fax:* 504-599-1390.

LOUISIANA STATE UNIVERSITY IN SHREVEPORT
Shreveport, LA

ABOUT THE INSTITUTION State-supported, coed. Awards: bachelor's and master's degrees and post-master's certificates. 40 undergraduate majors. Total enrollment: 4,401. Undergraduates: 3,753. Freshmen: 543.

GIFT AID (NEED-BASED) *Scholarships, grants, and awards:* Federal Pell, FSEOG, state, private.

GIFT AID (NON-NEED-BASED) *Scholarships, grants, and awards by category: Academic Interests/Achievement:* biological sciences, business, computer science, education, English, general academic interests/achievements, premedicine.

LOANS *Programs:* FFEL (Subsidized and Unsubsidized Stafford, PLUS).

WORK-STUDY Federal work-study jobs available. *State or other work-study/employment:* Part-time jobs available.

APPLYING FOR FINANCIAL AID *Required financial aid form:* FAFSA.

CONTACT Office of Student Financial Aid, Louisiana State University in Shreveport, One University Place, Shreveport, LA 71115-2399, 318-797-5363 or toll-free 800-229-5957 (in-state). *Fax:* 318-797-5366.

LOUISIANA TECH UNIVERSITY
Ruston, LA

Tuition & fees (LA res): $4375	Average undergraduate aid package: $5877

ABOUT THE INSTITUTION State-supported, coed. Awards: associate, bachelor's, master's, and doctoral degrees and first professional certificates. 79 undergraduate majors. Total enrollment: 11,691. Undergraduates: 9,318. Freshmen: 1,914. Both federal and institutional methodology are used as a basis for awarding need-based institutional aid.

UNDERGRADUATE EXPENSES for 2005–06 *Application fee:* $20. *Tuition, state resident:* full-time $3914. *Tuition, nonresident:* full-time $8819. *College room and board:* $4035; *room only:* $2130. *Payment plans:* Installment, deferred payment.

FRESHMAN FINANCIAL AID (Fall 2004, est.) 1583 applied for aid; of those 86% were deemed to have need. 91% of freshmen with need received aid; of those 18% had need fully met. *Average percent of need met:* 56% (excluding resources awarded to replace EFC). *Average financial aid package:* $5225 (excluding resources awarded to replace EFC). 17% of all full-time freshmen had no need and received non-need-based gift aid.

UNDERGRADUATE FINANCIAL AID (Fall 2004, est.) 7,451 applied for aid; of those 67% were deemed to have need. 85% of undergraduates with need received aid; of those 14% had need fully met. *Average percent of need met:* 52% (excluding resources awarded to replace EFC). *Average financial aid package:* $5877 (excluding resources awarded to replace EFC). 34% of all full-time undergraduates had no need and received non-need-based gift aid.

GIFT AID (NEED-BASED) *Total amount:* $16,829,427 (53% federal, 32% state, 11% institutional, 4% external sources). *Receiving aid:* Freshmen: 69% (1,128); All full-time undergraduates: 50% (3,741). *Average award:* Freshmen: $4332; Undergraduates: $4407. *Scholarships, grants, and awards:* Federal Pell, FSEOG, state, private, college/university gift aid from institutional funds.

GIFT AID (NON-NEED-BASED) *Total amount:* $8,094,768 (73% state, 21% institutional, 6% external sources). *Receiving aid:* Freshmen: 12% (204); Undergraduates: 7% (546). *Average Award:* Freshmen: $5135; Undergraduates: $5259. *Scholarships, grants, and awards by category: Academic Interests/Achievement:* 6,205 awards ($23,800,000 total): agriculture, architecture, biological sciences, business, computer science, education, engineering/technologies, English, foreign languages, general academic interests/achievements, health fields, home economics, humanities, library science, mathematics, military science, physical sciences, social sciences. *Creative Arts/Performance:* 424 awards ($497,259 total): debating, journalism/publications, music, performing arts, theater/drama. *Special Achievements/Activities:* 56 awards ($91,795 total): cheerleading/drum major. *Special Characteristics:* 389 awards ($1,774,998 total): children of faculty/staff, children with a deceased or disabled parent, out-of-state students, public servants, spouses of deceased or disabled public servants. *Tuition waivers:* Full or partial for children of alumni, employees or children of employees, senior citizens. *ROTC:* Army cooperative, Naval.

LOANS *Student loans:* $22,491,239 (69% need-based, 31% non-need-based). 83% of past graduating class borrowed through all loan programs. *Average indebtedness per student:* $16,641. *Average need-based loan:* Freshmen: $2022;

Undergraduates: $2975. *Parent loans:* $2,088,045 (20% need-based, 80% non-need-based). *Programs:* FFEL (Subsidized and Unsubsidized Stafford, PLUS), Perkins, state.

WORK-STUDY *Federal work-study:* Total amount: $838,001; 304 jobs averaging $2756. *State or other work-study/employment:* Total amount: $2,035,851 (100% non-need-based). 1,150 part-time jobs averaging $1770.

ATHLETIC AWARDS *Total amount:* $966,121 (86% need-based, 14% non-need-based).

APPLYING FOR FINANCIAL AID *Required financial aid forms:* FAFSA, institution's own form. *Financial aid deadline:* Continuous. *Notification date:* Continuous beginning 4/1. Students must reply within 4 weeks of notification.

CONTACT Financial Aid Office, Louisiana Tech University, PO Box 7925, Ruston, LA 71272, 318-257-2641 or toll-free 800-528-3241. *Fax:* 318-257-2628. *E-mail:* techaid@ltfa.latech.edu.

LOURDES COLLEGE
Sylvania, OH

Tuition & fees: $12,270	Average undergraduate aid package: $11,936

ABOUT THE INSTITUTION Independent Roman Catholic, coed. Awards: associate, bachelor's, and master's degrees. 21 undergraduate majors. Total enrollment: 1,460. Undergraduates: 1,390. Freshmen: 105. Federal methodology is used as a basis for awarding need-based institutional aid.

UNDERGRADUATE EXPENSES for 2005–06 *Application fee:* $25. *Tuition:* full-time $11,070; part-time $369 per credit hour. *Required fees:* full-time $1200; $40 per credit hour.

FRESHMAN FINANCIAL AID (Fall 2003) 34 applied for aid; of those 82% were deemed to have need. 100% of freshmen with need received aid. *Average financial aid package:* $12,480 (excluding resources awarded to replace EFC). 2% of all full-time freshmen had no need and received non-need-based gift aid.

UNDERGRADUATE FINANCIAL AID (Fall 2003) 487 applied for aid; of those 93% were deemed to have need. 100% of undergraduates with need received aid. *Average financial aid package:* $11,936 (excluding resources awarded to replace EFC). 2% of all full-time undergraduates had no need and received non-need-based gift aid.

GIFT AID (NEED-BASED) *Total amount:* $2,245,442 (53% federal, 22% state, 23% institutional, 2% external sources). *Receiving aid:* Freshmen: 57% (25); All full-time undergraduates: 72% (372). *Average award:* Freshmen: $5044; Undergraduates: $11,936. *Scholarships, grants, and awards:* Federal Pell, FSEOG, state, private, college/university gift aid from institutional funds.

GIFT AID (NON-NEED-BASED) *Total amount:* $2,182,632 (18% state, 76% institutional, 6% external sources). *Receiving aid:* Freshmen: 64% (28); Undergraduates: 71% (365). *Average Award:* Freshmen: $5980; Undergraduates: $4665. *Scholarships, grants, and awards by category:* Academic Interests/Achievement: 484 awards ($1,923,850 total): general academic interests/achievements. Creative Arts/Performance: art/fine arts, music. Special Achievements/Activities: general special achievements/activities. Special Characteristics: children of faculty/staff, international students, local/state students, members of minority groups. *ROTC:* Army cooperative, Air Force cooperative.

LOANS *Student loans:* $5,194,086 (100% need-based). *Average need-based loan:* Freshmen: $2344; Undergraduates: $4028. *Parent loans:* $205,230 (100% need-based). *Programs:* FFEL (Subsidized and Unsubsidized Stafford, PLUS), Perkins, state, college/university, alternative loans.

WORK-STUDY *Federal work-study:* Total amount: $100,400; 78 jobs averaging $1288.

APPLYING FOR FINANCIAL AID *Required financial aid form:* FAFSA. *Financial aid deadline (priority):* 3/1. *Notification date:* Continuous beginning 3/15. Students must reply within 2 weeks of notification.

CONTACT Greg Guzman, Director of Financial Aid, Lourdes College, 6832 Convent Boulevard, Sylvania, OH 43560-2898, 419-824-3732 or toll-free 800-878-3210 Ext. 1299. *Fax:* 419-882-3987. *E-mail:* finaid@lourdes.edu.

LOYOLA COLLEGE IN MARYLAND
Baltimore, MD

Tuition & fees: $28,170	Average undergraduate aid package: $19,090

ABOUT THE INSTITUTION Independent Roman Catholic (Jesuit), coed. Awards: bachelor's, master's, and doctoral degrees and post-master's certificates. 32 undergraduate majors. Total enrollment: 6,156. Undergraduates: 3,441. Freshmen: 953. Institutional methodology is used as a basis for awarding need-based institutional aid.

UNDERGRADUATE EXPENSES for 2004–05 *Application fee:* $30. *Comprehensive fee:* $37,129 includes full-time tuition ($27,570), mandatory fees ($600), and room and board ($8959). *College room only:* $6959. Full-time tuition and fees vary according to student level. Room and board charges vary according to board plan. *Part-time tuition:* $463 per credit. *Part-time fees:* $25 per term.

FRESHMAN FINANCIAL AID (Fall 2004, est.) 640 applied for aid; of those 78% were deemed to have need. 100% of freshmen with need received aid; of those 96% had need fully met. *Average percent of need met:* 96% (excluding resources awarded to replace EFC). *Average financial aid package:* $18,945 (excluding resources awarded to replace EFC). 8% of all full-time freshmen had no need and received non-need-based gift aid.

UNDERGRADUATE FINANCIAL AID (Fall 2004, est.) 2,279 applied for aid; of those 67% were deemed to have need. 100% of undergraduates with need received aid; of those 95% had need fully met. *Average percent of need met:* 97% (excluding resources awarded to replace EFC). *Average financial aid package:* $19,090 (excluding resources awarded to replace EFC). 12% of all full-time undergraduates had no need and received non-need-based gift aid.

GIFT AID (NEED-BASED) *Total amount:* $19,326,992 (7% federal, 3% state, 87% institutional, 3% external sources). *Receiving aid:* Freshmen: 38% (359); All full-time undergraduates: 32% (1,099). *Average award:* Freshmen: $11,600; Undergraduates: $11,810. *Scholarships, grants, and awards:* Federal Pell, FSEOG, state, private, college/university gift aid from institutional funds.

GIFT AID (NON-NEED-BASED) *Total amount:* $5,551,163 (6% federal, 1% state, 82% institutional, 11% external sources). *Receiving aid:* Freshmen: 22% (205); Undergraduates: 17% (588). *Average Award:* Freshmen: $10,530; Undergraduates: $10,925. *Scholarships, grants, and awards by category:* Academic Interests/Achievement: 685 awards ($6,646,720 total): general academic interests/achievements. Special Characteristics: 99 awards ($1,306,050 total): members of minority groups. *Tuition waivers:* Full or partial for employees or children of employees. *ROTC:* Army, Air Force cooperative.

LOANS *Student loans:* $11,221,008 (58% need-based, 42% non-need-based). 72% of past graduating class borrowed through all loan programs. *Average indebtedness per student:* $15,030. *Average need-based loan:* Freshmen: $5845; Undergraduates: $5390. *Programs:* Federal Direct (Subsidized and Unsubsidized Stafford), FFEL (PLUS), Perkins, college/university.

WORK-STUDY *Federal work-study:* Total amount: $745,960; 436 jobs averaging $1615. *State or other work-study/employment:* Total amount: $608,340 (58% need-based, 42% non-need-based). 83 part-time jobs averaging $9285.

ATHLETIC AWARDS *Total amount:* $3,517,366 (12% need-based, 88% non-need-based).

APPLYING FOR FINANCIAL AID *Required financial aid forms:* FAFSA, CSS Financial Aid PROFILE, noncustodial (divorced/separated) parent's statement, business/farm supplement. *Financial aid deadline:* 2/15. *Notification date:* 4/1. Students must reply by 5/1.

CONTACT Mr. Mark L. Lindenmeyer, Director of Financial Aid, Loyola College in Maryland, 4501 North Charles Street, Baltimore, MD 21210-2699, 410-617-2576 or toll-free 800-221-9107 Ext. 2252 (in-state). *Fax:* 410-617-5149.

LOYOLA MARYMOUNT UNIVERSITY
Los Angeles, CA

Tuition & fees: $25,756	Average undergraduate aid package: $17,254

ABOUT THE INSTITUTION Independent Roman Catholic, coed. Awards: bachelor's, master's, doctoral, and first professional degrees and post-bachelor's certificates. 48 undergraduate majors. Total enrollment: 8,855. Undergraduates: 5,721. Freshmen: 1,391. Both federal and institutional methodology are used as a basis for awarding need-based institutional aid.

UNDERGRADUATE EXPENSES for 2004–05 *Application fee:* $50. *Comprehensive fee:* $35,212 includes full-time tuition ($25,266), mandatory fees ($490), and room and board ($9456). *College room only:* $7206. Room and board charges vary according to board plan and housing facility. *Part-time tuition:* $1052 per unit. Part-time tuition and fees vary according to course load. *Payment plans:* Installment, deferred payment.

FRESHMAN FINANCIAL AID (Fall 2004, est.) 1222 applied for aid; of those 70% were deemed to have need. 86% of freshmen with need received aid; of those 22% had need fully met. *Average percent of need met:* 86% (excluding

resources awarded to replace EFC). *Average financial aid package:* $19,138 (excluding resources awarded to replace EFC). 4% of all full-time freshmen had no need and received non-need-based gift aid.

UNDERGRADUATE FINANCIAL AID (Fall 2004, est.) 4,129 applied for aid; of those 83% were deemed to have need. 96% of undergraduates with need received aid; of those 15% had need fully met. *Average percent of need met:* 76% (excluding resources awarded to replace EFC). *Average financial aid package:* $17,254 (excluding resources awarded to replace EFC). 2% of all full-time undergraduates had no need and received non-need-based gift aid.

GIFT AID (NEED-BASED) *Total amount:* $35,513,649 (12% federal, 27% state, 60% institutional, 1% external sources). *Receiving aid:* Freshmen: 44% (610); All full-time undergraduates: 42% (2,270). *Average award:* Freshmen: $11,423; Undergraduates: $9378. *Scholarships, grants, and awards:* Federal Pell, FSEOG, state, private, college/university gift aid from institutional funds.

GIFT AID (NON-NEED-BASED) *Total amount:* $2,515,648 (78% institutional, 22% external sources). *Receiving aid:* Freshmen: 22% (306); Undergraduates: 23% (1,259). *Average Award:* Freshmen: $15,781; Undergraduates: $9577. *Scholarships, grants, and awards by category:* Academic Interests/Achievement: general academic interests/achievements. Creative Arts/Performance: art/fine arts, debating, music. Special Achievements/Activities: community service, religious involvement. *Tuition waivers:* Full or partial for employees or children of employees. *ROTC:* Army cooperative, Air Force.

LOANS *Student loans:* $30,167,502 (85% need-based, 15% non-need-based). 76% of past graduating class borrowed through all loan programs. *Average indebtedness per student:* $21,164. *Average need-based loan:* Freshmen: $4400; Undergraduates: $5401. *Parent loans:* $14,016,525 (69% need-based, 31% non-need-based). *Programs:* FFEL (Subsidized and Unsubsidized Stafford, PLUS), Perkins, college/university.

WORK-STUDY *Federal work-study:* Total amount: $5,938,654; 1,600 jobs averaging $2000. *State or other work-study/employment:* Total amount: $900,885 (100% non-need-based). 579 part-time jobs averaging $2800.

ATHLETIC AWARDS *Total amount:* $4,933,473 (30% need-based, 70% non-need-based).

APPLYING FOR FINANCIAL AID *Required financial aid forms:* FAFSA, CSS Financial Aid PROFILE, state aid form. *Financial aid deadline:* 7/30 (priority: 2/15). *Notification date:* Continuous beginning 4/1. Students must reply by 5/1 or within 4 weeks of notification.

CONTACT Financial Aid Office, Loyola Marymount University, One LMU Drive, Los Angeles, CA 90045-8350, 310-338-2753 or toll-free 800-LMU-INFO. *E-mail:* finaid@lmu.edu.

LOYOLA UNIVERSITY CHICAGO
Chicago, IL

Tuition & fees: $23,836	Average undergraduate aid package: $16,465

ABOUT THE INSTITUTION Independent Roman Catholic (Jesuit), coed. Awards: bachelor's, master's, doctoral, and first professional degrees and post-bachelor's and post-master's certificates (also offers adult part-time program with significant enrollment not reflected in profile). 62 undergraduate majors. Total enrollment: 13,909. Undergraduates: 8,319. Freshmen: 1,787. Federal methodology is used as a basis for awarding need-based institutional aid.

UNDERGRADUATE EXPENSES for 2005–06 *Application fee:* $25. *Comprehensive fee:* $32,896 includes full-time tuition ($23,100), mandatory fees ($736), and room and board ($9060). *College room only:* $6200. *Part-time tuition:* $500 per semester hour.

FRESHMAN FINANCIAL AID (Fall 2003) 1659 applied for aid; of those 85% were deemed to have need. 100% of freshmen with need received aid; of those 6% had need fully met. *Average percent of need met:* 81% (excluding resources awarded to replace EFC). *Average financial aid package:* $15,997 (excluding resources awarded to replace EFC). 11% of all full-time freshmen had no need and received non-need-based gift aid.

UNDERGRADUATE FINANCIAL AID (Fall 2003) 5,399 applied for aid; of those 88% were deemed to have need. 100% of undergraduates with need received aid; of those 9% had need fully met. *Average percent of need met:* 73% (excluding resources awarded to replace EFC). *Average financial aid package:* $16,465 (excluding resources awarded to replace EFC). 8% of all full-time undergraduates had no need and received non-need-based gift aid.

GIFT AID (NEED-BASED) *Total amount:* $56,600,996 (12% federal, 16% state, 69% institutional, 3% external sources). *Receiving aid:* Freshmen: 67% (1,285); All full-time undergraduates: 69% (4,222). *Average award:* Freshmen: $12,743;

Undergraduates: $11,975. *Scholarships, grants, and awards:* Federal Pell, FSEOG, state, private, college/university gift aid from institutional funds.

GIFT AID (NON-NEED-BASED) *Total amount:* $6,854,115 (1% state, 91% institutional, 8% external sources). *Receiving aid:* Freshmen: 44% (851); Undergraduates: 62% (3,834). *Average Award:* Freshmen: $7205; Undergraduates: $8253. *Scholarships, grants, and awards by category:* Academic Interests/Achievement: 50 awards ($100,000 total): area/ethnic studies, biological sciences, business, communication, computer science, education, English, foreign languages, general academic interests/achievements, health fields, humanities, international studies, mathematics, physical sciences, premedicine, social sciences. Creative Arts/Performance: 75 awards ($150,000 total): art/fine arts, debating, journalism/publications, music, theater/drama. Special Achievements/Activities: 25 awards ($75,000 total): community service, general special achievements/activities, leadership, memberships. Special Characteristics: 10 awards ($20,000 total): adult students, ethnic background, general special characteristics, religious affiliation, veterans. *ROTC:* Army cooperative, Naval cooperative.

LOANS *Student loans:* $37,681,465 (63% need-based, 37% non-need-based). 53% of past graduating class borrowed through all loan programs. *Average indebtedness per student:* $18,575. *Average need-based loan:* Freshmen: $3637; Undergraduates: $5514. *Parent loans:* $7,830,019 (15% need-based, 85% non-need-based). *Programs:* Federal Direct (Subsidized and Unsubsidized Stafford, PLUS), FFEL (Subsidized and Unsubsidized Stafford, PLUS), Perkins, Federal Nursing.

WORK-STUDY *Federal work-study:* Total amount: $7,652,395; jobs available.

ATHLETIC AWARDS *Total amount:* $2,508,648 (22% need-based, 78% non-need-based).

APPLYING FOR FINANCIAL AID *Required financial aid form:* FAFSA. *Financial aid deadline (priority):* 3/1. *Notification date:* Continuous. Students must reply within 3 weeks of notification.

CONTACT Mr. Terry Richards, Associate Vice President of Enrollment Management, Loyola University Chicago, 6525 North Sheridan Road, Granada Center, Room 360, Chicago, IL 60626, 773-508-3155 or toll-free 800-262-2373. *Fax:* 773-508-3397. *E-mail:* lufinaid@luc.edu.

LOYOLA UNIVERSITY NEW ORLEANS
New Orleans, LA

Tuition & fees: $25,246	Average undergraduate aid package: $18,013

ABOUT THE INSTITUTION Independent Roman Catholic (Jesuit), coed. Awards: bachelor's, master's, and first professional degrees and post-bachelor's and post-master's certificates. 49 undergraduate majors. Total enrollment: 5,423. Undergraduates: 3,688. Freshmen: 815. Federal methodology is used as a basis for awarding need-based institutional aid.

UNDERGRADUATE EXPENSES for 2005–06 *Application fee:* $20. *Comprehensive fee:* $33,558 includes full-time tuition ($24,410), mandatory fees ($836), and room and board ($8312). *College room only:* $5166. *Part-time tuition:* $696 per credit hour.

FRESHMAN FINANCIAL AID (Fall 2003) 612 applied for aid; of those 79% were deemed to have need. 100% of freshmen with need received aid; of those 43% had need fully met. *Average percent of need met:* 86% (excluding resources awarded to replace EFC). *Average financial aid package:* $19,284 (excluding resources awarded to replace EFC). 25% of all full-time freshmen had no need and received non-need-based gift aid.

UNDERGRADUATE FINANCIAL AID (Fall 2003) 2,067 applied for aid; of those 80% were deemed to have need. 100% of undergraduates with need received aid; of those 41% had need fully met. *Average percent of need met:* 85% (excluding resources awarded to replace EFC). *Average financial aid package:* $18,013 (excluding resources awarded to replace EFC). 35% of all full-time undergraduates had no need and received non-need-based gift aid.

GIFT AID (NEED-BASED) *Total amount:* $20,907,608 (10% federal, 7% state, 81% institutional, 2% external sources). *Receiving aid:* Freshmen: 59% (481); All full-time undergraduates: 52% (1,629). *Average award:* Freshmen: $14,770; Undergraduates: $12,927. *Scholarships, grants, and awards:* Federal Pell, FSEOG, private, college/university gift aid from institutional funds.

GIFT AID (NON-NEED-BASED) *Total amount:* $14,064,121 (8% state, 89% institutional, 3% external sources). *Receiving aid:* Freshmen: 10% (81); Undergraduates: 9% (285). *Average Award:* Freshmen: $10,642; Undergraduates: $9669. *Scholarships, grants, and awards by category:* Academic Interests/Achievement: 766 awards ($6,926,625 total): general academic interests/achievements. Creative Arts/Performance: general creative arts/performance.

Loyola University New Orleans

Special Characteristics: 49 awards ($805,156 total): children of faculty/staff.
ROTC: Army cooperative, Naval cooperative, Air Force cooperative.
LOANS *Student loans:* $10,287,252 (67% need-based, 33% non-need-based). 61% of past graduating class borrowed through all loan programs. *Average indebtedness per student:* $18,543. *Average need-based loan:* Freshmen: $4730; Undergraduates: $5831. *Parent loans:* $4,202,961 (24% need-based, 76% non-need-based). *Programs:* FFEL (Subsidized and Unsubsidized Stafford, PLUS), Perkins.
WORK-STUDY *Federal work-study:* Total amount: $1,397,985; 764 jobs averaging $1858.
APPLYING FOR FINANCIAL AID *Required financial aid form:* FAFSA. *Financial aid deadline (priority):* 2/15. *Notification date:* Continuous beginning 3/1. Students must reply by 5/1 or within 2 weeks of notification.
CONTACT Catherine Simoneaux, Director of Scholarships and Financial Aid, Loyola University New Orleans, 6363 St. Charles Avenue, Box 206, New Orleans, LA 70118-6195, 504-865-3231 or toll-free 800-4-LOYOLA. *Fax:* 504-865-3233. *E-mail:* finaid@loyno.edu.

LUBBOCK CHRISTIAN UNIVERSITY
Lubbock, TX

Tuition & fees: $11,994	Average undergraduate aid package: $11,134

ABOUT THE INSTITUTION Independent religious, coed. Awards: bachelor's and master's degrees. 45 undergraduate majors. Total enrollment: 1,974. Undergraduates: 1,778. Freshmen: 270. Federal methodology is used as a basis for awarding need-based institutional aid.
UNDERGRADUATE EXPENSES for 2004–05 *Application fee:* $20. *Comprehensive fee:* $16,124 includes full-time tuition ($11,088), mandatory fees ($906), and room and board ($4130). Full-time tuition and fees vary according to program. Room and board charges vary according to board plan and housing facility. Part-time tuition and fees vary according to course load and program. *Payment plan:* Installment.
FRESHMAN FINANCIAL AID (Fall 2004, est.) 237 applied for aid; of those 84% were deemed to have need. 100% of freshmen with need received aid; of those 14% had need fully met. *Average percent of need met:* 79% (excluding resources awarded to replace EFC). *Average financial aid package:* $10,866 (excluding resources awarded to replace EFC). 18% of all full-time freshmen had no need and received non-need-based gift aid.
UNDERGRADUATE FINANCIAL AID (Fall 2004, est.) 1,007 applied for aid; of those 89% were deemed to have need. 100% of undergraduates with need received aid; of those 8% had need fully met. *Average percent of need met:* 73% (excluding resources awarded to replace EFC). *Average financial aid package:* $11,134 (excluding resources awarded to replace EFC). 15% of all full-time undergraduates had no need and received non-need-based gift aid.
GIFT AID (NEED-BASED) *Total amount:* $6,788,074 (31% federal, 32% state, 30% institutional, 7% external sources). *Receiving aid:* Freshmen: 80% (200); All full-time undergraduates: 78% (869). *Average award:* Freshmen: $7736; Undergraduates: $7049. *Scholarships, grants, and awards:* Federal Pell, FSEOG, state, college/university gift aid from institutional funds.
GIFT AID (NON-NEED-BASED) *Total amount:* $805,850 (1% state, 81% institutional, 18% external sources). *Receiving aid:* Freshmen: 10% (25); Undergraduates: 5% (57). *Average Award:* Freshmen: $10,180; Undergraduates: $10,018. *Scholarships, grants, and awards by category:* Academic Interests/Achievement: agriculture, business, communication, computer science, education, English, foreign languages, general academic interests/achievements, humanities, physical sciences, religion/biblical studies, social sciences. *Creative Arts/Performance:* art/fine arts, journalism/publications, music, performing arts, theater/drama. *Special Achievements/Activities:* 72 awards ($77,922 total): cheerleading/drum major, leadership. *Special Characteristics:* 55 awards ($345,369 total): children of faculty/staff, general special characteristics. *Tuition waivers:* Full or partial for employees or children of employees. *ROTC:* Army cooperative, Air Force cooperative.
LOANS *Student loans:* $11,306,985 (79% need-based, 21% non-need-based). 76% of past graduating class borrowed through all loan programs. *Average indebtedness per student:* $20,244. *Average need-based loan:* Freshmen: $2911; Undergraduates: $3809. *Parent loans:* $2,117,689 (32% need-based, 68% non-need-based). *Programs:* FFEL (Subsidized and Unsubsidized Stafford, PLUS), Perkins, state.
WORK-STUDY *Federal work-study:* Total amount: $936,376; 926 jobs averaging $2000. *State or other work-study/employment:* Total amount: $27,591 (40% need-based, 60% non-need-based). 91 part-time jobs averaging $303.

ATHLETIC AWARDS *Total amount:* $785,949 (46% need-based, 54% non-need-based).
APPLYING FOR FINANCIAL AID *Required financial aid forms:* FAFSA, institution's own form. *Financial aid deadline (priority):* 6/1. *Notification date:* Continuous.
CONTACT Amy Hardesty, Financial Aid Director, Lubbock Christian University, 5601 19th Street, Lubbock, TX 79407, 806-720-7176 or toll-free 800-933-7601. *Fax:* 806-720-7185. *E-mail:* amy.hardesty@lcu.edu.

LUTHER COLLEGE
Decorah, IA

Tuition & fees: $23,070	Average undergraduate aid package: $17,511

ABOUT THE INSTITUTION Independent religious, coed. Awards: bachelor's degrees. 44 undergraduate majors. Total enrollment: 2,573. Undergraduates: 2,573. Freshmen: 663. Federal methodology is used as a basis for awarding need-based institutional aid.
UNDERGRADUATE EXPENSES for 2004–05 *Application fee:* $25. *Comprehensive fee:* $27,240 includes full-time tuition ($23,070) and room and board ($4170). *College room only:* $2040. Full-time tuition and fees vary according to course load. Room and board charges vary according to board plan and housing facility. *Part-time tuition:* $824 per semester hour. Part-time tuition and fees vary according to course load. *Payment plan:* Installment.
FRESHMAN FINANCIAL AID (Fall 2004, est.) 586 applied for aid; of those 83% were deemed to have need. 100% of freshmen with need received aid; of those 68% had need fully met. *Average percent of need met:* 92% (excluding resources awarded to replace EFC). *Average financial aid package:* $18,496 (excluding resources awarded to replace EFC). 13% of all full-time freshmen had no need and received non-need-based gift aid.
UNDERGRADUATE FINANCIAL AID (Fall 2004, est.) 2,064 applied for aid; of those 86% were deemed to have need. 100% of undergraduates with need received aid; of those 29% had need fully met. *Average percent of need met:* 87% (excluding resources awarded to replace EFC). *Average financial aid package:* $17,511 (excluding resources awarded to replace EFC). 10% of all full-time undergraduates had no need and received non-need-based gift aid.
GIFT AID (NEED-BASED) *Total amount:* $21,082,196 (9% federal, 7% state, 80% institutional, 4% external sources). *Receiving aid:* Freshmen: 74% (487); All full-time undergraduates: 71% (1,768). *Average award:* Freshmen: $12,647; Undergraduates: $11,212. *Scholarships, grants, and awards:* Federal Pell, FSEOG, state, private, college/university gift aid from institutional funds.
GIFT AID (NON-NEED-BASED) *Total amount:* $4,685,499 (89% institutional, 11% external sources). *Receiving aid:* Freshmen: 61% (405); Undergraduates: 59% (1,462). *Average Award:* Freshmen: $7811; Undergraduates: $6944. *Scholarships, grants, and awards by category:* Academic Interests/Achievement: 1,159 awards ($6,887,674 total): general academic interests/achievements. *Creative Arts/Performance:* 592 awards ($1,206,411 total): music. *Special Characteristics:* 417 awards ($490,437 total): children and siblings of alumni, members of minority groups, religious affiliation. *Tuition waivers:* Full or partial for employees or children of employees.
LOANS *Student loans:* $9,539,439 (82% need-based, 18% non-need-based). 68% of past graduating class borrowed through all loan programs. *Average indebtedness per student:* $17,209. *Average need-based loan:* Freshmen: $4380; Undergraduates: $4890. *Parent loans:* $6,714,511 (36% need-based, 64% non-need-based). *Programs:* Federal Direct (Subsidized and Unsubsidized Stafford, PLUS), Perkins, college/university.
WORK-STUDY *Federal work-study:* Total amount: $1,219,867; 822 jobs averaging $1484. *State or other work-study/employment:* Total amount: $1,368,770 (15% need-based, 85% non-need-based). 787 part-time jobs averaging $1739.
APPLYING FOR FINANCIAL AID *Required financial aid forms:* FAFSA, institution's own form. *Financial aid deadline (priority):* 3/1. *Notification date:* Continuous beginning 3/15. Students must reply by 5/1.
CONTACT Ms. Janice Cordell, Director of Student Financial Planning, Luther College, 700 College Drive, Decorah, IA 52101-1045, 563-387-1018 or toll-free 800-458-8437. *E-mail:* cordellj@luther.edu.

LUTHER RICE BIBLE COLLEGE AND SEMINARY
Lithonia, GA

Tuition & fees: $3964	Average undergraduate aid package: $7220

ABOUT THE INSTITUTION Independent Baptist, coed. Awards: bachelor's, master's, and doctoral degrees. 2 undergraduate majors. Total enrollment: 1,600. Undergraduates: 655. Freshmen: 33. Both federal and institutional methodology are used as a basis for awarding need-based institutional aid.

UNDERGRADUATE EXPENSES for 2004–05 *Application fee:* $50. *Tuition:* full-time $3864; part-time $461 per course. *Required fees:* full-time $100; $50 per term part-time. *Payment plan:* Installment.

FRESHMAN FINANCIAL AID (Fall 2003) 26 applied for aid; of those 100% were deemed to have need. 38% of freshmen with need received aid; of those 100% had need fully met. *Average percent of need met:* 100% (excluding resources awarded to replace EFC). *Average financial aid package:* $7220 (excluding resources awarded to replace EFC).

UNDERGRADUATE FINANCIAL AID (Fall 2003) 26 applied for aid; of those 100% were deemed to have need. 38% of undergraduates with need received aid; of those 100% had need fully met. *Average percent of need met:* 100% (excluding resources awarded to replace EFC). *Average financial aid package:* $7220 (excluding resources awarded to replace EFC).

GIFT AID (NEED-BASED) *Total amount:* $186,086 (100% federal). *Receiving aid:* Freshmen: 35% (9); All full-time undergraduates: 8% (9). *Average award:* Freshmen: $3362; Undergraduates: $3362. *Scholarships, grants, and awards:* Federal Pell, FSEOG, college/university gift aid from institutional funds.

LOANS *Student loans:* $1,214,883 (60% need-based, 40% non-need-based). 11% of past graduating class borrowed through all loan programs. *Average indebtedness per student:* $12,551. *Average need-based loan:* Freshmen: $5641; Undergraduates: $5641. *Programs:* FFEL (Subsidized and Unsubsidized Stafford, PLUS).

WORK-STUDY *Federal work-study:* Total amount: $14,968; 2 jobs averaging $7484.

APPLYING FOR FINANCIAL AID *Required financial aid forms:* FAFSA, institution's own form. *Financial aid deadline:* Continuous. *Notification date:* Continuous. Students must reply within 2 weeks of notification.

CONTACT Gary W. Cook, Director of Financial Aid, Luther Rice Bible College and Seminary, 3038 Evans Mill Road, Lithonia, GA 30038-2418, 770-484-1204 Ext. 241 or toll-free 800-442-1577. *Fax:* 678-990-5388. *E-mail:* gcooke@lrs.edu.

LYCOMING COLLEGE
Williamsport, PA

Tuition & fees: $22,886	Average undergraduate aid package: $17,502

ABOUT THE INSTITUTION Independent United Methodist, coed. Awards: bachelor's degrees. 49 undergraduate majors. Total enrollment: 1,536. Undergraduates: 1,536. Freshmen: 401. Federal methodology is used as a basis for awarding need-based institutional aid.

UNDERGRADUATE EXPENSES for 2004–05 *Application fee:* $35. *Comprehensive fee:* $29,128 includes full-time tuition ($22,336), mandatory fees ($550), and room and board ($6242). *College room only:* $3196. Full-time tuition and fees vary according to course load. Room and board charges vary according to housing facility. *Part-time tuition:* $698 per course. *Payment plan:* Installment.

FRESHMAN FINANCIAL AID (Fall 2004, est.) 368 applied for aid; of those 90% were deemed to have need. 100% of freshmen with need received aid; of those 16% had need fully met. *Average percent of need met:* 77% (excluding resources awarded to replace EFC). *Average financial aid package:* $17,436 (excluding resources awarded to replace EFC). 12% of all full-time freshmen had no need and received non-need-based gift aid.

UNDERGRADUATE FINANCIAL AID (Fall 2004, est.) 1,332 applied for aid; of those 92% were deemed to have need. 100% of undergraduates with need received aid; of those 22% had need fully met. *Average percent of need met:* 77% (excluding resources awarded to replace EFC). *Average financial aid package:* $17,502 (excluding resources awarded to replace EFC). 13% of all full-time undergraduates had no need and received non-need-based gift aid.

GIFT AID (NEED-BASED) *Total amount:* $15,593,752 (7% federal, 13% state, 76% institutional, 4% external sources). *Receiving aid:* Freshmen: 83% (333); All full-time undergraduates: 82% (1,217). *Average award:* Freshmen: $14,036; Undergraduates: $13,304. *Scholarships, grants, and awards:* Federal Pell, FSEOG, state, private, college/university gift aid from institutional funds.

GIFT AID (NON-NEED-BASED) *Total amount:* $2,243,127 (1% state, 90% institutional, 9% external sources). *Receiving aid:* Freshmen: 8% (34); Undergraduates: 8% (124). *Average Award:* Freshmen: $8423; Undergraduates: $8640. *Scholarships, grants, and awards by category:* Academic Interests/Achievement: 818 awards ($6,549,585 total): biological sciences, business, communication, computer science, education, English, foreign languages, general

academic interests/achievements, health fields, humanities, international studies, mathematics, physical sciences, premedicine, religion/biblical studies, social sciences. *Creative Arts/Performance:* 213 awards ($340,525 total): art/fine arts, creative writing, music, theater/drama. *Special Achievements/Activities:* 53 awards ($86,000 total): general special achievements/activities, leadership. *Special Characteristics:* 64 awards ($1,154,139 total): children of educators, children of faculty/staff, relatives of clergy. *Tuition waivers:* Full or partial for employees or children of employees. *ROTC:* Army cooperative.

LOANS *Student loans:* $8,554,976 (73% need-based, 27% non-need-based). 84% of past graduating class borrowed through all loan programs. *Average indebtedness per student:* $23,364. *Average need-based loan:* Freshmen: $3424; Undergraduates: $4261. *Parent loans:* $4,130,050 (39% need-based, 61% non-need-based). *Programs:* FFEL (Subsidized and Unsubsidized Stafford, PLUS), Perkins, college/university.

WORK-STUDY *Federal work-study:* Total amount: $541,172; 510 jobs averaging $1060. *State or other work-study/employment:* Part-time jobs available.

APPLYING FOR FINANCIAL AID *Required financial aid forms:* FAFSA, institution's own form, state aid form. *Financial aid deadline (priority):* 3/1. *Notification date:* Continuous beginning 3/1. Students must reply by 5/1.

CONTACT Mrs. Jamie Lowthert, Director of Financial Aid, Lycoming College, 700 College Place, Long Hall, Williamsport, PA 17701-5192, 570-321-4040 or toll-free 800-345-3920 Ext. 4026. *Fax:* 570-321-4993. *E-mail:* lowthert@lycoming.edu.

LYME ACADEMY COLLEGE OF FINE ARTS
Old Lyme, CT

Tuition & fees: $16,916	Average undergraduate aid package: $9356

ABOUT THE INSTITUTION Independent, coed. Awards: bachelor's degrees. 3 undergraduate majors. Total enrollment: 160. Undergraduates: 160. Freshmen: 14. Both federal and institutional methodology are used as a basis for awarding need-based institutional aid.

UNDERGRADUATE EXPENSES for 2005–06 *Application fee:* $35. *Tuition:* full-time $16,416.

GIFT AID (NEED-BASED) *Total amount:* $172,636 (40% federal, 44% state, 16% external sources). *Scholarships, grants, and awards:* Federal Pell, FSEOG, state, private, college/university gift aid from institutional funds.

GIFT AID (NON-NEED-BASED) *Total amount:* $147,995 (100% institutional). *Scholarships, grants, and awards by category:* Creative Arts/Performance: art/fine arts.

LOANS *Student loans:* $372,783 (61% need-based, 39% non-need-based). 77% of past graduating class borrowed through all loan programs. *Parent loans:* $104,206 (100% non-need-based). *Programs:* FFEL (Subsidized and Unsubsidized Stafford, PLUS), Nellie Mae Loans, EXCEL Loans, TERI Loans, Connecticut Student Loan Foundation FFELP loans, alternative loans.

APPLYING FOR FINANCIAL AID *Required financial aid forms:* FAFSA, institution's own form, CSS Financial Aid PROFILE. *Financial aid deadline (priority):* 2/15. *Notification date:* Continuous beginning 2/1. Students must reply by 5/1 or within 2 weeks of notification.

CONTACT Mr. Jim Falconer, Director of Financial Aid, Lyme Academy College of Fine Arts, 84 Lyme Street, Old Lyme, CT 06371, 860-434-5232 Ext. 121. *Fax:* 860-434-8725. *E-mail:* jfalconer@lymeacademy.edu.

LYNCHBURG COLLEGE
Lynchburg, VA

Tuition & fees: $22,885	Average undergraduate aid package: $16,994

ABOUT THE INSTITUTION Independent religious, coed. Awards: bachelor's and master's degrees. 47 undergraduate majors. Total enrollment: 2,248. Undergraduates: 1,934. Freshmen: 568. Federal methodology is used as a basis for awarding need-based institutional aid.

UNDERGRADUATE EXPENSES for 2004–05 *Application fee:* $30. *Comprehensive fee:* $27,885 includes full-time tuition ($22,640), mandatory fees ($245), and room and board ($5000). *College room only:* $2900. Room and board charges vary according to board plan. *Part-time tuition:* $325 per credit hour. Part-time tuition and fees vary according to course load. *Payment plan:* Installment.

FRESHMAN FINANCIAL AID (Fall 2004, est.) 462 applied for aid; of those 82% were deemed to have need. 100% of freshmen with need received aid; of those 26% had need fully met. *Average percent of need met:* 90% (excluding resources

awarded to replace EFC). *Average financial aid package:* $17,808 (excluding resources awarded to replace EFC). 35% of all full-time freshmen had no need and received non-need-based gift aid.

UNDERGRADUATE FINANCIAL AID (Fall 2004, est.) 1,390 applied for aid; of those 84% were deemed to have need. 100% of undergraduates with need received aid; of those 7% had need fully met. *Average percent of need met:* 87% (excluding resources awarded to replace EFC). *Average financial aid package:* $16,994 (excluding resources awarded to replace EFC). 32% of all full-time undergraduates had no need and received non-need-based gift aid.

GIFT AID (NEED-BASED) *Total amount:* $14,725,312 (9% federal, 14% state, 74% institutional, 3% external sources). *Receiving aid:* Freshmen: 66% (377); All full-time undergraduates: 64% (1,169). *Average award:* Freshmen: $14,334; Undergraduates: $12,938. *Scholarships, grants, and awards:* Federal Pell, FSEOG, state, college/university gift aid from institutional funds.

GIFT AID (NON-NEED-BASED) *Total amount:* $6,109,364 (15% state, 81% institutional, 4% external sources). *Receiving aid:* Freshmen: 42% (241); Undergraduates: 41% (760). *Average Award: Freshmen:* $8238; *Undergraduates:* $7856. *Scholarships, grants, and awards by category: Academic Interests/Achievement:* general academic interests/achievements. *Special Characteristics:* children of faculty/staff. *Tuition waivers:* Full or partial for employees or children of employees, senior citizens.

LOANS *Student loans:* $7,601,318 (88% need-based, 12% non-need-based). 86% of past graduating class borrowed through all loan programs. *Average indebtedness per student:* $18,932. *Average need-based loan:* Freshmen: $3019; Undergraduates: $3459. *Parent loans:* $4,041,322 (76% need-based, 24% non-need-based). *Programs:* FFEL (Subsidized and Unsubsidized Stafford, PLUS), Perkins.

WORK-STUDY *Federal work-study:* Total amount: $187,700; 479 jobs averaging $1064. *State or other work-study/employment:* Total amount: $474,232 (42% need-based, 58% non-need-based). Part-time jobs available.

APPLYING FOR FINANCIAL AID *Required financial aid forms:* FAFSA, state aid form. *Financial aid deadline (priority):* 3/1. *Notification date:* Continuous beginning 3/10. Students must reply by 5/1 or within 2 weeks of notification.

CONTACT Mrs. Michelle Davis, Director of Financial Aid, Lynchburg College, 1501 Lakeside Drive, Lynchburg, VA 24501-3199, 434-544-8228 or toll-free 800-426-8101. *Fax:* 434-544-8653.

LYNDON STATE COLLEGE
Lyndonville, VT

ABOUT THE INSTITUTION State-supported, coed. Awards: associate, bachelor's, and master's degrees. 31 undergraduate majors. Total enrollment: 1,349. Undergraduates: 1,304. Freshmen: 345.

GIFT AID (NEED-BASED) *Scholarships, grants, and awards:* Federal Pell, FSEOG, state, private, college/university gift aid from institutional funds, Child-Care Grant Program, faculty/staff awards.

GIFT AID (NON-NEED-BASED) *Scholarships, grants, and awards by category: Academic Interests/Achievement:* business, education, general academic interests/ achievements, humanities. *Special Achievements/Activities:* community service, leadership. *Special Characteristics:* adult students, children of faculty/staff, siblings of current students.

LOANS *Programs:* Federal Direct (Subsidized and Unsubsidized Stafford, PLUS), Perkins.

WORK-STUDY Federal work-study jobs available.

APPLYING FOR FINANCIAL AID *Required financial aid form:* FAFSA.

CONTACT Ms. Terry Van Zile, Assistant Director of Financial Aid, Lyndon State College, PO Box 919, Lyndonville, VT 05851, 802-626-6217 or toll-free 800-225-1998 (in-state). *E-mail:* theresa.vanzile@lsc.vsc.edu.

LYNN UNIVERSITY
Boca Raton, FL

Tuition & fees: $25,850	Average undergraduate aid package: $19,332

ABOUT THE INSTITUTION Independent, coed. Awards: bachelor's, master's, and doctoral degrees and post-bachelor's certificates. 39 undergraduate majors. Total enrollment: 2,510. Undergraduates: 2,091. Freshmen: 597. Federal methodology is used as a basis for awarding need-based institutional aid.

UNDERGRADUATE EXPENSES for 2005–06 *Application fee:* $35. *Comprehensive fee:* $34,950 includes full-time tuition ($24,700), mandatory fees ($1150), and room and board ($9100). Room and board charges vary according to housing

facility. *Part-time tuition:* $725 per credit. Part-time tuition and fees vary according to class time and course load. *Payment plans:* Installment, deferred payment.

FRESHMAN FINANCIAL AID (Fall 2004, est.) 249 applied for aid; of those 82% were deemed to have need. 100% of freshmen with need received aid; of those 36% had need fully met. *Average percent of need met:* 71% (excluding resources awarded to replace EFC). *Average financial aid package:* $19,301 (excluding resources awarded to replace EFC). 67% of all full-time freshmen had no need and received non-need-based gift aid.

UNDERGRADUATE FINANCIAL AID (Fall 2004, est.) 803 applied for aid; of those 87% were deemed to have need. 99% of undergraduates with need received aid; of those 34% had need fully met. *Average percent of need met:* 72% (excluding resources awarded to replace EFC). *Average financial aid package:* $19,332 (excluding resources awarded to replace EFC). 35% of all full-time undergraduates had no need and received non-need-based gift aid.

GIFT AID (NEED-BASED) *Total amount:* $6,712,630 (19% federal, 12% state, 64% institutional, 5% external sources). *Receiving aid:* Freshmen: 32% (196); All full-time undergraduates: 41% (669). *Average award:* Freshmen: $11,346; Undergraduates: $11,283. *Scholarships, grants, and awards:* Federal Pell, FSEOG, state, private, college/university gift aid from institutional funds.

GIFT AID (NON-NEED-BASED) *Total amount:* $3,565,744 (13% state, 68% institutional, 19% external sources). *Receiving aid:* Freshmen: 1% (4); Undergraduates: 2% (35). *Average Award: Freshmen:* $10,251; *Undergraduates:* $10,440. *Scholarships, grants, and awards by category: Academic Interests/Achievement:* 530 awards ($3,339,431 total): business, communication, general academic interests/achievements. *Creative Arts/Performance:* 28 awards ($639,304 total): music. *Special Achievements/Activities:* 2 awards ($44,462 total): leadership, religious involvement. *Special Characteristics:* 44 awards ($390,960 total): children of faculty/staff, siblings of current students. *Tuition waivers:* Full or partial for employees or children of employees. *ROTC:* Air Force cooperative.

LOANS *Student loans:* $6,059,659 (75% need-based, 25% non-need-based). 68% of past graduating class borrowed through all loan programs. *Average indebtedness per student:* $21,852. *Average need-based loan:* Freshmen: $8751; Undergraduates: $9324. *Parent loans:* $4,977,818 (44% need-based, 56% non-need-based). *Programs:* FFEL (Subsidized and Unsubsidized Stafford, PLUS), Perkins, state, college/university.

WORK-STUDY *Federal work-study:* Total amount: $195,831; 175 jobs averaging $1119. *State or other work-study/employment:* Total amount: $209,851 (35% need-based, 65% non-need-based). 39 part-time jobs averaging $5432.

ATHLETIC AWARDS *Total amount:* $2,338,928 (43% need-based, 57% non-need-based).

APPLYING FOR FINANCIAL AID *Required financial aid forms:* FAFSA, institution's own form. *Financial aid deadline (priority):* 3/1. *Notification date:* Continuous. Students must reply within 2 weeks of notification.

CONTACT William Healy, Director of Student Financial Services, Lynn University, 3601 North Military Trail, Boca Raton, FL 33431-5598, 561-237-7814 or toll-free 800-888-5966 Ext. 1 (in-state), 800-888-5966 (out-of-state). *Fax:* 561-237-7189. *E-mail:* whealy@lynn.edu.

LYON COLLEGE
Batesville, AR

Tuition & fees: $13,905	Average undergraduate aid package: $13,982

ABOUT THE INSTITUTION Independent Presbyterian, coed. Awards: bachelor's degrees. 17 undergraduate majors. Total enrollment: 511. Undergraduates: 511. Freshmen: 144. Federal methodology is used as a basis for awarding need-based institutional aid.

UNDERGRADUATE EXPENSES for 2005–06 *Application fee:* $25. *One-time required fee:* $200. *Comprehensive fee:* $19,990 includes full-time tuition ($13,475), mandatory fees ($430), and room and board ($6085). *College room only:* $2500. Room and board charges vary according to housing facility. *Part-time tuition:* $560 per credit hour. Part-time tuition and fees vary according to course load. *Payment plan:* Installment.

FRESHMAN FINANCIAL AID (Fall 2004, est.) 109 applied for aid; of those 86% were deemed to have need. 100% of freshmen with need received aid; of those 29% had need fully met. *Average percent of need met:* 81% (excluding resources awarded to replace EFC). *Average financial aid package:* $13,809 (excluding resources awarded to replace EFC). 26% of all full-time freshmen had no need and received non-need-based gift aid.

UNDERGRADUATE FINANCIAL AID (Fall 2004, est.) 380 applied for aid; of those 88% were deemed to have need. 100% of undergraduates with need received aid; of those 29% had need fully met. *Average percent of need met:* 83% (excluding resources awarded to replace EFC). *Average financial aid package:* $13,982 (excluding resources awarded to replace EFC). 27% of all full-time undergraduates had no need and received non-need-based gift aid.

GIFT AID (NEED-BASED) *Total amount:* $3,156,162 (22% federal, 10% state, 64% institutional, 4% external sources). *Receiving aid:* Freshmen: 67% (94); All full-time undergraduates: 68% (333). *Average award:* Freshmen: $10,792; Undergraduates: $10,428. *Scholarships, grants, and awards:* Federal Pell, FSEOG, state, private, college/university gift aid from institutional funds.

GIFT AID (NON-NEED-BASED) *Total amount:* $1,244,381 (19% state, 77% institutional, 4% external sources). *Receiving aid:* Freshmen: 13% (19); Undergraduates: 12% (57). *Average Award: Freshmen:* $10,196; *Undergraduates:* $9733. *Scholarships, grants, and awards by category: Academic Interests/Achievement:* 565 awards ($2,549,050 total): general academic interests/achievements. *Creative Arts/Performance:* 31 awards ($86,240 total): art/fine arts. *Special Achievements/Activities:* 37 awards ($127,500 total): leadership. *Special Characteristics:* 45 awards ($170,016 total): children of faculty/staff, ethnic background, local/state students, members of minority groups, religious affiliation. *Tuition waivers:* Full or partial for employees or children of employees.

LOANS *Student loans:* $1,670,385 (79% need-based, 21% non-need-based). 93% of past graduating class borrowed through all loan programs. *Average indebtedness per student:* $13,423. *Average need-based loan:* Freshmen: $3138; Undergraduates: $4039. *Parent loans:* $408,890 (29% need-based, 71% non-need-based). *Programs:* FFEL (Subsidized and Unsubsidized Stafford, PLUS), Perkins.

WORK-STUDY *Federal work-study:* Total amount: $138,422; 123 jobs averaging $1125. *State or other work-study/employment:* Total amount: $45,210 (12% need-based, 88% non-need-based). 38 part-time jobs averaging $1171.

ATHLETIC AWARDS *Total amount:* $910,630 (30% need-based, 70% non-need-based).

APPLYING FOR FINANCIAL AID *Required financial aid form:* FAFSA. *Financial aid deadline (priority):* 3/15. *Notification date:* Continuous. Students must reply by 8/15.

CONTACT Ms. Louise Strauser, Assistant Director of Student Financial Assistance, Lyon College, 2300 Highland Road, Batesville, AR 72501, 870-698-4257 or toll-free 800-423-2542. *Fax:* 870-793-1791. *E-mail:* financialaid@lyon.edu.

MACALESTER COLLEGE
St. Paul, MN

Tuition & fees: $28,810	Average undergraduate aid package: $23,461

ABOUT THE INSTITUTION Independent Presbyterian, coed. Awards: bachelor's degrees. 38 undergraduate majors. Total enrollment: 1,900. Undergraduates: 1,900. Freshmen: 486. Institutional methodology is used as a basis for awarding need-based institutional aid.

UNDERGRADUATE EXPENSES for 2005–06 *Application fee:* $40. *Comprehensive fee:* $36,668 includes full-time tuition ($28,642), mandatory fees ($168), and room and board ($7858). *College room only:* $4084.

FRESHMAN FINANCIAL AID (Fall 2004, est.) 379 applied for aid; of those 92% were deemed to have need. 100% of freshmen with need received aid; of those 100% had need fully met. *Average percent of need met:* 100% (excluding resources awarded to replace EFC). *Average financial aid package:* $24,037 (excluding resources awarded to replace EFC). 5% of all full-time freshmen had no need and received non-need-based gift aid.

UNDERGRADUATE FINANCIAL AID (Fall 2004, est.) 1,364 applied for aid; of those 93% were deemed to have need. 100% of undergraduates with need received aid; of those 100% had need fully met. *Average percent of need met:* 100% (excluding resources awarded to replace EFC). *Average financial aid package:* $23,461 (excluding resources awarded to replace EFC). 6% of all full-time undergraduates had no need and received non-need-based gift aid.

GIFT AID (NEED-BASED) *Total amount:* $23,415,342 (4% federal, 2% state, 89% institutional, 5% external sources). *Receiving aid:* Freshmen: 72% (350); All full-time undergraduates: 69% (1,274). *Average award:* Freshmen: $20,010; Undergraduates: $18,351. *Scholarships, grants, and awards:* Federal Pell, FSEOG, state, private, college/university gift aid from institutional funds.

GIFT AID (NON-NEED-BASED) *Total amount:* $838,927 (1% federal, 1% state, 62% institutional, 36% external sources). *Average Award:* Freshmen: $4231; Undergraduates: $4988. *Scholarships, grants, and awards by category: Academic Interests/Achievement:* 326 awards ($2,280,084 total): general academic

interests/achievements. *Special Characteristics:* 140 awards ($458,000 total): ethnic background. *ROTC:* Naval cooperative, Air Force cooperative.

LOANS *Student loans:* $5,780,236 (77% need-based, 23% non-need-based). *Average need-based loan:* Freshmen: $2503; Undergraduates: $3302. *Parent loans:* $1,622,795 (100% non-need-based). *Programs:* FFEL (Subsidized and Unsubsidized Stafford, PLUS), Perkins, state.

WORK-STUDY *Federal work-study:* Total amount: $500,972; 310 jobs averaging $1616. *State or other work-study/employment:* Total amount: $1,871,064 (98% need-based, 2% non-need-based). 827 part-time jobs averaging $1803.

APPLYING FOR FINANCIAL AID *Required financial aid forms:* FAFSA, CSS Financial Aid PROFILE, noncustodial (divorced/separated) parent's statement. *Financial aid deadline (priority):* 2/9. *Notification date:* 4/1. Students must reply by 5/1.

CONTACT Financial Aid Office, Macalester College, 1600 Grand Avenue, St. Paul, MN 55105, 651-696-6214 or toll-free 800-231-7974. *Fax:* 651-696-6866. *E-mail:* finaid@macalester.edu.

MACHZIKEI HADATH RABBINICAL COLLEGE
Brooklyn, NY

CONTACT Rabbi Baruch Rozmarin, Director of Financial Aid, Machzikei Hadath Rabbinical College, 5407 16th Avenue, Brooklyn, NY 11204-1805, 718-854-8777.

MACMURRAY COLLEGE
Jacksonville, IL

Tuition & fees: $14,600	Average undergraduate aid package: $12,505

ABOUT THE INSTITUTION Independent United Methodist, coed. Awards: associate and bachelor's degrees. 39 undergraduate majors. Total enrollment: 667. Undergraduates: 667. Freshmen: 149. Federal methodology is used as a basis for awarding need-based institutional aid.

UNDERGRADUATE EXPENSES for 2004–05 *Comprehensive fee:* $20,220 includes full-time tuition ($14,500), mandatory fees ($100), and room and board ($5620). *College room only:* $2850. Room and board charges vary according to board plan and housing facility. *Part-time tuition:* $235 per credit hour. *Payment plan:* Installment.

FRESHMAN FINANCIAL AID (Fall 2004, est.) 145 applied for aid; of those 91% were deemed to have need. 100% of freshmen with need received aid; of those 11% had need fully met. *Average percent of need met:* 72% (excluding resources awarded to replace EFC). *Average financial aid package:* $11,539 (excluding resources awarded to replace EFC). 10% of all full-time freshmen had no need and received non-need-based gift aid.

UNDERGRADUATE FINANCIAL AID (Fall 2004, est.) 570 applied for aid; of those 90% were deemed to have need. 100% of undergraduates with need received aid; of those 21% had need fully met. *Average percent of need met:* 79% (excluding resources awarded to replace EFC). *Average financial aid package:* $12,505 (excluding resources awarded to replace EFC). 10% of all full-time undergraduates had no need and received non-need-based gift aid.

GIFT AID (NEED-BASED) *Total amount:* $5,249,701 (18% federal, 28% state, 52% institutional, 2% external sources). *Receiving aid:* Freshmen: 90% (132); All full-time undergraduates: 89% (513). *Average award:* Freshmen: $9096; Undergraduates: $9244. *Scholarships, grants, and awards:* Federal Pell, FSEOG, state, private, college/university gift aid from institutional funds.

GIFT AID (NON-NEED-BASED) *Total amount:* $536,633 (1% state, 91% institutional, 8% external sources). *Receiving aid:* Freshmen: 7% (10); Undergraduates: 8% (46). *Average Award:* Freshmen: $9968; *Undergraduates:* $8991. *Scholarships, grants, and awards by category: Academic Interests/Achievement:* 135 awards ($583,422 total): biological sciences, education, English, foreign languages, general academic interests/achievements, health fields, physical sciences, religion/biblical studies, social sciences. *Creative Arts/Performance:* 19 awards ($46,775 total): art/fine arts, music, theater/drama. *Special Achievements/Activities:* 19 awards ($43,800 total): leadership, religious involvement. *Special Characteristics:* 102 awards ($302,318 total): children and siblings of alumni, children of faculty/staff, international students, out-of-state students, previous college experience, religious affiliation, siblings of current students. *Tuition waivers:* Full or partial for minority students, children of alumni, employees or children of employees, senior citizens.

LOANS *Student loans:* $3,497,090 (74% need-based, 26% non-need-based). 97% of past graduating class borrowed through all loan programs. *Average indebtedness per student:* $17,477. *Average need-based loan:* Freshmen: $3013;

Undergraduates: $3790. *Parent loans:* $477,370 (50% need-based, 50% non-need-based). *Programs:* FFEL (Subsidized and Unsubsidized Stafford, PLUS), Perkins.

WORK-STUDY *Federal work-study:* Total amount: $44,701; 48 jobs averaging $1333. *State or other work-study/employment:* Total amount: $97,995 (74% need-based, 26% non-need-based). 86 part-time jobs averaging $1139.

APPLYING FOR FINANCIAL AID *Required financial aid form:* FAFSA. *Financial aid deadline (priority):* 5/31. *Notification date:* Continuous. Students must reply within 2 weeks of notification.

CONTACT Rhonda I. Cors, Vice President for Enrollment Management, MacMurray College, 447 East College Avenue, Jacksonville, IL 62650, 217-479-7056 or toll-free 800-252-7485 (in-state). *Fax:* 217-291-0702. *E-mail:* rhonda.cors@mac.edu.

MACON STATE COLLEGE
Macon, GA

Tuition & fees: N/R	Average undergraduate aid package: $5752

ABOUT THE INSTITUTION State-supported, coed. Awards: associate and bachelor's degrees. 58 undergraduate majors. Total enrollment: 5,733. Undergraduates: 5,733. Federal methodology is used as a basis for awarding need-based institutional aid.

FRESHMAN FINANCIAL AID (Fall 2003) 374 applied for aid; of those 100% were deemed to have need. 100% of freshmen with need received aid; of those 3% had need fully met. *Average percent of need met:* 32% (excluding resources awarded to replace EFC). *Average financial aid package:* $5220 (excluding resources awarded to replace EFC). 29% of all full-time freshmen had no need and received non-need-based gift aid.

UNDERGRADUATE FINANCIAL AID (Fall 2003) 1,222 applied for aid; of those 100% were deemed to have need. 100% of undergraduates with need received aid; of those 8% had need fully met. *Average percent of need met:* 38% (excluding resources awarded to replace EFC). *Average financial aid package:* $5752 (excluding resources awarded to replace EFC). 21% of all full-time undergraduates had no need and received non-need-based gift aid.

GIFT AID (NEED-BASED) *Total amount:* $4,867,506 (99% federal, 1% state). *Receiving aid:* Freshmen: 46% (292); All full-time undergraduates: 45% (966). *Average award:* Freshmen: $3171; Undergraduates: $2997. *Scholarships, grants, and awards:* Federal Pell, FSEOG, state, college/university gift aid from institutional funds, Georgia HOPE Scholarships.

GIFT AID (NON-NEED-BASED) *Total amount:* $2,783,897 (98% state, 1% institutional, 1% external sources). *Receiving aid:* Freshmen: 37% (235); Undergraduates: 24% (530). *Average Award:* Freshmen: $1800; Undergraduates: $1758. *Tuition waivers:* Full or partial for senior citizens.

LOANS *Student loans:* $7,321,489 (53% need-based, 47% non-need-based). 13% of past graduating class borrowed through all loan programs. *Average indebtedness per student:* $16,519. *Average need-based loan:* Freshmen: $2274; Undergraduates: $2777. *Parent loans:* $46,685 (100% non-need-based). *Programs:* FFEL (Subsidized and Unsubsidized Stafford, PLUS), state.

WORK-STUDY *Federal work-study:* Total amount: $179,810; 106 jobs available. *State or other work-study/employment:* Part-time jobs available.

APPLYING FOR FINANCIAL AID *Required financial aid forms:* FAFSA, state aid form. *Financial aid deadline (priority):* 4/1. *Notification date:* Continuous beginning 4/15.

CONTACT Office of Financial Aid, Macon State College, 100 College Station Drive, Macon, GA 31206, 478-471-2717 or toll-free 800-272-7619 Ext. 2800. *Fax:* 478-471-2790. *E-mail:* fainfo@mail.maconstate.edu.

MADONNA UNIVERSITY
Livonia, MI

CONTACT Financial Aid Secretary, Madonna University, 36600 Schoolcraft Road, Livonia, MI 48150-1173, 734-432-5663 or toll-free 800-852-4951.

MAGDALEN COLLEGE
Warner, NH

Tuition & fees: $9000	Average undergraduate aid package: $9433

ABOUT THE INSTITUTION Independent Roman Catholic, coed. Awards: associate and bachelor's degrees. 1 undergraduate major. Total enrollment: 65. Undergraduates: 65. Freshmen: 21. Institutional methodology is used as a basis for awarding need-based institutional aid.

UNDERGRADUATE EXPENSES for 2005–06 *Application fee:* $35. *Comprehensive fee:* $15,000 includes full-time tuition ($9000) and room and board ($6000).

FRESHMAN FINANCIAL AID (Fall 2003) 19 applied for aid; of those 100% were deemed to have need. 100% of freshmen with need received aid; of those 74% had need fully met. *Average percent of need met:* 100% (excluding resources awarded to replace EFC). *Average financial aid package:* $9208 (excluding resources awarded to replace EFC).

UNDERGRADUATE FINANCIAL AID (Fall 2003) 52 applied for aid; of those 100% were deemed to have need. 100% of undergraduates with need received aid; of those 50% had need fully met. *Average percent of need met:* 100% (excluding resources awarded to replace EFC). *Average financial aid package:* $9433 (excluding resources awarded to replace EFC).

GIFT AID (NEED-BASED) *Total amount:* $108,000 (99% institutional, 1% external sources). *Receiving aid:* Freshmen: 73% (19); All full-time undergraduates: 73% (52). *Average award:* Freshmen: $2110; Undergraduates: $2335. *Scholarships, grants, and awards:* private, college/university gift aid from institutional funds.

GIFT AID (NON-NEED-BASED) *Tuition waivers:* Full or partial for employees or children of employees.

LOANS *Student loans:* $164,000 (100% need-based). 60% of past graduating class borrowed through all loan programs. *Average indebtedness per student:* $11,215. *Average need-based loan:* Freshmen: $1650; Undergraduates: $4013. *Programs:* college/university, alternative loans.

WORK-STUDY *State or other work-study/employment:* Total amount: $14,800 (100% need-based). 11 part-time jobs averaging $1345.

APPLYING FOR FINANCIAL AID *Required financial aid form:* institution's own form. *Financial aid deadline:* Continuous. *Notification date:* 7/1. Students must reply within 4 weeks of notification.

CONTACT Gail Crowdes, Assistant to Executive Vice President, Magdalen College, 511 Kearsarge Mountain Road, Warner, NH 03278, 603-456-2656 or toll-free 877-498-1723 (out-of-state). *Fax:* 603-456-2660. *E-mail:* gcrowdes@magdalen.edu.

MAGNOLIA BIBLE COLLEGE
Kosciusko, MS

Tuition & fees: $6090	Average undergraduate aid package: $7543

ABOUT THE INSTITUTION Independent religious, coed, primarily men. Awards: bachelor's degrees. 1 undergraduate major. Total enrollment: 41. Undergraduates: 41. Freshmen: 1. Federal methodology is used as a basis for awarding need-based institutional aid.

UNDERGRADUATE EXPENSES for 2004–05 *Tuition:* full-time $6000; part-time $200 per semester hour. *Required fees:* full-time $90; $45 per term part-time. Room and board charges vary according to housing facility. *Payment plan:* Deferred payment.

GIFT AID (NEED-BASED) *Total amount:* $91,684 (57% federal, 5% state, 8% institutional, 30% external sources). *Receiving aid:* Freshmen: 100% (1); All full-time undergraduates: 52% (12). *Average award:* Freshmen: $6086; Undergraduates: $6811. *Scholarships, grants, and awards:* Federal Pell, FSEOG, state, college/university gift aid from institutional funds.

GIFT AID (NON-NEED-BASED) *Total amount:* $26,935 (15% state, 85% institutional). *Average Award:* Undergraduates: $2578. *Scholarships, grants, and awards by category:* Academic Interests/Achievement: 17 awards ($30,083 total): general academic interests/achievements, religion/biblical studies. *Special Characteristics:* 4 awards ($4790 total): children of faculty/staff, general special characteristics, spouses of current students. *Tuition waivers:* Full or partial for employees or children of employees.

LOANS *Student loans:* $6288 (90% need-based, 10% non-need-based). *Programs:* FFEL (Subsidized and Unsubsidized Stafford, PLUS).

APPLYING FOR FINANCIAL AID *Required financial aid form:* FAFSA. *Financial aid deadline (priority):* 8/1. *Notification date:* Continuous beginning 4/1. Students must reply within 4 weeks of notification.

CONTACT Allen Coker, Financial Aid Director, Magnolia Bible College, PO Box 1109, Kosciusko, MS 39090-1109, 662-289-2896 or toll-free 800-748-8655 (in-state). *Fax:* 662-289-1850. *E-mail:* acoker@magnolia.edu.

MAHARISHI UNIVERSITY OF MANAGEMENT
Fairfield, IA

Tuition & fees: $24,430	Average undergraduate aid package: N/A

ABOUT THE INSTITUTION Independent, coed. Awards: bachelor's, master's, and doctoral degrees and post-bachelor's certificates. 10 undergraduate majors. Total enrollment: 688. Undergraduates: 226. Freshmen: 30. Federal methodology is used as a basis for awarding need-based institutional aid.

UNDERGRADUATE EXPENSES for 2004–05 *Application fee:* $25. *One-time required fee:* $2500. *Comprehensive fee:* $30,430 includes full-time tuition ($24,000), mandatory fees ($430), and room and board ($6000). *College room only:* $2800. Full-time tuition and fees vary according to program. Room and board charges vary according to housing facility. *Part-time tuition:* $350 per unit. Part-time tuition and fees vary according to course load and program. *Payment plan:* Installment.

FRESHMAN FINANCIAL AID (Fall 2004, est.) 25 applied for aid; of those 96% were deemed to have need. 100% of freshmen with need received aid; of those 29% had need fully met. *Average percent of need met:* 83% (excluding resources awarded to replace EFC). 7% of all full-time freshmen had no need and received non-need-based gift aid.

UNDERGRADUATE FINANCIAL AID (Fall 2004, est.) 204 applied for aid; of those 100% were deemed to have need. 100% of undergraduates with need received aid; of those 27% had need fully met. *Average percent of need met:* 84% (excluding resources awarded to replace EFC). 3% of all full-time undergraduates had no need and received non-need-based gift aid.

GIFT AID (NEED-BASED) *Total amount:* $2,577,673 (21% federal, 7% state, 72% institutional). *Receiving aid:* Freshmen: 86% (24); All full-time undergraduates: 95% (203). *Scholarships, grants, and awards:* Federal Pell, FSEOG, state, private, college/university gift aid from institutional funds.

GIFT AID (NON-NEED-BASED) *Total amount:* $98,235 (100% institutional). *Average Award:* Freshmen: $1500; *Undergraduates:* $2561. *Scholarships, grants, and awards by category:* Academic Interests/Achievement: 9 awards ($62,512 total): general academic interests/achievements. *Creative Arts/Performance:* 5 awards ($5350 total): creative writing, music. *Special Characteristics:* 40 awards ($480,424 total): children of faculty/staff, ethnic background, veterans, veterans' children. *Tuition waivers:* Full or partial for employees or children of employees.

LOANS *Student loans:* $1,283,106 (85% need-based, 15% non-need-based). 82% of past graduating class borrowed through all loan programs. *Average indebtedness per student:* $22,133. *Parent loans:* $6800 (100% non-need-based). *Programs:* FFEL (Subsidized and Unsubsidized Stafford, PLUS), Perkins, college/university, alternative loans.

WORK-STUDY *Federal work-study:* Total amount: $129,290; 83 jobs averaging $1558. *State or other work-study/employment:* Total amount: $62,722 (100% need-based). 26 part-time jobs averaging $2412.

APPLYING FOR FINANCIAL AID *Required financial aid form:* FAFSA. *Financial aid deadline (priority):* 4/15. *Notification date:* Continuous. Students must reply by 5/30 or within 4 weeks of notification.

CONTACT Mr. Peter Lee, Associate Director of Financial Aid, Maharishi University of Management, 1000 North 4th Street, DB 1127, Fairfield, IA 52557-1127, 641-472-1156 or toll-free 800-369-6480. *Fax:* 641-472-1133. *E-mail:* finaid@mum.edu.

MAINE COLLEGE OF ART
Portland, ME

Tuition & fees: $22,443	Average undergraduate aid package: $13,791

ABOUT THE INSTITUTION Independent, coed. Awards: bachelor's and master's degrees. 9 undergraduate majors. Total enrollment: 465. Undergraduates: 431. Freshmen: 98. Federal methodology is used as a basis for awarding need-based institutional aid.

UNDERGRADUATE EXPENSES for 2004–05 *Application fee:* $40. *Comprehensive fee:* $30,849 includes full-time tuition ($21,850), mandatory fees ($593), and room and board ($8406). *College room only:* $5116. Full-time tuition and fees vary according to course load. Room and board charges vary according to board plan and housing facility. *Part-time tuition:* $910 per credit hour. Part-time tuition and fees vary according to course load. *Payment plan:* Installment.

FRESHMAN FINANCIAL AID (Fall 2004, est.) 93 applied for aid; of those 94% were deemed to have need. 100% of freshmen with need received aid; of those

7% had need fully met. *Average percent of need met:* 56% (excluding resources awarded to replace EFC). *Average financial aid package:* $13,856 (excluding resources awarded to replace EFC). 19% of all full-time freshmen had no need and received non-need-based gift aid.

UNDERGRADUATE FINANCIAL AID (Fall 2004, est.) 352 applied for aid; of those 94% were deemed to have need. 100% of undergraduates with need received aid; of those 9% had need fully met. *Average percent of need met:* 60% (excluding resources awarded to replace EFC). *Average financial aid package:* $13,791 (excluding resources awarded to replace EFC). 19% of all full-time undergraduates had no need and received non-need-based gift aid.

GIFT AID (NEED-BASED) *Total amount:* $3,227,401 (17% federal, 5% state, 75% institutional, 3% external sources). *Receiving aid:* Freshmen: 80% (87); All full-time undergraduates: 80% (328). *Average award:* Freshmen: $10,700; Undergraduates: $9492. *Scholarships, grants, and awards:* Federal Pell, FSEOG, state, private, college/university gift aid from institutional funds.

GIFT AID (NON-NEED-BASED) *Total amount:* $438,026 (96% institutional, 4% external sources). *Receiving aid:* Freshmen: 5% (5); Undergraduates: 4% (16). *Average Award:* Freshmen: $5571; *Undergraduates:* $6696. *Scholarships, grants, and awards by category:* Creative Arts/Performance: 419 awards ($2,015,271 total): art/fine arts. *Special Characteristics:* 2 awards ($43,700 total): children of faculty/staff. *Tuition waivers:* Full or partial for employees or children of employees.

LOANS *Student loans:* $3,013,958 (81% need-based, 19% non-need-based). 80% of past graduating class borrowed through all loan programs. *Average indebtedness per student:* $25,743. *Average need-based loan:* Freshmen: $3402; Undergraduates: $4378. *Parent loans:* $831,345 (62% need-based, 38% non-need-based). *Programs:* FFEL (Subsidized and Unsubsidized Stafford, PLUS), Perkins, alternative loans.

WORK-STUDY *Federal work-study:* Total amount: $155,174; 69 jobs averaging $2249.

APPLYING FOR FINANCIAL AID *Required financial aid form:* FAFSA. *Financial aid deadline (priority):* 3/1. *Notification date:* Continuous beginning 3/15. Students must reply within 2 weeks of notification.

CONTACT Michelle A. Leclerc, Director of Financial Aid, Maine College of Art, 97 Spring Street, Portland, ME 04101-3987, 207-775-3052 or toll-free 800-639-4808. *Fax:* 207-772-5069. *E-mail:* mleclerc@meca.edu.

MAINE MARITIME ACADEMY
Castine, ME

Tuition & fees (ME res): $7045	Average undergraduate aid package: $9479

ABOUT THE INSTITUTION State-supported, coed, primarily men. Awards: associate, bachelor's, and master's degrees. 12 undergraduate majors. Total enrollment: 861. Undergraduates: 846. Freshmen: 241. Federal methodology is used as a basis for awarding need-based institutional aid.

UNDERGRADUATE EXPENSES for 2004–05 *Application fee:* $15. *Tuition, state resident:* full-time $5960; part-time $200 per credit hour. *Tuition, nonresident:* full-time $11,700; part-time $380 per credit hour. Full-time tuition and fees vary according to program. Part-time tuition and fees vary according to program. *College room and board:* $6400; *room only:* $2300. Room and board charges vary according to board plan. New England Regional annual tuition cost: $8,940. *Payment plan:* Installment.

GIFT AID (NEED-BASED) *Total amount:* $1,890,598 (43% federal, 11% state, 35% institutional, 11% external sources). *Receiving aid:* Freshmen: 69% (145); All full-time undergraduates: 60% (440). *Average award:* Freshmen: $6099; Undergraduates: $5196. *Scholarships, grants, and awards:* Federal Pell, FSEOG, state, private, college/university gift aid from institutional funds.

GIFT AID (NON-NEED-BASED) *Total amount:* $205,186 (61% federal, 2% state, 24% institutional, 13% external sources). *Receiving aid:* Freshmen: 3% (6); Undergraduates: 2% (16). *Average Award:* Freshmen: $8400; *Undergraduates:* $10,134. *Scholarships, grants, and awards by category:* Academic Interests/Achievement: 72 awards ($180,000 total): biological sciences, business, engineering/technologies, general academic interests/achievements. *Special Characteristics:* 10 awards ($49,150 total): children of faculty/staff. *ROTC:* Army, Naval.

LOANS *Student loans:* $3,907,213 (69% need-based, 31% non-need-based). 60% of past graduating class borrowed through all loan programs. *Average indebtedness per student:* $25,866. *Average need-based loan:* Freshmen: $4828; Undergraduates: $5137. *Parent loans:* $645,991 (35% need-based, 65% non-need-based). *Programs:* FFEL (Subsidized and Unsubsidized Stafford, PLUS), Perkins, college/university, alternative loans.

APPLYING FOR FINANCIAL AID *Required financial aid form:* FAFSA. *Financial aid deadline (priority):* 4/15. *Notification date:* Continuous. Students must reply within 3 weeks of notification.
CONTACT Ms. Holly Bayle, Assistant Director of Financial Aid, Maine Maritime Academy, Pleasant Street, Castine, ME 04420, 207-326-2205 or toll-free 800-464-6565 (in-state), 800-227-8465 (out-of-state). *Fax:* 207-326-2515.

MALONE COLLEGE
Canton, OH

Tuition & fees: $15,880	Average undergraduate aid package: $11,799

ABOUT THE INSTITUTION Independent religious, coed. Awards: bachelor's and master's degrees and post-bachelor's certificates. 42 undergraduate majors. Total enrollment: 2,250. Undergraduates: 1,936. Freshmen: 403. Federal methodology is used as a basis for awarding need-based institutional aid.
UNDERGRADUATE EXPENSES for 2004–05 *Application fee:* $20. *Comprehensive fee:* $22,000 includes full-time tuition ($15,630), mandatory fees ($250), and room and board ($6120). *College room only:* $3250. Room and board charges vary according to board plan. *Part-time tuition:* $320 per semester hour. *Part-time fees:* $62.50 per term. Part-time tuition and fees vary according to course load. *Payment plan:* Installment.
FRESHMAN FINANCIAL AID (Fall 2004, est.) 375 applied for aid; of those 90% were deemed to have need. 100% of freshmen with need received aid; of those 18% had need fully met. *Average percent of need met:* 74% (excluding resources awarded to replace EFC). *Average financial aid package:* $12,626 (excluding resources awarded to replace EFC). 12% of all full-time freshmen had no need and received non-need-based gift aid.
UNDERGRADUATE FINANCIAL AID (Fall 2004, est.) 1,389 applied for aid; of those 90% were deemed to have need. 100% of undergraduates with need received aid; of those 19% had need fully met. *Average percent of need met:* 74% (excluding resources awarded to replace EFC). *Average financial aid package:* $11,799 (excluding resources awarded to replace EFC). 9% of all full-time undergraduates had no need and received non-need-based gift aid.
GIFT AID (NEED-BASED) *Total amount:* $8,742,600 (18% federal, 24% state, 51% institutional, 7% external sources). *Receiving aid:* Freshmen: 84% (337); All full-time undergraduates: 74% (1,245). *Average award:* Freshmen: $9187; Undergraduates: $8038. *Scholarships, grants, and awards:* Federal Pell, FSEOG, state, private, college/university gift aid from institutional funds.
GIFT AID (NON-NEED-BASED) *Total amount:* $1,273,868 (24% state, 68% institutional, 8% external sources). *Receiving aid:* Freshmen: 83% (333); Undergraduates: 71% (1,210). *Average Award:* Freshmen: $4409; Undergraduates: $4364. *Scholarships, grants, and awards by category: Academic Interests/Achievement:* 788 awards ($3,285,411 total): biological sciences, business, communication, computer science, education, English, foreign languages, general academic interests/achievements, health fields, humanities, international studies, mathematics, physical sciences, premedicine, religion/biblical studies, social sciences. *Creative Arts/Performance:* 79 awards ($79,400 total): debating, journalism/publications, music, theater/drama. *Special Achievements/Activities:* 163 awards ($247,308 total): community service, junior miss, leadership, religious involvement. *Special Characteristics:* 256 awards ($701,576 total): children and siblings of alumni, children of faculty/staff, international students, parents of current students, relatives of clergy, religious affiliation, siblings of current students, spouses of current students. *Tuition waivers:* Full or partial for employees or children of employees, senior citizens. *ROTC:* Army cooperative, Air Force cooperative.
LOANS *Student loans:* $7,078,344 (90% need-based, 10% non-need-based). 71% of past graduating class borrowed through all loan programs. *Average indebtedness per student:* $16,262. *Average need-based loan:* Freshmen: $2992; Undergraduates: $3610. *Parent loans:* $2,259,033 (91% need-based, 9% non-need-based). *Programs:* FFEL (Subsidized and Unsubsidized Stafford, PLUS), Perkins, state, college/university, alternative loans.
WORK-STUDY *Federal work-study:* Total amount: $562,700; 294 jobs averaging $1914. *State or other work-study/employment:* Total amount: $167,233 (73% need-based, 27% non-need-based). 71 part-time jobs averaging $2355.
ATHLETIC AWARDS *Total amount:* $1,474,619 (74% need-based, 26% non-need-based).
APPLYING FOR FINANCIAL AID *Required financial aid form:* FAFSA. *Financial aid deadline:* 7/31 (priority: 3/1). *Notification date:* Continuous. Students must reply within 2 weeks of notification.
CONTACT Mr. Michael Bole, Director of Financial Aid, Malone College, 515 25th Street, NW, Canton, OH 44709-3897, 330-471-8162 or toll-free 800-521-1146. *Fax:* 330-471-8478. *E-mail:* mbole@malone.edu.

MANCHESTER COLLEGE
North Manchester, IN

Tuition & fees: $19,360	Average undergraduate aid package: $17,269

ABOUT THE INSTITUTION Independent religious, coed. Awards: associate, bachelor's, and master's degrees. 59 undergraduate majors. Total enrollment: 1,068. Undergraduates: 1,056. Freshmen: 278. Federal methodology is used as a basis for awarding need-based institutional aid.
UNDERGRADUATE EXPENSES for 2005–06 *Application fee:* $20. *Comprehensive fee:* $26,270 includes full-time tuition ($18,750), mandatory fees ($610), and room and board ($6910). *College room only:* $4250. Room and board charges vary according to board plan and housing facility. *Payment plan:* Installment.
GIFT AID (NEED-BASED) *Total amount:* $10,652,587 (9% federal, 24% state, 64% institutional, 3% external sources). *Receiving aid:* Freshmen: 84% (233); All full-time undergraduates: 79% (793). *Average award:* Freshmen: $14,230; Undergraduates: $13,395. *Scholarships, grants, and awards:* Federal Pell, FSEOG, state, private, college/university gift aid from institutional funds.
GIFT AID (NON-NEED-BASED) *Total amount:* $1,903,843 (2% state, 95% institutional, 3% external sources). *Receiving aid:* Freshmen: 70% (194); Undergraduates: 56% (557). *Average Award:* Freshmen: $8250; Undergraduates: $7416. *Scholarships, grants, and awards by category: Academic Interests/Achievement:* business, English, foreign languages, general academic interests/achievements, humanities. *Special Characteristics:* children and siblings of alumni, ethnic background, international students, members of minority groups, previous college experience, religious affiliation. *Tuition waivers:* Full or partial for employees or children of employees.
LOANS *Student loans:* $2,693,208 (95% need-based, 5% non-need-based). 54% of past graduating class borrowed through all loan programs. *Average indebtedness per student:* $14,180. *Average need-based loan:* Freshmen: $1886; Undergraduates: $3661. *Parent loans:* $1,278,908 (89% need-based, 11% non-need-based). *Programs:* FFEL (Subsidized and Unsubsidized Stafford, PLUS), Perkins.
APPLYING FOR FINANCIAL AID *Required financial aid form:* FAFSA. *Financial aid deadline:* Continuous. *Notification date:* Continuous beginning 2/15.
CONTACT Ms. Gina Voelz, Director of Financial Aid, Manchester College, 604 East College Avenue, North Manchester, IN 46962-1225, 260-982-5066 or toll-free 800-852-3648. *Fax:* 260-982-6868. *E-mail:* glvoelz@manchester.edu.

MANHATTAN CHRISTIAN COLLEGE
Manhattan, KS

Tuition & fees: $9638	Average undergraduate aid package: $9695

ABOUT THE INSTITUTION Independent religious, coed. Awards: associate and bachelor's degrees. 9 undergraduate majors. Total enrollment: 331. Undergraduates: 331. Freshmen: 83. Federal methodology is used as a basis for awarding need-based institutional aid.
UNDERGRADUATE EXPENSES for 2005–06 *Application fee:* $25. *Comprehensive fee:* $15,228 includes full-time tuition ($9444), mandatory fees ($194), and room and board ($5590). Room and board charges vary according to board plan. *Part-time tuition:* $389 per hour. Part-time tuition and fees vary according to course load. *Payment plan:* Deferred payment.
FRESHMAN FINANCIAL AID (Fall 2003) 70 applied for aid; of those 83% were deemed to have need. 100% of freshmen with need received aid; of those 17% had need fully met. *Average percent of need met:* 75% (excluding resources awarded to replace EFC). *Average financial aid package:* $9334 (excluding resources awarded to replace EFC). 20% of all full-time freshmen had no need and received non-need-based gift aid.
UNDERGRADUATE FINANCIAL AID (Fall 2003) 256 applied for aid; of those 84% were deemed to have need. 100% of undergraduates with need received aid; of those 14% had need fully met. *Average percent of need met:* 71% (excluding resources awarded to replace EFC). *Average financial aid package:* $9695 (excluding resources awarded to replace EFC). 18% of all full-time undergraduates had no need and received non-need-based gift aid.
GIFT AID (NEED-BASED) *Total amount:* $882,466 (40% federal, 10% state, 50% institutional). *Receiving aid:* Freshmen: 76% (58); All full-time undergraduates: 53% (190). *Average award:* Freshmen: $6243; Undergraduates: $5277. *Scholarships, grants, and awards:* Federal Pell, FSEOG, state, private, college/university gift aid from institutional funds.
GIFT AID (NON-NEED-BASED) *Total amount:* $470,210 (1% state, 40% institutional, 59% external sources). *Receiving aid:* Freshmen: 76% (58);

Undergraduates: 43% (153). *Average Award:* Freshmen: $4260; *Undergraduates:* $3761. *Scholarships, grants, and awards by category:* Academic Interests/ Achievement: 186 awards ($439,063 total): general academic interests/ achievements, religion/biblical studies. *Creative Arts/Performance:* 8 awards ($4250 total): music. *Special Achievements/Activities:* 13 awards ($69,889 total): leadership. *Special Characteristics:* 8 awards ($30,068 total): children of faculty/staff. *Tuition waivers:* Full or partial for employees or children of employees, senior citizens. *ROTC:* Army cooperative, Air Force cooperative.

LOANS *Student loans:* $1,053,675 (69% need-based, 31% non-need-based). 75% of past graduating class borrowed through all loan programs. *Average indebtedness per student:* $12,046. *Average need-based loan:* Freshmen: $3325; Undergraduates: $4323. *Parent loans:* $111,776 (100% non-need-based). *Programs:* FFEL (Subsidized and Unsubsidized Stafford, PLUS), Perkins.

WORK-STUDY *Federal work-study:* Total amount: $74,825; 74 jobs averaging $1011.

APPLYING FOR FINANCIAL AID *Notification date:* Continuous beginning 3/5. Students must reply within 2 weeks of notification.

CONTACT Mrs. Margaret Carlisle, Director of Financial Aid, Manhattan Christian College, 1415 Anderson Avenue, Manhattan, KS 66502-4081, 785-539-3571 or toll-free 877-246-4622. *E-mail:* carlisle@mccks.edu.

MANHATTAN COLLEGE
Riverdale, NY

Tuition & fees: $20,600	Average undergraduate aid package: $16,455

ABOUT THE INSTITUTION Independent religious, coed. Awards: bachelor's and master's degrees and post-master's certificates. 41 undergraduate majors. Total enrollment: 3,301. Undergraduates: 2,905. Freshmen: 656. Both federal and institutional methodology are used as a basis for awarding need-based institutional aid.

UNDERGRADUATE EXPENSES for 2005–06 *Application fee:* $40. *Comprehensive fee:* $29,625 includes full-time tuition ($19,400), mandatory fees ($1200), and room and board ($9025). Full-time tuition and fees vary according to program. Room and board charges vary according to board plan. *Part-time tuition:* $550 per credit. *Payment plan:* Installment.

FRESHMAN FINANCIAL AID (Fall 2003) 555 applied for aid; of those 78% were deemed to have need. 100% of freshmen with need received aid; of those 7% had need fully met. *Average percent of need met:* 86% (excluding resources awarded to replace EFC). *Average financial aid package:* $13,099 (excluding resources awarded to replace EFC). 17% of all full-time freshmen had no need and received non-need-based gift aid.

UNDERGRADUATE FINANCIAL AID (Fall 2003) 2,170 applied for aid; of those 82% were deemed to have need. 100% of undergraduates with need received aid; of those 3% had need fully met. *Average percent of need met:* 71% (excluding resources awarded to replace EFC). *Average financial aid package:* $16,455 (excluding resources awarded to replace EFC). 14% of all full-time undergraduates had no need and received non-need-based gift aid.

GIFT AID (NEED-BASED) *Total amount:* $15,928,254 (15% federal, 16% state, 66% institutional, 3% external sources). *Receiving aid:* Freshmen: 57% (377); All full-time undergraduates: 60% (1,663). *Average award:* Freshmen: $10,332; Undergraduates: $9561. *Scholarships, grants, and awards:* Federal Pell, FSEOG, state, private, college/university gift aid from institutional funds.

GIFT AID (NON-NEED-BASED) *Total amount:* $2,919,127 (3% state, 97% institutional). *Receiving aid:* Freshmen: 25% (162); Undergraduates: 26% (718). *Average Award:* Freshmen: $7309; Undergraduates: $7082. *Scholarships, grants, and awards by category:* Academic Interests/Achievement: 600 awards ($1,600,000 total): biological sciences, business, computer science, foreign languages, general academic interests/achievements, mathematics, military science. *Creative Arts/Performance:* 30 awards ($25,000 total): music. *Special Achievements/Activities:* 300 awards ($1,200,000 total): community service, leadership. *Special Characteristics:* 35 awards ($580,000 total): children of faculty/staff. *Tuition waivers:* Full or partial for employees or children of employees. *ROTC:* Army cooperative, Air Force.

LOANS *Student loans:* $12,636,783 (44% need-based, 56% non-need-based). 79% of past graduating class borrowed through all loan programs. *Average indebtedness per student:* $15,715. *Average need-based loan:* Freshmen: $2317; Undergraduates: $3892. *Parent loans:* $5,706,465 (100% non-need-based). *Programs:* Federal Direct (Subsidized and Unsubsidized Stafford, PLUS), FFEL (Subsidized and Unsubsidized Stafford, PLUS), Perkins.

WORK-STUDY *Federal work-study:* Total amount: $576,021; 520 jobs averaging $1240. *State or other work-study/employment:* Total amount: $200,000 (100% non-need-based). 249 part-time jobs averaging $1506.

ATHLETIC AWARDS *Total amount:* $3,964,002 (29% need-based, 71% non-need-based).

APPLYING FOR FINANCIAL AID *Required financial aid forms:* FAFSA, institution's own form, state aid form. *Financial aid deadline (priority):* 3/1. *Notification date:* 4/1. Students must reply by 5/1.

CONTACT Mr. Edward Keough, Director of Student Financial Services, Manhattan College, 4513 Manhattan College Parkway, Riverdale, NY 10471, 718-862-7100 or toll-free 800-622-9235 (in-state). *Fax:* 718-862-8027. *E-mail:* finaid@manhattan.edu.

MANHATTAN SCHOOL OF MUSIC
New York, NY

Tuition & fees: $28,285	Average undergraduate aid package: $12,710

ABOUT THE INSTITUTION Independent, coed. Awards: bachelor's, master's, and doctoral degrees and post-bachelor's and post-master's certificates. 6 undergraduate majors. Total enrollment: 875. Undergraduates: 408. Freshmen: 103. Both federal and institutional methodology are used as a basis for awarding need-based institutional aid.

UNDERGRADUATE EXPENSES for 2005–06 *Application fee:* $100. *Comprehensive fee:* $40,785 includes full-time tuition ($26,000), mandatory fees ($2285), and room and board ($12,500). *College room only:* $8050. Full-time tuition and fees vary according to course load. Room and board charges vary according to board plan. *Part-time tuition:* $1100 per credit. Part-time tuition and fees vary according to course load. *Payment plans:* Installment, deferred payment.

FRESHMAN FINANCIAL AID (Fall 2003) 49 applied for aid; of those 71% were deemed to have need. 94% of freshmen with need received aid; of those 9% had need fully met. *Average percent of need met:* 51% (excluding resources awarded to replace EFC). *Average financial aid package:* $15,423 (excluding resources awarded to replace EFC). 31% of all full-time freshmen had no need and received non-need-based gift aid.

UNDERGRADUATE FINANCIAL AID (Fall 2003) 252 applied for aid; of those 100% were deemed to have need. 100% of undergraduates with need received aid; of those 5% had need fully met. *Average percent of need met:* 43% (excluding resources awarded to replace EFC). *Average financial aid package:* $12,710 (excluding resources awarded to replace EFC). 21% of all full-time undergraduates had no need and received non-need-based gift aid.

GIFT AID (NEED-BASED) *Total amount:* $2,315,795 (15% federal, 6% state, 74% institutional, 5% external sources). *Receiving aid:* Freshmen: 30% (31); All full-time undergraduates: 39% (164). *Average award:* Freshmen: $13,183; Undergraduates: $11,115. *Scholarships, grants, and awards:* Federal Pell, FSEOG, state, private, college/university gift aid from institutional funds.

GIFT AID (NON-NEED-BASED) *Total amount:* $114,127 (84% institutional, 16% external sources). *Receiving aid:* Freshmen: 2% (2); Undergraduates: 5% (21). *Average Award:* Freshmen: $12,593; Undergraduates: $13,803. *Scholarships, grants, and awards by category:* Creative Arts/Performance: 35 awards ($95,750 total): music. *Tuition waivers:* Full or partial for employees or children of employees.

LOANS *Student loans:* $1,572,868 (90% need-based, 10% non-need-based). 58% of past graduating class borrowed through all loan programs. *Average indebtedness per student:* $14,100. *Average need-based loan:* Freshmen: $3307; Undergraduates: $3997. *Parent loans:* $2,194,540 (79% need-based, 21% non-need-based). *Programs:* FFEL (Subsidized and Unsubsidized Stafford, PLUS), Perkins.

WORK-STUDY *Federal work-study:* Total amount: $80,975; 74 jobs averaging $1094.

APPLYING FOR FINANCIAL AID *Required financial aid forms:* FAFSA, institution's own form, CSS Financial Aid PROFILE, verification worksheet. *Financial aid deadline (priority):* 3/1. *Notification date:* 4/1. Students must reply by 5/1 or within 2 weeks of notification.

CONTACT Ms. Amy Anderson, Assistant Dean of Admission and Financial Aid, Manhattan School of Music, 120 Claremont Avenue, New York, NY 10027-4698, 212-749-2802 Ext. 4501. *Fax:* 212-749-3025. *E-mail:* aanderson@msmnyc.edu.

MANHATTANVILLE COLLEGE
Purchase, NY

Tuition & fees: $24,570	Average undergraduate aid package: $20,888

ABOUT THE INSTITUTION Independent, coed. Awards: bachelor's and master's degrees. 42 undergraduate majors. Total enrollment: 2,608. Undergraduates: 1,719. Freshmen: 440. Federal methodology is used as a basis for awarding need-based institutional aid.

UNDERGRADUATE EXPENSES for 2004–05 *Application fee:* $50. *Comprehensive fee:* $34,700 includes full-time tuition ($23,620), mandatory fees ($950), and room and board ($10,130). *College room only:* $6020. Room and board charges vary according to board plan. *Part-time tuition:* $540 per credit. *Part-time fees:* $35 per term. Part-time tuition and fees vary according to program. *Payment plans:* Installment, deferred payment.

GIFT AID (NEED-BASED) *Total amount:* $9,526,372 (13% federal, 18% state, 69% institutional). *Receiving aid:* Freshmen: 63% (262); All full-time undergraduates: 61% (908). *Average award:* Freshmen: $10,043; Undergraduates: $9040. *Scholarships, grants, and awards:* Federal Pell, FSEOG, state, private, college/university gift aid from institutional funds.

GIFT AID (NON-NEED-BASED) *Total amount:* $14,280,357 (99% institutional, 1% external sources). *Receiving aid:* Freshmen: 58% (242); Undergraduates: 57% (858). *Average Award: Freshmen:* $8337; *Undergraduates:* $8001. *Scholarships, grants, and awards by category: Academic Interests/Achievement:* 1,364 awards ($14,096,905 total): general academic interests/achievements. *Creative Arts/Performance:* 62 awards ($545,563 total): art/fine arts. *Special Achievements/Activities:* 142 awards ($272,500 total): community service. *Tuition waivers:* Full or partial for employees or children of employees, senior citizens.

LOANS *Student loans:* $7,622,210 (47% need-based, 53% non-need-based). 74% of past graduating class borrowed through all loan programs. *Average indebtedness per student:* $22,966. *Average need-based loan:* Freshmen: $3108; Undergraduates: $4095. *Parent loans:* $3,077,752 (100% non-need-based). *Programs:* FFEL (Subsidized and Unsubsidized Stafford, PLUS), Perkins.

APPLYING FOR FINANCIAL AID *Required financial aid forms:* FAFSA, state aid form. *Financial aid deadline (priority):* 3/1. *Notification date:* Continuous. Students must reply by 5/1 or within 2 weeks of notification.

CONTACT Maria A. Barlaam, Director of Financial Aid, Manhattanville College, 2900 Purchase Street, Purchase, NY 10577-2132, 914-323-5357 or toll-free 800-328-4553. *Fax:* 914-323-5382. *E-mail:* barlaamm@mville.edu.

MANNES COLLEGE OF MUSIC, NEW SCHOOL UNIVERSITY
New York, NY

ABOUT THE INSTITUTION Independent, coed. Awards: bachelor's and master's degrees and post-bachelor's certificates. 7 undergraduate majors. Total enrollment: 623. Undergraduates: 446. Freshmen: 34.

GIFT AID (NEED-BASED) *Scholarships, grants, and awards:* Federal Pell, FSEOG, private, college/university gift aid from institutional funds.

GIFT AID (NON-NEED-BASED) *Scholarships, grants, and awards by category: Academic Interests/Achievement:* general academic interests/achievements. *Creative Arts/Performance:* music. *Special Achievements/Activities:* general special achievements/activities.

LOANS *Programs:* FFEL (Subsidized and Unsubsidized Stafford, PLUS), Perkins.

WORK-STUDY *Federal work-study:* Total amount: $22,000; 19 jobs averaging $1911.

APPLYING FOR FINANCIAL AID *Required financial aid forms:* FAFSA, state aid form.

CONTACT Financial Aid Counselor, Mannes College of Music, New School University, 150 West 85th Street, New York, NY 10024-4402, 212-580-0210 or toll-free 800-292-3040. *Fax:* 212-580-1738.

MANSFIELD UNIVERSITY OF PENNSYLVANIA
Mansfield, PA

CONTACT Ms. Darcie Stephens, Director of Financial Aid, Mansfield University of Pennsylvania, 109 South Hall, Mansfield, PA 16933, 570-662-4854 or toll-free 800-577-6826. *Fax:* 570-662-4136.

MAPLE SPRINGS BAPTIST BIBLE COLLEGE AND SEMINARY
Capitol Heights, MD

CONTACT Ms. Fannie G. Thompson, Director of Business Affairs, Maple Springs Baptist Bible College and Seminary, 4130 Belt Road, Capitol Heights, MD 20743, 301-736-3631. *Fax:* 301-735-6507.

MARANATHA BAPTIST BIBLE COLLEGE
Watertown, WI

Tuition & fees: $8120	Average undergraduate aid package: $6811

ABOUT THE INSTITUTION Independent Baptist, coed. Awards: associate, bachelor's, and master's degrees. 19 undergraduate majors. Total enrollment: 904. Undergraduates: 850. Freshmen: 246. Federal methodology is used as a basis for awarding need-based institutional aid.

UNDERGRADUATE EXPENSES for 2004–05 *Application fee:* $40. *Comprehensive fee:* $12,820 includes full-time tuition ($7360), mandatory fees ($760), and room and board ($4700). Full-time tuition and fees vary according to course level. *Part-time tuition:* $230 per semester hour. Part-time tuition and fees vary according to course level.

FRESHMAN FINANCIAL AID (Fall 2003) 211 applied for aid; of those 79% were deemed to have need. 97% of freshmen with need received aid; of those 1% had need fully met. *Average percent of need met:* 52% (excluding resources awarded to replace EFC). *Average financial aid package:* $6455 (excluding resources awarded to replace EFC). 3% of all full-time freshmen had no need and received non-need-based gift aid.

UNDERGRADUATE FINANCIAL AID (Fall 2003) 718 applied for aid; of those 96% were deemed to have need. 97% of undergraduates with need received aid; of those 1% had need fully met. *Average percent of need met:* 52% (excluding resources awarded to replace EFC). *Average financial aid package:* $6811 (excluding resources awarded to replace EFC). 2% of all full-time undergraduates had no need and received non-need-based gift aid.

GIFT AID (NEED-BASED) *Total amount:* $1,596,079 (63% federal, 14% state, 12% institutional, 11% external sources). *Receiving aid:* Freshmen: 45% (101); All full-time undergraduates: 53% (456). *Average award:* Freshmen: $965; Undergraduates: $938. *Scholarships, grants, and awards:* Federal Pell, FSEOG, state, private, college/university gift aid from institutional funds.

GIFT AID (NON-NEED-BASED) *Total amount:* $26,825 (33% state, 34% institutional, 33% external sources). *Receiving aid:* Freshmen: 4% (9); Undergraduates: 2% (16). *Average Award: Freshmen:* $416; *Undergraduates:* $580. *Scholarships, grants, and awards by category: Academic Interests/Achievement:* 67 awards ($61,403 total): business, general academic interests/achievements, religion/biblical studies. *Special Characteristics:* 107 awards ($125,518 total): children and siblings of alumni, children of educators, children of faculty/staff, relatives of clergy, spouses of current students. *Tuition waivers:* Full or partial for employees or children of employees. *ROTC:* Air Force.

LOANS *Student loans:* $1,939,248 (91% need-based, 9% non-need-based). 44% of past graduating class borrowed through all loan programs. *Average indebtedness per student:* $13,587. *Average need-based loan:* Freshmen: $2703; Undergraduates: $3169. *Parent loans:* $415,334 (67% need-based, 33% non-need-based). *Programs:* FFEL (Subsidized and Unsubsidized Stafford, PLUS), state, alternative loans.

WORK-STUDY *State or other work-study/employment:* Total amount: $1,020,480 (100% need-based). 343 part-time jobs averaging $2975.

APPLYING FOR FINANCIAL AID *Required financial aid form:* FAFSA. *Financial aid deadline (priority):* 3/1. *Notification date:* Continuous. Students must reply within 2 weeks of notification.

CONTACT Mr. Bruce Roth, Associate Director of Financial Aid, Maranatha Baptist Bible College, 745 West Main Street, Watertown, WI 53094, 920-206-2318 or toll-free 800-622-2947. *Fax:* 920-261-9109. *E-mail:* financialaid@mbbc.edu.

MARIAN COLLEGE
Indianapolis, IN

ABOUT THE INSTITUTION Independent Roman Catholic, coed. Awards: associate, bachelor's, and master's degrees. 36 undergraduate majors. Total enrollment: 1,685. Undergraduates: 1,666. Freshmen: 269.

GIFT AID (NEED-BASED) *Scholarships, grants, and awards:* Federal Pell, FSEOG, state, private, college/university gift aid from institutional funds.

GIFT AID (NON-NEED-BASED) *Scholarships, grants, and awards by category: Academic Interests/Achievement:* general academic interests/achievements. *Creative Arts/Performance:* applied art and design, art/fine arts, music, performing arts, theater/drama. *Special Achievements/Activities:* community service, religious involvement. *Special Characteristics:* adult students, children and siblings of alumni, children of faculty/staff, international students, members of minority groups, religious affiliation, siblings of current students, spouses of current students.

LOANS *Programs:* FFEL (Subsidized and Unsubsidized Stafford, PLUS), Perkins, college/university.

WORK-STUDY *Federal work-study:* Total amount: $150,000; 200 jobs averaging $1500. *State or other work-study/employment:* Total amount: $56,500 (12% need-based, 88% non-need-based). Part-time jobs available.

APPLYING FOR FINANCIAL AID *Required financial aid forms:* FAFSA, institution's own form.

CONTACT Mr. John E. Shelton, Assistant Dean of Financial Aid, Marian College, 3200 Cold Spring Road, Indianapolis, IN 46222-1997, 317-955-6040 or toll-free 800-772-7264 (in-state). *Fax:* 317-955-6424. *E-mail:* jshelton@marian.edu.

MARIAN COLLEGE OF FOND DU LAC
Fond du Lac, WI

Tuition & fees: $15,825	Average undergraduate aid package: $14,670

ABOUT THE INSTITUTION Independent Roman Catholic, coed. Awards: bachelor's and master's degrees. 50 undergraduate majors. Total enrollment: 2,918. Undergraduates: 1,999. Freshmen: 270. Federal methodology is used as a basis for awarding need-based institutional aid.

UNDERGRADUATE EXPENSES for 2004–05 *Application fee:* $20. *Comprehensive fee:* $21,065 includes full-time tuition ($15,500), mandatory fees ($325), and room and board ($5240). *College room only:* $2750. Full-time tuition and fees vary according to class time and program. Room and board charges vary according to board plan and housing facility. *Part-time tuition:* $270 per credit. *Part-time fees:* $80 per term. Part-time tuition and fees vary according to class time, course load, and program. *Payment plan:* Installment.

FRESHMAN FINANCIAL AID (Fall 2004, est.) 263 applied for aid; of those 89% were deemed to have need. 100% of freshmen with need received aid; of those 29% had need fully met. *Average percent of need met:* 87% (excluding resources awarded to replace EFC). *Average financial aid package:* $13,981 (excluding resources awarded to replace EFC). 9% of all full-time freshmen had no need and received non-need-based gift aid.

UNDERGRADUATE FINANCIAL AID (Fall 2004, est.) 1,218 applied for aid; of those 88% were deemed to have need. 100% of undergraduates with need received aid; of those 36% had need fully met. *Average percent of need met:* 87% (excluding resources awarded to replace EFC). *Average financial aid package:* $14,670 (excluding resources awarded to replace EFC). 10% of all full-time undergraduates had no need and received non-need-based gift aid.

GIFT AID (NEED-BASED) *Total amount:* $10,504,742 (30% federal, 16% state, 53% institutional, 1% external sources). *Receiving aid:* Freshmen: 86% (233); All full-time undergraduates: 77% (1,011). *Average award:* Freshmen: $9650; Undergraduates: $9439. *Scholarships, grants, and awards:* Federal Pell, FSEOG, state, private, college/university gift aid from institutional funds, endowed scholarships.

GIFT AID (NON-NEED-BASED) *Total amount:* $782,175 (4% state, 92% institutional, 4% external sources). *Receiving aid:* Freshmen: 81% (218); Undergraduates: 67% (883). *Average Award:* Freshmen: $4186; Undergraduates: $4451. *Scholarships, grants, and awards by category: Academic Interests/ Achievement:* 1,012 awards ($4,209,388 total): general academic interests/ achievements. *Creative Arts/Performance:* 34 awards ($64,700 total): music. *Special Characteristics:* 74 awards ($203,929 total): children of faculty/staff, children with a deceased or disabled parent, siblings of current students. *Tuition waivers:* Full or partial for employees or children of employees, senior citizens. *ROTC:* Army.

LOANS *Student loans:* $7,344,856 (89% need-based, 11% non-need-based). 85% of past graduating class borrowed through all loan programs. *Average indebtedness per student:* $20,000. *Average need-based loan:* Freshmen: $2875; Undergraduates: $4307. *Parent loans:* $932,481 (65% need-based, 35% non-need-based). *Programs:* FFEL (Subsidized and Unsubsidized Stafford, PLUS), Perkins, Federal Nursing.

WORK-STUDY *Federal work-study:* Total amount: $1,036,402; 567 jobs averaging $1828. *State or other work-study/employment:* Total amount: $286,412 (100% non-need-based). 250 part-time jobs averaging $1000.

APPLYING FOR FINANCIAL AID *Required financial aid forms:* FAFSA, institution's own form. *Financial aid deadline (priority):* 3/1. *Notification date:* Continuous. Students must reply within 4 weeks of notification.

CONTACT Ms. Debra E. McKinney, Director of Financial Aid, Marian College of Fond du Lac, 45 South National Avenue, Fond du Lac, WI 54935-4699, 920-923-7614 or toll-free 800-2-MARIAN Ext. 7652 (in-state). *Fax:* 920-923-8767. *E-mail:* dmckinney@mariancollege.edu.

MARIETTA COLLEGE
Marietta, OH

Tuition & fees: $21,730	Average undergraduate aid package: $19,488

ABOUT THE INSTITUTION Independent, coed. Awards: associate, bachelor's, and master's degrees. 40 undergraduate majors. Total enrollment: 1,480. Undergraduates: 1,351. Freshmen: 439. Federal methodology is used as a basis for awarding need-based institutional aid.

UNDERGRADUATE EXPENSES for 2004–05 *Application fee:* $25. *Comprehensive fee:* $27,916 includes full-time tuition ($21,170), mandatory fees ($560), and room and board ($6186). *College room only:* $3304. Room and board charges vary according to board plan. *Part-time tuition:* $705 per credit. Part-time tuition and fees vary according to class time. *Payment plan:* Installment.

GIFT AID (NEED-BASED) *Total amount:* $6,743,806 (11% federal, 7% state, 82% institutional). *Receiving aid:* Freshmen: 69% (301); All full-time undergraduates: 63% (797). *Average award:* Freshmen: $9025; Undergraduates: $7941. *Scholarships, grants, and awards:* Federal Pell, FSEOG, state, private, college/ university gift aid from institutional funds.

GIFT AID (NON-NEED-BASED) *Total amount:* $7,160,594 (10% state, 84% institutional, 6% external sources). *Receiving aid:* Freshmen: 51% (223); Undergraduates: 52% (657). *Average Award:* Freshmen: $8145; Undergraduates: $944. *Scholarships, grants, and awards by category: Academic Interests/ Achievement:* 410 awards ($5,061,516 total): general academic interests/ achievements. *Creative Arts/Performance:* 55 awards ($112,750 total): art/fine arts. *Special Achievements/Activities:* 15 awards ($51,000 total): general special achievements/activities. *Special Characteristics:* 74 awards ($295,500 total): children and siblings of alumni, members of minority groups, siblings of current students. *Tuition waivers:* Full or partial for employees or children of employees.

LOANS *Student loans:* $4,317,467 (75% need-based, 25% non-need-based). 75% of past graduating class borrowed through all loan programs. *Average indebtedness per student:* $17,643. *Average need-based loan:* Freshmen: $3334; Undergraduates: $4269. *Parent loans:* $1,822,924 (100% non-need-based). *Programs:* Federal Direct (Subsidized and Unsubsidized Stafford, PLUS).

APPLYING FOR FINANCIAL AID *Required financial aid form:* FAFSA. *Financial aid deadline (priority):* 3/1. *Notification date:* 3/15. Students must reply within 2 weeks of notification.

CONTACT Mr. Gary Craig, Dean of Enrollment, Marietta College, 215 Fifth Street, Marietta, OH 45750-4000, 740-376-4712 or toll-free 800-331-7896. *Fax:* 740-376-4990. *E-mail:* finaid@marietta.edu.

MARIST COLLEGE
Poughkeepsie, NY

Tuition & fees: $21,015	Average undergraduate aid package: $12,685

ABOUT THE INSTITUTION Independent, coed. Awards: bachelor's and master's degrees. 49 undergraduate majors. Total enrollment: 5,646. Undergraduates: 4,800. Freshmen: 955. Federal methodology is used as a basis for awarding need-based institutional aid.

UNDERGRADUATE EXPENSES for 2005–06 *Application fee:* $40. *One-time required fee:* $25. *Comprehensive fee:* $30,233 includes full-time tuition ($20,535), mandatory fees ($480), and room and board ($9218). *College room only:* $5890. Room and board charges vary according to board plan and housing facility. *Part-time tuition:* $463 per credit. *Part-time fees:* $65 per term. *Payment plan:* Installment.

FRESHMAN FINANCIAL AID (Fall 2004, est.) 807 applied for aid; of those 74% were deemed to have need. 100% of freshmen with need received aid; of those 22% had need fully met. *Average percent of need met:* 77% (excluding resources awarded to replace EFC). *Average financial aid package:* $13,750 (excluding resources awarded to replace EFC). 23% of all full-time freshmen had no need and received non-need-based gift aid.

UNDERGRADUATE FINANCIAL AID (Fall 2004, est.) 3,299 applied for aid; of those 82% were deemed to have need. 100% of undergraduates with need received aid; of those 19% had need fully met. *Average percent of need met:* 67% (excluding resources awarded to replace EFC). *Average financial aid package:* $12,685 (excluding resources awarded to replace EFC). 15% of all full-time undergraduates had no need and received non-need-based gift aid.
GIFT AID (NEED-BASED) *Total amount:* $14,565,334 (16% federal, 20% state, 61% institutional, 3% external sources). *Receiving aid:* Freshmen: 63% (600); All full-time undergraduates: 59% (2,522). *Average award:* Freshmen: $9917; Undergraduates: $8520. *Scholarships, grants, and awards:* Federal Pell, FSEOG, state, private, college/university gift aid from institutional funds.
GIFT AID (NON-NEED-BASED) *Total amount:* $10,640,625 (98% institutional, 2% external sources). *Receiving aid:* Freshmen: 36% (341); Undergraduates: 26% (1,114). *Average Award:* Freshmen: $5704; Undergraduates: $5588. *Scholarships, grants, and awards by category: Academic Interests/Achievement:* general academic interests/achievements. *Creative Arts/Performance:* debating, music. *Special Achievements/Activities:* general special achievements/activities. *Tuition waivers:* Full or partial for employees or children of employees. *ROTC:* Army.
LOANS *Student loans:* $22,592,745 (47% need-based, 53% non-need-based). 63% of past graduating class borrowed through all loan programs. *Average indebtedness per student:* $27,013. *Average need-based loan:* Freshmen: $3544; Undergraduates: $4612. *Parent loans:* $7,665,220 (100% non-need-based). *Programs:* FFEL (Subsidized and Unsubsidized Stafford, PLUS), Perkins, alternative loans, Key Alternative Loans, CitiAssist Loans, TERI Loans, Signature Loans, EXCEL Loans.
WORK-STUDY *Federal work-study:* Total amount: $1,660,409; 744 jobs averaging $2232. *State or other work-study/employment:* Total amount: $486,950 (100% non-need-based). 506 part-time jobs available.
ATHLETIC AWARDS *Total amount:* $2,296,053 (100% non-need-based).
APPLYING FOR FINANCIAL AID *Required financial aid forms:* FAFSA, institution's own form. *Financial aid deadline:* 5/1 (priority: 2/15). *Notification date:* Continuous beginning 3/15. Students must reply by 5/1 or within 2 weeks of notification.
CONTACT Joseph R. Weglarz, Director of Financial Aid, Marist College, 3399 North Road, Poughkeepsie, NY 12601, 845-575-3230 or toll-free 800-436-5483. *Fax:* 845-575-3099. *E-mail:* joseph.weglarz@marist.edu.

MARLBORO COLLEGE
Marlboro, VT

Tuition & fees: $27,790   Average undergraduate aid package: $16,791

ABOUT THE INSTITUTION Independent, coed. Awards: bachelor's and master's degrees. 77 undergraduate majors. Total enrollment: 418. Undergraduates: 357. Freshmen: 102. Both federal and institutional methodology are used as a basis for awarding need-based institutional aid.
UNDERGRADUATE EXPENSES for 2005–06 *Application fee:* $50. *Comprehensive fee:* $35,980 includes full-time tuition ($26,940), mandatory fees ($850), and room and board ($8190). *College room only:* $4540. *Part-time tuition:* $890 per credit. *Payment plan:* Installment.
FRESHMAN FINANCIAL AID (Fall 2004, est.) 69 applied for aid; of those 87% were deemed to have need. 100% of freshmen with need received aid; of those 83% had need fully met. *Average percent of need met:* 88% (excluding resources awarded to replace EFC). *Average financial aid package:* $20,907 (excluding resources awarded to replace EFC). 13% of all full-time freshmen had no need and received non-need-based gift aid.
UNDERGRADUATE FINANCIAL AID (Fall 2004, est.) 281 applied for aid; of those 89% were deemed to have need. 100% of undergraduates with need received aid; of those 17% had need fully met. *Average percent of need met:* 82% (excluding resources awarded to replace EFC). *Average financial aid package:* $16,791 (excluding resources awarded to replace EFC). 14% of all full-time undergraduates had no need and received non-need-based gift aid.
GIFT AID (NEED-BASED) *Total amount:* $3,296,322 (11% federal, 3% state, 74% institutional, 12% external sources). *Receiving aid:* Freshmen: 65% (59); All full-time undergraduates: 62% (216). *Average award:* Freshmen: $15,969; Undergraduates: $13,256. *Scholarships, grants, and awards:* Federal Pell, FSEOG, state, private, college/university gift aid from institutional funds.
GIFT AID (NON-NEED-BASED) *Total amount:* $348,780 (47% institutional, 53% external sources). *Receiving aid:* Freshmen: 7% (6); Undergraduates: 3% (10). *Average Award:* Freshmen: $8191; Undergraduates: $10,539. *Scholarships, grants, and awards by category: Academic Interests/Achievement:* 35 awards

($350,000 total): general academic interests/achievements. *Creative Arts/Performance:* 1 award ($3000 total): general creative arts/performance. *Special Achievements/Activities:* 10 awards ($100,000 total): community service. *Tuition waivers:* Full or partial for employees or children of employees, senior citizens.
LOANS *Student loans:* $1,743,040 (84% need-based, 16% non-need-based). 80% of past graduating class borrowed through all loan programs. *Average indebtedness per student:* $18,212. *Average need-based loan:* Freshmen: $2483; Undergraduates: $3828. *Parent loans:* $1,694,787 (67% need-based, 33% non-need-based). *Programs:* FFEL (Subsidized and Unsubsidized Stafford, PLUS).
WORK-STUDY *Federal work-study:* Total amount: $352,919; 222 jobs averaging $1020. *State or other work-study/employment:* Total amount: $44,891 (44% need-based, 56% non-need-based). 3 part-time jobs averaging $1930.
APPLYING FOR FINANCIAL AID *Required financial aid forms:* FAFSA, CSS Financial Aid PROFILE, state aid form, noncustodial (divorced/separated) parent's statement. *Financial aid deadline:* 3/1. *Notification date:* 4/1. Students must reply by 5/1 or within 2 weeks of notification.
CONTACT Alan E. Young, Dean of Enrollment Management, Marlboro College, South Road, PO Box A, Marlboro, VT 05344-0300, 802-258-9261 or toll-free 800-343-0049. *Fax:* 802-258-9300. *E-mail:* finaid@marlboro.edu.

MARQUETTE UNIVERSITY
Milwaukee, WI

ABOUT THE INSTITUTION Independent Roman Catholic (Jesuit), coed. Awards: associate, bachelor's, master's, doctoral, and first professional degrees and post-master's certificates. 85 undergraduate majors. Total enrollment: 11,510. Undergraduates: 7,923. Freshmen: 1,807.
GIFT AID (NEED-BASED) *Scholarships, grants, and awards:* Federal Pell, FSEOG, state, private, college/university gift aid from institutional funds.
GIFT AID (NON-NEED-BASED) *Scholarships, grants, and awards by category: Academic Interests/Achievement:* biological sciences, business, communication, engineering/technologies, foreign languages, general academic interests/achievements, health fields, mathematics. *Creative Arts/Performance:* theater/drama. *Special Characteristics:* children of faculty/staff.
LOANS *Programs:* Federal Direct (Subsidized and Unsubsidized Stafford, PLUS), Perkins, Federal Nursing, state, college/university, alternative loans.
WORK-STUDY *Federal work-study:* Total amount: $1,536,596; 300 jobs averaging $2500. *State or other work-study/employment:* Total amount: $1,902,298 (100% non-need-based). Part-time jobs available.
APPLYING FOR FINANCIAL AID *Required financial aid form:* FAFSA.
CONTACT Daniel L. Goyette, Director of Financial Aid, Marquette University, Office of Student Financial Aid, 1212 Building, Room 415, Milwaukee, WI 53201-1881, 414-288-7390 or toll-free 800-222-6544. *Fax:* 414-288-1718. *E-mail:* financialaid@marquette.edu.

MARSHALL UNIVERSITY
Huntington, WV

Tuition & fees (WV res): $4296   Average undergraduate aid package: $6769

ABOUT THE INSTITUTION State-supported, coed. Awards: associate, bachelor's, master's, doctoral, and first professional degrees and post-master's certificates. 46 undergraduate majors. Total enrollment: 13,920. Undergraduates: 9,859. Freshmen: 1,799. Federal methodology is used as a basis for awarding need-based institutional aid.
UNDERGRADUATE EXPENSES for 2004–05 *Application fee:* $25. *Tuition, state resident:* full-time $3818; part-time $151 per semester hour. *Tuition, nonresident:* full-time $10,128; part-time $414 per semester hour. *Required fees:* full-time $478; $11.75 per semester hour. Full-time tuition and fees vary according to program and reciprocity agreements. Part-time tuition and fees vary according to program and reciprocity agreements. *College room and board:* $6060. Room and board charges vary according to board plan and housing facility. *Payment plans:* Installment, deferred payment.
FRESHMAN FINANCIAL AID (Fall 2004, est.) 1416 applied for aid; of those 70% were deemed to have need. 98% of freshmen with need received aid; of those 33% had need fully met. *Average percent of need met:* 52% (excluding resources awarded to replace EFC). *Average financial aid package:* $6841 (excluding resources awarded to replace EFC). 24% of all full-time freshmen had no need and received non-need-based gift aid.
UNDERGRADUATE FINANCIAL AID (Fall 2004, est.) 6,650 applied for aid; of those 76% were deemed to have need. 98% of undergraduates with need received aid; of those 36% had need fully met. *Average percent of need met:*

58% (excluding resources awarded to replace EFC). *Average financial aid package:* $6769 (excluding resources awarded to replace EFC). 17% of all full-time undergraduates had no need and received non-need-based gift aid.

GIFT AID (NEED-BASED) *Total amount:* $15,678,208 (74% federal, 26% state). *Receiving aid:* Freshmen: 38% (611); All full-time undergraduates: 37% (3,238). *Average award:* Freshmen: $4189; Undergraduates: $3930. *Scholarships, grants, and awards:* Federal Pell, FSEOG, state, private, college/university gift aid from institutional funds.

GIFT AID (NON-NEED-BASED) *Total amount:* $11,963,844 (55% state, 28% institutional, 17% external sources). *Receiving aid:* Freshmen: 33% (535); Undergraduates: 20% (1,720). *Average Award: Freshmen:* $4533; *Undergraduates:* $4758. *Scholarships, grants, and awards by category: Academic Interests/ Achievement:* 2,258 awards ($3,432,772 total): general academic interests/ achievements. *Creative Arts/Performance:* applied art and design, art/fine arts, cinema/film/broadcasting, creative writing, dance, debating, general creative arts/performance, journalism/publications, music, performing arts, theater/ drama. *Special Characteristics:* veterans' children. *Tuition waivers:* Full or partial for employees or children of employees. *ROTC:* Army.

LOANS *Student loans:* $27,423,652 (94% need-based, 6% non-need-based). 58% of past graduating class borrowed through all loan programs. *Average indebtedness per student:* $15,258. *Average need-based loan:* Freshmen: $3456; Undergraduates: $4683. *Parent loans:* $4,003,019 (100% non-need-based). *Programs:* Federal Direct (Subsidized and Unsubsidized Stafford, PLUS), Perkins, state, college/university.

WORK-STUDY *Federal work-study:* Total amount: $528,123; 330 jobs averaging $1600. *State or other work-study/employment:* Total amount: $357,352 (100% non-need-based). 54 part-time jobs averaging $6617.

ATHLETIC AWARDS *Total amount:* $3,409,729 (100% non-need-based).

APPLYING FOR FINANCIAL AID *Required financial aid form:* FAFSA. *Financial aid deadline (priority):* 3/1. *Notification date:* 4/15. Students must reply within 2 weeks of notification.

CONTACT Ms. Nadine A. Hamrick, Associate Director of Student Financial Aid, Marshall University, One John Marshall Drive, Huntington, WV 25755, 304-696-2277 or toll-free 800-642-3499 (in-state). *Fax:* 304-696-3242. *E-mail:* hamrick@ marshall.edu.

MARS HILL COLLEGE
Mars Hill, NC

Tuition & fees: $16,598	Average undergraduate aid package: $11,536

ABOUT THE INSTITUTION Independent Baptist, coed. Awards: bachelor's degrees. 61 undergraduate majors. Total enrollment: 1,378. Undergraduates: 1,378. Freshmen: 348. Federal methodology is used as a basis for awarding need-based institutional aid.

UNDERGRADUATE EXPENSES for 2005–06 *Application fee:* $25. *Comprehensive fee:* $22,734 includes full-time tuition ($15,252), mandatory fees ($1346), and room and board ($6136). *College room only:* $3112. *Part-time tuition:* $500 per credit hour.

GIFT AID (NEED-BASED) *Total amount:* $6,972,447 (21% federal, 26% state, 45% institutional, 8% external sources). *Receiving aid:* Freshmen: 99% (287); All full-time undergraduates: 75% (854). *Average award:* Freshmen: $9315; Undergraduates: $8813. *Scholarships, grants, and awards:* Federal Pell, FSEOG, state, private, college/university gift aid from institutional funds.

GIFT AID (NON-NEED-BASED) *Total amount:* $726,444 (1% federal, 20% state, 65% institutional, 14% external sources). *Receiving aid:* Freshmen: 11% (31); Undergraduates: 9% (97). *Average Award: Freshmen:* $8640; *Undergraduates:* $11,141. *Scholarships, grants, and awards by category: Academic Interests/ Achievement:* general academic interests/achievements. *Creative Arts/ Performance:* dance, music, theater/drama. *Special Achievements/Activities:* cheerleading/drum major. *Special Characteristics:* children of faculty/staff.

LOANS *Student loans:* $3,760,279 (81% need-based, 19% non-need-based). 87% of past graduating class borrowed through all loan programs. *Average indebtedness per student:* $9518. *Average need-based loan:* Freshmen: $2709; Undergraduates: $3448. *Parent loans:* $1,038,161 (40% need-based, 60% non-need-based). *Programs:* FFEL (Subsidized and Unsubsidized Stafford, PLUS), Perkins.

ATHLETIC AWARDS *Total amount:* $833,518 (84% need-based, 16% non-need-based).

APPLYING FOR FINANCIAL AID *Required financial aid forms:* FAFSA, state aid form. *Financial aid deadline (priority):* 4/15. *Notification date:* Continuous. Students must reply within 2 weeks of notification.

CONTACT Myrtle Martin, Director of Financial Aid, Mars Hill College, PO Box 370, Mars Hill, NC 28754, 828-689-1123 or toll-free 866-MHC-4-YOU. *Fax:* 828-689-1300.

MARTIN LUTHER COLLEGE
New Ulm, MN

ABOUT THE INSTITUTION Independent religious, coed. Awards: bachelor's degrees. 6 undergraduate majors. Total enrollment: 945. Undergraduates: 945. Freshmen: 185.

GIFT AID (NEED-BASED) *Scholarships, grants, and awards:* Federal Pell, FSEOG, state, private, college/university gift aid from institutional funds.

GIFT AID (NON-NEED-BASED) *Scholarships, grants, and awards by category: Academic Interests/Achievement:* general academic interests/achievements. *Creative Arts/Performance:* music. *Special Achievements/Activities:* general special achievements/activities. *Special Characteristics:* general special characteristics.

LOANS *Programs:* FFEL (Subsidized and Unsubsidized Stafford, PLUS), Perkins, state.

APPLYING FOR FINANCIAL AID *Required financial aid forms:* FAFSA, institution's own form, state aid form.

CONTACT Mr. Gene Slettedahl, Director of Financial Aid, Martin Luther College, 1995 Luther Court, New Ulm, MN 56073, 507-354-8221 Ext. 225. *Fax:* 507-354-8225. *E-mail:* slettega@mlc-wels.edu.

MARTIN METHODIST COLLEGE
Pulaski, TN

Tuition & fees: $13,650	Average undergraduate aid package: $5820

ABOUT THE INSTITUTION Independent United Methodist, coed. Awards: bachelor's degrees. 64 undergraduate majors. Total enrollment: 714. Undergraduates: 714. Freshmen: 209. Federal methodology is used as a basis for awarding need-based institutional aid.

UNDERGRADUATE EXPENSES for 2004–05 *Application fee:* $25. *Comprehensive fee:* $18,450 includes full-time tuition ($13,400), mandatory fees ($250), and room and board ($4800). Full-time tuition and fees vary according to class time. Room and board charges vary according to housing facility. *Part-time tuition:* $560 per credit hour. Part-time tuition and fees vary according to class time. *Payment plan:* Installment.

FRESHMAN FINANCIAL AID (Fall 2004, est.) 158 applied for aid; of those 70% were deemed to have need. 99% of freshmen with need received aid; of those 57% had need fully met. *Average percent of need met:* 89% (excluding resources awarded to replace EFC). *Average financial aid package:* $6750 (excluding resources awarded to replace EFC). 17% of all full-time freshmen had no need and received non-need-based gift aid.

UNDERGRADUATE FINANCIAL AID (Fall 2004, est.) 581 applied for aid; of those 67% were deemed to have need. 99% of undergraduates with need received aid; of those 81% had need fully met. *Average percent of need met:* 79% (excluding resources awarded to replace EFC). *Average financial aid package:* $5820 (excluding resources awarded to replace EFC). 13% of all full-time undergraduates had no need and received non-need-based gift aid.

GIFT AID (NEED-BASED) *Total amount:* $2,268,350 (37% federal, 28% state, 32% institutional, 3% external sources). *Receiving aid:* Freshmen: 66% (110); All full-time undergraduates: 54% (387). *Average award:* Freshmen: $3950; Undergraduates: $3620. *Scholarships, grants, and awards:* Federal Pell, FSEOG, state, private, college/university gift aid from institutional funds.

GIFT AID (NON-NEED-BASED) *Total amount:* $300,700 (40% state, 41% institutional, 19% external sources). *Receiving aid:* Freshmen: 25% (41); Undergraduates: 20% (141). *Average Award: Freshmen:* $1900; *Undergraduates:* $2400. *Scholarships, grants, and awards by category: Academic Interests/ Achievement:* 126 awards ($401,000 total): biological sciences, business, education, general academic interests/achievements, religion/biblical studies. *Creative Arts/Performance:* 61 awards ($134,300 total): art/fine arts, music, theater/ drama. *Special Achievements/Activities:* 8 awards ($8000 total): cheerleading/ drum major. *Special Characteristics:* 228 awards ($274,000 total): children of faculty/staff, local/state students, religious affiliation. *Tuition waivers:* Full or partial for employees or children of employees.

LOANS *Student loans:* $1,564,000 (67% need-based, 33% non-need-based). 64% of past graduating class borrowed through all loan programs. *Average indebtedness per student:* $14,200. *Average need-based loan:* Freshmen: $2224;

Undergraduates: $3250. *Parent loans:* $75,700 (17% need-based, 83% non-need-based). *Programs:* FFEL (Subsidized and Unsubsidized Stafford, PLUS), United Methodist Student Loans.

WORK-STUDY *Federal work-study:* Total amount: $50,499; 50 jobs averaging $1010. *State or other work-study/employment:* Total amount: $81,000 (59% need-based, 41% non-need-based). 61 part-time jobs averaging $1311.

ATHLETIC AWARDS *Total amount:* $1,351,200 (55% need-based, 45% non-need-based).

APPLYING FOR FINANCIAL AID *Required financial aid forms:* FAFSA, institution's own form. *Financial aid deadline (priority):* 2/1. *Notification date:* Continuous beginning 2/15. Students must reply within 4 weeks of notification.

CONTACT Ms. Anita Beecham, Financial Aid Assistant, Martin Methodist College, 433 West Madison Street, Pulaski, TN 38478-2716, 931-363-9808 or toll-free 800-467-1273. *Fax:* 931-363-9818. *E-mail:* abeecham@martinmethodist.edu.

MARTIN UNIVERSITY
Indianapolis, IN

Tuition & fees: $11,420	Average undergraduate aid package: $8779

ABOUT THE INSTITUTION Independent, coed. Awards: bachelor's and master's degrees. 28 undergraduate majors. Total enrollment: 571. Undergraduates: 465. Freshmen: 49. Federal methodology is used as a basis for awarding need-based institutional aid.

UNDERGRADUATE EXPENSES for 2005–06 *Application fee:* $25. *Tuition:* full-time $11,100; part-time $370 per credit. *Required fees:* full-time $320; $160 per term part-time.

FRESHMAN FINANCIAL AID (Fall 2004, est.) 22 applied for aid; of those 95% were deemed to have need. 100% of freshmen with need received aid; of those 10% had need fully met. *Average percent of need met:* 64% (excluding resources awarded to replace EFC). *Average financial aid package:* $7346 (excluding resources awarded to replace EFC).

UNDERGRADUATE FINANCIAL AID (Fall 2004, est.) 214 applied for aid; of those 96% were deemed to have need. 99% of undergraduates with need received aid; of those 1% had need fully met. *Average percent of need met:* 69% (excluding resources awarded to replace EFC). *Average financial aid package:* $8779 (excluding resources awarded to replace EFC).

GIFT AID (NEED-BASED) *Total amount:* $1,999,246 (52% federal, 46% state, 1% institutional, 1% external sources). *Receiving aid:* Freshmen: 65% (20); All full-time undergraduates: 78% (190). *Average award:* Freshmen: $6147; Undergraduates: $6705. *Scholarships, grants, and awards:* Federal Pell, FSEOG, state, private, college/university gift aid from institutional funds.

GIFT AID (NON-NEED-BASED) *Receiving aid:* Freshmen: 3% (1); Undergraduates: 1.

LOANS *Student loans:* $1,050,477 (95% need-based, 5% non-need-based). 91% of past graduating class borrowed through all loan programs. *Average indebtedness per student:* $27,193. *Average need-based loan:* Freshmen: $2625; Undergraduates: $3192. *Programs:* FFEL (Subsidized and Unsubsidized Stafford, PLUS), Charles E. Schell Foundation Loans.

WORK-STUDY *Federal work-study:* Total amount: $23,000; 9 jobs averaging $2445.

APPLYING FOR FINANCIAL AID *Required financial aid form:* FAFSA. *Financial aid deadline:* Continuous. *Notification date:* Continuous.

CONTACT Mason M. Moton, Director of Financial Aid, Martin University, 2171 Avondale Place, PO Box 18567, Indianapolis, IN 46218-3867, 317-543-3670. *Fax:* 317-543-4790. *E-mail:* mmoton@martin.edu.

MARY BALDWIN COLLEGE
Staunton, VA

Tuition & fees: $19,991	Average undergraduate aid package: $19,315

ABOUT THE INSTITUTION Independent, coed. Awards: bachelor's and master's degrees. 31 undergraduate majors. Total enrollment: 1,718. Undergraduates: 1,524. Freshmen: 256. Federal methodology is used as a basis for awarding need-based institutional aid.

UNDERGRADUATE EXPENSES for 2004–05 *Application fee:* $25. *Comprehensive fee:* $25,680 includes full-time tuition ($19,811), mandatory fees ($180), and room and board ($5689). *College room only:* $3554. Full-time tuition and fees vary according to degree level. Room and board charges vary according to

housing facility. *Part-time tuition:* $325 per credit hour. Part-time tuition and fees vary according to degree level. *Payment plan:* Installment.

FRESHMAN FINANCIAL AID (Fall 2004, est.) 244 applied for aid; of those 89% were deemed to have need. 99% of freshmen with need received aid; of those 45% had need fully met. *Average percent of need met:* 88% (excluding resources awarded to replace EFC). *Average financial aid package:* $20,796 (excluding resources awarded to replace EFC). 15% of all full-time freshmen had no need and received non-need-based gift aid.

UNDERGRADUATE FINANCIAL AID (Fall 2004, est.) 959 applied for aid; of those 90% were deemed to have need. 99% of undergraduates with need received aid; of those 47% had need fully met. *Average percent of need met:* 89% (excluding resources awarded to replace EFC). *Average financial aid package:* $19,315 (excluding resources awarded to replace EFC). 18% of all full-time undergraduates had no need and received non-need-based gift aid.

GIFT AID (NEED-BASED) *Total amount:* $9,499,808 (14% federal, 17% state, 65% institutional, 4% external sources). *Receiving aid:* Freshmen: 82% (215); All full-time undergraduates: 77% (844). *Average award:* Freshmen: $12,133; Undergraduates: $9826. *Scholarships, grants, and awards:* Federal Pell, FSEOG, state, private, college/university gift aid from institutional funds.

GIFT AID (NON-NEED-BASED) *Total amount:* $1,247,358 (20% state, 64% institutional, 16% external sources). *Receiving aid:* Freshmen: 82% (215); Undergraduates: 77% (850). *Average Award:* Freshmen: $12,831; Undergraduates: $12,257. *Scholarships, grants, and awards by category:* Academic Interests/Achievement: 755 awards ($4,147,754 total): general academic interests/achievements. *Special Achievements/Activities:* 31 awards ($62,000 total): leadership. *Special Characteristics:* 12 awards ($190,199 total): children of educators, children of faculty/staff. *Tuition waivers:* Full or partial for employees or children of employees. *ROTC:* Army, Naval cooperative, Air Force cooperative.

LOANS *Student loans:* $5,645,376 (100% need-based). 81% of past graduating class borrowed through all loan programs. *Average indebtedness per student:* $21,242. *Average need-based loan:* Freshmen: $1852; Undergraduates: $3185. *Parent loans:* $2,201,910 (97% need-based, 3% non-need-based). *Programs:* FFEL (Subsidized and Unsubsidized Stafford, PLUS), Perkins, alternative loans.

WORK-STUDY *Federal work-study:* Total amount: $605,496; 393 jobs averaging $1691. *State or other work-study/employment:* Total amount: $195,805 (77% need-based, 23% non-need-based). 72 part-time jobs averaging $1397.

APPLYING FOR FINANCIAL AID *Required financial aid forms:* FAFSA, state aid form (for VA residents only). *Financial aid deadline:* 5/15. *Notification date:* Continuous. Students must reply within 3 weeks of notification.

CONTACT Lisa Branson, Dean of Admissions and Financial Aid, Mary Baldwin College, Office of Financial Aid and Student Campus Employment, Staunton, VA 24401, 540-887-7022 or toll-free 800-468-2262. *Fax:* 540-887-7229. *E-mail:* lbranson@mbc.edu.

MARYGROVE COLLEGE
Detroit, MI

CONTACT Mr. Donald Hurt, Director of Financial Aid, Marygrove College, 8425 West McNichols Road, Detroit, MI 48221-2599, 313-862-8000 Ext. 436 or toll-free 866-313-1297.

MARYLAND INSTITUTE COLLEGE OF ART
Baltimore, MD

ABOUT THE INSTITUTION Independent, coed. Awards: bachelor's and master's degrees and post-bachelor's certificates. 16 undergraduate majors. Total enrollment: 1,608. Undergraduates: 1,402. Freshmen: 401.

GIFT AID (NEED-BASED) *Scholarships, grants, and awards:* Federal Pell, FSEOG, state, private, college/university gift aid from institutional funds.

GIFT AID (NON-NEED-BASED) *Scholarships, grants, and awards by category:* Academic Interests/Achievement: general academic interests/achievements. Creative Arts/Performance: applied art and design, art/fine arts. Special Characteristics: children of faculty/staff, international students, local/state students, religious affiliation.

LOANS *Programs:* FFEL (Subsidized and Unsubsidized Stafford, PLUS), Perkins. **WORK-STUDY** Federal work-study jobs available. *State or other work-study/employment:* Part-time jobs available.

APPLYING FOR FINANCIAL AID *Required financial aid forms:* FAFSA, institution's own form.

CONTACT Ms. Diane Prengaman, Associate Vice President for Financial Aid, Maryland Institute College of Art, 1300 Mount Royal Avenue, Baltimore, MD 21217, 410-225-2285. *Fax:* 410-225-2337. *E-mail:* dprengam@mica.edu.

MARYLHURST UNIVERSITY
Marylhurst, OR

Tuition & fees: $14,220	Average undergraduate aid package: $12,933

ABOUT THE INSTITUTION Independent Roman Catholic, coed. Awards: bachelor's and master's degrees and post-bachelor's certificates. 21 undergraduate majors. Total enrollment: 1,245. Undergraduates: 847. Freshmen: 23. Federal methodology is used as a basis for awarding need-based institutional aid.

UNDERGRADUATE EXPENSES for 2005–06 *Application fee:* $20. *Tuition:* full-time $13,860; part-time $308 per quarter hour. Full-time tuition and fees vary according to course load. Part-time tuition and fees vary according to course load. *Payment plans:* Installment, deferred payment.

FRESHMAN FINANCIAL AID (Fall 2003) 7 applied for aid; of those 100% were deemed to have need. 100% of freshmen with need received aid; of those 14% had need fully met. *Average percent of need met:* 47% (excluding resources awarded to replace EFC). *Average financial aid package:* $7380 (excluding resources awarded to replace EFC).

UNDERGRADUATE FINANCIAL AID (Fall 2003) 120 applied for aid; of those 97% were deemed to have need. 100% of undergraduates with need received aid; of those 4% had need fully met. *Average percent of need met:* 58% (excluding resources awarded to replace EFC). *Average financial aid package:* $12,933 (excluding resources awarded to replace EFC). 2% of all full-time undergraduates had no need and received non-need-based gift aid.

GIFT AID (NEED-BASED) *Total amount:* $1,423,086 (42% federal, 8% state, 39% institutional, 11% external sources). *Receiving aid:* Freshmen: 100% (7); All full-time undergraduates: 50% (102). *Average award:* Freshmen: $5533; Undergraduates: $7015. *Scholarships, grants, and awards:* Federal Pell, FSEOG, state, private, college/university gift aid from institutional funds, United Negro College Fund.

GIFT AID (NON-NEED-BASED) *Total amount:* $26,669 (100% institutional). *Receiving aid:* Freshmen: 14% (1); Undergraduates: 1% (2). *Tuition waivers:* Full or partial for employees or children of employees.

LOANS *Student loans:* $7,562,968 (50% need-based, 50% non-need-based). 60% of past graduating class borrowed through all loan programs. *Average indebtedness per student:* $17,906. *Average need-based loan:* Freshmen: $1586; Undergraduates: $5456. *Parent loans:* $170,500 (100% non-need-based). *Programs:* FFEL (Subsidized and Unsubsidized Stafford, PLUS), Perkins.

WORK-STUDY *Federal work-study:* Total amount: $94,623; 45 jobs available.

APPLYING FOR FINANCIAL AID *Required financial aid form:* FAFSA. *Financial aid deadline:* Continuous. *Notification date:* Continuous beginning 5/1.

CONTACT Marlena McKee-Flores, Office of Financial Aid, Marylhurst University, 17600 Pacific Highway, PO Box 261, Marylhurst, OR 97036, 503-699-6253 or toll-free 800-634-9982. *Fax:* 503-635-6585. *E-mail:* finaid@marylhurst.edu.

MARYMOUNT COLLEGE OF FORDHAM UNIVERSITY
Tarrytown, NY

Tuition & fees: $19,702	Average undergraduate aid package: $15,968

ABOUT THE INSTITUTION Independent, women only. Awards: associate and bachelor's degrees. 66 undergraduate majors. Total enrollment: 1,036. Freshmen: 255. Federal methodology is used as a basis for awarding need-based institutional aid.

UNDERGRADUATE EXPENSES for 2004–05 *Application fee:* $30. *Comprehensive fee:* $29,462 includes full-time tuition ($19,100), mandatory fees ($602), and room and board ($9760). Full-time tuition and fees vary according to student level. Room and board charges vary according to board plan and housing facility. *Part-time tuition:* $635 per credit hour. *Part-time fees:* $301 per term. Part-time tuition and fees vary according to class time. *Payment plans:* Installment, deferred payment.

FRESHMAN FINANCIAL AID (Fall 2003) 255 applied for aid; of those 91% were deemed to have need. 100% of freshmen with need received aid; of those 14% had need fully met. *Average percent of need met:* 70% (excluding resources awarded to replace EFC). *Average financial aid package:* $16,003 (excluding resources awarded to replace EFC). 18% of all full-time freshmen had no need and received non-need-based gift aid.

UNDERGRADUATE FINANCIAL AID (Fall 2003) 729 applied for aid; of those 90% were deemed to have need. 100% of undergraduates with need received aid; of those 16% had need fully met. *Average percent of need met:* 71%

(excluding resources awarded to replace EFC). *Average financial aid package:* $15,968 (excluding resources awarded to replace EFC). 25% of all full-time undergraduates had no need and received non-need-based gift aid.

GIFT AID (NEED-BASED) *Total amount:* $6,734,855 (18% federal, 19% state, 61% institutional, 2% external sources). *Receiving aid:* Freshmen: 81% (229); All full-time undergraduates: 67% (635). *Average award:* Freshmen: $11,779; Undergraduates: $10,406. *Scholarships, grants, and awards:* Federal Pell, FSEOG, state, private, college/university gift aid from institutional funds.

GIFT AID (NON-NEED-BASED) *Total amount:* $1,883,324 (97% institutional, 3% external sources). *Receiving aid:* Freshmen: 8% (22); Undergraduates: 5% (48). *Average Award:* Freshmen: $8690; Undergraduates: $7242. *Scholarships, grants, and awards by category:* Academic Interests/Achievement: 887 awards ($5,941,777 total): general academic interests/achievements, international studies. *Tuition waivers:* Full or partial for employees or children of employees.

LOANS *Student loans:* $4,856,195 (78% need-based, 22% non-need-based). 85% of past graduating class borrowed through all loan programs. *Average indebtedness per student:* $11,006. *Average need-based loan:* Freshmen: $4211; Undergraduates: $5752. *Parent loans:* $1,117,745 (44% need-based, 56% non-need-based). *Programs:* Federal Direct (Subsidized and Unsubsidized Stafford, PLUS), FFEL (Subsidized and Unsubsidized Stafford, PLUS), Perkins, alternative loans.

WORK-STUDY *Federal work-study:* Total amount: $210,820; 162 jobs averaging $1301. *State or other work-study/employment:* Total amount: $186,660 (71% need-based, 29% non-need-based). Part-time jobs available.

APPLYING FOR FINANCIAL AID *Required financial aid forms:* FAFSA, state aid form. *Financial aid deadline (priority):* 3/1. *Notification date:* Continuous beginning 4/1. Students must reply within 2 weeks of notification.

CONTACT Christine Engongoro, Campus Director, Student Financial Services, Marymount College of Fordham University, 100 Marymount Avenue, Tarrytown, NY 10591-3796, 914-332-8345 or toll-free 800-724-4312. *Fax:* 914-332-7421. *E-mail:* engongoro@fordham.edu.

MARYMOUNT MANHATTAN COLLEGE
New York, NY

Tuition & fees: $17,352	Average undergraduate aid package: N/A

ABOUT THE INSTITUTION Independent, coed. Awards: bachelor's degrees. 19 undergraduate majors. Total enrollment: 2,077. Undergraduates: 2,077. Freshmen: 454. Both federal and institutional methodology are used as a basis for awarding need-based institutional aid.

UNDERGRADUATE EXPENSES for 2004–05 *Application fee:* $60. *Comprehensive fee:* $29,718 includes full-time tuition ($16,606), mandatory fees ($746), and room and board ($12,366). *College room only:* $9066. Full-time tuition and fees vary according to course load. Room and board charges vary according to board plan and housing facility. *Part-time tuition:* $490 per credit. *Part-time fees:* $325 per term. Part-time tuition and fees vary according to course load. *Payment plan:* Installment.

GIFT AID (NEED-BASED) *Total amount:* $9,516,118 (18% federal, 14% state, 66% institutional, 2% external sources). *Receiving aid:* Freshmen: 65% (280); All full-time undergraduates: 68% (1,096). *Scholarships, grants, and awards:* Federal Pell, FSEOG, state, private, college/university gift aid from institutional funds.

GIFT AID (NON-NEED-BASED) *Total amount:* $1,459,892 (94% institutional, 6% external sources). *Receiving aid:* Freshmen: 37% (161); Undergraduates: 34% (550). *Scholarships, grants, and awards by category:* Academic Interests/Achievement: biological sciences, business, communication, education, English, general academic interests/achievements, humanities, international studies, premedicine, social sciences. *Creative Arts/Performance:* dance, theater/drama. *Special Achievements/Activities:* leadership. *Tuition waivers:* Full or partial for children of alumni, employees or children of employees, adult students, senior citizens.

LOANS *Student loans:* $9,074,971 (73% need-based, 27% non-need-based). 82% of past graduating class borrowed through all loan programs. *Average indebtedness per student:* $21,000. *Parent loans:* $12,807,758 (37% need-based, 63% non-need-based). *Programs:* FFEL (Subsidized and Unsubsidized Stafford, PLUS).

APPLYING FOR FINANCIAL AID *Required financial aid form:* FAFSA. *Financial aid deadline (priority):* 3/15. *Notification date:* Continuous. Students must reply within 4 weeks of notification.

CONTACT Maria DeInnocentiis, Director of Financial Aid, Marymount Manhattan College, 221 East 71st Street, New York, NY 10021-4597, 212-517-0480 or toll-free 800-MARYMOUNT (out-of-state). *Fax:* 212-517-0491.

MARYMOUNT UNIVERSITY
Arlington, VA

Tuition & fees: $17,090	Average undergraduate aid package: $13,276

ABOUT THE INSTITUTION Independent religious, coed. Awards: associate, bachelor's, master's, and doctoral degrees and post-bachelor's and post-master's certificates. 40 undergraduate majors. Total enrollment: 3,717. Undergraduates: 2,227. Freshmen: 422. Both federal and institutional methodology are used as a basis for awarding need-based institutional aid.
UNDERGRADUATE EXPENSES for 2004–05 *Application fee:* $35. *Comprehensive fee:* $24,610 includes full-time tuition ($16,952), mandatory fees ($138), and room and board ($7520). *Part-time tuition:* $549 per credit hour. *Part-time fees:* $5.75 per credit hour. *Payment plans:* Installment, deferred payment.
FRESHMAN FINANCIAL AID (Fall 2004, est.) 340 applied for aid; of those 79% were deemed to have need. 99% of freshmen with need received aid; of those 23% had need fully met. *Average percent of need met:* 79% (excluding resources awarded to replace EFC). *Average financial aid package:* $13,774 (excluding resources awarded to replace EFC). 19% of all full-time freshmen had no need and received non-need-based gift aid.
UNDERGRADUATE FINANCIAL AID (Fall 2004, est.) 1,259 applied for aid; of those 83% were deemed to have need. 98% of undergraduates with need received aid; of those 22% had need fully met. *Average percent of need met:* 73% (excluding resources awarded to replace EFC). *Average financial aid package:* $13,276 (excluding resources awarded to replace EFC). 17% of all full-time undergraduates had no need and received non-need-based gift aid.
GIFT AID (NEED-BASED) *Total amount:* $5,387,528 (28% federal, 1% state, 71% institutional). *Receiving aid:* Freshmen: 49% (204); All full-time undergraduates: 43% (758). *Average award:* Freshmen: $6959; Undergraduates: $6584. *Scholarships, grants, and awards:* Federal Pell, FSEOG, state, private, college/university gift aid from institutional funds, Federal Nursing.
GIFT AID (NON-NEED-BASED) *Total amount:* $6,290,377 (1% federal, 22% state, 76% institutional, 1% external sources). *Receiving aid:* Freshmen: 47% (195); Undergraduates: 38% (675). *Average Award:* *Freshmen:* $8392; *Undergraduates:* $7407. *Scholarships, grants, and awards by category:* *Academic Interests/Achievement:* 575 awards ($4,127,700 total): general academic interests/achievements. *Special Achievements/Activities:* 87 awards ($310,568 total): community service, leadership. *Special Characteristics:* 34 awards ($233,089 total): children and siblings of alumni, children of current students, children of faculty/staff, parents of current students, siblings of current students. *Tuition waivers:* Full or partial for children of alumni, employees or children of employees, senior citizens. *ROTC:* Army cooperative.
LOANS *Student loans:* $8,941,787 (42% need-based, 58% non-need-based). 70% of past graduating class borrowed through all loan programs. *Average indebtedness per student:* $21,981. *Average need-based loan:* Freshmen: $2722; Undergraduates: $3846. *Parent loans:* $3,801,267 (100% non-need-based). *Programs:* Federal Direct (Subsidized and Unsubsidized Stafford), FFEL (PLUS), Perkins.
WORK-STUDY *Federal work-study:* Total amount: $317,388; 180 jobs averaging $1763.
APPLYING FOR FINANCIAL AID *Required financial aid forms:* FAFSA, state aid form. *Financial aid deadline (priority):* 3/1. *Notification date:* Continuous beginning 3/15. Students must reply within 2 weeks of notification.
CONTACT Ms. Debbie A. Raines, Director of Financial Aid, Marymount University, 2807 North Glebe Road, Arlington, VA 22207-4299, 703-284-1530 or toll-free 800-548-7638. *Fax:* 703-516-4771. *E-mail:* admissions@marymount.edu.

MARYVILLE COLLEGE
Maryville, TN

Tuition & fees: $21,065	Average undergraduate aid package: $19,722

ABOUT THE INSTITUTION Independent Presbyterian, coed. Awards: bachelor's degrees. 49 undergraduate majors. Total enrollment: 1,080. Undergraduates: 1,080. Freshmen: 317. Federal methodology is used as a basis for awarding need-based institutional aid.
UNDERGRADUATE EXPENSES for 2004–05 *Application fee:* $25. *Comprehensive fee:* $27,565 includes full-time tuition ($20,465), mandatory fees ($600), and

room and board ($6500). *College room only:* $3200. Full-time tuition and fees vary according to course load. Room and board charges vary according to board plan, housing facility, and location. *Part-time tuition:* $853 per hour. *Part-time fees:* $12 per hour. Part-time tuition and fees vary according to course load. *Payment plan:* Installment.
FRESHMAN FINANCIAL AID (Fall 2004, est.) 317 applied for aid; of those 78% were deemed to have need. 100% of freshmen with need received aid; of those 20% had need fully met. *Average percent of need met:* 92% (excluding resources awarded to replace EFC). *Average financial aid package:* $21,071 (excluding resources awarded to replace EFC). 22% of all full-time freshmen had no need and received non-need-based gift aid.
UNDERGRADUATE FINANCIAL AID (Fall 2004, est.) 1,062 applied for aid; of those 76% were deemed to have need. 100% of undergraduates with need received aid; of those 38% had need fully met. *Average percent of need met:* 89% (excluding resources awarded to replace EFC). *Average financial aid package:* $19,722 (excluding resources awarded to replace EFC). 25% of all full-time undergraduates had no need and received non-need-based gift aid.
GIFT AID (NEED-BASED) *Total amount:* $10,580,868 (11% federal, 5% state, 84% institutional). *Receiving aid:* Freshmen: 78% (247); All full-time undergraduates: 76% (809). *Average award:* Freshmen: $17,247; Undergraduates: $14,916. *Scholarships, grants, and awards:* Federal Pell, FSEOG, state, private, college/university gift aid from institutional funds.
GIFT AID (NON-NEED-BASED) *Total amount:* $2,179,006 (29% institutional, 71% external sources). *Receiving aid:* Freshmen: 67% (213); Undergraduates: 41% (432). *Average Award:* Freshmen: $2543; Undergraduates: $1164. *Scholarships, grants, and awards by category:* Academic Interests/Achievement: 911 awards ($10,198,518 total): general academic interests/achievements. *Creative Arts/Performance:* 95 awards ($241,700 total): art/fine arts, music, theater/drama. *Special Achievements/Activities:* 118 awards ($302,460 total): community service, leadership. *Special Characteristics:* 192 awards ($962,198 total): children of faculty/staff, local/state students, members of minority groups, religious affiliation. *Tuition waivers:* Full or partial for employees or children of employees.
LOANS *Student loans:* $4,094,424 (59% need-based, 41% non-need-based). *Average need-based loan:* Freshmen: $2073; Undergraduates: $4046. *Parent loans:* $1,163,458 (100% non-need-based). *Programs:* FFEL (Subsidized and Unsubsidized Stafford, PLUS), Perkins, state, college/university.
WORK-STUDY *Federal work-study:* Total amount: $633,596; 404 jobs averaging $1513. *State or other work-study/employment:* Total amount: $229,262 (60% need-based, 40% non-need-based). 191 part-time jobs averaging $1231.
APPLYING FOR FINANCIAL AID *Required financial aid form:* FAFSA. *Financial aid deadline (priority):* 3/1. *Notification date:* Continuous beginning 3/15. Students must reply within 4 weeks of notification.
CONTACT Mr. Richard Brand, Director of Financial Aid, Maryville College, 502 East Lamar Alexander Parkway, Maryville, TN 37804-5907, 865-981-8100 or toll-free 800-597-2687. *E-mail:* richard.brand@maryvillecollege.edu.

MARYVILLE UNIVERSITY OF SAINT LOUIS
St. Louis, MO

Tuition & fees: $16,300	Average undergraduate aid package: $10,822

ABOUT THE INSTITUTION Independent, coed. Awards: bachelor's and master's degrees. 48 undergraduate majors. Total enrollment: 3,140. Undergraduates: 2,584. Freshmen: 324. Both federal and institutional methodology are used as a basis for awarding need-based institutional aid.
UNDERGRADUATE EXPENSES for 2004–05 *Application fee:* $25. *Comprehensive fee:* $23,300 includes full-time tuition ($16,000), mandatory fees ($300), and room and board ($7000). *College room only:* $6030. Full-time tuition and fees vary according to course load. Room and board charges vary according to housing facility. *Part-time tuition:* $485 per credit hour. *Part-time fees:* $75 per term. Part-time tuition and fees vary according to class time. *Payment plans:* Installment, deferred payment.
FRESHMAN FINANCIAL AID (Fall 2003) 298 applied for aid; of those 89% were deemed to have need. 100% of freshmen with need received aid; of those 15% had need fully met. *Average percent of need met:* 67% (excluding resources awarded to replace EFC). *Average financial aid package:* $12,787 (excluding resources awarded to replace EFC). 14% of all full-time freshmen had no need and received non-need-based gift aid.
UNDERGRADUATE FINANCIAL AID (Fall 2003) 1,301 applied for aid; of those 86% were deemed to have need. 99% of undergraduates with need received aid; of those 9% had need fully met. *Average percent of need met:* 42% (excluding resources awarded to replace EFC). *Average financial aid package:*

$10,822 (excluding resources awarded to replace EFC). 15% of all full-time undergraduates had no need and received non-need-based gift aid.

GIFT AID (NEED-BASED) *Total amount:* $8,437,441 (18% federal, 9% state, 72% institutional, 1% external sources). *Receiving aid:* Freshmen: 83% (265); All full-time undergraduates: 65% (1,034). *Average award:* Freshmen: $9806; Undergraduates: $5999. *Scholarships, grants, and awards:* Federal Pell, FSEOG, state, private, college/university gift aid from institutional funds.

GIFT AID (NON-NEED-BASED) *Total amount:* $2,566,477 (3% state, 82% institutional, 15% external sources). *Receiving aid:* Freshmen: 6% (20); Undergraduates: 5% (72). *Average Award:* Freshmen: $3558; *Undergraduates:* $6687. *Scholarships, grants, and awards by category: Academic Interests/ Achievement:* 970 awards ($3,849,748 total): education, general academic interests/achievements, health fields. *Creative Arts/Performance:* 27 awards ($53,250 total): art/fine arts. *Special Achievements/Activities:* 252 awards ($219,825 total): community service, general special achievements/activities, leadership. *Special Characteristics:* 35 awards ($45,468 total): children of current students, members of minority groups, parents of current students, religious affiliation, siblings of current students, spouses of current students, twins. *Tuition waivers:* Full or partial for employees or children of employees, senior citizens. *ROTC:* Army cooperative.

LOANS *Student loans:* $11,965,224 (61% need-based, 39% non-need-based). 82% of past graduating class borrowed through all loan programs. *Average indebtedness per student:* $11,167. *Average need-based loan:* Freshmen: $3039; Undergraduates: $4591. *Parent loans:* $2,860,217 (13% need-based, 87% non-need-based). *Programs:* Federal Direct (Subsidized and Unsubsidized Stafford, PLUS), Perkins, Sallie Mae Signature Loans, Keybank Loans, TERI Loans, Norwest Collegiate Loans, CitiAssist Loans, MOHELA ED Cash.

WORK-STUDY *Federal work-study:* Total amount: $193,959; 283 jobs averaging $914. *State or other work-study/employment:* Total amount: $344,653 (37% need-based, 63% non-need-based). 102 part-time jobs averaging $2950.

APPLYING FOR FINANCIAL AID *Required financial aid forms:* FAFSA, institution's own form. *Financial aid deadline (priority):* 4/1. *Notification date:* Continuous. Students must reply by 5/1 or within 2 weeks of notification.

CONTACT Ms. Martha Harbaugh, Director of Financial Aid, Maryville University of Saint Louis, 13550 Conway Road, St. Louis, MO 63141-7299, 314-529-9360 or toll-free 800-627-9855. *Fax:* 314-529-9199. *E-mail:* harbo@maryville.edu.

MARY WASHINGTON COLLEGE
Fredericksburg, VA

See University of Mary Washington.

MARYWOOD UNIVERSITY
Scranton, PA

ABOUT THE INSTITUTION Independent Roman Catholic, coed. Awards: associate, bachelor's, master's, and doctoral degrees and post-bachelor's and post-master's certificates. 86 undergraduate majors. Total enrollment: 3,127. Undergraduates: 1,811. Freshmen: 342.

GIFT AID (NEED-BASED) *Scholarships, grants, and awards:* Federal Pell, FSEOG, state, private, college/university gift aid from institutional funds.

GIFT AID (NON-NEED-BASED) *Scholarships, grants, and awards by category: Academic Interests/Achievement:* business, communication, education, foreign languages, general academic interests/achievements, health fields, mathematics, religion/biblical studies. *Creative Arts/Performance:* art/fine arts, cinema/ film/broadcasting, journalism/publications, music, performing arts, theater/ drama. *Special Achievements/Activities:* community service, general special achievements/activities, leadership. *Special Characteristics:* adult students, children and siblings of alumni, children of current students, children of faculty/staff, children of workers in trades, ethnic background, general special characteristics, international students, local/state students, religious affiliation, siblings of current students, spouses of current students.

LOANS *Programs:* FFEL (Subsidized and Unsubsidized Stafford, PLUS), Perkins, state, alternative loans.

WORK-STUDY *Federal work-study:* Total amount: $789,491; 643 jobs averaging $1724.

APPLYING FOR FINANCIAL AID *Required financial aid forms:* FAFSA, institution's own form.

CONTACT Mr. Stanley F. Skrutski, Director of Financial Aid, Marywood University, 2300 Adams Avenue, Scranton, PA 18509-1598, 570-348-6225 or toll-free 800-346-5014. *Fax:* 570-961-4739. *E-mail:* skrutski@ac.marywood.edu.

MASSACHUSETTS COLLEGE OF ART
Boston, MA

Tuition & fees (MA res): $6400	Average undergraduate aid package: $8599

ABOUT THE INSTITUTION State-supported, coed. Awards: bachelor's and master's degrees and post-bachelor's certificates. 16 undergraduate majors. Total enrollment: 2,049. Undergraduates: 1,917. Freshmen: 245. Federal methodology is used as a basis for awarding need-based institutional aid.

UNDERGRADUATE EXPENSES for 2004–05 *Application fee:* $30. *Tuition, state resident:* full-time $6400. *Tuition, nonresident:* full-time $17,700. Part-time tuition and fees vary according to class time, course load, and program. *College room and board:* $9737. Room and board charges vary according to housing facility. *Payment plan:* Installment.

FRESHMAN FINANCIAL AID (Fall 2004, est.) 200 applied for aid; of those 67% were deemed to have need. 100% of freshmen with need received aid. *Average financial aid package:* $6503 (excluding resources awarded to replace EFC).

UNDERGRADUATE FINANCIAL AID (Fall 2004, est.) 999 applied for aid; of those 81% were deemed to have need. 100% of undergraduates with need received aid. *Average financial aid package:* $8599 (excluding resources awarded to replace EFC).

GIFT AID (NEED-BASED) *Total amount:* $2,550,988 (50% federal, 36% state, 14% institutional). *Receiving aid:* Freshmen: 29% (72); All full-time undergraduates: 42% (562). *Average award:* Freshmen: $4410; Undergraduates: $4266. *Scholarships, grants, and awards:* Federal Pell, FSEOG, state, private, college/ university gift aid from institutional funds.

GIFT AID (NON-NEED-BASED) *Total amount:* $288,822 (100% external sources). *Receiving aid:* Freshmen: 22% (54); Undergraduates: 11% (146). *Scholarships, grants, and awards by category: Academic Interests/Achievement:* general academic interests/achievements. *Creative Arts/Performance:* applied art and design, art/fine arts. *Special Achievements/Activities:* community service, general special achievements/activities. *Special Characteristics:* children of faculty/staff, children of union members/company employees, veterans. *Tuition waivers:* Full or partial for employees or children of employees, senior citizens.

LOANS *Student loans:* $5,450,395 (63% need-based, 37% non-need-based). 59% of past graduating class borrowed through all loan programs. *Average indebtedness per student:* $18,337. *Average need-based loan:* Freshmen: $2768; Undergraduates: $4105. *Parent loans:* $4,632,682 (100% non-need-based). *Programs:* Federal Direct (Subsidized and Unsubsidized Stafford, PLUS), FFEL (Subsidized and Unsubsidized Stafford, PLUS), Perkins, state, college/university, alternative loans.

WORK-STUDY *Federal work-study:* Total amount: $314,172; 178 jobs averaging $1798.

APPLYING FOR FINANCIAL AID *Required financial aid form:* FAFSA. *Financial aid deadline (priority):* 3/15. *Notification date:* Continuous. Students must reply within 3 weeks of notification.

CONTACT Ken Berryhill, Director of Financial Aid, Massachusetts College of Art, 621 Huntington Avenue, Boston, MA 02115-5882, 617-879-7846. *Fax:* 617-566-4034. *E-mail:* kberryhill@massart.edu.

MASSACHUSETTS COLLEGE OF LIBERAL ARTS
North Adams, MA

ABOUT THE INSTITUTION State-supported, coed. Awards: bachelor's and master's degrees and post-bachelor's certificates. 41 undergraduate majors. Total enrollment: 1,811. Undergraduates: 1,458. Freshmen: 257.

GIFT AID (NEED-BASED) *Scholarships, grants, and awards:* Federal Pell, FSEOG, state, private, college/university gift aid from institutional funds.

GIFT AID (NON-NEED-BASED) *Scholarships, grants, and awards by category: Academic Interests/Achievement:* biological sciences, business, communication, computer science, education, English, general academic interests/ achievements, health fields, humanities, mathematics, physical sciences, social sciences. *Creative Arts/Performance:* applied art and design, art/fine arts, cinema/ film/broadcasting, journalism/publications, music, performing arts, theater/ drama. *Special Achievements/Activities:* general special achievements/activities, leadership, memberships. *Special Characteristics:* first-generation college students, handicapped students, local/state students, out-of-state students.

LOANS *Programs:* FFEL (Subsidized and Unsubsidized Stafford, PLUS), Perkins, state.

WORK-STUDY *Federal work-study:* Total amount: $254,954; jobs available. *State or other work-study/employment:* Total amount: $635,923 (100% non-need-based). Part-time jobs available.

APPLYING FOR FINANCIAL AID *Required financial aid forms:* FAFSA, institution's own form.

CONTACT Elizabeth M. Petri, Director of Financial Aid, Massachusetts College of Liberal Arts, 375 Church Street, Eldridge Hall, Room 112, North Adams, MA 01247, 413-662-5219 or toll-free 800-292-6632 (in-state). *E-mail:* epetri@mcla.edu.

MASSACHUSETTS COLLEGE OF PHARMACY AND HEALTH SCIENCES
Boston, MA

Tuition & fees: $20,220	Average undergraduate aid package: $12,189

ABOUT THE INSTITUTION Independent, coed. Awards: bachelor's, master's, doctoral, and first professional degrees and post-bachelor's and first professional certificates. 10 undergraduate majors. Total enrollment: 2,587. Undergraduates: 1,632. Freshmen: 308. Federal methodology is used as a basis for awarding need-based institutional aid.

UNDERGRADUATE EXPENSES for 2004–05 *Application fee:* $70. *Comprehensive fee:* $30,790 includes full-time tuition ($19,600), mandatory fees ($620), and room and board ($10,570). *College room only:* $7400. Full-time tuition and fees vary according to course level, course load, location, program, and student level. Room and board charges vary according to housing facility. *Part-time tuition:* $720 per credit. *Part-time fees:* $155 per term. *Payment plan:* Installment.

GIFT AID (NEED-BASED) *Total amount:* $7,384,955 (22% federal, 7% state, 66% institutional, 5% external sources). *Receiving aid:* Freshmen: 82% (244); All full-time undergraduates: 77% (1,120). *Average award:* Freshmen: $9335; Undergraduates: $6474. *Scholarships, grants, and awards:* Federal Pell, FSEOG, state, private, college/university gift aid from institutional funds.

GIFT AID (NON-NEED-BASED) *Total amount:* $336,314 (93% institutional, 7% external sources). *Receiving aid:* Freshmen: 2% (7); Undergraduates: 1% (15). *Average Award:* Freshmen: $10,068; Undergraduates: $13,940. *Scholarships, grants, and awards by category:* Academic Interests/Achievement: general academic interests/achievements. *Tuition waivers:* Full or partial for employees or children of employees. *ROTC:* Army cooperative, Air Force cooperative.

LOANS *Student loans:* $26,668,705 (84% need-based, 16% non-need-based). 75% of past graduating class borrowed through all loan programs. *Average need-based loan:* Freshmen: $6042; Undergraduates: $6476. *Parent loans:* $1,267,430 (55% need-based, 45% non-need-based). *Programs:* FFEL (Subsidized and Unsubsidized Stafford, PLUS), Perkins, state, Health Professions Student Loans (HPSL).

APPLYING FOR FINANCIAL AID *Required financial aid form:* FAFSA. *Financial aid deadline (priority):* 3/15. *Notification date:* Continuous. Students must reply by 5/1 or within 2 weeks of notification.

CONTACT Ms. Carrie Glass, Director of Student Financial Services, Massachusetts College of Pharmacy and Health Sciences, 179 Longwood Avenue, Boston, MA 02115-5896, 617-732-2199 or toll-free 617-732-2850 (in-state), 800-225-5506 (out-of-state). *Fax:* 617-732-2082. *E-mail:* carrie.glass@bos.mcphs.edu.

MASSACHUSETTS INSTITUTE OF TECHNOLOGY
Cambridge, MA

Tuition & fees: $30,800	Average undergraduate aid package: $24,875

ABOUT THE INSTITUTION Independent, coed. Awards: bachelor's, master's, and doctoral degrees. 33 undergraduate majors. Total enrollment: 10,320. Undergraduates: 4,136. Freshmen: 1,077. Institutional methodology is used as a basis for awarding need-based institutional aid.

UNDERGRADUATE EXPENSES for 2004–05 *Application fee:* $65. *Comprehensive fee:* $39,900 includes full-time tuition ($30,600), mandatory fees ($200), and room and board ($9100). *College room only:* $4900. Room and board charges vary according to board plan and housing facility. *Part-time tuition:* $482 per unit. Part-time tuition and fees vary according to course load. *Payment plan:* Installment.

FRESHMAN FINANCIAL AID (Fall 2003) 789 applied for aid; of those 83% were deemed to have need. 100% of freshmen with need received aid; of those 100% had need fully met. *Average percent of need met:* 100% (excluding resources awarded to replace EFC). *Average financial aid package:* $24,460 (excluding resources awarded to replace EFC).

UNDERGRADUATE FINANCIAL AID (Fall 2003) 2,816 applied for aid; of those 88% were deemed to have need. 100% of undergraduates with need received aid; of those 100% had need fully met. *Average percent of need met:* 100% (excluding resources awarded to replace EFC). *Average financial aid package:* $24,875 (excluding resources awarded to replace EFC).

GIFT AID (NEED-BASED) *Total amount:* $61,757,119 (8% federal, 1% state, 77% institutional, 14% external sources). *Receiving aid:* Freshmen: 63% (647); All full-time undergraduates: 59% (2,397). *Average award:* Freshmen: $22,589; Undergraduates: $22,225. *Scholarships, grants, and awards:* Federal Pell, FSEOG, state, private, college/university gift aid from institutional funds.

GIFT AID (NON-NEED-BASED) *Total amount:* $683,071 (20% federal, 80% external sources). *Tuition waivers:* Full or partial for employees or children of employees. *ROTC:* Army, Naval, Air Force.

LOANS *Student loans:* $11,118,420 (89% need-based, 11% non-need-based). 54% of past graduating class borrowed through all loan programs. *Average indebtedness per student:* $20,079. *Average need-based loan:* Freshmen: $3220; Undergraduates: $3931. *Parent loans:* $7,168,093 (100% non-need-based). *Programs:* Federal Direct (Subsidized and Unsubsidized Stafford, PLUS), Perkins, college/university.

WORK-STUDY *Federal work-study:* Total amount: $2,228,063; 958 jobs averaging $2325. *State or other work-study/employment:* Total amount: $1,638,189 (64% need-based, 36% non-need-based). 748 part-time jobs averaging $2190.

APPLYING FOR FINANCIAL AID *Required financial aid forms:* FAFSA, CSS Financial Aid PROFILE, noncustodial (divorced/separated) parent's statement, business/farm supplement, federal income tax form(s), W-2 forms. *Financial aid deadline:* 2/1 (priority: 2/1). *Notification date:* 3/15. Students must reply by 5/1.

CONTACT Student Financial Services, Massachusetts Institute of Technology, 77 Massachusetts Avenue, Room 11-320, Cambridge, MA 02139-4307, 617-253-4971. *Fax:* 617-253-9859. *E-mail:* finaid@mit.edu.

MASSACHUSETTS MARITIME ACADEMY
Buzzards Bay, MA

Tuition & fees (MA res): $4963	Average undergraduate aid package: $9013

ABOUT THE INSTITUTION State-supported, coed, primarily men. Awards: bachelor's and master's degrees and first professional certificates. 8 undergraduate majors. Total enrollment: 948. Undergraduates: 927. Freshmen: 275. Federal methodology is used as a basis for awarding need-based institutional aid.

UNDERGRADUATE EXPENSES for 2004–05 *Application fee:* $50. *Tuition, state resident:* full-time $1030; part-time $42 per credit. *Tuition, nonresident:* full-time $11,510. *Required fees:* full-time $3933; $151 per credit. *College room and board:* $6157; *room only:* $3086. *Payment plan:* Installment.

FRESHMAN FINANCIAL AID (Fall 2003) 246 applied for aid; of those 43% were deemed to have need. 100% of freshmen with need received aid; of those 24% had need fully met. *Average percent of need met:* 10% (excluding resources awarded to replace EFC). *Average financial aid package:* $7177 (excluding resources awarded to replace EFC). 18% of all full-time freshmen had no need and received non-need-based gift aid.

UNDERGRADUATE FINANCIAL AID (Fall 2003) 645 applied for aid; of those 65% were deemed to have need. 98% of undergraduates with need received aid; of those 44% had need fully met. *Average percent of need met:* 19% (excluding resources awarded to replace EFC). *Average financial aid package:* $9013 (excluding resources awarded to replace EFC). 15% of all full-time undergraduates had no need and received non-need-based gift aid.

GIFT AID (NEED-BASED) *Receiving aid:* Freshmen: 15% (41); All full-time undergraduates: 29% (279). *Average award:* Freshmen: $1943; Undergraduates: $1967. *Scholarships, grants, and awards:* Federal Pell, FSEOG, state, private, college/university gift aid from institutional funds.

GIFT AID (NON-NEED-BASED) *Receiving aid:* Freshmen: 18% (50); Undergraduates: 15% (146). *Average Award:* Freshmen: $1717; Undergraduates: $1239. *Scholarships, grants, and awards by category:* Academic Interests/Achievement: 107 awards ($186,132 total): general academic interests/achievements. Creative Arts/Performance: 2 awards ($2060 total): theater/drama. Special Achievements/Activities: 34 awards ($35,020 total): leadership. Special Characteristics: 27

awards ($83,877 total): children and siblings of alumni, children of faculty/staff, international students. *Tuition waivers:* Full or partial for employees or children of employees. *ROTC:* Army cooperative, Naval.

LOANS *Student loans:* $3,163,227 (42% need-based, 58% non-need-based). 82% of past graduating class borrowed through all loan programs. *Average indebtedness per student:* $12,125. *Average need-based loan:* Freshmen: $2625; Undergraduates: $3917. *Parent loans:* $954,734 (100% need-based). *Programs:* Federal Direct (Subsidized and Unsubsidized Stafford, PLUS).

WORK-STUDY *Federal work-study:* Total amount: $100,000; 166 jobs averaging $1500.

APPLYING FOR FINANCIAL AID *Required financial aid forms:* FAFSA, institution's own form. *Financial aid deadline (priority):* 4/30. *Notification date:* Continuous beginning 4/1.

CONTACT Mrs. Elizabeth Benway, Director of Financial Aid, Massachusetts Maritime Academy, 101 Academy Drive, Buzzards Bay, MA 02532, 508-830-5087 or toll-free 800-544-3411. *Fax:* 508-830-5077. *E-mail:* ebenway@maritime.edu.

THE MASTER'S COLLEGE AND SEMINARY
Santa Clarita, CA

ABOUT THE INSTITUTION Independent nondenominational, coed. Awards: bachelor's, master's, doctoral, and first professional degrees and first professional certificates. 46 undergraduate majors. Total enrollment: 1,523. Undergraduates: 1,134. Freshmen: 219.

GIFT AID (NEED-BASED) *Scholarships, grants, and awards:* Federal Pell, FSEOG, state, private, college/university gift aid from institutional funds.

GIFT AID (NON-NEED-BASED) *Scholarships, grants, and awards by category: Academic Interests/Achievement:* biological sciences, business, education, general academic interests/achievements, mathematics, physical sciences, religion/biblical studies, social sciences. *Creative Arts/Performance:* music. *Special Achievements/Activities:* leadership. *Special Characteristics:* children and siblings of alumni, children of faculty/staff, general special characteristics, international students, relatives of clergy.

LOANS *Programs:* FFEL (Subsidized and Unsubsidized Stafford, PLUS), Perkins, alternative loans.

WORK-STUDY *Federal work-study:* Total amount: $150,000; 45 jobs averaging $2666. *State or other work-study/employment:* Total amount: $896,650 (76% need-based, 24% non-need-based). Part-time jobs available.

APPLYING FOR FINANCIAL AID *Required financial aid forms:* FAFSA, institution's own form, state aid form.

CONTACT Karen Smith, Director of Financial Aid, The Master's College and Seminary, 21726 Placerita Canyon Road, Santa Clarita, CA 91321-1200, 661-259-3540 Ext. 3391 or toll-free 800-568-6248. *Fax:* 661-362-2693. *E-mail:* ksmith@masters.edu.

MAYVILLE STATE UNIVERSITY
Mayville, ND

ABOUT THE INSTITUTION State-supported, coed. Awards: associate and bachelor's degrees. 32 undergraduate majors. Total enrollment: 897. Undergraduates: 897. Freshmen: 164.

GIFT AID (NEED-BASED) *Scholarships, grants, and awards:* Federal Pell, FSEOG, state.

GIFT AID (NON-NEED-BASED) *Scholarships, grants, and awards by category: Academic Interests/Achievement:* biological sciences, business, education, English, general academic interests/achievements, library science, mathematics, physical sciences. *Creative Arts/Performance:* music. *Special Achievements/Activities:* leadership. *Special Characteristics:* children of union members/company employees, international students, local/state students, members of minority groups, out-of-state students.

LOANS *Programs:* FFEL (Subsidized and Unsubsidized Stafford, PLUS), Perkins, college/university.

APPLYING FOR FINANCIAL AID *Required financial aid form:* FAFSA.

CONTACT Ms. Shirley Hanson, Director of Student Financial Aid, Mayville State University, 330 3rd Street NE, Mayville, ND 58257-1299, 701-786-4767 or toll-free 800-437-4104. *E-mail:* s_hanson@mail.masu.nodak.edu.

McDANIEL COLLEGE
Westminster, MD

Tuition & fees: $24,800 | **Average undergraduate aid package: $19,963**

ABOUT THE INSTITUTION Independent, coed. Awards: bachelor's and master's degrees. 26 undergraduate majors. Total enrollment: 3,304. Undergraduates: 1,619. Freshmen: 357. Both federal and institutional methodology are used as a basis for awarding need-based institutional aid.

UNDERGRADUATE EXPENSES for 2004–05 *Application fee:* $50. *Comprehensive fee:* $30,400 includes full-time tuition ($24,500), mandatory fees ($300), and room and board ($5600). *College room only:* $3000. Room and board charges vary according to board plan and housing facility. *Part-time tuition:* $766 per credit. *Part-time fees:* $150 per term. *Payment plan:* Installment.

FRESHMAN FINANCIAL AID (Fall 2004, est.) 295 applied for aid; of those 84% were deemed to have need. 100% of freshmen with need received aid; of those 30% had need fully met. *Average percent of need met:* 94% (excluding resources awarded to replace EFC). *Average financial aid package:* $19,795 (excluding resources awarded to replace EFC). 25% of all full-time freshmen had no need and received non-need-based gift aid.

UNDERGRADUATE FINANCIAL AID (Fall 2004, est.) 1,159 applied for aid; of those 87% were deemed to have need. 100% of undergraduates with need received aid; of those 30% had need fully met. *Average percent of need met:* 93% (excluding resources awarded to replace EFC). *Average financial aid package:* $19,963 (excluding resources awarded to replace EFC). 24% of all full-time undergraduates had no need and received non-need-based gift aid.

GIFT AID (NEED-BASED) *Total amount:* $13,399,404 (7% federal, 8% state, 85% institutional). *Receiving aid:* Freshmen: 68% (241); All full-time undergraduates: 63% (981). *Average award:* Freshmen: $9098; Undergraduates: $8645. *Scholarships, grants, and awards:* Federal Pell, FSEOG, state, private, college/university gift aid from institutional funds.

GIFT AID (NON-NEED-BASED) *Total amount:* $5,699,752 (11% state, 85% institutional, 4% external sources). *Average Award:* Freshmen: $8965; Undergraduates: $13,007. *Scholarships, grants, and awards by category: Academic Interests/Achievement:* 1,140 awards ($10,417,355 total): general academic interests/achievements. *Special Achievements/Activities:* 4 awards ($8000 total): junior miss, leadership. *Special Characteristics:* 308 awards ($445,296 total): local/state students, previous college experience, siblings of current students. *Tuition waivers:* Full or partial for employees or children of employees. *ROTC:* Army.

LOANS *Student loans:* $6,440,297 (51% need-based, 49% non-need-based). 63% of past graduating class borrowed through all loan programs. *Average indebtedness per student:* $19,996. *Average need-based loan:* Freshmen: $3892; Undergraduates: $4981. *Parent loans:* $2,346,550 (100% non-need-based). *Programs:* FFEL (Subsidized and Unsubsidized Stafford, PLUS), Perkins, college/university.

WORK-STUDY *Federal work-study:* Total amount: $152,594; 193 jobs averaging $790. *State or other work-study/employment:* Total amount: $139,046 (100% non-need-based). 110 part-time jobs averaging $1264.

APPLYING FOR FINANCIAL AID *Required financial aid forms:* FAFSA, institution's own form, federal income tax form(s). *Financial aid deadline (priority):* 3/1. *Notification date:* Continuous. Students must reply by 5/1 or within 2 weeks of notification.

CONTACT Financial Aid Office, McDaniel College, 2 College Hill, Westminster, MD 21157-4390, 410-857-2233 or toll-free 800-638-5005. *Fax:* 410-857-2729. *E-mail:* finaid@mcdaniel.edu.

McKENDREE COLLEGE
Lebanon, IL

Tuition & fees: $16,600 | **Average undergraduate aid package: $13,846**

ABOUT THE INSTITUTION Independent religious, coed. Awards: bachelor's and master's degrees. 50 undergraduate majors. Total enrollment: 2,257. Undergraduates: 2,156. Freshmen: 339. Federal methodology is used as a basis for awarding need-based institutional aid.

UNDERGRADUATE EXPENSES for 2004–05 *Application fee:* $40. *Comprehensive fee:* $22,960 includes full-time tuition ($16,400), mandatory fees ($200), and room and board ($6360). *College room only:* $3360. Full-time tuition and fees vary according to location. Room and board charges vary according to board

McKendree College

plan and housing facility. *Part-time tuition:* $550 per hour. Part-time tuition and fees vary according to course load and location. *Payment plans:* Installment, deferred payment.

FRESHMAN FINANCIAL AID (Fall 2004, est.) 293 applied for aid; of those 90% were deemed to have need. 100% of freshmen with need received aid; of those 26% had need fully met. *Average percent of need met:* 84% (excluding resources awarded to replace EFC). *Average financial aid package:* $15,024 (excluding resources awarded to replace EFC). 19% of all full-time freshmen had no need and received non-need-based gift aid.

UNDERGRADUATE FINANCIAL AID (Fall 2004, est.) 1,128 applied for aid; of those 89% were deemed to have need. 100% of undergraduates with need received aid; of those 25% had need fully met. *Average percent of need met:* 81% (excluding resources awarded to replace EFC). *Average financial aid package:* $13,846 (excluding resources awarded to replace EFC). 20% of all full-time undergraduates had no need and received non-need-based gift aid.

GIFT AID (NEED-BASED) *Total amount:* $9,756,633 (15% federal, 23% state, 60% institutional, 2% external sources). *Receiving aid:* Freshmen: 78% (264); All full-time undergraduates: 78% (989). *Average award:* Freshmen: $12,735; Undergraduates: $10,940. *Scholarships, grants, and awards:* Federal Pell, FSEOG, state, private, college/university gift aid from institutional funds.

GIFT AID (NON-NEED-BASED) *Total amount:* $2,213,564 (2% state, 93% institutional, 5% external sources). *Receiving aid:* Freshmen: 15% (51); Undergraduates: 14% (177). *Average Award:* Freshmen: $9745; Undergraduates: $9433. *Scholarships, grants, and awards by category: Academic Interests/Achievement:* 853 awards ($3,913,446 total): biological sciences, business, general academic interests/achievements, religion/biblical studies. *Creative Arts/Performance:* 132 awards ($320,211 total): music. *Special Achievements/Activities:* 38 awards ($88,459 total): cheerleading/drum major, community service, leadership. *Special Characteristics:* 179 awards ($438,202 total): children of faculty/staff, general special characteristics, out-of-state students, religious affiliation. *Tuition waivers:* Full or partial for employees or children of employees. *ROTC:* Army cooperative, Air Force cooperative.

LOANS *Student loans:* $4,974,429 (71% need-based, 29% non-need-based). 58% of past graduating class borrowed through all loan programs. *Average indebtedness per student:* $16,240. *Average need-based loan:* Freshmen: $2116; Undergraduates: $3251. *Parent loans:* $1,657,829 (25% need-based, 75% non-need-based). *Programs:* FFEL (Subsidized and Unsubsidized Stafford, PLUS), Perkins.

WORK-STUDY *Federal work-study:* Total amount: $563,919; 441 jobs averaging $1276. *State or other work-study/employment:* Total amount: $202,427 (9% need-based, 91% non-need-based). 173 part-time jobs averaging $1164.

ATHLETIC AWARDS *Total amount:* $2,064,272 (54% need-based, 46% non-need-based).

APPLYING FOR FINANCIAL AID *Required financial aid forms:* FAFSA, institution's own form. *Financial aid deadline (priority):* 5/31. *Notification date:* Continuous beginning 3/1.

CONTACT Director of Financial Aid, McKendree College, 701 College Road, Lebanon, IL 62254-1299, 618-537-6827 or toll-free 800-232-7228 Ext. 6831. *Fax:* 618-537-6530.

McMURRY UNIVERSITY
Abilene, TX

Tuition & fees: $14,350	Average undergraduate aid package: $13,207

ABOUT THE INSTITUTION Independent United Methodist, coed. Awards: bachelor's degrees. 48 undergraduate majors. Total enrollment: 1,386. Undergraduates: 1,386. Freshmen: 282. Federal methodology is used as a basis for awarding need-based institutional aid.

UNDERGRADUATE EXPENSES for 2005–06 *Application fee:* $20. *Comprehensive fee:* $19,850 includes full-time tuition ($14,300), mandatory fees ($50), and room and board ($5500). *College room only:* $3000. Full-time tuition and fees vary according to course load. Room and board charges vary according to board plan and housing facility. *Part-time tuition:* $450 per semester hour. Part-time tuition and fees vary according to course load. *Payment plan:* Installment.

FRESHMAN FINANCIAL AID (Fall 2003) 262 applied for aid; of those 85% were deemed to have need. 100% of freshmen with need received aid; of those 7% had need fully met. *Average percent of need met:* 81% (excluding resources awarded to replace EFC). *Average financial aid package:* $13,062 (excluding resources awarded to replace EFC). 6% of all full-time freshmen had no need and received non-need-based gift aid.

UNDERGRADUATE FINANCIAL AID (Fall 2003) 1,047 applied for aid; of those 89% were deemed to have need. 100% of undergraduates with need received aid; of those 13% had need fully met. *Average percent of need met:* 78% (excluding resources awarded to replace EFC). *Average financial aid package:* $13,207 (excluding resources awarded to replace EFC). 6% of all full-time undergraduates had no need and received non-need-based gift aid.

GIFT AID (NEED-BASED) *Total amount:* $6,904,302 (25% federal, 31% state, 40% institutional, 4% external sources). *Receiving aid:* Freshmen: 78% (219); All full-time undergraduates: 74% (857). *Average award:* Freshmen: $8585; Undergraduates: $7018. *Scholarships, grants, and awards:* Federal Pell, FSEOG, state, private, college/university gift aid from institutional funds.

GIFT AID (NON-NEED-BASED) *Total amount:* $1,574,931 (6% federal, 9% state, 83% institutional, 2% external sources). *Receiving aid:* Freshmen: 23% (65); Undergraduates: 30% (351). *Average Award:* Freshmen: $4706; Undergraduates: $3986. *Scholarships, grants, and awards by category: Academic Interests/Achievement:* 766 awards ($2,509,532 total): general academic interests/achievements, religion/biblical studies. *Creative Arts/Performance:* 25 awards ($40,023 total): art/fine arts, music. *Special Achievements/Activities:* 37 awards ($40,050 total): general special achievements/activities, junior miss. *Special Characteristics:* 384 awards ($1,492,526 total): children of faculty/staff, international students, local/state students, out-of-state students, previous college experience, relatives of clergy, religious affiliation, veterans. *Tuition waivers:* Full or partial for employees or children of employees. *ROTC:* Air Force cooperative.

LOANS *Student loans:* $7,014,749 (43% need-based, 57% non-need-based). 69% of past graduating class borrowed through all loan programs. *Average indebtedness per student:* $28,368. *Average need-based loan:* Freshmen: $2870; Undergraduates: $3891. *Parent loans:* $1,169,306 (100% non-need-based). *Programs:* FFEL (Subsidized and Unsubsidized Stafford, PLUS), Perkins, state, Alternative Loan.

WORK-STUDY *Federal work-study:* Total amount: $292,181; 219 jobs averaging $929. *State or other work-study/employment:* Total amount: $124,764 (20% need-based, 80% non-need-based). 243 part-time jobs averaging $597.

APPLYING FOR FINANCIAL AID *Required financial aid forms:* FAFSA, institution's own form. *Financial aid deadline (priority):* 3/15. *Notification date:* Continuous beginning 2/1. Students must reply within 3 weeks of notification.

CONTACT Ms. Kathyrn Martin, Director of Financial Aid, McMurry University, Box 908, McMurry Station, Abilene, TX 79697, 325-793-4713 or toll-free 800-477-0077. *Fax:* 325-793-4718. *E-mail:* martink@mcmurryadm.mcm.edu.

McNEESE STATE UNIVERSITY
Lake Charles, LA

CONTACT Ms. Taina J. Savoit, Director of Financial Aid, McNeese State University, PO Box 93260, Lake Charles, LA 70609-3260, 337-475-5065 or toll-free 800-622-3352. *Fax:* 337-475-5068. *E-mail:* tsavoit@mail.mcneese.edu.

McPHERSON COLLEGE
McPherson, KS

Tuition & fees: $15,160	Average undergraduate aid package: $16,587

ABOUT THE INSTITUTION Independent religious, coed. Awards: associate and bachelor's degrees. 44 undergraduate majors. Total enrollment: 464. Undergraduates: 464. Freshmen: 115. Federal methodology is used as a basis for awarding need-based institutional aid.

UNDERGRADUATE EXPENSES for 2005–06 *Application fee:* $25. *Comprehensive fee:* $21,010 includes full-time tuition ($14,900), mandatory fees ($260), and room and board ($5850). *College room only:* $2400. *Part-time tuition:* $450 per credit hour.

GIFT AID (NEED-BASED) *Total amount:* $1,412,148 (43% federal, 15% state, 42% institutional). *Receiving aid:* Freshmen: 78% (90); All full-time undergraduates: 68% (289). *Average award:* Freshmen: $4701; Undergraduates: $4807. *Scholarships, grants, and awards:* Federal Pell, FSEOG, state, private, college/university gift aid from institutional funds.

GIFT AID (NON-NEED-BASED) *Total amount:* $2,302,607 (98% institutional, 2% external sources). *Receiving aid:* Freshmen: 84% (97); Undergraduates: 81% (343). *Average Award:* Freshmen: $5719; Undergraduates: $7527. *Scholarships, grants, and awards by category: Academic Interests/Achievement:* 397 awards ($1,088,782 total): general academic interests/achievements. *Special Characteristics:* 78 awards ($55,000 total): local/state students, religious affiliation.

LOANS *Student loans:* $2,427,314 (73% need-based, 27% non-need-based). 85% of past graduating class borrowed through all loan programs. *Average indebtedness per student:* $16,015. *Average need-based loan:* Freshmen: $5263; Undergraduates: $5683. *Parent loans:* $425,733 (100% non-need-based). *Programs:* FFEL (Subsidized and Unsubsidized Stafford, PLUS), Perkins.

APPLYING FOR FINANCIAL AID *Required financial aid forms:* FAFSA, state aid form. *Financial aid deadline (priority):* 4/1. *Notification date:* Continuous beginning 3/1. Students must reply within 4 weeks of notification.

CONTACT Ms. Carol L. Williams, Director of Admissions and Financial Aid, McPherson College, PO Box 1402, McPherson, KS 67460-1402, 316-241-0731 Ext. 1270 or toll-free 800-365-7402. *Fax:* 316-241-8443. *E-mail:* williamc@mcpherson.edu.

MEDAILLE COLLEGE
Buffalo, NY

ABOUT THE INSTITUTION Independent, coed. Awards: associate, bachelor's, and master's degrees. 30 undergraduate majors. Total enrollment: 2,526. Undergraduates: 1,708. Freshmen: 307.

GIFT AID (NEED-BASED) *Scholarships, grants, and awards:* Federal Pell, FSEOG, state, college/university gift aid from institutional funds.

GIFT AID (NON-NEED-BASED) *Scholarships, grants, and awards by category: Academic Interests/Achievement:* general academic interests/achievements. *Special Characteristics:* adult students.

LOANS *Programs:* FFEL (Subsidized and Unsubsidized Stafford, PLUS).

WORK-STUDY *Federal work-study:* Total amount: $127,000; 140 jobs averaging $1500.

APPLYING FOR FINANCIAL AID *Required financial aid forms:* FAFSA, institution's own form, state aid form.

CONTACT Ms. Jacqueline Matheny, Director of Enrollment Management and Admissions, Medaille College, 18 Agassiz Circle, Buffalo, NY 14214-2695, 716-884-3411 Ext. 203 or toll-free 800-292-1582 (in-state). *Fax:* 716-884-0291.

MEDCENTER ONE COLLEGE OF NURSING
Bismarck, ND

Tuition & fees: $8620	Average undergraduate aid package: $9281

ABOUT THE INSTITUTION Independent, coed, primarily women. Awards: bachelor's degrees. 1 undergraduate major. Total enrollment: 88. Undergraduates: 88. Federal methodology is used as a basis for awarding need-based institutional aid.

UNDERGRADUATE EXPENSES for 2004–05 *Application fee:* $40. *Tuition:* full-time $8000; part-time $334 per credit. *Required fees:* full-time $620; $5 per credit or $190 per term part-time. Part-time tuition and fees vary according to course load.

UNDERGRADUATE FINANCIAL AID (Fall 2003) 76 applied for aid; of those 87% were deemed to have need. 100% of undergraduates with need received aid; of those 82% had need fully met. *Average percent of need met:* 96% (excluding resources awarded to replace EFC). *Average financial aid package:* $9281 (excluding resources awarded to replace EFC). 8% of all full-time undergraduates had no need and received non-need-based gift aid.

GIFT AID (NEED-BASED) *Total amount:* $160,759 (77% federal, 7% state, 2% institutional, 14% external sources). *Receiving aid:* All full-time undergraduates: 60% (47). *Average award:* Undergraduates: $3045. *Scholarships, grants, and awards:* Federal Pell, FSEOG, state, private, college/university gift aid from institutional funds.

GIFT AID (NON-NEED-BASED) *Total amount:* $6407 (59% institutional, 41% external sources). *Receiving aid:* Undergraduates: 8% (6). *Average Award: Undergraduates:* $250. *Scholarships, grants, and awards by category: Academic Interests/Achievement:* 24 awards ($3350 total): general academic interests/achievements, health fields. *Special Achievements/Activities:* 16 awards ($1600 total): memberships. *Special Characteristics:* local/state students.

LOANS *Student loans:* $743,563 (31% need-based, 69% non-need-based). 100% of past graduating class borrowed through all loan programs. *Average indebtedness per student:* $10,993. *Average need-based loan:* Undergraduates: $3776. *Parent loans:* $8000 (100% non-need-based). *Programs:* FFEL (Subsidized and Unsubsidized Stafford, PLUS), Perkins, Federal Nursing, college/university.

WORK-STUDY *Federal work-study:* Total amount: $4261; 7 jobs averaging $1100.

APPLYING FOR FINANCIAL AID *Required financial aid forms:* FAFSA, institution's own form, institutional scholarship application form. *Financial aid deadline (priority):* 5/1. *Notification date:* 6/15. Students must reply within 2 weeks of notification.

CONTACT Ms. Janell Thomas, Financial Aid Director, Medcenter One College of Nursing, 512 North 7th Street, Bismarck, ND 58501-4494, 701-323-6270. *Fax:* 701-323-6967. *E-mail:* jthomas@mohs.org.

MEDCENTRAL COLLEGE OF NURSING
Mansfield, OH

CONTACT Financial Aid Office, MedCentral College of Nursing, 335 Glessner Avenue, Mansfield, OH 44903, 419-520-2600 or toll-free 877-656-4360.

MEDGAR EVERS COLLEGE OF THE CITY UNIVERSITY OF NEW YORK
Brooklyn, NY

Tuition & fees (NY res): $4230	Average undergraduate aid package: N/A

ABOUT THE INSTITUTION State and locally supported, coed. Awards: associate and bachelor's degrees. 19 undergraduate majors. Total enrollment: 5,098. Undergraduates: 5,098. Freshmen: 724. Federal methodology is used as a basis for awarding need-based institutional aid.

UNDERGRADUATE EXPENSES for 2004–05 *Application fee:* $60. *Tuition, state resident:* full-time $4000; part-time $170 per credit. *Tuition, nonresident:* full-time $8640; part-time $360 per credit. *Required fees:* full-time $230; $78.35 per term part-time. *Payment plans:* Installment, deferred payment.

GIFT AID (NEED-BASED) *Total amount:* $12,998,985 (57% federal, 43% state). *Receiving aid:* Freshmen: 71% (444); All full-time undergraduates: 64% (1,906). *Scholarships, grants, and awards:* Federal Pell, FSEOG, state, private, college/university gift aid from institutional funds.

GIFT AID (NON-NEED-BASED) *Total amount:* $12,500 (100% external sources). *Receiving aid:* Undergraduates: 5. *Scholarships, grants, and awards by category: Academic Interests/Achievement:* 5 awards ($10,128 total): general academic interests/achievements.

LOANS *Student loans:* $525,398 (100% need-based). *Programs:* Federal Direct (Subsidized and Unsubsidized Stafford, PLUS), FFEL (Subsidized and Unsubsidized Stafford, PLUS), Perkins.

WORK-STUDY *Federal work-study:* Total amount: $247,510; 516 jobs averaging $1300.

APPLYING FOR FINANCIAL AID *Required financial aid forms:* FAFSA, state aid form, University Financial Aid Information Supplemental Request (FASIR). *Financial aid deadline (priority):* 4/1. *Notification date:* Continuous beginning 9/1.

CONTACT Louise Martin, Director of Financial Aid, Medgar Evers College of the City University of New York, 1150 Carroll Street, Brooklyn, NY 11225, 718-270-6038. *E-mail:* louise@mec.cuny.edu.

MEDICAL COLLEGE OF GEORGIA
Augusta, GA

Tuition & fees (GA res): $3954	Average undergraduate aid package: $9164

ABOUT THE INSTITUTION State-supported, coed. Awards: bachelor's, master's, doctoral, and first professional degrees and post-bachelor's certificates. 10 undergraduate majors. Total enrollment: 2,115. Undergraduates: 725. Federal methodology is used as a basis for awarding need-based institutional aid.

UNDERGRADUATE EXPENSES for 2004–05 *Tuition, state resident:* full-time $3368; part-time $141 per hour. *Tuition, nonresident:* full-time $14,060; part-time $562 per hour. *Required fees:* full-time $586; $293 per term part-time. Full-time tuition and fees vary according to location. Part-time tuition and fees vary according to course load and location. *College room and board: room only:* $2334. Room and board charges vary according to housing facility.

UNDERGRADUATE FINANCIAL AID (Fall 2004, est.) 423 applied for aid; of those 89% were deemed to have need. 98% of undergraduates with need received aid; of those 12% had need fully met. *Average percent of need met:* 54% (excluding resources awarded to replace EFC). *Average financial aid package:* $9164 (excluding resources awarded to replace EFC). 23% of all full-time undergraduates had no need and received non-need-based gift aid.

GIFT AID (NEED-BASED) *Total amount:* $1,268,309 (36% federal, 51% state, 9% institutional, 4% external sources). *Receiving aid:* All full-time undergraduates: 49% (252). *Average award:* Undergraduates: $4408. *Scholarships, grants, and awards:* Federal Pell, FSEOG, state, private, college/university gift aid from institutional funds, Federal Nursing.

GIFT AID (NON-NEED-BASED) *Total amount:* $522,820 (98% state, 2% external sources). *Receiving aid:* Undergraduates: 4% (19). *Average Award:* Undergraduates: $7389. *Scholarships, grants, and awards by category:* Academic Interests/ Achievement: 452 awards ($3,835,863 total): health fields. *Special Characteristics:* 170 awards ($139,994 total): religious affiliation.

LOANS *Student loans:* $3,784,211 (77% need-based, 23% non-need-based). 89% of past graduating class borrowed through all loan programs. *Average indebtedness per student:* $20,453. *Average need-based loan:* Undergraduates: $6256. *Parent loans:* $55,902 (40% need-based, 60% non-need-based). *Programs:* FFEL (Subsidized and Unsubsidized Stafford, PLUS), Perkins, Federal Nursing, state, college/university.

WORK-STUDY *Federal work-study:* Total amount: $158,664; 98 jobs averaging $1892.

APPLYING FOR FINANCIAL AID *Required financial aid forms:* FAFSA, institution's own form. *Financial aid deadline (priority):* 3/31. *Notification date:* Continuous beginning 4/30. Students must reply within 2 weeks of notification.

CONTACT Cynthia Parks, Interim Director of Student Financial Aid, Medical College of Georgia, 2013 Administration Building, 1120 Fifteenth Street, Augusta, GA 30912-7320, 706-721-4901 or toll-free 800-519-3388 (in-state). *Fax:* 706-721-9407. *E-mail:* osfa@mail.mcg.edu.

MEDICAL UNIVERSITY OF SOUTH CAROLINA
Charleston, SC

Tuition & fees (SC res): $9446	Average undergraduate aid package: $6861

ABOUT THE INSTITUTION State-supported, coed. Awards: bachelor's, master's, doctoral, and first professional degrees and post-bachelor's certificates. 3 undergraduate majors. Total enrollment: 2,428. Undergraduates: 332. Federal methodology is used as a basis for awarding need-based institutional aid.

UNDERGRADUATE EXPENSES for 2004–05 *Application fee:* $75. *Tuition, state resident:* full-time $8368; part-time $728 per credit hour. *Tuition, nonresident:* full-time $22,144; part-time $2030 per credit hour. *Required fees:* full-time $1078; $1402 per term part-time. Full-time tuition and fees vary according to program. Part-time tuition and fees vary according to program. *Payment plan:* Installment.

UNDERGRADUATE FINANCIAL AID (Fall 2003) 60 applied for aid; of those 87% were deemed to have need. 94% of undergraduates with need received aid; of those 4% had need fully met. *Average percent of need met:* 54% (excluding resources awarded to replace EFC). *Average financial aid package:* $6861 (excluding resources awarded to replace EFC).

GIFT AID (NEED-BASED) *Total amount:* $522,398 (35% federal, 29% state, 1% institutional, 35% external sources). *Receiving aid:* Entering class: 89; All full-time undergraduates: 20. *Average award:* Freshmen: $5223; Undergraduates: $2876. *Scholarships, grants, and awards:* Federal Pell, FSEOG, state, private, college/university gift aid from institutional funds, Federal Nursing, Scholarships for Disadvantaged Students (SDS).

GIFT AID (NON-NEED-BASED) *Total amount:* $103,406 (6% federal, 60% state, 2% institutional, 32% external sources). *Receiving aid:* Freshmen: 9. *Average Award:* Freshmen: $1000. *Scholarships, grants, and awards by category:* Academic Interests/Achievement: general academic interests/achievements, health fields. *Special Characteristics:* ethnic background, general special characteristics, local/state students, members of minority groups. *Tuition waivers:* Full or partial for employees or children of employees, senior citizens.

LOANS *Student loans:* $3,122,971 (83% need-based, 17% non-need-based). 57% of past graduating class borrowed through all loan programs. *Average indebtedness per student:* $32,486. *Average need-based loan:* Freshmen: $6458; Undergraduates: $5738. *Parent loans:* $48,528 (23% need-based, 77% non-need-based). *Programs:* FFEL (Subsidized and Unsubsidized Stafford, PLUS), Perkins, Federal Nursing, state, Health Professions Loans, Loans for Disadvantaged Students program, Primary Care Loans, alternative loans, TERI Loans.

WORK-STUDY *Federal work-study:* Total amount: $14,838; jobs available.

APPLYING FOR FINANCIAL AID *Required financial aid forms:* FAFSA, institution's own form, income tax forms. *Financial aid deadline (priority):* 3/15.

CONTACT William H. Vandiver, Associate Director for Financial Aid Services, Medical University of South Carolina, 45 Courtenay Drive, PO Box 250176, Charleston, SC 29425, 843-792-2536. *Fax:* 843-792-2060. *E-mail:* vandivew@ musc.edu.

MEMPHIS COLLEGE OF ART
Memphis, TN

Tuition & fees: $15,860	Average undergraduate aid package: $7000

ABOUT THE INSTITUTION Independent, coed. Awards: bachelor's and master's degrees. 22 undergraduate majors. Total enrollment: 315. Undergraduates: 294. Freshmen: 60. Both federal and institutional methodology are used as a basis for awarding need-based institutional aid.

UNDERGRADUATE EXPENSES for 2004–05 *Application fee:* $25. *Comprehensive fee:* $23,260 includes full-time tuition ($15,800), mandatory fees ($60), and room and board ($7400). *College room only:* $5400. Room and board charges vary according to housing facility. *Part-time tuition:* $670 per credit hour. Part-time tuition and fees vary according to course load. *Payment plans:* Installment, deferred payment.

FRESHMAN FINANCIAL AID (Fall 2004, est.) 53 applied for aid; of those 91% were deemed to have need. 100% of freshmen with need received aid; of those 81% had need fully met. *Average percent of need met:* 90% (excluding resources awarded to replace EFC). *Average financial aid package:* $6500 (excluding resources awarded to replace EFC). 20% of all full-time freshmen had no need and received non-need-based gift aid.

UNDERGRADUATE FINANCIAL AID (Fall 2004, est.) 211 applied for aid; of those 100% were deemed to have need. 100% of undergraduates with need received aid; of those 56% had need fully met. *Average percent of need met:* 95% (excluding resources awarded to replace EFC). *Average financial aid package:* $7000 (excluding resources awarded to replace EFC). 24% of all full-time undergraduates had no need and received non-need-based gift aid.

GIFT AID (NEED-BASED) *Total amount:* $633,149 (69% federal, 23% state, 8% institutional). *Receiving aid:* Freshmen: 17% (10); All full-time undergraduates: 42% (118). *Average award:* Freshmen: $3000; Undergraduates: $3000. *Scholarships, grants, and awards:* Federal Pell, FSEOG, state, private, college/ university gift aid from institutional funds.

GIFT AID (NON-NEED-BASED) *Total amount:* $1,059,830 (5% state, 88% institutional, 7% external sources). *Receiving aid:* Freshmen: 80% (48); Undergraduates: 76% (211). *Average Award:* Freshmen: $3500; Undergraduates: $5500. *Scholarships, grants, and awards by category:* Academic Interests/Achievement: 275 awards ($863,750 total): general academic interests/achievements. Creative Arts/Performance: $863,750 total: applied art and design, art/fine arts. *Special Characteristics:* 13 awards ($13,500 total): previous college experience. *Tuition waivers:* Full or partial for employees or children of employees.

LOANS *Student loans:* $2,163,464 (37% need-based, 63% non-need-based). 90% of past graduating class borrowed through all loan programs. *Average indebtedness per student:* $20,000. *Average need-based loan:* Freshmen: $3500; Undergraduates: $5500. *Parent loans:* $932,350 (100% non-need-based). *Programs:* FFEL (Subsidized and Unsubsidized Stafford, PLUS), Perkins, college/university.

WORK-STUDY *Federal work-study:* Total amount: $65,000; 68 jobs averaging $1000. *State or other work-study/employment:* Total amount: $84,000 (100% non-need-based). 84 part-time jobs averaging $1000.

APPLYING FOR FINANCIAL AID *Required financial aid form:* FAFSA. *Financial aid deadline (priority):* 3/1. *Notification date:* Continuous. Students must reply within 3 weeks of notification.

CONTACT Cindy Stanley, Director of Financial Aid, Memphis College of Art, 1930 Poplar Avenue, Memphis, TN 38104-2764, 901-272-5136 or toll-free 800-727-1088. *Fax:* 901-272-5158.

MENLO COLLEGE
Atherton, CA

Tuition & fees: $24,450	Average undergraduate aid package: $17,705

ABOUT THE INSTITUTION Independent, coed. Awards: bachelor's degrees. 3 undergraduate majors. Total enrollment: 749. Undergraduates: 749. Freshmen: 192. Federal methodology is used as a basis for awarding need-based institutional aid.

UNDERGRADUATE EXPENSES for 2005–06 *Application fee:* $40. *Comprehensive fee:* $34,050 includes full-time tuition ($24,300), mandatory fees ($150), and room and board ($9600). Full-time tuition and fees vary according to program. Room and board charges vary according to housing facility. Part-time tuition and fees vary according to course load and program. *Payment plan:* Installment.
FRESHMAN FINANCIAL AID (Fall 2004, est.) 140 applied for aid; of those 88% were deemed to have need. 99% of freshmen with need received aid; of those 12% had need fully met. *Average percent of need met:* 72% (excluding resources awarded to replace EFC). *Average financial aid package:* $18,055 (excluding resources awarded to replace EFC). 34% of all full-time freshmen had no need and received non-need-based gift aid.
UNDERGRADUATE FINANCIAL AID (Fall 2004, est.) 484 applied for aid; of those 92% were deemed to have need. 100% of undergraduates with need received aid; of those 13% had need fully met. *Average percent of need met:* 72% (excluding resources awarded to replace EFC). *Average financial aid package:* $17,705 (excluding resources awarded to replace EFC). 26% of all full-time undergraduates had no need and received non-need-based gift aid.
GIFT AID (NEED-BASED) *Total amount:* $6,098,594 (11% federal, 12% state, 72% institutional, 5% external sources). *Receiving aid:* Freshmen: 57% (122); All full-time undergraduates: 58% (422). *Average award:* Freshmen: $15,455; Undergraduates: $14,284. *Scholarships, grants, and awards:* Federal Pell, FSEOG, state, college/university gift aid from institutional funds.
GIFT AID (NON-NEED-BASED) *Total amount:* $1,647,329 (1% federal, 96% institutional, 3% external sources). *Receiving aid:* Freshmen: 4% (9); Undergraduates: 4% (31). *Average Award:* Freshmen: $7967; *Undergraduates:* $10,125. *Scholarships, grants, and awards by category:* Academic Interests/Achievement: 521 awards ($3,838,000 total): general academic interests/achievements. Special Achievements/Activities: 403 awards ($3,351,000 total): community service. *Tuition waivers:* Full or partial for employees or children of employees. *ROTC:* Army cooperative.
LOANS *Student loans:* $3,135,308 (74% need-based, 26% non-need-based). 59% of past graduating class borrowed through all loan programs. *Average indebtedness per student:* $20,598. *Average need-based loan:* Freshmen: $2384; Undergraduates: $4053. *Parent loans:* $1,465,943 (51% need-based, 49% non-need-based). *Programs:* FFEL (Subsidized and Unsubsidized Stafford, PLUS).
WORK-STUDY *Federal work-study:* Total amount: $222,206; 287 jobs averaging $1000.
APPLYING FOR FINANCIAL AID *Required financial aid forms:* FAFSA, state aid form. *Financial aid deadline (priority):* 3/2. *Notification date:* Continuous beginning 3/15.
CONTACT Elinore Burkhardt, Director of Financial Aid, Menlo College, 1000 El Camino Real, Atherton, CA 94027-4301, 650-543-3880 or toll-free 800-556-3656. *Fax:* 650-543-4103.

MERCER UNIVERSITY
Macon, GA

Tuition & fees: $22,050	Average undergraduate aid package: $22,126

ABOUT THE INSTITUTION Independent Baptist, coed. Awards: bachelor's, master's, doctoral, and first professional degrees and post-bachelor's, post-master's, and first professional certificates. 49 undergraduate majors. Total enrollment: 7,180. Undergraduates: 4,628. Freshmen: 658. Federal methodology is used as a basis for awarding need-based institutional aid.
UNDERGRADUATE EXPENSES for 2004–05 *Application fee:* $50. *Comprehensive fee:* $29,110 includes full-time tuition ($22,050) and room and board ($7060). *College room only:* $3400. Full-time tuition and fees vary according to class time, course load, and location. Room and board charges vary according to board plan, housing facility, and location. *Part-time tuition:* $735 per credit hour. Part-time tuition and fees vary according to class time, course load, and location. *Payment plan:* Installment.
FRESHMAN FINANCIAL AID (Fall 2004, est.) 496 applied for aid; of those 80% were deemed to have need. 100% of freshmen with need received aid; of those 57% had need fully met. *Average percent of need met:* 95% (excluding resources awarded to replace EFC). *Average financial aid package:* $22,387 (excluding resources awarded to replace EFC). 29% of all full-time freshmen had no need and received non-need-based gift aid.
UNDERGRADUATE FINANCIAL AID (Fall 2004, est.) 1,824 applied for aid; of those 83% were deemed to have need. 100% of undergraduates with need received aid; of those 51% had need fully met. *Average percent of need met:* 90% (excluding resources awarded to replace EFC). *Average financial aid package:* $22,126 (excluding resources awarded to replace EFC). 31% of all full-time undergraduates had no need and received non-need-based gift aid.

GIFT AID (NEED-BASED) *Total amount:* $19,703,341 (11% federal, 12% state, 72% institutional, 5% external sources). *Receiving aid:* Freshmen: 69% (393); All full-time undergraduates: 66% (1,494). *Average award:* Freshmen: $14,046; Undergraduates: $13,293. *Scholarships, grants, and awards:* Federal Pell, FSEOG, state, college/university gift aid from institutional funds, Federal Nursing.
GIFT AID (NON-NEED-BASED) *Total amount:* $11,738,069 (19% state, 74% institutional, 7% external sources). *Receiving aid:* Freshmen: 31% (176); Undergraduates: 25% (572). *Average Award:* Freshmen: $14,411; Undergraduates: $13,852. *Scholarships, grants, and awards by category:* Academic Interests/Achievement: 2,341 awards ($15,659,608 total): biological sciences, business, education, engineering/technologies, English, foreign languages, general academic interests/achievements, international studies, military science, religion/biblical studies. Creative Arts/Performance: 148 awards ($406,915 total): art/fine arts, debating, music, theater/drama. Special Achievements/Activities: 15 awards ($143,655 total): community service, general special achievements/activities, junior miss, memberships. Special Characteristics: 1,772 awards ($7,612,555 total): adult students, children of faculty/staff, children of public servants, children of union members/company employees, general special characteristics, international students, local/state students, members of minority groups, relatives of clergy, religious affiliation, siblings of current students. *Tuition waivers:* Full or partial for employees or children of employees. *ROTC:* Army.
LOANS *Student loans:* $9,440,489 (64% need-based, 36% non-need-based). 72% of past graduating class borrowed through all loan programs. *Average indebtedness per student:* $13,974. *Average need-based loan:* Freshmen: $5130; Undergraduates: $6580. *Parent loans:* $3,108,823 (27% need-based, 73% non-need-based). *Programs:* Federal Direct (Subsidized and Unsubsidized Stafford, PLUS), Perkins, Federal Nursing, college/university.
WORK-STUDY *Federal work-study:* Total amount: $913,036; jobs available.
ATHLETIC AWARDS *Total amount:* $2,579,213 (27% need-based, 73% non-need-based).
APPLYING FOR FINANCIAL AID *Required financial aid forms:* FAFSA, institution's own form, state aid form (for GA residents only). *Financial aid deadline (priority):* 4/1. *Notification date:* Continuous beginning 3/15. Students must reply within 2 weeks of notification.
CONTACT Ms. Carol Williams, Associate Vice President, Financial Planning, Mercer University, 1400 Coleman Avenue, Macon, GA 31207-0003, 478-301-2670 or toll-free 800-840-8577. *Fax:* 478-301-2671. *E-mail:* williams_ck@mercer.edu.

MERCY COLLEGE
Dobbs Ferry, NY

Tuition & fees: $11,374	Average undergraduate aid package: N/A

ABOUT THE INSTITUTION Independent, coed. Awards: associate, bachelor's, and master's degrees. 54 undergraduate majors. Total enrollment: 10,395. Undergraduates: 6,208. Freshmen: 693. Federal methodology is used as a basis for awarding need-based institutional aid.
UNDERGRADUATE EXPENSES for 2004–05 *Application fee:* $35. *Comprehensive fee:* $19,800 includes full-time tuition ($11,230), mandatory fees ($144), and room and board ($8426). *Part-time tuition:* $472 per credit. *Part-time fees:* $6 per credit.
UNDERGRADUATE FINANCIAL AID (Fall 2004, est.) 8,950 applied for aid; of those 62% were deemed to have need. 100% of undergraduates with need received aid.
GIFT AID (NEED-BASED) *Total amount:* $21,469,555 (46% federal, 39% state, 15% institutional). *Scholarships, grants, and awards:* Federal Pell, FSEOG, state, private, college/university gift aid from institutional funds.
GIFT AID (NON-NEED-BASED) *Total amount:* $3,142,740 (39% institutional, 61% external sources). *Scholarships, grants, and awards by category:* Academic Interests/Achievement: general academic interests/achievements. *ROTC:* Air Force cooperative.
LOANS *Student loans:* $34,000,000 (100% need-based). *Parent loans:* $656,000 (100% non-need-based). *Programs:* FFEL (Subsidized and Unsubsidized Stafford, PLUS), Federal Nursing.
WORK-STUDY *Federal work-study:* Total amount: $734,000; jobs available.
ATHLETIC AWARDS *Total amount:* $593,895 (100% non-need-based).
APPLYING FOR FINANCIAL AID *Required financial aid forms:* FAFSA, state aid form. *Financial aid deadline (priority):* 5/1.

CONTACT Neal K. Harris, Director of Financial Aid, Mercy College, 28 Wells Avenue, 5th Floor, Yonkers, NY 00701, 800-MERCY-NY. *Fax:* 914-375-8582. *E-mail:* nharris@mercy.edu.

MERCY COLLEGE OF HEALTH SCIENCES
Des Moines, IA

Tuition & fees: $11,300	Average undergraduate aid package: $7670

ABOUT THE INSTITUTION Independent religious, coed, primarily women. Awards: associate and bachelor's degrees. 6 undergraduate majors. Total enrollment: 660. Undergraduates: 660. Freshmen: 69. Federal methodology is used as a basis for awarding need-based institutional aid.

UNDERGRADUATE EXPENSES for 2004–05 *Application fee:* $25. *Tuition:* full-time $11,300; part-time $375 per semester hour.

FRESHMAN FINANCIAL AID (Fall 2003) 56 applied for aid; of those 98% were deemed to have need. 96% of freshmen with need received aid. *Average percent of need met:* 30% (excluding resources awarded to replace EFC). *Average financial aid package:* $7615 (excluding resources awarded to replace EFC). 3% of all full-time freshmen had no need and received non-need-based gift aid.

UNDERGRADUATE FINANCIAL AID (Fall 2003) 331 applied for aid; of those 97% were deemed to have need. 94% of undergraduates with need received aid; of those 1% had need fully met. *Average percent of need met:* 29% (excluding resources awarded to replace EFC). *Average financial aid package:* $7670 (excluding resources awarded to replace EFC). 2% of all full-time undergraduates had no need and received non-need-based gift aid.

GIFT AID (NEED-BASED) *Total amount:* $1,720,105 (25% federal, 71% state, 4% institutional). *Receiving aid:* Freshmen: 62% (36); All full-time undergraduates: 58% (210). *Average award:* Freshmen: $3745; Undergraduates: $5132. *Scholarships, grants, and awards:* Federal Pell, FSEOG, state, private, college/university gift aid from institutional funds.

GIFT AID (NON-NEED-BASED) *Total amount:* $1,047,430 (4% state, 10% institutional, 86% external sources). *Receiving aid:* Freshmen: 53% (31); Undergraduates: 29% (105). *Average Award:* Freshmen: $750; Undergraduates: $6697. *Scholarships, grants, and awards by category:* Academic Interests/Achievement: 181 awards ($123,769 total): general academic interests/achievements, health fields. Special Achievements/Activities: 2 awards ($2000 total): community service. Special Characteristics: 149 awards ($605,461 total): children of union members/company employees, ethnic background, previous college experience.

LOANS *Student loans:* $5,628,539 (23% need-based, 77% non-need-based). 68% of past graduating class borrowed through all loan programs. *Average indebtedness per student:* $17,567. *Average need-based loan:* Freshmen: $2533; Undergraduates: $2492. *Parent loans:* $49,178 (100% non-need-based). *Programs:* FFEL (Subsidized and Unsubsidized Stafford, PLUS).

WORK-STUDY *Federal work-study:* Total amount: $21,602; 11 jobs averaging $1964.

APPLYING FOR FINANCIAL AID *Required financial aid form:* FAFSA. *Financial aid deadline:* 7/1. *Notification date:* Continuous beginning 1/15. Students must reply within 2 weeks of notification.

CONTACT Lisa Croat, Financial Aid Assistant Coordinator, Mercy College of Health Sciences, 928 Sixth Avenue, Des Moines, IA 50309, 515-643-6720 or toll-free 800-637-2994. *Fax:* 515-643-6702. *E-mail:* lcroat@mercydesmoines.org.

MERCYHURST COLLEGE
Erie, PA

Tuition & fees: $19,113	Average undergraduate aid package: $12,094

ABOUT THE INSTITUTION Independent Roman Catholic, coed. Awards: associate, bachelor's, and master's degrees and post-bachelor's certificates. 107 undergraduate majors. Total enrollment: 4,035. Undergraduates: 3,807. Freshmen: 1,036. Federal methodology is used as a basis for awarding need-based institutional aid.

UNDERGRADUATE EXPENSES for 2005–06 *Application fee:* $30. *Comprehensive fee:* $26,187 includes full-time tuition ($17,760), mandatory fees ($1353), and room and board ($7074). *College room only:* $3576. Full-time tuition and fees vary according to course load, degree level, and location. Room and board charges vary according to board plan and location. *Part-time tuition:* $592 per credit. Part-time tuition and fees vary according to course load and degree level. *Payment plan:* Installment.

FRESHMAN FINANCIAL AID (Fall 2004, est.) 960 applied for aid; of those 78% were deemed to have need. 100% of freshmen with need received aid; of those 80% had need fully met. *Average percent of need met:* 90% (excluding resources awarded to replace EFC). *Average financial aid package:* $12,403 (excluding resources awarded to replace EFC). 20% of all full-time freshmen had no need and received non-need-based gift aid.

UNDERGRADUATE FINANCIAL AID (Fall 2004, est.) 3,271 applied for aid; of those 79% were deemed to have need. 100% of undergraduates with need received aid; of those 80% had need fully met. *Average percent of need met:* 91% (excluding resources awarded to replace EFC). *Average financial aid package:* $12,094 (excluding resources awarded to replace EFC). 17% of all full-time undergraduates had no need and received non-need-based gift aid.

GIFT AID (NEED-BASED) *Total amount:* $21,269,751 (16% federal, 19% state, 63% institutional, 2% external sources). *Receiving aid:* Freshmen: 76% (740); All full-time undergraduates: 76% (2,493). *Average award:* Freshmen: $10,506; Undergraduates: $8617. *Scholarships, grants, and awards:* Federal Pell, FSEOG, state, private, college/university gift aid from institutional funds.

GIFT AID (NON-NEED-BASED) *Total amount:* $2,889,344 (2% federal, 2% state, 95% institutional, 1% external sources). *Receiving aid:* Freshmen: 58% (567); Undergraduates: 59% (1,958). *Average Award:* Freshmen: $8855; Undergraduates: $8220. *Scholarships, grants, and awards by category:* Academic Interests/Achievement: 694 awards ($3,108,164 total): biological sciences, business, communication, education, English, general academic interests/achievements, health fields, humanities, international studies, mathematics, physical sciences, premedicine, social sciences. Creative Arts/Performance: 87 awards ($866,237 total): applied art and design, art/fine arts, dance, music. Special Achievements/Activities: 242 awards ($934,341 total): community service, general special achievements/activities, leadership, religious involvement. Special Characteristics: 15 awards ($69,781 total): adult students, children and siblings of alumni, children of faculty/staff, local/state students, members of minority groups, siblings of current students. *Tuition waivers:* Full or partial for employees or children of employees. *ROTC:* Army cooperative, Air Force cooperative.

LOANS *Student loans:* $18,066,358 (92% need-based, 8% non-need-based). 95% of past graduating class borrowed through all loan programs. *Average indebtedness per student:* $22,000. *Average need-based loan:* Freshmen: $2816; Undergraduates: $3766. *Parent loans:* $3,627,662 (88% need-based, 12% non-need-based). *Programs:* FFEL (Subsidized and Unsubsidized Stafford, PLUS), Perkins, college/university.

WORK-STUDY *Federal work-study:* Total amount: $377,906; 271 jobs averaging $1372. *State or other work-study/employment:* Total amount: $1,692,441 (82% need-based, 18% non-need-based). 1,250 part-time jobs averaging $1171.

ATHLETIC AWARDS *Total amount:* $5,063,325 (61% need-based, 39% non-need-based).

APPLYING FOR FINANCIAL AID *Required financial aid forms:* FAFSA, institution's own form. *Financial aid deadline:* 5/1 (priority: 3/1). *Notification date:* Continuous.

CONTACT Mr. James Theeuwes, Director of Financial Aid, Mercyhurst College, 501 East 38th Street, Erie, PA 16546, 814-824-2288 or toll-free 800-825-1926 Ext. 2202. *Fax:* 814-824-2438. *E-mail:* jtheeuwes@mercyhurst.edu.

MEREDITH COLLEGE
Raleigh, NC

Tuition & fees: $19,950	Average undergraduate aid package: $14,010

ABOUT THE INSTITUTION Independent, women only. Awards: bachelor's and master's degrees and post-bachelor's certificates. 62 undergraduate majors. Total enrollment: 2,168. Undergraduates: 2,008. Freshmen: 407. Federal methodology is used as a basis for awarding need-based institutional aid.

UNDERGRADUATE EXPENSES for 2005–06 *Application fee:* $35. *Comprehensive fee:* $25,550 includes full-time tuition ($19,950) and room and board ($5600). *Part-time tuition:* $525 per credit hour.

FRESHMAN FINANCIAL AID (Fall 2004, est.) 315 applied for aid; of those 83% were deemed to have need. 100% of freshmen with need received aid; of those 16% had need fully met. *Average percent of need met:* 77% (excluding resources awarded to replace EFC). *Average financial aid package:* $13,995 (excluding resources awarded to replace EFC). 9% of all full-time freshmen had no need and received non-need-based gift aid.

UNDERGRADUATE FINANCIAL AID (Fall 2004, est.) 1,155 applied for aid; of those 88% were deemed to have need. 100% of undergraduates with need received aid; of those 12% had need fully met. *Average percent of need met:* 73% (excluding resources awarded to replace EFC). *Average financial aid*

package: $14,010 (excluding resources awarded to replace EFC). 6% of all full-time undergraduates had no need and received non-need-based gift aid.

GIFT AID (NEED-BASED) *Total amount:* $10,265,194 (15% federal, 33% state, 46% institutional, 6% external sources). *Receiving aid:* Freshmen: 66% (263); All full-time undergraduates: 64% (997). *Average award:* Freshmen: $10,847; Undergraduates: $10,068. *Scholarships, grants, and awards:* Federal Pell, FSEOG, state, private, college/university gift aid from institutional funds.

GIFT AID (NON-NEED-BASED) *Total amount:* $2,108,493 (48% state, 34% institutional, 18% external sources). *Receiving aid:* Freshmen: 8% (33); Undergraduates: 5% (70). *Average Award: Freshmen:* $5222; *Undergraduates:* $4730. *Scholarships, grants, and awards by category: Academic Interests/ Achievement:* 274 awards ($1,186,062 total): biological sciences, education, general academic interests/achievements, mathematics, religion/biblical studies. *Creative Arts/Performance:* 43 awards ($102,200 total): applied art and design, art/fine arts, creative writing, music. *Special Achievements/Activities:* 32 awards ($86,900 total): community service, leadership. *Special Characteristics:* 25 awards ($68,250 total): ethnic background, first-generation college students, religious affiliation. *ROTC:* Army cooperative, Air Force cooperative.

LOANS *Student loans:* $9,390,358 (73% need-based, 27% non-need-based). 60% of past graduating class borrowed through all loan programs. *Average indebtedness per student:* $18,133. *Average need-based loan:* Freshmen: $2894; Undergraduates: $3906. *Parent loans:* $1,867,866 (23% need-based, 77% non-need-based). *Programs:* FFEL (Subsidized and Unsubsidized Stafford, PLUS), Perkins, college/university.

WORK-STUDY *Federal work-study:* Total amount: $542,540; 518 jobs averaging $1217. *State or other work-study/employment:* Total amount: $6300 (27% need-based, 73% non-need-based). 4 part-time jobs averaging $1387.

APPLYING FOR FINANCIAL AID *Required financial aid form:* FAFSA. *Financial aid deadline (priority):* 2/15. *Notification date:* 3/15. Students must reply by 5/1 or within 2 weeks of notification.

CONTACT Ms. Patti Corjay, Director of Financial Assistance, Meredith College, 3800 Hillsborough Street, Raleigh, NC 27607-5298, 919-760-8565 or toll-free 800-MEREDITH. *Fax:* 919-760-2375. *E-mail:* corjayp@meredith.edu.

MERRIMACK COLLEGE
North Andover, MA

Tuition & fees: $22,100	Average undergraduate aid package: $17,000

ABOUT THE INSTITUTION Independent Roman Catholic, coed. Awards: associate, bachelor's, and master's degrees. 45 undergraduate majors. Total enrollment: 2,326. Undergraduates: 2,304. Freshmen: 509. Federal methodology is used as a basis for awarding need-based institutional aid.

UNDERGRADUATE EXPENSES for 2004–05 *Application fee:* $50. *Comprehensive fee:* $31,300 includes full-time tuition ($21,850), mandatory fees ($250), and room and board ($9200). *College room only:* $5200. Full-time tuition and fees vary according to program. Room and board charges vary according to board plan and housing facility. *Part-time tuition:* $805 per credit. *Part-time fees:* $35 per term. Part-time tuition and fees vary according to class time, course level, and course load. *Payment plans:* Installment, deferred payment.

GIFT AID (NEED-BASED) *Total amount:* $10,288,074 (6% federal, 7% state, 87% institutional). *Receiving aid:* Freshmen: 76% (387); All full-time undergraduates: 75% (1,520). *Average award:* Freshmen: $10,000; Undergraduates: $9000. *Scholarships, grants, and awards:* Federal Pell, FSEOG, state, private, college/university gift aid from institutional funds.

GIFT AID (NON-NEED-BASED) *Total amount:* $1,332,586 (75% institutional, 25% external sources). *Receiving aid:* Freshmen: 10% (50); Undergraduates: 10% (200). *Average Award: Freshmen:* $5000; *Undergraduates:* $2185. *Scholarships, grants, and awards by category: Academic Interests/Achievement:* 60 awards ($600,000 total): general academic interests/achievements. *Creative Arts/Performance:* 2 awards ($20,625 total): theater/drama. *Special Achievements/ Activities:* 20 awards ($200,000 total): leadership. *Special Characteristics:* 75 awards ($1,180,538 total): children and siblings of alumni, children of faculty/staff, relatives of clergy, siblings of current students. *Tuition waivers:* Full or partial for employees or children of employees, senior citizens. *ROTC:* Air Force cooperative.

LOANS *Student loans:* $9,187,016 (46% need-based, 54% non-need-based). 75% of past graduating class borrowed through all loan programs. *Average indebtedness per student:* $25,000. *Average need-based loan:* Freshmen: $4125; Undergraduates: $7000. *Parent loans:* $6,343,553 (100% non-need-based). *Programs:* FFEL (Subsidized and Unsubsidized Stafford, PLUS), Perkins, state, college/university, MEFA Loans, alternative loans.

ATHLETIC AWARDS *Total amount:* $2,577,690 (100% non-need-based).

APPLYING FOR FINANCIAL AID *Required financial aid forms:* FAFSA, noncustodial (divorced/separated) parent's statement, business/farm supplement. *Financial aid deadline:* 2/1. *Notification date:* Continuous beginning 3/1. Students must reply by 5/1.

CONTACT Christine A. Mordach, Director of Student Financial Aid and Scholarships, Merrimack College, 315 Turnpike Street, North Andover, MA 01845, 978-837-5186. *Fax:* 978-837-5067. *E-mail:* christine.mordach@merrimack.edu.

MESA STATE COLLEGE
Grand Junction, CO

Tuition & fees (CO res): $2724	Average undergraduate aid package: $6273

ABOUT THE INSTITUTION State-supported, coed. Awards: associate, bachelor's, and master's degrees. 67 undergraduate majors. Total enrollment: 6,235. Undergraduates: 6,192. Freshmen: 1,308. Federal methodology is used as a basis for awarding need-based institutional aid.

UNDERGRADUATE EXPENSES for 2004–05 *Application fee:* $30. *Tuition, state resident:* full-time $2063; part-time $93.79 per hour. *Tuition, nonresident:* full-time $8349; part-time $379.52 per hour. *Required fees:* full-time $661; $34.40 per hour. Part-time tuition and fees vary according to course load. *College room and board:* $6501; *room only:* $3260. Room and board charges vary according to board plan and housing facility. *Payment plan:* Installment.

GIFT AID (NEED-BASED) *Total amount:* $7,799,502 (76% federal, 24% state). *Receiving aid:* Freshmen: 38% (387); All full-time undergraduates: 44% (1,852). *Average award:* Freshmen: $3117; Undergraduates: $3514. *Scholarships, grants, and awards:* Federal Pell, FSEOG, state, private, college/university gift aid from institutional funds.

GIFT AID (NON-NEED-BASED) *Total amount:* $1,825,556 (7% federal, 9% state, 44% institutional, 40% external sources). *Receiving aid:* Freshmen: 13% (138); Undergraduates: 14% (577). *Average Award: Freshmen:* $3789; *Undergraduates:* $3914. *Scholarships, grants, and awards by category: Academic Interests/Achievement:* 698 awards ($828,986 total): biological sciences, business, communication, computer science, education, engineering/technologies, English, general academic interests/achievements, health fields, humanities, mathematics, physical sciences, social sciences. *Creative Arts/Performance:* 47 awards ($19,873 total): art/fine arts, creative writing, journalism/publications, music, theater/drama. *Special Achievements/Activities:* general special achievements/activities, hobbies/interests. *Special Characteristics:* 112 awards ($137,866 total): first-generation college students, international students, local/state students, members of minority groups, out-of-state students.

LOANS *Student loans:* $13,386,160 (57% need-based, 43% non-need-based). 60% of past graduating class borrowed through all loan programs. *Average indebtedness per student:* $16,522. *Average need-based loan:* Freshmen: $2330; Undergraduates: $3182. *Parent loans:* $1,430,696 (100% non-need-based). *Programs:* FFEL (Subsidized and Unsubsidized Stafford, PLUS), Perkins, college/university.

ATHLETIC AWARDS *Total amount:* $471,738 (100% non-need-based).

APPLYING FOR FINANCIAL AID *Required financial aid form:* FAFSA. *Financial aid deadline (priority):* 3/1. *Notification date:* Continuous beginning 4/1.

CONTACT Mr. Curt Martin, Director of Financial Aid, Mesa State College, 1100 North Avenue, Grand Junction, CO 81501-3122, 970-248-1396 or toll-free 800-982-MESA. *Fax:* 970-248-1191. *E-mail:* cmartin@mesastate.edu.

MESIVTA OF EASTERN PARKWAY RABBINICAL SEMINARY
Brooklyn, NY

CONTACT Rabbi Joseph Halberstadt, Dean, Mesivta of Eastern Parkway Rabbinical Seminary, 510 Dahill Road, Brooklyn, NY 11218-5559, 718-438-1002.

MESIVTA TIFERETH JERUSALEM OF AMERICA
New York, NY

CONTACT Rabbi Dickstein, Director of Financial Aid, Mesivta Tifereth Jerusalem of America, 141 East Broadway, New York, NY 10002-6301, 212-964-2830.

MESIVTA TORAH VODAATH RABBINICAL SEMINARY
Brooklyn, NY

CONTACT Mrs. Kayla Goldring, Director of Financial Aid, Mesivta Torah Vodaath Rabbinical Seminary, 425 East Ninth Street, Brooklyn, NY 11218-5209, 718-941-8000.

MESSENGER COLLEGE
Joplin, MO

Tuition & fees: $5410	Average undergraduate aid package: $7590

ABOUT THE INSTITUTION Independent Pentecostal, coed. Awards: associate and bachelor's degrees. 13 undergraduate majors. Total enrollment: 100. Undergraduates: 100. Freshmen: 31. Federal methodology is used as a basis for awarding need-based institutional aid.

UNDERGRADUATE EXPENSES for 2005–06 *Application fee:* $35. *Comprehensive fee:* $8910 includes full-time tuition ($4950), mandatory fees ($460), and room and board ($3500). Room and board charges vary according to housing facility. *Part-time tuition:* $165 per credit hour. *Payment plan:* Installment.

FRESHMAN FINANCIAL AID (Fall 2003) 29 applied for aid; of those 100% were deemed to have need. 97% of freshmen with need received aid. *Average percent of need met:* 58% (excluding resources awarded to replace EFC). *Average financial aid package:* $6642 (excluding resources awarded to replace EFC).

UNDERGRADUATE FINANCIAL AID (Fall 2003) 113 applied for aid; of those 98% were deemed to have need. 100% of undergraduates with need received aid. *Average percent of need met:* 63% (excluding resources awarded to replace EFC). *Average financial aid package:* $7590 (excluding resources awarded to replace EFC).

GIFT AID (NEED-BASED) *Total amount:* $240,470 (94% federal, 1% institutional, 5% external sources). *Receiving aid:* Freshmen: 76% (22); All full-time undergraduates: 86% (100). *Average award:* Freshmen: $3500; Undergraduates: $3600. *Scholarships, grants, and awards:* Federal Pell, FSEOG, private.

GIFT AID (NON-NEED-BASED) *Scholarships, grants, and awards by category:* Academic Interests/Achievement: education, general academic interests/achievements, religion/biblical studies. *Special Achievements/Activities:* religious involvement. *Special Characteristics:* religious affiliation. *Tuition waivers:* Full or partial for employees or children of employees.

LOANS *Student loans:* $388,502 (100% need-based). 100% of past graduating class borrowed through all loan programs. *Average indebtedness per student:* $17,348. *Average need-based loan:* Freshmen: $2625; Undergraduates: $3875. *Parent loans:* $17,400 (92% need-based, 8% non-need-based). *Programs:* FFEL (Subsidized and Unsubsidized Stafford, PLUS).

WORK-STUDY *Federal work-study:* Total amount: $28,831; 27 jobs averaging $1068.

APPLYING FOR FINANCIAL AID *Required financial aid form:* FAFSA. *Financial aid deadline:* Continuous. *Notification date:* Continuous.

CONTACT Sharon Shackelford, Financial Aid Director, Messenger College, 300 East 50th Street, Joplin, MO 64804, 417-624-7070 Ext. 308 or toll-free 800-385-8940 (in-state). *Fax:* 417-624-5070.

MESSIAH COLLEGE
Grantham, PA

Tuition & fees: $20,790	Average undergraduate aid package: $13,585

ABOUT THE INSTITUTION Independent interdenominational, coed. Awards: bachelor's degrees. 61 undergraduate majors. Total enrollment: 2,917. Undergraduates: 2,917. Freshmen: 690. Federal methodology is used as a basis for awarding need-based institutional aid.

UNDERGRADUATE EXPENSES for 2004–05 *Application fee:* $30. *Comprehensive fee:* $27,350 includes full-time tuition ($20,120), mandatory fees ($670), and room and board ($6560). *College room only:* $3400. Room and board charges vary according to board plan, housing facility, and location. *Part-time tuition:* $840 per credit. *Part-time fees:* $28 per credit. *Payment plan:* Installment.

FRESHMAN FINANCIAL AID (Fall 2004, est.) 604 applied for aid; of those 85% were deemed to have need. 100% of freshmen with need received aid; of those 26% had need fully met. *Average percent of need met:* 67% (excluding resources

awarded to replace EFC). *Average financial aid package:* $13,648 (excluding resources awarded to replace EFC). 10% of all full-time freshmen had no need and received non-need-based gift aid.

UNDERGRADUATE FINANCIAL AID (Fall 2004, est.) 2,316 applied for aid; of those 89% were deemed to have need. 100% of undergraduates with need received aid; of those 22% had need fully met. *Average percent of need met:* 66% (excluding resources awarded to replace EFC). *Average financial aid package:* $13,585 (excluding resources awarded to replace EFC). 18% of all full-time undergraduates had no need and received non-need-based gift aid.

GIFT AID (NEED-BASED) *Total amount:* $9,775,531 (17% federal, 23% state, 60% institutional). *Receiving aid:* Freshmen: 62% (428); All full-time undergraduates: 64% (1,829). *Average award:* Freshmen: $4431; Undergraduates: $4738. *Scholarships, grants, and awards:* Federal Pell, FSEOG, state, private, college/university gift aid from institutional funds.

GIFT AID (NON-NEED-BASED) *Total amount:* $12,902,440 (1% federal, 1% state, 88% institutional, 10% external sources). *Receiving aid:* Freshmen: 61% (419); Undergraduates: 58% (1,657). *Average Award:* Freshmen: $6530; Undergraduates: $5372. *Scholarships, grants, and awards by category:* Academic Interests/Achievement: general academic interests/achievements. Creative Arts/Performance: art/fine arts, music, theater/drama. Special Achievements/Activities: leadership. Special Characteristics: adult students, children and siblings of alumni, children of faculty/staff, relatives of clergy, religious affiliation, siblings of current students, spouses of current students. *Tuition waivers:* Full or partial for minority students, children of alumni, employees or children of employees, adult students, senior citizens.

LOANS *Student loans:* $16,954,214 (45% need-based, 55% non-need-based). 65% of past graduating class borrowed through all loan programs. *Average indebtedness per student:* $23,287. *Average need-based loan:* Freshmen: $2525; Undergraduates: $4011. *Parent loans:* $3,879,439 (100% non-need-based). *Programs:* Federal Direct (Subsidized and Unsubsidized Stafford, PLUS), Perkins, Federal Nursing.

WORK-STUDY *Federal work-study:* Total amount: $1,391,566; 755 jobs averaging $1821. *State or other work-study/employment:* Total amount: $1,695,421 (13% need-based, 87% non-need-based). 734 part-time jobs averaging $2296.

APPLYING FOR FINANCIAL AID *Required financial aid form:* FAFSA. *Financial aid deadline (priority):* 4/1. *Notification date:* Continuous. Students must reply by 5/1 or within 4 weeks of notification.

CONTACT Mr. Michael Strite, Assistant Director of Financial Aid, Messiah College, PO Box 3006, One College Avenue, Grantham, PA 17027, 717-691-6007 or toll-free 800-233-4220. *Fax:* 717-796-4791. *E-mail:* mstrite@messiah.edu.

METHODIST COLLEGE
Fayetteville, NC

Tuition & fees: $17,850	Average undergraduate aid package: $12,707

ABOUT THE INSTITUTION Independent United Methodist, coed. Awards: associate, bachelor's, and master's degrees. 56 undergraduate majors. Total enrollment: 2,257. Undergraduates: 2,195. Freshmen: 518. Federal methodology is used as a basis for awarding need-based institutional aid.

UNDERGRADUATE EXPENSES for 2005–06 *Application fee:* $25. *Comprehensive fee:* $24,620 includes full-time tuition ($17,580), mandatory fees ($270), and room and board ($6770). Full-time tuition and fees vary according to class time. Room and board charges vary according to board plan and housing facility. *Part-time tuition:* $570 per semester hour. Part-time tuition and fees vary according to class time. *Payment plans:* Installment, deferred payment.

GIFT AID (NEED-BASED) *Total amount:* $8,187,103 (22% federal, 16% state, 62% institutional). *Receiving aid:* Freshmen: 76% (292); All full-time undergraduates: 69% (1,107). *Average award:* Freshmen: $7814; Undergraduates: $6520. *Scholarships, grants, and awards:* Federal Pell, FSEOG, state, private, college/university gift aid from institutional funds.

GIFT AID (NON-NEED-BASED) *Total amount:* $5,882,623 (38% federal, 28% state, 30% institutional, 4% external sources). *Receiving aid:* Freshmen: 58% (223); Undergraduates: 59% (949). *Average Award:* Freshmen: $1403; Undergraduates: $4295. *Scholarships, grants, and awards by category:* Academic Interests/Achievement: 147 awards ($496,612 total): English, general academic interests/achievements. Creative Arts/Performance: 126 awards ($84,588 total): debating, music, theater/drama. Special Achievements/Activities: 32 awards ($12,600 total): cheerleading/drum major, leadership. Special Characteristics: 405 awards ($690,209 total): children and siblings of alumni, children of faculty/staff, relatives of clergy, religious affiliation. *Tuition waivers:* Full or partial for employees or children of employees, senior citizens. *ROTC:* Army, Air Force cooperative.

LOANS *Student loans:* $8,494,574 (49% need-based, 51% non-need-based). 77% of past graduating class borrowed through all loan programs. *Average indebtedness per student:* $18,656. *Average need-based loan:* Freshmen: $2441; Undergraduates: $3454. *Parent loans:* $2,370,011 (100% non-need-based). *Programs:* FFEL (Subsidized and Unsubsidized Stafford, PLUS), Perkins.
APPLYING FOR FINANCIAL AID *Required financial aid form:* FAFSA. *Financial aid deadline:* Continuous. *Notification date:* Continuous beginning 3/3. Students must reply within 2 weeks of notification.
CONTACT Financial Aid Office, Methodist College, 5400 Ramsey Street, Fayetteville, NC 28311-1420, 910-630-7307 or toll-free 800-488-7110 Ext. 7027. *Fax:* 910-630-7285.

METROPOLITAN COLLEGE
Oklahoma City, OK

CONTACT Office of Financial Aid, Metropolitan College, 1900 Northwest Expressway, Suite R302, Oklahoma City, OK 73118, 405-843-1000. *Fax:* 405-843-2325.

METROPOLITAN COLLEGE
Tulsa, OK

CONTACT Office of Financial Aid, Metropolitan College, 10820 East 45th Street, Suite 101B, Tulsa, OK 74136, 918-627-9429. *Fax:* 918-627-2122.

METROPOLITAN COLLEGE OF COURT REPORTING
Phoenix, AZ

CONTACT Financial Aid Director, Metropolitan College of Court Reporting, 4640 East Elwood Street, #12, Phoenix, AZ 85040, 480-955-5900. *Fax:* 480-894-8999.

METROPOLITAN COLLEGE OF COURT REPORTING
Albuquerque, NM

CONTACT Director of Financial Aid, Metropolitan College of Court Reporting, 1717 Louisiana Boulevard NE, Suite 207, Albuquerque, NM 87110-7027, 505-888-3400. *Fax:* 505-254-3738.

METROPOLITAN COLLEGE OF NEW YORK
New York, NY

CONTACT Rosibel Gomez, Financial Aid Director, Metropolitan College of New York, 75 Varick Street, New York, NY 10013-1919, 212-343-1234 Ext. 5004 or toll-free 800-33-THINK Ext. 5001 (in-state). *Fax:* 212-343-7399.

METROPOLITAN STATE COLLEGE OF DENVER
Denver, CO

Tuition & fees (CO res): $2859   **Average undergraduate aid package:** $6580

ABOUT THE INSTITUTION State-supported, coed. Awards: bachelor's degrees. 49 undergraduate majors. Total enrollment: 20,761. Undergraduates: 20,761. Freshmen: 2,490. Federal methodology is used as a basis for awarding need-based institutional aid.
UNDERGRADUATE EXPENSES for 2005–06 *Application fee:* $25. *Tuition, state resident:* full-time $2283. *Tuition, nonresident:* full-time $9366. Full-time tuition and fees vary according to course load and location. Part-time tuition and fees vary according to course load and location. *Payment plans:* Installment, deferred payment.
GIFT AID (NEED-BASED) *Total amount:* $18,869,894 (62% federal, 24% state, 12% institutional, 2% external sources). *Receiving aid:* Freshmen: 30% (541); All full-time undergraduates: 31% (3,555). *Average award:* Freshmen: $4043; Undergraduates: $4335. *Scholarships, grants, and awards:* Federal Pell, FSEOG, state, private, college/university gift aid from institutional funds.

GIFT AID (NON-NEED-BASED) *Total amount:* $969,229 (3% federal, 37% state, 37% institutional, 23% external sources). *Receiving aid:* Freshmen: 3% (47); Undergraduates: 2% (186). *Average Award:* Freshmen: $1715; Undergraduates: $1802. *Scholarships, grants, and awards by category:* Academic Interests/Achievement: 1,317 awards ($1,632,596 total): biological sciences, business, communication, computer science, education, engineering/technologies, English, foreign languages, general academic interests/achievements, health fields, humanities, mathematics, physical sciences, social sciences. *Creative Arts/Performance:* 62 awards ($45,859 total): art/fine arts, music, theater/drama. *Special Achievements/Activities:* 52 awards ($100,690 total): general special achievements/activities. *Tuition waivers:* Full or partial for senior citizens. *ROTC:* Army cooperative, Air Force cooperative.
LOANS *Student loans:* $40,618,483 (84% need-based, 16% non-need-based). 52% of past graduating class borrowed through all loan programs. *Average indebtedness per student:* $10,366. *Average need-based loan:* Freshmen: $2327; Undergraduates: $3656. *Parent loans:* $552,093 (56% need-based, 44% non-need-based). *Programs:* FFEL (Subsidized and Unsubsidized Stafford, PLUS), Perkins.
ATHLETIC AWARDS *Total amount:* $815,480 (100% non-need-based).
APPLYING FOR FINANCIAL AID *Required financial aid form:* FAFSA. *Financial aid deadline:* Continuous. *Notification date:* Continuous beginning 4/1.
CONTACT Office of Financial Aid, Metropolitan State College of Denver, PO Box 173362, Denver, CO 80217-3362, 303-556-8593. *Fax:* 303-556-4927.

METROPOLITAN STATE UNIVERSITY
St. Paul, MN

ABOUT THE INSTITUTION State-supported, coed. Awards: bachelor's and master's degrees (offers primarily part-time evening degree programs). 44 undergraduate majors. Total enrollment: 6,516. Undergraduates: 5,901. Freshmen: 87.
GIFT AID (NEED-BASED) *Scholarships, grants, and awards:* Federal Pell, FSEOG, state, private, college/university gift aid from institutional funds.
GIFT AID (NON-NEED-BASED) *Scholarships, grants, and awards by category:* Academic Interests/Achievement: education, general academic interests/achievements.
LOANS *Programs:* FFEL (Subsidized and Unsubsidized Stafford, PLUS), state.
APPLYING FOR FINANCIAL AID *Required financial aid forms:* FAFSA, federal income tax form(s).
CONTACT Mr. Michael Uran, Director of Financial Aid, Metropolitan State University, Founder's Hall, Room 105, 700 East 7th Street, St. Paul, MN 55106-5000, 651-793-1414. *E-mail:* finaid@metrostate.edu.

MIAMI INTERNATIONAL UNIVERSITY OF ART & DESIGN
Miami, FL

CONTACT Mitzie Forrest, Financial Aid Director, Miami International University of Art & Design, 1737 Bayshore Drive, Miami, FL 33132, 800-225-9023 Ext. 125 or toll-free 800-225-9023. *Fax:* 305-374-7946.

MIAMI UNIVERSITY
Oxford, OH

Tuition & fees (OH res): $9642   **Average undergraduate aid package:** $15,358

ABOUT THE INSTITUTION State-related, coed. Awards: associate, bachelor's, master's, and doctoral degrees and post-master's certificates. 106 undergraduate majors. Total enrollment: 17,151. Undergraduates: 15,059. Freshmen: 3,426. Federal methodology is used as a basis for awarding need-based institutional aid.
UNDERGRADUATE EXPENSES for 2004–05 *Application fee:* $45. *Tuition, state resident:* full-time $8236; part-time $760 per credit hour. *Tuition, nonresident:* full-time $18,236. *Required fees:* full-time $1406; $59 per credit hour. *College room and board:* $7010; *room only:* $3510. Room and board charges vary according to board plan and housing facility. Ohio residents receive $9,750 in resident scholarships. *Payment plan:* Installment.
FRESHMAN FINANCIAL AID (Fall 2004, est.) 2347 applied for aid; of those 69% were deemed to have need. 99% of freshmen with need received aid; of those 32% had need fully met. *Average percent of need met:* 70% (excluding

resources awarded to replace EFC). *Average financial aid package:* $15,101 (excluding resources awarded to replace EFC). 35% of all full-time freshmen had no need and received non-need-based gift aid.

UNDERGRADUATE FINANCIAL AID (Fall 2004, est.) 7,418 applied for aid; of those 80% were deemed to have need. 100% of undergraduates with need received aid; of those 27% had need fully met. *Average percent of need met:* 77% (excluding resources awarded to replace EFC). *Average financial aid package:* $15,358 (excluding resources awarded to replace EFC). 40% of all full-time undergraduates had no need and received non-need-based gift aid.

GIFT AID (NEED-BASED) *Total amount:* $10,787,060 (45% federal, 10% state, 45% institutional). *Receiving aid:* Freshmen: 15% (514); All full-time undergraduates: 15% (2,250). *Average award:* Freshmen: $5139; Undergraduates: $4350. *Scholarships, grants, and awards:* Federal Pell, FSEOG, state, private, college/university gift aid from institutional funds.

GIFT AID (NON-NEED-BASED) *Total amount:* $130,894,133 (1% state, 94% institutional, 5% external sources). *Receiving aid:* Freshmen: 43% (1,477); Undergraduates: 37% (5,381). *Average Award:* Freshmen: $10,462; Undergraduates: $11,132. *Scholarships, grants, and awards by category: Academic Interests/Achievement:* architecture, education, engineering/technologies, general academic interests/achievements. *Creative Arts/Performance:* art/fine arts, music, theater/drama. *Special Achievements/Activities:* general special achievements/activities, leadership. *Special Characteristics:* children of faculty/staff, local/state students, members of minority groups, out-of-state students. *Tuition waivers:* Full or partial for employees or children of employees. *ROTC:* Army cooperative, Naval, Air Force.

LOANS *Student loans:* $49,625,878 (35% need-based, 65% non-need-based). 47% of past graduating class borrowed through all loan programs. *Average indebtedness per student:* $19,718. *Average need-based loan:* Freshmen: $2585; Undergraduates: $3825. *Parent loans:* $1,472,347 (100% non-need-based). *Programs:* Federal Direct (Subsidized and Unsubsidized Stafford, PLUS), Perkins, Federal Nursing, college/university, alternative loans.

WORK-STUDY *Federal work-study:* Total amount: $1,569,175; 951 jobs averaging $1650.

ATHLETIC AWARDS *Total amount:* $2,488,888 (100% non-need-based).

APPLYING FOR FINANCIAL AID *Required financial aid form:* FAFSA. *Financial aid deadline (priority):* 2/15. *Notification date:* Continuous beginning 3/31. Students must reply by 5/1 or within 3 weeks of notification.

CONTACT Chuck Knepfle, Office of Student Financial Aid, Miami University, Campus Avenue Building, Oxford, OH 45056-3427, 513-529-8734. *Fax:* 513-529-8713. *E-mail:* financialaid@muohio.edu.

MICHIGAN JEWISH INSTITUTE
Oak Park, MI

CONTACT Financial Aid Office, Michigan Jewish Institute, 25401 Coolidge Highway, Oak Park, MI 48237-1304, 248-414-6900.

MICHIGAN STATE UNIVERSITY
East Lansing, MI

Tuition & fees (MI res): $7000	Average undergraduate aid package: $8022

ABOUT THE INSTITUTION State-supported, coed. Awards: bachelor's, master's, doctoral, and first professional degrees and post-master's certificates. 130 undergraduate majors. Total enrollment: 44,836. Undergraduates: 35,408. Freshmen: 7,607. Federal methodology is used as a basis for awarding need-based institutional aid.

UNDERGRADUATE EXPENSES for 2004–05 *Application fee:* $35. *Tuition, state resident:* full-time $6188; part-time $206.25 per credit. *Tuition, nonresident:* full-time $17,033; part-time $567.75 per credit. *Required fees:* full-time $812; $812 per year part-time. Full-time tuition and fees vary according to course load, degree level, program, and student level. Part-time tuition and fees vary according to course load, degree level, program, and student level. *College room and board:* $5458; *room only:* $2364. Room and board charges vary according to board plan and housing facility. *Payment plan:* Deferred payment.

FRESHMAN FINANCIAL AID (Fall 2004, est.) 5146 applied for aid; of those 59% were deemed to have need. 100% of freshmen with need received aid; of those 30% had need fully met. *Average percent of need met:* 79% (excluding resources awarded to replace EFC). *Average financial aid package:* $8044 (excluding resources awarded to replace EFC). 9% of all full-time freshmen had no need and received non-need-based gift aid.

UNDERGRADUATE FINANCIAL AID (Fall 2004, est.) 18,519 applied for aid; of those 69% were deemed to have need. 100% of undergraduates with need received aid; of those 28% had need fully met. *Average percent of need met:* 75% (excluding resources awarded to replace EFC). *Average financial aid package:* $8022 (excluding resources awarded to replace EFC). 8% of all full-time undergraduates had no need and received non-need-based gift aid.

GIFT AID (NEED-BASED) *Total amount:* $36,709,798 (54% federal, 1% state, 45% institutional). *Receiving aid:* Freshmen: 25% (1,852); All full-time undergraduates: 28% (8,885). *Average award:* Freshmen: $3831; Undergraduates: $3562. *Scholarships, grants, and awards:* Federal Pell, FSEOG, state, private, college/university gift aid from institutional funds, United Negro College Fund, Federal Nursing.

GIFT AID (NON-NEED-BASED) *Total amount:* $66,294,442 (3% federal, 57% state, 22% institutional, 18% external sources). *Receiving aid:* Freshmen: 36% (2,656); Undergraduates: 25% (7,841). *Average Award:* Freshmen: $3118; Undergraduates: $2990. *Scholarships, grants, and awards by category: Academic Interests/Achievement:* agriculture, architecture, biological sciences, business, computer science, education, engineering/technologies, general academic interests/achievements, military science, social sciences. *Creative Arts/Performance:* creative writing, debating, journalism/publications, music, performing arts, theater/drama. *Special Achievements/Activities:* community service, hobbies/interests, junior miss, leadership, memberships, religious involvement. *Special Characteristics:* children and siblings of alumni, children of faculty/staff, children of union members/company employees, ethnic background, first-generation college students, members of minority groups, out-of-state students, public servants, religious affiliation, spouses of deceased or disabled public servants, veterans, veterans' children. *Tuition waivers:* Full or partial for employees or children of employees. *ROTC:* Army, Air Force.

LOANS *Student loans:* $102,288,006 (53% need-based, 47% non-need-based). 57% of past graduating class borrowed through all loan programs. *Average indebtedness per student:* $21,037. *Average need-based loan:* Freshmen: $2573; Undergraduates: $3726. *Parent loans:* $39,682,085 (10% need-based, 90% non-need-based). *Programs:* FFEL (Subsidized and Unsubsidized Stafford, PLUS), Perkins, Federal Nursing, state, college/university.

WORK-STUDY *Federal work-study:* Total amount: $2,950,000; 1,634 jobs averaging $1545. *State or other work-study/employment:* Total amount: $912,939 (100% need-based). 393 part-time jobs averaging $1968.

ATHLETIC AWARDS *Total amount:* $6,665,105 (29% need-based, 71% non-need-based).

APPLYING FOR FINANCIAL AID *Required financial aid form:* FAFSA. *Financial aid deadline:* 6/30 (priority: 3/1). *Notification date:* Continuous beginning 3/15. Students must reply within 4 weeks of notification.

CONTACT Mr. Keith Williams, Associate Director, Michigan State University, 252 Student Services Building, East Lansing, MI 48824-1113, 517-353-5940. *Fax:* 517-432-1155. *E-mail:* willi398@msu.edu.

MICHIGAN TECHNOLOGICAL UNIVERSITY
Houghton, MI

Tuition & fees (MI res): $7610	Average undergraduate aid package: $9061

ABOUT THE INSTITUTION State-supported, coed. Awards: associate, bachelor's, master's, and doctoral degrees. 57 undergraduate majors. Total enrollment: 6,540. Undergraduates: 5,709. Freshmen: 1,227. Federal methodology is used as a basis for awarding need-based institutional aid.

UNDERGRADUATE EXPENSES for 2004–05 *Application fee:* $40. *Tuition, state resident:* full-time $6978; part-time $232.60 per credit hour. *Tuition, nonresident:* full-time $18,150; part-time $605 per credit hour. *Required fees:* full-time $632; $632 per term part-time. Full-time tuition and fees vary according to course load. Part-time tuition and fees vary according to course load. *College room and board:* $6096; *room only:* $2965. Room and board charges vary according to board plan and housing facility. *Payment plan:* Installment.

FRESHMAN FINANCIAL AID (Fall 2004, est.) 1022 applied for aid; of those 65% were deemed to have need. 99% of freshmen with need received aid; of those 36% had need fully met. *Average percent of need met:* 79% (excluding resources awarded to replace EFC). *Average financial aid package:* $9010 (excluding resources awarded to replace EFC). 41% of all full-time freshmen had no need and received non-need-based gift aid.

UNDERGRADUATE FINANCIAL AID (Fall 2004, est.) 3,809 applied for aid; of those 76% were deemed to have need. 96% of undergraduates with need received aid; of those 39% had need fully met. *Average percent of need met:* 75% (excluding resources awarded to replace EFC). *Average financial aid*

package: $9061 (excluding resources awarded to replace EFC). 35% of all full-time undergraduates had no need and received non-need-based gift aid.

GIFT AID (NEED-BASED) *Total amount:* $13,588,921 (24% federal, 17% state, 47% institutional, 12% external sources). *Receiving aid:* Freshmen: 48% (582); All full-time undergraduates: 43% (2,453). *Average award:* Freshmen: $5439; Undergraduates: $4847. *Scholarships, grants, and awards:* Federal Pell, FSEOG, state, private, college/university gift aid from institutional funds.

GIFT AID (NON-NEED-BASED) *Total amount:* $7,239,074 (10% state, 50% institutional, 40% external sources). *Receiving aid:* Freshmen: 41% (504); Undergraduates: 28% (1,573). *Average Award: Freshmen:* $2372; *Undergraduates:* $2179. *Scholarships, grants, and awards by category: Academic Interests/Achievement:* 1,069 awards ($1,441,922 total): biological sciences, business, communication, computer science, education, engineering/technologies, general academic interests/achievements, humanities, mathematics, physical sciences, premedicine, social sciences. *Special Achievements/Activities:* 25 awards ($10,000 total): leadership. *Special Characteristics:* 2,276 awards ($7,159,867 total): children and siblings of alumni, children of faculty/staff, ethnic background, general special characteristics, international students, local/state students, members of minority groups, out-of-state students, previous college experience. *Tuition waivers:* Full or partial for employees or children of employees, senior citizens. *ROTC:* Army, Air Force.

LOANS *Student loans:* $18,491,909 (79% need-based, 21% non-need-based). 59% of past graduating class borrowed through all loan programs. *Average indebtedness per student:* $17,000. *Average need-based loan:* Freshmen: $3369; Undergraduates: $4374. *Parent loans:* $2,869,630 (58% need-based, 42% non-need-based). *Programs:* Federal Direct (Subsidized and Unsubsidized Stafford, PLUS), Perkins, state, college/university, alternative loans.

WORK-STUDY *Federal work-study:* Total amount: $306,788; 231 jobs averaging $1407. *State or other work-study/employment:* Total amount: $3,857,165 (2% need-based, 98% non-need-based). 2,491 part-time jobs averaging $1550.

ATHLETIC AWARDS *Total amount:* $1,597,860 (26% need-based, 74% non-need-based).

APPLYING FOR FINANCIAL AID *Required financial aid form:* FAFSA. *Financial aid deadline (priority):* 2/18. *Notification date:* Continuous beginning 3/1. Students must reply within 4 weeks of notification.

CONTACT Adrene Remali, Manager of Information Systems, Michigan Technological University, 1400 Townsend Drive, Houghton, MI 49931-1295, 906-487-3222 or toll-free 888-MTU-1885. *Fax:* 906-487-3042. *E-mail:* adrene@mtu.edu.

MID-AMERICA CHRISTIAN UNIVERSITY
Oklahoma City, OK

CONTACT Mr. Todd Martin, Director of Financial Aid, Mid-America Christian University, 3500 Southwest 119th Street, Oklahoma City, OK 73170-4504, 405-691-3800. *Fax:* 405-692-3165. *E-mail:* tmartin@mabc.edu.

MIDAMERICA NAZARENE UNIVERSITY
Olathe, KS

Tuition & fees: $14,780	Average undergraduate aid package: $8719

ABOUT THE INSTITUTION Independent religious, coed. Awards: associate, bachelor's, and master's degrees. 41 undergraduate majors. Total enrollment: 1,985. Undergraduates: 1,466. Freshmen: 250. Federal methodology is used as a basis for awarding need-based institutional aid.

UNDERGRADUATE EXPENSES for 2005–06 *Application fee:* $15. *Comprehensive fee:* $20,570 includes full-time tuition ($13,830), mandatory fees ($950), and room and board ($5790). *Part-time tuition:* $561 per semester hour. *Part-time fees:* $500 per term.

GIFT AID (NEED-BASED) *Total amount:* $4,147,713 (30% federal, 13% state, 50% institutional, 7% external sources). *Receiving aid:* Freshmen: 78% (195); All full-time undergraduates: 68% (898). *Average award:* Freshmen: $9820; Undergraduates: $6671. *Scholarships, grants, and awards:* Federal Pell, FSEOG, state, private, college/university gift aid from institutional funds.

GIFT AID (NON-NEED-BASED) *Total amount:* $744,182 (85% institutional, 15% external sources). *Receiving aid:* Freshmen: 6% (14); Undergraduates: 6% (81). *Average Award: Freshmen:* $2663; *Undergraduates:* $2891. *Scholarships, grants, and awards by category: Academic Interests/Achievement:* agriculture, general academic interests/achievements, health fields. *Creative Arts/Performance:* cinema/film/broadcasting, music. *Special Achievements/*

Activities: cheerleading/drum major, leadership. *Special Characteristics:* children of faculty/staff, general special characteristics, relatives of clergy, religious affiliation. *ROTC:* Army cooperative, Air Force cooperative.

LOANS *Student loans:* $8,305,600 (52% need-based, 48% non-need-based). 72% of past graduating class borrowed through all loan programs. *Average indebtedness per student:* $17,421. *Average need-based loan:* Freshmen: $4624; Undergraduates: $4621. *Parent loans:* $835,381 (85% need-based, 15% non-need-based). *Programs:* FFEL (Subsidized and Unsubsidized Stafford, PLUS), Perkins, Federal Nursing.

ATHLETIC AWARDS *Total amount:* $1,385,963 (77% need-based, 23% non-need-based).

APPLYING FOR FINANCIAL AID *Required financial aid forms:* FAFSA, institution's own form. *Financial aid deadline (priority):* 3/1. *Notification date:* Continuous. Students must reply within 2 weeks of notification.

CONTACT Rhonda L. Cole, Director of Student Financial Services, MidAmerica Nazarene University, 2030 East College Way, Olathe, KS 66062-1899, 913-791-3298 or toll-free 800-800-8887. *Fax:* 913-791-3482. *E-mail:* rcole@mnu.edu.

MID-CONTINENT UNIVERSITY
Mayfield, KY

Tuition & fees: $9350	Average undergraduate aid package: $5947

ABOUT THE INSTITUTION Independent Southern Baptist, coed. Awards: associate and bachelor's degrees. 13 undergraduate majors. Total enrollment: 814. Undergraduates: 814. Freshmen: 83. Federal methodology is used as a basis for awarding need-based institutional aid.

UNDERGRADUATE EXPENSES for 2004–05 *Application fee:* $20. *Comprehensive fee:* $14,835 includes full-time tuition ($8100), mandatory fees ($1250), and room and board ($5485). Full-time tuition and fees vary according to course load and program. Room and board charges vary according to board plan and housing facility. *Part-time tuition:* $270 per credit hour. Part-time tuition and fees vary according to course load and program.

FRESHMAN FINANCIAL AID (Fall 2004, est.) 76 applied for aid; of those 84% were deemed to have need. 100% of freshmen with need received aid; of those 17% had need fully met. *Average percent of need met:* 60% (excluding resources awarded to replace EFC). *Average financial aid package:* $5496 (excluding resources awarded to replace EFC). 40% of all full-time freshmen had no need and received non-need-based gift aid.

UNDERGRADUATE FINANCIAL AID (Fall 2004, est.) 769 applied for aid; of those 80% were deemed to have need. 97% of undergraduates with need received aid; of those 17% had need fully met. *Average percent of need met:* 62% (excluding resources awarded to replace EFC). *Average financial aid package:* $5947 (excluding resources awarded to replace EFC). 18% of all full-time undergraduates had no need and received non-need-based gift aid.

GIFT AID (NEED-BASED) *Total amount:* $2,469,025 (38% federal, 52% state, 4% institutional, 6% external sources). *Receiving aid:* Freshmen: 69% (59); All full-time undergraduates: 64% (525). *Average award:* Freshmen: $4270; Undergraduates: $4514. *Scholarships, grants, and awards:* Federal Pell, FSEOG, state, private, college/university gift aid from institutional funds.

GIFT AID (NON-NEED-BASED) *Total amount:* $55,000 (100% state). *Receiving aid:* Freshmen: 24% (20); Undergraduates: 10% (85). *Average Award: Freshmen:* $5938; *Undergraduates:* $5458. *Scholarships, grants, and awards by category: Academic Interests/Achievement:* 25 awards ($20,000 total): education, English, general academic interests/achievements, humanities, religion/biblical studies, social sciences. *Special Characteristics:* 4 awards ($2000 total): children and siblings of alumni, children of faculty/staff, children of union members/company employees, married students, relatives of clergy. *Tuition waivers:* Full or partial for employees or children of employees.

LOANS *Student loans:* $2,090,977 (69% need-based, 31% non-need-based). 75% of past graduating class borrowed through all loan programs. *Average indebtedness per student:* $6738. *Average need-based loan:* Freshmen: $1953; Undergraduates: $2697. *Parent loans:* $33,138 (100% need-based). *Programs:* Federal Direct (Subsidized and Unsubsidized Stafford, PLUS), FFEL (Subsidized and Unsubsidized Stafford, PLUS).

WORK-STUDY *Federal work-study:* Total amount: $53,445; 40 jobs averaging $1650. *State or other work-study/employment:* Part-time jobs available.

ATHLETIC AWARDS *Total amount:* $360,000 (100% need-based).

APPLYING FOR FINANCIAL AID *Required financial aid forms:* FAFSA, institution's own form. *Financial aid deadline (priority):* 3/15. *Notification date:* Continuous. Students must reply within 2 weeks of notification.

CONTACT Kent Youngblood, Director of Financial Aid, Mid-Continent University, 99 Powell Road East, Mayfield, KY 42066, 270-251-9400 Ext. 260. *Fax:* 270-251-9475. *E-mail:* kyoungblood@midcontinent.edu.

MIDDLEBURY COLLEGE
Middlebury, VT

Comprehensive fee: $40,400	Average undergraduate aid package: $26,732

ABOUT THE INSTITUTION Independent, coed. Awards: bachelor's, master's, and doctoral degrees. 48 undergraduate majors. Total enrollment: 2,357. Undergraduates: 2,357. Freshmen: 577. Both federal and institutional methodology are used as a basis for awarding need-based institutional aid.

UNDERGRADUATE EXPENSES for 2004–05 *Application fee:* $55. *Comprehensive fee:* $40,400. *Part-time tuition:* $3900 per credit. *Payment plan:* Tuition prepayment.

FRESHMAN FINANCIAL AID (Fall 2004, est.) 276 applied for aid; of those 77% were deemed to have need. 100% of freshmen with need received aid; of those 100% had need fully met. *Average percent of need met:* 100% (excluding resources awarded to replace EFC). *Average financial aid package:* $28,752 (excluding resources awarded to replace EFC).

UNDERGRADUATE FINANCIAL AID (Fall 2004, est.) 1,088 applied for aid; of those 90% were deemed to have need. 100% of undergraduates with need received aid; of those 100% had need fully met. *Average percent of need met:* 100% (excluding resources awarded to replace EFC). *Average financial aid package:* $26,732 (excluding resources awarded to replace EFC).

GIFT AID (NEED-BASED) *Total amount:* $23,432,749 (4% federal, 1% state, 92% institutional, 3% external sources). *Receiving aid:* Freshmen: 37% (213); All full-time undergraduates: 42% (976). *Average award:* Freshmen: $23,650; Undergraduates: $23,160. *Scholarships, grants, and awards:* Federal Pell, FSEOG, state, private, college/university gift aid from institutional funds.

GIFT AID (NON-NEED-BASED) *Tuition waivers:* Full or partial for employees or children of employees. *ROTC:* Army cooperative.

LOANS *Student loans:* $4,506,027 (80% need-based, 20% non-need-based). 53% of past graduating class borrowed through all loan programs. *Average indebtedness per student:* $19,012. *Average need-based loan:* Freshmen: $2971; Undergraduates: $3690. *Parent loans:* $3,868,959 (100% non-need-based). *Programs:* Federal Direct (Subsidized and Unsubsidized Stafford, PLUS), Perkins, college/university.

WORK-STUDY *Federal work-study:* Total amount: $281,206; 503 jobs averaging $1529. *State or other work-study/employment:* Total amount: $754,311 (100% need-based). 114 part-time jobs averaging $1601.

APPLYING FOR FINANCIAL AID *Required financial aid forms:* FAFSA, CSS Financial Aid PROFILE, noncustodial (divorced/separated) parent's statement, business/farm supplement, federal income tax return. *Financial aid deadline (priority):* 12/31. *Notification date:* 4/1. Students must reply by 5/1.

CONTACT Marguerite Corbin, Financial Aid Assistant, Middlebury College, Emma Willard House, Middlebury, VT 05753, 802-443-5158. *E-mail:* financialaid@middlebury.edu.

MIDDLE TENNESSEE STATE UNIVERSITY
Murfreesboro, TN

Tuition & fees (TN res): $4230	Average undergraduate aid package: $4318

ABOUT THE INSTITUTION State-supported, coed. Awards: associate, bachelor's, master's, and doctoral degrees and post-bachelor's and post-master's certificates. 61 undergraduate majors. Total enrollment: 22,322. Undergraduates: 20,288. Freshmen: 3,143. Federal methodology is used as a basis for awarding need-based institutional aid.

UNDERGRADUATE EXPENSES for 2004–05 *Application fee:* $25. *Tuition, state resident:* full-time $3352; part-time $147 per semester hour. *Tuition, nonresident:* full-time $11,840; part-time $515 per semester hour. Part-time tuition and fees vary according to course load. *College room and board:* $4814; *room only:* $2576. Room and board charges vary according to board plan and housing facility. *Payment plan:* Deferred payment.

GIFT AID (NEED-BASED) *Total amount:* $20,253,538 (73% federal, 17% state, 10% external sources). *Receiving aid:* Freshmen: 31% (963); All full-time undergraduates: 27% (4,660). *Average award:* Freshmen: $2390; Undergraduates: $2156. *Scholarships, grants, and awards:* Federal Pell, FSEOG, state, private, college/university gift aid from institutional funds, Federal Nursing.

GIFT AID (NON-NEED-BASED) *Total amount:* $19,183,795 (58% state, 27% institutional, 15% external sources). *Receiving aid:* Freshmen: 47% (1,472); Undergraduates: 19% (3,180). *Average Award:* Freshmen: $4345; Undergraduates: $2330. *Scholarships, grants, and awards by category: Academic Interests/Achievement:* 2,542 awards ($5,138,004 total): agriculture, biological sciences, business, communication, computer science, education, engineering/technologies, English, foreign languages, general academic interests/achievements, health fields, home economics, humanities, international studies, mathematics, military science, physical sciences, premedicine, social sciences. *Creative Arts/Performance:* 484 awards ($27,245 total): dance, debating, journalism/publications, music, theater/drama. *Special Achievements/Activities:* 114 awards ($228,222 total): cheerleading/drum major, general special achievements/activities, leadership. *Special Characteristics:* 479 awards ($953,145 total): adult students, members of minority groups. *Tuition waivers:* Full or partial for employees or children of employees, senior citizens. *ROTC:* Army, Air Force cooperative.

LOANS *Student loans:* $50,106,606 (100% need-based). 7% of past graduating class borrowed through all loan programs. *Average indebtedness per student:* $19,574. *Average need-based loan:* Freshmen: $1557; Undergraduates: $4444. *Parent loans:* $7,053,094 (100% non-need-based). *Programs:* FFEL (Subsidized and Unsubsidized Stafford, PLUS), Perkins, college/university.

ATHLETIC AWARDS *Total amount:* $3,815,448 (100% non-need-based).

APPLYING FOR FINANCIAL AID *Required financial aid form:* FAFSA. *Financial aid deadline (priority):* 5/15. *Notification date:* Continuous beginning 4/15. Students must reply within 2 weeks of notification.

CONTACT David Hutton, Financial Aid Director, Middle Tennessee State University, 218 Cope Administration Building, Murfreesboro, TN 37132, 615-898-2830 or toll-free 800-331-MTSU (in-state), 800-433-MTSU (out-of-state). *Fax:* 615-898-5167.

MIDLAND LUTHERAN COLLEGE
Fremont, NE

Tuition & fees: $17,210	Average undergraduate aid package: $15,639

ABOUT THE INSTITUTION Independent Lutheran, coed. Awards: associate and bachelor's degrees. 57 undergraduate majors. Total enrollment: 955. Undergraduates: 955. Freshmen: 268. Both federal and institutional methodology are used as a basis for awarding need-based institutional aid.

UNDERGRADUATE EXPENSES for 2004–05 *Application fee:* $30. *Comprehensive fee:* $21,770 includes full-time tuition ($17,210) and room and board ($4560). *College room only:* $2010. Room and board charges vary according to board plan and housing facility. *Part-time tuition:* $720 per hour. Part-time tuition and fees vary according to course load. *Payment plan:* Installment.

GIFT AID (NEED-BASED) *Total amount:* $2,136,095 (56% federal, 10% state, 34% institutional). *Receiving aid:* Freshmen: 87% (222); All full-time undergraduates: 84% (775). *Average award:* Freshmen: $9746; Undergraduates: $9311. *Scholarships, grants, and awards:* Federal Pell, FSEOG, state, private, college/university gift aid from institutional funds.

GIFT AID (NON-NEED-BASED) *Total amount:* $486,517 (29% institutional, 71% external sources). *Average Award: Freshmen:* $8550; *Undergraduates:* $8083. *Scholarships, grants, and awards by category: Academic Interests/Achievement:* general academic interests/achievements. *Creative Arts/Performance:* art/fine arts, debating, journalism/publications, music, theater/drama. *Special Achievements/Activities:* community service, general special achievements/activities, leadership, religious involvement. *Special Characteristics:* children and siblings of alumni, handicapped students, international students, members of minority groups, religious affiliation, siblings of current students. *Tuition waivers:* Full or partial for employees or children of employees.

LOANS *Student loans:* $4,685,760 (87% need-based, 13% non-need-based). 87% of past graduating class borrowed through all loan programs. *Average indebtedness per student:* $19,698. *Average need-based loan:* Freshmen: $4991; Undergraduates: $6038. *Parent loans:* $1,335,113 (100% non-need-based). *Programs:* FFEL (Subsidized and Unsubsidized Stafford, PLUS), Perkins, college/university.

ATHLETIC AWARDS *Total amount:* $1,938,336 (78% need-based, 22% non-need-based).

APPLYING FOR FINANCIAL AID *Required financial aid form:* FAFSA. *Financial aid deadline:* Continuous. *Notification date:* Continuous beginning 3/1. Students must reply within 2 weeks of notification.

CONTACT Mr. Doug G. Watson, Associate Vice President, Midland Lutheran College, 900 North Clarkson Street, Fremont, NE 68025-4200, 402-721-5480 Ext. 6521 or toll-free 800-642-8382 Ext. 6501. *Fax:* 402-721-6513. *E-mail:* watson@mlc.edu.

MIDSTATE COLLEGE
Peoria, IL

CONTACT Janet Ozuna, Director of Financial Aid/Business Manager, Midstate College, 411 West Northmoor Road, Peoria, IL 61614, 309-692-4092. *Fax:* 309-692-3893.

MIDWAY COLLEGE
Midway, KY

Tuition & fees: $12,750	Average undergraduate aid package: $9342

ABOUT THE INSTITUTION Independent religious, women only. Awards: associate and bachelor's degrees. 18 undergraduate majors. Total enrollment: 1,271. Undergraduates: 1,271. Freshmen: 183. Federal methodology is used as a basis for awarding need-based institutional aid.

UNDERGRADUATE EXPENSES for 2004–05 *Application fee:* $25. *Comprehensive fee:* $18,550 includes full-time tuition ($12,600), mandatory fees ($150), and room and board ($5800). *College room only:* $2800. Full-time tuition and fees vary according to program. Room and board charges vary according to board plan and housing facility. *Part-time tuition:* $420 per semester hour. Part-time tuition and fees vary according to class time and course load. *Payment plan:* Deferred payment.

GIFT AID (NEED-BASED) *Total amount:* $4,895,008 (32% federal, 41% state, 16% institutional, 11% external sources). *Receiving aid:* Freshmen: 81% (115); All full-time undergraduates: 74% (639). *Average award:* Freshmen: $6972; Undergraduates: $6303. *Scholarships, grants, and awards:* Federal Pell, FSEOG, state, private, college/university gift aid from institutional funds.

GIFT AID (NON-NEED-BASED) *Total amount:* $69,320 (92% institutional, 8% external sources). *Average Award:* Freshmen: $2908; Undergraduates: $2811. *Scholarships, grants, and awards by category: Academic Interests/Achievement:* agriculture, business, general academic interests/achievements, health fields, premedicine. *Creative Arts/Performance:* art/fine arts, music. *Special Achievements/Activities:* general special achievements/activities, junior miss, leadership, religious involvement. *Special Characteristics:* children and siblings of alumni, children of faculty/staff, members of minority groups, relatives of clergy, religious affiliation, veterans. *Tuition waivers:* Full or partial for employees or children of employees, senior citizens. *ROTC:* Army cooperative.

LOANS *Student loans:* $4,628,417 (89% need-based, 11% non-need-based). 74% of past graduating class borrowed through all loan programs. *Average indebtedness per student:* $15,026. *Average need-based loan:* Freshmen: $3954; Undergraduates: $5247. *Parent loans:* $703,743 (80% need-based, 20% non-need-based). *Programs:* FFEL (Subsidized and Unsubsidized Stafford, PLUS), Perkins, college/university.

ATHLETIC AWARDS *Total amount:* $291,810 (93% need-based, 7% non-need-based).

APPLYING FOR FINANCIAL AID *Required financial aid forms:* FAFSA, institution's own form. *Financial aid deadline (priority):* 3/15. *Notification date:* Continuous. Students must reply within 4 weeks of notification.

CONTACT Katie Valentine, Director of Financial Aid, Midway College, 512 East Stephens Street, Midway, KY 40347-1120, 859-846-5410 or toll-free 800-755-0031. *Fax:* 859-846-5751. *E-mail:* kvalentine@midway.edu.

MIDWESTERN STATE UNIVERSITY
Wichita Falls, TX

Tuition & fees (TX res): $3740	Average undergraduate aid package: $6392

ABOUT THE INSTITUTION State-supported, coed. Awards: associate, bachelor's, and master's degrees. 45 undergraduate majors. Total enrollment: 6,348. Undergraduates: 5,606. Freshmen: 691. Federal methodology is used as a basis for awarding need-based institutional aid.

UNDERGRADUATE EXPENSES for 2004–05 *Application fee:* $25. *Tuition, state resident:* full-time $1440; part-time $48 per credit hour. *Tuition, nonresident:* full-time $9180; part-time $306 per credit hour. *Required fees:* full-time $2300; $132 per credit hour. Part-time tuition and fees vary according to course load.

College room and board: $4844; *room only:* $2400. Room and board charges vary according to board plan and housing facility. *Payment plan:* Installment.

FRESHMAN FINANCIAL AID (Fall 2004, est.) 78% of freshmen with need received aid; of those 2% had need fully met. *Average percent of need met:* 27% (excluding resources awarded to replace EFC). *Average financial aid package:* $3504 (excluding resources awarded to replace EFC). 9% of all full-time freshmen had no need and received non-need-based gift aid.

UNDERGRADUATE FINANCIAL AID (Fall 2004, est.) 95% of undergraduates with need received aid; of those 4% had need fully met. *Average percent of need met:* 39% (excluding resources awarded to replace EFC). *Average financial aid package:* $6392 (excluding resources awarded to replace EFC). 19% of all full-time undergraduates had no need and received non-need-based gift aid.

GIFT AID (NEED-BASED) *Total amount:* $6,908,386 (62% federal, 25% state, 6% institutional, 7% external sources). *Receiving aid:* Freshmen: 6% (40); All full-time undergraduates: 40% (1,569). *Average award:* Freshmen: $3392; Undergraduates: $4064. *Scholarships, grants, and awards:* Federal Pell, FSEOG, state, private, college/university gift aid from institutional funds.

GIFT AID (NON-NEED-BASED) *Total amount:* $1,278,966 (7% state, 55% institutional, 38% external sources). *Receiving aid:* Freshmen: 8% (54); Undergraduates: 18% (700). *Average Award:* Freshmen: $2188; Undergraduates: $2006. *Scholarships, grants, and awards by category: Academic Interests/Achievement:* 207 awards ($110,168 total): business, computer science, education, English, general academic interests/achievements, health fields, mathematics, social sciences. *Creative Arts/Performance:* 49 awards ($281,850 total): art/fine arts, general creative arts/performance, music, theater/drama. *Special Achievements/Activities:* 232 awards ($280,634 total): cheerleading/drum major, general special achievements/activities, leadership, memberships. *Special Characteristics:* 113 awards ($135,726 total): children of faculty/staff, general special characteristics, handicapped students, international students, out-of-state students, veterans. *Tuition waivers:* Full or partial for employees or children of employees, senior citizens. *ROTC:* Air Force cooperative.

LOANS *Student loans:* $11,106,258 (82% need-based, 18% non-need-based). 47% of past graduating class borrowed through all loan programs. *Average indebtedness per student:* $12,000. *Average need-based loan:* Freshmen: $2454; Undergraduates: $3344. *Parent loans:* $2,427,898 (42% need-based, 58% non-need-based). *Programs:* FFEL (Subsidized and Unsubsidized Stafford, PLUS), Perkins, state, college/university.

WORK-STUDY *Federal work-study:* Total amount: $131,664; 51 jobs averaging $1291. *State or other work-study/employment:* Total amount: $45,838 (100% need-based). 16 part-time jobs averaging $1432.

ATHLETIC AWARDS *Total amount:* $717,482 (33% need-based, 67% non-need-based).

APPLYING FOR FINANCIAL AID *Required financial aid forms:* FAFSA, institution's own form. *Financial aid deadline (priority):* 5/1. *Notification date:* Continuous. Students must reply within 2 weeks of notification.

CONTACT Ms. Kathy Pennartz, Director of Financial Aid, Midwestern State University, 3410 Taft Boulevard, Wichita Falls, TX 76308-2099, 940-397-4214 or toll-free 800-842-1922. *Fax:* 940-397-4852. *E-mail:* financial-aid@mwsu.edu.

MIDWESTERN UNIVERSITY, GLENDALE CAMPUS
Glendale, AZ

Tuition & fees: $15,556	Average undergraduate aid package: $25,210

ABOUT THE INSTITUTION Independent, coed. Awards: bachelor's, master's, and doctoral degrees and post-bachelor's certificates. Total enrollment: 1,117. Undergraduates: 45. Federal methodology is used as a basis for awarding need-based institutional aid.

UNDERGRADUATE EXPENSES for 2004–05 *Comprehensive fee:* $24,341 includes full-time tuition ($15,306), mandatory fees ($250), and room and board ($8785). *College room only:* $5670.

UNDERGRADUATE FINANCIAL AID (Fall 2003) 117 applied for aid; of those 97% were deemed to have need. 100% of undergraduates with need received aid; of those 1% had need fully met. *Average percent of need met:* 33% (excluding resources awarded to replace EFC). *Average financial aid package:* $25,210 (excluding resources awarded to replace EFC).

GIFT AID (NEED-BASED) *Total amount:* $274,081 (91% federal, 8% state, 1% external sources). *Receiving aid:* All full-time undergraduates: 43% (53). *Average award:* Undergraduates: $2404. *Scholarships, grants, and awards:* Federal Pell, FSEOG, state, private, college/university gift aid from institutional funds.

GIFT AID (NON-NEED-BASED) *Total amount:* $102,252 (82% federal, 17% state, 1% external sources). *Receiving aid:* Undergraduates: 6% (7). *Scholarships, grants, and awards by category: Academic Interests/Achievement:* health fields.

LOANS *Student loans:* $2,734,555 (22% need-based, 78% non-need-based). 91% of past graduating class borrowed through all loan programs. *Average indebtedness per student:* $52,677. *Average need-based loan:* Undergraduates: $4799. *Parent loans:* $30,382 (100% non-need-based). *Programs:* FFEL (Subsidized and Unsubsidized Stafford, PLUS), Perkins, alternative loans.

WORK-STUDY *Federal work-study:* Total amount: $64,364; 28 jobs averaging $2299.

APPLYING FOR FINANCIAL AID *Required financial aid forms:* FAFSA, institution's own form. *Financial aid deadline:* Continuous.

CONTACT Lynette Whitcomb, Administrative Assistant, Office of Student Financial Services, Midwestern University, Glendale Campus, 19555 North 59th Avenue, Glendale, AZ 85308, 623-572-3321 or toll-free 888-247-9277 (in-state), 888-247-9271 (out-of-state). *Fax:* 623-572-3283. *E-mail:* az_fin_aid@arizona.midwestern.edu.

MIDWIVES COLLEGE OF UTAH
Orem, UT

CONTACT Financial Aid Office, Midwives College of Utah, 282 North State Street, Orem, UT 84057, 801-764-9068 or toll-free 888-489-1238.

MILES COLLEGE
Fairfield, AL

ABOUT THE INSTITUTION Independent Christian Methodist Episcopal, coed. Awards: bachelor's degrees. 25 undergraduate majors. Total enrollment: 1,716. Undergraduates: 1,716. Freshmen: 437.

GIFT AID (NEED-BASED) *Scholarships, grants, and awards:* Federal Pell, FSEOG, state, private, college/university gift aid from institutional funds, United Negro College Fund.

GIFT AID (NON-NEED-BASED) *Scholarships, grants, and awards by category: Academic Interests/Achievement:* general academic interests/achievements. *Creative Arts/Performance:* general creative arts/performance. *Special Achievements/Activities:* cheerleading/drum major, general special achievements/activities, leadership, religious involvement. *Special Characteristics:* children of faculty/staff, general special characteristics, handicapped students, local/state students, veterans.

LOANS *Programs:* Federal Direct (Subsidized and Unsubsidized Stafford, PLUS), Perkins.

APPLYING FOR FINANCIAL AID *Required financial aid forms:* FAFSA, state aid form.

CONTACT P. N. Lanier, Financial Aid Administrator, Miles College, PO Box 3800, Birmingham, AL 35208, 205-929-1663 or toll-free 800-445-0708. *Fax:* 205-929-1668. *E-mail:* pnlani@netscape.net.

MILLERSVILLE UNIVERSITY OF PENNSYLVANIA
Millersville, PA

Tuition & fees (PA res): $6081	Average undergraduate aid package: $6171

ABOUT THE INSTITUTION State-supported, coed. Awards: associate, bachelor's, and master's degrees and post-bachelor's and post-master's certificates. 48 undergraduate majors. Total enrollment: 7,998. Undergraduates: 6,991. Freshmen: 1,409. Federal methodology is used as a basis for awarding need-based institutional aid.

UNDERGRADUATE EXPENSES for 2004–05 *Application fee:* $35. *Tuition, state resident:* full-time $4810; part-time $200 per credit. *Tuition, nonresident:* full-time $12,026; part-time $501 per credit. *Required fees:* full-time $1271; $74 per credit. Part-time tuition and fees vary according to course load. *College room and board:* $5642; *room only:* $3308. Room and board charges vary according to board plan. *Payment plan:* Installment.

GIFT AID (NEED-BASED) *Total amount:* $8,864,043 (38% federal, 52% state, 7% institutional, 3% external sources). *Receiving aid:* Freshmen: 43% (577); All full-time undergraduates: 38% (2,321). *Average award:* Freshmen: $4243;

Undergraduates: $3654. *Scholarships, grants, and awards:* Federal Pell, FSEOG, state, private, college/university gift aid from institutional funds, SICO Scholarships.

GIFT AID (NON-NEED-BASED) *Total amount:* $2,021,421 (2% state, 43% institutional, 55% external sources). *Receiving aid:* Freshmen: 10% (127); Undergraduates: 7% (435). *Average Award:* Freshmen: $2109; *Undergraduates:* $2342. *Scholarships, grants, and awards by category: Academic Interests/Achievement:* 368 awards ($872,333 total): biological sciences, business, communication, computer science, education, English, foreign languages, general academic interests/achievements, health fields, humanities, mathematics, physical sciences, social sciences. *Creative Arts/Performance:* 30 awards ($13,385 total): art/fine arts, music. *Special Achievements/Activities:* 2 awards ($1850 total): community service. *Special Characteristics:* 147 awards ($508,367 total): children of union members/company employees, international students. *Tuition waivers:* Full or partial for employees or children of employees, senior citizens. *ROTC:* Army.

LOANS *Student loans:* $18,825,884 (52% need-based, 48% non-need-based). 62% of past graduating class borrowed through all loan programs. *Average indebtedness per student:* $14,969. *Average need-based loan:* Freshmen: $2568; Undergraduates: $3373. *Parent loans:* $2,983,120 (100% non-need-based). *Programs:* FFEL (Subsidized and Unsubsidized Stafford, PLUS), Perkins, college/university.

ATHLETIC AWARDS *Total amount:* $267,013 (17% need-based, 83% non-need-based).

APPLYING FOR FINANCIAL AID *Required financial aid form:* FAFSA. *Financial aid deadline:* 3/15. *Notification date:* Continuous beginning 3/19. Students must reply within 2 weeks of notification.

CONTACT Mr. Dwight Horsey, Director of Financial Aid, Millersville University of Pennsylvania, PO Box 1002, Millersville, PA 17551-0302, 717-872-3026 or toll-free 800-MU-ADMIT (out-of-state). *Fax:* 717-871-2248. *E-mail:* dwight.horsey@millersville.edu.

MILLIGAN COLLEGE
Milligan College, TN

Tuition & fees: $16,360	Average undergraduate aid package: $15,539

ABOUT THE INSTITUTION Independent Christian, coed. Awards: bachelor's and master's degrees. 26 undergraduate majors. Total enrollment: 914. Undergraduates: 753. Freshmen: 191. Federal methodology is used as a basis for awarding need-based institutional aid.

UNDERGRADUATE EXPENSES for 2004–05 *Application fee:* $30. *Comprehensive fee:* $20,960 includes full-time tuition ($15,850), mandatory fees ($510), and room and board ($4600). *College room only:* $2250. Room and board charges vary according to board plan and housing facility. *Part-time tuition:* $275 per credit. *Part-time fees:* $142 per term. Part-time tuition and fees vary according to course load. *Payment plan:* Installment.

FRESHMAN FINANCIAL AID (Fall 2003) 150 applied for aid; of those 99% were deemed to have need. 100% of freshmen with need received aid; of those 23% had need fully met. *Average percent of need met:* 87% (excluding resources awarded to replace EFC). *Average financial aid package:* $15,122 (excluding resources awarded to replace EFC). 9% of all full-time freshmen had no need and received non-need-based gift aid.

UNDERGRADUATE FINANCIAL AID (Fall 2003) 613 applied for aid; of those 100% were deemed to have need. 100% of undergraduates with need received aid; of those 21% had need fully met. *Average percent of need met:* 72% (excluding resources awarded to replace EFC). *Average financial aid package:* $15,539 (excluding resources awarded to replace EFC). 5% of all full-time undergraduates had no need and received non-need-based gift aid.

GIFT AID (NEED-BASED) *Total amount:* $4,286,035 (15% federal, 8% state, 63% institutional, 14% external sources). *Receiving aid:* Freshmen: 76% (149); All full-time undergraduates: 80% (590). *Average award:* Freshmen: $7825; Undergraduates: $7179. *Scholarships, grants, and awards:* Federal Pell, FSEOG, state, college/university gift aid from institutional funds.

GIFT AID (NON-NEED-BASED) *Total amount:* $382,975 (86% institutional, 14% external sources). *Receiving aid:* Freshmen: 41% (80); Undergraduates: 33% (240). *Average Award:* Freshmen: $1485; Undergraduates: $1632. *Scholarships, grants, and awards by category: Academic Interests/Achievement:* 780 awards ($2,681,194 total): communication, computer science, general academic interests/achievements, health fields, mathematics, religion/biblical studies. *Creative Arts/Performance:* 27 awards ($24,850 total): art/fine arts, music. *Special Achievements/Activities:* 21 awards ($44,000 total): community service.

Special Characteristics: 14 awards ($172,490 total): children of faculty/staff. **Tuition waivers:** Full or partial for employees or children of employees. **ROTC:** Army cooperative.

LOANS Student loans: $2,967,094 (92% need-based, 8% non-need-based). 70% of past graduating class borrowed through all loan programs. Average indebtedness per student: $23,794. **Average need-based loan:** Freshmen: $2857; Undergraduates: $4160. **Parent loans:** $747,220 (85% need-based, 15% non-need-based). **Programs:** FFEL (Subsidized and Unsubsidized Stafford, PLUS), Perkins, Signature Loans.

WORK-STUDY Federal work-study: Total amount: $142,454; 162 jobs averaging $880. **State or other work-study/employment:** Total amount: $132,928 (68% need-based, 32% non-need-based). 147 part-time jobs averaging $904.

ATHLETIC AWARDS Total amount: $1,138,620 (93% need-based, 7% non-need-based).

APPLYING FOR FINANCIAL AID Required financial aid form: FAFSA. **Financial aid deadline (priority):** 3/1. **Notification date:** Continuous beginning 3/4. Students must reply within 2 weeks of notification.

CONTACT Becky Brewster, Director of Student Financial Services, Milligan College, PO Box 250, Milligan College, TN 37682, 423-461-8949 or toll-free 800-262-8337 (in-state). Fax: 423-929-2368. E-mail: rabrewster@milligan.edu.

MILLIKIN UNIVERSITY
Decatur, IL

ABOUT THE INSTITUTION Independent religious, coed. Awards: bachelor's and master's degrees. 51 undergraduate majors. Total enrollment: 2,672. Undergraduates: 2,645. Freshmen: 531.

GIFT AID (NEED-BASED) Scholarships, grants, and awards: Federal Pell, FSEOG, state, private, college/university gift aid from institutional funds.

GIFT AID (NON-NEED-BASED) Scholarships, grants, and awards by category: Academic Interests/Achievement: general academic interests/achievements. Creative Arts/Performance: art/fine arts, dance, music, theater/drama. Special Achievements/Activities: community service. Special Characteristics: children of union members/company employees, ethnic background, international students, relatives of clergy, religious affiliation.

LOANS Programs: FFEL (Subsidized and Unsubsidized Stafford, PLUS), Perkins.

APPLYING FOR FINANCIAL AID Required financial aid form: FAFSA.

CONTACT Director of Financial Aid, Millikin University, 1184 West Main Street, Decatur, IL 62522-2084, 217-424-6343 or toll-free 800-373-7733. Fax: 217-425-4669.

MILLSAPS COLLEGE
Jackson, MS

Tuition & fees: $20,690	Average undergraduate aid package: $17,064

ABOUT THE INSTITUTION Independent United Methodist, coed. Awards: bachelor's and master's degrees. 26 undergraduate majors. Total enrollment: 1,146. Undergraduates: 1,086. Freshmen: 278. Federal methodology is used as a basis for awarding need-based institutional aid.

UNDERGRADUATE EXPENSES for 2005–06 Application fee: $25. **Comprehensive fee:** $28,256 includes full-time tuition ($19,490), mandatory fees ($1200), and room and board ($7566). **College room only:** $4248. Room and board charges vary according to housing facility. **Part-time tuition:** $604 per credit hour. **Part-time fees:** $30 per credit hour. Part-time tuition and fees vary according to course load. **Payment plans:** Installment, deferred payment.

FRESHMAN FINANCIAL AID (Fall 2004, est.) 232 applied for aid; of those 78% were deemed to have need. 100% of freshmen with need received aid; of those 37% had need fully met. Average percent of need met: 91% (excluding resources awarded to replace EFC). Average financial aid package: $18,452 (excluding resources awarded to replace EFC). 33% of all full-time freshmen had no need and received non-need-based gift aid.

UNDERGRADUATE FINANCIAL AID (Fall 2004, est.) 706 applied for aid; of those 83% were deemed to have need. 99% of undergraduates with need received aid; of those 26% had need fully met. Average percent of need met: 81% (excluding resources awarded to replace EFC). Average financial aid package: $17,064 (excluding resources awarded to replace EFC). 40% of all full-time undergraduates had no need and received non-need-based gift aid.

GIFT AID (NEED-BASED) Total amount: $8,068,624 (12% federal, 4% state, 78% institutional, 6% external sources). **Receiving aid:** Freshmen: 65% (181); All full-time undergraduates: 55% (574). **Average award:** Freshmen: $15,206;

Undergraduates: $13,449. **Scholarships, grants, and awards:** Federal Pell, FSEOG, state, private, college/university gift aid from institutional funds.

GIFT AID (NON-NEED-BASED) Total amount: $5,027,662 (5% state, 85% institutional, 10% external sources). **Receiving aid:** Freshmen: 17% (47); Undergraduates: 12% (130). **Average Award:** Freshmen: $14,111; Undergraduates: $12,410. **Scholarships, grants, and awards by category:** Academic Interests/Achievement: 895 awards ($7,302,853 total): business, general academic interests/achievements. Creative Arts/Performance: 89 awards ($329,876 total): art/fine arts, music, theater/drama. Special Achievements/Activities: 886 awards ($7,255,797 total): community service, general special achievements/activities, hobbies/interests, leadership, religious involvement. Special Characteristics: 80 awards ($322,458 total): adult students, children of faculty/staff, ethnic background, first-generation college students, members of minority groups, relatives of clergy, religious affiliation. **Tuition waivers:** Full or partial for employees or children of employees. **ROTC:** Army cooperative.

LOANS Student loans: $4,021,835 (62% need-based, 38% non-need-based). 60% of past graduating class borrowed through all loan programs. Average indebtedness per student: $22,535. **Average need-based loan:** Freshmen: $3373; Undergraduates: $3903. **Parent loans:** $1,387,848 (15% need-based, 85% non-need-based). **Programs:** FFEL (Subsidized and Unsubsidized Stafford, PLUS), Perkins, college/university.

WORK-STUDY Federal work-study: Total amount: $415,787; 258 jobs averaging $1376. **State or other work-study/employment:** 320 part-time jobs averaging $788.

APPLYING FOR FINANCIAL AID Required financial aid forms: FAFSA, institution's own form, state aid form. **Financial aid deadline (priority):** 3/1. **Notification date:** Continuous beginning 3/15. Students must reply by 5/1 or within 2 weeks of notification.

CONTACT Patrick James, Director of Financial Aid, Millsaps College, 1701 North State Street, Jackson, MS 39210-0001, 601-974-1220 or toll-free 800-352-1050. Fax: 601-974-1224. E-mail: jamespg@millsaps.edu.

MILLS COLLEGE
Oakland, CA

ABOUT THE INSTITUTION Independent, women only. Awards: bachelor's, master's, and doctoral degrees and post-bachelor's certificates. 38 undergraduate majors. Total enrollment: 1,256. Undergraduates: 762. Freshmen: 136.

GIFT AID (NEED-BASED) Scholarships, grants, and awards: Federal Pell, FSEOG, state, private, college/university gift aid from institutional funds.

GIFT AID (NON-NEED-BASED) Scholarships, grants, and awards by category: Academic Interests/Achievement: biological sciences, computer science, general academic interests/achievements, mathematics, physical sciences, premedicine. Creative Arts/Performance: art/fine arts, music. Special Characteristics: children of faculty/staff.

LOANS Programs: FFEL (Subsidized and Unsubsidized Stafford, PLUS), Perkins, college/university.

WORK-STUDY Federal work-study: Total amount: $475,424; jobs available. **State or other work-study/employment:** Total amount: $470,925 (71% need-based, 29% non-need-based). Part-time jobs available.

APPLYING FOR FINANCIAL AID Required financial aid forms: FAFSA, institution's own form, state aid form, noncustodial (divorced/separated) parent's statement.

CONTACT The M Center/Financial Aid, Mills College, 5000 MacArthur Boulevard, Oakland, CA 94613, 510-430-2000 or toll-free 800-87-MILLS. E-mail: mcenter-finaid@mills.edu.

MILWAUKEE INSTITUTE OF ART AND DESIGN
Milwaukee, WI

Tuition & fees: $22,510	Average undergraduate aid package: $16,702

ABOUT THE INSTITUTION Independent, coed. Awards: bachelor's degrees. 9 undergraduate majors. Total enrollment: 636. Undergraduates: 636. Freshmen: 143. Federal methodology is used as a basis for awarding need-based institutional aid.

UNDERGRADUATE EXPENSES for 2005–06 Application fee: $25. **Comprehensive fee:** $29,310 includes full-time tuition ($22,200), mandatory fees ($310), and room and board ($6800). Room and board charges vary according to board plan. **Part-time tuition:** $740 per credit hour. Part-time tuition and fees vary according to course load. **Payment plan:** Deferred payment.

GIFT AID (NEED-BASED) *Total amount:* $4,379,537 (15% federal, 13% state, 68% institutional, 4% external sources). *Receiving aid:* Freshmen: 71% (135); All full-time undergraduates: 83% (444). *Average award:* Freshmen: $10,717; Undergraduates: $9236. *Scholarships, grants, and awards:* Federal Pell, FSEOG, state, private, college/university gift aid from institutional funds.

GIFT AID (NON-NEED-BASED) *Total amount:* $436,157 (97% institutional, 3% external sources). *Receiving aid:* Freshmen: 6% (11); Undergraduates: 4% (21). *Average Award:* Freshmen: $8152; Undergraduates: $8765. *Scholarships, grants, and awards by category:* Creative Arts/Performance: art/fine arts. *Special Characteristics:* children of faculty/staff, ethnic background, local/state students, members of minority groups. *Tuition waivers:* Full or partial for employees or children of employees.

LOANS *Student loans:* $5,047,558 (82% need-based, 18% non-need-based). 83% of past graduating class borrowed through all loan programs. *Average indebtedness per student:* $18,492. *Average need-based loan:* Freshmen: $6429; Undergraduates: $7465. *Parent loans:* $924,087 (50% need-based, 50% non-need-based). *Programs:* FFEL (Subsidized and Unsubsidized Stafford, PLUS), college/university, Norwest Collegiate Loans, Signature Loans.

APPLYING FOR FINANCIAL AID *Required financial aid form:* FAFSA. *Financial aid deadline:* 3/1. *Notification date:* 4/1. Students must reply by 5/1 or within 4 weeks of notification.

CONTACT Mr. Lloyd Mueller, Director of Financial Aid, Milwaukee Institute of Art and Design, 273 East Erie Street, Milwaukee, WI 53202-6003, 414-291-3272 or toll-free 888-749-MIAD. *Fax:* 414-291-8077. *E-mail:* llmuelle@miad.edu.

MILWAUKEE SCHOOL OF ENGINEERING
Milwaukee, WI

Tuition & fees: $23,955	Average undergraduate aid package: $14,971

ABOUT THE INSTITUTION Independent, coed. Awards: bachelor's and master's degrees. 16 undergraduate majors. Total enrollment: 2,363. Undergraduates: 2,089. Freshmen: 470. Federal methodology is used as a basis for awarding need-based institutional aid.

UNDERGRADUATE EXPENSES for 2005–06 *Application fee:* $25. *Comprehensive fee:* $29,847 includes full-time tuition ($23,955) and room and board ($5892). *College room only:* $3780. Room and board charges vary according to board plan and housing facility. *Part-time tuition:* $415 per quarter hour. Part-time tuition and fees vary according to course load. *Payment plan:* Installment.

FRESHMAN FINANCIAL AID (Fall 2003) 372 applied for aid; of those 91% were deemed to have need. 100% of freshmen with need received aid; of those 11% had need fully met. *Average percent of need met:* 68% (excluding resources awarded to replace EFC). *Average financial aid package:* $14,759 (excluding resources awarded to replace EFC). 33% of all full-time freshmen had no need and received non-need-based gift aid.

UNDERGRADUATE FINANCIAL AID (Fall 2003) 1,539 applied for aid; of those 93% were deemed to have need. 99% of undergraduates with need received aid; of those 13% had need fully met. *Average percent of need met:* 66% (excluding resources awarded to replace EFC). *Average financial aid package:* $14,971 (excluding resources awarded to replace EFC). 13% of all full-time undergraduates had no need and received non-need-based gift aid.

GIFT AID (NEED-BASED) *Total amount:* $17,501,818 (9% federal, 9% state, 79% institutional, 3% external sources). *Receiving aid:* Freshmen: 82% (336); All full-time undergraduates: 81% (1,421). *Average award:* Freshmen: $12,533; Undergraduates: $11,699. *Scholarships, grants, and awards:* Federal Pell, FSEOG, state, private, college/university gift aid from institutional funds.

GIFT AID (NON-NEED-BASED) *Total amount:* $2,547,522 (1% state, 93% institutional, 6% external sources). *Receiving aid:* Freshmen: 8% (31); Undergraduates: 7% (128). *Average Award:* Freshmen: $8852; Undergraduates: $11,984. *Scholarships, grants, and awards by category:* Academic Interests/Achievement: 2,350 awards ($15,625,146 total): business, communication, computer science, engineering/technologies, health fields. *Special Characteristics:* 21 awards ($308,245 total): children of faculty/staff. *Tuition waivers:* Full or partial for employees or children of employees. *ROTC:* Army cooperative, Naval cooperative, Air Force cooperative.

LOANS *Student loans:* $14,775,943 (74% need-based, 26% non-need-based). 74% of past graduating class borrowed through all loan programs. *Average indebtedness per student:* $31,253. *Average need-based loan:* Freshmen: $2335; Undergraduates: $3518. *Parent loans:* $2,460,434 (45% need-based, 55% non-need-based). *Programs:* FFEL (Subsidized and Unsubsidized Stafford, PLUS), Perkins, state, college/university.

WORK-STUDY *Federal work-study:* Total amount: $273,110; 208 jobs averaging $1313.

APPLYING FOR FINANCIAL AID *Required financial aid form:* FAFSA. *Financial aid deadline (priority):* 3/15. *Notification date:* Continuous beginning 3/1. Students must reply within 2 weeks of notification.

CONTACT Benjamin P. Dobner, Director of Student Financial Services, Milwaukee School of Engineering, 1025 North Broadway Street, Milwaukee, WI 53202-3109, 800-778-7223 or toll-free 800-332-6763. *Fax:* 414-277-6952. *E-mail:* finaid@msoe.edu.

MINNEAPOLIS COLLEGE OF ART AND DESIGN
Minneapolis, MN

ABOUT THE INSTITUTION Independent, coed. Awards: bachelor's and master's degrees and post-bachelor's certificates. 11 undergraduate majors. Total enrollment: 717. Undergraduates: 661. Freshmen: 107.

GIFT AID (NEED-BASED) *Scholarships, grants, and awards:* Federal Pell, FSEOG, state, private, college/university gift aid from institutional funds.

GIFT AID (NON-NEED-BASED) *Scholarships, grants, and awards by category:* Creative Arts/Performance: applied art and design, art/fine arts, cinema/film/broadcasting, general creative arts/performance.

LOANS *Programs:* FFEL (Subsidized and Unsubsidized Stafford, PLUS), Perkins, state, college/university.

WORK-STUDY *Federal work-study:* Total amount: $73,958; 61 jobs averaging $1843. *State or other work-study/employment:* Total amount: $280,189 (43% need-based, 57% non-need-based). 18 part-time jobs averaging $1753.

APPLYING FOR FINANCIAL AID *Required financial aid form:* FAFSA.

CONTACT Laura Link, Director of Financial Aid, Minneapolis College of Art and Design, 2501 Stevens Avenue South, Minneapolis, MN 55404-4347, 612-874-3733 or toll-free 800-874-6223. *Fax:* 612-874-3701. *E-mail:* laura_link@mead.edu.

MINNESOTA STATE UNIVERSITY MANKATO
Mankato, MN

Tuition & fees (MN res): $5088	Average undergraduate aid package: $6836

ABOUT THE INSTITUTION State-supported, coed. Awards: associate, bachelor's, and master's degrees and post-master's certificates. 127 undergraduate majors. Total enrollment: 14,153. Undergraduates: 12,466. Freshmen: 2,171. Federal methodology is used as a basis for awarding need-based institutional aid.

UNDERGRADUATE EXPENSES for 2004–05 *Application fee:* $20. *Tuition, state resident:* full-time $4376; part-time $175 per credit. *Tuition, nonresident:* full-time $9286; part-time $370.30 per credit. *Required fees:* full-time $712; $29.59 per credit. Full-time tuition and fees vary according to course load and reciprocity agreements. Part-time tuition and fees vary according to course load and reciprocity agreements. *College room and board:* $4716. Room and board charges vary according to board plan. *Payment plan:* Installment.

FRESHMAN FINANCIAL AID (Fall 2004, est.) 1728 applied for aid; of those 70% were deemed to have need. 99% of freshmen with need received aid; of those 41% had need fully met. *Average percent of need met:* 75% (excluding resources awarded to replace EFC). *Average financial aid package:* $6278 (excluding resources awarded to replace EFC). 7% of all full-time freshmen had no need and received non-need-based gift aid.

UNDERGRADUATE FINANCIAL AID (Fall 2004, est.) 8,252 applied for aid; of those 73% were deemed to have need. 99% of undergraduates with need received aid; of those 45% had need fully met. *Average percent of need met:* 79% (excluding resources awarded to replace EFC). *Average financial aid package:* $6836 (excluding resources awarded to replace EFC). 5% of all full-time undergraduates had no need and received non-need-based gift aid.

GIFT AID (NEED-BASED) *Total amount:* $14,471,469 (56% federal, 40% state, 4% institutional). *Receiving aid:* Freshmen: 34% (729); All full-time undergraduates: 34% (3,811). *Average award:* Freshmen: $3573; Undergraduates: $3475. *Scholarships, grants, and awards:* Federal Pell, FSEOG, state, private, college/university gift aid from institutional funds.

GIFT AID (NON-NEED-BASED) *Total amount:* $3,091,632 (36% federal, 1% state, 37% institutional, 26% external sources). *Receiving aid:* Freshmen: 18% (392); Undergraduates: 10% (1,080). *Average Award:* Freshmen: $1008; Undergraduates: $1732. *Scholarships, grants, and awards by category:* Academic Interests/Achievement: business, computer science, engineering/technologies, general academic interests/achievements, mathematics, physical sciences. Creative Arts/Performance: applied art and design, art/fine arts, creative writing, debating, music, theater/drama. *Special Achievements/Activities:* community service, leadership. *Special Characteristics:* children of union members/company employees, local/state students, out-of-state students. *Tuition waivers:* Full or partial for employees or children of employees, senior citizens. *ROTC:* Army.

LOANS *Student loans:* $47,487,934 (54% need-based, 46% non-need-based). 75% of past graduating class borrowed through all loan programs. *Average indebtedness per student:* $16,500. *Average need-based loan:* Freshmen: $3031; Undergraduates: $3918. *Parent loans:* $2,082,072 (100% non-need-based). *Programs:* FFEL (Subsidized and Unsubsidized Stafford, PLUS), Perkins, state, SELF Loans.

WORK-STUDY *Federal work-study:* Total amount: $1,131,837; 367 jobs averaging $3084. *State or other work-study/employment:* Total amount: $1,030,487 (100% need-based). 337 part-time jobs averaging $3057.

ATHLETIC AWARDS *Total amount:* $659,536 (100% non-need-based).

APPLYING FOR FINANCIAL AID *Required financial aid form:* FAFSA. *Financial aid deadline (priority):* 3/15. *Notification date:* Continuous beginning 3/30. Students must reply within 2 weeks of notification.

CONTACT Office of Student Financial Services, Minnesota State University Mankato, 120 Wigley Administration Center, Mankato, MN 56001, 507-389-1866 or toll-free 800-722-0544.

MINNESOTA STATE UNIVERSITY MOORHEAD
Moorhead, MN

Tuition & fees (MN res): $4894	Average undergraduate aid package: $4340

ABOUT THE INSTITUTION State-supported, coed. Awards: associate, bachelor's, and master's degrees and post-master's certificates. 85 undergraduate majors. Total enrollment: 7,642. Undergraduates: 7,211. Freshmen: 1,249. Federal methodology is used as a basis for awarding need-based institutional aid.

UNDERGRADUATE EXPENSES for 2004–05 *Application fee:* $20. *Tuition, state resident:* full-time $4172; part-time $139.06 per credit hour. *Tuition, nonresident:* full-time $4172; part-time $139.06 per credit hour. *Required fees:* full-time $722; $82.68 per credit hour. Full-time tuition and fees vary according to reciprocity agreements. Part-time tuition and fees vary according to reciprocity agreements. *College room and board:* $4530; *room only:* $2714. Room and board charges vary according to board plan and housing facility. *Payment plan:* Installment.

FRESHMAN FINANCIAL AID (Fall 2004, est.) 1059 applied for aid; of those 59% were deemed to have need. 100% of freshmen with need received aid. *Average financial aid package:* $3748 (excluding resources awarded to replace EFC). 12% of all full-time freshmen had no need and received non-need-based gift aid.

UNDERGRADUATE FINANCIAL AID (Fall 2004, est.) 5,834 applied for aid; of those 66% were deemed to have need. 100% of undergraduates with need received aid. *Average financial aid package:* $4340 (excluding resources awarded to replace EFC). 7% of all full-time undergraduates had no need and received non-need-based gift aid.

GIFT AID (NEED-BASED) *Total amount:* $8,139,491 (67% federal, 30% state, 1% institutional, 2% external sources). *Receiving aid:* Freshmen: 29% (352); All full-time undergraduates: 34% (2,125). *Average award:* Freshmen: $3479; Undergraduates: $3258. *Scholarships, grants, and awards:* Federal Pell, FSEOG, state, private, college/university gift aid from institutional funds.

GIFT AID (NON-NEED-BASED) *Total amount:* $1,594,979 (42% federal, 1% state, 20% institutional, 37% external sources). *Receiving aid:* Freshmen: 46% (557); Undergraduates: 20% (1,255). *Average Award:* Freshmen: $786; Undergraduates: $705. *Scholarships, grants, and awards by category:* Academic Interests/Achievement: 411 awards ($278,930 total): general academic interests/achievements. Creative Arts/Performance: 104 awards ($39,890 total): art/fine arts, creative writing, music, theater/drama. *Special Achievements/Activities:* community service, general special achievements/activities. *Special Characteristics:* 78 awards ($153,178 total): children of faculty/staff, members of minority groups. *Tuition waivers:* Full or partial for employees or children of employees, senior citizens. *ROTC:* Army cooperative, Air Force cooperative.

LOANS *Student loans:* $31,760,211 (43% need-based, 57% non-need-based). 65% of past graduating class borrowed through all loan programs. *Average indebtedness per student:* $19,209. *Average need-based loan:* Freshmen: $2664; Undergraduates: $3544. *Parent loans:* $650,208 (100% non-need-based). *Programs:* Federal Direct (Subsidized and Unsubsidized Stafford, PLUS), Perkins, state, alternative loans.

WORK-STUDY *Federal work-study:* Total amount: $441,601; 232 jobs averaging $1903. *State or other work-study/employment:* Total amount: $2,949,389 (16% need-based, 84% non-need-based). 1,047 part-time jobs averaging $2817.

ATHLETIC AWARDS *Total amount:* $146,565 (100% non-need-based).

APPLYING FOR FINANCIAL AID *Required financial aid form:* FAFSA. *Financial aid deadline (priority):* 2/15. *Notification date:* Continuous beginning 6/1. Students must reply within 2 weeks of notification.

CONTACT Ms. Carolyn Zehren, Director of Financial Aid, Minnesota State University Moorhead, 1104 7th Avenue South, Moorhead, MN 56563-0002, 218-477-2251 or toll-free 800-593-7246. *Fax:* 218-477-2058. *E-mail:* zehren@mnstate.edu.

MINOT STATE UNIVERSITY
Minot, ND

Tuition & fees (ND res): $3712	Average undergraduate aid package: $6564

ABOUT THE INSTITUTION State-supported, coed. Awards: associate, bachelor's, and master's degrees and post-master's certificates. 58 undergraduate majors. Total enrollment: 3,851. Undergraduates: 3,576. Freshmen: 572. Federal methodology is used as a basis for awarding need-based institutional aid.

UNDERGRADUATE EXPENSES for 2004–05 *Application fee:* $35. *Tuition, state resident:* full-time $3160; part-time $131.67 per semester hour. *Tuition, nonresident:* full-time $7885; part-time $351.55 per semester hour. *Required fees:* full-time $552; $23 per semester hour. Full-time tuition and fees vary according to course load and location. Part-time tuition and fees vary according to location. *College room and board:* $3592; *room only:* $1440. Room and board charges vary according to board plan and housing facility. *Payment plan:* Installment.

GIFT AID (NEED-BASED) *Total amount:* $3,958,027 (80% federal, 4% state, 3% institutional, 13% external sources). *Receiving aid:* Freshmen: 49% (261); All full-time undergraduates: 46% (1,770). *Average award:* Freshmen: $1496; Undergraduates: $1935. *Scholarships, grants, and awards:* Federal Pell, FSEOG, state, private, college/university gift aid from institutional funds, Federal Nursing.

GIFT AID (NON-NEED-BASED) *Total amount:* $2,626,801 (3% federal, 1% state, 11% institutional, 85% external sources). *Receiving aid:* Freshmen: 16% (84); Undergraduates: 7% (267). *Scholarships, grants, and awards by category:* Academic Interests/Achievement: 1,155 awards ($735,555 total): business, communication, computer science, education, English, general academic interests/achievements, health fields, humanities, mathematics, social sciences. Creative Arts/Performance: $122,181 total: music, theater/drama. *Special Characteristics:* 154 awards ($301,083 total): ethnic background, international students, local/state students, members of minority groups, out-of-state students, veterans, veterans' children. *Tuition waivers:* Full or partial for employees or children of employees.

LOANS *Student loans:* $8,966,170 (66% need-based, 34% non-need-based). 97% of past graduating class borrowed through all loan programs. *Average indebtedness per student:* $15,575. *Average need-based loan:* Freshmen: $1474; Undergraduates: $1421. *Parent loans:* $844,791 (100% non-need-based). *Programs:* FFEL (Subsidized and Unsubsidized Stafford, PLUS), Perkins, Federal Nursing, college/university.

ATHLETIC AWARDS *Total amount:* $145,292 (100% non-need-based).

APPLYING FOR FINANCIAL AID *Required financial aid form:* FAFSA. *Financial aid deadline (priority):* 3/15. *Notification date:* Continuous beginning 4/1. Students must reply within 2 weeks of notification.

CONTACT Mr. Dale Gehring, Director of Financial Aid, Minot State University, 500 University Avenue, West, Minot, ND 58707-0002, 701-858-3862 or toll-free 800-777-0750 Ext. 3350. *Fax:* 701-858-4310. *E-mail:* dale.gehring@minotstateu.edu.

MIRRER YESHIVA
Brooklyn, NY

CONTACT Financial Aid Office, Mirrer Yeshiva, 1795 Ocean Parkway, Brooklyn, NY 11223-2010, 718-645-0536.

MISSISSIPPI COLLEGE
Clinton, MS

Tuition & fees: $12,058	Average undergraduate aid package: $13,680

ABOUT THE INSTITUTION Independent Southern Baptist, coed. Awards: bachelor's, master's, and first professional degrees and post-bachelor's certificates. 60 undergraduate majors. Total enrollment: 3,588. Undergraduates: 2,422. Freshmen: 394. Federal methodology is used as a basis for awarding need-based institutional aid.

UNDERGRADUATE EXPENSES for 2005–06 *Application fee:* $25. *Comprehensive fee:* $17,752 includes full-time tuition ($11,400), mandatory fees ($658), and room and board ($5694). *College room only:* $2944. Full-time tuition and fees vary according to course load. Room and board charges vary according to board plan and housing facility. *Part-time tuition:* $355 per credit hour. *Part-time fees:* $133 per term. Part-time tuition and fees vary according to course load. *Payment plans:* Installment, deferred payment.

FRESHMAN FINANCIAL AID (Fall 2003) 373 applied for aid; of those 53% were deemed to have need. 100% of freshmen with need received aid; of those 42% had need fully met. *Average percent of need met:* 84% (excluding resources awarded to replace EFC). *Average financial aid package:* $13,187 (excluding resources awarded to replace EFC). 47% of all full-time freshmen had no need and received non-need-based gift aid.

UNDERGRADUATE FINANCIAL AID (Fall 2003) 1,861 applied for aid; of those 59% were deemed to have need. 99% of undergraduates with need received aid; of those 39% had need fully met. *Average percent of need met:* 82% (excluding resources awarded to replace EFC). *Average financial aid package:* $13,680 (excluding resources awarded to replace EFC). 40% of all full-time undergraduates had no need and received non-need-based gift aid.

GIFT AID (NEED-BASED) *Total amount:* $8,823,261 (29% federal, 8% state, 61% institutional, 2% external sources). *Receiving aid:* Freshmen: 34% (129); All full-time undergraduates: 44% (831). *Average award:* Freshmen: $10,421; Undergraduates: $8413. *Scholarships, grants, and awards:* Federal Pell, FSEOG, state, private, college/university gift aid from institutional funds.

GIFT AID (NON-NEED-BASED) *Total amount:* $9,782,029 (10% state, 86% institutional, 4% external sources). *Receiving aid:* Freshmen: 18% (69); Undergraduates: 12% (230). *Average Award:* Freshmen: $10,216; Undergraduates: $9801. *Scholarships, grants, and awards by category:* Academic Interests/Achievement: $5,846,861 total: general academic interests/achievements. Creative Arts/Performance: $210,054 total: applied art and design, art/fine arts, music. Special Achievements/Activities: $2,813,157 total: general special achievements/activities, leadership, religious involvement. Special Characteristics: $2,382,281 total: children and siblings of alumni, children of faculty/staff, general special characteristics, relatives of clergy. *Tuition waivers:* Full or partial for employees or children of employees. *ROTC:* Army cooperative.

LOANS *Student loans:* $9,036,606 (81% need-based, 19% non-need-based). 50% of past graduating class borrowed through all loan programs. *Average indebtedness per student:* $18,182. *Average need-based loan:* Freshmen: $3912; Undergraduates: $6116. *Parent loans:* $754,958 (100% non-need-based). *Programs:* FFEL (Subsidized and Unsubsidized Stafford, PLUS), Perkins, Federal Nursing, college/university.

WORK-STUDY *Federal work-study:* Total amount: $223,289; 219 jobs averaging $1019.

APPLYING FOR FINANCIAL AID *Required financial aid form:* FAFSA. *Financial aid deadline (priority):* 3/1. *Notification date:* Continuous beginning 4/15.

CONTACT Mary Givhan, Director of Financial Aid, Mississippi College, PO Box 4035, Clinton, MS 39058, 601-925-3319 or toll-free 800-738-1236. *E-mail:* givhan@mc.edu.

MISSISSIPPI STATE UNIVERSITY
Mississippi State, MS

Tuition & fees (MS res): $4106   Average undergraduate aid package: $8565

ABOUT THE INSTITUTION State-supported, coed. Awards: bachelor's, master's, doctoral, and first professional degrees and post-master's certificates. 71 undergraduate majors. Total enrollment: 15,934. Undergraduates: 12,495. Freshmen: 1,753. Federal methodology is used as a basis for awarding need-based institutional aid.

UNDERGRADUATE EXPENSES for 2004–05 *Tuition, state resident:* full-time $4106; part-time $171.25 per hour. *Tuition, nonresident:* full-time $9306; part-time $388 per hour. Part-time tuition and fees vary according to course load. *College room and board:* $5994; *room only:* $2454. Room and board charges vary according to board plan and housing facility.

FRESHMAN FINANCIAL AID (Fall 2003) 1100 applied for aid; of those 85% were deemed to have need. 97% of freshmen with need received aid; of those 33% had need fully met. *Average percent of need met:* 62% (excluding resources

awarded to replace EFC). *Average financial aid package:* $6470 (excluding resources awarded to replace EFC). 15% of all full-time freshmen had no need and received non-need-based gift aid.

UNDERGRADUATE FINANCIAL AID (Fall 2003) 7,624 applied for aid; of those 85% were deemed to have need. 98% of undergraduates with need received aid; of those 45% had need fully met. *Average percent of need met:* 70% (excluding resources awarded to replace EFC). *Average financial aid package:* $8565 (excluding resources awarded to replace EFC). 12% of all full-time undergraduates had no need and received non-need-based gift aid.

GIFT AID (NEED-BASED) *Total amount:* $20,215,242 (59% federal, 10% state, 17% institutional, 14% external sources). *Receiving aid:* Freshmen: 48% (824); All full-time undergraduates: 45% (5,491). *Average award:* Freshmen: $3231; Undergraduates: $3358. *Scholarships, grants, and awards:* Federal Pell, FSEOG, state, private, college/university gift aid from institutional funds.

GIFT AID (NON-NEED-BASED) *Total amount:* $8,237,675 (32% state, 52% institutional, 16% external sources). *Receiving aid:* Freshmen: 7% (111); Undergraduates: 3% (366). *Average Award:* Freshmen: $2594; Undergraduates: $2358. *Scholarships, grants, and awards by category:* Academic Interests/Achievement: agriculture, architecture, area/ethnic studies, biological sciences, business, communication, computer science, education, engineering/technologies, English, foreign languages, general academic interests/achievements, health fields, home economics, humanities, international studies, library science, mathematics, military science, physical sciences, premedicine, religion/biblical studies, social sciences. Creative Arts/Performance: applied art and design, art/fine arts, cinema/film/broadcasting, creative writing, dance, debating, general creative arts/performance, journalism/publications, music, performing arts, theater/drama. Special Achievements/Activities: cheerleading/drum major, general special achievements/activities, leadership, memberships. Special Characteristics: adult students, children and siblings of alumni, children of educators, children of faculty/staff, children of public servants, first-generation college students, handicapped students, local/state students, out-of-state students, previous college experience, spouses of deceased or disabled public servants. *Tuition waivers:* Full or partial for children of alumni, employees or children of employees, senior citizens. *ROTC:* Army, Air Force.

LOANS *Student loans:* $32,675,838 (89% need-based, 11% non-need-based). 51% of past graduating class borrowed through all loan programs. *Average indebtedness per student:* $17,910. *Average need-based loan:* Freshmen: $2631; Undergraduates: $3827. *Parent loans:* $3,289,395 (28% need-based, 72% non-need-based). *Programs:* FFEL (Subsidized and Unsubsidized Stafford, PLUS), Perkins, state, college/university.

WORK-STUDY *Federal work-study:* Total amount: $2,350,363; 879 jobs averaging $2674.

ATHLETIC AWARDS Total amount: $2,580,808 (100% non-need-based).

APPLYING FOR FINANCIAL AID *Required financial aid forms:* FAFSA, state grant/scholarship application. *Financial aid deadline (priority):* 2/1. *Notification date:* Continuous beginning 2/15. Students must reply within 3 weeks of notification.

CONTACT Mr. Bruce Crain, Director of Financial Aid, Mississippi State University, PO Box 6035, Mississippi State, MS 39762, 662-325-2450. *Fax:* 662-325-0702. *E-mail:* bruce@saffairs.msstate.edu.

MISSISSIPPI UNIVERSITY FOR WOMEN
Columbus, MS

Tuition & fees (MS res): $3495   Average undergraduate aid package: $8925

ABOUT THE INSTITUTION State-supported, coed, primarily women. Awards: associate, bachelor's, and master's degrees. 39 undergraduate majors. Total enrollment: 2,328. Undergraduates: 2,166. Federal methodology is used as a basis for awarding need-based institutional aid.

UNDERGRADUATE EXPENSES for 2004–05 *Tuition, state resident:* full-time $3495; part-time $145.67 per semester hour. *Tuition, nonresident:* full-time $8442; part-time $351.79 per semester hour. *College room and board:* $3778. Room and board charges vary according to housing facility.

FRESHMAN FINANCIAL AID (Fall 2003) 402 applied for aid; of those 96% were deemed to have need. 100% of freshmen with need received aid; of those 52% had need fully met. *Average percent of need met:* 78% (excluding resources awarded to replace EFC). *Average financial aid package:* $7512 (excluding resources awarded to replace EFC). 22% of all full-time freshmen had no need and received non-need-based gift aid.

UNDERGRADUATE FINANCIAL AID (Fall 2003) 1,569 applied for aid; of those 70% were deemed to have need. 100% of undergraduates with need received aid; of those 66% had need fully met. *Average percent of need met:* 78%

(excluding resources awarded to replace EFC). *Average financial aid package:* $8925 (excluding resources awarded to replace EFC). 14% of all full-time undergraduates had no need and received non-need-based gift aid.
GIFT AID (NEED-BASED) *Total amount:* $3,062,280 (99% federal, 1% state). *Receiving aid:* Freshmen: 21% (124); All full-time undergraduates: 49% (1,098). *Average award:* Freshmen: $2125; Undergraduates: $2475. *Scholarships, grants, and awards:* Federal Pell, FSEOG, state, private, college/university gift aid from institutional funds, United Negro College Fund.
GIFT AID (NON-NEED-BASED) *Total amount:* $4,295,070 (18% state, 75% institutional, 7% external sources). *Receiving aid:* Freshmen: 38% (221); Undergraduates: 33% (745). *Average Award:* Freshmen: $1575; Undergraduates: $2350. *Scholarships, grants, and awards by category: Academic Interests/ Achievement:* 285 awards ($974,290 total): biological sciences, business, communication, computer science, education, English, general academic interests/ achievements, health fields, home economics, humanities, mathematics, physical sciences. *Creative Arts/Performance:* 95 awards ($215,742 total): art/fine arts, dance, journalism/publications, music, performing arts, theater/drama. *Special Achievements/Activities:* 12 awards ($17,190 total): junior miss, leadership. *Special Characteristics:* 57 awards ($64,290 total): adult students, children and siblings of alumni, children of faculty/staff, ethnic background, international students, members of minority groups, out-of-state students, parents of current students. *ROTC:* Army cooperative, Air Force cooperative.
LOANS *Student loans:* $6,184,181 (57% need-based, 43% non-need-based). 78% of past graduating class borrowed through all loan programs. *Average indebtedness per student:* $20,704. *Average need-based loan:* Freshmen: $2174; Undergraduates: $3700. *Parent loans:* $72,256 (100% non-need-based). *Programs:* FFEL (Subsidized and Unsubsidized Stafford, PLUS), Perkins.
WORK-STUDY *Federal work-study:* Total amount: $186,163; 120 jobs averaging $3000. *State or other work-study/employment:* Total amount: $276,123 (100% non-need-based). 210 part-time jobs averaging $3000.
ATHLETIC AWARDS *Total amount:* $52,204 (100% non-need-based).
APPLYING FOR FINANCIAL AID *Required financial aid forms:* FAFSA, state aid form, scholarship application form(s). *Financial aid deadline (priority):* 3/15. *Notification date:* Continuous beginning 4/1.
CONTACT Don Rainer, Director of Financial Aid, Mississippi University for Women, 1100 College Street, MUW 1614, Columbus, MS 39701-4044, 662-329-7114 or toll-free 877-GO 2 THE W. *Fax:* 662-329-7325. *E-mail:* finaid@ muw.edu.

MISSISSIPPI VALLEY STATE UNIVERSITY
Itta Bena, MS

CONTACT Mr. Darrell G. Boyd, Director of Student Financial Aid, Mississippi Valley State University, 14000 Highway 82W #7268, Itta Bena, MS 38941-1400, 662-254-3765 or toll-free 800-844-6885 (in-state). *Fax:* 662-254-3759. *E-mail:* dboyd@mvsu.edu.

MISSOURI BAPTIST UNIVERSITY
St. Louis, MO

Tuition & fees: $13,030   **Average undergraduate aid package: $7947**

ABOUT THE INSTITUTION Independent Southern Baptist, coed. Awards: associate, bachelor's, and master's degrees and post-bachelor's certificates. 33 undergraduate majors. Total enrollment: 4,058. Undergraduates: 3,336. Freshmen: 230. Both federal and institutional methodology are used as a basis for awarding need-based institutional aid.
UNDERGRADUATE EXPENSES for 2004–05 *Application fee:* $25. *Comprehensive fee:* $18,830 includes full-time tuition ($12,480), mandatory fees ($550), and room and board ($5800). Full-time tuition and fees vary according to course load, degree level, and location. Room and board charges vary according to housing facility. *Part-time tuition:* $435 per credit. Part-time tuition and fees vary according to course load, degree level, and location. *Payment plan:* Installment.
UNDERGRADUATE FINANCIAL AID (Fall 2003) 1,158 applied for aid; of those 100% were deemed to have need. 100% of undergraduates with need received aid. *Average percent of need met:* 28% (excluding resources awarded to replace EFC). *Average financial aid package:* $7947 (excluding resources awarded to replace EFC). 7% of all full-time undergraduates had no need and received non-need-based gift aid.
GIFT AID (NEED-BASED) *Total amount:* $1,791,360 (54% federal, 13% state, 33% institutional). *Receiving aid:* All full-time undergraduates: 66% (821).

Average award: Undergraduates: $4957. *Scholarships, grants, and awards:* Federal Pell, FSEOG, state, private, college/university gift aid from institutional funds.
GIFT AID (NON-NEED-BASED) *Total amount:* $1,594,769 (3% state, 77% institutional, 20% external sources). *Receiving aid:* Undergraduates: 21% (257). *Average Award:* Undergraduates: $2990. *Scholarships, grants, and awards by category: Academic Interests/Achievement:* 379 awards ($1,332,577 total): general academic interests/achievements, religion/biblical studies. *Creative Arts/ Performance:* 94 awards ($138,521 total): music, theater/drama. *Special Achievements/Activities:* 270 awards ($268,857 total): cheerleading/drum major, religious involvement. *Special Characteristics:* 146 awards ($546,129 total): children and siblings of alumni, children of current students, children of faculty/ staff, parents of current students, public servants, relatives of clergy, religious affiliation, siblings of current students. *Tuition waivers:* Full or partial for children of alumni, employees or children of employees, senior citizens. *ROTC:* Army cooperative.
LOANS *Student loans:* $3,972,126 (62% need-based, 38% non-need-based). 65% of past graduating class borrowed through all loan programs. *Average indebtedness per student:* $18,728. *Average need-based loan:* Undergraduates: $3732. *Parent loans:* $440,606 (100% need-based). *Programs:* FFEL (Subsidized and Unsubsidized Stafford, PLUS).
WORK-STUDY *Federal work-study:* Total amount: $60,593; 61 jobs averaging $993. *State or other work-study/employment:* Total amount: $403 (100% need-based). 1 part-time job averaging $403.
ATHLETIC AWARDS *Total amount:* $2,347,575 (100% non-need-based).
APPLYING FOR FINANCIAL AID *Required financial aid forms:* FAFSA, institution's own form. *Financial aid deadline (priority):* 4/1. *Notification date:* Continuous beginning 4/15. Students must reply within 2 weeks of notification.
CONTACT Bob Miller, Director of Financial Services, Missouri Baptist University, One College Park Drive, St. Louis, MO 63141, 314-392-2366 or toll-free 877-434-1115 Ext. 2290. *Fax:* 314-434-7596. *E-mail:* millerb@mobap.edu.

MISSOURI SOUTHERN STATE UNIVERSITY
Joplin, MO

Tuition & fees (MO res): $3976   **Average undergraduate aid package: $6722**

ABOUT THE INSTITUTION State-supported, coed. Awards: associate, bachelor's, and master's degrees. 56 undergraduate majors. Total enrollment: 5,256. Undergraduates: 5,256. Freshmen: 777. Federal methodology is used as a basis for awarding need-based institutional aid.
UNDERGRADUATE EXPENSES for 2004–05 *Application fee:* $15. *Tuition, state resident:* full-time $3810; part-time $127 per credit. *Tuition, nonresident:* full-time $7620; part-time $254 per credit. *Required fees:* full-time $166; $83 per term part-time. Full-time tuition and fees vary according to course load. *College room and board:* $4770. Room and board charges vary according to board plan and housing facility. *Payment plans:* Installment, deferred payment.
FRESHMAN FINANCIAL AID (Fall 2003) 626 applied for aid. *Average percent of need met:* 70% (excluding resources awarded to replace EFC). *Average financial aid package:* $5591 (excluding resources awarded to replace EFC). 26% of all full-time freshmen had no need and received non-need-based gift aid.
UNDERGRADUATE FINANCIAL AID (Fall 2003) 3,209 applied for aid; of those 87% were deemed to have need. 100% of undergraduates with need received aid. *Average percent of need met:* 69% (excluding resources awarded to replace EFC). *Average financial aid package:* $6722 (excluding resources awarded to replace EFC). 17% of all full-time undergraduates had no need and received non-need-based gift aid.
GIFT AID (NEED-BASED) *Total amount:* $6,135,195 (95% federal, 5% state). *Receiving aid:* Freshmen: 83% (573); All full-time undergraduates: 66% (2,331). *Average award:* Freshmen: $3699; Undergraduates: $4636. *Scholarships, grants, and awards:* Federal Pell, FSEOG, state, private, college/university gift aid from institutional funds.
GIFT AID (NON-NEED-BASED) *Total amount:* $2,164,797 (12% state, 59% institutional, 29% external sources). *Receiving aid:* Freshmen: 8% (53); Undergraduates: 51% (1,789). *Average Award:* Freshmen: $2209; Undergraduates: $2560. *Scholarships, grants, and awards by category: Academic Interests/ Achievement:* 585 awards ($1,467,110 total): general academic interests/ achievements. *Creative Arts/Performance:* 190 awards ($192,811 total): art/fine arts, debating, journalism/publications, music, theater/drama. *Special Achievements/ Activities:* 12 awards ($6000 total): general special achievements/activities, leadership. *Special Characteristics:* 155 awards ($224,897 total): children and siblings of alumni, children of faculty/staff, ethnic background, local/state students. *Tuition waivers:* Full or partial for employees or children of employees.

LOANS *Student loans:* $14,636,130 (53% need-based, 47% non-need-based). 59% of past graduating class borrowed through all loan programs. *Average indebtedness per student:* $16,137. *Average need-based loan:* Freshmen: $1847; Undergraduates: $3249. *Parent loans:* $196,411 (100% non-need-based). *Programs:* Federal Direct (Subsidized and Unsubsidized Stafford, PLUS), Perkins, state.

WORK-STUDY *Federal work-study:* Total amount: $283,247; 149 jobs averaging $1575. *State or other work-study/employment:* Total amount: $457,656 (100% non-need-based). 438 part-time jobs averaging $1401.

ATHLETIC AWARDS *Total amount:* $953,045 (100% non-need-based).

APPLYING FOR FINANCIAL AID *Required financial aid form:* FAFSA. *Financial aid deadline (priority):* 2/15. *Notification date:* Continuous. Students must reply within 3 weeks of notification.

CONTACT Mr. James E. Gilbert, Director of Financial Aid, Missouri Southern State University, 3950 East Newman Road, Joplin, MO 64801-1595, 417-625-9325 or toll-free 866-818-MSSU. *Fax:* 417-625-3121. *E-mail:* gilbert-j@mssu.edu.

MISSOURI STATE UNIVERSITY
Springfield, MO

Tuition & fees (MO res): $5128	Average undergraduate aid package: $5959

ABOUT THE INSTITUTION State-supported, coed. Awards: bachelor's, master's, and doctoral degrees and post-bachelor's certificates. 91 undergraduate majors. Total enrollment: 19,114. Undergraduates: 16,269. Freshmen: 2,709. Federal methodology is used as a basis for awarding need-based institutional aid.

UNDERGRADUATE EXPENSES for 2004–05 *Application fee:* $30. *Tuition, state resident:* full-time $4620; part-time $154 per credit hour. *Tuition, nonresident:* full-time $9240; part-time $308 per credit hour. Full-time tuition and fees vary according to course load and degree level. Part-time tuition and fees vary according to course load and degree level. *College room and board:* $4660; *room only:* $3249. Room and board charges vary according to board plan and housing facility. *Payment plan:* Deferred payment.

FRESHMAN FINANCIAL AID (Fall 2004, est.) 1945 applied for aid; of those 67% were deemed to have need. 99% of freshmen with need received aid; of those 22% had need fully met. *Average percent of need met:* 58% (excluding resources awarded to replace EFC). *Average financial aid package:* $5342 (excluding resources awarded to replace EFC). 38% of all full-time freshmen had no need and received non-need-based gift aid.

UNDERGRADUATE FINANCIAL AID (Fall 2004, est.) 9,156 applied for aid; of those 76% were deemed to have need. 98% of undergraduates with need received aid; of those 22% had need fully met. *Average percent of need met:* 62% (excluding resources awarded to replace EFC). *Average financial aid package:* $5959 (excluding resources awarded to replace EFC). 31% of all full-time undergraduates had no need and received non-need-based gift aid.

GIFT AID (NEED-BASED) *Total amount:* $19,485,566 (56% federal, 11% state, 26% institutional, 7% external sources). *Receiving aid:* Freshmen: 42% (970); All full-time undergraduates: 42% (4,726). *Average award:* Freshmen: $4452; Undergraduates: $4115. *Scholarships, grants, and awards:* Federal Pell, FSEOG, state, private, college/university gift aid from institutional funds.

GIFT AID (NON-NEED-BASED) *Total amount:* $10,196,921 (12% state, 74% institutional, 14% external sources). *Receiving aid:* Freshmen: 7% (154); Undergraduates: 4% (454). *Average Award:* Freshmen: $7866; Undergraduates: $6989. *Scholarships, grants, and awards by category: Academic Interests/Achievement:* 6,888 awards ($10,500,000 total): agriculture, biological sciences, business, communication, computer science, education, foreign languages, general academic interests/achievements, health fields, home economics, mathematics, military science, physical sciences, premedicine, religion/biblical studies, social sciences. *Creative Arts/Performance:* applied art and design, art/fine arts, dance, debating, general creative arts/performance, journalism/publications, music, performing arts, theater/drama. *Special Achievements/Activities:* cheerleading/drum major, general special achievements/activities, hobbies/interests, memberships, rodeo. *Special Characteristics:* adult students, children and siblings of alumni, children of faculty/staff, ethnic background, first-generation college students, general special characteristics, handicapped students, international students, members of minority groups, out-of-state students, spouses of deceased or disabled public servants, veterans. *Tuition waivers:* Full or partial for children of alumni, employees or children of employees, senior citizens. *ROTC:* Army.

LOANS *Student loans:* $43,797,787 (68% need-based, 32% non-need-based). 59% of past graduating class borrowed through all loan programs. *Average indebtedness per student:* $13,381. *Average need-based loan:* Freshmen: $2451;

Undergraduates: $3637. *Parent loans:* $16,020,721 (21% need-based, 79% non-need-based). *Programs:* FFEL (Subsidized and Unsubsidized Stafford, PLUS), Perkins, state, college/university.

WORK-STUDY *Federal work-study:* Total amount: $665,560; 449 jobs averaging $1748. *State or other work-study/employment:* Total amount: $3,802,104 (100% non-need-based). 1,336 part-time jobs averaging $2924.

ATHLETIC AWARDS *Total amount:* $3,234,238 (24% need-based, 76% non-need-based).

APPLYING FOR FINANCIAL AID *Required financial aid form:* FAFSA. *Financial aid deadline (priority):* 3/30. *Notification date:* 4/1.

CONTACT David G. King, Assistant Director of Financial Aid, Missouri State University, 901 South National Avenue, Springfield, MO 65804, 417-836-5262 or toll-free 800-492-7900.

MISSOURI TECH
St. Louis, MO

ABOUT THE INSTITUTION Proprietary, coed, primarily men. Awards: associate and bachelor's degrees. 7 undergraduate majors. Total enrollment: 201. Undergraduates: 201. Freshmen: 11.

GIFT AID (NEED-BASED) *Scholarships, grants, and awards:* Federal Pell, private, college/university gift aid from institutional funds.

GIFT AID (NON-NEED-BASED) *Scholarships, grants, and awards by category: Academic Interests/Achievement:* general academic interests/achievements.

LOANS *Programs:* FFEL (Subsidized and Unsubsidized Stafford, PLUS), college/university.

APPLYING FOR FINANCIAL AID *Required financial aid forms:* FAFSA, institution's own form.

CONTACT Director of Financial Aid, Missouri Tech, 1167 Corporate Lake Drive, St. Louis, MO 63132-1716, 314-569-3600. *Fax:* 314-569-1167. *E-mail:* contact@motech.edu.

MISSOURI VALLEY COLLEGE
Marshall, MO

Tuition & fees: $13,500	Average undergraduate aid package: $12,141

ABOUT THE INSTITUTION Independent religious, coed. Awards: associate and bachelor's degrees. 40 undergraduate majors. Total enrollment: 1,623. Undergraduates: 1,623. Freshmen: 405. Federal methodology is used as a basis for awarding need-based institutional aid.

UNDERGRADUATE EXPENSES for 2004–05 *Application fee:* $15. *Comprehensive fee:* $18,700 includes full-time tuition ($13,000), mandatory fees ($500), and room and board ($5200). *Part-time tuition:* $350 per credit hour. *Payment plan:* Installment.

FRESHMAN FINANCIAL AID (Fall 2004, est.) 372 applied for aid; of those 100% were deemed to have need. 100% of freshmen with need received aid. *Average percent of need met:* 80% (excluding resources awarded to replace EFC). *Average financial aid package:* $11,402 (excluding resources awarded to replace EFC).

UNDERGRADUATE FINANCIAL AID (Fall 2004, est.) 1,411 applied for aid; of those 100% were deemed to have need. 100% of undergraduates with need received aid. *Average percent of need met:* 80% (excluding resources awarded to replace EFC). *Average financial aid package:* $12,141 (excluding resources awarded to replace EFC).

GIFT AID (NEED-BASED) *Total amount:* $10,700,947 (19% federal, 6% state, 75% institutional). *Receiving aid:* Freshmen: 99% (372); All full-time undergraduates: 100% (1,411). *Average award:* Freshmen: $9750; Undergraduates: $9999. *Scholarships, grants, and awards:* Federal Pell, FSEOG, state, private, college/university gift aid from institutional funds.

GIFT AID (NON-NEED-BASED) *Total amount:* $7380 (100% external sources). *Receiving aid:* Freshmen: 99% (372); Undergraduates: 100% (1,411). *Scholarships, grants, and awards by category: Academic Interests/Achievement:* 213 awards ($275,140 total): biological sciences, business, communication, computer science, education, English, humanities, mathematics, military science, physical sciences, premedicine, social sciences. *Creative Arts/Performance:* 46 awards ($118,880 total): dance, journalism/publications, music, performing arts, theater/drama. *Special Achievements/Activities:* 33 awards ($45,590 total): cheerleading/drum major, community service, general special achievements/activities, hobbies/interests, junior miss, leadership, rodeo. *Special Characteristics:* 39 awards

($153,880 total): children and siblings of alumni, children of faculty/staff. *Tuition waivers:* Full or partial for children of alumni, employees or children of employees, senior citizens. *ROTC:* Army cooperative.
LOANS *Student loans:* $5,210,946 (60% need-based, 40% non-need-based). 80% of past graduating class borrowed through all loan programs. *Average indebtedness per student:* $13,400. *Average need-based loan:* Freshmen: $1703; Undergraduates: $2455. *Parent loans:* $475,974 (100% non-need-based). *Programs:* FFEL (Subsidized and Unsubsidized Stafford, PLUS), Perkins.
WORK-STUDY *Federal work-study:* Total amount: $221,349; 146 jobs averaging $1860. *State or other work-study/employment:* Total amount: $810,840 (100% need-based). 530 part-time jobs averaging $1860.
ATHLETIC AWARDS *Total amount:* $4,007,224 (100% need-based).
APPLYING FOR FINANCIAL AID *Required financial aid form:* FAFSA. *Financial aid deadline:* 9/15 (priority: 3/20). *Notification date:* Continuous beginning 10/1. Students must reply within 4 weeks of notification.
CONTACT Jennifer Malotte, Director of Financial Aid, Missouri Valley College, 500 East College, Marshall, MO 65340-3197, 660-831-4176. *Fax:* 660-831-4003. *E-mail:* malottej@moval.edu.

MISSOURI WESTERN STATE COLLEGE
St. Joseph, MO

ABOUT THE INSTITUTION State-supported, coed. Awards: associate and bachelor's degrees. 40 undergraduate majors. Total enrollment: 5,065. Undergraduates: 5,065. Freshmen: 1,079.
GIFT AID (NEED-BASED) *Scholarships, grants, and awards:* Federal Pell, FSEOG, state, private, college/university gift aid from institutional funds.
GIFT AID (NON-NEED-BASED) *Scholarships, grants, and awards by category: Academic Interests/Achievement:* biological sciences, business, communication, computer science, education, engineering/technologies, English, general academic interests/achievements, health fields, humanities, mathematics, military science, physical sciences, social sciences. *Creative Arts/Performance:* art/fine arts, dance, music. *Special Achievements/Activities:* cheerleading/drum major, community service, general special achievements/activities, leadership. *Special Characteristics:* children of faculty/staff, members of minority groups, out-of-state students.
LOANS *Programs:* FFEL (Subsidized and Unsubsidized Stafford, PLUS), Perkins.
WORK-STUDY Federal work-study jobs available. *State or other work-study/employment:* Part-time jobs available.
APPLYING FOR FINANCIAL AID *Required financial aid forms:* FAFSA, institution's own form.
CONTACT Angela Beam, Director of Financial Aid, Missouri Western State College, 4525 Downs Drive, St. Joseph, MO 64507-2294, 816-271-4361 or toll-free 800-662-7041 Ext. 60. *Fax:* 816-271-5833.

MITCHELL COLLEGE
New London, CT

Tuition & fees: $20,705	Average undergraduate aid package: $16,357

ABOUT THE INSTITUTION Independent, coed. Awards: associate and bachelor's degrees. 20 undergraduate majors. Total enrollment: 555. Undergraduates: 555. Freshmen: 191. Federal methodology is used as a basis for awarding need-based institutional aid.
UNDERGRADUATE EXPENSES for 2005–06 *Application fee:* $30. *Comprehensive fee:* $30,035 includes full-time tuition ($19,405), mandatory fees ($1300), and room and board ($9330). *College room only:* $4850. *Part-time tuition:* $275 per credit hour. *Part-time fees:* $35 per term. *Payment plan:* Installment.
FRESHMAN FINANCIAL AID (Fall 2004, est.) 211 applied for aid; of those 100% were deemed to have need. 100% of freshmen with need received aid. *Average percent of need met:* 79% (excluding resources awarded to replace EFC). *Average financial aid package:* $13,783 (excluding resources awarded to replace EFC). 12% of all full-time freshmen had no need and received non-need-based gift aid.
UNDERGRADUATE FINANCIAL AID (Fall 2004, est.) 491 applied for aid; of those 84% were deemed to have need. *Average percent of need met:* 89% (excluding resources awarded to replace EFC). *Average financial aid package:* $16,357 (excluding resources awarded to replace EFC). 11% of all full-time undergraduates had no need and received non-need-based gift aid.
GIFT AID (NEED-BASED) *Receiving aid:* Freshmen: 93% (211). *Average award:* Freshmen: $7453; Undergraduates: $8058. *Scholarships, grants, and awards:* Federal Pell, FSEOG, state, college/university gift aid from institutional funds.

GIFT AID (NON-NEED-BASED) *Receiving aid:* Freshmen: 87% (196); Undergraduates: 60% (368). *Average Award:* Freshmen: $2676; Undergraduates: $2890. *Tuition waivers:* Full or partial for children of alumni, employees or children of employees.
LOANS *Student loans:* $2,519,747 (100% need-based). *Average need-based loan:* Freshmen: $2625; Undergraduates: $2904. *Parent loans:* $1,206,724 (100% need-based). *Programs:* FFEL (Subsidized and Unsubsidized Stafford, PLUS), Perkins, alternative loans.
WORK-STUDY *Federal work-study:* Total amount: $42,230; 44 jobs averaging $1000. *State or other work-study/employment:* Total amount: $2,561,977 (100% need-based).
ATHLETIC AWARDS *Total amount:* $237,000 (100% non-need-based).
APPLYING FOR FINANCIAL AID *Required financial aid form:* FAFSA. *Financial aid deadline (priority):* 4/1. *Notification date:* Continuous. Students must reply within 3 weeks of notification.
CONTACT Jacklyn Stoltz, Director of Financial Aid, Mitchell College, 437 Pequot Avenue, New London, CT 06320-4498, 800-443-2811. *Fax:* 860-444-1209. *E-mail:* stoltz_j@mitchell.edu.

MOLLOY COLLEGE
Rockville Centre, NY

Tuition & fees: $15,850	Average undergraduate aid package: $9362

ABOUT THE INSTITUTION Independent, coed. Awards: associate, bachelor's, and master's degrees and post-master's certificates. 44 undergraduate majors. Total enrollment: 3,352. Undergraduates: 2,512. Freshmen: 326. Federal methodology is used as a basis for awarding need-based institutional aid.
UNDERGRADUATE EXPENSES for 2004–05 *Application fee:* $30. *Tuition:* full-time $15,150; part-time $505 per credit. *Payment plan:* Installment.
FRESHMAN FINANCIAL AID (Fall 2003) 258 applied for aid; of those 85% were deemed to have need. 100% of freshmen with need received aid; of those 20% had need fully met. *Average percent of need met:* 59% (excluding resources awarded to replace EFC). *Average financial aid package:* $9221 (excluding resources awarded to replace EFC). 32% of all full-time freshmen had no need and received non-need-based gift aid.
UNDERGRADUATE FINANCIAL AID (Fall 2003) 1,435 applied for aid; of those 87% were deemed to have need. 100% of undergraduates with need received aid; of those 16% had need fully met. *Average percent of need met:* 56% (excluding resources awarded to replace EFC). *Average financial aid package:* $9362 (excluding resources awarded to replace EFC). 17% of all full-time undergraduates had no need and received non-need-based gift aid.
GIFT AID (NEED-BASED) *Total amount:* $6,875,104 (33% federal, 34% state, 31% institutional, 2% external sources). *Receiving aid:* Freshmen: 58% (204); All full-time undergraduates: 70% (1,070). *Average award:* Freshmen: $6724; Undergraduates: $5551. *Scholarships, grants, and awards:* Federal Pell, FSEOG, state, private, college/university gift aid from institutional funds.
GIFT AID (NON-NEED-BASED) *Total amount:* $712,400 (9% state, 75% institutional, 16% external sources). *Receiving aid:* Freshmen: 5% (19); Undergraduates: 4% (65). *Average Award:* Freshmen: $6297; Undergraduates: $9207. *Scholarships, grants, and awards by category: Academic Interests/Achievement:* general academic interests/achievements. *Creative Arts/Performance:* 27 awards ($71,524 total): art/fine arts, music, performing arts. *Special Characteristics:* 23 awards ($5250 total): siblings of current students. *Tuition waivers:* Full or partial for employees or children of employees. *ROTC:* Army cooperative, Naval cooperative, Air Force cooperative.
LOANS *Student loans:* $13,829,833 (79% need-based, 21% non-need-based). *Average need-based loan:* Freshmen: $3162; Undergraduates: $4735. *Parent loans:* $3,659,378 (47% need-based, 53% non-need-based). *Programs:* FFEL (Subsidized and Unsubsidized Stafford, PLUS), Perkins.
WORK-STUDY *Federal work-study:* Total amount: $369,480; 236 jobs averaging $1566.
ATHLETIC AWARDS *Total amount:* $842,024 (100% non-need-based).
APPLYING FOR FINANCIAL AID *Required financial aid forms:* FAFSA, state aid form. *Financial aid deadline (priority):* 5/1.
CONTACT Ana C. Lockward, Director of Financial Aid, Molloy College, 1000 Hempstead Avenue, PO Box 5002, Rockville Centre, NY 11571, 516-678-5000 Ext. 6221 or toll-free 888-4MOLLOY. *Fax:* 516-256-2292. *E-mail:* alockward@molloy.edu.

MONMOUTH COLLEGE
Monmouth, IL

ABOUT THE INSTITUTION Independent religious, coed. Awards: bachelor's degrees. 38 undergraduate majors. Total enrollment: 1,253. Undergraduates: 1,253. Freshmen: 389.

GIFT AID (NEED-BASED) *Scholarships, grants, and awards:* Federal Pell, FSEOG, state, private, college/university gift aid from institutional funds.

GIFT AID (NON-NEED-BASED) *Scholarships, grants, and awards by category: Academic Interests/Achievement:* general academic interests/achievements. *Creative Arts/Performance:* art/fine arts, music, theater/drama. *Special Achievements/Activities:* general special achievements/activities.

LOANS *Programs:* FFEL (Subsidized and Unsubsidized Stafford, PLUS), Perkins.

WORK-STUDY *Federal work-study:* Total amount: $195,538; jobs available. *State or other work-study/employment:* Total amount: $177,824 (100% non-need-based). Part-time jobs available.

APPLYING FOR FINANCIAL AID *Required financial aid form:* FAFSA.

CONTACT Ms. Jayne Whiteside, Director of Financial Aid, Monmouth College, 700 East Broadway, Monmouth, IL 61462-1998, 309-457-2129 or toll-free 800-747-2687. *Fax:* 309-457-2152. *E-mail:* jayne@monm.edu.

MONMOUTH UNIVERSITY
West Long Branch, NJ

Tuition & fees: $19,704	Average undergraduate aid package: $17,835

ABOUT THE INSTITUTION Independent, coed. Awards: associate, bachelor's, and master's degrees and post-master's certificates. 33 undergraduate majors. Total enrollment: 6,329. Undergraduates: 4,501. Freshmen: 951. Federal methodology is used as a basis for awarding need-based institutional aid.

UNDERGRADUATE EXPENSES for 2004–05 *Application fee:* $35. *Comprehensive fee:* $27,615 includes full-time tuition ($19,108), mandatory fees ($596), and room and board ($7911). *College room only:* $4229. Room and board charges vary according to board plan and housing facility. *Part-time tuition:* $553 per credit hour. *Part-time fees:* $149 per term. *Payment plan:* Installment.

FRESHMAN FINANCIAL AID (Fall 2004, est.) 801 applied for aid; of those 77% were deemed to have need. 100% of freshmen with need received aid; of those 16% had need fully met. *Average percent of need met:* 77% (excluding resources awarded to replace EFC). *Average financial aid package:* $11,462 (excluding resources awarded to replace EFC). 27% of all full-time freshmen had no need and received non-need-based gift aid.

UNDERGRADUATE FINANCIAL AID (Fall 2004, est.) 3,188 applied for aid; of those 83% were deemed to have need. 100% of undergraduates with need received aid; of those 7% had need fully met. *Average percent of need met:* 74% (excluding resources awarded to replace EFC). *Average financial aid package:* $17,835 (excluding resources awarded to replace EFC). 27% of all full-time undergraduates had no need and received non-need-based gift aid.

GIFT AID (NEED-BASED) *Total amount:* $9,559,495 (32% federal, 63% state, 5% institutional). *Receiving aid:* Freshmen: 27% (260); All full-time undergraduates: 28% (1,119). *Average award:* Freshmen: $9032; Undergraduates: $7951. *Scholarships, grants, and awards:* Federal Pell, FSEOG, state, private, college/university gift aid from institutional funds.

GIFT AID (NON-NEED-BASED) *Total amount:* $17,246,550 (97% institutional, 3% external sources). *Receiving aid:* Freshmen: 55% (524); Undergraduates: 55% (2,209). *Average Award:* Freshmen: $5240; Undergraduates: $4722. *Scholarships, grants, and awards by category: Academic Interests/Achievement:* 3,856 awards ($22,899,121 total): business, communication, computer science, education, general academic interests/achievements, health fields, humanities, mathematics. *Special Characteristics:* 270 awards ($612,929 total): adult students, children and siblings of alumni, children of faculty/staff, children of public servants, first-generation college students, general special characteristics, international students, local/state students, out-of-state students, veterans. *Tuition waivers:* Full or partial for employees or children of employees, senior citizens. *ROTC:* Air Force cooperative.

LOANS *Student loans:* $28,918,929 (36% need-based, 64% non-need-based). 66% of past graduating class borrowed through all loan programs. *Average indebtedness per student:* $27,600. *Average need-based loan:* Freshmen: $2977; Undergraduates: $4580. *Parent loans:* $5,860,478 (100% non-need-based). *Programs:* Federal Direct (Subsidized and Unsubsidized Stafford, PLUS), Perkins, state.

WORK-STUDY *Federal work-study:* Total amount: $350,000; jobs available (averaging $1200).

ATHLETIC AWARDS *Total amount:* $2,198,613 (100% non-need-based).

APPLYING FOR FINANCIAL AID *Required financial aid form:* FAFSA. *Financial aid deadline:* Continuous. *Notification date:* Continuous beginning 2/1. Students must reply within 2 weeks of notification.

CONTACT Ms. Claire Alasio, Director of Financial Aid, Monmouth University, 400 Cedar Avenue, West Long Branch, NJ 07764-1898, 732-571-3463 or toll-free 800-543-9671. *Fax:* 732-263-5577. *E-mail:* finaid@monmouth.edu.

MONTANA STATE UNIVERSITY
Bozeman, MT

Tuition & fees (MT res): $4577	Average undergraduate aid package: $7307

ABOUT THE INSTITUTION State-supported, coed. Awards: bachelor's, master's, and doctoral degrees and post-master's certificates. 49 undergraduate majors. Total enrollment: 12,003. Undergraduates: 10,668. Freshmen: 2,184. Federal methodology is used as a basis for awarding need-based institutional aid.

UNDERGRADUATE EXPENSES for 2004–05 *Application fee:* $30. *Tuition, state resident:* full-time $4577. *Tuition, nonresident:* full-time $14,177. Full-time tuition and fees vary according to course load. Part-time tuition and fees vary according to course load. *College room and board:* $5500. Room and board charges vary according to board plan and housing facility. *Payment plans:* Installment, deferred payment.

GIFT AID (NEED-BASED) *Total amount:* $14,395,880 (65% federal, 5% state, 12% institutional, 18% external sources). *Receiving aid:* Freshmen: 44% (886); All full-time undergraduates: 40% (3,689). *Average award:* Freshmen: $3678; Undergraduates: $3817. *Scholarships, grants, and awards:* Federal Pell, FSEOG, state, private, college/university gift aid from institutional funds, Federal Nursing.

GIFT AID (NON-NEED-BASED) *Total amount:* $5,987,277 (100% external sources). *Receiving aid:* Freshmen: 22% (448); Undergraduates: 12% (1,085). *Average Award:* Freshmen: $4263; Undergraduates: $4336. *Scholarships, grants, and awards by category: Academic Interests/Achievement:* agriculture, architecture, area/ethnic studies, biological sciences, business, communication, computer science, education, engineering/technologies, English, foreign languages, general academic interests/achievements, health fields, home economics, humanities, mathematics, military science, physical sciences, social sciences. *Creative Arts/Performance:* art/fine arts, cinema/film/broadcasting, dance, music, theater/drama. *Special Achievements/Activities:* general special achievements/activities. *Special Characteristics:* general special characteristics. *Tuition waivers:* Full or partial for minority students, employees or children of employees, senior citizens. *ROTC:* Army, Air Force.

LOANS *Student loans:* $32,483,127 (57% need-based, 43% non-need-based). 63% of past graduating class borrowed through all loan programs. *Average indebtedness per student:* $17,193. *Average need-based loan:* Freshmen: $3427; Undergraduates: $4220. *Parent loans:* $4,340,585 (16% need-based, 84% non-need-based). *Programs:* Federal Direct (Subsidized and Unsubsidized Stafford, PLUS), Perkins, Federal Nursing, college/university, Freeborn Loans.

ATHLETIC AWARDS *Total amount:* $2,739,202 (89% need-based, 11% non-need-based).

APPLYING FOR FINANCIAL AID *Required financial aid form:* FAFSA. *Financial aid deadline (priority):* 3/1. *Notification date:* Continuous beginning 4/1. Students must reply within 3 weeks of notification.

CONTACT Brandi Payne, Director of Financial Aid Services, Montana State University, Strand Union Building, Room 135, PO Box 174160, Bozeman, MT 59717-4160, 406-994-2845 or toll-free 888-MSU-CATS. *Fax:* 406-994-6962.

MONTANA STATE UNIVERSITY–BILLINGS
Billings, MT

Tuition & fees (MT res): $4550	Average undergraduate aid package: $7430

ABOUT THE INSTITUTION State-supported, coed. Awards: associate, bachelor's, and master's degrees and post-bachelor's and post-master's certificates. 70 undergraduate majors. Total enrollment: 4,702. Undergraduates: 4,230. Freshmen: 824. Federal methodology is used as a basis for awarding need-based institutional aid.

UNDERGRADUATE EXPENSES for 2004–05 *Application fee:* $30. *Tuition, state resident:* full-time $4550; part-time $125 per credit hour. *Tuition, nonresident:* full-time $12,831; part-time $356 per credit hour. Full-time tuition and fees vary according to course load, degree level, and location. Part-time tuition and fees vary according to course load, degree level, and location. *College room and board:* $4500. Room and board charges vary according to board plan and housing facility. *Payment plan:* Installment.

GIFT AID (NEED-BASED) *Total amount:* $6,529,038 (82% federal, 4% state, 7% institutional, 7% external sources). *Receiving aid:* Freshmen: 52% (379); All full-time undergraduates: 53% (1,661). *Average award:* Freshmen: $4041; Undergraduates: $4328. *Scholarships, grants, and awards:* Federal Pell, FSEOG, state, private, college/university gift aid from institutional funds.

GIFT AID (NON-NEED-BASED) *Total amount:* $289,437 (59% institutional, 41% external sources). *Receiving aid:* Freshmen: 29% (215); Undergraduates: 26% (815). *Average Award:* Freshmen: $4130; Undergraduates: $8712. *Scholarships, grants, and awards by category: Academic Interests/Achievement:* biological sciences, business, communication, computer science, education, engineering/technologies, English, general academic interests/achievements, health fields, humanities, mathematics, physical sciences, premedicine, social sciences. *Creative Arts/Performance:* art/fine arts, music, theater/drama. *Special Achievements/Activities:* cheerleading/drum major, general special achievements/activities. *Special Characteristics:* adult students, children and siblings of alumni, children of faculty/staff, children of union members/company employees, ethnic background, first-generation college students, local/state students, members of minority groups, out-of-state students, veterans. *Tuition waivers:* Full or partial for minority students, employees or children of employees, senior citizens.

LOANS *Student loans:* $14,743,506 (58% need-based, 42% non-need-based). 67% of past graduating class borrowed through all loan programs. *Average indebtedness per student:* $14,220. *Average need-based loan:* Freshmen: $2162; Undergraduates: $3199. *Parent loans:* $241,438 (100% non-need-based). *Programs:* FFEL (Subsidized and Unsubsidized Stafford, PLUS), Perkins, college/university.

ATHLETIC AWARDS *Total amount:* $441,848 (94% need-based, 6% non-need-based).

APPLYING FOR FINANCIAL AID *Required financial aid form:* FAFSA. *Financial aid deadline (priority):* 3/1. *Notification date:* Continuous beginning 4/1. Students must reply within 3 weeks of notification.

CONTACT Melina Hawkins, Director of Financial Aid, Montana State University–Billings, 1500 University Drive, Billings, MT 59101, 406-657-2188 or toll-free 800-565-6782. *E-mail:* mhawkins@msubillings.edu.

MONTANA STATE UNIVERSITY–NORTHERN
Havre, MT

CONTACT Kris Dramstad, Director of Financial Aid, Montana State University–Northern, PO Box 7751, Havre, MT 59501, 406-265-3787 or toll-free 800-662-6132 (in-state).

MONTANA TECH OF THE UNIVERSITY OF MONTANA
Butte, MT

Tuition & fees: N/R	Average undergraduate aid package: $7000

ABOUT THE INSTITUTION State-supported, coed. Awards: associate, bachelor's, and master's degrees and post-bachelor's certificates. 53 undergraduate majors. Total enrollment: 2,188. Undergraduates: 2,089. Freshmen: 394. Federal methodology is used as a basis for awarding need-based institutional aid.

UNDERGRADUATE EXPENSES for 2005–06 *Application fee:* $30. *One-time required fee:* $15. *Tuition, state resident:* part-time $312 per credit. *Tuition, nonresident:* part-time $695 per credit. *Required fees:* $43 per credit or $49. *College room and board:* $5128; *room only:* $2184.

FRESHMAN FINANCIAL AID (Fall 2004, est.) 200 applied for aid; of those 75% were deemed to have need. 93% of freshmen with need received aid; of those 50% had need fully met. *Average percent of need met:* 50% (excluding resources awarded to replace EFC). *Average financial aid package:* $5000 (excluding resources awarded to replace EFC). 9% of all full-time freshmen had no need and received non-need-based gift aid.

UNDERGRADUATE FINANCIAL AID (Fall 2004, est.) 1,500 applied for aid; of those 87% were deemed to have need. 92% of undergraduates with need received aid; of those 58% had need fully met. *Average percent of need met:* 60% (excluding resources awarded to replace EFC). *Average financial aid package:* $7000 (excluding resources awarded to replace EFC). 5% of all full-time undergraduates had no need and received non-need-based gift aid.

GIFT AID (NEED-BASED) *Total amount:* $1,790,000 (84% federal, 8% state, 6% institutional, 2% external sources). *Receiving aid:* Freshmen: 29% (100);

All full-time undergraduates: 47% (900). *Average award:* Freshmen: $1000; Undergraduates: $1000. *Scholarships, grants, and awards:* Federal Pell, FSEOG, state, private, college/university gift aid from institutional funds.

GIFT AID (NON-NEED-BASED) *Total amount:* $1,190,000 (71% institutional, 29% external sources). *Receiving aid:* Freshmen: 9% (30); Undergraduates: 5% (100). *Average Award:* Freshmen: $2500; Undergraduates: $4000. *Scholarships, grants, and awards by category: Academic Interests/Achievement:* 350 awards ($600,000 total): business, computer science, engineering/technologies, general academic interests/achievements, health fields, mathematics, physical sciences. *Special Achievements/Activities:* $50,000 total: general special achievements/activities. *Special Characteristics:* $50,000 total: general special characteristics.

LOANS *Student loans:* $7,000,000 (71% need-based, 29% non-need-based). 75% of past graduating class borrowed through all loan programs. *Average indebtedness per student:* $17,000. *Average need-based loan:* Freshmen: $2500; Undergraduates: $5000. *Parent loans:* $50,000 (100% need-based). *Programs:* FFEL (Subsidized and Unsubsidized Stafford, PLUS), Perkins, college/university.

WORK-STUDY *Federal work-study:* Total amount: $175,000; 100 jobs averaging $2000. *State or other work-study/employment:* Total amount: $125,000 (100% need-based). 25 part-time jobs averaging $2000.

ATHLETIC AWARDS *Total amount:* $300,000 (100% non-need-based).

APPLYING FOR FINANCIAL AID *Required financial aid forms:* FAFSA, institution's own form. *Financial aid deadline (priority):* 3/1. *Notification date:* Continuous beginning 3/15. Students must reply within 3 weeks of notification.

CONTACT Mike Richardson, Director of Financial Aid, Montana Tech of The University of Montana, West Park Street, Butte, MT 59701-8997, 406-496-4212 or toll-free 800-445-TECH Ext. 1. *Fax:* 406-496-4705.

MONTCLAIR STATE UNIVERSITY
Montclair, NJ

Tuition & fees (NJ res): $7026	Average undergraduate aid package: $9163

ABOUT THE INSTITUTION State-supported, coed. Awards: bachelor's, master's, and doctoral degrees and post-bachelor's and post-master's certificates. 76 undergraduate majors. Total enrollment: 15,637. Undergraduates: 11,818. Freshmen: 1,785. Federal methodology is used as a basis for awarding need-based institutional aid.

UNDERGRADUATE EXPENSES for 2004–05 *Application fee:* $55. *Tuition, state resident:* full-time $5168; part-time $172.26 per credit. *Tuition, nonresident:* full-time $8836; part-time $294.47 per credit. *Required fees:* full-time $1858; $60.79 per credit or $17 per term part-time. *College room and board:* $8212; *room only:* $5442. Room and board charges vary according to board plan and housing facility. *Payment plan:* Installment.

FRESHMAN FINANCIAL AID (Fall 2004, est.) 1344 applied for aid; of those 71% were deemed to have need. 96% of freshmen with need received aid; of those 42% had need fully met. *Average percent of need met:* 84% (excluding resources awarded to replace EFC). *Average financial aid package:* $9082 (excluding resources awarded to replace EFC). 9% of all full-time freshmen had no need and received non-need-based gift aid.

UNDERGRADUATE FINANCIAL AID (Fall 2004, est.) 6,248 applied for aid; of those 77% were deemed to have need. 95% of undergraduates with need received aid; of those 43% had need fully met. *Average percent of need met:* 84% (excluding resources awarded to replace EFC). *Average financial aid package:* $9163 (excluding resources awarded to replace EFC). 3% of all full-time undergraduates had no need and received non-need-based gift aid.

GIFT AID (NEED-BASED) *Total amount:* $18,640,766 (48% federal, 52% state). *Receiving aid:* Freshmen: 34% (603); All full-time undergraduates: 31% (2,987). *Average award:* Freshmen: $2729; Undergraduates: $2766. *Scholarships, grants, and awards:* Federal Pell, FSEOG, state, college/university gift aid from institutional funds.

GIFT AID (NON-NEED-BASED) *Total amount:* $5,021,305 (23% state, 68% institutional, 9% external sources). *Receiving aid:* Freshmen: 10% (174); Undergraduates: 6% (562). *Average Award:* Freshmen: $1836; Undergraduates: $2908. *Scholarships, grants, and awards by category: Academic Interests/Achievement:* 932 awards ($2,950,847 total): biological sciences, business, communication, education, English, foreign languages, general academic interests/achievements, home economics, humanities, mathematics, physical sciences, religion/biblical studies, social sciences. *Creative Arts/Performance:* 35 awards ($61,800 total): art/fine arts, cinema/film/broadcasting, dance, music, performing arts, theater/drama. *Special Achievements/Activities:* 102 awards ($461,611 total): community service, leadership. *Special Characteristics:* 2 awards ($3932

Montclair State University

total): children with a deceased or disabled parent. *Tuition waivers:* Full or partial for employees or children of employees, senior citizens. *ROTC:* Air Force cooperative.

LOANS *Student loans:* $33,564,901 (51% need-based, 49% non-need-based). 52% of past graduating class borrowed through all loan programs. *Average indebtedness per student:* $16,694. *Average need-based loan:* Freshmen: $2568; Undergraduates: $3581. *Parent loans:* $5,299,921 (100% non-need-based). *Programs:* FFEL (Subsidized and Unsubsidized Stafford, PLUS), Perkins, state, private educational loans.

WORK-STUDY *Federal work-study:* Total amount: $410,272; 443 jobs averaging $926. *State or other work-study/employment:* Total amount: $2,633,078 (100% non-need-based). 1,188 part-time jobs averaging $2216.

APPLYING FOR FINANCIAL AID *Required financial aid form:* FAFSA. *Financial aid deadline (priority):* 3/1. *Notification date:* Continuous beginning 4/1. Students must reply within 2 weeks of notification.

CONTACT Frank A. Cuozzo, Director of Financial Aid, Montclair State University, College Hall, Room 321, Upper Montclair, NJ 07043, 973-655-7022 or toll-free 800-331-9205. *Fax:* 973-655-7712. *E-mail:* cuozzof@mail.montclair.edu.

MONTREAT COLLEGE
Montreat, NC

Tuition & fees: $15,560	Average undergraduate aid package: $13,417

ABOUT THE INSTITUTION Independent religious, coed. Awards: associate, bachelor's, and master's degrees. 14 undergraduate majors. Total enrollment: 1,035. Undergraduates: 943. Freshmen: 126. Federal methodology is used as a basis for awarding need-based institutional aid.

UNDERGRADUATE EXPENSES for 2005–06 *Application fee:* $15. *Comprehensive fee:* $20,568 includes full-time tuition ($15,560) and room and board ($5008). *Part-time tuition:* $480 per credit hour.

FRESHMAN FINANCIAL AID (Fall 2004, est.) 130 applied for aid; of those 72% were deemed to have need. 100% of freshmen with need received aid; of those 12% had need fully met. *Average percent of need met:* 82% (excluding resources awarded to replace EFC). *Average financial aid package:* $11,143 (excluding resources awarded to replace EFC). 26% of all full-time freshmen had no need and received non-need-based gift aid.

UNDERGRADUATE FINANCIAL AID (Fall 2004, est.) 1,012 applied for aid; of those 80% were deemed to have need. 100% of undergraduates with need received aid; of those 22% had need fully met. *Average percent of need met:* 83% (excluding resources awarded to replace EFC). *Average financial aid package:* $13,417 (excluding resources awarded to replace EFC). 29% of all full-time undergraduates had no need and received non-need-based gift aid.

GIFT AID (NEED-BASED) *Total amount:* $4,161,480 (21% federal, 40% state, 33% institutional, 6% external sources). *Receiving aid:* Freshmen: 69% (93); All full-time undergraduates: 71% (766). *Average award:* Freshmen: $8012; Undergraduates: $6116. *Scholarships, grants, and awards:* Federal Pell, FSEOG, state, private, college/university gift aid from institutional funds.

GIFT AID (NON-NEED-BASED) *Receiving aid:* Freshmen: 6% (8); Undergraduates: 4% (44). *Average Award:* Freshmen: $4876; Undergraduates: $4983. *Scholarships, grants, and awards by category:* Academic Interests/Achievement: general academic interests/achievements. Creative Arts/Performance: 22 awards ($18,800 total): art/fine arts, music, theater/drama. Special Achievements/Activities: 1 award ($2000 total): leadership. Special Characteristics: 43 awards ($129,376 total): children and siblings of alumni, children of faculty/staff, international students, relatives of clergy.

LOANS *Student loans:* $3,600,222 (100% need-based). 88% of past graduating class borrowed through all loan programs. *Average indebtedness per student:* $18,512. *Average need-based loan:* Freshmen: $2546; Undergraduates: $5500. *Parent loans:* $244,777 (100% need-based). *Programs:* FFEL (Subsidized and Unsubsidized Stafford, PLUS), Perkins.

WORK-STUDY *Federal work-study:* Total amount: $122,304; 81 jobs averaging $1510. *State or other work-study/employment:* Total amount: $99,822 (44% need-based, 56% non-need-based). 41 part-time jobs averaging $1360.

ATHLETIC AWARDS *Total amount:* $307,152 (100% need-based).

APPLYING FOR FINANCIAL AID *Required financial aid forms:* FAFSA, institution's own form, state aid form (for NC residents only). *Financial aid deadline (priority):* 3/15. *Notification date:* Continuous beginning 1/15. Students must reply within 2 weeks of notification.

CONTACT Mr. James P. Devine, Director of Financial Aid, Montreat College, PO Box 1267, Montreat, NC 28757-1267, 828-669-8012 Ext. 3795 or toll-free 800-622-6968 (in-state). *Fax:* 828-669-0120. *E-mail:* jdevine@montreat.edu.

MONTSERRAT COLLEGE OF ART
Beverly, MA

ABOUT THE INSTITUTION Independent, coed. Awards: bachelor's degrees and post-bachelor's certificates. 10 undergraduate majors. Total enrollment: 353. Undergraduates: 332.

GIFT AID (NEED-BASED) *Scholarships, grants, and awards:* Federal Pell, FSEOG, state, private, college/university gift aid from institutional funds.

GIFT AID (NON-NEED-BASED) *Scholarships, grants, and awards by category:* Creative Arts/Performance: applied art and design, art/fine arts. Special Characteristics: siblings of current students.

LOANS *Programs:* FFEL (Subsidized and Unsubsidized Stafford, PLUS), state, alternative loans.

WORK-STUDY *Federal work-study:* Total amount: $43,529; 33 jobs averaging $1000.

APPLYING FOR FINANCIAL AID *Required financial aid form:* FAFSA.

CONTACT Creda Carney, Director of Financial Aid, Montserrat College of Art, 23 Essex Street, PO Box 26, Beverly, MA 01915, 978-922-8222 Ext. 1155 or toll-free 800-836-0487. *Fax:* 978-922-4268. *E-mail:* finaid@montserrat.edu.

MOODY BIBLE INSTITUTE
Chicago, IL

ABOUT THE INSTITUTION Independent nondenominational, coed. Awards: bachelor's, master's, and first professional degrees. 9 undergraduate majors. Total enrollment: 2,687. Undergraduates: 2,402. Freshmen: 250.

GIFT AID (NEED-BASED) *Scholarships, grants, and awards:* private, college/university gift aid from institutional funds.

LOANS *Programs:* alternative loans.

APPLYING FOR FINANCIAL AID *Required financial aid form:* institution's own form.

CONTACT Daniel R. Ward, Director of Financial Aid, Moody Bible Institute, 820 North LaSalle Boulevard, Chicago, IL 60610-3284, 312-329-4178 or toll-free 800-967-4MBI. *Fax:* 312-329-4197. *E-mail:* daniel.ward@moody.edu.

MOORE COLLEGE OF ART & DESIGN
Philadelphia, PA

Tuition & fees: $22,091	Average undergraduate aid package: $12,889

ABOUT THE INSTITUTION Independent, women only. Awards: bachelor's degrees and post-bachelor's certificates. 9 undergraduate majors. Total enrollment: 531. Undergraduates: 501. Freshmen: 82. Federal methodology is used as a basis for awarding need-based institutional aid.

UNDERGRADUATE EXPENSES for 2005–06 *Application fee:* $35. *Comprehensive fee:* $30,745 includes full-time tuition ($22,091) and room and board ($8654). *College room only:* $5227. Room and board charges vary according to housing facility. *Part-time tuition:* $855 per credit. *Part-time fees:* $175 per term. Part-time tuition and fees vary according to course load. *Payment plan:* Installment.

FRESHMAN FINANCIAL AID (Fall 2004, est.) 80 applied for aid; of those 84% were deemed to have need. 100% of freshmen with need received aid; of those 6% had need fully met. *Average percent of need met:* 50% (excluding resources awarded to replace EFC). *Average financial aid package:* $10,964 (excluding resources awarded to replace EFC). 33% of all full-time freshmen had no need and received non-need-based gift aid.

UNDERGRADUATE FINANCIAL AID (Fall 2004, est.) 427 applied for aid; of those 91% were deemed to have need. 100% of undergraduates with need received aid; of those 7% had need fully met. *Average percent of need met:* 53% (excluding resources awarded to replace EFC). *Average financial aid package:* $12,889 (excluding resources awarded to replace EFC). 22% of all full-time undergraduates had no need and received non-need-based gift aid.

GIFT AID (NEED-BASED) *Total amount:* $3,288,276 (22% federal, 12% state, 60% institutional, 6% external sources). *Receiving aid:* Freshmen: 65% (67); All full-time undergraduates: 75% (386). *Average award:* Freshmen: $7860; Undergraduates: $8111. *Scholarships, grants, and awards:* Federal Pell, FSEOG, state, private, college/university gift aid from institutional funds.

GIFT AID (NON-NEED-BASED) *Total amount:* $534,274 (95% institutional, 5% external sources). *Receiving aid:* Freshmen: 2% (2); Undergraduates: 4% (18). *Average Award:* Freshmen: $7716; Undergraduates: $8290. *Scholarships, grants,*

and awards by category: Academic Interests/Achievement: 450 awards ($2,000,000 total): general academic interests/achievements. **Tuition waivers:** Full or partial for employees or children of employees.

LOANS Student loans: $4,789,723 (82% need-based, 18% non-need-based). 80% of past graduating class borrowed through all loan programs. Average indebtedness per student: $25,000. **Average need-based loan:** Freshmen: $3156; Undergraduates: $4661. **Parent loans:** $1,872,054 (48% need-based, 52% non-need-based). **Programs:** FFEL (Subsidized and Unsubsidized Stafford, PLUS), Perkins.

WORK-STUDY Federal work-study: Total amount: $112,449; 110 jobs averaging $1020. **State or other work-study/employment:** Part-time jobs available.

APPLYING FOR FINANCIAL AID Required financial aid form: FAFSA. **Financial aid deadline (priority):** 3/1. **Notification date:** Continuous beginning 3/1. Students must reply within 2 weeks of notification.

CONTACT Rochelle Iannuzzi, Director of Financial Aid, Moore College of Art & Design, 20th and the Parkway, Philadelphia, PA 19103-1179, 215-568-4515 Ext. 4042 or toll-free 800-523-2025. Fax: 215-568-8017. E-mail: riannuzzi@moore.edu.

MORAVIAN COLLEGE
Bethlehem, PA

Tuition & fees: $23,574	Average undergraduate aid package: $15,775

ABOUT THE INSTITUTION Independent religious, coed. Awards: bachelor's, master's, and first professional degrees and post-bachelor's certificates. 56 undergraduate majors. Total enrollment: 2,078. Undergraduates: 1,828. Freshmen: 383. Both federal and institutional methodology are used as a basis for awarding need-based institutional aid.

UNDERGRADUATE EXPENSES for 2004–05 Application fee: $40. **Comprehensive fee:** $30,884 includes full-time tuition ($23,184), mandatory fees ($390), and room and board ($7310). **College room only:** $4105. Room and board charges vary according to board plan and housing facility. **Part-time tuition:** $725 per credit. Part-time tuition and fees vary according to class time. **Payment plan:** Installment.

FRESHMAN FINANCIAL AID (Fall 2003) 343 applied for aid; of those 87% were deemed to have need. 100% of freshmen with need received aid; of those 18% had need fully met. Average percent of need met: 79% (excluding resources awarded to replace EFC). Average financial aid package: $16,116 (excluding resources awarded to replace EFC). 18% of all full-time freshmen had no need and received non-need-based gift aid.

UNDERGRADUATE FINANCIAL AID (Fall 2003) 1,252 applied for aid; of those 90% were deemed to have need. 100% of undergraduates with need received aid; of those 22% had need fully met. Average percent of need met: 77% (excluding resources awarded to replace EFC). Average financial aid package: $15,775 (excluding resources awarded to replace EFC). 19% of all full-time undergraduates had no need and received non-need-based gift aid.

GIFT AID (NEED-BASED) Total amount: $12,258,278 (8% federal, 13% state, 76% institutional, 3% external sources). **Receiving aid:** Freshmen: 77% (294); All full-time undergraduates: 75% (1,105). **Average award:** Freshmen: $11,896; Undergraduates: $11,149. **Scholarships, grants, and awards:** Federal Pell, FSEOG, state, private, college/university gift aid from institutional funds.

GIFT AID (NON-NEED-BASED) Total amount: $2,336,614 (1% state, 89% institutional, 10% external sources). **Receiving aid:** Freshmen: 10% (38); Undergraduates: 9% (126). **Average Award:** Freshmen: $12,813; Undergraduates: $11,556. **Scholarships, grants, and awards by category:** Academic Interests/Achievement: 734 awards ($5,672,075 total): foreign languages, general academic interests/achievements, physical sciences. Creative Arts/Performance: 10 awards ($31,500 total): music. Special Achievements/Activities: 21 awards ($89,400 total): religious involvement. Special Characteristics: 201 awards ($1,188,974 total): adult students, children and siblings of alumni, children of educators, children of faculty/staff, ethnic background, international students, relatives of clergy, religious affiliation. **Tuition waivers:** Full or partial for children of alumni, employees or children of employees. **ROTC:** Army cooperative.

LOANS Student loans: $9,668,118 (61% need-based, 39% non-need-based). **Average need-based loan:** Freshmen: $3463; Undergraduates: $4070. **Parent loans:** $2,627,267 (36% need-based, 64% non-need-based). **Programs:** FFEL (Subsidized and Unsubsidized Stafford, PLUS), Perkins.

WORK-STUDY Federal work-study: Total amount: $1,278,460; jobs available. **State or other work-study/employment:** Total amount: $581,086 (5% need-based, 95% non-need-based). Part-time jobs available.

APPLYING FOR FINANCIAL AID Required financial aid forms: FAFSA, CSS Financial Aid PROFILE, state aid form, noncustodial (divorced/separated) parent's statement, business/farm supplement. **Financial aid deadline (priority):** 2/15. **Notification date:** 4/1. Students must reply by 5/1 or within 2 weeks of notification.

CONTACT Mr. Stephen C. Cassel, Director of Financial Aid, Moravian College, 1200 Main Street, Bethlehem, PA 18018-6650, 610-861-1330 or toll-free 800-441-3191. Fax: 610-861-1346. E-mail: cassels@moravian.edu.

MOREHEAD STATE UNIVERSITY
Morehead, KY

Tuition & fees (KY res): $3840	Average undergraduate aid package: $7129

ABOUT THE INSTITUTION State-supported, coed. Awards: associate, bachelor's, and master's degrees and post-master's certificates. 51 undergraduate majors. Total enrollment: 9,293. Undergraduates: 7,757. Freshmen: 1,284. Federal methodology is used as a basis for awarding need-based institutional aid.

UNDERGRADUATE EXPENSES for 2004–05 Tuition, state resident: full-time $3840; part-time $160 per credit hour. **Tuition, nonresident:** full-time $10,200; part-time $425 per credit hour. Full-time tuition and fees vary according to course load and reciprocity agreements. **College room and board:** $4410. Room and board charges vary according to board plan and housing facility. **Payment plans:** Installment, deferred payment.

FRESHMAN FINANCIAL AID (Fall 2004, est.) 1112 applied for aid; of those 81% were deemed to have need. 99% of freshmen with need received aid; of those 35% had need fully met. Average percent of need met: 86% (excluding resources awarded to replace EFC). Average financial aid package: $6464 (excluding resources awarded to replace EFC). 22% of all full-time freshmen had no need and received non-need-based gift aid.

UNDERGRADUATE FINANCIAL AID (Fall 2004, est.) 5,175 applied for aid; of those 84% were deemed to have need. 99% of undergraduates with need received aid; of those 41% had need fully met. Average percent of need met: 86% (excluding resources awarded to replace EFC). Average financial aid package: $7129 (excluding resources awarded to replace EFC). 18% of all full-time undergraduates had no need and received non-need-based gift aid.

GIFT AID (NEED-BASED) Total amount: $14,483,460 (78% federal, 22% state). **Receiving aid:** Freshmen: 53% (666); All full-time undergraduates: 51% (3,273). **Average award:** Freshmen: $3929; Undergraduates: $4019. **Scholarships, grants, and awards:** Federal Pell, FSEOG, state, private, college/university gift aid from institutional funds.

GIFT AID (NON-NEED-BASED) Total amount: $7,231,139 (49% state, 41% institutional, 10% external sources). **Receiving aid:** Freshmen: 56% (700); Undergraduates: 35% (2,210). **Average Award:** Freshmen: $2348; Undergraduates: $2750. **Scholarships, grants, and awards by category:** Academic Interests/Achievement: 1,450 awards ($2,181,736 total): agriculture, biological sciences, business, education, general academic interests/achievements, humanities, physical sciences, social sciences. Creative Arts/Performance: 124 awards ($123,932 total): art/fine arts, cinema/film/broadcasting, debating, journalism/publications, music, theater/drama. Special Achievements/Activities: 169 awards ($108,234 total): cheerleading/drum major, leadership. Special Characteristics: 334 awards ($239,638 total): adult students, children and siblings of alumni, local/state students, members of minority groups, out-of-state students. **Tuition waivers:** Full or partial for children of alumni, employees or children of employees, senior citizens. **ROTC:** Army.

LOANS Student loans: $17,455,863 (54% need-based, 46% non-need-based). 60% of past graduating class borrowed through all loan programs. Average indebtedness per student: $14,972. **Average need-based loan:** Freshmen: $2272; Undergraduates: $3007. **Parent loans:** $1,420,929 (100% non-need-based). **Programs:** Federal Direct (Subsidized and Unsubsidized Stafford, PLUS), Perkins, college/university.

WORK-STUDY Federal work-study: Total amount: $864,846; 632 jobs averaging $1368. **State or other work-study/employment:** Total amount: $834,074 (100% non-need-based). 599 part-time jobs averaging $1392.

ATHLETIC AWARDS Total amount: $973,583 (100% non-need-based).

APPLYING FOR FINANCIAL AID Required financial aid forms: FAFSA, institution's own form. **Financial aid deadline (priority):** 3/15. **Notification date:** Continuous.

CONTACT Carol Becker, Director of Financial Aid, Morehead State University, 301 Howell-McDowell Administration Building, Morehead, KY 40351, 606-783-2011 or toll-free 800-585-6781. Fax: 606-783-2293. E-mail: c.becker@moreheadstate.edu.

MOREHOUSE COLLEGE
Atlanta, GA

Tuition & fees: $15,740	Average undergraduate aid package: $11,079

ABOUT THE INSTITUTION Independent, men only. Awards: bachelor's degrees. 33 undergraduate majors. Total enrollment: 2,891. Undergraduates: 2,891. Freshmen: 707. Federal methodology is used as a basis for awarding need-based institutional aid.

UNDERGRADUATE EXPENSES for 2004–05 *Application fee:* $45. *Comprehensive fee:* $24,488 includes full-time tuition ($14,318), mandatory fees ($1422), and room and board ($8748). *College room only:* $4982. Room and board charges vary according to board plan. *Part-time tuition:* $597 per semester hour.

FRESHMAN FINANCIAL AID (Fall 2003) 696 applied for aid; of those 99% were deemed to have need. 97% of freshmen with need received aid; of those 2% had need fully met. *Average percent of need met:* 22% (excluding resources awarded to replace EFC). *Average financial aid package:* $11,054 (excluding resources awarded to replace EFC). 39% of all full-time freshmen had no need and received non-need-based gift aid.

UNDERGRADUATE FINANCIAL AID (Fall 2003) 2,519 applied for aid; of those 100% were deemed to have need. 98% of undergraduates with need received aid; of those 2% had need fully met. *Average percent of need met:* 25% (excluding resources awarded to replace EFC). *Average financial aid package:* $11,079 (excluding resources awarded to replace EFC). 38% of all full-time undergraduates had no need and received non-need-based gift aid.

GIFT AID (NEED-BASED) *Total amount:* $3,828,110 (100% federal). *Receiving aid:* Freshmen: 38% (281); All full-time undergraduates: 37% (1,023). *Average award:* Freshmen: $3807; Undergraduates: $3561. *Scholarships, grants, and awards:* Federal Pell, FSEOG, state, private, United Negro College Fund.

GIFT AID (NON-NEED-BASED) *Total amount:* $14,253,434 (11% state, 78% institutional, 11% external sources). *Receiving aid:* Freshmen: 73% (537); Undergraduates: 72% (1,977). *Average Award:* Freshmen: $11,678; Undergraduates: $10,593. *Scholarships, grants, and awards by category:* Academic Interests/Achievement: business, general academic interests/achievements, military science. Creative Arts/Performance: music. Special Achievements/Activities: community service, leadership, religious involvement. Special Characteristics: children of faculty/staff. *Tuition waivers:* Full or partial for employees or children of employees. *ROTC:* Army, Naval, Air Force.

LOANS *Student loans:* $15,356,019 (43% need-based, 57% non-need-based). 53% of past graduating class borrowed through all loan programs. *Average indebtedness per student:* $18,000. *Average need-based loan:* Freshmen: $2827; Undergraduates: $3864. *Parent loans:* $13,016,462 (100% non-need-based). *Programs:* Federal Direct (Subsidized and Unsubsidized Stafford, PLUS), FFEL (Subsidized and Unsubsidized Stafford, PLUS), Perkins, state, college/university.

WORK-STUDY *Federal work-study:* Total amount: $595,976; jobs available. *State or other work-study/employment:* Total amount: $298,970 (100% non-need-based). Part-time jobs available.

ATHLETIC AWARDS *Total amount:* $1,382,955 (100% non-need-based).

APPLYING FOR FINANCIAL AID *Required financial aid forms:* FAFSA, institution's own form, CSS Financial Aid PROFILE. *Financial aid deadline (priority):* 4/1. *Notification date:* 5/1.

CONTACT James A. Stotts, Director of Financial Aid, Morehouse College, 830 Westview Drive, SW, Atlanta, GA 30314, 404-681-2800 Ext. 2638 or toll-free 800-851-1254. *Fax:* 404-215-2711. *E-mail:* jstotts@morehouse.edu.

MORGAN STATE UNIVERSITY
Baltimore, MD

CONTACT Director of Financial Aid, Morgan State University, 1700 East Cold Spring Lane, Baltimore, MD 21251, 443-885-3170 or toll-free 800-332-6674.

MORNINGSIDE COLLEGE
Sioux City, IA

Tuition & fees: $17,170	Average undergraduate aid package: $17,038

ABOUT THE INSTITUTION Independent religious, coed. Awards: bachelor's and master's degrees. 43 undergraduate majors. Total enrollment: 1,204. Undergraduates: 1,037. Freshmen: 317. Federal methodology is used as a basis for awarding need-based institutional aid.

UNDERGRADUATE EXPENSES for 2004–05 *Application fee:* $25. *Comprehensive fee:* $22,570 includes full-time tuition ($16,260), mandatory fees ($910), and room and board ($5400). *College room only:* $2830. Full-time tuition and fees vary according to program. Room and board charges vary according to housing facility. *Part-time tuition:* $525 per semester hour. Part-time tuition and fees vary according to course load. *Payment plan:* Installment.

FRESHMAN FINANCIAL AID (Fall 2004, est.) 307 applied for aid; of those 91% were deemed to have need. 99% of freshmen with need received aid; of those 56% had need fully met. *Average percent of need met:* 83% (excluding resources awarded to replace EFC). *Average financial aid package:* $17,655 (excluding resources awarded to replace EFC). 11% of all full-time freshmen had no need and received non-need-based gift aid.

UNDERGRADUATE FINANCIAL AID (Fall 2004, est.) 935 applied for aid; of those 92% were deemed to have need. 99% of undergraduates with need received aid; of those 52% had need fully met. *Average percent of need met:* 81% (excluding resources awarded to replace EFC). *Average financial aid package:* $17,038 (excluding resources awarded to replace EFC). 11% of all full-time undergraduates had no need and received non-need-based gift aid.

GIFT AID (NEED-BASED) *Total amount:* $4,204,329 (32% federal, 40% state, 28% institutional). *Receiving aid:* Freshmen: 76% (241); All full-time undergraduates: 73% (716). *Average award:* Freshmen: $5850; Undergraduates: $5837. *Scholarships, grants, and awards:* Federal Pell, FSEOG, state, private, college/university gift aid from institutional funds.

GIFT AID (NON-NEED-BASED) *Total amount:* $5,294,163 (2% state, 89% institutional, 9% external sources). *Receiving aid:* Freshmen: 87% (276); Undergraduates: 84% (821). *Average Award:* Freshmen: $6528; Undergraduates: $6570. *Scholarships, grants, and awards by category:* Academic Interests/Achievement: 732 awards ($2,346,427 total): biological sciences, business, communication, computer science, education, English, foreign languages, general academic interests/achievements, health fields, humanities, mathematics, physical sciences, premedicine, religion/biblical studies, social sciences. Creative Arts/Performance: 181 awards ($470,649 total): art/fine arts, music, theater/drama. Special Achievements/Activities: 254 awards ($517,343 total): general special achievements/activities. Special Characteristics: 935 awards ($1,552,541 total): children and siblings of alumni, children of faculty/staff, first-generation college students, international students, local/state students, out-of-state students, relatives of clergy, religious affiliation. *Tuition waivers:* Full or partial for children of alumni, employees or children of employees, senior citizens. *ROTC:* Army cooperative.

LOANS *Student loans:* $7,366,822 (46% need-based, 54% non-need-based). 91% of past graduating class borrowed through all loan programs. *Average indebtedness per student:* $25,677. *Average need-based loan:* Freshmen: $3676; Undergraduates: $4456. *Parent loans:* $328,109 (100% non-need-based). *Programs:* FFEL (Subsidized and Unsubsidized Stafford, PLUS), Perkins, state, college/university, private loans.

WORK-STUDY *Federal work-study:* Total amount: $348,577; 378 jobs averaging $922. *State or other work-study/employment:* Total amount: $3,966,562 (94% need-based, 6% non-need-based). 177 part-time jobs averaging $1301.

ATHLETIC AWARDS *Total amount:* $1,181,354 (100% non-need-based).

APPLYING FOR FINANCIAL AID *Required financial aid form:* FAFSA. *Financial aid deadline (priority):* 3/1. *Notification date:* Continuous beginning 3/31.

CONTACT Karen K. Gagnon, Director of Student Financial Planning, Morningside College, 1501 Morningside Avenue, Sioux City, IA 51106, 712-274-5159 or toll-free 800-831-0806 Ext. 5111. *Fax:* 712-274-5605. *E-mail:* gagnon@morningside.edu.

MORRIS COLLEGE
Sumter, SC

Tuition & fees: $7985	Average undergraduate aid package: $12,100

ABOUT THE INSTITUTION Independent religious, coed. Awards: bachelor's degrees. 23 undergraduate majors. Total enrollment: 897. Undergraduates: 897. Freshmen: 255. Federal methodology is used as a basis for awarding need-based institutional aid.

UNDERGRADUATE EXPENSES for 2004–05 *Application fee:* $20. *Comprehensive fee:* $11,709 includes full-time tuition ($7750), mandatory fees ($235), and room and board ($3724). *Part-time tuition:* $315 per credit hour. *Part-time fees:* $45 per term. *Payment plan:* Installment.

GIFT AID (NEED-BASED) *Total amount:* $4,369,088 (67% federal, 28% state, 1% institutional, 4% external sources). *Receiving aid:* Freshmen: 91% (212); All full-time undergraduates: 96% (859). *Average award:* Freshmen: $8500;

Undergraduates: $7400. *Scholarships, grants, and awards:* Federal Pell, FSEOG, state, private, college/university gift aid from institutional funds, United Negro College Fund.

GIFT AID (NON-NEED-BASED) *Receiving aid:* Freshmen: 11% (25); Undergraduates: 6% (50). *Scholarships, grants, and awards by category: Academic Interests/Achievement:* 150 awards ($250,000 total): biological sciences, business, communication, computer science, education, general academic interests/achievements, humanities, mathematics, military science, physical sciences, premedicine, religion/biblical studies. *Creative Arts/Performance:* 10 awards ($9000 total): art/fine arts, creative writing, journalism/publications, performing arts. *Special Achievements/Activities:* 20 awards ($3000 total): cheerleading/drum major. *Special Characteristics:* 125 awards ($59,600 total): first-generation college students, veterans. *ROTC:* Army.

LOANS *Student loans:* $2,718,866 (100% need-based). 98% of past graduating class borrowed through all loan programs. *Average indebtedness per student:* $17,125. *Average need-based loan:* Freshmen: $2625; Undergraduates: $3900. *Parent loans:* $450,660 (100% need-based). *Programs:* Federal Direct (Subsidized and Unsubsidized Stafford, PLUS), FFEL (PLUS), Perkins.

ATHLETIC AWARDS *Total amount:* $126,225 (37% need-based, 63% non-need-based).

APPLYING FOR FINANCIAL AID *Required financial aid forms:* FAFSA, institution's own form. *Financial aid deadline (priority):* 3/30. *Notification date:* Continuous beginning 6/1. Students must reply within 2 weeks of notification.

CONTACT Ms. Sandra S. Gibson, Director of Financial Aid, Morris College, 100 West College Street, Sumter, SC 29150-3599, 803-934-3238 or toll-free 866-853-1345. *Fax:* 803-773-3687.

MORRISON UNIVERSITY
Reno, NV

ABOUT THE INSTITUTION Proprietary, coed. Awards: associate, bachelor's, and master's degrees. 9 undergraduate majors. Total enrollment: 130. Undergraduates: 110.

GIFT AID (NEED-BASED) *Scholarships, grants, and awards:* Federal Pell, state.

GIFT AID (NON-NEED-BASED) *Scholarships, grants, and awards by category: Academic Interests/Achievement:* business. *Special Characteristics:* general special characteristics.

LOANS *Programs:* FFEL (Subsidized and Unsubsidized Stafford, PLUS), alternative loans.

APPLYING FOR FINANCIAL AID *Required financial aid form:* FAFSA.

CONTACT Kim Droniak, Financial Aid Administrator, Morrison University, 140 Washington Street, Reno, NV 89503-5600, 775-850-0700 or toll-free 800-369-6144. *Fax:* 775-850-0711.

MOUNTAIN STATE UNIVERSITY
Beckley, WV

Tuition & fees: $5400	Average undergraduate aid package: $6262

ABOUT THE INSTITUTION Independent, coed. Awards: associate, bachelor's, and master's degrees. 45 undergraduate majors. Total enrollment: 4,107. Undergraduates: 3,742. Freshmen: 388. Federal methodology is used as a basis for awarding need-based institutional aid.

UNDERGRADUATE EXPENSES for 2004–05 *Application fee:* $25. *Comprehensive fee:* $10,840 includes full-time tuition ($4200), mandatory fees ($1200), and room and board ($5440). *College room only:* $2810. Full-time tuition and fees vary according to program. Room and board charges vary according to board plan. *Part-time tuition:* $175 per credit. *Part-time fees:* $50 per credit. Part-time tuition and fees vary according to program. *Payment plan:* Installment.

FRESHMAN FINANCIAL AID (Fall 2003) 268 applied for aid; of those 85% were deemed to have need. 100% of freshmen with need received aid. *Average percent of need met:* 42% (excluding resources awarded to replace EFC). *Average financial aid package:* $5281 (excluding resources awarded to replace EFC). 2% of all full-time freshmen had no need and received non-need-based gift aid.

UNDERGRADUATE FINANCIAL AID (Fall 2003) 2,259 applied for aid; of those 91% were deemed to have need. 100% of undergraduates with need received aid; of those 4% had need fully met. *Average percent of need met:* 49% (excluding resources awarded to replace EFC). *Average financial aid package:* $6262 (excluding resources awarded to replace EFC). 1% of all full-time undergraduates had no need and received non-need-based gift aid.

MOUNT ALOYSIUS COLLEGE
Cresson, PA

Tuition & fees: $14,530	Average undergraduate aid package: $9500

ABOUT THE INSTITUTION Independent Roman Catholic, coed. Awards: associate, bachelor's, and master's degrees and post-bachelor's certificates. 34 undergraduate majors. Total enrollment: 1,500. Undergraduates: 1,451. Freshmen: 277. Federal methodology is used as a basis for awarding need-based institutional aid.

UNDERGRADUATE EXPENSES for 2004–05 *Application fee:* $30. *Comprehensive fee:* $20,490 includes full-time tuition ($14,100), mandatory fees ($430), and room and board ($5960). *College room only:* $2980. Full-time tuition and fees vary according to class time, course load, and program. Room and board charges vary according to board plan. *Part-time tuition:* $450 per credit. *Part-time fees:* $110 per term. Part-time tuition and fees vary according to class time, course load, and program. *Payment plans:* Installment, deferred payment.

FRESHMAN FINANCIAL AID (Fall 2004, est.) 279 applied for aid; of those 96% were deemed to have need. 100% of freshmen with need received aid. *Average percent of need met:* 88% (excluding resources awarded to replace EFC). *Average financial aid package:* $9500 (excluding resources awarded to replace EFC).

UNDERGRADUATE FINANCIAL AID (Fall 2004, est.) 1,102 applied for aid; of those 99% were deemed to have need. 100% of undergraduates with need received aid. *Average percent of need met:* 83% (excluding resources awarded to replace EFC). *Average financial aid package:* $9500 (excluding resources awarded to replace EFC).

GIFT AID (NEED-BASED) *Total amount:* $7,301,326 (35% federal, 32% state, 31% institutional, 2% external sources). *Receiving aid:* Freshmen: 89% (249); All full-time undergraduates: 96% (1,072). *Average award:* Freshmen: $3000; Undergraduates: $2500. *Scholarships, grants, and awards:* Federal Pell, FSEOG, state, private, college/university gift aid from institutional funds.

GIFT AID (NON-NEED-BASED) *Receiving aid:* Freshmen: 4% (10); Undergraduates: 2% (20). *Scholarships, grants, and awards by category: Creative Arts/Performance:* 13 awards ($13,000 total): music, performing arts. *Special Achievements/Activities:* 24 awards ($174,000 total): leadership. *Special Characteristics:* 81 awards ($45,500 total): children of current students, parents of current students, religious affiliation, siblings of current students, spouses of current students, twins. *Tuition waivers:* Full or partial for employees or children of employees.

LOANS *Student loans:* $6,153,187 (100% need-based). 81% of past graduating class borrowed through all loan programs. *Average indebtedness per student:*

GIFT AID (NEED-BASED) *Total amount:* $6,772,080 (79% federal, 19% state, 1% institutional, 1% external sources). *Receiving aid:* Freshmen: 70% (208); All full-time undergraduates: 62% (1,545). *Average award:* Freshmen: $3549; Undergraduates: $3926. *Scholarships, grants, and awards:* Federal Pell, FSEOG, state, private, college/university gift aid from institutional funds, Federal Nursing.

GIFT AID (NON-NEED-BASED) *Total amount:* $283,288 (47% state, 53% institutional). *Receiving aid:* Freshmen: 4% (12); Undergraduates: 2% (60). *Average Award:* Freshmen: $3255; Undergraduates: $3889. *Scholarships, grants, and awards by category: Academic Interests/Achievement:* 38 awards ($148,393 total): general academic interests/achievements. *Tuition waivers:* Full or partial for employees or children of employees, senior citizens.

LOANS *Student loans:* $16,451,618 (50% need-based, 50% non-need-based). 73% of past graduating class borrowed through all loan programs. *Average indebtedness per student:* $24,870. *Average need-based loan:* Freshmen: $2578; Undergraduates: $3859. *Parent loans:* $142,388 (100% non-need-based). *Programs:* FFEL (Subsidized and Unsubsidized Stafford, PLUS), private education loans.

WORK-STUDY *Federal work-study:* Total amount: $275,633; 164 jobs averaging $1680.

ATHLETIC AWARDS *Total amount:* $284,555 (100% non-need-based).

APPLYING FOR FINANCIAL AID *Required financial aid form:* FAFSA. *Financial aid deadline:* Continuous. *Notification date:* Continuous beginning 4/1. Students must reply within 2 weeks of notification.

CONTACT Ms. Sue Pack, Director of Financial Aid, Mountain State University, PO Box 9003, Beckley, WV 25802, 304-929-1595 or toll-free 800-766-6067 Ext. 1433. *Fax:* 304-929-1390. *E-mail:* spack@mountainstate.edu.

$17,313. **Parent loans:** $1,415,820 (100% need-based). **Programs:** FFEL (Subsidized and Unsubsidized Stafford, PLUS), Perkins, Federal Nursing, alternative loans.
WORK-STUDY *Federal work-study:* Total amount: $215,785; 200 jobs averaging $1070.
ATHLETIC AWARDS *Total amount:* $11,600 (100% need-based).
APPLYING FOR FINANCIAL AID *Required financial aid form:* FAFSA. *Financial aid deadline (priority):* 2/15. *Notification date:* Continuous beginning 3/15. Students must reply within 4 weeks of notification.
CONTACT Mrs. Stacy L. Schenk, Director of Financial Aid, Mount Aloysius College, 7373 Admiral Peary Highway, Cresson, PA 16630-1900, 814-886-6357 or toll-free 888-823-2220. *Fax:* 814-886-6463. *E-mail:* sschenk@mtaloy.edu.

MOUNT ANGEL SEMINARY
Saint Benedict, OR

CONTACT Dorene Preis, Director of Student Financial Aid/Registrar, Mount Angel Seminary, 1 Abbey Drive, Saint Benedict, OR 97373, 503-845-3951. *Fax:* 503-845-3126. *E-mail:* dpreis@mtangel.edu.

MOUNT CARMEL COLLEGE OF NURSING
Columbus, OH

ABOUT THE INSTITUTION Independent, coed, primarily women. Awards: bachelor's and master's degrees and post-bachelor's certificates. Total enrollment: 573. Undergraduates: 550. Freshmen: 55.
GIFT AID (NEED-BASED) *Scholarships, grants, and awards:* Federal Pell, FSEOG, state, private, college/university gift aid from institutional funds.
GIFT AID (NON-NEED-BASED) *Scholarships, grants, and awards by category: Academic Interests/Achievement:* general academic interests/achievements. *Special Achievements/Activities:* community service. *Special Characteristics:* members of minority groups.
LOANS *Programs:* FFEL (Subsidized and Unsubsidized Stafford, PLUS), Perkins, Federal Nursing, state, college/university.
WORK-STUDY *State or other work-study/employment:* Total amount: $19,274 (100% need-based). 27 part-time jobs averaging $1930.
APPLYING FOR FINANCIAL AID *Required financial aid forms:* FAFSA, institution's own form.
CONTACT Carol Graham, Director of Financial Aid, Mount Carmel College of Nursing, 127 South Davis Avenue, Columbus, OH 43222, 614-234-5800 Ext. 5177. *E-mail:* cgraham@mchs.com.

MOUNT HOLYOKE COLLEGE
South Hadley, MA

Tuition & fees: $30,938	Average undergraduate aid package: $26,176

ABOUT THE INSTITUTION Independent, women only. Awards: bachelor's and master's degrees and post-bachelor's certificates. 48 undergraduate majors. Total enrollment: 2,073. Undergraduates: 2,071. Freshmen: 558. Both federal and institutional methodology are used as a basis for awarding need-based institutional aid.
UNDERGRADUATE EXPENSES for 2004–05 *Application fee:* $55. *Comprehensive fee:* $39,998 includes full-time tuition ($30,770), mandatory fees ($168), and room and board ($9060). *College room only:* $4430. Room and board charges vary according to board plan and housing facility. *Part-time tuition:* $965 per credit hour. *Part-time fees:* $168 per year. *Payment plans:* Tuition prepayment, installment.
FRESHMAN FINANCIAL AID (Fall 2004, est.) 432 applied for aid; of those 81% were deemed to have need. 100% of freshmen with need received aid; of those 100% had need fully met. *Average percent of need met:* 100% (excluding resources awarded to replace EFC). *Average financial aid package:* $26,119 (excluding resources awarded to replace EFC). 6% of all full-time freshmen had no need and received non-need-based gift aid.
UNDERGRADUATE FINANCIAL AID (Fall 2004, est.) 1,659 applied for aid; of those 90% were deemed to have need. 100% of undergraduates with need received aid; of those 100% had need fully met. *Average percent of need met:* 100% (excluding resources awarded to replace EFC). *Average financial aid package:* $26,176 (excluding resources awarded to replace EFC). 5% of all full-time undergraduates had no need and received non-need-based gift aid.

GIFT AID (NEED-BASED) *Total amount:* $30,207,702 (6% federal, 1% state, 91% institutional, 2% external sources). *Receiving aid:* Freshmen: 61% (344); All full-time undergraduates: 6% (149). *Average award:* Freshmen: $22,357; Undergraduates: $21,188. *Scholarships, grants, and awards:* Federal Pell, FSEOG, state, private, college/university gift aid from institutional funds.
GIFT AID (NON-NEED-BASED) *Total amount:* $1,430,001 (91% institutional, 9% external sources). *Receiving aid:* Freshmen: 4% (20); Undergraduates: 2% (47). *Average Award: Freshmen:* $12,916; *Undergraduates:* $10,337. *Scholarships, grants, and awards by category: Academic Interests/Achievement:* 123 awards ($1,271,451 total): general academic interests/achievements. *Tuition waivers:* Full or partial for employees or children of employees. *ROTC:* Army cooperative, Air Force cooperative.
LOANS *Student loans:* $8,597,024 (81% need-based, 19% non-need-based). 69% of past graduating class borrowed through all loan programs. *Average indebtedness per student:* $20,039. *Average need-based loan:* Freshmen: $3321; Undergraduates: $4925. *Parent loans:* $6,047,061 (100% non-need-based). *Programs:* Federal Direct (Subsidized and Unsubsidized Stafford, PLUS), Perkins, state, college/university.
WORK-STUDY *Federal work-study:* Total amount: $972,248; 844 jobs averaging $1590. *State or other work-study/employment:* Total amount: $742,122 (100% need-based). 448 part-time jobs averaging $1645.
APPLYING FOR FINANCIAL AID *Required financial aid forms:* FAFSA, CSS Financial Aid PROFILE, noncustodial (divorced/separated) parent's statement, business/farm supplement, federal income tax form(s), W-2 forms. *Financial aid deadline:* 2/1 (priority: 1/15). *Notification date:* 4/1. Students must reply by 5/1.
CONTACT Ms. Kathy Blaisdell, Director of Financial Assistance, Mount Holyoke College, 50 College Street, South Hadley, MA 01075-1492, 413-538-2291. *Fax:* 413-538-2512. *E-mail:* kblaisde@mtholyoke.edu.

MOUNT IDA COLLEGE
Newton, MA

Tuition & fees: $19,096	Average undergraduate aid package: $11,070

ABOUT THE INSTITUTION Independent, coed. Awards: associate and bachelor's degrees. 24 undergraduate majors. Total enrollment: 1,297. Undergraduates: 1,297. Freshmen: 378. Federal methodology is used as a basis for awarding need-based institutional aid.
UNDERGRADUATE EXPENSES for 2005–06 *Application fee:* $35. *Comprehensive fee:* $28,926 includes full-time tuition ($18,500), mandatory fees ($596), and room and board ($9830). *Part-time tuition:* $515 per credit hour. *Part-time fees:* $15 per credit.
FRESHMAN FINANCIAL AID (Fall 2004, est.) 341 applied for aid; of those 90% were deemed to have need. 99% of freshmen with need received aid; of those 7% had need fully met. *Average percent of need met:* 49% (excluding resources awarded to replace EFC). *Average financial aid package:* $10,362 (excluding resources awarded to replace EFC). 22% of all full-time freshmen had no need and received non-need-based gift aid.
UNDERGRADUATE FINANCIAL AID (Fall 2004, est.) 968 applied for aid; of those 94% were deemed to have need. 99% of undergraduates with need received aid; of those 5% had need fully met. *Average percent of need met:* 49% (excluding resources awarded to replace EFC). *Average financial aid package:* $11,070 (excluding resources awarded to replace EFC). 16% of all full-time undergraduates had no need and received non-need-based gift aid.
GIFT AID (NEED-BASED) *Total amount:* $7,041,443 (21% federal, 7% state, 69% institutional, 3% external sources). *Receiving aid:* Freshmen: 74% (297); All full-time undergraduates: 79% (860). *Average award:* Freshmen: $8030; Undergraduates: $7902. *Scholarships, grants, and awards:* Federal Pell, FSEOG, state, private, college/university gift aid from institutional funds.
GIFT AID (NON-NEED-BASED) *Total amount:* $503,569 (3% state, 87% institutional, 10% external sources). *Receiving aid:* Freshmen: 5% (19); Undergraduates: 4% (39). *Average Award: Freshmen:* $6509; *Undergraduates:* $6496. *Scholarships, grants, and awards by category: Creative Arts/Performance:* 55 awards ($53,730 total): applied art and design, art/fine arts, general creative arts/performance. *Special Achievements/Activities:* 927 awards ($3,106,155 total): community service, general special achievements/activities, leadership.
LOANS *Student loans:* $9,757,274 (81% need-based, 19% non-need-based). 57% of past graduating class borrowed through all loan programs. *Average indebtedness per student:* $31,105. *Average need-based loan:* Freshmen: $2368;

Undergraduates: $3355. *Parent loans:* $2,769,660 (61% need-based, 39% non-need-based). *Programs:* FFEL (Subsidized and Unsubsidized Stafford, PLUS), state, signature loans.

WORK-STUDY *Federal work-study:* Total amount: $259,837; 290 jobs averaging $896. *State or other work-study/employment:* Part-time jobs available.

APPLYING FOR FINANCIAL AID *Required financial aid form:* FAFSA. *Financial aid deadline (priority):* 5/1. *Notification date:* Continuous beginning 2/1.

CONTACT Linda Mularczyk, Director of Financial Aid, Mount Ida College, 777 Dedham Street, Newton, MA 02459-3310, 617-928-4099. *Fax:* 617-332-7869. *E-mail:* finserv@mountida.edu.

MOUNT MARTY COLLEGE
Yankton, SD

Tuition & fees: $14,936   **Average undergraduate aid package: $12,537**

ABOUT THE INSTITUTION Independent Roman Catholic, coed. Awards: associate, bachelor's, and master's degrees and post-bachelor's certificates. 30 undergraduate majors. Total enrollment: 1,163. Undergraduates: 1,075. Freshmen: 171. Federal methodology is used as a basis for awarding need-based institutional aid.

UNDERGRADUATE EXPENSES for 2004–05 *Application fee:* $35. *Comprehensive fee:* $19,700 includes full-time tuition ($13,256), mandatory fees ($1680), and room and board ($4764). Full-time tuition and fees vary according to course load and location. *Part-time tuition:* $200 per credit hour. *Part-time fees:* $25 per credit. Part-time tuition and fees vary according to course load and location. *Payment plan:* Installment.

FRESHMAN FINANCIAL AID (Fall 2004, est.) 127 applied for aid; of those 91% were deemed to have need. 100% of freshmen with need received aid; of those 19% had need fully met. *Average percent of need met:* 76% (excluding resources awarded to replace EFC). *Average financial aid package:* $12,776 (excluding resources awarded to replace EFC). 11% of all full-time freshmen had no need and received non-need-based gift aid.

UNDERGRADUATE FINANCIAL AID (Fall 2004, est.) 485 applied for aid; of those 93% were deemed to have need. 100% of undergraduates with need received aid; of those 20% had need fully met. *Average percent of need met:* 73% (excluding resources awarded to replace EFC). *Average financial aid package:* $12,537 (excluding resources awarded to replace EFC). 10% of all full-time undergraduates had no need and received non-need-based gift aid.

GIFT AID (NEED-BASED) *Total amount:* $3,173,015 (26% federal, 1% state, 66% institutional, 7% external sources). *Receiving aid:* Freshmen: 89% (116); All full-time undergraduates: 87% (449). *Average award:* Freshmen: $9128; Undergraduates: $8018. *Scholarships, grants, and awards:* Federal Pell, FSEOG, state, private, college/university gift aid from institutional funds.

GIFT AID (NON-NEED-BASED) *Total amount:* $177,030 (2% state, 94% institutional, 4% external sources). *Receiving aid:* Freshmen: 85% (111); Undergraduates: 78% (405). *Average Award:* Freshmen: $7777; Undergraduates: $6407. *Scholarships, grants, and awards by category:* Academic Interests/Achievement: 435 awards ($1,126,364 total): general academic interests/achievements. Creative Arts/Performance: 64 awards ($36,970 total): creative writing, music, theater/drama. Special Achievements/Activities: 141 awards ($256,708 total): leadership, memberships, religious involvement. Special Characteristics: 71 awards ($265,056 total): children of current students, children of faculty/staff, international students, parents of current students, religious affiliation, siblings of current students, spouses of current students. *Tuition waivers:* Full or partial for employees or children of employees. *ROTC:* Army cooperative.

LOANS *Student loans:* $3,653,193 (69% need-based, 31% non-need-based). 83% of past graduating class borrowed through all loan programs. *Average indebtedness per student:* $21,134. *Average need-based loan:* Freshmen: $3205; Undergraduates: $4508. *Parent loans:* $946,417 (12% need-based, 88% non-need-based). *Programs:* FFEL (Subsidized and Unsubsidized Stafford, PLUS), Perkins, Federal Nursing.

WORK-STUDY *Federal work-study:* Total amount: $261,157; 237 jobs averaging $1000. *State or other work-study/employment:* Total amount: $57,928 (100% non-need-based). 61 part-time jobs averaging $1000.

ATHLETIC AWARDS *Total amount:* $448,402 (31% need-based, 69% non-need-based).

APPLYING FOR FINANCIAL AID *Required financial aid forms:* FAFSA, institution's own form. *Financial aid deadline (priority):* 3/1. *Notification date:* Continuous beginning 3/15. Students must reply within 2 weeks of notification.

CONTACT Mr. Ken Kocer, Director of Financial Assistance, Mount Marty College, 1105 West 8th Street, Yankton, SD 57078-3724, 605-668-1589 or toll-free 800-658-4552. *Fax:* 605-668-1585. *E-mail:* kkocer@mtmc.edu.

MOUNT MARY COLLEGE
Milwaukee, WI

Tuition & fees: $16,155   **Average undergraduate aid package: $11,229**

ABOUT THE INSTITUTION Independent Roman Catholic, women only. Awards: bachelor's and master's degrees and post-bachelor's certificates. 47 undergraduate majors. Total enrollment: 1,632. Undergraduates: 1,404. Freshmen: 140. Federal methodology is used as a basis for awarding need-based institutional aid.

UNDERGRADUATE EXPENSES for 2004–05 *Application fee:* $25. *Comprehensive fee:* $21,505 includes full-time tuition ($15,975), mandatory fees ($180), and room and board ($5350). Room and board charges vary according to board plan. *Part-time tuition:* $466 per credit. *Part-time fees:* $45 per term. Part-time tuition and fees vary according to course load. *Payment plan:* Installment.

FRESHMAN FINANCIAL AID (Fall 2004, est.) 111 applied for aid; of those 89% were deemed to have need. 100% of freshmen with need received aid; of those 18% had need fully met. *Average percent of need met:* 73% (excluding resources awarded to replace EFC). *Average financial aid package:* $11,881 (excluding resources awarded to replace EFC). 23% of all full-time freshmen had no need and received non-need-based gift aid.

UNDERGRADUATE FINANCIAL AID (Fall 2004, est.) 632 applied for aid; of those 90% were deemed to have need. 100% of undergraduates with need received aid; of those 17% had need fully met. *Average percent of need met:* 69% (excluding resources awarded to replace EFC). *Average financial aid package:* $11,229 (excluding resources awarded to replace EFC). 17% of all full-time undergraduates had no need and received non-need-based gift aid.

GIFT AID (NEED-BASED) *Total amount:* $5,041,749 (26% federal, 19% state, 54% institutional, 1% external sources). *Receiving aid:* Freshmen: 73% (99); All full-time undergraduates: 67% (560). *Average award:* Freshmen: $8260; Undergraduates: $6580. *Scholarships, grants, and awards:* Federal Pell, FSEOG, state, private, college/university gift aid from institutional funds, Metropolitan Milwaukee Association of Commerce Awards.

GIFT AID (NON-NEED-BASED) *Total amount:* $692,503 (1% state, 95% institutional, 4% external sources). *Receiving aid:* Freshmen: 7% (9); Undergraduates: 4% (36). *Average Award:* Freshmen: $5367; Undergraduates: $6625. *Scholarships, grants, and awards by category:* Academic Interests/Achievement: 240 awards ($807,959 total): business, communication, education, English, general academic interests/achievements, health fields, home economics, humanities, mathematics, physical sciences, social sciences. Creative Arts/Performance: 27 awards ($23,550 total): applied art and design, art/fine arts, music. Special Achievements/Activities: 7 awards ($47,722 total): general special achievements/activities, leadership. Special Characteristics: 37 awards ($222,930 total): children of faculty/staff, international students, parents of current students, siblings of current students. *Tuition waivers:* Full or partial for employees or children of employees, senior citizens. *ROTC:* Army cooperative.

LOANS *Student loans:* $7,143,832 (78% need-based, 22% non-need-based). 77% of past graduating class borrowed through all loan programs. *Average indebtedness per student:* $21,345. *Average need-based loan:* Freshmen: $2941; Undergraduates: $4376. *Parent loans:* $784,697 (41% need-based, 59% non-need-based). *Programs:* FFEL (Subsidized and Unsubsidized Stafford, PLUS), Perkins, state.

WORK-STUDY *Federal work-study:* Total amount: $94,765; 144 jobs averaging $1200. *State or other work-study/employment:* Total amount: $113,076 (100% non-need-based). 51 part-time jobs averaging $1800.

APPLYING FOR FINANCIAL AID *Required financial aid form:* FAFSA. *Financial aid deadline (priority):* 3/1. *Notification date:* Continuous. Students must reply within 2 weeks of notification.

CONTACT Debra Duff, Director of Financial Aid, Mount Mary College, 2900 North Menomonee River Parkway, Milwaukee, WI 53222-4597, 414-256-1258. *Fax:* 414-443-3602. *E-mail:* finaid@mtmary.edu.

MOUNT MERCY COLLEGE
Cedar Rapids, IA

Tuition & fees: $18,840   **Average undergraduate aid package: $14,145**

ABOUT THE INSTITUTION Independent Roman Catholic, coed. Awards: bachelor's degrees. 37 undergraduate majors. Total enrollment: 1,486. Undergraduates: 1,486. Freshmen: 214. Federal methodology is used as a basis for awarding need-based institutional aid.

UNDERGRADUATE EXPENSES for 2005–06 *Application fee:* $20. *Comprehensive fee:* $24,520 includes full-time tuition ($18,030), mandatory fees ($810), and room and board ($5680). Full-time tuition and fees vary according to course load. Room and board charges vary according to board plan and housing facility. *Part-time tuition:* $500 per credit hour. Part-time tuition and fees vary according to course load. *Payment plan:* Installment.

FRESHMAN FINANCIAL AID (Fall 2003) 205 applied for aid; of those 88% were deemed to have need. 100% of freshmen with need received aid; of those 46% had need fully met. *Average percent of need met:* 86% (excluding resources awarded to replace EFC). *Average financial aid package:* $15,046 (excluding resources awarded to replace EFC). 16% of all full-time freshmen had no need and received non-need-based gift aid.

UNDERGRADUATE FINANCIAL AID (Fall 2003) 867 applied for aid; of those 91% were deemed to have need. 100% of undergraduates with need received aid; of those 35% had need fully met. *Average percent of need met:* 81% (excluding resources awarded to replace EFC). *Average financial aid package:* $14,145 (excluding resources awarded to replace EFC). 13% of all full-time undergraduates had no need and received non-need-based gift aid.

GIFT AID (NEED-BASED) *Total amount:* $7,583,620 (14% federal, 25% state, 58% institutional, 3% external sources). *Receiving aid:* Freshmen: 84% (180); All full-time undergraduates: 86% (781). *Average award:* Freshmen: $10,762; Undergraduates: $9081. *Scholarships, grants, and awards:* Federal Pell, FSEOG, state, college/university gift aid from institutional funds.

GIFT AID (NON-NEED-BASED) *Total amount:* $1,014,810 (2% state, 91% institutional, 7% external sources). *Receiving aid:* Freshmen: 10% (22); Undergraduates: 8% (75). *Average Award:* Freshmen: $11,667; Undergraduates: $9878. *Scholarships, grants, and awards by category: Academic Interests/Achievement:* 823 awards ($4,361,023 total): general academic interests/achievements. *Creative Arts/Performance:* 49 awards ($45,100 total): art/fine arts, music, theater/drama. *Special Achievements/Activities:* 256 awards ($268,750 total): leadership. *Special Characteristics:* 23 awards ($1100 total): previous college experience. *Tuition waivers:* Full or partial for employees or children of employees.

LOANS *Student loans:* $7,220,149 (69% need-based, 31% non-need-based). 84% of past graduating class borrowed through all loan programs. *Average indebtedness per student:* $19,930. *Average need-based loan:* Freshmen: $3911; Undergraduates: $5167. *Parent loans:* $323,782 (29% need-based, 71% non-need-based). *Programs:* Federal Direct (Subsidized and Unsubsidized Stafford, PLUS), Perkins, state, college/university.

WORK-STUDY *Federal work-study:* Total amount: $483,176; 322 jobs averaging $1461. *State or other work-study/employment:* Total amount: $189,380 (26% need-based, 74% non-need-based). 102 part-time jobs averaging $1067.

APPLYING FOR FINANCIAL AID *Required financial aid form:* FAFSA. *Financial aid deadline (priority):* 3/1. *Notification date:* Continuous beginning 3/15. Students must reply by 5/1 or within 3 weeks of notification.

CONTACT Lois M. Mulbrook, Director of Financial Aid, Mount Mercy College, 1330 Elmhurst Drive, NE, Cedar Rapids, IA 52402-4797, 319-368-6467 or toll-free 800-248-4504. *Fax:* 319-364-3546. *E-mail:* lmmulbro@mtmercy.edu.

MOUNT OLIVE COLLEGE
Mount Olive, NC

Tuition & fees: $11,800	Average undergraduate aid package: $6701

ABOUT THE INSTITUTION Independent Free Will Baptist, coed. Awards: associate and bachelor's degrees. 22 undergraduate majors. Total enrollment: 2,582. Undergraduates: 2,582. Freshmen: 277. Federal methodology is used as a basis for awarding need-based institutional aid.

UNDERGRADUATE EXPENSES for 2005–06 *Application fee:* $20. *Comprehensive fee:* $16,600 includes full-time tuition ($11,520), mandatory fees ($280), and room and board ($4800). *College room only:* $2000. Full-time tuition and fees vary according to location. Room and board charges vary according to board plan and housing facility. *Part-time tuition:* $215 per credit hour. Part-time tuition and fees vary according to course load and location. *Payment plan:* Installment.

FRESHMAN FINANCIAL AID (Fall 2003) 383 applied for aid; of those 59% were deemed to have need. 94% of freshmen with need received aid; of those 17% had need fully met. *Average percent of need met:* 65% (excluding resources

awarded to replace EFC). *Average financial aid package:* $7067 (excluding resources awarded to replace EFC). 11% of all full-time freshmen had no need and received non-need-based gift aid.

UNDERGRADUATE FINANCIAL AID (Fall 2003) 1,660 applied for aid; of those 75% were deemed to have need. 94% of undergraduates with need received aid; of those 18% had need fully met. *Average percent of need met:* 64% (excluding resources awarded to replace EFC). *Average financial aid package:* $6701 (excluding resources awarded to replace EFC). 11% of all full-time undergraduates had no need and received non-need-based gift aid.

GIFT AID (NEED-BASED) *Total amount:* $5,994,033 (34% federal, 58% state, 2% institutional, 6% external sources). *Receiving aid:* Freshmen: 34% (209); All full-time undergraduates: 49% (1,160). *Average award:* Freshmen: $5846; Undergraduates: $4861. *Scholarships, grants, and awards:* Federal Pell, FSEOG, state, private, college/university gift aid from institutional funds.

GIFT AID (NON-NEED-BASED) *Total amount:* $1,383,225 (46% state, 2% institutional, 52% external sources). *Receiving aid:* Freshmen: 3% (20); Undergraduates: 3% (79). *Average Award: Freshmen:* $2382; *Undergraduates:* $3678. *Scholarships, grants, and awards by category: Academic Interests/Achievement:* 63 awards ($218,526 total): general academic interests/achievements, mathematics. *Creative Arts/Performance:* 53 awards ($84,955 total): art/fine arts, music. *Special Achievements/Activities:* 144 awards ($272,701 total): leadership. *Special Characteristics:* 47 awards ($129,839 total): children of faculty/staff, religious affiliation. *Tuition waivers:* Full or partial for employees or children of employees, senior citizens.

LOANS *Student loans:* $6,199,716 (68% need-based, 32% non-need-based). 73% of past graduating class borrowed through all loan programs. *Average indebtedness per student:* $8818. *Average need-based loan:* Freshmen: $1733; Undergraduates: $2423. *Parent loans:* $142,582 (34% need-based, 66% non-need-based). *Programs:* FFEL (Subsidized and Unsubsidized Stafford, PLUS), Perkins.

WORK-STUDY *Federal work-study:* Total amount: $111,339; 120 jobs averaging $719.

ATHLETIC AWARDS *Total amount:* $599,687 (59% need-based, 41% non-need-based).

APPLYING FOR FINANCIAL AID *Required financial aid forms:* FAFSA, state aid form. *Financial aid deadline (priority):* 3/1. *Notification date:* Continuous beginning 3/15. Students must reply within 2 weeks of notification.

CONTACT Ms. Karen Britt Statler, Director of Financial Aid, Mount Olive College, 634 Henderson Street, Mount Olive, NC 28365, 919-658-2502 Ext. 3006 or toll-free 800-653-0854 (in-state). *Fax:* 919-658-9816.

MOUNT SAINT MARY COLLEGE
Newburgh, NY

Tuition & fees: $15,690	Average undergraduate aid package: $11,273

ABOUT THE INSTITUTION Independent, coed. Awards: bachelor's and master's degrees. 33 undergraduate majors. Total enrollment: 2,621. Undergraduates: 2,099. Freshmen: 422. Both federal and institutional methodology are used as a basis for awarding need-based institutional aid.

UNDERGRADUATE EXPENSES for 2004–05 *Application fee:* $35. *Comprehensive fee:* $23,330 includes full-time tuition ($15,180), mandatory fees ($510), and room and board ($7640). *College room only:* $4300. Full-time tuition and fees vary according to degree level. Room and board charges vary according to board plan, gender, housing facility, location, and student level. *Part-time tuition:* $506 per credit hour. *Part-time fees:* $35 per term. Part-time tuition and fees vary according to degree level. *Payment plan:* Installment.

FRESHMAN FINANCIAL AID (Fall 2004, est.) 419 applied for aid; of those 77% were deemed to have need. 99% of freshmen with need received aid; of those 23% had need fully met. *Average percent of need met:* 63% (excluding resources awarded to replace EFC). *Average financial aid package:* $10,694 (excluding resources awarded to replace EFC).

UNDERGRADUATE FINANCIAL AID (Fall 2004, est.) 1,558 applied for aid; of those 80% were deemed to have need. 98% of undergraduates with need received aid; of those 24% had need fully met. *Average percent of need met:* 65% (excluding resources awarded to replace EFC). *Average financial aid package:* $11,273 (excluding resources awarded to replace EFC).

GIFT AID (NEED-BASED) *Total amount:* $7,562,176 (24% federal, 30% state, 44% institutional, 2% external sources). *Receiving aid:* Freshmen: 69% (291); All full-time undergraduates: 63% (1,052). *Average award:* Freshmen: $6794; Undergraduates: $3007. *Scholarships, grants, and awards:* Federal Pell, FSEOG, state, private, college/university gift aid from institutional funds, Federal Nursing.

GIFT AID (NON-NEED-BASED) *Scholarships, grants, and awards by category:* *Academic Interests/Achievement:* 226 awards ($1,068,062 total): general academic interests/achievements. *Special Characteristics:* 96 awards ($706,927 total): children of faculty/staff. *Tuition waivers:* Full or partial for employees or children of employees. *ROTC:* Army cooperative.
LOANS *Student loans:* $12,742,731 (41% need-based, 59% non-need-based). 70% of past graduating class borrowed through all loan programs. *Average indebtedness per student:* $20,000. *Average need-based loan:* Freshmen: $2538; Undergraduates: $4002. *Parent loans:* $3,181,176 (100% need-based). *Programs:* FFEL (Subsidized and Unsubsidized Stafford, PLUS), Perkins, Federal Nursing.
WORK-STUDY *Federal work-study:* Total amount: $293,046; 219 jobs available. *State or other work-study/employment:* Total amount: $65,000 (100% need-based). 35 part-time jobs available.
APPLYING FOR FINANCIAL AID *Required financial aid forms:* FAFSA, institution's own form. *Financial aid deadline (priority):* 2/15. *Notification date:* Continuous beginning 3/1. Students must reply within 2 weeks of notification.
CONTACT Susan F. Twomey, Director of Financial Aid, Mount Saint Mary College, 330 Powell Avenue, Newburgh, NY 12550-3494, 845-561-0800 or toll-free 888-937-6762. *Fax:* 845-569-3302. *E-mail:* twomey@msmc.edu.

MOUNT ST. MARY'S COLLEGE
Los Angeles, CA

ABOUT THE INSTITUTION Independent Roman Catholic, coed, primarily women. Awards: associate, bachelor's, and master's degrees and post-bachelor's certificates. 40 undergraduate majors. Total enrollment: 2,257. Undergraduates: 1,804. Freshmen: 398.
GIFT AID (NEED-BASED) *Scholarships, grants, and awards:* Federal Pell, FSEOG, state, private, college/university gift aid from institutional funds.
GIFT AID (NON-NEED-BASED) *Scholarships, grants, and awards by category:* *Academic Interests/Achievement:* education, general academic interests/ achievements. *Special Achievements/Activities:* community service, leadership. *Special Characteristics:* children and siblings of alumni.
LOANS *Programs:* FFEL (Subsidized and Unsubsidized Stafford, PLUS), Federal Nursing, college/university.
WORK-STUDY *Federal work-study:* Total amount: $664,421; jobs available. *State or other work-study/employment:* Total amount: $727,751 (88% need-based, 12% non-need-based). Part-time jobs available.
APPLYING FOR FINANCIAL AID *Required financial aid forms:* FAFSA, institution's own form, state aid form.
CONTACT La Royce Dodd, Financial Aid Director, Mount St. Mary's College, 12001 Chalon Road, Los Angeles, CA 90049, 310-954-4192 or toll-free 800-999-9893.

MOUNT ST. MARY'S UNIVERSITY
Emmitsburg, MD

Tuition & fees: $22,900	Average undergraduate aid package: $15,552

ABOUT THE INSTITUTION Independent Roman Catholic, coed. Awards: bachelor's, master's, and first professional degrees and post-bachelor's certificates. 27 undergraduate majors. Total enrollment: 2,125. Undergraduates: 1,612. Freshmen: 392. Federal methodology is used as a basis for awarding need-based institutional aid.
UNDERGRADUATE EXPENSES for 2005–06 *Application fee:* $35. *Comprehensive fee:* $30,930 includes full-time tuition ($22,500), mandatory fees ($400), and room and board ($8030). *College room only:* $3930. Room and board charges vary according to board plan. *Part-time tuition:* $750 per credit. *Part-time fees:* $6 per credit. *Payment plan:* Installment.
FRESHMAN FINANCIAL AID (Fall 2004, est.) 332 applied for aid; of those 80% were deemed to have need. 100% of freshmen with need received aid; of those 26% had need fully met. *Average percent of need met:* 81% (excluding resources awarded to replace EFC). *Average financial aid package:* $15,428 (excluding resources awarded to replace EFC). 29% of all full-time freshmen had no need and received non-need-based gift aid.
UNDERGRADUATE FINANCIAL AID (Fall 2004, est.) 1,040 applied for aid; of those 84% were deemed to have need. 100% of undergraduates with need received aid; of those 28% had need fully met. *Average percent of need met:* 80% (excluding resources awarded to replace EFC). *Average financial aid package:* $15,552 (excluding resources awarded to replace EFC). 31% of all full-time undergraduates had no need and received non-need-based gift aid.

GIFT AID (NEED-BASED) *Total amount:* $9,483,046 (9% federal, 10% state, 78% institutional, 3% external sources). *Receiving aid:* Freshmen: 68% (266); All full-time undergraduates: 61% (864). *Average award:* Freshmen: $11,917; Undergraduates: $11,802. *Scholarships, grants, and awards:* Federal Pell, FSEOG, state, private, college/university gift aid from institutional funds.
GIFT AID (NON-NEED-BASED) *Total amount:* $4,565,635 (4% federal, 4% state, 88% institutional, 4% external sources). *Receiving aid:* Freshmen: 15% (58); Undergraduates: 12% (164). *Average Award:* Freshmen: $13,173; Undergraduates: $11,650. *Scholarships, grants, and awards by category:* *Academic Interests/Achievement:* 1,231 awards ($8,838,770 total): general academic interests/achievements. *Creative Arts/Performance:* 17 awards ($36,400 total): art/fine arts, journalism/publications. *Special Characteristics:* 152 awards ($724,665 total): children of faculty/staff, members of minority groups, siblings of current students. *Tuition waivers:* Full or partial for employees or children of employees. *ROTC:* Army cooperative.
LOANS *Student loans:* $6,046,724 (61% need-based, 39% non-need-based). 65% of past graduating class borrowed through all loan programs. *Average indebtedness per student:* $16,213. *Average need-based loan:* Freshmen: $3680; Undergraduates: $4299. *Parent loans:* $2,438,989 (24% need-based, 76% non-need-based). *Programs:* FFEL (Subsidized and Unsubsidized Stafford, PLUS), Perkins.
WORK-STUDY *Federal work-study:* Total amount: $254,678; 225 jobs averaging $1131. *State or other work-study/employment:* Total amount: $150,000 (100% non-need-based). 195 part-time jobs averaging $769.
ATHLETIC AWARDS *Total amount:* $1,746,450 (30% need-based, 70% non-need-based).
APPLYING FOR FINANCIAL AID *Required financial aid forms:* FAFSA, institution's own form. *Financial aid deadline:* 2/15. *Notification date:* Continuous. Students must reply by 5/1.
CONTACT Mr. David C. Reeder, Director of Financial Aid, Mount St. Mary's University, 16300 Old Emmitsburg Road, Emmitsburg, MD 21727-7799, 301-447-5207 or toll-free 800-448-4347. *Fax:* 301-447-5755. *E-mail:* reeder@msmary.edu.

MT. SIERRA COLLEGE
Monrovia, CA

CONTACT Financial Aid Office, Mt. Sierra College, 101 East Huntington Drive, Monrovia, CA 91016, 888-828-8800 or toll-free 888-828-8800.

MOUNT UNION COLLEGE
Alliance, OH

Tuition & fees: $18,810	Average undergraduate aid package: $14,714

ABOUT THE INSTITUTION Independent United Methodist, coed. Awards: bachelor's degrees. 44 undergraduate majors. Total enrollment: 2,333. Undergraduates: 2,333. Freshmen: 547. Federal methodology is used as a basis for awarding need-based institutional aid.
UNDERGRADUATE EXPENSES for 2004–05 *Application fee:* $20. *Comprehensive fee:* $24,440 includes full-time tuition ($18,560), mandatory fees ($250), and room and board ($5630). *College room only:* $2360. Room and board charges vary according to housing facility. *Part-time tuition:* $775 per semester hour. *Part-time fees:* $50 per term. *Payment plans:* Tuition prepayment, installment.
FRESHMAN FINANCIAL AID (Fall 2003) 541 applied for aid; of those 91% were deemed to have need. 100% of freshmen with need received aid; of those 20% had need fully met. *Average percent of need met:* 81% (excluding resources awarded to replace EFC). *Average financial aid package:* $14,736 (excluding resources awarded to replace EFC). 15% of all full-time freshmen had no need and received non-need-based gift aid.
UNDERGRADUATE FINANCIAL AID (Fall 2003) 1,815 applied for aid; of those 93% were deemed to have need. 100% of undergraduates with need received aid; of those 19% had need fully met. *Average percent of need met:* 81% (excluding resources awarded to replace EFC). *Average financial aid package:* $14,714 (excluding resources awarded to replace EFC). 17% of all full-time undergraduates had no need and received non-need-based gift aid.
GIFT AID (NEED-BASED) *Total amount:* $17,603,770 (12% federal, 14% state, 71% institutional, 3% external sources). *Receiving aid:* Freshmen: 83% (493); All full-time undergraduates: 81% (1,684). *Average award:* Freshmen: $10,885; Undergraduates: $10,412. *Scholarships, grants, and awards:* Federal Pell, FSEOG, state, private, college/university gift aid from institutional funds.

GIFT AID (NON-NEED-BASED) *Total amount:* $2,117,385 (18% state, 74% institutional, 8% external sources). *Receiving aid:* Freshmen: 5% (29); Undergraduates: 6% (115). *Average Award:* Freshmen: $7629; *Undergraduates:* $7842. *Scholarships, grants, and awards by category: Academic Interests/ Achievement:* 1,034 awards ($5,229,396 total): general academic interests/ achievements. *Creative Arts/Performance:* 156 awards ($424,359 total): art/fine arts, cinema/film/broadcasting, debating, journalism/publications, music, theater/ drama. *Special Characteristics:* 154 awards ($994,721 total): children and siblings of alumni, children of faculty/staff, ethnic background, international students, relatives of clergy. *Tuition waivers:* Full or partial for children of alumni, employees or children of employees, adult students. *ROTC:* Army cooperative, Air Force cooperative.

LOANS *Student loans:* $10,383,536 (75% need-based, 25% non-need-based). 77% of past graduating class borrowed through all loan programs. *Average indebtedness per student:* $15,944. *Average need-based loan:* Freshmen: $4022; Undergraduates: $4521. *Parent loans:* $2,506,197 (37% need-based, 63% non-need-based). *Programs:* FFEL (Subsidized and Unsubsidized Stafford, PLUS), Perkins, alternative loans.

WORK-STUDY *Federal work-study:* Total amount: $168,810; 1,284 jobs averaging $1112. *State or other work-study/employment:* Total amount: $598,727 (45% need-based, 55% non-need-based). 270 part-time jobs averaging $1349.

APPLYING FOR FINANCIAL AID *Required financial aid forms:* FAFSA, institution's own form. *Financial aid deadline:* Continuous. *Notification date:* Continuous beginning 3/15. Students must reply within 4 weeks of notification.

CONTACT Mrs. Sandra S. Pittenger, Director of Student Financial Services, Mount Union College, 1972 Clark Avenue, Alliance, OH 44601-3993, 330-823-2674 or toll-free 800-334-6682 (in-state), 800-992-6682 (out-of-state). *Fax:* 330-829-2814. *E-mail:* pittenss@muc.edu.

MOUNT VERNON NAZARENE UNIVERSITY
Mount Vernon, OH

Tuition & fees: $14,976	Average undergraduate aid package: $10,581

ABOUT THE INSTITUTION Independent Nazarene, coed. Awards: associate, bachelor's, and master's degrees. 67 undergraduate majors. Total enrollment: 2,455. Undergraduates: 2,166. Freshmen: 304. Federal methodology is used as a basis for awarding need-based institutional aid.

UNDERGRADUATE EXPENSES for 2004–05 *Application fee:* $25. *Comprehensive fee:* $19,710 includes full-time tuition ($14,482), mandatory fees ($494), and room and board ($4734). *College room only:* $2619. Full-time tuition and fees vary according to course load, program, and reciprocity agreements. Room and board charges vary according to housing facility. *Part-time tuition:* $517 per credit hour. Part-time tuition and fees vary according to course load, program, and reciprocity agreements. *Payment plan:* Installment.

FRESHMAN FINANCIAL AID (Fall 2003) 351 applied for aid; of those 86% were deemed to have need. 100% of freshmen with need received aid; of those 28% had need fully met. *Average percent of need met:* 77% (excluding resources awarded to replace EFC). *Average financial aid package:* $10,969 (excluding resources awarded to replace EFC). 13% of all full-time freshmen had no need and received non-need-based gift aid.

UNDERGRADUATE FINANCIAL AID (Fall 2003) 1,325 applied for aid; of those 78% were deemed to have need. 100% of undergraduates with need received aid; of those 27% had need fully met. *Average percent of need met:* 83% (excluding resources awarded to replace EFC). *Average financial aid package:* $10,581 (excluding resources awarded to replace EFC). 42% of all full-time undergraduates had no need and received non-need-based gift aid.

GIFT AID (NEED-BASED) *Total amount:* $3,588,838 (44% federal, 19% state, 19% institutional, 18% external sources). *Receiving aid:* Freshmen: 81% (303); All full-time undergraduates: 54% (1,036). *Average award:* Freshmen: $5508; Undergraduates: $5355. *Scholarships, grants, and awards:* Federal Pell, FSEOG, state, private, college/university gift aid from institutional funds.

GIFT AID (NON-NEED-BASED) *Total amount:* $4,576,714 (37% state, 58% institutional, 5% external sources). *Receiving aid:* Freshmen: 11% (42); Undergraduates: 8% (149). *Average Award:* Freshmen: $1405; *Undergraduates:* $1406. *Scholarships, grants, and awards by category: Academic Interests/ Achievement:* 553 awards ($1,066,600 total): business, computer science, education, general academic interests/achievements, health fields, home economics, religion/biblical studies. *Creative Arts/Performance:* 16 awards ($7600 total): music. *Special Achievements/Activities:* 62 awards ($52,882 total): general special achievements/activities, junior miss, religious involvement. *Special Characteristics:* 658 awards ($1,386,320 total): children of faculty/staff, international students, local/state students, relatives of clergy, religious affiliation,

siblings of current students, spouses of current students, veterans, veterans' children. *Tuition waivers:* Full or partial for employees or children of employees, senior citizens.

LOANS *Student loans:* $9,499,808 (69% need-based, 31% non-need-based). 80% of past graduating class borrowed through all loan programs. *Average indebtedness per student:* $17,796. *Average need-based loan:* Freshmen: $1073; Undergraduates: $831. *Parent loans:* $2,551,919 (100% non-need-based). *Programs:* FFEL (Subsidized and Unsubsidized Stafford, PLUS), Perkins, alternative loans.

WORK-STUDY *Federal work-study:* Total amount: $257,969; 180 jobs averaging $1472. *State or other work-study/employment:* Total amount: $414,551 (96% need-based, 4% non-need-based). 317 part-time jobs averaging $1534.

ATHLETIC AWARDS *Total amount:* $419,980 (18% need-based, 82% non-need-based).

APPLYING FOR FINANCIAL AID *Required financial aid forms:* FAFSA, institution's own form. *Financial aid deadline (priority):* 3/15. *Notification date:* Continuous. Students must reply within 2 weeks of notification.

CONTACT Steve Tracht, Financial Planning Counselor, Mount Vernon Nazarene University, 800 Martinsburg Road, Mount Vernon, OH 43050-9500, 740-392-6868 Ext. 4525 or toll-free 866-462-6868. *Fax:* 740-393-0511. *E-mail:* stracht@ mvnu.edu.

MUHLENBERG COLLEGE
Allentown, PA

ABOUT THE INSTITUTION Independent religious, coed. Awards: bachelor's degrees. 41 undergraduate majors. Total enrollment: 2,446. Undergraduates: 2,446. Freshmen: 559.

GIFT AID (NEED-BASED) *Scholarships, grants, and awards:* Federal Pell, FSEOG, state, private, college/university gift aid from institutional funds.

GIFT AID (NON-NEED-BASED) *Scholarships, grants, and awards by category: Academic Interests/Achievement:* general academic interests/achievements. *Creative Arts/Performance:* art/fine arts, dance, music, performing arts, theater/ drama. *Special Achievements/Activities:* leadership, memberships. *Special Characteristics:* relatives of clergy.

LOANS *Programs:* FFEL (Subsidized and Unsubsidized Stafford, PLUS), Perkins.

WORK-STUDY *Federal work-study:* Total amount: $250,000; jobs available. *State or other work-study/employment:* Total amount: $204,055 (26% need-based, 74% non-need-based). Part-time jobs available.

APPLYING FOR FINANCIAL AID *Required financial aid forms:* FAFSA, institution's own form, CSS Financial Aid PROFILE, noncustodial (divorced/separated) parent's statement, business/farm supplement.

CONTACT Mr. Greg Mitton, Director of Financial Aid, Muhlenberg College, 2400 Chew Street, Allentown, PA 18104-5586, 484-664-3175. *Fax:* 484-664-3234. *E-mail:* mitton@muhlenberg.edu.

MULTNOMAH BIBLE COLLEGE AND BIBLICAL SEMINARY
Portland, OR

Tuition & fees: $11,090	Average undergraduate aid package: $7858

ABOUT THE INSTITUTION Independent interdenominational, coed. Awards: bachelor's, master's, and first professional degrees and post-bachelor's certificates. 13 undergraduate majors. Total enrollment: 763. Undergraduates: 566. Freshmen: 95. Federal methodology is used as a basis for awarding need-based institutional aid.

UNDERGRADUATE EXPENSES for 2004–05 *Application fee:* $40. *Comprehensive fee:* $15,980 includes full-time tuition ($11,090) and room and board ($4890). Room and board charges vary according to board plan and housing facility. *Part-time tuition:* $460 per semester hour. Part-time tuition and fees vary according to course load. *Payment plan:* Installment.

FRESHMAN FINANCIAL AID (Fall 2004, est.) 74 applied for aid; of those 82% were deemed to have need. 100% of freshmen with need received aid; of those 11% had need fully met. *Average percent of need met:* 48% (excluding resources awarded to replace EFC). *Average financial aid package:* $6272 (excluding resources awarded to replace EFC). 21% of all full-time freshmen had no need and received non-need-based gift aid.

UNDERGRADUATE FINANCIAL AID (Fall 2004, est.) 451 applied for aid; of those 90% were deemed to have need. 100% of undergraduates with need received aid; of those 6% had need fully met. *Average percent of need met:*

57% (excluding resources awarded to replace EFC). *Average financial aid package:* $7858 (excluding resources awarded to replace EFC). 14% of all full-time undergraduates had no need and received non-need-based gift aid.

GIFT AID (NEED-BASED) *Total amount:* $1,639,345 (42% federal, 45% institutional, 13% external sources). *Receiving aid:* Freshmen: 76% (59); All full-time undergraduates: 79% (374). *Average award:* Freshmen: $3891; Undergraduates: $4262. *Scholarships, grants, and awards:* Federal Pell, FSEOG, private, college/university gift aid from institutional funds.

GIFT AID (NON-NEED-BASED) *Total amount:* $183,076 (30% institutional, 70% external sources). *Receiving aid:* Freshmen: 4% (3); Undergraduates: 1% (6). *Average Award:* Freshmen: $9605; Undergraduates: $9903. *Scholarships, grants, and awards by category: Academic Interests/Achievement:* 71 awards ($177,370 total): communication, general academic interests/achievements, religion/biblical studies. *Special Characteristics:* children of current students, international students, religious affiliation, siblings of current students. *Tuition waivers:* Full or partial for employees or children of employees.

LOANS *Student loans:* $2,517,739 (87% need-based, 13% non-need-based). 82% of past graduating class borrowed through all loan programs. *Average indebtedness per student:* $19,783. *Average need-based loan:* Freshmen: $2334; Undergraduates: $3633. *Parent loans:* $887,503 (100% non-need-based). *Programs:* FFEL (Subsidized and Unsubsidized Stafford, PLUS).

WORK-STUDY *Federal work-study:* Total amount: $165,136; 85 jobs averaging $2000.

APPLYING FOR FINANCIAL AID *Required financial aid forms:* FAFSA, institution's own form. *Financial aid deadline (priority):* 3/1. *Notification date:* Continuous beginning 4/1. Students must reply within 3 weeks of notification.

CONTACT Mr. David Allen, Director of Financial Aid, Multnomah Bible College and Biblical Seminary, 8435 Northeast Glisan Street, Portland, OR 97220-5898, 503-251-5335 or toll-free 800-275-4672. *Fax:* 503-254-1268.

MURRAY STATE UNIVERSITY
Murray, KY

Tuition & fees (KY res): $3984	Average undergraduate aid package: $4612

ABOUT THE INSTITUTION State-supported, coed. Awards: bachelor's and master's degrees and post-master's certificates. 114 undergraduate majors. Total enrollment: 10,120. Undergraduates: 8,363. Freshmen: 1,426. Federal methodology is used as a basis for awarding need-based institutional aid.

UNDERGRADUATE EXPENSES for 2004–05 *Application fee:* $25. *Tuition, state resident:* full-time $3420; part-time $143 per hour. *Tuition, nonresident:* full-time $5600; part-time $272 per hour. *Required fees:* full-time $564; $23 per hour. Full-time tuition and fees vary according to reciprocity agreements. Part-time tuition and fees vary according to reciprocity agreements. *College room and board:* $4510; *room only:* $2256. Room and board charges vary according to board plan. *Payment plan:* Installment.

GIFT AID (NEED-BASED) *Total amount:* $10,776,635 (65% federal, 16% state, 11% institutional, 8% external sources). *Receiving aid:* Freshmen: 34% (479); All full-time undergraduates: 30% (2,106). *Average award:* Freshmen: $2257; Undergraduates: $2181. *Scholarships, grants, and awards:* Federal Pell, FSEOG, state, private, college/university gift aid from institutional funds.

GIFT AID (NON-NEED-BASED) *Total amount:* $8,593,846 (47% state, 36% institutional, 17% external sources). *Receiving aid:* Freshmen: 24% (345); Undergraduates: 21% (1,487). *Average Award:* Freshmen: $2517; Undergraduates: $2553. *Scholarships, grants, and awards by category: Academic Interests/Achievement:* 2,580 awards ($2,920,000 total): agriculture, biological sciences, business, communication, computer science, education, engineering/technologies, English, foreign languages, general academic interests/achievements, health fields, humanities, international studies, library science, mathematics. *Creative Arts/Performance:* 130 awards ($101,000 total): applied art and design, art/fine arts, creative writing, dance, debating, general creative arts/performance, journalism/publications, music, theater/drama. *Special Achievements/Activities:* 291 awards ($376,000 total): general special achievements/activities, junior miss, leadership, rodeo. *Special Characteristics:* 1,180 awards ($2,315,000 total): adult students, children and siblings of alumni, children of faculty/staff, general special characteristics, handicapped students, international students, local/state students, members of minority groups. *Tuition waivers:* Full or partial for children of alumni, employees or children of employees, senior citizens. *ROTC:* Army cooperative.

LOANS *Student loans:* $19,722,687 (61% need-based, 39% non-need-based). 54% of past graduating class borrowed through all loan programs. *Average indebtedness per student:* $14,488. *Average need-based loan:* Freshmen: $1350;

Undergraduates: $1950. *Parent loans:* $1,268,509 (100% non-need-based). *Programs:* FFEL (Subsidized and Unsubsidized Stafford, PLUS), Perkins, Federal Nursing, college/university.

ATHLETIC AWARDS *Total amount:* $2,344,565 (30% need-based, 70% non-need-based).

APPLYING FOR FINANCIAL AID *Required financial aid forms:* FAFSA, institution's own form. *Financial aid deadline (priority):* 4/1. *Notification date:* Continuous beginning 4/15.

CONTACT Charles Vinson, Director of Student Financial Aid, Murray State University, B2 Sparks Hall, Murray, KY 42071-0009, 270-762-2546 or toll-free 800-272-4678. *Fax:* 270-762-3116. *E-mail:* charles.vinson@murraystate.edu.

MUSICIANS INSTITUTE
Hollywood, CA

ABOUT THE INSTITUTION Proprietary, coed. Awards: associate and bachelor's degrees. 1 undergraduate major. Total enrollment: 650. Undergraduates: 650.

GIFT AID (NEED-BASED) *Scholarships, grants, and awards:* Federal Pell, FSEOG, state.

LOANS *Programs:* FFEL (Subsidized and Unsubsidized Stafford, PLUS), alternative loans.

APPLYING FOR FINANCIAL AID *Required financial aid form:* FAFSA.

CONTACT Director of Financial Aid, Musicians Institute, 1655 North McCadden Place, Hollywood, CA 90028, 323-462-1384 or toll-free 800-255-PLAY.

MUSKINGUM COLLEGE
New Concord, OH

Tuition & fees: $15,630	Average undergraduate aid package: $14,009

ABOUT THE INSTITUTION Independent religious, coed. Awards: bachelor's and master's degrees. 59 undergraduate majors. Total enrollment: 2,142. Undergraduates: 1,622. Freshmen: 386. Federal methodology is used as a basis for awarding need-based institutional aid.

UNDERGRADUATE EXPENSES for 2004–05 *Comprehensive fee:* $21,830 includes full-time tuition ($14,920), mandatory fees ($710), and room and board ($6200). Room and board charges vary according to board plan and housing facility. *Part-time tuition:* $280 per credit hour. Part-time tuition and fees vary according to course load. *Payment plan:* Installment.

GIFT AID (NEED-BASED) *Total amount:* $12,568,000 (11% federal, 19% state, 67% institutional, 3% external sources). *Receiving aid:* Freshmen: 79% (368); All full-time undergraduates: 77% (1,225). *Average award:* Freshmen: $11,221; Undergraduates: $10,461. *Scholarships, grants, and awards:* Federal Pell, FSEOG, state, private, college/university gift aid from institutional funds.

GIFT AID (NON-NEED-BASED) *Total amount:* $1,900,100 (20% state, 78% institutional, 2% external sources). *Receiving aid:* Freshmen: 78% (364); Undergraduates: 77% (1,214). *Average Award:* Freshmen: $4607; Undergraduates:* $5092. *Scholarships, grants, and awards by category: Academic Interests/Achievement:* 620 awards ($3,750,000 total): biological sciences, computer science, general academic interests/achievements, mathematics, physical sciences, premedicine. *Creative Arts/Performance:* 190 awards ($282,000 total): art/fine arts, debating, journalism/publications, music, theater/drama. *Special Characteristics:* 905 awards ($955,000 total): children and siblings of alumni, ethnic background, local/state students, members of minority groups, religious affiliation, siblings of current students. *Tuition waivers:* Full or partial for employees or children of employees, senior citizens.

LOANS *Student loans:* $6,713,750 (65% need-based, 35% non-need-based). 76% of past graduating class borrowed through all loan programs. *Average indebtedness per student:* $17,027. *Average need-based loan:* Freshmen: $3356; Undergraduates: $4121. *Parent loans:* $3,071,700 (100% non-need-based). *Programs:* FFEL (Subsidized and Unsubsidized Stafford, PLUS), Perkins.

APPLYING FOR FINANCIAL AID *Required financial aid form:* FAFSA. *Financial aid deadline (priority):* 3/15. *Notification date:* Continuous beginning 3/1. Students must reply by 5/1.

CONTACT Mr. Jeff Zellers, Dean of Enrollment, Muskingum College, 163 Stormont Street, New Concord, OH 43762, 740-826-8139 or toll-free 800-752-6082. *Fax:* 740-826-8100. *E-mail:* jzellers@muskingum.edu.

NAES COLLEGE
Chicago, IL

ABOUT THE INSTITUTION Independent, coed. Awards: bachelor's degrees. 1 undergraduate major. Total enrollment: 70. Undergraduates: 70. Freshmen: 1.

GIFT AID (NEED-BASED) *Scholarships, grants, and awards:* Federal Pell, FSEOG, state, private, college/university gift aid from institutional funds, tribal scholarships.

APPLYING FOR FINANCIAL AID *Required financial aid form:* FAFSA.

CONTACT Ms. Yvonne Fuerte, Financial Aid Officer, NAES College, 2838 West Peterson Avenue, Chicago, IL 60659-3813, 773-761-5000 Ext. 23. *Fax:* 773-761-3808.

NAROPA UNIVERSITY
Boulder, CO

Tuition & fees: $16,548	Average undergraduate aid package: $16,641

ABOUT THE INSTITUTION Independent, coed. Awards: bachelor's, master's, and first professional degrees and post-bachelor's and post-master's certificates. 9 undergraduate majors. Total enrollment: 1,219. Undergraduates: 470. Freshmen: 54. Federal methodology is used as a basis for awarding need-based institutional aid.

UNDERGRADUATE EXPENSES for 2004–05 *Application fee:* $50. *Comprehensive fee:* $23,784 includes full-time tuition ($15,988), mandatory fees ($560), and room and board ($7236). *College room only:* $4437. Full-time tuition and fees vary according to course load. Room and board charges vary according to board plan. *Part-time tuition:* $571 per semester hour. *Part-time fees:* $280 per term. Part-time tuition and fees vary according to course load. *Payment plan:* Installment.

FRESHMAN FINANCIAL AID (Fall 2004, est.) 34 applied for aid; of those 76% were deemed to have need. 100% of freshmen with need received aid; of those 12% had need fully met. *Average percent of need met:* 61% (excluding resources awarded to replace EFC). *Average financial aid package:* $15,239 (excluding resources awarded to replace EFC).

UNDERGRADUATE FINANCIAL AID (Fall 2004, est.) 294 applied for aid; of those 91% were deemed to have need. 100% of undergraduates with need received aid; of those 4% had need fully met. *Average percent of need met:* 70% (excluding resources awarded to replace EFC). *Average financial aid package:* $16,641 (excluding resources awarded to replace EFC).

GIFT AID (NEED-BASED) *Total amount:* $2,067,825 (30% federal, 67% institutional, 3% external sources). *Receiving aid:* Freshmen: 46% (24); All full-time undergraduates: 58% (227). *Average award:* Freshmen: $10,940; Undergraduates: $8729. *Scholarships, grants, and awards:* Federal Pell, FSEOG, private, college/university gift aid from institutional funds.

GIFT AID (NON-NEED-BASED) *Tuition waivers:* Full or partial for employees or children of employees.

LOANS *Student loans:* $2,309,145 (95% need-based, 5% non-need-based). 70% of past graduating class borrowed through all loan programs. *Average indebtedness per student:* $20,768. *Average need-based loan:* Freshmen: $5841; Undergraduates: $7809. *Parent loans:* $1,784,157 (52% need-based, 48% non-need-based). *Programs:* FFEL (Subsidized and Unsubsidized Stafford, PLUS), Perkins.

WORK-STUDY *Federal work-study:* Total amount: $748,982; 189 jobs averaging $3963. *State or other work-study/employment:* Total amount: $57,658 (100% need-based). 10 part-time jobs averaging $5766.

APPLYING FOR FINANCIAL AID *Required financial aid form:* FAFSA. *Financial aid deadline (priority):* 3/1. *Notification date:* Continuous. Students must reply within 4 weeks of notification.

CONTACT Financial Aid Office, Naropa University, 2130 Arapahoe Avenue, Boulder, CO 80302-6697, 303-546-3534 or toll-free 800-772-0410 (out-of-state). *Fax:* 303-442-0792. *E-mail:* finaid@naropa.edu.

NATIONAL AMERICAN UNIVERSITY
Colorado Springs, CO

CONTACT Financial Aid Coordinator, National American University, 2577 North Chelton Road, Colorado Springs, CO 80909, 719-471-4205.

NATIONAL AMERICAN UNIVERSITY
Denver, CO

CONTACT Cheryl Schunneman, Director of Financial Aid, National American University, 321 Kansas City Street, Rapid City, SD 57701, 605-394-4800.

NATIONAL AMERICAN UNIVERSITY
Roseville, MN

CONTACT Financial Aid Office, National American University, 1500 West Highway 36, Roseville, MN 55113-4035, 651-644-1265.

NATIONAL AMERICAN UNIVERSITY
Kansas City, MO

CONTACT Mary Anderson, Coordinator of Financial Aid, National American University, 4200 Blue Ridge, Kansas City, MO 64133, 816-353-4554. *Fax:* 816-353-1176.

NATIONAL AMERICAN UNIVERSITY
Albuquerque, NM

CONTACT Director of Financial Aid, National American University, 321 Kansas City Street, Rapid City, SD 57701, 605-394-4800 or toll-free 800-843-8892.

NATIONAL AMERICAN UNIVERSITY
Rapid City, SD

CONTACT Financial Aid Director, National American University, PO Box 1780, Rapid City, SD 57709-1780, 605-721-5213 or toll-free 800-843-8892.

NATIONAL AMERICAN UNIVERSITY–SIOUX FALLS BRANCH
Sioux Falls, SD

CONTACT Ms. Rhonda Kohnen, Financial Aid Coordinator, National American University–Sioux Falls Branch, 2801 South Kiwanis Avenue, Suite 100, Sioux Falls, SD 57105-4293, 605-334-5430 or toll-free 800-388-5430 (out-of-state). *Fax:* 605-334-1575. *E-mail:* rkohnen@national.edu.

THE NATIONAL HISPANIC UNIVERSITY
San Jose, CA

Tuition & fees: N/R	Average undergraduate aid package: N/A

ABOUT THE INSTITUTION Independent, coed. Awards: associate and bachelor's degrees and post-bachelor's certificates. 5 undergraduate majors. Total enrollment: 469. Undergraduates: 293. Freshmen: 34. Federal methodology is used as a basis for awarding need-based institutional aid.

FRESHMAN FINANCIAL AID (Fall 2004, est.) 20 applied for aid; of those 95% were deemed to have need. 100% of freshmen with need received aid. *Average percent of need met:* 25% (excluding resources awarded to replace EFC).

UNDERGRADUATE FINANCIAL AID (Fall 2004, est.) 109 applied for aid; of those 89% were deemed to have need. 93% of undergraduates with need received aid. *Average percent of need met:* 30% (excluding resources awarded to replace EFC). 9% of all full-time undergraduates had no need and received non-need-based gift aid.

GIFT AID (NEED-BASED) *Total amount:* $601,000 (72% federal, 14% state, 14% institutional). *Receiving aid:* Freshmen: 95% (19); All full-time undergraduates: 60% (85). *Average award:* Freshmen: $1900; Undergraduates: $2500. *Scholarships, grants, and awards:* Federal Pell, FSEOG, state, private, college/university gift aid from institutional funds.

GIFT AID (NON-NEED-BASED) *Total amount:* $220,000 (100% institutional). *Receiving aid:* Undergraduates: 7% (10). *Average Award:* Undergraduates: $3000. *Scholarships, grants, and awards by category: Academic Interests/Achievement:* business, computer science, education. *Special Characteristics:* veterans, veterans' children.

LOANS *Student loans:* $385,000 (68% need-based, 32% non-need-based). *Average need-based loan:* Undergraduates: $3300. *Parent loans:* $5500 (100% non-need-based). *Programs:* FFEL (Subsidized and Unsubsidized Stafford, PLUS).
WORK-STUDY *Federal work-study:* Total amount: $12,000; 3 jobs averaging $3000.
APPLYING FOR FINANCIAL AID *Required financial aid form:* FAFSA. *Financial aid deadline:* Continuous. *Notification date:* Continuous beginning 6/1. Students must reply by 8/1 or within 2 weeks of notification.
CONTACT Takeo Kubo, Director of Financial Aid and Scholarship, The National Hispanic University, 14271 Story Road, San Jose, CA 95127-3823, 408-273-2708. *Fax:* 408-254-1369. *E-mail:* tkubo@nhu.edu.

NATIONAL-LOUIS UNIVERSITY
Chicago, IL

ABOUT THE INSTITUTION Independent, coed. Awards: bachelor's, master's, and doctoral degrees and post-bachelor's and post-master's certificates. 26 undergraduate majors. Total enrollment: 7,665. Undergraduates: 2,534. Freshmen: 67.
GIFT AID (NEED-BASED) *Scholarships, grants, and awards:* Federal Pell, FSEOG, state, private, college/university gift aid from institutional funds.
GIFT AID (NON-NEED-BASED) *Scholarships, grants, and awards by category:* Academic Interests/Achievement: general academic interests/achievements.
LOANS *Programs:* FFEL (Subsidized and Unsubsidized Stafford, PLUS), Perkins.
WORK-STUDY Federal work-study jobs available.
APPLYING FOR FINANCIAL AID *Required financial aid form:* FAFSA.
CONTACT Toni Todd, Student Finance Officer, National-Louis University, 1000 Capitol Drive, Wheeling, IL 60090, 847-465-0575 Ext. 5350 or toll-free 888-NLU-TODAY (in-state), 800-443-5522 (out-of-state).

NATIONAL UNIVERSITY
La Jolla, CA

ABOUT THE INSTITUTION Independent, coed. Awards: associate, bachelor's, and master's degrees and post-bachelor's certificates. 28 undergraduate majors. Total enrollment: 25,684. Undergraduates: 5,820. Freshmen: 228.
GIFT AID (NEED-BASED) *Scholarships, grants, and awards:* Federal Pell, FSEOG, state, private, college/university gift aid from institutional funds.
GIFT AID (NON-NEED-BASED) *Scholarships, grants, and awards by category:* Academic Interests/Achievement: general academic interests/achievements. Special Achievements/Activities: leadership.
LOANS *Programs:* Federal Direct (Subsidized and Unsubsidized Stafford), FFEL (Subsidized and Unsubsidized Stafford, PLUS), Perkins, college/university.
APPLYING FOR FINANCIAL AID *Required financial aid forms:* FAFSA, institution's own form.
CONTACT Financial Aid Office, National University, 11255 North Torrey Pines Road, La Jolla, CA 92037-1011, 858-642-8500 or toll-free 800-NAT-UNIV. *Fax:* 858-642-8720.

NAZARENE BIBLE COLLEGE
Colorado Springs, CO

Tuition & fees: $7340	Average undergraduate aid package: N/A

ABOUT THE INSTITUTION Independent religious, coed. Awards: associate and bachelor's degrees. 6 undergraduate majors. Total enrollment: 566. Undergraduates: 566. Freshmen: 32. Federal methodology is used as a basis for awarding need-based institutional aid.
UNDERGRADUATE EXPENSES for 2004–05 *Application fee:* $20. *Tuition:* full-time $7040; part-time $220 per semester hour. *Required fees:* full-time $300; $10 per term part-time. *Payment plan:* Installment.
FRESHMAN FINANCIAL AID (Fall 2003) 27 applied for aid; of those 100% were deemed to have need. 100% of freshmen with need received aid.
UNDERGRADUATE FINANCIAL AID (Fall 2003) 180 applied for aid; of those 100% were deemed to have need. 100% of undergraduates with need received aid.
GIFT AID (NEED-BASED) *Total amount:* $800,757 (83% federal, 16% institutional, 1% external sources). *Receiving aid:* Freshmen: 66% (19); All full-time undergraduates: 48% (98). *Scholarships, grants, and awards:* Federal Pell, FSEOG, college/university gift aid from institutional funds.

GIFT AID (NON-NEED-BASED) *Receiving aid:* Freshmen: 66% (19); Undergraduates: 48% (98). *Scholarships, grants, and awards by category:* Academic Interests/Achievement: 72 awards ($25,101 total): religion/biblical studies. *Tuition waivers:* Full or partial for employees or children of employees.
LOANS *Student loans:* $1,703,877 (64% need-based, 36% non-need-based). 72% of past graduating class borrowed through all loan programs. *Average indebtedness per student:* $19,141. *Parent loans:* $12,867 (100% non-need-based). *Programs:* FFEL (Subsidized and Unsubsidized Stafford, PLUS), Perkins, college/university.
WORK-STUDY *Federal work-study:* Total amount: $18,549; 8 jobs averaging $2300.
APPLYING FOR FINANCIAL AID *Required financial aid form:* FAFSA. *Financial aid deadline:* Continuous. *Notification date:* Continuous beginning 2/1.
CONTACT Mr. Malcolm Britton, Director of Financial Aid, Nazarene Bible College, 1111 Academy Park Loop, Colorado Springs, CO 80910-3717, 719-884-5051 or toll-free 800-873-3873. *Fax:* 719-884-5199.

NAZARETH COLLEGE OF ROCHESTER
Rochester, NY

Tuition & fees: $18,776	Average undergraduate aid package: $14,497

ABOUT THE INSTITUTION Independent, coed. Awards: bachelor's and master's degrees and post-master's certificates. 70 undergraduate majors. Total enrollment: 3,140. Undergraduates: 2,035. Freshmen: 449. Institutional methodology is used as a basis for awarding need-based institutional aid.
UNDERGRADUATE EXPENSES for 2005–06 *Application fee:* $40. *Comprehensive fee:* $26,616 includes full-time tuition ($18,040), mandatory fees ($736), and room and board ($7840). *College room only:* $4420. Room and board charges vary according to board plan and housing facility. *Part-time tuition:* $439 per credit hour. *Part-time fees:* $516 per year. *Payment plan:* Installment.
FRESHMAN FINANCIAL AID (Fall 2004, est.) 348 applied for aid; of those 87% were deemed to have need. 100% of freshmen with need received aid. *Average percent of need met:* 83% (excluding resources awarded to replace EFC). *Average financial aid package:* $14,219 (excluding resources awarded to replace EFC). 20% of all full-time freshmen had no need and received non-need-based gift aid.
UNDERGRADUATE FINANCIAL AID (Fall 2004, est.) 1,565 applied for aid; of those 90% were deemed to have need. 100% of undergraduates with need received aid. *Average percent of need met:* 80% (excluding resources awarded to replace EFC). *Average financial aid package:* $14,497 (excluding resources awarded to replace EFC). 14% of all full-time undergraduates had no need and received non-need-based gift aid.
GIFT AID (NEED-BASED) *Total amount:* $14,006,901 (12% federal, 19% state, 66% institutional, 3% external sources). *Receiving aid:* Freshmen: 79% (303); All full-time undergraduates: 80% (1,396). *Average award:* Freshmen: $9785; Undergraduates: $9354. *Scholarships, grants, and awards:* Federal Pell, FSEOG, state, private, college/university gift aid from institutional funds.
GIFT AID (NON-NEED-BASED) *Total amount:* $2,208,139 (6% state, 87% institutional, 7% external sources). *Receiving aid:* Freshmen: 9% (36); Undergraduates: 6% (100). *Average Award:* Freshmen: $7311; Undergraduates: $6424. *Scholarships, grants, and awards by category:* Academic Interests/Achievement: 736 awards ($4,178,099 total): general academic interests/achievements. Creative Arts/Performance: 106 awards ($252,050 total): art/fine arts, music, theater/drama. Special Characteristics: 186 awards ($831,614 total): children and siblings of alumni, children of faculty/staff, siblings of current students. *Tuition waivers:* Full or partial for minority students, children of alumni, employees or children of employees. *ROTC:* Army cooperative, Air Force cooperative.
LOANS *Student loans:* $11,759,253 (76% need-based, 24% non-need-based). 83% of past graduating class borrowed through all loan programs. *Average indebtedness per student:* $23,316. *Average need-based loan:* Freshmen: $3016; Undergraduates: $4670. *Parent loans:* $3,474,821 (30% need-based, 70% non-need-based). *Programs:* FFEL (Subsidized and Unsubsidized Stafford, PLUS), Perkins.
WORK-STUDY *Federal work-study:* Total amount: $1,009,600; 631 jobs averaging $1600.
APPLYING FOR FINANCIAL AID *Required financial aid form:* FAFSA. *Financial aid deadline (priority):* 2/15. *Notification date:* Continuous beginning 3/8. Students must reply by 5/1 or within 2 weeks of notification.

CONTACT Dr. Bruce C. Woolley, Director of Financial Aid, Nazareth College of Rochester, 4245 East Avenue, Rochester, NY 14618-3790, 585-389-2310 or toll-free 800-462-3944 (in-state). *Fax:* 585-389-2317. *E-mail:* bwoolle5@naz.edu.

NEBRASKA CHRISTIAN COLLEGE
Norfolk, NE

Tuition & fees: $6380	Average undergraduate aid package: N/A

ABOUT THE INSTITUTION Independent religious, coed. Awards: associate and bachelor's degrees. 10 undergraduate majors. Total enrollment: 167. Undergraduates: 167. Freshmen: 60. Both federal and institutional methodology are used as a basis for awarding need-based institutional aid.

UNDERGRADUATE EXPENSES for 2004–05 *Application fee:* $25. *Comprehensive fee:* $10,130 includes full-time tuition ($5760), mandatory fees ($620), and room and board ($3750). *Part-time tuition:* $192 per credit hour. *Payment plan:* Installment.

FRESHMAN FINANCIAL AID (Fall 2003) 44 applied for aid; of those 82% were deemed to have need. 100% of freshmen with need received aid. 18% of all full-time freshmen had no need and received non-need-based gift aid.

UNDERGRADUATE FINANCIAL AID (Fall 2003) 147 applied for aid; of those 88% were deemed to have need. 100% of undergraduates with need received aid. 11% of all full-time undergraduates had no need and received non-need-based gift aid.

GIFT AID (NEED-BASED) *Total amount:* $656,540 (37% federal, 4% state, 32% institutional, 27% external sources). *Receiving aid:* Freshmen: 64% (28); All full-time undergraduates: 56% (82). *Scholarships, grants, and awards:* Federal Pell, FSEOG, state, private, college/university gift aid from institutional funds.

GIFT AID (NON-NEED-BASED) *Average Award:* Freshmen: $1999; Undergraduates: $2215. *Scholarships, grants, and awards by category:* Academic Interests/Achievement: 131 awards ($195,595 total): general academic interests/achievements. Special Characteristics: 17 awards ($12,096 total): children of faculty/staff, international students, relatives of clergy. *Tuition waivers:* Full or partial for employees or children of employees.

LOANS *Student loans:* $434,574 (100% need-based). 80% of past graduating class borrowed through all loan programs. *Average indebtedness per student:* $11,593. *Average need-based loan:* Freshmen: $2358; Undergraduates: $2958. *Parent loans:* $15,585 (100% need-based). *Programs:* FFEL (Subsidized and Unsubsidized Stafford, PLUS).

WORK-STUDY *Federal work-study:* Total amount: $15,389; 13 jobs averaging $1183.

APPLYING FOR FINANCIAL AID *Required financial aid forms:* FAFSA, institution's own form. *Financial aid deadline (priority):* 6/1. *Notification date:* Continuous.

CONTACT Linda Bigbee, Director of Financial Aid, Nebraska Christian College, 1800 Syracuse Avenue, Norfolk, NE 68701-2458, 402-379-5017. *Fax:* 402-379-5100. *E-mail:* lbigbee@nechristian.edu.

NEBRASKA METHODIST COLLEGE
Omaha, NE

ABOUT THE INSTITUTION Independent religious, coed, primarily women. Awards: associate, bachelor's, and master's degrees and post-master's certificates. 6 undergraduate majors. Total enrollment: 564. Undergraduates: 512. Freshmen: 37.

GIFT AID (NEED-BASED) *Scholarships, grants, and awards:* Federal Pell, FSEOG, state, private, college/university gift aid from institutional funds.

GIFT AID (NON-NEED-BASED) *Scholarships, grants, and awards by category:* Academic Interests/Achievement: general academic interests/achievements.

LOANS *Programs:* FFEL (Subsidized and Unsubsidized Stafford, PLUS), Perkins, Federal Nursing, college/university, alternative loans.

WORK-STUDY *State or other work-study/employment:* Total amount: $5600 (2% need-based, 98% non-need-based). 3 part-time jobs averaging $1600.

APPLYING FOR FINANCIAL AID *Required financial aid forms:* FAFSA, institution's own form.

CONTACT Ms. Brenda Boyd, Financial Aid Coordinator, Nebraska Methodist College, 8501 West Dodge Road, Omaha, NE 68114-3426, 402-354-4874 or toll-free 800-335-5510. *Fax:* 402-354-8893. *E-mail:* bboyd@methodistcollege.edu.

NEBRASKA WESLEYAN UNIVERSITY
Lincoln, NE

Tuition & fees: $17,390	Average undergraduate aid package: $12,263

ABOUT THE INSTITUTION Independent United Methodist, coed. Awards: bachelor's and master's degrees and post-master's certificates. 52 undergraduate majors. Total enrollment: 1,953. Undergraduates: 1,797. Freshmen: 428. Federal methodology is used as a basis for awarding need-based institutional aid.

UNDERGRADUATE EXPENSES for 2004–05 *Application fee:* $20. *Comprehensive fee:* $22,020 includes full-time tuition ($17,090), mandatory fees ($300), and room and board ($4630). Room and board charges vary according to board plan and housing facility. *Part-time tuition:* $645 per hour. Part-time tuition and fees vary according to class time, course load, degree level, location, and program. *Payment plans:* Installment, deferred payment.

FRESHMAN FINANCIAL AID (Fall 2003) 377 applied for aid; of those 84% were deemed to have need. 100% of freshmen with need received aid; of those 15% had need fully met. *Average percent of need met:* 75% (excluding resources awarded to replace EFC). *Average financial aid package:* $12,068 (excluding resources awarded to replace EFC). 25% of all full-time freshmen had no need and received non-need-based gift aid.

UNDERGRADUATE FINANCIAL AID (Fall 2003) 1,282 applied for aid; of those 87% were deemed to have need. 100% of undergraduates with need received aid; of those 18% had need fully met. *Average percent of need met:* 74% (excluding resources awarded to replace EFC). *Average financial aid package:* $12,263 (excluding resources awarded to replace EFC). 22% of all full-time undergraduates had no need and received non-need-based gift aid.

GIFT AID (NEED-BASED) *Total amount:* $9,251,467 (13% federal, 4% state, 79% institutional, 4% external sources). *Receiving aid:* Freshmen: 73% (316); All full-time undergraduates: 70% (1,098). *Average award:* Freshmen: $9164; Undergraduates: $8195. *Scholarships, grants, and awards:* Federal Pell, FSEOG, state, private, college/university gift aid from institutional funds.

GIFT AID (NON-NEED-BASED) *Total amount:* $2,097,215 (93% institutional, 7% external sources). *Receiving aid:* Freshmen: 7% (29); Undergraduates: 4% (68). *Average Award:* Freshmen: $5965; Undergraduates: $5270. *Scholarships, grants, and awards by category:* Academic Interests/Achievement: 1,186 awards ($4,800,300 total): general academic interests/achievements. Creative Arts/Performance: 111 awards ($128,025 total): art/fine arts, music, theater/drama. Special Characteristics: 188 awards ($885,873 total): children of faculty/staff, members of minority groups, relatives of clergy, siblings of current students. *Tuition waivers:* Full or partial for employees or children of employees, adult students, senior citizens. *ROTC:* Army cooperative, Air Force cooperative.

LOANS *Student loans:* $5,601,601 (81% need-based, 19% non-need-based). 69% of past graduating class borrowed through all loan programs. *Average indebtedness per student:* $16,790. *Average need-based loan:* Freshmen: $3456; Undergraduates: $4015. *Parent loans:* $3,377,569 (38% need-based, 62% non-need-based). *Programs:* FFEL (Subsidized and Unsubsidized Stafford, PLUS), Perkins.

WORK-STUDY *Federal work-study:* Total amount: $110,000; jobs available. *State or other work-study/employment:* Total amount: $446,000 (66% need-based, 34% non-need-based). Part-time jobs available.

APPLYING FOR FINANCIAL AID *Required financial aid form:* FAFSA. *Financial aid deadline:* Continuous. *Notification date:* Continuous beginning 3/1. Students must reply within 4 weeks of notification.

CONTACT Mr. Claire Fredstrom, Director of Financial Aid, Nebraska Wesleyan University, 5000 Saint Paul Avenue, Lincoln, NE 68504, 402-465-2212 or toll-free 800-541-3818. *Fax:* 402-465-2179. *E-mail:* cdf@nebrwesleyan.edu.

NER ISRAEL RABBINICAL COLLEGE
Baltimore, MD

CONTACT Mr. Moshe Pelberg, Financial Aid Administrator, Ner Israel Rabbinical College, 400 Mount Wilson Lane, Baltimore, MD 21208, 410-484-7200.

NEUMANN COLLEGE
Aston, PA

Tuition & fees: $17,190	Average undergraduate aid package: $17,000

ABOUT THE INSTITUTION Independent Roman Catholic, coed. Awards: associate, bachelor's, and master's degrees. 18 undergraduate majors. Total enrollment: 2,682. Undergraduates: 2,197. Freshmen: 462. Federal methodology is used as a basis for awarding need-based institutional aid.

UNDERGRADUATE EXPENSES for 2004–05 *Application fee:* $35. *Comprehensive fee:* $24,930 includes full-time tuition ($16,590), mandatory fees ($600), and room and board ($7740). *College room only:* $4600. *Part-time tuition:* $380 per credit. *Payment plan:* Installment.

FRESHMAN FINANCIAL AID (Fall 2003) 416 applied for aid; of those 96% were deemed to have need. 100% of freshmen with need received aid; of those 62% had need fully met. *Average percent of need met:* 65% (excluding resources awarded to replace EFC). *Average financial aid package:* $17,000 (excluding resources awarded to replace EFC).

UNDERGRADUATE FINANCIAL AID (Fall 2003) 1,392 applied for aid; of those 95% were deemed to have need. 100% of undergraduates with need received aid; of those 68% had need fully met. *Average percent of need met:* 65% (excluding resources awarded to replace EFC). *Average financial aid package:* $17,000 (excluding resources awarded to replace EFC).

GIFT AID (NEED-BASED) *Total amount:* $14,126,107 (13% federal, 14% state, 72% institutional, 1% external sources). *Receiving aid:* Freshmen: 76% (353); All full-time undergraduates: 75% (1,234). *Average award:* Freshmen: $17,000; Undergraduates: $17,000. *Scholarships, grants, and awards:* Federal Pell, FSEOG, state, private, college/university gift aid from institutional funds.

GIFT AID (NON-NEED-BASED) *Scholarships, grants, and awards by category: Creative Arts/Performance:* 1 award ($1000 total): music. *Special Characteristics:* 29 awards ($254,386 total): children of faculty/staff. *Tuition waivers:* Full or partial for employees or children of employees. *ROTC:* Army cooperative.

LOANS *Student loans:* $10,103,962 (100% need-based). 70% of past graduating class borrowed through all loan programs. *Average indebtedness per student:* $18,000. *Average need-based loan:* Freshmen: $6625; Undergraduates: $7500. *Parent loans:* $2,871,920 (100% need-based). *Programs:* Federal Direct (Subsidized and Unsubsidized Stafford, PLUS), FFEL (Subsidized and Unsubsidized Stafford, PLUS), Perkins, Federal Nursing.

WORK-STUDY *Federal work-study:* Total amount: $200,000; 120 jobs averaging $1200. *State or other work-study/employment:* Part-time jobs available.

APPLYING FOR FINANCIAL AID *Required financial aid form:* FAFSA. *Financial aid deadline:* Continuous.

CONTACT Joseph Henderson, Director of Financial Aid, Neumann College, One Neumann Drive, Aston, PA 19014-1298, 610-558-5519 or toll-free 800-963-8626.

NEVADA STATE COLLEGE AT HENDERSON
Henderson, NV

CONTACT Financial Aid Office, Nevada State College at Henderson, 1125 Nevada State Drive, Henderson, NV 89015, 702-992-2000.

NEWBERRY COLLEGE
Newberry, SC

CONTACT Ms. Cathryn Stockweather, Director of Financial Aid, Newberry College, 2100 College Street, Newberry, SC 29108, 803-321-5120 or toll-free 800-845-4955 Ext. 5127. *Fax:* 803-321-5627. *E-mail:* cstockweather@newberry.edu.

NEWBURY COLLEGE
Brookline, MA

ABOUT THE INSTITUTION Independent, coed. Awards: associate and bachelor's degrees. 29 undergraduate majors. Total enrollment: 1,161. Undergraduates: 1,161. Freshmen: 400.

GIFT AID (NEED-BASED) *Scholarships, grants, and awards:* Federal Pell, FSEOG, state, private, college/university gift aid from institutional funds.

LOANS *Programs:* FFEL (Subsidized and Unsubsidized Stafford, PLUS), alternative loans, Meta Loans, Signature Loans, Nellie Mae Loans.

APPLYING FOR FINANCIAL AID *Required financial aid form:* FAFSA.

CONTACT Financial Aid Office, Newbury College, 129 Fisher Avenue, Brookline, MA 02445-5796, 617-730-7101 or toll-free 800-NEWBURY. *Fax:* 617-731-9618.

NEW COLLEGE OF CALIFORNIA
San Francisco, CA

CONTACT Director of Student Financial Aid, New College of California, 50 Fell Street, San Francisco, CA 94102-5206, 415-241-1300 Ext. 338 or toll-free 888-437-3460.

NEW COLLEGE OF FLORIDA
Sarasota, FL

Tuition & fees (FL res): $3483   **Average undergraduate aid package: $10,858**

ABOUT THE INSTITUTION State-supported, coed. Awards: bachelor's degrees. 39 undergraduate majors. Total enrollment: 692. Undergraduates: 692. Freshmen: 189. Federal methodology is used as a basis for awarding need-based institutional aid.

UNDERGRADUATE EXPENSES for 2004–05 *Application fee:* $30. *Tuition, state resident:* full-time $3483. *Tuition, nonresident:* full-time $18,543. *College room and board:* $5965; *room only:* $3710. Room and board charges vary according to board plan and housing facility. *Payment plans:* Tuition prepayment, installment, deferred payment.

FRESHMAN FINANCIAL AID (Fall 2004, est.) 118 applied for aid; of those 55% were deemed to have need. 100% of freshmen with need received aid; of those 57% had need fully met. *Average percent of need met:* 93% (excluding resources awarded to replace EFC). *Average financial aid package:* $10,983 (excluding resources awarded to replace EFC). 53% of all full-time freshmen had no need and received non-need-based gift aid.

UNDERGRADUATE FINANCIAL AID (Fall 2004, est.) 368 applied for aid; of those 73% were deemed to have need. 99% of undergraduates with need received aid; of those 60% had need fully met. *Average percent of need met:* 91% (excluding resources awarded to replace EFC). *Average financial aid package:* $10,858 (excluding resources awarded to replace EFC). 46% of all full-time undergraduates had no need and received non-need-based gift aid.

GIFT AID (NEED-BASED) *Total amount:* $1,562,126 (26% federal, 36% state, 35% institutional, 3% external sources). *Receiving aid:* Freshmen: 34% (65); All full-time undergraduates: 38% (261). *Average award:* Freshmen: $7556; Undergraduates: $6864. *Scholarships, grants, and awards:* Federal Pell, state, private, college/university gift aid from institutional funds.

GIFT AID (NON-NEED-BASED) *Total amount:* $1,896,090 (1% federal, 58% state, 37% institutional, 4% external sources). *Receiving aid:* Freshmen: 8% (16); Undergraduates: 6% (41). *Average Award:* Freshmen: $3600; *Undergraduates:* $3463. *Scholarships, grants, and awards by category: Academic Interests/ Achievement:* 530 awards ($1,816,460 total): general academic interests/achievements. *Special Characteristics:* 103 awards ($476,895 total): out-of-state students.

LOANS *Student loans:* $1,189,983 (59% need-based, 41% non-need-based). 44% of past graduating class borrowed through all loan programs. *Average indebtedness per student:* $15,045. *Average need-based loan:* Freshmen: $2417; Undergraduates: $3359. *Parent loans:* $278,419 (16% need-based, 84% non-need-based). *Programs:* FFEL (Subsidized and Unsubsidized Stafford, PLUS).

WORK-STUDY *State or other work-study/employment:* Total amount: $124,169 (100% need-based). 48 part-time jobs averaging $2587.

APPLYING FOR FINANCIAL AID *Required financial aid form:* FAFSA. *Financial aid deadline (priority):* 3/1. *Notification date:* Continuous beginning 3/1. Students must reply by 5/1 or within 4 weeks of notification.

CONTACT Monica Mattscheck, Director of Financial Aid, New College of Florida, 5700 North Tamiami Trail, PME 119, Sarasota, FL 34243-2197, 941-359-4255. *Fax:* 941-359-4229. *E-mail:* ncfinaid@ncf.edu.

NEW ENGLAND COLLEGE
Henniker, NH

Tuition & fees: $23,010   **Average undergraduate aid package: $16,475**

ABOUT THE INSTITUTION Independent, coed. Awards: associate, bachelor's, and master's degrees. 37 undergraduate majors. Total enrollment: 1,329. Undergraduates: 936. Freshmen: 313. Federal methodology is used as a basis for awarding need-based institutional aid.

UNDERGRADUATE EXPENSES for 2005–06 *Application fee:* $30. *Comprehensive fee:* $31,466 includes full-time tuition ($22,366), mandatory fees ($644), and room and board ($8456). *College room only:* $4398. Full-time tuition and fees vary according to course load, degree level, and location. Room and board charges vary according to board plan and housing facility. *Part-time tuition:* $1065 per credit. *Part-time fees:* $198 per term. Part-time tuition and fees vary according to degree level and location. *Payment plan:* Installment.

FRESHMAN FINANCIAL AID (Fall 2004, est.) 231 applied for aid; of those 89% were deemed to have need. 99% of freshmen with need received aid; of those 37% had need fully met. *Average percent of need met:* 81% (excluding resources awarded to replace EFC). *Average financial aid package:* $15,738 (excluding resources awarded to replace EFC). 19% of all full-time freshmen had no need and received non-need-based gift aid.

UNDERGRADUATE FINANCIAL AID (Fall 2004, est.) 645 applied for aid; of those 92% were deemed to have need. 99% of undergraduates with need received aid; of those 32% had need fully met. *Average percent of need met:* 80% (excluding resources awarded to replace EFC). *Average financial aid package:* $16,475 (excluding resources awarded to replace EFC). 19% of all full-time undergraduates had no need and received non-need-based gift aid.

GIFT AID (NEED-BASED) *Total amount:* $5,223,561 (15% federal, 2% state, 82% institutional, 1% external sources). *Receiving aid:* Freshmen: 65% (194); All full-time undergraduates: 65% (572). *Average award:* Freshmen: $10,670; Undergraduates: $10,010. *Scholarships, grants, and awards:* Federal Pell, FSEOG, state, private, college/university gift aid from institutional funds.

GIFT AID (NON-NEED-BASED) *Total amount:* $2,124,694 (95% institutional, 5% external sources). *Receiving aid:* Freshmen: 4% (12); Undergraduates: 4% (39). *Average Award:* Freshmen: $8302; Undergraduates: $8328. *Scholarships, grants, and awards by category: Academic Interests/Achievement:* 20 awards ($157,000 total): biological sciences, business, communication, education, engineering/technologies, English, general academic interests/achievements, humanities, international studies, mathematics, social sciences. *Creative Arts/Performance:* 3 awards ($18,750 total): applied art and design, art/fine arts, creative writing, theater/drama. *Special Achievements/Activities:* 23 awards ($156,175 total): community service, leadership. *Special Characteristics:* 82 awards ($853,908 total): children and siblings of alumni, children of educators, children of faculty/staff, ethnic background, international students, local/state students, parents of current students, siblings of current students. *Tuition waivers:* Full or partial for children of alumni, employees or children of employees, adult students, senior citizens. *ROTC:* Army cooperative, Air Force cooperative.

LOANS *Student loans:* $5,539,341 (55% need-based, 45% non-need-based). 69% of past graduating class borrowed through all loan programs. *Average indebtedness per student:* $35,748. *Average need-based loan:* Freshmen: $7302; Undergraduates: $7373. *Parent loans:* $1,750,172 (22% need-based, 78% non-need-based). *Programs:* FFEL (Subsidized and Unsubsidized Stafford, PLUS), Perkins, state.

WORK-STUDY *Federal work-study:* Total amount: $610,220; 434 jobs averaging $1524. *State or other work-study/employment:* Total amount: $40,000 (27% need-based, 73% non-need-based). 55 part-time jobs averaging $1094.

APPLYING FOR FINANCIAL AID *Required financial aid forms:* FAFSA, institution's own form. *Financial aid deadline (priority):* 4/1. *Notification date:* Continuous beginning 1/2. Students must reply within 2 weeks of notification.

CONTACT Mr. Ray Nault, Student Financial Services, New England College, 7 Main Street, Henniker, NH 03242-3293, 603-428-2226 or toll-free 800-521-7642. *Fax:* 603-428-2404.

NEW ENGLAND CONSERVATORY OF MUSIC
Boston, MA

Tuition & fees: $27,500	Average undergraduate aid package: $17,064

ABOUT THE INSTITUTION Independent, coed. Awards: bachelor's, master's, and doctoral degrees and post-bachelor's certificates. 8 undergraduate majors. Total enrollment: 792. Undergraduates: 406. Freshmen: 100. Federal methodology is used as a basis for awarding need-based institutional aid.

UNDERGRADUATE EXPENSES for 2005–06 *Application fee:* $100. *Comprehensive fee:* $38,450 includes full-time tuition ($27,500) and room and board ($10,950). *Part-time tuition:* $900 per credit.

FRESHMAN FINANCIAL AID (Fall 2004, est.) 81 applied for aid; of those 79% were deemed to have need. 100% of freshmen with need received aid; of those 16% had need fully met. *Average percent of need met:* 54% (excluding resources awarded to replace EFC). *Average financial aid package:* $14,468 (excluding resources awarded to replace EFC). 41% of all full-time freshmen had no need and received non-need-based gift aid.

UNDERGRADUATE FINANCIAL AID (Fall 2004, est.) 247 applied for aid; of those 82% were deemed to have need. 100% of undergraduates with need received aid; of those 15% had need fully met. *Average percent of need met:* 62% (excluding resources awarded to replace EFC). *Average financial aid package:* $17,064 (excluding resources awarded to replace EFC). 39% of all full-time undergraduates had no need and received non-need-based gift aid.

GIFT AID (NEED-BASED) *Total amount:* $2,874,324 (11% federal, 1% state, 84% institutional, 4% external sources). *Receiving aid:* Freshmen: 47% (51); All full-time undergraduates: 59% (196). *Average award:* Freshmen: $10,831; Undergraduates: $12,121. *Scholarships, grants, and awards:* Federal Pell, FSEOG, state, private, college/university gift aid from institutional funds.

GIFT AID (NON-NEED-BASED) *Total amount:* $882,316 (100% institutional). *Receiving aid:* Freshmen: 20% (22); Undergraduates: 21% (71). *Average Award:* Freshmen: $3780; Undergraduates: $5212. *Scholarships, grants, and awards by category: Creative Arts/Performance:* music, theater/drama.

LOANS *Student loans:* $1,311,972 (72% need-based, 28% non-need-based). 58% of past graduating class borrowed through all loan programs. *Average indebtedness per student:* $23,869. *Average need-based loan:* Freshmen: $3653; Undergraduates: $4720. *Parent loans:* $889,342 (51% need-based, 49% non-need-based). *Programs:* FFEL (Subsidized and Unsubsidized Stafford, PLUS), Perkins, state.

WORK-STUDY *Federal work-study:* Total amount: $290,445; 283 jobs averaging $1611. *State or other work-study/employment:* Part-time jobs available.

APPLYING FOR FINANCIAL AID *Required financial aid forms:* FAFSA, institution's own form. *Financial aid deadline (priority):* 2/1. *Notification date:* Continuous beginning 4/1. Students must reply by 5/1 or within 2 weeks of notification.

CONTACT Kenneth T. Ferreira Jr., Director of Financial Aid, New England Conservatory of Music, 290 Huntington Avenue, Boston, MA 02115, 617-585-1110. *Fax:* 617-585-1115. *E-mail:* kferreira@newenglandconservatory.edu.

THE NEW ENGLAND INSTITUTE OF ART
Brookline, MA

CONTACT Ms. Merry Kerber, Director of Financial Aid, The New England Institute of Art, 142 Berkeley Street, Boston, MA 02116-5100, 617-267-7910 or toll-free 800-903=4425 (in-state).

NEW ENGLAND SCHOOL OF COMMUNICATIONS
Bangor, ME

Tuition & fees: $10,045	Average undergraduate aid package: $6320

ABOUT THE INSTITUTION Independent, coed. Awards: associate and bachelor's degrees. 20 undergraduate majors. Total enrollment: 281. Undergraduates: 281. Freshmen: 107. Federal methodology is used as a basis for awarding need-based institutional aid.

UNDERGRADUATE EXPENSES for 2005–06 *Application fee:* $15. *Comprehensive fee:* $15,895 includes full-time tuition ($8890), mandatory fees ($1155), and room and board ($5850). *Part-time tuition:* $275 per credit. Part-time tuition and fees vary according to course load. *Payment plan:* Installment.

FRESHMAN FINANCIAL AID (Fall 2003) 93 applied for aid; of those 95% were deemed to have need. 100% of freshmen with need received aid; of those 35% had need fully met. *Average percent of need met:* 86% (excluding resources awarded to replace EFC). *Average financial aid package:* $4023 (excluding resources awarded to replace EFC).

UNDERGRADUATE FINANCIAL AID (Fall 2003) 186 applied for aid; of those 95% were deemed to have need. 100% of undergraduates with need received aid; of those 39% had need fully met. *Average percent of need met:* 90% (excluding resources awarded to replace EFC). *Average financial aid package:* $6320 (excluding resources awarded to replace EFC).

GIFT AID (NEED-BASED) *Total amount:* $601,497 (73% federal, 18% state, 1% institutional, 8% external sources). *Receiving aid:* Freshmen: 53% (52); All full-time undergraduates: 48% (97). *Average award:* Freshmen: $4000; Undergraduates: $6000. *Scholarships, grants, and awards:* Federal Pell, state, private, college/university gift aid from institutional funds.

GIFT AID (NON-NEED-BASED) *Receiving aid:* Freshmen: 20% (20); Undergraduates: 17% (34). *Scholarships, grants, and awards by category: Academic Interests/Achievement:* 10 awards ($6000 total): communication. *Creative Arts/Performance:* 1 award ($1050 total). *Special Achievements/Activities:* 3 awards ($1000 total): general special achievements/activities. *Tuition waivers:* Full or partial for employees or children of employees.

LOANS *Student loans:* $1,317,246 (87% need-based, 13% non-need-based). 91% of past graduating class borrowed through all loan programs. *Average indebtedness per student:* $21,000. *Average need-based loan:* Freshmen: $2625; Undergraduates: $3100. *Parent loans:* $213,429 (100% need-based). *Programs:* FFEL (Subsidized and Unsubsidized Stafford, PLUS), alternative loans.

WORK-STUDY *State or other work-study/employment:* Total amount: $8360 (100% need-based). 6 part-time jobs averaging $2200.

APPLYING FOR FINANCIAL AID *Required financial aid form:* FAFSA. *Financial aid deadline (priority):* 5/1. *Notification date:* Continuous beginning 5/1. Students must reply within 4 weeks of notification.

CONTACT Ms. Nicole Rediker, Director of Financial Aid, New England School of Communications, One College Circle, Bangor, ME 04401, 888-877-1876. *Fax:* 207-947-3987.

NEW HAMPSHIRE INSTITUTE OF ART
Manchester, NH

ABOUT THE INSTITUTION Proprietary, coed. Awards: bachelor's degrees. 1 undergraduate major. Total enrollment: 180. Undergraduates: 180. Freshmen: 60.

GIFT AID (NEED-BASED) *Scholarships, grants, and awards:* Federal Pell, FSEOG, state, private, college/university gift aid from institutional funds.

GIFT AID (NON-NEED-BASED) *Scholarships, grants, and awards by category:* Creative Arts/Performance: art/fine arts.

LOANS *Programs:* FFEL (Subsidized and Unsubsidized Stafford, PLUS), alternative loans.

WORK-STUDY Federal work-study jobs available.

APPLYING FOR FINANCIAL AID *Required financial aid form:* FAFSA.

CONTACT Linda Lavallee, Director of Financial Aid, New Hampshire Institute of Art, 148 Concord Street, Manchester, NH 03104-4858, 603-623-0313 Ext. 577 or toll-free 866-241-4918 (in-state). *Fax:* 603-647-0658. *E-mail:* llavallee@nhia. edu.

NEW JERSEY CITY UNIVERSITY
Jersey City, NJ

Tuition & fees (NJ res): $6550	Average undergraduate aid package: $7654

ABOUT THE INSTITUTION State-supported, coed. Awards: bachelor's and master's degrees and post-master's certificates. 27 undergraduate majors. Total enrollment: 8,799. Undergraduates: 6,018. Freshmen: 635. Federal methodology is used as a basis for awarding need-based institutional aid.

UNDERGRADUATE EXPENSES for 2004–05 *Application fee:* $35. *Tuition, state resident:* full-time $4860; part-time $162 per credit hour. *Tuition, nonresident:* full-time $9540; part-time $318 per credit hour. *Required fees:* full-time $1690; $54.70 per credit. *College room and board:* $6958; *room only:* $4410.

FRESHMAN FINANCIAL AID (Fall 2003) 570 applied for aid; of those 88% were deemed to have need. 95% of freshmen with need received aid; of those 92% had need fully met. *Average percent of need met:* 68% (excluding resources awarded to replace EFC). *Average financial aid package:* $7983 (excluding resources awarded to replace EFC). 8% of all full-time freshmen had no need and received non-need-based gift aid.

UNDERGRADUATE FINANCIAL AID (Fall 2003) 2,727 applied for aid; of those 91% were deemed to have need. 96% of undergraduates with need received aid; of those 88% had need fully met. *Average percent of need met:* 70% (excluding resources awarded to replace EFC). *Average financial aid package:* $7654 (excluding resources awarded to replace EFC). 7% of all full-time undergraduates had no need and received non-need-based gift aid.

GIFT AID (NEED-BASED) *Total amount:* $14,137,201 (57% federal, 43% state). *Receiving aid:* Freshmen: 58% (383); All full-time undergraduates: 46% (1,886). *Average award:* Freshmen: $6020; Undergraduates: $5562. *Scholarships, grants, and awards:* Federal Pell, FSEOG, state, private, college/university gift aid from institutional funds.

GIFT AID (NON-NEED-BASED) *Total amount:* $990,707 (91% institutional, 9% external sources). *Receiving aid:* Freshmen: 8% (55); Undergraduates: 6% (265). *Average Award:* Freshmen: $3154; Undergraduates: $2591. *Scholarships, grants, and awards by category:* Academic Interests/Achievement: biological sciences, business, communication, education, general academic interests/achievements, mathematics. *Creative Arts/Performance:* art/fine arts, dance, music.

LOANS *Student loans:* $12,838,225 (56% need-based, 44% non-need-based). *Average need-based loan:* Freshmen: $2412; Undergraduates: $3262. *Parent loans:* $453,565 (100% need-based). *Programs:* FFEL (Subsidized and Unsubsidized Stafford, PLUS), Perkins, state.

WORK-STUDY *Federal work-study:* Total amount: $792,265; jobs available.

APPLYING FOR FINANCIAL AID *Required financial aid form:* FAFSA. *Financial aid deadline (priority):* 4/15. *Notification date:* Continuous beginning 4/1.

CONTACT Ms. Carmen Panlilio, Financial Aid Office, New Jersey City University, 2039 Kennedy Boulevard, Jersey City, NJ 07305-1597, 201-200-3173 or toll-free 888-441-NJCU.

NEW JERSEY INSTITUTE OF TECHNOLOGY
Newark, NJ

Tuition & fees (NJ res): $9180	Average undergraduate aid package: $12,676

ABOUT THE INSTITUTION State-supported, coed. Awards: bachelor's, master's, and doctoral degrees and post-bachelor's certificates. 29 undergraduate majors. Total enrollment: 8,249. Undergraduates: 5,366. Freshmen: 673. Federal methodology is used as a basis for awarding need-based financial aid.

UNDERGRADUATE EXPENSES for 2004–05 *Application fee:* $35. *Tuition, state resident:* full-time $7918; part-time $300 per credit. *Tuition, nonresident:* full-time $13,716; part-time $587 per credit. *Required fees:* full-time $1262; $61 per credit or $82 per term part-time. Full-time tuition and fees vary according to course load and degree level. Part-time tuition and fees vary according to course load and degree level. *College room and board:* $8242; *room only:* $5744. Room and board charges vary according to board plan and housing facility. *Payment plan:* Installment.

FRESHMAN FINANCIAL AID (Fall 2004, est.) 666 applied for aid; of those 60% were deemed to have need. 100% of freshmen with need received aid; of those 19% had need fully met. *Average percent of need met:* 87% (excluding resources awarded to replace EFC). *Average financial aid package:* $13,149 (excluding resources awarded to replace EFC). 55% of all full-time freshmen had no need and received non-need-based gift aid.

UNDERGRADUATE FINANCIAL AID (Fall 2004, est.) 4,022 applied for aid; of those 58% were deemed to have need. 100% of undergraduates with need received aid; of those 12% had need fully met. *Average percent of need met:* 82% (excluding resources awarded to replace EFC). *Average financial aid package:* $12,676 (excluding resources awarded to replace EFC). 18% of all full-time undergraduates had no need and received non-need-based gift aid.

GIFT AID (NEED-BASED) *Total amount:* $12,318,271 (34% federal, 56% state, 2% institutional, 8% external sources). *Receiving aid:* Freshmen: 46% (310); All full-time undergraduates: 43% (1,718). *Average award:* Freshmen: $4678; Undergraduates: $2262. *Scholarships, grants, and awards:* Federal Pell, FSEOG, state, private, college/university gift aid from institutional funds.

GIFT AID (NON-NEED-BASED) *Total amount:* $7,129,452 (11% state, 76% institutional, 13% external sources). *Receiving aid:* Freshmen: 30% (198); Undergraduates: 18% (714). *Average Award:* Freshmen: $3818; Undergraduates: $4210. *Scholarships, grants, and awards by category:* Academic Interests/Achievement: architecture, general academic interests/achievements. *Special Characteristics:* out-of-state students. *Tuition waivers:* Full or partial for employees or children of employees. *ROTC:* Air Force.

LOANS *Student loans:* $12,179,308 (56% need-based, 44% non-need-based). 45% of past graduating class borrowed through all loan programs. *Average indebtedness per student:* $15,000. *Average need-based loan:* Freshmen: $2929; Undergraduates: $4071. *Parent loans:* $1,978,307 (100% non-need-based). *Programs:* Federal Direct (Subsidized and Unsubsidized Stafford, PLUS), Perkins, state, college/university.

WORK-STUDY *Federal work-study:* Total amount: $558,057; jobs available. *State or other work-study/employment:* Total amount: $404,000 (100% non-need-based). Part-time jobs available.

ATHLETIC AWARDS *Total amount:* $723,377 (100% non-need-based).

APPLYING FOR FINANCIAL AID *Required financial aid form:* FAFSA. *Financial aid deadline:* 5/15 (priority: 3/15). *Notification date:* Continuous beginning 3/1. Students must reply within 2 weeks of notification.

CONTACT Ms. Kathy Bialk, Director of Financial Aid, New Jersey Institute of Technology, University Heights, Newark, NJ 07102, 973-596-3478 or toll-free 800-925-NJIT. *Fax:* 973-802-1854. *E-mail:* kathy.j.bialk@njit.edu.

NEW LIFE THEOLOGICAL SEMINARY
Charlotte, NC

CONTACT Financial Aid Office, New Life Theological Seminary, PO Box 790106, Charlotte, NC 28206-7901, 704-334-6882.

NEWMAN UNIVERSITY
Wichita, KS

ABOUT THE INSTITUTION Independent Roman Catholic, coed. Awards: associate, bachelor's, and master's degrees. 34 undergraduate majors. Total enrollment: 2,179. Undergraduates: 1,843.
GIFT AID (NEED-BASED) *Scholarships, grants, and awards:* Federal Pell, FSEOG, state, private, college/university gift aid from institutional funds.
GIFT AID (NON-NEED-BASED) *Scholarships, grants, and awards by category: Academic Interests/Achievement:* general academic interests/achievements. *Creative Arts/Performance:* debating, music, theater/drama. *Special Achievements/Activities:* community service, leadership, memberships, religious involvement. *Special Characteristics:* children and siblings of alumni, out-of-state students, religious affiliation, siblings of current students.
LOANS *Programs:* FFEL (Subsidized and Unsubsidized Stafford, PLUS), Perkins.
APPLYING FOR FINANCIAL AID *Required financial aid forms:* FAFSA, institution's own form.
CONTACT April Davis, Senior Financial Aid Counselor, Newman University, 3100 McCormick Avenue, Wichita, KS 67213, 316-942-4291 Ext. 2103 or toll-free 877-NEWMANU Ext. 2144. *Fax:* 316-942-4483.

NEW MEXICO HIGHLANDS UNIVERSITY
Las Vegas, NM

Tuition & fees (NM res): $2300 **Average undergraduate aid package: $8183**

ABOUT THE INSTITUTION State-supported, coed. Awards: associate, bachelor's, and master's degrees. 45 undergraduate majors. Total enrollment: 3,671. Undergraduates: 1,931. Freshmen: 260. Federal methodology is used as a basis for awarding need-based institutional aid.
UNDERGRADUATE EXPENSES for 2004–05 *Application fee:* $15. *Tuition, state resident:* full-time $2280; part-time $95 per hour. *Tuition, nonresident:* full-time $9624; part-time $401 per hour. *College room and board:* $4274; *room only:* $2218.
GIFT AID (NEED-BASED) *Total amount:* $4,693,922 (85% federal, 6% state, 9% external sources). *Receiving aid:* Freshmen: 81% (207); All full-time undergraduates: 62% (931). *Average award:* Freshmen: $4766; Undergraduates: $4588. *Scholarships, grants, and awards:* Federal Pell, FSEOG, state, private, college/university gift aid from institutional funds.
GIFT AID (NON-NEED-BASED) *Total amount:* $1,896,739 (46% federal, 26% state, 18% institutional, 10% external sources). *Receiving aid:* Freshmen: 75% (192); Undergraduates: 43% (646). *Average Award:* Freshmen: $2158; Undergraduates: $2015. *Scholarships, grants, and awards by category: Academic Interests/Achievement:* 238 awards ($189,632 total): biological sciences, business, communication, computer science, education, engineering/technologies, English, foreign languages, general academic interests/achievements, health fields, humanities, mathematics, physical sciences, social sciences. *Creative Arts/Performance:* 41 awards ($28,400 total): art/fine arts, music, performing arts, theater/drama. *Special Characteristics:* 263 awards ($212,536 total): children of faculty/staff, children with a deceased or disabled parent, first-generation college students, international students.
LOANS *Student loans:* $8,123,069 (68% need-based, 32% non-need-based). 44% of past graduating class borrowed through all loan programs. *Average indebtedness per student:* $12,147. *Average need-based loan:* Freshmen: $1339; Undergraduates: $2867. *Parent loans:* $72,051 (100% non-need-based). *Programs:* FFEL (Subsidized and Unsubsidized Stafford, PLUS), Perkins, state.
ATHLETIC AWARDS *Total amount:* $470,862 (100% non-need-based).
APPLYING FOR FINANCIAL AID *Required financial aid form:* FAFSA. *Financial aid deadline (priority):* 3/1. *Notification date:* Continuous beginning 5/15. Students must reply within 2 weeks of notification.
CONTACT Eileen Sedillo, Director, Financial Aid & Scholarship, New Mexico Highlands University, Box 9000, Las Vegas, NM 87701, 505-454-3430 or toll-free 800-338-6648. *Fax:* 505-454-3398. *E-mail:* sedillo_e@nmhu.edu.

NEW MEXICO INSTITUTE OF MINING AND TECHNOLOGY
Socorro, NM

Tuition & fees (NM res): $3280 **Average undergraduate aid package: $7849**

ABOUT THE INSTITUTION State-supported, coed. Awards: associate, bachelor's, master's, and doctoral degrees. 38 undergraduate majors. Total enrollment: 1,806. Undergraduates: 1,341. Freshmen: 259. Federal methodology is used as a basis for awarding need-based institutional aid.
UNDERGRADUATE EXPENSES for 2004–05 *Application fee:* $15. *Tuition, state resident:* full-time $2307; part-time $96.11 per credit hour. *Tuition, nonresident:* full-time $8938; part-time $372.41 per credit hour. *Required fees:* full-time $973; $32.97 per credit hour or $107.32 per term part-time. Part-time tuition and fees vary according to course load. *College room and board:* $4670; *room only:* $1920. Room and board charges vary according to board plan and housing facility. *Payment plan:* Deferred payment.
FRESHMAN FINANCIAL AID (Fall 2004, est.) 279 applied for aid; of those 40% were deemed to have need. 96% of freshmen with need received aid; of those 55% had need fully met. *Average percent of need met:* 94% (excluding resources awarded to replace EFC). *Average financial aid package:* $7921 (excluding resources awarded to replace EFC). 40% of all full-time freshmen had no need and received non-need-based gift aid.
UNDERGRADUATE FINANCIAL AID (Fall 2004, est.) 941 applied for aid; of those 47% were deemed to have need. 97% of undergraduates with need received aid; of those 55% had need fully met. *Average percent of need met:* 94% (excluding resources awarded to replace EFC). *Average financial aid package:* $7849 (excluding resources awarded to replace EFC). 36% of all full-time undergraduates had no need and received non-need-based gift aid.
GIFT AID (NEED-BASED) *Total amount:* $1,386,498 (76% federal, 24% state). *Receiving aid:* Freshmen: 19% (62); All full-time undergraduates: 28% (297). *Average award:* Freshmen: $4444; Undergraduates: $4094. *Scholarships, grants, and awards:* Federal Pell, FSEOG, state, private, college/university gift aid from institutional funds, New Mexico Scholar Program, Legislative Endowment Scholarships.
GIFT AID (NON-NEED-BASED) *Total amount:* $2,429,349 (30% state, 70% institutional). *Receiving aid:* Freshmen: 25% (82); Undergraduates: 24% (258). *Average Award:* Freshmen: $3789; Undergraduates: $4097. *Scholarships, grants, and awards by category: Academic Interests/Achievement:* communication, engineering/technologies, general academic interests/achievements, physical sciences. *Special Characteristics:* children of faculty/staff. *Tuition waivers:* Full or partial for employees or children of employees, senior citizens.
LOANS *Student loans:* $1,419,816 (100% need-based). 62% of past graduating class borrowed through all loan programs. *Average indebtedness per student:* $8788. *Average need-based loan:* Freshmen: $3470; Undergraduates: $4120. *Parent loans:* $163,614 (100% need-based). *Programs:* FFEL (Subsidized and Unsubsidized Stafford, PLUS), Perkins.
WORK-STUDY *Federal work-study:* Total amount: $268,407; jobs available. *State or other work-study/employment:* Total amount: $132,035 (31% need-based, 69% non-need-based). Part-time jobs available.
APPLYING FOR FINANCIAL AID *Required financial aid forms:* FAFSA, institution's own form. *Financial aid deadline (priority):* 6/1. *Notification date:* Continuous beginning 5/1. Students must reply within 2 weeks of notification.
CONTACT Ms. Annette Kaus, Director of Financial Aid, New Mexico Institute of Mining and Technology, Financial Aid Office, 801 Leroy Place, Socorro, NM 87801, 505-835-5333 or toll-free 800-428-TECH. *Fax:* 505-835-5959. *E-mail:* akaus@admin.nmt.edu.

NEW MEXICO STATE UNIVERSITY
Las Cruces, NM

Tuition & fees (NM res): $3666 **Average undergraduate aid package: $8555**

ABOUT THE INSTITUTION State-supported, coed. Awards: associate, bachelor's, master's, and doctoral degrees and post-master's certificates. 81 undergraduate majors. Total enrollment: 16,428. Undergraduates: 12,975. Freshmen: 2,111. Federal methodology is used as a basis for awarding need-based institutional aid.
UNDERGRADUATE EXPENSES for 2004–05 *Application fee:* $15. *Tuition, state resident:* full-time $2628; part-time $152.75 per credit. *Tuition, nonresident:* full-time $11,172; part-time $508.75 per credit. *College room and board:*

$5046; *room only:* $2926. Room and board charges vary according to board plan and gender. *Payment plans:* Installment, deferred payment.

FRESHMAN FINANCIAL AID (Fall 2004, est.) 1547 applied for aid; of those 81% were deemed to have need. 97% of freshmen with need received aid; of those 19% had need fully met. *Average percent of need met:* 68% (excluding resources awarded to replace EFC). *Average financial aid package:* $7924 (excluding resources awarded to replace EFC). 29% of all full-time freshmen had no need and received non-need-based gift aid.

UNDERGRADUATE FINANCIAL AID (Fall 2004, est.) 7,525 applied for aid; of those 87% were deemed to have need. 96% of undergraduates with need received aid; of those 23% had need fully met. *Average percent of need met:* 71% (excluding resources awarded to replace EFC). *Average financial aid package:* $8555 (excluding resources awarded to replace EFC). 21% of all full-time undergraduates had no need and received non-need-based gift aid.

GIFT AID (NEED-BASED) *Total amount:* $26,901,023 (57% federal, 26% state, 12% institutional, 5% external sources). *Receiving aid:* Freshmen: 56% (1,172); All full-time undergraduates: 53% (5,746). *Average award:* Freshmen: $6305; Undergraduates: $5952. *Scholarships, grants, and awards:* Federal Pell, FSEOG, state, private, college/university gift aid from institutional funds.

GIFT AID (NON-NEED-BASED) *Total amount:* $8,647,120 (1% federal, 59% state, 29% institutional, 11% external sources). *Receiving aid:* Freshmen: 7% (152); Undergraduates: 6% (652). *Average Award:* Freshmen: $3078; Undergraduates: $3027. *Scholarships, grants, and awards by category: Academic Interests/ Achievement:* agriculture, biological sciences, business, communication, computer science, education, engineering/technologies, English, foreign languages, general academic interests/achievements, health fields, home economics, humanities, mathematics, military science, physical sciences, social sciences. *Creative Arts/ Performance:* applied art and design, art/fine arts, general creative arts/ performance, journalism/publications, music, performing arts, theater/drama. *Special Achievements/Activities:* leadership, rodeo. *Special Characteristics:* adult students, children and siblings of alumni, children of faculty/staff, children of public servants, children of union members/company employees, children of workers in trades, children with a deceased or disabled parent, ethnic background, handicapped students, international students, local/state students, married students, members of minority groups, out-of-state students, previous college experience, spouses of current students, veterans, veterans' children. *Tuition waivers:* Full or partial for employees or children of employees, senior citizens. *ROTC:* Army, Air Force.

LOANS *Student loans:* $26,007,879 (79% need-based, 21% non-need-based). *Average need-based loan:* Freshmen: $2767; Undergraduates: $3907. *Parent loans:* $1,108,393 (29% need-based, 71% non-need-based). *Programs:* FFEL (Subsidized and Unsubsidized Stafford, PLUS), Perkins, state.

WORK-STUDY *Federal work-study:* Total amount: $1,022,652; 409 jobs available. *State or other work-study/employment:* Total amount: $1,104,928 (66% need-based, 34% non-need-based). 420 part-time jobs available.

ATHLETIC AWARDS *Total amount:* $2,241,716 (39% need-based, 61% non-need-based).

APPLYING FOR FINANCIAL AID *Required financial aid forms:* FAFSA, institution's own form. *Financial aid deadline (priority):* 3/1.

CONTACT Tyler Pruett, Director of Financial Aid, New Mexico State University, Box 30001, Department 5100, Las Cruces, NM 88003-8001, 505-646-4105 or toll-free 800-662-6678. *Fax:* 505-646-7381.

NEW ORLEANS BAPTIST THEOLOGICAL SEMINARY
New Orleans, LA

ABOUT THE INSTITUTION Independent Southern Baptist, coed, primarily men. Awards: associate, bachelor's, master's, doctoral, and first professional degrees. 1 undergraduate major. Total enrollment: 2,712. Undergraduates: 1,063.

GIFT AID (NEED-BASED) *Scholarships, grants, and awards:* private, college/ university gift aid from institutional funds.

LOANS *Programs:* Signature Loans.

APPLYING FOR FINANCIAL AID *Required financial aid form:* institution's own form.

CONTACT Financial Aid Office, New Orleans Baptist Theological Seminary, 3939 Gentilly Boulevard, New Orleans, LA 70126-4858, 504-282-4455 Ext. 3348 or toll-free 800-662-8701. *E-mail:* financialaid@nobts.edu.

NEW SAINT ANDREWS COLLEGE
Moscow, ID

CONTACT Financial Aid Office, New Saint Andrews College, PO Box 9025, Moscow, ID 83843, 208-882-1566.

NEW SCHOOL BACHELOR'S PROGRAM, NEW SCHOOL UNIVERSITY
New York, NY

ABOUT THE INSTITUTION Independent, coed. Awards: bachelor's, master's, and doctoral degrees. 1 undergraduate major. Total enrollment: 1,809. Undergraduates: 989. Entering class: 4.

GIFT AID (NEED-BASED) *Scholarships, grants, and awards:* Federal Pell, FSEOG, state, private, college/university gift aid from institutional funds.

GIFT AID (NON-NEED-BASED) *Scholarships, grants, and awards by category: Creative Arts/Performance:* performing arts.

LOANS *Programs:* FFEL (Subsidized and Unsubsidized Stafford, PLUS), Perkins, college/university.

WORK-STUDY *Federal work-study:* Total amount: $38,000; jobs available.

APPLYING FOR FINANCIAL AID *Required financial aid forms:* FAFSA, state aid form.

CONTACT Financial Aid Counselor, New School Bachelor's Program, New School University, 65 Fifth Avenue, New York, NY 10003, 212-229-8930. *Fax:* 212-229-5919.

NEWSCHOOL OF ARCHITECTURE & DESIGN
San Diego, CA

CONTACT Ms. Cara E. Baker, Director of Financial Aid, Newschool of Architecture & Design, 1249 F Street, San Diego, CA 92101-6634, 619-235-4100 Ext. 103. *Fax:* 619-235-4651. *E-mail:* cbaker@newschoolarch.edu.

NEW YORK INSTITUTE OF TECHNOLOGY
Old Westbury, NY

Tuition & fees: $18,190	Average undergraduate aid package: $10,846

ABOUT THE INSTITUTION Independent, coed. Awards: associate, bachelor's, master's, doctoral, and first professional degrees and post-bachelor's and post-master's certificates. 70 undergraduate majors. Total enrollment: 9,387. Undergraduates: 5,602. Freshmen: 874. Federal methodology is used as a basis for awarding need-based institutional aid.

UNDERGRADUATE EXPENSES for 2004–05 *Application fee:* $50. *Comprehensive fee:* $25,970 includes full-time tuition ($17,840), mandatory fees ($350), and room and board ($7780). *College room only:* $4080. Full-time tuition and fees vary according to course load and program. Room and board charges vary according to board plan, housing facility, and location. *Part-time tuition:* $594 per credit. *Part-time fees:* $150 per term. Part-time tuition and fees vary according to course load. *Payment plan:* Installment.

FRESHMAN FINANCIAL AID (Fall 2003) 714 applied for aid; of those 85% were deemed to have need. 99% of freshmen with need received aid. *Average financial aid package:* $11,471 (excluding resources awarded to replace EFC). 13% of all full-time freshmen had no need and received non-need-based gift aid.

UNDERGRADUATE FINANCIAL AID (Fall 2003) 3,307 applied for aid; of those 86% were deemed to have need. 99% of undergraduates with need received aid. *Average financial aid package:* $10,846 (excluding resources awarded to replace EFC). 12% of all full-time undergraduates had no need and received non-need-based gift aid.

GIFT AID (NEED-BASED) *Total amount:* $13,853,808 (39% federal, 40% state, 21% institutional). *Receiving aid:* Freshmen: 65% (518); All full-time undergraduates: 60% (2,461). *Average award:* Freshmen: $5429; Undergraduates: $5425. *Scholarships, grants, and awards:* Federal Pell, FSEOG, state, private, college/ university gift aid from institutional funds.

GIFT AID (NON-NEED-BASED) *Total amount:* $8,920,627 (2% federal, 1% state, 97% institutional). *Receiving aid:* Freshmen: 49% (392); Undergraduates: 37% (1,498). *Average Award:* Freshmen: $7534; Undergraduates: $6437. *Scholarships, grants, and awards by category: Academic Interests/Achievement:*

general academic interests/achievements. *Special Characteristics:* children and siblings of alumni, children of educators, children of faculty/staff, children of public servants, local/state students, previous college experience, public servants, spouses of deceased or disabled public servants, veterans. *Tuition waivers:* Full or partial for employees or children of employees, senior citizens. *ROTC:* Army, Air Force.

LOANS *Student loans:* $18,732,310 (53% need-based, 47% non-need-based). 75% of past graduating class borrowed through all loan programs. *Average indebtedness per student:* $17,125. *Average need-based loan:* Freshmen: $3844; Undergraduates: $4154. *Parent loans:* $5,030,655 (100% non-need-based). *Programs:* FFEL (Subsidized and Unsubsidized Stafford, PLUS), Perkins, Federal Nursing, alternative loans.

WORK-STUDY *Federal work-study:* Total amount: $829,284; jobs available. *State or other work-study/employment:* Total amount: $72,660 (100% non-need-based). Part-time jobs available.

ATHLETIC AWARDS *Total amount:* $1,812,429 (100% non-need-based).

APPLYING FOR FINANCIAL AID *Required financial aid form:* FAFSA. *Financial aid deadline (priority):* 2/1. *Notification date:* Continuous beginning 2/15. Students must reply by 5/1 or within 2 weeks of notification.

CONTACT Clair Jacobi, Director of Financial Aid Office, New York Institute of Technology, PO Box 8000, Old Westbury, NY 11568-8000, 516-686-1085 or toll-free 800-345-NYIT. *Fax:* 516-686-3835. *E-mail:* owfinaid@nyit.edu.

NEW YORK SCHOOL OF INTERIOR DESIGN
New York, NY

Tuition & fees: $19,050	Average undergraduate aid package: $8500

ABOUT THE INSTITUTION Independent, coed, primarily women. Awards: associate, bachelor's, and master's degrees. 1 undergraduate major. Total enrollment: 784. Undergraduates: 769. Freshmen: 100. Federal methodology is used as a basis for awarding need-based institutional aid.

UNDERGRADUATE EXPENSES for 2005–06 *Application fee:* $50. *Tuition:* full-time $18,880; part-time $590 per credit. *Required fees:* full-time $170; $85 per term part-time. Full-time tuition and fees vary according to course load. Part-time tuition and fees vary according to course load. *Payment plan:* Installment.

FRESHMAN FINANCIAL AID (Fall 2004, est.) 28 applied for aid; of those 100% were deemed to have need. 100% of freshmen with need received aid. *Average percent of need met:* 50% (excluding resources awarded to replace EFC). *Average financial aid package:* $6500 (excluding resources awarded to replace EFC).

UNDERGRADUATE FINANCIAL AID (Fall 2004, est.) 69 applied for aid; of those 100% were deemed to have need. 100% of undergraduates with need received aid. *Average percent of need met:* 50% (excluding resources awarded to replace EFC). *Average financial aid package:* $8500 (excluding resources awarded to replace EFC).

GIFT AID (NEED-BASED) *Total amount:* $342,263 (33% federal, 28% state, 35% institutional, 4% external sources). *Receiving aid:* Freshmen: 44% (21); All full-time undergraduates: 35% (60). *Average award:* Freshmen: $5000; Undergraduates: $5000. *Scholarships, grants, and awards:* Federal Pell, FSEOG, state, college/university gift aid from institutional funds.

GIFT AID (NON-NEED-BASED) *Total amount:* $42,000 (100% institutional). *Receiving aid:* Undergraduates: 1% (2). *Tuition waivers:* Full or partial for employees or children of employees.

LOANS *Student loans:* $1,023,029 (38% need-based, 62% non-need-based). 15% of past graduating class borrowed through all loan programs. *Average indebtedness per student:* $13,250. *Average need-based loan:* Freshmen: $2625; Undergraduates: $3000. *Parent loans:* $450,637 (100% need-based). *Programs:* FFEL (Subsidized and Unsubsidized Stafford, PLUS).

WORK-STUDY *Federal work-study:* Total amount: $33,203; 28 jobs averaging $3000.

APPLYING FOR FINANCIAL AID *Required financial aid forms:* FAFSA, institution's own form. *Financial aid deadline (priority):* 5/1. *Notification date:* Continuous. Students must reply within 2 weeks of notification.

CONTACT Nina Bunchuk, Director of Financial Aid, New York School of Interior Design, 170 East 70th Street, New York, NY 10021-5110, 212-472-1500 Ext. 212 or toll-free 800-336-9743 Ext. 204. *Fax:* 212-472-1867. *E-mail:* nina@nysid.edu.

NEW YORK UNIVERSITY
New York, NY

Tuition & fees: $30,094	Average undergraduate aid package: $18,692

ABOUT THE INSTITUTION Independent, coed. Awards: associate, bachelor's, master's, doctoral, and first professional degrees and post-bachelor's, post-master's, and first professional certificates. 116 undergraduate majors. Total enrollment: 39,408. Undergraduates: 20,212. Freshmen: 4,603. Federal methodology is used as a basis for awarding need-based institutional aid.

UNDERGRADUATE EXPENSES for 2004–05 *Application fee:* $65. *Comprehensive fee:* $41,484 includes full-time tuition ($28,328), mandatory fees ($1766), and room and board ($11,390). Full-time tuition and fees vary according to program. Room and board charges vary according to board plan and housing facility. *Part-time tuition:* $835 per credit. *Part-time fees:* $52 per credit; $262 per term. Part-time tuition and fees vary according to program. *Payment plans:* Tuition prepayment, installment, deferred payment.

FRESHMAN FINANCIAL AID (Fall 2004, est.) 3244 applied for aid; of those 81% were deemed to have need. 100% of freshmen with need received aid. *Average percent of need met:* 68% (excluding resources awarded to replace EFC). *Average financial aid package:* $19,543 (excluding resources awarded to replace EFC). 10% of all full-time freshmen had no need and received non-need-based gift aid.

UNDERGRADUATE FINANCIAL AID (Fall 2004, est.) 11,795 applied for aid; of those 87% were deemed to have need. 100% of undergraduates with need received aid. *Average percent of need met:* 64% (excluding resources awarded to replace EFC). *Average financial aid package:* $18,692 (excluding resources awarded to replace EFC). 11% of all full-time undergraduates had no need and received non-need-based gift aid.

GIFT AID (NEED-BASED) *Total amount:* $125,303,775 (12% federal, 10% state, 73% institutional, 5% external sources). *Receiving aid:* Freshmen: 56% (2,470); All full-time undergraduates: 53% (9,594). *Average award:* Freshmen: $13,629; Undergraduates: $12,963. *Scholarships, grants, and awards:* Federal Pell, FSEOG, state, private, college/university gift aid from institutional funds.

GIFT AID (NON-NEED-BASED) *Total amount:* $18,270,928 (79% institutional, 21% external sources). *Average Award:* Freshmen: $6799; Undergraduates: $6924. *Scholarships, grants, and awards by category:* Academic Interests/Achievement: 2,191 awards ($14,147,406 total): general academic interests/achievements. *Tuition waivers:* Full or partial for employees or children of employees.

LOANS *Student loans:* $101,167,057 (87% need-based, 13% non-need-based). 60% of past graduating class borrowed through all loan programs. *Average indebtedness per student:* $27,639. *Average need-based loan:* Freshmen: $4351; Undergraduates: $5117. *Parent loans:* $83,347,816 (80% need-based, 20% non-need-based). *Programs:* FFEL (Subsidized and Unsubsidized Stafford, PLUS), Perkins, Federal Nursing.

WORK-STUDY *Federal work-study:* Total amount: $7,700,000; 3,338 jobs averaging $2309.

APPLYING FOR FINANCIAL AID *Required financial aid forms:* FAFSA, state aid form. *Financial aid deadline (priority):* 2/15. *Notification date:* 4/1.

CONTACT Financial Aid Office, New York University, 25 West Fourth Street, New York, NY 10012-1199, 212-998-4444. *Fax:* 212-995-4661. *E-mail:* financial.aid@nyu.edu.

NIAGARA UNIVERSITY
Niagara Falls, NY

Tuition & fees: $18,420	Average undergraduate aid package: $17,851

ABOUT THE INSTITUTION Independent religious, coed. Awards: associate, bachelor's, and master's degrees and post-master's certificates. 56 undergraduate majors. Total enrollment: 3,807. Undergraduates: 2,943. Freshmen: 738. Federal methodology is used as a basis for awarding need-based institutional aid.

UNDERGRADUATE EXPENSES for 2004–05 *Application fee:* $30. *Comprehensive fee:* $26,470 includes full-time tuition ($17,700), mandatory fees ($720), and room and board ($8050). *Part-time tuition:* $590 per credit hour. *Part-time fees:* $20 per term. *Payment plans:* Installment, deferred payment.

FRESHMAN FINANCIAL AID (Fall 2004, est.) 686 applied for aid; of those 91% were deemed to have need. 100% of freshmen with need received aid; of those 45% had need fully met. *Average percent of need met:* 85% (excluding resources

awarded to replace EFC). *Average financial aid package:* $17,257 (excluding resources awarded to replace EFC). 18% of all full-time freshmen had no need and received non-need-based gift aid.

UNDERGRADUATE FINANCIAL AID (Fall 2004, est.) 2,666 applied for aid; of those 83% were deemed to have need. 100% of undergraduates with need received aid; of those 31% had need fully met. *Average percent of need met:* 87% (excluding resources awarded to replace EFC). *Average financial aid package:* $17,851 (excluding resources awarded to replace EFC). 15% of all full-time undergraduates had no need and received non-need-based gift aid.

GIFT AID (NEED-BASED) *Total amount:* $25,038,958 (11% federal, 15% state, 72% institutional, 2% external sources). *Receiving aid:* Freshmen: 80% (585); All full-time undergraduates: 78% (2,113). *Average award:* Freshmen: $13,666; Undergraduates: $12,608. *Scholarships, grants, and awards:* Federal Pell, FSEOG, state, private, college/university gift aid from institutional funds.

GIFT AID (NON-NEED-BASED) *Total amount:* $3,707,289 (5% state, 93% institutional, 2% external sources). *Receiving aid:* Freshmen: 15% (107); Undergraduates: 20% (555). *Average Award:* Freshmen: $8097; Undergraduates: $7850. *Scholarships, grants, and awards by category: Academic Interests/Achievement:* 2,496 awards ($17,272,137 total): general academic interests/achievements. *Creative Arts/Performance:* 51 awards ($178,338 total): theater/drama. *Special Achievements/Activities:* 10 awards ($20,000 total): community service. *Special Characteristics:* 93 awards ($1,405,268 total): children of faculty/staff, relatives of clergy. *Tuition waivers:* Full or partial for employees or children of employees, senior citizens. *ROTC:* Army.

LOANS *Student loans:* $12,915,260 (67% need-based, 33% non-need-based). 79% of past graduating class borrowed through all loan programs. *Average indebtedness per student:* $16,621. *Average need-based loan:* Freshmen: $5660; Undergraduates: $5591. *Parent loans:* $2,903,552 (81% need-based, 19% non-need-based). *Programs:* FFEL (Subsidized and Unsubsidized Stafford, PLUS), Perkins, college/university.

WORK-STUDY *Federal work-study:* Total amount: $1,089,702; 461 jobs averaging $2172. *State or other work-study/employment:* Total amount: $87,865 (100% non-need-based). 28 part-time jobs averaging $2890.

ATHLETIC AWARDS *Total amount:* $2,754,294 (25% need-based, 75% non-need-based).

APPLYING FOR FINANCIAL AID *Required financial aid forms:* FAFSA, state aid form. *Financial aid deadline (priority):* 2/15. *Notification date:* Continuous beginning 3/15. Students must reply within 3 weeks of notification.

CONTACT Mrs. Maureen E. Salfi, Director of Financial Aid, Niagara University, Financial Aid Office, Niagara University, NY 14109, 716-286-8686 or toll-free 800-462-2111. *Fax:* 716-286-8678. *E-mail:* finaid@niagara.edu.

NICHOLLS STATE UNIVERSITY
Thibodaux, LA

Tuition & fees (LA res): $3240	Average undergraduate aid package: $5329

ABOUT THE INSTITUTION State-supported, coed. Awards: associate, bachelor's, and master's degrees and post-master's certificates. 54 undergraduate majors. Total enrollment: 7,473. Undergraduates: 6,784. Freshmen: 1,640. Federal methodology is used as a basis for awarding need-based institutional aid.

UNDERGRADUATE EXPENSES for 2004–05 *Application fee:* $20. *Tuition, state resident:* full-time $2135. *Tuition, nonresident:* full-time $8688. Part-time tuition and fees vary according to course load. *College room and board:* $3534; *room only:* $1800. *Payment plan:* Deferred payment.

FRESHMAN FINANCIAL AID (Fall 2003) 1232 applied for aid; of those 61% were deemed to have need. 99% of freshmen with need received aid; of those 16% had need fully met. *Average percent of need met:* 87% (excluding resources awarded to replace EFC). *Average financial aid package:* $4911 (excluding resources awarded to replace EFC). 3% of all full-time freshmen had no need and received non-need-based gift aid.

UNDERGRADUATE FINANCIAL AID (Fall 2003) 4,191 applied for aid; of those 63% were deemed to have need. 98% of undergraduates with need received aid; of those 22% had need fully met. *Average percent of need met:* 90% (excluding resources awarded to replace EFC). *Average financial aid package:* $5329 (excluding resources awarded to replace EFC). 2% of all full-time undergraduates had no need and received non-need-based gift aid.

GIFT AID (NEED-BASED) *Total amount:* $6,880,636 (84% federal, 12% state, 2% institutional, 2% external sources). *Receiving aid:* Freshmen: 46% (640); All full-time undergraduates: 40% (2,129). *Average award:* Freshmen: $3008; Undergraduates: $3015. *Scholarships, grants, and awards:* Federal Pell, FSEOG, state, private, college/university gift aid from institutional funds.

GIFT AID (NON-NEED-BASED) *Total amount:* $3,733,238 (81% state, 9% institutional, 10% external sources). *Receiving aid:* Freshmen: 13% (180); Undergraduates: 9% (474). *Average Award:* Freshmen: $2820; Undergraduates: $2727. *Scholarships, grants, and awards by category: Academic Interests/Achievement:* 179 awards ($442,451 total): general academic interests/achievements. *Creative Arts/Performance:* music. *Special Characteristics:* 449 awards ($624,014 total): children of faculty/staff, public servants. *Tuition waivers:* Full or partial for employees or children of employees.

LOANS *Student loans:* $10,302,505 (39% need-based, 61% non-need-based). *Average need-based loan:* Freshmen: $2300; Undergraduates: $2914. *Parent loans:* $300,568 (4% need-based, 96% non-need-based). *Programs:* FFEL (Subsidized and Unsubsidized Stafford, PLUS), Perkins.

WORK-STUDY *Federal work-study:* Total amount: $237,421; 240 jobs averaging $989. *State or other work-study/employment:* Total amount: $1,082,903 (5% need-based, 95% non-need-based). 627 part-time jobs averaging $1727.

ATHLETIC AWARDS *Total amount:* $917,403 (24% need-based, 76% non-need-based).

APPLYING FOR FINANCIAL AID *Required financial aid forms:* FAFSA, institution's own form, state aid form, noncustodial (divorced/separated) parent's statement. *Financial aid deadline:* 4/19 (priority: 4/8). *Notification date:* Continuous. Students must reply within 2 weeks of notification.

CONTACT Colette Lagarde, Office of Financial Aid, Nicholls State University, East Elkins Hall, PO Box 2005, Thibodaux, LA 70310, 985-448-4048 or toll-free 877-NICHOLLS. *Fax:* 985-448-4124. *E-mail:* colette.lagarde@nicholls.edu.

NICHOLS COLLEGE
Dudley, MA

Tuition & fees: $20,810	Average undergraduate aid package: $15,230

ABOUT THE INSTITUTION Independent, coed. Awards: associate, bachelor's, and master's degrees. 14 undergraduate majors. Total enrollment: 1,792. Undergraduates: 1,432. Freshmen: 313. Federal methodology is used as a basis for awarding need-based institutional aid.

UNDERGRADUATE EXPENSES for 2004–05 *Application fee:* $25. *Comprehensive fee:* $28,862 includes full-time tuition ($20,560), mandatory fees ($250), and room and board ($8052). *Part-time tuition:* $775 per credit. Part-time tuition and fees vary according to course load. *Payment plan:* Installment.

GIFT AID (NEED-BASED) *Total amount:* $6,145,018 (11% federal, 6% state, 76% institutional, 7% external sources). *Receiving aid:* Freshmen: 81% (252); All full-time undergraduates: 77% (692). *Average award:* Freshmen: $10,677; Undergraduates: $8752. *Scholarships, grants, and awards:* Federal Pell, FSEOG, state, private, college/university gift aid from institutional funds.

GIFT AID (NON-NEED-BASED) *Total amount:* $1,409,394 (1% state, 81% institutional, 18% external sources). *Receiving aid:* Freshmen: 4% (13); Undergraduates: 5% (46). *Average Award:* Freshmen: $9839; Undergraduates: $10,319. *Scholarships, grants, and awards by category: Academic Interests/Achievement:* 678 awards ($3,966,677 total): general academic interests/achievements. *Special Characteristics:* 33 awards ($180,440 total): children and siblings of alumni, children of faculty/staff, siblings of current students. *Tuition waivers:* Full or partial for employees or children of employees. *ROTC:* Army cooperative.

LOANS *Student loans:* $6,155,319 (72% need-based, 28% non-need-based). 86% of past graduating class borrowed through all loan programs. *Average indebtedness per student:* $26,626. *Average need-based loan:* Freshmen: $2420; Undergraduates: $6661. *Parent loans:* $2,739,902 (44% need-based, 56% non-need-based). *Programs:* FFEL (Subsidized and Unsubsidized Stafford, PLUS), state.

APPLYING FOR FINANCIAL AID *Required financial aid form:* FAFSA. *Financial aid deadline (priority):* 3/1. *Notification date:* Continuous beginning 3/25. Students must reply within 2 weeks of notification.

CONTACT Ms. Diane L. Gillespie, Director of Financial Aid, Nichols College, PO Box 5000, Dudley, MA 01571, 508-213-2276 or toll-free 800-470-3379. *Fax:* 508-943-9885. *E-mail:* diane.gillespie@nichols.edu.

NORFOLK STATE UNIVERSITY
Norfolk, VA

Tuition & fees (VA res): $4295	Average undergraduate aid package: $8884

Norfolk State University

ABOUT THE INSTITUTION State-supported, coed. Awards: associate, bachelor's, master's, and doctoral degrees. 34 undergraduate majors. Total enrollment: 6,846. Undergraduates: 6,039. Freshmen: 1,154. Federal methodology is used as a basis for awarding need-based institutional aid.

UNDERGRADUATE EXPENSES for 2004–05 *Application fee:* $25. *Tuition, state resident:* full-time $2220; part-time $74 per credit hour. *Tuition, nonresident:* full-time $12,180; part-time $406 per credit hour. *Required fees:* full-time $2075; $116 per credit hour. Full-time tuition and fees vary according to course load. Part-time tuition and fees vary according to course load. *College room and board:* $6236; *room only:* $3942. Room and board charges vary according to board plan. *Payment plans:* Installment, deferred payment.

GIFT AID (NEED-BASED) *Total amount:* $16,257,047 (48% federal, 25% state, 14% institutional, 13% external sources). *Receiving aid:* Freshmen: 72% (694); All full-time undergraduates: 68% (3,017). *Average award:* Freshmen: $5521; Undergraduates: $5020. *Scholarships, grants, and awards:* Federal Pell, FSEOG, state, private, college/university gift aid from institutional funds.

GIFT AID (NON-NEED-BASED) *Receiving aid:* Freshmen: 17% (169); Undergraduates: 13% (596). *Scholarships, grants, and awards by category:* Creative Arts/Performance: music, performing arts. *Special Achievements/Activities:* general special achievements/activities. *Tuition waivers:* Full or partial for employees or children of employees, senior citizens. *ROTC:* Army, Naval.

LOANS *Student loans:* $27,047,159 (100% need-based). 85% of past graduating class borrowed through all loan programs. *Average indebtedness per student:* $15,467. *Average need-based loan:* Freshmen: $2918; Undergraduates: $3977. *Parent loans:* $3,728,070 (100% need-based). *Programs:* Federal Direct (Subsidized and Unsubsidized Stafford), FFEL (PLUS), Perkins, state, alternative loans.

ATHLETIC AWARDS *Total amount:* $1,135,640 (100% need-based).

APPLYING FOR FINANCIAL AID *Required financial aid form:* FAFSA. *Financial aid deadline:* 5/31. *Notification date:* 6/15. Students must reply within 2 weeks of notification.

CONTACT Mrs. Estherine Harding, Director of Financial Aid, Norfolk State University, 700 Park Avenue, Norfolk, VA 23504-3907, 757-823-8381. *Fax:* 757-823-9059. *E-mail:* ejharding@nsu.edu.

NORTH CAROLINA AGRICULTURAL AND TECHNICAL STATE UNIVERSITY
Greensboro, NC

Tuition & fees (NC res): $3066	Average undergraduate aid package: $5238

ABOUT THE INSTITUTION State-supported, coed. Awards: bachelor's, master's, and doctoral degrees. 59 undergraduate majors. Total enrollment: 9,115. Undergraduates: 7,982. Freshmen: 2,043. Federal methodology is used as a basis for awarding need-based institutional aid.

UNDERGRADUATE EXPENSES for 2004–05 *Application fee:* $35. *Tuition, state resident:* full-time $1769; part-time $361.80 per credit hour. *Tuition, nonresident:* full-time $11,211; part-time $1,542.05 per credit hour. *College room and board:* $5070; *room only:* $2700.

FRESHMAN FINANCIAL AID (Fall 2003) 1650 applied for aid; of those 81% were deemed to have need. 98% of freshmen with need received aid; of those 3% had need fully met. *Average percent of need met:* 53% (excluding resources awarded to replace EFC). *Average financial aid package:* $5026 (excluding resources awarded to replace EFC). 2% of all full-time freshmen had no need and received non-need-based gift aid.

UNDERGRADUATE FINANCIAL AID (Fall 2003) 5,990 applied for aid; of those 84% were deemed to have need. 96% of undergraduates with need received aid; of those 6% had need fully met. *Average percent of need met:* 54% (excluding resources awarded to replace EFC). *Average financial aid package:* $5238 (excluding resources awarded to replace EFC). 4% of all full-time undergraduates had no need and received non-need-based gift aid.

GIFT AID (NEED-BASED) *Total amount:* $12,965,430 (72% federal, 28% state). *Receiving aid:* Freshmen: 61% (1,071); All full-time undergraduates: 51% (3,652). *Average award:* Freshmen: $3420; Undergraduates: $3287. *Scholarships, grants, and awards:* Federal Pell, FSEOG, state, private, college/university gift aid from institutional funds, Federal Nursing.

GIFT AID (NON-NEED-BASED) *Total amount:* $12,150,554 (13% state, 46% institutional, 41% external sources). *Receiving aid:* Freshmen: 45% (794); Undergraduates: 36% (2,563). *Average Award:* Freshmen: $3356; Undergraduates: $4169. *Scholarships, grants, and awards by category:* Academic Interests/

Achievement: military science. *Creative Arts/Performance:* music, theater/drama. *Special Characteristics:* ethnic background, handicapped students, members of minority groups. *ROTC:* Army, Air Force.

LOANS *Student loans:* $30,497,787 (75% need-based, 25% non-need-based). 71% of past graduating class borrowed through all loan programs. *Average indebtedness per student:* $16,044. *Average need-based loan:* Freshmen: $3087; Undergraduates: $4913. *Parent loans:* $3,255,677 (100% non-need-based). *Programs:* Federal Direct (Subsidized and Unsubsidized Stafford, PLUS), Perkins, state, Federal Direct Loan subsidized and unsubsidized.

WORK-STUDY *Federal work-study:* Total amount: $432,004; jobs available. *State or other work-study/employment:* Part-time jobs available.

ATHLETIC AWARDS *Total amount:* $1,311,231 (100% non-need-based).

APPLYING FOR FINANCIAL AID *Required financial aid form:* FAFSA. *Financial aid deadline (priority):* 3/15. *Notification date:* Continuous beginning 4/1. Students must reply within 2 weeks of notification.

CONTACT Mrs. Sherri Avent, Director of Student Financial Aid, North Carolina Agricultural and Technical State University, 1601 East Market Street, Dowdy Administration Building, Greensboro, NC 27411, 336-334-7973 or toll-free 800-443-8964 (in-state). *Fax:* 336-334-7954.

NORTH CAROLINA CENTRAL UNIVERSITY
Durham, NC

CONTACT Sharon J. Oliver, Director of Scholarships and Student Aid, North Carolina Central University, 106 Student Services Building, Durham, NC 27707-3129, 919-530-7412 or toll-free 877-667-7533.

NORTH CAROLINA SCHOOL OF THE ARTS
Winston-Salem, NC

Tuition & fees (NC res): $4306	Average undergraduate aid package: $10,101

ABOUT THE INSTITUTION State-supported, coed. Awards: bachelor's and master's degrees and post-master's certificates. 9 undergraduate majors. Total enrollment: 817. Undergraduates: 738. Freshmen: 200. Federal methodology is used as a basis for awarding need-based institutional aid.

UNDERGRADUATE EXPENSES for 2004–05 *Application fee:* $50. *Tuition, state resident:* full-time $2755. *Tuition, nonresident:* full-time $14,035. Full-time tuition and fees vary according to program. Part-time tuition and fees vary according to course load. *College room and board:* $5700; *room only:* $3035. Room and board charges vary according to board plan and housing facility. *Payment plan:* Installment.

FRESHMAN FINANCIAL AID (Fall 2003) 136 applied for aid; of those 87% were deemed to have need. 100% of freshmen with need received aid; of those 8% had need fully met. *Average percent of need met:* 73% (excluding resources awarded to replace EFC). *Average financial aid package:* $9792 (excluding resources awarded to replace EFC). 6% of all full-time freshmen had no need and received non-need-based gift aid.

UNDERGRADUATE FINANCIAL AID (Fall 2003) 486 applied for aid; of those 83% were deemed to have need. 100% of undergraduates with need received aid; of those 10% had need fully met. *Average percent of need met:* 73% (excluding resources awarded to replace EFC). *Average financial aid package:* $10,101 (excluding resources awarded to replace EFC). 11% of all full-time undergraduates had no need and received non-need-based gift aid.

GIFT AID (NEED-BASED) *Total amount:* $1,720,710 (32% federal, 23% state, 39% institutional, 6% external sources). *Receiving aid:* Freshmen: 68% (117); All full-time undergraduates: 57% (399). *Average award:* Freshmen: $3754; Undergraduates: $4313. *Scholarships, grants, and awards:* Federal Pell, FSEOG, state, private, college/university gift aid from institutional funds.

GIFT AID (NON-NEED-BASED) *Total amount:* $251,541 (5% state, 75% institutional, 20% external sources). *Receiving aid:* Freshmen: 1% (2); Undergraduates: 1% (7). *Average Award:* Freshmen: $3521; Undergraduates: $2946. *Scholarships, grants, and awards by category:* Creative Arts/Performance: applied art and design, cinema/film/broadcasting, dance, music, performing arts, theater/drama.

LOANS *Student loans:* $2,358,168 (76% need-based, 24% non-need-based). 53% of past graduating class borrowed through all loan programs. *Average indebtedness per student:* $19,384. *Average need-based loan:* Freshmen: $2467; Undergraduates: $3643. *Parent loans:* $1,537,228 (48% need-based, 52% non-need-based). *Programs:* Federal Direct (Subsidized and Unsubsidized Stafford, PLUS), Perkins.

WORK-STUDY *Federal work-study:* Total amount: $54,080; 138 jobs averaging $392.

APPLYING FOR FINANCIAL AID *Required financial aid form:* FAFSA. *Financial aid deadline (priority):* 3/1. *Notification date:* Continuous beginning 4/10. Students must reply within 2 weeks of notification.

CONTACT Jane C. Kamiab, Director of Financial Aid, North Carolina School of the Arts, 1533 South Main Street, Winston-Salem, NC 27127, 336-770-3297. *Fax:* 336-770-1489.

NORTH CAROLINA STATE UNIVERSITY
Raleigh, NC

Tuition & fees (NC res): $4667	Average undergraduate aid package: $8410

ABOUT THE INSTITUTION State-supported, coed. Awards: associate, bachelor's, master's, doctoral, and first professional degrees and first professional certificates. 121 undergraduate majors. Total enrollment: 29,957. Undergraduates: 22,754. Freshmen: 3,957. Both federal and institutional methodology are used as a basis for awarding need-based institutional aid.

UNDERGRADUATE EXPENSES for 2005–06 *Application fee:* $55. *Tuition, state resident:* full-time $3505. *Tuition, nonresident:* full-time $15,403. Full-time tuition and fees vary according to program. Part-time tuition and fees vary according to course load and program. *College room and board:* $6851; *room only:* $4183. Room and board charges vary according to board plan and housing facility. *Payment plan:* Installment.

FRESHMAN FINANCIAL AID (Fall 2004, est.) 2613 applied for aid; of those 64% were deemed to have need. 99% of freshmen with need received aid; of those 38% had need fully met. *Average percent of need met:* 84% (excluding resources awarded to replace EFC). *Average financial aid package:* $8137 (excluding resources awarded to replace EFC). 27% of all full-time freshmen had no need and received non-need-based gift aid.

UNDERGRADUATE FINANCIAL AID (Fall 2004, est.) 10,165 applied for aid; of those 74% were deemed to have need. 98% of undergraduates with need received aid; of those 41% had need fully met. *Average percent of need met:* 82% (excluding resources awarded to replace EFC). *Average financial aid package:* $8410 (excluding resources awarded to replace EFC). 21% of all full-time undergraduates had no need and received non-need-based gift aid.

GIFT AID (NEED-BASED) *Total amount:* $42,187,243 (27% federal, 18% state, 47% institutional, 8% external sources). *Receiving aid:* Freshmen: 41% (1,599); All full-time undergraduates: 38% (7,014). *Average award:* Freshmen: $6200; Undergraduates: $5925. *Scholarships, grants, and awards:* Federal Pell, FSEOG, state, private, college/university gift aid from institutional funds.

GIFT AID (NON-NEED-BASED) *Total amount:* $14,657,398 (1% federal, 4% state, 63% institutional, 32% external sources). *Receiving aid:* Freshmen: 4% (161); Undergraduates: 3% (501). *Average Award:* Freshmen: $6252; Undergraduates: $7306. *Scholarships, grants, and awards by category: Academic Interests/Achievement:* agriculture, biological sciences, business, education, engineering/technologies, general academic interests/achievements, humanities, mathematics, physical sciences, social sciences. *Tuition waivers:* Full or partial for employees or children of employees, senior citizens. *ROTC:* Army, Naval, Air Force.

LOANS *Student loans:* $40,484,917 (57% need-based, 43% non-need-based). 40% of past graduating class borrowed through all loan programs. *Average indebtedness per student:* $17,291. *Average need-based loan:* Freshmen: $2209; Undergraduates: $3155. *Parent loans:* $12,121,824 (11% need-based, 89% non-need-based). *Programs:* FFEL (Subsidized and Unsubsidized Stafford, PLUS), Perkins, state, college/university.

WORK-STUDY *Federal work-study:* Total amount: $842,889; 582 jobs averaging $1448. *State or other work-study/employment:* Total amount: $1,245,283 (45% need-based, 55% non-need-based). 218 part-time jobs averaging $5712.

ATHLETIC AWARDS *Total amount:* $5,729,141 (33% need-based, 67% non-need-based).

APPLYING FOR FINANCIAL AID *Required financial aid forms:* FAFSA, institution's own form. *Financial aid deadline (priority):* 3/1. *Notification date:* Continuous.

CONTACT Ms. Julia Rice Mallette, Director of Scholarships and Financial Aid, North Carolina State University, 2016 Harris Hall, Box 7302, Raleigh, NC 27695-7302, 919-515-2334. *Fax:* 919-515-8422. *E-mail:* julie_mallette@ncsu.edu.

NORTH CAROLINA WESLEYAN COLLEGE
Rocky Mount, NC

ABOUT THE INSTITUTION Independent religious, coed. Awards: bachelor's degrees (also offers adult part-time degree program with significant enrollment not reflected in profile). 26 undergraduate majors. Total enrollment: 1,776. Undergraduates: 1,776. Freshmen: 321.

GIFT AID (NEED-BASED) *Scholarships, grants, and awards:* Federal Pell, FSEOG, state, private, college/university gift aid from institutional funds.

GIFT AID (NON-NEED-BASED) *Scholarships, grants, and awards by category: Academic Interests/Achievement:* general academic interests/achievements. *Special Characteristics:* general special characteristics.

LOANS *Programs:* FFEL (Subsidized and Unsubsidized Stafford, PLUS), Perkins, alternative loans.

APPLYING FOR FINANCIAL AID *Required financial aid form:* FAFSA.

CONTACT Director of Financial Aid, North Carolina Wesleyan College, 3400 North Wesleyan Boulevard, Rocky Mount, NC 27804, 252-985-5290 or toll-free 800-488-6292.

NORTH CENTRAL COLLEGE
Naperville, IL

Tuition & fees: $20,400	Average undergraduate aid package: $18,447

ABOUT THE INSTITUTION Independent United Methodist, coed. Awards: bachelor's and master's degrees. 50 undergraduate majors. Total enrollment: 2,377. Undergraduates: 2,036. Freshmen: 381. Federal methodology is used as a basis for awarding need-based institutional aid.

UNDERGRADUATE EXPENSES for 2004–05 *Application fee:* $25. *Comprehensive fee:* $27,147 includes full-time tuition ($20,160), mandatory fees ($240), and room and board ($6747). Room and board charges vary according to housing facility. *Part-time tuition:* $505 per semester hour. *Part-time fees:* $20 per term. *Payment plan:* Installment.

FRESHMAN FINANCIAL AID (Fall 2004, est.) 324 applied for aid; of those 87% were deemed to have need. 100% of freshmen with need received aid; of those 52% had need fully met. *Average percent of need met:* 92% (excluding resources awarded to replace EFC). *Average financial aid package:* $20,112 (excluding resources awarded to replace EFC). 21% of all full-time freshmen had no need and received non-need-based gift aid.

UNDERGRADUATE FINANCIAL AID (Fall 2004, est.) 1,382 applied for aid; of those 87% were deemed to have need. 100% of undergraduates with need received aid; of those 42% had need fully met. *Average percent of need met:* 86% (excluding resources awarded to replace EFC). *Average financial aid package:* $18,447 (excluding resources awarded to replace EFC). 21% of all full-time undergraduates had no need and received non-need-based gift aid.

GIFT AID (NEED-BASED) *Total amount:* $13,582,985 (6% federal, 18% state, 74% institutional, 2% external sources). *Receiving aid:* Freshmen: 73% (280); All full-time undergraduates: 66% (1,169). *Average award:* Freshmen: $12,815; Undergraduates: $11,338. *Scholarships, grants, and awards:* Federal Pell, FSEOG, state, private, college/university gift aid from institutional funds.

GIFT AID (NON-NEED-BASED) *Total amount:* $3,458,136 (96% institutional, 4% external sources). *Receiving aid:* Freshmen: 21% (80); Undergraduates: 21% (375). *Average Award:* Freshmen: $8416; Undergraduates: $7604. *Scholarships, grants, and awards by category: Academic Interests/Achievement:* 1,315 awards ($7,940,902 total): biological sciences, business, communication, computer science, education, English, foreign languages, general academic interests/achievements, humanities, international studies, mathematics, physical sciences, premedicine, religion/biblical studies, social sciences. *Creative Arts/Performance:* 193 awards ($229,376 total): art/fine arts, cinema/film/broadcasting, debating, journalism/publications, music, theater/drama. *Special Achievements/Activities:* 75 awards ($63,342 total): community service, religious involvement. *Special Characteristics:* 150 awards ($1,083,899 total): adult students, children of faculty/staff, international students, relatives of clergy. *Tuition waivers:* Full or partial for employees or children of employees, senior citizens. *ROTC:* Army cooperative, Air Force cooperative.

LOANS *Student loans:* $7,864,202 (66% need-based, 34% non-need-based). 67% of past graduating class borrowed through all loan programs. *Average indebtedness per student:* $13,527. *Average need-based loan:* Freshmen: $4715; Undergraduates: $5993. *Parent loans:* $1,407,935 (100% need-based). *Programs:* FFEL (Subsidized and Unsubsidized Stafford, PLUS), Perkins, state, college/university.

WORK-STUDY *Federal work-study:* Total amount: $151,620; 217 jobs averaging $698. *State or other work-study/employment:* Total amount: $184,917 (47% need-based, 53% non-need-based). Part-time jobs available.

APPLYING FOR FINANCIAL AID *Required financial aid forms:* FAFSA, institution's own form, federal income tax form(s). *Financial aid deadline:* Continuous. *Notification date:* Continuous beginning 3/1. Students must reply within 4 weeks of notification.
CONTACT Ms. Katherine A. Edmunds, Director of Financial Aid, North Central College, 30 North Brainard Street, PO Box 3065, Naperville, IL 60566-7065, 630-637-5600 or toll-free 800-411-1861. *Fax:* 630-637-5608. *E-mail:* kaedmunds@noctrl.edu.

NORTH CENTRAL UNIVERSITY
Minneapolis, MN

Tuition & fees: $11,284	Average undergraduate aid package: N/A

ABOUT THE INSTITUTION Independent religious, coed. Awards: associate and bachelor's degrees. 31 undergraduate majors. Total enrollment: 1,241. Undergraduates: 1,241. Freshmen: 250. Federal methodology is used as a basis for awarding need-based institutional aid.
UNDERGRADUATE EXPENSES for 2004–05 *Application fee:* $25. *One-time required fee:* $100. *Comprehensive fee:* $15,634 includes full-time tuition ($10,530), mandatory fees ($754), and room and board ($4350). *College room only:* $1990. Room and board charges vary according to board plan and housing facility. *Payment plan:* Installment.
GIFT AID (NEED-BASED) *Total amount:* $5,012,510 (24% federal, 16% state, 54% institutional, 6% external sources). *Scholarships, grants, and awards:* Federal Pell, FSEOG, state, private, college/university gift aid from institutional funds.
GIFT AID (NON-NEED-BASED) *Scholarships, grants, and awards by category:* Academic Interests/Achievement: 428 awards ($519,007 total): general academic interests/achievements. Creative Arts/Performance: 39 awards ($39,000 total): music. Special Achievements/Activities: 985 awards ($876,062 total): community service, general special achievements/activities, leadership, memberships, religious involvement. Special Characteristics: 255 awards ($662,491 total): children of faculty/staff, general special characteristics, international students, relatives of clergy, religious affiliation. *Tuition waivers:* Full or partial for employees or children of employees, senior citizens. *ROTC:* Army cooperative, Air Force cooperative.
LOANS *Student loans:* $6,493,482 (49% need-based, 51% non-need-based). 79% of past graduating class borrowed through all loan programs. *Average indebtedness per student:* $21,965. *Parent loans:* $470,762 (77% need-based, 23% non-need-based). *Programs:* FFEL (Subsidized and Unsubsidized Stafford, PLUS), Perkins, state, alternative loans.
WORK-STUDY *Federal work-study:* Total amount: $139,075; 80 jobs averaging $1738. *State or other work-study/employment:* Total amount: $47,750 (100% need-based). 38 part-time jobs averaging $1257.
APPLYING FOR FINANCIAL AID *Required financial aid form:* FAFSA. *Financial aid deadline:* Continuous. *Notification date:* Continuous beginning 3/19. Students must reply within 2 weeks of notification.
CONTACT Mrs. Donna Jager, Director of Financial Aid, North Central University, 910 Elliot Avenue, Minneapolis, MN 55404-1322, 612-343-4485 or toll-free 800-289-6222. *Fax:* 612-343-8067. *E-mail:* finaid@northcentral.edu.

NORTH DAKOTA STATE UNIVERSITY
Fargo, ND

Tuition & fees (area res): $4775	Average undergraduate aid package: $5487

ABOUT THE INSTITUTION State-supported, coed. Awards: bachelor's, master's, doctoral, and first professional degrees and post-master's certificates. 96 undergraduate majors. Total enrollment: 12,026. Undergraduates: 10,549. Freshmen: 2,161. Federal methodology is used as a basis for awarding need-based institutional aid.
UNDERGRADUATE EXPENSES for 2004–05 *Application fee:* $35. *One-time required fee:* $45. *Tuition, area resident:* full-time $3981; part-time $165.88 per credit. *Tuition, nonresident:* full-time $10,629; part-time $442.88 per credit. *Required fees:* full-time $794; $31.32 per credit. Full-time tuition and fees vary according to reciprocity agreements. Part-time tuition and fees vary according to course load and reciprocity agreements. *College room and board:* $4727; *room only:* $1882. Room and board charges vary according to board plan and housing facility. Minnesota resident, $4,476 per year. *Payment plan:* Installment.
FRESHMAN FINANCIAL AID (Fall 2004, est.) 1532 applied for aid; of those 69% were deemed to have need. 100% of freshmen with need received aid; of those 31% had need fully met. *Average percent of need met:* 75% (excluding resources awarded to replace EFC). *Average financial aid package:* $5603 (excluding resources awarded to replace EFC). 34% of all full-time freshmen had no need and received non-need-based gift aid.
UNDERGRADUATE FINANCIAL AID (Fall 2004, est.) 6,681 applied for aid; of those 77% were deemed to have need. 100% of undergraduates with need received aid; of those 28% had need fully met. *Average percent of need met:* 72% (excluding resources awarded to replace EFC). *Average financial aid package:* $5487 (excluding resources awarded to replace EFC). 17% of all full-time undergraduates had no need and received non-need-based gift aid.
GIFT AID (NEED-BASED) *Total amount:* $9,954,710 (72% federal, 4% state, 20% institutional, 4% external sources). *Receiving aid:* Freshmen: 47% (844); All full-time undergraduates: 37% (3,189). *Average award:* Freshmen: $3550; Undergraduates: $2944. *Scholarships, grants, and awards:* Federal Pell, FSEOG, state, private, college/university gift aid from institutional funds, diversity waivers.
GIFT AID (NON-NEED-BASED) *Total amount:* $1,646,621 (3% federal, 6% state, 77% institutional, 14% external sources). *Receiving aid:* Freshmen: 21% (382); Undergraduates: 11% (991). *Average Award:* Freshmen: $2066; Undergraduates: $1703. *Scholarships, grants, and awards by category:* Academic Interests/Achievement: 2,600 awards ($3,673,253 total): agriculture, architecture, biological sciences, business, communication, computer science, education, engineering/technologies, English, general academic interests/achievements, health fields, home economics, humanities, mathematics, military science, physical sciences, premedicine, social sciences. Creative Arts/Performance: 106 awards ($73,923 total): art/fine arts, debating, journalism/publications, music, theater/drama. Special Achievements/Activities: memberships, religious involvement. Special Characteristics: 774 awards ($1,329,577 total): children of faculty/staff, ethnic background. *Tuition waivers:* Full or partial for minority students, children of alumni, employees or children of employees, senior citizens. *ROTC:* Army, Air Force.
LOANS *Student loans:* $32,990,096 (78% need-based, 22% non-need-based). 68% of past graduating class borrowed through all loan programs. *Average indebtedness per student:* $22,675. *Average need-based loan:* Freshmen: $2913; Undergraduates: $3838. *Parent loans:* $1,178,091 (61% need-based, 39% non-need-based). *Programs:* FFEL (Subsidized and Unsubsidized Stafford, PLUS), Perkins, Federal Nursing, alternative loans.
WORK-STUDY *Federal work-study:* Total amount: $1,706,669; 853 jobs averaging $1774.
ATHLETIC AWARDS *Total amount:* $786,858 (57% need-based, 43% non-need-based).
APPLYING FOR FINANCIAL AID *Required financial aid form:* FAFSA. *Financial aid deadline (priority):* 3/15. *Notification date:* Continuous.
CONTACT James Kennedy, Director of Financial Aid, North Dakota State University, PO Box 5315, Fargo, ND 58105, 701-231-7536 or toll-free 800-488-NDSU. *Fax:* 701-231-6126. *E-mail:* james.kennedy@ndsu.nodak.edu.

NORTHEASTERN ILLINOIS UNIVERSITY
Chicago, IL

Tuition & fees (IL res): $4235	Average undergraduate aid package: $6043

ABOUT THE INSTITUTION State-supported, coed. Awards: bachelor's and master's degrees. 42 undergraduate majors. Total enrollment: 12,164. Undergraduates: 9,305. Freshmen: 1,062. Federal methodology is used as a basis for awarding need-based institutional aid.
UNDERGRADUATE EXPENSES for 2004–05 *Application fee:* $25. *Tuition, state resident:* full-time $3720; part-time $124 per credit hour. *Tuition, nonresident:* full-time $7440; part-time $248 per credit hour. Full-time tuition and fees vary according to student level.
FRESHMAN FINANCIAL AID (Fall 2004, est.) 689 applied for aid; of those 73% were deemed to have need. 98% of freshmen with need received aid; of those 6% had need fully met. *Average percent of need met:* 61% (excluding resources awarded to replace EFC). *Average financial aid package:* $5324 (excluding resources awarded to replace EFC). 1% of all full-time freshmen had no need and received non-need-based gift aid.
UNDERGRADUATE FINANCIAL AID (Fall 2004, est.) 3,208 applied for aid; of those 80% were deemed to have need. 96% of undergraduates with need received aid; of those 16% had need fully met. *Average percent of need met:* 62% (excluding resources awarded to replace EFC). *Average financial aid package:* $6043 (excluding resources awarded to replace EFC). 2% of all full-time undergraduates had no need and received non-need-based gift aid.

GIFT AID (NEED-BASED) *Total amount:* $14,250,000 (60% federal, 40% state). *Receiving aid:* Freshmen: 46% (450); All full-time undergraduates: 42% (2,163). *Average award:* Freshmen: $5001; Undergraduates: $4462. *Scholarships, grants, and awards:* Federal Pell, FSEOG, state, private, college/university gift aid from institutional funds.

GIFT AID (NON-NEED-BASED) *Total amount:* $1,557,000 (72% state, 10% institutional, 18% external sources). *Receiving aid:* Freshmen: 3% (28); Undergraduates: 3% (168). *Average Award:* Freshmen: $860; Undergraduates: $1080. *Scholarships, grants, and awards by category: Academic Interests/Achievement:* 297 awards ($380,711 total): biological sciences, business, communication, computer science, education, English, foreign languages, general academic interests/achievements, mathematics, physical sciences, social sciences. *Creative Arts/Performance:* 94 awards ($159,082 total): art/fine arts, creative writing, dance, journalism/publications, music, performing arts, theater/drama. *Special Achievements/Activities:* 7 awards ($10,739 total): general special achievements/activities, leadership. *Special Characteristics:* 91 awards ($89,329 total): adult students, children of faculty/staff, general special characteristics. *ROTC:* Army cooperative, Air Force cooperative.

LOANS *Student loans:* $7,776,000 (63% need-based, 37% non-need-based). 29% of past graduating class borrowed through all loan programs. *Average indebtedness per student:* $10,941. *Average need-based loan:* Freshmen: $2300; Undergraduates: $3731. *Parent loans:* $60,000 (100% non-need-based). *Programs:* FFEL (Subsidized and Unsubsidized Stafford, PLUS), Perkins.

WORK-STUDY *Federal work-study:* Total amount: $482,000; 250 jobs averaging $1928. *State or other work-study/employment:* Total amount: $944,700 (100% non-need-based). 448 part-time jobs averaging $1863.

APPLYING FOR FINANCIAL AID *Required financial aid forms:* FAFSA, institution's own form. *Financial aid deadline (priority):* 3/1. *Notification date:* Continuous beginning 4/1. Students must reply within 3 weeks of notification.

CONTACT Financial Aid Office, Northeastern Illinois University, 5500 North St. Louis Avenue, Chicago, IL 60625, 773-442-5000. *Fax:* 773-442-5040. *E-mail:* financialaid@neiu.edu.

NORTHEASTERN STATE UNIVERSITY
Tahlequah, OK

Tuition & fees (OK res): $3000	Average undergraduate aid package: $7771

ABOUT THE INSTITUTION State-supported, coed. Awards: bachelor's, master's, and first professional degrees. 65 undergraduate majors. Total enrollment: 9,562. Undergraduates: 8,543. Freshmen: 1,302. Federal methodology is used as a basis for awarding need-based institutional aid.

UNDERGRADUATE EXPENSES for 2004–05 *Tuition, state resident:* full-time $3000; part-time $100 per credit hour. *Tuition, nonresident:* full-time $7350; part-time $245 per credit hour. Full-time tuition and fees vary according to course level, course load, and location. Part-time tuition and fees vary according to course level and course load. *College room and board:* $3080. Room and board charges vary according to board plan and housing facility.

FRESHMAN FINANCIAL AID (Fall 2003) 1126 applied for aid; of those 71% were deemed to have need. 98% of freshmen with need received aid; of those 14% had need fully met. *Average percent of need met:* 64% (excluding resources awarded to replace EFC). *Average financial aid package:* $6477 (excluding resources awarded to replace EFC). 2% of all full-time freshmen had no need and received non-need-based gift aid.

UNDERGRADUATE FINANCIAL AID (Fall 2003) 5,649 applied for aid; of those 79% were deemed to have need. 99% of undergraduates with need received aid; of those 17% had need fully met. *Average percent of need met:* 68% (excluding resources awarded to replace EFC). *Average financial aid package:* $7771 (excluding resources awarded to replace EFC). 2% of all full-time undergraduates had no need and received non-need-based gift aid.

GIFT AID (NEED-BASED) *Total amount:* $14,850,195 (83% federal, 11% state, 2% institutional, 4% external sources). *Receiving aid:* Freshmen: 49% (612); All full-time undergraduates: 54% (3,444). *Average award:* Freshmen: $3274; Undergraduates: $3415. *Scholarships, grants, and awards:* Federal Pell, FSEOG, state, private, college/university gift aid from institutional funds.

GIFT AID (NON-NEED-BASED) *Total amount:* $1,248,885 (35% institutional, 65% external sources). *Receiving aid:* Freshmen: 58% (725); Undergraduates: 63% (4,047). *Average Award:* Freshmen: $1863; Undergraduates: $2108. *Scholarships, grants, and awards by category: Academic Interests/Achievement:* 1,267 awards ($1,417,805 total): biological sciences, business, communication, computer science, education, English, foreign languages, general academic interests/achievements, health fields, home economics, humanities, library science, mathematics, physical sciences, premedicine, social sciences. *Creative*

Arts/Performance: 221 awards ($189,635 total): applied art and design, art/fine arts, dance, debating, journalism/publications, music, performing arts, theater/drama. *Special Achievements/Activities:* 38 awards ($33,080 total): cheerleading/drum major, community service, junior miss, leadership. *Special Characteristics:* 69 awards ($56,785 total): children and siblings of alumni, children of faculty/staff, children with a deceased or disabled parent, spouses of deceased or disabled public servants. *Tuition waivers:* Full or partial for employees or children of employees, senior citizens. *ROTC:* Army.

LOANS *Student loans:* $30,880,755 (56% need-based, 44% non-need-based). 63% of past graduating class borrowed through all loan programs. *Average indebtedness per student:* $16,047. *Average need-based loan:* Freshmen: $2079; Undergraduates: $3488. *Parent loans:* $1,030,221 (100% non-need-based). *Programs:* FFEL (Subsidized and Unsubsidized Stafford, PLUS), Perkins, college/university.

WORK-STUDY *Federal work-study:* Total amount: $556,867; 328 jobs averaging $2600. *State or other work-study/employment:* Total amount: $1,467,194 (100% non-need-based). 768 part-time jobs averaging $3000.

ATHLETIC AWARDS *Total amount:* $815,335 (100% non-need-based).

APPLYING FOR FINANCIAL AID *Required financial aid forms:* FAFSA, institution's own form. *Financial aid deadline (priority):* 4/1. *Notification date:* Continuous beginning 2/1. Students must reply within 2 weeks of notification.

CONTACT Teri Cochran, Director of Student Financial Services, Northeastern State University, 715 North Grand Avenue, Tahlequah, OK 74464-2399, 918-456-5511 Ext. 3410 or toll-free 800-722-9614 (in-state). *Fax:* 918-458-2510. *E-mail:* kindlet@nsuok.edu.

NORTHEASTERN UNIVERSITY
Boston, MA

Tuition & fees: $27,080	Average undergraduate aid package: $15,974

ABOUT THE INSTITUTION Independent, coed. Awards: bachelor's, master's, doctoral, and first professional degrees and post-master's certificates. 84 undergraduate majors. Total enrollment: 18,979. Undergraduates: 2,778. Freshmen: 2,778. Both federal and institutional methodology are used as a basis for awarding need-based institutional aid.

UNDERGRADUATE EXPENSES for 2004–05 *Application fee:* $50. *Comprehensive fee:* $37,260 includes full-time tuition ($26,750), mandatory fees ($330), and room and board ($10,180). *College room only:* $5440. Room and board charges vary according to board plan and housing facility. *Payment plans:* Installment, deferred payment.

FRESHMAN FINANCIAL AID (Fall 2004, est.) 2281 applied for aid; of those 84% were deemed to have need. 99% of freshmen with need received aid; of those 14% had need fully met. *Average percent of need met:* 68% (excluding resources awarded to replace EFC). *Average financial aid package:* $17,725 (excluding resources awarded to replace EFC). 19% of all full-time freshmen had no need and received non-need-based gift aid.

UNDERGRADUATE FINANCIAL AID (Fall 2004, est.) 10,842 applied for aid; of those 87% were deemed to have need. 99% of undergraduates with need received aid; of those 15% had need fully met. *Average percent of need met:* 61% (excluding resources awarded to replace EFC). *Average financial aid package:* $15,974 (excluding resources awarded to replace EFC). 15% of all full-time undergraduates had no need and received non-need-based gift aid.

GIFT AID (NEED-BASED) *Total amount:* $100,883,433 (9% federal, 4% state, 84% institutional, 3% external sources). *Receiving aid:* Freshmen: 67% (1,855); All full-time undergraduates: 60% (8,833). *Average award:* Freshmen: $13,965; Undergraduates: $11,737. *Scholarships, grants, and awards:* Federal Pell, FSEOG, state, private, college/university gift aid from institutional funds, Federal Nursing, Scholarships for Disadvantaged Students (SDS).

GIFT AID (NON-NEED-BASED) *Total amount:* $20,012,743 (92% institutional, 8% external sources). *Receiving aid:* Freshmen: 7% (199); Undergraduates: 6% (849). *Average Award:* Freshmen: $13,349; Undergraduates: $12,932. *Scholarships, grants, and awards by category: Academic Interests/Achievement:* 5,093 awards ($42,647,920 total): engineering/technologies, general academic interests/achievements. *Creative Arts/Performance:* 18 awards ($183,337 total): music. *Special Characteristics:* 62 awards ($324,375 total): international students. *Tuition waivers:* Full or partial for employees or children of employees, senior citizens. *ROTC:* Army, Naval cooperative, Air Force cooperative.

LOANS *Student loans:* $92,254,152 (71% need-based, 29% non-need-based). *Average need-based loan:* Freshmen: $3588; Undergraduates: $4763. *Parent loans:* $21,310,691 (41% need-based, 59% non-need-based). *Programs:* FFEL

(Subsidized and Unsubsidized Stafford, PLUS), Perkins, Federal Nursing, state, TERI Loans, Massachusetts No-Interest Loans (NIL), MEFA Loans, CitiAssist Loans.

WORK-STUDY *Federal work-study:* Total amount: $5,984,650; 3,479 jobs averaging $1448.

ATHLETIC AWARDS *Total amount:* $7,995,483 (43% need-based, 57% non-need-based).

APPLYING FOR FINANCIAL AID *Required financial aid forms:* FAFSA, CSS Financial Aid PROFILE. *Financial aid deadline (priority):* 2/15. *Notification date:* Continuous. Students must reply by 5/1.

CONTACT Mr. M. Seamus Harreys, Dean of Student Financial Services, Northeastern University, 360 Huntington Avenue, Boston, MA 02115, 617-373-3190. *Fax:* 617-373-8735. *E-mail:* sfs@neu.edu.

NORTHERN ARIZONA UNIVERSITY
Flagstaff, AZ

Tuition & fees (AZ res): $4073	Average undergraduate aid package: $7943

ABOUT THE INSTITUTION State-supported, coed. Awards: bachelor's, master's, doctoral, and first professional degrees and post-bachelor's and post-master's certificates. 105 undergraduate majors. Total enrollment: 19,147. Undergraduates: 13,333. Freshmen: 2,528. Federal methodology is used as a basis for awarding need-based institutional aid.

UNDERGRADUATE EXPENSES for 2004–05 *Application fee:* $25. *Tuition, state resident:* full-time $3983; part-time $208 per credit. *Tuition, nonresident:* full-time $12,503; part-time $524 per credit. *Required fees:* full-time $90; $23 per term part-time. Full-time tuition and fees vary according to program. Part-time tuition and fees vary according to program. *College room and board:* $5785; *room only:* $3160. Room and board charges vary according to board plan and housing facility.

FRESHMAN FINANCIAL AID (Fall 2003) 1681 applied for aid; of those 63% were deemed to have need. 99% of freshmen with need received aid; of those 24% had need fully met. *Average percent of need met:* 70% (excluding resources awarded to replace EFC). *Average financial aid package:* $6597 (excluding resources awarded to replace EFC). 2% of all full-time freshmen had no need and received non-need-based gift aid.

UNDERGRADUATE FINANCIAL AID (Fall 2003) 7,715 applied for aid; of those 76% were deemed to have need. 99% of undergraduates with need received aid; of those 25% had need fully met. *Average percent of need met:* 70% (excluding resources awarded to replace EFC). *Average financial aid package:* $7943 (excluding resources awarded to replace EFC). 4% of all full-time undergraduates had no need and received non-need-based gift aid.

GIFT AID (NEED-BASED) *Total amount:* $29,312,548 (47% federal, 1% state, 41% institutional, 11% external sources). *Receiving aid:* Freshmen: 29% (607); All full-time undergraduates: 36% (3,977). *Average award:* Freshmen: $4355; Undergraduates: $4501. *Scholarships, grants, and awards:* Federal Pell, FSEOG, state, private, college/university gift aid from institutional funds, Federal Nursing.

GIFT AID (NON-NEED-BASED) *Total amount:* $7,736,246 (6% federal, 78% institutional, 16% external sources). *Receiving aid:* Freshmen: 33% (708); Undergraduates: 23% (2,592). *Average Award:* Freshmen: $1486; Undergraduates: $1217. *Scholarships, grants, and awards by category: Academic Interests/ Achievement:* 655 awards ($795,426 total): biological sciences, business, communication, computer science, education, engineering/technologies, English, foreign languages, general academic interests/achievements, health fields, home economics, humanities, international studies, mathematics, military science, physical sciences, premedicine, religion/biblical studies, social sciences. *Creative Arts/Performance:* 306 awards ($913,495 total): art/fine arts, cinema/film/ broadcasting, creative writing, debating, journalism/publications, music, performing arts, theater/drama. *Special Characteristics:* 1,713 awards ($1,559,708 total): children and siblings of alumni, children of educators, children of faculty/staff, children of public servants, first-generation college students, handicapped students, international students, local/state students, out-of-state students, spouses of deceased or disabled public servants. *Tuition waivers:* Full or partial for employees or children of employees. *ROTC:* Army, Air Force.

LOANS *Student loans:* $38,065,393 (83% need-based, 17% non-need-based). 50% of past graduating class borrowed through all loan programs. *Average indebtedness per student:* $17,901. *Average need-based loan:* Freshmen: $2522; Undergraduates: $3715. *Parent loans:* $5,794,138 (59% need-based, 41% non-need-based). *Programs:* Federal Direct (Subsidized and Unsubsidized Stafford, PLUS), Perkins, Federal Nursing, college/university.

WORK-STUDY *Federal work-study:* Total amount: $897,316; 588 jobs averaging $1526. *State or other work-study/employment:* Total amount: $7,438,568 (51% need-based, 49% non-need-based). 3,041 part-time jobs averaging $2446.

ATHLETIC AWARDS *Total amount:* $2,756,623 (47% need-based, 53% non-need-based).

APPLYING FOR FINANCIAL AID *Required financial aid form:* FAFSA. *Financial aid deadline (priority):* 2/14. *Notification date:* Continuous beginning 3/15.

CONTACT Terri Eckel, Associate Director, Financial Aid, Northern Arizona University, Box 4108, Flagstaff, AZ 86011-4108, 928-523-4108 or toll-free 888-MORE-NAU. *Fax:* 928-523-1551.

NORTHERN ILLINOIS UNIVERSITY
De Kalb, IL

Tuition & fees (IL res): $5760	Average undergraduate aid package: $9042

ABOUT THE INSTITUTION State-supported, coed. Awards: bachelor's, master's, doctoral, and first professional degrees. 61 undergraduate majors. Total enrollment: 24,818. Undergraduates: 18,029. Freshmen: 2,951. Federal methodology is used as a basis for awarding need-based institutional aid.

UNDERGRADUATE EXPENSES for 2004–05 *Tuition, state resident:* full-time $4830. *Tuition, nonresident:* full-time $9690. Full-time tuition and fees vary according to course load. Part-time tuition and fees vary according to course load. *College room and board:* $5740. Room and board charges vary according to board plan and housing facility. *Payment plan:* Installment.

FRESHMAN FINANCIAL AID (Fall 2003) 2791 applied for aid; of those 70% were deemed to have need. 95% of freshmen with need received aid; of those 42% had need fully met. *Average percent of need met:* 77% (excluding resources awarded to replace EFC). *Average financial aid package:* $8636 (excluding resources awarded to replace EFC). 4% of all full-time freshmen had no need and received non-need-based gift aid.

UNDERGRADUATE FINANCIAL AID (Fall 2003) 12,400 applied for aid; of those 70% were deemed to have need. 97% of undergraduates with need received aid; of those 42% had need fully met. *Average percent of need met:* 79% (excluding resources awarded to replace EFC). *Average financial aid package:* $9042 (excluding resources awarded to replace EFC). 4% of all full-time undergraduates had no need and received non-need-based gift aid.

GIFT AID (NEED-BASED) *Total amount:* $32,354,157 (45% federal, 55% state). *Receiving aid:* Freshmen: 38% (1,234); All full-time undergraduates: 34% (5,563). *Average award:* Freshmen: $6275; Undergraduates: $5498. *Scholarships, grants, and awards:* Federal Pell, FSEOG, state, private, college/ university gift aid from institutional funds, Federal Nursing.

GIFT AID (NON-NEED-BASED) *Total amount:* $7,194,260 (10% federal, 49% state, 17% institutional, 24% external sources). *Receiving aid:* Freshmen: 38% (1,234); Undergraduates: 20% (3,222). *Average Award: Freshmen:* $2014; *Undergraduates:* $2207. *Scholarships, grants, and awards by category: Academic Interests/Achievement:* business, engineering/technologies, foreign languages, general academic interests/achievements. *Creative Arts/Performance:* applied art and design, art/fine arts, creative writing, dance, journalism/ publications, music, performing arts, theater/drama. *Special Achievements/ Activities:* leadership. *Special Characteristics:* adult students, children of faculty/ staff, ethnic background, international students, members of minority groups, veterans. *Tuition waivers:* Full or partial for minority students, employees or children of employees. *ROTC:* Army, Air Force cooperative.

LOANS *Student loans:* $51,978,768 (57% need-based, 43% non-need-based). 55% of past graduating class borrowed through all loan programs. *Average indebtedness per student:* $15,052. *Average need-based loan:* Freshmen: $2426; Undergraduates: $3852. *Parent loans:* $8,659,199 (100% non-need-based). *Programs:* FFEL (Subsidized and Unsubsidized Stafford, PLUS), Perkins, college/ university.

WORK-STUDY *Federal work-study:* Total amount: $575,943; 436 jobs averaging $1320. *State or other work-study/employment:* Total amount: $5,942,048 (100% non-need-based). 3,763 part-time jobs averaging $1579.

ATHLETIC AWARDS *Total amount:* $3,402,007 (100% non-need-based).

APPLYING FOR FINANCIAL AID *Required financial aid forms:* FAFSA, institution's own form. *Financial aid deadline (priority):* 3/1. *Notification date:* 3/26. Students must reply within 2 weeks of notification.

CONTACT Ms. Kathleen D. Brunson, Director of Student Financial Aid, Northern Illinois University, De Kalb, IL 60115-2854, 815-753-1395 or toll-free 800-892-3050 (in-state). *Fax:* 815-753-9475.

NORTHERN KENTUCKY UNIVERSITY
Highland Heights, KY

Tuition & fees (KY res): $4368   **Average undergraduate aid package: $7079**

ABOUT THE INSTITUTION State-supported, coed. Awards: associate, bachelor's, master's, and first professional degrees. 74 undergraduate majors. Total enrollment: 13,908. Undergraduates: 12,057. Freshmen: 2,071. Federal methodology is used as a basis for awarding need-based institutional aid.

UNDERGRADUATE EXPENSES for 2004–05 *Application fee:* $30. *Tuition, state resident:* full-time $4368; part-time $182 per credit hour. *Tuition, nonresident:* full-time $9096; part-time $379 per credit hour. Full-time tuition and fees vary according to location. Part-time tuition and fees vary according to location. *College room and board:* $4660; *room only:* $2580. Room and board charges vary according to board plan, housing facility, and location. *Payment plan:* Installment.

FRESHMAN FINANCIAL AID (Fall 2003) 1841 applied for aid; of those 80% were deemed to have need. 100% of freshmen with need received aid. *Average percent of need met:* 90% (excluding resources awarded to replace EFC). *Average financial aid package:* $5624 (excluding resources awarded to replace EFC). 22% of all full-time freshmen had no need and received non-need-based gift aid.

UNDERGRADUATE FINANCIAL AID (Fall 2003) 6,710 applied for aid; of those 80% were deemed to have need. 100% of undergraduates with need received aid. *Average percent of need met:* 85% (excluding resources awarded to replace EFC). *Average financial aid package:* $7079 (excluding resources awarded to replace EFC). 15% of all full-time undergraduates had no need and received non-need-based gift aid.

GIFT AID (NEED-BASED) *Total amount:* $9,531,169 (81% federal, 19% state). *Receiving aid:* Freshmen: 46% (883); All full-time undergraduates: 36% (3,221). *Average award:* Freshmen: $4368; Undergraduates: $4368. *Scholarships, grants, and awards:* Federal Pell, FSEOG, state, private.

GIFT AID (NON-NEED-BASED) *Total amount:* $10,360,674 (38% state, 55% institutional, 7% external sources). *Receiving aid:* Freshmen: 18% (343); Undergraduates: 17% (1,558). *Average Award:* Freshmen: $3766; Undergraduates: $3766. *Scholarships, grants, and awards by category: Academic Interests/Achievement:* 1,418 awards ($4,484,257 total): general academic interests/achievements. *Creative Arts/Performance:* 100 awards ($131,033 total): art/fine arts. *Special Characteristics:* 188 awards ($725,775 total): general special characteristics, members of minority groups, spouses of deceased or disabled public servants, veterans' children. *Tuition waivers:* Full or partial for employees or children of employees, senior citizens. *ROTC:* Army, Air Force cooperative.

LOANS *Student loans:* $26,611,918 (96% need-based, 4% non-need-based). 29% of past graduating class borrowed through all loan programs. *Average indebtedness per student:* $18,758. *Average need-based loan:* Freshmen: $2625; Undergraduates: $5306. *Parent loans:* $2,789,351 (100% non-need-based). *Programs:* FFEL (Subsidized and Unsubsidized Stafford, PLUS), Perkins, alternative loans.

WORK-STUDY *Federal work-study:* Total amount: $459,053; 283 jobs averaging $1622. *State or other work-study/employment:* Total amount: $1,764,800 (100% non-need-based). 782 part-time jobs averaging $1749.

ATHLETIC AWARDS *Total amount:* $617,269 (100% non-need-based).

APPLYING FOR FINANCIAL AID *Required financial aid form:* FAFSA. *Financial aid deadline (priority):* 3/1. *Notification date:* Continuous beginning 4/1. Students must reply within 3 weeks of notification.

CONTACT Mr. Robert F. Sprague, Director of Student Financial Assistance, Northern Kentucky University, 416 Administrative Center, Nunn Drive, Highland Heights, KY 41099, 859-572-5143 or toll-free 800-637-9948. *Fax:* 859-572-6997. *E-mail:* ofa@nku.edu.

NORTHERN MICHIGAN UNIVERSITY
Marquette, MI

Tuition & fees (MI res): $5434   **Average undergraduate aid package: $7466**

ABOUT THE INSTITUTION State-supported, coed. Awards: associate, bachelor's, and master's degrees and post-bachelor's and post-master's certificates. 153 undergraduate majors. Total enrollment: 9,846. Undergraduates: 9,118. Freshmen: 1,692. Federal methodology is used as a basis for awarding need-based institutional aid.

UNDERGRADUATE EXPENSES for 2004–05 *Application fee:* $30. *One-time required fee:* $100. *Tuition, state resident:* full-time $4776; part-time $199 per credit hour. *Tuition, nonresident:* full-time $8184; part-time $341 per credit hour. *Required fees:* full-time $658; $30 per term part-time. Part-time tuition and fees vary according to location. *College room and board:* $6182. Room and board charges vary according to board plan and housing facility. *Payment plans:* Installment, deferred payment.

FRESHMAN FINANCIAL AID (Fall 2004, est.) 1659 applied for aid; of those 64% were deemed to have need. 98% of freshmen with need received aid; of those 6% had need fully met. *Average percent of need met:* 76% (excluding resources awarded to replace EFC). *Average financial aid package:* $7505 (excluding resources awarded to replace EFC).

UNDERGRADUATE FINANCIAL AID (Fall 2004, est.) 6,859 applied for aid; of those 70% were deemed to have need. 98% of undergraduates with need received aid; of those 6% had need fully met. *Average percent of need met:* 74% (excluding resources awarded to replace EFC). *Average financial aid package:* $7466 (excluding resources awarded to replace EFC). 1% of all full-time undergraduates had no need and received non-need-based gift aid.

GIFT AID (NEED-BASED) *Total amount:* $11,290,988 (72% federal, 10% state, 17% institutional, 1% external sources). *Receiving aid:* Freshmen: 50% (827); All full-time undergraduates: 48% (3,569). *Average award:* Freshmen: $4091; Undergraduates: $3888. *Scholarships, grants, and awards:* Federal Pell, FSEOG, state, private, college/university gift aid from institutional funds.

GIFT AID (NON-NEED-BASED) *Total amount:* $8,912,071 (12% state, 69% institutional, 19% external sources). *Receiving aid:* Undergraduates: 1% (59). *Average Award:* Undergraduates: $21,548. *Scholarships, grants, and awards by category: Academic Interests/Achievement:* business, engineering/technologies, general academic interests/achievements, health fields, military science, premedicine. *Creative Arts/Performance:* applied art and design, music, theater/drama. *Special Achievements/Activities:* leadership. *Special Characteristics:* adult students, children of union members/company employees, members of minority groups, out-of-state students. *Tuition waivers:* Full or partial for employees or children of employees, senior citizens. *ROTC:* Army.

LOANS *Student loans:* $22,126,045 (61% need-based, 39% non-need-based). 72% of past graduating class borrowed through all loan programs. *Average indebtedness per student:* $15,776. *Average need-based loan:* Freshmen: $3368; Undergraduates: $3788. *Parent loans:* $2,056,926 (100% non-need-based). *Programs:* Federal Direct (Subsidized and Unsubsidized Stafford, PLUS), Perkins, state.

WORK-STUDY *Federal work-study:* Total amount: $2,949,514; jobs available. *State or other work-study/employment:* Total amount: $405,017 (100% need-based). Part-time jobs available.

ATHLETIC AWARDS *Total amount:* $1,455,021 (100% non-need-based).

APPLYING FOR FINANCIAL AID *Required financial aid form:* FAFSA. *Financial aid deadline (priority):* 2/20. *Notification date:* Continuous beginning 4/1. Students must reply within 2 weeks of notification.

CONTACT Carol Waldmann, Acting Director of Financial Aid, Northern Michigan University, 1401 Presque Isle Avenue, Marquette, MI 49855, 906-227-1564 or toll-free 800-682-9797 Ext. 1 (in-state), 800-682-9797 (out-of-state). *Fax:* 906-227-2321. *E-mail:* fao@nmu.edu.

NORTHERN STATE UNIVERSITY
Aberdeen, SD

Tuition & fees (SD res): $4448   **Average undergraduate aid package: $6009**

ABOUT THE INSTITUTION State-supported, coed. Awards: associate, bachelor's, and master's degrees and post-bachelor's certificates. 53 undergraduate majors. Total enrollment: 2,346. Undergraduates: 2,218. Freshmen: 400. Federal methodology is used as a basis for awarding need-based institutional aid.

UNDERGRADUATE EXPENSES for 2004–05 *Application fee:* $15. *Tuition, state resident:* full-time $2223; part-time $74.10 per credit hour. *Tuition, nonresident:* full-time $7066; part-time $235.55 per credit hour. *Required fees:* full-time $2225; $74.17 per credit hour. Full-time tuition and fees vary according to course level, course load, and reciprocity agreements. Part-time tuition and fees vary according to course level, course load, and reciprocity agreements. *College room and board:* $3733; *room only:* $1980. Room and board charges vary according to board plan. *Payment plan:* Installment.

FRESHMAN FINANCIAL AID (Fall 2004, est.) 299 applied for aid; of those 84% were deemed to have need. 99% of freshmen with need received aid; of those 100% had need fully met. *Average financial aid package:* $5642 (excluding resources awarded to replace EFC). 7% of all full-time freshmen had no need and received non-need-based gift aid.

UNDERGRADUATE FINANCIAL AID (Fall 2004, est.) 1,259 applied for aid; of those 83% were deemed to have need. 99% of undergraduates with need received aid; of those 100% had need fully met. *Average financial aid package:* $6009 (excluding resources awarded to replace EFC). 5% of all full-time undergraduates had no need and received non-need-based gift aid.

GIFT AID (NEED-BASED) *Total amount:* $2,532,516 (90% federal, 10% state). *Receiving aid:* Freshmen: 56% (211); All full-time undergraduates: 50% (791). *Average award:* Freshmen: $2481; Undergraduates: $2527. *Scholarships, grants, and awards:* Federal Pell, FSEOG, state, private.

GIFT AID (NON-NEED-BASED) *Total amount:* $848,275 (59% institutional, 41% external sources). *Receiving aid:* Freshmen: 59% (226); Undergraduates: 53% (847). *Average Award:* Freshmen: $1573; Undergraduates: $1294. *Scholarships, grants, and awards by category: Academic Interests/Achievement:* 224 awards ($110,974 total): biological sciences, business, education, English, foreign languages, general academic interests/achievements, humanities, international studies, mathematics, physical sciences, social sciences. *Creative Arts/Performance:* 105 awards ($52,262 total): art/fine arts, music, theater/drama. *Special Achievements/Activities:* 37 awards ($12,425 total): leadership.

LOANS *Student loans:* $7,950,738 (54% need-based, 46% non-need-based). 79% of past graduating class borrowed through all loan programs. *Average indebtedness per student:* $19,330. *Average need-based loan:* Freshmen: $3278; Undergraduates: $3378. *Parent loans:* $234,943 (100% non-need-based). *Programs:* FFEL (Subsidized and Unsubsidized Stafford, PLUS), Perkins, college/university, SELF Loans, alternative loans.

WORK-STUDY *Federal work-study:* Total amount: $632,900; 382 jobs averaging $1657. *State or other work-study/employment:* Total amount: $465,900 (100% non-need-based). 376 part-time jobs averaging $1239.

ATHLETIC AWARDS *Total amount:* $428,600 (100% non-need-based).

APPLYING FOR FINANCIAL AID *Required financial aid form:* FAFSA. *Financial aid deadline (priority):* 3/1. *Notification date:* 4/15. Students must reply within 2 weeks of notification.

CONTACT Ms. Sharon Kienow, Director of Financial Aid, Northern State University, 1200 South Jay Street, Aberdeen, SD 57401-7198, 605-626-2640 or toll-free 800-678-5330. *Fax:* 605-626-2587. *E-mail:* kienows@northern.edu.

NORTHFACE UNIVERSITY
Salt Lake City, UT

CONTACT Financial Aid Office, Northface University, 2755 East Cottonwood Parkway, Suite 600, Salt Lake City, UT 84121, 801-438-1100 or toll-free 866-622-3448.

NORTH GEORGIA COLLEGE & STATE UNIVERSITY
Dahlonega, GA

ABOUT THE INSTITUTION State-supported, coed. Awards: associate, bachelor's, and master's degrees and post-bachelor's and post-master's certificates. 48 undergraduate majors. Total enrollment: 4,552. Undergraduates: 4,014. Freshmen: 750.

GIFT AID (NEED-BASED) *Scholarships, grants, and awards:* Federal Pell, FSEOG, state, private, college/university gift aid from institutional funds.

GIFT AID (NON-NEED-BASED) *Scholarships, grants, and awards by category: Academic Interests/Achievement:* biological sciences, business, education, English, general academic interests/achievements, health fields, humanities, mathematics, military science, physical sciences, premedicine. *Creative Arts/Performance:* applied art and design, general creative arts/performance, music. *Special Achievements/Activities:* cheerleading/drum major, community service, general special achievements/activities, leadership. *Special Characteristics:* general special characteristics.

LOANS *Programs:* FFEL (Subsidized and Unsubsidized Stafford, PLUS), Perkins, state, college/university.

APPLYING FOR FINANCIAL AID *Required financial aid forms:* FAFSA, institution's own form.

CONTACT Charles Hawkins, Director, Institutional Research and Planning, North Georgia College & State University, 110 Barnes Hall, Dahlonega, GA 30597-1001, 706-864-1840 or toll-free 800-498-9581. *Fax:* 706-864-1411. *E-mail:* chawkins@ngcsu.edu.

NORTH GREENVILLE COLLEGE
Tigerville, SC

Tuition & fees: $10,350	Average undergraduate aid package: $8000

ABOUT THE INSTITUTION Independent Southern Baptist, coed. Awards: associate and bachelor's degrees. 30 undergraduate majors. Total enrollment: 1,766. Undergraduates: 1,766. Freshmen: 474. Federal methodology is used as a basis for awarding need-based institutional aid.

UNDERGRADUATE EXPENSES for 2005–06 *Application fee:* $25. *Comprehensive fee:* $16,300 includes full-time tuition ($10,350) and room and board ($5950). *Part-time tuition:* $200 per hour. Part-time tuition and fees vary according to course load. *Payment plan:* Installment.

FRESHMAN FINANCIAL AID (Fall 2004, est.) 427 applied for aid; of those 44% were deemed to have need. 100% of freshmen with need received aid; of those 40% had need fully met. *Average percent of need met:* 70% (excluding resources awarded to replace EFC). *Average financial aid package:* $8100 (excluding resources awarded to replace EFC). 11% of all full-time freshmen had no need and received non-need-based gift aid.

UNDERGRADUATE FINANCIAL AID (Fall 2004, est.) 1,387 applied for aid; of those 43% were deemed to have need. 100% of undergraduates with need received aid; of those 46% had need fully met. *Average percent of need met:* 71% (excluding resources awarded to replace EFC). *Average financial aid package:* $8000 (excluding resources awarded to replace EFC). 10% of all full-time undergraduates had no need and received non-need-based gift aid.

GIFT AID (NEED-BASED) *Total amount:* $10,156,609 (18% federal, 19% state, 59% institutional, 4% external sources). *Receiving aid:* Freshmen: 40% (187); All full-time undergraduates: 38% (596). *Average award:* Freshmen: $1000; Undergraduates: $1100. *Scholarships, grants, and awards:* Federal Pell, FSEOG, state, private, college/university gift aid from institutional funds.

GIFT AID (NON-NEED-BASED) *Total amount:* $2,958,375 (100% state). *Average Award:* Freshmen: $500; Undergraduates: $500. *Scholarships, grants, and awards by category: Academic Interests/Achievement:* communication, education, general academic interests/achievements, military science, religion/biblical studies. *Creative Arts/Performance:* art/fine arts, journalism/publications, music, theater/drama. *Special Achievements/Activities:* $4900 total: cheerleading/drum major, junior miss, religious involvement. *Special Characteristics:* $225,000 total: children of faculty/staff, relatives of clergy, siblings of current students. *Tuition waivers:* Full or partial for employees or children of employees. *ROTC:* Army cooperative.

LOANS *Student loans:* $4,200,000 (64% need-based, 36% non-need-based). 60% of past graduating class borrowed through all loan programs. *Average indebtedness per student:* $10,000. *Average need-based loan:* Freshmen: $2625; Undergraduates: $3500. *Parent loans:* $1,002,743 (100% need-based). *Programs:* FFEL (Subsidized and Unsubsidized Stafford, PLUS), Perkins, state, college/university.

WORK-STUDY *Federal work-study:* Total amount: $150,000; 173 jobs averaging $1000. *State or other work-study/employment:* Total amount: $110,000 (100% non-need-based). 76 part-time jobs averaging $1000.

ATHLETIC AWARDS *Total amount:* $925,000 (100% need-based).

APPLYING FOR FINANCIAL AID *Required financial aid form:* FAFSA. *Financial aid deadline (priority):* 6/30. *Notification date:* Continuous.

CONTACT Ms. Shirley Eskew, Assistant Director of Financial Aid, North Greenville College, PO Box 1892, Tigerville, SC 29688-1892, 864-977-7057 or toll-free 800-468-6642 Ext. 7001. *Fax:* 864-977-7177.

NORTHLAND COLLEGE
Ashland, WI

Tuition & fees: $19,715	Average undergraduate aid package: $15,708

ABOUT THE INSTITUTION Independent religious, coed. Awards: bachelor's degrees. 54 undergraduate majors. Total enrollment: 717. Undergraduates: 717. Freshmen: 125. Federal methodology is used as a basis for awarding need-based institutional aid.

UNDERGRADUATE EXPENSES for 2005–06 *Comprehensive fee:* $25,325 includes full-time tuition ($19,135), mandatory fees ($580), and room and board ($5610). *College room only:* $2270. Room and board charges vary according to board plan and housing facility. *Part-time tuition:* $330 per credit. Part-time tuition and fees vary according to course load. *Payment plan:* Installment.

FRESHMAN FINANCIAL AID (Fall 2004, est.) 122 applied for aid; of those 89% were deemed to have need. 100% of freshmen with need received aid; of those 15% had need fully met. *Average percent of need met:* 83% (excluding resources awarded to replace EFC). *Average financial aid package:* $16,085 (excluding resources awarded to replace EFC). 3% of all full-time freshmen had no need and received non-need-based gift aid.

UNDERGRADUATE FINANCIAL AID (Fall 2004, est.) 622 applied for aid; of those 92% were deemed to have need. 100% of undergraduates with need received aid; of those 17% had need fully met. *Average percent of need met:* 88% (excluding resources awarded to replace EFC). *Average financial aid package:* $15,708 (excluding resources awarded to replace EFC). 8% of all full-time undergraduates had no need and received non-need-based gift aid.

GIFT AID (NEED-BASED) *Total amount:* $5,977,499 (15% federal, 7% state, 75% institutional, 3% external sources). *Receiving aid:* Freshmen: 83% (106); All full-time undergraduates: 83% (557). *Average award:* Freshmen: $11,340; Undergraduates: $10,746. *Scholarships, grants, and awards:* Federal Pell, FSEOG, state, private, college/university gift aid from institutional funds, Bureau of Indian Affairs Grants.

GIFT AID (NON-NEED-BASED) *Total amount:* $196,330 (1% state, 96% institutional, 3% external sources). *Receiving aid:* Freshmen: 1% (1); Undergraduates: 1% (4). *Average Award:* Freshmen: $9567; Undergraduates: $8088. *Scholarships, grants, and awards by category: Academic Interests/ Achievement:* 314 awards ($1,708,620 total): general academic interests/ achievements. *Creative Arts/Performance:* 32 awards ($10,738 total): music. *Special Achievements/Activities:* 73 awards ($130,900 total): leadership. *Special Characteristics:* 30 awards ($42,950 total): ethnic background. *Tuition waivers:* Full or partial for employees or children of employees.

LOANS *Student loans:* $3,551,806 (64% need-based, 36% non-need-based). 84% of past graduating class borrowed through all loan programs. *Average indebtedness per student:* $20,164. *Average need-based loan:* Freshmen: $3464; Undergraduates: $4062. *Parent loans:* $1,311,219 (83% need-based, 17% non-need-based). *Programs:* Federal Direct (Subsidized and Unsubsidized Stafford, PLUS), FFEL (Subsidized and Unsubsidized Stafford, PLUS), Perkins.

WORK-STUDY *Federal work-study:* Total amount: $469,067; 304 jobs averaging $1543. *State or other work-study/employment:* Total amount: $404,476 (68% need-based, 32% non-need-based). 280 part-time jobs averaging $1445.

APPLYING FOR FINANCIAL AID *Required financial aid form:* FAFSA. *Financial aid deadline (priority):* 4/15. *Notification date:* Continuous beginning 3/1. Students must reply by 5/1 or within 4 weeks of notification.

CONTACT Tracy K. Steine, Director of Financial Aid, Northland College, 1411 Ellis Avenue, Ashland, WI 54806, 715-682-1255 or toll-free 800-753-1840 (in-state), 800-753-1040 (out-of-state). *Fax:* 715-682-1308. *E-mail:* tsteine@northland.edu.

NORTH PARK UNIVERSITY
Chicago, IL

CONTACT Dr. Lucy Shaker, Director of Financial Aid, North Park University, 3225 West Foster Avenue, Chicago, IL 60625-4895, 773-244-5526 or toll-free 800-888-NPC8. *Fax:* 773-244-4953.

NORTHWEST CHRISTIAN COLLEGE
Eugene, OR

ABOUT THE INSTITUTION Independent Christian, coed. Awards: associate, bachelor's, and master's degrees and post-bachelor's certificates. 15 undergraduate majors. Total enrollment: 459. Undergraduates: 393. Freshmen: 52.

GIFT AID (NEED-BASED) *Scholarships, grants, and awards:* Federal Pell, FSEOG, state, private, college/university gift aid from institutional funds.

GIFT AID (NON-NEED-BASED) *Scholarships, grants, and awards by category: Academic Interests/Achievement:* general academic interests/achievements. *Creative Arts/Performance:* general creative arts/performance, music. *Special Achievements/Activities:* general special achievements/activities, leadership, religious involvement. *Special Characteristics:* children of faculty/staff, relatives of clergy, religious affiliation.

LOANS *Programs:* FFEL (Subsidized and Unsubsidized Stafford, PLUS), Perkins.

WORK-STUDY *Federal work-study:* Total amount: $369,933; 150 jobs averaging $2466. *State or other work-study/employment:* Total amount: $69,600 (55% need-based, 45% non-need-based). 15 part-time jobs averaging $2560.

APPLYING FOR FINANCIAL AID *Required financial aid form:* FAFSA.

CONTACT Jocelyn Hubbs, Assistant Director, Northwest Christian College, 828 East 11th Avenue, Eugene, OR 97401-3727, 541-684-7218 or toll-free 877-463-6622. *Fax:* 541-684-7323. *E-mail:* jocelynh@nwcc.edu.

NORTHWEST COLLEGE OF ART
Poulsbo, WA

Tuition & fees: $14,400	Average undergraduate aid package: N/A

ABOUT THE INSTITUTION Proprietary, coed. Awards: bachelor's degrees. 2 undergraduate majors. Federal methodology is used as a basis for awarding need-based institutional aid.

UNDERGRADUATE EXPENSES for 2005–06 *Application fee:* $50. *Tuition:* full-time $14,300; part-time $625 per credit. Part-time tuition and fees vary according to course load. *Payment plans:* Guaranteed tuition, installment.

GIFT AID (NEED-BASED) *Scholarships, grants, and awards:* Federal Pell, state, private, college/university gift aid from institutional funds.

GIFT AID (NON-NEED-BASED) *Scholarships, grants, and awards by category: Creative Arts/Performance:* applied art and design, art/fine arts. *Tuition waivers:* Full or partial for employees or children of employees.

LOANS *Programs:* FFEL (Subsidized and Unsubsidized Stafford, PLUS), alternative loans.

APPLYING FOR FINANCIAL AID *Required financial aid form:* FAFSA. *Financial aid deadline:* 5/1.

CONTACT Ms. Kim Y. Perigard, Director of Financial Aid, Northwest College of Art, 16464 State Highway 305, Poulsbo, WA 98370, 360-779-9993 or toll-free 800-769-ARTS.

NORTHWESTERN COLLEGE
Orange City, IA

Tuition & fees: $16,360	Average undergraduate aid package: $14,719

ABOUT THE INSTITUTION Independent religious, coed. Awards: bachelor's degrees. 38 undergraduate majors. Total enrollment: 1,284. Undergraduates: 1,284. Freshmen: 357. Federal methodology is used as a basis for awarding need-based institutional aid.

UNDERGRADUATE EXPENSES for 2004–05 *Application fee:* $25. *Comprehensive fee:* $21,016 includes full-time tuition ($16,360) and room and board ($4656). *College room only:* $1980. Room and board charges vary according to housing facility. Part-time tuition and fees vary according to course load. *Payment plan:* Installment.

FRESHMAN FINANCIAL AID (Fall 2003) 288 applied for aid; of those 90% were deemed to have need. 100% of freshmen with need received aid; of those 49% had need fully met. *Average percent of need met:* 85% (excluding resources awarded to replace EFC). *Average financial aid package:* $14,798 (excluding resources awarded to replace EFC). 8% of all full-time freshmen had no need and received non-need-based gift aid.

UNDERGRADUATE FINANCIAL AID (Fall 2003) 1,125 applied for aid; of those 90% were deemed to have need. 97% of undergraduates with need received aid; of those 48% had need fully met. *Average percent of need met:* 80% (excluding resources awarded to replace EFC). *Average financial aid package:* $14,719 (excluding resources awarded to replace EFC). 8% of all full-time undergraduates had no need and received non-need-based gift aid.

GIFT AID (NEED-BASED) *Total amount:* $4,243,548 (32% federal, 38% state, 30% institutional). *Receiving aid:* Freshmen: 69% (216); All full-time undergraduates: 67% (827). *Average award:* Freshmen: $5138; Undergraduates: $4787. *Scholarships, grants, and awards:* Federal Pell, FSEOG, state, private, college/university gift aid from institutional funds.

GIFT AID (NON-NEED-BASED) *Total amount:* $4,606,234 (2% state, 91% institutional, 7% external sources). *Receiving aid:* Freshmen: 76% (236); Undergraduates: 71% (874). *Average Award:* Freshmen: $1500; Undergraduates: $2000. *Scholarships, grants, and awards by category: Academic Interests/ Achievement:* 801 awards ($2,935,467 total): biological sciences, business, communication, computer science, education, engineering/technologies, English, foreign languages, general academic interests/achievements, health fields, humanities, mathematics, physical sciences, premedicine, religion/biblical studies, social sciences. *Creative Arts/Performance:* 236 awards ($264,867 total): art/fine arts, journalism/publications, music, theater/drama. *Special Characteristics:* 637 awards ($1,210,413 total): adult students, children and siblings of alumni, children of faculty/staff, ethnic background, first-generation college students, handicapped

Northwestern College

students, international students, religious affiliation, siblings of current students. *Tuition waivers:* Full or partial for employees or children of employees.
LOANS *Student loans:* $6,867,678 (89% need-based, 11% non-need-based). 72% of past graduating class borrowed through all loan programs. *Average indebtedness per student:* $19,523. *Average need-based loan:* Freshmen: $3215; Undergraduates: $3172. *Parent loans:* $827,473 (100% non-need-based). *Programs:* FFEL (Subsidized and Unsubsidized Stafford, PLUS), Perkins, college/university, alternative loans.
WORK-STUDY *Federal work-study:* Total amount: $320,166; 338 jobs averaging $1000. *State or other work-study/employment:* Total amount: $333,159 (100% non-need-based). 301 part-time jobs averaging $1000.
ATHLETIC AWARDS *Total amount:* $717,075 (100% non-need-based).
APPLYING FOR FINANCIAL AID *Required financial aid form:* FAFSA. *Financial aid deadline (priority):* 4/1. *Notification date:* Continuous beginning 3/15. Students must reply within 3 weeks of notification.
CONTACT Mr. Gerry Korver, Director of Financial Aid, Northwestern College, 101 Seventh Street, SW, Orange City, IA 51041-1996, 712-707-7131 or toll-free 800-747-4757. *Fax:* 712-707-7164.

NORTHWESTERN COLLEGE
St. Paul, MN

Tuition & fees: $18,370	Average undergraduate aid package: $12,734

ABOUT THE INSTITUTION Independent nondenominational, coed. Awards: associate and bachelor's degrees. 46 undergraduate majors. Total enrollment: 2,734. Undergraduates: 2,734. Freshmen: 426. Federal methodology is used as a basis for awarding need-based institutional aid.
UNDERGRADUATE EXPENSES for 2004–05 *Application fee:* $30. *Comprehensive fee:* $24,390 includes full-time tuition ($18,370) and room and board ($6020). *College room only:* $3300. Full-time tuition and fees vary according to course load. Room and board charges vary according to board plan. *Part-time tuition:* $775 per credit. Part-time tuition and fees vary according to course load. *Payment plan:* Installment.
FRESHMAN FINANCIAL AID (Fall 2003) 425 applied for aid; of those 90% were deemed to have need. 100% of freshmen with need received aid; of those 8% had need fully met. *Average percent of need met:* 70% (excluding resources awarded to replace EFC). *Average financial aid package:* $13,197 (excluding resources awarded to replace EFC). 10% of all full-time freshmen had no need and received non-need-based gift aid.
UNDERGRADUATE FINANCIAL AID (Fall 2003) 1,830 applied for aid; of those 86% were deemed to have need. 100% of undergraduates with need received aid; of those 9% had need fully met. *Average percent of need met:* 72% (excluding resources awarded to replace EFC). *Average financial aid package:* $12,734 (excluding resources awarded to replace EFC). 11% of all full-time undergraduates had no need and received non-need-based gift aid.
GIFT AID (NEED-BASED) *Total amount:* $8,899,036 (24% federal, 25% state, 51% institutional). *Receiving aid:* Freshmen: 87% (378); All full-time undergraduates: 77% (1,503). *Average award:* Freshmen: $10,356; Undergraduates: $9263. *Scholarships, grants, and awards:* Federal Pell, FSEOG, state, private, college/university gift aid from institutional funds.
GIFT AID (NON-NEED-BASED) *Total amount:* $5,611,139 (88% institutional, 12% external sources). *Receiving aid:* Freshmen: 79% (342); Undergraduates: 62% (1,204). *Average Award:* Freshmen: $4236; Undergraduates: $4926. *Scholarships, grants, and awards by category:* Academic Interests/Achievement: 1,222 awards ($3,300,089 total): biological sciences, general academic interests/achievements. Creative Arts/Performance: 108 awards ($135,500 total): music, theater/drama. Special Achievements/Activities: 215 awards ($229,451 total): leadership. Special Characteristics: 584 awards ($2,391,837 total): children of faculty/staff, ethnic background, international students, relatives of clergy, siblings of current students. *Tuition waivers:* Full or partial for children of alumni, employees or children of employees, senior citizens. *ROTC:* Army cooperative, Air Force cooperative.
LOANS *Student loans:* $10,660,999 (56% need-based, 44% non-need-based). 56% of past graduating class borrowed through all loan programs. *Average indebtedness per student:* $19,238. *Average need-based loan:* Freshmen: $3362; Undergraduates: $4245. *Parent loans:* $1,683,714 (100% non-need-based). *Programs:* FFEL (Subsidized and Unsubsidized Stafford, PLUS), Perkins, state.
WORK-STUDY *Federal work-study:* Total amount: $325,691; 200 jobs averaging $1628. *State or other work-study/employment:* Total amount: $527,455 (100% need-based). 183 part-time jobs averaging $1748.

APPLYING FOR FINANCIAL AID *Required financial aid forms:* FAFSA, institution's own form. *Financial aid deadline:* 6/1 (priority: 3/1). *Notification date:* Continuous. Students must reply within 2 weeks of notification.
CONTACT Mr. Richard L. Blatchley, Director of Financial Aid, Northwestern College, 3003 Snelling Avenue North, St. Paul, MN 55113-1598, 651-631-5321 or toll-free 800-827-6827. *Fax:* 651-628-3332. *E-mail:* rlb@nwc.edu.

NORTHWESTERN OKLAHOMA STATE UNIVERSITY
Alva, OK

Tuition & fees (OK res): $3000	Average undergraduate aid package: $4673

ABOUT THE INSTITUTION State-supported, coed. Awards: bachelor's and master's degrees and post-bachelor's and post-master's certificates. 37 undergraduate majors. Total enrollment: 2,129. Undergraduates: 1,882. Freshmen: 316. Federal methodology is used as a basis for awarding need-based institutional aid.
UNDERGRADUATE EXPENSES for 2004–05 *Application fee:* $15. *Tuition, state resident:* full-time $2985; part-time $99.50 per credit hour. *Tuition, nonresident:* full-time $7395; part-time $246.50 per credit hour. Full-time tuition and fees vary according to course load, location, and student level. Part-time tuition and fees vary according to course load, location, and student level. *College room and board:* $2920; *room only:* $1000. Room and board charges vary according to board plan. *Payment plan:* Installment.
FRESHMAN FINANCIAL AID (Fall 2003) 212 applied for aid; of those 69% were deemed to have need. 99% of freshmen with need received aid; of those 46% had need fully met. *Average percent of need met:* 80% (excluding resources awarded to replace EFC). *Average financial aid package:* $4732 (excluding resources awarded to replace EFC). 34% of all full-time freshmen had no need and received non-need-based gift aid.
UNDERGRADUATE FINANCIAL AID (Fall 2003) 1,004 applied for aid; of those 78% were deemed to have need. 99% of undergraduates with need received aid; of those 53% had need fully met. *Average percent of need met:* 75% (excluding resources awarded to replace EFC). *Average financial aid package:* $4673 (excluding resources awarded to replace EFC). 16% of all full-time undergraduates had no need and received non-need-based gift aid.
GIFT AID (NEED-BASED) *Total amount:* $2,880,627 (77% federal, 16% state, 7% institutional). *Receiving aid:* Freshmen: 48% (128); All full-time undergraduates: 49% (647). *Average award:* Freshmen: $4263; Undergraduates: $3823. *Scholarships, grants, and awards:* Federal Pell, FSEOG, state, college/university gift aid from institutional funds.
GIFT AID (NON-NEED-BASED) *Total amount:* $734,233 (35% state, 42% institutional, 23% external sources). *Receiving aid:* Freshmen: 9% (23); Undergraduates: 5% (66). *Average Award:* Freshmen: $1150; Undergraduates: $1265. *Scholarships, grants, and awards by category:* Academic Interests/Achievement: 342 awards ($396,874 total): agriculture, biological sciences, business, communication, computer science, education, English, foreign languages, general academic interests/achievements, health fields, humanities, international studies, library science, mathematics, physical sciences, premedicine, social sciences. Creative Arts/Performance: 68 awards ($48,187 total): art/fine arts, cinema/film/broadcasting, dance, debating, general creative arts/performance, journalism/publications, music, theater/drama. Special Achievements/Activities: 95 awards ($111,556 total): cheerleading/drum major, general special achievements/activities, leadership, memberships, rodeo. Special Characteristics: 44 awards ($47,010 total): children and siblings of alumni, children of faculty/staff. *Tuition waivers:* Full or partial for employees or children of employees, senior citizens.
LOANS *Student loans:* $3,185,395 (54% need-based, 46% non-need-based). 61% of past graduating class borrowed through all loan programs. *Average indebtedness per student:* $9456. *Average need-based loan:* Freshmen: $1469; Undergraduates: $2308. *Parent loans:* $47,396 (100% non-need-based). *Programs:* FFEL (Subsidized and Unsubsidized Stafford, PLUS), Perkins.
WORK-STUDY *Federal work-study:* Total amount: $189,153; 174 jobs averaging $1087. *State or other work-study/employment:* Total amount: $186,227 (100% non-need-based). 203 part-time jobs averaging $917.
ATHLETIC AWARDS *Total amount:* $314,505 (48% need-based, 52% non-need-based).
APPLYING FOR FINANCIAL AID *Required financial aid forms:* FAFSA, institution's own form, institutional scholarship application form. *Financial aid deadline (priority):* 3/1. *Notification date:* Continuous beginning 6/1. Students must reply by 8/15.

CONTACT Irala K. Magee, Director of Financial Aid, Northwestern Oklahoma State University, 709 Oklahoma Boulevard, Alva, OK 73717-2799, 580-327-1700 Ext. 8542. *Fax:* 580-327-8177. *E-mail:* ikmagee@nwosu.edu.

NORTHWESTERN STATE UNIVERSITY OF LOUISIANA
Natchitoches, LA

Tuition & fees (LA res): $3241 **Average undergraduate aid package: $5200**

ABOUT THE INSTITUTION State-supported, coed. Awards: associate, bachelor's, and master's degrees and post-master's certificates. 39 undergraduate majors. Total enrollment: 10,546. Undergraduates: 9,414. Freshmen: 1,977. Both federal and institutional methodology are used as a basis for awarding need-based institutional aid.

UNDERGRADUATE EXPENSES for 2004–05 *Application fee:* $20. *Tuition, state resident:* full-time $2144; part-time $227 per credit. *Tuition, nonresident:* full-time $8222; part-time $480 per credit. Full-time tuition and fees vary according to course load. Part-time tuition and fees vary according to course load. *College room and board:* $3426; *room only:* $1850. Room and board charges vary according to board plan, housing facility, and location. *Payment plan:* Installment.

FRESHMAN FINANCIAL AID (Fall 2003) 1537 applied for aid; of those 74% were deemed to have need. 100% of freshmen with need received aid. *Average percent of need met:* 35% (excluding resources awarded to replace EFC). *Average financial aid package:* $4536 (excluding resources awarded to replace EFC). 26% of all full-time freshmen had no need and received non-need-based gift aid.

UNDERGRADUATE FINANCIAL AID (Fall 2003) 5,574 applied for aid; of those 72% were deemed to have need. 100% of undergraduates with need received aid; of those .4% had need fully met. *Average percent of need met:* 38% (excluding resources awarded to replace EFC). *Average financial aid package:* $5200 (excluding resources awarded to replace EFC). 23% of all full-time undergraduates had no need and received non-need-based gift aid.

GIFT AID (NEED-BASED) *Total amount:* $12,326,819 (99% federal, 1% state). *Receiving aid:* Freshmen: 54% (984); All full-time undergraduates: 48% (3,320). *Average award:* Freshmen: $4043; Undergraduates: $3983. *Scholarships, grants, and awards:* Federal Pell, FSEOG, state, private, college/university gift aid from institutional funds, United Negro College Fund, Federal Nursing, third party scholarships.

GIFT AID (NON-NEED-BASED) *Total amount:* $8,190,727 (63% state, 21% institutional, 16% external sources). *Receiving aid:* Freshmen: 23% (413); Undergraduates: 19% (1,341). *Average Award:* Freshmen: $3296; Undergraduates: $3366. *Scholarships, grants, and awards by category: Academic Interests/Achievement:* 2,171 awards ($1,659,264 total): biological sciences, education, general academic interests/achievements, humanities, mathematics, physical sciences. *Creative Arts/Performance:* 561 awards ($598,210 total): art/fine arts, cinema/film/broadcasting, creative writing, dance, journalism/publications, music, performing arts, theater/drama. *Special Achievements/Activities:* 137 awards ($122,992 total): cheerleading/drum major, general special achievements/activities, leadership, memberships. *Special Characteristics:* 1,590 awards ($2,455,465 total): adult students, children of faculty/staff, children of public servants, general special characteristics, international students, out-of-state students, public servants, veterans, veterans' children. *Tuition waivers:* Full or partial for employees or children of employees, senior citizens. *ROTC:* Army.

LOANS *Student loans:* $23,831,954 (54% need-based, 46% non-need-based). 64% of past graduating class borrowed through all loan programs. *Average indebtedness per student:* $13,606. *Average need-based loan:* Freshmen: $2239; Undergraduates: $3075. *Parent loans:* $224,026 (100% non-need-based). *Programs:* FFEL (Subsidized and Unsubsidized Stafford, PLUS), Perkins.

WORK-STUDY *Federal work-study:* Total amount: $268,106; 375 jobs averaging $715. *State or other work-study/employment:* Total amount: $970,685 (100% non-need-based). 859 part-time jobs averaging $1130.

ATHLETIC AWARDS *Total amount:* $1,575,048 (100% non-need-based).

APPLYING FOR FINANCIAL AID *Required financial aid forms:* FAFSA, institution's own form. *Financial aid deadline (priority):* 5/1. *Notification date:* Continuous. Students must reply within 4 weeks of notification.

CONTACT Mrs. Misti Chelette, Director of Financial Aid, Northwestern State University of Louisiana, 103 Roy Hall, Natchitoches, LA 71497, 318-357-5961 or toll-free 800-327-1903. *Fax:* 318-357-5488. *E-mail:* nsufinaid@nsula.edu.

NORTHWESTERN UNIVERSITY
Evanston, IL

Tuition & fees: $31,789 **Average undergraduate aid package: $24,761**

ABOUT THE INSTITUTION Independent, coed. Awards: bachelor's, master's, doctoral, and first professional degrees and post-master's certificates. 112 undergraduate majors. Total enrollment: 16,663. Undergraduates: 8,031. Freshmen: 1,915. Both federal and institutional methodology are used as a basis for awarding need-based institutional aid.

UNDERGRADUATE EXPENSES for 2005–06 *Application fee:* $65. *Comprehensive fee:* $41,662 includes full-time tuition ($31,644), mandatory fees ($145), and room and board ($9873). *College room only:* $5613. Room and board charges vary according to board plan and housing facility. *Part-time tuition:* $3754 per course. *Payment plan:* Installment.

FRESHMAN FINANCIAL AID (Fall 2004, est.) 1090 applied for aid; of those 77% were deemed to have need. 100% of freshmen with need received aid; of those 100% had need fully met. *Average percent of need met:* 100% (excluding resources awarded to replace EFC). *Average financial aid package:* $24,897 (excluding resources awarded to replace EFC). 3% of all full-time freshmen had no need and received non-need-based gift aid.

UNDERGRADUATE FINANCIAL AID (Fall 2004, est.) 3,857 applied for aid; of those 87% were deemed to have need. 100% of undergraduates with need received aid; of those 100% had need fully met. *Average percent of need met:* 100% (excluding resources awarded to replace EFC). *Average financial aid package:* $24,761 (excluding resources awarded to replace EFC). 1% of all full-time undergraduates had no need and received non-need-based gift aid.

GIFT AID (NEED-BASED) *Total amount:* $64,540,405 (7% federal, 3% state, 85% institutional, 5% external sources). *Receiving aid:* Freshmen: 42% (807); All full-time undergraduates: 41% (3,220). *Average award:* Freshmen: $22,009; Undergraduates: $20,074. *Scholarships, grants, and awards:* Federal Pell, FSEOG, state, private, college/university gift aid from institutional funds.

GIFT AID (NON-NEED-BASED) *Total amount:* $1,609,686 (6% state, 18% institutional, 76% external sources). *Average Award:* Freshmen: $2360; Undergraduates: $3423. *Tuition waivers:* Full or partial for employees or children of employees. *ROTC:* Army cooperative, Naval, Air Force cooperative.

LOANS *Student loans:* $15,070,858 (87% need-based, 13% non-need-based). 50% of past graduating class borrowed through all loan programs. *Average indebtedness per student:* $15,136. *Average need-based loan:* Freshmen: $2424; Undergraduates: $4148. *Parent loans:* $22,903,374 (100% non-need-based). *Programs:* FFEL (Subsidized and Unsubsidized Stafford, PLUS), Perkins, college/university.

WORK-STUDY *Federal work-study:* Total amount: $2,900,000; 1,690 jobs averaging $1715. *State or other work-study/employment:* Total amount: $2,530,544 (100% need-based). 1,162 part-time jobs averaging $2500.

ATHLETIC AWARDS *Total amount:* $9,932,541 (100% non-need-based).

APPLYING FOR FINANCIAL AID *Required financial aid forms:* FAFSA, CSS Financial Aid PROFILE, noncustodial (divorced/separated) parent's statement, business/farm supplement, federal income tax form(s). *Financial aid deadline (priority):* 2/1. *Notification date:* 4/1. Students must reply by 5/1 or within 2 weeks of notification.

CONTACT Mr. Allen Lentino, Senior Associate Director of Admission and Financial Aid, Northwestern University, 1801 Hinman Avenue, Evanston, IL 60208, 847-491-8443. *Fax:* 847-467-1317. *E-mail:* a-lentino@northwestern.edu.

NORTHWEST MISSOURI STATE UNIVERSITY
Maryville, MO

CONTACT Mr. Del Morley, Director of Financial Assistance, Northwest Missouri State University, 800 University Drive, Maryville, MO 64468-6001, 660-562-1138 or toll-free 800-633-1175.

NORTHWEST NAZARENE UNIVERSITY
Nampa, ID

Tuition & fees: $17,730 **Average undergraduate aid package: $13,185**

Northwest Nazarene University

ABOUT THE INSTITUTION Independent religious, coed. Awards: bachelor's and master's degrees. 64 undergraduate majors. Total enrollment: 1,578. Undergraduates: 1,163. Freshmen: 276. Federal methodology is used as a basis for awarding need-based institutional aid.

UNDERGRADUATE EXPENSES for 2005–06 *Application fee:* $25. *Comprehensive fee:* $22,590 includes full-time tuition ($17,280), mandatory fees ($450), and room and board ($4860). Room and board charges vary according to board plan and student level. *Part-time tuition:* $749 per credit. *Part-time fees:* $75 per term. Part-time tuition and fees vary according to course load. *Payment plans:* Tuition prepayment, installment.

FRESHMAN FINANCIAL AID (Fall 2004, est.) 224 applied for aid; of those 88% were deemed to have need. 100% of freshmen with need received aid; of those 21% had need fully met. *Average percent of need met:* 79% (excluding resources awarded to replace EFC). *Average financial aid package:* $13,238 (excluding resources awarded to replace EFC). 11% of all full-time freshmen had no need and received non-need-based gift aid.

UNDERGRADUATE FINANCIAL AID (Fall 2004, est.) 823 applied for aid; of those 87% were deemed to have need. 100% of undergraduates with need received aid; of those 22% had need fully met. *Average percent of need met:* 78% (excluding resources awarded to replace EFC). *Average financial aid package:* $13,185 (excluding resources awarded to replace EFC). 10% of all full-time undergraduates had no need and received non-need-based gift aid.

GIFT AID (NEED-BASED) *Total amount:* $1,982,640 (58% federal, 4% state, 17% institutional, 21% external sources). *Receiving aid:* Freshmen: 58% (144); All full-time undergraduates: 52% (507). *Average award:* Freshmen: $2723; Undergraduates: $2915. *Scholarships, grants, and awards:* Federal Pell, FSEOG, state, private, college/university gift aid from institutional funds.

GIFT AID (NON-NEED-BASED) *Total amount:* $460,025 (2% federal, 2% state, 82% institutional, 14% external sources). *Receiving aid:* Freshmen: 78% (196); Undergraduates: 74% (718). *Average Award: Freshmen:* $7797; *Undergraduates:* $8743. *Scholarships, grants, and awards by category: Academic Interests/Achievement:* 624 awards ($998,589 total): biological sciences, business, computer science, education, English, general academic interests/achievements, health fields, mathematics, military science, physical sciences, premedicine, religion/biblical studies, social sciences. *Creative Arts/Performance:* 86 awards ($50,900 total): art/fine arts, debating, general creative arts/performance, journalism/publications, music, performing arts, theater/drama. *Special Achievements/Activities:* 10 awards ($2600 total): cheerleading/drum major, general special achievements/activities, leadership, religious involvement. *Special Characteristics:* 856 awards ($2,286,957 total): children and siblings of alumni, children of educators, children of faculty/staff, ethnic background, international students, members of minority groups, out-of-state students, relatives of clergy, religious affiliation, siblings of current students, veterans. *Tuition waivers:* Full or partial for employees or children of employees. *ROTC:* Army.

LOANS *Student loans:* $5,205,234 (93% need-based, 7% non-need-based). 88% of past graduating class borrowed through all loan programs. *Average indebtedness per student:* $20,923. *Average need-based loan:* Freshmen: $3875; Undergraduates: $4834. *Parent loans:* $1,717,650 (85% need-based, 15% non-need-based). *Programs:* FFEL (Subsidized and Unsubsidized Stafford, PLUS), Perkins, college/university.

WORK-STUDY *Federal work-study:* Total amount: $447,156; 325 jobs averaging $1376.

ATHLETIC AWARDS *Total amount:* $595,766 (79% need-based, 21% non-need-based).

APPLYING FOR FINANCIAL AID *Required financial aid forms:* FAFSA, institution's own form. *Financial aid deadline (priority):* 3/1. *Notification date:* Continuous beginning 4/1. Students must reply within 3 weeks of notification.

CONTACT Mr. Wes Maggard, Director of Financial Aid, Northwest Nazarene University, 623 Holly Street, Nampa, ID 83686, 208-467-8774 or toll-free 877-NNU-4YOU. *Fax:* 208-467-8375. *E-mail:* mwmaggard@nnu.edu.

NORTHWEST UNIVERSITY
Kirkland, WA

Tuition & fees: $15,944	Average undergraduate aid package: $10,917

ABOUT THE INSTITUTION Independent religious, coed. Awards: associate, bachelor's, and master's degrees. 38 undergraduate majors. Total enrollment: 1,180. Undergraduates: 1,068. Freshmen: 132. Federal methodology is used as a basis for awarding need-based institutional aid.

UNDERGRADUATE EXPENSES for 2005–06 *Application fee:* $30. *Comprehensive fee:* $22,394 includes full-time tuition ($15,300), mandatory fees ($644), and room and board ($6450). *College room only:* $3225. Full-time tuition and fees

vary according to program. Room and board charges vary according to board plan and housing facility. *Part-time tuition:* $640 per credit. *Part-time fees:* $20 per credit. Part-time tuition and fees vary according to course load. *Payment plan:* Installment.

FRESHMAN FINANCIAL AID (Fall 2004, est.) 123 applied for aid; of those 83% were deemed to have need. 100% of freshmen with need received aid; of those 19% had need fully met. *Average percent of need met:* 72% (excluding resources awarded to replace EFC). *Average financial aid package:* $10,991 (excluding resources awarded to replace EFC). 18% of all full-time freshmen had no need and received non-need-based gift aid.

UNDERGRADUATE FINANCIAL AID (Fall 2004, est.) 860 applied for aid; of those 88% were deemed to have need. 99% of undergraduates with need received aid; of those 19% had need fully met. *Average percent of need met:* 69% (excluding resources awarded to replace EFC). *Average financial aid package:* $10,917 (excluding resources awarded to replace EFC). 15% of all full-time undergraduates had no need and received non-need-based gift aid.

GIFT AID (NEED-BASED) *Total amount:* $4,011,672 (24% federal, 15% state, 52% institutional, 9% external sources). *Receiving aid:* Freshmen: 74% (102); All full-time undergraduates: 74% (705). *Average award:* Freshmen: $7822; Undergraduates: $7060. *Scholarships, grants, and awards:* Federal Pell, FSEOG, state, private, college/university gift aid from institutional funds.

GIFT AID (NON-NEED-BASED) *Total amount:* $670,915 (2% state, 79% institutional, 19% external sources). *Receiving aid:* Freshmen: 12% (16); Undergraduates: 7% (66). *Average Award:* Freshmen: $8565; *Undergraduates:* $10,082. *Scholarships, grants, and awards by category: Academic Interests/Achievement:* 201 awards ($350,750 total): general academic interests/achievements. *Creative Arts/Performance:* 98 awards ($225,000 total): debating, journalism/publications, music, theater/drama. *Special Achievements/Activities:* 108 awards ($501,200 total): general special achievements/activities, leadership, religious involvement. *Special Characteristics:* 392 awards ($50,000 total): children of current students, children of faculty/staff, general special characteristics, international students, married students, parents of current students, relatives of clergy, religious affiliation, siblings of current students, spouses of current students. *Tuition waivers:* Full or partial for employees or children of employees, senior citizens. *ROTC:* Army cooperative.

LOANS *Student loans:* $5,547,835 (72% need-based, 28% non-need-based). 89% of past graduating class borrowed through all loan programs. *Average indebtedness per student:* $20,138. *Average need-based loan:* Freshmen: $2938; Undergraduates: $3960. *Parent loans:* $1,131,315 (44% need-based, 56% non-need-based). *Programs:* FFEL (Subsidized and Unsubsidized Stafford, PLUS), Perkins, state, alternative loans.

WORK-STUDY *Federal work-study:* Total amount: $128,502; 80 jobs averaging $2200. *State or other work-study/employment:* Total amount: $179,798 (88% need-based, 12% non-need-based). 32 part-time jobs averaging $3150.

ATHLETIC AWARDS *Total amount:* $480,622 (57% need-based, 43% non-need-based).

APPLYING FOR FINANCIAL AID *Required financial aid forms:* FAFSA, institution's own form. *Financial aid deadline (priority):* 3/1. *Notification date:* Continuous beginning 4/1. Students must reply within 4 weeks of notification.

CONTACT Ms. Lana J. Walter, Director of Financial Aid, Northwest University, PO Box 579, Kirkland, WA 98083-0579, 425-889-5336 or toll-free 800-669-3781. *Fax:* 425-889-5224. *E-mail:* lana.walter@ncag.edu.

NORTHWOOD UNIVERSITY
Midland, MI

Tuition & fees: $15,183	Average undergraduate aid package: $12,779

ABOUT THE INSTITUTION Independent, coed. Awards: associate, bachelor's, and master's degrees. 15 undergraduate majors. Total enrollment: 3,748. Undergraduates: 3,432. Freshmen: 439. Federal methodology is used as a basis for awarding need-based institutional aid.

UNDERGRADUATE EXPENSES for 2005–06 *Application fee:* $25. *Comprehensive fee:* $21,879 includes full-time tuition ($14,625), mandatory fees ($558), and room and board ($6696). *College room only:* $3405. Room and board charges vary according to board plan. *Part-time tuition:* $304 per credit. *Payment plan:* Installment.

FRESHMAN FINANCIAL AID (Fall 2004, est.) 339 applied for aid; of those 82% were deemed to have need. 100% of freshmen with need received aid; of those 27% had need fully met. *Average percent of need met:* 84% (excluding resources awarded to replace EFC). *Average financial aid package:* $13,794 (excluding resources awarded to replace EFC). 25% of all full-time freshmen had no need and received non-need-based gift aid.

UNDERGRADUATE FINANCIAL AID (Fall 2004, est.) 1,230 applied for aid; of those 84% were deemed to have need. 100% of undergraduates with need received aid; of those 27% had need fully met. *Average percent of need met:* 79% (excluding resources awarded to replace EFC). *Average financial aid package:* $12,779 (excluding resources awarded to replace EFC). 27% of all full-time undergraduates had no need and received non-need-based gift aid.

GIFT AID (NEED-BASED) *Total amount:* $7,634,497 (20% federal, 22% state, 55% institutional, 3% external sources). *Receiving aid:* Freshmen: 57% (249); All full-time undergraduates: 52% (908). *Average award:* Freshmen: $5847; Undergraduates: $5147. *Scholarships, grants, and awards:* Federal Pell, FSEOG, state, private, college/university gift aid from institutional funds.

GIFT AID (NON-NEED-BASED) *Total amount:* $2,810,403 (7% state, 91% institutional, 2% external sources). *Receiving aid:* Freshmen: 56% (245); Undergraduates: 44% (773). *Average Award: Freshmen:* $4072; *Undergraduates:* $3959. *Scholarships, grants, and awards by category: Academic Interests/Achievement:* 1,906 awards ($4,833,494 total): business, general academic interests/achievements. *Special Characteristics:* 149 awards ($656,273 total): children and siblings of alumni, children of faculty/staff, siblings of current students. *Tuition waivers:* Full or partial for children of alumni, employees or children of employees.

LOANS *Student loans:* $8,728,012 (62% need-based, 38% non-need-based). 55% of past graduating class borrowed through all loan programs. *Average indebtedness per student:* $13,782. *Average need-based loan:* Freshmen: $2431; Undergraduates: $3729. *Parent loans:* $1,535,202 (28% need-based, 72% non-need-based). *Programs:* FFEL (Subsidized and Unsubsidized Stafford, PLUS), state.

WORK-STUDY *Federal work-study:* Total amount: $454,474; 266 jobs averaging $1709. *State or other work-study/employment:* Total amount: $458,720 (100% need-based). 269 part-time jobs averaging $1705.

ATHLETIC AWARDS *Total amount:* $1,767,174 (37% need-based, 63% non-need-based).

APPLYING FOR FINANCIAL AID *Required financial aid form:* FAFSA. *Financial aid deadline:* Continuous. *Notification date:* Continuous beginning 3/1.

CONTACT Terri Mieler, Director of Financial Aid, Northwood University, 4000 Whiting Drive, Midland, MI 48640-2398, 989-837-4301 or toll-free 800-457-7878. *Fax:* 989-837-4130. *E-mail:* mieler@northwood.edu.

NORTHWOOD UNIVERSITY, FLORIDA CAMPUS
West Palm Beach, FL

Tuition & fees: $15,183	Average undergraduate aid package: $12,792

ABOUT THE INSTITUTION Independent, coed. Awards: associate and bachelor's degrees. 11 undergraduate majors. Total enrollment: 956. Undergraduates: 956. Freshmen: 193. Both federal and institutional methodology are used as a basis for awarding need-based institutional aid.

UNDERGRADUATE EXPENSES for 2005–06 *Application fee:* $25. *Comprehensive fee:* $22,440 includes full-time tuition ($14,625), mandatory fees ($558), and room and board ($7257). *College room only:* $3696. Room and board charges vary according to board plan. *Part-time tuition:* $304 per credit. *Payment plan:* Installment.

FRESHMAN FINANCIAL AID (Fall 2004, est.) 131 applied for aid; of those 85% were deemed to have need. 100% of freshmen with need received aid; of those 18% had need fully met. *Average percent of need met:* 72% (excluding resources awarded to replace EFC). *Average financial aid package:* $12,200 (excluding resources awarded to replace EFC). 27% of all full-time freshmen had no need and received non-need-based gift aid.

UNDERGRADUATE FINANCIAL AID (Fall 2004, est.) 407 applied for aid; of those 89% were deemed to have need. 100% of undergraduates with need received aid; of those 17% had need fully met. *Average percent of need met:* 73% (excluding resources awarded to replace EFC). *Average financial aid package:* $12,792 (excluding resources awarded to replace EFC). 27% of all full-time undergraduates had no need and received non-need-based gift aid.

GIFT AID (NEED-BASED) *Total amount:* $2,254,735 (28% federal, 6% state, 65% institutional, 1% external sources). *Receiving aid:* Freshmen: 49% (94); All full-time undergraduates: 43% (307). *Average award:* Freshmen: $6632; Undergraduates: $6310. *Scholarships, grants, and awards:* Federal Pell, FSEOG, state, private, college/university gift aid from institutional funds.

GIFT AID (NON-NEED-BASED) *Total amount:* $1,743,657 (4% state, 94% institutional, 2% external sources). *Receiving aid:* Freshmen: 46% (88); Undergraduates: 38% (268). *Average Award: Freshmen:* $4207; *Undergradu-*

ates: $4114. *Scholarships, grants, and awards by category: Academic Interests/Achievement:* 628 awards ($1,537,347 total): business, general academic interests/achievements. *Special Achievements/Activities:* 58 awards ($66,882 total): memberships. *Special Characteristics:* 38 awards ($123,620 total): children and siblings of alumni, children of faculty/staff, siblings of current students. *Tuition waivers:* Full or partial for children of alumni, employees or children of employees.

LOANS *Student loans:* $2,580,896 (71% need-based, 29% non-need-based). 27% of past graduating class borrowed through all loan programs. *Average indebtedness per student:* $19,968. *Average need-based loan:* Freshmen: $2127; Undergraduates: $3262. *Parent loans:* $737,112 (37% need-based, 63% non-need-based). *Programs:* FFEL (Subsidized and Unsubsidized Stafford, PLUS).

WORK-STUDY *Federal work-study:* Total amount: $199,712; 97 jobs averaging $2059.

ATHLETIC AWARDS *Total amount:* $716,254 (25% need-based, 75% non-need-based).

APPLYING FOR FINANCIAL AID *Required financial aid form:* FAFSA. *Financial aid deadline (priority):* 4/15. *Notification date:* Continuous beginning 3/1.

CONTACT Ms. Teresa A. Palmer, Director of Financial Aid, Northwood University, Florida Campus, 2600 North Military Trail, West Palm Beach, FL 33409-2911, 561-478-5590 or toll-free 800-458-8325. *Fax:* 561-681-7990. *E-mail:* palmer@northwood.edu.

NORTHWOOD UNIVERSITY, TEXAS CAMPUS
Cedar Hill, TX

Tuition & fees: $15,183	Average undergraduate aid package: $14,109

ABOUT THE INSTITUTION Independent, coed. Awards: associate and bachelor's degrees. 13 undergraduate majors. Total enrollment: 1,139. Undergraduates: 1,139. Freshmen: 149. Federal methodology is used as a basis for awarding need-based institutional aid.

UNDERGRADUATE EXPENSES for 2005–06 *Application fee:* $25. *Comprehensive fee:* $22,032 includes full-time tuition ($14,625), mandatory fees ($558), and room and board ($6849). *College room only:* $3153. Room and board charges vary according to board plan and housing facility. *Part-time tuition:* $304 per credit. *Payment plan:* Installment.

FRESHMAN FINANCIAL AID (Fall 2004, est.) 138 applied for aid; of those 87% were deemed to have need. 100% of freshmen with need received aid; of those 28% had need fully met. *Average percent of need met:* 28% (excluding resources awarded to replace EFC). *Average financial aid package:* $13,650 (excluding resources awarded to replace EFC). 18% of all full-time freshmen had no need and received non-need-based gift aid.

UNDERGRADUATE FINANCIAL AID (Fall 2004, est.) 506 applied for aid; of those 87% were deemed to have need. 100% of undergraduates with need received aid; of those 26% had need fully met. *Average percent of need met:* 26% (excluding resources awarded to replace EFC). *Average financial aid package:* $14,109 (excluding resources awarded to replace EFC). 22% of all full-time undergraduates had no need and received non-need-based gift aid.

GIFT AID (NEED-BASED) *Total amount:* $3,601,403 (24% federal, 75% institutional, 1% external sources). *Receiving aid:* Freshmen: 66% (97); All full-time undergraduates: 59% (360). *Average award:* Freshmen: $4901; Undergraduates: $5101. *Scholarships, grants, and awards:* Federal Pell, FSEOG, private, college/university gift aid from institutional funds.

GIFT AID (NON-NEED-BASED) *Total amount:* $827,334 (97% institutional, 3% external sources). *Receiving aid:* Freshmen: 80% (118); Undergraduates: 68% (415). *Average Award: Freshmen:* $5472; *Undergraduates:* $4438. *Scholarships, grants, and awards by category: Academic Interests/Achievement:* 570 awards ($2,202,576 total): business, general academic interests/achievements. *Special Achievements/Activities:* 478 awards ($539,609 total): general special achievements/activities, memberships. *Special Characteristics:* 32 awards ($116,588 total): children and siblings of alumni, children of faculty/staff, siblings of current students. *Tuition waivers:* Full or partial for children of alumni, employees or children of employees.

LOANS *Student loans:* $3,063,061 (75% need-based, 25% non-need-based). 44% of past graduating class borrowed through all loan programs. *Average indebtedness per student:* $19,157. *Average need-based loan:* Freshmen: $2469; Undergraduates: $3663. *Parent loans:* $787,254 (23% need-based, 77% non-need-based). *Programs:* FFEL (Subsidized and Unsubsidized Stafford, PLUS).

WORK-STUDY *Federal work-study:* Total amount: $744,756; 351 jobs averaging $2122.

Northwood University, Texas Campus

ATHLETIC AWARDS *Total amount:* $634,292 (63% need-based, 37% non-need-based).

APPLYING FOR FINANCIAL AID *Required financial aid form:* FAFSA. *Financial aid deadline:* Continuous. *Notification date:* Continuous beginning 3/1.

CONTACT Michael Rhodes, Director of Financial Aid, Northwood University, Texas Campus, 1114 West FM 1382, Cedar Hill, TX 75104, 972-293-5479 or toll-free 800-927-9663. *Fax:* 972-293-7196. *E-mail:* rhodes@northwood.edu.

NORWICH UNIVERSITY
Northfield, VT

CONTACT Director of Student Financial Planning, Norwich University, 158 Harmon Drive, Northfield, VT 05663, 802-485-2015 or toll-free 800-468-6679.

NOTRE DAME COLLEGE
South Euclid, OH

ABOUT THE INSTITUTION Independent Roman Catholic, coed. Awards: associate, bachelor's, and master's degrees and post-bachelor's certificates. 33 undergraduate majors. Total enrollment: 1,299. Undergraduates: 999. Freshmen: 174.

GIFT AID (NEED-BASED) *Scholarships, grants, and awards:* Federal Pell, FSEOG, state, private, college/university gift aid from institutional funds.

GIFT AID (NON-NEED-BASED) *Scholarships, grants, and awards by category: Academic Interests/Achievement:* biological sciences, computer science, general academic interests/achievements, mathematics. *Special Characteristics:* children and siblings of alumni, children of current students, children of faculty/staff, international students, parents of current students, relatives of clergy, siblings of current students, twins.

LOANS *Programs:* FFEL (Subsidized and Unsubsidized Stafford, PLUS), Perkins.

APPLYING FOR FINANCIAL AID *Required financial aid form:* FAFSA.

CONTACT Ms. Mary E. McCrystal, Financial Aid Director, Notre Dame College, 4545 College Road, South Euclid, OH 44121-4293, 216-381-1680 Ext. 263 or toll-free 800-632-1680. *Fax:* 216-381-3802. *E-mail:* mmccrystal@ndc.edu.

NOTRE DAME DE NAMUR UNIVERSITY
Belmont, CA

CONTACT Ms. Kathleen Kelly, Director of Financial Aid, Notre Dame de Namur University, 1500 Ralston Avenue, Belmont, CA 94002, 650-508-3509 or toll-free 800-263-0545.

NOVA SOUTHEASTERN UNIVERSITY
Fort Lauderdale, FL

Tuition & fees: $15,820	Average undergraduate aid package: $14,653

ABOUT THE INSTITUTION Independent, coed. Awards: associate, bachelor's, master's, doctoral, and first professional degrees and post-master's and first professional certificates. 29 undergraduate majors. Total enrollment: 25,430. Undergraduates: 5,355. Freshmen: 420. Federal methodology is used as a basis for awarding need-based institutional aid.

UNDERGRADUATE EXPENSES for 2004–05 *Application fee:* $50. *Comprehensive fee:* $23,946 includes full-time tuition ($15,600), mandatory fees ($220), and room and board ($8126). *College room only:* $5662. Full-time tuition and fees vary according to class time and program. Room and board charges vary according to board plan and housing facility. *Part-time tuition:* $520 per credit hour. Part-time tuition and fees vary according to class time, course load, and program. *Payment plans:* Installment, deferred payment.

FRESHMAN FINANCIAL AID (Fall 2004, est.) 380 applied for aid; of those 81% were deemed to have need. 100% of freshmen with need received aid; of those 6% had need fully met. *Average financial aid package:* $15,923 (excluding resources awarded to replace EFC). 10% of all full-time freshmen had no need and received non-need-based gift aid.

UNDERGRADUATE FINANCIAL AID (Fall 2004, est.) 3,330 applied for aid; of those 77% were deemed to have need. 100% of undergraduates with need received aid; of those 5% had need fully met. *Average percent of need met:* 64% (excluding resources awarded to replace EFC). *Average financial aid package:* $14,653 (excluding resources awarded to replace EFC). 8% of all full-time undergraduates had no need and received non-need-based gift aid.

GIFT AID (NEED-BASED) *Total amount:* $13,861,733 (51% federal, 22% state, 27% institutional). *Receiving aid:* Freshmen: 79% (301); All full-time undergraduates: 73% (2,447). *Average award:* Freshmen: $9297; Undergraduates: $7551. *Scholarships, grants, and awards:* Federal Pell, FSEOG, state, private, college/university gift aid from institutional funds.

GIFT AID (NON-NEED-BASED) *Total amount:* $6,930,499 (85% state, 15% institutional). *Receiving aid:* Freshmen: 76% (292); Undergraduates: 66% (2,219). *Average Award:* Freshmen: $3638; Undergraduates: $3595. *Scholarships, grants, and awards by category: Academic Interests/Achievement:* 1,082 awards ($3,493,093 total): general academic interests/achievements. *Special Achievements/Activities:* 25 awards ($87,750 total): leadership. *Special Characteristics:* 38 awards ($291,220 total): children of faculty/staff. *Tuition waivers:* Full or partial for employees or children of employees.

LOANS *Student loans:* $32,556,644 (45% need-based, 55% non-need-based). 62% of past graduating class borrowed through all loan programs. *Average indebtedness per student:* $26,658. *Average need-based loan:* Freshmen: $2905; Undergraduates: $5192. *Parent loans:* $875,854 (91% need-based, 9% non-need-based). *Programs:* FFEL (Subsidized and Unsubsidized Stafford, PLUS), Perkins, college/university.

WORK-STUDY *Federal work-study:* Total amount: $7,599,975; 1,018 jobs averaging $6284. *State or other work-study/employment:* Total amount: $847,414 (100% non-need-based). 261 part-time jobs averaging $3029.

ATHLETIC AWARDS *Total amount:* $1,743,419 (100% non-need-based).

APPLYING FOR FINANCIAL AID *Required financial aid forms:* FAFSA, institution's own form. *Financial aid deadline (priority):* 4/15. *Notification date:* Continuous beginning 3/15. Students must reply within 4 weeks of notification.

CONTACT Peggy Loewy-Wellisch, Associate Vice President for Student Financial Services & Registration, Nova Southeastern University, 3301 College Avenue, Fort Lauderdale, FL 33314, 954-262-7439 or toll-free 800-541-NOVA. *Fax:* 954-262-3967. *E-mail:* wellisch@nova.edu.

NYACK COLLEGE
Nyack, NY

Tuition & fees: $15,550	Average undergraduate aid package: $13,207

ABOUT THE INSTITUTION Independent religious, coed. Awards: associate, bachelor's, master's, and first professional degrees. 29 undergraduate majors. Total enrollment: 2,908. Undergraduates: 2,056. Freshmen: 277. Both federal and institutional methodology are used as a basis for awarding need-based institutional aid.

UNDERGRADUATE EXPENSES for 2005–06 *Application fee:* $25. *Comprehensive fee:* $23,150 includes full-time tuition ($14,750), mandatory fees ($800), and room and board ($7600). Full-time tuition and fees vary according to location and program. Room and board charges vary according to board plan and housing facility. *Part-time tuition:* $600 per credit. *Part-time fees:* $200 per term. Part-time tuition and fees vary according to course load, location, and program. *Payment plan:* Installment.

FRESHMAN FINANCIAL AID (Fall 2003) 291 applied for aid; of those 96% were deemed to have need. 99% of freshmen with need received aid; of those 17% had need fully met. *Average percent of need met:* 62% (excluding resources awarded to replace EFC). *Average financial aid package:* $12,709 (excluding resources awarded to replace EFC). 21% of all full-time freshmen had no need and received non-need-based gift aid.

UNDERGRADUATE FINANCIAL AID (Fall 2003) 1,367 applied for aid; of those 96% were deemed to have need. 100% of undergraduates with need received aid; of those 18% had need fully met. *Average percent of need met:* 62% (excluding resources awarded to replace EFC). *Average financial aid package:* $13,207 (excluding resources awarded to replace EFC). 14% of all full-time undergraduates had no need and received non-need-based gift aid.

GIFT AID (NEED-BASED) *Total amount:* $11,242,930 (27% federal, 22% state, 50% institutional, 1% external sources). *Receiving aid:* Freshmen: 75% (276); All full-time undergraduates: 83% (1,290). *Average award:* Freshmen: $8909; Undergraduates: $8456. *Scholarships, grants, and awards:* Federal Pell, FSEOG, state, private, college/university gift aid from institutional funds.

GIFT AID (NON-NEED-BASED) *Total amount:* $1,055,384 (2% state, 93% institutional, 5% external sources). *Receiving aid:* Freshmen: 4% (15); Undergraduates: 4% (55). *Average Award:* Freshmen: $4595; Undergraduates: $5847. *Scholarships, grants, and awards by category: Academic Interests/Achievement:* 371 awards ($738,854 total): general academic interests/achievements. *Creative Arts/Performance:* 111 awards ($213,500 total): journalism/publications, music, performing arts, theater/drama. *Special Achievements/Activities:* 1,199 awards ($1,232,870 total): general special achievements/

activities, leadership, religious involvement. *Special Characteristics:* 989 awards ($2,284,185 total): children and siblings of alumni, children of faculty/staff, general special characteristics, international students, local/state students, out-of-state students, relatives of clergy, religious affiliation, spouses of current students. *Tuition waivers:* Full or partial for employees or children of employees.
LOANS *Student loans:* $10,886,183 (86% need-based, 14% non-need-based). 79% of past graduating class borrowed through all loan programs. *Average indebtedness per student:* $20,915. *Average need-based loan:* Freshmen: $3615; Undergraduates: $4678. *Parent loans:* $1,209,866 (61% need-based, 39% non-need-based). *Programs:* FFEL (Subsidized and Unsubsidized Stafford, PLUS), Perkins.
WORK-STUDY *Federal work-study:* Total amount: $279,836; 151 jobs averaging $1828. *State or other work-study/employment:* Total amount: $74,614 (99% need-based, 1% non-need-based). 47 part-time jobs averaging $1571.
ATHLETIC AWARDS *Total amount:* $1,045,238 (76% need-based, 24% non-need-based).
APPLYING FOR FINANCIAL AID *Required financial aid forms:* FAFSA, state aid form. *Financial aid deadline (priority):* 3/1. *Notification date:* Continuous. Students must reply by 4/1 or within 4 weeks of notification.
CONTACT Andres Valenzuela, Director of Student Financial Services, Nyack College, 1 South Boulevard, Nyack, NY 10960-3698, 845-358-1710 or toll-free 800-33-NYACK. *Fax:* 845-358-7016. *E-mail:* sfs@nyack.edu.

OAK HILLS CHRISTIAN COLLEGE
Bemidji, MN

ABOUT THE INSTITUTION Independent interdenominational, coed. Awards: associate and bachelor's degrees. 8 undergraduate majors. Total enrollment: 171. Undergraduates: 171. Freshmen: 61.
GIFT AID (NEED-BASED) *Scholarships, grants, and awards:* Federal Pell, FSEOG, state, private, college/university gift aid from institutional funds.
GIFT AID (NON-NEED-BASED) *Scholarships, grants, and awards by category: Academic Interests/Achievement:* general academic interests/achievements, religion/biblical studies. *Special Characteristics:* children and siblings of alumni, children of faculty/staff, international students, out-of-state students, siblings of current students, spouses of current students.
LOANS *Programs:* FFEL (Subsidized and Unsubsidized Stafford, PLUS), state, alternative loans.
APPLYING FOR FINANCIAL AID *Required financial aid forms:* FAFSA, institution's own form.
CONTACT Daniel Hovestol, Financial Aid Director, Oak Hills Christian College, 1600 Oak Hills Road, SW, Bemidji, MN 56601-8832, 218-751-8671 Ext. 1220 or toll-free 888-751-8670 Ext. 285. *Fax:* 218-444-1311. *E-mail:* ohfinaid@oakhills.edu.

OAKLAND CITY UNIVERSITY
Oakland City, IN

Tuition & fees: $13,560   **Average undergraduate aid package:** N/A

ABOUT THE INSTITUTION Independent General Baptist, coed. Awards: associate, bachelor's, master's, doctoral, and first professional degrees. 59 undergraduate majors. Total enrollment: 1,928. Undergraduates: 1,596. Freshmen: 375. Federal methodology is used as a basis for awarding need-based institutional aid.
UNDERGRADUATE EXPENSES for 2005–06 *Application fee:* $35. *Comprehensive fee:* $18,590 includes full-time tuition ($13,200), mandatory fees ($360), and room and board ($5030). *College room only:* $1630. Full-time tuition and fees vary according to location and program. Room and board charges vary according to housing facility. *Part-time tuition:* $440 per hour. *Part-time fees:* $15 per hour. Part-time tuition and fees vary according to location and program. *Payment plans:* Installment, deferred payment.
FRESHMAN FINANCIAL AID (Fall 2004, est.) *Average percent of need met:* 90% (excluding resources awarded to replace EFC).
UNDERGRADUATE FINANCIAL AID (Fall 2004, est.) *Average percent of need met:* 90% (excluding resources awarded to replace EFC).
GIFT AID (NEED-BASED) *Total amount:* $5,750,000 (22% federal, 78% state). *Scholarships, grants, and awards:* Federal Pell, FSEOG, state, private, college/university gift aid from institutional funds.
GIFT AID (NON-NEED-BASED) *Total amount:* $95,000 (53% institutional, 47% external sources). *Scholarships, grants, and awards by category: Academic Interests/Achievement:* 200 awards: general academic interests/achievements.

Creative Arts/Performance: art/fine arts, music. *Special Achievements/Activities:* religious involvement. *Special Characteristics:* children and siblings of alumni, children of faculty/staff, ethnic background, international students, members of minority groups, religious affiliation. *Tuition waivers:* Full or partial for minority students, employees or children of employees, senior citizens.
LOANS *Parent loans:* $120,000 (100% need-based). *Programs:* FFEL (Subsidized and Unsubsidized Stafford, PLUS), Perkins, college/university.
WORK-STUDY *Federal work-study:* 150 jobs averaging $1600. *State or other work-study/employment:* 4 part-time jobs averaging $1500.
APPLYING FOR FINANCIAL AID *Required financial aid form:* FAFSA. *Financial aid deadline (priority):* 3/10. *Notification date:* Continuous beginning 5/15.
CONTACT Mrs. Caren K. Richeson, Director of Financial Aid, Oakland City University, 138 North Lucretia Street, Oakland City, IN 47660-1099, 812-749-1224 or toll-free 800-737-5125. *Fax:* 812-749-1438.

OAKLAND UNIVERSITY
Rochester, MI

Tuition & fees (MI res): $5354   **Average undergraduate aid package:** $5674

ABOUT THE INSTITUTION State-supported, coed. Awards: bachelor's, master's, and doctoral degrees and post-bachelor's and post-master's certificates. 89 undergraduate majors. Total enrollment: 16,901. Undergraduates: 13,114. Freshmen: 2,053. Federal methodology is used as a basis for awarding need-based institutional aid.
UNDERGRADUATE EXPENSES for 2004–05 *Application fee:* $40. *Tuition, state resident:* full-time $4868; part-time $162.25 per credit hour. *Tuition, nonresident:* full-time $11,468; part-time $382.25 per credit hour. *Required fees:* full-time $486; $243 per term part-time. Full-time tuition and fees vary according to program and student level. Part-time tuition and fees vary according to program and student level. *College room and board:* $5820. Room and board charges vary according to housing facility. *Payment plans:* Installment, deferred payment.
FRESHMAN FINANCIAL AID (Fall 2003) 1059 applied for aid; of those 65% were deemed to have need. 95% of freshmen with need received aid; of those 38% had need fully met. *Average percent of need met:* 88% (excluding resources awarded to replace EFC). *Average financial aid package:* $5564 (excluding resources awarded to replace EFC). 15% of all full-time freshmen had no need and received non-need-based gift aid.
UNDERGRADUATE FINANCIAL AID (Fall 2003) 4,393 applied for aid; of those 69% were deemed to have need. 95% of undergraduates with need received aid; of those 45% had need fully met. *Average percent of need met:* 88% (excluding resources awarded to replace EFC). *Average financial aid package:* $5674 (excluding resources awarded to replace EFC). 6% of all full-time undergraduates had no need and received non-need-based gift aid.
GIFT AID (NEED-BASED) *Total amount:* $7,368,138 (78% federal, 9% state, 13% institutional). *Receiving aid:* Freshmen: 27% (488); All full-time undergraduates: 20% (1,850). *Average award:* Freshmen: $3451; Undergraduates: $3226. *Scholarships, grants, and awards:* Federal Pell, FSEOG, state, private, college/university gift aid from institutional funds.
GIFT AID (NON-NEED-BASED) *Total amount:* $7,327,005 (25% state, 75% external sources). *Receiving aid:* Freshmen: 19% (352); Undergraduates: 7% (687). *Average Award:* Freshmen: $2091; Undergraduates: $2900. *Scholarships, grants, and awards by category: Academic Interests/Achievement:* 989 awards ($2,855,460 total): area/ethnic studies, biological sciences, business, education, engineering/technologies, English, foreign languages, general academic interests/achievements, health fields, humanities. *Creative Arts/Performance:* 62 awards ($94,200 total): dance, music, performing arts. *Special Characteristics:* 153 awards ($992,742 total): adult students, ethnic background, out-of-state students. *Tuition waivers:* Full or partial for employees or children of employees. *ROTC:* Air Force cooperative.
LOANS *Student loans:* $23,220,090 (44% need-based, 56% non-need-based). 45% of past graduating class borrowed through all loan programs. *Average indebtedness per student:* $15,513. *Average need-based loan:* Freshmen: $2224; Undergraduates: $3425. *Parent loans:* $1,277,575 (100% need-based). *Programs:* Federal Direct (Subsidized and Unsubsidized Stafford, PLUS), Perkins, state, alternative loans.
WORK-STUDY *Federal work-study:* Total amount: $306,679; 249 jobs averaging $1260. *State or other work-study/employment:* Total amount: $87,645 (100% need-based). 77 part-time jobs averaging $1155.
ATHLETIC AWARDS *Total amount:* $1,429,907 (100% non-need-based).
APPLYING FOR FINANCIAL AID *Required financial aid form:* FAFSA. *Financial aid deadline (priority):* 2/15. *Notification date:* Continuous beginning 3/15.

CONTACT Ms. Cindy Hermsen, Director of Financial Aid, Oakland University, 120 North Foundation Hall, Rochester, MI 48309-4481, 248-370-2550 or toll-free 800-OAK-UNIV. *E-mail:* finaid@oakland.edu.

OAKWOOD COLLEGE
Huntsville, AL

CONTACT Financial Aid Director, Oakwood College, 7000 Adventist Boulevard, Huntsville, AL 35896, 256-726-7210 or toll-free 800-358-3978 (in-state).

OBERLIN COLLEGE
Oberlin, OH

Tuition & fees: $31,163	Average undergraduate aid package: $23,508

ABOUT THE INSTITUTION Independent, coed. Awards: bachelor's and master's degrees and post-bachelor's certificates. 54 undergraduate majors. Total enrollment: 2,827. Undergraduates: 2,807. Freshmen: 740. Both federal and institutional methodology are used as a basis for awarding need-based institutional aid.

UNDERGRADUATE EXPENSES for 2004–05 *Application fee:* $35. *Comprehensive fee:* $38,806 includes full-time tuition ($30,975), mandatory fees ($188), and room and board ($7643). *College room only:* $4020. Full-time tuition and fees vary according to course load. Room and board charges vary according to board plan and housing facility. *Part-time tuition:* $1290 per credit. Part-time tuition and fees vary according to course load. *Payment plan:* Installment.

FRESHMAN FINANCIAL AID (Fall 2004, est.) 552 applied for aid; of those 82% were deemed to have need. 100% of freshmen with need received aid; of those 100% had need fully met. *Average percent of need met:* 100% (excluding resources awarded to replace EFC). *Average financial aid package:* $22,771 (excluding resources awarded to replace EFC). 11% of all full-time freshmen had no need and received non-need-based gift aid.

UNDERGRADUATE FINANCIAL AID (Fall 2004, est.) 1,873 applied for aid; of those 88% were deemed to have need. 100% of undergraduates with need received aid; of those 100% had need fully met. *Average percent of need met:* 100% (excluding resources awarded to replace EFC). *Average financial aid package:* $23,508 (excluding resources awarded to replace EFC). 10% of all full-time undergraduates had no need and received non-need-based gift aid.

GIFT AID (NEED-BASED) *Total amount:* $34,735,188 (5% federal, 1% state, 89% institutional, 5% external sources). *Receiving aid:* Freshmen: 54% (398); All full-time undergraduates: 54% (1,473). *Average award:* Freshmen: $18,041; Undergraduates: $18,033. *Scholarships, grants, and awards:* Federal Pell, FSEOG, state, private, college/university gift aid from institutional funds.

GIFT AID (NON-NEED-BASED) *Total amount:* $3,667,500 (89% institutional, 11% external sources). *Receiving aid:* Freshmen: 33% (244); Undergraduates: 31% (841). *Average Award:* Freshmen: $11,495; Undergraduates: $11,922. *Scholarships, grants, and awards by category: Academic Interests/Achievement:* 404 awards ($3,238,846 total): general academic interests/achievements, physical sciences. *Creative Arts/Performance:* 350 awards ($3,022,596 total): music. *Tuition waivers:* Full or partial for employees or children of employees.

LOANS *Student loans:* $7,855,064 (93% need-based, 7% non-need-based). 62% of past graduating class borrowed through all loan programs. *Average indebtedness per student:* $17,800. *Average need-based loan:* Freshmen: $3612; Undergraduates: $4187. *Parent loans:* $2,567,186 (100% need-based). *Programs:* FFEL (Subsidized and Unsubsidized Stafford, PLUS), Perkins, college/university.

WORK-STUDY *Federal work-study:* Total amount: $2,236,891; jobs available (averaging $1650). *State or other work-study/employment:* Part-time jobs available (averaging $1650).

APPLYING FOR FINANCIAL AID *Required financial aid forms:* FAFSA, CSS Financial Aid PROFILE, noncustodial (divorced/separated) parent's statement. *Financial aid deadline (priority):* 1/15. *Notification date:* 4/1. Students must reply by 5/1 or within 2 weeks of notification.

CONTACT Office of Financial Aid, Oberlin College, Carnegie Building 123, 52 West Lorain Street, Oberlin, OH 44074, 800-693-3173 or toll-free 800-622-OBIE. *Fax:* 440-775-8249. *E-mail:* financial.aid@oberlin.edu.

OCCIDENTAL COLLEGE
Los Angeles, CA

ABOUT THE INSTITUTION Independent, coed. Awards: bachelor's and master's degrees. 32 undergraduate majors. Total enrollment: 1,887. Undergraduates: 1,866. Freshmen: 496.

GIFT AID (NEED-BASED) *Scholarships, grants, and awards:* Federal Pell, FSEOG, state, private, college/university gift aid from institutional funds.

GIFT AID (NON-NEED-BASED) *Scholarships, grants, and awards by category: Academic Interests/Achievement:* general academic interests/achievements. *Creative Arts/Performance:* music. *Special Achievements/Activities:* general special achievements/activities, leadership. *Special Characteristics:* children of educators, children of faculty/staff.

LOANS *Programs:* FFEL (Subsidized and Unsubsidized Stafford, PLUS), Perkins, college/university.

WORK-STUDY *Federal work-study:* Total amount: $1,376,392; 767 jobs averaging $2175. *State or other work-study/employment:* Total amount: $358,359 (54% need-based, 46% non-need-based). 127 part-time jobs averaging $2005.

APPLYING FOR FINANCIAL AID *Required financial aid forms:* FAFSA, CSS Financial Aid PROFILE, state aid form, noncustodial (divorced/separated) parent's statement, business/farm supplement, income tax form(s), W-2 forms.

CONTACT Maureen McRae Levy, Director of Financial Aid, Occidental College, 1600 Campus Road, Los Angeles, CA 90041, 323-259-2548 or toll-free 800-825-5262. *Fax:* 323-341-4961. *E-mail:* finaid@oxy.edu.

OGLALA LAKOTA COLLEGE
Kyle, SD

Tuition & fees: N/R	Average undergraduate aid package: N/A

ABOUT THE INSTITUTION State and locally supported, coed. Awards: associate, bachelor's, and master's degrees. 23 undergraduate majors. Total enrollment: 1,000. Both federal and institutional methodology are used as a basis for awarding need-based institutional aid.

GIFT AID (NEED-BASED) *Scholarships, grants, and awards:* Federal Pell, FSEOG, private, college/university gift aid from institutional funds.

GIFT AID (NON-NEED-BASED) *Scholarships, grants, and awards by category: Academic Interests/Achievement:* business, education, health fields, social sciences.

WORK-STUDY Federal work-study jobs available.

APPLYING FOR FINANCIAL AID *Required financial aid form:* FAFSA. *Financial aid deadline:* Continuous. *Notification date:* Continuous beginning 10/21.

CONTACT Financial Aid Director, Oglala Lakota College, 490 Piya Wiconi Road, Kyle, SD 57752-0490, 605-455-6000.

OGLETHORPE UNIVERSITY
Atlanta, GA

Tuition & fees: $22,300	Average undergraduate aid package: $20,779

ABOUT THE INSTITUTION Independent, coed. Awards: bachelor's and master's degrees. 31 undergraduate majors. Total enrollment: 1,053. Undergraduates: 972. Freshmen: 223. Federal methodology is used as a basis for awarding need-based institutional aid.

UNDERGRADUATE EXPENSES for 2005–06 *Application fee:* $35. *Comprehensive fee:* $30,300 includes full-time tuition ($22,200), mandatory fees ($100), and room and board ($8000). Room and board charges vary according to board plan and housing facility. *Part-time tuition:* $925 per credit hour. Part-time tuition and fees vary according to program. *Payment plans:* Tuition prepayment, installment.

FRESHMAN FINANCIAL AID (Fall 2003) 150 applied for aid; of those 77% were deemed to have need. 100% of freshmen with need received aid; of those 66% had need fully met. *Average percent of need met:* 93% (excluding resources awarded to replace EFC). *Average financial aid package:* $23,190 (excluding resources awarded to replace EFC). 29% of all full-time freshmen had no need and received non-need-based gift aid.

UNDERGRADUATE FINANCIAL AID (Fall 2003) 525 applied for aid; of those 85% were deemed to have need. 100% of undergraduates with need received aid; of those 32% had need fully met. *Average percent of need met:* 86% (excluding resources awarded to replace EFC). *Average financial aid package:* $20,779 (excluding resources awarded to replace EFC). 34% of all full-time undergraduates had no need and received non-need-based gift aid.

GIFT AID (NEED-BASED) *Total amount:* $5,495,303 (12% federal, 15% state, 73% institutional). *Receiving aid:* Freshmen: 69% (115); All full-time undergraduates: 58% (444). *Average award:* Freshmen: $14,140; Undergraduates: $12,198. *Scholarships, grants, and awards:* Federal Pell, FSEOG, state, private, college/university gift aid from institutional funds.

GIFT AID (NON-NEED-BASED) *Total amount:* $4,221,449 (12% state, 76% institutional, 12% external sources). *Receiving aid:* Freshmen: 59% (99); Undergraduates: 58% (444). *Average Award:* Freshmen: $11,336; Undergraduates: $10,542. *Scholarships, grants, and awards by category:* Academic Interests/Achievement: general academic interests/achievements. *Creative Arts/Performance:* journalism/publications, music, performing arts, theater/drama. *Special Achievements/Activities:* community service, religious involvement. *Tuition waivers:* Full or partial for employees or children of employees.

LOANS *Student loans:* $3,048,208 (38% need-based, 62% non-need-based). 64% of past graduating class borrowed through all loan programs. *Average indebtedness per student:* $16,273. *Average need-based loan:* Freshmen: $1072; Undergraduates: $2288. *Parent loans:* $569,630 (100% non-need-based). *Programs:* Federal Direct (Subsidized and Unsubsidized Stafford, PLUS), FFEL (Subsidized and Unsubsidized Stafford, PLUS), Perkins.

WORK-STUDY *Federal work-study:* Total amount: $393,499; jobs available. *State or other work-study/employment:* Total amount: $121,015 (100% need-based). Part-time jobs available.

APPLYING FOR FINANCIAL AID *Required financial aid forms:* FAFSA, institution's own form, state aid form. *Financial aid deadline:* 9/1 (priority: 3/1). *Notification date:* Continuous.

CONTACT Mr. Patrick Bonones, Director of Financial Aid, Oglethorpe University, 4484 Peachtree Road NE, Atlanta, GA 30319, 404-364-8307 or toll-free 800-428-4484.

OHIO DOMINICAN UNIVERSITY
Columbus, OH

CONTACT Ms. Cynthia A. Hahn, Director of Financial Aid, Ohio Dominican University, 1216 Sunbury Road, Columbus, OH 43219, 614-251-4778 or toll-free 800-854-2670. *Fax:* 614-251-4456. *E-mail:* fin-aid@ohiodominican.edu.

OHIO NORTHERN UNIVERSITY
Ada, OH

Tuition & fees: $25,815	Average undergraduate aid package: $21,922

ABOUT THE INSTITUTION Independent religious, coed. Awards: bachelor's, master's, and first professional degrees and post-bachelor's certificates. 111 undergraduate majors. Total enrollment: 3,495. Undergraduates: 2,607. Freshmen: 753. Federal methodology is used as a basis for awarding need-based institutional aid.

UNDERGRADUATE EXPENSES for 2004–05 *Application fee:* $30. *Comprehensive fee:* $32,175 includes full-time tuition ($25,605), mandatory fees ($210), and room and board ($6360). *College room only:* $3180. Full-time tuition and fees vary according to course load, degree level, program, and student level. Room and board charges vary according to board plan and housing facility. *Part-time tuition:* $711 per quarter hour. *Part-time fees:* $20 per term. Part-time tuition and fees vary according to course load, degree level, program, and student level. *Payment plan:* Installment.

GIFT AID (NEED-BASED) *Total amount:* $28,672,478 (7% federal, 10% state, 81% institutional, 2% external sources). *Receiving aid:* Freshmen: 52% (388); All full-time undergraduates: 56% (1,344). *Average award:* Freshmen: $9194; Undergraduates: $9800. *Scholarships, grants, and awards:* Federal Pell, FSEOG, state, private, college/university gift aid from institutional funds.

GIFT AID (NON-NEED-BASED) *Total amount:* $8,145,492 (1% federal, 8% state, 80% institutional, 11% external sources). *Receiving aid:* Freshmen: 82% (616); Undergraduates: 79% (1,905). *Average Award:* Freshmen: $13,060; Undergraduates: $12,137. *Scholarships, grants, and awards by category:* Academic Interests/Achievement: 1,272 awards ($14,765,492 total): biological sciences, business, communication, computer science, education, engineering/technologies, English, foreign languages, general academic interests/achievements, health fields, humanities, international studies, mathematics, physical sciences, premedicine, religion/biblical studies, social sciences. *Creative Arts/Performance:* 173 awards ($835,090 total): applied art and design, art/fine arts, dance, journalism/publications, music, performing arts, theater/drama. *Special Achievements/Activities:* 235 awards ($2,113,067 total): community service, general special achievements/activities, junior miss, leadership. *Special Characteristics:* 156 awards ($359,011 total): children of faculty/staff, international students, relatives of clergy, religious affiliation, siblings of current students. *Tuition waivers:* Full or partial for employees or children of employees. *ROTC:* Army cooperative, Air Force cooperative.

LOANS *Student loans:* $18,179,327 (61% need-based, 39% non-need-based). 74% of past graduating class borrowed through all loan programs. *Average indebtedness per student:* $29,874. *Average need-based loan:* Freshmen: $4357; Undergraduates: $5055. *Parent loans:* $1,760,260 (20% need-based, 80% non-need-based). *Programs:* FFEL (Subsidized and Unsubsidized Stafford, PLUS), Perkins, Federal Nursing, college/university.

APPLYING FOR FINANCIAL AID *Required financial aid forms:* FAFSA, institution's own form. *Financial aid deadline:* 6/1 (priority: 4/15). *Notification date:* Continuous beginning 3/1. Students must reply within 2 weeks of notification.

CONTACT Mr. Wendell Schick, Director of Financial Aid, Ohio Northern University, 525 South Main Street, Ada, OH 45810, 419-772-2272 or toll-free 888-408-4ONU. *Fax:* 419-772-2313. *E-mail:* w-schick@onu.edu.

THE OHIO STATE UNIVERSITY
Columbus, OH

Tuition & fees (OH res): $7479	Average undergraduate aid package: $9149

ABOUT THE INSTITUTION State-supported, coed. Awards: associate, bachelor's, master's, doctoral, and first professional degrees and post-bachelor's and post-master's certificates. 170 undergraduate majors. Total enrollment: 50,995. Undergraduates: 37,509. Freshmen: 6,057. Federal methodology is used as a basis for awarding need-based institutional aid.

UNDERGRADUATE EXPENSES for 2004–05 *Application fee:* $40. *Tuition, state resident:* full-time $7479. *Tuition, nonresident:* full-time $18,066. Full-time tuition and fees vary according to course load, program, reciprocity agreements, and student level. Part-time tuition and fees vary according to course load, program, reciprocity agreements, and student level. *College room and board:* $6909. Room and board charges vary according to board plan and housing facility. *Payment plan:* Installment.

FRESHMAN FINANCIAL AID (Fall 2004, est.) 4743 applied for aid; of those 70% were deemed to have need. 100% of freshmen with need received aid; of those 28% had need fully met. *Average percent of need met:* 70% (excluding resources awarded to replace EFC). *Average financial aid package:* $8939 (excluding resources awarded to replace EFC). 26% of all full-time freshmen had no need and received non-need-based gift aid.

UNDERGRADUATE FINANCIAL AID (Fall 2004, est.) 21,792 applied for aid; of those 79% were deemed to have need. 100% of undergraduates with need received aid; of those 22% had need fully met. *Average percent of need met:* 68% (excluding resources awarded to replace EFC). *Average financial aid package:* $9149 (excluding resources awarded to replace EFC). 16% of all full-time undergraduates had no need and received non-need-based gift aid.

GIFT AID (NEED-BASED) *Total amount:* $72,701,501 (31% federal, 13% state, 49% institutional, 7% external sources). *Receiving aid:* Freshmen: 52% (3,126); All full-time undergraduates: 45% (15,123). *Average award:* Freshmen: $5702; Undergraduates: $4917. *Scholarships, grants, and awards:* Federal Pell, FSEOG, state, private, college/university gift aid from institutional funds.

GIFT AID (NON-NEED-BASED) *Total amount:* $32,763,123 (12% state, 71% institutional, 17% external sources). *Receiving aid:* Freshmen: 6% (354); Undergraduates: 2% (807). *Average Award:* Freshmen: $3244; Undergraduates: $3816. *Scholarships, grants, and awards by category:* Academic Interests/Achievement: agriculture, architecture, area/ethnic studies, biological sciences, business, communication, computer science, education, engineering/technologies, English, foreign languages, general academic interests/achievements, health fields, home economics, humanities, international studies, mathematics, military science, physical sciences, premedicine, social sciences. *Creative Arts/Performance:* creative writing, dance, journalism/publications, music, performing arts, theater/drama. *Special Achievements/Activities:* cheerleading/drum major, hobbies/interests, leadership, memberships. *Special Characteristics:* adult students, children and siblings of alumni, children of faculty/staff, children of public servants, children of union members/company employees, children of workers in trades, children with a deceased or disabled parent, ethnic background, handicapped students, members of minority groups, out-of-state students, previous college experience. *Tuition waivers:* Full or partial for employees or children of employees, senior citizens. *ROTC:* Army, Naval, Air Force.

LOANS *Student loans:* $128,470,072 (71% need-based, 29% non-need-based). 54% of past graduating class borrowed through all loan programs. *Average indebtedness per student:* $15,963. *Average need-based loan:* Freshmen: $3317; Undergraduates: $4254. *Parent loans:* $46,209,153 (100% non-need-based). *Programs:* Federal Direct (Subsidized and Unsubsidized Stafford, PLUS), Perkins, Federal Nursing, college/university.

WORK-STUDY *Federal work-study:* Total amount: $12,853,146; 4,303 jobs averaging $3322.

The Ohio State University

ATHLETIC AWARDS *Total amount:* $9,293,431 (100% non-need-based).

APPLYING FOR FINANCIAL AID *Required financial aid form:* FAFSA. *Financial aid deadline (priority):* 3/1. *Notification date:* 4/5. Students must reply by 5/1 or within 4 weeks of notification.

CONTACT Ms. Natala Hart, Director of Student Financial Aid, The Ohio State University, 517 Lincoln Tower, 1800 Cannon Drive, Columbus, OH 43210-1230, 614-292-3600. *Fax:* 614-292-9264. *E-mail:* finaid@fa.adm.ohio-state.edu.

OHIO UNIVERSITY
Athens, OH

Tuition & fees (OH res): $7770	Average undergraduate aid package: $7430

ABOUT THE INSTITUTION State-supported, coed. Awards: associate, bachelor's, master's, doctoral, and first professional degrees. 204 undergraduate majors. Total enrollment: 20,096. Undergraduates: 16,937. Freshmen: 3,791. Federal methodology is used as a basis for awarding need-based institutional aid.

UNDERGRADUATE EXPENSES for 2004–05 *Application fee:* $45. *Tuition, state resident:* full-time $7770; part-time $248 per quarter hour. *Tuition, nonresident:* full-time $16,734; part-time $543 per quarter hour. *College room and board:* $7539; *room only:* $3708. Room and board charges vary according to board plan. *Payment plan:* Installment.

FRESHMAN FINANCIAL AID (Fall 2004, est.) 3032 applied for aid; of those 65% were deemed to have need. 97% of freshmen with need received aid; of those 9% had need fully met. *Average percent of need met:* 47% (excluding resources awarded to replace EFC). *Average financial aid package:* $6321 (excluding resources awarded to replace EFC). 8% of all full-time freshmen had no need and received non-need-based gift aid.

UNDERGRADUATE FINANCIAL AID (Fall 2004, est.) 11,144 applied for aid; of those 72% were deemed to have need. 97% of undergraduates with need received aid; of those 11% had need fully met. *Average percent of need met:* 54% (excluding resources awarded to replace EFC). *Average financial aid package:* $7430 (excluding resources awarded to replace EFC). 8% of all full-time undergraduates had no need and received non-need-based gift aid.

GIFT AID (NEED-BASED) *Total amount:* $13,449,195 (63% federal, 18% state, 19% institutional). *Receiving aid:* Freshmen: 23% (877); All full-time undergraduates: 23% (3,681). *Average award:* Freshmen: $3552; Undergraduates: $3726. *Scholarships, grants, and awards:* Federal Pell, FSEOG, state, private, college/university gift aid from institutional funds.

GIFT AID (NON-NEED-BASED) *Total amount:* $14,972,612 (8% state, 75% institutional, 17% external sources). *Receiving aid:* Freshmen: 18% (696); Undergraduates: 14% (2,183). *Average Award:* Freshmen: $4606; Undergraduates: $4317. *Scholarships, grants, and awards by category: Academic Interests/ Achievement:* area/ethnic studies, biological sciences, business, communication, computer science, education, engineering/technologies, English, foreign languages, general academic interests/achievements, health fields, home economics, humanities, international studies, mathematics, military science, physical sciences, premedicine, social sciences. *Creative Arts/Performance:* applied art and design, art/fine arts, cinema/film/broadcasting, dance, debating, journalism/ publications, music, performing arts, theater/drama. *Special Characteristics:* children of faculty/staff, members of minority groups. *Tuition waivers:* Full or partial for employees or children of employees. *ROTC:* Army, Air Force.

LOANS *Student loans:* $51,841,167 (54% need-based, 46% non-need-based). 59% of past graduating class borrowed through all loan programs. *Average indebtedness per student:* $17,192. *Average need-based loan:* Freshmen: $2671; Undergraduates: $4018. *Parent loans:* $23,808,552 (100% non-need-based). *Programs:* Federal Direct (Subsidized and Unsubsidized Stafford, PLUS), Perkins, state, college/university.

WORK-STUDY *Federal work-study:* Total amount: $1,192,933; jobs available. *State or other work-study/employment:* Total amount: $11,080,069 (100% non-need-based). Part-time jobs available.

ATHLETIC AWARDS *Total amount:* $4,738,752 (100% non-need-based).

APPLYING FOR FINANCIAL AID *Required financial aid form:* FAFSA. *Financial aid deadline (priority):* 3/15. *Notification date:* 4/1.

CONTACT Ms. Sondra Williams, Director of Financial Aid, Ohio University, 020 Chubb Hall, Athens, OH 45701-2979, 740-593-4141. *Fax:* 740-593-4140. *E-mail:* willias1@ohio.edu.

OHIO UNIVERSITY–CHILLICOTHE
Chillicothe, OH

Tuition & fees: N/R	Average undergraduate aid package: $6700

ABOUT THE INSTITUTION State-supported, coed. Awards: associate, bachelor's, and master's degrees (offers first 2 years of most bachelor's degree programs available at the main campus in Athens; also offers several bachelor's degree programs that can be completed at this campus and several programs exclusive to this campus; also offers some graduate programs). 14 undergraduate majors. Total enrollment: 2,000. Undergraduates: 1,960. Federal methodology is used as a basis for awarding need-based institutional aid.

FRESHMAN FINANCIAL AID (Fall 2004, est.) 263 applied for aid; of those 83% were deemed to have need. 98% of freshmen with need received aid; of those 10% had need fully met. *Average percent of need met:* 52% (excluding resources awarded to replace EFC). *Average financial aid package:* $5419 (excluding resources awarded to replace EFC). 7% of all full-time freshmen had no need and received non-need-based gift aid.

UNDERGRADUATE FINANCIAL AID (Fall 2004, est.) 955 applied for aid; of those 86% were deemed to have need. 98% of undergraduates with need received aid; of those 10% had need fully met. *Average percent of need met:* 55% (excluding resources awarded to replace EFC). *Average financial aid package:* $6700 (excluding resources awarded to replace EFC). 4% of all full-time undergraduates had no need and received non-need-based gift aid.

GIFT AID (NEED-BASED) *Total amount:* $3,051,735 (73% federal, 24% state, 3% institutional). *Receiving aid:* Freshmen: 59% (160); All full-time undergraduates: 56% (613). *Average award:* Freshmen: $4222; Undergraduates: $4645. *Scholarships, grants, and awards:* Federal Pell, FSEOG, state, college/university gift aid from institutional funds.

GIFT AID (NON-NEED-BASED) *Total amount:* $292,342 (7% state, 62% institutional, 31% external sources). *Receiving aid:* Freshmen: 10% (27); Undergraduates: 6% (66). *Average Award:* Freshmen: $2113; Undergraduates: $2545. *Scholarships, grants, and awards by category: Academic Interests/ Achievement:* general academic interests/achievements. *Special Characteristics:* children of faculty/staff. *Tuition waivers:* Full or partial for employees or children of employees, senior citizens. *ROTC:* Army cooperative, Air Force cooperative.

LOANS *Student loans:* $5,278,273 (53% need-based, 47% non-need-based). 59% of past graduating class borrowed through all loan programs. *Average indebtedness per student:* $17,192. *Average need-based loan:* Freshmen: $2541; Undergraduates: $3432. *Parent loans:* $71,110 (100% non-need-based). *Programs:* Federal Direct (Subsidized and Unsubsidized Stafford, PLUS), Perkins, state, college/university.

WORK-STUDY *Federal work-study:* Total amount: $4635; jobs available.

APPLYING FOR FINANCIAL AID *Required financial aid form:* FAFSA. *Financial aid deadline (priority):* 3/15. *Notification date:* 4/1.

CONTACT Ms. Sondra Williams, Director of Financial Aid, Ohio University–Chillicothe, 020 Chubb Hall, Athens, OH 45701-2979, 740-593-4141 or toll-free 877-462-6824 (in-state). *Fax:* 740-593-4140. *E-mail:* willias1@ohio.edu.

OHIO UNIVERSITY–EASTERN
St. Clairsville, OH

Tuition & fees: N/R	Average undergraduate aid package: $6374

ABOUT THE INSTITUTION State-supported, coed. Awards: associate and bachelor's degrees (also offers some graduate courses). 77 undergraduate majors. Total enrollment: 1,118. Undergraduates: 931. Freshmen: 210. Federal methodology is used as a basis for awarding need-based institutional aid.

FRESHMAN FINANCIAL AID (Fall 2004, est.) 113 applied for aid; of those 80% were deemed to have need. 97% of freshmen with need received aid; of those 15% had need fully met. *Average percent of need met:* 59% (excluding resources awarded to replace EFC). *Average financial aid package:* $4705 (excluding resources awarded to replace EFC). 7% of all full-time freshmen had no need and received non-need-based gift aid.

UNDERGRADUATE FINANCIAL AID (Fall 2004, est.) 503 applied for aid; of those 86% were deemed to have need. 97% of undergraduates with need received aid; of those 14% had need fully met. *Average percent of need met:* 60% (excluding resources awarded to replace EFC). *Average financial aid package:* $6374 (excluding resources awarded to replace EFC). 5% of all full-time undergraduates had no need and received non-need-based gift aid.

GIFT AID (NEED-BASED) *Total amount:* $1,213,181 (72% federal, 20% state, 8% institutional). *Receiving aid:* Freshmen: 36% (50); All full-time undergradu-

ates: 54% (300). *Average award:* Freshmen: $4159; Undergraduates: $3868. *Scholarships, grants, and awards:* Federal Pell, FSEOG, state, private, college/university gift aid from institutional funds.

GIFT AID (NON-NEED-BASED) *Total amount:* $354,527 (2% state, 89% institutional, 9% external sources). *Receiving aid:* Freshmen: 23% (31); Undergraduates: 18% (103). *Average Award: Freshmen:* $2169; *Undergraduates:* $2596. *Scholarships, grants, and awards by category: Academic Interests/Achievement:* area/ethnic studies, biological sciences, business, communication, computer science, education, engineering/technologies, English, foreign languages, general academic interests/achievements, health fields, home economics, humanities, international studies, mathematics, military science, physical sciences, premedicine, social sciences. *Creative Arts/Performance:* applied art and design, art/fine arts, cinema/film/broadcasting, dance, debating, journalism/publications, music, performing arts, theater/drama. *Special Characteristics:* children of faculty/staff. *Tuition waivers:* Full or partial for employees or children of employees.

LOANS *Student loans:* $2,214,455 (62% need-based, 38% non-need-based). *Average need-based loan:* Freshmen: $2594; Undergraduates: $3895. *Parent loans:* $31,227 (100% non-need-based). *Programs:* Federal Direct (Subsidized and Unsubsidized Stafford, PLUS), Perkins, state, college/university.

WORK-STUDY *Federal work-study:* Total amount: $33,604; jobs available.

APPLYING FOR FINANCIAL AID *Required financial aid form:* FAFSA. *Financial aid deadline (priority):* 3/15. *Notification date:* 4/1.

CONTACT Ms. Sondra Williams, Director of Financial Aid, Ohio University–Eastern, 020 Chubb Hall, Athens, OH 45701-2979, 740-593-4141 or toll-free 800-648-3331 (in-state). *Fax:* 740-593-4140. *E-mail:* willias1@ohio.edu.

OHIO UNIVERSITY–LANCASTER
Lancaster, OH

Tuition & fees: N/R   **Average undergraduate aid package:** $6476

ABOUT THE INSTITUTION State-supported, coed. Awards: associate, bachelor's, and master's degrees. 20 undergraduate majors. Total enrollment: 1,744. Undergraduates: 1,617. Freshmen: 308. Federal methodology is used as a basis for awarding need-based institutional aid.

FRESHMAN FINANCIAL AID (Fall 2004, est.) 233 applied for aid; of those 71% were deemed to have need. 95% of freshmen with need received aid; of those 15% had need fully met. *Average percent of need met:* 54% (excluding resources awarded to replace EFC). *Average financial aid package:* $5063 (excluding resources awarded to replace EFC). 8% of all full-time freshmen had no need and received non-need-based gift aid.

UNDERGRADUATE FINANCIAL AID (Fall 2004, est.) 803 applied for aid; of those 80% were deemed to have need. 97% of undergraduates with need received aid; of those 13% had need fully met. *Average percent of need met:* 56% (excluding resources awarded to replace EFC). *Average financial aid package:* $6476 (excluding resources awarded to replace EFC). 4% of all full-time undergraduates had no need and received non-need-based gift aid.

GIFT AID (NEED-BASED) *Total amount:* $2,100,914 (72% federal, 22% state, 6% institutional). *Receiving aid:* Freshmen: 38% (108); All full-time undergraduates: 49% (443). *Average award:* Freshmen: $3897; Undergraduates: $4287. *Scholarships, grants, and awards:* Federal Pell, FSEOG, state, private, college/university gift aid from institutional funds.

GIFT AID (NON-NEED-BASED) *Total amount:* $338,394 (9% state, 72% institutional, 19% external sources). *Receiving aid:* Freshmen: 8% (24); Undergraduates: 8% (71). *Average Award:* Freshmen: $3792; *Undergraduates:* $3184. *Scholarships, grants, and awards by category: Academic Interests/Achievement:* general academic interests/achievements. *Creative Arts/Performance:* journalism/publications. *Special Characteristics:* children of faculty/staff, members of minority groups. *ROTC:* Army cooperative, Air Force cooperative.

LOANS *Student loans:* $4,351,137 (54% need-based, 46% non-need-based). *Average need-based loan:* Freshmen: $2583; Undergraduates: $3595. *Parent loans:* $103,863 (100% non-need-based). *Programs:* Federal Direct (Subsidized and Unsubsidized Stafford, PLUS), Perkins, state, college/university.

WORK-STUDY *Federal work-study:* Total amount: $9785; jobs available.

APPLYING FOR FINANCIAL AID *Required financial aid form:* FAFSA. *Financial aid deadline (priority):* 3/15. *Notification date:* 4/1.

CONTACT Ms. Sondra Williams, Director of Financial Aid, Ohio University–Lancaster, 020 Chubb Hall, Athens, OH 45701-2979, 740-593-4141 or toll-free 888-446-4468 Ext. 215. *Fax:* 740-593-4140. *E-mail:* willias1@ohio.edu.

OHIO UNIVERSITY–SOUTHERN CAMPUS
Ironton, OH

Tuition & fees (OH res): $4026   **Average undergraduate aid package:** $7049

ABOUT THE INSTITUTION State-supported, coed. Awards: associate, bachelor's, and master's degrees. 20 undergraduate majors. Total enrollment: 1,746. Undergraduates: 1,630. Freshmen: 348. Federal methodology is used as a basis for awarding need-based institutional aid.

UNDERGRADUATE EXPENSES for 2004–05 *Application fee:* $20. *Tuition, state resident:* full-time $4026. *Tuition, nonresident:* full-time $5676. Full-time tuition and fees vary according to student level. Part-time tuition and fees vary according to student level. *Payment plan:* Installment.

FRESHMAN FINANCIAL AID (Fall 2004, est.) 285 applied for aid; of those 91% were deemed to have need. 99% of freshmen with need received aid; of those 6% had need fully met. *Average percent of need met:* 58% (excluding resources awarded to replace EFC). *Average financial aid package:* $6317 (excluding resources awarded to replace EFC). 3% of all full-time freshmen had no need and received non-need-based gift aid.

UNDERGRADUATE FINANCIAL AID (Fall 2004, est.) 1,078 applied for aid; of those 93% were deemed to have need. 98% of undergraduates with need received aid; of those 6% had need fully met. *Average percent of need met:* 57% (excluding resources awarded to replace EFC). *Average financial aid package:* $7049 (excluding resources awarded to replace EFC). 2% of all full-time undergraduates had no need and received non-need-based gift aid.

GIFT AID (NEED-BASED) *Total amount:* $3,769,440 (76% federal, 20% state, 4% institutional). *Receiving aid:* Freshmen: 70% (217); All full-time undergraduates: 68% (816). *Average award:* Freshmen: $4257; Undergraduates: $4381. *Scholarships, grants, and awards:* Federal Pell, FSEOG, state, private, college/university gift aid from institutional funds.

GIFT AID (NON-NEED-BASED) *Total amount:* $265,470 (11% state, 69% institutional, 20% external sources). *Receiving aid:* Freshmen: 15% (45); Undergraduates: 12% (149). *Average Award: Freshmen:* $1960; *Undergraduates:* $1097. *Scholarships, grants, and awards by category: Academic Interests/Achievement:* general academic interests/achievements. *Special Characteristics:* children of faculty/staff. *Tuition waivers:* Full or partial for employees or children of employees, senior citizens.

LOANS *Student loans:* $5,782,087 (56% need-based, 44% non-need-based). *Average need-based loan:* Freshmen: $2663; Undergraduates: $3446. *Parent loans:* $91,270 (100% non-need-based). *Programs:* Federal Direct (Subsidized and Unsubsidized Stafford, PLUS), Perkins, state, college/university.

WORK-STUDY *Federal work-study:* Total amount: $19,965; jobs available.

APPLYING FOR FINANCIAL AID *Required financial aid form:* FAFSA. *Financial aid deadline (priority):* 4/1. *Notification date:* 4/1.

CONTACT Ms. Sondra Williams, Director of Financial Aid, Ohio University–Southern Campus, 020 Chubb Hall, Athens, OH 45701-2979, 740-593-4141 or toll-free 800-626-0513. *Fax:* 740-593-4140. *E-mail:* willias1@ohio.edu.

OHIO UNIVERSITY–ZANESVILLE
Zanesville, OH

Tuition & fees (OH res): $4263   **Average undergraduate aid package:** $6474

ABOUT THE INSTITUTION State-supported, coed. Awards: associate, bachelor's, and master's degrees (offers first 2 years of most bachelor's degree programs available at the main campus in Athens; also offers several bachelor's degree programs that can be completed at this campus; also offers some graduate courses). 9 undergraduate majors. Total enrollment: 1,877. Undergraduates: 1,834. Federal methodology is used as a basis for awarding need-based institutional aid.

UNDERGRADUATE EXPENSES for 2004–05 *Application fee:* $20. *Tuition, state resident:* full-time $4263. *Tuition, nonresident:* full-time $8511. Full-time tuition and fees vary according to course level. Part-time tuition and fees vary according to course level.

FRESHMAN FINANCIAL AID (Fall 2004, est.) 315 applied for aid; of those 77% were deemed to have need. 99% of freshmen with need received aid; of those 23% had need fully met. *Average percent of need met:* 61% (excluding resources awarded to replace EFC). *Average financial aid package:* $5638 (excluding resources awarded to replace EFC). 15% of all full-time freshmen had no need and received non-need-based gift aid.

UNDERGRADUATE FINANCIAL AID (Fall 2004, est.) 1,119 applied for aid; of those 82% were deemed to have need. 98% of undergraduates with need

Ohio University–Zanesville

Ohio University–Zanesville

received aid; of those 18% had need fully met. *Average percent of need met:* 59% (excluding resources awarded to replace EFC). *Average financial aid package:* $6474 (excluding resources awarded to replace EFC). 9% of all full-time undergraduates had no need and received non-need-based gift aid.

GIFT AID (NEED-BASED) *Total amount:* $2,893,320 (73% federal, 21% state, 6% institutional). *Receiving aid:* Freshmen: 49% (154); All full-time undergraduates: 53% (627). *Average award:* Freshmen: $3952; Undergraduates: $4273. *Scholarships, grants, and awards:* Federal Pell, FSEOG, state, private, college/university gift aid from institutional funds.

GIFT AID (NON-NEED-BASED) *Total amount:* $1,087,626 (4% state, 81% institutional, 15% external sources). *Receiving aid:* Freshmen: 38% (121); Undergraduates: 22% (260). *Average Award:* Freshmen: $3026; Undergraduates:* $2895. *Scholarships, grants, and awards by category: Academic Interests/Achievement:* general academic interests/achievements. *Special Characteristics:* children of faculty/staff. *Tuition waivers:* Full or partial for employees or children of employees, senior citizens.

LOANS *Student loans:* $5,038,929 (56% need-based, 44% non-need-based). *Average need-based loan:* Freshmen: $2381; Undergraduates: $3431. *Parent loans:* $100,112 (100% non-need-based). *Programs:* Federal Direct (Subsidized and Unsubsidized Stafford, PLUS), Perkins, state, college/university.

WORK-STUDY *Federal work-study:* Total amount: $55,234; jobs available.

APPLYING FOR FINANCIAL AID *Required financial aid form:* FAFSA. *Financial aid deadline (priority):* 4/1. *Notification date:* 4/1.

CONTACT Ms. Sondra Williams, Director of Financial Aid, Ohio University–Zanesville, 020 Chubb Hall, Athens, OH 45701-2979, 740-593-4141. *Fax:* 740-593-4140. *E-mail:* willias1@ohio.edu.

OHIO VALLEY UNIVERSITY
Vienna, WV

Tuition & fees: $12,012	Average undergraduate aid package: $8784

ABOUT THE INSTITUTION Independent religious, coed. Awards: associate and bachelor's degrees. 19 undergraduate majors. Total enrollment: 520. Undergraduates: 520. Freshmen: 95. Federal methodology is used as a basis for awarding need-based institutional aid.

UNDERGRADUATE EXPENSES for 2004–05 *Application fee:* $20. *Comprehensive fee:* $17,392 includes full-time tuition ($10,740), mandatory fees ($1272), and room and board ($5380). *College room only:* $2930. Full-time tuition and fees vary according to course load. Room and board charges vary according to board plan. *Part-time tuition:* $392 per credit hour. *Part-time fees:* $55 per credit hour. Part-time tuition and fees vary according to course load. *Payment plan:* Installment.

FRESHMAN FINANCIAL AID (Fall 2004, est.) 109 applied for aid; of those 89% were deemed to have need. 100% of freshmen with need received aid; of those 14% had need fully met. *Average percent of need met:* 57% (excluding resources awarded to replace EFC). *Average financial aid package:* $8368 (excluding resources awarded to replace EFC). 23% of all full-time freshmen had no need and received non-need-based gift aid.

UNDERGRADUATE FINANCIAL AID (Fall 2004, est.) 433 applied for aid; of those 90% were deemed to have need. 99% of undergraduates with need received aid; of those 20% had need fully met. *Average percent of need met:* 65% (excluding resources awarded to replace EFC). *Average financial aid package:* $8784 (excluding resources awarded to replace EFC). 19% of all full-time undergraduates had no need and received non-need-based gift aid.

GIFT AID (NEED-BASED) *Total amount:* $1,997,539 (34% federal, 10% state, 53% institutional, 3% external sources). *Receiving aid:* Freshmen: 66% (90); All full-time undergraduates: 72% (358). *Average award:* Freshmen: $6239; Undergraduates: $5624. *Scholarships, grants, and awards:* Federal Pell, FSEOG, state, private, college/university gift aid from institutional funds.

GIFT AID (NON-NEED-BASED) *Total amount:* $334,021 (1% federal, 14% state, 76% institutional, 9% external sources). *Receiving aid:* Freshmen: 10% (13); Undergraduates: 11% (57). *Average Award:* Freshmen: $5120; Undergraduates:* $6587. *Scholarships, grants, and awards by category: Academic Interests/Achievement:* 250 awards ($330,479 total): education, English, general academic interests/achievements, religion/biblical studies. *Creative Arts/Performance:* 38 awards ($57,750 total): general creative arts/performance, journalism/publications, music, performing arts, theater/drama. *Special Achievements/Activities:* 41 awards ($46,170 total): community service, general special achievements/activities, leadership, religious involvement. *Special Characteristics:* 95 awards ($228,304 total): adult students, children of faculty/staff, ethnic background, general special

characteristics, international students, local/state students, relatives of clergy, religious affiliation. *Tuition waivers:* Full or partial for employees or children of employees, senior citizens. *ROTC:* Air Force cooperative.

LOANS *Student loans:* $2,167,028 (81% need-based, 19% non-need-based). 93% of past graduating class borrowed through all loan programs. *Average indebtedness per student:* $17,119. *Average need-based loan:* Freshmen: $2712; Undergraduates: $3604. *Parent loans:* $1,891,850 (100% non-need-based). *Programs:* FFEL (Subsidized and Unsubsidized Stafford, PLUS), Perkins.

WORK-STUDY *Federal work-study:* Total amount: $121,048; 181 jobs averaging $800. *State or other work-study/employment:* Total amount: $80,778 (100% non-need-based). 102 part-time jobs averaging $800.

ATHLETIC AWARDS *Total amount:* $596,749 (100% non-need-based).

APPLYING FOR FINANCIAL AID *Required financial aid form:* FAFSA. *Financial aid deadline (priority):* 3/1. *Notification date:* Continuous beginning 3/15. Students must reply within 4 weeks of notification.

CONTACT Marjorie W. Lyons, Director of Financial Aid, Ohio Valley University, 1 Campus View Drive, Vienna, WV 26105-8000, 304-865-6077 or toll-free 877-446-8668 Ext. 6200 (out-of-state). *Fax:* 304-865-6001. *E-mail:* mlyons@ovc.edu.

OHIO WESLEYAN UNIVERSITY
Delaware, OH

Tuition & fees: $26,820	Average undergraduate aid package: $22,722

ABOUT THE INSTITUTION Independent United Methodist, coed. Awards: bachelor's degrees. 86 undergraduate majors. Total enrollment: 1,944. Undergraduates: 1,944. Freshmen: 563. Federal methodology is used as a basis for awarding need-based institutional aid.

UNDERGRADUATE EXPENSES for 2004–05 *Application fee:* $35. *Comprehensive fee:* $34,150 includes full-time tuition ($26,460), mandatory fees ($360), and room and board ($7330). *College room only:* $3640. Room and board charges vary according to board plan. *Part-time tuition:* $2880 per course. *Payment plan:* Installment.

GIFT AID (NEED-BASED) *Total amount:* $17,326,642 (8% federal, 6% state, 84% institutional, 2% external sources). *Receiving aid:* Freshmen: 60% (338); All full-time undergraduates: 57% (1,085). *Average award:* Freshmen: $21,926; Undergraduates: $21,548. *Scholarships, grants, and awards:* Federal Pell, FSEOG, state, private, college/university gift aid from institutional funds.

GIFT AID (NON-NEED-BASED) *Total amount:* $11,021,554 (4% state, 94% institutional, 2% external sources). *Receiving aid:* Freshmen: 14% (81); Undergraduates: 10% (195). *Average Award:* Freshmen: $12,119; Undergraduates:* $12,296. *Scholarships, grants, and awards by category: Academic Interests/Achievement:* 949 awards ($18,687,367 total): area/ethnic studies, biological sciences, business, communication, computer science, education, engineering/technologies, English, foreign languages, general academic interests/achievements, health fields, humanities, international studies, mathematics, physical sciences, premedicine, religion/biblical studies, social sciences. *Creative Arts/Performance:* 44 awards ($1,232,072 total): art/fine arts, dance, music, theater/drama. *Special Achievements/Activities:* 42 awards ($605,581 total): community service, leadership, religious involvement. *Special Characteristics:* 735 awards ($10,269,965 total): children and siblings of alumni, children of faculty/staff, ethnic background, international students, local/state students, members of minority groups, out-of-state students, relatives of clergy, religious affiliation. *Tuition waivers:* Full or partial for children of alumni, employees or children of employees. *ROTC:* Army cooperative.

LOANS *Student loans:* $6,868,265 (63% need-based, 37% non-need-based). 61% of past graduating class borrowed through all loan programs. *Average indebtedness per student:* $21,841. *Average need-based loan:* Freshmen: $4606; Undergraduates: $4805. *Parent loans:* $3,336,876 (100% non-need-based). *Programs:* FFEL (Subsidized and Unsubsidized Stafford, PLUS), Perkins, state, college/university.

APPLYING FOR FINANCIAL AID *Required financial aid forms:* FAFSA, institution's own form. *Financial aid deadline:* 5/1 (priority: 3/1). *Notification date:* Continuous beginning 2/1. Students must reply by 5/1 or within 2 weeks of notification.

CONTACT Mr. Gregory W. Matthews, Director of Financial Aid, Ohio Wesleyan University, 61 South Sandusky Street, Delaware, OH 43015, 740-368-3050 or toll-free 800-922-8953. *Fax:* 740-368-3066. *E-mail:* owfinaid@owu.edu.

OHR HAMEIR THEOLOGICAL SEMINARY
Peekskill, NY

CONTACT Financial Aid Office, Ohr Hameir Theological Seminary, Furnace Woods Road, Peekskill, NY 10566, 914-736-1500.

OHR SOMAYACH/JOSEPH TANENBAUM EDUCATIONAL CENTER
Monsey, NY

CONTACT Financial Aid Office, Ohr Somayach/Joseph Tanenbaum Educational Center, PO Box 334244, Route 306, Monsey, NY 10952-0334, 914-425-1370.

OKLAHOMA BAPTIST UNIVERSITY
Shawnee, OK

Tuition & fees: $13,162	Average undergraduate aid package: $10,644

ABOUT THE INSTITUTION Independent Southern Baptist, coed. Awards: bachelor's and master's degrees. 100 undergraduate majors. Total enrollment: 1,883. Undergraduates: 1,866. Freshmen: 411. Federal methodology is used as a basis for awarding need-based institutional aid.

UNDERGRADUATE EXPENSES for 2004–05 *Application fee:* $25. *Comprehensive fee:* $16,962 includes full-time tuition ($12,286), mandatory fees ($876), and room and board ($3800). *College room only:* $1750. Full-time tuition and fees vary according to course load. Room and board charges vary according to board plan and housing facility. *Part-time tuition:* $385 per credit hour. Part-time tuition and fees vary according to course load. *Payment plan:* Installment.

FRESHMAN FINANCIAL AID (Fall 2003) 391 applied for aid; of those 64% were deemed to have need. 100% of freshmen with need received aid; of those 62% had need fully met. *Average percent of need met:* 65% (excluding resources awarded to replace EFC). *Average financial aid package:* $10,630 (excluding resources awarded to replace EFC). 34% of all full-time freshmen had no need and received non-need-based gift aid.

UNDERGRADUATE FINANCIAL AID (Fall 2003) 1,398 applied for aid; of those 69% were deemed to have need. 100% of undergraduates with need received aid; of those 51% had need fully met. *Average percent of need met:* 70% (excluding resources awarded to replace EFC). *Average financial aid package:* $10,644 (excluding resources awarded to replace EFC). 29% of all full-time undergraduates had no need and received non-need-based gift aid.

GIFT AID (NEED-BASED) *Total amount:* $1,805,140 (68% federal, 15% state, 17% institutional). *Receiving aid:* Freshmen: 53% (218); All full-time undergraduates: 57% (865). *Average award:* Freshmen: $3330; Undergraduates: $3301. *Scholarships, grants, and awards:* Federal Pell, FSEOG, state, private, college/university gift aid from institutional funds.

GIFT AID (NON-NEED-BASED) *Total amount:* $6,612,370 (1% state, 82% institutional, 17% external sources). *Receiving aid:* Freshmen: 55% (225); Undergraduates: 54% (821). *Average Award:* Freshmen: $4716; Undergraduates:* $4398. *Scholarships, grants, and awards by category:* Academic Interests/Achievement: general academic interests/achievements, religion/biblical studies. *Creative Arts/Performance:* art/fine arts, music, performing arts. *Special Achievements/Activities:* leadership, religious involvement. *Special Characteristics:* children and siblings of alumni, children of faculty/staff, general special characteristics, local/state students, out-of-state students, relatives of clergy, religious affiliation. *Tuition waivers:* Full or partial for employees or children of employees, senior citizens. *ROTC:* Air Force cooperative.

LOANS *Student loans:* $4,046,143 (53% need-based, 47% non-need-based). 61% of past graduating class borrowed through all loan programs. *Average indebtedness per student:* $14,510. *Average need-based loan:* Freshmen: $3199; Undergraduates: $3834. *Parent loans:* $1,508,384 (100% non-need-based). *Programs:* FFEL (Subsidized and Unsubsidized Stafford, PLUS), Perkins.

WORK-STUDY *Federal work-study:* Total amount: $196,000; 303 jobs averaging $834. *State or other work-study/employment:* Total amount: $300,000 (100% non-need-based). Part-time jobs available.

ATHLETIC AWARDS *Total amount:* $997,887 (100% non-need-based).

APPLYING FOR FINANCIAL AID *Required financial aid form:* FAFSA. *Financial aid deadline (priority):* 3/1. *Notification date:* Continuous. Students must reply by 5/1 or within 2 weeks of notification.

CONTACT Student Financial Services, Oklahoma Baptist University, 500 West University, Shawnee, OK 74804, 405-878-2016 or toll-free 800-654-3285.

OKLAHOMA CHRISTIAN UNIVERSITY
Oklahoma City, OK

ABOUT THE INSTITUTION Independent religious, coed. Awards: bachelor's and master's degrees. 54 undergraduate majors. Total enrollment: 1,947. Undergraduates: 572. Freshmen: 572.

GIFT AID (NEED-BASED) *Scholarships, grants, and awards:* Federal Pell, FSEOG, state, private, college/university gift aid from institutional funds.

GIFT AID (NON-NEED-BASED) *Scholarships, grants, and awards by category:* Academic Interests/Achievement: biological sciences, business, communication, computer science, education, engineering/technologies, general academic interests/achievements, health fields, international studies, mathematics, physical sciences, premedicine, religion/biblical studies, social sciences. *Creative Arts/Performance:* applied art and design, journalism/publications, music, performing arts, theater/drama. *Special Achievements/Activities:* cheerleading/drum major, general special achievements/activities, hobbies/interests, leadership, religious involvement. *Special Characteristics:* children and siblings of alumni, children of current students, children of educators, children of faculty/staff, general special characteristics, international students, members of minority groups, parents of current students, relatives of clergy, siblings of current students, spouses of current students.

LOANS *Programs:* FFEL (Subsidized and Unsubsidized Stafford, PLUS), Perkins, alternative loans.

WORK-STUDY *Federal work-study:* Total amount: $300,000; 200 jobs averaging $1500.

APPLYING FOR FINANCIAL AID *Required financial aid forms:* FAFSA, institution's own form.

CONTACT Missi Bryant, Director of Financial Services, Oklahoma Christian University, Box 11000, Oklahoma City, OK 73136-1100, 405-425-5190 or toll-free 800-877-5010 (in-state). *Fax:* 405-425-5197. *E-mail:* missi.bryant@oc.edu.

OKLAHOMA CITY UNIVERSITY
Oklahoma City, OK

Tuition & fees: $16,040	Average undergraduate aid package: $11,702

ABOUT THE INSTITUTION Independent United Methodist, coed. Awards: bachelor's, master's, and first professional degrees. 75 undergraduate majors. Total enrollment: 3,695. Undergraduates: 1,869. Freshmen: 324. Federal methodology is used as a basis for awarding need-based institutional aid.

UNDERGRADUATE EXPENSES for 2004–05 *Application fee:* $30. *Comprehensive fee:* $21,990 includes full-time tuition ($15,200), mandatory fees ($840), and room and board ($5950). *College room only:* $2900. Full-time tuition and fees vary according to program. Room and board charges vary according to board plan and housing facility. *Part-time tuition:* $518 per semester hour. *Part-time fees:* $100 per term. Part-time tuition and fees vary according to program. *Payment plans:* Installment, deferred payment.

FRESHMAN FINANCIAL AID (Fall 2003) 263 applied for aid; of those 79% were deemed to have need. 100% of freshmen with need received aid; of those 25% had need fully met. *Average percent of need met:* 72% (excluding resources awarded to replace EFC). *Average financial aid package:* $12,581 (excluding resources awarded to replace EFC). 16% of all full-time freshmen had no need and received non-need-based gift aid.

UNDERGRADUATE FINANCIAL AID (Fall 2003) 868 applied for aid; of those 81% were deemed to have need. 97% of undergraduates with need received aid; of those 18% had need fully met. *Average percent of need met:* 79% (excluding resources awarded to replace EFC). *Average financial aid package:* $11,702 (excluding resources awarded to replace EFC). 9% of all full-time undergraduates had no need and received non-need-based gift aid.

GIFT AID (NEED-BASED) *Total amount:* $7,308,851 (16% federal, 2% state, 76% institutional, 6% external sources). *Receiving aid:* Freshmen: 67% (201); All full-time undergraduates: 47% (640). *Average award:* Freshmen: $10,418; Undergraduates: $8155. *Scholarships, grants, and awards:* Federal Pell, FSEOG, state, private, college/university gift aid from institutional funds, United Negro College Fund, Federal Nursing, Native American Grants.

GIFT AID (NON-NEED-BASED) *Total amount:* $1,075,312 (1% state, 94% institutional, 5% external sources). *Receiving aid:* Freshmen: 11% (32); Undergraduates: 7% (99). *Average Award:* Freshmen: $9186; Undergraduates: $7046. *Scholarships, grants, and awards by category:* Academic Interests/Achievement: 1,091 awards ($2,703,698 total): business, communication, education, general academic interests/achievements, health fields, religion/biblical studies. *Creative Arts/Performance:* 203 awards ($788,230 total): applied art and design, art/fine arts, dance, music, performing arts, theater/drama. *Special Achievements/Activities:* 108 awards ($226,337 total): cheerleading/drum major, general special achievements/activities, junior miss, leadership, religious involvement. *Special Characteristics:* 97 awards ($849,480 total): children of faculty/staff, relatives of clergy. *Tuition waivers:* Full or partial for employees or children of employees. *ROTC:* Army cooperative, Air Force cooperative.

LOANS *Student loans:* $3,914,872 (52% need-based, 48% non-need-based). 43% of past graduating class borrowed through all loan programs. *Average indebtedness per student:* $20,584. *Average need-based loan:* Freshmen: $2227; Undergraduates: $3547. *Parent loans:* $2,047,351 (100% non-need-based). *Programs:* FFEL (Subsidized and Unsubsidized Stafford, PLUS), Perkins, Federal Nursing.

WORK-STUDY *Federal work-study:* Total amount: $349,910; 190 jobs averaging $1842. *State or other work-study/employment:* Total amount: $121,745 (100% non-need-based). 55 part-time jobs averaging $2214.

ATHLETIC AWARDS *Total amount:* $1,461,946 (100% non-need-based).

APPLYING FOR FINANCIAL AID *Required financial aid form:* FAFSA. *Financial aid deadline (priority):* 3/1. *Notification date:* Continuous beginning 2/24. Students must reply within 2 weeks of notification.

CONTACT Denise Flis, Financial Aid Director, Oklahoma City University, 2501 North Blackwelder, Oklahoma City, OK 73106-1493, 405-208-5848 or toll-free 800-633-7242. *Fax:* 405-208-5466. *E-mail:* dflis@okcu.edu.

OKLAHOMA PANHANDLE STATE UNIVERSITY
Goodwell, OK

Tuition & fees (OK res): $2720	Average undergraduate aid package: N/A

ABOUT THE INSTITUTION State-supported, coed. Awards: associate and bachelor's degrees. 32 undergraduate majors. Total enrollment: 1,237. Undergraduates: 1,237. Freshmen: 240. Both federal and institutional methodology are used as a basis for awarding need-based institutional aid.

UNDERGRADUATE EXPENSES for 2004–05 *Tuition, state resident:* full-time $2070; part-time $69 per hour. *Tuition, nonresident:* full-time $2790; part-time $93 per hour. *Required fees:* full-time $650; $18.50 per hour or $51 per term part-time. Full-time tuition and fees vary according to course level and program. Part-time tuition and fees vary according to course level. *College room and board:* $2810; *room only:* $930. Room and board charges vary according to board plan, housing facility, and student level. *Payment plan:* Installment.

GIFT AID (NEED-BASED) *Total amount:* $14,202,457 (10% federal, 1% state, 89% external sources). *Scholarships, grants, and awards:* Federal Pell, FSEOG, state, private, college/university gift aid from institutional funds.

GIFT AID (NON-NEED-BASED) *Scholarships, grants, and awards by category:* Academic Interests/Achievement: agriculture, education, English, general academic interests/achievements, health fields, mathematics, physical sciences. *Creative Arts/Performance:* art/fine arts, debating, music, performing arts, theater/drama. *Special Achievements/Activities:* cheerleading/drum major, general special achievements/activities, rodeo. *Special Characteristics:* children of faculty/staff, general special characteristics, local/state students, out-of-state students, veterans, veterans' children. *Tuition waivers:* Full or partial for employees or children of employees.

LOANS *Student loans:* $2,052,942 (100% need-based). *Parent loans:* $67,047 (100% need-based). *Programs:* FFEL (Subsidized and Unsubsidized Stafford, PLUS), Perkins.

ATHLETIC AWARDS *Total amount:* $312,485 (100% need-based).

APPLYING FOR FINANCIAL AID *Required financial aid form:* FAFSA. *Financial aid deadline (priority):* 3/15. *Notification date:* 5/1. Students must reply by 8/1.

CONTACT Ms. Mary Ellen Riley, Director of Financial Aid, Oklahoma Panhandle State University, PO Box 430, Goodwell, OK 73939-0430, 580-349-2611 Ext. 324 or toll-free 800-664-6778. *E-mail:* mriley@opsu.edu.

OKLAHOMA STATE UNIVERSITY
Stillwater, OK

Tuition & fees (OK res): $4071	Average undergraduate aid package: $8307

ABOUT THE INSTITUTION State-supported, coed. Awards: bachelor's, master's, doctoral, and first professional degrees and post-master's certificates. 128 undergraduate majors. Total enrollment: 23,626. Undergraduates: 18,789. Freshmen: 3,264. Federal methodology is used as a basis for awarding need-based institutional aid.

UNDERGRADUATE EXPENSES for 2004–05 *Application fee:* $40. *Tuition, state resident:* full-time $2910; part-time $97 per credit hour. *Tuition, nonresident:* full-time $10,200; part-time $340 per credit hour. *Required fees:* full-time $1161; $46.21 per credit hour. Full-time tuition and fees vary according to course level. Part-time tuition and fees vary according to course level. *College room and board:* $5602; *room only:* $2602. Room and board charges vary according to board plan, housing facility, and location. *Payment plan:* Installment.

FRESHMAN FINANCIAL AID (Fall 2003) 1954 applied for aid; of those 73% were deemed to have need. 98% of freshmen with need received aid; of those 18% had need fully met. *Average percent of need met:* 78% (excluding resources awarded to replace EFC). *Average financial aid package:* $7873 (excluding resources awarded to replace EFC). 27% of all full-time freshmen had no need and received non-need-based gift aid.

UNDERGRADUATE FINANCIAL AID (Fall 2003) 10,773 applied for aid; of those 80% were deemed to have need. 98% of undergraduates with need received aid; of those 23% had need fully met. *Average percent of need met:* 78% (excluding resources awarded to replace EFC). *Average financial aid package:* $8307 (excluding resources awarded to replace EFC). 23% of all full-time undergraduates had no need and received non-need-based gift aid.

GIFT AID (NEED-BASED) *Total amount:* $23,788,490 (60% federal, 18% state, 11% institutional, 11% external sources). *Receiving aid:* Freshmen: 33% (1,014); All full-time undergraduates: 36% (5,912). *Average award:* Freshmen: $3713; Undergraduates: $3439. *Scholarships, grants, and awards:* Federal Pell, FSEOG, state, private, college/university gift aid from institutional funds.

GIFT AID (NON-NEED-BASED) *Total amount:* $9,763,768 (27% federal, 22% state, 29% institutional, 22% external sources). *Receiving aid:* Freshmen: 27% (829); Undergraduates: 22% (3,538). *Average Award:* Freshmen: $2246; Undergraduates: $2832. *Scholarships, grants, and awards by category:* Academic Interests/Achievement: agriculture, architecture, area/ethnic studies, biological sciences, business, communication, computer science, education, engineering/technologies, English, foreign languages, general academic interests/ achievements, home economics, humanities, international studies, mathematics, military science, physical sciences, premedicine, social sciences. *Creative Arts/Performance:* general creative arts/performance, music. *Special Achievements/ Activities:* cheerleading/drum major, community service, general special achievements/activities, leadership. *Special Characteristics:* adult students, children and siblings of alumni, general special characteristics, out-of-state students. *Tuition waivers:* Full or partial for children of alumni. *ROTC:* Army, Air Force.

LOANS *Student loans:* $46,498,437 (60% need-based, 40% non-need-based). 54% of past graduating class borrowed through all loan programs. *Average indebtedness per student:* $17,067. *Average need-based loan:* Freshmen: $2720; Undergraduates: $3891. *Parent loans:* $19,721,436 (19% need-based, 81% non-need-based). *Programs:* Federal Direct (Subsidized and Unsubsidized Stafford, PLUS), Perkins, college/university.

WORK-STUDY *Federal work-study:* Total amount: $947,318; 600 jobs averaging $1750. *State or other work-study/employment:* Total amount: $7,576,697 (100% non-need-based). 2,750 part-time jobs averaging $2205.

ATHLETIC AWARDS *Total amount:* $2,499,091 (38% need-based, 62% non-need-based).

APPLYING FOR FINANCIAL AID *Required financial aid form:* FAFSA. *Financial aid deadline:* Continuous. *Notification date:* Continuous beginning 3/15. Students must reply within 2 weeks of notification.

CONTACT Office of Scholarships and Financial Aid, Oklahoma State University, 119 Student Union, Stillwater, OK 74078-5061, 405-744-6604 or toll-free 800-233-5019 (in-state), 800-852-1255 (out-of-state). *Fax:* 405-744-6438. *E-mail:* finaid@okstate.edu.

OKLAHOMA WESLEYAN UNIVERSITY
Bartlesville, OK

Tuition & fees: $13,750	Average undergraduate aid package: $6651

ABOUT THE INSTITUTION Independent religious, coed. Awards: associate, bachelor's, and master's degrees. 37 undergraduate majors. Total enrollment: 887. Undergraduates: 887. Freshmen: 112. Both federal and institutional methodology are used as a basis for awarding need-based institutional aid.

UNDERGRADUATE EXPENSES for 2005–06 *Application fee:* $25. *Comprehensive fee:* $18,950 includes full-time tuition ($12,900), mandatory fees ($850), and room and board ($5200). *College room only:* $2625. Full-time tuition and fees vary according to course load. Room and board charges vary according to board plan and housing facility. *Part-time tuition:* $475 per credit. *Part-time fees:* $50 per credit. *Payment plans:* Installment, deferred payment.

FRESHMAN FINANCIAL AID (Fall 2003) 79 applied for aid; of those 86% were deemed to have need. 99% of freshmen with need received aid; of those 13% had need fully met. *Average percent of need met:* 48% (excluding resources awarded to replace EFC). *Average financial aid package:* $7113 (excluding resources awarded to replace EFC). 13% of all full-time freshmen had no need and received non-need-based gift aid.

UNDERGRADUATE FINANCIAL AID (Fall 2003) 671 applied for aid; of those 90% were deemed to have need. 98% of undergraduates with need received aid; of those 26% had need fully met. *Average percent of need met:* 59% (excluding resources awarded to replace EFC). *Average financial aid package:* $6651 (excluding resources awarded to replace EFC). 7% of all full-time undergraduates had no need and received non-need-based gift aid.

GIFT AID (NEED-BASED) *Total amount:* $816,914 (84% federal, 11% state, 5% institutional). *Receiving aid:* Freshmen: 47% (40); All full-time undergraduates: 46% (321). *Average award:* Freshmen: $2414; Undergraduates: $4019. *Scholarships, grants, and awards:* Federal Pell, FSEOG, state, private, college/university gift aid from institutional funds.

GIFT AID (NON-NEED-BASED) *Total amount:* $954,751 (79% institutional, 21% external sources). *Receiving aid:* Freshmen: 70% (60); Undergraduates: 45% (317). *Average Award:* *Freshmen:* $2100; *Undergraduates:* $2341. *Scholarships, grants, and awards by category: Academic Interests/Achievement:* 201 awards ($383,721 total): biological sciences, computer science, education, general academic interests/achievements, religion/biblical studies. *Creative Arts/Performance:* 18 awards ($14,000 total): debating, music. *Special Achievements/Activities:* 184 awards ($104,123 total): religious involvement. *Special Characteristics:* 231 awards ($311,206 total): children and siblings of alumni, children of educators, children of faculty/staff, international students, relatives of clergy, religious affiliation. *Tuition waivers:* Full or partial for employees or children of employees, senior citizens.

LOANS *Student loans:* $2,858,793 (100% need-based). 78% of past graduating class borrowed through all loan programs. *Average indebtedness per student:* $15,123. *Average need-based loan:* Freshmen: $2625; Undergraduates: $4286. *Parent loans:* $382,220 (76% need-based, 24% non-need-based). *Programs:* FFEL (Subsidized and Unsubsidized Stafford, PLUS), Perkins, college/university.

WORK-STUDY *Federal work-study:* Total amount: $208,733; 130 jobs averaging $1596. *State or other work-study/employment:* Total amount: $15,000 (57% need-based, 43% non-need-based). 13 part-time jobs averaging $1550.

ATHLETIC AWARDS *Total amount:* $247,535 (100% non-need-based).

APPLYING FOR FINANCIAL AID *Required financial aid forms:* FAFSA, institution's own form. *Financial aid deadline (priority):* 3/31. *Notification date:* Continuous beginning 5/1. Students must reply within 1 week of notification.

CONTACT Lee Kanakis, Director of Financial Aid, Oklahoma Wesleyan University, 2201 Silver Lake Road, Bartlesville, OK 74006, 918-335-6282 or toll-free 866-222-8226 (in-state). *Fax:* 918-335-6811. *E-mail:* financialaid@okwu.edu.

OLD DOMINION UNIVERSITY
Norfolk, VA

Tuition & fees (VA res): $5268	Average undergraduate aid package: $6313

ABOUT THE INSTITUTION State-supported, coed. Awards: bachelor's, master's, and doctoral degrees and post-master's certificates. 69 undergraduate majors. Total enrollment: 20,595. Undergraduates: 14,417. Freshmen: 1,953. Federal methodology is used as a basis for awarding need-based institutional aid.

UNDERGRADUATE EXPENSES for 2004–05 *Application fee:* $40. *Tuition, state resident:* full-time $5100; part-time $170 per credit hour. *Tuition, nonresident:* full-time $14,520; part-time $484 per credit hour. *Required fees:* full-time $168; $84 per term part-time. Full-time tuition and fees vary according to course level, course load, and location. Part-time tuition and fees vary according to course level, course load, and location. *College room and board:* $5802; *room only:* $3342. Room and board charges vary according to board plan and housing facility. *Payment plans:* Installment, deferred payment.

FRESHMAN FINANCIAL AID (Fall 2004, est.) 1485 applied for aid; of those 91% were deemed to have need. 90% of freshmen with need received aid; of those 51% had need fully met. *Average percent of need met:* 65% (excluding resources awarded to replace EFC). *Average financial aid package:* $6039 (excluding resources awarded to replace EFC). 4% of all full-time freshmen had no need and received non-need-based gift aid.

UNDERGRADUATE FINANCIAL AID (Fall 2004, est.) 7,221 applied for aid; of those 84% were deemed to have need. 94% of undergraduates with need

received aid; of those 48% had need fully met. *Average percent of need met:* 69% (excluding resources awarded to replace EFC). *Average financial aid package:* $6313 (excluding resources awarded to replace EFC). 5% of all full-time undergraduates had no need and received non-need-based gift aid.

GIFT AID (NEED-BASED) *Total amount:* $18,891,988 (57% federal, 38% state, 4% institutional, 1% external sources). *Receiving aid:* Freshmen: 35% (663); All full-time undergraduates: 30% (3,049). *Average award:* Freshmen: $3991; Undergraduates: $3676. *Scholarships, grants, and awards:* Federal Pell, FSEOG, state, private, college/university gift aid from institutional funds, United Negro College Fund, Federal Nursing.

GIFT AID (NON-NEED-BASED) *Total amount:* $5,336,747 (2% state, 73% institutional, 25% external sources). *Receiving aid:* Freshmen: 26% (498); Undergraduates: 12% (1,232). *Average Award:* Freshmen: $3254; *Undergraduates:* $3296. *Scholarships, grants, and awards by category: Academic Interests/Achievement:* 1,344 awards ($2,960,336 total): biological sciences, business, engineering/technologies, English, general academic interests/achievements, health fields, humanities, military science, physical sciences. *Creative Arts/Performance:* 67 awards ($73,991 total): art/fine arts, dance, music, performing arts, theater/drama. *Special Achievements/Activities:* 23 awards ($27,552 total): cheerleading/drum major, community service, leadership, memberships. *Special Characteristics:* 32 awards ($133,404 total): children of faculty/staff, handicapped students, international students, local/state students, members of minority groups, previous college experience, veterans' children. *Tuition waivers:* Full or partial for employees or children of employees, senior citizens. *ROTC:* Army, Naval.

LOANS *Student loans:* $35,522,429 (58% need-based, 42% non-need-based). 81% of past graduating class borrowed through all loan programs. *Average indebtedness per student:* $16,775. *Average need-based loan:* Freshmen: $2527; Undergraduates: $3721. *Parent loans:* $4,759,043 (100% non-need-based). *Programs:* Federal Direct (Subsidized and Unsubsidized Stafford, PLUS), Perkins.

WORK-STUDY *Federal work-study:* Total amount: $1,385,747; jobs available.

ATHLETIC AWARDS *Total amount:* $1,707,574 (100% non-need-based).

APPLYING FOR FINANCIAL AID *Required financial aid form:* FAFSA. *Financial aid deadline:* 3/15 (priority: 2/15). *Notification date:* Continuous beginning 2/1. Students must reply within 2 weeks of notification.

CONTACT Betty Diamond, Director of Student Financial Aid, Old Dominion University, 121 Rollins Hall, Norfolk, VA 23529, 757-683-3690 or toll-free 800-348-7926. *E-mail:* bdiamond@odu.edu.

OLIVET COLLEGE
Olivet, MI

Tuition & fees: $16,464	Average undergraduate aid package: $12,816

ABOUT THE INSTITUTION Independent religious, coed. Awards: bachelor's and master's degrees. 38 undergraduate majors. Total enrollment: 1,069. Undergraduates: 1,023. Freshmen: 198. Federal methodology is used as a basis for awarding need-based institutional aid.

UNDERGRADUATE EXPENSES for 2005–06 *Application fee:* $25. *Comprehensive fee:* $21,944 includes full-time tuition ($15,970), mandatory fees ($494), and room and board ($5480). *College room only:* $2980. Full-time tuition and fees vary according to reciprocity agreements. Room and board charges vary according to board plan and housing facility. *Part-time tuition:* $515 per credit. Part-time tuition and fees vary according to course load and reciprocity agreements. *Payment plan:* Installment.

FRESHMAN FINANCIAL AID (Fall 2003) 267 applied for aid; of those 94% were deemed to have need. 100% of freshmen with need received aid; of those 11% had need fully met. *Average percent of need met:* 80% (excluding resources awarded to replace EFC). *Average financial aid package:* $12,733 (excluding resources awarded to replace EFC). 15% of all full-time freshmen had no need and received non-need-based gift aid.

UNDERGRADUATE FINANCIAL AID (Fall 2003) 927 applied for aid; of those 95% were deemed to have need. 99% of undergraduates with need received aid; of those 14% had need fully met. *Average percent of need met:* 79% (excluding resources awarded to replace EFC). *Average financial aid package:* $12,816 (excluding resources awarded to replace EFC). 12% of all full-time undergraduates had no need and received non-need-based gift aid.

GIFT AID (NEED-BASED) *Total amount:* $8,217,233 (21% federal, 17% state, 61% institutional, 1% external sources). *Receiving aid:* Freshmen: 84% (250); All full-time undergraduates: 87% (872). *Average award:* Freshmen: $10,012; Undergraduates: $9079. *Scholarships, grants, and awards:* Federal Pell, FSEOG, state, private, college/university gift aid from institutional funds.

GIFT AID (NON-NEED-BASED) *Total amount:* $968,807 (4% state, 94% institutional, 2% external sources). *Receiving aid:* Freshmen: 4% (11); Undergraduates: 4% (45). *Average Award: Freshmen:* $9131; *Undergraduates:* $9445. *Scholarships, grants, and awards by category: Academic Interests/Achievement:* 503 awards ($2,234,852 total): business, communication, education, English, foreign languages, general academic interests/achievements. *Creative Arts/Performance:* 50 awards ($97,050 total): art/fine arts, journalism/publications, music. *Special Achievements/Activities:* 138 awards ($641,200 total): community service, leadership, memberships. *Special Characteristics:* 390 awards ($1,796,073 total): children and siblings of alumni, children of faculty/staff, international students, religious affiliation, siblings of current students. *Tuition waivers:* Full or partial for employees or children of employees.

LOANS *Student loans:* $6,013,583 (78% need-based, 22% non-need-based). 89% of past graduating class borrowed through all loan programs. *Average indebtedness per student:* $23,258. *Average need-based loan:* Freshmen: $2452; Undergraduates: $3593. *Parent loans:* $315,736 (31% need-based, 69% non-need-based). *Programs:* FFEL (Subsidized and Unsubsidized Stafford, PLUS), Perkins, state, Key Alternative Loans, CitiAssist Loans MI-Loan, Signature Loan.

WORK-STUDY *Federal work-study:* Total amount: $176,843; 175 jobs averaging $1017. *State or other work-study/employment:* Total amount: $337,805 (100% need-based). 260 part-time jobs averaging $1135.

APPLYING FOR FINANCIAL AID *Required financial aid form:* FAFSA. *Financial aid deadline:* Continuous. *Notification date:* Continuous beginning 3/1.

CONTACT Mr. Douglas Gilbertson, Director of Admissions, Olivet College, 320 South Main Street, Olivet, MI 49076-9701, 800-456-7189 Ext. 7635 or toll-free 800-456-7189. *Fax:* 269-269-6617.

OLIVET NAZARENE UNIVERSITY
Bourbonnais, IL

Tuition & fees: $16,490	Average undergraduate aid package: $11,961

ABOUT THE INSTITUTION Independent religious, coed. Awards: associate, bachelor's, and master's degrees. 77 undergraduate majors. Total enrollment: 4,364. Undergraduates: 2,633. Freshmen: 703. Federal methodology is used as a basis for awarding need-based institutional aid.

UNDERGRADUATE EXPENSES for 2005–06 *Comprehensive fee:* $22,590 includes full-time tuition ($15,650), mandatory fees ($840), and room and board ($6100). *College room only:* $3050. Full-time tuition and fees vary according to course load. Room and board charges vary according to board plan. *Part-time tuition:* $652 per hour. *Part-time fees:* $10 per term. Part-time tuition and fees vary according to course load. *Payment plan:* Installment.

GIFT AID (NEED-BASED) *Total amount:* $10,867,493 (16% federal, 21% state, 55% institutional, 8% external sources). *Receiving aid:* Freshmen: 75% (501); All full-time undergraduates: 69% (1,603). *Average award:* Freshmen: $8680; Undergraduates: $7845. *Scholarships, grants, and awards:* Federal Pell, FSEOG, state, private, college/university gift aid from institutional funds.

GIFT AID (NON-NEED-BASED) *Total amount:* $4,450,921 (6% federal, 2% state, 81% institutional, 11% external sources). *Receiving aid:* Freshmen: 75% (501); Undergraduates: 69% (1,602). *Average Award: Freshmen:* $6787; *Undergraduates:* $7430. *Scholarships, grants, and awards by category: Academic Interests/Achievement:* general academic interests/achievements. *Creative Arts/Performance:* art/fine arts, music. *Special Achievements/Activities:* religious involvement. *Special Characteristics:* children of current students, children of faculty/staff, general special characteristics, international students, parents of current students, relatives of clergy, religious affiliation, siblings of current students, spouses of current students. *Tuition waivers:* Full or partial for employees or children of employees. *ROTC:* Army.

LOANS *Student loans:* $10,902,462 (46% need-based, 54% non-need-based). 70% of past graduating class borrowed through all loan programs. *Average indebtedness per student:* $19,189. *Average need-based loan:* Freshmen: $3312; Undergraduates: $4153. *Parent loans:* $4,653,927 (100% non-need-based). *Programs:* FFEL (Subsidized and Unsubsidized Stafford, PLUS), Perkins, alternative loans.

ATHLETIC AWARDS *Total amount:* $1,505,736 (67% need-based, 33% non-need-based).

APPLYING FOR FINANCIAL AID *Required financial aid forms:* FAFSA, institution's own form. *Financial aid deadline (priority):* 3/1. *Notification date:* Continuous beginning 2/1. Students must reply within 2 weeks of notification.

CONTACT Mr. Greg Bruner, Director of Financial Aid, Olivet Nazarene University, Box 6007, Bourbonnais, IL 60914, 815-939-5249 or toll-free 800-648-1463. *Fax:* 815-939-5074. *E-mail:* gbruner@olivet.edu.

O'MORE COLLEGE OF DESIGN
Franklin, TN

CONTACT Office of Financial Aid, O'More College of Design, 423 South Margin Street, Franklin, TN 37064-2816, 615-794-4254 Ext. 30.

ORAL ROBERTS UNIVERSITY
Tulsa, OK

Tuition & fees: $15,880	Average undergraduate aid package: $14,950

ABOUT THE INSTITUTION Independent interdenominational, coed. Awards: bachelor's, master's, doctoral, and first professional degrees. 66 undergraduate majors. Total enrollment: 3,828. Undergraduates: 3,303. Freshmen: 543. Federal methodology is used as a basis for awarding need-based financial aid.

UNDERGRADUATE EXPENSES for 2005–06 *Application fee:* $35. *Comprehensive fee:* $22,410 includes full-time tuition ($15,400), mandatory fees ($480), and room and board ($6530). *College room only:* $3280. Room and board charges vary according to board plan and housing facility. *Part-time tuition:* $642 per credit hour. *Payment plan:* Installment.

FRESHMAN FINANCIAL AID (Fall 2004, est.) 470 applied for aid; of those 86% were deemed to have need. 99% of freshmen with need received aid; of those 53% had need fully met. *Average percent of need met:* 86% (excluding resources awarded to replace EFC). *Average financial aid package:* $13,969 (excluding resources awarded to replace EFC). 22% of all full-time freshmen had no need and received non-need-based gift aid.

UNDERGRADUATE FINANCIAL AID (Fall 2004, est.) 1,978 applied for aid; of those 90% were deemed to have need. 100% of undergraduates with need received aid; of those 45% had need fully met. *Average percent of need met:* 89% (excluding resources awarded to replace EFC). *Average financial aid package:* $14,950 (excluding resources awarded to replace EFC). 18% of all full-time undergraduates had no need and received non-need-based gift aid.

GIFT AID (NEED-BASED) *Total amount:* $10,550,615 (27% federal, 3% state, 64% institutional, 6% external sources). *Receiving aid:* Freshmen: 67% (383); All full-time undergraduates: 64% (1,597). *Average award:* Freshmen: $8414; Undergraduates: $7577. *Scholarships, grants, and awards:* Federal Pell, FSEOG, state, private, college/university gift aid from institutional funds.

GIFT AID (NON-NEED-BASED) *Total amount:* $2,866,534 (2% state, 94% institutional, 4% external sources). *Receiving aid:* Freshmen: 24% (137); Undergraduates: 23% (569). *Average Award: Freshmen:* $7170; *Undergraduates:* $7029. *Scholarships, grants, and awards by category: Academic Interests/Achievement:* 1,504 awards ($6,526,699 total): biological sciences, business, communication, education, engineering/technologies, general academic interests/achievements, health fields, religion/biblical studies. *Creative Arts/Performance:* 263 awards ($569,637 total): applied art and design, art/fine arts, cinema/film/broadcasting, journalism/publications, music. *Special Achievements/Activities:* 480 awards ($887,157 total): cheerleading/drum major, community service, general special achievements/activities, leadership, memberships, religious involvement. *Special Characteristics:* 1,605 awards ($4,166,293 total): children and siblings of alumni, children of faculty/staff, general special characteristics, international students, relatives of clergy, siblings of current students. *Tuition waivers:* Full or partial for children of alumni, employees or children of employees. *ROTC:* Air Force cooperative.

LOANS *Student loans:* $12,198,663 (76% need-based, 24% non-need-based). 84% of past graduating class borrowed through all loan programs. *Average indebtedness per student:* $27,956. *Average need-based loan:* Freshmen: $6716; Undergraduates: $8629. *Parent loans:* $5,733,187 (62% need-based, 38% non-need-based). *Programs:* FFEL (Subsidized and Unsubsidized Stafford, PLUS), Perkins, college/university.

WORK-STUDY *Federal work-study:* Total amount: $605,610; 313 jobs averaging $1590. *State or other work-study/employment:* Total amount: $723,341 (100% non-need-based). 750 part-time jobs averaging $1500.

ATHLETIC AWARDS *Total amount:* $2,364,056 (31% need-based, 69% non-need-based).

APPLYING FOR FINANCIAL AID *Required financial aid form:* FAFSA. *Financial aid deadline (priority):* 3/15. *Notification date:* Students must reply by 7/15.

CONTACT Scott Carr, Director of Financial Aid, Oral Roberts University, PO Box 700540, Tulsa, OK 74170-0540, 918-495-6510 or toll-free 800-678-8876. *Fax:* 918-495-6803. *E-mail:* finaid@oru.edu.

OREGON COLLEGE OF ART & CRAFT
Portland, OR

ABOUT THE INSTITUTION Independent, coed. Awards: bachelor's degrees and post-bachelor's certificates. 2 undergraduate majors. Total enrollment: 143. Undergraduates: 129. Freshmen: 7.

GIFT AID (NEED-BASED) *Scholarships, grants, and awards:* Federal Pell, FSEOG, state, private, college/university gift aid from institutional funds.

GIFT AID (NON-NEED-BASED) *Scholarships, grants, and awards by category: Creative Arts/Performance:* art/fine arts.

LOANS *Programs:* FFEL (Subsidized and Unsubsidized Stafford, PLUS), state, alternative loans.

APPLYING FOR FINANCIAL AID *Required financial aid form:* FAFSA.

CONTACT Lisa Newman, Director of Financial Aid, Oregon College of Art & Craft, 8245 Southwest Barnes Road, Portland, OR 97225, 503-297-5544 Ext. 124 or toll-free 800-390-0632 Ext. 129. *Fax:* 503-297-9651. *E-mail:* lnewman@ocac.edu.

OREGON HEALTH & SCIENCE UNIVERSITY
Portland, OR

Tuition & fees (OR res): $9369   **Average undergraduate aid package:** $11,698

ABOUT THE INSTITUTION State-related, coed. Awards: bachelor's, master's, doctoral, and first professional degrees and post-bachelor's, post-master's, and first professional certificates. 5 undergraduate majors. Total enrollment: 1,849. Undergraduates: 657. Federal methodology is used as a basis for awarding need-based institutional aid.

UNDERGRADUATE EXPENSES for 2004–05 *Application fee:* $60. *Tuition, state resident:* full-time $7794; part-time $433 per credit hour. *Tuition, nonresident:* full-time $8989; part-time $499 per credit hour.

GIFT AID (NEED-BASED) *Total amount:* $1,376,024 (42% federal, 13% state, 12% institutional, 33% external sources). *Receiving aid:* All full-time undergraduates: 49% (216). *Average award:* Undergraduates: $5791. *Scholarships, grants, and awards:* Federal Pell, FSEOG, state, private, college/university gift aid from institutional funds, Health Profession Scholarships.

GIFT AID (NON-NEED-BASED) *Total amount:* $12,601 (14% institutional, 86% external sources). *Receiving aid:* Undergraduates: 2. *Average Award:* Undergraduates: $3146. *Scholarships, grants, and awards by category: Academic Interests/Achievement:* 165 awards ($1,154,728 total): health fields. *ROTC:* Army cooperative.

LOANS *Student loans:* $6,345,434 (85% need-based, 15% non-need-based). 71% of past graduating class borrowed through all loan programs. *Average indebtedness per student:* $25,960. *Average need-based loan:* Undergraduates: $6758. *Parent loans:* $759,020 (58% need-based, 42% non-need-based). *Programs:* Federal Direct (Subsidized and Unsubsidized Stafford, PLUS), Perkins, Federal Nursing, state, college/university, alternative loans.

APPLYING FOR FINANCIAL AID *Required financial aid forms:* FAFSA, institution's own form, OHSU does not have Freshman FA applicants. *Financial aid deadline:* Continuous. *Notification date:* 6/1. Students must reply within 4 weeks of notification.

CONTACT Ms. Cherie Honnell, Director of Financial Aid/Registrar, Oregon Health & Science University, 3181 SW Sam Jackson Park Road, L-109, Portland, OR 97239-3089, 503-494-7800. *Fax:* 503-494-4629. *E-mail:* finaid@ohsu.edu.

OREGON INSTITUTE OF TECHNOLOGY
Klamath Falls, OR

ABOUT THE INSTITUTION State-supported, coed. Awards: associate, bachelor's, and master's degrees. 19 undergraduate majors. Total enrollment: 3,373. Undergraduates: 3,366. Freshmen: 318.

GIFT AID (NEED-BASED) *Scholarships, grants, and awards:* Federal Pell, FSEOG, state, private, college/university gift aid from institutional funds.

GIFT AID (NON-NEED-BASED) *Scholarships, grants, and awards by category: Academic Interests/Achievement:* general academic interests/achievements. *Special Achievements/Activities:* general special achievements/activities. *Special Characteristics:* ethnic background, members of minority groups.

LOANS *Programs:* FFEL (Subsidized and Unsubsidized Stafford, PLUS), Perkins.

APPLYING FOR FINANCIAL AID *Required financial aid form:* FAFSA.

CONTACT Tracey Lehman, Financial Aid Director, Oregon Institute of Technology, 3201 Campus Drive, Klamath Falls, OR 97601-8801, 541-885-1280 or toll-free 800-422-2017 (in-state), 800-343-6653 (out-of-state). *Fax:* 541-885-1024. *E-mail:* marquitt@oit.edu.

OREGON STATE UNIVERSITY
Corvallis, OR

Tuition & fees (OR res): $5319   **Average undergraduate aid package:** $8673

ABOUT THE INSTITUTION State-supported, coed. Awards: bachelor's, master's, doctoral, and first professional degrees and post-bachelor's certificates. 121 undergraduate majors. Total enrollment: 19,162. Undergraduates: 15,713. Freshmen: 2,888. Federal methodology is used as a basis for awarding need-based institutional aid.

UNDERGRADUATE EXPENSES for 2004–05 *Application fee:* $50. *Tuition, state resident:* full-time $4113; part-time $108 per credit. *Tuition, nonresident:* full-time $16,461; part-time $451 per credit. Part-time tuition and fees vary according to course load. *College room and board:* $6786. Room and board charges vary according to board plan and housing facility. *Payment plan:* Deferred payment.

FRESHMAN FINANCIAL AID (Fall 2004, est.) 2124 applied for aid; of those 71% were deemed to have need. 97% of freshmen with need received aid; of those 25% had need fully met. *Average percent of need met:* 69% (excluding resources awarded to replace EFC). *Average financial aid package:* $8191 (excluding resources awarded to replace EFC). 1% of all full-time freshmen had no need and received non-need-based gift aid.

UNDERGRADUATE FINANCIAL AID (Fall 2004, est.) 9,333 applied for aid; of those 79% were deemed to have need. 98% of undergraduates with need received aid; of those 22% had need fully met. *Average percent of need met:* 66% (excluding resources awarded to replace EFC). *Average financial aid package:* $8673 (excluding resources awarded to replace EFC). 1% of all full-time undergraduates had no need and received non-need-based gift aid.

GIFT AID (NEED-BASED) *Total amount:* $23,475,509 (56% federal, 11% state, 21% institutional, 12% external sources). *Receiving aid:* Freshmen: 41% (1,135); All full-time undergraduates: 38% (5,249). *Average award:* Freshmen: $2344; Undergraduates: $2646. *Scholarships, grants, and awards:* Federal Pell, FSEOG, state.

GIFT AID (NON-NEED-BASED) *Total amount:* $6,526,079 (1% federal, 55% institutional, 44% external sources). *Receiving aid:* Freshmen: 2% (52); Undergraduates: 2% (224). *Average Award:* Freshmen: $2890; Undergraduates: $2716. *Scholarships, grants, and awards by category: Academic Interests/Achievement:* general academic interests/achievements. *Creative Arts/Performance:* music. *Special Achievements/Activities:* general special achievements/activities. *Special Characteristics:* general special characteristics. *Tuition waivers:* Full or partial for employees or children of employees. *ROTC:* Army, Naval, Air Force.

LOANS *Student loans:* $52,973,023 (82% need-based, 18% non-need-based). *Average need-based loan:* Freshmen: $2153; Undergraduates: $3213. *Parent loans:* $43,701,420 (53% need-based, 47% non-need-based). *Programs:* Federal Direct (Subsidized and Unsubsidized Stafford, PLUS), Perkins, college/university.

WORK-STUDY *Federal work-study:* Total amount: $3,860,325; jobs available.

ATHLETIC AWARDS *Total amount:* $5,934,732 (8% need-based, 92% non-need-based).

APPLYING FOR FINANCIAL AID *Required financial aid form:* FAFSA. *Financial aid deadline:* 5/1 (priority: 2/1). *Notification date:* Continuous beginning 4/1. Students must reply within 4 weeks of notification.

CONTACT Kate Peterson, Director, Financial Aid, Oregon State University, 218 Kerr Administration Building, Corvallis, OR 97331-2120, 541-737-2241 or toll-free 800-291-4192 (in-state).

OREGON STATE UNIVERSITY–CASCADES
Bend, OR

CONTACT Financial Aid Office, Oregon State University–Cascades, 2600 NW College Way, Bend, OR 97701, 541-322-3100.

OTIS COLLEGE OF ART AND DESIGN
Los Angeles, CA

Tuition & fees: $25,100	Average undergraduate aid package: $13,633

ABOUT THE INSTITUTION Independent, coed. Awards: bachelor's and master's degrees. 10 undergraduate majors. Total enrollment: 1,043. Undergraduates: 997. Freshmen: 124. Federal methodology is used as a basis for awarding need-based institutional aid.

UNDERGRADUATE EXPENSES for 2004–05 *Application fee:* $50. *Tuition:* full-time $24,500; part-time $817 per credit. *Payment plan:* Installment.

FRESHMAN FINANCIAL AID (Fall 2003) 100% of freshmen with need received aid. *Average percent of need met:* 42% (excluding resources awarded to replace EFC). *Average financial aid package:* $12,517 (excluding resources awarded to replace EFC). 6% of all full-time freshmen had no need and received non-need-based gift aid.

UNDERGRADUATE FINANCIAL AID (Fall 2003) 100% of undergraduates with need received aid. *Average percent of need met:* 44% (excluding resources awarded to replace EFC). *Average financial aid package:* $13,633 (excluding resources awarded to replace EFC). 2% of all full-time undergraduates had no need and received non-need-based gift aid.

GIFT AID (NEED-BASED) *Total amount:* $7,169,524 (20% federal, 19% state, 60% institutional, 1% external sources). *Receiving aid:* Freshmen: 87% (107); All full-time undergraduates: 69% (686). *Average award:* Freshmen: $10,550; Undergraduates: $9935. *Scholarships, grants, and awards:* Federal Pell, FSEOG, state, private, college/university gift aid from institutional funds.

GIFT AID (NON-NEED-BASED) *Total amount:* $378,108 (98% institutional, 2% external sources). *Average Award:* Freshmen: $4571; Undergraduates: $4250. *Scholarships, grants, and awards by category:* Academic Interests/Achievement: general academic interests/achievements. Creative Arts/Performance: applied art and design, art/fine arts. *Tuition waivers:* Full or partial for employees or children of employees.

LOANS *Student loans:* $4,648,363 (93% need-based, 7% non-need-based). 63% of past graduating class borrowed through all loan programs. *Average indebtedness per student:* $32,156. *Average need-based loan:* Freshmen: $2475; Undergraduates: $3919. *Parent loans:* $4,179,774 (38% need-based, 62% non-need-based). *Programs:* FFEL (Subsidized and Unsubsidized Stafford, PLUS).

WORK-STUDY *Federal work-study:* Total amount: $233,506; 212 jobs averaging $1102. *State or other work-study/employment:* Total amount: $21,000 (100% non-need-based). 22 part-time jobs averaging $955.

APPLYING FOR FINANCIAL AID *Required financial aid forms:* FAFSA, institution's own form. *Financial aid deadline (priority):* 2/16. *Notification date:* 3/1. Students must reply within 2 weeks of notification.

CONTACT Nasreen Zia, Associate Director of Financial Aid, Otis College of Art and Design, 9045 Lincoln Boulevard, Los Angeles, CA 90045-9785, 310-665-6880 or toll-free 800-527-OTIS. *Fax:* 310-665-6884. *E-mail:* otisaid@otis.edu.

OTTAWA UNIVERSITY
Ottawa, KS

CONTACT Financial Aid Coordinator, Ottawa University, 1001 South Cedar, Ottawa, KS 66067-3399, 785-242-5200 or toll-free 800-755-5200 Ext. 5559. *E-mail:* finaid@ottawa.edu.

OTTERBEIN COLLEGE
Westerville, OH

ABOUT THE INSTITUTION Independent United Methodist, coed. Awards: bachelor's and master's degrees. 60 undergraduate majors. Total enrollment: 3,090. Undergraduates: 2,330. Freshmen: 686.

GIFT AID (NEED-BASED) *Scholarships, grants, and awards:* Federal Pell, FSEOG, state, private, college/university gift aid from institutional funds, Federal Nursing.

GIFT AID (NON-NEED-BASED) *Scholarships, grants, and awards by category:* Academic Interests/Achievement: general academic interests/achievements. Creative Arts/Performance: art/fine arts, music, theater/drama. Special Achievements/Activities: community service, leadership. Special Characteristics: children and siblings of alumni, children of faculty/staff, general special characteristics, international students, members of minority groups, previous college experience, relatives of clergy, siblings of current students.

LOANS *Programs:* FFEL (Subsidized and Unsubsidized Stafford, PLUS), Perkins, Federal Nursing, state, college/university.

WORK-STUDY Federal work-study jobs available. *State or other work-study/employment:* Part-time jobs available.

APPLYING FOR FINANCIAL AID *Required financial aid form:* FAFSA.

CONTACT Mr. Thomas V. Yarnell, Director of Financial Aid, Otterbein College, One Otterbein College, Clippinger Hall, Westerville, OH 43081-2006, 614-823-1502 or toll-free 800-488-8144. *Fax:* 614-823-1200. *E-mail:* tyarnell@otterbein.edu.

OUACHITA BAPTIST UNIVERSITY
Arkadelphia, AR

Tuition & fees: $15,920	Average undergraduate aid package: $12,093

ABOUT THE INSTITUTION Independent Baptist, coed. Awards: associate and bachelor's degrees. 54 undergraduate majors. Total enrollment: 1,511. Undergraduates: 1,511. Freshmen: 380. Federal methodology is used as a basis for awarding need-based institutional aid.

UNDERGRADUATE EXPENSES for 2005–06 *Application fee:* $50. *Comprehensive fee:* $20,920 includes full-time tuition ($15,580), mandatory fees ($340), and room and board ($5000). *Part-time tuition:* $430 per semester hour.

FRESHMAN FINANCIAL AID (Fall 2004, est.) 303 applied for aid; of those 78% were deemed to have need. 100% of freshmen with need received aid; of those 39% had need fully met. *Average percent of need met:* 78% (excluding resources awarded to replace EFC). *Average financial aid package:* $11,306 (excluding resources awarded to replace EFC). 24% of all full-time freshmen had no need and received non-need-based gift aid.

UNDERGRADUATE FINANCIAL AID (Fall 2004, est.) 947 applied for aid; of those 81% were deemed to have need. 100% of undergraduates with need received aid; of those 43% had need fully met. *Average percent of need met:* 82% (excluding resources awarded to replace EFC). *Average financial aid package:* $12,093 (excluding resources awarded to replace EFC). 30% of all full-time undergraduates had no need and received non-need-based gift aid.

GIFT AID (NEED-BASED) *Total amount:* $7,062,312 (16% federal, 5% state, 77% institutional, 2% external sources). *Receiving aid:* Freshmen: 49% (187); All full-time undergraduates: 45% (645). *Average award:* Freshmen: $9387; Undergraduates: $9705. *Scholarships, grants, and awards:* Federal Pell, FSEOG, state, private, college/university gift aid from institutional funds.

GIFT AID (NON-NEED-BASED) *Total amount:* $3,261,729 (10% state, 85% institutional, 5% external sources). *Receiving aid:* Freshmen: 18% (69); Undergraduates: 14% (195). *Average Award:* Freshmen: $6640; Undergraduates: $5567. *Scholarships, grants, and awards by category:* Academic Interests/Achievement: 434 awards ($1,084,294 total): area/ethnic studies, biological sciences, business, communication, computer science, education, engineering/technologies, English, foreign languages, general academic interests/achievements, health fields, home economics, humanities, international studies, mathematics, physical sciences, premedicine, religion/biblical studies, social sciences. Creative Arts/Performance: 175 awards ($725,504 total): art/fine arts, journalism/publications, music, performing arts, theater/drama. Special Achievements/Activities: 806 awards ($3,317,674 total): general special achievements/activities. Special Characteristics: children of faculty/staff, ethnic background, first-generation college students, general special characteristics, international students, local/state students, married students, members of minority groups, out-of-state students, relatives of clergy, religious affiliation, twins. *ROTC:* Army.

LOANS *Student loans:* $3,138,125 (60% need-based, 40% non-need-based). 42% of past graduating class borrowed through all loan programs. *Average indebtedness per student:* $11,131. *Average need-based loan:* Freshmen: $3545; Undergraduates: $4284. *Parent loans:* $1,360,181 (23% need-based, 77% non-need-based). *Programs:* FFEL (Subsidized and Unsubsidized Stafford, PLUS), Perkins, college/university.

WORK-STUDY *Federal work-study:* Total amount: $514,057; 370 jobs averaging $1331. *State or other work-study/employment:* Total amount: $396,147 (11% need-based, 89% non-need-based). 297 part-time jobs averaging $1400.

ATHLETIC AWARDS *Total amount:* $2,079,404 (48% need-based, 52% non-need-based).

APPLYING FOR FINANCIAL AID *Required financial aid forms:* FAFSA, institution's own form. *Financial aid deadline:* 6/1 (priority: 2/15). *Notification date:* Continuous beginning 3/31. Students must reply by 5/1.

CONTACT Mr. Lane Smith, Director of Financial Aid, Ouachita Baptist University, Box 3774, Arkadelphia, AR 71998-0001, 870-245-5570 or toll-free 800-342-5628 (in-state). *Fax:* 870-245-5318. *E-mail:* smithl@obu.edu.

OUR LADY OF HOLY CROSS COLLEGE
New Orleans, LA

ABOUT THE INSTITUTION Independent Roman Catholic, coed. Awards: associate, bachelor's, and master's degrees and post-bachelor's certificates. 25 undergraduate majors. Total enrollment: 1,446. Undergraduates: 1,316. Freshmen: 124.

GIFT AID (NEED-BASED) *Scholarships, grants, and awards:* Federal Pell, FSEOG, state, private, college/university gift aid from institutional funds, Federal Nursing.

GIFT AID (NON-NEED-BASED) *Scholarships, grants, and awards by category:* *Academic Interests/Achievement:* general academic interests/achievements. *Special Characteristics:* children of faculty/staff, general special characteristics, relatives of clergy, religious affiliation.

LOANS *Programs:* FFEL (Subsidized and Unsubsidized Stafford, PLUS).

WORK-STUDY *Federal work-study:* Total amount: $34,162; 45 jobs averaging $2698.

APPLYING FOR FINANCIAL AID *Required financial aid forms:* FAFSA, institution's own form.

CONTACT Mrs. Johnell S. Armer, Director of Financial Aid, Our Lady of Holy Cross College, 4123 Woodland Drive, New Orleans, LA 70131-7399, 504-398-2165 or toll-free 800-259-7744 Ext. 175. *Fax:* 504-391-2421. *E-mail:* jarmer@olhcc.edu.

OUR LADY OF THE LAKE COLLEGE
Baton Rouge, LA

Tuition & fees: $7280	Average undergraduate aid package: N/A

ABOUT THE INSTITUTION Independent Roman Catholic, coed, primarily women. Awards: associate, bachelor's, and master's degrees. 14 undergraduate majors. Total enrollment: 1,990. Undergraduates: 1,990. Federal methodology is used as a basis for awarding need-based institutional aid.

UNDERGRADUATE EXPENSES for 2005–06 *Application fee:* $35. *Tuition:* full-time $6780; part-time $226 per credit hour. *Required fees:* full-time $500; $75 per term part-time. *Payment plans:* Installment, deferred payment.

GIFT AID (NEED-BASED) *Total amount:* $2,487,106 (69% federal, 26% state, 5% institutional). *Scholarships, grants, and awards:* Federal Pell, FSEOG, state, private, college/university gift aid from institutional funds.

GIFT AID (NON-NEED-BASED) *Total amount:* $780,283 (82% state, 17% institutional, 1% external sources). *Tuition waivers:* Full or partial for employees or children of employees. *ROTC:* Army cooperative, Air Force cooperative.

LOANS *Student loans:* $7,451,536 (100% need-based). 80% of past graduating class borrowed through all loan programs. *Average indebtedness per student:* $30,000. *Parent loans:* $143,402 (100% need-based). *Programs:* FFEL (Subsidized and Unsubsidized Stafford, PLUS).

WORK-STUDY *Federal work-study:* Total amount: $90,000; 25 jobs averaging $3600.

APPLYING FOR FINANCIAL AID *Required financial aid forms:* FAFSA, institution's own form. *Financial aid deadline (priority):* 5/1. *Notification date:* Continuous.

CONTACT Sharon Butler, Director of Financial Aid, Our Lady of the Lake College, 7434 Perkins Road, Baton Rouge, LA 70808, 225-768-1701 or toll-free 877-242-3509. *Fax:* 225-768-1726.

OUR LADY OF THE LAKE UNIVERSITY OF SAN ANTONIO
San Antonio, TX

ABOUT THE INSTITUTION Independent Roman Catholic, coed. Awards: bachelor's, master's, and doctoral degrees. 31 undergraduate majors. Total enrollment: 3,025. Undergraduates: 1,931. Freshmen: 222.

GIFT AID (NEED-BASED) *Scholarships, grants, and awards:* Federal Pell, FSEOG, state, private, college/university gift aid from institutional funds.

GIFT AID (NON-NEED-BASED) *Scholarships, grants, and awards by category:* *Academic Interests/Achievement:* general academic interests/achievements. *Creative Arts/Performance:* music. *Special Characteristics:* children of faculty/staff.

LOANS *Programs:* FFEL (Subsidized and Unsubsidized Stafford, PLUS), Perkins, state, alternative loans.

WORK-STUDY *Federal work-study:* Total amount: $448,365; 312 jobs averaging $1437. *State or other work-study/employment:* Total amount: $96,516 (100% need-based). 64 part-time jobs averaging $1508.

APPLYING FOR FINANCIAL AID *Required financial aid form:* FAFSA.

CONTACT Leah Garza, Director of Financial Aid, Our Lady of the Lake University of San Antonio, 411 Southwest 24th Street, San Antonio, TX 78207-4689, 210-434-6711 Ext. 2299 or toll-free 800-436-6558. *Fax:* 210-431-3958.

OZARK CHRISTIAN COLLEGE
Joplin, MO

CONTACT Jill Kaminsky, Application Processor, Ozark Christian College, 1111 North Main Street, Joplin, MO 64801-4804, 417-624-2518 Ext. 2017 or toll-free 800-299-4622. *Fax:* 417-624-0090. *E-mail:* finaid@occ.edu.

PACE UNIVERSITY
New York, NY

ABOUT THE INSTITUTION Independent, coed. Awards: associate, bachelor's, master's, doctoral, and first professional degrees and post-bachelor's, post-master's, and first professional certificates. 66 undergraduate majors. Total enrollment: 13,670. Undergraduates: 8,668. Freshmen: 1,462.

GIFT AID (NEED-BASED) *Scholarships, grants, and awards:* Federal Pell, FSEOG, state, private, college/university gift aid from institutional funds, United Negro College Fund, Federal Nursing.

GIFT AID (NON-NEED-BASED) *Scholarships, grants, and awards by category:* *Academic Interests/Achievement:* biological sciences, business, communication, education, English, foreign languages, general academic interests/achievements, health fields, physical sciences, social sciences. *Creative Arts/Performance:* creative writing, debating, theater/drama. *Special Achievements/Activities:* community service, general special achievements/activities, leadership. *Special Characteristics:* adult students, children of faculty/staff, children with a deceased or disabled parent, general special characteristics, international students, parents of current students, previous college experience, spouses of deceased or disabled public servants.

LOANS *Programs:* Federal Direct (Subsidized and Unsubsidized Stafford, PLUS), Perkins, Federal Nursing.

WORK-STUDY *Federal work-study:* Total amount: $3,650,240; 1,018 jobs averaging $3585.

APPLYING FOR FINANCIAL AID *Required financial aid forms:* FAFSA, state aid form.

CONTACT Mark Stephens, Pace University, 861 Bedford Road, Pleasantville, NY 10570, 212-773-3501 or toll-free 800-874-7223. *E-mail:* mstephens@pace.edu.

PACIFIC ISLANDS BIBLE COLLEGE
Mangilao, GU

CONTACT Financial Aid Office, Pacific Islands Bible College, PO Box 22619, Guam Main Facility, GU 96921-2619, 671-734-1812.

PACIFIC LUTHERAN UNIVERSITY
Tacoma, WA

Tuition & fees: $20,790	Average undergraduate aid package: $18,086

ABOUT THE INSTITUTION Independent religious, coed. Awards: bachelor's and master's degrees and post-bachelor's and post-master's certificates. 62 undergraduate majors. Total enrollment: 3,643. Undergraduates: 3,324. Freshmen: 701. Federal methodology is used as a basis for awarding need-based institutional aid.

UNDERGRADUATE EXPENSES for 2004–05 *Application fee:* $40. *Comprehensive fee:* $27,200 includes full-time tuition ($20,790) and room and board ($6410). *College room only:* $3150. Full-time tuition and fees vary according to course load. Room and board charges vary according to board plan and housing facility. *Part-time tuition:* $648 per semester hour. Part-time tuition and fees vary according to course load. *Payment plan:* Installment.

FRESHMAN FINANCIAL AID (Fall 2004, est.) 641 applied for aid; of those 79% were deemed to have need. 100% of freshmen with need received aid; of those 37% had need fully met. *Average percent of need met:* 93% (excluding resources

Pacific Lutheran University

awarded to replace EFC). *Average financial aid package:* $18,299 (excluding resources awarded to replace EFC). 18% of all full-time freshmen had no need and received non-need-based gift aid.

UNDERGRADUATE FINANCIAL AID (Fall 2004, est.) 2,535 applied for aid; of those 85% were deemed to have need. 99% of undergraduates with need received aid; of those 29% had need fully met. *Average percent of need met:* 88% (excluding resources awarded to replace EFC). *Average financial aid package:* $18,086 (excluding resources awarded to replace EFC). 20% of all full-time undergraduates had no need and received non-need-based gift aid.

GIFT AID (NEED-BASED) *Total amount:* $20,167,953 (12% federal, 11% state, 73% institutional, 4% external sources). *Receiving aid:* Freshmen: 56% (404); All full-time undergraduates: 53% (1,627). *Average award:* Freshmen: $7864; Undergraduates: $8781. *Scholarships, grants, and awards:* Federal Pell, FSEOG, state, private, college/university gift aid from institutional funds, Federal Nursing.

GIFT AID (NON-NEED-BASED) *Total amount:* $13,157,850 (1% state, 72% institutional, 27% external sources). *Receiving aid:* Freshmen: 36% (259); Undergraduates: 32% (994). *Average Award:* Freshmen: $6248; Undergraduates: $7602. *Scholarships, grants, and awards by category: Academic Interests/Achievement:* 1,421 awards ($11,311,760 total): general academic interests/achievements. *Creative Arts/Performance:* 218 awards ($756,068 total): art/fine arts, dance, debating, general creative arts/performance, music, theater/drama. *Special Achievements/Activities:* 32 awards ($55,750 total): leadership. *Special Characteristics:* 576 awards ($1,617,306 total): children and siblings of alumni, children of educators, children of faculty/staff, international students, previous college experience, relatives of clergy. *Tuition waivers:* Full or partial for employees or children of employees, senior citizens. *ROTC:* Army.

LOANS *Student loans:* $15,659,068 (87% need-based, 13% non-need-based). 60% of past graduating class borrowed through all loan programs. *Average indebtedness per student:* $24,244. *Average need-based loan:* Freshmen: $4245; Undergraduates: $7098. *Parent loans:* $6,729,253 (62% need-based, 38% non-need-based). *Programs:* FFEL (Subsidized and Unsubsidized Stafford, PLUS), Perkins, Federal Nursing, state, college/university.

WORK-STUDY *Federal work-study:* Total amount: $864,994; 654 jobs averaging $1322. *State or other work-study/employment:* Total amount: $2,800,000 (36% need-based, 64% non-need-based). 458 part-time jobs averaging $2183.

APPLYING FOR FINANCIAL AID *Required financial aid form:* FAFSA. *Financial aid deadline (priority):* 3/1. *Notification date:* Continuous beginning 3/15. Students must reply by 5/1 or within 4 weeks of notification.

CONTACT Ms. Joan Riley, Associate Director, Systems, Pacific Lutheran University, Tacoma, WA 98447, 253-535-7168 or toll-free 800-274-6758. *Fax:* 253-535-8406. *E-mail:* rileyjo@plu.edu.

PACIFIC NORTHWEST COLLEGE OF ART
Portland, OR

Tuition & fees: $16,080	Average undergraduate aid package: $16,683

ABOUT THE INSTITUTION Independent, coed. Awards: bachelor's degrees. 7 undergraduate majors. Total enrollment: 307. Undergraduates: 307. Freshmen: 33. Federal methodology is used as a basis for awarding need-based institutional aid.

UNDERGRADUATE EXPENSES for 2004–05 *Application fee:* $35. *Tuition:* full-time $15,500; part-time $670 per semester hour. *Required fees:* full-time $580; $25 per semester hour or $157 per term part-time. Part-time tuition and fees vary according to course load. *Payment plan:* Installment.

FRESHMAN FINANCIAL AID (Fall 2003) 25 applied for aid; of those 88% were deemed to have need. 100% of freshmen with need received aid; of those 18% had need fully met. *Average percent of need met:* 72% (excluding resources awarded to replace EFC). *Average financial aid package:* $15,764 (excluding resources awarded to replace EFC).

UNDERGRADUATE FINANCIAL AID (Fall 2003) 206 applied for aid; of those 85% were deemed to have need. 100% of undergraduates with need received aid; of those 16% had need fully met. *Average percent of need met:* 73% (excluding resources awarded to replace EFC). *Average financial aid package:* $16,683 (excluding resources awarded to replace EFC). 9% of all full-time undergraduates had no need and received non-need-based gift aid.

GIFT AID (NEED-BASED) *Total amount:* $1,145,557 (42% federal, 10% state, 48% institutional). *Receiving aid:* Freshmen: 67% (22); All full-time undergraduates: 66% (176). *Average award:* Freshmen: $3369; Undergraduates: $3847. *Scholarships, grants, and awards:* Federal Pell, FSEOG, state, private, college/university gift aid from institutional funds.

GIFT AID (NON-NEED-BASED) *Total amount:* $184,297 (94% institutional, 6% external sources). *Receiving aid:* Undergraduates: 1. *Average Award:* Undergraduates: $586. *Scholarships, grants, and awards by category: Academic Interests/Achievement:* general academic interests/achievements. *Creative Arts/Performance:* art/fine arts. *Tuition waivers:* Full or partial for employees or children of employees.

LOANS *Student loans:* $1,897,690 (46% need-based, 54% non-need-based). 73% of past graduating class borrowed through all loan programs. *Average indebtedness per student:* $18,917. *Average need-based loan:* Freshmen: $2596; Undergraduates: $3862. *Parent loans:* $499,085 (100% non-need-based). *Programs:* FFEL (Subsidized and Unsubsidized Stafford, PLUS).

WORK-STUDY *Federal work-study:* Total amount: $31,805; 33 jobs averaging $1200. *State or other work-study/employment:* Total amount: $22,400 (22% need-based, 78% non-need-based). 33 part-time jobs averaging $1200.

APPLYING FOR FINANCIAL AID *Required financial aid form:* FAFSA. *Financial aid deadline (priority):* 3/1. *Notification date:* Continuous beginning 4/1. Students must reply within 2 weeks of notification.

CONTACT Peggy Burgus, Director of Financial Aid, Pacific Northwest College of Art, 1241 Northwest Johnson Street, Portland, OR 97209, 503-821-8976. *Fax:* 503-821-8978.

PACIFIC OAKS COLLEGE
Pasadena, CA

ABOUT THE INSTITUTION Independent, coed, primarily women. Awards: bachelor's and master's degrees and post-bachelor's and post-master's certificates. 6 undergraduate majors. Total enrollment: 863. Undergraduates: 208. Entering class: .

GIFT AID (NEED-BASED) *Scholarships, grants, and awards:* Federal Pell, FSEOG, state, private, college/university gift aid from institutional funds.

LOANS *Programs:* FFEL (Subsidized and Unsubsidized Stafford, PLUS), Perkins.

APPLYING FOR FINANCIAL AID *Required financial aid forms:* FAFSA, institution's own form, federal income tax form(s).

CONTACT Trina Rodler/Yvette Tapia, Financial Aid Manager/Financial Aid Specialist, Pacific Oaks College, 5 Westmoreland Place, Pasadena, CA 91103, 626-397-1350 or toll-free 800-684-0900. *E-mail:* financial@pacificoaks.edu.

PACIFIC UNION COLLEGE
Angwin, CA

Tuition & fees: $18,054	Average undergraduate aid package: $14,265

ABOUT THE INSTITUTION Independent Seventh-day Adventist, coed. Awards: associate, bachelor's, and master's degrees. 81 undergraduate majors. Total enrollment: 1,547. Undergraduates: 1,545. Freshmen: 321. Federal methodology is used as a basis for awarding need-based institutional aid.

UNDERGRADUATE EXPENSES for 2004–05 *Application fee:* $30. *One-time required fee:* $30. *Comprehensive fee:* $23,190 includes full-time tuition ($17,934), mandatory fees ($120), and room and board ($5136). *College room only:* $3096. Full-time tuition and fees vary according to course load. *Part-time tuition:* $520 per credit. *Part-time fees:* $40 per term. Part-time tuition and fees vary according to course load. *Payment plans:* Guaranteed tuition, installment, deferred payment.

FRESHMAN FINANCIAL AID (Fall 2004, est.) 255 applied for aid; of those 81% were deemed to have need. 100% of freshmen with need received aid; of those 38% had need fully met. *Average percent of need met:* 70% (excluding resources awarded to replace EFC). *Average financial aid package:* $14,503 (excluding resources awarded to replace EFC).

UNDERGRADUATE FINANCIAL AID (Fall 2004, est.) 1,138 applied for aid; of those 83% were deemed to have need. 99% of undergraduates with need received aid; of those 35% had need fully met. *Average percent of need met:* 70% (excluding resources awarded to replace EFC). *Average financial aid package:* $14,265 (excluding resources awarded to replace EFC).

GIFT AID (NEED-BASED) *Total amount:* $10,418,951 (18% federal, 20% state, 59% institutional, 3% external sources). *Receiving aid:* Freshmen: 64% (206); All full-time undergraduates: 57% (931). *Average award:* Freshmen: $8949; Undergraduates: $6789. *Scholarships, grants, and awards:* Federal Pell, FSEOG, state, private, college/university gift aid from institutional funds.

GIFT AID (NON-NEED-BASED) *Total amount:* $1,357,943 (1% state, 97% institutional, 2% external sources). *Receiving aid:* Freshmen: 1% (2); Undergraduates: 2% (27). *Scholarships, grants, and awards by category: Academic Interests/Achievement:* education. *Special Achievements/Activities:*

community service, general special achievements/activities, leadership, religious involvement. *Special Characteristics:* $50,000 total: siblings of current students. *Tuition waivers:* Full or partial for employees or children of employees, senior citizens.
LOANS *Student loans:* $9,986,272 (46% need-based, 54% non-need-based). 90% of past graduating class borrowed through all loan programs. *Average indebtedness per student:* $14,000. *Parent loans:* $950,052 (100% non-need-based). *Programs:* FFEL (Subsidized and Unsubsidized Stafford, PLUS), Perkins, college/university.
WORK-STUDY *Federal work-study:* Total amount: $128,566; 196 jobs averaging $861.
APPLYING FOR FINANCIAL AID *Required financial aid forms:* FAFSA, institution's own form, state aid form. *Financial aid deadline (priority):* 3/2. *Notification date:* Continuous beginning 5/1. Students must reply within 3 weeks of notification.
CONTACT Glen Bobst Jr., Director of Student Financial Services, Pacific Union College, One Angwin Avenue, Angwin, CA 94508, 707-965-7321 or toll-free 800-862-7080. *Fax:* 707-965-6595. *E-mail:* gbobst@puc.edu.

PACIFIC UNIVERSITY
Forest Grove, OR

Tuition & fees: $20,664	Average undergraduate aid package: $16,927

ABOUT THE INSTITUTION Independent, coed. Awards: bachelor's, master's, doctoral, and first professional degrees. 48 undergraduate majors. Total enrollment: 2,521. Undergraduates: 1,232. Freshmen: 294. Federal methodology is used as a basis for awarding need-based institutional aid.
UNDERGRADUATE EXPENSES for 2004–05 *Application fee:* $30. *Comprehensive fee:* $26,428 includes full-time tuition ($20,104), mandatory fees ($560), and room and board ($5764). *College room only:* $2788. Room and board charges vary according to board plan and housing facility. Part-time tuition and fees vary according to course load. *Payment plans:* Installment, deferred payment.
FRESHMAN FINANCIAL AID (Fall 2004, est.) 267 applied for aid; of those 80% were deemed to have need. 100% of freshmen with need received aid; of those 35% had need fully met. *Average percent of need met:* 91% (excluding resources awarded to replace EFC). *Average financial aid package:* $17,781 (excluding resources awarded to replace EFC). 25% of all full-time freshmen had no need and received non-need-based gift aid.
UNDERGRADUATE FINANCIAL AID (Fall 2004, est.) 1,005 applied for aid; of those 86% were deemed to have need. 100% of undergraduates with need received aid; of those 35% had need fully met. *Average percent of need met:* 85% (excluding resources awarded to replace EFC). *Average financial aid package:* $16,927 (excluding resources awarded to replace EFC). 21% of all full-time undergraduates had no need and received non-need-based gift aid.
GIFT AID (NEED-BASED) *Total amount:* $9,605,343 (12% federal, 2% state, 78% institutional, 8% external sources). *Receiving aid:* Freshmen: 72% (213); All full-time undergraduates: 73% (845). *Average award:* Freshmen: $12,181; Undergraduates: $10,796. *Scholarships, grants, and awards:* Federal Pell, FSEOG, state, private, college/university gift aid from institutional funds.
GIFT AID (NON-NEED-BASED) *Total amount:* $2,529,796 (94% institutional, 6% external sources). *Receiving aid:* Freshmen: 12% (35); Undergraduates: 9% (105). *Average Award:* Freshmen: $9192; Undergraduates: $8417. *Scholarships, grants, and awards by category: Academic Interests/Achievement:* 979 awards ($7,656,669 total): business, education, English, foreign languages, general academic interests/achievements, humanities, mathematics, physical sciences, social sciences. *Creative Arts/Performance:* 106 awards ($188,646 total): art/fine arts, debating, journalism/publications, music, theater/drama. *Special Achievements/Activities:* 11 awards ($15,750 total): community service, memberships. *Special Characteristics:* 39 awards ($723,744 total): children and siblings of alumni, children of faculty/staff, general special characteristics, international students, relatives of clergy. *Tuition waivers:* Full or partial for employees or children of employees. *ROTC:* Army cooperative, Air Force cooperative.
LOANS *Student loans:* $7,286,715 (67% need-based, 33% non-need-based). 86% of past graduating class borrowed through all loan programs. *Average indebtedness per student:* $21,003. *Average need-based loan:* Freshmen: $5348; Undergraduates: $5463. *Parent loans:* $1,958,797 (22% need-based, 78% non-need-based). *Programs:* Federal Direct (Subsidized and Unsubsidized Stafford, PLUS), Perkins, alternative loans.
WORK-STUDY *Federal work-study:* Total amount: $1,070,222; 615 jobs averaging $1740. *State or other work-study/employment:* Total amount: $214,572 (25% need-based, 75% non-need-based). 182 part-time jobs averaging $1178.

APPLYING FOR FINANCIAL AID *Required financial aid form:* FAFSA. *Financial aid deadline (priority):* 2/15. *Notification date:* Continuous beginning 3/1.
CONTACT Dala Ramsey, Director of Financial Aid, Pacific University, 2043 College Way, Forest Grove, OR 97116-1797, 503-352-2871 or toll-free 877-722-8648. *Fax:* 503-352-2950. *E-mail:* dramsey@pacificu.edu.

PAIER COLLEGE OF ART, INC.
Hamden, CT

CONTACT Mr. John DeRose, Director of Financial Aid, Paier College of Art, Inc., 20 Gorham Avenue, Hamden, CT 06514-3902, 203-287-3034. *Fax:* 203-287-3021. *E-mail:* paier.art@snet.net.

PAINE COLLEGE
Augusta, GA

CONTACT Ms. Gerri Bogan, Director of Financial Aid, Paine College, 1235 15th Street, Augusta, GA 30901, 706-821-8262 or toll-free 800-476-7703. *Fax:* 706-821-8691. *E-mail:* bogang@mail.paine.edu.

PALM BEACH ATLANTIC UNIVERSITY
West Palm Beach, FL

Tuition & fees: $17,342	Average undergraduate aid package: $11,999

ABOUT THE INSTITUTION Independent nondenominational, coed. Awards: associate, bachelor's, master's, and first professional degrees. 46 undergraduate majors. Total enrollment: 3,066. Undergraduates: 2,406. Freshmen: 450. Federal methodology is used as a basis for awarding need-based institutional aid.
UNDERGRADUATE EXPENSES for 2005–06 *Application fee:* $25. *Comprehensive fee:* $23,648 includes full-time tuition ($17,130), mandatory fees ($212), and room and board ($6306). *College room only:* $3350. Full-time tuition and fees vary according to course load, degree level, program, and reciprocity agreements. Room and board charges vary according to board plan and housing facility. *Part-time tuition:* $420 per credit. *Part-time fees:* $85 per term. Part-time tuition and fees vary according to course load, degree level, program, and reciprocity agreements. *Payment plan:* Installment.
FRESHMAN FINANCIAL AID (Fall 2004, est.) 371 applied for aid; of those 76% were deemed to have need. 100% of freshmen with need received aid; of those 26% had need fully met. *Average percent of need met:* 64% (excluding resources awarded to replace EFC). *Average financial aid package:* $11,322 (excluding resources awarded to replace EFC).
UNDERGRADUATE FINANCIAL AID (Fall 2004, est.) 1,836 applied for aid; of those 87% were deemed to have need. 100% of undergraduates with need received aid; of those 1% had need fully met. *Average percent of need met:* 74% (excluding resources awarded to replace EFC). *Average financial aid package:* $11,999 (excluding resources awarded to replace EFC). 10% of all full-time undergraduates had no need and received non-need-based gift aid.
GIFT AID (NEED-BASED) *Total amount:* $5,534,220 (39% federal, 6% state, 22% institutional, 33% external sources). *Receiving aid:* Freshmen: 36% (156); All full-time undergraduates: 45% (985). *Average award:* Freshmen: $3568; Undergraduates: $3636. *Scholarships, grants, and awards:* Federal Pell, FSEOG, state, private, college/university gift aid from institutional funds.
GIFT AID (NON-NEED-BASED) *Total amount:* $10,757,885 (42% state, 53% institutional, 5% external sources). *Receiving aid:* Freshmen: 62% (273); Undergraduates: 71% (1,571). *Average Award: Undergraduates:* $3846. *Scholarships, grants, and awards by category: Academic Interests/Achievement:* 1,573 awards ($3,824,924 total): general academic interests/achievements. *Creative Arts/Performance:* 138 awards ($377,959 total): art/fine arts, dance, music, performing arts, theater/drama. *Special Achievements/Activities:* 679 awards ($676,441 total): leadership, religious involvement. *Special Characteristics:* 137 awards ($667,735 total): children and siblings of alumni, children of current students, children of educators, children of faculty/staff, previous college experience, relatives of clergy, siblings of current students, spouses of current students. *Tuition waivers:* Full or partial for employees or children of employees.
LOANS *Student loans:* $14,404,038 (54% need-based, 46% non-need-based). 63% of past graduating class borrowed through all loan programs. *Average indebtedness per student:* $18,627. *Average need-based loan:* Freshmen: $2462; Undergraduates: $4070. *Parent loans:* $3,033,293 (100% non-need-based). *Programs:* FFEL (Subsidized and Unsubsidized Stafford, PLUS), Perkins, college/university.

WORK-STUDY *Federal work-study:* Total amount: $249,126; 238 jobs averaging $1047.

ATHLETIC AWARDS *Total amount:* $367,121 (100% non-need-based).

APPLYING FOR FINANCIAL AID *Required financial aid forms:* FAFSA, state aid form. *Financial aid deadline (priority):* 4/1. *Notification date:* Continuous. Students must reply by 5/1.

CONTACT Margherite Powell, Director of Financial Aid, Palm Beach Atlantic University, PO Box 24708, West Palm Beach, FL 33416-4708, 561-803-2000 or toll-free 800-238-3998. *Fax:* 561-803-2130. *E-mail:* margherite_powell@pba.edu.

PALMER COLLEGE OF CHIROPRACTIC
Davenport, IA

Tuition & fees: $5895	Average undergraduate aid package: N/A

ABOUT THE INSTITUTION Independent, coed. Awards: associate, master's, and first professional degrees. 2 undergraduate majors. Total enrollment: 1,669. Undergraduates: 97. Freshmen: 17. Federal methodology is used as a basis for awarding need-based institutional aid.

UNDERGRADUATE EXPENSES for 2004–05 *Application fee:* $50. *Tuition:* full-time $5640; part-time $137 per credit. *Required fees:* full-time $255; $100 per term part-time.

FRESHMAN FINANCIAL AID (Fall 2004, est.) 88 applied for aid; of those 100% were deemed to have need. 100% of freshmen with need received aid; of those 48% had need fully met. *Average percent of need met:* 65% (excluding resources awarded to replace EFC). *Average financial aid package:* $15,420 (excluding resources awarded to replace EFC).

GIFT AID (NEED-BASED) *Total amount:* $205,479 (83% federal, 14% institutional, 3% external sources). *Receiving aid:* Freshmen: 84% (76). *Average award:* Freshmen: $4050. *Scholarships, grants, and awards:* Federal Pell, FSEOG, state, private, college/university gift aid from institutional funds.

GIFT AID (NON-NEED-BASED) *Scholarships, grants, and awards by category: Academic Interests/Achievement:* biological sciences, general academic interests/achievements, health fields. *Tuition waivers:* Full or partial for employees or children of employees.

LOANS *Student loans:* $1,389,765 (100% need-based). 95% of past graduating class borrowed through all loan programs. *Average indebtedness per student:* $14,013. *Average need-based loan:* Freshmen: $5140. *Programs:* FFEL (Subsidized and Unsubsidized Stafford, PLUS), Perkins, state.

WORK-STUDY *Federal work-study:* Total amount: $13,100; 4 jobs averaging $2200.

APPLYING FOR FINANCIAL AID *Required financial aid form:* FAFSA. *Financial aid deadline:* Continuous. *Notification date:* Continuous beginning 1/3. Students must reply within 4 weeks of notification.

CONTACT Brenda Gran, Financial Planning Office, Palmer College of Chiropractic, 1000 Brady Street, Davenport, IA 52803, 563-884-5888 or toll-free 800-722-3648. *Fax:* 563-884-5299. *E-mail:* gran_b@palmer.edu.

PARK UNIVERSITY
Parkville, MO

Tuition & fees: $6048	Average undergraduate aid package: $6178

ABOUT THE INSTITUTION Independent, coed. Awards: associate, bachelor's, and master's degrees. 47 undergraduate majors. Total enrollment: 12,548. Undergraduates: 12,077. Freshmen: 127. Federal methodology is used as a basis for awarding need-based institutional aid.

UNDERGRADUATE EXPENSES for 2004–05 *Application fee:* $25. *Comprehensive fee:* $11,228 includes full-time tuition ($6048) and room and board ($5180). *College room only:* $2062. Room and board charges vary according to board plan and housing facility. *Part-time tuition:* $216 per credit. *Payment plan:* Installment.

FRESHMAN FINANCIAL AID (Fall 2003) 152 applied for aid; of those 93% were deemed to have need. 100% of freshmen with need received aid; of those 24% had need fully met. *Average percent of need met:* 73% (excluding resources awarded to replace EFC). *Average financial aid package:* $4180 (excluding resources awarded to replace EFC). 3% of all full-time freshmen had no need and received non-need-based gift aid.

UNDERGRADUATE FINANCIAL AID (Fall 2003) 6,277 applied for aid; of those 85% were deemed to have need. 93% of undergraduates with need received aid; of those 16% had need fully met. *Average percent of need met:* 69% (excluding resources awarded to replace EFC). *Average financial aid package:* $6178 (excluding resources awarded to replace EFC). 1% of all full-time undergraduates had no need and received non-need-based gift aid.

GIFT AID (NEED-BASED) *Total amount:* $6,219,725 (98% federal, 2% state). *Receiving aid:* Freshmen: 53% (100); All full-time undergraduates: 24% (2,555). *Average award:* Freshmen: $1900; Undergraduates: $5400. *Scholarships, grants, and awards:* Federal Pell, FSEOG, state, private, college/university gift aid from institutional funds.

GIFT AID (NON-NEED-BASED) *Total amount:* $4,749,012 (2% state, 14% institutional, 84% external sources). *Receiving aid:* Freshmen: 9% (16); Undergraduates: 14% (1,541). *Average Award: Freshmen:* $3500; *Undergraduates:* $5858. *Scholarships, grants, and awards by category: Academic Interests/Achievement:* 197 awards ($389,037 total): general academic interests/achievements. *Creative Arts/Performance:* 35 awards ($11,800 total): art/fine arts, theater/drama. *Special Achievements/Activities:* 8 awards ($8800 total): cheerleading/drum major. *Special Characteristics:* 263 awards ($438,170 total): children of faculty/staff, religious affiliation, siblings of current students. *Tuition waivers:* Full or partial for employees or children of employees, senior citizens. *ROTC:* Army.

LOANS *Student loans:* $18,540,912 (60% need-based, 40% non-need-based). 30% of past graduating class borrowed through all loan programs. *Average indebtedness per student:* $12,800. *Average need-based loan:* Freshmen: $2480; Undergraduates: $4541. *Parent loans:* $155,721 (100% non-need-based). *Programs:* FFEL (Subsidized and Unsubsidized Stafford, PLUS), Perkins, college/university.

WORK-STUDY *Federal work-study:* Total amount: $468,677; 209 jobs averaging $2875. *State or other work-study/employment:* Total amount: $331,426 (100% need-based). 103 part-time jobs averaging $2675.

ATHLETIC AWARDS *Total amount:* $849,798 (100% non-need-based).

APPLYING FOR FINANCIAL AID *Required financial aid forms:* FAFSA, institution's own form. *Financial aid deadline (priority):* 4/1. *Notification date:* Continuous. Students must reply within 2 weeks of notification.

CONTACT Ms. Cathy Colapietro, Director of Student Financial Services, Park University, 8700 NW River Park Drive, Parkville, MO 64152, 816-584-6728 or toll-free 800-745-7275. *Fax:* 816-741-9668.

PARSONS SCHOOL OF DESIGN, NEW SCHOOL UNIVERSITY
New York, NY

ABOUT THE INSTITUTION Independent, coed. Awards: associate, bachelor's, and master's degrees. 12 undergraduate majors. Total enrollment: 2,958. Undergraduates: 2,502. Freshmen: 309.

GIFT AID (NEED-BASED) *Scholarships, grants, and awards:* Federal Pell, FSEOG, state, private, college/university gift aid from institutional funds.

GIFT AID (NON-NEED-BASED) *Scholarships, grants, and awards by category: Academic Interests/Achievement:* general academic interests/achievements. *Creative Arts/Performance:* general creative arts/performance. *Special Achievements/Activities:* general special achievements/activities.

LOANS *Programs:* FFEL (Subsidized and Unsubsidized Stafford, PLUS), Perkins, college/university.

WORK-STUDY *Federal work-study:* Total amount: $375,125; jobs available. *State or other work-study/employment:* Part-time jobs available.

APPLYING FOR FINANCIAL AID *Required financial aid forms:* FAFSA, state aid form.

CONTACT Financial Aid Counselor, Parsons School of Design, New School University, 66 Fifth Avenue, New York, NY 10011, 212-229-8930 or toll-free 877-528-3321.

PATRICK HENRY COLLEGE
Purcellville, VA

CONTACT Financial Aid Office, Patrick Henry College, One Patrick Henry Circle, Purcellville, VA 20132, 540-338-1776.

PATTEN UNIVERSITY
Oakland, CA

CONTACT Mr. Robert A. Olivera, Dean of Enrollment Services, Patten University, 2433 Coolidge Avenue, Oakland, CA 94601-2699, 510-261-8500 Ext. 783. *Fax:* 510-534-8969. *E-mail:* oliverob@patten.edu.

PAUL QUINN COLLEGE
Dallas, TX

ABOUT THE INSTITUTION Independent African Methodist Episcopal, coed. Awards: bachelor's degrees. 18 undergraduate majors. Total enrollment: 871. Undergraduates: 871. Freshmen: 154.

GIFT AID (NEED-BASED) *Scholarships, grants, and awards:* Federal Pell, FSEOG, state, private, college/university gift aid from institutional funds, United Negro College Fund.

GIFT AID (NON-NEED-BASED) *Scholarships, grants, and awards by category:* Academic Interests/Achievement: general academic interests/achievements. Creative Arts/Performance: music, performing arts. Special Achievements/Activities: community service, general special achievements/activities, religious involvement. Special Characteristics: adult students, children of educators, children of faculty/staff, first-generation college students, local/state students, married students, out-of-state students, previous college experience, spouses of current students, twins, veterans.

LOANS *Programs:* FFEL (Subsidized and Unsubsidized Stafford, PLUS), alternative loans.

WORK-STUDY *Federal work-study:* Total amount: $123,055; 149 jobs averaging $826. *State or other work-study/employment:* Total amount: $9714 (100% need-based). 16 part-time jobs averaging $607.

APPLYING FOR FINANCIAL AID *Required financial aid form:* FAFSA.

CONTACT Khaleelah Ali, Assistant Director of Financial Aid, Paul Quinn College, 3837 Simpson Stuart Road, Dallas, TX 75241, 214-302-3530 or toll-free 800-237-2648. *Fax:* 214-302-3535. *E-mail:* kali@pqc.edu.

PAUL SMITH'S COLLEGE OF ARTS AND SCIENCES
Paul Smiths, NY

Tuition & fees: $17,110	Average undergraduate aid package: $5300

ABOUT THE INSTITUTION Independent, coed. Awards: associate and bachelor's degrees. 15 undergraduate majors. Total enrollment: 816. Undergraduates: 816. Freshmen: 242. Federal methodology is used as a basis for awarding need-based institutional aid.

UNDERGRADUATE EXPENSES for 2005–06 *Application fee:* $30. *Comprehensive fee:* $24,170 includes full-time tuition ($16,100), mandatory fees ($1010), and room and board ($7060). *College room only:* $3530. Full-time tuition and fees vary according to program. Room and board charges vary according to board plan. *Part-time tuition:* $505 per credit hour. Part-time tuition and fees vary according to course load and program. *Payment plan:* Installment.

FRESHMAN FINANCIAL AID (Fall 2003) 346 applied for aid; of those 97% were deemed to have need. 100% of freshmen with need received aid; of those 3% had need fully met. *Average percent of need met:* 85% (excluding resources awarded to replace EFC). *Average financial aid package:* $6500 (excluding resources awarded to replace EFC). 8% of all full-time freshmen had no need and received non-need-based gift aid.

UNDERGRADUATE FINANCIAL AID (Fall 2003) 861 applied for aid; of those 94% were deemed to have need. 100% of undergraduates with need received aid; of those 5% had need fully met. *Average percent of need met:* 85% (excluding resources awarded to replace EFC). *Average financial aid package:* $5300 (excluding resources awarded to replace EFC). 8% of all full-time undergraduates had no need and received non-need-based gift aid.

GIFT AID (NEED-BASED) *Total amount:* $6,530,963 (16% federal, 20% state, 64% institutional). *Receiving aid:* Freshmen: 86% (337); All full-time undergraduates: 91% (809). *Average award:* Freshmen: $4800; Undergraduates: $3034. *Scholarships, grants, and awards:* Federal Pell, FSEOG, state, private, college/university gift aid from institutional funds.

GIFT AID (NON-NEED-BASED) *Total amount:* $212,544 (4% institutional, 96% external sources). *Receiving aid:* Freshmen: 2% (9); Undergraduates: 6% (52). *Average Award:* Freshmen: $2169; Undergraduates: $2525. *Tuition waivers:* Full or partial for employees or children of employees.

LOANS *Student loans:* $5,631,567 (96% need-based, 4% non-need-based). 85% of past graduating class borrowed through all loan programs. *Average indebtedness per student:* $6625. *Average need-based loan:* Freshmen: $2625; Undergraduates: $6625. *Parent loans:* $1,405,088 (98% need-based, 2% non-need-based). *Programs:* FFEL (Subsidized and Unsubsidized Stafford, PLUS), Perkins.

WORK-STUDY *Federal work-study:* Total amount: $260,000; 814 jobs averaging $1588.

ATHLETIC AWARDS *Total amount:* $33,250 (100% need-based).

APPLYING FOR FINANCIAL AID *Required financial aid forms:* FAFSA, state aid form. *Financial aid deadline (priority):* 3/3. *Notification date:* Continuous. Students must reply within 4 weeks of notification.

CONTACT Mary Ellen Chamberlain, Director of Financial Aid, Paul Smith's College of Arts and Sciences, Routes 86 and 30, PO Box 265, Paul Smiths, NY 12970, 518-327-6220 or toll-free 800-421-2605. *Fax:* 518-327-6055. *E-mail:* chambem@paulsmiths.edu.

PEABODY CONSERVATORY OF MUSIC OF THE JOHNS HOPKINS UNIVERSITY
Baltimore, MD

Tuition & fees: $28,515	Average undergraduate aid package: $8999

ABOUT THE INSTITUTION Independent, coed. Awards: bachelor's, master's, and doctoral degrees and post-bachelor's certificates. 8 undergraduate majors. Total enrollment: 639. Undergraduates: 303. Freshmen: 78. Federal methodology is used as a basis for awarding need-based institutional aid.

UNDERGRADUATE EXPENSES for 2005–06 *Application fee:* $60. *Comprehensive fee:* $37,740 includes full-time tuition ($28,215), mandatory fees ($300), and room and board ($9225). Room and board charges vary according to board plan. *Part-time tuition:* $800 per semester hour. Part-time tuition and fees vary according to course load. *Payment plan:* Installment.

FRESHMAN FINANCIAL AID (Fall 2004, est.) 68 applied for aid; of those 82% were deemed to have need. 89% of freshmen with need received aid; of those 4% had need fully met. *Average percent of need met:* 45% (excluding resources awarded to replace EFC). *Average financial aid package:* $11,012 (excluding resources awarded to replace EFC). 7% of all full-time freshmen had no need and received non-need-based gift aid.

UNDERGRADUATE FINANCIAL AID (Fall 2004, est.) 200 applied for aid; of those 90% were deemed to have need. 94% of undergraduates with need received aid; of those 4% had need fully met. *Average percent of need met:* 34% (excluding resources awarded to replace EFC). *Average financial aid package:* $8999 (excluding resources awarded to replace EFC). 4% of all full-time undergraduates had no need and received non-need-based gift aid.

GIFT AID (NEED-BASED) *Total amount:* $1,256,277 (18% federal, 4% state, 78% institutional). *Receiving aid:* Freshmen: 43% (39); All full-time undergraduates: 43% (132). *Average award:* Freshmen: $6335; Undergraduates: $7339. *Scholarships, grants, and awards:* Federal Pell, FSEOG, state, private, college/university gift aid from institutional funds.

GIFT AID (NON-NEED-BASED) *Total amount:* $1,234,475 (1% state, 98% institutional, 1% external sources). *Receiving aid:* Freshmen: 19% (17); Undergraduates: 30% (94). *Average Award:* Freshmen: $11,833; Undergraduates: $10,653. *Scholarships, grants, and awards by category:* Creative Arts/Performance: 170 awards ($1,213,175 total): music.

LOANS *Student loans:* $1,676,910 (48% need-based, 52% non-need-based). 47% of past graduating class borrowed through all loan programs. *Average indebtedness per student:* $19,196. *Average need-based loan:* Freshmen: $4509; Undergraduates: $5610. *Parent loans:* $872,973 (100% non-need-based). *Programs:* Federal Direct (Subsidized and Unsubsidized Stafford), FFEL (PLUS), Perkins, college/university.

WORK-STUDY *Federal work-study:* Total amount: $218,753; 114 jobs averaging $1919. *State or other work-study/employment:* Total amount: $96,213 (100% non-need-based). 103 part-time jobs averaging $934.

APPLYING FOR FINANCIAL AID *Required financial aid form:* FAFSA. *Financial aid deadline (priority):* 3/1. *Notification date:* 4/1. Students must reply within 2 weeks of notification.

CONTACT George Tyree, Financial Aid Officer, Peabody Conservatory of Music of The Johns Hopkins University, 1 East Mount Vernon Place, Baltimore, MD 21202-2397, 410-659-8100 Ext. 3023 or toll-free 800-368-2521 (out-of-state). *Fax:* 410-659-8102. *E-mail:* finaid@peabody.jhu.edu.

PEACE COLLEGE
Raleigh, NC

Tuition & fees: $16,881	Average undergraduate aid package: $11,645

ABOUT THE INSTITUTION Independent religious, women only. Awards: bachelor's degrees. 11 undergraduate majors. Total enrollment: 701. Undergraduates: 701. Freshmen: 251. Federal methodology is used as a basis for awarding need-based institutional aid.

UNDERGRADUATE EXPENSES for 2004–05 *Application fee:* $25. *Comprehensive fee:* $23,407 includes full-time tuition ($16,881) and room and board ($6526). *Part-time tuition:* $400 per credit hour. *Payment plans:* Installment, deferred payment.

FRESHMAN FINANCIAL AID (Fall 2004, est.) 208 applied for aid; of those 84% were deemed to have need. 100% of freshmen with need received aid; of those 18% had need fully met. *Average percent of need met:* 75% (excluding resources awarded to replace EFC). *Average financial aid package:* $12,469 (excluding resources awarded to replace EFC). 32% of all full-time freshmen had no need and received non-need-based gift aid.

UNDERGRADUATE FINANCIAL AID (Fall 2004, est.) 531 applied for aid; of those 85% were deemed to have need. 100% of undergraduates with need received aid; of those 16% had need fully met. *Average percent of need met:* 70% (excluding resources awarded to replace EFC). *Average financial aid package:* $11,645 (excluding resources awarded to replace EFC). 34% of all full-time undergraduates had no need and received non-need-based gift aid.

GIFT AID (NEED-BASED) *Total amount:* $4,068,814 (16% federal, 31% state, 50% institutional, 3% external sources). *Receiving aid:* Freshmen: 68% (174); All full-time undergraduates: 66% (449). *Average award:* Freshmen: $10,450; Undergraduates: $8955. *Scholarships, grants, and awards:* Federal Pell, FSEOG, state, private, college/university gift aid from institutional funds, Federal Nursing.

GIFT AID (NON-NEED-BASED) *Total amount:* $1,327,787 (30% state, 63% institutional, 7% external sources). *Receiving aid:* Freshmen: 10% (25); Undergraduates: 8% (52). *Average Award:* Freshmen: $8287; Undergraduates: $7517. *Scholarships, grants, and awards by category:* Academic Interests/Achievement: 489 awards ($1,953,560 total): general academic interests/achievements. Creative Arts/Performance: 24 awards ($29,828 total): art/fine arts, music, theater/drama. Special Characteristics: 5 awards ($39,538 total): children of faculty/staff, relatives of clergy. *Tuition waivers:* Full or partial for employees or children of employees. *ROTC:* Army cooperative, Naval cooperative, Air Force cooperative.

LOANS *Student loans:* $2,579,286 (71% need-based, 29% non-need-based). 76% of past graduating class borrowed through all loan programs. *Average indebtedness per student:* $9250. *Average need-based loan:* Freshmen: $2240; Undergraduates: $2924. *Parent loans:* $1,450,628 (32% need-based, 68% non-need-based). *Programs:* FFEL (Subsidized and Unsubsidized Stafford, PLUS), alternative loans.

WORK-STUDY *Federal work-study:* Total amount: $160,888; 203 jobs averaging $793. *State or other work-study/employment:* Total amount: $24,133 (20% need-based, 80% non-need-based). 31 part-time jobs averaging $779.

APPLYING FOR FINANCIAL AID *Required financial aid form:* FAFSA. *Financial aid deadline:* Continuous. *Notification date:* Continuous.

CONTACT Angela Kirkley, Director of Financial Aid, Peace College, 15 East Peace Street, Raleigh, NC 27604, 919-508-2249 or toll-free 800-PEACE-47. *Fax:* 919-508-2325. *E-mail:* akirkley@peace.edu.

PEIRCE COLLEGE
Philadelphia, PA

Tuition & fees: $12,310	Average undergraduate aid package: $3500

ABOUT THE INSTITUTION Independent, coed. Awards: associate and bachelor's degrees and post-bachelor's certificates. 19 undergraduate majors. Total enrollment: 1,892. Undergraduates: 1,892. Freshmen: 256. Both federal and institutional methodology are used as a basis for awarding need-based institutional aid.

UNDERGRADUATE EXPENSES for 2004–05 *Application fee:* $50. *Tuition:* full-time $11,310; part-time $377 per credit hour. *Required fees:* full-time $1000; $100 per course. Full-time tuition and fees vary according to course load. Part-time tuition and fees vary according to course load. *Payment plan:* Installment.

GIFT AID (NEED-BASED) *Total amount:* $2,842,952 (57% federal, 40% state, 3% institutional). *Receiving aid:* Freshmen: 54% (30); All full-time undergradu-

ates: 36% (198). *Average award:* Freshmen: $1500; Undergraduates: $1000. *Scholarships, grants, and awards:* Federal Pell, FSEOG, state, private, college/university gift aid from institutional funds.

GIFT AID (NON-NEED-BASED) *Total amount:* $144,394 (100% institutional). *Average Award:* Freshmen: $1500; Undergraduates: $1000. *Scholarships, grants, and awards by category:* Academic Interests/Achievement: 63 awards ($144,394 total): general academic interests/achievements. Special Achievements/Activities: 11 awards ($12,700 total): community service, leadership, memberships. Special Characteristics: 15 awards ($22,815 total): children and siblings of alumni, children of public servants, parents of current students, previous college experience, public servants, siblings of current students, spouses of current students. *Tuition waivers:* Full or partial for children of alumni, employees or children of employees.

LOANS *Student loans:* $6,987,620 (50% need-based, 50% non-need-based). 80% of past graduating class borrowed through all loan programs. *Average indebtedness per student:* $13,000. *Average need-based loan:* Freshmen: $4000; Undergraduates: $4000. *Parent loans:* $38,365 (100% need-based). *Programs:* FFEL (Subsidized and Unsubsidized Stafford, PLUS).

APPLYING FOR FINANCIAL AID *Required financial aid forms:* FAFSA, institution's own form. *Financial aid deadline (priority):* 4/15. *Notification date:* 6/15. Students must reply within 3 weeks of notification.

CONTACT Lisa A. Gargiulo, Student Financial Services Manager, Peirce College, 1420 Pine Street, Philadelphia, PA 19102, 215-670-9370 or toll-free 877-670-9190 Ext. 9214. *Fax:* 215-545-3671. *E-mail:* lagargiulo@peirce.edu.

PENNSYLVANIA COLLEGE OF ART & DESIGN
Lancaster, PA

CONTACT J. David Hershey, Registrar/Director of Financial Aid, Pennsylvania College of Art & Design, 204 North Prince Street, PO Box 59, Lancaster, PA 17608-0059, 717-396-7833 Ext. 13. *Fax:* 717-396-1339. *E-mail:* finaid@psad.edu.

PENNSYLVANIA COLLEGE OF TECHNOLOGY
Williamsport, PA

Tuition & fees (PA res): $9480	Average undergraduate aid package: N/A

ABOUT THE INSTITUTION State-related, coed. Awards: associate and bachelor's degrees. 108 undergraduate majors. Total enrollment: 6,358. Undergraduates: 6,358. Freshmen: 1,705. Federal methodology is used as a basis for awarding need-based institutional aid.

UNDERGRADUATE EXPENSES for 2004–05 *Application fee:* $50. *Tuition, state resident:* full-time $8100; part-time $270 per credit. *Tuition, nonresident:* full-time $10,560; part-time $352 per credit. *Required fees:* full-time $1380; $46 per credit. Full-time tuition and fees vary according to course load and program. Part-time tuition and fees vary according to course load and program. *College room and board:* $5132; *room only:* $3832. Room and board charges vary according to board plan, housing facility, and location. *Payment plan:* Deferred payment.

GIFT AID (NEED-BASED) *Total amount:* $14,007,587 (42% federal, 52% state, 2% institutional, 4% external sources). *Scholarships, grants, and awards:* Federal Pell, FSEOG, state, private, college/university gift aid from institutional funds.

GIFT AID (NON-NEED-BASED) *Tuition waivers:* Full or partial for employees or children of employees. *ROTC:* Army cooperative.

LOANS *Student loans:* $26,723,318 (100% need-based). *Parent loans:* $6,283,551 (100% need-based). *Programs:* FFEL (Subsidized and Unsubsidized Stafford, PLUS).

WORK-STUDY *Federal work-study:* Total amount: $414,888; 324 jobs averaging $1281. *State or other work-study/employment:* Total amount: $290,396 (100% need-based). 260 part-time jobs averaging $1117.

APPLYING FOR FINANCIAL AID *Required financial aid forms:* FAFSA, institution's own form. *Financial aid deadline (priority):* 4/1. *Notification date:* Continuous beginning 6/1. Students must reply within 2 weeks of notification.

CONTACT Dennis L. Correll, Director of Financial Aid, Pennsylvania College of Technology, One College Avenue, # 108, Williamsport, PA 17701, 570-326-3761 Ext. 7048 or toll-free 800-367-9222 (in-state). *Fax:* 570-321-5552. *E-mail:* dcorrell@pct.edu.

THE PENNSYLVANIA STATE UNIVERSITY ABINGTON COLLEGE
Abington, PA

Tuition & fees (PA res): $9614   **Average undergraduate aid package: $9271**

ABOUT THE INSTITUTION State-related, coed. Awards: associate and bachelor's degrees. 120 undergraduate majors. Total enrollment: 3,143. Undergraduates: 3,143. Freshmen: 692. Federal methodology is used as a basis for awarding need-based institutional aid.

UNDERGRADUATE EXPENSES for 2004–05 *Application fee:* $50. *Tuition, state resident:* full-time $9180; part-time $371 per credit. *Tuition, nonresident:* full-time $14,040; part-time $585 per credit. *Required fees:* full-time $434; $73 per term part-time. Full-time tuition and fees vary according to course level, location, program, and student level. Part-time tuition and fees vary according to course level, course load, location, program, and student level. *Payment plan:* Deferred payment.

FRESHMAN FINANCIAL AID (Fall 2003) 624 applied for aid; of those 78% were deemed to have need. 98% of freshmen with need received aid; of those 3% had need fully met. *Average percent of need met:* 63% (excluding resources awarded to replace EFC). *Average financial aid package:* $8371 (excluding resources awarded to replace EFC). 5% of all full-time freshmen had no need and received non-need-based gift aid.

UNDERGRADUATE FINANCIAL AID (Fall 2003) 1,779 applied for aid; of those 77% were deemed to have need. 98% of undergraduates with need received aid; of those 6% had need fully met. *Average percent of need met:* 66% (excluding resources awarded to replace EFC). *Average financial aid package:* $9271 (excluding resources awarded to replace EFC). 4% of all full-time undergraduates had no need and received non-need-based gift aid.

GIFT AID (NEED-BASED) *Total amount:* $5,794,213 (49% federal, 34% state, 17% institutional). *Receiving aid:* Freshmen: 51% (400); All full-time undergraduates: 47% (1,098). *Average award:* Freshmen: $4819; Undergraduates: $4690. *Scholarships, grants, and awards:* Federal Pell, FSEOG, state, private, college/university gift aid from institutional funds.

GIFT AID (NON-NEED-BASED) *Total amount:* $659,573 (56% institutional, 44% external sources). *Receiving aid:* Freshmen: 15% (113); Undergraduates: 14% (323). *Average Award:* Freshmen: $2043; Undergraduates: $2341. *Scholarships, grants, and awards by category:* Academic Interests/Achievement: general academic interests/achievements. Special Characteristics: general special characteristics. *Tuition waivers:* Full or partial for employees or children of employees, senior citizens. *ROTC:* Army, Air Force cooperative.

LOANS *Student loans:* $7,326,068 (58% need-based, 42% non-need-based). 70% of past graduating class borrowed through all loan programs. *Average indebtedness per student:* $18,200. *Average need-based loan:* Freshmen: $2416; Undergraduates: $3276. *Parent loans:* $1,109,770 (100% non-need-based). *Programs:* FFEL (Subsidized and Unsubsidized Stafford, PLUS), Perkins, college/university, alternative loans.

WORK-STUDY *Federal work-study:* Total amount: $125,668; 112 jobs averaging $1099. *State or other work-study/employment:* Part-time jobs available.

APPLYING FOR FINANCIAL AID *Required financial aid form:* FAFSA. *Financial aid deadline:* Continuous. *Notification date:* Continuous beginning 2/15.

CONTACT Debbie Meditz, Assistant Student Aid Coordinator, The Pennsylvania State University Abington College, 106 Sutherland Building, 1600 Woodland Road, Abington, PA 19001, 215-881-7348. *Fax:* 215-881-7655. *E-mail:* dlm175@psu.edu.

THE PENNSYLVANIA STATE UNIVERSITY ALTOONA COLLEGE
Altoona, PA

Tuition & fees (PA res): $10,026   **Average undergraduate aid package: $11,650**

ABOUT THE INSTITUTION State-related, coed. Awards: associate and bachelor's degrees. 120 undergraduate majors. Total enrollment: 3,766. Undergraduates: 3,762. Freshmen: 1,271. Federal methodology is used as a basis for awarding need-based institutional aid.

UNDERGRADUATE EXPENSES for 2004–05 *Application fee:* $50. *Tuition, state resident:* full-time $9582; part-time $399 per credit. *Tuition, nonresident:* full-time $14,696; part-time $612 per credit. *Required fees:* full-time $444; $75 per term part-time. Full-time tuition and fees vary according to course level, location, program, and student level. Part-time tuition and fees vary according

to course level, course load, location, program, and student level. *College room and board:* $6230; *room only:* $3250. Room and board charges vary according to board plan and housing facility. *Payment plan:* Deferred payment.

FRESHMAN FINANCIAL AID (Fall 2003) 1101 applied for aid; of those 78% were deemed to have need. 98% of freshmen with need received aid; of those 5% had need fully met. *Average percent of need met:* 64% (excluding resources awarded to replace EFC). *Average financial aid package:* $10,905 (excluding resources awarded to replace EFC). 3% of all full-time freshmen had no need and received non-need-based gift aid.

UNDERGRADUATE FINANCIAL AID (Fall 2003) 2,713 applied for aid; of those 84% were deemed to have need. 99% of undergraduates with need received aid; of those 7% had need fully met. *Average percent of need met:* 68% (excluding resources awarded to replace EFC). *Average financial aid package:* $11,650 (excluding resources awarded to replace EFC). 3% of all full-time undergraduates had no need and received non-need-based gift aid.

GIFT AID (NEED-BASED) *Total amount:* $8,322,605 (46% federal, 51% state, 3% institutional). *Receiving aid:* Freshmen: 46% (607); All full-time undergraduates: 50% (1,681). *Average award:* Freshmen: $4186; Undergraduates: $4396. *Scholarships, grants, and awards:* Federal Pell, FSEOG, state, private, college/university gift aid from institutional funds.

GIFT AID (NON-NEED-BASED) *Total amount:* $1,059,337 (50% institutional, 50% external sources). *Receiving aid:* Freshmen: 19% (247); Undergraduates: 19% (655). *Average Award:* Freshmen: $2036; Undergraduates: $2950. *Scholarships, grants, and awards by category:* Academic Interests/Achievement: general academic interests/achievements. Special Characteristics: general special characteristics. *Tuition waivers:* Full or partial for employees or children of employees, senior citizens. *ROTC:* Army, Air Force.

LOANS *Student loans:* $11,595,730 (65% need-based, 35% non-need-based). 70% of past graduating class borrowed through all loan programs. *Average indebtedness per student:* $18,200. *Average need-based loan:* Freshmen: $2673; Undergraduates: $3462. *Parent loans:* $4,384,642 (100% non-need-based). *Programs:* FFEL (Subsidized and Unsubsidized Stafford, PLUS), Perkins, college/university, alternative loans.

WORK-STUDY *Federal work-study:* Total amount: $665,477; 423 jobs averaging $1557. *State or other work-study/employment:* Total amount: $132,034 (100% need-based). 29 part-time jobs averaging $4779.

APPLYING FOR FINANCIAL AID *Required financial aid form:* FAFSA. *Financial aid deadline:* Continuous. *Notification date:* Continuous beginning 2/15.

CONTACT Mr. David Pearlman, Assistant Director of Student Affairs, The Pennsylvania State University Altoona College, W111 Smith Building, Altoona, PA 16601-3760, 814-949-5055 or toll-free 800-848-9843. *Fax:* 814-949-5536. *E-mail:* dpp1@psu.edu.

THE PENNSYLVANIA STATE UNIVERSITY AT ERIE, THE BEHREND COLLEGE
Erie, PA

Tuition & fees (PA res): $10,026   **Average undergraduate aid package: $11,874**

ABOUT THE INSTITUTION State-related, coed. Awards: associate, bachelor's, and master's degrees. 131 undergraduate majors. Total enrollment: 3,593. Undergraduates: 3,440. Freshmen: 854. Federal methodology is used as a basis for awarding need-based institutional aid.

UNDERGRADUATE EXPENSES for 2004–05 *Application fee:* $50. *Tuition, state resident:* full-time $9582; part-time $399 per credit. *Tuition, nonresident:* full-time $15,466; part-time $644 per credit. *Required fees:* full-time $444; $75 per term part-time. Full-time tuition and fees vary according to course level, location, program, and student level. Part-time tuition and fees vary according to course level, course load, location, program, and student level. *College room and board:* $6230; *room only:* $3250. Room and board charges vary according to board plan and housing facility. *Payment plan:* Deferred payment.

FRESHMAN FINANCIAL AID (Fall 2003) 733 applied for aid; of those 78% were deemed to have need. 99% of freshmen with need received aid; of those 7% had need fully met. *Average percent of need met:* 66% (excluding resources awarded to replace EFC). *Average financial aid package:* $11,240 (excluding resources awarded to replace EFC). 5% of all full-time freshmen had no need and received non-need-based gift aid.

UNDERGRADUATE FINANCIAL AID (Fall 2003) 2,661 applied for aid; of those 84% were deemed to have need. 99% of undergraduates with need received aid; of those 8% had need fully met. *Average percent of need met:* 71% (excluding resources awarded to replace EFC). *Average financial aid package:*

$11,874 (excluding resources awarded to replace EFC). 5% of all full-time undergraduates had no need and received non-need-based gift aid.

GIFT AID (NEED-BASED) *Total amount:* $8,248,335 (36% federal, 49% state, 15% institutional). *Receiving aid:* Freshmen: 48% (399); All full-time undergraduates: 49% (1,577). *Average award:* Freshmen: $3960; Undergraduates: $4107. *Scholarships, grants, and awards:* Federal Pell, FSEOG, state, private, college/university gift aid from institutional funds.

GIFT AID (NON-NEED-BASED) *Total amount:* $2,262,625 (52% institutional, 48% external sources). *Receiving aid:* Freshmen: 27% (224); Undergraduates: 25% (815). *Average Award: Freshmen:* $2679; *Undergraduates:* $3526. **Scholarships, grants, and awards by category:** *Academic Interests/Achievement:* general academic interests/achievements. *Special Characteristics:* general special characteristics. *Tuition waivers:* Full or partial for employees or children of employees, senior citizens. *ROTC:* Army cooperative.

LOANS *Student loans:* $11,813,760 (68% need-based, 32% non-need-based). 70% of past graduating class borrowed through all loan programs. *Average indebtedness per student:* $18,600. *Average need-based loan:* Freshmen: $2663; Undergraduates: $3867. *Parent loans:* $4,640,013 (100% non-need-based). *Programs:* FFEL (Subsidized and Unsubsidized Stafford, PLUS), Perkins, college/university, alternative loans.

WORK-STUDY *Federal work-study:* Total amount: $499,246; 380 jobs averaging $1302. *State or other work-study/employment:* Total amount: $188,059 (100% need-based). 49 part-time jobs averaging $4755.

APPLYING FOR FINANCIAL AID *Required financial aid form:* FAFSA. *Financial aid deadline:* Continuous. *Notification date:* Continuous beginning 2/15.

CONTACT Ms. Jane Brady, Assistant Director of Admissions and Financial Aid, The Pennsylvania State University at Erie, The Behrend College, 5091 Station Road, Erie, PA 16563, 814-898-6162 or toll-free 866-374-3378. *Fax:* 814-898-7595. *E-mail:* jub9@psu.edu.

THE PENNSYLVANIA STATE UNIVERSITY BERKS CAMPUS OF THE BERKS–LEHIGH VALLEY COLLEGE
Reading, PA

Tuition & fees (PA res): $10,026   Average undergraduate aid package: $10,354

ABOUT THE INSTITUTION State-related, coed. Awards: associate and bachelor's degrees. 125 undergraduate majors. Total enrollment: 2,416. Undergraduates: 2,382. Freshmen: 797. Federal methodology is used as a basis for awarding need-based institutional aid.

UNDERGRADUATE EXPENSES for 2004–05 *Application fee:* $50. *Tuition, state resident:* full-time $9582; part-time $399 per credit. *Tuition, nonresident:* full-time $14,696; part-time $612 per credit. *Required fees:* full-time $444; $75 per term part-time. Full-time tuition and fees vary according to course level, location, program, and student level. Part-time tuition and fees vary according to course level, course load, location, program, and student level. *College room and board:* $6810; *room only:* $3830. Room and board charges vary according to board plan and housing facility. *Payment plan:* Deferred payment.

FRESHMAN FINANCIAL AID (Fall 2003) 585 applied for aid; of those 71% were deemed to have need. 97% of freshmen with need received aid; of those 7% had need fully met. *Average percent of need met:* 62% (excluding resources awarded to replace EFC). *Average financial aid package:* $9668 (excluding resources awarded to replace EFC). 4% of all full-time freshmen had no need and received non-need-based gift aid.

UNDERGRADUATE FINANCIAL AID (Fall 2003) 1,513 applied for aid; of those 76% were deemed to have need. 98% of undergraduates with need received aid; of those 8% had need fully met. *Average percent of need met:* 65% (excluding resources awarded to replace EFC). *Average financial aid package:* $10,354 (excluding resources awarded to replace EFC). 5% of all full-time undergraduates had no need and received non-need-based gift aid.

GIFT AID (NEED-BASED) *Total amount:* $3,843,940 (39% federal, 46% state, 15% institutional). *Receiving aid:* Freshmen: 37% (281); All full-time undergraduates: 39% (784). *Average award:* Freshmen: $4147; Undergraduates: $4151. *Scholarships, grants, and awards:* Federal Pell, FSEOG, state, private, college/university gift aid from institutional funds.

GIFT AID (NON-NEED-BASED) *Total amount:* $787,325 (39% institutional, 61% external sources). *Receiving aid:* Freshmen: 17% (127); Undergraduates: 19% (378). *Average Award: Freshmen:* $3116; *Undergraduates:* $3329. **Scholarships, grants, and awards by category:** *Academic Interests/Achievement:* general

academic interests/achievements. *Special Characteristics:* general special characteristics. *Tuition waivers:* Full or partial for employees or children of employees, senior citizens.

LOANS *Student loans:* $5,765,524 (60% need-based, 40% non-need-based). 70% of past graduating class borrowed through all loan programs. *Average indebtedness per student:* $18,600. *Average need-based loan:* Freshmen: $2665; Undergraduates: $3295. *Parent loans:* $2,309,490 (100% non-need-based). *Programs:* FFEL (Subsidized and Unsubsidized Stafford, PLUS), Perkins, college/university, alternative loans.

WORK-STUDY *Federal work-study:* Total amount: $88,226; 81 jobs averaging $1089. *State or other work-study/employment:* Total amount: $88,121 (100% need-based). 25 part-time jobs averaging $5987.

APPLYING FOR FINANCIAL AID *Required financial aid form:* FAFSA. *Financial aid deadline:* Continuous. *Notification date:* Continuous beginning 2/15.

CONTACT Maryann Hubick, Financial Aid Coordinator, The Pennsylvania State University Berks Campus of the Berks–Lehigh Valley College, Perkins Student Center, Room 6, Reading, PA 19610-6009, 610-396-6071. *Fax:* 610-396-6077. *E-mail:* mxh61@psu.edu.

THE PENNSYLVANIA STATE UNIVERSITY HARRISBURG CAMPUS OF THE CAPITAL COLLEGE
Middletown, PA

Tuition & fees (PA res): $10,016   Average undergraduate aid package: $12,442

ABOUT THE INSTITUTION State-related, coed. Awards: associate, bachelor's, master's, and doctoral degrees and post-bachelor's certificates. 28 undergraduate majors. Total enrollment: 3,729. Undergraduates: 2,047. Freshmen: 164. Federal methodology is used as a basis for awarding need-based institutional aid.

UNDERGRADUATE EXPENSES for 2004–05 *Application fee:* $50. *Tuition, state resident:* full-time $9582; part-time $399 per credit. *Tuition, nonresident:* full-time $15,466; part-time $644 per credit. *Required fees:* full-time $434; $73 per term part-time. Full-time tuition and fees vary according to course level, location, program, and student level. Part-time tuition and fees vary according to course level, course load, location, program, and student level. *College room and board:* $7650; *room only:* $4670. Room and board charges vary according to board plan and housing facility. *Payment plan:* Deferred payment.

FRESHMAN FINANCIAL AID (Fall 2003) 49 applied for aid; of those 78% were deemed to have need. 97% of freshmen with need received aid; of those 16% had need fully met. *Average percent of need met:* 65% (excluding resources awarded to replace EFC). *Average financial aid package:* $9559 (excluding resources awarded to replace EFC). 5% of all full-time freshmen had no need and received non-need-based gift aid.

UNDERGRADUATE FINANCIAL AID (Fall 2003) 991 applied for aid; of those 87% were deemed to have need. 99% of undergraduates with need received aid; of those 11% had need fully met. *Average percent of need met:* 72% (excluding resources awarded to replace EFC). *Average financial aid package:* $12,442 (excluding resources awarded to replace EFC). 4% of all full-time undergraduates had no need and received non-need-based gift aid.

GIFT AID (NEED-BASED) *Total amount:* $3,676,608 (48% federal, 46% state, 6% institutional). *Receiving aid:* Freshmen: 43% (24); All full-time undergraduates: 53% (653). *Average award:* Freshmen: $3256; Undergraduates: $4530. *Scholarships, grants, and awards:* Federal Pell, FSEOG, state, private, college/university gift aid from institutional funds.

GIFT AID (NON-NEED-BASED) *Total amount:* $538,705 (36% institutional, 64% external sources). *Receiving aid:* Freshmen: 30% (17); Undergraduates: 22% (267). *Average Award: Freshmen:* $3146; *Undergraduates:* $4704. **Scholarships, grants, and awards by category:** *Academic Interests/Achievement:* general academic interests/achievements. *Special Characteristics:* general special characteristics. *Tuition waivers:* Full or partial for employees or children of employees, senior citizens. *ROTC:* Army cooperative.

LOANS *Student loans:* $6,896,701 (59% need-based, 41% non-need-based). 70% of past graduating class borrowed through all loan programs. *Average indebtedness per student:* $18,600. *Average need-based loan:* Freshmen: $2777; Undergraduates: $4655. *Parent loans:* $675,857 (100% non-need-based). *Programs:* FFEL (Subsidized and Unsubsidized Stafford, PLUS), Perkins, college/university, alternative loans.

WORK-STUDY *Federal work-study:* Total amount: $100,574; 80 jobs averaging $1206. *State or other work-study/employment:* Total amount: $7420 (100% need-based). 3 part-time jobs averaging $3710.

APPLYING FOR FINANCIAL AID *Required financial aid form:* FAFSA. *Financial aid deadline:* Continuous. *Notification date:* Continuous beginning 2/15.

CONTACT Ms. Carolyn Julian, Student Aid Adviser, The Pennsylvania State University Harrisburg Campus of the Capital College, W112 Olmstead, 777 West Harrisburg Pike, Middletown, PA 17057-4898, 717-948-6307 or toll-free 800-222-2056. *Fax:* 717-948-6008. *E-mail:* czb3@psu.edu.

THE PENNSYLVANIA STATE UNIVERSITY, LEHIGH VALLEY CAMPUS OF THE BERKS-LEHIGH VALLEY COLLEGE
Fogelsville, PA

Tuition & fees (PA res): $9624   **Average undergraduate aid package: $9068**

ABOUT THE INSTITUTION State-related, coed. Awards: associate and bachelor's degrees. 119 undergraduate majors. Total enrollment: 680. Undergraduates: 644. Freshmen: 166. Federal methodology is used as a basis for awarding need-based institutional aid.

UNDERGRADUATE EXPENSES for 2004–05 *Application fee:* $50. *Tuition, state resident:* full-time $9180; part-time $371 per credit. *Tuition, nonresident:* full-time $14,040; part-time $585 per credit. *Required fees:* full-time $444; $75 per term part-time. Full-time tuition and fees vary according to course level, location, program, and student level. Part-time tuition and fees vary according to course level, course load, location, program, and student level. *Payment plan:* Deferred payment.

FRESHMAN FINANCIAL AID (Fall 2003) 158 applied for aid; of those 74% were deemed to have need. 98% of freshmen with need received aid; of those 4% had need fully met. *Average percent of need met:* 61% (excluding resources awarded to replace EFC). *Average financial aid package:* $7962 (excluding resources awarded to replace EFC). 4% of all full-time freshmen had no need and received non-need-based gift aid.

UNDERGRADUATE FINANCIAL AID (Fall 2003) 391 applied for aid; of those 77% were deemed to have need. 99% of undergraduates with need received aid; of those 7% had need fully met. *Average percent of need met:* 67% (excluding resources awarded to replace EFC). *Average financial aid package:* $9068 (excluding resources awarded to replace EFC). 6% of all full-time undergraduates had no need and received non-need-based gift aid.

GIFT AID (NEED-BASED) *Total amount:* $1,240,780 (45% federal, 41% state, 14% institutional). *Receiving aid:* Freshmen: 52% (99); All full-time undergraduates: 47% (244). *Average award:* Freshmen: $4067; Undergraduates: $4017. *Scholarships, grants, and awards:* Federal Pell, FSEOG, state, private, college/university gift aid from institutional funds.

GIFT AID (NON-NEED-BASED) *Total amount:* $180,124 (59% institutional, 41% external sources). *Receiving aid:* Freshmen: 15% (28); Undergraduates: 17% (89). *Average Award:* Freshmen: $940; *Undergraduates:* $1379. *Scholarships, grants, and awards by category:* Academic Interests/Achievement: general academic interests/achievements. *Special Characteristics:* general special characteristics. *Tuition waivers:* Full or partial for employees or children of employees, senior citizens.

LOANS *Student loans:* $1,577,238 (61% need-based, 39% non-need-based). 70% of past graduating class borrowed through all loan programs. *Average indebtedness per student:* $18,600. *Average need-based loan:* Freshmen: $2494; Undergraduates: $3196. *Parent loans:* $266,175 (100% non-need-based). *Programs:* FFEL (Subsidized and Unsubsidized Stafford, PLUS), Perkins, college/university, alternative loans.

WORK-STUDY *Federal work-study:* Total amount: $38,022; 31 jobs averaging $1172. *State or other work-study/employment:* Part-time jobs available.

APPLYING FOR FINANCIAL AID *Required financial aid form:* FAFSA. *Financial aid deadline:* Continuous. *Notification date:* Continuous beginning 2/15.

CONTACT Ms. Joan Willertz, Financial Aid Coordinator, The Pennsylvania State University, Lehigh Valley Campus of the Berks-Lehigh Valley College, Room 103, Academic Building, Fogelsville, PA 18051, 610-285-5000. *Fax:* 610-285-5220. *E-mail:* jcw4@psu.edu.

THE PENNSYLVANIA STATE UNIVERSITY SCHUYLKILL CAMPUS OF THE CAPITAL COLLEGE
Schuylkill Haven, PA

Tuition & fees (PA res): $9604   **Average undergraduate aid package: $11,204**

ABOUT THE INSTITUTION State-related, coed. Awards: associate and bachelor's degrees (bachelor's degree programs completed at the Harrisburg campus). 124 undergraduate majors. Total enrollment: 969. Undergraduates: 924. Freshmen: 277. Federal methodology is used as a basis for awarding need-based institutional aid.

UNDERGRADUATE EXPENSES for 2004–05 *Application fee:* $50. *Tuition, state resident:* full-time $9180; part-time $371 per credit. *Tuition, nonresident:* full-time $14,040; part-time $585 per credit. *Required fees:* full-time $424; $71 per term part-time. Full-time tuition and fees vary according to course level, location, program, and student level. Part-time tuition and fees vary according to course level, course load, location, program, and student level. *College room and board: room only:* $3996. Room and board charges vary according to board plan and housing facility. *Payment plan:* Deferred payment.

FRESHMAN FINANCIAL AID (Fall 2003) 267 applied for aid; of those 83% were deemed to have need. 98% of freshmen with need received aid; of those 4% had need fully met. *Average percent of need met:* 61% (excluding resources awarded to replace EFC). *Average financial aid package:* $10,846 (excluding resources awarded to replace EFC). 5% of all full-time freshmen had no need and received non-need-based gift aid.

UNDERGRADUATE FINANCIAL AID (Fall 2003) 665 applied for aid; of those 85% were deemed to have need. 99% of undergraduates with need received aid; of those 7% had need fully met. *Average percent of need met:* 68% (excluding resources awarded to replace EFC). *Average financial aid package:* $11,204 (excluding resources awarded to replace EFC). 4% of all full-time undergraduates had no need and received non-need-based gift aid.

GIFT AID (NEED-BASED) *Total amount:* $2,564,768 (48% federal, 35% state, 17% institutional). *Receiving aid:* Freshmen: 63% (185); All full-time undergraduates: 65% (475). *Average award:* Freshmen: $4514; Undergraduates: $4384. *Scholarships, grants, and awards:* Federal Pell, FSEOG, state, private, college/university gift aid from institutional funds.

GIFT AID (NON-NEED-BASED) *Total amount:* $382,151 (42% institutional, 58% external sources). *Receiving aid:* Freshmen: 26% (77); Undergraduates: 26% (194). *Average Award:* Freshmen: $1219; *Undergraduates:* $2087. *Scholarships, grants, and awards by category:* Academic Interests/Achievement: general academic interests/achievements. *Special Characteristics:* general special characteristics. *Tuition waivers:* Full or partial for employees or children of employees, senior citizens.

LOANS *Student loans:* $2,958,103 (60% need-based, 40% non-need-based). 70% of past graduating class borrowed through all loan programs. *Average indebtedness per student:* $18,600. *Average need-based loan:* Freshmen: $2682; Undergraduates: $3285. *Parent loans:* $740,388 (100% non-need-based). *Programs:* FFEL (Subsidized and Unsubsidized Stafford, PLUS), Perkins, college/university, alternative loans.

WORK-STUDY *Federal work-study:* Total amount: $126,992; 115 jobs averaging $1104. *State or other work-study/employment:* Total amount: $20,629 (100% need-based). 7 part-time jobs averaging $2947.

APPLYING FOR FINANCIAL AID *Required financial aid form:* FAFSA. *Financial aid deadline:* Continuous. *Notification date:* Continuous beginning 2/15.

CONTACT Tammie Durham, Student Aid and Admissions Coordinator, The Pennsylvania State University Schuylkill Campus of the Capital College, 200 University Drive, Schuylkill Haven, PA 17972-2208, 570-385-6244. *Fax:* 570-385-3672. *E-mail:* tld145@psu.edu.

THE PENNSYLVANIA STATE UNIVERSITY UNIVERSITY PARK CAMPUS
State College, PA

Tuition & fees (PA res): $10,856   **Average undergraduate aid package: $12,802**

ABOUT THE INSTITUTION State-related, coed. Awards: associate, bachelor's, master's, and doctoral degrees and post-bachelor's certificates. 124 undergraduate majors. Total enrollment: 41,289. Undergraduates: 34,824. Freshmen: 5,907. Federal methodology is used as a basis for awarding need-based institutional aid.

UNDERGRADUATE EXPENSES for 2004–05 *Application fee:* $50. *Tuition, state resident:* full-time $10,408; part-time $434 per credit. *Tuition, nonresident:* full-time $20,336; part-time $847 per credit. *Required fees:* full-time $448; $75 per term part-time. *College room and board:* $6230; *room only:* $3250.

FRESHMAN FINANCIAL AID (Fall 2003) 4472 applied for aid; of those 65% were deemed to have need. 97% of freshmen with need received aid; of those 9% had need fully met. *Average percent of need met:* 66% (excluding resources awarded to replace EFC). *Average financial aid package:* $12,630 (excluding resources awarded to replace EFC). 13% of all full-time freshmen had no need and received non-need-based gift aid.

UNDERGRADUATE FINANCIAL AID (Fall 2003) 21,940 applied for aid; of those 76% were deemed to have need. 98% of undergraduates with need received aid; of those 12% had need fully met. *Average percent of need met:* 70% (excluding resources awarded to replace EFC). *Average financial aid package:* $12,802 (excluding resources awarded to replace EFC). 11% of all full-time undergraduates had no need and received non-need-based gift aid.

GIFT AID (NEED-BASED) *Total amount:* $62,369,051 (35% federal, 37% state, 28% institutional). *Receiving aid:* Freshmen: 27% (1,609); All full-time undergraduates: 30% (10,054). *Average award:* Freshmen: $4707; Undergraduates: $4381. *Scholarships, grants, and awards:* Federal Pell, FSEOG, state, private, college/university gift aid from institutional funds.

GIFT AID (NON-NEED-BASED) *Total amount:* $23,300,164 (67% institutional, 33% external sources). *Receiving aid:* Freshmen: 23% (1,399); Undergraduates: 20% (6,742). *Average Award:* Freshmen: $3807; Undergraduates: $3887. *Scholarships, grants, and awards by category: Academic Interests/Achievement:* general academic interests/achievements. *Special Characteristics:* general special characteristics. *ROTC:* Army, Naval, Air Force.

LOANS *Student loans:* $95,293,186 (65% need-based, 35% non-need-based). 70% of past graduating class borrowed through all loan programs. *Average indebtedness per student:* $18,600. *Average need-based loan:* Freshmen: $2807; Undergraduates: $4221. *Parent loans:* $47,102,830 (100% non-need-based). *Programs:* FFEL (Subsidized and Unsubsidized Stafford, PLUS), Perkins, college/university, alternative loans.

WORK-STUDY *Federal work-study:* Total amount: $2,850,125; 2,125 jobs averaging $1327. *State or other work-study/employment:* Total amount: $978,031 (100% need-based). 286 part-time jobs averaging $4845.

ATHLETIC AWARDS *Total amount:* $8,098,656 (100% non-need-based).

APPLYING FOR FINANCIAL AID *Required financial aid form:* FAFSA. *Financial aid deadline:* Continuous. *Notification date:* Continuous beginning 2/15.

CONTACT Ms. Anna Griswold, Assistant Vice Provost for Student Aid, The Pennsylvania State University University Park Campus, 311 Shields Building, University Park, PA 16802, 814-863-0507. *Fax:* 814-863-0322. *E-mail:* amg5@psu.edu.

PEPPERDINE UNIVERSITY
Malibu, CA

Tuition & fees: $28,720	Average undergraduate aid package: $26,482

ABOUT THE INSTITUTION Independent religious, coed. Awards: bachelor's, master's, doctoral, and first professional degrees and post-master's certificates. 43 undergraduate majors. Total enrollment: 7,919. Undergraduates: 3,201. Freshmen: 727. Federal methodology is used as a basis for awarding need-based institutional aid.

UNDERGRADUATE EXPENSES for 2004–05 *Application fee:* $55. *Comprehensive fee:* $37,360 includes full-time tuition ($28,630), mandatory fees ($90), and room and board ($8640). *College room only:* $5540. Room and board charges vary according to board plan and housing facility. *Part-time tuition:* $890 per unit. *Payment plans:* Installment, deferred payment.

FRESHMAN FINANCIAL AID (Fall 2004, est.) 499 applied for aid; of those 84% were deemed to have need. 98% of freshmen with need received aid; of those 44% had need fully met. *Average percent of need met:* 90% (excluding resources awarded to replace EFC). *Average financial aid package:* $27,105 (excluding resources awarded to replace EFC). 7% of all full-time freshmen had no need and received non-need-based gift aid.

UNDERGRADUATE FINANCIAL AID (Fall 2004, est.) 1,899 applied for aid; of those 87% were deemed to have need. 99% of undergraduates with need received aid; of those 27% had need fully met. *Average percent of need met:* 87% (excluding resources awarded to replace EFC). *Average financial aid*

package: $26,482 (excluding resources awarded to replace EFC). 10% of all full-time undergraduates had no need and received non-need-based gift aid.

GIFT AID (NEED-BASED) *Total amount:* $28,097,869 (11% federal, 10% state, 68% institutional, 11% external sources). *Receiving aid:* Freshmen: 52% (379); All full-time undergraduates: 56% (1,492). *Average award:* Freshmen: $19,996; Undergraduates: $19,351. *Scholarships, grants, and awards:* Federal Pell, FSEOG, state, private, college/university gift aid from institutional funds.

GIFT AID (NON-NEED-BASED) *Total amount:* $8,229,860 (85% institutional, 15% external sources). *Receiving aid:* Freshmen: 10% (74); Undergraduates: 15% (402). *Average Award:* Freshmen: $21,569; Undergraduates: $19,024. *Scholarships, grants, and awards by category: Academic Interests/Achievement:* 394 awards ($888,794 total): biological sciences, business, communication, education, general academic interests/achievements, humanities, international studies, religion/biblical studies, social sciences. *Creative Arts/Performance:* 1,049 awards ($1,007,169 total): art/fine arts, debating, journalism/publications, music, performing arts, theater/drama. *Special Characteristics:* general special characteristics. *Tuition waivers:* Full or partial for employees or children of employees. *ROTC:* Army cooperative, Air Force cooperative.

LOANS *Student loans:* $14,281,371 (80% need-based, 20% non-need-based). 59% of past graduating class borrowed through all loan programs. *Average indebtedness per student:* $29,148. *Average need-based loan:* Freshmen: $6114; Undergraduates: $6532. *Parent loans:* $11,146,760 (65% need-based, 35% non-need-based). *Programs:* FFEL (Subsidized and Unsubsidized Stafford, PLUS), Perkins, college/university.

WORK-STUDY *Federal work-study:* Total amount: $985,000; 785 jobs averaging $1809. *State or other work-study/employment:* Total amount: $611,082 (18% need-based, 82% non-need-based). 284 part-time jobs averaging $1999.

ATHLETIC AWARDS *Total amount:* $3,557,130 (15% need-based, 85% non-need-based).

APPLYING FOR FINANCIAL AID *Required financial aid forms:* FAFSA, institution's own form. *Financial aid deadline:* 2/15 (priority: 2/15). *Notification date:* 4/15. Students must reply within 2 weeks of notification.

CONTACT Janet Lockhart, Director of Financial Assistance, Pepperdine University, 24255 Pacific Coast Highway, Malibu, CA 90263-4301, 310-506-4301. *Fax:* 310-506-4746. *E-mail:* finaid2@pepperdine.edu.

PERU STATE COLLEGE
Peru, NE

Tuition & fees (NE res): $3534	Average undergraduate aid package: N/A

ABOUT THE INSTITUTION State-supported, coed. Awards: bachelor's and master's degrees. 44 undergraduate majors. Total enrollment: 1,683. Undergraduates: 1,493. Freshmen: 219. Federal methodology is used as a basis for awarding need-based institutional aid.

UNDERGRADUATE EXPENSES for 2004–05 *Tuition, area resident:* part-time $95 per credit hour. *Tuition, state resident:* full-time $2850; part-time $190 per credit hour. *Tuition, nonresident:* full-time $5700. Full-time tuition and fees vary according to course load, location, and reciprocity agreements. Part-time tuition and fees vary according to course load, location, and reciprocity agreements. *College room and board:* $4486. Room and board charges vary according to board plan and housing facility. *Payment plan:* Deferred payment.

GIFT AID (NEED-BASED) *Total amount:* $1,329,196 (90% federal, 10% state). *Scholarships, grants, and awards:* Federal Pell, FSEOG, state, college/university gift aid from institutional funds.

GIFT AID (NON-NEED-BASED) *Total amount:* $752,702 (54% institutional, 46% external sources). *Scholarships, grants, and awards by category: Academic Interests/Achievement:* biological sciences, business, computer science, education, English, general academic interests/achievements, humanities, mathematics, physical sciences, premedicine, social sciences. *Creative Arts/Performance:* art/fine arts, music. *Special Achievements/Activities:* cheerleading/drum major, leadership, memberships. *Special Characteristics:* adult students, children of faculty/staff, ethnic background, first-generation college students, international students, local/state students, out-of-state students, previous college experience, veterans, veterans' children. *Tuition waivers:* Full or partial for employees or children of employees. *ROTC:* Army cooperative, Air Force cooperative.

LOANS *Student loans:* $3,127,087 (55% need-based, 45% non-need-based). *Parent loans:* $142,693 (100% non-need-based). *Programs:* FFEL (Subsidized and Unsubsidized Stafford, PLUS).

WORK-STUDY *Federal work-study:* Total amount: $125,000; jobs available.

ATHLETIC AWARDS *Total amount:* $217,691 (100% non-need-based).

APPLYING FOR FINANCIAL AID *Required financial aid forms:* FAFSA, institution's own form. *Financial aid deadline (priority):* 3/1. *Notification date:* Continuous beginning 3/15. Students must reply within 2 weeks of notification.
CONTACT Diana Lind, Director of Financial Aid, Peru State College, PO Box 10, Peru, NE 68421, 402-872-2228 or toll-free 800-742-4412 (in-state). *Fax:* 402-872-2419. *E-mail:* finaid@oakmail.peru.edu.

PFEIFFER UNIVERSITY
Misenheimer, NC

Tuition & fees: $14,570	Average undergraduate aid package: $11,678

ABOUT THE INSTITUTION Independent United Methodist, coed. Awards: bachelor's and master's degrees. 45 undergraduate majors. Total enrollment: 2,027. Undergraduates: 1,188. Freshmen: 170. Institutional methodology is used as a basis for awarding need-based institutional aid.
UNDERGRADUATE EXPENSES for 2004–05 *Application fee:* $25. *Comprehensive fee:* $20,400 includes full-time tuition ($14,570) and room and board ($5830). *College room only:* $3030. Full-time tuition and fees vary according to course load. Room and board charges vary according to housing facility. *Part-time tuition:* $330 per credit hour. Part-time tuition and fees vary according to course load. *Payment plan:* Installment.
GIFT AID (NEED-BASED) *Total amount:* $6,438,340 (21% federal, 29% state, 45% institutional, 5% external sources). *Receiving aid:* Freshmen: 81% (158); All full-time undergraduates: 69% (546). *Average award:* Freshmen: $9140; Undergraduates: $8567. *Scholarships, grants, and awards:* Federal Pell, FSEOG, state, private, college/university gift aid from institutional funds, United Negro College Fund.
GIFT AID (NON-NEED-BASED) *Total amount:* $1,292,777 (33% state, 51% institutional, 16% external sources). *Receiving aid:* Freshmen: 15% (30); Undergraduates: 12% (97). *Average Award:* Freshmen: $5932; Undergraduates: $5699. *Scholarships, grants, and awards by category:* Academic Interests/Achievement: general academic interests/achievements. Creative Arts/Performance: music. Special Achievements/Activities: leadership, religious involvement. Special Characteristics: children and siblings of alumni. *Tuition waivers:* Full or partial for employees or children of employees. *ROTC:* Army cooperative.
LOANS *Student loans:* $4,870,829 (67% need-based, 33% non-need-based). 77% of past graduating class borrowed through all loan programs. *Average indebtedness per student:* $16,700. *Average need-based loan:* Freshmen: $2895; Undergraduates: $3557. *Parent loans:* $672,629 (26% need-based, 74% non-need-based). *Programs:* FFEL (Subsidized and Unsubsidized Stafford, PLUS), Perkins, state, college/university.
ATHLETIC AWARDS *Total amount:* $717,761 (55% need-based, 45% non-need-based).
APPLYING FOR FINANCIAL AID *Required financial aid forms:* FAFSA, state aid form, noncustodial (divorced/separated) parent's statement. *Financial aid deadline (priority):* 4/15. *Notification date:* Continuous beginning 3/1.
CONTACT Amy Brown, Director of Financial Aid, Pfeiffer University, PO Box 960, Misenheimer, NC 28109, 704-463-1360 Ext. 2074 or toll-free 800-338-2060. *Fax:* 704-463-1363. *E-mail:* abrown@pfieffer.edu.

PHILADELPHIA BIBLICAL UNIVERSITY
Langhorne, PA

Tuition & fees: $14,500	Average undergraduate aid package: $10,811

ABOUT THE INSTITUTION Independent nondenominational, coed. Awards: bachelor's, master's, and first professional degrees. 11 undergraduate majors. Total enrollment: 1,372. Undergraduates: 1,022. Freshmen: 185. Federal methodology is used as a basis for awarding need-based institutional aid.
UNDERGRADUATE EXPENSES for 2005–06 *Application fee:* $25. *Comprehensive fee:* $20,600 includes full-time tuition ($14,180), mandatory fees ($320), and room and board ($6100). *College room only:* $3100. Full-time tuition and fees vary according to course load, location, and program. Room and board charges vary according to board plan, housing facility, and location. *Part-time tuition:* $427 per credit. Part-time tuition and fees vary according to course load, location, and program. *Payment plan:* Installment.
FRESHMAN FINANCIAL AID (Fall 2004, est.) 154 applied for aid; of those 94% were deemed to have need. 100% of freshmen with need received aid; of those 17% had need fully met. *Average percent of need met:* 68% (excluding resources

awarded to replace EFC). *Average financial aid package:* $10,346 (excluding resources awarded to replace EFC). 10% of all full-time freshmen had no need and received non-need-based gift aid.
UNDERGRADUATE FINANCIAL AID (Fall 2004, est.) 696 applied for aid; of those ·92% were deemed to have need. 100% of undergraduates with need received aid; of those 20% had need fully met. *Average percent of need met:* 70% (excluding resources awarded to replace EFC). *Average financial aid package:* $10,811 (excluding resources awarded to replace EFC). 15% of all full-time undergraduates had no need and received non-need-based gift aid.
GIFT AID (NEED-BASED) *Total amount:* $5,130,733 (20% federal, 11% state, 64% institutional, 5% external sources). *Receiving aid:* Freshmen: 74% (134); All full-time undergraduates: 65% (590). *Average award:* Freshmen: $7984; Undergraduates: $7796. *Scholarships, grants, and awards:* Federal Pell, FSEOG, state, private, college/university gift aid from institutional funds.
GIFT AID (NON-NEED-BASED) *Total amount:* $731,074 (6% federal, 3% state, 84% institutional, 7% external sources). *Receiving aid:* Freshmen: 3% (6); Undergraduates: 4% (32). *Average Award:* Freshmen: $7462; Undergraduates: $7064. *Scholarships, grants, and awards by category:* Academic Interests/Achievement: 275 awards ($1,131,645 total): general academic interests/achievements. Creative Arts/Performance: 57 awards ($88,170 total): music. Special Achievements/Activities: 155 awards ($227,817 total): general special achievements/activities, leadership, religious involvement. Special Characteristics: 161 awards ($680,414 total): children and siblings of alumni, children of faculty/staff, international students, relatives of clergy, siblings of current students. *Tuition waivers:* Full or partial for children of alumni, employees or children of employees. *ROTC:* Air Force cooperative.
LOANS *Student loans:* $3,630,679 (76% need-based, 24% non-need-based). 67% of past graduating class borrowed through all loan programs. *Average indebtedness per student:* $13,700. *Average need-based loan:* Freshmen: $3369; Undergraduates: $4126. *Parent loans:* $950,441 (35% need-based, 65% non-need-based). *Programs:* FFEL (Subsidized and Unsubsidized Stafford, PLUS).
WORK-STUDY *Federal work-study:* Total amount: $111,825; 96 jobs averaging $1247.
APPLYING FOR FINANCIAL AID *Required financial aid form:* FAFSA. *Financial aid deadline (priority):* 5/1. *Notification date:* Continuous beginning 3/15.
CONTACT William Kellaris, Director of Financial Aid, Philadelphia Biblical University, 200 Manor Avenue, Langhorne, PA 19047-2990, 215-702-4243 or toll-free 800-366-0049. *E-mail:* bkellaris@pbu.edu.

PHILADELPHIA UNIVERSITY
Philadelphia, PA

Tuition & fees: $21,010	Average undergraduate aid package: $14,862

ABOUT THE INSTITUTION Independent, coed. Awards: associate, bachelor's, master's, and doctoral degrees and post-bachelor's and post-master's certificates. 32 undergraduate majors. Total enrollment: 3,212. Undergraduates: 2,695. Freshmen: 669. Federal methodology is used as a basis for awarding need-based institutional aid.
UNDERGRADUATE EXPENSES for 2004–05 *Application fee:* $35. *Comprehensive fee:* $28,792 includes full-time tuition ($20,940), mandatory fees ($70), and room and board ($7782). *College room only:* $3834. Full-time tuition and fees vary according to program. Room and board charges vary according to board plan and housing facility. *Part-time tuition:* $676 per credit. Part-time tuition and fees vary according to class time and program. *Payment plans:* Installment, deferred payment.
FRESHMAN FINANCIAL AID (Fall 2004, est.) 594 applied for aid; of those 87% were deemed to have need. 100% of freshmen with need received aid; of those 11% had need fully met. *Average percent of need met:* 76% (excluding resources awarded to replace EFC). *Average financial aid package:* $16,063 (excluding resources awarded to replace EFC). 22% of all full-time freshmen had no need and received non-need-based gift aid.
UNDERGRADUATE FINANCIAL AID (Fall 2004, est.) 1,927 applied for aid; of those 86% were deemed to have need. 100% of undergraduates with need received aid; of those 11% had need fully met. *Average percent of need met:* 71% (excluding resources awarded to replace EFC). *Average financial aid package:* $14,862 (excluding resources awarded to replace EFC). 25% of all full-time undergraduates had no need and received non-need-based gift aid.
GIFT AID (NEED-BASED) *Total amount:* $15,097,917 (12% federal, 10% state, 75% institutional, 3% external sources). *Receiving aid:* Freshmen: 76% (512); All full-time undergraduates: 70% (1,652). *Average award:* Freshmen: $11,275; Undergraduates: $9499. *Scholarships, grants, and awards:* Federal Pell, FSEOG,

state, private, college/university gift aid from institutional funds, gifts scholarships from outside sources (non-endowed) for which university chooses recipient, also i.

GIFT AID (NON-NEED-BASED) *Total amount:* $2,564,093 (97% institutional, 3% external sources). *Receiving aid:* Freshmen: 6% (40); Undergraduates: 4% (106). *Average Award:* Freshmen: $4498; Undergraduates: $4058. *Scholarships, grants, and awards by category:* Academic Interests/Achievement: 2,163 awards ($8,814,180 total): general academic interests/achievements. *Tuition waivers:* Full or partial for employees or children of employees.

LOANS *Student loans:* $13,560,153 (75% need-based, 25% non-need-based). 74% of past graduating class borrowed through all loan programs. *Average indebtedness per student:* $24,422. *Average need-based loan:* Freshmen: $3117; Undergraduates: $4057. *Parent loans:* $7,188,845 (32% need-based, 68% non-need-based). *Programs:* FFEL (Subsidized and Unsubsidized Stafford, PLUS), Perkins, private loans.

WORK-STUDY *Federal work-study:* Total amount: $1,925,500; 850 jobs averaging $2000. *State or other work-study/employment:* Total amount: $293,373 (66% need-based, 34% non-need-based). Part-time jobs available.

ATHLETIC AWARDS *Total amount:* $1,445,224 (32% need-based, 68% non-need-based).

APPLYING FOR FINANCIAL AID *Required financial aid form:* FAFSA. *Financial aid deadline:* 4/15. *Notification date:* Continuous beginning 2/1. Students must reply within 3 weeks of notification.

CONTACT Ms. Lisa J. Cooper, Director of Financial Aid, Philadelphia University, School House Lane and Henry Avenue, Philadelphia, PA 19144-5497, 215-951-2940. Fax: 215-951-2907.

PHILANDER SMITH COLLEGE
Little Rock, AR

CONTACT Director of Financial Aid, Philander Smith College, 812 West 13th Street, Little Rock, AR 72202-3799, 501-370-5270 or toll-free 800-446-6772.

PIEDMONT BAPTIST COLLEGE
Winston-Salem, NC

CONTACT Ronnie Mathis, Director of Financial Aid, Piedmont Baptist College, 716 Franklin Street, Winston-Salem, NC 27101-5197, 336-725-8344 Ext. 2322 or toll-free 800-937-5097. Fax: 336-725-5522. E-mail: mathisr@pbc.edu.

PIEDMONT COLLEGE
Demorest, GA

Tuition & fees: $13,500	Average undergraduate aid package: $11,682

ABOUT THE INSTITUTION Independent religious, coed. Awards: bachelor's and master's degrees and post-master's certificates. 29 undergraduate majors. Total enrollment: 2,222. Undergraduates: 1,096. Freshmen: 180. Both federal and institutional methodology are used as a basis for awarding need-based institutional aid.

UNDERGRADUATE EXPENSES for 2004–05 *Comprehensive fee:* $18,200 includes full-time tuition ($13,500) and room and board ($4700). *College room only:* $2450. Full-time tuition and fees vary according to course load and program. Room and board charges vary according to housing facility. *Part-time tuition:* $562.50 per hour. Part-time tuition and fees vary according to course load and program. *Payment plan:* Installment.

GIFT AID (NEED-BASED) *Total amount:* $1,706,884 (65% federal, 33% institutional, 2% external sources). *Receiving aid:* Freshmen: 60% (100); All full-time undergraduates: 54% (507). *Average award:* Freshmen: $2498; Undergraduates: $2814. *Scholarships, grants, and awards:* Federal Pell, FSEOG, state, private, college/university gift aid from institutional funds.

GIFT AID (NON-NEED-BASED) *Total amount:* $6,127,040 (30% state, 66% institutional, 4% external sources). *Receiving aid:* Freshmen: 57% (96); Undergraduates: 70% (657). *Average Award:* Freshmen: $2486; Undergraduates: $2592. *Scholarships, grants, and awards by category:* Academic Interests/Achievement: 560 awards ($1,504,520 total): biological sciences, education, English, foreign languages, general academic interests/achievements, health fields, humanities, mathematics, premedicine, religion/biblical studies. Creative Arts/Performance: 58 awards ($66,000 total): art/fine arts, music, theater/drama. Special Achievements/Activities: 208 awards ($785,146 total): leadership.

Special Characteristics: 303 awards ($2,136,640 total): adult students, children of faculty/staff, international students, out-of-state students. *Tuition waivers:* Full or partial for employees or children of employees.

LOANS *Student loans:* $3,711,673 (61% need-based, 39% non-need-based). 68% of past graduating class borrowed through all loan programs. *Average indebtedness per student:* $15,537. *Average need-based loan:* Freshmen: $1923; Undergraduates: $5229. *Parent loans:* $1,224,475 (100% non-need-based). *Programs:* Federal Direct (Subsidized and Unsubsidized Stafford, PLUS), state.

APPLYING FOR FINANCIAL AID *Required financial aid forms:* FAFSA, state aid form. *Financial aid deadline (priority):* 5/1. *Notification date:* Continuous. Students must reply within 2 weeks of notification.

CONTACT Mrs. Kim Lovell, Director of Financial Aid, Piedmont College, PO Box 10, Demorest, GA 30535-0010, 706-778-3000 Ext. 1191 or toll-free 800-277-7020. Fax: 706-776-2811. E-mail: klovell@piedmont.edu.

PIKEVILLE COLLEGE
Pikeville, KY

Tuition & fees: $10,500	Average undergraduate aid package: $12,832

ABOUT THE INSTITUTION Independent religious, coed. Awards: associate, bachelor's, and first professional degrees and post-bachelor's certificates. 24 undergraduate majors. Total enrollment: 1,066. Undergraduates: 801. Freshmen: 177. Federal methodology is used as a basis for awarding need-based institutional aid.

UNDERGRADUATE EXPENSES for 2004–05 *Comprehensive fee:* $15,500 includes full-time tuition ($10,500) and room and board ($5000). *College room only:* $2500. Full-time tuition and fees vary according to course load. *Part-time tuition:* $438 per credit hour. *Payment plan:* Installment.

FRESHMAN FINANCIAL AID (Fall 2004, est.) 175 applied for aid; of those 85% were deemed to have need. 100% of freshmen with need received aid; of those 70% had need fully met. *Average percent of need met:* 97% (excluding resources awarded to replace EFC). *Average financial aid package:* $13,107 (excluding resources awarded to replace EFC). 10% of all full-time freshmen had no need and received non-need-based gift aid.

UNDERGRADUATE FINANCIAL AID (Fall 2004, est.) 743 applied for aid; of those 85% were deemed to have need. 100% of undergraduates with need received aid; of those 74% had need fully met. *Average percent of need met:* 95% (excluding resources awarded to replace EFC). *Average financial aid package:* $12,832 (excluding resources awarded to replace EFC). 8% of all full-time undergraduates had no need and received non-need-based gift aid.

GIFT AID (NEED-BASED) *Total amount:* $3,858,575 (44% federal, 49% state, 7% institutional). *Receiving aid:* Freshmen: 78% (136); All full-time undergraduates: 76% (571). *Average award:* Freshmen: $6908; Undergraduates: $6411. *Scholarships, grants, and awards:* Federal Pell, FSEOG, state, private, college/university gift aid from institutional funds.

GIFT AID (NON-NEED-BASED) *Total amount:* $2,551,781 (25% state, 72% institutional, 3% external sources). *Receiving aid:* Freshmen: 69% (120); Undergraduates: 74% (556). *Average Award:* Freshmen: $4698; Undergraduates: $4537. *Scholarships, grants, and awards by category:* Academic Interests/Achievement: 402 awards ($1,399,560 total): general academic interests/achievements. Creative Arts/Performance: 58 awards ($42,940 total): music. Special Characteristics: 36 awards ($168,670 total): children of faculty/staff, members of minority groups. *Tuition waivers:* Full or partial for employees or children of employees, senior citizens.

LOANS *Student loans:* $1,962,879 (96% need-based, 4% non-need-based). 69% of past graduating class borrowed through all loan programs. *Average indebtedness per student:* $14,012. *Average need-based loan:* Freshmen: $3030; Undergraduates: $3624. *Parent loans:* $19,726 (100% need-based). *Programs:* FFEL (Subsidized and Unsubsidized Stafford, PLUS), Perkins, college/university.

WORK-STUDY *Federal work-study:* Total amount: $335,813; 180 jobs averaging $1200.

ATHLETIC AWARDS *Total amount:* $1,055,890 (100% non-need-based).

APPLYING FOR FINANCIAL AID *Required financial aid forms:* FAFSA, institution's own form. *Financial aid deadline (priority):* 3/15. *Notification date:* Continuous beginning 1/15. Students must reply by 5/1.

CONTACT Melinda Lynch, Dean of Admissions and Student Financial Services, Pikeville College, 147 Sycamore Street, Pikeville, KY 41501, 606-218-5251 or toll-free 866-232-7700. Fax: 606-218-5255. E-mail: finaid@pc.edu.

PILLSBURY BAPTIST BIBLE COLLEGE
Owatonna, MN

CONTACT Financial Aid Administrator, Pillsbury Baptist Bible College, 315 South Grove Street, Owatonna, MN 55060-3097, 507-451-2710 or toll-free 800-747-4557. *Fax:* 507-451-6459. *E-mail:* pbbc@pillsbury.edu.

PINE MANOR COLLEGE
Chestnut Hill, MA

Tuition & fees: $14,794	Average undergraduate aid package: $14,730

ABOUT THE INSTITUTION Independent, women only. Awards: associate and bachelor's degrees. 16 undergraduate majors. Total enrollment: 478. Undergraduates: 478. Freshmen: 154. Federal methodology is used as a basis for awarding need-based institutional aid.

UNDERGRADUATE EXPENSES for 2004–05 *Application fee:* $25. *Comprehensive fee:* $23,794 includes full-time tuition ($14,544), mandatory fees ($250), and room and board ($9000). Full-time tuition and fees vary according to course load. *Part-time tuition:* $430 per credit. Part-time tuition and fees vary according to course load. *Payment plan:* Installment.

FRESHMAN FINANCIAL AID (Fall 2004, est.) 148 applied for aid; of those 95% were deemed to have need. 100% of freshmen with need received aid; of those 15% had need fully met. *Average percent of need met:* 77% (excluding resources awarded to replace EFC). *Average financial aid package:* $14,673 (excluding resources awarded to replace EFC).

UNDERGRADUATE FINANCIAL AID (Fall 2004, est.) 387 applied for aid; of those 94% were deemed to have need. 100% of undergraduates with need received aid; of those 16% had need fully met. *Average percent of need met:* 78% (excluding resources awarded to replace EFC). *Average financial aid package:* $14,730 (excluding resources awarded to replace EFC). 11% of all full-time undergraduates had no need and received non-need-based gift aid.

GIFT AID (NEED-BASED) *Total amount:* $3,908,186 (23% federal, 9% state, 67% institutional, 1% external sources). *Receiving aid:* Freshmen: 94% (141); All full-time undergraduates: 76% (362). *Average award:* Freshmen: $11,107; Undergraduates: $10,421. *Scholarships, grants, and awards:* Federal Pell, FSEOG, state, private, college/university gift aid from institutional funds.

GIFT AID (NON-NEED-BASED) *Total amount:* $390,291 (78% institutional, 22% external sources). *Receiving aid:* Freshmen: 19% (29); Undergraduates: 1% (4). *Average Award: Freshmen:* $6872; *Undergraduates:* $8299. *Scholarships, grants, and awards by category: Academic Interests/Achievement:* 54 awards ($185,121 total): biological sciences, education, general academic interests/achievements. *Special Achievements/Activities:* 44 awards ($166,000 total): general special achievements/activities, leadership. *Special Characteristics:* 2 awards ($3296 total): children and siblings of alumni, members of minority groups, siblings of current students. *Tuition waivers:* Full or partial for employees or children of employees.

LOANS *Student loans:* $2,498,983 (79% need-based, 21% non-need-based). 60% of past graduating class borrowed through all loan programs. *Average indebtedness per student:* $14,312. *Average need-based loan:* Freshmen: $2693; Undergraduates: $3575. *Parent loans:* $643,004 (100% need-based). *Programs:* FFEL (Subsidized and Unsubsidized Stafford, PLUS), state.

WORK-STUDY *Federal work-study:* Total amount: $85,000; 174 jobs averaging $843.

APPLYING FOR FINANCIAL AID *Required financial aid form:* FAFSA. *Financial aid deadline (priority):* 5/1. *Notification date:* Continuous beginning 3/1. Students must reply within 2 weeks of notification.

CONTACT Ms. Nancy Amaral, Director of Financial Aid, Pine Manor College, 400 Heath Street, Chestnut Hill, MA 02467, 617-731-7129 or toll-free 800-762-1357. *Fax:* 617-731-7102. *E-mail:* finaid@pmc.edu.

PITTSBURG STATE UNIVERSITY
Pittsburg, KS

Tuition & fees (KS res): $3294	Average undergraduate aid package: $6785

ABOUT THE INSTITUTION State-supported, coed. Awards: associate, bachelor's, and master's degrees. 109 undergraduate majors. Total enrollment: 6,537. Undergraduates: 5,493. Freshmen: 886. Federal methodology is used as a basis for awarding need-based institutional aid.

UNDERGRADUATE EXPENSES for 2004–05 *Application fee:* $30. *Tuition, state resident:* full-time $2632; part-time $88 per credit hour. *Tuition, nonresident:* full-time $8990; part-time $300 per credit hour. *Required fees:* full-time $662; $30 per credit hour. *College room and board:* $4234. Room and board charges vary according to board plan. *Payment plan:* Installment.

FRESHMAN FINANCIAL AID (Fall 2004, est.) 700 applied for aid; of those 74% were deemed to have need. 97% of freshmen with need received aid; of those 13% had need fully met. *Average percent of need met:* 89% (excluding resources awarded to replace EFC). *Average financial aid package:* $5988 (excluding resources awarded to replace EFC). 10% of all full-time freshmen had no need and received non-need-based gift aid.

UNDERGRADUATE FINANCIAL AID (Fall 2004, est.) 3,569 applied for aid; of those 81% were deemed to have need. 98% of undergraduates with need received aid; of those 13% had need fully met. *Average percent of need met:* 87% (excluding resources awarded to replace EFC). *Average financial aid package:* $6785 (excluding resources awarded to replace EFC). 8% of all full-time undergraduates had no need and received non-need-based gift aid.

GIFT AID (NEED-BASED) *Total amount:* $8,180,563 (62% federal, 6% state, 13% institutional, 19% external sources). *Receiving aid:* Freshmen: 49% (443); All full-time undergraduates: 46% (2,259). *Average award:* Freshmen: $3462; Undergraduates: $3165. *Scholarships, grants, and awards:* Federal Pell, FSEOG, state, private, college/university gift aid from institutional funds.

GIFT AID (NON-NEED-BASED) *Total amount:* $1,197,266 (1% federal, 67% institutional, 32% external sources). *Receiving aid:* Freshmen: 11% (103); Undergraduates: 5% (270). *Average Award:* Freshmen: $1418; *Undergraduates:* $1745. *Scholarships, grants, and awards by category: Academic Interests/Achievement:* 1,576 awards ($1,403,749 total): biological sciences, business, communication, computer science, education, engineering/technologies, English, foreign languages, general academic interests/achievements, health fields, home economics, mathematics, military science, physical sciences, social sciences. *Creative Arts/Performance:* 292 awards ($159,296 total): music. *Special Characteristics:* 86 awards ($27,100 total): children and siblings of alumni, general special characteristics. *Tuition waivers:* Full or partial for employees or children of employees. *ROTC:* Army.

LOANS *Student loans:* $12,682,884 (74% need-based, 26% non-need-based). 94% of past graduating class borrowed through all loan programs. *Average indebtedness per student:* $10,348. *Average need-based loan:* Freshmen: $2433; Undergraduates: $3762. *Parent loans:* $968,584 (5% need-based, 95% non-need-based). *Programs:* FFEL (Subsidized and Unsubsidized Stafford, PLUS), Perkins, Federal Nursing, college/university.

WORK-STUDY *Federal work-study:* Total amount: $430,941; 246 jobs averaging $1309. *State or other work-study/employment:* Total amount: $1,485,022 (22% need-based, 78% non-need-based). 1,019 part-time jobs averaging $1457.

ATHLETIC AWARDS *Total amount:* $820,853 (49% need-based, 51% non-need-based).

APPLYING FOR FINANCIAL AID *Required financial aid form:* FAFSA. *Financial aid deadline (priority):* 3/1. *Notification date:* Continuous. Students must reply within 2 weeks of notification.

CONTACT Marilyn Haverly, Director of Student Financial Assistance, Pittsburg State University, 1701 South Broadway, Pittsburg, KS 66762-5880, 316-235-4238 or toll-free 800-854-7488 Ext. 1. *Fax:* 316-235-4078. *E-mail:* mhaverly@pittstate.edu.

PITZER COLLEGE
Claremont, CA

Tuition & fees: $31,438	Average undergraduate aid package: $28,790

ABOUT THE INSTITUTION Independent, coed. Awards: bachelor's degrees. 47 undergraduate majors. Total enrollment: 927. Undergraduates: 927. Freshmen: 223. Both federal and institutional methodology are used as a basis for awarding need-based institutional aid.

UNDERGRADUATE EXPENSES for 2004–05 *Application fee:* $50. *Comprehensive fee:* $39,660 includes full-time tuition ($28,112), mandatory fees ($3326), and room and board ($8222). *College room only:* $5146. Full-time tuition and fees vary according to course load. Room and board charges vary according to board plan. *Part-time tuition:* $3514 per course. Part-time tuition and fees vary according to course load. *Payment plans:* Installment, deferred payment.

FRESHMAN FINANCIAL AID (Fall 2004, est.) 81 applied for aid; of those 77% were deemed to have need. 100% of freshmen with need received aid; of those 100% had need fully met. *Average percent of need met:* 100% (excluding

resources awarded to replace EFC). *Average financial aid package:* $28,203 (excluding resources awarded to replace EFC). 3% of all full-time freshmen had no need and received non-need-based gift aid.

UNDERGRADUATE FINANCIAL AID (Fall 2004, est.) 375 applied for aid; of those 93% were deemed to have need. 100% of undergraduates with need received aid; of those 100% had need fully met. *Average percent of need met:* 100% (excluding resources awarded to replace EFC). *Average financial aid package:* $28,790 (excluding resources awarded to replace EFC). 4% of all full-time undergraduates had no need and received non-need-based gift aid.

GIFT AID (NEED-BASED) *Total amount:* $8,261,288 (7% federal, 11% state, 80% institutional, 2% external sources). *Receiving aid:* Freshmen: 27% (60); All full-time undergraduates: 39% (340). *Average award:* Freshmen: $24,458; Undergraduates: $22,796. *Scholarships, grants, and awards:* Federal Pell, FSEOG, state, private, college/university gift aid from institutional funds.

GIFT AID (NON-NEED-BASED) *Total amount:* $408,510 (2% state, 78% institutional, 20% external sources). *Average Award:* Freshmen: $10,000; Undergraduates: $10,000. *Scholarships, grants, and awards by category: Academic Interests/Achievement:* 64 awards ($640,000 total): general academic interests/achievements. *Special Achievements/Activities:* community service, leadership. *Special Characteristics:* 18 awards ($90,000 total): members of minority groups. *Tuition waivers:* Full or partial for employees or children of employees. *ROTC:* Army cooperative, Air Force cooperative.

LOANS *Student loans:* $2,282,564 (66% need-based, 34% non-need-based). 60% of past graduating class borrowed through all loan programs. *Average indebtedness per student:* $20,900. *Average need-based loan:* Freshmen: $3148; Undergraduates: $5101. *Parent loans:* $1,088,952 (100% non-need-based). *Programs:* FFEL (Subsidized and Unsubsidized Stafford, PLUS), Perkins, college/university.

WORK-STUDY *Federal work-study:* Total amount: $767,070; 295 jobs averaging $2600.

APPLYING FOR FINANCIAL AID *Required financial aid forms:* FAFSA, CSS Financial Aid PROFILE, state aid form, noncustodial (divorced/separated) parent's statement, business/farm supplement. *Financial aid deadline:* 2/1. *Notification date:* 4/1. Students must reply by 5/1.

CONTACT Margaret Carothers, Director of Financial Aid, Pitzer College, 1050 North Mills Avenue, Claremont, CA 91711-6101, 909-621-8208 or toll-free 800-748-9371. *Fax:* 909-607-1205. *E-mail:* margaret_carothers@pitzer.edu.

PLATTSBURGH STATE UNIVERSITY OF NEW YORK
Plattsburgh, NY

See State University of New York at Plattsburgh.

PLYMOUTH STATE UNIVERSITY
Plymouth, NH

Tuition & fees (NH res): $6618   **Average undergraduate aid package: $7374**

ABOUT THE INSTITUTION State-supported, coed. Awards: bachelor's and master's degrees and post-bachelor's and post-master's certificates. 46 undergraduate majors. Total enrollment: 5,151. Undergraduates: 4,108. Freshmen: 1,055. Federal methodology is used as a basis for awarding need-based institutional aid.

UNDERGRADUATE EXPENSES for 2004–05 *Application fee:* $35. *Tuition, state resident:* full-time $5060; part-time $212 per credit hour. *Tuition, nonresident:* full-time $11,500; part-time $480 per credit hour. *Required fees:* full-time $1558; $71 per credit hour. Full-time tuition and fees vary according to reciprocity agreements. Part-time tuition and fees vary according to course load and reciprocity agreements. *College room and board:* $6322; *room only:* $4350. Room and board charges vary according to board plan and housing facility. *Payment plan:* Installment.

FRESHMAN FINANCIAL AID (Fall 2004, est.) 901 applied for aid; of those 72% were deemed to have need. 98% of freshmen with need received aid; of those 5% had need fully met. *Average percent of need met:* 61% (excluding resources awarded to replace EFC). *Average financial aid package:* $6831 (excluding resources awarded to replace EFC). 4% of all full-time freshmen had no need and received non-need-based gift aid.

UNDERGRADUATE FINANCIAL AID (Fall 2004, est.) 3,023 applied for aid; of those 75% were deemed to have need. 91% of undergraduates with need received aid; of those 4% had need fully met. *Average percent of need met:* 66% (excluding resources awarded to replace EFC). *Average financial aid*

package: $7374 (excluding resources awarded to replace EFC). 6% of all full-time undergraduates had no need and received non-need-based gift aid.

GIFT AID (NEED-BASED) *Total amount:* $5,780,364 (44% federal, 9% state, 47% institutional). *Receiving aid:* Freshmen: 38% (403); All full-time undergraduates: 34% (1,328). *Average award:* Freshmen: $4510; Undergraduates: $4283. *Scholarships, grants, and awards:* Federal Pell, FSEOG, state, private, college/university gift aid from institutional funds.

GIFT AID (NON-NEED-BASED) *Total amount:* $1,930,972 (70% institutional, 30% external sources). *Receiving aid:* Freshmen: 22% (231); Undergraduates: 15% (583). *Average Award:* Freshmen: $2207; Undergraduates: $2044. *Scholarships, grants, and awards by category: Academic Interests/Achievement:* 505 awards ($845,233 total): business, communication, education, English, general academic interests/achievements, health fields, mathematics, physical sciences, social sciences. *Creative Arts/Performance:* 20 awards ($40,000 total): creative writing, dance, music, theater/drama. *Special Characteristics:* 31 awards ($74,346 total): children of faculty/staff, international students. *Tuition waivers:* Full or partial for employees or children of employees, senior citizens. *ROTC:* Army cooperative, Air Force cooperative.

LOANS *Student loans:* $18,504,899 (47% need-based, 53% non-need-based). 64% of past graduating class borrowed through all loan programs. *Average indebtedness per student:* $22,916. *Average need-based loan:* Freshmen: $2713; Undergraduates: $3900. *Parent loans:* $5,456,564 (100% non-need-based). *Programs:* FFEL (Subsidized and Unsubsidized Stafford, PLUS), Perkins.

WORK-STUDY *Federal work-study:* Total amount: $2,360,485; 1,458 jobs averaging $1619.

APPLYING FOR FINANCIAL AID *Required financial aid form:* FAFSA. *Financial aid deadline (priority):* 3/1. *Notification date:* Continuous. Students must reply by 5/1.

CONTACT June Schlabach, Director of Financial Aid, Plymouth State University, 17 High Street, MSC 18, Plymouth, NH 03264-1595, 603-535-2338 or toll-free 800-842-6900. *Fax:* 603-535-2627. *E-mail:* jlschlabach@plymouth.edu.

POINT LOMA NAZARENE UNIVERSITY
San Diego, CA

ABOUT THE INSTITUTION Independent Nazarene, coed. Awards: bachelor's and master's degrees. 46 undergraduate majors. Total enrollment: 3,209. Undergraduates: 2,361. Freshmen: 535.

GIFT AID (NEED-BASED) *Scholarships, grants, and awards:* Federal Pell, FSEOG, state, private, college/university gift aid from institutional funds.

GIFT AID (NON-NEED-BASED) *Scholarships, grants, and awards by category: Academic Interests/Achievement:* biological sciences, business, communication, education, engineering/technologies, general academic interests/achievements, health fields, home economics, humanities, mathematics, religion/biblical studies, social sciences. *Creative Arts/Performance:* art/fine arts, debating, music, theater/drama. *Special Achievements/Activities:* general special achievements/activities. *Special Characteristics:* children and siblings of alumni, children of faculty/staff, local/state students, relatives of clergy, religious affiliation, siblings of current students.

LOANS *Programs:* FFEL (Subsidized and Unsubsidized Stafford, PLUS), Perkins, Federal Nursing, state, college/university.

APPLYING FOR FINANCIAL AID *Required financial aid forms:* FAFSA, institution's own form.

CONTACT Student Financial Services, Point Loma Nazarene University, 3900 Lomaland Drive, San Diego, CA 92106, 619-849-2538 or toll-free 800-733-7770. *Fax:* 619-849-7017.

POINT PARK UNIVERSITY
Pittsburgh, PA

Tuition & fees: $15,960   **Average undergraduate aid package: $12,451**

ABOUT THE INSTITUTION Independent, coed. Awards: associate, bachelor's, and master's degrees and post-bachelor's and post-master's certificates. 53 undergraduate majors. Total enrollment: 3,292. Undergraduates: 2,844. Freshmen: 393. Federal methodology is used as a basis for awarding need-based institutional aid.

UNDERGRADUATE EXPENSES for 2004–05 *Application fee:* $40. *Comprehensive fee:* $22,960 includes full-time tuition ($15,500), mandatory fees ($460), and room and board ($7000). *College room only:* $3300. Full-time tuition and fees vary according to program. Room and board charges vary according to board plan. *Part-time tuition:* $422 per credit. *Part-time fees:* $10 per credit. Part-time tuition and fees vary according to program. *Payment plans:* Installment, deferred payment.

FRESHMAN FINANCIAL AID (Fall 2004, est.) 360 applied for aid; of those 88% were deemed to have need. 99% of freshmen with need received aid; of those 24% had need fully met. *Average percent of need met:* 71% (excluding resources awarded to replace EFC). *Average financial aid package:* $12,843 (excluding resources awarded to replace EFC). 33% of all full-time freshmen had no need and received non-need-based gift aid.

UNDERGRADUATE FINANCIAL AID (Fall 2004, est.) 1,765 applied for aid; of those 92% were deemed to have need. 100% of undergraduates with need received aid; of those 19% had need fully met. *Average percent of need met:* 68% (excluding resources awarded to replace EFC). *Average financial aid package:* $12,451 (excluding resources awarded to replace EFC). 17% of all full-time undergraduates had no need and received non-need-based gift aid.

GIFT AID (NEED-BASED) *Total amount:* $12,400,713 (24% federal, 20% state, 47% institutional, 9% external sources). *Receiving aid:* Freshmen: 61% (308); All full-time undergraduates: 78% (1,553). *Average award:* Freshmen: $7630; Undergraduates: $6939. *Scholarships, grants, and awards:* Federal Pell, FSEOG, state, private, college/university gift aid from institutional funds.

GIFT AID (NON-NEED-BASED) *Total amount:* $1,900,917 (2% state, 74% institutional, 24% external sources). *Receiving aid:* Freshmen: 5% (25); Undergraduates: 5% (96). *Average Award: Freshmen:* $6349; *Undergraduates:* $7994. *Scholarships, grants, and awards by category: Academic Interests/ Achievement:* 736 awards ($1,594,250 total): general academic interests/ achievements. *Creative Arts/Performance:* 236 awards ($786,630 total): cinema/ film/broadcasting, dance, journalism/publications, performing arts, theater/ drama. *Special Achievements/Activities:* 707 awards ($653,250 total): community service, junior miss. *Special Characteristics:* 478 awards ($661,910 total): adult students, children and siblings of alumni, children of faculty/staff, international students, members of minority groups, previous college experience, siblings of current students. *Tuition waivers:* Full or partial for children of alumni, employees or children of employees. *ROTC:* Army cooperative, Air Force cooperative.

LOANS *Student loans:* $18,908,809 (79% need-based, 21% non-need-based). 83% of past graduating class borrowed through all loan programs. *Average indebtedness per student:* $20,551. *Average need-based loan:* Freshmen: $4366; Undergraduates: $5024. *Parent loans:* $2,844,861 (47% need-based, 53% non-need-based). *Programs:* FFEL (Subsidized and Unsubsidized Stafford, PLUS), Perkins.

WORK-STUDY *Federal work-study:* Total amount: $339,061; 213 jobs averaging $2205. *State or other work-study/employment:* Total amount: $2,273,569 (68% need-based, 32% non-need-based). 264 part-time jobs averaging $1965.

ATHLETIC AWARDS *Total amount:* $675,188 (63% need-based, 37% non-need-based).

APPLYING FOR FINANCIAL AID *Required financial aid form:* FAFSA. *Financial aid deadline:* 5/1 (priority: 5/1). *Notification date:* Continuous beginning 2/1. Students must reply by 8/30.

CONTACT Sandra M. Cronin, Director of Financial Aid, Point Park University, 201 Wood Street, Pittsburgh, PA 15222-1984, 412-392-3930 or toll-free 800-321-0129. *E-mail:* scronin@pointpark.edu.

POLYTECHNIC UNIVERSITY, BROOKLYN CAMPUS
Brooklyn, NY

Tuition & fees: $27,170	Average undergraduate aid package: $20,475

ABOUT THE INSTITUTION Independent, coed. Awards: bachelor's, master's, and doctoral degrees and post-bachelor's certificates. 14 undergraduate majors. Total enrollment: 2,819. Undergraduates: 1,543. Freshmen: 329. Federal methodology is used as a basis for awarding need-based institutional aid.

UNDERGRADUATE EXPENSES for 2004–05 *Application fee:* $50. *Comprehensive fee:* $35,170 includes full-time tuition ($26,200), mandatory fees ($970), and room and board ($8000). *College room only:* $6500. Full-time tuition and fees vary according to course load. Room and board charges vary according to housing facility. *Part-time tuition:* $835 per credit. *Part-time fees:* $300 per term. Part-time tuition and fees vary according to course load. *Payment plans:* Installment, deferred payment.

FRESHMAN FINANCIAL AID (Fall 2004, est.) 324 applied for aid; of those 85% were deemed to have need. 100% of freshmen with need received aid; of those 77% had need fully met. *Average percent of need met:* 91% (excluding resources awarded to replace EFC). *Average financial aid package:* $21,685 (excluding resources awarded to replace EFC). 15% of all full-time freshmen had no need and received non-need-based gift aid.

UNDERGRADUATE FINANCIAL AID (Fall 2004, est.) 1,428 applied for aid; of those 84% were deemed to have need. 100% of undergraduates with need received aid; of those 57% had need fully met. *Average percent of need met:* 89% (excluding resources awarded to replace EFC). *Average financial aid package:* $20,475 (excluding resources awarded to replace EFC). 16% of all full-time undergraduates had no need and received non-need-based gift aid.

GIFT AID (NEED-BASED) *Total amount:* $7,873,144 (40% federal, 20% state, 40% institutional). *Receiving aid:* Freshmen: 80% (262); All full-time undergraduates: 76% (1,120). *Average award:* Freshmen: $7346; Undergraduates: $6829. *Scholarships, grants, and awards:* Federal Pell, FSEOG, state, private, college/ university gift aid from institutional funds, United Negro College Fund.

GIFT AID (NON-NEED-BASED) *Total amount:* $15,689,443 (1% state, 95% institutional, 4% external sources). *Receiving aid:* Freshmen: 68% (223); Undergraduates: 62% (908). *Average Award: Freshmen:* $16,077; *Undergraduates:* $15,515. *Scholarships, grants, and awards by category: Academic Interests/Achievement:* computer science, engineering/technologies, general academic interests/achievements. *Special Characteristics:* members of minority groups. *Tuition waivers:* Full or partial for minority students, employees or children of employees. *ROTC:* Air Force cooperative.

LOANS *Student loans:* $7,410,779 (74% need-based, 26% non-need-based). 75% of past graduating class borrowed through all loan programs. *Average indebtedness per student:* $21,304. *Average need-based loan:* Freshmen: $5275; Undergraduates: $5485. *Parent loans:* $1,090,003 (100% need-based). *Programs:* FFEL (Subsidized and Unsubsidized Stafford, PLUS), Perkins, college/ university, alternative loans.

WORK-STUDY *Federal work-study:* Total amount: $328,100; 100 jobs averaging $3281.

APPLYING FOR FINANCIAL AID *Required financial aid forms:* FAFSA, state aid form. *Financial aid deadline:* Continuous. *Notification date:* Continuous beginning 2/15. Students must reply by 5/1 or within 2 weeks of notification.

CONTACT Mr. Nicholas Simos, Director of Financial Aid Services, Polytechnic University, Brooklyn Campus, 6 Metrotech Center, Brooklyn, NY 11201-2990, 718-260-3025 or toll-free 800-POLYTECH. *Fax:* 718-260-3062.

POLYTECHNIC UNIVERSITY OF PUERTO RICO
Hato Rey, PR

Tuition & fees: $5550	Average undergraduate aid package: $4363

ABOUT THE INSTITUTION Independent, coed. Awards: bachelor's and master's degrees. 13 undergraduate majors. Total enrollment: 5,674. Undergraduates: 5,018. Freshmen: 961. Federal methodology is used as a basis for awarding need-based institutional aid.

UNDERGRADUATE EXPENSES for 2005–06 *Application fee:* $30. *Tuition:* full-time $5220; part-time $145 per credit. *Required fees:* full-time $330; $110 per term part-time. Full-time tuition and fees vary according to program. Part-time tuition and fees vary according to program. *Payment plan:* Deferred payment.

FRESHMAN FINANCIAL AID (Fall 2003) 561 applied for aid; of those 99% were deemed to have need. 91% of freshmen with need received aid. *Average percent of need met:* 21% (excluding resources awarded to replace EFC). *Average financial aid package:* $3982 (excluding resources awarded to replace EFC).

UNDERGRADUATE FINANCIAL AID (Fall 2003) 2,206 applied for aid; of those 99% were deemed to have need. 92% of undergraduates with need received aid. *Average percent of need met:* 19% (excluding resources awarded to replace EFC). *Average financial aid package:* $4363 (excluding resources awarded to replace EFC).

GIFT AID (NEED-BASED) *Total amount:* $9,976,908 (90% federal, 7% state, 3% external sources). *Receiving aid:* Freshmen: 55% (360); All full-time undergraduates: 24% (637). *Average award:* Freshmen: $3988; Undergraduates: $4340. *Scholarships, grants, and awards:* Federal Pell, FSEOG, state.

GIFT AID (NON-NEED-BASED) *Total amount:* $112,340 (100% institutional). *Receiving aid:* Freshmen: 13% (85); Undergraduates: 10% (258). *Scholarships, grants, and awards by category: Academic Interests/Achievement:* architecture, business, engineering/technologies. *ROTC:* Army cooperative.

LOANS *Student loans:* $4,149,081 (82% need-based, 18% non-need-based). *Average need-based loan:* Freshmen: $849; Undergraduates: $2334. *Parent loans:* $281,506 (100% non-need-based). *Programs:* FFEL (Subsidized and Unsubsidized Stafford, PLUS).

WORK-STUDY *Federal work-study:* Total amount: $596,878; jobs available.
APPLYING FOR FINANCIAL AID *Required financial aid form:* FAFSA. *Financial aid deadline:* 5/15. *Notification date:* 7/15. Students must reply within 2 weeks of notification.
CONTACT Lidia L. Cruz, Financial Aid Administrator, Polytechnic University of Puerto Rico, 377 Ponce de Leon Avenue, Hato Rey, PR 00919, 787-754-8000 Ext. 253. *Fax:* 787-766-1163.

POMONA COLLEGE
Claremont, CA

Tuition & fees: $28,370	Average undergraduate aid package: $26,300

ABOUT THE INSTITUTION Independent, coed. Awards: bachelor's degrees. 53 undergraduate majors. Total enrollment: 1,562. Undergraduates: 1,562. Freshmen: 398. Both federal and institutional methodology are used as a basis for awarding need-based institutional aid.
UNDERGRADUATE EXPENSES for 2004–05 *Application fee:* $60. *Comprehensive fee:* $38,750 includes full-time tuition ($28,100), mandatory fees ($270), and room and board ($10,380). Room and board charges vary according to board plan. *Part-time tuition:* $4485 per credit. *Payment plan:* Installment.
FRESHMAN FINANCIAL AID (Fall 2003) 253 applied for aid; of those 82% were deemed to have need. 100% of freshmen with need received aid; of those 100% had need fully met. *Average percent of need met:* 100% (excluding resources awarded to replace EFC). *Average financial aid package:* $26,700 (excluding resources awarded to replace EFC).
UNDERGRADUATE FINANCIAL AID (Fall 2003) 946 applied for aid; of those 84% were deemed to have need. 100% of undergraduates with need received aid; of those 100% had need fully met. *Average percent of need met:* 100% (excluding resources awarded to replace EFC). *Average financial aid package:* $26,300 (excluding resources awarded to replace EFC).
GIFT AID (NEED-BASED) *Total amount:* $17,743,205 (5% federal, 5% state, 86% institutional, 4% external sources). *Receiving aid:* Freshmen: 52% (207); All full-time undergraduates: 52% (795). *Average award:* Freshmen: $23,950; Undergraduates: $22,400. *Scholarships, grants, and awards:* Federal Pell, FSEOG, state, private, college/university gift aid from institutional funds.
GIFT AID (NON-NEED-BASED) *Total amount:* $250,000 (100% external sources). *Tuition waivers:* Full or partial for employees or children of employees.
LOANS *Student loans:* $2,646,000 (85% need-based, 15% non-need-based). 60% of past graduating class borrowed through all loan programs. *Average indebtedness per student:* $15,600. *Average need-based loan:* Freshmen: $2000; Undergraduates: $2825. *Parent loans:* $206,000 (100% non-need-based). *Programs:* FFEL (Subsidized and Unsubsidized Stafford, PLUS), Perkins, college/university.
WORK-STUDY *Federal work-study:* Total amount: $255,465; 250 jobs averaging $1650. *State or other work-study/employment:* Total amount: $600,000 (100% need-based). 500 part-time jobs averaging $1650.
APPLYING FOR FINANCIAL AID *Required financial aid forms:* FAFSA, CSS Financial Aid PROFILE, state aid form, noncustodial (divorced/separated) parent's statement, business/farm supplement. *Financial aid deadline:* 2/1. *Notification date:* 4/10. Students must reply by 5/1.
CONTACT Patricia A. Coye, Director of Financial Aid, Pomona College, 550 North College Avenue, Room 117, Claremont, CA 91711, 909-621-8205. *Fax:* 909-607-7941. *E-mail:* financial_aid@pomadm.pomona.edu.

PONTIFICAL CATHOLIC UNIVERSITY OF PUERTO RICO
Ponce, PR

Tuition & fees: $4778	Average undergraduate aid package: $6550

ABOUT THE INSTITUTION Independent Roman Catholic, coed. Awards: associate, bachelor's, master's, doctoral, and first professional degrees (branch locations in Arecibo, Guayana, Mayagüez). 66 undergraduate majors. Total enrollment: 7,548. Undergraduates: 5,517. Freshmen: 1,133. Federal methodology is used as a basis for awarding need-based institutional aid.
UNDERGRADUATE EXPENSES for 2004–05 *Application fee:* $15. *Comprehensive fee:* $7918 includes full-time tuition ($4320), mandatory fees ($458), and room and board ($3140). *College room only:* $1100. Full-time tuition and fees vary according to course load. *Part-time tuition:* $135 per credit. Part-time tuition and fees vary according to course load. *Payment plan:* Deferred payment.

FRESHMAN FINANCIAL AID (Fall 2004, est.) 1047 applied for aid; of those 98% were deemed to have need. 97% of freshmen with need received aid; of those 8% had need fully met. *Average percent of need met:* 71% (excluding resources awarded to replace EFC). *Average financial aid package:* $6550 (excluding resources awarded to replace EFC).
UNDERGRADUATE FINANCIAL AID (Fall 2004, est.) 6,579 applied for aid; of those 99% were deemed to have need. 94% of undergraduates with need received aid; of those .3% had need fully met. *Average percent of need met:* 71% (excluding resources awarded to replace EFC). *Average financial aid package:* $6550 (excluding resources awarded to replace EFC).
GIFT AID (NEED-BASED) *Total amount:* $26,175,425 (96% federal, 4% state). *Receiving aid:* Freshmen: 84% (911); All full-time undergraduates: 82% (5,452). *Average award:* Freshmen: $3900; Undergraduates: $3961. *Scholarships, grants, and awards:* Federal Pell, FSEOG, state, private, college/university gift aid from institutional funds, Scholarships for Disadvantaged Students (SDS).
GIFT AID (NON-NEED-BASED) *Total amount:* $1,089,880 (95% institutional, 5% external sources). *Scholarships, grants, and awards by category:* Academic Interests/Achievement: 1,045 awards ($402,530 total): general academic interests/achievements. Creative Arts/Performance: 50 awards ($30,000 total): music, performing arts, theater/drama. Special Characteristics: 130 awards ($337,537 total): children of faculty/staff, first-generation college students, spouses of current students, veterans, veterans' children. *Tuition waivers:* Full or partial for employees or children of employees. *ROTC:* Army cooperative.
LOANS *Student loans:* $22,896,070 (100% need-based). 70% of past graduating class borrowed through all loan programs. *Average indebtedness per student:* $3500. *Average need-based loan:* Freshmen: $1968; Undergraduates: $4250. *Programs:* FFEL (Subsidized and Unsubsidized Stafford, PLUS), Perkins.
WORK-STUDY *Federal work-study:* Total amount: $1,445,724; 1,100 jobs averaging $750. *State or other work-study/employment:* Total amount: $40,000 (100% non-need-based). Part-time jobs available.
ATHLETIC AWARDS *Total amount:* $400,000 (100% non-need-based).
APPLYING FOR FINANCIAL AID *Required financial aid forms:* FAFSA, institution's own form, noncustodial (divorced/separated) parent's statement. *Financial aid deadline (priority):* 5/14. *Notification date:* 6/15. Students must reply within 4 weeks of notification.
CONTACT Mrs. Margaret Alustiza, Director of Financial Aid, Pontifical Catholic University of Puerto Rico, 2250 Las Americas Avenue, Suite 549, Ponce, PR 00717-0777, 787-841-2000 Ext. 1065 or toll-free 800-981-5040. *Fax:* 787-651-2041. *E-mail:* malustiza@pucpr.edu.

PONTIFICAL COLLEGE JOSEPHINUM
Columbus, OH

Tuition & fees: $14,635	Average undergraduate aid package: $14,762

ABOUT THE INSTITUTION Independent Roman Catholic, coed, primarily men. Awards: bachelor's, master's, and first professional degrees. 4 undergraduate majors. Total enrollment: 149. Undergraduates: 84. Freshmen: 8. Federal methodology is used as a basis for awarding need-based institutional aid.
UNDERGRADUATE EXPENSES for 2004–05 *Application fee:* $25. *Comprehensive fee:* $21,635 includes full-time tuition ($14,000), mandatory fees ($635), and room and board ($7000). *Part-time tuition:* $565 per credit hour. *Payment plans:* Installment, deferred payment.
FRESHMAN FINANCIAL AID (Fall 2003) 5 applied for aid; of those 100% were deemed to have need. 100% of freshmen with need received aid; of those 40% had need fully met. *Average percent of need met:* 82% (excluding resources awarded to replace EFC). *Average financial aid package:* $14,125 (excluding resources awarded to replace EFC).
UNDERGRADUATE FINANCIAL AID (Fall 2003) 44 applied for aid; of those 82% were deemed to have need. 100% of undergraduates with need received aid; of those 47% had need fully met. *Average percent of need met:* 82% (excluding resources awarded to replace EFC). *Average financial aid package:* $14,762 (excluding resources awarded to replace EFC). 7% of all full-time undergraduates had no need and received non-need-based gift aid.
GIFT AID (NEED-BASED) *Total amount:* $82,398 (63% federal, 31% state, 6% institutional). *Receiving aid:* Freshmen: 18% (2); All full-time undergraduates: 24% (16). *Average award:* Freshmen: $525; Undergraduates: $3148. *Scholarships, grants, and awards:* Federal Pell, FSEOG, state, private, college/university gift aid from institutional funds.
GIFT AID (NON-NEED-BASED) *Total amount:* $315,559 (8% state, 92% external sources). *Receiving aid:* Freshmen: 18% (2); Undergraduates: 24% (16). *Aver-*

age Award: Undergraduates: $2000. **Scholarships, grants, and awards by category:** *Special Characteristics:* local/state students.
LOANS *Student loans:* $128,186 (47% need-based, 53% non-need-based). 40% of past graduating class borrowed through all loan programs. *Average indebtedness per student:* $13,698. **Average need-based loan:** Undergraduates: $4157. *Programs:* FFEL (Subsidized and Unsubsidized Stafford, PLUS), Perkins.
WORK-STUDY *Federal work-study:* Total amount: $4892; 4 jobs averaging $507.
APPLYING FOR FINANCIAL AID *Required financial aid forms:* FAFSA, institution's own form. *Financial aid deadline (priority):* 9/2. *Notification date:* Continuous. Students must reply within 2 weeks of notification.
CONTACT Marky Leichtnam, Financial Aid Director, Pontifical College Josephinum, 7625 North High Street, Columbus, OH 43235-1498, 614-985-2212 or toll-free 888-252-5812. *Fax:* 614-885-2307. *E-mail:* mleichtnam@pcj.edu.

PORTLAND STATE UNIVERSITY
Portland, OR

Tuition & fees (OR res): $4311	Average undergraduate aid package: $7486

ABOUT THE INSTITUTION State-supported, coed. Awards: bachelor's, master's, and doctoral degrees and post-bachelor's certificates. 63 undergraduate majors. Total enrollment: 23,444. Undergraduates: 17,355. Freshmen: 1,363. Federal methodology is used as a basis for awarding need-based institutional aid.
UNDERGRADUATE EXPENSES for 2004–05 *Application fee:* $50. *Tuition, state resident:* full-time $3240; part-time $90 per credit. *Tuition, nonresident:* full-time $12,636; part-time $90 per credit. *Required fees:* full-time $1071; $17 per credit or $40 per term part-time. Full-time tuition and fees vary according to program. *College room and board:* $8310; *room only:* $6210. Room and board charges vary according to board plan and housing facility. *Payment plans:* Installment, deferred payment.
FRESHMAN FINANCIAL AID (Fall 2004, est.) 824 applied for aid; of those 75% were deemed to have need. 97% of freshmen with need received aid; of those 11% had need fully met. *Average percent of need met:* 48% (excluding resources awarded to replace EFC). *Average financial aid package:* $5739 (excluding resources awarded to replace EFC). 11% of all full-time freshmen had no need and received non-need-based gift aid.
UNDERGRADUATE FINANCIAL AID (Fall 2004, est.) 6,765 applied for aid; of those 84% were deemed to have need. 98% of undergraduates with need received aid; of those 12% had need fully met. *Average percent of need met:* 56% (excluding resources awarded to replace EFC). *Average financial aid package:* $7486 (excluding resources awarded to replace EFC). 2% of all full-time undergraduates had no need and received non-need-based gift aid.
GIFT AID (NEED-BASED) *Total amount:* $21,766,560 (76% federal, 11% state, 8% institutional, 5% external sources). *Receiving aid:* Freshmen: 30% (349); All full-time undergraduates: 36% (3,793). *Average award:* Freshmen: $3742; Undergraduates: $3939. *Scholarships, grants, and awards:* Federal Pell, FSEOG, state, private, college/university gift aid from institutional funds, United Negro College Fund.
GIFT AID (NON-NEED-BASED) *Total amount:* $2,032,867 (85% institutional, 15% external sources). *Receiving aid:* Freshmen: 8% (99); Undergraduates: 6% (604). *Average Award:* Freshmen: $1093; Undergraduates: $2318. *Scholarships, grants, and awards by category:* Academic Interests/Achievement: architecture, area/ethnic studies, business, computer science, education, engineering/technologies, foreign languages, general academic interests/achievements, humanities, international studies, physical sciences, social sciences. *Creative Arts/Performance:* art/fine arts, general creative arts/performance, music, theater/drama. *Special Achievements/Activities:* community service, general special achievements/activities, leadership, memberships. *Special Characteristics:* adult students, ethnic background, handicapped students, international students, members of minority groups, out-of-state students. *Tuition waivers:* Full or partial for minority students, employees or children of employees, senior citizens. *ROTC:* Army, Air Force cooperative.
LOANS *Student loans:* $51,687,945 (100% need-based). 61% of past graduating class borrowed through all loan programs. *Average indebtedness per student:* $17,278. *Average need-based loan:* Freshmen: $2714; Undergraduates: $4353. *Parent loans:* $5,052,062 (100% need-based). *Programs:* Federal Direct (Subsidized and Unsubsidized Stafford, PLUS), FFEL (Subsidized and Unsubsidized Stafford, PLUS), Perkins.
WORK-STUDY *Federal work-study:* Total amount: $2,038,933; 547 jobs averaging $3738.

ATHLETIC AWARDS *Total amount:* $2,044,857 (100% need-based).
APPLYING FOR FINANCIAL AID *Required financial aid form:* FAFSA. *Financial aid deadline:* Continuous. *Notification date:* Continuous. Students must reply within 4 weeks of notification.
CONTACT Mr. Gary Garoffolo, Interim Associate Director of Financial Aid, Portland State University, PO Box 751, Portland, OR 97207-0751, 503-725-5448 or toll-free 800-547-8887. *Fax:* 503-725-4882. *E-mail:* askfa@pdx.edu.

POST UNIVERSITY
Waterbury, CT

Tuition & fees: $18,800	Average undergraduate aid package: $10,827

ABOUT THE INSTITUTION Independent, coed. Awards: associate and bachelor's degrees and post-bachelor's certificates. 21 undergraduate majors. Total enrollment: 1,198. Undergraduates: 1,198. Freshmen: 221. Federal methodology is used as a basis for awarding need-based institutional aid.
UNDERGRADUATE EXPENSES for 2004–05 *Application fee:* $40. *Comprehensive fee:* $26,750 includes full-time tuition ($18,150), mandatory fees ($650), and room and board ($7950). *Part-time tuition:* $605 per credit. Part-time tuition and fees vary according to class time and course load. *Payment plan:* Installment.
FRESHMAN FINANCIAL AID (Fall 2004, est.) 184 applied for aid; of those 100% were deemed to have need. 100% of freshmen with need received aid. *Average percent of need met:* 79% (excluding resources awarded to replace EFC). *Average financial aid package:* $11,405 (excluding resources awarded to replace EFC). 8% of all full-time freshmen had no need and received non-need-based gift aid.
UNDERGRADUATE FINANCIAL AID (Fall 2004, est.) 613 applied for aid; of those 88% were deemed to have need. 100% of undergraduates with need received aid. *Average percent of need met:* 75% (excluding resources awarded to replace EFC). *Average financial aid package:* $10,827 (excluding resources awarded to replace EFC). 3% of all full-time undergraduates had no need and received non-need-based gift aid.
GIFT AID (NEED-BASED) *Total amount:* $6,759,873 (29% federal, 11% state, 59% institutional, 1% external sources). *Receiving aid:* Freshmen: 91% (184); All full-time undergraduates: 79% (542). *Average award:* Freshmen: $7500; Undergraduates: $6500. *Scholarships, grants, and awards:* Federal Pell, FSEOG, state, private, college/university gift aid from institutional funds.
GIFT AID (NON-NEED-BASED) *Average Award:* Freshmen: $4688; Undergraduates: $5736. *Scholarships, grants, and awards by category:* Academic Interests/Achievement: 7 awards ($80,800 total): business, international studies. *Special Achievements/Activities:* 14 awards ($29,500 total): community service, general special achievements/activities, leadership. *Special Characteristics:* 358 awards ($1,046,838 total): children and siblings of alumni, local/state students, members of minority groups, siblings of current students. *Tuition waivers:* Full or partial for employees or children of employees, senior citizens.
LOANS *Student loans:* $4,391,252 (100% need-based). 92% of past graduating class borrowed through all loan programs. *Average indebtedness per student:* $17,500. *Average need-based loan:* Freshmen: $2906; Undergraduates: $3303. *Parent loans:* $872,495 (100% need-based). *Programs:* FFEL (Subsidized and Unsubsidized Stafford, PLUS), Perkins, state, college/university.
WORK-STUDY *Federal work-study:* Total amount: $206,824; 330 jobs averaging $734. *State or other work-study/employment:* Total amount: $20,000 (100% need-based). 10 part-time jobs averaging $1750.
ATHLETIC AWARDS *Total amount:* $455,000 (71% need-based, 29% non-need-based).
APPLYING FOR FINANCIAL AID *Required financial aid form:* FAFSA. *Financial aid deadline (priority):* 3/1. *Notification date:* Continuous beginning 4/1. Students must reply within 4 weeks of notification.
CONTACT Patricia Del Buono, Associate Director of Financial Aid, Post University, 800 Country Club Road, Waterbury, CT 06723-2540, 203-596-4526 or toll-free 800-345-2562. *Fax:* 203-756-5810. *E-mail:* pdelbuono@teikyopost.edu.

POTOMAC COLLEGE
Washington, DC

CONTACT Phyllis Crews, Financial Aid Counselor, Potomac College, 4000 Chesapeake Street NW, Washington, DC 20016, 202-686-0876 or toll-free 888-686-0876. *Fax:* 202-686-0818. *E-mail:* pcrews@potomac.edu.

PRAIRIE VIEW A&M UNIVERSITY
Prairie View, TX

ABOUT THE INSTITUTION State-supported, coed. Awards: bachelor's, master's, and doctoral degrees. 41 undergraduate majors. Total enrollment: 8,350. Undergraduates: 6,324. Freshmen: 1,473.

GIFT AID (NEED-BASED) *Scholarships, grants, and awards:* Federal Pell, FSEOG, state, private, college/university gift aid from institutional funds.

GIFT AID (NON-NEED-BASED) *Scholarships, grants, and awards by category: Academic Interests/Achievement:* agriculture, architecture, education, general academic interests/achievements, premedicine. *Creative Arts/Performance:* art/fine arts, music, performing arts.

LOANS *Programs:* FFEL (Subsidized and Unsubsidized Stafford, PLUS), Perkins, state.

APPLYING FOR FINANCIAL AID *Required financial aid forms:* FAFSA, institution's own form.

CONTACT Mr. A. D. James Jr., Executive Director, Student Financial Services and Scholarships, Prairie View A&M University, PO Box 2967, Prairie View, TX 77446-2967, 936-857-2423. *Fax:* 936-857-2425. *E-mail:* ad_james@pvamu.edu.

PRATT INSTITUTE
Brooklyn, NY

ABOUT THE INSTITUTION Independent, coed. Awards: associate, bachelor's, master's, and first professional degrees. 29 undergraduate majors. Total enrollment: 4,540. Undergraduates: 3,068. Freshmen: 610.

GIFT AID (NEED-BASED) *Scholarships, grants, and awards:* Federal Pell, FSEOG, state, college/university gift aid from institutional funds.

GIFT AID (NON-NEED-BASED) *Scholarships, grants, and awards by category: Academic Interests/Achievement:* architecture. *Creative Arts/Performance:* applied art and design.

LOANS *Programs:* FFEL (Subsidized and Unsubsidized Stafford, PLUS), Perkins, college/university.

WORK-STUDY *Federal work-study:* Total amount: $606,724; 468 jobs averaging $1300.

APPLYING FOR FINANCIAL AID *Required financial aid forms:* FAFSA, institution's own form.

CONTACT Karen Price-Scott, Director of Financial Aid, Pratt Institute, 200 Willoughby Avenue, Brooklyn, NY 11205-3899, 718-636-3519 or toll-free 800-331-0834. *Fax:* 718-636-3739. *E-mail:* kpricesc@pratt.edu.

PRESBYTERIAN COLLEGE
Clinton, SC

ABOUT THE INSTITUTION Independent religious, coed. Awards: bachelor's degrees. 32 undergraduate majors. Total enrollment: 1,187. Undergraduates: 1,187. Freshmen: 344.

GIFT AID (NEED-BASED) *Scholarships, grants, and awards:* Federal Pell, FSEOG, state, private, college/university gift aid from institutional funds.

GIFT AID (NON-NEED-BASED) *Scholarships, grants, and awards by category: Academic Interests/Achievement:* general academic interests/achievements. *Creative Arts/Performance:* music. *Special Achievements/Activities:* leadership, religious involvement. *Special Characteristics:* children of faculty/staff, relatives of clergy, religious affiliation.

LOANS *Programs:* FFEL (Subsidized and Unsubsidized Stafford, PLUS), Perkins, college/university.

WORK-STUDY *Federal work-study:* Total amount: $187,500; 206 jobs averaging $910. *State or other work-study/employment:* Total amount: $150,000 (100% non-need-based). 200 part-time jobs averaging $750.

APPLYING FOR FINANCIAL AID *Required financial aid forms:* FAFSA, institution's own form.

CONTACT Ms. Judi Gillespie, Director of Financial Aid, Presbyterian College, 503 South Broad Street, Clinton, SC 29325, 864-833-8287 or toll-free 800-476-7272. *Fax:* 864-833-8481. *E-mail:* jgillesp@admin.presby.edu.

PRESCOTT COLLEGE
Prescott, AZ

Tuition & fees: $17,450	Average undergraduate aid package: $4560

ABOUT THE INSTITUTION Independent, coed. Awards: bachelor's and master's degrees. 49 undergraduate majors. Total enrollment: 1,036. Undergraduates: 805. Freshmen: 41. Federal methodology is used as a basis for awarding need-based institutional aid.

UNDERGRADUATE EXPENSES for 2005–06 *Application fee:* $25. *Tuition:* full-time $17,280; part-time $480 per credit hour. *Required fees:* full-time $170; $85 per term part-time.

GIFT AID (NEED-BASED) *Total amount:* $1,547,268 (66% federal, 3% state, 20% institutional, 11% external sources). *Receiving aid:* Freshmen: 26% (6); All full-time undergraduates: 53% (387). *Average award:* Freshmen: $2400; Undergraduates: $2725. *Scholarships, grants, and awards:* Federal Pell, FSEOG, state, private, college/university gift aid from institutional funds.

LOANS *Student loans:* $3,051,662 (56% need-based, 44% non-need-based). 66% of past graduating class borrowed through all loan programs. *Average indebtedness per student:* $14,255. *Average need-based loan:* Freshmen: $2150; Undergraduates: $3790. *Parent loans:* $1,280,396 (60% need-based, 40% non-need-based). *Programs:* FFEL (Subsidized and Unsubsidized Stafford, PLUS), Perkins, state, alternative loans.

APPLYING FOR FINANCIAL AID *Required financial aid form:* FAFSA. *Financial aid deadline:* Continuous. *Notification date:* Continuous beginning 4/1. Students must reply within 3 weeks of notification.

CONTACT Financial Aid Office, Prescott College, 220 Grove Avenue, Prescott, AZ 86301-2990, 928-350-1111 or toll-free 800-628-6364 (in-state), 800-628-6364-2100 (out-of-state). *Fax:* 928-776-5225. *E-mail:* finaid@prescott.edu.

PRESENTATION COLLEGE
Aberdeen, SD

Tuition & fees: $10,400	Average undergraduate aid package: $7514

ABOUT THE INSTITUTION Independent Roman Catholic, coed. Awards: associate and bachelor's degrees. 13 undergraduate majors. Total enrollment: 618. Undergraduates: 618. Freshmen: 162. Federal methodology is used as a basis for awarding need-based institutional aid.

UNDERGRADUATE EXPENSES for 2004–05 *Comprehensive fee:* $14,950 includes full-time tuition ($10,400) and room and board ($4550). *College room only:* $3800. Full-time tuition and fees vary according to course load, location, and program. Room and board charges vary according to board plan, housing facility, and student level. *Part-time tuition:* $395 per credit. Part-time tuition and fees vary according to course load, location, and program. *Payment plan:* Installment.

FRESHMAN FINANCIAL AID (Fall 2004, est.) 82 applied for aid; of those 83% were deemed to have need. 100% of freshmen with need received aid; of those 1% had need fully met. *Average percent of need met:* 52% (excluding resources awarded to replace EFC). *Average financial aid package:* $6069 (excluding resources awarded to replace EFC). 8% of all full-time freshmen had no need and received non-need-based gift aid.

UNDERGRADUATE FINANCIAL AID (Fall 2004, est.) 422 applied for aid; of those 93% were deemed to have need. 98% of undergraduates with need received aid; of those 15% had need fully met. *Average percent of need met:* 45% (excluding resources awarded to replace EFC). *Average financial aid package:* $7514 (excluding resources awarded to replace EFC). 5% of all full-time undergraduates had no need and received non-need-based gift aid.

GIFT AID (NEED-BASED) *Total amount:* $1,354,349 (68% federal, 5% state, 20% institutional, 7% external sources). *Receiving aid:* Freshmen: 69% (57); All full-time undergraduates: 60% (273). *Average award:* Freshmen: $3965; Undergraduates: $3992. *Scholarships, grants, and awards:* Federal Pell, FSEOG, private, college/university gift aid from institutional funds.

GIFT AID (NON-NEED-BASED) *Total amount:* $506,872 (100% institutional). *Receiving aid:* Freshmen: 40% (33); Undergraduates: 42% (189). *Average Award:* Freshmen: $2200; *Undergraduates:* $2518. *Scholarships, grants, and awards by category: Special Achievements/Activities:* 89 awards ($64,964 total): community service, general special achievements/activities, leadership, religious involvement. *Special Characteristics:* children of faculty/staff. *Tuition waivers:* Full or partial for employees or children of employees, senior citizens.

LOANS *Student loans:* $3,821,585 (39% need-based, 61% non-need-based). 98% of past graduating class borrowed through all loan programs. *Average*

indebtedness per student: $25,978. ***Average need-based loan:*** Freshmen: $2892; Undergraduates: $4094. ***Parent loans:*** $160,320 (100% non-need-based). ***Programs:*** FFEL (Subsidized and Unsubsidized Stafford, PLUS), Perkins, state, college/university.

WORK-STUDY *Federal work-study:* Total amount: $62,379; 42 jobs averaging $1500. ***State or other work-study/employment:*** Total amount: $29,182 (100% need-based). 19 part-time jobs averaging $1500.

APPLYING FOR FINANCIAL AID *Required financial aid forms:* FAFSA, state aid form. ***Financial aid deadline (priority):*** 3/1. ***Notification date:*** Continuous beginning 4/1. Students must reply within 2 weeks of notification.

CONTACT Ms. Valerie Weisser, Director of Financial Aid, Presentation College, 1500 North Main Street, Aberdeen, SD 57401-1299, 605-229-8427 or toll-free 800-437-6060. *Fax:* 605-229-8537. *E-mail:* weisserv@presentation.edu.

PRINCETON UNIVERSITY
Princeton, NJ

Tuition & fees: $29,910	Average undergraduate aid package: $25,369

ABOUT THE INSTITUTION Independent, coed. Awards: bachelor's, master's, and doctoral degrees. 35 undergraduate majors. Total enrollment: 6,836. Undergraduates: 4,801. Freshmen: 1,172. Both federal and institutional methodology are used as a basis for awarding need-based institutional aid.

UNDERGRADUATE EXPENSES for 2004–05 *Application fee:* $65. **Comprehensive fee:** $38,297 includes full-time tuition ($29,910) and room and board ($8387). ***College room only:*** $4315. Room and board charges vary according to board plan and student level. ***Payment plans:*** Installment, deferred payment.

FRESHMAN FINANCIAL AID (Fall 2003) 699 applied for aid; of those 88% were deemed to have need. 100% of freshmen with need received aid; of those 100% had need fully met. *Average percent of need met:* 100% (excluding resources awarded to replace EFC). *Average financial aid package:* $25,752 (excluding resources awarded to replace EFC).

UNDERGRADUATE FINANCIAL AID (Fall 2003) 2,508 applied for aid; of those 90% were deemed to have need. 100% of undergraduates with need received aid; of those 100% had need fully met. *Average percent of need met:* 100% (excluding resources awarded to replace EFC). *Average financial aid package:* $25,369 (excluding resources awarded to replace EFC).

GIFT AID (NEED-BASED) *Total amount:* $54,529,300 (4% federal, 1% state, 90% institutional, 5% external sources). ***Receiving aid:*** Freshmen: 52% (616); All full-time undergraduates: 49% (2,269). ***Average award:*** Freshmen: $24,172; Undergraduates: $24,032. ***Scholarships, grants, and awards:*** Federal Pell, FSEOG, state, private, college/university gift aid from institutional funds.

GIFT AID (NON-NEED-BASED) *Tuition waivers:* Full or partial for employees or children of employees. ***ROTC:*** Army, Air Force cooperative.

LOANS *Student loans:* 32% of past graduating class borrowed through all loan programs. *Average indebtedness per student:* $8050. ***Parent loans:*** $1,900,000 (100% non-need-based). ***Programs:*** FFEL (Subsidized and Unsubsidized Stafford, PLUS), Perkins, college/university.

WORK-STUDY *Federal work-study:* Total amount: $1,108,100; 830 jobs averaging $1335. ***State or other work-study/employment:*** Total amount: $956,900 (100% need-based). 840 part-time jobs averaging $1140.

APPLYING FOR FINANCIAL AID *Required financial aid forms:* FAFSA, institution's own form. ***Financial aid deadline (priority):*** 2/1. ***Notification date:*** 4/1. Students must reply by 5/1.

CONTACT Mr. Don Betterton, Director of Financial Aid, Princeton University, Box 591, Princeton, NJ 08544-1019, 609-258-3330.

PRINCIPIA COLLEGE
Elsah, IL

Tuition & fees: $20,415	Average undergraduate aid package: $18,456

ABOUT THE INSTITUTION Independent Christian Science, coed. Awards: bachelor's degrees. 28 undergraduate majors. Total enrollment: 542. Undergraduates: 542. Freshmen: 118. Institutional methodology is used as a basis for awarding need-based institutional aid.

UNDERGRADUATE EXPENSES for 2005–06 *Comprehensive fee:* $27,765 includes full-time tuition ($20,145), mandatory fees ($270), and room and board ($7350). ***College room only:*** $3480. ***Part-time tuition:*** $447 per quarter hour. ***Payment plan:*** Installment.

FRESHMAN FINANCIAL AID (Fall 2004, est.) 79 applied for aid; of those 92% were deemed to have need. 100% of freshmen with need received aid; of those 59% had need fully met. *Average percent of need met:* 96% (excluding resources awarded to replace EFC). *Average financial aid package:* $18,251 (excluding resources awarded to replace EFC). 32% of all full-time freshmen had no need and received non-need-based gift aid.

UNDERGRADUATE FINANCIAL AID (Fall 2004, est.) 338 applied for aid; of those 95% were deemed to have need. 100% of undergraduates with need received aid; of those 62% had need fully met. *Average percent of need met:* 98% (excluding resources awarded to replace EFC). *Average financial aid package:* $18,456 (excluding resources awarded to replace EFC). 23% of all full-time undergraduates had no need and received non-need-based gift aid.

GIFT AID (NEED-BASED) *Total amount:* $4,019,021 (100% institutional). ***Receiving aid:*** Freshmen: 52% (63); All full-time undergraduates: 54% (300). ***Average award:*** Freshmen: $10,840; Undergraduates: $12,314. ***Scholarships, grants, and awards:*** private, college/university gift aid from institutional funds.

GIFT AID (NON-NEED-BASED) *Total amount:* $2,403,890 (100% institutional). ***Receiving aid:*** Freshmen: 28% (34); Undergraduates: 22% (120). ***Average Award:*** Freshmen: $10,225; *Undergraduates:* $7914. ***Scholarships, grants, and awards by category:*** Academic Interests/Achievement: 105 awards ($2,340,890 total): general academic interests/achievements. *Special Characteristics:* 61 awards ($427,783 total): children and siblings of alumni, children of faculty/staff. ***Tuition waivers:*** Full or partial for employees or children of employees.

LOANS *Student loans:* $1,218,128 (100% need-based). 62% of past graduating class borrowed through all loan programs. *Average indebtedness per student:* $11,936. *Average need-based loan:* Freshmen: $4456; Undergraduates: $4259. ***Programs:*** college/university.

WORK-STUDY *State or other work-study/employment:* Total amount: $218,479 (100% need-based). 138 part-time jobs averaging $1583.

APPLYING FOR FINANCIAL AID *Required financial aid forms:* institution's own form, CSS Financial Aid PROFILE, income tax form(s). ***Financial aid deadline:*** 3/1. ***Notification date:*** Continuous beginning 3/15. Students must reply by 5/1 or within 4 weeks of notification.

CONTACT Sarah E. McGuigan, Director of Financial Aid, Principia College, 1 Maybeck Place, Elsah, IL 62028-9799, 618-374-5186 or toll-free 800-277-4648 Ext. 2802. *Fax:* 618-374-5906. *E-mail:* finaid@prin.edu.

PROVIDENCE COLLEGE
Providence, RI

Tuition & fees: $25,310	Average undergraduate aid package: $14,800

ABOUT THE INSTITUTION Independent Roman Catholic, coed. Awards: associate, bachelor's, and master's degrees. 37 undergraduate majors. Total enrollment: 5,366. Undergraduates: 4,488. Freshmen: 1,038. Both federal and institutional methodology are used as a basis for awarding need-based institutional aid.

UNDERGRADUATE EXPENSES for 2005–06 *Application fee:* $55. **Comprehensive fee:** $34,580 includes full-time tuition ($24,800), mandatory fees ($510), and room and board ($9270). ***College room only:*** $4970. Room and board charges vary according to board plan and housing facility. ***Part-time tuition:*** $232 per credit. ***Payment plan:*** Installment.

FRESHMAN FINANCIAL AID (Fall 2004, est.) 759 applied for aid; of those 74% were deemed to have need. 100% of freshmen with need received aid; of those 20% had need fully met. *Average percent of need met:* 88% (excluding resources awarded to replace EFC). *Average financial aid package:* $15,625 (excluding resources awarded to replace EFC). 10% of all full-time freshmen had no need and received non-need-based gift aid.

UNDERGRADUATE FINANCIAL AID (Fall 2004, est.) 2,615 applied for aid; of those 90% were deemed to have need. 100% of undergraduates with need received aid; of those 17% had need fully met. *Average percent of need met:* 86% (excluding resources awarded to replace EFC). *Average financial aid package:* $14,800 (excluding resources awarded to replace EFC). 10% of all full-time undergraduates had no need and received non-need-based gift aid.

GIFT AID (NEED-BASED) *Total amount:* $21,165,800 (9% federal, 2% state, 86% institutional, 3% external sources). ***Receiving aid:*** Freshmen: 51% (529); All full-time undergraduates: 57% (2,119). ***Average award:*** Freshmen: $11,000; Undergraduates: $9000. ***Scholarships, grants, and awards:*** Federal Pell, FSEOG, state, private, college/university gift aid from institutional funds.

GIFT AID (NON-NEED-BASED) *Total amount:* $5,800,750 (93% institutional, 7% external sources). ***Receiving aid:*** Freshmen: 4% (44); Undergraduates: 13% (470). ***Average Award:*** Freshmen: $9000; *Undergraduates:* $10,000.

Scholarships, grants, and awards by category: Academic Interests/Achievement: 400 awards ($3,750,000 total): business, general academic interests/achievements, military science, premedicine. *Creative Arts/Performance:* 5 awards ($15,000 total): theater/drama. *Special Achievements/Activities:* 12 awards ($60,000 total): community service. *Tuition waivers:* Full or partial for employees or children of employees. *ROTC:* Army.

LOANS *Student loans:* $11,985,000 (76% need-based, 24% non-need-based). 65% of past graduating class borrowed through all loan programs. *Average indebtedness per student:* $23,000. *Average need-based loan:* Freshmen: $4625; Undergraduates: $6150. *Programs:* Federal Direct (Subsidized and Unsubsidized Stafford, PLUS), FFEL (Subsidized and Unsubsidized Stafford, PLUS), Perkins.

WORK-STUDY *Federal work-study:* Total amount: $900,000; 700 jobs averaging $1800. *State or other work-study/employment:* Total amount: $993,000 (100% non-need-based). 700 part-time jobs averaging $1800.

ATHLETIC AWARDS *Total amount:* $3,666,000 (40% need-based, 60% non-need-based).

APPLYING FOR FINANCIAL AID *Required financial aid forms:* FAFSA, CSS Financial Aid PROFILE. *Financial aid deadline:* 2/1. *Notification date:* 4/1. Students must reply by 5/1.

CONTACT Mr. Herbert J. D'Arcy, Executive Director of Financial Aid, Providence College, River Avenue and Eaton Street, Providence, RI 02918, 401-865-2286 or toll-free 800-721-6444. *Fax:* 401-865-1186. *E-mail:* hdarcy@providence.edu.

PUGET SOUND CHRISTIAN COLLEGE
Everett, WA

ABOUT THE INSTITUTION Independent Christian, coed. Awards: associate and bachelor's degrees. 9 undergraduate majors. Total enrollment: 227. Undergraduates: 227. Freshmen: 38.

GIFT AID (NEED-BASED) *Scholarships, grants, and awards:* Federal Pell, FSEOG, private, college/university gift aid from institutional funds.

GIFT AID (NON-NEED-BASED) *Scholarships, grants, and awards by category: Academic Interests/Achievement:* general academic interests/achievements, religion/biblical studies. *Special Characteristics:* children of faculty/staff, relatives of clergy, spouses of current students.

LOANS *Programs:* FFEL (Subsidized and Unsubsidized Stafford, PLUS), alternative loans.

WORK-STUDY Federal work-study jobs available.

APPLYING FOR FINANCIAL AID *Required financial aid form:* FAFSA.

CONTACT Carlene Krause, Financial Aid Officer, Puget Sound Christian College, 7011 226th Place SW, Mountlake Terrace, WA 98043, 425-775-8686 Ext. 565 or toll-free 888-775-8699. *Fax:* 425-775-8688. *E-mail:* ckrause@pscc.edu.

PURCHASE COLLEGE, STATE UNIVERSITY OF NEW YORK
Purchase, NY

CONTACT Ms. Emilie B. Devine, Director of Financial Aid and Scholarships, Purchase College, State University of New York, 735 Anderson Hill Road, Purchase, NY 10577-1400, 914-251-6352. *E-mail:* emilie.devine@purchase.edu.

PURDUE UNIVERSITY
West Lafayette, IN

Tuition & fees (IN res): $6335	Average undergraduate aid package: $9426

ABOUT THE INSTITUTION State-supported, coed. Awards: associate, bachelor's, master's, doctoral, and first professional degrees. 84 undergraduate majors. Total enrollment: 38,653. Undergraduates: 30,747. Freshmen: 6,672. Federal methodology is used as a basis for awarding need-based institutional aid.

UNDERGRADUATE EXPENSES for 2005–06 *Application fee:* $30. *Tuition, state resident:* full-time $6335; part-time $227.10 per credit. *Tuition, nonresident:* full-time $19,822; part-time $658 per credit. Full-time tuition and fees vary according to course load and program. Part-time tuition and fees vary according to course load. *College room and board:* $7406. Room and board charges vary according to board plan and housing facility. *Payment plan:* Installment.

FRESHMAN FINANCIAL AID (Fall 2004, est.) 4817 applied for aid; of those 64% were deemed to have need. 95% of freshmen with need received aid; of those 31% had need fully met. *Average percent of need met:* 90% (excluding

resources awarded to replace EFC). *Average financial aid package:* $9990 (excluding resources awarded to replace EFC). 17% of all full-time freshmen had no need and received non-need-based gift aid.

UNDERGRADUATE FINANCIAL AID (Fall 2004, est.) 17,489 applied for aid; of those 70% were deemed to have need. 96% of undergraduates with need received aid; of those 35% had need fully met. *Average percent of need met:* 90% (excluding resources awarded to replace EFC). *Average financial aid package:* $9426 (excluding resources awarded to replace EFC). 13% of all full-time undergraduates had no need and received non-need-based gift aid.

GIFT AID (NEED-BASED) *Total amount:* $58,722,789 (43% federal, 27% state, 30% institutional). *Receiving aid:* Freshmen: 15% (1,022); All full-time undergraduates: 13% (3,886). *Average award:* Freshmen: $8946; Undergraduates: $7630. *Scholarships, grants, and awards:* Federal Pell, FSEOG, state, private, college/university gift aid from institutional funds.

GIFT AID (NON-NEED-BASED) *Total amount:* $8,964,444 (100% external sources). *Receiving aid:* Freshmen: 11% (750); Undergraduates: 6% (1,736). *Average Award:* Freshmen: $12,724; Undergraduates: $10,865. *Scholarships, grants, and awards by category: Academic Interests/Achievement:* agriculture, biological sciences, business, computer science, education, engineering/technologies, general academic interests/achievements, health fields, humanities, mathematics, military science, physical sciences. *Creative Arts/Performance:* music. *Special Achievements/Activities:* community service, leadership. *Special Characteristics:* children of faculty/staff. *Tuition waivers:* Full or partial for employees or children of employees, senior citizens. *ROTC:* Army, Naval, Air Force.

LOANS *Student loans:* $92,386,695 (56% need-based, 44% non-need-based). 49% of past graduating class borrowed through all loan programs. *Average indebtedness per student:* $17,510. *Average need-based loan:* Freshmen: $3005; Undergraduates: $4022. *Parent loans:* $130,376,382 (17% need-based, 83% non-need-based). *Programs:* FFEL (Subsidized and Unsubsidized Stafford, PLUS), Perkins, college/university, Federal Health Professions Loans.

WORK-STUDY *Federal work-study:* Total amount: $2,247,095; 1,290 jobs averaging $1742.

ATHLETIC AWARDS *Total amount:* $5,283,746 (100% non-need-based).

APPLYING FOR FINANCIAL AID *Required financial aid form:* FAFSA. *Financial aid deadline (priority):* 3/1. *Notification date:* 4/15.

CONTACT Division of Financial Aid, Purdue University, Schleman Hall of Student Services, Room 305, 475 Stadium Mall Drive, West Lafayette, IN 47907-2050, 765-494-5050.

PURDUE UNIVERSITY CALUMET
Hammond, IN

Tuition & fees (IN res): $4662	Average undergraduate aid package: $4586

ABOUT THE INSTITUTION State-supported, coed. Awards: associate, bachelor's, and master's degrees and post-bachelor's certificates. 76 undergraduate majors. Total enrollment: 9,222. Undergraduates: 8,283. Freshmen: 1,171. Federal methodology is used as a basis for awarding need-based institutional aid.

UNDERGRADUATE EXPENSES for 2005–06 *Tuition, state resident:* full-time $4316; part-time $154.15 per credit hour. *Tuition, nonresident:* full-time $10,096; part-time $360.60 per credit hour. *Required fees:* full-time $346; $13.40 per credit hour. Full-time tuition and fees vary according to program. Part-time tuition and fees vary according to course load and program. *College room and board: room only:* $3990. Room and board charges vary according to housing facility. *Payment plan:* Deferred payment.

FRESHMAN FINANCIAL AID (Fall 2003) 915 applied for aid; of those 82% were deemed to have need. 82% of freshmen with need received aid; of those 1% had need fully met. *Average percent of need met:* 19% (excluding resources awarded to replace EFC). *Average financial aid package:* $3211 (excluding resources awarded to replace EFC).

UNDERGRADUATE FINANCIAL AID (Fall 2003) 3,584 applied for aid; of those 81% were deemed to have need. 90% of undergraduates with need received aid; of those 1% had need fully met. *Average percent of need met:* 22% (excluding resources awarded to replace EFC). *Average financial aid package:* $4586 (excluding resources awarded to replace EFC). 2% of all full-time undergraduates had no need and received non-need-based gift aid.

GIFT AID (NEED-BASED) *Total amount:* $8,552,827 (65% federal, 34% state, 1% institutional). *Receiving aid:* Freshmen: 36% (470); All full-time undergraduates: 34% (1,863). *Average award:* Freshmen: $5143; Undergraduates: $6965. *Scholarships, grants, and awards:* Federal Pell, FSEOG, state, private, college/university gift aid from institutional funds.

GIFT AID (NON-NEED-BASED) *Total amount:* $1,368,914 (1% federal, 34% state, 45% institutional, 20% external sources). *Receiving aid:* Freshmen: 4% (53); Undergraduates: 7% (388). *Average Award: Undergraduates:* $3074. *Scholarships, grants, and awards by category: Academic Interests/Achievement:* 450 awards ($460,000 total): general academic interests/achievements. *Tuition waivers:* Full or partial for employees or children of employees, senior citizens. *ROTC:* Army cooperative.

LOANS *Student loans:* $10,781,107 (97% need-based, 3% non-need-based). 69% of past graduating class borrowed through all loan programs. *Average indebtedness per student:* $18,940. *Average need-based loan:* Freshmen: $2776; Undergraduates: $4922. *Parent loans:* $193,394 (100% non-need-based). *Programs:* Federal Direct (Subsidized and Unsubsidized Stafford, PLUS), Perkins.

WORK-STUDY *Federal work-study:* Total amount: $254,506; 138 jobs averaging $1936. *State or other work-study/employment:* Part-time jobs available.

ATHLETIC AWARDS *Total amount:* $52,275 (100% non-need-based).

APPLYING FOR FINANCIAL AID *Required financial aid form:* FAFSA. *Financial aid deadline (priority):* 3/10. *Notification date:* Continuous beginning 5/1. Students must reply within 2 weeks of notification.

CONTACT Ms. Chris Strug, Assistant Director of Financial Aid, Purdue University Calumet, 2200 169th Street, Hammond, IN 46323-2094, 219-989-2301 or toll-free 800-447-8738 (in-state). *Fax:* 219-989-2141. *E-mail:* finaid@calumet.purdue.edu.

PURDUE UNIVERSITY NORTH CENTRAL
Westville, IN

CONTACT Gerald Lewis, Director of Financial Aid, Purdue University North Central, 1401 South US Highway 421, Westville, IN 46391-9528, 219-785-5279 Ext. 5502 or toll-free 800-872-1231 (in-state). *Fax:* 219-785-5538.

QUEENS COLLEGE OF THE CITY UNIVERSITY OF NEW YORK
Flushing, NY

ABOUT THE INSTITUTION State and locally supported, coed. Awards: bachelor's and master's degrees and post-bachelor's and post-master's certificates. 72 undergraduate majors. Total enrollment: 17,395. Undergraduates: 12,628. Freshmen: 1,384.

GIFT AID (NEED-BASED) *Scholarships, grants, and awards:* Federal Pell, FSEOG, state, private, college/university gift aid from institutional funds.

GIFT AID (NON-NEED-BASED) *Scholarships, grants, and awards by category: Academic Interests/Achievement:* general academic interests/achievements. *Creative Arts/Performance:* music. *Special Achievements/Activities:* community service, leadership.

LOANS *Programs:* Federal Direct (Subsidized and Unsubsidized Stafford, PLUS), Perkins.

WORK-STUDY *Federal work-study:* Total amount: $1,625,048; 1,253 jobs averaging $1300.

APPLYING FOR FINANCIAL AID *Required financial aid forms:* FAFSA, institution's own form, state aid form.

CONTACT Office of Financial Aid Services, Queens College of the City University of New York, 65-30 Kissena Boulevard, Flushing, NY 11367-1597, 718-997-5100.

QUEENS UNIVERSITY OF CHARLOTTE
Charlotte, NC

ABOUT THE INSTITUTION Independent Presbyterian, coed. Awards: associate, bachelor's, and master's degrees and post-bachelor's certificates. 37 undergraduate majors. Total enrollment: 2,107. Undergraduates: 1,601. Freshmen: 245.

GIFT AID (NEED-BASED) *Scholarships, grants, and awards:* Federal Pell, FSEOG, state, private, college/university gift aid from institutional funds, United Negro College Fund.

GIFT AID (NON-NEED-BASED) *Scholarships, grants, and awards by category: Academic Interests/Achievement:* general academic interests/achievements. *Creative Arts/Performance:* art/fine arts, music, theater/drama. *Special Achievements/Activities:* community service, general special achievements/activities, leadership, religious involvement. *Special Characteristics:* adult students, children of current students, children of faculty/staff, first-generation college students, international students, members of minority groups, relatives of clergy, religious affiliation, siblings of current students.

LOANS *Programs:* FFEL (Subsidized and Unsubsidized Stafford, PLUS), Perkins.

APPLYING FOR FINANCIAL AID *Required financial aid form:* FAFSA.

CONTACT Lauren H. Mack, Director of Financial Aid, Queens University of Charlotte, 1900 Selwyn Avenue, Charlotte, NC 28274-0002, 704-337-2230 or toll-free 800-849-0202. *Fax:* 704-337-2416. *E-mail:* mackl@queens.edu.

QUINCY UNIVERSITY
Quincy, IL

Tuition & fees: $18,330	Average undergraduate aid package: $14,145

ABOUT THE INSTITUTION Independent Roman Catholic, coed. Awards: associate, bachelor's, and master's degrees. 40 undergraduate majors. Total enrollment: 1,294. Undergraduates: 1,086. Freshmen: 228. Federal methodology is used as a basis for awarding need-based institutional aid.

UNDERGRADUATE EXPENSES for 2005–06 *Application fee:* $25. *Comprehensive fee:* $24,920 includes full-time tuition ($17,800), mandatory fees ($530), and room and board ($6590). *College room only:* $3540. Room and board charges vary according to board plan and housing facility. *Part-time tuition:* $465 per credit hour. *Part-time fees:* $15 per credit hour. *Payment plan:* Installment.

FRESHMAN FINANCIAL AID (Fall 2003) 216 applied for aid; of those 84% were deemed to have need. 100% of freshmen with need received aid; of those 30% had need fully met. *Average percent of need met:* 84% (excluding resources awarded to replace EFC). *Average financial aid package:* $15,162 (excluding resources awarded to replace EFC). 13% of all full-time freshmen had no need and received non-need-based gift aid.

UNDERGRADUATE FINANCIAL AID (Fall 2003) 865 applied for aid; of those 88% were deemed to have need. 99% of undergraduates with need received aid; of those 39% had need fully met. *Average percent of need met:* 80% (excluding resources awarded to replace EFC). *Average financial aid package:* $14,145 (excluding resources awarded to replace EFC). 11% of all full-time undergraduates had no need and received non-need-based gift aid.

GIFT AID (NEED-BASED) *Total amount:* $6,013,535 (18% federal, 26% state, 55% institutional, 1% external sources). *Receiving aid:* Freshmen: 80% (181); All full-time undergraduates: 72% (732). *Average award:* Freshmen: $12,272; Undergraduates: $11,145. *Scholarships, grants, and awards:* Federal Pell, FSEOG, state, private, college/university gift aid from institutional funds.

GIFT AID (NON-NEED-BASED) *Total amount:* $1,673,264 (1% state, 96% institutional, 3% external sources). *Receiving aid:* Freshmen: 14% (31); Undergraduates: 11% (110). *Average Award:* Freshmen: $7276; Undergraduates: $6260. *Scholarships, grants, and awards by category: Academic Interests/Achievement:* 823 awards ($4,515,315 total): biological sciences, business, communication, computer science, education, English, general academic interests/achievements, health fields, international studies, mathematics, premedicine, religion/biblical studies, social sciences. *Creative Arts/Performance:* 44 awards ($56,041 total): art/fine arts, cinema/film/broadcasting, music. *Special Achievements/Activities:* 7 awards ($29,042 total): community service, leadership. *Special Characteristics:* 25 awards ($203,536 total): children of faculty/staff. *Tuition waivers:* Full or partial for employees or children of employees, senior citizens.

LOANS *Student loans:* $3,990,728 (64% need-based, 36% non-need-based). 80% of past graduating class borrowed through all loan programs. *Average indebtedness per student:* $16,837. *Average need-based loan:* Freshmen: $2817; Undergraduates: $4234. *Parent loans:* $1,165,872 (12% need-based, 88% non-need-based). *Programs:* FFEL (Subsidized and Unsubsidized Stafford, PLUS), Perkins.

WORK-STUDY *Federal work-study:* Total amount: $155,146; 569 jobs averaging $2000. *State or other work-study/employment:* Total amount: $24,958 (36% need-based, 64% non-need-based). 35 part-time jobs averaging $3000.

ATHLETIC AWARDS *Total amount:* $1,756,735 (18% need-based, 82% non-need-based).

APPLYING FOR FINANCIAL AID *Required financial aid form:* FAFSA. *Financial aid deadline (priority):* 3/15. *Notification date:* Continuous. Students must reply by 5/1 or within 2 weeks of notification.

CONTACT Shann Doerr, Director of Financial Aid, Quincy University, 1800 College Avenue, Quincy, IL 62301-2699, 217-228-5260 or toll-free 800-688-4295. *Fax:* 217-228-5635. *E-mail:* doerrsh@quincy.edu.

QUINNIPIAC UNIVERSITY
Hamden, CT

Tuition & fees: $24,340	Average undergraduate aid package: $13,160

Quinnipiac University

ABOUT THE INSTITUTION Independent, coed. Awards: bachelor's, master's, doctoral, and first professional degrees and post-bachelor's certificates. 62 undergraduate majors. Total enrollment: 7,220. Undergraduates: 5,464. Freshmen: 1,336. Federal methodology is used as a basis for awarding need-based institutional aid.

UNDERGRADUATE EXPENSES for 2005–06 *Application fee:* $45. *Comprehensive fee:* $34,640 includes full-time tuition ($23,360), mandatory fees ($980), and room and board ($10,300). Room and board charges vary according to housing facility. *Part-time tuition:* $570 per credit. *Part-time fees:* $30 per credit. Part-time tuition and fees vary according to course load. *Payment plans:* Installment, deferred payment.

FRESHMAN FINANCIAL AID (Fall 2004, est.) 1051 applied for aid; of those 78% were deemed to have need. 100% of freshmen with need received aid; of those 11% had need fully met. *Average percent of need met:* 64% (excluding resources awarded to replace EFC). *Average financial aid package:* $13,019 (excluding resources awarded to replace EFC). 9% of all full-time freshmen had no need and received non-need-based gift aid.

UNDERGRADUATE FINANCIAL AID (Fall 2004, est.) 3,599 applied for aid; of those 84% were deemed to have need. 100% of undergraduates with need received aid; of those 13% had need fully met. *Average percent of need met:* 66% (excluding resources awarded to replace EFC). *Average financial aid package:* $13,160 (excluding resources awarded to replace EFC). 9% of all full-time undergraduates had no need and received non-need-based gift aid.

GIFT AID (NEED-BASED) *Total amount:* $19,767,380 (9% federal, 12% state, 74% institutional, 5% external sources). *Receiving aid:* Freshmen: 60% (805); All full-time undergraduates: 57% (2,893). *Average award:* Freshmen: $9236; Undergraduates: $8937. *Scholarships, grants, and awards:* Federal Pell, FSEOG, state, private, college/university gift aid from institutional funds.

GIFT AID (NON-NEED-BASED) *Total amount:* $8,390,074 (98% institutional, 2% external sources). *Receiving aid:* Freshmen: 25% (340); Undergraduates: 23% (1,170). *Average Award: Freshmen:* $6116; *Undergraduates:* $5272. *Scholarships, grants, and awards by category: Academic Interests/Achievement:* 1,108 awards ($6,450,486 total): general academic interests/achievements. *Special Achievements/Activities:* 8 awards ($68,000 total): leadership. *Special Characteristics:* 662 awards ($2,699,766 total): children of faculty/staff, international students, members of minority groups, siblings of current students. *Tuition waivers:* Full or partial for employees or children of employees. *ROTC:* Army cooperative, Air Force cooperative.

LOANS *Student loans:* $18,503,668 (75% need-based, 25% non-need-based). 71% of past graduating class borrowed through all loan programs. *Average indebtedness per student:* $20,269. *Average need-based loan:* Freshmen: $2883; Undergraduates: $4087. *Parent loans:* $12,060,478 (100% non-need-based). *Programs:* FFEL (Subsidized and Unsubsidized Stafford, PLUS), Perkins, Federal Nursing.

WORK-STUDY *Federal work-study:* Total amount: $2,878,881; 1,443 jobs averaging $1978. *State or other work-study/employment:* Total amount: $57,150 (100% need-based). 41 part-time jobs averaging $1450.

ATHLETIC AWARDS *Total amount:* $4,644,526 (100% non-need-based).

APPLYING FOR FINANCIAL AID *Required financial aid form:* FAFSA. *Financial aid deadline (priority):* 3/1. *Notification date:* Continuous. Students must reply by 5/1 or within 2 weeks of notification.

CONTACT Mr. Dominic Yoia, Senior Director of Financial Aid, Quinnipiac University, 275 Mount Carmel Avenue, Hamden, CT 06518, 203-582-5224 or toll-free 800-462-1944 (out-of-state). *Fax:* 203-582-5238. *E-mail:* finaid@quinnipiac.edu.

RABBI JACOB JOSEPH SCHOOL
Edison, NJ

CONTACT Financial Aid Office, Rabbi Jacob Joseph School, One Plainfield Ave, Edison, NJ 08817, 908-985-6533.

RABBINICAL ACADEMY MESIVTA RABBI CHAIM BERLIN
Brooklyn, NY

CONTACT Office of Financial Aid, Rabbinical Academy Mesivta Rabbi Chaim Berlin, 1605 Coney Island Avenue, Brooklyn, NY 11230-4715, 718-377-0777.

RABBINICAL COLLEGE BETH SHRAGA
Monsey, NY

CONTACT Financial Aid Office, Rabbinical College Beth Shraga, 28 Saddle River Road, Monsey, NY 10952-3035, 914-356-1980.

RABBINICAL COLLEGE BOBOVER YESHIVA B'NEI ZION
Brooklyn, NY

CONTACT Financial Aid Office, Rabbinical College Bobover Yeshiva B'nei Zion, 1577 48th Street, Brooklyn, NY 11219, 718-438-2018.

RABBINICAL COLLEGE CH'SAN SOFER
Brooklyn, NY

CONTACT Financial Aid Office, Rabbinical College Ch'san Sofer, 1876 50th Street, Brooklyn, NY 11204, 718-236-1171.

RABBINICAL COLLEGE OF AMERICA
Morristown, NJ

CONTACT Financial Aid Office, Rabbinical College of America, 226 Sussex Avenue, Morristown, NJ 07960, 973-267-9404. *Fax:* 973-267-5208.

RABBINICAL COLLEGE OF LONG ISLAND
Long Beach, NY

CONTACT Rabbi Cone, Financial Aid Administrator, Rabbinical College of Long Island, 201 Magnolia Boulevard, Long Beach, NY 11561-3305, 516-431-7414.

RABBINICAL COLLEGE OF OHR SHIMON YISROEL
Brooklyn, NY

CONTACT Financial Aid Office, Rabbinical College of Ohr Shimon Yisroel, 215-217 Hewes Street, Brooklyn, NY 11211, 718-855-4092.

RABBINICAL COLLEGE OF TELSHE
Wickliffe, OH

CONTACT Financial Aid Office, Rabbinical College of Telshe, 28400 Euclid Avenue, Wickliffe, OH 44092-2523, 216-943-5300.

RABBINICAL SEMINARY ADAS YEREIM
Brooklyn, NY

CONTACT Mr. Israel Weingarten, Financial Aid Administrator, Rabbinical Seminary Adas Yereim, 185 Wilson Street, Brooklyn, NY 11211-7206, 718-388-1751.

RABBINICAL SEMINARY M'KOR CHAIM
Brooklyn, NY

CONTACT Financial Aid Office, Rabbinical Seminary M'kor Chaim, 1571 55th Street, Brooklyn, NY 11219, 718-851-0183.

RABBINICAL SEMINARY OF AMERICA
Flushing, NY

CONTACT Ms. Leah Eisenstein, Director of Financial Aid, Rabbinical Seminary of America, 92-15 69th Avenue, Forest Hills, NY 11375, 718-268-4700. *Fax:* 718-268-4684.

RADFORD UNIVERSITY
Radford, VA

Tuition & fees (VA res): $4762   **Average undergraduate aid package: $7736**

ABOUT THE INSTITUTION State-supported, coed. Awards: bachelor's and master's degrees and post-master's certificates. 43 undergraduate majors. Total enrollment: 9,329. Undergraduates: 8,356. Freshmen: 1,832. Federal methodology is used as a basis for awarding need-based institutional aid.

UNDERGRADUATE EXPENSES for 2004–05 *Application fee:* $35. *Tuition, state resident:* full-time $4762; part-time $198 per credit hour. *Tuition, nonresident:* full-time $11,762; part-time $490 per credit hour. *College room and board:* $5886; *room only:* $3154. Room and board charges vary according to board plan and housing facility. *Payment plan:* Installment.

FRESHMAN FINANCIAL AID (Fall 2003) 1193 applied for aid; of those 62% were deemed to have need. 96% of freshmen with need received aid; of those 64% had need fully met. *Average percent of need met:* 68% (excluding resources awarded to replace EFC). *Average financial aid package:* $6421 (excluding resources awarded to replace EFC). 23% of all full-time freshmen had no need and received non-need-based gift aid.

UNDERGRADUATE FINANCIAL AID (Fall 2003) 4,759 applied for aid; of those 68% were deemed to have need. 96% of undergraduates with need received aid; of those 65% had need fully met. *Average percent of need met:* 73% (excluding resources awarded to replace EFC). *Average financial aid package:* $7736 (excluding resources awarded to replace EFC). 23% of all full-time undergraduates had no need and received non-need-based gift aid.

GIFT AID (NEED-BASED) *Total amount:* $9,823,686 (47% federal, 39% state, 5% institutional, 9% external sources). *Receiving aid:* Freshmen: 27% (487); All full-time undergraduates: 27% (2,109). *Average award:* Freshmen: $3864; Undergraduates: $3717. *Scholarships, grants, and awards:* Federal Pell, FSEOG, state, private, college/university gift aid from institutional funds.

GIFT AID (NON-NEED-BASED) *Total amount:* $1,290,972 (6% state, 36% institutional, 58% external sources). *Receiving aid:* Freshmen: 12% (228); Undergraduates: 9% (693). *Average Award:* Freshmen: $5266; Undergraduates: $5566. *Scholarships, grants, and awards by category:* Academic Interests/Achievement: 379 awards ($841,530 total): area/ethnic studies, biological sciences, business, communication, computer science, education, English, general academic interests/achievements, health fields, humanities, library science, mathematics, military science, physical sciences, premedicine, social sciences. Creative Arts/Performance: 61 awards ($55,000 total): applied art and design, art/fine arts, cinema/film/broadcasting, dance, music, theater/drama. *Special Achievements/Activities:* 1 award ($500 total): leadership. *Special Characteristics:* 7 awards ($4750 total): children of faculty/staff. *Tuition waivers:* Full or partial for employees or children of employees. *ROTC:* Army, Naval cooperative.

LOANS *Student loans:* $20,559,368 (72% need-based, 28% non-need-based). 62% of past graduating class borrowed through all loan programs. *Average indebtedness per student:* $14,908. *Average need-based loan:* Freshmen: $2402; Undergraduates: $3257. *Parent loans:* $2,145,947 (89% need-based, 11% non-need-based). *Programs:* FFEL (Subsidized and Unsubsidized Stafford, PLUS), Perkins, Federal Nursing, state, college/university.

WORK-STUDY *Federal work-study:* Total amount: $527,837; 518 jobs averaging $1086. *State or other work-study/employment:* Total amount: $1,196,426 (45% need-based, 55% non-need-based). 600 part-time jobs averaging $1097.

ATHLETIC AWARDS *Total amount:* $570,444 (86% need-based, 14% non-need-based).

APPLYING FOR FINANCIAL AID *Required financial aid form:* FAFSA. *Financial aid deadline (priority):* 3/1. *Notification date:* 4/15. Students must reply within 2 weeks of notification.

CONTACT Mrs. Barbara Porter, Director of Financial Aid, Radford University, PO Box 6905, Radford, VA 24142, 540-831-5408 or toll-free 800-890-4265. *Fax:* 540-831-5138. *E-mail:* bporter@radford.edu.

RAMAPO COLLEGE OF NEW JERSEY
Mahwah, NJ

Tuition & fees (NJ res): $8081   **Average undergraduate aid package: $8928**

ABOUT THE INSTITUTION State-supported, coed. Awards: bachelor's and master's degrees. 40 undergraduate majors. Total enrollment: 5,617. Undergraduates: 5,278. Freshmen: 755. Federal methodology is used as a basis for awarding need-based institutional aid.

UNDERGRADUATE EXPENSES for 2004–05 *Application fee:* $55. *Tuition, state resident:* full-time $5640; part-time $176 per credit. *Tuition, nonresident:* full-time $10,192; part-time $319 per credit. *Required fees:* full-time $2441; $76 per credit or $1220 per term part-time. Part-time tuition and fees vary according to course load. *College room and board:* $8208; *room only:* $5628. Room and board charges vary according to board plan and housing facility. *Payment plans:* Installment, deferred payment.

FRESHMAN FINANCIAL AID (Fall 2003) 519 applied for aid; of those 70% were deemed to have need. 95% of freshmen with need received aid; of those 17% had need fully met. *Average percent of need met:* 88% (excluding resources awarded to replace EFC). *Average financial aid package:* $10,501 (excluding resources awarded to replace EFC). 19% of all full-time freshmen had no need and received non-need-based gift aid.

UNDERGRADUATE FINANCIAL AID (Fall 2003) 2,602 applied for aid; of those 76% were deemed to have need. 97% of undergraduates with need received aid; of those 16% had need fully met. *Average percent of need met:* 81% (excluding resources awarded to replace EFC). *Average financial aid package:* $8928 (excluding resources awarded to replace EFC). 13% of all full-time undergraduates had no need and received non-need-based gift aid.

GIFT AID (NEED-BASED) *Total amount:* $6,240,187 (44% federal, 46% state, 10% institutional). *Receiving aid:* Freshmen: 25% (179); All full-time undergraduates: 25% (998). *Average award:* Freshmen: $9743; Undergraduates: $6387. *Scholarships, grants, and awards:* Federal Pell, FSEOG, state, private, college/university gift aid from institutional funds.

GIFT AID (NON-NEED-BASED) *Total amount:* $4,128,309 (12% state, 79% institutional, 9% external sources). *Receiving aid:* Freshmen: 25% (178); Undergraduates: 21% (832). *Average Award:* Freshmen: $7328; Undergraduates: $6899. *Scholarships, grants, and awards by category:* Academic Interests/Achievement: 489 awards ($3,309,518 total): general academic interests/achievements. *Special Characteristics:* 71 awards ($925,414 total): international students, out-of-state students. *Tuition waivers:* Full or partial for minority students, employees or children of employees, senior citizens. *ROTC:* Air Force cooperative.

LOANS *Student loans:* $14,259,870 (46% need-based, 54% non-need-based). 35% of past graduating class borrowed through all loan programs. *Average indebtedness per student:* $15,666. *Average need-based loan:* Freshmen: $2570; Undergraduates: $3896. *Parent loans:* $2,727,609 (100% non-need-based). *Programs:* Federal Direct (Subsidized and Unsubsidized Stafford, PLUS), Perkins, state.

WORK-STUDY *Federal work-study:* Total amount: $193,789; 137 jobs averaging $1703. *State or other work-study/employment:* Total amount: $1,380,434 (100% non-need-based). 501 part-time jobs averaging $2105.

APPLYING FOR FINANCIAL AID *Required financial aid form:* FAFSA. *Financial aid deadline (priority):* 3/1. *Notification date:* Continuous beginning 4/1. Students must reply by 5/1 or within 2 weeks of notification.

CONTACT Bernice Mulch, Assistant Director of Financial Aid, Ramapo College of New Jersey, 505 Ramapo Valley Road, Mahwah, NJ 07430-1680, 201-684-7252 or toll-free 800-9RAMAPO (in-state). *Fax:* 201-684-7085. *E-mail:* finaid@ramapo.edu.

RANDOLPH-MACON COLLEGE
Ashland, VA

Tuition & fees: $22,625   **Average undergraduate aid package: $16,629**

ABOUT THE INSTITUTION Independent United Methodist, coed. Awards: bachelor's degrees. 30 undergraduate majors. Total enrollment: 1,127. Undergraduates: 1,127. Freshmen: 325. Federal methodology is used as a basis for awarding need-based institutional aid.

UNDERGRADUATE EXPENSES for 2004–05 *Application fee:* $30. *Comprehensive fee:* $29,135 includes full-time tuition ($21,990), mandatory fees ($635), and room and board ($6510). *College room only:* $3380. Room and board charges vary according to board plan and housing facility. *Part-time tuition:* $250 per credit hour. *Payment plan:* Installment.

FRESHMAN FINANCIAL AID (Fall 2004, est.) 257 applied for aid; of those 80% were deemed to have need. 100% of freshmen with need received aid; of those 39% had need fully met. *Average percent of need met:* 89% (excluding resources awarded to replace EFC). *Average financial aid package:* $17,305 (excluding resources awarded to replace EFC). 34% of all full-time freshmen had no need and received non-need-based gift aid.

UNDERGRADUATE FINANCIAL AID (Fall 2004, est.) 765 applied for aid; of those 84% were deemed to have need. 100% of undergraduates with need received aid; of those 28% had need fully met. *Average percent of need met:*

83% (excluding resources awarded to replace EFC). *Average financial aid package:* $16,629 (excluding resources awarded to replace EFC). 36% of all full-time undergraduates had no need and received non-need-based gift aid.

GIFT AID (NEED-BASED) *Total amount:* $7,410,432 (5% federal, 14% state, 74% institutional, 7% external sources). *Receiving aid:* Freshmen: 63% (206); All full-time undergraduates: 58% (639). *Average award:* Freshmen: $13,130; Undergraduates: $11,780. *Scholarships, grants, and awards:* Federal Pell, FSEOG, state, private, college/university gift aid from institutional funds.

GIFT AID (NON-NEED-BASED) *Total amount:* $3,653,313 (21% state, 68% institutional, 11% external sources). *Receiving aid:* Freshmen: 13% (41); Undergraduates: 8% (89). *Average Award: Freshmen:* $11,873; *Undergraduates:* $11,325. *Scholarships, grants, and awards by category: Academic Interests/Achievement:* 378 awards ($3,634,551 total): general academic interests/achievements, premedicine. *Special Achievements/Activities:* 228 awards ($1,069,430 total): general special achievements/activities. *Special Characteristics:* 129 awards ($706,326 total): children and siblings of alumni, children of faculty/staff, relatives of clergy, siblings of current students. *Tuition waivers:* Full or partial for employees or children of employees. *ROTC:* Army cooperative.

LOANS *Student loans:* $4,995,704 (66% need-based, 34% non-need-based). 64% of past graduating class borrowed through all loan programs. *Average indebtedness per student:* $18,031. *Average need-based loan:* Freshmen: $4302; Undergraduates: $4882. *Parent loans:* $2,873,427 (22% need-based, 78% non-need-based). *Programs:* FFEL (Subsidized and Unsubsidized Stafford, PLUS), Perkins, college/university.

WORK-STUDY *Federal work-study:* Total amount: $505,341; 233 jobs averaging $2169.

APPLYING FOR FINANCIAL AID *Required financial aid forms:* FAFSA, state aid form. *Financial aid deadline (priority):* 2/1. *Notification date:* 4/1. Students must reply by 5/1 or within 2 weeks of notification.

CONTACT Ms. Mary Neal, Director of Financial Aid, Randolph-Macon College, PO Box 5005, Ashland, VA 23005-5505, 804-752-7259 or toll-free 800-888-1762. *Fax:* 804-752-3719. *E-mail:* mneal@rmc.edu.

RANDOLPH-MACON WOMAN'S COLLEGE
Lynchburg, VA

Tuition & fees: $21,740	Average undergraduate aid package: $21,075

ABOUT THE INSTITUTION Independent Methodist, women only. Awards: bachelor's degrees. 37 undergraduate majors. Total enrollment: 732. Undergraduates: 732. Freshmen: 207. Federal methodology is used as a basis for awarding need-based institutional aid.

UNDERGRADUATE EXPENSES for 2004–05 *Application fee:* $35. *Comprehensive fee:* $29,970 includes full-time tuition ($21,360), mandatory fees ($380), and room and board ($8230). *Part-time tuition:* $890 per semester hour. *Part-time fees:* $45 per term. Part-time tuition and fees vary according to course load. *Payment plan:* Installment.

FRESHMAN FINANCIAL AID (Fall 2004, est.) 176 applied for aid; of those 85% were deemed to have need. 100% of freshmen with need received aid; of those 35% had need fully met. *Average percent of need met:* 88% (excluding resources awarded to replace EFC). *Average financial aid package:* $21,385 (excluding resources awarded to replace EFC). 28% of all full-time freshmen had no need and received non-need-based gift aid.

UNDERGRADUATE FINANCIAL AID (Fall 2004, est.) 537 applied for aid; of those 89% were deemed to have need. 100% of undergraduates with need received aid; of those 34% had need fully met. *Average percent of need met:* 88% (excluding resources awarded to replace EFC). *Average financial aid package:* $21,075 (excluding resources awarded to replace EFC). 29% of all full-time undergraduates had no need and received non-need-based gift aid.

GIFT AID (NEED-BASED) *Total amount:* $7,212,993 (9% federal, 6% state, 83% institutional, 2% external sources). *Receiving aid:* Freshmen: 72% (149); All full-time undergraduates: 70% (480). *Average award:* Freshmen: $16,877; Undergraduates: $15,202. *Scholarships, grants, and awards:* Federal Pell, FSEOG, state, private, college/university gift aid from institutional funds.

GIFT AID (NON-NEED-BASED) *Total amount:* $3,117,909 (9% state, 89% institutional, 2% external sources). *Receiving aid:* Freshmen: 13% (26); Undergraduates: 10% (69). *Average Award: Freshmen:* $13,229; *Undergraduates:* $13,000. *Scholarships, grants, and awards by category: Academic Interests/Achievement:* 460 awards ($4,256,929 total): biological sciences, education, English, general academic interests/achievements, mathematics, physical sciences, premedicine, social sciences. *Creative Arts/Performance:* 10 awards ($23,000 total): art/fine arts, creative writing, music, theater/drama. *Special Achievements/Activities:* 198 awards ($1,239,500 total): community service,

general special achievements/activities, leadership, religious involvement. *Special Characteristics:* 158 awards ($1,200,406 total): adult students, children of faculty/staff, international students, local/state students, relatives of clergy, religious affiliation, twins. *Tuition waivers:* Full or partial for employees or children of employees, adult students.

LOANS *Student loans:* $3,652,736 (68% need-based, 32% non-need-based). 68% of past graduating class borrowed through all loan programs. *Average indebtedness per student:* $22,869. *Average need-based loan:* Freshmen: $2454; Undergraduates: $4221. *Parent loans:* $766,855 (29% need-based, 71% non-need-based). *Programs:* FFEL (Subsidized and Unsubsidized Stafford, PLUS), Perkins.

WORK-STUDY *Federal work-study:* Total amount: $146,141; 79 jobs averaging $1860. *State or other work-study/employment:* Total amount: $640,599 (67% need-based, 33% non-need-based). 400 part-time jobs available.

APPLYING FOR FINANCIAL AID *Required financial aid forms:* FAFSA, state aid form. *Financial aid deadline (priority):* 3/1. *Notification date:* Continuous. Students must reply by 5/1 or within 2 weeks of notification.

CONTACT Sharon M. Wilkes, Director of Financial Planning and Assistance, Randolph-Macon Woman's College, 2500 Rivermont Avenue, Lynchburg, VA 24503-1526, 434-947-8128 or toll-free 800-745-7692. *Fax:* 434-947-8996. *E-mail:* swilkes@rmwc.edu.

REED COLLEGE
Portland, OR

Tuition & fees: $30,900	Average undergraduate aid package: $24,122

ABOUT THE INSTITUTION Independent, coed. Awards: bachelor's and master's degrees. 29 undergraduate majors. Total enrollment: 1,341. Undergraduates: 1,312. Freshmen: 338. Both federal and institutional methodology are used as a basis for awarding need-based institutional aid.

UNDERGRADUATE EXPENSES for 2004–05 *Application fee:* $40. *Comprehensive fee:* $38,970 includes full-time tuition ($30,670), mandatory fees ($230), and room and board ($8070). *College room only:* $4240. Full-time tuition and fees vary according to degree level. Room and board charges vary according to board plan and housing facility. *Part-time tuition:* $5100 per course. Part-time tuition and fees vary according to course level and degree level. *Payment plan:* Installment.

FRESHMAN FINANCIAL AID (Fall 2004, est.) 214 applied for aid; of those 68% were deemed to have need. 100% of freshmen with need received aid; of those 95% had need fully met. *Average percent of need met:* 100% (excluding resources awarded to replace EFC). *Average financial aid package:* $29,224 (excluding resources awarded to replace EFC).

UNDERGRADUATE FINANCIAL AID (Fall 2004, est.) 823 applied for aid; of those 87% were deemed to have need. 100% of undergraduates with need received aid; of those 89% had need fully met. *Average percent of need met:* 100% (excluding resources awarded to replace EFC). *Average financial aid package:* $24,122 (excluding resources awarded to replace EFC).

GIFT AID (NEED-BASED) *Total amount:* $14,435,930 (6% federal, 1% state, 91% institutional, 2% external sources). *Receiving aid:* Freshmen: 42% (141); All full-time undergraduates: 50% (640). *Average award:* Freshmen: $26,617; Undergraduates: $22,562. *Scholarships, grants, and awards:* Federal Pell, FSEOG, state, private, college/university gift aid from institutional funds.

GIFT AID (NON-NEED-BASED) *Total amount:* $66,706 (100% external sources). *Tuition waivers:* Full or partial for employees or children of employees.

LOANS *Student loans:* $3,170,026 (93% need-based, 7% non-need-based). 57% of past graduating class borrowed through all loan programs. *Average indebtedness per student:* $15,879. *Average need-based loan:* Freshmen: $2450; Undergraduates: $3928. *Parent loans:* $2,546,001 (100% non-need-based). *Programs:* FFEL (Subsidized and Unsubsidized Stafford, PLUS), Perkins.

WORK-STUDY *Federal work-study:* Total amount: $297,328; 447 jobs averaging $665. *State or other work-study/employment:* Total amount: $21,700 (100% need-based). 32 part-time jobs averaging $678.

APPLYING FOR FINANCIAL AID *Required financial aid forms:* FAFSA, institution's own form, CSS Financial Aid PROFILE, noncustodial (divorced/separated) parent's statement. *Financial aid deadline:* 2/1 (priority: 1/15). *Notification date:* 4/1. Students must reply by 5/1 or within 2 weeks of notification.

CONTACT Leslie Limper, Financial Aid Director, Reed College, 3203 Southeast Woodstock Boulevard, Portland, OR 97202-8199, 503-777-7223 or toll-free 800-547-4750 (out-of-state). *Fax:* 503-788-6682. *E-mail:* financial.aid@reed.edu.

REFORMED BIBLE COLLEGE
Grand Rapids, MI

Tuition & fees: $10,920	Average undergraduate aid package: $8480

ABOUT THE INSTITUTION Independent religious, coed. Awards: associate and bachelor's degrees and post-bachelor's certificates. 21 undergraduate majors. Total enrollment: 289. Undergraduates: 289. Federal methodology is used as a basis for awarding need-based institutional aid.

UNDERGRADUATE EXPENSES for 2004–05 *Application fee:* $25. *Comprehensive fee:* $16,420 includes full-time tuition ($10,400), mandatory fees ($520), and room and board ($5500). *College room only:* $2500. Full-time tuition and fees vary according to course load and student level. Room and board charges vary according to board plan, housing facility, and student level. *Part-time tuition:* $435 per credit hour. Part-time tuition and fees vary according to course load. *Payment plan:* Installment.

FRESHMAN FINANCIAL AID (Fall 2004, est.) 39 applied for aid; of those 64% were deemed to have need. 100% of freshmen with need received aid; of those 20% had need fully met. *Average percent of need met:* 52% (excluding resources awarded to replace EFC). *Average financial aid package:* $8969 (excluding resources awarded to replace EFC). 33% of all full-time freshmen had no need and received non-need-based gift aid.

UNDERGRADUATE FINANCIAL AID (Fall 2004, est.) 223 applied for aid; of those 87% were deemed to have need. 100% of undergraduates with need received aid; of those 16% had need fully met. *Average percent of need met:* 50% (excluding resources awarded to replace EFC). *Average financial aid package:* $8480 (excluding resources awarded to replace EFC). 12% of all full-time undergraduates had no need and received non-need-based gift aid.

GIFT AID (NEED-BASED) *Total amount:* $892,771 (26% federal, 29% state, 42% institutional, 3% external sources). *Receiving aid:* Freshmen: 52% (22); All full-time undergraduates: 79% (188). *Average award:* Freshmen: $4925; Undergraduates: $4409. *Scholarships, grants, and awards:* Federal Pell, FSEOG, state, college/university gift aid from institutional funds.

GIFT AID (NON-NEED-BASED) *Total amount:* $47,235 (32% state, 67% institutional, 1% external sources). *Receiving aid:* Freshmen: 10% (4); Undergraduates: 9% (21). *Average Award:* Freshmen: $500; Undergraduates: $500. *Scholarships, grants, and awards by category:* Academic Interests/Achievement: 98 awards ($57,575 total): general academic interests/achievements. *Special Achievements/Activities:* 19 awards ($43,750 total): leadership, religious involvement. *Special Characteristics:* 27 awards ($190,836 total): children of faculty/staff, international students, spouses of current students. *Tuition waivers:* Full or partial for employees or children of employees.

LOANS *Student loans:* $1,065,508 (68% need-based, 32% non-need-based). 63% of past graduating class borrowed through all loan programs. *Average indebtedness per student:* $11,065. *Average need-based loan:* Freshmen: $2419; Undergraduates: $3190. *Parent loans:* $58,400 (65% need-based, 35% non-need-based). *Programs:* FFEL (Subsidized and Unsubsidized Stafford, PLUS).

WORK-STUDY *Federal work-study:* Total amount: $35,996; 47 jobs averaging $1000. *State or other work-study/employment:* Total amount: $6193 (100% need-based). 5 part-time jobs averaging $1250.

APPLYING FOR FINANCIAL AID *Required financial aid forms:* FAFSA, institution's own form. *Financial aid deadline (priority):* 3/1. *Notification date:* 4/1. Students must reply within 2 weeks of notification.

CONTACT Ms. Agnes Russell, Director of Financial Aid, Reformed Bible College, 3333 East Beltline NE, Grand Rapids, MI 49525-9749, 616-988-3656 or toll-free 800-511-3749. *Fax:* 616-222-3045. *E-mail:* amr@reformed.edu.

REGENT UNIVERSITY
Virginia Beach, VA

CONTACT Financial Aid Office, Regent University, 1000 Regent University Drive, Virginia Beach, VA 23464-9800, 757-226-4000 or toll-free 800-373-5504.

REGIS COLLEGE
Weston, MA

Tuition & fees: $20,500	Average undergraduate aid package: $17,940

ABOUT THE INSTITUTION Independent Roman Catholic, women only. Awards: associate, bachelor's, and master's degrees and post-master's certificates. 18 undergraduate majors. Total enrollment: 1,271. Undergraduates: 897. Freshmen: 158. Both federal and institutional methodology are used as a basis for awarding need-based institutional aid.

UNDERGRADUATE EXPENSES for 2004–05 *Application fee:* $30. *Comprehensive fee:* $29,860 includes full-time tuition ($20,500) and room and board ($9360). *College room only:* $4760. *Part-time tuition:* $2150 per course. Part-time tuition and fees vary according to class time. *Payment plan:* Installment.

FRESHMAN FINANCIAL AID (Fall 2003) 146 applied for aid; of those 91% were deemed to have need. 100% of freshmen with need received aid; of those 11% had need fully met. *Average percent of need met:* 64% (excluding resources awarded to replace EFC). *Average financial aid package:* $20,193 (excluding resources awarded to replace EFC). 6% of all full-time freshmen had no need and received non-need-based gift aid.

UNDERGRADUATE FINANCIAL AID (Fall 2003) 504 applied for aid; of those 92% were deemed to have need. 100% of undergraduates with need received aid; of those 15% had need fully met. *Average percent of need met:* 57% (excluding resources awarded to replace EFC). *Average financial aid package:* $17,940 (excluding resources awarded to replace EFC). 10% of all full-time undergraduates had no need and received non-need-based gift aid.

GIFT AID (NEED-BASED) *Total amount:* $4,054,518 (20% federal, 11% state, 65% institutional, 4% external sources). *Receiving aid:* Freshmen: 76% (118); All full-time undergraduates: 66% (386). *Average award:* Freshmen: $10,925; Undergraduates: $9242. *Scholarships, grants, and awards:* Federal Pell, FSEOG, state, private, college/university gift aid from institutional funds.

GIFT AID (NON-NEED-BASED) *Total amount:* $2,294,861 (100% institutional). *Receiving aid:* Freshmen: 42% (65); Undergraduates: 44% (259). *Average Award:* Freshmen: $9000; Undergraduates: $8985. *Scholarships, grants, and awards by category:* Academic Interests/Achievement: 327 awards ($2,294,861 total): general academic interests/achievements. *Special Achievements/Activities:* 31 awards ($67,000 total): community service. *Special Characteristics:* 46 awards ($275,029 total): adult students, children of faculty/staff, international students, relatives of clergy, religious affiliation, siblings of current students. *Tuition waivers:* Full or partial for employees or children of employees. *ROTC:* Army cooperative.

LOANS *Student loans:* $5,369,333 (70% need-based, 30% non-need-based). 87% of past graduating class borrowed through all loan programs. *Average indebtedness per student:* $20,174. *Average need-based loan:* Freshmen: $4371; Undergraduates: $4874. *Parent loans:* $1,416,919 (100% non-need-based). *Programs:* FFEL (Subsidized and Unsubsidized Stafford, PLUS), Perkins, state.

WORK-STUDY *Federal work-study:* Total amount: $720,897; 383 jobs averaging $2000. *State or other work-study/employment:* Total amount: $64,050 (100% non-need-based). 32 part-time jobs averaging $1500.

APPLYING FOR FINANCIAL AID *Required financial aid forms:* FAFSA, institution's own form. *Financial aid deadline (priority):* 2/15. *Notification date:* Continuous beginning 3/15. Students must reply by 5/1 or within 2 weeks of notification.

CONTACT Dee J. Ludwick, Director of Financial Aid, Regis College, Box 81, 235 Wellesley Street, Weston, MA 02493, 781-768-7180 or toll-free 866-438-7344. *Fax:* 781-768-7225. *E-mail:* finaid@regiscollege.edu.

REGIS UNIVERSITY
Denver, CO

Tuition & fees: $22,400	Average undergraduate aid package: $21,807

ABOUT THE INSTITUTION Independent Roman Catholic (Jesuit), coed. Awards: bachelor's, master's, and doctoral degrees. 33 undergraduate majors. Total enrollment: 16,335. Undergraduates: 8,159. Freshmen: 487. Federal methodology is used as a basis for awarding need-based institutional aid.

UNDERGRADUATE EXPENSES for 2004–05 *Application fee:* $40. *Comprehensive fee:* $30,270 includes full-time tuition ($22,200), mandatory fees ($200), and room and board ($7870). *College room only:* $4500. Full-time tuition and fees vary according to program. Room and board charges vary according to board plan and housing facility. *Part-time tuition:* $695 per hour. *Part-time fees:* $200 per year. Part-time tuition and fees vary according to program. *Payment plan:* Installment.

FRESHMAN FINANCIAL AID (Fall 2004, est.) 319 applied for aid; of those 84% were deemed to have need. 100% of freshmen with need received aid; of those 30% had need fully met. *Average percent of need met:* 99% (excluding resources awarded to replace EFC). *Average financial aid package:* $21,750 (excluding resources awarded to replace EFC). 32% of all full-time freshmen had no need and received non-need-based gift aid.

UNDERGRADUATE FINANCIAL AID (Fall 2004, est.) 1,020 applied for aid; of those 87% were deemed to have need. 100% of undergraduates with need received aid; of those 26% had need fully met. *Average percent of need met:* 96% (excluding resources awarded to replace EFC). *Average financial aid package:* $21,807 (excluding resources awarded to replace EFC). 29% of all full-time undergraduates had no need and received non-need-based gift aid.
GIFT AID (NEED-BASED) *Total amount:* $9,668,461 (14% federal, 16% state, 61% institutional, 9% external sources). *Receiving aid:* Freshmen: 65% (263); All full-time undergraduates: 56% (828). *Average award:* Freshmen: $12,663; Undergraduates: $11,655. *Scholarships, grants, and awards:* Federal Pell, FSEOG, state, private, college/university gift aid from institutional funds.
GIFT AID (NON-NEED-BASED) *Total amount:* $3,285,752 (1% state, 92% institutional, 7% external sources). *Receiving aid:* Freshmen: 15% (62); Undergraduates: 10% (144). *Average Award:* Freshmen $6303; *Undergraduates:* $6434. *Scholarships, grants, and awards by category:* Academic Interests/Achievement: biological sciences, general academic interests/achievements, physical sciences. *Creative Arts/Performance:* 6 awards ($66,600 total): debating. *Special Achievements/Activities:* 8 awards ($4000 total): leadership. *Special Characteristics:* children of faculty/staff, ethnic background, local/state students, members of minority groups. *Tuition waivers:* Full or partial for employees or children of employees. *ROTC:* Army cooperative, Air Force cooperative.
LOANS *Student loans:* $6,503,827 (70% need-based, 30% non-need-based). 65% of past graduating class borrowed through all loan programs. *Average indebtedness per student:* $22,000. *Average need-based loan:* Freshmen: $4604; Undergraduates: $5860. *Parent loans:* $10,786,025 (21% need-based, 79% non-need-based). *Programs:* FFEL (Subsidized and Unsubsidized Stafford, PLUS), Perkins, Federal Nursing.
WORK-STUDY *Federal work-study:* Total amount: $402,037; 320 jobs averaging $1256. *State or other work-study/employment:* Total amount: $975,914 (41% need-based, 59% non-need-based). 423 part-time jobs averaging $2307.
ATHLETIC AWARDS *Total amount:* $1,796,235 (55% need-based, 45% non-need-based).
APPLYING FOR FINANCIAL AID *Required financial aid form:* FAFSA. *Financial aid deadline (priority):* 3/5. *Notification date:* Continuous beginning 3/15.
CONTACT Ms. Lydia MacMillan, Associate Vice President for Enrollment Services/Director of Financial Aid, Regis University, 3333 Regis Boulevard, Denver, CO 80221-1099, 303-458-4162 or toll-free 800-388-2366 Ext. 4900. *Fax:* 303-964-5407. *E-mail:* lmacmill@regis.edu.

REINHARDT COLLEGE
Waleska, GA

Tuition & fees: $12,200	Average undergraduate aid package: $6570

ABOUT THE INSTITUTION Independent religious, coed. Awards: associate and bachelor's degrees. 22 undergraduate majors. Total enrollment: 1,096. Undergraduates: 1,096. Freshmen: 317. Federal methodology is used as a basis for awarding need-based institutional aid.
UNDERGRADUATE EXPENSES for 2004–05 *Application fee:* $25. *Comprehensive fee:* $17,962 includes full-time tuition ($12,000), mandatory fees ($200), and room and board ($5762). Full-time tuition and fees vary according to course load and location. Room and board charges vary according to board plan and housing facility. *Part-time tuition:* $400 per credit hour. Part-time tuition and fees vary according to course load and location. *Payment plan:* Installment.
UNDERGRADUATE FINANCIAL AID (Fall 2003) *Average financial aid package:* $6570 (excluding resources awarded to replace EFC).
GIFT AID (NEED-BASED) *Total amount:* $930,530 (91% federal, 9% institutional). *Scholarships, grants, and awards:* Federal Pell, FSEOG, state, private, college/university gift aid from institutional funds.
GIFT AID (NON-NEED-BASED) *Total amount:* $4,799,855 (41% state, 57% institutional, 2% external sources). *Scholarships, grants, and awards by category:* Academic Interests/Achievement: general academic interests/achievements. *Creative Arts/Performance:* art/fine arts. *Special Characteristics:* 24 awards ($108,891 total): children of faculty/staff. *Tuition waivers:* Full or partial for employees or children of employees.
LOANS *Student loans:* $3,458,786 (50% need-based, 50% non-need-based). *Parent loans:* $1,802,558 (100% non-need-based). *Programs:* FFEL (Subsidized and Unsubsidized Stafford, PLUS), alternative loans.
WORK-STUDY *Federal work-study:* Total amount: $56,360; 68 jobs averaging $1138. *State or other work-study/employment:* Total amount: $171,227 (100% non-need-based). 156 part-time jobs averaging $909.
ATHLETIC AWARDS *Total amount:* $513,010 (100% non-need-based).

APPLYING FOR FINANCIAL AID *Required financial aid forms:* FAFSA, institution's own form, state aid form. *Financial aid deadline (priority):* 6/1. *Notification date:* 4/1. Students must reply within 2 weeks of notification.
CONTACT Robert Gregory, Director of Financial Aid, Reinhardt College, 7300 Reinhardt College Circle, Waleska, GA 30183-2981, 770-720-5532 or toll-free 87-REINHARDT. *Fax:* 770-720-9126.

REMINGTON COLLEGE–COLORADO SPRINGS CAMPUS
Colorado Springs, CO

CONTACT Financial Aid Office, Remington College–Colorado Springs Campus, 6050 Erin Park Drive, #250, Colorado Springs, CO 80918, 719-532-1234.

REMINGTON COLLEGE–DENVER CAMPUS
Lakewood, CO

CONTACT Robert J. Lantzy, Director of Financial Services, Remington College–Denver Campus, 11011 West Sixth Avenue, Lakewood, CO 80215, 303-445-0500 or toll-free 800-999-5181. *Fax:* 303-445-0090. *E-mail:* rlantzy@edamerica.com.

REMINGTON COLLEGE–HONOLULU CAMPUS
Honolulu, HI

CONTACT Financial Aid Office, Remington College–Honolulu Campus, 1111 Bishop Street, Suite 400, Honolulu, HI 96813, 808-942-1000.

REMINGTON COLLEGE–SAN DIEGO CAMPUS
San Diego, CA

CONTACT Financial Aid Office, Remington College–San Diego Campus, 123 Camino de la Reina, North Building, Suite 100, San Diego, CA 92108, 619-686-8600 or toll-free 800-214-7001.

REMINGTON COLLEGE–TEMPE CAMPUS
Tempe, AZ

CONTACT Financial Aid Office, Remington College–Tempe Campus, 875 West Elliot Road, Suite 216, Tempe, AZ 85284, 480-834-1000 or toll-free 800-395-4322.

RENSSELAER POLYTECHNIC INSTITUTE
Troy, NY

Tuition & fees: $29,786	Average undergraduate aid package: $24,862

ABOUT THE INSTITUTION Independent, coed. Awards: bachelor's, master's, and doctoral degrees. 54 undergraduate majors. Total enrollment: 7,521. Undergraduates: 4,929. Freshmen: 1,079. Federal methodology is used as a basis for awarding need-based institutional aid.
UNDERGRADUATE EXPENSES for 2004–05 *Application fee:* $70. *Comprehensive fee:* $38,869 includes full-time tuition ($28,950), mandatory fees ($836), and room and board ($9083). *College room only:* $5101. Room and board charges vary according to board plan, housing facility, and location. *Part-time tuition:* $905 per credit hour. *Payment plan:* Installment.
FRESHMAN FINANCIAL AID (Fall 2004, est.) 1006 applied for aid; of those 77% were deemed to have need. 100% of freshmen with need received aid; of those 66% had need fully met. *Average percent of need met:* 94% (excluding resources awarded to replace EFC). *Average financial aid package:* $26,221 (excluding resources awarded to replace EFC). 20% of all full-time freshmen had no need and received non-need-based gift aid.
UNDERGRADUATE FINANCIAL AID (Fall 2004, est.) 4,546 applied for aid; of those 77% were deemed to have need. 100% of undergraduates with need received aid; of those 66% had need fully met. *Average percent of need met:* 92% (excluding resources awarded to replace EFC). *Average financial aid*

package: $24,862 (excluding resources awarded to replace EFC). 16% of all full-time undergraduates had no need and received non-need-based gift aid.

GIFT AID (NEED-BASED) *Total amount:* $59,457,485 (12% federal, 6% state, 79% institutional, 3% external sources). *Receiving aid:* Freshmen: 72% (772); All full-time undergraduates: 72% (3,489). *Average award:* Freshmen: $20,299; Undergraduates: $18,159. *Scholarships, grants, and awards:* Federal Pell, FSEOG, state, private, college/university gift aid from institutional funds, Gates Millennium Scholarships.

GIFT AID (NON-NEED-BASED) *Total amount:* $13,678,219 (13% federal, 86% institutional, 1% external sources). *Receiving aid:* Freshmen: 22% (234); Undergraduates: 22% (1,057). *Average Award:* Freshmen: $14,817; Undergraduates: $14,700. *Scholarships, grants, and awards by category: Academic Interests/Achievement:* general academic interests/achievements, humanities, mathematics, military science. *Creative Arts/Performance:* general creative arts/performance. *Special Achievements/Activities:* general special achievements/activities. *Special Characteristics:* children and siblings of alumni, children of faculty/staff, ethnic background, general special characteristics, members of minority groups. *Tuition waivers:* Full or partial for employees or children of employees. *ROTC:* Army, Naval, Air Force.

LOANS *Student loans:* $30,302,947 (77% need-based, 23% non-need-based). 74% of past graduating class borrowed through all loan programs. *Average indebtedness per student:* $25,000. *Average need-based loan:* Freshmen: $5959; Undergraduates: $6951. *Parent loans:* $8,249,921 (80% need-based, 20% non-need-based). *Programs:* FFEL (Subsidized and Unsubsidized Stafford, PLUS), Perkins, college/university.

WORK-STUDY *Federal work-study:* Total amount: $1,462,586; 1,337 jobs averaging $1088.

ATHLETIC AWARDS *Total amount:* $643,820 (100% non-need-based).

APPLYING FOR FINANCIAL AID *Required financial aid form:* FAFSA. *Financial aid deadline (priority):* 2/15. *Notification date:* 3/25.

CONTACT Mr. James Stevenson, Director of Financial Aid, Rensselaer Polytechnic Institute, Financial Aid Building, 110 8th Street, Troy, NY 12180-3590, 518-276-6813 or toll-free 800-448-6562. *Fax:* 518-276-4797. *E-mail:* stevej@rpi.edu.

RESEARCH COLLEGE OF NURSING
Kansas City, MO

Tuition & fees: $19,540 | Average undergraduate aid package: $21,196

ABOUT THE INSTITUTION Independent, coed, primarily women. Awards: bachelor's and master's degrees (bachelor's degree offered jointly with Rockhurst College). 1 undergraduate major. Total enrollment: 213. Undergraduates: 187. Freshmen: 35. Federal methodology is used as a basis for awarding need-based institutional aid.

UNDERGRADUATE EXPENSES for 2005–06 *Application fee:* $25. *Comprehensive fee:* $25,640 includes full-time tuition ($18,900), mandatory fees ($640), and room and board ($6100). *College room only:* $3100. Full-time tuition and fees vary according to program. Room and board charges vary according to board plan, housing facility, and location. *Part-time tuition:* $630 per credit hour. Part-time tuition and fees vary according to class time and program. *Payment plans:* Installment, deferred payment.

UNDERGRADUATE FINANCIAL AID (Fall 2004, est.) 90 applied for aid; of those 90% were deemed to have need. 100% of undergraduates with need received aid; of those 23% had need fully met. *Average percent of need met:* 60% (excluding resources awarded to replace EFC). *Average financial aid package:* $21,196 (excluding resources awarded to replace EFC). 27% of all full-time undergraduates had no need and received non-need-based gift aid.

GIFT AID (NEED-BASED) *Total amount:* $357,504 (15% federal, 4% state, 81% institutional). *Receiving aid:* All full-time undergraduates: 52% (77). *Average award:* Undergraduates: $2000. *Scholarships, grants, and awards:* Federal Pell, FSEOG, state, private, college/university gift aid from institutional funds.

GIFT AID (NON-NEED-BASED) *Total amount:* $1,541,596 (100% institutional). *Receiving aid:* Undergraduates: 19% (28). *Average Award:* Undergraduates: $15,700. *Scholarships, grants, and awards by category: Academic Interests/Achievement:* 123 awards ($1,671,742 total): general academic interests/achievements, health fields. *Special Characteristics:* children and siblings of alumni, children of educators, children of faculty/staff, siblings of current students. *Tuition waivers:* Full or partial for employees or children of employees, senior citizens. *ROTC:* Army cooperative.

LOANS *Student loans:* $662,065 (45% need-based, 55% non-need-based). 75% of past graduating class borrowed through all loan programs. *Average indebtedness per student:* $12,740. *Average need-based loan:* Undergradu-

ates: $4580. *Parent loans:* $20,370 (100% need-based). *Programs:* FFEL (Subsidized and Unsubsidized Stafford, PLUS), Perkins, Federal Nursing, college/university.

APPLYING FOR FINANCIAL AID *Required financial aid form:* FAFSA. *Financial aid deadline (priority):* 3/15. *Notification date:* Continuous. Students must reply within 2 weeks of notification.

CONTACT Ms. Stacie Withers, Financial Aid Director, Research College of Nursing, 2300 East Meyer Boulevard, Kansas City, MO 64132, 816-276-4728 or toll-free 800-842-6776. *Fax:* 816-276-3526. *E-mail:* stacie.withers@hcamidwest.com.

REVANS UNIVERSITY–THE UNIVERSITY OF ACTION LEARNING
Boulder, CO

CONTACT Financial Aid Office, Revans University–The University of Action Learning, 1650 38th Street, Suite 205W, Boulder, CO 80301, 303-442-6907.

RHODE ISLAND COLLEGE
Providence, RI

CONTACT Office of Financial Aid, Rhode Island College, 600 Mount Pleasant Avenue, Providence, RI 02908, 401-456-8033 or toll-free 800-669-5760.

RHODE ISLAND SCHOOL OF DESIGN
Providence, RI

Tuition & fees: $27,975 | Average undergraduate aid package: $15,300

ABOUT THE INSTITUTION Independent, coed. Awards: bachelor's, master's, and first professional degrees. 17 undergraduate majors. Total enrollment: 2,282. Undergraduates: 1,882. Freshmen: 398. Both federal and institutional methodology are used as a basis for awarding need-based institutional aid.

UNDERGRADUATE EXPENSES for 2004–05 *Application fee:* $50. *Comprehensive fee:* $35,697 includes full-time tuition ($27,510), mandatory fees ($465), and room and board ($7722). *College room only:* $4324. Room and board charges vary according to board plan and housing facility. *Payment plan:* Installment.

FRESHMAN FINANCIAL AID (Fall 2003) 232 applied for aid; of those 82% were deemed to have need. 96% of freshmen with need received aid; of those 13% had need fully met. *Average percent of need met:* 67% (excluding resources awarded to replace EFC). *Average financial aid package:* $11,450 (excluding resources awarded to replace EFC). 1% of all full-time freshmen had no need and received non-need-based gift aid.

UNDERGRADUATE FINANCIAL AID (Fall 2003) 1,140 applied for aid; of those 81% were deemed to have need. 99% of undergraduates with need received aid; of those 10% had need fully met. *Average percent of need met:* 69% (excluding resources awarded to replace EFC). *Average financial aid package:* $15,300 (excluding resources awarded to replace EFC). 2% of all full-time undergraduates had no need and received non-need-based gift aid.

GIFT AID (NEED-BASED) *Total amount:* $9,549,000 (12% federal, 1% state, 84% institutional, 3% external sources). *Receiving aid:* Freshmen: 29% (113); All full-time undergraduates: 42% (812). *Average award:* Freshmen: $12,500; Undergraduates: $9200. *Scholarships, grants, and awards:* Federal Pell, FSEOG, state, private, college/university gift aid from institutional funds.

GIFT AID (NON-NEED-BASED) *Total amount:* $286,000 (77% institutional, 23% external sources). *Receiving aid:* Freshmen: 1% (3); Undergraduates: 2% (35). *Average Award:* Freshmen: $5000. *Scholarships, grants, and awards by category: Academic Interests/Achievement:* 35 awards ($45,000 total): general academic interests/achievements. *Creative Arts/Performance:* 4 awards ($10,000 total): applied art and design, art/fine arts. *Tuition waivers:* Full or partial for employees or children of employees.

LOANS *Student loans:* $7,287,000 (69% need-based, 31% non-need-based). 56% of past graduating class borrowed through all loan programs. *Average indebtedness per student:* $21,700. *Average need-based loan:* Freshmen: $3050; Undergraduates: $5600. *Parent loans:* $6,242,000 (100% non-need-based). *Programs:* FFEL (Subsidized and Unsubsidized Stafford, PLUS), Perkins, college/university.

WORK-STUDY *Federal work-study:* Total amount: $722,000; 469 jobs averaging $1364. *State or other work-study/employment:* Total amount: $925,000 (100% non-need-based). 350 part-time jobs averaging $1400.

APPLYING FOR FINANCIAL AID *Required financial aid forms:* FAFSA, CSS Financial Aid PROFILE. *Financial aid deadline (priority):* 2/15. *Notification date:* 4/1. Students must reply by 5/1 or within 4 weeks of notification.

CONTACT Mr. Peter R. Riefler, Director of Financial Aid, Rhode Island School of Design, 2 College Street, Providence, RI 02903-2784, 401-454-6636 or toll-free 800-364-7473. *Fax:* 401-454-6412.

RHODES COLLEGE
Memphis, TN

CONTACT Forrest M. Stuart, Director of Financial Aid, Rhodes College, 2000 North Parkway, Memphis, TN 38112-1690, 901-843-3810 or toll-free 800-844-5969 (out-of-state). *Fax:* 901-843-3435. *E-mail:* stuart@rhodes.edu.

RICE UNIVERSITY
Houston, TX

Tuition & fees: $21,206	Average undergraduate aid package: $18,360

ABOUT THE INSTITUTION Independent, coed. Awards: bachelor's, master's, and doctoral degrees. 59 undergraduate majors. Total enrollment: 4,973. Undergraduates: 3,025. Freshmen: 726. Institutional methodology is used as a basis for awarding need-based institutional aid.

UNDERGRADUATE EXPENSES for 2004–05 *Application fee:* $50. *Comprehensive fee:* $29,586 includes full-time tuition ($20,350), mandatory fees ($856), and room and board ($8380). *College room only:* $5200. Full-time tuition and fees vary according to student level. Room and board charges vary according to board plan. *Payment plan:* Installment.

FRESHMAN FINANCIAL AID (Fall 2004, est.) 538 applied for aid; of those 44% were deemed to have need. 100% of freshmen with need received aid; of those 100% had need fully met. *Average percent of need met:* 100% (excluding resources awarded to replace EFC). *Average financial aid package:* $19,565 (excluding resources awarded to replace EFC). 24% of all full-time freshmen had no need and received non-need-based gift aid.

UNDERGRADUATE FINANCIAL AID (Fall 2004, est.) 1,557 applied for aid; of those 62% were deemed to have need. 100% of undergraduates with need received aid; of those 100% had need fully met. *Average percent of need met:* 100% (excluding resources awarded to replace EFC). *Average financial aid package:* $18,360 (excluding resources awarded to replace EFC). 20% of all full-time undergraduates had no need and received non-need-based gift aid.

GIFT AID (NEED-BASED) *Total amount:* $15,271,486 (8% federal, 15% state, 63% institutional, 14% external sources). *Receiving aid:* Freshmen: 32% (233); All full-time undergraduates: 33% (966). *Average award:* Freshmen: $17,262; Undergraduates: $15,483. *Scholarships, grants, and awards:* Federal Pell, FSEOG, state, private, college/university gift aid from institutional funds.

GIFT AID (NON-NEED-BASED) *Total amount:* $4,248,190 (83% institutional, 17% external sources). *Receiving aid:* Freshmen: 10% (70); Undergraduates: 12% (342). *Average Award:* Freshmen: $5558; Undergraduates: $5335. *Scholarships, grants, and awards by category: Academic Interests/Achievement:* architecture, area/ethnic studies, biological sciences, computer science, engineering/technologies, English, foreign languages, general academic interests/achievements, humanities, international studies, mathematics, physical sciences, social sciences. *Creative Arts/Performance:* applied art and design, art/fine arts, creative writing, debating, journalism/publications, music, performing arts. *Special Achievements/Activities:* community service, general special achievements/activities, leadership. *Special Characteristics:* children and siblings of alumni, children of faculty/staff, ethnic background, general special characteristics, international students. *Tuition waivers:* Full or partial for employees or children of employees. *ROTC:* Army cooperative, Naval, Air Force cooperative.

LOANS *Student loans:* $2,939,113 (64% need-based, 36% non-need-based). 38% of past graduating class borrowed through all loan programs. *Average indebtedness per student:* $13,452. *Average need-based loan:* Freshmen: $2532; Undergraduates: $3069. *Parent loans:* $3,964,252 (100% non-need-based). *Programs:* FFEL (Subsidized and Unsubsidized Stafford, PLUS), Perkins, college/university.

WORK-STUDY *Federal work-study:* Total amount: $1,032,128; 655 jobs averaging $1800. *State or other work-study/employment:* Part-time jobs available.

ATHLETIC AWARDS *Total amount:* $6,242,499 (100% non-need-based).

APPLYING FOR FINANCIAL AID *Required financial aid forms:* FAFSA, CSS Financial Aid PROFILE, noncustodial (divorced/separated) parent's statement, business/farm supplement. *Financial aid deadline:* Continuous. *Notification date:* 4/15. Students must reply by 5/1.

CONTACT Office of Student Financial Services, Rice University, 116 Allen Center, MS 12, 6100 Main Street, Houston, TX 77005, 713-348-4958 or toll-free 800-527-OWLS. *Fax:* 713-348-2139.

THE RICHARD STOCKTON COLLEGE OF NEW JERSEY
Pomona, NJ

Tuition & fees (NJ res): $7203	Average undergraduate aid package: $10,764

ABOUT THE INSTITUTION State-supported, coed. Awards: bachelor's and master's degrees and post-bachelor's certificates. 31 undergraduate majors. Total enrollment: 7,004. Undergraduates: 6,580. Freshmen: 826. Federal methodology is used as a basis for awarding need-based institutional aid.

UNDERGRADUATE EXPENSES for 2004–05 *Application fee:* $50. *Tuition, state resident:* full-time $5091; part-time $159 per credit. *Tuition, nonresident:* full-time $8256; part-time $258 per credit. *Required fees:* full-time $2112; $66 per credit. *College room and board:* $7252; *room only:* $4750. Room and board charges vary according to board plan and housing facility. *Payment plan:* Installment.

FRESHMAN FINANCIAL AID (Fall 2004, est.) 651 applied for aid; of those 69% were deemed to have need. 98% of freshmen with need received aid; of those 69% had need fully met. *Average percent of need met:* 58% (excluding resources awarded to replace EFC). *Average financial aid package:* $11,367 (excluding resources awarded to replace EFC). 8% of all full-time freshmen had no need and received non-need-based gift aid.

UNDERGRADUATE FINANCIAL AID (Fall 2004, est.) 3,889 applied for aid; of those 76% were deemed to have need. 97% of undergraduates with need received aid; of those 61% had need fully met. *Average percent of need met:* 61% (excluding resources awarded to replace EFC). *Average financial aid package:* $10,764 (excluding resources awarded to replace EFC). 6% of all full-time undergraduates had no need and received non-need-based gift aid.

GIFT AID (NEED-BASED) *Total amount:* $10,535,344 (42% federal, 49% state, 7% institutional, 2% external sources). *Receiving aid:* Freshmen: 28% (223); All full-time undergraduates: 29% (1,575). *Average award:* Freshmen: $6346; Undergraduates: $5780. *Scholarships, grants, and awards:* Federal Pell, FSEOG, state, college/university gift aid from institutional funds.

GIFT AID (NON-NEED-BASED) *Total amount:* $988,880 (14% state, 65% institutional, 21% external sources). *Receiving aid:* Freshmen: 17% (139); Undergraduates: 9% (477). *Average Award:* Freshmen: $2404; Undergraduates: $2202. *Scholarships, grants, and awards by category: Academic Interests/Achievement:* 302 awards ($500,800 total): area/ethnic studies, biological sciences, business, computer science, education, general academic interests/achievements, health fields, humanities, mathematics, physical sciences, social sciences. *Creative Arts/Performance:* 25 awards ($82,150 total): applied art and design, art/fine arts, creative writing, dance, journalism/publications, music, performing arts, theater/drama. *Special Achievements/Activities:* 4 awards ($3500 total): community service, general special achievements/activities, leadership. *Special Characteristics:* 82 awards ($305,150 total): adult students, children of faculty/staff, children of union members/company employees, ethnic background, general special characteristics, international students, local/state students, members of minority groups, previous college experience. *Tuition waivers:* Full or partial for employees or children of employees, senior citizens.

LOANS *Student loans:* $21,108,273 (74% need-based, 26% non-need-based). 69% of past graduating class borrowed through all loan programs. *Average indebtedness per student:* $15,835. *Average need-based loan:* Freshmen: $2603; Undergraduates: $3787. *Parent loans:* $5,990,995 (34% need-based, 66% non-need-based). *Programs:* FFEL (Subsidized and Unsubsidized Stafford, PLUS), Perkins, state.

WORK-STUDY *Federal work-study:* Total amount: $503,328; 313 jobs averaging $1608. *State or other work-study/employment:* Total amount: $885,535 (100% non-need-based). 703 part-time jobs averaging $1260.

APPLYING FOR FINANCIAL AID *Required financial aid form:* FAFSA. *Financial aid deadline (priority):* 3/1. *Notification date:* Continuous beginning 4/1. Students must reply within 2 weeks of notification.

CONTACT Ms. Jeanne L. Lewis, Director of Financial Aid, The Richard Stockton College of New Jersey, Jimmie Leeds Road, Pomona, NJ 08240-9988, 609-652-4203. *Fax:* 609-626-5517. *E-mail:* iaprod91@stockton.edu.

RIDER UNIVERSITY
Lawrenceville, NJ

Tuition & fees: $23,470   **Average undergraduate aid package: $17,651**

ABOUT THE INSTITUTION Independent, coed. Awards: associate, bachelor's, and master's degrees and post-master's certificates. 52 undergraduate majors. Total enrollment: 5,502. Undergraduates: 4,268. Freshmen: 902. Federal methodology is used as a basis for awarding need-based institutional aid.

UNDERGRADUATE EXPENSES for 2005–06 *Application fee:* $40. *Comprehensive fee:* $32,310 includes full-time tuition ($22,910), mandatory fees ($560), and room and board ($8840). *College room only:* $4940. *Part-time tuition:* $770 per credit. *Part-time fees:* $35 per course.

FRESHMAN FINANCIAL AID (Fall 2004, est.) 768 applied for aid; of those 84% were deemed to have need. 100% of freshmen with need received aid; of those 20% had need fully met. *Average percent of need met:* 73% (excluding resources awarded to replace EFC). *Average financial aid package:* $18,235 (excluding resources awarded to replace EFC). 15% of all full-time freshmen had no need and received non-need-based gift aid.

UNDERGRADUATE FINANCIAL AID (Fall 2004, est.) 2,798 applied for aid; of those 86% were deemed to have need. 100% of undergraduates with need received aid; of those 21% had need fully met. *Average percent of need met:* 74% (excluding resources awarded to replace EFC). *Average financial aid package:* $17,651 (excluding resources awarded to replace EFC). 16% of all full-time undergraduates had no need and received non-need-based gift aid.

GIFT AID (NEED-BASED) *Total amount:* $25,734,919 (11% federal, 21% state, 66% institutional, 2% external sources). *Receiving aid:* Freshmen: 71% (629); All full-time undergraduates: 67% (2,358). *Average award:* Freshmen: $12,970; Undergraduates: $11,970. *Scholarships, grants, and awards:* Federal Pell, FSEOG, state, private, college/university gift aid from institutional funds.

GIFT AID (NON-NEED-BASED) *Total amount:* $5,541,345 (1% state, 93% institutional, 6% external sources). *Receiving aid:* Freshmen: 10% (86); Undergraduates: 10% (353). *Average Award:* Freshmen: $8473; Undergraduates: $7875. *Scholarships, grants, and awards by category: Academic Interests/Achievement:* 1,128 awards ($9,641,568 total): general academic interests/achievements. *Creative Arts/Performance:* 9 awards ($169,370 total): theater/drama. *Special Characteristics:* 14 awards ($186,354 total): members of minority groups. *ROTC:* Army cooperative.

LOANS *Student loans:* $27,212,635 (61% need-based, 39% non-need-based). 66% of past graduating class borrowed through all loan programs. *Average indebtedness per student:* $27,113. *Average need-based loan:* Freshmen: $3535; Undergraduates: $4206. *Parent loans:* $5,605,003 (30% need-based, 70% non-need-based). *Programs:* FFEL (Subsidized and Unsubsidized Stafford, PLUS), Perkins, state, college/university, alternative loans.

WORK-STUDY *Federal work-study:* Total amount: $3,496,593; 1,711 jobs averaging $2141.

ATHLETIC AWARDS *Total amount:* $2,666,772 (47% need-based, 53% non-need-based).

APPLYING FOR FINANCIAL AID *Required financial aid form:* FAFSA. *Financial aid deadline:* 6/1 (priority: 3/1). *Notification date:* Continuous beginning 4/15. **CONTACT** John J. Williams, Student Financial Services Office, Rider University, 2083 Lawrenceville Road, Lawrenceville, NJ 08648-3001, 609-896-5360 or toll-free 800-257-9026. *Fax:* 609-219-4487. *E-mail:* finaid@rider.edu.

RINGLING SCHOOL OF ART AND DESIGN
Sarasota, FL

Tuition & fees: $20,195   **Average undergraduate aid package: $8830**

ABOUT THE INSTITUTION Independent, coed. Awards: bachelor's degrees. 6 undergraduate majors. Total enrollment: 1,008. Undergraduates: 1,008. Freshmen: 201. Federal methodology is used as a basis for awarding need-based institutional aid.

UNDERGRADUATE EXPENSES for 2004–05 *Application fee:* $35. *Comprehensive fee:* $29,006 includes full-time tuition ($19,995), mandatory fees ($200), and room and board ($8811). *College room only:* $4727. Full-time tuition and fees vary according to course load, program, and student level. Room and board charges vary according to board plan and housing facility. *Part-time tuition:* $950 per credit hour. Part-time tuition and fees vary according to course load, program, and student level. *Payment plan:* Installment.

FRESHMAN FINANCIAL AID (Fall 2004, est.) 152 applied for aid; of those 83% were deemed to have need. 100% of freshmen with need received aid; of those

6% had need fully met. *Average percent of need met:* 31% (excluding resources awarded to replace EFC). *Average financial aid package:* $8038 (excluding resources awarded to replace EFC). 21% of all full-time freshmen had no need and received non-need-based gift aid.

UNDERGRADUATE FINANCIAL AID (Fall 2004, est.) 720 applied for aid; of those 88% were deemed to have need. 100% of undergraduates with need received aid; of those 3% had need fully met. *Average percent of need met:* 32% (excluding resources awarded to replace EFC). *Average financial aid package:* $8830 (excluding resources awarded to replace EFC). 15% of all full-time undergraduates had no need and received non-need-based gift aid.

GIFT AID (NEED-BASED) *Total amount:* $3,099,687 (31% federal, 39% state, 20% institutional, 10% external sources). *Receiving aid:* Freshmen: 51% (100); All full-time undergraduates: 63% (507). *Average award:* Freshmen: $7127; Undergraduates: $5991. *Scholarships, grants, and awards:* Federal Pell, FSEOG, state, private, college/university gift aid from institutional funds.

GIFT AID (NON-NEED-BASED) *Total amount:* $321,688 (74% state, 12% institutional, 14% external sources). *Receiving aid:* Freshmen: 3% (5); Undergraduates: 2% (12). *Average Award: Freshmen:* $8712; *Undergraduates:* $12,567. *Scholarships, grants, and awards by category: Academic Interests/Achievement:* 1 award ($18,000 total): general academic interests/achievements. *Creative Arts/Performance:* applied and design, art/fine arts. *Tuition waivers:* Full or partial for employees or children of employees.

LOANS *Student loans:* $8,141,610 (82% need-based, 18% non-need-based). 72% of past graduating class borrowed through all loan programs. *Average indebtedness per student:* $26,099. *Average need-based loan:* Freshmen: $2568; Undergraduates: $3939. *Parent loans:* $3,610,778 (60% need-based, 40% non-need-based). *Programs:* FFEL (Subsidized and Unsubsidized Stafford, PLUS), alternative loans.

WORK-STUDY *Federal work-study:* Total amount: $205,264; 100 jobs averaging $2034. *State or other work-study/employment:* Part-time jobs available.

APPLYING FOR FINANCIAL AID *Required financial aid form:* FAFSA. *Financial aid deadline (priority):* 3/1. *Notification date:* Continuous beginning 3/15. Students must reply within 2 weeks of notification.

CONTACT Heidi Neale, Financial Aid Counselor, Ringling School of Art and Design, 2700 North Tamiami Trail, Sarasota, FL 34234, 941-351-5100 or toll-free 800-255-7695. *Fax:* 941-359-7517.

RIPON COLLEGE
Ripon, WI

Tuition & fees: $20,730   **Average undergraduate aid package: $17,891**

ABOUT THE INSTITUTION Independent, coed. Awards: bachelor's degrees. 38 undergraduate majors. Total enrollment: 927. Undergraduates: 927. Freshmen: 202. Federal methodology is used as a basis for awarding need-based institutional aid.

UNDERGRADUATE EXPENSES for 2004–05 *Application fee:* $30. *Comprehensive fee:* $26,090 includes full-time tuition ($20,490), mandatory fees ($240), and room and board ($5360). *College room only:* $2530. *Part-time tuition:* $825 per credit. *Payment plans:* Guaranteed tuition, installment.

FRESHMAN FINANCIAL AID (Fall 2004, est.) 186 applied for aid; of those 90% were deemed to have need. 99% of freshmen with need received aid; of those 35% had need fully met. *Average percent of need met:* 96% (excluding resources awarded to replace EFC). *Average financial aid package:* $18,306 (excluding resources awarded to replace EFC). 19% of all full-time freshmen had no need and received non-need-based gift aid.

UNDERGRADUATE FINANCIAL AID (Fall 2004, est.) 755 applied for aid; of those 91% were deemed to have need. 100% of undergraduates with need received aid; of those 41% had need fully met. *Average percent of need met:* 95% (excluding resources awarded to replace EFC). *Average financial aid package:* $17,891 (excluding resources awarded to replace EFC). 16% of all full-time undergraduates had no need and received non-need-based gift aid.

GIFT AID (NEED-BASED) *Total amount:* $9,385,750 (8% federal, 9% state, 69% institutional, 14% external sources). *Receiving aid:* Freshmen: 80% (167); All full-time undergraduates: 74% (684). *Average award:* Freshmen: $14,512; Undergraduates: $13,796. *Scholarships, grants, and awards:* Federal Pell, FSEOG, state, private, college/university gift aid from institutional funds.

GIFT AID (NON-NEED-BASED) *Total amount:* $2,292,922 (85% institutional, 15% external sources). *Receiving aid:* Freshmen: 12% (26); Undergraduates: 15% (137). *Average Award: Freshmen:* $12,946; *Undergraduates:* $13,806. *Scholarships, grants, and awards by category: Academic Interests/Achievement:* 480 awards ($3,911,715 total): biological sciences, business, computer sci-

ence, education, English, foreign languages, general academic interests/ achievements, humanities, mathematics, military science, physical sciences, premedicine, religion/biblical studies, social sciences. *Creative Arts/Performance:* 97 awards ($349,000 total): art/fine arts, debating, music, theater/drama. *Special Achievements/Activities:* 202 awards ($858,000 total): general special achievements/ activities, leadership, memberships. *Special Characteristics:* 326 awards ($1,875,301 total): children and siblings of alumni, children of faculty/staff, general special characteristics, international students, local/state students, members of minority groups, out-of-state students, previous college experience, religious affiliation, siblings of current students. *Tuition waivers:* Full or partial for children of alumni, employees or children of employees. *ROTC:* Army. **LOANS** *Student loans:* $4,099,535 (63% need-based, 37% non-need-based). 90% of past graduating class borrowed through all loan programs. *Average indebtedness per student:* $19,067. *Average need-based loan:* Freshmen: $3516; Undergraduates: $4465. *Parent loans:* $680,443 (9% need-based, 91% non-need-based). *Programs:* FFEL (Subsidized and Unsubsidized Stafford, PLUS), Perkins, alternative loans. **WORK-STUDY** *Federal work-study:* Total amount: $434,274; 210 jobs averaging $1313. *State or other work-study/employment:* Total amount: $661,593 (2% need-based, 98% non-need-based). 397 part-time jobs averaging $1634. **APPLYING FOR FINANCIAL AID** *Required financial aid form:* FAFSA. *Financial aid deadline (priority):* 3/1. *Notification date:* Continuous. Students must reply within 2 weeks of notification.
CONTACT Steven Schuetz, Director of Financial Aid, Ripon College, 300 Seward Street, Ripon, WI 54971, 920-748-8101 or toll-free 800-947-4766. *Fax:* 920-748-8335. *E-mail:* financialaid@ripon.edu.

RIVIER COLLEGE
Nashua, NH

ABOUT THE INSTITUTION Independent Roman Catholic, coed. Awards: associate, bachelor's, and master's degrees and post-bachelor's and post-master's certificates. 41 undergraduate majors. Total enrollment: 2,289. Undergraduates: 1,469. Freshmen: 239.
GIFT AID (NEED-BASED) *Scholarships, grants, and awards:* Federal Pell, FSEOG, state, private, college/university gift aid from institutional funds.
GIFT AID (NON-NEED-BASED) *Scholarships, grants, and awards by category:* Academic Interests/Achievement: biological sciences, business, communication, computer science, education, English, foreign languages, general academic interests/achievements, humanities, mathematics, premedicine, social sciences. *Creative Arts/Performance:* applied art and design, art/fine arts, journalism/ publications. *Special Achievements/Activities:* general special achievements/ activities. *Special Characteristics:* children and siblings of alumni, members of minority groups, religious affiliation, siblings of current students.
LOANS *Programs:* FFEL (Subsidized and Unsubsidized Stafford, PLUS), Perkins.
WORK-STUDY *Federal work-study:* Total amount: $539,382; 256 jobs averaging $1926. *State or other work-study/employment:* Total amount: $163,795 (100% non-need-based). 90 part-time jobs averaging $1849.
APPLYING FOR FINANCIAL AID *Required financial aid form:* FAFSA.
CONTACT Valerie Patnaude, Director of Financial Aid, Rivier College, 420 Main Street, Nashua, NH 03060-5086, 603-897-8533 or toll-free 800-44RIVIER. *Fax:* 603-897-8810. *E-mail:* vpatnaude@rivier.edu.

ROANOKE BIBLE COLLEGE
Elizabeth City, NC

Tuition & fees: $8225	Average undergraduate aid package: $6614

ABOUT THE INSTITUTION Independent Christian, coed. Awards: associate and bachelor's degrees. 4 undergraduate majors. Total enrollment: 177. Undergraduates: 177. Freshmen: 30. Federal methodology is used as a basis for awarding need-based institutional aid.
UNDERGRADUATE EXPENSES for 2005–06 *Application fee:* $25. *Comprehensive fee:* $12,985 includes full-time tuition ($7360), mandatory fees ($865), and room and board ($4760). *College room only:* $2640. Room and board charges vary according to board plan. *Part-time tuition:* $230 per credit hour. *Payment plan:* Deferred payment.
FRESHMAN FINANCIAL AID (Fall 2003) 40 applied for aid; of those 82% were deemed to have need. 100% of freshmen with need received aid; of those 18% had need fully met. *Average percent of need met:* 57% (excluding resources

awarded to replace EFC). *Average financial aid package:* $6228 (excluding resources awarded to replace EFC). 14% of all full-time freshmen had no need and received non-need-based gift aid.
UNDERGRADUATE FINANCIAL AID (Fall 2003) 141 applied for aid; of those 86% were deemed to have need. 100% of undergraduates with need received aid; of those 10% had need fully met. *Average percent of need met:* 54% (excluding resources awarded to replace EFC). *Average financial aid package:* $6614 (excluding resources awarded to replace EFC). 12% of all full-time undergraduates had no need and received non-need-based gift aid.
GIFT AID (NEED-BASED) *Total amount:* $511,078 (43% federal, 53% institutional, 4% external sources). *Receiving aid:* Freshmen: 67% (33); All full-time undergraduates: 70% (121). *Average award:* Freshmen: $4171; Undergraduates: $3869. *Scholarships, grants, and awards:* Federal Pell, FSEOG, state, private, college/university gift aid from institutional funds.
GIFT AID (NON-NEED-BASED) *Total amount:* $70,689 (98% institutional, 2% external sources). *Receiving aid:* Freshmen: 8% (4); Undergraduates: 4% (7). *Average Award:* Freshmen: $1816; Undergraduates: $2181. *Scholarships, grants, and awards by category:* Academic Interests/Achievement: 28 awards ($87,000 total): general academic interests/achievements, religion/biblical studies. *Special Achievements/Activities:* 24 awards ($58,610 total): general special achievements/ activities, religious involvement. *Special Characteristics:* 54 awards ($52,437 total): children and siblings of alumni, children of faculty/staff, general special characteristics, handicapped students, international students, married students, spouses of current students.
LOANS *Student loans:* $574,929 (80% need-based, 20% non-need-based). 63% of past graduating class borrowed through all loan programs. *Average indebtedness per student:* $16,111. *Average need-based loan:* Freshmen: $2393; Undergraduates: $6719. *Parent loans:* $103,730 (61% need-based, 39% non-need-based). *Programs:* FFEL (Subsidized and Unsubsidized Stafford, PLUS), alternative loans.
WORK-STUDY *Federal work-study:* Total amount: $15,629; 24 jobs averaging $651.
APPLYING FOR FINANCIAL AID *Required financial aid forms:* FAFSA, institution's own form. *Financial aid deadline (priority):* 3/15. *Notification date:* Continuous beginning 4/1. Students must reply within 2 weeks of notification.
CONTACT Mrs. Julie Ann Fields, Director of Admissions and Financial Aid, Roanoke Bible College, 715 North Poindexter Street, Elizabeth City, NC 27909, 252-334-2019 or toll-free 800-RBC-8980. *Fax:* 252-334-2064. *E-mail:* jaf@ roanokebible.edu.

ROANOKE COLLEGE
Salem, VA

Tuition & fees: $22,109	Average undergraduate aid package: $18,394

ABOUT THE INSTITUTION Independent religious, coed. Awards: bachelor's degrees. 30 undergraduate majors. Total enrollment: 1,850. Undergraduates: 1,850. Freshmen: 484. Federal methodology is used as a basis for awarding need-based institutional aid.
UNDERGRADUATE EXPENSES for 2004–05 *Application fee:* $30. *Comprehensive fee:* $29,021 includes full-time tuition ($21,504), mandatory fees ($605), and room and board ($6912). *College room only:* $3350. Room and board charges vary according to housing facility. *Part-time tuition:* $1020 per course. *Payment plan:* Installment.
FRESHMAN FINANCIAL AID (Fall 2003) 389 applied for aid; of those 99% were deemed to have need. 100% of freshmen with need received aid; of those 23% had need fully met. *Average percent of need met:* 93% (excluding resources awarded to replace EFC). *Average financial aid package:* $18,596 (excluding resources awarded to replace EFC). 17% of all full-time freshmen had no need and received non-need-based gift aid.
UNDERGRADUATE FINANCIAL AID (Fall 2003) 1,387 applied for aid; of those 92% were deemed to have need. 100% of undergraduates with need received aid; of those 30% had need fully met. *Average percent of need met:* 88% (excluding resources awarded to replace EFC). *Average financial aid package:* $18,394 (excluding resources awarded to replace EFC). 24% of all full-time undergraduates had no need and received non-need-based gift aid.
GIFT AID (NEED-BASED) *Total amount:* $15,811,094 (6% federal, 11% state, 80% institutional, 3% external sources). *Receiving aid:* Freshmen: 67% (323); All full-time undergraduates: 64% (1,110). *Average award:* Freshmen: $15,749; Undergraduates: $14,459. *Scholarships, grants, and awards:* Federal Pell, FSEOG, state, private, college/university gift aid from institutional funds.

GIFT AID (NON-NEED-BASED) *Total amount:* $5,622,216 (10% state, 86% institutional, 4% external sources). *Receiving aid:* Freshmen: 72% (348); Undergraduates: 61% (1,061). *Average Award:* Freshmen: $8757; *Undergraduates:* $9187. *Scholarships, grants, and awards by category: Academic Interests/ Achievement:* general academic interests/achievements. *Creative Arts/ Performance:* art/fine arts, music. *Special Characteristics:* local/state students, members of minority groups, religious affiliation. *Tuition waivers:* Full or partial for employees or children of employees, senior citizens.

LOANS *Student loans:* $6,822,801 (89% need-based, 11% non-need-based). 70% of past graduating class borrowed through all loan programs. *Average indebtedness per student:* $17,803. *Average need-based loan:* Freshmen: $3011; Undergraduates: $4307. *Parent loans:* $2,257,579 (81% need-based, 19% non-need-based). *Programs:* FFEL (Subsidized and Unsubsidized Stafford, PLUS), Perkins, college/university.

WORK-STUDY *Federal work-study:* Total amount: $891,004; 620 jobs averaging $1409.

APPLYING FOR FINANCIAL AID *Required financial aid forms:* FAFSA, state aid form. *Financial aid deadline (priority):* 3/1. *Notification date:* Continuous beginning 11/1. Students must reply within 2 weeks of notification.

CONTACT Mr. Thomas S. Blair Jr., Director of Financial Aid, Roanoke College, 221 College Lane, Salem, VA 24153-3794, 540-375-2235 or toll-free 800-388-2276. *E-mail:* finaid@roanoke.edu.

ROBERT MORRIS COLLEGE
Chicago, IL

Tuition & fees: $14,250	Average undergraduate aid package: $10,818

ABOUT THE INSTITUTION Independent, coed. Awards: associate and bachelor's degrees. 19 undergraduate majors. Total enrollment: 5,520. Undergraduates: 5,520. Freshmen: 1,384. Federal methodology is used as a basis for awarding need-based institutional aid.

UNDERGRADUATE EXPENSES for 2004–05 *Application fee:* $30. *Comprehensive fee:* $20,640 includes full-time tuition ($14,250) and room and board ($6390). *College room only:* $4590. Full-time tuition and fees vary according to program. Room and board charges vary according to board plan and housing facility. *Part-time tuition:* $1580 per course. Part-time tuition and fees vary according to course load and program. *Payment plan:* Installment.

GIFT AID (NEED-BASED) *Total amount:* $26,412,309 (43% federal, 51% state, 4% institutional, 2% external sources). *Receiving aid:* Freshmen: 83% (1,151); All full-time undergraduates: 90% (4,559). *Average award:* Freshmen: $7958; Undergraduates: $8059. *Scholarships, grants, and awards:* Federal Pell, FSEOG, state, private, college/university gift aid from institutional funds.

GIFT AID (NON-NEED-BASED) *Total amount:* $556,112 (1% federal, 99% institutional). *Receiving aid:* Freshmen: 2% (30); Undergraduates: 2% (114). *Average Award:* Freshmen: $8764; Undergraduates: $8181. *Scholarships, grants, and awards by category: Academic Interests/Achievement:* business, computer science, general academic interests/achievements, health fields. *Creative Arts/ Performance:* applied art and design, journalism/publications. *Special Achievements/ Activities:* community service, general special achievements/activities. *Special Characteristics:* children of faculty/staff, general special characteristics, out-of-state students, veterans. *Tuition waivers:* Full or partial for employees or children of employees. *ROTC:* Army cooperative.

LOANS *Student loans:* $26,074,260 (93% need-based, 7% non-need-based). 91% of past graduating class borrowed through all loan programs. *Average indebtedness per student:* $16,666. *Average need-based loan:* Freshmen: $2685; Undergraduates: $3492. *Parent loans:* $2,882,016 (66% need-based, 34% non-need-based). *Programs:* FFEL (Subsidized and Unsubsidized Stafford, PLUS), Perkins.

ATHLETIC AWARDS *Total amount:* $1,809,996 (77% need-based, 23% non-need-based).

APPLYING FOR FINANCIAL AID *Required financial aid form:* FAFSA. *Financial aid deadline:* Continuous. *Notification date:* Continuous.

CONTACT Gabriel Hennessey, Assistant Director of Financial Services, Robert Morris College, 401 South State Street, Suite 140, Chicago, IL 60605, 312-935-4075 or toll-free 800-RMC-5960. *Fax:* 312-935-4074. *E-mail:* ghennessey@ robertmorris.edu.

ROBERT MORRIS UNIVERSITY
Moon Township, PA

Tuition & fees: $14,226	Average undergraduate aid package: $11,964

ABOUT THE INSTITUTION Independent, coed. Awards: bachelor's, master's, and doctoral degrees and post-bachelor's certificates. 33 undergraduate majors. Total enrollment: 4,971. Undergraduates: 3,861. Freshmen: 686. Federal methodology is used as a basis for awarding need-based institutional aid.

UNDERGRADUATE EXPENSES for 2004–05 *Application fee:* $30. *Comprehensive fee:* $21,512 includes full-time tuition ($14,226) and room and board ($7286). *College room only:* $4386. Room and board charges vary according to board plan and housing facility. *Part-time tuition:* $427 per credit. Part-time tuition and fees vary according to course load. *Payment plans:* Installment, deferred payment.

FRESHMAN FINANCIAL AID (Fall 2004, est.) 630 applied for aid; of those 85% were deemed to have need. 100% of freshmen with need received aid; of those 25% had need fully met. *Average percent of need met:* 74% (excluding resources awarded to replace EFC). *Average financial aid package:* $12,345 (excluding resources awarded to replace EFC). 19% of all full-time freshmen had no need and received non-need-based gift aid.

UNDERGRADUATE FINANCIAL AID (Fall 2004, est.) 2,426 applied for aid; of those 90% were deemed to have need. 100% of undergraduates with need received aid; of those 22% had need fully met. *Average percent of need met:* 68% (excluding resources awarded to replace EFC). *Average financial aid package:* $11,964 (excluding resources awarded to replace EFC). 15% of all full-time undergraduates had no need and received non-need-based gift aid.

GIFT AID (NEED-BASED) *Total amount:* $12,422,964 (23% federal, 32% state, 42% institutional, 3% external sources). *Receiving aid:* Freshmen: 78% (530); All full-time undergraduates: 67% (1,970). *Average award:* Freshmen: $7744; Undergraduates: $6463. *Scholarships, grants, and awards:* Federal Pell, FSEOG, state, private, college/university gift aid from institutional funds.

GIFT AID (NON-NEED-BASED) *Total amount:* $1,801,615 (2% state, 87% institutional, 11% external sources). *Receiving aid:* Freshmen: 7% (49); Undergraduates: 4% (119). *Average Award:* Freshmen: $9003; *Undergraduates:* $8632. *Scholarships, grants, and awards by category: Academic Interests/Achievement:* general academic interests/achievements. *Creative Arts/ Performance:* general creative arts/performance. *Special Achievements/Activities:* general special achievements/activities. *Special Characteristics:* children of faculty/ staff, ethnic background, members of minority groups, out-of-state students. *Tuition waivers:* Full or partial for employees or children of employees. *ROTC:* Army cooperative, Air Force cooperative.

LOANS *Student loans:* $22,982,010 (78% need-based, 22% non-need-based). *Average need-based loan:* Freshmen: $3882; Undergraduates: $5591. *Parent loans:* $4,136,109 (48% need-based, 52% non-need-based). *Programs:* FFEL (Subsidized and Unsubsidized Stafford, PLUS), Perkins, alternative loans.

WORK-STUDY *Federal work-study:* Total amount: $2,226,966; jobs available. *State or other work-study/employment:* Part-time jobs available.

ATHLETIC AWARDS *Total amount:* $2,083,802 (54% need-based, 46% non-need-based).

APPLYING FOR FINANCIAL AID *Required financial aid form:* FAFSA. *Financial aid deadline (priority):* 5/1. *Notification date:* Continuous. Students must reply within 2 weeks of notification.

CONTACT Ms. Shari Payne, Director, Financial Aid, Robert Morris University, 6001 University Boulevard, Moon Township, PA 15108-1189, 412-299-2450 or toll-free 800-762-0097. *Fax:* 412-262-8601. *E-mail:* finaid@rmu.edu.

ROBERTS WESLEYAN COLLEGE
Rochester, NY

Tuition & fees: $19,324	Average undergraduate aid package: $14,700

ABOUT THE INSTITUTION Independent religious, coed. Awards: associate, bachelor's, and master's degrees. 55 undergraduate majors. Total enrollment: 1,926. Undergraduates: 1,376. Freshmen: 258. Federal methodology is used as a basis for awarding need-based institutional aid.

UNDERGRADUATE EXPENSES for 2005–06 *Application fee:* $35. *Comprehensive fee:* $24,352 includes full-time tuition ($18,350), mandatory fees ($974), and room and board ($5028). *College room only:* $2026. Room and board charges vary according to board plan. *Part-time tuition:* $402 per credit. Part-time tuition and fees vary according to course load. *Payment plan:* Installment.

FRESHMAN FINANCIAL AID (Fall 2003) 220 applied for aid; of those 95% were deemed to have need. 100% of freshmen with need received aid; of those 14% had need fully met. *Average percent of need met:* 82% (excluding resources awarded to replace EFC). *Average financial aid package:* $15,150 (excluding resources awarded to replace EFC). 13% of all full-time freshmen had no need and received non-need-based gift aid.

UNDERGRADUATE FINANCIAL AID (Fall 2003) 874 applied for aid; of those 95% were deemed to have need. 100% of undergraduates with need received aid; of those 18% had need fully met. *Average percent of need met:* 79% (excluding resources awarded to replace EFC). *Average financial aid package:* $14,700 (excluding resources awarded to replace EFC). 13% of all full-time undergraduates had no need and received non-need-based gift aid.

GIFT AID (NEED-BASED) *Total amount:* $8,149,078 (18% federal, 20% state, 52% institutional, 10% external sources). *Receiving aid:* Freshmen: 87% (209); All full-time undergraduates: 87% (825). *Average award:* Freshmen: $10,563; Undergraduates: $9397. *Scholarships, grants, and awards:* Federal Pell, FSEOG, state, private, college/university gift aid from institutional funds.

GIFT AID (NON-NEED-BASED) *Total amount:* $1,021,177 (3% state, 54% institutional, 43% external sources). *Receiving aid:* Freshmen: 4% (9); Undergraduates: 5% (47). *Average Award:* Freshmen: $9170; Undergraduates: $8578. *Scholarships, grants, and awards by category:* Creative Arts/Performance: 152 awards ($253,150 total): art/fine arts, music. *Special Achievements/Activities:* 314 awards ($248,050 total): general special achievements/activities, leadership. *Special Characteristics:* 569 awards ($994,189 total): children and siblings of alumni, children of faculty/staff, international students, out-of-state students, relatives of clergy, religious affiliation, siblings of current students, spouses of current students. *Tuition waivers:* Full or partial for employees or children of employees. *ROTC:* Army cooperative, Air Force cooperative.

LOANS *Student loans:* $6,023,432 (84% need-based, 16% non-need-based). 93% of past graduating class borrowed through all loan programs. *Average need-based loan:* Freshmen: $4124; Undergraduates: $5005. *Parent loans:* $1,613,117 (56% need-based, 44% non-need-based). *Programs:* FFEL (Subsidized and Unsubsidized Stafford, PLUS), Perkins.

WORK-STUDY *Federal work-study:* Total amount: $623,017; 652 jobs averaging $956. *State or other work-study/employment:* Total amount: $95,422 (5% need-based, 95% non-need-based). 51 part-time jobs averaging $1693.

ATHLETIC AWARDS *Total amount:* $552,644 (63% need-based, 37% non-need-based).

APPLYING FOR FINANCIAL AID *Required financial aid form:* FAFSA. *Financial aid deadline (priority):* 3/15. *Notification date:* Continuous beginning 3/15. Students must reply by 5/1 or within 2 weeks of notification.

CONTACT Mr. Stephen Field, Director of Student Financial Services, Roberts Wesleyan College, 2301 Westside Drive, Rochester, NY 14624-1997, 585-594-6391 or toll-free 800-777-4RWC. *Fax:* 585-594-6036. *E-mail:* fields@roberts.edu.

ROCHESTER COLLEGE
Rochester Hills, MI

Tuition & fees: $11,456	Average undergraduate aid package: $2539

ABOUT THE INSTITUTION Independent religious, coed. Awards: associate and bachelor's degrees. 24 undergraduate majors. Total enrollment: 1,011. Undergraduates: 1,011. Freshmen: 111. Both federal and institutional methodology are used as a basis for awarding need-based institutional aid.

UNDERGRADUATE EXPENSES for 2004–05 *Application fee:* $25. *Comprehensive fee:* $17,772 includes full-time tuition ($10,580), mandatory fees ($876), and room and board ($6316). Room and board charges vary according to board plan and housing facility. *Part-time fees:* $171 per term. Part-time tuition and fees vary according to course load. *Payment plan:* Installment.

FRESHMAN FINANCIAL AID (Fall 2004, est.) 170 applied for aid; of those 100% were deemed to have need. 75% of freshmen with need received aid. *Average percent of need met:* 82% (excluding resources awarded to replace EFC). *Average financial aid package:* $2556 (excluding resources awarded to replace EFC). 65% of all full-time freshmen had no need and received non-need-based gift aid.

UNDERGRADUATE FINANCIAL AID (Fall 2004, est.) 552 applied for aid; of those 100% were deemed to have need. 84% of undergraduates with need received aid. *Average percent of need met:* 82% (excluding resources awarded

to replace EFC). *Average financial aid package:* $2539 (excluding resources awarded to replace EFC). 69% of all full-time undergraduates had no need and received non-need-based gift aid.

GIFT AID (NEED-BASED) *Total amount:* $1,401,739 (64% federal, 36% state). *Receiving aid:* Freshmen: 36% (62); All full-time undergraduates: 45% (246). *Average award:* Freshmen: $3186; Undergraduates: $2967. *Scholarships, grants, and awards:* Federal Pell, FSEOG, state, private, college/university gift aid from institutional funds.

GIFT AID (NON-NEED-BASED) *Total amount:* $1,611,678 (6% state, 94% institutional). *Receiving aid:* Freshmen: 72% (123); Undergraduates: 78% (428). *Average Award:* Freshmen: $4673; Undergraduates: $4455. *Scholarships, grants, and awards by category:* Academic Interests/Achievement: 362 awards ($510,817 total): business, computer science, education, general academic interests/achievements, mathematics, religion/biblical studies. *Creative Arts/Performance:* 87 awards ($93,102 total): journalism/publications, music, theater/drama. *Special Achievements/Activities:* 302 awards ($396,265 total): general special achievements/activities, leadership. *Special Characteristics:* 336 awards ($571,353 total): adult students, children and siblings of alumni, children of faculty/staff, first-generation college students, general special characteristics, out-of-state students, previous college experience, relatives of clergy, siblings of current students. *Tuition waivers:* Full or partial for children of alumni, employees or children of employees, senior citizens.

LOANS *Student loans:* $1,952,403 (57% need-based, 43% non-need-based). *Average need-based loan:* Freshmen: $2862; Undergraduates: $3243. *Parent loans:* $412,887 (100% non-need-based). *Programs:* Federal Direct (Subsidized and Unsubsidized Stafford, PLUS), Perkins.

WORK-STUDY *Federal work-study:* Total amount: $145,934; 93 jobs averaging $1500. *State or other work-study/employment:* Total amount: $75,342 (100% non-need-based). 106 part-time jobs averaging $1000.

ATHLETIC AWARDS *Total amount:* $226,319 (100% non-need-based).

APPLYING FOR FINANCIAL AID *Required financial aid forms:* FAFSA, institution's own form. *Financial aid deadline (priority):* 3/15. *Notification date:* Continuous beginning 3/15. Students must reply by 9/1.

CONTACT Burt Rutledge, Director of Financial Aid, Rochester College, 800 West Avon Road, Rochester Hills, MI 48307, 248-218-2028 or toll-free 800-521-6010. *Fax:* 248-218-2035. *E-mail:* brutledge@rc.edu.

ROCHESTER INSTITUTE OF TECHNOLOGY
Rochester, NY

Tuition & fees: $22,413	Average undergraduate aid package: $16,300

ABOUT THE INSTITUTION Independent, coed. Awards: associate, bachelor's, master's, and doctoral degrees and post-bachelor's and post-master's certificates. 119 undergraduate majors. Total enrollment: 14,552. Undergraduates: 12,304. Freshmen: 2,259. Both federal and institutional methodology are used as a basis for awarding need-based institutional aid.

UNDERGRADUATE EXPENSES for 2004–05 *Application fee:* $50. *Comprehensive fee:* $30,549 includes full-time tuition ($22,056), mandatory fees ($357), and room and board ($8136). *College room only:* $4653. Full-time tuition and fees vary according to course load, program, and student level. Room and board charges vary according to board plan and housing facility. *Part-time tuition:* $491 per credit hour. *Part-time fees:* $29 per term. Part-time tuition and fees vary according to course load, program, and student level. *Payment plans:* Tuition prepayment, installment, deferred payment.

FRESHMAN FINANCIAL AID (Fall 2003) 1837 applied for aid; of those 84% were deemed to have need. 100% of freshmen with need received aid; of those 84% had need fully met. *Average percent of need met:* 90% (excluding resources awarded to replace EFC). *Average financial aid package:* $16,800 (excluding resources awarded to replace EFC). 10% of all full-time freshmen had no need and received non-need-based gift aid.

UNDERGRADUATE FINANCIAL AID (Fall 2003) 8,100 applied for aid; of those 90% were deemed to have need. 100% of undergraduates with need received aid; of those 85% had need fully met. *Average percent of need met:* 90% (excluding resources awarded to replace EFC). *Average financial aid package:* $16,300 (excluding resources awarded to replace EFC). 9% of all full-time undergraduates had no need and received non-need-based gift aid.

GIFT AID (NEED-BASED) *Total amount:* $68,999,300 (14% federal, 12% state, 72% institutional, 2% external sources). *Receiving aid:* Freshmen: 67% (1,470); All full-time undergraduates: 67% (6,825). *Average award:* Freshmen: $10,300; Undergraduates: $9900. *Scholarships, grants, and awards:* Federal Pell, FSEOG, state, private, college/university gift aid from institutional funds.

GIFT AID (NON-NEED-BASED) *Total amount:* $19,027,000 (9% federal, 30% state, 46% institutional, 15% external sources). *Receiving aid:* Freshmen: 25% (550); Undergraduates: 24% (2,425). *Average Award:* Freshmen: $6100; Undergraduates: $5800. *Scholarships, grants, and awards by category:* *Academic Interests/Achievement:* 3,000 awards ($16,736,000 total): biological sciences, business, communication, computer science, engineering/technologies, general academic interests/achievements, health fields, international studies, mathematics, military science, physical sciences, premedicine, social sciences. *Creative Arts/Performance:* 310 awards ($1,903,000 total): applied art and design, art/fine arts, cinema/film/broadcasting. *Special Achievements/Activities:* community service, leadership. *Special Characteristics:* children of faculty/staff, international students, members of minority groups, veterans. *Tuition waivers:* Full or partial for employees or children of employees. *ROTC:* Army, Naval cooperative, Air Force.

LOANS *Student loans:* $53,102,500 (60% need-based, 40% non-need-based). 89% of past graduating class borrowed through all loan programs. *Average need-based loan:* Freshmen: $4400; Undergraduates: $4700. *Parent loans:* $12,529,900 (33% need-based, 67% non-need-based). *Programs:* Federal Direct (Subsidized and Unsubsidized Stafford, PLUS), Perkins, alternative loans, RIT loans.

WORK-STUDY *Federal work-study:* Total amount: $2,729,700; 2,060 jobs averaging $1330. *State or other work-study/employment:* Total amount: $8,348,000 (100% non-need-based). 4,700 part-time jobs averaging $1780.

APPLYING FOR FINANCIAL AID *Required financial aid form:* FAFSA. *Financial aid deadline (priority):* 3/1. *Notification date:* Continuous beginning 3/15. Students must reply by 5/1 or within 2 weeks of notification.

CONTACT Mrs. Verna Hazen, Director of Financial Aid and Scholarships, Rochester Institute of Technology, Office of Financial Aid and Scholarships, 56 Lomb Drive, Rochester, NY 14623-5604, 585-475-2186. *Fax:* 585-475-7270. *E-mail:* finaid@rit.edu.

ROCKFORD COLLEGE
Rockford, IL

ABOUT THE INSTITUTION Independent, coed. Awards: bachelor's and master's degrees. 50 undergraduate majors. Total enrollment: 1,280. Undergraduates: 976. Freshmen: 131.

GIFT AID (NEED-BASED) *Scholarships, grants, and awards:* Federal Pell, FSEOG, state, private, college/university gift aid from institutional funds.

GIFT AID (NON-NEED-BASED) *Scholarships, grants, and awards by category:* *Academic Interests/Achievement:* biological sciences, business, education, English, foreign languages, general academic interests/achievements, mathematics, physical sciences, premedicine, social sciences. *Creative Arts/Performance:* dance, music, performing arts, theater/drama. *Special Achievements/Activities:* community service, leadership. *Special Characteristics:* children and siblings of alumni, children of current students, children of educators, children of faculty/staff, children of workers in trades, general special characteristics, handicapped students, international students, out-of-state students, parents of current students, relatives of clergy, siblings of current students.

LOANS *Programs:* FFEL (Subsidized and Unsubsidized Stafford, PLUS), Perkins, college/university, alternative loans.

WORK-STUDY *Federal work-study:* Total amount: $136,000; jobs available. *State or other work-study/employment:* Total amount: $50,000 (100% non-need-based). Part-time jobs available.

APPLYING FOR FINANCIAL AID *Required financial aid form:* FAFSA.

CONTACT Mrs. Stacey Zimmerman, Financial Aid Specialist, Rockford College, 5050 East State Street, Rockford, IL 61108, 815-226-3396 or toll-free 800-892-2984. *Fax:* 815-394-5174.

ROCKHURST UNIVERSITY
Kansas City, MO

Tuition & fees: $18,560	Average undergraduate aid package: $18,167

ABOUT THE INSTITUTION Independent Roman Catholic (Jesuit), coed. Awards: bachelor's, master's, and doctoral degrees and post-bachelor's certificates. 40 undergraduate majors. Total enrollment: 2,764. Undergraduates: 1,962. Freshmen: 305. Federal methodology is used as a basis for awarding need-based institutional aid.

UNDERGRADUATE EXPENSES for 2004–05 *Application fee:* $25. *Comprehensive fee:* $24,060 includes full-time tuition ($17,950), mandatory fees ($610), and room and board ($5500). Full-time tuition and fees vary according to class time

and course load. Room and board charges vary according to board plan and housing facility. *Part-time tuition:* $600 per semester hour. *Part-time fees:* $25 per term. Part-time tuition and fees vary according to class time and course load. *Payment plans:* Installment, deferred payment.

FRESHMAN FINANCIAL AID (Fall 2004, est.) 303 applied for aid; of those 90% were deemed to have need. 100% of freshmen with need received aid; of those 4% had need fully met. *Average percent of need met:* 100% (excluding resources awarded to replace EFC). *Average financial aid package:* $19,108 (excluding resources awarded to replace EFC). 7% of all full-time freshmen had no need and received non-need-based gift aid.

UNDERGRADUATE FINANCIAL AID (Fall 2004, est.) 1,148 applied for aid; of those 84% were deemed to have need. 95% of undergraduates with need received aid; of those 4% had need fully met. *Average percent of need met:* 93% (excluding resources awarded to replace EFC). *Average financial aid package:* $18,167 (excluding resources awarded to replace EFC). 10% of all full-time undergraduates had no need and received non-need-based gift aid.

GIFT AID (NEED-BASED) *Total amount:* $7,620,836 (12% federal, 6% state, 80% institutional, 2% external sources). *Receiving aid:* Freshmen: 60% (184); All full-time undergraduates: 53% (661). *Average award:* Freshmen: $5850; Undergraduates: $6011. *Scholarships, grants, and awards:* Federal Pell, FSEOG, state, private, college/university gift aid from institutional funds.

GIFT AID (NON-NEED-BASED) *Total amount:* $2,401,575 (5% state, 93% institutional, 2% external sources). *Receiving aid:* Freshmen: 89% (272); Undergraduates: 73% (906). *Average Award:* Freshmen: $8473; Undergraduates: $8146. *Scholarships, grants, and awards by category:* *Academic Interests/Achievement:* 841 awards ($4,049,542 total): biological sciences, business, communication, computer science, English, foreign languages, general academic interests/achievements, health fields, humanities, mathematics, physical sciences, premedicine, religion/biblical studies, social sciences. *Creative Arts/Performance:* 27 awards ($39,625 total): creative writing, music, performing arts, theater/drama. *Special Achievements/Activities:* 130 awards ($177,000 total): community service, leadership. *Special Characteristics:* 173 awards ($713,320 total): children and siblings of alumni, children of faculty/staff, siblings of current students. *Tuition waivers:* Full or partial for children of alumni, employees or children of employees, senior citizens. *ROTC:* Army cooperative.

LOANS *Student loans:* $4,941,962 (60% need-based, 40% non-need-based). 79% of past graduating class borrowed through all loan programs. *Average indebtedness per student:* $25,823. *Average need-based loan:* Freshmen: $2319; Undergraduates: $2031. *Parent loans:* $1,081,796 (62% need-based, 38% non-need-based). *Programs:* FFEL (Subsidized and Unsubsidized Stafford, PLUS), Perkins.

WORK-STUDY *Federal work-study:* Total amount: $220,873; 198 jobs averaging $1500. *State or other work-study/employment:* Total amount: $57,335 (53% need-based, 47% non-need-based). 57 part-time jobs averaging $1200.

ATHLETIC AWARDS *Total amount:* $1,650,520 (35% need-based, 65% non-need-based).

APPLYING FOR FINANCIAL AID *Required financial aid form:* FAFSA. *Financial aid deadline:* 6/1 (priority: 3/1). *Notification date:* Continuous. Students must reply within 4 weeks of notification.

CONTACT Ms. Carla Boren, Director of Financial Aid, Rockhurst University, 1100 Rockhurst Road, Kansas City, MO 64110-2561, 816-501-4100 or toll-free 800-842-6776. *Fax:* 816-501-4241. *E-mail:* carla.boren@rockhurst.edu.

ROCKY MOUNTAIN COLLEGE
Billings, MT

ABOUT THE INSTITUTION Independent interdenominational, coed. Awards: associate, bachelor's, and master's degrees. 50 undergraduate majors. Total enrollment: 988. Undergraduates: 946. Freshmen: 229.

GIFT AID (NEED-BASED) *Scholarships, grants, and awards:* Federal Pell, FSEOG, state, private, college/university gift aid from institutional funds.

GIFT AID (NON-NEED-BASED) *Scholarships, grants, and awards by category:* *Academic Interests/Achievement:* biological sciences, business, education, English, general academic interests/achievements, health fields, humanities, mathematics, physical sciences, premedicine, religion/biblical studies, social sciences. *Creative Arts/Performance:* art/fine arts, creative writing, debating, music, theater/drama. *Special Achievements/Activities:* general special achievements/activities, leadership, religious involvement. *Special Characteristics:* children and siblings of alumni, children of faculty/staff, international students, members of minority groups, religious affiliation, siblings of current students, spouses of current students.

LOANS *Programs:* FFEL (Subsidized and Unsubsidized Stafford, PLUS), Perkins.

WORK-STUDY *Federal work-study:* Total amount: $136,736; 353 jobs averaging $387. *State or other work-study/employment:* Total amount: $288,432 (100% non-need-based). 216 part-time jobs averaging $1335.

APPLYING FOR FINANCIAL AID *Required financial aid forms:* FAFSA, institution's own form.

CONTACT Lisa Browning, Financial Aid Director, Rocky Mountain College, 1511 Poly Drive, Billings, MT 59102-1796, 406-657-1031 or toll-free 800-877-6259. *Fax:* 406-238-7351. *E-mail:* browninl@rocky.edu.

ROCKY MOUNTAIN COLLEGE OF ART & DESIGN
Lakewood, CO

Tuition & fees: $16,490	Average undergraduate aid package: $5260

ABOUT THE INSTITUTION Proprietary, coed. Awards: bachelor's degrees. 7 undergraduate majors. Total enrollment: 503. Undergraduates: 503. Freshmen: 54. Federal methodology is used as a basis for awarding need-based institutional aid.

UNDERGRADUATE EXPENSES for 2004–05 *Application fee:* $50. *Tuition:* full-time $16,400. Room and board charges vary according to housing facility. *Payment plan:* Installment.

FRESHMAN FINANCIAL AID (Fall 2003) 77 applied for aid; of those 94% were deemed to have need. 100% of freshmen with need received aid; of those 36% had need fully met. *Average percent of need met:* 38% (excluding resources awarded to replace EFC). *Average financial aid package:* $3694 (excluding resources awarded to replace EFC). 1% of all full-time freshmen had no need and received non-need-based gift aid.

UNDERGRADUATE FINANCIAL AID (Fall 2003) 397 applied for aid; of those 94% were deemed to have need. 100% of undergraduates with need received aid; of those 22% had need fully met. *Average percent of need met:* 56% (excluding resources awarded to replace EFC). *Average financial aid package:* $5260 (excluding resources awarded to replace EFC). 4% of all full-time undergraduates had no need and received non-need-based gift aid.

GIFT AID (NEED-BASED) *Total amount:* $634,801 (77% federal, 22% state, 1% external sources). *Receiving aid:* Freshmen: 70% (54); All full-time undergraduates: 60% (240). *Average award:* Freshmen: $2435; Undergraduates: $3841. *Scholarships, grants, and awards:* Federal Pell, FSEOG, state.

GIFT AID (NON-NEED-BASED) *Total amount:* $823,371 (94% institutional, 6% external sources). *Receiving aid:* Freshmen: 35% (27); Undergraduates: 52% (205). *Average Award:* Freshmen: $3750; Undergraduates: $2433. *Scholarships, grants, and awards by category:* Academic Interests/Achievement: 315 awards ($772,838 total): general academic interests/achievements. *Creative Arts/Performance:* applied art and design, art/fine arts. *Special Characteristics:* children of faculty/staff. *Tuition waivers:* Full or partial for employees or children of employees.

LOANS *Student loans:* $2,809,556 (100% need-based). *Average need-based loan:* Freshmen: $2298; Undergraduates: $3895. *Parent loans:* $1,017,120 (100% non-need-based). *Programs:* FFEL (Subsidized and Unsubsidized Stafford, PLUS), alternative loans.

WORK-STUDY *Federal work-study:* Total amount: $13,250; 3 jobs averaging $4417. *State or other work-study/employment:* Total amount: $32,500 (100% need-based). 9 part-time jobs averaging $3611.

APPLYING FOR FINANCIAL AID *Required financial aid forms:* FAFSA, state aid form. *Financial aid deadline (priority):* 4/1. *Notification date:* Continuous beginning 4/1. Students must reply within 2 weeks of notification.

CONTACT David Nelson, Director of Financial Aid, Rocky Mountain College of Art & Design, 1600 Pierce Street, Lakewood, CO 80214, 303-753-6046 Ext. 8551 or toll-free 800-888-ARTS. *Fax:* 303-759-4970. *E-mail:* dnelson@rmcad.edu.

ROGERS STATE UNIVERSITY
Claremore, OK

ABOUT THE INSTITUTION State-supported, coed. Awards: associate and bachelor's degrees. 35 undergraduate majors. Total enrollment: 3,300. Undergraduates: 3,300. Freshmen: 763.

GIFT AID (NEED-BASED) *Scholarships, grants, and awards:* Federal Pell, FSEOG, state, private, college/university gift aid from institutional funds.

LOANS *Programs:* FFEL (Subsidized and Unsubsidized Stafford, PLUS), alternative loans.

APPLYING FOR FINANCIAL AID *Required financial aid forms:* FAFSA, institution's own form.

CONTACT Cynthia Hoyt, Director of Financial Aid, Rogers State University, 1701 West Will Rogers Boulevard, Claremore, OK 74017-3252, 918-343-7553 or toll-free 800-256-7511. *Fax:* 918-343-7598. *E-mail:* finaid@rsu.edu.

ROGER WILLIAMS UNIVERSITY
Bristol, RI

Tuition & fees: $22,866	Average undergraduate aid package: $17,796

ABOUT THE INSTITUTION Independent, coed. Awards: associate, bachelor's, master's, and first professional degrees. 48 undergraduate majors. Total enrollment: 5,070. Undergraduates: 4,190. Freshmen: 1,059. Institutional methodology is used as a basis for awarding need-based institutional aid.

UNDERGRADUATE EXPENSES for 2005–06 *Application fee:* $50. *Comprehensive fee:* $33,103 includes full-time tuition ($21,848), mandatory fees ($1018), and room and board ($10,237). *College room only:* $5355. Full-time tuition and fees vary according to class time, course load, and program. Room and board charges vary according to board plan and housing facility. *Part-time tuition:* $910 per credit. Part-time tuition and fees vary according to class time. *Payment plans:* Installment, deferred payment.

GIFT AID (NEED-BASED) *Total amount:* $21,811,061 (7% federal, 2% state, 88% institutional, 3% external sources). *Receiving aid:* Freshmen: 57% (602); All full-time undergraduates: 37% (1,315). *Average award:* Freshmen: $9618; Undergraduates: $9801. *Scholarships, grants, and awards:* Federal Pell, FSEOG, state, private, college/university gift aid from institutional funds.

GIFT AID (NON-NEED-BASED) *Total amount:* $1,726,534 (97% institutional, 3% external sources). *Receiving aid:* Freshmen: 30% (319); Undergraduates: 16% (559). *Average Award:* Freshmen: $5435; Undergraduates: $5871. *Scholarships, grants, and awards by category:* Academic Interests/Achievement: 1,469 awards ($10,448,308 total): general academic interests/achievements. *Tuition waivers:* Full or partial for employees or children of employees. *ROTC:* Army.

LOANS *Student loans:* $20,394,313 (92% need-based, 8% non-need-based). 70% of past graduating class borrowed through all loan programs. *Average indebtedness per student:* $17,125. *Average need-based loan:* Freshmen: $3825; Undergraduates: $6157. *Parent loans:* $8,328,223 (86% need-based, 14% non-need-based). *Programs:* FFEL (Subsidized and Unsubsidized Stafford, PLUS), Perkins, state.

APPLYING FOR FINANCIAL AID *Required financial aid forms:* FAFSA, CSS Financial Aid PROFILE. *Financial aid deadline:* 2/1. *Notification date:* Continuous beginning 3/15. Students must reply within 2 weeks of notification.

CONTACT Ms. Tracy DaCosta, Associate Dean of Enrollment Management, Roger Williams University, 1 Old Ferry Road, Bristol, RI 02809, 401-254-3100 or toll-free 800-458-7144 (out-of-state). *Fax:* 401-254-3356.

ROLLINS COLLEGE
Winter Park, FL

Tuition & fees: $27,700	Average undergraduate aid package: $26,666

ABOUT THE INSTITUTION Independent, coed. Awards: bachelor's and master's degrees. 32 undergraduate majors. Total enrollment: 2,571. Undergraduates: 1,759. Freshmen: 486. Federal methodology is used as a basis for awarding need-based institutional aid.

UNDERGRADUATE EXPENSES for 2004–05 *Application fee:* $40. *Comprehensive fee:* $36,270 includes full-time tuition ($26,910), mandatory fees ($790), and room and board ($8570). *College room only:* $5000. *Payment plan:* Installment.

FRESHMAN FINANCIAL AID (Fall 2004, est.) 255 applied for aid; of those 80% were deemed to have need. 100% of freshmen with need received aid; of those 40% had need fully met. *Average percent of need met:* 92% (excluding resources awarded to replace EFC). *Average financial aid package:* $23,737 (excluding resources awarded to replace EFC). 21% of all full-time freshmen had no need and received non-need-based gift aid.

UNDERGRADUATE FINANCIAL AID (Fall 2004, est.) 832 applied for aid; of those 88% were deemed to have need. 100% of undergraduates with need received aid; of those 47% had need fully met. *Average percent of need met:* 93% (excluding resources awarded to replace EFC). *Average financial aid package:* $26,666 (excluding resources awarded to replace EFC). 12% of all full-time undergraduates had no need and received non-need-based gift aid.

GIFT AID (NEED-BASED) *Total amount:* $13,849,473 (7% federal, 14% state, 78% institutional, 1% external sources). *Receiving aid:* Freshmen: 40% (195);

All full-time undergraduates: 40% (705). *Average award:* Freshmen: $20,277; Undergraduates: $21,699. *Scholarships, grants, and awards:* Federal Pell, FSEOG, state, private, college/university gift aid from institutional funds.

GIFT AID (NON-NEED-BASED) *Total amount:* $4,166,385 (40% state, 57% institutional, 3% external sources). *Receiving aid:* Freshmen: 6% (27); Undergraduates: 4% (64). *Average Award:* Freshmen: $9461; Undergraduates: $8439. *Scholarships, grants, and awards by category: Academic Interests/Achievement:* 514 awards ($4,384,118 total): computer science, engineering/technologies, general academic interests/achievements, mathematics, physical sciences. *Creative Arts/Performance:* 104 awards ($469,421 total): art/fine arts, music, theater/drama. *Tuition waivers:* Full or partial for employees or children of employees.

LOANS *Student loans:* $4,142,900 (69% need-based, 31% non-need-based). 49% of past graduating class borrowed through all loan programs. *Average indebtedness per student:* $14,018. *Average need-based loan:* Freshmen: $3822; Undergraduates: $4844. *Parent loans:* $2,317,717 (14% need-based, 86% non-need-based). *Programs:* Federal Direct (Subsidized and Unsubsidized Stafford, PLUS), Perkins, college/university.

WORK-STUDY *Federal work-study:* Total amount: $378,674; jobs available (averaging $1202).

ATHLETIC AWARDS *Total amount:* $1,931,838 (16% need-based, 84% non-need-based).

APPLYING FOR FINANCIAL AID *Required financial aid forms:* FAFSA, institution's own form. *Financial aid deadline:* 3/1 (priority: 2/15). *Notification date:* Continuous beginning 3/1.

CONTACT Mr. Phil Asbury, Director of Student Financial Aid, Rollins College, 1000 Holt Avenue, #2721, Winter Park, FL 32789-4499, 407-646-2395. *Fax:* 407-646-2173. *E-mail:* pasbury@rollins.edu.

ROOSEVELT UNIVERSITY
Chicago, IL

ABOUT THE INSTITUTION Independent, coed. Awards: bachelor's, master's, and doctoral degrees and post-bachelor's certificates. 86 undergraduate majors. Total enrollment: 7,385. Undergraduates: 4,103. Freshmen: 275.

GIFT AID (NEED-BASED) *Scholarships, grants, and awards:* Federal Pell, FSEOG, state, private, college/university gift aid from institutional funds.

GIFT AID (NON-NEED-BASED) *Scholarships, grants, and awards by category: Academic Interests/Achievement:* general academic interests/achievements. *Creative Arts/Performance:* music, theater/drama. *Special Achievements/Activities:* general special achievements/activities. *Special Characteristics:* general special characteristics.

LOANS *Programs:* FFEL (Subsidized and Unsubsidized Stafford, PLUS).

WORK-STUDY *Federal work-study:* Total amount: $558,837; jobs available. *State or other work-study/employment:* Total amount: $597,216 (100% need-based).

APPLYING FOR FINANCIAL AID *Required financial aid forms:* FAFSA, institution's own form.

CONTACT Mr. Walter J. H. O'Neill, Director of Financial Aid, Roosevelt University, 430 South Michigan Avenue, Chicago, IL 60605-1394, 312-341-2090 or toll-free 877-APPLYRU. *Fax:* 312-341-3545. *E-mail:* woneill@roosevelt.edu.

ROSE-HULMAN INSTITUTE OF TECHNOLOGY
Terre Haute, IN

Tuition & fees: $26,136	Average undergraduate aid package: $15,690

ABOUT THE INSTITUTION Independent, coed, primarily men. Awards: bachelor's and master's degrees. 15 undergraduate majors. Total enrollment: 1,904. Undergraduates: 1,765. Freshmen: 473. Federal methodology is used as a basis for awarding need-based institutional aid.

UNDERGRADUATE EXPENSES for 2004–05 *Application fee:* $40. *One-time required fee:* $3125. *Comprehensive fee:* $33,201 includes full-time tuition ($25,686), mandatory fees ($450), and room and board ($7065). *College room only:* $4035. Full-time tuition and fees vary according to course load. Room and board charges vary according to board plan. *Part-time tuition:* $738 per credit. Part-time tuition and fees vary according to course load. *Payment plans:* Tuition prepayment, installment.

FRESHMAN FINANCIAL AID (Fall 2003) 419 applied for aid; of those 82% were deemed to have need. 100% of freshmen with need received aid; of those 12%

had need fully met. *Average percent of need met:* 87% (excluding resources awarded to replace EFC). *Average financial aid package:* $17,842 (excluding resources awarded to replace EFC). 24% of all full-time freshmen had no need and received non-need-based gift aid.

UNDERGRADUATE FINANCIAL AID (Fall 2003) 1,441 applied for aid; of those 86% were deemed to have need. 100% of undergraduates with need received aid; of those 11% had need fully met. *Average percent of need met:* 81% (excluding resources awarded to replace EFC). *Average financial aid package:* $15,690 (excluding resources awarded to replace EFC). 26% of all full-time undergraduates had no need and received non-need-based gift aid.

GIFT AID (NEED-BASED) *Total amount:* $16,111,227 (7% federal, 9% state, 59% institutional, 25% external sources). *Receiving aid:* Freshmen: 72% (341); All full-time undergraduates: 69% (1,216). *Average award:* Freshmen: $14,489; Undergraduates: $13,248. *Scholarships, grants, and awards:* Federal Pell, FSEOG, state, college/university gift aid from institutional funds.

GIFT AID (NON-NEED-BASED) *Total amount:* $5,675,312 (1% state, 71% institutional, 28% external sources). *Average Award:* Freshmen: $8009; Undergraduates: $6927. *Tuition waivers:* Full or partial for employees or children of employees. *ROTC:* Army, Air Force.

LOANS *Student loans:* $11,153,287 (91% need-based, 9% non-need-based). 77% of past graduating class borrowed through all loan programs. *Average indebtedness per student:* $27,745. *Average need-based loan:* Freshmen: $7774; Undergraduates: $4770. *Parent loans:* $5,654,996 (86% need-based, 14% non-need-based). *Programs:* Federal Direct (Subsidized and Unsubsidized Stafford, PLUS), Perkins.

WORK-STUDY *Federal work-study:* Total amount: $775,381; 493 jobs averaging $1579. *State or other work-study/employment:* Total amount: $799,681 (91% need-based, 9% non-need-based). 514 part-time jobs averaging $1548.

APPLYING FOR FINANCIAL AID *Required financial aid form:* FAFSA. *Financial aid deadline (priority):* 3/1. *Notification date:* 3/10.

CONTACT Melinda L. Middleton, Director of Financial Aid, Rose-Hulman Institute of Technology, 5500 Wabash Avenue, Box #5, Terre Haute, IN 47803, 812-877-8259 or toll-free 800-248-7448. *Fax:* 812-877-8746. *E-mail:* melinda.middleton@rose-hulman.edu.

ROSEMONT COLLEGE
Rosemont, PA

Tuition & fees: $19,365	Average undergraduate aid package: $19,465

ABOUT THE INSTITUTION Independent Roman Catholic, women only. Awards: bachelor's and master's degrees and post-bachelor's certificates. 24 undergraduate majors. Total enrollment: 1,083. Undergraduates: 666. Freshmen: 109. Federal methodology is used as a basis for awarding need-based institutional aid.

UNDERGRADUATE EXPENSES for 2004–05 *Application fee:* $35. *Comprehensive fee:* $27,765 includes full-time tuition ($18,500), mandatory fees ($865), and room and board ($8400). Room and board charges vary according to housing facility. *Part-time tuition:* $725 per credit. *Part-time fees:* $105 per course. *Payment plan:* Installment.

FRESHMAN FINANCIAL AID (Fall 2004, est.) 106 applied for aid; of those 92% were deemed to have need. 100% of freshmen with need received aid; of those 28% had need fully met. *Average percent of need met:* 77% (excluding resources awarded to replace EFC). *Average financial aid package:* $18,345 (excluding resources awarded to replace EFC). 12% of all full-time freshmen had no need and received non-need-based gift aid.

UNDERGRADUATE FINANCIAL AID (Fall 2004, est.) 309 applied for aid; of those 90% were deemed to have need. 96% of undergraduates with need received aid; of those 28% had need fully met. *Average percent of need met:* 77% (excluding resources awarded to replace EFC). *Average financial aid package:* $19,465 (excluding resources awarded to replace EFC). 13% of all full-time undergraduates had no need and received non-need-based gift aid.

GIFT AID (NEED-BASED) *Total amount:* $3,626,534 (12% federal, 14% state, 71% institutional, 3% external sources). *Receiving aid:* Freshmen: 88% (98); All full-time undergraduates: 55% (222). *Average award:* Freshmen: $16,507; Undergraduates: $16,213. *Scholarships, grants, and awards:* Federal Pell, FSEOG, state, private, college/university gift aid from institutional funds.

GIFT AID (NON-NEED-BASED) *Total amount:* $829,331 (98% institutional, 2% external sources). *Receiving aid:* Freshmen: 16% (18); Undergraduates: 9% (37). *Average Award:* Freshmen: $10,327; Undergraduates: $10,643. *Scholarships, grants, and awards by category: Academic Interests/Achievement:* 104 awards ($807,890 total): general academic interests/achievements. *Creative*

Arts/Performance: 1 award ($4000 total): art/fine arts. *Special Achievements/Activities:* community service, general special achievements/activities. *Special Characteristics:* 16 awards ($148,650 total): children and siblings of alumni, children of educators, children of faculty/staff, relatives of clergy, siblings of current students. *Tuition waivers:* Full or partial for employees or children of employees, senior citizens. *ROTC:* Army cooperative.

LOANS *Student loans:* $2,995,943 (48% need-based, 52% non-need-based). 82% of past graduating class borrowed through all loan programs. *Average indebtedness per student:* $20,506. *Average need-based loan:* Freshmen: $3108; Undergraduates: $3932. *Parent loans:* $566,772 (65% need-based, 35% non-need-based). *Programs:* FFEL (Subsidized and Unsubsidized Stafford, PLUS), Perkins.

WORK-STUDY *Federal work-study:* Total amount: $147,298; 111 jobs averaging $2000. *State or other work-study/employment:* 41 part-time jobs averaging $1000.

APPLYING FOR FINANCIAL AID *Required financial aid form:* FAFSA. *Financial aid deadline (priority):* 2/15. *Notification date:* Continuous beginning 2/1. Students must reply by 5/1 or within 4 weeks of notification.

CONTACT Melissa Walsh, Director of Financial Aid, Rosemont College, 1400 Montgomery Avenue, Rosemont, PA 19010, 610-527-0200 Ext. 2220 or toll-free 800-331-0708. *Fax:* 610-527-0341. *E-mail:* mwalsh@rosemont.edu.

ROWAN UNIVERSITY
Glassboro, NJ

Tuition & fees (NJ res): $7970	Average undergraduate aid package: $6213

ABOUT THE INSTITUTION State-supported, coed. Awards: bachelor's, master's, and doctoral degrees. 38 undergraduate majors. Total enrollment: 9,688. Undergraduates: 8,383. Freshmen: 1,254. Federal methodology is used as a basis for awarding need-based institutional aid.

UNDERGRADUATE EXPENSES for 2004–05 *Application fee:* $50. *Tuition, state resident:* full-time $5828; part-time $224 per semester hour. *Tuition, nonresident:* full-time $11,656; part-time $448 per semester hour. *Required fees:* full-time $2142; $85.80 per semester hour. *College room and board:* $7642. Room and board charges vary according to board plan and housing facility. *Payment plan:* Deferred payment.

FRESHMAN FINANCIAL AID (Fall 2003) 1025 applied for aid; of those 100% were deemed to have need. 100% of freshmen with need received aid; of those 35% had need fully met. *Average percent of need met:* 52% (excluding resources awarded to replace EFC). *Average financial aid package:* $6017 (excluding resources awarded to replace EFC). 1% of all full-time freshmen had no need and received non-need-based gift aid.

UNDERGRADUATE FINANCIAL AID (Fall 2003) 5,282 applied for aid; of those 100% were deemed to have need. 100% of undergraduates with need received aid; of those 38% had need fully met. *Average percent of need met:* 50% (excluding resources awarded to replace EFC). *Average financial aid package:* $6213 (excluding resources awarded to replace EFC). 1% of all full-time undergraduates had no need and received non-need-based gift aid.

GIFT AID (NEED-BASED) *Total amount:* $16,925,065 (33% federal, 34% state, 29% institutional, 4% external sources). *Receiving aid:* Freshmen: 53% (660); All full-time undergraduates: 57% (3,272). *Average award:* Freshmen: $4901; Undergraduates: $5000. *Scholarships, grants, and awards:* Federal Pell, FSEOG, state, private, college/university gift aid from institutional funds.

GIFT AID (NON-NEED-BASED) *Total amount:* $168,490 (7% state, 69% institutional, 24% external sources). *Receiving aid:* Freshmen: 43% (534); Undergraduates: 41% (2,374). *Average Award:* Freshmen: $881; Undergraduates: $1933. *Scholarships, grants, and awards by category:* Academic Interests/Achievement: general academic interests/achievements. Creative Arts/Performance: general creative arts/performance, music. Special Characteristics: handicapped students, international students, members of minority groups. *Tuition waivers:* Full or partial for employees or children of employees. *ROTC:* Army cooperative.

LOANS *Student loans:* $32,775,786 (70% need-based, 30% non-need-based). 97% of past graduating class borrowed through all loan programs. *Average indebtedness per student:* $9575. *Average need-based loan:* Freshmen: $2302; Undergraduates: $3400. *Parent loans:* $12,951,423 (100% need-based). *Programs:* Federal Direct (Subsidized and Unsubsidized Stafford, PLUS), state.

WORK-STUDY *Federal work-study:* Total amount: $551,692; 617 jobs averaging $899. *State or other work-study/employment:* Total amount: $1,730,548 (51% need-based, 49% non-need-based). 537 part-time jobs averaging $1638.

APPLYING FOR FINANCIAL AID *Required financial aid form:* FAFSA. *Financial aid deadline:* Continuous. *Notification date:* Continuous beginning 3/15.

CONTACT Luis Tavarez, Director of Financial Aid, Rowan University, 201 Mullica Hill Road, Savitz Hall, Glassboro, NJ 08028-1701, 856-256-4276 or toll-free 800-447-1165 (in-state). *Fax:* 856-256-4413. *E-mail:* tavarez@rowan.edu.

RUSH UNIVERSITY
Chicago, IL

ABOUT THE INSTITUTION Independent, coed. Awards: bachelor's, master's, doctoral, and first professional degrees and post-master's certificates. 3 undergraduate majors. Total enrollment: 1,362. Undergraduates: 212.

GIFT AID (NEED-BASED) *Scholarships, grants, and awards:* Federal Pell, FSEOG, state, private, college/university gift aid from institutional funds.

GIFT AID (NON-NEED-BASED) *Scholarships, grants, and awards by category:* Academic Interests/Achievement: general academic interests/achievements. Special Characteristics: children of faculty/staff, members of minority groups.

LOANS *Programs:* FFEL (Subsidized and Unsubsidized Stafford, PLUS), Perkins, Federal Nursing, state, college/university, credit-based loans.

WORK-STUDY *Federal work-study:* Total amount: $9467; 10 jobs averaging $950. *State or other work-study/employment:* Total amount: $109,656 (77% need-based, 23% non-need-based). 50 part-time jobs averaging $4500.

APPLYING FOR FINANCIAL AID *Required financial aid forms:* FAFSA, institution's own form.

CONTACT Mr. Robert A. Dame, Director of Student Financial Aid, Rush University, 600 South Paulina Street, Suite 440, Chicago, IL 60612-3832, 312-942-6256. *Fax:* 312-942-2219.

RUSSELL SAGE COLLEGE
Troy, NY

Tuition & fees: $22,270	Average undergraduate aid package: N/A

ABOUT THE INSTITUTION Independent, women only. Awards: bachelor's degrees. 25 undergraduate majors. Total enrollment: 837. Undergraduates: 837. Freshmen: 138. Federal methodology is used as a basis for awarding need-based institutional aid.

UNDERGRADUATE EXPENSES for 2004–05 *Application fee:* $30. *Comprehensive fee:* $29,320 includes full-time tuition ($21,500), mandatory fees ($770), and room and board ($7050). *College room only:* $3350. *Part-time tuition:* $715 per credit hour. *Payment plans:* Installment, deferred payment.

GIFT AID (NEED-BASED) *Total amount:* $4,562,176 (20% federal, 29% state, 45% institutional, 6% external sources). *Receiving aid:* Freshmen: 88% (84); All full-time undergraduates: 93% (663). *Scholarships, grants, and awards:* Federal Pell, FSEOG, state, private, college/university gift aid from institutional funds, Federal Nursing.

GIFT AID (NON-NEED-BASED) *Total amount:* $3,416,240 (100% institutional). *Receiving aid:* Freshmen: 57% (55); Undergraduates: 54% (389). *Average Award:* Freshmen: $8100; Undergraduates: $9600. *Scholarships, grants, and awards by category:* Academic Interests/Achievement: 467 awards ($2,934,740 total): general academic interests/achievements. Special Characteristics: 43 awards ($39,000 total): children and siblings of alumni. *Tuition waivers:* Full or partial for employees or children of employees. *ROTC:* Army cooperative, Air Force cooperative.

LOANS *Student loans:* $4,331,649 (57% need-based, 43% non-need-based). 89% of past graduating class borrowed through all loan programs. *Average indebtedness per student:* $19,200. *Parent loans:* $520,305 (100% need-based). *Programs:* FFEL (Subsidized and Unsubsidized Stafford, PLUS), Perkins.

APPLYING FOR FINANCIAL AID *Required financial aid forms:* FAFSA, state aid form. *Financial aid deadline (priority):* 3/1. *Notification date:* Continuous beginning 3/15. Students must reply within 2 weeks of notification.

CONTACT James Dease, Director of Financial Aid, Russell Sage College, 45 Ferry Street, Troy, NY 12180, 518-244-4525 or toll-free 888-VERY-SAGE (in-state), 888-VERY SAGE (out-of-state). *Fax:* 518-244-2460. *E-mail:* deasej@sage.edu.

RUST COLLEGE
Holly Springs, MS

Tuition & fees: $6060	Average undergraduate aid package: $5067

ABOUT THE INSTITUTION Independent United Methodist, coed. Awards: associate and bachelor's degrees. 20 undergraduate majors. Total enrollment: 1,001. Undergraduates: 1,001. Freshmen: 288. Both federal and institutional methodology are used as a basis for awarding need-based institutional aid.

UNDERGRADUATE EXPENSES for 2005–06 *Application fee:* $10. *Comprehensive fee:* $8660 includes full-time tuition ($6000), mandatory fees ($60), and room and board ($2600). *College room only:* $1162. *Part-time tuition:* $260 per credit hour. Part-time tuition and fees vary according to class time and course load. *Payment plans:* Installment, deferred payment.

FRESHMAN FINANCIAL AID (Fall 2004, est.) 255 applied for aid; of those 100% were deemed to have need. 100% of freshmen with need received aid; of those 59% had need fully met. *Average percent of need met:* 59% (excluding resources awarded to replace EFC). *Average financial aid package:* $6985 (excluding resources awarded to replace EFC). 11% of all full-time freshmen had no need and received non-need-based gift aid.

UNDERGRADUATE FINANCIAL AID (Fall 2004, est.) 806 applied for aid; of those 100% were deemed to have need. 100% of undergraduates with need received aid; of those 60% had need fully met. *Average percent of need met:* 60% (excluding resources awarded to replace EFC). *Average financial aid package:* $5067 (excluding resources awarded to replace EFC). 13% of all full-time undergraduates had no need and received non-need-based gift aid.

GIFT AID (NEED-BASED) *Total amount:* $3,172,213 (82% federal, 12% institutional, 6% external sources). *Receiving aid:* Freshmen: 89% (255); All full-time undergraduates: 88% (741). *Average award:* Freshmen: $6139; Undergraduates: $4281. *Scholarships, grants, and awards:* Federal Pell, FSEOG, state, private, college/university gift aid from institutional funds, United Negro College Fund.

GIFT AID (NON-NEED-BASED) *Total amount:* $640,901 (3% state, 64% institutional, 33% external sources). *Receiving aid:* Freshmen: 59% (170); Undergraduates: 55% (459). *Average Award:* Freshmen: $3898; Undergraduates: $2795. *Scholarships, grants, and awards by category:* Academic Interests/ Achievement: 117 awards ($37,557 total): general academic interests/ achievements. Creative Arts/Performance: 33 awards ($24,225 total): music, theater/drama. Special Characteristics: 289 awards ($346,817 total): children of faculty/staff, ethnic background, general special characteristics, international students, local/state students, members of minority groups, relatives of clergy, religious affiliation, siblings of current students, veterans. *Tuition waivers:* Full or partial for employees or children of employees, senior citizens. *ROTC:* Army.

LOANS *Student loans:* $1,683,081 (88% need-based, 12% non-need-based). 55% of past graduating class borrowed through all loan programs. *Average indebtedness per student:* $9314. *Average need-based loan:* Freshmen: $1793; Undergraduates: $2158. *Parent loans:* $23,787 (100% non-need-based). *Programs:* FFEL (Subsidized and Unsubsidized Stafford, PLUS), United Methodist Student Loans.

WORK-STUDY *Federal work-study:* Total amount: $368,600; 492 jobs averaging $714. *State or other work-study/employment:* Total amount: $108,808 (100% non-need-based). 189 part-time jobs averaging $546.

APPLYING FOR FINANCIAL AID *Required financial aid forms:* FAFSA, institution's own form, state aid form, noncustodial (divorced/separated) parent's statement, business/farm supplement. *Financial aid deadline (priority):* 4/1. *Notification date:* 6/1. Students must reply within 2 weeks of notification.

CONTACT Mrs. Helen L. Street, Director of Financial Aid, Rust College, 150 Rust Avenue, Holly Springs, MS 38635, 662-252-8000 Ext. 4061 or toll-free 888-886-8492 Ext. 4065. *Fax:* 662-252-8895.

RUTGERS, THE STATE UNIVERSITY OF NEW JERSEY, CAMDEN
Camden, NJ

Tuition & fees (NJ res): $8389	Average undergraduate aid package: $9516

ABOUT THE INSTITUTION State-supported, coed. Awards: bachelor's, master's, and first professional degrees. 33 undergraduate majors. Total enrollment: 5,563. Undergraduates: 4,007. Freshmen: 456. Federal methodology is used as a basis for awarding need-based institutional aid.

UNDERGRADUATE EXPENSES for 2004–05 *Application fee:* $50. *Tuition, state resident:* full-time $6793; part-time $219 per credit hour. *Tuition, nonresident:* full-time $13,828; part-time $448 per credit hour. *Required fees:* full-time $1596; $315.50 per term part-time. *College room and board:* $7862; *room only:* $5452.

FRESHMAN FINANCIAL AID (Fall 2003) 382 applied for aid; of those 74% were deemed to have need. 99% of freshmen with need received aid; of those 36%

---

had need fully met. *Average percent of need met:* 85% (excluding resources awarded to replace EFC). *Average financial aid package:* $9682 (excluding resources awarded to replace EFC). 5% of all full-time freshmen had no need and received non-need-based gift aid.

UNDERGRADUATE FINANCIAL AID (Fall 2003) 2,410 applied for aid; of those 81% were deemed to have need. 99% of undergraduates with need received aid; of those 44% had need fully met. *Average percent of need met:* 85% (excluding resources awarded to replace EFC). *Average financial aid package:* $9516 (excluding resources awarded to replace EFC). 3% of all full-time undergraduates had no need and received non-need-based gift aid.

GIFT AID (NEED-BASED) *Total amount:* $11,158,838 (31% federal, 49% state, 18% institutional, 2% external sources). *Receiving aid:* Freshmen: 45% (202); All full-time undergraduates: 46% (1,407). *Average award:* Freshmen: $7208; Undergraduates: $6611. *Scholarships, grants, and awards:* Federal Pell, FSEOG, state, private, college/university gift aid from institutional funds.

GIFT AID (NON-NEED-BASED) *Total amount:* $788,059 (89% institutional, 11% external sources). *Receiving aid:* Freshmen: 20% (91); Undergraduates: 12% (366). *Average Award:* Freshmen: $4445; Undergraduates: $4428. *Scholarships, grants, and awards by category:* Academic Interests/Achievement: 512 awards ($1,593,836 total): general academic interests/achievements. Creative Arts/Performance: general creative arts/performance. Special Characteristics: 42 awards ($217,119 total): children of faculty/staff. *ROTC:* Army cooperative, Air Force cooperative.

LOANS *Student loans:* $14,406,491 (81% need-based, 19% non-need-based). 64% of past graduating class borrowed through all loan programs. *Average indebtedness per student:* $16,203. *Average need-based loan:* Freshmen: $2499; Undergraduates: $3680. *Parent loans:* $743,867 (63% need-based, 37% non-need-based). *Programs:* Federal Direct (Subsidized and Unsubsidized Stafford, PLUS), Perkins, state, college/university, alternative loans.

WORK-STUDY *Federal work-study:* Total amount: $587,480; 330 jobs averaging $1780.

APPLYING FOR FINANCIAL AID *Required financial aid form:* FAFSA. *Financial aid deadline (priority):* 3/15. *Notification date:* Continuous. Students must reply within 2 weeks of notification.

CONTACT Ms. Marlene Martin, Assistant Funds Manager, Rutgers, The State University of New Jersey, Camden, 620 George Street, New Brunswick, NJ 08901, 732-932-7868. *E-mail:* mgmartin@rci.rutgers.edu.

RUTGERS, THE STATE UNIVERSITY OF NEW JERSEY, NEWARK
Newark, NJ

Tuition & fees (NJ res): $8209	Average undergraduate aid package: $9725

ABOUT THE INSTITUTION State-supported, coed. Awards: bachelor's, master's, doctoral, and first professional degrees. 51 undergraduate majors. Total enrollment: 10,293. Undergraduates: 6,608. Freshmen: 794. Federal methodology is used as a basis for awarding need-based institutional aid.

UNDERGRADUATE EXPENSES for 2004–05 *Application fee:* $50. *Tuition, state resident:* full-time $6793; part-time $219 per credit. *Tuition, nonresident:* full-time $13,828; part-time $448 per credit. *Required fees:* full-time $1416; $238 per term part-time. *College room and board:* $8570; *room only:* $5386. Room and board charges vary according to board plan and housing facility. *Payment plan:* Installment.

FRESHMAN FINANCIAL AID (Fall 2003) 626 applied for aid; of those 84% were deemed to have need. 97% of freshmen with need received aid; of those 27% had need fully met. *Average percent of need met:* 81% (excluding resources awarded to replace EFC). *Average financial aid package:* $9856 (excluding resources awarded to replace EFC). 3% of all full-time freshmen had no need and received non-need-based gift aid.

UNDERGRADUATE FINANCIAL AID (Fall 2003) 3,709 applied for aid; of those 88% were deemed to have need. 98% of undergraduates with need received aid; of those 31% had need fully met. *Average percent of need met:* 81% (excluding resources awarded to replace EFC). *Average financial aid package:* $9725 (excluding resources awarded to replace EFC). 4% of all full-time undergraduates had no need and received non-need-based gift aid.

GIFT AID (NEED-BASED) *Total amount:* $20,790,187 (34% federal, 48% state, 17% institutional, 1% external sources). *Receiving aid:* Freshmen: 51% (406); All full-time undergraduates: 51% (2,554). *Average award:* Freshmen: $7237; Undergraduates: $6892. *Scholarships, grants, and awards:* Federal Pell, FSEOG, state, private, college/university gift aid from institutional funds, Outside Scholarships.

GIFT AID (NON-NEED-BASED) *Total amount:* $1,135,268 (92% institutional, 8% external sources). *Receiving aid:* Freshmen: 21% (162); Undergraduates: 13% (643). *Average Award: Freshmen:* $2836; *Undergraduates:* $3770. *Scholarships, grants, and awards by category:* Academic Interests/Achievement: 853 awards ($2,738,824 total): general academic interests/achievements. *Creative Arts/Performance:* general creative arts/performance. *Special Characteristics:* 21 awards ($136,843 total): children of faculty/staff. *Tuition waivers:* Full or partial for employees or children of employees. *ROTC:* Army, Air Force.

LOANS *Student loans:* $17,277,428 (87% need-based, 13% non-need-based). 75% of past graduating class borrowed through all loan programs. *Average indebtedness per student:* $15,495. *Average need-based loan:* Freshmen: $2029; Undergraduates: $3656. *Parent loans:* $808,203 (70% need-based, 30% non-need-based). *Programs:* Federal Direct (Subsidized and Unsubsidized Stafford, PLUS), Perkins, state, college/university, alternative loans.

WORK-STUDY *Federal work-study:* Total amount: $1,298,834; 673 jobs averaging $1930.

ATHLETIC AWARDS *Total amount:* $84,210 (64% need-based, 36% non-need-based).

APPLYING FOR FINANCIAL AID *Required financial aid form:* FAFSA. *Financial aid deadline (priority):* 3/15. *Notification date:* Continuous.

CONTACT Ms. Marlene Martin, Assistant Funds Manager, Rutgers, The State University of New Jersey, Newark, 620 George Street, New Brunswick, NJ 08901, 732-932-7868. *E-mail:* mgmartin@rci.rutgers.edu.

RUTGERS, THE STATE UNIVERSITY OF NEW JERSEY, NEW BRUNSWICK/PISCATAWAY
New Brunswick, NJ

Tuition & fees (NJ res): $8564	Average undergraduate aid package: $10,745

ABOUT THE INSTITUTION State-supported, coed. Awards: bachelor's, master's, doctoral, and first professional degrees. 122 undergraduate majors. Total enrollment: 34,696. Undergraduates: 26,813. Freshmen: 4,847. Federal methodology is used as a basis for awarding need-based institutional aid.

UNDERGRADUATE EXPENSES for 2004–05 *Application fee:* $50. *Tuition, state resident:* full-time $6793; part-time $219 per credit hour. *Tuition, nonresident:* full-time $13,828; part-time $448 per credit hour. Part-time tuition and fees vary according to course level. *College room and board:* $8357; *room only:* $5107. Room and board charges vary according to board plan and housing facility. *Payment plan:* Installment.

FRESHMAN FINANCIAL AID (Fall 2003) 3697 applied for aid; of those 72% were deemed to have need. 98% of freshmen with need received aid; of those 36% had need fully met. *Average percent of need met:* 85% (excluding resources awarded to replace EFC). *Average financial aid package:* $10,709 (excluding resources awarded to replace EFC). 14% of all full-time freshmen had no need and received non-need-based gift aid.

UNDERGRADUATE FINANCIAL AID (Fall 2003) 15,796 applied for aid; of those 79% were deemed to have need. 99% of undergraduates with need received aid; of those 34% had need fully met. *Average percent of need met:* 83% (excluding resources awarded to replace EFC). *Average financial aid package:* $10,745 (excluding resources awarded to replace EFC). 11% of all full-time undergraduates had no need and received non-need-based gift aid.

GIFT AID (NEED-BASED) *Total amount:* $70,563,285 (31% federal, 45% state, 22% institutional, 2% external sources). *Receiving aid:* Freshmen: 35% (1,680); All full-time undergraduates: 34% (8,237). *Average award:* Freshmen: $7585; Undergraduates: $7247. *Scholarships, grants, and awards:* Federal Pell, FSEOG, state, private, college/university gift aid from institutional funds.

GIFT AID (NON-NEED-BASED) *Total amount:* $9,406,056 (87% institutional, 13% external sources). *Receiving aid:* Freshmen: 19% (897); Undergraduates: 13% (3,135). *Average Award: Freshmen:* $4843; *Undergraduates:* $5202. *Scholarships, grants, and awards by category:* Academic Interests/Achievement: 5,560 awards ($21,410,325 total): general academic interests/achievements. Creative Arts/Performance: 67 awards ($138,847 total): general creative arts/performance. *Special Characteristics:* 442 awards ($3,109,869 total): children of faculty/staff. *Tuition waivers:* Full or partial for employees or children of employees. *ROTC:* Army, Air Force.

LOANS *Student loans:* $86,798,405 (80% need-based, 20% non-need-based). 56% of past graduating class borrowed through all loan programs. *Average indebtedness per student:* $15,863. *Average need-based loan:* Freshmen: $2881;

Undergraduates: $4101. *Parent loans:* $9,981,571 (69% need-based, 31% non-need-based). *Programs:* Federal Direct (Subsidized and Unsubsidized Stafford, PLUS), Perkins, state, college/university.

WORK-STUDY *Federal work-study:* Total amount: $5,034,803; 2,646 jobs averaging $1903.

ATHLETIC AWARDS *Total amount:* $4,432,681 (42% need-based, 58% non-need-based).

APPLYING FOR FINANCIAL AID *Required financial aid form:* FAFSA. *Financial aid deadline:* Continuous. *Notification date:* Continuous beginning 2/1. Students must reply within 2 weeks of notification.

CONTACT Ms. Marlene Martin, Assistant Funds Manager, Rutgers, The State University of New Jersey, New Brunswick/Piscataway, 620 George Street, New Brunswick, NJ 08901, 732-932-7868. *E-mail:* mgmartin@rci.rutgers.edu.

SACRED HEART MAJOR SEMINARY
Detroit, MI

CONTACT Financial Aid Office, Sacred Heart Major Seminary, 2701 Chicago Boulevard, Detroit, MI 48206-1799, 313-883-8500. *Fax:* 313-868-6440.

SACRED HEART UNIVERSITY
Fairfield, CT

ABOUT THE INSTITUTION Independent Roman Catholic, coed. Awards: associate, bachelor's, master's, and doctoral degrees and post-bachelor's and post-master's certificates (also offers part-time program with significant enrollment not reflected in profile). 68 undergraduate majors. Total enrollment: 5,454. Undergraduates: 4,081. Freshmen: 877.

GIFT AID (NEED-BASED) *Scholarships, grants, and awards:* Federal Pell, FSEOG, state, private, college/university gift aid from institutional funds, Federal Nursing.

GIFT AID (NON-NEED-BASED) *Scholarships, grants, and awards by category:* Academic Interests/Achievement: biological sciences, business, communication, computer science, education, English, general academic interests/achievements, health fields, humanities, mathematics, premedicine. Creative Arts/Performance: applied art and design, art/fine arts, cinema/film/broadcasting, journalism/publications, music. *Special Achievements/Activities:* community service, general special achievements/activities, hobbies/interests, leadership, religious involvement. *Special Characteristics:* adult students, children and siblings of alumni, children of faculty/staff, children of union members/company employees, ethnic background, general special characteristics, members of minority groups, siblings of current students.

LOANS *Programs:* FFEL (Subsidized and Unsubsidized Stafford, PLUS), Perkins, state, alternative loans.

WORK-STUDY *Federal work-study:* Total amount: $579,410; 439 jobs averaging $1320. *State or other work-study/employment:* Total amount: $745,953 (34% need-based, 66% non-need-based). 672 part-time jobs averaging $1109.

APPLYING FOR FINANCIAL AID *Required financial aid forms:* FAFSA, CSS Financial Aid PROFILE.

CONTACT Ms. Julie B. Savino, Dean of University Financial Assistance, Sacred Heart University, 5151 Park Avenue, Fairfield, CT 06432-1000, 203-371-7980. *Fax:* 203-365-7608. *E-mail:* savinoj@sacredheart.edu.

SAGE COLLEGE OF ALBANY
Albany, NY

Tuition & fees: $16,020	Average undergraduate aid package: N/A

ABOUT THE INSTITUTION Independent, coed. Awards: associate and bachelor's degrees. 17 undergraduate majors. Total enrollment: 1,051. Undergraduates: 1,051. Freshmen: 94. Federal methodology is used as a basis for awarding need-based institutional aid.

UNDERGRADUATE EXPENSES for 2004–05 *Application fee:* $30. *Comprehensive fee:* $23,170 includes full-time tuition ($15,250), mandatory fees ($770), and room and board ($7150). *College room only:* $3450. Room and board charges vary according to board plan and location. *Part-time tuition:* $510 per credit hour. *Payment plans:* Installment, deferred payment.

GIFT AID (NEED-BASED) *Total amount:* $2,142,603 (27% federal, 48% state, 25% institutional). *Receiving aid:* Freshmen: 44% (53); All full-time undergraduates: 40% (176). *Scholarships, grants, and awards:* Federal Pell, FSEOG, state, private, college/university gift aid from institutional funds.

GIFT AID (NON-NEED-BASED) *Total amount:* $589,973 (95% institutional, 5% external sources). *Receiving aid:* Freshmen: 36% (44); Undergraduates: 45% (200). *Average Award: Freshmen:* $3600; *Undergraduates:* $3600. *Scholarships, grants, and awards by category: Academic Interests/Achievement:* 202 awards ($558,250 total). *Tuition waivers:* Full or partial for employees or children of employees.

LOANS *Student loans:* $1,931,815 (59% need-based, 41% non-need-based). 89% of past graduating class borrowed through all loan programs. *Average indebtedness per student:* $8600. *Parent loans:* $209,903 (100% non-need-based). *Programs:* FFEL (Subsidized and Unsubsidized Stafford, PLUS), Perkins, alternative loans.

ATHLETIC AWARDS *Total amount:* $45,522 (100% non-need-based).

APPLYING FOR FINANCIAL AID *Required financial aid forms:* FAFSA, state aid form. *Financial aid deadline (priority):* 3/1. *Notification date:* Continuous beginning 3/15. Students must reply within 2 weeks of notification.

CONTACT James K. Dease, Director of Financial Aid and Student Services, Sage College of Albany, 45 Ferry Street, Troy, NY 12180, 518-244-4525 or toll-free 888-VERY-SAGE. *Fax:* 518-244-2460. *E-mail:* deasej@sage.edu.

SAGINAW VALLEY STATE UNIVERSITY
University Center, MI

ABOUT THE INSTITUTION State-supported, coed. Awards: bachelor's and master's degrees and post-master's certificates. 47 undergraduate majors. Total enrollment: 9,448. Undergraduates: 7,789. Freshmen: 1,241.

GIFT AID (NEED-BASED) *Scholarships, grants, and awards:* Federal Pell, FSEOG, state, private, college/university gift aid from institutional funds.

GIFT AID (NON-NEED-BASED) *Scholarships, grants, and awards by category: Academic Interests/Achievement:* biological sciences, business, communication, computer science, education, engineering/technologies, general academic interests/achievements, health fields, international studies, mathematics, physical sciences, premedicine, social sciences. *Creative Arts/Performance:* music. *Special Characteristics:* children of faculty/staff, international students, out-of-state students.

LOANS *Programs:* Federal Direct (Subsidized and Unsubsidized Stafford, PLUS), state.

APPLYING FOR FINANCIAL AID *Required financial aid forms:* FAFSA, state aid form.

CONTACT Robert Lemuel, Director of Scholarships and Financial Aid, Saginaw Valley State University, 7400 Bay Road, University Center, MI 48710, 989-964-4103 or toll-free 800-968-9500. *Fax:* 989-790-0180.

ST. AMBROSE UNIVERSITY
Davenport, IA

Tuition & fees: $17,565	Average undergraduate aid package: $14,398

ABOUT THE INSTITUTION Independent Roman Catholic, coed. Awards: bachelor's, master's, and doctoral degrees and post-bachelor's and post-master's certificates. 72 undergraduate majors. Total enrollment: 3,534. Undergraduates: 2,639. Freshmen: 488. Federal methodology is used as a basis for awarding need-based institutional aid.

UNDERGRADUATE EXPENSES for 2004–05 *Application fee:* $25. *One-time required fee:* $100. *Comprehensive fee:* $24,200 includes full-time tuition ($17,565) and room and board ($6635). *College room only:* $3380. Full-time tuition and fees vary according to course load and location. Room and board charges vary according to board plan and housing facility. *Part-time tuition:* $547 per semester hour. Part-time tuition and fees vary according to course load and location. *Payment plan:* Installment.

FRESHMAN FINANCIAL AID (Fall 2004, est.) 481 applied for aid; of those 78% were deemed to have need. 100% of freshmen with need received aid; of those 29% had need fully met. *Average percent of need met:* 10% (excluding resources awarded to replace EFC). *Average financial aid package:* $14,468 (excluding resources awarded to replace EFC). 13% of all full-time freshmen had no need and received non-need-based gift aid.

UNDERGRADUATE FINANCIAL AID (Fall 2004, est.) 2,078 applied for aid; of those 79% were deemed to have need. 99% of undergraduates with need received aid; of those 28% had need fully met. *Average percent of need met:* 12% (excluding resources awarded to replace EFC). *Average financial aid package:* $14,398 (excluding resources awarded to replace EFC). 10% of all full-time undergraduates had no need and received non-need-based gift aid.

GIFT AID (NEED-BASED) *Total amount:* $12,950,857 (15% federal, 18% state, 65% institutional, 2% external sources). *Receiving aid:* Freshmen: 44% (214); All full-time undergraduates: 50% (1,074). *Average award:* Freshmen: $4714; Undergraduates: $4695. *Scholarships, grants, and awards:* Federal Pell, FSEOG, state, private, college/university gift aid from institutional funds.

GIFT AID (NON-NEED-BASED) *Total amount:* $1,220,235 (3% state, 95% institutional, 2% external sources). *Receiving aid:* Freshmen: 76% (370); Undergraduates: 71% (1,513). *Average Award: Freshmen:* $6812; *Undergraduates:* $5719. *Scholarships, grants, and awards by category: Academic Interests/Achievement:* 340 awards ($1,252,419 total): general academic interests/achievements, international studies. *Creative Arts/Performance:* 30 awards ($50,897 total): art/fine arts, dance, music, theater/drama. *Special Characteristics:* 35 awards ($280,658 total): children of faculty/staff, international students, members of minority groups. *Tuition waivers:* Full or partial for minority students, children of alumni, employees or children of employees, senior citizens.

LOANS *Student loans:* $14,980,282 (92% need-based, 8% non-need-based). 70% of past graduating class borrowed through all loan programs. *Average indebtedness per student:* $28,075. *Average need-based loan:* Freshmen: $2925; Undergraduates: $4315. *Parent loans:* $1,512,397 (77% need-based, 23% non-need-based). *Programs:* FFEL (Subsidized and Unsubsidized Stafford, PLUS), Perkins, state.

WORK-STUDY *Federal work-study:* Total amount: $964,601; 742 jobs averaging $1300. *State or other work-study/employment:* Total amount: $168,524 (70% need-based, 30% non-need-based). 116 part-time jobs averaging $1441.

ATHLETIC AWARDS *Total amount:* $1,563,483 (71% need-based, 29% non-need-based).

APPLYING FOR FINANCIAL AID *Required financial aid form:* FAFSA. *Financial aid deadline (priority):* 3/15. *Notification date:* Continuous beginning 3/1. Students must reply within 2 weeks of notification.

CONTACT Ms. Julie Haack, Director of Financial Aid, St. Ambrose University, 518 West Locust Street, Davenport, IA 52803, 563-333-6314 or toll-free 800-383-2627. *Fax:* 563-333-6243. *E-mail:* haackjuliea@sau.edu.

ST. ANDREWS PRESBYTERIAN COLLEGE
Laurinburg, NC

Tuition & fees: $15,725	Average undergraduate aid package: $12,496

ABOUT THE INSTITUTION Independent Presbyterian, coed. Awards: bachelor's degrees. 26 undergraduate majors. Total enrollment: 741. Undergraduates: 741. Freshmen: 206. Federal methodology is used as a basis for awarding need-based institutional aid.

UNDERGRADUATE EXPENSES for 2004–05 *Application fee:* $30. *Comprehensive fee:* $21,355 includes full-time tuition ($15,125), mandatory fees ($600), and room and board ($5630). *College room only:* $2310. Full-time tuition and fees vary according to location. *Part-time tuition:* $410 per credit. Part-time tuition and fees vary according to location. *Payment plan:* Installment.

FRESHMAN FINANCIAL AID (Fall 2004, est.) 172 applied for aid; of those 84% were deemed to have need. 100% of freshmen with need received aid; of those 20% had need fully met. *Average percent of need met:* 73% (excluding resources awarded to replace EFC). *Average financial aid package:* $12,205 (excluding resources awarded to replace EFC). 35% of all full-time freshmen had no need and received non-need-based gift aid.

UNDERGRADUATE FINANCIAL AID (Fall 2004, est.) 524 applied for aid; of those 84% were deemed to have need. 100% of undergraduates with need received aid; of those 23% had need fully met. *Average percent of need met:* 75% (excluding resources awarded to replace EFC). *Average financial aid package:* $12,496 (excluding resources awarded to replace EFC). 35% of all full-time undergraduates had no need and received non-need-based gift aid.

GIFT AID (NEED-BASED) *Total amount:* $3,810,180 (19% federal, 15% state, 60% institutional, 6% external sources). *Receiving aid:* Freshmen: 63% (144); All full-time undergraduates: 63% (436). *Average award:* Freshmen: $9590; Undergraduates: $9481. *Scholarships, grants, and awards:* Federal Pell, FSEOG, state, private, college/university gift aid from institutional funds.

GIFT AID (NON-NEED-BASED) *Total amount:* $1,836,211 (12% state, 83% institutional, 5% external sources). *Receiving aid:* Freshmen: 9% (21); Undergraduates: 10% (71). *Average Award: Freshmen:* $9086; *Undergraduates:* $8549. *Scholarships, grants, and awards by category: Academic Interests/Achievement:* general academic interests/achievements. *Creative Arts/Performance:* 5 awards ($4750 total): performing arts. *Special Achievements/Activities:* community service, general special achievements/activities, leadership.

St. Andrews Presbyterian College

Special Characteristics: children and siblings of alumni, local/state students. *Tuition waivers:* Full or partial for employees or children of employees, adult students, senior citizens.

LOANS *Student loans:* $2,053,826 (71% need-based, 29% non-need-based). 78% of past graduating class borrowed through all loan programs. *Average indebtedness per student:* $13,581. *Average need-based loan:* Freshmen: $2222; Undergraduates: $3068. *Parent loans:* $545,252 (86% need-based, 14% non-need-based). *Programs:* FFEL (Subsidized and Unsubsidized Stafford, PLUS).

WORK-STUDY *Federal work-study:* Total amount: $306,935; 220 jobs averaging $1800. *State or other work-study/employment:* Total amount: $28,800 (100% non-need-based). 75 part-time jobs averaging $1800.

ATHLETIC AWARDS *Total amount:* $757,191 (52% need-based, 48% non-need-based).

APPLYING FOR FINANCIAL AID *Required financial aid forms:* FAFSA, state aid form. *Financial aid deadline:* Continuous. *Notification date:* Continuous beginning 2/1. Students must reply within 2 weeks of notification.

CONTACT Kimberly Driggers, Director of Student Financial Planning, St. Andrews Presbyterian College, 1700 Dogwood Mile, Laurinburg, NC 28352, 910-277-5562 or toll-free 800-763-0198. *Fax:* 910-277-5206.

SAINT ANSELM COLLEGE
Manchester, NH

Tuition & fees: $24,660	Average undergraduate aid package: $18,215

ABOUT THE INSTITUTION Independent Roman Catholic, coed. Awards: bachelor's degrees. 29 undergraduate majors. Total enrollment: 1,987. Undergraduates: 1,987. Freshmen: 516. Federal methodology is used as a basis for awarding need-based institutional aid.

UNDERGRADUATE EXPENSES for 2005–06 *Application fee:* $50. *Comprehensive fee:* $33,730 includes full-time tuition ($23,990), mandatory fees ($670), and room and board ($9070). *Part-time tuition:* $2400 per course.

FRESHMAN FINANCIAL AID (Fall 2004, est.) 447 applied for aid; of those 86% were deemed to have need. 99% of freshmen with need received aid; of those 19% had need fully met. *Average percent of need met:* 82% (excluding resources awarded to replace EFC). *Average financial aid package:* $18,025 (excluding resources awarded to replace EFC). 17% of all full-time freshmen had no need and received non-need-based gift aid.

UNDERGRADUATE FINANCIAL AID (Fall 2004, est.) 1,583 applied for aid; of those 89% were deemed to have need. 100% of undergraduates with need received aid; of those 20% had need fully met. *Average percent of need met:* 83% (excluding resources awarded to replace EFC). *Average financial aid package:* $18,215 (excluding resources awarded to replace EFC). 16% of all full-time undergraduates had no need and received non-need-based gift aid.

GIFT AID (NEED-BASED) *Total amount:* $17,039,648 (6% federal, 1% state, 91% institutional, 2% external sources). *Receiving aid:* Freshmen: 74% (382); All full-time undergraduates: 71% (1,389). *Average award:* Freshmen: $13,349; Undergraduates: $12,712. *Scholarships, grants, and awards:* Federal Pell, FSEOG, state, private, college/university gift aid from institutional funds.

GIFT AID (NON-NEED-BASED) *Total amount:* $1,895,268 (97% institutional, 3% external sources). *Receiving aid:* Freshmen: 59% (306); Undergraduates: 44% (850). *Average Award:* Freshmen: $12,085; Undergraduates: $11,951. *Scholarships, grants, and awards by category: Academic Interests/Achievement:* 661 awards ($3,432,750 total): general academic interests/achievements. *Special Characteristics:* 141 awards ($2,002,241 total): children of educators, children of faculty/staff, siblings of current students. *ROTC:* Army cooperative, Air Force cooperative.

LOANS *Student loans:* $12,574,478 (66% need-based, 34% non-need-based). 81% of past graduating class borrowed through all loan programs. *Average indebtedness per student:* $23,437. *Average need-based loan:* Freshmen: $3512; Undergraduates: $5200. *Parent loans:* $4,711,273 (19% need-based, 81% non-need-based). *Programs:* FFEL (Subsidized and Unsubsidized Stafford, PLUS), Perkins, GATE Loans.

WORK-STUDY *Federal work-study:* Total amount: $1,155,825; 1,173 jobs averaging $987. *State or other work-study/employment:* Total amount: $31,000 (100% non-need-based). 17 part-time jobs averaging $1941.

ATHLETIC AWARDS *Total amount:* $608,258 (24% need-based, 76% non-need-based).

APPLYING FOR FINANCIAL AID *Required financial aid forms:* FAFSA, CSS Financial Aid PROFILE, federal income tax form(s). *Financial aid deadline:* 3/15 (priority: 3/1). *Notification date:* Continuous beginning 3/10. Students must reply by 5/1 or within 2 weeks of notification.

CONTACT Elizabeth Keuffel, Director of Financial Aid, Saint Anselm College, 100 Saint Anselm Drive, Manchester, NH 03102-1310, 603-641-7110 or toll-free 888-4ANSELM. *Fax:* 603-656-6015. *E-mail:* financial_aid@anselm.edu.

SAINT ANTHONY COLLEGE OF NURSING
Rockford, IL

ABOUT THE INSTITUTION Independent Roman Catholic, coed, primarily women. Awards: bachelor's degrees. 1 undergraduate major. Total enrollment: 112. Undergraduates: 112.

GIFT AID (NEED-BASED) *Scholarships, grants, and awards:* Federal Pell, state, private, college/university gift aid from institutional funds.

LOANS *Programs:* FFEL (Subsidized and Unsubsidized Stafford, PLUS), alternative loans.

APPLYING FOR FINANCIAL AID *Required financial aid forms:* FAFSA, institution's own form.

CONTACT Mrs. Lisa Ruch, Financial Aid Officer, Saint Anthony College of Nursing, 5658 East State Street, Rockford, IL 61108-2468, 815-395-5089. *Fax:* 815-395-2275. *E-mail:* lisaruch@sacn.edu.

ST. AUGUSTINE COLLEGE
Chicago, IL

Tuition & fees: $7128	Average undergraduate aid package: N/A

ABOUT THE INSTITUTION Independent, coed. Awards: associate and bachelor's degrees (offers bilingual Spanish/English degree programs). 16 undergraduate majors. Total enrollment: 1,582. Undergraduates: 1,582. Freshmen: 410. Both federal and institutional methodology are used as a basis for awarding need-based institutional aid.

UNDERGRADUATE EXPENSES for 2005–06 *Tuition:* full-time $7128; part-time $297 per credit. *Payment plan:* Installment.

FRESHMAN FINANCIAL AID (Fall 2003) 504 applied for aid; of those 81% were deemed to have need. 100% of freshmen with need received aid. *Average percent of need met:* 75% (excluding resources awarded to replace EFC). 1% of all full-time freshmen had no need and received non-need-based gift aid.

UNDERGRADUATE FINANCIAL AID (Fall 2003) 2,025 applied for aid; of those 84% were deemed to have need. 100% of undergraduates with need received aid. *Average percent of need met:* 75% (excluding resources awarded to replace EFC). 4% of all full-time undergraduates had no need and received non-need-based gift aid.

GIFT AID (NEED-BASED) *Total amount:* $9,311,124 (46% federal, 48% state, 6% institutional). *Receiving aid:* Freshmen: 55% (402); All full-time undergraduates: 79% (1,616). *Average award:* Freshmen: $6387; Undergraduates: $5762. *Scholarships, grants, and awards:* Federal Pell, FSEOG, state, private, college/university gift aid from institutional funds.

GIFT AID (NON-NEED-BASED) *Total amount:* $185,339 (100% institutional). *Average Award:* Freshmen: $2495; Undergraduates: $2233. *Scholarships, grants, and awards by category: Academic Interests/Achievement:* 19 awards ($45,738 total): business, computer science, education, general academic interests/achievements, health fields, humanities, social sciences. *Special Characteristics:* 64 awards ($139,601 total): children of faculty/staff. *Tuition waivers:* Full or partial for employees or children of employees.

LOANS *Programs:* Perkins, alternative loans.

WORK-STUDY *Federal work-study:* Total amount: $175,554; 57 jobs averaging $3080. *State or other work-study/employment:* Part-time jobs available.

APPLYING FOR FINANCIAL AID *Required financial aid forms:* FAFSA, institution's own form. *Financial aid deadline:* Continuous. *Notification date:* Continuous. Students must reply within 4 weeks of notification.

CONTACT Mrs. Maria Zambonino, Director of Financial Aid, St. Augustine College, 1345 W Angyle, Chicago, IL 60640, 773-878-3813. *Fax:* 773-878-9032. *E-mail:* mzambonino@hotmail.com.

SAINT AUGUSTINE'S COLLEGE
Raleigh, NC

CONTACT Ms. Wanda C. White, Director of Financial Aid, Saint Augustine's College, 1315 Oakwood Avenue, Raleigh, NC 27610-2298, 919-516-4131 or toll-free 800-948-1126. *Fax:* 919-516-4338. *E-mail:* wwhite@es.st-aug.edu.

ST. BONAVENTURE UNIVERSITY
St. Bonaventure, NY

Tuition & fees: $19,485	Average undergraduate aid package: $15,422

ABOUT THE INSTITUTION Independent religious, coed. Awards: bachelor's and master's degrees and post-bachelor's and post-master's certificates. 58 undergraduate majors. Total enrollment: 2,806. Undergraduates: 2,291. Freshmen: 596. Federal methodology is used as a basis for awarding need-based institutional aid.

UNDERGRADUATE EXPENSES for 2004–05 *Application fee:* $30. *Comprehensive fee:* $26,395 includes full-time tuition ($18,650), mandatory fees ($835), and room and board ($6910). *College room only:* $3530. Room and board charges vary according to board plan and housing facility. *Payment plans:* Tuition prepayment, installment, deferred payment.

FRESHMAN FINANCIAL AID (Fall 2004, est.) 503 applied for aid; of those 85% were deemed to have need. 100% of freshmen with need received aid; of those 28% had need fully met. *Average percent of need met:* 84% (excluding resources awarded to replace EFC). *Average financial aid package:* $16,294 (excluding resources awarded to replace EFC). 22% of all full-time freshmen had no need and received non-need-based gift aid.

UNDERGRADUATE FINANCIAL AID (Fall 2004, est.) 1,773 applied for aid; of those 86% were deemed to have need. 100% of undergraduates with need received aid; of those 30% had need fully met. *Average percent of need met:* 82% (excluding resources awarded to replace EFC). *Average financial aid package:* $15,422 (excluding resources awarded to replace EFC). 21% of all full-time undergraduates had no need and received non-need-based gift aid.

GIFT AID (NEED-BASED) *Total amount:* $13,003,237 (15% federal, 18% state, 66% institutional, 1% external sources). *Receiving aid:* Freshmen: 75% (430); All full-time undergraduates: 71% (1,518). *Average award:* Freshmen: $11,967; Undergraduates: $10,825. *Scholarships, grants, and awards:* Federal Pell, FSEOG, state, private, college/university gift aid from institutional funds.

GIFT AID (NON-NEED-BASED) *Total amount:* $6,129,242 (5% federal, 1% state, 92% institutional, 2% external sources). *Receiving aid:* Freshmen: 11% (64); Undergraduates: 11% (241). *Average Award: Freshmen:* $7721; *Undergraduates:* $6777. *Scholarships, grants, and awards by category: Academic Interests/Achievement:* 1,000 awards ($5,500,000 total): business, general academic interests/achievements. *Creative Arts/Performance:* 40 awards ($40,000 total): journalism/publications, music, performing arts. *Special Characteristics:* children of faculty/staff, local/state students, members of minority groups, relatives of clergy, religious affiliation, siblings of current students. *Tuition waivers:* Full or partial for employees or children of employees, senior citizens. *ROTC:* Army.

LOANS *Student loans:* $12,473,469 (73% need-based, 27% non-need-based). 75% of past graduating class borrowed through all loan programs. *Average indebtedness per student:* $17,500. *Average need-based loan:* Freshmen: $3551; Undergraduates: $4211. *Parent loans:* $4,070,627 (25% need-based, 75% non-need-based). *Programs:* FFEL (Subsidized and Unsubsidized Stafford, PLUS), Perkins, college/university.

WORK-STUDY *Federal work-study:* Total amount: $629,707; 525 jobs averaging $1200. *State or other work-study/employment:* Part-time jobs available.

ATHLETIC AWARDS *Total amount:* $1,943,337 (29% need-based, 71% non-need-based).

APPLYING FOR FINANCIAL AID *Required financial aid forms:* FAFSA, institution's own form, state aid form. *Financial aid deadline (priority):* 2/1. *Notification date:* Continuous beginning 4/1. Students must reply by 5/1 or within 3 weeks of notification.

CONTACT Ms. Elizabeth T. Rankin, Director of Financial Aid, St. Bonaventure University, Route 417, St. Bonaventure, NY 14778-2284, 716-375-2528 or toll-free 800-462-5050. *Fax:* 716-375-2087. *E-mail:* erankin@sbu.edu.

ST. CHARLES BORROMEO SEMINARY, OVERBROOK
Wynnewood, PA

CONTACT Ms. Bonnie L. Behm, Coordinator of Financial Aid, St. Charles Borromeo Seminary, Overbrook, 100 East Wynnewood Road, Wynnewood, PA 19096-3099, 610-785-6582. *Fax:* 610-667-3971. *E-mail:* finaid.scs@erols.com.

ST. CLOUD STATE UNIVERSITY
St. Cloud, MN

Tuition & fees (MN res): $5176	Average undergraduate aid package: $10,897

ABOUT THE INSTITUTION State-supported, coed. Awards: associate, bachelor's, and master's degrees and post-bachelor's certificates. 141 undergraduate majors. Total enrollment: 15,608. Undergraduates: 14,209. Freshmen: 2,205. Federal methodology is used as a basis for awarding need-based institutional aid.

UNDERGRADUATE EXPENSES for 2004–05 *Application fee:* $20. *Tuition, state resident:* full-time $4577; part-time $153 per credit. *Tuition, nonresident:* full-time $9935; part-time $331 per credit. *Required fees:* full-time $599; $25 per credit. Full-time tuition and fees vary according to course load and reciprocity agreements. Part-time tuition and fees vary according to course load and reciprocity agreements. *College room and board:* $4088; *room only:* $2804. Room and board charges vary according to board plan and housing facility. *Payment plan:* Installment.

FRESHMAN FINANCIAL AID (Fall 2004, est.) 1586 applied for aid; of those 69% were deemed to have need. 100% of freshmen with need received aid; of those 58% had need fully met. *Average percent of need met:* 81% (excluding resources awarded to replace EFC). *Average financial aid package:* $10,431 (excluding resources awarded to replace EFC). 9% of all full-time freshmen had no need and received non-need-based gift aid.

UNDERGRADUATE FINANCIAL AID (Fall 2004, est.) 8,129 applied for aid; of those 74% were deemed to have need. 100% of undergraduates with need received aid; of those 47% had need fully met. *Average percent of need met:* 84% (excluding resources awarded to replace EFC). *Average financial aid package:* $10,897 (excluding resources awarded to replace EFC). 1% of all full-time undergraduates had no need and received non-need-based gift aid.

GIFT AID (NEED-BASED) *Total amount:* $16,075,239 (55% federal, 37% state, 5% institutional, 3% external sources). *Receiving aid:* Freshmen: 38% (840); All full-time undergraduates: 32% (4,514). *Average award:* Freshmen: $3821; Undergraduates: $2738. *Scholarships, grants, and awards:* Federal Pell, FSEOG, state, private, college/university gift aid from institutional funds.

GIFT AID (NON-NEED-BASED) *Total amount:* $2,927,383 (20% federal, 34% state, 27% institutional, 19% external sources). *Receiving aid:* Freshmen: 16% (343); Undergraduates: 11% (1,607). *Average Award: Freshmen:* $1677; *Undergraduates:* $1534. *Scholarships, grants, and awards by category: Academic Interests/Achievement:* biological sciences, business, communication, computer science, education, engineering/technologies, English, general academic interests/achievements, international studies, mathematics, physical sciences, social sciences. *Creative Arts/Performance:* applied art and design, art/fine arts, cinema/film/broadcasting, journalism/publications, music, performing arts, theater/drama. *Special Achievements/Activities:* general special achievements/activities. *Special Characteristics:* children of faculty/staff, children of union members/company employees, local/state students, members of minority groups, out-of-state students. *Tuition waivers:* Full or partial for employees or children of employees, senior citizens. *ROTC:* Army.

LOANS *Student loans:* $63,492,030 (45% need-based, 55% non-need-based). 59% of past graduating class borrowed through all loan programs. *Average indebtedness per student:* $19,588. *Average need-based loan:* Freshmen: $3861; Undergraduates: $4178. *Parent loans:* $1,116,978 (6% need-based, 94% non-need-based). *Programs:* FFEL (Subsidized and Unsubsidized Stafford, PLUS), Perkins, state.

WORK-STUDY *Federal work-study:* Total amount: $1,494,229; jobs available. *State or other work-study/employment:* Total amount: $1,753,258 (100% need-based). Part-time jobs available.

ATHLETIC AWARDS *Total amount:* $925,193 (24% need-based, 76% non-need-based).

APPLYING FOR FINANCIAL AID *Required financial aid forms:* FAFSA, institution's own form. *Financial aid deadline (priority):* 4/15. *Notification date:* 5/15.

CONTACT Frank P. Morrissey, Associate Director of Scholarships and Financial Aid, St. Cloud State University, 106 Administrative Services, 720 4th Avenue South, St. Cloud, MN 56301-4498, 320-308-2047 or toll-free 877-654-7278. *Fax:* 320-308-5424. *E-mail:* fpmorrissey@stcloudstate.edu.

ST. EDWARD'S UNIVERSITY
Austin, TX

Tuition & fees: $17,320	Average undergraduate aid package: $12,340

St. Edward's University

ABOUT THE INSTITUTION Independent Roman Catholic, coed. Awards: bachelor's and master's degrees and post-bachelor's certificates. 47 undergraduate majors. Total enrollment: 4,651. Undergraduates: 3,731. Freshmen: 606. Federal methodology is used as a basis for awarding need-based institutional aid.

UNDERGRADUATE EXPENSES for 2005–06 *Application fee:* $45. *Tuition:* full-time $17,320; part-time $578 per hour. Room and board charges vary according to board plan and housing facility. *Payment plans:* Installment, deferred payment.

FRESHMAN FINANCIAL AID (Fall 2004, est.) 499 applied for aid; of those 77% were deemed to have need. 100% of freshmen with need received aid; of those 15% had need fully met. *Average percent of need met:* 79% (excluding resources awarded to replace EFC). *Average financial aid package:* $12,797 (excluding resources awarded to replace EFC). 18% of all full-time freshmen had no need and received non-need-based gift aid.

UNDERGRADUATE FINANCIAL AID (Fall 2004, est.) 1,948 applied for aid; of those 84% were deemed to have need. 99% of undergraduates with need received aid; of those 15% had need fully met. *Average percent of need met:* 71% (excluding resources awarded to replace EFC). *Average financial aid package:* $12,340 (excluding resources awarded to replace EFC). 9% of all full-time undergraduates had no need and received non-need-based gift aid.

GIFT AID (NEED-BASED) *Total amount:* $14,701,553 (24% federal, 27% state, 49% institutional). *Receiving aid:* Freshmen: 62% (372); All full-time undergraduates: 54% (1,458). *Average award:* Freshmen: $11,274; Undergraduates: $9141. *Scholarships, grants, and awards:* Federal Pell, FSEOG, state, private, college/university gift aid from institutional funds, endowed scholarships.

GIFT AID (NON-NEED-BASED) *Total amount:* $3,024,418 (82% institutional, 18% external sources). *Receiving aid:* Freshmen: 35% (211); Undergraduates: 25% (670). *Average Award:* Freshmen: $5845; Undergraduates: $5550. *Scholarships, grants, and awards by category:* Academic Interests/Achievement: 668 awards ($3,492,790 total): biological sciences, business, communication, computer science, education, English, foreign languages, general academic interests/achievements, humanities, international studies, mathematics, military science, physical sciences, religion/biblical studies, social sciences. *Creative Arts/Performance:* 29 awards ($78,550 total): theater/drama. *Special Achievements/Activities:* 88 awards ($141,696 total): cheerleading/drum major, community service, general special achievements/activities, leadership. *Special Characteristics:* 52 awards ($423,201 total): adult students, children of faculty/staff, religious affiliation. *Tuition waivers:* Full or partial for employees or children of employees. *ROTC:* Army cooperative, Air Force cooperative.

LOANS *Student loans:* $15,582,238 (48% need-based, 52% non-need-based). 65% of past graduating class borrowed through all loan programs. *Average indebtedness per student:* $23,476. *Average need-based loan:* Freshmen: $3012; Undergraduates: $4232. *Parent loans:* $4,869,359 (100% non-need-based). *Programs:* FFEL (Subsidized and Unsubsidized Stafford, PLUS), Perkins, state, alternative loans.

WORK-STUDY *Federal work-study:* Total amount: $533,039; 350 jobs averaging $1523. *State or other work-study/employment:* Total amount: $40,750 (100% need-based). 17 part-time jobs averaging $1882.

ATHLETIC AWARDS *Total amount:* $1,326,508 (100% non-need-based).

APPLYING FOR FINANCIAL AID *Required financial aid form:* FAFSA. *Financial aid deadline:* 4/15 (priority: 3/1). *Notification date:* Continuous beginning 2/15. Students must reply by 5/1 or within 4 weeks of notification.

CONTACT Office of Student Financial Services, St. Edward's University, 3001 South Congress Avenue, Austin, TX 78704-6489, 512-448-8523 or toll-free 800-555-0164. *Fax:* 512-416-5837. *E-mail:* stufinaid@admin.stedwards.edu.

ST. FRANCIS COLLEGE
Brooklyn Heights, NY

Tuition & fees: $11,785	Average undergraduate aid package: $6373

ABOUT THE INSTITUTION Independent Roman Catholic, coed. Awards: associate and bachelor's degrees. 35 undergraduate majors. Total enrollment: 2,326. Undergraduates: 2,326. Freshmen: 489. Federal methodology is used as a basis for awarding need-based institutional aid.

UNDERGRADUATE EXPENSES for 2004–05 *Application fee:* $35. *One-time required fee:* $25. *Comprehensive fee:* $19,785 includes full-time tuition ($11,420), mandatory fees ($365), and room and board ($8000). *College room only:* $6500. Full-time tuition and fees vary according to course level, course load, degree level, program, and student level. *Part-time tuition:* $395 per credit. *Part-time fees:* $70 per term. Part-time tuition and fees vary according to course level, course load, degree level, program, and student level. *Payment plans:* Installment, deferred payment.

FRESHMAN FINANCIAL AID (Fall 2004, est.) 447 applied for aid; of those 89% were deemed to have need. 100% of freshmen with need received aid; of those 72% had need fully met. *Average percent of need met:* 85% (excluding resources awarded to replace EFC). *Average financial aid package:* $9680 (excluding resources awarded to replace EFC).

UNDERGRADUATE FINANCIAL AID (Fall 2004, est.) 1,807 applied for aid; of those 89% were deemed to have need. 100% of undergraduates with need received aid; of those 52% had need fully met. *Average percent of need met:* 85% (excluding resources awarded to replace EFC). *Average financial aid package:* $6373 (excluding resources awarded to replace EFC).

GIFT AID (NEED-BASED) *Total amount:* $9,736,616 (24% federal, 35% state, 40% institutional, 1% external sources). *Receiving aid:* Freshmen: 68% (323); All full-time undergraduates: 70% (1,383). *Average award:* Freshmen: $2389; Undergraduates: $3201. *Scholarships, grants, and awards:* Federal Pell, FSEOG, state, private, college/university gift aid from institutional funds.

GIFT AID (NON-NEED-BASED) *Receiving aid:* Freshmen: 38% (182); Undergraduates: 34% (671). *Scholarships, grants, and awards by category:* Academic Interests/Achievement: 827 awards ($4,976,000 total): general academic interests/achievements. *Special Characteristics:* children of public servants, handicapped students, public servants. *Tuition waivers:* Full or partial for employees or children of employees.

LOANS *Student loans:* $3,983,558 (100% need-based). 29% of past graduating class borrowed through all loan programs. *Average need-based loan:* Freshmen: $940; Undergraduates: $2244. *Parent loans:* $713,072 (100% need-based). *Programs:* FFEL (Subsidized and Unsubsidized Stafford, PLUS), Perkins.

WORK-STUDY *Federal work-study:* Total amount: $212,415; 161 jobs averaging $2200.

ATHLETIC AWARDS *Total amount:* $713,812 (100% need-based).

APPLYING FOR FINANCIAL AID *Required financial aid forms:* FAFSA, state aid form. *Financial aid deadline (priority):* 2/15. *Notification date:* Continuous. Students must reply within 2 weeks of notification.

CONTACT Joseph Cummings, Director of Student Financial Services, St. Francis College, 180 Remsen Street, Brooklyn Heights, NY 11201-4398, 718-489-5390. *Fax:* 718-522-1274. *E-mail:* jcummings@stfranciscollege.edu.

SAINT FRANCIS MEDICAL CENTER COLLEGE OF NURSING
Peoria, IL

Tuition & fees: $10,778	Average undergraduate aid package: $12,100

ABOUT THE INSTITUTION Independent Roman Catholic, coed, primarily women. Awards: bachelor's and master's degrees. 1 undergraduate major. Total enrollment: 272. Undergraduates: 220. Federal methodology is used as a basis for awarding need-based institutional aid.

UNDERGRADUATE EXPENSES for 2004–05 *Application fee:* $50. *Tuition:* full-time $10,338; part-time $412 per semester hour. *Required fees:* full-time $440; $220 per term part-time. Full-time tuition and fees vary according to course load. Part-time tuition and fees vary according to course load. *Payment plans:* Installment, deferred payment.

UNDERGRADUATE FINANCIAL AID (Fall 2004, est.) 160 applied for aid; of those 81% were deemed to have need. 100% of undergraduates with need received aid; of those 33% had need fully met. *Average percent of need met:* 80% (excluding resources awarded to replace EFC). *Average financial aid package:* $12,100 (excluding resources awarded to replace EFC). 25% of all full-time undergraduates had no need and received non-need-based gift aid.

GIFT AID (NEED-BASED) *Total amount:* $1,028,343 (19% federal, 47% state, 25% institutional, 9% external sources). *Receiving aid:* All full-time undergraduates: 67% (122). *Average award:* Undergraduates: $7888. *Scholarships, grants, and awards:* Federal Pell, state, private, college/university gift aid from institutional funds.

GIFT AID (NON-NEED-BASED) *Total amount:* $317,984 (5% state, 88% institutional, 7% external sources). *Receiving aid:* Undergraduates: 4% (7). *Average Award:* Undergraduates: $6111. *Scholarships, grants, and awards by category:* Academic Interests/Achievement: 113 awards ($35,877 total): general academic interests/achievements, health fields. *Tuition waivers:* Full or partial for employees or children of employees.

LOANS *Student loans:* $729,616 (82% need-based, 18% non-need-based). 65% of past graduating class borrowed through all loan programs. *Average indebtedness per student:* $12,363. *Average need-based loan:* Undergraduates: $5996. *Parent loans:* $16,433 (36% need-based, 64% non-need-based). *Programs:* FFEL (Subsidized and Unsubsidized Stafford, PLUS), college/university.

APPLYING FOR FINANCIAL AID *Required financial aid forms:* FAFSA, institution's own form. *Financial aid deadline (priority):* 3/1. *Notification date:* Continuous beginning 5/1.

CONTACT Ms. Kathy Casey, Director of Student Finance and Systems, Saint Francis Medical Center College of Nursing, 511 Northeast Greenleaf Street, Peoria, IL 61603-3783, 309-655-2291. *E-mail:* kathy.casey@osfhealthcare.org.

SAINT FRANCIS UNIVERSITY
Loretto, PA

ABOUT THE INSTITUTION Independent Roman Catholic, coed. Awards: associate, bachelor's, and master's degrees. 71 undergraduate majors. Total enrollment: 1,846. Undergraduates: 1,332. Freshmen: 326.

GIFT AID (NEED-BASED) *Scholarships, grants, and awards:* Federal Pell, FSEOG, state, private, college/university gift aid from institutional funds.

GIFT AID (NON-NEED-BASED) *Scholarships, grants, and awards by category:* *Academic Interests/Achievement:* business, general academic interests/achievements, physical sciences. *Creative Arts/Performance:* music. *Special Achievements/Activities:* cheerleading/drum major, community service, junior miss, memberships, religious involvement. *Special Characteristics:* adult students, children of faculty/staff, siblings of current students.

LOANS *Programs:* FFEL (Subsidized and Unsubsidized Stafford, PLUS), Perkins, alternative loans.

WORK-STUDY *Federal work-study:* Total amount: $675,071; 724 jobs averaging $1000. *State or other work-study/employment:* Total amount: $28,000 (18% need-based, 82% non-need-based). 30 part-time jobs averaging $991.

APPLYING FOR FINANCIAL AID *Required financial aid form:* FAFSA.

CONTACT Vincent Frank, Director of Financial Aid, Saint Francis University, PO Box 600, Loretto, PA 15940-0600, 814-472-3010 or toll-free 800-342-5732. *Fax:* 814-472-3335. *E-mail:* vfrank@francis.edu.

ST. GREGORY'S UNIVERSITY
Shawnee, OK

Tuition & fees: $11,076	Average undergraduate aid package: $8906

ABOUT THE INSTITUTION Independent Roman Catholic, coed. Awards: associate and bachelor's degrees. 46 undergraduate majors. Total enrollment: 722. Undergraduates: 722. Freshmen: 107. Federal methodology is used as a basis for awarding need-based institutional aid.

UNDERGRADUATE EXPENSES for 2004–05 *Application fee:* $25. *Comprehensive fee:* $15,964 includes full-time tuition ($10,260), mandatory fees ($816), and room and board ($4888). Room and board charges vary according to board plan and housing facility. *Part-time tuition:* $342 per hour. Part-time tuition and fees vary according to course load and reciprocity agreements. *Payment plans:* Installment, deferred payment.

FRESHMAN FINANCIAL AID (Fall 2003) 92 applied for aid; of those 100% were deemed to have need. 100% of freshmen with need received aid; of those 15% had need fully met. *Average percent of need met:* 69% (excluding resources awarded to replace EFC). *Average financial aid package:* $8015 (excluding resources awarded to replace EFC). 1% of all full-time freshmen had no need and received non-need-based gift aid.

UNDERGRADUATE FINANCIAL AID (Fall 2003) 393 applied for aid; of those 100% were deemed to have need. 99% of undergraduates with need received aid; of those 23% had need fully met. *Average percent of need met:* 77% (excluding resources awarded to replace EFC). *Average financial aid package:* $8906 (excluding resources awarded to replace EFC). 17% of all full-time undergraduates had no need and received non-need-based gift aid.

GIFT AID (NEED-BASED) *Total amount:* $1,595,495 (49% federal, 12% state, 31% institutional, 8% external sources). *Receiving aid:* Freshmen: 46% (43); All full-time undergraduates: 46% (220). *Average award:* Freshmen: $6236; Undergraduates: $7252. *Scholarships, grants, and awards:* Federal Pell, FSEOG, state, private, college/university gift aid from institutional funds.

GIFT AID (NON-NEED-BASED) *Total amount:* $660,882 (92% institutional, 8% external sources). *Receiving aid:* Freshmen: 91% (85); Undergraduates: 63% (299). *Average Award:* Freshmen: $2206; Undergraduates: $5340. *Scholarships, grants, and awards by category:* *Academic Interests/Achievement:* 231 awards ($811,210 total): general academic interests/achievements. *Creative Arts/Performance:* 34 awards ($40,474 total): art/fine arts, dance, journalism/

publications, music, theater/drama. *Special Achievements/Activities:* 8 awards ($10,187 total): religious involvement. *Special Characteristics:* 159 awards ($90,116 total): ethnic background, handicapped students, international students, religious affiliation. *Tuition waivers:* Full or partial for employees or children of employees, adult students, senior citizens. *ROTC:* Army cooperative, Air Force cooperative.

LOANS *Student loans:* $2,428,186 (75% need-based, 25% non-need-based). 39% of past graduating class borrowed through all loan programs. *Average indebtedness per student:* $9845. *Average need-based loan:* Freshmen: $2027; Undergraduates: $3729. *Parent loans:* $279,160 (58% need-based, 42% non-need-based). *Programs:* FFEL (Subsidized and Unsubsidized Stafford, PLUS), Perkins, alternative loans.

WORK-STUDY *Federal work-study:* Total amount: $45,617; 43 jobs averaging $1143. *State or other work-study/employment:* Total amount: $58,110 (100% non-need-based). 28 part-time jobs averaging $2688.

ATHLETIC AWARDS *Total amount:* $1,166,840 (54% need-based, 46% non-need-based).

APPLYING FOR FINANCIAL AID *Required financial aid forms:* FAFSA, institution's own form. *Financial aid deadline:* Continuous. *Notification date:* Continuous beginning 2/15. Students must reply within 2 weeks of notification.

CONTACT Jonna Raney, Director of Financial Aid, St. Gregory's University, 1900 West MacArthur Drive, Shawnee, OK 74804, 405-878-5412 or toll-free 888-STGREGS. *Fax:* 405-878-5403. *E-mail:* jlraney@stgregorys.edu.

ST. JOHN FISHER COLLEGE
Rochester, NY

Tuition & fees: $18,450	Average undergraduate aid package: $14,981

ABOUT THE INSTITUTION Independent religious, coed. Awards: bachelor's and master's degrees and post-bachelor's certificates. 37 undergraduate majors. Total enrollment: 3,376. Undergraduates: 2,605. Freshmen: 531. Federal methodology is used as a basis for awarding need-based institutional aid.

UNDERGRADUATE EXPENSES for 2004–05 *Application fee:* $25. *One-time required fee:* $300. *Comprehensive fee:* $26,350 includes full-time tuition ($18,200), mandatory fees ($250), and room and board ($7900). *College room only:* $5100. Room and board charges vary according to board plan. *Part-time tuition:* $500 per credit hour. *Part-time fees:* $25 per term. Part-time tuition and fees vary according to course load. *Payment plans:* Installment, deferred payment.

FRESHMAN FINANCIAL AID (Fall 2004, est.) 502 applied for aid; of those 88% were deemed to have need. 100% of freshmen with need received aid; of those 9% had need fully met. *Average percent of need met:* 84% (excluding resources awarded to replace EFC). *Average financial aid package:* $16,098 (excluding resources awarded to replace EFC). 13% of all full-time freshmen had no need and received non-need-based gift aid.

UNDERGRADUATE FINANCIAL AID (Fall 2004, est.) 2,218 applied for aid; of those 91% were deemed to have need. 100% of undergraduates with need received aid; of those 54% had need fully met. *Average percent of need met:* 78% (excluding resources awarded to replace EFC). *Average financial aid package:* $14,981 (excluding resources awarded to replace EFC). 12% of all full-time undergraduates had no need and received non-need-based gift aid.

GIFT AID (NEED-BASED) *Total amount:* $21,270,692 (12% federal, 17% state, 70% institutional, 1% external sources). *Receiving aid:* Freshmen: 83% (442); All full-time undergraduates: 83% (1,978). *Average award:* Freshmen: $11,728; Undergraduates: $9734. *Scholarships, grants, and awards:* Federal Pell, FSEOG, state, private, college/university gift aid from institutional funds, Federal Nursing.

GIFT AID (NON-NEED-BASED) *Total amount:* $61,645 (13% state, 87% external sources). *Receiving aid:* Freshmen: 60% (320); Undergraduates: 55% (1,326). *Average Award:* Freshmen: $5449; Undergraduates: $4854. *Scholarships, grants, and awards by category:* *Academic Interests/Achievement:* 1,113 awards ($5,825,625 total): biological sciences, business, English, foreign languages, general academic interests/achievements, humanities, mathematics, physical sciences. *Special Achievements/Activities:* 127 awards ($1,028,805 total): community service. *Special Characteristics:* 119 awards ($930,845 total): children and siblings of alumni, ethnic background, first-generation college students, local/state students, members of minority groups. *Tuition waivers:* Full or partial for employees or children of employees. *ROTC:* Army cooperative, Naval cooperative, Air Force cooperative.

LOANS *Student loans:* $20,002,862 (81% need-based, 19% non-need-based). 76% of past graduating class borrowed through all loan programs. *Average indebtedness per student:* $22,747. *Average need-based loan:* Freshmen: $4433;

St. John Fisher College

Undergraduates: $6314. *Parent loans:* $6,316,673 (100% non-need-based). *Programs:* FFEL (Subsidized and Unsubsidized Stafford, PLUS), Perkins.

WORK-STUDY *Federal work-study:* Total amount: $350,000; 1,657 jobs averaging $1621.

APPLYING FOR FINANCIAL AID *Required financial aid forms:* FAFSA, state aid form. *Financial aid deadline (priority):* 2/15. *Notification date:* Continuous beginning 3/21. Students must reply by 5/1 or within 3 weeks of notification.

CONTACT Mrs. Angela Monnat, Director of Financial Aid, St. John Fisher College, 3690 East Avenue, Rochester, NY 14618-3597, 585-385-8042 or toll-free 800-444-4640. *Fax:* 585-385-8044. *E-mail:* amonnat@sjfc.edu.

ST. JOHN'S COLLEGE
Springfield, IL

Tuition & fees: $9786	Average undergraduate aid package: $13,113

ABOUT THE INSTITUTION Independent Roman Catholic, coed, primarily women. Awards: bachelor's degrees. 1 undergraduate major. Total enrollment: 82. Undergraduates: 82. Federal methodology is used as a basis for awarding need-based institutional aid.

UNDERGRADUATE EXPENSES for 2004-05 *Application fee:* $35. *Tuition:* full-time $9504; part-time $396 per credit hour. Full-time tuition and fees vary according to course load. Part-time tuition and fees vary according to course load. *Payment plan:* Installment.

UNDERGRADUATE FINANCIAL AID (Fall 2003) 68 applied for aid; of those 85% were deemed to have need. 100% of undergraduates with need received aid; of those 64% had need fully met. *Average percent of need met:* 61% (excluding resources awarded to replace EFC). *Average financial aid package:* $13,113 (excluding resources awarded to replace EFC).

GIFT AID (NEED-BASED) *Receiving aid:* All full-time undergraduates: 70% (57). *Average award:* Undergraduates: $1630. *Scholarships, grants, and awards:* Federal Pell, FSEOG, state, private, college/university gift aid from institutional funds.

GIFT AID (NON-NEED-BASED) *Receiving aid:* Undergraduates: 56% (45). *Scholarships, grants, and awards by category: Academic Interests/Achievement:* health fields.

LOANS *Student loans:* $566,187 (63% need-based, 37% non-need-based). 60% of past graduating class borrowed through all loan programs. *Average need-based loan:* Undergraduates: $4479. *Parent loans:* $28,959 (100% need-based). *Programs:* FFEL (Subsidized and Unsubsidized Stafford, PLUS), Federal Nursing, affiliate hospital offers scholarship/loan in exchange for work after graduation.

WORK-STUDY *Federal work-study:* Total amount: $7488; 4 jobs averaging $1872.

APPLYING FOR FINANCIAL AID *Required financial aid forms:* FAFSA, institution's own form.

CONTACT Mary M. Deatherage, Financial Aid Officer, St. John's College, 421 North Ninth Street, Springfield, IL 62702, 217-544-6464 Ext. 44705. *Fax:* 217-757-6870. *E-mail:* mdeather@st-johns.org.

ST. JOHN'S COLLEGE
Annapolis, MD

ABOUT THE INSTITUTION Independent, coed. Awards: bachelor's and master's degrees. 3 undergraduate majors. Total enrollment: 564. Undergraduates: 473. Freshmen: 133.

GIFT AID (NEED-BASED) *Scholarships, grants, and awards:* Federal Pell, FSEOG, state, college/university gift aid from institutional funds.

LOANS *Programs:* FFEL (Subsidized and Unsubsidized Stafford, PLUS), Perkins, college/university.

WORK-STUDY *Federal work-study:* Total amount: $335,000; 136 jobs averaging $2460. *State or other work-study/employment:* Total amount: $50,000 (100% non-need-based). 20 part-time jobs averaging $2460.

APPLYING FOR FINANCIAL AID *Required financial aid forms:* FAFSA, CSS Financial Aid PROFILE, noncustodial (divorced/separated) parent's statement, business/farm supplement.

CONTACT Ms. Caroline Christensen, Director of Financial Aid, St. John's College, PO Box 2800, Annapolis, MD 21404, 410-626-2502 or toll-free 800-727-9238. *Fax:* 410-626-2885. *E-mail:* c-christensen@sjca.edu.

ST. JOHN'S COLLEGE
Santa Fe, NM

ABOUT THE INSTITUTION Independent, coed. Awards: bachelor's and master's degrees. 22 undergraduate majors. Total enrollment: 518. Undergraduates: 414. Freshmen: 115.

GIFT AID (NEED-BASED) *Scholarships, grants, and awards:* Federal Pell, FSEOG, state, private, college/university gift aid from institutional funds.

GIFT AID (NON-NEED-BASED) *Scholarships, grants, and awards by category: Special Characteristics:* children of faculty/staff.

LOANS *Programs:* FFEL (Subsidized and Unsubsidized Stafford, PLUS), Perkins, state, college/university.

APPLYING FOR FINANCIAL AID *Required financial aid forms:* FAFSA, CSS Financial Aid PROFILE, noncustodial (divorced/separated) parent's statement, business/farm supplement.

CONTACT Michael Rodriguez, Director of Financial Aid, St. John's College, 1160 Camino Cruz Blanca, Santa Fe, NM 87505, 505-984-6058 or toll-free 800-331-5232. *Fax:* 505-984-6003. *E-mail:* faid@mail.sjcsf.edu.

SAINT JOHN'S UNIVERSITY
Collegeville, MN

Tuition & fees: $22,148	Average undergraduate aid package: $18,845

ABOUT THE INSTITUTION Independent Roman Catholic, coed, primarily men. Awards: bachelor's, master's, and first professional degrees (coordinate with College of Saint Benedict for women). 51 undergraduate majors. Total enrollment: 2,015. Undergraduates: 1,895. Freshmen: 512. Federal methodology is used as a basis for awarding need-based institutional aid.

UNDERGRADUATE EXPENSES for 2004-05 *Comprehensive fee:* $28,266 includes full-time tuition ($21,758), mandatory fees ($390), and room and board ($6118). *College room only:* $3008. Room and board charges vary according to board plan and housing facility. *Part-time tuition:* $907 per credit. *Part-time fees:* $195 per term. Part-time tuition and fees vary according to course load. *Payment plans:* Tuition prepayment, installment.

FRESHMAN FINANCIAL AID (Fall 2004, est.) 396 applied for aid; of those 83% were deemed to have need. 100% of freshmen with need received aid; of those 57% had need fully met. *Average percent of need met:* 96% (excluding resources awarded to replace EFC). *Average financial aid package:* $18,607 (excluding resources awarded to replace EFC). 30% of all full-time freshmen had no need and received non-need-based gift aid.

UNDERGRADUATE FINANCIAL AID (Fall 2004, est.) 1,413 applied for aid; of those 78% were deemed to have need. 100% of undergraduates with need received aid; of those 50% had need fully met. *Average percent of need met:* 84% (excluding resources awarded to replace EFC). *Average financial aid package:* $18,845 (excluding resources awarded to replace EFC). 31% of all full-time undergraduates had no need and received non-need-based gift aid.

GIFT AID (NEED-BASED) *Total amount:* $12,600,929 (11% federal, 12% state, 74% institutional, 3% external sources). *Receiving aid:* Freshmen: 64% (327); All full-time undergraduates: 50% (910). *Average award:* Freshmen: $13,411; Undergraduates: $8927. *Scholarships, grants, and awards:* Federal Pell, FSEOG, state, private, college/university gift aid from institutional funds.

GIFT AID (NON-NEED-BASED) *Total amount:* $4,979,155 (6% federal, 93% institutional, 1% external sources). *Receiving aid:* Freshmen: 57% (293); Undergraduates: 50% (910). *Average Award:* Freshmen: $6526; Undergraduates: $6143. *Scholarships, grants, and awards by category: Academic Interests/Achievement:* 910 awards ($4,643,896 total): general academic interests/achievements. *Creative Arts/Performance:* 152 awards ($228,500 total): art/fine arts, music, theater/drama. *Special Characteristics:* 58 awards ($774,229 total): international students. *Tuition waivers:* Full or partial for employees or children of employees. *ROTC:* Army.

LOANS *Student loans:* $6,857,342 (88% need-based, 12% non-need-based). 73% of past graduating class borrowed through all loan programs. *Average indebtedness per student:* $23,924. *Average need-based loan:* Freshmen: $3850; Undergraduates: $4489. *Parent loans:* $1,572,011 (64% need-based, 36% non-need-based). *Programs:* FFEL (Subsidized and Unsubsidized Stafford, PLUS), Perkins, state, SELF Loans, alternative loans.

WORK-STUDY *Federal work-study:* Total amount: $355,381; 157 jobs averaging $2263. *State or other work-study/employment:* Total amount: $1,990,732 (78% need-based, 22% non-need-based). 1,007 part-time jobs averaging $1977.

APPLYING FOR FINANCIAL AID *Required financial aid forms:* FAFSA, institution's own form, federal income tax form(s). *Financial aid deadline (priority):* 3/15. *Notification date:* Continuous beginning 3/15. Students must reply by 5/1 or within 3 weeks of notification.

CONTACT Ms. Mary Dehler, Associate Director of Financial Aid, Saint John's University, PO Box 5000, Collegeville, MN 56321-5000, 320-363-3664 or toll-free 800-544-1489. *Fax:* 320-363-3102. *E-mail:* mdehler@csbsju.edu.

ST. JOHN'S UNIVERSITY
Jamaica, NY

Tuition & fees: $23,280 **Average undergraduate aid package: $16,670**

ABOUT THE INSTITUTION Independent religious, coed. Awards: associate, bachelor's, master's, doctoral, and first professional degrees and post-bachelor's and post-master's certificates. 105 undergraduate majors. Total enrollment: 19,813. Undergraduates: 14,848. Freshmen: 3,005. Federal methodology is used as a basis for awarding need-based institutional aid.

UNDERGRADUATE EXPENSES for 2005–06 *Application fee:* $30. *Comprehensive fee:* $34,280 includes full-time tuition ($22,800), mandatory fees ($480), and room and board ($11,000). *College room only:* $6900. Full-time tuition and fees vary according to class time, course level, course load, program, and student level. Room and board charges vary according to board plan and housing facility. *Part-time tuition:* $760 per credit. *Part-time fees:* $165 per term. Part-time tuition and fees vary according to class time, course level, course load, program, and student level. *Payment plans:* Guaranteed tuition, installment, deferred payment.

GIFT AID (NEED-BASED) *Total amount:* $59,355,987 (28% federal, 34% state, 38% institutional). *Receiving aid:* Freshmen: 75% (2,223); All full-time undergraduates: 72% (8,474). *Average award:* Freshmen: $8344; Undergraduates: $7162. *Scholarships, grants, and awards:* Federal Pell, FSEOG, state, private, college/university gift aid from institutional funds.

GIFT AID (NON-NEED-BASED) *Total amount:* $48,614,046 (1% federal, 1% state, 90% institutional, 8% external sources). *Receiving aid:* Freshmen: 79% (2,340); Undergraduates: 51% (5,972). *Average Award:* Freshmen: $7286; Undergraduates: $8186. *Scholarships, grants, and awards by category: Academic Interests/Achievement:* 5,273 awards ($34,457,465 total): biological sciences, business, communication, computer science, education, general academic interests/achievements, health fields, mathematics, military science. *Creative Arts/Performance:* 157 awards ($211,425 total): art/fine arts, cinema/film/broadcasting, dance, debating, journalism/publications, music. *Special Achievements/Activities:* 278 awards ($314,655 total): cheerleading/drum major, community service, general special achievements/activities, hobbies/interests, leadership, religious involvement. *Special Characteristics:* 3,295 awards ($10,782,523 total): children of faculty/staff, general special characteristics, local/state students, relatives of clergy, religious affiliation. *Tuition waivers:* Full or partial for employees or children of employees. *ROTC:* Army.

LOANS *Student loans:* $53,936,938 (73% need-based, 27% non-need-based). 69% of past graduating class borrowed through all loan programs. *Average indebtedness per student:* $18,196. *Average need-based loan:* Freshmen: $3154; Undergraduates: $4322. *Parent loans:* $22,013,075 (100% non-need-based). *Programs:* FFEL (Subsidized and Unsubsidized Stafford, PLUS), Perkins.

ATHLETIC AWARDS *Total amount:* $3,929,112 (100% non-need-based).

APPLYING FOR FINANCIAL AID *Required financial aid form:* FAFSA. *Financial aid deadline (priority):* 1/1. *Notification date:* Continuous beginning 3/15. Students must reply within 2 weeks of notification.

CONTACT Mr. Jorge Rodriguez, Assistant Vice President/Executive Director of Financial Aid, St. John's University, 8000 Utopia Parkway, Queens, NY 11439, 718-990-2000 or toll-free 888-9STJOHNS (in-state), 888-9ST JOHNS (out-of-state). *Fax:* 718-990-5945. *E-mail:* financialaid@stjohns.edu.

ST. JOHN VIANNEY COLLEGE SEMINARY
Miami, FL

CONTACT Ms. Bonnie DeAngulo, Director of Financial Aid, St. John Vianney College Seminary, 2900 Southwest 87th Avenue, Miami, FL 33165-3244, 305-223-4561 Ext. 10.

SAINT JOSEPH COLLEGE
West Hartford, CT

Tuition & fees: $21,970 **Average undergraduate aid package: $17,325**

ABOUT THE INSTITUTION Independent Roman Catholic, women only. Awards: bachelor's and master's degrees. 34 undergraduate majors. Total enrollment: 1,792. Undergraduates: 1,172. Freshmen: 232. Federal methodology is used as a basis for awarding need-based institutional aid.

UNDERGRADUATE EXPENSES for 2004–05 *Application fee:* $35. *Comprehensive fee:* $31,195 includes full-time tuition ($21,370), mandatory fees ($600), and room and board ($9225). *College room only:* $4345. Room and board charges vary according to board plan. *Part-time tuition:* $515 per credit. *Part-time fees:* $60 per course. *Payment plan:* Installment.

GIFT AID (NEED-BASED) *Total amount:* $8,940,176 (13% federal, 13% state, 74% institutional). *Receiving aid:* Freshmen: 86% (162); All full-time undergraduates: 82% (707). *Average award:* Freshmen: $13,874; Undergraduates: $11,628. *Scholarships, grants, and awards:* Federal Pell, FSEOG, state, private, college/university gift aid from institutional funds.

GIFT AID (NON-NEED-BASED) *Total amount:* $412,223 (16% state, 66% institutional, 18% external sources). *Receiving aid:* Freshmen: 9% (17); Undergraduates: 8% (69). *Average Award:* Freshmen: $9188; Undergraduates: $10,190. *Scholarships, grants, and awards by category: Academic Interests/Achievement:* 176 awards ($477,995 total): general academic interests/achievements. *Special Characteristics:* 14 awards ($14,000 total): siblings of current students. *Tuition waivers:* Full or partial for employees or children of employees.

LOANS *Student loans:* $7,716,221 (71% need-based, 29% non-need-based). 82% of past graduating class borrowed through all loan programs. *Average indebtedness per student:* $14,859. *Average need-based loan:* Freshmen: $3997; Undergraduates: $6058. *Parent loans:* $1,082,515 (100% non-need-based). *Programs:* FFEL (Subsidized and Unsubsidized Stafford, PLUS), Perkins, state, Connecticut Family Education Loan Program.

APPLYING FOR FINANCIAL AID *Required financial aid form:* FAFSA. *Financial aid deadline (priority):* 3/15. *Notification date:* Continuous. Students must reply within 2 weeks of notification.

CONTACT Mr. Philip T. Malinoski, Student Financial Services Director, Saint Joseph College, 1678 Asylum Avenue, West Hartford, CT 06117, 860-231-5319. *E-mail:* pmalinoski@sjc.edu.

SAINT JOSEPH'S COLLEGE
Rensselaer, IN

Tuition & fees: $19,160 **Average undergraduate aid package: $13,800**

ABOUT THE INSTITUTION Independent Roman Catholic, coed. Awards: associate, bachelor's, and master's degrees. 35 undergraduate majors. Total enrollment: 1,010. Undergraduates: 1,010. Freshmen: 207. Federal methodology is used as a basis for awarding need-based institutional aid.

UNDERGRADUATE EXPENSES for 2004–05 *Application fee:* $25. *Comprehensive fee:* $25,460 includes full-time tuition ($19,000), mandatory fees ($160), and room and board ($6300). Room and board charges vary according to housing facility. *Part-time tuition:* $640 per credit.

FRESHMAN FINANCIAL AID (Fall 2003) 258 applied for aid; of those 80% were deemed to have need. 100% of freshmen with need received aid; of those 40% had need fully met. *Average percent of need met:* 80% (excluding resources awarded to replace EFC). *Average financial aid package:* $13,400 (excluding resources awarded to replace EFC). 5% of all full-time freshmen had no need and received non-need-based gift aid.

UNDERGRADUATE FINANCIAL AID (Fall 2003) 776 applied for aid; of those 85% were deemed to have need. 100% of undergraduates with need received aid; of those 45% had need fully met. *Average percent of need met:* 85% (excluding resources awarded to replace EFC). *Average financial aid package:* $13,800 (excluding resources awarded to replace EFC). 6% of all full-time undergraduates had no need and received non-need-based gift aid.

GIFT AID (NEED-BASED) *Total amount:* $5,696,552 (13% federal, 24% state, 63% institutional). *Receiving aid:* Freshmen: 64% (165); All full-time undergraduates: 60% (508). *Average award:* Freshmen: $4400; Undergraduates: $4500. *Scholarships, grants, and awards:* Federal Pell, FSEOG, state, private, college/university gift aid from institutional funds.

GIFT AID (NON-NEED-BASED) *Total amount:* $958,644 (66% institutional, 34% external sources). *Receiving aid:* Freshmen: 68% (175); Undergraduates: 35%

(297). *Average Award:* Freshmen: $2100; *Undergraduates:* $5000. **Scholarships, grants, and awards by category:** *Academic Interests/Achievement:* 355 awards ($2,236,875 total): general academic interests/achievements. *Creative Arts/Performance:* 143 awards ($228,138 total): cinema/film/broadcasting, music, theater/drama. *Special Achievements/Activities:* 15 awards ($18,625 total): cheerleading/drum major. *Special Characteristics:* 99 awards ($351,766 total): children and siblings of alumni, children of faculty/staff, members of minority groups, siblings of current students. *Tuition waivers:* Full or partial for minority students, children of alumni, employees or children of employees.

LOANS *Student loans:* $3,672,015 (57% need-based, 43% non-need-based). 83% of past graduating class borrowed through all loan programs. *Average indebtedness per student:* $18,500. *Average need-based loan:* Freshmen: $3100; Undergraduates: $4000. *Parent loans:* $1,642,733 (30% need-based, 70% non-need-based). *Programs:* FFEL (Subsidized and Unsubsidized Stafford, PLUS), Perkins.

WORK-STUDY *Federal work-study:* Total amount: $76,909; 112 jobs averaging $687.

ATHLETIC AWARDS *Total amount:* $1,994,903 (60% need-based, 40% non-need-based).

APPLYING FOR FINANCIAL AID *Required financial aid form:* FAFSA. *Financial aid deadline (priority):* 3/1. *Notification date:* Continuous. Students must reply by 5/1 or within 2 weeks of notification.

CONTACT Debra Sizemore, Director of Student Financial Services, Saint Joseph's College, US Highway 231, PO Box 971, Rensselaer, IN 47978, 219-866-6163 or toll-free 800-447-8781 (out-of-state). *Fax:* 219-866-6144. *E-mail:* debbie@saintjoe.edu.

ST. JOSEPH'S COLLEGE, NEW YORK
Brooklyn, NY

Tuition & fees: $11,430	Average undergraduate aid package: $11,000

ABOUT THE INSTITUTION Independent, coed. Awards: bachelor's and master's degrees. 22 undergraduate majors. Total enrollment: 1,313. Undergraduates: 1,148. Freshmen: 152. Federal methodology is used as a basis for awarding need-based institutional aid.

UNDERGRADUATE EXPENSES for 2004–05 *Application fee:* $25. *Tuition:* full-time $11,078; part-time $357 per credit. *Required fees:* full-time $352; $11 per credit or $30 per term part-time. *Payment plan:* Installment.

FRESHMAN FINANCIAL AID (Fall 2004, est.) 128 applied for aid; of those 66% were deemed to have need. 100% of freshmen with need received aid; of those 71% had need fully met. *Average percent of need met:* 85% (excluding resources awarded to replace EFC). *Average financial aid package:* $13,000 (excluding resources awarded to replace EFC). 25% of all full-time freshmen had no need and received non-need-based gift aid.

UNDERGRADUATE FINANCIAL AID (Fall 2004, est.) 600 applied for aid; of those 67% were deemed to have need. 100% of undergraduates with need received aid; of those 69% had need fully met. *Average percent of need met:* 75% (excluding resources awarded to replace EFC). *Average financial aid package:* $11,000 (excluding resources awarded to replace EFC). 19% of all full-time undergraduates had no need and received non-need-based gift aid.

GIFT AID (NEED-BASED) *Total amount:* $3,176,795 (33% federal, 39% state, 28% institutional). *Receiving aid:* Freshmen: 60% (85); All full-time undergraduates: 60% (400). *Average award:* Freshmen: $10,000; Undergraduates: $7000. *Scholarships, grants, and awards:* Federal Pell, FSEOG, state, private, college/university gift aid from institutional funds.

GIFT AID (NON-NEED-BASED) *Total amount:* $1,112,005 (1% state, 96% institutional, 3% external sources). *Receiving aid:* Freshmen: 50% (70); Undergraduates: 38% (250). *Average Award:* Freshmen: $4500; Undergraduates: $4500. *Scholarships, grants, and awards by category:* Academic Interests/Achievement: 360 awards ($1,350,000 total): general academic interests/achievements. *Special Characteristics:* 14 awards ($36,000 total): children and siblings of alumni, children of faculty/staff. *Tuition waivers:* Full or partial for employees or children of employees.

LOANS *Student loans:* $3,093,673 (45% need-based, 55% non-need-based). 43% of past graduating class borrowed through all loan programs. *Average indebtedness per student:* $16,681. *Average need-based loan:* Freshmen: $2500; Undergraduates: $3600. *Parent loans:* $283,937 (100% need-based). *Programs:* FFEL (Subsidized and Unsubsidized Stafford, PLUS), Perkins.

WORK-STUDY *Federal work-study:* Total amount: $74,655; 53 jobs averaging $1600. *State or other work-study/employment:* Total amount: $4770 (100% non-need-based). 3 part-time jobs averaging $1600.

APPLYING FOR FINANCIAL AID *Required financial aid forms:* FAFSA, institution's own form, state aid form. *Financial aid deadline (priority):* 2/25. *Notification date:* Continuous beginning 4/15. Students must reply by 5/1 or within 3 weeks of notification.

CONTACT Ms. Carol Sullivan, Director of Financial Aid, St. Joseph's College, New York, 245 Clinton Avenue, Brooklyn, NY 11205-3688, 718-636-6808. *Fax:* 718-636-6827. *E-mail:* csullivan@sjcny.edu.

SAINT JOSEPH'S COLLEGE OF MAINE
Standish, ME

Tuition & fees: $19,615	Average undergraduate aid package: $16,335

ABOUT THE INSTITUTION Independent religious, coed. Awards: bachelor's and master's degrees (profile does not include enrollment in distance learning master's program). 52 undergraduate majors. Total enrollment: 986. Undergraduates: 986. Freshmen: 291. Both federal and institutional methodology are used as a basis for awarding need-based institutional aid.

UNDERGRADUATE EXPENSES for 2004–05 *Application fee:* $40. *Comprehensive fee:* $27,775 includes full-time tuition ($18,950), mandatory fees ($665), and room and board ($8160). Full-time tuition and fees vary according to program. *Part-time tuition:* $325 per hour. *Part-time fees:* $125 per year. Part-time tuition and fees vary according to course load and program. *Payment plan:* Installment.

FRESHMAN FINANCIAL AID (Fall 2004, est.) 267 applied for aid; of those 93% were deemed to have need. 100% of freshmen with need received aid; of those 27% had need fully met. *Average percent of need met:* 81% (excluding resources awarded to replace EFC). *Average financial aid package:* $16,616 (excluding resources awarded to replace EFC). 14% of all full-time freshmen had no need and received non-need-based gift aid.

UNDERGRADUATE FINANCIAL AID (Fall 2004, est.) 875 applied for aid; of those 93% were deemed to have need. 100% of undergraduates with need received aid; of those 32% had need fully met. *Average percent of need met:* 79% (excluding resources awarded to replace EFC). *Average financial aid package:* $16,335 (excluding resources awarded to replace EFC). 14% of all full-time undergraduates had no need and received non-need-based gift aid.

GIFT AID (NEED-BASED) *Total amount:* $8,310,995 (10% federal, 3% state, 78% institutional, 9% external sources). *Receiving aid:* Freshmen: 86% (247); All full-time undergraduates: 84% (814). *Average award:* Freshmen: $11,701; Undergraduates: $10,191. *Scholarships, grants, and awards:* Federal Pell, FSEOG, state, private, college/university gift aid from institutional funds, Federal Nursing.

GIFT AID (NON-NEED-BASED) *Total amount:* $1,257,917 (84% institutional, 16% external sources). *Receiving aid:* Freshmen: 9% (27); Undergraduates: 7% (71). *Average Award:* Freshmen: $11,547; Undergraduates: $10,581. *Scholarships, grants, and awards by category:* Academic Interests/Achievement: 453 awards ($3,060,919 total): general academic interests/achievements. *Special Achievements/Activities:* 130 awards ($923,185 total): community service, religious involvement. *Special Characteristics:* 38 awards ($365,843 total): children of faculty/staff, siblings of current students, spouses of current students. *Tuition waivers:* Full or partial for employees or children of employees. *ROTC:* Army cooperative.

LOANS *Student loans:* $7,190,855 (69% need-based, 31% non-need-based). 96% of past graduating class borrowed through all loan programs. *Average indebtedness per student:* $24,301. *Average need-based loan:* Freshmen: $4818; Undergraduates: $6314. *Parent loans:* $1,981,603 (39% need-based, 61% non-need-based). *Programs:* FFEL (Subsidized and Unsubsidized Stafford, PLUS), Perkins, Federal Nursing, state.

WORK-STUDY *Federal work-study:* Total amount: $492,700; 416 jobs averaging $1184.

APPLYING FOR FINANCIAL AID *Required financial aid forms:* FAFSA, institution's own form. *Financial aid deadline (priority):* 3/1. *Notification date:* Continuous. Students must reply within 2 weeks of notification.

CONTACT Office of Financial Aid, Saint Joseph's College of Maine, 278 Whites Bridge Road, Standish, ME 04084-5263, 800-752-1266 or toll-free 800-338-7057. *Fax:* 207-893-6699. *E-mail:* finaid@sjcme.edu.

ST. JOSEPH'S COLLEGE, SUFFOLK CAMPUS
Patchogue, NY

Tuition & fees: $11,954	Average undergraduate aid package: $8228

ABOUT THE INSTITUTION Independent, coed. Awards: bachelor's and master's degrees (master's degree in education only). 32 undergraduate majors. Total enrollment: 4,005. Undergraduates: 3,789. Freshmen: 459. Federal methodology is used as a basis for awarding need-based institutional aid.

UNDERGRADUATE EXPENSES for 2005–06 *Application fee:* $25. *Tuition:* full-time $11,612; part-time $376 per credit. *Required fees:* full-time $342; $11 per credit or $104 per term part-time. Part-time tuition and fees vary according to course load. *Payment plan:* Installment.

FRESHMAN FINANCIAL AID (Fall 2004, est.) 374 applied for aid; of those 56% were deemed to have need. 100% of freshmen with need received aid; of those 51% had need fully met. *Average percent of need met:* 49% (excluding resources awarded to replace EFC). *Average financial aid package:* $8302 (excluding resources awarded to replace EFC). 25% of all full-time freshmen had no need and received non-need-based gift aid.

UNDERGRADUATE FINANCIAL AID (Fall 2004, est.) 2,277 applied for aid; of those 68% were deemed to have need. 100% of undergraduates with need received aid; of those 59% had need fully met. *Average percent of need met:* 56% (excluding resources awarded to replace EFC). *Average financial aid package:* $8228 (excluding resources awarded to replace EFC). 19% of all full-time undergraduates had no need and received non-need-based gift aid.

GIFT AID (NEED-BASED) *Total amount:* $8,048,384 (25% federal, 40% state, 35% institutional). *Receiving aid:* Freshmen: 47% (211); All full-time undergraduates: 55% (1,546). *Average award:* Freshmen: $6658; Undergraduates: $5206. *Scholarships, grants, and awards:* Federal Pell, FSEOG, state, private, college/university gift aid from institutional funds.

GIFT AID (NON-NEED-BASED) *Total amount:* $2,810,828 (2% state, 95% institutional, 3% external sources). *Receiving aid:* Freshmen: 26% (118); Undergraduates: 26% (731). *Average Award: Freshmen:* $5656; *Undergraduates:* $5101. *Scholarships, grants, and awards by category: Academic Interests/Achievement:* 751 awards ($4,017,325 total): general academic interests/achievements. *Tuition waivers:* Full or partial for employees or children of employees, senior citizens. *ROTC:* Army cooperative, Air Force cooperative.

LOANS *Student loans:* $13,485,790 (47% need-based, 53% non-need-based). 73% of past graduating class borrowed through all loan programs. *Average indebtedness per student:* $16,047. *Average need-based loan:* Freshmen: $2547; Undergraduates: $4203. *Parent loans:* $4,513,851 (100% non-need-based). *Programs:* FFEL (Subsidized and Unsubsidized Stafford, PLUS), Perkins.

WORK-STUDY *Federal work-study:* Total amount: $100,076; 46 jobs averaging $2125. *State or other work-study/employment:* Total amount: $161,669 (100% non-need-based). 74 part-time jobs averaging $2185.

APPLYING FOR FINANCIAL AID *Required financial aid forms:* FAFSA, institution's own form, state aid form. *Financial aid deadline (priority):* 2/25. *Notification date:* 4/15. Students must reply within 3 weeks of notification.

CONTACT Joan Farley, Associate Director of Financial Aid, St. Joseph's College, Suffolk Campus, 155 West Roe Boulevard, Patchogue, NY 11772-2399, 631-447-3214 or toll-free 866-AT ST JOE (in-state). *Fax:* 631-447-1734.

SAINT JOSEPH SEMINARY COLLEGE
Saint Benedict, LA

CONTACT Betty Anne Burns, Financial Aid Officer, Saint Joseph Seminary College, Saint Benedict, LA 70457, 985-867-2229. *Fax:* 985-867-2270.

SAINT JOSEPH'S UNIVERSITY
Philadelphia, PA

ABOUT THE INSTITUTION Independent Roman Catholic (Jesuit), coed. Awards: bachelor's, master's, and doctoral degrees and post-bachelor's and post-master's certificates. 48 undergraduate majors. Total enrollment: 7,730. Undergraduates: 4,978. Freshmen: 1,213.

GIFT AID (NEED-BASED) *Scholarships, grants, and awards:* Federal Pell, FSEOG, state, private, college/university gift aid from institutional funds.

GIFT AID (NON-NEED-BASED) *Scholarships, grants, and awards by category: Academic Interests/Achievement:* general academic interests/achievements. *Creative Arts/Performance:* debating, theater/drama. *Special Characteristics:* members of minority groups.

LOANS *Programs:* FFEL (Subsidized and Unsubsidized Stafford, PLUS), Perkins.

APPLYING FOR FINANCIAL AID *Required financial aid form:* FAFSA.

CONTACT Eileen M. Tucker, Director of Financial Assistance, Saint Joseph's University, 5600 City Avenue, Philadelphia, PA 19131-1395, 610-660-1556 or toll-free 888-BEAHAWK (in-state). *Fax:* 610-660-1342. *E-mail:* tucker@sju.edu.

ST. LAWRENCE UNIVERSITY
Canton, NY

Tuition & fees: $30,480	Average undergraduate aid package: $26,013

ABOUT THE INSTITUTION Independent, coed. Awards: bachelor's and master's degrees and post-master's certificates. 33 undergraduate majors. Total enrollment: 2,277. Undergraduates: 2,133. Freshmen: 566. Both federal and institutional methodology are used as a basis for awarding need-based institutional aid.

UNDERGRADUATE EXPENSES for 2004–05 *Application fee:* $50. *Comprehensive fee:* $38,235 includes full-time tuition ($30,270), mandatory fees ($210), and room and board ($7755). *College room only:* $4170. Room and board charges vary according to board plan. *Part-time tuition:* $3785 per course. *Payment plans:* Installment, deferred payment.

FRESHMAN FINANCIAL AID (Fall 2003) 429 applied for aid; of those 91% were deemed to have need. 98% of freshmen with need received aid; of those 39% had need fully met. *Average percent of need met:* 91% (excluding resources awarded to replace EFC). *Average financial aid package:* $26,725 (excluding resources awarded to replace EFC). 10% of all full-time freshmen had no need and received non-need-based gift aid.

UNDERGRADUATE FINANCIAL AID (Fall 2003) 1,620 applied for aid; of those 92% were deemed to have need. 99% of undergraduates with need received aid; of those 37% had need fully met. *Average percent of need met:* 90% (excluding resources awarded to replace EFC). *Average financial aid package:* $26,013 (excluding resources awarded to replace EFC). 10% of all full-time undergraduates had no need and received non-need-based gift aid.

GIFT AID (NEED-BASED) *Total amount:* $27,208,590 (5% federal, 6% state, 85% institutional, 4% external sources). *Receiving aid:* Freshmen: 66% (372); All full-time undergraduates: 69% (1,451). *Average award:* Freshmen: $20,310; Undergraduates: $18,585. *Scholarships, grants, and awards:* Federal Pell, FSEOG, state, college/university gift aid from institutional funds.

GIFT AID (NON-NEED-BASED) *Total amount:* $2,279,543 (100% institutional). *Receiving aid:* Freshmen: 11% (65); Undergraduates: 10% (210). *Average Award: Freshmen:* $9318; *Undergraduates:* $9151. *Scholarships, grants, and awards by category: Academic Interests/Achievement:* 729 awards ($8,752,195 total): general academic interests/achievements. *Special Achievements/Activities:* 21 awards ($157,500 total): community service. *Special Characteristics:* 264 awards ($657,500 total): children and siblings of alumni, siblings of current students. *Tuition waivers:* Full or partial for employees or children of employees. *ROTC:* Army cooperative, Air Force cooperative.

LOANS *Student loans:* $9,274,981 (88% need-based, 12% non-need-based). 70% of past graduating class borrowed through all loan programs. *Average indebtedness per student:* $23,091. *Average need-based loan:* Freshmen: $5093; Undergraduates: $6134. *Programs:* Federal Direct (Subsidized and Unsubsidized Stafford), FFEL (Subsidized and Unsubsidized Stafford, PLUS), Perkins, college/university.

WORK-STUDY *Federal work-study:* Total amount: $1,302,164; 931 jobs averaging $1402. *State or other work-study/employment:* Total amount: $665,339 (100% non-need-based). 483 part-time jobs averaging $1366.

ATHLETIC AWARDS *Total amount:* $1,190,327 (100% non-need-based).

APPLYING FOR FINANCIAL AID *Required financial aid forms:* FAFSA, institution's own form, noncustodial (divorced/separated) parent's statement, either institution's own financial aid form or CSS/Financial Aid PROFILE, income tax returns/w2s. *Financial aid deadline:* 2/15. *Notification date:* 3/30. Students must reply by 5/1 or within 2 weeks of notification.

CONTACT Mrs. Patricia J. B. Farmer, Director of Financial Aid, St. Lawrence University, Payson Hall, Park Street, Canton, NY 13617-1455, 315-229-5265 or toll-free 800-285-1856. *Fax:* 315-229-5502. *E-mail:* pfarmer@stlawu.edu.

SAINT LEO UNIVERSITY
Saint Leo, FL

Tuition & fees: $14,080	Average undergraduate aid package: $15,130

ABOUT THE INSTITUTION Independent Roman Catholic, coed. Awards: associate, bachelor's, and master's degrees. 31 undergraduate majors. Total enrollment: 1,825. Undergraduates: 1,241. Freshmen: 396. Federal methodology is used as a basis for awarding need-based institutional aid.

UNDERGRADUATE EXPENSES for 2004–05 *Application fee:* $35. *Comprehensive fee:* $21,340 includes full-time tuition ($13,650), mandatory fees ($430), and room and board ($7260). *College room only:* $3820. Full-time tuition and fees vary according to location. Room and board charges vary according to board plan and housing facility. Part-time tuition and fees vary according to location. *Payment plan:* Installment.

FRESHMAN FINANCIAL AID (Fall 2004, est.) 358 applied for aid; of those 80% were deemed to have need. 100% of freshmen with need received aid; of those 33% had need fully met. *Average percent of need met:* 85% (excluding resources awarded to replace EFC). *Average financial aid package:* $14,259 (excluding resources awarded to replace EFC). 26% of all full-time freshmen had no need and received non-need-based gift aid.

UNDERGRADUATE FINANCIAL AID (Fall 2004, est.) 1,079 applied for aid; of those 81% were deemed to have need. 99% of undergraduates with need received aid; of those 40% had need fully met. *Average percent of need met:* 86% (excluding resources awarded to replace EFC). *Average financial aid package:* $15,130 (excluding resources awarded to replace EFC). 23% of all full-time undergraduates had no need and received non-need-based gift aid.

GIFT AID (NEED-BASED) *Total amount:* $8,338,587 (16% federal, 24% state, 55% institutional, 5% external sources). *Receiving aid:* Freshmen: 73% (287); All full-time undergraduates: 72% (860). *Average award:* Freshmen: $10,180; Undergraduates: $10,553. *Scholarships, grants, and awards:* Federal Pell, FSEOG, state, private, college/university gift aid from institutional funds, United Negro College Fund.

GIFT AID (NON-NEED-BASED) *Total amount:* $2,540,443 (25% state, 64% institutional, 11% external sources). *Receiving aid:* Freshmen: 11% (45); Undergraduates: 11% (127). *Average Award:* Freshmen: $5696; Undergraduates: $5554. *Tuition waivers:* Full or partial for employees or children of employees. *ROTC:* Army, Air Force cooperative.

LOANS *Student loans:* $5,990,930 (65% need-based, 35% non-need-based). 72% of past graduating class borrowed through all loan programs. *Average indebtedness per student:* $15,714. *Average need-based loan:* Freshmen: $2748; Undergraduates: $3640. *Parent loans:* $1,745,536 (50% need-based, 50% non-need-based). *Programs:* FFEL (Subsidized and Unsubsidized Stafford, PLUS), Perkins.

WORK-STUDY *Federal work-study:* Total amount: $1,032,545; 501 jobs averaging $2061.

ATHLETIC AWARDS *Total amount:* $985,686 (62% need-based, 38% non-need-based).

APPLYING FOR FINANCIAL AID *Required financial aid form:* FAFSA. *Financial aid deadline (priority):* 3/1. *Notification date:* 3/1.

CONTACT Office of Student Financial Services, Saint Leo University, PO Box 6665, MC 2228, Saint Leo, FL 33574-6665, 800-240-7658 or toll-free 800-334-5532. *Fax:* 352-588-8403. *E-mail:* finaid@saintleo.edu.

ST. LOUIS CHRISTIAN COLLEGE
Florissant, MO

Tuition & fees: $7730	Average undergraduate aid package: $6755

ABOUT THE INSTITUTION Independent Christian, coed. Awards: associate and bachelor's degrees. 6 undergraduate majors. Total enrollment: 213. Undergraduates: 213. Freshmen: 26. Federal methodology is used as a basis for awarding need-based institutional aid.

UNDERGRADUATE EXPENSES for 2004–05 *Comprehensive fee:* $12,910 includes full-time tuition ($7680), mandatory fees ($50), and room and board ($5180). Room and board charges vary according to housing facility. *Part-time tuition:* $240 per hour. *Payment plan:* Installment.

FRESHMAN FINANCIAL AID (Fall 2004, est.) 21 applied for aid; of those 86% were deemed to have need. 100% of freshmen with need received aid; of those 39% had need fully met. *Average percent of need met:* 88% (excluding resources

awarded to replace EFC). *Average financial aid package:* $8245 (excluding resources awarded to replace EFC). 23% of all full-time freshmen had no need and received non-need-based gift aid.

UNDERGRADUATE FINANCIAL AID (Fall 2004, est.) 111 applied for aid; of those 100% were deemed to have need. 88% of undergraduates with need received aid; of those 24% had need fully met. *Average percent of need met:* 84% (excluding resources awarded to replace EFC). *Average financial aid package:* $6755 (excluding resources awarded to replace EFC). 12% of all full-time undergraduates had no need and received non-need-based gift aid.

GIFT AID (NEED-BASED) *Total amount:* $567,299 (38% federal, 44% institutional, 18% external sources). *Receiving aid:* Freshmen: 65% (17); All full-time undergraduates: 61% (75). *Average award:* Freshmen: $6626; Undergraduates: $4500. *Scholarships, grants, and awards:* Federal Pell, FSEOG, private, college/university gift aid from institutional funds.

GIFT AID (NON-NEED-BASED) *Total amount:* $47,250 (79% institutional, 21% external sources). *Average Award:* Freshmen: $2649; Undergraduates: $2125. *Scholarships, grants, and awards by category: Academic Interests/Achievement:* 24 awards ($93,060 total): general academic interests/achievements. *Special Achievements/Activities:* 80 awards ($138,794 total): leadership, religious involvement. *Special Characteristics:* 77 awards ($84,493 total): children and siblings of alumni, children of faculty/staff, general special characteristics, religious affiliation. *Tuition waivers:* Full or partial for employees or children of employees.

LOANS *Student loans:* $613,483 (91% need-based, 9% non-need-based). 50% of past graduating class borrowed through all loan programs. *Average indebtedness per student:* $13,977. *Average need-based loan:* Freshmen: $1443; Undergraduates: $2104. *Parent loans:* $65,000 (75% need-based, 25% non-need-based). *Programs:* FFEL (Subsidized and Unsubsidized Stafford, PLUS).

WORK-STUDY *Federal work-study:* Total amount: $17,245; 16 jobs averaging $1078. *State or other work-study/employment:* Total amount: $105,000 (100% non-need-based). 21 part-time jobs averaging $5000.

APPLYING FOR FINANCIAL AID *Required financial aid forms:* FAFSA, institution's own form. *Financial aid deadline (priority):* 5/1. *Notification date:* Continuous. Students must reply within 2 weeks of notification.

CONTACT Mrs. Catherine Wilhoit, Director of Financial Aid, St. Louis Christian College, 1360 Grandview Drive, Florissant, MO 63033-6499, 314-837-6777 Ext. 1101 or toll-free 800-887-SLCC. *Fax:* 314-837-8291.

SAINT LOUIS UNIVERSITY
St. Louis, MO

Tuition & fees: $23,558	Average undergraduate aid package: $18,257

ABOUT THE INSTITUTION Independent Roman Catholic (Jesuit), coed. Awards: bachelor's, master's, doctoral, and first professional degrees and post-bachelor's and post-master's certificates. 73 undergraduate majors. Total enrollment: 11,422. Undergraduates: 7,086. Freshmen: 1,595. Federal methodology is used as a basis for awarding need-based institutional aid.

UNDERGRADUATE EXPENSES for 2004–05 *Application fee:* $25. *Comprehensive fee:* $31,338 includes full-time tuition ($23,360), mandatory fees ($198), and room and board ($7780). *College room only:* $4320. Full-time tuition and fees vary according to location and program. Room and board charges vary according to board plan, housing facility, and location. *Part-time tuition:* $815 per credit hour. *Part-time fees:* $70 per term. Part-time tuition and fees vary according to location and program. *Payment plan:* Installment.

GIFT AID (NEED-BASED) *Total amount:* $50,460,418 (11% federal, 7% state, 78% institutional, 4% external sources). *Receiving aid:* Freshmen: 72% (961); All full-time undergraduates: 67% (4,098). *Average award:* Freshmen: $13,191; Undergraduates: $12,200. *Scholarships, grants, and awards:* Federal Pell, FSEOG, state, private, college/university gift aid from institutional funds.

GIFT AID (NON-NEED-BASED) *Total amount:* $10,074,487 (6% federal, 2% state, 78% institutional, 14% external sources). *Receiving aid:* Freshmen: 4% (60); Undergraduates: 5% (275). *Average Award:* Freshmen: $7679; Undergraduates: $8483. *Scholarships, grants, and awards by category: Academic Interests/Achievement:* 907 awards ($6,500,934 total): area/ethnic studies, biological sciences, business, communication, computer science, education, engineering/technologies, English, foreign languages, general academic interests/achievements, health fields, humanities, international studies, mathematics, military science, physical sciences, premedicine, religion/biblical studies, social sciences. *Creative Arts/Performance:* 21 awards ($18,700 total): art/fine arts, music, performing arts, theater/drama. *Special Achievements/Activities:* 183 awards ($1,826,327 total): cheerleading/drum major, community service, general special achievements/activities, leadership, memberships. *Special Characteristics:*

423 awards ($3,445,748 total): children of faculty/staff, first-generation college students, general special characteristics, international students, members of minority groups, previous college experience, siblings of current students. *Tuition waivers:* Full or partial for employees or children of employees. *ROTC:* Army cooperative, Air Force.

LOANS *Student loans:* $32,739,854 (89% need-based, 11% non-need-based). 68% of past graduating class borrowed through all loan programs. *Average indebtedness per student:* $22,534. *Average need-based loan:* Freshmen: $3505; Undergraduates: $5080. *Parent loans:* $11,080,522 (59% need-based, 41% non-need-based). *Programs:* FFEL (Subsidized and Unsubsidized Stafford, PLUS), Perkins, Federal Nursing.

ATHLETIC AWARDS *Total amount:* $3,057,988 (56% need-based, 44% non-need-based).

APPLYING FOR FINANCIAL AID *Required financial aid form:* FAFSA. *Financial aid deadline (priority):* 3/1. *Notification date:* Continuous beginning 3/1. Students must reply by 5/1 or within 4 weeks of notification.

CONTACT Cari Wickliffe, Director of Scholarship and Financial Aid, Saint Louis University, 221 North Grand Boulevard, Room 121, St. Louis, MO 63103-2097, 314-977-234750 or toll-free 800-758-3678 (out-of-state). *Fax:* 314-977-3437. *E-mail:* wicklics@slu.edu.

SAINT LUKE'S COLLEGE
Kansas City, MO

ABOUT THE INSTITUTION Independent Episcopal, coed. Awards: bachelor's degrees. 1 undergraduate major. Total enrollment: 109. Undergraduates: 109.

GIFT AID (NEED-BASED) *Scholarships, grants, and awards:* Federal Pell, FSEOG, state, private, college/university gift aid from institutional funds.

GIFT AID (NON-NEED-BASED) *Scholarships, grants, and awards by category:* Special Characteristics: ethnic background.

LOANS *Programs:* FFEL (Subsidized and Unsubsidized Stafford, PLUS), Perkins, Federal Nursing, college/university.

WORK-STUDY *Federal work-study:* Total amount: $10,000; jobs available.

APPLYING FOR FINANCIAL AID *Required financial aid forms:* FAFSA, institution's own form.

CONTACT Jeff Gannon, Director of Financial Aid, Saint Luke's College, 8320 Ward Parkway, Suite 300, Kansas City, MO 64114, 816-932-2194. *Fax:* 816-932-9064. *E-mail:* jgannon@saint-lukes.org.

SAINT MARTIN'S COLLEGE
Lacey, WA

Tuition & fees: $19,980	Average undergraduate aid package: $17,157

ABOUT THE INSTITUTION Independent Roman Catholic, coed. Awards: bachelor's and master's degrees and post-bachelor's certificates. 31 undergraduate majors. Total enrollment: 1,512. Undergraduates: 1,251. Freshmen: 126. Federal methodology is used as a basis for awarding need-based institutional aid.

UNDERGRADUATE EXPENSES for 2005–06 *Application fee:* $35. *Comprehensive fee:* $26,180 includes full-time tuition ($19,690), mandatory fees ($290), and room and board ($6200). *College room only:* $2790. Room and board charges vary according to board plan. *Part-time tuition:* $656 per credit. *Part-time fees:* $130 per term. Part-time tuition and fees vary according to course load. *Payment plan:* Installment.

FRESHMAN FINANCIAL AID (Fall 2004, est.) 109 applied for aid; of those 87% were deemed to have need. 100% of freshmen with need received aid; of those 34% had need fully met. *Average percent of need met:* 90% (excluding resources awarded to replace EFC). *Average financial aid package:* $19,697 (excluding resources awarded to replace EFC). 20% of all full-time freshmen had no need and received non-need-based gift aid.

UNDERGRADUATE FINANCIAL AID (Fall 2004, est.) 704 applied for aid; of those 91% were deemed to have need. 100% of undergraduates with need received aid; of those 32% had need fully met. *Average percent of need met:* 84% (excluding resources awarded to replace EFC). *Average financial aid package:* $17,157 (excluding resources awarded to replace EFC). 12% of all full-time undergraduates had no need and received non-need-based gift aid.

GIFT AID (NEED-BASED) *Total amount:* $7,457,147 (17% federal, 15% state, 47% institutional, 21% external sources). *Receiving aid:* Freshmen: 80% (95); All full-time undergraduates: 85% (625). *Average award:* Freshmen: $14,222; Undergraduates: $10,874. *Scholarships, grants, and awards:* Federal Pell, FSEOG, state, private, college/university gift aid from institutional funds.

GIFT AID (NON-NEED-BASED) *Total amount:* $798,258 (2% state, 73% institutional, 25% external sources). *Receiving aid:* Freshmen: 8% (9); Undergraduates: 7% (52). *Average Award:* Freshmen: $10,401; Undergraduates: $10,770. *Scholarships, grants, and awards by category:* Academic Interests/Achievement: business, education, engineering/technologies, general academic interests/achievements, humanities. Creative Arts/Performance: music, performing arts, theater/drama. Special Achievements/Activities: community service, leadership, memberships. Special Characteristics: children and siblings of alumni, children of current students, children of faculty/staff, ethnic background, general special characteristics, international students, local/state students, members of minority groups, religious affiliation, siblings of current students, spouses of current students. *Tuition waivers:* Full or partial for children of alumni, employees or children of employees. *ROTC:* Army cooperative.

LOANS *Student loans:* $6,780,313 (75% need-based, 25% non-need-based). 52% of past graduating class borrowed through all loan programs. *Average indebtedness per student:* $24,715. *Average need-based loan:* Freshmen: $4243; Undergraduates: $5280. *Parent loans:* $755,366 (26% need-based, 74% non-need-based). *Programs:* Federal Direct (Subsidized and Unsubsidized Stafford), FFEL (PLUS), Perkins, college/university.

WORK-STUDY *Federal work-study:* Total amount: $468,390; 210 jobs averaging $1875. *State or other work-study/employment:* Total amount: $948,093 (93% need-based, 7% non-need-based). 389 part-time jobs averaging $1893.

ATHLETIC AWARDS *Total amount:* $465,671 (66% need-based, 34% non-need-based).

APPLYING FOR FINANCIAL AID *Required financial aid forms:* FAFSA, admissions application. *Financial aid deadline (priority):* 3/1. *Notification date:* Continuous beginning 3/15. Students must reply within 3 weeks of notification.

CONTACT Rebecca Wonderly, Director of Financial Aid, Saint Martin's College, 5300 Pacific Avenue, SE, Lacey, WA 98503-1297, 360-438-4463 or toll-free 800-368-8803. *Fax:* 360-459-4124. *E-mail:* rwonderly@stmartins.edu.

SAINT MARY-OF-THE-WOODS COLLEGE
Saint Mary-of-the-Woods, IN

CONTACT Ms. Jan Benton, Director of Financial Aid, Saint Mary-of-the-Woods College, 106 Guerin Hall, Saint Mary-of-the-Woods, IN 47876, 812-535-5106 or toll-free 800-926-SMWC. *Fax:* 812-535-4900. *E-mail:* jbenton@smwc.edu.

SAINT MARY'S COLLEGE
Notre Dame, IN

ABOUT THE INSTITUTION Independent Roman Catholic, women only. Awards: bachelor's degrees. 36 undergraduate majors. Total enrollment: 1,418. Undergraduates: 1,418. Freshmen: 350.

GIFT AID (NEED-BASED) *Scholarships, grants, and awards:* Federal Pell, FSEOG, state, private, college/university gift aid from institutional funds.

GIFT AID (NON-NEED-BASED) *Scholarships, grants, and awards by category:* Academic Interests/Achievement: general academic interests/achievements. Creative Arts/Performance: art/fine arts, music, theater/drama. Special Achievements/Activities: community service. Special Characteristics: children of faculty/staff, siblings of current students.

LOANS *Programs:* FFEL (Subsidized and Unsubsidized Stafford, PLUS), Perkins, college/university.

WORK-STUDY *Federal work-study:* Total amount: $328,084; 273 jobs averaging $1201. *State or other work-study/employment:* Total amount: $1,348,385 (49% need-based, 51% non-need-based). 455 part-time jobs averaging $1446.

APPLYING FOR FINANCIAL AID *Required financial aid forms:* FAFSA, CSS Financial Aid PROFILE.

CONTACT Mrs. Mary Nucciarone, Director of Financial Aid, Saint Mary's College, 141 Le Mans Hall, Notre Dame, IN 46556, 574-284-4557 or toll-free 800-551-7621. *Fax:* 574-284-4707. *E-mail:* mnucciar@saintmarys.edu.

SAINT MARY'S COLLEGE OF CALIFORNIA
Moraga, CA

Tuition & fees: $25,150	Average undergraduate aid package: $21,145

ABOUT THE INSTITUTION Independent Roman Catholic, coed. Awards: bachelor's, master's, and doctoral degrees. 69 undergraduate majors. Total enrollment: 4,536. Undergraduates: 3,330. Freshmen: 611. Federal methodology is used as a basis for awarding need-based institutional aid.

Saint Mary's College of California

UNDERGRADUATE EXPENSES for 2004–05 *Application fee:* $55. *Comprehensive fee:* $34,680 includes full-time tuition ($25,000), mandatory fees ($150), and room and board ($9530). *College room only:* $5320. Full-time tuition and fees vary according to program. Room and board charges vary according to board plan and housing facility. *Part-time tuition:* $3125 per course. *Payment plan:* Installment.

FRESHMAN FINANCIAL AID (Fall 2004, est.) 457 applied for aid; of those 86% were deemed to have need. 99% of freshmen with need received aid; of those 12% had need fully met. *Average percent of need met:* 74% (excluding resources awarded to replace EFC). *Average financial aid package:* $20,850 (excluding resources awarded to replace EFC). 4% of all full-time freshmen had no need and received non-need-based gift aid.

UNDERGRADUATE FINANCIAL AID (Fall 2004, est.) 1,667 applied for aid; of those 91% were deemed to have need. 99% of undergraduates with need received aid; of those 11% had need fully met. *Average percent of need met:* 76% (excluding resources awarded to replace EFC). *Average financial aid package:* $21,145 (excluding resources awarded to replace EFC). 4% of all full-time undergraduates had no need and received non-need-based gift aid.

GIFT AID (NEED-BASED) *Total amount:* $21,953,611 (12% federal, 26% state, 61% institutional, 1% external sources). *Receiving aid:* Freshmen: 62% (373); All full-time undergraduates: 55% (1,349). *Average award:* Freshmen: $16,389; Undergraduates: $16,861. *Scholarships, grants, and awards:* Federal Pell, FSEOG, state, private, college/university gift aid from institutional funds.

GIFT AID (NON-NEED-BASED) *Total amount:* $901,728 (70% institutional, 30% external sources). *Receiving aid:* Freshmen: 7% (41); Undergraduates: 7% (168). *Average Award:* Freshmen: $7605; Undergraduates: $6684. *Scholarships, grants, and awards by category: Academic Interests/Achievement:* 244 awards ($1,371,841 total): general academic interests/achievements. *Special Achievements/Activities:* 32 awards ($210,000 total): memberships. *Special Characteristics:* 52 awards ($1,039,466 total): children and siblings of alumni, children of educators, children of faculty/staff, general special characteristics, relatives of clergy. *Tuition waivers:* Full or partial for employees or children of employees. *ROTC:* Army cooperative, Air Force cooperative.

LOANS *Student loans:* $12,361,928 (72% need-based, 28% non-need-based). 70% of past graduating class borrowed through all loan programs. *Average indebtedness per student:* $19,510. *Average need-based loan:* Freshmen: $3078; Undergraduates: $4590. *Parent loans:* $4,547,455 (15% need-based, 85% non-need-based). *Programs:* FFEL (Subsidized and Unsubsidized Stafford, PLUS), Perkins.

WORK-STUDY *Federal work-study:* Total amount: $1,040,220; 520 jobs averaging $2000.

ATHLETIC AWARDS *Total amount:* $3,129,041 (46% need-based, 54% non-need-based).

APPLYING FOR FINANCIAL AID *Required financial aid forms:* FAFSA, state aid form. *Financial aid deadline:* 3/2. *Notification date:* Continuous beginning 4/15. Students must reply by 5/1 or within 2 weeks of notification.

CONTACT Linda Judge, Acting Director of Financial Aid, Saint Mary's College of California, PO Box 4530, Moraga, CA 94575, 925-631-4370 or toll-free 800-800-4SMC. *Fax:* 925-376-2965. *E-mail:* finaid@stmarys-ca.edu.

ST. MARY'S COLLEGE OF MARYLAND
St. Mary's City, MD

Tuition & fees (MD res): $9680　　　　**Average undergraduate aid package: $6250**

ABOUT THE INSTITUTION State-supported, coed. Awards: bachelor's degrees. 24 undergraduate majors. Total enrollment: 1,935. Undergraduates: 1,935. Freshmen: 431. Federal methodology is used as a basis for awarding need-based institutional aid.

UNDERGRADUATE EXPENSES for 2004–05 *Application fee:* $40. *Tuition, state resident:* full-time $8092; part-time $150 per credit. *Tuition, nonresident:* full-time $15,572; part-time $150 per credit. Part-time tuition and fees vary according to course load. *College room and board:* $7400; *room only:* $4165. Room and board charges vary according to board plan, housing facility, and student level. *Payment plan:* Installment.

FRESHMAN FINANCIAL AID (Fall 2004, est.) 304 applied for aid; of those 64% were deemed to have need. 100% of freshmen with need received aid. *Average percent of need met:* 59% (excluding resources awarded to replace EFC). *Average financial aid package:* $7495 (excluding resources awarded to replace EFC). 32% of all full-time freshmen had no need and received non-need-based gift aid.

UNDERGRADUATE FINANCIAL AID (Fall 2004, est.) 1,127 applied for aid; of those 73% were deemed to have need. 100% of undergraduates with need received aid. *Average percent of need met:* 62% (excluding resources awarded to replace EFC). *Average financial aid package:* $6250 (excluding resources awarded to replace EFC). 24% of all full-time undergraduates had no need and received non-need-based gift aid.

GIFT AID (NEED-BASED) *Total amount:* $3,223,766 (21% federal, 27% state, 41% institutional, 11% external sources). *Receiving aid:* Freshmen: 19% (84); All full-time undergraduates: 19% (342). *Average award:* Freshmen: $3000; Undergraduates: $4000. *Scholarships, grants, and awards:* Federal Pell, FSEOG, state, private, college/university gift aid from institutional funds.

GIFT AID (NON-NEED-BASED) *Total amount:* $3,554,152 (19% state, 73% institutional, 8% external sources). *Receiving aid:* Freshmen: 19% (84); Undergraduates: 19% (342). *Average Award:* Freshmen: $3000; Undergraduates: $4000. *Scholarships, grants, and awards by category: Academic Interests/Achievement:* 819 awards ($2,896,408 total): general academic interests/achievements. *Special Characteristics:* 156 awards ($479,776 total): children and siblings of alumni, children of faculty/staff. *Tuition waivers:* Full or partial for employees or children of employees, senior citizens.

LOANS *Student loans:* $4,407,477 (46% need-based, 54% non-need-based). 69% of past graduating class borrowed through all loan programs. *Average indebtedness per student:* $17,125. *Average need-based loan:* Freshmen: $2625; Undergraduates: $5500. *Parent loans:* $5,069,241 (100% non-need-based). *Programs:* FFEL (Subsidized and Unsubsidized Stafford, PLUS), Perkins.

WORK-STUDY *Federal work-study:* Total amount: $123,976; 105 jobs averaging $794. *State or other work-study/employment:* Part-time jobs available.

APPLYING FOR FINANCIAL AID *Required financial aid form:* FAFSA. *Financial aid deadline:* 3/1. *Notification date:* 4/1. Students must reply by 5/1.

CONTACT Tim Wolfe, Director of Financial Aid, St. Mary's College of Maryland, 18952 East Fisher Road, St. Mary's City, MD 20686-3001, 240-895-3000 or toll-free 800-492-7181. *Fax:* 240-895-4959. *E-mail:* tawolfe@smcm.edu.

SAINT MARY'S UNIVERSITY OF MINNESOTA
Winona, MN

Tuition & fees: $17,925　　　　**Average undergraduate aid package: $15,380**

ABOUT THE INSTITUTION Independent Roman Catholic, coed. Awards: bachelor's, master's, and doctoral degrees and post-bachelor's and post-master's certificates. 62 undergraduate majors. Total enrollment: 4,861. Undergraduates: 1,644. Freshmen: 362. Both federal and institutional methodology are used as a basis for awarding need-based institutional aid.

UNDERGRADUATE EXPENSES for 2004–05 *Application fee:* $25. *Comprehensive fee:* $23,375 includes full-time tuition ($17,480), mandatory fees ($445), and room and board ($5450). *College room only:* $3050. Full-time tuition and fees vary according to course load and program. Room and board charges vary according to housing facility. *Part-time tuition:* $580 per credit. Part-time tuition and fees vary according to course load and program. *Payment plan:* Installment.

FRESHMAN FINANCIAL AID (Fall 2004, est.) 294 applied for aid; of those 86% were deemed to have need. 100% of freshmen with need received aid; of those 70% had need fully met. *Average percent of need met:* 75% (excluding resources awarded to replace EFC). *Average financial aid package:* $16,252 (excluding resources awarded to replace EFC). 17% of all full-time freshmen had no need and received non-need-based gift aid.

UNDERGRADUATE FINANCIAL AID (Fall 2004, est.) 1,035 applied for aid; of those 71% were deemed to have need. 100% of undergraduates with need received aid; of those 77% had need fully met. *Average percent of need met:* 71% (excluding resources awarded to replace EFC). *Average financial aid package:* $15,380 (excluding resources awarded to replace EFC). 13% of all full-time undergraduates had no need and received non-need-based gift aid.

GIFT AID (NEED-BASED) *Total amount:* $9,048,866 (9% federal, 10% state, 78% institutional, 3% external sources). *Receiving aid:* Freshmen: 70% (253); All full-time undergraduates: 55% (737). *Average award:* Freshmen: $8057; Undergraduates: $7016. *Scholarships, grants, and awards:* Federal Pell, FSEOG, state, private, college/university gift aid from institutional funds.

GIFT AID (NON-NEED-BASED) *Average Award:* Freshmen: $5924; Undergraduates: $5198. *Scholarships, grants, and awards by category: Academic Interests/Achievement:* 598 awards ($2,869,850 total): general academic interests/achievements. *Creative Arts/Performance:* 86 awards ($132,500 total): music, theater/drama. *Special Achievements/Activities:* 344 awards ($624,163 total):

leadership. *Special Characteristics:* 159 awards ($929,478 total): children and siblings of alumni, children of faculty/staff, members of minority groups. *Tuition waivers:* Full or partial for employees or children of employees. *ROTC:* Army cooperative.

LOANS *Student loans:* $6,790,992 (100% need-based). 71% of past graduating class borrowed through all loan programs. *Average indebtedness per student:* $22,530. *Average need-based loan:* Freshmen: $3605; Undergraduates: $4462. *Parent loans:* $1,197,959 (100% need-based). *Programs:* FFEL (Subsidized and Unsubsidized Stafford, PLUS), Perkins, state.

WORK-STUDY *Federal work-study:* Total amount: $260,878; 194 jobs averaging $1298. *State or other work-study/employment:* Total amount: $463,669 (100% need-based). 382 part-time jobs averaging $1214.

APPLYING FOR FINANCIAL AID *Required financial aid form:* FAFSA. *Financial aid deadline (priority):* 3/15. *Notification date:* Continuous. Students must reply within 3 weeks of notification.

CONTACT Ms. Jayne P. Wobig, Director of Financial Aid, Saint Mary's University of Minnesota, 700 Terrace Heights, #5, Winona, MN 55987-1399, 507-457-1437 or toll-free 800-635-5987. *Fax:* 507-457-6698. *E-mail:* jwobig@smumn.edu.

ST. MARY'S UNIVERSITY OF SAN ANTONIO
San Antonio, TX

Tuition & fees: $17,756	Average undergraduate aid package: $14,188

ABOUT THE INSTITUTION Independent Roman Catholic, coed. Awards: bachelor's, master's, doctoral, and first professional degrees. 46 undergraduate majors. Total enrollment: 4,110. Undergraduates: 2,531. Freshmen: 466. Federal methodology is used as a basis for awarding need-based institutional aid.

UNDERGRADUATE EXPENSES for 2004–05 *Application fee:* $30. *Comprehensive fee:* $24,254 includes full-time tuition ($17,256), mandatory fees ($500), and room and board ($6498). *College room only:* $3802. Full-time tuition and fees vary according to course load. Room and board charges vary according to board plan, housing facility, and student level. *Part-time tuition:* $517 per credit hour. *Part-time fees:* $250 per term. Part-time tuition and fees vary according to course load. *Payment plan:* Installment.

FRESHMAN FINANCIAL AID (Fall 2004, est.) 395 applied for aid; of those 92% were deemed to have need. 100% of freshmen with need received aid; of those 30% had need fully met. *Average percent of need met:* 74% (excluding resources awarded to replace EFC). *Average financial aid package:* $15,462 (excluding resources awarded to replace EFC). 6% of all full-time freshmen had no need and received non-need-based gift aid.

UNDERGRADUATE FINANCIAL AID (Fall 2004, est.) 1,830 applied for aid; of those 91% were deemed to have need. 100% of undergraduates with need received aid; of those 24% had need fully met. *Average percent of need met:* 69% (excluding resources awarded to replace EFC). *Average financial aid package:* $14,188 (excluding resources awarded to replace EFC). 6% of all full-time undergraduates had no need and received non-need-based gift aid.

GIFT AID (NEED-BASED) *Total amount:* $11,786,189 (29% federal, 48% state, 23% institutional). *Receiving aid:* Freshmen: 68% (314); All full-time undergraduates: 63% (1,443). *Average award:* Freshmen: $8648; Undergraduates: $7972. *Scholarships, grants, and awards:* Federal Pell, FSEOG, state, private, college/university gift aid from institutional funds.

GIFT AID (NON-NEED-BASED) *Total amount:* $12,775,488 (8% federal, 86% institutional, 6% external sources). *Receiving aid:* Freshmen: 48% (224); Undergraduates: 44% (1,017). *Average Award:* Freshmen: $10,424; Undergraduates: $9464. *Scholarships, grants, and awards by category:* Academic Interests/Achievement: 926 awards ($7,055,782 total): general academic interests/achievements, military science. Creative Arts/Performance: 69 awards ($197,728 total): music. Special Achievements/Activities: 24 awards ($36,590 total): cheerleading/drum major. *Tuition waivers:* Full or partial for employees or children of employees. *ROTC:* Army.

LOANS *Student loans:* $12,747,253 (56% need-based, 44% non-need-based). 77% of past graduating class borrowed through all loan programs. *Average indebtedness per student:* $23,447. *Average need-based loan:* Freshmen: $4224; Undergraduates: $4952. *Parent loans:* $1,053,523 (100% non-need-based). *Programs:* FFEL (Subsidized and Unsubsidized Stafford, PLUS), Perkins, state, alternative loans.

WORK-STUDY *Federal work-study:* Total amount: $1,509,795; 535 jobs averaging $2822. *State or other work-study/employment:* Total amount: $386,260 (100% non-need-based). 184 part-time jobs averaging $2099.

ATHLETIC AWARDS *Total amount:* $1,645,737 (100% non-need-based).

APPLYING FOR FINANCIAL AID *Required financial aid form:* FAFSA. *Financial aid deadline:* Continuous. *Notification date:* 3/15. Students must reply within 2 weeks of notification.

CONTACT Mr. David R. Krause, Director of Financial Assistance, St. Mary's University of San Antonio, One Camino Santa Maria, San Antonio, TX 78228-8541, 210-436-3141 or toll-free 800-FOR-STMU. *Fax:* 210-431-2221. *E-mail:* dkrause@alvin.stmarytx.edu.

SAINT MICHAEL'S COLLEGE
Colchester, VT

Tuition & fees: $25,535	Average undergraduate aid package: $18,408

ABOUT THE INSTITUTION Independent Roman Catholic, coed. Awards: bachelor's and master's degrees and post-bachelor's and post-master's certificates. 35 undergraduate majors. Total enrollment: 2,424. Undergraduates: 1,983. Freshmen: 518. Both federal and institutional methodology are used as a basis for awarding need-based institutional aid.

UNDERGRADUATE EXPENSES for 2004–05 *Application fee:* $45. *Comprehensive fee:* $31,785 includes full-time tuition ($25,325), mandatory fees ($210), and room and board ($6250). Room and board charges vary according to housing facility. *Part-time tuition:* $845 per semester hour. *Payment plan:* Installment.

FRESHMAN FINANCIAL AID (Fall 2004, est.) 418 applied for aid; of those 82% were deemed to have need. 100% of freshmen with need received aid; of those 25% had need fully met. *Average percent of need met:* 84% (excluding resources awarded to replace EFC). *Average financial aid package:* $18,366 (excluding resources awarded to replace EFC). 10% of all full-time freshmen had no need and received non-need-based gift aid.

UNDERGRADUATE FINANCIAL AID (Fall 2004, est.) 1,447 applied for aid; of those 87% were deemed to have need. 100% of undergraduates with need received aid; of those 29% had need fully met. *Average percent of need met:* 86% (excluding resources awarded to replace EFC). *Average financial aid package:* $18,408 (excluding resources awarded to replace EFC). 15% of all full-time undergraduates had no need and received non-need-based gift aid.

GIFT AID (NEED-BASED) *Total amount:* $15,372,872 (8% federal, 4% state, 84% institutional, 4% external sources). *Receiving aid:* Freshmen: 64% (329); All full-time undergraduates: 63% (1,205). *Average award:* Freshmen: $13,255; Undergraduates: $12,911. *Scholarships, grants, and awards:* Federal Pell, FSEOG, state, private, college/university gift aid from institutional funds.

GIFT AID (NON-NEED-BASED) *Total amount:* $2,772,217 (97% institutional, 3% external sources). *Receiving aid:* Freshmen: 14% (74); Undergraduates: 6% (123). *Average Award:* Freshmen: $7483; Undergraduates: $6784. *Scholarships, grants, and awards by category:* Academic Interests/Achievement: general academic interests/achievements. Creative Arts/Performance: art/fine arts. Special Characteristics: local/state students, members of minority groups, out-of-state students, religious affiliation, siblings of current students. *Tuition waivers:* Full or partial for employees or children of employees. *ROTC:* Army cooperative, Air Force cooperative.

LOANS *Student loans:* $7,672,701 (54% need-based, 46% non-need-based). 76% of past graduating class borrowed through all loan programs. *Average indebtedness per student:* $19,437. *Average need-based loan:* Freshmen: $4175; Undergraduates: $4924. *Parent loans:* $5,882,814 (100% non-need-based). *Programs:* FFEL (Subsidized and Unsubsidized Stafford, PLUS), Perkins.

WORK-STUDY *Federal work-study:* Total amount: $400,950; 150 jobs averaging $2000. *State or other work-study/employment:* Total amount: $974,425 (100% need-based). Part-time jobs available (averaging $1500).

ATHLETIC AWARDS *Total amount:* $635,700 (100% non-need-based).

APPLYING FOR FINANCIAL AID *Required financial aid form:* federal income tax forms (student and parent). *Financial aid deadline (priority):* 3/15. *Notification date:* 4/1. Students must reply by 5/1 or within 2 weeks of notification.

CONTACT Mrs. Nelberta B. Lunde, Director of Financial Aid, Saint Michael's College, Winooski Park, Colchester, VT 05439, 802-654-3243 or toll-free 800-762-8000. *Fax:* 802-654-2591. *E-mail:* finaid@smcvt.edu.

ST. NORBERT COLLEGE
De Pere, WI

Tuition & fees: $21,510	Average undergraduate aid package: $16,729

ABOUT THE INSTITUTION Independent Roman Catholic, coed. Awards: bachelor's and master's degrees. 37 undergraduate majors. Total enrollment: 2,103. Undergraduates: 2,020. Freshmen: 525. Federal methodology is used as a basis for awarding need-based institutional aid.

UNDERGRADUATE EXPENSES for 2004–05 *Application fee:* $25. *Comprehensive fee:* $27,490 includes full-time tuition ($21,210), mandatory fees ($300), and room and board ($5980). *College room only:* $3160. Full-time tuition and fees vary according to course load. Room and board charges vary according to board plan, housing facility, and student level. *Part-time tuition:* $2651 per course. Part-time tuition and fees vary according to course load. *Payment plans:* Installment, deferred payment.

FRESHMAN FINANCIAL AID (Fall 2004, est.) 416 applied for aid; of those 83% were deemed to have need. 100% of freshmen with need received aid; of those 36% had need fully met. *Average percent of need met:* 88% (excluding resources awarded to replace EFC). *Average financial aid package:* $16,937 (excluding resources awarded to replace EFC). 29% of all full-time freshmen had no need and received non-need-based gift aid.

UNDERGRADUATE FINANCIAL AID (Fall 2004, est.) 1,464 applied for aid; of those 86% were deemed to have need. 100% of undergraduates with need received aid; of those 39% had need fully met. *Average percent of need met:* 86% (excluding resources awarded to replace EFC). *Average financial aid package:* $16,729 (excluding resources awarded to replace EFC). 31% of all full-time undergraduates had no need and received non-need-based gift aid.

GIFT AID (NEED-BASED) *Total amount:* $14,503,885 (9% federal, 10% state, 78% institutional, 3% external sources). *Receiving aid:* Freshmen: 66% (344); All full-time undergraduates: 64% (1,253). *Average award:* Freshmen: $12,740; Undergraduates: $11,568. *Scholarships, grants, and awards:* Federal Pell, FSEOG, state, private, college/university gift aid from institutional funds.

GIFT AID (NON-NEED-BASED) *Total amount:* $3,722,270 (1% federal, 93% institutional, 6% external sources). *Receiving aid:* Freshmen: 9% (49); Undergraduates: 7% (133). *Average Award:* Freshmen: $10,414; Undergraduates: $9848. *Scholarships, grants, and awards by category:* Academic Interests/Achievement: 1,469 awards ($7,371,738 total): general academic interests/achievements. Creative Arts/Performance: 71 awards ($125,600 total): art/fine arts, music, theater/drama. Special Characteristics: 170 awards ($1,545,411 total): children of faculty/staff, children with a deceased or disabled parent, ethnic background, international students. *Tuition waivers:* Full or partial for employees or children of employees. *ROTC:* Army.

LOANS *Student loans:* $9,686,162 (87% need-based, 13% non-need-based). 68% of past graduating class borrowed through all loan programs. *Average indebtedness per student:* $20,770. *Average need-based loan:* Freshmen: $3881; Undergraduates: $5114. *Parent loans:* $1,670,164 (73% need-based, 27% non-need-based). *Programs:* Federal Direct (Subsidized and Unsubsidized Stafford, PLUS), Perkins, college/university.

WORK-STUDY *Federal work-study:* Total amount: $665,531; 502 jobs averaging $828. *State or other work-study/employment:* Total amount: $1,290,290 (56% need-based, 44% non-need-based). 938 part-time jobs averaging $1159.

APPLYING FOR FINANCIAL AID *Required financial aid forms:* FAFSA, institution's own form. *Financial aid deadline (priority):* 3/1. *Notification date:* Continuous beginning 3/15. Students must reply within 2 weeks of notification.

CONTACT Mr. Jeffrey A. Zahn, Director of Financial Aid, St. Norbert College, 100 Grant Street, De Pere, WI 54115-2099, 920-403-3071 or toll-free 800-236-4878. *Fax:* 920-403-3062. *E-mail:* jeff.zahn@snc.edu.

ST. OLAF COLLEGE
Northfield, MN

Tuition & fees: $26,500	Average undergraduate aid package: $19,797

ABOUT THE INSTITUTION Independent Lutheran, coed. Awards: bachelor's degrees. 48 undergraduate majors. Total enrollment: 3,046. Undergraduates: 3,046. Freshmen: 777. Both federal and institutional methodology are used as a basis for awarding need-based institutional aid.

UNDERGRADUATE EXPENSES for 2005–06 *Application fee:* $35. *Comprehensive fee:* $32,800 includes full-time tuition ($26,500) and room and board ($6300). *College room only:* $3100. *Part-time tuition:* $828 per credit hour.

FRESHMAN FINANCIAL AID (Fall 2004, est.) 592 applied for aid; of those 81% were deemed to have need. 100% of freshmen with need received aid; of those 100% had need fully met. *Average percent of need met:* 100% (excluding resources awarded to replace EFC). *Average financial aid package:* $20,529 (excluding resources awarded to replace EFC). 19% of all full-time freshmen had no need and received non-need-based gift aid.

UNDERGRADUATE FINANCIAL AID (Fall 2004, est.) 2,019 applied for aid; of those 91% were deemed to have need. 100% of undergraduates with need received aid; of those 100% had need fully met. *Average percent of need met:* 100% (excluding resources awarded to replace EFC). *Average financial aid package:* $19,797 (excluding resources awarded to replace EFC). 18% of all full-time undergraduates had no need and received non-need-based gift aid.

GIFT AID (NEED-BASED) *Total amount:* $26,340,106 (7% federal, 6% state, 82% institutional, 5% external sources). *Receiving aid:* Freshmen: 62% (482); All full-time undergraduates: 62% (1,822). *Average award:* Freshmen: $15,540; Undergraduates: $14,513. *Scholarships, grants, and awards:* Federal Pell, FSEOG, state, private, college/university gift aid from institutional funds.

GIFT AID (NON-NEED-BASED) *Total amount:* $4,278,505 (1% federal, 87% institutional, 12% external sources). *Receiving aid:* Freshmen: 25% (195); Undergraduates: 26% (783). *Average Award:* Freshmen: $6902; Undergraduates: $6545. *Scholarships, grants, and awards by category:* Academic Interests/Achievement: 1,116 awards ($7,084,750 total): general academic interests/achievements. Creative Arts/Performance: 194 awards ($425,500 total): music. Special Achievements/Activities: 219 awards ($639,500 total): community service, religious involvement. Special Characteristics: 18 awards ($196,738 total): international students.

LOANS *Student loans:* $12,620,378 (61% need-based, 39% non-need-based). 74% of past graduating class borrowed through all loan programs. *Average indebtedness per student:* $18,855. *Average need-based loan:* Freshmen: $3747; Undergraduates: $4507. *Parent loans:* $8,135,316 (100% non-need-based). *Programs:* FFEL (Subsidized and Unsubsidized Stafford, PLUS), Perkins, Federal Nursing, state, college/university.

WORK-STUDY *Federal work-study:* Total amount: $2,123,555; 1,101 jobs averaging $1929. *State or other work-study/employment:* Total amount: $1,516,441 (77% need-based, 23% non-need-based). 949 part-time jobs averaging $1598.

APPLYING FOR FINANCIAL AID *Required financial aid forms:* FAFSA, CSS Financial Aid PROFILE, noncustodial (divorced/separated) parent's statement. *Financial aid deadline (priority):* 2/1. *Notification date:* Continuous beginning 3/1. Students must reply by 5/1 or within 2 weeks of notification.

CONTACT Ms. Katharine Ruby, Director of Financial Aid, St. Olaf College, 1520 Saint Olaf Avenue, Northfield, MN 55057-1098, 507-646-3019 or toll-free 800-800-3025. *E-mail:* ruby@stolaf.edu.

SAINT PAUL'S COLLEGE
Lawrenceville, VA

Tuition & fees: $9420	Average undergraduate aid package: $9879

ABOUT THE INSTITUTION Independent Episcopal, coed. Awards: bachelor's degrees. 13 undergraduate majors. Total enrollment: 531. Undergraduates: 531. Federal methodology is used as a basis for awarding need-based institutional aid.

UNDERGRADUATE EXPENSES for 2004–05 *Application fee:* $20. *Comprehensive fee:* $14,710 includes full-time tuition ($8960), mandatory fees ($460), and room and board ($5290). *College room only:* $2380.

FRESHMAN FINANCIAL AID (Fall 2004, est.) 231 applied for aid; of those 98% were deemed to have need. 100% of freshmen with need received aid; of those 2% had need fully met. *Average percent of need met:* 80% (excluding resources awarded to replace EFC). *Average financial aid package:* $9959 (excluding resources awarded to replace EFC).

UNDERGRADUATE FINANCIAL AID (Fall 2004, est.) 556 applied for aid; of those 96% were deemed to have need. 100% of undergraduates with need received aid; of those 7% had need fully met. *Average percent of need met:* 85% (excluding resources awarded to replace EFC). *Average financial aid package:* $9879 (excluding resources awarded to replace EFC).

GIFT AID (NEED-BASED) *Total amount:* $1,760,202 (87% federal, 3% state, 4% institutional, 6% external sources). *Receiving aid:* Freshmen: 77% (181); All full-time undergraduates: 71% (412). *Average award:* Freshmen: $2198; Undergraduates: $2561. *Scholarships, grants, and awards:* Federal Pell, FSEOG, state, private, college/university gift aid from institutional funds, United Negro College Fund.

GIFT AID (NON-NEED-BASED) *Total amount:* $1,059,313 (77% state, 22% institutional, 1% external sources). *Receiving aid:* Freshmen: 72% (170); Undergraduates: 69% (403). *Scholarships, grants, and awards by category:* Academic Interests/Achievement: general academic interests/achievements. Special Achievements/Activities: 99 awards ($110,747 total): general special achievements/activities. Special Characteristics: 19 awards ($57,030 total): children of faculty/staff, children of union members/company employees. *ROTC:* Army.

LOANS *Student loans:* $1,801,473 (99% need-based, 1% non-need-based). 75% of past graduating class borrowed through all loan programs. *Average indebtedness per student:* $10,783. *Average need-based loan:* Freshmen: $2355; Undergraduates: $2875. *Parent loans:* $491,405 (100% need-based). *Programs:* Federal Direct (Subsidized and Unsubsidized Stafford, PLUS), Perkins.

WORK-STUDY *Federal work-study:* Total amount: $331,599; 254 jobs averaging $1306.

ATHLETIC AWARDS *Total amount:* $165,961 (100% non-need-based).

APPLYING FOR FINANCIAL AID *Required financial aid forms:* FAFSA, state aid form. *Financial aid deadline:* Continuous. *Notification date:* Continuous beginning 1/15. Students must reply by 7/1 or within 4 weeks of notification.

CONTACT Office of Financial Aid, Saint Paul's College, 115 College Drive, Lawrenceville, VA 23868-1202, 434-848-6495 or toll-free 800-678-7071. *Fax:* 434-848-6498. *E-mail:* aid@saintpauls.edu.

ST. PETERSBURG THEOLOGICAL SEMINARY
St. Petersburg, FL

CONTACT Financial Aid Office, St. Petersburg Theological Seminary, 10830 Navajo Drive, St. Petersburg, FL 33708, 727-399-0276.

SAINT PETER'S COLLEGE
Jersey City, NJ

ABOUT THE INSTITUTION Independent Roman Catholic (Jesuit), coed. Awards: associate, bachelor's, and master's degrees. 46 undergraduate majors. Total enrollment: 3,282. Undergraduates: 2,000.

GIFT AID (NEED-BASED) *Scholarships, grants, and awards:* Federal Pell, FSEOG, state, private, college/university gift aid from institutional funds.

GIFT AID (NON-NEED-BASED) *Scholarships, grants, and awards by category: Academic Interests/Achievement:* general academic interests/achievements. *Special Achievements/Activities:* leadership. *Special Characteristics:* children of faculty/staff, general special characteristics, relatives of clergy, religious affiliation.

LOANS *Programs:* FFEL (Subsidized and Unsubsidized Stafford, PLUS), Perkins, state.

APPLYING FOR FINANCIAL AID *Required financial aid form:* FAFSA.

CONTACT Director of Financial Aid, Saint Peter's College, 2641 Kennedy Boulevard, Jersey City, NJ 07306, 201-915-4929 or toll-free 888-SPC-9933. *Fax:* 201-434-6878.

ST. THOMAS AQUINAS COLLEGE
Sparkill, NY

CONTACT Margaret McGrail, Director of Financial Aid, St. Thomas Aquinas College, 125 Route 340, Sparkill, NY 10976, 914-398-4097 or toll-free 800-999-STAC.

ST. THOMAS UNIVERSITY
Miami Gardens, FL

Tuition & fees: $17,010	Average undergraduate aid package: $11,270

ABOUT THE INSTITUTION Independent Roman Catholic, coed. Awards: bachelor's, master's, and first professional degrees and post-bachelor's and post-master's certificates. 28 undergraduate majors. Total enrollment: 2,630. Undergraduates: 1,169. Freshmen: 192. Federal methodology is used as a basis for awarding need-based institutional aid.

UNDERGRADUATE EXPENSES for 2004–05 *Application fee:* $40. *Comprehensive fee:* $27,730 includes full-time tuition ($17,010) and room and board ($10,720). Room and board charges vary according to board plan and housing facility. *Part-time tuition:* $567 per credit. *Payment plan:* Installment.

FRESHMAN FINANCIAL AID (Fall 2004, est.) 160 applied for aid; of those 90% were deemed to have need. 100% of freshmen with need received aid. *Average percent of need met:* 80% (excluding resources awarded to replace EFC). *Average financial aid package:* $13,670 (excluding resources awarded to replace EFC). 19% of all full-time freshmen had no need and received non-need-based gift aid.

UNDERGRADUATE FINANCIAL AID (Fall 2004, est.) 884 applied for aid; of those 83% were deemed to have need. 100% of undergraduates with need

received aid. *Average percent of need met:* 66% (excluding resources awarded to replace EFC). *Average financial aid package:* $11,270 (excluding resources awarded to replace EFC). 14% of all full-time undergraduates had no need and received non-need-based gift aid.

GIFT AID (NEED-BASED) *Total amount:* $6,125,520 (29% federal, 6% state, 64% institutional, 1% external sources). *Receiving aid:* Freshmen: 65% (124); All full-time undergraduates: 54% (587). *Average award:* Freshmen: $1300; Undergraduates: $1100. *Scholarships, grants, and awards:* Federal Pell, FSEOG, state, private, college/university gift aid from institutional funds.

GIFT AID (NON-NEED-BASED) *Total amount:* $1,825,318 (100% state). *Average Award:* Freshmen: $6500; Undergraduates: $6100. *Scholarships, grants, and awards by category: Academic Interests/Achievement:* 857 awards ($3,872,588 total): general academic interests/achievements. *Tuition waivers:* Full or partial for minority students, children of alumni, employees or children of employees. *ROTC:* Army cooperative, Air Force cooperative.

LOANS *Student loans:* $7,327,361 (52% need-based, 48% non-need-based). 52% of past graduating class borrowed through all loan programs. *Average indebtedness per student:* $12,000. *Average need-based loan:* Freshmen: $3040; Undergraduates: $3424. *Parent loans:* $640,643 (100% need-based). *Programs:* FFEL (Subsidized and Unsubsidized Stafford, PLUS), Perkins.

WORK-STUDY *Federal work-study:* Total amount: $421,553; 227 jobs averaging $2325. *State or other work-study/employment:* 47 part-time jobs averaging $3277.

ATHLETIC AWARDS *Total amount:* $671,589 (100% need-based).

APPLYING FOR FINANCIAL AID *Required financial aid forms:* FAFSA, state aid form. *Financial aid deadline (priority):* 4/1. *Notification date:* Continuous beginning 3/1. Students must reply within 2 weeks of notification.

CONTACT Ms. Anh Do, Director of Financial Aid, St. Thomas University, 16400 Northwest 32nd Avenue, Miami, FL 33054-6459, 305-628-6547 or toll-free 800-367-9010. *Fax:* 305-628-6754. *E-mail:* ado@stu.edu.

SAINT VINCENT COLLEGE
Latrobe, PA

Tuition & fees: $20,822	Average undergraduate aid package: $16,118

ABOUT THE INSTITUTION Independent Roman Catholic, coed. Awards: bachelor's and master's degrees and post-bachelor's certificates. 43 undergraduate majors. Total enrollment: 1,490. Undergraduates: 1,409. Freshmen: 332. Federal methodology is used as a basis for awarding need-based institutional aid.

UNDERGRADUATE EXPENSES for 2004–05 *Application fee:* $25. *Comprehensive fee:* $27,246 includes full-time tuition ($20,312), mandatory fees ($510), and room and board ($6424). *College room only:* $3204. Room and board charges vary according to student level. *Part-time tuition:* $635 per credit hour. *Part-time fees:* $45 per term. *Payment plan:* Installment.

FRESHMAN FINANCIAL AID (Fall 2004, est.) 329 applied for aid; of those 86% were deemed to have need. 100% of freshmen with need received aid; of those 18% had need fully met. *Average percent of need met:* 87% (excluding resources awarded to replace EFC). *Average financial aid package:* $14,065 (excluding resources awarded to replace EFC). 14% of all full-time freshmen had no need and received non-need-based gift aid.

UNDERGRADUATE FINANCIAL AID (Fall 2004, est.) 1,214 applied for aid; of those 84% were deemed to have need. 100% of undergraduates with need received aid; of those 17% had need fully met. *Average percent of need met:* 77% (excluding resources awarded to replace EFC). *Average financial aid package:* $16,118 (excluding resources awarded to replace EFC). 14% of all full-time undergraduates had no need and received non-need-based gift aid.

GIFT AID (NEED-BASED) *Total amount:* $11,333,016 (9% federal, 17% state, 72% institutional, 2% external sources). *Receiving aid:* Freshmen: 84% (282); All full-time undergraduates: 82% (1,025). *Average award:* Freshmen: $11,129; Undergraduates: $10,967. *Scholarships, grants, and awards:* Federal Pell, FSEOG, state, private, college/university gift aid from institutional funds, United Negro College Fund.

GIFT AID (NON-NEED-BASED) *Total amount:* $1,679,660 (95% institutional, 5% external sources). *Receiving aid:* Freshmen: 26% (87); Undergraduates: 22% (270). *Average Award:* Freshmen: $8842; Undergraduates: $7071. *Scholarships, grants, and awards by category: Academic Interests/Achievement:* 769 awards ($4,615,326 total): biological sciences, business, computer science, general academic interests/achievements, mathematics, physical sciences, social sciences. *Creative Arts/Performance:* 2 awards ($6500 total): music. *Special Achievements/Activities:* 831 awards ($1,291,000 total): leadership. *Special*

Characteristics: 76 awards ($248,916 total): international students, members of minority groups. *Tuition waivers:* Full or partial for employees or children of employees, senior citizens. *ROTC:* Air Force cooperative.

LOANS *Student loans:* $4,492,111 (72% need-based, 28% non-need-based). *Average need-based loan:* Freshmen: $1817; Undergraduates: $3086. *Parent loans:* $1,580,716 (100% non-need-based). *Programs:* FFEL (Subsidized and Unsubsidized Stafford, PLUS), Perkins.

WORK-STUDY *Federal work-study:* Total amount: $687,443; 372 jobs averaging $1840. *State or other work-study/employment:* Total amount: $58,842 (100% need-based). 448 part-time jobs averaging $1524.

ATHLETIC AWARDS *Total amount:* $1,311,087 (60% need-based, 40% non-need-based).

APPLYING FOR FINANCIAL AID *Required financial aid forms:* FAFSA, state aid form. *Financial aid deadline:* 5/1 (priority: 3/1). *Notification date:* Continuous. Students must reply within 2 weeks of notification.

CONTACT Thomas Ball, Director of Financial Aid, Saint Vincent College, 300 Fraser Purchase Road, Latrobe, PA 15650, 724-537-4540 or toll-free 800-782-5549. *Fax:* 724-532-5069. *E-mail:* admission@stvincent.edu.

SAINT XAVIER UNIVERSITY
Chicago, IL

Tuition & fees: $17,330	Average undergraduate aid package: $14,910

ABOUT THE INSTITUTION Independent Roman Catholic, coed. Awards: bachelor's and master's degrees and post-bachelor's and post-master's certificates. 39 undergraduate majors. Total enrollment: 5,722. Undergraduates: 3,075. Freshmen: 414. Federal methodology is used as a basis for awarding need-based institutional aid.

UNDERGRADUATE EXPENSES for 2004–05 *Application fee:* $25. *Comprehensive fee:* $24,054 includes full-time tuition ($17,150), mandatory fees ($180), and room and board ($6724). *College room only:* $3836. Full-time tuition and fees vary according to course load. Room and board charges vary according to board plan. *Part-time tuition:* $575 per credit hour. Part-time tuition and fees vary according to course load. *Payment plan:* Installment.

GIFT AID (NEED-BASED) *Total amount:* $15,440,226 (23% federal, 24% state, 53% institutional). *Receiving aid:* Freshmen: 82% (340); All full-time undergraduates: 82% (1,882). *Average award:* Freshmen: $10,853; Undergraduates: $8610. *Scholarships, grants, and awards:* Federal Pell, FSEOG, state, private, college/university gift aid from institutional funds.

GIFT AID (NON-NEED-BASED) *Total amount:* $2,386,956 (2% state, 81% institutional, 17% external sources). *Receiving aid:* Freshmen: 79% (326); Undergraduates: 77% (1,773). *Average Award:* Freshmen: $6041; Undergraduates: $4287. *Scholarships, grants, and awards by category: Academic Interests/Achievement:* 2,289 awards ($7,248,562 total): general academic interests/achievements. *Creative Arts/Performance:* 60 awards ($203,149 total): music. *Special Achievements/Activities:* leadership. *Special Characteristics:* 55 awards ($607,218 total): children of faculty/staff. *Tuition waivers:* Full or partial for employees or children of employees, senior citizens. *ROTC:* Air Force cooperative.

LOANS *Student loans:* $15,337,565 (90% need-based, 10% non-need-based). 72% of past graduating class borrowed through all loan programs. *Average indebtedness per student:* $19,134. *Average need-based loan:* Freshmen: $2714; Undergraduates: $3930. *Parent loans:* $1,994,519 (34% need-based, 66% non-need-based). *Programs:* FFEL (Subsidized and Unsubsidized Stafford, PLUS), Perkins.

ATHLETIC AWARDS *Total amount:* $1,451,362 (69% need-based, 31% non-need-based).

APPLYING FOR FINANCIAL AID *Required financial aid form:* FAFSA. *Financial aid deadline (priority):* 3/1. *Notification date:* Continuous beginning 2/15. Students must reply by 5/1 or within 2 weeks of notification.

CONTACT Ms. Susan Swisher, Director of Financial Aid, Saint Xavier University, 3700 West 103rd Street, Chicago, IL 60655-3105, 773-298-3070 or toll-free 800-462-9288. *Fax:* 773-779-3084. *E-mail:* swisher@sxu.edu.

SALEM COLLEGE
Winston-Salem, NC

CONTACT Julie Setzer, Director of Financial Aid, Salem College, PO Box 10548, Winston-Salem, NC 27108, 336-721-2808 or toll-free 800-327-2536. *Fax:* 336-917-5584.

SALEM INTERNATIONAL UNIVERSITY
Salem, WV

ABOUT THE INSTITUTION Independent, coed. Awards: associate, bachelor's, and master's degrees. 27 undergraduate majors. Total enrollment: 568. Undergraduates: 443. Freshmen: 51.

GIFT AID (NEED-BASED) *Scholarships, grants, and awards:* Federal Pell, FSEOG, state, private, college/university gift aid from institutional funds.

GIFT AID (NON-NEED-BASED) *Scholarships, grants, and awards by category: Academic Interests/Achievement:* agriculture, biological sciences, business, communication, computer science, education, general academic interests/achievements, humanities. *Creative Arts/Performance:* cinema/film/broadcasting. *Special Characteristics:* out-of-state students, religious affiliation.

LOANS *Programs:* FFEL (Subsidized and Unsubsidized Stafford, PLUS), Perkins.

WORK-STUDY *Federal work-study:* Total amount: $353,671; 194 jobs averaging $1823. *State or other work-study/employment:* Total amount: $22,355 (100% non-need-based). 15 part-time jobs averaging $1490.

APPLYING FOR FINANCIAL AID *Required financial aid form:* FAFSA.

CONTACT Mrs. Charlotte Lake, Director of Financial Aid, Salem International University, 223 West Main Street, Salem, WV 26426-0500, 304-782-5303 or toll-free 800-283-4562. *Fax:* 304-782-5559. *E-mail:* lake@salemiu.edu.

SALEM STATE COLLEGE
Salem, MA

Tuition & fees (MA res): $5284	Average undergraduate aid package: $6512

ABOUT THE INSTITUTION State-supported, coed. Awards: bachelor's and master's degrees and post-master's certificates. 60 undergraduate majors. Total enrollment: 9,347. Undergraduates: 6,771. Freshmen: 1,058. Federal methodology is used as a basis for awarding need-based institutional aid.

UNDERGRADUATE EXPENSES for 2004–05 *Application fee:* $25. *Tuition, state resident:* full-time $910; part-time $37.92 per credit. *Tuition, nonresident:* full-time $7050; part-time $293.75 per credit. *Required fees:* full-time $4,374; $182.24 per credit or $13.50. Full-time tuition and fees vary according to class time. Part-time tuition and fees vary according to class time. *College room and board:* $7350. Room and board charges vary according to board plan and housing facility. *Payment plans:* Installment, deferred payment.

FRESHMAN FINANCIAL AID (Fall 2004, est.) 751 applied for aid; of those 77% were deemed to have need. 98% of freshmen with need received aid; of those 3% had need fully met. *Average percent of need met:* 59% (excluding resources awarded to replace EFC). *Average financial aid package:* $6084 (excluding resources awarded to replace EFC).

UNDERGRADUATE FINANCIAL AID (Fall 2004, est.) 2,950 applied for aid; of those 80% were deemed to have need. 99% of undergraduates with need received aid; of those 4% had need fully met. *Average percent of need met:* 66% (excluding resources awarded to replace EFC). *Average financial aid package:* $6512 (excluding resources awarded to replace EFC).

GIFT AID (NEED-BASED) *Total amount:* $7,899,687 (51% federal, 41% state, 2% institutional, 6% external sources). *Receiving aid:* Freshmen: 45% (458); All full-time undergraduates: 37% (1,806). *Average award:* Freshmen: $8054; Undergraduates: $8568. *Scholarships, grants, and awards:* Federal Pell, FSEOG, state, private, college/university gift aid from institutional funds.

GIFT AID (NON-NEED-BASED) *Scholarships, grants, and awards by category: Academic Interests/Achievement:* general academic interests/achievements. *Creative Arts/Performance:* applied art and design, art/fine arts, creative writing, dance, music, performing arts, theater/drama. *Special Achievements/Activities:* general special achievements/activities, memberships. *Special Characteristics:* adult students, children and siblings of alumni, children of faculty/staff, children of public servants, children of union members/company employees, first-generation college students, general special characteristics, members of minority groups, public servants, veterans, veterans' children. *Tuition waivers:* Full or partial for employees or children of employees, senior citizens.

LOANS *Student loans:* $12,493,932 (89% need-based, 11% non-need-based). *Average need-based loan:* Freshmen: $8430; Undergraduates: $8855. *Parent loans:* $2,019,791 (100% non-need-based). *Programs:* Federal Direct (Subsidized and Unsubsidized Stafford), FFEL (PLUS), Perkins, Federal Nursing, state, TERI Loans, MEFA Loans, CitiAssist Loans, Signature Loans.

WORK-STUDY *Federal work-study:* Total amount: $381,822; 726 jobs averaging $2000.

APPLYING FOR FINANCIAL AID *Required financial aid form:* FAFSA. *Financial aid deadline (priority):* 4/1. *Notification date:* Continuous beginning 4/1. Students must reply within 2 weeks of notification.

CONTACT Mary Benda, Director of Financial Aid, Salem State College, 352 Lafayette Street, Salem, MA 01970-5353, 978-542-6139. *Fax:* 978-542-6876.

SALISBURY UNIVERSITY
Salisbury, MD

Tuition & fees (MD res): $5976	Average undergraduate aid package: $5839

ABOUT THE INSTITUTION State-supported, coed. Awards: bachelor's and master's degrees. 42 undergraduate majors. Total enrollment: 6,942. Undergraduates: 6,366. Freshmen: 986. Federal methodology is used as a basis for awarding need-based institutional aid.

UNDERGRADUATE EXPENSES for 2004–05 *Application fee:* $45. *Tuition, state resident:* full-time $4546; part-time $188 per credit hour. *Tuition, nonresident:* full-time $12,124; part-time $487 per credit hour. *Required fees:* full-time $1430; $8 per credit hour. *College room and board:* $7050; *room only:* $3450. Room and board charges vary according to board plan and housing facility. *Payment plan:* Installment.

FRESHMAN FINANCIAL AID (Fall 2003) 621 applied for aid; of those 68% were deemed to have need. 100% of freshmen with need received aid; of those 11% had need fully met. *Average percent of need met:* 54% (excluding resources awarded to replace EFC). *Average financial aid package:* $5036 (excluding resources awarded to replace EFC). 15% of all full-time freshmen had no need and received non-need-based gift aid.

UNDERGRADUATE FINANCIAL AID (Fall 2003) 3,268 applied for aid; of those 72% were deemed to have need. 100% of undergraduates with need received aid; of those 19% had need fully met. *Average percent of need met:* 58% (excluding resources awarded to replace EFC). *Average financial aid package:* $5839 (excluding resources awarded to replace EFC). 6% of all full-time undergraduates had no need and received non-need-based gift aid.

GIFT AID (NEED-BASED) *Total amount:* $5,023,288 (54% federal, 33% state, 11% institutional, 2% external sources). *Receiving aid:* Freshmen: 26% (248); All full-time undergraduates: 18% (949). *Average award:* Freshmen: $4437; Undergraduates: $5418. *Scholarships, grants, and awards:* Federal Pell, FSEOG, state, college/university gift aid from institutional funds.

GIFT AID (NON-NEED-BASED) *Total amount:* $4,270,436 (57% state, 23% institutional, 20% external sources). *Receiving aid:* Freshmen: 17% (161); Undergraduates: 12% (656). *Average Award:* Freshmen: $3040; Undergraduates: $8128. *Scholarships, grants, and awards by category:* Academic Interests/Achievement: $867,987 total: biological sciences, business, communication, computer science, education, English, foreign languages, general academic interests/achievements, health fields, humanities, mathematics, physical sciences, premedicine, social sciences. *Tuition waivers:* Full or partial for employees or children of employees, senior citizens. *ROTC:* Army cooperative.

LOANS *Student loans:* $14,536,637 (49% need-based, 51% non-need-based). 53% of past graduating class borrowed through all loan programs. *Average indebtedness per student:* $16,557. *Average need-based loan:* Freshmen: $2436; Undergraduates: $3587. *Parent loans:* $10,836,809 (100% non-need-based). *Programs:* Federal Direct (Subsidized and Unsubsidized Stafford, PLUS), Perkins.

WORK-STUDY *Federal work-study:* Total amount: $152,908; 81 jobs averaging $1887. *State or other work-study/employment:* Part-time jobs available.

APPLYING FOR FINANCIAL AID *Required financial aid form:* FAFSA. *Financial aid deadline (priority):* 2/1. *Notification date:* Continuous beginning 4/1. Students must reply by 5/1.

CONTACT Ms. Beverly N. Horner, Director of Financial Aid, Salisbury University, 1101 Camden Avenue, Salisbury, MD 21801-6837, 410-543-6025 or toll-free 888-543-0148. *E-mail:* bnhorner@salisbury.edu.

SALVE REGINA UNIVERSITY
Newport, RI

Tuition & fees: $22,200	Average undergraduate aid package: $16,444

ABOUT THE INSTITUTION Independent Roman Catholic, coed. Awards: associate, bachelor's, master's, and doctoral degrees and post-bachelor's and post-master's certificates. 42 undergraduate majors. Total enrollment: 2,479. Undergraduates: 2,069. Freshmen: 558. Both federal and institutional methodology are used as a basis for awarding need-based institutional aid.

UNDERGRADUATE EXPENSES for 2004–05 *Application fee:* $40. *Comprehensive fee:* $31,200 includes full-time tuition ($21,750), mandatory fees ($450), and room and board ($9000). Room and board charges vary according to board plan. *Part-time tuition:* $725 per credit. *Part-time fees:* $40 per term. Part-time tuition and fees vary according to course load. *Payment plan:* Installment.

GIFT AID (NEED-BASED) *Total amount:* $13,511,974 (8% federal, 2% state, 87% institutional, 3% external sources). *Receiving aid:* Freshmen: 67% (374); All full-time undergraduates: 63% (1,229). *Average award:* Freshmen: $12,778; Undergraduates: $11,292. *Scholarships, grants, and awards:* Federal Pell, FSEOG, state, private, college/university gift aid from institutional funds.

GIFT AID (NON-NEED-BASED) *Total amount:* $1,010,285 (1% state, 85% institutional, 14% external sources). *Receiving aid:* Freshmen: 3% (16); Undergraduates: 2% (48). *Average Award:* Freshmen: $11,364; Undergraduates: $11,435. *Scholarships, grants, and awards by category:* Academic Interests/Achievement: 496 awards ($3,003,400 total): general academic interests/achievements. *Tuition waivers:* Full or partial for employees or children of employees. *ROTC:* Army cooperative.

LOANS *Student loans:* $11,157,454 (68% need-based, 32% non-need-based). 82% of past graduating class borrowed through all loan programs. *Average indebtedness per student:* $25,485. *Average need-based loan:* Freshmen: $3676; Undergraduates: $5187. *Parent loans:* $5,175,638 (37% need-based, 63% non-need-based). *Programs:* FFEL (Subsidized and Unsubsidized Stafford, PLUS), Perkins, Federal Nursing, college/university, alternative loans.

APPLYING FOR FINANCIAL AID *Required financial aid forms:* FAFSA, CSS Financial Aid PROFILE, noncustodial (divorced/separated) parent's statement, business/farm supplement. *Financial aid deadline (priority):* 3/1. *Notification date:* Continuous beginning 2/15. Students must reply by 5/1 or within 2 weeks of notification.

CONTACT Aida Mirante, Director of Financial Aid, Salve Regina University, 100 Ochre Point Avenue, Newport, RI 02840-4192, 401-341-2901 or toll-free 888-GO SALVE. *Fax:* 401-341-2928. *E-mail:* srufa@salve.edu.

SAMFORD UNIVERSITY
Birmingham, AL

Tuition & fees: $13,944	Average undergraduate aid package: $10,608

ABOUT THE INSTITUTION Independent Baptist, coed. Awards: associate, bachelor's, master's, doctoral, and first professional degrees and post-master's certificates. 69 undergraduate majors. Total enrollment: 4,416. Undergraduates: 2,856. Freshmen: 671. Federal methodology is used as a basis for awarding need-based institutional aid.

UNDERGRADUATE EXPENSES for 2004–05 *Application fee:* $25. *Comprehensive fee:* $19,450 includes full-time tuition ($13,944) and room and board ($5506). *College room only:* $2682. Full-time tuition and fees vary according to course load. Room and board charges vary according to board plan and housing facility. *Part-time tuition:* $463 per semester hour. Part-time tuition and fees vary according to course load.

FRESHMAN FINANCIAL AID (Fall 2003) 453 applied for aid; of those 65% were deemed to have need. 99% of freshmen with need received aid; of those 25% had need fully met. *Average percent of need met:* 69% (excluding resources awarded to replace EFC). *Average financial aid package:* $10,272 (excluding resources awarded to replace EFC). 23% of all full-time freshmen had no need and received non-need-based gift aid.

UNDERGRADUATE FINANCIAL AID (Fall 2003) 1,499 applied for aid; of those 74% were deemed to have need. 100% of undergraduates with need received aid; of those 23% had need fully met. *Average percent of need met:* 69% (excluding resources awarded to replace EFC). *Average financial aid package:* $10,608 (excluding resources awarded to replace EFC). 22% of all full-time undergraduates had no need and received non-need-based gift aid.

GIFT AID (NEED-BASED) *Total amount:* $5,797,372 (21% federal, 2% state, 62% institutional, 15% external sources). *Receiving aid:* Freshmen: 41% (277); All full-time undergraduates: 37% (995). *Average award:* Freshmen: $6605; Undergraduates: $5757. *Scholarships, grants, and awards:* Federal Pell, FSEOG, state, private, college/university gift aid from institutional funds.

GIFT AID (NON-NEED-BASED) *Total amount:* $2,929,756 (2% state, 74% institutional, 24% external sources). *Average Award:* Freshmen: $2801; Undergraduates: $3661. *Scholarships, grants, and awards by category:* Academic Interests/Achievement: 330 awards ($1,065,977 total): general academic interests/achievements. Creative Arts/Performance: 32 awards ($57,075 total): music. Special Characteristics: 139 awards ($811,089 total): children of faculty/staff, relatives of clergy. *Tuition waivers:* Full or partial for employees or children of employees. *ROTC:* Army cooperative, Air Force.

LOANS *Student loans:* $6,670,521 (52% need-based, 48% non-need-based). 49% of past graduating class borrowed through all loan programs. *Average indebtedness per student:* $15,959. *Average need-based loan:* Freshmen: $2351; Undergraduates: $3358. *Parent loans:* $5,763,144 (100% non-need-based). *Programs:* FFEL (Subsidized and Unsubsidized Stafford, PLUS), Perkins, college/university.

WORK-STUDY *Federal work-study:* Total amount: $837,389; 400 jobs averaging $1800. *State or other work-study/employment:* Total amount: $345,374 (53% need-based, 47% non-need-based). 750 part-time jobs averaging $1800.

ATHLETIC AWARDS *Total amount:* $3,118,855 (29% need-based, 71% non-need-based).

APPLYING FOR FINANCIAL AID *Required financial aid form:* FAFSA. *Financial aid deadline (priority):* 3/1. *Notification date:* 5/1.

CONTACT Ms. Ann P. Campbell, Director of Financial Aid, Samford University, 800 Lakeshore Drive, Birmingham, AL 35229-0002, 205-726-2905 or toll-free 800-888-7218. *Fax:* 205-726-2738. *E-mail:* apcampbe@samford.edu.

SAM HOUSTON STATE UNIVERSITY
Huntsville, TX

Tuition & fees (TX res): $4260	Average undergraduate aid package: $14,534

ABOUT THE INSTITUTION State-supported, coed. Awards: bachelor's, master's, and doctoral degrees. 96 undergraduate majors. Total enrollment: 14,371. Undergraduates: 12,297. Freshmen: 2,134. Federal methodology is used as a basis for awarding need-based institutional aid.

UNDERGRADUATE EXPENSES for 2004–05 *Application fee:* $35. *Tuition, state resident:* full-time $3030; part-time $101 per hour. *Tuition, nonresident:* full-time $10,770; part-time $359 per hour. *Required fees:* full-time $1230; $444 per term part-time. Full-time tuition and fees vary according to course load. Part-time tuition and fees vary according to course load. *College room and board:* $4336; *room only:* $2224. Room and board charges vary according to board plan and housing facility. *Payment plan:* Installment.

FRESHMAN FINANCIAL AID (Fall 2004, est.) 134 applied for aid; of those 100% were deemed to have need. 100% of freshmen with need received aid; of those 16% had need fully met. *Average percent of need met:* 85% (excluding resources awarded to replace EFC). *Average financial aid package:* $13,407 (excluding resources awarded to replace EFC). 31% of all full-time freshmen had no need and received non-need-based gift aid.

UNDERGRADUATE FINANCIAL AID (Fall 2004, est.) 493 applied for aid; of those 100% were deemed to have need. 99% of undergraduates with need received aid; of those 17% had need fully met. *Average percent of need met:* 83% (excluding resources awarded to replace EFC). *Average financial aid package:* $14,534 (excluding resources awarded to replace EFC). 55% of all full-time undergraduates had no need and received non-need-based gift aid.

GIFT AID (NEED-BASED) *Total amount:* $1,565,671 (47% federal, 1% state, 52% institutional). *Receiving aid:* Freshmen: 50% (95); All full-time undergraduates: 38% (285). *Average award:* Freshmen: $3672; Undergraduates: $4016. *Scholarships, grants, and awards:* Federal Pell, FSEOG, state, private, college/university gift aid from institutional funds.

GIFT AID (NON-NEED-BASED) *Total amount:* $4,457,909 (4% state, 86% institutional, 10% external sources). *Receiving aid:* Freshmen: 68% (130); Undergraduates: 62% (468). *Average Award:* Freshmen: $5818; Undergraduates:* $6297. *Scholarships, grants, and awards by category:* Academic Interests/Achievement: agriculture, biological sciences, business, communication, computer science, education, engineering/technologies, English, foreign languages, general academic interests/achievements, home economics, humanities, library science, mathematics, military science, physical sciences, social sciences. Special Achievements/Activities: cheerleading/drum major, general special achievements/activities, leadership, rodeo. Special Characteristics: general special characteristics, handicapped students. *ROTC:* Army.

LOANS *Student loans:* $3,502,794 (48% need-based, 52% non-need-based). 94% of past graduating class borrowed through all loan programs. *Average indebtedness per student:* $26,340. *Average need-based loan:* Freshmen: $3512; Undergraduates: $4552. *Parent loans:* $831,132 (100% non-need-based). *Programs:* FFEL (Subsidized and Unsubsidized Stafford, PLUS), Perkins.

WORK-STUDY *Federal work-study:* Total amount: $162,935; jobs available. *State or other work-study/employment:* Total amount: $69,596 (26% need-based, 74% non-need-based). Part-time jobs available.

ATHLETIC AWARDS *Total amount:* $895,006 (100% non-need-based).

APPLYING FOR FINANCIAL AID *Required financial aid forms:* FAFSA, institution's own form. *Financial aid deadline (priority):* 2/15. *Notification date:* Continuous beginning 12/1. Students must reply within 3 weeks of notification.

CONTACT Patricia Mabry, Director of Financial Aid, Sam Houston State University, 1903 University Avenue, Estill Building, 2nd Floor, Huntsville, TX 77341, 936-294-1724 or toll-free 866-232-7528 Ext. 1828.

SAMUEL MERRITT COLLEGE
Oakland, CA

CONTACT Anne-Marie Larroque, Assistant Director, Financial Aid Office, Samuel Merritt College, 450 30th Street, Room 2710, Oakland, CA 94609, 510-869-6131 or toll-free 800-607-MERRITT. *Fax:* 510-869-6683. *E-mail:* alarroque@samuelmerritt.edu.

SAN DIEGO STATE UNIVERSITY
San Diego, CA

ABOUT THE INSTITUTION State-supported, coed. Awards: bachelor's, master's, and doctoral degrees and post-bachelor's and post-master's certificates. 125 undergraduate majors. Total enrollment: 32,936. Undergraduates: 26,853. Freshmen: 4,140.

GIFT AID (NEED-BASED) *Scholarships, grants, and awards:* Federal Pell, FSEOG, state, private, college/university gift aid from institutional funds, Federal Nursing.

GIFT AID (NON-NEED-BASED) *Scholarships, grants, and awards by category:* Academic Interests/Achievement: general academic interests/achievements. Creative Arts/Performance: art/fine arts, creative writing, dance, journalism/publications, music, performing arts, theater/drama. Special Achievements/Activities: community service, leadership. Special Characteristics: children and siblings of alumni, children of faculty/staff, children of public servants, handicapped students, local/state students.

LOANS *Programs:* Federal Direct (Subsidized and Unsubsidized Stafford, PLUS), Perkins, college/university.

WORK-STUDY *Federal work-study:* Total amount: $2,919,000; jobs available.

APPLYING FOR FINANCIAL AID *Required financial aid forms:* FAFSA, state aid form.

CONTACT Ms. Chrys Dutton, Director of Financial Aid and Scholarships, San Diego State University, 5500 Campanile Drive, SSW-3605, San Diego, CA 92182-7436, 619-594-6323.

SAN FRANCISCO ART INSTITUTE
San Francisco, CA

ABOUT THE INSTITUTION Independent, coed. Awards: bachelor's and master's degrees and post-bachelor's certificates. 9 undergraduate majors. Total enrollment: 655. Undergraduates: 407. Freshmen: 39.

GIFT AID (NEED-BASED) *Scholarships, grants, and awards:* Federal Pell, FSEOG, state, college/university gift aid from institutional funds.

GIFT AID (NON-NEED-BASED) *Scholarships, grants, and awards by category:* Creative Arts/Performance: art/fine arts.

LOANS *Programs:* Federal Direct (Subsidized and Unsubsidized Stafford, PLUS), alternative loans.

WORK-STUDY Federal work-study jobs available.

APPLYING FOR FINANCIAL AID *Required financial aid form:* FAFSA.

CONTACT Director of Financial Aid, San Francisco Art Institute, 800 Chestnut Street, San Francisco, CA 94133-2299, 415-749-4560 or toll-free 800-345-SFAI. *Fax:* 415-351-3503.

SAN FRANCISCO CONSERVATORY OF MUSIC
San Francisco, CA

ABOUT THE INSTITUTION Independent, coed. Awards: bachelor's and master's degrees. 7 undergraduate majors. Total enrollment: 287. Undergraduates: 158.

GIFT AID (NEED-BASED) *Scholarships, grants, and awards:* Federal Pell, FSEOG, state, private, college/university gift aid from institutional funds.

GIFT AID (NON-NEED-BASED) *Scholarships, grants, and awards by category:* Creative Arts/Performance: music.

LOANS *Programs:* FFEL (Subsidized and Unsubsidized Stafford, PLUS), Perkins.

WORK-STUDY *Federal work-study:* Total amount: $70,000; 34 jobs averaging $2058. *State or other work-study/employment:* Total amount: $71,000 (43% need-based, 57% non-need-based). 33 part-time jobs averaging $2151.

APPLYING FOR FINANCIAL AID *Required financial aid forms:* FAFSA, institution's own form.

CONTACT Doris Howard, Financial Aid Manager, San Francisco Conservatory of Music, 1201 Ortega Street, San Francisco, CA 94122-4411, 415-759-3414. *Fax:* 415-759-3499.

SAN FRANCISCO STATE UNIVERSITY
San Francisco, CA

Tuition & fees (CA res): $3066	Average undergraduate aid package: $8638

ABOUT THE INSTITUTION State-supported, coed. Awards: bachelor's, master's, and doctoral degrees and post-bachelor's certificates. 91 undergraduate majors. Total enrollment: 28,804. Undergraduates: 22,291. Freshmen: 2,895. Federal methodology is used as a basis for awarding need-based institutional aid.

UNDERGRADUATE EXPENSES for 2005–06 *Application fee:* $55. *Tuition, state resident:* full-time $0. *Tuition, nonresident:* full-time $12,690. *College room and board:* $8870; *room only:* $5640.

FRESHMAN FINANCIAL AID (Fall 2003) 1502 applied for aid; of those 77% were deemed to have need. 91% of freshmen with need received aid; of those 21% had need fully met. *Average percent of need met:* 70% (excluding resources awarded to replace EFC). *Average financial aid package:* $8377 (excluding resources awarded to replace EFC). 1% of all full-time freshmen had no need and received non-need-based gift aid.

UNDERGRADUATE FINANCIAL AID (Fall 2003) 8,399 applied for aid; of those 91% were deemed to have need. 95% of undergraduates with need received aid; of those 15% had need fully met. *Average percent of need met:* 69% (excluding resources awarded to replace EFC). *Average financial aid package:* $8638 (excluding resources awarded to replace EFC). 1% of all full-time undergraduates had no need and received non-need-based gift aid.

GIFT AID (NEED-BASED) *Total amount:* $43,997,574 (48% federal, 43% state, 5% institutional, 4% external sources). *Receiving aid:* Freshmen: 35% (801); All full-time undergraduates: 35% (5,358). *Average award:* Freshmen: $6136; Undergraduates: $5280. *Scholarships, grants, and awards:* Federal Pell, FSEOG, state, private, college/university gift aid from institutional funds.

GIFT AID (NON-NEED-BASED) *Total amount:* $168,408 (46% federal, 54% external sources). *Receiving aid:* Freshmen: 1% (24); Undergraduates: 45. *Average Award:* Freshmen: $1062; Undergraduates: $1053. *ROTC:* Army cooperative, Naval cooperative, Air Force cooperative.

LOANS *Student loans:* $49,627,822 (88% need-based, 12% non-need-based). 44% of past graduating class borrowed through all loan programs. *Average indebtedness per student:* $16,088. *Average need-based loan:* Freshmen: $2689; Undergraduates: $4814. *Parent loans:* $12,671,904 (47% need-based, 53% non-need-based). *Programs:* Federal Direct (Subsidized and Unsubsidized Stafford), FFEL (PLUS), Perkins.

WORK-STUDY *Federal work-study:* Total amount: $1,578,397; jobs available. *State or other work-study/employment:* Part-time jobs available.

ATHLETIC AWARDS *Total amount:* $182,112 (95% need-based, 5% non-need-based).

APPLYING FOR FINANCIAL AID *Required financial aid form:* FAFSA. *Financial aid deadline (priority):* 3/3. *Notification date:* Continuous beginning 2/15. Students must reply within 3 weeks of notification.

CONTACT Associate Director of Financial Aid, San Francisco State University, 1600 Holloway Avenue, San Francisco, CA 94132-1722, 415-338-7000.

SAN JOSE STATE UNIVERSITY
San Jose, CA

Tuition & fees: N/R	Average undergraduate aid package: $8037

ABOUT THE INSTITUTION State-supported, coed. Awards: bachelor's and master's degrees. 89 undergraduate majors. Total enrollment: 29,044. Undergraduates: 21,663. Freshmen: 2,393. Federal methodology is used as a basis for awarding need-based institutional aid.

UNDERGRADUATE EXPENSES for 2004–05 *Application fee:* $55. *Tuition, nonresident:* part-time $339 per unit. *Required fees:* $983 per term part-time. Full-time tuition and fees vary according to course load. Part-time tuition and fees vary according to course load. Room and board charges vary according to board plan and housing facility. *Payment plan:* Installment.

FRESHMAN FINANCIAL AID (Fall 2003) 1265 applied for aid; of those 75% were deemed to have need. 92% of freshmen with need received aid; of those 13% had need fully met. *Average percent of need met:* 75% (excluding resources awarded to replace EFC). *Average financial aid package:* $7861 (excluding resources awarded to replace EFC). 1% of all full-time freshmen had no need and received non-need-based gift aid.

UNDERGRADUATE FINANCIAL AID (Fall 2003) 9,104 applied for aid; of those 88% were deemed to have need. 94% of undergraduates with need received aid; of those 18% had need fully met. *Average percent of need met:* 75% (excluding resources awarded to replace EFC). *Average financial aid package:* $8037 (excluding resources awarded to replace EFC). 1% of all full-time undergraduates had no need and received non-need-based gift aid.

GIFT AID (NEED-BASED) *Total amount:* $36,821,383 (49% federal, 45% state, 4% institutional, 2% external sources). *Receiving aid:* Freshmen: 39% (720); All full-time undergraduates: 30% (5,365). *Average award:* Freshmen: $5611; Undergraduates: $5286. *Scholarships, grants, and awards:* Federal Pell, FSEOG, state, private, college/university gift aid from institutional funds.

GIFT AID (NON-NEED-BASED) *Total amount:* $76,571 (30% federal, 33% state, 30% institutional, 7% external sources). *Receiving aid:* Freshmen: 2; Undergraduates: 2. *Average Award:* Freshmen: $3187; Undergraduates: $1597. *Scholarships, grants, and awards by category:* Academic Interests/Achievement: general academic interests/achievements. *Tuition waivers:* Full or partial for employees or children of employees. *ROTC:* Army, Air Force.

LOANS *Student loans:* $30,002,613 (100% need-based). 26% of past graduating class borrowed through all loan programs. *Average indebtedness per student:* $12,810. *Average need-based loan:* Freshmen: $2369; Undergraduates: $3849. *Parent loans:* $1,086,743 (56% need-based, 44% non-need-based). *Programs:* FFEL (Subsidized and Unsubsidized Stafford, PLUS), Perkins, college/university.

WORK-STUDY *Federal work-study:* Total amount: $12,718,434; 590 jobs averaging $2410.

ATHLETIC AWARDS *Total amount:* $722,625 (100% need-based).

APPLYING FOR FINANCIAL AID *Required financial aid form:* FAFSA. *Financial aid deadline (priority):* 3/2. *Notification date:* Continuous beginning 5/1.

CONTACT Colleen S. Brown, Director of Financial Aid, San Jose State University, One Washington Square, Student Services Center 200, San Jose, CA 95192-0036, 408-924-6060. *E-mail:* brownc@sjsu.edu.

SANTA CLARA UNIVERSITY
Santa Clara, CA

ABOUT THE INSTITUTION Independent Roman Catholic (Jesuit), coed. Awards: bachelor's, master's, doctoral, and first professional degrees and post-bachelor's, post-master's, and first professional certificates. 41 undergraduate majors. Total enrollment: 7,908. Undergraduates: 4,434. Freshmen: 1,172.

GIFT AID (NEED-BASED) *Scholarships, grants, and awards:* Federal Pell, FSEOG, state, private, college/university gift aid from institutional funds.

GIFT AID (NON-NEED-BASED) *Scholarships, grants, and awards by category:* Academic Interests/Achievement: business, engineering/technologies, general academic interests/achievements, military science. Creative Arts/Performance: dance, debating, music, theater/drama. Special Characteristics: children and siblings of alumni, children of faculty/staff, children with a deceased or disabled parent, handicapped students.

LOANS *Programs:* Federal Direct (Subsidized and Unsubsidized Stafford, PLUS), Perkins, alternative loans.

WORK-STUDY *Federal work-study:* Total amount: $1,065,881; 487 jobs averaging $2201.

APPLYING FOR FINANCIAL AID *Required financial aid forms:* FAFSA, CSS Financial Aid PROFILE.

CONTACT Marta I. Chaskelmann, Technical Specialist, Santa Clara University, 500 El Camino Real, Santa Clara, CA 95053, 408-551-6088. *Fax:* 408-551-6085. *E-mail:* mchaskelmann@scu.edu.

SARAH LAWRENCE COLLEGE
Bronxville, NY

Tuition & fees: $32,416	Average undergraduate aid package: $28,686

ABOUT THE INSTITUTION Independent, coed. Awards: bachelor's and master's degrees. 112 undergraduate majors. Total enrollment: 1,574. Undergraduates: 1,260. Freshmen: 329. Both federal and institutional methodology are used as a basis for awarding need-based institutional aid.

UNDERGRADUATE EXPENSES for 2004–05 *Application fee:* $60. *Comprehensive fee:* $43,854 includes full-time tuition ($31,680), mandatory fees ($736), and room and board ($11,438). *College room only:* $7238. Full-time tuition and fees vary according to course load. Room and board charges vary according to board plan. *Part-time tuition:* $1056 per credit. *Part-time fees:* $368 per term. Part-time tuition and fees vary according to course load. *Payment plan:* Installment.

FRESHMAN FINANCIAL AID (Fall 2004, est.) 213 applied for aid; of those 77% were deemed to have need. 100% of freshmen with need received aid; of those 75% had need fully met. *Average percent of need met:* 91% (excluding resources awarded to replace EFC). *Average financial aid package:* $25,919 (excluding resources awarded to replace EFC). 10% of all full-time freshmen had no need and received non-need-based gift aid.

UNDERGRADUATE FINANCIAL AID (Fall 2004, est.) 689 applied for aid; of those 84% were deemed to have need. 100% of undergraduates with need received aid; of those 81% had need fully met. *Average percent of need met:* 95% (excluding resources awarded to replace EFC). *Average financial aid package:* $28,686 (excluding resources awarded to replace EFC). 5% of all full-time undergraduates had no need and received non-need-based gift aid.

GIFT AID (NEED-BASED) *Total amount:* $11,628,336 (6% federal, 2% state, 91% institutional, 1% external sources). *Receiving aid:* Freshmen: 45% (149); All full-time undergraduates: 47% (541). *Average award:* Freshmen: $20,321; Undergraduates: $20,799. *Scholarships, grants, and awards:* Federal Pell, FSEOG, state, private, college/university gift aid from institutional funds.

GIFT AID (NON-NEED-BASED) *Total amount:* $22,000 (27% state, 68% institutional, 5% external sources). *Receiving aid:* Undergraduates: 1% (10). *Average Award:* Freshmen: $3006; Undergraduates: $5976. *Tuition waivers:* Full or partial for employees or children of employees.

LOANS *Student loans:* $2,887,078 (92% need-based, 8% non-need-based). 58% of past graduating class borrowed through all loan programs. *Average indebtedness per student:* $15,121. *Average need-based loan:* Freshmen: $2314; Undergraduates: $1722. *Parent loans:* $4,563,461 (100% non-need-based). *Programs:* FFEL (Subsidized and Unsubsidized Stafford, PLUS), Perkins, college/university, Achiever Loans, Signature Loans, CitiAssist Loans.

WORK-STUDY *Federal work-study:* Total amount: $851,976; 477 jobs averaging $1786. *State or other work-study/employment:* Total amount: $167,043 (100% non-need-based). 99 part-time jobs averaging $1687.

APPLYING FOR FINANCIAL AID *Required financial aid forms:* FAFSA, CSS Financial Aid PROFILE, state aid form, noncustodial (divorced/separated) parent's statement. *Financial aid deadline:* 2/1. *Notification date:* 4/1. Students must reply by 5/1.

CONTACT Ms. Heather McDonnell, Director of Financial Aid, Sarah Lawrence College, One Mead Way, Bronxville, NY 10708, 914-395-2570 or toll-free 800-888-2858. *Fax:* 914-395-2676. *E-mail:* hmcdonn@sarahlawrence.edu.

SAVANNAH COLLEGE OF ART AND DESIGN
Savannah, GA

Tuition & fees: $22,100	Average undergraduate aid package: $8100

ABOUT THE INSTITUTION Independent, coed. Awards: bachelor's and master's degrees and post-bachelor's certificates. 22 undergraduate majors. Total enrollment: 6,776. Undergraduates: 5,741. Freshmen: 1,303. Federal methodology is used as a basis for awarding need-based institutional aid.

UNDERGRADUATE EXPENSES for 2005–06 *Application fee:* $50. *Comprehensive fee:* $30,800 includes full-time tuition ($21,600), mandatory fees ($500), and room and board ($8700). *College room only:* $5550. *Part-time tuition:* $2400 per course.

FRESHMAN FINANCIAL AID (Fall 2004, est.) 906 applied for aid; of those 81% were deemed to have need. 99% of freshmen with need received aid; of those 41% had need fully met. *Average percent of need met:* 10% (excluding resources awarded to replace EFC). *Average financial aid package:* $7900 (excluding resources awarded to replace EFC). 32% of all full-time freshmen had no need and received non-need-based gift aid.

UNDERGRADUATE FINANCIAL AID (Fall 2004, est.) 3,358 applied for aid; of those 83% were deemed to have need. 96% of undergraduates with need received aid; of those 36% had need fully met. *Average percent of need met:* 13% (excluding resources awarded to replace EFC). *Average financial aid package:* $8100 (excluding resources awarded to replace EFC). 27% of all full-time undergraduates had no need and received non-need-based gift aid.

GIFT AID (NEED-BASED) *Total amount:* $3,002,267 (95% federal, 2% state, 3% institutional). *Receiving aid:* Freshmen: 15% (201); All full-time undergradu-

ates: 15% (801). *Average award:* Freshmen: $2800; Undergraduates: $3300. *Scholarships, grants, and awards:* Federal Pell, FSEOG, state, private, college/university gift aid from institutional funds.

GIFT AID (NON-NEED-BASED) *Total amount:* $16,882,410 (9% state, 84% institutional, 7% external sources). *Receiving aid:* Freshmen: 47% (612); Undergraduates: 41% (2,136). *Average Award:* Freshmen: $4032; Undergraduates: $3651. *Scholarships, grants, and awards by category: Academic Interests/ Achievement:* architecture, general academic interests/achievements, humanities. *Creative Arts/Performance:* art/fine arts, general creative arts/performance. *Special Achievements/Activities:* general special achievements/activities. *Special Characteristics:* general special characteristics.

LOANS *Student loans:* $14,534,844 (71% need-based, 29% non-need-based). 60% of past graduating class borrowed through all loan programs. *Average indebtedness per student:* $20,000. *Average need-based loan:* Freshmen: $2600; Undergraduates: $3900. *Parent loans:* $30,768,362 (100% non-need-based). *Programs:* Federal Direct (Subsidized and Unsubsidized Stafford, PLUS), Perkins.

WORK-STUDY *Federal work-study:* Total amount: $134,106; 39 jobs averaging $3439. *State or other work-study/employment:* Total amount: $329,298 (100% non-need-based). 152 part-time jobs averaging $2166.

ATHLETIC AWARDS *Total amount:* $978,813 (100% non-need-based).

APPLYING FOR FINANCIAL AID *Required financial aid forms:* FAFSA, institution's own form, state aid form. *Financial aid deadline (priority):* 4/1. *Notification date:* Continuous. Students must reply within 4 weeks of notification.

CONTACT Ms. Cindy Bradley, Director of Financial Aid, Savannah College of Art and Design, PO Box 3146, 342 Bull Street, Savannah, GA 31402-3146, 912-525-6119 or toll-free 800-869-7223. *Fax:* 912-525-6263. *E-mail:* cbradley@scad.edu.

SAVANNAH STATE UNIVERSITY
Savannah, GA

ABOUT THE INSTITUTION State-supported, coed. Awards: bachelor's and master's degrees. 28 undergraduate majors. Total enrollment: 2,800. Undergraduates: 2,665. Freshmen: 628.

GIFT AID (NEED-BASED) *Scholarships, grants, and awards:* Federal Pell, FSEOG, state, private, college/university gift aid from institutional funds.

GIFT AID (NON-NEED-BASED) *Scholarships, grants, and awards by category: Academic Interests/Achievement:* biological sciences, business, computer science, engineering/technologies, English, general academic interests/achievements, humanities, mathematics, military science, physical sciences, social sciences. *Creative Arts/Performance:* music.

LOANS *Programs:* Federal Direct (Subsidized and Unsubsidized Stafford, PLUS), Perkins, state, college/university.

WORK-STUDY Federal work-study jobs available.

APPLYING FOR FINANCIAL AID *Required financial aid form:* FAFSA.

CONTACT Mark Adkins, Director of Financial Aid, Savannah State University, PO Box 20523, Savannah, GA 31404, 912-356-2253 or toll-free 800-788-0478. *Fax:* 912-353-3150. *E-mail:* finaid@savstate.edu.

SCHOOL OF THE ART INSTITUTE OF CHICAGO
Chicago, IL

Tuition & fees: $27,150	Average undergraduate aid package: $19,566

ABOUT THE INSTITUTION Independent, coed. Awards: bachelor's and master's degrees. 35 undergraduate majors. Total enrollment: 2,660. Undergraduates: 2,093. Freshmen: 330. Federal methodology is used as a basis for awarding need-based institutional aid.

UNDERGRADUATE EXPENSES for 2005–06 *Application fee:* $65. *Tuition:* full-time $27,150; part-time $905 per credit hour. Room and board charges vary according to housing facility. *Payment plans:* Installment, deferred payment.

GIFT AID (NEED-BASED) *Total amount:* $12,008,220 (14% federal, 7% state, 77% institutional, 2% external sources). *Receiving aid:* Freshmen: 56% (184); All full-time undergraduates: 52% (977). *Average award:* Freshmen: $12,382; Undergraduates: $10,816. *Scholarships, grants, and awards:* Federal Pell, FSEOG, state, private, college/university gift aid from institutional funds.

GIFT AID (NON-NEED-BASED) *Total amount:* $1,125,940 (2% state, 94% institutional, 4% external sources). *Receiving aid:* Freshmen: 16% (51); Undergraduates: 16% (303). *Average Award:* Freshmen: $4513; Undergraduates: $4557. *Scholarships, grants, and awards by category: Academic Interests/*

Achievement: general academic interests/achievements. *Creative Arts/ Performance:* art/fine arts. *Tuition waivers:* Full or partial for employees or children of employees.

LOANS *Student loans:* $10,419,148 (79% need-based, 21% non-need-based). 63% of past graduating class borrowed through all loan programs. *Average indebtedness per student:* $26,011. *Average need-based loan:* Freshmen: $3528; Undergraduates: $4840. *Parent loans:* $3,438,046 (84% need-based, 16% non-need-based). *Programs:* FFEL (Subsidized and Unsubsidized Stafford, PLUS), Perkins.

APPLYING FOR FINANCIAL AID *Required financial aid forms:* FAFSA, institution's own form, federal income tax form(s). *Financial aid deadline (priority):* 3/15. *Notification date:* Continuous beginning 4/1. Students must reply within 4 weeks of notification.

CONTACT Financial Aid Office, School of the Art Institute of Chicago, 37 South Wabash, Chicago, IL 60603-3103, 312-899-5106 or toll-free 800-232-SAIC.

SCHOOL OF THE MUSEUM OF FINE ARTS, BOSTON
Boston, MA

Tuition & fees: $24,290	Average undergraduate aid package: $13,890

ABOUT THE INSTITUTION Independent, coed. Awards: bachelor's and master's degrees and post-bachelor's certificates. 21 undergraduate majors. Total enrollment: 780. Undergraduates: 664. Freshmen: 163. Federal methodology is used as a basis for awarding need-based institutional aid.

UNDERGRADUATE EXPENSES for 2004–05 *Application fee:* $60. *Tuition:* full-time $22,490; part-time $1410 per credit hour. *Required fees:* full-time $1800; $400 per term part-time. Full-time tuition and fees vary according to course load, degree level, and program. Part-time tuition and fees vary according to class time, course load, and program. Room and board charges vary according to housing facility. *Payment plan:* Installment.

FRESHMAN FINANCIAL AID (Fall 2004, est.) 124 applied for aid; of those 95% were deemed to have need. 100% of freshmen with need received aid; of those 7% had need fully met. *Average percent of need met:* 43% (excluding resources awarded to replace EFC). *Average financial aid package:* $18,420 (excluding resources awarded to replace EFC). 2% of all full-time freshmen had no need and received non-need-based gift aid.

UNDERGRADUATE FINANCIAL AID (Fall 2004, est.) 475 applied for aid; of those 97% were deemed to have need. 100% of undergraduates with need received aid; of those 6% had need fully met. *Average percent of need met:* 59% (excluding resources awarded to replace EFC). *Average financial aid package:* $13,890 (excluding resources awarded to replace EFC). 2% of all full-time undergraduates had no need and received non-need-based gift aid.

GIFT AID (NEED-BASED) *Total amount:* $4,510,266 (16% federal, 2% state, 79% institutional, 3% external sources). *Receiving aid:* Freshmen: 66% (104); All full-time undergraduates: 74% (409). *Average award:* Freshmen: $10,521; Undergraduates: $7892. *Scholarships, grants, and awards:* Federal Pell, FSEOG, state, private, college/university gift aid from institutional funds.

GIFT AID (NON-NEED-BASED) *Total amount:* $443,227 (100% institutional). *Receiving aid:* Freshmen: 28% (45); Undergraduates: 7% (40). *Average Award:* Freshmen: $3667; Undergraduates: $5235. *Scholarships, grants, and awards by category:* Creative Arts/Performance: art/fine arts. *Special Characteristics:* general special characteristics. *Tuition waivers:* Full or partial for employees or children of employees.

LOANS *Student loans:* $3,075,311 (100% need-based). 47% of past graduating class borrowed through all loan programs. *Average indebtedness per student:* $20,554. *Average need-based loan:* Freshmen: $2553; Undergraduates: $3715. *Parent loans:* $2,466,592 (100% need-based). *Programs:* FFEL (Subsidized and Unsubsidized Stafford, PLUS), state.

WORK-STUDY *Federal work-study:* Total amount: $220,192; 184 jobs averaging $1785.

APPLYING FOR FINANCIAL AID *Required financial aid forms:* FAFSA, institution's own form. *Financial aid deadline (priority):* 3/15. *Notification date:* 4/1.

CONTACT Ms. Elizabeth Goreham, Director of Financial Aid, School of the Museum of Fine Arts, Boston, 230 The Fenway, Boston, MA 02115, 617-369-3684 or toll-free 800-643-6078 (in-state). *Fax:* 617-369-3041.

SCHOOL OF VISUAL ARTS
New York, NY

Tuition & fees: $19,620	Average undergraduate aid package: $12,102

ABOUT THE INSTITUTION Proprietary, coed. Awards: bachelor's and master's degrees. 15 undergraduate majors. Total enrollment: 3,442. Undergraduates: 3,050. Freshmen: 489. Federal methodology is used as a basis for awarding need-based institutional aid.

UNDERGRADUATE EXPENSES for 2004–05 *Application fee:* $50. *Comprehensive fee:* $30,870 includes full-time tuition ($19,120), mandatory fees ($500), and room and board ($11,250). *College room only:* $7000. Room and board charges vary according to board plan, gender, housing facility, and location. *Part-time tuition:* $640 per credit. *Payment plan:* Installment.

GIFT AID (NEED-BASED) *Total amount:* $7,471,800 (36% federal, 24% state, 37% institutional, 3% external sources). *Receiving aid:* Freshmen: 44% (217); All full-time undergraduates: 41% (1,210). *Average award:* Freshmen: $6495; Undergraduates: $6135. *Scholarships, grants, and awards:* Federal Pell, FSEOG, state, private, college/university gift aid from institutional funds.

GIFT AID (NON-NEED-BASED) *Total amount:* $832,550 (5% state, 81% institutional, 14% external sources). *Receiving aid:* Freshmen: 10% (51); Undergraduates: 8% (246). *Average Award:* Freshmen: $7574; Undergraduates: $7057. *Scholarships, grants, and awards by category:* Creative Arts/ Performance: 195 awards ($711,025 total): art/fine arts. *Tuition waivers:* Full or partial for employees or children of employees.

LOANS *Student loans:* $19,277,319 (75% need-based, 25% non-need-based). 66% of past graduating class borrowed through all loan programs. *Average indebtedness per student:* $30,600. *Average need-based loan:* Freshmen: $2697; Undergraduates: $4300. *Parent loans:* $9,086,199 (48% need-based, 52% non-need-based). *Programs:* FFEL (Subsidized and Unsubsidized Stafford, PLUS), Perkins, alternative loans.

APPLYING FOR FINANCIAL AID *Required financial aid forms:* FAFSA, state aid form. *Financial aid deadline:* 2/12 (priority: 2/1). *Notification date:* Continuous beginning 2/15. Students must reply within 3 weeks of notification.

CONTACT Javier Vega, Director of Financial Aid, School of Visual Arts, 209 East 23rd Street, New York, NY 10010, 212-592-2030 or toll-free 800-436-4204. *Fax:* 212-592-2029. *E-mail:* jvega@sva.edu.

SCHREINER UNIVERSITY
Kerrville, TX

Tuition & fees: $14,443	Average undergraduate aid package: $12,868

ABOUT THE INSTITUTION Independent Presbyterian, coed. Awards: associate, bachelor's, and master's degrees and post-bachelor's certificates. 33 undergraduate majors. Total enrollment: 842. Undergraduates: 793. Freshmen: 212. Federal methodology is used as a basis for awarding need-based institutional aid.

UNDERGRADUATE EXPENSES for 2004–05 *Application fee:* $25. *Comprehensive fee:* $21,323 includes full-time tuition ($14,043), mandatory fees ($400), and room and board ($6880). *College room only:* $3580. Room and board charges vary according to board plan and housing facility. *Part-time tuition:* $599 per credit. *Payment plan:* Installment.

FRESHMAN FINANCIAL AID (Fall 2004, est.) 168 applied for aid; of those 88% were deemed to have need. 100% of freshmen with need received aid; of those 12% had need fully met. *Average percent of need met:* 68% (excluding resources awarded to replace EFC). *Average financial aid package:* $11,999 (excluding resources awarded to replace EFC). 19% of all full-time freshmen had no need and received non-need-based gift aid.

UNDERGRADUATE FINANCIAL AID (Fall 2004, est.) 642 applied for aid; of those 89% were deemed to have need. 100% of undergraduates with need received aid; of those 14% had need fully met. *Average percent of need met:* 73% (excluding resources awarded to replace EFC). *Average financial aid package:* $12,868 (excluding resources awarded to replace EFC). 16% of all full-time undergraduates had no need and received non-need-based gift aid.

GIFT AID (NEED-BASED) *Total amount:* $5,776,728 (19% federal, 21% state, 56% institutional, 4% external sources). *Receiving aid:* Freshmen: 70% (144); All full-time undergraduates: 79% (564). *Average award:* Freshmen: $9792; Undergraduates: $9911. *Scholarships, grants, and awards:* Federal Pell, FSEOG, state, private, college/university gift aid from institutional funds.

GIFT AID (NON-NEED-BASED) *Total amount:* $987,598 (1% federal, 4% state, 83% institutional, 12% external sources). *Receiving aid:* Freshmen: 8% (16); Undergraduates: 8% (58). *Average Award:* Freshmen: $14,838; *Undergradu-*

ates: $13,913. *Scholarships, grants, and awards by category:* Academic Interests/Achievement: 297 awards ($1,261,709 total): biological sciences, business, education, English, general academic interests/achievements, mathematics, physical sciences, religion/biblical studies, social sciences. *Creative Arts/Performance:* 37 awards ($44,750 total): art/fine arts, journalism/publications, music, theater/drama. *Special Achievements/Activities:* 9 awards ($63,000 total): community service, leadership, religious involvement. *Special Characteristics:* 374 awards ($855,073 total): children of faculty/staff, ethnic background, general special characteristics, international students, local/state students, religious affiliation. *Tuition waivers:* Full or partial for employees or children of employees.
LOANS *Student loans:* $4,049,807 (77% need-based, 23% non-need-based). 90% of past graduating class borrowed through all loan programs. *Average indebtedness per student:* $19,132. *Average need-based loan:* Freshmen: $2367; Undergraduates: $3224. *Parent loans:* $2,120,126 (32% need-based, 68% non-need-based). *Programs:* FFEL (Subsidized and Unsubsidized Stafford, PLUS), state, Sallie Mae Signature Loan, alternative loans.
WORK-STUDY *Federal work-study:* Total amount: $176,600; 110 jobs averaging $897. *State or other work-study/employment:* Total amount: $128,994 (2% need-based, 98% non-need-based). 170 part-time jobs averaging $638.
APPLYING FOR FINANCIAL AID *Required financial aid forms:* FAFSA, institution's own form. *Financial aid deadline:* 8/1 (priority: 4/1). *Notification date:* Continuous beginning 12/15. Students must reply within 2 weeks of notification.
CONTACT Toni Bryant, Director of Financial Aid, Schreiner University, 2100 Memorial Boulevard, Kerrville, TX 78028, 830-792-7217 or toll-free 800-343-4919. *Fax:* 830-792-7226. *E-mail:* finaid@schreiner.edu.

SCRIPPS COLLEGE
Claremont, CA

Tuition & fees: $29,000	Average undergraduate aid package: $26,573

ABOUT THE INSTITUTION Independent, women only. Awards: bachelor's degrees and post-bachelor's certificates. 57 undergraduate majors. Total enrollment: 839. Undergraduates: 822. Freshmen: 201. Both federal and institutional methodology are used as a basis for awarding need-based institutional aid.
UNDERGRADUATE EXPENSES for 2004–05 *Application fee:* $50. *Comprehensive fee:* $38,000 includes full-time tuition ($28,860), mandatory fees ($140), and room and board ($9000). *College room only:* $4800. Full-time tuition and fees vary according to program. Room and board charges vary according to board plan. *Part-time tuition:* $3,608 per course. Part-time tuition and fees vary according to program. *Payment plan:* Installment.
FRESHMAN FINANCIAL AID (Fall 2004, est.) 136 applied for aid; of those 67% were deemed to have need. 100% of freshmen with need received aid; of those 100% had need fully met. *Average percent of need met:* 100% (excluding resources awarded to replace EFC). *Average financial aid package:* $26,411 (excluding resources awarded to replace EFC). 7% of all full-time freshmen had no need and received non-need-based gift aid.
UNDERGRADUATE FINANCIAL AID (Fall 2004, est.) 467 applied for aid; of those 80% were deemed to have need. 100% of undergraduates with need received aid; of those 100% had need fully met. *Average percent of need met:* 100% (excluding resources awarded to replace EFC). *Average financial aid package:* $26,573 (excluding resources awarded to replace EFC). 8% of all full-time undergraduates had no need and received non-need-based gift aid.
GIFT AID (NEED-BASED) *Total amount:* $8,378,171 (5% federal, 8% state, 84% institutional, 3% external sources). *Receiving aid:* Freshmen: 40% (90); All full-time undergraduates: 46% (372). *Average award:* Freshmen: $22,251; Undergraduates: $21,781. *Scholarships, grants, and awards:* Federal Pell, FSEOG, state, private, college/university gift aid from institutional funds.
GIFT AID (NON-NEED-BASED) *Total amount:* $1,092,415 (1% state, 92% institutional, 7% external sources). *Receiving aid:* Freshmen: 6% (14); Undergraduates: 4% (32). *Average Award:* Freshmen: $14,364; Undergraduates: $15,022. *Scholarships, grants, and awards by category:* Academic Interests/Achievement: 134 awards ($1,862,577 total): general academic interests/achievements. *Tuition waivers:* Full or partial for employees or children of employees. *ROTC:* Army cooperative, Air Force cooperative.
LOANS *Student loans:* $2,251,432 (52% need-based, 48% non-need-based). 45% of past graduating class borrowed through all loan programs. *Average indebtedness per student:* $12,076. *Average need-based loan:* Freshmen: $3166; Undergraduates: $3647. *Parent loans:* $1,396,584 (100% non-need-based). *Programs:* FFEL (Subsidized and Unsubsidized Stafford, PLUS), Perkins, college/university.
WORK-STUDY *Federal work-study:* Total amount: $526,260; 323 jobs averaging $1629.

APPLYING FOR FINANCIAL AID *Required financial aid forms:* FAFSA, CSS Financial Aid PROFILE, noncustodial (divorced/separated) parent's statement, business/farm supplement, verification worksheet, federal income tax form(s). *Financial aid deadline (priority):* 1/15. *Notification date:* 4/1. Students must reply by 5/1 or within 2 weeks of notification.
CONTACT Sean Smith, Director of Financial Aid, Scripps College, 1030 Columbia Avenue, PMB 1293, Claremont, CA 91711-3948, 909-621-8275 or toll-free 800-770-1333. *Fax:* 909-607-7742. *E-mail:* finaid@scrippscollege.edu.

SEATTLE PACIFIC UNIVERSITY
Seattle, WA

Tuition & fees: $20,466	Average undergraduate aid package: $16,829

ABOUT THE INSTITUTION Independent Free Methodist, coed. Awards: bachelor's, master's, and doctoral degrees and post-master's certificates. 54 undergraduate majors. Total enrollment: 3,779. Undergraduates: 2,934. Freshmen: 635. Federal methodology is used as a basis for awarding need-based institutional aid.
UNDERGRADUATE EXPENSES for 2004–05 *Application fee:* $45. *Comprehensive fee:* $27,834 includes full-time tuition ($20,139), mandatory fees ($327), and room and board ($7368). *College room only:* $3951. Room and board charges vary according to board plan and housing facility. *Part-time tuition:* $560 per credit. Part-time tuition and fees vary according to course load. *Payment plan:* Installment.
FRESHMAN FINANCIAL AID (Fall 2004, est.) 505 applied for aid; of those 78% were deemed to have need. 100% of freshmen with need received aid; of those 22% had need fully met. *Average percent of need met:* 79% (excluding resources awarded to replace EFC). *Average financial aid package:* $16,260 (excluding resources awarded to replace EFC). 25% of all full-time freshmen had no need and received non-need-based gift aid.
UNDERGRADUATE FINANCIAL AID (Fall 2004, est.) 1,995 applied for aid; of those 85% were deemed to have need. 99% of undergraduates with need received aid; of those 19% had need fully met. *Average percent of need met:* 81% (excluding resources awarded to replace EFC). *Average financial aid package:* $16,829 (excluding resources awarded to replace EFC). 26% of all full-time undergraduates had no need and received non-need-based gift aid.
GIFT AID (NEED-BASED) *Total amount:* $19,398,860 (11% federal, 7% state, 75% institutional, 7% external sources). *Receiving aid:* Freshmen: 62% (386); All full-time undergraduates: 61% (1,645). *Average award:* Freshmen: $14,825; Undergraduates: $13,868. *Scholarships, grants, and awards:* Federal Pell, FSEOG, state, private, college/university gift aid from institutional funds, Federal Nursing.
GIFT AID (NON-NEED-BASED) *Total amount:* $5,094,934 (1% state, 91% institutional, 8% external sources). *Average Award:* Freshmen: $8054; Undergraduates: $8208. *Scholarships, grants, and awards by category:* Academic Interests/Achievement: 646 awards ($3,190,941 total): engineering/technologies, general academic interests/achievements. *Creative Arts/Performance:* 29 awards ($37,333 total): art/fine arts, performing arts. *Special Characteristics:* 221 awards ($755,733 total): children and siblings of alumni, children of faculty/staff, general special characteristics, international students, relatives of clergy, religious affiliation. *Tuition waivers:* Full or partial for employees or children of employees, senior citizens. *ROTC:* Army cooperative, Naval cooperative, Air Force cooperative.
LOANS *Student loans:* $12,813,907 (88% need-based, 12% non-need-based). 66% of past graduating class borrowed through all loan programs. *Average indebtedness per student:* $21,805. *Average need-based loan:* Freshmen: $4661; Undergraduates: $5584. *Parent loans:* $3,737,197 (77% need-based, 23% non-need-based). *Programs:* FFEL (Subsidized and Unsubsidized Stafford, PLUS), Perkins, Federal Nursing, college/university.
WORK-STUDY *Federal work-study:* Total amount: $540,824; 375 jobs averaging $1442. *State or other work-study/employment:* Total amount: $794,345 (100% need-based). 413 part-time jobs averaging $1923.
ATHLETIC AWARDS *Total amount:* $1,438,595 (58% need-based, 42% non-need-based).
APPLYING FOR FINANCIAL AID *Required financial aid form:* FAFSA. *Financial aid deadline (priority):* 4/1. *Notification date:* Continuous. Students must reply by 5/1 or within 4 weeks of notification.
CONTACT Mr. Jordan Grant, Director of Student Financial Services, Seattle Pacific University, 3307 Third Avenue West, Seattle, WA 98119-1997, 206-281-2469 or toll-free 800-366-3344. *E-mail:* grantj@spu.edu.

SEATTLE UNIVERSITY
Seattle, WA

ABOUT THE INSTITUTION Independent Roman Catholic, coed. Awards: bachelor's, master's, doctoral, and first professional degrees and post-bachelor's and post-master's certificates. 56 undergraduate majors. Total enrollment: 6,810. Undergraduates: 3,911. Freshmen: 722.

GIFT AID (NEED-BASED) *Scholarships, grants, and awards:* Federal Pell, FSEOG, state, private, college/university gift aid from institutional funds.

GIFT AID (NON-NEED-BASED) *Scholarships, grants, and awards by category: Academic Interests/Achievement:* general academic interests/achievements. *Creative Arts/Performance:* music. *Special Achievements/Activities:* leadership. *Special Characteristics:* children and siblings of alumni, children of educators, children of faculty/staff, members of minority groups.

LOANS *Programs:* Federal Direct (Subsidized and Unsubsidized Stafford, PLUS), Perkins, Federal Nursing, alternative loans.

WORK-STUDY *Federal work-study:* Total amount: $2,388,189; 704 jobs averaging $3899. *State or other work-study/employment:* Total amount: $3,015,374 (100% need-based). 830 part-time jobs averaging $5119.

APPLYING FOR FINANCIAL AID *Required financial aid form:* FAFSA.

CONTACT Mr. James White, Director of Student Financial Services, Seattle University, Broadway & Madison, Seattle, WA 98122-4460, 206-296-2000 or toll-free 800-542-0833 (in-state), 800-426-7123 (out-of-state). *Fax:* 206-296-5755. *E-mail:* financial-aid@seattleu.edu.

SETON HALL UNIVERSITY
South Orange, NJ

Tuition & fees: $23,460	Average undergraduate aid package: $14,664

ABOUT THE INSTITUTION Independent Roman Catholic, coed. Awards: bachelor's, master's, doctoral, and first professional degrees and post-master's certificates. 50 undergraduate majors. Total enrollment: 9,824. Undergraduates: 5,414. Freshmen: 1,238. Federal methodology is used as a basis for awarding need-based institutional aid.

UNDERGRADUATE EXPENSES for 2005–06 *Application fee:* $45. *Comprehensive fee:* $33,622 includes full-time tuition ($21,510), mandatory fees ($1950), and room and board ($10,162). *College room only:* $6470. *Part-time tuition:* $717 per credit. *Part-time fees:* $185 per term.

FRESHMAN FINANCIAL AID (Fall 2004, est.) 1080 applied for aid; of those 86% were deemed to have need. 97% of freshmen with need received aid; of those 20% had need fully met. *Average percent of need met:* 74% (excluding resources awarded to replace EFC). *Average financial aid package:* $15,530 (excluding resources awarded to replace EFC). 14% of all full-time freshmen had no need and received non-need-based gift aid.

UNDERGRADUATE FINANCIAL AID (Fall 2004, est.) 3,604 applied for aid; of those 86% were deemed to have need. 98% of undergraduates with need received aid; of those 19% had need fully met. *Average percent of need met:* 68% (excluding resources awarded to replace EFC). *Average financial aid package:* $14,664 (excluding resources awarded to replace EFC). 15% of all full-time undergraduates had no need and received non-need-based gift aid.

GIFT AID (NEED-BASED) *Total amount:* $27,586,269 (15% federal, 24% state, 60% institutional, 1% external sources). *Receiving aid:* Freshmen: 47% (577); All full-time undergraduates: 37% (1,806). *Average award:* Freshmen: $5179; Undergraduates: $4651. *Scholarships, grants, and awards:* Federal Pell, FSEOG, state, private, college/university gift aid from institutional funds.

GIFT AID (NON-NEED-BASED) *Total amount:* $11,873,274 (2% federal, 12% state, 85% institutional, 1% external sources). *Receiving aid:* Freshmen: 49% (601); Undergraduates: 34% (1,643). *Average Award:* Freshmen: $11,366; Undergraduates: $11,243. *Scholarships, grants, and awards by category: Academic Interests/Achievement:* 2,136 awards ($19,048,912 total): biological sciences, business, education, general academic interests/achievements, health fields, military science, physical sciences, premedicine. *Creative Arts/Performance:* 23 awards ($85,500 total): art/fine arts, cinema/film/broadcasting, debating, journalism/publications, music. *Special Achievements/Activities:* 15 awards ($87,906 total): community service, leadership. *Special Characteristics:* 431 awards ($3,205,356 total): children and siblings of alumni, children of faculty/staff, children of union members/company employees, ethnic background, members of minority groups, relatives of clergy, siblings of current students. *ROTC:* Army, Air Force cooperative.

LOANS *Student loans:* $31,940,094 (72% need-based, 28% non-need-based). 68% of past graduating class borrowed through all loan programs. *Average*

indebtedness per student: $29,108. *Average need-based loan:* Freshmen: $2533; Undergraduates: $3198. *Parent loans:* $17,517,586 (100% non-need-based). *Programs:* FFEL (Subsidized and Unsubsidized Stafford, PLUS), Perkins, state.

WORK-STUDY *Federal work-study:* Total amount: $1,070,739; 807 jobs averaging $1930. *State or other work-study/employment:* Total amount: $699,459 (36% need-based, 64% non-need-based). 1,116 part-time jobs averaging $1289.

ATHLETIC AWARDS *Total amount:* $4,428,769 (100% non-need-based).

APPLYING FOR FINANCIAL AID *Required financial aid form:* FAFSA. *Financial aid deadline (priority):* 2/15. *Notification date:* Continuous beginning 3/15. Students must reply by 5/1 or within 4 weeks of notification.

CONTACT Office of Enrollment Services, Seton Hall University, 400 South Orange Avenue, South Orange, NJ 07079, 973-761-9350 or toll-free 800-THE HALL (out-of-state). *Fax:* 973-275-2040. *E-mail:* thehall@shu.edu.

SETON HILL UNIVERSITY
Greensburg, PA

Tuition & fees: $20,630	Average undergraduate aid package: $17,589

ABOUT THE INSTITUTION Independent Roman Catholic, coed. Awards: bachelor's and master's degrees and post-bachelor's and post-master's certificates. 87 undergraduate majors. Total enrollment: 1,706. Undergraduates: 1,347. Freshmen: 296. Federal methodology is used as a basis for awarding need-based institutional aid.

UNDERGRADUATE EXPENSES for 2004–05 *Application fee:* $35. *Comprehensive fee:* $27,050 includes full-time tuition ($20,630) and room and board ($6420). Room and board charges vary according to board plan and housing facility. *Part-time tuition:* $545 per credit. *Part-time fees:* $55 per term. Part-time tuition and fees vary according to course load. *Payment plans:* Installment, deferred payment.

FRESHMAN FINANCIAL AID (Fall 2004, est.) 287 applied for aid; of those 93% were deemed to have need. 100% of freshmen with need received aid; of those 16% had need fully met. *Average percent of need met:* 85% (excluding resources awarded to replace EFC). *Average financial aid package:* $16,039 (excluding resources awarded to replace EFC). 5% of all full-time freshmen had no need and received non-need-based gift aid.

UNDERGRADUATE FINANCIAL AID (Fall 2004, est.) 824 applied for aid; of those 96% were deemed to have need. 100% of undergraduates with need received aid; of those 19% had need fully met. *Average percent of need met:* 80% (excluding resources awarded to replace EFC). *Average financial aid package:* $17,589 (excluding resources awarded to replace EFC). 6% of all full-time undergraduates had no need and received non-need-based gift aid.

GIFT AID (NEED-BASED) *Total amount:* $9,042,915 (10% federal, 16% state, 69% institutional, 5% external sources). *Receiving aid:* Freshmen: 91% (268); All full-time undergraduates: 85% (795). *Average award:* Freshmen: $12,300; Undergraduates: $11,500. *Scholarships, grants, and awards:* Federal Pell, FSEOG, state, private, college/university gift aid from institutional funds, United Negro College Fund.

GIFT AID (NON-NEED-BASED) *Total amount:* $490,566 (100% institutional). *Receiving aid:* Freshmen: 9% (28); Undergraduates: 9% (85). *Average Award:* Freshmen: $10,144; Undergraduates: $6186. *Scholarships, grants, and awards by category: Academic Interests/Achievement:* 285 awards ($1,948,345 total): biological sciences, business, communication, computer science, education, English, foreign languages, general academic interests/achievements, home economics, humanities, mathematics, physical sciences, premedicine, religion/biblical studies, social sciences. *Creative Arts/Performance:* 33 awards ($23,425 total): applied art and design, art/fine arts, creative writing, journalism/publications, music, performing arts, theater/drama. *Special Achievements/Activities:* 313 awards ($442,930 total): community service, general special achievements/activities, leadership, religious involvement. *Special Characteristics:* 76 awards ($739,499 total): adult students, children and siblings of alumni, children of faculty/staff, children with a deceased or disabled parent, international students, parents of current students, siblings of current students. *Tuition waivers:* Full or partial for employees or children of employees. *ROTC:* Army cooperative.

LOANS *Student loans:* $3,462,579 (66% need-based, 34% non-need-based). 67% of past graduating class borrowed through all loan programs. *Average indebtedness per student:* $25,787. *Average need-based loan:* Freshmen: $3625; Undergraduates: $3685. *Parent loans:* $1,152,680 (80% need-based, 20% non-need-based). *Programs:* FFEL (Subsidized and Unsubsidized Stafford, PLUS), Perkins, college/university, alternative loans.

WORK-STUDY *Federal work-study:* Total amount: $592,297; 479 jobs averaging $1236. *State or other work-study/employment:* Total amount: $208,370 (85% need-based, 15% non-need-based). 136 part-time jobs averaging $1300.

ATHLETIC AWARDS *Total amount:* $1,977,432 (66% need-based, 34% non-need-based).

APPLYING FOR FINANCIAL AID *Required financial aid forms:* FAFSA, institution's own form. *Financial aid deadline (priority):* 5/1. *Notification date:* Continuous. Students must reply within 2 weeks of notification.

CONTACT Maryann Dudas, Director of Financial Aid, Seton Hill University, Seton Hill Drive, Greensburg, PA 15601, 724-838-4293 or toll-free 800-826-6234. *Fax:* 724-830-1292. *E-mail:* dudas@setonhill.edu.

SHASTA BIBLE COLLEGE
Redding, CA

ABOUT THE INSTITUTION Independent nondenominational, coed. Awards: associate, bachelor's, and master's degrees. 3 undergraduate majors. Total enrollment: 123. Undergraduates: 90. Freshmen: 9.

GIFT AID (NEED-BASED) *Scholarships, grants, and awards:* Federal Pell, FSEOG, state, private, college/university gift aid from institutional funds.

GIFT AID (NON-NEED-BASED) *Scholarships, grants, and awards by category: Academic Interests/Achievement:* education. *Creative Arts/Performance:* general creative arts/performance. *Special Achievements/Activities:* general special achievements/activities. *Special Characteristics:* relatives of clergy, veterans.

WORK-STUDY *Federal work-study:* Total amount: $8253; 7 jobs averaging $1449. *State or other work-study/employment:* Total amount: $23,688 (100% non-need-based). 14 part-time jobs averaging $1692.

APPLYING FOR FINANCIAL AID *Required financial aid forms:* FAFSA, institution's own form, state aid form.

CONTACT Jeff Hage, Financial Aid Administrator, Shasta Bible College, 2951 Goodwater Avenue, Redding, CA 96002, 530-221-4275 or toll-free 800-800-45BC (in-state), 800-800-6929 (out-of-state). *Fax:* 530-221-6929. *E-mail:* finaid@shasta.edu.

SHAWNEE STATE UNIVERSITY
Portsmouth, OH

Tuition & fees (OH res): $5202	Average undergraduate aid package: $3972

ABOUT THE INSTITUTION State-supported, coed. Awards: associate and bachelor's degrees. 66 undergraduate majors. Total enrollment: 3,798. Undergraduates: 3,798. Freshmen: 746. Federal methodology is used as a basis for awarding need-based institutional aid.

UNDERGRADUATE EXPENSES for 2004–05 *Tuition, state resident:* full-time $4608; part-time $128 per credit hour. *Tuition, nonresident:* full-time $8208; part-time $228 per credit hour. *Required fees:* full-time $594; $16.50 per credit hour. Full-time tuition and fees vary according to course load, reciprocity agreements, and student level. Part-time tuition and fees vary according to course load, reciprocity agreements, and student level. *College room and board:* $6510; *room only:* $4281. Room and board charges vary according to board plan and housing facility. *Payment plan:* Installment.

FRESHMAN FINANCIAL AID (Fall 2004, est.) 526 applied for aid; of those 68% were deemed to have need. 94% of freshmen with need received aid; of those 100% had need fully met. *Average percent of need met:* 80% (excluding resources awarded to replace EFC). *Average financial aid package:* $3881 (excluding resources awarded to replace EFC).

UNDERGRADUATE FINANCIAL AID (Fall 2004, est.) 2,591 applied for aid; of those 70% were deemed to have need. 97% of undergraduates with need received aid; of those 100% had need fully met. *Average percent of need met:* 70% (excluding resources awarded to replace EFC). *Average financial aid package:* $3972 (excluding resources awarded to replace EFC).

GIFT AID (NEED-BASED) *Total amount:* $5,889,701 (67% federal, 22% state, 3% institutional, 8% external sources). *Receiving aid:* Freshmen: 58% (307); All full-time undergraduates: 65% (1,702). *Average award:* Freshmen: $2788; Undergraduates: $2620. *Scholarships, grants, and awards:* Federal Pell, FSEOG, state, private, college/university gift aid from institutional funds.

GIFT AID (NON-NEED-BASED) *Total amount:* $1,321,790 (9% state, 62% institutional, 29% external sources). *Receiving aid:* Freshmen: 30% (160); Undergraduates: 28% (724). *Scholarships, grants, and awards by category: Academic Interests/Achievement:* general academic interests/achievements. *Creative Arts/Performance:* art/fine arts, performing arts. *Special Achievements/Activities:* memberships. *Special Characteristics:* ethnic background, first-

generation college students, handicapped students, local/state students, members of minority groups, veterans. *Tuition waivers:* Full or partial for employees or children of employees, senior citizens.

LOANS *Student loans:* $5,211,243 (100% need-based). 56% of past graduating class borrowed through all loan programs. *Average indebtedness per student:* $10,944. *Parent loans:* $296,598 (100% need-based). *Programs:* FFEL (Subsidized and Unsubsidized Stafford, PLUS), college/university.

WORK-STUDY *Federal work-study:* Total amount: $209,898; 104 jobs averaging $2018.

ATHLETIC AWARDS *Total amount:* $113,813 (100% non-need-based).

APPLYING FOR FINANCIAL AID *Required financial aid forms:* FAFSA, institution's own form. *Financial aid deadline (priority):* 4/1. *Notification date:* 6/1.

CONTACT Patricia Moore, Director of Financial Aid, Shawnee State University, 940 Second Street, Portsmouth, OH 45662-4344, 740-351-3245 or toll-free 800-959-2SSU. *E-mail:* pmoore@shawnee.edu.

SHAW UNIVERSITY
Raleigh, NC

Tuition & fees: $9438	Average undergraduate aid package: $8145

ABOUT THE INSTITUTION Independent Baptist, coed. Awards: associate, bachelor's, master's, and first professional degrees. 33 undergraduate majors. Total enrollment: 2,709. Undergraduates: 2,516. Freshmen: 449. Federal methodology is used as a basis for awarding need-based institutional aid.

UNDERGRADUATE EXPENSES for 2004–05 *Application fee:* $25. *Comprehensive fee:* $15,488 includes full-time tuition ($7800), mandatory fees ($1638), and room and board ($6050). *College room only:* $2840. *Part-time tuition:* $325 per semester hour. *Part-time fees:* $460 per term.

GIFT AID (NEED-BASED) *Total amount:* $11,063,516 (56% federal, 37% state, 6% institutional, 1% external sources). *Receiving aid:* Freshmen: 88% (462); All full-time undergraduates: 90% (1,966). *Average award:* Freshmen: $6045; Undergraduates: $5019. *Scholarships, grants, and awards:* Federal Pell, FSEOG, state, private, college/university gift aid from institutional funds, United Negro College Fund.

GIFT AID (NON-NEED-BASED) *Total amount:* $590,243 (99% institutional, 1% external sources). *Receiving aid:* Freshmen: 10% (53); Undergraduates: 8% (176). *Average Award:* Freshmen: $6481; *Undergraduates:* $9581. *Scholarships, grants, and awards by category: Academic Interests/Achievement:* biological sciences, computer science, education, engineering/technologies, general academic interests/achievements, mathematics, physical sciences. *Creative Arts/Performance:* 104 awards ($475,372 total): music, performing arts. *Special Characteristics:* 30 awards ($135,128 total): children of faculty/staff, general special characteristics. *ROTC:* Army cooperative, Air Force cooperative.

LOANS *Student loans:* $12,250,212 (60% need-based, 40% non-need-based). 98% of past graduating class borrowed through all loan programs. *Average indebtedness per student:* $17,125. *Average need-based loan:* Freshmen: $3056; Undergraduates: $3708. *Parent loans:* $1,222,074 (100% non-need-based). *Programs:* Federal Direct (Subsidized and Unsubsidized Stafford, PLUS), Perkins, college/university, state loans (for Education majors).

ATHLETIC AWARDS *Total amount:* $886,830 (100% non-need-based).

APPLYING FOR FINANCIAL AID *Required financial aid forms:* FAFSA, institution's own form, state aid form. *Financial aid deadline:* 6/1 (priority: 3/1). *Notification date:* Continuous.

CONTACT Kamesia Ewing, Director of Financial Aid, Shaw University, 118 East South Street, Raleigh, NC 27601-2399, 919-546-8565 or toll-free 800-214-6683. *Fax:* 919-546-8356.

SHELDON JACKSON COLLEGE
Sitka, AK

ABOUT THE INSTITUTION Independent religious, coed. Awards: associate and bachelor's degrees. 10 undergraduate majors. Total enrollment: 274. Undergraduates: 274. Freshmen: 39.

GIFT AID (NEED-BASED) *Scholarships, grants, and awards:* Federal Pell, FSEOG, state, private, college/university gift aid from institutional funds.

GIFT AID (NON-NEED-BASED) *Scholarships, grants, and awards by category: Academic Interests/Achievement:* biological sciences, business, education, general academic interests/achievements, social sciences. *Creative Arts/Performance:* music, theater/drama. *Special Achievements/Activities:* religious involvement.

Special Characteristics: adult students, children and siblings of alumni, children of faculty/staff, ethnic background, local/state students, members of minority groups, religious affiliation, siblings of current students.
LOANS *Programs:* FFEL (Subsidized and Unsubsidized Stafford, PLUS), Perkins, state.
WORK-STUDY *Federal work-study:* Total amount: $110,199; 52 jobs averaging $2119. *State or other work-study/employment:* Total amount: $35,000 (100% non-need-based). 32 part-time jobs averaging $1094.
APPLYING FOR FINANCIAL AID *Required financial aid form:* FAFSA.
CONTACT Ms. Louise Driver, Financial Aid Director, Sheldon Jackson College, 801 Lincoln Street, Sitka, AK 99835-7699, 800-747-5206 or toll-free 800-478-4556. *Fax:* 907-747-6366. *E-mail:* ldriver@sj-alaska.edu.

SHENANDOAH UNIVERSITY
Winchester, VA

Tuition & fees: $19,240	Average undergraduate aid package: $13,220

ABOUT THE INSTITUTION Independent United Methodist, coed. Awards: associate, bachelor's, master's, doctoral, and first professional degrees and post-bachelor's and post-master's certificates. 34 undergraduate majors. Total enrollment: 3,000. Undergraduates: 1,538. Freshmen: 326. Federal methodology is used as a basis for awarding need-based institutional aid.
UNDERGRADUATE EXPENSES for 2004–05 *Application fee:* $30. *Comprehensive fee:* $26,330 includes full-time tuition ($19,090), mandatory fees ($150), and room and board ($7090). Full-time tuition and fees vary according to course load and location. Room and board charges vary according to board plan. *Part-time tuition:* $585 per credit hour. Part-time tuition and fees vary according to course load and location. *Payment plan:* Installment.
FRESHMAN FINANCIAL AID (Fall 2004, est.) 245 applied for aid; of those 100% were deemed to have need. 100% of freshmen with need received aid; of those 20% had need fully met. *Average percent of need met:* 84% (excluding resources awarded to replace EFC). *Average financial aid package:* $13,596 (excluding resources awarded to replace EFC). 14% of all full-time freshmen had no need and received non-need-based gift aid.
UNDERGRADUATE FINANCIAL AID (Fall 2004, est.) 875 applied for aid; of those 100% were deemed to have need. 100% of undergraduates with need received aid; of those 20% had need fully met. *Average percent of need met:* 84% (excluding resources awarded to replace EFC). *Average financial aid package:* $13,220 (excluding resources awarded to replace EFC). 11% of all full-time undergraduates had no need and received non-need-based gift aid.
GIFT AID (NEED-BASED) *Total amount:* $2,811,563 (47% federal, 2% state, 39% institutional, 12% external sources). *Receiving aid:* Freshmen: 39% (128); All full-time undergraduates: 55% (785). *Average award:* Freshmen: $4897; Undergraduates: $6817. *Scholarships, grants, and awards:* Federal Pell, FSEOG, state, private, college/university gift aid from institutional funds, Federal Nursing.
GIFT AID (NON-NEED-BASED) *Total amount:* $7,475,749 (23% state, 76% institutional, 1% external sources). *Receiving aid:* Freshmen: 32% (106); Undergraduates: 34% (484). *Average Award:* Freshmen: $4232; Undergraduates: $3733. *Scholarships, grants, and awards by category: Academic Interests/Achievement:* 621 awards ($2,222,691 total): business, general academic interests/achievements. *Creative Arts/Performance:* 336 awards ($1,150,274 total): dance, music, performing arts, theater/drama. *Special Characteristics:* 205 awards ($858,514 total): children of faculty/staff, local/state students, relatives of clergy, religious affiliation. *Tuition waivers:* Full or partial for employees or children of employees.
LOANS *Student loans:* $6,863,650 (62% need-based, 38% non-need-based). 85% of past graduating class borrowed through all loan programs. *Average indebtedness per student:* $19,518. *Average need-based loan:* Freshmen: $3677; Undergraduates: $5615. *Parent loans:* $4,572,508 (71% need-based, 29% non-need-based). *Programs:* Federal Direct (Subsidized and Unsubsidized Stafford, PLUS), Perkins, Federal Nursing, college/university.
WORK-STUDY *Federal work-study:* Total amount: $696,654; 461 jobs averaging $1475. *State or other work-study/employment:* Total amount: $313,792 (100% non-need-based). 209 part-time jobs averaging $1500.
APPLYING FOR FINANCIAL AID *Required financial aid forms:* FAFSA, state aid form. *Financial aid deadline (priority):* 2/15. *Notification date:* Continuous beginning 3/15. Students must reply within 2 weeks of notification.
CONTACT Nancy Bragg, Director of Financial Aid, Shenandoah University, 1460 University Drive, Winchester, VA 22601-5195, 540-665-4538 or toll-free 800-432-2266. *Fax:* 540-665-5433. *E-mail:* nbragg@su.edu.

SHEPHERD UNIVERSITY
Shepherdstown, WV

Tuition & fees (WV res): $3654	Average undergraduate aid package: $7797

ABOUT THE INSTITUTION State-supported, coed. Awards: associate, bachelor's, and master's degrees. 35 undergraduate majors. Total enrollment: 5,206. Undergraduates: 5,141. Freshmen: 843. Federal methodology is used as a basis for awarding need-based institutional aid.
UNDERGRADUATE EXPENSES for 2004–05 *Application fee:* $35. *Tuition, state resident:* full-time $3654. *Tuition, nonresident:* full-time $9234. Full-time tuition and fees vary according to degree level, program, and reciprocity agreements. Part-time tuition and fees vary according to degree level and program. *College room and board:* $5574. Room and board charges vary according to board plan and housing facility. *Payment plan:* Installment.
FRESHMAN FINANCIAL AID (Fall 2004, est.) 652 applied for aid; of those 65% were deemed to have need. 95% of freshmen with need received aid; of those 24% had need fully met. *Average percent of need met:* 69% (excluding resources awarded to replace EFC). *Average financial aid package:* $6341 (excluding resources awarded to replace EFC). 18% of all full-time freshmen had no need and received non-need-based gift aid.
UNDERGRADUATE FINANCIAL AID (Fall 2004, est.) 2,644 applied for aid; of those 63% were deemed to have need. 96% of undergraduates with need received aid; of those 24% had need fully met. *Average percent of need met:* 73% (excluding resources awarded to replace EFC). *Average financial aid package:* $7797 (excluding resources awarded to replace EFC). 16% of all full-time undergraduates had no need and received non-need-based gift aid.
GIFT AID (NEED-BASED) *Total amount:* $3,728,979 (75% federal, 19% state, 6% institutional). *Receiving aid:* Freshmen: 28% (217); All full-time undergraduates: 28% (888). *Average award:* Freshmen: $3201; Undergraduates: $3444. *Scholarships, grants, and awards:* Federal Pell, FSEOG, state, private, college/university gift aid from institutional funds.
GIFT AID (NON-NEED-BASED) *Total amount:* $2,743,002 (41% state, 50% institutional, 9% external sources). *Receiving aid:* Freshmen: 15% (113); Undergraduates: 10% (327). *Average Award:* Freshmen: $6263; Undergraduates: $7490. *Scholarships, grants, and awards by category: Academic Interests/Achievement:* 231 awards: biological sciences, business, communication, computer science, education, engineering/technologies, English, foreign languages, general academic interests/achievements, health fields, home economics, humanities, mathematics, physical sciences, premedicine, social sciences. *Creative Arts/Performance:* 49 awards: applied art and design, art/fine arts, music, performing arts. *Special Achievements/Activities:* 39 awards: leadership. *Special Characteristics:* 24 awards: ethnic background, members of minority groups, veterans' children. *Tuition waivers:* Full or partial for minority students, senior citizens.
LOANS *Student loans:* $10,484,048 (48% need-based, 52% non-need-based). 67% of past graduating class borrowed through all loan programs. *Average indebtedness per student:* $13,695. *Average need-based loan:* Freshmen: $2326; Undergraduates: $3552. *Parent loans:* $2,076,666 (100% non-need-based). *Programs:* Federal Direct (Subsidized and Unsubsidized Stafford, PLUS), Perkins, Federal Nursing.
WORK-STUDY *Federal work-study:* Total amount: $214,072; 183 jobs averaging $1500. *State or other work-study/employment:* Total amount: $867,706 (100% need-based). 325 part-time jobs averaging $3000.
ATHLETIC AWARDS *Total amount:* $488,693 (100% non-need-based).
APPLYING FOR FINANCIAL AID *Required financial aid forms:* FAFSA, state aid form. *Financial aid deadline (priority):* 3/1. *Notification date:* Continuous beginning 3/25. Students must reply within 2 weeks of notification.
CONTACT Financial Aid Office, Shepherd University, PO Box 3210, Shepherdstown, WV 25443-3210, 304-876-5470 or toll-free 800-344-5231. *Fax:* 304-876-5238. *E-mail:* faoweb@shepherd.edu.

SHIMER COLLEGE
Waukegan, IL

Tuition & fees: $17,645	Average undergraduate aid package: $16,000

ABOUT THE INSTITUTION Independent, coed. Awards: bachelor's degrees and post-bachelor's certificates. 7 undergraduate majors. Total enrollment: 138. Undergraduates: 126. Freshmen: 26. Federal methodology is used as a basis for awarding need-based institutional aid.

UNDERGRADUATE EXPENSES for 2004–05 *Application fee:* $25. *Comprehensive fee:* $20,545 includes full-time tuition ($16,870), mandatory fees ($775), and room and board ($2900). Full-time tuition and fees vary according to class time and course load. Room and board charges vary according to housing facility. *Part-time tuition:* $640 per credit hour. *Part-time fees:* $250 per term. Part-time tuition and fees vary according to class time and course load. *Payment plan:* Installment.

UNDERGRADUATE FINANCIAL AID (Fall 2004, est.) 120 applied for aid; of those 92% were deemed to have need. 100% of undergraduates with need received aid. *Average percent of need met:* 75% (excluding resources awarded to replace EFC). *Average financial aid package:* $16,000 (excluding resources awarded to replace EFC). 1% of all full-time undergraduates had no need and received non-need-based gift aid.

GIFT AID (NEED-BASED) *Total amount:* $660,815 (26% federal, 26% state, 48% institutional). *Receiving aid:* All full-time undergraduates: 51% (71). *Average award:* Undergraduates: $4000. *Scholarships, grants, and awards:* Federal Pell, FSEOG, state, private, college/university gift aid from institutional funds.

GIFT AID (NON-NEED-BASED) *Total amount:* $11,551 (100% external sources). *Average Award:* Undergraduates: $18,165. *Scholarships, grants, and awards by category:* Academic Interests/Achievement: 2 awards ($36,330 total): general academic interests/achievements. *Creative Arts/Performance:* 4 awards ($2000 total): art/fine arts, creative writing, theater/drama. *Special Achievements/Activities:* 2 awards ($2000 total): hobbies/interests. *Special Characteristics:* 2 awards ($1000 total): children and siblings of alumni, out-of-state students. *Tuition waivers:* Full or partial for employees or children of employees, adult students, senior citizens.

LOANS *Student loans:* $641,088 (100% need-based). *Average need-based loan:* Undergraduates: $4200. *Parent loans:* $116,993 (100% non-need-based). *Programs:* FFEL (Subsidized and Unsubsidized Stafford, PLUS), Perkins, Sallie Mae Signature Loans, TERI Loans.

WORK-STUDY *Federal work-study:* Total amount: $98,177; 54 jobs averaging $1500. *State or other work-study/employment:* Total amount: $17,192 (100% non-need-based). 12 part-time jobs averaging $1500.

APPLYING FOR FINANCIAL AID *Required financial aid forms:* FAFSA, institution's own form. *Financial aid deadline:* Continuous. *Notification date:* Continuous.

CONTACT Janet Henthorn, Director of Financial Aid, Shimer College, PO Box 500, Waukegan, IL 60079-0500, 847-249-7180 or toll-free 800-215-7173. Fax: 847-249-8798.

SHIPPENSBURG UNIVERSITY OF PENNSYLVANIA
Shippensburg, PA

Tuition & fees (PA res): $5986	Average undergraduate aid package: $6059

ABOUT THE INSTITUTION State-supported, coed. Awards: bachelor's and master's degrees and post-master's certificates. 31 undergraduate majors. Total enrollment: 7,653. Undergraduates: 6,579. Freshmen: 1,462. Federal methodology is used as a basis for awarding need-based institutional aid.

UNDERGRADUATE EXPENSES for 2004–05 *Application fee:* $30. *Tuition, state resident:* full-time $4810; part-time $200 per credit hour. *Tuition, nonresident:* full-time $12,026; part-time $501 per credit hour. *Required fees:* full-time $1176; $20 per credit hour or $127 per term part-time. *College room and board:* $5274; *room only:* $3190. Room and board charges vary according to board plan and housing facility. *Payment plan:* Installment.

FRESHMAN FINANCIAL AID (Fall 2004, est.) 1217 applied for aid; of those 67% were deemed to have need. 92% of freshmen with need received aid; of those 13% had need fully met. *Average percent of need met:* 61% (excluding resources awarded to replace EFC). *Average financial aid package:* $5364 (excluding resources awarded to replace EFC). 8% of all full-time freshmen had no need and received non-need-based gift aid.

UNDERGRADUATE FINANCIAL AID (Fall 2004, est.) 4,612 applied for aid; of those 71% were deemed to have need. 96% of undergraduates with need received aid; of those 21% had need fully met. *Average percent of need met:* 69% (excluding resources awarded to replace EFC). *Average financial aid package:* $6059 (excluding resources awarded to replace EFC). 30% of all full-time undergraduates had no need and received non-need-based gift aid.

GIFT AID (NEED-BASED) *Total amount:* $8,651,004 (41% federal, 49% state, 4% institutional, 6% external sources). *Receiving aid:* Freshmen: 41% (599); All full-time undergraduates: 38% (2,361). *Average award:* Freshmen: $3791;

Undergraduates: $3840. *Scholarships, grants, and awards:* Federal Pell, FSEOG, state, private, college/university gift aid from institutional funds.

GIFT AID (NON-NEED-BASED) *Total amount:* $917,083 (5% federal, 1% state, 44% institutional, 50% external sources). *Receiving aid:* Freshmen: 3% (45); Undergraduates: 3% (187). *Average Award:* Freshmen: $2368; *Undergraduates:* $695. *Scholarships, grants, and awards by category:* Academic Interests/Achievement: 351 awards ($735,480 total): biological sciences, business, communication, computer science, education, English, general academic interests/achievements, social sciences. *Tuition waivers:* Full or partial for employees or children of employees, senior citizens. *ROTC:* Army.

LOANS *Student loans:* $19,696,551 (58% need-based, 42% non-need-based). 68% of past graduating class borrowed through all loan programs. *Average indebtedness per student:* $16,819. *Average need-based loan:* Freshmen: $2630; Undergraduates: $3410. *Parent loans:* $5,945,130 (22% need-based, 78% non-need-based). *Programs:* FFEL (Subsidized and Unsubsidized Stafford, PLUS), Perkins, college/university, alternative loans.

WORK-STUDY *Federal work-study:* Total amount: $430,172; 294 jobs averaging $1463. *State or other work-study/employment:* Total amount: $551,425 (58% need-based, 42% non-need-based). 432 part-time jobs averaging $1276.

ATHLETIC AWARDS *Total amount:* $505,015 (40% need-based, 60% non-need-based).

APPLYING FOR FINANCIAL AID *Required financial aid form:* FAFSA. *Financial aid deadline (priority):* 3/15. *Notification date:* Continuous. Students must reply within 2 weeks of notification.

CONTACT Mr. Peter D'Annibale, Director of Financial Aid and Scholarships, Shippensburg University of Pennsylvania, 1871 Old Main Drive, Shippensburg, PA 17257-2299, 717-477-1131 or toll-free 800-822-8028 (in-state). Fax: 717-477-4028. E-mail: finaid@ship.edu.

SHORTER COLLEGE
Rome, GA

Tuition & fees: $12,770	Average undergraduate aid package: $10,329

ABOUT THE INSTITUTION Independent Baptist, coed. Awards: bachelor's degrees. 38 undergraduate majors. Total enrollment: 896. Undergraduates: 896. Freshmen: 226. Federal methodology is used as a basis for awarding need-based institutional aid.

UNDERGRADUATE EXPENSES for 2004–05 *Application fee:* $25. *Comprehensive fee:* $18,670 includes full-time tuition ($12,500), mandatory fees ($270), and room and board ($5900). *College room only:* $3300. Full-time tuition and fees vary according to course load. Room and board charges vary according to board plan and housing facility. *Part-time tuition:* $285 per semester hour. *Payment plan:* Installment.

FRESHMAN FINANCIAL AID (Fall 2004, est.) 179 applied for aid; of those 82% were deemed to have need. 100% of freshmen with need received aid; of those 26% had need fully met. *Average percent of need met:* 66% (excluding resources awarded to replace EFC). *Average financial aid package:* $10,104 (excluding resources awarded to replace EFC). 30% of all full-time freshmen had no need and received non-need-based gift aid.

UNDERGRADUATE FINANCIAL AID (Fall 2004, est.) 666 applied for aid; of those 85% were deemed to have need. 100% of undergraduates with need received aid; of those 24% had need fully met. *Average percent of need met:* 62% (excluding resources awarded to replace EFC). *Average financial aid package:* $10,329 (excluding resources awarded to replace EFC). 33% of all full-time undergraduates had no need and received non-need-based gift aid.

GIFT AID (NEED-BASED) *Total amount:* $3,952,720 (17% federal, 35% state, 46% institutional, 2% external sources). *Receiving aid:* Freshmen: 65% (146); All full-time undergraduates: 67% (561). *Average award:* Freshmen: $8352; Undergraduates: $7712. *Scholarships, grants, and awards:* Federal Pell, FSEOG, state, private, college/university gift aid from institutional funds.

GIFT AID (NON-NEED-BASED) *Total amount:* $2,603,328 (37% state, 60% institutional, 3% external sources). *Receiving aid:* Freshmen: 13% (29); Undergraduates: 12% (101). *Average Award:* Freshmen: $11,394; *Undergraduates:* $9766. *Scholarships, grants, and awards by category:* Academic Interests/Achievement: 1,147 awards ($1,392,067 total): English, foreign languages, general academic interests/achievements, religion/biblical studies. *Creative Arts/Performance:* 191 awards ($141,596 total): art/fine arts, music, theater/drama. *Special Achievements/Activities:* 786 awards ($246,052 total): religious involvement. *Special Characteristics:* 651 awards ($272,320 total): children of faculty/staff, children of union members/company employees, local/state students, out-of-state students, religious affiliation, siblings of current students. *Tuition waivers:* Full or partial for employees or children of employees, senior citizens.

LOANS *Student loans:* $2,428,895 (77% need-based, 23% non-need-based). 59% of past graduating class borrowed through all loan programs. *Average indebtedness per student:* $10,516. *Average need-based loan:* Freshmen: $2654; Undergraduates: $3615. *Parent loans:* $1,829,232 (48% need-based, 52% non-need-based). *Programs:* FFEL (Subsidized and Unsubsidized Stafford, PLUS), Perkins, college/university.

WORK-STUDY *Federal work-study:* Total amount: $129,549; 91 jobs averaging $1286. *State or other work-study/employment:* Total amount: $78,879 (100% non-need-based). 99 part-time jobs averaging $702.

ATHLETIC AWARDS *Total amount:* $964,957 (42% need-based, 58% non-need-based).

APPLYING FOR FINANCIAL AID *Financial aid deadline:* Continuous. *Notification date:* Continuous beginning 3/1. Students must reply within 2 weeks of notification.

CONTACT Dr. Philip Hawkins, Director of Financial Aid, Shorter College, 315 Shorter Avenue, Rome, GA 30165, 706-233-7227 or toll-free 800-868-6980. *Fax:* 706-233-7314. *E-mail:* phawkins@shorter.edu.

SH'OR YOSHUV RABBINICAL COLLEGE
Lawrence, NY

CONTACT Office of Financial Aid, Sh'or Yoshuv Rabbinical College, 1526 Central Avenue, Far Rockaway, NY 11691-4002, 718-327-2048.

SIENA COLLEGE
Loudonville, NY

ABOUT THE INSTITUTION Independent Roman Catholic, coed. Awards: bachelor's degrees. 27 undergraduate majors. Total enrollment: 3,338. Undergraduates: 3,338. Freshmen: 716.

GIFT AID (NEED-BASED) *Scholarships, grants, and awards:* Federal Pell, FSEOG, state, private, college/university gift aid from institutional funds, Siena Grants, Franciscan Community Grants.

GIFT AID (NON-NEED-BASED) *Scholarships, grants, and awards by category: Academic Interests/Achievement:* biological sciences, business, communication, computer science, education, English, foreign languages, general academic interests/achievements, health fields, home economics, humanities, international studies, mathematics, military science, physical sciences, premedicine, religion/biblical studies, social sciences. *Creative Arts/Performance:* creative writing, general creative arts/performance, journalism/publications, music, performing arts, theater/drama. *Special Achievements/Activities:* community service, general special achievements/activities, hobbies/interests, leadership, memberships, religious involvement. *Special Characteristics:* adult students, children and siblings of alumni, children of faculty/staff, children of public servants, children of union members/company employees, children of workers in trades, children with a deceased or disabled parent, ethnic background, general special characteristics, local/state students, out-of-state students, previous college experience, relatives of clergy, religious affiliation, veterans' children.

LOANS *Programs:* FFEL (Subsidized and Unsubsidized Stafford, PLUS), Perkins.

APPLYING FOR FINANCIAL AID *Required financial aid forms:* FAFSA, state aid form.

CONTACT Mary K. Lawyer, Assistant Vice President for Financial Aid, Siena College, 515 Loudon Road, Loudonville, NY 12211-1462, 518-783-2427 or toll-free 888-AT-SIENA. *Fax:* 518-783-2410. *E-mail:* aid@siena.edu.

SIENA HEIGHTS UNIVERSITY
Adrian, MI

CONTACT Office of Financial Aid, Siena Heights University, 1247 East Siena Heights Drive, Adrian, MI 49221, 517-264-7130 or toll-free 800-521-0009.

SIERRA NEVADA COLLEGE
Incline Village, NV

Tuition & fees: $19,650   **Average undergraduate aid package: $14,000**

ABOUT THE INSTITUTION Independent, coed. Awards: bachelor's and master's degrees. 11 undergraduate majors. Total enrollment: 492. Undergraduates: 302. Freshmen: 67. Federal methodology is used as a basis for awarding need-based institutional aid.

UNDERGRADUATE EXPENSES for 2004–05 *Comprehensive fee:* $27,100 includes full-time tuition ($19,500), mandatory fees ($150), and room and board ($7450). Full-time tuition and fees vary according to course load, location, and program. Room and board charges vary according to gender. *Part-time tuition:* $850 per hour. *Part-time fees:* $75 per term. Part-time tuition and fees vary according to course load, location, and program. *Payment plans:* Installment, deferred payment.

FRESHMAN FINANCIAL AID (Fall 2003) 72 applied for aid; of those 100% were deemed to have need. 100% of freshmen with need received aid. *Average percent of need met:* 60% (excluding resources awarded to replace EFC). *Average financial aid package:* $14,000 (excluding resources awarded to replace EFC). 14% of all full-time freshmen had no need and received non-need-based gift aid.

UNDERGRADUATE FINANCIAL AID (Fall 2003) 203 applied for aid; of those 100% were deemed to have need. 100% of undergraduates with need received aid. *Average percent of need met:* 60% (excluding resources awarded to replace EFC). *Average financial aid package:* $14,000 (excluding resources awarded to replace EFC). 12% of all full-time undergraduates had no need and received non-need-based gift aid.

GIFT AID (NEED-BASED) *Total amount:* $3,311,690 (17% federal, 82% institutional, 1% external sources). *Receiving aid:* Freshmen: 84% (72); All full-time undergraduates: 70% (203). *Average award:* Freshmen: $8000; Undergraduates: $6000. *Scholarships, grants, and awards:* Federal Pell, FSEOG, state, private, college/university gift aid from institutional funds.

GIFT AID (NON-NEED-BASED) *Total amount:* $80,800 (63% state, 37% external sources). *Receiving aid:* Freshmen: 67% (58); Undergraduates: 70% (203). *Average Award:* Freshmen: $8000; Undergraduates: $8000. *Scholarships, grants, and awards by category: Academic Interests/Achievement:* business, education, general academic interests/achievements, humanities. *Creative Arts/Performance:* art/fine arts, music. *Special Characteristics:* 17 awards ($56,503 total): ethnic background, local/state students, members of minority groups. *Tuition waivers:* Full or partial for employees or children of employees. *ROTC:* Army cooperative.

LOANS *Student loans:* $3,065,841 (100% need-based). 65% of past graduating class borrowed through all loan programs. *Average indebtedness per student:* $18,000. *Parent loans:* $564,734 (100% need-based). *Programs:* Federal Direct (Subsidized and Unsubsidized Stafford, PLUS), alternative loans.

WORK-STUDY *Federal work-study:* Total amount: $125,000; 63 jobs averaging $2000. *State or other work-study/employment:* 2 part-time jobs averaging $2500.

ATHLETIC AWARDS *Total amount:* $135,500 (100% non-need-based).

APPLYING FOR FINANCIAL AID *Required financial aid forms:* FAFSA, institution's own form. *Financial aid deadline (priority):* 6/1. *Notification date:* Continuous. Students must reply within 4 weeks of notification.

CONTACT Dorothy Caruso, Director of Financial Aid, Sierra Nevada College, 999 Tahoe Boulevard, Incline Village, NV 89451, 775-831-1314 Ext. 4066 or toll-free 775-831-1314 (in-state). *Fax:* 775-831-1347. *E-mail:* dcaruso@sierranevada.edu.

SILICON VALLEY UNIVERSITY
San Jose, CA

CONTACT Financial Aid Office, Silicon Valley University, 3590 North First Street, Suite 320, San Jose, CA 95134, 408-435-8989.

SILVER LAKE COLLEGE
Manitowoc, WI

Tuition & fees: $16,000   **Average undergraduate aid package: $11,043**

ABOUT THE INSTITUTION Independent Roman Catholic, coed. Awards: associate, bachelor's, and master's degrees and post-bachelor's certificates. 24 undergraduate majors. Total enrollment: 1,034. Undergraduates: 756. Freshmen: 28. Federal methodology is used as a basis for awarding need-based institutional aid.

UNDERGRADUATE EXPENSES for 2005–06 *Application fee:* $35. *Tuition:* full-time $16,000; part-time $500 per credit. Full-time tuition and fees vary according to location, program, and reciprocity agreements. Part-time tuition and fees vary according to course load, location, and program. Room and board charges vary according to board plan and housing facility. *Payment plans:* Installment, deferred payment.

FRESHMAN FINANCIAL AID (Fall 2004, est.) 23 applied for aid; of those 100% were deemed to have need. 100% of freshmen with need received aid; of those 4% had need fully met. *Average percent of need met:* 65% (excluding resources awarded to replace EFC). *Average financial aid package:* $13,107 (excluding resources awarded to replace EFC). 18% of all full-time freshmen had no need and received non-need-based gift aid.

UNDERGRADUATE FINANCIAL AID (Fall 2004, est.) 204 applied for aid; of those 89% were deemed to have need. 100% of undergraduates with need received aid; of those 15% had need fully met. *Average percent of need met:* 65% (excluding resources awarded to replace EFC). *Average financial aid package:* $11,043 (excluding resources awarded to replace EFC). 3% of all full-time undergraduates had no need and received non-need-based gift aid.

GIFT AID (NEED-BASED) *Total amount:* $1,570,706 (39% federal, 21% state, 37% institutional, 3% external sources). *Receiving aid:* Freshmen: 82% (23); All full-time undergraduates: 80% (167). *Average award:* Freshmen: $8586; Undergraduates: $6971. *Scholarships, grants, and awards:* Federal Pell, FSEOG, state, private, college/university gift aid from institutional funds.

GIFT AID (NON-NEED-BASED) *Total amount:* $62,785 (16% federal, 62% institutional, 22% external sources). *Receiving aid:* Undergraduates: 3% (7). *Average Award:* Freshmen: $5370; Undergraduates: $3996. *Scholarships, grants, and awards by category:* Academic Interests/Achievement: 82 awards ($260,195 total): general academic interests/achievements. *Creative Arts/Performance:* 13 awards ($12,250 total): applied art and design, music. *Special Achievements/ Activities:* 44 awards ($21,500 total): religious involvement. *Special Characteristics:* 1 award ($15,500 total): children of faculty/staff, international students. *Tuition waivers:* Full or partial for children of alumni, employees or children of employees, senior citizens.

LOANS *Student loans:* $1,593,897 (83% need-based, 17% non-need-based). 67% of past graduating class borrowed through all loan programs. *Average indebtedness per student:* $16,708. *Average need-based loan:* Freshmen: $2625; Undergraduates: $4172. *Parent loans:* $136,462 (46% need-based, 54% non-need-based). *Programs:* FFEL (Subsidized and Unsubsidized Stafford, PLUS).

WORK-STUDY *Federal work-study:* Total amount: $186,898; 107 jobs averaging $1747.

ATHLETIC AWARDS *Total amount:* $17,000 (88% need-based, 12% non-need-based).

APPLYING FOR FINANCIAL AID *Required financial aid form:* FAFSA. *Financial aid deadline (priority):* 3/15. *Notification date:* Continuous beginning 3/15. Students must reply within 2 weeks of notification.

CONTACT Michelle Leider, Associate Director of Financial Aid, Silver Lake College, 2406 South Alverno Road, Manitowoc, WI 54220-9319, 920-686-6205 or toll-free 800-236-4752 Ext. 175 (in-state). *Fax:* 920-684-7082. *E-mail:* mlleider@silver.sl.edu.

SIMMONS COLLEGE
Boston, MA

Tuition & fees: $25,440	Average undergraduate aid package: $15,854

ABOUT THE INSTITUTION Independent, women only. Awards: bachelor's, master's, and doctoral degrees and post-bachelor's and post-master's certificates. 52 undergraduate majors. Total enrollment: 4,549. Undergraduates: 1,812. Freshmen: 420. Federal methodology is used as a basis for awarding need-based institutional aid.

UNDERGRADUATE EXPENSES for 2005–06 *Application fee:* $35. *Comprehensive fee:* $35,640 includes full-time tuition ($24,680), mandatory fees ($760), and room and board ($10,200). Full-time tuition and fees vary according to course load. *Part-time tuition:* $770 per semester hour. Part-time tuition and fees vary according to course load. *Payment plan:* Installment.

FRESHMAN FINANCIAL AID (Fall 2004, est.) 336 applied for aid; of those 85% were deemed to have need. 100% of freshmen with need received aid; of those 6% had need fully met. *Average percent of need met:* 57% (excluding resources awarded to replace EFC). *Average financial aid package:* $15,314 (excluding resources awarded to replace EFC). 4% of all full-time freshmen had no need and received non-need-based gift aid.

UNDERGRADUATE FINANCIAL AID (Fall 2004, est.) 1,244 applied for aid; of those 90% were deemed to have need. 98% of undergraduates with need received aid; of those 4% had need fully met. *Average percent of need met:* 56% (excluding resources awarded to replace EFC). *Average financial aid package:* $15,854 (excluding resources awarded to replace EFC). 2% of all full-time undergraduates had no need and received non-need-based gift aid.

GIFT AID (NEED-BASED) *Total amount:* $13,097,875 (13% federal, 5% state, 82% institutional). *Receiving aid:* Freshmen: 64% (258); All full-time undergraduates: 66% (1,055). *Average award:* Freshmen: $9177; Undergraduates: $11,574. *Scholarships, grants, and awards:* Federal Pell, FSEOG, state, private, college/university gift aid from institutional funds.

GIFT AID (NON-NEED-BASED) *Receiving aid:* Freshmen: 29% (118); Undergraduates: 15% (233). *Average Award:* Freshmen: $10,823; Undergraduates: $12,780. *Scholarships, grants, and awards by category:* Academic Interests/Achievement: 95 awards ($1,207,832 total): general academic interests/achievements. *Special Achievements/Activities:* 226 awards ($1,072,500 total): community service, general special achievements/activities. *Special Characteristics:* 81 awards ($153,500 total): children and siblings of alumni, general special characteristics. *Tuition waivers:* Full or partial for employees or children of employees, adult students, senior citizens. *ROTC:* Army cooperative, Naval cooperative, Air Force cooperative.

LOANS *Student loans:* $6,663,237 (74% need-based, 26% non-need-based). 90% of past graduating class borrowed through all loan programs. *Average indebtedness per student:* $26,300. *Average need-based loan:* Freshmen: $3127; Undergraduates: $3040. *Parent loans:* $3,938,806 (100% need-based). *Programs:* FFEL (Subsidized and Unsubsidized Stafford, PLUS), Perkins, state, college/university.

WORK-STUDY *Federal work-study:* Total amount: $1,400,000; jobs available (averaging $2500).

APPLYING FOR FINANCIAL AID *Required financial aid form:* FAFSA. *Financial aid deadline (priority):* 2/15. *Notification date:* 3/15.

CONTACT Diane M. Hallisey, Director of Student Financial Services, Simmons College, 300 The Fenway, Boston, MA 02115, 617-521-2001 or toll-free 800-345-8468 (out-of-state). *Fax:* 617-521-3195. *E-mail:* hallisey@simmons.edu.

SIMON'S ROCK COLLEGE OF BARD
Great Barrington, MA

Tuition & fees: $31,187	Average undergraduate aid package: $18,892

ABOUT THE INSTITUTION Independent, coed. Awards: associate and bachelor's degrees. 71 undergraduate majors. Total enrollment: 386. Undergraduates: 386. Freshmen: 136. Both federal and institutional methodology are used as a basis for awarding need-based institutional aid.

UNDERGRADUATE EXPENSES for 2004–05 *Application fee:* $40. *Comprehensive fee:* $39,275 includes full-time tuition ($30,687), mandatory fees ($500), and room and board ($8088). Full-time tuition and fees vary according to course load and program. *Part-time tuition:* $1200 per credit hour. *Part-time fees:* $600. Part-time tuition and fees vary according to course load and program. *Payment plan:* Installment.

FRESHMAN FINANCIAL AID (Fall 2004, est.) 120 applied for aid; of those 91% were deemed to have need. 100% of freshmen with need received aid; of those 17% had need fully met. *Average percent of need met:* 68% (excluding resources awarded to replace EFC). *Average financial aid package:* $19,644 (excluding resources awarded to replace EFC). 9% of all full-time freshmen had no need and received non-need-based gift aid.

UNDERGRADUATE FINANCIAL AID (Fall 2004, est.) 293 applied for aid; of those 86% were deemed to have need. 100% of undergraduates with need received aid; of those 15% had need fully met. *Average percent of need met:* 68% (excluding resources awarded to replace EFC). *Average financial aid package:* $18,892 (excluding resources awarded to replace EFC). 4% of all full-time undergraduates had no need and received non-need-based gift aid.

GIFT AID (NEED-BASED) *Total amount:* $2,031,613 (13% federal, 2% state, 85% institutional). *Receiving aid:* Freshmen: 55% (76); All full-time undergraduates: 48% (172). *Average award:* Freshmen: $10,818; Undergraduates: $9954. *Scholarships, grants, and awards:* Federal Pell, FSEOG, state, private, college/university gift aid from institutional funds.

GIFT AID (NON-NEED-BASED) *Total amount:* $2,238,210 (96% institutional, 4% external sources). *Receiving aid:* Freshmen: 36% (49); Undergraduates: 33% (118). *Average Award:* Freshmen: $25,000; Undergraduates: $22,250. *Scholarships, grants, and awards by category:* Academic Interests/Achievement: 158 awards ($2,145,725 total): general academic interests/achievements, social sciences. *Special Characteristics:* 74 awards ($1,078,000 total): children of faculty/staff, general special characteristics, local/state students, members of minority groups. *Tuition waivers:* Full or partial for minority students, employees or children of employees.

LOANS *Student loans:* $1,179,310 (63% need-based, 37% non-need-based). 82% of past graduating class borrowed through all loan programs. *Average indebtedness per student:* $14,000. *Average need-based loan:* Freshmen: $3443;

Undergraduates: $5037. *Parent loans:* $1,523,809 (100% non-need-based). *Programs:* FFEL (Subsidized and Unsubsidized Stafford, PLUS), Perkins, state, alternative loans.

WORK-STUDY *Federal work-study:* Total amount: $210,000; 96 jobs averaging $1500.

APPLYING FOR FINANCIAL AID *Required financial aid forms:* FAFSA, CSS Financial Aid PROFILE, noncustodial (divorced/separated) parent's statement, business/farm supplement, federal income tax form(s), federal verification worksheet. *Financial aid deadline (priority):* 4/15. *Notification date:* Continuous. Students must reply within 2 weeks of notification.

CONTACT Ms. Ann Gitto Murtagh, Director of Financial Aid, Simon's Rock College of Bard, 84 Alford Road, Great Barrington, MA 01230-9702, 413-528-0771 or toll-free 800-235-7186. *Fax:* 413-528-7339. *E-mail:* agitto@simons-rock.edu.

SIMPSON COLLEGE
Indianola, IA

Tuition & fees: $19,635 | Average undergraduate aid package: $18,015

ABOUT THE INSTITUTION Independent United Methodist, coed. Awards: bachelor's degrees and post-bachelor's certificates. 50 undergraduate majors. Total enrollment: 1,964. Undergraduates: 1,953. Freshmen: 405. Federal methodology is used as a basis for awarding need-based institutional aid.

UNDERGRADUATE EXPENSES for 2004–05 *Comprehensive fee:* $25,196 includes full-time tuition ($19,430), mandatory fees ($205), and room and board ($5561). *College room only:* $2669. Room and board charges vary according to board plan and housing facility. Part-time tuition and fees vary according to class time and course load. *Payment plan:* Installment.

FRESHMAN FINANCIAL AID (Fall 2004, est.) 394 applied for aid; of those 89% were deemed to have need. 100% of freshmen with need received aid; of those 21% had need fully met. *Average percent of need met:* 88% (excluding resources awarded to replace EFC). *Average financial aid package:* $18,739 (excluding resources awarded to replace EFC). 10% of all full-time freshmen had no need and received non-need-based gift aid.

UNDERGRADUATE FINANCIAL AID (Fall 2004, est.) 1,440 applied for aid; of those 88% were deemed to have need. 100% of undergraduates with need received aid; of those 24% had need fully met. *Average percent of need met:* 85% (excluding resources awarded to replace EFC). *Average financial aid package:* $18,015 (excluding resources awarded to replace EFC). 12% of all full-time undergraduates had no need and received non-need-based gift aid.

GIFT AID (NEED-BASED) *Total amount:* $16,300,815 (8% federal, 17% state, 71% institutional, 4% external sources). *Receiving aid:* Freshmen: 89% (352); All full-time undergraduates: 87% (1,266). *Average award:* Freshmen: $13,923; Undergraduates: $12,280. *Scholarships, grants, and awards:* Federal Pell, FSEOG, state, private, college/university gift aid from institutional funds.

GIFT AID (NON-NEED-BASED) *Total amount:* $1,773,834 (91% institutional, 9% external sources). *Receiving aid:* Freshmen: 7% (29); Undergraduates: 9% (129). *Average Award:* Freshmen: $6779; Undergraduates: $7917. *Scholarships, grants, and awards by category:* Academic Interests/Achievement: $5,342,564 total: general academic interests/achievements. Creative Arts/Performance: $511,490 total: art/fine arts, music, theater/drama. Special Achievements/Activities: $300,410 total: leadership, religious involvement. Special Characteristics: $1,430,894 total: adult students, children and siblings of alumni, children of educators, children of faculty/staff, international students, members of minority groups, relatives of clergy, religious affiliation, siblings of current students, twins. *Tuition waivers:* Full or partial for employees or children of employees.

LOANS *Student loans:* $9,709,892 (68% need-based, 32% non-need-based). 91% of past graduating class borrowed through all loan programs. *Average indebtedness per student:* $23,558. *Average need-based loan:* Freshmen: $3417; Undergraduates: $3771. *Parent loans:* $1,304,074 (24% need-based, 76% non-need-based). *Programs:* FFEL (Subsidized and Unsubsidized Stafford, PLUS), Perkins, state, college/university, alternative loans.

WORK-STUDY *Federal work-study:* Total amount: $282,949; 470 jobs averaging $602. *State or other work-study/employment:* Total amount: $474,421 (6% need-based, 94% non-need-based). 630 part-time jobs averaging $753.

APPLYING FOR FINANCIAL AID *Required financial aid form:* FAFSA. *Financial aid deadline:* Continuous. *Notification date:* Continuous beginning 3/15. Students must reply by 5/1 or within 3 weeks of notification.

CONTACT Tracie Pavon, Assistant Vice President of Financial Aid, Simpson College, 701 North C Street, Indianola, IA 50125-1297, 515-961-1630 Ext. 1596 or toll-free 800-362-2454. *Fax:* 515-961-1300. *E-mail:* pavon@simpson.edu.

SIMPSON UNIVERSITY
Redding, CA

Tuition & fees: $17,000 | Average undergraduate aid package: $7140

ABOUT THE INSTITUTION Independent religious, coed. Awards: associate, bachelor's, and master's degrees. 20 undergraduate majors. Total enrollment: 1,134. Undergraduates: 954. Freshmen: 186. Federal methodology is used as a basis for awarding need-based institutional aid.

UNDERGRADUATE EXPENSES for 2005–06 *Application fee:* $20. *Comprehensive fee:* $22,900 includes full-time tuition ($17,000) and room and board ($5900). Room and board charges vary according to board plan. *Part-time tuition:* $710 per credit hour. *Payment plans:* Installment, deferred payment.

GIFT AID (NEED-BASED) *Total amount:* $3,938,847 (33% federal, 57% state, 10% institutional). *Receiving aid:* Freshmen: 83% (150); All full-time undergraduates: 91% (840). *Average award:* Freshmen: $5890; Undergraduates: $3775. *Scholarships, grants, and awards:* Federal Pell, FSEOG, state, private, college/university gift aid from institutional funds.

GIFT AID (NON-NEED-BASED) *Total amount:* $2,899,246 (95% institutional, 5% external sources). *Receiving aid:* Freshmen: 83% (150); Undergraduates: 91% (843). *Average Award:* Freshmen: $5840; Undergraduates: $4870. *Scholarships, grants, and awards by category:* Academic Interests/Achievement: general academic interests/achievements. Creative Arts/Performance: music. Special Achievements/Activities: leadership, religious involvement. Special Characteristics: children of faculty/staff, general special characteristics, members of minority groups, out-of-state students, relatives of clergy, religious affiliation, siblings of current students, spouses of current students. *Tuition waivers:* Full or partial for employees or children of employees.

LOANS *Student loans:* $4,491,278 (67% need-based, 33% non-need-based). 89% of past graduating class borrowed through all loan programs. *Average indebtedness per student:* $17,600. *Average need-based loan:* Freshmen: $2625; Undergraduates: $4500. *Parent loans:* $1,706,973 (100% non-need-based). *Programs:* FFEL (Subsidized and Unsubsidized Stafford, PLUS), Perkins, alternative loans.

APPLYING FOR FINANCIAL AID *Required financial aid forms:* FAFSA, institution's own form. *Financial aid deadline (priority):* 3/2. *Notification date:* Continuous beginning 3/16. Students must reply within 3 weeks of notification.

CONTACT Mr. James Herberger, Director of Student Financial Services, Simpson University, 2211 College View Drive, Redding, CA 96003-8606, 530-224-5600 or toll-free 800-598-2493. *Fax:* 530-226-4870. *E-mail:* financialaid@simpsonuniveristy.edu.

SINTE GLESKA UNIVERSITY
Rosebud, SD

CONTACT Office of Financial Aid, Sinte Gleska University, PO Box 490, Rosebud, SD 57570-0490, 605-747-4258. *Fax:* 605-747-2098.

SI TANKA UNIVERSITY
Huron, SD

ABOUT THE INSTITUTION Proprietary, coed. Awards: associate and bachelor's degrees. 13 undergraduate majors. Total enrollment: 528. Undergraduates: 528. Freshmen: 175.

GIFT AID (NEED-BASED) *Scholarships, grants, and awards:* Federal Pell, FSEOG, college/university gift aid from institutional funds.

GIFT AID (NON-NEED-BASED) *Scholarships, grants, and awards by category:* Academic Interests/Achievement: general academic interests/achievements. Creative Arts/Performance: music. Special Achievements/Activities: cheerleading/drum major.

LOANS *Programs:* FFEL (Subsidized and Unsubsidized Stafford, PLUS), Perkins.

WORK-STUDY *Federal work-study:* Total amount: $120,022; jobs available.

APPLYING FOR FINANCIAL AID *Required financial aid form:* FAFSA.

CONTACT Kristy O'Kief, Financial Aid Director, Si Tanka University, 333 9th Street SW, Huron, SD 57350-2798, 605-353-2012 or toll-free 800-710-7159. *Fax:* 605-353-2413. *E-mail:* kokief@sitanka.edu.

SKIDMORE COLLEGE
Saratoga Springs, NY

Tuition & fees: $31,108   **Average undergraduate aid package: $25,312**

ABOUT THE INSTITUTION Independent, coed. Awards: bachelor's and master's degrees. 41 undergraduate majors. Total enrollment: 2,691. Undergraduates: 2,637. Freshmen: 676. Both federal and institutional methodology are used as a basis for awarding need-based institutional aid.

UNDERGRADUATE EXPENSES for 2004–05 *Application fee:* $60. *Comprehensive fee:* $39,818 includes full-time tuition ($30,800), mandatory fees ($308), and room and board ($8710). *College room only:* $4860. Full-time tuition and fees vary according to course load. Room and board charges vary according to board plan and housing facility. *Part-time tuition:* $1030 per credit hour. *Part-time fees:* $25 per term. Part-time tuition and fees vary according to course load. *Payment plans:* Tuition prepayment, installment.

FRESHMAN FINANCIAL AID (Fall 2004, est.) 320 applied for aid; of those 84% were deemed to have need. 100% of freshmen with need received aid; of those 94% had need fully met. *Average percent of need met:* 99% (excluding resources awarded to replace EFC). *Average financial aid package:* $25,406 (excluding resources awarded to replace EFC). 1% of all full-time freshmen had no need and received non-need-based gift aid.

UNDERGRADUATE FINANCIAL AID (Fall 2004, est.) 1,112 applied for aid; of those 91% were deemed to have need. 100% of undergraduates with need received aid; of those 91% had need fully met. *Average percent of need met:* 95% (excluding resources awarded to replace EFC). *Average financial aid package:* $25,312 (excluding resources awarded to replace EFC). 1% of all full-time undergraduates had no need and received non-need-based gift aid.

GIFT AID (NEED-BASED) *Total amount:* $19,795,500 (7% federal, 5% state, 88% institutional). *Receiving aid:* Freshmen: 40% (270); All full-time undergraduates: 43% (1,010). *Average award:* Freshmen: $21,445; Undergraduates: $19,817. *Scholarships, grants, and awards:* Federal Pell, FSEOG, state, college/university gift aid from institutional funds.

GIFT AID (NON-NEED-BASED) *Total amount:* $813,806 (5% state, 43% institutional, 52% external sources). *Receiving aid:* Freshmen: 16% (111); Undergraduates: 9% (216). *Average Award:* Freshmen: $10,000; Undergraduates: $10,000. *Scholarships, grants, and awards by category:* Academic Interests/Achievement: 19 awards ($190,000 total): biological sciences, computer science, mathematics, physical sciences. Creative Arts/Performance: 16 awards ($160,000 total): music. Special Characteristics: 31 awards ($635,000 total): children of faculty/staff. *Tuition waivers:* Full or partial for employees or children of employees. *ROTC:* Army cooperative, Air Force cooperative.

LOANS *Student loans:* $4,935,000 (82% need-based, 18% non-need-based). 48% of past graduating class borrowed through all loan programs. *Average indebtedness per student:* $15,942. *Average need-based loan:* Freshmen: $2724; Undergraduates: $3991. *Parent loans:* $6,000,000 (100% non-need-based). *Programs:* FFEL (Subsidized and Unsubsidized Stafford, PLUS), Perkins.

WORK-STUDY *Federal work-study:* Total amount: $550,000; 550 jobs averaging $1000. *State or other work-study/employment:* Total amount: $450,000 (100% non-need-based). 700 part-time jobs averaging $643.

APPLYING FOR FINANCIAL AID *Required financial aid forms:* FAFSA, CSS Financial Aid PROFILE. *Financial aid deadline:* 1/15. *Notification date:* 4/1. Students must reply by 5/1.

CONTACT Mr. Robert D. Shorb, Director of Student Aid and Family Finance, Skidmore College, 815 North Broadway, Saratoga Springs, NY 12866-1632, 518-580-5750 or toll-free 800-867-6007. *Fax:* 518-580-5752. *E-mail:* rshorb@skidmore.edu.

SLIPPERY ROCK UNIVERSITY OF PENNSYLVANIA
Slippery Rock, PA

Tuition & fees (PA res): $6096   **Average undergraduate aid package: $6620**

ABOUT THE INSTITUTION State-supported, coed. Awards: bachelor's, master's, and doctoral degrees and post-bachelor's certificates. 43 undergraduate majors. Total enrollment: 7,928. Undergraduates: 7,202. Freshmen: 1,543. Federal methodology is used as a basis for awarding need-based institutional aid.

UNDERGRADUATE EXPENSES for 2004–05 *Application fee:* $25. *Tuition, state resident:* full-time $4810; part-time $200 per credit. *Tuition, nonresident:* full-time $7216; part-time $301 per credit. *Required fees:* full-time $1286; $46 per credit or $34 per term part-time. Full-time tuition and fees vary according to course load and degree level. Part-time tuition and fees vary according to course load and degree level. *College room and board:* $4714; *room only:* $2560. Room and board charges vary according to board plan, housing facility, and location. *Payment plan:* Installment.

FRESHMAN FINANCIAL AID (Fall 2004, est.) 1431 applied for aid; of those 76% were deemed to have need. 98% of freshmen with need received aid; of those 41% had need fully met. *Average percent of need met:* 77% (excluding resources awarded to replace EFC). *Average financial aid package:* $6352 (excluding resources awarded to replace EFC). 18% of all full-time freshmen had no need and received non-need-based gift aid.

UNDERGRADUATE FINANCIAL AID (Fall 2004, est.) 5,838 applied for aid; of those 73% were deemed to have need. 97% of undergraduates with need received aid; of those 49% had need fully met. *Average percent of need met:* 80% (excluding resources awarded to replace EFC). *Average financial aid package:* $6620 (excluding resources awarded to replace EFC). 18% of all full-time undergraduates had no need and received non-need-based gift aid.

GIFT AID (NEED-BASED) *Total amount:* $11,487,270 (48% federal, 48% state, 4% external sources). *Receiving aid:* Freshmen: 55% (853); All full-time undergraduates: 46% (3,077). *Average award:* Freshmen: $3098; Undergraduates: $2810. *Scholarships, grants, and awards:* Federal Pell, FSEOG, state, private, college/university gift aid from institutional funds.

GIFT AID (NON-NEED-BASED) *Total amount:* $2,762,199 (22% institutional, 78% external sources). *Receiving aid:* Freshmen: 19% (297); Undergraduates: 13% (891). *Average award:* Freshmen: $3527; Undergraduates: $4829. *Scholarships, grants, and awards by category:* Academic Interests/Achievement: 443 awards ($431,755 total): biological sciences, business, communication, computer science, education, English, general academic interests/achievements, health fields, physical sciences, social sciences. Creative Arts/Performance: applied art and design, art/fine arts, dance, music, performing arts, theater/drama. Special Achievements/Activities: community service, general special achievements/activities, leadership. Special Characteristics: children and siblings of alumni, children of faculty/staff, children of union members/company employees, ethnic background, general special characteristics, local/state students, members of minority groups, out-of-state students, previous college experience. *Tuition waivers:* Full or partial for minority students, employees or children of employees, senior citizens. *ROTC:* Army.

LOANS *Student loans:* $24,625,019 (54% need-based, 46% non-need-based). 80% of past graduating class borrowed through all loan programs. *Average indebtedness per student:* $20,041. *Average need-based loan:* Freshmen: $2445; Undergraduates: $3087. *Parent loans:* $4,001,789 (100% non-need-based). *Programs:* FFEL (Subsidized and Unsubsidized Stafford, PLUS), Perkins.

WORK-STUDY *Federal work-study:* Total amount: $612,199; jobs available. *State or other work-study/employment:* Total amount: $1,648,509 (100% non-need-based). Part-time jobs available.

ATHLETIC AWARDS *Total amount:* $621,985 (100% non-need-based).

APPLYING FOR FINANCIAL AID *Required financial aid form:* FAFSA. *Financial aid deadline (priority):* 5/1. *Notification date:* Continuous.

CONTACT Ms. Patty A. Hladio, Director of Financial Aid, Slippery Rock University of Pennsylvania, 1 Morrow Way, Slippery Rock, PA 16057, 724-738-2044 or toll-free 800-SRU-9111. *Fax:* 724-738-2922. *E-mail:* financial.aid@sru.edu.

SMITH COLLEGE
Northampton, MA

ABOUT THE INSTITUTION Independent, women only. Awards: bachelor's, master's, and doctoral degrees and post-bachelor's and post-master's certificates. 51 undergraduate majors. Total enrollment: 3,159. Undergraduates: 2,682. Freshmen: 635.

GIFT AID (NEED-BASED) *Scholarships, grants, and awards:* Federal Pell, FSEOG, state, college/university gift aid from institutional funds.

GIFT AID (NON-NEED-BASED) *Scholarships, grants, and awards by category:* Academic Interests/Achievement: engineering/technologies, general academic interests/achievements. Special Characteristics: local/state students.

LOANS *Programs:* Federal Direct (Subsidized and Unsubsidized Stafford), FFEL (PLUS), Perkins, state, college/university.

WORK-STUDY *Federal work-study:* Total amount: $2,815,200; jobs available. *State or other work-study/employment:* Total amount: $446,634 (81% need-based, 19% non-need-based). 219 part-time jobs averaging $1961.

APPLYING FOR FINANCIAL AID *Required financial aid forms:* FAFSA, institution's own form, CSS Financial Aid PROFILE, noncustodial (divorced/separated) parent's statement, business/farm supplement.

CONTACT Deborah Luekens, Director of Student Financial Services, Smith College, College Hall, Northampton, MA 01063, 413-585-2530 or toll-free 800-383-3232. *Fax:* 413-585-2566. *E-mail:* sfs@smith.edu.

SOJOURNER-DOUGLASS COLLEGE
Baltimore, MD

ABOUT THE INSTITUTION Independent, coed, primarily women. Awards: bachelor's and master's degrees (offers only evening and weekend programs). 18 undergraduate majors. Total enrollment: 1,124. Undergraduates: 1,060. Freshmen: 169.

GIFT AID (NEED-BASED) *Scholarships, grants, and awards:* Federal Pell, FSEOG, state.

LOANS *Programs:* FFEL (Subsidized and Unsubsidized Stafford, PLUS), college/university.

WORK-STUDY *Federal work-study:* Total amount: $108,712; 15 jobs averaging $7800.

APPLYING FOR FINANCIAL AID *Required financial aid forms:* FAFSA, institution's own form.

CONTACT Ms. Rebecca Chalk, Financial Aid Director, Sojourner-Douglass College, 500 North Caroline Street, Baltimore, MD 21205, 410-276-0306 Ext. 260. *Fax:* 410-276-1593.

SOKA UNIVERSITY OF AMERICA
Aliso Viejo, CA

CONTACT Financial Aid Office, Soka University of America, 1 University Drive, Aliso Viejo, CA 92656, 949-480-4000.

SONOMA STATE UNIVERSITY
Rohnert Park, CA

Tuition & fees (CA res): $3408   **Average undergraduate aid package: $9497**

ABOUT THE INSTITUTION State-supported, coed. Awards: bachelor's and master's degrees. 61 undergraduate majors. Total enrollment: 7,977. Undergraduates: 6,798. Freshmen: 1,111. Federal methodology is used as a basis for awarding need-based institutional aid.

UNDERGRADUATE EXPENSES for 2004–05 *Application fee:* $55. *Tuition, state resident:* full-time $0. *Tuition, nonresident:* full-time $10,176; part-time $339 per unit. *Required fees:* full-time $3408; $1215 per term part-time. Full-time tuition and fees vary according to course load. Part-time tuition and fees vary according to course load. *College room and board:* $8805; *room only:* $6001. Room and board charges vary according to board plan and housing facility. *Payment plan:* Deferred payment.

FRESHMAN FINANCIAL AID (Fall 2004, est.) 502 applied for aid; of those 61% were deemed to have need. 92% of freshmen with need received aid; of those 79% had need fully met. *Average percent of need met:* 82% (excluding resources awarded to replace EFC). *Average financial aid package:* $9062 (excluding resources awarded to replace EFC). 3% of all full-time freshmen had no need and received non-need-based gift aid.

UNDERGRADUATE FINANCIAL AID (Fall 2004, est.) 3,075 applied for aid; of those 76% were deemed to have need. 94% of undergraduates with need received aid; of those 66% had need fully met. *Average percent of need met:* 79% (excluding resources awarded to replace EFC). *Average financial aid package:* $9497 (excluding resources awarded to replace EFC). 2% of all full-time undergraduates had no need and received non-need-based gift aid.

GIFT AID (NEED-BASED) *Total amount:* $8,603,694 (49% federal, 51% state). *Receiving aid:* Freshmen: 15% (165); All full-time undergraduates: 24% (1,414). *Average award:* Freshmen: $6055; Undergraduates: $5298. *Scholarships, grants, and awards:* Federal Pell, FSEOG, state, private, college/university gift aid from institutional funds.

GIFT AID (NON-NEED-BASED) *Total amount:* $1,321,483 (20% state, 20% institutional, 60% external sources). *Receiving aid:* Freshmen: 19% (203); Undergraduates: 26% (1,512). *Average Award:* Freshmen: $2225; Undergraduates: $2066. *Scholarships, grants, and awards by category:* Academic Interests/Achievement: 66 awards ($56,050 total): area/ethnic studies, biological sciences, business, communication, computer science, education, English, foreign languages, general academic interests/achievements, health fields, humanities, mathematics, physical sciences, premedicine, social sciences. *Creative Arts/Performance:* 35 awards ($40,975 total): applied art and design, art/fine arts, cinema/film/broadcasting, creative writing, dance, journalism/publications, music, performing arts, theater/drama. *Special Achievements/Activities:* 3 awards ($1750 total): community service, leadership, memberships. *Special Characteristics:* 73 awards ($82,850 total): adult students, children and siblings of alumni, children of educators, children of faculty/staff, children of public servants, children of union members/company employees, children of workers in trades, ethnic background, first-generation college students, general special characteristics, handicapped students, international students, local/state students, married students, members of minority groups, out-of-state students, previous college experience, veterans. *Tuition waivers:* Full or partial for employees or children of employees. *ROTC:* Army cooperative, Air Force cooperative.

LOANS *Student loans:* $15,821,106 (61% need-based, 39% non-need-based). 54% of past graduating class borrowed through all loan programs. *Average indebtedness per student:* $8775. *Average need-based loan:* Freshmen: $2574; Undergraduates: $4281. *Parent loans:* $7,730,131 (100% non-need-based). *Programs:* Federal Direct (Subsidized and Unsubsidized Stafford, PLUS), Perkins.

WORK-STUDY *Federal work-study:* Total amount: $1,092,457; 401 jobs averaging $2739. *State or other work-study/employment:* Total amount: $1,600,000 (100% non-need-based). 694 part-time jobs averaging $2305.

ATHLETIC AWARDS *Total amount:* $183,005 (100% non-need-based).

APPLYING FOR FINANCIAL AID *Required financial aid form:* FAFSA. *Financial aid deadline (priority):* 1/31. *Notification date:* Continuous beginning 3/15. Students must reply within 4 weeks of notification.

CONTACT Susan Gutierrez, Director of Financial Aid, Sonoma State University, 1801 East Cotati Avenue, Rohnert Park, CA 94928-3609, 707-664-2287. *Fax:* 707-664-4242. *E-mail:* susan.gutierrez@sonoma.edu.

SOUTH CAROLINA STATE UNIVERSITY
Orangeburg, SC

Tuition & fees (SC res): $6355   **Average undergraduate aid package: N/A**

ABOUT THE INSTITUTION State-supported, coed. Awards: bachelor's, master's, and doctoral degrees and post-bachelor's and post-master's certificates. 49 undergraduate majors. Total enrollment: 4,294. Undergraduates: 3,704. Freshmen: 960.

UNDERGRADUATE EXPENSES for 2004–05 *Application fee:* $25. *Tuition, state resident:* full-time $6170; part-time $257 per credit hour. *Tuition, nonresident:* full-time $12,978; part-time $541 per credit hour. Full-time tuition and fees vary according to course load, degree level, reciprocity agreements, and student level. Part-time tuition and fees vary according to course load, degree level, reciprocity agreements, and student level. *College room and board:* $5776; *room only:* $3468. Room and board charges vary according to board plan and housing facility. *Payment plan:* Deferred payment.

GIFT AID (NEED-BASED) *Total amount:* $8,186,099 (95% federal, 5% state). *Scholarships, grants, and awards:* Federal Pell, FSEOG, state, private, college/university gift aid from institutional funds.

GIFT AID (NON-NEED-BASED) *Total amount:* $5,015,373 (43% state, 33% institutional, 24% external sources). *Scholarships, grants, and awards by category:* Academic Interests/Achievement: general academic interests/achievements. *Creative Arts/Performance:* music. *Tuition waivers:* Full or partial for employees or children of employees, senior citizens. *ROTC:* Army, Air Force cooperative.

LOANS *Student loans:* $19,529,975 (57% need-based, 43% non-need-based). *Average indebtedness per student:* $17,000. *Parent loans:* $1,152,381 (100% non-need-based). *Programs:* FFEL (Subsidized and Unsubsidized Stafford, PLUS), Perkins, college/university.

ATHLETIC AWARDS *Total amount:* $1,486,119 (100% non-need-based).

APPLYING FOR FINANCIAL AID *Required financial aid form:* FAFSA. *Financial aid deadline (priority):* 5/1. *Notification date:* Continuous beginning 4/15. Students must reply within 2 weeks of notification.

CONTACT Sandra S. Davis, Director of Financial Aid, South Carolina State University, 300 College Street Northeast, Orangeburg, SC 29117-0001, 803-536-7067 or toll-free 800-260-5956. *Fax:* 803-536-8420. *E-mail:* sdavis@scsu.edu.

SOUTH DAKOTA SCHOOL OF MINES AND TECHNOLOGY
Rapid City, SD

Tuition & fees (SD res): $4534   **Average undergraduate aid package: $6205**

South Dakota School of Mines and Technology

ABOUT THE INSTITUTION State-supported, coed. Awards: associate, bachelor's, master's, and doctoral degrees. 17 undergraduate majors. Total enrollment: 2,353. Undergraduates: 2,042. Freshmen: 360. Federal methodology is used as a basis for awarding need-based institutional aid.

UNDERGRADUATE EXPENSES for 2004–05 *Application fee:* $20. *Tuition, state resident:* full-time $2223; part-time $74.10 per credit hour. *Tuition, nonresident:* full-time $7080; part-time $236 per credit hour. *Required fees:* full-time $2311; $82.20 per credit hour. Full-time tuition and fees vary according to course load, program, and reciprocity agreements. Part-time tuition and fees vary according to course load, program, and reciprocity agreements. *College room and board:* $3684; *room only:* $1661. Room and board charges vary according to board plan and housing facility. *Payment plan:* Installment.

FRESHMAN FINANCIAL AID (Fall 2003) 374 applied for aid; of those 63% were deemed to have need. 99% of freshmen with need received aid; of those 21% had need fully met. *Average percent of need met:* 68% (excluding resources awarded to replace EFC). *Average financial aid package:* $5434 (excluding resources awarded to replace EFC). 15% of all full-time freshmen had no need and received non-need-based gift aid.

UNDERGRADUATE FINANCIAL AID (Fall 2003) 1,541 applied for aid; of those 63% were deemed to have need. 99% of undergraduates with need received aid; of those 20% had need fully met. *Average percent of need met:* 70% (excluding resources awarded to replace EFC). *Average financial aid package:* $6205 (excluding resources awarded to replace EFC). 13% of all full-time undergraduates had no need and received non-need-based gift aid.

GIFT AID (NEED-BASED) *Total amount:* $2,407,812 (74% federal, 12% institutional, 14% external sources). *Receiving aid:* Freshmen: 38% (153); All full-time undergraduates: 36% (611). *Average award:* Freshmen: $3467; Undergraduates: $3175. *Scholarships, grants, and awards:* Federal Pell, FSEOG, state, private, college/university gift aid from institutional funds.

GIFT AID (NON-NEED-BASED) *Total amount:* $545,648 (1% federal, 54% institutional, 45% external sources). *Receiving aid:* Freshmen: 21% (87); Undergraduates: 11% (186). *Average Award:* Freshmen: $2135; Undergraduates: $2451. *Scholarships, grants, and awards by category:* Academic Interests/Achievement: 217 awards ($292,212 total): computer science, engineering/technologies, mathematics. *Tuition waivers:* Full or partial for senior citizens. *ROTC:* Army.

LOANS *Student loans:* $4,789,643 (99% need-based, 1% non-need-based). 89% of past graduating class borrowed through all loan programs. *Average indebtedness per student:* $12,975. *Average need-based loan:* Freshmen: $2201; Undergraduates: $3398. *Parent loans:* $745,006 (58% need-based, 42% non-need-based). *Programs:* FFEL (Subsidized and Unsubsidized Stafford, PLUS), Perkins.

WORK-STUDY *Federal work-study:* Total amount: $140,942; jobs available.

ATHLETIC AWARDS *Total amount:* $169,725 (40% need-based, 60% non-need-based).

APPLYING FOR FINANCIAL AID *Required financial aid forms:* FAFSA, freshmen scholarship application form. *Financial aid deadline (priority):* 3/15. *Notification date:* Continuous beginning 5/15. Students must reply within 3 weeks of notification.

CONTACT David W. Martin, Financial Aid Director, South Dakota School of Mines and Technology, 501 East Saint Joseph Street, Rapid City, SD 57701-3995, 605-394-2274 or toll-free 800-544-8162 Ext. 2414. *Fax:* 605-394-1268. *E-mail:* david.martin@sdsmt.edu.

SOUTH DAKOTA STATE UNIVERSITY
Brookings, SD

Tuition & fees (SD res): $4732	Average undergraduate aid package: $7182

ABOUT THE INSTITUTION State-supported, coed. Awards: associate, bachelor's, master's, doctoral, and first professional degrees and post-bachelor's and post-master's certificates. 80 undergraduate majors. Total enrollment: 10,884. Undergraduates: 9,572. Freshmen: 2,075. Federal methodology is used as a basis for awarding need-based institutional aid.

UNDERGRADUATE EXPENSES for 2005–06 *Application fee:* $20. *Tuition, state resident:* full-time $2291; part-time $76.35 per credit. *Tuition, nonresident:* full-time $7278; part-time $242.60 per credit. *Required fees:* full-time $2441; $81.35 per credit. Full-time tuition and fees vary according to course load and program. Part-time tuition and fees vary according to course load and program. *College room and board:* $4769; *room only:* $2113. Room and board charges vary according to board plan and housing facility. *Payment plans:* Installment, deferred payment.

FRESHMAN FINANCIAL AID (Fall 2004, est.) 1720 applied for aid; of those 85% were deemed to have need. 99% of freshmen with need received aid; of those 67% had need fully met. *Average percent of need met:* 88% (excluding resources awarded to replace EFC). *Average financial aid package:* $6121 (excluding resources awarded to replace EFC). 24% of all full-time freshmen had no need and received non-need-based gift aid.

UNDERGRADUATE FINANCIAL AID (Fall 2004, est.) 6,610 applied for aid; of those 92% were deemed to have need. 99% of undergraduates with need received aid; of those 78% had need fully met. *Average percent of need met:* 86% (excluding resources awarded to replace EFC). *Average financial aid package:* $7182 (excluding resources awarded to replace EFC). 12% of all full-time undergraduates had no need and received non-need-based gift aid.

GIFT AID (NEED-BASED) *Total amount:* $8,240,123 (94% federal, 4% institutional, 2% external sources). *Receiving aid:* Freshmen: 39% (782); All full-time undergraduates: 44% (3,410). *Average award:* Freshmen: $3122; Undergraduates: $3095. *Scholarships, grants, and awards:* Federal Pell, FSEOG, state, private, college/university gift aid from institutional funds, United Negro College Fund, Federal Nursing, agency awards.

GIFT AID (NON-NEED-BASED) *Total amount:* $6,037,958 (15% federal, 9% state, 55% institutional, 21% external sources). *Receiving aid:* Freshmen: 46% (916); Undergraduates: 43% (3,302). *Average Award:* Freshmen: $1031; Undergraduates: $982. *Scholarships, grants, and awards by category:* Academic Interests/Achievement: 2,064 awards ($2,114,314 total): agriculture, area/ethnic studies, biological sciences, business, communication, computer science, education, engineering/technologies, English, foreign languages, general academic interests/achievements, health fields, home economics, humanities, international studies, mathematics, military science, physical sciences, premedicine, social sciences. *Creative Arts/Performance:* 251 awards ($218,614 total): art/fine arts, debating, general creative arts/performance, journalism/publications, music, performing arts, theater/drama. *Special Achievements/Activities:* 76 awards ($59,722 total): community service, general special achievements/activities, hobbies/interests, junior miss, leadership, memberships, rodeo. *Special Characteristics:* 122 awards ($171,998 total): adult students, children of faculty/staff, children of workers in trades, ethnic background, first-generation college students, general special characteristics, handicapped students, international students, members of minority groups, veterans, veterans' children. *Tuition waivers:* Full or partial for children of alumni, employees or children of employees, senior citizens. *ROTC:* Army, Air Force.

LOANS *Student loans:* $40,968,361 (62% need-based, 38% non-need-based). 82% of past graduating class borrowed through all loan programs. *Average indebtedness per student:* $18,333. *Average need-based loan:* Freshmen: $2814; Undergraduates: $4392. *Parent loans:* $2,147,629 (100% non-need-based). *Programs:* FFEL (Subsidized and Unsubsidized Stafford, PLUS), Perkins, Federal Nursing, college/university, alternative loans from private sources.

WORK-STUDY *Federal work-study:* Total amount: $732,780; 705 jobs averaging $1039. *State or other work-study/employment:* Total amount: $2,896,132 (100% non-need-based). 2,173 part-time jobs averaging $1332.

ATHLETIC AWARDS *Total amount:* $977,553 (100% non-need-based).

APPLYING FOR FINANCIAL AID *Required financial aid form:* FAFSA. *Financial aid deadline (priority):* 3/15. *Notification date:* Continuous beginning 4/1. Students must reply within 3 weeks of notification.

CONTACT Mr. Jay Larsen, Director of Financial Aid, South Dakota State University, Box 2201 ADM 106, Brookings, SD 57007, 605-688-4703 or toll-free 800-952-3541. *Fax:* 605-688-5882. *E-mail:* jay.larsen@sdstate.edu.

SOUTHEASTERN BAPTIST COLLEGE
Laurel, MS

CONTACT Financial Aid Officer, Southeastern Baptist College, 4229 Highway 15 North, Laurel, MS 39440-1096, 601-426-6346.

SOUTHEASTERN BAPTIST THEOLOGICAL SEMINARY
Wake Forest, NC

CONTACT H. Allan Moseley, Vice President of Student Services / Dean of Students, Southeastern Baptist Theological Seminary, PO Box 1889, Wake Forest, NC 27588, 919-556-3101 Ext. 306 or toll-free 800-284-6317. *Fax:* 919-556-0998. *E-mail:* deanofstudents@sebts.edu.

SOUTHEASTERN BIBLE COLLEGE
Birmingham, AL

Tuition & fees: $6770	Average undergraduate aid package: $6457

ABOUT THE INSTITUTION Independent nondenominational, coed. Awards: associate and bachelor's degrees. 8 undergraduate majors. Total enrollment: 256. Undergraduates: 256. Freshmen: 28. Federal methodology is used as a basis for awarding need-based institutional aid.

UNDERGRADUATE EXPENSES for 2004–05 *Application fee:* $20. *Comprehensive fee:* $10,770 includes full-time tuition ($6600), mandatory fees ($170), and room and board ($4000). Full-time tuition and fees vary according to course load. *Part-time tuition:* $275 per semester hour. *Part-time fees:* $50 per term. Part-time tuition and fees vary according to course load. *Payment plan:* Installment.

GIFT AID (NEED-BASED) *Total amount:* $342,436 (100% federal). *Receiving aid:* Freshmen: 100% (46); All full-time undergraduates: 90% (182). *Average award:* Freshmen: $2000; Undergraduates: $4000. *Scholarships, grants, and awards:* Federal Pell, FSEOG.

GIFT AID (NON-NEED-BASED) *Total amount:* $168,000 (2% state, 68% institutional, 30% external sources). *Receiving aid:* Freshmen: 15% (7); Undergraduates: 20% (40). *Scholarships, grants, and awards by category: Academic Interests/Achievement:* general academic interests/achievements. *Creative Arts/Performance:* 1 award ($2000 total): music. *Special Characteristics:* children of faculty/staff, local/state students, relatives of clergy, veterans. *Tuition waivers:* Full or partial for children of alumni, employees or children of employees.

LOANS *Student loans:* $1,300,000 (100% need-based). 50% of past graduating class borrowed through all loan programs. *Average indebtedness per student:* $20,000. *Average need-based loan:* Freshmen: $2625; Undergraduates: $4250. *Parent loans:* $98,000 (100% non-need-based). *Programs:* FFEL (Subsidized and Unsubsidized Stafford, PLUS).

APPLYING FOR FINANCIAL AID *Required financial aid forms:* FAFSA, institution's own form, state aid form. *Financial aid deadline (priority):* 5/1. *Notification date:* Continuous. Students must reply within 2 weeks of notification.

CONTACT Ms. Joanne Belin, Financial Aid Administrator, Southeastern Bible College, 2545 Valleydale Road, Birmingham, AL 35244, 205-970-9215 or toll-free 800-749-8878 (in-state). *E-mail:* jbelin@sebc.edu.

SOUTHEASTERN COLLEGE OF THE ASSEMBLIES OF GOD
Lakeland, FL

Tuition & fees: $10,140	Average undergraduate aid package: $7027

ABOUT THE INSTITUTION Independent religious, coed. Awards: bachelor's degrees. 23 undergraduate majors. Total enrollment: 1,964. Undergraduates: 1,964. Federal methodology is used as a basis for awarding need-based institutional aid.

UNDERGRADUATE EXPENSES for 2004–05 *Application fee:* $40. *Comprehensive fee:* $15,610 includes full-time tuition ($9900), mandatory fees ($240), and room and board ($5470). Full-time tuition and fees vary according to program. Room and board charges vary according to board plan and housing facility. *Part-time tuition:* $413 per credit. Part-time tuition and fees vary according to course load, program, and reciprocity agreements. *Payment plan:* Installment.

FRESHMAN FINANCIAL AID (Fall 2003) 319 applied for aid; of those 82% were deemed to have need. 97% of freshmen with need received aid; of those 9% had need fully met. *Average percent of need met:* 53% (excluding resources awarded to replace EFC). *Average financial aid package:* $6212 (excluding resources awarded to replace EFC). 29% of all full-time freshmen had no need and received non-need-based gift aid.

UNDERGRADUATE FINANCIAL AID (Fall 2003) 1,360 applied for aid; of those 84% were deemed to have need. 97% of undergraduates with need received aid; of those 11% had need fully met. *Average percent of need met:* 58% (excluding resources awarded to replace EFC). *Average financial aid package:* $7027 (excluding resources awarded to replace EFC). 22% of all full-time undergraduates had no need and received non-need-based gift aid.

GIFT AID (NEED-BASED) *Total amount:* $5,084,865 (34% federal, 37% state, 22% institutional, 7% external sources). *Receiving aid:* Freshmen: 52% (231); All full-time undergraduates: 65% (1,015). *Average award:* Freshmen: $4528; Undergraduates: $4714. *Scholarships, grants, and awards:* Federal Pell, FSEOG, state, private, college/university gift aid from institutional funds.

GIFT AID (NON-NEED-BASED) *Total amount:* $1,392,237 (52% state, 37% institutional, 11% external sources). *Receiving aid:* Freshmen: 4% (16); Undergraduates: 5% (79). *Average Award:* Freshmen: $6155; *Undergraduates:* $7802. *Scholarships, grants, and awards by category: Academic Interests/Achievement:* 748 awards ($966,625 total): communication, general academic interests/achievements, religion/biblical studies. *Creative Arts/Performance:* 181 awards ($211,236 total): journalism/publications, music, theater/drama. *Special Achievements/Activities:* religious involvement. *Special Characteristics:* children of faculty/staff, general special characteristics, siblings of current students. *Tuition waivers:* Full or partial for employees or children of employees. *ROTC:* Army cooperative, Air Force cooperative.

LOANS *Student loans:* $8,279,295 (68% need-based, 32% non-need-based). 93% of past graduating class borrowed through all loan programs. *Average indebtedness per student:* $18,480. *Average need-based loan:* Freshmen: $2447; Undergraduates: $3223. *Parent loans:* $2,250,904 (39% need-based, 61% non-need-based). *Programs:* FFEL (Subsidized and Unsubsidized Stafford, PLUS), Perkins.

WORK-STUDY *Federal work-study:* Total amount: $98,209; 101 jobs averaging $972.

APPLYING FOR FINANCIAL AID *Required financial aid forms:* FAFSA, institution's own form, state aid form (for FL residents only). *Financial aid deadline (priority):* 4/15. *Notification date:* Continuous beginning 3/1. Students must reply by 5/1 or within 4 weeks of notification.

CONTACT Ms. Carol B. Bradley, Financial Aid Director, Southeastern College of the Assemblies of God, 1000 Longfellow Boulevard, Lakeland, FL 33801-6099, 863-667-5000 or toll-free 800-500-8760. *Fax:* 863-667-5200. *E-mail:* c_bradly@secollege.edu.

SOUTHEASTERN LOUISIANA UNIVERSITY
Hammond, LA

Tuition & fees (LA res): $3191	Average undergraduate aid package: $6033

ABOUT THE INSTITUTION State-supported, coed. Awards: associate, bachelor's, and master's degrees. 45 undergraduate majors. Total enrollment: 15,472. Undergraduates: 13,664. Freshmen: 2,539. Federal methodology is used as a basis for awarding need-based institutional aid.

UNDERGRADUATE EXPENSES for 2004–05 *Application fee:* $20. *Tuition, state resident:* full-time $3191; part-time $133 per credit hour. *Tuition, nonresident:* full-time $8519; part-time $355 per credit hour. Full-time tuition and fees vary according to course load. Part-time tuition and fees vary according to course load. *College room and board:* $4290; *room only:* $2300. Room and board charges vary according to board plan and housing facility. *Payment plans:* Installment, deferred payment.

FRESHMAN FINANCIAL AID (Fall 2003) 1956 applied for aid; of those 88% were deemed to have need. 92% of freshmen with need received aid. *Average financial aid package:* $4005 (excluding resources awarded to replace EFC). 44% of all full-time freshmen had no need and received non-need-based gift aid.

UNDERGRADUATE FINANCIAL AID (Fall 2003) 8,727 applied for aid; of those 90% were deemed to have need. 81% of undergraduates with need received aid. *Average financial aid package:* $6033 (excluding resources awarded to replace EFC). 32% of all full-time undergraduates had no need and received non-need-based gift aid.

GIFT AID (NEED-BASED) *Total amount:* $16,897,337 (99% federal, 1% state). *Receiving aid:* Freshmen: 37% (879); All full-time undergraduates: 41% (4,649). *Average award:* Freshmen: $3076; Undergraduates: $3011. *Scholarships, grants, and awards:* Federal Pell, FSEOG, state, private, college/university gift aid from institutional funds, Federal Nursing.

GIFT AID (NON-NEED-BASED) *Total amount:* $5,323,751 (85% state, 12% institutional, 3% external sources). *Receiving aid:* Freshmen: 33% (795); Undergraduates: 12% (1,314). *Average Award:* Freshmen: $2379; *Undergraduates:* $2307. *Scholarships, grants, and awards by category: Academic Interests/Achievement:* biological sciences, business, communication, education, engineering/technologies, English, general academic interests/achievements, health fields, mathematics, social sciences. *Creative Arts/Performance:* debating, music. *Special Achievements/Activities:* cheerleading/drum major, leadership, memberships, rodeo. *Special Characteristics:* adult students, children and siblings of alumni, children of faculty/staff, children of public servants, children of union members/company employees, ethnic background, international students, local/state students, members of minority groups, out-of-state students, religious affiliation, veterans' children. *Tuition waivers:* Full or partial for employees or children of employees, senior citizens. *ROTC:* Army cooperative.

Southeastern Louisiana University

LOANS *Student loans:* $32,530,695 (61% need-based, 39% non-need-based). 58% of past graduating class borrowed through all loan programs. *Average indebtedness per student:* $12,527. *Average need-based loan:* Freshmen: $2081; Undergraduates: $3132. *Parent loans:* $653,950 (100% non-need-based). *Programs:* FFEL (Subsidized and Unsubsidized Stafford, PLUS), Perkins, college/university.

WORK-STUDY *Federal work-study:* Total amount: $563,177; 477 jobs averaging $1461. *State or other work-study/employment:* Total amount: $1,695,969 (100% non-need-based). 1,159 part-time jobs averaging $1596.

ATHLETIC AWARDS *Total amount:* $516,717 (100% non-need-based).

APPLYING FOR FINANCIAL AID *Required financial aid form:* FAFSA. *Financial aid deadline (priority):* 5/1. *Notification date:* Continuous. Students must reply within 2 weeks of notification.

CONTACT Sam Domiano, Director of New Student Enrollment and Student Aid, Southeastern Louisiana University, SLU 10768, Hammond, LA 70402, 985-549-5309 or toll-free 800-222-7358. *Fax:* 985-549-5077. *E-mail:* finaid@selu.edu.

SOUTHEASTERN OKLAHOMA STATE UNIVERSITY
Durant, OK

Tuition & fees (OK res): $3123   **Average undergraduate aid package:** $1254

ABOUT THE INSTITUTION State-supported, coed. Awards: bachelor's and master's degrees and post-master's certificates. 58 undergraduate majors. Total enrollment: 4,203. Undergraduates: 3,738. Freshmen: 646. Federal methodology is used as a basis for awarding need-based institutional aid.

UNDERGRADUATE EXPENSES for 2004–05 *Application fee:* $20. *Tuition, state resident:* full-time $2126; part-time $70.85 per credit hour. *Tuition, nonresident:* full-time $6455; part-time $215.15 per credit hour. *Required fees:* full-time $997; $28.70 per semester hour or $68 per term part-time. Full-time tuition and fees vary according to course level. Part-time tuition and fees vary according to course level and course load. *College room and board:* $3470; *room only:* $1850. Room and board charges vary according to board plan and housing facility.

FRESHMAN FINANCIAL AID (Fall 2003) 459 applied for aid; of those 99% were deemed to have need. 99% of freshmen with need received aid; of those 44% had need fully met. *Average percent of need met:* 74% (excluding resources awarded to replace EFC). *Average financial aid package:* $1043 (excluding resources awarded to replace EFC). 18% of all full-time freshmen had no need and received non-need-based gift aid.

UNDERGRADUATE FINANCIAL AID (Fall 2003) 1,486 applied for aid; of those 99% were deemed to have need. 97% of undergraduates with need received aid; of those 57% had need fully met. *Average percent of need met:* 75% (excluding resources awarded to replace EFC). *Average financial aid package:* $1254 (excluding resources awarded to replace EFC). 14% of all full-time undergraduates had no need and received non-need-based gift aid.

GIFT AID (NEED-BASED) *Total amount:* $5,424,097 (90% federal, 10% state). *Receiving aid:* Freshmen: 48% (268); All full-time undergraduates: 48% (955). *Average award:* Freshmen: $1200; Undergraduates: $1217. *Scholarships, grants, and awards:* Federal Pell, FSEOG, state.

GIFT AID (NON-NEED-BASED) *Total amount:* $1,734,914 (6% state, 13% institutional, 81% external sources). *Receiving aid:* Freshmen: 42% (236); Undergraduates: 27% (536). *Average Award:* Freshmen: $968; Undergraduates: $1024. *Scholarships, grants, and awards by category:* Academic Interests/Achievement: 199 awards ($140,068 total): biological sciences, business, computer science, education, engineering/technologies, general academic interests/achievements, mathematics, physical sciences, social sciences. *Creative Arts/Performance:* 28 awards ($21,385 total): music, theater/drama. *Special Achievements/Activities:* 13 awards ($19,594 total). *Special Characteristics:* 1,070 awards ($2,657,031 total): children and siblings of alumni, out-of-state students. *Tuition waivers:* Full or partial for minority students, children of alumni, employees or children of employees, senior citizens.

LOANS *Student loans:* $6,618,470 (76% need-based, 24% non-need-based). 29% of past graduating class borrowed through all loan programs. *Average indebtedness per student:* $6579. *Average need-based loan:* Freshmen: $1155; Undergraduates: $1898. *Parent loans:* $242,166 (100% non-need-based). *Programs:* FFEL (Subsidized and Unsubsidized Stafford, PLUS), Perkins.

WORK-STUDY *Federal work-study:* Total amount: $198,497; 362 jobs averaging $1189. *State or other work-study/employment:* Total amount: $775,667 (100% non-need-based). 857 part-time jobs averaging $1665.

ATHLETIC AWARDS *Total amount:* $508,314 (100% non-need-based).

APPLYING FOR FINANCIAL AID *Required financial aid forms:* FAFSA, institution's own form. *Financial aid deadline (priority):* 3/1. *Notification date:* Continuous beginning 5/1. Students must reply within 2 weeks of notification.

CONTACT Sherry Foster, Director of Student Financial Aid, Southeastern Oklahoma State University, 1405 North 4th Avenue, PMB 4113, Durant, OK 74701-0609, 580-745-2186 or toll-free 800-435-1327. *Fax:* 580-745-7469. *E-mail:* sfoster@sosu.edu.

SOUTHEASTERN UNIVERSITY
Washington, DC

CONTACT Hope Gibbs, Assistant Director of Financial Aid, Southeastern University, 501 I Street, SW, Washington, DC 20024-2788, 202-488-8162 Ext. 234. *E-mail:* hgibbs@admin.seu.edu.

SOUTHEAST MISSOURI STATE UNIVERSITY
Cape Girardeau, MO

Tuition & fees (MO res): $4875   **Average undergraduate aid package:** $6175

ABOUT THE INSTITUTION State-supported, coed. Awards: associate, bachelor's, and master's degrees and post-master's certificates. 69 undergraduate majors. Total enrollment: 9,618. Undergraduates: 8,460. Federal methodology is used as a basis for awarding need-based institutional aid.

UNDERGRADUATE EXPENSES for 2004–05 *Application fee:* $20. *Tuition, state resident:* full-time $4554; part-time $151.80 per credit. *Tuition, nonresident:* full-time $8139; part-time $267.30 per credit. *Required fees:* full-time $321; $10.70 per credit. Full-time tuition and fees vary according to course load and location. Part-time tuition and fees vary according to course load and location. *College room and board:* $5317; *room only:* $3335. Room and board charges vary according to board plan and housing facility. *Payment plans:* Installment, deferred payment.

FRESHMAN FINANCIAL AID (Fall 2003) 1073 applied for aid; of those 73% were deemed to have need. 99% of freshmen with need received aid; of those 17% had need fully met. *Average percent of need met:* 64% (excluding resources awarded to replace EFC). *Average financial aid package:* $5713 (excluding resources awarded to replace EFC). 20% of all full-time freshmen had no need and received non-need-based gift aid.

UNDERGRADUATE FINANCIAL AID (Fall 2003) 4,562 applied for aid; of those 77% were deemed to have need. 98% of undergraduates with need received aid; of those 17% had need fully met. *Average percent of need met:* 67% (excluding resources awarded to replace EFC). *Average financial aid package:* $6175 (excluding resources awarded to replace EFC). 12% of all full-time undergraduates had no need and received non-need-based gift aid.

GIFT AID (NEED-BASED) *Total amount:* $10,096,331 (58% federal, 11% state, 27% institutional, 4% external sources). *Receiving aid:* Freshmen: 45% (630); All full-time undergraduates: 38% (2,524). *Average award:* Freshmen: $3821; Undergraduates: $4040. *Scholarships, grants, and awards:* Federal Pell, FSEOG, state, private, college/university gift aid from institutional funds.

GIFT AID (NON-NEED-BASED) *Total amount:* $4,182,091 (7% federal, 10% state, 72% institutional, 11% external sources). *Receiving aid:* Freshmen: 6% (87); Undergraduates: 4% (262). *Average Award:* Freshmen: $2829; Undergraduates: $3417. *Scholarships, grants, and awards by category:* Academic Interests/Achievement: 796 awards ($2,477,470 total): agriculture, biological sciences, business, communication, computer science, education, English, foreign languages, general academic interests/achievements, health fields, home economics, humanities, international studies, mathematics, military science, physical sciences, premedicine, religion/biblical studies, social sciences. *Creative Arts/Performance:* 118 awards ($77,295 total): music, theater/drama. *Special Achievements/Activities:* 187 awards ($301,503 total): cheerleading/drum major, general special achievements/activities, leadership. *Special Characteristics:* 199 awards ($551,883 total): adult students, children of faculty/staff, first-generation college students, general special characteristics, international students, members of minority groups, out-of-state students, previous college experience. *Tuition waivers:* Full or partial for employees or children of employees, senior citizens. *ROTC:* Air Force.

LOANS *Student loans:* $20,957,038 (66% need-based, 34% non-need-based). 60% of past graduating class borrowed through all loan programs. *Average indebtedness per student:* $14,492. *Average need-based loan:* Freshmen: $2595; Undergraduates: $3493. *Parent loans:* $5,853,849 (18% need-based, 82% non-need-based). *Programs:* FFEL (Subsidized and Unsubsidized Stafford, PLUS), Perkins, state.

WORK-STUDY *Federal work-study:* Total amount: $455,620; 221 jobs averaging $1339. *State or other work-study/employment:* Total amount: $4,662,750 (14% need-based, 86% non-need-based). 1,613 part-time jobs averaging $1425.

ATHLETIC AWARDS *Total amount:* $1,929,304 (36% need-based, 64% non-need-based).

APPLYING FOR FINANCIAL AID *Required financial aid form:* FAFSA. *Financial aid deadline (priority):* 3/1. *Notification date:* Continuous beginning 4/1. Students must reply within 3 weeks of notification.

CONTACT Barbara Garner, Customer Service Supervisor, Southeast Missouri State University, One University Plaza, Cape Girardeau, MO 63701, 573-651-2840. *Fax:* 573-651-5006.

SOUTHERN ADVENTIST UNIVERSITY
Collegedale, TN

Tuition & fees: $14,020	Average undergraduate aid package: $9500

ABOUT THE INSTITUTION Independent Seventh-day Adventist, coed. Awards: associate, bachelor's, and master's degrees. 56 undergraduate majors. Total enrollment: 2,391. Undergraduates: 2,238. Federal methodology is used as a basis for awarding need-based institutional aid.

UNDERGRADUATE EXPENSES for 2005–06 *Application fee:* $25. *Comprehensive fee:* $18,500 includes full-time tuition ($13,580), mandatory fees ($440), and room and board ($4480). *College room only:* $2480. Room and board charges vary according to housing facility. *Part-time tuition:* $575 per semester hour. *Part-time fees:* $220 per term. Part-time tuition and fees vary according to course load. *Payment plans:* Tuition prepayment, installment, deferred payment.

FRESHMAN FINANCIAL AID (Fall 2004, est.) 475 applied for aid; of those 89% were deemed to have need. 100% of freshmen with need received aid; of those 12% had need fully met. *Average percent of need met:* 60% (excluding resources awarded to replace EFC). *Average financial aid package:* $8500 (excluding resources awarded to replace EFC). 35% of all full-time freshmen had no need and received non-need-based gift aid.

UNDERGRADUATE FINANCIAL AID (Fall 2004, est.) 1,526 applied for aid; of those 63% were deemed to have need. 100% of undergraduates with need received aid; of those 21% had need fully met. *Average percent of need met:* 67% (excluding resources awarded to replace EFC). *Average financial aid package:* $9500 (excluding resources awarded to replace EFC). 29% of all full-time undergraduates had no need and received non-need-based gift aid.

GIFT AID (NEED-BASED) *Total amount:* $4,530,286 (44% federal, 3% state, 53% institutional). *Receiving aid:* Freshmen: 74% (368); All full-time undergraduates: 35% (673). *Average award:* Freshmen: $4500; Undergraduates: $4000. *Scholarships, grants, and awards:* Federal Pell, FSEOG, state, private, college/university gift aid from institutional funds.

GIFT AID (NON-NEED-BASED) *Total amount:* $5,291,121 (4% state, 86% institutional, 10% external sources). *Receiving aid:* Freshmen: 76% (379); Undergraduates: 32% (611). *Average Award:* Freshmen: $3500; Undergraduates: $3100. *Scholarships, grants, and awards by category: Academic Interests/Achievement:* 1,006 awards ($1,426,168 total): business, communication, education, English, general academic interests/achievements, health fields, mathematics, religion/biblical studies. *Creative Arts/Performance:* 156 awards ($159,556 total): art/fine arts, journalism/publications, music, theater/drama. *Special Achievements/Activities:* 320 awards ($175,719 total): community service, general special achievements/activities, leadership, religious involvement. *Special Characteristics:* 521 awards ($424,212 total): children and siblings of alumni, general special characteristics, international students, local/state students, members of minority groups, out-of-state students, siblings of current students, spouses of current students. *Tuition waivers:* Full or partial for employees or children of employees, adult students, senior citizens.

LOANS *Student loans:* $7,037,534 (67% need-based, 33% non-need-based). 64% of past graduating class borrowed through all loan programs. *Average indebtedness per student:* $15,500. *Average need-based loan:* Freshmen: $3700; Undergraduates: $4300. *Parent loans:* $1,000,000 (40% need-based, 60% non-need-based). *Programs:* FFEL (Subsidized and Unsubsidized Stafford, PLUS), Perkins, Federal Nursing, college/university.

WORK-STUDY *Federal work-study:* Total amount: $250,000; 396 jobs averaging $2158. *State or other work-study/employment:* Part-time jobs available.

APPLYING FOR FINANCIAL AID *Required financial aid forms:* FAFSA, state aid form. *Financial aid deadline (priority):* 3/1. *Notification date:* Continuous beginning 2/15. Students must reply within 2 weeks of notification.

CONTACT Mr. Marc Grundy, Director of Student Finance Office, Southern Adventist University, PO Box 370, Collegedale, TN 37315-0370, 423-236-2875 or toll-free 800-768-8437. *Fax:* 423-236-1835.

SOUTHERN ARKANSAS UNIVERSITY– MAGNOLIA
Magnolia, AR

Tuition & fees (AR res): $3858	Average undergraduate aid package: $6298

ABOUT THE INSTITUTION State-supported, coed. Awards: associate, bachelor's, and master's degrees. 45 undergraduate majors. Total enrollment: 3,057. Undergraduates: 2,803. Freshmen: 651. Federal methodology is used as a basis for awarding need-based institutional aid.

UNDERGRADUATE EXPENSES for 2004–05 *Tuition, state resident:* full-time $3528; part-time $126 per credit hour. *Tuition, nonresident:* full-time $5348; part-time $191 per credit hour. *Required fees:* full-time $330; $330 per year part-time. Full-time tuition and fees vary according to course load. Part-time tuition and fees vary according to course load. *College room and board:* $3600. *Payment plans:* Installment, deferred payment.

FRESHMAN FINANCIAL AID (Fall 2004, est.) 463 applied for aid; of those 85% were deemed to have need. 93% of freshmen with need received aid; of those 100% had need fully met. *Average percent of need met:* 100% (excluding resources awarded to replace EFC). *Average financial aid package:* $5711 (excluding resources awarded to replace EFC). 25% of all full-time freshmen had no need and received non-need-based gift aid.

UNDERGRADUATE FINANCIAL AID (Fall 2004, est.) 1,787 applied for aid; of those 89% were deemed to have need. 94% of undergraduates with need received aid; of those 100% had need fully met. *Average percent of need met:* 100% (excluding resources awarded to replace EFC). *Average financial aid package:* $6298 (excluding resources awarded to replace EFC). 16% of all full-time undergraduates had no need and received non-need-based gift aid.

GIFT AID (NEED-BASED) *Total amount:* $5,163,753 (88% federal, 12% state). *Receiving aid:* Freshmen: 52% (318); All full-time undergraduates: 52% (1,256). *Average award:* Freshmen: $3504; Undergraduates: $3382. *Scholarships, grants, and awards:* Federal Pell, FSEOG, state, private, college/university gift aid from institutional funds.

GIFT AID (NON-NEED-BASED) *Total amount:* $2,843,578 (96% institutional, 4% external sources). *Receiving aid:* Freshmen: 39% (236); Undergraduates: 27% (644). *Average Award:* Freshmen: $2569; Undergraduates: $2759. *Scholarships, grants, and awards by category: Academic Interests/Achievement:* 640 awards ($2,061,034 total): agriculture, general academic interests/achievements. *Creative Arts/Performance:* 32 awards ($69,011 total): art/fine arts, dance, music, theater/drama. *Special Achievements/Activities:* 70 awards ($139,013 total): cheerleading/drum major, leadership, rodeo. *Special Characteristics:* 521 awards ($666,123 total): adult students, children and siblings of alumni, children of faculty/staff, members of minority groups, out-of-state students. *Tuition waivers:* Full or partial for children of alumni, employees or children of employees, senior citizens.

LOANS *Student loans:* $6,105,000 (61% need-based, 39% non-need-based). 45% of past graduating class borrowed through all loan programs. *Average indebtedness per student:* $22,124. *Average need-based loan:* Freshmen: $2034; Undergraduates: $3062. *Parent loans:* $127,000 (100% non-need-based). *Programs:* FFEL (Subsidized and Unsubsidized Stafford, PLUS), Perkins.

WORK-STUDY *Federal work-study:* Total amount: $704,549; 1,129 jobs averaging $2155. *State or other work-study/employment:* Total amount: $659,822 (100% non-need-based). 319 part-time jobs averaging $2278.

ATHLETIC AWARDS *Total amount:* $546,407 (100% non-need-based).

APPLYING FOR FINANCIAL AID *Required financial aid form:* FAFSA. *Financial aid deadline (priority):* 7/1. *Notification date:* Continuous beginning 4/1. Students must reply within 2 weeks of notification.

CONTACT Ms. Bronwyn C. Sneed, Director of Student Aid, Southern Arkansas University–Magnolia, PO Box 9344, Magnolia, AR 71754-9344, 870-235-4023 or toll-free 800-332-7286 (in-state). *Fax:* 870-235-4913. *E-mail:* bcsneed@saumag.edu.

SOUTHERN BAPTIST THEOLOGICAL SEMINARY
Louisville, KY

Tuition & fees: N/R **Average undergraduate aid package:** $159

ABOUT THE INSTITUTION Independent Southern Baptist, coed. Awards: associate and bachelor's degrees. Total enrollment: 475. Undergraduates: 475. Institutional methodology is used as a basis for awarding need-based institutional aid.

UNDERGRADUATE FINANCIAL AID (Fall 2003) 247 applied for aid; of those 67% were deemed to have need. 100% of undergraduates with need received aid. *Average percent of need met:* 4% (excluding resources awarded to replace EFC). *Average financial aid package:* $159 (excluding resources awarded to replace EFC).

GIFT AID (NEED-BASED) *Total amount:* $108,620 (24% institutional, 76% external sources). *Receiving aid:* All full-time undergraduates: 25% (165). *Scholarships, grants, and awards:* state, private, college/university gift aid from institutional funds, all other sources aid as long as the school does not need to participate in Title IV program.

LOANS *Student loans:* $150,953 (100% need-based). *Programs:* college/university, Non-Title IV loan programs such as Sallie Mae "Signature" Loan and Nellie Mae "Excel" loan.

APPLYING FOR FINANCIAL AID *Required financial aid form:* scholarship application form(s). *Financial aid deadline (priority):* 7/15. *Notification date:* 8/1.

CONTACT Mrs. Teresa M. Crosby, Assistant Director of Student Life, Southern Baptist Theological Seminary, Financial Aid Office, 2825 Lexington Road, Louisville, KY 40280, 502-897-4206. *Fax:* 502-897-4031. *E-mail:* financialaid@sbts.edu.

SOUTHERN CALIFORNIA BIBLE COLLEGE & SEMINARY
El Cajon, CA

CONTACT Financial Aid Office, Southern California Bible College & Seminary, 2075 East Madison Avenue, El Cajon, CA 92019, 619-442-9841.

SOUTHERN CALIFORNIA INSTITUTE OF ARCHITECTURE
Los Angeles, CA

Tuition & fees: $18,446 **Average undergraduate aid package:** $11,946

ABOUT THE INSTITUTION Independent, coed. Awards: bachelor's, master's, and first professional degrees. 1 undergraduate major. Total enrollment: 447. Undergraduates: 183. Freshmen: 5. Federal methodology is used as a basis for awarding need-based institutional aid.

UNDERGRADUATE EXPENSES for 2004–05 *Application fee:* $60. *Tuition:* full-time $18,376.

GIFT AID (NEED-BASED) *Total amount:* $808,107 (59% federal, 32% state, 8% institutional, 1% external sources). *Receiving aid:* Freshmen: 65% (53); All full-time undergraduates: 78% (159). *Average award:* Freshmen: $4293; Undergraduates: $4293. *Scholarships, grants, and awards:* Federal Pell, FSEOG, state, private, college/university gift aid from institutional funds.

GIFT AID (NON-NEED-BASED) *Total amount:* $22,876 (100% federal). *Average Award:* Freshmen: $4750; Undergraduates: $2239. *Scholarships, grants, and awards by category:* Academic Interests/Achievement: 35 awards ($137,000 total): architecture.

LOANS *Student loans:* $2,659,192 (30% need-based, 70% non-need-based). 97% of past graduating class borrowed through all loan programs. *Average indebtedness per student:* $33,000. *Average need-based loan:* Freshmen: $4574; Undergraduates: $5500. *Parent loans:* $426,195 (100% non-need-based). *Programs:* FFEL (Subsidized and Unsubsidized Stafford, PLUS), alternative loans.

APPLYING FOR FINANCIAL AID *Required financial aid forms:* FAFSA, institution's own form. *Financial aid deadline (priority):* 3/2. *Notification date:* 4/1. Students must reply within 4 weeks of notification.

CONTACT Lina Johnson, Financial Aid Director, Southern California Institute of Architecture, 960 East 3rd Street, Los Angeles, CA 90013, 213-613-2200 Ext. 345 or toll-free 800-774-7242. *Fax:* 213-613-2260. *E-mail:* financialaid@sciarc.edu.

SOUTHERN CHRISTIAN UNIVERSITY
Montgomery, AL

Tuition & fees: $10,040 **Average undergraduate aid package:** $8500

ABOUT THE INSTITUTION Independent religious, coed. Awards: bachelor's, master's, doctoral, and first professional degrees. 7 undergraduate majors. Total enrollment: 705. Undergraduates: 370. Freshmen: 13. Federal methodology is used as a basis for awarding need-based institutional aid.

UNDERGRADUATE EXPENSES for 2004–05 *Application fee:* $50. *Tuition:* full-time $9240; part-time $385 per credit hour. *Required fees:* full-time $800; $400 per term part-time. Part-time tuition and fees vary according to course load. *Payment plan:* Tuition prepayment.

UNDERGRADUATE FINANCIAL AID (Fall 2003) 330 applied for aid; of those 91% were deemed to have need. 100% of undergraduates with need received aid; of those 92% had need fully met. *Average percent of need met:* 85% (excluding resources awarded to replace EFC). *Average financial aid package:* $8500 (excluding resources awarded to replace EFC). 5% of all full-time undergraduates had no need and received non-need-based gift aid.

GIFT AID (NEED-BASED) *Total amount:* $719,776 (91% federal, 3% institutional, 6% external sources). *Receiving aid:* All full-time undergraduates: 73% (270). *Average award:* Undergraduates: $6500. *Scholarships, grants, and awards:* Federal Pell, FSEOG, state, private, college/university gift aid from institutional funds.

GIFT AID (NON-NEED-BASED) *Total amount:* $2,054,155 (100% institutional). *Receiving aid:* Undergraduates: 14% (50). *Average Award:* Undergraduates: $4000. *Scholarships, grants, and awards by category:* Special Achievements/Activities: religious involvement. *Special Characteristics:* children of faculty/staff, veterans. *Tuition waivers:* Full or partial for employees or children of employees, senior citizens.

LOANS *Student loans:* $6,258,646 (49% need-based, 51% non-need-based). 85% of past graduating class borrowed through all loan programs. *Average indebtedness per student:* $18,000. *Average need-based loan:* Undergraduates: $5500. *Programs:* FFEL (Subsidized and Unsubsidized Stafford, PLUS).

WORK-STUDY *Federal work-study:* Total amount: $7644; jobs available.

APPLYING FOR FINANCIAL AID *Required financial aid forms:* FAFSA, institution's own form. *Financial aid deadline:* Continuous. *Notification date:* 8/31. Students must reply within 2 weeks of notification.

CONTACT Rosemary Kennington, Financial Aid Director, Southern Christian University, 1200 Taylor Road, Montgomery, AL 36117, 334-387-3877 Ext. 7527 or toll-free 800-351-4040 Ext. 213. *Fax:* 334-387-3878. *E-mail:* financialaid@southernchristian.edu.

SOUTHERN CONNECTICUT STATE UNIVERSITY
New Haven, CT

Tuition & fees (CT res): $5814 **Average undergraduate aid package:** $6988

ABOUT THE INSTITUTION State-supported, coed. Awards: bachelor's, master's, and doctoral degrees and post-master's certificates. 58 undergraduate majors. Total enrollment: 12,177. Undergraduates: 8,314. Freshmen: 1,419. Federal methodology is used as a basis for awarding need-based institutional aid.

UNDERGRADUATE EXPENSES for 2005–06 *Application fee:* $50. *Tuition, state resident:* full-time $3034; part-time $307 per credit. *Tuition, nonresident:* full-time $9820; part-time $307 per credit. *Required fees:* full-time $2780; $63 per term part-time. *College room and board:* $7698; *room only:* $5558. Room and board charges vary according to housing facility. *Payment plan:* Installment.

FRESHMAN FINANCIAL AID (Fall 2004, est.) 1142 applied for aid; of those 61% were deemed to have need. 95% of freshmen with need received aid; of those 25% had need fully met. *Average percent of need met:* 81% (excluding resources awarded to replace EFC). *Average financial aid package:* $7318 (excluding resources awarded to replace EFC). 6% of all full-time freshmen had no need and received non-need-based gift aid.

UNDERGRADUATE FINANCIAL AID (Fall 2004, est.) 4,939 applied for aid; of those 65% were deemed to have need. 95% of undergraduates with need

received aid; of those 24% had need fully met. *Average percent of need met:* 78% (excluding resources awarded to replace EFC). *Average financial aid package:* $6988 (excluding resources awarded to replace EFC). 4% of all full-time undergraduates had no need and received non-need-based gift aid.

GIFT AID (NEED-BASED) *Total amount:* $10,371,510 (48% federal, 51% state, 1% external sources). *Receiving aid:* Freshmen: 37% (520); All full-time undergraduates: 37% (2,458). *Average award:* Freshmen: $4937; Undergraduates: $4432. *Scholarships, grants, and awards:* Federal Pell, FSEOG, state, college/university gift aid from institutional funds.

GIFT AID (NON-NEED-BASED) *Total amount:* $1,614,728 (1% federal, 5% state, 56% institutional, 38% external sources). *Receiving aid:* Freshmen: 12% (164); Undergraduates: 7% (466). *Average Award:* Freshmen: $2631; Undergraduates:* $3176. *Scholarships, grants, and awards by category: Special Characteristics:* children of faculty/staff, veterans. *Tuition waivers:* Full or partial for employees or children of employees, senior citizens. *ROTC:* Army cooperative, Air Force cooperative.

LOANS *Student loans:* $19,773,378 (38% need-based, 62% non-need-based). *Average need-based loan:* Freshmen: $2613; Undergraduates: $3134. *Parent loans:* $5,718,153 (100% non-need-based). *Programs:* FFEL (Subsidized and Unsubsidized Stafford, PLUS), Perkins, alternative loans.

WORK-STUDY *Federal work-study:* Total amount: $420,281; 139 jobs averaging $3086. *State or other work-study/employment:* Total amount: $7767 (100% need-based). 3 part-time jobs averaging $2589.

ATHLETIC AWARDS *Total amount:* $737,163 (1% need-based, 99% non-need-based).

APPLYING FOR FINANCIAL AID *Required financial aid forms:* FAFSA, institution's own form, federal income tax form(s). *Financial aid deadline (priority):* 4/14. *Notification date:* Continuous. Students must reply within 2 weeks of notification.

CONTACT Avon Dennis, Director of Financial Aid, Southern Connecticut State University, Wintergreen Building, 501 Crescent Street, New Haven, CT 06515-1355, 203-392-5448. *Fax:* 203-392-5229. *E-mail:* dennisa1@southernet.edu.

SOUTHERN ILLINOIS UNIVERSITY CARBONDALE
Carbondale, IL

Tuition & fees (IL res): $6341	Average undergraduate aid package: $8117

ABOUT THE INSTITUTION State-supported, coed. Awards: associate, bachelor's, master's, doctoral, and first professional degrees and post-bachelor's and first professional certificates. 85 undergraduate majors. Total enrollment: 21,589. Undergraduates: 16,872. Freshmen: 2,678. Federal methodology is used as a basis for awarding need-based institutional aid.

UNDERGRADUATE EXPENSES for 2004–05 *Application fee:* $30. *Tuition, state resident:* full-time $4920; part-time $164 per semester hour. *Tuition, nonresident:* full-time $12,300; part-time $410 per semester hour. Full-time tuition and fees vary according to course load and student level. Part-time tuition and fees vary according to course load and student level. *College room and board:* $5200; *room only:* $2640. Room and board charges vary according to board plan and housing facility. *Payment plans:* Guaranteed tuition, installment.

FRESHMAN FINANCIAL AID (Fall 2003) 2049 applied for aid; of those 75% were deemed to have need. 98% of freshmen with need received aid; of those 78% had need fully met. *Average percent of need met:* 92% (excluding resources awarded to replace EFC). *Average financial aid package:* $7363 (excluding resources awarded to replace EFC). 6% of all full-time freshmen had no need and received non-need-based gift aid.

UNDERGRADUATE FINANCIAL AID (Fall 2003) 10,483 applied for aid; of those 82% were deemed to have need. 97% of undergraduates with need received aid; of those 83% had need fully met. *Average percent of need met:* 95% (excluding resources awarded to replace EFC). *Average financial aid package:* $8117 (excluding resources awarded to replace EFC). 7% of all full-time undergraduates had no need and received non-need-based gift aid.

GIFT AID (NEED-BASED) *Total amount:* $30,044,899 (52% federal, 42% state, 4% institutional, 2% external sources). *Receiving aid:* Freshmen: 46% (1,193); All full-time undergraduates: 46% (6,796). *Average award:* Freshmen: $4689; Undergraduates: $4420. *Scholarships, grants, and awards:* Federal Pell, FSEOG, state, private, college/university gift aid from institutional funds.

GIFT AID (NON-NEED-BASED) *Total amount:* $13,319,540 (41% federal, 18% state, 27% institutional, 14% external sources). *Receiving aid:* Freshmen: 33% (853); Undergraduates: 30% (4,345). *Average Award:* Freshmen: $3545; Undergraduates: $3102. *Scholarships, grants, and awards by category: Academic Interests/Achievement:* 3,169 awards ($6,284,354 total): agriculture,

architecture, area/ethnic studies, biological sciences, business, communication, computer science, education, engineering/technologies, English, foreign languages, general academic interests/achievements, health fields, home economics, humanities, international studies, mathematics, military science, physical sciences, premedicine, religion/biblical studies, social sciences. *Creative Arts/ Performance:* 130 awards ($357,294 total): applied art and design, art/fine arts, cinema/film/broadcasting, creative writing, dance, debating, general creative arts/performance, journalism/publications, music, performing arts, theater/drama. *Special Achievements/Activities:* 67 awards ($132,423 total): cheerleading/drum major, community service, general special achievements/activities, leadership. *Special Characteristics:* 199 awards ($265,937 total): children and siblings of alumni, children of educators, children of faculty/staff, children of public servants, children with a deceased or disabled parent, general special characteristics, handicapped students, international students, public servants, spouses of deceased or disabled public servants, veterans. *Tuition waivers:* Full or partial for employees or children of employees, senior citizens. *ROTC:* Army, Air Force.

LOANS *Student loans:* $38,006,261 (66% need-based, 34% non-need-based). 37% of past graduating class borrowed through all loan programs. *Average indebtedness per student:* $13,712. *Average need-based loan:* Freshmen: $2631; Undergraduates: $3496. *Parent loans:* $4,281,917 (10% need-based, 90% non-need-based). *Programs:* Federal Direct (Subsidized and Unsubsidized Stafford, PLUS), Perkins, college/university.

WORK-STUDY *Federal work-study:* Total amount: $1,842,151; 1,898 jobs averaging $1205. *State or other work-study/employment:* Total amount: $3,587,007 (14% need-based, 86% non-need-based). 4,351 part-time jobs averaging $1680.

ATHLETIC AWARDS *Total amount:* $2,241,145 (25% need-based, 75% non-need-based).

APPLYING FOR FINANCIAL AID *Required financial aid form:* FAFSA. *Financial aid deadline (priority):* 4/1. *Notification date:* Continuous. Students must reply within 3 weeks of notification.

CONTACT Ms. Donna Williams, Interim Director of Financial Aid, Southern Illinois University Carbondale, Woody Hall, Third Floor, B-Wing, Carbondale, IL 62901-4702, 618-453-4334 Ext. 22. *Fax:* 618-453-4606. *E-mail:* donnawms@siu.edu.

SOUTHERN ILLINOIS UNIVERSITY EDWARDSVILLE
Edwardsville, IL

Tuition & fees (IL res): $5179	Average undergraduate aid package: $8073

ABOUT THE INSTITUTION State-supported, coed. Awards: bachelor's, master's, and first professional degrees and post-bachelor's, post-master's, and first professional certificates. 43 undergraduate majors. Total enrollment: 13,493. Undergraduates: 10,811. Freshmen: 1,723. Federal methodology is used as a basis for awarding need-based institutional aid.

UNDERGRADUATE EXPENSES for 2005–06 *Application fee:* $30. *Tuition, state resident:* full-time $4320; part-time $144 per semester hour. *Tuition, nonresident:* full-time $10,800; part-time $360 per semester hour. *Required fees:* full-time $859; $366.50 per term part-time. Full-time tuition and fees vary according to course load. Part-time tuition and fees vary according to course load. *College room and board:* $5819; *room only:* $3389. Room and board charges vary according to board plan and housing facility. *Payment plan:* Installment.

FRESHMAN FINANCIAL AID (Fall 2003) 1225 applied for aid; of those 73% were deemed to have need. 95% of freshmen with need received aid; of those 23% had need fully met. *Average percent of need met:* 77% (excluding resources awarded to replace EFC). *Average financial aid package:* $7418 (excluding resources awarded to replace EFC). 12% of all full-time freshmen had no need and received non-need-based gift aid.

UNDERGRADUATE FINANCIAL AID (Fall 2003) 5,940 applied for aid; of those 77% were deemed to have need. 96% of undergraduates with need received aid; of those 22% had need fully met. *Average percent of need met:* 78% (excluding resources awarded to replace EFC). *Average financial aid package:* $8073 (excluding resources awarded to replace EFC). 11% of all full-time undergraduates had no need and received non-need-based gift aid.

GIFT AID (NEED-BASED) *Total amount:* $18,656,647 (49% federal, 45% state, 3% institutional, 3% external sources). *Receiving aid:* Freshmen: 38% (645); All full-time undergraduates: 38% (3,365). *Average award:* Freshmen: $5140; Undergraduates: $5173. *Scholarships, grants, and awards:* Federal Pell, FSEOG, state, private, college/university gift aid from institutional funds, Federal Nursing.

Southern Illinois University Edwardsville

GIFT AID (NON-NEED-BASED) *Total amount:* $2,140,900 (5% federal, 50% state, 18% institutional, 27% external sources). *Receiving aid:* Freshmen: 4% (74); Undergraduates: 2% (192). *Average Award: Freshmen:* $3179; *Undergraduates:* $3172. *Scholarships, grants, and awards by category: Academic Interests/Achievement:* business, education, general academic interests/achievements, health fields. *Creative Arts/Performance:* art/fine arts, dance, music, theater/drama. *Special Characteristics:* children of faculty/staff. *Tuition waivers:* Full or partial for employees or children of employees, senior citizens. *ROTC:* Army, Air Force.
LOANS *Student loans:* $22,055,842 (64% need-based, 36% non-need-based). 20% of past graduating class borrowed through all loan programs. *Average indebtedness per student:* $16,606. *Average need-based loan:* Freshmen: $2249; Undergraduates: $3230. *Parent loans:* $5,064,504 (18% need-based, 82% non-need-based). *Programs:* Federal Direct (Subsidized and Unsubsidized Stafford, PLUS), FFEL (PLUS), Perkins, Federal Nursing, college/university, alternative loans.
WORK-STUDY *Federal work-study:* Total amount: $1,085,097; 724 jobs averaging $1499. *State or other work-study/employment:* Total amount: $6,951,274 (10% need-based, 90% non-need-based). 1,307 part-time jobs averaging $5318.
ATHLETIC AWARDS *Total amount:* $289,912 (31% need-based, 69% non-need-based).
APPLYING FOR FINANCIAL AID *Required financial aid form:* FAFSA. *Financial aid deadline (priority):* 3/1. *Notification date:* Continuous beginning 3/15. Students must reply within 2 weeks of notification.
CONTACT Sharon Berry, Director of Financial Aid, Southern Illinois University Edwardsville, Campus Box 1060, Rendleman Hall, Room 2308, Edwardsville, IL 62026-1060, 618-650-3834 or toll-free 800-447-SIUE. Fax: 618-650-3885. E-mail: shaberr@siue.edu.

SOUTHERN METHODIST COLLEGE
Orangeburg, SC

Tuition & fees: $5200	Average undergraduate aid package: $2025

ABOUT THE INSTITUTION Independent religious, coed. Awards: associate and bachelor's degrees. 2 undergraduate majors. Total enrollment: 77. Undergraduates: 77. Freshmen: 5. Both federal and institutional methodology are used as a basis for awarding need-based institutional aid.
UNDERGRADUATE EXPENSES for 2005–06 *Application fee:* $25. *Comprehensive fee:* $9400 includes full-time tuition ($4600), mandatory fees ($600), and room and board ($4200). Full-time tuition and fees vary according to class time and course load. Room and board charges vary according to housing facility. *Part-time tuition:* $192 per semester hour. *Part-time fees:* $25 per semester hour. Part-time tuition and fees vary according to class time and course load.
GIFT AID (NEED-BASED) *Total amount:* $77,000 (97% institutional, 3% external sources). *Receiving aid:* Freshmen: 79% (11); All full-time undergraduates: 87% (87). *Average award:* Freshmen: $2625; Undergraduates: $5000. *Scholarships, grants, and awards:* Federal Pell, FSEOG, college/university gift aid from institutional funds.
GIFT AID (NON-NEED-BASED) *Scholarships, grants, and awards by category: Academic Interests/Achievement:* $4000 total: education, religion/biblical studies. *Special Achievements/Activities:* $4600 total: religious involvement. *Special Characteristics:* relatives of clergy. *Tuition waivers:* Full or partial for employees or children of employees, senior citizens.
LOANS *Student loans:* $200,000 (100% need-based). 48% of past graduating class borrowed through all loan programs. *Average indebtedness per student:* $12,600. *Average need-based loan:* Freshmen: $4000; Undergraduates: $4000. *Parent loans:* $4000 (100% need-based). *Programs:* Federal Direct (Subsidized and Unsubsidized Stafford, PLUS).
APPLYING FOR FINANCIAL AID *Required financial aid forms:* FAFSA, institution's own form. *Financial aid deadline:* 3/15. *Notification date:* Continuous beginning 4/5. Students must reply within 2 weeks of notification.
CONTACT Terry H. Lynch, Financial Aid Officer, Southern Methodist College, PO Box 1027, 541 Broughton Street, Orangeburg, SC 29116, 803-534-7826 Ext. 1326 or toll-free 800-360-1503. Fax: 803-534-7827. E-mail: tlynch@smcollege.edu.

SOUTHERN METHODIST UNIVERSITY
Dallas, TX

Tuition & fees: $26,880	Average undergraduate aid package: $22,937

ABOUT THE INSTITUTION Independent religious, coed. Awards: bachelor's, master's, doctoral, and first professional degrees and post-bachelor's certificates. 65 undergraduate majors. Total enrollment: 10,901. Undergraduates: 6,208. Freshmen: 1,313. Both federal and institutional methodology are used as a basis for awarding need-based institutional aid.
UNDERGRADUATE EXPENSES for 2005–06 *Application fee:* $50. *Comprehensive fee:* $36,088 includes full-time tuition ($23,846), mandatory fees ($3034), and room and board ($9208). *College room only:* $5508. Full-time tuition and fees vary according to class time. Room and board charges vary according to board plan and housing facility. *Part-time tuition:* $996 per credit hour. *Part-time fees:* $127 per credit hour. Part-time tuition and fees vary according to class time and course load. *Payment plans:* Tuition prepayment, installment.
FRESHMAN FINANCIAL AID (Fall 2004, est.) 651 applied for aid; of those 75% were deemed to have need. 99% of freshmen with need received aid; of those 71% had need fully met. *Average percent of need met:* 91% (excluding resources awarded to replace EFC). *Average financial aid package:* $22,731 (excluding resources awarded to replace EFC). 34% of all full-time freshmen had no need and received non-need-based gift aid.
UNDERGRADUATE FINANCIAL AID (Fall 2004, est.) 2,681 applied for aid; of those 85% were deemed to have need. 99% of undergraduates with need received aid; of those 36% had need fully met. *Average percent of need met:* 91% (excluding resources awarded to replace EFC). *Average financial aid package:* $22,937 (excluding resources awarded to replace EFC). 24% of all full-time undergraduates had no need and received non-need-based gift aid.
GIFT AID (NEED-BASED) *Total amount:* $37,526,196 (10% federal, 15% state, 74% institutional, 1% external sources). *Receiving aid:* Freshmen: 29% (376); All full-time undergraduates: 33% (1,930). *Average award:* Freshmen: $15,278; Undergraduates: $14,425. *Scholarships, grants, and awards:* Federal Pell, FSEOG, state, private, college/university gift aid from institutional funds.
GIFT AID (NON-NEED-BASED) *Total amount:* $11,829,893 (95% institutional, 5% external sources). *Receiving aid:* Freshmen: 28% (373); Undergraduates: 26% (1,508). *Average Award: Freshmen:* $6511; *Undergraduates:* $6267. *Scholarships, grants, and awards by category: Academic Interests/Achievement:* area/ethnic studies, biological sciences, business, communication, computer science, engineering/technologies, English, foreign languages, general academic interests/achievements, humanities, international studies, mathematics, physical sciences, religion/biblical studies, social sciences. *Creative Arts/Performance:* art/fine arts, cinema/film/broadcasting, creative writing, dance, journalism/publications, music, theater/drama. *Special Achievements/Activities:* general special achievements/activities. *Special Characteristics:* children of faculty/staff, relatives of clergy. *Tuition waivers:* Full or partial for employees or children of employees. *ROTC:* Army, Air Force cooperative.
LOANS *Student loans:* $12,966,786 (66% need-based, 34% non-need-based). 52% of past graduating class borrowed through all loan programs. *Average indebtedness per student:* $16,906. *Average need-based loan:* Freshmen: $2529; Undergraduates: $3767. *Parent loans:* $12,446,009 (36% need-based, 64% non-need-based). *Programs:* FFEL (Subsidized and Unsubsidized Stafford, PLUS), Perkins, state, college/university.
WORK-STUDY *Federal work-study:* Total amount: $3,195,100; 1,568 jobs averaging $2500. *State or other work-study/employment:* Total amount: $146,064 (38% need-based, 62% non-need-based). 55 part-time jobs averaging $2000.
ATHLETIC AWARDS *Total amount:* $7,363,269 (42% need-based, 58% non-need-based).
APPLYING FOR FINANCIAL AID *Required financial aid forms:* FAFSA, CSS Financial Aid PROFILE, noncustodial (divorced/separated) parent's statement, business/farm supplement. *Financial aid deadline (priority):* 2/15. *Notification date:* Continuous beginning 3/15.
CONTACT Marc Peterson, Director of Financial Aid, Southern Methodist University, PO Box 750181, Dallas, TX 75275, 214-768-1588 or toll-free 800-323-0672.

SOUTHERN NAZARENE UNIVERSITY
Bethany, OK

ABOUT THE INSTITUTION Independent Nazarene, coed. Awards: associate, bachelor's, and master's degrees. 70 undergraduate majors. Total enrollment: 2,177. Undergraduates: 1,780. Freshmen: 310.
GIFT AID (NEED-BASED) *Scholarships, grants, and awards:* Federal Pell, FSEOG, state, private, college/university gift aid from institutional funds.
GIFT AID (NON-NEED-BASED) *Scholarships, grants, and awards by category: Academic Interests/Achievement:* biological sciences, business, communication, education, English, general academic interests/achievements, mathemat-

ics, religion/biblical studies. *Creative Arts/Performance:* music, performing arts. *Special Characteristics:* children and siblings of alumni, children of faculty/staff, local/state students, religious affiliation.
LOANS *Programs:* FFEL (Subsidized and Unsubsidized Stafford, PLUS), Perkins.
APPLYING FOR FINANCIAL AID *Required financial aid forms:* FAFSA, institution's own form.
CONTACT Mr. Chuck Kietzman, Director of Financial Assistance, Southern Nazarene University, 6729 Northwest 39th Expressway, Bethany, OK 73008, 405-491-6310 or toll-free 800-648-9899. *Fax:* 405-717-6271. *E-mail:* ckietzma@ snu.edu.

SOUTHERN NEW HAMPSHIRE UNIVERSITY
Manchester, NH

Tuition & fees: $19,314	Average undergraduate aid package: $14,545

ABOUT THE INSTITUTION Independent, coed. Awards: associate, bachelor's, master's, and doctoral degrees and post-bachelor's certificates. 36 undergraduate majors. Total enrollment: 3,887. Undergraduates: 1,844. Freshmen: 403. Federal methodology is used as a basis for awarding need-based institutional aid.
UNDERGRADUATE EXPENSES for 2004–05 *Application fee:* $35. *Comprehensive fee:* $27,180 includes full-time tuition ($18,984), mandatory fees ($330), and room and board ($7866). *College room only:* $5626. Full-time tuition and fees vary according to class time. Room and board charges vary according to board plan and housing facility. *Part-time tuition:* $791 per credit. Part-time tuition and fees vary according to class time. *Payment plans:* Installment, deferred payment.
FRESHMAN FINANCIAL AID (Fall 2004, est.) 420 applied for aid; of those 89% were deemed to have need. 100% of freshmen with need received aid; of those 12% had need fully met. *Average percent of need met:* 75% (excluding resources awarded to replace EFC). *Average financial aid package:* $14,536 (excluding resources awarded to replace EFC). 9% of all full-time freshmen had no need and received non-need-based gift aid.
UNDERGRADUATE FINANCIAL AID (Fall 2004, est.) 1,352 applied for aid; of those 89% were deemed to have need. 100% of undergraduates with need received aid; of those 11% had need fully met. *Average percent of need met:* 75% (excluding resources awarded to replace EFC). *Average financial aid package:* $14,545 (excluding resources awarded to replace EFC). 12% of all full-time undergraduates had no need and received non-need-based gift aid.
GIFT AID (NEED-BASED) *Total amount:* $10,249,782 (13% federal, 2% state, 85% institutional). *Receiving aid:* Freshmen: 60% (288); All full-time undergraduates: 55% (915). *Average award:* Freshmen: $7806; Undergraduates: $7660. *Scholarships, grants, and awards:* Federal Pell, FSEOG, state, private, college/university gift aid from institutional funds.
GIFT AID (NON-NEED-BASED) *Total amount:* $1,380,077 (72% institutional, 28% external sources). *Receiving aid:* Freshmen: 67% (321); Undergraduates: 70% (1,158). *Average Award:* Freshmen: $3933; Undergraduates: $3451. *Scholarships, grants, and awards by category: Academic Interests/Achievement:* 528 awards ($2,075,313 total): general academic interests/achievements. *Special Achievements/Activities:* 389 awards ($418,750 total): leadership, memberships. *Special Characteristics:* 90 awards ($85,600 total): children and siblings of alumni, children of faculty/staff, general special characteristics, international students, local/state students, previous college experience, siblings of current students, veterans, veterans' children. *Tuition waivers:* Full or partial for employees or children of employees. *ROTC:* Army cooperative, Air Force cooperative.
LOANS *Student loans:* $10,746,991 (87% need-based, 13% non-need-based). 53% of past graduating class borrowed through all loan programs. *Average indebtedness per student:* $22,200. *Average need-based loan:* Freshmen: $4256; Undergraduates: $5216. *Parent loans:* $41,222,264 (100% non-need-based). *Programs:* FFEL (Subsidized and Unsubsidized Stafford, PLUS), Perkins.
WORK-STUDY *Federal work-study:* Total amount: $3950; 568 jobs averaging $695.
ATHLETIC AWARDS *Total amount:* $1,530,637 (100% non-need-based).
APPLYING FOR FINANCIAL AID *Required financial aid form:* FAFSA. *Financial aid deadline (priority):* 3/15. *Notification date:* Continuous beginning 3/1. Students must reply within 3 weeks of notification.
CONTACT Financial Aid Office, Southern New Hampshire University, 2500 North River Road, Manchester, NH 03106, 603-645-9645 or toll-free 800-642-4968. *Fax:* 603-645-9639. *E-mail:* finaid@snhu.edu.

SOUTHERN OREGON UNIVERSITY
Ashland, OR

Tuition & fees (OR res): $4863	Average undergraduate aid package: $7587

ABOUT THE INSTITUTION State-supported, coed. Awards: bachelor's and master's degrees and post-bachelor's certificates. 40 undergraduate majors. Total enrollment: 5,162. Undergraduates: 4,672. Freshmen: 806. Federal methodology is used as a basis for awarding need-based institutional aid.
UNDERGRADUATE EXPENSES for 2005–06 *Application fee:* $50. *Tuition, state resident:* full-time $3738; part-time $98 per credit. *Tuition, nonresident:* full-time $14,565; part-time $98 per credit. *Required fees:* full-time $1125; $25 per credit. Full-time tuition and fees vary according to course load, location, and reciprocity agreements. Part-time tuition and fees vary according to course load, location, and reciprocity agreements. *College room and board:* $7560; *room only:* $4536. Room and board charges vary according to board plan and housing facility. *Payment plan:* Deferred payment.
FRESHMAN FINANCIAL AID (Fall 2004, est.) 495 applied for aid; of those 80% were deemed to have need. 99% of freshmen with need received aid; of those 7% had need fully met. *Average percent of need met:* 56% (excluding resources awarded to replace EFC). *Average financial aid package:* $6516 (excluding resources awarded to replace EFC). 15% of all full-time freshmen had no need and received non-need-based gift aid.
UNDERGRADUATE FINANCIAL AID (Fall 2004, est.) 2,487 applied for aid; of those 87% were deemed to have need. 98% of undergraduates with need received aid; of those 9% had need fully met. *Average percent of need met:* 56% (excluding resources awarded to replace EFC). *Average financial aid package:* $7587 (excluding resources awarded to replace EFC). 10% of all full-time undergraduates had no need and received non-need-based gift aid.
GIFT AID (NEED-BASED) *Total amount:* $7,616,302 (58% federal, 10% state, 22% institutional, 10% external sources). *Receiving aid:* Freshmen: 44% (327); All full-time undergraduates: 47% (1,728). *Average award:* Freshmen: $5200; Undergraduates: $4961. *Scholarships, grants, and awards:* Federal Pell, FSEOG, state, private, college/university gift aid from institutional funds.
GIFT AID (NON-NEED-BASED) *Total amount:* $945,778 (1% state, 80% institutional, 19% external sources). *Receiving aid:* Freshmen: 3% (19); Undergraduates: 2% (68). *Average Award: Freshmen:* $7318; *Undergraduates:* $8113. *Scholarships, grants, and awards by category: Academic Interests/ Achievement:* 400 awards ($711,391 total): biological sciences, business, English, general academic interests/achievements, health fields, humanities, mathematics, physical sciences, social sciences. *Creative Arts/Performance:* 47 awards ($33,286 total): art/fine arts, journalism/publications, music, theater/drama. *Special Achievements/Activities:* 4 awards ($5000 total): community service, leadership, memberships. *Special Characteristics:* 90 awards ($324,968 total): adult students, ethnic background, general special characteristics, international students, local/state students. *Tuition waivers:* Full or partial for employees or children of employees, senior citizens.
LOANS *Student loans:* $12,691,788 (84% need-based, 16% non-need-based). 61% of past graduating class borrowed through all loan programs. *Average indebtedness per student:* $19,375. *Average need-based loan:* Freshmen: $2576; Undergraduates: $4013. *Parent loans:* $6,229,494 (41% need-based, 59% non-need-based). *Programs:* Federal Direct (Subsidized and Unsubsidized Stafford, PLUS), Perkins, state, college/university.
WORK-STUDY *Federal work-study:* Total amount: $333,611; 371 jobs averaging $899.
ATHLETIC AWARDS *Total amount:* $212,287 (48% need-based, 52% non-need-based).
APPLYING FOR FINANCIAL AID *Required financial aid form:* FAFSA. *Financial aid deadline (priority):* 3/1. *Notification date:* Continuous beginning 4/1. Students must reply within 2 weeks of notification.
CONTACT Peggy K. Nitsos, Director of Financial Aid, Southern Oregon University, 1250 Siskiyou Boulevard, Ashland, OR 97520, 541-552-6754 or toll-free 800-482-7672 (in-state). *Fax:* 541-552-6035. *E-mail:* nitsos@sou.edu.

SOUTHERN POLYTECHNIC STATE UNIVERSITY
Marietta, GA

Tuition & fees (GA res): $2892	Average undergraduate aid package: $2406

Southern Polytechnic State University

ABOUT THE INSTITUTION State-supported, coed. Awards: associate, bachelor's, and master's degrees and post-bachelor's certificates. 23 undergraduate majors. Total enrollment: 3,801. Undergraduates: 3,255. Freshmen: 463. Federal methodology is used as a basis for awarding need-based institutional aid.

UNDERGRADUATE EXPENSES for 2004–05 *Application fee:* $20. *Tuition, state resident:* full-time $2428; part-time $102 per credit hour. *Tuition, nonresident:* full-time $9710; part-time $405 per credit hour. *College room and board:* $4946; *room only:* $2740. Room and board charges vary according to board plan.

FRESHMAN FINANCIAL AID (Fall 2003) 299 applied for aid; of those 50% were deemed to have need. 97% of freshmen with need received aid; of those 22% had need fully met. *Average percent of need met:* 68% (excluding resources awarded to replace EFC). *Average financial aid package:* $2209 (excluding resources awarded to replace EFC).

UNDERGRADUATE FINANCIAL AID (Fall 2003) 1,181 applied for aid; of those 65% were deemed to have need. 97% of undergraduates with need received aid; of those 21% had need fully met. *Average percent of need met:* 93% (excluding resources awarded to replace EFC). *Average financial aid package:* $2406 (excluding resources awarded to replace EFC).

GIFT AID (NEED-BASED) *Total amount:* $1,712,538 (98% federal, 1% state, 1% external sources). *Receiving aid:* Freshmen: 21% (88); All full-time undergraduates: 23% (452). *Average award:* Freshmen: $2561; Undergraduates: $2539. *Scholarships, grants, and awards:* Federal Pell, FSEOG, state, private, college/university gift aid from institutional funds.

GIFT AID (NON-NEED-BASED) *Total amount:* $2,774,861 (93% state, 7% external sources). *Receiving aid:* Freshmen: 30% (129); Undergraduates: 18% (352). *Scholarships, grants, and awards by category:* Academic Interests/Achievement: general academic interests/achievements. *Tuition waivers:* Full or partial for employees or children of employees, senior citizens. *ROTC:* Army cooperative, Naval cooperative, Air Force cooperative.

LOANS *Student loans:* $5,242,593 (48% need-based, 52% non-need-based). 89% of past graduating class borrowed through all loan programs. *Average indebtedness per student:* $4063. *Average need-based loan:* Freshmen: $2114; Undergraduates: $3595. *Parent loans:* $237,050 (100% non-need-based). *Programs:* FFEL (Subsidized and Unsubsidized Stafford, PLUS), state.

WORK-STUDY *Federal work-study:* Total amount: $80,654; jobs available.

ATHLETIC AWARDS *Total amount:* $176,442 (100% non-need-based).

APPLYING FOR FINANCIAL AID *Required financial aid form:* FAFSA. *Financial aid deadline:* Continuous. *Notification date:* Continuous beginning 6/1. Students must reply by 8/15.

CONTACT Gary W. Bush, Director of Financial Aid, Southern Polytechnic State University, 1100 South Marietta Parkway, Marietta, GA 30060-2896, 678-915-7290 or toll-free 800-635-3204. *Fax:* 678-915-4227. *E-mail:* gbush@spsu.edu.

SOUTHERN UNIVERSITY AND AGRICULTURAL AND MECHANICAL COLLEGE
Baton Rouge, LA

Tuition & fees (LA res): $3440	Average undergraduate aid package: $7098

ABOUT THE INSTITUTION State-supported, coed. Awards: associate, bachelor's, master's, and doctoral degrees. 46 undergraduate majors. Total enrollment: 9,400. Undergraduates: 8,023. Freshmen: 1,505. Federal methodology is used as a basis for awarding need-based institutional aid.

UNDERGRADUATE EXPENSES for 2004–05 *Application fee:* $5. *Tuition, state resident:* full-time $3440. *Tuition, nonresident:* full-time $9232. Full-time tuition and fees vary according to course load and location. Part-time tuition and fees vary according to course load and location. *College room and board:* $4310. Room and board charges vary according to board plan and housing facility.

FRESHMAN FINANCIAL AID (Fall 2003) 1081 applied for aid; of those 85% were deemed to have need. 95% of freshmen with need received aid; of those 9% had need fully met. *Average percent of need met:* 61% (excluding resources awarded to replace EFC). *Average financial aid package:* $6792 (excluding resources awarded to replace EFC). 1% of all full-time freshmen had no need and received non-need-based gift aid.

UNDERGRADUATE FINANCIAL AID (Fall 2003) 6,123 applied for aid; of those 90% were deemed to have need. 90% of undergraduates with need received aid; of those 9% had need fully met. *Average percent of need met:* 61% (excluding resources awarded to replace EFC). *Average financial aid package:*

$7098 (excluding resources awarded to replace EFC). 3% of all full-time undergraduates had no need and received non-need-based gift aid.

GIFT AID (NEED-BASED) *Total amount:* $27,618,000 (65% federal, 19% state, 16% institutional). *Receiving aid:* Freshmen: 69% (788); All full-time undergraduates: 69% (4,463). *Average award:* Freshmen: $3140; Undergraduates: $3680. *Scholarships, grants, and awards:* Federal Pell, FSEOG, state, private, college/university gift aid from institutional funds.

GIFT AID (NON-NEED-BASED) *Total amount:* $9,800,000 (54% state, 46% institutional). *Receiving aid:* Freshmen: 28% (320); Undergraduates: 28% (1,808). *Average Award:* Freshmen: $2625; Undergraduates: $4280. *Scholarships, grants, and awards by category:* Academic Interests/Achievement: 207 awards ($862,790 total): general academic interests/achievements. *Tuition waivers:* Full or partial for children of alumni, employees or children of employees, senior citizens. *ROTC:* Army, Naval, Air Force cooperative.

LOANS *Student loans:* $44,911,000 (100% need-based). 90% of past graduating class borrowed through all loan programs. *Average indebtedness per student:* $23,000. *Average need-based loan:* Freshmen: $2625; Undergraduates: $4280. *Parent loans:* $2,040,000 (100% need-based). *Programs:* Federal Direct (Subsidized and Unsubsidized Stafford, PLUS), FFEL (Subsidized and Unsubsidized Stafford, PLUS), college/university.

WORK-STUDY *Federal work-study:* Total amount: $1,250,000; 900 jobs averaging $1800. *State or other work-study/employment:* Total amount: $1,500,000 (50% need-based, 50% non-need-based). 300 part-time jobs averaging $2500.

APPLYING FOR FINANCIAL AID *Required financial aid forms:* FAFSA, institution's own form. *Financial aid deadline (priority):* 5/15. *Notification date:* Continuous beginning 6/30. Students must reply within 3 weeks of notification.

CONTACT Mr. Phillip Rodgers Sr., Director of Financial Aid, Southern University and Agricultural and Mechanical College, PO Box 9961, Baton Rouge, LA 70813, 225-771-2790 or toll-free 800-256-1531. *Fax:* 225-771-5898. *E-mail:* phillip_rodgers@cxs.subr.edu.

SOUTHERN UNIVERSITY AT NEW ORLEANS
New Orleans, LA

ABOUT THE INSTITUTION State-supported, coed. Awards: associate, bachelor's, and master's degrees. 20 undergraduate majors. Total enrollment: 5,000.

GIFT AID (NEED-BASED) *Scholarships, grants, and awards:* Federal Pell, FSEOG, state.

GIFT AID (NON-NEED-BASED) *Scholarships, grants, and awards by category:* Academic Interests/Achievement: biological sciences, physical sciences. Creative Arts/Performance: music.

LOANS *Programs:* Federal Direct (Subsidized and Unsubsidized Stafford), FFEL (Subsidized and Unsubsidized Stafford).

WORK-STUDY Federal work-study jobs available.

APPLYING FOR FINANCIAL AID *Required financial aid form:* FAFSA.

CONTACT Director of Financial Aid, Southern University at New Orleans, 6400 Press Drive, New Orleans, LA 70126, 504-286-5263. *Fax:* 504-286-5213.

SOUTHERN UTAH UNIVERSITY
Cedar City, UT

Tuition & fees (UT res): $3054	Average undergraduate aid package: $3699

ABOUT THE INSTITUTION State-supported, coed. Awards: associate, bachelor's, and master's degrees. 49 undergraduate majors. Total enrollment: 6,672. Undergraduates: 6,381. Freshmen: 971. Federal methodology is used as a basis for awarding need-based institutional aid.

UNDERGRADUATE EXPENSES for 2004–05 *Application fee:* $25. *Tuition, state resident:* full-time $2588; part-time $129 per credit hour. *Tuition, nonresident:* full-time $8542; part-time $427 per credit hour. Part-time tuition and fees vary according to course load. *College room and board:* $5400; *room only:* $2400. Room and board charges vary according to board plan and housing facility. *Payment plan:* Installment.

FRESHMAN FINANCIAL AID (Fall 2004, est.) 382 applied for aid; of those 85% were deemed to have need. 100% of freshmen with need received aid; of those 25% had need fully met. *Average percent of need met:* 75% (excluding resources awarded to replace EFC). *Average financial aid package:* $3299 (excluding resources awarded to replace EFC). 24% of all full-time freshmen had no need and received non-need-based gift aid.

UNDERGRADUATE FINANCIAL AID (Fall 2004, est.) 2,469 applied for aid; of those 94% were deemed to have need. 100% of undergraduates with need received aid; of those 37% had need fully met. *Average percent of need met:*

84% (excluding resources awarded to replace EFC). *Average financial aid package:* $3699 (excluding resources awarded to replace EFC). 16% of all full-time undergraduates had no need and received non-need-based gift aid.

GIFT AID (NEED-BASED) *Total amount:* $8,316,964 (84% federal, 16% institutional). *Receiving aid:* Freshmen: 22% (198); All full-time undergraduates: 42% (1,757). *Average award:* Freshmen: $2766; Undergraduates: $3020. *Scholarships, grants, and awards:* Federal Pell, FSEOG, state, private, college/university gift aid from institutional funds.

GIFT AID (NON-NEED-BASED) *Total amount:* $304,734 (100% federal). *Receiving aid:* Freshmen: 20% (187); Undergraduates: 33% (1,362). *Average Award:* Freshmen: $3274; Undergraduates: $3507. *Scholarships, grants, and awards by category: Academic Interests/Achievement:* business, communication, education, general academic interests/achievements. *Creative Arts/Performance:* dance, general creative arts/performance, journalism/publications, music, performing arts, theater/drama. *Special Achievements/Activities:* cheerleading/drum major, general special achievements/activities, leadership. *Special Characteristics:* ethnic background. *Tuition waivers:* Full or partial for employees or children of employees. *ROTC:* Army.

LOANS *Student loans:* $7,918,767 (77% need-based, 23% non-need-based). 62% of past graduating class borrowed through all loan programs. *Average indebtedness per student:* $11,359. *Average need-based loan:* Freshmen: $2465; Undergraduates: $3481. *Parent loans:* $403,396 (100% need-based). *Programs:* FFEL (Subsidized and Unsubsidized Stafford, PLUS), Perkins, college/university.

WORK-STUDY *Federal work-study:* Total amount: $284,348; jobs available. *State or other work-study/employment:* Total amount: $148,073 (100% need-based). Part-time jobs available.

ATHLETIC AWARDS *Total amount:* $1,061,150 (100% non-need-based).

APPLYING FOR FINANCIAL AID *Required financial aid forms:* FAFSA, institution's own form, institutional verification form. *Financial aid deadline:* Continuous. *Notification date:* Continuous beginning 2/1.

CONTACT Paul Morris, Director of Financial Aid, Southern Utah University, 351 West Center Street, Cedar City, UT 84720-2498, 435-586-7734. *Fax:* 435-586-7736. *E-mail:* morris@suu.edu.

SOUTHERN VERMONT COLLEGE
Bennington, VT

Tuition & fees: $14,373	Average undergraduate aid package: $11,899

ABOUT THE INSTITUTION Independent, coed. Awards: associate and bachelor's degrees. 15 undergraduate majors. Total enrollment: 464. Undergraduates: 464. Both federal and institutional methodology are used as a basis for awarding need-based institutional aid.

UNDERGRADUATE EXPENSES for 2005–06 *Application fee:* $30. *Comprehensive fee:* $21,317 includes full-time tuition ($14,373) and room and board ($6944). *College room only:* $3230. *Part-time tuition:* $399 per credit.

GIFT AID (NEED-BASED) *Total amount:* $2,212,056 (26% federal, 16% state, 54% institutional, 4% external sources). *Receiving aid:* Freshmen: 69% (59); All full-time undergraduates: 68% (252). *Average award:* Freshmen: $9700; Undergraduates: $3375. *Scholarships, grants, and awards:* Federal Pell, FSEOG, state, private, college/university gift aid from institutional funds.

GIFT AID (NON-NEED-BASED) *Total amount:* $208,517 (82% institutional, 18% external sources). *Receiving aid:* Freshmen: 1% (1); Undergraduates: 1% (2). *Average Award:* Freshmen: $3250; Undergraduates: $2800. *Scholarships, grants, and awards by category: Academic Interests/Achievement:* 79 awards ($218,750 total): general academic interests/achievements. *Special Achievements/Activities:* 5 awards ($5000 total): community service, leadership. *Special Characteristics:* children of faculty/staff.

LOANS *Student loans:* $1,966,419 (78% need-based, 22% non-need-based). 54% of past graduating class borrowed through all loan programs. *Average indebtedness per student:* $18,778. *Average need-based loan:* Freshmen: $2380; Undergraduates: $4168. *Parent loans:* $460,294 (32% need-based, 68% non-need-based). *Programs:* FFEL (Subsidized and Unsubsidized Stafford, PLUS).

APPLYING FOR FINANCIAL AID *Required financial aid forms:* FAFSA, institution's own form. *Financial aid deadline (priority):* 5/1. *Notification date:* Continuous. Students must reply within 2 weeks of notification.

CONTACT Office of Financial Aid Services, Southern Vermont College, PO Box 2000, Winooski, VT 05404, 877-563-6076 or toll-free 800-378-2782. *Fax:* 802-654-3765. *E-mail:* svc@vsac.org.

SOUTHERN VIRGINIA UNIVERSITY
Buena Vista, VA

Tuition & fees: $14,640	Average undergraduate aid package: $11,766

ABOUT THE INSTITUTION Independent Latter-day Saints, coed. Awards: bachelor's degrees. 14 undergraduate majors. Total enrollment: 579. Undergraduates: 579. Freshmen: 271. Federal methodology is used as a basis for awarding need-based institutional aid.

UNDERGRADUATE EXPENSES for 2004–05 *Application fee:* $35. *Comprehensive fee:* $19,940 includes full-time tuition ($14,640) and room and board ($5300). *Part-time tuition:* $475 per credit hour. *Payment plan:* Installment.

FRESHMAN FINANCIAL AID (Fall 2004, est.) 211 applied for aid; of those 86% were deemed to have need. 100% of freshmen with need received aid; of those 14% had need fully met. *Average percent of need met:* 68% (excluding resources awarded to replace EFC). *Average financial aid package:* $10,371 (excluding resources awarded to replace EFC). 11% of all full-time freshmen had no need and received non-need-based gift aid.

UNDERGRADUATE FINANCIAL AID (Fall 2004, est.) 509 applied for aid; of those 92% were deemed to have need. 100% of undergraduates with need received aid; of those 15% had need fully met. *Average percent of need met:* 75% (excluding resources awarded to replace EFC). *Average financial aid package:* $11,766 (excluding resources awarded to replace EFC). 7% of all full-time undergraduates had no need and received non-need-based gift aid.

GIFT AID (NEED-BASED) *Total amount:* $3,336,873 (24% federal, 6% state, 65% institutional, 5% external sources). *Receiving aid:* Freshmen: 65% (175); All full-time undergraduates: 78% (462). *Average award:* Freshmen: $8312; Undergraduates: $8734. *Scholarships, grants, and awards:* Federal Pell, FSEOG, state, private, college/university gift aid from institutional funds.

GIFT AID (NON-NEED-BASED) *Total amount:* $1,012,604 (9% state, 91% institutional). *Receiving aid:* Freshmen: 7% (19); Undergraduates: 7% (42). *Average Award:* Freshmen: $5585; Undergraduates: $5760. *Scholarships, grants, and awards by category: Academic Interests/Achievement:* 561 awards ($2,412,823 total): general academic interests/achievements. *Creative Arts/Performance:* 36 awards ($29,750 total): art/fine arts. *Special Achievements/Activities:* 139 awards ($201,840 total): religious involvement. *Special Characteristics:* 79 awards ($442,433 total): children of faculty/staff, international students. *Tuition waivers:* Full or partial for employees or children of employees. *ROTC:* Army cooperative.

LOANS *Student loans:* $2,309,412 (77% need-based, 23% non-need-based). 54% of past graduating class borrowed through all loan programs. *Average indebtedness per student:* $13,152. *Average need-based loan:* Freshmen: $2320; Undergraduates: $4200. *Parent loans:* $1,043,768 (42% need-based, 58% non-need-based). *Programs:* FFEL (Subsidized and Unsubsidized Stafford, PLUS), alternative loans.

WORK-STUDY *Federal work-study:* Total amount: $94,677; 117 jobs averaging $1000.

ATHLETIC AWARDS *Total amount:* $44,250 (64% need-based, 36% non-need-based).

APPLYING FOR FINANCIAL AID *Required financial aid forms:* FAFSA, Virginia Tuition Assistance Grant (VA residents only). *Financial aid deadline (priority):* 4/15. *Notification date:* Continuous beginning 2/1. Students must reply by 5/1 or within 2 weeks of notification.

CONTACT Jessica Massie, Financial Aid Specialist, Southern Virginia University, One University Hill Drive, Buena Vista, VA 24416, 540-261-4351 or toll-free 800-229-8420. *Fax:* 540-261-8559. *E-mail:* finaid@southernvirginia.edu.

SOUTHERN WESLEYAN UNIVERSITY
Central, SC

Tuition & fees: $14,750	Average undergraduate aid package: $8112

ABOUT THE INSTITUTION Independent religious, coed. Awards: associate, bachelor's, and master's degrees. 34 undergraduate majors. Total enrollment: 2,632. Undergraduates: 2,047. Freshmen: 123. Federal methodology is used as a basis for awarding need-based institutional aid.

UNDERGRADUATE EXPENSES for 2004–05 *Application fee:* $25. *Comprehensive fee:* $19,950 includes full-time tuition ($14,300), mandatory fees ($450), and room and board ($5200). Full-time tuition and fees vary according to course load, degree level, and program. Room and board charges vary according to

Southern Wesleyan University

board plan and housing facility. *Part-time tuition:* $440 per credit hour. *Part-time fees:* $162 per term. Part-time tuition and fees vary according to course load and degree level. *Payment plan:* Installment.

GIFT AID (NEED-BASED) *Total amount:* $4,506,952 (36% federal, 19% state, 27% institutional, 18% external sources). *Receiving aid:* Freshmen: 78% (97); All full-time undergraduates: 35% (907). *Average award:* Freshmen: $9749; Undergraduates: $5410. *Scholarships, grants, and awards:* Federal Pell, FSEOG, state, private, college/university gift aid from institutional funds.

GIFT AID (NON-NEED-BASED) *Total amount:* $961,832 (27% state, 47% institutional, 26% external sources). *Receiving aid:* Freshmen: 13% (16); Undergraduates: 3% (88). *Average Award:* Freshmen: $8198; *Undergraduates:* $6052. *Scholarships, grants, and awards by category: Academic Interests/Achievement:* biological sciences, business, computer science, education, English, general academic interests/achievements, humanities, mathematics, physical sciences, premedicine, religion/biblical studies, social sciences. *Creative Arts/Performance:* art/fine arts, creative writing, journalism/publications, music, theater/drama. *Special Achievements/Activities:* community service, leadership, religious involvement. *Special Characteristics:* children of faculty/staff, ethnic background, members of minority groups, relatives of clergy, religious affiliation, siblings of current students. *Tuition waivers:* Full or partial for employees or children of employees, senior citizens. *ROTC:* Army cooperative, Air Force cooperative.

LOANS *Student loans:* $7,892,799 (78% need-based, 22% non-need-based). 97% of past graduating class borrowed through all loan programs. *Average indebtedness per student:* $22,648. *Average need-based loan:* Freshmen: $3478; Undergraduates: $3734. *Parent loans:* $683,306 (32% need-based, 68% non-need-based). *Programs:* FFEL (Subsidized and Unsubsidized Stafford, PLUS), Perkins.

ATHLETIC AWARDS *Total amount:* $763,250 (71% need-based, 29% non-need-based).

APPLYING FOR FINANCIAL AID *Required financial aid forms:* FAFSA, institution's own form. *Financial aid deadline (priority):* 3/31. *Notification date:* Continuous. Students must reply within 2 weeks of notification.

CONTACT Mrs. Rita Martin, Financial Aid Associate, Southern Wesleyan University, 907 Wesleyan Drive, Central, SC 29630-1020, 800-289-1292 Ext. 5517 or toll-free 800-289-1292 Ext. 5550. *Fax:* 864-644-5970. *E-mail:* finaid@swu.edu.

SOUTH UNIVERSITY
Montgomery, AL

Tuition & fees: $11,085	Average undergraduate aid package: $5600

ABOUT THE INSTITUTION Proprietary, coed. Awards: associate and bachelor's degrees. 8 undergraduate majors. Total enrollment: 354. Undergraduates: 354. Freshmen: 40. Federal methodology is used as a basis for awarding need-based institutional aid.

UNDERGRADUATE EXPENSES for 2004–05 *Application fee:* $25. *Tuition:* full-time $11,085; part-time $2895 per term. Full-time tuition and fees vary according to course load. Part-time tuition and fees vary according to course load. *Payment plans:* Installment, deferred payment.

FRESHMAN FINANCIAL AID (Fall 2003) 47 applied for aid; of those 96% were deemed to have need. 100% of freshmen with need received aid. *Average percent of need met:* 40% (excluding resources awarded to replace EFC). *Average financial aid package:* $5600 (excluding resources awarded to replace EFC).

UNDERGRADUATE FINANCIAL AID (Fall 2003) 221 applied for aid; of those 95% were deemed to have need. 100% of undergraduates with need received aid. *Average percent of need met:* 40% (excluding resources awarded to replace EFC). *Average financial aid package:* $5600 (excluding resources awarded to replace EFC).

GIFT AID (NEED-BASED) *Total amount:* $1,181,038 (100% federal). *Receiving aid:* Freshmen: 89% (42); All full-time undergraduates: 92% (204). *Average award:* Freshmen: $3000; Undergraduates: $3000. *Scholarships, grants, and awards:* Federal Pell, FSEOG, state.

GIFT AID (NON-NEED-BASED) *Total amount:* $39,665 (100% external sources). *Tuition waivers:* Full or partial for employees or children of employees.

LOANS *Student loans:* $3,613,423 (100% need-based). 95% of past graduating class borrowed through all loan programs. *Average indebtedness per student:* $9600. *Average need-based loan:* Freshmen: $2625; Undergraduates: $2625. *Parent loans:* $265,123 (100% need-based). *Programs:* Federal Direct (Subsidized and Unsubsidized Stafford), FFEL (Subsidized and Unsubsidized Stafford, PLUS), Perkins, college/university.

WORK-STUDY *Federal work-study:* Total amount: $46,458; 21 jobs averaging $2213.

APPLYING FOR FINANCIAL AID *Required financial aid form:* FAFSA. *Financial aid deadline:* Continuous. *Notification date:* Continuous beginning 9/1.

CONTACT Financial Aid Office, South University, 5355 Vaughn Road, Montgomery, AL 36116-1120, 334-395-8800. *Fax:* 334-395-8859.

SOUTH UNIVERSITY
Savannah, GA

Tuition & fees: $11,085	Average undergraduate aid package: N/A

ABOUT THE INSTITUTION Proprietary, coed. Awards: associate, bachelor's, master's, and doctoral degrees. 9 undergraduate majors. Total enrollment: 801. Undergraduates: 579. Freshmen: 232. Federal methodology is used as a basis for awarding need-based institutional aid.

UNDERGRADUATE EXPENSES for 2004–05 *Application fee:* $25. *Tuition:* full-time $11,085. *Payment plan:* Installment.

FRESHMAN FINANCIAL AID (Fall 2003) 36 applied for aid; of those 100% were deemed to have need. 100% of freshmen with need received aid; of those 47% had need fully met. *Average percent of need met:* 80% (excluding resources awarded to replace EFC).

UNDERGRADUATE FINANCIAL AID (Fall 2003) 382 applied for aid; of those 73% were deemed to have need. 100% of undergraduates with need received aid. *Average percent of need met:* 85% (excluding resources awarded to replace EFC).

GIFT AID (NEED-BASED) *Total amount:* $4,192,799 (98% federal, 2% external sources). *Receiving aid:* Freshmen: 62% (29). *Scholarships, grants, and awards:* Federal Pell, FSEOG, state, private, college/university gift aid from institutional funds.

GIFT AID (NON-NEED-BASED) *Total amount:* $602,978 (95% state, 5% external sources). *Receiving aid:* Undergraduates: 48% (186). *Scholarships, grants, and awards by category: Academic Interests/Achievement:* business, general academic interests/achievements, health fields. *Tuition waivers:* Full or partial for employees or children of employees.

LOANS *Student loans:* $7,274,620 (61% need-based, 39% non-need-based). 83% of past graduating class borrowed through all loan programs. *Parent loans:* $365,079 (49% need-based, 51% non-need-based). *Programs:* FFEL (Subsidized and Unsubsidized Stafford, PLUS), Perkins, state.

WORK-STUDY *Federal work-study:* Total amount: $142,454; jobs available (averaging $2000).

APPLYING FOR FINANCIAL AID *Required financial aid forms:* FAFSA, state aid form. *Financial aid deadline (priority):* 5/31. *Notification date:* Continuous. Students must reply within 4 weeks of notification.

CONTACT Ms. Anne Gaglia, Director of Financial Services, South University, 709 Mall Boulevard, Savannah, GA 31406-4881, 912-201-8011 or toll-free 866-629-2901. *Fax:* 912-201-8072. *E-mail:* gaglia@southuniversity.edu.

SOUTHWEST BAPTIST UNIVERSITY
Bolivar, MO

Tuition & fees: $13,250	Average undergraduate aid package: $10,321

ABOUT THE INSTITUTION Independent Southern Baptist, coed. Awards: associate, bachelor's, and master's degrees and post-master's certificates. 55 undergraduate majors. Total enrollment: 3,445. Undergraduates: 2,746. Freshmen: 420. Federal methodology is used as a basis for awarding need-based institutional aid.

UNDERGRADUATE EXPENSES for 2005–06 *Application fee:* $25. *Comprehensive fee:* $17,200 includes full-time tuition ($12,450), mandatory fees ($800), and room and board ($3950). *College room only:* $1950. Full-time tuition and fees vary according to course load and location. Room and board charges vary according to board plan and housing facility. Part-time tuition and fees vary according to course load and location. *Payment plan:* Installment.

FRESHMAN FINANCIAL AID (Fall 2004, est.) 343 applied for aid; of those 85% were deemed to have need. 99% of freshmen with need received aid; of those 24% had need fully met. *Average percent of need met:* 72% (excluding resources awarded to replace EFC). *Average financial aid package:* $10,652 (excluding resources awarded to replace EFC). 22% of all full-time freshmen had no need and received non-need-based gift aid.

UNDERGRADUATE FINANCIAL AID (Fall 2004, est.) 1,475 applied for aid; of those 89% were deemed to have need. 99% of undergraduates with need received aid; of those 18% had need fully met. *Average percent of need met:* 68% (excluding resources awarded to replace EFC). *Average financial aid package:* $10,321 (excluding resources awarded to replace EFC). 21% of all full-time undergraduates had no need and received non-need-based gift aid.
GIFT AID (NEED-BASED) *Total amount:* $3,408,710 (83% federal, 16% state, 1% institutional). *Receiving aid:* Freshmen: 35% (138); All full-time undergraduates: 43% (786). *Average award:* Freshmen: $3685; Undergraduates: $3669. *Scholarships, grants, and awards:* Federal Pell, FSEOG, state, private, college/university gift aid from institutional funds.
GIFT AID (NON-NEED-BASED) *Total amount:* $6,621,924 (3% state, 86% institutional, 11% external sources). *Receiving aid:* Freshmen: 66% (258); Undergraduates: 57% (1,041). *Average Award: Freshmen:* $5058; *Undergraduates:* $4929. *Scholarships, grants, and awards by category: Academic Interests/Achievement:* 1,372 awards ($2,709,691 total): general academic interests/achievements. *Creative Arts/Performance:* 155 awards ($162,113 total): art/fine arts, debating, general creative arts/performance, music, theater/drama. *Special Achievements/Activities:* 296 awards ($546,250 total): religious involvement. *Special Characteristics:* 1,782 awards ($1,734,491 total): general special characteristics, local/state students, relatives of clergy. *Tuition waivers:* Full or partial for employees or children of employees. *ROTC:* Army cooperative.
LOANS *Student loans:* $8,626,951 (100% need-based). 72% of past graduating class borrowed through all loan programs. *Average indebtedness per student:* $11,159. *Average need-based loan:* Freshmen: $3795; Undergraduates: $4308. *Parent loans:* $942,017 (100% need-based). *Programs:* FFEL (Subsidized and Unsubsidized Stafford, PLUS), Perkins, Federal Nursing, state, alternative loans.
WORK-STUDY *Federal work-study:* Total amount: $525,241; 513 jobs averaging $1024.
ATHLETIC AWARDS *Total amount:* $1,521,525 (100% non-need-based).
APPLYING FOR FINANCIAL AID *Required financial aid forms:* FAFSA, institution's own form. *Financial aid deadline (priority):* 3/15. *Notification date:* Continuous beginning 3/1. Students must reply within 2 weeks of notification.
CONTACT Mr. Brad Gamble, Director of Financial Aid, Southwest Baptist University, 1600 University Avenue, Bolivar, MO 65613-2597, 417-328-1822 or toll-free 800-526-5859. *Fax:* 417-328-1514.

SOUTHWESTERN ADVENTIST UNIVERSITY
Keene, TX

ABOUT THE INSTITUTION Independent Seventh-day Adventist, coed. Awards: associate, bachelor's, and master's degrees. 29 undergraduate majors. Total enrollment: 1,191. Undergraduates: 1,163. Freshmen: 168.
GIFT AID (NEED-BASED) *Scholarships, grants, and awards:* Federal Pell, FSEOG, state, private, college/university gift aid from institutional funds.
GIFT AID (NON-NEED-BASED) *Scholarships, grants, and awards by category: Academic Interests/Achievement:* business, communication, computer science, education, English, general academic interests/achievements, humanities, physical sciences, premedicine, religion/biblical studies, social sciences. *Creative Arts/Performance:* music, theater/drama. *Special Achievements/Activities:* community service, general special achievements/activities, leadership, religious involvement. *Special Characteristics:* children of faculty/staff, married students, siblings of current students.
LOANS *Programs:* FFEL (Subsidized and Unsubsidized Stafford, PLUS), Perkins, state.
WORK-STUDY Federal work-study jobs available. *State or other work-study/employment:* Part-time jobs available.
APPLYING FOR FINANCIAL AID *Required financial aid forms:* FAFSA, institution's own form.
CONTACT Student Financial Services, Southwestern Adventist University, PO Box 567, Keene, TX 76059, 817-645-3921 Ext. 262 or toll-free 800-433-2240. *Fax:* 817-556-4744.

SOUTHWESTERN ASSEMBLIES OF GOD UNIVERSITY
Waxahachie, TX

CONTACT Financial Aid Office, Southwestern Assemblies of God University, 1200 Sycamore Street, Waxahachie, TX 75165-2397, 972-937-4010 Ext. 1140 or toll-free 888-937-7248. *Fax:* 972-937-4001. *E-mail:* finaid@sagu.edu.

SOUTHWESTERN CHRISTIAN COLLEGE
Terrell, TX

CONTACT Financial Aid Office, Southwestern Christian College, PO Box 10, Terrell, TX 75160, 972-524-3341. *Fax:* 972-563-7133.

SOUTHWESTERN CHRISTIAN UNIVERSITY
Bethany, OK

Tuition & fees: N/R	Average undergraduate aid package: $8925

ABOUT THE INSTITUTION Independent religious, coed. Awards: associate, bachelor's, and master's degrees. 10 undergraduate majors. Total enrollment: 199. Undergraduates: 128. Freshmen: 32. Federal methodology is used as a basis for awarding need-based institutional aid.
FRESHMAN FINANCIAL AID (Fall 2004, est.) 57 applied for aid; of those 95% were deemed to have need. 100% of freshmen with need received aid; of those 50% had need fully met. *Average percent of need met:* 69% (excluding resources awarded to replace EFC). *Average financial aid package:* $7495 (excluding resources awarded to replace EFC). 8% of all full-time freshmen had no need and received non-need-based gift aid.
UNDERGRADUATE FINANCIAL AID (Fall 2004, est.) 153 applied for aid; of those 99% were deemed to have need. 100% of undergraduates with need received aid; of those 29% had need fully met. *Average percent of need met:* 69% (excluding resources awarded to replace EFC). *Average financial aid package:* $8925 (excluding resources awarded to replace EFC). 4% of all full-time undergraduates had no need and received non-need-based gift aid.
GIFT AID (NEED-BASED) *Total amount:* $535,000 (56% federal, 6% state, 34% institutional, 4% external sources). *Receiving aid:* Freshmen: 84% (52); All full-time undergraduates: 80% (127). *Average award:* Freshmen: $2525; Undergraduates: $2250. *Scholarships, grants, and awards:* Federal Pell, FSEOG, state, private, college/university gift aid from institutional funds.
GIFT AID (NON-NEED-BASED) *Total amount:* $80,000 (25% federal, 7% state, 62% institutional, 6% external sources). *Receiving aid:* Freshmen: 42% (26); Undergraduates: 36% (57). *Average Award: Freshmen:* $1500; *Undergraduates:* $2100. *Scholarships, grants, and awards by category: Academic Interests/Achievement:* 70 awards ($90,000 total): business, education, general academic interests/achievements, religion/biblical studies. *Creative Arts/Performance:* 12 awards ($15,000 total): music, theater/drama. *Special Achievements/Activities:* cheerleading/drum major, religious involvement. *Special Characteristics:* 50 awards ($50,000 total): children and siblings of alumni, children of faculty/staff, relatives of clergy, religious affiliation.
LOANS *Student loans:* $700,000 (93% need-based, 7% non-need-based). 70% of past graduating class borrowed through all loan programs. *Average indebtedness per student:* $16,500. *Average need-based loan:* Freshmen: $2725; Undergraduates: $4000. *Parent loans:* $60,000 (100% need-based). *Programs:* FFEL (Subsidized and Unsubsidized Stafford, PLUS).
WORK-STUDY *Federal work-study:* Total amount: $70,000; 60 jobs averaging $1500. *State or other work-study/employment:* Total amount: $10,000 (100% non-need-based). 10 part-time jobs averaging $1000.
APPLYING FOR FINANCIAL AID *Required financial aid form:* FAFSA. *Financial aid deadline (priority):* 8/1. *Notification date:* Continuous.
CONTACT Mr. Mark Arthur, Financial Aid Director, Southwestern Christian University, PO Box 340, Bethany, OK 73008, 405-789-7661 Ext. 3456. *Fax:* 405-495-0078. *E-mail:* mark@swcu.edu.

SOUTHWESTERN COLLEGE
Phoenix, AZ

Tuition & fees: $11,570	Average undergraduate aid package: $5500

ABOUT THE INSTITUTION Independent Conservative Baptist, coed. Awards: associate and bachelor's degrees. 7 undergraduate majors. Total enrollment: 267. Undergraduates: 267. Freshmen: 29. Federal methodology is used as a basis for awarding need-based institutional aid.
UNDERGRADUATE EXPENSES for 2005–06 *Application fee:* $25. *Comprehensive fee:* $15,930 includes full-time tuition ($11,130), mandatory fees ($440), and room and board ($4360). *College room only:* $3360. Full-time tuition and fees vary according to course load and program. Room and board charges vary

according to housing facility. *Part-time tuition:* $464 per credit hour. *Part-time fees:* $220 per term. Part-time tuition and fees vary according to course load and program. *Payment plan:* Installment.

FRESHMAN FINANCIAL AID (Fall 2003) 35 applied for aid; of those 100% were deemed to have need. 100% of freshmen with need received aid. *Average percent of need met:* 10% (excluding resources awarded to replace EFC). *Average financial aid package:* $3800 (excluding resources awarded to replace EFC). 13% of all full-time freshmen had no need and received non-need-based gift aid.

UNDERGRADUATE FINANCIAL AID (Fall 2003) 147 applied for aid; of those 100% were deemed to have need. 100% of undergraduates with need received aid. *Average percent of need met:* 3% (excluding resources awarded to replace EFC). *Average financial aid package:* $5500 (excluding resources awarded to replace EFC). 37% of all full-time undergraduates had no need and received non-need-based gift aid.

GIFT AID (NEED-BASED) *Total amount:* $287,517 (94% federal, 1% state, 5% external sources). *Receiving aid:* Freshmen: 70% (28). *Average award:* Freshmen: $1200; Undergraduates: $1400. *Scholarships, grants, and awards:* Federal Pell, FSEOG, state, private, college/university gift aid from institutional funds.

GIFT AID (NON-NEED-BASED) *Total amount:* $303,475 (100% institutional). *Receiving aid:* Freshmen: 88% (35); Undergraduates: 55% (147). *Average Award:* Freshmen: $1600; Undergraduates: $1100. *Scholarships, grants, and awards by category:* Academic Interests/Achievement: 335 awards ($277,850 total): general academic interests/achievements. *Creative Arts/Performance:* 26 awards ($37,750 total): music. *Special Characteristics:* 11 awards ($15,400 total): children and siblings of alumni, children of faculty/staff, spouses of current students. *Tuition waivers:* Full or partial for employees or children of employees. *ROTC:* Air Force cooperative.

LOANS *Student loans:* $845,410 (100% need-based). 82% of past graduating class borrowed through all loan programs. *Average indebtedness per student:* $17,125. *Average need-based loan:* Freshmen: $4150; Undergraduates: $4500. *Parent loans:* $320,330 (100% need-based). *Programs:* FFEL (Subsidized and Unsubsidized Stafford, PLUS), Perkins.

WORK-STUDY *Federal work-study:* Total amount: $46,340; 20 jobs averaging $2000.

APPLYING FOR FINANCIAL AID *Required financial aid form:* FAFSA. *Financial aid deadline (priority):* 3/15. *Notification date:* Students must reply by 6/1.

CONTACT Mr. Pete Leonard, Director of Admissions and Financial Aid, Southwestern College, 2625 East Cactus Road, Phoenix, AZ 85032-7097, 602-992-6101 Ext. 114 or toll-free 800-247-2697. *Fax:* 602-404-2159.

SOUTHWESTERN COLLEGE
Winfield, KS

Tuition & fees: $16,118	Average undergraduate aid package: $14,836

ABOUT THE INSTITUTION Independent United Methodist, coed. Awards: bachelor's and master's degrees. 37 undergraduate majors. Total enrollment: 1,410. Undergraduates: 1,242. Freshmen: 141. Federal methodology is used as a basis for awarding need-based institutional aid.

UNDERGRADUATE EXPENSES for 2005–06 *Application fee:* $20. *Tuition:* full-time $16,118; part-time $671 per semester hour. Full-time tuition and fees vary according to degree level and location. Part-time tuition and fees vary according to degree level and location. Room and board charges vary according to board plan, housing facility, and location. *Payment plan:* Installment.

FRESHMAN FINANCIAL AID (Fall 2004, est.) 134 applied for aid; of those 92% were deemed to have need. 100% of freshmen with need received aid; of those 25% had need fully met. *Average percent of need met:* 84% (excluding resources awarded to replace EFC). *Average financial aid package:* $15,344 (excluding resources awarded to replace EFC). 13% of all full-time freshmen had no need and received non-need-based gift aid.

UNDERGRADUATE FINANCIAL AID (Fall 2004, est.) 505 applied for aid; of those 92% were deemed to have need. 100% of undergraduates with need received aid; of those 11% had need fully met. *Average percent of need met:* 74% (excluding resources awarded to replace EFC). *Average financial aid package:* $14,836 (excluding resources awarded to replace EFC). 18% of all full-time undergraduates had no need and received non-need-based gift aid.

GIFT AID (NEED-BASED) *Total amount:* $4,303,041 (28% federal, 10% state, 55% institutional, 7% external sources). *Receiving aid:* Freshmen: 87% (123); All full-time undergraduates: 81% (462). *Average award:* Freshmen: $10,006; Undergraduates: $8513. *Scholarships, grants, and awards:* Federal Pell, FSEOG, state, private, college/university gift aid from institutional funds.

GIFT AID (NON-NEED-BASED) *Total amount:* $739,486 (83% institutional, 17% external sources). *Receiving aid:* Freshmen: 87% (123); Undergraduates: 80% (460). *Average Award:* Freshmen: $5733; Undergraduates: $6785. *Scholarships, grants, and awards by category:* Academic Interests/Achievement: 477 awards ($1,456,665 total): biological sciences, business, communication, general academic interests/achievements, health fields, humanities, religion/biblical studies, social sciences. *Creative Arts/Performance:* 98 awards ($207,850 total): cinema/film/broadcasting, dance, debating, journalism/publications, music, performing arts, theater/drama. *Special Achievements/Activities:* 255 awards ($351,124 total): cheerleading/drum major, community service, general special achievements/activities, leadership, memberships, religious involvement. *Special Characteristics:* 33 awards ($203,212 total): children and siblings of alumni, children of current students, children of faculty/staff, ethnic background, international students, local/state students, members of minority groups, relatives of clergy, religious affiliation, siblings of current students, spouses of current students, twins. *Tuition waivers:* Full or partial for employees or children of employees, senior citizens.

LOANS *Student loans:* $6,311,970 (86% need-based, 14% non-need-based). 66% of past graduating class borrowed through all loan programs. *Average indebtedness per student:* $17,907. *Average need-based loan:* Freshmen: $4438; Undergraduates: $5652. *Parent loans:* $1,118,318 (32% need-based, 68% non-need-based). *Programs:* Federal Direct (Subsidized and Unsubsidized Stafford, PLUS), FFEL (Subsidized and Unsubsidized Stafford, PLUS), Perkins.

WORK-STUDY *Federal work-study:* Total amount: $116,052; 234 jobs averaging $496. *State or other work-study/employment:* Total amount: $86,758 (100% non-need-based). 107 part-time jobs averaging $810.

ATHLETIC AWARDS *Total amount:* $599,375 (78% need-based, 22% non-need-based).

APPLYING FOR FINANCIAL AID *Required financial aid forms:* FAFSA, institution's own form. *Financial aid deadline (priority):* 4/1. *Notification date:* Continuous beginning 2/1. Students must reply within 4 weeks of notification.

CONTACT Director of Financial Aid, Southwestern College, 100 College Street, Winfield, KS 67156-2499, 620-229-6215 or toll-free 800-846-1543. *Fax:* 620-229-6363. *E-mail:* finaid@sckans.edu.

SOUTHWESTERN OKLAHOMA STATE UNIVERSITY
Weatherford, OK

CONTACT Mr. Thomas M. Ratliff, Director of Student Financial Services, Southwestern Oklahoma State University, 100 Campus Drive, Weatherford, OK 73096-3098, 580-774-3786. *Fax:* 580-774-7066. *E-mail:* ratlift@swosu.edu.

SOUTHWESTERN UNIVERSITY
Georgetown, TX

Tuition & fees: $20,220	Average undergraduate aid package: $16,577

ABOUT THE INSTITUTION Independent Methodist, coed. Awards: bachelor's degrees. 38 undergraduate majors. Total enrollment: 1,276. Undergraduates: 1,276. Freshmen: 366. Both federal and institutional methodology are used as a basis for awarding need-based institutional aid.

UNDERGRADUATE EXPENSES for 2004–05 *Application fee:* $40. *Comprehensive fee:* $26,579 includes full-time tuition ($20,220) and room and board ($6359). *College room only:* $3023. Room and board charges vary according to board plan, housing facility, and student level. *Part-time tuition:* $845 per semester hour. *Payment plans:* Installment, deferred payment.

GIFT AID (NEED-BASED) *Total amount:* $8,155,982 (9% federal, 16% state, 67% institutional, 8% external sources). *Receiving aid:* Freshmen: 46% (169); All full-time undergraduates: 50% (624). *Average award:* Freshmen: $13,812; Undergraduates: $12,445. *Scholarships, grants, and awards:* Federal Pell, FSEOG, state, private, college/university gift aid from institutional funds.

GIFT AID (NON-NEED-BASED) *Total amount:* $2,919,688 (1% federal, 89% institutional, 10% external sources). *Receiving aid:* Freshmen: 30% (108); Undergraduates: 24% (298). *Average Award:* Freshmen: $8285; Undergraduates: $7397. *Scholarships, grants, and awards by category:* Academic Interests/Achievement: 624 awards ($3,679,910 total): general academic interests/achievements. *Creative Arts/Performance:* 133 awards ($467,320 total): art/fine arts, music, performing arts, theater/drama. *Special Characteristics:* 55 awards ($370,260 total): children of faculty/staff, relatives of clergy. *Tuition waivers:* Full or partial for employees or children of employees.

LOANS *Student loans:* $3,760,375 (89% need-based, 11% non-need-based). 49% of past graduating class borrowed through all loan programs. *Average indebtedness per student:* $18,393. *Average need-based loan:* Freshmen: $4335; Undergraduates: $4658. *Parent loans:* $7,961,128 (49% need-based, 51% non-need-based). *Programs:* FFEL (Subsidized and Unsubsidized Stafford, PLUS), Perkins, state, college/university.

APPLYING FOR FINANCIAL AID *Required financial aid form:* FAFSA. *Financial aid deadline:* 3/1 (priority: 3/1). *Notification date:* Continuous beginning 3/21. Students must reply by 5/1 or within 2 weeks of notification.

CONTACT Mr. James P. Gaeta, Director of Financial Aid, Southwestern University, PO Box 770, Georgetown, TX 78627-0770, 512-863-1259 or toll-free 800-252-3166. *E-mail:* gaetaj@southwestern.edu.

SOUTHWEST MINNESOTA STATE UNIVERSITY
Marshall, MN

Tuition & fees (MN res): $5294	Average undergraduate aid package: $6424

ABOUT THE INSTITUTION State-supported, coed. Awards: associate, bachelor's, and master's degrees. 50 undergraduate majors. Total enrollment: 5,636. Undergraduates: 5,167. Freshmen: 1,232. Federal methodology is used as a basis for awarding need-based institutional aid.

UNDERGRADUATE EXPENSES for 2004–05 *Application fee:* $20. *Tuition, state resident:* full-time $4538. *Tuition, nonresident:* full-time $4538. *College room and board:* $4806.

GIFT AID (NEED-BASED) *Total amount:* $3,671,740 (59% federal, 39% state, 2% institutional). *Receiving aid:* Freshmen: 42% (241); All full-time undergraduates: 46% (1,060). *Average award:* Freshmen: $3368; Undergraduates: $3330. *Scholarships, grants, and awards:* Federal Pell, FSEOG, state, private, college/university gift aid from institutional funds.

GIFT AID (NON-NEED-BASED) *Total amount:* $1,546,538 (1% federal, 62% institutional, 37% external sources). *Receiving aid:* Freshmen: 36% (208); Undergraduates: 27% (616). *Average Award:* Freshmen: $1653; Undergraduates: $1624. *Scholarships, grants, and awards by category: Academic Interests/Achievement:* 1,048 awards ($881,055 total): agriculture, biological sciences, business, communication, computer science, education, English, general academic interests/achievements, mathematics, physical sciences, social sciences. *Creative Arts/Performance:* 62 awards ($37,891 total): art/fine arts, music, theater/drama. *Special Achievements/Activities:* 278 awards ($429,245 total): general special achievements/activities. *Special Characteristics:* 104 awards ($286,554 total): children and siblings of alumni, children of union members/company employees, first-generation college students, handicapped students, international students, local/state students, members of minority groups, previous college experience, veterans, veterans' children.

LOANS *Student loans:* $9,216,958 (47% need-based, 53% non-need-based). 84% of past graduating class borrowed through all loan programs. *Average indebtedness per student:* $17,038. *Average need-based loan:* Freshmen: $2469; Undergraduates: $3237. *Parent loans:* $256,738 (100% non-need-based). *Programs:* FFEL (Subsidized and Unsubsidized Stafford, PLUS), Perkins, state. **ATHLETIC AWARDS** *Total amount:* $403,945 (100% non-need-based).

APPLYING FOR FINANCIAL AID *Required financial aid forms:* FAFSA, institution's own form. *Financial aid deadline (priority):* 3/1. *Notification date:* Continuous beginning 5/1.

CONTACT David Vikander, Director of Financial Aid, Southwest Minnesota State University, 1501 State Street, Marshall, MN 56258, 507-537-6281 or toll-free 800-642-0684. *Fax:* 507-537-6275. *E-mail:* v.kander@southwestmsu.edu.

SOUTHWEST MISSOURI STATE UNIVERSITY
Springfield, MO

See Missouri State University.

SPALDING UNIVERSITY
Louisville, KY

ABOUT THE INSTITUTION Independent religious, coed. Awards: associate, bachelor's, master's, and doctoral degrees and post-master's certificates. 32 undergraduate majors. Total enrollment: 1,679. Undergraduates: 970. Freshmen: 145.

GIFT AID (NEED-BASED) *Scholarships, grants, and awards:* Federal Pell, FSEOG, state, private, college/university gift aid from institutional funds.

GIFT AID (NON-NEED-BASED) *Scholarships, grants, and awards by category: Academic Interests/Achievement:* general academic interests/achievements. *Creative Arts/Performance:* applied art and design, art/fine arts, creative writing. *Special Achievements/Activities:* community service, general special achievements/activities, leadership. *Special Characteristics:* children and siblings of alumni, children of faculty/staff, first-generation college students, general special characteristics, international students, siblings of current students, spouses of current students.

LOANS *Programs:* FFEL (Subsidized and Unsubsidized Stafford, PLUS), Perkins, Federal Nursing, college/university.

WORK-STUDY Federal work-study jobs available. *State or other work-study/employment:* Part-time jobs available.

APPLYING FOR FINANCIAL AID *Required financial aid form:* FAFSA.

CONTACT Director of Student Financial Services, Spalding University, 851 South Fourth Street, Louisville, KY 40203, 502-588-7185 or toll-free 800-896-8941 Ext. 2111. *Fax:* 502-585-7128. *E-mail:* onestop@spalding.edu.

SPELMAN COLLEGE
Atlanta, GA

Tuition & fees: $15,945	Average undergraduate aid package: $4473

ABOUT THE INSTITUTION Independent, women only. Awards: bachelor's degrees. 25 undergraduate majors. Total enrollment: 2,186. Undergraduates: 2,186. Freshmen: 595. Federal methodology is used as a basis for awarding need-based institutional aid.

UNDERGRADUATE EXPENSES for 2005–06 *Application fee:* $35. *Comprehensive fee:* $24,400 includes full-time tuition ($13,525), mandatory fees ($2420), and room and board ($8455). *Part-time tuition:* $565 per credit hour.

FRESHMAN FINANCIAL AID (Fall 2004, est.) 543 applied for aid; of those 84% were deemed to have need. 100% of freshmen with need received aid; of those 5% had need fully met. *Average percent of need met:* 25% (excluding resources awarded to replace EFC). *Average financial aid package:* $5663 (excluding resources awarded to replace EFC). 11% of all full-time freshmen had no need and received non-need-based gift aid.

UNDERGRADUATE FINANCIAL AID (Fall 2004, est.) 1,976 applied for aid; of those 90% were deemed to have need. 100% of undergraduates with need received aid; of those 10% had need fully met. *Average percent of need met:* 25% (excluding resources awarded to replace EFC). *Average financial aid package:* $4473 (excluding resources awarded to replace EFC). 12% of all full-time undergraduates had no need and received non-need-based gift aid.

GIFT AID (NEED-BASED) *Total amount:* $3,834,675 (75% federal, 25% state). *Receiving aid:* Freshmen: 50% (300); All full-time undergraduates: 62% (1,292). *Average award:* Freshmen: $2000; Undergraduates: $2000. *Scholarships, grants, and awards:* Federal Pell, FSEOG, state, private, college/university gift aid from institutional funds, United Negro College Fund.

GIFT AID (NON-NEED-BASED) *Total amount:* $9,095,989 (3% state, 69% institutional, 28% external sources). *Receiving aid:* Freshmen: 18% (107); Undergraduates: 41% (860). *Average Award:* Freshmen: $10,055; Undergraduates: $9727. *Scholarships, grants, and awards by category: Academic Interests/Achievement:* 276 awards ($2,561,803 total): biological sciences, general academic interests/achievements, mathematics, physical sciences. *Creative Arts/Performance:* 11 awards ($14,365 total): dance, music, theater/drama. *Special Achievements/Activities:* 80 awards ($483,823 total): community service. *Special Characteristics:* 1 award ($5000 total). *ROTC:* Army cooperative, Air Force cooperative.

LOANS *Student loans:* $10,516,821 (85% need-based, 15% non-need-based). 82% of past graduating class borrowed through all loan programs. *Average indebtedness per student:* $16,700. *Parent loans:* $10,249,026 (85% need-based, 15% non-need-based). *Programs:* FFEL (Subsidized and Unsubsidized Stafford, PLUS), Perkins.

WORK-STUDY *Federal work-study:* Total amount: $221,802; 172 jobs averaging $882. *State or other work-study/employment:* Total amount: $125,000 (84% need-based, 16% non-need-based). 200 part-time jobs averaging $625.

APPLYING FOR FINANCIAL AID *Required financial aid form:* FAFSA. *Financial aid deadline (priority):* 3/1. *Notification date:* 2/15.

CONTACT Lenora J. Jackson, Director, Student Financial Services, Spelman College, 350 Spelman Lane, SW, PO Box 771, Atlanta, GA 30314-4399, 404-270-5212 or toll-free 800-982-2411. *Fax:* 404-270-5220. *E-mail:* lenoraj@spelman.edu.

SPRING ARBOR UNIVERSITY
Spring Arbor, MI

Tuition & fees: $16,096	Average undergraduate aid package: $12,733

ABOUT THE INSTITUTION Independent Free Methodist, coed. Awards: associate, bachelor's, and master's degrees. 35 undergraduate majors. Total enrollment: 3,511. Undergraduates: 2,510. Freshmen: 301. Federal methodology is used as a basis for awarding need-based institutional aid.

UNDERGRADUATE EXPENSES for 2004–05 *Application fee:* $50. *Comprehensive fee:* $21,706 includes full-time tuition ($15,700), mandatory fees ($396), and room and board ($5610). *College room only:* $2640. Room and board charges vary according to board plan, housing facility, and location. *Part-time tuition:* $305 per credit. *Part-time fees:* $306 per semester hour. Part-time tuition and fees vary according to course load. *Payment plans:* Installment, deferred payment.

FRESHMAN FINANCIAL AID (Fall 2003) 282 applied for aid; of those 86% were deemed to have need. 100% of freshmen with need received aid; of those 69% had need fully met. *Average percent of need met:* 95% (excluding resources awarded to replace EFC). *Average financial aid package:* $16,141 (excluding resources awarded to replace EFC). 11% of all full-time freshmen had no need and received non-need-based gift aid.

UNDERGRADUATE FINANCIAL AID (Fall 2003) 1,671 applied for aid; of those 85% were deemed to have need. 96% of undergraduates with need received aid; of those 14% had need fully met. *Average percent of need met:* 79% (excluding resources awarded to replace EFC). *Average financial aid package:* $12,733 (excluding resources awarded to replace EFC). 5% of all full-time undergraduates had no need and received non-need-based gift aid.

GIFT AID (NEED-BASED) *Total amount:* $10,336,597 (18% federal, 15% state, 66% institutional, 1% external sources). *Receiving aid:* Freshmen: 78% (237); All full-time undergraduates: 58% (1,169). *Average award:* Freshmen: $9282; Undergraduates: $7551. *Scholarships, grants, and awards:* Federal Pell, FSEOG, state, private, college/university gift aid from institutional funds.

GIFT AID (NON-NEED-BASED) *Total amount:* $838,581 (1% federal, 55% state, 44% external sources). *Receiving aid:* Freshmen: 53% (163); Undergraduates: 20% (408). *Average Award:* Freshmen: $1428; Undergraduates: $1510. *Scholarships, grants, and awards by category: Academic Interests/Achievement:* 856 awards ($2,792,219 total): general academic interests/achievements. *Creative Arts/Performance:* 123 awards ($89,464 total): art/fine arts, music. *Special Achievements/Activities:* 1 award ($6000 total): junior miss. *Special Characteristics:* 310 awards ($1,696,210 total): children of faculty/staff, international students, members of minority groups, out-of-state students, relatives of clergy, religious affiliation. *Tuition waivers:* Full or partial for employees or children of employees, senior citizens. *ROTC:* Army cooperative.

LOANS *Student loans:* $13,117,170 (50% need-based, 50% non-need-based). 82% of past graduating class borrowed through all loan programs. *Average indebtedness per student:* $11,634. *Average need-based loan:* Freshmen: $3694; Undergraduates: $3912. *Parent loans:* $1,107,890 (100% need-based). *Programs:* FFEL (Subsidized and Unsubsidized Stafford, PLUS), Perkins, state, MI-Loan Program, alternative loans.

WORK-STUDY *Federal work-study:* Total amount: $61,525; 401 jobs averaging $750. *State or other work-study/employment:* 9 part-time jobs averaging $700.

ATHLETIC AWARDS *Total amount:* $367,635 (100% need-based).

APPLYING FOR FINANCIAL AID *Required financial aid form:* FAFSA. *Financial aid deadline (priority):* 3/1. *Notification date:* Continuous beginning 4/1. Students must reply within 2 weeks of notification.

CONTACT Lois M. Hardy, Director of Financial Aid, Spring Arbor University, 106 East Main Street, Spring Arbor, MI 49283-9799, 517-750-6468 or toll-free 800-968-0011. *Fax:* 517-750-6620.

SPRINGFIELD COLLEGE
Springfield, MA

ABOUT THE INSTITUTION Independent, coed. Awards: bachelor's, master's, and doctoral degrees and post-bachelor's certificates. 52 undergraduate majors. Total enrollment: 3,119. Undergraduates: 2,238. Freshmen: 553.

GIFT AID (NEED-BASED) *Scholarships, grants, and awards:* Federal Pell, FSEOG, state, private, college/university gift aid from institutional funds, Project Spirit.

GIFT AID (NON-NEED-BASED) *Scholarships, grants, and awards by category: Academic Interests/Achievement:* general academic interests/achievements.

LOANS *Programs:* FFEL (Subsidized and Unsubsidized Stafford, PLUS), Perkins, state, alternative loans.

WORK-STUDY *Federal work-study:* Total amount: $1,744,541; 1,080 jobs averaging $1600. *State or other work-study/employment:* Total amount: $89,468 (48% need-based, 52% non-need-based). 80 part-time jobs averaging $1118.

APPLYING FOR FINANCIAL AID *Required financial aid forms:* FAFSA, CSS Financial Aid PROFILE, state aid form, federal income tax form(s).

CONTACT Edward J. Ciosek, Director of Financial Aid, Springfield College, 263 Alden Street, Springfield, MA 01109-3797, 413-748-3108 or toll-free 800-343-1257 (out-of-state). *Fax:* 413-748-3462. *E-mail:* edward_j_ciosek@spfldcol.edu.

SPRING HILL COLLEGE
Mobile, AL

Tuition & fees: $19,950	Average undergraduate aid package: $16,829

ABOUT THE INSTITUTION Independent Roman Catholic (Jesuit), coed. Awards: associate, bachelor's, and master's degrees and post-bachelor's certificates. 41 undergraduate majors. Total enrollment: 1,427. Undergraduates: 1,212. Freshmen: 309. Federal methodology is used as a basis for awarding need-based institutional aid.

UNDERGRADUATE EXPENSES for 2004–05 *Application fee:* $25. *Comprehensive fee:* $27,142 includes full-time tuition ($18,722), mandatory fees ($1228), and room and board ($7192). *College room only:* $3640. Room and board charges vary according to board plan and housing facility. *Part-time tuition:* $741 per semester hour. *Part-time fees:* $40 per semester hour. *Payment plan:* Installment.

FRESHMAN FINANCIAL AID (Fall 2004, est.) 253 applied for aid; of those 81% were deemed to have need. 100% of freshmen with need received aid; of those 21% had need fully met. *Average percent of need met:* 84% (excluding resources awarded to replace EFC). *Average financial aid package:* $19,016 (excluding resources awarded to replace EFC). 31% of all full-time freshmen had no need and received non-need-based gift aid.

UNDERGRADUATE FINANCIAL AID (Fall 2004, est.) 849 applied for aid; of those 84% were deemed to have need. 100% of undergraduates with need received aid; of those 21% had need fully met. *Average percent of need met:* 77% (excluding resources awarded to replace EFC). *Average financial aid package:* $16,829 (excluding resources awarded to replace EFC). 25% of all full-time undergraduates had no need and received non-need-based gift aid.

GIFT AID (NEED-BASED) *Total amount:* $9,293,351 (12% federal, 2% state, 84% institutional, 2% external sources). *Receiving aid:* Freshmen: 65% (201); All full-time undergraduates: 65% (695). *Average award:* Freshmen: $15,092; Undergraduates: $12,504. *Scholarships, grants, and awards:* Federal Pell, FSEOG, state, private, college/university gift aid from institutional funds, Whitehead Scholarships, foundation scholarships, endowed scholarships.

GIFT AID (NON-NEED-BASED) *Total amount:* $2,961,269 (3% state, 94% institutional, 3% external sources). *Receiving aid:* Freshmen: 32% (98); Undergraduates: 29% (314). *Average Award:* Freshmen: $10,544; Undergraduates: $9046. *Scholarships, grants, and awards by category: Academic Interests/Achievement:* 273 awards ($2,263,550 total): general academic interests/achievements. *Special Achievements/Activities:* 258 awards ($999,709 total): community service. *Special Characteristics:* 65 awards ($413,246 total): children of faculty/staff, siblings of current students. *Tuition waivers:* Full or partial for employees or children of employees. *ROTC:* Army cooperative, Air Force cooperative.

LOANS *Student loans:* $4,571,280 (58% need-based, 42% non-need-based). 72% of past graduating class borrowed through all loan programs. *Average indebtedness per student:* $12,041. *Average need-based loan:* Freshmen: $3328; Undergraduates: $4044. *Parent loans:* $2,121,526 (20% need-based, 80% non-need-based). *Programs:* FFEL (Subsidized and Unsubsidized Stafford, PLUS), Perkins, Key Corp Loans, Signature Loans, CitiAssist Loans, Chase Extra Loans.

WORK-STUDY *Federal work-study:* Total amount: $257,791; 220 jobs averaging $1172. *State or other work-study/employment:* Total amount: $90,893 (100% non-need-based). 90 part-time jobs averaging $1010.

ATHLETIC AWARDS *Total amount:* $1,161,935 (40% need-based, 60% non-need-based).

APPLYING FOR FINANCIAL AID *Required financial aid forms:* FAFSA, institution's own form, state aid form. *Financial aid deadline:* Continuous. *Notification date:* Continuous beginning 2/15. Students must reply by 5/1 or within 2 weeks of notification.

CONTACT Art Weeden, Director of Financial Aid, Spring Hill College, 4000 Dauphin Street, Mobile, AL 36608-1791, 251-380-3460 or toll-free 800-SHC-6704. *Fax:* 251-460-2176. *E-mail:* aweeden@shc.edu.

STANFORD UNIVERSITY
Stanford, CA

Tuition & fees: $29,847	Average undergraduate aid package: $26,768

ABOUT THE INSTITUTION Independent, coed. Awards: bachelor's, master's, doctoral, and first professional degrees. 57 undergraduate majors. Total enrollment: 18,836. Undergraduates: 6,555. Freshmen: 1,645. Both federal and institutional methodology are used as a basis for awarding need-based institutional aid.

UNDERGRADUATE EXPENSES for 2004–05 *Application fee:* $75. *Comprehensive fee:* $39,347 includes full-time tuition ($29,847) and room and board ($9500). *College room only:* $5012. Room and board charges vary according to board plan.

FRESHMAN FINANCIAL AID (Fall 2003) 1054 applied for aid; of those 74% were deemed to have need. 98% of freshmen with need received aid; of those 95% had need fully met. *Average percent of need met:* 100% (excluding resources awarded to replace EFC). *Average financial aid package:* $26,893 (excluding resources awarded to replace EFC). 5% of all full-time freshmen had no need and received non-need-based gift aid.

UNDERGRADUATE FINANCIAL AID (Fall 2003) 3,750 applied for aid; of those 86% were deemed to have need. 98% of undergraduates with need received aid; of those 96% had need fully met. *Average percent of need met:* 100% (excluding resources awarded to replace EFC). *Average financial aid package:* $26,768 (excluding resources awarded to replace EFC). 10% of all full-time undergraduates had no need and received non-need-based gift aid.

GIFT AID (NEED-BASED) *Total amount:* $71,959,047 (6% federal, 7% state, 80% institutional, 7% external sources). *Receiving aid:* Freshmen: 46% (761); All full-time undergraduates: 46% (3,070). *Average award:* Freshmen: $23,883; Undergraduates: $22,949. *Scholarships, grants, and awards:* Federal Pell, FSEOG, state, private, college/university gift aid from institutional funds.

GIFT AID (NON-NEED-BASED) *Total amount:* $8,563,652 (10% federal, 2% state, 25% institutional, 63% external sources). *Receiving aid:* Freshmen: 2% (34); Undergraduates: 2% (107). *Average Award:* Freshmen: $2759; Undergraduates: $3132. *Tuition waivers:* Full or partial for employees or children of employees. *ROTC:* Army cooperative, Naval cooperative, Air Force cooperative.

LOANS *Student loans:* $12,418,816 (84% need-based, 16% non-need-based). 47% of past graduating class borrowed through all loan programs. *Average indebtedness per student:* $15,590. *Average need-based loan:* Freshmen: $2585; Undergraduates: $2637. *Parent loans:* $9,741,090 (100% non-need-based). *Programs:* FFEL (Subsidized and Unsubsidized Stafford, PLUS), Perkins, GATE Loans.

WORK-STUDY *Federal work-study:* Total amount: $1,722,245; 705 jobs averaging $2443. *State or other work-study/employment:* Total amount: $1,838,134 (94% need-based, 6% non-need-based). 925 part-time jobs averaging $1862.

ATHLETIC AWARDS *Total amount:* $11,809,170 (7% need-based, 93% non-need-based).

APPLYING FOR FINANCIAL AID *Required financial aid forms:* FAFSA, CSS Financial Aid PROFILE, noncustodial (divorced/separated) parent's statement. *Financial aid deadline (priority):* 2/1. *Notification date:* Continuous beginning 4/3. Students must reply by 5/1.

CONTACT Financial Aid Office, Stanford University, 520 Lasuen Mall, Old Union Building, Room 322, Stanford, CA 94305-3021, 650-723-3058. *Fax:* 650-725-0540. *E-mail:* financialaid@lists.stanford.edu.

STATE UNIVERSITY OF NEW YORK AT ALBANY
Albany, NY

See University at Albany, State University of New York.

STATE UNIVERSITY OF NEW YORK AT BINGHAMTON
Binghamton, NY

Tuition & fees (NY res): $5756	Average undergraduate aid package: $11,089

ABOUT THE INSTITUTION State-supported, coed. Awards: bachelor's, master's, and doctoral degrees and post-master's certificates. 53 undergraduate majors.

Total enrollment: 13,860. Undergraduates: 11,034. Freshmen: 2,160. Federal methodology is used as a basis for awarding need-based institutional aid.

UNDERGRADUATE EXPENSES for 2004–05 *Application fee:* $40. *Tuition, state resident:* full-time $4350; part-time $181 per credit hour. *Tuition, nonresident:* full-time $10,610; part-time $442 per credit hour. *College room and board:* $7710; *room only:* $4736. Room and board charges vary according to board plan and housing facility. *Payment plan:* Installment.

FRESHMAN FINANCIAL AID (Fall 2004, est.) 1701 applied for aid; of those 60% were deemed to have need. 99% of freshmen with need received aid; of those 78% had need fully met. *Average percent of need met:* 81% (excluding resources awarded to replace EFC). *Average financial aid package:* $10,531 (excluding resources awarded to replace EFC). 4% of all full-time freshmen had no need and received non-need-based gift aid.

UNDERGRADUATE FINANCIAL AID (Fall 2004, est.) 7,317 applied for aid; of those 73% were deemed to have need. 99% of undergraduates with need received aid; of those 71% had need fully met. *Average percent of need met:* 81% (excluding resources awarded to replace EFC). *Average financial aid package:* $11,089 (excluding resources awarded to replace EFC). 3% of all full-time undergraduates had no need and received non-need-based gift aid.

GIFT AID (NEED-BASED) *Total amount:* $25,151,750 (40% federal, 52% state, 2% institutional, 6% external sources). *Receiving aid:* Freshmen: 41% (890); All full-time undergraduates: 44% (4,742). *Average award:* Freshmen: $5045; Undergraduates: $4798. *Scholarships, grants, and awards:* Federal Pell, FSEOG, state, private, college/university gift aid from institutional funds.

GIFT AID (NON-NEED-BASED) *Total amount:* $3,008,637 (23% state, 77% institutional). *Receiving aid:* Freshmen: 11% (248); Undergraduates: 10% (1,111). *Average Award:* Freshmen: $710; Undergraduates: $3479. *Scholarships, grants, and awards by category:* Academic Interests/Achievement: 425 awards ($862,252 total): biological sciences, business, computer science, engineering/technologies, English, foreign languages, general academic interests/achievements, health fields, international studies, mathematics, physical sciences, premedicine. Creative Arts/Performance: 24 awards ($25,245 total): creative writing, general creative arts/performance, music, performing arts, theater/drama. Special Achievements/Activities: 33 awards ($67,048 total): community service, general special achievements/activities, leadership, memberships. Special Characteristics: 80 awards ($170,963 total): children with a deceased or disabled parent, ethnic background, local/state students, members of minority groups, out-of-state students. *Tuition waivers:* Full or partial for employees or children of employees. *ROTC:* Air Force cooperative.

LOANS *Student loans:* $37,107,335 (100% need-based). 61% of past graduating class borrowed through all loan programs. *Average indebtedness per student:* $14,656. *Average need-based loan:* Freshmen: $3042; Undergraduates: $4296. *Parent loans:* $42,725,089 (100% need-based). *Programs:* Federal Direct (Subsidized and Unsubsidized Stafford, PLUS), Perkins, Federal Nursing, college/university.

WORK-STUDY *Federal work-study:* Total amount: $2,350,318; 988 jobs averaging $1287.

ATHLETIC AWARDS *Total amount:* $1,997,388 (100% non-need-based).

APPLYING FOR FINANCIAL AID *Required financial aid forms:* FAFSA, state aid form. *Financial aid deadline (priority):* 3/1. *Notification date:* Continuous beginning 3/15. Students must reply within 2 weeks of notification.

CONTACT Mr. Dennis Chavez, Director of Student Financial Aid and Employment, State University of New York at Binghamton, PO Box 6011, Binghamton, NY 13902-6011, 607-777-2428.

STATE UNIVERSITY OF NEW YORK AT NEW PALTZ
New Paltz, NY

Tuition & fees (NY res): $5220	Average undergraduate aid package: $2446

ABOUT THE INSTITUTION State-supported, coed. Awards: bachelor's and master's degrees and post-master's certificates. 74 undergraduate majors. Total enrollment: 7,603. Undergraduates: 6,191. Freshmen: 813. Both federal and institutional methodology are used as a basis for awarding need-based institutional aid.

UNDERGRADUATE EXPENSES for 2004–05 *Application fee:* $40. *Tuition, state resident:* full-time $4350; part-time $181 per credit. *Tuition, nonresident:* full-time $10,300; part-time $429 per credit. *Required fees:* full-time $870; $25.70 per credit or $125 per term part-time. *College room and board:* $6860; *room only:* $4240. Room and board charges vary according to board plan. *Payment plan:* Installment.

FRESHMAN FINANCIAL AID (Fall 2003) 790 applied for aid; of those 67% were deemed to have need. 99% of freshmen with need received aid; of those 24% had need fully met. *Average percent of need met:* 73% (excluding resources awarded to replace EFC). *Average financial aid package:* $2090 (excluding resources awarded to replace EFC). 5% of all full-time freshmen had no need and received non-need-based gift aid.

UNDERGRADUATE FINANCIAL AID (Fall 2003) 4,167 applied for aid; of those 73% were deemed to have need. 99% of undergraduates with need received aid; of those 29% had need fully met. *Average percent of need met:* 74% (excluding resources awarded to replace EFC). *Average financial aid package:* $2446 (excluding resources awarded to replace EFC). 3% of all full-time undergraduates had no need and received non-need-based gift aid.

GIFT AID (NEED-BASED) *Total amount:* $12,573,409 (43% federal, 56% state, 1% institutional). *Receiving aid:* Freshmen: 50% (458); All full-time undergraduates: 49% (2,660). *Average award:* Freshmen: $2229; Undergraduates: $2229. *Scholarships, grants, and awards:* Federal Pell, FSEOG, state, private, college/university gift aid from institutional funds.

GIFT AID (NON-NEED-BASED) *Total amount:* $1,048,919 (25% federal, 13% state, 10% institutional, 52% external sources). *Receiving aid:* Freshmen: 10% (92); Undergraduates: 6% (310). *Average Award:* Freshmen: $1083; Undergraduates:* $1525. *Scholarships, grants, and awards by category:* Academic Interests/Achievement: 91 awards ($135,640 total): computer science, education, engineering/technologies, English, health fields, humanities, mathematics, physical sciences, premedicine. *Special Characteristics:* members of minority groups.

LOANS *Student loans:* $15,772,030 (62% need-based, 38% non-need-based). 75% of past graduating class borrowed through all loan programs. *Average indebtedness per student:* $18,900. *Average need-based loan:* Freshmen: $2014; Undergraduates: $859. *Parent loans:* $4,204,286 (100% non-need-based). *Programs:* FFEL (Subsidized and Unsubsidized Stafford, PLUS), Perkins, Private.

WORK-STUDY *Federal work-study:* Total amount: $840,242; 986 jobs averaging $852. *State or other work-study/employment:* Total amount: $503,391 (100% non-need-based). 478 part-time jobs averaging $1053.

APPLYING FOR FINANCIAL AID *Required financial aid forms:* FAFSA, state aid form. *Financial aid deadline (priority):* 3/15. *Notification date:* Continuous beginning 4/1. Students must reply within 4 weeks of notification.

CONTACT Mr. Daniel Sistarenik, Director of Financial Aid, State University of New York at New Paltz, 75 South Manheim Boulevard, Suite 2, New Paltz, NY 12561-2437, 845-257-3250 or toll-free 888-639-7589 (in-state). *Fax:* 845-257-3568.

STATE UNIVERSITY OF NEW YORK AT OSWEGO
Oswego, NY

Tuition & fees (NY res): $5238	Average undergraduate aid package: $8625

ABOUT THE INSTITUTION State-supported, coed. Awards: bachelor's and master's degrees and post-master's certificates. 64 undergraduate majors. Total enrollment: 8,289. Undergraduates: 7,059. Freshmen: 1,377. Federal methodology is used as a basis for awarding need-based institutional aid.

UNDERGRADUATE EXPENSES for 2004–05 *Application fee:* $40. *Tuition, state resident:* full-time $4350; part-time $181 per credit hour. *Tuition, nonresident:* full-time $10,160; part-time $429 per credit hour. *Required fees:* full-time $888; $34.14 per credit hour. Part-time tuition and fees vary according to class time and location. *College room and board:* $7890; *room only:* $4790. Room and board charges vary according to board plan, housing facility, and location. *Payment plan:* Installment.

FRESHMAN FINANCIAL AID (Fall 2004, est.) 1222 applied for aid; of those 76% were deemed to have need. 97% of freshmen with need received aid; of those 28% had need fully met. *Average percent of need met:* 76% (excluding resources awarded to replace EFC). *Average financial aid package:* $7779 (excluding resources awarded to replace EFC). 19% of all full-time freshmen had no need and received non-need-based gift aid.

UNDERGRADUATE FINANCIAL AID (Fall 2004, est.) 5,551 applied for aid; of those 79% were deemed to have need. 98% of undergraduates with need received aid; of those 34% had need fully met. *Average percent of need met:* 84% (excluding resources awarded to replace EFC). *Average financial aid package:* $8625 (excluding resources awarded to replace EFC). 16% of all full-time undergraduates had no need and received non-need-based gift aid.

GIFT AID (NEED-BASED) *Total amount:* $16,041,681 (43% federal, 50% state, 5% institutional, 2% external sources). *Receiving aid:* Freshmen: 62% (847); All full-time undergraduates: 61% (3,955). *Average award:* Freshmen: $4453;

Undergraduates: $3737. *Scholarships, grants, and awards:* Federal Pell, FSEOG, state, private, college/university gift aid from institutional funds.

GIFT AID (NON-NEED-BASED) *Total amount:* $922,888 (5% federal, 1% state, 82% institutional, 12% external sources). *Receiving aid:* Freshmen: 25% (343); Undergraduates: 14% (914). *Average Award:* Freshmen: $3571; Undergraduates:* $5350. *Scholarships, grants, and awards by category:* Academic Interests/Achievement: 1,671 awards ($1,970,432 total): area/ethnic studies, biological sciences, business, communication, computer science, education, English, foreign languages, general academic interests/achievements, humanities, international studies, mathematics, physical sciences, premedicine, social sciences. *ROTC:* Army cooperative.

LOANS *Student loans:* $29,284,962 (82% need-based, 18% non-need-based). 80% of past graduating class borrowed through all loan programs. *Average indebtedness per student:* $18,094. *Average need-based loan:* Freshmen: $3319; Undergraduates: $4831. *Parent loans:* $4,756,659 (63% need-based, 37% non-need-based). *Programs:* FFEL (Subsidized and Unsubsidized Stafford, PLUS), Perkins.

WORK-STUDY *Federal work-study:* Total amount: $621,917; 574 jobs averaging $1083. *State or other work-study/employment:* Total amount: $1,788,908 (78% need-based, 22% non-need-based). 1,260 part-time jobs averaging $1113.

APPLYING FOR FINANCIAL AID *Required financial aid forms:* FAFSA, state aid form. *Financial aid deadline (priority):* 4/1. *Notification date:* Continuous beginning 3/1. Students must reply by 5/1 or within 3 weeks of notification.

CONTACT Mark C. Humbert, Director of Financial Aid, State University of New York at Oswego, 206 Culkin Hall, Oswego, NY 13126, 315-312-2248. *Fax:* 315-312-3696.

STATE UNIVERSITY OF NEW YORK AT PLATTSBURGH
Plattsburgh, NY

Tuition & fees (NY res): $5268	Average undergraduate aid package: $9139

ABOUT THE INSTITUTION State-supported, coed. Awards: bachelor's and master's degrees and post-master's certificates. 47 undergraduate majors. Total enrollment: 5,909. Undergraduates: 5,275. Freshmen: 863. Federal methodology is used as a basis for awarding need-based institutional aid.

UNDERGRADUATE EXPENSES for 2004–05 *Application fee:* $40. *Tuition, state resident:* full-time $4350; part-time $181 per credit hour. *Tuition, nonresident:* full-time $10,610; part-time $442 per credit hour. *Required fees:* full-time $918; $37.50 per credit hour. Part-time tuition and fees vary according to course load. *College room and board:* $6712; *room only:* $4200. Room and board charges vary according to board plan. *Payment plans:* Installment, deferred payment.

FRESHMAN FINANCIAL AID (Fall 2004, est.) 704 applied for aid; of those 71% were deemed to have need. 100% of freshmen with need received aid; of those 28% had need fully met. *Average percent of need met:* 85% (excluding resources awarded to replace EFC). *Average financial aid package:* $8156 (excluding resources awarded to replace EFC). 28% of all full-time freshmen had no need and received non-need-based gift aid.

UNDERGRADUATE FINANCIAL AID (Fall 2004, est.) 3,873 applied for aid; of those 79% were deemed to have need. 99% of undergraduates with need received aid; of those 31% had need fully met. *Average percent of need met:* 89% (excluding resources awarded to replace EFC). *Average financial aid package:* $9139 (excluding resources awarded to replace EFC). 25% of all full-time undergraduates had no need and received non-need-based gift aid.

GIFT AID (NEED-BASED) *Total amount:* $11,182,151 (42% federal, 46% state, 8% institutional, 4% external sources). *Receiving aid:* Freshmen: 56% (474); All full-time undergraduates: 56% (2,751). *Average award:* Freshmen: $4199; Undergraduates: $3997. *Scholarships, grants, and awards:* Federal Pell, FSEOG, state, private, college/university gift aid from institutional funds, Scholarships for Disadvantaged Students (SDS), Empire State Minority Honors Scholarships.

GIFT AID (NON-NEED-BASED) *Total amount:* $2,195,694 (1% federal, 16% state, 79% institutional, 4% external sources). *Receiving aid:* Freshmen: 20% (174); Undergraduates: 17% (854). *Average Award:* Freshmen: $3798; Undergraduates: $4741. *Scholarships, grants, and awards by category:* Academic Interests/Achievement: 672 awards ($1,109,386 total): area/ethnic studies, biological sciences, business, communication, computer science, education, engineering/technologies, English, general academic interests/achievements, health fields, home economics, humanities, international studies, mathematics, physical sciences, premedicine, social sciences. *Creative Arts/Performance:* 16 awards ($15,850 total): art/fine arts, journalism/publications, music, theater/

drama. *Special Achievements/Activities:* 17 awards ($3000 total): community service, general special achievements/activities, leadership. *Special Characteristics:* 1,067 awards ($1,684,815 total): international students, out-of-state students. *Tuition waivers:* Full or partial for employees or children of employees.
LOANS *Student loans:* $20,469,085 (82% need-based, 18% non-need-based). 72% of past graduating class borrowed through all loan programs. *Average indebtedness per student:* $16,956. *Average need-based loan:* Freshmen: $4296; Undergraduates: $5440. *Parent loans:* $3,806,036 (67% need-based, 33% non-need-based). *Programs:* Federal Direct (Subsidized and Unsubsidized Stafford, PLUS), Perkins, Federal Nursing, college/university, alternative loans, short-term emergency loans from Student Association.
WORK-STUDY *Federal work-study:* Total amount: $725,917; 464 jobs averaging $1564.
APPLYING FOR FINANCIAL AID *Required financial aid forms:* FAFSA, state aid form. *Financial aid deadline (priority):* 3/1. *Notification date:* Continuous beginning 3/15. Students must reply within 6 weeks of notification.
CONTACT Mr. Todd Moravec, Financial Aid Director, State University of New York at Plattsburgh, 101 Broad Street, Kehoe Administration Building 406, Plattsburgh, NY 12901-2681, 518-564-2072 or toll-free 888-673-0012 (in-state). *Fax:* 518-564-4079. *E-mail:* todd.moravec@plattsburgh.edu.

STATE UNIVERSITY OF NEW YORK COLLEGE AT BROCKPORT
Brockport, NY

Tuition & fees (NY res): $5263   **Average undergraduate aid package: $7019**

ABOUT THE INSTITUTION State-supported, coed. Awards: bachelor's and master's degrees and post-bachelor's and post-master's certificates. 112 undergraduate majors. Total enrollment: 8,595. Undergraduates: 6,980. Freshmen: 1,055. Federal methodology is used as a basis for awarding need-based institutional aid.
UNDERGRADUATE EXPENSES for 2004–05 *Application fee:* $40. *Tuition, state resident:* full-time $4350; part-time $181 per credit hour. *Tuition, nonresident:* full-time $10,300; part-time $429 per credit hour. *Required fees:* full-time $913; $37.85 per credit hour. Part-time tuition and fees vary according to course load. *College room and board:* $7226; *room only:* $4500. Room and board charges vary according to board plan and housing facility. *Payment plans:* Installment, deferred payment.
FRESHMAN FINANCIAL AID (Fall 2003) 948 applied for aid; of those 78% were deemed to have need. 99% of freshmen with need received aid; of those 50% had need fully met. *Average percent of need met:* 80% (excluding resources awarded to replace EFC). *Average financial aid package:* $7053 (excluding resources awarded to replace EFC). 7% of all full-time freshmen had no need and received non-need-based gift aid.
UNDERGRADUATE FINANCIAL AID (Fall 2003) 5,977 applied for aid; of those 81% were deemed to have need. 99% of undergraduates with need received aid; of those 52% had need fully met. *Average percent of need met:* 75% (excluding resources awarded to replace EFC). *Average financial aid package:* $7019 (excluding resources awarded to replace EFC). 3% of all full-time undergraduates had no need and received non-need-based gift aid.
GIFT AID (NEED-BASED) *Total amount:* $13,938,781 (47% federal, 53% state). *Receiving aid:* Freshmen: 65% (678); All full-time undergraduates: 57% (4,208). *Average award:* Freshmen: $3253; Undergraduates: $3222. *Scholarships, grants, and awards:* Federal Pell, FSEOG, state, private, college/university gift aid from institutional funds.
GIFT AID (NON-NEED-BASED) *Total amount:* $4,382,080 (19% federal, 4% state, 74% institutional, 3% external sources). *Receiving aid:* Freshmen: 24% (253); Undergraduates: 8% (601). *Average Award: Freshmen:* $5808; *Undergraduates:* $5099. *Scholarships, grants, and awards by category: Academic Interests/Achievement:* 600 awards ($2,000,000 total): biological sciences, business, communication, computer science, education, English, foreign languages, general academic interests/achievements, health fields, international studies, mathematics, military science, physical sciences, social sciences. *Creative Arts/Performance:* 23 awards ($10,000 total): art/fine arts, creative writing, dance, general creative arts/performance, journalism/publications, performing arts, theater/drama. *Special Achievements/Activities:* 2 awards ($1000 total): leadership. *Special Characteristics:* 50 awards ($500,000 total): children and siblings of alumni, ethnic background, first-generation college students, general special characteristics, international students, local/state students, married students, members of minority groups, out-of-state students. *Tuition waivers:* Full or partial for employees or children of employees, senior citizens. *ROTC:* Army, Naval cooperative, Air Force cooperative.

LOANS *Student loans:* $36,114,934 (52% need-based, 48% non-need-based). 77% of past graduating class borrowed through all loan programs. *Average indebtedness per student:* $17,918. *Average need-based loan:* Freshmen: $3613; Undergraduates: $4162. *Parent loans:* $2,636,499 (100% non-need-based). *Programs:* Federal Direct (Subsidized and Unsubsidized Stafford, PLUS), Perkins, Federal Nursing, alternative loans.
WORK-STUDY *Federal work-study:* Total amount: $760,101; 539 jobs averaging $1381. *State or other work-study/employment:* Total amount: $1,963,483 (100% non-need-based). 1,440 part-time jobs averaging $1422.
APPLYING FOR FINANCIAL AID *Required financial aid forms:* FAFSA, state aid form. *Financial aid deadline (priority):* 3/15. *Notification date:* Continuous.
CONTACT Mr. J. Scott Atkinson, Associate Vice President for Enrollment Management and Student Affairs, State University of New York College at Brockport, 350 New Campus Drive, Brockport, NY 14420-2937, 585-395-2501. *Fax:* 585-395-5445. *E-mail:* satkinson@brockport.edu.

STATE UNIVERSITY OF NEW YORK COLLEGE AT CORTLAND
Cortland, NY

ABOUT THE INSTITUTION State-supported, coed. Awards: bachelor's and master's degrees and post-bachelor's and post-master's certificates. 57 undergraduate majors. Total enrollment: 7,331. Undergraduates: 5,950. Freshmen: 1,086.
GIFT AID (NEED-BASED) *Scholarships, grants, and awards:* Federal Pell, FSEOG, state, private, college/university gift aid from institutional funds.
GIFT AID (NON-NEED-BASED) *Scholarships, grants, and awards by category: Academic Interests/Achievement:* general academic interests/achievements. *Creative Arts/Performance:* music, theater/drama. *Special Achievements/Activities:* general special achievements/activities, leadership. *Special Characteristics:* children and siblings of alumni, members of minority groups.
LOANS *Programs:* Federal Direct (Subsidized and Unsubsidized Stafford, PLUS), FFEL (Subsidized and Unsubsidized Stafford, PLUS), Perkins.
APPLYING FOR FINANCIAL AID *Required financial aid form:* FAFSA.
CONTACT Financial Aid Office, State University of New York College at Cortland, PO Box 2000, Cortland, NY 13045-0900, 607-753-4717. *Fax:* 607-753-5990.

STATE UNIVERSITY OF NEW YORK COLLEGE AT GENESEO
Geneseo, NY

Tuition & fees (NY res): $5435   **Average undergraduate aid package: $9123**

ABOUT THE INSTITUTION State-supported, coed. Awards: bachelor's and master's degrees. 45 undergraduate majors. Total enrollment: 5,573. Undergraduates: 5,375. Freshmen: 1,030. Federal methodology is used as a basis for awarding need-based institutional aid.
UNDERGRADUATE EXPENSES for 2004–05 *Application fee:* $40. *Tuition, state resident:* full-time $4350; part-time $181 per credit hour. *Tuition, nonresident:* full-time $10,610; part-time $429 per credit hour. *Required fees:* full-time $1085; $44.20 per credit hour. Part-time tuition and fees vary according to course load. *College room and board:* $6820. Room and board charges vary according to board plan and housing facility. *Payment plans:* Installment, deferred payment.
FRESHMAN FINANCIAL AID (Fall 2004, est.) 860 applied for aid; of those 53% were deemed to have need. 100% of freshmen with need received aid; of those 75% had need fully met. *Average percent of need met:* 78% (excluding resources awarded to replace EFC). *Average financial aid package:* $8552 (excluding resources awarded to replace EFC). 2% of all full-time freshmen had no need and received non-need-based gift aid.
UNDERGRADUATE FINANCIAL AID (Fall 2004, est.) 3,928 applied for aid; of those 64% were deemed to have need. 100% of undergraduates with need received aid; of those 90% had need fully met. *Average percent of need met:* 90% (excluding resources awarded to replace EFC). *Average financial aid package:* $9123 (excluding resources awarded to replace EFC). 9% of all full-time undergraduates had no need and received non-need-based gift aid.
GIFT AID (NEED-BASED) *Total amount:* $8,272,973 (39% federal, 61% state). *Receiving aid:* Freshmen: 40% (407); All full-time undergraduates: 47% (2,476). *Average award:* Freshmen: $2509; Undergraduates: $2698. *Scholarships, grants, and awards:* Federal Pell, FSEOG, state, private, college/university gift aid from institutional funds.

State University of New York College at Geneseo

GIFT AID (NON-NEED-BASED) *Total amount:* $1,094,645 (2% federal, 44% state, 54% institutional). *Receiving aid:* Freshmen: 2% (20); Undergraduates: 7% (371). *Average Award:* Freshmen: $1900; Undergraduates: $1520. *Scholarships, grants, and awards by category: Academic Interests/Achievement:* 431 awards ($393,050 total): area/ethnic studies, biological sciences, business, communication, computer science, education, English, foreign languages, general academic interests/achievements, humanities, mathematics, physical sciences, premedicine, social sciences. *Creative Arts/Performance:* 31 awards ($14,600 total): applied art and design, art/fine arts, creative writing, dance, general creative arts/performance, journalism/publications, music, performing arts, theater/drama. *Special Achievements/Activities:* 10 awards ($6100 total): community service, general special achievements/activities, leadership. *Special Characteristics:* 48 awards ($23,405 total): local/state students, members of minority groups. *Tuition waivers:* Full or partial for senior citizens. *ROTC:* Army cooperative, Air Force cooperative.
LOANS *Student loans:* $18,249,146 (55% need-based, 45% non-need-based). 73% of past graduating class borrowed through all loan programs. *Average indebtedness per student:* $15,800. *Average need-based loan:* Freshmen: $3159; Undergraduates: $4431. *Parent loans:* $2,776,635 (100% non-need-based). *Programs:* FFEL (Subsidized and Unsubsidized Stafford, PLUS), Perkins, state, alternative loans.
WORK-STUDY *Federal work-study:* Total amount: $565,000; 458 jobs averaging $1233.
APPLYING FOR FINANCIAL AID *Required financial aid forms:* FAFSA, state aid form. *Financial aid deadline (priority):* 2/15. *Notification date:* Continuous beginning 3/15. Students must reply by 5/1 or within 3 weeks of notification.
CONTACT Archie Cureton, Director of Financial Aid, State University of New York College at Geneseo, 1 College Circle, Erwin Hall 104, Geneseo, NY 14454, 585-245-5731 or toll-free 866-245-5211. *Fax:* 585-245-5717. *E-mail:* cureton@geneseo.edu.

STATE UNIVERSITY OF NEW YORK COLLEGE AT OLD WESTBURY
Old Westbury, NY

Tuition & fees (NY res): $5072	Average undergraduate aid package: $7212

ABOUT THE INSTITUTION State-supported, coed. Awards: bachelor's and master's degrees. 35 undergraduate majors. Total enrollment: 3,359. Undergraduates: 3,340. Freshmen: 390. Both federal and institutional methodology are used as a basis for awarding need-based institutional aid.
UNDERGRADUATE EXPENSES for 2004–05 *Application fee:* $40. *Tuition, state resident:* full-time $4350; part-time $181 per credit. *Tuition, nonresident:* full-time $10,610; part-time $429 per credit. *Required fees:* full-time $722; $113.50 per term part-time. Part-time tuition and fees vary according to course load. *College room and board:* $7914; *room only:* $5624. Room and board charges vary according to board plan and housing facility. *Payment plan:* Installment.
GIFT AID (NEED-BASED) *Total amount:* $8,264,735 (49% federal, 50% state, 1% institutional). *Receiving aid:* Freshmen: 72% (276); All full-time undergraduates: 59% (1,524). *Average award:* Freshmen: $6178; Undergraduates: $4931. *Scholarships, grants, and awards:* Federal Pell, FSEOG, state, private, college/university gift aid from institutional funds.
GIFT AID (NON-NEED-BASED) *Total amount:* $60,230 (5% institutional, 95% external sources). *Receiving aid:* Freshmen: 6% (24); Undergraduates: 2% (54). *Average Award:* Freshmen: $250; Undergraduates: $4622. *Scholarships, grants, and awards by category: Academic Interests/Achievement:* biological sciences, health fields, physical sciences. *Tuition waivers:* Full or partial for senior citizens. *ROTC:* Army cooperative, Air Force cooperative.
LOANS *Student loans:* $5,167,318 (95% need-based, 5% non-need-based). 49% of past graduating class borrowed through all loan programs. *Average indebtedness per student:* $14,064. *Average need-based loan:* Freshmen: $1876; Undergraduates: $2549. *Parent loans:* $815,911 (74% need-based, 26% non-need-based). *Programs:* FFEL (Subsidized and Unsubsidized Stafford, PLUS), Perkins.
APPLYING FOR FINANCIAL AID *Required financial aid forms:* FAFSA, institution's own form, income documentation. *Financial aid deadline (priority):* 4/14. *Notification date:* Continuous beginning 4/25. Students must reply within 2 weeks of notification.
CONTACT Ms. Dee Darrell, Financial Aid Assistant, State University of New York College at Old Westbury, PO Box 210, Old Westbury, NY 11568-0210, 516-876-3222. *Fax:* 516-876-3008. *E-mail:* finaid@oldwestbury.edu.

STATE UNIVERSITY OF NEW YORK COLLEGE AT ONEONTA
Oneonta, NY

Tuition & fees: N/R	Average undergraduate aid package: $9068

ABOUT THE INSTITUTION State-supported, coed. Awards: bachelor's and master's degrees and post-master's certificates. 71 undergraduate majors. Total enrollment: 5,806. Undergraduates: 5,605. Freshmen: 1,057. Federal methodology is used as a basis for awarding need-based institutional aid.
UNDERGRADUATE EXPENSES for 2005–06 *Application fee:* $40. *Payment plan:* Installment.
FRESHMAN FINANCIAL AID (Fall 2004, est.) 895 applied for aid; of those 71% were deemed to have need. 97% of freshmen with need received aid; of those 14% had need fully met. *Average percent of need met:* 61% (excluding resources awarded to replace EFC). *Average financial aid package:* $7844 (excluding resources awarded to replace EFC). 21% of all full-time freshmen had no need and received non-need-based gift aid.
UNDERGRADUATE FINANCIAL AID (Fall 2004, est.) 4,269 applied for aid; of those 77% were deemed to have need. 98% of undergraduates with need received aid; of those 18% had need fully met. *Average percent of need met:* 66% (excluding resources awarded to replace EFC). *Average financial aid package:* $9068 (excluding resources awarded to replace EFC). 19% of all full-time undergraduates had no need and received non-need-based gift aid.
GIFT AID (NEED-BASED) *Total amount:* $12,761,909 (39% federal, 49% state, 7% institutional, 5% external sources). *Receiving aid:* Freshmen: 53% (559); All full-time undergraduates: 53% (2,817). *Average award:* Freshmen: $3871; Undergraduates: $3759. *Scholarships, grants, and awards:* Federal Pell, FSEOG, state, private, college/university gift aid from institutional funds.
GIFT AID (NON-NEED-BASED) *Total amount:* $230,500 (56% institutional, 44% external sources). *Average Award:* Freshmen: $3779; Undergraduates: $4750. *Scholarships, grants, and awards by category: Academic Interests/Achievement:* 45 awards ($40,000 total): biological sciences, education, general academic interests/achievements, home economics, international studies, physical sciences, premedicine. *Creative Arts/Performance:* 18 awards ($10,000 total): journalism/publications, music. *Special Achievements/Activities:* 37 awards ($31,500 total): community service, general special achievements/activities, leadership. *Special Characteristics:* 33 awards ($37,000 total): adult students, children and siblings of alumni, ethnic background, general special characteristics, handicapped students, international students, local/state students, members of minority groups. *Tuition waivers:* Full or partial for employees or children of employees.
LOANS *Student loans:* $22,684,937 (55% need-based, 45% non-need-based). 68% of past graduating class borrowed through all loan programs. *Average indebtedness per student:* $16,904. *Average need-based loan:* Freshmen: $3294; Undergraduates: $4226. *Parent loans:* $8,000,335 (100% need-based). *Programs:* FFEL (Subsidized and Unsubsidized Stafford, PLUS), Perkins.
WORK-STUDY *Federal work-study:* Total amount: $474,727; 395 jobs averaging $1200. *State or other work-study/employment:* Part-time jobs available.
ATHLETIC AWARDS *Total amount:* $90,400 (24% need-based, 76% non-need-based).
APPLYING FOR FINANCIAL AID *Required financial aid forms:* FAFSA, state aid form. *Financial aid deadline (priority):* 3/15. *Notification date:* Continuous.
CONTACT Mr. Bill Goodhue, Director of Financial Aid, State University of New York College at Oneonta, Ravine Parkway, Oneonta, NY 13820, 607-436-2992 or toll-free 800-SUNY-123. *Fax:* 607-436-2659. *E-mail:* goodhucw@oneonta.edu.

STATE UNIVERSITY OF NEW YORK COLLEGE AT POTSDAM
Potsdam, NY

Tuition & fees (NY res): $5250	Average undergraduate aid package: $11,330

ABOUT THE INSTITUTION State-supported, coed. Awards: bachelor's and master's degrees. 53 undergraduate majors. Total enrollment: 4,311. Undergraduates: 3,539. Freshmen: 753. Federal methodology is used as a basis for awarding need-based institutional aid.
UNDERGRADUATE EXPENSES for 2004–05 *Application fee:* $40. *Tuition, state resident:* full-time $4350; part-time $181 per credit hour. *Tuition, nonresident:*

full-time $10,610; part-time $442 per credit hour. **Required fees:** full-time $900; $41.80 per credit hour. **College room and board:** $7270; **room only:** $4220. Room and board charges vary according to board plan and housing facility. **Payment plan:** Installment.

FRESHMAN FINANCIAL AID (Fall 2004, est.) 675 applied for aid; of those 75% were deemed to have need. 100% of freshmen with need received aid; of those 79% had need fully met. *Average percent of need met:* 79% (excluding resources awarded to replace EFC). *Average financial aid package:* $11,810 (excluding resources awarded to replace EFC). 12% of all full-time freshmen had no need and received non-need-based gift aid.

UNDERGRADUATE FINANCIAL AID (Fall 2004, est.) 2,866 applied for aid; of those 80% were deemed to have need. 99% of undergraduates with need received aid; of those 79% had need fully met. *Average percent of need met:* 79% (excluding resources awarded to replace EFC). *Average financial aid package:* $11,330 (excluding resources awarded to replace EFC). 5% of all full-time undergraduates had no need and received non-need-based gift aid.

GIFT AID (NEED-BASED) Total amount: $8,365,637 (46% federal, 54% state). **Receiving aid:** Freshmen: 65% (488); All full-time undergraduates: 62% (2,115). **Average award:** Freshmen: $4967; Undergraduates: $4396. **Scholarships, grants, and awards:** Federal Pell, FSEOG, state, private, college/university gift aid from institutional funds, VESID Awards, Veterans Administration Rehabilitation Awards, Bureau of Indian Affairs Grant.

GIFT AID (NON-NEED-BASED) Total amount: $3,277,807 (11% federal, 4% state, 74% institutional, 11% external sources). **Receiving aid:** Freshmen: 32% (241); Undergraduates: 26% (869). **Average Award:** *Freshmen:* $6990; *Undergraduates:* $7137. **Scholarships, grants, and awards by category:** *Academic Interests/Achievement:* 374 awards ($954,684 total): biological sciences, business, communication, computer science, education, engineering/technologies, English, foreign languages, general academic interests/achievements, humanities, mathematics, physical sciences, social sciences. *Creative Arts/Performance:* 114 awards ($111,865 total): art/fine arts, dance, music, performing arts, theater/drama. *Special Achievements/Activities:* 189 awards ($320,770 total): community service, general special achievements/activities, leadership. *Special Characteristics:* 153 awards ($67,900 total): adult students, children and siblings of alumni, children of faculty/staff, ethnic background, handicapped students, local/state students, members of minority groups, previous college experience. **ROTC:** Army cooperative, Air Force cooperative.

LOANS Student loans: $14,615,059 (56% need-based, 44% non-need-based). 81% of past graduating class borrowed through all loan programs. *Average indebtedness per student:* $17,019. **Average need-based loan:** Freshmen: $3470; Undergraduates: $4170. **Parent loans:** $5,613,311 (100% non-need-based). **Programs:** Federal Direct (Subsidized and Unsubsidized Stafford, PLUS), Perkins, college/university, alternative loans.

WORK-STUDY Federal work-study: Total amount: $697,523; 386 jobs averaging $1000.

APPLYING FOR FINANCIAL AID Required financial aid forms: FAFSA, state aid form. **Financial aid deadline:** 5/1 (priority: 3/1). **Notification date:** Continuous beginning 2/1. Students must reply within 18 weeks of notification.

CONTACT Susan C. Aldrich, Director of Financial Aid, State University of New York College at Potsdam, 44 Pierrepont Avenue, Potsdam, NY 13676, 315-267-2162 or toll-free 877-POTSDAM. *Fax:* 315-267-3067. *E-mail:* aldricsc@potsdam.edu.

STATE UNIVERSITY OF NEW YORK COLLEGE OF AGRICULTURE AND TECHNOLOGY AT COBLESKILL
Cobleskill, NY

Tuition & fees (NY res): $5345   **Average undergraduate aid package: $5640**

ABOUT THE INSTITUTION State-supported, coed. Awards: associate and bachelor's degrees. 44 undergraduate majors. Total enrollment: 2,510. Undergraduates: 2,510. Freshmen: 979. Federal methodology is used as a basis for awarding need-based institutional aid.

UNDERGRADUATE EXPENSES for 2005–06 Application fee: $40. **Tuition, state resident:** full-time $4350. **Tuition, nonresident:** full-time $10,610. Full-time tuition and fees vary according to course level and degree level. Part-time tuition and fees vary according to course level and degree level. **College room and board:** $7270; **room only:** $4300. Room and board charges vary according to board plan and housing facility. **Payment plan:** Installment.

FRESHMAN FINANCIAL AID (Fall 2004, est.) 752 applied for aid; of those 83% were deemed to have need. 100% of freshmen with need received aid; of those 13% had need fully met. *Average percent of need met:* 43% (excluding resources awarded to replace EFC). *Average financial aid package:* $5640 (excluding resources awarded to replace EFC). 12% of all full-time freshmen had no need and received non-need-based gift aid.

UNDERGRADUATE FINANCIAL AID (Fall 2004, est.) 2,312 applied for aid; of those 84% were deemed to have need. 99% of undergraduates with need received aid; of those 9% had need fully met. *Average percent of need met:* 48% (excluding resources awarded to replace EFC). *Average financial aid package:* $5640 (excluding resources awarded to replace EFC).

GIFT AID (NEED-BASED) Receiving aid: Freshmen: 9% (94); All full-time undergraduates: 11% (260). **Average award:** Freshmen: $1136; Undergraduates: $1218. **Scholarships, grants, and awards:** Federal Pell, FSEOG, state, private, college/university gift aid from institutional funds.

GIFT AID (NON-NEED-BASED) Tuition waivers: Full or partial for employees or children of employees.

LOANS Student loans: $9,600,954 (54% need-based, 46% non-need-based). **Average need-based loan:** Freshmen: $2393; Undergraduates: $2398. **Parent loans:** $2,664,793 (100% non-need-based). **Programs:** FFEL (Subsidized and Unsubsidized Stafford, PLUS), Perkins.

WORK-STUDY Federal work-study: Total amount: $195,555; 160 jobs averaging $750. **State or other work-study/employment:** Part-time jobs available.

APPLYING FOR FINANCIAL AID Required financial aid forms: FAFSA, state aid form. **Financial aid deadline:** 3/15. **Notification date:** 4/15. Students must reply within 2 weeks of notification.

CONTACT Richard Young, Director of Financial Aid, State University of New York College of Agriculture and Technology at Cobleskill, Knapp Hall, Cobleskill, NY 12043, 518-255-5623 or toll-free 800-295-8988. *Fax:* 518-255-5844.

STATE UNIVERSITY OF NEW YORK COLLEGE OF ENVIRONMENTAL SCIENCE AND FORESTRY
Syracuse, NY

Tuition & fees (NY res): $4991   **Average undergraduate aid package: $8300**

ABOUT THE INSTITUTION State-supported, coed. Awards: associate, bachelor's, master's, and doctoral degrees. 44 undergraduate majors. Total enrollment: 2,046. Undergraduates: 1,537. Freshmen: 228. Federal methodology is used as a basis for awarding need-based institutional aid.

UNDERGRADUATE EXPENSES for 2004–05 Application fee: $40. **Tuition, state resident:** full-time $4350; part-time $181 per credit hour. **Tuition, nonresident:** full-time $10,610; part-time $442 per credit hour. **Required fees:** full-time $641; $16.10 per credit hour or $19.10 per year part-time. Full-time tuition and fees vary according to location. Part-time tuition and fees vary according to course load and location. **College room and board:** $9790; **room only:** $4890. Room and board charges vary according to board plan, housing facility, and location. **Payment plans:** Installment, deferred payment.

FRESHMAN FINANCIAL AID (Fall 2004, est.) 202 applied for aid; of those 62% were deemed to have need. 100% of freshmen with need received aid; of those 100% had need fully met. *Average percent of need met:* 100% (excluding resources awarded to replace EFC). *Average financial aid package:* $8300 (excluding resources awarded to replace EFC). 11% of all full-time freshmen had no need and received non-need-based gift aid.

UNDERGRADUATE FINANCIAL AID (Fall 2004, est.) 1,064 applied for aid; of those 83% were deemed to have need. 100% of undergraduates with need received aid; of those 100% had need fully met. *Average percent of need met:* 100% (excluding resources awarded to replace EFC). *Average financial aid package:* $8300 (excluding resources awarded to replace EFC). 11% of all full-time undergraduates had no need and received non-need-based gift aid.

GIFT AID (NEED-BASED) Total amount: $3,281,289 (35% federal, 41% state, 18% institutional, 6% external sources). **Receiving aid:** Freshmen: 56% (126); All full-time undergraduates: 67% (878). **Average award:** Freshmen: $4500; Undergraduates: $5300. **Scholarships, grants, and awards:** Federal Pell, FSEOG, state, private, college/university gift aid from institutional funds.

GIFT AID (NON-NEED-BASED) Total amount: $310,000 (26% federal, 16% state, 32% institutional, 26% external sources). **Receiving aid:** Freshmen: 15% (35); Undergraduates: 9% (120). **Average Award:** Freshmen: $2500; Undergraduates: $2500. **Scholarships, grants, and awards by category:** *Academic Interests/Achievement:* 48 awards ($50,000 total): agriculture, architecture, biological sciences, engineering/technologies, physical sciences, premedicine. *Special Achievements/Activities:* leadership. *Special Characteristics:* 42 awards ($90,000 total): members of minority groups. *ROTC:* Army cooperative, Air Force cooperative.

LOANS *Student loans:* $5,883,500 (61% need-based, 39% non-need-based). 92% of past graduating class borrowed through all loan programs. *Average indebtedness per student:* $19,000. *Average need-based loan:* Freshmen: $2625; Undergraduates: $5500. *Parent loans:* $2,241,800 (100% non-need-based). *Programs:* FFEL (Subsidized and Unsubsidized Stafford, PLUS), Perkins, college/university.

WORK-STUDY *Federal work-study:* Total amount: $326,000; 310 jobs averaging $1200. *State or other work-study/employment:* Total amount: $110,000 (100% non-need-based). 118 part-time jobs averaging $1000.

APPLYING FOR FINANCIAL AID *Required financial aid forms:* FAFSA, state aid form. *Financial aid deadline (priority):* 3/1. *Notification date:* 4/1. Students must reply within 2 weeks of notification.

CONTACT Mr. John E. View, Director of Financial Aid, State University of New York College of Environmental Science and Forestry, One Forestry Drive, 115 Bray Hall, Syracuse, NY 13210-2779, 315-470-6671 or toll-free 800-777-7373. *Fax:* 315-470-4734. *E-mail:* jeview@esf.edu.

STATE UNIVERSITY OF NEW YORK DOWNSTATE MEDICAL CENTER
Brooklyn, NY

ABOUT THE INSTITUTION State-supported, coed. Awards: bachelor's, master's, doctoral, and first professional degrees and post-bachelor's and post-master's certificates. 6 undergraduate majors. Total enrollment: 1,569. Undergraduates: 354.

GIFT AID (NEED-BASED) *Scholarships, grants, and awards:* Federal Pell, FSEOG, state.

LOANS *Programs:* FFEL (Subsidized and Unsubsidized Stafford), Perkins, Federal Nursing.

CONTACT Office of Financial Aid, State University of New York Downstate Medical Center, 450 Clarkson Avenue, Brooklyn, NY 11203-2098, 718-270-2488.

STATE UNIVERSITY OF NEW YORK, FREDONIA
Fredonia, NY

Tuition & fees (NY res): $5391	Average undergraduate aid package: $6542

ABOUT THE INSTITUTION State-supported, coed. Awards: bachelor's and master's degrees. 74 undergraduate majors. Total enrollment: 5,359. Undergraduates: 4,954. Freshmen: 1,140. Federal methodology is used as a basis for awarding need-based institutional aid.

UNDERGRADUATE EXPENSES for 2005–06 *Application fee:* $40. *Tuition, state resident:* full-time $4350; part-time $181 per credit hour. *Tuition, nonresident:* full-time $10,300; part-time $429 per credit hour. *Required fees:* full-time $1041; $43 per credit hour. *College room and board:* $6940; *room only:* $4350. Room and board charges vary according to board plan and housing facility. *Payment plan:* Installment.

FRESHMAN FINANCIAL AID (Fall 2004, est.) 814 applied for aid; of those 63% were deemed to have need. 100% of freshmen with need received aid; of those 80% had need fully met. *Average percent of need met:* 67% (excluding resources awarded to replace EFC). *Average financial aid package:* $4830 (excluding resources awarded to replace EFC). 21% of all full-time freshmen had no need and received non-need-based gift aid.

UNDERGRADUATE FINANCIAL AID (Fall 2004, est.) 3,953 applied for aid; of those 58% were deemed to have need. 100% of undergraduates with need received aid; of those 80% had need fully met. *Average percent of need met:* 75% (excluding resources awarded to replace EFC). *Average financial aid package:* $6542 (excluding resources awarded to replace EFC). 17% of all full-time undergraduates had no need and received non-need-based gift aid.

GIFT AID (NEED-BASED) *Total amount:* $10,164,376 (37% federal, 52% state, 6% institutional, 5% external sources). *Receiving aid:* Freshmen: 22% (236); All full-time undergraduates: 28% (1,314). *Average award:* Freshmen: $3207; Undergraduates: $2868. *Scholarships, grants, and awards:* Federal Pell, FSEOG, state, private, college/university gift aid from institutional funds.

GIFT AID (NON-NEED-BASED) *Receiving aid:* Freshmen: 21% (230); Undergraduates: 17% (792). *Average Award:* Freshmen: $1313; Undergraduates: $1520. *Scholarships, grants, and awards by category: Academic Interests/Achievement:* 229 awards ($388,100 total): biological sciences, business, communication, education, English, foreign languages, general academic interests/achievements, humanities, international studies, mathematics, physical sciences, social sciences. *Creative Arts/Performance:* 55 awards ($73,000 total): applied art and design, dance, music, performing arts, theater/drama. *Special Achievements/Activities:* 30 awards ($20,000 total): general special achievements/activities, leadership. *Special Characteristics:* 56 awards ($83,800 total): children and siblings of alumni, ethnic background, general special characteristics, international students, local/state students, members of minority groups, out-of-state students, previous college experience, veterans, veterans' children.

LOANS *Student loans:* $33,081,862 (67% need-based, 33% non-need-based). 80% of past graduating class borrowed through all loan programs. *Average indebtedness per student:* $12,288. *Average need-based loan:* Freshmen: $3235; Undergraduates: $4143. *Parent loans:* $2,793,652 (100% non-need-based). *Programs:* FFEL (Subsidized and Unsubsidized Stafford, PLUS), Perkins.

WORK-STUDY *Federal work-study:* Total amount: $272,731; 267 jobs averaging $1400.

APPLYING FOR FINANCIAL AID *Required financial aid forms:* FAFSA, state aid form. *Financial aid deadline (priority):* 2/1. *Notification date:* Continuous beginning 3/15.

CONTACT Mr. Daniel M. Tramuta, Director of Financial Aid, State University of New York, Fredonia, Maytum Hall, 212, Fredonia, NY 14063, 716-673-3253 or toll-free 800-252-1212. *Fax:* 716-673-3785. *E-mail:* tramuta@fredonia.edu.

STATE UNIVERSITY OF NEW YORK INSTITUTE OF TECHNOLOGY
Utica, NY

Tuition & fees (NY res): $5244	Average undergraduate aid package: $7608

ABOUT THE INSTITUTION State-supported, coed. Awards: bachelor's and master's degrees and post-master's certificates. 19 undergraduate majors. Total enrollment: 2,432. Undergraduates: 1,876. Freshmen: 81. Federal methodology is used as a basis for awarding need-based institutional aid.

UNDERGRADUATE EXPENSES for 2005–06 *Application fee:* $30. *Tuition, state resident:* full-time $4350; part-time $181 per credit hour. *Tuition, nonresident:* full-time $10,610; part-time $442 per credit hour. *Required fees:* full-time $894; $53 per credit hour. *College room and board:* $7160.

FRESHMAN FINANCIAL AID (Fall 2003) 93 applied for aid; of those 72% were deemed to have need. 100% of freshmen with need received aid; of those 30% had need fully met. *Average percent of need met:* 85% (excluding resources awarded to replace EFC). *Average financial aid package:* $6131 (excluding resources awarded to replace EFC). 17% of all full-time freshmen had no need and received non-need-based gift aid.

UNDERGRADUATE FINANCIAL AID (Fall 2003) 1,059 applied for aid; of those 90% were deemed to have need. 98% of undergraduates with need received aid; of those 28% had need fully met. *Average percent of need met:* 77% (excluding resources awarded to replace EFC). *Average financial aid package:* $7608 (excluding resources awarded to replace EFC).

GIFT AID (NEED-BASED) *Total amount:* $3,561,388 (53% federal, 44% state, 3% institutional). *Receiving aid:* Freshmen: 63% (66); All full-time undergraduates: 71% (908). *Average award:* Freshmen: $1203; Undergraduates: $1466. *Scholarships, grants, and awards:* Federal Pell, FSEOG, state.

GIFT AID (NON-NEED-BASED) *Total amount:* $868,450 (9% federal, 12% state, 45% institutional, 34% external sources). *Receiving aid:* Freshmen: 39% (41); Undergraduates: 26% (335). *Average Award:* Freshmen: $3263. *Scholarships, grants, and awards by category: Academic Interests/Achievement:* computer science, engineering/technologies, general academic interests/achievements. *Special Characteristics:* local/state students, members of minority groups, previous college experience. *ROTC:* Army cooperative, Air Force cooperative.

LOANS *Student loans:* $6,923,785 (58% need-based, 42% non-need-based). 54% of past graduating class borrowed through all loan programs. *Average indebtedness per student:* $14,189. *Average need-based loan:* Freshmen: $1903; Undergraduates: $3759. *Parent loans:* $853,889 (80% need-based, 20% non-need-based). *Programs:* Federal Direct (Subsidized and Unsubsidized Stafford, PLUS), Perkins, Federal Nursing, college/university.

WORK-STUDY *Federal work-study:* Total amount: $142,767; 100 jobs averaging $1350. *State or other work-study/employment:* Part-time jobs available.

APPLYING FOR FINANCIAL AID *Required financial aid forms:* FAFSA, institution's own form, state aid form. *Financial aid deadline:* Continuous. *Notification date:* Continuous. Students must reply within 2 weeks of notification.
CONTACT Mr. Stewart Richards, Director of Financial Aid, State University of New York Institute of Technology, PO Box 3050, Utica, NY 13504-3050, 315-792-7210 or toll-free 800-SUNYTEC. *Fax:* 315-792-7220. *E-mail:* finaid@sunyit.edu.

STATE UNIVERSITY OF NEW YORK MARITIME COLLEGE
Throggs Neck, NY

CONTACT Ms. Madeline Aponte, Director of Financial Aid, State University of New York Maritime College, 6 Pennyfield Avenue, Throgs Neck, NY 10465-4198, 718-409-7267 or toll-free 800-654-1874 (in-state), 800-642-1874 (out-of-state). *Fax:* 718-409-7275. *E-mail:* finaid@sunymaritime.edu.

STATE UNIVERSITY OF NEW YORK UPSTATE MEDICAL UNIVERSITY
Syracuse, NY

Tuition & fees (NY res): $9166	Average undergraduate aid package: $18,332

ABOUT THE INSTITUTION State-supported, coed. Awards: bachelor's, master's, doctoral, and first professional degrees and post-master's certificates. 9 undergraduate majors. Total enrollment: 1,180. Undergraduates: 258. Entering class: . Federal methodology is used as a basis for awarding need-based institutional aid.
UNDERGRADUATE EXPENSES for 2004–05 *Application fee:* $30. *Tuition, state resident:* full-time $8700; part-time $181 per credit hour. *Tuition, nonresident:* full-time $21,220; part-time $442 per credit hour. *College room and board: room only:* $3586. *Payment plan:* Installment.
UNDERGRADUATE FINANCIAL AID (Fall 2003) 161 applied for aid; of those 100% were deemed to have need. 100% of undergraduates with need received aid; of those 99% had need fully met. *Average percent of need met:* 100% (excluding resources awarded to replace EFC). *Average financial aid package:* $18,332 (excluding resources awarded to replace EFC).
GIFT AID (NEED-BASED) *Total amount:* $495,434 (47% federal, 29% state, 10% institutional, 14% external sources). *Receiving aid:* All full-time undergraduates: 56% (139). *Average award:* Undergraduates: $3047. *Scholarships, grants, and awards:* Federal Pell, FSEOG, state, college/university gift aid from institutional funds.
GIFT AID (NON-NEED-BASED) *Total amount:* $132,632 (1% federal, 11% state, 88% institutional). *Receiving aid:* Undergraduates: 14% (34). *Scholarships, grants, and awards by category:* Academic Interests/Achievement: health fields.
LOANS *Student loans:* $1,074,545 (68% need-based, 32% non-need-based). 46% of past graduating class borrowed through all loan programs. *Average indebtedness per student:* $9680. *Average need-based loan:* Undergraduates: $8000. *Programs:* FFEL (Subsidized and Unsubsidized Stafford, PLUS), Perkins.
WORK-STUDY *Federal work-study:* Total amount: $70,200; jobs available.
APPLYING FOR FINANCIAL AID *Required financial aid form:* FAFSA. *Financial aid deadline:* 4/1 (priority: 3/1). *Notification date:* Continuous beginning 5/1. Students must reply within 3 weeks of notification.
CONTACT Office of Financial Aid, State University of New York Upstate Medical University, 155 Elizabeth Blackwell Street, Syracuse, NY 13210-2375, 315-464-4329 or toll-free 800-736-2171. *E-mail:* finaid@upstate.edu.

STEPHEN F. AUSTIN STATE UNIVERSITY
Nacogdoches, TX

Tuition & fees (TX res): $4298	Average undergraduate aid package: $4506

ABOUT THE INSTITUTION State-supported, coed. Awards: bachelor's, master's, and doctoral degrees. 73 undergraduate majors. Total enrollment: 11,287. Undergraduates: 9,568. Freshmen: 1,684. Federal methodology is used as a basis for awarding need-based institutional aid.
UNDERGRADUATE EXPENSES for 2004–05 *Application fee:* $25. *Tuition, state resident:* full-time $3360; part-time $145 per credit hour. *Tuition, nonresident:* full-time $11,100; part-time $403 per credit hour. *Required fees:* full-time $938; $33 per credit hour. Full-time tuition and fees vary according to course

load. Part-time tuition and fees vary according to course load. *College room and board:* $5012. Room and board charges vary according to board plan and housing facility. *Payment plan:* Installment.
FRESHMAN FINANCIAL AID (Fall 2003) 1199 applied for aid; of those 65% were deemed to have need. 99% of freshmen with need received aid; of those 31% had need fully met. *Average percent of need met:* 65% (excluding resources awarded to replace EFC). *Average financial aid package:* $4481 (excluding resources awarded to replace EFC). 11% of all full-time freshmen had no need and received non-need-based gift aid.
UNDERGRADUATE FINANCIAL AID (Fall 2003) 5,255 applied for aid; of those 76% were deemed to have need. 98% of undergraduates with need received aid; of those 23% had need fully met. *Average percent of need met:* 67% (excluding resources awarded to replace EFC). *Average financial aid package:* $4506 (excluding resources awarded to replace EFC). 5% of all full-time undergraduates had no need and received non-need-based gift aid.
GIFT AID (NEED-BASED) *Total amount:* $16,251,609 (61% federal, 23% state, 16% institutional). *Receiving aid:* Freshmen: 39% (592); All full-time undergraduates: 43% (3,131). *Average award:* Freshmen: $1340; Undergraduates: $1626. *Scholarships, grants, and awards:* Federal Pell, FSEOG, state, private, college/university gift aid from institutional funds.
GIFT AID (NON-NEED-BASED) *Total amount:* $6,103,002 (54% institutional, 46% external sources). *Receiving aid:* Freshmen: 27% (417); Undergraduates: 19% (1,418). *Average Award:* Freshmen: $3399; Undergraduates: $3012. *Scholarships, grants, and awards by category:* Academic Interests/Achievement: agriculture, biological sciences, business, communication, computer science, education, general academic interests/achievements, health fields, home economics, mathematics, military science, physical sciences, premedicine. *Creative Arts/Performance:* applied art and design, art/fine arts, journalism/publications, music, theater/drama. *Special Achievements/Activities:* cheerleading/drum major, general special achievements/activities, hobbies/interests, leadership, rodeo. *Special Characteristics:* adult students, children of union members/company employees, first-generation college students, general special characteristics, local/state students, previous college experience, religious affiliation. *Tuition waivers:* Full or partial for employees or children of employees. *ROTC:* Army.
LOANS *Student loans:* $35,214,326 (55% need-based, 45% non-need-based). 62% of past graduating class borrowed through all loan programs. *Average indebtedness per student:* $16,624. *Average need-based loan:* Freshmen: $1238; Undergraduates: $2066. *Parent loans:* $2,095,850 (100% non-need-based). *Programs:* FFEL (Subsidized and Unsubsidized Stafford, PLUS), Perkins, state, college/university, alternative loans.
WORK-STUDY *Federal work-study:* Total amount: $647,732; 421 jobs averaging $1539. *State or other work-study/employment:* Total amount: $110,240 (100% need-based). 100 part-time jobs averaging $1102.
ATHLETIC AWARDS *Total amount:* $1,615,811 (100% non-need-based).
APPLYING FOR FINANCIAL AID *Required financial aid forms:* FAFSA, institution's own form. *Financial aid deadline:* 4/15 (priority: 4/1). *Notification date:* Continuous beginning 5/1. Students must reply within 3 weeks of notification.
CONTACT Office of Financial Aid, Stephen F. Austin State University, PO Box 13052, SFA Station, Nacogdoches, TX 75962, 936-468-2403 or toll-free 800-731-2902. *Fax:* 936-468-1048. *E-mail:* finaid@sfasu.edu.

STEPHENS COLLEGE
Columbia, MO

Tuition & fees: $19,300	Average undergraduate aid package: $16,141

ABOUT THE INSTITUTION Independent, women only. Awards: bachelor's and master's degrees and post-bachelor's certificates. 35 undergraduate majors. Total enrollment: 705. Undergraduates: 633. Freshmen: 157. Federal methodology is used as a basis for awarding need-based institutional aid.
UNDERGRADUATE EXPENSES for 2005–06 *Application fee:* $25. *Comprehensive fee:* $26,930 includes full-time tuition ($19,300) and room and board ($7630). *College room only:* $4540. Room and board charges vary according to board plan. *Payment plan:* Installment.
GIFT AID (NEED-BASED) *Total amount:* $3,840,753 (14% federal, 4% state, 80% institutional, 2% external sources). *Receiving aid:* Freshmen: 54% (84); All full-time undergraduates: 53% (279). *Average award:* Freshmen: $6604; Undergraduates: $5657. *Scholarships, grants, and awards:* Federal Pell, FSEOG, state, private, college/university gift aid from institutional funds.
GIFT AID (NON-NEED-BASED) *Total amount:* $1,281,487 (1% state, 97% institutional, 2% external sources). *Receiving aid:* Freshmen: 68% (106); Undergraduates: 61% (318). *Average Award:* Freshmen: $7486; Undergradu-

Stephens College

ates: $7623. **Scholarships, grants, and awards by category:** *Academic Interests/ Achievement:* 392 awards ($2,971,800 total): general academic interests/ achievements. *Creative Arts/Performance:* 74 awards ($335,410 total): dance, performing arts, theater/drama. *Special Achievements/Activities:* 313 awards ($567,390 total): leadership. *Special Characteristics:* 120 awards ($187,138 total): children of faculty/staff, local/state students, siblings of current students. **Tuition waivers:** Full or partial for employees or children of employees. **ROTC:** Army cooperative, Air Force cooperative.

LOANS *Student loans:* $1,755,321 (64% need-based, 36% non-need-based). 48% of past graduating class borrowed through all loan programs. *Average indebtedness per student:* $6073. **Average need-based loan:** Freshmen: $3452; Undergraduates: $4210. **Parent loans:** $1,053,784 (26% need-based, 74% non-need-based). **Programs:** FFEL (Subsidized and Unsubsidized Stafford, PLUS), Perkins, state, alternative loans.

ATHLETIC AWARDS *Total amount:* $57,900 (66% need-based, 34% non-need-based).

APPLYING FOR FINANCIAL AID *Required financial aid form:* FAFSA. **Financial aid deadline (priority):** 3/15. **Notification date:** Continuous beginning 2/15. Students must reply within 2 weeks of notification.

CONTACT Mrs. Rachel Touchatt, Financial Aid Director, Stephens College, 1200 East Broadway, Campus Box 2124, Columbia, MO 65215-0002, 800-876-7207. *Fax:* 573-876-7237. *E-mail:* finaid@stephens.edu.

STERLING COLLEGE
Sterling, KS

Tuition & fees: $13,907	Average undergraduate aid package: $15,375

ABOUT THE INSTITUTION Independent Presbyterian, coed. Awards: bachelor's degrees. 19 undergraduate majors. Total enrollment: 487. Undergraduates: 487. Freshmen: 136. Federal methodology is used as a basis for awarding need-based institutional aid.

UNDERGRADUATE EXPENSES for 2004–05 *Application fee:* $25. **Comprehensive fee:** $19,696 includes full-time tuition ($13,807), mandatory fees ($100), and room and board ($5789). Room and board charges vary according to board plan and housing facility. **Part-time tuition:** $275 per semester hour. **Part-time fees:** $50 per term. Part-time tuition and fees vary according to course load. **Payment plan:** Installment.

FRESHMAN FINANCIAL AID (Fall 2004, est.) 118 applied for aid; of those 86% were deemed to have need. 100% of freshmen with need received aid; of those 39% had need fully met. *Average percent of need met:* 97% (excluding resources awarded to replace EFC). *Average financial aid package:* $15,803 (excluding resources awarded to replace EFC). 14% of all full-time freshmen had no need and received non-need-based gift aid.

UNDERGRADUATE FINANCIAL AID (Fall 2004, est.) 449 applied for aid; of those 81% were deemed to have need. 100% of undergraduates with need received aid; of those 48% had need fully met. *Average financial aid package:* $15,375 (excluding resources awarded to replace EFC). 17% of all full-time undergraduates had no need and received non-need-based gift aid.

GIFT AID (NEED-BASED) *Receiving aid:* Freshmen: 83% (98); All full-time undergraduates: 79% (353). *Average award:* Freshmen: $7732; Undergraduates: $7863. **Scholarships, grants, and awards:** Federal Pell, FSEOG, state, private, college/university gift aid from institutional funds.

GIFT AID (NON-NEED-BASED) *Average Award:* Freshmen: $3969; Undergraduates: $6817. **Scholarships, grants, and awards by category:** *Academic Interests/ Achievement:* $701,937 total: general academic interests/achievements. *Creative Arts/Performance:* $894,652 total: art/fine arts, debating, general creative arts/ performance, music, theater/drama. *Special Characteristics:* $121,252 total: children and siblings of alumni, siblings of current students, twins. **Tuition waivers:** Full or partial for employees or children of employees, senior citizens.

LOANS *Student loans:* 79% of past graduating class borrowed through all loan programs. *Average indebtedness per student:* $9647. **Average need-based loan:** Freshmen: $3736; Undergraduates: $4214. **Programs:** FFEL (Subsidized and Unsubsidized Stafford, PLUS), Perkins, college/university.

WORK-STUDY *Federal work-study:* 169 jobs averaging $501. **State or other work-study/employment:** 196 part-time jobs averaging $808.

APPLYING FOR FINANCIAL AID *Required financial aid form:* FAFSA. **Financial aid deadline (priority):** 4/1. **Notification date:** Continuous. Students must reply within 2 weeks of notification.

CONTACT Ms. Jodi Lightner, Director of Financial Aid, Sterling College, PO Box 98, Sterling, KS 67579-0098, 620-278-4207 or toll-free 800-346-1017. *Fax:* 620-278-4416. *E-mail:* jlightner@sterling.edu.

STERLING COLLEGE
Craftsbury Common, VT

Tuition & fees: $16,434	Average undergraduate aid package: $14,413

ABOUT THE INSTITUTION Independent, coed. Awards: associate and bachelor's degrees. 85 undergraduate majors. Total enrollment: 92. Undergraduates: 92. Freshmen: 18. Both federal and institutional methodology are used as a basis for awarding need-based institutional aid.

UNDERGRADUATE EXPENSES for 2004–05 *Application fee:* $35. **Comprehensive fee:** $22,516 includes full-time tuition ($16,134), mandatory fees ($300), and room and board ($6082). **College room only:** $2720. Full-time tuition and fees vary according to course load. Room and board charges vary according to board plan. **Part-time tuition:** $490 per credit. **Part-time fees:** $490 per credit. Part-time tuition and fees vary according to course load. **Payment plan:** Installment.

FRESHMAN FINANCIAL AID (Fall 2004, est.) 17 applied for aid; of those 82% were deemed to have need. 100% of freshmen with need received aid. *Average percent of need met:* 77% (excluding resources awarded to replace EFC). *Average financial aid package:* $13,979 (excluding resources awarded to replace EFC). 11% of all full-time freshmen had no need and received non-need-based gift aid.

UNDERGRADUATE FINANCIAL AID (Fall 2004, est.) 67 applied for aid; of those 90% were deemed to have need. 100% of undergraduates with need received aid; of those 3% had need fully met. *Average percent of need met:* 74% (excluding resources awarded to replace EFC). *Average financial aid package:* $14,413 (excluding resources awarded to replace EFC). 6% of all full-time undergraduates had no need and received non-need-based gift aid.

GIFT AID (NEED-BASED) *Total amount:* $556,115 (23% federal, 9% state, 65% institutional, 3% external sources). *Receiving aid:* Freshmen: 78% (14); All full-time undergraduates: 69% (60). *Average award:* Freshmen: $9779; Undergraduates: $9320. **Scholarships, grants, and awards:** Federal Pell, FSEOG, state, private, college/university gift aid from institutional funds.

GIFT AID (NON-NEED-BASED) *Total amount:* $6000 (100% institutional). *Average Award:* Freshmen: $1000; Undergraduates: $1200. **Scholarships, grants, and awards by category:** *Academic Interests/Achievement:* 6 awards ($14,500 total): general academic interests/achievements. *Special Achievements/Activities:* 11 awards ($1300 total): general special achievements/activities. *Special Characteristics:* 27 awards ($18,375 total): general special characteristics, local/ state students, previous college experience. **Tuition waivers:** Full or partial for employees or children of employees.

LOANS *Student loans:* $355,288 (97% need-based, 3% non-need-based). 33% of past graduating class borrowed through all loan programs. *Average indebtedness per student:* $13,200. **Average need-based loan:** Freshmen: $2625; Undergraduates: $3333. **Parent loans:** $134,345 (55% need-based, 45% non-need-based). **Programs:** FFEL (Subsidized and Unsubsidized Stafford, PLUS).

WORK-STUDY *Federal work-study:* Total amount: $11,474; 29 jobs averaging $396. **State or other work-study/employment:** Total amount: $110,188 (81% need-based, 19% non-need-based). 67 part-time jobs averaging $1645.

APPLYING FOR FINANCIAL AID *Required financial aid forms:* FAFSA, institution's own form, state aid form. **Financial aid deadline:** Continuous. **Notification date:** Continuous beginning 1/31. Students must reply by 5/1 or within 2 weeks of notification.

CONTACT Barbara Stuart, Associate Director of Financial Aid, Sterling College, PO Box 72, Craftsbury Common, VT 05827, 800-648-3591 Ext. 2 or toll-free 800-648-3591 Ext. 1. *Fax:* 802-586-2596. *E-mail:* bstuart@sterlingcollege.edu.

STETSON UNIVERSITY
DeLand, FL

Tuition & fees: $24,135	Average undergraduate aid package: $20,853

ABOUT THE INSTITUTION Independent, coed. Awards: bachelor's, master's, and first professional degrees and post-master's and first professional certificates. 59 undergraduate majors. Total enrollment: 3,577. Undergraduates: 2,230. Freshmen: 600. Federal methodology is used as a basis for awarding need-based institutional aid.

UNDERGRADUATE EXPENSES for 2004–05 *Application fee:* $40. **Comprehensive fee:** $31,195 includes full-time tuition ($22,730), mandatory fees ($1405), and room and board ($7060). **College room only:** $3960. Full-time tuition and fees vary according to course load and student level. Room and board charges vary according to board plan and housing facility. *Part-time tuition:* $725 per credit hour. Part-time tuition and fees vary according to course load. *Payment plan:* Installment.

FRESHMAN FINANCIAL AID (Fall 2004, est.) 428 applied for aid; of those 81% were deemed to have need. 100% of freshmen with need received aid; of those 36% had need fully met. *Average percent of need met:* 87% (excluding resources awarded to replace EFC). *Average financial aid package:* $21,857 (excluding resources awarded to replace EFC). 39% of all full-time freshmen had no need and received non-need-based gift aid.

UNDERGRADUATE FINANCIAL AID (Fall 2004, est.) 1,330 applied for aid; of those 87% were deemed to have need. 100% of undergraduates with need received aid; of those 32% had need fully met. *Average percent of need met:* 83% (excluding resources awarded to replace EFC). *Average financial aid package:* $20,853 (excluding resources awarded to replace EFC). 37% of all full-time undergraduates had no need and received non-need-based gift aid.

GIFT AID (NEED-BASED) *Total amount:* $12,532,700 (14% federal, 4% state, 82% institutional). *Receiving aid:* Freshmen: 58% (345); All full-time undergraduates: 54% (1,144). *Average award:* Freshmen: $17,501; Undergraduates: $15,574. *Scholarships, grants, and awards:* Federal Pell, FSEOG, state, private, college/university gift aid from institutional funds.

GIFT AID (NON-NEED-BASED) *Total amount:* $14,433,849 (44% state, 52% institutional, 4% external sources). *Receiving aid:* Freshmen: 58% (345); Undergraduates: 54% (1,135). *Average Award: Freshmen:* $10,354; *Undergraduates:* $9461. *Scholarships, grants, and awards by category: Academic Interests/ Achievement:* area/ethnic studies, biological sciences, business, communication, computer science, education, English, foreign languages, general academic interests/achievements, humanities, mathematics, military science, physical sciences, premedicine, religion/biblical studies, social sciences. *Creative Arts/ Performance:* applied art and design, art/fine arts, music, theater/drama. *Special Achievements/Activities:* cheerleading/drum major, community service, general special achievements/activities, leadership, religious involvement. *Special Characteristics:* children and siblings of alumni, children of faculty/staff, ethnic background, general special characteristics, international students, local/state students, members of minority groups. *Tuition waivers:* Full or partial for employees or children of employees. *ROTC:* Army cooperative.

LOANS *Student loans:* $6,775,881 (66% need-based, 34% non-need-based). 55% of past graduating class borrowed through all loan programs. *Average indebtedness per student:* $21,500. *Average need-based loan:* Freshmen: $4087; Undergraduates: $5261. *Parent loans:* $1,393,074 (82% need-based, 18% non-need-based). *Programs:* FFEL (Subsidized and Unsubsidized Stafford, PLUS), Perkins, college/university.

WORK-STUDY *Federal work-study:* Total amount: $1,379,493; 594 jobs averaging $2322. *State or other work-study/employment:* Total amount: $594,732 (59% need-based, 41% non-need-based). 189 part-time jobs averaging $2011.

ATHLETIC AWARDS *Total amount:* $2,637,308 (40% need-based, 60% non-need-based).

APPLYING FOR FINANCIAL AID *Required financial aid forms:* FAFSA, institution's own form. *Financial aid deadline (priority):* 3/15. *Notification date:* Continuous.

CONTACT Terry Whittum, Dean of Admissions and Financial Aid, Stetson University, 421 North Woodland Boulevard, DeLand, FL 32723, 386-822-7120 or toll-free 800-688-0101. *Fax:* 386-822-7126. *E-mail:* finaid@stetson.edu.

STEVENS INSTITUTE OF TECHNOLOGY
Hoboken, NJ

Tuition & fees: $29,760	Average undergraduate aid package: $19,538

ABOUT THE INSTITUTION Independent, coed. Awards: bachelor's, master's, and doctoral degrees and post-bachelor's certificates. 32 undergraduate majors. Total enrollment: 4,634. Undergraduates: 1,730. Freshmen: 438. Federal methodology is used as a basis for awarding need-based institutional aid.

UNDERGRADUATE EXPENSES for 2004–05 *Application fee:* $45. *Comprehensive fee:* $38,686 includes full-time tuition ($28,800), mandatory fees ($960), and room and board ($8926). *College room only:* $4620. Full-time tuition and fees vary according to student level. Room and board charges vary according to board plan and housing facility. *Part-time tuition:* $960 per credit. *Payment plan:* Installment.

FRESHMAN FINANCIAL AID (Fall 2004, est.) 398 applied for aid; of those 84% were deemed to have need. 100% of freshmen with need received aid; of those 24% had need fully met. *Average percent of need met:* 83% (excluding resources awarded to replace EFC). *Average financial aid package:* $24,557 (excluding resources awarded to replace EFC). 10% of all full-time freshmen had no need and received non-need-based gift aid.

UNDERGRADUATE FINANCIAL AID (Fall 2004, est.) 1,606 applied for aid; of those 89% were deemed to have need. 86% of undergraduates with need received aid; of those 18% had need fully met. *Average percent of need met:* 85% (excluding resources awarded to replace EFC). *Average financial aid package:* $19,538 (excluding resources awarded to replace EFC). 14% of all full-time undergraduates had no need and received non-need-based gift aid.

GIFT AID (NEED-BASED) *Total amount:* $11,150,000 (11% federal, 16% state, 73% institutional). *Receiving aid:* Freshmen: 55% (253); All full-time undergraduates: 53% (924). *Average award:* Freshmen: $15,021; Undergraduates: $12,871. *Scholarships, grants, and awards:* Federal Pell, FSEOG, state, private, college/university gift aid from institutional funds.

GIFT AID (NON-NEED-BASED) *Total amount:* $11,910,000 (2% state, 92% institutional, 6% external sources). *Receiving aid:* Freshmen: 64% (292); Undergraduates: 50% (856). *Average Award: Freshmen:* $11,909; *Undergraduates:* $9973. *Scholarships, grants, and awards by category: Academic Interests/ Achievement:* 1,450 awards ($10,800,000 total): business, computer science, engineering/technologies, general academic interests/achievements, humanities, mathematics, physical sciences, premedicine. *Creative Arts/Performance:* 52 awards ($154,500 total): music, performing arts, theater/drama. *Special Characteristics:* 85 awards ($920,000 total): children and siblings of alumni, children of educators, children of faculty/staff, international students, local/state students, members of minority groups. *Tuition waivers:* Full or partial for employees or children of employees. *ROTC:* Army cooperative, Air Force cooperative.

LOANS *Student loans:* $6,500,000 (72% need-based, 28% non-need-based). 68% of past graduating class borrowed through all loan programs. *Average indebtedness per student:* $14,113. *Average need-based loan:* Freshmen: $3655; Undergraduates: $4203. *Parent loans:* $3,100,000 (100% non-need-based). *Programs:* Federal Direct (Subsidized and Unsubsidized Stafford, PLUS), Perkins, state, Sallie Mae Signature Loans, TERI Loans, NJ Class Loans, CitiAssist Loans.

WORK-STUDY *Federal work-study:* Total amount: $500,000; 818 jobs averaging $1269.

APPLYING FOR FINANCIAL AID *Required financial aid form:* FAFSA. *Financial aid deadline (priority):* 2/15. *Notification date:* Continuous beginning 3/30. Students must reply by 5/1.

CONTACT Ms. Adrienne Hynek, Associate Director of Financial Aid, Stevens Institute of Technology, Castle Point on Hudson, Hoboken, NJ 07030, 201-216-5555 or toll-free 800-458-5323. *Fax:* 201-216-8050. *E-mail:* ahynek@stevens.edu.

STILLMAN COLLEGE
Tuscaloosa, AL

CONTACT Jacqueline S. Morris, Director of Financial Aid, Stillman College, PO Box 1430, Tuscaloosa, AL 35403, 205-366-8950 or toll-free 800-841-5722. *Fax:* 205-247-8106.

STONEHILL COLLEGE
Easton, MA

Tuition & fees: $23,008	Average undergraduate aid package: $17,306

ABOUT THE INSTITUTION Independent Roman Catholic, coed. Awards: bachelor's and master's degrees. 31 undergraduate majors. Total enrollment: 2,490. Undergraduates: 2,466. Freshmen: 614. Both federal and institutional methodology are used as a basis for awarding need-based institutional aid.

UNDERGRADUATE EXPENSES for 2004–05 *Application fee:* $50. *Comprehensive fee:* $33,214 includes full-time tuition ($22,068), mandatory fees ($940), and room and board ($10,206). *Part-time tuition:* $800 per course. *Part-time fees:* $25 per term. *Payment plans:* Tuition prepayment, installment.

FRESHMAN FINANCIAL AID (Fall 2004, est.) 525 applied for aid; of those 78% were deemed to have need. 100% of freshmen with need received aid; of those 27% had need fully met. *Average percent of need met:* 82% (excluding resources awarded to replace EFC). *Average financial aid package:* $17,171 (excluding resources awarded to replace EFC). 24% of all full-time freshmen had no need and received non-need-based gift aid.

UNDERGRADUATE FINANCIAL AID (Fall 2004, est.) 1,992 applied for aid; of those 87% were deemed to have need. 85% of undergraduates with need received aid; of those 19% had need fully met. *Average percent of need met:* 81% (excluding resources awarded to replace EFC). *Average financial aid*

package: $17,306 (excluding resources awarded to replace EFC). 22% of all full-time undergraduates had no need and received non-need-based gift aid.

GIFT AID (NEED-BASED) *Total amount:* $16,642,026 (6% federal, 5% state, 85% institutional, 4% external sources). *Receiving aid:* Freshmen: 64% (391); All full-time undergraduates: 67% (1,477). *Average award:* Freshmen: $13,373; Undergraduates: $12,518. *Scholarships, grants, and awards:* Federal Pell, FSEOG, state, private, college/university gift aid from institutional funds.

GIFT AID (NON-NEED-BASED) *Total amount:* $2,614,156 (3% federal, 85% institutional, 12% external sources). *Receiving aid:* Freshmen: 8% (47); Undergraduates: 6% (134). *Average Award:* Freshmen: $10,812; *Undergraduates:* $16,406. *Scholarships, grants, and awards by category: Academic Interests/Achievement:* 1,339 awards ($6,775,501 total): general academic interests/achievements. *Special Characteristics:* 165 awards ($1,898,907 total): children of faculty/staff, members of minority groups, relatives of clergy, siblings of current students. *Tuition waivers:* Full or partial for employees or children of employees. *ROTC:* Army.

LOANS *Student loans:* $10,945,989 (69% need-based, 31% non-need-based). 68% of past graduating class borrowed through all loan programs. *Average indebtedness per student:* $16,615. *Average need-based loan:* Freshmen: $4366; Undergraduates: $5164. *Parent loans:* $7,140,582 (27% need-based, 73% non-need-based). *Programs:* Federal Direct (Subsidized and Unsubsidized Stafford, PLUS), Perkins, state.

WORK-STUDY *Federal work-study:* Total amount: $1,672,348; 910 jobs averaging $1728. *State or other work-study/employment:* Total amount: $243,800 (1% need-based, 99% non-need-based). 218 part-time jobs averaging $1118.

ATHLETIC AWARDS *Total amount:* $1,310,101 (58% need-based, 42% non-need-based).

APPLYING FOR FINANCIAL AID *Required financial aid forms:* FAFSA, CSS Financial Aid PROFILE, noncustodial (divorced/separated) parent's statement, business/farm supplement. *Financial aid deadline (priority):* 2/1. *Notification date:* 4/1. Students must reply by 5/1.

CONTACT Rhonda Nickley, Staff Assistant, Stonehill College, 320 Washington Street, Easton, MA 02357, 508-565-1088. *Fax:* 508-565-1426. *E-mail:* finaid@stonehill.edu.

STONY BROOK UNIVERSITY, STATE UNIVERSITY OF NEW YORK
Stony Brook, NY

Tuition & fees (NY res): $5389	Average undergraduate aid package: $8555

ABOUT THE INSTITUTION State-supported, coed. Awards: bachelor's, master's, doctoral, and first professional degrees and post-bachelor's, post-master's, and first professional certificates. 54 undergraduate majors. Total enrollment: 21,685. Undergraduates: 13,858. Freshmen: 2,139. Federal methodology is used as a basis for awarding need-based institutional aid.

UNDERGRADUATE EXPENSES for 2004–05 *Application fee:* $40. *Tuition, state resident:* full-time $4350; part-time $181 per credit. *Tuition, nonresident:* full-time $10,610; part-time $442 per credit. *Required fees:* full-time $1039; $50.20 per credit. *College room and board:* $7730. Room and board charges vary according to board plan and housing facility. *Payment plan:* Installment.

FRESHMAN FINANCIAL AID (Fall 2003) 1721 applied for aid; of those 73% were deemed to have need. 98% of freshmen with need received aid; of those 15% had need fully met. *Average percent of need met:* 70% (excluding resources awarded to replace EFC). *Average financial aid package:* $8394 (excluding resources awarded to replace EFC). 21% of all full-time freshmen had no need and received non-need-based gift aid.

UNDERGRADUATE FINANCIAL AID (Fall 2003) 9,044 applied for aid; of those 81% were deemed to have need. 98% of undergraduates with need received aid; of those 16% had need fully met. *Average percent of need met:* 71% (excluding resources awarded to replace EFC). *Average financial aid package:* $8555 (excluding resources awarded to replace EFC). 8% of all full-time undergraduates had no need and received non-need-based gift aid.

GIFT AID (NEED-BASED) *Total amount:* $34,582,543 (48% federal, 52% state). *Receiving aid:* Freshmen: 53% (1,144); All full-time undergraduates: 53% (6,593). *Average award:* Freshmen: $5658; Undergraduates: $5123. *Scholarships, grants, and awards:* Federal Pell, FSEOG, state, private, college/university gift aid from institutional funds.

GIFT AID (NON-NEED-BASED) *Total amount:* $5,051,314 (8% federal, 14% state, 57% institutional, 21% external sources). *Receiving aid:* Freshmen: 14% (302); Undergraduates: 7% (855). *Average Award:* Freshmen: $2638; *Undergraduates:* $2746. *Scholarships, grants, and awards by category: Academic Interests/*

Achievement: 1,046 awards ($2,850,841 total): area/ethnic studies, biological sciences, business, computer science, engineering/technologies, general academic interests/achievements, health fields, physical sciences, social sciences. *Creative Arts/Performance:* 6 awards ($10,120 total): music, theater/drama. *Special Achievements/Activities:* general special achievements/activities. *ROTC:* Army cooperative, Air Force cooperative.

LOANS *Student loans:* $39,678,990 (89% need-based, 11% non-need-based). 58% of past graduating class borrowed through all loan programs. *Average indebtedness per student:* $13,912. *Average need-based loan:* Freshmen: $2762; Undergraduates: $3970. *Parent loans:* $4,205,764 (100% non-need-based). *Programs:* FFEL (Subsidized and Unsubsidized Stafford, PLUS), Perkins.

WORK-STUDY *Federal work-study:* Total amount: $1,197,755; 607 jobs averaging $1972. *State or other work-study/employment:* Total amount: $3,290,867 (100% non-need-based). 1,590 part-time jobs averaging $2070.

ATHLETIC AWARDS *Total amount:* $2,196,004 (12% need-based, 88% non-need-based).

APPLYING FOR FINANCIAL AID *Required financial aid form:* FAFSA. *Financial aid deadline (priority):* 3/1. *Notification date:* Continuous beginning 3/7. Students must reply within 2 weeks of notification.

CONTACT Jacqueline Pascariello, Director of Financial Aid and Student Employment, Stony Brook University, State University of New York, 180 Administration Building, Stony Brook, NY 11794-0851, 631-632-6840 or toll-free 800-872-7869 (out-of-state). *Fax:* 631-632-9525.

STRATFORD UNIVERSITY
Falls Church, VA

CONTACT Financial Aid Office, Stratford University, 7777 Leesburg Pike, Suite 100 South, Falls Church, VA 22043, 703-821-8570 or toll-free 800-444-0804.

STRAYER UNIVERSITY
Washington, DC

ABOUT THE INSTITUTION Proprietary, coed. Awards: associate, bachelor's, and master's degrees and post-bachelor's certificates. 11 undergraduate majors. Total enrollment: 20,138. Undergraduates: 15,972.

GIFT AID (NEED-BASED) *Scholarships, grants, and awards:* Federal Pell, FSEOG, state.

GIFT AID (NON-NEED-BASED) *Scholarships, grants, and awards by category: Academic Interests/Achievement:* business, computer science, general academic interests/achievements. *Special Achievements/Activities:* general special achievements/activities.

LOANS *Programs:* Federal Direct (Subsidized and Unsubsidized Stafford, PLUS), FFEL (Subsidized and Unsubsidized Stafford, PLUS), Perkins, college/university, credit-based loans (for tuition and fees).

WORK-STUDY Federal work-study jobs available.

APPLYING FOR FINANCIAL AID *Required financial aid form:* FAFSA.

CONTACT Ms. Marjorie Arrington, Director of Financial Aid, Strayer University, 1133 15th Street, NW, Washington, DC 20005-2603, 703-558-7020 or toll-free 888-4-STRAYER. *Fax:* 703-741-3710. *E-mail:* ma@strayer.edu.

SUFFOLK UNIVERSITY
Boston, MA

Tuition & fees: $19,870	Average undergraduate aid package: $11,956

ABOUT THE INSTITUTION Independent, coed. Awards: associate, bachelor's, master's, doctoral, and first professional degrees and post-bachelor's, post-master's, and first professional certificates (doctoral degree in law). 68 undergraduate majors. Total enrollment: 8,188. Undergraduates: 4,477. Freshmen: 1,027. Both federal and institutional methodology are used as a basis for awarding need-based institutional aid.

UNDERGRADUATE EXPENSES for 2004–05 *Application fee:* $50. *Comprehensive fee:* $31,281 includes full-time tuition ($19,790), mandatory fees ($80), and room and board ($11,411). Room and board charges vary according to board plan and housing facility. *Part-time tuition:* $521 per credit. *Part-time fees:* $10 per term. *Payment plans:* Installment, deferred payment.

FRESHMAN FINANCIAL AID (Fall 2004, est.) 905 applied for aid; of those 66% were deemed to have need. 99% of freshmen with need received aid; of those 8% had need fully met. *Average percent of need met:* 57% (excluding resources

awarded to replace EFC). *Average financial aid package:* $10,960 (excluding resources awarded to replace EFC). 8% of all full-time freshmen had no need and received non-need-based gift aid.

UNDERGRADUATE FINANCIAL AID (Fall 2004, est.) 2,917 applied for aid; of those 71% were deemed to have need. 99% of undergraduates with need received aid; of those 12% had need fully met. *Average percent of need met:* 62% (excluding resources awarded to replace EFC). *Average financial aid package:* $11,956 (excluding resources awarded to replace EFC). 8% of all full-time undergraduates had no need and received non-need-based gift aid.

GIFT AID (NEED-BASED) *Total amount:* $10,679,881 (27% federal, 10% state, 59% institutional, 4% external sources). *Receiving aid:* Freshmen: 51% (521); All full-time undergraduates: 47% (1,726). *Average award:* Freshmen: $6175; Undergraduates: $6289. *Scholarships, grants, and awards:* Federal Pell, FSEOG, state, private, college/university gift aid from institutional funds.

GIFT AID (NON-NEED-BASED) *Total amount:* $3,688,182 (2% state, 96% institutional, 2% external sources). *Receiving aid:* Freshmen: 15% (151); Undergraduates: 19% (713). *Average Award:* Freshmen: $4931; Undergraduates: $5300. *Scholarships, grants, and awards by category: Academic Interests/Achievement:* 975 awards ($2,751,229 total): general academic interests/achievements. *Special Achievements/Activities:* 5 awards ($13,000 total): community service. *Special Characteristics:* 273 awards ($460,574 total): children and siblings of alumni, children of faculty/staff, siblings of current students. *Tuition waivers:* Full or partial for employees or children of employees, senior citizens. *ROTC:* Army cooperative.

LOANS *Student loans:* $19,925,799 (54% need-based, 46% non-need-based). 61% of past graduating class borrowed through all loan programs. *Average indebtedness per student:* $19,376. *Average need-based loan:* Freshmen: $3615; Undergraduates: $4485. *Parent loans:* $10,898,301 (100% non-need-based). *Programs:* Federal Direct (Subsidized and Unsubsidized Stafford, PLUS), Perkins, state, college/university.

WORK-STUDY *Federal work-study:* Total amount: $2,214,570; 834 jobs averaging $2047. *State or other work-study/employment:* Total amount: $519,282 (100% non-need-based). 211 part-time jobs averaging $1704.

APPLYING FOR FINANCIAL AID *Required financial aid forms:* FAFSA, institution's own form. *Financial aid deadline (priority):* 3/1. *Notification date:* Continuous. Students must reply within 2 weeks of notification.

CONTACT Ms. Christine A. Perry, Director of Financial Aid, Suffolk University, 8 Ashburton Place, Boston, MA 02108, 617-573-8470 or toll-free 800-6-SUFFOLK. *Fax:* 617-720-3579. *E-mail:* finaid@suffolk.edu.

SULLIVAN UNIVERSITY
Louisville, KY

ABOUT THE INSTITUTION Proprietary, coed. Awards: associate, bachelor's, and master's degrees. 12 undergraduate majors. Total enrollment: 4,928. Undergraduates: 4,639.

GIFT AID (NEED-BASED) *Scholarships, grants, and awards:* Federal Pell, FSEOG, state, private, college/university gift aid from institutional funds.

GIFT AID (NON-NEED-BASED) *Scholarships, grants, and awards by category: Creative Arts/Performance:* general creative arts/performance.

LOANS *Programs:* Federal Direct (Subsidized and Unsubsidized Stafford, PLUS), FFEL (Subsidized and Unsubsidized Stafford, PLUS), Perkins, college/university, alternative loans.

APPLYING FOR FINANCIAL AID *Required financial aid forms:* FAFSA, institution's own form.

CONTACT Charlene Geiser, Financial Planning Office, Sullivan University, 3101 Bardstown Road, Louisville, KY 40205, 502-456-6504 Ext. 311 or toll-free 800-844-1354. *Fax:* 502-456-0040. *E-mail:* cgeiser@sullivan.edu.

SUL ROSS STATE UNIVERSITY
Alpine, TX

CONTACT Ms. Rena Gallego, Director of Financial Assistance and Recruiting, Sul Ross State University, PO Box C-113, Alpine, TX 79832, 915-837-8059 or toll-free 888-722-7778.

SUSQUEHANNA UNIVERSITY
Selinsgrove, PA

Tuition & fees: $24,810	Average undergraduate aid package: $17,743

ABOUT THE INSTITUTION Independent religious, coed. Awards: bachelor's degrees (also offers evening associate degree program limited to local adult students). 53 undergraduate majors. Total enrollment: 2,071. Undergraduates: 2,071. Freshmen: 535. Both federal and institutional methodology are used as a basis for awarding need-based institutional aid.

UNDERGRADUATE EXPENSES for 2004–05 *Application fee:* $35. *Comprehensive fee:* $31,650 includes full-time tuition ($24,500), mandatory fees ($310), and room and board ($6840). *College room only:* $3620. *Part-time tuition:* $780 per semester hour. *Payment plans:* Tuition prepayment, installment.

FRESHMAN FINANCIAL AID (Fall 2004, est.) 426 applied for aid; of those 79% were deemed to have need. 99% of freshmen with need received aid; of those 26% had need fully met. *Average percent of need met:* 82% (excluding resources awarded to replace EFC). *Average financial aid package:* $17,336 (excluding resources awarded to replace EFC). 28% of all full-time freshmen had no need and received non-need-based gift aid.

UNDERGRADUATE FINANCIAL AID (Fall 2004, est.) 1,429 applied for aid; of those 86% were deemed to have need. 100% of undergraduates with need received aid; of those 24% had need fully met. *Average percent of need met:* 83% (excluding resources awarded to replace EFC). *Average financial aid package:* $17,743 (excluding resources awarded to replace EFC). 28% of all full-time undergraduates had no need and received non-need-based gift aid.

GIFT AID (NEED-BASED) *Total amount:* $16,869,844 (6% federal, 9% state, 81% institutional, 4% external sources). *Receiving aid:* Freshmen: 63% (334); All full-time undergraduates: 63% (1,220). *Average award:* Freshmen: $14,380; Undergraduates: $13,961. *Scholarships, grants, and awards:* Federal Pell, FSEOG, state, private, college/university gift aid from institutional funds.

GIFT AID (NON-NEED-BASED) *Total amount:* $5,649,904 (1% state, 94% institutional, 5% external sources). *Receiving aid:* Freshmen: 12% (65); Undergraduates: 10% (193). *Average Award:* Freshmen: $10,849; Undergraduates: $11,878. *Scholarships, grants, and awards by category: Academic Interests/Achievement:* 694 awards ($7,348,120 total): biological sciences, business, general academic interests/achievements, mathematics, physical sciences, premedicine. *Creative Arts/Performance:* 94 awards ($236,750 total): creative writing, music. *Special Achievements/Activities:* 644 awards ($4,193,050 total): general special achievements/activities. *Special Characteristics:* 131 awards ($1,535,500 total): children of educators, children of faculty/staff, members of minority groups, relatives of clergy. *Tuition waivers:* Full or partial for employees or children of employees. *ROTC:* Army cooperative.

LOANS *Student loans:* $7,308,511 (65% need-based, 35% non-need-based). 90% of past graduating class borrowed through all loan programs. *Average indebtedness per student:* $18,119. *Average need-based loan:* Freshmen: $3140; Undergraduates: $3737. *Parent loans:* $4,543,280 (29% need-based, 71% non-need-based). *Programs:* FFEL (Subsidized and Unsubsidized Stafford, PLUS), Perkins, college/university.

WORK-STUDY *Federal work-study:* Total amount: $1,424,825; 905 jobs averaging $1574. *State or other work-study/employment:* Total amount: $244,195 (46% need-based, 54% non-need-based). 64 part-time jobs averaging $3816.

APPLYING FOR FINANCIAL AID *Required financial aid forms:* FAFSA, CSS Financial Aid PROFILE, business/farm supplement, income tax form(s). *Financial aid deadline (priority):* 3/1. *Notification date:* Continuous. Students must reply by 5/1.

CONTACT Helen S. Nunn, Director of Financial Aid, Susquehanna University, 514 University Avenue, Selinsgrove, PA 17870, 570-372-4450 or toll-free 800-326-9672. *Fax:* 570-372-2722. *E-mail:* nunn@susqu.edu.

SWARTHMORE COLLEGE
Swarthmore, PA

Tuition & fees: $30,094	Average undergraduate aid package: $27,421

ABOUT THE INSTITUTION Independent, coed. Awards: bachelor's degrees. 42 undergraduate majors. Total enrollment: 1,474. Undergraduates: 1,474. Freshmen: 366. Institutional methodology is used as a basis for awarding need-based institutional aid.

UNDERGRADUATE EXPENSES for 2004–05 *Application fee:* $60. *Comprehensive fee:* $39,408 includes full-time tuition ($29,782), mandatory fees ($312), and room and board ($9314). *College room only:* $4536. Room and board charges vary according to board plan. *Payment plan:* Installment.

FRESHMAN FINANCIAL AID (Fall 2004, est.) 240 applied for aid; of those 81% were deemed to have need. 100% of freshmen with need received aid; of those 100% had need fully met. *Average percent of need met:* 100% (excluding

resources awarded to replace EFC). *Average financial aid package:* $27,396 (excluding resources awarded to replace EFC). 1% of all full-time freshmen had no need and received non-need-based gift aid.

UNDERGRADUATE FINANCIAL AID (Fall 2004, est.) 807 applied for aid; of those 86% were deemed to have need. 100% of undergraduates with need received aid; of those 100% had need fully met. *Average percent of need met:* 100% (excluding resources awarded to replace EFC). *Average financial aid package:* $27,421 (excluding resources awarded to replace EFC). 1% of all full-time undergraduates had no need and received non-need-based gift aid.

GIFT AID (NEED-BASED) *Total amount:* $16,506,555 (5% federal, 1% state, 91% institutional, 3% external sources). *Receiving aid:* Freshmen: 53% (195); All full-time undergraduates: 48% (697). *Average award:* Freshmen: $24,421; Undergraduates: $23,604. *Scholarships, grants, and awards:* Federal Pell, FSEOG, state, private, college/university gift aid from institutional funds.

GIFT AID (NON-NEED-BASED) *Total amount:* $624,149 (1% state, 52% institutional, 47% external sources). *Average Award:* Freshmen: $29,782; *Undergraduates:* $29,782. *Scholarships, grants, and awards by category: Academic Interests/Achievement:* 11 awards ($327,602 total): general academic interests/achievements. *Tuition waivers:* Full or partial for employees or children of employees. *ROTC:* Army cooperative, Air Force cooperative.

LOANS *Student loans:* $2,056,931 (76% need-based, 24% non-need-based). 35% of past graduating class borrowed through all loan programs. *Average indebtedness per student:* $13,134. *Average need-based loan:* Freshmen: $2047; Undergraduates: $3061. *Parent loans:* $2,201,388 (100% non-need-based). *Programs:* FFEL (Subsidized and Unsubsidized Stafford, PLUS), Perkins, state, college/university.

WORK-STUDY *Federal work-study:* Total amount: $725,678; 625 jobs averaging $1512. *State or other work-study/employment:* Total amount: $605,587 (63% need-based, 37% non-need-based). Part-time jobs available.

APPLYING FOR FINANCIAL AID *Required financial aid forms:* FAFSA, institution's own form, CSS Financial Aid PROFILE, state aid form, noncustodial (divorced/separated) parent's statement, business/farm supplement, federal tax return, W2 statement, year-end paycheck stub. *Financial aid deadline (priority):* 2/15. *Notification date:* 4/1. Students must reply by 5/1.

CONTACT Laura Talbot, Director of Financial Aid, Swarthmore College, 500 College Avenue, Swarthmore, PA 19081-1397, 610-328-8358 or toll-free 800-667-3110. *Fax:* 610-328-8673. *E-mail:* finaid@swarthmore.edu.

SWEDISH INSTITUTE, COLLEGE OF HEALTH SCIENCES
New York, NY

CONTACT Financial Aid Office, Swedish Institute, College of Health Sciences, 226 West 26th Street, New York, NY 10001-6700, 212-924-5900.

SWEET BRIAR COLLEGE
Sweet Briar, VA

Tuition & fees: $22,430	Average undergraduate aid package: $14,778

ABOUT THE INSTITUTION Independent, women only. Awards: bachelor's and master's degrees. 36 undergraduate majors. Total enrollment: 738. Undergraduates: 728. Freshmen: 170. Federal methodology is used as a basis for awarding need-based institutional aid.

UNDERGRADUATE EXPENSES for 2005–06 *Application fee:* $25. *Comprehensive fee:* $31,460 includes full-time tuition ($22,230), mandatory fees ($200), and room and board ($9030). *College room only:* $3630. Full-time tuition and fees vary according to program. *Part-time tuition:* $740 per credit hour. Part-time tuition and fees vary according to program. *Payment plan:* Installment.

FRESHMAN FINANCIAL AID (Fall 2004, est.) 123 applied for aid; of those 100% were deemed to have need. 98% of freshmen with need received aid; of those 79% had need fully met. *Average percent of need met:* 30% (excluding resources awarded to replace EFC). *Average financial aid package:* $14,279 (excluding resources awarded to replace EFC). 38% of all full-time freshmen had no need and received non-need-based gift aid.

UNDERGRADUATE FINANCIAL AID (Fall 2004, est.) 346 applied for aid; of those 100% were deemed to have need. 99% of undergraduates with need received aid; of those 93% had need fully met. *Average percent of need met:* 33% (excluding resources awarded to replace EFC). *Average financial aid package:* $14,778 (excluding resources awarded to replace EFC). 42% of all full-time undergraduates had no need and received non-need-based gift aid.

GIFT AID (NEED-BASED) *Total amount:* $3,901,813 (8% federal, 15% state, 74% institutional, 3% external sources). *Receiving aid:* Freshmen: 54% (91); All full-time undergraduates: 51% (268). *Average award:* Freshmen: $13,154; Undergraduates: $12,930. *Scholarships, grants, and awards:* Federal Pell, FSEOG, state, private, college/university gift aid from institutional funds.

GIFT AID (NON-NEED-BASED) *Total amount:* $2,785,303 (8% state, 91% institutional, 1% external sources). *Receiving aid:* Freshmen: 38% (64); Undergraduates: 42% (221). *Average Award:* Freshmen: $10,684; *Undergraduates:* $10,627. *Scholarships, grants, and awards by category: Academic Interests/Achievement:* 428 awards ($3,614,440 total): general academic interests/achievements, premedicine. *Creative Arts/Performance:* 1 award ($860 total): art/fine arts, general creative arts/performance, music. *Special Characteristics:* 144 awards ($1,124,452 total): adult students, general special characteristics, international students, local/state students. *Tuition waivers:* Full or partial for employees or children of employees, adult students, senior citizens.

LOANS *Student loans:* $1,003,319 (91% need-based, 9% non-need-based). 63% of past graduating class borrowed through all loan programs. *Average indebtedness per student:* $17,101. *Average need-based loan:* Freshmen: $3675; Undergraduates: $4828. *Parent loans:* $1,449,695 (71% need-based, 29% non-need-based). *Programs:* Federal Direct (Subsidized and Unsubsidized Stafford, PLUS), Perkins, college/university.

WORK-STUDY *Federal work-study:* Total amount: $37,706; 76 jobs averaging $987. *State or other work-study/employment:* Total amount: $36,776 (99% need-based, 1% non-need-based). 75 part-time jobs averaging $906.

APPLYING FOR FINANCIAL AID *Required financial aid forms:* FAFSA, noncustodial (divorced/separated) parent's statement, business/farm supplement. *Financial aid deadline (priority):* 3/1. *Notification date:* Continuous beginning 3/1. Students must reply by 5/1 or within 2 weeks of notification.

CONTACT Bobbi Carpenter, Director of Financial Aid, Sweet Briar College, Box AS, Sweet Briar, VA 24595, 800-381-6156 or toll-free 800-381-6142. *Fax:* 434-381-6450. *E-mail:* bcarpenter@sbc.edu.

SYRACUSE UNIVERSITY
Syracuse, NY

Tuition & fees: $26,734	Average undergraduate aid package: $18,822

ABOUT THE INSTITUTION Independent, coed. Awards: bachelor's, master's, doctoral, and first professional degrees and post-master's certificates. 141 undergraduate majors. Total enrollment: 16,753. Undergraduates: 10,750. Freshmen: 2,671. Both federal and institutional methodology are used as a basis for awarding need-based institutional aid.

UNDERGRADUATE EXPENSES for 2004–05 *Application fee:* $60. *Comprehensive fee:* $36,704 includes full-time tuition ($25,720), mandatory fees ($1014), and room and board ($9970). *College room only:* $5400. Room and board charges vary according to board plan and housing facility. *Part-time tuition:* $1120 per credit hour. *Payment plan:* Installment.

FRESHMAN FINANCIAL AID (Fall 2004, est.) 1987 applied for aid; of those 82% were deemed to have need. 100% of freshmen with need received aid; of those 65% had need fully met. *Average percent of need met:* 82% (excluding resources awarded to replace EFC). *Average financial aid package:* $19,900 (excluding resources awarded to replace EFC). 13% of all full-time freshmen had no need and received non-need-based gift aid.

UNDERGRADUATE FINANCIAL AID (Fall 2004, est.) 7,157 applied for aid; of those 88% were deemed to have need. 100% of undergraduates with need received aid; of those 65% had need fully met. *Average percent of need met:* 80% (excluding resources awarded to replace EFC). *Average financial aid package:* $18,822 (excluding resources awarded to replace EFC). 16% of all full-time undergraduates had no need and received non-need-based gift aid.

GIFT AID (NEED-BASED) *Total amount:* $92,594,340 (9% federal, 8% state, 80% institutional, 3% external sources). *Receiving aid:* Freshmen: 54% (1,444); All full-time undergraduates: 52% (5,588). *Average award:* Freshmen: $14,588; Undergraduates: $13,661. *Scholarships, grants, and awards:* Federal Pell, FSEOG, state, college/university gift aid from institutional funds.

GIFT AID (NON-NEED-BASED) *Total amount:* $14,415,230 (95% institutional, 5% external sources). *Receiving aid:* Freshmen: 3% (88); Undergraduates: 2% (248). *Average Award:* Freshmen: $9300; *Undergraduates:* $8140. *Scholarships, grants, and awards by category: Academic Interests/Achievement:* general academic interests/achievements. *Creative Arts/Performance:* art/fine arts, music. *Tuition waivers:* Full or partial for employees or children of employees. *ROTC:* Army, Air Force.

LOANS *Student loans:* $45,074,842 (91% need-based, 9% non-need-based). 70% of past graduating class borrowed through all loan programs. *Average*

indebtedness per student: $19,200. *Average need-based loan:* Freshmen: $4100; Undergraduates: $5300. *Parent loans:* $25,144,215 (75% need-based, 25% non-need-based). *Programs:* FFEL (Subsidized and Unsubsidized Stafford, PLUS), Perkins.

WORK-STUDY *Federal work-study:* Total amount: $3,293,000; jobs available (averaging $1500). *State or other work-study/employment:* Part-time jobs available.

ATHLETIC AWARDS *Total amount:* $9,918,027 (47% need-based, 53% non-need-based).

APPLYING FOR FINANCIAL AID *Required financial aid forms:* FAFSA, CSS Financial Aid PROFILE, noncustodial (divorced/separated) parent's statement, business/farm supplement. *Financial aid deadline (priority):* 2/1. *Notification date:* 4/1. Students must reply by 5/1.

CONTACT Mr. Christopher Walsh, Executive Director of Financial Aid, Syracuse University, 200 Archbold Gymnasium, Syracuse, NY 13244-1140, 315-443-1513. *E-mail:* finmail@syr.edu.

TABOR COLLEGE
Hillsboro, KS

| Tuition & fees: $15,060 | Average undergraduate aid package: $14,517 |

ABOUT THE INSTITUTION Independent Mennonite Brethren, coed. Awards: associate, bachelor's, and master's degrees. 53 undergraduate majors. Total enrollment: 606. Undergraduates: 586. Freshmen: 139. Federal methodology is used as a basis for awarding need-based institutional aid.

UNDERGRADUATE EXPENSES for 2004–05 *Application fee:* $20. *Comprehensive fee:* $20,470 includes full-time tuition ($14,700), mandatory fees ($360), and room and board ($5410). *College room only:* $2100. Full-time tuition and fees vary according to course load. Room and board charges vary according to board plan, housing facility, and location. *Part-time tuition:* $583 per credit hour. Part-time tuition and fees vary according to course load. *Payment plan:* Installment.

FRESHMAN FINANCIAL AID (Fall 2003) 86 applied for aid; of those 84% were deemed to have need. 100% of freshmen with need received aid; of those 15% had need fully met. *Average percent of need met:* 79% (excluding resources awarded to replace EFC). *Average financial aid package:* $14,608 (excluding resources awarded to replace EFC). 17% of all full-time freshmen had no need and received non-need-based gift aid.

UNDERGRADUATE FINANCIAL AID (Fall 2003) 442 applied for aid; of those 82% were deemed to have need. 100% of undergraduates with need received aid; of those 31% had need fully met. *Average percent of need met:* 87% (excluding resources awarded to replace EFC). *Average financial aid package:* $14,517 (excluding resources awarded to replace EFC). 16% of all full-time undergraduates had no need and received non-need-based gift aid.

GIFT AID (NEED-BASED) *Total amount:* $948,094 (62% federal, 38% state). *Receiving aid:* Freshmen: 79% (69); All full-time undergraduates: 69% (314). *Average award:* Freshmen: $3981; Undergraduates: $3570. *Scholarships, grants, and awards:* Federal Pell, FSEOG, state, private, college/university gift aid from institutional funds.

GIFT AID (NON-NEED-BASED) *Total amount:* $2,160,076 (88% institutional, 12% external sources). *Receiving aid:* Freshmen: 79% (69); Undergraduates: 72% (327). *Average Award:* Freshmen: $4939; Undergraduates: $4620. *Scholarships, grants, and awards by category: Academic Interests/Achievement:* 433 awards ($1,912,996 total): biological sciences, business, communication, computer science, education, English, general academic interests/achievements, humanities, mathematics, premedicine, religion/biblical studies, social sciences. *Creative Arts/Performance:* 121 awards ($132,485 total): music, performing arts, theater/drama. *Special Achievements/Activities:* 486 awards ($430,329 total): cheerleading/drum major, general special achievements/activities, religious involvement. *Special Characteristics:* children and siblings of alumni, children of faculty/staff, general special characteristics, international students, local/state students, out-of-state students, religious affiliation. *Tuition waivers:* Full or partial for employees or children of employees.

LOANS *Student loans:* $2,574,582 (100% need-based). 82% of past graduating class borrowed through all loan programs. *Average indebtedness per student:* $20,077. *Average need-based loan:* Freshmen: $4650; Undergraduates: $6171. *Parent loans:* $250,899 (100% need-based). *Programs:* FFEL (Subsidized and Unsubsidized Stafford, PLUS), Perkins.

WORK-STUDY *Federal work-study:* Total amount: $109,367; 128 jobs averaging $675. *State or other work-study/employment:* Total amount: $5400 (100% need-based). 275 part-time jobs averaging $527.

ATHLETIC AWARDS *Total amount:* $457,936 (100% non-need-based).

APPLYING FOR FINANCIAL AID *Required financial aid forms:* FAFSA, state aid form, admissions application. *Financial aid deadline:* 8/15 (priority: 3/1). *Notification date:* Continuous beginning 3/15. Students must reply within 4 weeks of notification.

CONTACT Mr. Bruce Jost, Director of Student Financial Assistance, Tabor College, 400 South Jefferson, Hillsboro, KS 67063, 620-947-3121 Ext. 1726 or toll-free 800-822-6799. *Fax:* 620-947-6276. *E-mail:* brucej@tabor.edu.

TALLADEGA COLLEGE
Talladega, AL

| Tuition & fees: $7128 | Average undergraduate aid package: $5000 |

ABOUT THE INSTITUTION Independent, coed. Awards: bachelor's degrees. 33 undergraduate majors. Total enrollment: 362. Undergraduates: 362. Freshmen: 109. Federal methodology is used as a basis for awarding need-based institutional aid.

UNDERGRADUATE EXPENSES for 2004–05 *Application fee:* $25. *One-time required fee:* $150. *Comprehensive fee:* $11,548 includes full-time tuition ($6720), mandatory fees ($408), and room and board ($4420). *College room only:* $1600. *Part-time tuition:* $280 per credit hour. *Part-time fees:* $204 per term. Part-time tuition and fees vary according to course load. *Payment plan:* Installment.

FRESHMAN FINANCIAL AID (Fall 2003) 98 applied for aid; of those 77% were deemed to have need. 100% of freshmen with need received aid; of those 100% had need fully met. *Average percent of need met:* 90% (excluding resources awarded to replace EFC). *Average financial aid package:* $4586 (excluding resources awarded to replace EFC). 27% of all full-time freshmen had no need and received non-need-based gift aid.

UNDERGRADUATE FINANCIAL AID (Fall 2003) 407 applied for aid; of those 92% were deemed to have need. 100% of undergraduates with need received aid; of those 27% had need fully met. *Average percent of need met:* 90% (excluding resources awarded to replace EFC). *Average financial aid package:* $5000 (excluding resources awarded to replace EFC).

GIFT AID (NEED-BASED) *Total amount:* $12,517,325 (100% federal). *Receiving aid:* Freshmen: 66% (75); All full-time undergraduates: 92% (375). *Average award:* Freshmen: $2025; Undergraduates: $3025. *Scholarships, grants, and awards:* Federal Pell, FSEOG, state, private, college/university gift aid from institutional funds, United Negro College Fund.

GIFT AID (NON-NEED-BASED) *Total amount:* $3,461,670 (8% institutional, 92% external sources). *Receiving aid:* Freshmen: 66% (75); Undergraduates: 92% (375). *Average Award:* Freshmen: $1500; Undergraduates: $5774. *Scholarships, grants, and awards by category: Academic Interests/Achievement:* general academic interests/achievements. *Tuition waivers:* Full or partial for employees or children of employees. *ROTC:* Army cooperative.

LOANS *Student loans:* $1,289,333 (100% need-based). *Average indebtedness per student:* $12,790. *Average need-based loan:* Freshmen: $2547; Undergraduates: $5335. *Parent loans:* $242,561 (100% need-based). *Programs:* Federal Direct (Subsidized and Unsubsidized Stafford, PLUS), FFEL (Subsidized and Unsubsidized Stafford, PLUS), Perkins, college/university.

WORK-STUDY *Federal work-study:* Total amount: $162,608; 141 jobs averaging $691.

ATHLETIC AWARDS *Total amount:* $74,991 (100% need-based).

APPLYING FOR FINANCIAL AID *Required financial aid forms:* FAFSA, institution's own form. *Financial aid deadline:* 6/30 (priority: 4/15). *Notification date:* Continuous beginning 4/15. Students must reply within 2 weeks of notification.

CONTACT K. Michael Francois, Director of Financial Aid, Talladega College, 627 West Battle Street, Talladega, AL 35160, 256-761-6341 or toll-free 800-762-2468 (in-state), 800-633-2440 (out-of-state). *Fax:* 256-761-6462.

TALMUDICAL ACADEMY OF NEW JERSEY
Adelphia, NJ

CONTACT Office of Financial Aid, Talmudical Academy of New Jersey, Route 524, Adelphia, NJ 07710, 732-431-1600.

TALMUDICAL INSTITUTE OF UPSTATE NEW YORK
Rochester, NY

ABOUT THE INSTITUTION Independent Jewish, men only. Awards: also offers some graduate courses. 2 undergraduate majors. Total enrollment: 30. Undergraduates: 22. Freshmen: 5.
GIFT AID (NEED-BASED) *Scholarships, grants, and awards:* Federal Pell, FSEOG.
GIFT AID (NON-NEED-BASED) *Scholarships, grants, and awards by category:* Academic Interests/Achievement: religion/biblical studies.
WORK-STUDY *Federal work-study:* 5 jobs available.
APPLYING FOR FINANCIAL AID *Required financial aid form:* FAFSA.
CONTACT Mrs. Ella Berenstein, Financial Aid Administrator, Talmudical Institute of Upstate New York, 769 Park Avenue, Rochester, NY 14607-3046, 716-473-2810.

TALMUDICAL SEMINARY OHOLEI TORAH
Brooklyn, NY

CONTACT Financial Aid Administrator, Talmudical Seminary Oholei Torah, 667 Eastern Parkway, Brooklyn, NY 11213-3310, 718-774-5050.

TALMUDICAL YESHIVA OF PHILADELPHIA
Philadelphia, PA

CONTACT Rabbi Uri Mandelbaum, Director of Student Financial Aid/Registrar, Talmudical Yeshiva of Philadelphia, 6063 Drexel Road, Philadelphia, PA 19131-1296, 215-473-1212. *E-mail:* typp@juno.com.

TALMUDIC COLLEGE OF FLORIDA
Miami Beach, FL

CONTACT Rabbi Ira Hill, Director of Financial Aid, Talmudic College of Florida, 1910 Alton Road, Miami Beach, FL 33139, 305-534-7050 or toll-free 888-825-6834. *Fax:* 305-534-8444.

TARLETON STATE UNIVERSITY
Stephenville, TX

Tuition & fees (TX res): $3835	Average undergraduate aid package: $8162

ABOUT THE INSTITUTION State-supported, coed. Awards: associate, bachelor's, master's, and doctoral degrees. 68 undergraduate majors. Total enrollment: 8,985. Undergraduates: 7,405. Freshmen: 1,162. Federal methodology is used as a basis for awarding need-based institutional aid.
UNDERGRADUATE EXPENSES for 2005–06 *Application fee:* $25. *Tuition, state resident:* full-time $3000; part-time $100 per credit hour. *Tuition, nonresident:* full-time $10,740; part-time $358 per credit hour. *Required fees:* full-time $835; $30.50 per hour or $21. Full-time tuition and fees vary according to course load. Part-time tuition and fees vary according to course load. *College room and board:* $5900; *room only:* $3500. Room and board charges vary according to board plan and housing facility. *Payment plan:* Installment.
FRESHMAN FINANCIAL AID (Fall 2003) 1009 applied for aid; of those 90% were deemed to have need. 100% of freshmen with need received aid; of those 59% had need fully met. *Average percent of need met:* 50% (excluding resources awarded to replace EFC). *Average financial aid package:* $7874 (excluding resources awarded to replace EFC). 29% of all full-time freshmen had no need and received non-need-based gift aid.
UNDERGRADUATE FINANCIAL AID (Fall 2003) 4,916 applied for aid; of those 96% were deemed to have need. 100% of undergraduates with need received aid; of those 52% had need fully met. *Average percent of need met:* 60% (excluding resources awarded to replace EFC). *Average financial aid package:* $8162 (excluding resources awarded to replace EFC). 17% of all full-time undergraduates had no need and received non-need-based gift aid.
GIFT AID (NEED-BASED) *Total amount:* $9,842,061 (73% federal, 16% state, 11% institutional). *Receiving aid:* Freshmen: 33% (434); All full-time undergraduates: 40% (2,770). *Average award:* Freshmen: $3811; Undergraduates: $3272. *Scholarships, grants, and awards:* Federal Pell, FSEOG, state, private, college/university gift aid from institutional funds.

GIFT AID (NON-NEED-BASED) *Total amount:* $3,725,200 (50% institutional, 50% external sources). *Receiving aid:* Freshmen: 26% (351); Undergraduates: 23% (1,639). *Average Award:* Freshmen: $4101; Undergraduates: $3959. *Scholarships, grants, and awards by category:* Academic Interests/Achievement: general academic interests/achievements. Creative Arts/Performance: music, theater/drama. Special Achievements/Activities: rodeo. Special Characteristics: children of faculty/staff. *Tuition waivers:* Full or partial for employees or children of employees, senior citizens. *ROTC:* Army.
LOANS *Student loans:* $24,091,919 (54% need-based, 46% non-need-based). 60% of past graduating class borrowed through all loan programs. *Average indebtedness per student:* $16,776. *Average need-based loan:* Freshmen: $2204; Undergraduates: $3347. *Parent loans:* $3,234,487 (100% non-need-based). *Programs:* FFEL (Subsidized and Unsubsidized Stafford, PLUS), college/university.
WORK-STUDY *Federal work-study:* Total amount: $185,812; 73 jobs available. *State or other work-study/employment:* Total amount: $1,751,745 (2% need-based, 98% non-need-based). 10 part-time jobs averaging $3300.
ATHLETIC AWARDS *Total amount:* $694,535 (100% non-need-based).
APPLYING FOR FINANCIAL AID *Required financial aid forms:* FAFSA, institution's own form. *Financial aid deadline (priority):* 6/1. *Notification date:* Continuous. Students must reply within 2 weeks of notification.
CONTACT Ms. Betty Murray, Director of Student Financial Aid, Tarleton State University, Box T-0310, Stephenville, TX 76402, 254-968-9070 or toll-free 800-687-8236 (in-state). *Fax:* 254-968-9600. *E-mail:* finaid@tarleton.edu.

TAYLOR UNIVERSITY
Upland, IN

Tuition & fees: $20,746	Average undergraduate aid package: $13,875

ABOUT THE INSTITUTION Independent interdenominational, coed. Awards: associate, bachelor's, and master's degrees. 73 undergraduate majors. Total enrollment: 1,866. Undergraduates: 1,853. Freshmen: 478. Both federal and institutional methodology are used as a basis for awarding need-based institutional aid.
UNDERGRADUATE EXPENSES for 2005–06 *Application fee:* $25. *Comprehensive fee:* $26,376 includes full-time tuition ($20,520), mandatory fees ($226), and room and board ($5630). *College room only:* $2732. Full-time tuition and fees vary according to course load. Room and board charges vary according to housing facility. *Part-time tuition:* $696 per credit. *Part-time fees:* $64 per year. Part-time tuition and fees vary according to course load. *Payment plan:* Installment.
FRESHMAN FINANCIAL AID (Fall 2004, est.) 380 applied for aid; of those 76% were deemed to have need. 100% of freshmen with need received aid; of those 23% had need fully met. *Average percent of need met:* 77% (excluding resources awarded to replace EFC). *Average financial aid package:* $14,337 (excluding resources awarded to replace EFC). 21% of all full-time freshmen had no need and received non-need-based gift aid.
UNDERGRADUATE FINANCIAL AID (Fall 2004, est.) 1,244 applied for aid; of those 82% were deemed to have need. 100% of undergraduates with need received aid; of those 24% had need fully met. *Average percent of need met:* 78% (excluding resources awarded to replace EFC). *Average financial aid package:* $13,875 (excluding resources awarded to replace EFC). 23% of all full-time undergraduates had no need and received non-need-based gift aid.
GIFT AID (NEED-BASED) *Total amount:* $8,643,252 (11% federal, 12% state, 66% institutional, 11% external sources). *Receiving aid:* Freshmen: 58% (278); All full-time undergraduates: 52% (953). *Average award:* Freshmen: $10,921; Undergraduates: $10,270. *Scholarships, grants, and awards:* Federal Pell, FSEOG, state, private, college/university gift aid from institutional funds.
GIFT AID (NON-NEED-BASED) *Total amount:* $2,254,847 (2% state, 74% institutional, 24% external sources). *Receiving aid:* Freshmen: 7% (33); Undergraduates: 5% (99). *Average Award:* Freshmen: $3575; Undergraduates: $3471. *Scholarships, grants, and awards by category:* Academic Interests/Achievement: 787 awards ($2,145,137 total): general academic interests/achievements. Creative Arts/Performance: 89 awards ($116,115 total): music, theater/drama. Special Achievements/Activities: 84 awards ($375,757 total): leadership. Special Characteristics: 632 awards ($1,813,571 total): children and siblings of alumni, children of faculty/staff, ethnic background, international students, religious affiliation. *Tuition waivers:* Full or partial for employees or children of employees, senior citizens.
LOANS *Student loans:* $6,513,876 (68% need-based, 32% non-need-based). 56% of past graduating class borrowed through all loan programs. *Average indebtedness per student:* $16,014. *Average need-based loan:* Freshmen: $3974;

Undergraduates: $4433. *Parent loans:* $12,405,852 (26% need-based, 74% non-need-based). *Programs:* FFEL (Subsidized and Unsubsidized Stafford, PLUS), Perkins, college/university.

WORK-STUDY *Federal work-study:* Total amount: $355,969; 720 jobs averaging $467.

ATHLETIC AWARDS *Total amount:* $876,721 (61% need-based, 39% non-need-based).

APPLYING FOR FINANCIAL AID *Required financial aid forms:* FAFSA, institution's own form. *Financial aid deadline:* 3/10. *Notification date:* Continuous beginning 3/1. Students must reply by 5/1.

CONTACT Mr. Timothy A. Nace, Director of Financial Aid, Taylor University, 236 West Reade Avenue, Upland, IN 46989-1001, 765-998-5358 or toll-free 800-882-3456. *Fax:* 765-998-4910. *E-mail:* tmnace@taylor.edu.

TAYLOR UNIVERSITY FORT WAYNE
Fort Wayne, IN

Tuition & fees: $17,714	Average undergraduate aid package: $15,843

ABOUT THE INSTITUTION Independent interdenominational, coed. Awards: associate, bachelor's, and master's degrees and post-bachelor's certificates. 20 undergraduate majors. Total enrollment: 619. Undergraduates: 587. Freshmen: 109. Both federal and institutional methodology are used as a basis for awarding need-based institutional aid.

UNDERGRADUATE EXPENSES for 2005–06 *Application fee:* $20. *Comprehensive fee:* $22,674 includes full-time tuition ($17,600), mandatory fees ($114), and room and board ($4960). *College room only:* $2160. Room and board charges vary according to board plan. Part-time tuition and fees vary according to course load. *Payment plan:* Installment.

FRESHMAN FINANCIAL AID (Fall 2004, est.) 93 applied for aid; of those 95% were deemed to have need. 100% of freshmen with need received aid; of those 35% had need fully met. *Average percent of need met:* 87% (excluding resources awarded to replace EFC). *Average financial aid package:* $15,432 (excluding resources awarded to replace EFC). 4% of all full-time freshmen had no need and received non-need-based gift aid.

UNDERGRADUATE FINANCIAL AID (Fall 2004, est.) 351 applied for aid; of those 93% were deemed to have need. 100% of undergraduates with need received aid; of those 34% had need fully met. *Average percent of need met:* 86% (excluding resources awarded to replace EFC). *Average financial aid package:* $15,843 (excluding resources awarded to replace EFC). 7% of all full-time undergraduates had no need and received non-need-based gift aid.

GIFT AID (NEED-BASED) *Total amount:* $3,701,790 (18% federal, 28% state, 52% institutional, 2% external sources). *Receiving aid:* Freshmen: 88% (87); All full-time undergraduates: 86% (324). *Average award:* Freshmen: $10,829; Undergraduates: $11,288. *Scholarships, grants, and awards:* Federal Pell, FSEOG, state, private, college/university gift aid from institutional funds, endowed-donor scholarships.

GIFT AID (NON-NEED-BASED) *Total amount:* $201,457 (2% federal, 12% state, 81% institutional, 5% external sources). *Receiving aid:* Freshmen: 6% (6); Undergraduates: 5% (19). *Average Award:* Freshmen: $2880; Undergraduates: $4523. *Scholarships, grants, and awards by category: Academic Interests/Achievement:* 171 awards ($495,862 total): business, computer science, general academic interests/achievements. *Creative Arts/Performance:* 9 awards ($18,255 total). *Special Achievements/Activities:* 30 awards ($41,997 total): leadership. *Special Characteristics:* 325 awards ($444,026 total): children and siblings of alumni, children of faculty/staff, general special characteristics, local/state students, relatives of clergy, spouses of current students. *Tuition waivers:* Full or partial for children of alumni, employees or children of employees, senior citizens.

LOANS *Student loans:* $2,235,644 (80% need-based, 20% non-need-based). 78% of past graduating class borrowed through all loan programs. *Average indebtedness per student:* $13,562. *Average need-based loan:* Freshmen: $3927; Undergraduates: $4201. *Parent loans:* $456,407 (29% need-based, 71% non-need-based). *Programs:* FFEL (Subsidized and Unsubsidized Stafford, PLUS), Perkins, college/university.

WORK-STUDY *Federal work-study:* Total amount: $269,070; 95 jobs available.

ATHLETIC AWARDS *Total amount:* $10,500 (62% need-based, 38% non-need-based).

APPLYING FOR FINANCIAL AID *Required financial aid forms:* FAFSA, institution's own form. *Financial aid deadline (priority):* 3/1. *Notification date:* Continuous beginning 3/1. Students must reply by 5/1 or within 2 weeks of notification.

CONTACT Mr. Paul Johnston, Director of Financial Aid, Taylor University Fort Wayne, 1025 West Rudisill Boulevard, Fort Wayne, IN 46807-2197, 260-744-8644 or toll-free 800-233-3922. *Fax:* 260-744-8660. *E-mail:* pljohnston@tayloru.edu.

TEIKYO LORETTO HEIGHTS UNIVERSITY
Denver, CO

CONTACT Financial Aid Office, Teikyo Loretto Heights University, 3001 South Federal Boulevard, Denver, CO 80236, 303-936-4200.

TEIKYO POST UNIVERSITY
Waterbury, CT

See Post University.

TELSHE YESHIVA–CHICAGO
Chicago, IL

CONTACT Office of Financial Aid, Telshe Yeshiva–Chicago, 3535 West Foster Avenue, Chicago, IL 60625-5598, 773-463-7738.

TEMPLE BAPTIST COLLEGE
Cincinnati, OH

CONTACT Financial Aid Office, Temple Baptist College, 11965 Kenn Road, Cincinnati, OH 45240, 513-851-3800.

TEMPLE UNIVERSITY
Philadelphia, PA

Tuition & fees (PA res): $9102	Average undergraduate aid package: $12,190

ABOUT THE INSTITUTION State-related, coed. Awards: associate, bachelor's, master's, doctoral, and first professional degrees and post-master's and first professional certificates. 118 undergraduate majors. Total enrollment: 33,552. Undergraduates: 23,429. Freshmen: 3,815. Federal methodology is used as a basis for awarding need-based institutional aid.

UNDERGRADUATE EXPENSES for 2004–05 *Application fee:* $35. *Tuition, state resident:* full-time $8622; part-time $334 per credit hour. *Tuition, nonresident:* full-time $15,788; part-time $562 per credit hour. Full-time tuition and fees vary according to course load, location, program, and reciprocity agreements. Part-time tuition and fees vary according to course load, location, program, and reciprocity agreements. *College room and board:* $7522; *room only:* $4876. Room and board charges vary according to board plan and housing facility. *Payment plan:* Installment.

FRESHMAN FINANCIAL AID (Fall 2004, est.) 3380 applied for aid; of those 76% were deemed to have need. 98% of freshmen with need received aid; of those 30% had need fully met. *Average percent of need met:* 86% (excluding resources awarded to replace EFC). *Average financial aid package:* $12,488 (excluding resources awarded to replace EFC). 22% of all full-time freshmen had no need and received non-need-based gift aid.

UNDERGRADUATE FINANCIAL AID (Fall 2004, est.) 17,069 applied for aid; of those 78% were deemed to have need. 95% of undergraduates with need received aid; of those 37% had need fully met. *Average percent of need met:* 89% (excluding resources awarded to replace EFC). *Average financial aid package:* $12,190 (excluding resources awarded to replace EFC). 20% of all full-time undergraduates had no need and received non-need-based gift aid.

GIFT AID (NEED-BASED) *Total amount:* $57,306,726 (41% federal, 28% state, 31% institutional). *Receiving aid:* Freshmen: 70% (2,518); All full-time undergraduates: 67% (12,606). *Average award:* Freshmen: $5010; Undergraduates: $4452. *Scholarships, grants, and awards:* Federal Pell, FSEOG, state, private, college/university gift aid from institutional funds, Federal Nursing.

GIFT AID (NON-NEED-BASED) *Total amount:* $35,166,359 (16% institutional, 84% external sources). *Receiving aid:* Freshmen: 41% (1,483); Undergraduates: 29% (5,522). *Average Award:* Freshmen: $3613; Undergraduates: $3818. *Scholarships, grants, and awards by category: Academic Interests/Achievement:* general academic interests/achievements. *Creative Arts/Performance:* general creative arts/performance, music, performing arts. *Special Achievements/Activities:* cheerleading/drum major. *Special Characteristics:* general special characteristics. *Tuition waivers:* Full or partial for employees or children of employees. *ROTC:* Army, Naval cooperative, Air Force cooperative.

LOANS *Student loans:* $86,350,391 (65% need-based, 35% non-need-based). 72% of past graduating class borrowed through all loan programs. *Average indebtedness per student:* $23,772. *Average need-based loan:* Freshmen: $2778; Undergraduates: $3527. *Parent loans:* $696,659 (100% non-need-based). *Programs:* FFEL (Subsidized and Unsubsidized Stafford, PLUS), Perkins, Federal Nursing, college/university.

WORK-STUDY *Federal work-study:* Total amount: $3,066,696; jobs available.

ATHLETIC AWARDS *Total amount:* $5,607,514 (100% non-need-based).

APPLYING FOR FINANCIAL AID *Required financial aid form:* FAFSA. *Financial aid deadline (priority):* 3/1. *Notification date:* Continuous. Students must reply by 5/1 or within 3 weeks of notification.

CONTACT Dr. John F. Morris, Director of Finance and Accounting, Temple University, Conwell Hall, Ground Floor, 1801 North Broad Street, Philadelphia, PA 19122-6096, 215-204-8760 or toll-free 888-340-2222. *Fax:* 215-204-2016. *E-mail:* john.morris@temple.edu.

TENNESSEE STATE UNIVERSITY
Nashville, TN

ABOUT THE INSTITUTION State-supported, coed. Awards: associate, bachelor's, master's, and doctoral degrees. 59 undergraduate majors. Total enrollment: 9,100. Undergraduates: 7,257. Freshmen: 1,228.

GIFT AID (NEED-BASED) *Scholarships, grants, and awards:* Federal Pell, FSEOG, state, private, college/university gift aid from institutional funds.

GIFT AID (NON-NEED-BASED) *Scholarships, grants, and awards by category:* Academic Interests/Achievement: general academic interests/achievements. Creative Arts/Performance: music. Special Achievements/Activities: general special achievements/activities. Special Characteristics: local/state students, members of minority groups.

LOANS *Programs:* Federal Direct (Subsidized and Unsubsidized Stafford), FFEL (Subsidized and Unsubsidized Stafford, PLUS), Perkins, college/university.

WORK-STUDY *Federal work-study:* Total amount: $2,018,268; jobs available (averaging $2000). *State or other work-study/employment:* Part-time jobs available.

APPLYING FOR FINANCIAL AID *Required financial aid form:* FAFSA.

CONTACT Mary Chambliss, Director of Financial Aid, Tennessee State University, 3500 John Merritt Boulevard, Nashville, TN 37209-1561, 615-963-5701. *Fax:* 615-963-5108.

TENNESSEE TECHNOLOGICAL UNIVERSITY
Cookeville, TN

Tuition & fees (TN res): $3998	Average undergraduate aid package: $3870

ABOUT THE INSTITUTION State-supported, coed. Awards: bachelor's, master's, and doctoral degrees and post-bachelor's certificates. 67 undergraduate majors. Total enrollment: 9,217. Undergraduates: 7,224. Freshmen: 1,485. Federal methodology is used as a basis for awarding need-based institutional aid.

UNDERGRADUATE EXPENSES for 2004–05 *Application fee:* $15. *Tuition, state resident:* full-time $3998; part-time $147 per hour. *Tuition, nonresident:* full-time $12,486; part-time $515 per hour. *Required fees:* $42 per hour. Full-time tuition and fees vary according to program. Part-time tuition and fees vary according to course load and program. *College room and board:* $5270; *room only:* $2520. Room and board charges vary according to board plan and housing facility. *Payment plan:* Installment.

FRESHMAN FINANCIAL AID (Fall 2003) 612 applied for aid; of those 61% were deemed to have need. 96% of freshmen with need received aid; of those 21% had need fully met. *Average percent of need met:* 81% (excluding resources awarded to replace EFC). *Average financial aid package:* $5443 (excluding resources awarded to replace EFC). 10% of all full-time freshmen had no need and received non-need-based gift aid.

UNDERGRADUATE FINANCIAL AID (Fall 2003) 4,757 applied for aid; of those 58% were deemed to have need. 98% of undergraduates with need received aid; of those 26% had need fully met. *Average percent of need met:* 77% (excluding resources awarded to replace EFC). *Average financial aid package:* $3870 (excluding resources awarded to replace EFC). 19% of all full-time undergraduates had no need and received non-need-based gift aid.

GIFT AID (NEED-BASED) *Total amount:* $7,381,272 (81% federal, 19% state). *Receiving aid:* Freshmen: 17% (233); All full-time undergraduates: 27% (1,712).

Average award: Freshmen: $2710; Undergraduates: $2768. *Scholarships, grants, and awards:* Federal Pell, FSEOG, state, private, college/university gift aid from institutional funds, United Negro College Fund.

GIFT AID (NON-NEED-BASED) *Total amount:* $6,115,975 (12% state, 63% institutional, 25% external sources). *Receiving aid:* Freshmen: 8% (112); Undergraduates: 13% (814). *Average Award:* Freshmen: $3364; Undergraduates: $3030. *Scholarships, grants, and awards by category:* Academic Interests/Achievement: 1,726 awards ($1,892,381 total): agriculture, biological sciences, business, communication, computer science, education, engineering/technologies, English, foreign languages, general academic interests/achievements, health fields, home economics, humanities, international studies, mathematics, military science, physical sciences, premedicine, social sciences. Creative Arts/Performance: 148 awards ($190,896 total): art/fine arts, debating, music. Special Achievements/Activities: 2,664 awards ($4,392,375 total): cheerleading/drum major, general special achievements/activities. Special Characteristics: 1,431 awards ($1,898,876 total): children and siblings of alumni, children of educators, children of faculty/staff, children of public servants, ethnic background, first-generation college students, local/state students, members of minority groups, out-of-state students, public servants. *Tuition waivers:* Full or partial for employees or children of employees. *ROTC:* Army, Air Force cooperative.

LOANS *Student loans:* $15,945,907 (66% need-based, 34% non-need-based). 37% of past graduating class borrowed through all loan programs. *Average indebtedness per student:* $13,747. *Average need-based loan:* Freshmen: $1366; Undergraduates: $3061. *Parent loans:* $1,014,926 (100% non-need-based). *Programs:* Federal Direct (Subsidized and Unsubsidized Stafford), FFEL (PLUS), Perkins, college/university.

WORK-STUDY *Federal work-study:* Total amount: $695,872; 553 jobs averaging $1350. *State or other work-study/employment:* Total amount: $3,299,182 (100% non-need-based). Part-time jobs available.

ATHLETIC AWARDS *Total amount:* $2,546,688 (100% non-need-based).

APPLYING FOR FINANCIAL AID *Required financial aid forms:* FAFSA, income tax form(s), scholarship application prior to 12/15. *Financial aid deadline (priority):* 3/15. *Notification date:* Continuous beginning 4/15. Students must reply within 2 weeks of notification.

CONTACT Dr. Raymond L. Holbrook, Director of Student Financial Aid, Tennessee Technological University, Box 5076, 1000 North Dixie Avenue, Roaden University Center, Room 214, Cookeville, TN 38505, 931-372-3073 or toll-free 800-255-8881. *Fax:* 931-372-6309. *E-mail:* rholbrook@tntech.edu.

TENNESSEE TEMPLE UNIVERSITY
Chattanooga, TN

ABOUT THE INSTITUTION Independent Baptist, coed. Awards: associate, bachelor's, and master's degrees. 30 undergraduate majors. Total enrollment: 427. Undergraduates: 137. Freshmen: 137.

GIFT AID (NEED-BASED) *Scholarships, grants, and awards:* Federal Pell, FSEOG, state, private, college/university gift aid from institutional funds.

GIFT AID (NON-NEED-BASED) *Scholarships, grants, and awards by category:* Academic Interests/Achievement: general academic interests/achievements. Creative Arts/Performance: music. Special Achievements/Activities: leadership, religious involvement. Special Characteristics: children and siblings of alumni, children of faculty/staff, local/state students, siblings of current students, spouses of current students.

LOANS *Programs:* FFEL (Subsidized and Unsubsidized Stafford, PLUS), Perkins.

WORK-STUDY *Federal work-study:* Total amount: $93,112; 54 jobs averaging $1724. *State or other work-study/employment:* Total amount: $60,564 (100% need-based). 36 part-time jobs averaging $1682.

APPLYING FOR FINANCIAL AID *Required financial aid forms:* FAFSA, institution's own form.

CONTACT Mr. Michael Sapienza, Director of Financial Aid, Tennessee Temple University, 1815 Union Avenue, Chattanooga, TN 37404-3587, 423-493-4208 or toll-free 800-553-4050. *Fax:* 423-493-4497. *E-mail:* michaels@mail.tntemple.edu.

TENNESSEE WESLEYAN COLLEGE
Athens, TN

Tuition & fees: $13,550	Average undergraduate aid package: $10,908

ABOUT THE INSTITUTION Independent United Methodist, coed. Awards: bachelor's degrees (profile includes information for both the main and branch campuses). 40 undergraduate majors. Total enrollment: 815. Undergraduates: 815. Freshmen: 166. Federal methodology is used as a basis for awarding need-based institutional aid.

UNDERGRADUATE EXPENSES for 2005–06 *Application fee:* $25. *Comprehensive fee:* $18,650 includes full-time tuition ($13,000), mandatory fees ($550), and room and board ($5100). Full-time tuition and fees vary according to location. Room and board charges vary according to housing facility. *Part-time tuition:* $375 per semester hour. *Part-time fees:* $180 per term. Part-time tuition and fees vary according to class time and location. *Payment plans:* Installment, deferred payment.

FRESHMAN FINANCIAL AID (Fall 2004, est.) 162 applied for aid; of those 82% were deemed to have need. 100% of freshmen with need received aid; of those 18% had need fully met. *Average percent of need met:* 73% (excluding resources awarded to replace EFC). *Average financial aid package:* $10,846 (excluding resources awarded to replace EFC). 17% of all full-time freshmen had no need and received non-need-based gift aid.

UNDERGRADUATE FINANCIAL AID (Fall 2004, est.) 622 applied for aid; of those 88% were deemed to have need. 100% of undergraduates with need received aid; of those 17% had need fully met. *Average percent of need met:* 70% (excluding resources awarded to replace EFC). *Average financial aid package:* $10,908 (excluding resources awarded to replace EFC). 14% of all full-time undergraduates had no need and received non-need-based gift aid.

GIFT AID (NEED-BASED) *Total amount:* $3,651,676 (26% federal, 29% state, 39% institutional, 6% external sources). *Receiving aid:* Freshmen: 82% (133); All full-time undergraduates: 79% (544). *Average award:* Freshmen: $9360; Undergraduates: $8172. *Scholarships, grants, and awards:* Federal Pell, FSEOG, state, private, college/university gift aid from institutional funds, Federal Nursing.

GIFT AID (NON-NEED-BASED) *Total amount:* $583,582 (27% state, 63% institutional, 10% external sources). *Receiving aid:* Freshmen: 13% (22); Undergraduates: 9% (59). *Average Award:* Freshmen: $7302; Undergraduates: $6109. *Scholarships, grants, and awards by category:* Academic Interests/Achievement: 435 awards ($1,222,530 total): biological sciences, business, communication, computer science, education, English, foreign languages, general academic interests/achievements, health fields, humanities, international studies, mathematics, physical sciences, premedicine, religion/biblical studies, social sciences. Creative Arts/Performance: 18 awards ($53,400 total): music. Special Achievements/Activities: 50 awards ($107,330 total): cheerleading/drum major, general special achievements/activities, junior miss, memberships, religious involvement. Special Characteristics: 87 awards ($212,557 total): children of faculty/staff, general special characteristics, international students, members of minority groups, relatives of clergy, religious affiliation. *Tuition waivers:* Full or partial for employees or children of employees.

LOANS *Student loans:* $2,843,192 (82% need-based, 18% non-need-based). 87% of past graduating class borrowed through all loan programs. *Average indebtedness per student:* $18,159. *Average need-based loan:* Freshmen: $2172; Undergraduates: $3627. *Parent loans:* $381,968 (34% need-based, 66% non-need-based). *Programs:* FFEL (Subsidized and Unsubsidized Stafford, PLUS), Perkins, state, United Methodist Student Loans.

WORK-STUDY *Federal work-study:* Total amount: $70,481; 103 jobs averaging $678. *State or other work-study/employment:* Total amount: $24,856 (7% need-based, 93% non-need-based). 39 part-time jobs averaging $837.

ATHLETIC AWARDS *Total amount:* $1,474,965 (61% need-based, 39% non-need-based).

APPLYING FOR FINANCIAL AID *Required financial aid forms:* FAFSA, institution's own form. *Financial aid deadline:* Continuous. *Notification date:* Continuous beginning 2/15. Students must reply within 2 weeks of notification.

CONTACT Ms. Bobbie Pennington, Financial Aid Officer, Tennessee Wesleyan College, PO Box 40, Athens, TN 37371-0040, 423-746-5215 or toll-free 800-PICK-TWC. *Fax:* 423-744-9968. *E-mail:* bpennington@twcnet.edu.

TEXAS A&M INTERNATIONAL UNIVERSITY
Laredo, TX

ABOUT THE INSTITUTION State-supported, coed. Awards: bachelor's, master's, and doctoral degrees. 34 undergraduate majors. Total enrollment: 4,078. Undergraduates: 3,116. Freshmen: 497.

GIFT AID (NEED-BASED) *Scholarships, grants, and awards:* Federal Pell, FSEOG, state, college/university gift aid from institutional funds.

GIFT AID (NON-NEED-BASED) *Scholarships, grants, and awards by category:* Academic Interests/Achievement: general academic interests/achievements. Creative Arts/Performance: art/fine arts, dance, music, performing arts.

LOANS *Programs:* FFEL (Subsidized and Unsubsidized Stafford, PLUS), college/university, Hinson-Hazelwood Loan Program.

APPLYING FOR FINANCIAL AID *Required financial aid form:* FAFSA.

CONTACT Laura Elizondo, Director of Financial Aid, Texas A&M International University, 5201 University Boulevard, Laredo, TX 78041, 956-326-2225 or toll-free 888-489-2648. *Fax:* 956-326-2224. *E-mail:* laura@tamiu.edu.

TEXAS A&M UNIVERSITY
College Station, TX

Tuition & fees (TX res): $5955	Average undergraduate aid package: $8781

ABOUT THE INSTITUTION State-supported, coed. Awards: bachelor's, master's, doctoral, and first professional degrees and post-bachelor's certificates. 107 undergraduate majors. Total enrollment: 44,435. Undergraduates: 35,732. Freshmen: 7,068. Federal methodology is used as a basis for awarding need-based institutional aid.

UNDERGRADUATE EXPENSES for 2004–05 *Application fee:* $50. *Tuition, state resident:* full-time $3675; part-time $122.50 per semester hour. *Tuition, nonresident:* full-time $11,415; part-time $380.50 per semester hour. Full-time tuition and fees vary according to course load, location, and program. *College room and board:* $6887; *room only:* $3704. Room and board charges vary according to board plan, housing facility, and location. *Payment plan:* Installment.

FRESHMAN FINANCIAL AID (Fall 2003) 4198 applied for aid; of those 62% were deemed to have need. 98% of freshmen with need received aid; of those 97% had need fully met. *Average percent of need met:* 65% (excluding resources awarded to replace EFC). *Average financial aid package:* $10,049 (excluding resources awarded to replace EFC). 40% of all full-time freshmen had no need and received non-need-based gift aid.

UNDERGRADUATE FINANCIAL AID (Fall 2003) 20,833 applied for aid; of those 56% were deemed to have need. 98% of undergraduates with need received aid; of those 74% had need fully met. *Average percent of need met:* 64% (excluding resources awarded to replace EFC). *Average financial aid package:* $8781 (excluding resources awarded to replace EFC). 32% of all full-time undergraduates had no need and received non-need-based gift aid.

GIFT AID (NEED-BASED) *Total amount:* $18,324,037 (100% federal). *Receiving aid:* Freshmen: 38% (2,518); All full-time undergraduates: 35% (11,239). *Average award:* Freshmen: $10,105; Undergraduates: $8880. *Scholarships, grants, and awards:* Federal Pell, FSEOG, state, private, college/university gift aid from institutional funds.

GIFT AID (NON-NEED-BASED) *Total amount:* $49,826,372 (1% federal, 37% state, 8% institutional, 54% external sources). *Receiving aid:* Freshmen: 37% (2,469); Undergraduates: 31% (10,167). *Average Award:* Freshmen: $6406; Undergraduates: $6370. *Scholarships, grants, and awards by category:* Academic Interests/Achievement: agriculture, architecture, biological sciences, business, computer science, education, engineering/technologies, general academic interests/achievements, health fields, physical sciences. Creative Arts/Performance: journalism/publications, performing arts, theater/drama. Special Achievements/Activities: general special achievements/activities, leadership, memberships, rodeo. Special Characteristics: children of faculty/staff, veterans, veterans' children. ROTC: Army, Naval, Air Force.

LOANS *Student loans:* $37,876,962 (95% need-based, 5% non-need-based). 32% of past graduating class borrowed through all loan programs. *Average indebtedness per student:* $15,927. *Average need-based loan:* Freshmen: $3059; Undergraduates: $4153. *Parent loans:* $18,746,792 (39% need-based, 61% non-need-based). *Programs:* FFEL (Subsidized and Unsubsidized Stafford, PLUS), Perkins, state, college/university.

WORK-STUDY *Federal work-study:* Total amount: $2,740,236; 1,047 jobs averaging $1278. *State or other work-study/employment:* Total amount: $403,638 (100% need-based). 4,500 part-time jobs averaging $2599.

ATHLETIC AWARDS *Total amount:* $3,343,386 (34% need-based, 66% non-need-based).

APPLYING FOR FINANCIAL AID *Required financial aid forms:* FAFSA, institution's own form. *Financial aid deadline:* Continuous. *Notification date:* Continuous beginning 4/1. Students must reply within 4 weeks of notification.

CONTACT Mrs. Debra J. Lagrone, Associate Director of Student Financial Aid, Texas A&M University, Department of Student Financial Aid, PO Box 30016, College Station, TX 77842-3016, 979-845-3236. *Fax:* 979-847-9061.

TEXAS A&M UNIVERSITY AT GALVESTON
Galveston, TX

Tuition & fees (TX res): $4682	Average undergraduate aid package: $9681

ABOUT THE INSTITUTION State-supported, coed. Awards: bachelor's and master's degrees. 12 undergraduate majors. Total enrollment: 1,615. Undergraduates: 1,577. Freshmen: 380. Federal methodology is used as a basis for awarding need-based institutional aid.

UNDERGRADUATE EXPENSES for 2005–06 *Application fee:* $35. *Tuition, state resident:* full-time $3675; part-time $48 per hour. *Tuition, nonresident:* full-time $11,415; part-time $306 per hour. *Required fees:* full-time $1007; $504 per term part-time. Full-time tuition and fees vary according to course load and program. Part-time tuition and fees vary according to course load and program. *College room and board:* $4870; *room only:* $1958. Room and board charges vary according to board plan and housing facility. *Payment plan:* Installment.

FRESHMAN FINANCIAL AID (Fall 2004, est.) 269 applied for aid; of those 84% were deemed to have need. 94% of freshmen with need received aid; of those 35% had need fully met. *Average percent of need met:* 13% (excluding resources awarded to replace EFC). *Average financial aid package:* $9335 (excluding resources awarded to replace EFC). 12% of all full-time freshmen had no need and received non-need-based gift aid.

UNDERGRADUATE FINANCIAL AID (Fall 2004, est.) 836 applied for aid; of those 93% were deemed to have need. 95% of undergraduates with need received aid; of those 37% had need fully met. *Average percent of need met:* 23% (excluding resources awarded to replace EFC). *Average financial aid package:* $9681 (excluding resources awarded to replace EFC). 8% of all full-time undergraduates had no need and received non-need-based gift aid.

GIFT AID (NEED-BASED) *Total amount:* $1,295,193 (68% federal, 21% state, 11% institutional). *Receiving aid:* Freshmen: 28% (122); All full-time undergraduates: 29% (427). *Average award:* Freshmen: $3987; Undergraduates: $4014. *Scholarships, grants, and awards:* Federal Pell, FSEOG, state, private, college/university gift aid from institutional funds.

GIFT AID (NON-NEED-BASED) *Total amount:* $303,435 (20% state, 80% institutional). *Receiving aid:* Freshmen: 13% (57); Undergraduates: 9% (137). *Average Award:* Freshmen: $2256; Undergraduates: $2099. *Scholarships, grants, and awards by category:* Academic Interests/Achievement: 100 awards ($100,000 total): general academic interests/achievements. Special Achievements/Activities: 35 awards ($42,000 total): leadership. *ROTC:* Naval.

LOANS *Student loans:* $5,499,233 (28% need-based, 72% non-need-based). 70% of past graduating class borrowed through all loan programs. *Average indebtedness per student:* $10,857. *Average need-based loan:* Freshmen: $1912; Undergraduates: $2744. *Parent loans:* $3,043,794 (100% non-need-based). *Programs:* FFEL (Subsidized and Unsubsidized Stafford, PLUS), Perkins, college/university, alternative loans.

WORK-STUDY *Federal work-study:* Total amount: $71,130; jobs available (averaging $1871).

APPLYING FOR FINANCIAL AID *Required financial aid form:* FAFSA. *Financial aid deadline:* Continuous. *Notification date:* 3/15. Students must reply within 3 weeks of notification.

CONTACT Dennis Carlton, Director for Financial Aid, Texas A&M University at Galveston, PO Box 1675, Galveston, TX 77553-1675, 409-740-4500 or toll-free 87—SEAAGGIE. *Fax:* 409-740-4959. *E-mail:* carltond@tamug.tamu.edu.

TEXAS A&M UNIVERSITY–COMMERCE
Commerce, TX

Tuition & fees (TX res): $4178	Average undergraduate aid package: $7040

ABOUT THE INSTITUTION State-supported, coed. Awards: bachelor's, master's, and doctoral degrees. 67 undergraduate majors. Total enrollment: 6,317. Undergraduates: 5,387. Freshmen: 813. Federal methodology is used as a basis for awarding need-based institutional aid.

UNDERGRADUATE EXPENSES for 2004–05 *Application fee:* $25. *Tuition, state resident:* full-time $3224; part-time $203 per credit hour. *Tuition, nonresident:* full-time $9764; part-time $461 per credit hour. Full-time tuition and fees vary according to course load. Part-time tuition and fees vary according to course load. *College room and board:* $5246; *room only:* $2750. Room and board charges vary according to board plan and housing facility. *Payment plan:* Installment.

FRESHMAN FINANCIAL AID (Fall 2003) 353 applied for aid; of those 82% were deemed to have need. 98% of freshmen with need received aid; of those 20% had need fully met. *Average percent of need met:* 70% (excluding resources awarded to replace EFC). *Average financial aid package:* $6570 (excluding resources awarded to replace EFC). 20% of all full-time freshmen had no need and received non-need-based gift aid.

UNDERGRADUATE FINANCIAL AID (Fall 2003) 3,101 applied for aid; of those 85% were deemed to have need. 97% of undergraduates with need received aid; of those 21% had need fully met. *Average percent of need met:* 71% (excluding resources awarded to replace EFC). *Average financial aid package:* $7040 (excluding resources awarded to replace EFC). 14% of all full-time undergraduates had no need and received non-need-based gift aid.

GIFT AID (NEED-BASED) *Total amount:* $10,614,893 (61% federal, 26% state, 9% institutional, 4% external sources). *Receiving aid:* Freshmen: 60% (273); All full-time undergraduates: 56% (2,326). *Average award:* Freshmen: $5457; Undergraduates: $4753. *Scholarships, grants, and awards:* Federal Pell, FSEOG, state, private, college/university gift aid from institutional funds.

GIFT AID (NON-NEED-BASED) *Total amount:* $1,311,722 (18% state, 65% institutional, 17% external sources). *Average Award:* Freshmen: $1985; Undergraduates: $1777. *Scholarships, grants, and awards by category:* Academic Interests/Achievement: agriculture, general academic interests/ achievements. Creative Arts/Performance: art/fine arts, journalism/publications, music, theater/drama. Special Achievements/Activities: cheerleading/drum major, general special achievements/activities, leadership. *Tuition waivers:* Full or partial for senior citizens.

LOANS *Student loans:* $12,785,054 (88% need-based, 12% non-need-based). 59% of past graduating class borrowed through all loan programs. *Average indebtedness per student:* $16,236. *Average need-based loan:* Freshmen: $2372; Undergraduates: $3390. *Parent loans:* $557,002 (58% need-based, 42% non-need-based). *Programs:* Federal Direct (Subsidized and Unsubsidized Stafford), FFEL (Subsidized and Unsubsidized Stafford, PLUS), Perkins, state.

WORK-STUDY *Federal work-study:* Total amount: $228,781; 129 jobs averaging $1730. *State or other work-study/employment:* Total amount: $46,780 (100% need-based). 34 part-time jobs averaging $1371.

ATHLETIC AWARDS *Total amount:* $529,655 (68% need-based, 32% non-need-based).

APPLYING FOR FINANCIAL AID *Required financial aid forms:* FAFSA, institution's own form. *Financial aid deadline (priority):* 4/1. *Notification date:* Continuous. Students must reply within 2 weeks of notification.

CONTACT Ms. Smithenia Harris, Interim Director of Financial Aid, Texas A&M University–Commerce, PO Box 3011, Commerce, TX 75429, 903-886-5096 or toll-free 800-331-3878.

TEXAS A&M UNIVERSITY–CORPUS CHRISTI
Corpus Christi, TX

ABOUT THE INSTITUTION State-supported, coed. Awards: bachelor's, master's, and doctoral degrees. 31 undergraduate majors. Total enrollment: 8,227. Undergraduates: 6,581. Freshmen: 1,155.

GIFT AID (NEED-BASED) *Scholarships, grants, and awards:* Federal Pell, FSEOG, state, college/university gift aid from institutional funds.

GIFT AID (NON-NEED-BASED) *Scholarships, grants, and awards by category:* Academic Interests/Achievement: general academic interests/achievements. Creative Arts/Performance: art/fine arts.

LOANS *Programs:* FFEL (Subsidized and Unsubsidized Stafford, PLUS), Perkins, college/university.

APPLYING FOR FINANCIAL AID *Required financial aid forms:* FAFSA, institution's own form.

CONTACT Financial Aid Adviser, Texas A&M University–Corpus Christi, 6300 Ocean Drive, Corpus Christi, TX 78412-5503, 361-825-2338 or toll-free 800-482-6822. *Fax:* 361-825-6095. *E-mail:* faoweb@mail.tamucc.edu.

TEXAS A&M UNIVERSITY–KINGSVILLE
Kingsville, TX

ABOUT THE INSTITUTION State-supported, coed. Awards: bachelor's, master's, and doctoral degrees and post-bachelor's certificates. 72 undergraduate majors. Total enrollment: 7,126. Undergraduates: 5,645. Freshmen: 887.

GIFT AID (NEED-BASED) *Scholarships, grants, and awards:* Federal Pell, FSEOG, state, private, college/university gift aid from institutional funds.

GIFT AID (NON-NEED-BASED) *Scholarships, grants, and awards by category:* Special Achievements/Activities: rodeo. Special Characteristics: general special characteristics.

LOANS *Programs:* FFEL (Subsidized and Unsubsidized Stafford, PLUS), Perkins, alternative loans.

APPLYING FOR FINANCIAL AID *Required financial aid form:* FAFSA.

CONTACT Roel M. Villarreal, Director, Financial Aid, Texas A&M University–Kingsville, 700 University Boulevard, Kingsville, TX 78363, 361-593-2174 or toll-free 800-687-6000. *Fax:* 361-593-3026.

TEXAS A&M UNIVERSITY–TEXARKANA
Texarkana, TX

Tuition & fees (TX res): $2340	Average undergraduate aid package: N/A

ABOUT THE INSTITUTION State-supported, coed. Awards: bachelor's and master's degrees. 19 undergraduate majors. Total enrollment: 1,559. Undergraduates: 984. Federal methodology is used as a basis for awarding need-based institutional aid.

UNDERGRADUATE EXPENSES for 2004–05 *Tuition, state resident:* full-time $1968; part-time $82 per credit hour. *Tuition, nonresident:* full-time $9160; part-time $340 per credit hour. *Required fees:* full-time $372; $15 per credit hour or $6 per term part-time. Full-time tuition and fees vary according to course level, course load, and student level. Part-time tuition and fees vary according to course level, course load, and student level. *Payment plan:* Installment.

GIFT AID (NEED-BASED) *Total amount:* $1,155,059 (73% federal, 22% state, 5% external sources). *Scholarships, grants, and awards:* Federal Pell, FSEOG, state, private, college/university gift aid from institutional funds.

GIFT AID (NON-NEED-BASED) *Total amount:* $256,182 (100% institutional). *Scholarships, grants, and awards by category: Academic Interests/Achievement:* business, education, English, general academic interests/achievements, mathematics, social sciences. *Special Achievements/Activities:* community service, general special achievements/activities, leadership, memberships. *Tuition waivers:* Full or partial for senior citizens.

LOANS *Student loans:* $1,111,093 (71% need-based, 29% non-need-based). *Parent loans:* $1455 (100% non-need-based). *Programs:* FFEL (Subsidized and Unsubsidized Stafford, PLUS), college/university.

WORK-STUDY *Federal work-study:* Total amount: $17,850; jobs available.

APPLYING FOR FINANCIAL AID *Required financial aid forms:* FAFSA, institution's own form, state aid form. *Financial aid deadline (priority):* 5/1. *Notification date:* Continuous beginning 6/1. Students must reply within 6 weeks of notification.

CONTACT Marilyn Raney, Director of Financial Aid and Veterans' Services, Texas A&M University–Texarkana, 2600 North Robison Road, Texarkana, TX 75505, 903-223-3060. *Fax:* 903-223-3118. *E-mail:* marilyn.raney@tamut.edu.

TEXAS CHIROPRACTIC COLLEGE
Pasadena, TX

ABOUT THE INSTITUTION Independent, coed. Awards: first professional degrees. 2 undergraduate majors. Total enrollment: 517. Undergraduates: 55.

GIFT AID (NEED-BASED) *Scholarships, grants, and awards:* Federal Pell, FSEOG, state, private, college/university gift aid from institutional funds.

GIFT AID (NON-NEED-BASED) *Scholarships, grants, and awards by category: Academic Interests/Achievement:* general academic interests/achievements. *Special Characteristics:* children of faculty/staff, spouses of current students.

LOANS *Programs:* FFEL (Subsidized and Unsubsidized Stafford, PLUS), state, college/university, Chiroloans, alternative loans.

WORK-STUDY *Federal work-study:* Total amount: $5200; jobs available.

APPLYING FOR FINANCIAL AID *Required financial aid forms:* FAFSA, institution's own form, verification worksheet, income tax form(s).

CONTACT Arthur Goudeau, Financial Aid Director, Texas Chiropractic College, 5912 Spencer Highway, Pasadena, TX 77505, 281-998-6022 or toll-free 800-468-6839. *Fax:* 281-991-5237. *E-mail:* agoudeau@txchiro.edu.

TEXAS CHRISTIAN UNIVERSITY
Fort Worth, TX

Tuition & fees: $19,740	Average undergraduate aid package: $14,037

ABOUT THE INSTITUTION Independent religious, coed. Awards: bachelor's, master's, doctoral, and first professional degrees and post-bachelor's and first professional certificates. 86 undergraduate majors. Total enrollment: 8,632. Undergraduates: 7,154. Freshmen: 1,607. Federal methodology is used as a basis for awarding need-based institutional aid.

UNDERGRADUATE EXPENSES for 2004–05 *Application fee:* $40. *Comprehensive fee:* $25,620 includes full-time tuition ($19,700), mandatory fees ($40), and room and board ($5880). *College room only:* $3880. Room and board charges vary according to board plan and housing facility. *Payment plan:* Installment.

FRESHMAN FINANCIAL AID (Fall 2004, est.) 935 applied for aid; of those 73% were deemed to have need. 99% of freshmen with need received aid; of those 52% had need fully met. *Average percent of need met:* 71% (excluding resources awarded to replace EFC). *Average financial aid package:* $13,314 (excluding resources awarded to replace EFC). 24% of all full-time freshmen had no need and received non-need-based gift aid.

UNDERGRADUATE FINANCIAL AID (Fall 2004, est.) 3,698 applied for aid; of those 79% were deemed to have need. 99% of undergraduates with need received aid; of those 43% had need fully met. *Average percent of need met:* 67% (excluding resources awarded to replace EFC). *Average financial aid package:* $14,037 (excluding resources awarded to replace EFC). 22% of all full-time undergraduates had no need and received non-need-based gift aid.

GIFT AID (NEED-BASED) *Total amount:* $24,212,723 (12% federal, 20% state, 61% institutional, 7% external sources). *Receiving aid:* Freshmen: 40% (636); All full-time undergraduates: 38% (2,573). *Average award:* Freshmen: $9529; Undergraduates: $9867. *Scholarships, grants, and awards:* Federal Pell, FSEOG, state, private, college/university gift aid from institutional funds, United Negro College Fund.

GIFT AID (NON-NEED-BASED) *Total amount:* $16,036,657 (80% institutional, 20% external sources). *Receiving aid:* Freshmen: 15% (244); Undergraduates: 12% (814). *Average Award:* Freshmen: $7445; Undergraduates: $8209. *Scholarships, grants, and awards by category: Academic Interests/Achievement:* 2,071 awards ($12,097,000 total): education, engineering/technologies, general academic interests/achievements, international studies, military science, premedicine, religion/biblical studies. *Creative Arts/Performance:* 244 awards ($1,470,000 total): art/fine arts, cinema/film/broadcasting, dance, journalism/publications, music, performing arts, theater/drama. *Special Achievements/Activities:* 400 awards ($2,264,000 total): general special achievements/activities, leadership. *Special Characteristics:* 722 awards ($7,311,000 total): adult students, children of faculty/staff, children of union members/company employees, international students, local/state students, relatives of clergy, religious affiliation. *Tuition waivers:* Full or partial for employees or children of employees. *ROTC:* Army, Air Force.

LOANS *Student loans:* $24,182,095 (78% need-based, 22% non-need-based). *Average need-based loan:* Freshmen: $4305; Undergraduates: $5317. *Parent loans:* $19,401,047 (4% need-based, 96% non-need-based). *Programs:* FFEL (Subsidized and Unsubsidized Stafford, PLUS), Perkins, Federal Nursing, state, college/university.

WORK-STUDY *Federal work-study:* Total amount: $3,048,857; 1,296 jobs averaging $2313. *State or other work-study/employment:* Total amount: $60,000 (100% need-based). 25 part-time jobs averaging $2400.

ATHLETIC AWARDS *Total amount:* $6,939,883 (30% need-based, 70% non-need-based).

APPLYING FOR FINANCIAL AID *Required financial aid forms:* FAFSA, institution's own form. *Financial aid deadline (priority):* 5/1. *Notification date:* Continuous.

CONTACT Michael Scott, Director, Scholarships and Student Financial Aid, Texas Christian University, PO Box 297012, Fort Worth, TX 76129-0002, 817-257-7858 or toll-free 800-828-3764. *Fax:* 817-257-7462. *E-mail:* m.scott@tcu.edu.

TEXAS COLLEGE
Tyler, TX

ABOUT THE INSTITUTION Independent religious, coed. Awards: bachelor's degrees and post-bachelor's certificates. 14 undergraduate majors. Total enrollment: 757. Undergraduates: 752. Freshmen: 244.

GIFT AID (NEED-BASED) *Scholarships, grants, and awards:* Federal Pell, FSEOG, state, college/university gift aid from institutional funds, United Negro College Fund.

GIFT AID (NON-NEED-BASED) *Scholarships, grants, and awards by category: Special Achievements/Activities:* leadership.

LOANS *Programs:* Federal Direct (Subsidized and Unsubsidized Stafford, PLUS), FFEL (Subsidized and Unsubsidized Stafford, PLUS), state.

APPLYING FOR FINANCIAL AID *Required financial aid forms:* FAFSA, institution's own form.

CONTACT Mrs. Ruth Jordan, Financial Aid Office, Texas College, 2404 North Grand Avenue, Tyler, TX 75702, 903-593-8311 Ext. 2210 or toll-free 800-306-6299 (out-of-state). *Fax:* 903-596-0001. *E-mail:* rjordanW@texascollege.edu.

TEXAS LUTHERAN UNIVERSITY
Seguin, TX

Tuition & fees: $16,600   **Average undergraduate aid package: $12,130**

ABOUT THE INSTITUTION Independent religious, coed. Awards: bachelor's degrees and post-bachelor's certificates. 42 undergraduate majors. Total enrollment: 1,414. Undergraduates: 1,414. Freshmen: 399. Federal methodology is used as a basis for awarding need-based institutional aid.

UNDERGRADUATE EXPENSES for 2004–05 *Application fee:* $25. *Comprehensive fee:* $21,630 includes full-time tuition ($16,480), mandatory fees ($120), and room and board ($5030). *College room only:* $2340. Full-time tuition and fees vary according to course load. Room and board charges vary according to board plan, housing facility, and location. *Part-time tuition:* $550 per credit hour. *Part-time fees:* $60 per term. Part-time tuition and fees vary according to course load. *Payment plan:* Installment.

FRESHMAN FINANCIAL AID (Fall 2003) 336 applied for aid; of those 85% were deemed to have need. 100% of freshmen with need received aid; of those 27% had need fully met. *Average percent of need met:* 76% (excluding resources awarded to replace EFC). *Average financial aid package:* $12,643 (excluding resources awarded to replace EFC). 20% of all full-time freshmen had no need and received non-need-based gift aid.

UNDERGRADUATE FINANCIAL AID (Fall 2003) 1,031 applied for aid; of those 87% were deemed to have need. 100% of undergraduates with need received aid; of those 23% had need fully met. *Average percent of need met:* 70% (excluding resources awarded to replace EFC). *Average financial aid package:* $12,130 (excluding resources awarded to replace EFC). 26% of all full-time undergraduates had no need and received non-need-based gift aid.

GIFT AID (NEED-BASED) *Total amount:* $8,275,794 (16% federal, 27% state, 53% institutional, 4% external sources). *Receiving aid:* Freshmen: 66% (238); All full-time undergraduates: 62% (763). *Average award:* Freshmen: $6121; Undergraduates: $5592. *Scholarships, grants, and awards:* Federal Pell, FSEOG, state, private, college/university gift aid from institutional funds.

GIFT AID (NON-NEED-BASED) *Total amount:* $1,884,020 (95% institutional, 5% external sources). *Receiving aid:* Freshmen: 78% (280); Undergraduates: 70% (863). *Average Award:* Freshmen: $5470; Undergraduates: $5308. *Scholarships, grants, and awards by category: Academic Interests/Achievement:* 717 awards ($3,477,945 total): general academic interests/achievements. *Creative Arts/Performance:* 250 awards ($453,608 total): journalism/publications, music, theater/drama. *Special Achievements/Activities:* 236 awards ($455,529 total): general special achievements/activities, leadership, religious involvement. *Special Characteristics:* 666 awards ($925,093 total): children and siblings of alumni, children of faculty/staff, first-generation college students, general special characteristics, international students, religious affiliation. *Tuition waivers:* Full or partial for children of alumni, employees or children of employees. *ROTC:* Army cooperative, Air Force cooperative.

LOANS *Student loans:* $7,111,240 (88% need-based, 12% non-need-based). 72% of past graduating class borrowed through all loan programs. *Average indebtedness per student:* $25,050. *Average need-based loan:* Freshmen: $2909; Undergraduates: $2689. *Parent loans:* $3,382,314 (68% need-based, 32% non-need-based). *Programs:* FFEL (Subsidized and Unsubsidized Stafford, PLUS), Perkins, alternative loans.

WORK-STUDY *Federal work-study:* Total amount: $83,209; 342 jobs averaging $1000. *State or other work-study/employment:* Total amount: $387,327 (4% need-based, 96% non-need-based). 16 part-time jobs averaging $1030.

APPLYING FOR FINANCIAL AID *Required financial aid form:* FAFSA. *Financial aid deadline (priority):* 4/1. *Notification date:* Continuous beginning 3/1. Students must reply within 2 weeks of notification.

CONTACT Debbie Mattke, Assistant Director Financial Aid, Texas Lutheran University, 1000 West Court Street, Seguin, TX 78155-5999, 830-372-8075 or toll-free 800-771-8521. *Fax:* 830-372-8096. *E-mail:* dmattke@tlu.edu.

TEXAS SOUTHERN UNIVERSITY
Houston, TX

ABOUT THE INSTITUTION State-supported, coed. Awards: bachelor's, master's, doctoral, and first professional degrees. 106 undergraduate majors. Total enrollment: 11,635. Undergraduates: 9,585. Freshmen: 2,113.

GIFT AID (NEED-BASED) *Scholarships, grants, and awards:* Federal Pell, FSEOG, state, private, college/university gift aid from institutional funds, United Negro College Fund, Federal Nursing.

GIFT AID (NON-NEED-BASED) *Scholarships, grants, and awards by category: Academic Interests/Achievement:* business, communication, engineering/technologies, general academic interests/achievements.

LOANS *Programs:* FFEL (Subsidized and Unsubsidized Stafford, PLUS), Perkins.

WORK-STUDY *Federal work-study:* Total amount: $559,768; 225 jobs averaging $4000. *State or other work-study/employment:* Total amount: $77,226 (100% need-based). 29 part-time jobs averaging $4000.

APPLYING FOR FINANCIAL AID *Required financial aid forms:* FAFSA, institution's own form.

CONTACT Financial Aid Office, Texas Southern University, 3100 Cleburne, Houston, TX 77004-4584, 713-313-7011. *Fax:* 713-313-1858.

TEXAS STATE UNIVERSITY-SAN MARCOS
San Marcos, TX

Tuition & fees (TX res): $4680   **Average undergraduate aid package: $8997**

ABOUT THE INSTITUTION State-supported, coed. Awards: bachelor's, master's, and doctoral degrees and post-bachelor's certificates. 92 undergraduate majors. Total enrollment: 26,783. Undergraduates: 22,402. Freshmen: 2,801. Federal methodology is used as a basis for awarding need-based institutional aid.

UNDERGRADUATE EXPENSES for 2004–05 *Application fee:* $40. *Tuition, state resident:* full-time $3270; part-time $109 per semester hour. *Tuition, nonresident:* full-time $11,010; part-time $367 per semester hour. *Required fees:* full-time $1410; $36 per semester hour or $247 per term part-time. Full-time tuition and fees vary according to course load. Part-time tuition and fees vary according to course load. *College room and board:* $5456; *room only:* $3370. Room and board charges vary according to board plan and housing facility. *Payment plan:* Installment.

FRESHMAN FINANCIAL AID (Fall 2004, est.) 1937 applied for aid; of those 66% were deemed to have need. 94% of freshmen with need received aid; of those 12% had need fully met. *Average percent of need met:* 64% (excluding resources awarded to replace EFC). *Average financial aid package:* $8229 (excluding resources awarded to replace EFC). 15% of all full-time freshmen had no need and received non-need-based gift aid.

UNDERGRADUATE FINANCIAL AID (Fall 2004, est.) 11,220 applied for aid; of those 84% were deemed to have need. 95% of undergraduates with need received aid; of those 15% had need fully met. *Average percent of need met:* 66% (excluding resources awarded to replace EFC). *Average financial aid package:* $8997 (excluding resources awarded to replace EFC). 14% of all full-time undergraduates had no need and received non-need-based gift aid.

GIFT AID (NEED-BASED) *Total amount:* $22,973,007 (69% federal, 31% state). *Receiving aid:* Freshmen: 20% (590); All full-time undergraduates: 30% (5,480). *Average award:* Freshmen: $4215; Undergraduates: $3814. *Scholarships, grants, and awards:* Federal Pell, FSEOG, state, college/university gift aid from institutional funds.

GIFT AID (NON-NEED-BASED) *Total amount:* $14,639,928 (11% institutional, 89% external sources). *Receiving aid:* Freshmen: 18% (518); Undergraduates: 12% (2,121). *Average Award:* Freshmen: $7694; Undergraduates: $7617. *Scholarships, grants, and awards by category: Academic Interests/Achievement:* agriculture, business, education, English, general academic interests/achievements, home economics, international studies, military science. *Creative Arts/Performance:* applied art and design, journalism/publications, music, theater/drama. *Special Characteristics:* children and siblings of alumni, first-generation college students, handicapped students. *Tuition waivers:* Full or partial for employees or children of employees. *ROTC:* Army, Air Force.

LOANS *Student loans:* $59,417,691 (58% need-based, 42% non-need-based). 59% of past graduating class borrowed through all loan programs. *Average indebtedness per student:* $16,161. *Average need-based loan:* Freshmen: $2395; Undergraduates: $3820. *Parent loans:* $11,564,090 (100% non-need-based). *Programs:* Federal Direct (Subsidized and Unsubsidized Stafford, PLUS), FFEL (Subsidized and Unsubsidized Stafford, PLUS), Perkins, state, college/university.

WORK-STUDY *Federal work-study:* Total amount: $1,212,874; 737 jobs averaging $1646. *State or other work-study/employment:* Total amount: $99,432 (100% need-based). 126 part-time jobs averaging $789.

ATHLETIC AWARDS *Total amount:* $2,088,545 (100% non-need-based).

APPLYING FOR FINANCIAL AID *Required financial aid form:* FAFSA. *Financial aid deadline (priority):* 4/1. *Notification date:* Continuous. Students must reply within 3 weeks of notification.

CONTACT Ms. Mariko Gomez, Director of Financial Aid, Texas State University-San Marcos, 601 University Drive, San Marcos, TX 78666-4602, 512-245-2315. *Fax:* 512-245-7920. *E-mail:* mg01@txstate.edu.

TEXAS TECH UNIVERSITY
Lubbock, TX

Tuition & fees (TX res): $5848   **Average undergraduate aid package: $6485**

ABOUT THE INSTITUTION State-supported, coed. Awards: bachelor's, master's, doctoral, and first professional degrees. 112 undergraduate majors. Total enrollment: 28,325. Undergraduates: 23,329. Freshmen: 3,951. Federal methodology is used as a basis for awarding need-based institutional aid.

UNDERGRADUATE EXPENSES for 2004–05 *Application fee:* $50. *Tuition, state resident:* full-time $3720; part-time $124 per credit hour. *Tuition, nonresident:* full-time $11,460; part-time $382 per credit hour. *Required fees:* full-time $2128; $54 per credit hour or $284. Full-time tuition and fees vary according to course load, program, and reciprocity agreements. Part-time tuition and fees vary according to course load, program, and reciprocity agreements. *College room and board:* $6421; *room only:* $3631. Room and board charges vary according to board plan and housing facility. *Payment plan:* Installment.

FRESHMAN FINANCIAL AID (Fall 2003) 3048 applied for aid; of those 57% were deemed to have need. 96% of freshmen with need received aid. *Average financial aid package:* $5875 (excluding resources awarded to replace EFC). 44% of all full-time freshmen had no need and received non-need-based gift aid.

UNDERGRADUATE FINANCIAL AID (Fall 2003) 13,082 applied for aid; of those 67% were deemed to have need. 98% of undergraduates with need received aid. *Average financial aid package:* $6485 (excluding resources awarded to replace EFC). 27% of all full-time undergraduates had no need and received non-need-based gift aid.

GIFT AID (NEED-BASED) *Total amount:* $24,022,596 (54% federal, 9% state, 37% institutional). *Receiving aid:* Freshmen: 29% (1,124); All full-time undergraduates: 27% (5,707). *Average award:* Freshmen: $4485; Undergraduates: $3281. *Scholarships, grants, and awards:* Federal Pell, FSEOG, state, private, college/university gift aid from institutional funds.

GIFT AID (NON-NEED-BASED) *Total amount:* $8,231,300 (2% federal, 57% institutional, 41% external sources). *Receiving aid:* Freshmen: 23% (873); Undergraduates: 13% (2,705). *Average Award:* Freshmen: $2396; Undergraduates: $2204. *Scholarships, grants, and awards by category:* Academic Interests/Achievement: agriculture, architecture, biological sciences, business, communication, computer science, education, engineering/technologies, English, foreign languages, general academic interests/achievements, home economics, international studies, mathematics, military science, physical sciences, premedicine, social sciences. *Creative Arts/Performance:* applied art and design, art/fine arts, dance, journalism/publications, music, performing arts, theater/drama. *Special Achievements/Activities:* community service, memberships, rodeo. *Special Characteristics:* children of faculty/staff, first-generation college students, handicapped students, out-of-state students, veterans, veterans' children. *Tuition waivers:* Full or partial for employees or children of employees, senior citizens. *ROTC:* Army, Air Force.

LOANS *Student loans:* $52,923,192 (52% need-based, 48% non-need-based). 57% of past graduating class borrowed through all loan programs. *Average indebtedness per student:* $19,972. *Average need-based loan:* Freshmen: $2310; Undergraduates: $3662. *Parent loans:* $25,368,497 (100% need-based). *Programs:* FFEL (Subsidized and Unsubsidized Stafford, PLUS), Perkins, state, college/university.

WORK-STUDY *Federal work-study:* Total amount: $692,066; 445 jobs averaging $1555.

ATHLETIC AWARDS *Total amount:* $2,845,449 (100% non-need-based).

APPLYING FOR FINANCIAL AID *Required financial aid form:* FAFSA. *Financial aid deadline (priority):* 5/1. *Notification date:* Continuous. Students must reply within 2 weeks of notification.

CONTACT Becky Wilson, Director of Financial Aid, Interim, Texas Tech University, PO Box 45011, Lubbock, TX 79409-5011, 806-742-3681. *Fax:* 806-742-0880.

TEXAS WESLEYAN UNIVERSITY
Fort Worth, TX

Tuition & fees: $13,000   **Average undergraduate aid package: N/A**

ABOUT THE INSTITUTION Independent United Methodist, coed. Awards: bachelor's, master's, and first professional degrees. 70 undergraduate majors. Total enrollment: 2,742. Undergraduates: 1,491. Freshmen: 161. Federal methodology is used as a basis for awarding need-based institutional aid.

UNDERGRADUATE EXPENSES for 2004–05 *Application fee:* $25. *Comprehensive fee:* $18,400 includes full-time tuition ($11,950), mandatory fees ($1050), and room and board ($5400). *College room only:* $1730. Full-time tuition and fees vary according to program. Room and board charges vary according to board plan and student level. *Part-time tuition:* $395 per credit. *Part-time fees:* $40 per credit. Part-time tuition and fees vary according to program. *Payment plans:* Installment, deferred payment.

FRESHMAN FINANCIAL AID (Fall 2004, est.) 149 applied for aid; of those 78% were deemed to have need. 100% of freshmen with need received aid. *Average percent of need met:* 73% (excluding resources awarded to replace EFC).

UNDERGRADUATE FINANCIAL AID (Fall 2004, est.) 974 applied for aid; of those 82% were deemed to have need. 100% of undergraduates with need received aid. *Average percent of need met:* 74% (excluding resources awarded to replace EFC).

GIFT AID (NEED-BASED) *Total amount:* $3,848,924 (48% federal, 49% state, 3% institutional). *Receiving aid:* Freshmen: 72% (109). *Average award:* Freshmen: $1100. *Scholarships, grants, and awards:* Federal Pell, FSEOG, state, private, college/university gift aid from institutional funds.

GIFT AID (NON-NEED-BASED) *Total amount:* $2,635,803 (94% institutional, 6% external sources). *Receiving aid:* Freshmen: 69% (104); Undergraduates: 60% (580). *Scholarships, grants, and awards by category:* Academic Interests/Achievement: general academic interests/achievements. *Creative Arts/Performance:* art/fine arts, general creative arts/performance. *Special Achievements/Activities:* cheerleading/drum major, general special achievements/activities, leadership, religious involvement. *Special Characteristics:* relatives of clergy, religious affiliation. *Tuition waivers:* Full or partial for employees or children of employees. *ROTC:* Army cooperative, Air Force cooperative.

LOANS *Student loans:* $6,896,462 (50% need-based, 50% non-need-based). *Parent loans:* $171,295 (100% non-need-based). *Programs:* FFEL (Subsidized and Unsubsidized Stafford, PLUS), state, college/university.

WORK-STUDY *Federal work-study:* Total amount: $250,000; jobs available (averaging $2400). *State or other work-study/employment:* Total amount: $32,779 (100% need-based). Part-time jobs available (averaging $2400).

ATHLETIC AWARDS *Total amount:* $508,584 (100% non-need-based).

APPLYING FOR FINANCIAL AID *Required financial aid forms:* FAFSA, institution's own form. *Financial aid deadline:* Continuous. *Notification date:* Continuous. Students must reply within 4 weeks of notification.

CONTACT Mrs. Dean Carpenter, Director of Financial Aid, Texas Wesleyan University, 1201 Wesleyan Street, Fort Worth, TX 76105-1536, 817-531-4420 or toll-free 800-580-8980 (in-state). *Fax:* 817-531-4231. *E-mail:* finaid@txwes.edu.

TEXAS WOMAN'S UNIVERSITY
Denton, TX

ABOUT THE INSTITUTION State-supported, coed, primarily women. Awards: bachelor's, master's, and doctoral degrees and post-master's certificates. 46 undergraduate majors. Total enrollment: 10,750. Undergraduates: 5,826. Freshmen: 650.

GIFT AID (NEED-BASED) *Scholarships, grants, and awards:* Federal Pell, FSEOG, state, private, college/university gift aid from institutional funds.

GIFT AID (NON-NEED-BASED) *Scholarships, grants, and awards by category:* Academic Interests/Achievement: biological sciences, business, communication, computer science, education, English, foreign languages, general academic interests/achievements, health fields, home economics, humanities, library science, mathematics, physical sciences, premedicine, social sciences. *Creative Arts/Performance:* applied art and design, art/fine arts, cinema/film/broadcasting, dance, journalism/publications, music, theater/drama. *Special Characteristics:* international students.

LOANS *Programs:* FFEL (Subsidized and Unsubsidized Stafford, PLUS), Perkins, Federal Nursing, state, college/university, alternative loans.

WORK-STUDY *Federal work-study:* Total amount: $111,490; 131 jobs averaging $1702. *State or other work-study/employment:* Total amount: $1,180,525 (2% need-based, 98% non-need-based). 481 part-time jobs averaging $3144.

APPLYING FOR FINANCIAL AID *Required financial aid forms:* FAFSA, institution's own form.

CONTACT Mr. Governor Jackson, Director of Financial Aid, Texas Woman's University, PO Box 425408, Denton, TX 76204-5408, 940-898-3051 or toll-free 888-948-9984. *Fax:* 940-898-3068. *E-mail:* gjackson@twu.edu.

THIEL COLLEGE
Greenville, PA

Tuition & fees: $16,390	Average undergraduate aid package: $14,916

ABOUT THE INSTITUTION Independent religious, coed. Awards: associate and bachelor's degrees. 37 undergraduate majors. Total enrollment: 1,245. Undergraduates: 1,245. Freshmen: 369. Federal methodology is used as a basis for awarding need-based institutional aid.

UNDERGRADUATE EXPENSES for 2004–05 *Application fee:* $25. *Comprehensive fee:* $22,974 includes full-time tuition ($15,000), mandatory fees ($1390), and room and board ($6584). *College room only:* $3396. Full-time tuition and fees vary according to course load. Room and board charges vary according to board plan and housing facility. *Part-time tuition:* $400 per credit hour. Part-time tuition and fees vary according to course load. *Payment plan:* Installment.

FRESHMAN FINANCIAL AID (Fall 2004, est.) 358 applied for aid; of those 89% were deemed to have need. 100% of freshmen with need received aid; of those 16% had need fully met. *Average percent of need met:* 82% (excluding resources awarded to replace EFC). *Average financial aid package:* $14,675 (excluding resources awarded to replace EFC). 14% of all full-time freshmen had no need and received non-need-based gift aid.

UNDERGRADUATE FINANCIAL AID (Fall 2004, est.) 1,132 applied for aid; of those 90% were deemed to have need. 100% of undergraduates with need received aid; of those 18% had need fully met. *Average percent of need met:* 81% (excluding resources awarded to replace EFC). *Average financial aid package:* $14,916 (excluding resources awarded to replace EFC). 12% of all full-time undergraduates had no need and received non-need-based gift aid.

GIFT AID (NEED-BASED) *Total amount:* $9,665,268 (17% federal, 19% state, 62% institutional, 2% external sources). *Receiving aid:* Freshmen: 86% (319); All full-time undergraduates: 86% (1,018). *Average award:* Freshmen: $10,541; Undergraduates: $10,025. *Scholarships, grants, and awards:* Federal Pell, FSEOG, state, private, college/university gift aid from institutional funds.

GIFT AID (NON-NEED-BASED) *Total amount:* $668,734 (100% institutional). *Receiving aid:* Freshmen: 86% (319); Undergraduates: 86% (1,018). *Average Award:* Freshmen: $4810; Undergraduates: $4676. *Scholarships, grants, and awards by category: Academic Interests/Achievement:* biological sciences, business, computer science, education, English, general academic interests/achievements, mathematics, physical sciences, religion/biblical studies. *Creative Arts/Performance:* 10 awards ($5750 total): music. *Special Achievements/Activities:* leadership. *Special Characteristics:* children and siblings of alumni, children of faculty/staff, relatives of clergy, religious affiliation, siblings of current students. *Tuition waivers:* Full or partial for employees or children of employees, senior citizens.

LOANS *Student loans:* $4,311,897 (100% need-based). 89% of past graduating class borrowed through all loan programs. *Average indebtedness per student:* $19,559. *Average need-based loan:* Freshmen: $3634; Undergraduates: $4236. *Parent loans:* $1,631,333 (92% need-based, 8% non-need-based). *Programs:* FFEL (Subsidized and Unsubsidized Stafford, PLUS), Perkins, college/university.

WORK-STUDY *Federal work-study:* Total amount: $126,636; 154 jobs averaging $1013. *State or other work-study/employment:* Total amount: $633,010 (86% need-based, 14% non-need-based). 416 part-time jobs averaging $1014.

APPLYING FOR FINANCIAL AID *Required financial aid forms:* FAFSA, state aid form. *Financial aid deadline (priority):* 3/15. *Notification date:* Continuous beginning 2/15. Students must reply within 2 weeks of notification.

CONTACT Ms. Cynthia H. Farrell, Director of Financial Aid, Thiel College, 75 College Avenue, Greenville, PA 16125-2181, 724-589-2178 or toll-free 800-248-4435. *Fax:* 724-589-2850. *E-mail:* cfarrell@thiel.edu.

THOMAS AQUINAS COLLEGE
Santa Paula, CA

Tuition & fees: $18,600	Average undergraduate aid package: $15,826

ABOUT THE INSTITUTION Independent Roman Catholic, coed. Awards: bachelor's degrees. 4 undergraduate majors. Total enrollment: 331. Undergraduates: 331. Freshmen: 104. Both federal and institutional methodology are used as a basis for awarding need-based institutional aid.

UNDERGRADUATE EXPENSES for 2005–06 *Comprehensive fee:* $24,400 includes full-time tuition ($18,600) and room and board ($5800).

FRESHMAN FINANCIAL AID (Fall 2004, est.) 75 applied for aid; of those 87% were deemed to have need. 100% of freshmen with need received aid; of those

100% had need fully met. *Average percent of need met:* 100% (excluding resources awarded to replace EFC). *Average financial aid package:* $15,164 (excluding resources awarded to replace EFC).

UNDERGRADUATE FINANCIAL AID (Fall 2004, est.) 236 applied for aid; of those 89% were deemed to have need. 100% of undergraduates with need received aid; of those 100% had need fully met. *Average percent of need met:* 100% (excluding resources awarded to replace EFC). *Average financial aid package:* $15,826 (excluding resources awarded to replace EFC).

GIFT AID (NEED-BASED) *Total amount:* $2,124,596 (11% federal, 18% state, 67% institutional, 4% external sources). *Receiving aid:* Freshmen: 57% (59); All full-time undergraduates: 58% (193). *Average award:* Freshmen: $10,913; Undergraduates: $10,975. *Scholarships, grants, and awards:* Federal Pell, state, private, college/university gift aid from institutional funds.

GIFT AID (NON-NEED-BASED) *Total amount:* $59,337 (12% state, 88% external sources). *Receiving aid:* Freshmen: 2% (2); Undergraduates: 1% (3).

LOANS *Student loans:* $852,983 (79% need-based, 21% non-need-based). 78% of past graduating class borrowed through all loan programs. *Average indebtedness per student:* $14,000. *Average need-based loan:* Freshmen: $2613; Undergraduates: $3351. *Parent loans:* $174,151 (25% need-based, 75% non-need-based). *Programs:* FFEL (Subsidized and Unsubsidized Stafford, PLUS), college/university, Canada Student Loans.

WORK-STUDY *State or other work-study/employment:* Total amount: $592,057 (96% need-based, 4% non-need-based). 193 part-time jobs averaging $3068.

APPLYING FOR FINANCIAL AID *Required financial aid forms:* FAFSA, institution's own form, state aid form, noncustodial (divorced/separated) parent's statement, income tax returns. *Financial aid deadline:* Continuous. *Notification date:* Continuous beginning 1/1. Students must reply within 4 weeks of notification.

CONTACT Mr. Gregory Becher, Director of Financial Aid, Thomas Aquinas College, 10000 North Ojai Road, Santa Paula, CA 93060-9980, 805-525-4419 Ext. 308 or toll-free 800-634-9797. *Fax:* 805-525-9342. *E-mail:* gbecher@thomasaquinas.edu.

THOMAS COLLEGE
Waterville, ME

ABOUT THE INSTITUTION Independent, coed. Awards: associate, bachelor's, and master's degrees. 27 undergraduate majors. Total enrollment: 870. Undergraduates: 737. Freshmen: 186.

GIFT AID (NEED-BASED) *Scholarships, grants, and awards:* Federal Pell, FSEOG, state, private, college/university gift aid from institutional funds.

GIFT AID (NON-NEED-BASED) *Scholarships, grants, and awards by category: Academic Interests/Achievement:* general academic interests/achievements. *Special Achievements/Activities:* leadership.

LOANS *Programs:* Federal Direct (Subsidized and Unsubsidized Stafford, PLUS), Perkins.

WORK-STUDY *Federal work-study:* Total amount: $198,931; 108 jobs averaging $1700.

APPLYING FOR FINANCIAL AID *Required financial aid form:* FAFSA.

CONTACT Jami Jandreau, Student Financial Services Assistant, Thomas College, 180 West River Road, Waterville, ME 04901-5097, 800-339-7001. *Fax:* 207-859-1114. *E-mail:* sfsassistant@thomas.edu.

THOMAS EDISON STATE COLLEGE
Trenton, NJ

Tuition & fees: N/R	Average undergraduate aid package: N/A

ABOUT THE INSTITUTION State-supported, coed. Awards: associate, bachelor's, and master's degrees (offers only distance learning degree programs). 79 undergraduate majors. Total enrollment: 11,000. Undergraduates: 10,750. Federal methodology is used as a basis for awarding need-based institutional aid.

UNDERGRADUATE EXPENSES for 2004–05 *Application fee:* $75. *Tuition, state resident:* part-time $3490 per year. *Tuition, nonresident:* part-time $5015 per year.

GIFT AID (NEED-BASED) *Total amount:* $1,333,080 (92% federal, 8% state). *Scholarships, grants, and awards:* Federal Pell, state, private.

LOANS *Student loans:* $4,432,218 (100% need-based). *Programs:* FFEL (Subsidized and Unsubsidized Stafford, PLUS).

APPLYING FOR FINANCIAL AID *Required financial aid forms:* FAFSA, institution's own form. *Financial aid deadline:* Continuous. *Notification date:* Continuous. Students must reply within 9 weeks of notification.

CONTACT Financial Aid Office, Thomas Edison State College, 101 West State Street, Trenton, NJ 08608, 609-633-9658 or toll-free 888-442-8372. *Fax:* 609-633-6489.

THOMAS JEFFERSON UNIVERSITY
Philadelphia, PA

Tuition & fees: $20,914	Average undergraduate aid package: N/A

ABOUT THE INSTITUTION Independent, coed. Awards: bachelor's, master's, and doctoral degrees and post-bachelor's certificates. 8 undergraduate majors. Total enrollment: 2,457. Undergraduates: 908. Freshmen: 108. Both federal and institutional methodology are used as a basis for awarding need-based institutional aid.

UNDERGRADUATE EXPENSES for 2004–05 *Application fee:* $50. *Comprehensive fee:* $28,897 includes full-time tuition ($20,914) and room and board ($7983). *College room only:* $4068. Full-time tuition and fees vary according to course level. Room and board charges vary according to housing facility. Part-time tuition and fees vary according to course level. *Payment plan:* Installment.

FRESHMAN FINANCIAL AID (Fall 2004, est.) 53 applied for aid; of those 92% were deemed to have need. 100% of freshmen with need received aid; of those 4% had need fully met.

UNDERGRADUATE FINANCIAL AID (Fall 2004, est.) 525 applied for aid; of those 93% were deemed to have need. 100% of undergraduates with need received aid; of those 6% had need fully met. 2% of all full-time undergraduates had no need and received non-need-based gift aid.

GIFT AID (NEED-BASED) *Total amount:* $3,031,540 (19% federal, 13% state, 17% institutional, 51% external sources). *Receiving aid:* Freshmen: 57% (33); All full-time undergraduates: 45% (253). *Scholarships, grants, and awards:* Federal Pell, FSEOG, state, private, college/university gift aid from institutional funds, Scholarships for Disadvantaged Students (SDS).

GIFT AID (NON-NEED-BASED) *Total amount:* $437,436 (11% institutional, 89% external sources). *Receiving aid:* Freshmen: 2% (1); Undergraduates: 2% (10). *Average Award:* Undergraduates: $5000. *Scholarships, grants, and awards by category:* Academic Interests/Achievement: 55 awards ($270,000 total): general academic interests/achievements, health fields. *Special Characteristics:* members of minority groups, veterans. *Tuition waivers:* Full or partial for employees or children of employees. *ROTC:* Air Force cooperative.

LOANS *Student loans:* $8,457,331 (88% need-based, 12% non-need-based). 75% of past graduating class borrowed through all loan programs. *Average indebtedness per student:* $24,703. *Average need-based loan:* Undergraduates: $10,993. *Parent loans:* $555,470 (100% non-need-based). *Programs:* FFEL (Subsidized and Unsubsidized Stafford, PLUS), Perkins, Federal Nursing, college/university.

WORK-STUDY *Federal work-study:* Total amount: $91,281; 116 jobs averaging $2000.

APPLYING FOR FINANCIAL AID *Required financial aid forms:* FAFSA, institution's own form, parent and student income tax returns. *Financial aid deadline (priority):* 4/1. *Notification date:* Continuous. Students must reply within 2 weeks of notification.

CONTACT Susan Batchelor, University Director of Financial Aid, Thomas Jefferson University, 1025 Walnut Street, Room G-1, College Building, Philadelphia, PA 19107, 215-955-2867 or toll-free 877-533-3247. *E-mail:* financial.aid@jefferson.edu.

THOMAS MORE COLLEGE
Crestview Hills, KY

Tuition & fees: $18,320	Average undergraduate aid package: $15,810

ABOUT THE INSTITUTION Independent Roman Catholic, coed. Awards: associate, bachelor's, and master's degrees. 39 undergraduate majors. Total enrollment: 1,465. Undergraduates: 1,339. Federal methodology is used as a basis for awarding need-based institutional aid.

UNDERGRADUATE EXPENSES for 2005–06 *Application fee:* $25. *Comprehensive fee:* $24,420 includes full-time tuition ($17,600), mandatory fees ($720), and room and board ($6100). *College room only:* $2900. Full-time tuition and fees vary according to program. Room and board charges vary according to board plan and housing facility. *Part-time tuition:* $450 per credit hour. *Part-time fees:* $30 per credit hour; $15 per term. Part-time tuition and fees vary according to course load and program. *Payment plans:* Installment, deferred payment.

FRESHMAN FINANCIAL AID (Fall 2004, est.) 167 applied for aid; of those 100% were deemed to have need. 100% of freshmen with need received aid; of those 100% had need fully met. *Average percent of need met:* 87% (excluding resources awarded to replace EFC). *Average financial aid package:* $16,376 (excluding resources awarded to replace EFC). 9% of all full-time freshmen had no need and received non-need-based gift aid.

UNDERGRADUATE FINANCIAL AID (Fall 2004, est.) 800 applied for aid; of those 100% were deemed to have need. 100% of undergraduates with need received aid; of those 99% had need fully met. *Average percent of need met:* 80% (excluding resources awarded to replace EFC). *Average financial aid package:* $15,810 (excluding resources awarded to replace EFC). 13% of all full-time undergraduates had no need and received non-need-based gift aid.

GIFT AID (NEED-BASED) *Total amount:* $1,721,686 (45% federal, 55% state). *Receiving aid:* Freshmen: 88% (155); All full-time undergraduates: 65% (697). *Average award:* Freshmen: $4086; Undergraduates: $4503. *Scholarships, grants, and awards:* Federal Pell, FSEOG, state, private, college/university gift aid from institutional funds.

GIFT AID (NON-NEED-BASED) *Total amount:* $5,316,779 (9% state, 87% institutional, 4% external sources). *Receiving aid:* Freshmen: 95% (167); Undergraduates: 74% (790). *Average Award:* Freshmen: $5102; Undergraduates: $6366. *Scholarships, grants, and awards by category:* Academic Interests/Achievement: 362 awards ($1,543,390 total): general academic interests/achievements. *Creative Arts/Performance:* 17 awards ($21,937 total): art/fine arts, theater/drama. *Special Achievements/Activities:* religious involvement. *Special Characteristics:* 208 awards ($550,471 total): adult students, children and siblings of alumni, children of faculty/staff, religious affiliation. *Tuition waivers:* Full or partial for children of alumni, employees or children of employees. *ROTC:* Army cooperative, Air Force cooperative.

LOANS *Student loans:* $5,019,849 (56% need-based, 44% non-need-based). 67% of past graduating class borrowed through all loan programs. *Average indebtedness per student:* $23,318. *Average need-based loan:* Freshmen: $1962; Undergraduates: $2414. *Parent loans:* $1,095,610 (100% non-need-based). *Programs:* FFEL (Subsidized and Unsubsidized Stafford, PLUS), Perkins, Federal Nursing, college/university.

WORK-STUDY *Federal work-study:* Total amount: $123,437; 247 jobs averaging $2100. *State or other work-study/employment:* Total amount: $141,070 (100% non-need-based). 89 part-time jobs averaging $2100.

APPLYING FOR FINANCIAL AID *Required financial aid forms:* FAFSA, institution's own form. *Financial aid deadline (priority):* 3/15. *Notification date:* Continuous beginning 3/1. Students must reply by 5/1.

CONTACT Ms. Linda Hayes, Director of Financial Aid, Thomas More College, 333 Thomas More Parkway, Crestview Hills, KY 41017-3495, 859-344-3531 or toll-free 800-825-4557. *Fax:* 859-344-3638. *E-mail:* linda.hayes@thomasmore.edu.

THOMAS MORE COLLEGE OF LIBERAL ARTS
Merrimack, NH

Tuition & fees: $10,650	Average undergraduate aid package: $11,177

ABOUT THE INSTITUTION Independent religious, coed. Awards: bachelor's degrees. 4 undergraduate majors. Total enrollment: 86. Undergraduates: 86. Freshmen: 21. Federal methodology is used as a basis for awarding need-based institutional aid.

UNDERGRADUATE EXPENSES for 2005–06 *Comprehensive fee:* $18,650 includes full-time tuition ($10,600), mandatory fees ($50), and room and board ($8000). *Part-time tuition:* $175 per credit hour. *Payment plan:* Installment.

FRESHMAN FINANCIAL AID (Fall 2004, est.) 19 applied for aid; of those 63% were deemed to have need. 100% of freshmen with need received aid; of those 8% had need fully met. *Average percent of need met:* 70% (excluding resources awarded to replace EFC). *Average financial aid package:* $10,782 (excluding resources awarded to replace EFC). 18% of all full-time freshmen had no need and received non-need-based gift aid.

UNDERGRADUATE FINANCIAL AID (Fall 2004, est.) 79 applied for aid; of those 71% were deemed to have need. 100% of undergraduates with need received aid; of those 5% had need fully met. *Average percent of need met:* 70% (excluding resources awarded to replace EFC). *Average financial aid package:* $11,177 (excluding resources awarded to replace EFC). 26% of all full-time undergraduates had no need and received non-need-based gift aid.

GIFT AID (NEED-BASED) *Total amount:* $386,713 (25% federal, 1% state, 73% institutional, 1% external sources). *Receiving aid:* Freshmen: 55% (12); All full-time undergraduates: 65% (56). **Average award:** Freshmen: $6204; Undergraduates: $6461. **Scholarships, grants, and awards:** Federal Pell, FSEOG, state, private, college/university gift aid from institutional funds.

GIFT AID (NON-NEED-BASED) Total amount: $117,400 (100% institutional). **Average Award:** Freshmen: $7075; Undergraduates: $4957. **Scholarships, grants, and awards by category:** Academic Interests/Achievement: 52 awards ($162,160 total): general academic interests/achievements. **Tuition waivers:** Full or partial for employees or children of employees.

LOANS Student loans: $286,675 (84% need-based, 16% non-need-based). 77% of past graduating class borrowed through all loan programs. *Average indebtedness per student:* $19,363. **Average need-based loan:** Freshmen: $2625; Undergraduates: $3780. **Parent loans:** $88,490 (14% need-based, 86% non-need-based). **Programs:** FFEL (Subsidized and Unsubsidized Stafford, PLUS).

WORK-STUDY State or other work-study/employment: Total amount: $81,570 (75% need-based, 25% non-need-based). 37 part-time jobs averaging $2205.

APPLYING FOR FINANCIAL AID Required financial aid form: FAFSA. **Financial aid deadline:** Continuous. **Notification date:** Continuous beginning 5/15. Students must reply within 2 weeks of notification.

CONTACT Mrs. Pam Bernstein, Business Manager, Thomas More College of Liberal Arts, 6 Manchester Street, Merrimack, NH 03054-4818, 603-880-8308 or toll-free 800-880-8308. *Fax:* 603-546-0034. *E-mail:* thomasmorecollege@hotmail.com.

THOMAS UNIVERSITY
Thomasville, GA

Tuition & fees: $10,720	Average undergraduate aid package: $5119

ABOUT THE INSTITUTION Independent, coed. Awards: associate, bachelor's, and master's degrees and post-bachelor's certificates. 23 undergraduate majors. Total enrollment: 783. Undergraduates: 688. Freshmen: 80. Federal methodology is used as a basis for awarding need-based institutional aid.

UNDERGRADUATE EXPENSES for 2005–06 Application fee: $25. **Tuition:** full-time $10,200; part-time $348 per semester hour. **Required fees:** full-time $520; $180 per term part-time.

GIFT AID (NEED-BASED) Total amount: $1,277,466 (100% federal). **Receiving aid:** Freshmen: 55% (37); All full-time undergraduates: 42% (306). **Average award:** Freshmen: $2963; Undergraduates: $2652. **Scholarships, grants, and awards:** Federal Pell, FSEOG, state, private, college/university gift aid from institutional funds.

GIFT AID (NON-NEED-BASED) Total amount: $1,782,283 (48% state, 52% institutional). **Receiving aid:** Freshmen: 85% (57); Undergraduates: 53% (390). **Scholarships, grants, and awards by category:** Academic Interests/Achievement: 28 awards ($26,800 total): biological sciences, business, education, English, general academic interests/achievements, health fields, international studies, physical sciences, social sciences. Creative Arts/Performance: art/fine arts, music, performing arts. Special Achievements/Activities: 6 awards ($9000 total): junior miss. Special Characteristics: 681 awards ($158,948 total): children of faculty/staff, out-of-state students, veterans. **Tuition waivers:** Full or partial for employees or children of employees, senior citizens.

LOANS Student loans: $3,886,526 (52% need-based, 48% non-need-based). 51% of past graduating class borrowed through all loan programs. *Average indebtedness per student:* $12,000. **Average need-based loan:** Freshmen: $2578; Undergraduates: $3475. **Parent loans:** $10,116 (100% non-need-based). **Programs:** FFEL (Subsidized and Unsubsidized Stafford, PLUS), state, alternative loans.

ATHLETIC AWARDS Total amount: $546,572 (100% non-need-based).

APPLYING FOR FINANCIAL AID Required financial aid forms: FAFSA, institution's own form, state aid form. **Financial aid deadline:** Continuous. **Notification date:** Continuous.

CONTACT Ms. Angela Keys, Director of Financial Aid, Thomas University, 1501 Millpond Road, Thomasville, GA 31792-7499, 229-226-1621 Ext. 216 or toll-free 800-538-9784. *Fax:* 229-227-6919. *E-mail:* akeys@thomasu.edu.

TIFFIN UNIVERSITY
Tiffin, OH

Tuition & fees: $14,280	Average undergraduate aid package: $11,693

ABOUT THE INSTITUTION Independent, coed. Awards: associate, bachelor's, and master's degrees. 20 undergraduate majors. Total enrollment: 1,407. Undergraduates: 1,026. Freshmen: 262. Federal methodology is used as a basis for awarding need-based institutional aid.

UNDERGRADUATE EXPENSES for 2004–05 Application fee: $20. **Comprehensive fee:** $20,430 includes full-time tuition ($14,280) and room and board ($6150). **College room only:** $3200. Room and board charges vary according to board plan and housing facility. **Part-time tuition:** $476 per credit hour. **Payment plan:** Installment.

GIFT AID (NEED-BASED) Total amount: $4,821,271 (27% federal, 30% state, 40% institutional, 3% external sources). **Receiving aid:** Freshmen: 84% (218); All full-time undergraduates: 68% (591). **Average award:** Freshmen: $6781; Undergraduates: $7054. **Scholarships, grants, and awards:** Federal Pell, FSEOG, state, private, college/university gift aid from institutional funds.

GIFT AID (NON-NEED-BASED) Receiving aid: Freshmen: 81% (210); Undergraduates: 76% (657). **Average Award:** Freshmen: $3981; Undergraduates: $2409. **Scholarships, grants, and awards by category:** Academic Interests/Achievement: 457 awards ($1,145,211 total): business, general academic interests/achievements, international studies. Creative Arts/Performance: 56 awards ($108,775 total): music. Special Achievements/Activities: 52 awards ($71,500 total): cheerleading/drum major, general special achievements/activities, leadership. Special Characteristics: 541 awards ($2,087,052 total): children and siblings of alumni, children of faculty/staff, general special characteristics, international students, local/state students, out-of-state students, public servants, veterans' children. **Tuition waivers:** Full or partial for employees or children of employees, senior citizens. **ROTC:** Army cooperative, Air Force cooperative.

LOANS Student loans: $6,123,571 (100% need-based). 82% of past graduating class borrowed through all loan programs. *Average indebtedness per student:* $17,125. **Average need-based loan:** Freshmen: $2175; Undergraduates: $3975. **Parent loans:** $219,633 (100% need-based). **Programs:** Federal Direct (Subsidized and Unsubsidized Stafford, PLUS), Perkins, college/university, alternative loans.

ATHLETIC AWARDS Total amount: $1,484,493 (100% need-based).

APPLYING FOR FINANCIAL AID Required financial aid form: FAFSA. **Financial aid deadline:** Continuous. **Notification date:** Continuous beginning 2/15. Students must reply within 2 weeks of notification.

CONTACT Tera Van Doren, Director of Financial Aid, Tiffin University, 155 Miami Street, Tiffin, OH 44883-2161, 419-448-3357 or toll-free 800-968-6446. *Fax:* 419-443-5006. *E-mail:* vandorent@tiffin.edu.

TOCCOA FALLS COLLEGE
Toccoa Falls, GA

Tuition & fees: $12,050	Average undergraduate aid package: $9876

ABOUT THE INSTITUTION Independent interdenominational, coed. Awards: associate and bachelor's degrees. 19 undergraduate majors. Total enrollment: 829. Undergraduates: 829. Freshmen: 160. Federal methodology is used as a basis for awarding need-based institutional aid.

UNDERGRADUATE EXPENSES for 2005–06 Application fee: $20. **One-time required fee:** $475. **Comprehensive fee:** $16,650 includes full-time tuition ($12,050) and room and board ($4600). Full-time tuition and fees vary according to course load. Room and board charges vary according to board plan. **Part-time tuition:** $502 per credit hour. Part-time tuition and fees vary according to course load. **Payment plan:** Installment.

FRESHMAN FINANCIAL AID (Fall 2004, est.) 142 applied for aid; of those 87% were deemed to have need. 100% of freshmen with need received aid; of those 16% had need fully met. *Average percent of need met:* 56% (excluding resources awarded to replace EFC). *Average financial aid package:* $8967 (excluding resources awarded to replace EFC). 16% of all full-time freshmen had no need and received non-need-based gift aid.

UNDERGRADUATE FINANCIAL AID (Fall 2004, est.) 686 applied for aid; of those 89% were deemed to have need. 100% of undergraduates with need received aid; of those 13% had need fully met. *Average percent of need met:* 60% (excluding resources awarded to replace EFC). *Average financial aid package:* $9876 (excluding resources awarded to replace EFC). 19% of all full-time undergraduates had no need and received non-need-based gift aid.

GIFT AID (NEED-BASED) Total amount: $1,817,284 (53% federal, 1% state, 46% institutional). **Receiving aid:** Freshmen: 60% (96); All full-time undergraduates: 61% (475). **Average award:** Freshmen: $3368; Undergraduates: $3563. **Scholarships, grants, and awards:** Federal Pell, FSEOG, state, private, college/university gift aid from institutional funds.

GIFT AID (NON-NEED-BASED) *Total amount:* $2,645,720 (36% state, 58% institutional, 6% external sources). *Receiving aid:* Freshmen: 58% (94); Undergraduates: 63% (487). *Average Award: Freshmen:* $5144; *Undergraduates:* $4806. *Scholarships, grants, and awards by category: Academic Interests/ Achievement:* 228 awards ($952,415 total): business, communication, education, general academic interests/achievements, religion/biblical studies. *Creative Arts/Performance:* 40 awards ($71,350 total): music. *Special Achievements/ Activities:* 57 awards ($177,880 total): leadership. *Special Characteristics:* 253 awards ($462,712 total): children of faculty/staff, ethnic background, general special characteristics, international students, married students, relatives of clergy, religious affiliation, siblings of current students. *Tuition waivers:* Full or partial for employees or children of employees.

LOANS *Student loans:* $2,923,753 (55% need-based, 45% non-need-based). 62% of past graduating class borrowed through all loan programs. *Average indebtedness per student:* $17,145. *Average need-based loan:* Freshmen: $2743; Undergraduates: $3838. *Parent loans:* $843,626 (100% non-need-based). *Programs:* FFEL (Subsidized and Unsubsidized Stafford, PLUS), Perkins, college/ university.

WORK-STUDY *Federal work-study:* Total amount: $644,884; 355 jobs averaging $1804. *State or other work-study/employment:* Total amount: $166,500 (100% non-need-based). 89 part-time jobs averaging $1871.

APPLYING FOR FINANCIAL AID *Required financial aid form:* FAFSA. *Financial aid deadline (priority):* 5/1. *Notification date:* Continuous beginning 3/15. Students must reply within 2 weeks of notification.

CONTACT Vince Welch, Director of Financial Aid, Toccoa Falls College, PO Box 800900, Toccoa Falls, GA 30598, 706-886-7299 Ext. 5234. *E-mail:* vwelch@tfc. edu.

TORAH TEMIMAH TALMUDICAL SEMINARY
Brooklyn, NY

CONTACT Financial Aid Office, Torah Temimah Talmudical Seminary, 507 Ocean Parkway, Brooklyn, NY 11218-5913, 718-853-8500.

TOUGALOO COLLEGE
Tougaloo, MS

ABOUT THE INSTITUTION Independent religious, coed. Awards: associate and bachelor's degrees. 23 undergraduate majors. Total enrollment: 940. Undergraduates: 940. Freshmen: 222.

GIFT AID (NEED-BASED) *Scholarships, grants, and awards:* Federal Pell, FSEOG, state, private, college/university gift aid from institutional funds, United Negro College Fund.

GIFT AID (NON-NEED-BASED) *Scholarships, grants, and awards by category: Academic Interests/Achievement:* general academic interests/achievements. *Creative Arts/Performance:* music. *Special Characteristics:* general special characteristics.

LOANS *Programs:* Federal Direct (Subsidized and Unsubsidized Stafford, PLUS), FFEL (Subsidized and Unsubsidized Stafford, PLUS).

APPLYING FOR FINANCIAL AID *Required financial aid forms:* FAFSA, institution's own form.

CONTACT Director of Financial Aid, Tougaloo College, 500 West County Line Road, Tougaloo, MS 39174, 601-977-6134 or toll-free 888-42GALOO. *Fax:* 601-977-6164.

TOURO COLLEGE
New York, NY

ABOUT THE INSTITUTION Independent, coed. Awards: associate, bachelor's, master's, doctoral, and first professional degrees and post-master's certificates. 43 undergraduate majors. Total enrollment: 11,447. Undergraduates: 7,393. Freshmen: 3,389.

GIFT AID (NEED-BASED) *Scholarships, grants, and awards:* Federal Pell, FSEOG, state, private, college/university gift aid from institutional funds.

GIFT AID (NON-NEED-BASED) *Scholarships, grants, and awards by category: Academic Interests/Achievement:* general academic interests/achievements. *Special Characteristics:* children of faculty/staff.

LOANS *Programs:* FFEL (Subsidized and Unsubsidized Stafford, PLUS), Perkins, alternative loans.

APPLYING FOR FINANCIAL AID *Required financial aid forms:* FAFSA, institution's own form.

CONTACT Office of Financial Aid, Touro College, 27 West 23rd Street, New York, NY 10010, 212-463-0400.

TOURO UNIVERSITY INTERNATIONAL
Cypress, CA

CONTACT Financial Aid Office, Touro University International, 5665 Plaza Drive, 3rd Floor, Cypress, CA 90630, 714-816-0366.

TOWSON UNIVERSITY
Towson, MD

Tuition & fees (MD res): $6672	Average undergraduate aid package: $7508

ABOUT THE INSTITUTION State-supported, coed. Awards: bachelor's, master's, and doctoral degrees and post-bachelor's and post-master's certificates. 54 undergraduate majors. Total enrollment: 17,667. Undergraduates: 14,311. Freshmen: 2,097. Federal methodology is used as a basis for awarding need-based institutional aid.

UNDERGRADUATE EXPENSES for 2004–05 *Application fee:* $45. *Tuition, state resident:* full-time $4890; part-time $212 per credit. *Tuition, nonresident:* full-time $13,570; part-time $508 per credit. *Required fees:* full-time $1782; $69 per credit. Full-time tuition and fees vary according to course load. *College room and board:* $6468; *room only:* $3816. Room and board charges vary according to board plan and housing facility. *Payment plan:* Installment.

FRESHMAN FINANCIAL AID (Fall 2004, est.) 1587 applied for aid; of those 61% were deemed to have need. 93% of freshmen with need received aid; of those 18% had need fully met. *Average percent of need met:* 58% (excluding resources awarded to replace EFC). *Average financial aid package:* $5930 (excluding resources awarded to replace EFC). 12% of all full-time freshmen had no need and received non-need-based gift aid.

UNDERGRADUATE FINANCIAL AID (Fall 2004, est.) 8,591 applied for aid; of those 63% were deemed to have need. 95% of undergraduates with need received aid; of those 21% had need fully met. *Average percent of need met:* 66% (excluding resources awarded to replace EFC). *Average financial aid package:* $7508 (excluding resources awarded to replace EFC). 12% of all full-time undergraduates had no need and received non-need-based gift aid.

GIFT AID (NEED-BASED) *Total amount:* $18,911,255 (34% federal, 32% state, 32% institutional, 2% external sources). *Receiving aid:* Freshmen: 22% (466); All full-time undergraduates: 25% (3,048). *Average award:* Freshmen: $5275; Undergraduates: $4895. *Scholarships, grants, and awards:* Federal Pell, FSEOG, state, private, college/university gift aid from institutional funds.

GIFT AID (NON-NEED-BASED) *Total amount:* $9,327,210 (25% state, 64% institutional, 11% external sources). *Receiving aid:* Freshmen: 17% (353); Undergraduates: 13% (1,553). *Average Award: Freshmen:* $4104; *Undergraduates:* $4353. *Scholarships, grants, and awards by category: Academic Interests/ Achievement:* general academic interests/achievements. *Creative Arts/ Performance:* art/fine arts, dance, music, theater/drama. *Tuition waivers:* Full or partial for employees or children of employees, senior citizens. *ROTC:* Army cooperative, Air Force cooperative.

LOANS *Student loans:* $26,743,253 (68% need-based, 32% non-need-based). 52% of past graduating class borrowed through all loan programs. *Average indebtedness per student:* $15,575. *Average need-based loan:* Freshmen: $2850; Undergraduates: $3938. *Parent loans:* $22,455,093 (26% need-based, 74% non-need-based). *Programs:* Federal Direct (Subsidized and Unsubsidized Stafford, PLUS), Perkins.

WORK-STUDY *Federal work-study:* Total amount: $944,854; jobs available. *State or other work-study/employment:* Part-time jobs available.

ATHLETIC AWARDS *Total amount:* $3,031,359 (19% need-based, 81% non-need-based).

APPLYING FOR FINANCIAL AID *Required financial aid form:* FAFSA. *Financial aid deadline:* 3/1 (priority: 1/31). *Notification date:* Continuous beginning 4/10. Students must reply within 2 weeks of notification.

CONTACT Vince Pecora, Director of Financial Aid, Towson University, 8000 York Road, Towson, MD 21252-0001, 410-704-4236 or toll-free 888-4TOWSON. *E-mail:* finaid@towson.edu.

TRANSYLVANIA UNIVERSITY
Lexington, KY

Tuition & fees: $19,650	Average undergraduate aid package: $16,309

ABOUT THE INSTITUTION Independent religious, coed. Awards: bachelor's degrees. 29 undergraduate majors. Total enrollment: 1,114. Undergraduates: 1,114. Freshmen: 321. Federal methodology is used as a basis for awarding need-based institutional aid.

UNDERGRADUATE EXPENSES for 2005–06 *Application fee:* $30. *Comprehensive fee:* $26,240 includes full-time tuition ($19,650) and room and board ($6590). Room and board charges vary according to board plan and location. *Part-time tuition:* $2100 per course. *Part-time fees:* $84 per course. *Payment plan:* Installment.

FRESHMAN FINANCIAL AID (Fall 2004, est.) 256 applied for aid; of those 75% were deemed to have need. 100% of freshmen with need received aid; of those 23% had need fully met. *Average percent of need met:* 87% (excluding resources awarded to replace EFC). *Average financial aid package:* $16,510 (excluding resources awarded to replace EFC). 40% of all full-time freshmen had no need and received non-need-based gift aid.

UNDERGRADUATE FINANCIAL AID (Fall 2004, est.) 756 applied for aid; of those 84% were deemed to have need. 100% of undergraduates with need received aid; of those 27% had need fully met. *Average percent of need met:* 87% (excluding resources awarded to replace EFC). *Average financial aid package:* $16,309 (excluding resources awarded to replace EFC). 41% of all full-time undergraduates had no need and received non-need-based gift aid.

GIFT AID (NEED-BASED) *Total amount:* $7,691,477 (8% federal, 26% state, 63% institutional, 3% external sources). *Receiving aid:* Freshmen: 60% (192); All full-time undergraduates: 58% (634). *Average award:* Freshmen: $12,579; Undergraduates: $12,173. *Scholarships, grants, and awards:* Federal Pell, FSEOG, state, private, college/university gift aid from institutional funds.

GIFT AID (NON-NEED-BASED) *Total amount:* $4,305,626 (17% state, 79% institutional, 4% external sources). *Receiving aid:* Freshmen: 8% (27); Undergraduates: 8% (89). *Average Award:* Freshmen: $10,525; Undergraduates: $10,501. *Scholarships, grants, and awards by category: Academic Interests/Achievement:* 1,072 awards ($6,800,278 total): computer science, general academic interests/achievements. *Creative Arts/Performance:* 48 awards ($113,490 total): art/fine arts, music. *Special Achievements/Activities:* 271 awards ($459,079 total): cheerleading/drum major, general special achievements/activities, religious involvement. *Special Characteristics:* 131 awards ($511,458 total): children of faculty/staff, members of minority groups, out-of-state students, relatives of clergy, religious affiliation. *Tuition waivers:* Full or partial for employees or children of employees. *ROTC:* Army cooperative, Air Force cooperative.

LOANS *Student loans:* $3,277,002 (69% need-based, 31% non-need-based). 64% of past graduating class borrowed through all loan programs. *Average indebtedness per student:* $15,874. *Average need-based loan:* Freshmen: $3713; Undergraduates: $4083. *Parent loans:* $1,340,436 (19% need-based, 81% non-need-based). *Programs:* FFEL (Subsidized and Unsubsidized Stafford, PLUS), Perkins, college/university.

WORK-STUDY *Federal work-study:* Total amount: $441,023; 367 jobs averaging $1201. *State or other work-study/employment:* Total amount: $296,417 (32% need-based, 68% non-need-based). 50 part-time jobs averaging $5928.

APPLYING FOR FINANCIAL AID *Required financial aid form:* FAFSA. *Financial aid deadline (priority):* 3/1. *Notification date:* Continuous beginning 3/15. Students must reply within 2 weeks of notification.

CONTACT Mr. Dave Cecil, Director of Financial Aid, Transylvania University, 300 North Broadway, Lexington, KY 40508-1797, 859-233-8239 or toll-free 800-872-6798. *Fax:* 859-281-3650. *E-mail:* dcecil@transy.edu.

TREVECCA NAZARENE UNIVERSITY
Nashville, TN

Tuition & fees: $12,792	Average undergraduate aid package: $8457

ABOUT THE INSTITUTION Independent Nazarene, coed. Awards: associate, bachelor's, master's, and doctoral degrees and post-master's certificates. 36 undergraduate majors. Total enrollment: 2,089. Undergraduates: 1,241. Freshmen: 237. Federal methodology is used as a basis for awarding need-based institutional aid.

UNDERGRADUATE EXPENSES for 2004–05 *Application fee:* $25. *Comprehensive fee:* $18,660 includes full-time tuition ($12,792) and room and board ($5868).

College room only: $2648. Full-time tuition and fees vary according to course load. Room and board charges vary according to board plan. *Part-time tuition:* $492 per semester hour. Part-time tuition and fees vary according to course load. *Payment plan:* Installment.

FRESHMAN FINANCIAL AID (Fall 2003) 213 applied for aid; of those 85% were deemed to have need. 70% of freshmen with need received aid; of those 33% had need fully met. *Average percent of need met:* 53% (excluding resources awarded to replace EFC). *Average financial aid package:* $10,578 (excluding resources awarded to replace EFC). 36% of all full-time freshmen had no need and received non-need-based gift aid.

UNDERGRADUATE FINANCIAL AID (Fall 2003) 1,049 applied for aid; of those 86% were deemed to have need. 81% of undergraduates with need received aid; of those 16% had need fully met. *Average percent of need met:* 54% (excluding resources awarded to replace EFC). *Average financial aid package:* $8457 (excluding resources awarded to replace EFC). 28% of all full-time undergraduates had no need and received non-need-based gift aid.

GIFT AID (NEED-BASED) *Total amount:* $4,198,044 (28% federal, 6% state, 62% institutional, 4% external sources). *Receiving aid:* Freshmen: 58% (128); All full-time undergraduates: 67% (594). *Average award:* Freshmen: $8791; Undergraduates: $6356. *Scholarships, grants, and awards:* Federal Pell, FSEOG, state, private, college/university gift aid from institutional funds.

GIFT AID (NON-NEED-BASED) *Total amount:* $1,916,173 (93% institutional, 7% external sources). *Receiving aid:* Freshmen: 15% (32); Undergraduates: 9% (79). *Average Award:* Freshmen: $7065; Undergraduates: $8289. *Scholarships, grants, and awards by category: Academic Interests/Achievement:* business, communication, education, general academic interests/achievements, physical sciences, religion/biblical studies, social sciences. *Creative Arts/Performance:* music. *Special Achievements/Activities:* general special achievements/activities, memberships. *Special Characteristics:* children and siblings of alumni, general special characteristics, handicapped students, relatives of clergy, religious affiliation. *Tuition waivers:* Full or partial for employees or children of employees, senior citizens. *ROTC:* Army cooperative.

LOANS *Student loans:* $5,722,373 (72% need-based, 28% non-need-based). 79% of past graduating class borrowed through all loan programs. *Average indebtedness per student:* $6544. *Average need-based loan:* Freshmen: $2923; Undergraduates: $4116. *Parent loans:* $1,355,827 (31% need-based, 69% non-need-based). *Programs:* FFEL (Subsidized and Unsubsidized Stafford, PLUS), Perkins.

WORK-STUDY *Federal work-study:* Total amount: $54,089; jobs available. *State or other work-study/employment:* Part-time jobs available.

ATHLETIC AWARDS *Total amount:* $165,348 (30% need-based, 70% non-need-based).

APPLYING FOR FINANCIAL AID *Required financial aid form:* FAFSA. *Financial aid deadline (priority):* 3/1. *Notification date:* Continuous beginning 3/20.

CONTACT Eddie White, Assistant Director of Financial Aid, Trevecca Nazarene University, 333 Murfreesboro Road, Nashville, TN 37210-2834, 615-248-1242 or toll-free 888-210-4TNU. *Fax:* 615-248-7728. *E-mail:* ewhite@trevecca.edu.

TRINITY BAPTIST COLLEGE
Jacksonville, FL

CONTACT Mr. Donald Schaffer, Financial Aid Administrator, Trinity Baptist College, 800 Hammond Boulevard, Jacksonville, FL 32221, 904-596-2445 or toll-free 800-786-2206 (out-of-state). *Fax:* 904-596-2531. *E-mail:* financialaid@tbc.edu.

TRINITY BIBLE COLLEGE
Ellendale, ND

ABOUT THE INSTITUTION Independent Assemblies of God, coed. Awards: associate and bachelor's degrees. 8 undergraduate majors. Total enrollment: 307. Undergraduates: 307. Freshmen: 73.

GIFT AID (NEED-BASED) *Scholarships, grants, and awards:* Federal Pell, FSEOG, state, private, college/university gift aid from institutional funds.

GIFT AID (NON-NEED-BASED) *Scholarships, grants, and awards by category: Academic Interests/Achievement:* business, education, general academic interests/achievements, religion/biblical studies. *Creative Arts/Performance:* art/fine arts, creative writing, music, theater/drama. *Special Achievements/Activities:* community service, general special achievements/activities, leadership, religious involvement. *Special Characteristics:* children and siblings of alumni, children of current students, children of faculty/staff, general special characteristics, inter-

national students, married students, parents of current students, relatives of clergy, siblings of current students, spouses of current students.
LOANS *Programs:* FFEL (Subsidized and Unsubsidized Stafford, PLUS), Perkins, alternative loans.
WORK-STUDY *Federal work-study:* Total amount: $173,751; 162 jobs averaging $1073.
APPLYING FOR FINANCIAL AID *Required financial aid form:* FAFSA.
CONTACT Rhonda Miller, Financial Aid Associate, Trinity Bible College, 50 South 6th Avenue, Ellendale, ND 58436-7150, 888-822-2329 Ext. 2781 or toll-free 888-TBC-2DAY. *Fax:* 701-349-5786. *E-mail:* financialaid@trinitybiblecollege.edu.

TRINITY CHRISTIAN COLLEGE
Palos Heights, IL

ABOUT THE INSTITUTION Independent Christian Reformed, coed. Awards: bachelor's degrees. 61 undergraduate majors. Total enrollment: 1,234. Undergraduates: 1,234. Freshmen: 218.
GIFT AID (NEED-BASED) *Scholarships, grants, and awards:* Federal Pell, FSEOG, state, private, college/university gift aid from institutional funds.
GIFT AID (NON-NEED-BASED) *Scholarships, grants, and awards by category:* Academic Interests/Achievement: business, English, general academic interests/achievements, health fields, mathematics. *Creative Arts/Performance:* journalism/publications, music, theater/drama. *Special Achievements/Activities:* general special achievements/activities, leadership. *Special Characteristics:* children and siblings of alumni, children of faculty/staff, local/state students, members of minority groups, out-of-state students.
LOANS *Programs:* FFEL (Subsidized and Unsubsidized Stafford, PLUS), Perkins, Federal Nursing.
APPLYING FOR FINANCIAL AID *Required financial aid forms:* FAFSA, institution's own form.
CONTACT L. Denise Coleman, Director of Financial Aid, Trinity Christian College, 6601 West College Drive, Palos Heights, IL 60463-0929, 708-239-4706 or toll-free 800-748-0085. *E-mail:* financial.aid@trnty.edu.

TRINITY COLLEGE
Washington, DC

See Trinity (Washington) University.

TRINITY COLLEGE
Hartford, CT

Tuition & fees: $31,940	Average undergraduate aid package: $24,377

ABOUT THE INSTITUTION Independent, coed. Awards: bachelor's and master's degrees. 44 undergraduate majors. Total enrollment: 2,371. Undergraduates: 2,188. Freshmen: 550. Both federal and institutional methodology are used as a basis for awarding need-based institutional aid.
UNDERGRADUATE EXPENSES for 2004–05 *Application fee:* $50. *Comprehensive fee:* $40,200 includes full-time tuition ($30,380), mandatory fees ($1560), and room and board ($8260). *College room only:* $5310. Full-time tuition and fees vary according to program. Room and board charges vary according to board plan. Part-time tuition and fees vary according to program. *Payment plan:* Installment.
FRESHMAN FINANCIAL AID (Fall 2003) 248 applied for aid; of those 80% were deemed to have need. 100% of freshmen with need received aid; of those 100% had need fully met. *Average percent of need met:* 100% (excluding resources awarded to replace EFC). *Average financial aid package:* $23,890 (excluding resources awarded to replace EFC).
UNDERGRADUATE FINANCIAL AID (Fall 2003) 938 applied for aid; of those 92% were deemed to have need. 100% of undergraduates with need received aid; of those 100% had need fully met. *Average percent of need met:* 100% (excluding resources awarded to replace EFC). *Average financial aid package:* $24,377 (excluding resources awarded to replace EFC). 1% of all full-time undergraduates had no need and received non-need-based gift aid.
GIFT AID (NEED-BASED) *Total amount:* $19,511,942 (5% federal, 3% state, 88% institutional, 4% external sources). *Receiving aid:* Freshmen: 34% (185); All full-time undergraduates: 44% (812). *Average award:* Freshmen: $21,727; Undergraduates: $21,494. *Scholarships, grants, and awards:* Federal Pell, FSEOG, state, private, college/university gift aid from institutional funds.

Trinity College of Nursing and Health Sciences

GIFT AID (NON-NEED-BASED) *Total amount:* $163,390 (100% institutional). *Receiving aid:* Undergraduates: 5. *Average Award:* Undergraduates: $12,096. *Scholarships, grants, and awards by category:* Academic Interests/Achievement: 3 awards ($3000 total): general academic interests/achievements. *Special Achievements/Activities:* 2 awards ($57,480 total): leadership. *Tuition waivers:* Full or partial for employees or children of employees, adult students. *ROTC:* Army cooperative.
LOANS *Student loans:* $5,095,473 (59% need-based, 41% non-need-based). 49% of past graduating class borrowed through all loan programs. *Average indebtedness per student:* $16,100. *Average need-based loan:* Freshmen: $2868; Undergraduates: $4051. *Parent loans:* $4,016,564 (100% non-need-based). *Programs:* FFEL (Subsidized and Unsubsidized Stafford, PLUS), Perkins, college/university, alternative loans.
WORK-STUDY *Federal work-study:* Total amount: $354,341; 638 jobs averaging $1530. *State or other work-study/employment:* Total amount: $10,058 (100% need-based). 12 part-time jobs averaging $838.
APPLYING FOR FINANCIAL AID *Required financial aid forms:* FAFSA, CSS Financial Aid PROFILE, noncustodial (divorced/separated) parent's statement, business/farm supplement, federal income tax form(s). *Financial aid deadline:* 3/1 (priority: 2/1). *Notification date:* 4/1. Students must reply by 5/1 or within 2 weeks of notification.
CONTACT Ms. Kelly O'Brien, Director of Financial Aid, Trinity College, 300 Summit Street, Hartford, CT 06106-3100, 860-297-2046. *Fax:* 860-987-6296.

TRINITY COLLEGE OF FLORIDA
New Port Richey, FL

Tuition & fees: $7860	Average undergraduate aid package: $7500

ABOUT THE INSTITUTION Independent nondenominational, coed. Awards: associate and bachelor's degrees. 8 undergraduate majors. Total enrollment: 203. Undergraduates: 203. Freshmen: 34. Federal methodology is used as a basis for awarding need-based institutional aid.
UNDERGRADUATE EXPENSES for 2004–05 *Application fee:* $25. *Comprehensive fee:* $12,530 includes full-time tuition ($7450), mandatory fees ($410), and room and board ($4670). *Part-time tuition:* $310 per credit hour. *Part-time fees:* $205 per term. Part-time tuition and fees vary according to course load. *Payment plan:* Deferred payment.
GIFT AID (NEED-BASED) *Total amount:* $378,752 (76% federal, 11% state, 7% institutional, 6% external sources). *Receiving aid:* Freshmen: 86% (31); All full-time undergraduates: 87% (120). *Average award:* Freshmen: $3105; Undergraduates: $3375. *Scholarships, grants, and awards:* Federal Pell, FSEOG, state, private, college/university gift aid from institutional funds.
GIFT AID (NON-NEED-BASED) *Total amount:* $153,211 (60% state, 20% institutional, 20% external sources). *Receiving aid:* Freshmen: 69% (25); Undergraduates: 71% (98). *Average Award:* Freshmen: $500; Undergraduates: $500. *Scholarships, grants, and awards by category:* Academic Interests/Achievement: religion/biblical studies. *Special Achievements/Activities:* community service, leadership, religious involvement. *Tuition waivers:* Full or partial for children of alumni, employees or children of employees, senior citizens.
LOANS *Student loans:* $508,670 (100% need-based). *Average need-based loan:* Freshmen: $4500; Undergraduates: $4500. *Parent loans:* $61,044 (100% need-based). *Programs:* FFEL (Subsidized and Unsubsidized Stafford, PLUS).
APPLYING FOR FINANCIAL AID *Required financial aid forms:* FAFSA, institution's own form. *Financial aid deadline (priority):* 4/1. *Notification date:* Continuous.
CONTACT Sue Wayne, Director of Financial Aid, Trinity College of Florida, 2430 Welbilt Boulevard, New Port Richey, FL 34655, 727-376-6911 Ext. 310 or toll-free 800-388-0869. *Fax:* 727-376-0781.

TRINITY COLLEGE OF NURSING AND HEALTH SCIENCES
Rock Island, IL

CONTACT Nick Shinstine, Assistant Director of Learner Services, Trinity College of Nursing and Health Sciences, 2122 25th Avenue, Rock Island, IL 61201, 309-779-7704. *Fax:* 309-779-7748. *E-mail:* shinstinen@trinityqc.com.

TRINITY INTERNATIONAL UNIVERSITY
Deerfield, IL

Tuition & fees: $18,150	Average undergraduate aid package: $14,236

ABOUT THE INSTITUTION Independent religious, coed. Awards: bachelor's, master's, doctoral, and first professional degrees and post-bachelor's certificates. 38 undergraduate majors. Total enrollment: 2,815. Undergraduates: 1,309. Freshmen: 401. Federal methodology is used as a basis for awarding need-based institutional aid.

UNDERGRADUATE EXPENSES for 2004–05 *Application fee:* $25. *Comprehensive fee:* $24,230 includes full-time tuition ($17,900), mandatory fees ($250), and room and board ($6080). *College room only:* $3240. Full-time tuition and fees vary according to location. Room and board charges vary according to board plan. *Part-time tuition:* $747 per hour. *Part-time fees:* $125 per term. Part-time tuition and fees vary according to location. *Payment plan:* Installment.

FRESHMAN FINANCIAL AID (Fall 2004, est.) 208 applied for aid; of those 82% were deemed to have need. 100% of freshmen with need received aid; of those 7% had need fully met. *Average percent of need met:* 15% (excluding resources awarded to replace EFC). *Average financial aid package:* $14,291 (excluding resources awarded to replace EFC). 5% of all full-time freshmen had no need and received non-need-based gift aid.

UNDERGRADUATE FINANCIAL AID (Fall 2004, est.) 945 applied for aid; of those 88% were deemed to have need. 100% of undergraduates with need received aid; of those 11% had need fully met. *Average percent of need met:* 21% (excluding resources awarded to replace EFC). *Average financial aid package:* $14,236 (excluding resources awarded to replace EFC). 5% of all full-time undergraduates had no need and received non-need-based gift aid.

GIFT AID (NEED-BASED) *Total amount:* $4,896,927 (26% federal, 24% state, 50% institutional). *Receiving aid:* Freshmen: 30% (115); All full-time undergraduates: 52% (612). *Average award:* Freshmen: $7651; Undergraduates: $7638. *Scholarships, grants, and awards:* Federal Pell, FSEOG, state, private, college/university gift aid from institutional funds.

GIFT AID (NON-NEED-BASED) *Total amount:* $1,342,583 (93% institutional, 7% external sources). *Receiving aid:* Freshmen: 34% (130); Undergraduates: 50% (580). *Average Award:* Freshmen: $3605; Undergraduates: $2712. *Scholarships, grants, and awards by category: Academic Interests/Achievement:* 211 awards ($573,000 total): general academic interests/achievements. *Creative Arts/Performance:* 60 awards ($301,630 total): music. *Special Achievements/Activities:* 115 awards ($45,000 total): leadership, religious involvement. *Special Characteristics:* 196 awards ($113,238 total): children and siblings of alumni, members of minority groups, religious affiliation. *Tuition waivers:* Full or partial for employees or children of employees.

LOANS *Student loans:* $4,959,525 (57% need-based, 43% non-need-based). 76% of past graduating class borrowed through all loan programs. *Average indebtedness per student:* $16,500. *Average need-based loan:* Freshmen: $3070; Undergraduates: $4451. *Parent loans:* $1,186,560 (100% need-based). *Programs:* Federal Direct (Subsidized and Unsubsidized Stafford, PLUS), Perkins.

WORK-STUDY *Federal work-study:* Total amount: $720,897; 374 jobs averaging $1926.

ATHLETIC AWARDS *Total amount:* $2,157,893 (100% need-based).

APPLYING FOR FINANCIAL AID *Required financial aid form:* FAFSA. *Financial aid deadline (priority):* 4/1. *Notification date:* Continuous beginning 2/15. Students must reply within 4 weeks of notification.

CONTACT Mr. Ron Campbell, Director of Enrollment Services for Financial Aid and Undergraduate Admission, Trinity International University, 2065 Half Day Road, Deerfield, IL 60015-1284, 847-317-8060 or toll-free 800-822-3225 (out-of-state). Fax: 847-317-7081. E-mail: finaid@tiu.edu.

TRINITY LIFE BIBLE COLLEGE
Sacramento, CA

CONTACT Financial Aid Office, Trinity Life Bible College, 5225 Hillsdale Boulevard, Sacramento, CA 95842, 916-348-4689.

TRINITY LUTHERAN COLLEGE
Issaquah, WA

Tuition & fees: $11,334	Average undergraduate aid package: N/A

ABOUT THE INSTITUTION Independent Lutheran, coed. Awards: associate and bachelor's degrees and post-bachelor's certificates. 3 undergraduate majors. Total enrollment: 156. Undergraduates: 156. Freshmen: 19. Federal methodology is used as a basis for awarding need-based institutional aid.

UNDERGRADUATE EXPENSES for 2004–05 *Application fee:* $30. *Comprehensive fee:* $16,954 includes full-time tuition ($10,984), mandatory fees ($350), and room and board ($5620). *Part-time tuition:* $290 per credit hour. *Part-time fees:* $7 per credit hour.

GIFT AID (NEED-BASED) *Total amount:* $211,558 (64% federal, 36% institutional). *Scholarships, grants, and awards:* Federal Pell, FSEOG, college/university gift aid from institutional funds.

GIFT AID (NON-NEED-BASED) *Total amount:* $105,880 (100% institutional). *Scholarships, grants, and awards by category: Academic Interests/Achievement:* general academic interests/achievements, religion/biblical studies. *Creative Arts/Performance:* general creative arts/performance, music. *Special Achievements/Activities:* leadership, religious involvement. *Special Characteristics:* international students, relatives of clergy, religious affiliation.

LOANS *Student loans:* $460,867 (100% need-based). *Parent loans:* $135,172 (100% need-based). *Programs:* FFEL (Subsidized and Unsubsidized Stafford, PLUS), college/university.

WORK-STUDY *Federal work-study:* Total amount: $25,103; 42 jobs averaging $597.

APPLYING FOR FINANCIAL AID *Required financial aid forms:* FAFSA, institution's own form. *Financial aid deadline (priority):* 3/1. *Notification date:* Continuous. Students must reply within 4 weeks of notification.

CONTACT Ms. Susan Dalgleish, Director of Financial Aid, Trinity Lutheran College, 4221 228th Avenue SE, Issaquah, WA 98029-9299, 425-961-5514 or toll-free 800-843-5659. Fax: 425-392-0404. E-mail: finaid@tlc.edu.

TRINITY UNIVERSITY
San Antonio, TX

Tuition & fees: $20,010	Average undergraduate aid package: $15,486

ABOUT THE INSTITUTION Independent religious, coed. Awards: bachelor's and master's degrees. 49 undergraduate majors. Total enrollment: 2,718. Undergraduates: 2,487. Freshmen: 641. Federal methodology is used as a basis for awarding need-based institutional aid.

UNDERGRADUATE EXPENSES for 2004–05 *Application fee:* $40. *Comprehensive fee:* $28,215 includes full-time tuition ($19,860), mandatory fees ($150), and room and board ($8205). *College room only:* $4775. Full-time tuition and fees vary according to course load. Room and board charges vary according to board plan. *Part-time tuition:* $827.50 per semester hour. *Part-time fees:* $6.25 per semester hour. Part-time tuition and fees vary according to course load. *Payment plan:* Installment.

FRESHMAN FINANCIAL AID (Fall 2003) 388 applied for aid; of those 70% were deemed to have need. 99% of freshmen with need received aid; of those 65% had need fully met. *Average percent of need met:* 90% (excluding resources awarded to replace EFC). *Average financial aid package:* $16,046 (excluding resources awarded to replace EFC). 44% of all full-time freshmen had no need and received non-need-based gift aid.

UNDERGRADUATE FINANCIAL AID (Fall 2003) 1,276 applied for aid; of those 78% were deemed to have need. 99% of undergraduates with need received aid; of those 63% had need fully met. *Average percent of need met:* 86% (excluding resources awarded to replace EFC). *Average financial aid package:* $15,486 (excluding resources awarded to replace EFC). 37% of all full-time undergraduates had no need and received non-need-based gift aid.

GIFT AID (NEED-BASED) *Total amount:* $10,972,144 (12% federal, 20% state, 62% institutional, 6% external sources). *Receiving aid:* Freshmen: 41% (258); All full-time undergraduates: 39% (929). *Average award:* Freshmen: $11,811; Undergraduates: $10,905. *Scholarships, grants, and awards:* Federal Pell, FSEOG, state, private, college/university gift aid from institutional funds.

GIFT AID (NON-NEED-BASED) *Total amount:* $6,047,286 (5% state, 90% institutional, 5% external sources). *Receiving aid:* Freshmen: 34% (218); Undergraduates: 25% (600). *Average Award:* Freshmen: $6264; Undergraduates: $6358. *Scholarships, grants, and awards by category: Academic Interests/Achievement:* general academic interests/achievements. *Creative Arts/Performance:* music. *Special Achievements/Activities:* general special achievements/activities. *Tuition waivers:* Full or partial for employees or children of employees. *ROTC:* Air Force cooperative.

LOANS *Student loans:* $7,848,784 (42% need-based, 58% non-need-based). *Average need-based loan:* Freshmen: $3490; Undergraduates: $4215. *Parent*

loans: $5,820,845 (100% non-need-based). **Programs:** FFEL (Subsidized and Unsubsidized Stafford, PLUS), Perkins, state, college/university.

WORK-STUDY *Federal work-study:* Total amount: $736,207; jobs available. *State or other work-study/employment:* Total amount: $20,000 (100% need-based). 10 part-time jobs averaging $1435.

APPLYING FOR FINANCIAL AID *Required financial aid form:* FAFSA. *Financial aid deadline:* 4/1 (priority: 2/1). *Notification date:* Continuous. Students must reply by 5/1.

CONTACT Director of Financial Aid, Trinity University, 715 Stadium Drive, San Antonio, TX 78212-7200, 210-999-8315 or toll-free 800-TRINITY. *Fax:* 210-999-8316. *E-mail:* financialaid@trinity.edu.

TRINITY (WASHINGTON) UNIVERSITY
Washington, DC

Tuition & fees: $17,360	Average undergraduate aid package: $15,034

ABOUT THE INSTITUTION Independent Roman Catholic, women only. Awards: bachelor's and master's degrees and post-bachelor's certificates. 27 undergraduate majors. Total enrollment: 1,672. Undergraduates: 968. Freshmen: 182. Federal methodology is used as a basis for awarding need-based institutional aid.

UNDERGRADUATE EXPENSES for 2005–06 *Application fee:* $35. *Comprehensive fee:* $24,934 includes full-time tuition ($17,200), mandatory fees ($160), and room and board ($7574). *College room only:* $3350. Full-time tuition and fees vary according to class time. Room and board charges vary according to board plan and housing facility. *Part-time tuition:* $555 per credit hour. Part-time tuition and fees vary according to class time. *Payment plans:* Installment, deferred payment.

FRESHMAN FINANCIAL AID (Fall 2004, est.) 137 applied for aid; of those 98% were deemed to have need. 100% of freshmen with need received aid; of those 12% had need fully met. *Average percent of need met:* 70% (excluding resources awarded to replace EFC). *Average financial aid package:* $15,793 (excluding resources awarded to replace EFC). 4% of all full-time freshmen had no need and received non-need-based gift aid.

UNDERGRADUATE FINANCIAL AID (Fall 2004, est.) 507 applied for aid; of those 96% were deemed to have need. 99% of undergraduates with need received aid; of those 11% had need fully met. *Average percent of need met:* 65% (excluding resources awarded to replace EFC). *Average financial aid package:* $15,034 (excluding resources awarded to replace EFC). 6% of all full-time undergraduates had no need and received non-need-based gift aid.

GIFT AID (NEED-BASED) *Total amount:* $5,747,992 (23% federal, 12% state, 59% institutional, 6% external sources). *Receiving aid:* Freshmen: 93% (134); All full-time undergraduates: 86% (472). *Average award:* Freshmen: $12,481; Undergraduates: $11,261. *Scholarships, grants, and awards:* Federal Pell, FSEOG, state, private, college/university gift aid from institutional funds.

GIFT AID (NON-NEED-BASED) *Total amount:* $277,526 (7% state, 82% institutional, 11% external sources). *Receiving aid:* Freshmen: 8% (11); Undergraduates: 3% (19). *Average Award:* Freshmen: $10,658; Undergraduates: $11,242. *Scholarships, grants, and awards by category:* Academic Interests/Achievement: 147 awards ($1,142,300 total): biological sciences, general academic interests/achievements. Special Achievements/Activities: 11 awards ($44,000 total): memberships. Special Characteristics: 12 awards ($29,134 total): children and siblings of alumni, siblings of current students. *Tuition waivers:* Full or partial for employees or children of employees. *ROTC:* Army cooperative.

LOANS *Student loans:* $5,400,922 (86% need-based, 14% non-need-based). 78% of past graduating class borrowed through all loan programs. *Average indebtedness per student:* $29,875. *Average need-based loan:* Freshmen: $3714; Undergraduates: $4389. *Parent loans:* $411,576 (44% need-based, 56% non-need-based). *Programs:* FFEL (Subsidized and Unsubsidized Stafford, PLUS), Perkins.

WORK-STUDY *Federal work-study:* Total amount: $163,075; 122 jobs averaging $1300. *State or other work-study/employment:* Total amount: $16,925 (100% non-need-based).

APPLYING FOR FINANCIAL AID *Required financial aid form:* FAFSA. *Financial aid deadline (priority):* 3/1. *Notification date:* Continuous beginning 2/1. Students must reply within 2 weeks of notification.

CONTACT Catherine H. Geier, Director of Student Financial Services, Trinity (Washington) University, 125 Michigan Avenue, NE, Washington, DC 20017-1094, 202-884-9530 or toll-free 800-IWANTTC. *Fax:* 202-884-9524. *E-mail:* financialaid@trinitydc.edu.

TRI-STATE BIBLE COLLEGE
South Point, OH

CONTACT Financial Aid Office, Tri-State Bible College, 506 Margaret Street, PO Box 445, South Point, OH 45680-8402, 740-377-2520.

TRI-STATE UNIVERSITY
Angola, IN

Tuition & fees: $20,200	Average undergraduate aid package: $13,128

ABOUT THE INSTITUTION Independent, coed. Awards: associate, bachelor's, and master's degrees. 42 undergraduate majors. Total enrollment: 1,232. Undergraduates: 1,225. Freshmen: 300. Federal methodology is used as a basis for awarding need-based institutional aid.

UNDERGRADUATE EXPENSES for 2005–06 *Application fee:* $20. *Comprehensive fee:* $26,200 includes full-time tuition ($20,200) and room and board ($6000). *Part-time tuition:* $630 per semester hour. *Payment plan:* Installment.

FRESHMAN FINANCIAL AID (Fall 2004, est.) 271 applied for aid; of those 100% were deemed to have need. 100% of freshmen with need received aid; of those 89% had need fully met. *Average percent of need met:* 48% (excluding resources awarded to replace EFC). *Average financial aid package:* $18,596 (excluding resources awarded to replace EFC). 4% of all full-time freshmen had no need and received non-need-based gift aid.

UNDERGRADUATE FINANCIAL AID (Fall 2004, est.) 1,016 applied for aid; of those 100% were deemed to have need. 100% of undergraduates with need received aid; of those 91% had need fully met. *Average percent of need met:* 76% (excluding resources awarded to replace EFC). *Average financial aid package:* $13,128 (excluding resources awarded to replace EFC). 6% of all full-time undergraduates had no need and received non-need-based gift aid.

GIFT AID (NEED-BASED) *Total amount:* $3,549,713 (27% federal, 45% state, 28% institutional). *Receiving aid:* Freshmen: 55% (157); All full-time undergraduates: 29% (294). *Average award:* Freshmen: $3250; Undergraduates: $3393. *Scholarships, grants, and awards:* Federal Pell, FSEOG, state, private, college/university gift aid from institutional funds.

GIFT AID (NON-NEED-BASED) *Total amount:* $6,334,802 (97% institutional, 3% external sources). *Receiving aid:* Freshmen: 90% (259); Undergraduates: 99% (1,012). *Average Award:* Freshmen: $4415; Undergraduates: $3732. *Scholarships, grants, and awards by category:* Academic Interests/Achievement: general academic interests/achievements. Special Characteristics: children of faculty/staff. *Tuition waivers:* Full or partial for employees or children of employees.

LOANS *Student loans:* $3,586,416 (69% need-based, 31% non-need-based). 62% of past graduating class borrowed through all loan programs. *Average indebtedness per student:* $15,240. *Average need-based loan:* Freshmen: $2682; Undergraduates: $3839. *Parent loans:* $3,217,349 (100% non-need-based). *Programs:* FFEL (Subsidized and Unsubsidized Stafford, PLUS), alternative loans.

WORK-STUDY *Federal work-study:* Total amount: $882,465; 502 jobs averaging $1639.

APPLYING FOR FINANCIAL AID *Required financial aid form:* FAFSA. *Financial aid deadline:* 3/10 (priority: 3/10). *Notification date:* Continuous beginning 2/1. Students must reply by 4/15 or within 2 weeks of notification.

CONTACT Kim Bennett, Director of Financial Aid, Tri-State University, 1 University Avenue, Angola, IN 46703-1764, 260-665-4175 or toll-free 800-347-4TSU. *Fax:* 260-665-4511. *E-mail:* admit@tristate.edu.

TROY UNIVERSITY
Troy, AL

Tuition & fees (AL res): $4162	Average undergraduate aid package: $3320

ABOUT THE INSTITUTION State-supported, coed. Awards: associate, bachelor's, and master's degrees and post-master's certificates. 45 undergraduate majors. Total enrollment: 8,847. Undergraduates: 5,487. Freshmen: 1,074. Federal methodology is used as a basis for awarding need-based institutional aid.

UNDERGRADUATE EXPENSES for 2004–05 *Application fee:* $20. *Tuition, state resident:* full-time $3850; part-time $163 per credit hour. *Tuition, nonresident:* full-time $7700; part-time $326 per credit hour. *Required fees:* full-time $312;

Troy University

$13 per credit hour. **College room and board:** $4812; **room only:** $2300. Room and board charges vary according to board plan and housing facility. **Payment plan:** Installment.

FRESHMAN FINANCIAL AID (Fall 2004, est.) 535 applied for aid; of those 89% were deemed to have need. 100% of freshmen with need received aid; of those 100% had need fully met. *Average financial aid package:* $2970 (excluding resources awarded to replace EFC). 25% of all full-time freshmen had no need and received non-need-based gift aid.

UNDERGRADUATE FINANCIAL AID (Fall 2004, est.) 2,303 applied for aid; of those 98% were deemed to have need. 100% of undergraduates with need received aid; of those 100% had need fully met. *Average financial aid package:* $3320 (excluding resources awarded to replace EFC). 20% of all full-time undergraduates had no need and received non-need-based gift aid.

GIFT AID (NEED-BASED) Total amount: $7,432,911 (100% federal). **Receiving aid:** Freshmen: 35% (338); All full-time undergraduates: 39% (1,696). **Average award:** Freshmen: $3234; Undergraduates: $3209. **Scholarships, grants, and awards:** Federal Pell, FSEOG, state, private, college/university gift aid from institutional funds.

GIFT AID (NON-NEED-BASED) Total amount: $5,784,487 (100% institutional). **Receiving aid:** Freshmen: 18% (173); Undergraduates: 16% (677). **Average Award:** Freshmen: $2332; Undergraduates: $2729. **Scholarships, grants, and awards by category:** *Academic Interests/Achievement:* general academic interests/achievements. *Creative Arts/Performance:* music, theater/drama. *Special Achievements/Activities:* leadership. *Special Characteristics:* general special characteristics. **Tuition waivers:** Full or partial for employees or children of employees. **ROTC:** Army, Air Force.

LOANS Student loans: $21,435,284 (56% need-based, 44% non-need-based). *Average indebtedness per student:* $14,564. **Average need-based loan:** Freshmen: $2499; Undergraduates: $3392. **Parent loans:** $3,939,842 (100% need-based). **Programs:** FFEL (Subsidized and Unsubsidized Stafford, PLUS), Perkins.

WORK-STUDY Federal work-study: Total amount: $633,180.

ATHLETIC AWARDS Total amount: $2,923,989 (100% non-need-based).

APPLYING FOR FINANCIAL AID Required financial aid forms: FAFSA, institution's own form. **Financial aid deadline (priority):** 5/1. **Notification date:** Continuous beginning 6/1. Students must reply within 2 weeks of notification.

CONTACT Ms. Carol Supri, Director of Financial Aid, Troy University, 131 Adams Administration Bldg., Troy, AL 36082, 334-670-3186 or toll-free 800-551-9716. *Fax:* 334-670-3702. *E-mail:* csupri@troy.edu.

TROY UNIVERSITY DOTHAN
Dothan, AL

Tuition & fees (AL res): $4162 | **Average undergraduate aid package: N/A**

ABOUT THE INSTITUTION State-supported, coed. Awards: associate, bachelor's, and master's degrees and post-master's certificates. 20 undergraduate majors. Total enrollment: 1,894. Undergraduates: 1,538. Freshmen: 82. Federal methodology is used as a basis for awarding need-based institutional aid.

UNDERGRADUATE EXPENSES for 2004–05 Application fee: $20. **Tuition, state resident:** full-time $3850; part-time $163 per credit hour. **Tuition, nonresident:** full-time $7700; part-time $326 per credit hour. **Required fees:** full-time $312; $312 per year part-time. **Payment plans:** Installment, deferred payment.

FRESHMAN FINANCIAL AID (Fall 2004, est.) 58 applied for aid; of those 100% were deemed to have need. 100% of freshmen with need received aid; of those 100% had need fully met.

UNDERGRADUATE FINANCIAL AID (Fall 2004, est.) 700 applied for aid; of those 100% were deemed to have need. 100% of undergraduates with need received aid; of those 100% had need fully met.

GIFT AID (NEED-BASED) Total amount: $2,098,393 (100% federal). **Receiving aid:** Freshmen: 34% (21); All full-time undergraduates: 41% (311). **Average award:** Freshmen: $3364; Undergraduates: $3146. **Scholarships, grants, and awards:** Federal Pell, FSEOG, state, private, college/university gift aid from institutional funds.

GIFT AID (NON-NEED-BASED) Receiving aid: Freshmen: 28% (17); Undergraduates: 9% (68). **Scholarships, grants, and awards by category:** *Academic Interests/Achievement:* general academic interests/achievements. **Tuition waivers:** Full or partial for employees or children of employees.

LOANS Student loans: $10,081,034 (100% need-based). 50% of past graduating class borrowed through all loan programs. *Average indebtedness per student:* $6038. **Average need-based loan:** Freshmen: $2125; Undergraduates: $3000. **Programs:** FFEL (Subsidized and Unsubsidized Stafford, PLUS).

WORK-STUDY Federal work-study: Total amount: $96,300; 21 jobs averaging $2140.

APPLYING FOR FINANCIAL AID Required financial aid forms: FAFSA, institution's own form. **Financial aid deadline (priority):** 3/1. **Notification date:** Continuous beginning 2/1. Students must reply within 2 weeks of notification.

CONTACT Jonua Byrd, Director of Financial Aid and Veterans' Affairs, Troy University Dothan, PO Box 8368, Dothan, AL 36304-8368, 334-983-6556 Ext. 255. *Fax:* 334-983-6322. *E-mail:* jbbyrd@troy.edu.

TROY UNIVERSITY MONTGOMERY
Montgomery, AL

Tuition & fees (AL res): $3920 | **Average undergraduate aid package: $3213**

ABOUT THE INSTITUTION State-supported, coed. Awards: associate, bachelor's, and master's degrees and post-master's certificates. 14 undergraduate majors. Total enrollment: 4,313. Undergraduates: 3,665. Freshmen: 321. Federal methodology is used as a basis for awarding need-based institutional aid.

UNDERGRADUATE EXPENSES for 2004–05 Application fee: $20. **Tuition, state resident:** full-time $3850; part-time $163 per semester hour. **Tuition, nonresident:** full-time $7700; part-time $326 per semester hour. **Required fees:** full-time $70; $35. Full-time tuition and fees vary according to program. **Payment plan:** Installment.

FRESHMAN FINANCIAL AID (Fall 2003) 73 applied for aid; of those 100% were deemed to have need. 100% of freshmen with need received aid. *Average financial aid package:* $3213 (excluding resources awarded to replace EFC).

UNDERGRADUATE FINANCIAL AID (Fall 2003) 86 applied for aid; of those 100% were deemed to have need. 100% of undergraduates with need received aid. *Average financial aid package:* $3213 (excluding resources awarded to replace EFC).

GIFT AID (NEED-BASED) Total amount: $3,827,598 (100% federal). **Receiving aid:** Freshmen: 46% (52); All full-time undergraduates: 45% (59). **Average award:** Freshmen: $3516; Undergraduates: $3490. **Scholarships, grants, and awards:** Federal Pell, FSEOG, state, college/university gift aid from institutional funds.

GIFT AID (NON-NEED-BASED) Scholarships, grants, and awards by category: *Academic Interests/Achievement:* general academic interests/achievements. **Tuition waivers:** Full or partial for employees or children of employees. **ROTC:** Army cooperative, Air Force cooperative.

LOANS Student loans: $5,057,254 (100% need-based). **Parent loans:** $87,420 (100% need-based). **Programs:** FFEL (Subsidized and Unsubsidized Stafford, PLUS), Perkins.

WORK-STUDY Federal work-study: Total amount: $27,820; jobs available.

APPLYING FOR FINANCIAL AID Required financial aid form: FAFSA. **Financial aid deadline (priority):** 5/1.

CONTACT Mr. John A. Brown, Director of Financial Aid, Troy University Montgomery, TSUM, PO Drawer 4419, 231 Montgomery Street, Montgomery, AL 36103-4419, 334-241-9520 or toll-free 800-355-TSUM. *Fax:* 334-241-5427. *E-mail:* jab@troy.edu.

TRUMAN STATE UNIVERSITY
Kirksville, MO

Tuition & fees (MO res): $5812 | **Average undergraduate aid package: $5842**

ABOUT THE INSTITUTION State-supported, coed. Awards: bachelor's and master's degrees. 56 undergraduate majors. Total enrollment: 5,862. Undergraduates: 5,616. Freshmen: 1,480. Federal methodology is used as a basis for awarding need-based institutional aid.

UNDERGRADUATE EXPENSES for 2005–06 Tuition, state resident: full-time $5740; part-time $239 per credit hour. **Tuition, nonresident:** full-time $9920; part-time $413 per credit hour. Part-time tuition and fees vary according to course load. **College room and board:** $5380. Room and board charges vary according to housing facility. **Payment plan:** Installment.

FRESHMAN FINANCIAL AID (Fall 2003) 738 applied for aid; of those 60% were deemed to have need. 100% of freshmen with need received aid; of those 57% had need fully met. *Average percent of need met:* 82% (excluding resources awarded to replace EFC). *Average financial aid package:* $6454 (excluding resources awarded to replace EFC). 61% of all full-time freshmen had no need and received non-need-based gift aid.

UNDERGRADUATE FINANCIAL AID (Fall 2003) 3,190 applied for aid; of those 69% were deemed to have need. 100% of undergraduates with need received aid; of those 64% had need fully met. *Average percent of need met:* 80% (excluding resources awarded to replace EFC). *Average financial aid package:* $5842 (excluding resources awarded to replace EFC). 42% of all full-time undergraduates had no need and received non-need-based gift aid.

GIFT AID (NEED-BASED) *Total amount:* $2,617,979 (76% federal, 15% state, 9% institutional). *Receiving aid:* Freshmen: 15% (194); All full-time undergraduates: 17% (892). *Average award:* Freshmen: $3114; Undergraduates: $3063. *Scholarships, grants, and awards:* Federal Pell, FSEOG, state, private, college/university gift aid from institutional funds.

GIFT AID (NON-NEED-BASED) *Total amount:* $18,134,356 (13% state, 76% institutional, 11% external sources). *Receiving aid:* Freshmen: 31% (409); Undergraduates: 30% (1,580). *Average Award: Freshmen:* $4002; *Undergraduates:* $3902. *Scholarships, grants, and awards by category: Academic Interests/Achievement:* 3,530 awards ($11,716,625 total): biological sciences, business, communication, education, English, foreign languages, general academic interests/achievements, mathematics, military science, physical sciences, premedicine, social sciences. *Creative Arts/Performance:* 135 awards ($115,434 total): art/fine arts, debating, music, theater/drama. *Special Achievements/Activities:* 386 awards ($929,844 total): leadership. *Special Characteristics:* 285 awards ($904,662 total): children and siblings of alumni, children of faculty/staff, ethnic background, international students. *Tuition waivers:* Full or partial for employees or children of employees, senior citizens. *ROTC:* Army.

LOANS *Student loans:* $10,442,648 (54% need-based, 46% non-need-based). 43% of past graduating class borrowed through all loan programs. *Average indebtedness per student:* $16,208. *Average need-based loan:* Freshmen: $2893; Undergraduates: $3868. *Parent loans:* $1,283,285 (100% non-need-based). *Programs:* FFEL (Subsidized and Unsubsidized Stafford, PLUS), Perkins, Federal Nursing, state, college/university.

WORK-STUDY *Federal work-study:* Total amount: $244,583; 291 jobs averaging $842. *State or other work-study/employment:* Total amount: $1,686,506 (100% non-need-based). 1,914 part-time jobs averaging $1028.

ATHLETIC AWARDS *Total amount:* $1,076,455 (100% non-need-based).

APPLYING FOR FINANCIAL AID *Required financial aid forms:* FAFSA, institution's own form. *Financial aid deadline (priority):* 4/1. *Notification date:* Continuous beginning 4/1. Students must reply within 4 weeks of notification.

CONTACT Ms. Melinda Wood, Director of Financial Aid, Truman State University, 103 McClain Hall, Kirksville, MO 63501-4221, 660-785-4130 or toll-free 800-892-7792 (in-state). *Fax:* 660-785-7389. *E-mail:* mwood@truman.edu.

TUFTS UNIVERSITY
Medford, MA

Tuition & fees: $31,248	Average undergraduate aid package: $24,230

ABOUT THE INSTITUTION Independent, coed. Awards: bachelor's, master's, doctoral, and first professional degrees and post-master's certificates. 64 undergraduate majors. Total enrollment: 9,693. Undergraduates: 4,913. Freshmen: 1,273. Both federal and institutional methodology are used as a basis for awarding need-based institutional aid.

UNDERGRADUATE EXPENSES for 2004–05 *Application fee:* $60. *Comprehensive fee:* $40,278 includes full-time tuition ($30,482), mandatory fees ($766), and room and board ($9030). *College room only:* $4641. Room and board charges vary according to board plan. *Payment plans:* Tuition prepayment, installment.

FRESHMAN FINANCIAL AID (Fall 2004, est.) 632 applied for aid; of those 78% were deemed to have need. 100% of freshmen with need received aid; of those 100% had need fully met. *Average percent of need met:* 100% (excluding resources awarded to replace EFC). *Average financial aid package:* $22,304 (excluding resources awarded to replace EFC). 2% of all full-time freshmen had no need and received non-need-based gift aid.

UNDERGRADUATE FINANCIAL AID (Fall 2004, est.) 2,206 applied for aid; of those 88% were deemed to have need. 100% of undergraduates with need received aid; of those 100% had need fully met. *Average percent of need met:* 100% (excluding resources awarded to replace EFC). *Average financial aid package:* $24,230 (excluding resources awarded to replace EFC). 2% of all full-time undergraduates had no need and received non-need-based gift aid.

GIFT AID (NEED-BASED) *Total amount:* $37,671,817 (7% federal, 2% state, 87% institutional, 4% external sources). *Receiving aid:* Freshmen: 36% (459); All full-time undergraduates: 37% (1,796). *Average award:* Freshmen: $20,049; Undergraduates: $21,037. *Scholarships, grants, and awards:* Federal Pell, FSEOG, state, private, college/university gift aid from institutional funds.

GIFT AID (NON-NEED-BASED) *Total amount:* $213,500 (22% federal, 18% institutional, 60% external sources). *Average Award: Freshmen:* $500; *Undergraduates:* $500. *Scholarships, grants, and awards by category: Academic Interests/Achievement:* 145 awards ($162,000 total): general academic interests/achievements. *Special Characteristics:* children of faculty/staff. *Tuition waivers:* Full or partial for employees or children of employees. *ROTC:* Army cooperative, Naval cooperative, Air Force cooperative.

LOANS *Student loans:* $7,736,184 (89% need-based, 11% non-need-based). 39% of past graduating class borrowed through all loan programs. *Average indebtedness per student:* $14,683. *Average need-based loan:* Freshmen: $2911; Undergraduates: $4219. *Parent loans:* $9,993,926 (100% non-need-based). *Programs:* FFEL (Subsidized and Unsubsidized Stafford, PLUS), Perkins, state, college/university.

WORK-STUDY *Federal work-study:* Total amount: $2,529,567; 1,725 jobs averaging $1466. *State or other work-study/employment:* Total amount: $51,100 (100% need-based). 27 part-time jobs averaging $1892.

APPLYING FOR FINANCIAL AID *Required financial aid forms:* FAFSA, CSS Financial Aid PROFILE, noncustodial (divorced/separated) parent's statement, business/farm supplement, federal income tax form(s). *Financial aid deadline:* 2/15. *Notification date:* 4/5. Students must reply by 5/1.

CONTACT Patricia C. Reilly, Director of Financial Aid, Tufts University, Dowling Hall, Medford, MA 02155, 617-627-2000. *Fax:* 617-627-3987. *E-mail:* patricia.reilly@tufts.edu.

TULANE UNIVERSITY
New Orleans, LA

CONTACT Ms. Elaine Rivera, Director of Financial Aid, Tulane University, 6823 St. Charles Avenue, New Orleans, LA 70118-5669, 504-865-5723 or toll-free 800-873-9283. *E-mail:* finaid@tulane.edu.

TUSCULUM COLLEGE
Greeneville, TN

Tuition & fees: $15,110	Average undergraduate aid package: $9972

ABOUT THE INSTITUTION Independent Presbyterian, coed. Awards: bachelor's and master's degrees. 27 undergraduate majors. Total enrollment: 2,305. Undergraduates: 2,053. Freshmen: 357. Federal methodology is used as a basis for awarding need-based institutional aid.

UNDERGRADUATE EXPENSES for 2004–05 *Comprehensive fee:* $21,060 includes full-time tuition ($14,810), mandatory fees ($300), and room and board ($5950). Full-time tuition and fees vary according to degree level, program, and reciprocity agreements. Room and board charges vary according to housing facility. *Part-time tuition:* $680 per semester hour. Part-time tuition and fees vary according to degree level, program, and reciprocity agreements. *Payment plan:* Installment.

FRESHMAN FINANCIAL AID (Fall 2004, est.) 330 applied for aid; of those 98% were deemed to have need. 100% of freshmen with need received aid; of those 24% had need fully met. *Average percent of need met:* 70% (excluding resources awarded to replace EFC). *Average financial aid package:* $12,929 (excluding resources awarded to replace EFC). 21% of all full-time freshmen had no need and received non-need-based gift aid.

UNDERGRADUATE FINANCIAL AID (Fall 2004, est.) 1,728 applied for aid; of those 75% were deemed to have need. 100% of undergraduates with need received aid; of those 21% had need fully met. *Average percent of need met:* 72% (excluding resources awarded to replace EFC). *Average financial aid package:* $9972 (excluding resources awarded to replace EFC). 14% of all full-time undergraduates had no need and received non-need-based gift aid.

GIFT AID (NEED-BASED) *Total amount:* $8,370,756 (28% federal, 12% state, 60% institutional). *Receiving aid:* Freshmen: 81% (288); All full-time undergraduates: 39% (803). *Average award:* Freshmen: $2032; Undergraduates: $2000. *Scholarships, grants, and awards:* Federal Pell, FSEOG, state, private, college/university gift aid from institutional funds.

GIFT AID (NON-NEED-BASED) *Total amount:* $2,039,130 (22% state, 64% institutional, 14% external sources). *Receiving aid:* Freshmen: 38% (135); Undergraduates: 37% (751). *Average Award: Freshmen:* $6440; *Undergraduates:* $5553. *Scholarships, grants, and awards by category: Academic Interests/Achievement:* general academic interests/achievements. *Creative Arts/Performance:* music. *Special Achievements/Activities:* cheerleading/drum major, community service, leadership. *Special Characteristics:* adult students, children of faculty/staff, local/state students. *Tuition waivers:* Full or partial for employees or children of employees.

LOANS *Student loans:* $11,851,704 (48% need-based, 52% non-need-based). 58% of past graduating class borrowed through all loan programs. *Average indebtedness per student:* $14,633. *Average need-based loan:* Freshmen: $2769; Undergraduates: $4007. *Parent loans:* $989,763 (100% non-need-based). *Programs:* FFEL (Subsidized and Unsubsidized Stafford, PLUS), Perkins.

WORK-STUDY *Federal work-study:* Total amount: $396,257; 221 jobs averaging $1074. *State or other work-study/employment:* 266 part-time jobs averaging $776.

ATHLETIC AWARDS *Total amount:* $1,035,870 (100% non-need-based).

APPLYING FOR FINANCIAL AID *Required financial aid form:* FAFSA. *Financial aid deadline (priority):* 2/15. *Notification date:* Continuous beginning 3/1. Students must reply within 3 weeks of notification.

CONTACT Mr. J. Pat Shannon, Director of Financial Aid, Tusculum College, 5049 Tusculum Station, Greeneville, TN 37743-9997, 423-636-7300 Ext. 5373 or toll-free 800-729-0256. *Fax:* 801-697-6885. *E-mail:* pshannon@tusculum.edu.

TUSKEGEE UNIVERSITY
Tuskegee, AL

Tuition & fees: $11,590	Average undergraduate aid package: $13,824

ABOUT THE INSTITUTION Independent, coed. Awards: bachelor's, master's, doctoral, and first professional degrees. 43 undergraduate majors. Total enrollment: 2,870. Undergraduates: 2,481. Freshmen: 709. Federal methodology is used as a basis for awarding need-based institutional aid.

UNDERGRADUATE EXPENSES for 2004–05 *Application fee:* $25. *Comprehensive fee:* $17,530 includes full-time tuition ($11,290), mandatory fees ($300), and room and board ($5940). *College room only:* $3170. Full-time tuition and fees vary according to course load and program. Room and board charges vary according to housing facility. *Part-time tuition:* $460 per credit hour. *Part-time fees:* $150 per term. Part-time tuition and fees vary according to course load and program. *Payment plan:* Installment.

FRESHMAN FINANCIAL AID (Fall 2003) 635 applied for aid; of those 85% were deemed to have need. 92% of freshmen with need received aid; of those 70% had need fully met. *Average percent of need met:* 85% (excluding resources awarded to replace EFC). *Average financial aid package:* $13,824 (excluding resources awarded to replace EFC).

UNDERGRADUATE FINANCIAL AID (Fall 2003) 2,519 applied for aid; of those 85% were deemed to have need. 92% of undergraduates with need received aid; of those 70% had need fully met. *Average percent of need met:* 85% (excluding resources awarded to replace EFC). *Average financial aid package:* $13,824 (excluding resources awarded to replace EFC).

GIFT AID (NEED-BASED) *Total amount:* $5,459,147 (98% federal, 2% institutional). *Receiving aid:* Freshmen: 56% (422); All full-time undergraduates: 61% (1,675). *Average award:* Freshmen: $8000; Undergraduates: $8000. *Scholarships, grants, and awards:* Federal Pell, FSEOG, state, private, college/university gift aid from institutional funds, United Negro College Fund, Federal Nursing.

GIFT AID (NON-NEED-BASED) *Total amount:* $3,408,097 (45% institutional, 55% external sources). *Receiving aid:* Freshmen: 36% (273); Undergraduates: 35% (951). *Average Award:* Freshmen: $6000; Undergraduates: $6000. *Scholarships, grants, and awards by category:* Academic Interests/Achievement: 1,714 awards ($9,086,319 total): general academic interests/achievements. *Creative Arts/Performance:* 108 awards ($68,400 total): music. *Special Characteristics:* 36 awards ($157,002 total): children of faculty/staff, local/state students. *Tuition waivers:* Full or partial for employees or children of employees. *ROTC:* Army, Air Force.

LOANS *Student loans:* $16,456,358 (53% need-based, 47% non-need-based). 91% of past graduating class borrowed through all loan programs. *Average indebtedness per student:* $30,000. *Average need-based loan:* Freshmen: $5625; Undergraduates: $6006. *Parent loans:* $3,098,631 (100% non-need-based). *Programs:* FFEL (Subsidized and Unsubsidized Stafford, PLUS), Perkins.

WORK-STUDY *Federal work-study:* Total amount: $830,097; 525 jobs averaging $1879. *State or other work-study/employment:* Total amount: $1,318,823 (100% non-need-based). 425 part-time jobs averaging $4739.

ATHLETIC AWARDS *Total amount:* $1,145,218 (100% non-need-based).

APPLYING FOR FINANCIAL AID *Required financial aid forms:* FAFSA, institution's own form, CSS Financial Aid PROFILE. *Financial aid deadline (priority):* 3/31. *Notification date:* Continuous beginning 4/15. Students must reply within 2 weeks of notification.

CONTACT Mr. A. D. James Jr., Director of Student Financial Services, Tuskegee University, Office of Student Financial Services, Tuskegee, AL 36088, 334-727-8201 or toll-free 800-622-6531. *Fax:* 334-724-4227. *E-mail:* jamesad@tuskegee.edu.

UNION COLLEGE
Barbourville, KY

Tuition & fees: $13,750	Average undergraduate aid package: $12,426

ABOUT THE INSTITUTION Independent United Methodist, coed. Awards: bachelor's and master's degrees. 21 undergraduate majors. Total enrollment: 1,047. Undergraduates: 571. Freshmen: 130. Federal methodology is used as a basis for awarding need-based institutional aid.

UNDERGRADUATE EXPENSES for 2004–05 *Application fee:* $20. *Comprehensive fee:* $18,150 includes full-time tuition ($13,750) and room and board ($4400). Room and board charges vary according to board plan and housing facility. *Part-time tuition:* $240 per hour. *Payment plan:* Installment.

FRESHMAN FINANCIAL AID (Fall 2004, est.) 147 applied for aid; of those 93% were deemed to have need. 100% of freshmen with need received aid; of those 23% had need fully met. *Average percent of need met:* 69% (excluding resources awarded to replace EFC). *Average financial aid package:* $10,993 (excluding resources awarded to replace EFC). 6% of all full-time freshmen had no need and received non-need-based gift aid.

UNDERGRADUATE FINANCIAL AID (Fall 2004, est.) 563 applied for aid; of those 96% were deemed to have need. 99% of undergraduates with need received aid; of those 26% had need fully met. *Average percent of need met:* 75% (excluding resources awarded to replace EFC). *Average financial aid package:* $12,426 (excluding resources awarded to replace EFC). 5% of all full-time undergraduates had no need and received non-need-based gift aid.

GIFT AID (NEED-BASED) *Total amount:* $2,935,765 (40% federal, 45% state, 15% institutional). *Receiving aid:* Freshmen: 92% (135); All full-time undergraduates: 92% (526). *Average award:* Freshmen: $7485; Undergraduates: $7170. *Scholarships, grants, and awards:* Federal Pell, FSEOG, state, college/university gift aid from institutional funds.

GIFT AID (NON-NEED-BASED) *Total amount:* $54,418 (100% state). *Receiving aid:* Freshmen: 12% (18); Undergraduates: 14% (81). *Average Award:* Freshmen: $8314; Undergraduates: $8961. *Scholarships, grants, and awards by category:* Academic Interests/Achievement: 350 awards ($684,101 total): general academic interests/achievements. *Creative Arts/Performance:* 7 awards ($19,400 total): music. *Special Achievements/Activities:* 17 awards ($15,150 total): cheerleading/drum major. *Special Characteristics:* 53 awards ($45,624 total): children and siblings of alumni, religious affiliation. *Tuition waivers:* Full or partial for minority students, children of alumni, employees or children of employees, senior citizens. *ROTC:* Army cooperative.

LOANS *Student loans:* $2,761,732 (86% need-based, 14% non-need-based). 90% of past graduating class borrowed through all loan programs. *Average indebtedness per student:* $11,253. *Average need-based loan:* Freshmen: $3334; Undergraduates: $4470. *Parent loans:* $203,648 (100% need-based). *Programs:* FFEL (Subsidized and Unsubsidized Stafford, PLUS), Perkins, college/university.

WORK-STUDY *Federal work-study:* Total amount: $181,000; 181 jobs averaging $1000. *State or other work-study/employment:* Part-time jobs available.

ATHLETIC AWARDS *Total amount:* $1,455,095 (100% need-based).

APPLYING FOR FINANCIAL AID *Required financial aid form:* FAFSA. *Financial aid deadline (priority):* 3/15. *Notification date:* Continuous beginning 4/1. Students must reply within 2 weeks of notification.

CONTACT Mrs. Sue Buttery, Associate Dean of Financial Aid and Admission, Union College, 310 College Street, Barbourville, KY 40906-1499, 606-546-1224 or toll-free 800-489-8646. *Fax:* 606-546-1556. *E-mail:* sbuttery@unionky.edu.

UNION COLLEGE
Lincoln, NE

ABOUT THE INSTITUTION Independent Seventh-day Adventist, coed. Awards: associate, bachelor's, and master's degrees. 54 undergraduate majors. Total enrollment: 936. Undergraduates: 912. Freshmen: 191.

GIFT AID (NEED-BASED) *Scholarships, grants, and awards:* Federal Pell, FSEOG, state, private, college/university gift aid from institutional funds.

GIFT AID (NON-NEED-BASED) *Scholarships, grants, and awards by category:* *Academic Interests/Achievement:* general academic interests/achievements. *Creative Arts/Performance:* music. *Special Achievements/Activities:* community service, leadership, religious involvement.

LOANS *Programs:* FFEL (Subsidized and Unsubsidized Stafford, PLUS), Perkins, Federal Nursing, college/university.

WORK-STUDY *Federal work-study:* Total amount: $314,000; 172 jobs averaging $1663.

APPLYING FOR FINANCIAL AID *Required financial aid form:* FAFSA.

CONTACT Mr. John C. Burdick, IV, Director of Financial Aid, Union College, 3800 South 48th Street, Lincoln, NE 68506-4300, 800-228-4600. *Fax:* 402-486-2895. *E-mail:* financialaid@ucollege.edu.

UNION COLLEGE
Schenectady, NY

Comprehensive fee: $38,703	Average undergraduate aid package: $24,227

ABOUT THE INSTITUTION Independent, coed. Awards: bachelor's degrees. 26 undergraduate majors. Total enrollment: 2,192. Undergraduates: 2,192. Freshmen: 552. Both federal and institutional methodology are used as a basis for awarding need-based institutional aid.

UNDERGRADUATE EXPENSES for 2004–05 *Application fee:* $50. *Comprehensive fee:* $38,703. *Payment plan:* Installment.

FRESHMAN FINANCIAL AID (Fall 2003) 333 applied for aid; of those 81% were deemed to have need. 100% of freshmen with need received aid; of those 100% had need fully met. *Average percent of need met:* 100% (excluding resources awarded to replace EFC). *Average financial aid package:* $25,751 (excluding resources awarded to replace EFC). 10% of all full-time freshmen had no need and received non-need-based gift aid.

UNDERGRADUATE FINANCIAL AID (Fall 2003) 1,153 applied for aid; of those 90% were deemed to have need. 100% of undergraduates with need received aid; of those 95% had need fully met. *Average percent of need met:* 100% (excluding resources awarded to replace EFC). *Average financial aid package:* $24,227 (excluding resources awarded to replace EFC). 5% of all full-time undergraduates had no need and received non-need-based gift aid.

GIFT AID (NEED-BASED) *Total amount:* $21,099,524 (7% federal, 7% state, 84% institutional, 2% external sources). *Receiving aid:* Freshmen: 48% (269); All full-time undergraduates: 48% (1,018). *Average award:* Freshmen: $18,404; Undergraduates: $20,630. *Scholarships, grants, and awards:* Federal Pell, FSEOG, state, private, college/university gift aid from institutional funds.

GIFT AID (NON-NEED-BASED) *Total amount:* $2,051,136 (10% federal, 2% state, 88% institutional). *Receiving aid:* Freshmen: 1% (3); Undergraduates: 6. *Average Award:* Freshmen: $10,850; Undergraduates: $12,200. *Scholarships, grants, and awards by category:* Academic Interests/Achievement: 90 awards ($900,000 total): general academic interests/achievements. *Tuition waivers:* Full or partial for employees or children of employees, senior citizens. *ROTC:* Army cooperative, Air Force cooperative.

LOANS *Student loans:* $4,193,077 (96% need-based, 4% non-need-based). 50% of past graduating class borrowed through all loan programs. *Average indebtedness per student:* $16,705. *Average need-based loan:* Freshmen: $2848; Undergraduates: $4437. *Parent loans:* $2,849,571 (100% need-based). *Programs:* FFEL (Subsidized and Unsubsidized Stafford, PLUS), Perkins, college/university.

WORK-STUDY *Federal work-study:* Total amount: $756,359; 594 jobs averaging $1275. *State or other work-study/employment:* Total amount: $42,466 (100% need-based). 36 part-time jobs averaging $1596.

APPLYING FOR FINANCIAL AID *Required financial aid forms:* FAFSA, CSS Financial Aid PROFILE, state aid form, noncustodial (divorced/separated) parent's statement, business/farm supplement. *Financial aid deadline:* 2/1. *Notification date:* 4/1. Students must reply by 5/1.

CONTACT Ms. Beth Post, Director of Financial Aid, Union College, Grant Hall, Schenectady, NY 12308-2311, 518-388-6123 or toll-free 888-843-6688 (in-state). *Fax:* 518-388-8052. *E-mail:* financialaid@union.edu.

UNION INSTITUTE & UNIVERSITY
Cincinnati, OH

CONTACT Ms. Rebecca Zackerman, Director of Financial Aid, Union Institute & University, 440 East McMillan Street, Cincinnati, OH 45206-1925, 513-861-6400 or toll-free 800-486-3116. *Fax:* 513-861-0779. *E-mail:* bzackerman@tui.edu.

UNION UNIVERSITY
Jackson, TN

Tuition & fees: $15,370	Average undergraduate aid package: $10,492

ABOUT THE INSTITUTION Independent Southern Baptist, coed. Awards: associate, bachelor's, master's, and doctoral degrees and post-master's certificates. 66 undergraduate majors. Total enrollment: 2,843. Undergraduates: 2,074. Freshmen: 439. Federal methodology is used as a basis for awarding need-based institutional aid.

UNDERGRADUATE EXPENSES for 2004–05 *Application fee:* $25. *Comprehensive fee:* $20,340 includes full-time tuition ($14,850), mandatory fees ($520), and room and board ($4970). *College room only:* $2990. Full-time tuition and fees vary according to class time, course load, location, and program. Room and board charges vary according to board plan and location. *Part-time tuition:* $495 per credit hour. *Payment plans:* Tuition prepayment, installment, deferred payment.

FRESHMAN FINANCIAL AID (Fall 2003) 388 applied for aid; of those 100% were deemed to have need. 66% of freshmen with need received aid. *Average financial aid package:* $10,402 (excluding resources awarded to replace EFC).

UNDERGRADUATE FINANCIAL AID (Fall 2003) 1,414 applied for aid; of those 61% were deemed to have need. 99% of undergraduates with need received aid. *Average financial aid package:* $10,492 (excluding resources awarded to replace EFC).

GIFT AID (NEED-BASED) *Total amount:* $3,250,703 (35% federal, 16% state, 44% institutional, 5% external sources). *Receiving aid:* Freshmen: 45% (182); All full-time undergraduates: 42% (620). *Average award:* Freshmen: $2585; Undergraduates: $3719. *Scholarships, grants, and awards:* Federal Pell, FSEOG, state, private, college/university gift aid from institutional funds.

GIFT AID (NON-NEED-BASED) *Total amount:* $5,970,786 (94% institutional, 6% external sources). *Receiving aid:* Freshmen: 49% (200); Undergraduates: 55% (820). *Average Award:* Freshmen: $5475; Undergraduates: $4884. *Scholarships, grants, and awards by category:* Academic Interests/Achievement: 1,050 awards ($3,386,984 total): business, communication, education, general academic interests/achievements, mathematics, premedicine, religion/biblical studies. *Creative Arts/Performance:* 102 awards ($147,300 total): art/fine arts, cinema/film/broadcasting, journalism/publications, music, theater/drama. *Special Achievements/Activities:* 640 awards ($704,254 total): cheerleading/drum major, leadership. *Special Characteristics:* 433 awards ($1,546,126 total): children and siblings of alumni, children of faculty/staff, ethnic background, relatives of clergy, religious affiliation, siblings of current students. *Tuition waivers:* Full or partial for employees or children of employees.

LOANS *Student loans:* $8,432,613 (46% need-based, 54% non-need-based). 11% of past graduating class borrowed through all loan programs. *Average indebtedness per student:* $15,328. *Average need-based loan:* Freshmen: $2655; Undergraduates: $3782. *Parent loans:* $1,370,783 (100% non-need-based). *Programs:* FFEL (Subsidized and Unsubsidized Stafford, PLUS), Perkins, college/university, alternative loans.

WORK-STUDY *Federal work-study:* Total amount: $125,000; 127 jobs averaging $985. *State or other work-study/employment:* Total amount: $159,913 (100% non-need-based). 111 part-time jobs averaging $1440.

ATHLETIC AWARDS *Total amount:* $1,291,400 (100% non-need-based).

APPLYING FOR FINANCIAL AID *Required financial aid forms:* FAFSA, institution's own form. *Financial aid deadline (priority):* 1/15. *Notification date:* Continuous beginning 2/1. Students must reply by 5/1 or within 2 weeks of notification.

CONTACT John Brandt, Director of Financial Aid, Union University, 1050 Union University Drive, Jackson, TN 38305-3697, 731-661-5015 or toll-free 800-33-UNION. *Fax:* 731-661-5570. *E-mail:* jbrandt@uu.edu.

UNITED TALMUDICAL SEMINARY
Brooklyn, NY

CONTACT Financial Aid Office, United Talmudical Seminary, 82 Lee Avenue, Brooklyn, NY 11211-7900, 718-963-9770 Ext. 309.

UNITY COLLEGE
Unity, ME

Tuition & fees: $17,680	Average undergraduate aid package: $12,979

ABOUT THE INSTITUTION Independent, coed. Awards: associate and bachelor's degrees. 14 undergraduate majors. Total enrollment: 521. Undergraduates: 521. Freshmen: 159. Federal methodology is used as a basis for awarding need-based institutional aid.

UNDERGRADUATE EXPENSES for 2005–06 *Application fee:* $25. *Comprehensive fee:* $24,310 includes full-time tuition ($16,740), mandatory fees ($940), and room and board ($6630). Part-time tuition and fees vary according to course load. *Payment plan:* Installment.

FRESHMAN FINANCIAL AID (Fall 2004, est.) 149 applied for aid; of those 85% were deemed to have need. 100% of freshmen with need received aid; of those 26% had need fully met. *Average percent of need met:* 74% (excluding resources awarded to replace EFC). *Average financial aid package:* $13,214 (excluding resources awarded to replace EFC). 18% of all full-time freshmen had no need and received non-need-based gift aid.

UNDERGRADUATE FINANCIAL AID (Fall 2004, est.) 474 applied for aid; of those 88% were deemed to have need. 100% of undergraduates with need received aid; of those 27% had need fully met. *Average percent of need met:* 75% (excluding resources awarded to replace EFC). *Average financial aid package:* $12,979 (excluding resources awarded to replace EFC). 17% of all full-time undergraduates had no need and received non-need-based gift aid.

GIFT AID (NEED-BASED) *Total amount:* $2,885,773 (25% federal, 6% state, 64% institutional, 5% external sources). *Receiving aid:* Freshmen: 80% (127); All full-time undergraduates: 78% (407). *Average award:* Freshmen: $8490; Undergraduates: $7082. *Scholarships, grants, and awards:* Federal Pell, FSEOG, state, private, college/university gift aid from institutional funds.

GIFT AID (NON-NEED-BASED) *Total amount:* $315,110 (1% federal, 86% institutional, 13% external sources). *Receiving aid:* Freshmen: 3% (5); Undergraduates: 2% (13). *Average Award:* Freshmen: $7808; Undergraduates: $8845. *Scholarships, grants, and awards by category: Academic Interests/Achievement:* 229 awards ($822,650 total): general academic interests/achievements. *Special Achievements/Activities:* 91 awards ($88,000 total): community service, leadership. *Special Characteristics:* 50 awards ($118,295 total): children of educators, general special characteristics, local/state students, members of minority groups. *Tuition waivers:* Full or partial for employees or children of employees. *ROTC:* Army cooperative.

LOANS *Student loans:* $3,824,280 (71% need-based, 29% non-need-based). *Average need-based loan:* Freshmen: $4315; Undergraduates: $5366. *Parent loans:* $551,774 (38% need-based, 62% non-need-based). *Programs:* FFEL (Subsidized and Unsubsidized Stafford, PLUS), Perkins.

WORK-STUDY *Federal work-study:* Total amount: $488,261; 296 jobs averaging $1650. *State or other work-study/employment:* Total amount: $11,900 (8% need-based, 92% non-need-based). 9 part-time jobs averaging $1233.

APPLYING FOR FINANCIAL AID *Required financial aid form:* FAFSA. *Financial aid deadline:* Continuous. *Notification date:* Continuous beginning 3/10. Students must reply within 2 weeks of notification.

CONTACT Mr. Rand E. Newell, Director of Financial Aid, Unity College, 90 Quaker Hill Road, Unity, ME 04988, 207-948-3131 Ext. 201. *Fax:* 207-948-6277. *E-mail:* rnewell@unity.edu.

UNIVERSIDAD ADVENTISTA DE LAS ANTILLAS
Mayagüez, PR

CONTACT Mr. Heriberto Juarbe, Director of Financial Aid, Universidad Adventista de las Antillas, Box 118, Mayagüez, PR 00681-0118, 787-834-9595 Ext. 2200. *Fax:* 787-834-9597.

UNIVERSIDAD DEL ESTE
Carolina, PR

CONTACT Mr. Clotilde Santiago, Director of Financial Aid, Universidad del Este, Apartado 2010, Carolina, PR 00928, 787-257-7373 Ext. 3300.

UNIVERSIDAD DEL TURABO
Gurabo, PR

CONTACT Ms. Ivette Vázquez Ríos, Directora Oficina de Asistencia Económica, Universidad del Turabo, Apartado 3030, Gurabo, PR 00778-3030, 787-743-7979 Ext. 4352. *Fax:* 787-743-7979.

UNIVERSIDAD FLET
Miami, FL

CONTACT Financial Aid Office, Universidad FLET, 14540 SW 136th Street, Suite 200, Miami, FL 33186, 305-232-5880 or toll-free 888-376-3538.

UNIVERSIDAD METROPOLITANA
Río Piedras, PR

CONTACT Economic Assistant Director, Universidad Metropolitana, Call Box 21150, Rio Piedras, PR 00928-1150, 787-766-1717 Ext. 6586 or toll-free 800-747-8362 (out-of-state).

UNIVERSITY AT ALBANY, STATE UNIVERSITY OF NEW YORK
Albany, NY

Tuition & fees (NY res): $5810   **Average undergraduate aid package:** $8651

ABOUT THE INSTITUTION State-supported, coed. Awards: bachelor's, master's, and doctoral degrees and post-master's certificates. 69 undergraduate majors. Total enrollment: 16,293. Undergraduates: 11,388. Freshmen: 2,020. Federal methodology is used as a basis for awarding need-based institutional aid.

UNDERGRADUATE EXPENSES for 2004–05 *Application fee:* $40. *Tuition, state resident:* full-time $4350; part-time $181 per credit. *Tuition, nonresident:* full-time $10,610; part-time $442 per credit. Part-time tuition and fees vary according to course load. *College room and board:* $7540; *room only:* $4560. Room and board charges vary according to board plan and housing facility. *Payment plan:* Installment.

GIFT AID (NEED-BASED) *Total amount:* $25,267,225 (41% federal, 51% state, 7% institutional, 1% external sources). *Receiving aid:* Freshmen: 50% (1,000); All full-time undergraduates: 50% (5,224). *Average award:* Freshmen: $5312; Undergraduates: $4932. *Scholarships, grants, and awards:* Federal Pell, FSEOG, state, private, college/university gift aid from institutional funds.

GIFT AID (NON-NEED-BASED) *Total amount:* $3,970,530 (2% federal, 22% state, 61% institutional, 15% external sources). *Receiving aid:* Freshmen: 4% (76); Undergraduates: 2% (256). *Average Award:* Freshmen: $3487; *Undergraduates:* $3534. *Scholarships, grants, and awards by category: Academic Interests/Achievement:* 1,230 awards ($4,173,503 total): area/ethnic studies, general academic interests/achievements. *Special Characteristics:* 274 awards ($1,423,050 total): ethnic background, out-of-state students. *Tuition waivers:* Full or partial for senior citizens. *ROTC:* Army, Air Force cooperative.

LOANS *Student loans:* $37,243,900 (55% need-based, 45% non-need-based). 73% of past graduating class borrowed through all loan programs. *Average indebtedness per student:* $16,033. *Average need-based loan:* Freshmen: $3334; Undergraduates: $4162. *Parent loans:* $6,724,266 (100% non-need-based). *Programs:* FFEL (Subsidized and Unsubsidized Stafford, PLUS), Perkins.

ATHLETIC AWARDS *Total amount:* $2,300,591 (28% need-based, 72% non-need-based).

APPLYING FOR FINANCIAL AID *Required financial aid forms:* FAFSA, NY state residents should apply for TAP online at www.hesc.com. *Financial aid deadline:* 4/15. *Notification date:* Continuous beginning 3/15. Students must reply by 5/1 or within 2 weeks of notification.

CONTACT Brenda Wright, Assistant Director of Financial Aid, University at Albany, State University of New York, 1400 Washington Avenue, Campus Center B52, Albany, NY 12222-0001, 518-442-5757 or toll-free 800-293-7869 (in-state). *Fax:* 518-442-5295.

UNIVERSITY AT BUFFALO, THE STATE UNIVERSITY OF NEW YORK
Buffalo, NY

Tuition & fees (NY res): $5966   **Average undergraduate aid package:** $7132

ABOUT THE INSTITUTION State-supported, coed. Awards: bachelor's, master's, doctoral, and first professional degrees and post-master's and first professional certificates. 79 undergraduate majors. Total enrollment: 27,276. Undergraduates: 17,838. Freshmen: 3,183. Federal methodology is used as a basis for awarding need-based institutional aid.

UNDERGRADUATE EXPENSES for 2004–05 *Application fee:* $40. *Tuition, state resident:* full-time $4350; part-time $181 per credit hour. *Tuition, nonresident:* full-time $10,610; part-time $442 per credit hour. *Required fees:* full-time $1616; $72 per credit hour. Part-time tuition and fees vary according to course load. *College room and board:* $7226; *room only:* $4336. Room and board charges vary according to board plan and housing facility. *Payment plan:* Installment.

FRESHMAN FINANCIAL AID (Fall 2004, est.) 2577 applied for aid; of those 67% were deemed to have need. 96% of freshmen with need received aid; of those 65% had need fully met. *Average percent of need met:* 70% (excluding resources awarded to replace EFC). *Average financial aid package:* $5926 (excluding resources awarded to replace EFC). 21% of all full-time freshmen had no need and received non-need-based gift aid.

UNDERGRADUATE FINANCIAL AID (Fall 2004, est.) 11,918 applied for aid; of those 75% were deemed to have need. 97% of undergraduates with need received aid; of those 55% had need fully met. *Average percent of need met:* 71% (excluding resources awarded to replace EFC). *Average financial aid package:* $7132 (excluding resources awarded to replace EFC). 11% of all full-time undergraduates had no need and received non-need-based gift aid.

GIFT AID (NEED-BASED) *Total amount:* $42,125,390 (46% federal, 47% state, 5% institutional, 2% external sources). *Receiving aid:* Freshmen: 35% (1,099); All full-time undergraduates: 33% (5,398). *Average award:* Freshmen: $3130; Undergraduates: $3109. *Scholarships, grants, and awards:* Federal Pell, FSEOG, state, private, college/university gift aid from institutional funds, Federal Nursing.

GIFT AID (NON-NEED-BASED) *Total amount:* $3,887,665 (100% institutional). *Receiving aid:* Freshmen: 21% (678); Undergraduates: 11% (1,778). *Average Award:* Freshmen: $2511; Undergraduates: $2631. *Scholarships, grants, and awards by category:* Academic Interests/Achievement: general academic interests/achievements. *Creative Arts/Performance:* music. *Special Achievements/Activities:* general special achievements/activities. *Special Characteristics:* local/state students. *Tuition waivers:* Full or partial for minority students. *ROTC:* Army cooperative.

LOANS *Student loans:* $115,277,927 (100% need-based). 69% of past graduating class borrowed through all loan programs. *Average indebtedness per student:* $17,657. *Average need-based loan:* Freshmen: $2345; Undergraduates: $3143. *Parent loans:* $10,601,140 (100% non-need-based). *Programs:* Federal Direct (Subsidized and Unsubsidized Stafford, PLUS), Perkins, Federal Nursing, college/university.

WORK-STUDY *Federal work-study:* Total amount: $2,351,984; 2,185 jobs averaging $1076. *State or other work-study/employment:* Total amount: $5,223,682 (100% non-need-based). 913 part-time jobs averaging $5428.

ATHLETIC AWARDS *Total amount:* $4,224,440 (100% non-need-based).

APPLYING FOR FINANCIAL AID *Required financial aid form:* FAFSA. *Financial aid deadline (priority):* 3/1. *Notification date:* Continuous beginning 5/1.

CONTACT Customer Service Department, University at Buffalo, The State University of New York, 232 Capen Hall, Buffalo, NY 14260, 716-645-2450 or toll-free 888-UB-ADMIT. *Fax:* 716-645-7760. *E-mail:* src@buffalo.edu.

UNIVERSITY OF ADVANCING TECHNOLOGY
Tempe, AZ

CONTACT Director of Financial Aid, University of Advancing Technology, 2625 West Baseline Road, Tempe, AZ 85283-1042, 602-383-8228 or toll-free 800-658-5744 (out-of-state).

THE UNIVERSITY OF AKRON
Akron, OH

Tuition & fees (OH res): $7510	Average undergraduate aid package: $5999

ABOUT THE INSTITUTION State-supported, coed. Awards: associate, bachelor's, master's, doctoral, and first professional degrees and post-bachelor's and first professional certificates. 243 undergraduate majors. Total enrollment: 23,282. Undergraduates: 19,245. Freshmen: 3,284. Federal methodology is used as a basis for awarding need-based institutional aid.

UNDERGRADUATE EXPENSES for 2004–05 *Application fee:* $30. *Tuition, state resident:* full-time $6424; part-time $268 per credit. *Tuition, nonresident:* full-time $14,654; part-time $542 per credit. *Required fees:* full-time $1086; $45 per credit. Full-time tuition and fees vary according to course load, degree level, and location. Part-time tuition and fees vary according to course load,

degree level, and location. *College room and board:* $6660; *room only:* $4240. Room and board charges vary according to board plan and housing facility. *Payment plan:* Installment.

FRESHMAN FINANCIAL AID (Fall 2003) 2453 applied for aid; of those 87% were deemed to have need. 92% of freshmen with need received aid; of those 6% had need fully met. *Average percent of need met:* 37% (excluding resources awarded to replace EFC). *Average financial aid package:* $5263 (excluding resources awarded to replace EFC). 17% of all full-time freshmen had no need and received non-need-based gift aid.

UNDERGRADUATE FINANCIAL AID (Fall 2003) 9,870 applied for aid; of those 89% were deemed to have need. 95% of undergraduates with need received aid; of those 10% had need fully met. *Average percent of need met:* 41% (excluding resources awarded to replace EFC). *Average financial aid package:* $5999 (excluding resources awarded to replace EFC). 13% of all full-time undergraduates had no need and received non-need-based gift aid.

GIFT AID (NEED-BASED) *Total amount:* $24,810,517 (77% federal, 23% state). *Receiving aid:* Freshmen: 37% (1,109); All full-time undergraduates: 36% (4,805). *Average award:* Freshmen: $4544; Undergraduates: $4415. *Scholarships, grants, and awards:* Federal Pell, FSEOG, state.

GIFT AID (NON-NEED-BASED) *Total amount:* $11,425,316 (10% state, 71% institutional, 19% external sources). *Receiving aid:* Freshmen: 18% (542); Undergraduates: 14% (1,920). *Average Award:* Freshmen: $1887; Undergraduates: $1807. *Scholarships, grants, and awards by category:* Academic Interests/Achievement: 2,585 awards ($4,996,286 total): biological sciences, business, communication, computer science, education, engineering/technologies, English, foreign languages, general academic interests/achievements, health fields, home economics, humanities, international studies, mathematics, military science, physical sciences, premedicine, social sciences. *Creative Arts/Performance:* 220 awards ($291,907 total): applied art and design, art/fine arts, creative writing, dance, debating, general creative arts/performance, journalism/publications, music, performing arts, theater/drama. *Special Achievements/Activities:* 143 awards ($3,010,090 total): general special achievements/activities, leadership, memberships. *Special Characteristics:* 800 awards ($1,956,603 total): adult students, general special characteristics, handicapped students, local/state students, members of minority groups, out-of-state students. *Tuition waivers:* Full or partial for employees or children of employees, senior citizens. *ROTC:* Army, Air Force.

LOANS *Student loans:* $67,064,633 (85% need-based, 15% non-need-based). 58% of past graduating class borrowed through all loan programs. *Average indebtedness per student:* $15,036. *Average need-based loan:* Freshmen: $2861; Undergraduates: $3655. *Parent loans:* $8,463,337 (100% non-need-based). *Programs:* FFEL (Subsidized and Unsubsidized Stafford, PLUS), Perkins, Federal Nursing, college/university.

WORK-STUDY *Federal work-study:* Total amount: $1,419,754; 740 jobs averaging $1919. *State or other work-study/employment:* Total amount: $4,173,378 (100% non-need-based). 2,374 part-time jobs averaging $1758.

ATHLETIC AWARDS *Total amount:* $3,084,386 (100% non-need-based).

APPLYING FOR FINANCIAL AID *Required financial aid forms:* FAFSA, institution's own form. *Financial aid deadline:* 3/1 (priority: 2/1). *Notification date:* Continuous beginning 4/15. Students must reply within 2 weeks of notification.

CONTACT Mr. Doug McNutt, Director of Financial Aid, The University of Akron, Office of Student Financial Aid, Akron, OH 44325-6211, 330-972-6343 or toll-free 800-655-4884. *Fax:* 330-972-7139. *E-mail:* dmcnutt@uakron.edu.

THE UNIVERSITY OF ALABAMA
Tuscaloosa, AL

Tuition & fees (AL res): $4630	Average undergraduate aid package: $7902

ABOUT THE INSTITUTION State-supported, coed. Awards: bachelor's, master's, doctoral, and first professional degrees and post-bachelor's, post-master's, and first professional certificates. 72 undergraduate majors. Total enrollment: 20,929. Undergraduates: 16,568. Freshmen: 3,367. Federal methodology is used as a basis for awarding need-based institutional aid.

UNDERGRADUATE EXPENSES for 2004–05 *Application fee:* $25. *Tuition, state resident:* full-time $4630. *Tuition, nonresident:* full-time $12,664. Full-time tuition and fees vary according to course load. Part-time tuition and fees vary according to course load. *College room and board:* $4734; *room only:* $2982. Room and board charges vary according to board plan and housing facility. *Payment plans:* Installment, deferred payment.

FRESHMAN FINANCIAL AID (Fall 2003) 2244 applied for aid; of those 46% were deemed to have need. 98% of freshmen with need received aid; of those 31% had need fully met. *Average percent of need met:* 68% (excluding resources

The University of Alabama

awarded to replace EFC). *Average financial aid package:* $7414 (excluding resources awarded to replace EFC). 34% of all full-time freshmen had no need and received non-need-based gift aid.

UNDERGRADUATE FINANCIAL AID (Fall 2003) 10,487 applied for aid; of those 54% were deemed to have need. 99% of undergraduates with need received aid; of those 34% had need fully met. *Average percent of need met:* 74% (excluding resources awarded to replace EFC). *Average financial aid package:* $7902 (excluding resources awarded to replace EFC). 28% of all full-time undergraduates had no need and received non-need-based gift aid.

GIFT AID (NEED-BASED) *Total amount:* $11,863,261 (97% federal, 3% institutional). *Receiving aid:* Freshmen: 20% (602); All full-time undergraduates: 24% (3,449). *Average award:* Freshmen: $3662; Undergraduates: $3664. *Scholarships, grants, and awards:* Federal Pell, FSEOG, state, private, college/university gift aid from institutional funds, Federal Nursing.

GIFT AID (NON-NEED-BASED) *Total amount:* $18,838,251 (37% institutional, 63% external sources). *Receiving aid:* Freshmen: 9% (265); Undergraduates: 8% (1,137). *Average Award: Freshmen:* $4670; *Undergraduates:* $4659. *Scholarships, grants, and awards by category: Academic Interests/Achievement:* 4,538 awards ($7,950,079 total): area/ethnic studies, biological sciences, business, communication, computer science, education, engineering/technologies, English, foreign languages, general academic interests/achievements, home economics, library science, mathematics, military science, physical sciences, premedicine, social sciences. *Creative Arts/Performance:* 619 awards ($678,987 total): art/fine arts, cinema/film/broadcasting, creative writing, dance, debating, journalism/publications, music, theater/drama. *Special Achievements/Activities:* 297 awards ($871,160 total): cheerleading/drum major, community service, general special achievements/activities, hobbies/interests, junior miss. *Special Characteristics:* 139 awards ($258,354 total): children of union members/company employees, general special characteristics, international students, out-of-state students, spouses of deceased or disabled public servants. *Tuition waivers:* Full or partial for employees or children of employees. *ROTC:* Army, Air Force.

LOANS *Student loans:* $42,550,587 (51% need-based, 49% non-need-based). 53% of past graduating class borrowed through all loan programs. *Average indebtedness per student:* $18,989. *Average need-based loan:* Freshmen: $3220; Undergraduates: $5025. *Parent loans:* $7,248,144 (100% non-need-based). *Programs:* Federal Direct (Subsidized and Unsubsidized Stafford, PLUS), Perkins, college/university.

WORK-STUDY *Federal work-study:* Total amount: $1,885,453; 700 jobs averaging $3100. *State or other work-study/employment:* 1,500 part-time jobs averaging $4000.

ATHLETIC AWARDS *Total amount:* $4,095,304 (100% non-need-based).

APPLYING FOR FINANCIAL AID *Required financial aid form:* FAFSA. *Financial aid deadline (priority):* 3/1. *Notification date:* 4/1. Students must reply within 3 weeks of notification.

CONTACT Helen Leathers, Assistant Director of Financial Aid, The University of Alabama, Box 870162, Tuscaloosa, AL 35487-0162, 205-348-6756 or toll-free 800-933-BAMA. *Fax:* 205-348-2989. *E-mail:* helen.leathers@ua.edu.

THE UNIVERSITY OF ALABAMA AT BIRMINGHAM
Birmingham, AL

Tuition & fees (AL res): $4662	Average undergraduate aid package: $13,600

ABOUT THE INSTITUTION State-supported, coed. Awards: bachelor's, master's, doctoral, and first professional degrees and post-bachelor's and post-master's certificates. 48 undergraduate majors. Total enrollment: 16,694. Undergraduates: 11,441. Freshmen: 1,628. Institutional methodology is used as a basis for awarding need-based institutional aid.

UNDERGRADUATE EXPENSES for 2004–05 *Application fee:* $30. *Tuition, state resident:* full-time $4662. *Tuition, nonresident:* full-time $10,422. Full-time tuition and fees vary according to program. Part-time tuition and fees vary according to program. *College room and board: room only:* $3060. Room and board charges vary according to housing facility.

FRESHMAN FINANCIAL AID (Fall 2004, est.) 1226 applied for aid; of those 66% were deemed to have need. 99% of freshmen with need received aid; of those 13% had need fully met. *Average percent of need met:* 39% (excluding resources awarded to replace EFC). *Average financial aid package:* $10,410 (excluding resources awarded to replace EFC). 22% of all full-time freshmen had no need and received non-need-based gift aid.

UNDERGRADUATE FINANCIAL AID (Fall 2004, est.) 5,812 applied for aid; of those 73% were deemed to have need. 98% of undergraduates with need

---

received aid; of those 13% had need fully met. *Average percent of need met:* 42% (excluding resources awarded to replace EFC). *Average financial aid package:* $13,600 (excluding resources awarded to replace EFC). 16% of all full-time undergraduates had no need and received non-need-based gift aid.

GIFT AID (NEED-BASED) *Total amount:* $11,606,591 (98% federal, 2% institutional). *Receiving aid:* Freshmen: 32% (501); All full-time undergraduates: 34% (2,682). *Average award:* Freshmen: $3204; Undergraduates: $3345. *Scholarships, grants, and awards:* Federal Pell, FSEOG, state, private, college/university gift aid from institutional funds, United Negro College Fund.

GIFT AID (NON-NEED-BASED) *Total amount:* $4,472,949 (1% federal, 2% state, 69% institutional, 28% external sources). *Receiving aid:* Freshmen: 17% (256); Undergraduates: 14% (1,125). *Average Award:* Freshmen: $7335; *Undergraduates:* $8392. *Scholarships, grants, and awards by category: Academic Interests/Achievement:* business, communication, computer science, engineering/technologies, general academic interests/achievements, health fields, mathematics. *Creative Arts/Performance:* art/fine arts, music, performing arts, theater/drama. *Special Achievements/Activities:* cheerleading/drum major, junior miss, leadership, memberships, religious involvement. *Special Characteristics:* adult students, children and siblings of alumni, children of current students, children of educators, children of faculty/staff, children of public servants, children of union members/company employees, children of workers in trades, children with a deceased or disabled parent, ethnic background, first-generation college students, general special characteristics, handicapped students, local/state students, married students, members of minority groups, out-of-state students, parents of current students, previous college experience, public servants, relatives of clergy, religious affiliation, siblings of current students, spouses of current students, spouses of deceased or disabled public servants, twins, veterans, veterans' children. *Tuition waivers:* Full or partial for employees or children of employees. *ROTC:* Army, Air Force cooperative.

LOANS *Student loans:* $30,788,289 (70% need-based, 30% non-need-based). 54% of past graduating class borrowed through all loan programs. *Average indebtedness per student:* $17,594. *Average need-based loan:* Freshmen: $2962; Undergraduates: $4163. *Parent loans:* $4,621,761 (100% non-need-based). *Programs:* Federal Direct (Subsidized and Unsubsidized Stafford, PLUS), Perkins, state, college/university.

WORK-STUDY *Federal work-study:* Total amount: $2,120,284; jobs available.

ATHLETIC AWARDS *Total amount:* $3,671,711 (100% non-need-based).

APPLYING FOR FINANCIAL AID *Required financial aid forms:* FAFSA, institution's own form. *Financial aid deadline (priority):* 4/1. *Notification date:* Continuous beginning 4/1. Students must reply within 4 weeks of notification.

CONTACT Ms. Janet B. May, Financial Aid Director, The University of Alabama at Birmingham, Hill University Center 317, 1530 3rd Avenue South, Birmingham, AL 35294-1150, 205-934-8132 or toll-free 800-421-8743.

THE UNIVERSITY OF ALABAMA IN HUNTSVILLE
Huntsville, AL

Tuition & fees (AL res): $4516	Average undergraduate aid package: $5848

ABOUT THE INSTITUTION State-supported, coed. Awards: bachelor's, master's, and doctoral degrees and post-bachelor's and post-master's certificates. 29 undergraduate majors. Total enrollment: 7,036. Undergraduates: 5,523. Freshmen: 680. Both federal and institutional methodology are used as a basis for awarding need-based institutional aid.

UNDERGRADUATE EXPENSES for 2004–05 *Application fee:* $30. *Tuition, state resident:* full-time $4516; part-time $1013 per term. *Tuition, nonresident:* full-time $9518; part-time $2128 per term. Full-time tuition and fees vary according to course load. Part-time tuition and fees vary according to course load. *College room and board:* $5200; *room only:* $3600. Room and board charges vary according to board plan and housing facility. *Payment plan:* Deferred payment.

FRESHMAN FINANCIAL AID (Fall 2004, est.) 585 applied for aid; of those 44% were deemed to have need. 95% of freshmen with need received aid; of those 17% had need fully met. *Average percent of need met:* 52% (excluding resources awarded to replace EFC). *Average financial aid package:* $5508 (excluding resources awarded to replace EFC). 39% of all full-time freshmen had no need and received non-need-based gift aid.

UNDERGRADUATE FINANCIAL AID (Fall 2004, est.) 3,122 applied for aid; of those 54% were deemed to have need. 92% of undergraduates with need received aid; of those 17% had need fully met. *Average percent of need met:* 52% (excluding resources awarded to replace EFC). *Average financial aid*

---

package: $5848 (excluding resources awarded to replace EFC). 22% of all full-time undergraduates had no need and received non-need-based gift aid.

GIFT AID (NEED-BASED) *Total amount:* $4,788,027 (77% federal, 1% state, 15% institutional, 7% external sources). *Receiving aid:* Freshmen: 19% (127); All full-time undergraduates: 24% (942). *Average award:* Freshmen: $3132; Undergraduates: $3240. *Scholarships, grants, and awards:* Federal Pell, FSEOG, state, private, college/university gift aid from institutional funds.

GIFT AID (NON-NEED-BASED) *Total amount:* $2,172,079 (1% state, 75% institutional, 24% external sources). *Receiving aid:* Freshmen: 27% (179); Undergraduates: 15% (569). *Average Award:* Freshmen: $2680; *Undergraduates:* $2208. *Scholarships, grants, and awards by category: Academic Interests/Achievement:* 1,912 awards ($3,127,347 total): business, computer science, education, engineering/technologies, English, general academic interests/achievements, health fields, humanities, physical sciences, social sciences. *Creative Arts/Performance:* 56 awards ($23,725 total): art/fine arts, music. *Special Achievements/Activities:* 521 awards ($1,229,908 total): cheerleading/drum major, community service, general special achievements/activities, junior miss, leadership. *Special Characteristics:* 44 awards ($58,950 total): general special characteristics, local/state students, members of minority groups. *Tuition waivers:* Full or partial for employees or children of employees. *ROTC:* Army cooperative.

LOANS *Student loans:* $9,645,018 (100% need-based). 52% of past graduating class borrowed through all loan programs. *Average indebtedness per student:* $17,242. *Average need-based loan:* Freshmen: $2415; Undergraduates: $3618. *Parent loans:* $1,098,365 (100% need-based). *Programs:* Federal Direct (Subsidized and Unsubsidized Stafford, PLUS).

WORK-STUDY *Federal work-study:* Total amount: $260,506; 108 jobs averaging $2911.

ATHLETIC AWARDS *Total amount:* $1,164,203 (17% need-based, 83% non-need-based).

APPLYING FOR FINANCIAL AID *Required financial aid forms:* FAFSA, institution's own form. *Financial aid deadline:* 7/31 (priority: 4/1). *Notification date:* Continuous beginning 4/1. Students must reply within 2 weeks of notification.

CONTACT Mr. Andrew Weaver, Director of Student Financial Services, The University of Alabama in Huntsville, Office of Financial Aid, 301 Sparkman Drive, Huntsville, AL 35899, 256-824-6241 or toll-free 800-UAH-CALL. *Fax:* 256-824-6212. *E-mail:* finaid@email.uah.edu.

UNIVERSITY OF ALASKA ANCHORAGE
Anchorage, AK

Tuition & fees (AK res): $3465	Average undergraduate aid package: $9354

ABOUT THE INSTITUTION State-supported, coed. Awards: associate, bachelor's, and master's degrees. 67 undergraduate majors. Total enrollment: 16,261. Undergraduates: 15,481. Freshmen: 1,417. Federal methodology is used as a basis for awarding need-based institutional aid.

UNDERGRADUATE EXPENSES for 2005–06 *Application fee:* $40. *Tuition, state resident:* full-time $2952; part-time $116 per credit hour. *Tuition, nonresident:* full-time $9048; part-time $370 per credit hour. Full-time tuition and fees vary according to course level. Part-time tuition and fees vary according to course level. *College room and board:* $7810; *room only:* $4710. Room and board charges vary according to board plan and housing facility.

GIFT AID (NEED-BASED) *Total amount:* $8,034,714 (74% federal, 7% institutional, 19% external sources). *Receiving aid:* Freshmen: 23% (267); All full-time undergraduates: 25% (1,515). *Average award:* Freshmen: $3906; Undergraduates: $3813. *Scholarships, grants, and awards:* Federal Pell, FSEOG, state, private, college/university gift aid from institutional funds.

GIFT AID (NON-NEED-BASED) *Total amount:* $3,099,327 (77% institutional, 23% external sources). *Receiving aid:* Freshmen: 2% (18); Undergraduates: 1% (72). *Average Award:* Freshmen: $2755; *Undergraduates:* $2814. *Scholarships, grants, and awards by category: Academic Interests/Achievement:* biological sciences, business, communication, computer science, education, engineering/technologies, English, general academic interests/achievements, health fields, humanities, mathematics, social sciences. *Special Achievements/Activities:* general special achievements/activities. *Tuition waivers:* Full or partial for children of alumni, employees or children of employees, senior citizens. *ROTC:* Air Force.

LOANS *Student loans:* $25,978,897 (73% need-based, 27% non-need-based). 47% of past graduating class borrowed through all loan programs. *Average indebtedness per student:* $15,621. *Average need-based loan:* Freshmen: $5460; Undergraduates: $6559. *Programs:* FFEL (Subsidized and Unsubsidized Stafford, PLUS), state.

ATHLETIC AWARDS *Total amount:* $669,121 (8% need-based, 92% non-need-based).

APPLYING FOR FINANCIAL AID *Required financial aid form:* FAFSA. *Financial aid deadline:* 8/1 (priority: 4/1). *Notification date:* Continuous beginning 3/7. Students must reply within 4 weeks of notification.

CONTACT Theodore E. Malone, Director of Student Financial Aid, University of Alaska Anchorage, PO Box 141608, Anchorage, AK 99514-1608, 907-786-1520. *Fax:* 907-786-6122.

UNIVERSITY OF ALASKA FAIRBANKS
Fairbanks, AK

Tuition & fees (AK res): $4762	Average undergraduate aid package: $8906

ABOUT THE INSTITUTION State-supported, coed. Awards: associate, bachelor's, master's, and doctoral degrees. 71 undergraduate majors. Total enrollment: 8,693. Undergraduates: 7,610. Freshmen: 950. Federal methodology is used as a basis for awarding need-based institutional aid.

UNDERGRADUATE EXPENSES for 2005–06 *Application fee:* $40. *Tuition, state resident:* full-time $3480; part-time $116 per credit. *Tuition, nonresident:* full-time $11,100; part-time $370 per credit. Full-time tuition and fees vary according to course level, course load, and location. Part-time tuition and fees vary according to course level, course load, and location. *College room and board:* $5580; *room only:* $2990. Room and board charges vary according to board plan and housing facility. *Payment plan:* Installment.

FRESHMAN FINANCIAL AID (Fall 2004, est.) 790 applied for aid; of those 42% were deemed to have need. 93% of freshmen with need received aid; of those 30% had need fully met. *Average percent of need met:* 68% (excluding resources awarded to replace EFC). *Average financial aid package:* $8098 (excluding resources awarded to replace EFC). 21% of all full-time freshmen had no need and received non-need-based gift aid.

UNDERGRADUATE FINANCIAL AID (Fall 2004, est.) 3,357 applied for aid; of those 43% were deemed to have need. 96% of undergraduates with need received aid; of those 31% had need fully met. *Average percent of need met:* 70% (excluding resources awarded to replace EFC). *Average financial aid package:* $8906 (excluding resources awarded to replace EFC). 17% of all full-time undergraduates had no need and received non-need-based gift aid.

GIFT AID (NEED-BASED) *Total amount:* $3,859,628 (77% federal, 15% institutional, 8% external sources). *Receiving aid:* Freshmen: 28% (225); All full-time undergraduates: 29% (960). *Average award:* Freshmen: $3956; Undergraduates: $3803. *Scholarships, grants, and awards:* Federal Pell, FSEOG, private, college/university gift aid from institutional funds, Native Non-Profit Corporations.

GIFT AID (NON-NEED-BASED) *Total amount:* $2,170,094 (83% institutional, 17% external sources). *Receiving aid:* Freshmen: 5% (38); Undergraduates: 3% (112). *Average Award:* Freshmen: $3292; *Undergraduates:* $3339. *Scholarships, grants, and awards by category: Academic Interests/Achievement:* 37 awards ($180,166 total): general academic interests/achievements. *Creative Arts/Performance:* art/fine arts, creative writing, music, theater/drama. *Special Achievements/Activities:* 57 awards ($194,160 total): community service, general special achievements/activities. *Special Characteristics:* $749,084 total: children and siblings of alumni, children of faculty/staff. *Tuition waivers:* Full or partial for children of alumni, employees or children of employees, senior citizens. *ROTC:* Army.

LOANS *Student loans:* $14,282,979 (73% need-based, 27% non-need-based). 47% of past graduating class borrowed through all loan programs. *Average indebtedness per student:* $12,403. *Average need-based loan:* Freshmen: $6049; Undergraduates: $6830. *Parent loans:* $11,548,638 (98% need-based, 2% non-need-based). *Programs:* Federal Direct (Subsidized and Unsubsidized Stafford, PLUS), FFEL (Subsidized and Unsubsidized Stafford, PLUS), state, college/university.

WORK-STUDY *Federal work-study:* Total amount: $312,030; 95 jobs averaging $3284.

ATHLETIC AWARDS *Total amount:* $508,527 (15% need-based, 85% non-need-based).

APPLYING FOR FINANCIAL AID *Required financial aid form:* FAFSA. *Financial aid deadline (priority):* 7/1. *Notification date:* Continuous beginning 3/1. Students must reply within 2 weeks of notification.

CONTACT Tamara Hornbuckle, Financial Aid Officer, University of Alaska Fairbanks, 101 Eielson Building, PO Box 756360, Fairbanks, AK 99775-6360, 907-474-6628 or toll-free 800-478-1823. *Fax:* 907-474-7065. *E-mail:* fntmh@uaf.edu.

UNIVERSITY OF ALASKA SOUTHEAST
Juneau, AK

Tuition & fees (AK res): $3342   **Average undergraduate aid package: $6655**

ABOUT THE INSTITUTION State-supported, coed. Awards: associate, bachelor's, and master's degrees. 17 undergraduate majors. Total enrollment: 3,379. Undergraduates: 3,153. Freshmen: 179. Federal methodology is used as a basis for awarding need-based institutional aid.

UNDERGRADUATE EXPENSES for 2005–06 *Application fee:* $40. *Tuition, state resident:* full-time $2784; part-time $123 per credit hour. *Tuition, nonresident:* full-time $8880; part-time $376 per credit hour. *Required fees:* full-time $558; $10 per credit hour or $15. Full-time tuition and fees vary according to course level and course load. Part-time tuition and fees vary according to course level and course load. *College room and board:* $5370; *room only:* $3980. Room and board charges vary according to housing facility. *Payment plans:* Installment, deferred payment.

FRESHMAN FINANCIAL AID (Fall 2004, est.) 90 applied for aid; of those 58% were deemed to have need. 98% of freshmen with need received aid; of those 22% had need fully met. *Average percent of need met:* 60% (excluding resources awarded to replace EFC). *Average financial aid package:* $5901 (excluding resources awarded to replace EFC). 7% of all full-time freshmen had no need and received non-need-based gift aid.

UNDERGRADUATE FINANCIAL AID (Fall 2004, est.) 504 applied for aid; of those 63% were deemed to have need. 96% of undergraduates with need received aid; of those 20% had need fully met. *Average percent of need met:* 62% (excluding resources awarded to replace EFC). *Average financial aid package:* $6655 (excluding resources awarded to replace EFC). 6% of all full-time undergraduates had no need and received non-need-based gift aid.

GIFT AID (NEED-BASED) *Total amount:* $1,051,225 (70% federal, 8% institutional, 22% external sources). *Receiving aid:* Freshmen: 37% (40); All full-time undergraduates: 35% (215). *Average award:* Freshmen: $3890; Undergraduates: $3729. *Scholarships, grants, and awards:* Federal Pell, FSEOG, private, college/university gift aid from institutional funds.

GIFT AID (NON-NEED-BASED) *Total amount:* $366,018 (3% federal, 53% institutional, 44% external sources). *Receiving aid:* Freshmen: 7% (7); Undergraduates: 4% (26). *Average Award:* Freshmen: $3500; Undergraduates: $2868. *Scholarships, grants, and awards by category: Academic Interests/ Achievement:* 442 awards ($730,617 total): biological sciences, business, communication, education, general academic interests/achievements, social sciences. *Creative Arts/Performance:* 1 award ($500 total): performing arts. *Special Achievements/Activities:* 9 awards ($11,500 total): general special achievements/ activities, leadership. *Special Characteristics:* 4 awards ($4000 total): ethnic background. *Tuition waivers:* Full or partial for children of alumni, senior citizens.

LOANS *Student loans:* $2,736,669 (69% need-based, 31% non-need-based). 45% of past graduating class borrowed through all loan programs. *Average indebtedness per student:* $18,249. *Average need-based loan:* Freshmen: $3589; Undergraduates: $4226. *Parent loans:* $169,830 (34% need-based, 66% non-need-based). *Programs:* FFEL (Subsidized and Unsubsidized Stafford, PLUS), state.

WORK-STUDY *Federal work-study:* Total amount: $69,126; 27 jobs averaging $3195.

APPLYING FOR FINANCIAL AID *Required financial aid form:* FAFSA. *Financial aid deadline (priority):* 6/1. *Notification date:* Continuous. Students must reply within 3 weeks of notification.

CONTACT Ms. Barbara Carlson Burnett, Financial Aid Director, University of Alaska Southeast, 11120 Glacier Highway, Juneau, AK 99801-8680, 907-465-6296 or toll-free 877-465-4827. *Fax:* 907-465-1394. *E-mail:* barbara.burnett@uas.alaska.edu.

THE UNIVERSITY OF ARIZONA
Tucson, AZ

Tuition & fees (AZ res): $4093   **Average undergraduate aid package: $9993**

ABOUT THE INSTITUTION State-supported, coed. Awards: bachelor's, master's, doctoral, and first professional degrees and post-bachelor's certificates. 128 undergraduate majors. Total enrollment: 36,932. Undergraduates: 28,368. Freshmen: 5,725. Federal methodology is used as a basis for awarding need-based institutional aid.

UNDERGRADUATE EXPENSES for 2005–06 *Tuition, state resident:* full-time $3998; part-time $237 per unit. *Tuition, nonresident:* full-time $12,978; part-time $566 per unit. *College room and board:* $7108; *room only:* $3820.

GIFT AID (NEED-BASED) *Total amount:* $34,639,330 (64% federal, 1% state, 16% institutional, 19% external sources). *Scholarships, grants, and awards:* Federal Pell, FSEOG, state, private, college/university gift aid from institutional funds, Federal Nursing.

GIFT AID (NON-NEED-BASED) *Total amount:* $10,232,683 (46% institutional, 54% external sources). *Scholarships, grants, and awards by category: Academic Interests/Achievement:* agriculture, architecture, biological sciences, business, education, engineering/technologies, general academic interests/achievements, humanities, military science, physical sciences, religion/biblical studies. *Creative Arts/Performance:* art/fine arts, dance, music, performing arts, theater/drama. *Special Achievements/Activities:* leadership. *Special Characteristics:* children of faculty/staff, ethnic background, international students. *ROTC:* Army, Naval, Air Force.

LOANS *Student loans:* $58,957,437 (78% need-based, 22% non-need-based). 42% of past graduating class borrowed through all loan programs. *Average indebtedness per student:* $16,881. *Parent loans:* $18,522,639 (78% need-based, 22% non-need-based). *Programs:* FFEL (Subsidized and Unsubsidized Stafford, PLUS), Perkins, Federal Nursing, college/university.

APPLYING FOR FINANCIAL AID *Required financial aid form:* FAFSA. *Financial aid deadline (priority):* 3/1. *Notification date:* Continuous beginning 4/1.

CONTACT Student Financial Aid Office, The University of Arizona, PO Box 210066, Tucson, AZ 85721-0066, 520-621-1858. *Fax:* 520-621-9473. *E-mail:* askaid@arizona.edu.

UNIVERSITY OF ARKANSAS
Fayetteville, AR

ABOUT THE INSTITUTION State-supported, coed. Awards: bachelor's, master's, doctoral, and first professional degrees and post-bachelor's certificates. 115 undergraduate majors. Total enrollment: 17,269. Undergraduates: 13,817. Freshmen: 2,514.

GIFT AID (NEED-BASED) *Scholarships, grants, and awards:* Federal Pell, FSEOG, state, private, college/university gift aid from institutional funds.

GIFT AID (NON-NEED-BASED) *Scholarships, grants, and awards by category: Academic Interests/Achievement:* general academic interests/achievements. *Creative Arts/Performance:* music, theater/drama. *Special Achievements/Activities:* community service, general special achievements/activities, leadership. *Special Characteristics:* children and siblings of alumni, children of faculty/staff, ethnic background, international students, out-of-state students, previous college experience.

LOANS *Programs:* FFEL (Subsidized and Unsubsidized Stafford, PLUS), Perkins, state, college/university.

WORK-STUDY *Federal work-study:* Total amount: $1,100,000; 1,898 jobs averaging $2000.

APPLYING FOR FINANCIAL AID *Required financial aid form:* FAFSA.

CONTACT Ed Schroeder, Director of Financial Aid, University of Arkansas, 114 Silas H. Hunt Hall, Fayetteville, AR 72701-1201, 479-575-3277 or toll-free 800-377-5346 (in-state), 800-377-8632 (out-of-state). *E-mail:* edward@uark.edu.

UNIVERSITY OF ARKANSAS AT FORT SMITH
Fort Smith, AR

Tuition & fees (area res): $2280   **Average undergraduate aid package: $5568**

ABOUT THE INSTITUTION State and locally supported, coed. Awards: associate and bachelor's degrees. 28 undergraduate majors. Total enrollment: 6,623. Undergraduates: 6,623. Freshmen: 1,328. Federal methodology is used as a basis for awarding need-based institutional aid.

UNDERGRADUATE EXPENSES for 2004–05 *Tuition, area resident:* full-time $1740; part-time $58 per credit hour. *Tuition, state resident:* full-time $1890; part-time $63 per credit hour. *Tuition, nonresident:* full-time $6840; part-time $228 per credit hour. *Required fees:* full-time $540; $17 per credit hour or $15 per term part-time. Full-time tuition and fees vary according to course level. Part-time tuition and fees vary according to course level. *Payment plan:* Installment.

FRESHMAN FINANCIAL AID (Fall 2004, est.) 824 applied for aid; of those 82% were deemed to have need. 95% of freshmen with need received aid; of those 11% had need fully met. *Average percent of need met:* 66% (excluding resources awarded to replace EFC). *Average financial aid package:* $5372 (excluding resources awarded to replace EFC). 14% of all full-time freshmen had no need and received non-need-based gift aid.

UNDERGRADUATE FINANCIAL AID (Fall 2004, est.) 2,564 applied for aid; of those 87% were deemed to have need. 95% of undergraduates with need received aid; of those 10% had need fully met. *Average percent of need met:* 62% (excluding resources awarded to replace EFC). *Average financial aid package:* $5568 (excluding resources awarded to replace EFC). 9% of all full-time undergraduates had no need and received non-need-based gift aid.

GIFT AID (NEED-BASED) *Total amount:* $8,794,195 (88% federal, 10% state, 1% institutional, 1% external sources). *Receiving aid:* Freshmen: 48% (548); All full-time undergraduates: 49% (1,843). *Average award:* Freshmen: $3480; Undergraduates: $3504. *Scholarships, grants, and awards:* Federal Pell, FSEOG, state, private, college/university gift aid from institutional funds.

GIFT AID (NON-NEED-BASED) *Total amount:* $2,126,985 (3% federal, 5% state, 82% institutional, 10% external sources). *Receiving aid:* Freshmen: 18% (203); Undergraduates: 13% (468). *Average Award:* Freshmen: $2767; Undergraduates: $2643. *Scholarships, grants, and awards by category: Academic Interests/Achievement:* 350 awards ($569,000 total): biological sciences, business, computer science, education, engineering/technologies, English, health fields, mathematics, military science, social sciences. *Creative Arts/ Performance:* 70 awards ($77,825 total): music. *Special Achievements/Activities:* 15 awards ($16,000 total): cheerleading/drum major, general special achievements/ activities, leadership. *Special Characteristics:* 25 awards ($50,000 total): adult students, children of faculty/staff, children of workers in trades, general special characteristics, local/state students. *Tuition waivers:* Full or partial for employees or children of employees. *ROTC:* Air Force cooperative.

LOANS *Student loans:* $9,589,942 (52% need-based, 48% non-need-based). 27% of past graduating class borrowed through all loan programs. *Average indebtedness per student:* $7339. *Average need-based loan:* Freshmen: $2233; Undergraduates: $3183. *Parent loans:* $134,130 (100% non-need-based). *Programs:* FFEL (Subsidized and Unsubsidized Stafford, PLUS), state.

WORK-STUDY *Federal work-study:* Total amount: $633,531; 110 jobs averaging $3000. *State or other work-study/employment:* Total amount: $117,787 (61% need-based, 39% non-need-based). 94 part-time jobs averaging $3000.

ATHLETIC AWARDS *Total amount:* $208,934 (100% non-need-based).

APPLYING FOR FINANCIAL AID *Required financial aid forms:* FAFSA, institution's own form. *Financial aid deadline:* Continuous. *Notification date:* Continuous beginning 3/1. Students must reply within 4 weeks of notification.

CONTACT Scott A. Medlin, Financial Aid Director, University of Arkansas at Fort Smith, 5210 Grand Avenue, Fort Smith, AR 72913, 479-788-7093 or toll-free 888-512-5466. *Fax:* 479-788-7095. *E-mail:* smedlin@uafortsmith.edu.

UNIVERSITY OF ARKANSAS AT LITTLE ROCK
Little Rock, AR

ABOUT THE INSTITUTION State-supported, coed. Awards: associate, bachelor's, master's, doctoral, and first professional degrees and post-master's certificates. 55 undergraduate majors. Total enrollment: 11,757. Undergraduates: 9,330. Freshmen: 777.

GIFT AID (NEED-BASED) *Scholarships, grants, and awards:* Federal Pell, FSEOG, state, private, college/university gift aid from institutional funds.

GIFT AID (NON-NEED-BASED) *Scholarships, grants, and awards by category: Academic Interests/Achievement:* biological sciences, business, communication, computer science, education, engineering/technologies, English, foreign languages, general academic interests/achievements, health fields, humanities, international studies, mathematics, physical sciences, social sciences. *Creative Arts/Performance:* art/fine arts, music, theater/drama. *Special Achievements/ Activities:* community service, leadership, memberships. *Special Characteristics:* local/state students, members of minority groups, previous college experience.

LOANS *Programs:* FFEL (Subsidized and Unsubsidized Stafford, PLUS).

WORK-STUDY *Federal work-study:* Total amount: $343,259; jobs available.

APPLYING FOR FINANCIAL AID *Required financial aid form:* FAFSA.

CONTACT Financial Aid Office, University of Arkansas at Little Rock, 2801 South University Avenue, Little Rock, AR 72204-1099, 501-569-3127 or toll-free 800-482-8892 (in-state).

UNIVERSITY OF ARKANSAS AT MONTICELLO
Monticello, AR

Tuition & fees (AR res): $3765	Average undergraduate aid package: N/A

ABOUT THE INSTITUTION State-supported, coed. Awards: associate, bachelor's, and master's degrees and post-bachelor's certificates. 33 undergraduate majors. Total enrollment: 2,875. Undergraduates: 2,694. Freshmen: 751. Federal methodology is used as a basis for awarding need-based institutional aid.

UNDERGRADUATE EXPENSES for 2004–05 *Tuition, state resident:* full-time $2850; part-time $125.50 per hour. *Tuition, nonresident:* full-time $6420; part-time $244.50 per hour. *College room and board:* $3150. Room and board charges vary according to board plan and housing facility.

GIFT AID (NEED-BASED) *Scholarships, grants, and awards:* Federal Pell, FSEOG, state, private, college/university gift aid from institutional funds.

GIFT AID (NON-NEED-BASED) *Scholarships, grants, and awards by category: Academic Interests/Achievement:* 267 awards ($813,054 total): general academic interests/achievements. *Creative Arts/Performance:* 175 awards ($345,470 total): debating, music. *Special Achievements/Activities:* 125 awards ($133,654 total): cheerleading/drum major, general special achievements/activities, leadership, rodeo. *Special Characteristics:* 218 awards ($632,427 total): children of faculty/ staff, out-of-state students. *Tuition waivers:* Full or partial for employees or children of employees, senior citizens.

LOANS *Student loans:* $6,864,265 (71% need-based, 29% non-need-based). *Average indebtedness per student:* $13,599. *Parent loans:* $178,154 (100% non-need-based). *Programs:* FFEL (Subsidized and Unsubsidized Stafford, PLUS), Perkins.

WORK-STUDY *Federal work-study:* Total amount: $188,993; 194 jobs averaging $974. *State or other work-study/employment:* Total amount: $336,672 (100% non-need-based). 311 part-time jobs averaging $1082.

ATHLETIC AWARDS *Total amount:* $432,121 (68% need-based, 32% non-need-based).

APPLYING FOR FINANCIAL AID *Required financial aid forms:* FAFSA, institution's own form. *Financial aid deadline:* Continuous. *Notification date:* Continuous beginning 3/1. Students must reply within 2 weeks of notification.

CONTACT Susan Brewer, Director of Financial Aid, University of Arkansas at Monticello, PO Box 3470, Monticello, AR 71656, 870-460-1050 or toll-free 800-844-1826 (in-state). *Fax:* 870-460-1450. *E-mail:* brewers@uamont.edu.

UNIVERSITY OF ARKANSAS AT PINE BLUFF
Pine Bluff, AR

Tuition & fees (AR res): $4044	Average undergraduate aid package: $3202

ABOUT THE INSTITUTION State-supported, coed. Awards: associate, bachelor's, and master's degrees. 52 undergraduate majors. Total enrollment: 3,303. Undergraduates: 3,200. Freshmen: 699. Federal methodology is used as a basis for awarding need-based institutional aid.

UNDERGRADUATE EXPENSES for 2004–05 *Tuition, state resident:* full-time $3000; part-time $100 per credit hour. *Tuition, nonresident:* full-time $6975; part-time $232.50 per credit hour. Full-time tuition and fees vary according to location. Part-time tuition and fees vary according to location. *College room and board:* $5436. Room and board charges vary according to board plan and housing facility.

GIFT AID (NEED-BASED) *Receiving aid:* Freshmen: 73% (535); All full-time undergraduates: 68% (1,912). *Average award:* Freshmen: $3212; Undergraduates: $3218. *Scholarships, grants, and awards:* Federal Pell, FSEOG, state.

GIFT AID (NON-NEED-BASED) *Total amount:* $1,135,418 *Receiving aid:* Freshmen: 19% (136); Undergraduates: 14% (395). *Scholarships, grants, and awards by category: Academic Interests/Achievement:* agriculture, biological sciences, business, education, English, general academic interests/achievements, mathematics. *Creative Arts/Performance:* art/fine arts, music. *Special Achievements/ Activities:* leadership. *Tuition waivers:* Full or partial for employees or children of employees, senior citizens. *ROTC:* Army.

LOANS *Student loans:* $9,006,672 (66% need-based, 34% non-need-based). *Average need-based loan:* Freshmen: $2625; Undergraduates: $4506. *Parent loans:* $536,663 (100% non-need-based). *Programs:* FFEL (Subsidized and Unsubsidized Stafford, PLUS), signature loans.

ATHLETIC AWARDS *Total amount:* $1,067,578 (100% non-need-based).

APPLYING FOR FINANCIAL AID *Required financial aid forms:* FAFSA, institution's own form, verification worksheet. *Financial aid deadline (priority):* 4/1. *Notification date:* Continuous beginning 1/1. Students must reply within 2 weeks of notification.

CONTACT Mrs. Carolyn Iverson, Director of Financial Aid, University of Arkansas at Pine Bluff, 1200 North University Drive, PO Box 4985, Pine Bluff, AR 71601, 870-575-8303 or toll-free 800-264-6585. *Fax:* 870-575-4622. *E-mail:* iverson_c@uapb.edu.

UNIVERSITY OF ARKANSAS FOR MEDICAL SCIENCES
Little Rock, AR

Tuition & fees (AR res): $3672	Average undergraduate aid package: $3000

ABOUT THE INSTITUTION State-supported, coed. Awards: associate, bachelor's, master's, doctoral, and first professional degrees (bachelor's degree is upper-level). 10 undergraduate majors. Total enrollment: 2,016. Undergraduates: 683. Federal methodology is used as a basis for awarding need-based institutional aid.

UNDERGRADUATE EXPENSES for 2004–05 *Tuition, area resident:* part-time $145 per semester hour. *Tuition, state resident:* full-time $3672. *Tuition, nonresident:* full-time $8424. Full and part-time tuition varies by program.

UNDERGRADUATE FINANCIAL AID (Fall 2003) 576 applied for aid; of those 74% were deemed to have need. 100% of undergraduates with need received aid. *Average percent of need met:* 65% (excluding resources awarded to replace EFC). *Average financial aid package:* $3000 (excluding resources awarded to replace EFC).

GIFT AID (NEED-BASED) *Total amount:* $1,186,450 (65% federal, 26% state, 6% institutional, 3% external sources). *Average award:* Undergraduates: $500. *Scholarships, grants, and awards:* Federal Pell, FSEOG, state, private, college/university gift aid from institutional funds.

GIFT AID (NON-NEED-BASED) *ROTC:* Army cooperative.

LOANS *Student loans:* $2,877,259 (100% need-based). 73% of past graduating class borrowed through all loan programs. *Average indebtedness per student:* $7000. *Average need-based loan:* Undergraduates: $4000. *Parent loans:* $283,834 (100% non-need-based). *Programs:* FFEL (Subsidized and Unsubsidized Stafford, PLUS), Perkins, Federal Nursing.

WORK-STUDY *Federal work-study:* Total amount: $10,814; 9 jobs averaging $1201.

APPLYING FOR FINANCIAL AID *Required financial aid form:* FAFSA. *Financial aid deadline:* Continuous. *Notification date:* Continuous beginning 4/1. Students must reply within 2 weeks of notification.

CONTACT Mr. Paul Carter, Director of Financial Aid, University of Arkansas for Medical Sciences, 4301 West Markham Street, MS 601, Little Rock, AR 72205, 501-686-5454. *Fax:* 501-686-5661. *E-mail:* pvcarter@uams.edu.

UNIVERSITY OF BALTIMORE
Baltimore, MD

CONTACT Financial Aid Office, University of Baltimore, 1420 North Charles Street, CH 123, Baltimore, MD 21201-5779, 410-837-4763 or toll-free 877-APPLYUB. *Fax:* 410-837-5493.

UNIVERSITY OF BRIDGEPORT
Bridgeport, CT

Tuition & fees: $20,595	Average undergraduate aid package: N/A

ABOUT THE INSTITUTION Independent, coed. Awards: associate, bachelor's, master's, doctoral, and first professional degrees and post-master's certificates. 36 undergraduate majors. Total enrollment: 3,274. Undergraduates: 1,374. Freshmen: 255. Federal methodology is used as a basis for awarding need-based institutional aid.

UNDERGRADUATE EXPENSES for 2005–06 *Application fee:* $25. *Comprehensive fee:* $29,595 includes full-time tuition ($19,200), mandatory fees ($1395), and room and board ($9000). *College room only:* $4600. Full-time tuition and fees vary according to program. Room and board charges vary according to board

plan and student level. *Part-time tuition:* $640 per credit. *Part-time fees:* $60 per term. Part-time tuition and fees vary according to program. *Payment plans:* Installment, deferred payment.

FRESHMAN FINANCIAL AID (Fall 2004, est.) *Average percent of need met:* 75% (excluding resources awarded to replace EFC). *Average financial aid package:* $20,204 (excluding resources awarded to replace EFC).

UNDERGRADUATE FINANCIAL AID (Fall 2004, est.) *Average percent of need met:* 75% (excluding resources awarded to replace EFC).

GIFT AID (NEED-BASED) *Total amount:* $6,455,877 (34% federal, 6% state, 60% institutional). *Receiving aid:* Freshmen: 92% (230). *Average award:* Freshmen: $9527. *Scholarships, grants, and awards:* Federal Pell, FSEOG, state, college/university gift aid from institutional funds.

GIFT AID (NON-NEED-BASED) *Total amount:* $3,079,940 (97% institutional, 3% external sources). *Scholarships, grants, and awards by category:* Academic Interests/Achievement: general academic interests/achievements. Creative Arts/Performance: music. Special Achievements/Activities: leadership. Special Characteristics: children of faculty/staff, local/state students, parents of current students, siblings of current students, spouses of current students. *Tuition waivers:* Full or partial for employees or children of employees, senior citizens. *ROTC:* Army.

LOANS *Student loans:* $21,335,133 (47% need-based, 53% non-need-based). *Average need-based loan:* Freshmen: $6178. *Parent loans:* $2,589,034 (100% non-need-based). *Programs:* FFEL (Subsidized and Unsubsidized Stafford, PLUS), Perkins.

WORK-STUDY *Federal work-study:* Total amount: $532,892; jobs available.

ATHLETIC AWARDS *Total amount:* $1,386,848 (100% non-need-based).

APPLYING FOR FINANCIAL AID *Required financial aid forms:* FAFSA, institution's own form. *Financial aid deadline (priority):* 4/15. *Notification date:* Continuous beginning 4/1. Students must reply within 4 weeks of notification.

CONTACT Kathleen A. Gailor, Director of Financial Aid, University of Bridgeport, 126 Park Avenue, Bridgeport, CT 06604, 203-576-4568 or toll-free 800-EXCEL-UB (in-state), 800-243-9496 (out-of-state). *Fax:* 203-576-4570. *E-mail:* finaid@bridgeport.edu.

UNIVERSITY OF CALIFORNIA, BERKELEY
Berkeley, CA

Tuition & fees (CA res): $6730	Average undergraduate aid package: $14,361

ABOUT THE INSTITUTION State-supported, coed. Awards: bachelor's, master's, doctoral, and first professional degrees. 90 undergraduate majors. Total enrollment: 32,814. Undergraduates: 22,880. Freshmen: 3,672. Both federal and institutional methodology are used as a basis for awarding need-based institutional aid.

UNDERGRADUATE EXPENSES for 2004–05 *Application fee:* $55. *Tuition, state resident:* full-time $0. *Tuition, nonresident:* full-time $16,956. Full-time tuition and fees vary according to program. *College room and board:* $11,630. Room and board charges vary according to board plan and housing facility. *Payment plan:* Installment.

FRESHMAN FINANCIAL AID (Fall 2004, est.) 2732 applied for aid; of those 64% were deemed to have need. 97% of freshmen with need received aid; of those 44% had need fully met. *Average percent of need met:* 91% (excluding resources awarded to replace EFC). *Average financial aid package:* $15,425 (excluding resources awarded to replace EFC). 9% of all full-time freshmen had no need and received non-need-based gift aid.

UNDERGRADUATE FINANCIAL AID (Fall 2004, est.) 13,592 applied for aid; of those 81% were deemed to have need. 97% of undergraduates with need received aid; of those 48% had need fully met. *Average percent of need met:* 88% (excluding resources awarded to replace EFC). *Average financial aid package:* $14,361 (excluding resources awarded to replace EFC). 6% of all full-time undergraduates had no need and received non-need-based gift aid.

GIFT AID (NEED-BASED) *Total amount:* $108,004,022 (22% federal, 31% state, 43% institutional, 4% external sources). *Receiving aid:* Freshmen: 44% (1,593); All full-time undergraduates: 47% (10,134). *Average award:* Freshmen: $11,096; Undergraduates: $10,441. *Scholarships, grants, and awards:* Federal Pell, FSEOG, state, private, college/university gift aid from institutional funds.

GIFT AID (NON-NEED-BASED) *Total amount:* $10,432,600 (6% federal, 25% state, 41% institutional, 28% external sources). *Receiving aid:* Freshmen: 2% (69); Undergraduates: 1% (171). *Average Award:* Freshmen: $2393; Undergraduates: $2899. *Scholarships, grants, and awards by category:* Academic Interests/Achievement: engineering/technologies, general academic interests/achievements. *ROTC:* Army, Naval, Air Force.

LOANS *Student loans:* $42,038,164 (77% need-based, 23% non-need-based). 49% of past graduating class borrowed through all loan programs. *Average indebtedness per student:* $13,277. *Average need-based loan:* Freshmen: $4096; Undergraduates: $5014. *Parent loans:* $27,048,991 (16% need-based, 84% non-need-based). *Programs:* Federal Direct (Subsidized and Unsubsidized Stafford, PLUS), Perkins.

WORK-STUDY *Federal work-study:* Total amount: $4,992,300; jobs available. *State or other work-study/employment:* Total amount: $8,007,565 (100% need-based). Part-time jobs available.

ATHLETIC AWARDS *Total amount:* $6,832,504 (27% need-based, 73% non-need-based).

APPLYING FOR FINANCIAL AID *Required financial aid forms:* FAFSA, state aid form. *Financial aid deadline:* 3/2 (priority: 3/2). *Notification date:* 4/15.

CONTACT Sandy Jensen, Administrative Services Coordinator, University of California, Berkeley, 225 Sproul Hall, Berkeley, CA 94720-1960, 510-642-0649. *Fax:* 510-643-5526.

UNIVERSITY OF CALIFORNIA, DAVIS
Davis, CA

Tuition & fees (CA res): $6936	Average undergraduate aid package: $11,181

ABOUT THE INSTITUTION State-supported, coed. Awards: bachelor's, master's, doctoral, and first professional degrees and post-bachelor's and post-master's certificates. 73 undergraduate majors. Total enrollment: 30,229. Undergraduates: 23,472. Freshmen: 4,786. Both federal and institutional methodology are used as a basis for awarding need-based institutional aid.

UNDERGRADUATE EXPENSES for 2004–05 *Application fee:* $40. *Tuition, state resident:* full-time $0. *Tuition, nonresident:* full-time $15,855; part-time $2746 per term. *College room and board:* $10,234. Room and board charges vary according to board plan. *Payment plan:* Deferred payment.

FRESHMAN FINANCIAL AID (Fall 2004, est.) 2287 applied for aid; of those 71% were deemed to have need. 96% of freshmen with need received aid; of those 15% had need fully met. *Average percent of need met:* 76% (excluding resources awarded to replace EFC). *Average financial aid package:* $12,171 (excluding resources awarded to replace EFC). 13% of all full-time freshmen had no need and received non-need-based gift aid.

UNDERGRADUATE FINANCIAL AID (Fall 2004, est.) 12,534 applied for aid; of those 83% were deemed to have need. 96% of undergraduates with need received aid; of those 13% had need fully met. *Average percent of need met:* 75% (excluding resources awarded to replace EFC). *Average financial aid package:* $11,181 (excluding resources awarded to replace EFC). 6% of all full-time undergraduates had no need and received non-need-based gift aid.

GIFT AID (NEED-BASED) *Total amount:* $87,853,524 (26% federal, 36% state, 36% institutional, 2% external sources). *Receiving aid:* Freshmen: 49% (1,484); All full-time undergraduates: 43% (8,962). *Average award:* Freshmen: $9375; Undergraduates: $8594. *Scholarships, grants, and awards:* Federal Pell, FSEOG, state, private, college/university gift aid from institutional funds, Federal Nursing.

GIFT AID (NON-NEED-BASED) *Total amount:* $7,410,290 (3% federal, 15% state, 69% institutional, 13% external sources). *Receiving aid:* Freshmen: 2% (56); Undergraduates: 1% (125). *Average Award:* Freshmen: $2919; Undergraduates: $3854. *Scholarships, grants, and awards by category:* Academic Interests/Achievement: agriculture, general academic interests/achievements. *ROTC:* Army, Naval cooperative, Air Force cooperative.

LOANS *Student loans:* $40,398,269 (85% need-based, 15% non-need-based). 50% of past graduating class borrowed through all loan programs. *Average indebtedness per student:* $12,231. *Average need-based loan:* Freshmen: $4430; Undergraduates: $4557. *Parent loans:* $16,301,431 (16% need-based, 84% non-need-based). *Programs:* Federal Direct (Subsidized and Unsubsidized Stafford, PLUS), Perkins, Federal Nursing, state, college/university.

WORK-STUDY *Federal work-study:* Total amount: $1,222,395; jobs available. *State or other work-study/employment:* Total amount: $21,549 (100% need-based).

APPLYING FOR FINANCIAL AID *Required financial aid forms:* FAFSA, state aid form. *Financial aid deadline (priority):* 3/2. *Notification date:* Continuous beginning 3/15. Students must reply within 3 weeks of notification.

CONTACT Lora Jo Bossio, Director of Financial Aid, University of California, Davis, One Shields Avenue, 1100 Dutton Hall, Davis, CA 95616, 530-752-2396. *Fax:* 530-752-7339.

UNIVERSITY OF CALIFORNIA, IRVINE
Irvine, CA

Tuition & fees (CA res): $6313	Average undergraduate aid package: $12,291

ABOUT THE INSTITUTION State-supported, coed. Awards: bachelor's, master's, doctoral, and first professional degrees and post-bachelor's certificates. 66 undergraduate majors. Total enrollment: 24,307. Undergraduates: 19,862. Freshmen: 3,629. Federal methodology is used as a basis for awarding need-based institutional aid.

UNDERGRADUATE EXPENSES for 2005–06 *Application fee:* $40. *Tuition, state resident:* full-time $0. *Tuition, nonresident:* full-time $18,277. *College room and board:* $9176. Room and board charges vary according to board plan. *Payment plan:* Installment.

FRESHMAN FINANCIAL AID (Fall 2004, est.) 2745 applied for aid; of those 67% were deemed to have need. 92% of freshmen with need received aid; of those 35% had need fully met. *Average percent of need met:* 85% (excluding resources awarded to replace EFC). *Average financial aid package:* $11,999 (excluding resources awarded to replace EFC). 4% of all full-time freshmen had no need and received non-need-based gift aid.

UNDERGRADUATE FINANCIAL AID (Fall 2004, est.) 11,866 applied for aid; of those 82% were deemed to have need. 96% of undergraduates with need received aid; of those 28% had need fully met. *Average percent of need met:* 84% (excluding resources awarded to replace EFC). *Average financial aid package:* $12,291 (excluding resources awarded to replace EFC). 4% of all full-time undergraduates had no need and received non-need-based gift aid.

GIFT AID (NEED-BASED) *Total amount:* $74,120,441 (24% federal, 39% state, 35% institutional, 2% external sources). *Receiving aid:* Freshmen: 40% (1,455); All full-time undergraduates: 42% (8,060). *Average award:* Freshmen: $9236; Undergraduates: $9121. *Scholarships, grants, and awards:* Federal Pell, FSEOG, state, private, college/university gift aid from institutional funds.

GIFT AID (NON-NEED-BASED) *Total amount:* $7,681,456 (2% federal, 13% state, 76% institutional, 9% external sources). *Receiving aid:* Freshmen: 1% (39); Undergraduates: 94. *Average Award:* Freshmen: $7657; Undergraduates: $6861. *Scholarships, grants, and awards by category:* Academic Interests/Achievement: 783 awards ($5,207,357 total): computer science, general academic interests/achievements, humanities. *Creative Arts/Performance:* 66 awards ($139,487 total): art/fine arts, dance, general creative arts/performance, music. *ROTC:* Army cooperative, Air Force cooperative.

LOANS *Student loans:* $39,590,201 (79% need-based, 21% non-need-based). 55% of past graduating class borrowed through all loan programs. *Average indebtedness per student:* $13,226. *Average need-based loan:* Freshmen: $5130; Undergraduates: $5765. *Parent loans:* $30,061,737 (25% need-based, 75% non-need-based). *Programs:* Federal Direct (Subsidized and Unsubsidized Stafford, PLUS), Perkins, college/university, Private Loans.

WORK-STUDY *Federal work-study:* Total amount: $3,929,626; 2,610 jobs averaging $1506. *State or other work-study/employment:* Part-time jobs available.

ATHLETIC AWARDS *Total amount:* $2,177,890 (19% need-based, 81% non-need-based).

APPLYING FOR FINANCIAL AID *Required financial aid forms:* FAFSA, state aid form. *Financial aid deadline:* 5/2 (priority: 3/2). *Notification date:* Continuous beginning 4/1.

CONTACT Penny Harrell, Associate Director of Student Services, University of California, Irvine, Office of Financial Aid and Scholarships, 102 Administration Building, Irvine, CA 92697-2825, 949-824-8262. *Fax:* 949-824-4876. *E-mail:* finaid@uci.edu.

UNIVERSITY OF CALIFORNIA, LOS ANGELES
Los Angeles, CA

Tuition & fees (CA res): $6576	Average undergraduate aid package: $13,462

ABOUT THE INSTITUTION State-supported, coed. Awards: bachelor's, master's, doctoral, and first professional degrees. 150 undergraduate majors. Total enrollment: 24,946. Undergraduates: 24,946. Freshmen: 3,724. Both federal and institutional methodology are used as a basis for awarding need-based institutional aid.

University of California, Los Angeles

UNDERGRADUATE EXPENSES for 2004–05 *Application fee:* $55. *Tuition, state resident:* full-time $0. *Tuition, nonresident:* full-time $16,956. *College room and board:* $11,187. Room and board charges vary according to board plan and housing facility.

FRESHMAN FINANCIAL AID (Fall 2004, est.) 2371 applied for aid; of those 77% were deemed to have need. 100% of freshmen with need received aid; of those 48% had need fully met. *Average percent of need met:* 86% (excluding resources awarded to replace EFC). *Average financial aid package:* $14,143 (excluding resources awarded to replace EFC). 6% of all full-time freshmen had no need and received non-need-based gift aid.

UNDERGRADUATE FINANCIAL AID (Fall 2004, est.) 14,266 applied for aid; of those 90% were deemed to have need. 100% of undergraduates with need received aid; of those 51% had need fully met. *Average percent of need met:* 85% (excluding resources awarded to replace EFC). *Average financial aid package:* $13,462 (excluding resources awarded to replace EFC). 5% of all full-time undergraduates had no need and received non-need-based gift aid.

GIFT AID (NEED-BASED) *Total amount:* $121,269,522 (22% federal, 35% state, 39% institutional, 4% external sources). *Receiving aid:* Freshmen: 48% (1,770); All full-time undergraduates: 51% (12,153). *Average award:* Freshmen: $11,316; Undergraduates: $9950. *Scholarships, grants, and awards:* Federal Pell, FSEOG, state, private, college/university gift aid from institutional funds, United Negro College Fund, Federal Nursing, National Merit.

GIFT AID (NON-NEED-BASED) *Total amount:* $10,513,495 (3% federal, 18% state, 65% institutional, 14% external sources). *Receiving aid:* Freshmen: 2% (66); Undergraduates: 1% (151). *Average Award:* Freshmen: $6778; Undergraduates: $5588. *Scholarships, grants, and awards by category: Academic Interests/Achievement:* general academic interests/achievements. *Special Achievements/Activities:* general special achievements/activities. *Special Characteristics:* general special characteristics. *ROTC:* Army, Naval, Air Force.

LOANS *Student loans:* $54,345,295 (83% need-based, 17% non-need-based). 51% of past graduating class borrowed through all loan programs. *Average indebtedness per student:* $13,894. *Average need-based loan:* Freshmen: $4402; Undergraduates: $5166. *Parent loans:* $20,098,114 (20% need-based, 80% non-need-based). *Programs:* FFEL (Subsidized and Unsubsidized Stafford, PLUS), Perkins, Federal Nursing, state, college/university.

WORK-STUDY *Federal work-study:* Total amount: $6,343,253; 3,186 jobs averaging $1991. *State or other work-study/employment:* Total amount: $827,306 (100% need-based). 751 part-time jobs averaging $1102.

ATHLETIC AWARDS *Total amount:* $5,992,607 (34% need-based, 66% non-need-based).

APPLYING FOR FINANCIAL AID *Required financial aid form:* FAFSA. *Financial aid deadline (priority):* 3/2. *Notification date:* Continuous beginning 3/15.

CONTACT Ms. Yolanda Tan, Administrative Assistant, University of California, Los Angeles, Financial Aid Office, A-129 Murphy Hall, 405 Hilgard Avenue, Los Angeles, CA 90095-1435, 310-206-0404. *E-mail:* finaid@saonet.ucla.edu.

UNIVERSITY OF CALIFORNIA, RIVERSIDE
Riverside, CA

Tuition & fees (CA res): $6685   **Average undergraduate aid package:** $12,670

ABOUT THE INSTITUTION State-supported, coed. Awards: bachelor's, master's, and doctoral degrees. 59 undergraduate majors. Total enrollment: 17,104. Undergraduates: 15,089. Freshmen: 3,456. Federal methodology is used as a basis for awarding need-based institutional aid.

UNDERGRADUATE EXPENSES for 2004–05 *Application fee:* $55. *Tuition, state resident:* full-time $0. *Tuition, nonresident:* full-time $16,476. *College room and board:* $9800. Room and board charges vary according to board plan and housing facility. *Payment plan:* Deferred payment.

FRESHMAN FINANCIAL AID (Fall 2004, est.) 2398 applied for aid; of those 82% were deemed to have need. 96% of freshmen with need received aid; of those 52% had need fully met. *Average percent of need met:* 89% (excluding resources awarded to replace EFC). *Average financial aid package:* $13,876 (excluding resources awarded to replace EFC). 1% of all full-time freshmen had no need and received non-need-based gift aid.

UNDERGRADUATE FINANCIAL AID (Fall 2004, est.) 10,572 applied for aid; of those 87% were deemed to have need. 97% of undergraduates with need received aid; of those 45% had need fully met. *Average percent of need met:* 84% (excluding resources awarded to replace EFC). *Average financial aid package:* $12,670 (excluding resources awarded to replace EFC). 1% of all full-time undergraduates had no need and received non-need-based gift aid.

GIFT AID (NEED-BASED) *Total amount:* $71,451,513 (28% federal, 40% state, 31% institutional, 1% external sources). *Receiving aid:* Freshmen: 52% (1,621); All full-time undergraduates: 53% (7,738). *Average award:* Freshmen: $10,090; Undergraduates: $9130. *Scholarships, grants, and awards:* Federal Pell, FSEOG, state, private, college/university gift aid from institutional funds.

GIFT AID (NON-NEED-BASED) *Total amount:* $4,370,658 (5% federal, 6% state, 81% institutional, 8% external sources). *Receiving aid:* Freshmen: 1% (34); Undergraduates: 1% (100). *Average Award:* Freshmen: $6589; Undergraduates:* $6374. *Scholarships, grants, and awards by category: Academic Interests/Achievement:* agriculture, area/ethnic studies, biological sciences, business, education, engineering/technologies, English, general academic interests/achievements, humanities, mathematics, physical sciences, premedicine, social sciences. *Creative Arts/Performance:* art/fine arts, creative writing, dance, music, theater/drama. *ROTC:* Army cooperative, Air Force cooperative.

LOANS *Student loans:* $35,084,981 (85% need-based, 15% non-need-based). 65% of past graduating class borrowed through all loan programs. *Average indebtedness per student:* $14,119. *Average need-based loan:* Freshmen: $4827; Undergraduates: $5399. *Parent loans:* $19,226,641 (40% need-based, 60% non-need-based). *Programs:* Federal Direct (Subsidized and Unsubsidized Stafford, PLUS), Perkins, college/university.

WORK-STUDY *Federal work-study:* Total amount: $4,446,406; 1,504 jobs averaging $2956. *State or other work-study/employment:* Part-time jobs available.

ATHLETIC AWARDS *Total amount:* $1,637,708 (33% need-based, 67% non-need-based).

APPLYING FOR FINANCIAL AID *Required financial aid form:* FAFSA. *Financial aid deadline:* 3/2 (priority: 3/2). *Notification date:* Continuous beginning 3/1. Students must reply by 5/1 or within 3 weeks of notification.

CONTACT Ms. Sheryl Hayes, Director of Financial Aid, University of California, Riverside, 900 University Avenue, 1156 Hinderaker Hall, Riverside, CA 92521-0209, 909-787-3878. *E-mail:* finaid@pop.ucr.edu.

UNIVERSITY OF CALIFORNIA, SAN DIEGO
La Jolla, CA

Tuition & fees (CA res): $6224   **Average undergraduate aid package:** $12,837

ABOUT THE INSTITUTION State-supported, coed. Awards: bachelor's, master's, doctoral, and first professional degrees. 76 undergraduate majors. Total enrollment: 24,105. Undergraduates: 19,872. Freshmen: 3,799. Federal methodology is used as a basis for awarding need-based institutional aid.

UNDERGRADUATE EXPENSES for 2004–05 *Application fee:* $55. *One-time required fee:* $597. *Tuition, state resident:* full-time $0. *Tuition, nonresident:* full-time $16,476. Full-time tuition and fees vary according to location. *College room and board:* $8996. *Payment plans:* Installment, deferred payment.

GIFT AID (NEED-BASED) *Total amount:* $83,766,068 (25% federal, 39% state, 33% institutional, 3% external sources). *Receiving aid:* Freshmen: 51% (1,831); All full-time undergraduates: 46% (8,922). *Average award:* Freshmen: $9351; Undergraduates: $8970. *Scholarships, grants, and awards:* Federal Pell, FSEOG, state, private, college/university gift aid from institutional funds.

GIFT AID (NON-NEED-BASED) *Total amount:* $7,716,566 (6% federal, 16% state, 58% institutional, 20% external sources). *Receiving aid:* Freshmen: 1% (52); Undergraduates: 1% (109). *Average Award:* Freshmen: $9498; Undergraduates:* $6589. *Scholarships, grants, and awards by category: Academic Interests/Achievement:* 896 awards ($2,595,216 total): biological sciences, business, communication, computer science, engineering/technologies, general academic interests/achievements, mathematics, physical sciences, premedicine, social sciences. *Creative Arts/Performance:* 6 awards ($6600 total): applied art and design, cinema/film/broadcasting, dance, journalism/publications, performing arts. *Special Achievements/Activities:* 2 awards ($2000 total): community service, leadership. *Special Characteristics:* 116 awards ($284,353 total): ethnic background, first-generation college students, handicapped students, members of minority groups, veterans' children. *ROTC:* Army cooperative.

LOANS *Student loans:* $42,870,656 (83% need-based, 17% non-need-based). 51% of past graduating class borrowed through all loan programs. *Average indebtedness per student:* $14,535. *Average need-based loan:* Freshmen: $4489; Undergraduates: $5036. *Parent loans:* $15,645,689 (22% need-based, 78% non-need-based). *Programs:* FFEL (Subsidized and Unsubsidized Stafford, PLUS), Perkins, college/university, alternative loans.

APPLYING FOR FINANCIAL AID *Required financial aid forms:* FAFSA, state aid form. *Financial aid deadline (priority):* 3/2. *Notification date:* Continuous beginning 3/15.

CONTACT Mr. Vincent De Anda, Director of Financial Aid Office, University of California, San Diego, 9500 Gilman Drive-0013, La Jolla, CA 92093-0013, 858-534-3800. *Fax:* 858-534-5459. *E-mail:* vdeanda@ucsd.edu.

UNIVERSITY OF CALIFORNIA, SANTA BARBARA
Santa Barbara, CA

Tuition & fees (CA res): $6495	Average undergraduate aid package: $11,439

ABOUT THE INSTITUTION State-supported, coed. Awards: bachelor's, master's, and doctoral degrees and first professional certificates. 67 undergraduate majors. Total enrollment: 21,026. Undergraduates: 18,121. Freshmen: 3,895. Both federal and institutional methodology are used as a basis for awarding need-based institutional aid.

UNDERGRADUATE EXPENSES for 2004–05 *Application fee:* $40. *Tuition, state resident:* full-time $0. *Tuition, nonresident:* full-time $16,476. *College room and board:* $9897; *room only:* $7491.

FRESHMAN FINANCIAL AID (Fall 2003) 2921 applied for aid; of those 66% were deemed to have need. 96% of freshmen with need received aid; of those 39% had need fully met. *Average percent of need met:* 81% (excluding resources awarded to replace EFC). *Average financial aid package:* $11,572 (excluding resources awarded to replace EFC). 2% of all full-time freshmen had no need and received non-need-based gift aid.

UNDERGRADUATE FINANCIAL AID (Fall 2003) 10,369 applied for aid; of those 78% were deemed to have need. 97% of undergraduates with need received aid; of those 35% had need fully met. *Average percent of need met:* 81% (excluding resources awarded to replace EFC). *Average financial aid package:* $11,439 (excluding resources awarded to replace EFC). 2% of all full-time undergraduates had no need and received non-need-based gift aid.

GIFT AID (NEED-BASED) *Total amount:* $55,543,330 (27% federal, 37% state, 34% institutional, 2% external sources). *Receiving aid:* Freshmen: 45% (1,780); All full-time undergraduates: 43% (7,358). *Average award:* Freshmen: $7009; Undergraduates: $6960. *Scholarships, grants, and awards:* Federal Pell, FSEOG, state, college/university gift aid from institutional funds, endowed scholarships.

GIFT AID (NON-NEED-BASED) *Total amount:* $3,673,441 (5% federal, 31% state, 44% institutional, 20% external sources). *Receiving aid:* Freshmen: 1% (41); Undergraduates: 1% (91). *Average Award:* Freshmen: $3890; Undergraduates: $3913. *Scholarships, grants, and awards by category:* Academic Interests/Achievement: general academic interests/achievements. *Tuition waivers:* Full or partial for employees or children of employees. *ROTC:* Army.

LOANS *Student loans:* $35,071,200 (76% need-based, 24% non-need-based). *Average need-based loan:* Freshmen: $5016; Undergraduates: $5407. *Parent loans:* $25,585,398 (24% need-based, 76% non-need-based). *Programs:* Federal Direct (Subsidized and Unsubsidized Stafford, PLUS), Perkins.

WORK-STUDY *Federal work-study:* Total amount: $2,678,136; jobs available.

ATHLETIC AWARDS *Total amount:* $1,925,428 (26% need-based, 74% non-need-based).

APPLYING FOR FINANCIAL AID *Required financial aid form:* FAFSA. *Financial aid deadline (priority):* 3/2. *Notification date:* Continuous beginning 3/15. Students must reply by 8/15.

CONTACT Office of Financial Aid, University of California, Santa Barbara, Santa Barbara, CA 93106, 805-893-2432. *Fax:* 805-893-8793.

UNIVERSITY OF CALIFORNIA, SANTA CRUZ
Santa Cruz, CA

Tuition & fees (CA res): $7023	Average undergraduate aid package: $12,819

ABOUT THE INSTITUTION State-supported, coed. Awards: bachelor's, master's, and doctoral degrees and post-bachelor's certificates. 76 undergraduate majors. Total enrollment: 15,036. Undergraduates: 13,694. Freshmen: 3,162. Both federal and institutional methodology are used as a basis for awarding need-based institutional aid.

UNDERGRADUATE EXPENSES for 2004–05 *Application fee:* $55. *Tuition, state resident:* full-time $0. *Tuition, nonresident:* full-time $19,956. *College room and board:* $10,947. Room and board charges vary according to board plan and housing facility. *Payment plans:* Installment, deferred payment.

FRESHMAN FINANCIAL AID (Fall 2004, est.) 1799 applied for aid; of those 93% were deemed to have need. 96% of freshmen with need received aid; of those 33% had need fully met. *Average percent of need met:* 84% (excluding

resources awarded to replace EFC). *Average financial aid package:* $12,633 (excluding resources awarded to replace EFC). 1% of all full-time freshmen had no need and received non-need-based gift aid.

UNDERGRADUATE FINANCIAL AID (Fall 2004, est.) 7,309 applied for aid; of those 92% were deemed to have need. 96% of undergraduates with need received aid; of those 38% had need fully met. *Average percent of need met:* 84% (excluding resources awarded to replace EFC). *Average financial aid package:* $12,819 (excluding resources awarded to replace EFC). 1% of all full-time undergraduates had no need and received non-need-based gift aid.

GIFT AID (NEED-BASED) *Total amount:* $51,603,271 (21% federal, 32% state, 44% institutional, 3% external sources). *Receiving aid:* Freshmen: 46% (1,396); All full-time undergraduates: 43% (5,596). *Average award:* Freshmen: $8889; Undergraduates: $8967. *Scholarships, grants, and awards:* Federal Pell, FSEOG, state, private, college/university gift aid from institutional funds.

GIFT AID (NON-NEED-BASED) *Total amount:* $1,129,050 (3% federal, 24% state, 47% institutional, 26% external sources). *Receiving aid:* Freshmen: 1% (22); Undergraduates: 1% (67). *Average Award:* Freshmen: $5648; Undergraduates: $6081. *Tuition waivers:* Full or partial for employees or children of employees. *ROTC:* Army cooperative, Naval cooperative, Air Force cooperative.

LOANS *Student loans:* $29,719,548 (79% need-based, 21% non-need-based). 53% of past graduating class borrowed through all loan programs. *Average indebtedness per student:* $13,419. *Average need-based loan:* Freshmen: $4196; Undergraduates: $4672. *Parent loans:* $16,268,276 (8% need-based, 92% non-need-based). *Programs:* Federal Direct (Subsidized and Unsubsidized Stafford, PLUS), Perkins.

WORK-STUDY *Federal work-study:* Total amount: $7,986,809. *State or other work-study/employment:* Total amount: $1300 (100% need-based).

APPLYING FOR FINANCIAL AID *Required financial aid forms:* FAFSA, state aid form. *Financial aid deadline:* 3/2 (priority: 3/2). *Notification date:* 4/1. Students must reply within 4 weeks of notification.

CONTACT Ms. Ann Draper, Associate Director of Financial Aid, University of California, Santa Cruz, 201 Hahn Student Services Building, Santa Cruz, CA 95064, 831-459-4358. *Fax:* 831-459-4631. *E-mail:* ann@ucsc.edu.

UNIVERSITY OF CENTRAL ARKANSAS
Conway, AR

CONTACT Cheryl Lyons, Director of Student Aid, University of Central Arkansas, 201 Donaghey Avenue, Conway, AR 72035, 501-450-3140 or toll-free 800-243-8245 (in-state). *Fax:* 501-450-5168. *E-mail:* clyons@uca.edu.

UNIVERSITY OF CENTRAL FLORIDA
Orlando, FL

Tuition & fees (FL res): $3180	Average undergraduate aid package: $5397

ABOUT THE INSTITUTION State-supported, coed. Awards: associate, bachelor's, master's, and doctoral degrees and post-bachelor's certificates. 81 undergraduate majors. Total enrollment: 42,568. Undergraduates: 35,159. Freshmen: 5,965. Federal methodology is used as a basis for awarding need-based institutional aid.

UNDERGRADUATE EXPENSES for 2004–05 *Application fee:* $30. *Tuition, state resident:* full-time $2982; part-time $99.40 per credit. *Tuition, nonresident:* full-time $15,488; part-time $516.28 per credit. *Required fees:* full-time $198; $6 per credit. Full-time tuition and fees vary according to course load. Part-time tuition and fees vary according to course load. *College room and board:* $7232; *room only:* $4300. Room and board charges vary according to board plan and housing facility. *Payment plans:* Tuition prepayment, deferred payment.

FRESHMAN FINANCIAL AID (Fall 2003) 2933 applied for aid; of those 100% were deemed to have need. 97% of freshmen with need received aid; of those 54% had need fully met. *Average percent of need met:* 68% (excluding resources awarded to replace EFC). *Average financial aid package:* $4642 (excluding resources awarded to replace EFC). 14% of all full-time freshmen had no need and received non-need-based gift aid.

UNDERGRADUATE FINANCIAL AID (Fall 2003) 14,103 applied for aid; of those 97% were deemed to have need. 98% of undergraduates with need received aid; of those 52% had need fully met. *Average percent of need met:* 71% (excluding resources awarded to replace EFC). *Average financial aid package:* $5397 (excluding resources awarded to replace EFC). 6% of all full-time undergraduates had no need and received non-need-based gift aid.

GIFT AID (NEED-BASED) *Total amount:* $28,142,726 (67% federal, 16% state, 17% institutional). *Receiving aid:* Freshmen: 23% (914); All full-time undergradu-

ates: 26% (6,140). *Average award:* Freshmen: $3543; Undergraduates: $3709. *Scholarships, grants, and awards:* Federal Pell, FSEOG, state, private, college/university gift aid from institutional funds.

GIFT AID (NON-NEED-BASED) *Total amount:* $37,007,740 (77% state, 14% institutional, 9% external sources). *Receiving aid:* Freshmen: 66% (2,630); Undergraduates: 36% (8,555). *Average Award:* Freshmen: $1885; *Undergraduates:* $1728. *Scholarships, grants, and awards by category: Academic Interests/Achievement:* general academic interests/achievements. *Creative Arts/Performance:* music, theater/drama. *Special Achievements/Activities:* general special achievements/activities, leadership. *Special Characteristics:* members of minority groups. *Tuition waivers:* Full or partial for employees or children of employees, senior citizens. *ROTC:* Army, Air Force.

LOANS *Student loans:* $52,328,696 (62% need-based, 38% non-need-based). 36% of past graduating class borrowed through all loan programs. *Average indebtedness per student:* $12,780. *Average need-based loan:* Freshmen: $2416; Undergraduates: $3982. *Parent loans:* $2,952,100 (100% non-need-based). *Programs:* FFEL (Subsidized and Unsubsidized Stafford, PLUS), Perkins.

WORK-STUDY *Federal work-study:* Total amount: $1,128,379; jobs available. *State or other work-study/employment:* Part-time jobs available.

ATHLETIC AWARDS *Total amount:* $1,373,492 (100% non-need-based).

APPLYING FOR FINANCIAL AID *Required financial aid form:* FAFSA. *Financial aid deadline:* 6/30 (priority: 3/1). *Notification date:* Continuous beginning 3/15. Students must reply within 3 weeks of notification.

CONTACT Mr. Thomas S. Silarek, Coordinator, Student Financial Assistance, University of Central Florida, 4000 Central Florida Boulevard, Orlando, FL 32816-0113, 407-823-2827. *Fax:* 407-823-5241. *E-mail:* tsilarek@mail.ucf.edu.

UNIVERSITY OF CENTRAL OKLAHOMA
Edmond, OK

CONTACT Ms. Becky Garrett, Assistant Director, Technical Services, University of Central Oklahoma, 100 North University Drive, Edmond, OK 73034-5209, 405-974-3334 or toll-free 800-254-4215. *Fax:* 405-340-7658. *E-mail:* bgarrett@ucok.edu.

UNIVERSITY OF CHARLESTON
Charleston, WV

Tuition & fees: $20,200	Average undergraduate aid package: $17,320

ABOUT THE INSTITUTION Independent, coed. Awards: associate, bachelor's, and master's degrees. 34 undergraduate majors. Total enrollment: 941. Undergraduates: 901. Freshmen: 187. Federal methodology is used as a basis for awarding need-based institutional aid.

UNDERGRADUATE EXPENSES for 2005–06 *Application fee:* $25. *Comprehensive fee:* $27,600 includes full-time tuition ($20,200) and room and board ($7400). Room and board charges vary according to board plan and housing facility. *Part-time tuition:* $380 per credit. Part-time tuition and fees vary according to course load and program. *Payment plans:* Guaranteed tuition, installment.

FRESHMAN FINANCIAL AID (Fall 2004, est.) 139 applied for aid; of those 89% were deemed to have need. 100% of freshmen with need received aid; of those 40% had need fully met. *Average percent of need met:* 88% (excluding resources awarded to replace EFC). *Average financial aid package:* $18,750 (excluding resources awarded to replace EFC). 12% of all full-time freshmen had no need and received non-need-based gift aid.

UNDERGRADUATE FINANCIAL AID (Fall 2004, est.) 693 applied for aid; of those 91% were deemed to have need. 99% of undergraduates with need received aid; of those 35% had need fully met. *Average percent of need met:* 83% (excluding resources awarded to replace EFC). *Average financial aid package:* $17,320 (excluding resources awarded to replace EFC). 5% of all full-time undergraduates had no need and received non-need-based gift aid.

GIFT AID (NEED-BASED) *Receiving aid:* Freshmen: 63% (109); All full-time undergraduates: 78% (605). *Average award:* Freshmen: $5800; Undergraduates: $4810. *Scholarships, grants, and awards:* Federal Pell, FSEOG, state, private, college/university gift aid from institutional funds, Council of Independent Colleges Tuition Exchange grants, Tuition Exchange Inc. grants.

GIFT AID (NON-NEED-BASED) *Receiving aid:* Freshmen: 57% (98); Undergraduates: 69% (532). *Average Award:* Freshmen: $6150; Undergraduates: $4890. *Scholarships, grants, and awards by category: Academic Interests/Achievement:* general academic interests/achievements, military science. *Creative Arts/Performance:* 30 awards ($30,000 total): music. *Special Achievements/Activities:* cheerleading/drum major, community service, general special achievements/

activities, leadership. *Special Characteristics:* children and siblings of alumni, children of educators, children of faculty/staff, international students, local/state students. *Tuition waivers:* Full or partial for employees or children of employees, senior citizens. *ROTC:* Army.

LOANS *Student loans:* $5,826,560 (85% need-based, 15% non-need-based). 80% of past graduating class borrowed through all loan programs. *Average indebtedness per student:* $19,825. *Average need-based loan:* Freshmen: $6500; Undergraduates: $9210. *Parent loans:* $539,508 (100% need-based). *Programs:* FFEL (Subsidized and Unsubsidized Stafford, PLUS), Perkins, Federal Nursing, alternative loans.

WORK-STUDY *Federal work-study:* Total amount: $142,000; jobs available (averaging $975). *State or other work-study/employment:* Part-time jobs available (averaging $850).

ATHLETIC AWARDS *Total amount:* $1,895,894 (68% need-based, 32% non-need-based).

APPLYING FOR FINANCIAL AID *Required financial aid forms:* FAFSA, institution's own form. *Financial aid deadline (priority):* 3/1. *Notification date:* Continuous beginning 3/15. Students must reply by 5/1 or within 4 weeks of notification.

CONTACT Ms. Janet M. Ruge, Director of Financial Aid, University of Charleston, 2300 MacCorkle Avenue SE, Charleston, WV 25304-1099, 304-357-4759 or toll-free 800-995-GOUC. *Fax:* 304-357-4769. *E-mail:* janetruge@ucwv.edu.

UNIVERSITY OF CHICAGO
Chicago, IL

CONTACT Office of College Aid, University of Chicago, 1116 East 59th Street, Room 203, Chicago, IL 60637, 773-702-8666. *Fax:* 773-702-5846.

UNIVERSITY OF CINCINNATI
Cincinnati, OH

Tuition & fees (OH res): $8379	Average undergraduate aid package: $7790

ABOUT THE INSTITUTION State-supported, coed. Awards: associate, bachelor's, master's, doctoral, and first professional degrees and post-bachelor's certificates. 142 undergraduate majors. Total enrollment: 27,178. Undergraduates: 19,128. Freshmen: 3,714. Federal methodology is used as a basis for awarding need-based institutional aid.

UNDERGRADUATE EXPENSES for 2004–05 *Application fee:* $35. *Tuition, state resident:* full-time $7005; part-time $233 per credit hour. *Tuition, nonresident:* full-time $19,977; part-time $594 per credit hour. Full-time tuition and fees vary according to course load, degree level, location, program, and reciprocity agreements. Part-time tuition and fees vary according to course load, degree level, location, program, and reciprocity agreements. *College room and board:* $8004; *room only:* $5142. Room and board charges vary according to board plan and housing facility. *Payment plan:* Installment.

FRESHMAN FINANCIAL AID (Fall 2003) 2906 applied for aid; of those 81% were deemed to have need. 98% of freshmen with need received aid; of those 13% had need fully met. *Average percent of need met:* 51% (excluding resources awarded to replace EFC). *Average financial aid package:* $7182 (excluding resources awarded to replace EFC). 8% of all full-time freshmen had no need and received non-need-based gift aid.

UNDERGRADUATE FINANCIAL AID (Fall 2003) 9,334 applied for aid; of those 83% were deemed to have need. 98% of undergraduates with need received aid; of those 13% had need fully met. *Average percent of need met:* 54% (excluding resources awarded to replace EFC). *Average financial aid package:* $7790 (excluding resources awarded to replace EFC). 4% of all full-time undergraduates had no need and received non-need-based gift aid.

GIFT AID (NEED-BASED) *Total amount:* $47,240,486 (31% federal, 12% state, 49% institutional, 8% external sources). *Receiving aid:* Freshmen: 43% (1,621); All full-time undergraduates: 33% (5,190). *Average award:* Freshmen: $4135; Undergraduates: $4039. *Scholarships, grants, and awards:* Federal Pell, FSEOG, state, private, college/university gift aid from institutional funds, Federal Nursing.

GIFT AID (NON-NEED-BASED) *Total amount:* $2,897,828 (1% federal, 2% state, 87% institutional, 10% external sources). *Receiving aid:* Freshmen: 18% (679); Undergraduates: 8% (1,303). *Average Award:* Freshmen: $4470; *Undergraduates:* $4013. *Scholarships, grants, and awards by category: Academic Interests/Achievement:* architecture, area/ethnic studies, biological sciences, business, communication, computer science, education, engineering/technologies, English, foreign languages, general academic interests/achievements, health fields, humanities, mathematics, military science, physical sciences, premedicine, social sciences. *Creative Arts/Performance:* applied art and design, art/fine arts, music. *Special Achievements/Activities:* general special achievements/activities. *Special Characteristics:* children of faculty/staff, members of minority groups, out-of-state students. *Tuition waivers:* Full or partial for employees or children of employees. *ROTC:* Army, Air Force.

LOANS *Student loans:* $113,671,095 (38% need-based, 62% non-need-based). 61% of past graduating class borrowed through all loan programs. *Average indebtedness per student:* $22,425. *Average need-based loan:* Freshmen: $2235; Undergraduates: $3652. *Parent loans:* $48,683,014 (63% need-based, 37% non-need-based). *Programs:* FFEL (Subsidized and Unsubsidized Stafford, PLUS), Perkins, Federal Nursing, state, college/university.

WORK-STUDY *Federal work-study:* Total amount: $4,016,420; jobs available.

ATHLETIC AWARDS *Total amount:* $4,592,564 (96% need-based, 4% non-need-based).

APPLYING FOR FINANCIAL AID *Required financial aid form:* FAFSA. *Financial aid deadline:* Continuous. *Notification date:* Continuous beginning 3/15. Students must reply within 2 weeks of notification.

CONTACT Mrs. Martha Geiger, Student Financial Aid Associate Director, University of Cincinnati, 2624 Clifton Avenue, Cincinnati, OH 45221, 513-556-2441. *Fax:* 513-556-9171. *E-mail:* martha.geiger@uc.edu.

UNIVERSITY OF COLORADO AT BOULDER
Boulder, CO

Tuition & fees (CO res): $4341	Average undergraduate aid package: $9089

ABOUT THE INSTITUTION State-supported, coed. Awards: bachelor's, master's, doctoral, and first professional degrees. 64 undergraduate majors. Total enrollment: 31,943. Undergraduates: 26,182. Freshmen: 5,149. Federal methodology is used as a basis for awarding need-based institutional aid.

UNDERGRADUATE EXPENSES for 2004–05 *Application fee:* $50. *Tuition, state resident:* full-time $3480. *Tuition, nonresident:* full-time $20,592. Full-time tuition and fees vary according to program. Part-time tuition and fees vary according to course load and program. *College room and board:* $7564. Room and board charges vary according to board plan, location, and student level. *Payment plan:* Deferred payment.

FRESHMAN FINANCIAL AID (Fall 2004, est.) 3364 applied for aid; of those 59% were deemed to have need. 98% of freshmen with need received aid; of those 51% had need fully met. *Average percent of need met:* 91% (excluding resources awarded to replace EFC). *Average financial aid package:* $7187 (excluding resources awarded to replace EFC). 20% of all full-time freshmen had no need and received non-need-based gift aid.

UNDERGRADUATE FINANCIAL AID (Fall 2004, est.) 13,755 applied for aid; of those 58% were deemed to have need. 98% of undergraduates with need received aid; of those 53% had need fully met. *Average percent of need met:* 89% (excluding resources awarded to replace EFC). *Average financial aid package:* $9089 (excluding resources awarded to replace EFC). 16% of all full-time undergraduates had no need and received non-need-based gift aid.

GIFT AID (NEED-BASED) *Total amount:* $28,450,021 (43% federal, 13% state, 32% institutional, 12% external sources). *Receiving aid:* Freshmen: 22% (1,136); All full-time undergraduates: 20% (4,879). *Average award:* Freshmen: $5256; Undergraduates: $5251. *Scholarships, grants, and awards:* Federal Pell, FSEOG, state, private, college/university gift aid from institutional funds.

GIFT AID (NON-NEED-BASED) *Total amount:* $7,489,556 (34% federal, 14% state, 33% institutional, 19% external sources). *Receiving aid:* Freshmen: 1% (68); Undergraduates: 1% (158). *Average Award:* Freshmen: $3792; Undergraduates: $5496. *Scholarships, grants, and awards by category: Academic Interests/ Achievement:* architecture, area/ethnic studies, biological sciences, business, communication, computer science, education, engineering/technologies, English, foreign languages, general academic interests/achievements, health fields, humanities, international studies, mathematics, military science, physical sciences, premedicine, social sciences. *Creative Arts/Performance:* art/fine arts, cinema/film/broadcasting, creative writing, dance, journalism/publications, music, performing arts, theater/drama. *Special Achievements/Activities:* community service, general special achievements/activities, leadership. *Special Characteristics:* first-generation college students, general special characteristics, local/state students. *Tuition waivers:* Full or partial for senior citizens. *ROTC:* Army, Naval, Air Force.

LOANS *Student loans:* $57,536,528 (66% need-based, 34% non-need-based). 44% of past graduating class borrowed through all loan programs. *Average indebtedness per student:* $16,348. *Average need-based loan:* Freshmen: $3490; Undergraduates: $4989. *Parent loans:* $83,895,564 (44% need-based, 56% non-need-based). *Programs:* Federal Direct (Subsidized and Unsubsidized Stafford, PLUS), Perkins, college/university, alternative loans.

WORK-STUDY *Federal work-study:* Total amount: $1,074,889; 1,117 jobs averaging $1599. *State or other work-study/employment:* Total amount: $2,056,410 (98% need-based, 2% non-need-based). 875 part-time jobs averaging $2155.

ATHLETIC AWARDS *Total amount:* $4,145,238 (35% need-based, 65% non-need-based).

APPLYING FOR FINANCIAL AID *Required financial aid forms:* FAFSA, income tax form(s). *Financial aid deadline (priority):* 4/1. *Notification date:* Continuous. Students must reply within 3 weeks of notification.

CONTACT Gwen Eberhard, Director of Financial Aid, University of Colorado at Boulder, University Campus Box 77, Boulder, CO 80309, 303-492-8223. *Fax:* 303-492-0838. *E-mail:* finaid@colorado.edu.

UNIVERSITY OF COLORADO AT COLORADO SPRINGS
Colorado Springs, CO

Tuition & fees (CO res): $4106	Average undergraduate aid package: $7243

ABOUT THE INSTITUTION State-supported, coed. Awards: bachelor's, master's, and doctoral degrees. 34 undergraduate majors. Total enrollment: 7,629. Undergraduates: 6,005. Freshmen: 740. Federal methodology is used as a basis for awarding need-based institutional aid.

UNDERGRADUATE EXPENSES for 2004–05 *Application fee:* $50. *Tuition, state resident:* full-time $3286; part-time $162 per credit hour. *Tuition, nonresident:* full-time $15,264; part-time $832 per credit hour. *Required fees:* full-time $820; $410 per term part-time. Full-time tuition and fees vary according to program and student level. Part-time tuition and fees vary according to program and student level. *College room and board:* $6729. Room and board charges vary according to board plan and housing facility. *Payment plan:* Deferred payment.

FRESHMAN FINANCIAL AID (Fall 2004, est.) 574 applied for aid; of those 68% were deemed to have need. 78% of freshmen with need received aid; of those 10% had need fully met. *Average percent of need met:* 52% (excluding resources awarded to replace EFC). *Average financial aid package:* $5574 (excluding resources awarded to replace EFC). 19% of all full-time freshmen had no need and received non-need-based gift aid.

UNDERGRADUATE FINANCIAL AID (Fall 2004, est.) 3,601 applied for aid; of those 84% were deemed to have need. 82% of undergraduates with need received aid; of those 9% had need fully met. *Average percent of need met:* 59% (excluding resources awarded to replace EFC). *Average financial aid package:* $7243 (excluding resources awarded to replace EFC). 8% of all full-time undergraduates had no need and received non-need-based gift aid.

GIFT AID (NEED-BASED) *Total amount:* $10,704,038 (42% federal, 22% state, 27% institutional, 9% external sources). *Receiving aid:* Freshmen: 34% (236); All full-time undergraduates: 36% (1,707). *Average award:* Freshmen: $4117; Undergraduates: $4755. *Scholarships, grants, and awards:* Federal Pell, FSEOG, state, private, college/university gift aid from institutional funds.

GIFT AID (NON-NEED-BASED) *Average Award:* Freshmen: $1635; Undergraduates: $1956. *Scholarships, grants, and awards by category: Academic Interests/ Achievement:* biological sciences, business, computer science, education, engineering/technologies, English, general academic interests/achievements, health fields, mathematics, military science, physical sciences, premedicine. *Special Achievements/Activities:* community service, leadership. *Special Characteristics:* children and siblings of alumni, ethnic background, first-generation college students, general special characteristics, handicapped students, out-of-state students. *Tuition waivers:* Full or partial for employees or children of employees. *ROTC:* Army.

LOANS *Student loans:* $20,076,914 (100% need-based). 45% of past graduating class borrowed through all loan programs. *Average indebtedness per student:* $12,694. *Average need-based loan:* Freshmen: $2578; Undergraduates: $3614. *Parent loans:* $2,655,010 (100% need-based). *Programs:* FFEL (Subsidized and Unsubsidized Stafford, PLUS), Perkins, college/university.

WORK-STUDY *Federal work-study:* Total amount: $514,991; 144 jobs averaging $3576. *State or other work-study/employment:* Total amount: $904,282 (84% need-based, 16% non-need-based). 271 part-time jobs averaging $3337.

ATHLETIC AWARDS *Total amount:* $276,159 (100% need-based).

APPLYING FOR FINANCIAL AID *Required financial aid form:* FAFSA. *Financial aid deadline (priority):* 4/1. *Notification date:* Continuous beginning 4/15. Students must reply within 3 weeks of notification.

CONTACT Ms. Lee Ingalls-Noble, Director of Financial Aid, University of Colorado at Colorado Springs, 1420 Austin Bluffs Parkway, Colorado Springs, CO 80933-7150, 719-262-3466 or toll-free 800-990-8227 Ext. 3383.

UNIVERSITY OF COLORADO AT DENVER AND HEALTH SCIENCES CENTER-DOWNTOWN DENVER CAMPUS
Denver, CO

Tuition & fees (CO res): $4457   **Average undergraduate aid package: $6868**

ABOUT THE INSTITUTION State-supported, coed. Awards: bachelor's, master's, and doctoral degrees and post-master's certificates. 26 undergraduate majors. Total enrollment: 15,596. Undergraduates: 8,903. Freshmen: 645. Federal methodology is used as a basis for awarding need-based institutional aid.
UNDERGRADUATE EXPENSES for 2005–06 *Application fee:* $50. *Tuition, state resident:* full-time $3664; part-time $175 per semester hour. *Tuition, nonresident:* full-time $15,634; part-time $915 per semester hour. *Required fees:* full-time $793; $681 per year part-time. Full-time tuition and fees vary according to program and student level. Part-time tuition and fees vary according to program and student level. *Payment plans:* Installment, deferred payment.
FRESHMAN FINANCIAL AID (Fall 2003) 382 applied for aid; of those 65% were deemed to have need. 86% of freshmen with need received aid; of those 13% had need fully met. *Average percent of need met:* 64% (excluding resources awarded to replace EFC). *Average financial aid package:* $5318 (excluding resources awarded to replace EFC). 2% of all full-time freshmen had no need and received non-need-based gift aid.
UNDERGRADUATE FINANCIAL AID (Fall 2003) 2,566 applied for aid; of those 81% were deemed to have need. 93% of undergraduates with need received aid; of those 12% had need fully met. *Average percent of need met:* 73% (excluding resources awarded to replace EFC). *Average financial aid package:* $6868 (excluding resources awarded to replace EFC). 2% of all full-time undergraduates had no need and received non-need-based gift aid.
GIFT AID (NEED-BASED) *Total amount:* $6,661,370 (60% federal, 24% state, 12% institutional, 4% external sources). *Receiving aid:* Freshmen: 28% (173); All full-time undergraduates: 28% (1,333). *Average award:* Freshmen: $4659; Undergraduates: $4457. *Scholarships, grants, and awards:* Federal Pell, FSEOG, state, private, college/university gift aid from institutional funds.
GIFT AID (NON-NEED-BASED) *Total amount:* $598,275 (31% state, 42% institutional, 27% external sources). *Receiving aid:* Freshmen: 2% (10); Undergraduates: 1% (40). *Average Award:* Freshmen: $1817; Undergraduates: $1710. *Scholarships, grants, and awards by category:* Academic Interests/Achievement: 492 awards ($639,274 total): business, engineering/technologies, general academic interests/achievements. Creative Arts/Performance: 9 awards ($5911 total): general creative arts/performance. Special Achievements/Activities: 57 awards ($131,500 total): leadership. Special Characteristics: 333 awards ($516,709 total): children of faculty/staff, first-generation college students, general special characteristics, handicapped students, members of minority groups. *Tuition waivers:* Full or partial for employees or children of employees. *ROTC:* Army, Air Force cooperative.
LOANS *Student loans:* $11,895,731 (75% need-based, 25% non-need-based). 41% of past graduating class borrowed through all loan programs. *Average indebtedness per student:* $16,315. *Average need-based loan:* Freshmen: $2261; Undergraduates: $3449. *Parent loans:* $690,746 (27% need-based, 73% non-need-based). *Programs:* FFEL (Subsidized and Unsubsidized Stafford, PLUS), Perkins, alternative loans.
WORK-STUDY *Federal work-study:* Total amount: $537,397; 144 jobs averaging $3732. *State or other work-study/employment:* Total amount: $705,765 (85% need-based, 15% non-need-based). 193 part-time jobs averaging $3651.
APPLYING FOR FINANCIAL AID *Required financial aid forms:* FAFSA, institution's own form. *Financial aid deadline (priority):* 4/1. *Notification date:* Continuous beginning 5/1. Students must reply within 2 weeks of notification.
CONTACT Ellinor Miller, Director of Financial Aid, University of Colorado at Denver and Health Sciences Center—Downtown Denver Campus, PO Box 173364, Denver, CO 80217-3364, 303-556-2886. Fax: 303-556-2325.

UNIVERSITY OF COLORADO AT DENVER AND HEALTH SCIENCES CENTER-HEALTH SCIENCES PROGRAM
Denver, CO

Tuition & fees (CO res): $6560   **Average undergraduate aid package: $11,126**

ABOUT THE INSTITUTION State-supported, coed. Awards: bachelor's, master's, doctoral, and first professional degrees and post-master's and first professional certificates. 2 undergraduate majors. Total enrollment: 2,567. Undergraduates: 320. Federal methodology is used as a basis for awarding need-based institutional aid.
UNDERGRADUATE EXPENSES for 2004–05 *Application fee:* $50. *Tuition, state resident:* full-time $6180. *Tuition, nonresident:* full-time $21,600.
UNDERGRADUATE FINANCIAL AID (Fall 2004, est.) 376 applied for aid; of those 91% were deemed to have need. 96% of undergraduates with need received aid; of those 3% had need fully met. *Average percent of need met:* 80% (excluding resources awarded to replace EFC). *Average financial aid package:* $11,126 (excluding resources awarded to replace EFC).
GIFT AID (NEED-BASED) *Total amount:* $329,000 (78% federal, 18% state, 4% institutional). *Receiving aid:* All full-time undergraduates: 19% (90). *Average award:* Undergraduates: $5174. *Scholarships, grants, and awards:* Federal Pell, FSEOG, state, private, college/university gift aid from institutional funds.
GIFT AID (NON-NEED-BASED) *Total amount:* $230,500 (4% state, 15% institutional, 81% external sources). *Receiving aid:* Undergraduates: 12% (54). *Scholarships, grants, and awards by category:* Academic Interests/Achievement: health fields. *Special Characteristics:* children of faculty/staff, ethnic background, first-generation college students, general special characteristics, local/state students, previous college experience.
LOANS *Student loans:* $3,600,000 (92% need-based, 8% non-need-based). 93% of past graduating class borrowed through all loan programs. *Average indebtedness per student:* $21,592. *Average need-based loan:* Undergraduates: $8737. *Parent loans:* $190,000 (100% non-need-based). *Programs:* Federal Direct (Subsidized and Unsubsidized Stafford, PLUS), Perkins, Federal Nursing, college/university, Loans for Disadvantaged Students program, Health Professions Student Loans (HPSL).
WORK-STUDY *Federal work-study:* Total amount: $140,000; jobs available (averaging $3000). *State or other work-study/employment:* Total amount: $38,000 (100% need-based). Part-time jobs available (averaging $3000).
APPLYING FOR FINANCIAL AID *Required financial aid forms:* FAFSA, institution's own form. *Financial aid deadline:* Continuous.
CONTACT Student Financial Office, University of Colorado at Denver and Health Sciences Center—Health Sciences Program, 4200 East Ninth Avenue, Denver, CO 80262, 303-315-8364. *Fax:* 303-315-3350. *E-mail:* financial.aid@uchsc.edu.

UNIVERSITY OF CONNECTICUT
Storrs, CT

Tuition & fees (CT res): $7912   **Average undergraduate aid package: $8662**

ABOUT THE INSTITUTION State-supported, coed. Awards: associate, bachelor's, master's, doctoral, and first professional degrees and post-bachelor's and post-master's certificates. 96 undergraduate majors. Total enrollment: 22,694. Undergraduates: 15,751. Freshmen: 3,247. Federal methodology is used as a basis for awarding need-based institutional aid.
UNDERGRADUATE EXPENSES for 2005–06 *Application fee:* $70. *Tuition, state resident:* full-time $6096; part-time $254 per credit. *Tuition, nonresident:* full-time $18,600; part-time $775 per credit. *Required fees:* full-time $1816; $605 per term part-time. Part-time tuition and fees vary according to course load. *College room and board:* $7848; *room only:* $4104. Room and board charges vary according to board plan and housing facility. *Payment plans:* Installment, deferred payment.
FRESHMAN FINANCIAL AID (Fall 2004, est.) 2645 applied for aid; of those 61% were deemed to have need. 97% of freshmen with need received aid; of those 25% had need fully met. *Average percent of need met:* 71% (excluding resources awarded to replace EFC). *Average financial aid package:* $8604 (excluding resources awarded to replace EFC). 14% of all full-time freshmen had no need and received non-need-based gift aid.
UNDERGRADUATE FINANCIAL AID (Fall 2004, est.) 10,045 applied for aid; of those 72% were deemed to have need. 98% of undergraduates with need received aid; of those 30% had need fully met. *Average percent of need met:* 73% (excluding resources awarded to replace EFC). *Average financial aid package:* $8662 (excluding resources awarded to replace EFC). 12% of all full-time undergraduates had no need and received non-need-based gift aid.
GIFT AID (NEED-BASED) *Total amount:* $31,965,097 (22% federal, 16% state, 55% institutional, 7% external sources). *Receiving aid:* Freshmen: 35% (1,143); All full-time undergraduates: 36% (5,296). *Average award:* Freshmen: $5473; Undergraduates: $5508. *Scholarships, grants, and awards:* Federal Pell, FSEOG, state, private, college/university gift aid from institutional funds.

GIFT AID (NON-NEED-BASED) *Total amount:* $8,979,275 (80% institutional, 20% external sources). *Receiving aid:* Freshmen: 30% (983); Undergraduates: 20% (2,904). *Average Award: Freshmen:* $4867; *Undergraduates:* $5567. *Scholarships, grants, and awards by category: Academic Interests/Achievement:* 2,013 awards ($9,945,937 total): agriculture, biological sciences, business, computer science, education, engineering/technologies, English, foreign languages, general academic interests/achievements, health fields, humanities, international studies, mathematics, physical sciences, premedicine, religion/biblical studies, social sciences. *Creative Arts/Performance:* 98 awards ($183,850 total): art/fine arts, music, theater/drama. *Special Achievements/Activities:* 459 awards ($2,717,669 total): community service, leadership. *Special Characteristics:* 441 awards ($1,140,225 total): adult students, children of faculty/staff, veterans. *Tuition waivers:* Full or partial for employees or children of employees, senior citizens. *ROTC:* Army, Air Force.

LOANS *Student loans:* $43,220,002 (59% need-based, 41% non-need-based). 62% of past graduating class borrowed through all loan programs. *Average indebtedness per student:* $18,045. *Average need-based loan:* Freshmen: $2445; Undergraduates: $3276. *Parent loans:* $14,005,127 (47% need-based, 53% non-need-based). *Programs:* FFEL (Subsidized and Unsubsidized Stafford, PLUS), Perkins, state.

WORK-STUDY *Federal work-study:* Total amount: $2,479,424; 1,412 jobs averaging $1756. *State or other work-study/employment:* Total amount: $10,400,000 (100% non-need-based). 5,502 part-time jobs averaging $1890.

ATHLETIC AWARDS *Total amount:* $6,533,203 (33% need-based, 67% non-need-based).

APPLYING FOR FINANCIAL AID *Required financial aid form:* FAFSA. *Financial aid deadline (priority):* 3/1. *Notification date:* Continuous. Students must reply within 4 weeks of notification.

CONTACT Client Service Staff, University of Connecticut, 233 Glenbrook Road, Unit 4116, Storrs, CT 06269-4116, 860-486-2819.

UNIVERSITY OF DALLAS
Irving, TX

Tuition & fees: $20,411	Average undergraduate aid package: $14,390

ABOUT THE INSTITUTION Independent Roman Catholic, coed. Awards: bachelor's, master's, and doctoral degrees and post-bachelor's and post-master's certificates. 34 undergraduate majors. Total enrollment: 3,005. Undergraduates: 1,174. Freshmen: 243. Federal methodology is used as a basis for awarding need-based institutional aid.

UNDERGRADUATE EXPENSES for 2005–06 *Application fee:* $40. *Comprehensive fee:* $27,437 includes full-time tuition ($19,604), mandatory fees ($807), and room and board ($7026). *College room only:* $3296. Room and board charges vary according to board plan and housing facility. *Part-time tuition:* $823 per credit. *Part-time fees:* $807. *Payment plan:* Installment.

FRESHMAN FINANCIAL AID (Fall 2003) 263 applied for aid; of those 73% were deemed to have need. 100% of freshmen with need received aid; of those 25% had need fully met. *Average percent of need met:* 81% (excluding resources awarded to replace EFC). *Average financial aid package:* $15,167 (excluding resources awarded to replace EFC). 32% of all full-time freshmen had no need and received non-need-based gift aid.

UNDERGRADUATE FINANCIAL AID (Fall 2003) 897 applied for aid; of those 79% were deemed to have need. 100% of undergraduates with need received aid; of those 22% had need fully met. *Average percent of need met:* 76% (excluding resources awarded to replace EFC). *Average financial aid package:* $14,390 (excluding resources awarded to replace EFC). 30% of all full-time undergraduates had no need and received non-need-based gift aid.

GIFT AID (NEED-BASED) *Total amount:* $7,057,867 (11% federal, 16% state, 70% institutional, 3% external sources). *Receiving aid:* Freshmen: 64% (190); All full-time undergraduates: 62% (688). *Average award:* Freshmen: $11,320; Undergraduates: $10,197. *Scholarships, grants, and awards:* Federal Pell, FSEOG, state, private, college/university gift aid from institutional funds.

GIFT AID (NON-NEED-BASED) *Total amount:* $3,746,967 (97% institutional, 3% external sources). *Receiving aid:* Freshmen: 14% (41); Undergraduates: 9% (97). *Average Award:* Freshmen: $10,545; Undergraduates: $10,001. *Scholarships, grants, and awards by category: Academic Interests/Achievement:* $7,900,275 total: business, computer science, education, foreign languages, general academic interests/achievements, mathematics, physical sciences, religion/biblical studies. *Creative Arts/Performance:* $87,293 total: art/fine arts, performing arts. *Special Achievements/Activities:* $330,024 total: leadership, religious involvement. *Special Characteristics:* $181,698 total: children of faculty/

staff, members of minority groups, siblings of current students. *Tuition waivers:* Full or partial for employees or children of employees. *ROTC:* Army cooperative, Air Force cooperative.

LOANS *Student loans:* $5,086,254 (73% need-based, 27% non-need-based). 70% of past graduating class borrowed through all loan programs. *Average indebtedness per student:* $21,700. *Average need-based loan:* Freshmen: $3886; Undergraduates: $4264. *Parent loans:* $1,081,603 (34% need-based, 66% non-need-based). *Programs:* FFEL (Subsidized and Unsubsidized Stafford, PLUS), Perkins, state.

WORK-STUDY *Federal work-study:* Total amount: $422,861; 311 jobs averaging $1360. *State or other work-study/employment:* Total amount: $300,607 (27% need-based, 73% non-need-based). 343 part-time jobs available.

APPLYING FOR FINANCIAL AID *Required financial aid forms:* FAFSA, institution's own form. *Financial aid deadline (priority):* 3/1. *Notification date:* Continuous. Students must reply by 5/1 or within 2 weeks of notification.

CONTACT Curt Eley, Dean of Enrollment Management, University of Dallas, 1845 East Northgate Drive, Irving, TX 75062, 972-721-5266 or toll-free 800-628-6999. *Fax:* 972-721-5017. *E-mail:* ugadmis@udallas.edu.

UNIVERSITY OF DAYTON
Dayton, OH

Tuition & fees: $20,250	Average undergraduate aid package: $13,325

ABOUT THE INSTITUTION Independent Roman Catholic, coed. Awards: bachelor's, master's, doctoral, and first professional degrees and post-master's certificates. 75 undergraduate majors. Total enrollment: 10,495. Undergraduates: 7,158. Freshmen: 1,812. Both federal and institutional methodology are used as a basis for awarding need-based institutional aid.

UNDERGRADUATE EXPENSES for 2004–05 *One-time required fee:* $1200. *Comprehensive fee:* $26,550 includes full-time tuition ($19,570), mandatory fees ($680), and room and board ($6300). *College room only:* $3600. Full-time tuition and fees vary according to program. Room and board charges vary according to board plan, housing facility, and student level. *Part-time tuition:* $652 per credit hour. *Part-time fees:* $25 per term. Part-time tuition and fees vary according to course load and program. *Payment plan:* Deferred payment.

GIFT AID (NEED-BASED) *Total amount:* $34,043,182 (10% federal, 11% state, 75% institutional, 4% external sources). *Receiving aid:* Freshmen: 62% (1,164); All full-time undergraduates: 59% (3,911). *Average award:* Freshmen: $9505; Undergraduates: $8340. *Scholarships, grants, and awards:* Federal Pell, FSEOG, state, private, college/university gift aid from institutional funds.

GIFT AID (NON-NEED-BASED) *Total amount:* $13,053,667 (5% federal, 12% state, 77% institutional, 6% external sources). *Receiving aid:* Freshmen: 62% (1,164); Undergraduates: 59% (3,905). *Average Award: Freshmen:* $5519; *Undergraduates:* $4988. *Scholarships, grants, and awards by category: Academic Interests/Achievement:* 5,009 awards ($22,692,282 total): business, education, engineering/technologies, general academic interests/achievements, humanities. *Creative Arts/Performance:* 94 awards ($336,793 total): art/fine arts, music. *Special Achievements/Activities:* 140 awards ($241,130 total): general special achievements/activities. *Special Characteristics:* 10 awards ($97,586 total): religious affiliation. *Tuition waivers:* Full or partial for employees or children of employees, senior citizens. *ROTC:* Army, Air Force cooperative.

LOANS *Student loans:* $19,725,884 (79% need-based, 21% non-need-based). 61% of past graduating class borrowed through all loan programs. *Average indebtedness per student:* $21,273. *Average need-based loan:* Freshmen: $3683; Undergraduates: $4152. *Parent loans:* $6,375,176 (71% need-based, 29% non-need-based). *Programs:* FFEL (Subsidized and Unsubsidized Stafford, PLUS), Perkins, state, college/university.

ATHLETIC AWARDS *Total amount:* $2,057,027 (44% need-based, 56% non-need-based).

APPLYING FOR FINANCIAL AID *Required financial aid form:* FAFSA. *Financial aid deadline (priority):* 3/31. *Notification date:* Continuous.

CONTACT Jeff Daniels, Interim Director of Scholarships and Financial Aid, University of Dayton, 300 College Park Drive, Dayton, OH 45469-1305, 937-229-4311 or toll-free 800-837-7433. *Fax:* 937-229-4338. *E-mail:* jdaniels@udayton.edu.

UNIVERSITY OF DELAWARE
Newark, DE

Tuition & fees (DE res): $6954	Average undergraduate aid package: $10,200

University of Delaware

ABOUT THE INSTITUTION State-related, coed. Awards: associate, bachelor's, master's, and doctoral degrees (enrollment data for undergraduate students does not include non-degree-seeking students). 132 undergraduate majors. Total enrollment: 20,713. Undergraduates: 17,318. Freshmen: 3,385. Federal methodology is used as a basis for awarding need-based institutional aid.

UNDERGRADUATE EXPENSES for 2004–05 *Application fee:* $60. *Tuition, state resident:* full-time $6304; part-time $263 per credit. *Tuition, nonresident:* full-time $15,990; part-time $667 per credit. *Required fees:* full-time $650; $15 per term part-time. *College room and board:* $6458; *room only:* $3668. Room and board charges vary according to housing facility. *Payment plan:* Installment.

FRESHMAN FINANCIAL AID (Fall 2004, est.) 2582 applied for aid; of those 58% were deemed to have need. 100% of freshmen with need received aid; of those 45% had need fully met. *Average percent of need met:* 78% (excluding resources awarded to replace EFC). *Average financial aid package:* $9800 (excluding resources awarded to replace EFC). 25% of all full-time freshmen had no need and received non-need-based gift aid.

UNDERGRADUATE FINANCIAL AID (Fall 2004, est.) 8,773 applied for aid; of those 66% were deemed to have need. 100% of undergraduates with need received aid; of those 45% had need fully met. *Average percent of need met:* 78% (excluding resources awarded to replace EFC). *Average financial aid package:* $10,200 (excluding resources awarded to replace EFC). 22% of all full-time undergraduates had no need and received non-need-based gift aid.

GIFT AID (NEED-BASED) *Total amount:* $24,200,000 (21% federal, 24% state, 36% institutional, 19% external sources). *Receiving aid:* Freshmen: 36% (1,215); All full-time undergraduates: 30% (4,481). *Average award:* Freshmen: $6000; Undergraduates: $5800. *Scholarships, grants, and awards:* Federal Pell, FSEOG, state, private, college/university gift aid from institutional funds.

GIFT AID (NON-NEED-BASED) *Total amount:* $12,850,000 (7% state, 74% institutional, 19% external sources). *Receiving aid:* Freshmen: 14% (467); Undergraduates: 10% (1,562). *Average Award:* Freshmen: $4025; Undergraduates: $4050. *Scholarships, grants, and awards by category: Academic Interests/ Achievement:* agriculture, biological sciences, business, communication, computer science, education, engineering/technologies, English, foreign languages, general academic interests/achievements, health fields, humanities, international studies, mathematics, military science, physical sciences, premedicine, religion/ biblical studies, social sciences. *Creative Arts/Performance:* applied art and design, art/fine arts, music, theater/drama. *Special Achievements/Activities:* cheerleading/drum major, community service, general special achievements/ activities, leadership. *Special Characteristics:* children and siblings of alumni, children of faculty/staff, children of public servants, ethnic background, first-generation college students, general special characteristics, local/state students, members of minority groups. *Tuition waivers:* Full or partial for employees or children of employees, senior citizens. *ROTC:* Army, Air Force.

LOANS *Student loans:* $33,200,000 (72% need-based, 28% non-need-based). 38% of past graduating class borrowed through all loan programs. *Average indebtedness per student:* $14,639. *Average need-based loan:* Freshmen: $3895; Undergraduates: $4750. *Parent loans:* $20,650,000 (61% need-based, 39% non-need-based). *Programs:* Federal Direct (Subsidized and Unsubsidized Stafford, PLUS), Perkins, Federal Nursing.

WORK-STUDY *Federal work-study:* Total amount: $1,600,000; jobs available. *State or other work-study/employment:* Total amount: $377,000 (93% need-based, 7% non-need-based). Part-time jobs available.

ATHLETIC AWARDS *Total amount:* $4,800,000 (27% need-based, 73% non-need-based).

APPLYING FOR FINANCIAL AID *Required financial aid form:* FAFSA. *Financial aid deadline:* 3/15 (priority: 2/1). *Notification date:* Continuous. Students must reply by 5/1 or within 3 weeks of notification.

CONTACT Mr. Johnie A. Burton, Director of Scholarships and Financial Aid, University of Delaware, 224 Hullihen Hall, Newark, DE 19716, 302-831-8081. *E-mail:* jburton@udel.edu.

UNIVERSITY OF DENVER
Denver, CO

Tuition & fees: $26,610	Average undergraduate aid package: $18,539

ABOUT THE INSTITUTION Independent, coed. Awards: bachelor's, master's, doctoral, and first professional degrees. 67 undergraduate majors. Total enrollment: 9,808. Undergraduates: 4,669. Freshmen: 1,145. Federal methodology is used as a basis for awarding need-based institutional aid.

UNDERGRADUATE EXPENSES for 2004–05 *Application fee:* $50. *Comprehensive fee:* $34,973 includes full-time tuition ($25,956), mandatory fees ($654), and room and board ($8363). *College room only:* $5093. Full-time tuition and fees

vary according to class time, course load, and program. Room and board charges vary according to board plan and housing facility. *Part-time tuition:* $721 per quarter hour. Part-time tuition and fees vary according to class time, course load, and program. *Payment plan:* Deferred payment.

FRESHMAN FINANCIAL AID (Fall 2003) 612 applied for aid; of those 75% were deemed to have need. 100% of freshmen with need received aid; of those 15% had need fully met. *Average percent of need met:* 75% (excluding resources awarded to replace EFC). *Average financial aid package:* $19,204 (excluding resources awarded to replace EFC). 30% of all full-time freshmen had no need and received non-need-based gift aid.

UNDERGRADUATE FINANCIAL AID (Fall 2003) 2,108 applied for aid; of those 82% were deemed to have need. 99% of undergraduates with need received aid; of those 9% had need fully met. *Average percent of need met:* 70% (excluding resources awarded to replace EFC). *Average financial aid package:* $18,539 (excluding resources awarded to replace EFC). 29% of all full-time undergraduates had no need and received non-need-based gift aid.

GIFT AID (NEED-BASED) *Total amount:* $25,522,544 (8% federal, 5% state, 86% institutional, 1% external sources). *Receiving aid:* Freshmen: 44% (447); All full-time undergraduates: 43% (1,684). *Average award:* Freshmen: $14,582; Undergraduates: $13,359. *Scholarships, grants, and awards:* Federal Pell, FSEOG, state, private, college/university gift aid from institutional funds.

GIFT AID (NON-NEED-BASED) *Total amount:* $11,490,444 (85% institutional, 15% external sources). *Receiving aid:* Freshmen: 45% (458); Undergraduates: 44% (1,729). *Average Award:* Freshmen: $9182; *Undergraduates:* $7845. *Scholarships, grants, and awards by category: Creative Arts/Performance:* art/fine arts. *Tuition waivers:* Full or partial for employees or children of employees. *ROTC:* Army cooperative, Air Force cooperative.

LOANS *Student loans:* $12,655,493 (80% need-based, 20% non-need-based). 48% of past graduating class borrowed through all loan programs. *Average indebtedness per student:* $20,551. *Average need-based loan:* Freshmen: $3581; Undergraduates: $4655. *Parent loans:* $5,240,592 (25% need-based, 75% non-need-based). *Programs:* Federal Direct (Subsidized and Unsubsidized Stafford, PLUS), FFEL (Subsidized and Unsubsidized Stafford, PLUS), Perkins, college/university.

WORK-STUDY *Federal work-study:* Total amount: $505,562; 306 jobs averaging $1644. *State or other work-study/employment:* Total amount: $741,965 (64% need-based, 36% non-need-based). 418 part-time jobs averaging $1768.

ATHLETIC AWARDS *Total amount:* $4,891,699 (11% need-based, 89% non-need-based).

APPLYING FOR FINANCIAL AID *Required financial aid form:* FAFSA. *Financial aid deadline (priority):* 3/1. *Notification date:* Continuous beginning 3/15. Students must reply within 3 weeks of notification.

CONTACT Mr. Craig Johnson, Director of Financial Aid, University of Denver, Office of Financial Aid, Denver, CO 80208, 303-871-2337 or toll-free 800-525-9495 (out-of-state). *Fax:* 303-871-2341. *E-mail:* cjons26@du.edu.

UNIVERSITY OF DETROIT MERCY
Detroit, MI

Tuition & fees: $22,470	Average undergraduate aid package: $20,162

ABOUT THE INSTITUTION Independent Roman Catholic (Jesuit), coed. Awards: associate, bachelor's, master's, doctoral, and first professional degrees and post-bachelor's, post-master's, and first professional certificates. 64 undergraduate majors. Total enrollment: 5,521. Undergraduates: 3,311. Freshmen: 461. Federal methodology is used as a basis for awarding need-based institutional aid.

UNDERGRADUATE EXPENSES for 2005–06 *Application fee:* $25. *Comprehensive fee:* $29,798 includes full-time tuition ($21,900), mandatory fees ($570), and room and board ($7328). *College room only:* $4288. *Part-time tuition:* $535 per credit hour.

FRESHMAN FINANCIAL AID (Fall 2003) 407 applied for aid; of those 91% were deemed to have need. 100% of freshmen with need received aid; of those 30% had need fully met. *Average percent of need met:* 89% (excluding resources awarded to replace EFC). *Average financial aid package:* $22,914 (excluding resources awarded to replace EFC). 5% of all full-time freshmen had no need and received non-need-based gift aid.

UNDERGRADUATE FINANCIAL AID (Fall 2003) 1,528 applied for aid; of those 93% were deemed to have need. 100% of undergraduates with need received aid; of those 19% had need fully met. *Average percent of need met:* 80% (excluding resources awarded to replace EFC). *Average financial aid package:*

$20,162 (excluding resources awarded to replace EFC). 6% of all full-time undergraduates had no need and received non-need-based gift aid.
GIFT AID (NEED-BASED) *Total amount:* $21,473,320 (18% federal, 16% state, 64% institutional, 2% external sources). *Receiving aid:* Freshmen: 72% (318); All full-time undergraduates: 75% (1,303). *Average award:* Freshmen: $18,531; Undergraduates: $14,985. *Scholarships, grants, and awards:* Federal Pell, FSEOG, state, private, college/university gift aid from institutional funds.
GIFT AID (NON-NEED-BASED) *Total amount:* $4,625,057 (99% institutional, 1% external sources). *Average Award:* Freshmen: $13,773; *Undergraduates:* $12,108. *Scholarships, grants, and awards by category: Academic Interests/ Achievement:* general academic interests/achievements. *Creative Arts/ Performance:* theater/drama. *Special Achievements/Activities:* religious involvement. *Special Characteristics:* children and siblings of alumni, children of faculty/staff, members of minority groups.
LOANS *Student loans:* $40,700,194 (93% need-based, 7% non-need-based). *Average need-based loan:* Freshmen: $3579; Undergraduates: $4561. *Parent loans:* $1,555,247 (23% need-based, 77% non-need-based). *Programs:* FFEL (Subsidized and Unsubsidized Stafford, PLUS), Perkins, Federal Nursing.
WORK-STUDY *Federal work-study:* Total amount: $890,270; jobs available. *State or other work-study/employment:* Total amount: $1,183,042 (6% need-based, 94% non-need-based). Part-time jobs available.
ATHLETIC AWARDS *Total amount:* $2,349,734 (83% need-based, 17% non-need-based).
APPLYING FOR FINANCIAL AID *Required financial aid form:* FAFSA. *Financial aid deadline (priority):* 3/1. *Notification date:* Continuous. Students must reply within 3 weeks of notification.
CONTACT Sandy Ross, Director of Financial Aid and Scholarships, University of Detroit Mercy, 4001 West McNichols Road, PO Box 19900, Detroit, MI 48219-0900, 313-993-3350 or toll-free 800-635-5020 (out-of-state). *Fax:* 313-993-3347.

UNIVERSITY OF DUBUQUE
Dubuque, IA

Tuition & fees: $16,845	Average undergraduate aid package: $16,999

ABOUT THE INSTITUTION Independent Presbyterian, coed. Awards: associate, bachelor's, master's, doctoral, and first professional degrees. 32 undergraduate majors. Total enrollment: 1,380. Undergraduates: 1,120. Freshmen: 304. Federal methodology is used as a basis for awarding need-based institutional aid.
UNDERGRADUATE EXPENSES for 2005–06 *Application fee:* $25. *Comprehensive fee:* $22,545 includes full-time tuition ($16,660), mandatory fees ($185), and room and board ($5700). *College room only:* $2900. Room and board charges vary according to board plan and housing facility. *Part-time tuition:* $375 per credit. *Payment plan:* Installment.
FRESHMAN FINANCIAL AID (Fall 2004, est.) 294 applied for aid; of those 91% were deemed to have need. 100% of freshmen with need received aid; of those 54% had need fully met. *Average percent of need met:* 90% (excluding resources awarded to replace EFC). *Average financial aid package:* $17,697 (excluding resources awarded to replace EFC). 10% of all full-time freshmen had no need and received non-need-based gift aid.
UNDERGRADUATE FINANCIAL AID (Fall 2004, est.) 1,017 applied for aid; of those 92% were deemed to have need. 100% of undergraduates with need received aid; of those 50% had need fully met. *Average percent of need met:* 86% (excluding resources awarded to replace EFC). *Average financial aid package:* $16,999 (excluding resources awarded to replace EFC). 9% of all full-time undergraduates had no need and received non-need-based gift aid.
GIFT AID (NEED-BASED) *Total amount:* $8,608,312 (18% federal, 15% state, 58% institutional, 9% external sources). *Receiving aid:* Freshmen: 85% (260); All full-time undergraduates: 87% (903). *Average award:* Freshmen: $8820; Undergraduates: $8972. *Scholarships, grants, and awards:* Federal Pell, FSEOG, state, private, college/university gift aid from institutional funds.
GIFT AID (NON-NEED-BASED) *Total amount:* $709,615 (77% institutional, 23% external sources). *Receiving aid:* Freshmen: 5% (16); Undergraduates: 6% (59). *Average Award:* Freshmen: $15,121; Undergraduates: $15,527. *Scholarships, grants, and awards by category: Academic Interests/Achievement:* $456,500 total: general academic interests/achievements. *Special Characteristics:* children and siblings of alumni, children of educators, children of faculty/staff, ethnic background, members of minority groups, out-of-state students, relatives of clergy, religious affiliation, siblings of current students. *Tuition waivers:* Full or partial for children of alumni, employees or children of employees. *ROTC:* Army.

LOANS *Student loans:* $11,059,911 (81% need-based, 19% non-need-based). 97% of past graduating class borrowed through all loan programs. *Average indebtedness per student:* $26,500. *Average need-based loan:* Freshmen: $9528; Undergraduates: $8932. *Parent loans:* $289,929 (55% need-based, 45% non-need-based). *Programs:* FFEL (Subsidized and Unsubsidized Stafford, PLUS), Perkins, state, college/university.
WORK-STUDY *Federal work-study:* Total amount: $166,894; 175 jobs averaging $1500. *State or other work-study/employment:* Total amount: $150,000 (100% need-based). 150 part-time jobs averaging $1500.
APPLYING FOR FINANCIAL AID *Required financial aid form:* FAFSA. *Financial aid deadline:* Continuous. *Notification date:* Continuous beginning 3/1. Students must reply within 3 weeks of notification.
CONTACT Mr. Timothy Kremer, Director of Financial Aid, University of Dubuque, 2000 University Avenue, Dubuque, IA 52001-5050, 563-589-3170 or toll-free 800-722-5583 (in-state). *Fax:* 563-589-3690.

UNIVERSITY OF EVANSVILLE
Evansville, IN

Tuition & fees: $20,515	Average undergraduate aid package: $18,532

ABOUT THE INSTITUTION Independent religious, coed. Awards: associate, bachelor's, and master's degrees. 71 undergraduate majors. Total enrollment: 2,687. Undergraduates: 2,632. Freshmen: 636. Federal methodology is used as a basis for awarding need-based institutional aid.
UNDERGRADUATE EXPENSES for 2004–05 *Application fee:* $35. *Comprehensive fee:* $26,525 includes full-time tuition ($19,995), mandatory fees ($520), and room and board ($6010). *College room only:* $2820. Room and board charges vary according to board plan and housing facility. *Part-time tuition:* $550 per hour. *Part-time fees:* $35 per term. Part-time tuition and fees vary according to course load. *Payment plan:* Installment.
FRESHMAN FINANCIAL AID (Fall 2004, est.) 556 applied for aid; of those 84% were deemed to have need. 100% of freshmen with need received aid; of those 28% had need fully met. *Average percent of need met:* 92% (excluding resources awarded to replace EFC). *Average financial aid package:* $18,883 (excluding resources awarded to replace EFC). 22% of all full-time freshmen had no need and received non-need-based gift aid.
UNDERGRADUATE FINANCIAL AID (Fall 2004, est.) 2,249 applied for aid; of those 72% were deemed to have need. 100% of undergraduates with need received aid; of those 33% had need fully met. *Average percent of need met:* 90% (excluding resources awarded to replace EFC). *Average financial aid package:* $18,532 (excluding resources awarded to replace EFC). 22% of all full-time undergraduates had no need and received non-need-based gift aid.
GIFT AID (NEED-BASED) *Total amount:* $20,931,983 (11% federal, 20% state, 62% institutional, 7% external sources). *Receiving aid:* Freshmen: 71% (454); All full-time undergraduates: 67% (1,547). *Average award:* Freshmen: $15,190; Undergraduates: $13,909. *Scholarships, grants, and awards:* Federal Pell, FSEOG, state, private, college/university gift aid from institutional funds.
GIFT AID (NON-NEED-BASED) *Total amount:* $5,335,640 (88% institutional, 12% external sources). *Receiving aid:* Freshmen: 61% (390); Undergraduates: 49% (1,115). *Average Award:* Freshmen: $10,102; Undergraduates: $9203. *Scholarships, grants, and awards by category: Academic Interests/Achievement:* 752 awards ($4,556,643 total): biological sciences, business, communication, computer science, education, engineering/technologies, English, foreign languages, general academic interests/achievements, health fields, humanities, international studies, mathematics, physical sciences, premedicine, religion/biblical studies, social sciences. *Creative Arts/Performance:* 228 awards ($1,566,853 total): art/fine arts, music, theater/drama. *Special Achievements/Activities:* 145 awards ($592,040 total): leadership. *Special Characteristics:* 298 awards ($2,871,644 total): children and siblings of alumni, children of faculty/staff, international students, members of minority groups, religious affiliation, siblings of current students. *Tuition waivers:* Full or partial for minority students, children of alumni, employees or children of employees, senior citizens.
LOANS *Student loans:* $7,190,026 (92% need-based, 8% non-need-based). 67% of past graduating class borrowed through all loan programs. *Average indebtedness per student:* $21,512. *Average need-based loan:* Freshmen: $4019; Undergraduates: $4595. *Parent loans:* $4,120,232 (84% need-based, 16% non-need-based). *Programs:* FFEL (Subsidized and Unsubsidized Stafford, PLUS), Perkins, Federal Nursing, college/university.
WORK-STUDY *Federal work-study:* Total amount: $530,450; 412 jobs averaging $1288. *State or other work-study/employment:* Total amount: $100,850 (1% need-based, 99% non-need-based). 80 part-time jobs averaging $1260.

ATHLETIC AWARDS *Total amount:* $2,755,030 (41% need-based, 59% non-need-based).

APPLYING FOR FINANCIAL AID *Required financial aid form:* FAFSA. *Financial aid deadline (priority):* 3/1. *Notification date:* Continuous beginning 3/21. Students must reply by 5/1.

CONTACT Ms. JoAnn E. Laugel, Director of Financial Aid, University of Evansville, 1800 Lincoln Avenue, Evansville, IN 47722-0002, 812-479-2364 or toll-free 800-423-8633 Ext. 2468. *Fax:* 812-479-2028. *E-mail:* jl25@evansville.edu.

THE UNIVERSITY OF FINDLAY
Findlay, OH

Tuition & fees: $20,914	Average undergraduate aid package: $14,150

ABOUT THE INSTITUTION Independent religious, coed. Awards: associate, bachelor's, and master's degrees. 61 undergraduate majors. Total enrollment: 4,654. Undergraduates: 3,460. Freshmen: 1,045. Both federal and institutional methodology are used as a basis for awarding need-based institutional aid.

UNDERGRADUATE EXPENSES for 2004–05 *Comprehensive fee:* $28,188 includes full-time tuition ($19,996), mandatory fees ($918), and room and board ($7274). *College room only:* $3646. Full-time tuition and fees vary according to location and program. Room and board charges vary according to housing facility. *Part-time tuition:* $440 per semester hour. *Part-time fees:* $120 per term. Part-time tuition and fees vary according to location and program. *Payment plan:* Installment.

FRESHMAN FINANCIAL AID (Fall 2003) 490 applied for aid; of those 100% were deemed to have need. 84% of freshmen with need received aid; of those 20% had need fully met. *Average percent of need met:* 87% (excluding resources awarded to replace EFC). *Average financial aid package:* $15,500 (excluding resources awarded to replace EFC). 15% of all full-time freshmen had no need and received non-need-based gift aid.

UNDERGRADUATE FINANCIAL AID (Fall 2003) 1,875 applied for aid; of those 98% were deemed to have need. 100% of undergraduates with need received aid; of those 19% had need fully met. *Average percent of need met:* 84% (excluding resources awarded to replace EFC). *Average financial aid package:* $14,150 (excluding resources awarded to replace EFC). 16% of all full-time undergraduates had no need and received non-need-based gift aid.

GIFT AID (NEED-BASED) *Total amount:* $14,077,714 (17% federal, 8% state, 75% institutional). *Receiving aid:* Freshmen: 60% (412); All full-time undergraduates: 71% (1,820). *Average award:* Freshmen: $10,765; Undergraduates: $9100. *Scholarships, grants, and awards:* Federal Pell, FSEOG, state, college/university gift aid from institutional funds.

GIFT AID (NON-NEED-BASED) *Total amount:* $10,281,695 (19% state, 76% institutional, 5% external sources). *Receiving aid:* Freshmen: 10% (72); Undergraduates: 22% (565). *Average Award:* Freshmen: $8400; Undergraduates: $7200. *Scholarships, grants, and awards by category:* Academic Interests/Achievement: general academic interests/achievements. Creative Arts/Performance: music, theater/drama. Special Characteristics: children of faculty/staff. *Tuition waivers:* Full or partial for children of alumni, employees or children of employees, senior citizens. *ROTC:* Army cooperative, Air Force cooperative.

LOANS *Student loans:* $14,217,000 (43% need-based, 57% non-need-based). 85% of past graduating class borrowed through all loan programs. *Average indebtedness per student:* $17,000. *Average need-based loan:* Freshmen: $2500; Undergraduates: $4000. *Parent loans:* $2,149,244 (100% non-need-based). *Programs:* Federal Direct (Subsidized and Unsubsidized Stafford, PLUS), Perkins, college/university.

WORK-STUDY *Federal work-study:* Total amount: $325,000; 300 jobs averaging $830. *State or other work-study/employment:* Total amount: $300,000 (100% non-need-based). Part-time jobs available.

ATHLETIC AWARDS *Total amount:* $2,796,560 (100% non-need-based).

APPLYING FOR FINANCIAL AID *Required financial aid form:* FAFSA. *Financial aid deadline:* Continuous. *Notification date:* Continuous beginning 3/1.

CONTACT Mr. Arman Habegger, Director of Financial Aid, The University of Findlay, 1000 North Main Street, Findlay, OH 45840-3695, 419-434-4791 or toll-free 800-548-0932. *Fax:* 419-434-4898. *E-mail:* finaid@findlay.edu.

UNIVERSITY OF FLORIDA
Gainesville, FL

Tuition & fees (FL res): $2955	Average undergraduate aid package: $10,004

ABOUT THE INSTITUTION State-supported, coed. Awards: bachelor's, master's, doctoral, and first professional degrees. 98 undergraduate majors. Total enrollment: 47,858. Undergraduates: 33,982. Freshmen: 6,596. Federal methodology is used as a basis for awarding need-based institutional aid.

UNDERGRADUATE EXPENSES for 2004–05 *Application fee:* $30. *Tuition, state resident:* full-time $2955; part-time $98.50 per credit hour. *Tuition, nonresident:* full-time $15,827; part-time $527.58 per credit hour. *College room and board:* $6040; *room only:* $3780. Room and board charges vary according to board plan and housing facility. *Payment plan:* Tuition prepayment.

FRESHMAN FINANCIAL AID (Fall 2003) 4114 applied for aid; of those 61% were deemed to have need. 99% of freshmen with need received aid; of those 34% had need fully met. *Average percent of need met:* 85% (excluding resources awarded to replace EFC). *Average financial aid package:* $8995 (excluding resources awarded to replace EFC). 55% of all full-time freshmen had no need and received non-need-based gift aid.

UNDERGRADUATE FINANCIAL AID (Fall 2003) 16,565 applied for aid; of those 80% were deemed to have need. 99% of undergraduates with need received aid; of those 30% had need fully met. *Average percent of need met:* 84% (excluding resources awarded to replace EFC). *Average financial aid package:* $10,004 (excluding resources awarded to replace EFC). 48% of all full-time undergraduates had no need and received non-need-based gift aid.

GIFT AID (NEED-BASED) *Total amount:* $38,337,771 (63% federal, 14% state, 23% institutional). *Receiving aid:* Freshmen: 22% (1,473); All full-time undergraduates: 25% (8,364). *Average award:* Freshmen: $4333; Undergraduates: $4368. *Scholarships, grants, and awards:* Federal Pell, FSEOG, state, private, college/university gift aid from institutional funds.

GIFT AID (NON-NEED-BASED) *Total amount:* $101,396,523 (1% federal, 57% state, 16% institutional, 26% external sources). *Receiving aid:* Freshmen: 35% (2,313); Undergraduates: 28% (9,361). *Average Award:* Freshmen: $4589; Undergraduates: $3909. *Scholarships, grants, and awards by category:* Academic Interests/Achievement: agriculture, architecture, business, communication, computer science, education, engineering/technologies, general academic interests/achievements, health fields, military science. Creative Arts/Performance: art/fine arts, dance, general creative arts/performance, journalism/publications, music, performing arts, theater/drama. Special Achievements/Activities: community service, general special achievements/activities, leadership. Special Characteristics: children of faculty/staff, members of minority groups, out-of-state students. *Tuition waivers:* Full or partial for employees or children of employees, senior citizens. *ROTC:* Army, Air Force.

LOANS *Student loans:* $54,243,743 (55% need-based, 45% non-need-based). *Average need-based loan:* Freshmen: $2668; Undergraduates: $4138. *Parent loans:* $3,937,634 (100% non-need-based). *Programs:* Federal Direct (Subsidized and Unsubsidized Stafford, PLUS), Perkins, college/university.

WORK-STUDY *Federal work-study:* Total amount: $2,191,383; 1,507 jobs averaging $1454. *State or other work-study/employment:* Total amount: $7,660,235 (100% non-need-based). 4,517 part-time jobs averaging $1696.

ATHLETIC AWARDS *Total amount:* $3,102,897 (100% non-need-based).

APPLYING FOR FINANCIAL AID *Required financial aid form:* FAFSA. *Financial aid deadline (priority):* 3/15. *Notification date:* Continuous beginning 4/1.

CONTACT Ms. Karen L. Fooks, Director of Student Financial Affairs, University of Florida, S-107 Criser Hall, PO Box 114025, Gainesville, FL 32611-4025, 352-392-1271. *Fax:* 352-392-2861. *E-mail:* kfooks@ufl.edu.

UNIVERSITY OF GEORGIA
Athens, GA

Tuition & fees (GA res): $4628	Average undergraduate aid package: $7058

ABOUT THE INSTITUTION State-supported, coed. Awards: associate, bachelor's, master's, doctoral, and first professional degrees. 119 undergraduate majors. Total enrollment: 33,405. Undergraduates: 25,019. Freshmen: 4,513. Federal methodology is used as a basis for awarding need-based institutional aid.

UNDERGRADUATE EXPENSES for 2005–06 *Application fee:* $50. *Tuition, state resident:* full-time $3638; part-time $152 per credit. *Tuition, nonresident:* full-time $15,858; part-time $661 per credit. *Required fees:* full-time $990; $495 per term part-time. Full-time tuition and fees vary according to course load and reciprocity agreements. Part-time tuition and fees vary according to course load and reciprocity agreements. *College room and board:* $6376; *room only:* $3436. Room and board charges vary according to board plan and housing facility.

FRESHMAN FINANCIAL AID (Fall 2004, est.) 2684 applied for aid; of those 44% were deemed to have need. 99% of freshmen with need received aid; of those 40% had need fully met. *Average percent of need met:* 80% (excluding resources awarded to replace EFC). *Average financial aid package:* $6628 (excluding resources awarded to replace EFC). 6% of all full-time freshmen had no need and received non-need-based gift aid.

UNDERGRADUATE FINANCIAL AID (Fall 2004, est.) 10,192 applied for aid; of those 59% were deemed to have need. 98% of undergraduates with need received aid; of those 34% had need fully met. *Average percent of need met:* 74% (excluding resources awarded to replace EFC). *Average financial aid package:* $7058 (excluding resources awarded to replace EFC). 5% of all full-time undergraduates had no need and received non-need-based gift aid.

GIFT AID (NEED-BASED) *Total amount:* $26,728,690 (35% federal, 60% state, 2% institutional, 3% external sources). *Receiving aid:* Freshmen: 25% (1,107); All full-time undergraduates: 22% (5,066). *Average award:* Freshmen: $5768; Undergraduates: $5392. *Scholarships, grants, and awards:* Federal Pell, FSEOG, state, private, college/university gift aid from institutional funds.

GIFT AID (NON-NEED-BASED) *Total amount:* $59,005,534 (1% federal, 91% state, 4% institutional, 4% external sources). *Receiving aid:* Freshmen: 9% (383); Undergraduates: 5% (1,058). *Average Award:* Freshmen: $1811; Undergraduates: $1896. *Scholarships, grants, and awards by category:* Academic Interests/Achievement: 20,936 awards ($76,049,321 total): agriculture, business, education, general academic interests/achievements. Creative Arts/Performance: 140 awards ($123,075 total): music. Special Characteristics: 51 awards ($52,000 total): local/state students. *Tuition waivers:* Full or partial for senior citizens. *ROTC:* Army, Air Force.

LOANS *Student loans:* $35,316,997 (50% need-based, 50% non-need-based). 45% of past graduating class borrowed through all loan programs. *Average indebtedness per student:* $13,209. *Average need-based loan:* Freshmen: $2505; Undergraduates: $3686. *Parent loans:* $8,867,135 (21% need-based, 79% non-need-based). *Programs:* Federal Direct (Subsidized and Unsubsidized Stafford, PLUS), Perkins, state, college/university.

WORK-STUDY *Federal work-study:* Total amount: $1,068,671; 406 jobs averaging $2632.

ATHLETIC AWARDS *Total amount:* $4,819,906 (25% need-based, 75% non-need-based).

APPLYING FOR FINANCIAL AID *Required financial aid form:* FAFSA. *Financial aid deadline (priority):* 3/1. *Notification date:* Continuous beginning 3/1. Students must reply within 2 weeks of notification.

CONTACT Ms. Susan D. Little, Director of Student Affairs, University of Georgia, 220 Holmes/Hunter Academic Building, Athens, GA 30602-6114, 706-542-8208. *Fax:* 706-542-8217.

UNIVERSITY OF GREAT FALLS
Great Falls, MT

Tuition & fees: $14,000	Average undergraduate aid package: $10,938

ABOUT THE INSTITUTION Independent Roman Catholic, coed. Awards: associate, bachelor's, and master's degrees. 77 undergraduate majors. Total enrollment: 764. Undergraduates: 671. Freshmen: 119. Federal methodology is used as a basis for awarding need-based institutional aid.

UNDERGRADUATE EXPENSES for 2005–06 *Application fee:* $35. *Comprehensive fee:* $19,950 includes full-time tuition ($13,400), mandatory fees ($600), and room and board ($5950). *College room only:* $2440. Full-time tuition and fees vary according to course load, degree level, location, and reciprocity agreements. Room and board charges vary according to board plan and housing facility. *Part-time tuition:* $425 per credit. *Part-time fees:* $15 per credit. Part-time tuition and fees vary according to course load, degree level, and reciprocity agreements. *Payment plans:* Installment, deferred payment.

FRESHMAN FINANCIAL AID (Fall 2004, est.) 78 applied for aid; of those 100% were deemed to have need. 100% of freshmen with need received aid; of those 12% had need fully met. *Average percent of need met:* 70% (excluding resources awarded to replace EFC). *Average financial aid package:* $10,320 (excluding resources awarded to replace EFC). 6% of all full-time freshmen had no need and received non-need-based gift aid.

UNDERGRADUATE FINANCIAL AID (Fall 2004, est.) 367 applied for aid; of those 100% were deemed to have need. 100% of undergraduates with need received aid; of those 11% had need fully met. *Average percent of need met:* 70% (excluding resources awarded to replace EFC). *Average financial aid package:* $10,938 (excluding resources awarded to replace EFC). 5% of all full-time undergraduates had no need and received non-need-based gift aid.

GIFT AID (NEED-BASED) *Receiving aid:* Freshmen: 55% (60); All full-time undergraduates: 59% (274). *Average award:* Freshmen: $3208; Undergraduates: $3326. *Scholarships, grants, and awards:* Federal Pell, FSEOG, state, private, college/university gift aid from institutional funds.

GIFT AID (NON-NEED-BASED) *Total amount:* $1,583,069 (85% institutional, 15% external sources). *Receiving aid:* Freshmen: 67% (73); Undergraduates: 69% (321). *Average Award:* Freshmen: $3789; Undergraduates: $4456. *Scholarships, grants, and awards by category:* Academic Interests/Achievement: 311 awards ($857,000 total): biological sciences, business, communication, computer science, education, English, general academic interests/achievements, health fields, humanities, mathematics, physical sciences, premedicine, religion/biblical studies, social sciences. Creative Arts/Performance: 3 awards ($14,000 total): music. Special Achievements/Activities: 56 awards ($92,350 total): community service, general special achievements/activities, leadership, religious involvement. Special Characteristics: 99 awards ($250,164 total): children of current students, children of faculty/staff, ethnic background, first-generation college students, international students, parents of current students, religious affiliation, siblings of current students, spouses of current students. *Tuition waivers:* Full or partial for employees or children of employees, senior citizens.

LOANS *Student loans:* $2,903,593 (50% need-based, 50% non-need-based). 83% of past graduating class borrowed through all loan programs. *Average indebtedness per student:* $27,315. *Average need-based loan:* Freshmen: $2893; Undergraduates: $4016. *Parent loans:* $607,643 (45% need-based, 55% non-need-based). *Programs:* FFEL (Subsidized and Unsubsidized Stafford, PLUS), Perkins.

WORK-STUDY *Federal work-study:* Total amount: $114,481; 162 jobs averaging $2724. *State or other work-study/employment:* Part-time jobs available.

ATHLETIC AWARDS *Total amount:* $680,415 (30% need-based, 70% non-need-based).

APPLYING FOR FINANCIAL AID *Required financial aid form:* FAFSA. *Financial aid deadline:* Continuous. *Notification date:* Continuous beginning 3/1.

CONTACT Chris Steckmann, Director of Financial Aid, University of Great Falls, 1301 20th Street South, Great Falls, MT 59405, 406-791-5237 or toll-free 800-856-9544. *Fax:* 406-791-5242. *E-mail:* lhabel@ugf.edu.

UNIVERSITY OF GUAM
Mangilao, GU

CONTACT Office of Financial Aid, University of Guam, UOG Station, Mangilao, GU 96923, 671-735-2280.

UNIVERSITY OF HARTFORD
West Hartford, CT

Tuition & fees: $23,480	Average undergraduate aid package: $19,230

ABOUT THE INSTITUTION Independent, coed. Awards: associate, bachelor's, master's, and doctoral degrees and post-bachelor's and post-master's certificates. 86 undergraduate majors. Total enrollment: 7,246. Undergraduates: 5,566. Freshmen: 1,330. Federal methodology is used as a basis for awarding need-based institutional aid.

UNDERGRADUATE EXPENSES for 2004–05 *Application fee:* $35. *Comprehensive fee:* $32,476 includes full-time tuition ($22,290), mandatory fees ($1190), and room and board ($8996). *College room only:* $5548. Full-time tuition and fees vary according to program. Room and board charges vary according to board plan and housing facility. *Part-time tuition:* $320 per credit. Part-time tuition and fees vary according to course load and program. *Payment plans:* Tuition prepayment, installment.

FRESHMAN FINANCIAL AID (Fall 2003) 1116 applied for aid; of those 87% were deemed to have need. 100% of freshmen with need received aid; of those 26% had need fully met. *Average percent of need met:* 68% (excluding resources awarded to replace EFC). *Average financial aid package:* $17,211 (excluding resources awarded to replace EFC). 7% of all full-time freshmen had no need and received non-need-based gift aid.

UNDERGRADUATE FINANCIAL AID (Fall 2003) 3,252 applied for aid; of those 90% were deemed to have need. 99% of undergraduates with need received aid; of those 29% had need fully met. *Average percent of need met:* 74% (excluding resources awarded to replace EFC). *Average financial aid package:* $19,230 (excluding resources awarded to replace EFC). 8% of all full-time undergraduates had no need and received non-need-based gift aid.

GIFT AID (NEED-BASED) *Total amount:* $37,134,851 (7% federal, 6% state, 85% institutional, 2% external sources). *Receiving aid:* Freshmen: 56% (804);

All full-time undergraduates: 53% (2,398). *Average award:* Freshmen: $9623; Undergraduates: $10,189. *Scholarships, grants, and awards:* Federal Pell, FSEOG, state, private, college/university gift aid from institutional funds.

GIFT AID (NON-NEED-BASED) *Total amount:* $3,344,841 (96% institutional, 4% external sources). *Receiving aid:* Freshmen: 24% (347); Undergraduates: 23% (1,037). *Average Award:* Freshmen: $9183; Undergraduates: $8302. *Scholarships, grants, and awards by category: Academic Interests/Achievement:* 3,141 awards ($15,900,207 total): general academic interests/achievements, health fields, premedicine. *Creative Arts/Performance:* 535 awards ($4,735,860 total): art/fine arts, dance, music, performing arts, theater/drama. *Special Achievements/Activities:* community service. *Special Characteristics:* adult students, children of current students, children of faculty/staff, children of union members/company employees, children with a deceased or disabled parent, ethnic background, first-generation college students, handicapped students, international students, local/state students, members of minority groups, parents of current students, previous college experience, religious affiliation, siblings of current students, twins. *Tuition waivers:* Full or partial for employees or children of employees, senior citizens. *ROTC:* Army cooperative, Air Force cooperative.

LOANS *Student loans:* $25,869,599 (91% need-based, 9% non-need-based). 67% of past graduating class borrowed through all loan programs. *Average indebtedness per student:* $24,878. *Average need-based loan:* Freshmen: $3788; Undergraduates: $5185. *Parent loans:* $9,864,611 (100% need-based). *Programs:* FFEL (Subsidized and Unsubsidized Stafford, PLUS), Perkins.

WORK-STUDY *Federal work-study:* Total amount: $488,257; 400 jobs averaging $1554. *State or other work-study/employment:* Total amount: $792,225 (79% need-based, 21% non-need-based). 89 part-time jobs averaging $8901.

ATHLETIC AWARDS *Total amount:* $2,971,983 (35% need-based, 65% non-need-based).

APPLYING FOR FINANCIAL AID *Required financial aid form:* FAFSA. *Financial aid deadline (priority):* 2/1. *Notification date:* Continuous beginning 3/1. Students must reply by 5/1.

CONTACT University of Hartford, Office of Admission and Student Financial Assistance, University of Hartford, 200 Bloomfield Avenue, West Hartford, CT 06117-1599, 860-768-4296 or toll-free 800-947-4303. *Fax:* 860-768-4961. *E-mail:* finaid@hartford.edu.

UNIVERSITY OF HAWAII AT HILO
Hilo, HI

Tuition & fees (HI res): $2604	Average undergraduate aid package: $6647

ABOUT THE INSTITUTION State-supported, coed. Awards: bachelor's and master's degrees and post-bachelor's certificates. 29 undergraduate majors. Total enrollment: 3,288. Undergraduates: 3,081. Federal methodology is used as a basis for awarding need-based institutional aid.

UNDERGRADUATE EXPENSES for 2005–06 *Application fee:* $40. *Tuition, state resident:* full-time $2472; part-time $103 per credit hour. *Tuition, nonresident:* full-time $8040; part-time $335 per credit hour. *College room and board:* $5374; *room only:* $2774.

GIFT AID (NEED-BASED) *Total amount:* $3,810,521 (96% federal, 1% state, 3% institutional). *Receiving aid:* Freshmen: 32% (141); All full-time undergraduates: 40% (1,041). *Average award:* Freshmen: $3124; Undergraduates: $3713. *Scholarships, grants, and awards:* Federal Pell, FSEOG, state, private, college/university gift aid from institutional funds.

GIFT AID (NON-NEED-BASED) *Total amount:* $3,340,840 (10% institutional, 90% external sources). *Receiving aid:* Freshmen: 16% (70); Undergraduates: 12% (309). *Average Award:* Freshmen: $833; Undergraduates: $1266. *Scholarships, grants, and awards by category: Academic Interests/Achievement:* 21 awards ($16,500 total): agriculture, business, computer science, English, general academic interests/achievements, health fields, social sciences. *Creative Arts/Performance:* 1 award ($250 total): art/fine arts, music, performing arts, theater/drama. *Special Achievements/Activities:* 5 awards ($3000 total): community service, leadership.

LOANS *Student loans:* $6,716,408 (59% need-based, 41% non-need-based). 38% of past graduating class borrowed through all loan programs. *Average indebtedness per student:* $11,210. *Average need-based loan:* Freshmen: $2046; Undergraduates: $2135. *Parent loans:* $524,404 (100% non-need-based). *Programs:* FFEL (Subsidized and Unsubsidized Stafford, PLUS), Perkins, state.

ATHLETIC AWARDS *Total amount:* $64,681 (100% non-need-based).

APPLYING FOR FINANCIAL AID *Required financial aid form:* FAFSA. *Financial aid deadline (priority):* 3/1. *Notification date:* Continuous beginning 4/1. Students must reply within 3 weeks of notification.

CONTACT Financial Aid Coordinator, University of Hawaii at Hilo, 200 West Kawili Street, Hilo, HI 96720-4091, 808-974-7324 or toll-free 808-974-7414 (in-state), 800-897-4456 (out-of-state). *Fax:* 808-933-0861.

UNIVERSITY OF HAWAII AT MANOA
Honolulu, HI

Tuition & fees (HI res): $3504	Average undergraduate aid package: $5860

ABOUT THE INSTITUTION State-supported, coed. Awards: bachelor's, master's, doctoral, and first professional degrees and post-bachelor's certificates. 102 undergraduate majors. Total enrollment: 20,549. Undergraduates: 14,251. Freshmen: 2,019. Federal methodology is used as a basis for awarding need-based institutional aid.

UNDERGRADUATE EXPENSES for 2004–05 *Application fee:* $50. *Tuition, state resident:* full-time $3504; part-time $146 per credit hour. *Tuition, nonresident:* full-time $9984; part-time $416 per credit hour. Full-time tuition and fees vary according to class time, course load, and program. Part-time tuition and fees vary according to class time, course load, and program. *College room and board:* $5942; *room only:* $3498. Room and board charges vary according to board plan and housing facility.

FRESHMAN FINANCIAL AID (Fall 2003) 1191 applied for aid; of those 53% were deemed to have need. 93% of freshmen with need received aid; of those 26% had need fully met. *Average percent of need met:* 66% (excluding resources awarded to replace EFC). *Average financial aid package:* $5099 (excluding resources awarded to replace EFC). 11% of all full-time freshmen had no need and received non-need-based gift aid.

UNDERGRADUATE FINANCIAL AID (Fall 2003) 6,362 applied for aid; of those 61% were deemed to have need. 96% of undergraduates with need received aid; of those 32% had need fully met. *Average percent of need met:* 71% (excluding resources awarded to replace EFC). *Average financial aid package:* $5860 (excluding resources awarded to replace EFC). 9% of all full-time undergraduates had no need and received non-need-based gift aid.

GIFT AID (NEED-BASED) *Total amount:* $9,770,899 (89% federal, 1% state, 5% institutional, 5% external sources). *Receiving aid:* Freshmen: 26% (468); All full-time undergraduates: 26% (3,019). *Average award:* Freshmen: $3508; Undergraduates: $3444. *Scholarships, grants, and awards:* Federal Pell, FSEOG, state, private, college/university gift aid from institutional funds, Federal Nursing.

GIFT AID (NON-NEED-BASED) *Total amount:* $3,262,819 (12% institutional, 88% external sources). *Receiving aid:* Freshmen: 6% (113); Undergraduates: 5% (624). *Average Award:* Freshmen: $2402; Undergraduates: $2741. *Scholarships, grants, and awards by category: Academic Interests/Achievement:* general academic interests/achievements. *Creative Arts/Performance:* art/fine arts, dance, journalism/publications, music, performing arts, theater/drama. *Tuition waivers:* Full or partial for minority students, employees or children of employees. *ROTC:* Army, Air Force.

LOANS *Student loans:* $17,143,095 (60% need-based, 40% non-need-based). 21% of past graduating class borrowed through all loan programs. *Average indebtedness per student:* $5379. *Average need-based loan:* Freshmen: $2398; Undergraduates: $3465. *Parent loans:* $5,420,078 (100% non-need-based). *Programs:* FFEL (Subsidized and Unsubsidized Stafford, PLUS), Perkins, Federal Nursing, state, college/university.

WORK-STUDY *Federal work-study:* Total amount: $474,094; 280 jobs averaging $1693.

ATHLETIC AWARDS *Total amount:* $3,433,387 (1% need-based, 99% non-need-based).

APPLYING FOR FINANCIAL AID *Required financial aid forms:* FAFSA, institution's own form. *Financial aid deadline (priority):* 3/1. *Notification date:* Continuous beginning 3/28. Students must reply within 2 weeks of notification.

CONTACT Ms. Gail C. Koki, Director of Financial Aid Services, University of Hawaii at Manoa, 2600 Campus Road, Suite 112, Honolulu, HI 96822, 808-956-7251 or toll-free 800-823-9771. *Fax:* 808-956-3985. *E-mail:* finaid@hawaii.edu.

UNIVERSITY OF HAWAII–WEST OAHU
Pearl City, HI

ABOUT THE INSTITUTION State-supported, coed. Awards: bachelor's degrees. 18 undergraduate majors. Total enrollment: 831. Undergraduates: 831.

GIFT AID (NEED-BASED) *Scholarships, grants, and awards:* Federal Pell, FSEOG, state, college/university gift aid from institutional funds.

GIFT AID (NON-NEED-BASED) *Scholarships, grants, and awards by category: Academic Interests/Achievement:* general academic interests/achievements. *Special Achievements/Activities:* general special achievements/activities.

LOANS *Programs:* FFEL (Subsidized and Unsubsidized Stafford, PLUS).

APPLYING FOR FINANCIAL AID *Required financial aid forms:* FAFSA, institution's own form.

CONTACT Student Services Office, University of Hawaii–West Oahu, 96-129 Ala Ike, Pearl City, HI 96782-3366, 808-454-4700 or toll-free 808-454 Ext. 4700 (in-state). *Fax:* 808-453-6075.

UNIVERSITY OF HOUSTON
Houston, TX

CONTACT Financial Aid Office, University of Houston, 4800 Calhoun Road, Houston, TX 77204-2160, 713-743-1010. *Fax:* 713-743-9098.

UNIVERSITY OF HOUSTON–CLEAR LAKE
Houston, TX

ABOUT THE INSTITUTION State-supported, coed. Awards: bachelor's and master's degrees. 50 undergraduate majors. Total enrollment: 7,785. Undergraduates: 4,017. Entering class: .

GIFT AID (NEED-BASED) *Scholarships, grants, and awards:* Federal Pell, FSEOG, state, college/university gift aid from institutional funds.

GIFT AID (NON-NEED-BASED) *Scholarships, grants, and awards by category: Academic Interests/Achievement:* biological sciences, business, computer science, education, humanities, mathematics, social sciences. *Special Achievements/Activities:* community service, general special achievements/activities, leadership. *Special Characteristics:* veterans, veterans' children.

LOANS *Programs:* FFEL (Subsidized and Unsubsidized Stafford, PLUS), Perkins, state.

WORK-STUDY *Federal work-study:* Total amount: $69,945; 58 jobs available. *State or other work-study/employment:* Total amount: $7386 (77% need-based, 23% non-need-based). 5 part-time jobs available.

APPLYING FOR FINANCIAL AID *Required financial aid forms:* FAFSA, institution's own form.

CONTACT Lynda McKendree, Director of Financial Aid and Veterans' Affairs, University of Houston–Clear Lake, 2700 Bay Area Boulevard, Houston, TX 77058-1098, 281-283-2485. *Fax:* 281-283-2502. *E-mail:* mckendree@cl.uh.edu.

UNIVERSITY OF HOUSTON–DOWNTOWN
Houston, TX

Tuition & fees (TX res): $3934	Average undergraduate aid package: $4371

ABOUT THE INSTITUTION State-supported, coed. Awards: bachelor's and master's degrees. 28 undergraduate majors. Total enrollment: 11,408. Undergraduates: 11,261. Freshmen: 1,113. Federal methodology is used as a basis for awarding need-based institutional aid.

UNDERGRADUATE EXPENSES for 2004–05 *Application fee:* $25. *Tuition, state resident:* full-time $3170; part-time $106 per credit. *Tuition, nonresident:* full-time $9362; part-time $364 per credit. *Required fees:* full-time $764; $23 per credit or $37 per term part-time. *Payment plan:* Installment.

FRESHMAN FINANCIAL AID (Fall 2003) 751 applied for aid; of those 91% were deemed to have need. 89% of freshmen with need received aid; of those 7% had need fully met. *Average percent of need met:* 46% (excluding resources awarded to replace EFC). *Average financial aid package:* $4225 (excluding resources awarded to replace EFC). 17% of all full-time freshmen had no need and received non-need-based gift aid.

UNDERGRADUATE FINANCIAL AID (Fall 2003) 3,193 applied for aid; of those 89% were deemed to have need. 88% of undergraduates with need received aid; of those 14% had need fully met. *Average percent of need met:* 50% (excluding resources awarded to replace EFC). *Average financial aid package:* $4371 (excluding resources awarded to replace EFC). 8% of all full-time undergraduates had no need and received non-need-based gift aid.

GIFT AID (NEED-BASED) *Total amount:* $14,889,187 (69% federal, 14% state, 13% institutional, 4% external sources). *Receiving aid:* Freshmen: 52% (558); All full-time undergraduates: 37% (2,075). *Average award:* Freshmen: $3763;

Undergraduates: $3657. *Scholarships, grants, and awards:* Federal Pell, FSEOG, state, private, college/university gift aid from institutional funds.

GIFT AID (NON-NEED-BASED) *Total amount:* $1,412,233 (1% federal, 7% state, 64% institutional, 28% external sources). *Receiving aid:* Freshmen: 1% (8); Undergraduates: 1% (54). *Average Award:* Freshmen: $2194; Undergraduates: $3935. *Scholarships, grants, and awards by category: Academic Interests/Achievement:* general academic interests/achievements. *Special Achievements/Activities:* community service, general special achievements/activities, leadership. *Special Characteristics:* general special characteristics. *Tuition waivers:* Full or partial for senior citizens. *ROTC:* Army cooperative.

LOANS *Student loans:* $16,898,050 (69% need-based, 31% non-need-based). 43% of past graduating class borrowed through all loan programs. *Average indebtedness per student:* $10,372. *Average need-based loan:* Freshmen: $1814; Undergraduates: $2449. *Parent loans:* $80,937 (27% need-based, 73% non-need-based). *Programs:* FFEL (Subsidized and Unsubsidized Stafford, PLUS), state.

WORK-STUDY *Federal work-study:* Total amount: $397,300; 209 jobs averaging $1944. *State or other work-study/employment:* Total amount: $17,486 (100% need-based). 11 part-time jobs averaging $1592.

APPLYING FOR FINANCIAL AID *Required financial aid forms:* FAFSA, institution's own form. *Financial aid deadline (priority):* 4/1. *Notification date:* Continuous beginning 6/1. Students must reply within 4 weeks of notification.

CONTACT Office of Scholarships and Financial Aid, University of Houston–Downtown, One Main Street, Suite 330 South, Houston, TX 77002-1001, 713-221-8041. *Fax:* 713-221-8468. *E-mail:* uhd.finaid@dt.uh.edu.

UNIVERSITY OF HOUSTON–VICTORIA
Victoria, TX

Tuition & fees (TX res): $4290	Average undergraduate aid package: $6803

ABOUT THE INSTITUTION State-supported, coed. Awards: bachelor's and master's degrees. 10 undergraduate majors. Total enrollment: 2,418. Undergraduates: 1,208. Federal methodology is used as a basis for awarding need-based institutional aid.

UNDERGRADUATE EXPENSES for 2004–05 *Tuition, state resident:* full-time $4290; part-time $143 per semester hour. *Tuition, nonresident:* full-time $13,501; part-time $445 per semester hour. Full-time tuition and fees vary according to course load. Part-time tuition and fees vary according to course load. *Payment plan:* Installment.

UNDERGRADUATE FINANCIAL AID (Fall 2003) 440 applied for aid; of those 52% were deemed to have need. 96% of undergraduates with need received aid; of those 3% had need fully met. *Average percent of need met:* 57% (excluding resources awarded to replace EFC). *Average financial aid package:* $6803 (excluding resources awarded to replace EFC). 8% of all full-time undergraduates had no need and received non-need-based gift aid.

GIFT AID (NEED-BASED) *Total amount:* $2,023,791 (55% federal, 17% state, 14% institutional, 14% external sources). *Receiving aid:* All full-time undergraduates: 35% (202). *Average award:* Undergraduates: $3920. *Scholarships, grants, and awards:* Federal Pell, FSEOG, state, private, college/university gift aid from institutional funds.

GIFT AID (NON-NEED-BASED) *Total amount:* $218,086 (2% state, 61% institutional, 37% external sources). *Receiving aid:* Undergraduates: 1% (5). *Average Award:* Undergraduates: $3484. *Scholarships, grants, and awards by category: Academic Interests/Achievement:* 186 awards ($144,219 total): biological sciences, business, communication, computer science, education, general academic interests/achievements, humanities, mathematics, social sciences. *Special Achievements/Activities:* 2 awards ($2000 total): community service, leadership, memberships. *Special Characteristics:* 1 award ($500 total): first-generation college students. *Tuition waivers:* Full or partial for senior citizens.

LOANS *Student loans:* $3,281,906 (76% need-based, 24% non-need-based). 57% of past graduating class borrowed through all loan programs. *Average indebtedness per student:* $20,694. *Average need-based loan:* Undergraduates: $4137. *Parent loans:* $7688 (42% need-based, 58% non-need-based). *Programs:* FFEL (Subsidized and Unsubsidized Stafford, PLUS), state.

WORK-STUDY *Federal work-study:* Total amount: $38,218; 25 jobs averaging $1714. *State or other work-study/employment:* Total amount: $11,244 (81% need-based, 19% non-need-based). 6 part-time jobs averaging $1874.

APPLYING FOR FINANCIAL AID *Required financial aid forms:* FAFSA, institution's own form. *Financial aid deadline (priority):* 4/15. *Notification date:* Continuous beginning 5/20. Students must reply within 3 weeks of notification.

CONTACT Carolyn Mallory, Financial Aid Director, University of Houston–Victoria, 3007 North Ben Wilson, Victoria, TX 77901-5731, 361-570-4131 or toll-free 877-940-4848. *Fax:* 361-570-4132. *E-mail:* malloryc@uhv.edu.

UNIVERSITY OF IDAHO
Moscow, ID

Tuition & fees (ID res): $3632	Average undergraduate aid package: $9177

ABOUT THE INSTITUTION State-supported, coed. Awards: bachelor's, master's, doctoral, and first professional degrees and post-master's certificates. 109 undergraduate majors. Total enrollment: 12,824. Undergraduates: 9,550. Freshmen: 1,649. Federal methodology is used as a basis for awarding need-based institutional aid.

UNDERGRADUATE EXPENSES for 2004–05 *Application fee:* $40. *Tuition, state resident:* full-time $0. *Tuition, nonresident:* full-time $8020; part-time $123 per credit. *Required fees:* full-time $3632; $178 per credit. Full-time tuition and fees vary according to degree level and program. Part-time tuition and fees vary according to course load, degree level, and program. *College room and board:* $5034. Room and board charges vary according to board plan and housing facility. *Payment plans:* Installment, deferred payment.

FRESHMAN FINANCIAL AID (Fall 2003) 1302 applied for aid; of those 70% were deemed to have need. 99% of freshmen with need received aid; of those 32% had need fully met. *Average percent of need met:* 81% (excluding resources awarded to replace EFC). *Average financial aid package:* $7983 (excluding resources awarded to replace EFC). 38% of all full-time freshmen had no need and received non-need-based gift aid.

UNDERGRADUATE FINANCIAL AID (Fall 2003) 6,396 applied for aid; of those 81% were deemed to have need. 98% of undergraduates with need received aid; of those 30% had need fully met. *Average percent of need met:* 79% (excluding resources awarded to replace EFC). *Average financial aid package:* $9177 (excluding resources awarded to replace EFC). 26% of all full-time undergraduates had no need and received non-need-based gift aid.

GIFT AID (NEED-BASED) *Total amount:* $11,765,392 (86% federal, 2% state, 12% institutional). *Receiving aid:* Freshmen: 38% (609); All full-time undergraduates: 43% (3,644). *Average award:* Freshmen: $2997; Undergraduates: $2991. *Scholarships, grants, and awards:* Federal Pell, FSEOG, state, private, college/university gift aid from institutional funds.

GIFT AID (NON-NEED-BASED) *Total amount:* $7,890,220 (2% state, 84% institutional, 14% external sources). *Receiving aid:* Freshmen: 52% (828); Undergraduates: 44% (3,693). *Average Award:* Freshmen: $3327; Undergraduates: $3697. *Scholarships, grants, and awards by category: Academic Interests/Achievement:* 7,000 awards ($12,000,000 total): agriculture, architecture, biological sciences, business, communication, computer science, education, engineering/technologies, English, foreign languages, general academic interests/achievements, home economics, humanities, mathematics, military science, physical sciences, premedicine, social sciences. *Creative Arts/Performance:* 200 awards ($100,000 total): applied art and design, art/fine arts, creative writing, dance, general creative arts/performance, journalism/publications, music, performing arts, theater/drama. *Special Achievements/Activities:* 50 awards ($50,000 total): cheerleading/drum major, general special achievements/activities, junior miss, leadership, rodeo. *Special Characteristics:* 400 awards ($250,000 total): children and siblings of alumni, children of faculty/staff, ethnic background, first-generation college students, general special characteristics, handicapped students, international students, local/state students, members of minority groups, out-of-state students. *Tuition waivers:* Full or partial for minority students, children of alumni, employees or children of employees, senior citizens. *ROTC:* Army, Naval, Air Force cooperative.

LOANS *Student loans:* $33,698,580 (60% need-based, 40% non-need-based). 69% of past graduating class borrowed through all loan programs. *Average indebtedness per student:* $20,112. *Average need-based loan:* Freshmen: $3400; Undergraduates: $5806. *Parent loans:* $1,875,430 (100% non-need-based). *Programs:* Federal Direct (Subsidized and Unsubsidized Stafford, PLUS), Perkins, college/university.

WORK-STUDY *Federal work-study:* Total amount: $806,998; 498 jobs averaging $1483. *State or other work-study/employment:* Total amount: $406,275 (100% need-based). 231 part-time jobs averaging $1757.

ATHLETIC AWARDS *Total amount:* $2,892,206 (100% non-need-based).

APPLYING FOR FINANCIAL AID *Required financial aid form:* FAFSA. *Financial aid deadline (priority):* 2/15. *Notification date:* Continuous beginning 3/30. Students must reply within 3 weeks of notification.

CONTACT Mr. Dan Davenport, Director of Admissions and Financial Aid, University of Idaho, Financial Aid Office, Moscow, ID 83844-4291, 208-885-6312 or toll-free 888-884-3246. *Fax:* 208-885-5592. *E-mail:* dand@uidaho.edu.

UNIVERSITY OF ILLINOIS AT CHICAGO
Chicago, IL

Tuition & fees (IL res): $8502	Average undergraduate aid package: $11,750

ABOUT THE INSTITUTION State-supported, coed. Awards: bachelor's, master's, doctoral, and first professional degrees and first professional certificates. 77 undergraduate majors. Total enrollment: 24,810. Undergraduates: 15,457. Freshmen: 2,716. Federal methodology is used as a basis for awarding need-based institutional aid.

UNDERGRADUATE EXPENSES for 2005–06 *Application fee:* $40. *Tuition, state resident:* full-time $6194. *Tuition, nonresident:* full-time $18,584. *College room and board:* $7160. *Payment plan:* Installment.

FRESHMAN FINANCIAL AID (Fall 2003) 2326 applied for aid; of those 73% were deemed to have need. 95% of freshmen with need received aid; of those 54% had need fully met. *Average percent of need met:* 89% (excluding resources awarded to replace EFC). *Average financial aid package:* $11,550 (excluding resources awarded to replace EFC). 9% of all full-time freshmen had no need and received non-need-based gift aid.

UNDERGRADUATE FINANCIAL AID (Fall 2003) 10,151 applied for aid; of those 79% were deemed to have need. 96% of undergraduates with need received aid; of those 52% had need fully met. *Average percent of need met:* 89% (excluding resources awarded to replace EFC). *Average financial aid package:* $11,750 (excluding resources awarded to replace EFC). 7% of all full-time undergraduates had no need and received non-need-based gift aid.

GIFT AID (NEED-BASED) *Total amount:* $48,420,741 (32% federal, 45% state, 21% institutional, 2% external sources). *Receiving aid:* Freshmen: 43% (1,282); All full-time undergraduates: 44% (6,258). *Average award:* Freshmen: $7492; Undergraduates: $7059. *Scholarships, grants, and awards:* Federal Pell, FSEOG, state, private, college/university gift aid from institutional funds.

GIFT AID (NON-NEED-BASED) *Total amount:* $1,505,882 (3% federal, 62% state, 32% institutional, 3% external sources). *Receiving aid:* Freshmen: 14% (416); Undergraduates: 9% (1,313). *Average Award:* Freshmen: $2397; Undergraduates: $3060. *Scholarships, grants, and awards by category: Academic Interests/Achievement:* 170 awards ($478,951 total): architecture, general academic interests/achievements. *Creative Arts/Performance:* 125 awards ($303,998 total): applied art and design, art/fine arts, music, performing arts, theater/drama. *Special Achievements/Activities:* 107 awards ($2,071,011 total): general special achievements/activities. *Special Characteristics:* 634 awards ($2,255,920 total): children of faculty/staff, general special characteristics, members of minority groups, veterans, veterans' children. *Tuition waivers:* Full or partial for employees or children of employees, senior citizens. *ROTC:* Army, Naval cooperative, Air Force cooperative.

LOANS *Student loans:* $27,877,074 (99% need-based, 1% non-need-based). 45% of past graduating class borrowed through all loan programs. *Average indebtedness per student:* $17,000. *Average need-based loan:* Freshmen: $2917; Undergraduates: $4069. *Parent loans:* $2,582,590 (61% need-based, 39% non-need-based). *Programs:* Federal Direct (Subsidized and Unsubsidized Stafford, PLUS), Perkins, Federal Nursing, college/university.

WORK-STUDY *Federal work-study:* Total amount: $879,142; 514 jobs averaging $1700. *State or other work-study/employment:* Total amount: $6,895,801 (100% non-need-based). 2,635 part-time jobs averaging $2600.

ATHLETIC AWARDS *Total amount:* $2,071,011 (35% need-based, 65% non-need-based).

APPLYING FOR FINANCIAL AID *Required financial aid form:* FAFSA. *Financial aid deadline (priority):* 3/1. *Notification date:* Continuous beginning 4/1. Students must reply within 2 weeks of notification.

CONTACT Ms. Agnes Roche, Associate Director of Financial Aid, University of Illinois at Chicago, 1200 West Harrison, M/C 334, Chicago, IL 60607-7128, 312-996-5563. *Fax:* 312-996-3385. *E-mail:* aroche@uic.edu.

UNIVERSITY OF ILLINOIS AT SPRINGFIELD
Springfield, IL

Tuition & fees (IL res): $4962	Average undergraduate aid package: $7529

ABOUT THE INSTITUTION State-supported, coed. Awards: bachelor's, master's, and doctoral degrees and post-bachelor's and post-master's certificates. 27

undergraduate majors. Total enrollment: 4,396. Undergraduates: 2,507. Freshmen: 90. Federal methodology is used as a basis for awarding need-based institutional aid.

UNDERGRADUATE EXPENSES for 2004–05 *Application fee:* $40. *Tuition, state resident:* full-time $3728; part-time $125 per credit. *Tuition, nonresident:* full-time $11,183; part-time $373 per credit. *Required fees:* full-time $1234; $617 per term part-time. Full-time tuition and fees vary according to program. *College room and board: room only:* $2878. Room and board charges vary according to housing facility. *Payment plans:* Guaranteed tuition, installment.

GIFT AID (NEED-BASED) *Total amount:* $3,612,623 (48% federal, 43% state, 9% institutional). *Receiving aid:* Freshmen: 23% (27); All full-time undergraduates: 39% (569). *Average award:* Freshmen: $4927; Undergraduates: $4840. *Scholarships, grants, and awards:* Federal Pell, FSEOG, state, private, college/university gift aid from institutional funds.

GIFT AID (NON-NEED-BASED) *Total amount:* $1,828,932 (1% federal, 43% state, 47% institutional, 9% external sources). *Receiving aid:* Freshmen: 66% (77); Undergraduates: 20% (300). *Average Award:* Freshmen: $2885; Undergraduates: $3012. *Scholarships, grants, and awards by category: Academic Interests/Achievement:* 534 awards ($1,170,776 total): agriculture, biological sciences, business, communication, computer science, education, engineering/technologies, English, foreign languages, general academic interests/achievements, health fields, humanities, international studies, mathematics, social sciences. *Creative Arts/Performance:* art/fine arts, journalism/publications. *Special Achievements/Activities:* community service, leadership. *Special Characteristics:* 182 awards ($167,040 total): adult students, children of educators, children of faculty/staff, children of union members/company employees, children of workers in trades, children with a deceased or disabled parent, ethnic background, first-generation college students, general special characteristics, international students, local/state students, members of minority groups, out-of-state students, public servants, veterans, veterans' children. *Tuition waivers:* Full or partial for employees or children of employees, senior citizens.

LOANS *Student loans:* $5,975,096 (56% need-based, 44% non-need-based). 53% of past graduating class borrowed through all loan programs. *Average indebtedness per student:* $11,049. *Average need-based loan:* Freshmen: $2042; Undergraduates: $3922. *Parent loans:* $396,869 (100% non-need-based). *Programs:* FFEL (Subsidized and Unsubsidized Stafford, PLUS), Perkins, college/university.

ATHLETIC AWARDS *Total amount:* $409,465 (100% non-need-based).

APPLYING FOR FINANCIAL AID *Required financial aid forms:* FAFSA, institution's own form. *Financial aid deadline:* 11/15 (priority: 4/1). *Notification date:* Continuous. Students must reply within 3 weeks of notification.

CONTACT Mr. Gerard Joseph, Director of Financial Aid, University of Illinois at Springfield, One University Plaza, MS UHB 1042, Financial Aid Office, Room 1044, Springfield, IL 627-5407, 217-206-6724 or toll-free 888-977-4847. *Fax:* 217-206-7376. *E-mail:* finaid@uis.edu.

UNIVERSITY OF ILLINOIS AT URBANA–CHAMPAIGN
Champaign, IL

Tuition & fees (IL res): $8553	Average undergraduate aid package: $17,612

ABOUT THE INSTITUTION State-supported, coed. Awards: bachelor's, master's, doctoral, and first professional degrees and post-master's certificates. 125 undergraduate majors. Total enrollment: 40,694. Undergraduates: 29,639. Freshmen: 7,237. Federal methodology is used as a basis for awarding need-based institutional aid.

UNDERGRADUATE EXPENSES for 2005–06 *Application fee:* $40. *Tuition, state resident:* full-time $7042. *Tuition, nonresident:* full-time $21,128. Full-time tuition and fees vary according to course load, program, and student level. *College room and board:* $6710; *room only:* $2970. Room and board charges vary according to board plan and housing facility. *Payment plans:* Guaranteed tuition, installment.

FRESHMAN FINANCIAL AID (Fall 2003) 4854 applied for aid; of those 64% were deemed to have need. 95% of freshmen with need received aid; of those 54% had need fully met. *Average percent of need met:* 89% (excluding resources awarded to replace EFC). *Average financial aid package:* $16,848 (excluding resources awarded to replace EFC). 21% of all full-time freshmen had no need and received non-need-based gift aid.

UNDERGRADUATE FINANCIAL AID (Fall 2003) 16,416 applied for aid; of those 72% were deemed to have need. 96% of undergraduates with need received aid; of those 50% had need fully met. *Average percent of need met:* 89%

(excluding resources awarded to replace EFC). *Average financial aid package:* $17,612 (excluding resources awarded to replace EFC). 13% of all full-time undergraduates had no need and received non-need-based gift aid.

GIFT AID (NEED-BASED) *Total amount:* $57,273,422 (26% federal, 42% state, 24% institutional, 8% external sources). *Receiving aid:* Freshmen: 27% (1,798); All full-time undergraduates: 27% (7,467). *Average award:* Freshmen: $13,190; Undergraduates: $12,433. *Scholarships, grants, and awards:* Federal Pell, FSEOG, state, private, college/university gift aid from institutional funds, United Negro College Fund.

GIFT AID (NON-NEED-BASED) *Total amount:* $9,556,702 (2% federal, 19% state, 41% institutional, 38% external sources). *Receiving aid:* Freshmen: 29% (1,947); Undergraduates: 19% (5,377). *Average Award:* Freshmen: $5958; Undergraduates: $6634. *Tuition waivers:* Full or partial for employees or children of employees, senior citizens. *ROTC:* Army, Naval, Air Force.

LOANS *Student loans:* $48,921,024 (100% need-based). 56% of past graduating class borrowed through all loan programs. *Average indebtedness per student:* $15,100. *Average need-based loan:* Freshmen: $6264; Undergraduates: $7827. *Parent loans:* $27,457,089 (54% need-based, 46% non-need-based). *Programs:* Federal Direct (Subsidized and Unsubsidized Stafford, PLUS), Perkins, college/university, alternative loans.

WORK-STUDY *Federal work-study:* Total amount: $836,242; 1,702 jobs averaging $1421. *State or other work-study/employment:* Total amount: $16,668,397 (100% non-need-based). Part-time jobs available.

ATHLETIC AWARDS *Total amount:* $5,320,824 (26% need-based, 74% non-need-based).

APPLYING FOR FINANCIAL AID *Required financial aid form:* FAFSA. *Financial aid deadline (priority):* 3/15. *Notification date:* 3/15.

CONTACT Daniel Mann, Director of Student Financial Aid, University of Illinois at Urbana–Champaign, Student Services Arcade Building, 620 East John Street, Champaign, IL 61820-5711, 217-333-0100.

UNIVERSITY OF INDIANAPOLIS
Indianapolis, IN

Tuition & fees: $17,200	Average undergraduate aid package: $15,547

ABOUT THE INSTITUTION Independent religious, coed. Awards: associate, bachelor's, master's, and doctoral degrees. 69 undergraduate majors. Total enrollment: 4,188. Undergraduates: 3,145. Freshmen: 720. Federal methodology is used as a basis for awarding need-based institutional aid.

UNDERGRADUATE EXPENSES for 2004–05 *Application fee:* $20. *Comprehensive fee:* $23,350 includes full-time tuition ($17,200) and room and board ($6150). Full-time tuition and fees vary according to program. Room and board charges vary according to board plan and housing facility. Part-time tuition and fees vary according to class time. *Payment plan:* Deferred payment.

FRESHMAN FINANCIAL AID (Fall 2003) 556 applied for aid; of those 88% were deemed to have need. 100% of freshmen with need received aid; of those 27% had need fully met. *Average percent of need met:* 79% (excluding resources awarded to replace EFC). *Average financial aid package:* $14,673 (excluding resources awarded to replace EFC). 12% of all full-time freshmen had no need and received non-need-based gift aid.

UNDERGRADUATE FINANCIAL AID (Fall 2003) 1,288 applied for aid; of those 91% were deemed to have need. 99% of undergraduates with need received aid; of those 35% had need fully met. *Average percent of need met:* 85% (excluding resources awarded to replace EFC). *Average financial aid package:* $15,547 (excluding resources awarded to replace EFC). 11% of all full-time undergraduates had no need and received non-need-based gift aid.

GIFT AID (NEED-BASED) *Total amount:* $7,961,516 (32% federal, 60% state, 8% institutional). *Receiving aid:* Freshmen: 70% (425); All full-time undergraduates: 66% (1,028). *Average award:* Freshmen: $7502; Undergraduates: $8497. *Scholarships, grants, and awards:* Federal Pell, FSEOG, state, private, college/university gift aid from institutional funds.

GIFT AID (NON-NEED-BASED) *Total amount:* $9,724,572 (98% institutional, 2% external sources). *Receiving aid:* Freshmen: 77% (470); Undergraduates: 69% (1,068). *Average Award:* Freshmen: $7568; Undergraduates: $7725. *Scholarships, grants, and awards by category: Academic Interests/Achievement:* 1,277 awards ($6,021,362 total): business, communication, general academic interests/achievements, health fields, physical sciences, religion/biblical studies. *Creative Arts/Performance:* 158 awards ($509,376 total): art/fine arts, music, theater/drama. *Special Achievements/Activities:* 159 awards ($347,143 total): community service, memberships. *Special Characteristics:* 461 awards ($2,673,576 total): children of faculty/staff, ethnic background, international students, out-of-state students, relatives of clergy, religious affiliation. *Tuition waivers:* Full or partial for employees or children of employees, senior citizens. *ROTC:* Army cooperative.

LOANS *Student loans:* $18,899,382 (51% need-based, 49% non-need-based). 74% of past graduating class borrowed through all loan programs. *Average indebtedness per student:* $21,200. *Average need-based loan:* Freshmen: $2988; Undergraduates: $4451. *Parent loans:* $1,808,494 (83% need-based, 17% non-need-based). *Programs:* FFEL (Subsidized and Unsubsidized Stafford, PLUS), Perkins, Federal Nursing.

WORK-STUDY *Federal work-study:* Total amount: $335,114; 281 jobs averaging $1193.

ATHLETIC AWARDS *Total amount:* $2,664,572 (100% non-need-based).

APPLYING FOR FINANCIAL AID *Required financial aid forms:* FAFSA, institution's own form. *Financial aid deadline (priority):* 3/1. *Notification date:* Continuous.

CONTACT Ms. Linda B. Handy, Director of Financial Aid, University of Indianapolis, 1400 East Hanna Avenue, Indianapolis, IN 46227-3697, 317-788-3217 or toll-free 800-232-8634 Ext. 3216. *Fax:* 317-788-6136. *E-mail:* handy@uindy.edu.

THE UNIVERSITY OF IOWA
Iowa City, IA

ABOUT THE INSTITUTION State-supported, coed. Awards: bachelor's, master's, doctoral, and first professional degrees and post-master's and first professional certificates. 144 undergraduate majors. Total enrollment: 28,442. Undergraduates: 20,135. Freshmen: 4,017.

GIFT AID (NEED-BASED) *Scholarships, grants, and awards:* Federal Pell, FSEOG, state, private, college/university gift aid from institutional funds.

GIFT AID (NON-NEED-BASED) *Scholarships, grants, and awards by category:* *Academic Interests/Achievement:* business, engineering/technologies, general academic interests/achievements. *Creative Arts/Performance:* music, performing arts, theater/drama. *Special Achievements/Activities:* general special achievements/activities. *Special Characteristics:* general special characteristics.

LOANS *Programs:* Federal Direct (Subsidized and Unsubsidized Stafford, PLUS), Perkins, Federal Nursing, college/university.

WORK-STUDY *Federal work-study:* Total amount: $2,798,944; 1,200 jobs averaging $2500. *State or other work-study/employment:* Part-time jobs available.

APPLYING FOR FINANCIAL AID *Required financial aid forms:* FAFSA, institution's own form.

CONTACT Director of Student Financial Aid, The University of Iowa, 208 Calvin Hall, Iowa City, IA 52242, 319-335-1449 or toll-free 800-553-4692.

UNIVERSITY OF JUDAISM
Bel Air, CA

ABOUT THE INSTITUTION Independent Jewish, coed. Awards: bachelor's and master's degrees. 8 undergraduate majors. Total enrollment: 41. Undergraduates: 41. Freshmen: 31.

GIFT AID (NEED-BASED) *Scholarships, grants, and awards:* Federal Pell, FSEOG, state, private, college/university gift aid from institutional funds.

GIFT AID (NON-NEED-BASED) *Scholarships, grants, and awards by category:* *Academic Interests/Achievement:* general academic interests/achievements, premedicine. *Special Achievements/Activities:* leadership.

LOANS *Programs:* FFEL (Subsidized and Unsubsidized Stafford, PLUS), alternative loans.

WORK-STUDY Federal work-study jobs available. *State or other work-study/employment:* Part-time jobs available.

APPLYING FOR FINANCIAL AID *Required financial aid forms:* FAFSA, institution's own form, parent and student income tax returns.

CONTACT Director of Financial Aid, University of Judaism, 15600 Mulholland Drive, Bel Air, CA 90077-1599, 310-476-9777 Ext. 252 or toll-free 888-853-6763. *Fax:* 310-472-2374. *E-mail:* finaid@uj.edu.

UNIVERSITY OF KANSAS
Lawrence, KS

Tuition & fees (KS res): $4737	Average undergraduate aid package: $6610

ABOUT THE INSTITUTION State-supported, coed. Awards: bachelor's, master's, doctoral, and first professional degrees and post-master's certificates (University of Kansas is a single institution with academic programs and facilities at two primary locations: Lawrence and Kansas City. Undergraduate, graduate, and

professional education are the principal missions of the Lawrence campus, with medicine and related professional education the focus of the Kansas City campus). 104 undergraduate majors. Total enrollment: 28,905. Undergraduates: 21,343. Freshmen: 4,269. Federal methodology is used as a basis for awarding need-based institutional aid.

UNDERGRADUATE EXPENSES for 2004–05 *Application fee:* $30. *Tuition, state resident:* full-time $4163; part-time $138.75 per credit hour. *Tuition, nonresident:* full-time $12,117; part-time $403.90 per credit hour. *Required fees:* full-time $574; $48 per credit hour. Full-time tuition and fees vary according to program and reciprocity agreements. Part-time tuition and fees vary according to program and reciprocity agreements. *College room and board:* $5216; *room only:* $2576. Room and board charges vary according to board plan and housing facility. *Payment plan:* Installment.

FRESHMAN FINANCIAL AID (Fall 2003) 2513 applied for aid; of those 62% were deemed to have need. 95% of freshmen with need received aid; of those 23% had need fully met. *Average percent of need met:* 62% (excluding resources awarded to replace EFC). *Average financial aid package:* $5523 (excluding resources awarded to replace EFC). 10% of all full-time freshmen had no need and received non-need-based gift aid.

UNDERGRADUATE FINANCIAL AID (Fall 2003) 9,587 applied for aid; of those 70% were deemed to have need. 96% of undergraduates with need received aid; of those 27% had need fully met. *Average percent of need met:* 70% (excluding resources awarded to replace EFC). *Average financial aid package:* $6610 (excluding resources awarded to replace EFC). 11% of all full-time undergraduates had no need and received non-need-based gift aid.

GIFT AID (NEED-BASED) *Total amount:* $17,574,676 (49% federal, 8% state, 30% institutional, 13% external sources). *Receiving aid:* Freshmen: 31% (1,247); All full-time undergraduates: 28% (5,016). *Average award:* Freshmen: $3385; Undergraduates: $3353. *Scholarships, grants, and awards:* Federal Pell, FSEOG, state, private, college/university gift aid from institutional funds.

GIFT AID (NON-NEED-BASED) *Total amount:* $6,903,663 (87% institutional, 13% external sources). *Receiving aid:* Freshmen: 1; Undergraduates: 19. *Average Award:* Freshmen: $2298; Undergraduates: $4054. *Scholarships, grants, and awards by category:* *Academic Interests/Achievement:* architecture, area/ethnic studies, biological sciences, business, communication, computer science, education, engineering/technologies, English, foreign languages, general academic interests/achievements, health fields, humanities, international studies, library science, mathematics, military science, physical sciences, premedicine, religion/biblical studies, social sciences. *Creative Arts/Performance:* applied art and design, art/fine arts, cinema/film/broadcasting, creative writing, dance, debating, general creative arts/performance, journalism/publications, music, performing arts, theater/drama. *Special Achievements/Activities:* community service, general special achievements/activities, leadership. *Special Characteristics:* adult students, children of faculty/staff, ethnic background, first-generation college students, general special characteristics, international students, local/state students, married students, members of minority groups, out-of-state students, previous college experience. *Tuition waivers:* Full or partial for employees or children of employees. *ROTC:* Army, Naval, Air Force.

LOANS *Student loans:* $39,478,559 (54% need-based, 46% non-need-based). 38% of past graduating class borrowed through all loan programs. *Average indebtedness per student:* $16,945. *Average need-based loan:* Freshmen: $2544; Undergraduates: $3602. *Parent loans:* $17,746,377 (100% need-based). *Programs:* Federal Direct (Subsidized and Unsubsidized Stafford, PLUS), Perkins, college/university.

WORK-STUDY *Federal work-study:* Total amount: $835,259; 393 jobs averaging $2148. *State or other work-study/employment:* Total amount: $438,807 (100% non-need-based). 106 part-time jobs averaging $4412.

ATHLETIC AWARDS *Total amount:* $4,163,383 (38% need-based, 62% non-need-based).

APPLYING FOR FINANCIAL AID *Required financial aid form:* FAFSA. *Financial aid deadline (priority):* 3/1. *Notification date:* Continuous beginning 4/1. Students must reply within 2 weeks of notification.

CONTACT Ms. Brenda Maigaard, Director of Student Financial Aid, University of Kansas, Office of Student Financial Aid, 50 Strong Hall, 1450 Jayhawk Boulevard, Lawrence, KS 66045-7535, 785-864-4700 or toll-free 888-686-7323 (in-state). *Fax:* 785-864-5469. *E-mail:* osfa@ku.edu.

UNIVERSITY OF KENTUCKY
Lexington, KY

ABOUT THE INSTITUTION State-supported, coed. Awards: bachelor's, master's, doctoral, and first professional degrees and post-master's certificates. 80 undergraduate majors. Total enrollment: 25,686. Undergraduates: 18,434. Freshmen: 3,961.

GIFT AID (NEED-BASED) *Scholarships, grants, and awards:* Federal Pell, FSEOG, state, private, college/university gift aid from institutional funds.

GIFT AID (NON-NEED-BASED) *Scholarships, grants, and awards by category: Academic Interests/Achievement:* agriculture, architecture, biological sciences, business, communication, education, engineering/technologies, foreign languages, general academic interests/achievements, health fields, home economics, mathematics, military science, physical sciences. *Creative Arts/Performance:* applied art and design, art/fine arts, debating, general creative arts/performance, journalism/publications, music, performing arts. *Special Achievements/Activities:* cheerleading/drum major, general special achievements/activities, leadership. *Special Characteristics:* adult students, children and siblings of alumni, children of educators, children of faculty/staff, children of public servants, children of union members/company employees, children of workers in trades, children with a deceased or disabled parent, ethnic background, first-generation college students, general special characteristics, handicapped students, international students, members of minority groups, spouses of deceased or disabled public servants, veterans, veterans' children.

LOANS *Programs:* Federal Direct (Subsidized and Unsubsidized Stafford, PLUS), Perkins, Federal Nursing, college/university.

WORK-STUDY *Federal work-study:* Total amount: $715,623; jobs available. *State or other work-study/employment:* Part-time jobs available.

APPLYING FOR FINANCIAL AID *Required financial aid form:* FAFSA.

CONTACT Ms. Lynda S. George, Director of Financial Aid, University of Kentucky, 128 Funkhouser Building, Lexington, KY 40506-0054, 606-257-3172 Ext. 241 or toll-free 800-432-0967 (in-state). *Fax:* 606-257-4398. *E-mail:* lgeorge@email.uky.edu.

UNIVERSITY OF LA VERNE
La Verne, CA

Tuition & fees: $22,800	Average undergraduate aid package: $21,604

ABOUT THE INSTITUTION Independent, coed. Awards: associate, bachelor's, master's, doctoral, and first professional degrees and post-bachelor's and post-master's certificates (also offers continuing education program with significant enrollment not reflected in profile). 53 undergraduate majors. Total enrollment: 4,021. Undergraduates: 1,650. Freshmen: 379. Federal methodology is used as a basis for awarding need-based institutional aid.

UNDERGRADUATE EXPENSES for 2005–06 *Application fee:* $50. *One-time required fee:* $110. *Comprehensive fee:* $31,910 includes full-time tuition ($22,800) and room and board ($9110). *College room only:* $4490. Full-time tuition and fees vary according to course load, degree level, location, and program. Room and board charges vary according to board plan and housing facility. *Part-time tuition:* $650 per unit. Part-time tuition and fees vary according to course load, degree level, location, and program. *Payment plans:* Installment, deferred payment.

FRESHMAN FINANCIAL AID (Fall 2004, est.) 343 applied for aid; of those 91% were deemed to have need. 100% of freshmen with need received aid; of those 15% had need fully met. *Average financial aid package:* $21,985 (excluding resources awarded to replace EFC). 13% of all full-time freshmen had no need and received non-need-based gift aid.

UNDERGRADUATE FINANCIAL AID (Fall 2004, est.) 1,363 applied for aid; of those 93% were deemed to have need. 100% of undergraduates with need received aid; of those 19% had need fully met. *Average financial aid package:* $21,604 (excluding resources awarded to replace EFC). 13% of all full-time undergraduates had no need and received non-need-based gift aid.

GIFT AID (NEED-BASED) *Total amount:* $17,817,975 (8% federal, 19% state, 72% institutional, 1% external sources). *Receiving aid:* Freshmen: 80% (300); All full-time undergraduates: 79% (1,216). *Average award:* Freshmen: $10,572; Undergraduates: $10,995. *Scholarships, grants, and awards:* Federal Pell, FSEOG, state, private, college/university gift aid from institutional funds.

GIFT AID (NON-NEED-BASED) *Total amount:* $693,672 (91% institutional, 9% external sources). *Receiving aid:* Freshmen: 78% (294); Undergraduates: 72% (1,118). *Average Award:* Freshmen: $9204; *Undergraduates:* $7716. *Scholarships, grants, and awards by category: Academic Interests/Achievement:* 978

awards ($7,015,915 total): general academic interests/achievements. *Creative Arts/Performance:* 75 awards ($436,755 total): art/fine arts, debating, journalism/publications, music, theater/drama. *Special Achievements/Activities:* 19 awards ($103,180 total): community service, leadership. *Special Characteristics:* 244 awards ($732,244 total): children and siblings of alumni, children of faculty/staff, ethnic background, first-generation college students, general special characteristics, international students, religious affiliation. *Tuition waivers:* Full or partial for employees or children of employees.

LOANS *Student loans:* $3,534,472 (85% need-based, 15% non-need-based). *Average need-based loan:* Freshmen: $2907; Undergraduates: $3442. *Parent loans:* $1,646,943 (100% non-need-based). *Programs:* FFEL (Subsidized and Unsubsidized Stafford, PLUS), Perkins, college/university, alternative loans.

WORK-STUDY *Federal work-study:* Total amount: $616,481; 752 jobs averaging $1997. *State or other work-study/employment:* Part-time jobs available.

APPLYING FOR FINANCIAL AID *Required financial aid forms:* FAFSA, state aid form. *Financial aid deadline (priority):* 3/2. *Notification date:* Continuous beginning 3/12. Students must reply by 5/1 or within 1 week of notification.

CONTACT Leatha Webster, Director of Financial Aid, University of La Verne, 1950 3rd Street, La Verne, CA 91750-4443, 909-593-3511 Ext. 4180 or toll-free 800-876-4858. *Fax:* 909-392-2751. *E-mail:* websterl@ulv.edu.

UNIVERSITY OF LOUISIANA AT LAFAYETTE
Lafayette, LA

ABOUT THE INSTITUTION State-supported, coed. Awards: bachelor's, master's, and doctoral degrees and post-master's certificates. 89 undergraduate majors. Total enrollment: 16,563. Undergraduates: 15,043. Freshmen: 2,745.

GIFT AID (NEED-BASED) *Scholarships, grants, and awards:* Federal Pell, FSEOG, state, college/university gift aid from institutional funds.

GIFT AID (NON-NEED-BASED) *Scholarships, grants, and awards by category: Academic Interests/Achievement:* general academic interests/achievements. *Creative Arts/Performance:* general creative arts/performance. *Special Achievements/Activities:* general special achievements/activities.

LOANS *Programs:* FFEL (Subsidized and Unsubsidized Stafford, PLUS), Perkins, Federal Nursing.

WORK-STUDY *Federal work-study:* Total amount: $1,036,618; 775 jobs averaging $1338. *State or other work-study/employment:* Total amount: $288,390 (100% non-need-based). 507 part-time jobs averaging $569.

APPLYING FOR FINANCIAL AID *Required financial aid form:* FAFSA.

CONTACT Cindy S. Perez, Director of Financial Aid, University of Louisiana at Lafayette, 104 East University Avenue, Lafayette, LA 70504-1206, 337-482-6497 or toll-free 800-752-6553 (in-state). *Fax:* 337-482-6502. *E-mail:* cperez@louisiana.edu.

UNIVERSITY OF LOUISIANA AT MONROE
Monroe, LA

CONTACT Roslynn Pogue, Assistant Director, Financial Aid, University of Louisiana at Monroe, 700 University Avenue, Monroe, LA 71209, 318-342-5320 or toll-free 800-372-5272 (in-state), 800-372-5127 (out-of-state). *Fax:* 318-342-3539. *E-mail:* sspogue@ulm.edu.

UNIVERSITY OF LOUISVILLE
Louisville, KY

Tuition & fees (KY res): $5532	Average undergraduate aid package: $8173

ABOUT THE INSTITUTION State-supported, coed. Awards: associate, bachelor's, master's, doctoral, and first professional degrees and post-bachelor's and post-master's certificates. 50 undergraduate majors. Total enrollment: 20,731. Undergraduates: 14,872. Freshmen: 2,358. Federal methodology is used as a basis for awarding need-based institutional aid.

UNDERGRADUATE EXPENSES for 2005–06 *Application fee:* $30. *Tuition, state resident:* full-time $5532; part-time $231 per hour. *Tuition, nonresident:* full-time $15,092; part-time $629 per hour. Full-time tuition and fees vary according to reciprocity agreements. Part-time tuition and fees vary according to course load and reciprocity agreements. *College room and board:* $6036; *room only:* $4490. Room and board charges vary according to board plan and housing facility. *Payment plan:* Installment.

FRESHMAN FINANCIAL AID (Fall 2004, est.) 1602 applied for aid; of those 83% were deemed to have need. 99% of freshmen with need received aid; of

University of Louisville

those 17% had need fully met. *Average percent of need met:* 59% (excluding resources awarded to replace EFC). *Average financial aid package:* $8235 (excluding resources awarded to replace EFC). 19% of all full-time freshmen had no need and received non-need-based gift aid.

UNDERGRADUATE FINANCIAL AID (Fall 2004, est.) 6,666 applied for aid; of those 88% were deemed to have need. 97% of undergraduates with need received aid; of those 12% had need fully met. *Average percent of need met:* 58% (excluding resources awarded to replace EFC). *Average financial aid package:* $8173 (excluding resources awarded to replace EFC). 15% of all full-time undergraduates had no need and received non-need-based gift aid.

GIFT AID (NEED-BASED) *Total amount:* $29,136,114 (35% federal, 25% state, 33% institutional, 7% external sources). *Receiving aid:* Freshmen: 54% (1,247); All full-time undergraduates: 43% (4,811). *Average award:* Freshmen: $5927; Undergraduates: $5350. *Scholarships, grants, and awards:* Federal Pell, FSEOG, state, private, college/university gift aid from institutional funds.

GIFT AID (NON-NEED-BASED) *Total amount:* $15,185,374 (35% state, 57% institutional, 8% external sources). *Receiving aid:* Freshmen: 7% (159); Undergraduates: 3% (338). *Average Award:* Freshmen: $5120; Undergraduates: $4927. *Scholarships, grants, and awards by category: Academic Interests/ Achievement:* general academic interests/achievements. *Creative Arts/ Performance:* general creative arts/performance. *Special Achievements/Activities:* general special achievements/activities, memberships. *Special Characteristics:* general special characteristics. *Tuition waivers:* Full or partial for employees or children of employees, senior citizens. *ROTC:* Army, Air Force.

LOANS *Student loans:* $25,543,611 (89% need-based, 11% non-need-based). 42% of past graduating class borrowed through all loan programs. *Average indebtedness per student:* $14,721. *Average need-based loan:* Freshmen: $2825; Undergraduates: $4230. *Parent loans:* $1,917,211 (46% need-based, 54% non-need-based). *Programs:* FFEL (Subsidized and Unsubsidized Stafford, PLUS), Perkins, Federal Nursing, college/university.

WORK-STUDY *Federal work-study:* Total amount: $1,205,675; jobs available.

ATHLETIC AWARDS *Total amount:* $4,949,433 (36% need-based, 64% non-need-based).

APPLYING FOR FINANCIAL AID *Required financial aid form:* FAFSA. *Financial aid deadline (priority):* 3/15. *Notification date:* Continuous beginning 4/1. Students must reply by 5/1.

CONTACT Ms. Patricia O. Arauz, Director of Financial Aid, University of Louisville, 2301 South Third Street, Louisville, KY 40292-0001, 502-852-6145 or toll-free 502-852-6531 (in-state), 800-334-8635 (out-of-state). *Fax:* 502-852-0182. *E-mail:* finaid@louisville.edu.

UNIVERSITY OF MAINE
Orono, ME

Tuition & fees (ME res): $6328   **Average undergraduate aid package:** $9238

ABOUT THE INSTITUTION State-supported, coed. Awards: bachelor's, master's, and doctoral degrees and post-master's certificates. 82 undergraduate majors. Total enrollment: 11,358. Undergraduates: 9,085. Freshmen: 1,667. Federal methodology is used as a basis for awarding need-based institutional aid.

UNDERGRADUATE EXPENSES for 2004–05 *Application fee:* $40. *Tuition, state resident:* full-time $5040; part-time $168 per credit hour. *Tuition, nonresident:* full-time $14,370; part-time $479 per credit hour. Full-time tuition and fees vary according to reciprocity agreements. Part-time tuition and fees vary according to reciprocity agreements. *College room and board:* $6412; *room only:* $3238. Room and board charges vary according to board plan and housing facility. *Payment plan:* Installment.

GIFT AID (NEED-BASED) *Total amount:* $19,245,637 (45% federal, 11% state, 32% institutional, 12% external sources). *Receiving aid:* Freshmen: 57% (1,178); All full-time undergraduates: 45% (3,769). *Average award:* Freshmen: $5760; Undergraduates: $4963. *Scholarships, grants, and awards:* Federal Pell, FSEOG, state, private, college/university gift aid from institutional funds.

GIFT AID (NON-NEED-BASED) *Total amount:* $3,770,787 (22% institutional, 78% external sources). *Receiving aid:* Freshmen: 4% (83); Undergraduates: 3% (269). *Average Award:* Freshmen: $4043; Undergraduates: $5374. *Scholarships, grants, and awards by category: Academic Interests/Achievement:* 786 awards ($1,980,211 total): biological sciences, business, communication, computer science, education, engineering/technologies, English, general academic interests/achievements, humanities, mathematics, military science, physical sciences, social sciences. *Creative Arts/Performance:* applied art and design, art/fine arts, creative writing, journalism/publications, music, performing arts, theater/drama. *Special Achievements/Activities:* community service, general special achievements/activities, leadership, memberships. *Special Characteristics:* children

and siblings of alumni, children of faculty/staff, children of union members/ company employees, children with a deceased or disabled parent, ethnic background, international students, local/state students, members of minority groups, out-of-state students, previous college experience, public servants, veterans, veterans' children. *Tuition waivers:* Full or partial for employees or children of employees. *ROTC:* Army, Naval.

LOANS *Student loans:* $28,389,639 (70% need-based, 30% non-need-based). 72% of past graduating class borrowed through all loan programs. *Average indebtedness per student:* $19,795. *Average need-based loan:* Freshmen: $3319; Undergraduates: $4290. *Parent loans:* $4,078,310 (100% non-need-based). *Programs:* FFEL (Subsidized and Unsubsidized Stafford, PLUS), Perkins, state, college/university.

ATHLETIC AWARDS *Total amount:* $1,333,951 (100% need-based).

APPLYING FOR FINANCIAL AID *Required financial aid form:* FAFSA. *Financial aid deadline (priority):* 3/1. *Notification date:* Continuous beginning 3/15. Students must reply by 5/1 or within 2 weeks of notification.

CONTACT Ms. Peggy L. Crawford, Director of Student Aid, University of Maine, 5781 Wingate Hall, Orono, ME 04469, 207-581-1324 or toll-free 877-486-2364. *Fax:* 207-581-3261. *E-mail:* peggy.crawford@umit.maine.edu.

THE UNIVERSITY OF MAINE AT AUGUSTA
Augusta, ME

Tuition & fees (ME res): $4695   **Average undergraduate aid package:** $7474

ABOUT THE INSTITUTION State-supported, coed. Awards: associate and bachelor's degrees and post-bachelor's certificates (also offers some graduate courses and continuing education programs with significant enrollment not reflected in profile). 26 undergraduate majors. Total enrollment: 5,538. Undergraduates: 5,538. Freshmen: 604. Federal methodology is used as a basis for awarding need-based institutional aid.

UNDERGRADUATE EXPENSES for 2004–05 *Application fee:* $40. *Tuition, state resident:* full-time $3960; part-time $132 per credit. *Tuition, nonresident:* full-time $9600; part-time $320 per credit. *Required fees:* full-time $735; $24.50 per credit hour. Full-time tuition and fees vary according to reciprocity agreements. Part-time tuition and fees vary according to reciprocity agreements. *Payment plan:* Installment.

FRESHMAN FINANCIAL AID (Fall 2004, est.) 313 applied for aid; of those 99% were deemed to have need. 95% of freshmen with need received aid; of those 12% had need fully met. *Average percent of need met:* 63% (excluding resources awarded to replace EFC). *Average financial aid package:* $5866 (excluding resources awarded to replace EFC). 9% of all full-time freshmen had no need and received non-need-based gift aid.

UNDERGRADUATE FINANCIAL AID (Fall 2004, est.) 1,483 applied for aid; of those 98% were deemed to have need. 97% of undergraduates with need received aid; of those 16% had need fully met. *Average percent of need met:* 68% (excluding resources awarded to replace EFC). *Average financial aid package:* $7474 (excluding resources awarded to replace EFC). 7% of all full-time undergraduates had no need and received non-need-based gift aid.

GIFT AID (NEED-BASED) *Total amount:* $10,495,267 (69% federal, 14% state, 5% institutional, 12% external sources). *Receiving aid:* Freshmen: 74% (260); All full-time undergraduates: 78% (1,242). *Average award:* Freshmen: $4384; Undergraduates: $4667. *Scholarships, grants, and awards:* Federal Pell, FSEOG, state, private, college/university gift aid from institutional funds.

GIFT AID (NON-NEED-BASED) *Total amount:* $395,768 (80% institutional, 20% external sources). *Receiving aid:* Freshmen: 1% (4); Undergraduates: 2% (29). *Average Award:* Freshmen: $3482; Undergraduates: $3959. *Scholarships, grants, and awards by category: Academic Interests/Achievement:* 30 awards ($33,780 total): biological sciences, business, general academic interests/achievements, mathematics. *Creative Arts/Performance:* 11 awards ($14,623 total): music. *Special Achievements/Activities:* 44 awards ($52,064 total): general special achievements/activities, leadership. *Special Characteristics:* 125 awards ($332,953 total): children of faculty/staff, ethnic background, international students, local/ state students, veterans' children. *Tuition waivers:* Full or partial for employees or children of employees, senior citizens.

LOANS *Student loans:* $10,290,981 (74% need-based, 26% non-need-based). 61% of past graduating class borrowed through all loan programs. *Average indebtedness per student:* $12,911. *Average need-based loan:* Freshmen: $2541; Undergraduates: $3512. *Parent loans:* $88,006 (100% non-need-based). *Programs:* Federal Direct (Subsidized and Unsubsidized Stafford), FFEL (Subsidized and Unsubsidized Stafford, PLUS), Perkins, Federal Nursing.

WORK-STUDY *Federal work-study:* Total amount: $363,232; 241 jobs averaging $1507.

ATHLETIC AWARDS *Total amount:* $24,455 (100% non-need-based).

APPLYING FOR FINANCIAL AID *Required financial aid form:* FAFSA. *Financial aid deadline (priority):* 3/1. *Notification date:* Continuous beginning 3/15. Students must reply by 5/1 or within 2 weeks of notification.

CONTACT Sherry McCollett, Financial Aid Counselor, The University of Maine at Augusta, 46 University Drive, Augusta, ME 04330-9410, 207-621-3455 or toll-free 877-862-1234 Ext. 3185 (in-state). *Fax:* 207-621-3116. *E-mail:* sherrym@maine.edu.

UNIVERSITY OF MAINE AT FARMINGTON
Farmington, ME

Tuition & fees (ME res): $5240	Average undergraduate aid package: $8235

ABOUT THE INSTITUTION State-supported, coed. Awards: bachelor's degrees. 40 undergraduate majors. Total enrollment: 2,349. Undergraduates: 2,349. Freshmen: 515. Federal methodology is used as a basis for awarding need-based institutional aid.

UNDERGRADUATE EXPENSES for 2004–05 *Application fee:* $40. *Tuition, state resident:* full-time $4650; part-time $155 per credit hour. *Tuition, nonresident:* full-time $11,340; part-time $378 per credit hour. *Required fees:* full-time $590; $75 per term part-time. Full-time tuition and fees vary according to course load, reciprocity agreements, and student level. Part-time tuition and fees vary according to course load, reciprocity agreements, and student level. *College room and board:* $5700; *room only:* $3048. Room and board charges vary according to board plan and housing facility. *Payment plan:* Installment.

FRESHMAN FINANCIAL AID (Fall 2003) 469 applied for aid; of those 80% were deemed to have need. 99% of freshmen with need received aid; of those 23% had need fully met. *Average percent of need met:* 74% (excluding resources awarded to replace EFC). *Average financial aid package:* $7956 (excluding resources awarded to replace EFC). 3% of all full-time freshmen had no need and received non-need-based gift aid.

UNDERGRADUATE FINANCIAL AID (Fall 2003) 1,685 applied for aid; of those 83% were deemed to have need. 99% of undergraduates with need received aid; of those 25% had need fully met. *Average percent of need met:* 76% (excluding resources awarded to replace EFC). *Average financial aid package:* $8235 (excluding resources awarded to replace EFC). 2% of all full-time undergraduates had no need and received non-need-based gift aid.

GIFT AID (NEED-BASED) *Total amount:* $4,845,512 (55% federal, 15% state, 28% institutional, 2% external sources). *Receiving aid:* Freshmen: 64% (334); All full-time undergraduates: 55% (1,136). *Average award:* Freshmen: $4546; Undergraduates: $4050. *Scholarships, grants, and awards:* Federal Pell, FSEOG, state, private, college/university gift aid from institutional funds.

GIFT AID (NON-NEED-BASED) *Total amount:* $1,658,386 (1% state, 33% institutional, 66% external sources). *Receiving aid:* Freshmen: 17% (90); Undergraduates: 13% (278). *Average Award:* Freshmen: $2193; Undergraduates: $1993. *Scholarships, grants, and awards by category: Academic Interests/Achievement:* general academic interests/achievements. *Special Characteristics:* children of faculty/staff, members of minority groups, out-of-state students, veterans' children. *Tuition waivers:* Full or partial for minority students, employees or children of employees, senior citizens.

LOANS *Student loans:* $8,343,810 (63% need-based, 37% non-need-based). 76% of past graduating class borrowed through all loan programs. *Average indebtedness per student:* $15,841. *Average need-based loan:* Freshmen: $2880; Undergraduates: $3744. *Parent loans:* $696,158 (100% non-need-based). *Programs:* FFEL (Subsidized and Unsubsidized Stafford, PLUS), Perkins, college/university, Educators For Maine Loans.

WORK-STUDY *Federal work-study:* Total amount: $531,486; 525 jobs averaging $1013. *State or other work-study/employment:* Total amount: $744,148 (100% non-need-based). 529 part-time jobs available.

APPLYING FOR FINANCIAL AID *Required financial aid form:* FAFSA. *Financial aid deadline (priority):* 3/1. *Notification date:* Continuous beginning 3/15. Students must reply within 2 weeks of notification.

CONTACT Mr. Ronald P. Milliken, Director of Financial Aid, University of Maine at Farmington, 224 Main Street, Farmington, ME 04938-1990, 207-778-7105. *Fax:* 207-788-8178. *E-mail:* milliken@maine.edu.

UNIVERSITY OF MAINE AT FORT KENT
Fort Kent, ME

Tuition & fees (ME res): $4514	Average undergraduate aid package: $4995

ABOUT THE INSTITUTION State-supported, coed. Awards: associate and bachelor's degrees. 25 undergraduate majors. Total enrollment: 1,076. Undergraduates: 1,076. Federal methodology is used as a basis for awarding need-based institutional aid.

UNDERGRADUATE EXPENSES for 2004–05 *Application fee:* $40. *Tuition, state resident:* full-time $3960; part-time $132 per credit hour. *Tuition, nonresident:* full-time $9600; part-time $320 per credit hour. *Required fees:* full-time $554; $16.50 per credit hour. Full-time tuition and fees vary according to course load. Part-time tuition and fees vary according to course load. *College room and board:* $5600; *room only:* $3460. Room and board charges vary according to board plan and housing facility. *Payment plan:* Installment.

FRESHMAN FINANCIAL AID (Fall 2004, est.) 64% of freshmen with need received aid; of those 18% had need fully met. *Average percent of need met:* 72% (excluding resources awarded to replace EFC). *Average financial aid package:* $3648 (excluding resources awarded to replace EFC). 6% of all full-time freshmen had no need and received non-need-based gift aid.

UNDERGRADUATE FINANCIAL AID (Fall 2004, est.) 553 applied for aid; of those 83% were deemed to have need. 72% of undergraduates with need received aid; of those 29% had need fully met. *Average percent of need met:* 83% (excluding resources awarded to replace EFC). *Average financial aid package:* $4995 (excluding resources awarded to replace EFC). 5% of all full-time undergraduates had no need and received non-need-based gift aid.

GIFT AID (NEED-BASED) *Total amount:* $1,394,848 (63% federal, 14% state, 8% institutional, 15% external sources). *Receiving aid:* Freshmen: 52% (88); All full-time undergraduates: 38% (290). *Average award:* Freshmen: $3561; Undergraduates: $3704. *Scholarships, grants, and awards:* Federal Pell, FSEOG, state, private, college/university gift aid from institutional funds.

GIFT AID (NON-NEED-BASED) *Total amount:* $192,213 (13% institutional, 87% external sources). *Receiving aid:* Freshmen: 4% (7); Undergraduates: 3% (20). *Average Award:* Freshmen: $2819; Undergraduates: $3600. *Scholarships, grants, and awards by category: Academic Interests/Achievement:* business, computer science, education, English, foreign languages, general academic interests/achievements, health fields, humanities, mathematics, social sciences. *Creative Arts/Performance:* general creative arts/performance, performing arts. *Special Achievements/Activities:* general special achievements/activities. *Special Characteristics:* adult students, children of faculty/staff, general special characteristics, international students, members of minority groups. *Tuition waivers:* Full or partial for employees or children of employees.

LOANS *Student loans:* $1,811,578 (60% need-based, 40% non-need-based). 81% of past graduating class borrowed through all loan programs. *Average indebtedness per student:* $10,483. *Average need-based loan:* Freshmen: $2767; Undergraduates: $3639. *Parent loans:* $148,567 (100% non-need-based). *Programs:* FFEL (Subsidized and Unsubsidized Stafford, PLUS), Perkins, state.

WORK-STUDY *Federal work-study:* Total amount: $140,363; 119 jobs averaging $1500. *State or other work-study/employment:* Total amount: $48,687 (8% need-based, 92% non-need-based). 44 part-time jobs averaging $1500.

APPLYING FOR FINANCIAL AID *Required financial aid form:* FAFSA. *Financial aid deadline (priority):* 3/1. *Notification date:* Continuous beginning 3/1.

CONTACT Ellen Cost, Director of Financial Aid, University of Maine at Fort Kent, 23 University Drive, Fort Kent, ME 04743-1292, 207-834-7606 or toll-free 888-TRY-UMFK. *Fax:* 207-834-7841. *E-mail:* ecost@maine.edu.

UNIVERSITY OF MAINE AT MACHIAS
Machias, ME

CONTACT Ms. Stephanie Larrabee, Director of Financial Aid, University of Maine at Machias, 9 O'Brien Avenue, Machias, ME 04654, 207-255-1203 or toll-free 888-GOTOUMM. *Fax:* 207-255-4864.

UNIVERSITY OF MAINE AT PRESQUE ISLE
Presque Isle, ME

Tuition & fees (ME res): $4460	Average undergraduate aid package: $6480

ABOUT THE INSTITUTION State-supported, coed. Awards: associate and bachelor's degrees. 29 undergraduate majors. Total enrollment: 1,652. Undergraduates: 1,652. Freshmen: 244. Federal methodology is used as a basis for awarding need-based institutional aid.

UNDERGRADUATE EXPENSES for 2004–05 *Application fee:* $25. *Tuition, state resident:* full-time $3960; part-time $132 per credit hour. *Tuition, nonresident:* full-time $9900; part-time $330 per credit hour. *Required fees:* full-time $500; $18 per credit hour. Full-time tuition and fees vary according to course load and reciprocity agreements. Part-time tuition and fees vary according to course load and reciprocity agreements. **College room and board:** $5114; **room only:** $2920. Room and board charges vary according to board plan. **Payment plans:** Installment, deferred payment.

FRESHMAN FINANCIAL AID (Fall 2004, est.) 226 applied for aid; of those 81% were deemed to have need. 85% of freshmen with need received aid; of those 31% had need fully met. *Average percent of need met:* 81% (excluding resources awarded to replace EFC). *Average financial aid package:* $5932 (excluding resources awarded to replace EFC). 13% of all full-time freshmen had no need and received non-need-based gift aid.

UNDERGRADUATE FINANCIAL AID (Fall 2004, est.) 872 applied for aid; of those 87% were deemed to have need. 86% of undergraduates with need received aid; of those 38% had need fully met. *Average percent of need met:* 86% (excluding resources awarded to replace EFC). *Average financial aid package:* $6480 (excluding resources awarded to replace EFC). 8% of all full-time undergraduates had no need and received non-need-based gift aid.

GIFT AID (NEED-BASED) Total amount: $2,915,753 (68% federal, 14% state, 9% institutional, 9% external sources). **Receiving aid:** Freshmen: 57% (142); All full-time undergraduates: 51% (591). **Average award:** Freshmen: $4806; Undergraduates: $4567. **Scholarships, grants, and awards:** Federal Pell, FSEOG, state, private, college/university gift aid from institutional funds.

GIFT AID (NON-NEED-BASED) Total amount: $120,937 (37% institutional, 63% external sources). **Receiving aid:** Freshmen: 3% (8); Undergraduates: 2% (21). *Average Award:* Freshmen: $3019; Undergraduates: $3815. **Scholarships, grants, and awards by category:** Academic Interests/Achievement: 98 awards ($152,352 total): general academic interests/achievements. Creative Arts/Performance: 7 awards ($9320 total): art/fine arts. Special Achievements/Activities: 2 awards ($1000 total): community service. Special Characteristics: 122 awards ($305,393 total): children of faculty/staff, ethnic background, international students, veterans' children. **Tuition waivers:** Full or partial for minority students, employees or children of employees, senior citizens.

LOANS Student loans: $2,303,738 (69% need-based, 31% non-need-based). 44% of past graduating class borrowed through all loan programs. *Average indebtedness per student:* $11,254. **Average need-based loan:** Freshmen: $2670; Undergraduates: $3144. **Parent loans:** $224,541 (100% non-need-based). **Programs:** Federal Direct (Subsidized and Unsubsidized Stafford, PLUS), Perkins, state, college/university.

WORK-STUDY Federal work-study: Total amount: $448,569; 283 jobs averaging $1318.

APPLYING FOR FINANCIAL AID Required financial aid form: FAFSA. **Financial aid deadline (priority):** 4/1. **Notification date:** Continuous beginning 3/1. Students must reply within 2 weeks of notification.

CONTACT Ms. Barbara J. Bridges, Director of Financial Aid, University of Maine at Presque Isle, 181 Main Street, Presque Isle, ME 04769-2888, 207-768-9513. *Fax:* 207-768-9608. *E-mail:* bridges@umpi.maine.edu.

UNIVERSITY OF MANAGEMENT AND TECHNOLOGY
Arlington, VA

ABOUT THE INSTITUTION Proprietary, coed. Awards: associate, bachelor's, master's, and doctoral degrees and post-bachelor's and post-master's certificates. 6 undergraduate majors.

CONTACT Financial Aid Office, University of Management and Technology, 1901 North Fort Myer Drive, Arlington, VA 22209, 703-516-0035 or toll-free 800-924-4885 (in-state). *E-mail:* info@umtweb.edu.

UNIVERSITY OF MARY
Bismarck, ND

Tuition & fees: $10,817	Average undergraduate aid package: N/A

ABOUT THE INSTITUTION Independent Roman Catholic, coed. Awards: associate, bachelor's, master's, and doctoral degrees. 39 undergraduate majors. Total enrollment: 2,757. Undergraduates: 2,227. Freshmen: 413. Federal methodology is used as a basis for awarding need-based institutional aid.

UNDERGRADUATE EXPENSES for 2005–06 Application fee: $25. **Comprehensive fee:** $14,927 includes full-time tuition ($10,600), mandatory fees ($217), and room and board ($4110). **College room only:** $1910. Full-time tuition and fees vary according to course load and program. Room and board charges vary

according to board plan, housing facility, and location. **Part-time tuition:** $335 per credit. Part-time tuition and fees vary according to course load and degree level. **Payment plan:** Installment.

FRESHMAN FINANCIAL AID (Fall 2003) 377 applied for aid; of those 68% were deemed to have need. 100% of freshmen with need received aid; of those 19% had need fully met.

GIFT AID (NEED-BASED) Total amount: $7,025,438 (32% federal, 2% state, 60% institutional, 6% external sources). **Receiving aid:** Freshmen: 63% (255). **Scholarships, grants, and awards:** Federal Pell, FSEOG, state, private, college/university gift aid from institutional funds.

GIFT AID (NON-NEED-BASED) Receiving aid: Freshmen: 63% (255). **Scholarships, grants, and awards by category:** Academic Interests/Achievement: 1,440 awards ($3,931,866 total): general academic interests/achievements. Creative Arts/Performance: 53 awards ($280,700 total): debating, music, theater/drama. Special Characteristics: 135 awards ($323,662 total): children of faculty/staff. **Tuition waivers:** Full or partial for employees or children of employees, senior citizens.

LOANS Student loans: $11,159,041 (56% need-based, 44% non-need-based). **Parent loans:** $993,007 (100% need-based). **Programs:** FFEL (Subsidized and Unsubsidized Stafford, PLUS), Perkins, Federal Nursing, college/university.

WORK-STUDY Federal work-study: Total amount: $372,533; 402 jobs averaging $927. **State or other work-study/employment:** Total amount: $78,690 (100% non-need-based). 63 part-time jobs averaging $1249.

ATHLETIC AWARDS Total amount: $1,727,727 (100% need-based).

APPLYING FOR FINANCIAL AID Required financial aid form: FAFSA. **Financial aid deadline (priority):** 5/1. **Notification date:** Continuous. Students must reply within 2 weeks of notification.

CONTACT Dave Hanson, Director of Financial Aid, University of Mary, 7500 University Drive, Bismarck, ND 58504-9652, 701-255-7500 Ext. 8079 or toll-free 800-288-6279. *Fax:* 701-255-7687.

UNIVERSITY OF MARY HARDIN-BAYLOR
Belton, TX

Tuition & fees: $12,380	Average undergraduate aid package: $12,443

ABOUT THE INSTITUTION Independent Southern Baptist, coed. Awards: bachelor's and master's degrees. 56 undergraduate majors. Total enrollment: 2,713. Undergraduates: 2,582. Freshmen: 475. Federal methodology is used as a basis for awarding need-based institutional aid.

UNDERGRADUATE EXPENSES for 2004–05 Application fee: $35. **Comprehensive fee:** $16,380 includes full-time tuition ($11,400), mandatory fees ($980), and room and board ($4000). Room and board charges vary according to housing facility. **Part-time tuition:** $380 per semester hour. **Part-time fees:** $31 per semester hour; $25 per term. **Payment plans:** Tuition prepayment, installment.

FRESHMAN FINANCIAL AID (Fall 2004, est.) 452 applied for aid; of those 73% were deemed to have need. 100% of freshmen with need received aid; of those 15% had need fully met. *Average percent of need met:* 62% (excluding resources awarded to replace EFC). *Average financial aid package:* $9741 (excluding resources awarded to replace EFC). 22% of all full-time freshmen had no need and received non-need-based gift aid.

UNDERGRADUATE FINANCIAL AID (Fall 2004, est.) 2,006 applied for aid; of those 73% were deemed to have need. 100% of undergraduates with need received aid; of those 15% had need fully met. *Average percent of need met:* 74% (excluding resources awarded to replace EFC). *Average financial aid package:* $12,443 (excluding resources awarded to replace EFC). 22% of all full-time undergraduates had no need and received non-need-based gift aid.

GIFT AID (NEED-BASED) Total amount: $7,776,541 (36% federal, 50% state, 14% institutional). **Receiving aid:** Freshmen: 64% (309); All full-time undergraduates: 61% (1,362). **Average award:** Freshmen: $4995; Undergraduates: $4995. **Scholarships, grants, and awards:** Federal Pell, FSEOG, state, private, college/university gift aid from institutional funds.

GIFT AID (NON-NEED-BASED) Total amount: $3,637,446 (1% state, 75% institutional, 24% external sources). **Receiving aid:** Freshmen: 53% (255); Undergraduates: 50% (1,113). *Average Award:* Freshmen: $3186; Undergraduates: $3186. **Scholarships, grants, and awards by category:** Academic Interests/Achievement: 488 awards ($936,453 total): biological sciences, business, communication, computer science, education, English, foreign languages, general academic interests/achievements, health fields, humanities, international studies, mathematics, physical sciences, premedicine, religion/biblical studies, social sciences. Creative Arts/Performance: 125 awards ($230,484 total): art/fine arts, music. Special Achievements/Activities: 73 awards ($157,601 total): cheerleading/

drum major, community service, leadership, religious involvement. *Special Characteristics:* 345 awards ($984,825 total): children and siblings of alumni, children of faculty/staff, ethnic background, handicapped students, international students, local/state students, members of minority groups, out-of-state students, relatives of clergy, religious affiliation. *Tuition waivers:* Full or partial for employees or children of employees. *ROTC:* Air Force cooperative.

LOANS *Student loans:* $11,961,302 (59% need-based, 41% non-need-based). 80% of past graduating class borrowed through all loan programs. *Average indebtedness per student:* $15,819. *Average need-based loan:* Freshmen: $2453; Undergraduates: $4611. *Parent loans:* $2,000,494 (100% non-need-based). *Programs:* FFEL (Subsidized and Unsubsidized Stafford, PLUS), Perkins, state, college/university.

WORK-STUDY *Federal work-study:* Total amount: $519,430; 258 jobs averaging $2300. *State or other work-study/employment:* Total amount: $369,840 (37% need-based, 63% non-need-based). 198 part-time jobs averaging $2300.

APPLYING FOR FINANCIAL AID *Required financial aid form:* FAFSA. *Financial aid deadline (priority):* 3/1. *Notification date:* Continuous beginning 2/1. Students must reply within 2 weeks of notification.

CONTACT Ms. Kelly Graves, Assistant Director of Financial Aid, University of Mary Hardin-Baylor, Box 8080, UMHB Station, Belton, TX 76513, 254-295-4517 or toll-free 800-727-8642. *Fax:* 254-295-5049. *E-mail:* kgraves@umhb.edu.

UNIVERSITY OF MARYLAND, BALTIMORE COUNTY
Baltimore, MD

Tuition & fees (MD res): $8020	Average undergraduate aid package: $7090

ABOUT THE INSTITUTION State-supported, coed. Awards: bachelor's, master's, and doctoral degrees and post-bachelor's certificates. 52 undergraduate majors. Total enrollment: 11,852. Undergraduates: 9,668. Freshmen: 1,420. Federal methodology is used as a basis for awarding need-based institutional aid.

UNDERGRADUATE EXPENSES for 2004–05 *Application fee:* $50. *Tuition, state resident:* full-time $6120; part-time $255 per credit hour. *Tuition, nonresident:* full-time $13,720; part-time $571 per credit hour. *Required fees:* full-time $1900; $80 per credit hour. *College room and board:* $7620; *room only:* $4650. Room and board charges vary according to board plan and housing facility. *Payment plan:* Installment.

FRESHMAN FINANCIAL AID (Fall 2004, est.) 1204 applied for aid; of those 82% were deemed to have need. 80% of freshmen with need received aid; of those 72% had need fully met. *Average percent of need met:* 60% (excluding resources awarded to replace EFC). *Average financial aid package:* $7090 (excluding resources awarded to replace EFC). 17% of all full-time freshmen had no need and received non-need-based gift aid.

UNDERGRADUATE FINANCIAL AID (Fall 2004, est.) 6,368 applied for aid; of those 82% were deemed to have need. 80% of undergraduates with need received aid; of those 72% had need fully met. *Average percent of need met:* 60% (excluding resources awarded to replace EFC). *Average financial aid package:* $7090 (excluding resources awarded to replace EFC). 17% of all full-time undergraduates had no need and received non-need-based gift aid.

GIFT AID (NEED-BASED) *Total amount:* $11,022,320 (55% federal, 38% state, 7% institutional). *Receiving aid:* Freshmen: 27% (403); All full-time undergraduates: 27% (2,131). *Average award:* Freshmen: $4294; Undergraduates: $4294. *Scholarships, grants, and awards:* Federal Pell, FSEOG, state, private, college/university gift aid from institutional funds.

GIFT AID (NON-NEED-BASED) *Total amount:* $14,273,969 (4% federal, 11% state, 75% institutional, 10% external sources). *Receiving aid:* Freshmen: 25% (379); Undergraduates: 22% (1,723). *Average Award:* Freshmen: $6445; Undergraduates: $6445. *Scholarships, grants, and awards by category:* Academic Interests/Achievement: 878 awards ($4,687,479 total): biological sciences, computer science, engineering/technologies, English, foreign languages, general academic interests/achievements, humanities, mathematics, physical sciences. *Creative Arts/Performance:* 87 awards ($485,297 total): art/fine arts, cinema/film/broadcasting, creative writing, dance, music, performing arts, theater/drama. *Tuition waivers:* Full or partial for employees or children of employees, senior citizens. *ROTC:* Army cooperative.

LOANS *Student loans:* $23,613,690 (55% need-based, 45% non-need-based). 30% of past graduating class borrowed through all loan programs. *Average indebtedness per student:* $14,500. *Average need-based loan:* Freshmen: $2575; Undergraduates: $4564. *Parent loans:* $6,450,646 (100% non-need-based). *Programs:* FFEL (Subsidized and Unsubsidized Stafford, PLUS), Perkins.

WORK-STUDY *Federal work-study:* Total amount: $247,128; jobs available (averaging $2000).
ATHLETIC AWARDS *Total amount:* $3,001,345 (100% non-need-based).
APPLYING FOR FINANCIAL AID *Required financial aid form:* FAFSA. *Financial aid deadline (priority):* 2/15. *Notification date:* Continuous beginning 3/15. Students must reply within 2 weeks of notification.
CONTACT Stephanie Johnson, Director of Financial Aid, University of Maryland, Baltimore County, 1000 Hilltop Circle, Baltimore, MD 21250, 410-455-2387 or toll-free 800-UMBC-4U2 (in-state), 800-862-2402 (out-of-state). *Fax:* 410-455-1094. *E-mail:* finaid@umbc.edu.

UNIVERSITY OF MARYLAND, COLLEGE PARK
College Park, MD

Tuition & fees (MD res): $7410	Average undergraduate aid package: $12,132

ABOUT THE INSTITUTION State-supported, coed. Awards: bachelor's, master's, doctoral, and first professional degrees and post-bachelor's and post-master's certificates. 94 undergraduate majors. Total enrollment: 35,262. Undergraduates: 25,379. Freshmen: 4,063. Federal methodology is used as a basis for awarding need-based institutional aid.

UNDERGRADUATE EXPENSES for 2004–05 *Application fee:* $50. *Tuition, state resident:* full-time $6200; part-time $258 per credit hour. *Tuition, nonresident:* full-time $17,500; part-time $729 per credit hour. *Required fees:* full-time $1210; $276 per term part-time. Part-time tuition and fees vary according to course load. *College room and board:* $7931; *room only:* $4796. Room and board charges vary according to board plan. *Payment plans:* Installment, deferred payment.

FRESHMAN FINANCIAL AID (Fall 2003) 3337 applied for aid; of those 54% were deemed to have need. 92% of freshmen with need received aid; of those 31% had need fully met. *Average percent of need met:* 71% (excluding resources awarded to replace EFC). *Average financial aid package:* $11,800 (excluding resources awarded to replace EFC). 22% of all full-time freshmen had no need and received non-need-based gift aid.

UNDERGRADUATE FINANCIAL AID (Fall 2003) 15,238 applied for aid; of those 63% were deemed to have need. 94% of undergraduates with need received aid; of those 26% had need fully met. *Average percent of need met:* 68% (excluding resources awarded to replace EFC). *Average financial aid package:* $12,132 (excluding resources awarded to replace EFC). 15% of all full-time undergraduates had no need and received non-need-based gift aid.

GIFT AID (NEED-BASED) *Total amount:* $29,131,632 (41% federal, 28% state, 31% institutional). *Receiving aid:* Freshmen: 26% (1,054); All full-time undergraduates: 27% (6,156). *Average award:* Freshmen: $5762; Undergraduates: $4722. *Scholarships, grants, and awards:* Federal Pell, FSEOG, state, private, college/university gift aid from institutional funds.

GIFT AID (NON-NEED-BASED) *Total amount:* $28,678,390 (24% state, 52% institutional, 24% external sources). *Receiving aid:* Freshmen: 22% (884); Undergraduates: 14% (3,118). *Average Award:* Freshmen: $5145; Undergraduates: $5889. *Scholarships, grants, and awards by category:* Academic Interests/Achievement: 5,790 awards ($18,675,641 total): agriculture, architecture, biological sciences, business, communication, computer science, education, engineering/technologies, English, foreign languages, general academic interests/achievements, health fields, humanities, international studies, library science, mathematics, military science, physical sciences, premedicine, social sciences. *Creative Arts/Performance:* 193 awards ($600,222 total): applied art and design, art/fine arts, cinema/film/broadcasting, creative writing, dance, journalism/publications, music, performing arts, theater/drama. *Special Achievements/Activities:* 23 awards ($63,000 total): cheerleading/drum major, leadership. *Special Characteristics:* 384 awards ($1,613,750 total): adult students, out-of-state students. *Tuition waivers:* Full or partial for employees or children of employees. *ROTC:* Army, Naval cooperative, Air Force.

LOANS *Student loans:* $54,864,755 (73% need-based, 27% non-need-based). 34% of past graduating class borrowed through all loan programs. *Average indebtedness per student:* $14,076. *Average need-based loan:* Freshmen: $2437; Undergraduates: $3845. *Parent loans:* $19,571,516 (40% need-based, 60% non-need-based). *Programs:* FFEL (Subsidized and Unsubsidized Stafford, PLUS), Perkins, college/university.

WORK-STUDY *Federal work-study:* Total amount: $1,150,533; 801 jobs averaging $1436.
ATHLETIC AWARDS *Total amount:* $7,277,356 (100% non-need-based).

University of Maryland, College Park

APPLYING FOR FINANCIAL AID *Required financial aid form:* FAFSA. *Financial aid deadline (priority):* 2/15. *Notification date:* Continuous beginning 4/1.

CONTACT Sarah Bauder, Director of Financial Aid, University of Maryland, College Park, 0102 Lee Building, College Park, MD 20742, 301-314-9000 or toll-free 800-422-5867. *Fax:* 301-314-9587. *E-mail:* umfinaid@osfa.umd.edu.

UNIVERSITY OF MARYLAND EASTERN SHORE
Princess Anne, MD

Tuition & fees (MD res): $5558   **Average undergraduate aid package: $11,180**

ABOUT THE INSTITUTION State-supported, coed. Awards: bachelor's, master's, and doctoral degrees. 53 undergraduate majors. Total enrollment: 3,762. Undergraduates: 3,326. Freshmen: 846. Federal methodology is used as a basis for awarding need-based institutional aid.

UNDERGRADUATE EXPENSES for 2004–05 *Application fee:* $25. *Tuition, state resident:* full-time $3916; part-time $163 per credit hour. *Tuition, nonresident:* full-time $9779; part-time $353 per credit hour. *Required fees:* full-time $1642; $40 per term part-time. Part-time tuition and fees vary according to course load. *College room and board:* $5880; *room only:* $3280. Room and board charges vary according to board plan and housing facility. *Payment plans:* Installment, deferred payment.

FRESHMAN FINANCIAL AID (Fall 2003) 762 applied for aid; of those 82% were deemed to have need. 100% of freshmen with need received aid; of those 22% had need fully met. *Average percent of need met:* 73% (excluding resources awarded to replace EFC). *Average financial aid package:* $11,180 (excluding resources awarded to replace EFC). 8% of all full-time freshmen had no need and received non-need-based gift aid.

UNDERGRADUATE FINANCIAL AID (Fall 2003) 2,425 applied for aid; of those 82% were deemed to have need. 100% of undergraduates with need received aid; of those 16% had need fully met. *Average percent of need met:* 73% (excluding resources awarded to replace EFC). *Average financial aid package:* $11,180 (excluding resources awarded to replace EFC). 11% of all full-time undergraduates had no need and received non-need-based gift aid.

GIFT AID (NEED-BASED) *Total amount:* $8,069,301 (61% federal, 32% state, 7% institutional). *Receiving aid:* Freshmen: 66% (625); All full-time undergraduates: 65% (1,980). *Average award:* Freshmen: $6225; Undergraduates: $6225. *Scholarships, grants, and awards:* Federal Pell, FSEOG, state, college/university gift aid from institutional funds.

GIFT AID (NON-NEED-BASED) *Total amount:* $1,301,801 (54% institutional, 46% external sources). *Receiving aid:* Freshmen: 5% (47); Undergraduates: 7% (227). *Average Award:* Freshmen: $2465; Undergraduates: $2500. *Scholarships, grants, and awards by category:* Academic Interests/Achievement: 75 awards ($68,000 total): agriculture, business, computer science, education, engineering/technologies, English, general academic interests/achievements, health fields, home economics, mathematics, physical sciences, social sciences. Creative Arts/Performance: 25 awards ($25,000 total): art/fine arts, music, performing arts, theater/drama. Special Characteristics: 175 awards ($225,000 total): adult students, children of faculty/staff, first-generation college students, veterans. *Tuition waivers:* Full or partial for employees or children of employees, senior citizens.

LOANS *Student loans:* $12,791,439 (59% need-based, 41% non-need-based). 72% of past graduating class borrowed through all loan programs. *Average indebtedness per student:* $8500. *Average need-based loan:* Freshmen: $2600; Undergraduates: $5000. *Parent loans:* $5,310,745 (100% non-need-based). *Programs:* Federal Direct (Subsidized and Unsubsidized Stafford, PLUS), Perkins.

WORK-STUDY *Federal work-study:* Total amount: $319,460; 221 jobs averaging $1445. *State or other work-study/employment:* Total amount: $1,475,000 (100% non-need-based). Part-time jobs available.

ATHLETIC AWARDS *Total amount:* $764,276 (100% non-need-based).

APPLYING FOR FINANCIAL AID *Required financial aid form:* FAFSA. *Financial aid deadline (priority):* 3/1. *Notification date:* Continuous beginning 4/15.

CONTACT Mr. James W. Kellam, Director of Financial Aid, University of Maryland Eastern Shore, Backbone Road, Princess Anne, MD 21853-1299, 410-651-6172. *Fax:* 410-651-7670. *E-mail:* jwkellam@umes.edu.

UNIVERSITY OF MARYLAND UNIVERSITY COLLEGE
Adelphi, MD

Tuition & fees (MD res): $5424   **Average undergraduate aid package: $4692**

ABOUT THE INSTITUTION State-supported, coed. Awards: associate, bachelor's, master's, and doctoral degrees and post-bachelor's certificates (offers primarily part-time evening and weekend degree programs at more than 30 off-campus locations in Maryland and the Washington, DC area, and more than 180 military communities in Europe and Asia with military enrollment not reflected in this profile; associate of arts program available to military students only). 19 undergraduate majors. Total enrollment: 28,374. Undergraduates: 19,857. Freshmen: 558. Federal methodology is used as a basis for awarding need-based institutional aid.

UNDERGRADUATE EXPENSES for 2004–05 *Application fee:* $30. *Tuition, state resident:* full-time $5304; part-time $221 per semester hour. *Tuition, nonresident:* full-time $9768; part-time $407 per semester hour.

FRESHMAN FINANCIAL AID (Fall 2003) 51 applied for aid; of those 98% were deemed to have need. 74% of freshmen with need received aid. *Average percent of need met:* 16% (excluding resources awarded to replace EFC). *Average financial aid package:* $3252 (excluding resources awarded to replace EFC).

UNDERGRADUATE FINANCIAL AID (Fall 2003) 1,546 applied for aid; of those 93% were deemed to have need. 86% of undergraduates with need received aid; of those 2% had need fully met. *Average percent of need met:* 24% (excluding resources awarded to replace EFC). *Average financial aid package:* $4692 (excluding resources awarded to replace EFC).

GIFT AID (NEED-BASED) *Total amount:* $7,886,279 (73% federal, 9% state, 18% institutional). *Receiving aid:* Freshmen: 38% (27); All full-time undergraduates: 30% (740). *Average award:* Freshmen: $1562; Undergraduates: $1499. *Scholarships, grants, and awards:* Federal Pell, FSEOG, state, private, college/university gift aid from institutional funds.

GIFT AID (NON-NEED-BASED) *Total amount:* $211,005 (29% state, 40% institutional, 31% external sources). *Receiving aid:* Freshmen: 6% (4); Undergraduates: 1% (33). *Scholarships, grants, and awards by category:* Academic Interests/Achievement: general academic interests/achievements. Special Achievements/Activities: general special achievements/activities.

LOANS *Student loans:* $36,791,061 (49% need-based, 51% non-need-based). 89% of past graduating class borrowed through all loan programs. *Average indebtedness per student:* $1977. *Average need-based loan:* Freshmen: $1288; Undergraduates: $2155. *Parent loans:* $271,660 (100% non-need-based). *Programs:* Federal Direct (Subsidized and Unsubsidized Stafford, PLUS), Perkins.

WORK-STUDY *Federal work-study:* Total amount: $542,203; jobs available. *State or other work-study/employment:* Total amount: $153,448 (100% non-need-based). Part-time jobs available.

APPLYING FOR FINANCIAL AID *Required financial aid forms:* FAFSA, institution's own form. *Notification date:* Continuous beginning 5/1. Students must reply within 2 weeks of notification.

CONTACT Financial Aid Counselor, University of Maryland University College, 3501 University Boulevard East, Adelphi, MD 20783, 301-985-7510 or toll-free 800-888-8682 (in-state). *Fax:* 301-985-7462. *E-mail:* finaid@umuc.edu.

UNIVERSITY OF MARY WASHINGTON
Fredericksburg, VA

Tuition & fees (VA res): $5128   **Average undergraduate aid package: $5300**

ABOUT THE INSTITUTION State-supported, coed. Awards: bachelor's and master's degrees and post-bachelor's certificates. 40 undergraduate majors. Total enrollment: 4,792. Undergraduates: 4,220. Freshmen: 869. Federal methodology is used as a basis for awarding need-based institutional aid.

UNDERGRADUATE EXPENSES for 2004–05 *Application fee:* $35. *Tuition, state resident:* full-time $2544; part-time $129 per credit. *Tuition, nonresident:* full-time $10,950; part-time $529 per credit. Part-time tuition and fees vary according to course load. *College room and board:* $5744; *room only:* $3334. Room and board charges vary according to board plan and housing facility. *Payment plan:* Installment.

FRESHMAN FINANCIAL AID (Fall 2004, est.) 650 applied for aid; of those 63% were deemed to have need. 94% of freshmen with need received aid; of those 9% had need fully met. *Average percent of need met:* 60% (excluding resources

awarded to replace EFC). *Average financial aid package:* $4450 (excluding resources awarded to replace EFC). 16% of all full-time freshmen had no need and received non-need-based gift aid.

UNDERGRADUATE FINANCIAL AID (Fall 2004, est.) 2,501 applied for aid; of those 64% were deemed to have need. 88% of undergraduates with need received aid; of those 6% had need fully met. *Average percent of need met:* 56% (excluding resources awarded to replace EFC). *Average financial aid package:* $5300 (excluding resources awarded to replace EFC). 12% of all full-time undergraduates had no need and received non-need-based gift aid.

GIFT AID (NEED-BASED) *Total amount:* $3,050,000 (36% federal, 36% state, 16% institutional, 12% external sources). *Receiving aid:* Freshmen: 40% (350); All full-time undergraduates: 36% (1,292). *Average award:* Freshmen: $2825; Undergraduates: $3200. *Scholarships, grants, and awards:* Federal Pell, FSEOG, state, college/university gift aid from institutional funds.

GIFT AID (NON-NEED-BASED) *Total amount:* $822,000 (2% state, 62% institutional, 36% external sources). *Receiving aid:* Freshmen: 16% (140); Undergraduates: 8% (270). *Average Award:* Freshmen: $1080; Undergraduates: $1180. *Scholarships, grants, and awards by category:* Academic Interests/Achievement: 750 awards ($905,000 total): business, computer science, education, English, foreign languages, general academic interests/achievements, humanities, mathematics, physical sciences, religion/biblical studies, social sciences. *Creative Arts/Performance:* 65 awards ($120,000 total): art/fine arts, dance, journalism/publications, music, theater/drama. *Special Achievements/Activities:* 2 awards ($13,500 total): leadership. *Special Characteristics:* 15 awards ($36,000 total): adult students, children and siblings of alumni, children of faculty/staff, local/state students. *Tuition waivers:* Full or partial for senior citizens.

LOANS *Student loans:* $7,470,000 (46% need-based, 54% non-need-based). 72% of past graduating class borrowed through all loan programs. *Average indebtedness per student:* $12,665. *Average need-based loan:* Freshmen: $2515; Undergraduates: $4000. *Parent loans:* $3,500,000 (100% non-need-based). *Programs:* FFEL (Subsidized and Unsubsidized Stafford, PLUS), Perkins.

WORK-STUDY *Federal work-study:* Total amount: $52,000; 45 jobs averaging $1600. *State or other work-study/employment:* Total amount: $1,025,000 (100% non-need-based). 751 part-time jobs averaging $1480.

APPLYING FOR FINANCIAL AID *Required financial aid form:* FAFSA. *Financial aid deadline (priority):* 3/1. *Notification date:* 4/15. Students must reply by 5/1 or within 2 weeks of notification.

CONTACT Ms. Debra J. Harber, Associate Dean for Financial Aid, University of Mary Washington, 1301 College Avenue, Fredericksburg, VA 22401-5358, 540-654-2468 or toll-free 800-468-5614. *Fax:* 540-654-1858. *E-mail:* dharber@umw.edu.

UNIVERSITY OF MASSACHUSETTS AMHERST
Amherst, MA

Tuition & fees (MA res): $9008　　**Average undergraduate aid package: $10,347**

ABOUT THE INSTITUTION State-supported, coed. Awards: associate, bachelor's, master's, and doctoral degrees and post-master's certificates. 88 undergraduate majors. Total enrollment: 24,646. Undergraduates: 18,966. Freshmen: 4,340. Federal methodology is used as a basis for awarding need-based institutional aid.

UNDERGRADUATE EXPENSES for 2004–05 *Application fee:* $40. *Tuition, state resident:* full-time $1714; part-time $71.50 per credit. *Tuition, nonresident:* full-time $9937; part-time $414 per credit. *Required fees:* full-time $7294; $1564 per term part-time. Full-time tuition and fees vary according to course load, reciprocity agreements, and student level. Part-time tuition and fees vary according to course load. *College room and board:* $6189; *room only:* $3428. Room and board charges vary according to board plan and housing facility. *Payment plan:* Installment.

FRESHMAN FINANCIAL AID (Fall 2003) 2401 applied for aid; of those 68% were deemed to have need. 96% of freshmen with need received aid; of those 12% had need fully met. *Average percent of need met:* 83% (excluding resources awarded to replace EFC). *Average financial aid package:* $9173 (excluding resources awarded to replace EFC). 1% of all full-time freshmen had no need and received non-need-based gift aid.

UNDERGRADUATE FINANCIAL AID (Fall 2003) 11,513 applied for aid; of those 77% were deemed to have need. 97% of undergraduates with need received aid; of those 26% had need fully met. *Average percent of need met:* 88% (excluding resources awarded to replace EFC). *Average financial aid package:*

$10,347 (excluding resources awarded to replace EFC). 2% of all full-time undergraduates had no need and received non-need-based gift aid.

GIFT AID (NEED-BASED) *Total amount:* $41,457,429 (31% federal, 15% state, 46% institutional, 8% external sources). *Receiving aid:* Freshmen: 36% (1,507); All full-time undergraduates: 47% (8,157). *Average award:* Freshmen: $5009; Undergraduates: $5537. *Scholarships, grants, and awards:* Federal Pell, FSEOG, state, private, college/university gift aid from institutional funds.

GIFT AID (NON-NEED-BASED) *Total amount:* $4,620,516 (2% state, 45% institutional, 53% external sources). *Receiving aid:* Freshmen: 1% (46); Undergraduates: 2% (329). *Average Award:* Freshmen: $5291; Undergraduates: $5049. *Scholarships, grants, and awards by category:* Academic Interests/Achievement: agriculture, architecture, biological sciences, business, communication, computer science, education, engineering/technologies, English, general academic interests/achievements, health fields, humanities, mathematics, military science, physical sciences, premedicine, social sciences. *Creative Arts/Performance:* art/fine arts, dance, journalism/publications, music, theater/drama. *Special Achievements/Activities:* cheerleading/drum major, general special achievements/activities, leadership. *Special Characteristics:* children and siblings of alumni, children of faculty/staff, handicapped students, veterans. *Tuition waivers:* Full or partial for employees or children of employees, senior citizens. *ROTC:* Army, Air Force.

LOANS *Student loans:* $56,443,041 (62% need-based, 38% non-need-based). 42% of past graduating class borrowed through all loan programs. *Average indebtedness per student:* $12,677. *Average need-based loan:* Freshmen: $2931; Undergraduates: $3952. *Parent loans:* $15,008,417 (18% need-based, 82% non-need-based). *Programs:* Federal Direct (Subsidized and Unsubsidized Stafford, PLUS), Perkins, state.

WORK-STUDY *Federal work-study:* Total amount: $8,318,588; 4,940 jobs averaging $1684.

ATHLETIC AWARDS *Total amount:* $4,010,132 (34% need-based, 66% non-need-based).

APPLYING FOR FINANCIAL AID *Required financial aid form:* FAFSA. *Financial aid deadline (priority):* 3/1. *Notification date:* Continuous beginning 4/1.

CONTACT Office of Financial Aid Services, University of Massachusetts Amherst, 255 Whitmore Administration Building, Amherst, MA 01003, 413-545-0801.

UNIVERSITY OF MASSACHUSETTS BOSTON
Boston, MA

Tuition & fees (MA res): $8034　　**Average undergraduate aid package: $8292**

ABOUT THE INSTITUTION State-supported, coed. Awards: bachelor's, master's, and doctoral degrees and post-bachelor's and post-master's certificates. 39 undergraduate majors. Total enrollment: 11,682. Undergraduates: 8,832. Freshmen: 565. Federal methodology is used as a basis for awarding need-based institutional aid.

UNDERGRADUATE EXPENSES for 2004–05 *Application fee:* $40. *Tuition, area resident:* part-time $72 per credit hour. *Tuition, state resident:* full-time $8034; part-time $107 per credit hour. *Tuition, nonresident:* full-time $18,767; part-time $406.50 per credit hour. *Required fees:* $263 per credit hour. Full-time tuition and fees vary according to class time, course load, program, reciprocity agreements, and student level. Part-time tuition and fees vary according to class time, course load, program, reciprocity agreements, and student level. *Payment plan:* Installment.

FRESHMAN FINANCIAL AID (Fall 2003) 445 applied for aid; of those 85% were deemed to have need. 98% of freshmen with need received aid; of those 40% had need fully met. *Average percent of need met:* 86% (excluding resources awarded to replace EFC). *Average financial aid package:* $8087 (excluding resources awarded to replace EFC). 1% of all full-time freshmen had no need and received non-need-based gift aid.

UNDERGRADUATE FINANCIAL AID (Fall 2003) 4,012 applied for aid; of those 87% were deemed to have need. 98% of undergraduates with need received aid; of those 55% had need fully met. *Average percent of need met:* 89% (excluding resources awarded to replace EFC). *Average financial aid package:* $8292 (excluding resources awarded to replace EFC). 1% of all full-time undergraduates had no need and received non-need-based gift aid.

GIFT AID (NEED-BASED) *Total amount:* $16,542,598 (46% federal, 39% state, 13% institutional, 2% external sources). *Receiving aid:* Freshmen: 52% (296); All full-time undergraduates: 50% (2,725). *Average award:* Freshmen: $6046; Undergraduates: $5145. *Scholarships, grants, and awards:* Federal Pell, FSEOG, state, private, college/university gift aid from institutional funds.

University of Massachusetts Boston

GIFT AID (NON-NEED-BASED) *Total amount:* $246,470 (4% federal, 32% state, 39% institutional, 25% external sources). *Receiving aid:* Freshmen: 8% (44); Undergraduates: 5% (270). *Average Award: Freshmen:* $7042; *Undergraduates:* $2588. *Scholarships, grants, and awards by category: Academic Interests/Achievement:* general academic interests/achievements. *Special Achievements/Activities:* general special achievements/activities. *Tuition waivers:* Full or partial for employees or children of employees, senior citizens.

LOANS *Student loans:* $26,837,508 (74% need-based, 26% non-need-based). 84% of past graduating class borrowed through all loan programs. *Average indebtedness per student:* $14,805. *Average need-based loan:* Freshmen: $2009; Undergraduates: $3274. *Parent loans:* $779,862 (41% need-based, 59% non-need-based). *Programs:* Federal Direct (Subsidized and Unsubsidized Stafford, PLUS), Perkins, state.

WORK-STUDY *Federal work-study:* Total amount: $3,933,264; jobs available.

APPLYING FOR FINANCIAL AID *Required financial aid form:* FAFSA. *Financial aid deadline (priority):* 3/1. *Notification date:* Continuous beginning 4/1.

CONTACT Judy L. Keyes, Director of Financial Aid Services, University of Massachusetts Boston, 100 Morrissey Boulevard, Boston, MA 02125-3393, 617-287-6300. *Fax:* 617-287-6323. *E-mail:* judy.keyes@umb.edu.

UNIVERSITY OF MASSACHUSETTS DARTMOUTH
North Dartmouth, MA

Tuition & fees (MA res): $7802   **Average undergraduate aid package:** $7604

ABOUT THE INSTITUTION State-supported, coed. Awards: bachelor's, master's, and doctoral degrees and post-bachelor's and post-master's certificates. 48 undergraduate majors. Total enrollment: 8,299. Undergraduates: 7,290. Freshmen: 1,474. Federal methodology is used as a basis for awarding need-based institutional aid.

UNDERGRADUATE EXPENSES for 2004–05 *Application fee:* $35; $55 for nonresidents. *Tuition, state resident:* full-time $1417; part-time $59.04 per credit. *Tuition, nonresident:* full-time $10,917; part-time $454.88 per credit. *Required fees:* full-time $6385; $266.04 per credit. Full-time tuition and fees vary according to reciprocity agreements. Part-time tuition and fees vary according to course load and reciprocity agreements. *College room and board:* $7471; *room only:* $4297. Room and board charges vary according to board plan and housing facility. *Payment plan:* Installment.

FRESHMAN FINANCIAL AID (Fall 2003) 685 applied for aid; of those 73% were deemed to have need. 95% of freshmen with need received aid; of those 56% had need fully met. *Average percent of need met:* 86% (excluding resources awarded to replace EFC). *Average financial aid package:* $6931 (excluding resources awarded to replace EFC). 2% of all full-time freshmen had no need and received non-need-based gift aid.

UNDERGRADUATE FINANCIAL AID (Fall 2003) 4,594 applied for aid; of those 83% were deemed to have need. 97% of undergraduates with need received aid; of those 53% had need fully met. *Average percent of need met:* 86% (excluding resources awarded to replace EFC). *Average financial aid package:* $7604 (excluding resources awarded to replace EFC). 4% of all full-time undergraduates had no need and received non-need-based gift aid.

GIFT AID (NEED-BASED) *Total amount:* $13,147,904 (33% federal, 25% state, 36% institutional, 6% external sources). *Receiving aid:* Freshmen: 21% (353); All full-time undergraduates: 54% (3,262). *Average award:* Freshmen: $4828; Undergraduates: $4410. *Scholarships, grants, and awards:* Federal Pell, FSEOG, state, private, college/university gift aid from institutional funds.

GIFT AID (NON-NEED-BASED) *Total amount:* $830,212 (3% state, 64% institutional, 33% external sources). *Receiving aid:* Freshmen: 1% (23); Undergraduates: 3% (196). *Average Award: Freshmen:* $3300; *Undergraduates:* $2323. *Scholarships, grants, and awards by category: Academic Interests/Achievement:* 405 awards ($1,082,716 total): general academic interests/achievements. *Special Achievements/Activities:* 25 awards ($16,000 total): community service. *Special Characteristics:* 286 awards ($283,217 total): adult students, children of faculty/staff, children with a deceased or disabled parent, first-generation college students, members of minority groups, veterans. *Tuition waivers:* Full or partial for employees or children of employees, senior citizens. *ROTC:* Army cooperative.

LOANS *Student loans:* $24,238,831 (67% need-based, 33% non-need-based). 62% of past graduating class borrowed through all loan programs. *Average indebtedness per student:* $14,943. *Average need-based loan:* Freshmen: $3113;

Undergraduates: $3800. *Parent loans:* $2,638,742 (60% need-based, 40% non-need-based). *Programs:* Federal Direct (Subsidized and Unsubsidized Stafford, PLUS), Perkins, Federal Nursing, state.

WORK-STUDY *Federal work-study:* Total amount: $770,151; 718 jobs averaging $1072. *State or other work-study/employment:* Total amount: $2,700,000 (100% non-need-based). 950 part-time jobs averaging $2842.

APPLYING FOR FINANCIAL AID *Required financial aid form:* FAFSA. *Financial aid deadline (priority):* 3/1. *Notification date:* Continuous beginning 3/25.

CONTACT Bruce Palmer, Director of Financial Aid, University of Massachusetts Dartmouth, 285 Old Westport Road, North Dartmouth, MA 02747-2300, 508-999-8643. *Fax:* 508-999-8935. *E-mail:* financialaid@umassd.edu.

UNIVERSITY OF MASSACHUSETTS LOWELL
Lowell, MA

Tuition & fees (MA res): $7891   **Average undergraduate aid package:** $8084

ABOUT THE INSTITUTION State-supported, coed. Awards: associate, bachelor's, master's, and doctoral degrees and post-master's certificates. 38 undergraduate majors. Total enrollment: 11,089. Undergraduates: 8,662. Freshmen: 1,012. Federal methodology is used as a basis for awarding need-based institutional aid.

UNDERGRADUATE EXPENSES for 2004–05 *Application fee:* $20. *Tuition, state resident:* full-time $1454; part-time $60.58 per credit. *Tuition, nonresident:* full-time $8567; part-time $356.96 per credit. *Required fees:* full-time $6437; $279.87 per credit. *College room and board:* $6011; *room only:* $3567. Room and board charges vary according to board plan and housing facility. Full-time required fee for out of state students: $8084. *Payment plan:* Installment.

FRESHMAN FINANCIAL AID (Fall 2003) 765 applied for aid; of those 62% were deemed to have need. 96% of freshmen with need received aid; of those 83% had need fully met. *Average percent of need met:* 96% (excluding resources awarded to replace EFC). *Average financial aid package:* $8026 (excluding resources awarded to replace EFC). 3% of all full-time freshmen had no need and received non-need-based gift aid.

UNDERGRADUATE FINANCIAL AID (Fall 2003) 3,844 applied for aid; of those 72% were deemed to have need. 96% of undergraduates with need received aid; of those 81% had need fully met. *Average percent of need met:* 96% (excluding resources awarded to replace EFC). *Average financial aid package:* $8084 (excluding resources awarded to replace EFC). 4% of all full-time undergraduates had no need and received non-need-based gift aid.

GIFT AID (NEED-BASED) *Receiving aid:* Freshmen: 39% (392); All full-time undergraduates: 36% (2,092). *Average award:* Freshmen: $3778; Undergraduates: $3922. *Scholarships, grants, and awards:* Federal Pell, FSEOG, state, private, college/university gift aid from institutional funds.

GIFT AID (NON-NEED-BASED) *Receiving aid:* Freshmen: 9% (86); Undergraduates: 9% (529). *Average Award: Freshmen:* $2783; *Undergraduates:* $3473. *Scholarships, grants, and awards by category: Academic Interests/Achievement:* computer science, engineering/technologies, general academic interests/achievements, health fields, humanities. *Creative Arts/Performance:* music. *Special Achievements/Activities:* community service, general special achievements/activities. *Special Characteristics:* general special characteristics. *Tuition waivers:* Full or partial for employees or children of employees, senior citizens. *ROTC:* Air Force.

LOANS *Student loans:* $18,385,925 (44% need-based, 56% non-need-based). 62% of past graduating class borrowed through all loan programs. *Average indebtedness per student:* $15,167. *Average need-based loan:* Freshmen: $2356; Undergraduates: $3258. *Parent loans:* $2,764,320 (100% non-need-based). *Programs:* Federal Direct (Subsidized and Unsubsidized Stafford, PLUS), Perkins, state.

WORK-STUDY *Federal work-study:* Total amount: $213,741; 159 jobs averaging $2801. *State or other work-study/employment:* Total amount: $1,798,340 (100% non-need-based). 582 part-time jobs averaging $3092.

ATHLETIC AWARDS *Total amount:* $1,003,152 (100% non-need-based).

APPLYING FOR FINANCIAL AID *Required financial aid form:* FAFSA. *Financial aid deadline (priority):* 3/1. *Notification date:* Continuous beginning 3/24.

CONTACT Mr. Richard Barrett, Director of Financial Aid, University of Massachusetts Lowell, 883 Broadway Street, Room 102, Lowell, MA 01854, 978-934-4226 or toll-free 800-410-4607. *E-mail:* richard_barrett@uml.edu.

THE UNIVERSITY OF MEMPHIS
Memphis, TN

Tuition & fees (TN res): $4480 **Average undergraduate aid package: $3980**

ABOUT THE INSTITUTION State-supported, coed. Awards: bachelor's, master's, doctoral, and first professional degrees and post-bachelor's, post-master's, and first professional certificates. 65 undergraduate majors. Total enrollment: 20,668. Undergraduates: 15,928. Federal methodology is used as a basis for awarding need-based institutional aid.

UNDERGRADUATE EXPENSES for 2004–05 *Application fee:* $15. *Tuition, state resident:* full-time $3748; part-time $209 per credit hour. *Tuition, nonresident:* full-time $12,472; part-time $573 per credit hour. Full-time tuition and fees vary according to program and reciprocity agreements. Part-time tuition and fees vary according to course load and program. *College room and board:* $4920; *room only:* $2840. Room and board charges vary according to housing facility. *Payment plan:* Installment.

GIFT AID (NEED-BASED) *Total amount:* $26,324,059 (64% federal, 13% state, 22% institutional, 1% external sources). *Receiving aid:* Freshmen: 29% (533); All full-time undergraduates: 31% (3,499). *Average award:* Freshmen: $3071; Undergraduates: $2989. *Scholarships, grants, and awards:* Federal Pell, FSEOG, state, college/university gift aid from institutional funds.

GIFT AID (NON-NEED-BASED) *Total amount:* $4,676,041 (96% institutional, 4% external sources). *Receiving aid:* Freshmen: 16% (301); Undergraduates: 14% (1,539). *Average Award:* Freshmen: $4205; Undergraduates: $3744. *Scholarships, grants, and awards by category: Academic Interests/Achievement:* biological sciences, business, communication, education, engineering/ technologies, English, general academic interests/achievements, health fields, humanities, international studies, mathematics, military science, physical sciences, premedicine, social sciences. *Creative Arts/Performance:* art/fine arts, cinema/film/broadcasting, dance, journalism/publications, music. *Special Achievements/Activities:* cheerleading/drum major, general special achievements/ activities, leadership. *Special Characteristics:* adult students, children of educators, children of faculty/staff, children of public servants, handicapped students, members of minority groups, public servants. *Tuition waivers:* Full or partial for employees or children of employees, senior citizens. *ROTC:* Army, Naval, Air Force.

LOANS *Student loans:* $45,152,579 (54% need-based, 46% non-need-based). 30% of past graduating class borrowed through all loan programs. *Average indebtedness per student:* $21,454. *Average need-based loan:* Freshmen: $1568; Undergraduates: $3417. *Parent loans:* $2,292,504 (100% non-need-based). *Programs:* Federal Direct (Subsidized and Unsubsidized Stafford, PLUS), Perkins, college/university.

ATHLETIC AWARDS *Total amount:* $3,807,237 (66% need-based, 34% non-need-based).

APPLYING FOR FINANCIAL AID *Required financial aid form:* FAFSA. *Financial aid deadline (priority):* 3/1. *Notification date:* Continuous. Students must reply by 8/1.

CONTACT Richard Ritzman, Director of Student Financial Aid, The University of Memphis, Wilder Tower 103, Memphis, TN 38152, 901-678-3205. *Fax:* 901-678-3590. *E-mail:* rritzman@memphis.edu.

UNIVERSITY OF MIAMI
Coral Gables, FL

Tuition & fees: $27,840 **Average undergraduate aid package: $22,711**

ABOUT THE INSTITUTION Independent, coed. Awards: bachelor's, master's, doctoral, and first professional degrees and post-bachelor's and post-master's certificates. 116 undergraduate majors. Total enrollment: 15,250. Undergraduates: 10,104. Freshmen: 2,043. Federal methodology is used as a basis for awarding need-based institutional aid.

UNDERGRADUATE EXPENSES for 2004–05 *Application fee:* $65. *Comprehensive fee:* $36,442 includes full-time tuition ($27,384), mandatory fees ($456), and room and board ($8602). *College room only:* $5028. Full-time tuition and fees vary according to course load, location, and program. Room and board charges vary according to board plan and housing facility. Part-time tuition and fees vary according to course load, location, and program. *Payment plans:* Guaranteed tuition, tuition prepayment, installment, deferred payment.

FRESHMAN FINANCIAL AID (Fall 2003) 1407 applied for aid; of those 82% were deemed to have need. 100% of freshmen with need received aid; of those 31% had need fully met. *Average percent of need met:* 79% (excluding resources awarded to replace EFC). *Average financial aid package:* $22,858 (excluding resources awarded to replace EFC). 22% of all full-time freshmen had no need and received non-need-based gift aid.

UNDERGRADUATE FINANCIAL AID (Fall 2003) 5,515 applied for aid; of those 88% were deemed to have need. 100% of undergraduates with need received aid; of those 25% had need fully met. *Average percent of need met:* 77% (excluding resources awarded to replace EFC). *Average financial aid package:* $22,711 (excluding resources awarded to replace EFC). 22% of all full-time undergraduates had no need and received non-need-based gift aid.

GIFT AID (NEED-BASED) *Total amount:* $74,881,581 (9% federal, 18% state, 70% institutional, 3% external sources). *Receiving aid:* Freshmen: 55% (1,122); All full-time undergraduates: 52% (4,781). *Average award:* Freshmen: $17,860; Undergraduates: $16,943. *Scholarships, grants, and awards:* Federal Pell, FSEOG, state, private, college/university gift aid from institutional funds, Federal Nursing.

GIFT AID (NON-NEED-BASED) *Total amount:* $43,203,431 (1% federal, 26% state, 70% institutional, 3% external sources). *Receiving aid:* Freshmen: 14% (274); Undergraduates: 9% (786). *Average Award: Freshmen:* $13,779; *Undergraduates:* $13,660. *Scholarships, grants, and awards by category: Academic Interests/Achievement:* 4,472 awards ($56,423,175 total): biological sciences, business, communication, education, engineering/technologies, general academic interests/achievements, military science. *Creative Arts/Performance:* 422 awards ($5,723,916 total): art/fine arts, cinema/film/broadcasting, debating, music, performing arts, theater/drama. *Special Characteristics:* 1,358 awards ($19,089,633 total): children of faculty/staff, ethnic background, international students. *Tuition waivers:* Full or partial for employees or children of employees. *ROTC:* Army, Air Force.

LOANS *Student loans:* $47,106,426 (69% need-based, 31% non-need-based). 58% of past graduating class borrowed through all loan programs. *Average indebtedness per student:* $31,723. *Average need-based loan:* Freshmen: $3317; Undergraduates: $4776. *Parent loans:* $12,752,713 (34% need-based, 66% non-need-based). *Programs:* FFEL (Subsidized and Unsubsidized Stafford, PLUS), Perkins, Federal Nursing, Signature Loans, alternative loans.

WORK-STUDY *Federal work-study:* Total amount: $4,298,704; 2,096 jobs averaging $2051. *State or other work-study/employment:* Total amount: $1,000,589 (24% need-based, 76% non-need-based). 226 part-time jobs averaging $4427.

ATHLETIC AWARDS *Total amount:* $7,669,574 (39% need-based, 61% non-need-based).

APPLYING FOR FINANCIAL AID *Required financial aid form:* FAFSA. *Financial aid deadline (priority):* 2/15. *Notification date:* Continuous beginning 3/15.

CONTACT Mr. James M. Bauer, Director, Financial Assistance, University of Miami, Rhodes House, Building 37E, Coral Gables, FL 33124-5240, 305-284-5212. *Fax:* 305-284-4491. *E-mail:* jbauer@miami.edu.

UNIVERSITY OF MICHIGAN
Ann Arbor, MI

Tuition & fees (MI res): $8201 **Average undergraduate aid package: $11,306**

ABOUT THE INSTITUTION State-supported, coed. Awards: bachelor's, master's, doctoral, and first professional degrees and post-bachelor's and post-master's certificates. 143 undergraduate majors. Total enrollment: 39,533. Undergraduates: 24,828. Freshmen: 6,037. Federal methodology is used as a basis for awarding need-based institutional aid.

UNDERGRADUATE EXPENSES for 2004–05 *Application fee:* $40. *Tuition, state resident:* full-time $8014; part-time $308 per credit. *Tuition, nonresident:* full-time $25,840; part-time $1050 per credit. *Required fees:* full-time $187; $93.69 per term part-time. Full-time tuition and fees vary according to course load, degree level, program, and student level. Part-time tuition and fees vary according to course load, degree level, program, and student level. *College room and board:* $7030. Room and board charges vary according to board plan and housing facility. *Payment plan:* Installment.

FRESHMAN FINANCIAL AID (Fall 2003) 3350 applied for aid; of those 83% were deemed to have need. 100% of freshmen with need received aid; of those 90% had need fully met. *Average percent of need met:* 90% (excluding resources awarded to replace EFC). *Average financial aid package:* $8479 (excluding resources awarded to replace EFC). 23% of all full-time freshmen had no need and received non-need-based gift aid.

UNDERGRADUATE FINANCIAL AID (Fall 2003) 13,400 applied for aid; of those 80% were deemed to have need. 100% of undergraduates with need received aid; of those 90% had need fully met. *Average percent of need met:* 90% (excluding resources awarded to replace EFC). *Average financial aid package:*

University of Michigan

$11,306 (excluding resources awarded to replace EFC). 20% of all full-time undergraduates had no need and received non-need-based gift aid.

GIFT AID (NEED-BASED) *Total amount:* $46,184,301 (23% federal, 1% state, 76% institutional). *Receiving aid:* Freshmen: 24% (1,318); All full-time undergraduates: 24% (5,867). *Average award:* Freshmen: $7813; Undergraduates: $7872. *Scholarships, grants, and awards:* Federal Pell, FSEOG, state, private, college/university gift aid from institutional funds.

GIFT AID (NON-NEED-BASED) *Total amount:* $50,620,469 (7% federal, 17% state, 50% institutional, 26% external sources). *Receiving aid:* Freshmen: 25% (1,401); Undergraduates: 23% (5,605). *Average Award:* Freshmen: $4081; Undergraduates: $5203. *Scholarships, grants, and awards by category:* Academic Interests/Achievement: architecture, area/ethnic studies, biological sciences, business, communication, computer science, education, engineering/technologies, English, foreign languages, general academic interests/achievements, health fields, humanities, international studies, library science, mathematics, military science, physical sciences, premedicine, social sciences. *Creative Arts/Performance:* journalism/publications, music, theater/drama. *Special Achievements/Activities:* community service, general special achievements/activities, leadership. *Special Characteristics:* children of faculty/staff, children of workers in trades, handicapped students, international students, local/state students, members of minority groups, out-of-state students. *Tuition waivers:* Full or partial for senior citizens. *ROTC:* Army, Air Force.

LOANS *Student loans:* $77,799,923 (76% need-based, 24% non-need-based). 43% of past graduating class borrowed through all loan programs. *Average indebtedness per student:* $21,326. *Average need-based loan:* Freshmen: $4311; Undergraduates: $5814. *Parent loans:* $15,075,874 (100% non-need-based). *Programs:* Federal Direct (Subsidized and Unsubsidized Stafford, PLUS), Perkins, Federal Nursing, state, college/university, MI-Loan Program, Health Professions Student Loans (HPSL).

WORK-STUDY *Federal work-study:* Total amount: $11,595,249; 4,731 jobs averaging $2451. *State or other work-study/employment:* Total amount: $1,035,140 (100% need-based). 465 part-time jobs averaging $2226.

APPLYING FOR FINANCIAL AID *Required financial aid forms:* FAFSA, federal income tax form(s). *Financial aid deadline:* 4/30 (priority: 2/15). *Notification date:* Continuous beginning 3/15.

CONTACT Financial Aid Counseling and Advising Office, University of Michigan, 2011 Student Activities Building, Ann Arbor, MI 48109-1316, 734-763-6600. *Fax:* 734-647-3081. *E-mail:* financial.aid@umich.edu.

UNIVERSITY OF MICHIGAN–DEARBORN
Dearborn, MI

Tuition & fees (MI res): $6112   **Average undergraduate aid package:** $8654

ABOUT THE INSTITUTION State-supported, coed. Awards: bachelor's and master's degrees and post-bachelor's certificates. 60 undergraduate majors. Total enrollment: 8,631. Undergraduates: 6,449. Freshmen: 696. Federal methodology is used as a basis for awarding need-based institutional aid.

UNDERGRADUATE EXPENSES for 2004–05 *Application fee:* $30. *Tuition, state resident:* full-time $6002; part-time $228.80 per credit hour. *Tuition, nonresident:* full-time $13,273; part-time $519.45 per credit hour. Full-time tuition and fees vary according to course level, course load, program, and student level. Part-time tuition and fees vary according to course level, course load, program, and student level. *Payment plan:* Installment.

FRESHMAN FINANCIAL AID (Fall 2003) 480 applied for aid; of those 64% were deemed to have need. 100% of freshmen with need received aid; of those 2% had need fully met. *Average percent of need met:* 2% (excluding resources awarded to replace EFC). *Average financial aid package:* $8370 (excluding resources awarded to replace EFC). 45% of all full-time freshmen had no need and received non-need-based gift aid.

UNDERGRADUATE FINANCIAL AID (Fall 2003) 2,452 applied for aid; of those 75% were deemed to have need. 99% of undergraduates with need received aid; of those 4% had need fully met. *Average percent of need met:* 4% (excluding resources awarded to replace EFC). *Average financial aid package:* $8654 (excluding resources awarded to replace EFC). 16% of all full-time undergraduates had no need and received non-need-based gift aid.

GIFT AID (NEED-BASED) *Total amount:* $5,929,001 (71% federal, 8% state, 21% institutional). *Receiving aid:* Freshmen: 29% (215); All full-time undergraduates: 29% (1,274). *Average award:* Freshmen: $4100; Undergraduates: $4260. *Scholarships, grants, and awards:* Federal Pell, FSEOG, state, private, college/university gift aid from institutional funds.

GIFT AID (NON-NEED-BASED) *Total amount:* $4,661,470 (20% state, 44% institutional, 36% external sources). *Receiving aid:* Freshmen: 33% (241);

Undergraduates: 11% (483). *Average Award:* Freshmen: $3665; Undergraduates: $3928. *Scholarships, grants, and awards by category:* Academic Interests/Achievement: 282 awards ($841,960 total): biological sciences, business, computer science, engineering/technologies, general academic interests/achievements, international studies, mathematics, physical sciences, social sciences. *Creative Arts/Performance:* 54 awards ($41,068 total): art/fine arts, creative writing, journalism/publications. *Special Achievements/Activities:* 18 awards ($24,932 total): community service. *Special Characteristics:* 160 awards ($518,672 total): children and siblings of alumni, children of current students, ethnic background, general special characteristics, members of minority groups, previous college experience. *Tuition waivers:* Full or partial for employees or children of employees, senior citizens. *ROTC:* Army cooperative, Naval cooperative, Air Force cooperative.

LOANS *Student loans:* $18,112,230 (55% need-based, 45% non-need-based). 44% of past graduating class borrowed through all loan programs. *Average indebtedness per student:* $13,086. *Average need-based loan:* Freshmen: $2792; Undergraduates: $4147. *Parent loans:* $265,098 (100% non-need-based). *Programs:* Federal Direct (Subsidized and Unsubsidized Stafford, PLUS), Perkins, state, college/university.

WORK-STUDY *Federal work-study:* Total amount: $65,333; 47 jobs averaging $1390. *State or other work-study/employment:* Total amount: $34,424 (100% need-based). 20 part-time jobs averaging $1721.

ATHLETIC AWARDS *Total amount:* $65,000 (100% non-need-based).

APPLYING FOR FINANCIAL AID *Required financial aid form:* FAFSA. *Financial aid deadline (priority):* 3/15. *Notification date:* Continuous beginning 4/1. Students must reply within 3 weeks of notification.

CONTACT Mr. John A. Mason, Director of Financial Aid, University of Michigan–Dearborn, 4901 Evergreen Road, 1183 UC, Dearborn, MI 48128-1491, 313-593-5300. *Fax:* 313-593-5313. *E-mail:* jamason@umd.umich.edu.

UNIVERSITY OF MICHIGAN–FLINT
Flint, MI

Tuition & fees (MI res): $6018   **Average undergraduate aid package:** $6705

ABOUT THE INSTITUTION State-supported, coed. Awards: bachelor's, master's, and first professional degrees. 80 undergraduate majors. Total enrollment: 6,188. Undergraduates: 5,620. Freshmen: 553. Federal methodology is used as a basis for awarding need-based institutional aid.

UNDERGRADUATE EXPENSES for 2004–05 *Application fee:* $30. *Tuition, state resident:* full-time $5722; part-time $214 per credit. *Tuition, nonresident:* full-time $10,582; part-time $428 per credit. *Required fees:* full-time $296; $148 per term part-time. Full-time tuition and fees vary according to program. Part-time tuition and fees vary according to program. *Payment plan:* Deferred payment.

FRESHMAN FINANCIAL AID (Fall 2003) 285 applied for aid; of those 70% were deemed to have need. 99% of freshmen with need received aid; of those 7% had need fully met. *Average financial aid package:* $5608 (excluding resources awarded to replace EFC).

UNDERGRADUATE FINANCIAL AID (Fall 2003) 2,391 applied for aid; of those 81% were deemed to have need. 97% of undergraduates with need received aid; of those 1% had need fully met. *Average financial aid package:* $6705 (excluding resources awarded to replace EFC). 1% of all full-time undergraduates had no need and received non-need-based gift aid.

GIFT AID (NEED-BASED) *Total amount:* $7,918,661 (55% federal, 5% state, 38% institutional, 2% external sources). *Receiving aid:* Freshmen: 29% (122); All full-time undergraduates: 34% (1,163). *Average award:* Freshmen: $3478; Undergraduates: $3983. *Scholarships, grants, and awards:* Federal Pell, FSEOG, state, private, college/university gift aid from institutional funds.

GIFT AID (NON-NEED-BASED) *Total amount:* $613,950 (100% state). *Receiving aid:* Freshmen: 36% (150); Undergraduates: 18% (615). *Average Award:* Undergraduates: $1799. *Scholarships, grants, and awards by category:* Academic Interests/Achievement: biological sciences, business, communication, computer science, education, engineering/technologies, English, foreign languages, general academic interests/achievements, health fields, humanities, international studies, mathematics, physical sciences, premedicine, social sciences. *Creative Arts/Performance:* art/fine arts, music, theater/drama. *Special Achievements/Activities:* community service, hobbies/interests, leadership. *Special Characteristics:* children and siblings of alumni, children of union members/company employees, ethnic background, general special characteristics, handicapped students, international students, members of minority groups. *Tuition waivers:* Full or partial for minority students, employees or children of employees, senior citizens.

LOANS *Student loans:* $17,191,883 (52% need-based, 48% non-need-based). 66% of past graduating class borrowed through all loan programs. *Average indebtedness per student:* $20,010. *Average need-based loan:* Freshmen: $2699; Undergraduates: $3897. *Parent loans:* $190,350 (100% non-need-based). **Programs:** Federal Direct (Subsidized and Unsubsidized Stafford, PLUS), Perkins. **WORK-STUDY** *Federal work-study:* Total amount: $557,648; 428 jobs averaging $2000. *State or other work-study/employment:* Total amount: $160,359 (100% need-based). 59 part-time jobs averaging $2000.
APPLYING FOR FINANCIAL AID *Required financial aid form:* FAFSA. *Financial aid deadline (priority):* 3/1. *Notification date:* Continuous beginning 3/15. Students must reply within 4 weeks of notification.
CONTACT Financial Aid Office, University of Michigan–Flint, Room 277 UPAV, Flint, MI 48502-1950, 810-762-3444 or toll-free 800-942-5636 (in-state).

UNIVERSITY OF MINNESOTA, CROOKSTON
Crookston, MN

ABOUT THE INSTITUTION State-supported, coed. Awards: associate and bachelor's degrees. 32 undergraduate majors. Total enrollment: 2,088. Undergraduates: 2,088. Freshmen: 215.
GIFT AID (NEED-BASED) *Scholarships, grants, and awards:* Federal Pell, FSEOG, state, college/university gift aid from institutional funds.
GIFT AID (NON-NEED-BASED) *Scholarships, grants, and awards by category:* Academic Interests/Achievement: agriculture, business, communication, computer science, engineering/technologies, general academic interests/achievements, health fields. *Special Achievements/Activities:* general special achievements/ activities, leadership. *Special Characteristics:* children and siblings of alumni, children of faculty/staff, ethnic background, general special characteristics, members of minority groups, out-of-state students, previous college experience.
LOANS *Programs:* Federal Direct (Subsidized and Unsubsidized Stafford, PLUS), Perkins, state, college/university.
APPLYING FOR FINANCIAL AID *Required financial aid form:* FAFSA.
CONTACT Associate Director of Financial Aid, University of Minnesota, Crookston, 170 Owen Hall, Crookston, MN 56716-5001, 218-281-8576 or toll-free 800-862-6466. *Fax:* 218-281-8575.

UNIVERSITY OF MINNESOTA, DULUTH
Duluth, MN

ABOUT THE INSTITUTION State-supported, coed. Awards: bachelor's, master's, and first professional degrees. 68 undergraduate majors. Total enrollment: 10,366. Undergraduates: 9,490. Freshmen: 2,248.
GIFT AID (NEED-BASED) *Scholarships, grants, and awards:* Federal Pell, FSEOG, state, private, college/university gift aid from institutional funds.
LOANS *Programs:* Federal Direct (Subsidized and Unsubsidized Stafford, PLUS), Perkins, state, college/university, Primary Care Loans.
WORK-STUDY *Federal work-study:* Total amount: $482,219; 243 jobs averaging $1961. *State or other work-study/employment:* Total amount: $377,718 (100% need-based). 185 part-time jobs averaging $2002.
APPLYING FOR FINANCIAL AID *Required financial aid form:* FAFSA.
CONTACT Ms. Brenda Herzig, Director of Financial Aid, University of Minnesota, Duluth, 10 University Drive, 184 Darland Administration Building, Duluth, MN 55812-2496, 218-726-8000 or toll-free 800-232-1339. *Fax:* 218-726-8219.

UNIVERSITY OF MINNESOTA, MORRIS
Morris, MN

Tuition & fees (MN res): $9056   **Average undergraduate aid package: $12,065**

ABOUT THE INSTITUTION State-supported, coed. Awards: bachelor's degrees. 42 undergraduate majors. Total enrollment: 1,836. Undergraduates: 1,836. Freshmen: 386. Federal methodology is used as a basis for awarding need-based institutional aid.
UNDERGRADUATE EXPENSES for 2004–05 *Application fee:* $35. *Tuition, state resident:* full-time $7668; part-time $255.60 per credit. *Tuition, nonresident:* full-time $7668; part-time $255.60 per credit. *Required fees:* full-time $1388; $10 per credit. Full-time tuition and fees vary according to reciprocity agreements. Part-time tuition and fees vary according to course load and reciprocity agreements. *College room and board:* $5250; *room only:* $2510. Room and board charges vary according to board plan and housing facility. *Payment plans:* Installment, deferred payment.

FRESHMAN FINANCIAL AID (Fall 2004, est.) 331 applied for aid; of those 78% were deemed to have need. 98% of freshmen with need received aid; of those 47% had need fully met. *Average percent of need met:* 82% (excluding resources awarded to replace EFC). *Average financial aid package:* $11,970 (excluding resources awarded to replace EFC). 20% of all full-time freshmen had no need and received non-need-based gift aid.
UNDERGRADUATE FINANCIAL AID (Fall 2004, est.) 1,349 applied for aid; of those 82% were deemed to have need. 100% of undergraduates with need received aid; of those 43% had need fully met. *Average percent of need met:* 83% (excluding resources awarded to replace EFC). *Average financial aid package:* $12,065 (excluding resources awarded to replace EFC). 18% of all full-time undergraduates had no need and received non-need-based gift aid.
GIFT AID (NEED-BASED) *Total amount:* $5,588,806 (31% federal, 32% state, 26% institutional, 11% external sources). *Receiving aid:* Freshmen: 62% (237); All full-time undergraduates: 60% (970). *Average award:* Freshmen: $6333; Undergraduates: $5669. *Scholarships, grants, and awards:* Federal Pell, FSEOG, state, private, college/university gift aid from institutional funds.
GIFT AID (NON-NEED-BASED) *Total amount:* $940,129 (75% institutional, 25% external sources). *Receiving aid:* Freshmen: 26% (100); Undergraduates: 22% (349). *Average Award:* Freshmen: $3310; Undergraduates: $3374. *Scholarships, grants, and awards by category:* Academic Interests/Achievement: 1,066 awards ($1,716,192 total): general academic interests/achievements. *Creative Arts/Performance:* 23 awards ($3910 total): music. *Special Achievements/ Activities:* 41 awards ($33,925 total): general special achievements/activities. *Special Characteristics:* 72 awards ($134,475 total): ethnic background, international students, members of minority groups, veterans, veterans' children. *Tuition waivers:* Full or partial for senior citizens.
LOANS *Student loans:* $7,884,154 (82% need-based, 18% non-need-based). 91% of past graduating class borrowed through all loan programs. *Average indebtedness per student:* $15,490. *Average need-based loan:* Freshmen: $6106; Undergraduates: $6989. *Parent loans:* $249,664 (100% non-need-based). *Programs:* Federal Direct (Subsidized and Unsubsidized Stafford, PLUS), Perkins, state, college/university, SELF Loans.
WORK-STUDY *Federal work-study:* Total amount: $301,383; 487 jobs averaging $734. *State or other work-study/employment:* Total amount: $473,170 (51% need-based, 49% non-need-based). 531 part-time jobs averaging $900.
ATHLETIC AWARDS *Total amount:* $15,400 (100% non-need-based).
APPLYING FOR FINANCIAL AID *Required financial aid form:* FAFSA. *Financial aid deadline (priority):* 3/1. *Notification date:* Continuous beginning 3/15. Students must reply within 3 weeks of notification.
CONTACT Ms. Pam Engebretson, Director of Financial Aid, University of Minnesota, Morris, 600 East 4th Street, Morris, MN 56267, 320-589-6035 or toll-free 800-992-8863. *Fax:* 320-589-1673. *E-mail:* engebrpj@morris.umn.edu.

UNIVERSITY OF MINNESOTA, TWIN CITIES CAMPUS
Minneapolis, MN

Tuition & fees (MN res): $8030   **Average undergraduate aid package: $9027**

ABOUT THE INSTITUTION State-supported, coed. Awards: bachelor's, master's, doctoral, and first professional degrees and post-bachelor's and post-master's certificates. 132 undergraduate majors. Total enrollment: 50,954. Undergraduates: 32,716. Freshmen: 5,588. Federal methodology is used as a basis for awarding need-based institutional aid.
UNDERGRADUATE EXPENSES for 2004–05 *Application fee:* $45. *Tuition, state resident:* full-time $6678; part-time $257 per credit. *Tuition, nonresident:* full-time $18,308; part-time $704 per credit. Full-time tuition and fees vary according to program and reciprocity agreements. Part-time tuition and fees vary according to course load, program, and reciprocity agreements. *College room and board:* $6458; *room only:* $3730. Room and board charges vary according to board plan, housing facility, and location. *Payment plans:* Guaranteed tuition, installment.
FRESHMAN FINANCIAL AID (Fall 2003) 3806 applied for aid; of those 72% were deemed to have need. 98% of freshmen with need received aid; of those 45% had need fully met. *Average percent of need met:* 82% (excluding resources awarded to replace EFC). *Average financial aid package:* $9377 (excluding resources awarded to replace EFC). 15% of all full-time freshmen had no need and received non-need-based gift aid.
UNDERGRADUATE FINANCIAL AID (Fall 2003) 16,775 applied for aid; of those 78% were deemed to have need. 98% of undergraduates with need received aid; of those 35% had need fully met. *Average percent of need met:* 76%

University of Minnesota, Twin Cities Campus

(excluding resources awarded to replace EFC). *Average financial aid package:* $9027 (excluding resources awarded to replace EFC). 10% of all full-time undergraduates had no need and received non-need-based gift aid.

GIFT AID (NEED-BASED) *Total amount:* $57,403,834 (33% federal, 27% state, 34% institutional, 6% external sources). *Receiving aid:* Freshmen: 40% (2,072); All full-time undergraduates: 36% (9,079). *Average award:* Freshmen: $6463; Undergraduates: $6074. *Scholarships, grants, and awards:* Federal Pell, FSEOG, state, private, college/university gift aid from institutional funds, Federal Nursing.

GIFT AID (NON-NEED-BASED) *Total amount:* $11,128,118 (82% institutional, 18% external sources). *Receiving aid:* Freshmen: 7% (384); Undergraduates: 5% (1,177). *Average Award:* Freshmen: $3892; Undergraduates: $4238. *Scholarships, grants, and awards by category: Academic Interests/Achievement:* agriculture, architecture, area/ethnic studies, biological sciences, business, communication, computer science, education, engineering/technologies, English, foreign languages, general academic interests/achievements, health fields, home economics, humanities, international studies, library science, mathematics, military science, physical sciences, premedicine, religion/biblical studies, social sciences. *Creative Arts/Performance:* general creative arts/performance. *Special Achievements/Activities:* hobbies/interests, leadership. *Special Characteristics:* general special characteristics. *Tuition waivers:* Full or partial for senior citizens. *ROTC:* Army, Air Force.

LOANS *Student loans:* $79,727,306 (81% need-based, 19% non-need-based). *Average need-based loan:* Freshmen: $4508; Undergraduates: $5720. *Parent loans:* $43,834,126 (100% non-need-based). *Programs:* Federal Direct (Subsidized and Unsubsidized Stafford, PLUS), Perkins, Federal Nursing, state, college/university, Health Professions Loans, alternative loans.

WORK-STUDY *Federal work-study:* Total amount: $5,212,980; jobs available. *State or other work-study/employment:* Total amount: $4,864,887 (100% need-based). Part-time jobs available.

ATHLETIC AWARDS *Total amount:* $5,775,150 (100% non-need-based).

APPLYING FOR FINANCIAL AID *Required financial aid form:* FAFSA. *Financial aid deadline (priority):* 1/15. *Notification date:* Continuous.

CONTACT Mr. John Kellogg, Analyst, Office of Institutional Research and Reporting, University of Minnesota, Twin Cities Campus, 318 Morrill Hall, 100 Church Street SE, Minneapolis, MN 55455, 612-625-3387 or toll-free 800-752-1000. *E-mail:* j-kell@umn.edu.

UNIVERSITY OF MISSISSIPPI
Oxford, MS

Tuition & fees (MS res): $4110   **Average undergraduate aid package:** $7532

ABOUT THE INSTITUTION State-supported, coed. Awards: bachelor's, master's, doctoral, and first professional degrees. 63 undergraduate majors. Total enrollment: 14,497. Undergraduates: 11,820. Freshmen: 2,276. Federal methodology is used as a basis for awarding need-based institutional aid.

UNDERGRADUATE EXPENSES for 2004–05 *Application fee:* $25; $40 for nonresidents. *Tuition, state resident:* full-time $4110. *Tuition, nonresident:* full-time $9264. *College room and board:* $5610; *room only:* $2800. *Payment plan:* Tuition prepayment.

FRESHMAN FINANCIAL AID (Fall 2003) 1328 applied for aid; of those 64% were deemed to have need. 98% of freshmen with need received aid; of those 20% had need fully met. *Average percent of need met:* 59% (excluding resources awarded to replace EFC). *Average financial aid package:* $6938 (excluding resources awarded to replace EFC). 15% of all full-time freshmen had no need and received non-need-based gift aid.

UNDERGRADUATE FINANCIAL AID (Fall 2003) 5,471 applied for aid; of those 75% were deemed to have need. 97% of undergraduates with need received aid; of those 18% had need fully met. *Average percent of need met:* 64% (excluding resources awarded to replace EFC). *Average financial aid package:* $7532 (excluding resources awarded to replace EFC). 10% of all full-time undergraduates had no need and received non-need-based gift aid.

GIFT AID (NEED-BASED) *Total amount:* $9,577,017 (81% federal, 3% state, 16% institutional). *Receiving aid:* Freshmen: 21% (496); All full-time undergraduates: 24% (2,416). *Average award:* Freshmen: $4148; Undergraduates: $3779. *Scholarships, grants, and awards:* Federal Pell, FSEOG, state, private, college/university gift aid from institutional funds.

GIFT AID (NON-NEED-BASED) *Total amount:* $19,734,173 (1% federal, 22% state, 54% institutional, 23% external sources). *Receiving aid:* Freshmen: 26% (609); Undergraduates: 25% (2,521). *Average Award:* Freshmen: $3972; Undergraduates: $3623. *Scholarships, grants, and awards by category: Academic Interests/Achievement:* business, education, engineering/technologies,

general academic interests/achievements, international studies, military science. *Creative Arts/Performance:* art/fine arts, journalism/publications, music, theater/drama. *Special Achievements/Activities:* cheerleading/drum major, general special achievements/activities, leadership. *Special Characteristics:* children and siblings of alumni, children of faculty/staff, handicapped students, local/state students, out-of-state students, spouses of current students. *Tuition waivers:* Full or partial for children of alumni, employees or children of employees, senior citizens. *ROTC:* Army, Air Force.

LOANS *Student loans:* $24,601,566 (48% need-based, 52% non-need-based). *Average need-based loan:* Freshmen: $2303; Undergraduates: $3704. *Parent loans:* $5,168,350 (100% non-need-based). *Programs:* FFEL (Subsidized and Unsubsidized Stafford, PLUS), Perkins, college/university.

WORK-STUDY *Federal work-study:* Total amount: $622,190; 506 jobs averaging $1230.

ATHLETIC AWARDS *Total amount:* $3,506,963 (100% non-need-based).

APPLYING FOR FINANCIAL AID *Required financial aid form:* FAFSA. *Financial aid deadline (priority):* 2/15. *Notification date:* Continuous beginning 4/15. Students must reply within 3 weeks of notification.

CONTACT Ms. Laura Diven-Brown, Director of Financial Aid, University of Mississippi, 257 Martindale Center, University, MS 38677, 662-915-5788 or toll-free 800-653-6477 (in-state). *Fax:* 662-915-1164. *E-mail:* ldivenbr@olemiss.edu.

UNIVERSITY OF MISSISSIPPI MEDICAL CENTER
Jackson, MS

CONTACT Minetta Veazey, Administrative Secretary, University of Mississippi Medical Center, 2500 North State Street, Jackson, MS 39216, 601-984-1117. *Fax:* 601-984-6984. *E-mail:* mveazey@registrar.umsmed.edu.

UNIVERSITY OF MISSOURI–COLUMBIA
Columbia, MO

Tuition & fees (MO res): $7100   **Average undergraduate aid package:** $10,048

ABOUT THE INSTITUTION State-supported, coed. Awards: bachelor's, master's, doctoral, and first professional degrees and post-master's certificates. 124 undergraduate majors. Total enrollment: 28,257. Undergraduates: 22,137. Freshmen: 4,509. Federal methodology is used as a basis for awarding need-based institutional aid.

UNDERGRADUATE EXPENSES for 2004–05 *Application fee:* $35. *Tuition, state resident:* full-time $6276; part-time $209.20 per credit hour. *Tuition, nonresident:* full-time $15,723; part-time $524.10 per credit hour. *Required fees:* full-time $824; $31.60 per credit hour. Full-time tuition and fees vary according to course load and program. Part-time tuition and fees vary according to course load and program. *College room and board:* $6220. Room and board charges vary according to board plan and housing facility. *Payment plan:* Installment.

GIFT AID (NEED-BASED) *Total amount:* $36,615,779 (31% federal, 12% state, 41% institutional, 16% external sources). *Receiving aid:* Freshmen: 39% (1,790); All full-time undergraduates: 37% (7,227). *Average award:* Freshmen: $6049; Undergraduates: $5295. *Scholarships, grants, and awards:* Federal Pell, FSEOG, state, private, college/university gift aid from institutional funds, Federal Nursing.

GIFT AID (NON-NEED-BASED) *Total amount:* $20,572,826 (4% federal, 15% state, 50% institutional, 31% external sources). *Receiving aid:* Freshmen: 4% (180); Undergraduates: 3% (496). *Average Award:* Freshmen: $4207; Undergraduates: $4203. *Scholarships, grants, and awards by category: Academic Interests/Achievement:* agriculture, biological sciences, business, communication, computer science, education, engineering/technologies, English, foreign languages, general academic interests/achievements, health fields, home economics, mathematics, premedicine, religion/biblical studies, social sciences. *Creative Arts/Performance:* journalism/publications, music, theater/drama. *Special Achievements/Activities:* general special achievements/activities. *Special Characteristics:* children and siblings of alumni, international students, members of minority groups, out-of-state students. *Tuition waivers:* Full or partial for employees or children of employees, senior citizens. *ROTC:* Army, Naval, Air Force.

LOANS *Student loans:* $54,014,649 (67% need-based, 33% non-need-based). 55% of past graduating class borrowed through all loan programs. *Average indebtedness per student:* $16,704. *Average need-based loan:* Freshmen: $3197; Undergraduates: $4078. *Parent loans:* $12,069,544 (99% need-based, 1%

non-need-based). *Programs:* Federal Direct (Subsidized and Unsubsidized Stafford, PLUS), Perkins, Federal Nursing, state, college/university, Health Professions Loans, Primary Care Loans, alternative loans.
ATHLETIC AWARDS *Total amount:* $4,758,924 (34% need-based, 66% non-need-based).
APPLYING FOR FINANCIAL AID *Required financial aid form:* FAFSA. *Financial aid deadline (priority):* 3/1. *Notification date:* Continuous beginning 4/1. Students must reply within 4 weeks of notification.
CONTACT Lori A. Hartman, Associate Director, Student Financial Aid, University of Missouri–Columbia, 11 Jesse Hall, Columbia, MO 65211, 573-882-3569 or toll-free 800-225-6075 (in-state). *Fax:* 573-884-5335. *E-mail:* hartmanlo@missouri.edu.

UNIVERSITY OF MISSOURI–KANSAS CITY
Kansas City, MO

Tuition & fees (MO res): $7250   **Average undergraduate aid package:** $10,682

ABOUT THE INSTITUTION State-supported, coed. Awards: bachelor's, master's, doctoral, and first professional degrees and post-master's and first professional certificates. 55 undergraduate majors. Total enrollment: 14,256. Undergraduates: 9,393. Freshmen: 918. Federal methodology is used as a basis for awarding need-based institutional aid.
UNDERGRADUATE EXPENSES for 2005–06 *Application fee:* $35. *Tuition, state resident:* full-time $6495. *Tuition, nonresident:* full-time $16,272. Full-time tuition and fees vary according to course load, program, and student level. Part-time tuition and fees vary according to course load, program, and student level. *College room and board:* $7505; *room only:* $5100. Room and board charges vary according to board plan and housing facility. *Payment plan:* Installment.
FRESHMAN FINANCIAL AID (Fall 2004, est.) 845 applied for aid; of those 70% were deemed to have need. 99% of freshmen with need received aid; of those 64% had need fully met. *Average percent of need met:* 62% (excluding resources awarded to replace EFC). *Average financial aid package:* $11,914 (excluding resources awarded to replace EFC). 21% of all full-time freshmen had no need and received non-need-based gift aid.
UNDERGRADUATE FINANCIAL AID (Fall 2004, est.) 4,682 applied for aid; of those 74% were deemed to have need. 100% of undergraduates with need received aid; of those 46% had need fully met. *Average percent of need met:* 58% (excluding resources awarded to replace EFC). *Average financial aid package:* $10,682 (excluding resources awarded to replace EFC). 12% of all full-time undergraduates had no need and received non-need-based gift aid.
GIFT AID (NEED-BASED) *Total amount:* $11,283,143 (56% federal, 6% state, 33% institutional, 5% external sources). *Receiving aid:* Freshmen: 45% (408); All full-time undergraduates: 41% (2,225). *Average award:* Freshmen: $5372; Undergraduates: $4602. *Scholarships, grants, and awards:* Federal Pell, FSEOG, state, private, college/university gift aid from institutional funds, United Negro College Fund, Federal Nursing.
GIFT AID (NON-NEED-BASED) *Total amount:* $5,657,487 (4% federal, 7% state, 82% institutional, 7% external sources). *Receiving aid:* Freshmen: 42% (375); Undergraduates: 22% (1,163). *Average Award:* Freshmen: $4245; Undergraduates: $4122. *Scholarships, grants, and awards by category:* Academic Interests/Achievement: general academic interests/achievements. Creative Arts/Performance: debating, general creative arts/performance, music, performing arts. Special Achievements/Activities: general special achievements/activities. Special Characteristics: members of minority groups, out-of-state students. *Tuition waivers:* Full or partial for employees or children of employees. *ROTC:* Army, Air Force cooperative.
LOANS *Student loans:* $36,060,563 (71% need-based, 29% non-need-based). 82% of past graduating class borrowed through all loan programs. *Average indebtedness per student:* $15,704. *Average need-based loan:* Freshmen: $3815; Undergraduates: $6507. *Parent loans:* $1,458,448 (13% need-based, 87% non-need-based). *Programs:* FFEL (Subsidized and Unsubsidized Stafford, PLUS), Perkins, state, college/university.
WORK-STUDY *Federal work-study:* Total amount: $3,821,397; jobs available.
ATHLETIC AWARDS *Total amount:* $1,764,178 (18% need-based, 82% non-need-based).
APPLYING FOR FINANCIAL AID *Required financial aid form:* FAFSA. *Financial aid deadline (priority):* 3/1. *Notification date:* Continuous beginning 4/1.
CONTACT Jan Brandow, Financial Aid and Scholarships Office, University of Missouri–Kansas City, 5100 Rockhill Road, Kansas City, MO 64110-2499, 816-235-1154 or toll-free 800-775-8652 (out-of-state). *Fax:* 816-235-5511.

UNIVERSITY OF MISSOURI–ROLLA
Rolla, MO

ABOUT THE INSTITUTION State-supported, coed. Awards: bachelor's, master's, and doctoral degrees and post-bachelor's certificates. 40 undergraduate majors. Total enrollment: 5,407. Undergraduates: 4,121. Freshmen: 842.
GIFT AID (NEED-BASED) *Scholarships, grants, and awards:* Federal Pell, FSEOG, state, private, college/university gift aid from institutional funds, ROTC-Army and Air Force.
GIFT AID (NON-NEED-BASED) *Scholarships, grants, and awards by category:* Academic Interests/Achievement: biological sciences, business, computer science, education, engineering/technologies, English, general academic interests/achievements, humanities, mathematics, military science, physical sciences, premedicine, social sciences. Creative Arts/Performance: music, theater/drama. Special Characteristics: children and siblings of alumni, members of minority groups, out-of-state students.
LOANS *Programs:* Federal Direct (Subsidized and Unsubsidized Stafford), FFEL (PLUS), Perkins, state, college/university, alternative loans.
WORK-STUDY *Federal work-study:* Total amount: $368,000; 244 jobs averaging $1220. *State or other work-study/employment:* Total amount: $1,090,000 (100% non-need-based). 1,038 part-time jobs averaging $1145.
APPLYING FOR FINANCIAL AID *Required financial aid form:* FAFSA.
CONTACT Mr. Robert W. Whites, Director of Student Financial Assistance, University of Missouri–Rolla, G1 Parker Hall, Rolla, MO 65409, 573-341-4282 or toll-free 800-522-0938. *Fax:* 573-341-4274. *E-mail:* bobw@umr.edu.

UNIVERSITY OF MISSOURI–ST. LOUIS
St. Louis, MO

Tuition & fees (MO res): $7378   **Average undergraduate aid package:** $9207

ABOUT THE INSTITUTION State-supported, coed. Awards: bachelor's, master's, doctoral, and first professional degrees and post-bachelor's certificates. 70 undergraduate majors. Total enrollment: 15,512. Undergraduates: 12,586. Freshmen: 447. Federal methodology is used as a basis for awarding need-based institutional aid.
UNDERGRADUATE EXPENSES for 2004–05 *Application fee:* $35. *Tuition, state resident:* full-time $6276; part-time $209.20 per credit hour. *Tuition, nonresident:* full-time $15,723; part-time $524.10 per credit hour. *Required fees:* full-time $1102; $42.45 per credit hour. Full-time tuition and fees vary according to course load, program, and reciprocity agreements. Part-time tuition and fees vary according to course load, program, and reciprocity agreements. *College room and board:* $6194; *room only:* $4430. Room and board charges vary according to board plan and housing facility. *Payment plan:* Installment.
GIFT AID (NEED-BASED) *Total amount:* $10,149,329 (65% federal, 10% state, 19% institutional, 6% external sources). *Receiving aid:* Freshmen: 43% (171); All full-time undergraduates: 34% (1,891). *Average award:* Freshmen: $4165; Undergraduates: $3955. *Scholarships, grants, and awards:* Federal Pell, FSEOG, state, private, college/university gift aid from institutional funds, Federal Nursing.
GIFT AID (NON-NEED-BASED) *Total amount:* $2,586,128 (3% federal, 6% state, 83% institutional, 8% external sources). *Receiving aid:* Freshmen: 7% (29); Undergraduates: 2% (129). *Average Award:* Freshmen: $4384; Undergraduates: $4702. *Scholarships, grants, and awards by category:* Academic Interests/Achievement: biological sciences, business, communication, computer science, education, engineering/technologies, English, foreign languages, general academic interests/achievements, health fields, humanities, international studies, mathematics. Creative Arts/Performance: art/fine arts, music. Special Achievements/Activities: memberships. Special Characteristics: ethnic background, general special characteristics, local/state students, members of minority groups. *Tuition waivers:* Full or partial for employees or children of employees, senior citizens. *ROTC:* Army cooperative, Air Force cooperative.
LOANS *Student loans:* $34,811,122 (87% need-based, 13% non-need-based). 71% of past graduating class borrowed through all loan programs. *Average indebtedness per student:* $16,048. *Average need-based loan:* Freshmen: $2552; Undergraduates: $4247. *Parent loans:* $2,877,565 (59% need-based, 41% non-need-based). *Programs:* FFEL (Subsidized and Unsubsidized Stafford, PLUS), Perkins, Federal Nursing, state, college/university.
ATHLETIC AWARDS *Total amount:* $556,755 (52% need-based, 48% non-need-based).
APPLYING FOR FINANCIAL AID *Required financial aid form:* FAFSA. *Financial aid deadline (priority):* 4/1. *Notification date:* Continuous. Students must reply within 2 weeks of notification.

CONTACT Samantha Ruffini, Senior Associate Director, Student Financial Aid, University of Missouri–St. Louis, One University Boulevard, 327 MSC, St. Louis, MO 63121-4499, 314-516-6893 or toll-free 888-GO2-UMSL (in-state). *Fax:* 314-516-5408. *E-mail:* ruffinis@umsl.edu.

UNIVERSITY OF MOBILE
Mobile, AL

ABOUT THE INSTITUTION Independent Southern Baptist, coed. Awards: associate, bachelor's, and master's degrees. 31 undergraduate majors. Total enrollment: 1,864. Undergraduates: 1,653. Freshmen: 257.

GIFT AID (NEED-BASED) *Scholarships, grants, and awards:* Federal Pell, FSEOG, state, private, college/university gift aid from institutional funds.

GIFT AID (NON-NEED-BASED) *Scholarships, grants, and awards by category:* *Academic Interests/Achievement:* general academic interests/achievements, religion/biblical studies. *Creative Arts/Performance:* art/fine arts, general creative arts/performance, music. *Special Achievements/Activities:* cheerleading/drum major, community service, junior miss, leadership, religious involvement.

LOANS *Programs:* FFEL (Subsidized and Unsubsidized Stafford, PLUS), Perkins.

APPLYING FOR FINANCIAL AID *Required financial aid forms:* FAFSA, institution's own form, state aid form.

CONTACT Marie Thomas, Director of Financial Aid, University of Mobile, PO Box 13220, Mobile, AL 36663-0220, 251-442-2370 or toll-free 800-946-7267. *Fax:* 251-442-2498.

THE UNIVERSITY OF MONTANA–MISSOULA
Missoula, MT

ABOUT THE INSTITUTION State-supported, coed. Awards: associate, bachelor's, master's, doctoral, and first professional degrees and post-master's certificates. 115 undergraduate majors. Total enrollment: 13,558. Undergraduates: 11,431. Freshmen: 2,224.

GIFT AID (NEED-BASED) *Scholarships, grants, and awards:* Federal Pell, FSEOG, state, private, college/university gift aid from institutional funds.

GIFT AID (NON-NEED-BASED) *Scholarships, grants, and awards by category:* *Academic Interests/Achievement:* biological sciences, business, computer science, education, English, foreign languages, general academic interests/achievements, health fields, humanities, international studies, mathematics, military science, physical sciences, premedicine, social sciences. *Creative Arts/Performance:* art/fine arts, creative writing, dance, journalism/publications, music, performing arts, theater/drama. *Special Achievements/Activities:* cheerleading/drum major, leadership, rodeo. *Special Characteristics:* children and siblings of alumni, children with a deceased or disabled parent, general special characteristics, international students, members of minority groups, out-of-state students, veterans.

LOANS *Programs:* FFEL (Subsidized and Unsubsidized Stafford, PLUS), Perkins, college/university.

APPLYING FOR FINANCIAL AID *Required financial aid forms:* FAFSA, institution's own form.

CONTACT Mick Hanson, Director of Financial Aid, The University of Montana–Missoula, Arthur and University Avenues, Missoula, MT 59812-0002, 406-243-5373 or toll-free 800-462-8636. *Fax:* 406-243-4930. *E-mail:* faid@selway.umt.edu.

THE UNIVERSITY OF MONTANA–WESTERN
Dillon, MT

Tuition & fees (MT res): $3530	Average undergraduate aid package: $2649

ABOUT THE INSTITUTION State-supported, coed. Awards: associate and bachelor's degrees. 41 undergraduate majors. Total enrollment: 1,146. Undergraduates: 1,146. Freshmen: 240. Federal methodology is used as a basis for awarding need-based institutional aid.

UNDERGRADUATE EXPENSES for 2005–06 *Application fee:* $30. *Tuition, state resident:* full-time $2750; part-time $133 per credit. *Tuition, nonresident:* full-time $11,100; part-time $460 per credit. *Required fees:* full-time $780; $115 per credit or $371 per term part-time. Full-time tuition and fees vary according to course load. Part-time tuition and fees vary according to course load. *College room and board:* $4740; *room only:* $1890. Room and board charges vary according to board plan and housing facility. *Payment plan:* Deferred payment.

FRESHMAN FINANCIAL AID (Fall 2004, est.) 222 applied for aid; of those 86% were deemed to have need. 95% of freshmen with need received aid; of those 2% had need fully met. *Average percent of need met:* 16% (excluding resources awarded to replace EFC). *Average financial aid package:* $2263 (excluding resources awarded to replace EFC). 1% of all full-time freshmen had no need and received non-need-based gift aid.

UNDERGRADUATE FINANCIAL AID (Fall 2004, est.) 875 applied for aid; of those 92% were deemed to have need. 95% of undergraduates with need received aid; of those 2% had need fully met. *Average percent of need met:* 18% (excluding resources awarded to replace EFC). *Average financial aid package:* $2649 (excluding resources awarded to replace EFC). 1% of all full-time undergraduates had no need and received non-need-based gift aid.

GIFT AID (NEED-BASED) *Total amount:* $2,876,690 (87% federal, 3% state, 8% institutional, 2% external sources). *Receiving aid:* Freshmen: 65% (155); All full-time undergraduates: 73% (657). *Average award:* Freshmen: $2210; Undergraduates: $2256. *Scholarships, grants, and awards:* Federal Pell, FSEOG, state, private, college/university gift aid from institutional funds.

GIFT AID (NON-NEED-BASED) *Total amount:* $56,697 (47% institutional, 53% external sources). *Receiving aid:* Freshmen: 2% (6); Undergraduates: 3% (25). *Average Award:* Freshmen: $750; *Undergraduates:* $667. *Scholarships, grants, and awards by category:* *Academic Interests/Achievement:* 230 awards ($209,096 total): business, education, English, general academic interests/achievements, social sciences. *Creative Arts/Performance:* 20 awards ($20,500 total): art/fine arts. *Special Achievements/Activities:* 45 awards ($35,000 total): rodeo. *Special Characteristics:* 2 awards ($2000 total): members of minority groups. *Tuition waivers:* Full or partial for senior citizens.

LOANS *Student loans:* $3,100,941 (71% need-based, 29% non-need-based). 84% of past graduating class borrowed through all loan programs. *Average indebtedness per student:* $20,703. *Average need-based loan:* Freshmen: $2394; Undergraduates: $3485. *Parent loans:* $231,418 (85% need-based, 15% non-need-based). *Programs:* FFEL (Subsidized and Unsubsidized Stafford, PLUS), Perkins, college/university.

WORK-STUDY *Federal work-study:* Total amount: $247,405; 210 jobs averaging $1178. *State or other work-study/employment:* Total amount: $312,464 (10% need-based, 90% non-need-based). 187 part-time jobs averaging $1671.

ATHLETIC AWARDS *Total amount:* $97,500 (85% need-based, 15% non-need-based).

APPLYING FOR FINANCIAL AID *Required financial aid form:* FAFSA. *Financial aid deadline (priority):* 3/1. *Notification date:* Continuous. Students must reply within 2 weeks of notification.

CONTACT Arlene Williams, Financial Aid Director, The University of Montana–Western, 710 South Atlantic Street, Dillon, MT 59725, 406-683-7511 or toll-free 866-869-6668. *Fax:* 406-683-7493. *E-mail:* a_williams@umwestern.edu.

UNIVERSITY OF MONTEVALLO
Montevallo, AL

ABOUT THE INSTITUTION State-supported, coed. Awards: bachelor's and master's degrees and post-master's certificates. 49 undergraduate majors. Total enrollment: 3,061. Undergraduates: 2,614. Freshmen: 498.

GIFT AID (NEED-BASED) *Scholarships, grants, and awards:* Federal Pell, FSEOG, state, private, college/university gift aid from institutional funds.

GIFT AID (NON-NEED-BASED) *Scholarships, grants, and awards by category:* *Academic Interests/Achievement:* biological sciences, education, general academic interests/achievements, physical sciences. *Creative Arts/Performance:* art/fine arts, music. *Special Achievements/Activities:* junior miss. *Special Characteristics:* international students, out-of-state students, veterans, veterans' children.

LOANS *Programs:* Federal Direct (Subsidized and Unsubsidized Stafford, PLUS), FFEL (PLUS), Perkins.

WORK-STUDY *Federal work-study:* Total amount: $116,642; 136 jobs averaging $1410. *State or other work-study/employment:* Total amount: $631,023 (100% non-need-based). Part-time jobs available.

APPLYING FOR FINANCIAL AID *Required financial aid form:* FAFSA.

CONTACT Ms. Maria Parker, Director of Student Financial Aid, University of Montevallo, Station 6050, Montevallo, AL 35115, 205-665-6050 or toll-free 800-292-4349. *Fax:* 205-665-6047. *E-mail:* finaid@montevallo.edu.

UNIVERSITY OF NEBRASKA AT KEARNEY
Kearney, NE

Tuition & fees (NE res): $4260	Average undergraduate aid package: $6490

ABOUT THE INSTITUTION State-supported, coed. Awards: bachelor's and master's degrees and post-master's certificates. 41 undergraduate majors. Total enrollment: 6,382. Undergraduates: 5,380. Freshmen: 1,163. Federal methodology is used as a basis for awarding need-based institutional aid.

UNDERGRADUATE EXPENSES for 2004–05 *Application fee:* $45. *Tuition, state resident:* full-time $3495; part-time $117 per hour. *Tuition, nonresident:* full-time $7148; part-time $238 per hour. *Required fees:* full-time $765; $14 per hour. *College room and board:* $4990. Room and board charges vary according to board plan and housing facility. *Payment plan:* Installment.

FRESHMAN FINANCIAL AID (Fall 2003) 819 applied for aid; of those 76% were deemed to have need. 99% of freshmen with need received aid; of those 41% had need fully met. *Average percent of need met:* 78% (excluding resources awarded to replace EFC). *Average financial aid package:* $6543 (excluding resources awarded to replace EFC). 4% of all full-time freshmen had no need and received non-need-based gift aid.

UNDERGRADUATE FINANCIAL AID (Fall 2003) 3,539 applied for aid; of those 80% were deemed to have need. 98% of undergraduates with need received aid; of those 42% had need fully met. *Average percent of need met:* 79% (excluding resources awarded to replace EFC). *Average financial aid package:* $6490 (excluding resources awarded to replace EFC). 2% of all full-time undergraduates had no need and received non-need-based gift aid.

GIFT AID (NEED-BASED) *Total amount:* $8,597,647 (52% federal, 7% state, 28% institutional, 13% external sources). *Receiving aid:* Freshmen: 38% (373); All full-time undergraduates: 36% (1,758). *Average award:* Freshmen: $3501; Undergraduates: $3361. *Scholarships, grants, and awards:* Federal Pell, FSEOG, state, private, college/university gift aid from institutional funds.

GIFT AID (NON-NEED-BASED) *Receiving aid:* Freshmen: 46% (454); Undergraduates: 25% (1,204). *Average Award:* Freshmen: $1964; Undergraduates: $1920. *Scholarships, grants, and awards by category: Academic Interests/Achievement:* 3 awards ($2200 total): communication. *Creative Arts/Performance:* 89 awards ($63,874 total): applied art and design, art/fine arts, debating, journalism/publications, music. *Special Achievements/Activities:* 15 awards ($3120 total): cheerleading/drum major. *Special Characteristics:* 469 awards ($812,191 total): children of faculty/staff, ethnic background, first-generation college students, international students, out-of-state students, veterans, veterans' children. *Tuition waivers:* Full or partial for employees or children of employees.

LOANS *Student loans:* $13,266,939 (62% need-based, 38% non-need-based). 68% of past graduating class borrowed through all loan programs. *Average indebtedness per student:* $14,930. *Average need-based loan:* Freshmen: $2537; Undergraduates: $3429. *Parent loans:* $1,572,768 (100% non-need-based). *Programs:* FFEL (Subsidized and Unsubsidized Stafford, PLUS), Perkins.

WORK-STUDY *Federal work-study:* Total amount: $752,173; 325 jobs averaging $1088.

ATHLETIC AWARDS *Total amount:* $707,504 (100% need-based).

APPLYING FOR FINANCIAL AID *Required financial aid forms:* FAFSA, institution's own form, federal income tax form(s). *Financial aid deadline (priority):* 3/1. *Notification date:* 4/1. Students must reply within 3 weeks of notification.

CONTACT Financial Aid Office, University of Nebraska at Kearney, Memorial Student Affairs Building, 905 West 25th Street, Kearney, NE 68849-0001, 308-865-8520 or toll-free 800-532-7639. *Fax:* 308-865-8096.

UNIVERSITY OF NEBRASKA AT OMAHA
Omaha, NE

Tuition & fees (NE res): $4533	Average undergraduate aid package: N/A

ABOUT THE INSTITUTION State-supported, coed. Awards: bachelor's, master's, and doctoral degrees and post-bachelor's and post-master's certificates. 73 undergraduate majors. Total enrollment: 13,824. Undergraduates: 11,041. Freshmen: 1,643. Federal methodology is used as a basis for awarding need-based institutional aid.

UNDERGRADUATE EXPENSES for 2004–05 *Application fee:* $45. *Tuition, state resident:* full-time $3,938; part-time $131.25 per semester hour. *Tuition, nonresident:* full-time $11,602; part-time $386.75 per semester hour. *Required fees:* full-time $595; $15.50 per semester hour or $72 per term part-time. Full-time tuition and fees vary according to course load and student level. Part-time tuition and fees vary according to course load and student level. *College room and board:* $5960; *room only:* $3570. Room and board charges vary according to board plan. *Payment plans:* Installment, deferred payment.

FRESHMAN FINANCIAL AID (Fall 2003) 1116 applied for aid; of those 68% were deemed to have need. 100% of freshmen with need received aid.

UNDERGRADUATE FINANCIAL AID (Fall 2003) 5,477 applied for aid; of those 73% were deemed to have need. 99% of undergraduates with need received aid.

GIFT AID (NEED-BASED) *Total amount:* $11,243,762 (62% federal, 29% state, 9% institutional). *Receiving aid:* Freshmen: 29% (481); All full-time undergraduates: 40% (3,588). *Scholarships, grants, and awards:* Federal Pell, FSEOG, state, private, college/university gift aid from institutional funds.

GIFT AID (NON-NEED-BASED) *Total amount:* $11,590,748 (39% state, 43% institutional, 18% external sources). *Receiving aid:* Freshmen: 42% (690); Undergraduates: 39% (3,505). *Scholarships, grants, and awards by category: Academic Interests/Achievement:* biological sciences, business, communication, computer science, education, engineering/technologies, English, foreign languages, general academic interests/achievements, home economics, mathematics, physical sciences, premedicine, social sciences. *Creative Arts/Performance:* art/fine arts, creative writing, debating, journalism/publications, music, performing arts, theater/drama. *Special Achievements/Activities:* general special achievements/activities, leadership, memberships. *Special Characteristics:* adult students, children and siblings of alumni, children of faculty/staff, ethnic background, first-generation college students, handicapped students, international students, members of minority groups, out-of-state students, veterans' children. *Tuition waivers:* Full or partial for employees or children of employees. *ROTC:* Army cooperative, Air Force.

LOANS *Student loans:* $32,339,721 (52% need-based, 48% non-need-based). 47% of past graduating class borrowed through all loan programs. *Average indebtedness per student:* $22,000. *Parent loans:* $871,910 (100% non-need-based). *Programs:* FFEL (Subsidized and Unsubsidized Stafford, PLUS), Perkins, college/university.

WORK-STUDY *Federal work-study:* Total amount: $611,385; 359 jobs averaging $1703.

ATHLETIC AWARDS *Total amount:* $1,399,685 (100% non-need-based).

APPLYING FOR FINANCIAL AID *Required financial aid form:* FAFSA. *Financial aid deadline (priority):* 3/1. *Notification date:* Continuous beginning 4/1. Students must reply within 2 weeks of notification.

CONTACT Office of Financial Aid, University of Nebraska at Omaha, 103 Eppley Administration Building, 6001 Dodge Street, Omaha, NE 68182-0187, 402-554-2327 or toll-free 800-858-8648 (in-state). *Fax:* 402-554-3472. *E-mail:* finaid@unomaha.edu.

UNIVERSITY OF NEBRASKA–LINCOLN
Lincoln, NE

Tuition & fees (NE res): $5268	Average undergraduate aid package: $7647

ABOUT THE INSTITUTION State-supported, coed. Awards: associate, bachelor's, master's, doctoral, and first professional degrees and post-bachelor's and post-master's certificates. 128 undergraduate majors. Total enrollment: 21,792. Undergraduates: 17,137. Freshmen: 3,266. Both federal and institutional methodology are used as a basis for awarding need-based institutional aid.

UNDERGRADUATE EXPENSES for 2004–05 *Application fee:* $25. *Tuition, state resident:* full-time $4313; part-time $143.75 per credit hour. *Tuition, nonresident:* full-time $12,803; part-time $426.75 per credit hour. *Required fees:* full-time $955; $6 per credit hour or $187.35 per term part-time. Full-time tuition and fees vary according to course load. Part-time tuition and fees vary according to course load. *College room and board:* $6008; *room only:* $3239. Room and board charges vary according to board plan and housing facility.

FRESHMAN FINANCIAL AID (Fall 2003) 2425 applied for aid; of those 69% were deemed to have need. 99% of freshmen with need received aid; of those 25% had need fully met. *Average percent of need met:* 87% (excluding resources awarded to replace EFC). *Average financial aid package:* $7921 (excluding resources awarded to replace EFC). 12% of all full-time freshmen had no need and received non-need-based gift aid.

UNDERGRADUATE FINANCIAL AID (Fall 2003) 10,200 applied for aid; of those 74% were deemed to have need. 97% of undergraduates with need received aid; of those 26% had need fully met. *Average percent of need met:* 87% (excluding resources awarded to replace EFC). *Average financial aid package:* $7647 (excluding resources awarded to replace EFC). 6% of all full-time undergraduates had no need and received non-need-based gift aid.

GIFT AID (NEED-BASED) *Total amount:* $22,610,364 (44% federal, 6% state, 37% institutional, 13% external sources). *Receiving aid:* Freshmen: 38% (1,384); All full-time undergraduates: 33% (5,306). *Average award:* Freshmen: $4995; Undergraduates: $4488. *Scholarships, grants, and awards:* Federal Pell, FSEOG, state, private, college/university gift aid from institutional funds.

GIFT AID (NON-NEED-BASED) *Total amount:* $15,353,379 (2% federal, 76% institutional, 22% external sources). *Receiving aid:* Freshmen: 5% (185); Undergraduates: 3% (466). *Average Award:* Freshmen: $3908; Undergraduates: $4295. *Scholarships, grants, and awards by category: Academic Interests/ Achievement:* agriculture, architecture, biological sciences, business, computer science, education, engineering/technologies, English, foreign languages, general academic interests/achievements, health fields, home economics, humanities, international studies, mathematics, physical sciences, premedicine, social sciences. *Creative Arts/Performance:* art/fine arts, cinema/film/broadcasting, dance, journalism/publications, music, performing arts, theater/drama. *Special Achievements/Activities:* cheerleading/drum major, community service, leadership. *Special Characteristics:* children and siblings of alumni, ethnic background, handicapped students, international students, members of minority groups, out-of-state students, veterans' children. *Tuition waivers:* Full or partial for employees or children of employees. *ROTC:* Army, Naval, Air Force.

LOANS *Student loans:* $41,882,561 (65% need-based, 35% non-need-based). 60% of past graduating class borrowed through all loan programs. *Average indebtedness per student:* $16,703. *Average need-based loan:* Freshmen: $2891; Undergraduates: $3809. *Parent loans:* $17,400,878 (46% need-based, 54% non-need-based). *Programs:* Federal Direct (Subsidized and Unsubsidized Stafford, PLUS), Perkins, college/university.

WORK-STUDY *Federal work-study:* Total amount: $2,524,090; 1,364 jobs averaging $2121.

ATHLETIC AWARDS *Total amount:* $4,634,890 (100% non-need-based).

APPLYING FOR FINANCIAL AID *Required financial aid form:* FAFSA. *Financial aid deadline:* Continuous. *Notification date:* Continuous beginning 3/15.

CONTACT Ms. Jo Tederman, Assistant Director of Scholarships and Financial Aid, University of Nebraska–Lincoln, 16 Canfield Administration Building, PO Box 880411, Lincoln, NE 68588-0411, 402-472-2030 or toll-free 800-742-8800. *Fax:* 402-472-9826.

UNIVERSITY OF NEBRASKA MEDICAL CENTER
Omaha, NE

Tuition & fees (NE res): $6657 **Average undergraduate aid package: N/A**

ABOUT THE INSTITUTION State-supported, coed. Awards: bachelor's, master's, doctoral, and first professional degrees and post-bachelor's, post-master's, and first professional certificates. 7 undergraduate majors. Total enrollment: 2,904. Undergraduates: 779. Federal methodology is used as a basis for awarding need-based institutional aid.

UNDERGRADUATE EXPENSES for 2004–05 *Application fee:* $45. *Tuition, state resident:* full-time $5460; part-time $182 per credit hour. *Tuition, nonresident:* full-time $15,990; part-time $533 per credit hour. *Required fees:* full-time $1197; $2 per credit hour or $47.50 per term part-time. Full-time tuition and fees vary according to course level, course load, and program. Part-time tuition and fees vary according to program.

UNDERGRADUATE FINANCIAL AID (Fall 2003) 813 applied for aid; of those 100% were deemed to have need. 100% of undergraduates with need received aid. *Average percent of need met:* 60% (excluding resources awarded to replace EFC).

GIFT AID (NEED-BASED) *Total amount:* $2,100,928 (31% federal, 12% state, 39% institutional, 18% external sources). *Receiving aid:* All full-time undergraduates: 90% (813). *Average award:* Undergraduates: $3525. *Scholarships, grants, and awards:* Federal Pell, FSEOG, state, private, college/university gift aid from institutional funds.

GIFT AID (NON-NEED-BASED) *Tuition waivers:* Full or partial for children of alumni, employees or children of employees. *ROTC:* Army cooperative, Air Force cooperative.

LOANS *Student loans:* $5,477,842 (100% need-based). 91% of past graduating class borrowed through all loan programs. *Average need-based loan:* Undergraduates: $6700. *Parent loans:* $756,927 (100% need-based). *Programs:* FFEL (Subsidized and Unsubsidized Stafford, PLUS), Perkins, Federal Nursing, state, college/university.

WORK-STUDY *Federal work-study:* Total amount: $24,166; 38 jobs averaging $1515.

APPLYING FOR FINANCIAL AID *Required financial aid forms:* FAFSA, institution's own form. *Financial aid deadline (priority):* 2/1. *Notification date:* Continuous beginning 4/1. Students must reply within 2 weeks of notification.

CONTACT Judi Walker, Director of Financial Aid, University of Nebraska Medical Center, 984265 Nebraska Medical Center, Omaha, NE 68198-4265, 402-559-6409 or toll-free 800-626-8431 Ext. 6468. *Fax:* 402-559-6796. *E-mail:* jdwalker@unmc.edu.

UNIVERSITY OF NEVADA, LAS VEGAS
Las Vegas, NV

Tuition & fees (NV res): $3532 **Average undergraduate aid package: $6911**

ABOUT THE INSTITUTION State-supported, coed. Awards: bachelor's, master's, doctoral, and first professional degrees and post-bachelor's and post-master's certificates. 86 undergraduate majors. Total enrollment: 27,344. Undergraduates: 21,783. Freshmen: 3,271. Federal methodology is used as a basis for awarding need-based institutional aid.

UNDERGRADUATE EXPENSES for 2005–06 *Application fee:* $60. *Tuition, state resident:* full-time $3060; part-time $102 per credit hour. *Tuition, nonresident:* full-time $12,527; part-time $209 per credit hour. Full-time tuition and fees vary according to course load. Part-time tuition and fees vary according to course load. *College room and board:* $8326; *room only:* $5278. Room and board charges vary according to board plan. *Payment plan:* Deferred payment.

FRESHMAN FINANCIAL AID (Fall 2003) 1702 applied for aid; of those 78% were deemed to have need. 90% of freshmen with need received aid; of those 59% had need fully met. *Average percent of need met:* 68% (excluding resources awarded to replace EFC). *Average financial aid package:* $5681 (excluding resources awarded to replace EFC). 38% of all full-time freshmen had no need and received non-need-based gift aid.

UNDERGRADUATE FINANCIAL AID (Fall 2003) 7,594 applied for aid; of those 82% were deemed to have need. 92% of undergraduates with need received aid; of those 50% had need fully met. *Average percent of need met:* 74% (excluding resources awarded to replace EFC). *Average financial aid package:* $6911 (excluding resources awarded to replace EFC). 27% of all full-time undergraduates had no need and received non-need-based gift aid.

GIFT AID (NEED-BASED) *Total amount:* $14,308,000 (76% federal, 21% state, 2% institutional, 1% external sources). *Receiving aid:* Freshmen: 20% (561); All full-time undergraduates: 23% (3,356). *Average award:* Freshmen: $2913; Undergraduates: $3030. *Scholarships, grants, and awards:* Federal Pell, FSEOG, state, private, college/university gift aid from institutional funds.

GIFT AID (NON-NEED-BASED) *Total amount:* $16,260,000 (2% federal, 69% state, 29% external sources). *Receiving aid:* Freshmen: 27% (759); Undergraduates: 14% (2,030). *Average Award:* Freshmen: $1200; Undergraduates: $2094. *Scholarships, grants, and awards by category: Academic Interests/Achievement:* architecture, biological sciences, business, communication, computer science, education, engineering/technologies, English, general academic interests/ achievements, health fields, humanities, international studies, mathematics, physical sciences, premedicine, social sciences. *Creative Arts/Performance:* applied art and design, art/fine arts, cinema/film/broadcasting, dance, journalism/ publications, music, performing arts, theater/drama. *Special Achievements/ Activities:* cheerleading/drum major, community service, general special achievements/activities, hobbies/interests, leadership, memberships, rodeo. *Special Characteristics:* children and siblings of alumni, children of faculty/staff, children of public servants, children of workers in trades, ethnic background, first-generation college students, general special characteristics, handicapped students, international students, local/state students, members of minority groups, out-of-state students. *Tuition waivers:* Full or partial for children of alumni, employees or children of employees, senior citizens.

LOANS *Student loans:* $48,000,000 (65% need-based, 35% non-need-based). 47% of past graduating class borrowed through all loan programs. *Average indebtedness per student:* $12,900. *Average need-based loan:* Freshmen: $2517; Undergraduates: $3993. *Parent loans:* $6,200,000 (42% need-based, 58% non-need-based). *Programs:* Federal Direct (Subsidized and Unsubsidized Stafford, PLUS), Perkins, state, college/university.

WORK-STUDY *Federal work-study:* Total amount: $1,200,000; 300 jobs averaging $3100. *State or other work-study/employment:* Total amount: $1,000,000 (70% need-based, 30% non-need-based). 300 part-time jobs averaging $3000.

ATHLETIC AWARDS *Total amount:* $3,750,000 (100% non-need-based).

APPLYING FOR FINANCIAL AID *Required financial aid forms:* FAFSA, institution's own form. *Financial aid deadline (priority):* 2/1. *Notification date:* Continuous beginning 4/1. Students must reply within 2 weeks of notification.

CONTACT Director of Student Financial Services, University of Nevada, Las Vegas, 4505 Maryland Parkway, Box 452016, Las Vegas, NV 89154-2016, 702-895-3424. *Fax:* 702-895-1353.

UNIVERSITY OF NEVADA, RENO
Reno, NV

Tuition & fees (NV res): $3010   **Average undergraduate aid package: $7563**

ABOUT THE INSTITUTION State-supported, coed. Awards: bachelor's, master's, doctoral, and first professional degrees and post-bachelor's, post-master's, and first professional certificates. 97 undergraduate majors. Total enrollment: 15,950. Undergraduates: 12,524. Freshmen: 2,180. Federal methodology is used as a basis for awarding need-based institutional aid.

UNDERGRADUATE EXPENSES for 2004–05 *Application fee:* $60. *Tuition, state resident:* full-time $2850; part-time $95 per credit. *Tuition, nonresident:* full-time $11,524; part-time $195 per credit. Full-time tuition and fees vary according to course load. Part-time tuition and fees vary according to course load. *College room and board:* $7385; *room only:* $3990. Room and board charges vary according to board plan and housing facility. *Payment plan:* Deferred payment.

FRESHMAN FINANCIAL AID (Fall 2003) 1018 applied for aid; of those 63% were deemed to have need. 97% of freshmen with need received aid; of those 21% had need fully met. *Average percent of need met:* 64% (excluding resources awarded to replace EFC). *Average financial aid package:* $6228 (excluding resources awarded to replace EFC). 56% of all full-time freshmen had no need and received non-need-based gift aid.

UNDERGRADUATE FINANCIAL AID (Fall 2003) 4,067 applied for aid; of those 76% were deemed to have need. 97% of undergraduates with need received aid; of those 14% had need fully met. *Average percent of need met:* 62% (excluding resources awarded to replace EFC). *Average financial aid package:* $7563 (excluding resources awarded to replace EFC). 43% of all full-time undergraduates had no need and received non-need-based gift aid.

GIFT AID (NEED-BASED) *Total amount:* $11,184,205 (42% federal, 39% state, 13% institutional, 6% external sources). *Receiving aid:* Freshmen: 15% (306); All full-time undergraduates: 20% (1,927). *Average award:* Freshmen: $2805; Undergraduates: $3138. *Scholarships, grants, and awards:* Federal Pell, FSEOG, private, college/university gift aid from institutional funds.

GIFT AID (NON-NEED-BASED) *Total amount:* $12,738,334 (2% federal, 68% state, 21% institutional, 9% external sources). *Receiving aid:* Freshmen: 26% (549); Undergraduates: 21% (1,958). *Average Award: Freshmen:* $2797; *Undergraduates:* $2815. *Scholarships, grants, and awards by category: Academic Interests/Achievement:* agriculture, biological sciences, business, computer science, education, engineering/technologies, English, foreign languages, general academic interests/achievements, health fields, humanities, international studies, mathematics, military science, physical sciences, premedicine, social sciences. *Creative Arts/Performance:* applied art and design, art/fine arts, creative writing, dance, debating, general creative arts/performance, journalism/publications, music, performing arts, theater/drama. *Special Achievements/Activities:* cheerleading/drum major. *Special Characteristics:* adult students, children and siblings of alumni, ethnic background, first-generation college students, local/state students, married students, members of minority groups. *Tuition waivers:* Full or partial for children of alumni, employees or children of employees, senior citizens. *ROTC:* Army.

LOANS *Student loans:* $16,312,312 (84% need-based, 16% non-need-based). 44% of past graduating class borrowed through all loan programs. *Average indebtedness per student:* $16,273. *Average need-based loan:* Freshmen: $2445; Undergraduates: $4171. *Parent loans:* $1,725,190 (74% need-based, 26% non-need-based). *Programs:* FFEL (Subsidized and Unsubsidized Stafford, PLUS), Perkins, college/university.

WORK-STUDY *Federal work-study:* Total amount: $512,584; 210 jobs averaging $2464. *State or other work-study/employment:* Total amount: $33,559 (76% need-based, 24% non-need-based). 16 part-time jobs averaging $2115.

ATHLETIC AWARDS *Total amount:* $3,871,027 (17% need-based, 83% non-need-based).

APPLYING FOR FINANCIAL AID *Required financial aid form:* FAFSA. *Financial aid deadline (priority):* 2/1. *Notification date:* Continuous beginning 4/1. Students must reply within 2 weeks of notification.

CONTACT Dr. Nancee Langley, Director of Student Financial Aid, University of Nevada, Reno, Student Services Building, Room 316, Mail Stop 076, Reno, NV 89557, 775-784-4666 Ext. 3009 or toll-free 866-263-8232. Fax: 775-784-1025. E-mail: langley@unr.edu.

UNIVERSITY OF NEW ENGLAND
Biddeford, ME

Tuition & fees: $20,915   **Average undergraduate aid package: $18,320**

ABOUT THE INSTITUTION Independent, coed. Awards: associate, bachelor's, master's, and first professional degrees and post-bachelor's and post-master's certificates. 43 undergraduate majors. Total enrollment: 3,327. Undergraduates: 1,695. Freshmen: 491. Federal methodology is used as a basis for awarding need-based institutional aid.

UNDERGRADUATE EXPENSES for 2004–05 *Application fee:* $40. *Comprehensive fee:* $29,070 includes full-time tuition ($20,225), mandatory fees ($690), and room and board ($8155). Room and board charges vary according to housing facility. *Part-time tuition:* $725 per credit. *Payment plan:* Installment.

GIFT AID (NEED-BASED) *Total amount:* $11,271,213 (12% federal, 4% state, 77% institutional, 7% external sources). *Receiving aid:* Freshmen: 88% (429); All full-time undergraduates: 81% (1,126). *Average award:* Freshmen: $11,439; Undergraduates: $9769. *Scholarships, grants, and awards:* Federal Pell, FSEOG, state, private, college/university gift aid from institutional funds.

GIFT AID (NON-NEED-BASED) *Total amount:* $1,704,754 (93% institutional, 7% external sources). *Receiving aid:* Freshmen: 5% (24); Undergraduates: 4% (57). *Average Award: Freshmen:* $6149; *Undergraduates:* $6173. *Scholarships, grants, and awards by category: Academic Interests/Achievement:* 1,682 awards ($7,782,848 total): biological sciences, business, education, English, general academic interests/achievements, health fields, humanities, international studies, mathematics, physical sciences, premedicine, social sciences. *Special Achievements/Activities:* 16 awards ($13,500 total): general special achievements/activities, leadership. *Special Characteristics:* 11 awards ($12,750 total): children and siblings of alumni, siblings of current students. *Tuition waivers:* Full or partial for children of alumni, employees or children of employees. *ROTC:* Army cooperative.

LOANS *Student loans:* $14,253,693 (60% need-based, 40% non-need-based). 90% of past graduating class borrowed through all loan programs. *Average indebtedness per student:* $34,371. *Average need-based loan:* Freshmen: $4561; Undergraduates: $5624. *Parent loans:* $2,200,294 (20% need-based, 80% non-need-based). *Programs:* FFEL (Subsidized and Unsubsidized Stafford, PLUS), Perkins, Federal Nursing, state, college/university.

APPLYING FOR FINANCIAL AID *Required financial aid form:* FAFSA. *Financial aid deadline (priority):* 5/1. *Notification date:* Continuous beginning 2/1. Students must reply within 2 weeks of notification.

CONTACT John R. Bowie, Director of Financial Aid, University of New England, 11 Hills Beach Road, Biddeford, ME 04005, 207-283-0171 Ext. 2342 or toll-free 800-477-4UNE. Fax: 207-294-5946. E-mail: finaid@une.edu.

UNIVERSITY OF NEW HAMPSHIRE
Durham, NH

Tuition & fees (NH res): $9226   **Average undergraduate aid package: $14,867**

ABOUT THE INSTITUTION State-supported, coed. Awards: associate, bachelor's, master's, and doctoral degrees and post-master's certificates. 138 undergraduate majors. Total enrollment: 14,405. Undergraduates: 11,394. Freshmen: 2,572. Federal methodology is used as a basis for awarding need-based institutional aid.

UNDERGRADUATE EXPENSES for 2004–05 *Application fee:* $45. *Tuition, state resident:* full-time $7210; part-time $300 per credit. *Tuition, nonresident:* full-time $18,240; part-time $760 per credit. *Required fees:* full-time $2016; $15 per term part-time. Full-time tuition and fees vary according to program and reciprocity agreements. Part-time tuition and fees vary according to course load, program, and reciprocity agreements. *College room and board:* $6612; *room only:* $3858. Room and board charges vary according to board plan and housing facility. *Payment plan:* Installment.

FRESHMAN FINANCIAL AID (Fall 2004, est.) 1955 applied for aid; of those 76% were deemed to have need. 98% of freshmen with need received aid; of those 23% had need fully met. *Average percent of need met:* 83% (excluding resources awarded to replace EFC). *Average financial aid package:* $15,380 (excluding resources awarded to replace EFC). 21% of all full-time freshmen had no need and received non-need-based gift aid.

UNDERGRADUATE FINANCIAL AID (Fall 2004, est.) 7,357 applied for aid; of those 81% were deemed to have need. 99% of undergraduates with need received aid; of those 19% had need fully met. *Average percent of need met:* 78% (excluding resources awarded to replace EFC). *Average financial aid*

package: $14,867 (excluding resources awarded to replace EFC). 20% of all full-time undergraduates had no need and received non-need-based gift aid.

GIFT AID (NEED-BASED) *Total amount:* $27,021,529 (27% federal, 4% state, 52% institutional, 17% external sources). *Receiving aid:* Freshmen: 42% (1,010); All full-time undergraduates: 36% (3,728). *Average award:* Freshmen: $2877; Undergraduates: $2466. *Scholarships, grants, and awards:* Federal Pell, FSEOG, state, private, college/university gift aid from institutional funds.

GIFT AID (NON-NEED-BASED) *Total amount:* $12,151,670 (100% institutional). *Receiving aid:* Freshmen: 6% (149); Undergraduates: 3% (357). *Average Award:* Freshmen: $5274; Undergraduates: $5660. *Scholarships, grants, and awards by category: Academic Interests/Achievement:* agriculture, business, education, engineering/technologies, English, general academic interests/ achievements, health fields, humanities, mathematics, military science. *Creative Arts/Performance:* art/fine arts, dance, music, theater/drama. *Special Achievements/ Activities:* community service. *Special Characteristics:* children and siblings of alumni, children of faculty/staff, handicapped students, international students, local/state students. *Tuition waivers:* Full or partial for employees or children of employees, senior citizens. *ROTC:* Army, Air Force.

LOANS *Student loans:* $44,387,586 (68% need-based, 32% non-need-based). 68% of past graduating class borrowed through all loan programs. *Average indebtedness per student:* $22,354. *Average need-based loan:* Freshmen: $2414; Undergraduates: $3453. *Parent loans:* $14,104,036 (100% non-need-based). *Programs:* FFEL (Subsidized and Unsubsidized Stafford, PLUS), Perkins, state, college/university.

WORK-STUDY *Federal work-study:* Total amount: $6,658,408; 3,216 jobs averaging $1818. *State or other work-study/employment:* Total amount: $4,923,103 (100% non-need-based). 2,835 part-time jobs averaging $1744.

ATHLETIC AWARDS *Total amount:* $5,157,445 (100% non-need-based).

APPLYING FOR FINANCIAL AID *Required financial aid form:* FAFSA. *Financial aid deadline (priority):* 3/1. *Notification date:* Continuous beginning 3/1.

CONTACT Susan K. Allen, Director of Financial Aid, University of New Hampshire, 11 Garrison Avenue, Stoke Hall, Durham, NH 03824, 603-862-3600. *Fax:* 603-862-1947. *E-mail:* financial.aid@unh.edu.

UNIVERSITY OF NEW HAMPSHIRE AT MANCHESTER
Manchester, NH

Tuition & fees (NH res): $6593	Average undergraduate aid package: $7708

ABOUT THE INSTITUTION State-supported, coed. Awards: associate, bachelor's, and master's degrees. 13 undergraduate majors. Total enrollment: 1,215. Undergraduates: 1,048. Freshmen: 107. Federal methodology is used as a basis for awarding need-based institutional aid.

UNDERGRADUATE EXPENSES for 2004–05 *Application fee:* $35. *Tuition, state resident:* full-time $6390; part-time $266 per credit. *Tuition, nonresident:* full-time $16,170; part-time $674 per credit. Full-time tuition and fees vary according to course load and program. Part-time tuition and fees vary according to course load and program.

FRESHMAN FINANCIAL AID (Fall 2004, est.) 58 applied for aid; of those 57% were deemed to have need. 97% of freshmen with need received aid; of those 16% had need fully met. *Average percent of need met:* 55% (excluding resources awarded to replace EFC). *Average financial aid package:* $7264 (excluding resources awarded to replace EFC).

UNDERGRADUATE FINANCIAL AID (Fall 2004, est.) 452 applied for aid; of those 75% were deemed to have need. 94% of undergraduates with need received aid; of those 12% had need fully met. *Average percent of need met:* 56% (excluding resources awarded to replace EFC). *Average financial aid package:* $7708 (excluding resources awarded to replace EFC). 1% of all full-time undergraduates had no need and received non-need-based gift aid.

GIFT AID (NEED-BASED) *Total amount:* $515,899 (62% federal, 9% state, 7% institutional, 22% external sources). *Receiving aid:* Freshmen: 13% (11); All full-time undergraduates: 6% (67). *Average award:* Freshmen: $523; Undergraduates: $616. *Scholarships, grants, and awards:* Federal Pell, FSEOG, state, private, college/university gift aid from institutional funds.

GIFT AID (NON-NEED-BASED) *Total amount:* $65,450 (100% institutional). *Receiving aid:* Undergraduates: 4. *Average Award:* Undergraduates: $1625. *Scholarships, grants, and awards by category: Academic Interests/Achievement:* general academic interests/achievements. *Special Characteristics:* children of faculty/staff. *Tuition waivers:* Full or partial for employees or children of employees, senior citizens. *ROTC:* Army cooperative, Air Force cooperative.

LOANS *Student loans:* $1,921,293 (62% need-based, 38% non-need-based). 51% of past graduating class borrowed through all loan programs. *Average indebtedness per student:* $14,728. *Average need-based loan:* Freshmen: $2051; Undergraduates: $3511. *Parent loans:* $53,316 (100% non-need-based). *Programs:* FFEL (Subsidized and Unsubsidized Stafford, PLUS), Perkins, state, college/university.

WORK-STUDY *Federal work-study:* Total amount: $153,725; 86 jobs averaging $1764.

APPLYING FOR FINANCIAL AID *Required financial aid form:* FAFSA. *Financial aid deadline (priority):* 5/1. *Notification date:* Continuous beginning 4/1.

CONTACT Jodi Abad, Assistant Director of Financial Aid, University of New Hampshire at Manchester, French Hall, 400 Commercial Street, Manchester, NH 03101-1113, 603-641-4146. *Fax:* 603-641-4125.

UNIVERSITY OF NEW HAVEN
West Haven, CT

Tuition & fees: $22,982	Average undergraduate aid package: $17,042

ABOUT THE INSTITUTION Independent, coed. Awards: associate, bachelor's, and master's degrees and post-bachelor's certificates. 50 undergraduate majors. Total enrollment: 4,173. Undergraduates: 2,570. Freshmen: 590. Federal methodology is used as a basis for awarding need-based institutional aid.

UNDERGRADUATE EXPENSES for 2005–06 *Application fee:* $50. *Comprehensive fee:* $32,532 includes full-time tuition ($22,380), mandatory fees ($602), and room and board ($9550). *College room only:* $5796. Full-time tuition and fees vary according to course load. Room and board charges vary according to board plan and housing facility. *Part-time tuition:* $746 per credit hour. Part-time tuition and fees vary according to class time, course load, and location. *Payment plan:* Installment.

FRESHMAN FINANCIAL AID (Fall 2004, est.) 506 applied for aid; of those 89% were deemed to have need. 100% of freshmen with need received aid; of those 29% had need fully met. *Average percent of need met:* 79% (excluding resources awarded to replace EFC). *Average financial aid package:* $16,794 (excluding resources awarded to replace EFC). 14% of all full-time freshmen had no need and received non-need-based gift aid.

UNDERGRADUATE FINANCIAL AID (Fall 2004, est.) 1,693 applied for aid; of those 90% were deemed to have need. 100% of undergraduates with need received aid; of those 39% had need fully met. *Average percent of need met:* 79% (excluding resources awarded to replace EFC). *Average financial aid package:* $17,042 (excluding resources awarded to replace EFC). 11% of all full-time undergraduates had no need and received non-need-based gift aid.

GIFT AID (NEED-BASED) *Total amount:* $14,971,512 (11% federal, 10% state, 76% institutional, 3% external sources). *Receiving aid:* Freshmen: 75% (429); All full-time undergraduates: 69% (1,429). *Average award:* Freshmen: $12,372; Undergraduates: $11,121. *Scholarships, grants, and awards:* Federal Pell, FSEOG, state, private, college/university gift aid from institutional funds.

GIFT AID (NON-NEED-BASED) *Total amount:* $1,088,647 (100% institutional). *Receiving aid:* Freshmen: 7% (42); Undergraduates: 5% (103). *Average Award:* Freshmen: $13,527; Undergraduates: $14,673. *Scholarships, grants, and awards by category: Special Achievements/Activities:* general special achievements/ activities. *Tuition waivers:* Full or partial for employees or children of employees.

LOANS *Student loans:* $17,000,000 (35% need-based, 65% non-need-based). 83% of past graduating class borrowed through all loan programs. *Average indebtedness per student:* $29,200. *Average need-based loan:* Freshmen: $5319; Undergraduates: $7076. *Parent loans:* $4,041,084 (100% non-need-based). *Programs:* FFEL (Subsidized and Unsubsidized Stafford, PLUS), Perkins.

WORK-STUDY *Federal work-study:* Total amount: $198,000.

ATHLETIC AWARDS *Total amount:* $1,330,221 (49% need-based, 51% non-need-based).

APPLYING FOR FINANCIAL AID *Required financial aid forms:* FAFSA, institution's own form. *Financial aid deadline:* 3/1 (priority: 3/1). *Notification date:* Continuous beginning 3/15. Students must reply by 5/1 or within 2 weeks of notification.

CONTACT Mr. Christopher Hourigan, Director of Institutional Research, University of New Haven, 300 Boston Post Road, West Haven, CT 06516-1916, 203-932-7139 or toll-free 800-DIAL-UNH. *Fax:* 203-931-6050. *E-mail:* finaid@newhaven. edu.

UNIVERSITY OF NEW MEXICO
Albuquerque, NM

CONTACT Office of Student Financial Aid, University of New Mexico, Mesa Vista Hall North, Albuquerque, NM 87131, 505-277-2041 or toll-free 800-CALLUNM (in-state). *Fax:* 505-277-6326. *E-mail:* finaid@unm.edu.

UNIVERSITY OF NEW ORLEANS
New Orleans, LA

Tuition & fees (LA res): $3492   Average undergraduate aid package: $5910

ABOUT THE INSTITUTION State-supported, coed. Awards: bachelor's, master's, and doctoral degrees and post-bachelor's certificates. 50 undergraduate majors. Total enrollment: 17,350. Undergraduates: 13,225. Freshmen: 2,079. Federal methodology is used as a basis for awarding need-based institutional aid.

UNDERGRADUATE EXPENSES for 2005–06 Application fee: $20. **Tuition, state resident:** full-time $3184. **Tuition, nonresident:** full-time $10,228. **College room and board: room only:** $4122.

FRESHMAN FINANCIAL AID (Fall 2003) 1767 applied for aid; of those 100% were deemed to have need. 72% of freshmen with need received aid; of those 11% had need fully met. *Average percent of need met:* 64% (excluding resources awarded to replace EFC). *Average financial aid package:* $5331 (excluding resources awarded to replace EFC). 6% of all full-time freshmen had no need and received non-need-based gift aid.

UNDERGRADUATE FINANCIAL AID (Fall 2003) 7,565 applied for aid; of those 100% were deemed to have need. 74% of undergraduates with need received aid; of those 11% had need fully met. *Average percent of need met:* 70% (excluding resources awarded to replace EFC). *Average financial aid package:* $5910 (excluding resources awarded to replace EFC). 2% of all full-time undergraduates had no need and received non-need-based gift aid.

GIFT AID (NEED-BASED) Total amount: $13,695,884 (99% federal, 1% state). **Receiving aid:** Freshmen: 43% (839); All full-time undergraduates: 38% (3,650). **Average award:** Freshmen: $3231; Undergraduates: $3118. **Scholarships, grants, and awards:** Federal Pell, FSEOG, state, private, college/university gift aid from institutional funds.

GIFT AID (NON-NEED-BASED) Total amount: $6,642,105 (100% state). **Receiving aid:** Freshmen: 31% (606); Undergraduates: 16% (1,579). **Average Award:** Freshmen: $1471; Undergraduates: $1486. **Scholarships, grants, and awards by category:** Academic Interests/Achievement: 234 awards ($542,219 total): communication, computer science, education, foreign languages, general academic interests/achievements, international studies, mathematics, military science, physical sciences. Creative Arts/Performance: 62 awards ($244,951 total): general creative arts/performance, music. Special Achievements/Activities: 23 awards ($12,042 total). Special Characteristics: 2,528 awards ($6,834,854 total): adult students, children and siblings of alumni, children of public servants, children with a deceased or disabled parent, local/state students, out-of-state students, previous college experience, public servants, veterans' children. **ROTC:** Army cooperative, Naval cooperative, Air Force cooperative.

LOANS Student loans: $44,030,324 (54% need-based, 46% non-need-based). 36% of past graduating class borrowed through all loan programs. *Average indebtedness per student:* $22,272. **Average need-based loan:** Freshmen: $2477; Undergraduates: $3570. **Parent loans:** $875,237 (100% non-need-based). **Programs:** FFEL (Subsidized and Unsubsidized Stafford, PLUS), Perkins, college/university.

WORK-STUDY Federal work-study: Total amount: $417,646; 289 jobs averaging $1445. **State or other work-study/employment:** Total amount: $2,351,204 (100% non-need-based). 1,351 part-time jobs averaging $1741.

ATHLETIC AWARDS *Total amount:* $1,013,087 (100% non-need-based).

APPLYING FOR FINANCIAL AID Required financial aid forms: FAFSA, institution's own form. **Financial aid deadline (priority):** 5/15. **Notification date:** Continuous beginning 4/20. Students must reply within 4 weeks of notification.

CONTACT Ms. Emily London-Jones, Director of Student Financial Aid, University of New Orleans, Administration Building, Room 1005, New Orleans, LA 70148, 504-280-6687 or toll-free 800-256-5866 (out-of-state). *Fax:* 504-280-3973. *E-mail:* elondon@uno.edu.

UNIVERSITY OF NORTH ALABAMA
Florence, AL

Tuition & fees (AL res): $4096   Average undergraduate aid package: $3508

ABOUT THE INSTITUTION State-supported, coed. Awards: bachelor's and master's degrees and post-master's certificates. 38 undergraduate majors. Total enrollment: 5,961. Undergraduates: 5,200. Freshmen: 772. Federal methodology is used as a basis for awarding need-based institutional aid.

UNDERGRADUATE EXPENSES for 2004–05 Application fee: $25. **Tuition, state resident:** full-time $3528; part-time $139 per credit hour. **Tuition, nonresident:** full-time $7055; part-time $278 per credit hour. Part-time tuition and fees vary according to course load. **College room and board:** $4140; **room only:** $1960. Room and board charges vary according to board plan and housing facility. **Payment plan:** Installment.

FRESHMAN FINANCIAL AID (Fall 2003) 549 applied for aid; of those 75% were deemed to have need. 94% of freshmen with need received aid; of those 21% had need fully met. *Average percent of need met:* 35% (excluding resources awarded to replace EFC). *Average financial aid package:* $3516 (excluding resources awarded to replace EFC).

UNDERGRADUATE FINANCIAL AID (Fall 2003) 2,905 applied for aid; of those 92% were deemed to have need. 91% of undergraduates with need received aid; of those 39% had need fully met. *Average percent of need met:* 41% (excluding resources awarded to replace EFC). *Average financial aid package:* $3508 (excluding resources awarded to replace EFC).

GIFT AID (NEED-BASED) Total amount: $4,258,970 (100% federal). **Receiving aid:** Freshmen: 32% (262); All full-time undergraduates: 36% (1,559). **Average award:** Freshmen: $3297; Undergraduates: $2780. **Scholarships, grants, and awards:** Federal Pell, FSEOG, state, private, college/university gift aid from institutional funds.

GIFT AID (NON-NEED-BASED) Total amount: $3,270,818 (87% institutional, 13% external sources). **Scholarships, grants, and awards by category:** Academic Interests/Achievement: general academic interests/achievements. Creative Arts/Performance: art/fine arts, journalism/publications, music. Special Achievements/Activities: cheerleading/drum major, general special achievements/activities, leadership. Special Characteristics: children of faculty/staff, first-generation college students, general special characteristics, out-of-state students. **Tuition waivers:** Full or partial for employees or children of employees, senior citizens. **ROTC:** Army.

LOANS Student loans: $11,736,270 (54% need-based, 46% non-need-based). 38% of past graduating class borrowed through all loan programs. *Average indebtedness per student:* $15,835. **Average need-based loan:** Freshmen: $2983; Undergraduates: $4913. **Parent loans:** $434,993 (100% non-need-based). **Programs:** FFEL (Subsidized and Unsubsidized Stafford, PLUS), Perkins.

WORK-STUDY Federal work-study: Total amount: $371,552; 240 jobs averaging $1298.

ATHLETIC AWARDS *Total amount:* $1,037,680 (100% non-need-based).

APPLYING FOR FINANCIAL AID Required financial aid form: FAFSA. **Financial aid deadline (priority):** 4/1. **Notification date:** 5/31. Students must reply within 2 weeks of notification.

CONTACT Mr. Ben Baker, Director of Student Financial Services, University of North Alabama, UNA Box 5014, Florence, AL 35632-0001, 256-765-4278 or toll-free 800-TALKUNA. *Fax:* 256-765-4920. *E-mail:* bjbaker@una.edu.

THE UNIVERSITY OF NORTH CAROLINA AT ASHEVILLE
Asheville, NC

Tuition & fees (NC res): $3392   Average undergraduate aid package: $7383

ABOUT THE INSTITUTION State-supported, coed. Awards: bachelor's and master's degrees and post-bachelor's certificates. 28 undergraduate majors. Total enrollment: 3,607. Undergraduates: 3,572. Freshmen: 707. Federal methodology is used as a basis for awarding need-based institutional aid.

UNDERGRADUATE EXPENSES for 2004–05 Application fee: $50. **Tuition, state resident:** full-time $1897. **Tuition, nonresident:** full-time $11,097. Part-time tuition and fees vary according to course load. **College room and board:** $5212; **room only:** $2722. Room and board charges vary according to housing facility.

FRESHMAN FINANCIAL AID (Fall 2003) 418 applied for aid; of those 58% were deemed to have need. 98% of freshmen with need received aid; of those 24%

had need fully met. *Average percent of need met:* 71% (excluding resources awarded to replace EFC). *Average financial aid package:* $5944 (excluding resources awarded to replace EFC). 10% of all full-time freshmen had no need and received non-need-based gift aid.

UNDERGRADUATE FINANCIAL AID (Fall 2003) 1,787 applied for aid; of those 64% were deemed to have need. 97% of undergraduates with need received aid; of those 38% had need fully met. *Average percent of need met:* 79% (excluding resources awarded to replace EFC). *Average financial aid package:* $7383 (excluding resources awarded to replace EFC). 9% of all full-time undergraduates had no need and received non-need-based gift aid.

GIFT AID (NEED-BASED) *Total amount:* $3,822,728 (53% federal, 24% state, 19% institutional, 4% external sources). *Receiving aid:* Freshmen: 36% (215); All full-time undergraduates: 36% (965). *Average award:* Freshmen: $2843; Undergraduates: $3365. *Scholarships, grants, and awards:* Federal Pell, FSEOG, state, private, college/university gift aid from institutional funds.

GIFT AID (NON-NEED-BASED) *Total amount:* $949,661 (15% federal, 35% state, 36% institutional, 14% external sources). *Receiving aid:* Freshmen: 14% (82); Undergraduates: 9% (240). *Average Award:* Freshmen: $3154; Undergraduates: $2891. *Scholarships, grants, and awards by category: Academic Interests/Achievement:* 262 awards ($621,555 total): biological sciences, business, communication, computer science, education, engineering/technologies, English, general academic interests/achievements, health fields, mathematics, physical sciences, premedicine, social sciences. *Creative Arts/Performance:* 33 awards ($16,761 total): art/fine arts, general creative arts/performance, music, theater/drama. *Special Achievements/Activities:* 98 awards ($177,686 total): community service, general special achievements/activities, junior miss, leadership. *Special Characteristics:* 39 awards ($127,317 total): adult students, children and siblings of alumni, children of faculty/staff, ethnic background, first-generation college students, general special characteristics, handicapped students, international students, local/state students, members of minority groups, veterans, veterans' children. *Tuition waivers:* Full or partial for employees or children of employees, senior citizens.

LOANS *Student loans:* $5,879,877 (68% need-based, 32% non-need-based). 54% of past graduating class borrowed through all loan programs. *Average indebtedness per student:* $14,698. *Average need-based loan:* Freshmen: $2644; Undergraduates: $3539. *Parent loans:* $1,144,554 (19% need-based, 81% non-need-based). *Programs:* Federal Direct (Subsidized and Unsubsidized Stafford, PLUS), Perkins, state, college/university.

WORK-STUDY *Federal work-study:* Total amount: $121,089; 101 jobs averaging $1234. *State or other work-study/employment:* Total amount: $869,698 (10% need-based, 90% non-need-based). 637 part-time jobs averaging $1407.

ATHLETIC AWARDS *Total amount:* $827,508 (24% need-based, 76% non-need-based).

APPLYING FOR FINANCIAL AID *Required financial aid form:* FAFSA. *Financial aid deadline (priority):* 3/1. *Notification date:* Continuous beginning 3/15. Students must reply within 2 weeks of notification.

CONTACT Ms. Elizabeth D. Bartlett, Associate Director of Financial Aid, The University of North Carolina at Asheville, 1 University Heights, Asheville, NC 28804-8510, 828-232-6535 or toll-free 800-531-9842. *Fax:* 828-251-2294. *E-mail:* bbartlett@unca.edu.

THE UNIVERSITY OF NORTH CAROLINA AT CHAPEL HILL
Chapel Hill, NC

Tuition & fees (NC res): $4451	Average undergraduate aid package: $9430

ABOUT THE INSTITUTION State-supported, coed. Awards: bachelor's, master's, doctoral, and first professional degrees and post-master's certificates. 70 undergraduate majors. Total enrollment: 26,878. Undergraduates: 16,525. Freshmen: 3,589. Both federal and institutional methodology are used as a basis for awarding need-based institutional aid.

UNDERGRADUATE EXPENSES for 2004–05 *Application fee:* $60. *Tuition, state resident:* full-time $3205. *Tuition, nonresident:* full-time $16,303. Full-time tuition and fees vary according to program. Part-time tuition and fees vary according to course load and program. *College room and board:* $6245; *room only:* $3420. Room and board charges vary according to board plan, housing facility, and location. *Payment plans:* Installment, deferred payment.

FRESHMAN FINANCIAL AID (Fall 2003) 2611 applied for aid; of those 45% were deemed to have need. 97% of freshmen with need received aid; of those 78% had need fully met. *Average percent of need met:* 100% (excluding

resources awarded to replace EFC). *Average financial aid package:* $9100 (excluding resources awarded to replace EFC). 21% of all full-time freshmen had no need and received non-need-based gift aid.

UNDERGRADUATE FINANCIAL AID (Fall 2003) 9,570 applied for aid; of those 53% were deemed to have need. 98% of undergraduates with need received aid; of those 72% had need fully met. *Average percent of need met:* 100% (excluding resources awarded to replace EFC). *Average financial aid package:* $9430 (excluding resources awarded to replace EFC). 14% of all full-time undergraduates had no need and received non-need-based gift aid.

GIFT AID (NEED-BASED) *Total amount:* $33,699,059 (23% federal, 14% state, 54% institutional, 9% external sources). *Receiving aid:* Freshmen: 32% (1,125); All full-time undergraduates: 32% (4,893). *Average award:* Freshmen: $7091; Undergraduates: $6777. *Scholarships, grants, and awards:* Federal Pell, FSEOG, state, private, college/university gift aid from institutional funds, state grants.

GIFT AID (NON-NEED-BASED) *Total amount:* $13,353,427 (6% federal, 12% state, 33% institutional, 49% external sources). *Receiving aid:* Freshmen: 16% (561); Undergraduates: 10% (1,460). *Average Award:* Freshmen: $4206; Undergraduates: $5408. *Scholarships, grants, and awards by category: Academic Interests/Achievement:* business, communication, education, English, general academic interests/achievements, health fields, mathematics. *Creative Arts/Performance:* applied art and design, art/fine arts, journalism/publications, music, theater/drama. *Special Achievements/Activities:* community service, general special achievements/activities, leadership. *Special Characteristics:* children of faculty/staff, international students, out-of-state students, relatives of clergy, religious affiliation. *Tuition waivers:* Full or partial for employees or children of employees, senior citizens. *ROTC:* Army, Naval, Air Force.

LOANS *Student loans:* $24,006,299 (71% need-based, 29% non-need-based). 24% of past graduating class borrowed through all loan programs. *Average indebtedness per student:* $11,519. *Average need-based loan:* Freshmen: $2752; Undergraduates: $3761. *Parent loans:* $7,166,276 (37% need-based, 63% non-need-based). *Programs:* FFEL (Subsidized and Unsubsidized Stafford, PLUS), Perkins, state, college/university, alternative loans.

WORK-STUDY *Federal work-study:* Total amount: $1,454,839; 824 jobs averaging $1691.

ATHLETIC AWARDS *Total amount:* $5,832,149 (29% need-based, 71% non-need-based).

APPLYING FOR FINANCIAL AID *Required financial aid forms:* FAFSA, CSS Financial Aid PROFILE. *Financial aid deadline (priority):* 3/1. *Notification date:* Continuous beginning 3/15. Students must reply by 5/1.

CONTACT Ms. Shirley A. Ort, Director, Office of Scholarships and Student Aid, The University of North Carolina at Chapel Hill, PO Box 1080, Chapel Hill, NC 27514, 919-962-9246. *E-mail:* sao@unc.edu.

THE UNIVERSITY OF NORTH CAROLINA AT CHARLOTTE
Charlotte, NC

Tuition & fees (NC res): $3473	Average undergraduate aid package: $8527

ABOUT THE INSTITUTION State-supported, coed. Awards: bachelor's, master's, and doctoral degrees and post-master's certificates. 67 undergraduate majors. Total enrollment: 19,846. Undergraduates: 15,875. Freshmen: 2,629. Federal methodology is used as a basis for awarding need-based institutional aid.

UNDERGRADUATE EXPENSES for 2004–05 *Application fee:* $50. *Tuition, state resident:* full-time $2129; part-time $533 per term. *Tuition, nonresident:* full-time $12,241; part-time $3061 per term. *Required fees:* full-time $1344; $398 per term part-time. Full-time tuition and fees vary according to course load. Part-time tuition and fees vary according to course load. *College room and board:* $5304; *room only:* $2724. Room and board charges vary according to board plan and housing facility.

FRESHMAN FINANCIAL AID (Fall 2004, est.) 1770 applied for aid; of those 69% were deemed to have need. 94% of freshmen with need received aid; of those 25% had need fully met. *Average percent of need met:* 66% (excluding resources awarded to replace EFC). *Average financial aid package:* $7190 (excluding resources awarded to replace EFC). 18% of all full-time freshmen had no need and received non-need-based gift aid.

UNDERGRADUATE FINANCIAL AID (Fall 2004, est.) 7,689 applied for aid; of those 78% were deemed to have need. 96% of undergraduates with need received aid; of those 33% had need fully met. *Average percent of need met:* 64% (excluding resources awarded to replace EFC). *Average financial aid package:* $8527 (excluding resources awarded to replace EFC). 15% of all full-time undergraduates had no need and received non-need-based gift aid.

GIFT AID (NEED-BASED) *Total amount:* $19,703,469 (57% federal, 37% state, 2% institutional, 4% external sources). *Receiving aid:* Freshmen: 37% (995); All full-time undergraduates: 36% (4,626). *Average award:* Freshmen: $4323; Undergraduates: $4083. *Scholarships, grants, and awards:* Federal Pell, FSEOG, state, private, college/university gift aid from institutional funds.

GIFT AID (NON-NEED-BASED) *Total amount:* $1,644,722 (28% state, 25% institutional, 47% external sources). *Receiving aid:* Freshmen: 9% (240); Undergraduates: 5% (651). *Average Award: Freshmen:* $5854; *Undergraduates:* $5772. *Scholarships, grants, and awards by category: Academic Interests/ Achievement:* 170 awards ($528,000 total): architecture, business, computer science, education, engineering/technologies, general academic interests/ achievements, health fields, humanities, mathematics, military science. *Creative Arts/Performance:* 30 awards ($42,500 total): music, performing arts. *Special Characteristics:* 54 awards ($56,000 total): adult students. *Tuition waivers:* Full or partial for senior citizens. *ROTC:* Army, Air Force.

LOANS *Student loans:* $41,759,710 (52% need-based, 48% non-need-based). 56% of past graduating class borrowed through all loan programs. *Average indebtedness per student:* $17,730. *Average need-based loan:* Freshmen: $2768; Undergraduates: $3862. *Parent loans:* $6,026,987 (100% non-need-based). *Programs:* FFEL (Subsidized and Unsubsidized Stafford, PLUS), Perkins, state, college/university.

WORK-STUDY *Federal work-study:* Total amount: $679,643; 530 jobs averaging $1282. *State or other work-study/employment:* Total amount: $2,298,246 (100% non-need-based). 1,825 part-time jobs averaging $1611.

ATHLETIC AWARDS *Total amount:* $1,894,032 (34% need-based, 66% non-need-based).

APPLYING FOR FINANCIAL AID *Required financial aid form:* FAFSA. *Financial aid deadline (priority):* 4/1. *Notification date:* 4/2. Students must reply within 3 weeks of notification.

CONTACT Anthony D. Carter, Director of Financial Aid, The University of North Carolina at Charlotte, 9201 University City Boulevard, Charlotte, NC 28223-0001, 704-687-2461. *Fax:* 704-687-3132. *E-mail:* finaid@email.uncc.edu.

THE UNIVERSITY OF NORTH CAROLINA AT GREENSBORO
Greensboro, NC

Tuition & fees (NC res): $3435	Average undergraduate aid package: $6655

ABOUT THE INSTITUTION State-supported, coed. Awards: bachelor's, master's, and doctoral degrees. 103 undergraduate majors. Total enrollment: 14,328. Undergraduates: 11,106. Freshmen: 2,056. Federal methodology is used as a basis for awarding need-based institutional aid.

UNDERGRADUATE EXPENSES for 2004–05 *Application fee:* $35. *Tuition, state resident:* full-time $2028; part-time $253 per hour. *Tuition, nonresident:* full-time $12,996; part-time $1625 per hour. *Required fees:* full-time $1407; $2838 per term part-time. Part-time tuition and fees vary according to course load. *College room and board:* $5000; *room only:* $2800. Room and board charges vary according to board plan and housing facility. *Payment plan:* Installment.

FRESHMAN FINANCIAL AID (Fall 2004, est.) 1672 applied for aid; of those 67% were deemed to have need. 100% of freshmen with need received aid; of those 13% had need fully met. *Average percent of need met:* 67% (excluding resources awarded to replace EFC). *Average financial aid package:* $5860 (excluding resources awarded to replace EFC). 7% of all full-time freshmen had no need and received non-need-based gift aid.

UNDERGRADUATE FINANCIAL AID (Fall 2004, est.) 7,342 applied for aid; of those 70% were deemed to have need. 96% of undergraduates with need received aid; of those 17% had need fully met. *Average percent of need met:* 70% (excluding resources awarded to replace EFC). *Average financial aid package:* $6655 (excluding resources awarded to replace EFC). 8% of all full-time undergraduates had no need and received non-need-based gift aid.

GIFT AID (NEED-BASED) *Total amount:* $10,979,247 (86% federal, 8% state, 6% institutional). *Receiving aid:* Freshmen: 46% (997); All full-time undergraduates: 50% (4,903). *Average award:* Freshmen: $2129; Undergraduates: $2105. *Scholarships, grants, and awards:* Federal Pell, FSEOG, state, private, college/university gift aid from institutional funds.

GIFT AID (NON-NEED-BASED) *Total amount:* $9,596,361 (63% state, 33% institutional, 4% external sources). *Receiving aid:* Freshmen: 48% (1,044); Undergraduates: 50% (4,846). *Average Award: Freshmen:* $3893; *Undergraduates:* $3533. *Scholarships, grants, and awards by category: Academic Interests/ Achievement:* 320 awards ($600,000 total): biological sciences, business, communication, education, English, foreign languages, general academic interests/

achievements, health fields, home economics, humanities, library science, mathematics, physical sciences, premedicine, religion/biblical studies, social sciences. *Creative Arts/Performance:* 100 awards ($350,000 total): art/fine arts, cinema/film/broadcasting, dance, music, performing arts, theater/drama. *Special Achievements/Activities:* 25 awards ($30,000 total): community service, general special achievements/activities, junior miss, leadership, religious involvement. *Special Characteristics:* 500 awards ($500,000 total): adult students, ethnic background, general special characteristics, handicapped students, members of minority groups, out-of-state students, religious affiliation, veterans, veterans' children. *Tuition waivers:* Full or partial for employees or children of employees. *ROTC:* Army cooperative, Air Force cooperative.

LOANS *Student loans:* $31,152,684 (51% need-based, 49% non-need-based). 58% of past graduating class borrowed through all loan programs. *Average indebtedness per student:* $16,905. *Average need-based loan:* Freshmen: $2318; Undergraduates: $3433. *Parent loans:* $9,980,691 (100% non-need-based). *Programs:* FFEL (Subsidized and Unsubsidized Stafford, PLUS), Perkins, college/ university.

WORK-STUDY *Federal work-study:* Total amount: $557,498; 565 jobs averaging $1801.

ATHLETIC AWARDS *Total amount:* $1,517,964 (100% non-need-based).

APPLYING FOR FINANCIAL AID *Required financial aid form:* FAFSA. *Financial aid deadline (priority):* 3/1. *Notification date:* Continuous beginning 3/15. Students must reply within 3 weeks of notification.

CONTACT Mr. Bruce Cabiness, Associate Director of Financial Aid, The University of North Carolina at Greensboro, PO Box 26170, Greensboro, NC 27402-6170, 336-334-5702. *Fax:* 336-334-3010. *E-mail:* bruce_cabiness@uncg.edu.

THE UNIVERSITY OF NORTH CAROLINA AT PEMBROKE
Pembroke, NC

Tuition & fees (NC res): $2832	Average undergraduate aid package: $6598

ABOUT THE INSTITUTION State-supported, coed. Awards: bachelor's and master's degrees. 40 undergraduate majors. Total enrollment: 5,027. Undergraduates: 4,508. Freshmen: 760. Federal methodology is used as a basis for awarding need-based institutional aid.

UNDERGRADUATE EXPENSES for 2004–05 *Application fee:* $40. *Tuition, state resident:* full-time $1696. *Tuition, nonresident:* full-time $11,128. Full-time tuition and fees vary according to course load and location. Part-time tuition and fees vary according to course load and location. *College room and board:* $4560; *room only:* $2610. Room and board charges vary according to board plan and housing facility. *Payment plan:* Installment.

FRESHMAN FINANCIAL AID (Fall 2004, est.) 646 applied for aid; of those 92% were deemed to have need. 89% of freshmen with need received aid; of those 14% had need fully met. *Average percent of need met:* 64% (excluding resources awarded to replace EFC). *Average financial aid package:* $6136 (excluding resources awarded to replace EFC). 6% of all full-time freshmen had no need and received non-need-based gift aid.

UNDERGRADUATE FINANCIAL AID (Fall 2004, est.) 2,821 applied for aid; of those 87% were deemed to have need. 97% of undergraduates with need received aid; of those 17% had need fully met. *Average percent of need met:* 68% (excluding resources awarded to replace EFC). *Average financial aid package:* $6598 (excluding resources awarded to replace EFC). 3% of all full-time undergraduates had no need and received non-need-based gift aid.

GIFT AID (NEED-BASED) *Total amount:* $9,439,476 (61% federal, 27% state, 5% institutional, 7% external sources). *Receiving aid:* Freshmen: 63% (480); All full-time undergraduates: 63% (2,117). *Average award:* Freshmen: $4340; Undergraduates: $4118. *Scholarships, grants, and awards:* Federal Pell, FSEOG, state, private, college/university gift aid from institutional funds.

GIFT AID (NON-NEED-BASED) *Total amount:* $150,205 (100% institutional). *Receiving aid:* Freshmen: 4% (34); Undergraduates: 3% (90). *Average Award: Freshmen:* $1806; *Undergraduates:* $1313. *Scholarships, grants, and awards by category: Academic Interests/Achievement:* 64 awards ($107,905 total): business, communication, education, English, general academic interests/ achievements, health fields, physical sciences. *Creative Arts/Performance:* 42 awards ($22,650 total): journalism/publications, music. *Special Characteristics:* 9 awards ($19,500 total): children and siblings of alumni, general special characteristics. *Tuition waivers:* Full or partial for senior citizens. *ROTC:* Army, Air Force.

LOANS *Student loans:* $10,960,458 (68% need-based, 32% non-need-based). 66% of past graduating class borrowed through all loan programs. *Average*

The University of North Carolina at Pembroke

indebtedness per student: $12,844. *Average need-based loan:* Freshmen: $2452; Undergraduates: $3438. *Parent loans:* $1,004,440 (100% non-need-based). *Programs:* FFEL (Subsidized and Unsubsidized Stafford, PLUS), Perkins, college/university.

WORK-STUDY *Federal work-study:* Total amount: $348,741; 383 jobs averaging $1500. *State or other work-study/employment:* Total amount: $30,629 (100% need-based). 27 part-time jobs averaging $1500.

ATHLETIC AWARDS *Total amount:* $905,249 (100% need-based).

APPLYING FOR FINANCIAL AID *Required financial aid form:* FAFSA. *Financial aid deadline:* Continuous. *Notification date:* 4/15.

CONTACT Mildred Weber, Assistant Director of Financial Aid, The University of North Carolina at Pembroke, PO Box 1510, Pembroke, NC 28372-1510, 910-521-6612 or toll-free 800-949-UNCP.

THE UNIVERSITY OF NORTH CAROLINA AT WILMINGTON
Wilmington, NC

Tuition & fees (NC res): $3626   **Average undergraduate aid package: $6693**

ABOUT THE INSTITUTION State-supported, coed. Awards: bachelor's, master's, and doctoral degrees. 60 undergraduate majors. Total enrollment: 11,327. Undergraduates: 10,353. Freshmen: 1,897. Federal methodology is used as a basis for awarding need-based institutional aid.

UNDERGRADUATE EXPENSES for 2004–05 *Application fee:* $45. *Tuition, state resident:* full-time $1928. *Tuition, nonresident:* full-time $11,638. Full-time tuition and fees vary according to course load. Part-time tuition and fees vary according to course load. *College room and board:* $5800. Room and board charges vary according to board plan and housing facility. *Payment plan:* Installment.

FRESHMAN FINANCIAL AID (Fall 2004, est.) 1062 applied for aid; of those 58% were deemed to have need. 100% of freshmen with need received aid; of those 66% had need fully met. *Average percent of need met:* 87% (excluding resources awarded to replace EFC). *Average financial aid package:* $5552 (excluding resources awarded to replace EFC). 1% of all full-time freshmen had no need and received non-need-based gift aid.

UNDERGRADUATE FINANCIAL AID (Fall 2004, est.) 5,500 applied for aid; of those 66% were deemed to have need. 100% of undergraduates with need received aid; of those 64% had need fully met. *Average percent of need met:* 88% (excluding resources awarded to replace EFC). *Average financial aid package:* $6693 (excluding resources awarded to replace EFC). 1% of all full-time undergraduates had no need and received non-need-based gift aid.

GIFT AID (NEED-BASED) *Total amount:* $12,939,274 (46% federal, 39% state, 4% institutional, 11% external sources). *Receiving aid:* Freshmen: 24% (446); All full-time undergraduates: 31% (2,948). *Average award:* Freshmen: $4225; Undergraduates: $3852. *Scholarships, grants, and awards:* Federal Pell, FSEOG, state, private, college/university gift aid from institutional funds.

GIFT AID (NON-NEED-BASED) *Total amount:* $2,303,925 (41% state, 20% institutional, 39% external sources). *Receiving aid:* Freshmen: 3; Undergraduates: 6. *Average Award:* Freshmen: $1976; Undergraduates: $1369. *Scholarships, grants, and awards by category:* Academic Interests/Achievement: 133 awards ($275,315 total): biological sciences, business, communication, computer science, education, English, foreign languages, general academic interests/achievements, health fields, humanities, international studies, mathematics, physical sciences, religion/biblical studies, social sciences. *Creative Arts/Performance:* 21 awards ($14,500 total): art/fine arts, creative writing, music, theater/drama. *Special Achievements/Activities:* 63 awards ($14,430 total): cheerleading/drum major, general special achievements/activities, leadership. *Special Characteristics:* local/state students. *Tuition waivers:* Full or partial for employees or children of employees, senior citizens.

LOANS *Student loans:* $24,237,097 (55% need-based, 45% non-need-based). 49% of past graduating class borrowed through all loan programs. *Average indebtedness per student:* $15,046. *Average need-based loan:* Freshmen: $2827; Undergraduates: $4046. *Parent loans:* $15,489,674 (100% non-need-based). *Programs:* Federal Direct (Subsidized and Unsubsidized Stafford, PLUS), Perkins, state, college/university.

WORK-STUDY *Federal work-study:* Total amount: $671,098; 279 jobs averaging $3000. *State or other work-study/employment:* Part-time jobs available.

ATHLETIC AWARDS *Total amount:* $1,551,572 (29% need-based, 71% non-need-based).

APPLYING FOR FINANCIAL AID *Required financial aid forms:* FAFSA, institution's own form. *Financial aid deadline:* Continuous. *Notification date:* Continuous beginning 3/15. Students must reply within 3 weeks of notification.

CONTACT Emily Bliss, Director of Financial Aid and Veterans' Services Office, The University of North Carolina at Wilmington, 601 South College Road, Wilmington, NC 28403-5951, 910-962-3177 or toll-free 800-228-5571 (out-of-state). *Fax:* 910-962-3851. *E-mail:* finaid@uncw.edu.

UNIVERSITY OF NORTH DAKOTA
Grand Forks, ND

Tuition & fees (ND res): $4828   **Average undergraduate aid package: $8634**

ABOUT THE INSTITUTION State-supported, coed. Awards: bachelor's, master's, doctoral, and first professional degrees and post-master's certificates. 71 undergraduate majors. Total enrollment: 13,187. Undergraduates: 10,710. Freshmen: 2,200. Federal methodology is used as a basis for awarding need-based institutional aid.

UNDERGRADUATE EXPENSES for 2004–05 *Application fee:* $35. *Tuition, state resident:* full-time $4009; part-time $167.03 per credit hour. *Tuition, nonresident:* full-time $10,703; part-time $445.95 per credit hour. *Required fees:* full-time $819; $54.97 per credit hour. Full-time tuition and fees vary according to degree level, program, and reciprocity agreements. Part-time tuition and fees vary according to course load, degree level, program, and reciprocity agreements. *College room and board:* $4455; *room only:* $1825. Room and board charges vary according to board plan and housing facility. *Payment plan:* Deferred payment.

GIFT AID (NEED-BASED) *Total amount:* $17,150,661 (53% federal, 3% state, 27% institutional, 17% external sources). *Receiving aid:* Freshmen: 20% (548); All full-time undergraduates: 24% (2,014). *Average award:* Freshmen: $2967; Undergraduates: $3098. *Scholarships, grants, and awards:* Federal Pell, FSEOG, state, private, college/university gift aid from institutional funds.

GIFT AID (NON-NEED-BASED) *Total amount:* $2,297,098 (9% federal, 2% state, 62% institutional, 27% external sources). *Receiving aid:* Freshmen: 26% (688); Undergraduates: 18% (1,506). *Average Award:* Freshmen: $2960; Undergraduates: $2924. *Scholarships, grants, and awards by category:* Academic Interests/Achievement: 2,634 awards ($3,118,021 total): biological sciences, business, communication, computer science, education, engineering/technologies, English, foreign languages, general academic interests/achievements, health fields, humanities, international studies, mathematics, military science, physical sciences, premedicine, social sciences. *Creative Arts/Performance:* 113 awards ($70,185 total): art/fine arts, debating, music, theater/drama. *Special Achievements/Activities:* 590 awards ($1,571,474 total): general special achievements/activities, leadership, memberships. *Special Characteristics:* 302 awards ($985,693 total): children of faculty/staff, ethnic background, general special characteristics, handicapped students, international students, members of minority groups, veterans' children. *Tuition waivers:* Full or partial for minority students, employees or children of employees, senior citizens. *ROTC:* Army, Air Force.

LOANS *Student loans:* $50,159,079 (81% need-based, 19% non-need-based). 70% of past graduating class borrowed through all loan programs. *Average indebtedness per student:* $26,225. *Average need-based loan:* Freshmen: $3309; Undergraduates: $4260. *Parent loans:* $2,921,472 (64% need-based, 36% non-need-based). *Programs:* FFEL (Subsidized and Unsubsidized Stafford, PLUS), Perkins, Federal Nursing.

ATHLETIC AWARDS *Total amount:* $1,370,364 (31% need-based, 69% non-need-based).

APPLYING FOR FINANCIAL AID *Required financial aid form:* FAFSA. *Financial aid deadline (priority):* 3/15. *Notification date:* Continuous beginning 5/15. Students must reply within 4 weeks of notification.

CONTACT Ms. Robin Holden, Director of Student Financial Aid, University of North Dakota, Box 8371, Grand Forks, ND 58202, 701-777-3121 or toll-free 800-CALL UND. *Fax:* 701-777-2040. *E-mail:* robin.holden@mail.und.nodak.edu.

UNIVERSITY OF NORTHERN COLORADO
Greeley, CO

Tuition & fees (CO res): $3370   **Average undergraduate aid package: $9109**

ABOUT THE INSTITUTION State-supported, coed. Awards: bachelor's, master's, and doctoral degrees. 43 undergraduate majors. Total enrollment: 13,204. Undergraduates: 10,664. Freshmen: 2,140. Federal methodology is used as a basis for awarding need-based institutional aid.

UNDERGRADUATE EXPENSES for 2004–05 *Application fee:* $40. *Tuition, state resident:* full-time $2850; part-time $142.50 per credit hour. *Tuition, nonresident:* full-time $11,740; part-time $587 per credit hour. *Required fees:* full-time $520; $26 per credit hour. *College room and board:* $5954; *room only:* $2876. Room and board charges vary according to board plan and housing facility. *Payment plan:* Deferred payment.

FRESHMAN FINANCIAL AID (Fall 2003) 1781 applied for aid; of those 52% were deemed to have need. 99% of freshmen with need received aid; of those 46% had need fully met. *Average percent of need met:* 88% (excluding resources awarded to replace EFC). *Average financial aid package:* $7079 (excluding resources awarded to replace EFC). 10% of all full-time freshmen had no need and received non-need-based gift aid.

UNDERGRADUATE FINANCIAL AID (Fall 2003) 7,395 applied for aid; of those 57% were deemed to have need. 99% of undergraduates with need received aid; of those 57% had need fully met. *Average percent of need met:* 100% (excluding resources awarded to replace EFC). *Average financial aid package:* $9109 (excluding resources awarded to replace EFC). 8% of all full-time undergraduates had no need and received non-need-based gift aid.

GIFT AID (NEED-BASED) *Total amount:* $8,188,543 (73% federal, 27% state). *Receiving aid:* Freshmen: 19% (405); All full-time undergraduates: 23% (2,205). *Average award:* Freshmen: $3254; Undergraduates: $3503. *Scholarships, grants, and awards:* Federal Pell, FSEOG, state, private, college/university gift aid from institutional funds, Robert C. Byrd Scholarships.

GIFT AID (NON-NEED-BASED) *Total amount:* $8,266,554 (16% state, 27% institutional, 57% external sources). *Receiving aid:* Freshmen: 23% (491); Undergraduates: 18% (1,712). *Average Award:* Freshmen: $2247; Undergraduates: $2587. *Scholarships, grants, and awards by category: Academic Interests/Achievement:* 992 awards ($927,199 total): biological sciences, business, communication, education, English, general academic interests/achievements, health fields, home economics, mathematics, military science, physical sciences, social sciences. *Creative Arts/Performance:* 183 awards ($119,810 total): dance, music, performing arts, theater/drama. *Special Characteristics:* 3,392 awards ($6,560,074 total): adult students, children and siblings of alumni, children of faculty/staff, children of union members/company employees, ethnic background, general special characteristics, handicapped students, international students, local/state students, members of minority groups, out-of-state students, veterans. *ROTC:* Army, Air Force.

LOANS *Student loans:* $30,462,189 (47% need-based, 53% non-need-based). *Average need-based loan:* Freshmen: $2936; Undergraduates: $3728. *Parent loans:* $31,790,053 (100% non-need-based). *Programs:* FFEL (Subsidized and Unsubsidized Stafford, PLUS), Perkins, college/university.

WORK-STUDY *Federal work-study:* Total amount: $790,603; 350 jobs averaging $2259. *State or other work-study/employment:* Total amount: $7,576,827 (20% need-based, 80% non-need-based). 734 part-time jobs averaging $2049.

ATHLETIC AWARDS *Total amount:* $685,412 (100% non-need-based).

APPLYING FOR FINANCIAL AID *Required financial aid form:* FAFSA. *Financial aid deadline (priority):* 3/1. *Notification date:* Continuous beginning 4/15. Students must reply within 4 weeks of notification.

CONTACT Donni Clark, Director of Student Financial Resources, University of Northern Colorado, Carter Hall 1005, Campus Box 33, Greeley, CO 80639, 970-351-2502 or toll-free 888-700-4UNC (in-state). *Fax:* 970-351-3737. *E-mail:* sfr@unco.edu.

UNIVERSITY OF NORTHERN IOWA
Cedar Falls, IA

Tuition & fees (IA res): $5387	Average undergraduate aid package: $6907

ABOUT THE INSTITUTION State-supported, coed. Awards: bachelor's, master's, and doctoral degrees. 111 undergraduate majors. Total enrollment: 12,927. Undergraduates: 11,266. Freshmen: 1,700. Federal methodology is used as a basis for awarding need-based institutional aid.

UNDERGRADUATE EXPENSES for 2004–05 *Application fee:* $30. *Tuition, state resident:* full-time $4702; part-time $196 per hour. *Tuition, nonresident:* full-time $12,020; part-time $501 per hour. Full-time tuition and fees vary according to course load. Part-time tuition and fees vary according to course load. *College room and board:* $5261; *room only:* $2431. Room and board charges vary according to board plan and housing facility. *Payment plan:* Installment.

FRESHMAN FINANCIAL AID (Fall 2004, est.) 1417 applied for aid; of those 72% were deemed to have need. 95% of freshmen with need received aid; of those 20% had need fully met. *Average percent of need met:* 66% (excluding resources awarded to replace EFC). *Average financial aid package:* $5953 (excluding resources awarded to replace EFC). 13% of all full-time freshmen had no need and received non-need-based gift aid.

UNDERGRADUATE FINANCIAL AID (Fall 2004, est.) 7,798 applied for aid; of those 78% were deemed to have need. 96% of undergraduates with need received aid; of those 22% had need fully met. *Average percent of need met:* 63% (excluding resources awarded to replace EFC). *Average financial aid package:* $6907 (excluding resources awarded to replace EFC). 8% of all full-time undergraduates had no need and received non-need-based gift aid.

GIFT AID (NEED-BASED) *Total amount:* $11,871,109 (66% federal, 8% state, 26% institutional). *Receiving aid:* Freshmen: 37% (615); All full-time undergraduates: 30% (2,964). *Average award:* Freshmen: $2640; Undergraduates: $3140. *Scholarships, grants, and awards:* Federal Pell, FSEOG, state, private, college/university gift aid from institutional funds.

GIFT AID (NON-NEED-BASED) *Total amount:* $5,843,721 (7% state, 68% institutional, 25% external sources). *Receiving aid:* Freshmen: 28% (459); Undergraduates: 16% (1,561). *Average Award:* Freshmen: $2845; Undergraduates: $2964. *Scholarships, grants, and awards by category: Academic Interests/Achievement:* biological sciences, business, education, general academic interests/achievements, mathematics, physical sciences, social sciences. *Creative Arts/Performance:* applied art and design, art/fine arts, music, theater/drama. *Special Achievements/Activities:* leadership. *Special Characteristics:* general special characteristics, members of minority groups. *ROTC:* Army.

LOANS *Student loans:* $51,308,831 (52% need-based, 48% non-need-based). 76% of past graduating class borrowed through all loan programs. *Average indebtedness per student:* $18,397. *Average need-based loan:* Freshmen: $2646; Undergraduates: $4177. *Parent loans:* $10,166,553 (100% non-need-based). *Programs:* Federal Direct (Subsidized and Unsubsidized Stafford, PLUS), Perkins, state, alternative loans.

WORK-STUDY *Federal work-study:* Total amount: $1,270,047; 573 jobs averaging $1845. *State or other work-study/employment:* Total amount: $331,828 (64% need-based, 36% non-need-based). 145 part-time jobs averaging $1974.

ATHLETIC AWARDS *Total amount:* $2,648,950 (100% non-need-based).

APPLYING FOR FINANCIAL AID *Required financial aid form:* FAFSA. *Financial aid deadline:* Continuous. *Notification date:* Continuous beginning 3/1.

CONTACT Joyce Morrow, Associate Director of Financial Aid, University of Northern Iowa, 255 Gilchrist Hall, Cedar Falls, IA 50614-0024, 319-273-2700 or toll-free 800-772-2037. *Fax:* 319-273-6950. *E-mail:* joyce.morrow@uni.edu.

UNIVERSITY OF NORTHERN VIRGINIA
Manassas, VA

CONTACT Financial Aid Office, University of Northern Virginia, 10021 Balls Ford Road, Manassas, VA 20109, 703-392-0771.

UNIVERSITY OF NORTH FLORIDA
Jacksonville, FL

Tuition & fees (FL res): $3101	Average undergraduate aid package: $2286

ABOUT THE INSTITUTION State-supported, coed. Awards: associate, bachelor's, master's, and doctoral degrees and post-bachelor's and post-master's certificates (doctoral degree in education only). 50 undergraduate majors. Total enrollment: 14,534. Undergraduates: 12,669. Freshmen: 2,303. Federal methodology is used as a basis for awarding need-based institutional aid.

UNDERGRADUATE EXPENSES for 2004–05 *Application fee:* $30. *Tuition, state resident:* full-time $3101; part-time $103.37 per semester hour. *Tuition, nonresident:* full-time $14,851; part-time $495.02 per semester hour. *College room and board:* $6278; *room only:* $3768. Room and board charges vary according to housing facility. *Payment plan:* Deferred payment.

FRESHMAN FINANCIAL AID (Fall 2004, est.) 1891 applied for aid; of those 78% were deemed to have need. 99% of freshmen with need received aid; of those 19% had need fully met. *Average percent of need met:* 81% (excluding resources awarded to replace EFC). *Average financial aid package:* $2006 (excluding resources awarded to replace EFC). 17% of all full-time freshmen had no need and received non-need-based gift aid.

UNDERGRADUATE FINANCIAL AID (Fall 2004, est.) 7,033 applied for aid; of those 84% were deemed to have need. 99% of undergraduates with need received aid; of those 18% had need fully met. *Average percent of need met:*

75% (excluding resources awarded to replace EFC). *Average financial aid package:* $2286 (excluding resources awarded to replace EFC). 11% of all full-time undergraduates had no need and received non-need-based gift aid.

GIFT AID (NEED-BASED) *Total amount:* $20,753,016 (33% federal, 47% state, 18% institutional, 2% external sources). *Receiving aid:* Freshmen: 27% (588); All full-time undergraduates: 27% (2,387). *Average award:* Freshmen: $1790; Undergraduates: $1956. *Scholarships, grants, and awards:* Federal Pell, FSEOG, state, college/university gift aid from institutional funds, 2+2 Scholarships (jointly sponsored with Florida Community College at Jacksonville).

GIFT AID (NON-NEED-BASED) *Total amount:* $2,381,208 (1% federal, 64% state, 12% institutional, 23% external sources). *Receiving aid:* Freshmen: 58% (1,253); Undergraduates: 45% (4,048). *Average Award:* Freshmen: $2520; Undergraduates: $3197. *Scholarships, grants, and awards by category: Academic Interests/Achievement:* 584 awards ($1,255,620 total): business, computer science, education, engineering/technologies, general academic interests/achievements, health fields, international studies. *Creative Arts/ Performance:* 80 awards ($68,598 total): art/fine arts, music. *Special Achievements/ Activities:* 51 awards ($55,775 total): community service, general special achievements/activities, leadership. *Special Characteristics:* 144 awards ($644,571 total): first-generation college students, general special characteristics, international students, members of minority groups, out-of-state students. *Tuition waivers:* Full or partial for employees or children of employees, senior citizens. *ROTC:* Naval cooperative.

LOANS *Student loans:* $18,199,901 (87% need-based, 13% non-need-based). 40% of past graduating class borrowed through all loan programs. *Average indebtedness per student:* $12,698. *Average need-based loan:* Freshmen: $2422; Undergraduates: $3768. *Parent loans:* $1,697,505 (50% need-based, 50% non-need-based). *Programs:* FFEL (Subsidized and Unsubsidized Stafford, PLUS), Perkins.

WORK-STUDY *Federal work-study:* Total amount: $377,286; 127 jobs averaging $3210.

ATHLETIC AWARDS *Total amount:* $745,340 (82% need-based, 18% non-need-based).

APPLYING FOR FINANCIAL AID *Required financial aid forms:* FAFSA, financial aid transcript (for transfers). *Financial aid deadline (priority):* 4/1. *Notification date:* Continuous. Students must reply within 2 weeks of notification.

CONTACT Mrs. Janice Nowak, Director of Financial Aid, University of North Florida, 4567 St. Johns Bluff Road, South, Jacksonville, FL 32224-2645, 904-620-2604. *E-mail:* jnowak@unf.edu.

UNIVERSITY OF NORTH TEXAS
Denton, TX

Tuition & fees (TX res): $5561	Average undergraduate aid package: $7269

ABOUT THE INSTITUTION State-supported, coed. Awards: bachelor's, master's, and doctoral degrees and post-bachelor's certificates. 103 undergraduate majors. Total enrollment: 31,155. Undergraduates: 24,274. Freshmen: 3,456. Federal methodology is used as a basis for awarding need-based institutional aid.

UNDERGRADUATE EXPENSES for 2004–05 *Application fee:* $40. *Tuition, state resident:* full-time $3690; part-time $123 per credit hour. *Tuition, nonresident:* full-time $11,430; part-time $381 per credit hour. *Required fees:* full-time $1871; $483 per term part-time. Full-time tuition and fees vary according to course load. Part-time tuition and fees vary according to course load. *College room and board:* $5124; *room only:* $2890. Room and board charges vary according to board plan. *Payment plan:* Installment.

FRESHMAN FINANCIAL AID (Fall 2004, est.) 2200 applied for aid; of those 66% were deemed to have need. 98% of freshmen with need received aid; of those 22% had need fully met. *Average percent of need met:* 67% (excluding resources awarded to replace EFC). *Average financial aid package:* $6782 (excluding resources awarded to replace EFC). 9% of all full-time freshmen had no need and received non-need-based gift aid.

UNDERGRADUATE FINANCIAL AID (Fall 2004, est.) 11,735 applied for aid; of those 76% were deemed to have need. 97% of undergraduates with need received aid; of those 19% had need fully met. *Average percent of need met:* 65% (excluding resources awarded to replace EFC). *Average financial aid package:* $7269 (excluding resources awarded to replace EFC). 5% of all full-time undergraduates had no need and received non-need-based gift aid.

GIFT AID (NEED-BASED) *Total amount:* $37,305,363 (48% federal, 23% state, 24% institutional, 5% external sources). *Receiving aid:* Freshmen: 36% (1,168); All full-time undergraduates: 37% (7,061). *Average award:* Freshmen: $3646; Undergraduates: $3655. *Scholarships, grants, and awards:* Federal Pell, FSEOG, state, college/university gift aid from institutional funds.

GIFT AID (NON-NEED-BASED) *Total amount:* $1,719,734 (47% institutional, 53% external sources). *Receiving aid:* Freshmen: 14% (469); Undergraduates: 8% (1,615). *Average Award:* Freshmen: $1535; Undergraduates: $1482. *Scholarships, grants, and awards by category: Academic Interests/Achievement:* general academic interests/achievements. *Creative Arts/Performance:* dance, music, theater/drama. *Tuition waivers:* Full or partial for employees or children of employees, senior citizens. *ROTC:* Army cooperative, Naval.

LOANS *Student loans:* $73,836,321 (82% need-based, 18% non-need-based). 42% of past graduating class borrowed through all loan programs. *Average indebtedness per student:* $18,175. *Average need-based loan:* Freshmen: $2142; Undergraduates: $3728. *Parent loans:* $35,903,643 (53% need-based, 47% non-need-based). *Programs:* FFEL (Subsidized and Unsubsidized Stafford, PLUS), Perkins, state, college/university.

WORK-STUDY *Federal work-study:* Total amount: $2,825,012; jobs available. *State or other work-study/employment:* Total amount: $203,348 (100% need-based). Part-time jobs available.

ATHLETIC AWARDS *Total amount:* $2,507,913 (37% need-based, 63% non-need-based).

APPLYING FOR FINANCIAL AID *Required financial aid form:* FAFSA. *Financial aid deadline (priority):* 6/1. *Notification date:* Continuous.

CONTACT Mrs. Carolyn Cunningham, Director of Financial Aid, University of North Texas, PO Box 311370, Denton, TX 76203-1370, 940-565-2302 or toll-free 800-868-8211 (in-state). *Fax:* 940-565-2738.

UNIVERSITY OF NOTRE DAME
Notre Dame, IN

Tuition & fees: $29,512	Average undergraduate aid package: $25,061

ABOUT THE INSTITUTION Independent Roman Catholic, coed. Awards: bachelor's, master's, doctoral, and first professional degrees. 55 undergraduate majors. Total enrollment: 11,479. Undergraduates: 8,332. Freshmen: 1,985. Both federal and institutional methodology are used as a basis for awarding need-based institutional aid.

UNDERGRADUATE EXPENSES for 2004–05 *Application fee:* $50. *Comprehensive fee:* $36,930 includes full-time tuition ($29,070), mandatory fees ($442), and room and board ($7418). Room and board charges vary according to board plan and housing facility. *Part-time tuition:* $1211 per credit. *Payment plan:* Installment.

FRESHMAN FINANCIAL AID (Fall 2004, est.) 1381 applied for aid; of those 76% were deemed to have need. 100% of freshmen with need received aid; of those 84% had need fully met. *Average percent of need met:* 100% (excluding resources awarded to replace EFC). *Average financial aid package:* $24,700 (excluding resources awarded to replace EFC). 1% of all full-time freshmen had no need and received non-need-based gift aid.

UNDERGRADUATE FINANCIAL AID (Fall 2004, est.) 4,751 applied for aid; of those 84% were deemed to have need. 100% of undergraduates with need received aid; of those 100% had need fully met. *Average percent of need met:* 100% (excluding resources awarded to replace EFC). *Average financial aid package:* $25,061 (excluding resources awarded to replace EFC). 2% of all full-time undergraduates had no need and received non-need-based gift aid.

GIFT AID (NEED-BASED) *Total amount:* $67,230,624 (8% federal, 1% state, 86% institutional, 5% external sources). *Receiving aid:* Freshmen: 51% (1,017); All full-time undergraduates: 5% (383). *Average award:* Freshmen: $19,058; Undergraduates: $18,296. *Scholarships, grants, and awards:* Federal Pell, FSEOG, state, college/university gift aid from institutional funds.

GIFT AID (NON-NEED-BASED) *Total amount:* $11,991,490 (44% federal, 6% institutional, 50% external sources). *Receiving aid:* Freshmen: 23% (461); Undergraduates: 17% (1,404). *Average Award:* Freshmen: $5433; Undergraduates: $7630. *Scholarships, grants, and awards by category: Special Characteristics:* 266 awards ($6,930,704 total): children of faculty/staff. *Tuition waivers:* Full or partial for employees or children of employees. *ROTC:* Army, Naval, Air Force.

LOANS *Student loans:* $33,861,886 (52% need-based, 48% non-need-based). 56% of past graduating class borrowed through all loan programs. *Average indebtedness per student:* $25,986. *Average need-based loan:* Freshmen: $3603; Undergraduates: $5278. *Parent loans:* $7,352,469 (100% non-need-based). *Programs:* FFEL (Subsidized and Unsubsidized Stafford, PLUS), Perkins, private student loans.

WORK-STUDY *Federal work-study:* Total amount: $3,411,105; 1,752 jobs averaging $1947. *State or other work-study/employment:* Total amount: $7,651,390 (3% need-based, 97% non-need-based). 3,164 part-time jobs averaging $2418.

ATHLETIC AWARDS *Total amount:* $10,391,830 (18% need-based, 82% non-need-based).

APPLYING FOR FINANCIAL AID *Required financial aid forms:* FAFSA, CSS Financial Aid PROFILE, noncustodial (divorced/separated) parent's statement, business/farm supplement, income tax form(s), W-2 forms. *Financial aid deadline:* 2/15. *Notification date:* Continuous beginning 3/15. Students must reply by 5/1.

CONTACT Mr. Joseph A. Russo, Director of Financial Aid, University of Notre Dame, 115 Main Building, Notre Dame, IN 46556, 574-631-6436. *Fax:* 574-631-6899. *E-mail:* finaid.1@nd.edu.

UNIVERSITY OF OKLAHOMA
Norman, OK

Tuition & fees (OK res): $4140	Average undergraduate aid package: $8180

ABOUT THE INSTITUTION State-supported, coed. Awards: bachelor's, master's, doctoral, and first professional degrees and post-master's certificates. 103 undergraduate majors. Total enrollment: 24,551. Undergraduates: 20,297. Freshmen: 3,614. Federal methodology is used as a basis for awarding need-based institutional aid.

UNDERGRADUATE EXPENSES for 2004–05 *Application fee:* $40. *Tuition, state resident:* full-time $2778; part-time $92.60 per credit hour. *Tuition, nonresident:* full-time $10,296; part-time $343.20 per credit hour. *Required fees:* full-time $1362; $38.30 per credit hour or $106.50 per term part-time. Full-time tuition and fees vary according to course load, location, program, and reciprocity agreements. Part-time tuition and fees vary according to course load, location, program, and reciprocity agreements. *College room and board:* $5814; *room only:* $2924. Room and board charges vary according to board plan and housing facility. *Payment plan:* Installment.

FRESHMAN FINANCIAL AID (Fall 2003) 2126 applied for aid; of those 80% were deemed to have need. 100% of freshmen with need received aid; of those 47% had need fully met. *Average percent of need met:* 81% (excluding resources awarded to replace EFC). *Average financial aid package:* $7639 (excluding resources awarded to replace EFC). 13% of all full-time freshmen had no need and received non-need-based gift aid.

UNDERGRADUATE FINANCIAL AID (Fall 2003) 9,294 applied for aid; of those 90% were deemed to have need. 100% of undergraduates with need received aid; of those 47% had need fully met. *Average percent of need met:* 81% (excluding resources awarded to replace EFC). *Average financial aid package:* $8180 (excluding resources awarded to replace EFC). 11% of all full-time undergraduates had no need and received non-need-based gift aid.

GIFT AID (NEED-BASED) *Total amount:* $22,534,783 (61% federal, 21% state, 11% institutional, 7% external sources). *Receiving aid:* Freshmen: 9% (344); All full-time undergraduates: 15% (2,665). *Average award:* Freshmen: $3823; Undergraduates: $3662. *Scholarships, grants, and awards:* Federal Pell, FSEOG, state, private, college/university gift aid from institutional funds, United Negro College Fund.

GIFT AID (NON-NEED-BASED) *Total amount:* $9,308,567 (9% federal, 52% state, 24% institutional, 15% external sources). *Receiving aid:* Freshmen: 28% (1,060); Undergraduates: 22% (3,826). *Average Award:* Freshmen: $1080; *Undergraduates:* $1107. *Scholarships, grants, and awards by category: Academic Interests/Achievement:* 8,127 awards ($17,067,499 total): architecture, area/ethnic studies, biological sciences, business, communication, computer science, education, engineering/technologies, foreign languages, general academic interests/achievements, humanities, international studies, mathematics, physical sciences, social sciences. *Creative Arts/Performance:* 127 awards ($1,284,275 total): art/fine arts, dance, journalism/publications, music, performing arts, theater/drama. *Special Achievements/Activities:* 66 awards ($75,429 total): leadership. *Special Characteristics:* 918 awards ($2,070,792 total): children and siblings of alumni, members of minority groups, previous college experience. *Tuition waivers:* Full or partial for employees or children of employees, senior citizens. *ROTC:* Army, Naval, Air Force.

LOANS *Student loans:* $45,508,718 (99% need-based, 1% non-need-based). 51% of past graduating class borrowed through all loan programs. *Average indebtedness per student:* $17,723. *Average need-based loan:* Freshmen: $2979; Undergraduates: $4282. *Parent loans:* $9,776,080 (86% need-based, 14% non-need-based). *Programs:* FFEL (Subsidized and Unsubsidized Stafford, PLUS), Perkins, college/university, alternative loans.

WORK-STUDY *Federal work-study:* Total amount: $1,527,003; 657 jobs averaging $2324.

ATHLETIC AWARDS *Total amount:* $4,058,898 (37% need-based, 63% non-need-based).

APPLYING FOR FINANCIAL AID *Required financial aid form:* FAFSA. *Financial aid deadline:* Continuous. *Notification date:* Continuous beginning 3/15. Students must reply within 6 weeks of notification.

CONTACT Financial Aid Assistant, University of Oklahoma, 1000 Asp Avenue, Room 216, Norman, OK 73019-4078, 405-325-4521 or toll-free 800-234-6868. *Fax:* 405-325-0819. *E-mail:* financialaid@ou.edu.

UNIVERSITY OF OREGON
Eugene, OR

Tuition & fees (OR res): $5550	Average undergraduate aid package: $8016

ABOUT THE INSTITUTION State-supported, coed. Awards: bachelor's, master's, doctoral, and first professional degrees and post-bachelor's and post-master's certificates. 97 undergraduate majors. Total enrollment: 20,295. Undergraduates: 16,349. Freshmen: 3,183. Federal methodology is used as a basis for awarding need-based institutional aid.

UNDERGRADUATE EXPENSES for 2004–05 *Application fee:* $50. *Tuition, state resident:* full-time $4071; part-time $103 per credit hour. *Tuition, nonresident:* full-time $15,501; part-time $407 per credit hour. *Required fees:* full-time $1479; $346 per term part-time. Full-time tuition and fees vary according to class time, course load, degree level, program, and reciprocity agreements. Part-time tuition and fees vary according to class time, course load, degree level, and program. *College room and board:* $7331. Room and board charges vary according to board plan and housing facility. *Payment plan:* Installment.

GIFT AID (NEED-BASED) *Total amount:* $14,995,212 (83% federal, 16% state, 1% institutional). *Receiving aid:* Freshmen: 19% (583); All full-time undergraduates: 25% (3,650). *Average award:* Freshmen: $3937; Undergraduates: $3841. *Scholarships, grants, and awards:* Federal Pell, FSEOG, state, private, college/university gift aid from institutional funds.

GIFT AID (NON-NEED-BASED) *Total amount:* $9,107,970 (88% institutional, 12% external sources). *Receiving aid:* Freshmen: 18% (553); Undergraduates: 12% (1,764). *Average Award:* Freshmen: $1745; *Undergraduates:* $1875. *Scholarships, grants, and awards by category: Academic Interests/Achievement:* architecture, biological sciences, business, education, foreign languages, general academic interests/achievements, physical sciences, social sciences. *Creative Arts/Performance:* art/fine arts, dance, journalism/publications, music, performing arts, theater/drama. *Special Achievements/Activities:* general special achievements/activities. *Special Characteristics:* general special characteristics, international students, local/state students. *Tuition waivers:* Full or partial for employees or children of employees. *ROTC:* Army, Air Force cooperative.

LOANS *Student loans:* $42,743,847 (61% need-based, 39% non-need-based). 57% of past graduating class borrowed through all loan programs. *Average indebtedness per student:* $17,802. *Average need-based loan:* Freshmen: $3566; Undergraduates: $4490. *Parent loans:* $25,300,453 (23% need-based, 77% non-need-based). *Programs:* Federal Direct (Subsidized and Unsubsidized Stafford, PLUS), Perkins, college/university.

ATHLETIC AWARDS *Total amount:* $5,184,496 (100% non-need-based).

APPLYING FOR FINANCIAL AID *Required financial aid form:* FAFSA. *Financial aid deadline (priority):* 3/1. *Notification date:* Continuous beginning 4/1.

CONTACT Elizabeth Bickford, Director of Student Financial Aid, University of Oregon, 260 Oregon Hall, Eugene, OR 97403, 541-346-3221 or toll-free 800-232-3825 (in-state). *Fax:* 541-346-1175. *E-mail:* ebick@uoregon.edu.

UNIVERSITY OF PENNSYLVANIA
Philadelphia, PA

Tuition & fees: $30,716	Average undergraduate aid package: $26,052

ABOUT THE INSTITUTION Independent, coed. Awards: associate, bachelor's, master's, doctoral, and first professional degrees and post-bachelor's, post-master's, and first professional certificates (also offers evening program with significant enrollment not reflected in profile). 92 undergraduate majors. Total enrollment: 18,642. Undergraduates: 9,719. Freshmen: 2,419. Institutional methodology is used as a basis for awarding need-based institutional aid.

UNDERGRADUATE EXPENSES for 2004–05 *Application fee:* $70. *Comprehensive fee:* $39,634 includes full-time tuition ($27,544), mandatory fees ($3172), and room and board ($8918). *College room only:* $5336. Room and board charges vary according to board plan and housing facility. *Part-time tuition:* $3518 per term. *Part-time fees:* $370 per course. Part-time tuition and fees vary according to course load. *Payment plan:* Installment.

FRESHMAN FINANCIAL AID (Fall 2003) 1377 applied for aid; of those 80% were deemed to have need. 100% of freshmen with need received aid; of those 100% had need fully met. *Average percent of need met:* 100% (excluding resources awarded to replace EFC). *Average financial aid package:* $26,256 (excluding resources awarded to replace EFC).

UNDERGRADUATE FINANCIAL AID (Fall 2003) 4,872 applied for aid; of those 89% were deemed to have need. 100% of undergraduates with need received aid; of those 100% had need fully met. *Average percent of need met:* 100% (excluding resources awarded to replace EFC). *Average financial aid package:* $26,052 (excluding resources awarded to replace EFC).

GIFT AID (NEED-BASED) *Total amount:* $82,681,000 (7% federal, 2% state, 86% institutional, 5% external sources). *Receiving aid:* Freshmen: 42% (1,020); All full-time undergraduates: 39% (3,954). *Average award:* Freshmen: $21,970; Undergraduates: $20,697. *Scholarships, grants, and awards:* Federal Pell, FSEOG, state, private, college/university gift aid from institutional funds.

GIFT AID (NON-NEED-BASED) *Total amount:* $5,119,000 (1% federal, 99% external sources). *Tuition waivers:* Full or partial for employees or children of employees. *ROTC:* Army cooperative, Naval, Air Force cooperative.

LOANS *Student loans:* $31,996,000 (82% need-based, 18% non-need-based). 43% of past graduating class borrowed through all loan programs. *Average indebtedness per student:* $19,579. *Average need-based loan:* Freshmen: $3001; Undergraduates: $4212. *Parent loans:* $12,725,000 (61% need-based, 39% non-need-based). *Programs:* FFEL (Subsidized and Unsubsidized Stafford, PLUS), Perkins, Federal Nursing, college/university, supplemental third-party loans (guaranteed by institution).

WORK-STUDY *Federal work-study:* Total amount: $14,089,000; 3,954 jobs averaging $3563.

APPLYING FOR FINANCIAL AID *Required financial aid forms:* FAFSA, institution's own form, CSS Financial Aid PROFILE, state aid form, noncustodial (divorced/separated) parent's statement, business/farm supplement, federal income tax form(s). *Financial aid deadline (priority):* 2/15. *Notification date:* 4/1. Students must reply by 5/1.

CONTACT Mr. William Schilling, Director of Financial Aid, University of Pennsylvania, 212 Franklin Building, 3451 Walnut Street, Philadelphia, PA 19104-6270, 215-898-6784. *Fax:* 215-573-2208. *E-mail:* schilling@sfs.upenn.edu.

UNIVERSITY OF PHOENIX–ATLANTA CAMPUS
Atlanta, GA

Tuition & fees: $10,830	Average undergraduate aid package: $4298

ABOUT THE INSTITUTION Proprietary, coed. Awards: bachelor's degrees (courses conducted at 121 campuses and learning centers in 25 states). 12 undergraduate majors. Total enrollment: 2,031. Undergraduates: 1,293. Freshmen: 94. Both federal and institutional methodology are used as a basis for awarding need-based institutional aid.

UNDERGRADUATE EXPENSES for 2004–05 *Application fee:* $110. *Tuition:* full-time $10,830; part-time $361 per credit. *Payment plan:* Deferred payment.

FRESHMAN FINANCIAL AID (Fall 2003) *Average financial aid package:* $2834 (excluding resources awarded to replace EFC).

UNDERGRADUATE FINANCIAL AID (Fall 2003) *Average financial aid package:* $4298 (excluding resources awarded to replace EFC).

GIFT AID (NEED-BASED) *Total amount:* $7,064,158 (100% federal). *Receiving aid:* Freshmen: 3; All full-time undergraduates: 1,483. *Scholarships, grants, and awards:* Federal Pell, FSEOG, state.

GIFT AID (NON-NEED-BASED) *Total amount:* $8,464,984 (100% federal). *Receiving aid:* Freshmen: 3; Undergraduates: 1,521. *Scholarships, grants, and awards by category:* Academic Interests/Achievement: business, computer science, health fields. *Tuition waivers:* Full or partial for employees or children of employees.

LOANS *Programs:* Federal Direct (Unsubsidized Stafford, PLUS), Perkins.

APPLYING FOR FINANCIAL AID *Required financial aid form:* FAFSA. *Financial aid deadline:* Continuous. *Notification date:* Continuous.

CONTACT ACS/AFS, University of Phoenix–Atlanta Campus, 875 West Elliot Road, Suite 116, Tempe, AZ 85284, 480-735-3000 or toll-free 800-776-4867 (in-state), 800-228-7240 (out-of-state). *Fax:* 480-940-2060.

UNIVERSITY OF PHOENIX–BOSTON CAMPUS
Braintree, MA

ABOUT THE INSTITUTION Proprietary, coed. Awards: bachelor's and master's degrees (courses conducted at 121 campuses and learning centers in 25 states). 3 undergraduate majors. Total enrollment: 568. Undergraduates: 348. Freshmen: 22.

GIFT AID (NEED-BASED) *Scholarships, grants, and awards:* Federal Pell, FSEOG, state.

GIFT AID (NON-NEED-BASED) *Scholarships, grants, and awards by category:* Academic Interests/Achievement: business, computer science, health fields.

LOANS *Programs:* Federal Direct (Unsubsidized Stafford, PLUS), Perkins.

APPLYING FOR FINANCIAL AID *Required financial aid form:* FAFSA.

CONTACT ACS/AFS, University of Phoenix–Boston Campus, 875 West Elliot Road, Suite 116, Tempe, AZ 85284, 480-735-3000 or toll-free 800-228-7240. *Fax:* 480-940-2060.

UNIVERSITY OF PHOENIX–CENTRAL MASSACHUSETTS CAMPUS
Westborough, MA

CONTACT Financial Aid Office, University of Phoenix–Central Massachusetts Campus, One Research Drive, Westborough, MA 01581, 508-614-4100 or toll-free 800-776-4867 (in-state), 800-228-7240 (out-of-state).

UNIVERSITY OF PHOENIX–CENTRAL VALLEY CAMPUS
Fresno, CA

CONTACT Financial Aid Office, University of Phoenix–Central Valley Campus, 8355 N. Fresno Street, Suite 200, Fresno, CA 93720, toll-free 888-776-4867 (in-state), 888-228-7240 (out-of-state).

UNIVERSITY OF PHOENIX–CHARLOTTE CAMPUS
Charlotte, NC

CONTACT Financial Aid Office, University of Phoenix–Charlotte Campus, 3800 Arco Corporate Drive, Suite 100, Charlotte, NC 28273, 704-504-5409 or toll-free 800-776-4867 (in-state), 800-228-7240 (out-of-state).

UNIVERSITY OF PHOENIX–CHICAGO CAMPUS
Schaumburg, IL

Tuition & fees: $10,350	Average undergraduate aid package: $3242

ABOUT THE INSTITUTION Proprietary, coed. Awards: bachelor's and master's degrees (courses conducted at 121 campuses and learning centers in 25 states). 5 undergraduate majors. Total enrollment: 1,399. Undergraduates: 1,046. Freshmen: 81. Both federal and institutional methodology are used as a basis for awarding need-based institutional aid.

UNDERGRADUATE EXPENSES for 2004–05 *Application fee:* $110. *Tuition:* full-time $10,350; part-time $345 per credit. *Payment plan:* Deferred payment.

FRESHMAN FINANCIAL AID (Fall 2003) *Average financial aid package:* $2113 (excluding resources awarded to replace EFC).

UNDERGRADUATE FINANCIAL AID (Fall 2003) *Average financial aid package:* $3242 (excluding resources awarded to replace EFC).

GIFT AID (NEED-BASED) *Total amount:* $3,018,343 (100% federal). *Receiving aid:* Freshmen: 2; All full-time undergraduates: 792. *Scholarships, grants, and awards:* Federal Pell, FSEOG, state.

GIFT AID (NON-NEED-BASED) *Total amount:* $4,023,905 (100% federal). *Receiving aid:* Undergraduates: 837. *Scholarships, grants, and awards by category:* Academic Interests/Achievement: business, computer science. *Tuition waivers:* Full or partial for employees or children of employees.

LOANS *Programs:* Federal Direct (Unsubsidized Stafford, PLUS), Perkins.

APPLYING FOR FINANCIAL AID *Required financial aid form:* FAFSA. *Financial aid deadline:* Continuous. *Notification date:* Continuous.

CONTACT ACS/AFS, University of Phoenix–Chicago Campus, 875 West Elliot Road, Suite 116, Tempe, AZ 85284, 480-735-3000 or toll-free 800-776-4867 (in-state), 800-228-7240 (out-of-state). *Fax:* 480-940-2060.

UNIVERSITY OF PHOENIX–CINCINNATI CAMPUS
West Chester, OH

CONTACT Financial Aid Office, University of Phoenix–Cincinnati Campus, 9050 Centre Pointe Drive, West Chester, OH 45069, 513-772-9600 or toll-free 800-776-4867 (in-state), 800-228-7240 (out-of-state).

UNIVERSITY OF PHOENIX–CLEVELAND CAMPUS
Independence, OH

Tuition & fees: $10,740	Average undergraduate aid package: $3974

ABOUT THE INSTITUTION Proprietary, coed. Awards: bachelor's and master's degrees (courses conducted at 121 campuses and learning centers in 25 states). 5 undergraduate majors. Total enrollment: 824. Undergraduates: 614. Freshmen: 59. Both federal and institutional methodology are used as a basis for awarding need-based institutional aid.

UNDERGRADUATE EXPENSES for 2004–05 *Application fee:* $110. *Tuition:* full-time $10,740; part-time $358 per credit. *Payment plan:* Deferred payment.

FRESHMAN FINANCIAL AID (Fall 2003) *Average financial aid package:* $1406 (excluding resources awarded to replace EFC).

UNDERGRADUATE FINANCIAL AID (Fall 2003) *Average financial aid package:* $3974 (excluding resources awarded to replace EFC).

GIFT AID (NEED-BASED) *Total amount:* $2,696,234 (100% federal). *Receiving aid:* Freshmen: 3; All full-time undergraduates: 623. *Scholarships, grants, and awards:* Federal Pell, FSEOG, state.

GIFT AID (NON-NEED-BASED) *Total amount:* $2,895,001 (100% federal). *Receiving aid:* Freshmen: 1; Undergraduates: 603. *Scholarships, grants, and awards by category: Academic Interests/Achievement:* business, computer science, health fields, social sciences. *Tuition waivers:* Full or partial for employees or children of employees.

LOANS *Programs:* Federal Direct (Unsubsidized Stafford, PLUS), Perkins.

APPLYING FOR FINANCIAL AID *Required financial aid form:* FAFSA. *Financial aid deadline:* Continuous. *Notification date:* Continuous.

CONTACT ACS/AFS, University of Phoenix–Cleveland Campus, 875 West Elliot Road, Suite 116, Tempe, AZ 85284, 480-735-3000 or toll-free 800-776-4867 (in-state), 800-228-7240 (out-of-state). *Fax:* 480-940-2060.

UNIVERSITY OF PHOENIX–DENVER CAMPUS
Lone Tree, CO

Tuition & fees: $9000	Average undergraduate aid package: $4097

ABOUT THE INSTITUTION Proprietary, coed. Awards: bachelor's and master's degrees and post-master's certificates (courses conducted at 121 campuses and learning centers in 25 states). 8 undergraduate majors. Total enrollment: 3,364. Undergraduates: 1,896. Freshmen: 62. Both federal and institutional methodology are used as a basis for awarding need-based institutional aid.

UNDERGRADUATE EXPENSES for 2004–05 *Application fee:* $110. *Tuition:* full-time $9000; part-time $300 per credit. *Payment plan:* Deferred payment.

FRESHMAN FINANCIAL AID (Fall 2003) *Average financial aid package:* $7815 (excluding resources awarded to replace EFC).

UNDERGRADUATE FINANCIAL AID (Fall 2003) *Average financial aid package:* $4097 (excluding resources awarded to replace EFC).

GIFT AID (NEED-BASED) *Receiving aid:* Freshmen: 3; All full-time undergraduates: 2,477. *Scholarships, grants, and awards:* Federal Pell, FSEOG, state.

GIFT AID (NON-NEED-BASED) *Receiving aid:* Freshmen: 3; Undergraduates: 2,691. *Tuition waivers:* Full or partial for employees or children of employees.

LOANS *Programs:* Federal Direct (Unsubsidized Stafford, PLUS), Perkins.

APPLYING FOR FINANCIAL AID *Required financial aid form:* FAFSA. *Financial aid deadline:* Continuous. *Notification date:* Continuous.

CONTACT ACS/AFS, University of Phoenix–Denver Campus, 875 West Elliot Road, Suite 116, Tempe, AZ 85284, 480-735-3000 or toll-free 800-776-4867 (in-state), 800-228-7240 (out-of-state). *Fax:* 480-940-2060.

UNIVERSITY OF PHOENIX–COLUMBUS GEORGIA CAMPUS
Columbus, GA

CONTACT Financial Aid Office, University of Phoenix–Columbus Georgia Campus, 4747 Hamilton Road, Suite E, Columbus, GA 31904, 706-320-1262 or toll-free 800-776-4867 (in-state), 800-228-7240 (out-of-state).

UNIVERSITY OF PHOENIX–COLUMBUS OHIO CAMPUS
Columbus, OH

CONTACT Financial Aid Office, University of Phoenix–Columbus Ohio Campus, 8425 Pulsar Place, Columbus, OH 43240, 614-433-0095 or toll-free 800-776-4867 (in-state), 800-228-7240 (out-of-state).

UNIVERSITY OF PHOENIX–DALLAS CAMPUS
Dallas, TX

Tuition & fees: $11,010	Average undergraduate aid package: $3841

ABOUT THE INSTITUTION Proprietary, coed. Awards: bachelor's, master's, and doctoral degrees (courses conducted at 121 campuses and learning centers in 25 states). 5 undergraduate majors. Total enrollment: 2,546. Undergraduates: 1,987. Freshmen: 84. Both federal and institutional methodology are used as a basis for awarding need-based institutional aid.

UNDERGRADUATE EXPENSES for 2004–05 *Application fee:* $110. *Tuition:* full-time $11,010; part-time $367 per credit. *Payment plan:* Deferred payment.

FRESHMAN FINANCIAL AID (Fall 2003) *Average financial aid package:* $1273 (excluding resources awarded to replace EFC).

UNDERGRADUATE FINANCIAL AID (Fall 2003) *Average financial aid package:* $3841 (excluding resources awarded to replace EFC).

GIFT AID (NEED-BASED) *Receiving aid:* Freshmen: 1; All full-time undergraduates: 1,983. *Scholarships, grants, and awards:* Federal Pell, FSEOG, state.

GIFT AID (NON-NEED-BASED) *Receiving aid:* Freshmen: 1; Undergraduates: 2,058. *Scholarships, grants, and awards by category: Academic Interests/Achievement:* business, computer science, health fields, social sciences. *Tuition waivers:* Full or partial for employees or children of employees.

LOANS *Programs:* Federal Direct (Unsubsidized Stafford, PLUS), Perkins.

APPLYING FOR FINANCIAL AID *Required financial aid form:* FAFSA. *Financial aid deadline:* Continuous. *Notification date:* Continuous.

CONTACT ACS/AFS, University of Phoenix–Dallas Campus, 875 West Elliot Road, Suite 116, Tempe, AZ 85284, 480-735-3000 or toll-free 800-776-4867 (in-state), 800-228-7240 (out-of-state). *Fax:* 480-940-2060.

UNIVERSITY OF PHOENIX–FORT LAUDERDALE CAMPUS
Fort Lauderdale, FL

Tuition & fees: $10,170	Average undergraduate aid package: $4417

ABOUT THE INSTITUTION Proprietary, coed. Awards: bachelor's and master's degrees (courses conducted at 121 campuses and learning centers in 25 states). 8 undergraduate majors. Total enrollment: 2,586. Undergraduates: 1,891. Freshmen: 115. Both federal and institutional methodology are used as a basis for awarding need-based institutional aid.

UNDERGRADUATE EXPENSES for 2004–05 *Application fee:* $110. *Tuition:* full-time $10,170; part-time $339 per credit. *Payment plan:* Deferred payment.

FRESHMAN FINANCIAL AID (Fall 2003) *Average financial aid package:* $3351 (excluding resources awarded to replace EFC).

UNDERGRADUATE FINANCIAL AID (Fall 2003) *Average financial aid package:* $4417 (excluding resources awarded to replace EFC).
GIFT AID (NEED-BASED) *Receiving aid:* Freshmen: 4; All full-time undergraduates: 1,887. *Scholarships, grants, and awards:* Federal Pell, FSEOG, state.
GIFT AID (NON-NEED-BASED) *Receiving aid:* Freshmen: 5; Undergraduates: 1,904. *Scholarships, grants, and awards by category: Academic Interests/ Achievement:* business, computer science, health fields, social sciences. *Tuition waivers:* Full or partial for employees or children of employees.
LOANS *Programs:* Federal Direct (Unsubsidized Stafford, PLUS), Perkins.
APPLYING FOR FINANCIAL AID *Required financial aid form:* FAFSA. *Financial aid deadline:* Continuous. *Notification date:* Continuous.
CONTACT ACS/AFS, University of Phoenix–Fort Lauderdale Campus, 875 West Elliot Road, Suite 116, Tempe, AZ 85284, 480-735-3000 or toll-free 800-228-7240. *Fax:* 480-940-2060.

UNIVERSITY OF PHOENIX–HAWAII CAMPUS
Honolulu, HI

Tuition & fees: $10,650	Average undergraduate aid package: $4482

ABOUT THE INSTITUTION Proprietary, coed. Awards: bachelor's and master's degrees (courses conducted at 121 campuses and learning centers in 25 states). 12 undergraduate majors. Total enrollment: 1,480. Undergraduates: 965. Freshmen: 37. Both federal and institutional methodology are used as a basis for awarding need-based institutional aid.
UNDERGRADUATE EXPENSES for 2004–05 *Application fee:* $110. *Tuition:* full-time $10,650; part-time $355 per credit. *Payment plan:* Deferred payment.
FRESHMAN FINANCIAL AID (Fall 2003) *Average financial aid package:* $6297 (excluding resources awarded to replace EFC).
UNDERGRADUATE FINANCIAL AID (Fall 2003) *Average financial aid package:* $4482 (excluding resources awarded to replace EFC).
GIFT AID (NEED-BASED) *Receiving aid:* Freshmen: 4; All full-time undergraduates: 1,342. *Scholarships, grants, and awards:* Federal Pell, FSEOG, state.
GIFT AID (NON-NEED-BASED) *Receiving aid:* Freshmen: 4; Undergraduates: 1,319. *Tuition waivers:* Full or partial for employees or children of employees.
LOANS *Programs:* Federal Direct (Unsubsidized Stafford, PLUS), Perkins.
APPLYING FOR FINANCIAL AID *Required financial aid form:* FAFSA. *Financial aid deadline:* Continuous. *Notification date:* Continuous.
CONTACT ACS/AFS, University of Phoenix–Hawaii Campus, 875 West Elliot Road, Suite 116, Tempe, AZ 85284, 480-735-3000 or toll-free 800-776-4867 (in-state), 800-228-7240 (out-of-state). *Fax:* 480-940-2060.

UNIVERSITY OF PHOENIX–HOUSTON CAMPUS
Houston, TX

Tuition & fees: $11,010	Average undergraduate aid package: $4241

ABOUT THE INSTITUTION Proprietary, coed. Awards: bachelor's and master's degrees (courses conducted at 121 campuses and learning centers in 25 states). 6 undergraduate majors. Total enrollment: 4,297. Undergraduates: 3,416. Freshmen: 228. Both federal and institutional methodology are used as a basis for awarding need-based institutional aid.
UNDERGRADUATE EXPENSES for 2004–05 *Application fee:* $110. *Tuition:* full-time $11,010; part-time $367 per credit. *Payment plan:* Deferred payment.
FRESHMAN FINANCIAL AID (Fall 2003) *Average financial aid package:* $5516 (excluding resources awarded to replace EFC).
UNDERGRADUATE FINANCIAL AID (Fall 2003) *Average financial aid package:* $4241 (excluding resources awarded to replace EFC).
GIFT AID (NEED-BASED) *Receiving aid:* Freshmen: 7; All full-time undergraduates: 2,838. *Scholarships, grants, and awards:* Federal Pell, FSEOG, state.
GIFT AID (NON-NEED-BASED) *Receiving aid:* Freshmen: 6; Undergraduates: 2,938. *Scholarships, grants, and awards by category: Academic Interests/ Achievement:* business, computer science, health fields, social sciences. *Tuition waivers:* Full or partial for employees or children of employees.
LOANS *Programs:* Federal Direct (Unsubsidized Stafford, PLUS), Perkins.
APPLYING FOR FINANCIAL AID *Required financial aid form:* FAFSA. *Financial aid deadline:* Continuous. *Notification date:* Continuous.

CONTACT ACS/AFS, University of Phoenix–Houston Campus, 875 West Elliot Road, Suite 116, Tempe, AZ 85284, 480-735-3000 or toll-free 800-776-4867 (in-state), 800-228-7240 (out-of-state). *Fax:* 480-940-2060.

UNIVERSITY OF PHOENIX–IDAHO CAMPUS
Meridian, ID

Tuition & fees: $9450	Average undergraduate aid package: $3982

ABOUT THE INSTITUTION Proprietary, coed. Awards: bachelor's and master's degrees (courses conducted at 121 campuses and learning centers in 25 states). 6 undergraduate majors. Total enrollment: 713. Undergraduates: 600. Freshmen: 26. Both federal and institutional methodology are used as a basis for awarding need-based institutional aid.
UNDERGRADUATE EXPENSES for 2004–05 *Application fee:* $110. *Tuition:* full-time $9450; part-time $315 per credit. *Payment plan:* Deferred payment.
UNDERGRADUATE FINANCIAL AID (Fall 2003) *Average financial aid package:* $3982 (excluding resources awarded to replace EFC).
GIFT AID (NEED-BASED) *Receiving aid:* All full-time undergraduates: 532. *Scholarships, grants, and awards:* Federal Pell, FSEOG, state.
GIFT AID (NON-NEED-BASED) *Receiving aid:* Undergraduates: 498. *Scholarships, grants, and awards by category: Academic Interests/Achievement:* business, computer science. *Tuition waivers:* Full or partial for employees or children of employees.
LOANS *Programs:* Federal Direct (Unsubsidized Stafford, PLUS), Perkins.
APPLYING FOR FINANCIAL AID *Required financial aid form:* FAFSA. *Financial aid deadline:* Continuous. *Notification date:* Continuous.
CONTACT ACS/AFS, University of Phoenix–Idaho Campus, 875 West Elliot Road, Suite 116, Tempe, AZ 85284, 480-735-3000 or toll-free 800-776-4867 (in-state), 800-228-7240 (out-of-state). *Fax:* 480-940-2060.

UNIVERSITY OF PHOENIX–INDIANAPOLIS CAMPUS
Indianapolis, IN

CONTACT Financial Aid Office, University of Phoenix–Indianapolis Campus, 7999 Knue Road Drive, Suite 150, Indianapolis, IN 46250, 317-585-8610 or toll-free 800-776-4867 (in-state), 800-228-7240 (out-of-state).

UNIVERSITY OF PHOENIX–JACKSONVILLE CAMPUS
Jacksonville, FL

Tuition & fees: $10,170	Average undergraduate aid package: $4267

ABOUT THE INSTITUTION Proprietary, coed. Awards: bachelor's and master's degrees (courses conducted at 121 campuses and learning centers in 25 states). 10 undergraduate majors. Total enrollment: 2,122. Undergraduates: 1,605. Freshmen: 49. Both federal and institutional methodology are used as a basis for awarding need-based institutional aid.
UNDERGRADUATE EXPENSES for 2004–05 *Application fee:* $110. *Tuition:* full-time $10,170; part-time $339 per credit. *Payment plan:* Deferred payment.
FRESHMAN FINANCIAL AID (Fall 2003) *Average financial aid package:* $5123 (excluding resources awarded to replace EFC).
UNDERGRADUATE FINANCIAL AID (Fall 2003) *Average financial aid package:* $4267 (excluding resources awarded to replace EFC).
GIFT AID (NEED-BASED) *Receiving aid:* Freshmen: 6; All full-time undergraduates: 1,621. *Scholarships, grants, and awards:* Federal Pell, FSEOG, state.
GIFT AID (NON-NEED-BASED) *Receiving aid:* Freshmen: 6; Undergraduates: 1,623. *Scholarships, grants, and awards by category: Academic Interests/ Achievement:* business, computer science, health fields, social sciences. *Tuition waivers:* Full or partial for employees or children of employees.
LOANS *Programs:* Federal Direct (Unsubsidized Stafford, PLUS), Perkins.
APPLYING FOR FINANCIAL AID *Required financial aid form:* FAFSA. *Financial aid deadline:* Continuous. *Notification date:* Continuous.
CONTACT ACS/AFS, University of Phoenix–Jacksonville Campus, 875 West Elliot Road, Suite 116, Tempe, AZ 85284, 480-735-3000 or toll-free 800-776-4867 (in-state), 800-894-1758 (out-of-state). *Fax:* 480-940-2060.

UNIVERSITY OF PHOENIX–KANSAS CITY CAMPUS
Kansas City, MO

Tuition & fees: $10,350 **Average undergraduate aid package: $3971**

ABOUT THE INSTITUTION Proprietary, coed. Awards: bachelor's and master's degrees (courses conducted at 121 campuses and learning centers in 25 states). 8 undergraduate majors. Total enrollment: 1,016. Undergraduates: 742. Freshmen: 45. Both federal and institutional methodology are used as a basis for awarding need-based institutional aid.

UNDERGRADUATE EXPENSES for 2004–05 *Application fee:* $110. *Tuition:* full-time $10,350; part-time $345 per credit. *Payment plan:* Deferred payment.

UNDERGRADUATE FINANCIAL AID (Fall 2003) *Average financial aid package:* $3971 (excluding resources awarded to replace EFC).

GIFT AID (NEED-BASED) *Receiving aid:* All full-time undergraduates: 682. *Scholarships, grants, and awards:* Federal Pell, FSEOG, state.

GIFT AID (NON-NEED-BASED) *Receiving aid:* Undergraduates: 662. *Scholarships, grants, and awards by category: Academic Interests/Achievement:* business, computer science. *Tuition waivers:* Full or partial for employees or children of employees.

LOANS *Programs:* Federal Direct (Unsubsidized Stafford, PLUS), Perkins.

APPLYING FOR FINANCIAL AID *Required financial aid form:* FAFSA. *Financial aid deadline:* Continuous. *Notification date:* Continuous.

CONTACT ACS/AFS, University of Phoenix–Kansas City Campus, 875 West Elliot Road, Suite 116, Tempe, AZ 85284, 480-735-3000 or toll-free 800-776-4867 (in-state), 800-228-7240 (out-of-state). *Fax:* 480-940-2060.

UNIVERSITY OF PHOENIX–LITTLE ROCK CAMPUS
Little Rock, AR

CONTACT Financial Aid Office, University of Phoenix–Little Rock Campus, 10800 Financial Center Parkway, Little Rock, AR 72211, 501-225-9337 or toll-free 800-776-4867 (in-state), 800-228-7240 (out-of-state).

UNIVERSITY OF PHOENIX–LOUISIANA CAMPUS
Metairie, LA

Tuition & fees: $9330 **Average undergraduate aid package: $5095**

ABOUT THE INSTITUTION Proprietary, coed. Awards: bachelor's and master's degrees (courses conducted at 121 campuses and learning centers in 25 states). 7 undergraduate majors. Total enrollment: 2,585. Undergraduates: 1,904. Freshmen: 68. Both federal and institutional methodology are used as a basis for awarding need-based institutional aid.

UNDERGRADUATE EXPENSES for 2004–05 *Application fee:* $110. *Tuition:* full-time $9330; part-time $311 per credit. *Payment plan:* Deferred payment.

FRESHMAN FINANCIAL AID (Fall 2003) *Average financial aid package:* $6279 (excluding resources awarded to replace EFC).

UNDERGRADUATE FINANCIAL AID (Fall 2003) *Average financial aid package:* $5095 (excluding resources awarded to replace EFC).

GIFT AID (NEED-BASED) *Receiving aid:* Freshmen: 5; All full-time undergraduates: 2,220. *Scholarships, grants, and awards:* Federal Pell, FSEOG, state.

GIFT AID (NON-NEED-BASED) *Receiving aid:* Freshmen: 5; Undergraduates: 2,183. *Scholarships, grants, and awards by category: Academic Interests/Achievement:* business, computer science, health fields, social sciences. *Tuition waivers:* Full or partial for employees or children of employees.

LOANS *Programs:* Federal Direct (Unsubsidized Stafford, PLUS), Perkins.

APPLYING FOR FINANCIAL AID *Required financial aid form:* FAFSA. *Financial aid deadline:* Continuous. *Notification date:* Continuous.

CONTACT ACS/AFS, University of Phoenix–Louisiana Campus, 875 West Elliot Road, Suite 116, Tempe, AZ 85284, 480-735-3000 or toll-free 800-776-4867 (in-state), 800-228-7240 (out-of-state). *Fax:* 480-940-2060.

UNIVERSITY OF PHOENIX–MARYLAND CAMPUS
Columbia, MD

Tuition & fees: $10,800 **Average undergraduate aid package: $3933**

ABOUT THE INSTITUTION Proprietary, coed. Awards: bachelor's and master's degrees (courses conducted at 121 campuses and learning centers in 25 states). 5 undergraduate majors. Total enrollment: 2,132. Undergraduates: 1,516. Freshmen: 142. Both federal and institutional methodology are used as a basis for awarding need-based institutional aid.

UNDERGRADUATE EXPENSES for 2004–05 *Application fee:* $110. *Tuition:* full-time $10,800; part-time $360 per credit. *Payment plan:* Deferred payment.

FRESHMAN FINANCIAL AID (Fall 2003) *Average financial aid package:* $1674 (excluding resources awarded to replace EFC).

UNDERGRADUATE FINANCIAL AID (Fall 2003) *Average financial aid package:* $3933 (excluding resources awarded to replace EFC).

GIFT AID (NEED-BASED) *Receiving aid:* Freshmen: 5; All full-time undergraduates: 1,273. *Scholarships, grants, and awards:* Federal Pell, FSEOG, state.

GIFT AID (NON-NEED-BASED) *Receiving aid:* Freshmen: 5; Undergraduates: 1,266. *Scholarships, grants, and awards by category: Academic Interests/Achievement:* business, computer science. *Tuition waivers:* Full or partial for employees or children of employees.

LOANS *Programs:* Federal Direct (Unsubsidized Stafford, PLUS), Perkins.

APPLYING FOR FINANCIAL AID *Required financial aid form:* FAFSA. *Financial aid deadline:* Continuous. *Notification date:* Continuous.

CONTACT ACS/AFS, University of Phoenix–Maryland Campus, 875 West Elliot Road, Suite 116, Tempe, AZ 85284, 480-735-3000 or toll-free 800-776-4867 (in-state), 800-228-7240 (out-of-state). *Fax:* 480-940-2060.

UNIVERSITY OF PHOENIX–METRO DETROIT CAMPUS
Troy, MI

Tuition & fees: $11,790 **Average undergraduate aid package: $4178**

ABOUT THE INSTITUTION Proprietary, coed. Awards: bachelor's and master's degrees (courses conducted at 121 campuses and learning centers in 25 states). 8 undergraduate majors. Total enrollment: 3,948. Undergraduates: 2,919. Freshmen: 211. Both federal and institutional methodology are used as a basis for awarding need-based institutional aid.

UNDERGRADUATE EXPENSES for 2004–05 *Application fee:* $110. *Tuition:* full-time $11,790; part-time $393 per credit. *Payment plan:* Deferred payment.

FRESHMAN FINANCIAL AID (Fall 2003) *Average financial aid package:* $3538 (excluding resources awarded to replace EFC).

UNDERGRADUATE FINANCIAL AID (Fall 2003) *Average financial aid package:* $4178 (excluding resources awarded to replace EFC).

GIFT AID (NEED-BASED) *Receiving aid:* Freshmen: 22; All full-time undergraduates: 3,106. *Scholarships, grants, and awards:* Federal Pell, FSEOG, state.

GIFT AID (NON-NEED-BASED) *Receiving aid:* Freshmen: 19; Undergraduates: 3,109. *Scholarships, grants, and awards by category: Academic Interests/Achievement:* business, computer science, health fields, social sciences. *Tuition waivers:* Full or partial for employees or children of employees.

LOANS *Programs:* Federal Direct (Unsubsidized Stafford, PLUS), Perkins.

APPLYING FOR FINANCIAL AID *Required financial aid form:* FAFSA. *Financial aid deadline:* Continuous. *Notification date:* Continuous.

CONTACT ACS/AFS, University of Phoenix–Metro Detroit Campus, 875 West Elliot Road, Suite 116, Tempe, AZ 85284, 480-735-3000 or toll-free 800-776-4867 (in-state), 800-228-7240 (out-of-state). *Fax:* 480-940-2060.

UNIVERSITY OF PHOENIX–NASHVILLE CAMPUS
Nashville, TN

CONTACT Financial Aid Office, University of Phoenix–Nashville Campus, 616 Marriott Drive, Suite 150, Nashville, TN 37214, 615-872-0188 or toll-free 800-776-4867 (in-state), 800-228-7240 (out-of-state).

UNIVERSITY OF PHOENIX–NEVADA CAMPUS

Las Vegas, NV

Tuition & fees: $9300	Average undergraduate aid package: $4042

ABOUT THE INSTITUTION Proprietary, coed. Awards: bachelor's and master's degrees and post-master's certificates (courses conducted at 121 campuses and learning centers in 25 states). 7 undergraduate majors. Total enrollment: 4,125. Undergraduates: 2,914. Freshmen: 149. Both federal and institutional methodology are used as a basis for awarding need-based institutional aid.
UNDERGRADUATE EXPENSES for 2004–05 *Application fee:* $110. *Tuition:* full-time $9300; part-time $310 per credit. *Payment plan:* Deferred payment.
FRESHMAN FINANCIAL AID (Fall 2003) *Average financial aid package:* $4708 (excluding resources awarded to replace EFC).
UNDERGRADUATE FINANCIAL AID (Fall 2003) *Average financial aid package:* $4042 (excluding resources awarded to replace EFC).
GIFT AID (NEED-BASED) *Receiving aid:* Freshmen: 10; All full-time undergraduates: 3,252. *Scholarships, grants, and awards:* Federal Pell, FSEOG, state.
GIFT AID (NON-NEED-BASED) *Receiving aid:* Freshmen: 10; Undergraduates: 3,365. *Scholarships, grants, and awards by category:* Academic Interests/ Achievement: business, computer science, social sciences. *Tuition waivers:* Full or partial for employees or children of employees.
LOANS *Programs:* Federal Direct (Unsubsidized Stafford, PLUS), Perkins.
APPLYING FOR FINANCIAL AID *Required financial aid form:* FAFSA. *Financial aid deadline:* Continuous. *Notification date:* Continuous.
CONTACT ACS/AFS, University of Phoenix–Nevada Campus, 875 West Elliot Road, Suite 116, Tempe, AZ 85284, 480-735-3000 or toll-free 800-776-4867 (in-state), 800-228-7240 (out-of-state). *Fax:* 480-940-2060.

UNIVERSITY OF PHOENIX–NEW MEXICO CAMPUS

Albuquerque, NM

Tuition & fees: $8940	Average undergraduate aid package: $5232

ABOUT THE INSTITUTION Proprietary, coed. Awards: bachelor's and master's degrees (courses conducted at 121 campuses and learning centers in 25 states). 11 undergraduate majors. Total enrollment: 4,812. Undergraduates: 3,757. Freshmen: 218. Both federal and institutional methodology are used as a basis for awarding need-based institutional aid.
UNDERGRADUATE EXPENSES for 2004–05 *Application fee:* $110. *Tuition:* full-time $8940; part-time $298 per credit. *Payment plan:* Deferred payment.
FRESHMAN FINANCIAL AID (Fall 2003) *Average financial aid package:* $4544 (excluding resources awarded to replace EFC).
UNDERGRADUATE FINANCIAL AID (Fall 2003) *Average financial aid package:* $5232 (excluding resources awarded to replace EFC).
GIFT AID (NEED-BASED) *Receiving aid:* Freshmen: 61; All full-time undergraduates: 4,199. *Scholarships, grants, and awards:* Federal Pell, FSEOG, state.
GIFT AID (NON-NEED-BASED) *Receiving aid:* Freshmen: 46; Undergraduates: 4,064. *Scholarships, grants, and awards by category:* Academic Interests/ Achievement: business, computer science, health fields, social sciences. *Tuition waivers:* Full or partial for employees or children of employees.
LOANS *Programs:* Federal Direct (Unsubsidized Stafford, PLUS), Perkins.
APPLYING FOR FINANCIAL AID *Required financial aid form:* FAFSA. *Financial aid deadline:* Continuous. *Notification date:* Continuous.
CONTACT ACS/AFS, University of Phoenix–New Mexico Campus, 875 West Elliot Road, Suite 116, Tempe, AZ 85284, 480-735-3000 or toll-free 800-776-4867 (in-state), 800-228-7240 (out-of-state). *Fax:* 480-940-2060.

UNIVERSITY OF PHOENIX–NORTHERN CALIFORNIA CAMPUS

Pleasanton, CA

Tuition & fees: $12,630	Average undergraduate aid package: $3674

ABOUT THE INSTITUTION Proprietary, coed. Awards: associate, bachelor's, and master's degrees (courses conducted at 121 campuses and learning centers in

25 states). 10 undergraduate majors. Total enrollment: 5,707. Undergraduates: 4,261. Freshmen: 124. Both federal and institutional methodology are used as a basis for awarding need-based institutional aid.
UNDERGRADUATE EXPENSES for 2004–05 *Application fee:* $110. *Tuition:* full-time $12,630; part-time $421 per credit. *Payment plan:* Deferred payment.
FRESHMAN FINANCIAL AID (Fall 2003) *Average financial aid package:* $2727 (excluding resources awarded to replace EFC).
UNDERGRADUATE FINANCIAL AID (Fall 2003) *Average financial aid package:* $3674 (excluding resources awarded to replace EFC).
GIFT AID (NEED-BASED) *Receiving aid:* Freshmen: 4; All full-time undergraduates: 2,867. *Scholarships, grants, and awards:* Federal Pell, FSEOG, state.
GIFT AID (NON-NEED-BASED) *Receiving aid:* Freshmen: 3; Undergraduates: 3,189. *Scholarships, grants, and awards by category:* Academic Interests/ Achievement: business, computer science, health fields, social sciences. *Tuition waivers:* Full or partial for employees or children of employees.
LOANS *Programs:* Federal Direct (Unsubsidized Stafford, PLUS), Perkins.
APPLYING FOR FINANCIAL AID *Required financial aid form:* FAFSA. *Financial aid deadline:* Continuous. *Notification date:* Continuous.
CONTACT ACS/AFS, University of Phoenix–Northern California Campus, 875 West Elliot Road, Suite 116, Tempe, AZ 85284, 480-735-3000 or toll-free 877-4-STUDENT. *Fax:* 480-940-2060.

UNIVERSITY OF PHOENIX–NORTHERN VIRGINIA CAMPUS

Reston, VA

CONTACT Financial Aid Office, University of Phoenix–Northern Virginia Campus, 11730 Plaza American Drive, Suite 2000, Reston, VA 20190, 703-435-4402 or toll-free 800-776-4867 (in-state), 800-228-7240 (out-of-state).

UNIVERSITY OF PHOENIX–OKLAHOMA CITY CAMPUS

Oklahoma City, OK

Tuition & fees: $8910	Average undergraduate aid package: $4713

ABOUT THE INSTITUTION Proprietary, coed. Awards: bachelor's and master's degrees (courses conducted at 121 campuses and learning centers in 25 states). 8 undergraduate majors. Total enrollment: 1,049. Undergraduates: 824. Freshmen: 32. Both federal and institutional methodology are used as a basis for awarding need-based institutional aid.
UNDERGRADUATE EXPENSES for 2004–05 *Application fee:* $110. *Tuition:* full-time $8910; part-time $297 per credit. *Payment plan:* Deferred payment.
FRESHMAN FINANCIAL AID (Fall 2003) *Average financial aid package:* $3622 (excluding resources awarded to replace EFC).
UNDERGRADUATE FINANCIAL AID (Fall 2003) *Average financial aid package:* $4713 (excluding resources awarded to replace EFC).
GIFT AID (NEED-BASED) *Receiving aid:* Freshmen: 7; All full-time undergraduates: 977. *Scholarships, grants, and awards:* Federal Pell, FSEOG, state.
GIFT AID (NON-NEED-BASED) *Receiving aid:* Freshmen: 4; Undergraduates: 959. *Scholarships, grants, and awards by category:* Academic Interests/ Achievement: business, computer science, health fields, social sciences. *Tuition waivers:* Full or partial for employees or children of employees.
LOANS *Programs:* Federal Direct (Unsubsidized Stafford, PLUS), Perkins.
APPLYING FOR FINANCIAL AID *Required financial aid form:* FAFSA. *Financial aid deadline:* Continuous. *Notification date:* Continuous.
CONTACT ACS/AFS, University of Phoenix–Oklahoma City Campus, 875 West Elliot Road, Suite 116, Tempe, AZ 85284, 480-735-3000 or toll-free 800-776-4867 (in-state), 800-228-7240 (out-of-state). *Fax:* 480-940-2060.

UNIVERSITY OF PHOENIX ONLINE CAMPUS

Phoenix, AZ

Tuition & fees: $13,200	Average undergraduate aid package: $3361

ABOUT THE INSTITUTION Proprietary, coed. Awards: associate, bachelor's, master's, and doctoral degrees and post-bachelor's and post-master's certificates (courses conducted at 121 campuses and learning centers in 25 states). 8

undergraduate majors. Total enrollment: 115,796. Undergraduates: 75,852. Freshmen: 4,075. Both federal and institutional methodology are used as a basis for awarding need-based institutional aid.

UNDERGRADUATE EXPENSES for 2004–05 *Application fee:* $110. *Tuition:* full-time $13,200; part-time $440 per credit. *Payment plan:* Deferred payment.

FRESHMAN FINANCIAL AID (Fall 2003) *Average financial aid package:* $2910 (excluding resources awarded to replace EFC).

UNDERGRADUATE FINANCIAL AID (Fall 2003) *Average financial aid package:* $3361 (excluding resources awarded to replace EFC).

GIFT AID (NEED-BASED) *Receiving aid:* Freshmen: 173; All full-time undergraduates: 84,113. *Scholarships, grants, and awards:* Federal Pell, FSEOG, state.

GIFT AID (NON-NEED-BASED) *Receiving aid:* Freshmen: 103; Undergraduates: 77,867. *Scholarships, grants, and awards by category:* Academic Interests/ Achievement: business, computer science, health fields, social sciences. *Tuition waivers:* Full or partial for employees or children of employees.

LOANS *Programs:* Federal Direct (Unsubsidized Stafford, PLUS), Perkins.

APPLYING FOR FINANCIAL AID *Required financial aid form:* FAFSA. *Financial aid deadline:* Continuous. *Notification date:* Continuous.

CONTACT ACS/AFS, University of Phoenix Online Campus, 875 West Elliot Road, Suite 116, Tempe, AZ 85284, 480-735-3000 or toll-free 800-776-4867 (in-state), 800-228-7240 (out-of-state). *Fax:* 480-940-2060.

UNIVERSITY OF PHOENIX–OREGON CAMPUS
Portland, OR

Tuition & fees: $9960	Average undergraduate aid package: $4049

ABOUT THE INSTITUTION Proprietary, coed. Awards: bachelor's and master's degrees (courses conducted at 121 campuses and learning centers in 25 states). 7 undergraduate majors. Total enrollment: 2,130. Undergraduates: 1,694. Freshmen: 57. Both federal and institutional methodology are used as a basis for awarding need-based institutional aid.

UNDERGRADUATE EXPENSES for 2004–05 *Application fee:* $110. *Tuition:* full-time $9960; part-time $332 per credit. *Payment plan:* Deferred payment.

FRESHMAN FINANCIAL AID (Fall 2003) *Average financial aid package:* $2786 (excluding resources awarded to replace EFC).

UNDERGRADUATE FINANCIAL AID (Fall 2003) *Average financial aid package:* $4049 (excluding resources awarded to replace EFC).

GIFT AID (NEED-BASED) *Receiving aid:* Freshmen: 4; All full-time undergraduates: 1,464. *Scholarships, grants, and awards:* Federal Pell, FSEOG, state.

GIFT AID (NON-NEED-BASED) *Receiving aid:* Freshmen: 3; Undergraduates: 1,497. *Scholarships, grants, and awards by category:* Academic Interests/ Achievement: business, computer science, health fields, social sciences. *Tuition waivers:* Full or partial for employees or children of employees.

LOANS *Programs:* Federal Direct (Unsubsidized Stafford, PLUS), Perkins.

APPLYING FOR FINANCIAL AID *Required financial aid form:* FAFSA. *Financial aid deadline:* Continuous. *Notification date:* Continuous.

CONTACT ACS/AFS, University of Phoenix–Oregon Campus, 875 West Elliot Road, Suite 116, Tempe, AZ 85284, 480-735-3000 or toll-free 800-776-4867 (in-state), 800-228-7240 (out-of-state). *Fax:* 480-940-2060.

UNIVERSITY OF PHOENIX–ORLANDO CAMPUS
Maitland, FL

Tuition & fees: $10,170	Average undergraduate aid package: $4305

ABOUT THE INSTITUTION Proprietary, coed. Awards: bachelor's and master's degrees (courses conducted at 121 campuses and learning centers in 25 states). 9 undergraduate majors. Total enrollment: 2,142. Undergraduates: 1,475. Freshmen: 67. Both federal and institutional methodology are used as a basis for awarding need-based institutional aid.

UNDERGRADUATE EXPENSES for 2004–05 *Application fee:* $110. *Tuition:* full-time $10,170; part-time $339 per credit. *Payment plan:* Deferred payment.

FRESHMAN FINANCIAL AID (Fall 2003) *Average financial aid package:* $1739 (excluding resources awarded to replace EFC).

UNDERGRADUATE FINANCIAL AID (Fall 2003) *Average financial aid package:* $4305 (excluding resources awarded to replace EFC).

GIFT AID (NEED-BASED) *Receiving aid:* Freshmen: 4; All full-time undergraduates: 1,596. *Scholarships, grants, and awards:* Federal Pell, FSEOG, state.

GIFT AID (NON-NEED-BASED) *Receiving aid:* Freshmen: 3; Undergraduates: 1,628. *Scholarships, grants, and awards by category:* Academic Interests/ Achievement: business, computer science, health fields, social sciences. *Tuition waivers:* Full or partial for employees or children of employees.

LOANS *Programs:* Federal Direct (Unsubsidized Stafford, PLUS), Perkins.

APPLYING FOR FINANCIAL AID *Required financial aid form:* FAFSA. *Financial aid deadline:* Continuous. *Notification date:* Continuous.

CONTACT ACS/AFS, University of Phoenix–Orlando Campus, 875 West Elliot Road, Suite 116, Tempe, AZ 85284, 480-735-3000 or toll-free 800-776-4867 (in-state), 800-228-7240 (out-of-state). *Fax:* 480-940-2060.

UNIVERSITY OF PHOENIX–PHILADELPHIA CAMPUS
Wayne, PA

Tuition & fees: $12,000	Average undergraduate aid package: $4058

ABOUT THE INSTITUTION Proprietary, coed. Awards: bachelor's and master's degrees (courses conducted at 121 campuses and learning centers in 25 states). 4 undergraduate majors. Total enrollment: 1,704. Undergraduates: 1,209. Freshmen: 109. Both federal and institutional methodology are used as a basis for awarding need-based institutional aid.

UNDERGRADUATE EXPENSES for 2004–05 *Application fee:* $110. *Tuition:* full-time $12,000; part-time $400 per credit. *Payment plan:* Deferred payment.

FRESHMAN FINANCIAL AID (Fall 2003) *Average financial aid package:* $1334 (excluding resources awarded to replace EFC).

UNDERGRADUATE FINANCIAL AID (Fall 2003) *Average financial aid package:* $4058 (excluding resources awarded to replace EFC).

GIFT AID (NEED-BASED) *Receiving aid:* Freshmen: 1; All full-time undergraduates: 1,052. *Scholarships, grants, and awards:* Federal Pell, FSEOG, state.

GIFT AID (NON-NEED-BASED) *Receiving aid:* Freshmen: 1; Undergraduates: 1,069. *Scholarships, grants, and awards by category:* Academic Interests/ Achievement: business, computer science. *Tuition waivers:* Full or partial for employees or children of employees.

LOANS *Programs:* Federal Direct (Unsubsidized Stafford, PLUS), Perkins.

APPLYING FOR FINANCIAL AID *Required financial aid form:* FAFSA. *Financial aid deadline:* Continuous. *Notification date:* Continuous.

CONTACT ACS/AFS, University of Phoenix–Philadelphia Campus, 875 West Elliot Road, Suite 116, Tempe, AZ 85284, 480-735-3000 or toll-free 800-776-4867 (in-state), 800-228-7240 (out-of-state). *Fax:* 480-940-2060.

UNIVERSITY OF PHOENIX–PHOENIX CAMPUS
Phoenix, AZ

Tuition & fees: $9090	Average undergraduate aid package: $4191

ABOUT THE INSTITUTION Proprietary, coed. Awards: bachelor's and master's degrees and post-bachelor's and post-master's certificates (courses conducted at 121 campuses and learning centers in 25 states). 14 undergraduate majors. Total enrollment: 9,699. Undergraduates: 5,983. Freshmen: 219. Both federal and institutional methodology are used as a basis for awarding need-based institutional aid.

UNDERGRADUATE EXPENSES for 2004–05 *Application fee:* $110. *Tuition:* full-time $9090; part-time $303 per credit. *Payment plan:* Deferred payment.

FRESHMAN FINANCIAL AID (Fall 2003) *Average financial aid package:* $5072 (excluding resources awarded to replace EFC).

UNDERGRADUATE FINANCIAL AID (Fall 2003) *Average financial aid package:* $4191 (excluding resources awarded to replace EFC).

GIFT AID (NEED-BASED) *Receiving aid:* Freshmen: 42; All full-time undergraduates: 6,375. *Scholarships, grants, and awards:* Federal Pell, FSEOG, state.

GIFT AID (NON-NEED-BASED) *Receiving aid:* Freshmen: 46; Undergraduates: 6,457. *Scholarships, grants, and awards by category:* Academic Interests/ Achievement: business, computer science, health fields, social sciences. *Tuition waivers:* Full or partial for employees or children of employees.

LOANS *Programs:* Federal Direct (Unsubsidized Stafford, PLUS), Perkins.

APPLYING FOR FINANCIAL AID *Required financial aid form:* FAFSA. *Financial aid deadline:* Continuous. *Notification date:* Continuous.

CONTACT ACS/AFS, University of Phoenix–Phoenix Campus, 875 West Elliot Road, Suite 116, Tempe, AZ 85284, 480-735-3000 or toll-free 800-776-4867 (in-state), 800-228-7240 (out-of-state). *Fax:* 480-940-2060.

UNIVERSITY OF PHOENIX–PITTSBURGH CAMPUS
Pittsburgh, PA

Tuition & fees: $12,000	Average undergraduate aid package: $4072

ABOUT THE INSTITUTION Proprietary, coed. Awards: bachelor's and master's degrees (courses conducted at 121 campuses and learning centers in 25 states). 6 undergraduate majors. Total enrollment: 613. Undergraduates: 444. Freshmen: 32. Both federal and institutional methodology are used as a basis for awarding need-based institutional aid.

UNDERGRADUATE EXPENSES for 2004–05 *Application fee:* $110. *Tuition:* full-time $12,000; part-time $400 per credit. *Payment plan:* Deferred payment.

FRESHMAN FINANCIAL AID (Fall 2003) *Average financial aid package:* $5355 (excluding resources awarded to replace EFC).

UNDERGRADUATE FINANCIAL AID (Fall 2003) *Average financial aid package:* $4072 (excluding resources awarded to replace EFC).

GIFT AID (NEED-BASED) *Receiving aid:* Freshmen: 1; All full-time undergraduates: 444. *Scholarships, grants, and awards:* Federal Pell, FSEOG, state.

GIFT AID (NON-NEED-BASED) *Receiving aid:* Freshmen: 1; Undergraduates: 332. *Scholarships, grants, and awards by category:* Academic Interests/Achievement: business, computer science. *Tuition waivers:* Full or partial for employees or children of employees.

LOANS *Programs:* Federal Direct (Unsubsidized Stafford, PLUS), Perkins.

APPLYING FOR FINANCIAL AID *Required financial aid form:* FAFSA. *Financial aid deadline:* Continuous. *Notification date:* Continuous.

CONTACT ACS/AFS, University of Phoenix–Pittsburgh Campus, 875 West Elliot Road, Suite 116, Tempe, AZ 85284, 480-735-3000 or toll-free 800-776-4867 (in-state), 800-228-7240 (out-of-state). *Fax:* 480-940-2060.

UNIVERSITY OF PHOENIX–PUERTO RICO CAMPUS
Guaynabo, PR

Tuition & fees: $5910	Average undergraduate aid package: $5843

ABOUT THE INSTITUTION Proprietary, coed. Awards: bachelor's and master's degrees (courses conducted at 121 campuses and learning centers in 25 states). 4 undergraduate majors. Total enrollment: 2,326. Undergraduates: 600. Freshmen: 26. Both federal and institutional methodology are used as a basis for awarding need-based institutional aid.

UNDERGRADUATE EXPENSES for 2004–05 *Application fee:* $110. *Tuition:* full-time $5910; part-time $197 per credit. *Payment plan:* Deferred payment.

FRESHMAN FINANCIAL AID (Fall 2003) *Average financial aid package:* $8777 (excluding resources awarded to replace EFC).

UNDERGRADUATE FINANCIAL AID (Fall 2003) *Average financial aid package:* $5843 (excluding resources awarded to replace EFC).

GIFT AID (NEED-BASED) *Total amount:* $8,747,425 (100% federal). *Receiving aid:* Freshmen: 2; All full-time undergraduates: 1,474. *Scholarships, grants, and awards:* Federal Pell, FSEOG, state.

GIFT AID (NON-NEED-BASED) *Total amount:* $6,990,680 (100% federal). *Receiving aid:* Freshmen: 2; Undergraduates: 1,190. *Scholarships, grants, and awards by category:* Academic Interests/Achievement: business, computer science, social sciences. *Tuition waivers:* Full or partial for employees or children of employees.

LOANS *Programs:* Federal Direct (Unsubsidized Stafford, PLUS), Perkins.

APPLYING FOR FINANCIAL AID *Required financial aid form:* FAFSA. *Financial aid deadline:* Continuous. *Notification date:* Continuous.

CONTACT ACS/AFS, University of Phoenix–Puerto Rico Campus, 875 West Elliot Road, Suite 116, Tempe, AZ 85284, 480-735-3000 or toll-free 800-776-4867 (in-state), 800-228-7240 (out-of-state). *Fax:* 480-940-2060.

UNIVERSITY OF PHOENIX–RALEIGH CAMPUS
Raleigh, NC

CONTACT Financial Aid Office, University of Phoenix–Raleigh Campus, 5511 Capital Center Drive, Raleigh, NC 27606, toll-free 800-776-4867 (in-state), 800-228-7240 (out-of-state).

UNIVERSITY OF PHOENIX–RICHMOND CAMPUS
Richmond, VA

CONTACT Financial Aid Office, University of Phoenix–Richmond Campus, 6802 Paragon Place, Suite 420, Richmond, VA 23230, 804-288-3390 or toll-free 800-776-4867 (in-state), 800-228-7240 (out-of-state).

UNIVERSITY OF PHOENIX–SACRAMENTO CAMPUS
Sacramento, CA

Tuition & fees: $11,850	Average undergraduate aid package: $4366

ABOUT THE INSTITUTION Proprietary, coed. Awards: bachelor's and master's degrees (courses conducted at 121 campuses and learning centers in 25 states). 11 undergraduate majors. Total enrollment: 4,365. Undergraduates: 3,338. Freshmen: 152. Both federal and institutional methodology are used as a basis for awarding need-based institutional aid.

UNDERGRADUATE EXPENSES for 2004–05 *Application fee:* $110. *Tuition:* full-time $11,850; part-time $395 per credit. *Payment plan:* Deferred payment.

FRESHMAN FINANCIAL AID (Fall 2003) *Average financial aid package:* $6164 (excluding resources awarded to replace EFC).

UNDERGRADUATE FINANCIAL AID (Fall 2003) *Average financial aid package:* $4366 (excluding resources awarded to replace EFC).

GIFT AID (NEED-BASED) *Total amount:* $15,683,258 (100% federal). *Receiving aid:* Freshmen: 8; All full-time undergraduates: 3,381. *Scholarships, grants, and awards:* Federal Pell, FSEOG, state.

GIFT AID (NON-NEED-BASED) *Total amount:* $18,237,585 (95% federal, 5% state). *Receiving aid:* Freshmen: 9; Undergraduates: 3,472. *Scholarships, grants, and awards by category:* Academic Interests/Achievement: business, computer science, health fields, social sciences. *Tuition waivers:* Full or partial for employees or children of employees.

LOANS *Programs:* Federal Direct (Unsubsidized Stafford, PLUS), Perkins.

APPLYING FOR FINANCIAL AID *Required financial aid form:* FAFSA. *Financial aid deadline:* Continuous. *Notification date:* Continuous.

CONTACT ACS/AFS, University of Phoenix–Sacramento Campus, 875 West Elliot Road, Suite 116, Tempe, AZ 85284, 480-735-3000 or toll-free 800-776-4867 (in-state), 800-228-7240 (out-of-state). *Fax:* 480-940-2060.

UNIVERSITY OF PHOENIX–ST. LOUIS CAMPUS
St. Louis, MO

Tuition & fees: $12,060	Average undergraduate aid package: $3854

ABOUT THE INSTITUTION Proprietary, coed. Awards: bachelor's and master's degrees (courses conducted at 121 campuses and learning centers in 25 states). 7 undergraduate majors. Total enrollment: 892. Undergraduates: 738. Freshmen: 57. Both federal and institutional methodology are used as a basis for awarding need-based institutional aid.

UNDERGRADUATE EXPENSES for 2004–05 *Application fee:* $110. *Tuition:* full-time $12,060; part-time $402 per credit. *Payment plan:* Deferred payment.

FRESHMAN FINANCIAL AID (Fall 2003) *Average financial aid package:* $5757 (excluding resources awarded to replace EFC).

UNDERGRADUATE FINANCIAL AID (Fall 2003) *Average financial aid package:* $3854 (excluding resources awarded to replace EFC).

GIFT AID (NEED-BASED) *Receiving aid:* Freshmen: 1; All full-time undergraduates: 689. *Scholarships, grants, and awards:* Federal Pell, FSEOG, state.

GIFT AID (NON-NEED-BASED) *Receiving aid:* Freshmen: 1; Undergraduates: 663. *Scholarships, grants, and awards by category:* Academic Interests/Achievement: business, computer science. *Tuition waivers:* Full or partial for employees or children of employees.

LOANS *Programs:* Federal Direct (Unsubsidized Stafford, PLUS), Perkins.

APPLYING FOR FINANCIAL AID *Required financial aid form:* FAFSA. *Financial aid deadline:* Continuous. *Notification date:* Continuous.

CONTACT ACS/AFS, University of Phoenix–St. Louis Campus, 875 West Elliot Road, Suite 116, Tempe, AZ 85284, 480-735-3000 or toll-free 800-776-4867 (in-state), 800-228-7240 (out-of-state). *Fax:* 480-940-2060.

UNIVERSITY OF PHOENIX–SAN DIEGO CAMPUS
San Diego, CA

Tuition & fees: $11,370	Average undergraduate aid package: $3838

ABOUT THE INSTITUTION Proprietary, coed. Awards: bachelor's and master's degrees (courses conducted at 121 campuses and learning centers in 25 states). 9 undergraduate majors. Total enrollment: 4,761. Undergraduates: 3,697. Freshmen: 97. Both federal and institutional methodology are used as a basis for awarding need-based institutional aid.

UNDERGRADUATE EXPENSES for 2004–05 *Application fee:* $110. *Tuition:* full-time $11,370; part-time $379 per credit. *Payment plan:* Deferred payment.

FRESHMAN FINANCIAL AID (Fall 2003) *Average financial aid package:* $5761 (excluding resources awarded to replace EFC).

UNDERGRADUATE FINANCIAL AID (Fall 2003) *Average financial aid package:* $3838 (excluding resources awarded to replace EFC).

GIFT AID (NEED-BASED) *Receiving aid:* Freshmen: 16; All full-time undergraduates: 3,675. *Scholarships, grants, and awards:* Federal Pell, FSEOG, state.

GIFT AID (NON-NEED-BASED) *Receiving aid:* Freshmen: 17; Undergraduates: 3,825. *Scholarships, grants, and awards by category:* Academic Interests/Achievement: business, computer science, health fields, social sciences. *Tuition waivers:* Full or partial for employees or children of employees.

LOANS *Programs:* Federal Direct (Unsubsidized Stafford, PLUS), Perkins.

APPLYING FOR FINANCIAL AID *Required financial aid form:* FAFSA. *Financial aid deadline:* Continuous. *Notification date:* Continuous.

CONTACT ACS/AFS, University of Phoenix–San Diego Campus, 875 West Elliot Road, Suite 116, Tempe, AZ 85284, 480-735-3000 or toll-free 888-776-4867 (in-state), 888-228-7240 (out-of-state). *Fax:* 480-940-2060.

UNIVERSITY OF PHOENIX–SOUTHERN ARIZONA CAMPUS
Tucson, AZ

Tuition & fees: $8910	Average undergraduate aid package: $4617

ABOUT THE INSTITUTION Proprietary, coed. Awards: bachelor's and master's degrees and post-master's certificates (courses conducted at 121 campuses and learning centers in 25 states). 12 undergraduate majors. Total enrollment: 3,660. Undergraduates: 2,521. Freshmen: 90. Both federal and institutional methodology are used as a basis for awarding need-based institutional aid.

UNDERGRADUATE EXPENSES for 2004–05 *Application fee:* $110. *Tuition:* full-time $8910; part-time $297 per credit. *Payment plan:* Deferred payment.

FRESHMAN FINANCIAL AID (Fall 2003) *Average financial aid package:* $4208 (excluding resources awarded to replace EFC).

UNDERGRADUATE FINANCIAL AID (Fall 2003) *Average financial aid package:* $4617 (excluding resources awarded to replace EFC).

GIFT AID (NON-NEED-BASED) *Total amount:* $11,830,675 (99% federal, 1% state). *Receiving aid:* Freshmen: 16; Undergraduates: 2,403. *Tuition waivers:* Full or partial for employees or children of employees.

LOANS *Programs:* Federal Direct (Unsubsidized Stafford, PLUS), Perkins.

APPLYING FOR FINANCIAL AID *Required financial aid form:* FAFSA. *Financial aid deadline:* Continuous. *Notification date:* Continuous.

CONTACT ACS/AFS, University of Phoenix–Southern Arizona Campus, 875 West Elliot Road, Suite 116, Tempe, AZ 85284, 480-735-3000 or toll-free 800-776-4867 (in-state), 800-228-7240 (out-of-state). *Fax:* 480-940-2060.

UNIVERSITY OF PHOENIX–SOUTHERN CALIFORNIA CAMPUS
Costa Mesa, CA

Tuition & fees: $12,360	Average undergraduate aid package: $4198

ABOUT THE INSTITUTION Proprietary, coed. Awards: bachelor's and master's degrees (courses conducted at 121 campuses and learning centers in 25 states). 8 undergraduate majors. Total enrollment: 15,913. Undergraduates: 12,544. Freshmen: 477. Both federal and institutional methodology are used as a basis for awarding need-based institutional aid.

UNDERGRADUATE EXPENSES for 2004–05 *Application fee:* $110. *Tuition:* full-time $12,360; part-time $412 per credit. *Payment plan:* Deferred payment.

FRESHMAN FINANCIAL AID (Fall 2003) *Average financial aid package:* $4576 (excluding resources awarded to replace EFC).

UNDERGRADUATE FINANCIAL AID (Fall 2003) *Average financial aid package:* $4198 (excluding resources awarded to replace EFC).

GIFT AID (NEED-BASED) *Total amount:* $56,528,341 (100% federal). *Receiving aid:* Freshmen: 14; All full-time undergraduates: 12,618. *Scholarships, grants, and awards:* Federal Pell, FSEOG, state.

GIFT AID (NON-NEED-BASED) *Total amount:* $63,084,833 (97% federal, 3% state). *Receiving aid:* Freshmen: 15; Undergraduates: 12,939. *Tuition waivers:* Full or partial for employees or children of employees.

LOANS *Programs:* Federal Direct (Unsubsidized Stafford, PLUS), Perkins.

APPLYING FOR FINANCIAL AID *Required financial aid form:* FAFSA. *Financial aid deadline:* Continuous. *Notification date:* Continuous.

CONTACT ACS/AFS, University of Phoenix–Southern California Campus, 875 West Elliot Road, Suite 116, Tempe, AZ 85284, 480-735-3000 or toll-free 800-776-4867 (in-state), 800-228-7240 (out-of-state). *Fax:* 480-940-2060.

UNIVERSITY OF PHOENIX–SOUTHERN COLORADO CAMPUS
Colorado Springs, CO

Tuition & fees: $9000	Average undergraduate aid package: $4480

ABOUT THE INSTITUTION Proprietary, coed. Awards: bachelor's and master's degrees (courses conducted at 121 campuses and learning centers in 25 states). 9 undergraduate majors. Total enrollment: 1,410. Undergraduates: 896. Freshmen: 29. Both federal and institutional methodology are used as a basis for awarding need-based institutional aid.

UNDERGRADUATE EXPENSES for 2004–05 *Application fee:* $110. *Tuition:* full-time $9000; part-time $300 per credit. *Payment plan:* Deferred payment.

FRESHMAN FINANCIAL AID (Fall 2003) *Average financial aid package:* $5593 (excluding resources awarded to replace EFC).

UNDERGRADUATE FINANCIAL AID (Fall 2003) *Average financial aid package:* $4480 (excluding resources awarded to replace EFC).

GIFT AID (NEED-BASED) *Total amount:* $4,932,529 (100% federal). *Receiving aid:* Freshmen: 2; All full-time undergraduates: 1,101. *Scholarships, grants, and awards:* Federal Pell, FSEOG, state.

GIFT AID (NON-NEED-BASED) *Total amount:* $5,484,423 (100% federal). *Receiving aid:* Freshmen: 2; Undergraduates: 994. *Scholarships, grants, and awards by category:* Academic Interests/Achievement: business, computer science, health fields, social sciences. *Tuition waivers:* Full or partial for employees or children of employees.

LOANS *Programs:* Federal Direct (Unsubsidized Stafford, PLUS), Perkins.

APPLYING FOR FINANCIAL AID *Required financial aid form:* FAFSA. *Financial aid deadline:* Continuous. *Notification date:* Continuous.

CONTACT ACS/AFS, University of Phoenix–Southern Colorado Campus, 875 West Elliot Road, Suite 116, Tempe, AZ 85284, 480-735-3000 or toll-free 800-776-4867 (in-state), 800-228-7240 (out-of-state). *Fax:* 480-940-2060.

UNIVERSITY OF PHOENIX–SPOKANE CAMPUS
Spokane, WA

CONTACT Financial Aid Office, University of Phoenix–Spokane Campus, Rock Point Corporate Center, 1330 North Washington Street, Suite 2460, Spokane, WA 99201-2446, 509-327-2443 or toll-free 800-776-4867 (in-state), 800-228-7240 (out-of-state).

UNIVERSITY OF PHOENIX–SPRINGFIELD CAMPUS
Springfield, MO

CONTACT Financial Aid Office, University of Phoenix–Springfield Campus, 1260 E. Kingsley Street, Springfield, MO, toll-free 800-776-4867 (in-state), 800-228-7240 (out-of-state).

UNIVERSITY OF PHOENIX–TAMPA CAMPUS
Tampa, FL

Tuition & fees: $10,170	Average undergraduate aid package: $3885

ABOUT THE INSTITUTION Proprietary, coed. Awards: bachelor's and master's degrees (courses conducted at 121 campuses and learning centers in 25 states). 10 undergraduate majors. Total enrollment: 2,570. Undergraduates: 1,854. Freshmen: 113. Both federal and institutional methodology are used as a basis for awarding need-based institutional aid.

UNDERGRADUATE EXPENSES for 2004–05 *Application fee:* $110. *Tuition:* full-time $10,170; part-time $339 per credit. *Payment plan:* Deferred payment.

FRESHMAN FINANCIAL AID (Fall 2003) *Average financial aid package:* $4966 (excluding resources awarded to replace EFC).

UNDERGRADUATE FINANCIAL AID (Fall 2003) *Average financial aid package:* $3885 (excluding resources awarded to replace EFC).

GIFT AID (NEED-BASED) *Receiving aid:* Freshmen: 3; All full-time undergraduates: 1,811. *Scholarships, grants, and awards:* Federal Pell, FSEOG, state.

GIFT AID (NON-NEED-BASED) *Receiving aid:* Freshmen: 3; Undergraduates: 1,825. *Scholarships, grants, and awards by category: Academic Interests/Achievement:* business, computer science, health fields, social sciences. *Tuition waivers:* Full or partial for employees or children of employees.

LOANS *Programs:* Federal Direct (Unsubsidized Stafford, PLUS), Perkins.

APPLYING FOR FINANCIAL AID *Required financial aid form:* FAFSA. *Financial aid deadline:* Continuous. *Notification date:* Continuous.

CONTACT ACS/AFS, University of Phoenix–Tampa Campus, 875 West Elliot Road, Suite 116, Tempe, AZ 85284, 480-735-3000 or toll-free 800-776-4867 (in-state), 800-228-7240 (out-of-state). *Fax:* 480-940-2060.

UNIVERSITY OF PHOENIX–TULSA CAMPUS
Tulsa, OK

Tuition & fees: $8910	Average undergraduate aid package: $4794

ABOUT THE INSTITUTION Proprietary, coed. Awards: bachelor's and master's degrees (courses conducted at 121 campuses and learning centers in 25 states). 9 undergraduate majors. Total enrollment: 1,202. Undergraduates: 1,007. Freshmen: 63. Both federal and institutional methodology are used as a basis for awarding need-based institutional aid.

UNDERGRADUATE EXPENSES for 2004–05 *Application fee:* $110. *Tuition:* full-time $8910; part-time $297 per credit. *Payment plan:* Deferred payment.

FRESHMAN FINANCIAL AID (Fall 2003) *Average financial aid package:* $4280 (excluding resources awarded to replace EFC).

UNDERGRADUATE FINANCIAL AID (Fall 2003) *Average financial aid package:* $4794 (excluding resources awarded to replace EFC).

GIFT AID (NEED-BASED) *Receiving aid:* Freshmen: 4; All full-time undergraduates: 1,118. *Scholarships, grants, and awards:* Federal Pell, FSEOG, state.

GIFT AID (NON-NEED-BASED) *Receiving aid:* Freshmen: 3; Undergraduates: 1,081. *Scholarships, grants, and awards by category: Academic Interests/Achievement:* business, computer science, health fields, social sciences. *Tuition waivers:* Full or partial for employees or children of employees.

LOANS *Programs:* Federal Direct (Unsubsidized Stafford, PLUS), Perkins.

APPLYING FOR FINANCIAL AID *Required financial aid form:* FAFSA. *Financial aid deadline:* Continuous. *Notification date:* Continuous.

CONTACT ACS/AFS, University of Phoenix–Tulsa Campus, 875 West Elliot Road, Suite 116, Tempe, AZ 85284, 480-735-3000 or toll-free 800-776-4867 (in-state), 800-228-7240 (out-of-state). *Fax:* 480-940-2060.

UNIVERSITY OF PHOENIX–UTAH CAMPUS
Salt Lake City, UT

Tuition & fees: $9540	Average undergraduate aid package: $4623

ABOUT THE INSTITUTION Proprietary, coed. Awards: bachelor's and master's degrees (courses conducted at 121 campuses and learning centers in 25 states). 10 undergraduate majors. Total enrollment: 4,057. Undergraduates: 2,645. Freshmen: 171. Both federal and institutional methodology are used as a basis for awarding need-based institutional aid.

UNDERGRADUATE EXPENSES for 2004–05 *Application fee:* $110. *Tuition:* full-time $9540; part-time $318 per credit. *Payment plan:* Deferred payment.

FRESHMAN FINANCIAL AID (Fall 2003) *Average financial aid package:* $3612 (excluding resources awarded to replace EFC).

UNDERGRADUATE FINANCIAL AID (Fall 2003) *Average financial aid package:* $4623 (excluding resources awarded to replace EFC).

GIFT AID (NEED-BASED) *Receiving aid:* Freshmen: 17; All full-time undergraduates: 2,739. *Scholarships, grants, and awards:* Federal Pell, FSEOG, state.

GIFT AID (NON-NEED-BASED) *Receiving aid:* Freshmen: 10; Undergraduates: 2,598. *Scholarships, grants, and awards by category: Academic Interests/Achievement:* business, computer science, health fields, social sciences. *Tuition waivers:* Full or partial for employees or children of employees.

LOANS *Programs:* Federal Direct (Unsubsidized Stafford, PLUS), Perkins.

APPLYING FOR FINANCIAL AID *Required financial aid form:* FAFSA. *Financial aid deadline:* Continuous. *Notification date:* Continuous.

CONTACT ACS/AFS, University of Phoenix–Utah Campus, 875 West Elliot Road, Suite 116, Tempe, AZ 85284, 480-735-3000 or toll-free 800-776-4867 (in-state), 800-228-7240 (out-of-state). *Fax:* 480-940-2060.

UNIVERSITY OF PHOENIX–WASHINGTON CAMPUS
Seattle, WA

Tuition & fees: $10,290	Average undergraduate aid package: $3666

ABOUT THE INSTITUTION Proprietary, coed. Awards: bachelor's and master's degrees (courses conducted at 121 campuses and learning centers in 25 states). 10 undergraduate majors. Total enrollment: 2,197. Undergraduates: 1,707. Freshmen: 94. Both federal and institutional methodology are used as a basis for awarding need-based institutional aid.

UNDERGRADUATE EXPENSES for 2004–05 *Application fee:* $110. *Tuition:* full-time $10,290; part-time $343 per credit. *Payment plan:* Deferred payment.

FRESHMAN FINANCIAL AID (Fall 2003) *Average financial aid package:* $4669 (excluding resources awarded to replace EFC).

UNDERGRADUATE FINANCIAL AID (Fall 2003) *Average financial aid package:* $3666 (excluding resources awarded to replace EFC).

GIFT AID (NEED-BASED) *Total amount:* $5,682,961 (100% federal). *Receiving aid:* Freshmen: 1; All full-time undergraduates: 1,352. *Scholarships, grants, and awards:* Federal Pell, FSEOG, state.

GIFT AID (NON-NEED-BASED) *Total amount:* $7,086,866 (100% federal). *Receiving aid:* Freshmen: 2; Undergraduates: 1,468. *Scholarships, grants, and awards by category: Academic Interests/Achievement:* business, computer science, health fields, social sciences. *Tuition waivers:* Full or partial for employees or children of employees.

LOANS *Programs:* Federal Direct (Unsubsidized Stafford, PLUS), Perkins.

APPLYING FOR FINANCIAL AID *Required financial aid form:* FAFSA. *Financial aid deadline:* Continuous. *Notification date:* Continuous.

CONTACT ACS/AFS, University of Phoenix–Washington Campus, 875 West Elliot Road, Suite 116, Tempe, AZ 85284, 480-735-3000 or toll-free 800-776-4867 (in-state), 800-228-7240 (out-of-state). *Fax:* 480-940-2060.

UNIVERSITY OF PHOENIX–WEST MICHIGAN CAMPUS
Grand Rapids, MI

Tuition & fees: $11,520	Average undergraduate aid package: $4028

ABOUT THE INSTITUTION Proprietary, coed. Awards: bachelor's and master's degrees (courses conducted at 121 campuses and learning centers in 25 states). 9 undergraduate majors. Total enrollment: 1,167. Undergraduates: 921. Freshmen: 34. Both federal and institutional methodology are used as a basis for awarding need-based institutional aid.

UNDERGRADUATE EXPENSES for 2004–05 *Application fee:* $110. *Tuition:* full-time $11,520; part-time $384 per credit. *Payment plan:* Deferred payment.

FRESHMAN FINANCIAL AID (Fall 2003) *Average financial aid package:* $3772 (excluding resources awarded to replace EFC).

UNDERGRADUATE FINANCIAL AID (Fall 2003) *Average financial aid package:* $4028 (excluding resources awarded to replace EFC).

GIFT AID (NEED-BASED) *Total amount:* $4,153,226 (100% federal). *Receiving aid:* Freshmen: 6; All full-time undergraduates: 954. *Scholarships, grants, and awards:* Federal Pell, FSEOG, state.

GIFT AID (NON-NEED-BASED) *Total amount:* $4,287,577 (100% federal). *Receiving aid:* Freshmen: 3; Undergraduates: 928. *Scholarships, grants, and awards by category:* Academic Interests/Achievement: business, computer science, health fields, social sciences. *Tuition waivers:* Full or partial for employees or children of employees.

LOANS *Programs:* Federal Direct (Unsubsidized Stafford, PLUS), Perkins.

APPLYING FOR FINANCIAL AID *Required financial aid form:* FAFSA. *Financial aid deadline:* Continuous. *Notification date:* Continuous.

CONTACT ACS/AFS, University of Phoenix–West Michigan Campus, 875 West Elliot Road, Suite 116, Tempe, AZ 85284, 480-735-3000 or toll-free 800-776-4867 (in-state), 800-228-7240 (out-of-state). *Fax:* 480-940-2060.

UNIVERSITY OF PHOENIX–WICHITA CAMPUS
Wichita, KS

CONTACT Financial Aid Office, University of Phoenix–Wichita Campus, 3020 North Cypress Drive, Suite 150, Wichita, KS 67226, 316-630-8121 or toll-free 800-776-4867 (in-state), 800-228-7240 (out-of-state).

UNIVERSITY OF PHOENIX–WISCONSIN CAMPUS
Brookfield, WI

ABOUT THE INSTITUTION Proprietary, coed. Awards: bachelor's and master's degrees (courses conducted at 121 campuses and learning centers in 25 states). 5 undergraduate majors. Total enrollment: 1,296. Undergraduates: 985. Freshmen: 64.

GIFT AID (NEED-BASED) *Scholarships, grants, and awards:* Federal Pell, FSEOG, state.

LOANS *Programs:* Federal Direct (Unsubsidized Stafford, PLUS), Perkins.

APPLYING FOR FINANCIAL AID *Required financial aid form:* FAFSA.

CONTACT ACS/AFS, University of Phoenix–Wisconsin Campus, 875 West Elliot Road, Suite 116, Tempe, AZ 85284, 480-735-3000 or toll-free 800-776-4867 (in-state), 800-228-7240 (out-of-state). *Fax:* 480-940-2060.

UNIVERSITY OF PITTSBURGH
Pittsburgh, PA

ABOUT THE INSTITUTION State-related, coed. Awards: bachelor's, master's, doctoral, and first professional degrees and post-bachelor's and post-master's certificates. 86 undergraduate majors. Total enrollment: 26,731. Undergraduates: 17,181. Freshmen: 3,019.

GIFT AID (NEED-BASED) *Scholarships, grants, and awards:* Federal Pell, FSEOG, state, college/university gift aid from institutional funds.

GIFT AID (NON-NEED-BASED) *Scholarships, grants, and awards by category:* Academic Interests/Achievement: general academic interests/achievements. *Special Characteristics:* children of faculty/staff.

LOANS *Programs:* FFEL (Subsidized and Unsubsidized Stafford, PLUS), Perkins, Federal Nursing.

WORK-STUDY *Federal work-study:* Total amount: $2,399,736; 1,643 jobs averaging $1722.

APPLYING FOR FINANCIAL AID *Required financial aid forms:* FAFSA, institution's own form.

CONTACT Dr. Betsy A. Porter, Director, Office of Admissions and Financial Aid, University of Pittsburgh, 4227 Fifth Avenue, First Floor, Alumni Hall, Pittsburgh, PA 15260, 412-624-7488. *Fax:* 412-648-8815. *E-mail:* oafa@pitt.edu.

UNIVERSITY OF PITTSBURGH AT BRADFORD
Bradford, PA

Tuition & fees (PA res): $9980	Average undergraduate aid package: $11,495

ABOUT THE INSTITUTION State-related, coed. Awards: associate and bachelor's degrees. 27 undergraduate majors. Total enrollment: 1,460. Undergraduates: 1,460. Freshmen: 316. Federal methodology is used as a basis for awarding need-based institutional aid.

UNDERGRADUATE EXPENSES for 2004–05 *Application fee:* $35. *Tuition, state resident:* full-time $9330; part-time $333 per credit. *Tuition, nonresident:* full-time $19,200; part-time $685 per credit. *Required fees:* full-time $650; $95 per term part-time. Full-time tuition and fees vary according to course load and program. Part-time tuition and fees vary according to course load and program. *College room and board:* $6344; *room only:* $3600. Room and board charges vary according to board plan and housing facility. *Payment plan:* Installment.

FRESHMAN FINANCIAL AID (Fall 2004, est.) 275 applied for aid; of those 87% were deemed to have need. 100% of freshmen with need received aid; of those 18% had need fully met. *Average percent of need met:* 76% (excluding resources awarded to replace EFC). *Average financial aid package:* $11,495 (excluding resources awarded to replace EFC). 17% of all full-time freshmen had no need and received non-need-based gift aid.

UNDERGRADUATE FINANCIAL AID (Fall 2004, est.) 1,008 applied for aid; of those 87% were deemed to have need. 100% of undergraduates with need received aid; of those 22% had need fully met. *Average percent of need met:* 78% (excluding resources awarded to replace EFC). *Average financial aid package:* $11,495 (excluding resources awarded to replace EFC). 11% of all full-time undergraduates had no need and received non-need-based gift aid.

GIFT AID (NEED-BASED) *Total amount:* $2,897,577 (46% federal, 54% state). *Receiving aid:* Freshmen: 58% (175); All full-time undergraduates: 59% (622). *Average award:* Freshmen: $3000; Undergraduates: $3000. *Scholarships, grants, and awards:* Federal Pell, FSEOG, state, private, college/university gift aid from institutional funds.

GIFT AID (NON-NEED-BASED) *Total amount:* $3,640,387 (11% state, 64% institutional, 25% external sources). *Receiving aid:* Freshmen: 61% (184); Undergraduates: 58% (617). *Average Award:* Freshmen: $4000; Undergraduates: $4000. *Scholarships, grants, and awards by category:* Academic Interests/Achievement: biological sciences, business, communication, computer science, education, engineering/technologies, English, general academic interests/achievements, health fields, humanities, mathematics, physical sciences, social sciences. *Tuition waivers:* Full or partial for employees or children of employees. *ROTC:* Army cooperative.

LOANS *Student loans:* $6,647,114 (47% need-based, 53% non-need-based). 85% of past graduating class borrowed through all loan programs. *Average indebtedness per student:* $19,733. *Average need-based loan:* Freshmen: $2625; Undergraduates: $4281. *Parent loans:* $878,422 (100% non-need-based). *Programs:* FFEL (Subsidized and Unsubsidized Stafford, PLUS), Perkins.

WORK-STUDY *Federal work-study:* Total amount: $186,500; 200 jobs averaging $1400. *State or other work-study/employment:* Total amount: $100,000 (100% non-need-based). 10 part-time jobs averaging $1400.

APPLYING FOR FINANCIAL AID *Required financial aid form:* FAFSA. *Financial aid deadline (priority):* 3/1. *Notification date:* Continuous beginning 4/1. Students must reply within 4 weeks of notification.

CONTACT Melissa Ibañez, Director of Financial Aid, University of Pittsburgh at Bradford, 300 Campus Drive, Bradford, PA 16701-2812, 814-362-7550 or toll-free 800-872-1787. *Fax:* 814-362-7578. *E-mail:* ibanez@exchange.upb.pitt.edu.

UNIVERSITY OF PITTSBURGH AT GREENSBURG
Greensburg, PA

ABOUT THE INSTITUTION State-related, coed. Awards: bachelor's degrees. 22 undergraduate majors. Total enrollment: 1,860. Undergraduates: 1,860. Freshmen: 468.

GIFT AID (NEED-BASED) *Scholarships, grants, and awards:* Federal Pell, FSEOG, state, private, college/university gift aid from institutional funds, United Negro College Fund.

GIFT AID (NON-NEED-BASED) *Scholarships, grants, and awards by category:* *Academic Interests/Achievement:* general academic interests/achievements. *Special Achievements/Activities:* general special achievements/activities.

LOANS *Programs:* FFEL (Subsidized and Unsubsidized Stafford, PLUS), Perkins.

APPLYING FOR FINANCIAL AID *Required financial aid forms:* FAFSA, institution's own form, state aid form.

CONTACT Ms. Brandi S. Darr, Director of Admissions and Financial Aid, University of Pittsburgh at Greensburg, 1150 Mount Pleasant Road, Greensburg, PA 15601-5860, 724-836-7167. *E-mail:* upgadmit@pitt.edu.

UNIVERSITY OF PITTSBURGH AT JOHNSTOWN
Johnstown, PA

Tuition & fees (PA res): $9972	Average undergraduate aid package: $9144

ABOUT THE INSTITUTION State-related, coed. Awards: associate and bachelor's degrees. 50 undergraduate majors. Total enrollment: 3,209. Undergraduates: 3,209. Freshmen: 896. Federal methodology is used as a basis for awarding need-based institutional aid.

UNDERGRADUATE EXPENSES for 2004–05 *Application fee:* $35. *Tuition, state resident:* full-time $9330; part-time $333 per credit. *Tuition, nonresident:* full-time $19,200; part-time $685 per credit. Full-time tuition and fees vary according to program and student level. Part-time tuition and fees vary according to program and student level. *College room and board:* $5930; *room only:* $3600. Room and board charges vary according to board plan and housing facility. *Payment plan:* Installment.

FRESHMAN FINANCIAL AID (Fall 2004, est.) 775 applied for aid; of those 86% were deemed to have need. 93% of freshmen with need received aid; of those 10% had need fully met. *Average percent of need met:* 49% (excluding resources awarded to replace EFC). *Average financial aid package:* $8530 (excluding resources awarded to replace EFC). 4% of all full-time freshmen had no need and received non-need-based gift aid.

UNDERGRADUATE FINANCIAL AID (Fall 2004, est.) 2,651 applied for aid; of those 82% were deemed to have need. 93% of undergraduates with need received aid; of those 7% had need fully met. *Average percent of need met:* 52% (excluding resources awarded to replace EFC). *Average financial aid package:* $9144 (excluding resources awarded to replace EFC). 3% of all full-time undergraduates had no need and received non-need-based gift aid.

GIFT AID (NEED-BASED) *Total amount:* $7,189,574 (35% federal, 57% state, 5% institutional, 3% external sources). *Receiving aid:* Freshmen: 59% (510); All full-time undergraduates: 55% (1,623). *Average award:* Freshmen: $4191; Undergraduates: $4175. *Scholarships, grants, and awards:* Federal Pell, FSEOG, state, private, college/university gift aid from institutional funds.

GIFT AID (NON-NEED-BASED) *Total amount:* $1,442,037 (18% state, 82% institutional). *Receiving aid:* Freshmen: 38% (328); Undergraduates: 18% (543). *Average Award:* Freshmen: $2612; Undergraduates: $2557. *Scholarships, grants, and awards by category:* *Academic Interests/Achievement:* 166 awards ($541,734 total): general academic interests/achievements. *Special Achievements/Activities:* 144 awards ($179,750 total): leadership. *Special Characteristics:* 121 awards ($1,040,238 total): children of faculty/staff. *Tuition waivers:* Full or partial for employees or children of employees.

LOANS *Student loans:* $10,349,057 (55% need-based, 45% non-need-based). 85% of past graduating class borrowed through all loan programs. *Average indebtedness per student:* $18,601. *Average need-based loan:* Freshmen: $2416; Undergraduates: $3227. *Parent loans:* $4,461,870 (100% non-need-based). *Programs:* FFEL (Subsidized and Unsubsidized Stafford, PLUS), Perkins.

WORK-STUDY *Federal work-study:* Total amount: $507,947; 372 jobs averaging $1661. *State or other work-study/employment:* 332 part-time jobs averaging $941.

ATHLETIC AWARDS *Total amount:* $389,846 (100% non-need-based).

APPLYING FOR FINANCIAL AID *Required financial aid forms:* FAFSA, institution's own form. *Financial aid deadline (priority):* 4/1. *Notification date:* Continuous beginning 3/15. Students must reply within 2 weeks of notification.

CONTACT Ms. Julie A. Salem, Director of Student Financial Aid, University of Pittsburgh at Johnstown, 125 Biddle Hall, Johnstown, PA 15904-2990, 814-269-7045 or toll-free 800-765-4875. *Fax:* 814-269-7061. *E-mail:* jasalem@pitt.edu.

UNIVERSITY OF PORTLAND
Portland, OR

Tuition & fees: $24,900	Average undergraduate aid package: $20,606

ABOUT THE INSTITUTION Independent Roman Catholic, coed. Awards: bachelor's and master's degrees and post-master's certificates. 42 undergraduate majors. Total enrollment: 3,343. Undergraduates: 2,829. Freshmen: 750. Federal methodology is used as a basis for awarding need-based institutional aid.

UNDERGRADUATE EXPENSES for 2005–06 *Application fee:* $50. *Comprehensive fee:* $32,300 includes full-time tuition ($24,580), mandatory fees ($320), and room and board ($7400). *College room only:* $3700. Full-time tuition and fees vary according to program. Room and board charges vary according to board plan and housing facility. *Part-time tuition:* $778 per credit hour. Part-time tuition and fees vary according to program. *Payment plans:* Installment, deferred payment.

FRESHMAN FINANCIAL AID (Fall 2003) 632 applied for aid; of those 76% were deemed to have need. 100% of freshmen with need received aid; of those 31% had need fully met. *Average percent of need met:* 86% (excluding resources awarded to replace EFC). *Average financial aid package:* $19,726 (excluding resources awarded to replace EFC). 32% of all full-time freshmen had no need and received non-need-based gift aid.

UNDERGRADUATE FINANCIAL AID (Fall 2003) 1,939 applied for aid; of those 81% were deemed to have need. 99% of undergraduates with need received aid; of those 31% had need fully met. *Average percent of need met:* 83% (excluding resources awarded to replace EFC). *Average financial aid package:* $20,606 (excluding resources awarded to replace EFC). 36% of all full-time undergraduates had no need and received non-need-based gift aid.

GIFT AID (NEED-BASED) *Total amount:* $19,686,714 (8% federal, 2% state, 85% institutional, 5% external sources). *Receiving aid:* Freshmen: 64% (480); All full-time undergraduates: 57% (1,547). *Average award:* Freshmen: $13,807; Undergraduates: $13,764. *Scholarships, grants, and awards:* Federal Pell, FSEOG, state, private, college/university gift aid from institutional funds.

GIFT AID (NON-NEED-BASED) *Total amount:* $15,298,196 (1% federal, 78% institutional, 21% external sources). *Receiving aid:* Freshmen: 34% (251); Undergraduates: 24% (646). *Average Award:* Freshmen: $12,041; Undergraduates: $15,934. *Scholarships, grants, and awards by category:* *Academic Interests/Achievement:* biological sciences, business, communication, computer science, education, engineering/technologies, English, foreign languages, general academic interests/achievements, health fields, humanities, mathematics, military science, physical sciences, premedicine, religion/biblical studies, social sciences. *Creative Arts/Performance:* music, performing arts, theater/drama. *Special Achievements/Activities:* community service. *Special Characteristics:* children of faculty/staff, relatives of clergy. *Tuition waivers:* Full or partial for employees or children of employees. *ROTC:* Army, Air Force.

LOANS *Student loans:* $6,025,019 (91% need-based, 9% non-need-based). 67% of past graduating class borrowed through all loan programs. *Average indebtedness per student:* $18,972. *Average need-based loan:* Freshmen: $2944; Undergraduates: $5277. *Parent loans:* $3,502,005 (31% need-based, 69% non-need-based). *Programs:* FFEL (Subsidized and Unsubsidized Stafford, PLUS), Perkins, Federal Nursing, college/university.

WORK-STUDY *Federal work-study:* Total amount: $1,581,465; 900 jobs averaging $1750. *State or other work-study/employment:* Total amount: $14,940 (86% need-based, 14% non-need-based). 9 part-time jobs averaging $1660.

ATHLETIC AWARDS *Total amount:* $2,946,371 (21% need-based, 79% non-need-based).

APPLYING FOR FINANCIAL AID *Required financial aid forms:* FAFSA, institution's own form. *Financial aid deadline (priority):* 3/1. *Notification date:* Continuous beginning 3/15. Students must reply within 3 weeks of notification.

CONTACT Ms. Tracy Reisinger, Director of Financial Aid, University of Portland, 5000 North Willamette Boulevard, Portland, OR 97203-5798, 503-943-7311 or toll-free 888-627-5601 (out-of-state). *Fax:* 503-943-7508. *E-mail:* reisinge@up.edu.

UNIVERSITY OF PUERTO RICO, AGUADILLA UNIVERSITY COLLEGE
Aguadilla, PR

CONTACT Director of Financial Aid, University of Puerto Rico, Aguadilla University College, PO Box 250-160, Aguadilla, PR 00604-0160, 787-890-2681 Ext. 273.

UNIVERSITY OF PUERTO RICO AT ARECIBO
Arecibo, PR

CONTACT Mr. Luis Rodriguez, Director of Financial Aid, University of Puerto Rico at Arecibo, PO Box 4010, Arecibo, PR 00613, 787-878-2830 Ext. 2008.

UNIVERSITY OF PUERTO RICO AT BAYAMÓN
Bayamón, PR

CONTACT Financial Aid Director, University of Puerto Rico at Bayamón, 170 Carr 174 Parque Indust Minillas, Bayamon, PR 00959-1919, 787-786-2885 Ext. 2434.

UNIVERSITY OF PUERTO RICO AT HUMACAO
Humacao, PR

CONTACT Larry Cruz, Director of Financial Aid, University of Puerto Rico at Humacao, HUC Station, Humacao, PR 00791-4300, 787-850-9342.

UNIVERSITY OF PUERTO RICO AT PONCE
Ponce, PR

CONTACT Carmelo Vega Montes, Director of Financial Aid, University of Puerto Rico at Ponce, Box 7186, Ponce, PR 00732-7186, 787-844-8181. *Fax:* 787-840-8108.

UNIVERSITY OF PUERTO RICO AT UTUADO
Utuado, PR

CONTACT Edgar Salva, Director of Student Financial Assistance, University of Puerto Rico at Utuado, Call Box 2500, Utuado, PR 00641, 787-894-2828. *Fax:* 787-894-2891.

UNIVERSITY OF PUERTO RICO, CAYEY UNIVERSITY COLLEGE
Cayey, PR

CONTACT Mr. Hector Maldonado Otero, Director of Financial Aid, University of Puerto Rico, Cayey University College, Antonio Barcelo, Cayey, PR 00736, 787-738-2161. *Fax:* 787-263-0676.

UNIVERSITY OF PUERTO RICO, MAYAGÜEZ CAMPUS
Mayagüez, PR

Tuition & fees: N/R	Average undergraduate aid package: $3902

ABOUT THE INSTITUTION Commonwealth-supported, coed. Awards: bachelor's, master's, and doctoral degrees. 50 undergraduate majors. Total enrollment: 12,108. Undergraduates: 11,032. Freshmen: 2,158. Federal methodology is used as a basis for awarding need-based institutional aid.

UNDERGRADUATE EXPENSES for 2005–06 *Application fee:* $15.

GIFT AID (NEED-BASED) *Total amount:* $24,918,001 (1% federal, 10% state, 2% external sources). *Receiving aid:* Freshmen: 72% (1,555); All full-time undergraduates: 65% (7,218). *Average award:* Freshmen: $3902; Undergraduates: $3902. *Scholarships, grants, and awards:* Federal Pell, FSEOG, state, private, college/university gift aid from institutional funds.

GIFT AID (NON-NEED-BASED) *Total amount:* $117,500 (100% external sources). *Receiving aid:* Freshmen: 1% (25); Undergraduates: 1% (132). *Scholarships, grants, and awards by category: Academic Interests/Achievement:* military science. *Creative Arts/Performance:* 272 awards ($277,440 total): dance, music. *Special Achievements/Activities:* 15 awards ($16,200 total): cheerleading/drum major. *ROTC:* Army, Air Force.

LOANS *Student loans:* $7,738,548 (96% need-based, 4% non-need-based). 52% of past graduating class borrowed through all loan programs. *Average indebtedness per student:* $6400. *Average need-based loan:* Freshmen: $2625; Undergraduates: $3895. *Programs:* FFEL (Subsidized and Unsubsidized Stafford), college/university.

ATHLETIC AWARDS *Total amount:* $382,500 (100% non-need-based).

APPLYING FOR FINANCIAL AID *Required financial aid forms:* FAFSA, institution's own form, noncustodial (divorced/separated) parent's statement, business/farm supplement. *Financial aid deadline:* Continuous. *Notification date:* Continuous beginning 5/1. Students must reply within 2 weeks of notification.

CONTACT Ms. Ana I. Rodríguez, Director of Financial Aid, University of Puerto Rico, Mayagüez Campus, PO Box 9000, Mayagüez, PR 00681-9000, 787-265-3863. *Fax:* 787-265-1920. *E-mail:* a_rodriguez@rumad.uprm.edu.

UNIVERSITY OF PUERTO RICO, MEDICAL SCIENCES CAMPUS
San Juan, PR

Tuition & fees: N/R	Average undergraduate aid package: $5651

ABOUT THE INSTITUTION Commonwealth-supported, coed, primarily women. Awards: associate, bachelor's, master's, doctoral, and first professional degrees and post-bachelor's and first professional certificates (bachelor's degree is upper-level). 14 undergraduate majors. Total enrollment: 2,457. Undergraduates: 678. Entering class: . Both federal and institutional methodology are used as a basis for awarding need-based institutional aid.

UNDERGRADUATE FINANCIAL AID (Fall 2003) 340 applied for aid; of those 95% were deemed to have need. 100% of undergraduates with need received aid; of those 60% had need fully met. *Average percent of need met:* 65% (excluding resources awarded to replace EFC). *Average financial aid package:* $5651 (excluding resources awarded to replace EFC).

GIFT AID (NEED-BASED) *Total amount:* $1,567,025 (73% federal, 4% state, 23% institutional). *Receiving aid:* Entering class: 92% (122); All full-time undergraduates: 63% (324). *Average award:* Freshmen: $4292; Undergraduates: $4837. *Scholarships, grants, and awards:* Federal Pell, FSEOG, state, college/university gift aid from institutional funds, Department of Health and Human Services Scholarships.

LOANS *Student loans:* $233,470 (100% need-based). 20% of past graduating class borrowed through all loan programs. *Average indebtedness per student:* $3279. *Average need-based loan:* Freshmen: $679; Undergraduates: $2267. *Programs:* Perkins, alternative loans.

WORK-STUDY *Federal work-study:* Total amount: $30,408; 47 jobs averaging $618.

APPLYING FOR FINANCIAL AID *Required financial aid forms:* FAFSA, institution's own form. *Financial aid deadline:* 5/15. *Notification date:* Continuous beginning 8/1. Students must reply within 2 weeks of notification.

CONTACT Zoraida Figueroa, Financial Aid Director, University of Puerto Rico, Medical Sciences Campus, Terreno Centro Médico-Edificio Decanato Farmacia y Estudiantes, PO Box 365067, Rio Piedras, PR 00936-5067, 787-763-2525. *Fax:* 787-282-7117. *E-mail:* zfigueroa@rcm.upr.edu.

UNIVERSITY OF PUERTO RICO, RÍO PIEDRAS
San Juan, PR

CONTACT Mr. Efraim Williams, EDP Manager, University of Puerto Rico, Río Piedras, PO Box 23353, San Juan, PR 00931, 787-764-0000 Ext. 5573.

UNIVERSITY OF PUGET SOUND
Tacoma, WA

Tuition & fees: $26,880 **Average undergraduate aid package: $19,532**

ABOUT THE INSTITUTION Independent, coed. Awards: bachelor's, master's, and first professional degrees and post-master's certificates. 40 undergraduate majors. Total enrollment: 2,892. Undergraduates: 2,616. Freshmen: 671. Federal methodology is used as a basis for awarding need-based institutional aid.

UNDERGRADUATE EXPENSES for 2004–05 *Application fee:* $40. *Comprehensive fee:* $33,610 includes full-time tuition ($26,700), mandatory fees ($180), and room and board ($6730). *College room only:* $3680. Full-time tuition and fees vary according to course load. Room and board charges vary according to board plan and housing facility. *Part-time tuition:* $3370 per unit. Part-time tuition and fees vary according to course load. *Payment plans:* Installment, deferred payment.

FRESHMAN FINANCIAL AID (Fall 2004, est.) 510 applied for aid; of those 80% were deemed to have need. 100% of freshmen with need received aid; of those 35% had need fully met. *Average percent of need met:* 86% (excluding resources awarded to replace EFC). *Average financial aid package:* $20,408 (excluding resources awarded to replace EFC). 25% of all full-time freshmen had no need and received non-need-based gift aid.

UNDERGRADUATE FINANCIAL AID (Fall 2004, est.) 1,756 applied for aid; of those 88% were deemed to have need. 100% of undergraduates with need received aid; of those 27% had need fully met. *Average percent of need met:* 81% (excluding resources awarded to replace EFC). *Average financial aid package:* $19,532 (excluding resources awarded to replace EFC). 27% of all full-time undergraduates had no need and received non-need-based gift aid.

GIFT AID (NEED-BASED) *Total amount:* $20,667,545 (8% federal, 3% state, 84% institutional, 5% external sources). *Receiving aid:* Freshmen: 60% (400); All full-time undergraduates: 59% (1,507). *Average award:* Freshmen: $15,466; Undergraduates: $13,856. *Scholarships, grants, and awards:* Federal Pell, FSEOG, state, private, college/university gift aid from institutional funds.

GIFT AID (NON-NEED-BASED) *Total amount:* $5,018,179 (1% state, 94% institutional, 5% external sources). *Receiving aid:* Freshmen: 26% (175); Undergraduates: 28% (707). *Average Award:* Freshmen: $6766; Undergraduates: $6847. *Scholarships, grants, and awards by category: Academic Interests/Achievement:* 754 awards ($3,863,967 total): biological sciences, business, communication, computer science, English, foreign languages, general academic interests/achievements, humanities, international studies, mathematics, physical sciences, premedicine, social sciences. *Creative Arts/Performance:* 68 awards ($204,938 total): art/fine arts, debating, music, theater/drama. *Special Achievements/Activities:* 9 awards ($60,000 total): leadership, religious involvement. *Special Characteristics:* 27 awards ($480,455 total): children of faculty/staff, international students. *Tuition waivers:* Full or partial for employees or children of employees. *ROTC:* Army cooperative.

LOANS *Student loans:* $11,185,867 (92% need-based, 8% non-need-based). 63% of past graduating class borrowed through all loan programs. *Average indebtedness per student:* $24,387. *Average need-based loan:* Freshmen: $5098; Undergraduates: $5812. *Parent loans:* $4,243,662 (76% need-based, 24% non-need-based). *Programs:* FFEL (Subsidized and Unsubsidized Stafford, PLUS), Perkins, Alaska Loans.

WORK-STUDY *Federal work-study:* Total amount: $1,202,000; 596 jobs averaging $2017. *State or other work-study/employment:* Total amount: $1,772,233 (100% need-based). 799 part-time jobs averaging $2155.

APPLYING FOR FINANCIAL AID *Required financial aid form:* FAFSA. *Financial aid deadline:* Continuous. *Notification date:* Continuous beginning 3/15. Students must reply by 5/1.

CONTACT Maggie A. Mittuch, Director of Student Financial Services, University of Puget Sound, 1500 North Warner Street, Tacoma, WA 98416-1075, 253-879-3214 or toll-free 800-396-7191. *Fax:* 253-879-8508. *E-mail:* mmittuch@ups.edu.

UNIVERSITY OF REDLANDS
Redlands, CA

Tuition & fees: $25,524 **Average undergraduate aid package: $23,475**

ABOUT THE INSTITUTION Independent, coed. Awards: bachelor's and master's degrees and post-bachelor's and post-master's certificates. 42 undergraduate majors. Total enrollment: 2,451. Undergraduates: 2,352. Freshmen: 605. Federal methodology is used as a basis for awarding need-based institutional aid.

UNDERGRADUATE EXPENSES for 2004–05 *Application fee:* $45. *Comprehensive fee:* $34,220 includes full-time tuition ($25,224), mandatory fees ($300), and room and board ($8696). Room and board charges vary according to board plan and housing facility. *Part-time tuition:* $789 per credit. *Part-time fees:* $150 per term. Part-time tuition and fees vary according to course load. *Payment plan:* Installment.

FRESHMAN FINANCIAL AID (Fall 2004, est.) 499 applied for aid; of those 84% were deemed to have need. 100% of freshmen with need received aid; of those 47% had need fully met. *Average percent of need met:* 92% (excluding resources awarded to replace EFC). *Average financial aid package:* $23,508 (excluding resources awarded to replace EFC). 7% of all full-time freshmen had no need and received non-need-based gift aid.

UNDERGRADUATE FINANCIAL AID (Fall 2004, est.) 1,917 applied for aid; of those 85% were deemed to have need. 100% of undergraduates with need received aid; of those 37% had need fully met. *Average percent of need met:* 89% (excluding resources awarded to replace EFC). *Average financial aid package:* $23,475 (excluding resources awarded to replace EFC). 6% of all full-time undergraduates had no need and received non-need-based gift aid.

GIFT AID (NEED-BASED) *Total amount:* $28,777,529 (9% federal, 18% state, 71% institutional, 2% external sources). *Receiving aid:* Freshmen: 68% (412); All full-time undergraduates: 69% (1,593). *Average award:* Freshmen: $12,977; Undergraduates: $13,040. *Scholarships, grants, and awards:* Federal Pell, FSEOG, state, private, college/university gift aid from institutional funds.

GIFT AID (NON-NEED-BASED) *Total amount:* $2,511,673 (99% institutional, 1% external sources). *Receiving aid:* Freshmen: 39% (234); Undergraduates: 34% (795). *Average Award:* Freshmen: $10,311; Undergraduates: $9956. *Scholarships, grants, and awards by category: Academic Interests/Achievement:* 1,023 awards ($10,236,483 total): general academic interests/achievements. *Creative Arts/Performance:* 142 awards ($597,862 total): art/fine arts, creative writing, debating, music. *Special Achievements/Activities:* general special achievements/activities. *Special Characteristics:* international students. *Tuition waivers:* Full or partial for employees or children of employees.

LOANS *Student loans:* $8,647,421 (91% need-based, 9% non-need-based). 78% of past graduating class borrowed through all loan programs. *Average indebtedness per student:* $23,946. *Average need-based loan:* Freshmen: $4364; Undergraduates: $5090. *Parent loans:* $2,958,569 (76% need-based, 24% non-need-based). *Programs:* FFEL (Subsidized and Unsubsidized Stafford, PLUS), Perkins, college/university, alternative loans.

WORK-STUDY *Federal work-study:* Total amount: $2,089,588; 1,033 jobs averaging $2030. *State or other work-study/employment:* Total amount: $612,864 (74% need-based, 26% non-need-based). 368 part-time jobs averaging $1821.

APPLYING FOR FINANCIAL AID *Required financial aid forms:* FAFSA, state aid form. *Financial aid deadline (priority):* 2/15. *Notification date:* Continuous beginning 3/2.

CONTACT Ms. Bethann Corey, Director of Financial Aid, University of Redlands, PO Box 3080, Redlands, CA 92373-0999, 909-335-4047 or toll-free 800-455-5064. *Fax:* 909-335-4089. *E-mail:* bethann_corey@redlands.edu.

UNIVERSITY OF RHODE ISLAND
Kingston, RI

Tuition & fees (RI res): $6752 **Average undergraduate aid package: $10,136**

ABOUT THE INSTITUTION State-supported, coed. Awards: bachelor's, master's, doctoral, and first professional degrees and post-bachelor's certificates. 76 undergraduate majors. Total enrollment: 14,749. Undergraduates: 11,397. Freshmen: 2,542. Federal methodology is used as a basis for awarding need-based institutional aid.

UNDERGRADUATE EXPENSES for 2004–05 *Application fee:* $50. *Tuition, state resident:* full-time $4680; part-time $195 per credit. *Tuition, nonresident:* full-time $16,266; part-time $678 per credit. *Required fees:* full-time $2072; $62 per credit or $48 per term part-time. Full-time tuition and fees vary according to reciprocity agreements. Part-time tuition and fees vary according to reciprocity agreements. *College room and board:* $7810; *room only:* $4434. Room and board charges vary according to board plan and housing facility. *Payment plan:* Installment.

FRESHMAN FINANCIAL AID (Fall 2004, est.) 2159 applied for aid; of those 77% were deemed to have need. 76% of freshmen with need received aid; of those 77% had need fully met. *Average percent of need met:* 59% (excluding resources awarded to replace EFC). *Average financial aid package:* $9949 (excluding resources awarded to replace EFC). 7% of all full-time freshmen had no need and received non-need-based gift aid.

UNDERGRADUATE FINANCIAL AID (Fall 2004, est.) 8,111 applied for aid; of those 84% were deemed to have need. 73% of undergraduates with need received aid; of those 63% had need fully met. *Average percent of need met:* 57% (excluding resources awarded to replace EFC). *Average financial aid package:* $10,136 (excluding resources awarded to replace EFC). 4% of all full-time undergraduates had no need and received non-need-based gift aid.

GIFT AID (NEED-BASED) *Total amount:* $28,455,355 (26% federal, 11% state, 57% institutional, 6% external sources). *Receiving aid:* Freshmen: 51% (1,262); All full-time undergraduates: 51% (4,903). *Average award:* Freshmen: $5481; Undergraduates: $5306. *Scholarships, grants, and awards:* Federal Pell, FSEOG, state, private, college/university gift aid from institutional funds.

GIFT AID (NON-NEED-BASED) *Total amount:* $1,620,208 (89% institutional, 11% external sources). *Receiving aid:* Freshmen: 7% (179); Undergraduates: 5% (448). *Average Award:* Freshmen: $3356; *Undergraduates:* $3803. *Scholarships, grants, and awards by category: Academic Interests/Achievement:* general academic interests/achievements. *Creative Arts/Performance:* music. *Special Achievements/Activities:* general special achievements/activities. *Special Characteristics:* general special characteristics. *Tuition waivers:* Full or partial for minority students, employees or children of employees, senior citizens. *ROTC:* Army.

LOANS *Student loans:* $40,030,143 (82% need-based, 18% non-need-based). 64% of past graduating class borrowed through all loan programs. *Average indebtedness per student:* $14,000. *Average need-based loan:* Freshmen: $5178; Undergraduates: $5818. *Parent loans:* $13,170,969 (69% need-based, 31% non-need-based). *Programs:* Federal Direct (Subsidized and Unsubsidized Stafford, PLUS), Perkins, Federal Nursing, state, college/university.

WORK-STUDY *Federal work-study:* Total amount: $931,751; jobs available. *State or other work-study/employment:* Total amount: $6,200,000 (52% need-based, 48% non-need-based). Part-time jobs available.

ATHLETIC AWARDS *Total amount:* $4,708,224 (97% need-based, 3% non-need-based).

APPLYING FOR FINANCIAL AID *Required financial aid form:* FAFSA. *Financial aid deadline (priority):* 3/1. *Notification date:* Continuous beginning 3/31. Students must reply by 5/1 or within 2 weeks of notification.

CONTACT Mr. Horace J. Amaral Jr., Director of Enrollment Services, University of Rhode Island, Green Hall, Kingston, RI 02881, 401-874-9500.

UNIVERSITY OF RICHMOND
Richmond, VA

Tuition & fees: $27,850	Average undergraduate aid package: $20,539

ABOUT THE INSTITUTION Independent, coed. Awards: associate, bachelor's, master's, and first professional degrees and post-bachelor's certificates. 55 undergraduate majors. Total enrollment: 3,637. Undergraduates: 2,976. Freshmen: 765. Federal methodology is used as a basis for awarding need-based institutional aid.

UNDERGRADUATE EXPENSES for 2005–06 *Application fee:* $50. *Comprehensive fee:* $33,510 includes full-time tuition ($27,850) and room and board ($5660). *College room only:* $2582. Full-time tuition and fees vary according to course load and student level. Room and board charges vary according to board plan and housing facility. *Part-time tuition:* $1390 per semester hour. *Payment plans:* Installment, deferred payment.

FRESHMAN FINANCIAL AID (Fall 2004, est.) 432 applied for aid; of those 69% were deemed to have need. 99% of freshmen with need received aid; of those 81% had need fully met. *Average percent of need met:* 98% (excluding resources awarded to replace EFC). *Average financial aid package:* $20,250 (excluding resources awarded to replace EFC). 6% of all full-time freshmen had no need and received non-need-based gift aid.

UNDERGRADUATE FINANCIAL AID (Fall 2004, est.) 1,375 applied for aid; of those 75% were deemed to have need. 99% of undergraduates with need received aid; of those 76% had need fully met. *Average percent of need met:* 98% (excluding resources awarded to replace EFC). *Average financial aid package:* $20,539 (excluding resources awarded to replace EFC). 14% of all full-time undergraduates had no need and received non-need-based gift aid.

GIFT AID (NEED-BASED) *Total amount:* $16,399,409 (6% federal, 3% state, 89% institutional, 2% external sources). *Receiving aid:* Freshmen: 37% (283); All full-time undergraduates: 33% (989). *Average award:* Freshmen: $17,109; Undergraduates: $17,617. *Scholarships, grants, and awards:* Federal Pell, FSEOG, state, private, college/university gift aid from institutional funds.

GIFT AID (NON-NEED-BASED) *Total amount:* $7,923,057 (7% federal, 9% state, 77% institutional, 7% external sources). *Receiving aid:* Freshmen: 5%

(41); Undergraduates: 3% (104). *Average Award:* Freshmen: $22,051; *Undergraduates:* $13,778. *Scholarships, grants, and awards by category: Academic Interests/Achievement:* 226 awards ($4,412,148 total): biological sciences, computer science, general academic interests/achievements, mathematics, physical sciences. *Creative Arts/Performance:* 12 awards ($42,500 total): music. *Special Achievements/Activities:* 16 awards ($33,600 total): community service. *Special Characteristics:* 54 awards ($951,699 total): members of minority groups. *Tuition waivers:* Full or partial for employees or children of employees. *ROTC:* Army.

LOANS *Student loans:* $6,267,219 (35% need-based, 65% non-need-based). 42% of past graduating class borrowed through all loan programs. *Average indebtedness per student:* $16,900. *Average need-based loan:* Freshmen: $2821; Undergraduates: $3109. *Parent loans:* $3,912,641 (4% need-based, 96% non-need-based). *Programs:* Federal Direct (Subsidized and Unsubsidized Stafford, PLUS), Perkins, Charles B. Keesee Educational Loans (VA and NC residents).

WORK-STUDY *Federal work-study:* Total amount: $317,375; 239 jobs averaging $1325.

ATHLETIC AWARDS *Total amount:* $5,262,183 (15% need-based, 85% non-need-based).

APPLYING FOR FINANCIAL AID *Required financial aid forms:* FAFSA, institution's own form. *Financial aid deadline:* 2/25. *Notification date:* 4/1. Students must reply within 4 weeks of notification.

CONTACT Financial Aid Office, University of Richmond, Sarah Brunet Hall, 28 Westhampton Way, University of Richmond, VA 23173, 804-289-8438 or toll-free 800-700-1662. *Fax:* 804-287-6003. *E-mail:* finaid@richmond.edu.

UNIVERSITY OF RIO GRANDE
Rio Grande, OH

Tuition & fees (area res): $12,345	Average undergraduate aid package: $9651

ABOUT THE INSTITUTION Independent, coed. Awards: associate, bachelor's, and master's degrees. 67 undergraduate majors. Total enrollment: 2,522. Undergraduates: 2,259. Freshmen: 463. Federal methodology is used as a basis for awarding need-based institutional aid.

UNDERGRADUATE EXPENSES for 2004–05 *Application fee:* $25. *Tuition, area resident:* full-time $11,820. *Tuition, state resident:* full-time $12,030; part-time $488 per credit hour. *Tuition, nonresident:* full-time $13,050; part-time $539 per credit hour. *College room and board:* $6024. Room and board charges vary according to board plan.

FRESHMAN FINANCIAL AID (Fall 2003) 462 applied for aid; of those 84% were deemed to have need. 97% of freshmen with need received aid; of those 51% had need fully met. *Average percent of need met:* 72% (excluding resources awarded to replace EFC). *Average financial aid package:* $7343 (excluding resources awarded to replace EFC). 9% of all full-time freshmen had no need and received non-need-based gift aid.

UNDERGRADUATE FINANCIAL AID (Fall 2003) 1,511 applied for aid; of those 88% were deemed to have need. 97% of undergraduates with need received aid; of those 55% had need fully met. *Average percent of need met:* 73% (excluding resources awarded to replace EFC). *Average financial aid package:* $9651 (excluding resources awarded to replace EFC). 20% of all full-time undergraduates had no need and received non-need-based gift aid.

GIFT AID (NEED-BASED) *Total amount:* $3,655,262 (71% federal, 24% state, 3% institutional, 2% external sources). *Receiving aid:* Freshmen: 72% (364); All full-time undergraduates: 57% (1,015). *Average award:* Freshmen: $5453; Undergraduates: $4765. *Scholarships, grants, and awards:* Federal Pell, FSEOG, state, private, college/university gift aid from institutional funds.

GIFT AID (NON-NEED-BASED) *Total amount:* $2,350,684 (18% state, 72% institutional, 10% external sources). *Scholarships, grants, and awards by category: Academic Interests/Achievement:* biological sciences, business, communication, computer science, education, English, general academic interests/achievements, health fields, humanities, mathematics, physical sciences, social sciences. *Creative Arts/Performance:* art/fine arts, music. *Special Achievements/Activities:* cheerleading/drum major. *Special Characteristics:* children and siblings of alumni, children of faculty/staff, local/state students, out-of-state students. *Tuition waivers:* Full or partial for senior citizens. *ROTC:* Army cooperative.

LOANS *Student loans:* $5,648,837 (60% need-based, 40% non-need-based). 84% of past graduating class borrowed through all loan programs. *Average indebtedness per student:* $13,750. *Average need-based loan:* Freshmen: $2732; Undergraduates: $3733. *Parent loans:* $140,374 (100% non-need-based). *Programs:* Federal Direct (Subsidized and Unsubsidized Stafford, PLUS), Perkins.

WORK-STUDY *Federal work-study:* Total amount: $157,245; jobs available. *State or other work-study/employment:* Part-time jobs available.

ATHLETIC AWARDS *Total amount:* $512,997 (100% non-need-based).

APPLYING FOR FINANCIAL AID *Required financial aid form:* FAFSA. *Financial aid deadline:* Continuous. *Notification date:* Continuous beginning 2/1. Students must reply within 3 weeks of notification.

CONTACT Dr. John Hill, Director of Financial Aid, University of Rio Grande, 218 North College Avenue, Rio Grande, OH 45674, 740-245-7218 or toll-free 800-282-7201 (in-state). *Fax:* 740-245-7102.

UNIVERSITY OF ROCHESTER
Rochester, NY

Tuition & fees: $28,982	Average undergraduate aid package: $22,342

ABOUT THE INSTITUTION Independent, coed. Awards: bachelor's, master's, doctoral, and first professional degrees and post-bachelor's, post-master's, and first professional certificates. 50 undergraduate majors. Total enrollment: 8,365. Undergraduates: 4,535. Freshmen: 1,084. Institutional methodology is used as a basis for awarding need-based institutional aid.

UNDERGRADUATE EXPENSES for 2004–05 *Application fee:* $50. *Comprehensive fee:* $38,547 includes full-time tuition ($28,250), mandatory fees ($732), and room and board ($9565). *College room only:* $5460. Room and board charges vary according to board plan. *Part-time tuition:* $494 per credit hour. Part-time tuition and fees vary according to course load. *Payment plans:* Tuition prepayment, installment.

FRESHMAN FINANCIAL AID (Fall 2003) 730 applied for aid; of those 75% were deemed to have need. 100% of freshmen with need received aid; of those 100% had need fully met. *Average percent of need met:* 100% (excluding resources awarded to replace EFC). *Average financial aid package:* $22,572 (excluding resources awarded to replace EFC). 33% of all full-time freshmen had no need and received non-need-based gift aid.

UNDERGRADUATE FINANCIAL AID (Fall 2003) 2,525 applied for aid; of those 83% were deemed to have need. 100% of undergraduates with need received aid; of those 52% had need fully met. *Average percent of need met:* 86% (excluding resources awarded to replace EFC). *Average financial aid package:* $22,342 (excluding resources awarded to replace EFC). 34% of all full-time undergraduates had no need and received non-need-based gift aid.

GIFT AID (NEED-BASED) *Total amount:* $45,111,720 (5% federal, 7% state, 83% institutional, 5% external sources). *Receiving aid:* Freshmen: 56% (544); All full-time undergraduates: 55% (2,085). *Average award:* Freshmen: $19,369; Undergraduates: $17,869. *Scholarships, grants, and awards:* Federal Pell, FSEOG, state, college/university gift aid from institutional funds.

GIFT AID (NON-NEED-BASED) *Total amount:* $4,243,831 (2% state, 93% institutional, 5% external sources). *Receiving aid:* Freshmen: 13% (128); Undergraduates: 10% (381). *Average Award:* Freshmen: $7500; Undergraduates: $8313. *Scholarships, grants, and awards by category:* Academic Interests/Achievement: biological sciences, general academic interests/achievements, humanities, mathematics, physical sciences, social sciences. *Special Achievements/Activities:* leadership. *Special Characteristics:* children and siblings of alumni, children of faculty/staff, local/state students. *Tuition waivers:* Full or partial for children of alumni, employees or children of employees. *ROTC:* Naval, Air Force cooperative.

LOANS *Student loans:* $17,195,652 (87% need-based, 13% non-need-based). 68% of past graduating class borrowed through all loan programs. *Average indebtedness per student:* $19,782. *Average need-based loan:* Freshmen: $3339; Undergraduates: $4707. *Parent loans:* $6,235,196 (68% need-based, 32% non-need-based). *Programs:* Federal Direct (Subsidized and Unsubsidized Stafford, PLUS), Perkins, Federal Nursing, college/university, alternative loans.

WORK-STUDY *Federal work-study:* Total amount: $2,635,912; 1,232 jobs averaging $2139. *State or other work-study/employment:* Total amount: $513,134 (82% need-based, 18% non-need-based).

APPLYING FOR FINANCIAL AID *Required financial aid forms:* FAFSA, CSS Financial Aid PROFILE, state aid form, noncustodial (divorced/separated) parent's statement, business/farm supplement. *Financial aid deadline (priority):* 2/1. *Notification date:* 4/1. Students must reply by 5/1.

CONTACT Charles W. Puls, Director of Financial Aid, University of Rochester, Office of Financial Aid, 314 Meliora Hall, Box 270261, Rochester, NY 14627, 585-275-3226 or toll-free 888-822-2256. *Fax:* 585-756-7664. *E-mail:* cpuls@finaid.rochester.edu.

UNIVERSITY OF ST. FRANCIS
Joliet, IL

Tuition & fees: $17,670	Average undergraduate aid package: $13,698

ABOUT THE INSTITUTION Independent Roman Catholic, coed. Awards: bachelor's and master's degrees. 36 undergraduate majors. Total enrollment: 2,110. Undergraduates: 1,249. Freshmen: 157. Federal methodology is used as a basis for awarding need-based institutional aid.

UNDERGRADUATE EXPENSES for 2004–05 *Application fee:* $20. *Comprehensive fee:* $23,850 includes full-time tuition ($17,310), mandatory fees ($360), and room and board ($6180). Full-time tuition and fees vary according to course load and degree level. *Part-time tuition:* $500 per semester hour. *Part-time fees:* $15 per term. Part-time tuition and fees vary according to course load and degree level. *Payment plan:* Installment.

FRESHMAN FINANCIAL AID (Fall 2004, est.) 139 applied for aid; of those 86% were deemed to have need. 100% of freshmen with need received aid; of those 87% had need fully met. *Average percent of need met:* 85% (excluding resources awarded to replace EFC). *Average financial aid package:* $14,891 (excluding resources awarded to replace EFC). 22% of all full-time freshmen had no need and received non-need-based gift aid.

UNDERGRADUATE FINANCIAL AID (Fall 2004, est.) 968 applied for aid; of those 84% were deemed to have need. 100% of undergraduates with need received aid; of those 83% had need fully met. *Average percent of need met:* 83% (excluding resources awarded to replace EFC). *Average financial aid package:* $13,698 (excluding resources awarded to replace EFC). 21% of all full-time undergraduates had no need and received non-need-based gift aid.

GIFT AID (NEED-BASED) *Total amount:* $5,376,884 (18% federal, 34% state, 46% institutional, 2% external sources). *Receiving aid:* Freshmen: 76% (119); All full-time undergraduates: 63% (672). *Average award:* Freshmen: $8760; Undergraduates: $8276. *Scholarships, grants, and awards:* Federal Pell, FSEOG, state, private, college/university gift aid from institutional funds.

GIFT AID (NON-NEED-BASED) *Total amount:* $1,554,738 (1% state, 98% institutional, 1% external sources). *Receiving aid:* Freshmen: 73% (115); Undergraduates: 68% (730). *Average Award:* Freshmen: $6008; Undergraduates: $5086. *Scholarships, grants, and awards by category:* Academic Interests/Achievement: 1,796 awards ($3,510,642 total): biological sciences, education, general academic interests/achievements, health fields, social sciences. *Creative Arts/Performance:* 36 awards ($25,250 total): applied art and design, art/fine arts, music. *Special Achievements/Activities:* 441 awards ($2,418,766 total): community service, leadership, religious involvement. *Special Characteristics:* 269 awards ($222,079 total): children and siblings of alumni, children of educators, ethnic background, religious affiliation, siblings of current students. *Tuition waivers:* Full or partial for children of alumni, employees or children of employees.

LOANS *Student loans:* $5,091,766 (49% need-based, 51% non-need-based). 73% of past graduating class borrowed through all loan programs. *Average indebtedness per student:* $15,199. *Average need-based loan:* Freshmen: $3008; Undergraduates: $4172. *Parent loans:* $1,638,206 (36% need-based, 64% non-need-based). *Programs:* Federal Direct (Subsidized and Unsubsidized Stafford, PLUS), Perkins, alternative loans.

WORK-STUDY *Federal work-study:* Total amount: $371,308; 232 jobs averaging $1600. *State or other work-study/employment:* Total amount: $388,939 (100% non-need-based). 286 part-time jobs averaging $1360.

ATHLETIC AWARDS *Total amount:* $2,067,241 (52% need-based, 48% non-need-based).

APPLYING FOR FINANCIAL AID *Required financial aid forms:* FAFSA, institution's own form. *Financial aid deadline (priority):* 5/1. *Notification date:* Continuous. Students must reply within 3 weeks of notification.

CONTACT Mrs. Mary V. Shaw, Director of Financial Aid Services, University of St. Francis, 500 North Wilcox Street, Joliet, IL 60435-6188, 815-740-3403 or toll-free 800-735-3500. *Fax:* 815-740-3822. *E-mail:* mshaw@stfrancis.edu.

UNIVERSITY OF SAINT FRANCIS
Fort Wayne, IN

Tuition & fees: $16,460	Average undergraduate aid package: $13,031

ABOUT THE INSTITUTION Independent Roman Catholic, coed. Awards: associate, bachelor's, and master's degrees and post-bachelor's certificates. 54

undergraduate majors. Total enrollment: 1,883. Undergraduates: 1,650. Freshmen: 293. Federal methodology is used as a basis for awarding need-based institutional aid.

UNDERGRADUATE EXPENSES for 2004–05 *Application fee:* $20. *Comprehensive fee:* $21,910 includes full-time tuition ($15,800), mandatory fees ($660), and room and board ($5450). Full-time tuition and fees vary according to course load. Room and board charges vary according to housing facility. *Part-time tuition:* $500 per semester hour. Part-time tuition and fees vary according to course load. *Payment plans:* Installment, deferred payment.

FRESHMAN FINANCIAL AID (Fall 2004, est.) 292 applied for aid; of those 87% were deemed to have need. 100% of freshmen with need received aid; of those 30% had need fully met. *Average percent of need met:* 78% (excluding resources awarded to replace EFC). *Average financial aid package:* $12,856 (excluding resources awarded to replace EFC). 13% of all full-time freshmen had no need and received non-need-based gift aid.

UNDERGRADUATE FINANCIAL AID (Fall 2004, est.) 1,253 applied for aid; of those 89% were deemed to have need. 100% of undergraduates with need received aid; of those 26% had need fully met. *Average percent of need met:* 76% (excluding resources awarded to replace EFC). *Average financial aid package:* $13,031 (excluding resources awarded to replace EFC). 11% of all full-time undergraduates had no need and received non-need-based gift aid.

GIFT AID (NEED-BASED) *Total amount:* $9,079,699 (16% federal, 39% state, 35% institutional, 10% external sources). *Receiving aid:* Freshmen: 83% (253); All full-time undergraduates: 85% (1,104). *Average award:* Freshmen: $9906; Undergraduates: $9298. *Scholarships, grants, and awards:* Federal Pell, FSEOG, state, private, college/university gift aid from institutional funds.

GIFT AID (NON-NEED-BASED) *Total amount:* $975,114 (3% state, 62% institutional, 35% external sources). *Receiving aid:* Freshmen: 14% (44); Undergraduates: 10% (128). *Average Award:* Freshmen: $9843; Undergraduates: $10,117. *Scholarships, grants, and awards by category:* Academic Interests/Achievement: 468 awards ($1,695,331 total): biological sciences, general academic interests/achievements, health fields, physical sciences. *Creative Arts/Performance:* 170 awards ($430,235 total): art/fine arts, music. *Special Achievements/Activities:* 89 awards ($101,435 total): cheerleading/drum major, religious involvement. *Special Characteristics:* 148 awards ($362,326 total): children and siblings of alumni, children of faculty/staff, siblings of current students. *Tuition waivers:* Full or partial for children of alumni, employees or children of employees, senior citizens.

LOANS *Student loans:* $8,709,184 (74% need-based, 26% non-need-based). 81% of past graduating class borrowed through all loan programs. *Average indebtedness per student:* $20,005. *Average need-based loan:* Freshmen: $2545; Undergraduates: $3308. *Parent loans:* $1,511,743 (37% need-based, 63% non-need-based). *Programs:* FFEL (Subsidized and Unsubsidized Stafford, PLUS), Perkins.

WORK-STUDY *Federal work-study:* Total amount: $1,260,987; 954 jobs averaging $1444. *State or other work-study/employment:* Total amount: $32,752 (100% non-need-based). 16 part-time jobs averaging $2047.

ATHLETIC AWARDS *Total amount:* $2,073,896 (77% need-based, 23% non-need-based).

APPLYING FOR FINANCIAL AID *Required financial aid form:* FAFSA. *Financial aid deadline:* 6/30 (priority: 3/1). *Notification date:* Continuous. Students must reply within 2 weeks of notification.

CONTACT Sherri Shockey, Director of Financial Aid, University of Saint Francis, 2701 Spring Street, Fort Wayne, IN 46808, 260-434-3283 or toll-free 800-729-4732. *Fax:* 260-434-7526.

UNIVERSITY OF SAINT MARY
Leavenworth, KS

CONTACT Mrs. Judy Wiedower, Financial Aid Director, University of Saint Mary, 4100 South Fourth Street, Leavenworth, KS 66048, 913-758-6314 or toll-free 800-752-7043 (out-of-state). *Fax:* 913-758-6146. *E-mail:* wiedower@hub.smcks.edu.

UNIVERSITY OF ST. THOMAS
St. Paul, MN

Tuition & fees: $21,828	Average undergraduate aid package: $17,696

ABOUT THE INSTITUTION Independent Roman Catholic, coed. Awards: bachelor's, master's, doctoral, and first professional degrees and post-bachelor's and post-master's certificates. 83 undergraduate majors. Total enrollment: 10,474.

Undergraduates: 5,302. Freshmen: 1,162. Both federal and institutional methodology are used as a basis for awarding need-based institutional aid.

UNDERGRADUATE EXPENSES for 2004–05 *Comprehensive fee:* $28,370 includes full-time tuition ($21,440), mandatory fees ($388), and room and board ($6542). *College room only:* $4040. Full-time tuition and fees vary according to course load. Room and board charges vary according to board plan and housing facility. *Part-time tuition:* $670 per credit hour. Part-time tuition and fees vary according to course load. *Payment plans:* Installment, deferred payment.

FRESHMAN FINANCIAL AID (Fall 2004, est.) 865 applied for aid; of those 75% were deemed to have need. 100% of freshmen with need received aid; of those 29% had need fully met. *Average percent of need met:* 86% (excluding resources awarded to replace EFC). *Average financial aid package:* $17,086 (excluding resources awarded to replace EFC). 17% of all full-time freshmen had no need and received non-need-based gift aid.

UNDERGRADUATE FINANCIAL AID (Fall 2004, est.) 3,260 applied for aid; of those 79% were deemed to have need. 100% of undergraduates with need received aid; of those 27% had need fully met. *Average percent of need met:* 86% (excluding resources awarded to replace EFC). *Average financial aid package:* $17,696 (excluding resources awarded to replace EFC). 12% of all full-time undergraduates had no need and received non-need-based gift aid.

GIFT AID (NEED-BASED) *Total amount:* $24,562,170 (11% federal, 14% state, 72% institutional, 3% external sources). *Receiving aid:* Freshmen: 51% (640); All full-time undergraduates: 52% (2,465). *Average award:* Freshmen: $10,325; Undergraduates: $9341. *Scholarships, grants, and awards:* Federal Pell, FSEOG, state, private, college/university gift aid from institutional funds.

GIFT AID (NON-NEED-BASED) *Total amount:* $13,304,010 (2% state, 93% institutional, 5% external sources). *Receiving aid:* Freshmen: 14% (170); Undergraduates: 11% (505). *Average Award:* Freshmen: $8116; Undergraduates: $6945. *Scholarships, grants, and awards by category:* Academic Interests/Achievement: 2,008 awards ($10,275,649 total): biological sciences, business, education, English, general academic interests/achievements, humanities, international studies, mathematics, physical sciences, religion/biblical studies, social sciences. *Creative Arts/Performance:* 54 awards ($129,069 total): journalism/publications, music. *Special Characteristics:* 202 awards ($2,134,492 total): general special characteristics. *Tuition waivers:* Full or partial for employees or children of employees, senior citizens. *ROTC:* Army cooperative, Air Force.

LOANS *Student loans:* $22,639,046 (64% need-based, 36% non-need-based). 67% of past graduating class borrowed through all loan programs. *Average indebtedness per student:* $23,839. *Average need-based loan:* Freshmen: $3233; Undergraduates: $4442. *Parent loans:* $3,873,404 (22% need-based, 78% non-need-based). *Programs:* FFEL (Subsidized and Unsubsidized Stafford, PLUS), Perkins, state, alternative loans.

WORK-STUDY *Federal work-study:* Total amount: $2,568,479; 916 jobs averaging $2804. *State or other work-study/employment:* Total amount: $3,290,550 (100% need-based). 1,167 part-time jobs averaging $2820.

APPLYING FOR FINANCIAL AID *Required financial aid form:* FAFSA. *Financial aid deadline (priority):* 4/1. *Notification date:* Continuous beginning 3/1. Students must reply within 3 weeks of notification.

CONTACT Ms. Ginny Reese, Associate Director, Student Financial Services, University of St. Thomas, 2115 Summit Avenue, FOL100, St. Paul, MN 55105-1096, 651-962-6557 or toll-free 800-328-6819 Ext. 26150. *Fax:* 651-962-6599. *E-mail:* vmreese@stthomas.edu.

UNIVERSITY OF ST. THOMAS
Houston, TX

Tuition & fees: $16,312	Average undergraduate aid package: $11,396

ABOUT THE INSTITUTION Independent Roman Catholic, coed. Awards: bachelor's, master's, doctoral, and first professional degrees. 36 undergraduate majors. Total enrollment: 3,648. Undergraduates: 1,910. Freshmen: 303. Federal methodology is used as a basis for awarding need-based institutional aid.

UNDERGRADUATE EXPENSES for 2004–05 *Application fee:* $35. *Comprehensive fee:* $23,612 includes full-time tuition ($16,200), mandatory fees ($112), and room and board ($7300). *College room only:* $4000. Full-time tuition and fees vary according to course load. Room and board charges vary according to board plan and housing facility. *Part-time tuition:* $540 per credit hour. *Part-time fees:* $30 per term. Part-time tuition and fees vary according to course load. *Payment plans:* Installment, deferred payment.

FRESHMAN FINANCIAL AID (Fall 2004, est.) 210 applied for aid; of those 84% were deemed to have need. 99% of freshmen with need received aid; of those 7% had need fully met. *Average percent of need met:* 66% (excluding resources

awarded to replace EFC). *Average financial aid package:* $12,523 (excluding resources awarded to replace EFC). 27% of all full-time freshmen had no need and received non-need-based gift aid.

UNDERGRADUATE FINANCIAL AID (Fall 2004, est.) 869 applied for aid; of those 89% were deemed to have need. 99% of undergraduates with need received aid; of those 12% had need fully met. *Average percent of need met:* 65% (excluding resources awarded to replace EFC). *Average financial aid package:* $11,396 (excluding resources awarded to replace EFC). 19% of all full-time undergraduates had no need and received non-need-based gift aid.

GIFT AID (NEED-BASED) *Total amount:* $6,310,373 (22% federal, 32% state, 46% institutional). *Receiving aid:* Freshmen: 57% (171); All full-time undergraduates: 55% (727). *Average award:* Freshmen: $9753; Undergraduates: $8250. *Scholarships, grants, and awards:* Federal Pell, FSEOG, state, college/university gift aid from institutional funds.

GIFT AID (NON-NEED-BASED) *Total amount:* $2,449,915 (1% state, 81% institutional, 18% external sources). *Receiving aid:* Freshmen: 18% (55); Undergraduates: 11% (146). *Average Award: Freshmen:* $7761; *Undergraduates:* $6792. *Scholarships, grants, and awards by category: Academic Interests/ Achievement:* 315 awards ($1,990,331 total): biological sciences, English, foreign languages, general academic interests/achievements, mathematics, physical sciences, social sciences. *Creative Arts/Performance:* debating, music, theater/ drama. *Special Achievements/Activities:* community service. *Special Characteristics:* children of educators, children of faculty/staff, general special characteristics, international students, members of minority groups, relatives of clergy, religious affiliation. *Tuition waivers:* Full or partial for employees or children of employees, senior citizens. *ROTC:* Army cooperative.

LOANS *Student loans:* $4,581,137 (54% need-based, 46% non-need-based). 49% of past graduating class borrowed through all loan programs. *Average indebtedness per student:* $20,491. *Average need-based loan:* Freshmen: $2768; Undergraduates: $3865. *Parent loans:* $1,823,685 (100% non-need-based). *Programs:* FFEL (Subsidized and Unsubsidized Stafford, PLUS), Perkins.

WORK-STUDY *Federal work-study:* Total amount: $114,300; 39 jobs averaging $2931. *State or other work-study/employment:* Total amount: $15,000 (100% need-based). 5 part-time jobs averaging $3000.

APPLYING FOR FINANCIAL AID *Required financial aid form:* FAFSA. *Financial aid deadline (priority):* 3/1. *Notification date:* Continuous. Students must reply within 4 weeks of notification.

CONTACT Scott Moore, Dean of Scholarships and Financial Aid, University of St. Thomas, 3800 Montrose Boulevard, Houston, TX 77006-4696, 713-942-3465 or toll-free 800-856-8565. *Fax:* 713-525-2142. *E-mail:* finaid@stthom.edu.

UNIVERSITY OF SAN DIEGO
San Diego, CA

Tuition & fees: $26,856	Average undergraduate aid package: $21,804

ABOUT THE INSTITUTION Independent Roman Catholic, coed. Awards: bachelor's, master's, doctoral, and first professional degrees and post-bachelor's, post-master's, and first professional certificates. 34 undergraduate majors. Total enrollment: 7,486. Undergraduates: 4,908. Freshmen: 1,174. Both federal and institutional methodology are used as a basis for awarding need-based institutional aid.

UNDERGRADUATE EXPENSES for 2004–05 *Application fee:* $55. *Comprehensive fee:* $37,046 includes full-time tuition ($26,660), mandatory fees ($196), and room and board ($10,190). *College room only:* $7670. Room and board charges vary according to board plan and housing facility. *Part-time tuition:* $920 per unit. Part-time tuition and fees vary according to course load. *Payment plan:* Installment.

FRESHMAN FINANCIAL AID (Fall 2003) 830 applied for aid; of those 71% were deemed to have need. 100% of freshmen with need received aid; of those 58% had need fully met. *Average percent of need met:* 100% (excluding resources awarded to replace EFC). *Average financial aid package:* $20,708 (excluding resources awarded to replace EFC). 18% of all full-time freshmen had no need and received non-need-based gift aid.

UNDERGRADUATE FINANCIAL AID (Fall 2003) 3,420 applied for aid; of those 73% were deemed to have need. 100% of undergraduates with need received aid; of those 48% had need fully met. *Average percent of need met:* 100% (excluding resources awarded to replace EFC). *Average financial aid package:* $21,804 (excluding resources awarded to replace EFC). 15% of all full-time undergraduates had no need and received non-need-based gift aid.

GIFT AID (NEED-BASED) *Total amount:* $39,402,427 (10% federal, 15% state, 72% institutional, 3% external sources). *Receiving aid:* Freshmen: 55% (574); All full-time undergraduates: 51% (2,398). *Average award:* Freshmen: $17,508;

Undergraduates: $16,473. *Scholarships, grants, and awards:* Federal Pell, FSEOG, state, private, college/university gift aid from institutional funds.

GIFT AID (NON-NEED-BASED) *Total amount:* $6,913,404 (39% federal, 55% institutional, 6% external sources). *Receiving aid:* Freshmen: 20% (207); Undergraduates: 16% (736). *Average Award:* Freshmen: $6268; *Undergraduates:* $5241. *Scholarships, grants, and awards by category: Academic Interests/ Achievement:* 1,035 awards ($7,708,847 total): general academic interests/ achievements. *Creative Arts/Performance:* 15 awards ($95,150 total): music. *Special Characteristics:* 87 awards ($1,323,521 total): children of faculty/staff. *Tuition waivers:* Full or partial for employees or children of employees. *ROTC:* Army cooperative, Naval, Air Force cooperative.

LOANS *Student loans:* $14,893,836 (90% need-based, 10% non-need-based). 45% of past graduating class borrowed through all loan programs. *Average indebtedness per student:* $26,665. *Average need-based loan:* Freshmen: $2620; Undergraduates: $4347. *Parent loans:* $14,493,786 (77% need-based, 23% non-need-based). *Programs:* FFEL (Subsidized and Unsubsidized Stafford, PLUS), Perkins, Federal Nursing, college/university.

WORK-STUDY *Federal work-study:* Total amount: $2,086,640; 816 jobs averaging $2557. *State or other work-study/employment:* Total amount: $609,395 (65% need-based, 35% non-need-based). 117 part-time jobs averaging $5208.

ATHLETIC AWARDS *Total amount:* $2,903,622 (13% need-based, 87% non-need-based).

APPLYING FOR FINANCIAL AID *Required financial aid forms:* FAFSA, institution's own form. *Financial aid deadline (priority):* 2/20. *Notification date:* Continuous beginning 3/1. Students must reply within 3 weeks of notification.

CONTACT Judith Lewis Logue, Director of Financial Aid Services, University of San Diego, 5998 Alcala Park, San Diego, CA 92110-2492, 619-260-4514 or toll-free 800-248-4873.

UNIVERSITY OF SAN FRANCISCO
San Francisco, CA

Tuition & fees: $26,840	Average undergraduate aid package: $19,713

ABOUT THE INSTITUTION Independent Roman Catholic (Jesuit), coed. Awards: bachelor's, master's, doctoral, and first professional degrees and post-master's certificates. 64 undergraduate majors. Total enrollment: 8,271. Undergraduates: 4,967. Freshmen: 933. Federal methodology is used as a basis for awarding need-based institutional aid.

UNDERGRADUATE EXPENSES for 2005–06 *Application fee:* $55. *Comprehensive fee:* $37,080 includes full-time tuition ($26,680), mandatory fees ($160), and room and board ($10,240). *College room only:* $6500. Full-time tuition and fees vary according to program. Room and board charges vary according to board plan. *Part-time tuition:* $955 per credit. *Part-time fees:* $160 per year. *Payment plans:* Tuition prepayment, installment, deferred payment.

FRESHMAN FINANCIAL AID (Fall 2004, est.) 667 applied for aid; of those 85% were deemed to have need. 96% of freshmen with need received aid; of those 14% had need fully met. *Average percent of need met:* 70% (excluding resources awarded to replace EFC). *Average financial aid package:* $19,459 (excluding resources awarded to replace EFC). 6% of all full-time freshmen had no need and received non-need-based gift aid.

UNDERGRADUATE FINANCIAL AID (Fall 2004, est.) 2,750 applied for aid; of those 91% were deemed to have need. 98% of undergraduates with need received aid; of those 20% had need fully met. *Average percent of need met:* 74% (excluding resources awarded to replace EFC). *Average financial aid package:* $19,713 (excluding resources awarded to replace EFC). 7% of all full-time undergraduates had no need and received non-need-based gift aid.

GIFT AID (NEED-BASED) *Total amount:* $30,182,548 (11% federal, 22% state, 66% institutional, 1% external sources). *Receiving aid:* Freshmen: 49% (452); All full-time undergraduates: 50% (2,084). *Average award:* Freshmen: $16,227; Undergraduates: $14,336. *Scholarships, grants, and awards:* Federal Pell, FSEOG, state, private, college/university gift aid from institutional funds.

GIFT AID (NON-NEED-BASED) *Total amount:* $5,372,017 (15% federal, 70% institutional, 15% external sources). *Receiving aid:* Freshmen: 27% (250); Undergraduates: 11% (474). *Average Award: Freshmen:* $13,751; *Undergraduates:* $12,679. *Scholarships, grants, and awards by category: Academic Interests/Achievement:* general academic interests/achievements, military science. *Creative Arts/Performance:* general creative arts/performance. *Special Achievements/ Activities:* general special achievements/activities. *Tuition waivers:* Full or partial for employees or children of employees. *ROTC:* Army, Air Force cooperative.

LOANS *Student loans:* $19,867,802 (53% need-based, 47% non-need-based). 59% of past graduating class borrowed through all loan programs. *Average*

---

indebtedness per student: $24,718. ***Average need-based loan:*** Freshmen: $3693; Undergraduates: $4874. ***Parent loans:*** $13,459,467 (100% non-need-based). ***Programs:*** Federal Direct (Subsidized and Unsubsidized Stafford, PLUS), Perkins, Federal Nursing, college/university.

WORK-STUDY *Federal work-study:* Total amount: $2,342,460; 680 jobs averaging $3441. ***State or other work-study/employment:*** Total amount: $694,000 (100% non-need-based). 202 part-time jobs averaging $3428.

ATHLETIC AWARDS *Total amount:* $3,538,240 (100% non-need-based).

APPLYING FOR FINANCIAL AID *Required financial aid form:* FAFSA. ***Financial aid deadline (priority):*** 2/15. ***Notification date:*** Continuous beginning 4/1. Students must reply within 4 weeks of notification.

CONTACT Ms. Susan Murphy, Director of Financial Aid, University of San Francisco, 2130 Fulton Street, San Francisco, CA 94117-1080, 415-422-2620 or toll-free 415-422-6563 (in-state), 800-CALL USF (out-of-state). *Fax:* 415-422-6084. *E-mail:* murphy@usfca.edu.

UNIVERSITY OF SCIENCE AND ARTS OF OKLAHOMA
Chickasha, OK

Tuition & fees (OK res): $3180	Average undergraduate aid package: $6802

ABOUT THE INSTITUTION State-supported, coed. Awards: bachelor's degrees. 25 undergraduate majors. Total enrollment: 1,414. Undergraduates: 1,414. Freshmen: 262. Federal methodology is used as a basis for awarding need-based institutional aid.

UNDERGRADUATE EXPENSES for 2004–05 *Application fee:* $15. ***Tuition, state resident:*** full-time $2280; part-time $76 per hour. ***Tuition, nonresident:*** full-time $6600; part-time $220 per hour. ***Required fees:*** full-time $900; $30 per hour. Full-time tuition and fees vary according to course load. Part-time tuition and fees vary according to course load. ***College room and board:*** $3990; ***room only:*** $2100. Room and board charges vary according to board plan and housing facility. ***Payment plan:*** Installment.

FRESHMAN FINANCIAL AID (Fall 2004, est.) 211 applied for aid; of those 85% were deemed to have need. 100% of freshmen with need received aid; of those 19% had need fully met. *Average percent of need met:* 70% (excluding resources awarded to replace EFC). *Average financial aid package:* $6452 (excluding resources awarded to replace EFC). 18% of all full-time freshmen had no need and received non-need-based gift aid.

UNDERGRADUATE FINANCIAL AID (Fall 2004, est.) 820 applied for aid; of those 87% were deemed to have need. 100% of undergraduates with need received aid; of those 19% had need fully met. *Average percent of need met:* 70% (excluding resources awarded to replace EFC). *Average financial aid package:* $6802 (excluding resources awarded to replace EFC). 16% of all full-time undergraduates had no need and received non-need-based gift aid.

GIFT AID (NEED-BASED) *Total amount:* $2,992,882 (63% federal, 16% state, 6% institutional, 15% external sources). ***Receiving aid:*** Freshmen: 71% (177); All full-time undergraduates: 64% (671). ***Average award:*** Freshmen: $5168; Undergraduates: $4978. ***Scholarships, grants, and awards:*** Federal Pell, FSEOG, state, private, college/university gift aid from institutional funds, USAO Foundation Grants.

GIFT AID (NON-NEED-BASED) *Total amount:* $307,587 (25% state, 37% institutional, 38% external sources). ***Receiving aid:*** Freshmen: 7% (17); Undergraduates: 4% (46). ***Average Award:*** Freshmen: $3389; Undergraduates: $3343. ***Scholarships, grants, and awards by category:*** Academic Interests/Achievement: 109 awards ($135,242 total): general academic interests/achievements. Creative Arts/Performance: 27 awards ($26,500 total): art/fine arts, music, theater/drama. Special Achievements/Activities: 11 awards ($6768 total): cheerleading/drum major, leadership. Special Characteristics: 43 awards ($141,319 total): international students, out-of-state students, previous college experience. ***Tuition waivers:*** Full or partial for employees or children of employees, senior citizens.

LOANS *Student loans:* $2,063,960 (76% need-based, 24% non-need-based). 61% of past graduating class borrowed through all loan programs. *Average indebtedness per student:* $11,940. *Average need-based loan:* Freshmen: $2033; Undergraduates: $2702. ***Parent loans:*** $128,924 (16% need-based, 84% non-need-based). ***Programs:*** FFEL (Subsidized and Unsubsidized Stafford, PLUS), Perkins.

WORK-STUDY *Federal work-study:* Total amount: $267,502; 220 jobs averaging $1500.

ATHLETIC AWARDS *Total amount:* $492,164 (55% need-based, 45% non-need-based).

APPLYING FOR FINANCIAL AID *Required financial aid forms:* FAFSA, institution's own form. ***Financial aid deadline (priority):*** 3/15. ***Notification date:*** Continuous beginning 3/15. Students must reply within 4 weeks of notification.

CONTACT Nancy Moats, Director of Financial Aid, University of Science and Arts of Oklahoma, 1727 West Alabama, Chickasha, OK 73018-5322, 405-574-1251 or toll-free 800-933-8726 Ext. 1212. *Fax:* 405-574-1220.

THE UNIVERSITY OF SCRANTON
Scranton, PA

Tuition & fees: $22,474	Average undergraduate aid package: $15,558

ABOUT THE INSTITUTION Independent Roman Catholic (Jesuit), coed. Awards: associate, bachelor's, master's, and doctoral degrees and post-bachelor's and post-master's certificates. 55 undergraduate majors. Total enrollment: 4,795. Undergraduates: 4,045. Freshmen: 965. Federal methodology is used as a basis for awarding need-based institutional aid.

UNDERGRADUATE EXPENSES for 2004–05 *Application fee:* $40. ***Comprehensive fee:*** $31,998 includes full-time tuition ($22,214), mandatory fees ($260), and room and board ($9524). ***College room only:*** $5564. Room and board charges vary according to board plan and housing facility. ***Part-time tuition:*** $618 per credit. ***Part-time fees:*** $25 per term. ***Payment plan:*** Installment.

FRESHMAN FINANCIAL AID (Fall 2004, est.) 824 applied for aid; of those 84% were deemed to have need. 99% of freshmen with need received aid; of those 11% had need fully met. *Average percent of need met:* 77% (excluding resources awarded to replace EFC). *Average financial aid package:* $15,825 (excluding resources awarded to replace EFC). 9% of all full-time freshmen had no need and received non-need-based gift aid.

UNDERGRADUATE FINANCIAL AID (Fall 2004, est.) 2,961 applied for aid; of those 87% were deemed to have need. 97% of undergraduates with need received aid; of those 13% had need fully met. *Average percent of need met:* 72% (excluding resources awarded to replace EFC). *Average financial aid package:* $15,558 (excluding resources awarded to replace EFC). 6% of all full-time undergraduates had no need and received non-need-based gift aid.

GIFT AID (NEED-BASED) *Total amount:* $32,408,330 (7% federal, 9% state, 81% institutional, 3% external sources). ***Receiving aid:*** Freshmen: 68% (656); All full-time undergraduates: 64% (2,438). ***Average award:*** Freshmen: $12,204; Undergraduates: $11,250. ***Scholarships, grants, and awards:*** Federal Pell, FSEOG, state, private, college/university gift aid from institutional funds.

GIFT AID (NON-NEED-BASED) *Total amount:* $3,049,009 (76% institutional, 24% external sources). ***Receiving aid:*** Freshmen: 4% (39); Undergraduates: 5% (190). ***Average Award:*** Freshmen: $9163; Undergraduates: $7813. ***Scholarships, grants, and awards by category:*** Academic Interests/Achievement: 1,988 awards ($14,018,940 total): general academic interests/achievements, military science. ***Special Characteristics:*** children of educators, children of faculty/staff, members of minority groups, siblings of current students. ***Tuition waivers:*** Full or partial for employees or children of employees, senior citizens. ***ROTC:*** Army, Air Force cooperative.

LOANS *Student loans:* $17,572,662 (71% need-based, 29% non-need-based). 63% of past graduating class borrowed through all loan programs. *Average indebtedness per student:* $15,800. *Average need-based loan:* Freshmen: $3352; Undergraduates: $4375. ***Parent loans:*** $9,074,230 (31% need-based, 69% non-need-based). ***Programs:*** FFEL (Subsidized and Unsubsidized Stafford, PLUS), Perkins, Federal Nursing.

WORK-STUDY *Federal work-study:* Total amount: $1,744,021; 1,005 jobs averaging $1800. ***State or other work-study/employment:*** Total amount: $396,382 (16% need-based, 84% non-need-based). 255 part-time jobs averaging $1500.

APPLYING FOR FINANCIAL AID *Required financial aid form:* FAFSA. ***Financial aid deadline (priority):*** 2/15. ***Notification date:*** Continuous beginning 3/15. Students must reply by 5/1.

CONTACT Mr. William R. Burke, Director of Financial Aid, The University of Scranton, St. Thomas Hall 401, Scranton, PA 18510, 570-941-7887 or toll-free 888-SCRANTON. *Fax:* 570-941-4370. *E-mail:* finaid@scranton.edu.

UNIVERSITY OF SIOUX FALLS
Sioux Falls, SD

Tuition & fees: $14,900	Average undergraduate aid package: N/A

ABOUT THE INSTITUTION Independent American Baptist Churches in the USA, coed. Awards: associate, bachelor's, master's, and doctoral degrees. 57

undergraduate majors. Total enrollment: 1,586. Undergraduates: 1,304. Freshmen: 244. Federal methodology is used as a basis for awarding need-based institutional aid.

UNDERGRADUATE EXPENSES for 2004–05 *Application fee:* $25. *Comprehensive fee:* $19,250 includes full-time tuition ($14,900) and room and board ($4350). *College room only:* $1900. Full-time tuition and fees vary according to course load. Room and board charges vary according to board plan and housing facility. *Part-time tuition:* $250 per semester hour. Part-time tuition and fees vary according to course load. *Payment plan:* Installment.

GIFT AID (NEED-BASED) *Total amount:* $4,439,465 (23% federal, 77% institutional). *Scholarships, grants, and awards:* Federal Pell, FSEOG, private, college/university gift aid from institutional funds.

GIFT AID (NON-NEED-BASED) *Total amount:* $634,210 (100% external sources). *Scholarships, grants, and awards by category:* Academic Interests/Achievement: 477 awards ($1,337,300 total): biological sciences, business, communication, computer science, education, engineering/technologies, English, general academic interests/achievements, humanities, mathematics, physical sciences, premedicine, religion/biblical studies, social sciences. Creative Arts/Performance: 121 awards ($260,000 total): art/fine arts, music, theater/drama. Special Achievements/Activities: cheerleading/drum major, leadership. Special Characteristics: 487 awards ($684,135 total): children and siblings of alumni, children of faculty/staff, international students, local/state students, out-of-state students, religious affiliation, siblings of current students, spouses of current students. *Tuition waivers:* Full or partial for employees or children of employees.

LOANS *Student loans:* $7,875,012 (45% need-based, 55% non-need-based). *Parent loans:* $714,983 (100% non-need-based). *Programs:* FFEL (Subsidized and Unsubsidized Stafford, PLUS), Perkins, alternative loans.

WORK-STUDY *Federal work-study:* Total amount: $229,471; 130 jobs averaging $1200.

ATHLETIC AWARDS *Total amount:* $1,090,725 (100% non-need-based).

APPLYING FOR FINANCIAL AID *Required financial aid form:* FAFSA. *Financial aid deadline (priority):* 3/1. *Notification date:* Continuous. Students must reply within 2 weeks of notification.

CONTACT Rachel Gunn, Financial Aid Counselor, University of Sioux Falls, 1101 West 22nd Street, Sioux Falls, SD 57105-1699, 605-331-6623 or toll-free 800-888-1047. *Fax:* 605-331-6615. *E-mail:* rachel.gunn@usiouxfalls.edu.

UNIVERSITY OF SOUTH ALABAMA
Mobile, AL

ABOUT THE INSTITUTION State-supported, coed. Awards: bachelor's, master's, doctoral, and first professional degrees and post-bachelor's and post-master's certificates. 47 undergraduate majors. Total enrollment: 13,340. Undergraduates: 10,350. Freshmen: 1,422.

GIFT AID (NEED-BASED) *Scholarships, grants, and awards:* Federal Pell, FSEOG, state, college/university gift aid from institutional funds.

GIFT AID (NON-NEED-BASED) *Scholarships, grants, and awards by category:* Academic Interests/Achievement: business, computer science, general academic interests/achievements, humanities, international studies, military science. Creative Arts/Performance: art/fine arts, journalism/publications, music, theater/drama. Special Achievements/Activities: general special achievements/activities, hobbies/interests, junior miss, leadership. Special Characteristics: children and siblings of alumni, children of faculty/staff, members of minority groups.

LOANS *Programs:* FFEL (Subsidized and Unsubsidized Stafford, PLUS), Perkins.

WORK-STUDY *Federal work-study:* Total amount: $503,318; jobs available (averaging $3000). *State or other work-study/employment:* Part-time jobs available.

APPLYING FOR FINANCIAL AID *Required financial aid forms:* FAFSA, institution's own form.

CONTACT Financial Aid Office, University of South Alabama, 307 University Boulevard, Mobile, AL 36688-0002, 251-460-6231 or toll-free 800-872-5247. *Fax:* 251-460-6517.

UNIVERSITY OF SOUTH CAROLINA
Columbia, SC

Tuition & fees (SC res): $5778	Average undergraduate aid package: $9188

ABOUT THE INSTITUTION State-supported, coed. Awards: associate, bachelor's, master's, doctoral, and first professional degrees and post-bachelor's and post-master's certificates. 65 undergraduate majors. Total enrollment: 25,597. Undergraduates: 17,690. Freshmen: 3,404. Federal methodology is used as a basis for awarding need-based institutional aid.

UNDERGRADUATE EXPENSES for 2004–05 *Application fee:* $40. *Tuition, state resident:* full-time $5548; part-time $260 per credit hour. *Tuition, nonresident:* full-time $14,886; part-time $677 per credit hour. *Required fees:* full-time $230; $10 per credit hour. Full-time tuition and fees vary according to program and reciprocity agreements. *College room and board:* $5590; *room only:* $3280. Room and board charges vary according to board plan, housing facility, and location. *Payment plans:* Installment, deferred payment.

GIFT AID (NEED-BASED) *Total amount:* $40,514,683 (29% federal, 53% state, 10% institutional, 8% external sources). *Receiving aid:* Freshmen: 22% (750); All full-time undergraduates: 26% (3,811). *Average award:* Freshmen: $3524; Undergraduates: $3352. *Scholarships, grants, and awards:* Federal Pell, FSEOG, state, private, college/university gift aid from institutional funds, United Negro College Fund, Federal Nursing.

GIFT AID (NON-NEED-BASED) *Total amount:* $20,485,236 (67% state, 22% institutional, 11% external sources). *Receiving aid:* Freshmen: 42% (1,432); Undergraduates: 26% (3,802). *Average Award:* Freshmen: $5712; Undergraduates: $5990. *Scholarships, grants, and awards by category:* Academic Interests/Achievement: 3,776 awards ($7,883,424 total): area/ethnic studies, biological sciences, business, communication, computer science, education, engineering/technologies, English, foreign languages, general academic interests/achievements, health fields, humanities, international studies, library science, mathematics, military science, physical sciences, premedicine, religion/biblical studies, social sciences. Creative Arts/Performance: 496 awards ($570,749 total): art/fine arts, debating, journalism/publications, music, theater/drama. Special Achievements/Activities: 74 awards ($48,350 total): cheerleading/drum major, community service, general special achievements/activities, leadership, religious involvement. Special Characteristics: 968 awards ($2,915,706 total): adult students, children and siblings of alumni, children of faculty/staff, children of union members/company employees, children of workers in trades, children with a deceased or disabled parent, ethnic background, first-generation college students, general special characteristics, handicapped students, international students, local/state students, members of minority groups, out-of-state students, relatives of clergy, religious affiliation, spouses of deceased or disabled public servants. *Tuition waivers:* Full or partial for employees or children of employees, senior citizens. *ROTC:* Army, Air Force.

LOANS *Student loans:* $42,236,657 (48% need-based, 52% non-need-based). 51% of past graduating class borrowed through all loan programs. *Average indebtedness per student:* $17,828. *Average need-based loan:* Freshmen: $1854; Undergraduates: $3471. *Parent loans:* $7,157,682 (91% need-based, 9% non-need-based). *Programs:* FFEL (Subsidized and Unsubsidized Stafford, PLUS), Perkins, Federal Nursing.

ATHLETIC AWARDS *Total amount:* $4,293,189 (47% need-based, 53% non-need-based).

APPLYING FOR FINANCIAL AID *Required financial aid form:* FAFSA. *Financial aid deadline (priority):* 4/1. *Notification date:* Continuous beginning 4/1.

CONTACT Dr. Ed Miller, Financial Aid Director, University of South Carolina, 1714 College Street, Columbia, SC 29208, 803-777-8134 or toll-free 800-868-5872 (in-state). *Fax:* 803-777-0941.

UNIVERSITY OF SOUTH CAROLINA AIKEN
Aiken, SC

ABOUT THE INSTITUTION State-supported, coed. Awards: bachelor's and master's degrees. 19 undergraduate majors. Total enrollment: 3,382. Undergraduates: 3,268. Freshmen: 620.

GIFT AID (NEED-BASED) *Scholarships, grants, and awards:* Federal Pell, FSEOG, state.

GIFT AID (NON-NEED-BASED) *Scholarships, grants, and awards by category:* Academic Interests/Achievement: biological sciences, business, communication, computer science, education, engineering/technologies, English, general academic interests/achievements, humanities, mathematics, physical sciences, social sciences. Creative Arts/Performance: art/fine arts, creative writing, journalism/publications, music. Special Achievements/Activities: cheerleading/drum major.

LOANS *Programs:* FFEL (Subsidized and Unsubsidized Stafford, PLUS), Perkins.

WORK-STUDY Federal work-study jobs available. *State or other work-study/employment:* Part-time jobs available.

APPLYING FOR FINANCIAL AID *Required financial aid form:* FAFSA.

CONTACT Financial Aid Office, University of South Carolina Aiken, 471 University Parkway, Aiken, SC 29801, 803-641-3476 or toll-free 888-WOW-USCA.

UNIVERSITY OF SOUTH CAROLINA BEAUFORT
Beaufort, SC

ABOUT THE INSTITUTION State-supported, coed. Awards: associate and bachelor's degrees (offers courses for bachelor's degrees awarded by other University of South Carolina system schools). 1 undergraduate major. Total enrollment: 1,277. Undergraduates: 1,277. Freshmen: 178.

GIFT AID (NEED-BASED) *Scholarships, grants, and awards:* Federal Pell, FSEOG, state, private, college/university gift aid from institutional funds.

LOANS *Programs:* FFEL (Subsidized and Unsubsidized Stafford, PLUS), Perkins.

WORK-STUDY *Federal work-study:* 30 jobs averaging $3000.

APPLYING FOR FINANCIAL AID *Required financial aid form:* FAFSA.

CONTACT Sally Maybin, Financial Aid Director, University of South Carolina Beaufort, 801 Carteret Street, Beaufort, SC 29902, 843-521-3104. *Fax:* 843-521-4194. *E-mail:* smaybin@gwm.sc.edu.

UNIVERSITY OF SOUTH CAROLINA UPSTATE
Spartanburg, SC

Tuition & fees (SC res): $6186   **Average undergraduate aid package: $8244**

ABOUT THE INSTITUTION State-supported, coed. Awards: associate, bachelor's, and master's degrees. 20 undergraduate majors. Total enrollment: 4,376. Undergraduates: 4,277. Freshmen: 668. Federal methodology is used as a basis for awarding need-based institutional aid.

UNDERGRADUATE EXPENSES for 2004–05 *Application fee:* $35. *Tuition, state resident:* full-time $5860; part-time $257 per hour. *Tuition, nonresident:* full-time $12,104; part-time $532 per hour. *Required fees:* full-time $326; $11 per hour or $25 per term part-time. Full-time tuition and fees vary according to course load. Part-time tuition and fees vary according to course load. *College room and board:* $5140; *room only:* $3100. Room and board charges vary according to board plan and housing facility. *Payment plan:* Deferred payment.

FRESHMAN FINANCIAL AID (Fall 2003) 533 applied for aid; of those 81% were deemed to have need. 98% of freshmen with need received aid; of those 21% had need fully met. *Average percent of need met:* 36% (excluding resources awarded to replace EFC). *Average financial aid package:* $7613 (excluding resources awarded to replace EFC). 2% of all full-time freshmen had no need and received non-need-based gift aid.

UNDERGRADUATE FINANCIAL AID (Fall 2003) 2,542 applied for aid; of those 85% were deemed to have need. 98% of undergraduates with need received aid; of those 18% had need fully met. *Average percent of need met:* 47% (excluding resources awarded to replace EFC). *Average financial aid package:* $8244 (excluding resources awarded to replace EFC). 3% of all full-time undergraduates had no need and received non-need-based gift aid.

GIFT AID (NEED-BASED) *Total amount:* $4,891,966 (91% federal, 9% state). *Receiving aid:* Freshmen: 43% (283); All full-time undergraduates: 41% (1,405). *Average award:* Freshmen: $3048; Undergraduates: $3182. *Scholarships, grants, and awards:* Federal Pell, FSEOG, state, private, college/university gift aid from institutional funds.

GIFT AID (NON-NEED-BASED) *Total amount:* $4,779,888 (82% state, 9% institutional, 9% external sources). *Receiving aid:* Freshmen: 52% (343); Undergraduates: 20% (696). *Average Award:* Freshmen: $2410; *Undergraduates:* $3096. *Scholarships, grants, and awards by category: Academic Interests/Achievement:* 99 awards ($430,298 total): general academic interests/achievements. *Special Characteristics:* 45 awards ($32,775 total): first-generation college students. *Tuition waivers:* Full or partial for senior citizens. *ROTC:* Army cooperative.

LOANS *Student loans:* $13,786,157 (52% need-based, 48% non-need-based). 57% of past graduating class borrowed through all loan programs. *Average indebtedness per student:* $9760. *Average need-based loan:* Freshmen: $2363; Undergraduates: $3575. *Parent loans:* $603,011 (100% non-need-based). *Programs:* FFEL (Subsidized and Unsubsidized Stafford, PLUS), Perkins, state.

WORK-STUDY *Federal work-study:* Total amount: $185,456; 102 jobs averaging $1501. *State or other work-study/employment:* Total amount: $554,645 (100% non-need-based). 465 part-time jobs averaging $1240.

ATHLETIC AWARDS *Total amount:* $566,326 (100% non-need-based).

APPLYING FOR FINANCIAL AID *Required financial aid form:* FAFSA. *Financial aid deadline (priority):* 3/1. *Notification date:* Continuous beginning 4/1. Students must reply within 2 weeks of notification.

CONTACT Kim Jenerette, Director of Financial Aid, University of South Carolina Upstate, 800 University Way, Spartanburg, SC 29303, 864-503-5340 or toll-free 800-277-8727. *Fax:* 864-503-5974. *E-mail:* kjenerette@uscupstate.edu.

THE UNIVERSITY OF SOUTH DAKOTA
Vermillion, SD

Tuition & fees (SD res): $4749   **Average undergraduate aid package: $6032**

ABOUT THE INSTITUTION State-supported, coed. Awards: associate, bachelor's, master's, doctoral, and first professional degrees and post-bachelor's and post-master's certificates. 61 undergraduate majors. Total enrollment: 8,120. Undergraduates: 6,024. Freshmen: 1,057. Federal methodology is used as a basis for awarding need-based institutional aid.

UNDERGRADUATE EXPENSES for 2004–05 *Application fee:* $20. *Tuition, state resident:* full-time $2,371; part-time $74.10 per credit hour. *Tuition, nonresident:* full-time $7,538; part-time $235.55 per credit hour. *Required fees:* full-time $2,378; $74.30 per credit hour. Full-time tuition and fees vary according to course load and reciprocity agreements. Part-time tuition and fees vary according to course load and reciprocity agreements. *College room and board:* $3,741; *room only:* $1,937. Room and board charges vary according to board plan and housing facility. *Payment plan:* Deferred payment.

FRESHMAN FINANCIAL AID (Fall 2003) 825 applied for aid; of those 69% were deemed to have need. 99% of freshmen with need received aid; of those 84% had need fully met. *Average percent of need met:* 84% (excluding resources awarded to replace EFC). *Average financial aid package:* $5451 (excluding resources awarded to replace EFC). 30% of all full-time freshmen had no need and received non-need-based gift aid.

UNDERGRADUATE FINANCIAL AID (Fall 2003) 3,566 applied for aid; of those 100% were deemed to have need. 79% of undergraduates with need received aid; of those 73% had need fully met. *Average percent of need met:* 75% (excluding resources awarded to replace EFC). *Average financial aid package:* $6032 (excluding resources awarded to replace EFC). 19% of all full-time undergraduates had no need and received non-need-based gift aid.

GIFT AID (NEED-BASED) *Receiving aid:* Freshmen: 30% (294); All full-time undergraduates: 34% (1,483). *Average award:* Freshmen: $3093; Undergraduates: $3037. *Scholarships, grants, and awards:* Federal Pell, FSEOG, private, college/university gift aid from institutional funds, Federal Nursing.

GIFT AID (NON-NEED-BASED) *Receiving aid:* Freshmen: 36% (352); Undergraduates: 27% (1,159). *Average Award:* Freshmen: $5623; *Undergraduates:* $5643. *Scholarships, grants, and awards by category: Academic Interests/Achievement:* biological sciences, business, communication, computer science, education, English, foreign languages, general academic interests/achievements, humanities, mathematics, military science, premedicine, social sciences. *Creative Arts/Performance:* art/fine arts, creative writing, debating, music, theater/drama. *Tuition waivers:* Full or partial for employees or children of employees, senior citizens. *ROTC:* Army.

LOANS *Student loans:* $35,860,713 (58% need-based, 42% non-need-based). 80% of past graduating class borrowed through all loan programs. *Average indebtedness per student:* $18,810. *Average need-based loan:* Freshmen: $2714; Undergraduates: $3562. *Parent loans:* $1,434,084 (100% non-need-based). *Programs:* FFEL (Subsidized and Unsubsidized Stafford, PLUS), Perkins, Federal Nursing, alternative loans.

WORK-STUDY *Federal work-study:* Total amount: $780,301; 650 jobs averaging $1200. *State or other work-study/employment:* Total amount: $985,006 (100% non-need-based).

ATHLETIC AWARDS *Total amount:* $866,704 (100% non-need-based).

APPLYING FOR FINANCIAL AID *Required financial aid form:* FAFSA. *Financial aid deadline (priority):* 3/15. *Notification date:* Continuous beginning 4/1. Students must reply within 3 weeks of notification.

CONTACT Julie Pier, Director of Student Financial Aid, The University of South Dakota, Belbas Center, 414 East Clark Street, Vermillion, SD 57069-2390, 605-677-5446 or toll-free 877-269-6837. *Fax:* 605-677-5238.

UNIVERSITY OF SOUTHERN CALIFORNIA
Los Angeles, CA

Tuition & fees: $30,512   **Average undergraduate aid package: $26,812**

University of Southern California

ABOUT THE INSTITUTION Independent, coed. Awards: bachelor's, master's, doctoral, and first professional degrees and post-bachelor's, post-master's, and first professional certificates. 114 undergraduate majors. Total enrollment: 32,160. Undergraduates: 16,474. Freshmen: 2,770. Both federal and institutional methodology are used as a basis for awarding need-based institutional aid.

UNDERGRADUATE EXPENSES for 2004–05 *Application fee:* $65. *Comprehensive fee:* $39,500 includes full-time tuition ($29,988), mandatory fees ($524), and room and board ($8988). *College room only:* $4960. Full-time tuition and fees vary according to program. Room and board charges vary according to board plan and housing facility. *Part-time tuition:* $1010 per credit hour. *Part-time fees:* $524 per term. Part-time tuition and fees vary according to course load and program. *Payment plans:* Tuition prepayment, installment, deferred payment.

FRESHMAN FINANCIAL AID (Fall 2003) 1992 applied for aid; of those 72% were deemed to have need. 100% of freshmen with need received aid; of those 95% had need fully met. *Average percent of need met:* 100% (excluding resources awarded to replace EFC). *Average financial aid package:* $27,377 (excluding resources awarded to replace EFC). 24% of all full-time freshmen had no need and received non-need-based gift aid.

UNDERGRADUATE FINANCIAL AID (Fall 2003) 9,121 applied for aid; of those 82% were deemed to have need. 100% of undergraduates with need received aid; of those 92% had need fully met. *Average percent of need met:* 100% (excluding resources awarded to replace EFC). *Average financial aid package:* $26,812 (excluding resources awarded to replace EFC). 18% of all full-time undergraduates had no need and received non-need-based gift aid.

GIFT AID (NEED-BASED) *Total amount:* $144,128,291 (11% federal, 14% state, 71% institutional, 4% external sources). *Receiving aid:* Freshmen: 42% (1,259); All full-time undergraduates: 42% (6,644). *Average award:* Freshmen: $18,073; Undergraduates: $17,341. *Scholarships, grants, and awards:* Federal Pell, FSEOG, state, private, college/university gift aid from institutional funds.

GIFT AID (NON-NEED-BASED) *Total amount:* $32,727,010 (84% institutional, 16% external sources). *Receiving aid:* Freshmen: 31% (931); Undergraduates: 21% (3,344). *Average Award:* Freshmen: $10,484; *Undergraduates:* $11,494. *Scholarships, grants, and awards by category: Academic Interests/Achievement:* 4,932 awards ($47,019,676 total): general academic interests/achievements. *Creative Arts/Performance:* 18 awards ($315,840 total): debating. *Special Achievements/Activities:* 120 awards ($1,162,500 total): leadership. *Special Characteristics:* 923 awards ($11,872,982 total): children and siblings of alumni, children of faculty/staff, international students, members of minority groups. *Tuition waivers:* Full or partial for employees or children of employees. *ROTC:* Army, Air Force.

LOANS *Student loans:* $96,953,870 (40% need-based, 60% non-need-based). 57% of past graduating class borrowed through all loan programs. *Average indebtedness per student:* $18,968. *Average need-based loan:* Freshmen: $3756; Undergraduates: $6110. *Parent loans:* $32,976,841 (100% non-need-based). *Programs:* FFEL (Subsidized and Unsubsidized Stafford, PLUS), Perkins, 'Credit Ready' and 'Credit Based' loans.

WORK-STUDY *Federal work-study:* Total amount: $13,780,692; 4,984 jobs averaging $2764.

ATHLETIC AWARDS *Total amount:* $10,999,994 (28% need-based, 72% non-need-based).

APPLYING FOR FINANCIAL AID *Required financial aid forms:* FAFSA, CSS Financial Aid PROFILE, federal income tax form(s), W-2 forms. *Financial aid deadline (priority):* 1/20. *Notification date:* Continuous beginning 3/15. Students must reply by 5/1 or within 2 weeks of notification.

CONTACT Catherine C. Thomas, Associate Dean of Admissions and Financial Aid, University of Southern California, University Park Campus, Los Angeles, CA 90089-0914, 213-740-1111. *Fax:* 213-740-0680.

UNIVERSITY OF SOUTHERN INDIANA
Evansville, IN

Tuition & fees (IN res): $4077	Average undergraduate aid package: $5452

ABOUT THE INSTITUTION State-supported, coed. Awards: associate, bachelor's, and master's degrees and post-bachelor's certificates. 55 undergraduate majors. Total enrollment: 10,050. Undergraduates: 9,217. Freshmen: 2,104. Federal methodology is used as a basis for awarding need-based institutional aid.

UNDERGRADUATE EXPENSES for 2005–06 *Application fee:* $25. *Tuition, state resident:* full-time $4017; part-time $131.91 per semester hour. *Tuition, nonresident:* full-time $9582; part-time $319.41 per semester hour. *Required fees:* full-time $60; $22.75 per term part-time. Full-time tuition and fees vary according to course load and reciprocity agreements. Part-time tuition and fees vary according to course load and reciprocity agreements. *College room and*

board: $5480; *room only:* $3000. Room and board charges vary according to board plan and housing facility. *Payment plan:* Installment.

FRESHMAN FINANCIAL AID (Fall 2004, est.) 1776 applied for aid; of those 74% were deemed to have need. 94% of freshmen with need received aid; of those 12% had need fully met. *Average percent of need met:* 58% (excluding resources awarded to replace EFC). *Average financial aid package:* $5093 (excluding resources awarded to replace EFC). 10% of all full-time freshmen had no need and received non-need-based gift aid.

UNDERGRADUATE FINANCIAL AID (Fall 2004, est.) 5,957 applied for aid; of those 77% were deemed to have need. 93% of undergraduates with need received aid; of those 14% had need fully met. *Average percent of need met:* 57% (excluding resources awarded to replace EFC). *Average financial aid package:* $5452 (excluding resources awarded to replace EFC). 7% of all full-time undergraduates had no need and received non-need-based gift aid.

GIFT AID (NEED-BASED) *Total amount:* $13,068,758 (48% federal, 37% state, 10% institutional, 5% external sources). *Receiving aid:* Freshmen: 47% (949); All full-time undergraduates: 41% (3,020). *Average award:* Freshmen: $4383; Undergraduates: $4233. *Scholarships, grants, and awards:* Federal Pell, FSEOG, state, private, college/university gift aid from institutional funds.

GIFT AID (NON-NEED-BASED) *Total amount:* $2,081,507 (74% institutional, 26% external sources). *Receiving aid:* Freshmen: 7% (149); Undergraduates: 10% (722). *Average Award:* Freshmen: $2071; Undergraduates: $2139. *Scholarships, grants, and awards by category: Academic Interests/Achievement:* 698 awards ($889,854 total): biological sciences, business, education, engineering/technologies, general academic interests/achievements, health fields, humanities, mathematics, premedicine, social sciences. *Creative Arts/Performance:* 31 awards ($31,370 total): art/fine arts, creative writing, theater/drama. *Special Achievements/Activities:* 2 awards ($2000 total): leadership. *Special Characteristics:* 289 awards ($641,396 total): children of faculty/staff, members of minority groups, out-of-state students, spouses of current students, veterans' children. *Tuition waivers:* Full or partial for employees or children of employees, senior citizens. *ROTC:* Army.

LOANS *Student loans:* $18,379,970 (74% need-based, 26% non-need-based). 58% of past graduating class borrowed through all loan programs. *Average indebtedness per student:* $14,552. *Average need-based loan:* Freshmen: $2398; Undergraduates: $3108. *Parent loans:* $4,312,181 (61% need-based, 39% non-need-based). *Programs:* FFEL (Subsidized and Unsubsidized Stafford, PLUS), Perkins.

WORK-STUDY *Federal work-study:* Total amount: $335,070; 146 jobs averaging $1574.

ATHLETIC AWARDS *Total amount:* $696,569 (44% need-based, 56% non-need-based).

APPLYING FOR FINANCIAL AID *Required financial aid forms:* FAFSA, institution's own form. *Financial aid deadline:* 3/1. *Notification date:* Continuous beginning 4/15.

CONTACT Financial Aid Counselor, University of Southern Indiana, 8600 University Boulevard, Evansville, IN 47712-3590, 812-464-1767 or toll-free 800-467-1965. *Fax:* 812-465-7154. *E-mail:* finaid@usi.edu.

UNIVERSITY OF SOUTHERN MAINE
Portland, ME

Tuition & fees (ME res): $5510	Average undergraduate aid package: $8907

ABOUT THE INSTITUTION State-supported, coed. Awards: associate, bachelor's, master's, doctoral, and first professional degrees and post-master's certificates. 46 undergraduate majors. Total enrollment: 11,089. Undergraduates: 8,736. Freshmen: 931. Federal methodology is used as a basis for awarding need-based institutional aid.

UNDERGRADUATE EXPENSES for 2004–05 *Application fee:* $40. *Tuition, state resident:* full-time $4620; part-time $154 per credit hour. *Tuition, nonresident:* full-time $12,780; part-time $426 per credit hour. Full-time tuition and fees vary according to course load, degree level, and reciprocity agreements. Part-time tuition and fees vary according to course load, degree level, and reciprocity agreements. *College room and board:* $6908; *room only:* $3978. Room and board charges vary according to board plan, housing facility, and location. *Payment plan:* Installment.

FRESHMAN FINANCIAL AID (Fall 2004, est.) 773 applied for aid; of those 81% were deemed to have need. 96% of freshmen with need received aid; of those 12% had need fully met. *Average percent of need met:* 71% (excluding resources awarded to replace EFC). *Average financial aid package:* $7306 (excluding resources awarded to replace EFC). 11% of all full-time freshmen had no need and received non-need-based gift aid.

UNDERGRADUATE FINANCIAL AID (Fall 2004, est.) 4,066 applied for aid; of those 87% were deemed to have need. 97% of undergraduates with need received aid; of those 24% had need fully met. *Average percent of need met:* 78% (excluding resources awarded to replace EFC). *Average financial aid package:* $8907 (excluding resources awarded to replace EFC). 9% of all full-time undergraduates had no need and received non-need-based gift aid.

GIFT AID (NEED-BASED) *Total amount:* $11,704,921 (67% federal, 13% state, 11% institutional, 9% external sources). *Receiving aid:* Freshmen: 55% (474); All full-time undergraduates: 55% (2,537). *Average award:* Freshmen: $3898; Undergraduates: $3857. *Scholarships, grants, and awards:* Federal Pell, FSEOG, state, college/university gift aid from institutional funds.

GIFT AID (NON-NEED-BASED) *Total amount:* $1,665,322 (17% institutional, 83% external sources). *Receiving aid:* Freshmen: 3% (22); Undergraduates: 2% (79). *Average Award: Freshmen:* $2982; *Undergraduates:* $4360. *Scholarships, grants, and awards by category: Academic Interests/Achievement:* general academic interests/achievements. *Creative Arts/Performance:* music, theater/drama. *Special Achievements/Activities:* community service. *Special Characteristics:* children of faculty/staff, general special characteristics, local/state students, out-of-state students. *Tuition waivers:* Full or partial for minority students, employees or children of employees, senior citizens. *ROTC:* Army cooperative, Air Force cooperative.

LOANS *Student loans:* $25,464,886 (66% need-based, 34% non-need-based). 50% of past graduating class borrowed through all loan programs. *Average indebtedness per student:* $21,912. *Average need-based loan:* Freshmen: $3079; Undergraduates: $4355. *Parent loans:* $3,067,360 (100% non-need-based). *Programs:* FFEL (Subsidized and Unsubsidized Stafford, PLUS), Perkins, Federal Nursing, college/university.

WORK-STUDY *Federal work-study:* Total amount: $4,994,000; jobs available.

APPLYING FOR FINANCIAL AID *Required financial aid form:* FAFSA. *Financial aid deadline (priority):* 2/15. *Notification date:* Continuous beginning 3/15. Students must reply within 2 weeks of notification.

CONTACT Mr. Keith P. Dubois, Director of Student Financial Aid, University of Southern Maine, 96 Falmouth Street, PO Box 9300, Portland, ME 04104-9300, 207-780-5122 or toll-free 800-800-4USM Ext. 5670. *Fax:* 207-780-5143. *E-mail:* dubois@maine.edu.

UNIVERSITY OF SOUTHERN MISSISSIPPI
Hattiesburg, MS

Tuition & fees (MS res): $4106   **Average undergraduate aid package: $7177**

ABOUT THE INSTITUTION State-supported, coed. Awards: bachelor's, master's, and doctoral degrees. 66 undergraduate majors. Total enrollment: 15,253. Undergraduates: 12,520. Freshmen: 1,483. Federal methodology is used as a basis for awarding need-based institutional aid.

UNDERGRADUATE EXPENSES for 2004–05 *Tuition, state resident:* full-time $4106; part-time $172 per credit hour. *Tuition, nonresident:* full-time $9276; part-time $388 per credit hour. Part-time tuition and fees vary according to course load. *College room and board:* $5010; *room only:* $3010. Room and board charges vary according to housing facility. *Payment plan:* Installment.

FRESHMAN FINANCIAL AID (Fall 2003) 1200 applied for aid; of those 78% were deemed to have need. 98% of freshmen with need received aid; of those 17% had need fully met. *Average percent of need met:* 78% (excluding resources awarded to replace EFC). *Average financial aid package:* $6095 (excluding resources awarded to replace EFC). 13% of all full-time freshmen had no need and received non-need-based gift aid.

UNDERGRADUATE FINANCIAL AID (Fall 2003) 7,547 applied for aid; of those 84% were deemed to have need. 98% of undergraduates with need received aid; of those 35% had need fully met. *Average percent of need met:* 87% (excluding resources awarded to replace EFC). *Average financial aid package:* $7177 (excluding resources awarded to replace EFC). 8% of all full-time undergraduates had no need and received non-need-based gift aid.

GIFT AID (NEED-BASED) *Total amount:* $19,882,036 (79% federal, 8% state, 7% institutional, 6% external sources). *Receiving aid:* Freshmen: 42% (646); All full-time undergraduates: 45% (4,450). *Average award:* Freshmen: $3185; Undergraduates: $3196. *Scholarships, grants, and awards:* Federal Pell, FSEOG, state, private, college/university gift aid from institutional funds.

GIFT AID (NON-NEED-BASED) *Total amount:* $8,801,180 (1% federal, 34% state, 42% institutional, 23% external sources). *Receiving aid:* Freshmen: 32% (485); Undergraduates: 28% (2,845). *Average Award: Freshmen:* $2847; *Undergraduates:* $2290. *Scholarships, grants, and awards by category: Academic Interests/Achievement:* 1,925 awards ($3,245,981 total): general academic interests/achievements. *Creative Arts/Performance:* 376 awards

($602,051 total): art/fine arts, dance, music, theater/drama. *Special Achievements/Activities:* 226 awards ($276,050 total): cheerleading/drum major, leadership. *Special Characteristics:* 4,553 awards ($5,572,227 total): children and siblings of alumni, children of faculty/staff, ethnic background, local/state students, out-of-state students, veterans. *Tuition waivers:* Full or partial for children of alumni, employees or children of employees, senior citizens. *ROTC:* Army, Air Force.

LOANS *Student loans:* $42,810,618 (65% need-based, 35% non-need-based). 61% of past graduating class borrowed through all loan programs. *Average indebtedness per student:* $12,073. *Average need-based loan:* Freshmen: $2844; Undergraduates: $4264. *Parent loans:* $2,383,535 (20% need-based, 80% non-need-based). *Programs:* FFEL (Subsidized and Unsubsidized Stafford, PLUS), Perkins, Federal Nursing, college/university.

WORK-STUDY *Federal work-study:* Total amount: $448,792; 366 jobs averaging $1226.

ATHLETIC AWARDS *Total amount:* $2,893,646 (37% need-based, 63% non-need-based).

APPLYING FOR FINANCIAL AID *Required financial aid forms:* FAFSA, institution's own form, state aid form. *Financial aid deadline (priority):* 3/15. *Notification date:* Continuous. Students must reply within 2 weeks of notification.

CONTACT Kristi Motter, Director of Financial Aid, University of Southern Mississippi, Box 5101, Hattiesburg, MS 39406-5101, 601-266-4774. *E-mail:* kristi.motter@usm.edu.

UNIVERSITY OF SOUTH FLORIDA
Tampa, FL

Tuition & fees (FL res): $3164   **Average undergraduate aid package: $9439**

ABOUT THE INSTITUTION State-supported, coed. Awards: associate, bachelor's, master's, doctoral, and first professional degrees and post-bachelor's certificates. 84 undergraduate majors. Total enrollment: 42,238. Undergraduates: 33,266. Freshmen: 4,720. Federal methodology is used as a basis for awarding need-based institutional aid.

UNDERGRADUATE EXPENSES for 2004–05 *Application fee:* $30. *Tuition, state resident:* full-time $3090; part-time $103 per credit hour. *Tuition, nonresident:* full-time $15,960; part-time $532 per credit hour. *Required fees:* full-time $74; $37 per term part-time. Full-time tuition and fees vary according to course level, course load, and location. Part-time tuition and fees vary according to course level, course load, and location. *College room and board:* $6730; *room only:* $3519. Room and board charges vary according to board plan, housing facility, and location. *Payment plan:* Installment.

FRESHMAN FINANCIAL AID (Fall 2003) 2826 applied for aid; of those 74% were deemed to have need. 99% of freshmen with need received aid; of those 7% had need fully met. *Average percent of need met:* 32% (excluding resources awarded to replace EFC). *Average financial aid package:* $7268 (excluding resources awarded to replace EFC). 16% of all full-time freshmen had no need and received non-need-based gift aid.

UNDERGRADUATE FINANCIAL AID (Fall 2003) 12,018 applied for aid; of those 84% were deemed to have need. 99% of undergraduates with need received aid; of those 8% had need fully met. *Average percent of need met:* 32% (excluding resources awarded to replace EFC). *Average financial aid package:* $9439 (excluding resources awarded to replace EFC). 6% of all full-time undergraduates had no need and received non-need-based gift aid.

GIFT AID (NEED-BASED) *Total amount:* $33,577,091 (70% federal, 17% state, 13% institutional). *Receiving aid:* Freshmen: 27% (1,178); All full-time undergraduates: 33% (7,052). *Average award:* Freshmen: $3645; Undergraduates: $3667. *Scholarships, grants, and awards:* Federal Pell, FSEOG, state, private, college/university gift aid from institutional funds.

GIFT AID (NON-NEED-BASED) *Total amount:* $48,352,021 (73% state, 21% institutional, 6% external sources). *Receiving aid:* Freshmen: 25% (1,065); Undergraduates: 17% (3,553). *Average Award:* Freshmen: $4112; *Undergraduates:* $1626. *Scholarships, grants, and awards by category: Academic Interests/Achievement:* 1,635 awards ($2,140,548 total): architecture, biological sciences, business, communication, computer science, education, engineering/technologies, English, foreign languages, general academic interests/achievements, health fields, humanities, international studies, library science, mathematics, military science, physical sciences, premedicine, religion/biblical studies, social sciences. *Creative Arts/Performance:* 106 awards ($105,980 total): applied art and design, art/fine arts, cinema/film/broadcasting, creative writing, dance, debating, journalism/publications, music, performing arts, theater/

University of South Florida

drama. *Special Achievements/Activities:* general special achievements/activities. *Special Characteristics:* general special characteristics. *Tuition waivers:* Full or partial for senior citizens. *ROTC:* Army, Naval, Air Force.

LOANS *Student loans:* $71,630,765 (58% need-based, 42% non-need-based). 52% of past graduating class borrowed through all loan programs. *Average indebtedness per student:* $17,304. *Average need-based loan:* Freshmen: $2616; Undergraduates: $4913. *Parent loans:* $3,763,519 (100% non-need-based). *Programs:* FFEL (Subsidized and Unsubsidized Stafford, PLUS), Perkins, college/university.

WORK-STUDY *Federal work-study:* Total amount: $2,977,418; 880 jobs averaging $3600.

ATHLETIC AWARDS *Total amount:* $2,104,914 (100% non-need-based).

APPLYING FOR FINANCIAL AID *Required financial aid form:* FAFSA. *Financial aid deadline (priority):* 3/1. *Notification date:* Continuous beginning 3/28. Students must reply within 4 weeks of notification.

CONTACT Mr. Leonard Gude, Director of Student Financial Aid, University of South Florida, 4202 East Fowler Avenue, SVC 1102, Tampa, FL 33620-6960, 813-974-4700 or toll-free 877-USF-BULLS. *Fax:* 813-974-5144. *E-mail:* lgude@admin.usf.edu.

THE UNIVERSITY OF TAMPA
Tampa, FL

Tuition & fees: $18,172	Average undergraduate aid package: $14,398

ABOUT THE INSTITUTION Independent, coed. Awards: associate, bachelor's, and master's degrees. 45 undergraduate majors. Total enrollment: 4,879. Undergraduates: 4,348. Freshmen: 970. Federal methodology is used as a basis for awarding need-based institutional aid.

UNDERGRADUATE EXPENSES for 2004–05 *Application fee:* $35. *Comprehensive fee:* $24,838 includes full-time tuition ($17,250), mandatory fees ($922), and room and board ($6666). *College room only:* $3567. Full-time tuition and fees vary according to class time. Room and board charges vary according to board plan and housing facility. *Part-time tuition:* $368 per hour. *Part-time fees:* $35 per term. Part-time tuition and fees vary according to class time. *Payment plan:* Installment.

FRESHMAN FINANCIAL AID (Fall 2004, est.) 847 applied for aid; of those 66% were deemed to have need. 100% of freshmen with need received aid; of those 36% had need fully met. *Average percent of need met:* 84% (excluding resources awarded to replace EFC). *Average financial aid package:* $15,008 (excluding resources awarded to replace EFC). 27% of all full-time freshmen had no need and received non-need-based gift aid.

UNDERGRADUATE FINANCIAL AID (Fall 2004, est.) 2,750 applied for aid; of those 80% were deemed to have need. 100% of undergraduates with need received aid; of those 35% had need fully met. *Average percent of need met:* 83% (excluding resources awarded to replace EFC). *Average financial aid package:* $14,398 (excluding resources awarded to replace EFC). 8% of all full-time undergraduates had no need and received non-need-based gift aid.

GIFT AID (NEED-BASED) *Total amount:* $22,729,400 (15% federal, 13% state, 66% institutional, 6% external sources). *Receiving aid:* Freshmen: 56% (538); All full-time undergraduates: 56% (2,136). *Average award:* Freshmen: $6944; Undergraduates: $6810. *Scholarships, grants, and awards:* Federal Pell, FSEOG, state, private, college/university gift aid from institutional funds.

GIFT AID (NON-NEED-BASED) *Total amount:* $7,825,545 (23% state, 71% institutional, 6% external sources). *Receiving aid:* Freshmen: 55% (523); Undergraduates: 54% (2,068). *Average Award:* Freshmen: $6944; Undergraduates: $6668. *Scholarships, grants, and awards by category: Academic Interests/Achievement:* biological sciences, business, communication, education, general academic interests/achievements, health fields, military science, social sciences. *Creative Arts/Performance:* art/fine arts, creative writing, journalism/publications, music, performing arts. *Special Achievements/Activities:* general special achievements/activities, leadership. *Special Characteristics:* children and siblings of alumni, children of faculty/staff, international students. *Tuition waivers:* Full or partial for employees or children of employees. *ROTC:* Army, Air Force cooperative.

LOANS *Student loans:* $14,823,881 (59% need-based, 41% non-need-based). 71% of past graduating class borrowed through all loan programs. *Average indebtedness per student:* $24,402. *Average need-based loan:* Freshmen: $3029; Undergraduates: $3828. *Parent loans:* $7,566,976 (74% need-based, 26% non-need-based). *Programs:* FFEL (Subsidized and Unsubsidized Stafford, PLUS), Perkins, state, college/university.

WORK-STUDY *Federal work-study:* Total amount: $529,783; jobs available (averaging $2000).

ATHLETIC AWARDS *Total amount:* $629,106 (93% need-based, 7% non-need-based).

APPLYING FOR FINANCIAL AID *Required financial aid forms:* FAFSA, state aid form. *Financial aid deadline:* Continuous. *Notification date:* Continuous beginning 2/1. Students must reply within 3 weeks of notification.

CONTACT Financial Aid Office, The University of Tampa, 401 West Kennedy Boulevard, Tampa, FL 33606-1490, 813-253-6219 or toll-free 888-646-2438 (in-state), 888-MINARET (out-of-state). *Fax:* 813-254-4955. *E-mail:* finaid@ut.edu.

THE UNIVERSITY OF TENNESSEE
Knoxville, TN

ABOUT THE INSTITUTION State-supported, coed. Awards: bachelor's, master's, doctoral, and first professional degrees and post-bachelor's, post-master's, and first professional certificates. 92 undergraduate majors. Total enrollment: 27,764. Undergraduates: 19,634. Freshmen: 4,422.

GIFT AID (NEED-BASED) *Scholarships, grants, and awards:* Federal Pell, FSEOG, state, private, college/university gift aid from institutional funds, Federal Nursing.

GIFT AID (NON-NEED-BASED) *Scholarships, grants, and awards by category: Academic Interests/Achievement:* agriculture, architecture, biological sciences, business, communication, computer science, education, engineering/technologies, English, foreign languages, general academic interests/achievements, health fields, humanities, international studies, mathematics, military science, physical sciences, premedicine, social sciences. *Creative Arts/Performance:* applied art and design, art/fine arts, journalism/publications, music, theater/drama. *Special Achievements/Activities:* cheerleading/drum major, hobbies/interests, leadership. *Special Characteristics:* adult students, children of union members/company employees, ethnic background, first-generation college students, handicapped students, local/state students, members of minority groups, previous college experience, veterans' children.

LOANS *Programs:* FFEL (Subsidized and Unsubsidized Stafford, PLUS), Perkins, college/university.

WORK-STUDY *Federal work-study:* Total amount: $816,363; jobs available. *State or other work-study/employment:* Part-time jobs available.

APPLYING FOR FINANCIAL AID *Required financial aid form:* FAFSA.

CONTACT Office of Financial Aid and Scholarships, The University of Tennessee, 115 Student Services Building, Knoxville, TN 37996-0210, 865-974-3131 or toll-free 800-221-8657 (in-state). *Fax:* 865-974-2175. *E-mail:* finaid@utk.edu.

THE UNIVERSITY OF TENNESSEE AT CHATTANOOGA
Chattanooga, TN

Tuition & fees (TN res): $4928	Average undergraduate aid package: $8450

ABOUT THE INSTITUTION State-supported, coed. Awards: bachelor's, master's, doctoral, and first professional degrees and post-bachelor's and post-master's certificates. 44 undergraduate majors. Total enrollment: 8,844. Undergraduates: 7,405. Freshmen: 1,502. Both federal and institutional methodology are used as a basis for awarding need-based institutional aid.

UNDERGRADUATE EXPENSES for 2004–05 *Application fee:* $25. *Tuition, state resident:* full-time $4128; part-time $221 per hour. *Tuition, nonresident:* full-time $12,350; part-time $565 per hour. *College room and board:* $5808; *room only:* $3360. Room and board charges vary according to housing facility. *Payment plan:* Deferred payment.

FRESHMAN FINANCIAL AID (Fall 2004, est.) 1385 applied for aid; of those 50% were deemed to have need. 90% of freshmen with need received aid; of those 43% had need fully met. *Average percent of need met:* 84% (excluding resources awarded to replace EFC). *Average financial aid package:* $8875 (excluding resources awarded to replace EFC). 18% of all full-time freshmen had no need and received non-need-based gift aid.

UNDERGRADUATE FINANCIAL AID (Fall 2004, est.) 4,620 applied for aid; of those 86% were deemed to have need. 78% of undergraduates with need received aid; of those 19% had need fully met. *Average percent of need met:* 80% (excluding resources awarded to replace EFC). *Average financial aid package:* $8450 (excluding resources awarded to replace EFC). 13% of all full-time undergraduates had no need and received non-need-based gift aid.

GIFT AID (NEED-BASED) *Total amount:* $7,675,000 (76% federal, 24% state). *Receiving aid:* Freshmen: 34% (514); All full-time undergraduates: 38% (2,346). *Average award:* Freshmen: $3900; Undergraduates: $3600. *Scholarships, grants, and awards:* Federal Pell, FSEOG, state, private, college/university gift aid from institutional funds, Federal Nursing.

GIFT AID (NON-NEED-BASED) *Total amount:* $11,875,000 (49% state, 44% institutional, 7% external sources). *Receiving aid:* Freshmen: 35% (528); Undergraduates: 26% (1,625). *Average Award: Freshmen:* $2400; *Undergraduates:* $3400. *Scholarships, grants, and awards by category: Academic Interests/Achievement:* 600 awards ($625,000 total): general academic interests/achievements. *Creative Arts/Performance:* 150 awards ($100,000 total): art/fine arts, music, theater/drama. *Special Achievements/Activities:* 110 awards ($131,000 total): cheerleading/drum major, leadership. *Special Characteristics:* 250 awards ($845,000 total): members of minority groups. *Tuition waivers:* Full or partial for employees or children of employees, senior citizens.

LOANS *Student loans:* $18,525,000 (58% need-based, 42% non-need-based). 47% of past graduating class borrowed through all loan programs. *Average indebtedness per student:* $14,750. *Average need-based loan:* Freshmen: $2475; Undergraduates: $4450. *Parent loans:* $1,800,000 (100% non-need-based). *Programs:* FFEL (Subsidized and Unsubsidized Stafford, PLUS), Perkins.

WORK-STUDY *Federal work-study:* Total amount: $395,000; 220 jobs averaging $1795. *State or other work-study/employment:* Total amount: $750,000 (100% non-need-based). 400 part-time jobs averaging $1875.

ATHLETIC AWARDS *Total amount:* $2,325,000 (100% non-need-based).

APPLYING FOR FINANCIAL AID *Required financial aid forms:* FAFSA, institution's own form. *Financial aid deadline (priority):* 4/1. *Notification date:* Continuous. Students must reply by 5/1 or within 2 weeks of notification.

CONTACT Jonathan Looney, Financial Aid Director, The University of Tennessee at Chattanooga, 615 McCallie Avenue, Chattanooga, TN 37403-2598, 423-425-4677 or toll-free 800-UTC-MOCS (in-state). *Fax:* 423-425-2292. *E-mail:* jonathan-looney@utc.edu.

THE UNIVERSITY OF TENNESSEE AT MARTIN
Martin, TN

Tuition & fees (TN res): $4134	Average undergraduate aid package: $8183

ABOUT THE INSTITUTION State-supported, coed. Awards: bachelor's and master's degrees. 80 undergraduate majors. Total enrollment: 6,104. Undergraduates: 5,667. Freshmen: 1,201. Institutional methodology is used as a basis for awarding need-based institutional aid.

UNDERGRADUATE EXPENSES for 2004–05 *Application fee:* $25. *Tuition, state resident:* full-time $4134; part-time $183 per credit hour. *Tuition, nonresident:* full-time $12,388; part-time $197 per credit hour. *College room and board:* $4100; *room only:* $1960. Room and board charges vary according to board plan and housing facility. *Payment plan:* Deferred payment.

GIFT AID (NEED-BASED) *Total amount:* $8,605,111 (70% federal, 26% state, 4% external sources). *Receiving aid:* Freshmen: 42% (744); All full-time undergraduates: 39% (1,865). *Average award:* Freshmen: $4168; Undergraduates: $4036. *Scholarships, grants, and awards:* Federal Pell, FSEOG, state, private.

GIFT AID (NON-NEED-BASED) *Total amount:* $6,953,718 (49% state, 45% institutional, 6% external sources). *Receiving aid:* Freshmen: 40% (704); Undergraduates: 27% (1,323). *Average Award: Freshmen:* $4397; *Undergraduates:* $3901. *Scholarships, grants, and awards by category: Academic Interests/Achievement:* 1,356 awards ($1,811,550 total): agriculture, biological sciences, business, communication, computer science, education, engineering/technologies, English, general academic interests/achievements, health fields, home economics, humanities, mathematics, military science, physical sciences, premedicine, social sciences. *Creative Arts/Performance:* 175 awards ($127,130 total): art/fine arts, journalism/publications, music, theater/drama. *Special Achievements/Activities:* 454 awards ($566,410 total): cheerleading/drum major, general special achievements/activities, leadership, rodeo. *Special Characteristics:* 1,362 awards ($1,899,264 total): adult students, children of educators, children of faculty/staff, ethnic background, handicapped students, members of minority groups, out-of-state students. *Tuition waivers:* Full or partial for employees or children of employees, senior citizens. *ROTC:* Army.

LOANS *Student loans:* $12,449,038 (59% need-based, 41% non-need-based). 58% of past graduating class borrowed through all loan programs. *Average indebtedness per student:* $14,458. *Average need-based loan:* Freshmen: $2772;

Undergraduates: $3687. *Parent loans:* $996,709 (100% non-need-based). *Programs:* FFEL (Subsidized and Unsubsidized Stafford, PLUS), Perkins.

ATHLETIC AWARDS *Total amount:* $1,932,671 (100% non-need-based).

APPLYING FOR FINANCIAL AID *Required financial aid form:* FAFSA. *Financial aid deadline (priority):* 3/1. *Notification date:* 5/1. Students must reply within 2 weeks of notification.

CONTACT Sandra J. Neel, Director of Student Financial Assistance, The University of Tennessee at Martin, 205 Administration Building, Martin, TN 38238-1000, 731-881-7040 or toll-free 800-829-8861. *Fax:* 731-881-7036. *E-mail:* bmcclain@utm.edu.

THE UNIVERSITY OF TEXAS AT ARLINGTON
Arlington, TX

Tuition & fees (TX res): $5300	Average undergraduate aid package: $8480

ABOUT THE INSTITUTION State-supported, coed. Awards: bachelor's, master's, and doctoral degrees and post-bachelor's and post-master's certificates. 60 undergraduate majors. Total enrollment: 25,297. Undergraduates: 19,114. Freshmen: 1,789. Federal methodology is used as a basis for awarding need-based institutional aid.

UNDERGRADUATE EXPENSES for 2004–05 *Application fee:* $35. *Tuition, state resident:* full-time $3630; part-time $121 per credit hour. *Tuition, nonresident:* full-time $12,690; part-time $423 per credit hour. *Required fees:* full-time $1670; $59 per credit hour or $103 per term part-time. Full-time tuition and fees vary according to course level, course load, and program. Part-time tuition and fees vary according to course level, course load, and program. *College room and board:* $5212. Room and board charges vary according to board plan and housing facility. *Payment plan:* Installment.

GIFT AID (NEED-BASED) *Total amount:* $28,621,095 (52% federal, 28% state, 13% institutional, 7% external sources). *Receiving aid:* Freshmen: 39% (666); All full-time undergraduates: 36% (4,906). *Average award:* Freshmen: $4078; Undergraduates: $4275. *Scholarships, grants, and awards:* Federal Pell, FSEOG, state, private, college/university gift aid from institutional funds.

GIFT AID (NON-NEED-BASED) *Total amount:* $4,197,609 (57% institutional, 43% external sources). *Receiving aid:* Freshmen: 31% (539); Undergraduates: 17% (2,377). *Average Award: Freshmen:* $2292; *Undergraduates:* $2397. *Scholarships, grants, and awards by category: Academic Interests/Achievement:* 3,530 awards ($4,353,387 total): architecture, biological sciences, business, communication, education, engineering/technologies, English, foreign languages, general academic interests/achievements, health fields, humanities, international studies, mathematics, military science, physical sciences, social sciences. *Creative Arts/Performance:* 290 awards ($213,100 total): dance, journalism/publications, music, theater/drama. *Special Achievements/Activities:* 87 awards ($110,057 total): cheerleading/drum major, community service, general special achievements/activities, leadership. *Special Characteristics:* 94 awards ($114,512 total): first-generation college students, general special characteristics, handicapped students, international students. *Tuition waivers:* Full or partial for employees or children of employees. *ROTC:* Army, Air Force cooperative.

LOANS *Student loans:* $45,014,951 (80% need-based, 20% non-need-based). 50% of past graduating class borrowed through all loan programs. *Average indebtedness per student:* $13,319. *Average need-based loan:* Freshmen: $3762; Undergraduates: $5383. *Parent loans:* $3,510,024 (39% need-based, 61% non-need-based). *Programs:* FFEL (Subsidized and Unsubsidized Stafford, PLUS), Perkins, state, college/university.

ATHLETIC AWARDS *Total amount:* $1,320,484 (25% need-based, 75% non-need-based).

APPLYING FOR FINANCIAL AID *Required financial aid form:* FAFSA. *Financial aid deadline (priority):* 5/15. *Notification date:* Continuous beginning 5/1. Students must reply within 3 weeks of notification.

CONTACT Karen Krause, Director of Financial Aid, The University of Texas at Arlington, PO Box 19199, Arlington, TX 76019, 817-272-3568. *Fax:* 817-272-3555. *E-mail:* kkrause@uta.edu.

THE UNIVERSITY OF TEXAS AT AUSTIN
Austin, TX

Tuition & fees (TX res): $5735	Average undergraduate aid package: $9250

ABOUT THE INSTITUTION State-supported, coed. Awards: bachelor's, master's, doctoral, and first professional degrees. 104 undergraduate majors. Total enroll-

The University of Texas at Austin

ment: 50,377. Undergraduates: 37,377. Freshmen: 6,795. Federal methodology is used as a basis for awarding need-based institutional aid.

UNDERGRADUATE EXPENSES for 2004–05 *Application fee:* $50. *Tuition, state resident:* full-time $4260. *Tuition, nonresident:* full-time $12,960. Full-time tuition and fees vary according to course load and program. Part-time tuition and fees vary according to course load and program. *College room and board:* $6184; *room only:* $3569. Room and board charges vary according to board plan and housing facility. *Payment plan:* Installment.

FRESHMAN FINANCIAL AID (Fall 2004, est.) 4500 applied for aid; of those 86% were deemed to have need. 97% of freshmen with need received aid; of those 93% had need fully met. *Average percent of need met:* 95% (excluding resources awarded to replace EFC). *Average financial aid package:* $9150 (excluding resources awarded to replace EFC). 26% of all full-time freshmen had no need and received non-need-based gift aid.

UNDERGRADUATE FINANCIAL AID (Fall 2004, est.) 23,850 applied for aid; of those 75% were deemed to have need. 96% of undergraduates with need received aid; of those 90% had need fully met. *Average percent of need met:* 95% (excluding resources awarded to replace EFC). *Average financial aid package:* $9250 (excluding resources awarded to replace EFC). 28% of all full-time undergraduates had no need and received non-need-based gift aid.

GIFT AID (NEED-BASED) *Total amount:* $67,811,300 (33% federal, 22% state, 36% institutional, 9% external sources). *Receiving aid:* Freshmen: 48% (3,280); All full-time undergraduates: 36% (12,100). *Average award:* Freshmen: $6650; Undergraduates: $5850. *Scholarships, grants, and awards:* Federal Pell, FSEOG, state, private, college/university gift aid from institutional funds, Federal Nursing.

GIFT AID (NON-NEED-BASED) *Total amount:* $41,332,600 (1% federal, 1% state, 79% institutional, 19% external sources). *Average Award:* Freshmen: $3650; Undergraduates: $4280. *Scholarships, grants, and awards by category:* Academic Interests/Achievement: general academic interests/achievements. Creative Arts/Performance: general creative arts/performance. Special Achievements/Activities: general special achievements/activities. Special Characteristics: general special characteristics. *Tuition waivers:* Full or partial for employees or children of employees, senior citizens. *ROTC:* Army, Naval, Air Force.

LOANS *Student loans:* $95,357,300 (75% need-based, 25% non-need-based). 38% of past graduating class borrowed through all loan programs. *Average indebtedness per student:* $16,200. *Average need-based loan:* Freshmen: $3650; Undergraduates: $4920. *Parent loans:* $37,221,100 (30% need-based, 70% non-need-based). *Programs:* FFEL (Subsidized and Unsubsidized Stafford, PLUS), Perkins, state.

WORK-STUDY *Federal work-study:* Total amount: $2,469,000; 1,370 jobs averaging $1802. *State or other work-study/employment:* Total amount: $15,371,350 (2% need-based, 98% non-need-based). 300 part-time jobs averaging $1227.

APPLYING FOR FINANCIAL AID *Required financial aid form:* FAFSA. *Financial aid deadline (priority):* 4/1. *Notification date:* Continuous beginning 4/1. Students must reply within 4 weeks of notification.

CONTACT Don C. Davis, Associate Director of Student Financial Services, The University of Texas at Austin, PO Box 7758, UT Station, Austin, TX 78713-7758, 512-475-6282. *Fax:* 512-475-6296. *E-mail:* dondavis@mail.utexas.edu.

THE UNIVERSITY OF TEXAS AT BROWNSVILLE
Brownsville, TX

Tuition & fees (TX res): $2805   **Average undergraduate aid package: $3092**

ABOUT THE INSTITUTION State-supported, coed. Awards: associate, bachelor's, and master's degrees. 37 undergraduate majors. Total enrollment: 11,560. Undergraduates: 10,683. Entering class: 1,659. Federal methodology is used as a basis for awarding need-based institutional aid.

UNDERGRADUATE EXPENSES for 2004–05 *Tuition, state resident:* full-time $2064; part-time $86 per credit hour. *Tuition, nonresident:* full-time $8256; part-time $344 per credit hour. *Required fees:* full-time $741; $22 per credit hour or $107 per term part-time. *College room and board: room only:* $2300. *Payment plan:* Installment.

UNDERGRADUATE FINANCIAL AID (Fall 2004, est.) 3,570 applied for aid; of those 95% were deemed to have need. 98% of undergraduates with need received aid. *Average percent of need met:* 30% (excluding resources awarded to replace EFC). *Average financial aid package:* $3092 (excluding resources awarded to replace EFC). 1% of all full-time undergraduates had no need and received non-need-based gift aid.

GIFT AID (NEED-BASED) *Total amount:* $10,695,943 (87% federal, 13% state). *Receiving aid:* Entering class: 79% (979); All full-time undergraduates: 73%

(3,079). *Average award:* Freshmen: $2285; Undergraduates: $2308. *Scholarships, grants, and awards:* Federal Pell, FSEOG, state, private, college/university gift aid from institutional funds.

GIFT AID (NON-NEED-BASED) *Total amount:* $963,492 (18% state, 72% institutional, 10% external sources). *Receiving aid:* Freshmen: 31% (379); Undergraduates: 23% (970). *Average Award:* Freshmen: $1532; Undergraduates: $1212. *Scholarships, grants, and awards by category:* Academic Interests/Achievement: biological sciences, education, engineering/technologies, general academic interests/achievements, health fields, mathematics. Creative Arts/Performance: art/fine arts, music. Special Characteristics: general special characteristics. *Tuition waivers:* Full or partial for employees or children of employees.

LOANS *Student loans:* $7,711,693 (79% need-based, 21% non-need-based). *Average need-based loan:* Freshmen: $1265; Undergraduates: $1838. *Parent loans:* $21,600 (100% non-need-based). *Programs:* FFEL (Subsidized and Unsubsidized Stafford, PLUS), state, college/university.

WORK-STUDY *Federal work-study:* Total amount: $198,981; jobs available. *State or other work-study/employment:* Total amount: $84,735 (100% need-based). Part-time jobs available.

ATHLETIC AWARDS *Total amount:* $90,049 (100% non-need-based).

APPLYING FOR FINANCIAL AID *Required financial aid form:* FAFSA. *Financial aid deadline (priority):* 3/1. *Notification date:* 5/1. Students must reply by 7/1 or within 12 weeks of notification.

CONTACT Ms. Georgiana M. Velarde, Assistant Director of Financial Aid, The University of Texas at Brownsville, 80 Fort Brown, Tandy Building, Suite 206, Brownsville, TX 78520-4991, 956-544-8830 or toll-free 800-850-0160 (in-state). *Fax:* 956-544-8229. *E-mail:* gvelarde@utb.edu.

THE UNIVERSITY OF TEXAS AT DALLAS
Richardson, TX

Tuition & fees (TX res): $6363   **Average undergraduate aid package: $11,349**

ABOUT THE INSTITUTION State-supported, coed. Awards: bachelor's, master's, and doctoral degrees. 36 undergraduate majors. Total enrollment: 14,092. Undergraduates: 9,070. Freshmen: 1,102. Both federal and institutional methodology are used as a basis for awarding need-based institutional aid.

UNDERGRADUATE EXPENSES for 2004–05 *Application fee:* $50. *Tuition, state resident:* full-time $1440; part-time $48 per credit. *Tuition, nonresident:* full-time $9180; part-time $306 per credit. *Required fees:* full-time $4923; $159.60 per credit or $167 per term part-time. Full-time tuition and fees vary according to course load, degree level, program, and student level. Part-time tuition and fees vary according to course load, degree level, program, and student level. *College room and board:* $6244. Room and board charges vary according to board plan and housing facility. *Payment plan:* Installment.

GIFT AID (NEED-BASED) *Total amount:* $14,269,052 (54% federal, 38% state, 8% institutional). *Receiving aid:* Freshmen: 31% (329); All full-time undergraduates: 30% (1,894). *Average award:* Freshmen: $3996; Undergraduates: $6638. *Scholarships, grants, and awards:* Federal Pell, FSEOG, state, private, college/university gift aid from institutional funds.

GIFT AID (NON-NEED-BASED) *Total amount:* $12,276,348 (93% institutional, 7% external sources). *Receiving aid:* Freshmen: 15% (157); Undergraduates: 7% (424). *Average Award:* Freshmen: $7374; Undergraduates: $8774. *Scholarships, grants, and awards by category:* Academic Interests/Achievement: biological sciences, business, computer science, engineering/technologies, general academic interests/achievements, mathematics, physical sciences. Special Achievements/Activities: general special achievements/activities, leadership. Special Characteristics: adult students, children of public servants, general special characteristics, handicapped students, international students, local/state students, members of minority groups, out-of-state students, public servants, veterans, veterans' children. *Tuition waivers:* Full or partial for senior citizens. *ROTC:* Army cooperative, Air Force cooperative.

LOANS *Student loans:* $43,021,740 (46% need-based, 54% non-need-based). *Average need-based loan:* Freshmen: $4506; Undergraduates: $6729. *Parent loans:* $222,197,592 (100% non-need-based). *Programs:* FFEL (Subsidized and Unsubsidized Stafford, PLUS), Perkins, state, college/university.

APPLYING FOR FINANCIAL AID *Required financial aid form:* FAFSA. *Financial aid deadline (priority):* 4/12. *Notification date:* Continuous beginning 3/1. Students must reply within 3 weeks of notification.

CONTACT Maria Ramos, Director of Financial Aid, The University of Texas at Dallas, 2601 North Floyd Road, PO Box 830688, HH11, Richardson, TX 75083, 972-883-2941 or toll-free 800-889-2443. *Fax:* 972-883-2947. *E-mail:* ramos@utdallas.edu.

THE UNIVERSITY OF TEXAS AT EL PASO
El Paso, TX

Tuition & fees (TX res): $5064 | **Average undergraduate aid package: $8482**

ABOUT THE INSTITUTION State-supported, coed. Awards: bachelor's, master's, and doctoral degrees. 62 undergraduate majors. Total enrollment: 18,918. Undergraduates: 15,592. Freshmen: 2,534. Federal methodology is used as a basis for awarding need-based institutional aid.

UNDERGRADUATE EXPENSES for 2005–06 *Tuition, state resident:* full-time $3930; part-time $131 per credit hour. *Tuition, nonresident:* full-time $12,210. Part-time tuition and fees vary according to course load. *College room and board: room only:* $4095. Room and board charges vary according to housing facility. *Payment plan:* Installment.

FRESHMAN FINANCIAL AID (Fall 2003) 1899 applied for aid; of those 75% were deemed to have need. 98% of freshmen with need received aid; of those 16% had need fully met. *Average percent of need met:* 73% (excluding resources awarded to replace EFC). *Average financial aid package:* $6897 (excluding resources awarded to replace EFC). 9% of all full-time freshmen had no need and received non-need-based gift aid.

UNDERGRADUATE FINANCIAL AID (Fall 2003) 7,594 applied for aid; of those 78% were deemed to have need. 98% of undergraduates with need received aid; of those 37% had need fully met. *Average percent of need met:* 87% (excluding resources awarded to replace EFC). *Average financial aid package:* $8482 (excluding resources awarded to replace EFC). 7% of all full-time undergraduates had no need and received non-need-based gift aid.

GIFT AID (NEED-BASED) *Total amount:* $34,128,095 (72% federal, 19% state, 9% institutional). *Receiving aid:* Freshmen: 60% (1,335); All full-time undergraduates: 52% (5,524). *Average award:* Freshmen: $4183; Undergraduates: $4310. *Scholarships, grants, and awards:* Federal Pell, FSEOG, state, college/university gift aid from institutional funds, Federal Nursing.

GIFT AID (NON-NEED-BASED) *Total amount:* $4,236,700 (3% state, 78% institutional, 19% external sources). *Receiving aid:* Freshmen: 7% (162); Undergraduates: 5% (579). *Average Award:* Freshmen: $1278; Undergraduates: $1890. *Scholarships, grants, and awards by category: Academic Interests/Achievement:* biological sciences, business, communication, computer science, education, engineering/technologies, English, general academic interests/achievements, health fields, humanities, international studies, mathematics, military science, physical sciences. *Creative Arts/Performance:* applied art and design, art/fine arts, journalism/publications, music, performing arts, theater/drama. *Special Achievements/Activities:* cheerleading/drum major, leadership. *Special Characteristics:* ethnic background, international students, local/state students, members of minority groups, out-of-state students. *ROTC:* Army, Air Force.

LOANS *Student loans:* $39,274,875 (100% need-based). 42% of past graduating class borrowed through all loan programs. *Average indebtedness per student:* $6041. *Average need-based loan:* Freshmen: $2720; Undergraduates: $4556. *Parent loans:* $339,198 (100% non-need-based). *Programs:* FFEL (Subsidized and Unsubsidized Stafford, PLUS), Perkins, Federal Nursing, state, college/university.

WORK-STUDY *Federal work-study:* Total amount: $1,790,840; 854 jobs averaging $2097. *State or other work-study/employment:* Total amount: $161,460 (100% need-based). 63 part-time jobs averaging $2563.

ATHLETIC AWARDS *Total amount:* $2,698,334 (100% non-need-based).

APPLYING FOR FINANCIAL AID *Required financial aid forms:* FAFSA, institution's own form. *Financial aid deadline (priority):* 3/15. *Notification date:* 6/30. Students must reply within 2 weeks of notification.

CONTACT Mr. Raul Lerma, Director of Financial Aid, The University of Texas at El Paso, 500 West University Avenue, El Paso, TX 79968-0001, 915-747-7378 or toll-free 877-746-4636.

THE UNIVERSITY OF TEXAS AT SAN ANTONIO
San Antonio, TX

Tuition & fees (TX res): $5272 | **Average undergraduate aid package: $6136**

ABOUT THE INSTITUTION State-supported, coed. Awards: bachelor's, master's, and doctoral degrees. 63 undergraduate majors. Total enrollment: 26,175. Undergraduates: 22,537. Freshmen: 3,125. Federal methodology is used as a basis for awarding need-based institutional aid.

UNDERGRADUATE EXPENSES for 2004–05 *Application fee:* $30. *Tuition, state resident:* full-time $3720; part-time $124 per hour. *Tuition, nonresident:* full-time $11,460; part-time $382 per hour. *College room and board:* $5306; *room only:* $3114.

FRESHMAN FINANCIAL AID (Fall 2003) 3205 applied for aid; of those 72% were deemed to have need. 95% of freshmen with need received aid; of those 10% had need fully met. *Average percent of need met:* 66% (excluding resources awarded to replace EFC). *Average financial aid package:* $5761 (excluding resources awarded to replace EFC). 51% of all full-time freshmen had no need and received non-need-based gift aid.

UNDERGRADUATE FINANCIAL AID (Fall 2003) 13,916 applied for aid; of those 80% were deemed to have need. 97% of undergraduates with need received aid; of those 13% had need fully met. *Average percent of need met:* 59% (excluding resources awarded to replace EFC). *Average financial aid package:* $6136 (excluding resources awarded to replace EFC). 3% of all full-time undergraduates had no need and received non-need-based gift aid.

GIFT AID (NEED-BASED) *Total amount:* $33,057,795 (69% federal, 31% state). *Receiving aid:* Freshmen: 41% (1,786); All full-time undergraduates: 46% (8,537). *Average award:* Freshmen: $4225; Undergraduates: $3584. *Scholarships, grants, and awards:* Federal Pell, FSEOG, state, private, college/university gift aid from institutional funds.

GIFT AID (NON-NEED-BASED) *Total amount:* $12,435,650 (50% institutional, 50% external sources). *Receiving aid:* Freshmen: 14% (628); Undergraduates: 9% (1,689). *Average Award:* Freshmen: $1295; Undergraduates: $1466. *Scholarships, grants, and awards by category: Academic Interests/Achievement:* agriculture, architecture, area/ethnic studies, biological sciences, business, communication, computer science, education, engineering/technologies, English, foreign languages, general academic interests/achievements, humanities, mathematics, physical sciences, social sciences. *Creative Arts/Performance:* art/fine arts, debating, music. *Special Achievements/Activities:* general special achievements/activities. *Special Characteristics:* ethnic background, general special characteristics, handicapped students, local/state students, out-of-state students. *ROTC:* Army, Air Force.

LOANS *Student loans:* $80,634,444 (56% need-based, 44% non-need-based). 52% of past graduating class borrowed through all loan programs. *Average indebtedness per student:* $17,000. *Average need-based loan:* Freshmen: $2317; Undergraduates: $3579. *Parent loans:* $3,994,723 (100% non-need-based). *Programs:* FFEL (Subsidized and Unsubsidized Stafford, PLUS), Perkins, state, college/university.

WORK-STUDY *Federal work-study:* Total amount: $1,064,720; 393 jobs averaging $4000. *State or other work-study/employment:* Total amount: $400,399 (100% need-based). 293 part-time jobs averaging $4000.

ATHLETIC AWARDS *Total amount:* $1,394,147 (100% non-need-based).

APPLYING FOR FINANCIAL AID *Required financial aid forms:* FAFSA, institution's own form. *Financial aid deadline (priority):* 3/31. *Notification date:* Continuous beginning 4/1. Students must reply within 4 weeks of notification.

CONTACT Kim Canady, Assistant Director of Student Financial Aid, The University of Texas at San Antonio, 6900 North Loop 1604 West, San Antonio, TX 78249, 210-458-8000 or toll-free 800-669-0919. *Fax:* 210-458-4638. *E-mail:* financialaid@utsa.edu.

THE UNIVERSITY OF TEXAS AT TYLER
Tyler, TX

Tuition & fees (TX res): $4046 | **Average undergraduate aid package: $7221**

ABOUT THE INSTITUTION State-supported, coed. Awards: bachelor's and master's degrees. 33 undergraduate majors. Total enrollment: 5,303. Undergraduates: 4,086. Freshmen: 498. Federal methodology is used as a basis for awarding need-based institutional aid.

UNDERGRADUATE EXPENSES for 2004–05 *Tuition, state resident:* full-time $3304; part-time $110 per semester hour. *Tuition, nonresident:* full-time $9496; part-time $412 per semester hour. Full-time tuition and fees vary according to course load. *College room and board:* $5373. Room and board charges vary according to housing facility. *Payment plan:* Installment.

GIFT AID (NEED-BASED) *Total amount:* $7,119,468 (59% federal, 16% state, 20% institutional, 5% external sources). *Receiving aid:* Freshmen: 42% (206); All full-time undergraduates: 47% (1,461). *Average award:* Freshmen: $4782; Undergraduates: $4185. *Scholarships, grants, and awards:* Federal Pell, FSEOG, state, private, college/university gift aid from institutional funds, Texas Grant, Teach for Texas Conditional Prog, Institutional Grants (Education Affordability Prog).

GIFT AID (NON-NEED-BASED) *Total amount:* $2,381,554 (74% institutional, 26% external sources). *Receiving aid:* Freshmen: 15% (74); Undergraduates: 7% (203). *Average Award:* Freshmen: $2593; Undergraduates: $1965. *Scholarships, grants, and awards by category:* Academic Interests/Achievement: 7,325 awards ($9,022,790 total): engineering/technologies, general academic interests/achievements. *Tuition waivers:* Full or partial for employees or children of employees, senior citizens.

LOANS *Student loans:* $14,070,133 (66% need-based, 34% non-need-based). 54% of past graduating class borrowed through all loan programs. *Average indebtedness per student:* $14,967. *Average need-based loan:* Freshmen: $1652; Undergraduates: $3296. *Parent loans:* $3,769,268 (15% need-based, 85% non-need-based). *Programs:* FFEL (Subsidized and Unsubsidized Stafford, PLUS), state.

APPLYING FOR FINANCIAL AID *Required financial aid form:* FAFSA. *Financial aid deadline (priority):* 4/1. *Notification date:* Continuous beginning 4/15. Students must reply within 2 weeks of notification.

CONTACT Ms. Candice A. Garner, Associate Dean of Enrollment Management, The University of Texas at Tyler, 3900 University Boulevard, Tyler, TX 75799-0001, 903-566-7221 or toll-free 800-UTTYLER (in-state). *Fax:* 903-566-7183. *E-mail:* cgarner@uttyler.edu.

THE UNIVERSITY OF TEXAS HEALTH SCIENCE CENTER AT HOUSTON
Houston, TX

Tuition & fees (TX res): $5602   **Average undergraduate aid package: $15,838**

ABOUT THE INSTITUTION State-supported, coed. Awards: bachelor's, master's, doctoral, and first professional degrees and post-master's certificates. 2 undergraduate majors. Total enrollment: 3,399. Undergraduates: 381. Federal methodology is used as a basis for awarding need-based institutional aid.

UNDERGRADUATE EXPENSES for 2005–06 *Application fee:* $30. *Tuition, state resident:* full-time $4905; part-time $105 per hour. *Tuition, nonresident:* full-time $16,571; part-time $364.50 per hour. Part-time tuition and fees vary according to course load. *Payment plan:* Installment.

UNDERGRADUATE FINANCIAL AID (Fall 2004, est.) 265 applied for aid; of those 82% were deemed to have need. 100% of undergraduates with need received aid. *Average percent of need met:* 95% (excluding resources awarded to replace EFC). *Average financial aid package:* $15,838 (excluding resources awarded to replace EFC).

GIFT AID (NEED-BASED) *Total amount:* $748,703 (34% federal, 4% state, 52% institutional, 10% external sources). *Receiving aid:* All full-time undergraduates: 39% (148). *Average award:* Undergraduates: $5059. *Scholarships, grants, and awards:* Federal Pell, FSEOG, state, private, college/university gift aid from institutional funds.

GIFT AID (NON-NEED-BASED) *ROTC:* Army cooperative.

LOANS *Student loans:* $2,764,008 (100% need-based). 93% of past graduating class borrowed through all loan programs. *Average indebtedness per student:* $17,505. *Average need-based loan:* Undergraduates: $6200. *Parent loans:* $400,836 (100% need-based). *Programs:* FFEL (Subsidized and Unsubsidized Stafford, PLUS), Perkins, state, college/university, alternative loans.

APPLYING FOR FINANCIAL AID *Required financial aid forms:* FAFSA, institution's own form. *Financial aid deadline:* Continuous. *Notification date:* Continuous.

CONTACT Mr. Carl W. Gordon, Director of Student Financial Aid, The University of Texas Health Science Center at Houston, PO Box 20036, Houston, TX 77225-0036, 713-500-3860. *Fax:* 713-500-3863. *E-mail:* carl.w.gordon@uth.tmc.edu.

THE UNIVERSITY OF TEXAS HEALTH SCIENCE CENTER AT SAN ANTONIO
San Antonio, TX

CONTACT Robert T. Lawson, Financial Aid Administrator, The University of Texas Health Science Center at San Antonio, 7703 Floyd Curl Drive, MSC 7708, San Antonio, TX 78284, 210-567-0025. *Fax:* 210-567-6643.

THE UNIVERSITY OF TEXAS MEDICAL BRANCH
Galveston, TX

Tuition & fees (TX res): $3210   **Average undergraduate aid package: N/A**

ABOUT THE INSTITUTION State-supported, coed. Awards: bachelor's, master's, doctoral, and first professional degrees. 4 undergraduate majors. Total enrollment: 2,121. Undergraduates: 511. Entering class: . Federal methodology is used as a basis for awarding need-based institutional aid.

UNDERGRADUATE EXPENSES for 2004–05 *Application fee:* $25. *Tuition, state resident:* full-time $2640; part-time $88 per credit hour. *Tuition, nonresident:* full-time $10,380; part-time $346 per credit hour. *Required fees:* full-time $570; $15 per credit hour or $55 per term part-time. Full-time tuition and fees vary according to course load and program. Part-time tuition and fees vary according to course load and program. *College room and board: room only:* $2160. Room and board charges vary according to housing facility. *Payment plan:* Installment.

GIFT AID (NEED-BASED) *Total amount:* $1,002,658 (44% federal, 40% state, 12% institutional, 4% external sources). *Scholarships, grants, and awards:* Federal Pell, FSEOG, state, private, college/university gift aid from institutional funds.

GIFT AID (NON-NEED-BASED) *Total amount:* $19,467 (73% institutional, 27% external sources). *Scholarships, grants, and awards by category:* Academic Interests/Achievement: 10 awards ($14,167 total): health fields.

LOANS *Student loans:* $8,228,422 (96% need-based, 4% non-need-based). *Programs:* Federal Direct (Subsidized and Unsubsidized Stafford, PLUS), Perkins, Federal Nursing, state, college/university.

WORK-STUDY *Federal work-study:* Total amount: $33,485; 24 jobs available.

APPLYING FOR FINANCIAL AID *Required financial aid form:* FAFSA. *Financial aid deadline:* Continuous. *Notification date:* Continuous. Students must reply within 4 weeks of notification.

CONTACT Ms. Ellen Gomes, University Financial Aid Officer, The University of Texas Medical Branch, 301 University Boulevard, Galveston, TX 77555-1305, 409-772-1215. *Fax:* 409-772-4466. *E-mail:* enrollment.services@utmb.edu.

THE UNIVERSITY OF TEXAS OF THE PERMIAN BASIN
Odessa, TX

Tuition & fees: N/R   **Average undergraduate aid package: $6943**

ABOUT THE INSTITUTION State-supported, coed. Awards: bachelor's and master's degrees. 24 undergraduate majors. Total enrollment: 2,695. Undergraduates: 2,012. Freshmen: 226. Federal methodology is used as a basis for awarding need-based institutional aid.

GIFT AID (NEED-BASED) *Total amount:* $3,866,494 (79% federal, 21% state). *Receiving aid:* Freshmen: 78% (144); All full-time undergraduates: 75% (1,349). *Average award:* Freshmen: $6314; Undergraduates: $7095. *Scholarships, grants, and awards:* Federal Pell, FSEOG, state, private, college/university gift aid from institutional funds.

GIFT AID (NON-NEED-BASED) *Total amount:* $2,770,002 (19% federal, 57% institutional, 24% external sources). *Receiving aid:* Freshmen: 8% (15); Undergraduates: 2% (37). *Scholarships, grants, and awards by category:* Academic Interests/Achievement: 1,340 awards ($1,591,499 total): general academic interests/achievements. Creative Arts/Performance: 11 awards ($5346 total): art/fine arts, general creative arts/performance.

LOANS *Student loans:* $6,918,626 (57% need-based, 43% non-need-based). 22% of past graduating class borrowed through all loan programs. *Average indebtedness per student:* $15,424. *Average need-based loan:* Freshmen: $1703; Undergraduates: $1736. *Parent loans:* $21,825 (100% non-need-based). *Programs:* FFEL (Subsidized and Unsubsidized Stafford, PLUS), state, college/university.

ATHLETIC AWARDS *Total amount:* $142,186 (100% non-need-based).

APPLYING FOR FINANCIAL AID *Required financial aid forms:* FAFSA, institution's own form. *Financial aid deadline (priority):* 5/1. *Notification date:* Continuous.

CONTACT Mr. Robert L. Vasquez, Director of Financial Aid, The University of Texas of the Permian Basin, 4901 East University, Odessa, TX 79762-0001, 432-552-2620 or toll-free 866-552-UTPB. *Fax:* 432-552-2621. *E-mail:* vasquez_r@utpb.edu.

THE UNIVERSITY OF TEXAS–PAN AMERICAN
Edinburg, TX

Tuition & fees (TX res): $3152	Average undergraduate aid package: $6950

ABOUT THE INSTITUTION State-supported, coed. Awards: bachelor's, master's, and doctoral degrees and post-bachelor's and post-master's certificates. 58 undergraduate majors. Total enrollment: 17,030. Undergraduates: 14,788. Freshmen: 2,824. Federal methodology is used as a basis for awarding need-based institutional aid.

UNDERGRADUATE EXPENSES for 2004–05 *Tuition, state resident:* full-time $2504; part-time $86 per semester hour. *Tuition, nonresident:* full-time $10,244; part-time $344 per semester hour. *Required fees:* full-time $648; $75 per semester hour. *College room and board:* $4233; *room only:* $2406. Room and board charges vary according to board plan and housing facility. *Payment plan:* Installment.

FRESHMAN FINANCIAL AID (Fall 2003) 1553 applied for aid; of those 95% were deemed to have need. 100% of freshmen with need received aid; of those 4% had need fully met. *Average percent of need met:* 67% (excluding resources awarded to replace EFC). *Average financial aid package:* $5572 (excluding resources awarded to replace EFC). 5% of all full-time freshmen had no need and received non-need-based gift aid.

UNDERGRADUATE FINANCIAL AID (Fall 2003) 7,112 applied for aid; of those 96% were deemed to have need. 97% of undergraduates with need received aid; of those 6% had need fully met. *Average percent of need met:* 82% (excluding resources awarded to replace EFC). *Average financial aid package:* $6950 (excluding resources awarded to replace EFC). 5% of all full-time undergraduates had no need and received non-need-based gift aid.

GIFT AID (NEED-BASED) *Total amount:* $35,352,700 (61% federal, 33% state, 4% institutional, 2% external sources). *Receiving aid:* Freshmen: 86% (1,450); All full-time undergraduates: 80% (6,392). *Average award:* Freshmen: $5581; Undergraduates: $7001. *Scholarships, grants, and awards:* Federal Pell, FSEOG, state, private, college/university gift aid from institutional funds.

GIFT AID (NON-NEED-BASED) *Total amount:* $1,252,009 (7% federal, 1% state, 59% institutional, 33% external sources). *Receiving aid:* Freshmen: 1% (23); Undergraduates: 2% (124). *Average Award:* Freshmen: $3837; Undergraduates: $4082. *Scholarships, grants, and awards by category:* Academic Interests/Achievement: 1,386 awards ($2,914,023 total): biological sciences, business, communication, computer science, education, engineering/technologies, English, general academic interests/achievements, health fields, mathematics, military science, premedicine, social sciences. Creative Arts/Performance: 78 awards ($48,695 total): art/fine arts, dance, journalism/publications, music, theater/drama. Special Achievements/Activities: 213 awards ($274,341 total): cheerleading/drum major, community service, general special achievements/activities, leadership, memberships. Special Characteristics: 133 awards ($227,897 total): ethnic background, general special characteristics, international students, local/state students, out-of-state students, veterans. *Tuition waivers:* Full or partial for senior citizens. *ROTC:* Army.

LOANS *Student loans:* $15,638,292 (100% need-based). 83% of past graduating class borrowed through all loan programs. *Average indebtedness per student:* $12,080. *Average need-based loan:* Freshmen: $1208; Undergraduates: $3382. *Parent loans:* $88,065 (35% need-based, 65% non-need-based). *Programs:* FFEL (Subsidized and Unsubsidized Stafford, PLUS), Perkins, college/university.

WORK-STUDY *Federal work-study:* Total amount: $1,644,337; 848 jobs averaging $1939. *State or other work-study/employment:* Total amount: $155,625 (100% need-based). 133 part-time jobs averaging $1170.

ATHLETIC AWARDS *Total amount:* $710,197 (32% need-based, 68% non-need-based).

APPLYING FOR FINANCIAL AID *Required financial aid form:* FAFSA. *Financial aid deadline (priority):* 3/1. *Notification date:* Continuous beginning 3/15. Students must reply within 2 weeks of notification.

CONTACT Mrs. Michelle Alvarado, Director of Financial Aid, The University of Texas–Pan American, 1201 West University Drive, Edinburg, TX 78541, 956-381-2190. *Fax:* 956-381-2396. *E-mail:* michelle@panam.edu.

THE UNIVERSITY OF TEXAS SOUTHWESTERN MEDICAL CENTER AT DALLAS
Dallas, TX

Tuition & fees (TX res): $2820	Average undergraduate aid package: N/A

ABOUT THE INSTITUTION State-supported, coed. Awards: bachelor's, master's, doctoral, and first professional degrees and post-bachelor's certificates. 6 undergraduate majors. Total enrollment: 2,267. Undergraduates: 118. Federal methodology is used as a basis for awarding need-based institutional aid.

UNDERGRADUATE EXPENSES for 2005–06 *Application fee:* $10. *Tuition, state resident:* full-time $2820; part-time $48 per credit hour. *Tuition, nonresident:* full-time $11,880; part-time $350 per credit hour. Full-time tuition and fees vary according to course load. Part-time tuition and fees vary according to course load. *Payment plan:* Installment.

UNDERGRADUATE FINANCIAL AID (Fall 2003) 92 applied for aid; of those 100% were deemed to have need. 100% of undergraduates with need received aid.

GIFT AID (NEED-BASED) *Total amount:* $358,047 (44% federal, 2% state, 54% institutional). *Scholarships, grants, and awards:* Federal Pell, FSEOG, state, private, college/university gift aid from institutional funds.

GIFT AID (NON-NEED-BASED) *Total amount:* $42,100 (7% federal, 2% institutional, 91% external sources). *Average Award: Undergraduates:* $500. *Scholarships, grants, and awards by category:* Special Achievements/Activities: community service.

LOANS *Student loans:* $803,222 (59% need-based, 41% non-need-based). 86% of past graduating class borrowed through all loan programs. *Average indebtedness per student:* $34,946. *Parent loans:* $31,125 (100% non-need-based). *Programs:* FFEL (Subsidized and Unsubsidized Stafford, PLUS), Perkins, state, college/university, alternative loans.

WORK-STUDY *Federal work-study:* Total amount: $23,873; 8 jobs averaging $1458. *State or other work-study/employment:* Total amount: $2679 (100% need-based).

APPLYING FOR FINANCIAL AID *Required financial aid forms:* FAFSA, we do not enroll freshmen, they must have 60-90 hours prior to attending U T Southwestern. *Financial aid deadline (priority):* 3/15. *Notification date:* 4/15. Students must reply within 2 weeks of notification.

CONTACT Ms. June M. Perry, Associate Director of Student Financial Aid, The University of Texas Southwestern Medical Center at Dallas, 5323 Harry Hines Boulevard, Dallas, TX 75390-9064, 214-648-3611. *Fax:* 214-648-3289. *E-mail:* june.perry@utsouthwestern.edu.

THE UNIVERSITY OF THE ARTS
Philadelphia, PA

CONTACT Office of Financial Aid, The University of the Arts, 320 South Broad Street, Philadelphia, PA 19102-4944, 800-616-ARTS Ext. 6170 or toll-free 800-616-ARTS. *E-mail:* finaid@uarts.edu.

UNIVERSITY OF THE CUMBERLANDS
Williamsburg, KY

Tuition & fees: $12,658	Average undergraduate aid package: $13,000

ABOUT THE INSTITUTION Independent Kentucky Baptist, coed. Awards: associate, bachelor's, and master's degrees. 34 undergraduate majors. Total enrollment: 1,744. Undergraduates: 1,603. Freshmen: 422. Federal methodology is used as a basis for awarding need-based institutional aid.

UNDERGRADUATE EXPENSES for 2005–06 *Application fee:* $30. *Comprehensive fee:* $18,184 includes full-time tuition ($12,298), mandatory fees ($360), and room and board ($5526). *Part-time tuition:* $410 per hour. *Part-time fees:* $48.75 per term. Part-time tuition and fees vary according to course load. *Payment plan:* Installment.

FRESHMAN FINANCIAL AID (Fall 2004, est.) 388 applied for aid; of those 91% were deemed to have need. 100% of freshmen with need received aid; of those 54% had need fully met. *Average percent of need met:* 92% (excluding resources awarded to replace EFC). *Average financial aid package:* $13,864 (excluding resources awarded to replace EFC). 5% of all full-time freshmen had no need and received non-need-based gift aid.

University of the Cumberlands

UNDERGRADUATE FINANCIAL AID (Fall 2004, est.) 1,250 applied for aid; of those 93% were deemed to have need. 100% of undergraduates with need received aid; of those 45% had need fully met. *Average percent of need met:* 94% (excluding resources awarded to replace EFC). *Average financial aid package:* $13,000 (excluding resources awarded to replace EFC). 8% of all full-time undergraduates had no need and received non-need-based gift aid.
GIFT AID (NEED-BASED) *Receiving aid:* Freshmen: 62% (258); All full-time undergraduates: 63% (868). *Average award:* Freshmen: $5512; Undergraduates: $5090. *Scholarships, grants, and awards:* Federal Pell, FSEOG, state, private, college/university gift aid from institutional funds.
GIFT AID (NON-NEED-BASED) *Receiving aid:* Freshmen: 85% (350); Undergraduates: 75% (1,032). *Average Award:* Freshmen: $6912; Undergraduates: $6360. *Scholarships, grants, and awards by category: Academic Interests/Achievement:* 866 awards ($2,534,192 total): general academic interests/achievements. *Creative Arts/Performance:* 122 awards ($205,710 total): art/fine arts, debating, music, theater/drama. *Special Achievements/Activities:* 271 awards ($167,097 total): cheerleading/drum major, community service, religious involvement. *Special Characteristics:* 285 awards ($352,559 total): children and siblings of alumni, children of faculty/staff, relatives of clergy, siblings of current students. *Tuition waivers:* Full or partial for employees or children of employees. *ROTC:* Army.
LOANS *Student loans:* $4,726,771 (64% need-based, 36% non-need-based). 70% of past graduating class borrowed through all loan programs. *Average indebtedness per student:* $14,455. *Average need-based loan:* Freshmen: $3038; Undergraduates: $3658. *Parent loans:* $505,445 (100% non-need-based). *Programs:* FFEL (Subsidized and Unsubsidized Stafford, PLUS), Perkins, college/university.
WORK-STUDY *Federal work-study:* Total amount: $784,516; 456 jobs averaging $1720. *State or other work-study/employment:* Total amount: $349,733 (100% need-based). 198 part-time jobs averaging $1766.
ATHLETIC AWARDS *Total amount:* $2,070,458 (100% non-need-based).
APPLYING FOR FINANCIAL AID *Required financial aid form:* FAFSA. *Financial aid deadline (priority):* 3/1. *Notification date:* Continuous beginning 4/1. Students must reply within 2 weeks of notification.
CONTACT Mr. Steve Allen, Director of Student Financial Planning, University of the Cumberlands, 6190 College Station Drive, Williamsburg, KY 40769-1372, 606-549-2200 Ext. 4220 or toll-free 800-343-1609. *Fax:* 606-539-4220. *E-mail:* finaid@cumberlandcollege.edu.

UNIVERSITY OF THE DISTRICT OF COLUMBIA
Washington, DC

Tuition & fees (DC res): $2070	Average undergraduate aid package: $5927

ABOUT THE INSTITUTION District-supported, coed. Awards: associate, bachelor's, and master's degrees. 102 undergraduate majors. Total enrollment: 5,165. Undergraduates: 4,966. Freshmen: 1,058. Federal methodology is used as a basis for awarding need-based institutional aid.
UNDERGRADUATE EXPENSES for 2005–06 *Application fee:* $20. *Tuition, state resident:* full-time $1800; part-time $75 per credit. *Tuition, nonresident:* full-time $4440; part-time $185 per credit. *Required fees:* full-time $270; $135 per term part-time. Part-time tuition and fees vary according to course load. *Payment plans:* Installment, deferred payment.
FRESHMAN FINANCIAL AID (Fall 2004, est.) 663 applied for aid; of those 60% were deemed to have need. 69% of freshmen with need received aid; of those 35% had need fully met. *Average percent of need met:* 71% (excluding resources awarded to replace EFC). *Average financial aid package:* $4821 (excluding resources awarded to replace EFC). 3% of all full-time freshmen had no need and received non-need-based gift aid.
UNDERGRADUATE FINANCIAL AID (Fall 2004, est.) 2,280 applied for aid; of those 60% were deemed to have need. 83% of undergraduates with need received aid; of those 34% had need fully met. *Average financial aid package:* $5927 (excluding resources awarded to replace EFC). 2% of all full-time undergraduates had no need and received non-need-based gift aid.
GIFT AID (NEED-BASED) *Total amount:* $5,311,109 (91% federal, 7% state, 2% institutional). *Receiving aid:* Freshmen: 13% (127); All full-time undergraduates: 18% (673). *Average award:* Freshmen: $2746; Undergraduates: $2822. *Scholarships, grants, and awards:* Federal Pell, FSEOG, state, college/university gift aid from institutional funds.
GIFT AID (NON-NEED-BASED) *Total amount:* $384,855 (25% institutional, 75% external sources). *Receiving aid:* Freshmen: 6% (57); Undergraduates: 3% (103). *Average Award:* Freshmen: $3625; Undergraduates: $2147. *Scholar-*

ships, grants, and awards by category: *Academic Interests/Achievement:* general academic interests/achievements. *Creative Arts/Performance:* music. *Special Characteristics:* children of faculty/staff. *Tuition waivers:* Full or partial for employees or children of employees, senior citizens. *ROTC:* Army cooperative, Air Force cooperative.
LOANS *Student loans:* $4,841,198 (69% need-based, 31% non-need-based). 74% of past graduating class borrowed through all loan programs. *Average indebtedness per student:* $16,270. *Average need-based loan:* Freshmen: $2842; Undergraduates: $4447. *Parent loans:* $13,628 (100% need-based). *Programs:* FFEL (Subsidized and Unsubsidized Stafford, PLUS), Perkins, college/university.
WORK-STUDY *Federal work-study:* Total amount: $230,801; 110 jobs averaging $3000. *State or other work-study/employment:* Total amount: $175,000 (100% non-need-based). Part-time jobs available.
APPLYING FOR FINANCIAL AID *Required financial aid forms:* FAFSA, district aid form, loan request form. *Financial aid deadline (priority):* 3/31. *Notification date:* Continuous beginning 4/1. Students must reply within 2 weeks of notification.
CONTACT Alice Dais, Financial Aid Counselor, University of the District of Columbia, 4200 Connecticut Avenue NW, Washington, DC 20008-1175, 202-274-5060.

UNIVERSITY OF THE INCARNATE WORD
San Antonio, TX

Tuition & fees: $17,072	Average undergraduate aid package: $11,283

ABOUT THE INSTITUTION Independent Roman Catholic, coed. Awards: associate, bachelor's, master's, and doctoral degrees. 61 undergraduate majors. Total enrollment: 4,800. Undergraduates: 4,022. Freshmen: 486. Federal methodology is used as a basis for awarding need-based institutional aid.
UNDERGRADUATE EXPENSES for 2005–06 *Application fee:* $20. *One-time required fee:* $30. *Comprehensive fee:* $23,306 includes full-time tuition ($16,500), mandatory fees ($572), and room and board ($6234). *College room only:* $3750. Room and board charges vary according to board plan and housing facility. *Part-time tuition:* $525 per semester hour. *Part-time fees:* $270 per term. Part-time tuition and fees vary according to course load. *Payment plan:* Installment.
FRESHMAN FINANCIAL AID (Fall 2004, est.) 409 applied for aid; of those 83% were deemed to have need. 100% of freshmen with need received aid; of those 59% had need fully met. *Average percent of need met:* 75% (excluding resources awarded to replace EFC). *Average financial aid package:* $11,798 (excluding resources awarded to replace EFC). 14% of all full-time freshmen had no need and received non-need-based gift aid.
UNDERGRADUATE FINANCIAL AID (Fall 2004, est.) 1,795 applied for aid; of those 96% were deemed to have need. 100% of undergraduates with need received aid; of those 64% had need fully met. *Average percent of need met:* 71% (excluding resources awarded to replace EFC). *Average financial aid package:* $11,283 (excluding resources awarded to replace EFC). 15% of all full-time undergraduates had no need and received non-need-based gift aid.
GIFT AID (NEED-BASED) *Total amount:* $8,501,107 (48% federal, 43% state, 4% institutional, 5% external sources). *Receiving aid:* Freshmen: 72% (339); All full-time undergraduates: 68% (1,553). *Average award:* Freshmen: $8782; Undergraduates: $7471. *Scholarships, grants, and awards:* Federal Pell, FSEOG, state, private, college/university gift aid from institutional funds, United Negro College Fund, Federal Nursing.
GIFT AID (NON-NEED-BASED) *Total amount:* $5,872,729 (97% institutional, 3% external sources). *Receiving aid:* Freshmen: 34% (163); Undergraduates: 51% (1,175). *Average Award:* Freshmen: $6430; Undergraduates: $8180. *Scholarships, grants, and awards by category: Academic Interests/Achievement:* 1,447 awards ($4,323,736 total): general academic interests/achievements. *Creative Arts/Performance:* 83 awards ($159,095 total): art/fine arts, dance, music, theater/drama. *Special Achievements/Activities:* 23 awards ($31,225 total): religious involvement. *Special Characteristics:* 72 awards ($743,226 total): children of union members/company employees. *Tuition waivers:* Full or partial for employees or children of employees. *ROTC:* Army cooperative, Air Force cooperative.
LOANS *Student loans:* $18,143,459 (39% need-based, 61% non-need-based). 84% of past graduating class borrowed through all loan programs. *Average indebtedness per student:* $24,476. *Average need-based loan:* Freshmen: $2992; Undergraduates: $4252. *Parent loans:* $1,148,559 (15% need-based, 85% non-need-based). *Programs:* FFEL (Subsidized and Unsubsidized Stafford, PLUS), Perkins, Federal Nursing, state, alternative loans.

WORK-STUDY *Federal work-study:* Total amount: $704,017; 471 jobs averaging $1526. *State or other work-study/employment:* Total amount: $42,383 (100% need-based). 27 part-time jobs averaging $1569.

ATHLETIC AWARDS *Total amount:* $1,848,227 (65% need-based, 35% non-need-based).

APPLYING FOR FINANCIAL AID *Required financial aid form:* FAFSA. *Financial aid deadline (priority):* 4/1. *Notification date:* Continuous beginning 2/15. Students must reply within 2 weeks of notification.

CONTACT Ms. Amy Carcanagues, Director of Financial Assistance, University of the Incarnate Word, 4301 Broadway, Box 308, San Antonio, TX 78209, 210-829-6008 or toll-free 800-749-WORD. *Fax:* 210-283-5053. *E-mail:* amyc@universe.uiwtx.edu.

UNIVERSITY OF THE OZARKS
Clarksville, AR

Tuition & fees: $13,312	Average undergraduate aid package: $12,958

ABOUT THE INSTITUTION Independent Presbyterian, coed. Awards: bachelor's degrees. 36 undergraduate majors. Total enrollment: 628. Undergraduates: 628. Freshmen: 135. Both federal and institutional methodology are used as a basis for awarding need-based institutional aid.

UNDERGRADUATE EXPENSES for 2004–05 *Application fee:* $10. *Comprehensive fee:* $18,192 includes full-time tuition ($12,902), mandatory fees ($410), and room and board ($4880). Full-time tuition and fees vary according to course load. Room and board charges vary according to board plan and housing facility. *Part-time tuition:* $540 per credit. *Payment plan:* Installment.

FRESHMAN FINANCIAL AID (Fall 2004, est.) 82 applied for aid; of those 88% were deemed to have need. 100% of freshmen with need received aid; of those 12% had need fully met. *Average percent of need met:* 64% (excluding resources awarded to replace EFC). *Average financial aid package:* $12,787 (excluding resources awarded to replace EFC). 25% of all full-time freshmen had no need and received non-need-based gift aid.

UNDERGRADUATE FINANCIAL AID (Fall 2004, est.) 341 applied for aid; of those 90% were deemed to have need. 100% of undergraduates with need received aid; of those 6% had need fully met. *Average percent of need met:* 71% (excluding resources awarded to replace EFC). *Average financial aid package:* $12,958 (excluding resources awarded to replace EFC). 37% of all full-time undergraduates had no need and received non-need-based gift aid.

GIFT AID (NEED-BASED) *Total amount:* $3,215,635 (17% federal, 5% state, 76% institutional, 2% external sources). *Receiving aid:* Freshmen: 53% (72); All full-time undergraduates: 52% (308). *Average award:* Freshmen: $11,481; Undergraduates: $10,134. *Scholarships, grants, and awards:* Federal Pell, FSEOG, state, private, college/university gift aid from institutional funds.

GIFT AID (NON-NEED-BASED) *Total amount:* $1,731,618 (8% state, 82% institutional, 10% external sources). *Receiving aid:* Freshmen: 21% (29); Undergraduates: 18% (104). *Average Award:* Freshmen: $8571; Undergraduates: $7766. *Scholarships, grants, and awards by category: Academic Interests/Achievement:* 240 awards ($1,434,508 total): biological sciences, business, communication, education, English, general academic interests/achievements, humanities, mathematics, premedicine, religion/biblical studies, social sciences. *Creative Arts/Performance:* 19 awards ($44,116 total): art/fine arts, music, theater/drama. *Special Achievements/Activities:* 199 awards ($597,875 total): leadership. *Special Characteristics:* 191 awards ($623,054 total): children and siblings of alumni, children of faculty/staff, general special characteristics, international students, members of minority groups, relatives of clergy, religious affiliation, siblings of current students. *Tuition waivers:* Full or partial for employees or children of employees.

LOANS *Student loans:* $1,569,098 (51% need-based, 49% non-need-based). 44% of past graduating class borrowed through all loan programs. *Average indebtedness per student:* $12,160. *Average need-based loan:* Freshmen: $667; Undergraduates: $2630. *Parent loans:* $568,726 (20% need-based, 80% non-need-based). *Programs:* FFEL (Subsidized and Unsubsidized Stafford, PLUS), Perkins, college/university.

WORK-STUDY *Federal work-study:* Total amount: $75,394; 109 jobs averaging $1391. *State or other work-study/employment:* Total amount: $173,242 (100% non-need-based). 232 part-time jobs averaging $1625.

APPLYING FOR FINANCIAL AID *Required financial aid form:* FAFSA. *Financial aid deadline (priority):* 2/15. *Notification date:* Continuous beginning 3/15. Students must reply within 2 weeks of notification.

CONTACT Ms. Jana D. Hart, Director of Financial Aid, University of the Ozarks, 415 North College Avenue, Clarksville, AR 72830-2880, 479-979-1221 or toll-free 800-264-8636. *Fax:* 479-979-1355. *E-mail:* jhart@ozarks.edu.

UNIVERSITY OF THE PACIFIC
Stockton, CA

Tuition & fees: $24,750	Average undergraduate aid package: $22,114

ABOUT THE INSTITUTION Independent, coed. Awards: bachelor's, master's, doctoral, and first professional degrees. 54 undergraduate majors. Total enrollment: 6,268. Undergraduates: 3,459. Freshmen: 880. Federal methodology is used as a basis for awarding need-based institutional aid.

UNDERGRADUATE EXPENSES for 2004–05 *Application fee:* $50. *Comprehensive fee:* $32,608 includes full-time tuition ($24,320), mandatory fees ($430), and room and board ($7858). *College room only:* $3914. Room and board charges vary according to board plan and housing facility. *Part-time tuition:* $839 per unit. Part-time tuition and fees vary according to course load. *Payment plan:* Deferred payment.

FRESHMAN FINANCIAL AID (Fall 2004, est.) 741 applied for aid; of those 81% were deemed to have need. 100% of freshmen with need received aid; of those 31% had need fully met. *Average financial aid package:* $20,347 (excluding resources awarded to replace EFC). 17% of all full-time freshmen had no need and received non-need-based gift aid.

UNDERGRADUATE FINANCIAL AID (Fall 2004, est.) 2,574 applied for aid; of those 88% were deemed to have need. 100% of undergraduates with need received aid; of those 27% had need fully met. *Average financial aid package:* $22,114 (excluding resources awarded to replace EFC). 12% of all full-time undergraduates had no need and received non-need-based gift aid.

GIFT AID (NEED-BASED) *Total amount:* $36,175,911 (11% federal, 26% state, 63% institutional). *Receiving aid:* Freshmen: 67% (588); All full-time undergraduates: 64% (2,173). *Average award:* Freshmen: $16,710; Undergraduates: $17,092. *Scholarships, grants, and awards:* Federal Pell, FSEOG, state, private, college/university gift aid from institutional funds.

GIFT AID (NON-NEED-BASED) *Total amount:* $3,124,759 (100% institutional). *Average Award:* Freshmen: $7738; Undergraduates: $7784. *Scholarships, grants, and awards by category: Academic Interests/Achievement:* 1,196 awards ($9,285,739 total): general academic interests/achievements. *Creative Arts/Performance:* 97 awards ($539,670 total): music. *Special Achievements/Activities:* 30 awards ($73,500 total): religious involvement. *Tuition waivers:* Full or partial for employees or children of employees.

LOANS *Student loans:* $11,032,747 (93% need-based, 7% non-need-based). *Average need-based loan:* Freshmen: $3331; Undergraduates: $4955. *Parent loans:* $7,169,299 (80% need-based, 20% non-need-based). *Programs:* Federal Direct (Subsidized and Unsubsidized Stafford, PLUS), FFEL (Subsidized and Unsubsidized Stafford, PLUS), Perkins, state.

WORK-STUDY *Federal work-study:* Total amount: $3,039,583; 2,123 jobs averaging $1432. *State or other work-study/employment:* Part-time jobs available.

ATHLETIC AWARDS *Total amount:* $3,667,370 (35% need-based, 65% non-need-based).

APPLYING FOR FINANCIAL AID *Required financial aid form:* FAFSA. *Financial aid deadline (priority):* 2/15. *Notification date:* Continuous beginning 3/15.

CONTACT Director of Financial Aid, University of the Pacific, 3601 Pacific Avenue, Stockton, CA 95211-0197, 209-946-2421 or toll-free 800-959-2867.

UNIVERSITY OF THE SACRED HEART
San Juan, PR

CONTACT Ms. Maria Torres, Director of Financial Aid, University of the Sacred Heart, PO Box 12383, San Juan, PR 00914-0383, 787-728-1515 Ext. 3605.

UNIVERSITY OF THE SCIENCES IN PHILADELPHIA
Philadelphia, PA

ABOUT THE INSTITUTION Independent, coed. Awards: bachelor's, master's, doctoral, and first professional degrees. 16 undergraduate majors. Total enrollment: 2,824. Undergraduates: 1,964. Freshmen: 560.

GIFT AID (NEED-BASED) *Scholarships, grants, and awards:* Federal Pell, FSEOG, state, college/university gift aid from institutional funds.

GIFT AID (NON-NEED-BASED) *Scholarships, grants, and awards by category:* *Academic Interests/Achievement:* general academic interests/achievements.
LOANS *Programs:* FFEL (Subsidized and Unsubsidized Stafford, PLUS), Perkins, alternative loans.
WORK-STUDY Federal work-study jobs available. *State or other work-study/employment:* Part-time jobs available.
APPLYING FOR FINANCIAL AID *Required financial aid form:* FAFSA.
CONTACT Mr. Nick Flocco, Director of Financial Aid, University of the Sciences in Philadelphia, 600 South 43rd Street, Philadelphia, PA 19104-4495, 215-596-8894 or toll-free 888-996-8747 (in-state). *Fax:* 215-596-8554.

UNIVERSITY OF THE SOUTH
Sewanee, TN

Tuition & fees: $25,580	Average undergraduate aid package: $19,864

ABOUT THE INSTITUTION Independent Episcopal, coed. Awards: bachelor's, master's, doctoral, and first professional degrees and post-bachelor's, post-master's, and first professional certificates. 41 undergraduate majors. Total enrollment: 1,492. Undergraduates: 1,385. Freshmen: 398. Both federal and institutional methodology are used as a basis for awarding need-based institutional aid.
UNDERGRADUATE EXPENSES for 2004–05 *Application fee:* $45. *Comprehensive fee:* $32,700 includes full-time tuition ($25,374), mandatory fees ($206), and room and board ($7120). *College room only:* $3640. *Payment plans:* Installment, deferred payment.
FRESHMAN FINANCIAL AID (Fall 2003) 218 applied for aid; of those 64% were deemed to have need. 100% of freshmen with need received aid; of those 100% had need fully met. *Average percent of need met:* 100% (excluding resources awarded to replace EFC). *Average financial aid package:* $21,185 (excluding resources awarded to replace EFC). 17% of all full-time freshmen had no need and received non-need-based gift aid.
UNDERGRADUATE FINANCIAL AID (Fall 2003) 671 applied for aid; of those 96% were deemed to have need. 100% of undergraduates with need received aid; of those 100% had need fully met. *Average percent of need met:* 100% (excluding resources awarded to replace EFC). *Average financial aid package:* $19,864 (excluding resources awarded to replace EFC). 15% of all full-time undergraduates had no need and received non-need-based gift aid.
GIFT AID (NEED-BASED) *Total amount:* $9,445,332 (7% federal, 2% state, 86% institutional, 5% external sources). *Receiving aid:* Freshmen: 35% (138); All full-time undergraduates: 45% (612). *Average award:* Freshmen: $18,342; Undergraduates: $17,365. *Scholarships, grants, and awards:* Federal Pell, FSEOG, state, private, college/university gift aid from institutional funds.
GIFT AID (NON-NEED-BASED) *Total amount:* $2,970,243 (90% institutional, 10% external sources). *Average Award:* Freshmen: $10,638; Undergraduates: $12,221. *Scholarships, grants, and awards by category:* *Academic Interests/Achievement:* 292 awards ($2,965,530 total): general academic interests/achievements. *Special Characteristics:* 129 awards ($575,230 total): children of faculty/staff, ethnic background, members of minority groups, relatives of clergy. *Tuition waivers:* Full or partial for employees or children of employees.
LOANS *Student loans:* $2,042,150 (81% need-based, 19% non-need-based). 35% of past graduating class borrowed through all loan programs. *Average indebtedness per student:* $13,244. *Average need-based loan:* Freshmen: $3629; Undergraduates: $3338. *Parent loans:* $2,965,090 (44% need-based, 56% non-need-based). *Programs:* FFEL (Subsidized and Unsubsidized Stafford, PLUS), Perkins, state, college/university, alternative loans.
WORK-STUDY *Federal work-study:* Total amount: $400,850; 348 jobs averaging $1152. *State or other work-study/employment:* Total amount: $204,920 (35% need-based, 65% non-need-based). 152 part-time jobs averaging $1348.
APPLYING FOR FINANCIAL AID *Required financial aid forms:* FAFSA, institution's own form. *Financial aid deadline (priority):* 3/1. *Notification date:* 4/1. Students must reply within 4 weeks of notification.
CONTACT Mr. David R. Gelinas, Director of Financial Aid, University of the South, 735 University Avenue, Sewanee, TN 37383-1000, 931-598-1312 or toll-free 800-522-2234. *Fax:* 931-598-3273.

UNIVERSITY OF THE VIRGIN ISLANDS
Saint Thomas, VI

Tuition & fees (VI res): $3796	Average undergraduate aid package: $4230

ABOUT THE INSTITUTION Territory-supported, coed. Awards: associate, bachelor's, and master's degrees. 23 undergraduate majors. Total enrollment: 2,565. Undergraduates: 2,352. Freshmen: 449. Federal methodology is used as a basis for awarding need-based institutional aid.
UNDERGRADUATE EXPENSES for 2005–06 *Application fee:* $25. *Tuition, state resident:* full-time $3370; part-time $100 per credit. *Tuition, nonresident:* full-time $9370; part-time $300 per credit. *Required fees:* full-time $426; $276 per year part-time. Full-time tuition and fees vary according to course load, degree level, and program. Part-time tuition and fees vary according to course load, degree level, and program. *College room and board:* $7740; *room only:* $1100. Room and board charges vary according to board plan and housing facility.
FRESHMAN FINANCIAL AID (Fall 2004, est.) 270 applied for aid; of those 90% were deemed to have need. 90% of freshmen with need received aid; of those 2% had need fully met. *Average percent of need met:* 60% (excluding resources awarded to replace EFC). *Average financial aid package:* $4400 (excluding resources awarded to replace EFC).
UNDERGRADUATE FINANCIAL AID (Fall 2004, est.) 1,155 applied for aid; of those 90% were deemed to have need. 83% of undergraduates with need received aid; of those 1% had need fully met. *Average percent of need met:* 45% (excluding resources awarded to replace EFC). *Average financial aid package:* $4230 (excluding resources awarded to replace EFC).
GIFT AID (NEED-BASED) *Total amount:* $3,286,888 (82% federal, 18% institutional). *Receiving aid:* Freshmen: 62% (202); All full-time undergraduates: 68% (810). *Average award:* Freshmen: $3800; Undergraduates: $3300. *Scholarships, grants, and awards:* Federal Pell, FSEOG, state, college/university gift aid from institutional funds, Federal Nursing.
GIFT AID (NON-NEED-BASED) *Receiving aid:* Freshmen: 7% (24); Undergraduates: 6% (67). *Scholarships, grants, and awards by category:* *Special Characteristics:* 50 awards ($78,570 total): children of faculty/staff, veterans. *Tuition waivers:* Full or partial for employees or children of employees, senior citizens. *ROTC:* Army.
LOANS *Student loans:* $1,233,451 (77% need-based, 23% non-need-based). 4% of past graduating class borrowed through all loan programs. *Average indebtedness per student:* $4400. *Average need-based loan:* Freshmen: $1500; Undergraduates: $2300. *Parent loans:* $87,879 (100% need-based). *Programs:* Federal Direct (Subsidized and Unsubsidized Stafford, PLUS), Perkins, college/university.
WORK-STUDY *Federal work-study:* Total amount: $98,840; 90 jobs averaging $3000. *State or other work-study/employment:* Total amount: $75,000 (100% need-based). 50 part-time jobs averaging $3500.
ATHLETIC AWARDS *Total amount:* $15,365 (100% need-based).
APPLYING FOR FINANCIAL AID *Required financial aid form:* FAFSA. *Financial aid deadline (priority):* 3/1. *Notification date:* Continuous beginning 5/15. Students must reply within 2 weeks of notification.
CONTACT Mavis M. Gilchrist, Director of Financial Aid, University of the Virgin Islands, RR #2, Box 10,000, Kingshill, St. Croix, VI 00850, 340-692-4186. *Fax:* 340-692-4145. *E-mail:* mgilchr@uvi.edu.

UNIVERSITY OF THE WEST
Rosemead, CA

ABOUT THE INSTITUTION Independent, coed. Awards: bachelor's, master's, doctoral, and first professional degrees and post-master's certificates. 9 undergraduate majors.
GIFT AID (NEED-BASED) *Scholarships, grants, and awards:* private, college/university gift aid from institutional funds.
GIFT AID (NON-NEED-BASED) *Scholarships, grants, and awards by category:* *Academic Interests/Achievement:* business, religion/biblical studies, social sciences.
WORK-STUDY *State or other work-study/employment:* Total amount: $140,400 (100% need-based). 20 part-time jobs available.
APPLYING FOR FINANCIAL AID *Required financial aid form:* HLU scholarship application form.
CONTACT Dr. Teresa Ku, Director of Student Services, University of the West, 1409 Walnut Grove Avenue, Rosemead, CA 91770, 626-571-8811 Ext. 355. *Fax:* 626-571-1413. *E-mail:* naikuangk@hlu.edu.

THE UNIVERSITY OF TOLEDO
Toledo, OH

Tuition & fees (OH res): $7054	Average undergraduate aid package: $6583

ABOUT THE INSTITUTION State-supported, coed. Awards: associate, bachelor's, master's, doctoral, and first professional degrees and post-bachelor's and post-master's certificates. 173 undergraduate majors. Total enrollment: 19,480. Undergraduates: 16,366. Freshmen: 3,025. Federal methodology is used as a basis for awarding need-based institutional aid.

UNDERGRADUATE EXPENSES for 2004–05 *Application fee:* $40. *Tuition, state resident:* full-time $5990; part-time $294 per semester hour. *Tuition, nonresident:* full-time $14,801; part-time $661 per semester hour. Full-time tuition and fees vary according to course load, program, and reciprocity agreements. Part-time tuition and fees vary according to course load, program, and reciprocity agreements. *College room and board:* $7488. Room and board charges vary according to board plan, housing facility, and location. *Payment plan:* Installment.

FRESHMAN FINANCIAL AID (Fall 2004, est.) 2149 applied for aid; of those 79% were deemed to have need. 100% of freshmen with need received aid; of those 7% had need fully met. *Average percent of need met:* 47% (excluding resources awarded to replace EFC). *Average financial aid package:* $5925 (excluding resources awarded to replace EFC). 8% of all full-time freshmen had no need and received non-need-based gift aid.

UNDERGRADUATE FINANCIAL AID (Fall 2004, est.) 9,607 applied for aid; of those 81% were deemed to have need. 100% of undergraduates with need received aid; of those 8% had need fully met. *Average percent of need met:* 52% (excluding resources awarded to replace EFC). *Average financial aid package:* $6583 (excluding resources awarded to replace EFC). 7% of all full-time undergraduates had no need and received non-need-based gift aid.

GIFT AID (NEED-BASED) *Total amount:* $26,506,750 (53% federal, 17% state, 25% institutional, 5% external sources). *Receiving aid:* Freshmen: 45% (1,177); All full-time undergraduates: 41% (5,400). *Average award:* Freshmen: $4916; Undergraduates: $4577. *Scholarships, grants, and awards:* Federal Pell, FSEOG, state, private, college/university gift aid from institutional funds.

GIFT AID (NON-NEED-BASED) *Total amount:* $6,151,934 (14% state, 77% institutional, 9% external sources). *Receiving aid:* Freshmen: 11% (302); Undergraduates: 14% (1,841). *Average Award:* Freshmen: $3696; *Undergraduates:* $3079. *Scholarships, grants, and awards by category: Academic Interests/ Achievement:* 3,511 awards ($9,696,332 total): business, communication, education, engineering/technologies, English, foreign languages, general academic interests/achievements, health fields, humanities, international studies, library science, mathematics, physical sciences, premedicine, social sciences. *Creative Arts/Performance:* 83 awards ($148,442 total): applied art and design, art/fine arts, cinema/film/broadcasting, general creative arts/performance, music, performing arts, theater/drama. *Special Achievements/Activities:* 212 awards ($279,417 total): cheerleading/drum major, general special achievements/activities, leadership, memberships, religious involvement. *Special Characteristics:* 753 awards ($837,808 total): adult students, children and siblings of alumni, children of faculty/staff, children of public servants, children of union members/company employees, ethnic background, general special characteristics, handicapped students, international students, members of minority groups, previous college experience, public servants, veterans, veterans' children. *Tuition waivers:* Full or partial for employees or children of employees. *ROTC:* Army, Air Force cooperative.

LOANS *Student loans:* $58,418,318 (85% need-based, 15% non-need-based). 65% of past graduating class borrowed through all loan programs. *Average indebtedness per student:* $25,871. *Average need-based loan:* Freshmen: $2692; Undergraduates: $3526. *Parent loans:* $22,147,788 (77% need-based, 23% non-need-based). *Programs:* Federal Direct (Subsidized and Unsubsidized Stafford, PLUS), Perkins, state, alternative loans.

WORK-STUDY *Federal work-study:* Total amount: $1,283,268; 520 jobs averaging $2333.

ATHLETIC AWARDS *Total amount:* $3,191,154 (44% need-based, 56% non-need-based).

APPLYING FOR FINANCIAL AID *Required financial aid form:* FAFSA. *Financial aid deadline (priority):* 4/1. *Notification date:* Continuous beginning 3/15. Students must reply within 4 weeks of notification.

CONTACT Carolyn Baumgartner, Financial Aid Officer, The University of Toledo, 2801 West Bancroft Street, 1200 Rocket Hall, Toledo, OH 43606, 419-530-5812 or toll-free 800-5TOLEDO (in-state). *Fax:* 419-530-5835. *E-mail:* cbaumga@ utnet.utoledo.edu.

UNIVERSITY OF TULSA
Tulsa, OK

Tuition & fees: $17,630	Average undergraduate aid package: $19,097

ABOUT THE INSTITUTION Independent religious, coed. Awards: bachelor's, master's, doctoral, and first professional degrees and post-bachelor's and first professional certificates. 54 undergraduate majors. Total enrollment: 4,174. Undergraduates: 2,756. Freshmen: 681. Federal methodology is used as a basis for awarding need-based institutional aid.

UNDERGRADUATE EXPENSES for 2004–05 *Application fee:* $35. *One-time required fee:* $375. *Comprehensive fee:* $23,556 includes full-time tuition ($17,550), mandatory fees ($80), and room and board ($5926). *College room only:* $3216. Room and board charges vary according to board plan and housing facility. *Part-time tuition:* $630 per credit hour. *Part-time fees:* $3 per credit hour. *Payment plans:* Tuition prepayment, installment.

FRESHMAN FINANCIAL AID (Fall 2003) 553 applied for aid; of those 61% were deemed to have need. 100% of freshmen with need received aid; of those 76% had need fully met. *Average percent of need met:* 96% (excluding resources awarded to replace EFC). *Average financial aid package:* $19,568 (excluding resources awarded to replace EFC). 30% of all full-time freshmen had no need and received non-need-based gift aid.

UNDERGRADUATE FINANCIAL AID (Fall 2003) 2,124 applied for aid; of those 57% were deemed to have need. 99% of undergraduates with need received aid; of those 77% had need fully met. *Average percent of need met:* 96% (excluding resources awarded to replace EFC). *Average financial aid package:* $19,097 (excluding resources awarded to replace EFC). 27% of all full-time undergraduates had no need and received non-need-based gift aid.

GIFT AID (NEED-BASED) *Total amount:* $3,142,292 (60% federal, 11% state, 29% institutional). *Receiving aid:* Freshmen: 28% (163); All full-time undergraduates: 30% (727). *Average award:* Freshmen: $4120; Undergraduates: $4220. *Scholarships, grants, and awards:* Federal Pell, FSEOG, state, private, college/ university gift aid from institutional funds.

GIFT AID (NON-NEED-BASED) *Total amount:* $11,999,942 (1% federal, 9% state, 82% institutional, 8% external sources). *Receiving aid:* Freshmen: 53% (309); Undergraduates: 39% (943). *Average Award:* Freshmen: $9338; *Undergraduates:* $9334. *Scholarships, grants, and awards by category: Academic Interests/Achievement:* 1,086 awards ($5,308,004 total): biological sciences, business, communication, computer science, engineering/technologies, English, foreign languages, general academic interests/achievements, international studies, mathematics, premedicine, religion/biblical studies, social sciences. *Creative Arts/Performance:* 147 awards ($729,725 total): art/fine arts, music, performing arts, theater/drama. *Special Achievements/Activities:* 162 awards ($376,600 total): cheerleading/drum major, community service, leadership. *Special Characteristics:* 378 awards ($2,885,517 total): children and siblings of alumni, children of faculty/staff. *Tuition waivers:* Full or partial for employees or children of employees. *ROTC:* Air Force cooperative.

LOANS *Student loans:* $9,656,457 (59% need-based, 41% non-need-based). 65% of past graduating class borrowed through all loan programs. *Average indebtedness per student:* $22,330. *Average need-based loan:* Freshmen: $5076; Undergraduates: $6228. *Parent loans:* $2,889,774 (100% non-need-based). *Programs:* FFEL (Subsidized and Unsubsidized Stafford, PLUS), Perkins.

WORK-STUDY *Federal work-study:* Total amount: $1,305,149; 682 jobs averaging $2053. *State or other work-study/employment:* Total amount: $14,051 (100% non-need-based). 16 part-time jobs averaging $1100.

ATHLETIC AWARDS *Total amount:* $5,087,430 (100% non-need-based).

APPLYING FOR FINANCIAL AID *Required financial aid forms:* FAFSA, institution's own form. *Financial aid deadline (priority):* 4/1. *Notification date:* Continuous beginning 3/1. Students must reply by 5/1 or within 2 weeks of notification.

CONTACT Ms. Vicki Hendrickson, Director of Student Financial Services, University of Tulsa, 600 South College, Tulsa, OK 74104-3189, 918-631-2526 or toll-free 800-331-3050. *Fax:* 918-631-5105. *E-mail:* vicki-hendrickson@utulsa.edu.

UNIVERSITY OF UTAH
Salt Lake City, UT

Tuition & fees (UT res): $4000	Average undergraduate aid package: $7719

ABOUT THE INSTITUTION State-supported, coed. Awards: bachelor's, master's, doctoral, and first professional degrees and post-bachelor's and post-master's

University of Utah

certificates. 128 undergraduate majors. Total enrollment: 28,933. Undergraduates: 22,775. Freshmen: 2,769. Federal methodology is used as a basis for awarding need-based institutional aid.

UNDERGRADUATE EXPENSES for 2004–05 *Application fee:* $35. *Tuition, state resident:* full-time $3364; part-time $95 per credit. *Tuition, nonresident:* full-time $11,774; part-time $325 per credit. *Required fees:* full-time $636; $318 per term part-time. Full-time tuition and fees vary according to course level, course load, degree level, and program. Part-time tuition and fees vary according to course level, course load, degree level, and program. *College room and board:* $5726; *room only:* $2623. Room and board charges vary according to board plan and housing facility. *Payment plan:* Installment.

FRESHMAN FINANCIAL AID (Fall 2004, est.) 1282 applied for aid; of those 57% were deemed to have need. 99% of freshmen with need received aid; of those 13% had need fully met. *Average percent of need met:* 51% (excluding resources awarded to replace EFC). *Average financial aid package:* $6560 (excluding resources awarded to replace EFC). 7% of all full-time freshmen had no need and received non-need-based gift aid.

UNDERGRADUATE FINANCIAL AID (Fall 2004, est.) 8,525 applied for aid; of those 72% were deemed to have need. 99% of undergraduates with need received aid; of those 13% had need fully met. *Average percent of need met:* 54% (excluding resources awarded to replace EFC). *Average financial aid package:* $7719 (excluding resources awarded to replace EFC). 3% of all full-time undergraduates had no need and received non-need-based gift aid.

GIFT AID (NEED-BASED) *Total amount:* $20,121,000 (79% federal, 5% state, 5% institutional, 11% external sources). *Receiving aid:* Freshmen: 26% (571); All full-time undergraduates: 33% (4,703). *Average award:* Freshmen: $4318; Undergraduates: $4015. *Scholarships, grants, and awards:* Federal Pell, FSEOG, state, private, college/university gift aid from institutional funds.

GIFT AID (NON-NEED-BASED) *Total amount:* $956,000 (10% institutional, 90% external sources). *Receiving aid:* Freshmen: 1% (30); Undergraduates: 1% (79). *Average Award:* Freshmen: $3603; Undergraduates: $3411. *Scholarships, grants, and awards by category: Academic Interests/Achievement:* architecture, area/ethnic studies, biological sciences, business, communication, computer science, education, engineering/technologies, English, foreign languages, general academic interests/achievements, health fields, humanities, mathematics, physical sciences, social sciences. *Creative Arts/Performance:* art/fine arts, cinema/film/broadcasting, dance, music, theater/drama. *Special Achievements/Activities:* cheerleading/drum major, general special achievements/ activities, leadership. *Special Characteristics:* children of faculty/staff, children with a deceased or disabled parent, ethnic background, handicapped students, out-of-state students, spouses of deceased or disabled public servants. *Tuition waivers:* Full or partial for employees or children of employees, senior citizens. *ROTC:* Army, Naval, Air Force.

LOANS *Student loans:* $34,900,000 (86% need-based, 14% non-need-based). 41% of past graduating class borrowed through all loan programs. *Average indebtedness per student:* $11,496. *Average need-based loan:* Freshmen: $3560; Undergraduates: $4934. *Parent loans:* $329,000 (30% need-based, 70% non-need-based). *Programs:* FFEL (Subsidized and Unsubsidized Stafford, PLUS), Perkins, Federal Nursing, college/university, alternative loans.

WORK-STUDY *Federal work-study:* Total amount: $1,488,000; jobs available.

ATHLETIC AWARDS *Total amount:* $1,570,000 (70% need-based, 30% non-need-based).

APPLYING FOR FINANCIAL AID *Required financial aid form:* FAFSA. *Financial aid deadline (priority):* 3/15. *Notification date:* Continuous beginning 4/20. Students must reply within 6 weeks of notification.

CONTACT Amy Capps, Manager, University of Utah, 201 South 1460 East, Room 105, Salt Lake City, UT 84112-9055, 801-581-6211 or toll-free 800-444-8638. *Fax:* 801-585-6350. *E-mail:* fawin1@saff.utah.edu.

UNIVERSITY OF VERMONT
Burlington, VT

Tuition & fees (VT res): $10,226	Average undergraduate aid package: $14,960

ABOUT THE INSTITUTION State-supported, coed. Awards: bachelor's, master's, doctoral, and first professional degrees and post-bachelor's and post-master's certificates. 105 undergraduate majors. Total enrollment: 10,940. Undergraduates: 9,235. Freshmen: 1,960. Federal methodology is used as a basis for awarding need-based institutional aid.

UNDERGRADUATE EXPENSES for 2004–05 *Application fee:* $45. *One-time required fee:* $300. *Tuition, state resident:* full-time $9088; part-time $379 per credit. *Tuition, nonresident:* full-time $22,728; part-time $947 per credit. Part-time tuition and fees vary according to course load. *College room and board:*

$7016; *room only:* $4710. Room and board charges vary according to board plan. *Payment plans:* Installment, deferred payment.

FRESHMAN FINANCIAL AID (Fall 2003) 1379 applied for aid; of those 79% were deemed to have need. 99% of freshmen with need received aid; of those 82% had need fully met. *Average percent of need met:* 88% (excluding resources awarded to replace EFC). *Average financial aid package:* $16,231 (excluding resources awarded to replace EFC). 17% of all full-time freshmen had no need and received non-need-based gift aid.

UNDERGRADUATE FINANCIAL AID (Fall 2003) 5,006 applied for aid; of those 85% were deemed to have need. 99% of undergraduates with need received aid; of those 47% had need fully met. *Average percent of need met:* 82% (excluding resources awarded to replace EFC). *Average financial aid package:* $14,960 (excluding resources awarded to replace EFC). 12% of all full-time undergraduates had no need and received non-need-based gift aid.

GIFT AID (NEED-BASED) *Total amount:* $40,482,619 (15% federal, 8% state, 73% institutional, 4% external sources). *Receiving aid:* Freshmen: 52% (996); All full-time undergraduates: 50% (3,761). *Average award:* Freshmen: $11,576; Undergraduates: $10,079. *Scholarships, grants, and awards:* Federal Pell, FSEOG, state, private, college/university gift aid from institutional funds, Federal Nursing.

GIFT AID (NON-NEED-BASED) *Total amount:* $2,941,626 (75% institutional, 25% external sources). *Receiving aid:* Freshmen: 3% (56); Undergraduates: 2% (188). *Average Award:* Freshmen: $1763; Undergraduates: $2132. *Scholarships, grants, and awards by category: Academic Interests/Achievement:* 2,666 awards ($5,820,642 total): agriculture, business, engineering/technologies, foreign languages, general academic interests/achievements, mathematics, military science. *Creative Arts/Performance:* 5 awards ($15,000 total): music, theater/ drama. *Special Achievements/Activities:* 92 awards ($220,968 total): community service. *Special Characteristics:* 96 awards ($438,500 total): ethnic background, first-generation college students, international students. *Tuition waivers:* Full or partial for employees or children of employees, senior citizens. *ROTC:* Army.

LOANS *Student loans:* $30,107,090 (84% need-based, 16% non-need-based). 45% of past graduating class borrowed through all loan programs. *Average indebtedness per student:* $23,114. *Average need-based loan:* Freshmen: $5323; Undergraduates: $5980. *Parent loans:* $20,148,616 (24% need-based, 76% non-need-based). *Programs:* FFEL (Subsidized and Unsubsidized Stafford, PLUS), Perkins, Federal Nursing, state, college/university.

WORK-STUDY *Federal work-study:* Total amount: $3,356,641; 1,786 jobs averaging $2004.

ATHLETIC AWARDS *Total amount:* $2,347,615 (19% need-based, 81% non-need-based).

APPLYING FOR FINANCIAL AID *Required financial aid form:* FAFSA. *Financial aid deadline (priority):* 2/10. *Notification date:* Continuous beginning 3/15. Students must reply within 4 weeks of notification.

CONTACT Financial Aid Office, University of Vermont, 330 Waterman, South Prospect Street, Burlington, VT 05405-0160, 802-656-5700. *Fax:* 802-656-4076. *E-mail:* financialaid@uvm.edu.

UNIVERSITY OF VIRGINIA
Charlottesville, VA

Tuition & fees (VA res): $6790	Average undergraduate aid package: $13,449

ABOUT THE INSTITUTION State-supported, coed. Awards: bachelor's, master's, doctoral, and first professional degrees and post-master's certificates. 49 undergraduate majors. Total enrollment: 23,341. Undergraduates: 14,129. Freshmen: 3,096. Federal methodology is used as a basis for awarding need-based institutional aid.

UNDERGRADUATE EXPENSES for 2004–05 *Application fee:* $40. *Tuition, state resident:* full-time $5131. *Tuition, nonresident:* full-time $21,172. Part-time tuition and fees vary according to course load. *College room and board:* $5960; *room only:* $2970. Room and board charges vary according to board plan and housing facility. *Payment plan:* Installment.

FRESHMAN FINANCIAL AID (Fall 2004, est.) 1605 applied for aid; of those 45% were deemed to have need. 94% of freshmen with need received aid; of those 65% had need fully met. *Average percent of need met:* 94% (excluding resources awarded to replace EFC). *Average financial aid package:* $13,115 (excluding resources awarded to replace EFC). 26% of all full-time freshmen had no need and received non-need-based gift aid.

UNDERGRADUATE FINANCIAL AID (Fall 2004, est.) 5,033 applied for aid; of those 62% were deemed to have need. 93% of undergraduates with need

received aid; of those 64% had need fully met. *Average percent of need met:* 93% (excluding resources awarded to replace EFC). *Average financial aid package:* $13,449 (excluding resources awarded to replace EFC). 18% of all full-time undergraduates had no need and received non-need-based gift aid.

GIFT AID (NEED-BASED) *Total amount:* $25,301,075 (13% federal, 15% state, 65% institutional, 7% external sources). *Receiving aid:* Freshmen: 20% (605); All full-time undergraduates: 19% (2,532). *Average award:* Freshmen: $10,673; Undergraduates: $10,250. *Scholarships, grants, and awards:* Federal Pell, FSEOG, state, private, college/university gift aid from institutional funds.

GIFT AID (NON-NEED-BASED) *Total amount:* $5,109,673 (7% state, 31% institutional, 62% external sources). *Receiving aid:* Freshmen: 3% (101); Undergraduates: 2% (278). *Average Award:* Freshmen: $5605; Undergraduates:* $6006. *Scholarships, grants, and awards by category:* Academic Interests/ Achievement: general academic interests/achievements. *Tuition waivers:* Full or partial for employees or children of employees, senior citizens. *ROTC:* Army, Naval, Air Force.

LOANS *Student loans:* $16,162,057 (63% need-based, 37% non-need-based). 32% of past graduating class borrowed through all loan programs. *Average indebtedness per student:* $14,065. *Average need-based loan:* Freshmen: $3722; Undergraduates: $4409. *Parent loans:* $8,896,746 (2% need-based, 98% non-need-based). *Programs:* Federal Direct (Subsidized and Unsubsidized Stafford, PLUS), Perkins, Federal Nursing, college/university.

WORK-STUDY *Federal work-study:* Total amount: $1,045,300; 671 jobs averaging $1558.

ATHLETIC AWARDS *Total amount:* $6,806,940 (28% need-based, 72% non-need-based).

APPLYING FOR FINANCIAL AID *Required financial aid forms:* FAFSA, institution's own form. *Financial aid deadline (priority):* 3/1. *Notification date:* 4/5. Students must reply by 5/1.

CONTACT Ms. Yvonne B. Hubbard, Director, Student Financial Services, University of Virginia, PO Box 400207, Charlottesville, VA 22904-4207, 434-982-6000. *E-mail:* faid@virginia.edu.

THE UNIVERSITY OF VIRGINIA'S COLLEGE AT WISE
Wise, VA

Tuition & fees (VA res): $5081	Average undergraduate aid package: $5807

ABOUT THE INSTITUTION State-supported, coed. Awards: bachelor's degrees and post-bachelor's certificates. 24 undergraduate majors. Total enrollment: 1,836. Undergraduates: 1,836. Freshmen: 374. Federal methodology is used as a basis for awarding need-based institutional aid.

UNDERGRADUATE EXPENSES for 2005–06 *Application fee:* $25. *Tuition, state resident:* full-time $2984; part-time $123 per semester hour. *Tuition, nonresident:* full-time $13,062; part-time $539 per semester hour. *Required fees:* full-time $2097; $38 per semester hour or $14.25 per term part-time. *College room and board:* $6200; *room only:* $3488.

GIFT AID (NEED-BASED) *Total amount:* $3,337,994 (56% federal, 35% state, 6% institutional, 3% external sources). *Receiving aid:* Freshmen: 63% (234); All full-time undergraduates: 63% (896). *Average award:* Freshmen: $4186; Undergraduates: $3609. *Scholarships, grants, and awards:* Federal Pell, FSEOG, state, private, college/university gift aid from institutional funds.

GIFT AID (NON-NEED-BASED) *Total amount:* $746,150 (51% institutional, 49% external sources). *Receiving aid:* Freshmen: 49% (184); Undergraduates: 32% (453). *Average Award:* Freshmen: $1899; Undergraduates: $1899. *Scholarships, grants, and awards by category:* Academic Interests/Achievement: agriculture, biological sciences, business, computer science, education, English, general academic interests/achievements, health fields, humanities, mathematics, physical sciences, premedicine, social sciences. *Creative Arts/Performance:* creative writing, general creative arts/performance, journalism/publications, music, performing arts, theater/drama. *Special Achievements/Activities:* community service, religious involvement. *Special Characteristics:* children with a deceased or disabled parent, ethnic background, local/state students, veterans, veterans' children.

LOANS *Student loans:* $3,170,973 (65% need-based, 35% non-need-based). 68% of past graduating class borrowed through all loan programs. *Average indebtedness per student:* $8385. *Average need-based loan:* Freshmen: $2024; Undergraduates: $2852. *Parent loans:* $1,026,628 (100% non-need-based). *Programs:* FFEL (Subsidized and Unsubsidized Stafford, PLUS), Perkins, state, college/university.

ATHLETIC AWARDS *Total amount:* $191,533 (100% non-need-based).

APPLYING FOR FINANCIAL AID *Required financial aid form:* FAFSA. *Financial aid deadline (priority):* 4/1. *Notification date:* Continuous beginning 2/1. Students must reply within 4 weeks of notification.

CONTACT Bill Wendle, Director of Financial Aid, The University of Virginia's College at Wise, 1 College Avenue, Wise, VA 24293, 276-328-0103 or toll-free 888-282-9324. *Fax:* 276-328-0251. *E-mail:* wdw8m@uvawise.edu.

UNIVERSITY OF WASHINGTON
Seattle, WA

Tuition & fees (WA res): $5286	Average undergraduate aid package: $10,400

ABOUT THE INSTITUTION State-supported, coed. Awards: bachelor's, master's, doctoral, and first professional degrees. 155 undergraduate majors. Total enrollment: 39,246. Undergraduates: 28,362. Freshmen: 4,771. Federal methodology is used as a basis for awarding need-based institutional aid.

UNDERGRADUATE EXPENSES for 2004–05 *Application fee:* $37. *Tuition, state resident:* full-time $5286. *Tuition, nonresident:* full-time $17,916. *College room and board:* $7017. Room and board charges vary according to board plan and housing facility.

FRESHMAN FINANCIAL AID (Fall 2004, est.) 3215 applied for aid; of those 56% were deemed to have need. 94% of freshmen with need received aid; of those 53% had need fully met. *Average percent of need met:* 87% (excluding resources awarded to replace EFC). *Average financial aid package:* $9000 (excluding resources awarded to replace EFC).

UNDERGRADUATE FINANCIAL AID (Fall 2004, est.) 18,000 applied for aid; of those 73% were deemed to have need. 84% of undergraduates with need received aid; of those 44% had need fully met. *Average percent of need met:* 86% (excluding resources awarded to replace EFC). *Average financial aid package:* $10,400 (excluding resources awarded to replace EFC).

GIFT AID (NEED-BASED) *Total amount:* $58,833,900 (36% federal, 42% state, 18% institutional, 4% external sources). *Receiving aid:* Freshmen: 1,350; All full-time undergraduates: 8,108. *Average award:* Freshmen: $5700; Undergraduates: $7000. *Scholarships, grants, and awards:* Federal Pell, FSEOG, state, private, college/university gift aid from institutional funds.

GIFT AID (NON-NEED-BASED) *Total amount:* $9,539,300 (3% federal, 14% state, 54% institutional, 29% external sources). *Receiving aid:* Freshmen: 200; Undergraduates: 650. *Average Award:* Freshmen: $2800; Undergraduates: $3300. *Scholarships, grants, and awards by category:* Academic Interests/Achievement: architecture, biological sciences, business, communication, engineering/ technologies, English, foreign languages, general academic interests/ achievements, health fields, humanities, mathematics, physical sciences, social sciences. *Creative Arts/Performance:* art/fine arts, creative writing, dance, general creative arts/performance, journalism/publications, music, performing arts, theater/drama. *Special Achievements/Activities:* community service, general special achievements/activities, leadership. *Special Characteristics:* international students. *Tuition waivers:* Full or partial for senior citizens. *ROTC:* Army, Naval, Air Force.

LOANS *Student loans:* $66,000,000 (67% need-based, 33% non-need-based). 50% of past graduating class borrowed through all loan programs. *Average indebtedness per student:* $15,210. *Average need-based loan:* Freshmen: $3200; Undergraduates: $5000. *Parent loans:* $21,000,000 (29% need-based, 71% non-need-based). *Programs:* Federal Direct (Subsidized and Unsubsidized Stafford, PLUS), Perkins, Federal Nursing, college/university.

WORK-STUDY *Federal work-study:* Total amount: $2,300,000; 855 jobs averaging $2690. *State or other work-study/employment:* Total amount: $470,000 (100% need-based). 156 part-time jobs averaging $3000.

ATHLETIC AWARDS *Total amount:* $5,600,000 (36% need-based, 64% non-need-based).

APPLYING FOR FINANCIAL AID *Required financial aid form:* FAFSA. *Financial aid deadline (priority):* 2/28. *Notification date:* Continuous beginning 4/1. Students must reply within 3 weeks of notification.

CONTACT Office of Student Financial Aid, University of Washington, Box 355880, Seattle, WA 98195-5880, 206-543-6101. *E-mail:* osfa@u.washington.edu.

UNIVERSITY OF WASHINGTON, BOTHELL
Bothell, WA

CONTACT Financial Aid Office, University of Washington, Bothell, 18115 Campus Way NE, Bothell, WA 98011-8246, 425-352-5000.

UNIVERSITY OF WASHINGTON, TACOMA
Tacoma, WA

CONTACT Financial Aid Office, University of Washington, Tacoma, 1900 Commerce Street, Tacoma, WA 98402-3100, 253-692-4000 or toll-free 800-736-7750 (out-of-state).

THE UNIVERSITY OF WEST ALABAMA
Livingston, AL

ABOUT THE INSTITUTION State-supported, coed. Awards: associate, bachelor's, and master's degrees. 19 undergraduate majors. Total enrollment: 2,667. Undergraduates: 1,637. Freshmen: 264.

GIFT AID (NEED-BASED) *Scholarships, grants, and awards:* Federal Pell, FSEOG, state, private, college/university gift aid from institutional funds.

GIFT AID (NON-NEED-BASED) *Scholarships, grants, and awards by category: Academic Interests/Achievement:* business, computer science, education, English, general academic interests/achievements. *Creative Arts/Performance:* creative writing, dance, journalism/publications, music. *Special Achievements/Activities:* cheerleading/drum major, rodeo. *Special Characteristics:* children of faculty/staff, first-generation college students.

LOANS *Programs:* FFEL (Subsidized and Unsubsidized Stafford, PLUS), Perkins.

APPLYING FOR FINANCIAL AID *Required financial aid form:* FAFSA.

CONTACT Mrs. Pat Reedy, Director of Financial Aid, The University of West Alabama, Station 3, Livingston, AL 35470, 205-652-3576 or toll-free 800-621-7742 (in-state), 800-621-8044 (out-of-state).

UNIVERSITY OF WEST FLORIDA
Pensacola, FL

Tuition & fees (FL res): $3039   **Average undergraduate aid package: N/A**

ABOUT THE INSTITUTION State-supported, coed. Awards: associate, bachelor's, master's, and doctoral degrees. 56 undergraduate majors. Total enrollment: 9,518. Undergraduates: 7,974. Freshmen: 956. Federal methodology is used as a basis for awarding need-based institutional aid.

UNDERGRADUATE EXPENSES for 2004–05 *Application fee:* $30. *Tuition, state resident:* full-time $2045; part-time $68.16 per semester hour. *Tuition, nonresident:* full-time $14,552; part-time $485.04 per semester hour. *Required fees:* full-time $994; $33.15 per semester hour. Full-time tuition and fees vary according to location. Part-time tuition and fees vary according to location. *College room and board:* $6294. Room and board charges vary according to housing facility. *Payment plans:* Tuition prepayment, deferred payment.

GIFT AID (NEED-BASED) *Total amount:* $8,839,092 (74% federal, 16% state, 10% institutional). *Scholarships, grants, and awards:* Federal Pell, FSEOG, state, college/university gift aid from institutional funds.

GIFT AID (NON-NEED-BASED) *Total amount:* $7,090,954 (1% federal, 75% state, 16% institutional, 8% external sources). *Scholarships, grants, and awards by category: Academic Interests/Achievement:* 1,022 awards ($1,022,522 total): general academic interests/achievements. *Creative Arts/Performance:* 80 awards ($54,000 total): applied art and design, art/fine arts, music, theater/drama. *Special Characteristics:* 70 awards ($70,000 total): members of minority groups. *Tuition waivers:* Full or partial for employees or children of employees, senior citizens. *ROTC:* Army, Air Force.

LOANS *Student loans:* $18,247,589 (70% need-based, 30% non-need-based). *Parent loans:* $1,150,727 (100% non-need-based). *Programs:* Federal Direct (Subsidized and Unsubsidized Stafford, PLUS), Perkins, college/university.

WORK-STUDY *Federal work-study:* Total amount: $245,584; 178 jobs averaging $2350. *State or other work-study/employment:* 1,545 part-time jobs available.

ATHLETIC AWARDS *Total amount:* $803,413 (100% non-need-based).

APPLYING FOR FINANCIAL AID *Required financial aid forms:* FAFSA, institution's own form. *Financial aid deadline:* Continuous. *Notification date:* Continuous beginning 3/1.

CONTACT Ms. Georganne E. Major, Program Manager, University of West Florida, 11000 University Parkway, Pensacola, FL 32514-5750, 850-474-2397 or toll-free 800-263-1074. *E-mail:* gmajor@uwf.edu.

UNIVERSITY OF WEST GEORGIA
Carrollton, GA

Tuition & fees (GA res): $2906   **Average undergraduate aid package: $6771**

ABOUT THE INSTITUTION State-supported, coed. Awards: bachelor's, master's, and doctoral degrees and post-master's certificates. 54 undergraduate majors. Total enrollment: 10,216. Undergraduates: 8,279. Freshmen: 2,008. Federal methodology is used as a basis for awarding need-based institutional aid.

UNDERGRADUATE EXPENSES for 2004–05 *Application fee:* $20. *Tuition, state resident:* full-time $2322; part-time $97 per semester hour. *Tuition, nonresident:* full-time $9290; part-time $388 per semester hour. *Required fees:* full-time $584; $15.83 per semester hour or $102 per term part-time. Part-time tuition and fees vary according to course load. *College room and board:* $4550; *room only:* $2600. Room and board charges vary according to board plan and housing facility.

FRESHMAN FINANCIAL AID (Fall 2004, est.) 1344 applied for aid; of those 69% were deemed to have need. 99% of freshmen with need received aid; of those 28% had need fully met. *Average percent of need met:* 83% (excluding resources awarded to replace EFC). *Average financial aid package:* $6868 (excluding resources awarded to replace EFC). 1% of all full-time freshmen had no need and received non-need-based gift aid.

UNDERGRADUATE FINANCIAL AID (Fall 2004, est.) 4,791 applied for aid; of those 72% were deemed to have need. 95% of undergraduates with need received aid; of those 25% had need fully met. *Average percent of need met:* 68% (excluding resources awarded to replace EFC). *Average financial aid package:* $6771 (excluding resources awarded to replace EFC). 2% of all full-time undergraduates had no need and received non-need-based gift aid.

GIFT AID (NEED-BASED) *Total amount:* $13,116,804 (51% federal, 47% state, 1% institutional, 1% external sources). *Receiving aid:* Freshmen: 47% (865); All full-time undergraduates: 41% (2,834). *Average award:* Freshmen: $4615; Undergraduates: $4336. *Scholarships, grants, and awards:* Federal Pell, FSEOG, state, private, college/university gift aid from institutional funds.

GIFT AID (NON-NEED-BASED) *Total amount:* $7,252,965 (94% state, 4% institutional, 2% external sources). *Receiving aid:* Freshmen: 5% (97); Undergraduates: 4% (274). *Average Award:* Freshmen: $1434; Undergraduates: $1532. *Scholarships, grants, and awards by category: Academic Interests/Achievement:* biological sciences, business, communication, computer science, education, English, foreign languages, general academic interests/achievements, health fields, humanities, mathematics, physical sciences, social sciences. *Creative Arts/Performance:* art/fine arts, debating, journalism/publications, music, theater/drama. *Special Achievements/Activities:* community service, memberships, religious involvement. *Special Characteristics:* adult students, children and siblings of alumni, children of union members/company employees, ethnic background, handicapped students, international students, local/state students, members of minority groups, previous college experience. *Tuition waivers:* Full or partial for minority students, employees or children of employees, adult students, senior citizens. *ROTC:* Army.

LOANS *Student loans:* $12,526,265 (60% need-based, 40% non-need-based). 55% of past graduating class borrowed through all loan programs. *Average indebtedness per student:* $12,249. *Average need-based loan:* Freshmen: $1855; Undergraduates: $2819. *Parent loans:* $1,126,617 (100% non-need-based). *Programs:* Federal Direct (Subsidized and Unsubsidized Stafford, PLUS), Perkins, state, college/university.

WORK-STUDY *Federal work-study:* Total amount: $2,567,622; 538 jobs averaging $2400. *State or other work-study/employment:* Part-time jobs available.

ATHLETIC AWARDS *Total amount:* $643,451 (48% need-based, 52% non-need-based).

APPLYING FOR FINANCIAL AID *Required financial aid form:* FAFSA. *Financial aid deadline (priority):* 4/1. *Notification date:* Continuous. Students must reply within 5 weeks of notification.

CONTACT Kimberly Jordan, Director of Financial Aid, University of West Georgia, Aycock Hall, Carrollton, GA 30118, 678-839-6421. *Fax:* 678-839-6422. *E-mail:* kjordan@westga.edu.

UNIVERSITY OF WEST LOS ANGELES
Inglewood, CA

ABOUT THE INSTITUTION Independent, coed. Awards: bachelor's and first professional degrees and post-bachelor's certificates. 4 undergraduate majors. Total enrollment: 63. Undergraduates: 63.

GIFT AID (NEED-BASED) *Scholarships, grants, and awards:* Federal Pell, FSEOG, state, college/university gift aid from institutional funds.

GIFT AID (NON-NEED-BASED) *Scholarships, grants, and awards by category:* *Academic Interests/Achievement:* general academic interests/achievements. *Special Characteristics:* siblings of current students, spouses of current students.

LOANS *Programs:* FFEL (Subsidized and Unsubsidized Stafford), alternative loans.

APPLYING FOR FINANCIAL AID *Required financial aid form:* FAFSA.

CONTACT Roberto Quinones, Assistant Director of Financial Aid, University of West Los Angeles, 1155 West Arbor Vitae Street, Inglewood, CA 90301-2902, 310-342-5268. *Fax:* 310-342-5294.

UNIVERSITY OF WISCONSIN–EAU CLAIRE
Eau Claire, WI

Tuition & fees (WI res): $4864	Average undergraduate aid package: $6593

ABOUT THE INSTITUTION State-supported, coed. Awards: associate, bachelor's, and master's degrees and post-bachelor's and post-master's certificates. 48 undergraduate majors. Total enrollment: 10,540. Undergraduates: 10,034. Freshmen: 2,033. Federal methodology is used as a basis for awarding need-based institutional aid.

UNDERGRADUATE EXPENSES for 2004–05 *Application fee:* $35. *Tuition, state resident:* full-time $4864; part-time $202.50 per credit. *Tuition, nonresident:* full-time $14,910; part-time $621.09 per credit. Full-time tuition and fees vary according to reciprocity agreements. Part-time tuition and fees vary according to reciprocity agreements. *College room and board:* $4310; *room only:* $2480. Room and board charges vary according to board plan. *Payment plan:* Installment.

FRESHMAN FINANCIAL AID (Fall 2003) 1376 applied for aid; of those 57% were deemed to have need. 99% of freshmen with need received aid; of those 81% had need fully met. *Average percent of need met:* 96% (excluding resources awarded to replace EFC). *Average financial aid package:* $6182 (excluding resources awarded to replace EFC). 16% of all full-time freshmen had no need and received non-need-based gift aid.

UNDERGRADUATE FINANCIAL AID (Fall 2003) 5,985 applied for aid; of those 66% were deemed to have need. 99% of undergraduates with need received aid; of those 82% had need fully met. *Average percent of need met:* 96% (excluding resources awarded to replace EFC). *Average financial aid package:* $6593 (excluding resources awarded to replace EFC). 9% of all full-time undergraduates had no need and received non-need-based gift aid.

GIFT AID (NEED-BASED) *Total amount:* $9,594,255 (63% federal, 25% state, 4% institutional, 8% external sources). *Receiving aid:* Freshmen: 26% (480); All full-time undergraduates: 24% (2,183). *Average award:* Freshmen: $3847; Undergraduates: $4108. *Scholarships, grants, and awards:* Federal Pell, FSEOG, state, private, college/university gift aid from institutional funds, Federal Nursing.

GIFT AID (NON-NEED-BASED) *Total amount:* $1,465,888 (7% federal, 3% state, 35% institutional, 55% external sources). *Average Award: Freshmen:* $1528; *Undergraduates:* $1675. *Scholarships, grants, and awards by category: Academic Interests/Achievement:* biological sciences, business, communication, computer science, education, English, foreign languages, general academic interests/achievements, health fields, international studies, mathematics, physical sciences, premedicine, social sciences. *Creative Arts/Performance:* debating, music, theater/drama. *Special Achievements/Activities:* community service, general special achievements/activities, hobbies/interests, leadership, memberships. *Special Characteristics:* adult students, ethnic background, first-generation college students, general special characteristics, international students, local/state students, members of minority groups, previous college experience. *Tuition waivers:* Full or partial for minority students, senior citizens.

LOANS *Student loans:* $24,954,553 (59% need-based, 41% non-need-based). 65% of past graduating class borrowed through all loan programs. *Average indebtedness per student:* $16,237. *Average need-based loan:* Freshmen: $3324; Undergraduates: $3845. *Programs:* Federal Direct (Subsidized and Unsubsidized Stafford, PLUS), Perkins, college/university, alternative loans.

WORK-STUDY *Federal work-study:* Total amount: $3,006,034; 1,725 jobs averaging $1743. *State or other work-study/employment:* Total amount: $2,364,804 (38% need-based, 62% non-need-based). 2,120 part-time jobs averaging $1115.

APPLYING FOR FINANCIAL AID *Required financial aid form:* FAFSA. *Financial aid deadline (priority):* 4/15. *Notification date:* Continuous. Students must reply within 3 weeks of notification.

CONTACT Ms. Kathleen Sahlhoff, Director of Financial Aid, University of Wisconsin–Eau Claire, 115 Schofield Hall, Eau Claire, WI 54701, 715-836-3373. *Fax:* 715-836-3846.

UNIVERSITY OF WISCONSIN–GREEN BAY
Green Bay, WI

Tuition & fees (WI res): $5154	Average undergraduate aid package: $7477

ABOUT THE INSTITUTION State-supported, coed. Awards: associate, bachelor's, and master's degrees and post-bachelor's certificates. 36 undergraduate majors. Total enrollment: 5,706. Undergraduates: 5,489. Freshmen: 1,003. Federal methodology is used as a basis for awarding need-based institutional aid.

UNDERGRADUATE EXPENSES for 2004–05 *Application fee:* $35. *Tuition, state resident:* full-time $4000; part-time $167 per credit hour. *Tuition, nonresident:* full-time $14,046; part-time $585 per credit hour. *Required fees:* full-time $1154; $38 per credit. Full-time tuition and fees vary according to reciprocity agreements. Part-time tuition and fees vary according to reciprocity agreements. *College room and board:* $4716; *room only:* $2826. Room and board charges vary according to board plan and housing facility. *Payment plan:* Installment.

FRESHMAN FINANCIAL AID (Fall 2004, est.) 820 applied for aid; of those 72% were deemed to have need. 96% of freshmen with need received aid; of those 35% had need fully met. *Average percent of need met:* 74% (excluding resources awarded to replace EFC). *Average financial aid package:* $6975 (excluding resources awarded to replace EFC). 2% of all full-time freshmen had no need and received non-need-based gift aid.

UNDERGRADUATE FINANCIAL AID (Fall 2004, est.) 3,416 applied for aid; of those 76% were deemed to have need. 97% of undergraduates with need received aid; of those 42% had need fully met. *Average percent of need met:* 79% (excluding resources awarded to replace EFC). *Average financial aid package:* $7477 (excluding resources awarded to replace EFC). 1% of all full-time undergraduates had no need and received non-need-based gift aid.

GIFT AID (NEED-BASED) *Total amount:* $6,456,563 (52% federal, 32% state, 2% institutional, 14% external sources). *Receiving aid:* Freshmen: 38% (379); All full-time undergraduates: 32% (1,421). *Average award:* Freshmen: $4097; Undergraduates: $4237. *Scholarships, grants, and awards:* Federal Pell, FSEOG, state, college/university gift aid from institutional funds.

GIFT AID (NON-NEED-BASED) *Total amount:* $607,969 (10% state, 22% institutional, 68% external sources). *Receiving aid:* Freshmen: 19% (193); Undergraduates: 19% (870). *Average Award: Freshmen:* $1836; *Undergraduates:* $1978. *Scholarships, grants, and awards by category: Academic Interests/Achievement:* 65 awards ($141,946 total): area/ethnic studies, biological sciences, business, communication, engineering/technologies, general academic interests/achievements, physical sciences, social sciences. *Creative Arts/Performance:* art/fine arts, dance, music, theater/drama. *Special Achievements/Activities:* community service, leadership. *Special Characteristics:* adult students, children of public servants, ethnic background, veterans. *Tuition waivers:* Full or partial for senior citizens. *ROTC:* Army.

LOANS *Student loans:* $14,359,290 (57% need-based, 43% non-need-based). 57% of past graduating class borrowed through all loan programs. *Average indebtedness per student:* $9238. *Average need-based loan:* Freshmen: $2908; Undergraduates: $3930. *Parent loans:* $1,021,711 (100% non-need-based). *Programs:* FFEL (Subsidized and Unsubsidized Stafford, PLUS), Perkins.

WORK-STUDY *Federal work-study:* Total amount: $396,555; jobs available. *State or other work-study/employment:* Part-time jobs available.

ATHLETIC AWARDS *Total amount:* $1,688,014 (68% need-based, 32% non-need-based).

APPLYING FOR FINANCIAL AID *Required financial aid form:* FAFSA. *Financial aid deadline (priority):* 4/15. *Notification date:* Continuous. Students must reply within 3 weeks of notification.

CONTACT Mr. Ron Ronnenberg, Director of Financial Aid, University of Wisconsin–Green Bay, 2420 Nicolet Drive, Green Bay, WI 54311-7001, 920-465-2073 or toll-free 888-367-8942 (out-of-state). *E-mail:* ronnenbr@uwgb.edu.

UNIVERSITY OF WISCONSIN–LA CROSSE
La Crosse, WI

Tuition & fees (WI res): $4895	Average undergraduate aid package: $5499

University of Wisconsin–La Crosse

ABOUT THE INSTITUTION State-supported, coed. Awards: associate, bachelor's, and master's degrees. 51 undergraduate majors. Total enrollment: 8,511. Undergraduates: 7,844. Freshmen: 1,544. Federal methodology is used as a basis for awarding need-based institutional aid.

UNDERGRADUATE EXPENSES for 2004–05 *Application fee:* $35. *Tuition, state resident:* full-time $4895; part-time $204 per credit. *Tuition, nonresident:* full-time $14,941; part-time $623 per credit. Full-time tuition and fees vary according to program and reciprocity agreements. Part-time tuition and fees vary according to course load, program, and reciprocity agreements. *College room and board:* $4570; *room only:* $2530. Room and board charges vary according to board plan. *Payment plan:* Installment.

FRESHMAN FINANCIAL AID (Fall 2003) 1116 applied for aid; of those 80% were deemed to have need. 98% of freshmen with need received aid; of those 78% had need fully met. *Average percent of need met:* 81% (excluding resources awarded to replace EFC). *Average financial aid package:* $4316 (excluding resources awarded to replace EFC). 3% of all full-time freshmen had no need and received non-need-based gift aid.

UNDERGRADUATE FINANCIAL AID (Fall 2003) 5,487 applied for aid; of those 80% were deemed to have need. 98% of undergraduates with need received aid; of those 89% had need fully met. *Average percent of need met:* 82% (excluding resources awarded to replace EFC). *Average financial aid package:* $5499 (excluding resources awarded to replace EFC). 5% of all full-time undergraduates had no need and received non-need-based gift aid.

GIFT AID (NEED-BASED) *Total amount:* $7,347,525 (60% federal, 32% state, 5% institutional, 3% external sources). *Receiving aid:* Freshmen: 26% (402); All full-time undergraduates: 27% (2,023). *Average award:* Freshmen: $1419; Undergraduates: $1836. *Scholarships, grants, and awards:* Federal Pell, FSEOG, state, private, college/university gift aid from institutional funds.

GIFT AID (NON-NEED-BASED) *Total amount:* $2,339,093 (5% federal, 15% state, 4% institutional, 76% external sources). *Receiving aid:* Freshmen: 4% (64); Undergraduates: 6% (477). *Average Award:* Freshmen: $394; *Undergraduates:* $701. *Scholarships, grants, and awards by category: Academic Interests/Achievement:* 172 awards ($185,032 total): biological sciences, business, communication, computer science, education, English, foreign languages, general academic interests/achievements, health fields, mathematics, military science, physical sciences, social sciences. *Creative Arts/Performance:* 35 awards ($21,012 total): art/fine arts, music, theater/drama. *Special Characteristics:* 42 awards ($74,110 total): adult students, children and siblings of alumni, ethnic background, general special characteristics, members of minority groups, out-of-state students. *ROTC:* Army.

LOANS *Student loans:* $27,056,049 (57% need-based, 43% non-need-based). 60% of past graduating class borrowed through all loan programs. *Average indebtedness per student:* $14,481. *Average need-based loan:* Freshmen: $1901; Undergraduates: $3284. *Parent loans:* $1,406,271 (100% non-need-based). *Programs:* FFEL (Subsidized and Unsubsidized Stafford, PLUS), Perkins, college/university, alternative loans.

WORK-STUDY *Federal work-study:* Total amount: $459,243; 598 jobs averaging $768. *State or other work-study/employment:* Total amount: $2,588,725 (100% non-need-based). 1,072 part-time jobs averaging $2415.

APPLYING FOR FINANCIAL AID *Required financial aid forms:* FAFSA, institution's own form. *Financial aid deadline (priority):* 3/15. *Notification date:* Continuous. Students must reply by 5/10 or within 3 weeks of notification.

CONTACT Mr. James E. Finn, Director of Financial Aid, University of Wisconsin–La Crosse, 1725 State Street, La Crosse, WI 54601-3742, 608-785-8604. *Fax:* 608-785-8843. *E-mail:* finn.jame@uwlax.edu.

UNIVERSITY OF WISCONSIN–MADISON
Madison, WI

Tuition & fees (WI res): $5860	Average undergraduate aid package: $10,740

ABOUT THE INSTITUTION State-supported, coed. Awards: bachelor's, master's, doctoral, and first professional degrees and post-master's and first professional certificates. 138 undergraduate majors. Total enrollment: 41,169. Undergraduates: 29,766. Freshmen: 5,642. Both federal and institutional methodology are used as a basis for awarding need-based institutional aid.

UNDERGRADUATE EXPENSES for 2004–05 *Application fee:* $35. *Tuition, state resident:* full-time $5860. *Tuition, nonresident:* full-time $19,860. Full-time tuition and fees vary according to degree level and reciprocity agreements. Part-time tuition and fees vary according to course load, degree level, and reciprocity agreements. *College room and board:* $6250. Room and board charges vary according to board plan, housing facility, and location.

FRESHMAN FINANCIAL AID (Fall 2004, est.) 4151 applied for aid; of those 47% were deemed to have need. 94% of freshmen with need received aid; of those 35% had need fully met. *Average financial aid package:* $10,502 (excluding resources awarded to replace EFC). 21% of all full-time freshmen had no need and received non-need-based gift aid.

UNDERGRADUATE FINANCIAL AID (Fall 2004, est.) 14,093 applied for aid; of those 62% were deemed to have need. 95% of undergraduates with need received aid; of those 32% had need fully met. *Average financial aid package:* $10,740 (excluding resources awarded to replace EFC). 14% of all full-time undergraduates had no need and received non-need-based gift aid.

GIFT AID (NEED-BASED) *Total amount:* $21,830,585 (57% federal, 24% state, 19% institutional). *Receiving aid:* Freshmen: 11% (610); All full-time undergraduates: 12% (3,313). *Average award:* Freshmen: $7022; Undergraduates: $6689. *Scholarships, grants, and awards:* Federal Pell, FSEOG, state, private, college/university gift aid from institutional funds.

GIFT AID (NON-NEED-BASED) *Total amount:* $21,633,567 (5% federal, 20% state, 42% institutional, 33% external sources). *Receiving aid:* Freshmen: 19% (1,050); Undergraduates: 11% (2,944). *Average Award:* Freshmen: $2804; Undergraduates: $2762. *Scholarships, grants, and awards by category: Academic Interests/Achievement:* general academic interests/achievements. *Creative Arts/Performance:* general creative arts/performance. *Special Achievements/Activities:* general special achievements/activities. *Special Characteristics:* general special characteristics. *ROTC:* Army, Naval, Air Force.

LOANS *Student loans:* $67,521,230 (56% need-based, 44% non-need-based). 44% of past graduating class borrowed through all loan programs. *Average indebtedness per student:* $17,528. *Average need-based loan:* Freshmen: $4081; Undergraduates: $4397. *Parent loans:* $12,726,844 (100% non-need-based). *Programs:* FFEL (Subsidized and Unsubsidized Stafford, PLUS), Perkins, Federal Nursing, state, college/university.

WORK-STUDY *Federal work-study:* Total amount: $10,281,779; 3,894 jobs averaging $2640.

ATHLETIC AWARDS *Total amount:* $6,515,395 (100% non-need-based).

APPLYING FOR FINANCIAL AID *Required financial aid forms:* FAFSA, institution's own form. *Financial aid deadline:* Continuous. *Notification date:* Continuous beginning 4/1. Students must reply within 3 weeks of notification.

CONTACT Office of Student Financial Services, University of Wisconsin–Madison, 432 North Murray Street, Madison, WI 53706-1380, 608-262-3060. *Fax:* 608-262-9068. *E-mail:* finaid@das.wisc.edu.

UNIVERSITY OF WISCONSIN–MILWAUKEE
Milwaukee, WI

Tuition & fees (WI res): $5835	Average undergraduate aid package: $5503

ABOUT THE INSTITUTION State-supported, coed. Awards: bachelor's, master's, and doctoral degrees and post-bachelor's and post-master's certificates. 105 undergraduate majors. Total enrollment: 26,832. Undergraduates: 22,307. Freshmen: 3,821. Federal methodology is used as a basis for awarding need-based institutional aid.

UNDERGRADUATE EXPENSES for 2004–05 *Application fee:* $35. *Tuition, state resident:* full-time $5138; part-time $214.09 per credit. *Tuition, nonresident:* full-time $17,890; part-time $745.42 per credit. Full-time tuition and fees vary according to location, program, and reciprocity agreements. Part-time tuition and fees vary according to course load, location, program, and reciprocity agreements. *College room and board:* $4505; *room only:* $2670. Room and board charges vary according to board plan and housing facility. *Payment plan:* Installment.

FRESHMAN FINANCIAL AID (Fall 2003) 2714 applied for aid; of those 71% were deemed to have need. 93% of freshmen with need received aid; of those 27% had need fully met. *Average percent of need met:* 58% (excluding resources awarded to replace EFC). *Average financial aid package:* $4584 (excluding resources awarded to replace EFC). 3% of all full-time freshmen had no need and received non-need-based gift aid.

UNDERGRADUATE FINANCIAL AID (Fall 2003) 14,678 applied for aid; of those 76% were deemed to have need. 84% of undergraduates with need received aid; of those 43% had need fully met. *Average percent of need met:* 68% (excluding resources awarded to replace EFC). *Average financial aid package:* $5503 (excluding resources awarded to replace EFC). 2% of all full-time undergraduates had no need and received non-need-based gift aid.

GIFT AID (NEED-BASED) *Total amount:* $21,737,560 (65% federal, 34% state, 1% institutional). *Receiving aid:* Freshmen: 20% (768); All full-time undergradu-

ates: 23% (4,477). *Average award:* Freshmen: $4243; Undergraduates: $4275. *Scholarships, grants, and awards:* Federal Pell, FSEOG, state, private.

GIFT AID (NON-NEED-BASED) *Total amount:* $3,102,127 (4% state, 51% institutional, 45% external sources). *Receiving aid:* Freshmen: 10% (388); Undergraduates: 5% (1,021). *Average Award: Freshmen:* $1774; *Undergraduates:* $2242. *Scholarships, grants, and awards by category: Academic Interests/Achievement:* general academic interests/achievements. *Creative Arts/Performance:* general creative arts/performance. *Special Achievements/Activities:* general special achievements/activities. *Special Characteristics:* general special characteristics. *ROTC:* Army cooperative, Air Force cooperative.

LOANS *Student loans:* $63,006,838 (92% need-based, 8% non-need-based). 66% of past graduating class borrowed through all loan programs. *Average indebtedness per student:* $16,159. *Average need-based loan:* Freshmen: $2755; Undergraduates: $3601. *Parent loans:* $3,626,128 (100% non-need-based). *Programs:* Federal Direct (Subsidized and Unsubsidized Stafford, PLUS), Perkins, Federal Nursing, Alternative loans.

WORK-STUDY *Federal work-study:* Total amount: $1,294,293; jobs available.

ATHLETIC AWARDS *Total amount:* $300,421 (94% need-based, 6% non-need-based).

APPLYING FOR FINANCIAL AID *Required financial aid form:* FAFSA. *Financial aid deadline (priority):* 3/1. *Notification date:* Continuous beginning 3/20.

CONTACT Ms. Jane Hojan-Clark, Director of Financial Aid and Student Employment Services, University of Wisconsin–Milwaukee, Mellencamp Hall 162, Milwaukee, WI 53201, 414-229-6300. *E-mail:* jhojan@uwm.edu.

UNIVERSITY OF WISCONSIN–OSHKOSH
Oshkosh, WI

Tuition & fees (WI res): $4616	Average undergraduate aid package: $3080

ABOUT THE INSTITUTION State-supported, coed. Awards: associate, bachelor's, and master's degrees. 56 undergraduate majors. Total enrollment: 11,039. Undergraduates: 9,812. Freshmen: 1,722. Federal methodology is used as a basis for awarding need-based institutional aid.

UNDERGRADUATE EXPENSES for 2004–05 *Application fee:* $35. *Tuition, state resident:* full-time $4616; part-time $194 per credit hour. *Tuition, nonresident:* full-time $14,662; part-time $612 per credit hour. Full-time tuition and fees vary according to reciprocity agreements. Part-time tuition and fees vary according to reciprocity agreements. *College room and board:* $4630; *room only:* $2530. Room and board charges vary according to board plan and housing facility. *Payment plan:* Installment.

FRESHMAN FINANCIAL AID (Fall 2003) 1305 applied for aid; of those 70% were deemed to have need. 100% of freshmen with need received aid; of those 50% had need fully met. *Average percent of need met:* 50% (excluding resources awarded to replace EFC). *Average financial aid package:* $2500 (excluding resources awarded to replace EFC). 1% of all full-time freshmen had no need and received non-need-based gift aid.

UNDERGRADUATE FINANCIAL AID (Fall 2003) 6,864 applied for aid; of those 75% were deemed to have need. 100% of undergraduates with need received aid; of those 58% had need fully met. *Average percent of need met:* 53% (excluding resources awarded to replace EFC). *Average financial aid package:* $3080 (excluding resources awarded to replace EFC). 1% of all full-time undergraduates had no need and received non-need-based gift aid.

GIFT AID (NEED-BASED) *Total amount:* $9,895,000 (63% federal, 26% state, 6% institutional, 5% external sources). *Receiving aid:* Freshmen: 56% (914); All full-time undergraduates: 48% (4,118). *Average award:* Freshmen: $1800; Undergraduates: $2000. *Scholarships, grants, and awards:* Federal Pell, FSEOG, state, private, college/university gift aid from institutional funds, Federal Nursing.

GIFT AID (NON-NEED-BASED) *Receiving aid:* Freshmen: 56% (914); Undergraduates: 48% (4,118). *Average Award:* Freshmen: $4000; *Undergraduates:* $3333. *Scholarships, grants, and awards by category: Academic Interests/Achievement:* business, computer science, general academic interests/achievements, mathematics, physical sciences. *Creative Arts/Performance:* art/fine arts, debating, music, theater/drama. *Special Achievements/Activities:* general special achievements/activities. *Special Characteristics:* children and siblings of alumni, local/state students, members of minority groups. *ROTC:* Army.

LOANS *Student loans:* $26,750,000 (100% need-based). 70% of past graduating class borrowed through all loan programs. *Average indebtedness per student:* $14,000. *Average need-based loan:* Freshmen: $2500; Undergraduates: $3500. *Parent loans:* $4,725,000 (100% need-based). *Programs:* FFEL (Subsidized and Unsubsidized Stafford, PLUS), Perkins, Federal Nursing, state.

WORK-STUDY *Federal work-study:* Total amount: $925,000; jobs available. *State or other work-study/employment:* Total amount: $2,000,000 (100% non-need-based). Part-time jobs available.

APPLYING FOR FINANCIAL AID *Required financial aid form:* FAFSA. *Financial aid deadline (priority):* 3/15. *Notification date:* 4/25. Students must reply within 4 weeks of notification.

CONTACT Ms. Sheila Denney, Financial Aid Counselor, University of Wisconsin–Oshkosh, 800 Algoma Boulevard, Oshkosh, WI 54901, 920-424-3377. *E-mail:* denney@uwosh.edu.

UNIVERSITY OF WISCONSIN–PARKSIDE
Kenosha, WI

Tuition & fees (WI res): $4652	Average undergraduate aid package: $5953

ABOUT THE INSTITUTION State-supported, coed. Awards: bachelor's and master's degrees. 37 undergraduate majors. Total enrollment: 5,072. Undergraduates: 4,965. Freshmen: 990. Federal methodology is used as a basis for awarding need-based institutional aid.

UNDERGRADUATE EXPENSES for 2004–05 *Application fee:* $35. *One-time required fee:* $87. *Tuition, state resident:* full-time $4652; part-time $196 per credit hour. *Tuition, nonresident:* full-time $14,698; part-time $614 per credit hour. Full-time tuition and fees vary according to course load and reciprocity agreements. Part-time tuition and fees vary according to course load. *College room and board:* $5415; *room only:* $3515. Room and board charges vary according to board plan and housing facility. *Payment plan:* Installment.

FRESHMAN FINANCIAL AID (Fall 2004, est.) 422 applied for aid; of those 61% were deemed to have need. 93% of freshmen with need received aid; of those 45% had need fully met. *Average percent of need met:* 72% (excluding resources awarded to replace EFC). *Average financial aid package:* $5175 (excluding resources awarded to replace EFC). 6% of all full-time freshmen had no need and received non-need-based gift aid.

UNDERGRADUATE FINANCIAL AID (Fall 2004, est.) 2,597 applied for aid; of those 66% were deemed to have need. 95% of undergraduates with need received aid; of those 42% had need fully met. *Average percent of need met:* 78% (excluding resources awarded to replace EFC). *Average financial aid package:* $5953 (excluding resources awarded to replace EFC). 4% of all full-time undergraduates had no need and received non-need-based gift aid.

GIFT AID (NEED-BASED) *Total amount:* $6,126,987 (69% federal, 28% state, 3% institutional). *Receiving aid:* Freshmen: 21% (116); All full-time undergraduates: 26% (937). *Average award:* Freshmen: $4055; Undergraduates: $4098. *Scholarships, grants, and awards:* Federal Pell, FSEOG, state, private, college/university gift aid from institutional funds.

GIFT AID (NON-NEED-BASED) *Total amount:* $4,103,270 (6% federal, 61% state, 7% institutional, 26% external sources). *Receiving aid:* Freshmen: 14% (78); Undergraduates: 12% (429). *Average Award: Freshmen:* $1770; *Undergraduates:* $2105. *Scholarships, grants, and awards by category: Academic Interests/Achievement:* 160 awards ($170,000 total): biological sciences, business, communication, education, engineering/technologies, English, foreign languages, general academic interests/achievements, health fields, mathematics, physical sciences, premedicine. *Creative Arts/Performance:* 20 awards ($8000 total): applied art and design, art/fine arts, music, theater/drama. *Special Achievements/Activities:* 2 awards ($2000 total): community service, leadership. *Special Characteristics:* 160 awards ($170,000 total): adult students, children of union members/company employees, children of workers in trades, ethnic background, general special characteristics, international students, local/state students, members of minority groups. *Tuition waivers:* Full or partial for senior citizens. *ROTC:* Army cooperative.

LOANS *Student loans:* $9,416,122 (40% need-based, 60% non-need-based). 62% of past graduating class borrowed through all loan programs. *Average indebtedness per student:* $12,500. *Average need-based loan:* Freshmen: $2620; Undergraduates: $3405. *Parent loans:* $292,818 (100% non-need-based). *Programs:* FFEL (Subsidized and Unsubsidized Stafford, PLUS), Perkins, state.

WORK-STUDY *Federal work-study:* Total amount: $345,651; jobs available.

ATHLETIC AWARDS *Total amount:* $799,570 (76% need-based, 24% non-need-based).

APPLYING FOR FINANCIAL AID *Required financial aid form:* FAFSA. *Financial aid deadline:* Continuous. *Notification date:* Continuous beginning 4/1. Students must reply within 2 weeks of notification.

CONTACT Dr. Randall McCready, Director of Financial Aid and Scholarships, University of Wisconsin–Parkside, 900 Wood Road, Kenosha, WI 53141-2000, 262-595-2574. *E-mail:* randall.mccready@uwp.edu.

UNIVERSITY OF WISCONSIN–PLATTEVILLE
Platteville, WI

ABOUT THE INSTITUTION State-supported, coed. Awards: associate, bachelor's, and master's degrees. 48 undergraduate majors. Total enrollment: 6,158. Undergraduates: 5,607. Freshmen: 1,159.

GIFT AID (NEED-BASED) *Scholarships, grants, and awards:* Federal Pell, FSEOG, state, college/university gift aid from institutional funds.

GIFT AID (NON-NEED-BASED) *Scholarships, grants, and awards by category: Academic Interests/Achievement:* agriculture, biological sciences, business, communication, education, engineering/technologies, general academic interests/achievements, health fields, mathematics. *Creative Arts/Performance:* art/fine arts, music, theater/drama. *Special Achievements/Activities:* leadership.

LOANS *Programs:* FFEL (Subsidized and Unsubsidized Stafford, PLUS), Perkins.

APPLYING FOR FINANCIAL AID *Required financial aid form:* FAFSA.

CONTACT Elizabeth Tucker, Director of Financial Aid, University of Wisconsin–Platteville, 1 University Plaza, Platteville, WI 53818-3099, 608-342-1836 or toll-free 800-362-5515. *Fax:* 608-342-1281. *E-mail:* tucker@uwplatt.edu.

UNIVERSITY OF WISCONSIN–RIVER FALLS
River Falls, WI

ABOUT THE INSTITUTION State-supported, coed. Awards: bachelor's and master's degrees and post-master's certificates. 80 undergraduate majors. Total enrollment: 5,950. Undergraduates: 5,504. Freshmen: 1,212.

GIFT AID (NEED-BASED) *Scholarships, grants, and awards:* Federal Pell, FSEOG, state, private, college/university gift aid from institutional funds.

GIFT AID (NON-NEED-BASED) *Scholarships, grants, and awards by category: Academic Interests/Achievement:* agriculture, area/ethnic studies, biological sciences, business, communication, computer science, education, English, foreign languages, general academic interests/achievements, health fields, humanities, international studies, mathematics, physical sciences, premedicine, social sciences. *Creative Arts/Performance:* art/fine arts, music, theater/drama.

LOANS *Programs:* FFEL (Subsidized and Unsubsidized Stafford, PLUS), Perkins, state.

WORK-STUDY *Federal work-study:* Total amount: $1,219,498; jobs available (averaging $1200). *State or other work-study/employment:* Total amount: $800,000 (100% non-need-based). Part-time jobs available.

APPLYING FOR FINANCIAL AID *Required financial aid forms:* FAFSA, institution's own form.

CONTACT Mr. David Woodward, Director of Financial Aid, University of Wisconsin–River Falls, 410 South Third Street, River Falls, WI 54022-5001, 715-425-3272. *Fax:* 715-425-0708.

UNIVERSITY OF WISCONSIN–STEVENS POINT
Stevens Point, WI

Tuition & fees (WI res): $4704	Average undergraduate aid package: $6337

ABOUT THE INSTITUTION State-supported, coed. Awards: associate, bachelor's, and master's degrees. 56 undergraduate majors. Total enrollment: 9,023. Undergraduates: 8,560. Freshmen: 1,525. Federal methodology is used as a basis for awarding need-based institutional aid.

UNDERGRADUATE EXPENSES for 2004–05 *Application fee:* $50. *Tuition, state resident:* full-time $4000; part-time $166 per credit. *Tuition, nonresident:* full-time $14,046; part-time $585 per credit. *Required fees:* full-time $704; $63 per credit. Full-time tuition and fees vary according to course load and reciprocity agreements. Part-time tuition and fees vary according to course load and reciprocity agreements. *College room and board:* $4094; *room only:* $2406. Room and board charges vary according to housing facility. *Payment plan:* Installment.

FRESHMAN FINANCIAL AID (Fall 2003) 1254 applied for aid; of those 59% were deemed to have need. 94% of freshmen with need received aid; of those 51% had need fully met. *Average percent of need met:* 94% (excluding resources awarded to replace EFC). *Average financial aid package:* $5120 (excluding resources awarded to replace EFC). 5% of all full-time freshmen had no need and received non-need-based gift aid.

UNDERGRADUATE FINANCIAL AID (Fall 2003) 6,955 applied for aid; of those 58% were deemed to have need. 96% of undergraduates with need received aid; of those 53% had need fully met. *Average percent of need met:* 89% (excluding resources awarded to replace EFC). *Average financial aid package:* $6337 (excluding resources awarded to replace EFC). 6% of all full-time undergraduates had no need and received non-need-based gift aid.

GIFT AID (NEED-BASED) *Total amount:* $9,447,112 (68% federal, 27% state, 3% institutional, 2% external sources). *Receiving aid:* Freshmen: 24% (362); All full-time undergraduates: 26% (2,084). *Average award:* Freshmen: $3864; Undergraduates: $4300. *Scholarships, grants, and awards:* Federal Pell, FSEOG, state, college/university gift aid from institutional funds.

GIFT AID (NON-NEED-BASED) *Total amount:* $1,373,544 (8% state, 48% institutional, 44% external sources). *Receiving aid:* Freshmen: 5% (70); Undergraduates: 5% (423). *Average Award: Freshmen:* $2102; *Undergraduates:* $1730. *Scholarships, grants, and awards by category: Academic Interests/Achievement:* 327 awards ($216,190 total): agriculture, architecture, biological sciences, business, communication, computer science, education, engineering/technologies, English, foreign languages, general academic interests/achievements, health fields, home economics, humanities, international studies, mathematics, military science, physical sciences, premedicine, social sciences. *Creative Arts/Performance:* 46 awards ($25,300 total): applied art and design, creative writing, dance, music, performing arts, theater/drama. *Special Achievements/Activities:* 23 awards ($21,645 total): general special achievements/activities, leadership. *Special Characteristics:* 30 awards ($30,450 total): adult students, ethnic background, general special characteristics, international students, members of minority groups, out-of-state students, veterans. *Tuition waivers:* Full or partial for senior citizens. *ROTC:* Army.

LOANS *Student loans:* $19,891,887 (70% need-based, 30% non-need-based). 65% of past graduating class borrowed through all loan programs. *Average indebtedness per student:* $13,935. *Average need-based loan:* Freshmen: $2952; Undergraduates: $3900. *Parent loans:* $12,074,822 (100% non-need-based). *Programs:* Perkins, college/university.

WORK-STUDY *Federal work-study:* Total amount: $2,118,629; 934 jobs averaging $1300.

APPLYING FOR FINANCIAL AID *Required financial aid form:* FAFSA. *Financial aid deadline (priority):* 6/15. *Notification date:* Continuous. Students must reply within 4 weeks of notification.

CONTACT Mr. Paul Watson, Interim Director of Financial Aid, University of Wisconsin–Stevens Point, 105 Student Services Center, Stevens Point, WI 54481-3897, 715-346-4771. *Fax:* 715-346-3526. *E-mail:* pwatson@uwsp.edu.

UNIVERSITY OF WISCONSIN–STOUT
Menomonie, WI

Tuition & fees (WI res): $6262	Average undergraduate aid package: $7107

ABOUT THE INSTITUTION State-supported, coed. Awards: bachelor's and master's degrees and post-master's certificates. 29 undergraduate majors. Total enrollment: 7,547. Undergraduates: 6,972. Freshmen: 1,281. Federal methodology is used as a basis for awarding need-based institutional aid.

UNDERGRADUATE EXPENSES for 2004–05 *Application fee:* $35. *Tuition, state resident:* full-time $4455; part-time $186 per credit. *Tuition, nonresident:* full-time $14,780; part-time $530 per credit. *Required fees:* full-time $1807; $23 per credit. Full-time tuition and fees vary according to reciprocity agreements. Part-time tuition and fees vary according to reciprocity agreements. *College room and board:* $4334; *room only:* $2500. Room and board charges vary according to board plan. *Payment plan:* Installment.

FRESHMAN FINANCIAL AID (Fall 2004, est.) 970 applied for aid; of those 66% were deemed to have need. 100% of freshmen with need received aid; of those 55% had need fully met. *Average percent of need met:* 87% (excluding resources awarded to replace EFC). *Average financial aid package:* $6867 (excluding resources awarded to replace EFC). 10% of all full-time freshmen had no need and received non-need-based gift aid.

UNDERGRADUATE FINANCIAL AID (Fall 2004, est.) 4,562 applied for aid; of those 72% were deemed to have need. 100% of undergraduates with need received aid; of those 59% had need fully met. *Average percent of need met:* 90% (excluding resources awarded to replace EFC). *Average financial aid package:* $7107 (excluding resources awarded to replace EFC). 6% of all full-time undergraduates had no need and received non-need-based gift aid.

GIFT AID (NEED-BASED) *Total amount:* $7,129,964 (68% federal, 28% state, 4% external sources). *Receiving aid:* Freshmen: 24% (300); All full-time undergraduates: 26% (1,613). *Average award:* Freshmen: $4168; Undergraduates: $4230. *Scholarships, grants, and awards:* Federal Pell, FSEOG, state, private, college/university gift aid from institutional funds, Bureau of Indian Affairs Grants, GEAR UP grants.

GIFT AID (NON-NEED-BASED) *Total amount:* $1,587,481 (4% federal, 3% state, 22% institutional, 71% external sources). *Receiving aid:* Freshmen: 17% (220); Undergraduates: 9% (587). *Average Award:* Freshmen: $1966; *Undergraduates:* $2140. *Scholarships, grants, and awards by category: Academic Interests/ Achievement:* 290 awards ($239,275 total): business, education, engineering/ technologies, general academic interests/achievements, home economics, international studies, mathematics, physical sciences. *Creative Arts/Performance:* 11 awards ($10,900 total): applied art and design, art/fine arts, music. *Special Achievements/Activities:* 17 awards ($9175 total): general special achievements/ activities, memberships. *Special Characteristics:* 45 awards ($33,250 total): adult students, handicapped students, international students, local/state students, members of minority groups, out-of-state students, previous college experience, veterans, veterans' children.

LOANS *Student loans:* $24,762,937 (50% need-based, 50% non-need-based). 69% of past graduating class borrowed through all loan programs. *Average indebtedness per student:* $18,172. *Average need-based loan:* Freshmen: $3587; Undergraduates: $4031. *Parent loans:* $2,173,773 (100% non-need-based). *Programs:* FFEL (Subsidized and Unsubsidized Stafford, PLUS), Perkins, alternative loans.

WORK-STUDY *Federal work-study:* Total amount: $2,038,222; 1,352 jobs averaging $1448.

APPLYING FOR FINANCIAL AID *Required financial aid form:* FAFSA. *Financial aid deadline (priority):* 3/15. *Notification date:* Continuous beginning 4/1. Students must reply within 4 weeks of notification.

CONTACT Beth A. Resech, Director of Financial Aid, University of Wisconsin–Stout, 210 Bowman Hall, Menomonie, WI 54751, 715-232-1363 or toll-free 800-HI-STOUT (in-state). *Fax:* 715-232-5246. *E-mail:* resechb@uwstout.edu.

UNIVERSITY OF WISCONSIN–SUPERIOR
Superior, WI

Tuition & fees (WI res): $4808   **Average undergraduate aid package: $6836**

ABOUT THE INSTITUTION State-supported, coed. Awards: associate, bachelor's, master's, and first professional degrees and post-bachelor's certificates. 62 undergraduate majors. Total enrollment: 2,804. Undergraduates: 2,546. Freshmen: 344. Federal methodology is used as a basis for awarding need-based institutional aid.

UNDERGRADUATE EXPENSES for 2004–05 *Application fee:* $35. *Tuition, state resident:* full-time $4808; part-time $282.08 per credit. *Tuition, nonresident:* full-time $14,854; part-time $700.67 per credit. Full-time tuition and fees vary according to course load and reciprocity agreements. Part-time tuition and fees vary according to course load and reciprocity agreements. *College room and board:* $4342; *room only:* $2502. Room and board charges vary according to housing facility. *Payment plan:* Installment.

FRESHMAN FINANCIAL AID (Fall 2004, est.) 236 applied for aid; of those 77% were deemed to have need. 97% of freshmen with need received aid; of those 31% had need fully met. *Average financial aid package:* $6035 (excluding resources awarded to replace EFC). 4% of all full-time freshmen had no need and received non-need-based gift aid.

UNDERGRADUATE FINANCIAL AID (Fall 2004, est.) 1,486 applied for aid; of those 81% were deemed to have need. 98% of undergraduates with need received aid; of those 29% had need fully met. *Average financial aid package:* $6836 (excluding resources awarded to replace EFC). 2% of all full-time undergraduates had no need and received non-need-based gift aid.

GIFT AID (NEED-BASED) *Total amount:* $3,343,621 (73% federal, 27% state). *Receiving aid:* Freshmen: 33% (99); All full-time undergraduates: 34% (710). *Average award:* Freshmen: $4188; Undergraduates: $4190. *Scholarships, grants, and awards:* Federal Pell, FSEOG, state, private, college/university gift aid from institutional funds.

GIFT AID (NON-NEED-BASED) *Total amount:* $959,444 (1% state, 63% institutional, 36% external sources). *Receiving aid:* Freshmen: 24% (73); Undergraduates: 14% (291). *Average Award:* Freshmen: $2154; *Undergraduates:* $2378. *Scholarships, grants, and awards by category: Academic Interests/ Achievement:* biological sciences, business, communication, computer science, education, English, general academic interests/achievements, health fields, humanities, mathematics, physical sciences, social sciences. *Special Characteristics:* general special characteristics. *Tuition waivers:* Full or partial for minority students, senior citizens. *ROTC:* Air Force cooperative.

LOANS *Student loans:* $7,874,411 (53% need-based, 47% non-need-based). 68% of past graduating class borrowed through all loan programs. *Average need-based loan:* Freshmen: $2446; Undergraduates: $3512. *Parent loans:*

$377,895 (100% non-need-based). *Programs:* Federal Direct (Subsidized and Unsubsidized Stafford, PLUS), Perkins, state, college/university.

WORK-STUDY *Federal work-study:* Total amount: $362,871; 260 jobs averaging $1320. *State or other work-study/employment:* Part-time jobs available.

APPLYING FOR FINANCIAL AID *Required financial aid form:* FAFSA. *Financial aid deadline (priority):* 4/15. *Notification date:* Continuous.

CONTACT Financial Aid Office, University of Wisconsin–Superior, Belknap and Catlin, PO Box 2000, Superior, WI 54880-4500, 715-394-8200 or toll-free 715-394-8230 (in-state).

UNIVERSITY OF WISCONSIN–WHITEWATER
Whitewater, WI

Tuition & fees (WI res): $5080   **Average undergraduate aid package: $6080**

ABOUT THE INSTITUTION State-supported, coed. Awards: associate, bachelor's, and master's degrees. 56 undergraduate majors. Total enrollment: 10,938. Undergraduates: 9,533. Freshmen: 1,762. Federal methodology is used as a basis for awarding need-based institutional aid.

UNDERGRADUATE EXPENSES for 2005–06 *Application fee:* $35. *One-time required fee:* $100. *Tuition, state resident:* full-time $4370; part-time $186 per credit. *Tuition, nonresident:* full-time $14,965; part-time $663 per credit. *Required fees:* full-time $710; $28.75 per credit. Full-time tuition and fees vary according to degree level and reciprocity agreements. *College room and board:* $4210; *room only:* $2460. Room and board charges vary according to board plan. *Payment plan:* Installment.

FRESHMAN FINANCIAL AID (Fall 2004, est.) 1571 applied for aid; of those 67% were deemed to have need. 93% of freshmen with need received aid; of those 41% had need fully met. *Average percent of need met:* 68% (excluding resources awarded to replace EFC). *Average financial aid package:* $5360 (excluding resources awarded to replace EFC). 12% of all full-time freshmen had no need and received non-need-based gift aid.

UNDERGRADUATE FINANCIAL AID (Fall 2004, est.) 6,037 applied for aid; of those 71% were deemed to have need. 95% of undergraduates with need received aid; of those 51% had need fully met. *Average percent of need met:* 75% (excluding resources awarded to replace EFC). *Average financial aid package:* $6080 (excluding resources awarded to replace EFC). 8% of all full-time undergraduates had no need and received non-need-based gift aid.

GIFT AID (NEED-BASED) *Total amount:* $8,600,000 (64% federal, 36% state). *Receiving aid:* Freshmen: 27% (470); All full-time undergraduates: 22% (1,937). *Average award:* Freshmen: $4262; Undergraduates: $4199. *Scholarships, grants, and awards:* Federal Pell, FSEOG, state, private, college/university gift aid from institutional funds.

GIFT AID (NON-NEED-BASED) *Total amount:* $2,670,000 (2% federal, 4% state, 34% institutional, 60% external sources). *Receiving aid:* Freshmen: 15% (266); Undergraduates: 8% (660). *Average Award:* Freshmen: $1831; *Undergraduates:* $2254. *Scholarships, grants, and awards by category: Academic Interests/ Achievement:* 656 awards ($730,000 total): biological sciences, business, communication, computer science, education, English, foreign languages, general academic interests/achievements, humanities, mathematics, physical sciences, premedicine, social sciences. *Creative Arts/Performance:* art/fine arts, cinema/ film/broadcasting, creative writing, journalism/publications, music, theater/ drama. *Special Achievements/Activities:* leadership. *Special Characteristics:* adult students, ethnic background, handicapped students, international students, local/ state students, members of minority groups, out-of-state students. *Tuition waivers:* Full or partial for children of alumni, senior citizens. *ROTC:* Army, Air Force.

LOANS *Student loans:* $33,000,000 (52% need-based, 48% non-need-based). *Average need-based loan:* Freshmen: $2920; Undergraduates: $3739. *Parent loans:* $2,900,000 (100% non-need-based). *Programs:* Federal Direct (Subsidized and Unsubsidized Stafford, PLUS), Perkins.

WORK-STUDY *Federal work-study:* Total amount: $696,000; 575 jobs averaging $1210. *State or other work-study/employment:* Total amount: $4,000,000 (100% non-need-based). 2,100 part-time jobs averaging $1860.

APPLYING FOR FINANCIAL AID *Required financial aid form:* FAFSA. *Financial aid deadline (priority):* 3/15. *Notification date:* Continuous beginning 4/1. Students must reply within 2 weeks of notification.

CONTACT Ms. Carol Miller, Director of Financial Aid, University of Wisconsin–Whitewater, 800 West Main Street, Whitewater, WI 53190-1790, 262-472-1130. *Fax:* 262-472-5655.

UNIVERSITY OF WYOMING
Laramie, WY

Tuition & fees (WY res): $3243   **Average undergraduate aid package: $7910**

ABOUT THE INSTITUTION State-supported, coed. Awards: bachelor's, master's, doctoral, and first professional degrees and post-master's certificates. 78 undergraduate majors. Total enrollment: 13,207. Undergraduates: 9,589. Freshmen: 1,518. Federal methodology is used as a basis for awarding need-based institutional aid.

UNDERGRADUATE EXPENSES for 2004–05 *Application fee:* $30. *Tuition, state resident:* full-time $2610; part-time $87 per credit hour. *Tuition, nonresident:* full-time $8640; part-time $288 per credit hour. *Required fees:* full-time $633; $153 per term part-time. Full-time tuition and fees vary according to course load, location, program, and reciprocity agreements. Part-time tuition and fees vary according to course load, location, program, and reciprocity agreements. *College room and board:* $5953; *room only:* $2590. Room and board charges vary according to board plan and housing facility. *Payment plans:* Installment, deferred payment.

FRESHMAN FINANCIAL AID (Fall 2003) 1257 applied for aid; of those 67% were deemed to have need. 98% of freshmen with need received aid; of those 55% had need fully met. *Average percent of need met:* 75% (excluding resources awarded to replace EFC). *Average financial aid package:* $7834 (excluding resources awarded to replace EFC). 16% of all full-time freshmen had no need and received non-need-based gift aid.

UNDERGRADUATE FINANCIAL AID (Fall 2003) 5,888 applied for aid; of those 77% were deemed to have need. 98% of undergraduates with need received aid; of those 70% had need fully met. *Average percent of need met:* 75% (excluding resources awarded to replace EFC). *Average financial aid package:* $7910 (excluding resources awarded to replace EFC). 22% of all full-time undergraduates had no need and received non-need-based gift aid.

GIFT AID (NEED-BASED) *Total amount:* $8,338,955 (87% federal, 4% institutional, 9% external sources). *Receiving aid:* Freshmen: 19% (265); All full-time undergraduates: 20% (1,770). *Average award:* Freshmen: $1849; Undergraduates: $1932. *Scholarships, grants, and awards:* Federal Pell, FSEOG, state, private, college/university gift aid from institutional funds.

GIFT AID (NON-NEED-BASED) *Total amount:* $15,231,244 (13% federal, 45% state, 19% institutional, 23% external sources). *Receiving aid:* Freshmen: 23% (314); Undergraduates: 17% (1,505). *Average Award:* Freshmen: $1436; Undergraduates: $1435. *Scholarships, grants, and awards by category: Academic Interests/Achievement:* agriculture, business, communication, computer science, education, engineering/technologies, English, foreign languages, general academic interests/achievements, health fields, home economics, international studies, mathematics, military science, physical sciences, social sciences. *Creative Arts/Performance:* 436 awards ($517,944 total): dance, debating, music, theater/drama. *Special Achievements/Activities:* 217 awards ($248,200 total): cheerleading/drum major, junior miss, leadership, rodeo. *Special Characteristics:* adult students, children and siblings of alumni, ethnic background, first-generation college students, handicapped students, international students, local/state students, out-of-state students, veterans. *Tuition waivers:* Full or partial for children of alumni, employees or children of employees, senior citizens. *ROTC:* Army, Air Force.

LOANS *Student loans:* $18,924,769 (60% need-based, 40% non-need-based). 44% of past graduating class borrowed through all loan programs. *Average indebtedness per student:* $15,352. *Average need-based loan:* Freshmen: $2010; Undergraduates: $3526. *Parent loans:* $1,821,031 (100% non-need-based). *Programs:* FFEL (Subsidized and Unsubsidized Stafford, PLUS), Perkins, alternative loans.

WORK-STUDY *Federal work-study:* Total amount: $602,828; 464 jobs averaging $1299.

ATHLETIC AWARDS *Total amount:* $2,540,142 (100% non-need-based).

APPLYING FOR FINANCIAL AID *Required financial aid form:* FAFSA. *Financial aid deadline (priority):* 2/1. *Notification date:* Continuous beginning 3/15. Students must reply within 3 weeks of notification.

CONTACT Mr. David Gruen, Director of Student Financial Aid, University of Wyoming, Department 3335, 1000 East University Avenue, Laramie, WY 82071-3335, 307-766-2116 or toll-free 800-342-5996. *Fax:* 307-766-3800. *E-mail:* finaid@uwyo.edu.

UPPER IOWA UNIVERSITY
Fayette, IA

CONTACT Jobyna Johnston, Director of Financial Aid, Upper Iowa University, Parker Fox Hall, Box 1859, Fayette, IA 52142-1859, 563-425-5393 or toll-free 800-553-4150 Ext. 2. *Fax:* 563-425-5277. *E-mail:* jobyna@uiu.edu.

URBANA UNIVERSITY
Urbana, OH

Tuition & fees: $14,220   **Average undergraduate aid package: $13,421**

ABOUT THE INSTITUTION Independent, coed. Awards: associate, bachelor's, and master's degrees. 28 undergraduate majors. Total enrollment: 1,531. Undergraduates: 1,529. Federal methodology is used as a basis for awarding need-based institutional aid.

UNDERGRADUATE EXPENSES for 2004–05 *Application fee:* $25. *Comprehensive fee:* $19,900 includes full-time tuition ($14,220) and room and board ($5680). *College room only:* $1920. Full-time tuition and fees vary according to location. Room and board charges vary according to board plan, housing facility, location, and student level. *Part-time tuition:* $295 per semester hour. *Part-time fees:* $90 per term. Part-time tuition and fees vary according to location. *Payment plans:* Installment, deferred payment.

FRESHMAN FINANCIAL AID (Fall 2004, est.) 346 applied for aid; of those 98% were deemed to have need. 100% of freshmen with need received aid; of those 67% had need fully met. *Average percent of need met:* 35% (excluding resources awarded to replace EFC). *Average financial aid package:* $11,856 (excluding resources awarded to replace EFC).

UNDERGRADUATE FINANCIAL AID (Fall 2004, est.) 756 applied for aid; of those 98% were deemed to have need. 100% of undergraduates with need received aid; of those 87% had need fully met. *Average percent of need met:* 46% (excluding resources awarded to replace EFC). *Average financial aid package:* $13,421 (excluding resources awarded to replace EFC).

GIFT AID (NEED-BASED) *Total amount:* $1,755,406 (66% federal, 34% state). *Receiving aid:* Freshmen: 47% (174); All full-time undergraduates: 77% (601). *Average award:* Freshmen: $1809; Undergraduates: $2312. *Scholarships, grants, and awards:* Federal Pell, FSEOG, state, private, college/university gift aid from institutional funds.

GIFT AID (NON-NEED-BASED) *Total amount:* $1,838,890 (35% state, 61% institutional, 4% external sources). *Receiving aid:* Freshmen: 92% (339); Undergraduates: 95% (742). *Scholarships, grants, and awards by category: Academic Interests/Achievement:* 348 awards ($981,476 total): general academic interests/achievements. *Creative Arts/Performance:* 29 awards ($99,110 total): music. *Special Achievements/Activities:* community service, leadership, religious involvement. *Special Characteristics:* 56 awards ($292,888 total): children and siblings of alumni, children of faculty/staff, religious affiliation, spouses of current students. *Tuition waivers:* Full or partial for children of alumni, employees or children of employees, senior citizens.

LOANS *Student loans:* $5,719,416 (100% need-based). 82% of past graduating class borrowed through all loan programs. *Average indebtedness per student:* $19,281. *Average need-based loan:* Freshmen: $2625; Undergraduates: $4769. *Parent loans:* $1,286,237 (100% need-based). *Programs:* FFEL (Subsidized and Unsubsidized Stafford, PLUS), Perkins.

WORK-STUDY *Federal work-study:* Total amount: $246,691; 410 jobs averaging $1000.

ATHLETIC AWARDS *Total amount:* $2,155,795 (100% non-need-based).

APPLYING FOR FINANCIAL AID *Required financial aid forms:* FAFSA, institution's own form. *Financial aid deadline (priority):* 4/1. *Notification date:* Continuous. Students must reply within 4 weeks of notification.

CONTACT Mrs. Amy M. Barnhart, Director of Student Financial Services, Urbana University, 579 College Way, Urbana, OH 43078-2091, 937-484-1359 or toll-free 800-7-URBANA. *Fax:* 937-652-6870. *E-mail:* abarnhart@urbana.edu.

URSINUS COLLEGE
Collegeville, PA

Tuition & fees: $31,450   **Average undergraduate aid package: $22,129**

ABOUT THE INSTITUTION Independent, coed. Awards: bachelor's degrees. 36 undergraduate majors. Total enrollment: 1,499. Undergraduates: 1,499. Freshmen: 394. Both federal and institutional methodology are used as a basis for awarding need-based institutional aid.

UNDERGRADUATE EXPENSES for 2005–06 *Application fee:* $50. *Comprehensive fee:* $38,800 includes full-time tuition ($31,450) and room and board ($7350). *Part-time tuition:* $1048 per credit. *Payment plan:* Installment.

FRESHMAN FINANCIAL AID (Fall 2003) 433 applied for aid; of those 97% were deemed to have need. 100% of freshmen with need received aid; of those 60% had need fully met. *Average percent of need met:* 90% (excluding resources awarded to replace EFC). *Average financial aid package:* $22,606 (excluding resources awarded to replace EFC). 8% of all full-time freshmen had no need and received non-need-based gift aid.

UNDERGRADUATE FINANCIAL AID (Fall 2003) 1,412 applied for aid; of those 97% were deemed to have need. 100% of undergraduates with need received aid; of those 55% had need fully met. *Average percent of need met:* 90% (excluding resources awarded to replace EFC). *Average financial aid package:* $22,129 (excluding resources awarded to replace EFC). 8% of all full-time undergraduates had no need and received non-need-based gift aid.

GIFT AID (NEED-BASED) *Total amount:* $20,726,980 (6% federal, 6% state, 86% institutional, 2% external sources). *Receiving aid:* Freshmen: 83% (379); All full-time undergraduates: 76% (1,134). *Average award:* Freshmen: $17,048; Undergraduates: $15,874. *Scholarships, grants, and awards:* Federal Pell, FSEOG, state, private, college/university gift aid from institutional funds, Office of Vocational Rehabilitation Awards.

GIFT AID (NON-NEED-BASED) *Total amount:* $2,321,041 (100% institutional). *Receiving aid:* Freshmen: 7% (32); Undergraduates: 7% (105). *Average Award:* Freshmen: $11,500; Undergraduates: $11,500. *Scholarships, grants, and awards by category:* Academic Interests/Achievement: 118 awards ($2,321,041 total): general academic interests/achievements. *Creative Arts/Performance:* 12 awards ($100,000 total): art/fine arts, creative writing, music, theater/drama. *Special Achievements/Activities:* 60 awards ($350,000 total): leadership. *Special Characteristics:* 60 awards ($527,000 total): children of faculty/staff, international students, siblings of current students. *Tuition waivers:* Full or partial for employees or children of employees, senior citizens.

LOANS *Student loans:* $8,737,458 (100% need-based). 78% of past graduating class borrowed through all loan programs. *Average indebtedness per student:* $18,000. *Average need-based loan:* Freshmen: $4128; Undergraduates: $5155. *Parent loans:* $2,656,520 (100% need-based). *Programs:* FFEL (Subsidized and Unsubsidized Stafford, PLUS), Perkins, college/university.

WORK-STUDY *Federal work-study:* Total amount: $1,045,915; 637 jobs averaging $1540.

APPLYING FOR FINANCIAL AID *Required financial aid forms:* FAFSA, institution's own form, CSS Financial Aid PROFILE. *Financial aid deadline (priority):* 2/15. *Notification date:* 4/1. Students must reply by 5/1.

CONTACT Ms. Suzanne B. Sparrow, Financial Aid Officer, Ursinus College, PO Box 1000, Collegeville, PA 19426-1000, 610-409-3600 Ext. 2242. *Fax:* 610-409-3662. *E-mail:* ssparrowui@ursinus.edu.

URSULINE COLLEGE
Pepper Pike, OH

Tuition & fees: $18,150	Average undergraduate aid package: $15,511

ABOUT THE INSTITUTION Independent Roman Catholic, women only. Awards: bachelor's and master's degrees and post-master's certificates (applications from men are also accepted). 47 undergraduate majors. Total enrollment: 1,462. Undergraduates: 1,139. Freshmen: 124. Federal methodology is used as a basis for awarding need-based institutional aid.

UNDERGRADUATE EXPENSES for 2004–05 *Application fee:* $25. *Comprehensive fee:* $24,046 includes full-time tuition ($17,970), mandatory fees ($180), and room and board ($5896). *College room only:* $3012. Room and board charges vary according to board plan. *Part-time tuition:* $599 per credit hour. *Part-time fees:* $55 per term. *Payment plan:* Installment.

FRESHMAN FINANCIAL AID (Fall 2003) 118 applied for aid; of those 92% were deemed to have need. 100% of freshmen with need received aid; of those 19% had need fully met. *Average percent of need met:* 90% (excluding resources awarded to replace EFC). *Average financial aid package:* $16,371 (excluding resources awarded to replace EFC). 6% of all full-time freshmen had no need and received non-need-based gift aid.

UNDERGRADUATE FINANCIAL AID (Fall 2003) 621 applied for aid; of those 95% were deemed to have need. 100% of undergraduates with need received

aid; of those 22% had need fully met. *Average percent of need met:* 76% (excluding resources awarded to replace EFC). *Average financial aid package:* $15,511 (excluding resources awarded to replace EFC). 15% of all full-time undergraduates had no need and received non-need-based gift aid.

GIFT AID (NEED-BASED) *Total amount:* $3,768,972 (34% federal, 31% state, 30% institutional, 5% external sources). *Receiving aid:* Freshmen: 82% (101). *Average award:* Freshmen: $8464. *Scholarships, grants, and awards:* Federal Pell, FSEOG, state, private, college/university gift aid from institutional funds, United Negro College Fund.

GIFT AID (NON-NEED-BASED) *Total amount:* $882,479 (7% state, 88% institutional, 5% external sources). *Receiving aid:* Freshmen: 87% (107). *Average Award:* Freshmen: $3750; Undergraduates: $4124. *Scholarships, grants, and awards by category:* Academic Interests/Achievement: general academic interests/achievements. *Special Achievements/Activities:* community service, leadership. *Special Characteristics:* children and siblings of alumni, children of faculty/staff, relatives of clergy, religious affiliation, siblings of current students. *Tuition waivers:* Full or partial for employees or children of employees.

LOANS *Student loans:* $8,226,884 (67% need-based, 33% non-need-based). 44% of past graduating class borrowed through all loan programs. *Average indebtedness per student:* $21,680. *Average need-based loan:* Freshmen: $3323; Undergraduates: $4200. *Programs:* FFEL (Subsidized and Unsubsidized Stafford, PLUS), Perkins, college/university.

WORK-STUDY *Federal work-study:* Total amount: $104,719; jobs available.

ATHLETIC AWARDS *Total amount:* $204,400 (89% need-based, 11% non-need-based).

APPLYING FOR FINANCIAL AID *Required financial aid forms:* FAFSA, institution's own form. *Financial aid deadline (priority):* 3/1. *Notification date:* Continuous beginning 4/1. Students must reply within 4 weeks of notification.

CONTACT Ms. Mary Lynn Perri, Director of Financial Aid and Enrollment Services, Ursuline College, 2550 Lander Road, Mullen Building, Room 202b, Pepper Pike, OH 44124-4398, 440-646-8330 or toll-free 888-URSULINE.

UTAH STATE UNIVERSITY
Logan, UT

Tuition & fees (UT res): $3374	Average undergraduate aid package: $5000

ABOUT THE INSTITUTION State-supported, coed. Awards: associate, bachelor's, master's, and doctoral degrees and post-bachelor's and post-master's certificates. 121 undergraduate majors. Total enrollment: 16,130. Undergraduates: 13,585. Freshmen: 2,183. Federal methodology is used as a basis for awarding need-based institutional aid.

UNDERGRADUATE EXPENSES for 2004–05 *Application fee:* $40. *Tuition, state resident:* full-time $2850. *Tuition, nonresident:* full-time $9178. Full-time tuition and fees vary according to course load and student level. Part-time tuition and fees vary according to course load and student level. *College room and board:* $4230; *room only:* $1550. Room and board charges vary according to board plan and housing facility. *Payment plan:* Deferred payment.

FRESHMAN FINANCIAL AID (Fall 2003) 1045 applied for aid; of those 83% were deemed to have need. 95% of freshmen with need received aid; of those 13% had need fully met. *Average percent of need met:* 59% (excluding resources awarded to replace EFC). *Average financial aid package:* $3300 (excluding resources awarded to replace EFC). 16% of all full-time freshmen had no need and received non-need-based gift aid.

UNDERGRADUATE FINANCIAL AID (Fall 2003) 7,089 applied for aid; of those 92% were deemed to have need. 97% of undergraduates with need received aid; of those 13% had need fully met. *Average percent of need met:* 58% (excluding resources awarded to replace EFC). *Average financial aid package:* $5000 (excluding resources awarded to replace EFC). 9% of all full-time undergraduates had no need and received non-need-based gift aid.

GIFT AID (NEED-BASED) *Total amount:* $16,660,514 (98% federal, 2% state). *Receiving aid:* Freshmen: 22% (519); All full-time undergraduates: 36% (4,955). *Average award:* Freshmen: $2800; Undergraduates: $3100. *Scholarships, grants, and awards:* Federal Pell, FSEOG, state, private, college/university gift aid from institutional funds.

GIFT AID (NON-NEED-BASED) *Total amount:* $5,181,543 (84% institutional, 16% external sources). *Receiving aid:* Freshmen: 13% (309); Undergraduates: 12% (1,615). *Average Award:* Freshmen: $2500; Undergraduates: $2800. *Scholarships, grants, and awards by category:* Academic Interests/Achievement: 6,994 awards ($10,863,860 total): agriculture, architecture, biological sciences, business, communication, computer science, education, engineering/technologies, English, foreign languages, general academic interests/achievements, health fields, home economics, humanities, international studies, library science, mathematics, physical sciences, premedicine, social sciences. *Creative Arts/ Performance:* 158 awards ($174,225 total): applied art and design, art/fine arts, general creative arts/performance, journalism/publications, music, performing arts, theater/drama. *Tuition waivers:* Full or partial for minority students, children of alumni, employees or children of employees, adult students, senior citizens. *ROTC:* Army, Air Force.

LOANS *Student loans:* $22,018,600 (76% need-based, 24% non-need-based). 50% of past graduating class borrowed through all loan programs. *Average indebtedness per student:* $12,430. *Average need-based loan:* Freshmen: $2600; Undergraduates: $3850. *Parent loans:* $1,077,100 (100% non-need-based). *Programs:* FFEL (Subsidized and Unsubsidized Stafford, PLUS), Perkins, college/ university.

WORK-STUDY *Federal work-study:* Total amount: $1,101,823; 458 jobs averaging $2406. *State or other work-study/employment:* Total amount: $271,823 (100% need-based). 113 part-time jobs averaging $2406.

ATHLETIC AWARDS *Total amount:* $1,976,150 (100% non-need-based).

APPLYING FOR FINANCIAL AID *Required financial aid forms:* FAFSA, institution's own form. *Financial aid deadline:* Continuous. *Notification date:* Continuous beginning 4/1. Students must reply within 4 weeks of notification.

CONTACT Steve Sharp, Associate Director of Financial Aid, Utah State University, Old Main Hill, Logan, UT 84322, 435-797-1455 or toll-free 800-488-8108. *Fax:* 435-797-0654. *E-mail:* sjsharp@cc.usu.edu.

UTAH VALLEY STATE COLLEGE
Orem, UT

Tuition & fees (UT res): $2788   **Average undergraduate aid package: $6477**

ABOUT THE INSTITUTION State-supported, coed. Awards: associate and bachelor's degrees. 82 undergraduate majors. Total enrollment: 24,149. Undergraduates: 24,149. Freshmen: 2,733. Both federal and institutional methodology are used as a basis for awarding need-based institutional aid.

UNDERGRADUATE EXPENSES for 2004–05 *Application fee:* $30. *Tuition, state resident:* full-time $2788. *Tuition, nonresident:* full-time $8718. Full-time tuition and fees vary according to course level. Part-time tuition and fees vary according to course level and course load. *Payment plans:* Installment, deferred payment.

GIFT AID (NEED-BASED) *Total amount:* $15,256,420 (98% federal, 2% institutional). *Receiving aid:* Freshmen: 23% (179); All full-time undergraduates: 31% (3,359). *Average award:* Freshmen: $2889; Undergraduates: $2278. *Scholarships, grants, and awards:* Federal Pell, FSEOG, state, private, college/ university gift aid from institutional funds.

GIFT AID (NON-NEED-BASED) *Total amount:* $150,456 (100% external sources). *Receiving aid:* Freshmen: 1; Undergraduates: 38. *Average Award: Freshmen:* $1828; *Undergraduates:* $1603. *Tuition waivers:* Full or partial for employees or children of employees. *ROTC:* Army, Air Force cooperative.

LOANS *Student loans:* $24,015,191 (86% need-based, 14% non-need-based). 28% of past graduating class borrowed through all loan programs. *Average indebtedness per student:* $6273. *Average need-based loan:* Freshmen: $2123; Undergraduates: $1965. *Parent loans:* $519,160 (100% non-need-based). *Programs:* FFEL (Subsidized and Unsubsidized Stafford, PLUS), Perkins, college/ university.

ATHLETIC AWARDS *Total amount:* $30,784 (100% non-need-based).

APPLYING FOR FINANCIAL AID *Required financial aid forms:* FAFSA, institution's own form. *Financial aid deadline (priority):* 6/1. *Notification date:* Continuous beginning 1/1. Students must reply within 2 weeks of notification.

CONTACT Mr. Michael H. Johnson, Director of Financial Aid, Utah Valley State College, Mail Code—164, 800 West 1200 South Street, Orem, UT 84058-0001, 801-222-8442. *Fax:* 801-222-8448.

U.T.A. MESIVTA OF KIRYAS JOEL
Monroe, NY

CONTACT Financial Aid Office, U.T.A. Mesivta of Kiryas Joel, 33 Forest Road, Suite 101, Monroe, NY 10950, 845-873-9901.

UTICA COLLEGE
Utica, NY

Tuition & fees: $21,270   **Average undergraduate aid package: N/A**

ABOUT THE INSTITUTION Independent, coed. Awards: bachelor's, master's, and first professional degrees. 46 undergraduate majors. Total enrollment: 2,652. Undergraduates: 2,310. Freshmen: 487. Federal methodology is used as a basis for awarding need-based institutional aid.

UNDERGRADUATE EXPENSES for 2004–05 *Application fee:* $40. *Comprehensive fee:* $29,870 includes full-time tuition ($20,980), mandatory fees ($290), and room and board ($8600). *College room only:* $4500. Full-time tuition and fees vary according to class time and course load. Room and board charges vary according to board plan and housing facility. *Part-time tuition:* $702 per credit hour. *Part-time fees:* $45 per term. Part-time tuition and fees vary according to class time, course load, and degree level. *Payment plans:* Tuition prepayment, installment, deferred payment.

GIFT AID (NEED-BASED) *Total amount:* $23,431,988 (12% federal, 17% state, 69% institutional, 2% external sources). *Receiving aid:* Freshmen: 94% (458); All full-time undergraduates: 91% (1,802). *Average award:* Freshmen: $14,621; Undergraduates: $12,802. *Scholarships, grants, and awards:* Federal Pell, FSEOG, state, private, college/university gift aid from institutional funds, Federal Nursing.

GIFT AID (NON-NEED-BASED) *Total amount:* $647,250 (4% state, 95% institutional, 1% external sources). *Receiving aid:* Freshmen: 26% (127); Undergraduates: 21% (420). *Average Award: Freshmen:* $8375; *Undergraduates:* $8142. *Scholarships, grants, and awards by category:* Academic Interests/ Achievement: general academic interests/achievements. *Tuition waivers:* Full or partial for employees or children of employees, senior citizens. *ROTC:* Army, Air Force cooperative.

LOANS *Student loans:* $12,724,987 (96% need-based, 4% non-need-based). *Average need-based loan:* Freshmen: $3722; Undergraduates: $4447. *Parent loans:* $3,678,165 (93% need-based, 7% non-need-based). *Programs:* Federal Direct (Subsidized and Unsubsidized Stafford, PLUS), Perkins, GATE Loans.

APPLYING FOR FINANCIAL AID *Required financial aid forms:* FAFSA, state aid form. *Financial aid deadline (priority):* 2/15. *Notification date:* Continuous beginning 2/1. Students must reply by 5/1 or within 4 weeks of notification.

CONTACT Mrs. Elizabeth C. Wilson, Director of Financial Aid, Utica College, 1600 Burrstone Road, Utica, NY 13502-4892, 800-782-8884. *Fax:* 315-792-3368.

VALDOSTA STATE UNIVERSITY
Valdosta, GA

Tuition & fees (GA res): $2992   **Average undergraduate aid package: $8045**

ABOUT THE INSTITUTION State-supported, coed. Awards: associate, bachelor's, master's, and doctoral degrees and post-master's certificates. 88 undergraduate majors. Total enrollment: 10,400. Undergraduates: 9,013. Freshmen: 1,740. Federal methodology is used as a basis for awarding need-based institutional aid.

UNDERGRADUATE EXPENSES for 2004–05 *Application fee:* $20. *Tuition, state resident:* full-time $2322; part-time $97 per semester hour. *Tuition, nonresident:* full-time $9290; part-time $388 per semester hour. Part-time tuition and fees vary according to course load. *College room and board:* $5208; *room only:* $2664. Room and board charges vary according to board plan and housing facility.

FRESHMAN FINANCIAL AID (Fall 2003) 1645 applied for aid; of those 52% were deemed to have need. 100% of freshmen with need received aid; of those 84% had need fully met. *Average percent of need met:* 95% (excluding resources awarded to replace EFC). *Average financial aid package:* $7932 (excluding resources awarded to replace EFC). 2% of all full-time freshmen had no need and received non-need-based gift aid.

UNDERGRADUATE FINANCIAL AID (Fall 2003) 6,070 applied for aid; of those 59% were deemed to have need. 100% of undergraduates with need received aid; of those 71% had need fully met. *Average percent of need met:* 89% (excluding resources awarded to replace EFC). *Average financial aid package:* $8045 (excluding resources awarded to replace EFC). 2% of all full-time undergraduates had no need and received non-need-based gift aid.

GIFT AID (NEED-BASED) *Total amount:* $12,974,588 (57% federal, 41% state, 1% institutional, 1% external sources). *Receiving aid:* Freshmen: 29% (481); All full-time undergraduates: 30% (2,095). *Average award:* Freshmen: $967;

Undergraduates: $1522. *Scholarships, grants, and awards:* Federal Pell, FSEOG, state, private, college/university gift aid from institutional funds.
GIFT AID (NON-NEED-BASED) *Total amount:* $8,498,428 (95% state, 2% institutional, 3% external sources). *Receiving aid:* Freshmen: 44% (735); Undergraduates: 27% (1,882). *Average Award:* Freshmen: $1449; Undergraduates: $1411. *Scholarships, grants, and awards by category:* Academic Interests/Achievement: 4,586 awards ($13,108,473 total): biological sciences, business, communication, computer science, education, English, foreign languages, general academic interests/achievements, health fields, mathematics, military science, physical sciences, premedicine, social sciences. *Creative Arts/Performance:* 71 awards ($59,255 total): art/fine arts, music, theater/drama. *Special Achievements/Activities:* 86 awards ($89,610 total): community service, general special achievements/activities, hobbies/interests. *Special Characteristics:* 38 awards ($34,800 total): children of public servants, general special characteristics, international students, members of minority groups. *Tuition waivers:* Full or partial for employees or children of employees, senior citizens. *ROTC:* Air Force.
LOANS *Student loans:* $32,750,664 (46% need-based, 54% non-need-based). 55% of past graduating class borrowed through all loan programs. *Average indebtedness per student:* $17,595. *Average need-based loan:* Freshmen: $2344; Undergraduates: $3325. *Parent loans:* $17,724,184 (31% need-based, 69% non-need-based). *Programs:* Federal Direct (Subsidized and Unsubsidized Stafford, PLUS), college/university.
WORK-STUDY *Federal work-study:* Total amount: $438,317; 185 jobs averaging $2369.
ATHLETIC AWARDS *Total amount:* $882,903 (27% need-based, 73% non-need-based).
APPLYING FOR FINANCIAL AID *Required financial aid form:* FAFSA. *Financial aid deadline (priority):* 5/1. *Notification date:* Continuous beginning 5/15.
CONTACT Mr. Douglas R. Tanner, Director of Financial Aid, Valdosta State University, 1500 North Patterson Street, Valdosta, GA 31698, 229-333-5935 or toll-free 800-618-1878 Ext. 1. *Fax:* 229-333-5430.

VALLEY CITY STATE UNIVERSITY
Valley City, ND

Tuition & fees (ND res): $3130	Average undergraduate aid package: $6299

ABOUT THE INSTITUTION State-supported, coed. Awards: bachelor's degrees. 40 undergraduate majors. Total enrollment: 1,033. Undergraduates: 1,033. Freshmen: 171. Federal methodology is used as a basis for awarding need-based institutional aid.
UNDERGRADUATE EXPENSES for 2004–05 *Application fee:* $35. *Tuition, state resident:* full-time $3130; part-time $113.73 per semester hour. *Tuition, nonresident:* full-time $8357; part-time $303.63 per semester hour. *Required fees:* $5953 per semester hour. *College room and board:* $4074; *room only:* $1970. Room and board charges vary according to board plan.
FRESHMAN FINANCIAL AID (Fall 2004, est.) 129 applied for aid; of those 91% were deemed to have need. 100% of freshmen with need received aid; of those 27% had need fully met. *Average percent of need met:* 74% (excluding resources awarded to replace EFC). *Average financial aid package:* $5920 (excluding resources awarded to replace EFC). 30% of all full-time freshmen had no need and received non-need-based gift aid.
UNDERGRADUATE FINANCIAL AID (Fall 2004, est.) 639 applied for aid; of those 79% were deemed to have need. 98% of undergraduates with need received aid; of those 25% had need fully met. *Average percent of need met:* 75% (excluding resources awarded to replace EFC). *Average financial aid package:* $6299 (excluding resources awarded to replace EFC). 12% of all full-time undergraduates had no need and received non-need-based gift aid.
GIFT AID (NEED-BASED) *Total amount:* $1,177,339 (75% federal, 7% state, 13% institutional, 5% external sources). *Receiving aid:* Freshmen: 36% (60); All full-time undergraduates: 33% (279). *Average award:* Freshmen: $2933; Undergraduates: $3028. *Scholarships, grants, and awards:* Federal Pell, FSEOG, state, private, college/university gift aid from institutional funds.
GIFT AID (NON-NEED-BASED) *Total amount:* $154,927 (12% federal, 4% state, 61% institutional, 23% external sources). *Receiving aid:* Freshmen: 52% (87); Undergraduates: 33% (275). *Average Award:* Freshmen: $1575; Undergraduates: $1626. *Scholarships, grants, and awards by category:* Academic Interests/Achievement: 497 awards ($297,508 total): biological sciences, business, communication, computer science, education, English, general academic interests/achievements, library science, mathematics, physical sciences, social sciences. *Creative Arts/Performance:* 46 awards ($14,555 total): applied art and design, art/fine arts, journalism/publications, music, theater/drama. *Tuition waivers:* Full or partial for children of alumni, employees or children of employees.

LOANS *Student loans:* $2,239,053 (74% need-based, 26% non-need-based). 57% of past graduating class borrowed through all loan programs. *Average indebtedness per student:* $15,750. *Average need-based loan:* Freshmen: $2924; Undergraduates: $3686. *Parent loans:* $76,049 (65% need-based, 35% non-need-based). *Programs:* FFEL (Subsidized and Unsubsidized Stafford, PLUS), Perkins, college/university.
WORK-STUDY *Federal work-study:* Total amount: $92,860; 75 jobs averaging $1238. *State or other work-study/employment:* Total amount: $187,126 (100% non-need-based). 170 part-time jobs averaging $1101.
ATHLETIC AWARDS *Total amount:* $108,750 (61% need-based, 39% non-need-based).
APPLYING FOR FINANCIAL AID *Required financial aid form:* FAFSA. *Financial aid deadline (priority):* 3/15. *Notification date:* Continuous beginning 2/1. Students must reply within 2 weeks of notification.
CONTACT Betty Kuss Schumacher, Director of Financial Aid, Valley City State University, 101 College Street SW, Valley City, ND 58072, 701-845-7412 or toll-free 800-532-8641 Ext. 37101. *Fax:* 701-845-7410. *E-mail:* betty.schumacher@vcsu.edu.

VALLEY FORGE CHRISTIAN COLLEGE
Phoenixville, PA

Tuition & fees: $10,982	Average undergraduate aid package: $7644

ABOUT THE INSTITUTION Independent Assemblies of God, coed. Awards: associate and bachelor's degrees. 6 undergraduate majors. Total enrollment: 856. Undergraduates: 856. Freshmen: 169. Federal methodology is used as a basis for awarding need-based institutional aid.
UNDERGRADUATE EXPENSES for 2005–06 *Application fee:* $25. *Comprehensive fee:* $16,442 includes full-time tuition ($10,050), mandatory fees ($932), and room and board ($5460). *College room only:* $2460. Full-time tuition and fees vary according to course load. Room and board charges vary according to board plan and housing facility. *Part-time tuition:* $385 per credit. Part-time tuition and fees vary according to course load. *Payment plan:* Installment.
FRESHMAN FINANCIAL AID (Fall 2004, est.) 188 applied for aid; of those 91% were deemed to have need. 99% of freshmen with need received aid; of those 7% had need fully met. *Average percent of need met:* 51% (excluding resources awarded to replace EFC). *Average financial aid package:* $6538 (excluding resources awarded to replace EFC). 35% of all full-time freshmen had no need and received non-need-based gift aid.
UNDERGRADUATE FINANCIAL AID (Fall 2004, est.) 798 applied for aid; of those 90% were deemed to have need. 99% of undergraduates with need received aid; of those 13% had need fully met. *Average percent of need met:* 58% (excluding resources awarded to replace EFC). *Average financial aid package:* $7644 (excluding resources awarded to replace EFC). 18% of all full-time undergraduates had no need and received non-need-based gift aid.
GIFT AID (NEED-BASED) *Total amount:* $3,431,069 (32% federal, 19% state, 42% institutional, 7% external sources). *Receiving aid:* Freshmen: 60% (159); All full-time undergraduates: 75% (662). *Average award:* Freshmen: $4663; Undergraduates: $4671. *Scholarships, grants, and awards:* Federal Pell, FSEOG, state, private, college/university gift aid from institutional funds.
GIFT AID (NON-NEED-BASED) *Receiving aid:* Freshmen: 2% (6); Undergraduates: 3% (27). *Average Award:* Freshmen: $4166; Undergraduates: $6341. *Scholarships, grants, and awards by category:* Academic Interests/Achievement: 154 awards ($287,641 total): general academic interests/achievements. *Creative Arts/Performance:* 359 awards ($386,221 total): art/fine arts, music. *Special Achievements/Activities:* 507 awards ($342,574 total): general special achievements/activities, leadership. *Special Characteristics:* 213 awards ($241,039 total): children of current students, children of faculty/staff, general special characteristics, married students, relatives of clergy, siblings of current students, spouses of current students. *Tuition waivers:* Full or partial for employees or children of employees.
LOANS *Student loans:* $5,449,003 (44% need-based, 56% non-need-based). 94% of past graduating class borrowed through all loan programs. *Average indebtedness per student:* $26,691. *Average need-based loan:* Freshmen: $2341; Undergraduates: $3467. *Parent loans:* $1,287,029 (100% non-need-based). *Programs:* FFEL (Subsidized and Unsubsidized Stafford, PLUS), Perkins, state.
WORK-STUDY *Federal work-study:* Total amount: $74,619; 59 jobs averaging $1265.
APPLYING FOR FINANCIAL AID *Required financial aid form:* FAFSA. *Financial aid deadline (priority):* 5/1. *Notification date:* Continuous beginning 3/1. Students must reply within 3 weeks of notification.

CONTACT Mrs. Evie Meyer, Director of Financial Aid, Valley Forge Christian College, 1401 Charlestown Road, Phoenixville, PA 19460-2399, 610-917-1417 or toll-free 800-432-8322. *Fax:* 610-917-2069. *E-mail:* eemeyer@vfcc.edu.

VALPARAISO UNIVERSITY
Valparaiso, IN

Tuition & fees: $21,700	Average undergraduate aid package: $18,419

ABOUT THE INSTITUTION Independent religious, coed. Awards: associate, bachelor's, master's, and first professional degrees and post-bachelor's and post-master's certificates. 89 undergraduate majors. Total enrollment: 3,969. Undergraduates: 3,067. Freshmen: 759. Both federal and institutional methodology are used as a basis for awarding need-based institutional aid.

UNDERGRADUATE EXPENSES for 2004–05 *Application fee:* $30. *Comprehensive fee:* $27,540 includes full-time tuition ($21,000), mandatory fees ($700), and room and board ($5840). *College room only:* $3690. Room and board charges vary according to housing facility and student level. *Part-time tuition:* $925 per credit hour. *Part-time fees:* $60 per term. Part-time tuition and fees vary according to course load. *Payment plans:* Installment, deferred payment.

FRESHMAN FINANCIAL AID (Fall 2004, est.) 681 applied for aid; of those 80% were deemed to have need. 100% of freshmen with need received aid; of those 65% had need fully met. *Average percent of need met:* 95% (excluding resources awarded to replace EFC). *Average financial aid package:* $19,777 (excluding resources awarded to replace EFC). 22% of all full-time freshmen had no need and received non-need-based gift aid.

UNDERGRADUATE FINANCIAL AID (Fall 2004, est.) 2,354 applied for aid; of those 84% were deemed to have need. 100% of undergraduates with need received aid; of those 60% had need fully met. *Average percent of need met:* 93% (excluding resources awarded to replace EFC). *Average financial aid package:* $18,419 (excluding resources awarded to replace EFC). 22% of all full-time undergraduates had no need and received non-need-based gift aid.

GIFT AID (NEED-BASED) *Total amount:* $24,420,000 (11% federal, 9% state, 74% institutional, 6% external sources). *Receiving aid:* Freshmen: 73% (547); All full-time undergraduates: 67% (1,941). *Average award:* Freshmen: $14,458; Undergraduates: $12,778. *Scholarships, grants, and awards:* Federal Pell, FSEOG, state, private, college/university gift aid from institutional funds.

GIFT AID (NON-NEED-BASED) *Total amount:* $5,500,000 (91% institutional, 9% external sources). *Receiving aid:* Freshmen: 13% (95); Undergraduates: 11% (312). *Average Award:* Freshmen: $8425; Undergraduates: $8720. *Scholarships, grants, and awards by category:* Academic Interests/Achievement: 1,800 awards ($12,200,000 total): business, engineering/technologies, foreign languages, general academic interests/achievements, health fields, physical sciences, religion/biblical studies. *Creative Arts/Performance:* 130 awards ($140,000 total): art/fine arts, music, performing arts, theater/drama. *Special Achievements/Activities:* 400 awards ($1,100,000 total): general special achievements/activities, religious involvement. *Special Characteristics:* 1,900 awards ($4,544,000 total): children and siblings of alumni, children of faculty/staff, international students, relatives of clergy, religious affiliation. *Tuition waivers:* Full or partial for employees or children of employees. *ROTC:* Air Force.

LOANS *Student loans:* $14,760,000 (58% need-based, 42% non-need-based). 67% of past graduating class borrowed through all loan programs. *Average indebtedness per student:* $21,798. *Average need-based loan:* Freshmen: $4903; Undergraduates: $5128. *Parent loans:* $3,000,000 (100% non-need-based). *Programs:* Federal Direct (Subsidized and Unsubsidized Stafford, PLUS), Perkins, college/university.

WORK-STUDY *Federal work-study:* Total amount: $400,000; 437 jobs averaging $915. *State or other work-study/employment:* Total amount: $1,100,000 (9% need-based, 91% non-need-based). 850 part-time jobs averaging $1294.

ATHLETIC AWARDS *Total amount:* $2,050,000 (50% need-based, 50% non-need-based).

APPLYING FOR FINANCIAL AID *Required financial aid form:* FAFSA. *Financial aid deadline (priority):* 3/1. *Notification date:* Continuous. Students must reply by 5/1.

CONTACT Mr. David Fevig, Director of Financial Aid, Valparaiso University, 1700 Chapel Drive, Valparaiso, IN 46383-6493, 219-464-5015 or toll-free 888-GO-VALPO. *Fax:* 219-464-5012. *E-mail:* david.fevig@valpo.edu.

VANDERBILT UNIVERSITY
Nashville, TN

Tuition & fees: $29,990	Average undergraduate aid package: $30,338

ABOUT THE INSTITUTION Independent, coed. Awards: bachelor's, master's, doctoral, and first professional degrees. 56 undergraduate majors. Total enrollment: 11,294. Undergraduates: 6,272. Freshmen: 1,602. Both federal and institutional methodology are used as a basis for awarding need-based institutional aid.

UNDERGRADUATE EXPENSES for 2004–05 *Application fee:* $50. *Comprehensive fee:* $39,726 includes full-time tuition ($29,240), mandatory fees ($750), and room and board ($9736). *College room only:* $6336. Full-time tuition and fees vary according to course load. Room and board charges vary according to board plan and housing facility. *Part-time tuition:* $1213 per credit hour. Part-time tuition and fees vary according to course load. *Payment plans:* Tuition prepayment, installment, deferred payment.

FRESHMAN FINANCIAL AID (Fall 2004, est.) 833 applied for aid; of those 86% were deemed to have need. 99% of freshmen with need received aid; of those 100% had need fully met. *Average percent of need met:* 100% (excluding resources awarded to replace EFC). *Average financial aid package:* $30,404 (excluding resources awarded to replace EFC). 12% of all full-time freshmen had no need and received non-need-based gift aid.

UNDERGRADUATE FINANCIAL AID (Fall 2004, est.) 2,700 applied for aid; of those 92% were deemed to have need. 100% of undergraduates with need received aid; of those 99% had need fully met. *Average percent of need met:* 99% (excluding resources awarded to replace EFC). *Average financial aid package:* $30,338 (excluding resources awarded to replace EFC). 13% of all full-time undergraduates had no need and received non-need-based gift aid.

GIFT AID (NEED-BASED) *Total amount:* $66,693,576 (5% federal, 2% state, 90% institutional, 3% external sources). *Receiving aid:* Freshmen: 39% (617); All full-time undergraduates: 37% (2,320). *Average award:* Freshmen: $24,141; Undergraduates: $23,508. *Scholarships, grants, and awards:* Federal Pell, FSEOG, state, private, college/university gift aid from institutional funds.

GIFT AID (NON-NEED-BASED) *Total amount:* $15,288,655 (3% state, 84% institutional, 13% external sources). *Receiving aid:* Freshmen: 26% (424); Undergraduates: 18% (1,127). *Average Award:* Freshmen: $12,306; Undergraduates: $17,780. *Scholarships, grants, and awards by category:* Academic Interests/Achievement: education, engineering/technologies, general academic interests/achievements, humanities. *Creative Arts/Performance:* 52 awards ($344,234 total): journalism/publications, music. *Special Characteristics:* 144 awards ($3,191,412 total): local/state students, members of minority groups. *Tuition waivers:* Full or partial for employees or children of employees. *ROTC:* Army, Naval, Air Force cooperative.

LOANS *Student loans:* $11,804,251 (88% need-based, 12% non-need-based). 36% of past graduating class borrowed through all loan programs. *Average indebtedness per student:* $24,044. *Average need-based loan:* Freshmen: $2922; Undergraduates: $3794. *Parent loans:* $9,594,671 (48% need-based, 52% non-need-based). *Programs:* FFEL (Subsidized and Unsubsidized Stafford, PLUS), Perkins, Federal Nursing, college/university.

WORK-STUDY *Federal work-study:* Total amount: $2,012,209; jobs available.

ATHLETIC AWARDS *Total amount:* $7,143,019 (29% need-based, 71% non-need-based).

APPLYING FOR FINANCIAL AID *Required financial aid forms:* FAFSA, CSS Financial Aid PROFILE, noncustodial (divorced/separated) parent's statement. *Financial aid deadline (priority):* 2/1. *Notification date:* 4/1. Students must reply by 5/1.

CONTACT David Mohning, Director of Financial Aid, Vanderbilt University, 2309 West End Avenue, Nashville, TN 37235, 615-322-3591 or toll-free 800-288-0432. *Fax:* 615-343-8512. *E-mail:* finaid@vanderbilt.edu.

VANDERCOOK COLLEGE OF MUSIC
Chicago, IL

Tuition & fees: $16,610	Average undergraduate aid package: $7983

ABOUT THE INSTITUTION Independent, coed. Awards: bachelor's and master's degrees. 1 undergraduate major. Total enrollment: 188. Undergraduates: 123. Freshmen: 28. Both federal and institutional methodology are used as a basis for awarding need-based institutional aid.

UNDERGRADUATE EXPENSES for 2005–06 *Application fee:* $35. *Comprehensive fee:* $23,810 includes full-time tuition ($15,890), mandatory fees ($720), and room and board ($7200). Room and board charges vary according to board plan and housing facility. Part-time tuition and fees vary according to course load.

FRESHMAN FINANCIAL AID (Fall 2003) *Average percent of need met:* 90% (excluding resources awarded to replace EFC). 12% of all full-time freshmen had no need and received non-need-based gift aid.

UNDERGRADUATE FINANCIAL AID (Fall 2003) *Average financial aid package:* $7983 (excluding resources awarded to replace EFC).

GIFT AID (NEED-BASED) *Total amount:* $365,489 (23% federal, 55% state, 14% institutional, 8% external sources). *Scholarships, grants, and awards:* Federal Pell, state, private, college/university gift aid from institutional funds.

GIFT AID (NON-NEED-BASED) *Total amount:* $225,926 (77% state, 23% institutional). *Scholarships, grants, and awards by category: Academic Interests/ Achievement:* general academic interests/achievements. *Creative Arts/ Performance:* music. *Special Characteristics:* ethnic background.

LOANS *Student loans:* $559,693 (72% need-based, 28% non-need-based). *Average indebtedness per student:* $18,500. *Parent loans:* $256,972 (100% non-need-based). *Programs:* FFEL (Subsidized and Unsubsidized Stafford, PLUS), alternative loans.

WORK-STUDY *State or other work-study/employment:* Total amount: $32,000 (100% need-based). Part-time jobs available.

APPLYING FOR FINANCIAL AID *Required financial aid form:* FAFSA. *Financial aid deadline:* 4/30. *Notification date:* Continuous beginning 5/15. Students must reply within 2 weeks of notification.

CONTACT Mr. James P. Malley, Director of Undergraduate Admissions, VanderCook College of Music, 3140 South Federal Street, Chicago, IL 60616, 312-225-6288 Ext. 241 or toll-free 800-448-2655 Ext. 230. *Fax:* 312-225-5211. *E-mail:* admissions@vandercook.edu.

VANGUARD UNIVERSITY OF SOUTHERN CALIFORNIA
Costa Mesa, CA

Tuition & fees: $20,330	Average undergraduate aid package: $9700

ABOUT THE INSTITUTION Independent religious, coed. Awards: bachelor's and master's degrees. 37 undergraduate majors. Total enrollment: 2,195. Undergraduates: 1,800. Freshmen: 355. Federal methodology is used as a basis for awarding need-based institutional aid.

UNDERGRADUATE EXPENSES for 2005–06 *Application fee:* $45. *Comprehensive fee:* $27,086 includes full-time tuition ($19,900), mandatory fees ($430), and room and board ($6756). *College room only:* $3366. Room and board charges vary according to board plan and housing facility. *Part-time tuition:* $829 per credit hour. *Part-time fees:* $25 per term. *Payment plan:* Installment.

FRESHMAN FINANCIAL AID (Fall 2004, est.) 301 applied for aid; of those 89% were deemed to have need. 100% of freshmen with need received aid; of those 62% had need fully met. *Average percent of need met:* 72% (excluding resources awarded to replace EFC). *Average financial aid package:* $9700 (excluding resources awarded to replace EFC). 6% of all full-time freshmen had no need and received non-need-based gift aid.

UNDERGRADUATE FINANCIAL AID (Fall 2004, est.) 1,171 applied for aid; of those 90% were deemed to have need. 100% of undergraduates with need received aid; of those 55% had need fully met. *Average percent of need met:* 68% (excluding resources awarded to replace EFC). *Average financial aid package:* $9700 (excluding resources awarded to replace EFC). 15% of all full-time undergraduates had no need and received non-need-based gift aid.

GIFT AID (NEED-BASED) *Total amount:* $11,213,001 (13% federal, 27% state, 57% institutional, 3% external sources). *Receiving aid:* Freshmen: 77% (269); All full-time undergraduates: 77% (1,056). *Average award:* Freshmen: $6204; Undergraduates: $6204. *Scholarships, grants, and awards:* Federal Pell, FSEOG, state, private, college/university gift aid from institutional funds.

GIFT AID (NON-NEED-BASED) *Total amount:* $1,990,102 (92% institutional, 8% external sources). *Receiving aid:* Freshmen: 28% (97); Undergraduates: 28% (389). *Average Award:* Freshmen: $5037; Undergraduates: $5037. *Scholarships, grants, and awards by category: Academic Interests/Achievement:* 749 awards ($3,702,859 total): general academic interests/achievements. *Creative Arts/Performance:* 213 awards ($519,963 total): debating, music, theater/drama. *Special Characteristics:* 40 awards ($487,328 total): children of faculty/staff. *Tuition waivers:* Full or partial for employees or children of employees. *ROTC:* Air Force cooperative.

LOANS *Student loans:* $6,651,440 (75% need-based, 25% non-need-based). 75% of past graduating class borrowed through all loan programs. *Average*

indebtedness per student: $21,244. *Average need-based loan:* Freshmen: $3751; Undergraduates: $3751. *Parent loans:* $1,372,786 (67% need-based, 33% non-need-based). *Programs:* FFEL (Subsidized and Unsubsidized Stafford, PLUS), Perkins, college/university.

WORK-STUDY *Federal work-study:* Total amount: $245,146; 67 jobs averaging $3600. *State or other work-study/employment:* Total amount: $91,099 (74% need-based, 26% non-need-based).

ATHLETIC AWARDS *Total amount:* $1,313,696 (34% need-based, 66% non-need-based).

APPLYING FOR FINANCIAL AID *Required financial aid forms:* FAFSA, state aid form. *Financial aid deadline:* 3/2. *Notification date:* 3/15. Students must reply within 3 weeks of notification.

CONTACT Ms. Jennifer Purga, Director of Undergraduate Admissions, Vanguard University of Southern California, 55 Fair Drive, Costa Mesa, CA 92626-6597, 800-722-6279. *Fax:* 714-966-5471. *E-mail:* admissions@vanguard.edu.

VASSAR COLLEGE
Poughkeepsie, NY

Tuition & fees: $31,350	Average undergraduate aid package: $24,305

ABOUT THE INSTITUTION Independent, coed. Awards: bachelor's and master's degrees. 48 undergraduate majors. Total enrollment: 2,475. Undergraduates: 2,475. Freshmen: 654. Institutional methodology is used as a basis for awarding need-based institutional aid.

UNDERGRADUATE EXPENSES for 2004–05 *Application fee:* $60. *Comprehensive fee:* $39,030 includes full-time tuition ($30,895), mandatory fees ($455), and room and board ($7680). *College room only:* $4080. Room and board charges vary according to board plan and housing facility. *Part-time tuition:* $3635 per course. *Part-time fees:* $225 per year. Part-time tuition and fees vary according to course load. *Payment plan:* Installment.

FRESHMAN FINANCIAL AID (Fall 2003) 401 applied for aid; of those 75% were deemed to have need. 100% of freshmen with need received aid; of those 100% had need fully met. *Average percent of need met:* 100% (excluding resources awarded to replace EFC). *Average financial aid package:* $24,075 (excluding resources awarded to replace EFC).

UNDERGRADUATE FINANCIAL AID (Fall 2003) 1,542 applied for aid; of those 82% were deemed to have need. 100% of undergraduates with need received aid; of those 100% had need fully met. *Average percent of need met:* 100% (excluding resources awarded to replace EFC). *Average financial aid package:* $24,305 (excluding resources awarded to replace EFC).

GIFT AID (NEED-BASED) *Total amount:* $23,825,805 (5% federal, 3% state, 89% institutional, 3% external sources). *Receiving aid:* Freshmen: 47% (299); All full-time undergraduates: 52% (1,246). *Average award:* Freshmen: $20,302; Undergraduates: $19,511. *Scholarships, grants, and awards:* Federal Pell, FSEOG, state, private, college/university gift aid from institutional funds.

GIFT AID (NON-NEED-BASED) *Total amount:* $168,811 (13% federal, 37% state, 50% external sources). *Tuition waivers:* Full or partial for employees or children of employees.

LOANS *Student loans:* $6,900,183 (64% need-based, 36% non-need-based). 57% of past graduating class borrowed through all loan programs. *Average indebtedness per student:* $18,729. *Average need-based loan:* Freshmen: $2233; Undergraduates: $3009. *Parent loans:* $3,992,782 (100% non-need-based). *Programs:* FFEL (Subsidized and Unsubsidized Stafford, PLUS), Perkins, college/university.

WORK-STUDY *Federal work-study:* Total amount: $1,569,452; 933 jobs averaging $1682. *State or other work-study/employment:* Total amount: $483,990 (99% need-based, 1% non-need-based). 282 part-time jobs averaging $1658.

APPLYING FOR FINANCIAL AID *Required financial aid forms:* FAFSA, institution's own form, CSS Financial Aid PROFILE, state aid form, noncustodial (divorced/separated) parent's statement, business/farm supplement. *Financial aid deadline:* 2/1. *Notification date:* 4/2. Students must reply by 5/1.

CONTACT Mr. Michael P. Fraher, Director of Financial Aid, Vassar College, 124 Raymond Avenue, Poughkeepsie, NY 12604, 845-437-5322 or toll-free 800-827-7270. *E-mail:* mifraher@vassar.edu.

VAUGHN COLLEGE OF AERONAUTICS AND TECHNOLOGY
Flushing, NY

ABOUT THE INSTITUTION Independent, coed, primarily men. Awards: associate and bachelor's degrees. 9 undergraduate majors. Total enrollment: 1,244. Undergraduates: 1,244. Freshmen: 254.

GIFT AID (NEED-BASED) *Scholarships, grants, and awards:* Federal Pell, FSEOG, state, private, college/university gift aid from institutional funds.

GIFT AID (NON-NEED-BASED) *Scholarships, grants, and awards by category: Academic Interests/Achievement:* engineering/technologies, general academic interests/achievements.

LOANS *Programs:* FFEL (Subsidized and Unsubsidized Stafford, PLUS).

WORK-STUDY *Federal work-study:* 78 jobs averaging $2628. *State or other work-study/employment:* Part-time jobs available.

APPLYING FOR FINANCIAL AID *Required financial aid forms:* FAFSA, state aid form.

CONTACT Melanie Williams, Director of Financial Aid, Vaughn College of Aeronautics and Technology, 86-01 23rd Avenue, LaGuardia Airport, Flushing, NY 11369, 718-429-6600 Ext. 164 or toll-free 800-776-2376 Ext. 145 (in-state). *Fax:* 718-779-2231. *E-mail:* melanie@aero.edu.

VENNARD COLLEGE
University Park, IA

Tuition & fees: N/R	Average undergraduate aid package: $7000

ABOUT THE INSTITUTION Independent interdenominational, coed. Awards: associate and bachelor's degrees. 18 undergraduate majors. Total enrollment: 72. Undergraduates: 72. Freshmen: 10. Both federal and institutional methodology are used as a basis for awarding need-based institutional aid.

UNDERGRADUATE EXPENSES for 2004–05 *Application fee:* $20. Full-time (12+hours) tuition is $255 per credit hour. *Payment plan:* Installment.

FRESHMAN FINANCIAL AID (Fall 2003) *Average percent of need met:* 60% (excluding resources awarded to replace EFC). *Average financial aid package:* $7000 (excluding resources awarded to replace EFC). 8% of all full-time freshmen had no need and received non-need-based gift aid.

UNDERGRADUATE FINANCIAL AID (Fall 2003) *Average percent of need met:* 60% (excluding resources awarded to replace EFC). *Average financial aid package:* $7000 (excluding resources awarded to replace EFC). 5% of all full-time undergraduates had no need and received non-need-based gift aid.

GIFT AID (NEED-BASED) *Scholarships, grants, and awards:* Federal Pell, FSEOG, state, college/university gift aid from institutional funds.

GIFT AID (NON-NEED-BASED) *Tuition waivers:* Full or partial for employees or children of employees.

LOANS *Student loans: Average indebtedness per student:* $12,000.

WORK-STUDY *State or other work-study/employment:* Part-time jobs available.

APPLYING FOR FINANCIAL AID *Required financial aid forms:* FAFSA, institution's own form, scholarship application form(s). *Financial aid deadline (priority):* 4/1.

CONTACT Office of Financial Aid, Vennard College, PO Box 29, University Park, IA 52595, 641-673-8391 or toll-free 800-686-8391.

VERMONT TECHNICAL COLLEGE
Randolph Center, VT

Tuition & fees (VT res): $7502	Average undergraduate aid package: $8888

ABOUT THE INSTITUTION State-supported, coed. Awards: associate and bachelor's degrees. 27 undergraduate majors. Total enrollment: 1,332. Undergraduates: 1,332. Freshmen: 240. Federal methodology is used as a basis for awarding need-based institutional aid.

UNDERGRADUATE EXPENSES for 2004–05 *Application fee:* $34. *Tuition, state resident:* full-time $7186; part-time $302 per credit. *Tuition, nonresident:* full-time $13,670; part-time $572 per credit. *Required fees:* full-time $316; $50 per term part-time. Full-time tuition and fees vary according to course load and program. Part-time tuition and fees vary according to program. *College room and board:* $6454; *room only:* $3858. Room and board charges vary according to board plan. *Payment plans:* Installment, deferred payment.

FRESHMAN FINANCIAL AID (Fall 2003) 198 applied for aid; of those 88% were deemed to have need. 98% of freshmen with need received aid; of those 15% had need fully met. *Average percent of need met:* 73% (excluding resources awarded to replace EFC). *Average financial aid package:* $8666 (excluding resources awarded to replace EFC). 6% of all full-time freshmen had no need and received non-need-based gift aid.

UNDERGRADUATE FINANCIAL AID (Fall 2003) 778 applied for aid; of those 90% were deemed to have need. 98% of undergraduates with need received aid; of those 16% had need fully met. *Average percent of need met:* 77% (excluding resources awarded to replace EFC). *Average financial aid package:* $8888 (excluding resources awarded to replace EFC). 2% of all full-time undergraduates had no need and received non-need-based gift aid.

GIFT AID (NEED-BASED) *Total amount:* $2,229,781 (49% federal, 36% state, 15% institutional). *Receiving aid:* Freshmen: 59% (135); All full-time undergraduates: 57% (551). *Average award:* Freshmen: $3560; Undergraduates: $4630. *Scholarships, grants, and awards:* Federal Pell, FSEOG, state, private, college/university gift aid from institutional funds.

GIFT AID (NON-NEED-BASED) *Total amount:* $754,135 (22% institutional, 78% external sources). *Receiving aid:* Freshmen: 6% (14); Undergraduates: 12% (114). *Average Award:* Freshmen: $4600; Undergraduates: $3500. *Scholarships, grants, and awards by category: Academic Interests/Achievement:* 24 awards ($132,490 total): general academic interests/achievements. *Tuition waivers:* Full or partial for employees or children of employees. *ROTC:* Army cooperative.

LOANS *Student loans:* $4,012,028 (46% need-based, 54% non-need-based). 70% of past graduating class borrowed through all loan programs. *Average indebtedness per student:* $12,000. *Average need-based loan:* Freshmen: $1945; Undergraduates: $2440. *Parent loans:* $1,301,220 (100% non-need-based). *Programs:* Federal Direct (Subsidized and Unsubsidized Stafford, PLUS), FFEL (Subsidized and Unsubsidized Stafford, PLUS), Perkins.

WORK-STUDY *Federal work-study:* Total amount: $136,102; 168 jobs averaging $750. *State or other work-study/employment:* Part-time jobs available.

APPLYING FOR FINANCIAL AID *Required financial aid forms:* FAFSA, state aid form. *Financial aid deadline (priority):* 3/1. *Notification date:* 4/1. Students must reply within 2 weeks of notification.

CONTACT Catherine R. McCullough, Director of Financial Aid, Vermont Technical College, PO Box 500, Randolph Center, VT 05061-0500, 802-728-1248 or toll-free 800-442-VTC1. *Fax:* 802-728-1390.

VILLA JULIE COLLEGE
Stevenson, MD

Tuition & fees: $14,653	Average undergraduate aid package: $9542

ABOUT THE INSTITUTION Independent, coed. Awards: associate, bachelor's, and master's degrees. 48 undergraduate majors. Total enrollment: 2,740. Undergraduates: 2,659. Freshmen: 568. Both federal and institutional methodology are used as a basis for awarding need-based institutional aid.

UNDERGRADUATE EXPENSES for 2004–05 *Application fee:* $25. *Tuition:* full-time $13,715; part-time $390 per credit. *Required fees:* full-time $938; $70 per term part-time. *Payment plans:* Installment, deferred payment.

GIFT AID (NEED-BASED) *Total amount:* $7,450,164 (18% federal, 29% state, 53% institutional). *Receiving aid:* Freshmen: 55% (309); All full-time undergraduates: 50% (1,042). *Average award:* Freshmen: $7806; Undergraduates: $7203. *Scholarships, grants, and awards:* Federal Pell, FSEOG, state, private, college/university gift aid from institutional funds.

GIFT AID (NON-NEED-BASED) *Total amount:* $4,841,576 (17% state, 68% institutional, 15% external sources). *Receiving aid:* Freshmen: 46% (256); Undergraduates: 36% (741). *Average Award:* Freshmen: $6206; Undergraduates: $5600. *Scholarships, grants, and awards by category: Academic Interests/Achievement:* 1,186 awards ($4,771,286 total): business, computer science, general academic interests/achievements. *Creative Arts/Performance:* 26 awards ($182,575 total): art/fine arts, cinema/film/broadcasting. *Special Achievements/Activities:* 292 awards ($1,420,655 total): community service, general special achievements/activities, leadership. *Tuition waivers:* Full or partial for employees or children of employees. *ROTC:* Army cooperative.

LOANS *Student loans:* $7,934,463 (46% need-based, 54% non-need-based). 38% of past graduating class borrowed through all loan programs. *Average indebtedness per student:* $15,679. *Average need-based loan:* Freshmen: $2420; Undergraduates: $3481. *Parent loans:* $11,537,447 (100% non-need-based). *Programs:* FFEL (Subsidized and Unsubsidized Stafford, PLUS), Perkins.

APPLYING FOR FINANCIAL AID *Required financial aid form:* FAFSA. *Financial aid deadline (priority):* 2/15. *Notification date:* Continuous beginning 3/15. Students must reply within 2 weeks of notification.

CONTACT Ms. Debra Bottomms, Director of Financial Aid, Villa Julie College, 1525 Greenspring Valley Road, Stevenson, MD 21153, 443-334-2559 or toll-free 877-468-6852 (in-state), 877-468-3852 (out-of-state). *Fax:* 443-334-2600. *E-mail:* fa-deb1@mail.vjc.edu.

VILLANOVA UNIVERSITY
Villanova, PA

Tuition & fees: $27,850	Average undergraduate aid package: $20,271

ABOUT THE INSTITUTION Independent Roman Catholic, coed. Awards: associate, bachelor's, master's, doctoral, and first professional degrees. 44 undergraduate majors. Total enrollment: 10,626. Undergraduates: 7,292. Freshmen: 1,657. Federal methodology is used as a basis for awarding need-based institutional aid.

UNDERGRADUATE EXPENSES for 2004–05 *Application fee:* $70. *Comprehensive fee:* $36,917 includes full-time tuition ($27,175), mandatory fees ($675), and room and board ($9067). *College room only:* $4787. Full-time tuition and fees vary according to program and student level. Room and board charges vary according to board plan and housing facility. *Part-time tuition:* $580 per credit hour. *Part-time fees:* $280 per term. Part-time tuition and fees vary according to class time, course level, and program. *Payment plan:* Installment.

FRESHMAN FINANCIAL AID (Fall 2004, est.) 1096 applied for aid; of those 73% were deemed to have need. 99% of freshmen with need received aid; of those 19% had need fully met. *Average percent of need met:* 83% (excluding resources awarded to replace EFC). *Average financial aid package:* $22,208 (excluding resources awarded to replace EFC). 5% of all full-time freshmen had no need and received non-need-based gift aid.

UNDERGRADUATE FINANCIAL AID (Fall 2004, est.) 3,759 applied for aid; of those 81% were deemed to have need. 99% of undergraduates with need received aid; of those 15% had need fully met. *Average percent of need met:* 77% (excluding resources awarded to replace EFC). *Average financial aid package:* $20,271 (excluding resources awarded to replace EFC). 5% of all full-time undergraduates had no need and received non-need-based gift aid.

GIFT AID (NEED-BASED) *Total amount:* $40,076,448 (10% federal, 4% state, 82% institutional, 4% external sources). *Receiving aid:* Freshmen: 43% (718); All full-time undergraduates: 40% (2,658). *Average award:* Freshmen: $18,298; Undergraduates: $15,101. *Scholarships, grants, and awards:* Federal Pell, FSEOG, state, private, college/university gift aid from institutional funds, endowed and restricted grants.

GIFT AID (NON-NEED-BASED) *Total amount:* $6,561,850 (38% federal, 54% institutional, 8% external sources). *Receiving aid:* Freshmen: 17% (273); Undergraduates: 14% (918). *Average Award:* Freshmen: $9665; Undergraduates: $10,648. *Scholarships, grants, and awards by category:* Academic Interests/Achievement: 545 awards ($4,239,318 total): general academic interests/achievements, international studies, military science. *Special Achievements/Activities:* 18 awards ($18,500 total): general special achievements/activities. *Special Characteristics:* 271 awards ($6,506,207 total): children of educators, children of faculty/staff, general special characteristics, members of minority groups, religious affiliation. *Tuition waivers:* Full or partial for employees or children of employees, senior citizens. *ROTC:* Army cooperative, Naval, Air Force cooperative.

LOANS *Student loans:* $26,334,665 (83% need-based, 17% non-need-based). 55% of past graduating class borrowed through all loan programs. *Average indebtedness per student:* $29,675. *Average need-based loan:* Freshmen: $3089; Undergraduates: $4774. *Parent loans:* $15,939,443 (78% need-based, 22% non-need-based). *Programs:* FFEL (Subsidized and Unsubsidized Stafford, PLUS), Perkins, Federal Nursing, Villanova Loan.

WORK-STUDY *Federal work-study:* Total amount: $4,053,473; 1,975 jobs averaging $2052.

ATHLETIC AWARDS *Total amount:* $6,535,349 (30% need-based, 70% non-need-based).

APPLYING FOR FINANCIAL AID *Required financial aid forms:* FAFSA, institution's own form, W-2 forms, federal income tax forms. *Financial aid deadline (priority):* 2/7. *Notification date:* 4/1. Students must reply by 5/1.

CONTACT Bonnie Lee Behm, Director of Financial Assistance, Villanova University, 800 Lancaster Avenue, Villanova, PA 19085-1699, 610-519-4010. *Fax:* 610-519-7599.

VIRGINIA COLLEGE AT BIRMINGHAM
Birmingham, AL

ABOUT THE INSTITUTION Proprietary, coed. Awards: associate and bachelor's degrees. 19 undergraduate majors. Total enrollment: 2,407. Undergraduates: 2,407. Freshmen: 515.

GIFT AID (NEED-BASED) *Scholarships, grants, and awards:* Federal Pell, FSEOG, state, private, college/university gift aid from institutional funds.

LOANS *Programs:* Federal Direct (Subsidized and Unsubsidized Stafford, PLUS), alternative loans.

WORK-STUDY Federal work-study jobs available.

APPLYING FOR FINANCIAL AID *Required financial aid forms:* FAFSA, institution's own form.

CONTACT Vice President, Campus Administration, Virginia College at Birmingham, 65 Bagby Drive, Birmingham, AL 35209, 205-802-1200. *Fax:* 205-271-8273.

VIRGINIA COMMONWEALTH UNIVERSITY
Richmond, VA

Tuition & fees (VA res): $5385	Average undergraduate aid package: $7172

ABOUT THE INSTITUTION State-supported, coed. Awards: bachelor's, master's, doctoral, and first professional degrees and post-bachelor's and post-master's certificates. 51 undergraduate majors. Total enrollment: 28,462. Undergraduates: 19,180. Freshmen: 3,364. Federal methodology is used as a basis for awarding need-based institutional aid.

UNDERGRADUATE EXPENSES for 2005–06 *Application fee:* $30. *Tuition, state resident:* full-time $3969; part-time $165.40 per credit. *Tuition, nonresident:* full-time $16,732; part-time $668 per credit. *Required fees:* full-time $1416; $52.05 per credit. *College room and board:* $7042; *room only:* $4102. Room and board charges vary according to board plan. *Payment plan:* Installment.

GIFT AID (NEED-BASED) *Total amount:* $21,669,841 (54% federal, 45% state, 1% external sources). *Receiving aid:* Freshmen: 45% (1,468); All full-time undergraduates: 41% (5,669). *Average award:* Freshmen: $3585; Undergraduates: $3508. *Scholarships, grants, and awards:* Federal Pell, FSEOG, state, private, college/university gift aid from institutional funds, United Negro College Fund, Federal Nursing.

GIFT AID (NON-NEED-BASED) *Total amount:* $8,884,171 (40% federal, 2% state, 17% institutional, 41% external sources). *Receiving aid:* Freshmen: 14% (464); Undergraduates: 9% (1,282). *Average Award:* Freshmen: $3306; Undergraduates: $4156. *Scholarships, grants, and awards by category:* Academic Interests/Achievement: business, engineering/technologies, foreign languages, general academic interests/achievements, health fields, mathematics, military science. *Creative Arts/Performance:* applied art and design, art/fine arts, dance, music, performing arts, theater/drama. *Special Characteristics:* children of union members/company employees, general special characteristics, veterans' children. *Tuition waivers:* Full or partial for employees or children of employees, senior citizens. *ROTC:* Army cooperative.

LOANS *Student loans:* $46,180,811 (58% need-based, 42% non-need-based). 67% of past graduating class borrowed through all loan programs. *Average indebtedness per student:* $19,337. *Average need-based loan:* Freshmen: $2787; Undergraduates: $3834. *Parent loans:* $8,261,381 (100% non-need-based). *Programs:* Federal Direct (Subsidized and Unsubsidized Stafford, PLUS), Perkins, Federal Nursing, state, college/university.

ATHLETIC AWARDS *Total amount:* $1,787,562 (100% non-need-based).

APPLYING FOR FINANCIAL AID *Required financial aid form:* FAFSA. *Financial aid deadline (priority):* 3/1. *Notification date:* Continuous beginning 4/1. Students must reply within 4 weeks of notification.

CONTACT Susan Kadir, Director of Financial Aid, Virginia Commonwealth University, PO Box 843026, 901 W. Franklin Street, Richmond, VA 23284-3026, 804-828-6669 or toll-free 800-841-3638. *Fax:* 804-828-6186. *E-mail:* faidmail@vcu.edu.

VIRGINIA INTERMONT COLLEGE
Bristol, VA

Tuition & fees: $15,200	Average undergraduate aid package: $11,719

Virginia Intermont College

ABOUT THE INSTITUTION Independent religious, coed. Awards: associate and bachelor's degrees. 43 undergraduate majors. Total enrollment: 1,152. Undergraduates: 1,152. Freshmen: 104. Federal methodology is used as a basis for awarding need-based institutional aid.

UNDERGRADUATE EXPENSES for 2004–05 *Application fee:* $15. *Comprehensive fee:* $20,850 includes full-time tuition ($14,500), mandatory fees ($700), and room and board ($5650). *College room only:* $2750. Full-time tuition and fees vary according to class time and program. Room and board charges vary according to housing facility. *Part-time tuition:* $190 per credit. *Part-time fees:* $35 per credit. Part-time tuition and fees vary according to class time, course load, and program. *Payment plan:* Installment.

GIFT AID (NEED-BASED) *Total amount:* $1,423,971 (98% federal, 2% state). *Receiving aid:* Freshmen: 31% (68); All full-time undergraduates: 52% (517). *Average award:* Freshmen: $1809; Undergraduates: $1773. *Scholarships, grants, and awards:* Federal Pell, FSEOG, state, private, college/university gift aid from institutional funds.

GIFT AID (NON-NEED-BASED) *Total amount:* $3,771,089 (32% state, 64% institutional, 4% external sources). *Receiving aid:* Freshmen: 60% (130); Undergraduates: 51% (512). *Average Award:* Freshmen: $5140; Undergraduates: $5326. *Scholarships, grants, and awards by category: Academic Interests/Achievement:* general academic interests/achievements. *Creative Arts/Performance:* applied art and design, art/fine arts, dance, general creative arts/performance, performing arts, theater/drama. *Special Characteristics:* children of faculty/staff, first-generation college students, members of minority groups, religious affiliation. *Tuition waivers:* Full or partial for employees or children of employees, senior citizens.

LOANS *Student loans:* $5,143,781 (58% need-based, 42% non-need-based). 82% of past graduating class borrowed through all loan programs. *Average indebtedness per student:* $15,065. *Average need-based loan:* Freshmen: $2271; Undergraduates: $3357. *Parent loans:* $1,770,803 (100% need-based). *Programs:* FFEL (Subsidized and Unsubsidized Stafford, PLUS), Perkins, alternative loans.

ATHLETIC AWARDS *Total amount:* $2,212,519 (100% non-need-based).

APPLYING FOR FINANCIAL AID *Required financial aid forms:* FAFSA, state aid form. *Financial aid deadline:* Continuous. *Notification date:* Continuous beginning 3/15. Students must reply within 4 weeks of notification.

CONTACT Mrs. Nancy Roberts, Director of Financial Aid, Virginia Intermont College, 1013 Moore Street, Bristol, VA 24201-4298, 276-466-7873 or toll-free 800-451-1842. *Fax:* 276-669-5763.

VIRGINIA MILITARY INSTITUTE
Lexington, VA

Tuition & fees (VA res): $6529	Average undergraduate aid package: $12,502

ABOUT THE INSTITUTION State-supported, coed, primarily men. Awards: bachelor's degrees. 14 undergraduate majors. Total enrollment: 1,362. Undergraduates: 1,362. Freshmen: 363. Federal methodology is used as a basis for awarding need-based institutional aid.

UNDERGRADUATE EXPENSES for 2004–05 *Application fee:* $35. *One-time required fee:* $1525. *Tuition, state resident:* full-time $4050. *Tuition, nonresident:* full-time $17,512. *College room and board:* $5474. *Payment plan:* Installment.

FRESHMAN FINANCIAL AID (Fall 2003) 243 applied for aid; of those 80% were deemed to have need. 99% of freshmen with need received aid; of those 63% had need fully met. *Average percent of need met:* 93% (excluding resources awarded to replace EFC). *Average financial aid package:* $10,551 (excluding resources awarded to replace EFC). 14% of all full-time freshmen had no need and received non-need-based gift aid.

UNDERGRADUATE FINANCIAL AID (Fall 2003) 712 applied for aid; of those 81% were deemed to have need. 100% of undergraduates with need received aid; of those 63% had need fully met. *Average percent of need met:* 93% (excluding resources awarded to replace EFC). *Average financial aid package:* $12,502 (excluding resources awarded to replace EFC). 18% of all full-time undergraduates had no need and received non-need-based gift aid.

GIFT AID (NEED-BASED) *Total amount:* $3,808,080 (14% federal, 16% state, 62% institutional, 8% external sources). *Receiving aid:* Freshmen: 44% (182); All full-time undergraduates: 40% (549). *Average award:* Freshmen: $7459; Undergraduates: $7661. *Scholarships, grants, and awards:* Federal Pell, FSEOG, state, private, college/university gift aid from institutional funds.

GIFT AID (NON-NEED-BASED) *Total amount:* $4,948,222 (61% federal, 34% institutional, 5% external sources). *Receiving aid:* Freshmen: 7% (27);

Undergraduates: 6% (81). *Average Award:* Freshmen: $6755; Undergraduates: $6421. *Scholarships, grants, and awards by category: Academic Interests/Achievement:* 150 awards ($1,000,000 total): biological sciences, business, computer science, engineering/technologies, English, general academic interests/achievements, international studies, mathematics, military science, premedicine. *Creative Arts/Performance:* 12 awards ($6000 total): music. *Special Achievements/Activities:* 15 awards ($75,000 total): general special achievements/activities, leadership. *Special Characteristics:* 300 awards ($1,250,000 total): children and siblings of alumni, children of faculty/staff, general special characteristics, local/state students, out-of-state students. *ROTC:* Army, Naval, Air Force.

LOANS *Student loans:* $2,544,026 (51% need-based, 49% non-need-based). 29% of past graduating class borrowed through all loan programs. *Average indebtedness per student:* $14,456. *Average need-based loan:* Freshmen: $3400; Undergraduates: $3619. *Parent loans:* $1,734,580 (100% non-need-based). *Programs:* Federal Direct (Subsidized and Unsubsidized Stafford, PLUS), Perkins.

WORK-STUDY *Federal work-study:* Total amount: $49,439; 56 jobs averaging $883.

ATHLETIC AWARDS *Total amount:* $1,942,622 (27% need-based, 73% non-need-based).

APPLYING FOR FINANCIAL AID *Required financial aid forms:* FAFSA, institution's own form. *Financial aid deadline (priority):* 3/1. *Notification date:* Continuous beginning 3/15. Students must reply by 5/1.

CONTACT Col. Timothy P. Golden, Director of Financial Aid, Virginia Military Institute, 306 Carroll Hall, Lexington, VA 24450, 540-464-7208 or toll-free 800-767-4207. *Fax:* 540-464-7629. *E-mail:* goldentp@vmi.edu.

VIRGINIA POLYTECHNIC INSTITUTE AND STATE UNIVERSITY
Blacksburg, VA

Tuition & fees (VA res): $5836	Average undergraduate aid package: $7035

ABOUT THE INSTITUTION State-supported, coed. Awards: associate, bachelor's, master's, doctoral, and first professional degrees. 73 undergraduate majors. Total enrollment: 25,619. Undergraduates: 21,272. Freshmen: 5,911. Federal methodology is used as a basis for awarding need-based institutional aid.

UNDERGRADUATE EXPENSES for 2004–05 *Application fee:* $40. *Tuition, state resident:* full-time $4512; part-time $188 per credit hour. *Tuition, nonresident:* full-time $15,206; part-time $633.50 per credit hour. *Required fees:* full-time $1324; $156 per term part-time. *College room and board:* $4288; *room only:* $2150. Room and board charges vary according to board plan and location. *Payment plan:* Installment.

FRESHMAN FINANCIAL AID (Fall 2003) 3555 applied for aid; of those 66% were deemed to have need. 81% of freshmen with need received aid; of those 3% had need fully met. *Average percent of need met:* 71% (excluding resources awarded to replace EFC). *Average financial aid package:* $7593 (excluding resources awarded to replace EFC). 9% of all full-time freshmen had no need and received non-need-based gift aid.

UNDERGRADUATE FINANCIAL AID (Fall 2003) 13,158 applied for aid; of those 65% were deemed to have need. 90% of undergraduates with need received aid; of those 3% had need fully met. *Average percent of need met:* 75% (excluding resources awarded to replace EFC). *Average financial aid package:* $7035 (excluding resources awarded to replace EFC). 5% of all full-time undergraduates had no need and received non-need-based gift aid.

GIFT AID (NEED-BASED) *Total amount:* $24,090,766 (34% federal, 41% state, 25% institutional). *Receiving aid:* Freshmen: 30% (1,468); All full-time undergraduates: 28% (5,806). *Average award:* Freshmen: $5310; Undergraduates: $4371. *Scholarships, grants, and awards:* Federal Pell, FSEOG, state, private, college/university gift aid from institutional funds, United Negro College Fund, General Scholarship Program.

GIFT AID (NON-NEED-BASED) *Total amount:* $12,968,961 (100% external sources). *Receiving aid:* Freshmen: 8% (405); Undergraduates: 5% (1,127). *Average Award:* Freshmen: $1389; Undergraduates: $1615. *Scholarships, grants, and awards by category: Academic Interests/Achievement:* 639 awards ($1,197,861 total): agriculture, architecture, area/ethnic studies, biological sciences, business, communication, computer science, education, engineering/technologies, English, foreign languages, general academic interests/achievements, health fields, home economics, humanities, international studies, mathematics, military science, physical sciences, premedicine, religion/biblical studies, social sciences. *Creative Arts/Performance:* 462 awards ($542,476 total): applied art and design, art/fine arts, cinema/film/broadcasting, creative writing, journalism/publications, music, performing arts, theater/drama. *Special

Achievements/Activities: 312 awards: cheerleading/drum major, community service, general special achievements/activities, leadership, memberships, religious involvement. *Special Characteristics:* 290 awards ($200,000 total): children of faculty/staff, first-generation college students, local/state students, members of minority groups, out-of-state students, twins, veterans' children. *ROTC:* Army, Naval, Air Force.

LOANS *Student loans:* $50,488,632 (51% need-based, 49% non-need-based). 55% of past graduating class borrowed through all loan programs. *Average indebtedness per student:* $18,281. *Average need-based loan:* Freshmen: $3215; Undergraduates: $3743. *Parent loans:* $19,030,421 (100% non-need-based). *Programs:* Federal Direct (Subsidized and Unsubsidized Stafford, PLUS), Perkins, state, college/university, Health Professions Loans.

WORK-STUDY *Federal work-study:* Total amount: $1,113,130; 923 jobs averaging $1177. *State or other work-study/employment:* Total amount: $5,837,645 (100% non-need-based). 3,940 part-time jobs averaging $1482.

ATHLETIC AWARDS *Total amount:* $3,937,100 (100% non-need-based).

APPLYING FOR FINANCIAL AID *Required financial aid form:* FAFSA. *Financial aid deadline (priority):* 3/11. *Notification date:* Continuous beginning 4/1. Students must reply by 5/1 or within 4 weeks of notification.

CONTACT Dr. Barry Simmons, Director of Financial Aid, Virginia Polytechnic Institute and State University, 222 Burruss Hall, Blacksburg, VA 24061, 540-231-5179. *Fax:* 540-231-9139. *E-mail:* finaid@vt.edu.

VIRGINIA STATE UNIVERSITY
Petersburg, VA

ABOUT THE INSTITUTION State-supported, coed. Awards: bachelor's, master's, and doctoral degrees and post-master's certificates. 34 undergraduate majors. Total enrollment: 4,859. Undergraduates: 4,173. Freshmen: 1,027.

GIFT AID (NEED-BASED) *Scholarships, grants, and awards:* Federal Pell, FSEOG, state, private, college/university gift aid from institutional funds.

GIFT AID (NON-NEED-BASED) *Scholarships, grants, and awards by category: Academic Interests/Achievement:* agriculture, biological sciences, business, communication, computer science, education, engineering/technologies, general academic interests/achievements, health fields, home economics, mathematics, military science, premedicine, social sciences. *Creative Arts/Performance:* art/fine arts, music, performing arts. *Special Achievements/Activities:* community service, hobbies/interests, religious involvement. *Special Characteristics:* veterans.

LOANS *Programs:* Federal Direct (Subsidized and Unsubsidized Stafford, PLUS), FFEL (PLUS), Perkins, college/university.

WORK-STUDY *Federal work-study:* Total amount: $545,966; 340 jobs averaging $1600. *State or other work-study/employment:* Total amount: $499,724 (100% non-need-based). 225 part-time jobs averaging $2220.

APPLYING FOR FINANCIAL AID *Required financial aid forms:* FAFSA, institution's own form.

CONTACT Sylvia Blizzard, Interim Assistant Director of Student Services, Virginia State University, 102 Gandy Hall, PO Box 9031, Petersburg, VA 23806-2096, 804-524-5565 or toll-free 800-871-7611. *Fax:* 804-524-6818. *E-mail:* sblizzard@vsu.edu.

VIRGINIA UNION UNIVERSITY
Richmond, VA

Tuition & fees: $12,260	Average undergraduate aid package: $6804

ABOUT THE INSTITUTION Independent Baptist, coed. Awards: bachelor's, master's, doctoral, and first professional degrees. 22 undergraduate majors. Total enrollment: 1,777. Undergraduates: 1,400. Freshmen: 439. Federal methodology is used as a basis for awarding need-based institutional aid.

UNDERGRADUATE EXPENSES for 2004–05 *Application fee:* $15. *Comprehensive fee:* $17,696 includes full-time tuition ($11,090), mandatory fees ($1170), and room and board ($5436). *College room only:* $2536. Full-time tuition and fees vary according to course level and course load. *Part-time tuition:* $462 per credit hour. *Part-time fees:* $370 per term. Part-time tuition and fees vary according to course level and course load. *Payment plans:* Installment, deferred payment.

FRESHMAN FINANCIAL AID (Fall 2004, est.) 279 applied for aid; of those 95% were deemed to have need. 99% of freshmen with need received aid; of those 30% had need fully met. *Average percent of need met:* 58% (excluding resources awarded to replace EFC). *Average financial aid package:* $6983 (excluding resources awarded to replace EFC). 6% of all full-time freshmen had no need and received non-need-based gift aid.

UNDERGRADUATE FINANCIAL AID (Fall 2004, est.) 1,203 applied for aid; of those 92% were deemed to have need. 99% of undergraduates with need received aid; of those 33% had need fully met. *Average percent of need met:* 77% (excluding resources awarded to replace EFC). *Average financial aid package:* $6804 (excluding resources awarded to replace EFC). 5% of all full-time undergraduates had no need and received non-need-based gift aid.

GIFT AID (NEED-BASED) *Total amount:* $4,592,194 (70% federal, 4% state, 19% institutional, 7% external sources). *Receiving aid:* Freshmen: 60% (189); All full-time undergraduates: 74% (1,014). *Average award:* Freshmen: $4202; Undergraduates: $3784. *Scholarships, grants, and awards:* Federal Pell, FSEOG, state, private, college/university gift aid from institutional funds.

GIFT AID (NON-NEED-BASED) *Total amount:* $2,001,376 (1% federal, 78% state, 21% external sources). *Average Award:* Freshmen: $5617; Undergraduates: $9122. *Scholarships, grants, and awards by category: Academic Interests/Achievement:* 146 awards ($1,004,371 total): general academic interests/achievements. *Tuition waivers:* Full or partial for employees or children of employees. *ROTC:* Army cooperative.

LOANS *Student loans:* $7,041,622 (51% need-based, 49% non-need-based). 98% of past graduating class borrowed through all loan programs. *Average indebtedness per student:* $17,568. *Average need-based loan:* Freshmen: $2607; Undergraduates: $3233. *Parent loans:* $3,468,789 (100% non-need-based). *Programs:* Federal Direct (Subsidized and Unsubsidized Stafford), FFEL (PLUS), Perkins.

WORK-STUDY *Federal work-study:* Total amount: $487,829; 292 jobs averaging $1623.

ATHLETIC AWARDS *Total amount:* $912,706 (100% non-need-based).

APPLYING FOR FINANCIAL AID *Required financial aid forms:* FAFSA, state aid form. *Financial aid deadline (priority):* 5/1. *Notification date:* Continuous. Students must reply within 2 weeks of notification.

CONTACT Mrs. Phenie Golatt, Director of Financial Aid, Virginia Union University, 1500 North Lombardy Street, Richmond, VA 23220-1170, 804-257-5882 or toll-free 800-368-3227 (out-of-state). *E-mail:* pgolatt@vuu.edu.

VIRGINIA UNIVERSITY OF LYNCHBURG
Lynchburg, VA

CONTACT Financial Aid Office, Virginia University of Lynchburg, 2058 Garfield Avenue, Lynchburg, VA 24501-6417, 804-528-5276.

VIRGINIA WESLEYAN COLLEGE
Norfolk, VA

Tuition & fees: $20,448	Average undergraduate aid package: $13,762

ABOUT THE INSTITUTION Independent United Methodist, coed. Awards: bachelor's degrees. 42 undergraduate majors. Total enrollment: 1,442. Undergraduates: 1,442. Freshmen: 325. Federal methodology is used as a basis for awarding need-based institutional aid.

UNDERGRADUATE EXPENSES for 2004–05 *Application fee:* $40. *Comprehensive fee:* $27,048 includes full-time tuition ($20,448) and room and board ($6600). Full-tuition and fees vary according to class time. Room and board charges vary according to board plan and housing facility. *Part-time tuition:* $852 per semester hour. Part-time tuition and fees vary according to class time and course load. *Payment plans:* Installment, deferred payment.

FRESHMAN FINANCIAL AID (Fall 2003) 212 applied for aid; of those 99% were deemed to have need. 100% of freshmen with need received aid; of those 5% had need fully met. *Average percent of need met:* 66% (excluding resources awarded to replace EFC). *Average financial aid package:* $14,083 (excluding resources awarded to replace EFC). 26% of all full-time freshmen had no need and received non-need-based gift aid.

UNDERGRADUATE FINANCIAL AID (Fall 2003) 793 applied for aid; of those 100% were deemed to have need. 99% of undergraduates with need received aid; of those 5% had need fully met. *Average percent of need met:* 66% (excluding resources awarded to replace EFC). *Average financial aid package:* $13,762 (excluding resources awarded to replace EFC). 20% of all full-time undergraduates had no need and received non-need-based gift aid.

GIFT AID (NEED-BASED) *Total amount:* $1,174,823 (92% federal, 4% state, 4% institutional). *Receiving aid:* Freshmen: 26% (86); All full-time undergraduates: 30% (349). *Average award:* Freshmen: $3357; Undergraduates: $3292. *Scholarships, grants, and awards:* Federal Pell, FSEOG, state, college/university gift aid from institutional funds.

Virginia Wesleyan College

GIFT AID (NON-NEED-BASED) *Total amount:* $8,589,116 (19% state, 77% institutional, 4% external sources). *Receiving aid:* Freshmen: 64% (209); Undergraduates: 67% (786). *Average Award: Freshmen:* $6036; *Undergraduates:* $5663. *Scholarships, grants, and awards by category: Academic Interests/Achievement:* general academic interests/achievements. *Creative Arts/Performance:* art/fine arts, music. *Special Achievements/Activities:* leadership, religious involvement. *Special Characteristics:* children of educators, children of faculty/staff, relatives of clergy. *Tuition waivers:* Full or partial for employees or children of employees, senior citizens. *ROTC:* Army cooperative.

LOANS *Student loans:* $6,680,291 (46% need-based, 54% non-need-based). *Average need-based loan:* Freshmen: $3214; Undergraduates: $4082. *Parent loans:* $2,988,029 (100% non-need-based). *Programs:* FFEL (Subsidized and Unsubsidized Stafford, PLUS), Perkins, alternative loans.

WORK-STUDY *Federal work-study:* Total amount: $207,360; jobs available.

APPLYING FOR FINANCIAL AID *Required financial aid forms:* FAFSA, state aid form. *Financial aid deadline:* Continuous. *Notification date:* Continuous beginning 3/1. Students must reply by 5/1 or within 2 weeks of notification.

CONTACT Ms. Eugenia F. Hickman, Director of Financial Aid, Virginia Wesleyan College, 1584 Wesleyan Drive, Norfolk, VA 23502-5599, 757-455-3207 or toll-free 800-737-8684. *Fax:* 757-455-6779. *E-mail:* dhickman@vwc.edu.

VITERBO UNIVERSITY
La Crosse, WI

ABOUT THE INSTITUTION Independent Roman Catholic, coed. Awards: bachelor's and master's degrees. 50 undergraduate majors. Total enrollment: 2,690. Undergraduates: 1,922. Freshmen: 312.

GIFT AID (NEED-BASED) *Scholarships, grants, and awards:* Federal Pell, FSEOG, state, private, college/university gift aid from institutional funds.

GIFT AID (NON-NEED-BASED) *Scholarships, grants, and awards by category: Academic Interests/Achievement:* general academic interests/achievements, health fields, international studies. *Creative Arts/Performance:* art/fine arts, music, theater/drama. *Special Achievements/Activities:* general special achievements/activities. *Special Characteristics:* children and siblings of alumni, children of faculty/staff, international students, members of minority groups.

LOANS *Programs:* FFEL (Subsidized and Unsubsidized Stafford, PLUS), Perkins, Federal Nursing.

WORK-STUDY *Federal work-study:* Total amount: $566,186; 387 jobs averaging $1680. *State or other work-study/employment:* Total amount: $30,670 (35% need-based, 65% non-need-based). 19 part-time jobs averaging $1615.

APPLYING FOR FINANCIAL AID *Required financial aid forms:* FAFSA, institution's own form.

CONTACT Ms. Terry Norman, Director of Financial Aid, Viterbo University, 900 Viterbo Drive, La Crosse, WI 54601-4797, 608-796-3900 or toll-free 800-VITERBO Ext. 3010. *Fax:* 608-796-3050. *E-mail:* twnorman@viterbo.edu.

VOORHEES COLLEGE
Denmark, SC

Tuition & fees: $7276	Average undergraduate aid package: $7449

ABOUT THE INSTITUTION Independent Episcopal, coed. Awards: bachelor's degrees. 16 undergraduate majors. Total enrollment: 847. Undergraduates: 847. Freshmen: 156. Federal methodology is used as a basis for awarding need-based institutional aid.

UNDERGRADUATE EXPENSES for 2004–05 *Application fee:* $25. *Comprehensive fee:* $11,848 includes full-time tuition ($7106), mandatory fees ($170), and room and board ($4572). *College room only:* $1904. Room and board charges vary according to housing facility. *Part-time tuition:* $242 per quarter hour. *Payment plans:* Installment, deferred payment.

FRESHMAN FINANCIAL AID (Fall 2004, est.) 201 applied for aid; of those 97% were deemed to have need. 100% of freshmen with need received aid; of those 7% had need fully met. *Average percent of need met:* 52% (excluding resources awarded to replace EFC). *Average financial aid package:* $7569 (excluding resources awarded to replace EFC). 19% of all full-time freshmen had no need and received non-need-based gift aid.

UNDERGRADUATE FINANCIAL AID (Fall 2004, est.) 813 applied for aid; of those 97% were deemed to have need. 99% of undergraduates with need received aid; of those 8% had need fully met. *Average percent of need met:* 51% (excluding resources awarded to replace EFC). *Average financial aid package:* $7449 (excluding resources awarded to replace EFC). 8% of all full-time undergraduates had no need and received non-need-based gift aid.

GIFT AID (NEED-BASED) *Total amount:* $4,111,998 (60% federal, 18% state, 19% institutional, 3% external sources). *Receiving aid:* Freshmen: 78% (187); All full-time undergraduates: 85% (728). *Average award:* Freshmen: $5341; Undergraduates: $4805. *Scholarships, grants, and awards:* Federal Pell, FSEOG, state, private, college/university gift aid from institutional funds, United Negro College Fund.

GIFT AID (NON-NEED-BASED) *Receiving aid:* Freshmen: 5% (13); Undergraduates: 7% (61). *Average Award:* Freshmen: $9844; Undergraduates: $9582. *Scholarships, grants, and awards by category: Special Characteristics:* 5 awards ($4356 total): children of faculty/staff. *Tuition waivers:* Full or partial for employees or children of employees. *ROTC:* Army cooperative.

LOANS *Student loans:* $3,546,869 (100% need-based). 98% of past graduating class borrowed through all loan programs. *Average indebtedness per student:* $13,383. *Average need-based loan:* Freshmen: $1981; Undergraduates: $2840. *Parent loans:* $172,096 (100% need-based). *Programs:* FFEL (Subsidized and Unsubsidized Stafford, PLUS).

WORK-STUDY *Federal work-study:* Total amount: $321,361; 223 jobs averaging $2000. *State or other work-study/employment:* Part-time jobs available.

ATHLETIC AWARDS *Total amount:* $80,650 (100% need-based).

APPLYING FOR FINANCIAL AID *Required financial aid forms:* FAFSA, institution's own form. *Financial aid deadline (priority):* 4/15. *Notification date:* Continuous beginning 3/1.

CONTACT Augusta L. Kitchen, Director of Financial Aid, Voorhees College, PO Box 678, Denmark, SC 29042, 803-703-7109 Ext. 7106 or toll-free 800-446-6250. *Fax:* 803-793-0831. *E-mail:* akitchen@voorhees.edu.

WABASH COLLEGE
Crawfordsville, IN

Tuition & fees: $22,274	Average undergraduate aid package: $20,635

ABOUT THE INSTITUTION Independent, men only. Awards: bachelor's degrees. 24 undergraduate majors. Total enrollment: 857. Undergraduates: 857. Freshmen: 249. Both federal and institutional methodology are used as a basis for awarding need-based institutional aid.

UNDERGRADUATE EXPENSES for 2004–05 *Application fee:* $30. *Comprehensive fee:* $29,324 includes full-time tuition ($21,870), mandatory fees ($404), and room and board ($7050). *College room only:* $2610. Room and board charges vary according to board plan and housing facility. *Part-time tuition:* $3645 per course. Part-time tuition and fees vary according to course load. *Payment plans:* Tuition prepayment, installment.

FRESHMAN FINANCIAL AID (Fall 2004, est.) 203 applied for aid; of those 87% were deemed to have need. 100% of freshmen with need received aid; of those 100% had need fully met. *Average percent of need met:* 100% (excluding resources awarded to replace EFC). *Average financial aid package:* $21,453 (excluding resources awarded to replace EFC). 24% of all full-time freshmen had no need and received non-need-based gift aid.

UNDERGRADUATE FINANCIAL AID (Fall 2004, est.) 649 applied for aid; of those 89% were deemed to have need. 100% of undergraduates with need received aid; of those 100% had need fully met. *Average percent of need met:* 100% (excluding resources awarded to replace EFC). *Average financial aid package:* $20,635 (excluding resources awarded to replace EFC). 25% of all full-time undergraduates had no need and received non-need-based gift aid.

GIFT AID (NEED-BASED) *Total amount:* $8,258,569 (5% federal, 12% state, 77% institutional, 6% external sources). *Receiving aid:* Freshmen: 70% (175); All full-time undergraduates: 67% (572). *Average award:* Freshmen: $17,419; Undergraduates: $15,272. *Scholarships, grants, and awards:* Federal Pell, state, private, college/university gift aid from institutional funds.

GIFT AID (NON-NEED-BASED) *Total amount:* $3,559,747 (84% institutional, 16% external sources). *Receiving aid:* Freshmen: 20% (49); Undergraduates: 12% (104). *Average Award:* Freshmen: $12,291; *Undergraduates:* $16,584. *Scholarships, grants, and awards by category: Academic Interests/Achievement:* 619 awards ($4,835,260 total): education, general academic interests/achievements. *Creative Arts/Performance:* 48 awards ($195,501 total): art/fine arts, creative writing, journalism/publications, music, theater/drama. *Special Achievements/Activities:* 65 awards ($822,670 total): community service, leadership. *Special Characteristics:* 22 awards ($440,213 total): children of faculty/staff, international students. *Tuition waivers:* Full or partial for employees or children of employees. *ROTC:* Army cooperative.

LOANS *Student loans:* $3,875,146 (40% need-based, 60% non-need-based). 68% of past graduating class borrowed through all loan programs. *Average*

indebtedness per student: $16,004. *Average need-based loan:* Freshmen: $1557; Undergraduates: $2689. *Programs:* FFEL (Subsidized and Unsubsidized Stafford, PLUS), college/university.

WORK-STUDY *State or other work-study/employment:* Total amount: $1,076,780 (89% need-based, 11% non-need-based). 677 part-time jobs averaging $1956.

APPLYING FOR FINANCIAL AID *Required financial aid forms:* FAFSA, CSS Financial Aid PROFILE, federal income tax form(s), W-2 forms. *Financial aid deadline:* 3/1 (priority: 2/15). *Notification date:* 4/1. Students must reply by 5/1 or within 2 weeks of notification.

CONTACT Mr. Clint Gasaway, Financial Aid Director, Wabash College, PO Box 352, Crawfordsville, IN 47933-0352, 800-718-9746 or toll-free 800-345-5385. *Fax:* 765-361-6166. *E-mail:* financialaid@wabash.edu.

WAGNER COLLEGE
Staten Island, NY

ABOUT THE INSTITUTION Independent, coed. Awards: bachelor's and master's degrees and post-master's certificates. 34 undergraduate majors. Total enrollment: 2,259. Undergraduates: 1,929. Freshmen: 491.

GIFT AID (NEED-BASED) *Scholarships, grants, and awards:* Federal Pell, FSEOG, state, private, college/university gift aid from institutional funds.

GIFT AID (NON-NEED-BASED) *Scholarships, grants, and awards by category: Academic Interests/Achievement:* general academic interests/achievements. *Creative Arts/Performance:* music, theater/drama. *Special Achievements/Activities:* general special achievements/activities, leadership. *Special Characteristics:* children of faculty/staff, international students, siblings of current students.

LOANS *Programs:* FFEL (Subsidized and Unsubsidized Stafford, PLUS), Perkins, Federal Nursing, alternative loans.

WORK-STUDY *Federal work-study:* Total amount: $787,864; 670 jobs averaging $1176. *State or other work-study/employment:* Part-time jobs available.

APPLYING FOR FINANCIAL AID *Required financial aid forms:* FAFSA, state aid form.

CONTACT Mr. Angelo Araimo, Vice President for Enrollment and Planning, Wagner College, One Campus Road, Staten Island, NY 10301, 718-390-3411 or toll-free 800-221-1010 (out-of-state). *Fax:* 718-390-3105.

WAKE FOREST UNIVERSITY
Winston-Salem, NC

Tuition & fees: $30,210	Average undergraduate aid package: $22,883

ABOUT THE INSTITUTION Independent, coed. Awards: bachelor's, master's, doctoral, and first professional degrees. 37 undergraduate majors. Total enrollment: 6,504. Undergraduates: 4,128. Freshmen: 1,119. Both federal and institutional methodology are used as a basis for awarding need-based institutional aid.

UNDERGRADUATE EXPENSES for 2005–06 *Application fee:* $40. *Comprehensive fee:* $38,710 includes full-time tuition ($30,110), mandatory fees ($100), and room and board ($8500). *College room only:* $5200. Room and board charges vary according to board plan and housing facility. *Part-time tuition:* $1175 per hour. *Payment plan:* Installment.

GIFT AID (NEED-BASED) *Total amount:* $19,137,857 (8% federal, 11% state, 75% institutional, 6% external sources). *Receiving aid:* Freshmen: 37% (414); All full-time undergraduates: 33% (1,332). *Average award:* Freshmen: $16,769; Undergraduates: $16,492. *Scholarships, grants, and awards:* Federal Pell, FSEOG, state, private, college/university gift aid from institutional funds.

GIFT AID (NON-NEED-BASED) *Total amount:* $7,914,395 (1% federal, 15% state, 57% institutional, 27% external sources). *Receiving aid:* Freshmen: 6% (72); Undergraduates: 5% (215). *Average Award: Freshmen:* $10,040; *Undergraduates:* $10,466. *Scholarships, grants, and awards by category: Academic Interests/Achievement:* 619 awards ($3,151,247 total): biological sciences, business, education, English, foreign languages, general academic interests/achievements, international studies, mathematics, military science, physical sciences, premedicine, religion/biblical studies. *Creative Arts/Performance:* 109 awards ($816,465 total): art/fine arts, debating, general creative arts/performance, journalism/publications, music, theater/drama. *Special Achievements/Activities:* 21 awards ($40,220 total): cheerleading/drum major, community service, memberships. *Special Characteristics:* 495 awards ($5,740,272 total): children of faculty/staff, general special characteristics, members of minority groups, relatives of clergy, religious affiliation. *Tuition waivers:* Full or partial for employees or children of employees. *ROTC:* Army.

LOANS *Student loans:* $14,540,134 (62% need-based, 38% non-need-based). 37% of past graduating class borrowed through all loan programs. *Average indebtedness per student:* $26,151. *Average need-based loan:* Freshmen: $6030; Undergraduates: $6947. *Parent loans:* $7,933,563 (9% need-based, 91% non-need-based). *Programs:* FFEL (Subsidized and Unsubsidized Stafford, PLUS), Perkins, state, college/university, alternative loans.

ATHLETIC AWARDS *Total amount:* $7,528,171 (30% need-based, 70% non-need-based).

APPLYING FOR FINANCIAL AID *Required financial aid forms:* FAFSA, CSS Financial Aid PROFILE, state aid form, noncustodial (divorced/separated) parent's statement, federal income tax forms, W-2 form(s). *Financial aid deadline (priority):* 3/1. *Notification date:* Continuous beginning 4/1. Students must reply by 5/1 or within 4 weeks of notification.

CONTACT Office of Student Financial Aid, Wake Forest University, PO Box 7246, Winston-Salem, NC 27109-7246, 336-758-5154. *Fax:* 336-758-4924.

WALDEN UNIVERSITY
Minneapolis, MN

CONTACT Financial Aid Office, Walden University, 155 Fifth Avenue South, Minneapolis, MN 55401, 612-338-7224.

WALDORF COLLEGE
Forest City, IA

Tuition & fees: $14,200	Average undergraduate aid package: $14,273

ABOUT THE INSTITUTION Independent Lutheran, coed. Awards: bachelor's degrees. 31 undergraduate majors. Total enrollment: 629. Undergraduates: 629. Freshmen: 197. Federal methodology is used as a basis for awarding need-based institutional aid.

UNDERGRADUATE EXPENSES for 2004–05 *Comprehensive fee:* $18,600 includes full-time tuition ($13,500), mandatory fees ($700), and room and board ($4400). *College room only:* $2200. Full-time tuition and fees vary according to class time and course load. Room and board charges vary according to board plan and housing facility. *Part-time tuition:* $180 per credit. *Part-time fees:* $35 per credit. *Payment plans:* Installment, deferred payment.

FRESHMAN FINANCIAL AID (Fall 2003) 173 applied for aid; of those 92% were deemed to have need. 98% of freshmen with need received aid; of those 19% had need fully met. *Average percent of need met:* 83% (excluding resources awarded to replace EFC). *Average financial aid package:* $12,597 (excluding resources awarded to replace EFC). 17% of all full-time freshmen had no need and received non-need-based gift aid.

UNDERGRADUATE FINANCIAL AID (Fall 2003) 455 applied for aid; of those 93% were deemed to have need. 98% of undergraduates with need received aid; of those 16% had need fully met. *Average percent of need met:* 73% (excluding resources awarded to replace EFC). *Average financial aid package:* $14,273 (excluding resources awarded to replace EFC). 14% of all full-time undergraduates had no need and received non-need-based gift aid.

GIFT AID (NEED-BASED) *Total amount:* $3,537,653 (21% federal, 23% state, 44% institutional, 12% external sources). *Receiving aid:* Freshmen: 79% (156); All full-time undergraduates: 81% (411). *Average award:* Freshmen: $9140; Undergraduates: $10,146. *Scholarships, grants, and awards:* Federal Pell, FSEOG, state, private, college/university gift aid from institutional funds.

GIFT AID (NON-NEED-BASED) *Total amount:* $353,595 (1% state, 85% institutional, 14% external sources). *Receiving aid:* Freshmen: 9% (18); Undergraduates: 7% (37). *Average Award: Freshmen:* $9575; *Undergraduates:* $9512. *Scholarships, grants, and awards by category: Academic Interests/Achievement:* 363 awards ($1,111,413 total): communication, general academic interests/achievements. *Creative Arts/Performance:* 197 awards ($196,707 total): music, theater/drama. *Special Characteristics:* 125 awards ($228,384 total): children of faculty/staff, religious affiliation. *Tuition waivers:* Full or partial for employees or children of employees.

LOANS *Student loans:* $2,141,020 (82% need-based, 18% non-need-based). 76% of past graduating class borrowed through all loan programs. *Average indebtedness per student:* $15,873. *Average need-based loan:* Freshmen: $3347; Undergraduates: $4123. *Parent loans:* $1,725,174 (36% need-based, 64% non-need-based). *Programs:* Federal Direct (Subsidized and Unsubsidized Stafford, PLUS), Perkins, state, alternative loans.

WORK-STUDY *Federal work-study:* Total amount: $219,318; 228 jobs averaging $1842. *State or other work-study/employment:* Total amount: $41,533 (2% need-based, 98% non-need-based). 23 part-time jobs averaging $1239.

ATHLETIC AWARDS *Total amount:* $738,944 (79% need-based, 21% non-need-based).

APPLYING FOR FINANCIAL AID *Required financial aid form:* FAFSA. *Financial aid deadline (priority):* 3/1. *Notification date:* Continuous beginning 3/1. Students must reply within 2 weeks of notification.

CONTACT Duane Polsdofer, Director of Financial Aid, Waldorf College, 106 South 6th Street, Forest City, IA 50436, 641-585-8120 or toll-free 800-292-1903. *Fax:* 641-585-8125.

WALLA WALLA COLLEGE
College Place, WA

Tuition & fees: $17,829	Average undergraduate aid package: $16,623

ABOUT THE INSTITUTION Independent Seventh-day Adventist, coed. Awards: associate, bachelor's, and master's degrees. 64 undergraduate majors. Total enrollment: 1,968. Undergraduates: 1,718. Freshmen: 359. Both federal and institutional methodology are used as a basis for awarding need-based institutional aid.

UNDERGRADUATE EXPENSES for 2004–05 *Application fee:* $40. *Comprehensive fee:* $21,513 includes full-time tuition ($17,655), mandatory fees ($174), and room and board ($3684). *College room only:* $2250. Full-time tuition and fees vary according to course load, degree level, and location. Room and board charges vary according to housing facility and location. *Part-time tuition:* $462 per credit. *Part-time fees:* $58 per term. *Payment plan:* Installment.

FRESHMAN FINANCIAL AID (Fall 2003) 296 applied for aid; of those 71% were deemed to have need. 100% of freshmen with need received aid; of those 20% had need fully met. *Average percent of need met:* 86% (excluding resources awarded to replace EFC). *Average financial aid package:* $15,588 (excluding resources awarded to replace EFC). 27% of all full-time freshmen had no need and received non-need-based gift aid.

UNDERGRADUATE FINANCIAL AID (Fall 2003) 1,304 applied for aid; of those 77% were deemed to have need. 100% of undergraduates with need received aid; of those 17% had need fully met. *Average percent of need met:* 86% (excluding resources awarded to replace EFC). *Average financial aid package:* $16,623 (excluding resources awarded to replace EFC). 17% of all full-time undergraduates had no need and received non-need-based gift aid.

GIFT AID (NEED-BASED) *Total amount:* $9,561,200 (20% federal, 6% state, 50% institutional, 24% external sources). *Receiving aid:* Freshmen: 57% (175); All full-time undergraduates: 58% (824). *Average award:* Freshmen: $5369; Undergraduates: $6472. *Scholarships, grants, and awards:* Federal Pell, FSEOG, state, private, college/university gift aid from institutional funds.

GIFT AID (NON-NEED-BASED) *Total amount:* $1,816,582 (1% state, 40% institutional, 59% external sources). *Receiving aid:* Freshmen: 61% (187); Undergraduates: 51% (733). *Average Award:* Freshmen: $3482; Undergraduates: $2704. *Scholarships, grants, and awards by category:* Academic Interests/Achievement: 739 awards ($1,147,126 total): biological sciences, education, general academic interests/achievements, social sciences. *Creative Arts/Performance:* 68 awards ($41,581 total): general creative arts/performance, music. *Special Achievements/Activities:* 209 awards ($198,159 total): community service, leadership. *Special Characteristics:* 77 awards ($549,437 total): children of faculty/staff, ethnic background. *Tuition waivers:* Full or partial for employees or children of employees, senior citizens.

LOANS *Student loans:* $8,130,594 (91% need-based, 9% non-need-based). 78% of past graduating class borrowed through all loan programs. *Average indebtedness per student:* $22,235. *Average need-based loan:* Freshmen: $5085; Undergraduates: $5803. *Parent loans:* $1,270,526 (46% need-based, 54% non-need-based). *Programs:* FFEL (Subsidized and Unsubsidized Stafford, PLUS), Perkins, Federal Nursing, college/university.

WORK-STUDY *Federal work-study:* Total amount: $1,656,184; 753 jobs averaging $2356. *State or other work-study/employment:* Total amount: $116,391 (100% need-based). 94 part-time jobs averaging $2727.

APPLYING FOR FINANCIAL AID *Required financial aid forms:* FAFSA, institution's own form. *Financial aid deadline:* Continuous. *Notification date:* Continuous beginning 3/15.

CONTACT Ms. Nancy Caldera, Associate Director of Financial Aid, Walla Walla College, 204 South College Avenue, College Place, WA 99324-1198, 509-527-2315 or toll-free 800-541-8900. *Fax:* 509-527-2253. *E-mail:* caldna@wwc.edu.

WALSH COLLEGE OF ACCOUNTANCY AND BUSINESS ADMINISTRATION
Troy, MI

Tuition & fees: $7550	Average undergraduate aid package: $8432

ABOUT THE INSTITUTION Independent, coed. Awards: bachelor's and master's degrees. 5 undergraduate majors. Total enrollment: 3,105. Undergraduates: 909. Federal methodology is used as a basis for awarding need-based institutional aid.

UNDERGRADUATE EXPENSES for 2004–05 *Application fee:* $25. *Tuition:* full-time $7320; part-time $244 per credit. *Required fees:* full-time $230; $115 per term part-time. *Payment plan:* Deferred payment.

UNDERGRADUATE FINANCIAL AID (Fall 2003) 31 applied for aid; of those 84% were deemed to have need. 100% of undergraduates with need received aid. *Average percent of need met:* 21% (excluding resources awarded to replace EFC). *Average financial aid package:* $8432 (excluding resources awarded to replace EFC). 4% of all full-time undergraduates had no need and received non-need-based gift aid.

GIFT AID (NEED-BASED) *Total amount:* $597,691 (48% federal, 29% state, 21% institutional, 2% external sources). *Receiving aid:* All full-time undergraduates: 42% (22). *Average award:* Undergraduates: $2197. *Scholarships, grants, and awards:* Federal Pell, FSEOG, state, private, college/university gift aid from institutional funds.

GIFT AID (NON-NEED-BASED) *Total amount:* $164,352 (2% state, 98% institutional). *Receiving aid:* Undergraduates: 4% (2). *Average Award:* Undergraduates: $1750. *Scholarships, grants, and awards by category:* Academic Interests/Achievement: business. *Special Characteristics:* $135,000 total: previous college experience.

LOANS *Student loans:* $3,100,385 (93% need-based, 7% non-need-based). 45% of past graduating class borrowed through all loan programs. *Average indebtedness per student:* $8908. *Average need-based loan:* Undergraduates: $8431. *Parent loans:* $37,500 (60% need-based, 40% non-need-based). *Programs:* FFEL (Subsidized and Unsubsidized Stafford, PLUS), alternative loans.

WORK-STUDY Federal work-study jobs available. *State or other work-study/employment:* Total amount: $5866 (100% need-based). Part-time jobs available.

APPLYING FOR FINANCIAL AID *Required financial aid forms:* FAFSA, institution's own form. *Financial aid deadline:* Continuous. *Notification date:* Continuous beginning 6/1.

CONTACT Howard Thomas, Director of Student Financial Resources, Walsh College of Accountancy and Business Administration, 3838 Livernois Road, PO Box 7006, Troy, MI 48007-7006, 248-823-1285 or toll-free 800-925-7401 (in-state). *Fax:* 248-524-2520. *E-mail:* hthomas@walshcollege.edu.

WALSH UNIVERSITY
North Canton, OH

ABOUT THE INSTITUTION Independent Roman Catholic, coed. Awards: associate, bachelor's, and master's degrees. 37 undergraduate majors. Total enrollment: 1,951. Undergraduates: 1,694. Freshmen: 341.

GIFT AID (NEED-BASED) *Scholarships, grants, and awards:* Federal Pell, FSEOG, state, private, college/university gift aid from institutional funds.

GIFT AID (NON-NEED-BASED) *Scholarships, grants, and awards by category:* Academic Interests/Achievement: biological sciences, business, communication, computer science, education, English, foreign languages, general academic interests/achievements, health fields, humanities, international studies, mathematics, physical sciences, premedicine, religion/biblical studies, social sciences. *Creative Arts/Performance:* music. *Special Achievements/Activities:* leadership, religious involvement. *Special Characteristics:* children and siblings of alumni, children of faculty/staff, international students, local/state students, members of minority groups, out-of-state students, siblings of current students.

LOANS *Programs:* FFEL (Subsidized and Unsubsidized Stafford), Perkins, state, college/university.

WORK-STUDY *Federal work-study:* Total amount: $242,000; 182 jobs averaging $1480. *State or other work-study/employment:* Total amount: $54,200 (100% non-need-based). 30 part-time jobs averaging $1418.

APPLYING FOR FINANCIAL AID *Required financial aid forms:* FAFSA, institution's own form.

CONTACT Holly Van Gilder, Director of Financial Aid, Walsh University, 2020 East Maple NW, North Canton, OH 44720-3396, 330-490-7147 or toll-free 800-362-9846 (in-state), 800-362-8846 (out-of-state). *Fax:* 330-490-7372. *E-mail:* hvangilder@walsh.edu.

WARNER PACIFIC COLLEGE
Portland, OR

Tuition & fees: $18,020	Average undergraduate aid package: $13,229

ABOUT THE INSTITUTION Independent religious, coed. Awards: associate, bachelor's, and master's degrees and post-bachelor's certificates. 34 undergraduate majors. Total enrollment: 510. Undergraduates: 504. Freshmen: 68. Federal methodology is used as a basis for awarding need-based institutional aid.

UNDERGRADUATE EXPENSES for 2004–05 *Application fee:* $25. *Comprehensive fee:* $23,120 includes full-time tuition ($17,580), mandatory fees ($440), and room and board ($5100). Room and board charges vary according to board plan and housing facility. *Part-time tuition:* $390 per credit. Part-time tuition and fees vary according to course load. *Payment plan:* Installment.

FRESHMAN FINANCIAL AID (Fall 2004, est.) 71 applied for aid; of those 94% were deemed to have need. 100% of freshmen with need received aid; of those 10% had need fully met. *Average percent of need met:* 67% (excluding resources awarded to replace EFC). *Average financial aid package:* $12,558 (excluding resources awarded to replace EFC). 4% of all full-time freshmen had no need and received non-need-based gift aid.

UNDERGRADUATE FINANCIAL AID (Fall 2004, est.) 376 applied for aid; of those 93% were deemed to have need. 100% of undergraduates with need received aid; of those 11% had need fully met. *Average percent of need met:* 73% (excluding resources awarded to replace EFC). *Average financial aid package:* $13,229 (excluding resources awarded to replace EFC). 5% of all full-time undergraduates had no need and received non-need-based gift aid.

GIFT AID (NEED-BASED) *Receiving aid:* Freshmen: 72% (64); All full-time undergraduates: 74% (290). *Average award:* Freshmen: $5091; Undergraduates: $4432. *Scholarships, grants, and awards:* Federal Pell, FSEOG, state, private, college/university gift aid from institutional funds.

GIFT AID (NON-NEED-BASED) *Average Award:* Freshmen: $11,710; Undergraduates: $10,696. *Scholarships, grants, and awards by category:* Academic Interests/Achievement: 220 awards ($91,955 total): biological sciences, general academic interests/achievements, religion/biblical studies. *Creative Arts/Performance:* 49 awards ($94,123 total): music, theater/drama. *Special Achievements/Activities:* 69 awards ($91,950 total): leadership. *Special Characteristics:* 2,380 awards ($304,865 total): children and siblings of alumni, members of minority groups, religious affiliation. *Tuition waivers:* Full or partial for children of alumni, employees or children of employees. *ROTC:* Army cooperative, Air Force cooperative.

LOANS *Student loans:* $2,815,954 (53% need-based, 47% non-need-based). 83% of past graduating class borrowed through all loan programs. *Average indebtedness per student:* $20,787. *Average need-based loan:* Freshmen: $2951; Undergraduates: $4089. *Parent loans:* $427,436 (100% non-need-based). *Programs:* FFEL (Subsidized and Unsubsidized Stafford, PLUS), Perkins.

WORK-STUDY *Federal work-study:* Total amount: $296,532; 212 jobs averaging $1328. *State or other work-study/employment:* Part-time jobs available.

ATHLETIC AWARDS *Total amount:* $475,903 (100% non-need-based).

APPLYING FOR FINANCIAL AID *Required financial aid form:* FAFSA. *Financial aid deadline:* Continuous. *Notification date:* Continuous beginning 3/1. Students must reply within 2 weeks of notification.

CONTACT Cynthia Pollard, Director of Financial Aid, Warner Pacific College, 2219 Southeast 68th Avenue, Portland, OR 97215-4099, 503-517-1018 or toll-free 800-582-7885 (in-state), 800-804-1510 (out-of-state). *E-mail:* cpollard@warnerpacific.edu.

WARNER SOUTHERN COLLEGE
Lake Wales, FL

Tuition & fees: $11,990	Average undergraduate aid package: $10,127

ABOUT THE INSTITUTION Independent religious, coed. Awards: associate, bachelor's, and master's degrees. 27 undergraduate majors. Total enrollment: 1,024. Undergraduates: 973. Freshmen: 128. Both federal and institutional methodology are used as a basis for awarding need-based institutional aid.

UNDERGRADUATE EXPENSES for 2004–05 *Application fee:* $20. *Comprehensive fee:* $17,150 includes full-time tuition ($11,740), mandatory fees ($250), and room and board ($5160). *College room only:* $2080. Room and board charges vary according to board plan. *Part-time tuition:* $305 per hour. *Part-time fees:* $45 per term. *Payment plans:* Installment, deferred payment.

FRESHMAN FINANCIAL AID (Fall 2003) 113 applied for aid; of those 71% were deemed to have need. 100% of freshmen with need received aid. *Average financial aid package:* $19,722 (excluding resources awarded to replace EFC). 73% of all full-time freshmen had no need and received non-need-based gift aid.

UNDERGRADUATE FINANCIAL AID (Fall 2003) 794 applied for aid; of those 66% were deemed to have need. 100% of undergraduates with need received aid. *Average financial aid package:* $10,127 (excluding resources awarded to replace EFC). 16% of all full-time undergraduates had no need and received non-need-based gift aid.

GIFT AID (NEED-BASED) *Total amount:* $1,317,173 (88% federal, 12% state). *Receiving aid:* Freshmen: 50% (57); All full-time undergraduates: 43% (347). *Average award:* Freshmen: $3249; Undergraduates: $3129. *Scholarships, grants, and awards:* Federal Pell, FSEOG, state, private, college/university gift aid from institutional funds.

GIFT AID (NON-NEED-BASED) *Total amount:* $4,142,598 (36% state, 58% institutional, 6% external sources). *Receiving aid:* Freshmen: 71% (80); Undergraduates: 64% (516). *Average Award:* Freshmen: $3219; Undergraduates: $3771. *Scholarships, grants, and awards by category:* Academic Interests/Achievement: 122 awards ($343,023 total): business, communication, education, English, general academic interests/achievements, humanities. *Creative Arts/Performance:* 21 awards ($31,950 total): music. *Special Achievements/Activities:* 597 awards ($643,666 total): leadership, religious involvement. *Special Characteristics:* 300 awards ($627,615 total): children and siblings of alumni, children of educators, children of faculty/staff, international students, out-of-state students, previous college experience, relatives of clergy, siblings of current students, veterans, veterans' children. *Tuition waivers:* Full or partial for employees or children of employees.

LOANS *Student loans:* $5,066,168 (52% need-based, 48% non-need-based). 35% of past graduating class borrowed through all loan programs. *Average indebtedness per student:* $6846. *Average need-based loan:* Freshmen: $2372; Undergraduates: $4141. *Parent loans:* $147,691 (100% non-need-based). *Programs:* FFEL (Subsidized and Unsubsidized Stafford, PLUS), Perkins, alternative loans.

WORK-STUDY *Federal work-study:* Total amount: $85,532; 99 jobs averaging $1500. *State or other work-study/employment:* Total amount: $184,387 (15% need-based, 85% non-need-based). Part-time jobs available.

ATHLETIC AWARDS *Total amount:* $1,042,557 (100% non-need-based).

APPLYING FOR FINANCIAL AID *Required financial aid forms:* FAFSA, state aid form, verification form. *Financial aid deadline:* Continuous. *Notification date:* Continuous beginning 3/15. Students must reply within 4 weeks of notification.

CONTACT Student Financial Services, Warner Southern College, 13895 Highway 27, Lake Wales, FL 33859, 863-638-7202 or toll-free 800-949-7248 (in-state). *Fax:* 863-638-7603. *E-mail:* financialaid@warner.edu.

WARREN WILSON COLLEGE
Swannanoa, NC

Tuition & fees: $19,160	Average undergraduate aid package: $12,906

ABOUT THE INSTITUTION Independent religious, coed. Awards: bachelor's and master's degrees. 27 undergraduate majors. Total enrollment: 865. Undergraduates: 792. Freshmen: 210. Both federal and institutional methodology are used as a basis for awarding need-based institutional aid.

UNDERGRADUATE EXPENSES for 2005–06 *Comprehensive fee:* $24,620 includes full-time tuition ($18,910), mandatory fees ($250), and room and board ($5460). Full-time tuition and fees vary according to course load. Room and board charges vary according to board plan. Part-time tuition and fees vary according to course load. *Payment plan:* Installment.

FRESHMAN FINANCIAL AID (Fall 2004, est.) 148 applied for aid; of those 80% were deemed to have need. 100% of freshmen with need received aid; of those 17% had need fully met. *Average percent of need met:* 72% (excluding resources awarded to replace EFC). *Average financial aid package:* $13,074 (excluding resources awarded to replace EFC). 23% of all full-time freshmen had no need and received non-need-based gift aid.

UNDERGRADUATE FINANCIAL AID (Fall 2004, est.) 545 applied for aid; of those 83% were deemed to have need. 100% of undergraduates with need received aid; of those 20% had need fully met. *Average percent of need met:* 77% (excluding resources awarded to replace EFC). *Average financial aid*

package: $12,906 (excluding resources awarded to replace EFC). 14% of all full-time undergraduates had no need and received non-need-based gift aid.
GIFT AID (NEED-BASED) *Total amount:* $3,607,927 (17% federal, 7% state, 71% institutional, 5% external sources). *Receiving aid:* Freshmen: 49% (108); All full-time undergraduates: 49% (409). *Average award:* Freshmen: $9293; Undergraduates: $8109. *Scholarships, grants, and awards:* Federal Pell, FSEOG, state, college/university gift aid from institutional funds.
GIFT AID (NON-NEED-BASED) *Total amount:* $603,216 (12% state, 65% institutional, 23% external sources). *Receiving aid:* Freshmen: 27% (59); Undergraduates: 16% (138). *Average Award:* Freshmen: $2166; Undergraduates: $3217. *Scholarships, grants, and awards by category: Academic Interests/ Achievement:* 130 awards ($254,892 total): general academic interests/ achievements. *Creative Arts/Performance:* 19 awards ($11,750 total): art/fine arts, creative writing. *Special Achievements/Activities:* 42 awards ($60,500 total): community service, general special achievements/activities, leadership. *Special Characteristics:* 81 awards ($218,337 total): children of faculty/staff, general special characteristics, local/state students, previous college experience, religious affiliation. *Tuition waivers:* Full or partial for employees or children of employees.
LOANS *Student loans:* $2,106,419 (87% need-based, 13% non-need-based). 59% of past graduating class borrowed through all loan programs. *Average indebtedness per student:* $15,041. *Average need-based loan:* Freshmen: $2278; Undergraduates: $3386. *Parent loans:* $1,005,258 (71% need-based, 29% non-need-based). *Programs:* FFEL (Subsidized and Unsubsidized Stafford, PLUS), Perkins, college/university.
WORK-STUDY *Federal work-study:* Total amount: $750,000; 350 jobs averaging $2143. *State or other work-study/employment:* Total amount: $750,000 (33% need-based, 67% non-need-based). 375 part-time jobs averaging $2000.
APPLYING FOR FINANCIAL AID *Required financial aid forms:* FAFSA, institution's own form, state aid form. *Financial aid deadline (priority):* 4/1. *Notification date:* Continuous. Students must reply by 5/1 or within 3 weeks of notification.
CONTACT Admissions Office, Warren Wilson College, PO Box 9000, Asheville, NC 28815-9000, 800-934-3536. *Fax:* 828-298-1440.

WARTBURG COLLEGE
Waverly, IA

Tuition & fees: $19,700	Average undergraduate aid package: $17,996

ABOUT THE INSTITUTION Independent Lutheran, coed. Awards: bachelor's degrees. 52 undergraduate majors. Total enrollment: 1,804. Undergraduates: 1,804. Freshmen: 499. Federal methodology is used as a basis for awarding need-based institutional aid.
UNDERGRADUATE EXPENSES for 2004–05 *Application fee:* $20. *Comprehensive fee:* $25,215 includes full-time tuition ($19,230), mandatory fees ($470), and room and board ($5515). *College room only:* $2715. Room and board charges vary according to board plan and housing facility. *Part-time tuition:* $710 per credit. *Part-time fees:* $15 per term. Part-time tuition and fees vary according to course load. *Payment plan:* Installment.
FRESHMAN FINANCIAL AID (Fall 2004, est.) 432 applied for aid; of those 90% were deemed to have need. 100% of freshmen with need received aid; of those 69% had need fully met. *Average percent of need met:* 95% (excluding resources awarded to replace EFC). *Average financial aid package:* $18,541 (excluding resources awarded to replace EFC). 21% of all full-time freshmen had no need and received non-need-based gift aid.
UNDERGRADUATE FINANCIAL AID (Fall 2004, est.) 1,540 applied for aid; of those 89% were deemed to have need. 100% of undergraduates with need received aid; of those 68% had need fully met. *Average percent of need met:* 95% (excluding resources awarded to replace EFC). *Average financial aid package:* $17,996 (excluding resources awarded to replace EFC). 21% of all full-time undergraduates had no need and received non-need-based gift aid.
GIFT AID (NEED-BASED) *Total amount:* $16,203,852 (9% federal, 16% state, 65% institutional, 10% external sources). *Receiving aid:* Freshmen: 79% (386); All full-time undergraduates: 79% (1,369). *Average award:* Freshmen: $13,313; Undergraduates: $11,749. *Scholarships, grants, and awards:* Federal Pell, FSEOG, state, private, college/university gift aid from institutional funds.
GIFT AID (NON-NEED-BASED) *Total amount:* $4,160,494 (1% state, 81% institutional, 18% external sources). *Receiving aid:* Freshmen: 9% (42); Undergraduates: 9% (160). *Average Award:* Freshmen: $24,404; Undergraduates: $23,078. *Scholarships, grants, and awards by category: Academic Interests/Achievement:* biological sciences, business, communication, computer science, education, English, general academic interests/achievements, international studies, mathematics, physical sciences, religion/biblical studies. *Creative*

Arts/Performance: art/fine arts, journalism/publications, music. *Special Achievements/ Activities:* junior miss. *Special Characteristics:* children and siblings of alumni, children of faculty/staff, ethnic background, international students, members of minority groups, out-of-state students, religious affiliation, siblings of current students. *Tuition waivers:* Full or partial for employees or children of employees, senior citizens.
LOANS *Student loans:* $21,207,290 (40% need-based, 60% non-need-based). 96% of past graduating class borrowed through all loan programs. *Average indebtedness per student:* $28,129. *Average need-based loan:* Freshmen: $5270; Undergraduates: $6680. *Parent loans:* $886,185 (50% need-based, 50% non-need-based). *Programs:* FFEL (Subsidized and Unsubsidized Stafford, PLUS), Perkins, alternative loans.
WORK-STUDY *Federal work-study:* Total amount: $597,116; 401 jobs averaging $1489. *State or other work-study/employment:* Total amount: $1,023,809 (100% non-need-based). 631 part-time jobs averaging $1622.
APPLYING FOR FINANCIAL AID *Required financial aid form:* FAFSA. *Financial aid deadline (priority):* 3/1. *Notification date:* Continuous beginning 3/21. Students must reply within 2 weeks of notification.
CONTACT Ms. Jennifer Sassman, Director of Financial Aid, Wartburg College, 100 Wartburg Boulevard, PO Box 1003, Waverly, IA 50677-0903, 319-352-8262 or toll-free 800-772-2085. *Fax:* 319-352-8514. *E-mail:* jennifer.sassman@ wartburg.edu.

WASHBURN UNIVERSITY
Topeka, KS

CONTACT Annita Huff, Director of Financial Aid, Washburn University, 1700 SW College Avenue, Topeka, KS 66621, 785-231-1151 or toll-free 800-332-0291 (in-state). *E-mail:* zzahuff@washburn.edu.

WASHINGTON & JEFFERSON COLLEGE
Washington, PA

Tuition & fees: $24,620	Average undergraduate aid package: $15,658

ABOUT THE INSTITUTION Independent, coed. Awards: associate and bachelor's degrees. 25 undergraduate majors. Total enrollment: 1,355. Undergraduates: 1,355. Freshmen: 466. Both federal and institutional methodology are used as a basis for awarding need-based institutional aid.
UNDERGRADUATE EXPENSES for 2004–05 *Application fee:* $25. *Comprehensive fee:* $31,330 includes full-time tuition ($24,220), mandatory fees ($400), and room and board ($6710). *College room only:* $3700. Room and board charges vary according to board plan and housing facility. *Part-time tuition:* $757 per credit hour. *Payment plans:* Installment, deferred payment.
FRESHMAN FINANCIAL AID (Fall 2003) 304 applied for aid; of those 88% were deemed to have need. 100% of freshmen with need received aid; of those 29% had need fully met. *Average percent of need met:* 82% (excluding resources awarded to replace EFC). *Average financial aid package:* $17,146 (excluding resources awarded to replace EFC). 22% of all full-time freshmen had no need and received non-need-based gift aid.
UNDERGRADUATE FINANCIAL AID (Fall 2003) 1,007 applied for aid; of those 92% were deemed to have need. 99% of undergraduates with need received aid; of those 17% had need fully met. *Average percent of need met:* 74% (excluding resources awarded to replace EFC). *Average financial aid package:* $15,658 (excluding resources awarded to replace EFC). 24% of all full-time undergraduates had no need and received non-need-based gift aid.
GIFT AID (NEED-BASED) *Total amount:* $11,694,187 (8% federal, 11% state, 78% institutional, 3% external sources). *Receiving aid:* Freshmen: 77% (268); All full-time undergraduates: 75% (916). *Average award:* Freshmen: $10,871; Undergraduates: $9984. *Scholarships, grants, and awards:* Federal Pell, FSEOG, state, private, college/university gift aid from institutional funds.
GIFT AID (NON-NEED-BASED) *Total amount:* $1,875,310 (99% institutional, 1% external sources). *Receiving aid:* Freshmen: 35% (120); Undergraduates: 33% (407). *Average Award:* Freshmen: $7006; Undergraduates: $5928. *Scholarships, grants, and awards by category: Academic Interests/Achievement:* 850 awards ($6,168,750 total): business, general academic interests/achievements. *Special Characteristics:* 38 awards ($538,343 total): children and siblings of alumni, children of faculty/staff. *Tuition waivers:* Full or partial for employees or children of employees. *ROTC:* Army cooperative, Air Force cooperative.
LOANS *Student loans:* $7,976,934 (51% need-based, 49% non-need-based). 74% of past graduating class borrowed through all loan programs. *Average indebtedness per student:* $16,384. *Average need-based loan:* Freshmen: $2961;

Undergraduates: $3875. **Parent loans:** $1,304,290 (35% need-based, 65% non-need-based). **Programs:** FFEL (Subsidized and Unsubsidized Stafford, PLUS), Perkins, college/university.

WORK-STUDY Federal work-study: Total amount: $396,527; 474 jobs averaging $1500. **State or other work-study/employment:** Total amount: $323,686 (100% non-need-based). 255 part-time jobs averaging $1200.

APPLYING FOR FINANCIAL AID Required financial aid form: FAFSA. **Financial aid deadline (priority):** 2/15. **Notification date:** Continuous beginning 3/1. Students must reply by 5/1.

CONTACT Michelle Vettorel, Director of Financial Aid, Washington & Jefferson College, 60 South Lincoln Street, Washington, PA 15301-4801, 724-223-6528 or toll-free 888-WANDJAY. Fax: 724-223-6534. E-mail: mvettorel@washjeff.edu.

WASHINGTON AND LEE UNIVERSITY
Lexington, VA

Tuition & fees: $28,635	Average undergraduate aid package: $23,416

ABOUT THE INSTITUTION Independent, coed. Awards: bachelor's, master's, and first professional degrees. 39 undergraduate majors. Total enrollment: 2,166. Undergraduates: 1,760. Freshmen: 460. Both federal and institutional methodology are used as a basis for awarding need-based institutional aid.

UNDERGRADUATE EXPENSES for 2005–06 Application fee: $40. **Comprehensive fee:** $35,860 includes full-time tuition ($27,960), mandatory fees ($675), and room and board ($7225). **College room only:** $3425. Room and board charges vary according to housing facility and student level.

FRESHMAN FINANCIAL AID (Fall 2004, est.) 232 applied for aid; of those 74% were deemed to have need. 97% of freshmen with need received aid; of those 85% had need fully met. Average percent of need met: 99% (excluding resources awarded to replace EFC). Average financial aid package: $22,468 (excluding resources awarded to replace EFC). 7% of all full-time freshmen had no need and received non-need-based gift aid.

UNDERGRADUATE FINANCIAL AID (Fall 2004, est.) 630 applied for aid; of those 85% were deemed to have need. 99% of undergraduates with need received aid; of those 86% had need fully met. Average percent of need met: 99% (excluding resources awarded to replace EFC). Average financial aid package: $23,416 (excluding resources awarded to replace EFC). 14% of all full-time undergraduates had no need and received non-need-based gift aid.

GIFT AID (NEED-BASED) Total amount: $8,732,997 (4% federal, 2% state, 90% institutional, 4% external sources). **Receiving aid:** Freshmen: 27% (122); All full-time undergraduates: 24% (426). **Average award:** Freshmen: $19,728; Undergraduates: $18,370. **Scholarships, grants, and awards:** Federal Pell, FSEOG, state, private, college/university gift aid from institutional funds.

GIFT AID (NON-NEED-BASED) Total amount: $6,299,041 (1% federal, 7% state, 86% institutional, 6% external sources). **Receiving aid:** Freshmen: 11% (52); Undergraduates: 9% (162). **Average Award:** Freshmen: $12,091; Undergraduates: $12,571. **Scholarships, grants, and awards by category:** Academic Interests/Achievement: general academic interests/achievements. Special Characteristics: local/state students. **Tuition waivers:** Full or partial for employees or children of employees. **ROTC:** Army cooperative.

LOANS Student loans: $2,824,775 (68% need-based, 32% non-need-based). 35% of past graduating class borrowed through all loan programs. Average indebtedness per student: $17,374. **Average need-based loan:** Freshmen: $3273; Undergraduates: $4264. **Parent loans:** $3,158,057 (51% need-based, 49% non-need-based). **Programs:** FFEL (Subsidized and Unsubsidized Stafford, PLUS), Perkins, college/university.

WORK-STUDY Federal work-study: Total amount: $189,875; 142 jobs averaging $1337. **State or other work-study/employment:** Total amount: $418,950 (76% need-based, 24% non-need-based). 301 part-time jobs averaging $1392.

APPLYING FOR FINANCIAL AID Required financial aid forms: FAFSA, CSS Financial Aid PROFILE, noncustodial (divorced/separated) parent's statement, business/farm supplement. **Financial aid deadline (priority):** 2/1. **Notification date:** 4/3. Students must reply by 5/1.

CONTACT John DeCourcy, Director, Financial Aid, Washington and Lee University, Gilliam House, Letcher Avenue, Lexington, VA 24450, 540-458-8729. Fax: 540-458-8614.

WASHINGTON BIBLE COLLEGE
Lanham, MD

Tuition & fees: $14,880	Average undergraduate aid package: $5000

ABOUT THE INSTITUTION Independent nondenominational, coed. Awards: associate and bachelor's degrees. 8 undergraduate majors. Total enrollment: 331. Undergraduates: 331. Both federal and institutional methodology are used as a basis for awarding need-based institutional aid.

UNDERGRADUATE EXPENSES for 2004–05 Application fee: $25. **Comprehensive fee:** $20,130 includes full-time tuition ($14,500), mandatory fees ($380), and room and board ($5250). **College room only:** $3000. Room and board charges vary according to board plan. **Part-time tuition:** $335 per credit. **Part-time fees:** $335 per credit. Part-time tuition and fees vary according to course load and location. **Payment plans:** Installment, deferred payment.

GIFT AID (NEED-BASED) Total amount: $522,222 (47% federal, 17% state, 33% institutional, 3% external sources). **Receiving aid:** Freshmen: 34% (15); All full-time undergraduates: 40% (76). **Average award:** Freshmen: $500; Undergraduates: $500. **Scholarships, grants, and awards:** Federal Pell, FSEOG, state, private, college/university gift aid from institutional funds.

GIFT AID (NON-NEED-BASED) Total amount: $65,342 (7% state, 93% institutional). **Receiving aid:** Freshmen: 55% (24); Undergraduates: 10% (19). **Average Award:** Freshmen: $2130; Undergraduates: $2053. **Scholarships, grants, and awards by category:** Academic Interests/Achievement: 100 awards ($26,814 total): general academic interests/achievements. Special Achievements/Activities: 23 awards ($21,864 total): general special achievements/activities, leadership, religious involvement. Special Characteristics: 88 awards ($151,897 total): children of faculty/staff, international students, relatives of clergy, religious affiliation, spouses of current students. **Tuition waivers:** Full or partial for employees or children of employees.

LOANS Student loans: $545,422 (92% need-based, 8% non-need-based). 50% of past graduating class borrowed through all loan programs. Average indebtedness per student: $8000. **Average need-based loan:** Freshmen: $2625; Undergraduates: $4625. **Parent loans:** $87,942 (59% need-based, 41% non-need-based). **Programs:** FFEL (Subsidized and Unsubsidized Stafford, PLUS).

APPLYING FOR FINANCIAL AID Required financial aid forms: FAFSA, institution's own form, CSS Financial Aid PROFILE, verification worksheet. **Financial aid deadline (priority):** 6/1. **Notification date:** Continuous beginning 7/1. Students must reply within 2 weeks of notification.

CONTACT Nancy Minton, Director of Financial Aid, Washington Bible College, 6511 Princess Garden Parkway, Lanham, MD 20706-3599, 301-552-1400 Ext. 1243 or toll-free 877-793-7227 Ext. 1212. Fax: 301-614-1051. E-mail: nminton@bible.edu.

WASHINGTON COLLEGE
Chestertown, MD

Tuition & fees: $26,550	Average undergraduate aid package: $17,107

ABOUT THE INSTITUTION Independent, coed. Awards: bachelor's and master's degrees. 34 undergraduate majors. Total enrollment: 1,426. Undergraduates: 1,349. Freshmen: 302. Both federal and institutional methodology are used as a basis for awarding need-based institutional aid.

UNDERGRADUATE EXPENSES for 2004–05 Application fee: $40. **Comprehensive fee:** $32,550 includes full-time tuition ($25,990), mandatory fees ($560), and room and board ($6000). **College room only:** $2800. Full-time tuition and fees vary according to program and reciprocity agreements. Room and board charges vary according to board plan and housing facility. **Part-time tuition:** $4332 per course. Part-time tuition and fees vary according to course load and program. **Payment plans:** Tuition prepayment, installment.

FRESHMAN FINANCIAL AID (Fall 2004, est.) 201 applied for aid; of those 78% were deemed to have need. 100% of freshmen with need received aid; of those 75% had need fully met. Average percent of need met: 80% (excluding resources awarded to replace EFC). Average financial aid package: $16,300 (excluding resources awarded to replace EFC). 32% of all full-time freshmen had no need and received non-need-based gift aid.

UNDERGRADUATE FINANCIAL AID (Fall 2004, est.) 727 applied for aid; of those 85% were deemed to have need. 100% of undergraduates with need received aid; of those 72% had need fully met. Average percent of need met: 85% (excluding resources awarded to replace EFC). Average financial aid package: $17,107 (excluding resources awarded to replace EFC). 39% of all full-time undergraduates had no need and received non-need-based gift aid.

GIFT AID (NEED-BASED) Total amount: $8,088,022 (5% federal, 8% state, 87% institutional). **Receiving aid:** Freshmen: 48% (155); All full-time undergraduates: 47% (599). **Average award:** Freshmen: $14,946; Undergraduates: $15,134. **Scholarships, grants, and awards:** Federal Pell, FSEOG, state, private, college/university gift aid from institutional funds.

GIFT AID (NON-NEED-BASED) *Total amount:* $6,950,233 (5% state, 87% institutional, 8% external sources). *Receiving aid:* Freshmen: 36% (116); Undergraduates: 36% (456). *Average Award:* Freshmen: $10,870; Undergraduates: $12,228. *Scholarships, grants, and awards by category:* Academic Interests/Achievement: general academic interests/achievements. Creative Arts/Performance: 12 awards ($18,000 total): creative writing. Special Achievements/Activities: 653 awards ($6,530,000 total): memberships. Special Characteristics: 97 awards ($1,458,759 total): children of faculty/staff, children of union members/company employees, international students. *Tuition waivers:* Full or partial for minority students, employees or children of employees.

LOANS *Student loans:* $4,687,179 (45% need-based, 55% non-need-based). 57% of past graduating class borrowed through all loan programs. *Average indebtedness per student:* $19,434. *Average need-based loan:* Freshmen: $2625; Undergraduates: $3500. *Parent loans:* $4,341,015 (100% non-need-based). *Programs:* FFEL (Subsidized and Unsubsidized Stafford, PLUS), Perkins, college/university.

WORK-STUDY *Federal work-study:* Total amount: $372,375; 259 jobs averaging $1435.

APPLYING FOR FINANCIAL AID *Required financial aid forms:* FAFSA, institution's own form, federal income tax form(s). *Financial aid deadline (priority):* 2/15. *Notification date:* Continuous beginning 3/1. Students must reply by 5/1.

CONTACT Ms. Jean M. Narcum, Director of Financial Aid, Washington College, 300 Washington Avenue, Chestertown, MD 21620-1197, 410-778-7214 or toll-free 800-422-1782. *Fax:* 410-778-7287. *E-mail:* jnarcum2@washcoll.edu.

WASHINGTON STATE UNIVERSITY
Pullman, WA

Tuition & fees (WA res): $5358   **Average undergraduate aid package: $9702**

ABOUT THE INSTITUTION State-supported, coed. Awards: bachelor's, master's, doctoral, and first professional degrees and post-bachelor's certificates. 149 undergraduate majors. Total enrollment: 23,240. Undergraduates: 19,280. Freshmen: 3,108. Federal methodology is used as a basis for awarding need-based institutional aid.

UNDERGRADUATE EXPENSES for 2004–05 *Application fee:* $38. *Tuition, state resident:* full-time $4745; part-time $258 per credit. *Tuition, nonresident:* full-time $13,163; part-time $679 per credit. Part-time tuition and fees vary according to course load. *College room and board:* $6450; *room only:* $3622. Room and board charges vary according to board plan and housing facility. *Payment plan:* Installment.

FRESHMAN FINANCIAL AID (Fall 2003) 2152 applied for aid; of those 66% were deemed to have need. 98% of freshmen with need received aid; of those 33% had need fully met. *Average percent of need met:* 95% (excluding resources awarded to replace EFC). *Average financial aid package:* $8728 (excluding resources awarded to replace EFC). 14% of all full-time freshmen had no need and received non-need-based gift aid.

UNDERGRADUATE FINANCIAL AID (Fall 2003) 11,749 applied for aid; of those 78% were deemed to have need. 95% of undergraduates with need received aid; of those 35% had need fully met. *Average percent of need met:* 95% (excluding resources awarded to replace EFC). *Average financial aid package:* $9702 (excluding resources awarded to replace EFC). 5% of all full-time undergraduates had no need and received non-need-based gift aid.

GIFT AID (NEED-BASED) *Total amount:* $30,114,666 (46% federal, 41% state, 13% institutional). *Receiving aid:* Freshmen: 26% (781); All full-time undergraduates: 37% (5,781). *Average award:* Freshmen: $4567; Undergraduates: $5292. *Scholarships, grants, and awards:* Federal Pell, FSEOG, state, private, college/university gift aid from institutional funds.

GIFT AID (NON-NEED-BASED) *Total amount:* $11,738,561 (9% state, 41% institutional, 50% external sources). *Receiving aid:* Freshmen: 27% (816); Undergraduates: 26% (4,086). *Average Award:* Freshmen: $3732; Undergraduates: $3401. *Scholarships, grants, and awards by category:* Academic Interests/Achievement: agriculture, architecture, area/ethnic studies, biological sciences, business, communication, computer science, education, engineering/technologies, English, foreign languages, general academic interests/achievements, health fields, home economics, humanities, international studies, mathematics, military science, physical sciences, premedicine, social sciences. Creative Arts/Performance: applied art and design, art/fine arts, cinema/film/broadcasting, creative writing, general creative arts/performance, journalism/publications, music, performing arts, theater/drama. Special Achievements/Activities: community service, general special achievements/activities, junior miss, leadership, memberships, religious involvement, rodeo. Special Characteristics: children and siblings of alumni, children of faculty/staff, children of public servants, children with a

deceased or disabled parent, first-generation college students, handicapped students, international students, out-of-state students, public servants, religious affiliation, veterans. *Tuition waivers:* Full or partial for children of alumni, employees or children of employees. *ROTC:* Army, Naval, Air Force.

LOANS *Student loans:* $52,511,302 (59% need-based, 41% non-need-based). 46% of past graduating class borrowed through all loan programs. *Average indebtedness per student:* $20,216. *Average need-based loan:* Freshmen: $2914; Undergraduates: $4497. *Parent loans:* $21,730,263 (100% non-need-based). *Programs:* FFEL (Subsidized and Unsubsidized Stafford, PLUS), Perkins, Federal Nursing, college/university, alternative loans.

WORK-STUDY *Federal work-study:* Total amount: $795,196; 639 jobs averaging $1316. *State or other work-study/employment:* Total amount: $1,498,302 (100% need-based). 1,080 part-time jobs averaging $1425.

ATHLETIC AWARDS *Total amount:* $4,368,397 (100% non-need-based).

APPLYING FOR FINANCIAL AID *Required financial aid form:* FAFSA. *Financial aid deadline (priority):* 3/1. *Notification date:* 4/15.

CONTACT Financial Aid Office, Washington State University, Office of Student Financial Aid, PO Box 641068, Pullman, WA 99164-1068, 509-335-9711 or toll-free 888-468-6978. *E-mail:* finaid@wsu.edu.

WASHINGTON UNIVERSITY IN ST. LOUIS
St. Louis, MO

Tuition & fees: $32,042   **Average undergraduate aid package: $25,309**

ABOUT THE INSTITUTION Independent, coed. Awards: bachelor's, master's, doctoral, and first professional degrees and post-bachelor's certificates. 168 undergraduate majors. Total enrollment: 13,380. Undergraduates: 7,433. Freshmen: 1,452. Both federal and institutional methodology are used as a basis for awarding need-based institutional aid.

UNDERGRADUATE EXPENSES for 2005–06 *Application fee:* $55. *Comprehensive fee:* $42,106 includes full-time tuition ($31,100), mandatory fees ($942), and room and board ($10,064). *College room only:* $6096. Room and board charges vary according to board plan and housing facility. Part-time tuition and fees vary according to class time. *Payment plans:* Tuition prepayment, installment.

FRESHMAN FINANCIAL AID (Fall 2004, est.) 945 applied for aid; of those 58% were deemed to have need. 98% of freshmen with need received aid; of those 100% had need fully met. *Average percent of need met:* 100% (excluding resources awarded to replace EFC). *Average financial aid package:* $25,095 (excluding resources awarded to replace EFC). 18% of all full-time freshmen had no need and received non-need-based gift aid.

UNDERGRADUATE FINANCIAL AID (Fall 2004, est.) 4,191 applied for aid; of those 62% were deemed to have need. 99% of undergraduates with need received aid; of those 100% had need fully met. *Average percent of need met:* 100% (excluding resources awarded to replace EFC). *Average financial aid package:* $25,309 (excluding resources awarded to replace EFC). 14% of all full-time undergraduates had no need and received non-need-based gift aid.

GIFT AID (NEED-BASED) *Total amount:* $51,677,219 (5% federal, 2% state, 87% institutional, 6% external sources). *Receiving aid:* Freshmen: 36% (524); All full-time undergraduates: 43% (2,550). *Average award:* Freshmen: $21,754; Undergraduates: $20,266. *Scholarships, grants, and awards:* Federal Pell, FSEOG, state, private, college/university gift aid from institutional funds, United Negro College Fund.

GIFT AID (NON-NEED-BASED) *Total amount:* $5,970,674 (2% federal, 6% state, 82% institutional, 10% external sources). *Receiving aid:* Freshmen: 5% (72); Undergraduates: 3% (182). *Average Award:* Freshmen: $7414; Undergraduates: $6914. *Scholarships, grants, and awards by category:* Academic Interests/Achievement: architecture, biological sciences, business, communication, computer science, education, engineering/technologies, English, foreign languages, general academic interests/achievements, health fields, humanities, international studies, mathematics, military science, physical sciences, premedicine, religion/biblical studies, social sciences. Creative Arts/Performance: applied art and design, art/fine arts, cinema/film/broadcasting, creative writing, dance, music, performing arts, theater/drama. *Tuition waivers:* Full or partial for employees or children of employees. *ROTC:* Army, Air Force cooperative.

LOANS *Student loans:* $15,045,315 (94% need-based, 6% non-need-based). 41% of past graduating class borrowed through all loan programs. *Average need-based loan:* Freshmen: $4239; Undergraduates: $5971. *Parent loans:* $4,650,385 (58% need-based, 42% non-need-based). *Programs:* FFEL (Subsidized and Unsubsidized Stafford, PLUS), Perkins, state, college/university.

WORK-STUDY *Federal work-study:* Total amount: $2,318,275; 1,223 jobs averaging $1895.

APPLYING FOR FINANCIAL AID *Required financial aid forms:* FAFSA, CSS Financial Aid PROFILE, noncustodial (divorced/separated) parent's statement, student and parent 1040 tax return or signed waiver if there is no tax return. *Financial aid deadline:* 2/15. *Notification date:* 4/1. Students must reply by 5/1 or within 2 weeks of notification.

CONTACT Mr. William Witbrodt, Director of Financial Aid, Washington University in St. Louis, Campus Box 1041, One Brookings Drive, St. Louis, MO 63130-4899, 314-935-5900 or toll-free 800-638-0700. *Fax:* 314-935-4037. *E-mail:* financial@wustl.edu.

WATKINS COLLEGE OF ART AND DESIGN
Nashville, TN

ABOUT THE INSTITUTION Independent, coed. Awards: bachelor's degrees. 9 undergraduate majors. Total enrollment: 384. Undergraduates: 359. Freshmen: 23.

GIFT AID (NEED-BASED) *Scholarships, grants, and awards:* Federal Pell, FSEOG, state, college/university gift aid from institutional funds.

GIFT AID (NON-NEED-BASED) *Scholarships, grants, and awards by category:* *Creative Arts/Performance:* applied art and design, art/fine arts, cinema/film/broadcasting.

LOANS *Programs:* FFEL (Subsidized and Unsubsidized Stafford, PLUS).

WORK-STUDY *Federal work-study:* Total amount: $15,766; 15 jobs averaging $1500. *State or other work-study/employment:* Total amount: $20,000 (100% need-based). 15 part-time jobs averaging $1500.

APPLYING FOR FINANCIAL AID *Required financial aid forms:* FAFSA, institution's own form.

CONTACT Regina Gilbert, Financial Aid Director, Watkins College of Art and Design, 2298 Metrocenter Boulevard, Nashville, TN 37228, 615-383-4848. *Fax:* 615-383-4849. *E-mail:* rgilbert@watkins.edu.

WAYLAND BAPTIST UNIVERSITY
Plainview, TX

Tuition & fees: $9250	Average undergraduate aid package: $8863

ABOUT THE INSTITUTION Independent Baptist, coed. Awards: associate, bachelor's, and master's degrees (branch locations in Anchorage, AK; Amarillo, TX; Luke Airforce Base, AZ; Glorieta, NM; Aiea, HI; Lubbock, TX; San Antonio, TX; Wichita Falls, TX). 28 undergraduate majors. Total enrollment: 1,067. Undergraduates: 998. Freshmen: 215. Federal methodology is used as a basis for awarding need-based institutional aid.

UNDERGRADUATE EXPENSES for 2004–05 *Application fee:* $35. *Comprehensive fee:* $12,670 includes full-time tuition ($8850), mandatory fees ($400), and room and board ($3420). *College room only:* $1276. Full-time tuition and fees vary according to course load and location. Room and board charges vary according to board plan and housing facility. *Part-time tuition:* $295 per credit hour. *Part-time fees:* $50 per term. Part-time tuition and fees vary according to course load and location. *Payment plan:* Installment.

FRESHMAN FINANCIAL AID (Fall 2004, est.) 191 applied for aid; of those 82% were deemed to have need. 99% of freshmen with need received aid; of those 23% had need fully met. *Average percent of need met:* 77% (excluding resources awarded to replace EFC). *Average financial aid package:* $8453 (excluding resources awarded to replace EFC). 26% of all full-time freshmen had no need and received non-need-based gift aid.

UNDERGRADUATE FINANCIAL AID (Fall 2004, est.) 748 applied for aid; of those 87% were deemed to have need. 100% of undergraduates with need received aid; of those 27% had need fully met. *Average percent of need met:* 79% (excluding resources awarded to replace EFC). *Average financial aid package:* $8863 (excluding resources awarded to replace EFC). 20% of all full-time undergraduates had no need and received non-need-based gift aid.

GIFT AID (NEED-BASED) *Total amount:* $4,409,385 (34% federal, 31% state, 31% institutional, 4% external sources). *Receiving aid:* Freshmen: 72% (154); All full-time undergraduates: 76% (635). *Average award:* Freshmen: $6911; Undergraduates: $6511. *Scholarships, grants, and awards:* Federal Pell, FSEOG, state, private, college/university gift aid from institutional funds.

GIFT AID (NON-NEED-BASED) *Total amount:* $1,262,827 (1% federal, 90% institutional, 9% external sources). *Receiving aid:* Freshmen: 9% (20); Undergraduates: 8% (66). *Average Award:* Freshmen: $8110; Undergraduates: $8240. *Scholarships, grants, and awards by category:* Academic Interests/Achievement: 547 awards ($1,003,509 total): biological sciences, business, communication, education, English, general academic interests/achievements,

mathematics, physical sciences, religion/biblical studies, social sciences. *Creative Arts/Performance:* 115 awards ($143,375 total): art/fine arts, journalism/publications, music, theater/drama. *Special Achievements/Activities:* 6 awards ($2600 total): cheerleading/drum major, leadership, memberships, religious involvement. *Special Characteristics:* 260 awards ($253,290 total): children and siblings of alumni, children of faculty/staff, ethnic background, general special characteristics, local/state students, members of minority groups, relatives of clergy. *Tuition waivers:* Full or partial for employees or children of employees. *ROTC:* Army cooperative, Air Force cooperative.

LOANS *Student loans:* $3,647,817 (72% need-based, 28% non-need-based). *Average need-based loan:* Freshmen: $1953; Undergraduates: $2867. *Parent loans:* $197,939 (11% need-based, 89% non-need-based). *Programs:* FFEL (Subsidized and Unsubsidized Stafford, PLUS), Perkins, state.

WORK-STUDY *Federal work-study:* Total amount: $224,385; 182 jobs averaging $1320. *State or other work-study/employment:* Total amount: $31,921 (22% need-based, 78% non-need-based). 57 part-time jobs averaging $1162.

ATHLETIC AWARDS *Total amount:* $531,065 (100% non-need-based).

APPLYING FOR FINANCIAL AID *Required financial aid forms:* FAFSA, institution's own form. *Financial aid deadline (priority):* 5/1. *Notification date:* Continuous beginning 2/15. Students must reply within 4 weeks of notification.

CONTACT Karen LaQuey, Director of Financial Aid, Wayland Baptist University, 1900 West 7th Street, Plainview, TX 79072-6998, 806-291-3520 or toll-free 800-588-1928. *Fax:* 806-291-1956. *E-mail:* laquey@wbu.edu.

WAYNESBURG COLLEGE
Waynesburg, PA

Tuition & fees: $14,540	Average undergraduate aid package: $11,440

ABOUT THE INSTITUTION Independent religious, coed. Awards: associate, bachelor's, and master's degrees. 51 undergraduate majors. Total enrollment: 2,102. Undergraduates: 1,634. Freshmen: 366. Federal methodology is used as a basis for awarding need-based financial aid.

UNDERGRADUATE EXPENSES for 2004–05 *Application fee:* $20. *Comprehensive fee:* $20,340 includes full-time tuition ($14,200), mandatory fees ($340), and room and board ($5800). *College room only:* $2960. Full-time tuition and fees vary according to class time. Room and board charges vary according to board plan. *Part-time tuition:* $595 per credit. *Part-time fees:* $15 per credit. Part-time tuition and fees vary according to class time, course load, and location. *Payment plans:* Installment, deferred payment.

FRESHMAN FINANCIAL AID (Fall 2004, est.) 383 applied for aid; of those 91% were deemed to have need. 100% of freshmen with need received aid; of those 26% had need fully met. *Average percent of need met:* 78% (excluding resources awarded to replace EFC). *Average financial aid package:* $11,587 (excluding resources awarded to replace EFC). 10% of all full-time freshmen had no need and received non-need-based gift aid.

UNDERGRADUATE FINANCIAL AID (Fall 2004, est.) 1,348 applied for aid; of those 91% were deemed to have need. 99% of undergraduates with need received aid; of those 26% had need fully met. *Average percent of need met:* 78% (excluding resources awarded to replace EFC). *Average financial aid package:* $11,440 (excluding resources awarded to replace EFC). 10% of all full-time undergraduates had no need and received non-need-based gift aid.

GIFT AID (NEED-BASED) *Total amount:* $9,902,866 (17% federal, 21% state, 59% institutional, 3% external sources). *Receiving aid:* Freshmen: 75% (339); All full-time undergraduates: 77% (1,144). *Average award:* Freshmen: $9279; Undergraduates: $8519. *Scholarships, grants, and awards:* Federal Pell, FSEOG, state, private, college/university gift aid from institutional funds.

GIFT AID (NON-NEED-BASED) *Total amount:* $913,707 (1% federal, 4% state, 92% institutional, 3% external sources). *Receiving aid:* Freshmen: 7% (34); Undergraduates: 6% (82). *Average Award:* Freshmen: $7686; Undergraduates: $8723. *Scholarships, grants, and awards by category:* Academic Interests/Achievement: 60 awards ($2000 total): biological sciences, business, communication, computer science, education, English, general academic interests/achievements, international studies, mathematics, religion/biblical studies. *Creative Arts/Performance:* 4 awards ($2000 total): music. *Special Achievements/Activities:* 65 awards ($2100 total): community service. *Special Characteristics:* 50 awards ($500,000 total): children of faculty/staff. *Tuition waivers:* Full or partial for employees or children of employees. *ROTC:* Army cooperative.

LOANS *Student loans:* $8,165,117 (71% need-based, 29% non-need-based). 87% of past graduating class borrowed through all loan programs. *Average indebtedness per student:* $20,000. *Average need-based loan:* Freshmen: $2602;

Undergraduates: $3650. *Parent loans:* $1,507,397 (29% need-based, 71% non-need-based). *Programs:* FFEL (Subsidized and Unsubsidized Stafford, PLUS), Perkins, Federal Nursing.
WORK-STUDY *Federal work-study:* Total amount: $195,812; 268 jobs averaging $1187.
APPLYING FOR FINANCIAL AID *Required financial aid forms:* FAFSA, institution's own form. *Financial aid deadline:* Continuous. *Notification date:* Continuous beginning 2/15. Students must reply within 2 weeks of notification.
CONTACT Matthew C. Stokan, Director of Financial Aid, Waynesburg College, 51 West College Street, Waynesburg, PA 15370-1222, 724-852-3208 or toll-free 800-225-7393. *Fax:* 724-627-6416. *E-mail:* mstokan@waynesburg.edu.

WAYNE STATE COLLEGE
Wayne, NE

Tuition & fees (NE res): $3672   **Average undergraduate aid package: $3615**

ABOUT THE INSTITUTION State-supported, coed. Awards: bachelor's and master's degrees and post-master's certificates. 60 undergraduate majors. Total enrollment: 3,398. Undergraduates: 2,750. Freshmen: 564. Federal methodology is used as a basis for awarding need-based institutional aid.
UNDERGRADUATE EXPENSES for 2004–05 *Application fee:* $30. *Tuition, state resident:* full-time $2850; part-time $95 per credit hour. *Tuition, nonresident:* full-time $5700; part-time $190 per credit hour. *Required fees:* full-time $822; $33 per credit hour. Full-time tuition and fees vary according to course level and course load. Part-time tuition and fees vary according to course level and course load. *College room and board:* $4120; *room only:* $2000. Room and board charges vary according to board plan and housing facility. *Payment plan:* Installment.
GIFT AID (NEED-BASED) *Total amount:* $3,343,279 (88% federal, 10% state, 2% institutional). *Receiving aid:* Freshmen: 49% (296); All full-time undergraduates: 45% (1,163). *Average award:* Freshmen: $1385; Undergraduates: $1371. *Scholarships, grants, and awards:* Federal Pell, FSEOG, state, private, college/university gift aid from institutional funds.
GIFT AID (NON-NEED-BASED) *Total amount:* $1,079,930 (46% institutional, 54% external sources). *Receiving aid:* Freshmen: 20% (121); Undergraduates: 18% (454). *Scholarships, grants, and awards by category:* Academic Interests/Achievement: biological sciences, business, communication, computer science, education, English, foreign languages, general academic interests/achievements, health fields, home economics, humanities, mathematics, physical sciences, premedicine, social sciences. Creative Arts/Performance: art/fine arts, journalism/publications, music, theater/drama. Special Achievements/Activities: general special achievements/activities, leadership. Special Characteristics: children of faculty/staff, ethnic background, general special characteristics, local/state students, members of minority groups, out-of-state students, veterans, veterans' children. *Tuition waivers:* Full or partial for minority students, employees or children of employees. *ROTC:* Army cooperative.
LOANS *Student loans:* $7,119,083 (60% need-based, 40% non-need-based). *Average need-based loan:* Freshmen: $1362; Undergraduates: $1598. *Parent loans:* $206,559 (100% non-need-based). *Programs:* FFEL (Subsidized and Unsubsidized Stafford, PLUS), Perkins.
ATHLETIC AWARDS *Total amount:* $449,244 (100% non-need-based).
APPLYING FOR FINANCIAL AID *Required financial aid forms:* FAFSA, institution's own form. *Financial aid deadline (priority):* 5/1. *Notification date:* Continuous. Students must reply within 4 weeks of notification.
CONTACT Mrs. Kyle M. Rose, Director of Financial Aid, Wayne State College, 1111 Main Street, Wayne, NE 68787, 402-375-7230 or toll-free 800-228-9972 (in-state). *Fax:* 402-375-7204. *E-mail:* kyrose1@wsc.edu.

WAYNE STATE UNIVERSITY
Detroit, MI

Tuition & fees (MI res): $5399   **Average undergraduate aid package: $7254**

ABOUT THE INSTITUTION State-supported, coed. Awards: bachelor's, master's, doctoral, and first professional degrees and post-bachelor's and post-master's certificates. 88 undergraduate majors. Total enrollment: 33,314. Undergraduates: 20,712. Freshmen: 3,120. Federal methodology is used as a basis for awarding need-based institutional aid.
UNDERGRADUATE EXPENSES for 2004–05 *Application fee:* $30. *Tuition, state resident:* full-time $4773; part-time $159 per semester hour. *Tuition, nonresident:* full-time $10,941; part-time $365 per semester hour. *Required fees:* full-time

$626; $14.30 per semester hour or $98.50 per term part-time. Full-time tuition and fees vary according to student level. Part-time tuition and fees vary according to student level. *College room and board:* $6700. Room and board charges vary according to housing facility. *Payment plan:* Installment.
FRESHMAN FINANCIAL AID (Fall 2003) 1599 applied for aid; of those 87% were deemed to have need. 97% of freshmen with need received aid; of those 8% had need fully met. *Average percent of need met:* 53% (excluding resources awarded to replace EFC). *Average financial aid package:* $6609 (excluding resources awarded to replace EFC). 6% of all full-time freshmen had no need and received non-need-based gift aid.
UNDERGRADUATE FINANCIAL AID (Fall 2003) 6,863 applied for aid; of those 90% were deemed to have need. 96% of undergraduates with need received aid; of those 4% had need fully met. *Average percent of need met:* 58% (excluding resources awarded to replace EFC). *Average financial aid package:* $7254 (excluding resources awarded to replace EFC). 2% of all full-time undergraduates had no need and received non-need-based gift aid.
GIFT AID (NEED-BASED) *Total amount:* $22,106,120 (88% federal, 6% state, 6% institutional). *Receiving aid:* Freshmen: 43% (980); All full-time undergraduates: 40% (4,279). *Average award:* Freshmen: $3453; Undergraduates: $3631. *Scholarships, grants, and awards:* Federal Pell, FSEOG, state, private, college/university gift aid from institutional funds.
GIFT AID (NON-NEED-BASED) *Total amount:* $14,773,722 (14% state, 82% institutional, 4% external sources). *Receiving aid:* Freshmen: 37% (850); Undergraduates: 20% (2,124). *Average Award:* Freshmen: $3565; Undergraduates: $3626. *Scholarships, grants, and awards by category:* Academic Interests/Achievement: 1,373 awards ($7,337,108 total): general academic interests/achievements. Creative Arts/Performance: 305 awards ($586,818 total): art/fine arts, dance, debating, journalism/publications, music, theater/drama. Special Achievements/Activities: 38 awards ($16,208 total): general special achievements/activities. *Tuition waivers:* Full or partial for employees or children of employees, senior citizens. *ROTC:* Air Force cooperative.
LOANS *Student loans:* $46,576,507 (95% need-based, 5% non-need-based). 45% of past graduating class borrowed through all loan programs. *Average indebtedness per student:* $19,563. *Average need-based loan:* Freshmen: $2589; Undergraduates: $4148. *Parent loans:* $111,461 (100% need-based). *Programs:* FFEL (Subsidized and Unsubsidized Stafford, PLUS), Perkins, Federal Nursing, state, college/university.
WORK-STUDY *Federal work-study:* Total amount: $1,108,003; 375 jobs averaging $2954. *State or other work-study/employment:* Total amount: $331,627 (100% need-based). 189 part-time jobs averaging $1754.
ATHLETIC AWARDS *Total amount:* $1,848,967 (100% non-need-based).
APPLYING FOR FINANCIAL AID *Required financial aid forms:* FAFSA, income tax forms, W-2 forms. *Financial aid deadline (priority):* 3/1. *Notification date:* Continuous beginning 4/1. Students must reply within 2 weeks of notification.
CONTACT Catherine Kay, Interim Director of Scholarships and Financial Aid, Wayne State University, 3W HNJ Student Services Building, Detroit, MI 48202, 313-577-3378 or toll-free 877-978 Ext. 4636. *Fax:* 313-577-6648.

WEBBER INTERNATIONAL UNIVERSITY
Babson Park, FL

Tuition & fees: $12,900   **Average undergraduate aid package: $11,467**

ABOUT THE INSTITUTION Independent, coed. Awards: associate, bachelor's, and master's degrees. 11 undergraduate majors. Total enrollment: 641. Undergraduates: 585. Freshmen: 135. Federal methodology is used as a basis for awarding need-based institutional aid.
UNDERGRADUATE EXPENSES for 2004–05 *Application fee:* $35. *Comprehensive fee:* $17,410 includes full-time tuition ($12,300), mandatory fees ($600), and room and board ($4510). Full-time tuition and fees vary according to class time. Room and board charges vary according to board plan. *Part-time tuition:* $160 per credit hour. Part-time tuition and fees vary according to course load. *Payment plan:* Installment.
FRESHMAN FINANCIAL AID (Fall 2004, est.) 85 applied for aid; of those 87% were deemed to have need. 100% of freshmen with need received aid; of those 19% had need fully met. *Average percent of need met:* 62% (excluding resources awarded to replace EFC). *Average financial aid package:* $10,851 (excluding resources awarded to replace EFC). 41% of all full-time freshmen had no need and received non-need-based gift aid.
UNDERGRADUATE FINANCIAL AID (Fall 2004, est.) 384 applied for aid; of those 88% were deemed to have need. 100% of undergraduates with need received aid; of those 21% had need fully met. *Average percent of need met:*

77% (excluding resources awarded to replace EFC). *Average financial aid package:* $11,467 (excluding resources awarded to replace EFC). 37% of all full-time undergraduates had no need and received non-need-based gift aid.

GIFT AID (NEED-BASED) *Total amount:* $1,849,139 (39% federal, 48% state, 11% institutional, 2% external sources). *Receiving aid:* Freshmen: 55% (74); All full-time undergraduates: 63% (338). *Average award:* Freshmen: $8504; Undergraduates: $8475. *Scholarships, grants, and awards:* Federal Pell, FSEOG, state, private, college/university gift aid from institutional funds.

GIFT AID (NON-NEED-BASED) *Total amount:* $569,938 (61% state, 29% institutional, 10% external sources). *Average Award:* Freshmen: $4637; Undergraduates: $4467. *Scholarships, grants, and awards by category:* *Academic Interests/Achievement:* 180 awards ($238,300 total): business, general academic interests/achievements. *Creative Arts/Performance:* 40 awards ($37,250 total): general creative arts/performance, journalism/publications. *Special Achievements/Activities:* 394 awards ($1,471,285 total): cheerleading/drum major, community service, general special achievements/activities, leadership, memberships. *Special Characteristics:* 118 awards ($242,932 total): children and siblings of alumni, children of faculty/staff, first-generation college students, general special characteristics, international students, local/state students, siblings of current students. *Tuition waivers:* Full or partial for children of alumni, employees or children of employees, adult students, senior citizens.

LOANS *Student loans:* $1,482,042 (85% need-based, 15% non-need-based). 61% of past graduating class borrowed through all loan programs. *Average indebtedness per student:* $16,051. *Average need-based loan:* Freshmen: $2556; Undergraduates: $3705. *Parent loans:* $371,708 (83% need-based, 17% non-need-based). *Programs:* FFEL (Subsidized and Unsubsidized Stafford, PLUS), Perkins, alternative loans.

WORK-STUDY *Federal work-study:* Total amount: $38,983; 65 jobs averaging $637. *State or other work-study/employment:* Total amount: $59,017 (33% need-based, 67% non-need-based). 46 part-time jobs averaging $725.

ATHLETIC AWARDS *Total amount:* $1,414,388 (58% need-based, 42% non-need-based).

APPLYING FOR FINANCIAL AID *Required financial aid forms:* FAFSA, state aid form. *Financial aid deadline:* 8/1 (priority: 5/1). *Notification date:* Continuous. Students must reply within 4 weeks of notification.

CONTACT Ms. Kathleen Wilson, Director of Financial Aid, Webber International University, PO Box 96, Babson Park, FL 33827-0096, 863-638-2930 or toll-free 800-741-1844. *Fax:* 863-638-1317. *E-mail:* wilson@webber.edu.

WEBB INSTITUTE
Glen Cove, NY

ABOUT THE INSTITUTION Independent, coed. Awards: bachelor's degrees. 1 undergraduate major. Total enrollment: 76. Undergraduates: 76. Freshmen: 25.

GIFT AID (NEED-BASED) *Scholarships, grants, and awards:* Federal Pell, private, college/university gift aid from institutional funds.

LOANS *Programs:* FFEL (Subsidized and Unsubsidized Stafford, PLUS).

APPLYING FOR FINANCIAL AID *Required financial aid form:* FAFSA.

CONTACT William G. Murray, Director of Financial Aid, Webb Institute, Crescent Beach Road, Glen Cove, NY 11542-1398, 516-671-2213. *Fax:* 516-674-9838. *E-mail:* bmurray@webb-institute.edu.

WEBER STATE UNIVERSITY
Ogden, UT

CONTACT Mr. Richard O. Effiong, Financial Aid Director, Weber State University, 120 Student Service Center, 1136 University Circle, Ogden, UT 84408-1136, 801-626-7569 or toll-free 800-634-6568 (in-state), 800-848-7770 (out-of-state). *E-mail:* finaid@weber.edu.

WEBSTER UNIVERSITY
St. Louis, MO

Tuition & fees: $16,250   **Average undergraduate aid package: $16,687**

ABOUT THE INSTITUTION Independent, coed. Awards: bachelor's, master's, and doctoral degrees and post-bachelor's and post-master's certificates. 65 undergraduate majors. Total enrollment: 7,424. Undergraduates: 3,580. Freshmen: 454. Federal methodology is used as a basis for awarding need-based institutional aid.

UNDERGRADUATE EXPENSES for 2004–05 *Application fee:* $25. *Comprehensive fee:* $22,860 includes full-time tuition ($16,250) and room and board ($6610). *College room only:* $3260. Full-time tuition and fees vary according to program. Room and board charges vary according to board plan and housing facility. *Part-time tuition:* $445 per credit hour. Part-time tuition and fees vary according to location. *Payment plan:* Installment.

GIFT AID (NEED-BASED) *Total amount:* $16,431,763 (15% federal, 8% state, 60% institutional, 17% external sources). *Receiving aid:* Freshmen: 65% (295); All full-time undergraduates: 61% (1,545). *Average award:* Freshmen: $4928; Undergraduates: $4864. *Scholarships, grants, and awards:* Federal Pell, FSEOG, state, private, college/university gift aid from institutional funds.

GIFT AID (NON-NEED-BASED) *Total amount:* $3,306,768 (3% state, 78% institutional, 19% external sources). *Receiving aid:* Freshmen: 59% (268); Undergraduates: 44% (1,107). *Average Award:* Freshmen: $9834; Undergraduates: $8594. *Scholarships, grants, and awards by category:* *Academic Interests/Achievement:* 1,424 awards ($7,129,657 total): education, general academic interests/achievements, humanities, international studies. *Creative Arts/Performance:* 80 awards ($92,000 total): art/fine arts, debating, music, theater/drama. *Special Achievements/Activities:* 60 awards ($90,000 total): leadership. *Tuition waivers:* Full or partial for employees or children of employees. *ROTC:* Army cooperative, Air Force cooperative.

LOANS *Student loans:* $13,491,384 (91% need-based, 9% non-need-based). 52% of past graduating class borrowed through all loan programs. *Average indebtedness per student:* $17,502. *Average need-based loan:* Freshmen: $2562; Undergraduates: $4117. *Parent loans:* $2,241,178 (79% need-based, 21% non-need-based). *Programs:* FFEL (Subsidized and Unsubsidized Stafford, PLUS), Perkins.

APPLYING FOR FINANCIAL AID *Required financial aid forms:* FAFSA, institution's own form. *Financial aid deadline (priority):* 4/1. *Notification date:* Continuous beginning 2/10. Students must reply within 2 weeks of notification.

CONTACT Marilynn Shelton, Financial Aid Counselor, Webster University, Financial Aid Office, 470 East Lockwood Avenue, St. Louis, MO 63119, 314-968-6992 Ext. 7671 or toll-free 800-75-ENROL. *Fax:* 314-968-7125. *E-mail:* sheltoma@webster.edu.

WELLESLEY COLLEGE
Wellesley, MA

Tuition & fees: $29,796   **Average undergraduate aid package: $26,673**

ABOUT THE INSTITUTION Independent, women only. Awards: bachelor's degrees (double bachelor's degree with Massachusetts Institute of Technology). 54 undergraduate majors. Total enrollment: 2,289. Undergraduates: 2,289. Freshmen: 617. Both federal and institutional methodology are used as a basis for awarding need-based institutional aid.

UNDERGRADUATE EXPENSES for 2004–05 *Application fee:* $50. *Comprehensive fee:* $38,998 includes full-time tuition ($29,176), mandatory fees ($620), and room and board ($9202). *College room only:* $4662. Room and board charges vary according to board plan. *Payment plans:* Tuition prepayment, installment.

FRESHMAN FINANCIAL AID (Fall 2004, est.) 432 applied for aid; of those 81% were deemed to have need. 100% of freshmen with need received aid; of those 100% had need fully met. *Average percent of need met:* 100% (excluding resources awarded to replace EFC). *Average financial aid package:* $26,118 (excluding resources awarded to replace EFC).

UNDERGRADUATE FINANCIAL AID (Fall 2004, est.) 1,492 applied for aid; of those 87% were deemed to have need. 100% of undergraduates with need received aid; of those 100% had need fully met. *Average percent of need met:* 100% (excluding resources awarded to replace EFC). *Average financial aid package:* $26,673 (excluding resources awarded to replace EFC).

GIFT AID (NEED-BASED) *Total amount:* $29,990,712 (5% federal, 1% state, 90% institutional, 4% external sources). *Receiving aid:* Freshmen: 55% (341); All full-time undergraduates: 57% (1,259). *Average award:* Freshmen: $24,015; Undergraduates: $23,821. *Scholarships, grants, and awards:* Federal Pell, FSEOG, state, private, college/university gift aid from institutional funds.

GIFT AID (NON-NEED-BASED) *Total amount:* $482,395 (100% external sources). *Tuition waivers:* Full or partial for employees or children of employees. *ROTC:* Army cooperative, Air Force cooperative.

LOANS *Student loans:* $4,406,586 (75% need-based, 25% non-need-based). 50% of past graduating class borrowed through all loan programs. *Average indebtedness per student:* $11,621. *Average need-based loan:* Freshmen: $2488; Undergraduates: $3097. *Parent loans:* $4,949,406 (100% non-need-based). *Programs:* FFEL (Subsidized and Unsubsidized Stafford, PLUS), Perkins, state, college/university.

WORK-STUDY *Federal work-study:* Total amount: $940,683; 815 jobs averaging $1154. *State or other work-study/employment:* Total amount: $329,233 (100% need-based). 206 part-time jobs averaging $1598.

APPLYING FOR FINANCIAL AID *Required financial aid forms:* FAFSA, institution's own form, CSS Financial Aid PROFILE, noncustodial (divorced/separated) parent's statement, business/farm supplement, federal income tax form(s), W-2 forms. *Financial aid deadline (priority):* 1/15. *Notification date:* 4/1. Students must reply by 5/1.

CONTACT Ms. Kathryn Osmond, Director of Financial Aid, Wellesley College, 106 Central Street, Wellesley, MA 02481-8203, 781-283-2360. *Fax:* 781-283-3946. *E-mail:* finaid@wellesley.edu.

WELLS COLLEGE
Aurora, NY

Tuition & fees: $14,900   **Average undergraduate aid package: $17,045**

ABOUT THE INSTITUTION Independent, coed, primarily women. Awards: bachelor's degrees. 40 undergraduate majors. Total enrollment: 390. Undergraduates: 390. Freshmen: 87. Federal methodology is used as a basis for awarding need-based institutional aid.

UNDERGRADUATE EXPENSES for 2004–05 *Application fee:* $40. *Comprehensive fee:* $21,900 includes full-time tuition ($14,000), mandatory fees ($900), and room and board ($7000). *College room only:* $3500. *Part-time tuition:* $585 per credit hour. *Part-time fees:* $100 per credit hour. *Payment plan:* Installment.

FRESHMAN FINANCIAL AID (Fall 2004, est.) 80 applied for aid; of those 82% were deemed to have need. 100% of freshmen with need received aid; of those 26% had need fully met. *Average percent of need met:* 93% (excluding resources awarded to replace EFC). *Average financial aid package:* $16,594 (excluding resources awarded to replace EFC). 13% of all full-time freshmen had no need and received non-need-based gift aid.

UNDERGRADUATE FINANCIAL AID (Fall 2004, est.) 319 applied for aid; of those 86% were deemed to have need. 100% of undergraduates with need received aid; of those 34% had need fully met. *Average percent of need met:* 92% (excluding resources awarded to replace EFC). *Average financial aid package:* $17,045 (excluding resources awarded to replace EFC). 15% of all full-time undergraduates had no need and received non-need-based gift aid.

GIFT AID (NEED-BASED) *Total amount:* $3,109,595 (18% federal, 17% state, 62% institutional, 3% external sources). *Receiving aid:* Freshmen: 73% (66); All full-time undergraduates: 72% (273). *Average award:* Freshmen: $12,595; Undergraduates: $11,390. *Scholarships, grants, and awards:* Federal Pell, FSEOG, state, private, college/university gift aid from institutional funds.

GIFT AID (NON-NEED-BASED) *Total amount:* $329,779 (4% state, 81% institutional, 15% external sources). *Average Award:* Freshmen: $4750; Undergraduates: $4764. *Scholarships, grants, and awards by category:* Academic Interests/Achievement: 46 awards ($137,432 total): general academic interests/achievements. *Special Achievements/Activities:* 74 awards ($370,000 total): leadership. *Special Characteristics:* 6 awards ($15,000 total): children and siblings of alumni. *Tuition waivers:* Full or partial for children of alumni, employees or children of employees, senior citizens. *ROTC:* Air Force cooperative.

LOANS *Student loans:* $1,528,993 (78% need-based, 22% non-need-based). 90% of past graduating class borrowed through all loan programs. *Average indebtedness per student:* $17,125. *Average need-based loan:* Freshmen: $2626; Undergraduates: $4335. *Parent loans:* $397,371 (100% non-need-based). *Programs:* FFEL (Subsidized and Unsubsidized Stafford, PLUS), Perkins.

WORK-STUDY *Federal work-study:* Total amount: $110,000; 78 jobs averaging $1400. *State or other work-study/employment:* Total amount: $319,406 (82% need-based, 18% non-need-based). 222 part-time jobs averaging $1400.

APPLYING FOR FINANCIAL AID *Required financial aid form:* FAFSA. *Financial aid deadline (priority):* 2/15. *Notification date:* 3/1. Students must reply by 5/1.

CONTACT Ms. Cathleen A. Bellomo, Director of Financial Aid, Wells College, Route 90, Aurora, NY 13026, 315-364-3289 or toll-free 800-952-9355. *Fax:* 315-364-3227. *E-mail:* cbellomo@henry.wells.edu.

WENTWORTH INSTITUTE OF TECHNOLOGY
Boston, MA

Tuition & fees: $18,500   **Average undergraduate aid package: $7625**

ABOUT THE INSTITUTION Independent, coed. Awards: associate and bachelor's degrees. 21 undergraduate majors. Total enrollment: 3,597. Undergraduates: 3,597. Freshmen: 858. Federal methodology is used as a basis for awarding need-based institutional aid.

UNDERGRADUATE EXPENSES for 2005–06 *Application fee:* $30. *Comprehensive fee:* $27,500 includes full-time tuition ($18,500) and room and board ($9000). *Payment plan:* Installment.

FRESHMAN FINANCIAL AID (Fall 2004, est.) 852 applied for aid; of those 67% were deemed to have need. 100% of freshmen with need received aid; of those 4% had need fully met. *Average percent of need met:* 40% (excluding resources awarded to replace EFC). *Average financial aid package:* $8443 (excluding resources awarded to replace EFC). 19% of all full-time freshmen had no need and received non-need-based gift aid.

UNDERGRADUATE FINANCIAL AID (Fall 2004, est.) 3,192 applied for aid; of those 42% were deemed to have need. 100% of undergraduates with need received aid; of those 5% had need fully met. *Average percent of need met:* 46% (excluding resources awarded to replace EFC). *Average financial aid package:* $7625 (excluding resources awarded to replace EFC). 13% of all full-time undergraduates had no need and received non-need-based gift aid.

GIFT AID (NEED-BASED) *Total amount:* $4,240,713 (49% federal, 18% state, 15% institutional, 18% external sources). *Receiving aid:* Freshmen: 23% (195); All full-time undergraduates: 13% (412). *Average award:* Freshmen: $2163; Undergraduates: $2163. *Scholarships, grants, and awards:* Federal Pell, FSEOG, state, private, college/university gift aid from institutional funds.

GIFT AID (NON-NEED-BASED) *Total amount:* $8,387,446 (100% institutional). *Receiving aid:* Freshmen: 62% (528); Undergraduates: 3% (82). *Average Award:* Freshmen: $3657; Undergraduates: $3657. *Tuition waivers:* Full or partial for employees or children of employees. *ROTC:* Army cooperative, Air Force cooperative.

LOANS *Student loans:* $20,807,211 (38% need-based, 62% non-need-based). 80% of past graduating class borrowed through all loan programs. *Average indebtedness per student:* $20,928. *Average need-based loan:* Freshmen: $3076; Undergraduates: $4156. *Parent loans:* $3,634,699 (100% non-need-based). *Programs:* Federal Direct (Subsidized and Unsubsidized Stafford, PLUS), Perkins, state.

WORK-STUDY *Federal work-study:* Total amount: $1,281,374; 800 jobs averaging $1600.

APPLYING FOR FINANCIAL AID *Required financial aid forms:* FAFSA, state aid form. *Financial aid deadline (priority):* 3/1. *Notification date:* Continuous beginning 3/15. Students must reply within 2 weeks of notification.

CONTACT Traci Cady, Director of Financial Aid, Wentworth Institute of Technology, 550 Huntington Avenue, Boston, MA 02115-5998, 617-989-4037 or toll-free 800-556-0610. *Fax:* 617-989-4201.

WESLEYAN COLLEGE
Macon, GA

ABOUT THE INSTITUTION Independent United Methodist, women only. Awards: bachelor's and master's degrees. 30 undergraduate majors. Total enrollment: 639. Undergraduates: 567. Freshmen: 75.

GIFT AID (NEED-BASED) *Scholarships, grants, and awards:* Federal Pell, FSEOG, state, private, college/university gift aid from institutional funds.

GIFT AID (NON-NEED-BASED) *Scholarships, grants, and awards by category:* Academic Interests/Achievement: biological sciences, business, communication, education, English, foreign languages, general academic interests/achievements, humanities, mathematics, premedicine, religion/biblical studies, social sciences. Creative Arts/Performance: art/fine arts, music, theater/drama. Special Achievements/Activities: community service, general special achievements/activities, leadership, religious involvement. Special Characteristics: adult students, children and siblings of alumni, children of current students, children of faculty/staff, ethnic background, first-generation college students, general special characteristics, handicapped students, international students, out-of-state students, parents of current students, relatives of clergy, religious affiliation, siblings of current students, spouses of current students.

LOANS *Programs:* FFEL (Subsidized and Unsubsidized Stafford, PLUS), Perkins, college/university, CitiAssist Loans, TERI Loans.

WORK-STUDY *Federal work-study:* Total amount: $69,412; 97 jobs averaging $1200. *State or other work-study/employment:* Total amount: $181,622 (1% need-based, 99% non-need-based). 147 part-time jobs averaging $1200.

APPLYING FOR FINANCIAL AID *Required financial aid forms:* FAFSA, institution's own form, state aid form, noncustodial (divorced/separated) parent's statement.

CONTACT Sylvia M. Jones, Director of Financial Aid, Wesleyan College, 4760 Forsyth Road, Macon, GA 31210-4462, 478-757-5161 or toll-free 800-447-6610. *Fax:* 478-757-4030. *E-mail:* sjones@wesleyancollege.edu.

WESLEYAN UNIVERSITY
Middletown, CT

Tuition & fees: $31,670	Average undergraduate aid package: $27,667

ABOUT THE INSTITUTION Independent, coed. Awards: bachelor's, master's, and doctoral degrees and post-master's certificates. 46 undergraduate majors. Total enrollment: 3,217. Undergraduates: 2,777. Freshmen: 728. Both federal and institutional methodology are used as a basis for awarding need-based institutional aid.

UNDERGRADUATE EXPENSES for 2004–05 *Application fee:* $55. *One-time required fee:* $300. *Comprehensive fee:* $40,144 includes full-time tuition ($31,456), mandatory fees ($214), and room and board ($8474). *College room only:* $5132.

FRESHMAN FINANCIAL AID (Fall 2003) 395 applied for aid; of those 87% were deemed to have need. 100% of freshmen with need received aid; of those 100% had need fully met. *Average percent of need met:* 100% (excluding resources awarded to replace EFC). *Average financial aid package:* $27,948 (excluding resources awarded to replace EFC).

UNDERGRADUATE FINANCIAL AID (Fall 2003) 1,465 applied for aid; of those 91% were deemed to have need. 100% of undergraduates with need received aid; of those 100% had need fully met. *Average percent of need met:* 100% (excluding resources awarded to replace EFC). *Average financial aid package:* $27,667 (excluding resources awarded to replace EFC).

GIFT AID (NEED-BASED) *Total amount:* $28,641,118 (6% federal, 2% state, 88% institutional, 4% external sources). *Receiving aid:* Freshmen: 45% (327); All full-time undergraduates: 45% (1,251). *Average award:* Freshmen: $23,654; Undergraduates: $21,443. *Scholarships, grants, and awards:* Federal Pell, FSEOG, state, private, college/university gift aid from institutional funds.

GIFT AID (NON-NEED-BASED) *ROTC:* Air Force cooperative.

LOANS *Student loans:* $5,896,126 (100% need-based). 43% of past graduating class borrowed through all loan programs. *Average indebtedness per student:* $21,320. *Average need-based loan:* Freshmen: $2466; Undergraduates: $4427. *Programs:* FFEL (Subsidized and Unsubsidized Stafford, PLUS), Perkins, college/university.

WORK-STUDY *Federal work-study:* 1,014 jobs averaging $1808. *State or other work-study/employment:* Total amount: $2,223,350 (100% need-based). 223 part-time jobs averaging $1747.

APPLYING FOR FINANCIAL AID *Required financial aid forms:* FAFSA, CSS Financial Aid PROFILE, noncustodial (divorced/separated) parent's statement, business/farm supplement. *Financial aid deadline:* 2/1. *Notification date:* 4/1. Students must reply by 5/1 or within 2 weeks of notification.

CONTACT Ms. Karen Hook, Associate Director of Financial Aid, Wesleyan University, 237 High Street, Middletown, CT 06459-0260, 860-685-2800. *Fax:* 860-685-2801. *E-mail:* finaid@wesleyan.edu.

WESLEY COLLEGE
Dover, DE

Tuition & fees: $15,379	Average undergraduate aid package: $13,725

ABOUT THE INSTITUTION Independent United Methodist, coed. Awards: associate, bachelor's, and master's degrees and post-bachelor's and post-master's certificates. 18 undergraduate majors. Total enrollment: 2,037. Undergraduates: 1,901. Freshmen: 487. Federal methodology is used as a basis for awarding need-based institutional aid.

UNDERGRADUATE EXPENSES for 2004–05 *Application fee:* $25. *Comprehensive fee:* $22,339 includes full-time tuition ($14,600), mandatory fees ($779), and room and board ($6960). Full-time tuition and fees vary according to class time. Room and board charges vary according to board plan and housing facility. *Part-time tuition:* $529 per credit hour. *Payment plan:* Installment.

FRESHMAN FINANCIAL AID (Fall 2004, est.) 466 applied for aid; of those 83% were deemed to have need. 100% of freshmen with need received aid. *Average percent of need met:* 85% (excluding resources awarded to replace EFC). *Average financial aid package:* $14,000 (excluding resources awarded to replace EFC). 39% of all full-time freshmen had no need and received non-need-based gift aid.

UNDERGRADUATE FINANCIAL AID (Fall 2004, est.) 1,501 applied for aid; of those 91% were deemed to have need. 100% of undergraduates with need received aid. *Average percent of need met:* 80% (excluding resources awarded to replace EFC). *Average financial aid package:* $13,725 (excluding resources awarded to replace EFC). 27% of all full-time undergraduates had no need and received non-need-based gift aid.

GIFT AID (NEED-BASED) *Total amount:* $2,683,188 (41% federal, 6% state, 53% institutional). *Receiving aid:* Freshmen: 63% (305); All full-time undergraduates: 73% (1,133). *Average award:* Freshmen: $5500; Undergraduates: $5000. *Scholarships, grants, and awards:* Federal Pell, FSEOG, state, private, college/university gift aid from institutional funds.

GIFT AID (NON-NEED-BASED) *Total amount:* $4,561,659 (95% institutional, 5% external sources). *Receiving aid:* Freshmen: 37% (178); Undergraduates: 63% (974). *Average Award:* Freshmen: $2000; Undergraduates: $4500. *Scholarships, grants, and awards by category: Academic Interests/Achievement:* general academic interests/achievements. *Special Achievements/Activities:* community service, general special achievements/activities, leadership, religious involvement. *Tuition waivers:* Full or partial for employees or children of employees, senior citizens. *ROTC:* Army cooperative.

LOANS *Student loans:* $2,739,549 (100% need-based). 90% of past graduating class borrowed through all loan programs. *Average indebtedness per student:* $11,500. *Average need-based loan:* Freshmen: $2200; Undergraduates: $4250. *Parent loans:* $2,395,472 (30% need-based, 70% non-need-based). *Programs:* Federal Direct (Subsidized and Unsubsidized Stafford, PLUS), FFEL (Subsidized and Unsubsidized Stafford, PLUS), Perkins, state, college/university.

WORK-STUDY *Federal work-study:* Total amount: $128,700; 225 jobs averaging $2200. *State or other work-study/employment:* Part-time jobs available.

APPLYING FOR FINANCIAL AID *Required financial aid forms:* FAFSA, institution's own form. *Financial aid deadline (priority):* 4/15. *Notification date:* Continuous. Students must reply within 2 weeks of notification.

CONTACT James Marks, Director of Student Financial Planning, Wesley College, 120 North State Street, Dover, DE 19901-3875, 302-736-2334 or toll-free 800-937-5398 Ext. 2400 (out-of-state). *Fax:* 302-736-2594. *E-mail:* marksja@wesley.edu.

WESLEY COLLEGE
Florence, MS

Tuition & fees: $5100	Average undergraduate aid package: N/A

ABOUT THE INSTITUTION Independent Congregational Methodist, coed. Awards: bachelor's degrees. 2 undergraduate majors. Total enrollment: 80. Undergraduates: 80. Freshmen: 19. Federal methodology is used as a basis for awarding need-based institutional aid.

UNDERGRADUATE EXPENSES for 2004–05 *Application fee:* $20. *Comprehensive fee:* $8060 includes full-time tuition ($4600), mandatory fees ($500), and room and board ($2960). *College room only:* $900. *Part-time tuition:* $200 per credit hour.

GIFT AID (NEED-BASED) *Total amount:* $131,855 (95% federal, 2% state, 3% institutional). *Scholarships, grants, and awards:* Federal Pell, FSEOG, state, college/university gift aid from institutional funds.

GIFT AID (NON-NEED-BASED) *Total amount:* $16,900 (29% institutional, 71% external sources). *Scholarships, grants, and awards by category: Academic Interests/Achievement:* 2 awards ($2450 total): general academic interests/achievements. *Special Achievements/Activities:* 14 awards ($270 total): religious involvement.

LOANS *Student loans:* $195,645 (64% need-based, 36% non-need-based). 85% of past graduating class borrowed through all loan programs. *Parent loans:* $38,500 (100% need-based). *Programs:* Federal Direct (Subsidized and Unsubsidized Stafford, PLUS).

WORK-STUDY *Federal work-study:* Total amount: $25,296; 10 jobs averaging $2500.

APPLYING FOR FINANCIAL AID *Required financial aid form:* FAFSA. *Financial aid deadline (priority):* 8/20. *Notification date:* Continuous beginning 5/1. Students must reply within 2 weeks of notification.

CONTACT Director of Financial Aid, Wesley College, PO Box 1070, Florence, MS 39073-1070, 601-845-4086 or toll-free 800-748-9972. *Fax:* 601-845-2266.

WEST CHESTER UNIVERSITY OF PENNSYLVANIA
West Chester, PA

ABOUT THE INSTITUTION State-supported, coed. Awards: bachelor's and master's degrees and post-bachelor's certificates. 76 undergraduate majors. Total enrollment: 12,822. Undergraduates: 10,644. Freshmen: 1,879.

GIFT AID (NEED-BASED) *Scholarships, grants, and awards:* Federal Pell, FSEOG, state, college/university gift aid from institutional funds.

GIFT AID (NON-NEED-BASED) *Scholarships, grants, and awards by category: Academic Interests/Achievement:* business, general academic interests/achievements, mathematics, social sciences. *Creative Arts/Performance:* music, theater/drama. *Special Characteristics:* children of faculty/staff.

LOANS *Programs:* FFEL (Subsidized and Unsubsidized Stafford, PLUS), Perkins, Federal Nursing.

WORK-STUDY Federal work-study jobs available. *State or other work-study/ employment:* Part-time jobs available.

APPLYING FOR FINANCIAL AID *Required financial aid form:* FAFSA.

CONTACT Financial Aid Office, West Chester University of Pennsylvania, 138 E.O. Bull Center, West Chester, PA 19383, 610-436-2627 or toll-free 877-315-2165 (in-state). *Fax:* 610-436-2574.

WESTERN BAPTIST COLLEGE
Salem, OR

See Corban College.

WESTERN CAROLINA UNIVERSITY
Cullowhee, NC

Tuition & fees (NC res): $3449	Average undergraduate aid package: $7904

ABOUT THE INSTITUTION State-supported, coed. Awards: bachelor's, master's, and doctoral degrees and post-master's certificates. 66 undergraduate majors. Total enrollment: 8,396. Undergraduates: 6,785. Freshmen: 1,578. Federal methodology is used as a basis for awarding need-based institutional aid.

UNDERGRADUATE EXPENSES for 2004–05 *Application fee:* $40. *Tuition, state resident:* full-time $1651. *Tuition, nonresident:* full-time $11,087. Part-time tuition and fees vary according to course load. *College room and board:* $4028; *room only:* $2128. Room and board charges vary according to board plan and housing facility. *Payment plan:* Installment.

FRESHMAN FINANCIAL AID (Fall 2004, est.) 1109 applied for aid; of those 67% were deemed to have need. 100% of freshmen with need received aid; of those 71% had need fully met. *Average percent of need met:* 78% (excluding resources awarded to replace EFC). *Average financial aid package:* $6331 (excluding resources awarded to replace EFC). 14% of all full-time freshmen had no need and received non-need-based gift aid.

UNDERGRADUATE FINANCIAL AID (Fall 2004, est.) 3,964 applied for aid; of those 75% were deemed to have need. 99% of undergraduates with need received aid; of those 63% had need fully met. *Average percent of need met:* 76% (excluding resources awarded to replace EFC). *Average financial aid package:* $7904 (excluding resources awarded to replace EFC). 14% of all full-time undergraduates had no need and received non-need-based gift aid.

GIFT AID (NEED-BASED) *Total amount:* $11,010,317 (56% federal, 30% state, 9% institutional, 5% external sources). *Receiving aid:* Freshmen: 46% (730); All full-time undergraduates: 49% (2,849). *Average award:* Freshmen: $3751; Undergraduates: $4149. *Scholarships, grants, and awards:* Federal Pell, FSEOG, state, private, college/university gift aid from institutional funds.

GIFT AID (NON-NEED-BASED) *Total amount:* $2,940,110 (35% state, 36% institutional, 29% external sources). *Receiving aid:* Freshmen: 2% (27); Undergraduates: 3% (171). *Average Award:* Freshmen: $2245; Undergraduates: $2576. *Scholarships, grants, and awards by category: Academic Interests/ Achievement:* 671 awards ($969,037 total): biological sciences, business, communication, education, English, general academic interests/achievements, health fields, mathematics, social sciences. *Creative Arts/Performance:* 197 awards ($74,119 total): art/fine arts, music, theater/drama. *Special Characteristics:* 87 awards ($108,037 total): ethnic background, handicapped students, local/state students, members of minority groups. *Tuition waivers:* Full or partial for employees or children of employees, senior citizens.

LOANS *Student loans:* $17,990,498 (77% need-based, 23% non-need-based). 48% of past graduating class borrowed through all loan programs. *Average indebtedness per student:* $15,964. *Average need-based loan:* Freshmen: $1967; Undergraduates: $3421. *Parent loans:* $6,040,066 (54% need-based, 46% non-need-based). *Programs:* Federal Direct (Subsidized and Unsubsidized Stafford, PLUS), Perkins.

WORK-STUDY *Federal work-study:* Total amount: $469,000; 335 jobs averaging $1378.

ATHLETIC AWARDS *Total amount:* $1,678,945 (44% need-based, 56% non-need-based).

APPLYING FOR FINANCIAL AID *Required financial aid forms:* FAFSA, institution's own form. *Financial aid deadline (priority):* 3/31. *Notification date:* Continuous beginning 4/1.

CONTACT Ms. Nancy B. Dillard, Director of Financial Aid, Western Carolina University, 224 Killian Annex, Cullowhee, NC 28723, 828-227-7292 or toll-free 877-WCU4YOU. *Fax:* 828-227-7042. *E-mail:* dillard@wcu.edu.

WESTERN CONNECTICUT STATE UNIVERSITY
Danbury, CT

Tuition & fees (CT res): $5661	Average undergraduate aid package: $6712

ABOUT THE INSTITUTION State-supported, coed. Awards: associate, bachelor's, master's, and doctoral degrees. 40 undergraduate majors. Total enrollment: 5,884. Undergraduates: 5,137. Freshmen: 855. Federal methodology is used as a basis for awarding need-based institutional aid.

UNDERGRADUATE EXPENSES for 2004–05 *Application fee:* $40. *Tuition, state resident:* full-time $3010; part-time $287 per semester hour. *Tuition, nonresident:* full-time $9744; part-time $287 per semester hour. *Required fees:* full-time $2651; $60 per term part-time. Full-time tuition and fees vary according to reciprocity agreements. *College room and board:* $6582; *room only:* $5112. Room and board charges vary according to housing facility. *Payment plan:* Installment.

FRESHMAN FINANCIAL AID (Fall 2003) 594 applied for aid; of those 66% were deemed to have need. 94% of freshmen with need received aid; of those 33% had need fully met. *Average percent of need met:* 71% (excluding resources awarded to replace EFC). *Average financial aid package:* $6517 (excluding resources awarded to replace EFC). 1% of all full-time freshmen had no need and received non-need-based gift aid.

UNDERGRADUATE FINANCIAL AID (Fall 2003) 2,432 applied for aid; of those 67% were deemed to have need. 91% of undergraduates with need received aid; of those 25% had need fully met. *Average percent of need met:* 65% (excluding resources awarded to replace EFC). *Average financial aid package:* $6712 (excluding resources awarded to replace EFC). 1% of all full-time undergraduates had no need and received non-need-based gift aid.

GIFT AID (NEED-BASED) *Total amount:* $4,505,526 (41% federal, 59% state). *Receiving aid:* Freshmen: 34% (277); All full-time undergraduates: 31% (1,165). *Average award:* Freshmen: $4343; Undergraduates: $3691. *Scholarships, grants, and awards:* Federal Pell, FSEOG, state, private, college/university gift aid from institutional funds.

GIFT AID (NON-NEED-BASED) *Total amount:* $668,665 (35% institutional, 65% external sources). *Receiving aid:* Freshmen: 1% (8); Undergraduates: 1% (56). *Average Award:* Freshmen: $4237; Undergraduates: $4663. *Scholarships, grants, and awards by category: Academic Interests/Achievement:* 45 awards ($170,015 total): general academic interests/achievements. *Tuition waivers:* Full or partial for employees or children of employees, senior citizens. *ROTC:* Army cooperative, Air Force cooperative.

LOANS *Student loans:* $9,569,817 (62% need-based, 38% non-need-based). 47% of past graduating class borrowed through all loan programs. *Average indebtedness per student:* $6005. *Average need-based loan:* Freshmen: $3478; Undergraduates: $4155. *Parent loans:* $1,207,488 (100% non-need-based). *Programs:* FFEL (Subsidized and Unsubsidized Stafford, PLUS), Perkins.

WORK-STUDY *Federal work-study:* Total amount: $111,562; 78 jobs averaging $1180. *State or other work-study/employment:* Total amount: $1,153,122 (2% need-based, 98% non-need-based). 417 part-time jobs averaging $2273.

APPLYING FOR FINANCIAL AID *Required financial aid forms:* FAFSA, institution's own form. *Financial aid deadline:* 4/15 (priority: 3/15). *Notification date:* Continuous. Students must reply by 5/1 or within 2 weeks of notification.

CONTACT Nancy Barton, Director of Financial Aid, Western Connecticut State University, 181 White Street, Danbury, CT 06810-6860, 203-837-8580 or toll-free 877-837-9278. *Fax:* 203-837-8528. *E-mail:* bartonn@wcsu.edu.

WESTERN GOVERNORS UNIVERSITY
Salt Lake City, UT

CONTACT Stacey Ludwig-Hardman, Director of Academic Services, Western Governors University, 2040 East Murray Holladay Road, Suite #106, Salt Lake City, UT 84117, 801-274-3280 or toll-free 877-435-7948. *Fax:* 801-274-3305. *E-mail:* shardman@wgu.edu.

WESTERN ILLINOIS UNIVERSITY
Macomb, IL

Tuition & fees (IL res): $6183	Average undergraduate aid package: $7659

ABOUT THE INSTITUTION State-supported, coed. Awards: bachelor's and master's degrees and post-bachelor's and post-master's certificates. 53 undergraduate majors. Total enrollment: 13,558. Undergraduates: 11,310. Freshmen: 2,085. Federal methodology is used as a basis for awarding need-based institutional aid.

UNDERGRADUATE EXPENSES for 2004–05 *Application fee:* $30. *Tuition, state resident:* full-time $4537; part-time $151.25 per semester hour. *Tuition, nonresident:* full-time $9075; part-time $302.50 per semester hour. *Required fees:* full-time $1646; $38.59 per semester hour. Full-time tuition and fees vary according to location. Part-time tuition and fees vary according to location. *College room and board:* $5768; *room only:* $3428. Room and board charges vary according to housing facility. *Payment plan:* Guaranteed tuition.

FRESHMAN FINANCIAL AID (Fall 2004, est.) 1460 applied for aid; of those 73% were deemed to have need. 95% of freshmen with need received aid; of those 32% had need fully met. *Average percent of need met:* 62% (excluding resources awarded to replace EFC). *Average financial aid package:* $6168 (excluding resources awarded to replace EFC). 4% of all full-time freshmen had no need and received non-need-based gift aid.

UNDERGRADUATE FINANCIAL AID (Fall 2004, est.) 7,153 applied for aid; of those 95% were deemed to have need. 97% of undergraduates with need received aid; of those 32% had need fully met. *Average percent of need met:* 67% (excluding resources awarded to replace EFC). *Average financial aid package:* $7659 (excluding resources awarded to replace EFC). 5% of all full-time undergraduates had no need and received non-need-based gift aid.

GIFT AID (NEED-BASED) *Total amount:* $23,664,744 (44% federal, 47% state, 6% institutional, 3% external sources). *Receiving aid:* Freshmen: 33% (685); All full-time undergraduates: 39% (3,973). *Average award:* Freshmen: $4886; Undergraduates: $4889. *Scholarships, grants, and awards:* Federal Pell, FSEOG, state, private, college/university gift aid from institutional funds.

GIFT AID (NON-NEED-BASED) *Total amount:* $3,387,741 (32% federal, 26% state, 34% institutional, 8% external sources). *Average Award:* Freshmen: $2722; *Undergraduates:* $2138. *Scholarships, grants, and awards by category: Academic Interests/Achievement:* 1,928 awards ($1,286,792 total): agriculture, biological sciences, business, education, foreign languages, general academic interests/achievements, home economics, mathematics, physical sciences, social sciences. *Creative Arts/Performance:* 475 awards ($414,109 total): applied art and design, cinema/film/broadcasting, dance, debating, journalism/publications, music, performing arts, theater/drama. *Special Achievements/Activities:* 299 awards ($153,589 total): community service, leadership. *Special Characteristics:* 1,084 awards ($1,520,145 total): children of faculty/staff, general special characteristics, international students, members of minority groups, veterans' children. *Tuition waivers:* Full or partial for employees or children of employees, senior citizens. *ROTC:* Army.

LOANS *Student loans:* $32,588,123 (65% need-based, 35% non-need-based). 66% of past graduating class borrowed through all loan programs. *Average indebtedness per student:* $13,900. *Average need-based loan:* Freshmen: $2480; Undergraduates: $3540. *Parent loans:* $7,239,134 (69% need-based, 31% non-need-based). *Programs:* FFEL (Subsidized and Unsubsidized Stafford, PLUS), Perkins, college/university.

WORK-STUDY *Federal work-study:* Total amount: $343,109; 184 jobs averaging $1865. *State or other work-study/employment:* Total amount: $1,468,535 (68% need-based, 32% non-need-based). 1,761 part-time jobs averaging $834.

ATHLETIC AWARDS *Total amount:* $1,752,191 (43% need-based, 57% non-need-based).

APPLYING FOR FINANCIAL AID *Required financial aid form:* FAFSA. *Financial aid deadline (priority):* 2/15. *Notification date:* Continuous.

CONTACT Financial Aid Office, Western Illinois University, 1 University Circle, 127 Sherman Hall, Macomb, IL 61455-1390, 309-298-2446 or toll-free 877-742-5948. *Fax:* 309-298-2353. *E-mail:* financial_aid@doss.wiu.edu.

WESTERN KENTUCKY UNIVERSITY
Bowling Green, KY

Tuition & fees (KY res): $5391	Average undergraduate aid package: $6955

ABOUT THE INSTITUTION State-supported, coed. Awards: associate, bachelor's, and master's degrees and post-bachelor's, post-master's, and first professional certificates. 85 undergraduate majors. Total enrollment: 18,485. Undergraduates: 15,818. Freshmen: 2,983. Federal methodology is used as a basis for awarding need-based institutional aid.

UNDERGRADUATE EXPENSES for 2005–06 *Application fee:* $35. *Tuition, state resident:* full-time $5391; part-time $217 per hour. *Tuition, nonresident:* full-time $13,167; part-time $529 per hour. Full-time tuition and fees vary according to course load, location, program, and reciprocity agreements. Part-time tuition and fees vary according to course load, location, program, and reciprocity agreements. *College room and board:* $4778; *room only:* $2600. Room and board charges vary according to board plan and housing facility. *Payment plans:* Tuition prepayment, installment.

FRESHMAN FINANCIAL AID (Fall 2003) 2251 applied for aid; of those 71% were deemed to have need. 99% of freshmen with need received aid; of those 31% had need fully met. *Average percent of need met:* 31% (excluding resources awarded to replace EFC). *Average financial aid package:* $6308 (excluding resources awarded to replace EFC). 36% of all full-time freshmen had no need and received non-need-based gift aid.

UNDERGRADUATE FINANCIAL AID (Fall 2003) 9,077 applied for aid; of those 75% were deemed to have need. 98% of undergraduates with need received aid; of those 36% had need fully met. *Average percent of need met:* 36% (excluding resources awarded to replace EFC). *Average financial aid package:* $6955 (excluding resources awarded to replace EFC). 31% of all full-time undergraduates had no need and received non-need-based gift aid.

GIFT AID (NEED-BASED) *Total amount:* $17,287,525 (77% federal, 23% state). *Receiving aid:* Freshmen: 33% (976); All full-time undergraduates: 34% (4,333). *Average award:* Freshmen: $3541; Undergraduates: $3555. *Scholarships, grants, and awards:* Federal Pell, FSEOG, state, private, college/university gift aid from institutional funds, United Negro College Fund.

GIFT AID (NON-NEED-BASED) *Total amount:* $16,672,905 (11% federal, 46% state, 30% institutional, 13% external sources). *Receiving aid:* Freshmen: 42% (1,248); Undergraduates: 27% (3,500). *Average Award:* Freshmen: $2783; *Undergraduates:* $3025. *Scholarships, grants, and awards by category: Academic Interests/Achievement:* 1,377 awards ($3,749,061 total): agriculture, biological sciences, business, communication, education, engineering/technologies, English, foreign languages, general academic interests/achievements, health fields, home economics, library science, mathematics, military science, physical sciences, premedicine, religion/biblical studies, social sciences. *Creative Arts/Performance:* 247 awards ($288,225 total): art/fine arts, cinema/film/broadcasting, dance, debating, general creative arts/performance, journalism/publications, music, theater/drama. *Special Achievements/Activities:* 53 awards ($78,802 total): general special achievements/activities, leadership, memberships. *Special Characteristics:* 1,134 awards ($1,769,133 total): adult students, children and siblings of alumni, children of public servants, children of union members/company employees, ethnic background, general special characteristics, handicapped students, international students, local/state students, members of minority groups, out-of-state students, religious affiliation, veterans, veterans' children. *Tuition waivers:* Full or partial for employees or children of employees, senior citizens. *ROTC:* Army, Air Force cooperative.

LOANS *Student loans:* $27,359,975 (57% need-based, 43% non-need-based). 52% of past graduating class borrowed through all loan programs. *Average indebtedness per student:* $12,250. *Average need-based loan:* Freshmen: $2255; Undergraduates: $3127. *Parent loans:* $2,607,352 (100% non-need-based). *Programs:* FFEL (Subsidized and Unsubsidized Stafford, PLUS), Perkins, college/university, alternative loans.

WORK-STUDY *Federal work-study:* Total amount: $1,058,913; 729 jobs averaging $1453. *State or other work-study/employment:* Total amount: $3,150,990 (100% non-need-based). 1,469 part-time jobs averaging $1728.

ATHLETIC AWARDS *Total amount:* $2,011,714 (100% non-need-based).

APPLYING FOR FINANCIAL AID *Required financial aid form:* FAFSA. *Financial aid deadline (priority):* 4/1. *Notification date:* Continuous beginning 3/1.

CONTACT Cindy Burnette, Student Financial Assistance Director, Western Kentucky University, Potter Hall, Room 317, 1 Big Red Way, Bowling Green, KY 42101-3576, 270-745-2758 or toll-free 800-495-8463 (in-state). *Fax:* 270-745-6586. *E-mail:* cindy.burnette@wku.edu.

WESTERN MICHIGAN UNIVERSITY
Kalamazoo, MI

ABOUT THE INSTITUTION State-supported, coed. Awards: bachelor's, master's, and doctoral degrees and post-master's certificates. 149 undergraduate majors. Total enrollment: 27,829. Undergraduates: 22,502. Freshmen: 3,761.

GIFT AID (NEED-BASED) *Scholarships, grants, and awards:* Federal Pell, FSEOG, state, private, college/university gift aid from institutional funds.

GIFT AID (NON-NEED-BASED) *Scholarships, grants, and awards by category:* *Academic Interests/Achievement:* biological sciences, business, education, engineering/technologies, English, foreign languages, general academic interests/achievements, health fields, humanities, international studies, mathematics, military science, physical sciences, social sciences. *Creative Arts/Performance:* applied art and design, art/fine arts, dance, music, performing arts, theater/drama. *Special Achievements/Activities:* community service, general special achievements/activities, leadership, memberships. *Special Characteristics:* general special characteristics.

LOANS *Programs:* Federal Direct (Subsidized and Unsubsidized Stafford, PLUS), Perkins, alternative loans.

WORK-STUDY *Federal work-study:* Total amount: $750,000; jobs available. *State or other work-study/employment:* Total amount: $9,400,000 (5% need-based, 95% non-need-based). Part-time jobs available.

APPLYING FOR FINANCIAL AID *Required financial aid form:* FAFSA.

CONTACT Mr. David Ladd, Associate Director of Student Financial Aid, Western Michigan University, 1903 West Michigan Avenue, Faunce Student Services Building, Room 3306, Kalamazoo, MI 49008-5337, 269-387-6000 or toll-free 800-400-4968 (in-state). *E-mail:* david.ladd@wmich.edu.

WESTERN NEW ENGLAND COLLEGE
Springfield, MA

Tuition & fees: $21,986	Average undergraduate aid package: $13,198

ABOUT THE INSTITUTION Independent, coed. Awards: associate, bachelor's, master's, and first professional degrees. 28 undergraduate majors. Total enrollment: 4,025. Undergraduates: 3,038. Freshmen: 813. Federal methodology is used as a basis for awarding need-based institutional aid.

UNDERGRADUATE EXPENSES for 2004–05 *Application fee:* $50. *Comprehensive fee:* $30,510 includes full-time tuition ($20,570), mandatory fees ($1416), and room and board ($8524). Full-time tuition and fees vary according to program and student level. Room and board charges vary according to board plan and housing facility. *Part-time tuition:* $421 per credit hour. *Part-time fees:* $20 per term. Part-time tuition and fees vary according to program. *Payment plans:* Tuition prepayment, installment, deferred payment.

FRESHMAN FINANCIAL AID (Fall 2004, est.) 750 applied for aid; of those 81% were deemed to have need. 100% of freshmen with need received aid; of those 10% had need fully met. *Average percent of need met:* 67% (excluding resources awarded to replace EFC). *Average financial aid package:* $13,884 (excluding resources awarded to replace EFC). 10% of all full-time freshmen had no need and received non-need-based gift aid.

UNDERGRADUATE FINANCIAL AID (Fall 2004, est.) 2,185 applied for aid; of those 82% were deemed to have need. 99% of undergraduates with need received aid; of those 14% had need fully met. *Average percent of need met:* 67% (excluding resources awarded to replace EFC). *Average financial aid package:* $13,198 (excluding resources awarded to replace EFC). 8% of all full-time undergraduates had no need and received non-need-based gift aid.

GIFT AID (NEED-BASED) *Total amount:* $14,697,575 (9% federal, 4% state, 83% institutional, 4% external sources). *Receiving aid:* Freshmen: 74% (595); All full-time undergraduates: 71% (1,702). *Average award:* Freshmen: $8341; Undergraduates: $7925. *Scholarships, grants, and awards:* Federal Pell, FSEOG, state, private, college/university gift aid from institutional funds.

GIFT AID (NON-NEED-BASED) *Total amount:* $1,503,308 (86% institutional, 14% external sources). *Receiving aid:* Freshmen: 3% (24); Undergraduates: 3% (62). *Average Award:* Freshmen: $7041; Undergraduates: $6577. *Scholarships, grants, and awards by category:* *Academic Interests/Achievement:* general academic interests/achievements. *Special Achievements/Activities:* leadership. *Special Characteristics:* children of faculty/staff, children of union members/company employees, international students, local/state students, members of minority groups, out-of-state students, siblings of current students. *Tuition waivers:* Full or partial for employees or children of employees, senior citizens. *ROTC:* Army, Air Force cooperative.

LOANS *Student loans:* $17,088,963 (41% need-based, 59% non-need-based). 85% of past graduating class borrowed through all loan programs. *Average need-based loan:* Freshmen: $3345; Undergraduates: $3884. *Parent loans:* $6,847,074 (100% non-need-based). *Programs:* Federal Direct (Subsidized and Unsubsidized Stafford, PLUS), FFEL (PLUS), Perkins, state.

WORK-STUDY *Federal work-study:* Total amount: $1,683,253; 911 jobs averaging $1848. *State or other work-study/employment:* Total amount: $550,000 (100% non-need-based). Part-time jobs available.

APPLYING FOR FINANCIAL AID *Required financial aid forms:* FAFSA, federal income tax form(s). *Financial aid deadline:* Continuous. *Notification date:* 3/15. Students must reply by 5/1 or within 2 weeks of notification.

CONTACT Mrs. Kathy M. Chambers, Associate Director of Student Administrative Services, Western New England College, 1215 Wilbraham Road, Springfield, MA 01119-2684, 413-796-2080 or toll-free 800-325-1122 Ext. 1321. *Fax:* 413-796-2081. *E-mail:* finaid@wnec.edu.

WESTERN NEW MEXICO UNIVERSITY
Silver City, NM

Tuition & fees: N/R	Average undergraduate aid package: $5915

ABOUT THE INSTITUTION State-supported, coed. Awards: associate, bachelor's, and master's degrees. 53 undergraduate majors. Total enrollment: 3,074. Undergraduates: 2,555. Federal methodology is used as a basis for awarding need-based institutional aid.

FRESHMAN FINANCIAL AID (Fall 2003) 351 applied for aid; of those 87% were deemed to have need. 100% of freshmen with need received aid; of those 9% had need fully met. *Average percent of need met:* 62% (excluding resources awarded to replace EFC). *Average financial aid package:* $4744 (excluding resources awarded to replace EFC). 10% of all full-time freshmen had no need and received non-need-based gift aid.

UNDERGRADUATE FINANCIAL AID (Fall 2003) 1,349 applied for aid; of those 94% were deemed to have need. 100% of undergraduates with need received aid; of those 16% had need fully met. *Average percent of need met:* 68% (excluding resources awarded to replace EFC). *Average financial aid package:* $5915 (excluding resources awarded to replace EFC). 7% of all full-time undergraduates had no need and received non-need-based gift aid.

GIFT AID (NEED-BASED) *Total amount:* $4,827,501 (84% federal, 7% state, 9% institutional). *Receiving aid:* Freshmen: 73% (280); All full-time undergraduates: 71% (1,166). *Average award:* Freshmen: $2282; Undergraduates: $2434. *Scholarships, grants, and awards:* Federal Pell, FSEOG, state, private, college/university gift aid from institutional funds.

GIFT AID (NON-NEED-BASED) *Total amount:* $221,069 (100% external sources). *Receiving aid:* Freshmen: 5% (19); Undergraduates: 6% (93). *Average Award:* Freshmen: $1667; Undergraduates: $2457. *Scholarships, grants, and awards by category:* *Academic Interests/Achievement:* 422 awards ($562,383 total): general academic interests/achievements. *Creative Arts/Performance:* 53 awards ($22,772 total): performing arts. *Special Achievements/Activities:* 32 awards ($38,251 total): general special achievements/activities. *Special Characteristics:* 46 awards ($84,451 total): general special characteristics, veterans.

LOANS *Student loans:* $3,335,043 (100% need-based). 55% of past graduating class borrowed through all loan programs. *Average indebtedness per student:* $17,000. *Average need-based loan:* Freshmen: $2344; Undergraduates: $2980. *Parent loans:* $27,700 (100% need-based). *Programs:* FFEL (Subsidized and Unsubsidized Stafford, PLUS), Perkins, state, college/university.

WORK-STUDY *Federal work-study:* Total amount: $244,574; 134 jobs averaging $1825. *State or other work-study/employment:* Total amount: $357,048 (44% need-based, 56% non-need-based). 82 part-time jobs averaging $1937.

ATHLETIC AWARDS *Total amount:* $408,152 (100% non-need-based).

APPLYING FOR FINANCIAL AID *Required financial aid forms:* FAFSA, institution's own form. *Financial aid deadline (priority):* 4/1. *Notification date:* Continuous. Students must reply within 2 weeks of notification.

CONTACT Debra Reyes, Grant Counselor, Western New Mexico University, PO Box 680, Silver City, NM 88062, 505-538-6173 or toll-free 800-872-WNMU (in-state).

WESTERN OREGON UNIVERSITY
Monmouth, OR

Tuition & fees (OR res): $4332	Average undergraduate aid package: $6596

ABOUT THE INSTITUTION State-supported, coed. Awards: associate, bachelor's, and master's degrees and post-bachelor's certificates. 33 undergraduate majors. Total enrollment: 4,772. Undergraduates: 4,303. Freshmen: 827. Federal methodology is used as a basis for awarding need-based institutional aid.

UNDERGRADUATE EXPENSES for 2005–06 *Application fee:* $50. *Tuition, state resident:* full-time $3240; part-time $90 per credit. *Tuition, nonresident:* full-time $11,685; part-time $325 per credit. *College room and board:* $6276. Room and board charges vary according to board plan and housing facility. *Payment plan:* Deferred payment.

FRESHMAN FINANCIAL AID (Fall 2004, est.) 568 applied for aid; of those 78% were deemed to have need. 100% of freshmen with need received aid; of those 12% had need fully met. *Average percent of need met:* 64% (excluding resources awarded to replace EFC). *Average financial aid package:* $6155 (excluding resources awarded to replace EFC). 23% of all full-time freshmen had no need and received non-need-based gift aid.

UNDERGRADUATE FINANCIAL AID (Fall 2004, est.) 2,892 applied for aid; of those 83% were deemed to have need. 100% of undergraduates with need received aid; of those 11% had need fully met. *Average percent of need met:* 67% (excluding resources awarded to replace EFC). *Average financial aid package:* $6596 (excluding resources awarded to replace EFC). 20% of all full-time undergraduates had no need and received non-need-based gift aid.

GIFT AID (NEED-BASED) *Total amount:* $6,743,699 (62% federal, 13% state, 6% institutional, 19% external sources). *Receiving aid:* Freshmen: 58% (360); All full-time undergraduates: 57% (1,789). *Average award:* Freshmen: $4352; Undergraduates: $4095. *Scholarships, grants, and awards:* Federal Pell, FSEOG, state, private, college/university gift aid from institutional funds.

GIFT AID (NON-NEED-BASED) *Total amount:* $731,321 (1% state, 33% institutional, 66% external sources). *Receiving aid:* Freshmen: 4% (23); Undergraduates: 3% (84). *Average Award:* Freshmen: $7225; Undergraduates: $7295. *Scholarships, grants, and awards by category: Academic Interests/ Achievement:* 947 awards ($1,112,159 total): biological sciences, business, computer science, education, general academic interests/achievements, international studies, mathematics, physical sciences, social sciences. *Creative Arts/ Performance:* 41 awards ($30,706 total): art/fine arts, dance, music, performing arts. *Special Achievements/Activities:* 173 awards ($99,090 total): general special achievements/activities. *Tuition waivers:* Full or partial for employees or children of employees. *ROTC:* Army, Air Force cooperative.

LOANS *Student loans:* $15,935,767 (72% need-based, 28% non-need-based). 59% of past graduating class borrowed through all loan programs. *Average indebtedness per student:* $1791. *Average need-based loan:* Freshmen: $2620; Undergraduates: $3590. *Parent loans:* $6,090,330 (30% need-based, 70% non-need-based). *Programs:* Federal Direct (Subsidized and Unsubsidized Stafford, PLUS), Perkins, college/university.

WORK-STUDY *Federal work-study:* Total amount: $281,877; 958 jobs averaging $298.

ATHLETIC AWARDS *Total amount:* $211,537 (64% need-based, 36% non-need-based).

APPLYING FOR FINANCIAL AID *Required financial aid form:* FAFSA. *Financial aid deadline (priority):* 3/1. *Notification date:* Continuous beginning 3/19. Students must reply within 2 weeks of notification.

CONTACT Ms. Donna Fossum, Director of Financial Aid, Western Oregon University, 345 North Monmouth Avenue, Monmouth, OR 97361, 503-838-8475 or toll-free 877-877-1593. *Fax:* 503-838-8200. *E-mail:* fossumd@wou.edu.

WESTERN STATE COLLEGE OF COLORADO
Gunnison, CO

Tuition & fees (CO res): $2761   **Average undergraduate aid package: $8800**

ABOUT THE INSTITUTION State-supported, coed. Awards: bachelor's degrees. 53 undergraduate majors. Total enrollment: 2,270. Undergraduates: 2,270. Freshmen: 491. Federal methodology is used as a basis for awarding need-based institutional aid.

UNDERGRADUATE EXPENSES for 2004–05 *Application fee:* $40. *Tuition, state resident:* full-time $1980; part-time $90 per credit hour. *Tuition, nonresident:* full-time $9966; part-time $453 per credit hour. *Required fees:* full-time $781; $33.35 per credit hour. Full-time tuition and fees vary according to course load. Part-time tuition and fees vary according to course load. *College room and board:* $6705; *room only:* $3665. Room and board charges vary according to board plan and housing facility. *Payment plans:* Installment, deferred payment.

FRESHMAN FINANCIAL AID (Fall 2004, est.) 368 applied for aid; of those 80% were deemed to have need. 85% of freshmen with need received aid; of those 15% had need fully met. *Average percent of need met:* 45% (excluding resources awarded to replace EFC). *Average financial aid package:* $6625 (excluding resources awarded to replace EFC). 30% of all full-time freshmen had no need and received non-need-based gift aid.

UNDERGRADUATE FINANCIAL AID (Fall 2004, est.) 1,242 applied for aid; of those 60% were deemed to have need. 85% of undergraduates with need received aid; of those 16% had need fully met. *Average percent of need met:* 50% (excluding resources awarded to replace EFC). *Average financial aid package:* $8800 (excluding resources awarded to replace EFC). 25% of all full-time undergraduates had no need and received non-need-based gift aid.

GIFT AID (NEED-BASED) *Total amount:* $2,150,000 (70% federal, 22% state, 2% institutional, 6% external sources). *Receiving aid:* Freshmen: 30% (150); All full-time undergraduates: 26% (538). *Average award:* Freshmen: $2500; Undergraduates: $2500. *Scholarships, grants, and awards:* Federal Pell, FSEOG, state, private, college/university gift aid from institutional funds.

GIFT AID (NON-NEED-BASED) *Total amount:* $1,010,000 (11% state, 64% institutional, 25% external sources). *Receiving aid:* Freshmen: 15% (75); Undergraduates: 9% (180). *Average Award:* Freshmen: $1000; Undergraduates:* $1000. *Scholarships, grants, and awards by category: Academic Interests/ Achievement:* 175 awards ($150,000 total): general academic interests/ achievements. *Creative Arts/Performance:* 75 awards ($35,000 total): art/fine arts, music. *Special Achievements/Activities:* 50 awards ($75,000 total): leadership. *Tuition waivers:* Full or partial for employees or children of employees, senior citizens.

LOANS *Student loans:* $6,000,000 (60% need-based, 40% non-need-based). 60% of past graduating class borrowed through all loan programs. *Average indebtedness per student:* $15,000. *Average need-based loan:* Freshmen: $2625; Undergraduates: $5000. *Parent loans:* $1,600,000 (100% non-need-based). *Programs:* FFEL (Subsidized and Unsubsidized Stafford, PLUS), Perkins.

WORK-STUDY *Federal work-study:* Total amount: $210,000; 200 jobs averaging $1050. *State or other work-study/employment:* Total amount: $577,000 (36% need-based, 64% non-need-based). 161 part-time jobs averaging $1273.

ATHLETIC AWARDS *Total amount:* $500,000 (100% non-need-based).

APPLYING FOR FINANCIAL AID *Required financial aid form:* FAFSA. *Financial aid deadline (priority):* 4/1. *Notification date:* Continuous beginning 4/1. Students must reply within 3 weeks of notification.

CONTACT Marty Somero, Director, Financial Aid, Western State College of Colorado, Room 207, Taylor Hall, Gunnison, CO 81231, 970-943-3026 or toll-free 800-876-5309. *Fax:* 970-943-3086. *E-mail:* msomero@western.edu.

WESTERN WASHINGTON UNIVERSITY
Bellingham, WA

Tuition & fees (WA res): $4452   **Average undergraduate aid package: $8681**

ABOUT THE INSTITUTION State-supported, coed. Awards: bachelor's and master's degrees and post-bachelor's certificates. 116 undergraduate majors. Total enrollment: 14,190. Undergraduates: 12,862. Freshmen: 2,457. Federal methodology is used as a basis for awarding need-based institutional aid.

UNDERGRADUATE EXPENSES for 2004–05 *Application fee:* $38. *Tuition, state resident:* full-time $3885; part-time $130 per credit. *Tuition, nonresident:* full-time $13,272; part-time $442 per credit. *Required fees:* full-time $567; $189 per term part-time. Full-time tuition and fees vary according to location. Part-time tuition and fees vary according to location. *College room and board:* $6242; *room only:* $4101. Room and board charges vary according to board plan and housing facility. *Payment plan:* Installment.

FRESHMAN FINANCIAL AID (Fall 2004, est.) 1678 applied for aid; of those 57% were deemed to have need. 97% of freshmen with need received aid; of those 27% had need fully met. *Average percent of need met:* 86% (excluding resources awarded to replace EFC). *Average financial aid package:* $8304 (excluding resources awarded to replace EFC). 2% of all full-time freshmen had no need and received non-need-based gift aid.

UNDERGRADUATE FINANCIAL AID (Fall 2004, est.) 7,061 applied for aid; of those 71% were deemed to have need. 97% of undergraduates with need received aid; of those 30% had need fully met. *Average percent of need met:* 85% (excluding resources awarded to replace EFC). *Average financial aid package:* $8681 (excluding resources awarded to replace EFC). 2% of all full-time undergraduates had no need and received non-need-based gift aid.

GIFT AID (NEED-BASED) *Total amount:* $18,324,468 (42% federal, 38% state, 12% institutional, 8% external sources). *Receiving aid:* Freshmen: 32% (782);

Western Washington University

All full-time undergraduates: 32% (3,731). **Average award:** Freshmen: $5223; Undergraduates: $5170. **Scholarships, grants, and awards:** Federal Pell, FSEOG, state, private, college/university gift aid from institutional funds.

GIFT AID (NON-NEED-BASED) *Total amount:* $1,813,589 (5% federal, 26% state, 23% institutional, 46% external sources). *Receiving aid:* Freshmen: 2% (54); Undergraduates: 1% (126). *Average Award:* Freshmen: $1862; *Undergraduates:* $1633. *Scholarships, grants, and awards by category: Academic Interests/Achievement:* biological sciences, business, communication, computer science, education, engineering/technologies, English, foreign languages, general academic interests/achievements, health fields, humanities, library science, mathematics, physical sciences, premedicine, social sciences. *Creative Arts/Performance:* applied art and design, art/fine arts, cinema/film/broadcasting, creative writing, dance, general creative arts/performance, journalism/publications, music, performing arts, theater/drama. *Special Achievements/Activities:* community service, leadership, memberships. *Special Characteristics:* children of public servants, children of union members/company employees, ethnic background, general special characteristics, international students, local/state students, members of minority groups, previous college experience, veterans. *Tuition waivers:* Full or partial for employees or children of employees.

LOANS *Student loans:* $30,092,501 (64% need-based, 36% non-need-based). 58% of past graduating class borrowed through all loan programs. *Average indebtedness per student:* $15,139. *Average need-based loan:* Freshmen: $2817; Undergraduates: $4150. *Parent loans:* $18,231,990 (17% need-based, 83% non-need-based). *Programs:* Federal Direct (Subsidized and Unsubsidized Stafford, PLUS), FFEL (PLUS), Perkins, college/university, alternative loans.

WORK-STUDY *Federal work-study:* Total amount: $706,746; 264 jobs averaging $2677. *State or other work-study/employment:* Total amount: $1,031,595 (100% need-based). 312 part-time jobs averaging $3306.

ATHLETIC AWARDS *Total amount:* $690,259 (26% need-based, 74% non-need-based).

APPLYING FOR FINANCIAL AID *Required financial aid form:* FAFSA. *Financial aid deadline (priority):* 2/15. *Notification date:* 5/1. Students must reply within 3 weeks of notification.

CONTACT Ms. Fidele Dent, Office Support Supervisor II, Student Financial Resources, Western Washington University, OM 240 MS 9006, Bellingham, WA 98225-9006, 360-650-3470. *E-mail:* sfr@cc.wwu.edu.

WESTFIELD STATE COLLEGE
Westfield, MA

Tuition & fees (MA res): $4857   Average undergraduate aid package: $5534

ABOUT THE INSTITUTION State-supported, coed. Awards: bachelor's and master's degrees and post-bachelor's and post-master's certificates. 49 undergraduate majors. Total enrollment: 4,906. Undergraduates: 4,291. Freshmen: 857. Federal methodology is used as a basis for awarding need-based institutional aid.

UNDERGRADUATE EXPENSES for 2005–06 *Application fee:* $25. *Tuition, state resident:* full-time $970. *Tuition, nonresident:* full-time $7050. *College room and board:* $5742; *room only:* $3692.

FRESHMAN FINANCIAL AID (Fall 2003) 710 applied for aid; of those 64% were deemed to have need. 100% of freshmen with need received aid; of those 20% had need fully met. *Average percent of need met:* 81% (excluding resources awarded to replace EFC). *Average financial aid package:* $5244 (excluding resources awarded to replace EFC). 35% of all full-time freshmen had no need and received non-need-based gift aid.

UNDERGRADUATE FINANCIAL AID (Fall 2003) 2,614 applied for aid; of those 68% were deemed to have need. 100% of undergraduates with need received aid; of those 29% had need fully met. *Average percent of need met:* 80% (excluding resources awarded to replace EFC). *Average financial aid package:* $5534 (excluding resources awarded to replace EFC). 30% of all full-time undergraduates had no need and received non-need-based gift aid.

GIFT AID (NEED-BASED) *Total amount:* $5,494,880 (41% federal, 36% state, 17% institutional, 6% external sources). *Receiving aid:* Freshmen: 46% (337); All full-time undergraduates: 48% (1,319). *Average award:* Freshmen: $4038; Undergraduates: $3934. *Scholarships, grants, and awards:* Federal Pell, FSEOG, state, private, college/university gift aid from institutional funds.

GIFT AID (NON-NEED-BASED) *Total amount:* $287,191 (20% state, 17% institutional, 63% external sources). *Receiving aid:* Freshmen: 1% (10); Undergraduates: 1% (28). *Average Award:* Freshmen: $3816; *Undergraduates:* $4780. *Scholarships, grants, and awards by category: Academic Interests/Achievement:* $123,784 total: general academic interests/achievements. *Special Achievements/Activities:* community service. *ROTC:* Army cooperative, Air Force cooperative.

LOANS *Student loans:* $10,081,024 (49% need-based, 51% non-need-based). 86% of past graduating class borrowed through all loan programs. *Average indebtedness per student:* $12,731. *Average need-based loan:* Freshmen: $2306; Undergraduates: $2810. *Parent loans:* $774,895 (11% need-based, 89% non-need-based). *Programs:* FFEL (Subsidized and Unsubsidized Stafford, PLUS), Perkins, state.

WORK-STUDY *Federal work-study:* Total amount: $349,316; 339 jobs averaging $1126.

APPLYING FOR FINANCIAL AID *Required financial aid form:* FAFSA. *Financial aid deadline (priority):* 3/1. *Notification date:* 4/15.

CONTACT Catherine Ryan, Financial Aid Director, Westfield State College, 333 Western Avenue, Westfield, MA 01086, 413-572-5218 or toll-free 800-322-8401 (in-state).

WEST LIBERTY STATE COLLEGE
West Liberty, WV

Tuition & fees (WV res): $3380   Average undergraduate aid package: $5457

ABOUT THE INSTITUTION State-supported, coed. Awards: associate and bachelor's degrees. 35 undergraduate majors. Total enrollment: 2,374. Undergraduates: 2,374. Freshmen: 468. Federal methodology is used as a basis for awarding need-based institutional aid.

UNDERGRADUATE EXPENSES for 2005–06 *Tuition, state resident:* full-time $3380. *Tuition, nonresident:* full-time $8354. *College room and board:* $5006. Room and board charges vary according to board plan and housing facility. *Payment plans:* Installment, deferred payment.

FRESHMAN FINANCIAL AID (Fall 2004, est.) 430 applied for aid; of those 61% were deemed to have need. 95% of freshmen with need received aid; of those 59% had need fully met. *Average percent of need met:* 76% (excluding resources awarded to replace EFC). *Average financial aid package:* $4917 (excluding resources awarded to replace EFC). 8% of all full-time freshmen had no need and received non-need-based gift aid.

UNDERGRADUATE FINANCIAL AID (Fall 2004, est.) 1,744 applied for aid; of those 80% were deemed to have need. 97% of undergraduates with need received aid; of those 33% had need fully met. *Average percent of need met:* 73% (excluding resources awarded to replace EFC). *Average financial aid package:* $5457 (excluding resources awarded to replace EFC). 11% of all full-time undergraduates had no need and received non-need-based gift aid.

GIFT AID (NEED-BASED) *Total amount:* $3,239,042 (83% federal, 17% state). *Receiving aid:* Freshmen: 46% (204); All full-time undergraduates: 44% (887). *Average award:* Freshmen: $3807; Undergraduates: $3614. *Scholarships, grants, and awards:* Federal Pell, FSEOG, state, private, college/university gift aid from institutional funds.

GIFT AID (NON-NEED-BASED) *Total amount:* $1,327,218 (57% state, 30% institutional, 13% external sources). *Receiving aid:* Freshmen: 44% (195); Undergraduates: 21% (433). *Average Award:* Freshmen: $2684; *Undergraduates:* $2638. *Scholarships, grants, and awards by category: Academic Interests/Achievement:* 148 awards ($285,019 total): business, communication, education, English, general academic interests/achievements, health fields, mathematics, physical sciences. *Creative Arts/Performance:* 73 awards ($125,011 total): art/fine arts, music, theater/drama. *Special Achievements/Activities:* cheerleading/drum major. *Special Characteristics:* 7 awards ($5954 total): children and siblings of alumni, children of faculty/staff. *Tuition waivers:* Full or partial for employees or children of employees, senior citizens.

LOANS *Student loans:* $8,203,229 (53% need-based, 47% non-need-based). 64% of past graduating class borrowed through all loan programs. *Average indebtedness per student:* $13,800. *Average need-based loan:* Freshmen: $2582; Undergraduates: $3712. *Parent loans:* $945,089 (100% non-need-based). *Programs:* Federal Direct (Subsidized and Unsubsidized Stafford, PLUS), Perkins, Federal Nursing, alternative loans.

WORK-STUDY *Federal work-study:* Total amount: $133,700; 142 jobs averaging $941. *State or other work-study/employment:* Total amount: $215,541 (100% non-need-based). 61 part-time jobs averaging $3533.

ATHLETIC AWARDS *Total amount:* $450,201 (100% non-need-based).

APPLYING FOR FINANCIAL AID *Required financial aid form:* FAFSA. *Financial aid deadline (priority):* 3/1. *Notification date:* Continuous. Students must reply within 2 weeks of notification.

CONTACT Mr. Scott A. Cook, Director of Financial Aid, West Liberty State College, PO Box 295, West Liberty, WV 26074-0295, 304-336-8016 or toll-free 800-732-6204 Ext. 8076. *Fax:* 304-336-8088. *E-mail:* cookscot@wlsc.edu.

WESTMINSTER CHOIR COLLEGE OF RIDER UNIVERSITY
Princeton, NJ

ABOUT THE INSTITUTION Independent, coed. Awards: bachelor's and master's degrees. 10 undergraduate majors. Total enrollment: 438. Undergraduates: 320. Freshmen: 89.

GIFT AID (NEED-BASED) *Scholarships, grants, and awards:* Federal Pell, FSEOG, state, private, college/university gift aid from institutional funds.

GIFT AID (NON-NEED-BASED) *Scholarships, grants, and awards by category: Creative Arts/Performance:* music.

LOANS *Programs:* FFEL (Subsidized and Unsubsidized Stafford, PLUS), Perkins, state, college/university, alternative loans.

APPLYING FOR FINANCIAL AID *Required financial aid form:* FAFSA.

CONTACT Student Financial Services, Westminster Choir College of Rider University, 2083 Lawrenceville Road, Lawrenceville, NJ 08648, 609-896-5360 or toll-free 800-96-CHOIR. *Fax:* 609-219-4487. *E-mail:* finaid@rider.edu.

WESTMINSTER COLLEGE
Fulton, MO

Tuition & fees: $14,170   **Average undergraduate aid package:** $14,641

ABOUT THE INSTITUTION Independent religious, coed. Awards: bachelor's degrees. 28 undergraduate majors. Total enrollment: 867. Undergraduates: 867. Freshmen: 232. Both federal and institutional methodology are used as a basis for awarding need-based institutional aid.

UNDERGRADUATE EXPENSES for 2005–06 *Comprehensive fee:* $20,040 includes full-time tuition ($13,750), mandatory fees ($420), and room and board ($5870). *College room only:* $3020. Room and board charges vary according to board plan and housing facility. *Part-time tuition:* $710 per credit hour. *Part-time fees:* $210 per term. *Payment plan:* Installment.

FRESHMAN FINANCIAL AID (Fall 2004, est.) 167 applied for aid; of those 82% were deemed to have need. 100% of freshmen with need received aid; of those 63% had need fully met. *Average percent of need met:* 94% (excluding resources awarded to replace EFC). *Average financial aid package:* $13,217 (excluding resources awarded to replace EFC). 42% of all full-time freshmen had no need and received non-need-based gift aid.

UNDERGRADUATE FINANCIAL AID (Fall 2004, est.) 591 applied for aid; of those 87% were deemed to have need. 100% of undergraduates with need received aid; of those 64% had need fully met. *Average percent of need met:* 94% (excluding resources awarded to replace EFC). *Average financial aid package:* $14,641 (excluding resources awarded to replace EFC). 38% of all full-time undergraduates had no need and received non-need-based gift aid.

GIFT AID (NEED-BASED) *Total amount:* $8,189,857 (7% federal, 6% state, 83% institutional, 4% external sources). *Receiving aid:* Freshmen: 59% (137); All full-time undergraduates: 61% (511). *Average award:* Freshmen: $10,533; Undergraduates: $10,977. *Scholarships, grants, and awards:* Federal Pell, FSEOG, state, private, college/university gift aid from institutional funds.

GIFT AID (NON-NEED-BASED) *Average Award:* Freshmen: $7252; Undergraduates: $7543. *Scholarships, grants, and awards by category: Academic Interests/Achievement:* 464 awards ($3,451,704 total): general academic interests/achievements. *Special Achievements/Activities:* 248 awards ($696,934 total): leadership. *Special Characteristics:* 249 awards ($906,863 total): children and siblings of alumni, ethnic background, international students, local/state students, relatives of clergy, religious affiliation, siblings of current students. *Tuition waivers:* Full or partial for children of alumni, employees or children of employees. *ROTC:* Army cooperative, Air Force cooperative.

LOANS *Student loans:* $1,993,274 (53% need-based, 47% non-need-based). 54% of past graduating class borrowed through all loan programs. *Average indebtedness per student:* $15,843. *Average need-based loan:* Freshmen: $2432; Undergraduates: $3596. *Parent loans:* $1,084,763 (100% non-need-based). *Programs:* FFEL (Subsidized and Unsubsidized Stafford, PLUS), Perkins.

WORK-STUDY *Federal work-study:* Total amount: $87,843; 147 jobs averaging $598. *State or other work-study/employment:* Total amount: $178,566 (100% non-need-based). 100 part-time jobs averaging $1786.

APPLYING FOR FINANCIAL AID *Required financial aid form:* FAFSA. *Financial aid deadline (priority):* 2/15. *Notification date:* Continuous beginning 2/28. Students must reply within 3 weeks of notification.

CONTACT Ms. Aimee Bristow, Director of Financial Aid, Westminster College, 501 Westminster Avenue, Fulton, MO 65251-1299, 800-475-3361. *Fax:* 573-592-5255. *E-mail:* bristoa@westminster-mo.edu.

WESTMINSTER COLLEGE
New Wilmington, PA

Tuition & fees: $22,680   **Average undergraduate aid package:** $18,440

ABOUT THE INSTITUTION Independent religious, coed. Awards: bachelor's and master's degrees. 52 undergraduate majors. Total enrollment: 1,626. Undergraduates: 1,478. Freshmen: 375. Federal methodology is used as a basis for awarding need-based institutional aid.

UNDERGRADUATE EXPENSES for 2005–06 *Application fee:* $35. *Comprehensive fee:* $29,380 includes full-time tuition ($21,700), mandatory fees ($980), and room and board ($6700). *College room only:* $3500. Room and board charges vary according to board plan. *Part-time tuition:* $680 per semester hour. *Part-time fees:* $10 per semester hour. *Payment plan:* Installment.

FRESHMAN FINANCIAL AID (Fall 2004, est.) 350 applied for aid; of those 89% were deemed to have need. 100% of freshmen with need received aid; of those 22% had need fully met. *Average percent of need met:* 90% (excluding resources awarded to replace EFC). *Average financial aid package:* $18,644 (excluding resources awarded to replace EFC). 17% of all full-time freshmen had no need and received non-need-based gift aid.

UNDERGRADUATE FINANCIAL AID (Fall 2004, est.) 1,220 applied for aid; of those 91% were deemed to have need. 100% of undergraduates with need received aid; of those 21% had need fully met. *Average percent of need met:* 89% (excluding resources awarded to replace EFC). *Average financial aid package:* $18,440 (excluding resources awarded to replace EFC). 18% of all full-time undergraduates had no need and received non-need-based gift aid.

GIFT AID (NEED-BASED) *Total amount:* $15,518,493 (7% federal, 11% state, 77% institutional, 5% external sources). *Receiving aid:* Freshmen: 81% (310); All full-time undergraduates: 81% (1,105). *Average award:* Freshmen: $15,365; Undergraduates: $14,026. *Scholarships, grants, and awards:* Federal Pell, FSEOG, state, private, college/university gift aid from institutional funds.

GIFT AID (NON-NEED-BASED) *Total amount:* $2,066,344 (97% institutional, 3% external sources). *Receiving aid:* Freshmen: 80% (306); Undergraduates: 74% (1,002). *Average Award: Freshmen:* $8334; *Undergraduates:* $8297. *Scholarships, grants, and awards by category: Academic Interests/Achievement:* 1,198 awards ($8,350,731 total): general academic interests/achievements. *Creative Arts/Performance:* 157 awards ($174,250 total): cinema/film/broadcasting, general creative arts/performance, music, theater/drama. *Special Achievements/Activities:* leadership. *Special Characteristics:* 360 awards ($1,356,295 total): children and siblings of alumni, general special characteristics, international students, religious affiliation. *ROTC:* Army cooperative.

LOANS *Student loans:* $6,127,176 (95% need-based, 5% non-need-based). 73% of past graduating class borrowed through all loan programs. *Average indebtedness per student:* $17,930. *Average need-based loan:* Freshmen: $3669; Undergraduates: $4310. *Parent loans:* $1,735,867 (89% need-based, 11% non-need-based). *Programs:* FFEL (Subsidized and Unsubsidized Stafford, PLUS), Perkins, Resource Loans.

WORK-STUDY *Federal work-study:* Total amount: $480,649; 304 jobs averaging $1581. *State or other work-study/employment:* Total amount: $402,582 (72% need-based, 28% non-need-based). 233 part-time jobs averaging $1728.

APPLYING FOR FINANCIAL AID *Required financial aid forms:* FAFSA, institution's own form. *Financial aid deadline (priority):* 5/1. *Notification date:* Continuous. Students must reply within 3 weeks of notification.

CONTACT Mr. Robert A. Latta, Director of Financial Aid, Westminster College, South Market Street, New Wilmington, PA 16172-0001, 724-946-7102 or toll-free 800-942-8033 (in-state). *Fax:* 724-946-6171. *E-mail:* lattara@westminster.edu.

WESTMINSTER COLLEGE
Salt Lake City, UT

Tuition & fees: $18,476   **Average undergraduate aid package:** $15,651

ABOUT THE INSTITUTION Independent, coed. Awards: bachelor's and master's degrees and post-bachelor's certificates. 31 undergraduate majors. Total enrollment: 2,417. Undergraduates: 1,896. Freshmen: 320. Federal methodology is used as a basis for awarding need-based institutional aid.

UNDERGRADUATE EXPENSES for 2004–05 *Application fee:* $40. *Comprehensive fee:* $24,112 includes full-time tuition ($18,192), mandatory fees ($284), and room and board ($5636). Full-time tuition and fees vary according to course load. Room and board charges vary according to board plan. *Part-time tuition:* $758 per credit hour. *Part-time fees:* $107 per term. *Payment plans:* Installment, deferred payment.

FRESHMAN FINANCIAL AID (Fall 2004, est.) 244 applied for aid; of those 82% were deemed to have need. 100% of freshmen with need received aid; of those 85% had need fully met. *Average percent of need met:* 92% (excluding resources awarded to replace EFC). *Average financial aid package:* $15,920 (excluding resources awarded to replace EFC). 35% of all full-time freshmen had no need and received non-need-based gift aid.

UNDERGRADUATE FINANCIAL AID (Fall 2004, est.) 1,323 applied for aid; of those 89% were deemed to have need. 100% of undergraduates with need received aid; of those 46% had need fully met. *Average percent of need met:* 88% (excluding resources awarded to replace EFC). *Average financial aid package:* $15,651 (excluding resources awarded to replace EFC). 29% of all full-time undergraduates had no need and received non-need-based gift aid.

GIFT AID (NEED-BASED) *Total amount:* $11,242,082 (17% federal, 1% state, 68% institutional, 14% external sources). *Receiving aid:* Freshmen: 63% (199); All full-time undergraduates: 70% (1,169). *Average award:* Freshmen: $10,499; Undergraduates: $9154. *Scholarships, grants, and awards:* Federal Pell, FSEOG, state, private, college/university gift aid from institutional funds, United Negro College Fund, Federal Nursing.

GIFT AID (NON-NEED-BASED) *Total amount:* $4,191,789 (75% institutional, 25% external sources). *Receiving aid:* Freshmen: 8% (26); Undergraduates: 7% (112). *Average Award:* Freshmen: $8031; Undergraduates: $6998. *Scholarships, grants, and awards by category: Academic Interests/Achievement:* 1,688 awards ($10,451,520 total): biological sciences, business, communication, computer science, education, English, general academic interests/achievements, health fields, humanities, international studies, mathematics, military science, physical sciences, premedicine, social sciences. *Creative Arts/Performance:* 49 awards ($94,500 total): art/fine arts, journalism/publications, music, theater/drama. *Special Characteristics:* 82 awards ($215,000 total): adult students, children and siblings of alumni, children of faculty/staff, children of public servants, ethnic background, first-generation college students, handicapped students, international students, local/state students, members of minority groups, public servants, relatives of clergy, religious affiliation, siblings of current students, spouses of current students, veterans, veterans' children. *Tuition waivers:* Full or partial for employees or children of employees. *ROTC:* Army cooperative, Naval cooperative, Air Force cooperative.

LOANS *Student loans:* $9,048,536 (77% need-based, 23% non-need-based). 66% of past graduating class borrowed through all loan programs. *Average indebtedness per student:* $16,100. *Average need-based loan:* Freshmen: $3218; Undergraduates: $4122. *Parent loans:* $537,750 (47% need-based, 53% non-need-based). *Programs:* FFEL (Subsidized and Unsubsidized Stafford, PLUS), Perkins.

WORK-STUDY *Federal work-study:* Total amount: $508,400; 248 jobs averaging $2050. *State or other work-study/employment:* Total amount: $455,500 (100% non-need-based). Part-time jobs available.

APPLYING FOR FINANCIAL AID *Required financial aid form:* FAFSA. *Financial aid deadline (priority):* 4/15. *Notification date:* 3/15. Students must reply within 3 weeks of notification.

CONTACT Ruth Henneman, Director of Financial Aid, Westminster College, 1840 South 1300 East, Salt Lake City, UT 84105, 801-832-2500 or toll-free 800-748-4753 (out-of-state). *Fax:* 801-832-2506. *E-mail:* rhenneman@westminstercollege.edu.

WESTMONT COLLEGE
Santa Barbara, CA

Tuition & fees: $26,240	Average undergraduate aid package: $17,506

ABOUT THE INSTITUTION Independent nondenominational, coed. Awards: bachelor's degrees and post-bachelor's certificates. 43 undergraduate majors. Total enrollment: 1,376. Undergraduates: 1,369. Freshmen: 360. Federal methodology is used as a basis for awarding need-based institutional aid.

UNDERGRADUATE EXPENSES for 2004–05 *Application fee:* $50. *Comprehensive fee:* $34,850 includes full-time tuition ($25,544), mandatory fees ($696), and room and board ($8610). *College room only:* $5120. Room and board charges vary according to board plan. *Payment plan:* Installment.

FRESHMAN FINANCIAL AID (Fall 2004, est.) 266 applied for aid; of those 82% were deemed to have need. 100% of freshmen with need received aid; of those

11% had need fully met. *Average percent of need met:* 65% (excluding resources awarded to replace EFC). *Average financial aid package:* $16,706 (excluding resources awarded to replace EFC). 26% of all full-time freshmen had no need and received non-need-based gift aid.

UNDERGRADUATE FINANCIAL AID (Fall 2004, est.) 882 applied for aid; of those 85% were deemed to have need. 100% of undergraduates with need received aid; of those 7% had need fully met. *Average percent of need met:* 67% (excluding resources awarded to replace EFC). *Average financial aid package:* $17,506 (excluding resources awarded to replace EFC). 30% of all full-time undergraduates had no need and received non-need-based gift aid.

GIFT AID (NEED-BASED) *Total amount:* $8,602,993 (9% federal, 22% state, 67% institutional, 2% external sources). *Receiving aid:* Freshmen: 59% (211); All full-time undergraduates: 55% (746). *Average award:* Freshmen: $13,287; Undergraduates: $12,349. *Scholarships, grants, and awards:* Federal Pell, FSEOG, state, private, college/university gift aid from institutional funds.

GIFT AID (NON-NEED-BASED) *Total amount:* $2,909,753 (2% state, 97% institutional, 1% external sources). *Receiving aid:* Freshmen: 6% (23); Undergraduates: 3% (47). *Average Award:* Freshmen: $9626; Undergraduates: $9214. *Scholarships, grants, and awards by category: Academic Interests/Achievement:* 838 awards ($5,319,162 total): general academic interests/achievements. *Creative Arts/Performance:* 69 awards ($58,325 total): art/fine arts, music, theater/drama. *Special Achievements/Activities:* 11 awards ($21,000 total): general special achievements/activities, leadership. *Special Characteristics:* 235 awards ($1,339,225 total): children of faculty/staff, ethnic background, international students. *Tuition waivers:* Full or partial for employees or children of employees. *ROTC:* Army cooperative, Air Force cooperative.

LOANS *Student loans:* $5,161,472 (79% need-based, 21% non-need-based). 81% of past graduating class borrowed through all loan programs. *Average indebtedness per student:* $19,969. *Average need-based loan:* Freshmen: $3622; Undergraduates: $5282. *Parent loans:* $4,011,513 (50% need-based, 50% non-need-based). *Programs:* FFEL (Subsidized and Unsubsidized Stafford, PLUS), Perkins, college/university, Alternative Loans.

WORK-STUDY *Federal work-study:* Total amount: $210,397; 147 jobs averaging $1431.

ATHLETIC AWARDS *Total amount:* $608,614 (45% need-based, 55% non-need-based).

APPLYING FOR FINANCIAL AID *Required financial aid form:* FAFSA. *Financial aid deadline (priority):* 3/1. *Notification date:* 3/1. Students must reply by 5/1 or within 2 weeks of notification.

CONTACT Mrs. Diane L. Horvath, Director of Financial Aid, Westmont College, 955 La Paz Road, Santa Barbara, CA 93108, 888-963-4624 or toll-free 800-777-9011. *Fax:* 805-565-7157. *E-mail:* dhorvath@westmont.edu.

WEST SUBURBAN COLLEGE OF NURSING
Oak Park, IL

CONTACT Ms. Ruth Rehwaldt, Director of Financial Aid, West Suburban College of Nursing, 3 Erie Court, Oak Park, IL 60302, 708-287-8100.

WEST TEXAS A&M UNIVERSITY
Canyon, TX

Tuition & fees (TX res): $3472	Average undergraduate aid package: $5916

ABOUT THE INSTITUTION State-supported, coed. Awards: bachelor's, master's, and doctoral degrees. 59 undergraduate majors. Total enrollment: 7,299. Undergraduates: 5,822. Freshmen: 809. Federal methodology is used as a basis for awarding need-based institutional aid.

UNDERGRADUATE EXPENSES for 2004–05 *Application fee:* $25. *One-time required fee:* $10. *Tuition, state resident:* full-time $2580; part-time $86 per hour. *Tuition, nonresident:* full-time $10,320; part-time $344 per hour. *Required fees:* full-time $892; $26 per hour or $116 per term part-time. Full-time tuition and fees vary according to course load. *College room and board:* $4592; *room only:* $2090. Room and board charges vary according to board plan and housing facility. *Payment plan:* Installment.

FRESHMAN FINANCIAL AID (Fall 2004, est.) 608 applied for aid; of those 70% were deemed to have need. 99% of freshmen with need received aid; of those 93% had need fully met. *Average percent of need met:* 83% (excluding resources awarded to replace EFC). *Average financial aid package:* $5639 (excluding resources awarded to replace EFC). 20% of all full-time freshmen had no need and received non-need-based gift aid.

UNDERGRADUATE FINANCIAL AID (Fall 2004, est.) 3,490 applied for aid; of those 80% were deemed to have need. 98% of undergraduates with need received aid; of those 99% had need fully met. *Average percent of need met:* 70% (excluding resources awarded to replace EFC). *Average financial aid package:* $5916 (excluding resources awarded to replace EFC). 11% of all full-time undergraduates had no need and received non-need-based gift aid.
GIFT AID (NEED-BASED) *Total amount:* $8,234,096 (68% federal, 30% state, 2% institutional). *Receiving aid:* Freshmen: 47% (370); All full-time undergraduates: 48% (2,161). *Average award:* Freshmen: $3907; Undergraduates: $3664. *Scholarships, grants, and awards:* Federal Pell, FSEOG, state, college/university gift aid from institutional funds.
GIFT AID (NON-NEED-BASED) *Total amount:* $1,773,147 (55% institutional, 45% external sources). *Receiving aid:* Freshmen: 26% (206); Undergraduates: 16% (712). *Average Award:* Freshmen: $3184; Undergraduates: $4490. *Scholarships, grants, and awards by category: Academic Interests/Achievement:* 697 awards ($757,067 total): agriculture, biological sciences, business, communication, computer science, education, English, foreign languages, general academic interests/achievements, health fields, humanities, mathematics, physical sciences, social sciences. *Creative Arts/Performance:* 162 awards ($77,648 total): art/fine arts, dance, debating, journalism/publications, music, theater/drama. *Special Achievements/Activities:* 107 awards ($67,942 total): cheerleading/drum major, leadership, memberships, rodeo. *Special Characteristics:* 130 awards ($67,948 total): children of faculty/staff, first-generation college students, handicapped students.
LOANS *Student loans:* $13,717,595 (49% need-based, 51% non-need-based). 32% of past graduating class borrowed through all loan programs. *Average indebtedness per student:* $11,875. *Average need-based loan:* Freshmen: $1952; Undergraduates: $3721. *Parent loans:* $299,310 (100% non-need-based). *Programs:* FFEL (Subsidized and Unsubsidized Stafford, PLUS), Perkins, state, college/university.
WORK-STUDY *Federal work-study:* Total amount: $223,773; 123 jobs averaging $1821. *State or other work-study/employment:* Total amount: $39,456 (100% need-based). 44 part-time jobs averaging $897.
ATHLETIC AWARDS *Total amount:* $563,005 (100% non-need-based).
APPLYING FOR FINANCIAL AID *Required financial aid forms:* FAFSA, scholarship application form(s). *Financial aid deadline (priority):* 5/1. *Notification date:* Continuous. Students must reply within 2 weeks of notification.
CONTACT Mr. Jim Reed, Director of Financial Aid, West Texas A&M University, WTAMU Box 60939, Canyon, TX 79016-0001, 806-651-2055 or toll-free 800-99-WTAMU. *Fax:* 806-651-2924. *E-mail:* jreed@mail.wtamu.edu.

WEST VIRGINIA STATE UNIVERSITY
Institute, WV

CONTACT Mrs. Mary Blizzard, Director, Office of Student Financial Assistance, West Virginia State University, PO Box 1000, Ferrell Hall 324, Institute, WV 25112-1000, 304-766-3131 or toll-free 800-987-2112.

WEST VIRGINIA UNIVERSITY
Morgantown, WV

Tuition & fees (WV res): $3938   **Average undergraduate aid package:** $6837

ABOUT THE INSTITUTION State-supported, coed. Awards: bachelor's, master's, doctoral, and first professional degrees. 76 undergraduate majors. Total enrollment: 25,255. Undergraduates: 18,653. Freshmen: 4,359. Federal methodology is used as a basis for awarding need-based institutional aid.
UNDERGRADUATE EXPENSES for 2004–05 *Application fee:* $25. *Tuition, state resident:* full-time $3938; part-time $167 per credit hour. *Tuition, nonresident:* full-time $12,060; part-time $506 per credit hour. Full-time tuition and fees vary according to location, program, and reciprocity agreements. Part-time tuition and fees vary according to course load, location, program, and reciprocity agreements. *College room and board:* $6084; *room only:* $3212. Room and board charges vary according to board plan, housing facility, and location. *Payment plan:* Deferred payment.
FRESHMAN FINANCIAL AID (Fall 2004, est.) 2500 applied for aid; of those 80% were deemed to have need. 95% of freshmen with need received aid; of those 45% had need fully met. *Average percent of need met:* 89% (excluding resources awarded to replace EFC). *Average financial aid package:* $6156 (excluding resources awarded to replace EFC). 27% of all full-time freshmen had no need and received non-need-based gift aid.

UNDERGRADUATE FINANCIAL AID (Fall 2004, est.) 12,894 applied for aid; of those 70% were deemed to have need. 96% of undergraduates with need received aid; of those 26% had need fully met. *Average percent of need met:* 88% (excluding resources awarded to replace EFC). *Average financial aid package:* $6837 (excluding resources awarded to replace EFC). 37% of all full-time undergraduates had no need and received non-need-based gift aid.
GIFT AID (NEED-BASED) *Total amount:* $22,385,803 (59% federal, 33% state, 8% institutional). *Receiving aid:* Freshmen: 21% (929); All full-time undergraduates: 35% (6,187). *Average award:* Freshmen: $3139; Undergraduates: $3209. *Scholarships, grants, and awards:* Federal Pell, FSEOG, state, private, college/university gift aid from institutional funds.
GIFT AID (NON-NEED-BASED) *Total amount:* $16,969,980 (65% state, 26% institutional, 9% external sources). *Receiving aid:* Freshmen: 21% (909); Undergraduates: 24% (4,174). *Average Award:* Freshmen: $5342; Undergraduates: $3019. *Scholarships, grants, and awards by category: Academic Interests/Achievement:* 3,000 awards ($5,000,000 total): agriculture, architecture, area/ethnic studies, biological sciences, business, communication, computer science, education, engineering/technologies, English, foreign languages, general academic interests/achievements, health fields, home economics, humanities, international studies, library science, mathematics, military science, physical sciences, premedicine, religion/biblical studies, social sciences. *Creative Arts/Performance:* 100 awards ($660,000 total): art/fine arts, debating, music, theater/drama. *Special Achievements/Activities:* 12 awards ($35,000 total): general special achievements/activities, leadership. *Special Characteristics:* 500 awards ($1,100,000 total): children of faculty/staff, children of union members/company employees, children of workers in trades, ethnic background, general special characteristics, international students, local/state students, members of minority groups. *Tuition waivers:* Full or partial for employees or children of employees, senior citizens. *ROTC:* Army, Air Force.
LOANS *Student loans:* $52,823,642 (60% need-based, 40% non-need-based). 67% of past graduating class borrowed through all loan programs. *Average indebtedness per student:* $21,100. *Average need-based loan:* Freshmen: $3518; Undergraduates: $3975. *Parent loans:* $26,966,677 (100% non-need-based). *Programs:* Federal Direct (Subsidized and Unsubsidized Stafford, PLUS), Perkins, Federal Nursing, state, college/university.
WORK-STUDY *Federal work-study:* Total amount: $1,476,412; 2,000 jobs averaging $1480. *State or other work-study/employment:* Total amount: $1,405,663 (100% non-need-based). 1,230 part-time jobs averaging $1142.
ATHLETIC AWARDS *Total amount:* $4,330,753 (100% non-need-based).
APPLYING FOR FINANCIAL AID *Required financial aid form:* FAFSA. *Financial aid deadline:* 3/1 (priority: 2/15). *Notification date:* Continuous beginning 3/15. Students must reply within 2 weeks of notification.
CONTACT Kaye Widney, Director of Financial Aid, West Virginia University, PO Box 6004, Morgantown, WV 26506-6004, 304-293-5242 or toll-free 800-344-9881. *Fax:* 304-293-4890. *E-mail:* kaye.widney@mail.wvu.edu.

WEST VIRGINIA UNIVERSITY INSTITUTE OF TECHNOLOGY
Montgomery, WV

CONTACT Nina M. Morton, Director of Financial Aid, West Virginia University Institute of Technology, 405 Fayette Pike, Montgomery, WV 25136, 304-442-3032 or toll-free 888-554-8324.

WEST VIRGINIA WESLEYAN COLLEGE
Buckhannon, WV

Tuition & fees: $21,250   **Average undergraduate aid package:** $20,197

ABOUT THE INSTITUTION Independent religious, coed. Awards: bachelor's and master's degrees. 64 undergraduate majors. Total enrollment: 1,522. Undergraduates: 1,486. Freshmen: 350. Federal methodology is used as a basis for awarding need-based institutional aid.
UNDERGRADUATE EXPENSES for 2005–06 *Application fee:* $35. *Comprehensive fee:* $26,750 includes full-time tuition ($20,250), mandatory fees ($1000), and room and board ($5500). Full-time tuition and fees vary according to course load. Room and board charges vary according to board plan and housing facility. Part-time tuition and fees vary according to course load. *Payment plan:* Installment.
FRESHMAN FINANCIAL AID (Fall 2004, est.) 314 applied for aid; of those 89% were deemed to have need. 100% of freshmen with need received aid; of those 33% had need fully met. *Average percent of need met:* 89% (excluding resources

awarded to replace EFC). *Average financial aid package:* $20,276 (excluding resources awarded to replace EFC). 20% of all full-time freshmen had no need and received non-need-based gift aid.

UNDERGRADUATE FINANCIAL AID (Fall 2004, est.) 1,204 applied for aid; of those 91% were deemed to have need. 100% of undergraduates with need received aid; of those 45% had need fully met. *Average percent of need met:* 88% (excluding resources awarded to replace EFC). *Average financial aid package:* $20,197 (excluding resources awarded to replace EFC). 24% of all full-time undergraduates had no need and received non-need-based gift aid.

GIFT AID (NEED-BASED) *Total amount:* $15,394,863 (9% federal, 10% state, 77% institutional, 4% external sources). *Receiving aid:* Freshmen: 80% (278); All full-time undergraduates: 75% (1,099). *Average award:* Freshmen: $16,861; Undergraduates: $15,775. *Scholarships, grants, and awards:* Federal Pell, FSEOG, state, private, college/university gift aid from institutional funds.

GIFT AID (NON-NEED-BASED) *Total amount:* $3,021,600 (5% state, 93% institutional, 2% external sources). *Receiving aid:* Freshmen: 16% (56); Undergraduates: 13% (192). *Average Award:* Freshmen: $11,475; Undergraduates: $10,270. *Scholarships, grants, and awards by category:* Academic Interests/Achievement: general academic interests/achievements. *Creative Arts/Performance:* art/fine arts, music, theater/drama. *Special Achievements/Activities:* community service, leadership, religious involvement. *Special Characteristics:* children of faculty/staff, general special characteristics, international students, members of minority groups, relatives of clergy. *Tuition waivers:* Full or partial for employees or children of employees.

LOANS *Student loans:* $5,856,455 (82% need-based, 18% non-need-based). *Average need-based loan:* Freshmen: $3098; Undergraduates: $4371. *Parent loans:* $1,890,306 (100% non-need-based). *Programs:* FFEL (Subsidized and Unsubsidized Stafford, PLUS), Perkins, college/university.

WORK-STUDY *Federal work-study:* Total amount: $891,800; 696 jobs available. *State or other work-study/employment:* Total amount: $971,600 (15% need-based, 85% non-need-based). 652 part-time jobs available.

ATHLETIC AWARDS *Total amount:* $2,384,680 (64% need-based, 36% non-need-based).

APPLYING FOR FINANCIAL AID *Required financial aid form:* FAFSA. *Financial aid deadline (priority):* 2/15. *Notification date:* Continuous beginning 3/15. Students must reply within 4 weeks of notification.

CONTACT Mr. Robert N. Skinner, Director of Admission and Financial Aid, West Virginia Wesleyan College, 59 College Avenue, Buckhannon, WV 26201, 304-473-8510 or toll-free 800-722-9933 (out-of-state). *Fax:* 304-472-2571.

WESTWOOD COLLEGE–ATLANTA NORTHLAKE
Atlanta, GA

CONTACT Financial Aid Office, Westwood College–Atlanta Northlake, 2220 Parklake Drive, Suite 175, Atlanta, GA 30345, 404-962-2999.

WHEATON COLLEGE
Wheaton, IL

Tuition & fees: $20,000	Average undergraduate aid package: $18,371

ABOUT THE INSTITUTION Independent nondenominational, coed. Awards: bachelor's, master's, and doctoral degrees and post-bachelor's certificates. 40 undergraduate majors. Total enrollment: 2,898. Undergraduates: 2,440. Freshmen: 596. Institutional methodology is used as a basis for awarding need-based institutional aid.

UNDERGRADUATE EXPENSES for 2004–05 *Application fee:* $50. *Comprehensive fee:* $26,466 includes full-time tuition ($20,000) and room and board ($6466). *College room only:* $3784. Room and board charges vary according to board plan and housing facility. *Part-time tuition:* $834 per hour. Part-time tuition and fees vary according to course load. *Payment plans:* Installment, deferred payment.

FRESHMAN FINANCIAL AID (Fall 2004, est.) 455 applied for aid; of those 65% were deemed to have need. 100% of freshmen with need received aid; of those 20% had need fully met. *Average percent of need met:* 88% (excluding resources awarded to replace EFC). *Average financial aid package:* $18,243 (excluding resources awarded to replace EFC). 22% of all full-time freshmen had no need and received non-need-based gift aid.

UNDERGRADUATE FINANCIAL AID (Fall 2004, est.) 1,727 applied for aid; of those 70% were deemed to have need. 98% of undergraduates with need

received aid; of those 17% had need fully met. *Average percent of need met:* 85% (excluding resources awarded to replace EFC). *Average financial aid package:* $18,371 (excluding resources awarded to replace EFC). 19% of all full-time undergraduates had no need and received non-need-based gift aid.

GIFT AID (NEED-BASED) *Total amount:* $14,048,315 (10% federal, 4% state, 79% institutional, 7% external sources). *Receiving aid:* Freshmen: 39% (231); All full-time undergraduates: 41% (960). *Average award:* Freshmen: $13,226; Undergraduates: $12,212. *Scholarships, grants, and awards:* Federal Pell, FSEOG, state, college/university gift aid from institutional funds.

GIFT AID (NON-NEED-BASED) *Total amount:* $1,351,656 (4% federal, 1% state, 64% institutional, 31% external sources). *Receiving aid:* Freshmen: 21% (123); Undergraduates: 19% (434). *Average Award:* Freshmen: $2616; Undergraduates: $3761. *Scholarships, grants, and awards by category:* Academic Interests/Achievement: 19 awards ($50,447 total): English, general academic interests/achievements, physical sciences, premedicine. *Creative Arts/Performance:* 26 awards ($152,552 total): music. *Special Characteristics:* 1 award ($3738 total): handicapped students. *Tuition waivers:* Full or partial for employees or children of employees. *ROTC:* Army, Air Force cooperative.

LOANS *Student loans:* $7,324,781 (88% need-based, 12% non-need-based). 53% of past graduating class borrowed through all loan programs. *Average indebtedness per student:* $17,382. *Average need-based loan:* Freshmen: $4703; Undergraduates: $5458. *Parent loans:* $3,122,546 (56% need-based, 44% non-need-based). *Programs:* FFEL (Subsidized and Unsubsidized Stafford, PLUS), Perkins, college/university.

WORK-STUDY *Federal work-study:* Total amount: $451,234; 768 jobs averaging $825.

APPLYING FOR FINANCIAL AID *Required financial aid forms:* FAFSA, institution's own form. *Financial aid deadline (priority):* 2/15. *Notification date:* Continuous beginning 3/1.

CONTACT Mrs. Donna Peltz, Director of Financial Aid, Wheaton College, 501 College Avenue, Wheaton, IL 60187-5593, 630-752-5021 or toll-free 800-222-2419 (out-of-state). *E-mail:* finaid@wheaton.edu.

WHEATON COLLEGE
Norton, MA

Tuition & fees: $30,580	Average undergraduate aid package: $22,674

ABOUT THE INSTITUTION Independent, coed. Awards: bachelor's degrees. 36 undergraduate majors. Total enrollment: 1,538. Undergraduates: 1,538. Freshmen: 443. Institutional methodology is used as a basis for awarding need-based institutional aid.

UNDERGRADUATE EXPENSES for 2004–05 *Application fee:* $55. *Comprehensive fee:* $38,160 includes full-time tuition ($30,355), mandatory fees ($225), and room and board ($7580). *College room only:* $4000. *Payment plans:* Tuition prepayment, installment.

FRESHMAN FINANCIAL AID (Fall 2004, est.) 277 applied for aid; of those 77% were deemed to have need. 100% of freshmen with need received aid; of those 48% had need fully met. *Average percent of need met:* 93% (excluding resources awarded to replace EFC). *Average financial aid package:* $22,631 (excluding resources awarded to replace EFC). 14% of all full-time freshmen had no need and received non-need-based gift aid.

UNDERGRADUATE FINANCIAL AID (Fall 2004, est.) 957 applied for aid; of those 85% were deemed to have need. 100% of undergraduates with need received aid; of those 44% had need fully met. *Average percent of need met:* 93% (excluding resources awarded to replace EFC). *Average financial aid package:* $22,674 (excluding resources awarded to replace EFC). 13% of all full-time undergraduates had no need and received non-need-based gift aid.

GIFT AID (NEED-BASED) *Total amount:* $14,127,226 (6% federal, 3% state, 87% institutional, 4% external sources). *Receiving aid:* Freshmen: 47% (206); All full-time undergraduates: 49% (790). *Average award:* Freshmen: $18,322; Undergraduates: $17,162. *Scholarships, grants, and awards:* Federal Pell, FSEOG, state, private, college/university gift aid from institutional funds.

GIFT AID (NON-NEED-BASED) *Total amount:* $2,068,486 (92% institutional, 8% external sources). *Receiving aid:* Freshmen: 2; Undergraduates: 3. *Average Award:* Freshmen: $11,291; Undergraduates: $9287. *Scholarships, grants, and awards by category:* Academic Interests/Achievement: 466 awards ($3,686,350 total): general academic interests/achievements. *Tuition waivers:* Full or partial for employees or children of employees. *ROTC:* Army cooperative.

LOANS *Student loans:* $5,171,295 (71% need-based, 29% non-need-based). 69% of past graduating class borrowed through all loan programs. *Average indebtedness per student:* $22,052. *Average need-based loan:* Freshmen: $3568;

Undergraduates: $4826. *Parent loans:* $4,540,800 (100% non-need-based). *Programs:* FFEL (Subsidized and Unsubsidized Stafford, PLUS), Perkins, state, college/university, MEFA, TERI, Citi Assist, Signature, alternative loans.

WORK-STUDY *Federal work-study:* Total amount: $1,175,247; 698 jobs averaging $1688. *State or other work-study/employment:* Total amount: $510,140 (37% need-based, 63% non-need-based). 227 part-time jobs averaging $2247.

APPLYING FOR FINANCIAL AID *Required financial aid forms:* FAFSA, CSS Financial Aid PROFILE, noncustodial (divorced/separated) parent's statement, business/farm supplement, federal income tax form(s). *Financial aid deadline:* 2/1. *Notification date:* 4/1. Students must reply by 5/1.

CONTACT Ms. Susan Beard, Director of Financial Aid Programs, Wheaton College, East Main Street, Norton, MA 02766, 508-286-8232 or toll-free 800-394-6003. *Fax:* 508-286-3787. *E-mail:* sfs@wheatonma.edu.

WHEELING JESUIT UNIVERSITY
Wheeling, WV

Tuition & fees: $21,350	Average undergraduate aid package: $16,719

ABOUT THE INSTITUTION Independent Roman Catholic (Jesuit), coed. Awards: bachelor's, master's, and doctoral degrees. 54 undergraduate majors. Total enrollment: 1,699. Undergraduates: 1,232. Freshmen: 288. Both federal and institutional methodology are used as a basis for awarding need-based institutional aid.

UNDERGRADUATE EXPENSES for 2005–06 *Application fee:* $25. *Comprehensive fee:* $27,800 includes full-time tuition ($20,890), mandatory fees ($460), and room and board ($6450). *College room only:* $3070. Full-time tuition and fees vary according to course load and program. Room and board charges vary according to board plan, gender, and housing facility. *Part-time tuition:* $540 per credit hour. *Part-time fees:* $465 per term. Part-time tuition and fees vary according to class time and program. *Payment plan:* Installment.

FRESHMAN FINANCIAL AID (Fall 2004, est.) 276 applied for aid; of those 88% were deemed to have need. 100% of freshmen with need received aid; of those 42% had need fully met. *Average percent of need met:* 94% (excluding resources awarded to replace EFC). *Average financial aid package:* $18,884 (excluding resources awarded to replace EFC). 14% of all full-time freshmen had no need and received non-need-based gift aid.

UNDERGRADUATE FINANCIAL AID (Fall 2004, est.) 954 applied for aid; of those 87% were deemed to have need. 100% of undergraduates with need received aid; of those 37% had need fully met. *Average percent of need met:* 87% (excluding resources awarded to replace EFC). *Average financial aid package:* $16,719 (excluding resources awarded to replace EFC). 15% of all full-time undergraduates had no need and received non-need-based gift aid.

GIFT AID (NEED-BASED) *Total amount:* $3,003,617 (37% federal, 7% state, 56% institutional). *Receiving aid:* Freshmen: 69% (200); All full-time undergraduates: 58% (603). *Average award:* Freshmen: $5670; Undergraduates: $4870. *Scholarships, grants, and awards:* Federal Pell, FSEOG, state, private, college/university gift aid from institutional funds, Federal Nursing.

GIFT AID (NON-NEED-BASED) *Total amount:* $7,681,075 (2% federal, 5% state, 89% institutional, 4% external sources). *Receiving aid:* Freshmen: 84% (242); Undergraduates: 39% (413). *Average Award:* Freshmen: $9201; Undergraduates: $8672. *Scholarships, grants, and awards by category:* Academic Interests/Achievement: 772 awards ($5,735,144 total): biological sciences, business, communication, computer science, education, engineering/technologies, English, foreign languages, general academic interests/achievements, health fields, humanities, international studies, mathematics, physical sciences, premedicine, religion/biblical studies, social sciences. Creative Arts/Performance: 51 awards ($102,000 total): music. Special Achievements/Activities: 103 awards ($243,710 total): community service, general special achievements/activities, religious involvement. Special Characteristics: 461 awards ($1,435,663 total): children and siblings of alumni, children of faculty/staff, children of union members/company employees, general special characteristics, international students, religious affiliation. *Tuition waivers:* Full or partial for employees or children of employees, senior citizens.

LOANS *Student loans:* $5,639,348 (54% need-based, 46% non-need-based). 73% of past graduating class borrowed through all loan programs. *Average indebtedness per student:* $15,001. *Average need-based loan:* Freshmen: $3222; Undergraduates: $4404. *Parent loans:* $1,062,398 (100% non-need-based). *Programs:* Federal Direct (Subsidized and Unsubsidized Stafford, PLUS), Perkins, Federal Nursing, alternative loans.

WORK-STUDY *Federal work-study:* Total amount: $255,327; 194 jobs averaging $1316. *State or other work-study/employment:* Total amount: $300,634 (100% non-need-based). 207 part-time jobs averaging $1452.

ATHLETIC AWARDS *Total amount:* $601,460 (100% non-need-based).

APPLYING FOR FINANCIAL AID *Required financial aid forms:* FAFSA, institution's own form. *Financial aid deadline (priority):* 3/1. *Notification date:* Continuous beginning 3/15. Students must reply within 2 weeks of notification.

CONTACT Christie Tomczyk, Director of Financial Aid, Wheeling Jesuit University, 316 Washington Avenue, Wheeling, WV 26003-6295, 304-243-2304 or toll-free 800-624-6992 Ext. 2359. *Fax:* 304-243-4397. *E-mail:* finaid@wju.edu.

WHEELOCK COLLEGE
Boston, MA

CONTACT Joseph L. Chillo, Vice President for Enrollment Management, Wheelock College, 200 The Riverway, Boston, MA 02215-4176, 617-879-2205 or toll-free 800-734-5212 (out-of-state).

WHITMAN COLLEGE
Walla Walla, WA

Tuition & fees: $27,106	Average undergraduate aid package: $19,483

ABOUT THE INSTITUTION Independent, coed. Awards: bachelor's degrees. 29 undergraduate majors. Total enrollment: 1,481. Undergraduates: 1,481. Freshmen: 385. Both federal and institutional methodology are used as a basis for awarding need-based institutional aid.

UNDERGRADUATE EXPENSES for 2004–05 *Application fee:* $45. *Comprehensive fee:* $34,286 includes full-time tuition ($26,870), mandatory fees ($236), and room and board ($7180). *College room only:* $3300. Room and board charges vary according to board plan and housing facility. *Part-time tuition:* $1120 per credit. *Payment plan:* Deferred payment.

FRESHMAN FINANCIAL AID (Fall 2004, est.) 266 applied for aid; of those 70% were deemed to have need. 100% of freshmen with need received aid; of those 77% had need fully met. *Average percent of need met:* 94% (excluding resources awarded to replace EFC). *Average financial aid package:* $19,385 (excluding resources awarded to replace EFC). 48% of all full-time freshmen had no need and received non-need-based gift aid.

UNDERGRADUATE FINANCIAL AID (Fall 2004, est.) 919 applied for aid; of those 73% were deemed to have need. 100% of undergraduates with need received aid; of those 74% had need fully met. *Average percent of need met:* 93% (excluding resources awarded to replace EFC). *Average financial aid package:* $19,483 (excluding resources awarded to replace EFC). 34% of all full-time undergraduates had no need and received non-need-based gift aid.

GIFT AID (NEED-BASED) *Total amount:* $9,569,600 (6% federal, 2% state, 92% institutional). *Receiving aid:* Freshmen: 52% (183); All full-time undergraduates: 46% (668). *Average award:* Freshmen: $14,674; Undergraduates: $13,268. *Scholarships, grants, and awards:* Federal Pell, FSEOG, state, private, college/university gift aid from institutional funds.

GIFT AID (NON-NEED-BASED) *Total amount:* $6,065,655 (6% state, 85% institutional, 9% external sources). *Receiving aid:* Freshmen: 42% (149); Undergraduates: 23% (342). *Average Award:* Freshmen: $6850; Undergraduates: $7450. *Scholarships, grants, and awards by category:* Academic Interests/Achievement: 492 awards ($3,823,200 total): general academic interests/achievements. Creative Arts/Performance: 146 awards ($376,675 total): art/fine arts, debating, music, theater/drama. Special Characteristics: 66 awards ($1,347,000 total): ethnic background, international students. *Tuition waivers:* Full or partial for employees or children of employees.

LOANS *Student loans:* $2,799,105 (86% need-based, 14% non-need-based). 55% of past graduating class borrowed through all loan programs. *Average indebtedness per student:* $17,927. *Average need-based loan:* Freshmen: $3125; Undergraduates: $4364. *Parent loans:* $1,701,925 (100% non-need-based). *Programs:* FFEL (Subsidized and Unsubsidized Stafford, PLUS), Perkins, alternative loans.

WORK-STUDY *Federal work-study:* Total amount: $1,048,300; 483 jobs averaging $1989. *State or other work-study/employment:* Total amount: $283,850 (100% non-need-based). 220 part-time jobs averaging $1529.

APPLYING FOR FINANCIAL AID *Required financial aid forms:* FAFSA, CSS Financial Aid PROFILE. *Financial aid deadline (priority):* 11/15. *Notification date:* Continuous beginning 12/19. Students must reply within 3 weeks of notification.

CONTACT Tyson Hailow, Financial Aid Assistant, Whitman College, 515 Boyer Avenue, Walla Walla, WA 99362-2046, 509-527-5178 or toll-free 877-462-9448. *Fax:* 509-527-4967.

WHITTIER COLLEGE
Whittier, CA

Tuition & fees: $26,138	Average undergraduate aid package: $25,619

ABOUT THE INSTITUTION Independent, coed. Awards: bachelor's, master's, and first professional degrees. 25 undergraduate majors. Total enrollment: 1,307. Undergraduates: 1,307. Freshmen: 394. Both federal and institutional methodology are used as a basis for awarding need-based institutional aid.

UNDERGRADUATE EXPENSES for 2005–06 *Application fee:* $50. *Comprehensive fee:* $34,066 includes full-time tuition ($25,838), mandatory fees ($300), and room and board ($7928).

FRESHMAN FINANCIAL AID (Fall 2003) 370 applied for aid. of those 50% had need fully met. *Average percent of need met:* 100% (excluding resources awarded to replace EFC). *Average financial aid package:* $26,518 (excluding resources awarded to replace EFC). 18% of all full-time freshmen had no need and received non-need-based gift aid.

UNDERGRADUATE FINANCIAL AID (Fall 2003) 1,161 applied for aid. of those 47% had need fully met. *Average percent of need met:* 100% (excluding resources awarded to replace EFC). *Average financial aid package:* $25,619 (excluding resources awarded to replace EFC). 20% of all full-time undergraduates had no need and received non-need-based gift aid.

GIFT AID (NEED-BASED) *Total amount:* $7,310,833 (18% federal, 28% state, 54% institutional). *Receiving aid:* Freshmen: 50% (186); All full-time undergraduates: 56% (671). *Average award:* Freshmen: $10,946; Undergraduates: $12,005. *Scholarships, grants, and awards:* Federal Pell, FSEOG, state, private, college/university gift aid from institutional funds.

GIFT AID (NON-NEED-BASED) *Total amount:* $8,880,044 (98% institutional, 2% external sources). *Receiving aid:* Freshmen: 51% (189); Undergraduates: 50% (608). *Average Award:* Freshmen: $11,365; *Undergraduates:* $11,212. *Scholarships, grants, and awards by category: Academic Interests/Achievement:* general academic interests/achievements. *Creative Arts/Performance:* art/fine arts, music, theater/drama. *Special Characteristics:* children and siblings of alumni, children of faculty/staff, international students. *ROTC:* Army cooperative, Air Force cooperative.

LOANS *Student loans:* $5,433,186 (90% need-based, 10% non-need-based). 93% of past graduating class borrowed through all loan programs. *Average indebtedness per student:* $22,104. *Average need-based loan:* Freshmen: $4805. *Parent loans:* $1,642,187 (100% non-need-based). *Programs:* Federal Direct (PLUS), FFEL (Subsidized and Unsubsidized Stafford, PLUS), Perkins, alternative financing loans.

WORK-STUDY *Federal work-study:* Total amount: $1,199,929; jobs available. *State or other work-study/employment:* Total amount: $618,738 (100% non-need-based). Part-time jobs available.

APPLYING FOR FINANCIAL AID *Required financial aid forms:* FAFSA, CSS Financial Aid PROFILE. *Financial aid deadline:* 6/30 (priority: 3/1). *Notification date:* Continuous beginning 3/1. Students must reply within 2 weeks of notification.

CONTACT Mr. Vernon Bridges, Director of Student Financing, Whittier College, 13406 East Philadelphia Street, PO Box 634, Whittier, CA 90608-0634, 562-907-4285. *Fax:* 562-464-4560. *E-mail:* vbridges@whittier.edu.

WHITWORTH COLLEGE
Spokane, WA

Tuition & fees: $22,678	Average undergraduate aid package: $17,980

ABOUT THE INSTITUTION Independent Presbyterian, coed. Awards: bachelor's and master's degrees. 44 undergraduate majors. Total enrollment: 2,373. Undergraduates: 2,034. Freshmen: 471. Federal methodology is used as a basis for awarding need-based institutional aid.

UNDERGRADUATE EXPENSES for 2005–06 *Comprehensive fee:* $29,438 includes full-time tuition ($22,400), mandatory fees ($278), and room and board ($6760). Room and board charges vary according to board plan and housing facility. Part-time tuition and fees vary according to class time. *Payment plan:* Installment.

FRESHMAN FINANCIAL AID (Fall 2004, est.) 397 applied for aid; of those 82% were deemed to have need. 100% of freshmen with need received aid; of those 29% had need fully met. *Average percent of need met:* 86% (excluding resources awarded to replace EFC). *Average financial aid package:* $18,357 (excluding resources awarded to replace EFC). 28% of all full-time freshmen had no need and received non-need-based gift aid.

UNDERGRADUATE FINANCIAL AID (Fall 2004, est.) 1,612 applied for aid; of those 89% were deemed to have need. 100% of undergraduates with need received aid; of those 21% had need fully met. *Average percent of need met:* 84% (excluding resources awarded to replace EFC). *Average financial aid package:* $17,980 (excluding resources awarded to replace EFC). 21% of all full-time undergraduates had no need and received non-need-based gift aid.

GIFT AID (NEED-BASED) *Total amount:* $16,788,375 (11% federal, 9% state, 73% institutional, 7% external sources). *Receiving aid:* Freshmen: 69% (326); All full-time undergraduates: 68% (1,387). *Average award:* Freshmen: $13,031; Undergraduates: $12,079. *Scholarships, grants, and awards:* Federal Pell, FSEOG, state, private, college/university gift aid from institutional funds.

GIFT AID (NON-NEED-BASED) *Total amount:* $3,750,704 (4% federal, 2% state, 85% institutional, 9% external sources). *Receiving aid:* Freshmen: 7% (32); Undergraduates: 5% (99). *Average Award:* Freshmen: $7013; Undergraduates: $6711. *Scholarships, grants, and awards by category: Academic Interests/Achievement:* 1,481 awards ($7,065,544 total): biological sciences, computer science, general academic interests/achievements, military science, physical sciences. *Creative Arts/Performance:* 147 awards ($262,810 total): art/fine arts, journalism/publications, music, theater/drama. *Special Achievements/Activities:* 668 awards ($662,028 total): religious involvement. *Special Characteristics:* 499 awards ($872,610 total): children and siblings of alumni, ethnic background, international students, relatives of clergy, siblings of current students. *Tuition waivers:* Full or partial for employees or children of employees. *ROTC:* Army cooperative.

LOANS *Student loans:* $8,001,825 (80% need-based, 20% non-need-based). 71% of past graduating class borrowed through all loan programs. *Average indebtedness per student:* $17,014. *Average need-based loan:* Freshmen: $3722; Undergraduates: $4525. *Parent loans:* $2,533,149 (35% need-based, 65% non-need-based). *Programs:* Federal Direct (Subsidized and Unsubsidized Stafford, PLUS), Perkins, college/university.

WORK-STUDY *Federal work-study:* Total amount: $978,569; 485 jobs averaging $2003. *State or other work-study/employment:* Total amount: $825,388 (94% need-based, 6% non-need-based). 327 part-time jobs averaging $2886.

APPLYING FOR FINANCIAL AID *Required financial aid form:* FAFSA. *Financial aid deadline (priority):* 3/1. *Notification date:* Continuous beginning 4/1. Students must reply by 5/1 or within 4 weeks of notification.

CONTACT Ms. Wendy Z. Olson, Director of Financial Aid, Whitworth College, 300 West Hawthorne Road, Spokane, WA 99251-0001, 509-777-4306 or toll-free 800-533-4668 (out-of-state). *Fax:* 509-777-3725. *E-mail:* wolson@whitworth.edu.

WICHITA STATE UNIVERSITY
Wichita, KS

Tuition & fees (KS res): $3908	Average undergraduate aid package: $5207

ABOUT THE INSTITUTION State-supported, coed. Awards: associate, bachelor's, master's, and doctoral degrees and post-bachelor's and post-master's certificates. 59 undergraduate majors. Total enrollment: 14,297. Undergraduates: 11,199. Freshmen: 1,158. Federal methodology is used as a basis for awarding need-based institutional aid.

UNDERGRADUATE EXPENSES for 2004–05 *Application fee:* $30. *Tuition, state resident:* full-time $3150; part-time $105 per credit hour. *Tuition, nonresident:* full-time $11,362; part-time $353.45 per credit hour. *Required fees:* full-time $758; $24.15 per credit hour or $17. Full-time tuition and fees vary according to course load. *College room and board:* $4900. Room and board charges vary according to board plan and housing facility. *Payment plan:* Installment.

FRESHMAN FINANCIAL AID (Fall 2003) 945 applied for aid; of those 98% were deemed to have need. 98% of freshmen with need received aid; of those 6% had need fully met. *Average percent of need met:* 47% (excluding resources awarded to replace EFC). *Average financial aid package:* $6305 (excluding resources awarded to replace EFC). 14% of all full-time freshmen had no need and received non-need-based gift aid.

UNDERGRADUATE FINANCIAL AID (Fall 2003) 5,293 applied for aid; of those 99% were deemed to have need. 97% of undergraduates with need received aid; of those 7% had need fully met. *Average percent of need met:* 51% (excluding resources awarded to replace EFC). *Average financial aid package:* $5207 (excluding resources awarded to replace EFC). 9% of all full-time undergraduates had no need and received non-need-based gift aid.

GIFT AID (NEED-BASED) *Total amount:* $13,527,504 (90% federal, 10% state). *Receiving aid:* Freshmen: 41% (448); All full-time undergraduates: 33% (2,612).

Average award: Freshmen: $3260; Undergraduates: $3453. *Scholarships, grants, and awards:* Federal Pell, FSEOG, state, private, college/university gift aid from institutional funds, Bureau of Indian Affairs Grants.

GIFT AID (NON-NEED-BASED) *Total amount:* $4,938,529 (88% institutional, 12% external sources). *Receiving aid:* Freshmen: 35% (379); Undergraduates: 17% (1,304). *Average Award:* Freshmen: $1704; Undergraduates: $1419. *Scholarships, grants, and awards by category:* Academic Interests/Achievement: area/ethnic studies, biological sciences, business, communication, computer science, education, engineering/technologies, English, foreign languages, general academic interests/achievements, health fields, humanities, international studies, mathematics, physical sciences, premedicine, social sciences. *Creative Arts/Performance:* applied art and design, art/fine arts, dance, debating, journalism/publications, music, performing arts, theater/drama. *Special Achievements/Activities:* general special achievements/activities, leadership. *Special Characteristics:* adult students, first-generation college students, international students, members of minority groups. *Tuition waivers:* Full or partial for employees or children of employees, senior citizens.

LOANS *Student loans:* $44,416,998 (100% need-based). 52% of past graduating class borrowed through all loan programs. *Average indebtedness per student:* $18,510. *Average need-based loan:* Freshmen: $2316; Undergraduates: $4224. *Parent loans:* $1,057,404 (100% non-need-based). *Programs:* FFEL (Subsidized and Unsubsidized Stafford, PLUS), Perkins, college/university.

WORK-STUDY *Federal work-study:* Total amount: $1,074,997; 195 jobs averaging $2576. *State or other work-study/employment:* Total amount: $102,937 (100% need-based). Part-time jobs available.

ATHLETIC AWARDS *Total amount:* $1,783,009 (100% non-need-based).

APPLYING FOR FINANCIAL AID *Required financial aid forms:* FAFSA, state aid form, scholarship application form(s). *Financial aid deadline (priority):* 3/15. *Notification date:* Continuous beginning 4/1. Students must reply within 2 weeks of notification.

CONTACT Deborah D. Byers, Director of Financial Aid, Wichita State University, 1845 Fairmount, Wichita, KS 67260-0024, 316-978-3430 or toll-free 800-362-2594. *Fax:* 316-978-3396.

WIDENER UNIVERSITY
Chester, PA

ABOUT THE INSTITUTION Independent, coed. Awards: associate, bachelor's, master's, doctoral, and first professional degrees. 70 undergraduate majors. Total enrollment: 5,940. Undergraduates: 2,501. Freshmen: 730.

GIFT AID (NEED-BASED) *Scholarships, grants, and awards:* Federal Pell, FSEOG, state, private, college/university gift aid from institutional funds.

GIFT AID (NON-NEED-BASED) *Scholarships, grants, and awards by category:* Academic Interests/Achievement: biological sciences, business, communication, computer science, education, engineering/technologies, English, foreign languages, general academic interests/achievements, health fields, humanities, international studies, mathematics, military science, physical sciences, premedicine, social sciences. *Creative Arts/Performance:* music. *Special Achievements/Activities:* community service, general special achievements/activities, leadership. *Special Characteristics:* adult students, children of faculty/staff, ethnic background, international students, siblings of current students.

LOANS *Programs:* FFEL (Subsidized and Unsubsidized Stafford, PLUS), Perkins.

WORK-STUDY *Federal work-study:* Total amount: $2,541,630; jobs available (averaging $1080).

APPLYING FOR FINANCIAL AID *Required financial aid forms:* FAFSA, institution's own form.

CONTACT Walter Cathie, Dean of University Financial Aid, Widener University, One University Place, Chester, PA 19013-5792, 610-499-4174 or toll-free 888-WIDENER. *Fax:* 610-499-4687.

WILBERFORCE UNIVERSITY
Wilberforce, OH

CONTACT Director of Financial Aid, Wilberforce University, 1055 North Bickett Road, Wilberforce, OH 45384, 937-708-5727 or toll-free 800-367-8568. *Fax:* 937-376-4752.

WILEY COLLEGE
Marshall, TX

ABOUT THE INSTITUTION Independent religious, coed. Awards: associate and bachelor's degrees. 27 undergraduate majors. Total enrollment: 666. Undergraduates: 666. Freshmen: 165.

GIFT AID (NEED-BASED) *Scholarships, grants, and awards:* Federal Pell, FSEOG, state, private, college/university gift aid from institutional funds, United Negro College Fund.

GIFT AID (NON-NEED-BASED) *Scholarships, grants, and awards by category:* Academic Interests/Achievement: general academic interests/achievements. *Creative Arts/Performance:* music. *Special Achievements/Activities:* memberships. *Special Characteristics:* children of faculty/staff, relatives of clergy, religious affiliation.

LOANS *Programs:* FFEL (Subsidized and Unsubsidized Stafford, PLUS), Perkins, state.

WORK-STUDY *Federal work-study:* Total amount: $182,438; jobs available. *State or other work-study/employment:* Total amount: $58,724 (12% need-based, 88% non-need-based). Part-time jobs available.

APPLYING FOR FINANCIAL AID *Required financial aid forms:* FAFSA, institution's own form.

CONTACT Cecelia Jones, Interim Director of Financial Aid, Wiley College, 711 Wiley Avenue, Marshall, TX 75670-5199, 903-927-3210 or toll-free 800-658-6889. *Fax:* 903-927-3366.

WILKES UNIVERSITY
Wilkes-Barre, PA

Tuition & fees: $20,408	Average undergraduate aid package: $15,826

ABOUT THE INSTITUTION Independent, coed. Awards: bachelor's, master's, and first professional degrees. 35 undergraduate majors. Total enrollment: 4,364. Undergraduates: 2,108. Freshmen: 561. Federal methodology is used as a basis for awarding need-based institutional aid.

UNDERGRADUATE EXPENSES for 2004–05 *Application fee:* $35. *Comprehensive fee:* $29,332 includes full-time tuition ($19,428), mandatory fees ($980), and room and board ($8924). *College room only:* $5284. Room and board charges vary according to board plan and housing facility. *Part-time tuition:* $536 per credit. *Part-time fees:* $30 per credit. *Payment plans:* Installment, deferred payment.

FRESHMAN FINANCIAL AID (Fall 2004, est.) 539 applied for aid; of those 88% were deemed to have need. 100% of freshmen with need received aid; of those 17% had need fully met. *Average percent of need met:* 83% (excluding resources awarded to replace EFC). *Average financial aid package:* $16,751 (excluding resources awarded to replace EFC). 14% of all full-time freshmen had no need and received non-need-based gift aid.

UNDERGRADUATE FINANCIAL AID (Fall 2004, est.) 1,885 applied for aid; of those 90% were deemed to have need. 97% of undergraduates with need received aid; of those 24% had need fully met. *Average percent of need met:* 79% (excluding resources awarded to replace EFC). *Average financial aid package:* $15,826 (excluding resources awarded to replace EFC). 12% of all full-time undergraduates had no need and received non-need-based gift aid.

GIFT AID (NEED-BASED) *Total amount:* $19,357,846 (11% federal, 16% state, 72% institutional, 1% external sources). *Receiving aid:* Freshmen: 86% (472); All full-time undergraduates: 81% (1,644). *Average award:* Freshmen: $13,264; Undergraduates: $11,690. *Scholarships, grants, and awards:* Federal Pell, FSEOG, state, private, college/university gift aid from institutional funds.

GIFT AID (NON-NEED-BASED) *Total amount:* $1,973,268 (5% federal, 94% institutional, 1% external sources). *Receiving aid:* Freshmen: 86% (472); Undergraduates: 81% (1,644). *Average Award:* Freshmen: $9163; Undergraduates:* $7691. *Scholarships, grants, and awards by category:* Academic Interests/Achievement: biological sciences, business, communication, education, engineering/technologies, English, general academic interests/achievements, health fields, humanities, international studies, mathematics, premedicine, social sciences. *Creative Arts/Performance:* dance, journalism/publications, music, performing arts, theater/drama. *Special Achievements/Activities:* general special achievements/activities, leadership. *Special Characteristics:* adult students, children of faculty/staff. *Tuition waivers:* Full or partial for employees or children of employees. *ROTC:* Army cooperative, Air Force.

LOANS *Student loans:* $11,511,661 (94% need-based, 6% non-need-based). 82% of past graduating class borrowed through all loan programs. *Average indebtedness per student:* $20,711. *Average need-based loan:* Freshmen: $2116;

Undergraduates: $2932. *Parent loans:* $1,673,541 (85% need-based, 15% non-need-based). *Programs:* FFEL (Subsidized and Unsubsidized Stafford, PLUS), Perkins, Federal Nursing, state, college/university, Gulf Oil Loan Fund, Rulison Evans Loan Fund.

WORK-STUDY *Federal work-study:* Total amount: $1,703,432; 1,044 jobs averaging $1632. *State or other work-study/employment:* Total amount: $137,120 (57% need-based, 43% non-need-based). 74 part-time jobs averaging $1853.

APPLYING FOR FINANCIAL AID *Required financial aid forms:* FAFSA, institution's own form. *Financial aid deadline (priority):* 3/1. *Notification date:* Continuous.

CONTACT Mrs. Rachael L. Lohman, Director of Financial Aid, Wilkes University, 267 South Franklin Street, Wilkes-Barre, PA 18766, 570-408-4346 or toll-free 800-945-5378 Ext. 4400. *Fax:* 570-408-7808. *E-mail:* rachael@wilkes.edu.

WILLAMETTE UNIVERSITY
Salem, OR

ABOUT THE INSTITUTION Independent United Methodist, coed. Awards: bachelor's, master's, and first professional degrees and post-bachelor's and first professional certificates. 37 undergraduate majors. Total enrollment: 2,663. Undergraduates: 1,977. Freshmen: 511.

GIFT AID (NEED-BASED) *Scholarships, grants, and awards:* Federal Pell, FSEOG, state, private, college/university gift aid from institutional funds, United Negro College Fund.

GIFT AID (NON-NEED-BASED) *Scholarships, grants, and awards by category:* *Academic Interests/Achievement:* general academic interests/achievements. *Creative Arts/Performance:* debating, music, theater/drama. *Special Achievements/ Activities:* community service, leadership. *Special Characteristics:* international students, members of minority groups.

LOANS *Programs:* FFEL (Subsidized and Unsubsidized Stafford, PLUS), Perkins, state, alternative loans.

WORK-STUDY *Federal work-study:* Total amount: $1,427,012; 769 jobs averaging $1856.

APPLYING FOR FINANCIAL AID *Required financial aid forms:* FAFSA, CSS Financial Aid PROFILE.

CONTACT James Eddy, Director of Financial Aid, Willamette University, 900 State Street, Salem, OR 97301-3931, 503-370-6273 or toll-free 877-542-2787. *Fax:* 503-370-6588. *E-mail:* jeddy@willamette.edu.

WILLIAM CAREY COLLEGE
Hattiesburg, MS

Tuition & fees: $8415	Average undergraduate aid package: $10,500

ABOUT THE INSTITUTION Independent Southern Baptist, coed. Awards: bachelor's and master's degrees. 32 undergraduate majors. Total enrollment: 2,758. Undergraduates: 1,853. Freshmen: 125. Federal methodology is used as a basis for awarding need-based institutional aid.

UNDERGRADUATE EXPENSES for 2005–06 *Application fee:* $20. *Comprehensive fee:* $11,880 includes full-time tuition ($8100), mandatory fees ($315), and room and board ($3465). *College room only:* $1305. Full-time tuition and fees vary according to degree level and location. Room and board charges vary according to board plan, housing facility, and location. *Part-time tuition:* $270 per hour. *Part-time fees:* $105 per term. Part-time tuition and fees vary according to degree level and location. *Payment plan:* Deferred payment.

GIFT AID (NEED-BASED) *Total amount:* $2,700,000 (71% federal, 22% state, 7% external sources). *Receiving aid:* All full-time undergraduates: 96% (1,771). *Average award:* Undergraduates: $5500. *Scholarships, grants, and awards:* Federal Pell, FSEOG, state, private, college/university gift aid from institutional funds.

GIFT AID (NON-NEED-BASED) *Total amount:* $3,200,000 (100% institutional). *Receiving aid:* Undergraduates: 50% (922). *Average Award:* Undergraduates: $5000. *Scholarships, grants, and awards by category:* *Academic Interests/ Achievement:* 800 awards ($2,500,000 total): general academic interests/ achievements. *Creative Arts/Performance:* 50 awards ($150,000 total): art/fine arts, debating, journalism/publications, music, theater/drama. *Special Achievements/ Activities:* 200 awards ($50,000 total): cheerleading/drum major, junior miss, leadership, religious involvement. *Special Characteristics:* 180 awards ($250,000 total): children and siblings of alumni, children of educators, children of faculty/ staff, first-generation college students, international students, relatives of clergy, religious affiliation, veterans. *Tuition waivers:* Full or partial for employees or children of employees. *ROTC:* Army cooperative, Air Force cooperative.

LOANS *Student loans:* $12,000,000 (100% need-based). 80% of past graduating class borrowed through all loan programs. *Average indebtedness per student:* $15,000. *Average need-based loan:* Undergraduates: $4500. *Parent loans:* $150,000 (100% need-based). *Programs:* FFEL (Subsidized and Unsubsidized Stafford, PLUS), Perkins, college/university.

ATHLETIC AWARDS *Total amount:* $725,000 (100% non-need-based).

APPLYING FOR FINANCIAL AID *Required financial aid form:* FAFSA. *Financial aid deadline (priority):* 3/1. *Notification date:* Continuous beginning 5/1. Students must reply within 2 weeks of notification.

CONTACT Ms. Brenda Pittman, Associate Director of Financial Aid, William Carey College, 498 Tuscan Avenue, Hattiesburg, MS 39401-5499, 601-318-6153 or toll-free 800-962-5991 (in-state).

WILLIAM JESSUP UNIVERSITY
Rocklin, CA

CONTACT Kristi Kindberg, Financial Aid Administrator, William Jessup University, 790 South 12th Street, San Jose, CA 95112-2381, 408-278-4328 or toll-free 800-355-7522. *Fax:* 408-293-9299. *E-mail:* finaid@sjchristian.edu.

WILLIAM JEWELL COLLEGE
Liberty, MO

Tuition & fees: $17,500	Average undergraduate aid package: $14,468

ABOUT THE INSTITUTION Independent Baptist, coed. Awards: bachelor's degrees (also offers evening program with significant enrollment not reflected in profile). 42 undergraduate majors. Total enrollment: 1,310. Undergraduates: 1,310. Freshmen: 329. Federal methodology is used as a basis for awarding need-based institutional aid.

UNDERGRADUATE EXPENSES for 2004–05 *Application fee:* $25. *Comprehensive fee:* $22,600 includes full-time tuition ($17,500) and room and board ($5100). *College room only:* $2150. Full-time tuition and fees vary according to class time and course load. Room and board charges vary according to board plan and housing facility. Part-time tuition and fees vary according to class time. *Payment plans:* Tuition prepayment, installment.

FRESHMAN FINANCIAL AID (Fall 2004, est.) 278 applied for aid; of those 79% were deemed to have need. 100% of freshmen with need received aid. *Average financial aid package:* $15,111 (excluding resources awarded to replace EFC).

UNDERGRADUATE FINANCIAL AID (Fall 2004, est.) 1,004 applied for aid; of those 85% were deemed to have need. 100% of undergraduates with need received aid. *Average financial aid package:* $14,468 (excluding resources awarded to replace EFC).

GIFT AID (NEED-BASED) *Total amount:* $7,744,738 (13% federal, 9% state, 72% institutional, 6% external sources). *Receiving aid:* Freshmen: 66% (218); All full-time undergraduates: 66% (838). *Average award:* Freshmen: $11,457; Undergraduates: $10,882. *Scholarships, grants, and awards:* Federal Pell, FSEOG, state, college/university gift aid from institutional funds.

GIFT AID (NON-NEED-BASED) *Total amount:* $2,895,612 (4% state, 93% institutional, 3% external sources). *Scholarships, grants, and awards by category:* *Academic Interests/Achievement:* 222 awards ($1,168,442 total): education, general academic interests/achievements. *Creative Arts/Performance:* 78 awards ($173,525 total): art/fine arts, cinema/film/broadcasting, debating, journalism/publications, music, theater/drama. *Special Achievements/Activities:* 34 awards ($69,600 total): cheerleading/drum major, religious involvement. *Special Characteristics:* 187 awards ($400,861 total): children and siblings of alumni, children of faculty/staff, members of minority groups, out-of-state students, relatives of clergy, religious affiliation, siblings of current students. *Tuition waivers:* Full or partial for minority students, children of alumni, employees or children of employees, senior citizens.

LOANS *Student loans:* $5,633,025 (90% need-based, 10% non-need-based). 64% of past graduating class borrowed through all loan programs. *Average indebtedness per student:* $15,225. *Average need-based loan:* Freshmen: $3874; Undergraduates: $4619. *Parent loans:* $2,651,617 (71% need-based, 29% non-need-based). *Programs:* FFEL (Subsidized and Unsubsidized Stafford, PLUS), Perkins, Federal Nursing, non-Federal alternative loans (non-college).

WORK-STUDY *Federal work-study:* Total amount: $854,873; 529 jobs averaging $1629. *State or other work-study/employment:* Total amount: $100,500 (100% non-need-based). 63 part-time jobs averaging $1224.

ATHLETIC AWARDS *Total amount:* $1,876,509 (63% need-based, 37% non-need-based).

APPLYING FOR FINANCIAL AID *Required financial aid form:* FAFSA. *Financial aid deadline (priority):* 3/1. *Notification date:* Continuous beginning 1/1. Students must reply within 2 weeks of notification.

CONTACT Ms. Sue Armstrong, Director of Financial Aid and Scholarship Services, William Jewell College, 500 College Hill, Box 2005, T38, Brown Hall, Liberty, MO 64068, 816-415-5973 or toll-free 888-2JEWELL. *Fax:* 816-415-5006. *E-mail:* armstrongs@william.jewell.edu.

WILLIAM PATERSON UNIVERSITY OF NEW JERSEY
Wayne, NJ

Tuition & fees (NJ res): $7952	Average undergraduate aid package: $9511

ABOUT THE INSTITUTION State-supported, coed. Awards: bachelor's and master's degrees and post-bachelor's and post-master's certificates. 53 undergraduate majors. Total enrollment: 11,409. Undergraduates: 9,418. Freshmen: 1,520. Federal methodology is used as a basis for awarding need-based institutional aid.

UNDERGRADUATE EXPENSES for 2004–05 *Application fee:* $50. *Tuition, state resident:* full-time $7952; part-time $255 per credit. *Tuition, nonresident:* full-time $12,690; part-time $410 per credit. *College room and board:* $8340; *room only:* $5490. Room and board charges vary according to board plan and housing facility. *Payment plan:* Installment.

FRESHMAN FINANCIAL AID (Fall 2003) 1105 applied for aid; of those 75% were deemed to have need. 95% of freshmen with need received aid; of those 21% had need fully met. *Average percent of need met:* 84% (excluding resources awarded to replace EFC). *Average financial aid package:* $9641 (excluding resources awarded to replace EFC). 2% of all full-time freshmen had no need and received non-need-based gift aid.

UNDERGRADUATE FINANCIAL AID (Fall 2003) 5,129 applied for aid; of those 79% were deemed to have need. 94% of undergraduates with need received aid; of those 21% had need fully met. *Average percent of need met:* 83% (excluding resources awarded to replace EFC). *Average financial aid package:* $9511 (excluding resources awarded to replace EFC). 2% of all full-time undergraduates had no need and received non-need-based gift aid.

GIFT AID (NEED-BASED) *Total amount:* $12,820,000 (44% federal, 50% state, 6% institutional). *Receiving aid:* Freshmen: 33% (465); All full-time undergraduates: 29% (2,195). *Average award:* Freshmen: $6268; Undergraduates: $5745. *Scholarships, grants, and awards:* Federal Pell, FSEOG, state, college/university gift aid from institutional funds.

GIFT AID (NON-NEED-BASED) *Total amount:* $5,670,000 (7% state, 86% institutional, 7% external sources). *Receiving aid:* Freshmen: 18% (258); Undergraduates: 13% (1,021). *Average Award: Freshmen:* $5482; *Undergraduates:* $4191. *Scholarships, grants, and awards by category: Academic Interests/Achievement:* 844 awards ($4,959,434 total): general academic interests/achievements. *Creative Arts/Performance:* 12 awards ($3300 total): music. *Special Characteristics:* general special characteristics. *Tuition waivers:* Full or partial for employees or children of employees, senior citizens. *ROTC:* Air Force cooperative.

LOANS *Student loans:* $26,000,000 (46% need-based, 54% non-need-based). 48% of past graduating class borrowed through all loan programs. *Average indebtedness per student:* $10,868. *Average need-based loan:* Freshmen: $2661; Undergraduates: $3805. *Parent loans:* $6,000,000 (100% non-need-based). *Programs:* Federal Direct (Subsidized and Unsubsidized Stafford, PLUS), Perkins, NJ Class Loans.

WORK-STUDY *Federal work-study:* Total amount: $300,000; 220 jobs averaging $1136. *State or other work-study/employment:* Total amount: $275,000 (100% need-based). 192 part-time jobs averaging $1300.

APPLYING FOR FINANCIAL AID *Required financial aid form:* FAFSA. *Financial aid deadline:* 4/1 (priority: 4/1). *Notification date:* Continuous beginning 3/1. Students must reply within 2 weeks of notification.

CONTACT Robert Baumel, Director of Financial Aid, William Paterson University of New Jersey, 300 Pompton Road, Raubinger Hall, Wayne, NJ 07470, 973-720-2928 or toll-free 877-WPU-EXCEL (in-state). *E-mail:* baumelr@wpunj.edu.

WILLIAM PENN UNIVERSITY
Oskaloosa, IA

Tuition & fees: $14,604	Average undergraduate aid package: N/A

ABOUT THE INSTITUTION Independent religious, coed. Awards: associate and bachelor's degrees. 39 undergraduate majors. Total enrollment: 1,499. Undergraduates: 1,499. Freshmen: 230. Federal methodology is used as a basis for awarding need-based institutional aid.

UNDERGRADUATE EXPENSES for 2004–05 *Application fee:* $20. *Comprehensive fee:* $19,350 includes full-time tuition ($14,234), mandatory fees ($370), and room and board ($4746). *College room only:* $1852. Room and board charges vary according to board plan and housing facility. Part-time tuition and fees vary according to course load. *Payment plan:* Installment.

GIFT AID (NEED-BASED) *Total amount:* $7,754,155 (40% federal, 22% state, 21% institutional, 17% external sources). *Scholarships, grants, and awards:* Federal Pell, FSEOG, state, private, college/university gift aid from institutional funds.

GIFT AID (NON-NEED-BASED) *Total amount:* $806,094 (20% institutional, 80% external sources). *Scholarships, grants, and awards by category: Academic Interests/Achievement:* general academic interests/achievements. *Creative Arts/Performance:* art/fine arts, creative writing, journalism/publications, music, theater/drama. *Special Achievements/Activities:* junior miss, leadership, religious involvement. *Special Characteristics:* children and siblings of alumni. *Tuition waivers:* Full or partial for employees or children of employees, senior citizens.

LOANS *Student loans:* $5,621,855 (91% need-based, 9% non-need-based). 81% of past graduating class borrowed through all loan programs. *Average indebtedness per student:* $19,875. *Parent loans:* $634,399 (75% need-based, 25% non-need-based). *Programs:* FFEL (Subsidized and Unsubsidized Stafford, PLUS), Perkins, state.

ATHLETIC AWARDS *Total amount:* $2,839,430 (90% need-based, 10% non-need-based).

APPLYING FOR FINANCIAL AID *Required financial aid form:* FAFSA. *Financial aid deadline (priority):* 4/15. *Notification date:* Continuous. Students must reply within 2 weeks of notification.

CONTACT Cyndi Peiffer, Director of Financial Aid, William Penn University, 201 Trueblood Avenue, Oskaloosa, IA 52577-1799, 641-673-1060 or toll-free 800-779-7366. *Fax:* 641-673-1115. *E-mail:* peifferc@wmpenn.edu.

WILLIAMS BAPTIST COLLEGE
Walnut Ridge, AR

Tuition & fees: $8600	Average undergraduate aid package: $9494

ABOUT THE INSTITUTION Independent Southern Baptist, coed. Awards: associate and bachelor's degrees. 26 undergraduate majors. Total enrollment: 653. Undergraduates: 653. Freshmen: 121. Federal methodology is used as a basis for awarding need-based institutional aid.

UNDERGRADUATE EXPENSES for 2004–05 *Application fee:* $20. *Comprehensive fee:* $12,600 includes full-time tuition ($8000), mandatory fees ($600), and room and board ($4000). Room and board charges vary according to housing facility. Part-time tuition and fees vary according to course load. *Payment plan:* Installment.

FRESHMAN FINANCIAL AID (Fall 2003) 115 applied for aid; of those 71% were deemed to have need. 100% of freshmen with need received aid. *Average financial aid package:* $9893 (excluding resources awarded to replace EFC). 29% of all full-time freshmen had no need and received non-need-based gift aid.

UNDERGRADUATE FINANCIAL AID (Fall 2003) 529 applied for aid; of those 79% were deemed to have need. 100% of undergraduates with need received aid. *Average financial aid package:* $9494 (excluding resources awarded to replace EFC). 20% of all full-time undergraduates had no need and received non-need-based gift aid.

GIFT AID (NEED-BASED) *Total amount:* $1,318,282 (79% federal, 21% state). *Receiving aid:* Freshmen: 65% (75); All full-time undergraduates: 65% (347). *Average award:* Freshmen: $2911; Undergraduates: $2974. *Scholarships, grants, and awards:* Federal Pell, FSEOG, state, private, college/university gift aid from institutional funds.

GIFT AID (NON-NEED-BASED) *Total amount:* $1,495,312 (9% state, 77% institutional, 14% external sources). *Receiving aid:* Freshmen: 70% (81); Undergraduates: 71% (379). *Average Award: Freshmen:* $4941; *Undergraduates:* $4386. *Scholarships, grants, and awards by category: Academic Interests/Achievement:* 430 awards ($966,777 total): biological sciences, business, education, general academic interests/achievements, humanities, religion/biblical studies. *Creative Arts/Performance:* 40 awards ($55,400 total): art/fine arts, music. *Special Achievements/Activities:* 9 awards ($5100 total): cheerleading/drum major. *Special Characteristics:* 168 awards ($104,881 total): children of faculty/staff, international students, members of minority groups, relatives of clergy, religious affiliation. *Tuition waivers:* Full or partial for employees or children of employees, senior citizens. *ROTC:* Army cooperative.

LOANS *Student loans:* $1,808,328 (67% need-based, 33% non-need-based). 85% of past graduating class borrowed through all loan programs. *Average indebtedness per student:* $14,880. *Average need-based loan:* Freshmen: $1977; Undergraduates: $3462. *Parent loans:* $79,912 (100% non-need-based). *Programs:* Federal Direct (Subsidized and Unsubsidized Stafford, PLUS).

WORK-STUDY *Federal work-study:* Total amount: $245,524; 249 jobs averaging $977. *State or other work-study/employment:* Total amount: $43,152 (100% non-need-based). 42 part-time jobs averaging $962.

ATHLETIC AWARDS *Total amount:* $336,004 (100% non-need-based).

APPLYING FOR FINANCIAL AID *Required financial aid form:* FAFSA. *Financial aid deadline:* Continuous. *Notification date:* Continuous beginning 4/1. Students must reply within 2 weeks of notification.

CONTACT Barbara Turner, Director of Financial Aid, Williams Baptist College, 60 West Fulbright Avenue, PO Box 3661, Walnut Ridge, AR 72476, 870-759-4112 or toll-free 800-722-4434. *Fax:* 870-886-3924. *E-mail:* financialaid@wbcoll.edu.

WILLIAMS COLLEGE
Williamstown, MA

Tuition & fees: $29,990	Average undergraduate aid package: $27,840

ABOUT THE INSTITUTION Independent, coed. Awards: bachelor's and master's degrees. 33 undergraduate majors. Total enrollment: 2,050. Undergraduates: 1,991. Freshmen: 532. Institutional methodology is used as a basis for awarding need-based institutional aid.

UNDERGRADUATE EXPENSES for 2004–05 *Application fee:* $60. *Comprehensive fee:* $38,100 includes full-time tuition ($29,786), mandatory fees ($204), and room and board ($8110). *College room only:* $4060. Room and board charges vary according to board plan. *Payment plan:* Installment.

FRESHMAN FINANCIAL AID (Fall 2004, est.) 300 applied for aid; of those 76% were deemed to have need. 100% of freshmen with need received aid; of those 100% had need fully met. *Average percent of need met:* 100% (excluding resources awarded to replace EFC). *Average financial aid package:* $28,988 (excluding resources awarded to replace EFC).

UNDERGRADUATE FINANCIAL AID (Fall 2004, est.) 1,044 applied for aid; of those 78% were deemed to have need. 100% of undergraduates with need received aid; of those 100% had need fully met. *Average percent of need met:* 100% (excluding resources awarded to replace EFC). *Average financial aid package:* $27,840 (excluding resources awarded to replace EFC).

GIFT AID (NEED-BASED) *Total amount:* $19,619,195 (5% federal, 1% state, 90% institutional, 4% external sources). *Receiving aid:* Freshmen: 42% (225); All full-time undergraduates: 40% (789). *Average award:* Freshmen: $25,427; Undergraduates: $23,809. *Scholarships, grants, and awards:* Federal Pell, FSEOG, state, private, college/university gift aid from institutional funds.

GIFT AID (NON-NEED-BASED) *Total amount:* $960,636 (100% external sources).

LOANS *Student loans:* $2,155,387 (81% need-based, 19% non-need-based). 42% of past graduating class borrowed through all loan programs. *Average indebtedness per student:* $10,753. *Average need-based loan:* Freshmen: $2187; Undergraduates: $2860. *Parent loans:* $4,212,243 (100% non-need-based). *Programs:* Federal Direct (Subsidized and Unsubsidized Stafford, PLUS), Perkins, college/university.

WORK-STUDY *Federal work-study:* Total amount: $681,279; 444 jobs averaging $1572. *State or other work-study/employment:* Total amount: $530,404 (91% need-based, 9% non-need-based). 338 part-time jobs averaging $1589.

APPLYING FOR FINANCIAL AID *Required financial aid forms:* FAFSA, CSS Financial Aid PROFILE. *Financial aid deadline:* 2/1. *Notification date:* 4/1. Students must reply by 5/1.

CONTACT Paul J. Boyer, Director of Financial Aid, Williams College, PO Box 37, Williamstown, MA 01267, 413-597-4181. *Fax:* 413-597-2999. *E-mail:* paul.j.boyer@williams.edu.

WILLIAMSON CHRISTIAN COLLEGE
Franklin, TN

ABOUT THE INSTITUTION Independent interdenominational, coed. Awards: associate and bachelor's degrees. 5 undergraduate majors. Total enrollment: 70. Undergraduates: 70. Freshmen: 2.

GIFT AID (NEED-BASED) *Scholarships, grants, and awards:* Federal Pell, private, college/university gift aid from institutional funds.

LOANS *Programs:* FFEL (Subsidized and Unsubsidized Stafford, PLUS).

WORK-STUDY *Federal work-study:* 2 jobs averaging $2000.

APPLYING FOR FINANCIAL AID *Required financial aid forms:* FAFSA, institution's own form.

CONTACT Jeanie Maguire, Director of Financial Aid, Williamson Christian College, 200 Seaboard Lane, Franklin, TN 37067, 615-771-7821. *Fax:* 615-771-7810. *E-mail:* info@williamsoncc.edu.

WILLIAM WOODS UNIVERSITY
Fulton, MO

Tuition & fees: $14,720	Average undergraduate aid package: $14,783

ABOUT THE INSTITUTION Independent religious, coed. Awards: associate, bachelor's, and master's degrees. 46 undergraduate majors. Total enrollment: 2,191. Undergraduates: 1,012. Freshmen: 196. Federal methodology is used as a basis for awarding need-based institutional aid.

UNDERGRADUATE EXPENSES for 2004–05 *Application fee:* $25. *Comprehensive fee:* $20,420 includes full-time tuition ($14,300), mandatory fees ($420), and room and board ($5700). Full-time tuition and fees vary according to program. Room and board charges vary according to board plan. *Part-time tuition:* $465 per credit hour. *Part-time fees:* $15 per term. *Payment plan:* Installment.

FRESHMAN FINANCIAL AID (Fall 2004, est.) 176 applied for aid; of those 58% were deemed to have need. 100% of freshmen with need received aid; of those 29% had need fully met. *Average percent of need met:* 84% (excluding resources awarded to replace EFC). *Average financial aid package:* $13,382 (excluding resources awarded to replace EFC). 38% of all full-time freshmen had no need and received non-need-based gift aid.

UNDERGRADUATE FINANCIAL AID (Fall 2004, est.) 697 applied for aid; of those 56% were deemed to have need. 100% of undergraduates with need received aid; of those 39% had need fully met. *Average percent of need met:* 89% (excluding resources awarded to replace EFC). *Average financial aid package:* $14,783 (excluding resources awarded to replace EFC). 33% of all full-time undergraduates had no need and received non-need-based gift aid.

GIFT AID (NEED-BASED) *Total amount:* $1,402,037 (62% federal, 16% state, 22% institutional). *Receiving aid:* Freshmen: 32% (62); All full-time undergraduates: 34% (266). *Average award:* Freshmen: $1937; Undergraduates: $1967. *Scholarships, grants, and awards:* Federal Pell, FSEOG, state, college/university gift aid from institutional funds.

GIFT AID (NON-NEED-BASED) *Total amount:* $4,850,207 (1% state, 93% institutional, 6% external sources). *Receiving aid:* Freshmen: 52% (102); Undergraduates: 47% (365). *Average Award:* Freshmen: $3732; Undergraduates: $3946. *Scholarships, grants, and awards by category:* Academic Interests/Achievement: 383 awards ($1,282,958 total): general academic interests/achievements, health fields. Creative Arts/Performance: 31 awards ($103,500 total): art/fine arts, journalism/publications, performing arts, theater/drama. Special Achievements/Activities: 645 awards ($2,692,437 total): general special achievements/activities, leadership. Special Characteristics: 169 awards ($331,700 total): children and siblings of alumni, children of faculty/staff, relatives of clergy, religious affiliation, siblings of current students. *Tuition waivers:* Full or partial for children of alumni, employees or children of employees, senior citizens. *ROTC:* Army cooperative, Naval cooperative, Air Force cooperative.

LOANS *Student loans:* $3,320,366 (53% need-based, 47% non-need-based). 48% of past graduating class borrowed through all loan programs. *Average indebtedness per student:* $13,873. *Average need-based loan:* Freshmen: $2393; Undergraduates: $3191. *Parent loans:* $645,695 (100% non-need-based). *Programs:* FFEL (Subsidized and Unsubsidized Stafford, PLUS), Perkins, college/university.

WORK-STUDY *Federal work-study:* Total amount: $331,520; 282 jobs averaging $1177. *State or other work-study/employment:* Total amount: $160,724 (12% need-based, 88% non-need-based). 170 part-time jobs averaging $974.

ATHLETIC AWARDS *Total amount:* $1,047,775 (100% non-need-based).

APPLYING FOR FINANCIAL AID *Required financial aid forms:* FAFSA, institution's own form. *Financial aid deadline (priority):* 3/1. *Notification date:* Continuous beginning 3/15. Students must reply within 3 weeks of notification.

CONTACT Mrs. Liz Bennett, Director of Student Financial Services, William Woods University, One University Avenue, Fulton, MO 65251, 573-592-4232 or toll-free 800-995-3159 Ext. 4221. *Fax:* 573-592-1180.

WILMINGTON COLLEGE
New Castle, DE

Tuition & fees: $7340	Average undergraduate aid package: $5770

ABOUT THE INSTITUTION Independent, coed. Awards: associate, bachelor's, master's, and doctoral degrees and post-bachelor's and post-master's certificates. 23 undergraduate majors. Total enrollment: 7,156. Undergraduates: 4,391. Freshmen: 356. Federal methodology is used as a basis for awarding need-based institutional aid.

UNDERGRADUATE EXPENSES for 2004–05 *Application fee:* $25. *Tuition:* full-time $7290; part-time $243 per credit. *Required fees:* full-time $50; $25 per term part-time. Full-time tuition and fees vary according to course load, degree level, and location. Part-time tuition and fees vary according to course load, degree level, and location. *Payment plan:* Installment.

FRESHMAN FINANCIAL AID (Fall 2004, est.) 168 applied for aid; of those 74% were deemed to have need. 100% of freshmen with need received aid. *Average percent of need met:* 42% (excluding resources awarded to replace EFC). *Average financial aid package:* $4409 (excluding resources awarded to replace EFC). 2% of all full-time freshmen had no need and received non-need-based gift aid.

UNDERGRADUATE FINANCIAL AID (Fall 2004, est.) 1,217 applied for aid; of those 74% were deemed to have need. 94% of undergraduates with need received aid. *Average percent of need met:* 48% (excluding resources awarded to replace EFC). *Average financial aid package:* $5770 (excluding resources awarded to replace EFC). 3% of all full-time undergraduates had no need and received non-need-based gift aid.

GIFT AID (NEED-BASED) *Total amount:* $2,860,000 (91% federal, 9% state). *Receiving aid:* Freshmen: 33% (90); All full-time undergraduates: 16% (338). *Average award:* Freshmen: $2768; Undergraduates: $2464. *Scholarships, grants, and awards:* Federal Pell, FSEOG, state, college/university gift aid from institutional funds, Federal Nursing.

GIFT AID (NON-NEED-BASED) *Total amount:* $406,591 (86% institutional, 14% external sources). *Receiving aid:* Freshmen: 5% (15); Undergraduates: 6% (118). *Average Award:* Freshmen: $250; Undergraduates: $1100. *Scholarships, grants, and awards by category: Academic Interests/Achievement:* $20,430 total: education. *Tuition waivers:* Full or partial for employees or children of employees. *ROTC:* Army cooperative, Air Force cooperative.

LOANS *Student loans:* $26,165,638 (98% need-based, 2% non-need-based). 58% of past graduating class borrowed through all loan programs. *Average indebtedness per student:* $17,486. *Average need-based loan:* Freshmen: $2567; Undergraduates: $3889. *Parent loans:* $241,492 (100% need-based). *Programs:* FFEL (Subsidized and Unsubsidized Stafford, PLUS), alternative loans.

WORK-STUDY *Federal work-study:* Total amount: $134,000; 25 jobs averaging $2000.

ATHLETIC AWARDS *Total amount:* $432,080 (100% need-based).

APPLYING FOR FINANCIAL AID *Required financial aid form:* FAFSA. *Financial aid deadline (priority):* 4/30. *Notification date:* Continuous beginning 5/1.

CONTACT J. Lynn Iocono, Director of Financial Aid, Wilmington College, 320 DuPont Highway, New Castle, DE 19720, 302-328-9437 or toll-free 877-967-5464. *Fax:* 302-328-5902.

WILMINGTON COLLEGE
Wilmington, OH

Tuition & fees: $18,728	Average undergraduate aid package: $17,080

ABOUT THE INSTITUTION Independent Friends, coed. Awards: bachelor's and master's degrees. 42 undergraduate majors. Total enrollment: 1,755. Undergraduates: 1,701. Freshmen: 332. Federal methodology is used as a basis for awarding need-based institutional aid.

UNDERGRADUATE EXPENSES for 2004–05 *Comprehensive fee:* $25,446 includes full-time tuition ($18,292), mandatory fees ($436), and room and board ($6718). Room and board charges vary according to board plan and housing facility. Part-time tuition and fees vary according to course load. *Payment plan:* Installment.

FRESHMAN FINANCIAL AID (Fall 2003) 296 applied for aid; of those 92% were deemed to have need. 100% of freshmen with need received aid; of those 51% had need fully met. *Average percent of need met:* 90% (excluding resources awarded to replace EFC). *Average financial aid package:* $17,400 (excluding resources awarded to replace EFC). 14% of all full-time freshmen had no need and received non-need-based gift aid.

UNDERGRADUATE FINANCIAL AID (Fall 2003) 1,067 applied for aid; of those 94% were deemed to have need. 100% of undergraduates with need received aid; of those 54% had need fully met. *Average percent of need met:* 92% (excluding resources awarded to replace EFC). *Average financial aid package:* $17,080 (excluding resources awarded to replace EFC). 14% of all full-time undergraduates had no need and received non-need-based gift aid.

GIFT AID (NEED-BASED) *Total amount:* $11,172,204 (13% federal, 16% state, 67% institutional, 4% external sources). *Receiving aid:* Freshmen: 89% (273); All full-time undergraduates: 86% (998). *Average award:* Freshmen: $12,640; Undergraduates: $11,159. *Scholarships, grants, and awards:* Federal Pell, FSEOG, state, college/university gift aid from institutional funds.

GIFT AID (NON-NEED-BASED) *Total amount:* $1,215,554 (16% state, 74% institutional, 10% external sources). *Receiving aid:* Freshmen: 6% (18); Undergraduates: 5% (58). *Average Award:* Freshmen: $6350; Undergraduates: $5729. *Scholarships, grants, and awards by category: Academic Interests/Achievement:* 839 awards ($4,979,022 total): agriculture, biological sciences, business, communication, education, general academic interests/achievements, international studies, mathematics, physical sciences, premedicine, religion/biblical studies. *Creative Arts/Performance:* 2 awards ($4000 total): theater/drama. *Special Achievements/Activities:* 7 awards ($37,100 total): leadership. *Special Characteristics:* 88 awards ($159,878 total): children and siblings of alumni, members of minority groups, religious affiliation, siblings of current students. *Tuition waivers:* Full or partial for employees or children of employees.

LOANS *Student loans:* $6,924,263 (72% need-based, 28% non-need-based). 84% of past graduating class borrowed through all loan programs. *Average indebtedness per student:* $21,932. *Average need-based loan:* Freshmen: $4499; Undergraduates: $5630. *Parent loans:* $1,189,143 (20% need-based, 80% non-need-based). *Programs:* FFEL (Subsidized and Unsubsidized Stafford, PLUS), Perkins.

WORK-STUDY *Federal work-study:* Total amount: $685,408; 518 jobs averaging $1342.

APPLYING FOR FINANCIAL AID *Required financial aid form:* FAFSA. *Financial aid deadline (priority):* 3/15. *Notification date:* Continuous beginning 3/1. Students must reply within 3 weeks of notification.

CONTACT Donna Barton, Coordinator of Financial Aid, Wilmington College, Pyle Center Box 1184, Wilmington, OH 45177, 937-382-6661 Ext. 466 or toll-free 800-341-9318. *Fax:* 937-383-8564.

WILSON COLLEGE
Chambersburg, PA

Tuition & fees: $18,408	Average undergraduate aid package: $16,104

ABOUT THE INSTITUTION Independent religious, women only. Awards: associate and bachelor's degrees. 25 undergraduate majors. Total enrollment: 776. Undergraduates: 776. Freshmen: 72. Both federal and institutional methodology are used as a basis for awarding need-based institutional aid.

UNDERGRADUATE EXPENSES for 2004–05 *Application fee:* $30. *Comprehensive fee:* $25,716 includes full-time tuition ($17,948), mandatory fees ($460), and room and board ($7308). *College room only:* $3765. Room and board charges vary according to board plan. *Part-time tuition:* $1795 per course. *Part-time fees:* $15. Part-time tuition and fees vary according to course load. *Payment plan:* Installment.

FRESHMAN FINANCIAL AID (Fall 2004, est.) 65 applied for aid; of those 86% were deemed to have need. 98% of freshmen with need received aid; of those 11% had need fully met. *Average percent of need met:* 68% (excluding resources awarded to replace EFC). *Average financial aid package:* $14,736 (excluding resources awarded to replace EFC). 22% of all full-time freshmen had no need and received non-need-based gift aid.

UNDERGRADUATE FINANCIAL AID (Fall 2004, est.) 292 applied for aid; of those 87% were deemed to have need. 99% of undergraduates with need received aid; of those 16% had need fully met. *Average percent of need met:* 78% (excluding resources awarded to replace EFC). *Average financial aid package:* $16,104 (excluding resources awarded to replace EFC). 24% of all full-time undergraduates had no need and received non-need-based gift aid.

GIFT AID (NEED-BASED) *Total amount:* $3,518,061 (15% federal, 16% state, 67% institutional, 2% external sources). *Receiving aid:* Freshmen: 74% (55); All full-time undergraduates: 72% (246). *Average award:* Freshmen: $12,107; Undergraduates: $12,633. *Scholarships, grants, and awards:* Federal Pell, FSEOG, state, private, college/university gift aid from institutional funds.

GIFT AID (NON-NEED-BASED) *Total amount:* $886,697 (4% federal, 4% state, 89% institutional, 3% external sources). *Receiving aid:* Freshmen: 7% (5); Undergraduates: 6% (21). *Average Award:* Freshmen: $12,845; *Undergradu-*

ates: $13,919. **Scholarships, grants, and awards by category:** *Academic Interests/Achievement:* 207 awards ($830,000 total): biological sciences, communication, computer science, education, English, foreign languages, general academic interests/achievements, humanities, international studies, mathematics, physical sciences, premedicine, religion/biblical studies, social sciences. *Creative Arts/Performance:* 1 award ($1800 total): music. *Special Achievements/Activities:* 26 awards ($129,488 total): community service. *Special Characteristics:* 76 awards ($300,000 total): adult students, children and siblings of alumni, children of current students, children of faculty/staff, international students, local/state students, relatives of clergy, religious affiliation, veterans. **Tuition waivers:** Full or partial for children of alumni, employees or children of employees. **ROTC:** Army cooperative.

LOANS *Student loans:* $2,725,946 (69% need-based, 31% non-need-based). 83% of past graduating class borrowed through all loan programs. *Average indebtedness per student:* $22,208. **Average need-based loan:** Freshmen: $2444; Undergraduates: $4064. **Parent loans:** $793,727 (36% need-based, 64% non-need-based). **Programs:** FFEL (Subsidized and Unsubsidized Stafford, PLUS), Perkins, college/university.

WORK-STUDY *Federal work-study:* Total amount: $23,150; 44 jobs averaging $1340. **State or other work-study/employment:** Total amount: $132,789 (40% need-based, 60% non-need-based). 124 part-time jobs averaging $1340.

APPLYING FOR FINANCIAL AID *Required financial aid forms:* FAFSA, institution's own form. **Financial aid deadline (priority):** 4/30. **Notification date:** Continuous. Students must reply within 2 weeks of notification.

CONTACT Linda Brittain, Associate Dean of Enrollment, Wilson College, 1015 Philadelphia Avenue, Chambersburg, PA 17201-1285, 717-262-2016 or toll-free 800-421-8402. *Fax:* 717-262-2546. *E-mail:* finaid@wilson.edu.

WINGATE UNIVERSITY
Wingate, NC

Tuition & fees: $16,000	Average undergraduate aid package: $12,748

ABOUT THE INSTITUTION Independent Baptist, coed. Awards: bachelor's, master's, and first professional degrees. 53 undergraduate majors. Total enrollment: 1,560. Undergraduates: 1,331. Freshmen: 358. Both federal and institutional methodology are used as a basis for awarding need-based institutional aid.

UNDERGRADUATE EXPENSES for 2004–05 *Application fee:* $25. **Comprehensive fee:** $22,200 includes full-time tuition ($15,000), mandatory fees ($1000), and room and board ($6200). **Part-time tuition:** $495 per credit hour. **Payment plan:** Installment.

FRESHMAN FINANCIAL AID (Fall 2003) 361 applied for aid; of those 73% were deemed to have need. 100% of freshmen with need received aid; of those 1% had need fully met. *Average percent of need met:* 53% (excluding resources awarded to replace EFC). *Average financial aid package:* $12,008 (excluding resources awarded to replace EFC). 39% of all full-time freshmen had no need and received non-need-based gift aid.

UNDERGRADUATE FINANCIAL AID (Fall 2003) 1,273 applied for aid; of those 68% were deemed to have need. 100% of undergraduates with need received aid; of those 1% had need fully met. *Average percent of need met:* 56% (excluding resources awarded to replace EFC). *Average financial aid package:* $12,748 (excluding resources awarded to replace EFC). 2% of all full-time undergraduates had no need and received non-need-based gift aid.

GIFT AID (NEED-BASED) *Total amount:* $3,396,087 (29% federal, 24% state, 47% institutional). *Receiving aid:* Freshmen: 53% (198); All full-time undergraduates: 52% (665). *Average award:* Freshmen: $3920; Undergraduates: $4134. **Scholarships, grants, and awards:** Federal Pell, FSEOG, state, private, college/university gift aid from institutional funds.

GIFT AID (NON-NEED-BASED) *Total amount:* $6,621,107 (18% state, 75% institutional, 7% external sources). *Receiving aid:* Freshmen: 70% (261); Undergraduates: 65% (828). *Average Award:* Freshmen: $5202; Undergraduates: $4918. **Scholarships, grants, and awards by category:** *Academic Interests/Achievement:* 759 awards ($2,755,006 total): general academic interests/achievements. *Creative Arts/Performance:* 124 awards ($90,565 total): music. *Special Achievements/Activities:* 43 awards ($45,400 total): religious involvement. *Special Characteristics:* 26 awards ($12,250 total): children and siblings of alumni, relatives of clergy, religious affiliation. **Tuition waivers:** Full or partial for employees or children of employees. **ROTC:** Army cooperative, Air Force cooperative.

LOANS *Student loans:* $3,805,722 (57% need-based, 43% non-need-based). 88% of past graduating class borrowed through all loan programs. *Average*

---

indebtedness per student: $24,000. **Average need-based loan:** Freshmen: $2307; Undergraduates: $3359. **Programs:** FFEL (Subsidized and Unsubsidized Stafford, PLUS).

WORK-STUDY *Federal work-study:* Total amount: $233,501; jobs available. **State or other work-study/employment:** Total amount: $143,836 (100% non-need-based). 373 part-time jobs averaging $560.

ATHLETIC AWARDS *Total amount:* $1,511,842 (100% non-need-based).

APPLYING FOR FINANCIAL AID *Required financial aid form:* FAFSA. **Financial aid deadline (priority):** 5/1. **Notification date:** Continuous. Students must reply within 4 weeks of notification.

CONTACT Teresa G. Williams, Director of Financial Planning, Wingate University, Campus Box 3001, Wingate, NC 28174, 704-233-8209 or toll-free 800-755-5550. *Fax:* 704-233-9396. *E-mail:* tgwilliam@wingate.edu.

WINONA STATE UNIVERSITY
Winona, MN

Tuition & fees (MN res): $6420	Average undergraduate aid package: $5540

ABOUT THE INSTITUTION State-supported, coed. Awards: associate, bachelor's, and master's degrees and post-master's certificates. 112 undergraduate majors. Total enrollment: 8,236. Undergraduates: 7,569. Freshmen: 1,552. Federal methodology is used as a basis for awarding need-based institutional aid.

UNDERGRADUATE EXPENSES for 2004–05 *Application fee:* $20. **Tuition, state resident:** full-time $4620. **Tuition, nonresident:** full-time $9160. **College room and board:** $4960. Room and board charges vary according to board plan and housing facility.

GIFT AID (NEED-BASED) *Total amount:* $6,771,094 (57% federal, 40% state, 3% institutional). *Receiving aid:* Freshmen: 28% (448); All full-time undergraduates: 30% (2,029). *Average award:* Freshmen: $2870; Undergraduates: $2991. **Scholarships, grants, and awards:** Federal Pell, FSEOG, state, private, college/university gift aid from institutional funds.

GIFT AID (NON-NEED-BASED) *Total amount:* $5,148,825 (64% institutional, 36% external sources). *Receiving aid:* Freshmen: 31% (499); Undergraduates: 18% (1,192). *Average Award:* Freshmen: $1423; Undergraduates: $2006. **Scholarships, grants, and awards by category:** *Academic Interests/Achievement:* 2,767 awards ($2,269,993 total): general academic interests/achievements. *Creative Arts/Performance:* 45 awards ($12,350 total): art/fine arts, debating, music, theater/drama. *Special Characteristics:* 2,386 awards ($2,323,306 total): children and siblings of alumni, children of faculty/staff, local/state students, members of minority groups, out-of-state students. **ROTC:** Army cooperative.

LOANS *Student loans:* $30,461,252 (40% need-based, 60% non-need-based). 81% of past graduating class borrowed through all loan programs. *Average indebtedness per student:* $14,987. **Average need-based loan:** Freshmen: $2310; Undergraduates: $3280. **Parent loans:** $973,170 (100% non-need-based). **Programs:** FFEL (Subsidized and Unsubsidized Stafford, PLUS), Perkins, state, college/university.

ATHLETIC AWARDS *Total amount:* $316,915 (100% non-need-based).

APPLYING FOR FINANCIAL AID *Required financial aid form:* FAFSA. **Financial aid deadline:** Continuous. **Notification date:** 5/1. Students must reply within 3 weeks of notification.

CONTACT Cindy Groth, Counselor, Winona State University, PO Box 5838, Winona, MN 55987-5838, 507-457-5090 Ext. 5561 or toll-free 800-DIAL WSU.

WINSTON-SALEM BIBLE COLLEGE
Winston-Salem, NC

CONTACT Financial Aid Office, Winston-Salem Bible College, 4117 Northampton Drive, PO Box 777, Winston-Salem, NC 27102-0777, 336-744-0900.

WINSTON-SALEM STATE UNIVERSITY
Winston-Salem, NC

Tuition & fees (NC res): $2734	Average undergraduate aid package: $3356

ABOUT THE INSTITUTION State-supported, coed. Awards: bachelor's and master's degrees. 41 undergraduate majors. Total enrollment: 4,805. Undergraduates: 4,568. Freshmen: 901. Federal methodology is used as a basis for awarding need-based institutional aid.

UNDERGRADUATE EXPENSES for 2004–05 *Application fee:* $30. **Tuition, state resident:** full-time $1510. **Tuition, nonresident:** full-time $10,003. Full-time tuition and fees vary according to degree level. Part-time tuition and fees vary according to course load and location. *College room and board:* $5135; *room only:* $3030. Room and board charges vary according to board plan and housing facility. *Payment plan:* Installment.

FRESHMAN FINANCIAL AID (Fall 2003) 698 applied for aid; of those 96% were deemed to have need. 95% of freshmen with need received aid; of those 3% had need fully met. *Average percent of need met:* 77% (excluding resources awarded to replace EFC). *Average financial aid package:* $3471 (excluding resources awarded to replace EFC). 3% of all full-time freshmen had no need and received non-need-based gift aid.

UNDERGRADUATE FINANCIAL AID (Fall 2003) 3,055 applied for aid; of those 97% were deemed to have need. 93% of undergraduates with need received aid; of those 4% had need fully met. *Average percent of need met:* 75% (excluding resources awarded to replace EFC). *Average financial aid package:* $3356 (excluding resources awarded to replace EFC). 3% of all full-time undergraduates had no need and received non-need-based gift aid.

GIFT AID (NEED-BASED) *Total amount:* $9,306,090 (80% federal, 20% state). *Receiving aid:* Freshmen: 56% (492); All full-time undergraduates: 80% (2,633). *Average award:* Freshmen: $2660; Undergraduates: $2527. *Scholarships, grants, and awards:* Federal Pell, FSEOG, state, private, college/university gift aid from institutional funds, United Negro College Fund.

GIFT AID (NON-NEED-BASED) *Total amount:* $1,934,967 (24% state, 28% institutional, 48% external sources). *Receiving aid:* Freshmen: 5% (41); Undergraduates: 5% (178). *Average Award:* Freshmen: $2507; Undergraduates: $3107. *Scholarships, grants, and awards by category:* Academic Interests/Achievement: 341 awards ($1,124,101 total): business, computer science, education, general academic interests/achievements, health fields, mathematics. Creative Arts/Performance: 83 awards ($889,404 total): music. Special Achievements/Activities: cheerleading/drum major. *Tuition waivers:* Full or partial for employees or children of employees, senior citizens. *ROTC:* Army, Air Force.

LOANS *Student loans:* $14,970,593 (55% need-based, 45% non-need-based). 83% of past graduating class borrowed through all loan programs. *Average indebtedness per student:* $10,800. *Average need-based loan:* Freshmen: $2469; Undergraduates: $3317. *Parent loans:* $1,626,620 (100% non-need-based). *Programs:* FFEL (Subsidized and Unsubsidized Stafford, PLUS), Perkins, state, college/university.

WORK-STUDY *Federal work-study:* Total amount: $560,657; 378 jobs averaging $1585. *State or other work-study/employment:* Total amount: $308,975 (100% non-need-based). 163 part-time jobs averaging $2473.

ATHLETIC AWARDS *Total amount:* $334,368 (100% non-need-based).

APPLYING FOR FINANCIAL AID *Required financial aid form:* FAFSA. *Financial aid deadline:* 4/1 (priority: 3/1). *Notification date:* 5/15. Students must reply within 2 weeks of notification.

CONTACT Mr. Theodore Hindsman, Director of Financial Aid Office, Winston-Salem State University, 601 Martin Luther King Jr. Drive, PO Box 19524, Winston-Salem, NC 27110-0003, 336-750-3280 or toll-free 800-257-4052. *Fax:* 336-750-3297.

WINTHROP UNIVERSITY
Rock Hill, SC

Tuition & fees (SC res): $7836	Average undergraduate aid package: $8945

ABOUT THE INSTITUTION State-supported, coed. Awards: bachelor's and master's degrees. 32 undergraduate majors. Total enrollment: 6,447. Undergraduates: 5,213. Freshmen: 1,001. Federal methodology is used as a basis for awarding need-based institutional aid.

UNDERGRADUATE EXPENSES for 2004–05 *Application fee:* $40. *Tuition, state resident:* full-time $7816; part-time $326 per semester hour. *Tuition, nonresident:* full-time $14,410; part-time $601 per semester hour. *Required fees:* full-time $20; $10 per term part-time. Full-time tuition and fees vary according to degree level. Part-time tuition and fees vary according to degree level. *College room and board:* $4992; *room only:* $3060. Room and board charges vary according to board plan and housing facility. *Payment plan:* Installment.

FRESHMAN FINANCIAL AID (Fall 2003) 794 applied for aid; of those 75% were deemed to have need. 100% of freshmen with need received aid; of those 18% had need fully met. *Average percent of need met:* 82% (excluding resources awarded to replace EFC). *Average financial aid package:* $8318 (excluding resources awarded to replace EFC). 16% of all full-time freshmen had no need and received non-need-based gift aid.

UNDERGRADUATE FINANCIAL AID (Fall 2003) 3,336 applied for aid; of those 82% were deemed to have need. 95% of undergraduates with need received

aid; of those 23% had need fully met. *Average percent of need met:* 64% (excluding resources awarded to replace EFC). *Average financial aid package:* $8945 (excluding resources awarded to replace EFC). 11% of all full-time undergraduates had no need and received non-need-based gift aid.

GIFT AID (NEED-BASED) *Total amount:* $12,064,160 (37% federal, 49% state, 11% institutional, 3% external sources). *Receiving aid:* Freshmen: 58% (579); All full-time undergraduates: 45% (2,073). *Average award:* Freshmen: $6343; Undergraduates: $5819. *Scholarships, grants, and awards:* Federal Pell, FSEOG, state, private, college/university gift aid from institutional funds.

GIFT AID (NON-NEED-BASED) *Total amount:* $8,504,350 (53% state, 35% institutional, 12% external sources). *Receiving aid:* Freshmen: 6% (55); Undergraduates: 3% (144). *Average Award:* Freshmen: $4838; Undergraduates: $6545. *Scholarships, grants, and awards by category:* Academic Interests/Achievement: 375 awards ($1,192,819 total): general academic interests/achievements. Creative Arts/Performance: 125 awards ($117,848 total): art/fine arts, dance, music, performing arts, theater/drama. Special Characteristics: 11 awards ($3780 total): children of faculty/staff. *Tuition waivers:* Full or partial for employees or children of employees, senior citizens.

LOANS *Student loans:* $21,504,649 (51% need-based, 49% non-need-based). 60% of past graduating class borrowed through all loan programs. *Average indebtedness per student:* $17,800. *Average need-based loan:* Freshmen: $2857; Undergraduates: $4884. *Parent loans:* $2,899,690 (100% non-need-based). *Programs:* Federal Direct (Subsidized and Unsubsidized Stafford), FFEL (PLUS), Perkins.

WORK-STUDY *Federal work-study:* Total amount: $220,000; 250 jobs averaging $880. *State or other work-study/employment:* Total amount: $1,452,449 (100% non-need-based). Part-time jobs available (averaging $1000).

ATHLETIC AWARDS *Total amount:* $1,129,703 (40% need-based, 60% non-need-based).

APPLYING FOR FINANCIAL AID *Required financial aid form:* FAFSA. *Financial aid deadline (priority):* 3/1. *Notification date:* Continuous beginning 3/15. Students must reply within 2 weeks of notification.

CONTACT Ms. Geneva Drakeford, Assistant Director, Office of Financial Aid, Winthrop University, 119 Tillman Hall, Rock Hill, SC 29733, 803-323-2189 or toll-free 800-763-0230. *Fax:* 803-323-2557. *E-mail:* finaid@winthrop.edu.

WISCONSIN LUTHERAN COLLEGE
Milwaukee, WI

ABOUT THE INSTITUTION Independent religious, coed. Awards: bachelor's degrees. 20 undergraduate majors. Total enrollment: 706. Undergraduates: 706. Freshmen: 207.

GIFT AID (NEED-BASED) *Scholarships, grants, and awards:* Federal Pell, FSEOG, state, private, college/university gift aid from institutional funds.

GIFT AID (NON-NEED-BASED) *Scholarships, grants, and awards by category:* Academic Interests/Achievement: biological sciences, business, communication, education, general academic interests/achievements, international studies, mathematics, social sciences. Creative Arts/Performance: art/fine arts, music, theater/drama. Special Achievements/Activities: general special achievements/activities, leadership. Special Characteristics: children of faculty/staff, international students, members of minority groups.

LOANS *Programs:* FFEL (Subsidized and Unsubsidized Stafford, PLUS), state, alternative loans.

WORK-STUDY *Federal work-study:* Total amount: $405,977; 250 jobs averaging $1624. *State or other work-study/employment:* Total amount: $112,800 (33% need-based, 67% non-need-based). 23 part-time jobs averaging $4904.

APPLYING FOR FINANCIAL AID *Required financial aid forms:* FAFSA, institution's own form, business/farm supplement.

CONTACT Mrs. Linda Loeffel, Director of Financial Aid, Wisconsin Lutheran College, 8800 West Bluemound Road, Milwaukee, WI 53226-4699, 414-443-8842 or toll-free 888-WIS LUTH. *Fax:* 414-443-8514. *E-mail:* linda_loeffel@wlc.edu.

WITTENBERG UNIVERSITY
Springfield, OH

Tuition & fees: $26,196	Average undergraduate aid package: $20,750

ABOUT THE INSTITUTION Independent religious, coed. Awards: bachelor's and master's degrees. 40 undergraduate majors. Total enrollment: 2,190. Undergraduates: 2,177. Freshmen: 578. Federal methodology is used as a basis for awarding need-based institutional aid.

UNDERGRADUATE EXPENSES for 2004–05 *Application fee:* $40. *Comprehensive fee:* $32,882 includes full-time tuition ($26,040), mandatory fees ($156), and room and board ($6686). *College room only:* $3454. Room and board charges vary according to board plan. *Part-time tuition:* $826 per hour. Part-time tuition and fees vary according to course load. *Payment plan:* Installment.

FRESHMAN FINANCIAL AID (Fall 2003) 507 applied for aid; of those 85% were deemed to have need. 100% of freshmen with need received aid. *Average financial aid package:* $20,994 (excluding resources awarded to replace EFC). 24% of all full-time freshmen had no need and received non-need-based gift aid.

UNDERGRADUATE FINANCIAL AID (Fall 2003) 1,714 applied for aid; of those 87% were deemed to have need. 100% of undergraduates with need received aid. *Average financial aid package:* $20,750 (excluding resources awarded to replace EFC). 25% of all full-time undergraduates had no need and received non-need-based gift aid.

GIFT AID (NEED-BASED) *Total amount:* $24,253,803 (7% federal, 8% state, 81% institutional, 4% external sources). *Receiving aid:* Freshmen: 75% (431); All full-time undergraduates: 72% (1,491). *Average award:* Freshmen: $17,153; Undergraduates: $16,355. *Scholarships, grants, and awards:* Federal Pell, FSEOG, state, private, college/university gift aid from institutional funds.

GIFT AID (NON-NEED-BASED) *Total amount:* $5,300,011 (6% state, 92% institutional, 2% external sources). *Average Award:* Freshmen: $10,612; *Undergraduates:* $10,047. *Scholarships, grants, and awards by category:* Academic Interests/Achievement: general academic interests/achievements. Creative Arts/Performance: art/fine arts, dance, music, theater/drama. Special Achievements/Activities: community service, general special achievements/activities, leadership. Special Characteristics: adult students, children and siblings of alumni, children of faculty/staff, ethnic background, international students, local/state students, members of minority groups, relatives of clergy, religious affiliation. *Tuition waivers:* Full or partial for minority students, children of alumni, employees or children of employees, adult students, senior citizens. *ROTC:* Army cooperative, Air Force cooperative.

LOANS *Student loans:* $9,564,683 (92% need-based, 8% non-need-based). 69% of past graduating class borrowed through all loan programs. *Average indebtedness per student:* $21,799. *Average need-based loan:* Freshmen: $3796; Undergraduates: $4564. *Parent loans:* $3,625,508 (85% need-based, 15% non-need-based). *Programs:* FFEL (Subsidized and Unsubsidized Stafford, PLUS), Perkins, college/university, alternative loans.

WORK-STUDY *Federal work-study:* Total amount: $1,065,732; 690 jobs averaging $1545. *State or other work-study/employment:* Total amount: $1,175,240 (63% need-based, 37% non-need-based). 791 part-time jobs averaging $1486.

APPLYING FOR FINANCIAL AID *Required financial aid form:* FAFSA. *Financial aid deadline (priority):* 3/15. *Notification date:* Continuous beginning 3/1. Students must reply by 5/1 or within 2 weeks of notification.

CONTACT Mr. J. Randy Green, Director of Financial Aid, Wittenberg University, PO Box 720, Springfield, OH 45501-0720, 937-327-7321 or toll-free 800-677-7558 Ext. 6314. *Fax:* 937-327-6379. *E-mail:* jgreen@wittenberg.edu.

WOFFORD COLLEGE
Spartanburg, SC

Tuition & fees: $22,300	Average undergraduate aid package: $22,163

ABOUT THE INSTITUTION Independent religious, coed. Awards: bachelor's degrees. 30 undergraduate majors. Total enrollment: 1,161. Undergraduates: 1,161. Freshmen: 323. Federal methodology is used as a basis for awarding need-based institutional aid.

UNDERGRADUATE EXPENSES for 2004–05 *Application fee:* $40. *Comprehensive fee:* $28,740 includes full-time tuition ($21,480), mandatory fees ($820), and room and board ($6440). *College room only:* $3475. *Part-time tuition:* $805 per hour. *Payment plan:* Installment.

GIFT AID (NEED-BASED) *Total amount:* $8,270,070 (7% federal, 28% state, 62% institutional, 3% external sources). *Receiving aid:* Freshmen: 52% (168); All full-time undergraduates: 54% (621). *Average award:* Freshmen: $10,122; Undergraduates: $10,687. *Scholarships, grants, and awards:* Federal Pell, FSEOG, state, private, college/university gift aid from institutional funds.

GIFT AID (NON-NEED-BASED) *Total amount:* $5,128,803 (1% federal, 35% state, 58% institutional, 6% external sources). *Receiving aid:* Freshmen: 28% (89); Undergraduates: 29% (338). *Average Award:* Freshmen: $8268; *Undergraduates:* $8998. *Scholarships, grants, and awards by category:* Academic Interests/Achievement: general academic interests/achievements. Creative Arts/Performance: music. Special Achievements/Activities: cheerleading/drum major, community service, general special achievements/activities, leadership, religious

involvement. *Special Characteristics:* children of faculty/staff, general special characteristics, relatives of clergy. *Tuition waivers:* Full or partial for employees or children of employees. *ROTC:* Army.

LOANS *Student loans:* $2,324,629 (64% need-based, 36% non-need-based). 64% of past graduating class borrowed through all loan programs. *Average indebtedness per student:* $12,281. *Average need-based loan:* Freshmen: $3685; Undergraduates: $4469. *Parent loans:* $1,685,099 (20% need-based, 80% non-need-based). *Programs:* FFEL (Subsidized and Unsubsidized Stafford, PLUS), Perkins, state.

ATHLETIC AWARDS *Total amount:* $3,032,476 (37% need-based, 63% non-need-based).

APPLYING FOR FINANCIAL AID *Required financial aid form:* FAFSA. *Financial aid deadline (priority):* 3/15. *Notification date:* Continuous beginning 3/31. Students must reply by 5/1.

CONTACT Donna D. Hawkins, Director of Financial Aid, Wofford College, Campus PO Box 171, 429 North Church Street, Spartanburg, SC 29303-3663, 864-597-4160. *Fax:* 864-597-4149. *E-mail:* hawkinsdd@wofford.edu.

WOODBURY COLLEGE
Montpelier, VT

CONTACT Kathleen Moore, Admissions Director, Woodbury College, 660 Elm Street, Montpelier, VT 05602, 800-639-6039 Ext. 329 or toll-free 800-639-6039 (in-state). *E-mail:* admissions@woodbury-college.edu.

WOODBURY UNIVERSITY
Burbank, CA

Tuition & fees: $21,314	Average undergraduate aid package: $16,234

ABOUT THE INSTITUTION Independent, coed. Awards: bachelor's and master's degrees. 15 undergraduate majors. Total enrollment: 1,446. Undergraduates: 1,270. Freshmen: 123. Federal methodology is used as a basis for awarding need-based institutional aid.

UNDERGRADUATE EXPENSES for 2004–05 *Application fee:* $35. *Comprehensive fee:* $29,016 includes full-time tuition ($21,074), mandatory fees ($240), and room and board ($7702). *College room only:* $4514. Full-time tuition and fees vary according to program. Room and board charges vary according to board plan and housing facility. *Part-time tuition:* $688 per credit. Part-time tuition and fees vary according to class time, course load, and program. *Payment plans:* Installment, deferred payment.

FRESHMAN FINANCIAL AID (Fall 2004, est.) 110 applied for aid; of those 93% were deemed to have need. 100% of freshmen with need received aid; of those 2% had need fully met. *Average percent of need met:* 64% (excluding resources awarded to replace EFC). *Average financial aid package:* $17,208 (excluding resources awarded to replace EFC). 29% of all full-time freshmen had no need and received non-need-based gift aid.

UNDERGRADUATE FINANCIAL AID (Fall 2004, est.) 825 applied for aid; of those 94% were deemed to have need. 100% of undergraduates with need received aid; of those 3% had need fully met. *Average percent of need met:* 60% (excluding resources awarded to replace EFC). *Average financial aid package:* $16,234 (excluding resources awarded to replace EFC). 15% of all full-time undergraduates had no need and received non-need-based gift aid.

GIFT AID (NEED-BASED) *Total amount:* $10,043,371 (19% federal, 30% state, 50% institutional, 1% external sources). *Receiving aid:* Freshmen: 71% (101); All full-time undergraduates: 81% (742). *Average award:* Freshmen: $15,153; Undergraduates: $12,761. *Scholarships, grants, and awards:* Federal Pell, FSEOG, state, private, college/university gift aid from institutional funds.

GIFT AID (NON-NEED-BASED) *Total amount:* $771,333 (3% state, 91% institutional, 6% external sources). *Receiving aid:* Freshmen: 1% (1); Undergraduates: 1% (7). *Average Award:* Freshmen: $9206; *Undergraduates:* $11,044. *Scholarships, grants, and awards by category:* Academic Interests/Achievement: 645 awards ($3,271,215 total): general academic interests/achievements. Creative Arts/Performance: 2 awards ($33,267 total): applied art and design. *Tuition waivers:* Full or partial for employees or children of employees.

LOANS *Student loans:* $8,387,274 (85% need-based, 15% non-need-based). *Average need-based loan:* Freshmen: $2545; Undergraduates: $4420. *Parent loans:* $2,729,822 (58% need-based, 42% non-need-based). *Programs:* FFEL (Subsidized and Unsubsidized Stafford, PLUS), Perkins, alternative loans.

WORK-STUDY *Federal work-study:* Total amount: $155,913; 100 jobs averaging $1500.

APPLYING FOR FINANCIAL AID *Required financial aid forms:* FAFSA, institution's own form. *Financial aid deadline:* Continuous. *Notification date:* Continuous beginning 3/15. Students must reply within 2 weeks of notification.
CONTACT Celeastia Williams, Director of Enrollment Services, Woodbury University, 7500 Glenoaks Boulevard, Burbank, CA 91510, 818-767-0888 Ext. 273 or toll-free 800-784-WOOD. *Fax:* 818-767-4816.

WORCESTER POLYTECHNIC INSTITUTE
Worcester, MA

Tuition & fees: $30,130	Average undergraduate aid package: $20,980

ABOUT THE INSTITUTION Independent, coed. Awards: bachelor's, master's, and doctoral degrees and post-bachelor's and post-master's certificates. 48 undergraduate majors. Total enrollment: 3,817. Undergraduates: 2,868. Freshmen: 748. Both federal and institutional methodology are used as a basis for awarding need-based institutional aid.
UNDERGRADUATE EXPENSES for 2004–05 *Application fee:* $60. *Comprehensive fee:* $39,294 includes full-time tuition ($29,930), mandatory fees ($200), and room and board ($9164). *College room only:* $5288. Room and board charges vary according to board plan and housing facility. *Payment plans:* Installment, deferred payment.
FRESHMAN FINANCIAL AID (Fall 2004, est.) 99% of freshmen with need received aid; of those 42% had need fully met. *Average percent of need met:* 99% (excluding resources awarded to replace EFC). *Average financial aid package:* $20,839 (excluding resources awarded to replace EFC). 15% of all full-time freshmen had no need and received non-need-based gift aid.
UNDERGRADUATE FINANCIAL AID (Fall 2004, est.) 99% of undergraduates with need received aid; of those 29% had need fully met. *Average percent of need met:* 91% (excluding resources awarded to replace EFC). *Average financial aid package:* $20,980 (excluding resources awarded to replace EFC). 11% of all full-time undergraduates had no need and received non-need-based gift aid.
GIFT AID (NEED-BASED) *Total amount:* $32,910,310 (6% federal, 4% state, 84% institutional, 6% external sources). *Receiving aid:* Freshmen: 73% (544); All full-time undergraduates: 71% (1,919). *Average award:* Freshmen: $17,392; Undergraduates: $16,006. *Scholarships, grants, and awards:* Federal Pell, FSEOG, state, private, college/university gift aid from institutional funds.
GIFT AID (NON-NEED-BASED) *Total amount:* $6,564,795 (73% institutional, 27% external sources). *Receiving aid:* Freshmen: 22% (165); Undergraduates: 14% (374). *Average Award:* Freshmen: $18,252; Undergraduates: $19,160. *Scholarships, grants, and awards by category: Academic Interests/Achievement:* 594 awards ($7,956,838 total): general academic interests/achievements, premedicine. *Special Characteristics:* 22 awards ($116,510 total): children of workers in trades. *Tuition waivers:* Full or partial for employees or children of employees. *ROTC:* Army, Naval cooperative, Air Force.
LOANS *Student loans:* $19,104,224 (58% need-based, 42% non-need-based). 76% of past graduating class borrowed through all loan programs. *Average indebtedness per student:* $30,016. *Average need-based loan:* Freshmen: $4549; Undergraduates: $6168. *Parent loans:* $5,334,645 (100% non-need-based). *Programs:* FFEL (Subsidized and Unsubsidized Stafford, PLUS), Perkins, state, college/university.
WORK-STUDY *Federal work-study:* Total amount: $552,763; 653 jobs averaging $660. *State or other work-study/employment:* Part-time jobs available.
APPLYING FOR FINANCIAL AID *Required financial aid forms:* FAFSA, CSS Financial Aid PROFILE, noncustodial (divorced/separated) parent's statement, federal income tax form(s) and W-2 statements. *Financial aid deadline:* 3/1 (priority: 3/1). *Notification date:* 4/1. Students must reply by 5/1.
CONTACT Office of Financial Aid, Worcester Polytechnic Institute, 100 Institute Road, Worcester, MA 01609-2280, 508-831-5469. *Fax:* 508-831-5039. *E-mail:* finaid@wpi.edu.

WORCESTER STATE COLLEGE
Worcester, MA

Tuition & fees (MA res): $4579	Average undergraduate aid package: $6868

ABOUT THE INSTITUTION State-supported, coed. Awards: bachelor's and master's degrees and post-bachelor's certificates. 23 undergraduate majors. Total enrollment: 5,404. Undergraduates: 4,554. Freshmen: 632. Federal methodology is used as a basis for awarding need-based institutional aid.
UNDERGRADUATE EXPENSES for 2004–05 *Application fee:* $20. *Tuition, state resident:* full-time $970; part-time $40.42 per credit. *Tuition, nonresident:*

full-time $7050; part-time $293.75 per credit. *Required fees:* full-time $3609; $145.79 per credit. Full-time tuition and fees vary according to class time, course load, and reciprocity agreements. Part-time tuition and fees vary according to class time, course load, and reciprocity agreements. *College room and board:* $6896; *room only:* $4596. Room and board charges vary according to board plan and housing facility. *Payment plan:* Deferred payment.
FRESHMAN FINANCIAL AID (Fall 2003) 477 applied for aid; of those 66% were deemed to have need. 96% of freshmen with need received aid; of those 45% had need fully met. *Average percent of need met:* 75% (excluding resources awarded to replace EFC). *Average financial aid package:* $5494 (excluding resources awarded to replace EFC). 3% of all full-time freshmen had no need and received non-need-based gift aid.
UNDERGRADUATE FINANCIAL AID (Fall 2003) 1,920 applied for aid; of those 72% were deemed to have need. 95% of undergraduates with need received aid; of those 48% had need fully met. *Average percent of need met:* 79% (excluding resources awarded to replace EFC). *Average financial aid package:* $6868 (excluding resources awarded to replace EFC). 1% of all full-time undergraduates had no need and received non-need-based gift aid.
GIFT AID (NEED-BASED) *Total amount:* $3,746,794 (62% federal, 38% state). *Receiving aid:* Freshmen: 42% (259); All full-time undergraduates: 34% (1,052). *Average award:* Freshmen: $1717; Undergraduates: $1836. *Scholarships, grants, and awards:* Federal Pell, FSEOG, state, private, college/university gift aid from institutional funds.
GIFT AID (NON-NEED-BASED) *Total amount:* $1,426,093 (11% federal, 7% state, 54% institutional, 28% external sources). *Receiving aid:* Freshmen: 12% (75); Undergraduates: 7% (222). *Average Award:* Freshmen: $2199; Undergraduates: $1541. *Scholarships, grants, and awards by category: Academic Interests/Achievement:* biological sciences, business, education, English, foreign languages, health fields. *Creative Arts/Performance:* art/fine arts. *Special Achievements/Activities:* community service, general special achievements/activities. *Special Characteristics:* children and siblings of alumni, children of faculty/staff, children with a deceased or disabled parent, general special characteristics, handicapped students, local/state students, veterans. *Tuition waivers:* Full or partial for employees or children of employees, senior citizens. *ROTC:* Army cooperative, Naval cooperative, Air Force cooperative.
LOANS *Student loans:* $3,366,260 (42% need-based, 58% non-need-based). *Average indebtedness per student:* $11,843. *Average need-based loan:* Freshmen: $1022; Undergraduates: $1532. *Parent loans:* $589,747 (100% non-need-based). *Programs:* FFEL (Subsidized and Unsubsidized Stafford, PLUS), Perkins, Massachusetts No-Interest Loans (NIL).
WORK-STUDY *Federal work-study:* Total amount: $240,160; jobs available.
APPLYING FOR FINANCIAL AID *Required financial aid forms:* FAFSA, institution's own form. *Financial aid deadline (priority):* 3/1. *Notification date:* Continuous. Students must reply within 2 weeks of notification.
CONTACT Jayne McGinn, Director of Financial Aid, Worcester State College, 486 Chandler Street, Worcester, MA 01602, 508-929-8058 or toll-free 866-WSC-CALL. *Fax:* 508-929-8194. *E-mail:* jmcginn@worcester.edu.

WRIGHT STATE UNIVERSITY
Dayton, OH

CONTACT Mr. David R. Darr, Director of Financial Aid, Wright State University, Colonel Glenn Highway, Dayton, OH 45435, 937-873-5721 or toll-free 800-247-1770.

XAVIER UNIVERSITY
Cincinnati, OH

Tuition & fees: $20,400	Average undergraduate aid package: $13,874

ABOUT THE INSTITUTION Independent Roman Catholic, coed. Awards: associate, bachelor's, master's, and doctoral degrees and post-bachelor's and post-master's certificates. 53 undergraduate majors. Total enrollment: 6,668. Undergraduates: 3,943. Freshmen: 878. Federal methodology is used as a basis for awarding need-based institutional aid.
UNDERGRADUATE EXPENSES for 2004–05 *Application fee:* $35. *Comprehensive fee:* $28,650 includes full-time tuition ($20,100), mandatory fees ($300), and room and board ($8250). *College room only:* $4580. Full-time tuition and fees vary according to program. Room and board charges vary according to board plan and housing facility. *Part-time tuition:* $405 per credit hour. Part-time tuition and fees vary according to course load. *Payment plans:* Installment, deferred payment.

FRESHMAN FINANCIAL AID (Fall 2004, est.) 710 applied for aid; of those 76% were deemed to have need. 100% of freshmen with need received aid; of those 32% had need fully met. *Average percent of need met:* 74% (excluding resources awarded to replace EFC). *Average financial aid package:* $13,488 (excluding resources awarded to replace EFC). 35% of all full-time freshmen had no need and received non-need-based gift aid.

UNDERGRADUATE FINANCIAL AID (Fall 2004, est.) 2,130 applied for aid; of those 81% were deemed to have need. 99% of undergraduates with need received aid; of those 29% had need fully met. *Average percent of need met:* 72% (excluding resources awarded to replace EFC). *Average financial aid package:* $13,874 (excluding resources awarded to replace EFC). 34% of all full-time undergraduates had no need and received non-need-based gift aid.

GIFT AID (NEED-BASED) *Total amount:* $17,186,906 (10% federal, 10% state, 73% institutional, 7% external sources). *Receiving aid:* Freshmen: 61% (535); All full-time undergraduates: 50% (1,674). *Average award:* Freshmen: $10,297; Undergraduates: $9986. *Scholarships, grants, and awards:* Federal Pell, FSEOG, state, private, college/university gift aid from institutional funds.

GIFT AID (NON-NEED-BASED) *Total amount:* $9,761,193 (9% state, 77% institutional, 14% external sources). *Receiving aid:* Freshmen: 17% (149); Undergraduates: 11% (365). *Average Award:* Freshmen: $10,010; Undergraduates: $8890. *Scholarships, grants, and awards by category:* Academic Interests/Achievement: 2,009 awards ($12,509,968 total): foreign languages, general academic interests/achievements, mathematics, military science, physical sciences, social sciences. *Creative Arts/Performance:* 158 awards ($408,800 total): art/fine arts, music, performing arts, theater/drama. *Special Characteristics:* 325 awards ($1,174,200 total): international students, members of minority groups, siblings of current students. *Tuition waivers:* Full or partial for employees or children of employees, senior citizens. *ROTC:* Army, Air Force cooperative.

LOANS *Student loans:* $13,146,970 (70% need-based, 30% non-need-based). 63% of past graduating class borrowed through all loan programs. *Average indebtedness per student:* $19,750. *Average need-based loan:* Freshmen: $3298; Undergraduates: $4301. *Parent loans:* $4,498,441 (30% need-based, 70% non-need-based). *Programs:* FFEL (Subsidized and Unsubsidized Stafford, PLUS), Perkins.

WORK-STUDY *Federal work-study:* Total amount: $1,288,291; 642 jobs averaging $2007. *State or other work-study/employment:* Total amount: $141,826 (5% need-based, 95% non-need-based). 74 part-time jobs averaging $1917.

ATHLETIC AWARDS *Total amount:* $2,779,489 (31% need-based, 69% non-need-based).

APPLYING FOR FINANCIAL AID *Required financial aid form:* FAFSA. *Financial aid deadline (priority):* 2/15. *Notification date:* Continuous beginning 3/1. Students must reply by 5/1.

CONTACT Office of Financial Aid, Xavier University, 3800 Victory Parkway, Cincinnati, OH 45207-5411, 513-745-3142 or toll-free 800-344-4698. *Fax:* 513-745-2806.

XAVIER UNIVERSITY OF LOUISIANA
New Orleans, LA

Tuition & fees: $12,200	Average undergraduate aid package: $4551

ABOUT THE INSTITUTION Independent Roman Catholic, coed. Awards: bachelor's, master's, and first professional degrees. 54 undergraduate majors. Total enrollment: 4,121. Undergraduates: 3,290. Freshmen: 1,001. Federal methodology is used as a basis for awarding need-based institutional aid.

UNDERGRADUATE EXPENSES for 2004–05 *Application fee:* $25. *Comprehensive fee:* $19,300 includes full-time tuition ($11,300), mandatory fees ($900), and room and board ($7100). Room and board charges vary according to location. *Part-time tuition:* $475 per credit hour. *Payment plan:* Installment.

FRESHMAN FINANCIAL AID (Fall 2004, est.) 947 applied for aid; of those 84% were deemed to have need. 100% of freshmen with need received aid; of those 1% had need fully met. *Average percent of need met:* 74% (excluding resources awarded to replace EFC). *Average financial aid package:* $3921 (excluding resources awarded to replace EFC). 7% of all full-time freshmen had no need and received non-need-based gift aid.

UNDERGRADUATE FINANCIAL AID (Fall 2004, est.) 3,128 applied for aid; of those 87% were deemed to have need. 99% of undergraduates with need received aid; of those .4% had need fully met. *Average percent of need met:* 77% (excluding resources awarded to replace EFC). *Average financial aid package:* $4551 (excluding resources awarded to replace EFC). 3% of all full-time undergraduates had no need and received non-need-based gift aid.

GIFT AID (NEED-BASED) *Total amount:* $7,675,345 (88% federal, 12% state). *Scholarships, grants, and awards:* Federal Pell, FSEOG, state, private, college/university gift aid from institutional funds, United Negro College Fund.

GIFT AID (NON-NEED-BASED) *Total amount:* $8,652,494 (96% institutional, 4% external sources). *Receiving aid:* Freshmen: 35% (345); Undergraduates: 23% (806). *Average Award:* Freshmen: $3215; Undergraduates: $3152. *Scholarships, grants, and awards by category:* Academic Interests/Achievement: biological sciences, business, computer science, education, engineering/technologies, foreign languages, general academic interests/achievements, humanities, mathematics, physical sciences, premedicine, social sciences. *Creative Arts/Performance:* art/fine arts, music, performing arts. *Special Achievements/Activities:* religious involvement. *Special Characteristics:* children of faculty/staff. *Tuition waivers:* Full or partial for employees or children of employees. *ROTC:* Army cooperative, Naval cooperative, Air Force cooperative.

LOANS *Student loans:* $23,217,790 (56% need-based, 44% non-need-based). 74% of past graduating class borrowed through all loan programs. *Average indebtedness per student:* $20,083. *Average need-based loan:* Freshmen: $2340; Undergraduates: $5241. *Parent loans:* $9,854,660 (100% non-need-based). *Programs:* Federal Direct (Subsidized and Unsubsidized Stafford, PLUS), FFEL (Subsidized and Unsubsidized Stafford, PLUS), Perkins.

WORK-STUDY *Federal work-study:* Total amount: $289,318; jobs available.

ATHLETIC AWARDS *Total amount:* $943,439 (100% non-need-based).

APPLYING FOR FINANCIAL AID *Required financial aid form:* FAFSA. *Financial aid deadline (priority):* 1/1. *Notification date:* Continuous beginning 4/1.

CONTACT Mrs. Mildred Higgins, Financial Aid Director, Xavier University of Louisiana, One Drexel Drive, New Orleans, LA 70125-1098, 504-520-7517 or toll-free 877-XAVIERU.

YALE UNIVERSITY
New Haven, CT

Tuition & fees: $29,820	Average undergraduate aid package: $26,978

ABOUT THE INSTITUTION Independent, coed. Awards: bachelor's, master's, doctoral, and first professional degrees and post-master's certificates. 67 undergraduate majors. Total enrollment: 11,441. Undergraduates: 5,319. Freshmen: 1,307. Both federal and institutional methodology are used as a basis for awarding need-based institutional aid.

UNDERGRADUATE EXPENSES for 2004–05 *Application fee:* $65. *Comprehensive fee:* $38,850 includes full-time tuition ($29,820) and room and board ($9030). *College room only:* $4930. *Payment plan:* Installment.

FRESHMAN FINANCIAL AID (Fall 2003) 808 applied for aid; of those 73% were deemed to have need. 100% of freshmen with need received aid; of those 100% had need fully met. *Average percent of need met:* 100% (excluding resources awarded to replace EFC). *Average financial aid package:* $26,995 (excluding resources awarded to replace EFC).

UNDERGRADUATE FINANCIAL AID (Fall 2003) 2,595 applied for aid; of those 81% were deemed to have need. 100% of undergraduates with need received aid; of those 100% had need fully met. *Average percent of need met:* 100% (excluding resources awarded to replace EFC). *Average financial aid package:* $26,978 (excluding resources awarded to replace EFC).

GIFT AID (NEED-BASED) *Total amount:* $51,088,855 (6% federal, 1% state, 87% institutional, 6% external sources). *Receiving aid:* Freshmen: 43% (582); All full-time undergraduates: 40% (2,096). *Average award:* Freshmen: $24,685; Undergraduates: $23,574. *Scholarships, grants, and awards:* Federal Pell, FSEOG, state, private, college/university gift aid from institutional funds, United Negro College Fund, Alumni Club awards.

GIFT AID (NON-NEED-BASED) *ROTC:* Army cooperative, Air Force cooperative.

LOANS *Student loans:* $5,429,898 (100% need-based). 39% of past graduating class borrowed through all loan programs. *Average indebtedness per student:* $16,911. *Average need-based loan:* Freshmen: $1573; Undergraduates: $2591. *Parent loans:* $4,895,514 (100% need-based). *Programs:* FFEL (Subsidized and Unsubsidized Stafford, PLUS), Perkins, state, college/university.

WORK-STUDY *Federal work-study:* Total amount: $2,197,962; 1,202 jobs averaging $1829. *State or other work-study/employment:* Total amount: $879,805 (100% need-based). 334 part-time jobs averaging $2634.

APPLYING FOR FINANCIAL AID *Required financial aid forms:* FAFSA, CSS Financial Aid PROFILE, state aid form, noncustodial (divorced/separated) parent's statement, business/farm supplement, income tax form(s). *Financial aid deadline (priority):* 3/1. *Notification date:* 4/1. Students must reply by 5/1 or within 1 week of notification.

CONTACT Myra Baas Smith, University Director of Financial Aid, Yale University, PO Box 208288, New Haven, CT 06520-8288, 203-432-0372. *Fax:* 203-432-0359. *E-mail:* myra.smith@yale.edu.

YESHIVA AND KOLEL BAIS MEDRASH ELYON
Monsey, NY

CONTACT Financial Aid Office, Yeshiva and Kolel Bais Medrash Elyon, 73 Main Street, Monsey, NY 10952, 845-356-7064.

YESHIVA AND KOLLEL HARBOTZAS TORAH
Brooklyn, NY

CONTACT Financial Aid Office, Yeshiva And Kollel Harbotzas Torah, 1049 East 15th Street, Brooklyn, NY 11230, 718-692-0208.

YESHIVA BETH MOSHE
Scranton, PA

CONTACT Financial Aid Office, Yeshiva Beth Moshe, 930 Hickory Street, Scranton, PA 18505-2124, 717-346-1747.

YESHIVA COLLEGE OF THE NATION'S CAPITAL
Silver Spring, MD

CONTACT Financial Aid Office, Yeshiva College of the Nation's Capital, 1216 Arcola Avenue, Silver Spring, MD 20902, 301-593-2534.

YESHIVA DERECH CHAIM
Brooklyn, NY

CONTACT Financial Aid Office, Yeshiva Derech Chaim, 1573 39th Street, Brooklyn, NY 11218, 718-438-5426.

YESHIVA D'MONSEY RABBINICAL COLLEGE
Monsey, NY

CONTACT Financial Aid Office, Yeshiva D'Monsey Rabbinical College, 2 Roman Boulevard, Monsey, NY 10952, 914-352-5852.

YESHIVA GEDDOLAH OF GREATER DETROIT RABBINICAL COLLEGE
Oak Park, MI

CONTACT Rabbi P. Rushnawitz, Executive Administrator, Yeshiva Geddolah of Greater Detroit Rabbinical College, 24600 Greenfield Road, Oak Park, MI 48237-1544, 810-968-3360. *Fax:* 810-968-8613.

YESHIVA GEDOLAH IMREI YOSEF D'SPINKA
Brooklyn, NY

CONTACT Financial Aid Office, Yeshiva Gedolah Imrei Yosef D'Spinka, 1466 56th Street, Brooklyn, NY 11219, 718-851-8721.

YESHIVA GEDOLAH RABBINICAL COLLEGE
Miami Beach, FL

CONTACT Financial Aid Office, Yeshiva Gedolah Rabbinical College, 1140 Alton Road, Miami Beach, FL 33139, 305-673-5664.

YESHIVA KARLIN STOLIN RABBINICAL INSTITUTE
Brooklyn, NY

ABOUT THE INSTITUTION Independent Jewish, men only. 3 undergraduate majors. Total enrollment: 53. Undergraduates: 38. Freshmen: 14.
GIFT AID (NEED-BASED) *Scholarships, grants, and awards:* Federal Pell, FSEOG.
LOANS *Programs:* Perkins.
APPLYING FOR FINANCIAL AID *Required financial aid forms:* FAFSA, institution's own form.
CONTACT Mr. Daniel Ross, Financial Aid Administrator, Yeshiva Karlin Stolin Rabbinical Institute, 1818 Fifty-fourth Street, Brooklyn, NY 11204, 718-232-7800 Ext. 116. *Fax:* 718-331-4833.

YESHIVA OF NITRA RABBINICAL COLLEGE
Mount Kisco, NY

CONTACT Mr. Yosef Rosen, Financial Aid Administrator, Yeshiva of Nitra Rabbinical College, 194 Division Avenue, Mount Kisco, NY 10549, 718-384-5460. *Fax:* 718-387-9400.

YESHIVA OF THE TELSHE ALUMNI
Riverdale, NY

CONTACT Financial Aid Office, Yeshiva of the Telshe Alumni, 4904 Independence Avenue, Riverdale, NY 10471, 718-601-3523.

YESHIVA OHR ELCHONON CHABAD/WEST COAST TALMUDICAL SEMINARY
Los Angeles, CA

CONTACT Ms. Hendy Tauber, Director of Financial Aid, Yeshiva Ohr Elchonon Chabad/West Coast Talmudical Seminary, 7215 Waring Avenue, Los Angeles, CA 90046-7660, 213-937-3763. *Fax:* 213-937-9456.

YESHIVA SHAAREI TORAH OF ROCKLAND
Suffern, NY

CONTACT Financial Aid Office, Yeshiva Shaarei Torah of Rockland, 91 West Carlton Road, Suffern, NY 10901, 845-352-3431.

YESHIVA SHAAR HATORAH TALMUDIC RESEARCH INSTITUTE
Kew Gardens, NY

CONTACT Mr. Yoel Yankelewitz, Executive Director, Financial Aid, Yeshiva Shaar Hatorah Talmudic Research Institute, 117-06 84th Avenue, Kew Gardens, NY 11418-1469, 718-846-1940.

YESHIVAS NOVOMINSK
Brooklyn, NY

CONTACT Financial Aid Office, Yeshivas Novominsk, 1569 47th Street, Brooklyn, NY 11219, 718-438-2727.

YESHIVATH VIZNITZ
Monsey, NY

CONTACT Financial Aid Office, Yeshivath Viznitz, Phyllis Terrace, PO Box 446, Monsey, NY 10952, 914-356-1010.

YESHIVATH ZICHRON MOSHE
South Fallsburg, NY

CONTACT Ms. Miryom R. Miller, Director of Financial Aid, Yeshivath Zichron Moshe, Laurel Park Road, South Fallsburg, NY 12779, 914-434-5240. *Fax:* 914-434-1009. *E-mail:* lehus@aol.com.

YESHIVAT MIKDASH MELECH
Brooklyn, NY
CONTACT Financial Aid Office, Yeshivat Mikdash Melech, 1326 Ocean Parkway, Brooklyn, NY 11230-5601, 718-339-1090.

YESHIVA TORAS CHAIM TALMUDICAL SEMINARY
Denver, CO
CONTACT Office of Financial Aid, Yeshiva Toras Chaim Talmudical Seminary, 1400 Quitman Street, Denver, CO 80204-1415, 303-629-8200.

YESHIVA UNIVERSITY
New York, NY
CONTACT Jean Belmont, Director of Student Finances, Yeshiva University, 500 West 185th Street, Room 121, New York, NY 10033-3201, 212-960-5269. *Fax:* 212-960-0037. *E-mail:* jbelmont@ymail.yu.edu.

YORK COLLEGE
York, NE

Tuition & fees: $11,930 | **Average undergraduate aid package: $10,149**

ABOUT THE INSTITUTION Independent religious, coed. Awards: associate and bachelor's degrees. 38 undergraduate majors. Total enrollment: 444. Undergraduates: 444. Freshmen: 108. Institutional methodology is used as a basis for awarding need-based institutional aid.

UNDERGRADUATE EXPENSES for 2004–05 *Application fee:* $20. *Comprehensive fee:* $15,730 includes full-time tuition ($10,900), mandatory fees ($1030), and room and board ($3800). *College room only:* $1500. Full-time tuition and fees vary according to course load. Room and board charges vary according to board plan and housing facility. *Part-time tuition:* $340 per credit hour. *Part-time fees:* $50 per credit hour. Part-time tuition and fees vary according to course load. *Payment plan:* Installment.

FRESHMAN FINANCIAL AID (Fall 2004, est.) *Average percent of need met:* 80% (excluding resources awarded to replace EFC). 17% of all full-time freshmen had no need and received non-need-based gift aid.

UNDERGRADUATE FINANCIAL AID (Fall 2004, est.) 387 applied for aid; of those 93% were deemed to have need. 100% of undergraduates with need received aid; of those 4% had need fully met. *Average percent of need met:* 80% (excluding resources awarded to replace EFC). *Average financial aid package:* $10,149 (excluding resources awarded to replace EFC). 6% of all full-time undergraduates had no need and received non-need-based gift aid.

GIFT AID (NEED-BASED) *Total amount:* $1,287,933 (44% federal, 3% state, 48% institutional, 5% external sources). *Receiving aid:* All full-time undergraduates: 46% (204). *Average award:* Undergraduates: $5542. *Scholarships, grants, and awards:* Federal Pell, FSEOG, state, private, college/university gift aid from institutional funds.

GIFT AID (NON-NEED-BASED) *Receiving aid:* Undergraduates: 81% (359). *Average Award:* Undergraduates: $4107. *Scholarships, grants, and awards by category:* Academic Interests/Achievement: 304 awards ($486,530 total): biological sciences, business, communication, computer science, education, English, general academic interests/achievements, mathematics, premedicine, religion/biblical studies. *Creative Arts/Performance:* 107 awards ($121,395 total): music, theater/drama. *Special Achievements/Activities:* 217 awards ($172,565 total): leadership. *Special Characteristics:* 136 awards ($267,840 total): children and siblings of alumni, children of faculty/staff, previous college experience, siblings of current students. *Tuition waivers:* Full or partial for employees or children of employees. *ROTC:* Army cooperative, Naval cooperative, Air Force cooperative.

LOANS *Student loans:* $2,179,916 (62% need-based, 38% non-need-based). 85% of past graduating class borrowed through all loan programs. *Average indebtedness per student:* $19,556. *Average need-based loan:* Undergraduates: $4200. *Parent loans:* $542,013 (100% non-need-based). *Programs:* FFEL (Subsidized and Unsubsidized Stafford, PLUS), Perkins, alternative loans.

WORK-STUDY *Federal work-study:* Total amount: $78,774; 160 jobs averaging $820. *State or other work-study/employment:* Total amount: $44,228 (100% non-need-based).

ATHLETIC AWARDS *Total amount:* $765,138 (100% non-need-based).

APPLYING FOR FINANCIAL AID *Required financial aid form:* FAFSA. *Financial aid deadline (priority):* 4/30. *Notification date:* Continuous beginning 3/1. Students must reply within 4 weeks of notification.

CONTACT Deb Lowry, Director of Financial Aid, York College, 1125 East 8th Street, York, NE 68467, 402-363-5624 or toll-free 800-950-9675. *Fax:* 402-363-5623.

YORK COLLEGE OF PENNSYLVANIA
York, PA

Tuition & fees: $9184 | **Average undergraduate aid package: $6773**

ABOUT THE INSTITUTION Independent, coed. Awards: associate, bachelor's, and master's degrees. 66 undergraduate majors. Total enrollment: 5,687. Undergraduates: 5,379. Freshmen: 1,075. Federal methodology is used as a basis for awarding need-based institutional aid.

UNDERGRADUATE EXPENSES for 2004–05 *Application fee:* $30. *Comprehensive fee:* $15,434 includes full-time tuition ($8600), mandatory fees ($584), and room and board ($6250). *College room only:* $3475. Full-time tuition and fees vary according to course load and program. Room and board charges vary according to housing facility. *Part-time tuition:* $260 per credit hour. Part-time tuition and fees vary according to course load and program. *Payment plans:* Tuition prepayment, installment.

FRESHMAN FINANCIAL AID (Fall 2004, est.) 879 applied for aid; of those 64% were deemed to have need. 98% of freshmen with need received aid; of those 22% had need fully met. *Average percent of need met:* 74% (excluding resources awarded to replace EFC). *Average financial aid package:* $6442 (excluding resources awarded to replace EFC). 14% of all full-time freshmen had no need and received non-need-based gift aid.

UNDERGRADUATE FINANCIAL AID (Fall 2004, est.) 3,234 applied for aid; of those 69% were deemed to have need. 99% of undergraduates with need received aid; of those 20% had need fully met. *Average percent of need met:* 72% (excluding resources awarded to replace EFC). *Average financial aid package:* $6773 (excluding resources awarded to replace EFC). 9% of all full-time undergraduates had no need and received non-need-based gift aid.

GIFT AID (NEED-BASED) *Total amount:* $7,854,768 (28% federal, 31% state, 36% institutional, 5% external sources). *Receiving aid:* Freshmen: 43% (441); All full-time undergraduates: 37% (1,587). *Average award:* Freshmen: $3850; Undergraduates: $3809. *Scholarships, grants, and awards:* Federal Pell, FSEOG, state, private, college/university gift aid from institutional funds.

GIFT AID (NON-NEED-BASED) *Total amount:* $1,096,813 (3% state, 83% institutional, 14% external sources). *Receiving aid:* Freshmen: 18% (190); Undergraduates: 11% (482). *Average Award:* Freshmen: $2807; Undergraduates: $3068. *Scholarships, grants, and awards by category:* Academic Interests/Achievement: 519 awards ($1,534,085 total): general academic interests/achievements. *Creative Arts/Performance:* 22 awards ($26,330 total): music. *Special Achievements/Activities:* 14 awards ($37,272 total): community service, memberships. *Special Characteristics:* 37 awards ($51,910 total): children and siblings of alumni, children of union members/company employees, international students, members of minority groups. *Tuition waivers:* Full or partial for employees or children of employees. *ROTC:* Army cooperative.

LOANS *Student loans:* $14,842,893 (52% need-based, 48% non-need-based). 66% of past graduating class borrowed through all loan programs. *Average indebtedness per student:* $17,818. *Average need-based loan:* Freshmen: $2475; Undergraduates: $3617. *Parent loans:* $3,614,885 (46% need-based, 54% non-need-based). *Programs:* Federal Direct (Subsidized and Unsubsidized Stafford, PLUS), FFEL (Subsidized and Unsubsidized Stafford, PLUS), Perkins, Federal Nursing, college/university.

WORK-STUDY *Federal work-study:* Total amount: $355,428; 252 jobs averaging $1375. *State or other work-study/employment:* Total amount: $77,600 (26% need-based, 74% non-need-based). 62 part-time jobs averaging $1209.

APPLYING FOR FINANCIAL AID *Required financial aid form:* FAFSA. *Financial aid deadline (priority):* 3/1. *Notification date:* Continuous beginning 3/1. Students must reply within 4 weeks of notification.

CONTACT Calvin Williams, Director of Financial Aid, York College of Pennsylvania, Country Club Road, York, PA 17405-7199, 717-849-1682 or toll-free 800-455-8018. *Fax:* 717-849-1607. *E-mail:* financialaid@ycp.edu.

YORK COLLEGE OF THE CITY UNIVERSITY OF NEW YORK
Jamaica, NY

CONTACT Randy Punter, Acting Director of Student Financial Services, York College of the City University of New York, 94-20 Guy R. Brewer Boulevard, Jamaica, NY 11451-0001, 718-262-2238.

YOUNGSTOWN STATE UNIVERSITY
Youngstown, OH

Tuition & fees (OH res): $5884	Average undergraduate aid package: N/A

ABOUT THE INSTITUTION State-supported, coed. Awards: associate, bachelor's, master's, and doctoral degrees and post-bachelor's certificates. 165 undergraduate majors. Total enrollment: 13,092. Undergraduates: 11,796. Freshmen: 2,157. Federal methodology is used as a basis for awarding need-based institutional aid.

UNDERGRADUATE EXPENSES for 2004–05 *Application fee:* $30. *Tuition, state resident:* full-time $5655; part-time $235.62 per credit. *Tuition, nonresident:* full-time $10,863; part-time $452.62 per credit. *Required fees:* full-time $229; $9.54 per credit. Full-time tuition and fees vary according to course load. Part-time tuition and fees vary according to course load. *College room and board:* $6100. Room and board charges vary according to board plan and housing facility. *Payment plan:* Installment.

GIFT AID (NEED-BASED) *Total amount:* $16,842,556 (74% federal, 20% state, 6% institutional). *Scholarships, grants, and awards:* Federal Pell, FSEOG, state, private, college/university gift aid from institutional funds.

GIFT AID (NON-NEED-BASED) *Total amount:* $11,350,920 (2% federal, 25% state, 42% institutional, 31% external sources). *Scholarships, grants, and awards by category: Academic Interests/Achievement:* business, computer science, education, engineering/technologies, English, general academic interests/achievements, health fields, humanities, military science. *Creative Arts/Performance:* music, theater/drama. *Special Achievements/Activities:* cheerleading/drum major, leadership. *Special Characteristics:* adult students, children and siblings of alumni, children of faculty/staff, children of union members/company employees, children of workers in trades, children with a deceased or disabled parent, handicapped students, members of minority groups, spouses of deceased or disabled public servants, veterans, veterans' children. *Tuition waivers:* Full or partial for employees or children of employees, senior citizens. *ROTC:* Army, Air Force cooperative.

LOANS *Student loans:* $42,696,153 (95% need-based, 5% non-need-based). *Parent loans:* $3,863,750 (100% non-need-based). *Programs:* FFEL (Subsidized and Unsubsidized Stafford, PLUS), Perkins, state, Charles E. Schell Foundation Loans.

WORK-STUDY *Federal work-study:* Total amount: $1,245,562; 657 jobs averaging $1896. *State or other work-study/employment:* Part-time jobs available.

ATHLETIC AWARDS *Total amount:* $2,397,293 (100% non-need-based).

APPLYING FOR FINANCIAL AID *Required financial aid forms:* FAFSA, institution's own form. *Financial aid deadline (priority):* 2/15. *Notification date:* 5/1. Students must reply within 4 weeks of notification.

CONTACT Ms. Beth Bartlett, Administrative Assistant, Youngstown State University, One University Plaza, Youngstown, OH 44555, 330-941-3504 or toll-free 877-468-6978. *Fax:* 330-941-1659. *E-mail:* babartlett@ysu.edu.

ZION BIBLE INSTITUTE
Barrington, RI

CONTACT Financial Aid Office, Zion Bible Institute, 27 Middle Highway, Barrington, RI 02806, 401-246-0900 or toll-free 800-356-4014.

Appendix

State Scholarship and Grant Programs

Each state government has established one or more state-administered financial aid programs for qualified students. In many instances, these state programs are restricted to legal residents of the state. However, they often are available to out-of-state students who will be or are attending colleges or universities within the state. In addition to residential status, other qualifications frequently exist.

Gift aid and forgivable loan programs open to undergraduate students for all states and the District of Columbia are described on the following pages. They are arranged in alphabetical order, first by state name, then by program name. The annotation for each program provides information about the program, eligibility, and the contact addresses for applications or further information. Unless otherwise stated, this information refers to awards for 2004-05. Information is provided by the state-sponsoring agency in response to *Thomson Peterson's Annual Survey of Non-institutional Aid*, which was conducted between November 2004 and March 2005. Information is accurate when Peterson's receives it. However, it is always advisable to check with the sponsor to ascertain that the information remains correct.

You should write to the address given for each program to request that award details for 2005-06 be sent to you as soon as they are available. Descriptive information, brochures, and application forms for state scholarship programs are usually available from the financial aid offices of public colleges or universities within the specific state. High school guidance offices often have information and relevant forms for awards for which high school seniors may be eligible. Increasingly, state government agencies are putting state scholarship information on state government agency Web sites. In searching state government Web sites, however, you should be aware that the higher education agency in many states is separate from the state's general education office, which is often responsible only for elementary and secondary education. Also, the page at public university Web sites that provides information about student financial aid frequently has a list of state-sponsored scholarships and financial aid programs. College and university Web sites can be easily accessed through at www.petersons.com.

Names of scholarship programs are frequently used inconsistently or become abbreviated in popular usage. Many programs have variant names by which they are known. The program's sponsor has approved the title of the program that Peterson's uses in this guide, yet this name may differ from the program's official name or from its most commonly used name.

In addition to the grant aid and forgivable loan programs listed on the following pages, states may also offer internship or work-study programs, graduate fellowships and grants, or low-interest loans. If you are interested in learning more about these other kinds of programs, the state education office that supplies information or applications for the undergraduate scholarship programs listed here should be able to provide information about other kinds of higher education financial aid programs that are sponsored by the state.

ALABAMA

Alabama G.I. Dependents Scholarship Program. Full scholarship for dependents of Alabama disabled, prisoner of war, or missing-in-action veterans. Child or stepchild must initiate training before 26th birthday; age 30 deadline may apply in certain situations. No age deadline for spouses or widows. Contact for application procedures and deadline. *Award:* Scholarship for use in freshman, sophomore, junior, senior, or graduate year; renewable. *Award amount:* varies. *Number of awards:* varies. *Eligibility Requirements:* Applicant must be enrolled or expecting to enroll full or part-time at a two-year, four-year, or technical institution or university; resident of Alabama and studying in Alabama. Available to U.S. and non-U.S. citizens. Applicant or parent must meet one or more of the following requirements: general military experience; retired from active duty; disabled or killed as a result of military service; prisoner of war; or missing in action. *Application Requirements:* Application. *Deadline:* varies.

Contact: Willie E. Moore, Scholarship Administrator, Alabama Department of Veterans Affairs, PO Box 1509, Montgomery, AL 36102-1509. *E-mail:* wmoore@va.state.al.us. *Phone:* 334-242-5077. *Fax:* 334-242-5102. *Web site:* www.va.state.al.us/scholarship.htm.

Alabama National Guard Educational Assistance Program. Renewable award aids Alabama residents who are members of the Alabama National Guard and are enrolled in an accredited college in Alabama. Forms must be signed by a representative of the Alabama Military Department and financial aid officer. Recipient must be in a degree-seeking program. *Award:* Grant for use in freshman, sophomore, junior, senior, or graduate year; renewable. *Award amount:* up to $1000. *Number of awards:* varies. *Eligibility Requirements:* Applicant must be enrolled or expecting to enroll full or part-time at a two-year, four-year, or technical institution or university; resident of Alabama and studying in Alabama. Available to U.S. citizens. Applicant must have served in the Air Force National Guard or Army National Guard. *Application Requirements:* Application. *Deadline:* continuous.

Contact: Dr. William Wall, Associate Executive Director for Student Assistance, Alabama Commission on Higher Education, PO Box 302000, Montgomery, AL 36130-2000. *Web site:* www.ache.state.al.us.

Alabama Scholarship for Dependents of Blind Parents. Scholarship given to defray the cost of books and fees for children of blind parents. Must be accepted or enrolled in a Alabama state supported school. Must be Alabama resident. Financial need is considered. Family income must be less than 1.3 times the federal poverty guideline for size of family unit. *Award:* Scholarship for use in freshman, sophomore, junior, or senior year; renewable. *Award amount:* varies. *Number of awards:* varies. *Eligibility Requirements:* Applicant must be age 28 or under; enrolled or expecting to enroll full-time at a two-year, four-year, or technical institution or university; resident of Alabama and studying in Alabama. Available to U.S. citizens. *Application Requirements:* Application, financial need analysis. *Deadline:* continuous.

Contact: Deborah Culver, Coordinator of Blind Services, Alabama Department of Rehabilitation Services, Alabama Scholarship for Dependents of Blind Parents, 2129 East South Boulevard, Montgomery, AL 36111. *Phone:* 800-441-7607. *Web site:* www.rehab.state.al.us.

Alabama Student Grant Program. Renewable awards available to Alabama residents for undergraduate study at certain independent colleges within the state. Both full- and half-time students are eligible. Deadlines: September 15, January 15, and February 15. *Award:* Grant for use in freshman, sophomore, junior, or senior year; renewable. *Award amount:* up to $1200. *Number of awards:* varies. *Eligibility Requirements:* Applicant must be enrolled or expecting to enroll full or part-time at a four-year institution or university; resident of Alabama and studying in Alabama. Available to U.S. citizens. *Application Requirements:* Application. *Deadline:* varies.

Contact: Dr. William Wall, Associate Executive Director for Student Assistance, ACHE, Alabama Commission on Higher Education, PO Box 302000, Montgomery, AL 36130-2000. *Web site:* www.ache.state.al.us.

American Legion Department of Alabama Scholarship Program. One-time award for Alabama residents directly related to any war veteran. Parents must be legal residents of Alabama. Send self-addressed stamped envelope to receive scholarship application, list of available schools, and instructions. *Award:* Scholarship for use in freshman, sophomore, junior, or senior year; not renewable. *Award amount:* $850. *Number of awards:* 150. *Eligibility Requirements:* Applicant must be enrolled or expecting to enroll full-time at a two-year or four-year institution or university; resident of Alabama and studying in Alabama. Available to U.S. citizens. *Application Requirements:* Application, photo, references, self-addressed stamped envelope, test scores, transcript. *Deadline:* May 1.

Contact: Braxton Bridgers, Department Adjutant, American Legion, Department of Alabama, PO Box 1069, Montgomery, AL 36101-1069. *E-mail:* allegion@bellsouth.net. *Phone:* 334-262-6638. *Web site:* www.americanlegionalabama.org/.

Math and Science Scholarship Program for Alabama Teachers. For students pursuing teaching certificates in mathematics, general science, biology, or physics. Applicants must agree to teach for five years (if a position is offered) in a targeted system with critical needs. Renewable if recipient continues to meet the requirements. Minimum 2.5 GPA required. Must attend school in Alabama. *Academic Fields/Career Goals:* Biology; Earth Science; Meteorology/Atmospheric Science; Natural Sciences; Physical Sciences and Math. *Award:* Forgivable loan for use in junior, senior, or graduate year; renewable. *Award amount:* $2000–$12,000. *Eligibility Requirements:* Applicant must be enrolled or expecting to enroll full or part-time at a four-year institution or university and studying in Alabama. Applicant must have 2.5 GPA or higher. Available to U.S. citizens. *Application Requirements:* Application. *Deadline:* varies.

Contact: Alabama State Department of Education, PO Box 302101, Montgomery, AL 36130-2101. *Phone:* 334-242-9935. *Web site:* www.alsde.edu.

Police Officers and Firefighters Survivors Education Assistance Program-Alabama. Provides tuition, fees, books, and supplies to dependents of full-time police officers and firefighters killed in the line of duty. Must attend any Alabama public college as an undergraduate. Must be Alabama resident. Renewable. *Award:* Grant for use in freshman, sophomore, junior, or senior year; renewable. *Award amount:* $2000–$5000. *Number of awards:* 15–30. *Eligibility Requirements:* Applicant must be enrolled or expecting to enroll full or part-time at a two-year, four-year, or technical institution or university; single; resident of Alabama and studying in Alabama. Applicant or parent of applicant must have employment or volunteer experience in police/firefighting. Available to U.S. citizens. *Application Requirements:* Application, transcript. *Deadline:* continuous.

Contact: Dr. William Wall, Associate Executive Director for Student Assistance, ACHE, Alabama Commission on Higher Education, PO Box 302000, Montgomery, AL 36130-2000. *Web site:* www.ache.state.al.us.

ALASKA

A.W. "Winn" Brindle Memorial Education Loans. Renewable loan for study of approved curriculum in fisheries, seafood processing, food technology or related fields for Alaska residents. Must maintain good standing at institution. Eligible for up to 50% forgiveness if recipient returns to Alaska for employment in fisheries-related field. *Academic Fields/Career Goals:* Agribusiness; Animal/Veterinary Sciences; Biology; Food Science/Nutrition; Natural Resources. *Award:* Forgivable loan for use in freshman, sophomore, junior, senior, or graduate year; renewable. *Eligibility Requirements:* Applicant must be enrolled or expecting to enroll full-time at a two-year, four-year, or technical institution or university and resident of Alaska. Available to U.S. citizens. *Application Requirements:* Application, essay. *Deadline:* May 15.

Contact: Lori Stedman, Administrative Assistant, Special Programs, Alaska Commission on Postsecondary Education, 3030 Vintage Boulevard, Juneau, AK 99801-7100. *Phone:* 907-465-6741. *Fax:* 907-465-5316. *Web site:* www.state.ak.us/acpe/.

Alaska Commission on Postsecondary Education Teacher Education Loan. Renewable loans for graduates of an Alaskan high school pursuing teaching careers in rural elementary and secondary schools in Alaska. Must be nominated by rural school district. Eligible for 100% forgiveness if loan recipient teaches in rural Alaska upon graduation. Several awards of up to $7500 each. Must maintain good standing at institution. *Academic Fields/Career Goals:* Education. *Award:* Forgivable loan for use in freshman, sophomore, junior, or senior year; renewable. *Award amount:* up to $7500. *Number of awards:* varies. *Eligibility Requirements:* Applicant must be enrolled or expecting to enroll full-time at a four-year institution or university. Available to U.S. citizens. *Application Requirements:* Application, transcript. *Deadline:* July 1.

Contact: Lori Stedman, Administrative Assistant, Special Programs, Alaska Commission on Postsecondary Education, 3030 Vintage Boulevard, Juneau, AK 99801-7100. *Phone:* 907-465-6741. *Fax:* 907-465-5316. *Web site:* www.state.ak.us/acpe/.

Western Undergraduate Exchange (WUE) Program. Program allowing Alaska residents to enroll at two-or four-year institutions in participating states at a reduced tuition level, which is the in-state tuition plus a percentage of that amount. To be used for full-time undergraduate studies. See Web site at http://www.state.ak.us/acpe for further information, a list of eligible institutions, and deadlines. *Award:* Grant for use in freshman, sophomore, junior, or senior year; renewable. *Award amount:* varies. *Number of awards:* varies. *Eligibility Requirements:*

Applicant must be enrolled or expecting to enroll full-time at a two-year or four-year institution or university; resident of Alaska and studying in Arizona, Colorado, Hawaii, Idaho, Montana, Nevada, New Mexico, North Dakota, Oregon, South Dakota, Utah, or Washington. Available to U.S. citizens. *Application Requirements: Deadline:* varies.

Contact: Program Office, Alaska Commission on Postsecondary Education. *Phone:* 800-441-2962. *Web site:* www.state.ak.us/acpe/.

ARIZONA

Arizona Private Postsecondary Education Student Financial Assistance Program. Provides grants to financially needy Arizona Community College graduates to attend a private postsecondary baccalaureate degree-granting institution. *Award:* Forgivable loan for use in junior or senior year; renewable. *Award amount:* $750–$1500. *Number of awards:* varies. *Eligibility Requirements:* Applicant must be enrolled or expecting to enroll full-time at a four-year institution or university; resident of Arizona and studying in Arizona. Available to U.S. citizens. *Application Requirements:* Financial need analysis, transcript, promissory note. *Deadline:* continuous.

Contact: Danny Lee, PFAP Program Manager, Arizona Commission for Postsecondary Education, 2020 North Central Avenue, Suite 550, Phoenix, AZ 85004-4503. *E-mail:* dan_lee@azhighered.org. *Phone:* 602-258-2435 Ext. 103. *Fax:* 602-258-2483. *Web site:* www.azhighered.org.

Leveraging Educational Assistance Partnership. LEAP provides grants to financially needy students who enroll in and attend postsecondary education or training in Arizona schools. LEAP Program was formerly known as the State Student Incentive Grant or SSIG Program. *Award:* Grant for use in freshman, sophomore, junior, senior, or graduate year; not renewable. *Award amount:* $100–$2500. *Number of awards:* varies. *Eligibility Requirements:* Applicant must be enrolled or expecting to enroll full or part-time at a two-year, four-year, or technical institution or university; resident of Arizona and studying in Arizona. Available to U.S. citizens. *Application Requirements:* Financial need analysis. *Deadline:* continuous.

Contact: Mila A. Zaporteza, Business Manager/LEAP Financial Aid Manager, Arizona Commission for Postsecondary Education, 2020 North Central Avenue, Suite 550, Phoenix, AZ 85004-4503. *E-mail:* mila@azhighered.org. *Phone:* 602-258-2435 Ext. 102. *Fax:* 602-258-2483. *Web site:* www.azhighered.org.

ARKANSAS

Arkansas Academic Challenge Scholarship Program. Awards for Arkansas residents who are graduating high school seniors to study at an Arkansas institution. Must have at least a 2.75 GPA, meet minimum ACT composite score standards, and have financial need. Renewable up to three additional years. *Award:* Scholarship for use in freshman, sophomore, junior, or senior year; renewable. *Award amount:* $2000–$3000. *Eligibility Requirements:* Applicant must be high school student; planning to enroll or expecting to enroll full-time at a two-year or four-year institution or university; resident of Arkansas and studying in Arkansas. Available to U.S. citizens. *Application Requirements:* Application, financial need analysis, test scores, transcript. *Deadline:* June 1.

Contact: Elyse Price, Assistant Coordinator, Arkansas Department of Higher Education, 114 East Capitol, Little Rock, AR 72201. *Phone:* 501-371-2050. *Fax:* 501-371-2001. *Web site:* www.arscholarships.com.

Arkansas Health Education Grant Program (ARHEG). Award provides assistance to Arkansas residents pursuing professional degrees in dentistry, optometry, veterinary medicine, podiatry, chiropractic medicine, or osteopathic medicine at out-of-state, accredited institutions (programs that are unavailable in Arkansas). *Academic Fields/Career Goals:* Animal/Veterinary Sciences; Dental Health/Services; Health and Medical Sciences. *Award:* Grant for use in sophomore, junior, senior, or graduate year; renewable. *Award amount:* $5000–$14,600. *Number of awards:* 258–288. *Eligibility Requirements:* Applicant must be enrolled or expecting to enroll full-time at a four-year institution or university and resident of Arkansas. Available to U.S. citizens. *Application Requirements:* Application, affidavit of Arkansas residency. *Deadline:* continuous.

Contact: Ms. Judy McAinsh, Coordinator, Arkansas Health Education Grant Program, Arkansas Department of Higher Education, 114 East Capitol, Little Rock, AR 72201-3818. *E-mail:* judym@adhe.arknet.edu. *Phone:* 501-371-2013. *Fax:* 501-371-2002. *Web site:* www.arscholarships.com.

Arkansas Minority Teacher Scholars Program. Renewable award for Native-American, African-American, Hispanic and Asian-American students who have completed at least 60 semester hours and are enrolled full-time in a teacher education program in Arkansas. Award may be renewed for one year. Must be Arkansas resident with minimum 2.5 GPA. Must teach for three to five years in Arkansas to repay scholarship funds received. Must pass PPST exam. *Academic Fields/Career Goals:* Education. *Award:* Forgivable loan for use in junior or senior year; renewable. *Award amount:* up to $5000. *Number of awards:* up to 100. *Eligibility Requirements:* Applicant must be American Indian/Alaska Native, Asian/Pacific Islander, Black (non-Hispanic), or Hispanic; enrolled or expecting to enroll full-time at a four-year institution or university; resident of Arkansas and studying in Arkansas. Applicant must have 2.5 GPA or higher. Available to U.S. citizens. *Application Requirements:* Application, transcript. *Deadline:* June 1.

Contact: Lillian Williams, Assistant Coordinator, Arkansas Department of Higher Education, 114 East Capitol, Little Rock, AR 72201. *Phone:* 501-371-2050. *Fax:* 501-371-2001. *Web site:* www.arscholarships.com.

Arkansas Student Assistance Grant Program. Award for Arkansas residents attending a college within the state. Must be enrolled full-time, have financial need, and maintain satisfactory progress. One-time award for undergraduate use only. Application is the FAFSA. *Award:* Grant for use in freshman, sophomore, junior, or senior year; not renewable. *Award amount:* $600. *Number of awards:* 600–5500. *Eligibility Requirements:* Applicant must be enrolled or expecting to enroll full-time at a two-year, four-year, or technical institution or university; resident of Arkansas and studying in Arkansas. Available to U.S. citizens. *Application Requirements:* Application, financial need analysis, FAFSA. *Deadline:* April 1.

Contact: Mr. Philip Axelroth, Assistant Coordinator, Arkansas Department of Higher Education, 114 East Capitol, Little Rock, AR 72201. *Phone:* 501-371-2050. *Fax:* 501-371-2001. *Web site:* www.arscholarships.com.

Emergency Secondary Education Loan Program. Must be Arkansas resident enrolled full-time in approved Arkansas institution. Renewable award for students majoring in secondary math, chemistry, physics, biology, physical science, general science, special education, or foreign language. Must teach in Arkansas at least five years. Must rank in upper half of class or have a minimum 2.5 GPA. *Academic Fields/Career Goals:* Biology; Education; Foreign Language; Physical Sciences and Math; Special Education. *Award:* Forgivable loan for use in sophomore, junior, senior, or graduate year; renewable. *Award amount:* up to $2500. *Number of awards:* up to 50. *Eligibility Requirements:* Applicant must be enrolled or expecting to enroll full-time at a two-year or four-year institution or

university; resident of Arkansas and studying in Arkansas. Applicant must have 2.5 GPA or higher. Available to U.S. citizens. *Application Requirements:* Application, transcript. *Deadline:* April 1.

Contact: Lillian K. Williams, Assistant Coordinator, Arkansas Department of Higher Education, 114 East Capitol, Little Rock, AR 72201. *Phone:* 501-371-2050. *Fax:* 501-371-2001. *Web site:* www.arscholarships.com.

Governor's Scholars-Arkansas. Awards for outstanding Arkansas high school seniors. Must be an Arkansas resident and have a high school GPA of at least 3.5 or have scored at least 27 on the ACT. Award is $4000 per year for four years of full-time undergraduate study. Applicants who attain 32 or above on ACT, 1410 or above on SAT and have an academic 3.50 GPA, or are selected as National Merit or National Achievement finalists may receive an award equal to tuition, mandatory fees, room, and board up to $10,000 per year at any Arkansas institution. *Award:* Scholarship for use in freshman, sophomore, junior, or senior year; renewable. *Award amount:* $4000–$10,000. *Number of awards:* 75–250. *Eligibility Requirements:* Applicant must be high school student; planning to enroll or expecting to enroll full-time at a two-year or four-year institution or university; resident of Arkansas and studying in Arkansas. Applicant must have 3.5 GPA or higher. Available to U.S. citizens. *Application Requirements:* Application, test scores, transcript. *Deadline:* February 1.

Contact: Philip Axelroth, Assistant Coordinator of Financial Aid, Arkansas Department of Higher Education, 114 East Capitol, Little Rock, AR 72201. *E-mail:* phila@adhe.arknet.edu. *Phone:* 501-371-2050. *Fax:* 501-371-2001. *Web site:* www.arscholarships.com.

Law Enforcement Officers' Dependents Scholarship-Arkansas. For dependents, under 23 years old, of Arkansas law-enforcement officers killed or permanently disabled in the line of duty. Renewable award is a waiver of tuition, fees, and room at two- or four-year Arkansas institution. Submit birth certificate, death certificate, and claims commission report of findings of fact. Proof of disability from State Claims Commission may also be submitted. *Award:* Scholarship for use in freshman, sophomore, junior, or senior year; renewable. *Award amount:* $2000–$2500. *Number of awards:* 27–32. *Eligibility Requirements:* Applicant must be age 22 or under; enrolled or expecting to enroll full or part-time at a two-year or four-year institution or university; resident of Arkansas and studying in Arkansas. Applicant or parent of applicant must have employment or volunteer experience in

police/firefighting. Available to U.S. citizens. *Application Requirements:* Application. *Deadline:* continuous.

Contact: Lillian Williams, Assistant Coordinator, Arkansas Department of Higher Education, 114 East Capitol, Little Rock, AR 72201. *E-mail:* lillianw@adhe.arknet.edu. *Phone:* 501-371-2050. *Fax:* 501-371-2001. *Web site:* www.arscholarships.com.

Missing in Action/Killed in Action Dependent's Scholarship-Arkansas. Available to Arkansas residents whose parent or spouse was classified either as missing in action, killed in action, or a prisoner-of-war. Must attend state-supported institution in Arkansas. Renewable waiver of tuition, fees, room and board. Submit proof of casualty. *Award:* Scholarship for use in freshman, sophomore, junior, or senior year; renewable. *Award amount:* up to $2500. *Eligibility Requirements:* Applicant must be enrolled or expecting to enroll full-time at a two-year, four-year, or technical institution or university; resident of Arkansas and studying in Arkansas. Available to U.S. citizens. Applicant or parent must meet one or more of the following requirements: general military experience; retired from active duty; disabled or killed as a result of military service; prisoner of war; or missing in action. *Application Requirements:* Application, report of casualty. *Deadline:* continuous.

Contact: Lillian K. Williams, Assistant Coordinator, Arkansas Department of Higher Education, 114 East Capitol, Little Rock, AR 72201. *Phone:* 501-371-2050. *Fax:* 501-371-2001. *Web site:* www.arscholarships.com.

Second Effort Scholarship. Awarded to those scholars who achieved one of the 10 highest scores on the Arkansas High School Diploma Test (GED). Must be at least age 18 and not have graduated from high school. Students do not apply for this award, they are contacted by the Arkansas Department of Higher Education. *Award:* Scholarship for use in freshman, sophomore, junior, or senior year; renewable. *Award amount:* up to $1000. *Number of awards:* 10. *Eligibility Requirements:* Applicant must be age 18; enrolled or expecting to enroll full or part-time at a two-year or four-year institution or university; resident of Arkansas and studying in Arkansas. Applicant must have 2.5 GPA or higher. *Application Requirements:* Application.

Contact: Arkansas Department of Higher Education. *Phone:* 501-371-2050. *Fax:* 501-371-2001. *Web site:* www.arscholarships.com.

CALIFORNIA

Assumption Programs of Loans for Education. The APLE is a competitive teacher loan assumption program designed to encourage outstanding students and out-of-state teachers to become California teachers within subject areas where a teacher shortage has been identified or in schools meeting specific criteria identified annually. Participants may receive up to $19,000 towards outstanding student loans. *Award:* Forgivable loan for use in junior, senior, or graduate year; renewable. *Award amount:* $11,000–$19,000. *Number of awards:* up to 7700. *Eligibility Requirements:* Applicant must be enrolled or expecting to enroll full or part-time at a four-year institution or university; resident of California and studying in California. Available to U.S. citizens. *Application Requirements:* Application, references. *Deadline:* June 30.

Contact: California Student Aid Commission, PO Box 419027, Rancho Cordova, CA 95741-9027. *E-mail:* custsvcs@csac.ca.gov. *Phone:* 916-526-7590. *Fax:* 916-526-8002. *Web site:* www.csac.ca.gov.

Cal Grant C. Award for California residents who are enrolled in a short-term vocational training program. Program must lead to a recognized degree or certificate. Course length must be a minimum of 4 months and no longer than 24 months. Students must be attending an approved California institution and show financial need. *Award:* Grant for use in freshman, sophomore, junior, or senior year; renewable. *Award amount:* $576–$3168. *Number of awards:* up to 7761. *Eligibility Requirements:* Applicant must be enrolled or expecting to enroll full or part-time at a two-year or technical institution; resident of California and studying in California. Available to U.S. citizens. *Application Requirements:* Application, financial need analysis, GPA verification. *Deadline:* March 2.

Contact: California Student Aid Commission, PO Box 419027, Rancho Cordova, CA 95741-9027. *E-mail:* custsvs@csac.ca.gov. *Phone:* 916-526-7590. *Fax:* 916-526-8002. *Web site:* www.csac.ca.gov.

Child Development Teacher and Supervisor Grant Program. Award is for those students pursuing an approved course of study leading to a Child Development Permit issued by the California Commission on Teacher Credentialing. In exchange for each year funding is received, recipients agree to provide one year of service in a licensed childcare center. *Award:* Grant for use in freshman, sophomore, junior, or senior year; renewable. *Award amount:*

$1000–$2000. *Number of awards:* up to 300. *Eligibility Requirements:* Applicant must be enrolled or expecting to enroll full or part-time at a two-year, four-year, or technical institution or university; resident of California and studying in California. Available to U.S. citizens. *Application Requirements:* Application, financial need analysis, references, FAFSA. *Deadline:* June 1.

Contact: California Student Aid Commission, PO Box 419027, Rancho Cordova, CA 95741-9027. *E-mail:* custsvcs@csac.ca.gov. *Phone:* 916-526-7590. *Fax:* 916-526-8002. *Web site:* www.csac.ca.gov.

Competitive Cal Grant A. Award for California residents who are not recent high school graduates attending an approved college or university within the state. Must show financial need and meet minimum 3.0 GPA requirement. *Award:* Grant for use in freshman, sophomore, junior, or senior year; renewable. *Award amount:* $2046–$9708. *Number of awards:* up to 22,500. *Eligibility Requirements:* Applicant must be enrolled or expecting to enroll full or part-time at a two-year, four-year, or technical institution or university; resident of California and studying in California. Applicant must have 3.0 GPA or higher. Available to U.S. citizens. *Application Requirements:* Application, financial need analysis, GPA verification. *Deadline:* March 2.

Contact: California Student Aid Commission, PO Box 419027, Rancho Cordova, CA 95741-9027. *E-mail:* custsvcs@csac.ca.gov. *Phone:* 916-526-7590. *Fax:* 916-526-8002. *Web site:* www.csac.ca.gov.

Competitive Cal Grant B. Award is for California residents who are not recent high school graduates attending an approved college or university within the state. Must show financial need and meet the minimum 2.0 GPA requirement. *Award:* Grant for use in freshman, sophomore, or junior year; renewable. *Award amount:* $700–$11,259. *Number of awards:* up to 22,500. *Eligibility Requirements:* Applicant must be enrolled or expecting to enroll full or part-time at a two-year, four-year, or technical institution or university; resident of California and studying in California. Available to U.S. citizens. *Application Requirements:* Application, financial need analysis, GPA verification. *Deadline:* March 2.

Contact: California Student Aid Commission, PO Box 419027, Rancho Cordova, CA 95741-9027. *E-mail:* custsvcs@csac.ca.gov. *Phone:* 916-526-7590. *Fax:* 916-526-8002. *Web site:* www.csac.ca.gov.

Cooperative Agencies Resources for Education Program. Renewable award available to California resident attending a two-year California community college. Must have no more than 70 degree-applicable units, currently receive CALWORKS/TANF, and have at least one child under 14 years of age. Must be in EOPS, single head of household, and 18 or older. Contact local college EOPS-CARE office. *Award:* Grant for use in freshman or sophomore year; renewable. *Number of awards:* 11,000. *Eligibility Requirements:* Applicant must be age 18; enrolled or expecting to enroll full-time at a two-year institution; single; resident of California and studying in California. Available to U.S. citizens. *Application Requirements:* Application, financial need analysis, test scores, transcript. *Deadline:* continuous.

Contact: Local Community College EOPS/CARE Program, California Community Colleges, 1102 Q Street, Sacramento, CA 95814-6511. *Web site:* www.cccco.edu.

Entitlement Cal Grant A. Award is for California residents who are recent high school graduates attending an approved college or university within the state. Must show financial need and meet the minimum 3.0 GPA requirement. *Award:* Grant for use in freshman, sophomore, junior, or senior year; renewable. *Award amount:* $2046–$9708. *Number of awards:* varies. *Eligibility Requirements:* Applicant must be enrolled or expecting to enroll full or part-time at a two-year, four-year, or technical institution or university; resident of California and studying in California. Applicant must have 3.0 GPA or higher. Available to U.S. citizens. *Application Requirements:* Application, financial need analysis, GPA verification. *Deadline:* March 2.

Contact: California Student Aid Commission, PO Box 419027, Rancho Cordova, CA 95741-9027. *E-mail:* custsvcs@csac.ca.gov. *Phone:* 916-526-7590. *Fax:* 916-526-8002. *Web site:* www.csac.ca.gov.

Entitlement Cal Grant B. Award for California residents who are high school graduates attending an approved college or university within the state. Must show financial need and meet the minimum 2.0 GPA requirement. *Award:* Grant for use in freshman, sophomore, junior, or senior year; renewable. *Award amount:* $700–$11,259. *Number of awards:* varies. *Eligibility Requirements:* Applicant must be enrolled or expecting to enroll full or part-time at a two-year, four-year, or technical institution or university; resident of California and studying in California. Available to U.S.

citizens. *Application Requirements:* Application, financial need analysis. *Deadline:* March 2.

Contact: California Student Aid Commission, PO Box 419027, Rancho Cordova, CA 95741-9027. *E-mail:* custsvcs@csac.ca.gov. *Phone:* 916-526-7590. *Fax:* 916-526-8002. *Web site:* www.csac.ca.gov.

Law Enforcement Personnel Development Scholarship. The Law Enforcement Personnel Dependents Scholarship Program provides college grants to needy dependents of California law enforcement officers, officers and employees of the Department of Corrections and Department of Youth Authority, and firefighters killed or disabled in the line of duty. *Award:* Grant for use in freshman, sophomore, junior, or senior year; renewable. *Award amount:* $100–$11,259. *Number of awards:* varies. *Eligibility Requirements:* Applicant must be enrolled or expecting to enroll full or part-time at a two-year, four-year, or technical institution or university; resident of California and studying in California. Applicant or parent of applicant must have employment or volunteer experience in police/firefighting. Available to U.S. citizens. *Application Requirements:* Application, financial need analysis. *Deadline:* continuous.

Contact: California Student Aid Commission, PO Box 419027, Rancho Cordova, CA 95741-9027. *E-mail:* custsvcs@csac.ca.gov. *Phone:* 916-526-7590. *Fax:* 916-526-8002. *Web site:* www.csac.ca.gov.

COLORADO

Colorado Leveraging Educational Assistance Partnership (CLEAP) and SLEAP. Renewable awards for Colorado residents who are attending Colorado state-supported postsecondary institutions at the undergraduate level. Must document financial need. Contact colleges for complete information and deadlines. *Award:* Grant for use in freshman, sophomore, junior, or senior year; not renewable. *Award amount:* $50–$900. *Number of awards:* 5000. *Eligibility Requirements:* Applicant must be enrolled or expecting to enroll full or part-time at a two-year, four-year, or technical institution or university; resident of Colorado and studying in Colorado. Available to U.S. citizens. *Application Requirements:* Application, financial need analysis. *Deadline:* varies.

Contact: Financial Aid Office at college/institution, Colorado Commission on Higher Education, 1380 Lawrence Street, Suite 1200, Denver, CO 80204-2059. *Web site:* www.state.co.us/cche.

Colorado Student Grant. Assists Colorado residents attending eligible public, private, or vocational institutions within the state. Application deadlines vary by institution. Renewable award for undergraduates. Contact the financial aid office at the college/institution for more information and an application. *Award:* Grant for use in freshman, sophomore, junior, or senior year; renewable. *Award amount:* $500–$5000. *Number of awards:* varies. *Eligibility Requirements:* Applicant must be enrolled or expecting to enroll full or part-time at a two-year, four-year, or technical institution or university; resident of Colorado and studying in Colorado. *Application Requirements:* Application, financial need analysis. *Deadline:* varies.

Contact: Financial Aid Office at college/institution, Colorado Commission on Higher Education, 1380 Lawrence Street, Suite 1200, Denver, CO 80204-2059. *Web site:* www.state.co.us/cche.

Colorado Undergraduate Merit Scholarships. Renewable awards for students attending Colorado state-supported institutions at the undergraduate level. Must demonstrate superior scholarship or talent. Contact college financial aid office for complete information and deadlines. *Award:* Scholarship for use in freshman, sophomore, junior, or senior year; renewable. *Award amount:* $1230. *Number of awards:* 10,823. *Eligibility Requirements:* Applicant must be enrolled or expecting to enroll full or part-time at a two-year, four-year, or technical institution or university; resident of Colorado and studying in Colorado. Applicant must have 3.0 GPA or higher. *Application Requirements:* Application, test scores, transcript. *Deadline:* varies.

Contact: Financial Aid Office at college/institution, Colorado Commission on Higher Education, 1380 Lawrence Street, Suite 1200, Denver, CO 80204-2059. *Web site:* www.state.co.us/cche.

Department of Military Affairs Colorado National Guard State Tuition Assistance Program. Applicant must be member of Colorado National Guard for six months. Applicant must maintain 2.0 GPA during Tuition Assistance Program. Please refer to Web site http://www.coloradoguard.com. *Award:* Forgivable loan for use in freshman, sophomore, junior, or senior year; renewable. *Award amount:* varies. *Number of awards:* varies. *Eligibility Requirements:* Applicant must be enrolled or expecting to enroll full or part-time at a two-year, four-year, or technical institution or university; resident of Colorado and studying in Colorado. Available to U.S. citizens. Applicant or parent must meet one or more

of the following requirements: Air Force National Guard or Army National Guard experience; retired from active duty; disabled or killed as a result of military service; prisoner of war; or missing in action. *Application Requirements:* Application, financial need analysis. *Deadline:* varies.

Contact: See Web site., Department of Military Affairs. *Web site:* www.coloradoguard.com.

Governor's Opportunity Scholarship. Scholarship available for the most needy first-time freshmen whose parents' adjusted gross income is less than $26,000. Must be U.S. citizen or permanent legal resident. Work-study is part of the program. *Award:* Scholarship for use in freshman, sophomore, junior, or senior year; renewable. *Award amount:* $5665. *Number of awards:* up to 1052. *Eligibility Requirements:* Applicant must be high school student; planning to enroll or expecting to enroll full-time at a two-year, four-year, or technical institution or university; resident of Colorado and studying in Colorado. Available to U.S. citizens. *Application Requirements:* Application, financial need analysis, test scores, transcript. *Deadline:* continuous.

Contact: Financial Aid Office at college/institution, Colorado Commission on Higher Education, 1380 Lawrence Street, Suite 1200, Denver, CO 80204-2059. *Web site:* www.state.co.us/cche.

Western Undergraduate Exchange Program. Residents of Alaska, Arizona, Colorado, Hawaii, Idaho, Montana, Nevada, New Mexico, North Dakota, Oregon, South Dakota, Utah, Washington and Wyoming can enroll in designated two- and four-year undergraduate programs at public institutions in participating states at reduced tuition level (resident tuition plus half). Contact Western Interstate Commission for Higher Education for list and deadlines. *Award:* Scholarship for use in freshman, sophomore, junior, or senior year; renewable. *Eligibility Requirements:* Applicant must be enrolled or expecting to enroll full or part-time at a two-year or four-year institution; resident of Alaska, Arizona, Colorado, Hawaii, Idaho, Montana, Nevada, New Mexico, North Dakota, Oregon, South Dakota, Utah, Washington, or Wyoming and studying in Alaska, Colorado, Hawaii, Idaho, Montana, Nevada, New Mexico, North Dakota, Oregon, South Dakota, Utah, or Wyoming. Available to U.S. citizens. *Application Requirements:* Application.

Contact: Ms. Sandy Jackson, Program Coordinator, Western Interstate Commission for Higher Education, PO Box 9752, Boulder, CO 80301-9752. *E-mail:* info-sep@wiche.

edu. *Phone:* 303-541-0214. *Fax:* 303-541-0291. *Web site:* www.wiche.edu/sep.

CONNECTICUT

Aid for Public College Students Grant Program/Connecticut. Award for students at Connecticut public college or university. Must be state residents and enrolled at least half-time. Renewable award based on financial need and academic progress. Application deadlines vary by institution. Apply at college financial aid office. *Award:* Grant for use in freshman, sophomore, junior, or senior year; renewable. *Award amount:* varies. *Number of awards:* varies. *Eligibility Requirements:* Applicant must be enrolled or expecting to enroll full or part-time at a two-year or four-year institution or university; resident of Connecticut and studying in Connecticut. *Application Requirements:* Application, financial need analysis, transcript. *Deadline:* varies.

Contact: John Siegrist, Financial Aid Office, Connecticut Department of Higher Education, 61 Woodland Street, Hartford, CT 06105-2326. *Phone:* 860-947-1855. *Fax:* 860-947-1311. *Web site:* www.ctdhe.org.

Capitol Scholarship Program. Award for Connecticut residents attending eligible institutions in Connecticut or in a state with reciprocity with Connecticut (Delaware, Maine, Massachusetts, New Hampshire, Pennsylvania, Rhode Island, Vermont, or Washington, D.C). Must be U.S. citizen or permanent resident alien who is a high school senior or graduate. Must rank in top 20% of class or score at least 1200 on SAT. Must show financial need. *Award:* Scholarship for use in freshman, sophomore, junior, or senior year; renewable. *Award amount:* up to $2000. *Number of awards:* varies. *Eligibility Requirements:* Applicant must be enrolled or expecting to enroll at a two-year or four-year institution or university; resident of Connecticut and studying in Connecticut, Delaware, District of Columbia, Maine, Massachusetts, New Hampshire, Pennsylvania, Rhode Island, or Vermont. Applicant must have 3.5 GPA or higher. Available to U.S. citizens. *Application Requirements:* Application, financial need analysis, test scores. *Deadline:* February 15.

Contact: John Siegrist, Financial Aid Office, Connecticut Department of Higher Education, 61 Woodland Street, Hartford, CT 06105-2326. *Phone:* 860-947-1855. *Fax:* 860-947-1311. *Web site:* www.ctdhe.org.

Connecticut Army National Guard 100% Tuition Waiver. 100% Tuition Waiver Program is for any active member of the Connecticut Army National Guard in good standing. Must be a resident of Connecticut attending any Connecticut state (public) university, community-technical college or regional vocational-technical school. *Award:* Scholarship for use in freshman, sophomore, junior, or senior year; not renewable. *Award amount:* varies. *Number of awards:* varies. *Eligibility Requirements:* Applicant must be age 17-65; enrolled or expecting to enroll full or part-time at a two-year, four-year, or technical institution or university; resident of Connecticut and studying in Connecticut. Available to U.S. and non-U.S. citizens. Applicant must have served in the Army National Guard. *Application Requirements:* Application. *Deadline:* continuous.

Contact: Education Services Officer, Connecticut Army National Guard. *E-mail:* education@ct.ngb.army.mil. *Phone:* 860-524-4816. *Web site:* www.ct.ngb.army.mil/armyguard/join/tuition.asp.

Connecticut Independent College Student Grants. Award for Connecticut residents attending an independent college or university within the state on at least a half-time basis. Renewable awards based on financial need. Application deadline varies by institution. Apply at college financial aid office. *Award:* Grant for use in freshman, sophomore, junior, or senior year; renewable. *Award amount:* up to $7700. *Number of awards:* varies. *Eligibility Requirements:* Applicant must be enrolled or expecting to enroll full or part-time at a two-year or four-year institution or university; resident of Connecticut and studying in Connecticut. *Application Requirements:* Application, financial need analysis, transcript. *Deadline:* varies.

Contact: John Siegrist, Financial Aid Office, Connecticut Department of Higher Education, 61 Woodland Street, Hartford, CT 06105-2326. *Phone:* 860-947-1855. *Fax:* 860-947-1311. *Web site:* www.ctdhe.org.

Connecticut Special Education Teacher Incentive Grant. Renewable award for upper-level undergraduates or graduate students in special education programs. Must be in a program at a Connecticut college or university, or be a Connecticut resident enrolled in an approved out-of-state program. Priority is placed on minority and bilingual candidates. Application deadline is October 1. Must be nominated by the education dean of institution attended. *Academic Fields/Career Goals:* Special Education. *Award:* Grant for use in junior, senior, or graduate year; renewable. *Award amount:* $2000–$5000. *Number of awards:* varies. *Eligibility Requirements:* Applicant must be enrolled or expecting to enroll full or part-time at a four-year institution or university. *Application Requirements:* Application. *Deadline:* October 1.

Contact: John Siegrist, Financial Aid Office, Connecticut Department of Higher Education, 61 Woodland Street, Hartford, CT 06105-2326. *Phone:* 860-947-1855. *Fax:* 860-947-1311. *Web site:* www.ctdhe.org.

Connecticut Tuition Waiver for Senior Citizens. Renewable tuition waiver for a Connecticut senior citizen age 62 or older to use at an accredited two- or four-year public institution in Connecticut. Must show financial need and prove senior citizen status. Award for undergraduate study only. Must be enrolled in credit courses. *Award:* Grant for use in freshman, sophomore, junior, or senior year; renewable. *Award amount:* varies. *Number of awards:* varies. *Eligibility Requirements:* Applicant must be age 62; enrolled or expecting to enroll at a two-year or four-year institution; resident of Connecticut and studying in Connecticut. *Application Requirements:* Application, financial need analysis. *Deadline:* continuous.

Contact: John Siegrist, Financial Aid Office, Connecticut Department of Higher Education, 61 Woodland Street, Hartford, CT 06105-2326. *Phone:* 860-947-1855. *Fax:* 860-947-1311. *Web site:* www.ctdhe.org.

Connecticut Tuition Waiver for Veterans. Renewable tuition waiver for a Connecticut veteran to use at an accredited two-or four-year public institution in Connecticut. Military separation papers are required; see application for qualifications of service. *Award:* Grant for use in freshman, sophomore, junior, or senior year; renewable. *Award amount:* varies. *Number of awards:* varies. *Eligibility Requirements:* Applicant must be enrolled or expecting to enroll at a two-year or four-year institution; resident of Connecticut and studying in Connecticut. Applicant or parent must meet one or more of the following requirements: general military experience; retired from active duty; disabled or killed as a result of military service; prisoner of war; or missing in action. *Application Requirements:* Application, financial need analysis, military discharge papers. *Deadline:* continuous.

Contact: John Siegrist, Financial Aid Office, Connecticut Department of Higher Education, 61 Woodland Street, Hartford, CT 06105-2326. *Phone:* 860-947-1855. *Fax:* 860-947-1311. *Web site:* www.ctdhe.org.

Tuition Set-Aside Aid—Connecticut. Need-based program that assists Connecticut residents who are enrolled at state-supported colleges and universities in Connecticut. Award amounts are variable but do not exceed student's financial need. Deadlines vary by institution. Apply at college financial aid office. *Award:* Grant for use in freshman, sophomore, junior, or senior year; not renewable. *Award amount:* varies. *Number of awards:* varies. *Eligibility Requirements:* Applicant must be enrolled or expecting to enroll at a two-year or four-year institution or university; resident of Connecticut and studying in Connecticut. *Application Requirements:* Application, financial need analysis. *Deadline:* varies.

Contact: John Siegrist, Financial Aid Office, Connecticut Department of Higher Education, 61 Woodland Street, Hartford, CT 06105-2326. *Phone:* 860-947-1855. *Fax:* 860-947-1311. *Web site:* www.ctdhe.org.

DELAWARE

Christa McAuliffe Teacher Scholarship Loan-Delaware. Award for Delaware residents who are pursuing teaching careers. Must agree to teach in Delaware public schools as repayment of loan. Minimum award is $1000 and is renewable for up to four years. Available only at Delaware colleges. Based on academic merit. Must be ranked in upper half of class, and have a score of 1050 on SAT or 25 on the ACT. *Academic Fields/Career Goals:* Education. *Award:* Forgivable loan for use in freshman, sophomore, junior, or senior year; renewable. *Award amount:* $1000–$5000. *Number of awards:* 1–60. *Eligibility Requirements:* Applicant must be enrolled or expecting to enroll full-time at a four-year institution or university; resident of Delaware and studying in Delaware. Applicant must have 2.5 GPA or higher. Available to U.S. citizens. *Application Requirements:* Application, essay, test scores, transcript. *Deadline:* March 31.

Contact: Donna Myers, Higher Education Analyst, Delaware Higher Education Commission, 820 North French Street, 5th Floor, Wilmington, DE 19711-3509. *E-mail:* dhec@ doe.k12.de.us. *Phone:* 302-577-3240. *Fax:* 302-577-6765. *Web site:* www.doe.state.de. us/high-ed.

Delaware Nursing Incentive Scholarship Loan. Award for Delaware residents pursuing a nursing career. Must be repaid with nursing practice at a Delaware state-owned hospital. Based on academic merit. Must have minimum 2.5 GPA. Renewable for up to four years. *Academic Fields/Career Goals:* Nursing. *Award:* Forgivable loan for use in freshman, sophomore, junior, or senior year; renewable. *Award amount:* $1000–$5000. *Number of awards:* 1–40. *Eligibility Requirements:* Applicant must be enrolled or expecting to enroll full-time at a two-year or four-year institution or university and resident of Delaware. Applicant must have 2.5 GPA or higher.

Available to U.S. citizens. *Application Requirements:* Application, essay, test scores, transcript. *Deadline:* March 31.

Contact: Donna Myers, Higher Education Analyst, Delaware Higher Education Commission, 820 North French Street, 5th Floor, Wilmington, DE 19711-3509. *E-mail:* dhec@ doe.k12.de.us. *Phone:* 302-577-3240. *Fax:* 302-577-6765. *Web site:* www.doe.state.de. us/high-ed.

Delaware Solid Waste Authority John P. "Pat" Healy Scholarship. Scholarships given to residents of Delaware who are high school seniors or freshmen or sophomores in college. Must be majoring in either environmental engineering or environmental sciences in a Delaware college. Must file the Free Application for Federal Student Aid (FAFSA). Scholarships are automatically renewed for three years if a 3.0 GPA is maintained. Deadline: March 15. *Award:* Scholarship for use in freshman or sophomore year; renewable. *Award amount:* $2000. *Number of awards:* 1. *Eligibility Requirements:* Applicant must be enrolled or expecting to enroll full-time at a two-year or four-year institution or university; resident of Delaware and studying in Delaware. Applicant must have 3.0 GPA or higher. *Application Requirements:* Financial need analysis, FAFSA. *Deadline:* March 15.

Contact: Donna Myers, Higher Education Analyst, Delaware Higher Education Commission, 820 North French Street, 5th Floor, Wilmington, DE 19711-3509. *E-mail:* dhec@ doe.k12.de.us. *Phone:* 302-577-3240. *Fax:* 302-577-6765. *Web site:* www.doe.state.de. us/high-ed.

Diamond State Scholarship. Renewable award for Delaware high school seniors enrolling full-time at an accredited college or university. Must be ranked in upper quarter of class and score 1200 on SAT or 27 on the ACT. *Award:* Scholarship for use in freshman year; renewable. *Award amount:* $1250. *Number of awards:* 50–200. *Eligibility Requirements:* Applicant must be high school student; planning to enroll or expecting to enroll full-time at a four-year institution or university and resident of Delaware. Applicant must have 3.5 GPA or higher. Available to U.S. citizens. *Application Requirements:* Application, essay, test scores, transcript. *Deadline:* March 31.

Contact: Donna Myers, Higher Education Analyst, Delaware Higher Education Commission, 820 North French Street, 5th Floor, Wilmington, DE 19711-3509. *E-mail:* dhec@ doe.k12.de.us. *Phone:* 302-577-3240. *Fax:* 302-577-6765. *Web site:* www.doe.state.de. us/high-ed.

Educational Benefits for Children of Deceased Military and State Police. Renewable award for Delaware residents who are children of state or military police who were killed in the line of duty. Must attend a Delaware institution unless program of study is not available. Funds cover tuition and fees at Delaware institutions. The amount varies at non-Delaware institutions. Must submit proof of service and related death. Must be ages 16-24 at time of application. Deadline is three weeks before classes begin. *Award:* Grant for use in freshman, sophomore, junior, or senior year; renewable. *Award amount:* $6255. *Number of awards:* 1–10. *Eligibility Requirements:* Applicant must be age 16-24; enrolled or expecting to enroll full-time at a two-year or four-year institution or university and resident of Delaware. Applicant or parent of applicant must have employment or volunteer experience in police/firefighting. Available to U.S. citizens. Applicant or parent must meet one or more of the following requirements: general military experience; retired from active duty; disabled or killed as a result of military service; prisoner of war; or missing in action. *Application Requirements:* Application, verification of service-related death. *Deadline:* continuous.

Contact: Donna Myers, Higher Education Analyst, Delaware Higher Education Commission, 820 North French Street, 5th Floor, Wilmington, DE 19711-3509. *E-mail:* dhec@ doe.k12.de.us. *Phone:* 302-577-3240. *Fax:* 302-577-6765. *Web site:* www.doe.state.de. us/high-ed.

Legislative Essay Scholarship. Must be a senior in high school and Delaware resident. Submit an essay of 500 to 2000 words on a designated historical topic (changes annually). Deadline: November 16. For more information visit: http://www.doe.state.de.us/high-ed. *Award:* Scholarship for use in freshman year; not renewable. *Award amount:* $500–$5500. *Number of awards:* 62. *Eligibility Requirements:* Applicant must be high school student; planning to enroll or expecting to enroll full or part-time at a two-year, four-year, or technical institution or university and resident of Delaware. Available to U.S. citizens. *Application Requirements:* Application, applicant must enter a contest, essay. *Deadline:* November 16.

Contact: Donna Myers, Higher Education Analyst, Delaware Higher Education Commission, 820 North French Street, 5th Floor, Wilmington, DE 19711-3509. *E-mail:* dhec@ doe.k12.de.us. *Phone:* 302-577-3240. *Fax:* 302-577-6765. *Web site:* www.doe.state.de. us/high-ed.

Scholarship Incentive Program-Delaware. One-time award for Delaware residents with financial need. May be used at an institution in Delaware or Pennsylvania, or at another out-of-state institution if a program is not available at a publicly-supported school in Delaware. Must have minimum 2.5 GPA. *Award:* Grant for use in freshman, sophomore, junior, or senior year; not renewable. *Award amount:* $700–$2200. *Number of awards:* 1000–1300. *Eligibility Requirements:* Applicant must be enrolled or expecting to enroll full-time at a two-year or four-year institution or university; resident of Delaware and studying in Delaware or Pennsylvania. Applicant must have 2.5 GPA or higher. Available to U.S. citizens. *Application Requirements:* Application, financial need analysis, transcript. *Deadline:* April 15.

Contact: Donna Myers, Higher Education Analyst, Delaware Higher Education Commission, 820 North French Street, 5th Floor, Wilmington, DE 19711-3509. *E-mail:* dhec@doe.k12.de.us. *Phone:* 302-577-3240. *Fax:* 302-577-6765. *Web site:* www.doe.state.de.us/high-ed.

State Tuition Assistance. Award providing tuition assistance for any member of the Air or Army National Guard attending a Delaware two-year or four-year college. Awards are renewable. Applicant's minimum GPA must be 2.0. For full- or part-time study. Amount of award varies. *Award:* Scholarship for use in freshman, sophomore, junior, or senior year; renewable. *Award amount:* varies. *Number of awards:* varies. *Eligibility Requirements:* Applicant must be enrolled or expecting to enroll full or part-time at a two-year or four-year institution or university and studying in Delaware. Available to U.S. citizens. Applicant must have served in the Air Force National Guard or Army National Guard. *Application Requirements:* Application, transcript. *Deadline:* varies.

Contact: TSgt. Robert L. Csizmadia, State Tuition Assistance Manager, Delaware National Guard, First Regiment Road, Wilmington, DE 19808-2191. *E-mail:* robert.csizmadi@de.ngb.army.mil. *Phone:* 302-326-7012. *Fax:* 302-326-7055. *Web site:* www.delawarenationalguard.com.

DISTRICT OF COLUMBIA

American Council of the Blind Scholarships. Merit-based award available to undergraduate, graduate, vocational or technical students who are legally blind in both eyes. Submit certificate of legal blindness and proof of acceptance at an accredited postsecondary institution. *Award:* Scholarship for use in freshman, sophomore, junior, senior, or graduate year; not renewable. *Award amount:* $500–$5000. *Number of awards:* 28. *Eligibility Requirements:* Applicant must be enrolled or expecting to enroll full-time at a two-year, four-year, or technical institution or university. Applicant must be visually impaired. Applicant must have 3.5 GPA or higher. *Application Requirements:* Application, autobiography, essay, references, transcript. *Deadline:* March 1.

Contact: Terry Pacheco, Affiliate and Membership Services, American Council of the Blind, 1155 15th Street, NW, Suite 1004, Washington, DC 20005. *E-mail:* info@acb.org. *Phone:* 202-467-5081. *Fax:* 202-467-5085. *Web site:* www.acb.org.

DC Leveraging Educational Assistance Partnership Program (LEAP). Available to Washington, D.C. residents who have financial need. Must also apply for the Federal Pell Grant. Must attend an eligible college at least half time. Contact financial aid office or local library for more information. Proof of residency may be required. Deadline is last Friday in June. *Award:* Scholarship for use in freshman, sophomore, junior, or senior year; not renewable. *Award amount:* $500–$1500. *Number of awards:* 1200–1500. *Eligibility Requirements:* Applicant must be enrolled or expecting to enroll full or part-time at a two-year, four-year, or technical institution or university and resident of District of Columbia. Available to U.S. citizens. *Application Requirements:* Application, financial need analysis, Student Aid Report (SAR). *Deadline:* June 28.

Contact: Angela M. March, Program Manager, District of Columbia State Education Office, 441 4th Street NW, Suite 350 North, Washington, DC 20001. *E-mail:* angela.march@dc.gov. *Phone:* 202-727-6436. *Fax:* 202-727-2019. *Web site:* www.seo.dc.gov.

FLORIDA

Critical Teacher Shortage Student Loan Forgiveness Program-Florida. Eligible Florida teachers may receive up to $5,000 for repayment of undergraduate and graduate educational loans which lead to certification in critical teacher shortage subject area. Must teach full-time at a Florida public school in a critical area for a minimum of ninety days to be eligible. Visit Web site for further information. *Award:* Forgivable loan for use in freshman, sophomore, junior, senior, or graduate year; not renewable. *Award amount:* up to $5000. *Number of awards:* varies. *Eligibility Requirements:* Applicant must be enrolled or expecting to enroll at a two-year or four-year institution or university; resident of Florida and study-

ing in Florida. Applicant or parent of applicant must have employment or volunteer experience in teaching. Available to U.S. citizens. *Application Requirements:* Application, transcript. *Deadline:* July 15.

Contact: Scholarship Information, Florida Department of Education, Office of Student Financial Assistance, 1940 North Monroe, Suite 70, Tallahassee, FL 32303-4759. *E-mail:* osfa@fldoe.org. *Phone:* 888-827-2004. *Web site:* www.floridastudentfinancialaid.org.

Critical Teacher Shortage Tuition Reimbursement-Florida. One-time awards for full-time Florida public school employees who are certified to teach in Florida and are teaching, or preparing to teach, in critical teacher shortage subject areas. Must earn minimum grade of 3.0 in approved courses. May receive tuition reimbursement up to 9 semester hours or equivalent per academic year, not to exceed $78 per semester hour, for maximum 36 hours. Must be resident of Florida. *Academic Fields/Career Goals:* Education. *Award:* Scholarship for use in freshman, sophomore, junior, senior, or graduate year; not renewable. *Award amount:* up to $234. *Number of awards:* 1000–1200. *Eligibility Requirements:* Applicant must be enrolled or expecting to enroll part-time at a two-year or four-year institution or university; resident of Florida and studying in Florida. Applicant or parent of applicant must have employment or volunteer experience in teaching. Applicant must have 3.0 GPA or higher. Available to U.S. citizens. *Application Requirements:* Application, financial need analysis. *Deadline:* September 15.

Contact: Scholarship Information, Florida Department of Education, Office of Student Financial Assistance, 1940 North Monroe, Suite 70, Tallahassee, FL 32303-4759. *E-mail:* osfa@fldoe.org. *Phone:* 888-827-2004. *Web site:* www.floridastudentfinancialaid.org.

Florida Bright Futures Scholarship Program. Reward for Florida high school graduates who demonstrate high academic achievement, participate in community service projects, and enroll in eligible Florida postsecondary institutions. There are three award levels. Each has different academic criteria and awards a different amount. Top ranked scholars from each county will receive additional $1500. Web site at http://www.firn.edu/doe contains complete information and application which must be completed and submitted to high school guidance counselor prior to graduation. *Award:* Scholarship for use in freshman, sophomore, junior, or senior year; renewable. *Award amount:* varies. *Number of awards:* varies. *Eligibility Requirements:* Applicant must be high school student; planning to enroll or expecting to enroll full or part-time at a two-year, four-year, or technical institution or university; resident of Florida and studying in Florida. Available to U.S. citizens. *Application Requirements:* Application, financial need analysis, test scores, transcript.

Contact: Scholarship Information, Florida Department of Education, Office of Student Financial Assistance, 1940 North Monroe, Suite 70, Tallahassee, FL 32303-4759. *E-mail:* osfa@fldoe.org. *Phone:* 888-827-2004. *Web site:* www.floridastudentfinancialaid.org.

Florida Space Research and Education Grant Program. One-time award for aerospace and technology research. Grant is for research in Florida only. Submit research proposal with budget. Application deadline is March 1. Applicants must be from a university, college, or industry in Florida. *Award:* Grant for use in freshman, sophomore, junior, senior, graduate, or postgraduate years; not renewable. *Award amount:* $10,000–$30,000. *Number of awards:* 9–12. *Eligibility Requirements:* Applicant must be enrolled or expecting to enroll full or part-time at a two-year, four-year, or technical institution or university and studying in Florida. Available to U.S. citizens. *Application Requirements:* Proposal with budget. *Deadline:* March 1.

Contact: Dr. Jaydeep Mukherjee, Administrator, NASA Florida Space Grant Consortium, Mail Stop: FSGC, Kennedy Space Center, FL 32899. *E-mail:* jmukherj@mail.ucf.edu. *Phone:* 321-452-4301. *Fax:* 321-449-0739. *Web site:* fsgc.engr.ucf.edu.

Nursing Scholarship Program. Provides financial assistance for Florida residents who are full- or part-time nursing students enrolled in an approved nursing program in Florida. Awards are for a maximum of two years and must be repaid through full-time service at an approved/designated site, in a medically underserved area in Florida. *Academic Fields/Career Goals:* Nursing. *Award:* Scholarship for use in junior, senior, or graduate year; renewable. *Award amount:* $8000–$12,000. *Number of awards:* 15–30. *Eligibility Requirements:* Applicant must be enrolled or expecting to enroll full or part-time at a two-year or four-year institution or university; resident of Florida and studying in Florida. Available to U.S. and non-U.S. citizens. *Application Requirements:* Application. *Deadline:* varies.

Contact: Thomas P. Gabriele, Program Coordinator, Florida Department of Health, Office of Public Health Nursing, 4052 Bald Cypress Way, Mail Bin C-27, Tallahassee, FL 32399-1708. *Phone:* 800-342-8660 Ext. 3503. *Fax:* 850-922-6296.

Rosewood Family Scholarship Fund. Renewable award for eligible minority students to attend a Florida public postsecondary institution on a full-time basis. Preference given to direct descendants of African-American Rosewood families affected by the incidents of January 1923. Must be Black, Hispanic, Asian, Pacific Islander, American-Indian, or Alaska Native. Free Application for Federal Student Aid (and Student Aid Report for nonresidents of Florida) must be processed by May 15. *Award:* Scholarship for use in freshman, sophomore, junior, or senior year; renewable. *Award amount:* up to $4000. *Number of awards:* up to 25. *Eligibility Requirements:* Applicant must be American Indian/Alaska Native, Asian/Pacific Islander, Black (non-Hispanic), or Hispanic; enrolled or expecting to enroll full-time at a two-year, four-year, or technical institution or university and studying in Florida. Available to U.S. citizens. *Application Requirements:* Application, financial need analysis. *Deadline:* April 1.

Contact: Scholarship Information, Florida Department of Education, Office of Student Financial Assistance, 1940 North Monroe, Suite 70, Tallahassee, FL 32303-4759. *E-mail:* osfa@fldoe.org. *Phone:* 888-827-2004. *Web site:* www.floridastudentfinancialaid.org.

Scholarships for Children of Deceased or Disabled Veterans or Children of Servicemen Classified as POW or MIA. Scholarship provides full tuition assistance for children of deceased or disabled veterans or of servicemen classified as POW or MIA who are in full-time attendance at eligible public or non-public Florida institutions. Service connection must be as specified under Florida statute. Amount of payment to non-public institutions is equal to cost at public institutions at the comparable level. Must be between 16 and 22. Qualified veteran and applicant must meet residency requirements. *Award:* Scholarship for use in freshman, sophomore, junior, or senior year; renewable. *Number of awards:* 160. *Eligibility Requirements:* Applicant must be age 16-22; enrolled or expecting to enroll full-time at a two-year, four-year, or technical institution or university; resident of Florida and studying in Florida. Available to U.S. citizens. Applicant or parent must meet one or more of the following requirements: general military experience; retired from active duty; disabled or killed as a result of military service; prisoner of war; or missing in action. *Application Requirements:* Application, financial need analysis. *Deadline:* May 1.

Contact: Scholarship Information, Florida Department of Education, Office of Student

Financial Assistance, 1940 North Monroe, Suite 70, Tallahassee, FL 32303-4759. *E-mail:* osfa@fldoe.org. *Phone:* 888-827-2004. *Web site:* www.floridastudentfinancialaid.org.

William L. Boyd IV Florida Resident Access Grant. Awards given to Florida residents attending an independent nonprofit college or university in Florida for undergraduate study. Cannot have previously received bachelor's degree. Must enroll minimum 12 credit hours. Deadline set by eligible postsecondary financial aid offices. Contact financial aid administrator for application information. Reapply for renewal. *Award:* Grant for use in freshman, sophomore, junior, or senior year; not renewable. *Award amount:* up to $2686. *Number of awards:* varies. *Eligibility Requirements:* Applicant must be enrolled or expecting to enroll full-time at a four-year institution or university; resident of Florida and studying in Florida. Available to U.S. citizens. *Application Requirements:* Application. *Deadline:* April 1.

Contact: Scholarship Information, Florida Department of Education, Office of Student Financial Assistance, 1940 North Monroe, Suite 70, Tallahassee, FL 32303-4759. *E-mail:* osfa@fldoe.org. *Phone:* 888-827-2004. *Web site:* www.floridastudentfinancialaid.org.

GEORGIA

Department of Human Resources Federal Stafford Loan with the Service Cancelable Loan Option. Forgivable loans of $4000 are awarded to current Department of Human Resources employees who will be enrolled in a baccalaureate or advanced nursing degree program at an eligible participating school in Georgia. Loans are cancelled upon two calendar years of service as a registered nurse for the Georgia DHR or any Georgia county board of health. *Academic Fields/Career Goals:* Nursing. *Award:* Forgivable loan for use in freshman, sophomore, junior, senior, or graduate year; not renewable. *Award amount:* $4000. *Number of awards:* varies. *Eligibility Requirements:* Applicant must be enrolled or expecting to enroll full or part-time at a four-year institution or university; resident of Georgia and studying in Georgia. Available to U.S. citizens. *Application Requirements:* Application, financial need analysis. *Deadline:* June 4.

Contact: Peggy Matthews, Manager/GSFA Originations, State of Georgia, 2082 East Exchange Place, Suite 230, Tucker, GA 30084-5305. *E-mail:* peggy@gsfc.org. *Phone:* 770-724-9230. *Fax:* 770-724-9225. *Web site:* www.gsfc.org.

GAE GFIE Scholarship for Aspiring Teachers.

Up to ten $1000 scholarships will be awarded to graduating seniors who currently attend a fully accredited public Georgia high school and will attend a fully accredited Georgia college or university within the next 12 months. Must have a 3.0 GPA. Must submit three letters of recommendation. Must have plans to enter the teaching profession. *Academic Fields/Career Goals:* Education. *Award:* Scholarship for use in freshman year; not renewable. *Award amount:* $1000. *Number of awards:* up to 10. *Eligibility Requirements:* Applicant must be high school student; planning to enroll or expecting to enroll at a two-year or four-year institution or university; resident of Georgia and studying in Georgia. Applicant must have 3.0 GPA or higher. Available to U.S. citizens. *Application Requirements:* Application, transcript. *Deadline:* March 15.

Contact: Sally Bennett, Professional Development Specialist, Georgia Association of Educators, 100 Crescent Centre Parkway, Suite 500, Tucker, GA 30084-7049. *E-mail:* sally.bennett@gae.org. *Phone:* 678-837-1103. *Web site:* www.gae.org.

Georgia Leveraging Educational Assistance Partnership Grant Program.

Based on financial need. Recipients must be eligible for the Federal Pell Grant. Renewable award for Georgia residents enrolled in a state postsecondary institution. Must be U.S. citizen. *Award:* Grant for use in freshman, sophomore, junior, or senior year; renewable. *Award amount:* $370. *Number of awards:* 3000–3500. *Eligibility Requirements:* Applicant must be enrolled or expecting to enroll full or part-time at a two-year, four-year, or technical institution or university; resident of Georgia and studying in Georgia. Available to U.S. citizens. *Application Requirements:* Application, financial need analysis. *Deadline:* continuous.

Contact: William Flook, Director of Scholarships and Grants, Georgia Student Finance Commission, 2082 East Exchange Place, Suite 100, Tucker, GA 30084. *Phone:* 770-724-9052. *Fax:* 770-724-9031. *Web site:* www.gsfc.org.

Georgia National Guard Service Cancelable Loan Program.

Forgivable loans will be awarded to residents of Georgia maintaining good military standing as an eligible member of the Georgia National Guard who are enrolled at least half-time in an undergraduate degree program at an eligible college, university or technical school within the state of Georgia. *Award:* Forgivable loan for use in freshman, sophomore, junior, or senior year; not renewable. *Award amount:* $150–$1821. *Number of awards:* 200–250. *Eligibility Requirements:* Applicant must be enrolled or expecting to enroll full or part-time at a two-year, four-year, or technical institution or university; resident of Georgia and studying in Georgia. Available to U.S. citizens. Applicant must have served in the Air Force National Guard or Army National Guard. *Application Requirements:* Application, financial need analysis. *Deadline:* June 4.

Contact: Peggy Matthews, Manager/GSFA Originations, State of Georgia, 2082 East Exchange Place, Suite 230, Tucker, GA 30084-5305. *E-mail:* peggy@gsfc.org. *Phone:* 770-724-9230. *Fax:* 770-724-9225. *Web site:* www.gsfc.org.

Georgia PROMISE Teacher Scholarship Program.

Renewable, forgivable loans for junior undergraduates at Georgia colleges who have been accepted for enrollment into a teacher education program leading to initial certification. Minimum cumulative 3.0 GPA required. Recipient must teach at a Georgia public school for one year for each $1500 awarded. Available to seniors for renewal only. Write for deadlines. *Academic Fields/Career Goals:* Education. *Award:* Forgivable loan for use in junior or senior year; renewable. *Award amount:* $3000–$6000. *Number of awards:* 700–1400. *Eligibility Requirements:* Applicant must be enrolled or expecting to enroll full or part-time at a four-year institution or university and studying in Georgia. Applicant must have 3.0 GPA or higher. Available to U.S. citizens. *Application Requirements:* Application, transcript. *Deadline:* continuous.

Contact: Stan DeWitt, Manager of Teacher Scholarships, Georgia Student Finance Commission, 2082 East Exchange Place, Suite 100, Tucker, GA 30084. *Phone:* 770-724-9060. *Fax:* 770-724-9031. *Web site:* www.gsfc.org.

Georgia Public Safety Memorial Grant/Law Enforcement Personnel Department Grant.

Award for children of Georgia law enforcement officers, prison guards, or fire fighters killed or permanently disabled in the line of duty. Must attend an accredited postsecondary Georgia school. Complete the Law Enforcement Personnel Dependents application. *Award:* Grant for use in freshman, sophomore, junior, or senior year; renewable. *Award amount:* $2000. *Number of awards:* 20–40. *Eligibility Requirements:* Applicant must be enrolled or expecting to enroll full-time at a two-year, four-year, or technical institution or university; resident of Georgia and studying in Georgia. Applicant or parent of applicant must have employment or volunteer experience in police/firefighting. Available to U.S. citizens. *Application Requirements:* Application. *Deadline:* continuous.

Contact: William Flook, Director of Scholarships and Grants Division, Georgia Student Finance Commission, 2082 East Exchange Place, Suite 100, Tucker, GA 30084. *Phone:* 770-724-9052. *Fax:* 770-724-9031. *Web site:* www.gsfc.org.

Georgia Tuition Equalization Grant (GTEG).

Award for Georgia residents pursuing undergraduate study at an accredited two- or four-year Georgia private institution. Complete the Georgia Student Grant Application. Award is $909 per academic year. Deadlines vary. *Award:* Grant for use in freshman, sophomore, junior, or senior year; renewable. *Award amount:* $909. *Number of awards:* 25,000–32,000. *Eligibility Requirements:* Applicant must be enrolled or expecting to enroll full-time at a two-year or four-year institution or university; resident of Georgia and studying in Georgia. Available to U.S. citizens. *Application Requirements:* Application. *Deadline:* continuous.

Contact: William Flook, Director of Scholarships and Grants Division, Georgia Student Finance Commission, 2082 East Exchange Place, Suite 100, Tucker, GA 30084. *Phone:* 770-724-9052. *Fax:* 770-724-9031. *Web site:* www.gsfc.org.

Governor's Scholarship-Georgia.

Award to assist students selected as Georgia scholars, STAR students, valedictorians, and salutatorians. For use at two- and four-year colleges and universities in Georgia. Recipients are selected as entering freshmen. Renewable award of up to $1000. Minimum 3.5 GPA required. *Award:* Scholarship for use in freshman, sophomore, junior, or senior year; renewable. *Award amount:* up to $1000. *Number of awards:* 2000–3000. *Eligibility Requirements:* Applicant must be high school student; planning to enroll or expecting to enroll full-time at a two-year or four-year institution or university; resident of Georgia and studying in Georgia. Applicant must have 3.5 GPA or higher. Available to U.S. citizens. *Application Requirements:* Application, transcript. *Deadline:* continuous.

Contact: William Flook, Director of Scholarships and Grants Division, Georgia Student Finance Commission, 2082 East Exchange Place, Suite 100, Tucker, GA 30084. *Phone:* 770-724-9052. *Fax:* 770-724-9031. *Web site:* www.gsfc.org.

HOPE—Helping Outstanding Pupils Educationally.

Grant program for Georgia residents who are college undergraduates to attend an accredited two- or four-year Georgia institution. Tuition and fees may be covered by the grant. Minimum 3.0 GPA required. Renewable if student maintains grades and reapplies. Write for deadlines.

Award: Scholarship for use in freshman, sophomore, junior, or senior year; renewable. *Award amount:* $300–$3900. *Number of awards:* 140,000–170,000. *Eligibility Requirements:* Applicant must be enrolled or expecting to enroll full or part-time at a two-year or four-year institution or university; resident of Georgia and studying in Georgia. Applicant must have 3.0 GPA or higher. Available to U.S. citizens. *Application Requirements:* Application. *Deadline:* continuous.

Contact: William Flook, Director of Scholarships and Grants Division, Georgia Student Finance Commission, 2082 East Exchange Place, Suite 100, Tucker, GA 30084. *Phone:* 770-724-9052. *Fax:* 770-724-9031. *Web site:* www.gsfc.org.

Intellectual Capital Partnership Program, ICAPP. Forgivable loans will be awarded to undergraduate students who are residents of Georgia studying high-tech related fields at a Georgia institution. Repayment for every $2500 that is awarded is one-year service in a high-tech field in Georgia. Can be enrolled in a certificate or degree program. *Academic Fields/Career Goals:* Trade/Technical Specialties. *Award:* Forgivable loan for use in freshman, sophomore, junior, or senior year; not renewable. *Award amount:* $7000–$10,000. *Number of awards:* up to 328. *Eligibility Requirements:* Applicant must be enrolled or expecting to enroll full or part-time at a two-year or four-year institution or university; resident of Georgia and studying in Georgia. Available to U.S. citizens. *Application Requirements:* Application, financial need analysis. *Deadline:* June 3.

Contact: Peggy Matthews, Manager/GSFA Originations, State of Georgia, 2082 East Exchange Place, Suite 230, Tucker, GA 30084-5305. *E-mail:* peggy@gsfc.org. *Phone:* 770-724-9230. *Fax:* 770-724-9225. *Web site:* www.gsfc.org.

Ladders in Nursing Career Service Cancelable Loan Program. Forgivable loans of $3,000 are awarded to students who agree to serve for one calendar year at an approved site within the state of Georgia. Eligible applicants will be residents of Georgia who are studying nursing at a Georgia institution. *Academic Fields/Career Goals:* Nursing. *Award:* Forgivable loan for use in freshman, sophomore, junior, senior, or graduate year; not renewable. *Award amount:* $3000. *Number of awards:* varies. *Eligibility Requirements:* Applicant must be enrolled or expecting to enroll full or part-time at a two-year, four-year, or technical institution or university; resident of Georgia and studying in Georgia. Avail-

able to U.S. citizens. *Application Requirements:* Application, financial need analysis. *Deadline:* June 3.

Contact: Peggy Matthews, Manager/GSFA Originations, State of Georgia, 2082 East Exchange Place, Suite 230, Tucker, GA 30084-5305. *E-mail:* peggy@gsfc.org. *Phone:* 770-724-9230. *Fax:* 770-724-9225. *Web site:* www.gsfc.org.

Northeast Georgia Pilot Nurse Service Cancelable Loan. Up to 100 forgivable loans between $2,500 and $4,500 will be awarded to undergraduate students who are residents of Georgia studying nursing at a four-year school in Georgia. Loans can be repaid by working as a nurse in northeast Georgia. *Academic Fields/Career Goals:* Nursing. *Award:* Forgivable loan for use in freshman, sophomore, junior, or senior year; not renewable. *Award amount:* $2500–$4500. *Number of awards:* up to 100. *Eligibility Requirements:* Applicant must be enrolled or expecting to enroll full-time at a four-year institution; resident of Georgia and studying in Georgia. Available to U.S. citizens. *Application Requirements:* Application, financial need analysis. *Deadline:* June 3.

Contact: Peggy Matthews, Manager/GSFA Originations, State of Georgia, 2082 East Exchange Place, Suite 230, Tucker, GA 30084-5305. *E-mail:* peggy@gsfc.org. *Phone:* 770-724-9230. *Fax:* 770-724-9225. *Web site:* www.gsfc.org.

Registered Nurse Service Cancelable Loan Program. Forgivable loans will be awarded to undergraduate students who are residents of Georgia studying nursing in a two-year or four-year school in Georgia. Loans can be repaid by working as a registered nurse in the state of Georgia. *Academic Fields/Career Goals:* Nursing. *Award:* Forgivable loan for use in freshman, sophomore, junior, or senior year; not renewable. *Award amount:* $200–$4500. *Number of awards:* varies. *Eligibility Requirements:* Applicant must be enrolled or expecting to enroll full or part-time at a two-year or four-year institution; resident of Georgia and studying in Georgia. Available to U.S. citizens. *Application Requirements:* Application, financial need analysis. *Deadline:* June 3.

Contact: Peggy Matthews, Manager/GSFA Originations, State of Georgia, 2082 East Exchange Place, Suite 230, Tucker, GA 30084-5305. *E-mail:* peggy@gsfc.org. *Phone:* 770-724-9230. *Fax:* 770-724-9225. *Web site:* www.gsfc.org.

Robert C. Byrd Honors Scholarship-Georgia. Complete the application provided by the Georgia Department of Education. Renewable awards for outstanding graduat-

ing Georgia high school seniors to be used for full-time undergraduate study at eligible U.S. institution. *Award:* Scholarship for use in freshman, sophomore, junior, or senior year; renewable. *Award amount:* $1500. *Number of awards:* 600–700. *Eligibility Requirements:* Applicant must be high school student; planning to enroll or expecting to enroll full-time at a two-year or four-year institution or university and resident of Georgia. Available to U.S. citizens. *Application Requirements:* Application, transcript. *Deadline:* April 1.

Contact: William Flook, Director of Scholarships and Grants Division, Georgia Student Finance Commission, 2082 East Exchange Place, Suite 100, Tucker, GA 30084. *Phone:* 770-724-9052. *Fax:* 770-724-9031. *Web site:* www.gsfc.org.

Service-Cancelable Stafford Loan-Georgia. To assist Georgia students enrolled in critical fields of study in allied health (e.g., nursing, physical therapy). For use at GSFA-approved schools. $3500 forgivable loan for dentistry students only. Contact school financial aid officer for more details. *Academic Fields/Career Goals:* Dental Health/Services; Health and Medical Sciences; Nursing; Therapy/Rehabilitation. *Award:* Forgivable loan for use in freshman, sophomore, junior, senior, or graduate year; not renewable. *Award amount:* $2000–$4500. *Number of awards:* 500–1200. *Eligibility Requirements:* Applicant must be enrolled or expecting to enroll full or part-time at a two-year, four-year, or technical institution or university; resident of Georgia and studying in Georgia. Available to U.S. citizens. *Application Requirements:* Application, financial need analysis. *Deadline:* continuous.

Contact: Peggy Matthews, Manager/GSFA Originations, State of Georgia, 2082 East Exchange Place, Suite 230, Tucker, GA 30084-5305. *E-mail:* peggy@gsfc.org. *Phone:* 770-724-9230. *Fax:* 770-724-9225. *Web site:* www.gsfc.org.

HAWAII

Hawaii State Student Incentive Grant. Grants are given to residents of Hawaii who are enrolled in a participating Hawaiian state school. Funds are for undergraduate tuition only. Applicants must submit a financial need analysis. *Award:* Grant for use in freshman, sophomore, junior, or senior year; renewable. *Award amount:* varies. *Number of awards:* varies. *Eligibility Requirements:* Applicant must be enrolled or expecting to enroll full or part-time at a two-year, four-year, or technical institution or university; resident of Hawaii and studying in Hawaii. Available to U.S. citizens. *Application Requirements:* Financial need analysis. *Deadline:* varies.

Contact: Jo Ann Yoshida, Financial Aid Specialist, Hawaii State Postsecondary Education Commission, University of Hawaii, Honolulu, HI 96822. *E-mail:* iha@hawaii. edu. *Phone:* 808-956-6066.

Kumu Kahua Theater/UHM Theater Department Playwriting Contest, Hawaii Prize. Contest for residents and non-residents of Hawaii. Contestants will be judged on full-length plays dealing with some aspect of the Hawaii experience or plays set in Hawaii. Submissions should be a minimum of 50 pages in standard form. Write for details. *Award:* Prize for use in freshman, sophomore, junior, senior, graduate, or postgraduate years; not renewable. *Award amount:* $500. *Number of awards:* 1. *Eligibility Requirements:* Applicant must be enrolled or expecting to enroll at an institution or university and must have an interest in writing. Available to U.S. and non-U.S. citizens. *Application Requirements:* Applicant must enter a contest, 3 copies of manuscript. *Deadline:* January 2.

Contact: Kumu Kahua Playwriting Contest, Kumu Kahua Theatre, 46 Merchant Street, Honolulu, HI 96813. *E-mail:* info@kumukahua. com.

Kumu Kahua Theater/UHM Theater Department Playwriting Contest, Pacific Rim Prize. Contest for residents and non-residents of Hawaii. Play must be set in or deal with the Pacific Islands, the Pacific Rim, or the Pacific/Asian-American experience. Restricted to full-length plays of a minimum of 50 pages in standard form. Write for details. *Award:* Prize for use in freshman, sophomore, junior, senior, graduate, or postgraduate years; not renewable. *Award amount:* $400. *Number of awards:* 1. *Eligibility Requirements:* Applicant must be enrolled or expecting to enroll at an institution or university and must have an interest in writing. Available to U.S. and non-U.S. citizens. *Application Requirements:* Applicant must enter a contest, 3 copies of manuscript. *Deadline:* January 2.

Contact: Kuma Kahua Playwriting Contest, Kumu Kahua Theatre, 46 Merchant Street, Honolulu, HI 96813. *E-mail:* info@kumukahua. com.

Kumu Kahua Theater/UHM Theater Department Playwriting Contest, Resident Prize. Contest for residents in Hawaii. Play may be any length on any topic. Write for details. *Award:* Prize for use in freshman, sophomore, junior, senior, graduate, or postgraduate years; not renewable. *Award amount:* $200. *Number of awards:* 1.

Eligibility Requirements: Applicant must be enrolled or expecting to enroll at an institution or university; resident of Hawaii and must have an interest in writing. Available to U.S. citizens. *Application Requirements:* Applicant must enter a contest, 3 copies of manuscript. *Deadline:* January 2.

Contact: Kuma Kahua Playwriting Contest, Kumu Kahua Theatre, 46 Merchant Street, Honolulu, HI 96813. *E-mail:* info@kumukahua. com.

IDAHO

Education Incentive Loan Forgiveness Contract-Idaho. Renewable award assists Idaho residents enrolling in teacher education or nursing programs within state. Must rank in top 15% of high school graduating class, have a 3.0 GPA or above, and agree to work in Idaho for two years. Deadlines vary. Contact financial aid office at institution of choice. *Academic Fields/Career Goals:* Education; Nursing. *Award:* Forgivable loan for use in freshman, sophomore, junior, or senior year; renewable. *Award amount:* varies. *Number of awards:* 13–45. *Eligibility Requirements:* Applicant must be enrolled or expecting to enroll full-time at a two-year or four-year institution or university; resident of Idaho and studying in Idaho. Applicant must have 3.0 GPA or higher. Available to U.S. citizens. *Application Requirements:* Application, test scores, transcript. *Deadline:* varies.

Contact: Financial Aid Office, Idaho State Board of Education. *Web site:* www. idahoboardofed.org.

Idaho Minority and "At Risk" Student Scholarship. Renewable award for Idaho residents who are disabled or members of a minority group and have financial need. Must attend one of eight postsecondary institutions in the state for undergraduate study. Deadlines vary by institution. Must be a U.S. citizen and be a graduate of an Idaho high school. Contact college financial aid office. *Award:* Scholarship for use in freshman, sophomore, junior, or senior year; renewable. *Award amount:* $3000. *Number of awards:* 35–40. *Eligibility Requirements:* Applicant must be American Indian/Alaska Native, Black (non-Hispanic), or Hispanic; enrolled or expecting to enroll full-time at a two-year, four-year, or technical institution or university; resident of Idaho and studying in Idaho. Applicant must be hearing impaired, physically disabled, or visually impaired. Available to U.S. citizens. *Application Requirements:* Application, financial need analysis, transcript. *Deadline:* varies.

Contact: Financial Aid Office, Idaho State Board of Education. *Web site:* www. idahoboardofed.org.

Idaho Promise Category A Scholarship Program. Renewable award available to Idaho residents who are graduating high school seniors. Must attend an approved Idaho institute of higher education full-time. Based on class rank (must be verified by school official), GPA, and ACT scores. Professional-technical student applicants must take COMPASS. *Award:* Scholarship for use in freshman, sophomore, junior, or senior year; renewable. *Award amount:* $3000. *Number of awards:* 25–30. *Eligibility Requirements:* Applicant must be high school student; planning to enroll or expecting to enroll full-time at a two-year, four-year, or technical institution or university; resident of Idaho and studying in Idaho. Applicant must have 3.5 GPA or higher. Available to U.S. citizens. *Application Requirements:* Application, test scores. *Deadline:* December 15.

Contact: Lynn Humphrey, Manager, Student Aid Programs, Idaho State Board of Education, PO Box 83720, Boise, ID 83720-0037. *E-mail:* lhumphre@osbe.state.id.us. *Phone:* 208-334-2270. *Fax:* 208-334-2632. *Web site:* www.idahoboardofed.org.

Idaho Promise Category B Scholarship Program. Available to Idaho residents entering college for the first time prior to the age of 22. Must have completed high school or its equivalent in Idaho and have a minimum GPA of 3.0 or an ACT score of 20 or higher. Scholarship limited to two years or 4 semesters. *Award:* Scholarship for use in freshman or sophomore year; renewable. *Award amount:* $500. *Number of awards:* varies. *Eligibility Requirements:* Applicant must be age 21 or under; enrolled or expecting to enroll full-time at a two-year, four-year, or technical institution or university; resident of Idaho and studying in Idaho. Applicant must have 3.0 GPA or higher. Available to U.S. citizens. *Application Requirements:* Application, transcript. *Deadline:* continuous.

Contact: Lynn Humphrey, Manager, Student Aid Programs, Idaho State Board of Education, PO Box 83720, Boise, ID 83720-0037. *Phone:* 208-334-2270. *Fax:* 208-334-2632. *Web site:* www.idahoboardofed.org.

Leveraging Educational Assistance State Partnership Program (LEAP). One-time award assists students attending participating Idaho trade schools, colleges, and universities majoring in any field except theology or divinity. Must be U.S. citizen or permanent resident, and show financial need. Application deadlines vary by institution. *Award:* Grant for use in fresh-man, sophomore, junior, senior, or gradu-ate year; not renewable. *Award amount:* $400–$5000. *Number of awards:* varies. *Eligibility Requirements:* Applicant must be enrolled or expecting to enroll full or part-time at a two-year, four-year, or techni-cal institution or university; resident of Idaho and studying in Idaho. Available to U.S. citizens. *Application Requirements:* Application, financial need analysis, self-addressed stamped envelope. *Deadline:* continuous.

Contact: Lynn Humphrey, Manager, Student Aid Programs, Idaho State Board of Educa-tion, PO Box 83720, Boise, ID 83720-0037. *Phone:* 208-334-2270. *Fax:* 208-334-2632. *Web site:* www.idahoboardofed.org.

ILLINOIS

Golden Apple Scholars of Illinois. 100 scholars are selected annually. Scholars receive $7,000 a year for 4 years. Applicants must be between 17 and 21 and maintain a GPA of 2.5. Eligible applicants must be residents of Illinois studying in Illinois. The deadline is December 1. Recipients must agree to teach in high-need Illinois schools. *Academic Fields/Career Goals:* Education. *Award:* Forgivable loan for use in freshman, sophomore, junior, or senior year; renewable. *Award amount:* $7000. *Number of awards:* up to 100. *Eligibility Requirements:* Applicant must be age 17-21; enrolled or expecting to enroll full-time at a four-year institution or university; resident of Illinois and studying in Illinois. Applicant must have 2.5 GPA or higher. Available to U.S. and non-U.S. citizens. *Application Requirements:* Application, autobiography, essay, interview, photo, references, test scores, transcript. *Deadline:* December 1.

Contact: Pat Kilduff, Director of Recruit-ment and Placement, Golden Apple Founda-tion, 8 South Michigan Avenue, Suite 700, Chicago, IL 60603-3318. *E-mail:* kilduff@goldenapple.org. *Phone:* 312-407-0006 Ext. 105. *Fax:* 312-407-0344. *Web site:* www.goldenapple.org.

Grant Program for Dependents of Police, Fire, or Correctional Officers. Award for dependents of police, fire, and corrections officers killed or disabled in line of duty. Provides for tuition and fees at approved Illinois institutions. Must be resident of Illinois. Continuous deadline. Provide proof of status. For information and application, go to Web site: http://www.collegezone. *Award:* Grant for use in freshman, sophomore, junior, senior, graduate, or postgraduate years; renewable. *Award amount:* $3000–$4000. *Number of awards:*

50–55. *Eligibility Requirements:* Applicant must be enrolled or expecting to enroll at a two-year, four-year, or technical institution or university; resident of Illinois and study-ing in Illinois. Applicant or parent of applicant must have employment or volunteer experience in police/firefighting. Available to U.S. citizens. *Application Requirements:* Application, proof of status. *Deadline:* continuous.

Contact: College Zone Counselor, Illinois Student Assistance Commission (ISAC), 1755 Lake Cook Road, Deerfield, IL 60015-5209. *E-mail:* collegezone@isac.org. *Phone:* 800-899-4722. *Web site:* www.collegezone.org.

Higher Education License Plate Program—HELP. Need-based grants for students at Illinois institutions participat-ing in program whose funds are raised by sale of special license plates commemorat-ing the institutions. Deadline: June 30. Must be Illinois resident. May be eligible to receive the grant for the equivalent of 10 semesters of full-time enrollment. *Award:* Grant for use in freshman, sophomore, junior, or senior year; not renewable. *Award amount:* up to $2000. *Number of awards:* 175–200. *Eligibility Requirements:* Applicant must be enrolled or expecting to enroll full or part-time at a two-year or four-year institution or university; resident of Illinois and studying in Illinois. Available to U.S. citizens. *Application Requirements:* Financial need analysis, FAFSA. *Deadline:* June 30.

Contact: College Zone Counselor, Illinois Student Assistance Commission (ISAC), 1755 Lake Cook Road, Deerfield, IL 60015-5209. *E-mail:* collegezone@isac.org. *Phone:* 800-899-4722. *Web site:* www.collegezone.org.

Illinois College Savings Bond Bonus Incentive Grant Program. Program offers holders of Illinois College Savings Bonds a $20 grant for each year of bond maturity payable upon bond redemption if at least 70% of proceeds are used to attend college in Illinois. May not be used by students attending religious or divinity schools. *Award:* Grant for use in freshman, sophomore, junior, senior, graduate, or postgraduate years; not renewable. *Award amount:* $40–$440. *Number of awards:* 1200–1400. *Eligibility Requirements:* Applicant must be enrolled or expecting to enroll full or part-time at a two-year, four-year, or technical institution or university and studying in Illinois. Available to U.S. citizens. *Application Requirements:* Application. *Deadline:* continuous.

Contact: College Zone Counselor, Illinois Student Assistance Commission (ISAC), 1755 Lake Cook Road, Deerfield, IL 60015-5209. *E-mail:* collegezone@isac.org. *Phone:* 800-899-4722. *Web site:* www.collegezone.org.

Illinois Future Teachers Corps Program. Scholarships available for students plan-ning to become teachers in Illinois. Students must be Illinois residents enrolled or accepted as a junior or above in a Teacher Educa-tion Program at an Illinois college or university. By receiving award, students agree to teach for 5 years at either a public, private, or parochial Illinois preschool, or at a public elementary or secondary school. For an application and further information, visit http://www.collegezone.com. *Academic Fields/Career Goals:* Education. *Award:* Forgivable loan for use in junior, senior, or graduate year; renewable. *Award amount:* $5000–$15,000. *Number of awards:* 1150. *Eligibility Requirements:* Applicant must be enrolled or expecting to enroll full or part-time at a four-year institution or university; resident of Illinois and studying in Illinois. Available to U.S. citizens. *Application Requirements:* Application, financial need analysis, FAFSA. *Deadline:* March 1.

Contact: College Zone Counselor, Illinois Student Assistance Commission (ISAC), 1755 Lake Cook Road, Deerfield, IL 60015-5209. *E-mail:* collegezone@isac.org. *Phone:* 800-899-4722. *Web site:* www.collegezone.org.

Illinois Incentive for Access Program. Award for eligible first-time freshmen enrolling in approved Illinois institutions. One-time grant of up to $500 may be used for any educational expense. Using the FAFSA, applicants are encouraged to apply as quickly as possible after January 1st preceding the academic year. *Award:* Grant for use in freshman year; not renewable. *Award amount:* $300–$500. *Number of awards:* 19,000–22,000. *Eligibility Require-ments:* Applicant must be enrolled or expecting to enroll full or part-time at a two-year, four-year, or technical institution or university; resident of Illinois and study-ing in Illinois. Available to U.S. citizens. *Application Requirements:* Financial need analysis, FAFSA online. *Deadline:* continuous.

Contact: College Zone Counselor, Illinois Student Assistance Commission (ISAC), 1755 Lake Cook Road, Deerfield, IL 60015-5209. *E-mail:* collegezone@isac.org. *Phone:* 800-899-4722. *Web site:* www.collegezone.org.

Illinois Monetary Award Program. Award for eligible students attending Illinois public universities, private colleges and universi-ties, community colleges, and some proprietary institutions. Applicable only to tuition and fees. Based on financial need. Applicants are encouraged to apply as soon after January 1st as possible. *Award:* Grant for use in freshman, sophomore, junior, or senior year; not renewable. *Award amount:*

up to $4968. *Number of awards:* 135,000–145,000. *Eligibility Requirements:* Applicant must be enrolled or expecting to enroll full or part-time at a two-year, four-year, or technical institution or university; resident of Illinois and studying in Illinois. Available to U.S. citizens. *Application Requirements:* Financial need analysis, FAFSA online. *Deadline:* continuous.

Contact: College Zone Counselor, Illinois Student Assistance Commission (ISAC), 1755 Lake Cook Road, Deerfield, IL 60015-5209. *E-mail:* collegezone@isac.org. *Phone:* 800-899-4722. *Web site:* www.collegezone.org.

Illinois National Guard Grant Program. Award for qualified National Guard personnel which pays tuition and fees at Illinois public universities and community colleges. Must provide documentation of service. Applications are due October 1 of the academic year for full year, March 1 for second/third term, or June 15 for the summer term. *Award:* Grant for use in freshman, sophomore, junior, senior, graduate, or postgraduate years; renewable. *Award amount:* $1300–$1700. *Number of awards:* 2000–3000. *Eligibility Requirements:* Applicant must be enrolled or expecting to enroll full or part-time at a two-year or four-year institution or university; resident of Illinois and studying in Illinois. Available to U.S. citizens. Applicant must have served in the Air Force National Guard or Army National Guard. *Application Requirements:* Application, documentation of service. *Deadline:* varies.

Contact: College Zone Counselor, Illinois Student Assistance Commission (ISAC), 1755 Lake Cook Road, Deerfield, IL 60015-5209. *E-mail:* collegezone@isac.org. *Phone:* 800-899-4722. *Web site:* www.collegezone.org.

Illinois Student-to-Student Program of Matching Grants. Award provides matching funds for need-based grants at participating Illinois public universities and community colleges. Deadlines are set by each institution. Contact financial aid office at the institution in which you are enrolled for eligibility. *Award:* Grant for use in freshman, sophomore, junior, or senior year; not renewable. *Award amount:* $300–$500. *Number of awards:* 2000–4000. *Eligibility Requirements:* Applicant must be enrolled or expecting to enroll full or part-time at a two-year or four-year institution or university; resident of Illinois and studying in Illinois. Available to U.S. citizens. *Application Requirements:* Application, financial need analysis. *Deadline:* varies.

Contact: College Zone Counselor, Illinois Student Assistance Commission (ISAC), 1755 Lake Cook Road, Deerfield, IL 60015-5209.

E-mail: collegezone@isac.org. *Phone:* 800-899-4722. *Web site:* www.collegezone.org.

Illinois Veteran Grant Program—IVG. Award for qualified veterans for tuition and fees at Illinois public universities and community colleges. Must provide documentation of service (DD214). Deadline is continuous. *Award:* Grant for use in freshman, sophomore, junior, senior, or graduate year; renewable. *Award amount:* $1400–$1600. *Number of awards:* 11,000–13,000. *Eligibility Requirements:* Applicant must be enrolled or expecting to enroll full or part-time at a two-year or four-year institution or university; resident of Illinois and studying in Illinois. Available to U.S. citizens. Applicant must have general military experience. *Application Requirements:* Application, documentation of service. *Deadline:* continuous.

Contact: College Zone Counselor, Illinois Student Assistance Commission (ISAC), 1755 Lake Cook Road, Deerfield, IL 60015-5209. *E-mail:* collegezone@isac.org. *Phone:* 800-899-4722. *Web site:* www.collegezone.org.

Merit Recognition Scholarship (MRS) Program. Award for Illinois high school seniors graduating in the top 4% of their class and attending Illinois postsecondary institution or one of the nation's four approved Military Service Academies. Students scoring in the top 4% in one of the college entrance tests among Illinois residents are also eligible. Contact for application procedures. *Award:* Scholarship for use in freshman year; not renewable. *Award amount:* up to $1000. *Number of awards:* 5000–6000. *Eligibility Requirements:* Applicant must be high school student; planning to enroll or expecting to enroll full or part-time at a two-year or four-year institution or university; resident of Illinois and studying in Illinois. Applicant must have 3.5 GPA or higher. Available to U.S. citizens. *Application Requirements:* Application. *Deadline:* continuous.

Contact: College Zone Counselor, Illinois Student Assistance Commission (ISAC), 1755 Lake Cook Road, Deerfield, IL 60015-5209. *E-mail:* collegezone@isac.org. *Phone:* 800-899-4722. *Web site:* www.collegezone.org.

MIA/POW Scholarships. One-time award for spouse, child, or step-child of veterans who are missing in action or were a prisoner of war. Must be enrolled at a state-supported school in Illinois. Candidate must be U.S. citizen. Must apply and be accepted before beginning of school. Also for children and spouses of veterans who are determined to be 100% disabled as established by the Veterans Administration. *Award:* Scholarship for use in freshman, sophomore, junior,

senior, or graduate year; renewable. *Award amount:* varies. *Number of awards:* varies. *Eligibility Requirements:* Applicant must be enrolled or expecting to enroll full or part-time at a two-year or four-year institution or university; resident of Illinois and studying in Illinois. Available to U.S. citizens. Applicant or parent must meet one or more of the following requirements: general military experience; retired from active duty; disabled or killed as a result of military service; prisoner of war; or missing in action. *Application Requirements:* Application. *Deadline:* continuous.

Contact: Ms. Tracy Mahan, Grants Section, Illinois Department of Veterans' Affairs, 833 South Spring Street, Springfield, IL 62794-9432. *Phone:* 217-782-3564. *Fax:* 217-782-4161. *Web site:* www.state.il.us/agency/dva.

Minority Teachers of Illinois Scholarship Program. Award for minority students planning to teach at an approved Illinois preschool, elementary, or secondary school. Deadline: March 1. Must be Illinois resident. *Academic Fields/Career Goals:* Education; Special Education. *Award:* Forgivable loan for use in freshman, sophomore, junior, senior, graduate, or postgraduate years; renewable. *Award amount:* up to $5000. *Number of awards:* 450–550. *Eligibility Requirements:* Applicant must be American Indian/Alaska Native, Asian/Pacific Islander, Black (non-Hispanic), or Hispanic; enrolled or expecting to enroll full or part-time at a two-year or four-year institution or university; resident of Illinois and studying in Illinois. Applicant must have 2.5 GPA or higher. Available to U.S. citizens. *Application Requirements:* Application. *Deadline:* March 1.

Contact: College Zone Counselor, Illinois Student Assistance Commission (ISAC), 1755 Lake Cook Road, Deerfield, IL 60015-5209. *E-mail:* collegezone@isac.org. *Phone:* 800-899-4722. *Web site:* www.collegezone.org.

Veterans' Children Educational Opportunities. Award is provided to each child age 18 or younger of a veteran who died or became totally disabled as a result of service during World War I, World War II, Korean, or Vietnam War. Must be an Illinois resident and studying in Illinois. Death must be service-connected. Disability must be rated 100% for two or more years. *Award:* Grant for use in freshman year; not renewable. *Award amount:* up to $250. *Number of awards:* varies. *Eligibility Requirements:* Applicant must be age 10-18; enrolled or expecting to enroll at an institution or university; resident of Illinois and studying in Illinois. Available to U.S. citizens. Applicant or parent must meet one or more of the following requirements: general military experience; retired from active duty; disabled or killed as a result of military service; prisoner of war; or missing in action. *Application Requirements:* Application. *Deadline:* June 30.

Contact: Ms. Tracy Mahan, Grants Section, Illinois Department of Veterans' Affairs, 833 South Spring Street, Springfield, IL 62794-9432. *Phone:* 217-782-3564. *Fax:* 217-782-4161. *Web site:* www.state.il.us/agency/dva.

INDIANA

Charles A. Holt Indiana Wildlife Federation Endowment Scholarship. A $1000 scholarship will be awarded to an Indiana resident accepted for the study or already enrolled for the study of resource conservation or environmental education at the undergraduate level. For more details see Web site: http://www.indianawildlife.org. *Academic Fields/Career Goals:* Natural Resources. *Award:* Scholarship for use in sophomore, junior, or senior year; not renewable. *Award amount:* $1000. *Number of awards:* 1. *Eligibility Requirements:* Applicant must be enrolled or expecting to enroll full-time at a four-year institution or university; resident of Indiana and studying in Indiana. Available to U.S. citizens. *Application Requirements:* Application. *Deadline:* April 30.

Contact: Application available at Web site., Indiana Wildlife Federation Endowment. *Web site:* indianawildlife.org.

Child of Disabled Veteran Grant or Purple Heart Recipient Grant. Free tuition at Indiana state-supported colleges or universities for children of disabled veterans or Purple Heart recipients. Must submit Form DD214 or service record. *Award:* Grant for use in freshman, sophomore, junior, senior, graduate, or postgraduate years; renewable. *Award amount:* varies. *Number of awards:* varies. *Eligibility Requirements:* Applicant must be enrolled or expecting to enroll full or part-time at a two-year or four-year institution or university; resident of Indiana and studying in Indiana. Available to U.S. citizens. Applicant or parent must meet one or more of the following requirements: general military experience; retired from active duty; disabled or killed as a result of military service; prisoner of war; or missing in action. *Application Requirements:* Application. *Deadline:* continuous.

Contact: Jon Brinkley, State Service Officer, Indiana Department of Veterans' Affairs, 302 West Washington Street, Room E-120, Indianapolis, IN 46204-2738. *E-mail:*

jbrinkley@dva.state.in.us. *Phone:* 317-232-3910. *Fax:* 317-232-7721. *Web site:* www.ai.org/veteran/index.html.

Culture Connection Foundation Scholarship. Scholarships available for students in single parent families. May be used for undergraduate or graduate study. Those interested in foreign languages, culture, and ethnic studies are encouraged to apply. Application deadline is August 1. *Academic Fields/Career Goals:* African Studies; Anthropology; Area/Ethnic Studies; Art History; Asian Studies; Education; European Studies; Foreign Language; International Studies; Law/Legal Services. *Award:* Scholarship for use in freshman, sophomore, junior, senior, or graduate year; renewable. *Award amount:* $4700. *Number of awards:* 1000. *Eligibility Requirements:* Applicant must be enrolled or expecting to enroll full or part-time at a two-year, four-year, or technical institution or university and single. Applicant must have 2.5 GPA or higher. Available to U.S. and non-U.S. citizens. *Application Requirements:* Application, essay, financial need analysis, interview, references, self-addressed stamped envelope, test scores, transcript, birth certificate, divorce decree. *Deadline:* August 1.

Contact: Anna Leis, National Program Director, Culture Connection, 8888 Keystone Crossing, Suite 1300, Indianapolis, IN 46240. *E-mail:* annaleis@thecultureconnection.com. *Phone:* 317-547-7055. *Fax:* 317-547-7083. *Web site:* www.thecultureconnection.com.

Department of Veterans Affairs Free Tuition for Children of POW/MIA's in Vietnam. Renewable award for residents of Indiana who are the children of veterans declared missing in action or prisoner-of-war after January 1, 1960. Provides tuition at Indiana state-supported institutions for undergraduate study. *Award:* Grant for use in freshman, sophomore, junior, senior, graduate, or postgraduate years; renewable. *Award amount:* varies. *Number of awards:* varies. *Eligibility Requirements:* Applicant must be enrolled or expecting to enroll at a two-year or four-year institution or university; resident of Indiana and studying in Indiana. Available to U.S. citizens. Applicant or parent must meet one or more of the following requirements: general military experience; retired from active duty; disabled or killed as a result of military service; prisoner of war; or missing in action. *Application Requirements:* Application. *Deadline:* continuous.

Contact: Jon Brinkley, State Service Officer, Indiana Department of Veterans' Affairs, 302 West Washington Street, Room E-120, Indianapolis, IN 46204-2738. *E-mail:* jbrinkley@dva.state.in.us. *Phone:* 317-232-

3910. *Fax:* 317-232-7721. *Web site:* www.ai.org/veteran/index.html.

Hoosier Scholar Award. The Hoosier Scholar Award is a $500 nonrenewable award. Based on the size of the senior class, one to three scholars are selected by the guidance counselor(s) of each accredited high school in Indiana. The award is based on academic merit and may be used for any educational expense at an eligible Indiana institution of higher education. *Award:* Scholarship for use in freshman year; not renewable. *Award amount:* $500. *Number of awards:* 790–840. *Eligibility Requirements:* Applicant must be high school student; planning to enroll or expecting to enroll full-time at a two-year or four-year institution or university; resident of Indiana and studying in Indiana. Applicant must have 3.5 GPA or higher. Available to U.S. citizens. *Application Requirements:* References. *Deadline:* March 10.

Contact: Ms. Ada Sparkman, Program Coordinator, State Student Assistance Commission of Indiana (SSACI), 150 West Market Street, Suite 500, Indianapolis, IN 46204-2805. *Phone:* 317-232-2350. *Fax:* 317-232-3260. *Web site:* www.ssaci.in.gov.

Indiana Freedom of Choice Grant. The Freedom of Choice Grant is a need-based, tuition-restricted program for students attending Indiana private institutions seeking a first undergraduate degree. It is awarded in addition to the Higher Education Award. Students (and parents of dependent students) who are U.S. citizens and Indiana residents must file the FAFSA yearly by the March 10 deadline. *Award:* Grant for use in freshman, sophomore, junior, or senior year; not renewable. *Award amount:* $200–$5915. *Number of awards:* 10,000–11,830. *Eligibility Requirements:* Applicant must be enrolled or expecting to enroll full-time at a four-year institution or university; resident of Indiana and studying in Indiana. Available to U.S. citizens. *Application Requirements:* Application, financial need analysis, FAFSA. *Deadline:* March 10.

Contact: Grants Counselor, State Student Assistance Commission of Indiana (SSACI), 150 West Market Street, Suite 500, Indianapolis, IN 46204-2805. *E-mail:* grants@ssaci.state.in.us. *Phone:* 317-232-2350. *Fax:* 317-232-3260. *Web site:* www.ssaci.in.gov.

Indiana Higher Education Award. The Higher Education Award is a need-based, tuition-restricted program for students attending Indiana public, private, or proprietary institutions seeking a first undergraduate degree. Students (and parents of dependent students) who are U.S. citizens and Indiana residents must file the FAFSA yearly by the March 10 deadline. *Award:* Grant for use in freshman, sophomore, junior, or senior year; not renewable. *Award amount:* $200–$4700. *Number of awards:* 38,000–43,660. *Eligibility Requirements:* Applicant must be enrolled or expecting to enroll full-time at a two-year, four-year, or technical institution or university; resident of Indiana and studying in Indiana. Available to U.S. citizens. *Application Requirements:* Application, financial need analysis, FAFSA. *Deadline:* March 10.

Contact: Grants Counselor, State Student Assistance Commission of Indiana (SSACI), 150 West Market Street, Suite 500, Indianapolis, IN 46204-2805. *E-mail:* grants@ssaci.state. in.us. *Phone:* 317-232-2350. *Fax:* 317-232-3260. *Web site:* www.ssaci.in.gov.

Indiana Minority Teacher and Special Education Services Scholarship Program. For Black or Hispanic students seeking teaching certification or for students seeking special education teaching certification or occupational or physical therapy certification. Must be a U.S. citizen and Indiana resident enrolled full-time in an eligible Indiana institution. Must teach in an Indiana-accredited elementary or secondary school after graduation. Contact institution for application and deadline. Minimum 2.0 GPA required. *Academic Fields/Career Goals:* Education; Special Education; Therapy/Rehabilitation. *Award:* Scholarship for use in freshman, sophomore, junior, or senior year; not renewable. *Award amount:* $1000–$4000. *Number of awards:* 280–370. *Eligibility Requirements:* Applicant must be Black (non-Hispanic) or Hispanic; enrolled or expecting to enroll full-time at a four-year institution or university; resident of Indiana and studying in Indiana. Available to U.S. citizens. *Application Requirements:* Application, financial need analysis. *Deadline:* continuous.

Contact: Ms. Yvonne Heflin, Director, Special Programs, State Student Assistance Commission of Indiana (SSACI), 150 West Market Street, Suite 500, Indianapolis, IN 46204-2805. *E-mail:* grants@ssaci.state.in. us. *Phone:* 317-232-2350. *Fax:* 317-232-3260. *Web site:* www.ssaci.in.gov.

Indiana National Guard Supplemental Grant. The award is a supplement to the Indiana Higher Education Grant program. Applicants must be members of the Indiana National Guard. All Guard paperwork must be completed prior to the start of each semester. The FAFSA must be received by March 10. Award covers certain tuition and fees at select public colleges. *Award:* Grant for use in freshman, sophomore, junior, or senior year; not renewable. *Award amount:* $200–$6516. *Number of awards:* 503–925.

Eligibility Requirements: Applicant must be enrolled or expecting to enroll full or part-time at a two-year or four-year institution or university; resident of Indiana and studying in Indiana. Available to U.S. citizens. Applicant must have served in the Air Force National Guard or Army National Guard. *Application Requirements:* Application. *Deadline:* March 10.

Contact: Grants Counselor, State Student Assistance Commission of Indiana (SSACI), 150 West Market Street, Suite 500, Indianapolis, IN 46204-2805. *E-mail:* grants@ssaci.state. in.us. *Phone:* 317-232-2350. *Fax:* 317-232-2360. *Web site:* www.ssaci.in.gov.

Indiana Nursing Scholarship Fund. Need-based tuition funding for nursing students enrolled full- or part-time at an eligible Indiana institution. Must be a U.S. citizen and an Indiana resident and have a minimum 2.0 GPA or meet the minimum requirements for the nursing program. Upon graduation, recipients must practice as a nurse in an Indiana health care setting for two years. *Academic Fields/Career Goals:* Nursing. *Award:* Scholarship for use in freshman, sophomore, junior, or senior year; not renewable. *Award amount:* $200–$5000. *Number of awards:* 490–690. *Eligibility Requirements:* Applicant must be enrolled or expecting to enroll full or part-time at a two-year or four-year institution or university; resident of Indiana and studying in Indiana. Available to U.S. citizens. *Application Requirements:* Application, financial need analysis. *Deadline:* continuous.

Contact: Ms. Yvonne Heflin, Director, Special Programs, State Student Assistance Commission of Indiana (SSACI), 150 West Market Street, Suite 500, Indianapolis, IN 46204-2805. *Phone:* 317-232-2350. *Fax:* 317-232-3260. *Web site:* www.ssaci.in.gov.

Part-time Grant Program. Program is designed to encourage part-time undergraduates to start and complete their associate or baccalaureate degrees or certificates by subsidizing part-time tuition costs. It is a term-based award that is based on need. State residency requirements must be met and a FAFSA must be filed. Eligibility is determined at the institutional level subject to approval by SSACI. *Award:* Grant for use in freshman, sophomore, junior, or senior year; not renewable. *Award amount:* $50–$4000. *Number of awards:* 4680–6700. *Eligibility Requirements:* Applicant must be enrolled or expecting to enroll part-time at a two-year, four-year, or technical institution or university; resident of Indiana and studying in Indiana. Available to U.S. citizens. *Application Requirements:* Application, financial need analysis. *Deadline:* continuous.

Contact: Grants Counselor, State Student Assistance Commission of Indiana (SSACI), 150 West Market Street, Suite 500, Indianapolis, IN 46204-2805. *E-mail:* grants@ssaci.state. in.us. *Phone:* 317-232-2350. *Fax:* 317-232-3260. *Web site:* www.ssaci.in.gov.

Twenty-first Century Scholars Award. Income-eligible 7th graders who enroll in the program, fulfill a pledge of good citizenship, and complete the Affirmation Form are guaranteed tuition for four years at any participating public institution. If the student attends a private institution, the state will award an amount comparable to that of a public institution. If the student attends a participating proprietary school, the state will award a tuition scholarship equal to that of Ivy Tech State College. FAFSA and affirmation form must be filed yearly by March 10. Applicant must be resident of Indiana. *Award:* Scholarship for use in freshman, sophomore, junior, or senior year; not renewable. *Award amount:* $1000–$6516. *Number of awards:* 2800–8100. *Eligibility Requirements:* Applicant must be enrolled or expecting to enroll full-time at a two-year, four-year, or technical institution or university; resident of Indiana and studying in Indiana. Applicant must have 2.5 GPA or higher. Available to U.S. citizens. *Application Requirements:* Application, financial need analysis, affirmation form. *Deadline:* March 10.

Contact: Twenty-first Century Scholars Program Counselors, State Student Assistance Commission of Indiana (SSACI), 150 West Market Street, Suite 500, Indianapolis, IN 46204-2805. *Phone:* 317-233-2100. *Fax:* 317-232-3260. *Web site:* www.ssaci.in.gov.

IOWA

Governor Terry E. Branstad Iowa State Fair Scholarship. Up to four scholarships ranging from $500 to $1000 will be awarded to students graduating from an Iowa high school. Must actively participate at the Iowa State Fair. For more details see Web site: http://www.iowacollegeaid.org. *Award:* Scholarship for use in freshman year; not renewable. *Award amount:* $500–$1000. *Number of awards:* up to 4. *Eligibility Requirements:* Applicant must be high school student; planning to enroll or expecting to enroll at an institution or university; resident of Iowa and studying in Iowa. Available to U.S. citizens. *Application Requirements:* Application, essay, financial need analysis, references, transcript. *Deadline:* May 1.

Contact: Brenda Easter, Director, Special Programs, Iowa College Student Aid Commission, 200 10th Street, 4th Floor, Des

Moines, IA 50309-3609. *Phone:* 515-242-3380. *Fax:* 515-242-3388. *Web site:* www.iowacollegeaid.org.

Iowa Foster Child Grants. Grants renewable up to four years will be awarded to students graduating from an Iowa high school who are in Iowa foster care under the care and custody of the Iowa Department of Human Service. Must have a minimum GPA of 2.25 and have applied to an accredited Iowa college or university. For more details see Web site: http://www.iowacollegeaid.org. *Award:* Grant for use in freshman year; renewable. *Award amount:* $2000–$4200. *Number of awards:* varies. *Eligibility Requirements:* Applicant must be high school student; planning to enroll or expecting to enroll at a two-year or four-year institution or university; resident of Iowa and studying in Iowa. Available to U.S. citizens. *Application Requirements:* Application. *Deadline:* April 15.

Contact: Brenda Easter, Director, Special Programs, Iowa College Student Aid Commission, 200 10th Street, 4th Floor, Des Moines, IA 50309-3609. *Phone:* 515-242-3380. *Fax:* 515-242-3388. *Web site:* www.iowacollegeaid.org.

Iowa Grants. Statewide need-based program to assist high-need Iowa residents. Recipients must demonstrate a high level of financial need to receive awards ranging from $100 to $1,000. Awards are prorated for students enrolled for less than full-time. Awards must be used at Iowa postsecondary institutions. *Award:* Grant for use in freshman, sophomore, junior, or senior year; not renewable. *Award amount:* $100–$1000. *Number of awards:* varies. *Eligibility Requirements:* Applicant must be enrolled or expecting to enroll full or part-time at a two-year, four-year, or technical institution or university; resident of Iowa and studying in Iowa. Available to U.S. citizens. *Application Requirements:* Application, financial need analysis. *Deadline:* continuous.

Contact: Julie Leeper, Director, State Student Aid Programs, Iowa College Student Aid Commission, 200 10th Street, 4th Floor, Des Moines, IA 50309-3609. *E-mail:* icsac@max.state.ia.us. *Phone:* 515-242-3370. *Fax:* 515-242-3388. *Web site:* www.iowacollegeaid.org.

Iowa National Guard Education Assistance Program. Program provides postsecondary tuition assistance to members of Iowa National Guard Units. Must study at a postsecondary institution in Iowa. Contact for additional information. *Award:* Grant for use in freshman, sophomore, junior, or senior year; not renewable. *Award amount:* up to $1200. *Number of awards:* varies.

Eligibility Requirements: Applicant must be enrolled or expecting to enroll full or part-time at a two-year, four-year, or technical institution or university; resident of Iowa and studying in Iowa. Available to U.S. citizens. Applicant must have served in the Air Force National Guard or Army National Guard. *Application Requirements:* Application. *Deadline:* continuous.

Contact: Julie Leeper, Director, State Student Aid Programs, Iowa College Student Aid Commission, 200 10th Street, 4th Floor, Des Moines, IA 50309-3609. *E-mail:* icsac@max.state.ia.us. *Phone:* 515-242-3370. *Fax:* 515-242-3388. *Web site:* www.iowacollegeaid.org.

Iowa Teacher Forgivable Loan Program. Forgivable loan assists students who will teach in Iowa secondary schools. Must be an Iowa resident attending an Iowa postsecondary institution. Contact for additional information. *Academic Fields/Career Goals:* Education. *Award:* Forgivable loan for use in freshman, sophomore, junior, or senior year; not renewable. *Award amount:* $2686. *Number of awards:* varies. *Eligibility Requirements:* Applicant must be enrolled or expecting to enroll full or part-time at a four-year institution or university; resident of Iowa and studying in Iowa. Applicant or parent of applicant must have employment or volunteer experience in teaching. Available to U.S. citizens. *Application Requirements:* Application, financial need analysis. *Deadline:* continuous.

Contact: Brenda Easter, Special Programs Administrator, Iowa College Student Aid Commission, 200 10th Street, 4th Floor, Des Moines, IA 50309-3609. *E-mail:* icsac@max.state.ia.us. *Phone:* 515-242-3380. *Fax:* 515-242-3388. *Web site:* www.iowacollegeaid.org.

Iowa Tuition Grant Program. Program assists students who attend independent postsecondary institutions in Iowa. Iowa residents currently enrolled, or planning to enroll, for at least three semester hours at one of the eligible Iowa postsecondary institutions may apply. Awards currently range from $100 to $4000. Grants may not exceed the difference between independent college and university tuition and fees and the average tuition and fees at the three public Regent universities. *Award:* Grant for use in freshman, sophomore, junior, or senior year; not renewable. *Award amount:* $100–$4000. *Number of awards:* varies. *Eligibility Requirements:* Applicant must be enrolled or expecting to enroll full or part-time at a two-year or four-year institution; resident of Iowa and studying in Iowa. Available to U.S. citizens. *Application*

Requirements: Application, financial need analysis. *Deadline:* July 1.

Contact: Julie Leeper, Director, State Student Aid Programs, Iowa College Student Aid Commission, 200 10th Street, 4th Floor, Des Moines, IA 50309-3609. *E-mail:* icsac@max.state.ia.us. *Phone:* 515-242-3370. *Fax:* 515-242-3388. *Web site:* www.iowacollegeaid.org.

Iowa Vocational Rehabilitation. Provides vocational rehabilitation services to individuals with disabilities who need these services in order to maintain, retain, or obtain employment compatible with their disabilities. Must be Iowa resident. *Award:* Grant for use in freshman, sophomore, junior, senior, graduate, or postgraduate years; renewable. *Award amount:* $500–$4000. *Number of awards:* up to 5000. *Eligibility Requirements:* Applicant must be enrolled or expecting to enroll full or part-time at a two-year, four-year, or technical institution or university and resident of Iowa. Applicant must be hearing impaired, learning disabled, physically disabled, or visually impaired. Available to U.S. and non-U.S. citizens. *Application Requirements:* Application, interview. *Deadline:* continuous.

Contact: Ralph Childers, Policy and Workforce Initiatives Coordinator, Iowa Division of Vocational Rehabilitation Services, Division of Vocational Rehabilitation Services, 510 East 12th Street, Des Moines, IA 50319. *E-mail:* rchilders@dvrs.state.ia.us. *Phone:* 515-281-4151. *Fax:* 515-281-4703. *Web site:* www.dvrs.state.ia.us.

Iowa Vocational-Technical Tuition Grant Program. Program provides need-based financial assistance to Iowa residents enrolled in career education (vocational-technical), and career option programs at Iowa area community colleges. Grants range from $150 to $650, depending on the length of program, financial need, and available funds. *Award:* Grant for use in freshman or sophomore year; not renewable. *Award amount:* $150–$650. *Number of awards:* varies. *Eligibility Requirements:* Applicant must be enrolled or expecting to enroll full or part-time at a technical institution; resident of Iowa and studying in Iowa. Available to U.S. citizens. *Application Requirements:* Application, financial need analysis. *Deadline:* July 1.

Contact: Julie Leeper, Director, State Student Aid Programs, Iowa College Student Aid Commission, 200 10th Street, 4th Floor, Des Moines, IA 50309-3609. *E-mail:* icsac@max.state.ia.us. *Phone:* 515-242-3370. *Fax:* 515-242-3388. *Web site:* www.iowacollegeaid.org.

State of Iowa Scholarship Program. Program provides recognition and financial honorarium to Iowa's academically talented high school seniors. Honorary scholarships are presented to all qualified candidates. Approximately 1700 top-ranking candidates are designated State of Iowa Scholars every March, from an applicant pool of nearly 5000 high school seniors. Must be used at an Iowa postsecondary institution. Minimum 3.5 GPA required. *Award:* Scholarship for use in freshman year; not renewable. *Award amount:* up to $400. *Number of awards:* up to 1700. *Eligibility Requirements:* Applicant must be high school student; planning to enroll or expecting to enroll full-time at a two-year, four-year, or technical institution or university; resident of Iowa and studying in Iowa. Applicant must have 3.5 GPA or higher. Available to U.S. citizens. *Application Requirements:* Application, test scores. *Deadline:* November 1.

Contact: Julie Leeper, Director, State Student Aid Programs, Iowa College Student Aid Commission, 200 10th Street, 4th Floor, Des Moines, IA 50309-3609. *E-mail:* icsac@max.state.ia.us. *Phone:* 515-242-3370. *Fax:* 515-242-3388. *Web site:* www.iowacollegeaid.org.

KANSAS

Kansas Educational Benefits for Children of MIA, POW, and Deceased Veterans of the Vietnam War. Full-tuition scholarship awarded to students who are children of veterans. Must show proof of parent's status as missing in action, prisoner of war, or killed in action in the Vietnam War. Kansas residence required of veteran at time of entry to service. Must attend a state-supported postsecondary school. *Award:* Scholarship for use in freshman, sophomore, junior, or senior year; not renewable. *Eligibility Requirements:* Applicant must be enrolled or expecting to enroll at a two-year, four-year, or technical institution or university and studying in Kansas. Available to U.S. citizens. Applicant or parent must meet one or more of the following requirements: general military experience; retired from active duty; disabled or killed as a result of military service; prisoner of war; or missing in action. *Application Requirements:* Application, report of casualty, birth certificate, school acceptance letter. *Deadline:* continuous.

Contact: Tony Floyd, Program Director, Kansas Commission on Veterans Affairs, 700 Southwest Jackson, Jayhawk Tower, #701, Topeka, KS 66603. *E-mail:* kcva004@ink.org. *Phone:* 785-291-3422. *Fax:* 785-296-1462. *Web site:* www.kcva.org.

Kansas National Guard Educational Assistance Award Program. Service scholarship for enlisted soldiers in the Kansas National Guard. Pays up to 100% of tuition and fees based on funding. Must attend a state-supported institution. Recipients will be required to serve in the KNG for three months for every semester of benefits after the last payment of state tuition assistance. Must not have over 15 years of service at time of application. Deadlines are January 15 and August 20. Contact KNG Education Services Specialist for further information. Must be Kansas resident. *Award:* Scholarship for use in freshman, sophomore, junior, or senior year; not renewable. *Award amount:* $250–$3500. *Number of awards:* up to 400. *Eligibility Requirements:* Applicant must be enrolled or expecting to enroll full or part-time at a two-year, four-year, or technical institution or university; resident of Kansas and studying in Kansas. Available to U.S. citizens. Applicant must have served in the Air Force National Guard or Army National Guard. *Application Requirements:* Application. *Deadline:* varies.

Contact: Steve Finch, Education Services Specialist, Kansas National Guard Educational Assistance Program, Attn: AGKS-DOP-ESO, The Adjutant General of Kansas, 2800 South West Topeka Boulevard, Topeka, KS 66611-1287. *E-mail:* steve.finch@ks.ngb.army.mil. *Phone:* 785-274-1060. *Fax:* 785-274-1609.

KENTUCKY

College Access Program (CAP) Grant. Award for U.S. citizen and Kentucky resident with no previous college degree. Provides $58 per semester hour for a minimum of six hours per semester. Applicants seeking degrees in religion are not eligible. Must demonstrate financial need and submit Free Application for Federal Student Aid. Priority deadline is March 15. *Award:* Grant for use in freshman, sophomore, junior, or senior year; not renewable. *Award amount:* up to $1400. *Number of awards:* 35,000–40,000. *Eligibility Requirements:* Applicant must be enrolled or expecting to enroll full or part-time at a two-year, four-year, or technical institution or university; resident of Kentucky and studying in Kentucky. Available to U.S. citizens. *Application Requirements:* Financial need analysis. *Deadline:* continuous.

Contact: Michael D. Morgan, Program Coordinator, Kentucky Higher Education Assistance Authority (KHEAA), PO Box 798, Frankfort, KY 40602-0798. *E-mail:* mmorgan@kheaa.com. *Phone:* 502-696-7394. *Fax:* 502-696-7373. *Web site:* www.kheaa.com.

Early Childhood Development Scholarship. Scholarship with conditional service commitment for part-time students currently employed by participating ECD facility or providing training in ECD for an approved organization. *Academic Fields/Career Goals:* Child and Family Studies; Education. *Award:* Scholarship for use in freshman, sophomore, junior, or senior year; not renewable. *Award amount:* up to $1400. *Number of awards:* 900–1000. *Eligibility Requirements:* Applicant must be enrolled or expecting to enroll part-time at a four-year institution or university; resident of Kentucky and studying in Kentucky. Available to U.S. citizens. *Application Requirements:* Application, resume. *Deadline:* continuous.

Contact: Early Childhood Development Authority, Kentucky Higher Education Assistance Authority (KHEAA), 275 East Main Street, 2W-E, Frankfort, KY 40621. *Phone:* 502-564-8099. *Web site:* www.kheaa.com.

Environmental Protection Scholarships. Renewable awards for college juniors, seniors, and graduate students for tuition, fees, and room and board at a Kentucky state university. Awards of $4000 to $5000 per semester for up to four semesters. Minimum 2.5 GPA required. Must agree to work full-time for the Kentucky Natural Resources and Environmental Protection Cabinet upon graduation. Interview is required. *Academic Fields/Career Goals:* Chemical Engineering; Civil Engineering; Earth Science; Materials Science, Engineering, and Metallurgy. *Award:* Forgivable loan for use in junior, senior, or graduate year; renewable. *Award amount:* $4000–$5000. *Number of awards:* 3–5. *Eligibility Requirements:* Applicant must be enrolled or expecting to enroll full-time at a four-year institution or university and studying in Kentucky. Applicant must have 2.5 GPA or higher. Available to U.S. and non-U.S. citizens. *Application Requirements:* Application, essay, interview, references, transcript, non-U.S. citizens must have valid work permit. *Deadline:* February 15.

Contact: James Kipp, Scholarship Program Coordinator, Kentucky Natural Resources and Environmental Protection Cabinet, 233 Mining/Mineral Resources Building, Lexington, KY 40506-0107. *E-mail:* kipp@uky.edu. *Phone:* 859-257-1299. *Fax:* 859-323-1049. *Web site:* www.uky.edu/waterresources.

Kentucky Department of Vocational Rehabilitation. Kentucky Department of Vocational Rehabilitation provides services necessary to secure employment. Eligible individual must possess physical or mental impairment that results in a substantial impediment to employment; benefit from vocational rehabilitation services in terms of an employment outcome; and require vocational rehabilitation services to prepare for, enter, or retain employment. *Award:* Grant for use in freshman, sophomore, junior, senior, graduate, or postgraduate years; renewable. *Award amount:* varies. *Number of awards:* varies. *Eligibility Requirements:* Applicant must be enrolled or expecting to enroll full or part-time at a two-year, four-year, or technical institution or university and resident of Kentucky. Applicant must be learning disabled or physically disabled. Available to U.S. citizens. *Application Requirements:* Application, financial need analysis, interview, test scores, transcript. *Deadline:* continuous.

Contact: Ms. Marian Spencer, Program Administrator, Kentucky Department of Vocational Rehabilitation, 209 St. Clair Street, Frankfort, KY 40601. *E-mail:* marianu. spencer@mail.state.ky.us. *Phone:* 502-564-4440. *Fax:* 502-564-6745. *Web site:* www. ihdi.uky.edu/.

Kentucky Educational Excellence Scholarship (KEES). Annual award based on GPA and highest ACT or SAT score received by high school graduation. Awards are renewable if required cumulative GPA maintained at a Kentucky postsecondary school. Must be a Kentucky resident, and a graduate of a Kentucky high school. *Award:* Scholarship for use in freshman, sophomore, junior, or senior year; renewable. *Award amount:* $125–$2500. *Number of awards:* 55,000–60,000. *Eligibility Requirements:* Applicant must be high school student; planning to enroll or expecting to enroll full or part-time at a two-year, four-year, or technical institution or university; resident of Kentucky and studying in Kentucky. Applicant must have 2.5 GPA or higher. Available to U.S. citizens. *Application Requirements:* Test scores, transcript. *Deadline:* continuous.

Contact: Tim Phelps, Student Aid Branch Manager, Kentucky Higher Education Assistance Authority (KHEAA), PO Box 798, Frankfort, KY 40602-0798. *E-mail:* tphelps@ kheaa.com. *Phone:* 502-696-7393. *Fax:* 502-696-7373. *Web site:* www.kheaa.com.

Kentucky Minority Educator Recruitment and Retention (KMERR) Scholarship. Scholarship for minority teacher candidates who rank in the upper half of their class or have a minimum 2.5 GPA. Must be a U.S. citizen and Kentucky resident enrolled in one of Kentucky's eight public institutions. Must teach one semester in Kentucky for each semester the scholarship is received. *Academic Fields/Career Goals:* Education. *Award:* Forgivable loan for use in freshman, sophomore, junior, or senior year; renewable. *Award amount:* $2500–$5000. *Number of awards:* 300.

Eligibility Requirements: Applicant must be American Indian/Alaska Native, Asian/Pacific Islander, Black (non-Hispanic), or Hispanic; enrolled or expecting to enroll full-time at a four-year institution or university; resident of Kentucky and studying in Kentucky. Applicant must have 2.5 GPA or higher. Available to U.S. citizens. *Application Requirements:* Application, essay, references, test scores, transcript. *Deadline:* continuous.

Contact: Robby Morton, Director, Kentucky Department of Education, 500 Mero Street, 17th Floor, Frankfort, KY 40601. *E-mail:* rmorton@kde.state.ky.us. *Phone:* 502-564-1479. *Fax:* 502-564-6952. *Web site:* www. kde.state.ky.us.

Kentucky National Guard Tuition Assistance Program. Members of Kentucky National Guard in good standing are eligible for awards equal to in-state tuition for full or part-time study at any Kentucky public postsecondary institution. *Award:* Grant for use in freshman, sophomore, junior, or senior year; not renewable. *Award amount:* varies. *Number of awards:* 800–1000. *Eligibility Requirements:* Applicant must be enrolled or expecting to enroll full or part-time at a two-year, four-year, or technical institution or university and studying in Kentucky. Available to U.S. citizens. Applicant must have served in the Air Force National Guard or Army National Guard. *Application Requirements:* Application. *Deadline:* continuous.

Contact: Kentucky National Guard, Kentucky Higher Education Assistance Authority (KHEAA), 100 Minuteman Parkway, Frankfort, KY 40601. *Phone:* 800-464-8273. *Web site:* www.kheaa.com.

Kentucky National Guard Tuition Award Program. Tuition award available to all members of the Kentucky National Guard. Award is for study at state institutions. Members must be in good standing to be eligible for awards. Applications deadlines are April 1 and October 1. Completed AGO-18-7 required. Undergraduate study given priority. *Award:* Scholarship for use in freshman, sophomore, junior, or senior year; not renewable. *Award amount:* varies. *Number of awards:* varies. *Eligibility Requirements:* Applicant must be enrolled or expecting to enroll full or part-time at a two-year, four-year, or technical institution or university and studying in Kentucky. Available to U.S. citizens. Applicant must have served in the Air Force National Guard or Army National Guard. *Application Requirements:* AGO-18-7. *Deadline:* varies.

Contact: Michelle Kelley, Administration Specialist, Kentucky National Guard, Education Office, 100 Minuteman Parkway, Frankfort,

KY 40601. *E-mail:* kelleyam@bng.dma.state. ky.us. *Phone:* 502-607-1039. *Fax:* 502-607-1264.

Kentucky Teacher Scholarship Program. Award for Kentucky resident attending Kentucky institutions and pursuing initial teacher certification. Must teach one semester for each semester of award received. In critical shortage areas, must teach one semester for every two semesters of award received. Repayment obligation if teaching requirement not met. Submit Free Application for Federal Student Aid and Teacher Scholarship Application by May 1. *Academic Fields/Career Goals:* Education. *Award:* Forgivable loan for use in freshman, sophomore, junior, senior, or graduate year; renewable. *Award amount:* $250–$5000. *Number of awards:* 600–700. *Eligibility Requirements:* Applicant must be enrolled or expecting to enroll full-time at a two-year or four-year institution or university; resident of Kentucky and studying in Kentucky. Available to U.S. citizens. *Application Requirements:* Application, financial need analysis. *Deadline:* May 1.

Contact: Tim Phelps, Student Aid Branch Manager, Kentucky Higher Education Assistance Authority (KHEAA), PO Box 798, Frankfort, KY 40602-0798. *E-mail:* tphelps@ kheaa.com. *Phone:* 502-696-7393. *Fax:* 502-696-7373. *Web site:* www.kheaa.com.

Kentucky Transportation Cabinet Civil Engineering Scholarship Program. Scholarships are available to eligible applicants at 4 universities in Kentucky. Our mission is to continually pursue statewide recruitment and retention of bright, motivated civil engineers in the Kentucky Transportation Cabinet. *Academic Fields/Career Goals:* Civil Engineering. *Award:* Scholarship for use in freshman, sophomore, junior, senior, or graduate year; renewable. *Award amount:* $7200–$8000. *Number of awards:* 10–20. *Eligibility Requirements:* Applicant must be enrolled or expecting to enroll full-time at an institution or university; resident of Kentucky and studying in Kentucky. Available to U.S. and non-U.S. citizens. *Application Requirements:* Application, essay, interview, references, test scores, transcript. *Deadline:* March 1.

Contact: Jo Anne Tingle, Scholarship Program Manager, Kentucky Transportation Cabinet, Attn: Scholarship Program Manager, SHE's Office, Suite E6-S1-00, 200 Metro Street, Frankfort, KY 40622. *E-mail:* jo.tingle@ ky.gov. *Phone:* 502-564-3730. *Fax:* 502-564-2277. *Web site:* www.transportation.ky.gov/.

Kentucky Tuition Grant (KTG). Available to Kentucky residents who are full-time undergraduates at an independent college within the state. Must not be enrolled in a religion program. Based on financial need. Submit Free Application for Federal Student Aid. Priority deadline is March 15. *Award:* Grant for use in freshman, sophomore, junior, or senior year; not renewable. *Award amount:* $200–$2400. *Number of awards:* 10,000–12,000. *Eligibility Requirements:* Applicant must be enrolled or expecting to enroll full-time at a two-year or four-year institution or university; resident of Kentucky and studying in Kentucky. Available to U.S. citizens. *Application Requirements:* Financial need analysis. *Deadline:* continuous.

Contact: Tim Phelps, Student Aid Branch Manager, Kentucky Higher Education Assistance Authority (KHEAA), PO Box 798, Frankfort, KY 40602-0798. *E-mail:* tphelps@kheaa.com. *Phone:* 502-696-7393. *Fax:* 502-696-7373. *Web site:* www.kheaa.com.

Minority Educator Recruitment and Retention Scholarship. Conversion loan/scholarship providing up to $5,000 per academic year to minority students majoring in teacher education pursuing initial teacher certification. Must be repaid with interest if scholarship requirements not met. *Academic Fields/Career Goals:* Education; Special Education. *Award:* Forgivable loan for use in freshman, sophomore, junior, senior, or graduate year; not renewable. *Award amount:* up to $5000. *Number of awards:* 200–300. *Eligibility Requirements:* Applicant must be American Indian/Alaska Native, Asian/Pacific Islander, Black (non-Hispanic), or Hispanic; enrolled or expecting to enroll full-time at a four-year institution or university; resident of Kentucky and studying in Kentucky. Applicant must have 2.5 GPA or higher. Available to U.S. citizens. *Application Requirements:* Application. *Deadline:* continuous.

Contact: Dr. Lucian Yates III, Director, MERR, KY Department of Education, Kentucky Higher Education Assistance Authority (KHEAA), 500 Metro Street, Frankfort, KY 40601. *Phone:* 502-564-1479. *Web site:* www.kheaa.com.

LOUISIANA

Leveraging Educational Assistance Program (LEAP). LEAP program provides federal and state funds to provide need-based grants to academically qualified students. Individual award determined by Financial Aid Office and governed by number of applicants and availability of funds. File FAFSA by school deadline to apply each year. For Louisiana students attending Louisiana postsecondary institutions. *Award:* Grant for use in freshman, sophomore, junior, or senior year; not renewable. *Award amount:* $200–$2000. *Number of awards:* 3000. *Eligibility Requirements:* Applicant must be enrolled or expecting to enroll full or part-time at a two-year, four-year, or technical institution or university; resident of Louisiana and studying in Louisiana. Available to U.S. citizens. *Application Requirements:* Application, financial need analysis. *Deadline:* varies.

Contact: Public Information, Louisiana Office of Student Financial Assistance, PO Box 91202, Baton Rouge, LA 70821-9202. *E-mail:* custserv@osfa.state.la.us. *Phone:* 800-259-5626 Ext. 1012. *Fax:* 225-922-0790. *Web site:* www.osfa.state.la.us.

Louisiana Department of Veterans Affairs State Aid Program. Tuition exemption at any state supported college, university, or technical institute for children (dependents between the ages of 18-25) of veterans that are rated 90% or above service connected disabled by the U.S. Department of Veterans Affairs. Tuition exemption also available for the surviving spouse and children (dependents between he ages of 18-25) of veterans who died on active duty, in line of duty, or where death was the result of a disability incurred in or aggravated by military service. For residents of Louisiana who are attending a Louisiana institution. *Award:* Grant for use in freshman, sophomore, junior, senior, graduate, or postgraduate years; renewable. *Award amount:* varies. *Number of awards:* varies. *Eligibility Requirements:* Applicant must be enrolled or expecting to enroll full-time at a two-year, four-year, or technical institution or university; resident of Louisiana and studying in Louisiana. Available to U.S. citizens. Applicant or parent must meet one or more of the following requirements: general military experience; retired from active duty; disabled or killed as a result of military service; prisoner of war; or missing in action. *Application Requirements:* Application. *Deadline:* continuous.

Contact: Richard Blackwell, Veterans Affairs Regional Manager, Louisiana Department of Veteran Affairs, PO Box 94095, Capitol Station, Baton Rouge, LA 70804-4095. *E-mail:* rblackwell@vetaffairs.com. *Phone:* 225-922-0500 Ext. 203. *Fax:* 225-922-0511. *Web site:* www.gov.state.la.us/depts/veteraaffairs.htm.

Louisiana National Guard State Tuition Exemption Program. Renewable award for college undergraduates to receive tuition exemption upon satisfactory performance in the Louisiana National Guard. Applicant must attend a state-funded institution in Louisiana, be a resident and registered voter in Louisiana, meet the academic and residency requirements of the university attended, and provide documentation of Louisiana National Guard enlistment. The exemption can be used for up to 15 semesters. Minimum 2.5 GPA required. *Award:* Scholarship for use in freshman, sophomore, junior, or senior year; renewable. *Award amount:* varies. *Number of awards:* varies. *Eligibility Requirements:* Applicant must be enrolled or expecting to enroll full or part-time at a two-year, four-year, or technical institution or university; resident of Louisiana and studying in Louisiana. Applicant must have 2.5 GPA or higher. Available to U.S. citizens. Applicant must have served in the Air Force National Guard or Army National Guard. *Application Requirements:* *Deadline:* continuous.

Contact: Maj. Jona M. Hughes, Education Services Officers, Louisiana National Guard—State of Louisiana, Joint Task Force LA, Building 35, Jackson Barracks, JI-PD, New Orleans, LA 70146-0330. *E-mail:* hughesj@la-arng.ngb.army.mil. *Phone:* 504-278-8531 Ext. 8304. *Fax:* 504-278-8025. *Web site:* www.la.ngb.army.mil.

Rockefeller State Wildlife Scholarship. For Louisiana residents attending a public college within the state studying wildlife, forestry, or marine sciences full-time. Renewable up to five years as an undergraduate and two years as a graduate. Must have at least a 2.5 GPA and have taken the ACT or SAT. *Academic Fields/Career Goals:* Animal/Veterinary Sciences; Applied Sciences; Marine Biology; Natural Resources. *Award:* Scholarship for use in freshman, sophomore, junior, senior, or graduate year; renewable. *Award amount:* $1000. *Number of awards:* 60. *Eligibility Requirements:* Applicant must be enrolled or expecting to enroll full-time at a four-year institution or university; resident of Louisiana and studying in Louisiana. Applicant must have 2.5 GPA or higher. Available to U.S. citizens. *Application Requirements:* Application, test scores, transcript. *Deadline:* July 1.

Contact: Public Information, Louisiana Office of Student Financial Assistance, PO Box 91202, Baton Rouge, LA 70821-9202. *E-mail:* custserv@osfa.state.la.us. *Phone:* 800-259-5626 Ext. 1012. *Fax:* 225-922-0790. *Web site:* www.osfa.state.la.us.

TOPS Alternate Performance Award. Program awards an amount equal to tuition plus a $400 annual stipend to students attending a Louisiana public institution, or an amount equal to the weighted average public tuition plus a $400 annual stipend to students attending a LAICU private institution. Must have a minimum high school GPA of 3.0 based on TOPS core curriculum, ACT score of 24, completion of 10 honors courses, and completion of a 16.5 unit core curriculum. Must be a resident of Louisiana. *Award:* Scholarship for use in freshman, sophomore, junior, or senior year; renewable. *Award amount:* varies. *Number of awards:* varies. *Eligibility Requirements:* Applicant must be high school student; planning to enroll or expecting to enroll full-time at a two-year, four-year, or technical institution or university; resident of Louisiana and studying in Louisiana. Applicant must have 3.0 GPA or higher. Available to U.S. citizens. *Application Requirements:* Application, test scores. *Deadline:* July 1.

Contact: Public Information Representative, Louisiana Office of Student Financial Assistance, PO Box 91202, Baton Rouge, LA 70821-9202. *E-mail:* custserv@osfa.state. la.us. *Phone:* 800-259-5626 Ext. 1012. *Fax:* 225-922-0790. *Web site:* www.osfa.state.la. us.

TOPS Honors Award. Program awards an amount equal to tuition plus an $800 per year stipend to students attending a Louisiana public institution, or an amount equal to the weighted average public tuition plus an $800 per year stipend to students attending a LAICU private institution. Must have a minimum high school GPA of 3.5 based on TOPS core curriculum, ACT score of 27, and complete a 16.5 unit core curriculum. Must be resident of Louisiana. *Award:* Scholarship for use in freshman, sophomore, junior, or senior year; renewable. *Award amount:* $1541–$3894. *Number of awards:* varies. *Eligibility Requirements:* Applicant must be high school student; planning to enroll or expecting to enroll full-time at a two-year, four-year, or technical institution or university; resident of Louisiana and studying in Louisiana. Applicant must have 3.5 GPA or higher. Available to U.S. citizens. *Application Requirements:* Application, test scores. *Deadline:* July 1.

Contact: Public Information, Louisiana Office of Student Financial Assistance, PO Box 91202, Baton Rouge, LA 70821-9202. *E-mail:* custserv@osfa.state.la.us. *Phone:* 800-259-5626 Ext. 1012. *Fax:* 225-922-0790. *Web site:* www.osfa.state.la.us.

TOPS Opportunity Award. Program awards an amount equal to tuition to students attending a Louisiana public institution, or an amount equal to the weighted average public tuition to students attending a LAICU private institution. Must have a minimum high school GPA of 2.5 based on the TOPS core curriculum, the prior year's state average ACT score, and complete a 16.5 unit core curriculum. Must be a Louisiana

resident. *Award:* Scholarship for use in freshman, sophomore, junior, or senior year; renewable. *Award amount:* $741–$3094. *Number of awards:* varies. *Eligibility Requirements:* Applicant must be high school student; planning to enroll or expecting to enroll full-time at a two-year, four-year, or technical institution or university; resident of Louisiana and studying in Louisiana. Applicant must have 2.5 GPA or higher. Available to U.S. citizens. *Application Requirements:* Application, test scores. *Deadline:* July 1.

Contact: Public Information, Louisiana Office of Student Financial Assistance, PO Box 91202, Baton Rouge, LA 70821-9202. *E-mail:* custserv@osfa.state.la.us. *Phone:* 800-259-5626 Ext. 1012. *Fax:* 225-922-0790. *Web site:* www.osfa.state.la.us.

TOPS Performance Award. Program awards an amount equal to tuition plus a $400 annual stipend to students attending a Louisiana public institution, or an amount equal to the weighted average public tuition plus a $400 annual stipend to students attending a LAICU private institution. Must have a minimum high school GPA of 3.5 based on the TOPS core curriculum, an ACT score of 23 and completion of a 16.5 unit core curriculum. Must be a Louisiana resident. *Award:* Scholarship for use in freshman, sophomore, junior, or senior year; renewable. *Award amount:* $1141–$3494. *Number of awards:* varies. *Eligibility Requirements:* Applicant must be high school student; planning to enroll or expecting to enroll full-time at a two-year, four-year, or technical institution or university; resident of Louisiana and studying in Louisiana. Applicant must have 3.5 GPA or higher. Available to U.S. citizens. *Application Requirements:* Application, test scores. *Deadline:* July 1.

Contact: Public Information, Louisiana Office of Student Financial Assistance, PO Box 91202, Baton Rouge, LA 70821-9202. *E-mail:* custserv@osfa.state.la.us. *Phone:* 800-259-5626 Ext. 1012. *Fax:* 225-922-0790. *Web site:* www.osfa.state.la.us.

TOPS Tech Award. Program awards an amount equal to tuition for up to two years of technical training at a Louisiana postsecondary institution that offers a vocational or technical education certificate or diploma program, or a non-academic degree program. Must have a 2.5 high school GPA based on TOPS Tech core curriculum, an ACT score of 17, and complete the TOPS-Tech core curriculum. Must be a Louisiana resident. *Award:* Scholarship for use in freshman or sophomore year; renewable. *Award amount:* $741–$1592. *Number of awards:* varies. *Eligibility Require-*

ments: Applicant must be high school student; planning to enroll or expecting to enroll full-time at a technical institution; resident of Louisiana and studying in Louisiana. Applicant must have 2.5 GPA or higher. Available to U.S. citizens. *Application Requirements:* Application, test scores. *Deadline:* July 1.

Contact: Public Information, Louisiana Office of Student Financial Assistance, PO Box 91202, Baton Rouge, LA 70821-9202. *E-mail:* custserv@osfa.state.la.us. *Phone:* 800-259-5626 Ext. 1012. *Fax:* 225-922-0790. *Web site:* www.osfa.state.la.us.

MAINE

Early College Program. For high school students who have not made plans for college but are academically capable of success in college. Recipients are selected by their school principal or director. Refer to Web site: http://www.mccs.me.edu/scholarships.html. Students must be entering a Maine Community College. *Award:* Scholarship for use in freshman year. *Award amount:* up to $2000. *Number of awards:* up to 200. *Eligibility Requirements:* Applicant must be high school student; planning to enroll or expecting to enroll at a two-year institution; resident of Maine and studying in Maine. *Application Requirements:* *Deadline:* varies.

Contact: Maine Community College Financial Aid Department., Maine Community College System. *Web site:* www.mccs.me. edu.

Educators for Maine Program. Loans for residents of Maine who are high school seniors, college students, or college graduates with a minimum 3.0 GPA, studying or preparing to study teacher education. Loan is forgivable if student teaches in Maine upon graduation. Awards are based on merit. *Academic Fields/Career Goals:* Education. *Award:* Forgivable loan for use in freshman, sophomore, junior, senior, or graduate year; not renewable. *Award amount:* $2000–$3000. *Number of awards:* varies. *Eligibility Requirements:* Applicant must be enrolled or expecting to enroll full-time at a two-year or four-year institution or university and resident of Maine. Applicant must have 3.0 GPA or higher. Available to U.S. citizens. *Application Requirements:* Application, essay, test scores, transcript. *Deadline:* April 1.

Contact: Trisha Malloy, Program Officer, Finance Authority of Maine, 5 Community Drive, Augusta, ME 04332-0949. *E-mail:* trisha@famemaine.com. *Phone:* 800-228-3734. *Fax:* 207-623-0095. *Web site:* www. famemaine.com.

George J. Mitchell Peace Scholarship.

An annual exchange and scholarship to Ireland for students from the Maine Community College System and the University of Maine System. Scholarship will provide opportunity for student to study at a university or institute of technology in Ireland. Refer to Web site for details: http://www.mccs.me.edu. *Award:* Scholarship for use in freshman, sophomore, junior, or senior year. *Award amount:* varies. *Number of awards:* varies. *Eligibility Requirements:* Applicant must be enrolled or expecting to enroll full-time at a two-year institution or university; resident of Maine and studying in Maine. *Application Requirements: Deadline:* February 15.

Contact: Maine Community College or University Financial Aid Department., Maine Community College System. *Web site:* www.mccs.me.edu.

Maine Community College Scholarship.

Participating high schools and technical centers/regions identify students to apply for the scholarship during their junior year. Students must be both nominated by their school and accepted into a Maine community college program of study. Award is $500 per semester, $1000 per year for a one-year program and a maximum of $2000 for a two-year program, so long as student meets program requirements. For details see Web site: http://www.ccd.me.edu/scholarship. *Award:* Scholarship for use in freshman or sophomore year; renewable. *Award amount:* $500–$2000. *Number of awards:* varies. *Eligibility Requirements:* Applicant must be high school student; planning to enroll or expecting to enroll at a two-year or technical institution; resident of Maine and studying in Maine. *Application Requirements: Deadline:* varies.

Contact: Dorry French, Maine Community College System, 2 Fort Road, South Portland, ME 04106. *E-mail:* dfrench@ccd.me.edu. *Phone:* 207-767-5210 Ext. 4117. *Web site:* www.mccs.me.edu.

Maine State Grant.

Scholarships for residents of Maine attending an eligible school, full time, in Connecticut, Maine, Massachusetts, New Hampshire, Pennsylvania, Rhode Island, Washington, D.C., or Vermont. Award based on need. Must apply annually. Complete Free Application for Federal Student Aid to apply. One-time award of $500-$1250 for undergraduate study. *Award:* Grant for use in freshman, sophomore, junior, or senior year; not renewable. *Award amount:* $500–$1250. *Number of awards:* 8900–12,500. *Eligibility Requirements:* Applicant must be enrolled or expecting to enroll full-time at a two-

year, four-year, or technical institution or university; resident of Maine and studying in Connecticut, District of Columbia, Maine, Massachusetts, New Hampshire, Pennsylvania, Rhode Island, or Vermont. *Application Requirements:* Application, financial need analysis, FAFSA. *Deadline:* May 1.

Contact: Claude Roy, Program Officer, Finance Authority of Maine, 5 Community Drive, Augusta, ME 04332-0949. *E-mail:* claude@famemaine.com. *Phone:* 800-228-3734. *Fax:* 207-623-0095. *Web site:* www.famemaine.com.

Quality Child Care Program Education Scholarship Program.

Open to residents of Maine who are taking a minimum of one childhood education course or are pursuing a child development associate certificate, associate's degree, baccalaureate degree, or post-baccalaureate teacher certification in child care-related fields. Scholarships of up to $500 per course or $2,000 per year available. See Web site for information (http://www.famemaine.com). *Academic Fields/Career Goals:* Education. *Award:* Scholarship for use in sophomore, junior, senior, or graduate year; not renewable. *Award amount:* $500–$2000. *Number of awards:* varies. *Eligibility Requirements:* Applicant must be enrolled or expecting to enroll at a two-year or four-year institution or university and resident of Maine. Available to U.S. citizens. *Application Requirements:* Application, financial need analysis. *Deadline:* continuous.

Contact: Trisha Malloy, Program Officer, Finance Authority of Maine, 5 Community Drive, Augusta, ME 04332-0949. *E-mail:* trisha@famemaine.com. *Phone:* 800-228-3734. *Fax:* 207-623-0095. *Web site:* www.famemaine.com.

Tuition Waiver Programs.

Provides tuition waivers for children and spouses of EMS personnel, firefighters, and law enforcement officers who have been killed in the line of duty and for students who were foster children under the custody of the Department of Human Services when they graduated from high school. Waivers valid at the University of Maine System, the Maine Technical College System, and Maine Maritime Academy. *Award:* Grant for use in freshman, sophomore, junior, or senior year; not renewable. *Award amount:* varies. *Number of awards:* varies. *Eligibility Requirements:* Applicant must be enrolled or expecting to enroll at an institution or university; resident of Maine and studying in Maine. Applicant or parent of applicant must have employment or volunteer experience in designated career field or police/firefighting. Available to U.S. citizens.

Application Requirements: Application. *Deadline:* continuous.

Contact: Trisha Malloy, Program Officer, Finance Authority of Maine, 5 Community Drive, Augusta, ME 04332. *E-mail:* trisha@famemaine.com. *Phone:* 207-623-3263. *Fax:* 207-623-0095. *Web site:* www.famemaine.com.

Veterans Dependents Educational Benefits-Maine.

Tuition waiver award for dependents or spouses of veterans who were prisoners of war, missing in action, or permanently disabled as a result of service. Veteran must have been Maine resident at service entry for five years preceding application. For use at Maine University system, technical colleges and Maine Maritime. Must be high school graduate. Must submit birth certificate and proof of VA disability of veteran. Award renewable for eight semesters for those under 22 years of age. *Award:* Scholarship for use in freshman, sophomore, junior, or senior year; renewable. *Award amount:* varies. *Number of awards:* varies. *Eligibility Requirements:* Applicant must be age 21 or under; enrolled or expecting to enroll full or part-time at a technical institution or university; resident of Maine and studying in Maine. Available to U.S. citizens. Applicant or parent must meet one or more of the following requirements: general military experience; retired from active duty; disabled or killed as a result of military service; prisoner of war; or missing in action. *Application Requirements:* Application. *Deadline:* continuous.

Contact: Roland Lapointe, Director, Maine Bureau of Veterans Services, State House Station 117, Augusta, ME 04333-0117. *E-mail:* mvs@me.ngb.army.mil. *Phone:* 207-626-4464. *Fax:* 207-626-4471. *Web site:* www.state.me.us.

MARYLAND

Child Care Provider Program-Maryland.

Forgivable loan provides assistance for Maryland undergraduates attending a Maryland institution and pursuing studies in a child development program or an early childhood education program. Must serve as a professional day care provider in Maryland for one year for each year award received. Must maintain minimum 2.0 GPA. Contact for further information. *Academic Fields/Career Goals:* Education. *Award:* Forgivable loan for use in freshman, sophomore, junior, or senior year; renewable. *Award amount:* $500–$2000. *Number of awards:* 100–150. *Eligibility Requirements:* Applicant must be enrolled or expecting to enroll full or part-time at a two-year or four-year institution or university; resident of Maryland and studying in Maryland. Available to U.S. citizens. *Application Requirements:* Application, transcript. *Deadline:* June 15.

Contact: Margaret Crutchley, Office of Student Financial Assistance, Maryland Higher Education Commission, 839 Bestgate Road, Suite 400, Annapolis, MD 21401-3013. *E-mail:* ofsamail@mhec.state.md.us. *Phone:* 410-260-4545. *Fax:* 410-260-3203. *Web site:* www.mhec.state.md.us.

Delegate Scholarship Program-Maryland. Delegate scholarships help Maryland residents attending Maryland degree-granting institutions, certain career schools, or nursing diploma schools. May attend out-of-state institution if Maryland Higher Education Commission deems major to be unique and not offered at a Maryland institution. Free Application for Federal Student Aid may be required. Students interested in this program should apply by contacting their legislative district delegate. *Award:* Scholarship for use in freshman, sophomore, junior, senior, or graduate year; not renewable. *Award amount:* $200–$7200. *Number of awards:* up to 3500. *Eligibility Requirements:* Applicant must be enrolled or expecting to enroll full or part-time at a two-year, four-year, or technical institution or university; resident of Maryland and studying in Maryland. Available to U.S. citizens. *Application Requirements:* Application, financial need analysis. *Deadline:* continuous.

Contact: Barbara Fantom, Office of Student Financial Assistance, Maryland Higher Education Commission, 839 Bestgage Road, Suite 400, Annapolis, MD 21401-3013. *E-mail:* osfamail@mhec.state.md.us. *Phone:* 410-260-4547. *Fax:* 410-260-3200. *Web site:* www.mhec.state.md.us.

Developmental Disabilities, Mental Health, Child Welfare and Juvenile Justice Workforce Tuition Assistance Program. Provides tuition assistance to students who are service employees who provide direct support or care to individuals with developmental disabilities or mental disorders. Must be a Maryland resident attending a Maryland college. Minimum 2.0 GPA. *Academic Fields/Career Goals:* Health and Medical Sciences; Nursing; Social Services; Special Education; Therapy/Rehabilitation. *Award:* Forgivable loan for use in freshman, sophomore, junior, senior, or graduate year; renewable. *Award amount:* $500–$3000. *Number of awards:* 300–400. *Eligibility Requirements:* Applicant must be enrolled or expecting to enroll full or part-time at a two-year or four-year institution or university; resident of Maryland and studying in Maryland. Applicant or

parent of applicant must have employment or volunteer experience in designated career field. Available to U.S. citizens. *Application Requirements:* Application, transcript. *Deadline:* July 1.

Contact: Gerrie Rogers, Office of Student Financial Assistance, Maryland Higher Education Commission, 839 Bestgate Road, Suite 400, Annapolis, MD 21401. *E-mail:* osfamail@mhec.state.md.us. *Phone:* 410-260-4574. *Fax:* 410-260-3203. *Web site:* www.mhec.state.md.us.

Distinguished Scholar Award-Maryland. Renewable award for Maryland students enrolled full-time at Maryland institutions. National Merit Scholar Finalists automatically offered award. Others may qualify for the award in satisfying criteria of a minimum 3.7 GPA or in combination with high test scores, or for Talent in Arts competition in categories of music, drama, dance, or visual arts. Must maintain annual 3.0 GPA in college for award to be renewed. Contact for further details. *Award:* Scholarship for use in freshman, sophomore, junior, or senior year; renewable. *Award amount:* up to $3000. *Number of awards:* up to 2000. *Eligibility Requirements:* Applicant must be high school student; planning to enroll or expecting to enroll full-time at a two-year or four-year institution or university; resident of Maryland and studying in Maryland. Available to U.S. citizens. *Application Requirements:* Application, test scores, transcript. *Deadline:* varies.

Contact: Monica Tipton, Office of Student Financial Assistance, Maryland Higher Education Commission, 839 Bestgate Road, Suite 400, Annapolis, MD 21401-3013. *E-mail:* ofsamail@mhec.state.md.us. *Phone:* 410-260-4568. *Fax:* 410-260-3200. *Web site:* www.mhec.state.md.us.

Distinguished Scholar-Teacher Education Awards. Up to $3,000 award for Maryland high school seniors who have received the Distinguished Scholar Award. Recipient must enroll as a full-time undergraduate in a Maryland institution and pursue a program of study leading to a Maryland teaching certificate. Must maintain annual 3.0 GPA for renewal. Must teach in a Maryland public school one year for each year award is received. *Academic Fields/ Career Goals:* Education. *Award:* Forgivable loan for use in freshman, sophomore, junior, or senior year; renewable. *Award amount:* up to $3000. *Number of awards:* 20–80. *Eligibility Requirements:* Applicant must be high school student; planning to enroll or expecting to enroll full-time at a two-year or four-year institution or university; resident of Maryland and studying in Maryland. Applicant must have 3.0 GPA

or higher. Available to U.S. citizens. *Application Requirements:* Application, test scores, transcript, must be recipient of the Distinguished Scholar Award. *Deadline:* continuous.

Contact: Monica Tipton, Office of Student Financial Assistance, Maryland Higher Education Commission, 839 Bestgate Road, Suite 400, Annapolis, MD 21401-3013. *E-mail:* ofsamail@mhec.state.md.us. *Phone:* 410-260-4568. *Fax:* 410-260-3200. *Web site:* www.mhec.state.md.us.

Educational Assistance Grants-Maryland. Award for Maryland residents accepted or enrolled in a full-time undergraduate degree or certificate program at a Maryland institution or hospital nursing school. Must submit financial aid form by March 1. Must earn 2.0 GPA in college to maintain award. *Award:* Grant for use in freshman, sophomore, junior, or senior year; renewable. *Award amount:* $400–$2700. *Number of awards:* 11,000–20,000. *Eligibility Requirements:* Applicant must be enrolled or expecting to enroll full-time at a two-year or four-year institution or university; resident of Maryland and studying in Maryland. Available to U.S. citizens. *Application Requirements:* Application, financial need analysis. *Deadline:* March 1.

Contact: Barbara Fantom, Office of Student Financial Assistance, Maryland Higher Education Commission, 839 Bestgate Road, Suite 400, Annapolis, MD 21401-3013. *E-mail:* osfamail@mhec.state.md.us. *Phone:* 410-260-4547. *Fax:* 410-260-3200. *Web site:* www.mhec.state.md.us.

Edward T. Conroy Memorial Scholarship Program. Scholarship for dependents of deceased or 100% disabled U.S. Armed Forces personnel; the son, daughter, or surviving spouse of a victim of the September 11, 2001, terrorist attacks who died as a result of the attacks on the World Trade Center in New York City, the attack on the Pentagon in Virginia, or the crash of United Airlines Flight 93 in Pennsylvania; a POW/MIA of the Vietnam Conflict or his/her son or daughter; the son, daughter or surviving spouse (who has not remarried), of a state or local public safety employee or volunteer who died in the line of duty; or a state or local public safety employee or volunteer who was 100% disabled in the line of duty. Must be Maryland resident at time of disability. Submit applicable VA certification. Must be at least 16 years of age and attend Maryland institution. *Award:* Scholarship for use in freshman, sophomore, junior, senior, or graduate year; renewable. *Award amount:* up to $7200. *Number of awards:* up to 70. *Eligibility Requirements:* Applicant must be age 16-24; enrolled or expecting to enroll full or part-time at a two-year or four-year institution or university; resident of Maryland and studying in Maryland. Available to U.S. citizens. *Application Requirements:* Application, birth and death certificate, and disability papers. *Deadline:* July 30.

Contact: Margaret Crutchley, Office of Student Financial Assistance, Maryland Higher Education Commission, 839 Bestgate Road, Suite 400, Annapolis, MD 21401-3013. *E-mail:* osfamail@mhec.state.md.us. *Phone:* 410-260-4545. *Fax:* 410-260-3203. *Web site:* www.mhec.state.md.us.

Firefighter, Ambulance, and Rescue Squad Member Tuition Reimbursement Program-Maryland. Award intended to reimburse members of rescue organizations serving Maryland communities for tuition costs of course work towards a degree or certificate in fire service or medical technology. Must attend a two- or four-year school in Maryland. Minimum 2.0 GPA. *Academic Fields/Career Goals:* Fire Sciences; Health and Medical Sciences; Trade/Technical Specialties. *Award:* Scholarship for use in freshman, sophomore, junior, or senior year; not renewable. *Award amount:* $200–$4000. *Number of awards:* 100–300. *Eligibility Requirements:* Applicant must be enrolled or expecting to enroll full or part-time at a two-year or four-year institution or university; resident of Maryland and studying in Maryland. Applicant or parent of applicant must have employment or volunteer experience in police/firefighting. Available to U.S. citizens. *Application Requirements:* Application, transcript. *Deadline:* July 1.

Contact: Gerrie Rogers, Office of Student Financial Assistance, Maryland Higher Education Commission, 839 Bestgate Road, Suite 400, Annapolis, MD 21401-3013. *E-mail:* ofsamail@mhec.state.md.us. *Phone:* 410-260-4574. *Fax:* 410-260-3203. *Web site:* www.mhec.state.md.us.

Graduate and Professional Scholarship Program-Maryland. Graduate and professional scholarships provide need-based financial assistance to students attending a Maryland school of medicine, dentistry, law, pharmacy, social work, or nursing. Funds are provided to specific Maryland colleges and universities. Students must demonstrate financial need and be Maryland residents. Contact institution financial aid office for more information. *Academic Fields/Career Goals:* Dental Health/Services; Health and Medical Sciences; Law/Legal Services; Nursing; Social Services. *Award:* Scholarship for use in freshman, sophomore, junior, senior, graduate, or postgraduate years; renewable. *Award amount:* $1000–$5000.

Number of awards: 40–200. *Eligibility Requirements:* Applicant must be enrolled or expecting to enroll full or part-time at a four-year institution or university; resident of Maryland and studying in Maryland. Available to U.S. citizens. *Application Requirements:* Application, financial need analysis. *Deadline:* March 1.

Contact: institution financial aid office, Maryland Higher Education Commission. *Web site:* www.mhec.state.md.us.

Guaranteed Access Grant-Maryland. Award for Maryland resident enrolling full-time in an undergraduate program at a Maryland institution. Must be under 22 at time of first award and begin college within one year of completing high school in Maryland with a minimum 2.5 GPA. Must have an annual family income less than 130% of the federal poverty level guideline. *Award:* Grant for use in freshman, sophomore, junior, or senior year; renewable. *Award amount:* $400–$11,600. *Number of awards:* up to 1000. *Eligibility Requirements:* Applicant must be enrolled or expecting to enroll full-time at a two-year or four-year institution or university; resident of Maryland and studying in Maryland. Applicant must have 2.5 GPA or higher. Available to U.S. citizens. *Application Requirements:* Application, financial need analysis, transcript. *Deadline:* continuous.

Contact: Theresa Lowe, Office of Student Financial Assistance, Maryland Higher Education Commission, 839 Bestgate Road, Suite 400, Annapolis, MD 21401-3013. *E-mail:* osfamail@mhec.state.md.us. *Phone:* 410-260-4555. *Fax:* 410-260-3200. *Web site:* www.mhec.state.md.us.

J.F. Tolbert Memorial Student Grant Program. Available to Maryland residents attending a private career school in Maryland with at least 18 clock hours per week. *Award:* Grant for use in freshman or sophomore year; not renewable. *Award amount:* up to $400. *Number of awards:* 1000. *Eligibility Requirements:* Applicant must be enrolled or expecting to enroll at a technical institution; resident of Maryland and studying in Maryland. Available to U.S. citizens. *Application Requirements:* Application, financial need analysis. *Deadline:* continuous.

Contact: Carla Rich, Office of Student Financial Assistance, Maryland Higher Education Commission, 839 Bestgate Road, Suite 400, Annapolis, MD 21401-3013. *E-mail:* osfamail@mhec.state.md.us. *Phone:* 410-260-4513. *Fax:* 410-260-3200. *Web site:* www.mhec.state.md.us.

Janet L. Hoffmann Loan Assistance Repayment Program. Provides assistance

for repayment of loan debt to Maryland residents working full-time in nonprofit organizations and state or local governments. Must submit Employment Verification Form and Lender Verification Form. *Academic Fields/Career Goals:* Education; Law/Legal Services; Nursing; Social Services; Therapy/Rehabilitation. *Award:* Grant for use in freshman, sophomore, junior, senior, or graduate year; not renewable. *Award amount:* up to $7500. *Number of awards:* up to 400. *Eligibility Requirements:* Applicant must be enrolled or expecting to enroll at an institution or university; resident of Maryland and studying in Maryland. Available to U.S. citizens. *Application Requirements:* Application, transcript, IRS 1040 form. *Deadline:* September 30.

Contact: Marie Janiszewski, Office of Student Financial Assistance, Maryland Higher Education Commission, 839 Bestgate Road, Suite 400, Annapolis, MD 21401. *E-mail:* osfamail@mhec.state.md.us. *Phone:* 410-260-4569. *Fax:* 410-260-3203. *Web site:* www.mhec.state.md.us.

Maryland State Nursing Scholarship and Living Expenses Grant. Renewable grant for Maryland residents enrolled in a two- or four-year Maryland institution nursing degree program. Recipients must agree to serve as a full-time nurse in a Maryland shortage area and must maintain a 3.0 GPA in college. Application deadline is June 30. Submit Free Application for Federal Student Aid. *Academic Fields/Career Goals:* Nursing. *Award:* Forgivable loan for use in freshman, sophomore, junior, senior, or graduate year; renewable. *Award amount:* $200–$3000. *Number of awards:* up to 600. *Eligibility Requirements:* Applicant must be enrolled or expecting to enroll full or part-time at a two-year or four-year institution or university; resident of Maryland and studying in Maryland. Applicant must have 3.0 GPA or higher. Available to U.S. citizens. *Application Requirements:* Application, financial need analysis, transcript. *Deadline:* June 30.

Contact: Marie Janiszewski, Office of Student Financial Assistance, Maryland Higher Education Commission, 839 Bestgate Road, Suite 400, Annapolis, MD 21401-3013. *E-mail:* ofsamail@mhec.state.md.us. *Phone:* 410-260-4569. *Fax:* 410-260-3203. *Web site:* www.mhec.state.md.us.

Part-time Grant Program-Maryland. Funds provided to Maryland colleges and universities. Eligible students must be enrolled on a part-time basis (6-11 credits) in an undergraduate degree program. Must demonstrate financial need and also be Maryland resident. Contact financial aid office at institution for more information.

Award: Grant for use in freshman, sophomore, junior, or senior year; renewable. *Award amount:* $200–$1000. *Number of awards:* 1800–9000. *Eligibility Requirements:* Applicant must be enrolled or expecting to enroll part-time at a two-year or four-year institution or university; resident of Maryland and studying in Maryland. Available to U.S. citizens. *Application Requirements:* Application, financial need analysis. *Deadline:* March 1.

Contact: Maryland Higher Education Commission, 839 Bestgate Road, Suite 400, Annapolis, MD 21401-3013. *Web site:* www.mhec.state.md.us.

Physical and Occupational Therapists and Assistants Grant Program. For Maryland residents training as physical, occupational therapists or therapy assistants at Maryland postsecondary institutions. Recipients must provide one year of service for each full, or partial, year of award. Service must be to handicapped children in a Maryland facility that has, or accommodates and provides services to, such children. Minimum 2.0 GPA. *Academic Fields/Career Goals:* Therapy/Rehabilitation. *Award:* Forgivable loan for use in freshman, sophomore, junior, senior, or graduate year; renewable. *Award amount:* up to $2000. *Number of awards:* up to 10. *Eligibility Requirements:* Applicant must be enrolled or expecting to enroll full-time at a two-year or four-year institution or university; resident of Maryland and studying in Maryland. Available to U.S. citizens. *Application Requirements:* Application, transcript. *Deadline:* July 1.

Contact: Gerrie Rogers, Office of Student Financial Assistance, Maryland Higher Education Commission, 839 Bestgate Road, Suite 400, Annapolis, MD 21401. *E-mail:* ssamail@mhec.state.md.us. *Phone:* 410-260-4574. *Fax:* 410-260-3203. *Web site:* www.mhec.state.md.us.

Senatorial Scholarships-Maryland. Renewable award for Maryland residents attending a Maryland degree-granting institution, nursing diploma school, or certain private career schools. May be used out-of-state only if Maryland Higher Education Commission deems major to be unique and not offered at Maryland institution. *Award:* Scholarship for use in freshman, sophomore, junior, senior, or graduate year; renewable. *Award amount:* $200–$2000. *Number of awards:* up to 7000. *Eligibility Requirements:* Applicant must be enrolled or expecting to enroll full or part-time at a two-year, four-year, or technical institution or university; resident of Maryland and studying in Maryland. Available to U.S. citizens. *Application Requirements:* Financial need analysis, test scores, application to Legislative District Senator. *Deadline:* March 1.

Contact: Barbara Fantom, Office of Student Financial Assistance, Maryland Higher Education Commission, 839 Bestgate Road, Suite 400, Annapolis, MD 21401-3013. *E-mail:* osfamail@mhec.state.md.us. *Phone:* 410-260-4547. *Fax:* 410-260-3202. *Web site:* www.mhec.state.md.us.

Sharon Christa McAuliffe Teacher Education-Critical Shortage Grant Program. Renewable awards for Maryland residents who are college juniors, seniors, or graduate students enrolled in a Maryland teacher education program. Must agree to enter profession in a subject designated as a critical shortage area. Must teach in Maryland for one year for each award year. Renewable for one year. *Academic Fields/Career Goals:* Education. *Award:* Forgivable loan for use in junior, senior, or graduate year; renewable. *Award amount:* $200–$14,775. *Number of awards:* up to 137. *Eligibility Requirements:* Applicant must be enrolled or expecting to enroll full or part-time at a four-year institution or university; resident of Maryland and studying in Maryland. Applicant must have 3.0 GPA or higher. Available to U.S. citizens. *Application Requirements:* Application, essay, resume, transcript. *Deadline:* December 31.

Contact: Margaret Crutchley, Office of Student Financial Assistance, Maryland Higher Education Commission, 839 Bestgate Road, Suite 400, Annapolis, MD 21401-3013. *E-mail:* ofsamail@mhec.state.md.us. *Phone:* 410-260-4545. *Fax:* 410-260-3203. *Web site:* www.mhec.state.md.us.

Tuition Reduction for Non-Resident Nursing Students. Forgivable loan is available to nonresidents of Maryland who attend a two-year or four-year public institution in Maryland. The loan will be renewed provided student maintains academic requirements designated by institution attended. Loan recipient must agree to serve as a full-time nurse in a hospital or related institution for an equal amount of years as tuition was paid by Maryland Higher Education Commission. Loan recipient will pay tuition of Maryland resident. *Academic Fields/Career Goals:* Nursing. *Award:* Forgivable loan for use in freshman, sophomore, junior, or senior year; renewable. *Award amount:* varies. *Number of awards:* varies. *Eligibility Requirements:* Applicant must be enrolled or expecting to enroll full or part-time at a two-year or four-year institution and studying in Maryland. *Application Requirements:* Application. *Deadline:* varies.

Contact: Financial Aid Office of your school, Maryland Higher Education Commission. *Web site:* www.mhec.state.md.us.

Tuition Waiver for Foster Care Recipients. Applicant must be a high school graduate or recipient of a GED under the age of 21. Applicant must either have resided in a foster care home in Maryland at time of high school graduation or GED reception, or until 14th birthday and had been adopted after 14th birthday. Applicant, if status approved, will be exempt from paying tuition and mandatory fees at a public college in Maryland. *Award:* Scholarship for use in freshman, sophomore, junior, or senior year; renewable. *Award amount:* varies. *Number of awards:* varies. *Eligibility Requirements:* Applicant must be age 20 or under; enrolled or expecting to enroll full or part-time at a two-year or four-year institution or university and studying in Maryland. Available to U.S. citizens. *Application Requirements:* Application, financial need analysis. *Deadline:* March 1.

Contact: Inquire at financial aid office of your school., Maryland Higher Education Commission. *Web site:* www.mhec.state.md.us.

William Kapell International Piano Competition and Festival. Quadrennial international piano competition for ages 18-31. $80 application fee. Competition takes place at the Clarice Smith Performing Arts Center at the University of Maryland July 16-25, 2003. Next competition will be in 2007. *Academic Fields/Career Goals:* Performing Arts. *Award:* Prize for use in freshman, sophomore, junior, senior, graduate, or postgraduate years; not renewable. *Award amount:* $1000–$20,000. *Number of awards:* up to 12. *Eligibility Requirements:* Applicant must be age 18-31; enrolled or expecting to enroll at an institution or university and must have an interest in music. Available to U.S. and non-U.S. citizens. *Application Requirements:* Application, applicant must enter a contest, autobiography, photo, portfolio, references, CD of performance. *Fee:* $80. *Deadline:* December 1.

Contact: Dr. Christopher Patton, Coordinator, Clarice Smith Performing Arts Center at Maryland, Suite 3800, University of Maryland, College Park, MD 20742-1625. *E-mail:* kapell@deans.umd.edu. *Phone:* 301-405-8174. *Fax:* 301-405-5977. *Web site:* www.claricesmithcenter.umd.edu.

MASSACHUSETTS

Christian A. Herter Memorial Scholarship. Renewable award for Massachusetts residents who are in the 10th-11th grades and whose socio-economic backgrounds and environment may inhibit their ability to attain educational goals. Must exhibit severe personal or family-related difficulties, medical problems, or have overcome a personal obstacle. Provides up to 50% of the student's calculated need, as determined by Federal methodology, at the college of their choice within the continental U.S. *Award:* Scholarship for use in freshman, sophomore, junior, or senior year; renewable. *Award amount:* varies. *Number of awards:* 25. *Eligibility Requirements:* Applicant must be high school student; planning to enroll or expecting to enroll full-time at a two-year, four-year, or technical institution or university and resident of Massachusetts. Applicant must have 2.5 GPA or higher. Available to U.S. citizens. *Application Requirements:* Application, autobiography, financial need analysis, interview, references. *Deadline:* March 31.

Contact: Ken Smith, Massachusetts Office of Student Financial Assistance, 454 Broadway, Suite 200, Revere, MA 02151. *E-mail:* osfa@osfa.mass.edu. *Phone:* 617-727-9420. *Fax:* 617-727-0667. *Web site:* www.osfa.mass.edu.

Higher Education Coordinating Council-Tuition Waiver Program. Renewable award is tuition exemption for up to four years. Available to active members of Air Force, Army, Navy, Marines, or Coast Guard who are residents of Massachusetts. For use at a Massachusetts college or university. Deadlines vary. Contact veterans coordinator at college. *Award:* Scholarship for use in freshman, sophomore, junior, or senior year; renewable. *Award amount:* varies. *Number of awards:* varies. *Eligibility Requirements:* Applicant must be enrolled or expecting to enroll full or part-time at a two-year or four-year institution or university; resident of Massachusetts and studying in Massachusetts. Available to U.S. citizens. Applicant must have served in the Air Force, Army, Coast Guard, Marine Corp, or Navy. *Application Requirements:* Application, financial need analysis. *Deadline:* varies.

Contact: College financial aid office, Massachusetts Office of Student Financial Assistance. *Web site:* www.osfa.mass.edu.

Massachusetts Assistance for Student Success Program. Provides need-based financial assistance to Massachusetts residents to attend undergraduate postsecondary institutions in Connecticut, Maine, Massachusetts, New Hampshire, Pennsylvania, Rhode Island, Vermont, and District of Columbia. High school seniors may apply. Timely filing of FAFSA required. *Award:* Grant for use in

freshman, sophomore, junior, or senior year; not renewable. *Award amount:* $300–$2300. *Number of awards:* 25,000–30,000. *Eligibility Requirements:* Applicant must be enrolled or expecting to enroll full-time at a two-year, four-year, or technical institution or university; resident of Massachusetts and studying in Connecticut, District of Columbia, Maine, Massachusetts, New Hampshire, Pennsylvania, Rhode Island, or Vermont. Available to U.S. citizens. *Application Requirements:* Financial need analysis, FAFSA. *Deadline:* May 1.

Contact: Robert Brun, Director of Scholarships and Grants, Massachusetts Office of Student Financial Assistance, 454 Broadway, Suite 200, Revere, MA 02151. *Phone:* 617-727-9420. *Fax:* 617-727-0667. *Web site:* www.osfa.mass.edu.

Massachusetts Cash Grant Program. A need-based grant to assist with mandatory fees and non-state supported tuition, this supplemental award is available to Massachusetts residents who are undergraduates at public two-year colleges, four-year colleges and universities in Massachusetts. Must file FAFSA before May 1. Contact college financial aid office for information. *Award:* Grant for use in freshman, sophomore, junior, or senior year; not renewable. *Award amount:* $150–$1900. *Number of awards:* varies. *Eligibility Requirements:* Applicant must be enrolled or expecting to enroll full-time at a two-year or four-year institution or university; resident of Massachusetts and studying in Massachusetts. Available to U.S. citizens. *Application Requirements:* Financial need analysis, FAFSA. *Deadline:* continuous.

Contact: College financial aid office, Massachusetts Office of Student Financial Assistance. *Web site:* www.osfa.mass.edu.

Massachusetts Gilbert Matching Student Grant Program. Must be permanent Massachusetts resident for at least one year and attending an independent, regionally accredited Massachusetts school or school of nursing full time. File the Free Application for Federal Student Aid after January 1. Contact college financial aid office for complete details and deadlines. *Academic Fields/Career Goals:* Nursing. *Award:* Grant for use in freshman, sophomore, junior, or senior year; not renewable. *Award amount:* $200–$2500. *Number of awards:* varies. *Eligibility Requirements:* Applicant must be enrolled or expecting to enroll full-time at a four-year institution or university; resident of Massachusetts and studying in Massachusetts. Available to U.S. citizens. *Application Requirements:* Financial need analysis, FAFSA. *Deadline:* varies.

Contact: College financial aid office, Massachusetts Office of Student Financial Assistance. *Web site:* www.osfa.mass.edu.

Massachusetts Part-time Grant Program. Award for permanent Massachusetts resident for at least one year enrolled part-time in a state-approved postsecondary school. Recipient must not have first bachelor's degree. FAFSA must be filed before May 1. Contact college financial aid office for further information. *Award:* Grant for use in freshman, sophomore, junior, or senior year; not renewable. *Award amount:* $150–$1150. *Number of awards:* varies. *Eligibility Requirements:* Applicant must be enrolled or expecting to enroll part-time at a two-year, four-year, or technical institution or university; resident of Massachusetts and studying in Massachusetts. Available to U.S. citizens. *Application Requirements:* Financial need analysis, FAFSA. *Deadline:* May 1.

Contact: College financial aid office, Massachusetts Office of Student Financial Assistance. *Web site:* www.osfa.mass.edu.

Massachusetts Public Service Grant Program. Scholarships for children and/or spouses of deceased members of fire, police, and corrections departments who were killed in the line of duty. For Massachusetts residents attending Massachusetts institutions. *Award:* Grant for use in freshman, sophomore, junior, or senior year; not renewable. *Award amount:* $720–$1714. *Number of awards:* varies. *Eligibility Requirements:* Applicant must be enrolled or expecting to enroll full-time at a four-year institution or university; resident of Massachusetts and studying in Massachusetts. Applicant or parent of applicant must have employment or volunteer experience in police/firefighting. Available to U.S. citizens. *Application Requirements:* Application, financial need analysis, FAFSA. *Deadline:* May 1.

Contact: Alison Leary, Massachusetts Office of Student Financial Assistance, 454 Broadway, Suite 200, Revere, MA 02151. *E-mail:* osfa@osfa.mass.edu. *Phone:* 617-727-9420. *Fax:* 617-727-0667. *Web site:* www.osfa.mass.edu.

New England Regional Student Program (New England Board of Higher Education). For residents of Connecticut, Maine, Massachusetts, New Hampshire, Rhode Island, and Vermont. Through Regional Student Program, students pay reduced out-of-state tuition at public colleges or universities in other New England states when enrolling in certain majors not offered at public institutions in home state. *Award:* Scholarship for use in freshman, sophomore, junior, senior, or graduate year; renewable. *Award amount:* varies. *Number* *of awards:* varies. *Eligibility Requirements:* Applicant must be enrolled or expecting to enroll full or part-time at a two-year or four-year institution or university; resident of Connecticut, Maine, Massachusetts, New Hampshire, Rhode Island, or Vermont and studying in Connecticut, Maine, Massachusetts, New Hampshire, Rhode Island, or Vermont. Available to U.S. citizens. *Application Requirements:* College application. *Deadline:* continuous.

Contact: Wendy Lindsay, Director of Regional Student Program, New England Board of Higher Education, 45 Temple Place, Boston, MA 02111-1305. *E-mail:* rsp@nebhe.org. *Phone:* 617-357-9620 Ext. 111. *Fax:* 617-338-1577. *Web site:* www.nebhe.org.

Paraprofessional Teacher Preparation Grant. Grant providing financial aid assistance to Massachusetts residents who are currently employed as paraprofessionals in Massachusetts public schools and wish to obtain higher education and become certified as full time teachers. *Academic Fields/Career Goals:* Education. *Award:* Grant for use in freshman, sophomore, junior, or senior year. *Award amount:* $750–$6500. *Number of awards:* varies. *Eligibility Requirements:* Applicant must be enrolled or expecting to enroll full or part-time at a two-year or four-year institution or university and resident of Massachusetts. Available to U.S. citizens. *Application Requirements:* Application. *Deadline:* varies.

Contact: Clantha McCurdy, Associate Vice Chancellor, Massachusetts Office of Student Financial Assistance, 454 Broadway, Suite 200, Revere, MA 02151. *E-mail:* cmccurdy@osfa.mass.edu. *Phone:* 617-727-9420. *Fax:* 617-727-0667. *Web site:* www.osfa.mass.edu.

Performance Bonus Grant Program. One-time award to residents of Massachusetts enrolled in a Massachusetts postsecondary institution. Minimum 3.0 GPA required. Timely filing of FAFSA required. Must be sophomore, junior or senior level undergraduate. *Award:* Grant for use in sophomore, junior, or senior year; not renewable. *Award amount:* $350–$500. *Number of awards:* varies. *Eligibility Requirements:* Applicant must be enrolled or expecting to enroll full-time at a two-year or four-year institution or university; resident of Massachusetts and studying in Massachusetts. Applicant must have 3.0 GPA or higher. Available to U.S. citizens. *Application Requirements:* Financial need analysis, FAFSA. *Deadline:* May 1.

Contact: Scholarship Information, Massachusetts Office of Student Financial Assistance, 454 Broadway, Suite 200, Revere, MA 02151. *Phone:* 617-727-9420. *Fax:* 617-727-0667. *Web site:* www.osfa.mass.edu.

Tomorrow's Teachers Scholarship Program. Tuition waver for graduating high school senior ranking in top 25% of class. Must be a resident of Massachusetts and pursue a bachelor's degree at a public college or university in the Commonwealth. Must commit to teach for four years in a Massachusetts public school. *Academic Fields/Career Goals:* Education. *Award:* Scholarship for use in freshman, sophomore, junior, or senior year; renewable. *Award amount:* varies. *Number of awards:* varies. *Eligibility Requirements:* Applicant must be high school student; planning to enroll or expecting to enroll full-time at a four-year institution or university; resident of Massachusetts and studying in Massachusetts. Applicant must have 3.5 GPA or higher. Available to U.S. citizens. *Application Requirements:* Application, essay, references, transcript. *Deadline:* February 15.

Contact: Alison Leary, Massachusetts Office of Student Financial Assistance, 454 Broadway, Suite 200, Revere, MA 02151. *E-mail:* osfa@osfa.mass.edu. *Phone:* 617-727-9420. *Fax:* 617-727-0667. *Web site:* www.osfa.mass.edu.

Tuition Waiver (General)-Massachusetts. Need-based tuition waiver for full-time students. Must attend a Massachusetts public institution of higher education and be a permanent Massachusetts resident. File the Free Application for Federal Student Aid after January 1. Award is for undergraduate use. Contact school financial aid office for more information. *Award:* Scholarship for use in freshman, sophomore, junior, or senior year; renewable. *Award amount:* $175–$1300. *Number of awards:* varies. *Eligibility Requirements:* Applicant must be enrolled or expecting to enroll full-time at a two-year or four-year institution or university; resident of Massachusetts and studying in Massachusetts. Available to U.S. citizens. *Application Requirements:* Application, financial need analysis, FAFSA. *Deadline:* May 1.

Contact: College financial aid office, Massachusetts Office of Student Financial Assistance. *Web site:* www.osfa.mass.edu.

MICHIGAN

Michigan Adult Part-time Grant. Grant for part-time, needy, independent undergraduates at an approved, degree-granting Michigan college or university. Eligibility is limited to two years. Must be Michigan resident. Deadlines determined by college. *Award:* Grant for use in freshman, sophomore, junior, or senior year; not renewable. *Award amount:* up to $600. *Number of awards:* varies. *Eligibility Requirements:* Applicant must be enrolled or

expecting to enroll part-time at a two-year or four-year institution or university; resident of Michigan and studying in Michigan. Available to U.S. citizens. *Application Requirements:* Application, financial need analysis.

Contact: Program Director, Michigan Bureau of Student Financial Assistance, PO Box 30466, Lansing, MI 48909-7966. *Web site:* www.michigan.gov/mistudentaid.

Michigan Competitive Scholarship. Awards limited to tuition. Must maintain a C average and meet the college's academic progress requirements. Must file Free Application for Federal Student Aid. Deadline: March 1. Must be Michigan resident. Renewable award of $1300 for undergraduate study at a Michigan institution. *Award:* Scholarship for use in freshman, sophomore, junior, or senior year; renewable. *Award amount:* $100–$1300. *Number of awards:* varies. *Eligibility Requirements:* Applicant must be enrolled or expecting to enroll at a two-year or four-year institution or university; resident of Michigan and studying in Michigan. Available to U.S. citizens. *Application Requirements:* Application, financial need analysis, test scores, FAFSA. *Deadline:* March 1.

Contact: Scholarship and Grant Director, Michigan Bureau of Student Financial Assistance, PO Box 30466, Lansing, MI 48909. *Web site:* www.michigan.gov/mistudentaid.

Michigan Educational Opportunity Grant. Need-based program for Michigan residents who are at least half-time undergraduates attending public Michigan colleges. Must maintain good academic standing. Deadline determined by college. Award of up to $1000. *Award:* Grant for use in freshman, sophomore, junior, or senior year; not renewable. *Award amount:* up to $1000. *Number of awards:* varies. *Eligibility Requirements:* Applicant must be enrolled or expecting to enroll full or part-time at a two-year or four-year institution or university; resident of Michigan and studying in Michigan. Available to U.S. citizens. *Application Requirements:* Application, financial need analysis. *Deadline:* varies.

Contact: Program Director, Michigan Bureau of Student Financial Assistance, PO Box 30466, Lansing, MI 48909-7966. *Web site:* www.michigan.gov/mistudentaid.

Michigan Indian Tuition Waiver. Renewable award provides free tuition for Native-American of one-quarter or more blood degree who attend a Michigan public college or university. Must be a Michigan resident for at least one year. For more details and deadlines contact college financial aid office. *Award:* Scholarship for use in freshman, sophomore, junior, senior, graduate, or postgraduate years; renewable. *Award amount:* varies. *Number of awards:* varies. *Eligibility Requirements:* Applicant must be American Indian/Alaska Native; enrolled or expecting to enroll full or part-time at a two-year or four-year institution or university; resident of Michigan and studying in Michigan. Available to U.S. and Canadian citizens. *Application Requirements:* Application, driver's license. *Deadline:* continuous.

Contact: Christin McKerchie, Executive Assistant to Programs, Inter-Tribal Council of Michigan, Inc., 405 East Easterday Avenue, Sault Ste. Marie, MI 49783. *E-mail:* christin@itcmi.org. *Phone:* 906-632-6896. *Fax:* 906-632-1810. *Web site:* www.itcmi.org.

Michigan Merit Award. Scholarship for students scoring well on state's standardized assessment tests. Students will have four years from high school graduation to use the award. *Award:* Scholarship for use in freshman year; not renewable. *Award amount:* $1000–$2500. *Number of awards:* varies. *Eligibility Requirements:* Applicant must be high school student; planning to enroll or expecting to enroll full or part-time at a two-year, four-year, or technical institution or university and resident of Michigan. Available to U.S. citizens. *Application Requirements:* Test scores.

Contact: Program Director, Michigan Bureau of Student Financial Assistance, PO Box 30466, Lansing, MI 48909-7966. *Web site:* www.michigan.gov/mistudentaid.

Michigan Nursing Scholarship. For students enrolled in an LPN, associate degree in nursing, or bachelor of science in nursing programs. Colleges determine application procedure and select recipients. Recipients must fulfill in-state work commitment or repay scholarship. *Academic Fields/Career Goals:* Nursing. *Award:* Scholarship for use in freshman, sophomore, junior, or senior year; renewable. *Award amount:* up to $4000. *Number of awards:* varies. *Eligibility Requirements:* Applicant must be enrolled or expecting to enroll full or part-time at a two-year or four-year institution or university; resident of Michigan and studying in Michigan. Available to U.S. citizens.

Contact: Program Director, Michigan Bureau of Student Financial Assistance, PO Box 30466, Lansing, MI 48909-7966. *Web site:* www.michigan.gov/mistudentaid.

Michigan Tuition Grants. Need-based program. Students must attend a Michigan private, nonprofit, degree-granting college. Must file the Free Application for Federal Student Aid and meet the college's academic progress requirements. Deadline: March 1. Must be Michigan resident. Renewable award of $2000. *Award:* Grant for use in freshman, sophomore, junior, or senior year; renewable. *Award amount:* $100–$2750. *Number of awards:* varies. *Eligibility Requirements:* Applicant must be enrolled or expecting to enroll at a two-year or four-year institution or university; resident of Michigan and studying in Michigan. Available to U.S. citizens. *Application Requirements:* Application, financial need analysis, FAFSA. *Deadline:* March 1.

Contact: Scholarship and Grant Director, Michigan Bureau of Student Financial Assistance, PO Box 30466, Lansing, MI 48909-7966. *Web site:* www.michigan.gov/mistudentaid.

Michigan Veterans Trust Fund Tuition Grant Program. Tuition grant of $2,800 for children of Michigan veterans who died on active duty or subsequently declared 100% disabled as the result of service-connected illness or injury. Must be 17 to 25 years old, be a Michigan resident, and attend a private or public institution in Michigan. *Award:* Grant for use in freshman, sophomore, junior, or senior year; renewable. *Award amount:* up to $2800. *Number of awards:* varies. *Eligibility Requirements:* Applicant must be age 17-25; enrolled or expecting to enroll full-time at a two-year, four-year, or technical institution or university; resident of Michigan and studying in Michigan. Applicant or parent must meet one or more of the following requirements: general military experience; retired from active duty; disabled or killed as a result of military service; prisoner of war; or missing in action. *Application Requirements:* Application. *Deadline:* continuous.

Contact: Phyllis Ochis, Department of Military and Veterans Affairs, Michigan Veterans Trust Fund, 2500 South Washington Avenue, Lansing, MI 48913. *Phone:* 517-483-5469. *Web site:* www.michigan.gov/dmva.

Tuition Incentive Program (TIP)-Michigan. Award for Michigan residents who receive or have received Medicaid for required period of time through the Family Independence Agency. Scholarship provides two years tuition towards an associate's degree at a Michigan college or university. Apply before graduating from high school or earning General Education Development diploma. *Award:* Scholarship for use in freshman or sophomore year; renewable. *Number of awards:* varies. *Eligibility Requirements:* Applicant must be high school student; planning to enroll or expecting to enroll full or part-time at a two-year or four-year institution or university; resident of Michigan and studying in Michigan. Available to U.S. citizens. *Application Requirements:* Application, financial need analysis. *Deadline:* continuous.

Contact: Program Director, Michigan Bureau of Student Financial Assistance, PO Box 30466, Lansing, MI 48909. *Web site:* www.michigan.gov/mistudentaid.

MINNESOTA

Donaldson Company, Inc. Scholarship Program. Scholarships for children of U.S. employees of Donaldson Company, Inc. Any form of accredited postsecondary education is eligible. Application deadline is March 12. *Award:* Scholarship for use in freshman, sophomore, junior, or senior year; renewable. *Award amount:* $1000–$3000. *Eligibility Requirements:* Applicant must be enrolled or expecting to enroll full-time at a two-year, four-year, or technical institution or university. Applicant or parent of applicant must be affiliated with Donaldson Company. Available to U.S. citizens. *Application Requirements:* Application, essay, financial need analysis, references, transcript. *Deadline:* March 12.

Contact: Norm Linnell, Vice President, General Counsel, and Secretary, Donaldson Company, PO Box 1299, Minneapolis, MN 55440. *E-mail:* nlinnell@mail.donaldson.com. *Phone:* 952-887-3631. *Fax:* 952-887-3005. *Web site:* www.donaldson.com.

Leadership, Excellence and Dedicated Service Scholarship. Awarded to high school seniors who enlist in the Minnesota National Guard. The award recognizes demonstrated leadership, community services and potential for success in the Minnesota National Guard. For more information, applicant may contact any Minnesota army national guard recruiter at 1-800-go-guard or visit the Web site http://www.dma.state.mn.us. *Award:* Scholarship for use in freshman year; not renewable. *Award amount:* $1000. *Number of awards:* 30. *Eligibility Requirements:* Applicant must be high school student and planning to enroll or expecting to enroll full or part-time at a two-year, four-year, or technical institution or university. Available to U.S. and non-U.S. citizens. Applicant must have served in the Air Force National Guard or Army National Guard. *Application Requirements:* Essay, resume, references, transcript. *Deadline:* March 15.

Contact: Barbara O'Reilly, Education Services Officer, Minnesota Department of Military Affairs, Veterans Services Building, 20 West 12th Street, St. Paul, MN 55155-

2098. *E-mail:* barbara.oreilly@mn.ngb.army. mil. *Phone:* 651-282-4508. *Web site:* www. dma.state.mn.us.

Minnesota Educational Assistance for War Orphans. War orphans may qualify for $750 per year. Must have lost parent through service-related death. Children of deceased veterans may qualify for free tuition at State university, college, or vocational or technical schools, but not at University of Minnesota. Must have been resident of Minnesota for at least two years. *Award:* Grant for use in freshman, sophomore, junior, or senior year; renewable. *Award amount:* $750. *Number of awards:* varies. *Eligibility Requirements:* Applicant must be enrolled or expecting to enroll full or part-time at a two-year, four-year, or technical institution or university; resident of Minnesota and studying in Minnesota. Available to U.S. citizens. Applicant or parent must meet one or more of the following requirements: general military experience; retired from active duty; disabled or killed as a result of military service; prisoner of war; or missing in action. *Application Requirements:* Application, financial need analysis. *Deadline:* continuous.

Contact: Terrence Logan, Management Analyst IV, Minnesota Department of Veterans' Affairs, 20 West 12th Street, Second Floor, St. Paul, MN 55155-2079. *Phone:* 651-296-2562. *Fax:* 651-296-3954.

Minnesota Indian Scholarship Program. One time award for Minnesota Native-American. Applicant must be one quarter Native-American and a resident of Minnesota. Must re-apply for scholarship annually. *Award:* Scholarship for use in freshman, sophomore, junior, or senior year; not renewable. *Award amount:* up to $3300. *Number of awards:* varies. *Eligibility Requirements:* Applicant must be American Indian/Alaska Native; enrolled or expecting to enroll full or part-time at a two-year, four-year, or technical institution or university; resident of Minnesota and studying in Minnesota. Available to U.S. citizens. *Application Requirements:* Application, financial need analysis. *Deadline:* July 1.

Contact: Lea Perkins, Director, Minnesota Indian Scholarship Office, Minnesota Department of Education, 1500 Highway 36W, Roseville, MN 55113-4266. *E-mail:* cfl. indianeducation@state.mn.us. *Phone:* 800-657-3927. *Web site:* www.mheso.state.mn.us.

Minnesota Nurses Loan Forgiveness Program. This program offers loan repayment to registered nurse and licensed practical nurse students who agree to practice in a Minnesota nursing home or an Intermediate Care Facility for persons with mental retardation for a minimum 3-year service obligation after completion of training. Candidates must apply while still in school. *Academic Fields/Career Goals:* Health and Medical Sciences; Nursing. *Award:* Grant for use in freshman, sophomore, junior, or senior year; not renewable. *Award amount:* $3000–$4000. *Number of awards:* 25–35. *Eligibility Requirements:* Applicant must be enrolled or expecting to enroll full or part-time at a two-year, four-year, or technical institution or university. Available to U.S. citizens. *Application Requirements:* Application, essay, resume. *Deadline:* continuous.

Contact: Karen Welter, Minnesota Department of Health, 121 East Seventh Place, Suite 460, PO Box 64975, St. Paul, MN 55164-0975. *E-mail:* karen.welter@health.state.mn. us. *Phone:* 651-282-6302. *Web site:* www. health.state.mn.us.

Minnesota Reciprocal Agreement. Renewable tuition waiver for Minnesota residents. Waives all or part of non-resident tuition surcharge at public institutions in Iowa, Kansas, Michigan, Missouri, Nebraska, North Dakota, South Dakota, and Wisconsin. Deadline is last day of academic term. *Award:* Scholarship for use in freshman, sophomore, junior, senior, graduate, or postgraduate years; renewable. *Award amount:* varies. *Number of awards:* varies. *Eligibility Requirements:* Applicant must be enrolled or expecting to enroll full or part-time at a two-year, four-year, or technical institution or university; resident of Minnesota and studying in Iowa, Kansas, Michigan, Missouri, Nebraska, North Dakota, South Dakota, or Wisconsin. Available to U.S. citizens. *Application Requirements:* Application. *Deadline:* varies.

Contact: Minnesota Higher Education Services Office, 1450 Energy Park Drive, Suite 350, St. Paul, MN 55108-5227. *Phone:* 651-642-0567 Ext. 1. *Web site:* www.mheso. state.mn.us.

Minnesota Safety Officers' Survivor Program. Grant for eligible survivors of Minnesota public safety officer killed in the line of duty. Safety officers who have been permanently or totally disabled in the line of duty are also eligible. Must be used at a Minnesota institution participating in State Grant Program. Write for details. Must submit proof of death or disability and Public Safety Officers Benefit Fund Certificate. Must apply each year. Can be renewed for four years. *Award:* Grant for use in freshman, sophomore, junior, or senior year; not renewable. *Award amount:* up to $8096. *Eligibility Requirements:* Applicant must be enrolled or expecting to enroll full or part-time at a two-year, four-year, or technical institution or university and studying in Minnesota. Applicant or parent of applicant must have employment or volunteer experience in police/firefighting. Available to U.S. citizens. *Application Requirements:* Application, proof of death/disability. *Deadline:* continuous.

Contact: Minnesota Higher Education Services Office, 1450 Energy Park Drive, Suite 350, St. Paul, MN 55108-5227. *Phone:* 651-642-0567 Ext. 1. *Web site:* www.mheso. state.mn.us.

Minnesota State Grant Program. Need-based grant program available for Minnesota residents attending Minnesota colleges. Student covers 46% of cost with remainder covered by Pell Grant, parent contribution and state grant. Students apply with FAFSA and college administers the program on campus. *Award:* Grant for use in freshman, sophomore, junior, or senior year; not renewable. *Award amount:* $100–$7662. *Number of awards:* 71,000–75,000. *Eligibility Requirements:* Applicant must be age 17; enrolled or expecting to enroll full or part-time at a two-year, four-year, or technical institution or university; resident of Minnesota and studying in Minnesota. Available to U.S. citizens. *Application Requirements:* Application, financial need analysis. *Deadline:* varies.

Contact: Minnesota Higher Education Services Office, 1450 Energy Park Drive, Suite 350, St. Paul, MN 55108. *Phone:* 651-642-0567 Ext. 1. *Web site:* www.mheso.state. mn.us.

Minnesota State Veterans' Dependents Assistance Program. Tuition assistance to dependents of persons considered to be prisoner-of-war or missing in action after August 1, 1958. Must be Minnesota resident attending Minnesota two- or four-year school. *Award:* Scholarship for use in freshman, sophomore, junior, or senior year; renewable. *Award amount:* varies. *Number of awards:* varies. *Eligibility Requirements:* Applicant must be enrolled or expecting to enroll at a two-year or four-year institution; resident of Minnesota and studying in Minnesota. Available to U.S. citizens. Applicant or parent must meet one or more of the following requirements: general military experience; retired from active duty; disabled or killed as a result of military service; prisoner of war; or missing in action. *Application Requirements:* Application. *Deadline:* continuous.

Contact: Minnesota Higher Education Services Office, 1450 Energy Park Drive, Suite 350, St. Paul, MN 55108-5227. *Web site:* www.mheso.state.mn.us.

Minnesota VA Educational Assistance for Veterans. One-time $750 stipend given to veterans who have used up all other federal funds, yet have time remaining on their delimiting period. Applicant must be a Minnesota resident and must be attending a Minnesota college or university, but not the University of Minnesota. *Award:* Grant for use in freshman, sophomore, junior, or senior year; not renewable. *Award amount:* $750. *Number of awards:* varies. *Eligibility Requirements:* Applicant must be enrolled or expecting to enroll full or part-time at a two-year, four-year, or technical institution or university; resident of Minnesota and studying in Minnesota. Available to U.S. citizens. Applicant must have general military experience. *Application Requirements:* Application, financial need analysis. *Deadline:* continuous.

Contact: Terrence Logan, Management Analyst IV, Minnesota Department of Veterans' Affairs, 20 West 12th Street, Second Floor, St. Paul, MN 55155-2079. *Phone:* 651-296-2562. *Fax:* 651-296-3954.

Postsecondary Child Care Grant Program-Minnesota. One-time grant available for students not receiving MFIP. Based on financial need. Cannot exceed actual child care costs or maximum award chart (based on income). Must be Minnesota resident. For use at Minnesota two- or four-year school, including public technical colleges. *Award:* Grant for use in freshman, sophomore, junior, or senior year; not renewable. *Award amount:* $100–$2200. *Number of awards:* varies. *Eligibility Requirements:* Applicant must be enrolled or expecting to enroll full or part-time at a two-year, four-year, or technical institution or university; resident of Minnesota and studying in Minnesota. Available to U.S. citizens. *Application Requirements:* Application, financial need analysis. *Deadline:* continuous.

Contact: Minnesota Higher Education Services Office, 1450 Energy Park Drive, Suite 350, St. Paul, MN 55108-5227. *Phone:* 651-642-0567 Ext. 1. *Web site:* www.mheso. state.mn.us.

MISSISSIPPI

Critical Needs Teacher Loan/Scholarship. Eligible applicants will agree to employment immediately upon degree completion as a full-time classroom teacher in a public school located in a critical teacher shortage area in the state of Mississippi. Must verify the intention to pursue a first bachelor's degree in teacher education. Award covers tuition and required fees, average cost of room and meals plus a $500 allowance for books. Must be enrolled at a Mississippi college or university. *Academic Fields/Career Goals:* Education; Psychology; Therapy/Rehabilitation. *Award:* Forgivable loan for use in junior or senior year; not renewable. *Number of awards:* varies. *Eligibility Requirements:* Applicant must be enrolled or expecting to enroll full or part-time at a four-year institution or university and studying in Mississippi. Applicant must have 2.5 GPA or higher. Available to U.S. citizens. *Application Requirements:* Application, test scores, transcript. *Deadline:* March 31.

Contact: Mississippi Student Financial Aid, Mississippi State Student Financial Aid, 3825 Ridgewood Road, Jackson, MS 39211-6453. *E-mail:* sfa@ihl.state.ms.us. *Phone:* 800-327-2980. *Web site:* www.mississippiuniversities. com.

Higher Education Legislative Plan (HELP). Eligible applicant must be resident of Mississippi and be freshmen and/or sophomore student who graduated from high school within the immediate past two years. Must demonstrate need as determined by the results of the Free Application for Federal Student Aid, documenting an average family adjusted gross income of $36,500 or less over the prior two years. Must be enrolled full-time at a Mississippi college or university, have a cumulative grade point average of 2.5 and have scored 20 on the ACT. *Award:* Scholarship for use in freshman or sophomore year; renewable. *Number of awards:* varies. *Eligibility Requirements:* Applicant must be enrolled or expecting to enroll full-time at a four-year institution or university; resident of Mississippi and studying in Mississippi. Applicant must have 2.5 GPA or higher. Available to U.S. citizens. *Application Requirements:* Application, financial need analysis, test scores, transcript, FAFSA. *Deadline:* March 31.

Contact: Mississippi Student Financial Aid, Mississippi State Student Financial Aid, 3825 Ridgewood Road, Jackson, MS 39211-6453. *E-mail:* sfa@ihl.state.ms.us. *Phone:* 800-327-2980. *Web site:* www.mississippiuniversities. com.

Mississippi Law Enforcement Officers and Firemen Scholarship Program. Award for dependents and spouses of policemen or firemen who were killed or disabled in the line of duty. Must be a Mississippi resident and attend a state-supported college or university. The award is a full tuition waiver. Contact for deadline. *Award:* Scholarship for use in freshman, sophomore, junior, or senior year; renewable. *Number of awards:* varies. *Eligibility Requirements:* Applicant must be enrolled or expecting to enroll full-time at a two-year or four-year institution or university; resident of Mississippi and studying in Mississippi. Applicant or parent of applicant must have employment or volunteer experience in police/firefighting. Available to U.S. citizens. *Application Requirements:* Application, driver's license, references. *Deadline:* continuous.

Contact: Susan Eckels, Program Administrator, Mississippi State Student Financial Aid, 3825 Ridgewood Road, Jackson, MS 39211-6453. *E-mail:* sme@ihl.state.ms.us. *Phone:* 601-432-6997. *Web site:* www. mississippiuniversities.com.

Mississippi Eminent Scholars Grant. Award for high-school seniors who are residents of Mississippi. Applicants must achieve a grade point average of 3.5 after a minimum of seven semesters in high school and must have scored 29 on the ACT. Must enroll full-time at an eligible Mississippi college or university. *Award:* Grant for use in freshman, sophomore, junior, or senior year; renewable. *Award amount:* up to $2500. *Number of awards:* varies. *Eligibility Requirements:* Applicant must be high school student; planning to enroll or expecting to enroll full-time at a four-year institution or university; resident of Mississippi and studying in Mississippi. Applicant must have 3.5 GPA or higher. Available to U.S. citizens. *Application Requirements:* Application, test scores, transcript. *Deadline:* September 15.

Contact: Mississippi Student Financial Aid, Mississippi State Student Financial Aid, 3825 Ridgewood Road, Jackson, MS 39211-6453. *E-mail:* sfa@ihl.state.ms.us. *Phone:* 800-327-2980. *Web site:* www.mississippiuniversities. com.

Mississippi Health Care Professions Loan/Scholarship Program. Renewable award for junior and senior undergraduates studying psychology, speech pathology or occupational therapy. Must be Mississippi residents attending four-year universities in Mississippi. Must fulfill work obligation in Mississippi or pay back as loan. Renewable award for graduate student enrolled in physical therapy. *Academic Fields/Career Goals:* Health and Medical Sciences; Psychology; Therapy/Rehabilitation. *Award:* Forgivable loan for use in junior, senior, or graduate year; renewable. *Award amount:* $1500–$6000. *Number of awards:* varies. *Eligibility Requirements:* Applicant must be enrolled or expecting to enroll full-time at a four-year institution or university; resident of Mississippi and studying in Mississippi. Available to U.S. citizens. *Application Requirements:* Application, driver's license, references, transcript. *Deadline:* March 31.

Contact: Susan Eckels, Program Administrator, Mississippi State Student Financial Aid, 3825 Ridgewood Road, Jackson, MS 39211-6453. *E-mail:* sme@ihl.state.ms.us. *Phone:* 601-432-6997. *Web site:* www.mississippiuniversities.com.

Mississippi Leveraging Educational Assistance Partnership (LEAP). Award for Mississippi residents enrolled for full-time study at a Mississippi college or university. Based on financial need. Deadline varies with each institution. Contact college financial aid office. *Award:* Grant for use in freshman, sophomore, junior, or senior year; not renewable. *Award amount:* $100–$1500. *Number of awards:* varies. *Eligibility Requirements:* Applicant must be enrolled or expecting to enroll full-time at a two-year or four-year institution or university; resident of Mississippi and studying in Mississippi. Available to U.S. citizens. *Application Requirements:* Application, financial need analysis, FAFSA. *Deadline:* continuous.

Contact: Student Financial Aid Office, Mississippi State Student Financial Aid. *Web site:* www.mississippiuniversities.com.

Mississippi Resident Tuition Assistance Grant. Must be a resident of Mississippi enrolled full-time at an eligible Mississippi college or university. Must maintain a minimum 2.5 GPA each semester. MTAG awards may be up to $500 per academic year for freshmen and sophomores and $1,000 per academic year for juniors and seniors. Funds will be made available to eligible participants for eight (8) semesters or the normal time required to complete the degree program, whichever comes first. Refer to Web site for application information http://www.mississippiuniversities.com *Award:* Grant for use in freshman, sophomore, junior, or senior year; renewable. *Award amount:* $500–$1000. *Eligibility Requirements:* Applicant must be enrolled or expecting to enroll full-time at a two-year or four-year institution or university; resident of Mississippi and studying in Mississippi. Applicant must have 2.5 GPA or higher. Available to U.S. citizens. *Application Requirements:* Application, test scores, transcript. *Deadline:* September 15.

Contact: Mississippi Student Financial Aid, Mississippi State Student Financial Aid, 3825 Ridgewood Road, Jackson, MS 39211-6453. *E-mail:* sfa@ihl.state.ms.us. *Phone:* 800-327-2980. *Web site:* www.mississippiuniversities.com.

Nursing Education Loan/Scholarship-BSN. Renewable award for Mississippi undergraduates in junior or senior year pursuing nursing programs in Mississippi in order to earn BSN degree. Include transcript and references with application. Must agree to employment in professional nursing (patient care) in Mississippi. *Academic Fields/Career Goals:* Nursing. *Award:* Forgivable loan for use in junior or senior year; renewable. *Award amount:* up to $8000. *Number of awards:* varies. *Eligibility Requirements:* Applicant must be enrolled or expecting to enroll full or part-time at a four-year institution or university; resident of Mississippi and studying in Mississippi. Applicant must have 2.5 GPA or higher. Available to U.S. citizens. *Application Requirements:* Application, driver's license, financial need analysis, references, transcript. *Deadline:* March 31.

Contact: Board of Trustees, Mississippi State Student Financial Aid, 3825 Ridgewood road, Jackson, MS 39211-6453. *Web site:* www.mississippiuniversities.com.

William Winter Teacher Scholar Loan Program. Awarded to Mississippi residents pursuing a teaching career. Must be enrolled full-time in a program leading to a Class A certification and maintain a 2.5 GPA. Must agree to teach one year for each year award is received. *Academic Fields/Career Goals:* Education. *Award:* Forgivable loan for use in junior or senior year; renewable. *Award amount:* $500–$8000. *Number of awards:* varies. *Eligibility Requirements:* Applicant must be enrolled or expecting to enroll full-time at a two-year or four-year institution or university; resident of Mississippi and studying in Mississippi. Applicant must have 2.5 GPA or higher. Available to U.S. citizens. *Application Requirements:* Application, driver's license, references, transcript. *Deadline:* March 31.

Contact: Board of Trustees, Mississippi State Student Financial Aid, 3825 Ridgewood Road, Jackson, MS 39211-6453. *Web site:* www.mississippiuniversities.com.

MISSOURI

Charles Gallagher Student Assistance Program. Available to Missouri residents attending Missouri colleges or universities full-time. Must be undergraduates with financial need. May reapply for up to a maximum of ten semesters. Free Application for Federal Student Aid (FAFSA) or a renewal must be received by the federal processor by April 1 to be considered. *Award:* Grant for use in freshman, sophomore, junior, or senior year; not renewable. *Award amount:* $100–$1500. *Number of awards:* varies. *Eligibility Requirements:* Applicant must be enrolled or expecting to enroll full-time at a two-year, four-year, or technical institution or university; resident of Missouri and studying in Missouri. Available to U.S. citizens. *Application Requirements:* Financial need analysis. *Deadline:* April 1.

Contact: MDHE Information Center, Missouri Department of Higher Education, 3515 Amazonas Drive, Jefferson City, MO 65109. *E-mail:* icweb@dhe.mo.gov. *Phone:* 800-473-6757 Ext. 1. *Fax:* 573-751-6635. *Web site:* www.dhe.mo.gov.

Marguerite Ross Barnett Memorial Scholarship. Applicant must be employed (at least 20 hours per week) and attending school part-time. Must be Missouri resident and enrolled at a participating Missouri postsecondary school. Awards not available during summer term. Minimum age is 18. *Award:* Scholarship for use in freshman, sophomore, junior, or senior year; not renewable. *Award amount:* $900–$1700. *Number of awards:* varies. *Eligibility Requirements:* Applicant must be age 18; enrolled or expecting to enroll part-time at a two-year or four-year institution or university; resident of Missouri and studying in Missouri. Available to U.S. citizens. *Application Requirements:* Application, financial need analysis. *Deadline:* April 1.

Contact: MDHE Information Center, Missouri Department of Higher Education, 3515 Amazonas Drive, Jefferson City, MO 65109. *E-mail:* icweb@dhe.mo.gov. *Phone:* 800-473-6757 Ext. 1. *Fax:* 573-751-6635. *Web site:* www.dhe.mo.gov.

Missouri College Guarantee Program. Available to Missouri residents attending Missouri colleges full-time. Minimum 2.5 GPA required. Must have participated in high school extracurricular activities. *Award:* Scholarship for use in freshman, sophomore, junior, or senior year; not renewable. *Award amount:* $100–$4900. *Number of awards:* varies. *Eligibility Requirements:* Applicant must be enrolled or expecting to enroll full-time at a two-year or four-year institution or university; resident of Missouri and studying in Missouri. Applicant must have 2.5 GPA or higher. Available to U.S. citizens. *Application Requirements:* Financial need analysis, test scores. *Deadline:* April 1.

Contact: MDHE Information Center, Missouri Department of Higher Education, 3515 Amazonas Drive, Jefferson City, MO 65109. *E-mail:* icweb@dhe.mo.gov. *Phone:* 800-473-6757 Ext. 1. *Fax:* 573-751-6635. *Web site:* www.dhe.mo.gov.

Missouri Higher Education Academic Scholarship (Bright Flight). Awards of $2000 for Missouri high school seniors. Must be in top 3% of Missouri SAT or ACT scorers. Must attend Missouri institution as full-time undergraduate. May reapply for up to ten semesters. Must be Missouri resident and U.S. citizen. *Award:* Scholarship for use in freshman, sophomore, junior, or senior year; not renewable. *Award amount:* $2000. *Number of awards:* varies. *Eligibility Requirements:* Applicant must be high school student; planning to enroll or expecting to enroll full-time at a two-year, four-year, or technical institution or university; resident of Missouri and studying in Missouri. Available to U.S. citizens. *Application Requirements:* Test scores. *Deadline:* July 31.

Contact: MDHE Information Center, Missouri Department of Higher Education, 3515 Amazonas Drive, Jefferson City, MO 65109. *E-mail:* icweb@dhe.mo.gov. *Phone:* 800-473-6757 Ext. 1. *Fax:* 573-751-6635. *Web site:* www.dhe.mo.gov.

Missouri Minority Teaching Scholarship. Award may be used any year up to four years at an approved, participating Missouri institution. Scholarship is for minority Missouri residents in teaching programs. Recipients must commit to teach for five years in a Missouri public elementary or secondary school. Graduate students must teach math or science. Otherwise, award must be repaid. *Academic Fields/Career Goals:* Education. *Award:* Scholarship for use in freshman, sophomore, junior, senior, or graduate year; renewable. *Award amount:* $3000. *Number of awards:* 100. *Eligibility Requirements:* Applicant must be American Indian/Alaska Native, Asian/Pacific Islander, Black (non-Hispanic), or Hispanic; enrolled or expecting to enroll full-time at a two-year or four-year institution or university; resident of Missouri and studying in Missouri. Applicant must have 3.0 GPA or higher. Available to U.S. citizens. *Application Requirements:* Application, essay, financial need analysis, resume, references, test scores, transcript. *Deadline:* February 15.

Contact: Laura Harrison, Administrative Assistant II, Missouri Department of Elementary and Secondary Education, PO Box 480, Jefferson City, MO 65102-0480. *E-mail:* laura. harrison@dese.mo.gov. *Phone:* 573-751-1668. *Fax:* 573-526-3580. *Web site:* www.dese.state. mo.us.

Missouri Teacher Education Scholarship (General). Nonrenewable award for Missouri high school seniors or Missouri resident college students. Must attend approved teacher training program at a participating Missouri institution. Must rank in top 15 % of high school class on ACT/SAT. Merit-based award. Recipients must commit to teach in Missouri for five years at a public elementary or secondary school or award must be repaid. *Academic Fields/Career Goals:* Education. *Award:* Scholar-

ship for use in freshman, sophomore, junior, or senior year; not renewable. *Award amount:* $2000. *Number of awards:* 200–240. *Eligibility Requirements:* Applicant must be enrolled or expecting to enroll full-time at a two-year or four-year institution or university; resident of Missouri and studying in Missouri. Applicant must have 3.5 GPA or higher. Available to U.S. citizens. *Application Requirements:* Application, essay, resume, references, test scores, transcript. *Deadline:* February 15.

Contact: Laura Harrison, Administrative Assistant II, Missouri Department of Elementary and Secondary Education, PO Box 480, Jefferson City, MO 65102-0480. *E-mail:* laura. harrison@dese.mo.gov. *Phone:* 573-751-1668. *Fax:* 573-526-3580. *Web site:* www.dese.state. mo.us.

National Farmworker Jobs Program. The grant is from the Department of Labor. Renewable grant to low income seasonal farm workers and their dependents for tuition assistance. Must be a resident of Missouri. Must be paid wages for doing farm work. High school seniors may apply. Must attend a Missouri school. Minimum 2.5 GPA required. *Award:* Grant for use in freshman, sophomore, junior, or senior year; renewable. *Award amount:* up to $3000. *Number of awards:* varies. *Eligibility Requirements:* Applicant must be age 16; enrolled or expecting to enroll at a two-year, four-year, or technical institution or university; resident of Missouri and studying in Missouri. Applicant or parent of applicant must have employment or volunteer experience in agriculture, farming, or migrant worker. Applicant must have 2.5 GPA or higher. *Application Requirements:* Application. *Deadline:* continuous.

Contact: Lynn Hatfield, Program Director, Rural Missouri, Inc., 1014 Northeast Drive, Jefferson City, MO 65109. *E-mail:* lynn@rmiinc.org. *Phone:* 800-234-4971. *Fax:* 573-635-5636. *Web site:* www.rmiinc.org.

Primary Care Resource Initiative for Missouri Loan Program. Forgivable loans for Missouri residents attending Missouri institutions pursuing a degree as a primary care physician or dentist, studying for a bachelors degree as a dental hygienist, or a master of science degree in nursing leading to certification as an Advanced Practice Nurse. To be forgiven participant must work in a Missouri health professional shortage area. *Academic Fields/Career Goals:* Dental Health/Services; Health and Medical Sciences; Nursing. *Award:* Forgivable loan for use in freshman, sophomore, junior, senior, graduate, or postgraduate years; not renewable. *Award amount:* $3000–$25,000. *Number of awards:* varies. *Eligibility Require-

ments:* Applicant must be enrolled or expecting to enroll full or part-time at a four-year institution or university; resident of Missouri and studying in Missouri. Available to U.S. citizens. *Application Requirements:* Application, driver's license. *Deadline:* July 1.

Contact: Kristie Frank, Health Program Representative, Missouri Department of Health and Senior Services, PO Box 570, Jefferson City, MO 65102-0570. *E-mail:* frank@dhss. mo.gov. *Phone:* 800-891-7415. *Fax:* 573-522-8146. *Web site:* www.dhss.state.mo.us.

MONTANA

Indian Student Fee Waiver. Fee waiver awarded by the Montana University System to undergraduate and graduate students meeting the criteria. Amount varies depending upon the tuition and registration fee at each participating college. Students must provide documentation of one-fourth Indian blood or more; must be a resident of Montana for at least one year prior to enrolling in school and must demonstrate financial need. Full-or part-time study qualifies. Complete and submit the FAFSA by March 1 and a Montana Indian Fee Waiver application form. Contact the financial aid office at the college of attendance to determine eligibility. *Award:* Scholarship for use in freshman, sophomore, junior, senior, or graduate year; renewable. *Award amount:* $2000. *Number of awards:* 600. *Eligibility Requirements:* Applicant must be American Indian/Alaska Native; enrolled or expecting to enroll full or part-time at a two-year or four-year institution or university; resident of Montana and studying in Montana. Available to U.S. citizens. *Application Requirements:* Application, financial need analysis, FAFSA. *Deadline:* March 1.

Contact: Sally Speer, Grants and Scholarship Coordinator, Montana Guaranteed Student Loan Program, Office of Commissioner of Higher Education, 2500 Broadway, PO Box 203101, Helena, MT 59620-3101. *E-mail:* sspeer@mgslp.state.mt.us. *Phone:* 406-444-0638. *Fax:* 406-444-1869. *Web site:* www. mgslp.state.mt.us.

Life Member Montana Federation of Garden Clubs Scholarship. Applicant must be at least a sophomore, majoring in conservation, horticulture, park or forestry, floriculture, greenhouse management, land management, or related subjects. Must be in need of assistance. Must have a potential for a successful future. Must be ranked in upper half of class or have a minimum 2.8 GPA. Must be a Montana resident and all study must be done in Montana. Deadline: May 1. *Academic Fields/Career Goals:*

Biology; Earth Science; Horticulture/ Floriculture; Landscape Architecture. *Award:* Scholarship for use in sophomore, junior, or senior year; not renewable. *Award amount:* $1000. *Number of awards:* 1. *Eligibility Requirements:* Applicant must be enrolled or expecting to enroll full-time at a four-year institution or university; resident of Montana and studying in Montana. Available to U.S. citizens. *Application Requirements:* Autobiography, financial need analysis, photo, references, transcript. *Deadline:* May 1.

Contact: Elizabeth Kehmeier, Life Members Scholarship Chairman, Montana Federation of Garden Clubs, 214 Wyant Lane, Hamilton, MT 59840. *E-mail:* elizabethhammt@aol. com. *Phone:* 406-363-5693.

Montana Higher Education Opportunity Grant. This grant is awarded based on need to undergraduate students attending either part-time or full-time who are residents of Montana and attending participating Montana schools. Awards are limited to the most needy students. A specific major or program of study is not required. This grant does not need to be repaid, and students may apply each year. Apply by filing a Free Application for Federal Student Aid by March 1 and contacting the financial aid office at the admitting college. *Award:* Grant for use in freshman, sophomore, junior, or senior year; not renewable. *Award amount:* $400–$600. *Number of awards:* up to 800. *Eligibility Requirements:* Applicant must be enrolled or expecting to enroll full or part-time at a two-year or four-year institution or university; resident of Montana and studying in Montana. Available to U.S. citizens. *Application Requirements:* Financial need analysis, FAFSA. *Deadline:* March 1.

Contact: Sally Speer, Grants and Scholarship Coordinator, Montana Guaranteed Student Loan Program, Office of Commissioner of Higher Education, 2500 Broadway, PO Box 203101, Helena, MT 59620-3101. *E-mail:* sspeer@mgslp.state.mt.us. *Phone:* 406-444-0638. *Fax:* 406-444-1869. *Web site:* www. mgslp.state.mt.us.

Montana Tuition Assistance Program-Baker Grant. Need-based grant for Montana residents attending participating Montana schools who have earned at least $2,575 during the previous calendar year. Must be enrolled full time. Grant does not need to be repaid. Award covers the first undergraduate degree or certificate. Apply by filing a Free Application for Federal Student Aid by March 1 and contacting the financial aid office at the admitting college. *Award:* Grant for use in freshman, sophomore, junior, or senior year; not renewable. *Award amount:* $100–$1000. *Number of awards:*

varies. *Eligibility Requirements:* Applicant must be enrolled or expecting to enroll full-time at a two-year or four-year institution or university; resident of Montana and studying in Montana. Available to U.S. citizens. *Application Requirements:* Financial need analysis, FAFSA. *Deadline:* March 1.

Contact: Sally Speer, Grants and Scholarship Coordinator, Montana Guaranteed Student Loan Program, Office of Commissioner of Higher Education, 2500 Broadway, PO Box 203101, Helena, MT 59620-3101. *E-mail:* sspeer@mgslp.state.mt.us. *Phone:* 406-444-0638. *Fax:* 406-444-1869. *Web site:* www. mgslp.state.mt.us.

Montana University System Honor Scholarship. Scholarship provides a four-year renewable fee waiver of tuition and registration and is awarded to graduating high school seniors from accredited high schools in Montana. 300-400 scholarships are awarded each year averaging $2,000-$3,000 per recipient. The value of the award varies, depending on the tuition and registration fee at each participating Montana university or college. Must have a minimum 3.5 GPA, meet all college preparatory requirements, and be enrolled in an accredited high school for at least three years prior to graduation. Awarded to highest-ranking student in class attending a participating school. Contact high school counselor to apply. Deadline: January 31. *Award:* Scholarship for use in freshman, sophomore, junior, or senior year; renewable. *Award amount:* $2000–$3000. *Number of awards:* 300–400. *Eligibility Requirements:* Applicant must be high school student; planning to enroll or expecting to enroll full or part-time at a two-year or four-year institution or university; resident of Montana and studying in Montana. Applicant must have 3.5 GPA or higher. Available to U.S. citizens. *Application Requirements:* Application, transcript. *Deadline:* January 31.

Contact: High School Counselor, Montana Guaranteed Student Loan Program, Office of Commissioner of Higher Education. *Web site:* www.mgslp.state.mt.us.

NEBRASKA

Nebraska National Guard Tuition Credit. Renewable award for members of the Nebraska National Guard. Pays 75% of enlisted soldier's tuition until he or she has received a baccalaureate degree. *Award:* Scholarship for use in freshman, sophomore, junior, or senior year; renewable. *Number of awards:* up to 1200. *Eligibility Requirements:* Applicant must be enrolled or expecting to enroll full or part-time at a two-year, four-year, or technical institution

or university; resident of Nebraska and studying in Nebraska. Applicant must have served in the Air Force National Guard or Army National Guard. *Application Requirements:* Application. *Deadline:* continuous.

Contact: Cindy York, Administrative Assistant, Nebraska National Guard, 1300 Military Road, Lincoln, NE 68508-1090. *Phone:* 402-309-7143. *Fax:* 402-309-7128. *Web site:* www.neguard.com.

Nebraska State Grant. Available to undergraduates attending a participating postsecondary institution in Nebraska. Available to Pell Grant recipients only. Nebraska residency required. Awards determined by each participating institution. Contact financial aid office at institution for application and additional information. *Award:* Grant for use in freshman, sophomore, junior, or senior year; not renewable. *Award amount:* $100–$1032. *Number of awards:* varies. *Eligibility Requirements:* Applicant must be enrolled or expecting to enroll full or part-time at a two-year, four-year, or technical institution or university; resident of Nebraska and studying in Nebraska. Available to U.S. citizens. *Application Requirements:* Application, financial need analysis. *Deadline:* continuous.

Contact: Financial Aid Office at college or university, State of Nebraska Coordinating Commission for Postsecondary Education. *Web site:* www.ccpe.state.ne.us.

NEVADA

Nevada Student Incentive Grant. Award available to Nevada residents for use at an accredited Nevada college or university. Must show financial need. Any field of study eligible. High school students may not apply. One-time award of up to $5000. Contact financial aid office at local college. *Award:* Grant for use in freshman, sophomore, junior, or senior year; not renewable. *Award amount:* $100–$5000. *Number of awards:* 400–800. *Eligibility Requirements:* Applicant must be enrolled or expecting to enroll full or part-time at a two-year, four-year, or technical institution or university; resident of Nevada and studying in Nevada. Available to U.S. citizens. *Application Requirements:* Application, financial need analysis. *Deadline:* continuous.

Contact: Financial Aid Office at local college, Nevada Department of Education, 700 East 5th Street, Carson City, NV 89701.

NEW HAMPSHIRE

Leveraged Incentive Grant Program. Award open to New Hampshire residents attending school in New Hampshire. Must be in sophomore, junior, or senior year. Award based on financial need and merit. Contact financial aid office for more information and deadline. *Award:* Grant for use in sophomore, junior, or senior year; not renewable. *Award amount:* $200–$7500. *Number of awards:* varies. *Eligibility Requirements:* Applicant must be enrolled or expecting to enroll full-time at a two-year or four-year institution or university; resident of New Hampshire and studying in New Hampshire. Available to U.S. citizens. *Application Requirements:* Application, financial need analysis. *Deadline:* varies.

Contact: Financial Aid Office, New Hampshire Postsecondary Education Commission. *Web site:* www.state.nh.us/postsecondary.

New Hampshire Incentive Program (NHIP). One-time grants for New Hampshire residents attending school in New Hampshire, Connecticut, Maine, Massachusetts, Rhode Island, or Vermont. Must have financial need. Deadline is May 1. Complete Free Application for Federal Student Aid. Grant is not automatically renewable. Applicant must reapply. *Award:* Grant for use in freshman, sophomore, junior, or senior year; not renewable. *Award amount:* $125–$1000. *Number of awards:* 3000–4300. *Eligibility Requirements:* Applicant must be enrolled or expecting to enroll full or part-time at a two-year, four-year, or technical institution or university; resident of New Hampshire and studying in Connecticut, Maine, Massachusetts, New Hampshire, Rhode Island, or Vermont. Available to U.S. citizens. *Application Requirements:* Application, financial need analysis. *Deadline:* May 1.

Contact: Sherrie Tucker, Program Assistant, New Hampshire Postsecondary Education Commission, 3 Barrell Court, Suite 300, Concord, NH 03301-8512. *E-mail:* stucker@pec.state.nh.us. *Phone:* 603-271-2555 Ext. 355. *Fax:* 603-271-2696. *Web site:* www.state.nh.us/postsecondary.

Scholarships for Orphans of Veterans-New Hampshire. Awards for New Hampshire residents whose parent died as a result of service in WWI, WWII, the Korean Conflict, or the Southeast Asian Conflict. Parent must have been a New Hampshire resident at time of death. Possible full tuition and $1000 per year with automatic renewal on reapplication. Contact department for application deadlines. Must be under 26. Must include proof of eligibility and proof of parent's death. *Award:* Scholarship for use in freshman, sophomore, junior, or senior year; renewable. *Award amount:* varies. *Number of awards:* 1–10. *Eligibility Requirements:* Applicant must be age 16-25; enrolled or expecting to enroll

full-time at a two-year or four-year institution or university and resident of New Hampshire. Available to U.S. citizens. Applicant or parent must meet one or more of the following requirements: general military experience; retired from active duty; disabled or killed as a result of military service; prisoner of war; or missing in action. *Application Requirements:* Application, VA approval. *Deadline:* varies.

Contact: Melanie K. Deshaies, Program Assistant, New Hampshire Postsecondary Education Commission, 3 Barrell Court, Suite 300, Concord, NH 03301-8543. *E-mail:* mdeshaies@pec.state.nh.us. *Phone:* 603-271-2555 Ext. 356. *Fax:* 603-271-2696. *Web site:* www.state.nh.us/postsecondary.

Workforce Incentive Program. The Workforce Incentive Program links higher education with critical workforce needs. There are two components to the program: an incentive for students to study in particular areas (forgivable loan) and assistance for employees in critical workforce shortage areas (loan repayment). Critical shortage areas are: nursing, special education, and foreign language education. Please refer to Web site for further details: http://www.state.nh.us/postsecondary. *Academic Fields/Career Goals:* Education; Foreign Language; Nursing; Special Education. *Award:* Forgivable loan for use in freshman, sophomore, junior, senior, graduate, or postgraduate years. *Award amount:* varies. *Number of awards:* varies. *Eligibility Requirements:* Applicant must be enrolled or expecting to enroll at an institution or university and studying in New Hampshire. Available to U.S. citizens. *Application Requirements:* Application. *Deadline:* varies.

Contact: Judith A. Knapp, Student Financial Assistant Coordinator, New Hampshire Postsecondary Education Commission, 3 Barrell Court, Suite 300, Concord, NH 03301-8543. *E-mail:* jknapp@pec.state.nh.us. *Phone:* 603-271-2555. *Fax:* 603-271-2696. *Web site:* www.state.nh.us/postsecondary.

NEW JERSEY

Dana Christmas Scholarship for Heroism. Honors young New Jersey residents for acts of heroism. Scholarship is a non-renewable award of up to $10000 for up to five recipients. This scholarship may be used for undergraduate or graduate study. *Award:* Scholarship for use in freshman, sophomore, junior, senior, or graduate year; not renewable. *Award amount:* up to $10,000. *Number of awards:* up to 5. *Eligibility Requirements:* Applicant must be age 21 or under; enrolled or expecting to enroll full or part-time at a four-year

institution or university and resident of New Jersey. Available to U.S. citizens. *Application Requirements:* Application. *Deadline:* October 15.

Contact: Gisele Joachim, Director of Financial Aid Services, New Jersey Higher Education Student Assistance Authority, PO Box 540, Trenton, NJ 08625. *Phone:* 800-792-8670. *Fax:* 609-588-7389. *Web site:* www.hesaa.org.

Edward J. Bloustein Distinguished Scholars. Renewable scholarship for students who place in the top 10% of their classes and have a minimum combined SAT score of 1260, or are ranked first, second or third in their class as of the end of the junior year. Must be New Jersey resident. Must attend a New Jersey two-year college, four-year college or university, or approved programs at proprietary institutions. Secondary schools forward to HESAA the names and class standings for all nominees. *Award:* Scholarship for use in freshman, sophomore, junior, or senior year; renewable. *Award amount:* $950. *Number of awards:* varies. *Eligibility Requirements:* Applicant must be high school student; planning to enroll or expecting to enroll full-time at a two-year or four-year institution or university; resident of New Jersey and studying in New Jersey. Available to U.S. citizens. *Application Requirements:* Test scores, nominated by high school. *Deadline:* October 1.

Contact: Carol Muka, Assistant Director of Grants and Scholarships, New Jersey Higher Education Student Assistance Authority, PO Box 540, Trenton, NJ 08625. *Phone:* 800-792-8670. *Fax:* 609-588-2228. *Web site:* www.hesaa.org.

New Jersey Educational Opportunity Fund Grants. Grants up to $4150 per year. Must be a New Jersey resident for at least twelve consecutive months and attend a New Jersey institution. Must be from a disadvantaged background as defined by EOF guidelines. EOF grant applicants must also apply for financial aid. EOF recipients may qualify for the Martin Luther King Physician/Dentistry Scholarships for graduate study at a professional institution. *Academic Fields/Career Goals:* Dental Health/Services; Health and Medical Sciences. *Award:* Grant for use in freshman, sophomore, junior, senior, or graduate year; renewable. *Award amount:* up to $4150. *Number of awards:* varies. *Eligibility Requirements:* Applicant must be enrolled or expecting to enroll full-time at a four-year institution or university; resident of New Jersey and studying in New Jersey. Available to U.S. citizens. *Application*

Requirements: Application, financial need analysis. *Deadline:* continuous.

Contact: Sandra Rollins, Associate Director of Financial Aid, University of Medicine and Dentistry of NJ School of Osteopathic Medicine, 40 East Laurel Road, Primary Care Center 119, Stratford, NJ 08084. *E-mail:* rollins@umdnj.edu. *Phone:* 856-566-6008. *Fax:* 856-566-6015. *Web site:* www.umdnj.edu/studentfinancialaid.

New Jersey War Orphans Tuition Assistance. Renewable award for New Jersey residents who are high school seniors ages 16-21 and who are children of veterans killed or disabled in duty, missing in action, or prisoner-of-war. For use at a two- or four-year college or university. Write for more information. Deadlines: October 1 for fall semester and March 1 for spring semester. *Award:* Scholarship for use in freshman, sophomore, junior, or senior year; renewable. *Award amount:* $2000–$8000. *Number of awards:* varies. *Eligibility Requirements:* Applicant must be high school student; age 16-21; planning to enroll or expecting to enroll full-time at a two-year or four-year institution or university and resident of New Jersey. Applicant or parent must meet one or more of the following requirements: general military experience; retired from active duty; disabled or killed as a result of military service; prisoner of war; or missing in action. *Application Requirements:* Application, transcript. *Deadline:* varies.

Contact: Patricia Richter, Grants Manager, New Jersey Department of Military and Veterans Affairs, PO Box 340, Trenton, NJ 08625-0340. *E-mail:* patricia.richter@njdmava.state.nj.us. *Phone:* 609-530-6854. *Fax:* 609-530-6970. *Web site:* www.state.nj.us/military.

New Jersey World Trade Center Scholarship. Established by the legislature to aid the dependent children and surviving spouses of NJ residents who were killed in the terrorist attacks, or who are missing and officially presumed dead as a direct result of the attacks; applies to in-state and out-of-state institutions for students seeking undergraduate degrees. *Award:* Scholarship for use in freshman, sophomore, junior, or senior year; renewable. *Award amount:* up to $6500. *Number of awards:* varies. *Eligibility Requirements:* Applicant must be enrolled or expecting to enroll full-time at a two-year or four-year institution or university and resident of New Jersey. Available to U.S. citizens. *Application Requirements:* Application. *Deadline:* October 1.

Contact: Giselle Joachim, Director of Financial Aid Services, New Jersey Higher Education Student Assistance Authority, PO Box 540, Trenton, NJ 08625. *Phone:* 800-792-8670. *Fax:* 609-588-7389. *Web site:* www.hesaa.org.

NJSA Scholarship Program. One-time award for legal residents of New Jersey enrolled in an accredited architecture program. Minimum 2.5 GPA required. Must show evidence of financial need, scholarship, and promise in architecture. Submit portfolio and $5 application fee. *Academic Fields/Career Goals:* Architecture. *Award:* Scholarship for use in sophomore, junior, senior, or graduate year; not renewable. *Award amount:* $1500–$3000. *Number of awards:* 5–8. *Eligibility Requirements:* Applicant must be enrolled or expecting to enroll full-time at a four-year, or technical institution or university and resident of New Jersey. Applicant must have 2.5 GPA or higher. Available to U.S. citizens. *Application Requirements:* Application, essay, financial need analysis, portfolio, references, transcript. *Fee:* $5. *Deadline:* April 25.

Contact: Robert Zaccone, President, AIA New Jersey Scholarship Foundation, Inc., 212 White Avenue, Old Tappan, NJ 07675-7411. *Fax:* 201-767-5541.

Outstanding Scholar Recruitment Program. Students who meet the eligibility criteria and enroll as first-time freshmen at participating New Jersey institutions receive annual scholarship awards of $2500 to $7500. The award amounts vary on a sliding scale depending on class rank and combined SAT scores. Must maintain a B average for renewal. Deadline October 1 for Fall term, March 1 for Spring term. *Award:* Scholarship for use in freshman, sophomore, junior, or senior year; renewable. *Award amount:* $2500–$7500. *Number of awards:* varies. *Eligibility Requirements:* Applicant must be high school student; planning to enroll or expecting to enroll at an institution or university; resident of New Jersey and studying in New Jersey. Available to U.S. citizens. *Application Requirements:* Test scores. *Deadline:* varies.

Contact: Carol Muka, Assistant Director of Grants and Scholarships, New Jersey Higher Education Student Assistance Authority, PO Box 540, Trenton, NJ 08625. *Phone:* 800-792-8670. *Fax:* 609-588-2228. *Web site:* www.hesaa.org.

Part-time Tuition Aid Grant (TAG) for County Colleges. Provides financial aid to eligible part-time undergraduate students enrolled for 6-11 credits at participating NJ community colleges. *Award:* Grant for use in freshman or sophomore year; renewable. *Award amount:* $116–$375. *Number of awards:* varies. *Eligibility Requirements:* Applicant must be enrolled or expecting to enroll part-time at a two-year institution; resident of New Jersey and studying in New Jersey. Available to U.S. citizens. *Application Requirements:* Application, financial need analysis. *Deadline:* varies.

Contact: Sherri Fox, Acting Director of Grants and Scholarships, New Jersey Higher Education Student Assistance Authority, PO Box 540, Trenton, NJ 08625. *Phone:* 800-792-8670. *Fax:* 609-588-2228. *Web site:* www.hesaa.org.

Richard G. McCormick Prize. Award to the author of an outstanding book on New Jersey history published during the preceding two years. Offered only in odd-numbered years. Nomination form is on the Web site. Must be nominated. *Academic Fields/Career Goals:* History. *Award:* Prize for use in freshman, sophomore, junior, senior, graduate, or postgraduate years; not renewable. *Award amount:* $1000. *Number of awards:* 1. *Eligibility Requirements:* Applicant must be enrolled or expecting to enroll at an institution or university. Available to U.S. citizens. *Application Requirements:* Application, nomination, one copy of book. *Deadline:* January 2.

Contact: Mary R. Murrin, Director, Grants Program, New Jersey Historical Commission, Attn: Grants and Prizes, 225 West State Street, PO Box 305, Trenton, NJ 08625-0305. *E-mail:* mary.murrin@sos.state.nj.us. *Phone:* 609-984-0954. *Fax:* 609-633-8168. *Web site:* www.state.nj.us/state/history/grants.html.

Survivor Tuition Benefits Program. Provides tuition for spouses and dependents of law enforcement officers, fire, or emergency services personnel killed in the line of duty. Recipients must be enrolled in an undergraduate degree program at a college or university in New Jersey as either half-time or full-time students. Deadline October 1 for Fall term, March 1 for Spring term. *Award:* Scholarship for use in freshman, sophomore, junior, or senior year; renewable. *Number of awards:* varies. *Eligibility Requirements:* Applicant must be enrolled or expecting to enroll full or part-time at a two-year or four-year institution or university; resident of New Jersey and studying in New Jersey. Applicant or parent of applicant must have employment or volunteer experience in police/firefighting. Available to U.S. citizens. *Application Requirements:* Application. *Deadline:* varies.

Contact: Carol Muka, Assistant Director of Grants and Scholarships, New Jersey Higher Education Student Assistance Authority, PO Box 540, Trenton, NJ 08625. *Phone:* 800-792-8670. *Fax:* 609-588-2228. *Web site:* www.hesaa.org.

Tuition Aid Grant. The Tuition Aid Grant (TAG) program provides financial aid to eligible undergraduate students attending participating in-state institutions. *Award:* Grant for use in freshman, sophomore, junior, or senior year; renewable. *Award amount:* $868–$7272. *Number of awards:* varies. *Eligibility Requirements:* Applicant must be enrolled or expecting to enroll full-time at a two-year or four-year institution or university; resident of New Jersey and studying in New Jersey. Available to U.S. citizens. *Application Requirements:* Application, financial need analysis. *Deadline:* varies.

Contact: Sherri Fox, Acting Director of Grants and Scholarships, New Jersey Higher Education Student Assistance Authority, PO Box 540, Trenton, NJ 08625. *Phone:* 800-792-8670. *Fax:* 609-588-2228. *Web site:* www.hesaa.org.

Tuition Assistance for Children of POW/MIAs. Assists children of military service personnel declared missing in action or prisoner-of-war after January 1, 1960. Must be a resident of New Jersey. Renewable grants provide tuition for undergraduate study in New Jersey. Apply by October 1 for fall, March 1 for spring. Must be high school senior to apply. *Award:* Scholarship for use in freshman, sophomore, junior, or senior year; renewable. *Award amount:* $500. *Number of awards:* varies. *Eligibility Requirements:* Applicant must be high school student; planning to enroll or expecting to enroll full-time at a two-year or four-year institution; resident of New Jersey and studying in New Jersey. Applicant must have 2.5 GPA or higher. Available to U.S. citizens. Applicant or parent must meet one or more of the following requirements: general military experience; retired from active duty; disabled or killed as a result of military service; prisoner of war; or missing in action. *Application Requirements:* Application, transcript. *Deadline:* varies.

Contact: Patricia Richter, Grants Manager, New Jersey Department of Military and Veterans Affairs, PO Box 340, Trenton, NJ 08625-0340. *E-mail:* patricia.richter@njdmava. state.nj.us. *Phone:* 609-530-6854. *Fax:* 609-530-6970. *Web site:* www.state.nj.us/military.

Urban Scholars. Renewable scholarship to high achieving students attending public secondary schools in the State's urban and economically distressed areas of New Jersey. Students must rank in the top 10% of their class and have a GPA of at least 3.0 at the end of their junior year. Must be

New Jersey resident. Must attend a New Jersey two-year college, four-year college or university, or approved programs at proprietary institutions. Students do not apply directly for scholarship consideration. Secondary schools forward to HESAA the names and class standing for all nominees. *Award:* Scholarship for use in freshman, sophomore, junior, or senior year; renewable. *Award amount:* $950. *Number of awards:* varies. *Eligibility Requirements:* Applicant must be high school student; planning to enroll or expecting to enroll full-time at a two-year or four-year institution or university; resident of New Jersey and studying in New Jersey. Applicant must have 3.0 GPA or higher. Available to U.S. citizens. *Application Requirements:* Test scores, nominated by school. *Deadline:* October 1.

Contact: Carol Muka, Assistant Director of Grants and Scholarships, New Jersey Higher Education Student Assistance Authority, PO Box 540, Trenton, NJ 08625. *Phone:* 800-792-8670. *Fax:* 609-588-2228. *Web site:* www.hesaa.org.

Veterans' Tuition Credit Program-New Jersey. Award for veterans who served in the armed forces between December 31, 1960, and May 7, 1975. Must have been a New Jersey resident at time of induction or discharge or for one year prior to application. Apply by October 1 for fall, March 1 for spring. Renewable award of $200-$400. *Award:* Scholarship for use in freshman, sophomore, junior, or senior year; renewable. *Award amount:* $200–$400. *Number of awards:* varies. *Eligibility Requirements:* Applicant must be enrolled or expecting to enroll full or part-time at a two-year, four-year, or technical institution or university. Available to U.S. citizens. Applicant must have general military experience. *Application Requirements:* Application. *Deadline:* varies.

Contact: Patricia Richter, Grants Manager, New Jersey Department of Military and Veterans Affairs, PO Box 340, Trenton, NJ 08625-0340. *E-mail:* patricia.richter@njdmava. state.nj.us. *Phone:* 609-530-6854. *Fax:* 609-530-6970. *Web site:* www.state.nj.us/military.

NEW MEXICO

Allied Health Student Loan Program-New Mexico. Renewable loans for New Mexico residents enrolled in an undergraduate allied health program. Loans can be forgiven through service in a medically underserved area or can be repaid. Penalties apply for failure to provide service. May borrow up to $12,000 per year for four years. *Academic Fields/Career Goals:* Dental Health/Services; Health and Medi-

cal Sciences; Nursing; Social Sciences; Therapy/Rehabilitation. *Award:* Forgivable loan for use in freshman, sophomore, junior, or senior year; renewable. *Award amount:* up to $12,000. *Number of awards:* 1–40. *Eligibility Requirements:* Applicant must be enrolled or expecting to enroll full or part-time at a two-year or four-year institution or university; resident of New Mexico and studying in New Mexico. Available to U.S. citizens. *Application Requirements:* Application, financial need analysis, transcript, FAFSA. *Deadline:* July 1.

Contact: Maria Barele, Financial Specialist, New Mexico Commission on Higher Education, PO Box 15910, Santa Fe, NM 87506-5910. *Phone:* 505-827-4026. *Fax:* 505-827-7392. *Web site:* www.nmche.org.

Children of Deceased Veterans Scholarship-New Mexico. Award for New Mexico residents who are children of veterans killed or disabled as a result of service, prisoner of war, or veterans missing-in-action. Must be between ages 16 to 26. For use at New Mexico schools for undergraduate study. Submit parent's death certificate and DD form 214. *Award:* Scholarship for use in freshman, sophomore, junior, or senior year; renewable. *Award amount:* $250–$600. *Eligibility Requirements:* Applicant must be age 16-26; enrolled or expecting to enroll full or part-time at an institution or university; resident of New Mexico and studying in New Mexico. Applicant or parent must meet one or more of the following requirements: general military experience; retired from active duty; disabled or killed as a result of military service; prisoner of war; or missing in action. *Application Requirements:* Application, transcript. *Deadline:* continuous.

Contact: Alan Martinez, Manager of State Benefits, New Mexico Veterans' Service Commission, PO Box 2324, Sante Fe, NM 87504. *Phone:* 505-827-6300. *Fax:* 505-827-6372. *Web site:* www.state.nm.us/veterans.

Legislative Endowment Scholarships. Awards for undergraduate students with substantial financial need who are attending public postsecondary institutions in New Mexico. Preference given to returning adult students at two-year and four-year institutions and students transferring from two-year to four-year institutions. Deadline set by each institution. Must be resident of New Mexico. Contact financial aid office of any New Mexico public postsecondary institution to apply. *Award:* Scholarship for use in freshman, sophomore, junior, or senior year; not renewable. *Award amount:* $1000–$2500. *Eligibility Requirements:* Applicant must be enrolled or expecting to enroll full or part-time at a two-year or four-year institution or university; resident of New Mexico and studying in New Mexico. Available to U.S. citizens. *Application Requirements:* Application, financial need analysis, FAFSA.

Contact: Maria Barele, Financial Specialist, New Mexico Commission on Higher Education, PO Box 15910, Santa Fe, NM 87506-5910. *Phone:* 505-827-7383. *Fax:* 505-827-7392. *Web site:* www.nmche.org.

Lottery Success Scholarships. Awards equal to 100% of tuition at New Mexico public postsecondary institution. Must have New Mexico high school degree and be enrolled at New Mexico public college or university in first regular semester following high school graduation. Must obtain 2.5 GPA during this semester. May be eligible for up to eight consecutive semesters of support. Deadlines vary by institution. Apply through financial aid office of any New Mexico public postsecondary institution. *Award:* Scholarship for use in freshman, sophomore, junior, or senior year; renewable. *Eligibility Requirements:* Applicant must be enrolled or expecting to enroll full-time at a two-year or four-year institution; resident of New Mexico and studying in New Mexico. Applicant must have 2.5 GPA or higher. Available to U.S. citizens. *Application Requirements:* Application.

Contact: Maria Barele, Financial Specialist, New Mexico Commission on Higher Education, PO Box 15910, Santa Fe, NM 87506-5910. *Phone:* 505-827-4026. *Fax:* 505-827-7392. *Web site:* www.nmche.org.

New Mexico Competitive Scholarship. Scholarship available to encourage out-of-state students who have demonstrated high academic achievement to enroll in public institutions of higher education in New Mexico. One-time award for undergraduate students. Deadlines set by each institution. Contact financial aid office of any New Mexico public postsecondary institution to apply. *Award:* Scholarship for use in freshman, sophomore, junior, or senior year; not renewable. *Award amount:* $100. *Eligibility Requirements:* Applicant must be enrolled or expecting to enroll full or part-time at a two-year or four-year institution or university and studying in New Mexico. Applicant must have 3.0 GPA or higher. Available to U.S. citizens. *Application Requirements:* Application, essay, references, test scores.

Contact: Maria Barele, Financial Specialist, New Mexico Commission on Higher Education, PO Box 15910, Santa Fe, NM 87506-5910. *Phone:* 505-827-4026. *Fax:* 505-827-7392. *Web site:* www.nmche.org.

New Mexico Scholars' Program. Several scholarships to encourage New Mexico high school graduates to enroll in college at a public or selected private nonprofit postsecondary institution in New Mexico before their 22nd birthday. Selected private colleges are College of Santa Fe, St. John's College in Santa Fe, and College of the Southwest. Must have graduated in top 5% of their class or obtained an ACT score of 25 or SAT score of 1140. One-time scholarship for tuition, books, and fees. Contact financial aid office at college to apply. *Award:* Scholarship for use in freshman, sophomore, junior, or senior year; not renewable. *Eligibility Requirements:* Applicant must be age 22 or under; enrolled or expecting to enroll full or part-time at a two-year or four-year institution; resident of New Mexico and studying in New Mexico. Available to U.S. citizens. *Application Requirements:* Application, financial need analysis, test scores, FAFSA.

Contact: Maria Barele, Financial Specialist, New Mexico Commission on Higher Education, PO Box 15910, Santa Fe, NM 87506-5910. *Phone:* 505-827-4026. *Fax:* 505-827-7392. *Web site:* www.nmche.org.

New Mexico Student Incentive Grant. Several grants available for resident undergraduate students attending public and selected private nonprofit institutions in New Mexico. Must demonstrate financial need. To apply contact financial aid office at any public or private nonprofit postsecondary institution in New Mexico. *Award:* Grant for use in freshman, sophomore, junior, or senior year; not renewable. *Award amount:* $200–$2500. *Eligibility Requirements:* Applicant must be enrolled or expecting to enroll at a two-year or four-year institution or university; resident of New Mexico and studying in New Mexico. Available to U.S. citizens. *Application Requirements:* Application, financial need analysis, FAFSA.

Contact: Maria Barele, Financial Specialist, New Mexico Commission on Higher Education, PO Box 15910, Santa Fe, NM 87506-5910. *Phone:* 505-827-4026. *Fax:* 505-827-7392. *Web site:* www.nmche.org.

New Mexico Vietnam Veterans' Scholarship. Renewable award for Vietnam veterans who are New Mexico residents attending state-sponsored schools. Must have been awarded the Vietnam Campaign medal. Submit DD214. Must include discharge papers. *Award:* Scholarship for use in freshman, sophomore, junior, or senior year; renewable. *Award amount:* up to $1554. *Eligibility Requirements:* Applicant must be enrolled or expecting to enroll at an institution or university; resident of New Mexico and studying in New Mexico. Available to U.S. citizens. Applicant must have general military experience. *Application Requirements:* Application. *Deadline:* continuous.

Contact: Alan Martinez, Manager State Benefits, New Mexico Veterans' Service Commission, PO Box 2324, Sante Fe, NM 87504. *Phone:* 505-827-6300. *Fax:* 505-827-6372. *Web site:* www.state.nm.us/veterans.

Nursing Student Loan-For-Service Program. Award for New Mexico residents accepted or enrolled in nursing program at New Mexico public postsecondary institution. Must practice as nurse in designated health professional shortage area in New Mexico. Award dependent upon financial need but may not exceed $12,000. Deadline: July 1. *Academic Fields/Career Goals:* Nursing. *Award:* Forgivable loan for use in freshman, sophomore, junior, or senior year; not renewable. *Award amount:* up to $12,000. *Eligibility Requirements:* Applicant must be enrolled or expecting to enroll full or part-time at a two-year or four-year institution; resident of New Mexico and studying in New Mexico. Available to U.S. citizens. *Application Requirements:* Application, financial need analysis, FAFSA. *Deadline:* July 1.

Contact: Maria Barele, Financial Specialist, New Mexico Commission on Higher Education, PO Box 15910, Santa Fe, NM 87506-5910. *Phone:* 505-827-4026. *Fax:* 505-827-7392. *Web site:* www.nmche.org.

3% Scholarship Program. Award equal to tuition and required fees for New Mexico residents who are undergraduate students attending public postsecondary institutions in New Mexico. Contact financial aid office of any public postsecondary institution in New Mexico for deadline. *Award:* Scholarship for use in freshman, sophomore, junior, senior, or graduate year; not renewable. *Eligibility Requirements:* Applicant must be enrolled or expecting to enroll full or part-time at a two-year or four-year institution or university; resident of New Mexico and studying in New Mexico. Available to U.S. citizens. *Application Requirements:* Application.

Contact: Maria Barele, Financial Specialist, New Mexico Commission on Higher Education, PO Box 15910, Santa Fe, NM 87506-5910. *Phone:* 505-827-4026. *Fax:* 505-827-7392. *Web site:* www.nmche.org.

Vietnam Veterans' Scholarship Program. Award for New Mexico residents who are Vietnam veterans enrolled in undergraduate or master's-level course work at public or selected private New Mexico postsecondary institutions. Award may include tuition, required fees, and book allowance. Contact financial aid office of any public or eligible private New Mexico postsecondary institution for deadline. *Award:* Scholarship for use in freshman, sophomore, junior, senior, or graduate year; not renewable. *Eligibility Requirements:* Applicant must be enrolled or expecting to enroll full or part-time at a two-year or four-year institution; resident of New Mexico and studying in New Mexico. Available to U.S. citizens. Applicant must have general military experience. *Application Requirements:* Application, certification by the NM Veteran's commission.

Contact: Maria Barele, Financial Specialist, New Mexico Commission on Higher Education, PO Box 15910, Santa Fe, NM 87506-5910. *Phone:* 505-827-4026. *Fax:* 505-827-7392. *Web site:* www.nmche.org.

NEW YORK

Department of Education Scholarship for Programs in China. Scholarships offered to students who are pursuing Chinese language programs in China. Must be a U.S. citizen enrolled in a CIEE program. Students must have the equivalent of two years study in Chinese language documented. Deadlines are April 15 and November 15. For more details see Web site: http://www.ciee.org. *Academic Fields/Career Goals:* Education. *Award:* Scholarship for use in junior, senior, or graduate year; not renewable. *Award amount:* $500–$6000. *Number of awards:* 10–20. *Eligibility Requirements:* Applicant must be enrolled or expecting to enroll full-time at a four-year institution or university and must have an interest in foreign language. Applicant must have 3.0 GPA or higher. Available to U.S. citizens. *Application Requirements:* Application, essay, financial need analysis, references, transcript. *Deadline:* varies.

Contact: Scholarship Committee, Council for International Educational Exchange, 7 Custom House Street, 3rd Floor, Portland, ME 04101. *E-mail:* scholarships@ciee.org. *Web site:* www.ciee.org/study.

New York Aid for Part-time Study (APTS). Renewable scholarship provides tuition assistance to part-time students who are New York residents attending New York accredited institutions. Deadlines and award amounts vary. Must be U.S. citizen. *Award:* Grant for use in freshman, sophomore, junior, or senior year; renewable. *Award amount:* up to $2000. *Number of awards:* varies. *Eligibility Requirements:* Applicant must be enrolled or expecting to enroll part-time at a two-year or four-year institution; resident of New York and studying in New York. Available to U.S. citizens. *Application Requirements:* Application.

Contact: Student Information, New York State Higher Education Services Corporation, 99 Washington Avenue, Room 1320, Albany, NY 12255. *Phone:* 518-473-3887. *Fax:* 518-474-2839. *Web site:* www.hesc.org.

New York Educational Opportunity Program (EOP). Renewable award for New York resident attending New York college/university for undergraduate study. For educationally and economically disadvantaged students; includes educational assistance such as tutoring. Contact prospective college for information. *Award:* Scholarship for use in freshman, sophomore, junior, or senior year; renewable. *Award amount:* varies. *Number of awards:* varies. *Eligibility Requirements:* Applicant must be enrolled or expecting to enroll full-time at a two-year or four-year institution or university; resident of New York and studying in New York. Available to U.S. citizens. *Application Requirements:* Application, financial need analysis, transcript.

Contact: Student Information, New York State Higher Education Services Corporation, 99 Washington Avenue, Room 1320, Albany, NY 12255. *Web site:* www.hesc.org.

New York Lottery Leaders of Tomorrow (Lot) Scholarship. The goal of this program is to reinforce the lottery's education mission by awarding four-year scholarships, $1000 per year for up to four years. One scholarship is available to every New York high school, public or private, that awards a high school diploma. *Award:* Scholarship for use in freshman, sophomore, junior, or senior year; renewable. *Award amount:* $1000. *Number of awards:* varies. *Eligibility Requirements:* Applicant must be high school student; planning to enroll or expecting to enroll full-time at a two-year, four-year, or technical institution or university; resident of New York and studying in New York. Applicant must have 3.0 GPA or higher. Available to U.S. citizens. *Application Requirements:* Application, essay, transcript. *Deadline:* varies.

Contact: Betsey Morgan, Program Coordinator, CASDA-LOT (Capital Area School Development Association), The University at Albany East Campus, One University Place—A-409, Rensselaer, NY 12144-3456. *E-mail:* casdalot@uamail.albany.edu. *Phone:* 518-525-2788. *Fax:* 518-525-2797. *Web site:* www.nylottery.org/lot.

New York State Aid to Native Americans. Award for enrolled members of a New York State tribe and their children who are attending or planning to attend a New York State college and who are New York State residents. Award for full-time-students up to $1550 annually; part-time awards approximately $65 per credit hour. *Award:* Scholarship for use in freshman, sophomore, junior, or senior year; not renewable. *Award amount:* up to $1550. *Number of awards:* varies. *Eligibility Requirements:* Applicant must be American Indian/Alaska Native; enrolled or expecting to enroll full or part-time at a two-year, four-year, or technical institution or university; resident of New York and studying in New York. *Application Requirements:* Application. *Deadline:* July 15.

Contact: Native American Education Unit, New York State Education Department, New York State Higher Education Services Corporation, EBA Room 374, Albany, NY 12234. *Phone:* 518-474-0537. *Web site:* www.hesc.org.

New York State Tuition Assistance Program. Award for New York state residents attending a New York postsecondary institution. Must be full-time student in approved program with tuition over $200 per year. Must show financial need and not be in default in any other state program. Renewable award of $500-$5000. *Award:* Grant for use in freshman, sophomore, junior, or senior year; renewable. *Award amount:* $500–$5000. *Number of awards:* 350,000–360,000. *Eligibility Requirements:* Applicant must be enrolled or expecting to enroll full-time at a two-year or four-year institution or university; resident of New York and studying in New York. *Application Requirements:* Application, financial need analysis. *Deadline:* May 1.

Contact: Student Information, New York State Higher Education Services Corporation, 99 Washington Avenue, Room 1320, Albany, NY 12255. *Web site:* www.hesc.org.

New York Vietnam Veterans Tuition Awards. Scholarship for veterans who served in Vietnam. Must be a New York resident attending a New York institution. Renewable award of $500-$1000. Deadline: May 1. Must establish eligibility by September 1. *Award:* Scholarship for use in freshman, sophomore, junior, or senior year; renewable. *Award amount:* $500–$1000. *Number of awards:* varies. *Eligibility Requirements:* Applicant must be enrolled or expecting to enroll full or part-time at a two-year, four-year, or technical institution or university; resident of New York and studying in New York. Applicant must have served in the Air Force, Army, Marine Corp, or Navy. *Application Requirements:* Application, financial need analysis. *Deadline:* May 1.

Contact: Student Information, New York State Higher Education Services Corporation, 99 Washington Avenue, Room 1320, Albany, NY 12255. *Web site:* www.hesc.org.

Regents Award for Child of Veteran. Award for students whose parent, as a result of service in U.S. Armed Forces during war or national emergency, died; suffered a 40% or more disability; or is classified as missing in action or a prisoner of war. Veteran must be current New York State resident or have been so at time of death. Must be New York resident attending, or planning to attend, college in New York State. Must establish eligibility before applying for payment. *Award:* Scholarship for use in freshman, sophomore, junior, or senior year; not renewable. *Award amount:* $450. *Number of awards:* varies. *Eligibility Requirements:* Applicant must be enrolled or expecting to enroll full-time at a two-year or four-year institution or university; resident of New York and studying in New York. Available to U.S. citizens. Applicant or parent must meet one or more of the following requirements: general military experience; retired from active duty; disabled or killed as a result of military service; prisoner of war; or missing in action. *Application Requirements:* Application, proof of eligibility. *Deadline:* May 1.

Contact: Student Information, New York State Higher Education Services Corporation, 99 Washington Avenue, Room 1320, Albany, NY 12255. *Web site:* www.hesc.org.

Regents Professional Opportunity Scholarship. Scholarship for New York residents beginning or already enrolled in an approved degree-bearing program of study in New York that leads to licensure in a particular profession. See the Web site for the list of eligible professions. Must be U.S. citizen or permanent resident. Award recipients must agree to practice upon licensure in their profession in New York for 12 months for each annual payment received. Priority given to economically disadvantaged members of minority groups underrepresented in the professions. *Academic Fields/Career Goals:* Accounting; Architecture; Dental Health/Services; Engineering/Technology; Health and Medical Sciences; Interior Design; Landscape Architecture; Law/Legal Services; Nursing; Pharmacy; Psychology; Social Services. *Award:* Scholarship for use in freshman, sophomore, junior, senior, or graduate year. *Award amount:* $1000–$5000. *Number of awards:* 220. *Eligibility Requirements:* Applicant must be enrolled or expecting to enroll full-time at a two-year or four-year institution or university; resident of New York and studying in New York. Available to U.S. citizens. *Application Requirements: Deadline:* May 3.

Contact: Lewis J. Hall, Coordinator, New York State Education Department, Room 1078 EBA, Albany, NY 12234. *Phone:* 518-486-1319. *Fax:* 518-486-5346. *Web site:* www.highered.nysed.gov.

Regents Professional Opportunity Scholarships. Award for New York State residents pursuing career in certain licensed professions. Must attend New York State college. Priority given to economically disadvantaged members of minority group underrepresented in chosen profession and graduates of SEEK, College Discovery, EOP, and HEOP. Must work in New York State in chosen profession one year for each annual payment. *Award:* Scholarship for use in freshman, sophomore, junior, senior, or graduate year; not renewable. *Award amount:* $1000–$5000. *Number of awards:* 220. *Eligibility Requirements:* Applicant must be enrolled or expecting to enroll full-time at a two-year or four-year institution or university; resident of New York and studying in New York. Available to U.S. citizens. *Application Requirements:* Application. *Deadline:* May 3.

Contact: Scholarship Processing Unit-New York State Education Department, New York State Higher Education Services Corporation, EBA Room 1078, Albany, NY 12234. *Phone:* 518-486-1319. *Web site:* www.hesc.org.

Scholarship for Academic Excellence. Renewable award for New York residents. Scholarship winners must attend a college or university in New York. 2000 scholarships are for $1500 and 6000 are for $500. The selection criteria used are based on Regents test scores and rank in class. Must be U.S. citizen or permanent resident. *Award:* Scholarship for use in freshman, sophomore, junior, or senior year; renewable. *Award amount:* $500–$1500. *Number of awards:* up to 8000. *Eligibility Requirements:* Applicant must be high school student; planning to enroll or expecting to enroll full-time at a two-year or four-year institution or university; resident of New York and studying in New York. Applicant must have 3.5 GPA or higher. Available to U.S. citizens. *Application Requirements:* Application. *Deadline:* December 19.

Contact: Lewis J. Hall, Coordinator, New York State Education Department, Room 1078 EBA, Albany, NY 12234. *Phone:* 518-486-1319. *Fax:* 518-486-5346. *Web site:* www.highered.nysed.gov.

Scholarships for Academic Excellence. Renewable awards of up to $1500 for academically outstanding New York State high school graduates planning to attend an approved postsecondary institution in New York State. For full-time study only. Contact high school guidance counselor to apply. *Award:* Scholarship for use in freshman, sophomore, junior, or senior year; renewable. *Award amount:* $500–$1500. *Number of awards:* 8000. *Eligibility Requirements:* Applicant must be high school student; planning to enroll or expecting to enroll full-time at a four-year institution or university; resident of New York and studying in New York. Available to U.S. citizens. *Application Requirements:* Application. *Deadline:* December 19.

Contact: Student Information, New York State Higher Education Services Corporation, 99 Washington Avenue, Room 1320, Albany, NY 12255. *Web site:* www.hesc.org.

World Trade Center Memorial Scholarship. Renewable awards of up to the average cost of attendance at a State University of New York four-year college. Available to the families and financial dependents of victims who died or were severely and permanently disabled as a result of the Sept. 11, 2001 terrorist attacks on the U.S. and the rescue and recovery efforts. *Award:* Scholarship for use in freshman, sophomore, junior, or senior year; renewable. *Award amount:* varies. *Number of awards:* varies. *Eligibility Requirements:* Applicant must be enrolled or expecting to enroll full-time at a two-year or four-year institution or university; resident of New York and studying in New York. Available to U.S. citizens. *Application Requirements:* Application. *Deadline:* May 1.

Contact: HESC Scholarship Unit, New York State Higher Education Services Corporation, 99 Washington Avenue, Room 1320, Albany, NY 12255. *Phone:* 518-402-6494. *Web site:* www.hesc.org.

NORTH CAROLINA

Governor James G. Martin College Scholarships. Awarded to high school seniors who are residents of North Carolina with a minimum 3.5 GPA. Must enroll full-time and maintain a C average. Must attend a participating North Carolina four-year institution. Renewable up to five years. Based on academic merit, community service, and leadership. *Award:* Scholarship for use in freshman, junior, or senior year; renewable. *Award amount:* up to $1000. *Number of awards:* up to 25. *Eligibility Requirements:* Applicant must be high school student; planning to enroll or expecting to enroll full-time at a four-year institution or university; resident of North Carolina and studying in North Carolina. Applicant or parent of applicant must have employment or volunteer experience in community service. Available to U.S. citizens. *Application Requirements:*

Application, essay, photo, references, test scores, transcript. *Deadline:* March 15.

Contact: Sharon Scott, Assistant, Scholarship and Grant Division, North Carolina State Education Assistance Authority, PO Box 13663, Research Triangle Park, NC 27709-3663. *Web site:* www.cfnc.org.

Incentive Scholarship for Certain Constituent Institutions.
Scholarship aid to well-prepared, in-state students who want to attend one of UNC constituent universities on a full-time basis. *Award:* Scholarship for use in freshman, sophomore, junior, or senior year. *Award amount:* $2000–$3000. *Number of awards:* varies. *Eligibility Requirements:* Applicant must be enrolled or expecting to enroll full-time at an institution or university; resident of North Carolina and studying in North Carolina. *Application Requirements: Deadline:* varies.

Contact: Bill Carswell, Manager of Scholarship and Grant Division, North Carolina State Education Assistance Authority, PO Box 13663, Research Triangle Park, NC 27709-3663. *E-mail:* carswellb@ncseaa.edu. *Phone:* 919-549-8614. *Fax:* 919-248-4687. *Web site:* www.cfnc.org.

North Carolina Community College Grant Program.
Annual award for North Carolina residents enrolled at least part-time in a North Carolina community college curriculum program. Priority given to those enrolled in college transferable curriculum programs, persons seeking new job skills, women in non-traditional curricula, and those participating in an ABE, GED, or high school diploma program. Contact financial aid office of institution the student attends for information and deadline. Must complete Free Application for Federal Student Aid. *Award:* Grant for use in freshman or sophomore year; renewable. *Award amount:* $683. *Number of awards:* varies. *Eligibility Requirements:* Applicant must be enrolled or expecting to enroll full or part-time at a two-year or technical institution; resident of North Carolina and studying in North Carolina. Available to U.S. citizens. *Application Requirements:* Financial need analysis, FAFSA. *Deadline:* varies.

Contact: Bill Carswell, Manager, Scholarship and Grants Division, North Carolina State Education Assistance Authority, PO Box 13663, Research Triangle Park, NC 27709-3663. *Web site:* www.cfnc.org.

North Carolina Division of Services for the Blind Rehabilitation Services.
Financial assistance is available for North Carolina residents who are blind or visually impaired and who require vocational rehabilitation to help find employment. Tuition and other assistance provided based on need. Open to U.S. citizens and legal residents of United States. Applicants goal must be to work after receiving vocational services. To apply, contact the local DSB office and apply for vocational rehabilitation services. *Award:* Scholarship for use in freshman, sophomore, junior, or senior year; renewable. *Award amount:* varies. *Number of awards:* varies. *Eligibility Requirements:* Applicant must be enrolled or expecting to enroll full or part-time at a two-year, four-year, or technical institution or university and resident of North Carolina. Applicant must be visually impaired. Available to U.S. citizens. *Application Requirements:* Application, financial need analysis, interview, proof of eligibility. *Deadline:* continuous.

Contact: JoAnn Strader, Chief of Rehabilitation Field Services, North Carolina Division of Services for the Blind, 2601 Mail Service Center, Raleigh, NC 27699-2601. *E-mail:* joann.strader@ncmail.net. *Fax:* 919-715-8771.

North Carolina Legislative Tuition Grant Program (NCLTG).
Renewable aid for North Carolina residents attending approved private colleges or universities within the state. Must be enrolled full-time in an undergraduate program not leading to a religious vocation. Contact college financial aid office for deadlines. *Award:* Grant for use in freshman, sophomore, junior, or senior year; renewable. *Award amount:* $1500–$1800. *Number of awards:* varies. *Eligibility Requirements:* Applicant must be enrolled or expecting to enroll full-time at a two-year or four-year institution or university; resident of North Carolina and studying in North Carolina. Available to U.S. citizens. *Application Requirements:* Application. *Deadline:* varies.

Contact: Bill Carswell, Manager of Scholarship and Grant Division, North Carolina State Education Assistance Authority, PO Box 13663, Research Triangle Park, NC 27709-3663. *Web site:* www.cfnc.org.

North Carolina National Guard Tuition Assistance Program.
For members of the North Carolina Air and Army National Guard who will remain in the service for two years following the period for which assistance is provided. Applicants must reapply for each academic period. For use at approved North Carolina institutions. Deadline: last day of late registration period set by the school. Applicant must currently be serving in the Air National Guard or Army National Guard. Annual maximum (July 1 through June 30) of $2000. Career maximum of $8000. *Award:* Grant for use in freshman, sophomore, junior, senior, or graduate year; not renewable. *Award amount:* up to $2000. *Number of awards:*

varies. *Eligibility Requirements:* Applicant must be enrolled or expecting to enroll full or part-time at a two-year, four-year, or technical institution or university and studying in North Carolina. Available to U.S. citizens. Applicant must have served in the Air Force National Guard or Army National Guard. *Application Requirements:* Application. *Deadline:* varies.

Contact: Capt. Miriam Gray, Education Services Officer, North Carolina National Guard, 4105 Reedy Creek Road, Raleigh, NC 27607-6410. *E-mail:* miriam.gray@nc.ngb.army.mil. *Phone:* 800-621-4136 Ext. 6272. *Fax:* 919-664-6520. *Web site:* www.nc.ngb.army.mil/education.

North Carolina Police Corps Scholarship.
Selected participants must attend a four-year institution full-time. May receive up to $6667 per year with a maximum of $30,000. Must complete 24-week training course receiving $450 per week while in residence and serve four years in selected law enforcement agency. Must have physical, background investigation, drug test, and psychological evaluation. *Academic Fields/Career Goals:* Criminal Justice/Criminology; Law Enforcement/Police Administration. *Award:* Scholarship for use in freshman, sophomore, junior, senior, or graduate year; renewable. *Award amount:* $5000–$6667. *Number of awards:* 15–30. *Eligibility Requirements:* Applicant must be enrolled or expecting to enroll full-time at a four-year institution or university. Available to U.S. citizens. *Application Requirements:* Application, autobiography, essay, interview, photo, references, test scores, transcript. *Deadline:* November 15.

Contact: Neil Woodcock, Director, NC Police Corps, North Carolina Police Corps, NC Department of Crime Control and Public Safety, 4710 Mail Service Center, Raleigh, NC 27699-4710. *E-mail:* nwoodcock@ncpolicecorps.org. *Phone:* 919-773-2823. *Fax:* 919-773-2845. *Web site:* www.ncpolicecorps.org.

North Carolina Sheriffs' Association Undergraduate Criminal Justice Scholarships.
One-time award for full-time North Carolina resident undergraduate students majoring in criminal justice at a University of North Carolina school. Priority given to child of any North Carolina law enforcement officer. Letter of recommendation from county sheriff required. *Academic Fields/Career Goals:* Criminal Justice/Criminology; Law Enforcement/Police Administration. *Award:* Scholarship for use in freshman, sophomore, junior, or senior year; not renewable. *Award amount:* $1000–$2000. *Number of awards:* up to 10. *Eligibility Requirements:* Applicant must

be enrolled or expecting to enroll full-time at a four-year institution; resident of North Carolina and studying in North Carolina. Applicant or parent of applicant must have employment or volunteer experience in police/firefighting. Available to U.S. citizens. *Application Requirements:* Application, essay, financial need analysis, references, transcript. *Deadline:* continuous.

Contact: Sharon Scott, Assistant, Scholarship and Grant Division, North Carolina State Education Assistance Authority, PO Box 13663, Research Triangle Park, NC 27709-3663. *Web site:* www.cfnc.org.

North Carolina Student Incentive Grant (NCSIG). Renewable award for North Carolina residents who are enrolled full-time in an undergraduate program not leading to a religious vocation at a North Carolina postsecondary institution. Must demonstrate substantial financial need. Must complete Free Application for Student Aid. Must be U.S. citizen and must maintain satisfactory academic progress. Offered by NCSEAA through College Foundation, Inc. Visit Web site at http://www.cfnc.org. *Award:* Grant for use in freshman, sophomore, junior, or senior year; renewable. *Award amount:* up to $700. *Number of awards:* varies. *Eligibility Requirements:* Applicant must be enrolled or expecting to enroll full-time at a two-year or four-year institution or university; resident of North Carolina and studying in North Carolina. Available to U.S. citizens. *Application Requirements:* Application, financial need analysis. *Deadline:* March 15.

Contact: Bill Carswell, Manager of Scholarship and Grant Division, North Carolina State Education Assistance Authority, PO Box 13663, Research Triangle Park, NC 27709-3663. *Web site:* www.cfnc.org.

North Carolina Student Loan Program for Health, Science, and Mathematics. Renewable award for North Carolina residents studying health-related fields, or science or math education. Based on merit, need, and promise of service as a health professional or educator in an underserved area of North Carolina. Need two co-signers. Submit surety statement. *Academic Fields/ Career Goals:* Dental Health/Services; Health Administration; Health and Medical Sciences; Nursing; Physical Sciences and Math; Therapy/Rehabilitation. *Award:* Forgivable loan for use in freshman, sophomore, junior, senior, or graduate year; renewable. *Award amount:* $3000–$8000. *Eligibility Requirements:* Applicant must be enrolled or expecting to enroll full-time at a two-year or four-year institution or university and resident of North Carolina. Available to U.S. citizens. *Application*

Requirements: Application, financial need analysis, transcript. *Deadline:* June 1.

Contact: Edna Williams, Manager, Selection and Origination, HSM Loan Program, North Carolina State Education Assistance Authority, PO Box 14223, Research Triangle Park, NC 27709-4223. *Phone:* 919-549-8614. *Web site:* www.cfnc.org.

North Carolina Teaching Fellows Scholarship Program. Renewable award for North Carolina high school seniors pursuing teaching careers. Must agree to teach in a North Carolina public or government school for four years or repay award. Must attend one of the 14 approved schools in North Carolina. Merit-based. Must interview at the local level and at the regional level as a finalist. Application available online only: http://www.teachingfellows.org. *Academic Fields/Career Goals:* Education. *Award:* Forgivable loan for use in freshman, sophomore, junior, or senior year; renewable. *Award amount:* $6500. *Number of awards:* up to 400. *Eligibility Requirements:* Applicant must be high school student; planning to enroll or expecting to enroll full-time at a four-year institution; resident of North Carolina and studying in North Carolina. Applicant must have 3.5 GPA or higher. Available to U.S. citizens. *Application Requirements:* Application, essay, interview, references, test scores, transcript. *Deadline:* varies.

Contact: Ms. Sherry Woodruff, Program Officer, North Carolina Teaching Fellows Commission, 3739 National Drive, Suite 210, Raleigh, NC 27612. *E-mail:* tfellows@ncforum.org. *Phone:* 919-781-6833 Ext. 103. *Fax:* 919-781-6527. *Web site:* www.teachingfellows.org.

North Carolina Veterans' Scholarships Class I-A. Renewable awards for children of veterans who were killed or died in wartime service or died as a result of service-connected condition incurred in wartime service as defined in the law. Parent must have been a North Carolina resident at time of entry into service. Duration of the scholarship is four academic years (8 semesters) if used within 8 years. Free tuition, a room allowance, a board allowance, and exemption from certain mandatory fees as set forth in the law in Public, Community & Technical Colleges/ Institutions. Award is $4500 per nine-month academic year in Private Colleges & Junior Colleges. No limit on number awarded each year. See Web site for details and where to procure an application. *Award:* Scholarship for use in freshman, sophomore, junior, or senior year; renewable. *Award amount:* varies. *Number of awards:* varies. *Eligibility Requirements:* Applicant must be enrolled

or expecting to enroll full or part-time at a two-year, four-year, or technical institution or university and studying in North Carolina. Available to U.S. citizens. Applicant or parent must meet one or more of the following requirements: general military experience; retired from active duty; disabled or killed as a result of military service; prisoner of war; or missing in action. *Application Requirements:* Application, financial need analysis, interview, transcript. *Deadline:* continuous.

Contact: Charles F. Smith, Director, North Carolina Division of Veterans' Affairs, 325 North Salisbury Street, Raleigh, NC 27603. *Phone:* 919-733-3851. *Fax:* 919-733-2834. *Web site:* www.doa.state.nc.us/doa/vets/synopsis.htm.

North Carolina Veterans' Scholarships Class I-B. Renewable awards for children of veterans rated by U.S. DVA as 100% disabled due to wartime service as defined in the law, and currently or at time of death drawing compensation for such disability. Parent must have been a North Carolina resident at time of entry into service. Duration of the scholarship is four academic years (8 semesters) if used within 8 years. Free tuition and exemption from certain mandatory fees as set forth in the law in Public, Community & Technical Colleges/ Institutions. See Web site for details and where to procure an application. $1500 per nine month academic year in Private Colleges & Junior Colleges. No limit on number awarded each year. *Award:* Scholarship for use in freshman, sophomore, junior, or senior year; renewable. *Award amount:* varies. *Number of awards:* varies. *Eligibility Requirements:* Applicant must be enrolled or expecting to enroll full or part-time at a two-year, four-year, or technical institution or university and studying in North Carolina. Available to U.S. citizens. Applicant or parent must meet one or more of the following requirements: general military experience; retired from active duty; disabled or killed as a result of military service; prisoner of war; or missing in action. *Application Requirements:* Application, financial need analysis, interview, transcript. *Deadline:* continuous.

Contact: Charles F. Smith, Director, North Carolina Division of Veterans' Affairs, 325 North Salisbury Street, Raleigh, NC 27603. *Phone:* 919-733-3851. *Fax:* 919-733-2834. *Web site:* www.doa.state.nc.us/doa/vets/synopsis.htm.

North Carolina Veterans' Scholarships Class II. Renewable awards for children of veterans rated by U.S. DVA as much as 20% but less than 100% disabled due to wartime service as defined in the law, or awarded Purple Heart Medal for wounds received. Parent must have been a North Carolina resident at time of entry into service. Duration of the scholarship is four academic years (8 semesters) if used within 8 years. Free tuition and exemption from certain mandatory fees as set forth in the law in Public, Community & Technical Colleges/Institutions. See Web site for details and where to procure an application. $4500 per nine month academic year in Private Colleges & Junior Colleges. Up to 100 awarded each year. Deadline is March 31. *Award:* Scholarship for use in freshman, sophomore, junior, or senior year; renewable. *Award amount:* varies. *Number of awards:* up to 100. *Eligibility Requirements:* Applicant must be enrolled or expecting to enroll full or part-time at a two-year, four-year, or technical institution or university and studying in North Carolina. Available to U.S. citizens. Applicant or parent must meet one or more of the following requirements: general military experience; retired from active duty; disabled or killed as a result of military service; prisoner of war; or missing in action. *Application Requirements:* Application, financial need analysis, interview, transcript. *Deadline:* March 31.

Contact: Charles F. Smith, Director, North Carolina Division of Veterans' Affairs, 325 North Salisbury Street, Raleigh, NC 27603. *Phone:* 919-733-3851. *Fax:* 919-733-2834. *Web site:* www.doa.state.nc.us/doa/vets/synopsis. htm.

North Carolina Veterans' Scholarships Class III.
Renewable awards for children of a veteran who died or was, at time of death, drawing a pension for total and permanent disability as rated by U.S. DVA, was honorably discharged and does not a qualify for Class I, II, or IV, scholarships, or served in a combat zone or waters adjacent to a combat zone and received a campaign badge or medal and does not qualify under Class I, II, IV, or V. Parent must have been a North Carolina resident at time of entry into service. Duration of the scholarship is four academic years (8 semesters) if used within eight years. Free tuition and exemption from certain mandatory fees as set forth in the law in Public, Community & Technical Colleges/ Institutions. $4500 per nine month academic year in Private Colleges & Junior Colleges. See Web site for details and where to procure an application. Up to 100 awarded each year. Deadline is March 31. *Award:* Scholarship for use in freshman, sophomore, junior, or senior year; renewable. *Award amount:* varies. *Number of awards:* up to 100. *Eligibility Requirements:* Applicant must be enrolled or expecting to enroll full

or part-time at a two-year, four-year, or technical institution or university and studying in North Carolina. Available to U.S. citizens. Applicant or parent must meet one or more of the following requirements: general military experience; retired from active duty; disabled or killed as a result of military service; prisoner of war; or missing in action. *Application Requirements:* Application, financial need analysis, interview, transcript. *Deadline:* March 31.

Contact: Charles F. Smith, Director, North Carolina Division of Veterans' Affairs, 325 North Salisbury Street, Raleigh, NC 27603. *Phone:* 919-733-3851. *Fax:* 919-733-2834. *Web site:* www.doa.state.nc.us/doa/vets/synopsis. htm.

North Carolina Veterans' Scholarships Class IV.
Renewable awards for children of a veteran who was a POW or MIA. Parent must have been a North Carolina resident at time of entry into service. Duration of the scholarship is four academic years (8 semesters) if used within eight years. No limit on number awarded per year. The student receives free tuition, a room allowance, a board allowance, and exemption from certain mandatory fees as set forth in the law in public, community, and technical colleges or institutions. The scholarship is $4500 per nine-month academic year in private colleges and junior colleges. *Award:* Scholarship for use in freshman, sophomore, junior, or senior year; renewable. *Award amount:* varies. *Number of awards:* varies. *Eligibility Requirements:* Applicant must be enrolled or expecting to enroll full or part-time at a two-year, four-year, or technical institution or university and studying in North Carolina. Available to U.S. citizens. Applicant or parent must meet one or more of the following requirements: general military experience; retired from active duty; disabled or killed as a result of military service; prisoner of war; or missing in action. *Application Requirements:* Application, financial need analysis, interview, transcript. *Deadline:* March 31.

Contact: Charles F. Smith, Director, North Carolina Division of Veterans' Affairs, 325 North Salisbury Street, Raleigh, NC 27603. *Phone:* 919-733-3851. *Fax:* 919-733-2834. *Web site:* www.doa.state.nc.us/doa/vets/synopsis. htm.

Nurse Education Scholarship Loan Program (NESLP).
Must be U.S. citizen and North Carolina resident. Award available through financial aid offices of North Carolina colleges and universities that offer nurse education programs to prepare students for licensure in the state as LPN or RN. Recipients enter contract with the State of North Carolina to work full time as a

licensed nurse. Loans not repaid through service must be repaid in cash. Award based upon financial need. Maximum award for students enrolled in Associate Degree Nursing and Practical Nurse Education programs is $3000. Maximum award for students enrolled in a Baccalaureate program is $5000. *Academic Fields/Career Goals:* Nursing. *Award:* Forgivable loan for use in freshman, sophomore, junior, or senior year; renewable. *Award amount:* $3000–$5000. *Number of awards:* varies. *Eligibility Requirements:* Applicant must be enrolled or expecting to enroll at a four-year institution or university; resident of North Carolina and studying in North Carolina. Available to U.S. citizens. *Application Requirements:* Application, financial need analysis. *Deadline:* continuous.

Contact: Financial Aid Office, North Carolina State Education Assistance Authority. *Web site:* www.cfnc.org.

State Contractual Scholarship Fund Program-North Carolina.
Renewable award for North Carolina residents already attending an approved private college or university in the state in pursuit of an undergraduate degree. Must have financial need. Contact college financial aid office for deadline and information. May not be enrolled in a program leading to a religious vocation. *Award:* Scholarship for use in freshman, sophomore, junior, or senior year; renewable. *Award amount:* up to $1100. *Number of awards:* varies. *Eligibility Requirements:* Applicant must be enrolled or expecting to enroll full or part-time at a two-year or four-year institution or university; resident of North Carolina and studying in North Carolina. Available to U.S. citizens. *Application Requirements:* Financial need analysis. *Deadline:* varies.

Contact: Bill Carswell, Manager of Scholarship and Grant Division, North Carolina State Education Assistance Authority, PO Box 13663, Research Triangle Park, NC 27709-3663. *Web site:* www.cfnc.org.

Teacher Assistant Scholarship Program.
Funding to attend a public or private four-year college or university in North Carolina with an approved teacher education program. Applicant must be employed full-time as a teacher assistant in an instructional area while pursuing licensure and maintain employment to remain eligible. Refer to Web site for further details: http://www. ncseaa.edu/tas.htm *Academic Fields/Career Goals:* Education. *Award:* Scholarship for use in freshman, sophomore, junior, or senior year. *Award amount:* $1600–$4800. *Number of awards:* varies. *Eligibility Requirements:* Applicant must be enrolled or

expecting to enroll at a four-year institution or university; resident of North Carolina and studying in North Carolina. Applicant must have 2.5 GPA or higher. *Application Requirements: Deadline:* varies.

Contact: See Web site: http://www.ncseaa. edu/tas.htm, North Carolina State Education Assistance Authority. *Web site:* www.cfnc. org.

University of North Carolina Need-Based Grant. Must be enrolled in at least 6 credit hours at one of 16 UNC system universities. Eligibility based on need; applicant must have submitted Free Application for Federal Student Aid. Award varies, consideration for grant automatic when FAFSA is filed. Late applications may be denied due to insufficient funds. *Award:* Grant for use in freshman, sophomore, junior, or senior year; renewable. *Award amount:* varies. *Number of awards:* varies. *Eligibility Requirements:* Applicant must be enrolled or expecting to enroll full or part-time at an institution or university and studying in North Carolina. Available to U.S. citizens. *Application Requirements:* Financial need analysis, FAFSA. *Deadline:* varies.

Contact: Bill Carswell, Manager of Scholarship and Grant Division, North Carolina State Education Assistance Authority, PO Box 13663, Research Triangle Park, NC 27709-3663. *E-mail:* carswellb@ncseaa.edu. *Phone:* 919-549-8614. *Fax:* 919-248-4687. *Web site:* www.cfnc.org.

NORTH DAKOTA

North Dakota Department of Transportation Engineering Grant. Educational grants for civil or construction engineering, or civil engineering technology, are awarded to students who have completed one year of course study at an institution of higher learning in North Dakota. Recipients must agree to work for the Department for a period of time at least equal to the grant period or repay the grant at 6% interest. Minimum 2.0 GPA required. *Academic Fields/Career Goals:* Civil Engineering; Engineering/Technology. *Award:* Grant for use in sophomore, junior, or senior year; renewable. *Award amount:* $1000–$6000. *Number of awards:* varies. *Eligibility Requirements:* Applicant must be enrolled or expecting to enroll full-time at a four-year, or technical institution and studying in North Dakota. Available to U.S. citizens. *Application Requirements:* Application, financial need analysis, interview, transcript. *Deadline:* continuous.

Contact: Lorrie Pavlicek, Human Resources Manager, North Dakota Department of Transportation, 503 38th Street South, Fargo,

ND 58103. *E-mail:* lpavlice@state.nd.us. *Phone:* 701-239-8934. *Fax:* 701-239-8939. *Web site:* www.state.nd.us/dot/.

North Dakota Indian Scholarship Program. Assists Native-American North Dakota residents in obtaining a college education. Priority given to full-time undergraduate students and those having a 3.5 GPA or higher. Certification of tribal enrollment required. For use at North Dakota institution. *Award:* Scholarship for use in freshman, sophomore, junior, senior, or graduate year; renewable. *Award amount:* $600–$900. *Number of awards:* up to 150. *Eligibility Requirements:* Applicant must be American Indian/Alaska Native; enrolled or expecting to enroll at a two-year or four-year institution or university; resident of North Dakota and studying in North Dakota. Applicant must have 3.5 GPA or higher. *Application Requirements:* Application, financial need analysis, transcript, proof of tribal enrollment. *Deadline:* July 15.

Contact: Rhonda Schauer, Coordinator of American Indian Higher Education, State of North Dakota, 600 East Boulevard, Department 215, Bismarck, ND 58505-0230. *Phone:* 701-328-9661. *Web site:* www.ndus.nodak. edu.

North Dakota Scholars Program. Provides scholarships equal to cost of tuition at the public colleges in North Dakota for North Dakota residents. Must score at or above the 95th percentile on ACT and rank in top twenty percent of high school graduation class. Must take ACT in fall. For high school seniors with a minimum 3.5 GPA. Application deadline is the October or June ACT test date. *Award:* Scholarship for use in freshman, sophomore, junior, or senior year; renewable. *Award amount:* varies. *Number of awards:* 20. *Eligibility Requirements:* Applicant must be high school student; planning to enroll or expecting to enroll full-time at a two-year or four-year institution or university; resident of North Dakota and studying in North Dakota. Applicant must have 3.5 GPA or higher. Available to U.S. citizens. *Application Requirements:* Test scores. *Deadline:* varies.

Contact: Peggy Wipf, Director of Financial Aid, State of North Dakota, 600 East Boulevard, Department 215, Bismarck, ND 58505-0230. *Phone:* 701-328-4114. *Web site:* www.ndus. nodak.edu.

North Dakota Student Financial Assistance Grants. Aids North Dakota residents attending an approved college or university in North Dakota. Must be enrolled in a program of at least nine months in length. *Award:* Grant for use in freshman,

sophomore, junior, or senior year; not renewable. *Award amount:* up to $600. *Number of awards:* 2500–2600. *Eligibility Requirements:* Applicant must be enrolled or expecting to enroll full-time at a two-year or four-year institution or university; resident of North Dakota and studying in North Dakota. Available to U.S. citizens. *Application Requirements:* Financial need analysis, FAFSA. *Deadline:* March 15.

Contact: Peggy Wipf, Director of Financial Aid, State of North Dakota, 600 East Boulevard, Department 215, Bismarck, ND 58505-0230. *Phone:* 701-328-4114. *Web site:* www.ndus. nodak.edu.

OHIO

Accountancy Board of Ohio Educational Assistance Program. Program intended for minority students or students with financial need. Applicant must be enrolled as accounting major at an accredited Ohio college or university in a five-year degree program. Applicant must be an Ohio resident. Please refer to Web site for further details: http:// acc.ohio.gov/educasst.html. *Academic Fields/ Career Goals:* Accounting. *Award:* Scholarship for use in sophomore, junior, or senior year; not renewable. *Award amount:* $7700. *Number of awards:* varies. *Eligibility Requirements:* Applicant must be enrolled or expecting to enroll at a four-year institution or university; resident of Ohio and studying in Ohio. Available to U.S. citizens. *Application Requirements:* Application, financial need analysis, transcript, FAFSA. *Deadline:* varies.

Contact: Kay Sedgmer, Scholarship Secretary, Accountancy Board of Ohio, Accountancy Board of Ohio, 77 South High Street, 18th Floor, Columbus, OH 43266-0301. *E-mail:* kay.sedgmer@acc.state.oh.us. *Phone:* 614-466-4135. *Fax:* 614-466-2628. *Web site:* acc.ohio.gov/.

Ohio Academic Scholarship Program. Award for academically outstanding Ohio residents planning to attend an approved Ohio college. Must be a high school senior intending to enroll full-time. Award is renewable for up to four years. Must rank in upper quarter of class or have a minimum GPA of 3.5. *Award:* Scholarship for use in freshman, sophomore, junior, or senior year; renewable. *Award amount:* $2205. *Number of awards:* 1000. *Eligibility Requirements:* Applicant must be high school student; planning to enroll or expecting to enroll full-time at a two-year or four-year institution; resident of Ohio and studying in Ohio. Applicant must have 3.5 GPA or higher. Available to U.S. citizens. *Application*

Requirements: Application, test scores, transcript. *Deadline:* February 23.

Contact: Sarina Wilks, Program Administrator, Ohio Board of Regents, PO Box 182452, Columbus, OH 43218-2452. *E-mail:* swilks@regents.state.oh.us. *Phone:* 614-752-9528. *Fax:* 614-752-5903. *Web site:* www.regents.state.oh.us.

Ohio Instructional Grant. Award for low- and middle-income Ohio residents attending an approved college or school in Ohio or Pennsylvania. Must be enrolled full-time and have financial need. Average award is $630. May be used for any course of study except theology. *Award:* Grant for use in freshman, sophomore, junior, or senior year; renewable. *Award amount:* $78–$5466. *Number of awards:* varies. *Eligibility Requirements:* Applicant must be enrolled or expecting to enroll full-time at a two-year or four-year institution or university; resident of Ohio and studying in Ohio or Pennsylvania. Available to U.S. citizens. *Application Requirements:* Application, financial need analysis. *Deadline:* October 1.

Contact: Charles Shahid, Assistant Director, Ohio Board of Regents, PO Box 182452, Columbus, OH 43218-2452. *E-mail:* cshahid@regents.state.oh.us. *Phone:* 614-644-5959. *Fax:* 614-752-5903. *Web site:* www.regents.state.oh.us.

Ohio Missing in Action and Prisoners of War Orphans Scholarship. Renewable award aids children of Vietnam conflict servicemen who have been classified as missing in action or prisoner of war. Must be an Ohio resident, be 16-21, and be enrolled full-time at an Ohio college. Full tuition awards. *Award:* Scholarship for use in freshman, sophomore, junior, or senior year; renewable. *Award amount:* varies. *Number of awards:* 1–5. *Eligibility Requirements:* Applicant must be age 16-21; enrolled or expecting to enroll full-time at a two-year or four-year institution; resident of Ohio and studying in Ohio. Available to U.S. citizens. Applicant or parent must meet one or more of the following requirements: general military experience; retired from active duty; disabled or killed as a result of military service; prisoner of war; or missing in action. *Application Requirements:* Application. *Deadline:* July 1.

Contact: Sarina Wilks, Program Administrator, Ohio Board of Regents, PO Box 182452, Columbus, OH 43218-2452. *E-mail:* swilks@regents.state.oh.us. *Phone:* 614-752-9528. *Fax:* 614-752-5903. *Web site:* www.regents.state.oh.us.

Ohio National Guard Scholarship Program. Scholarships are for undergraduate studies at an approved Ohio postsecondary institution. Applicants must enlist for six years of Selective Service Reserve Duty in the Ohio National Guard. Scholarship pays 100% instructional and general fees for public institutions and an average of cost of public schools is available for private schools. Must be 18 years of age or older. Award is renewable. Deadlines: July 1, November 1, February 1, April 1. *Award:* Scholarship for use in freshman, sophomore, junior, or senior year; renewable. *Award amount:* up to $3000. *Number of awards:* 3500–8000. *Eligibility Requirements:* Applicant must be age 18; enrolled or expecting to enroll full or part-time at a two-year, four-year, or technical institution or university and studying in Ohio. Available to U.S. citizens. Applicant must have served in the Air Force National Guard or Army National Guard. *Application Requirements:* Application. *Deadline:* varies.

Contact: Mrs. Toni Davis, Grants Administrator, Ohio National Guard, 2825 West Dublin Granville Road, Columbus, OH 43235-2789. *E-mail:* toni.davis@tagoh.org. *Phone:* 614-336-7032. *Fax:* 614-336-7318.

Ohio Safety Officers College Memorial Fund. Renewable award covering up to full tuition is available to children and surviving spouses of peace officers and fire fighters killed in the line of duty in any state. Children must be under 26 years of age. Must be an Ohio resident and enroll full-time or part-time at an Ohio college or university. *Award:* Scholarship for use in freshman, sophomore, junior, or senior year; renewable. *Award amount:* varies. *Number of awards:* 50–65. *Eligibility Requirements:* Applicant must be age 25 or under; enrolled or expecting to enroll full or part-time at a two-year or four-year institution or university; resident of Ohio and studying in Ohio. Applicant or parent of applicant must have employment or volunteer experience in police/firefighting. Available to U.S. citizens. *Application Requirements:* Deadline: continuous.

Contact: Barbara Metheney, Program Administrator, Ohio Board of Regents, PO Box 182452, Columbus, OH 43218-2452. *E-mail:* bmethene@regents.state.oh.us. *Phone:* 614-752-9535. *Fax:* 614-752-5903. *Web site:* www.regents.state.oh.us.

Ohio Student Choice Grant Program. Renewable award available to Ohio residents attending private colleges within the state. Must be enrolled full-time in a bachelor's degree program. Do not apply to state. Check with financial aid office of college. *Award:* Grant for use in freshman, sophomore, junior, or senior year; renewable. *Award amount:* up to $1002. *Number of awards:* varies. *Eligibility Requirements:*

Applicant must be enrolled or expecting to enroll full-time at a four-year institution; resident of Ohio and studying in Ohio. Available to U.S. citizens. *Application Requirements: Deadline:* continuous.

Contact: Barbara Metheney, Program Administrator, Ohio Board of Regents, PO Box 182452, Columbus, OH 43218-2452. *E-mail:* bmetheney@regents.state.oh.us. *Phone:* 614-752-9535. *Fax:* 614-752-5903. *Web site:* www.regents.state.oh.us.

Ohio War Orphans Scholarship. Aids Ohio residents attending an eligible college in Ohio. Must be between the ages of 16-21, the child of a disabled or deceased veteran, and enrolled full-time. Renewable up to five years. Amount of award varies. Must include Form DD214. *Award:* Scholarship for use in freshman, sophomore, junior, or senior year; renewable. *Award amount:* varies. *Number of awards:* 300–450. *Eligibility Requirements:* Applicant must be age 16-21; enrolled or expecting to enroll full-time at a two-year or four-year institution; resident of Ohio and studying in Ohio. Available to U.S. citizens. Applicant or parent must meet one or more of the following requirements: general military experience; retired from active duty; disabled or killed as a result of military service; prisoner of war; or missing in action. *Application Requirements:* Application. *Deadline:* July 1.

Contact: Sarina Wilks, Program Administrator, Ohio Board of Regents, PO Box 182452, Columbus, OH 43218-2452. *E-mail:* swilks@regents.state.oh.us. *Phone:* 614-752-9528. *Fax:* 614-752-5903. *Web site:* www.regents.state.oh.us.

Part-time Student Instructional Grant. Renewable grants for part-time undergraduates who are Ohio residents. Award amounts vary. Must attend an Ohio institution. *Award:* Grant for use in freshman, sophomore, or junior year; renewable. *Award amount:* varies. *Number of awards:* varies. *Eligibility Requirements:* Applicant must be enrolled or expecting to enroll part-time at a two-year or four-year institution or university; resident of Ohio and studying in Ohio. Available to U.S. citizens. *Application Requirements:* Application, financial need analysis. *Deadline:* continuous.

Contact: Barbara Metheney, Program Administrator, Ohio Board of Regents, PO Box 182452, Columbus, OH 43218-2452. *E-mail:* bmethene@regents.state.oh.us. *Phone:* 614-752-9535. *Fax:* 614-752-5903. *Web site:* www.regents.state.oh.us.

Robert C. Byrd Honors Scholarship. Renewable award for graduating high school seniors who demonstrate outstanding academic achievement. Each Ohio high school receives applications by January of each year. School can submit one application for every 200 students in the senior class. Application deadline is the second Friday in March. *Award:* Scholarship for use in freshman, sophomore, junior, or senior year; renewable. *Award amount:* up to $1500. *Number of awards:* varies. *Eligibility Requirements:* Applicant must be high school student; planning to enroll or expecting to enroll at a two-year or four-year institution or university and resident of Ohio. Applicant must have 3.5 GPA or higher. Available to U.S. citizens. *Application Requirements:* Application, test scores. *Deadline:* varies.

Contact: Byrd Program Office, Ohio Department of Education, 25 South Front Street, Second Floor, Columbus, OH 43215. *Phone:* 614-466-4590. *Web site:* www.ode.state.oh.us.

OKLAHOMA

Academic Scholars Program. Encourages students of high academic ability to attend institutions in Oklahoma. Renewable up to four years. ACT or SAT scores must fall between 99.5 and 100th percentiles, or applicant must be designated as a National Merit scholar or finalist. *Award:* Scholarship for use in freshman, sophomore, junior, or senior year; renewable. *Award amount:* $3500–$5500. *Number of awards:* varies. *Eligibility Requirements:* Applicant must be high school student; planning to enroll or expecting to enroll full-time at a two-year or four-year institution or university and studying in Oklahoma. Available to U.S. and non-U.S. citizens. *Application Requirements:* Application, test scores, transcript. *Deadline:* continuous.

Contact: Oklahoma State Regents for Higher Education, PO Box 108850, Oklahoma City, OK 73101-8850. *E-mail:* studentinfo@osrhe.edu. *Phone:* 800-858-1840. *Fax:* 405-225-9230. *Web site:* www.okhighered.org.

Future Teacher Scholarship-Oklahoma. Open to outstanding Oklahoma high school graduates who agree to teach in shortage areas. Must rank in top 15% of graduating class or score above 85th percentile on ACT or similar test, or be accepted in an educational program. Students nominated by institution. Reapply to renew. Must attend college/university in Oklahoma. Contact institution's financial aid office for application deadline. *Academic Fields/Career Goals:* Education. *Award:* Scholarship for use in freshman, sophomore, junior, senior, or graduate year; not renewable. *Award amount:* up to $1500. *Number of awards:* varies. *Eligibility Requirements:* Applicant must be enrolled or expecting to enroll full or part-time at a two-year or four-year institution or university; resident of Oklahoma and studying in Oklahoma. Available to U.S. and non-U.S. citizens. *Application Requirements:* Application, essay, test scores, transcript. *Deadline:* continuous.

Contact: Oklahoma State Regents for Higher Education, PO Box 108850, Oklahoma City, OK 73101-8850. *Phone:* 800-858-1840. *Fax:* 405-225-9230. *Web site:* www.okhighered.org.

Oklahoma Tuition Aid Grant. Award for Oklahoma residents enrolled at an Oklahoma institution at least part time each semester in a degree program. May be enrolled in two- or four-year or approved vocational-technical institution. Award of up to $1000 per year. Application is made through FAFSA. *Award:* Grant for use in freshman, sophomore, junior, senior, or graduate year; renewable. *Award amount:* $200–$1000. *Number of awards:* 23,000. *Eligibility Requirements:* Applicant must be enrolled or expecting to enroll full or part-time at a two-year, four-year, or technical institution or university; resident of Oklahoma and studying in Oklahoma. Available to U.S. citizens. *Application Requirements:* Application, financial need analysis, FAFSA. *Deadline:* April 30.

Contact: Oklahoma State Regents for Higher Education, PO Box 3020, Oklahoma City, OK 73101-3020. *E-mail:* otaginfo@otag.org. *Phone:* 405-225-9456. *Fax:* 405-225-9392. *Web site:* www.okhighered.org.

Regional University Baccalaureate Scholarship. Renewable award for Oklahoma residents attending one of 11 participating Oklahoma public universities. Must have an ACT composite score of at least 30 or be a National Merit semifinalist or commended student. In addition to the award amount, each recipient will receive a resident tuition waiver from the institution. Must maintain a 3.25 GPA. Deadlines vary depending upon the institution attended. *Award:* Scholarship for use in freshman, sophomore, junior, or senior year; renewable. *Award amount:* $3000. *Number of awards:* varies. *Eligibility Requirements:* Applicant must be enrolled or expecting to enroll full-time at an institution or university; resident of Oklahoma and studying in Oklahoma. Available to U.S. and non-U.S. citizens. *Application Requirements:* Application. *Deadline:* varies.

Contact: Oklahoma State Regents for Higher Education, PO Box 108850, Oklahoma City, OK 73101-8850. *E-mail:* studentinfo@osrhe.edu. *Phone:* 800-858-1840. *Fax:* 405-225-9230. *Web site:* www.okhighered.org.

OREGON

American Ex-Prisoner of War Scholarships: Peter Connacher Memorial Scholarship. Renewable award for American prisoners-of-war and their descendants. Written proof of prisoner-of-war status and discharge papers from the U.S. Armed Forces must accompany application. Statement of relationship between applicant and former prisoner-of-war is required. See Web site at http://www.osac.state.or.us for details. *Award:* Scholarship for use in freshman, sophomore, junior, or senior year; renewable. *Award amount:* $1150. *Number of awards:* 4. *Eligibility Requirements:* Applicant must be enrolled or expecting to enroll at a two-year or four-year institution and resident of Oregon. Available to U.S. citizens. Applicant or parent must meet one or more of the following requirements: general military experience; retired from active duty; disabled or killed as a result of military service; prisoner of war; or missing in action. *Application Requirements:* Application, essay, financial need analysis, transcript. *Deadline:* March 1.

Contact: Director of Grant Programs, Oregon Student Assistance Commission, 1500 Valley River Drive, Suite 100, Eugene, OR 97401-7020. *E-mail:* awardinfo@mercury.osac.state.or.us. *Phone:* 800-452-8807 Ext. 7395. *Web site:* www.osac.state.or.us.

Children, Adult, and Family Services Scholarship. One-time award for graduating high school seniors, GED recipients, and college students currently or formerly in foster care or an Independent Living Program (ILP) financially supported through the Oregon State Office for Services to Children and Families. Must attend an Oregon public college. Visit Web site for more details (http://www.osac.state.or.us). Award varies between $500-$5000. *Award:* Scholarship for use in freshman, sophomore, junior, senior, or graduate year; not renewable. *Award amount:* $500–$5000. *Number of awards:* varies. *Eligibility Requirements:* Applicant must be enrolled or expecting to enroll at a two-year or four-year institution; resident of Oregon and studying in Oregon. Available to U.S. citizens. *Application Requirements:* Application, essay, financial need analysis, references, transcript, activity chart. *Deadline:* March 1.

Contact: Director of Grant Programs, Oregon Student Assistance Commission, 1500 Valley River Drive, Suite 100, Eugene, OR 97401-7020. *E-mail:* awardinfo@mercury.osac.state.or.us. *Phone:* 800-452-8807 Ext. 7395. *Web site:* www.osac.state.or.us.

Dorothy Campbell Memorial Scholarship. Renewable award for female Oregon high school senior with a minimum 2.75 GPA. Must submit essay describing strong, continuing interest in golf and the contribution that sport has made to applicant's development. *Award:* Scholarship for use in freshman, sophomore, junior, or senior year; renewable. *Award amount:* $1500. *Number of awards:* 2. *Eligibility Requirements:* Applicant must be high school student; planning to enroll or expecting to enroll at a four-year institution; female; resident of Oregon; studying in Oregon and must have an interest in golf. Available to U.S. citizens. *Application Requirements:* Application, essay, financial need analysis, test scores, transcript, activity chart. *Deadline:* March 1.

Contact: Director of Grant Programs, Oregon Student Assistance Commission, 1500 Valley River Drive, Suite 100, Eugene, OR 97401-7020. *E-mail:* awardinfo@mercury. osac.state.or.us. *Phone:* 800-452-8807 Ext. 7395. *Web site:* www.osac.state.or.us.

Glenn Jackson Scholars Scholarships (OCF). Award for graduating high school seniors who are dependents of employees or retirees of Oregon Department of Transportation or Parks and Recreation Department. Employees must have worked in their department at least three years. Award for maximum twelve undergraduate quarters or six quarters at a two-year institution. Must be U.S. citizen or permanent resident. Visit Web site (http://www.osac. state.or.us) for more details. *Award:* Scholarship for use in freshman, sophomore, junior, or senior year; renewable. *Award amount:* $2500. *Number of awards:* 2. *Eligibility Requirements:* Applicant must be high school student; planning to enroll or expecting to enroll at a four-year institution and resident of Oregon. Applicant or parent of applicant must be affiliated with Oregon Department of Transportation Parks and Recreation. Applicant or parent of applicant must have employment or volunteer experience in designated career field. Available to U.S. citizens. *Application Requirements:* Application, essay, financial need analysis, references, transcript, activity chart. *Deadline:* March 1.

Contact: Director of Grant Programs, Oregon Student Assistance Commission, 1500 Valley River Drive, Suite 100, Eugene, OR 97401-7020. *E-mail:* awardinfo@mercury. osac.state.or.us. *Phone:* 800-452-8807 Ext. 7395. *Web site:* www.osac.state.or.us.

Lawrence R. Foster Memorial Scholarship. One-time award to students enrolled or planning to enroll in a public health degree program. First preference given to those working in the public health field and those pursuing a graduate degree in public health. Undergraduates entering junior or senior year health programs may apply if seeking a public health career, and not private practice. Prefer applicants from diverse cultures. Must provide 3 references. Additional essay required. Must be resident of Oregon. *Academic Fields/Career Goals:* Health and Medical Sciences. *Award:* Scholarship for use in junior, senior, graduate, or postgraduate years; not renewable. *Award amount:* $4167. *Number of awards:* 6. *Eligibility Requirements:* Applicant must be enrolled or expecting to enroll at a four-year institution and resident of Oregon. Available to U.S. citizens. *Application Requirements:* Application, essay, financial need analysis, references, transcript, activity chart. *Deadline:* March 1.

Contact: Director of Grant Programs, Oregon Student Assistance Commission, 1500 Valley River Drive, Suite 100, Eugene, OR 97401-7020. *E-mail:* awardinfo@mercury. osac.state.or.us. *Phone:* 800-452-8807 Ext. 7395. *Web site:* www.osac.state.or.us.

Oregon Occupational Safety and Health Division Workers Memorial Scholarship. Available to Oregon residents who are the dependents or spouses of an Oregon worker who was killed or permanently disabled on the job. Submit essay of 500 words or less titled "How has the injury or death of your parent or spouse affected or influenced your decision to further your education?" See Web site for more details. (http://www.osac. state.or.us) *Award:* Scholarship for use in freshman, sophomore, junior, senior, or graduate year; not renewable. *Award amount:* $4786. *Number of awards:* 1. *Eligibility Requirements:* Applicant must be enrolled or expecting to enroll at a two-year or four-year institution and resident of Oregon. Applicant or parent of applicant must have employment or volunteer experience in designated career field. Available to U.S. citizens. *Application Requirements:* Application, essay, financial need analysis, test scores, transcript, workers compensation claim number. *Deadline:* March 1.

Contact: Director of Grant Programs, Oregon Student Assistance Commission, 1500 Valley River Drive, Suite 100, Eugene, OR 97401-7020. *E-mail:* awardinfo@mercury. osac.state.or.us. *Phone:* 800-452-8807 Ext. 7395. *Web site:* www.osac.state.or.us.

Oregon Scholarship Fund Community College Student Award. Scholarship open to Oregon residents enrolled or planning to enroll in Oregon community college programs. May apply for one additional year. *Award:* Scholarship for use in freshman or sophomore year; not renewable. *Award amount:* $500. *Number of awards:* varies. *Eligibility Requirements:* Applicant must be enrolled or expecting to enroll at a two-year institution; resident of Oregon and studying in Oregon. Available to U.S. citizens. *Application Requirements:* Application, essay, financial need analysis, transcript, activity chart. *Deadline:* March 1.

Contact: Director of Grant Programs, Oregon Student Assistance Commission, 1500 Valley River Drive, Suite 100, Eugene, OR 97401-7020. *E-mail:* awardinfo@mercury. osac.state.or.us. *Phone:* 800-452-8807 Ext. 7395. *Web site:* www.osac.state.or.us.

Oregon Scholarship Fund Transfer Student Award. Award open to Oregon residents who are currently enrolled in their second year at a community college and are planning to transfer to a four-year college in Oregon. Prior recipients may apply for one additional year. *Award:* Scholarship for use in junior or senior year; not renewable. *Award amount:* $500. *Number of awards:* varies. *Eligibility Requirements:* Applicant must be enrolled or expecting to enroll at a four-year institution; resident of Oregon and studying in Oregon. Available to U.S. citizens. *Application Requirements:* Application, essay, financial need analysis, transcript, activity chart. *Deadline:* March 1.

Contact: Director of Grant Programs, Oregon Student Assistance Commission, 1500 Valley River Drive, Suite 100, Eugene, OR 97401-7020. *E-mail:* awardinfo@mercury. osac.state.or.us. *Phone:* 800-452-8807 Ext. 7395. *Web site:* www.osac.state.or.us.

Oregon Student Assistance Commission Employee and Dependent Scholarship. One-time award for current permanent employee of the Oregon Student Assistance Commission or legally dependent children of employee. Also available to dependent children of an employee who retires, is permanently disabled, or deceased directly from employment at OSAC. Dependent must enroll full time. Employee may enroll part time. *Award:* Scholarship for use in freshman, sophomore, junior, or senior year; not renewable. *Award amount:* $500. *Number of awards:* 7. *Eligibility Requirements:* Applicant must be enrolled or expecting to enroll full or part-time at an institution or university and resident of Oregon. *Application Requirements:* Application, essay, financial need analysis, transcript. *Deadline:* March 1.

Contact: Director of Grant Programs, Oregon Student Assistance Commission, 1500 Valley River Drive, Suite 100, Eugene, OR 97401-7020. *E-mail:* awardinfo@mercury. osac.state.or.us. *Phone:* 800-452-8807 Ext. 7395. *Web site:* www.osac.state.or.us.

Oregon Trucking Association Scholarship. One scholarship available to a child of an Oregon Trucking Association member, or child of employee of member. Applicants must be Oregon residents who are graduating high school seniors from an Oregon high school. One-time award. *Award:* Scholarship for use in freshman year; not renewable. *Award amount:* $750. *Number of awards:* 4. *Eligibility Requirements:* Applicant must be high school student; planning to enroll or expecting to enroll at a four-year institution and resident of Oregon. Applicant or parent of applicant must have employment or volunteer experience in designated career field. Available to U.S. citizens. *Application Requirements:* Application, essay, financial need analysis, references, transcript, activity chart. *Deadline:* March 1.

Contact: Director of Grant Programs, Oregon Student Assistance Commission, 1500 Valley River Drive, Suite 100, Eugene, OR 97401-7020. *E-mail:* awardinfo@mercury. osac.state.or.us. *Phone:* 800-452-8807 Ext. 7395. *Web site:* www.osac.state.or.us.

Oregon Veterans' Education Aid. To be eligible, veteran must have served in U.S. armed forces 90 days and been discharged under honorable conditions; U.S. citizen and Oregon resident; Korean War veteran or received campaign or expeditionary medal or ribbon awarded by U.S. armed forces for services after June 30, 1958. Full-time students receive $50/month, part-time students receive $35/month. *Award:* Grant for use in freshman, sophomore, junior, senior, graduate, or postgraduate years; renewable. *Award amount:* varies. *Number of awards:* varies. *Eligibility Requirements:* Applicant must be enrolled or expecting to enroll full or part-time at a two-year, four-year, or technical institution or university; resident of Oregon and studying in Oregon. Available to U.S. citizens. Applicant must have general military experience. *Application Requirements:* Application, certified copy of DD Form 214. *Deadline:* continuous.

Contact: Ruth Sherman, Educational Aid Coordinator, Oregon Department of Veterans' Affairs, 700 Summer Street, NE, Salem, OR 97301-1289. *E-mail:* shermar@odva.state.or. us. *Phone:* 503-373-2085. *Fax:* 503-373-2392. *Web site:* www.odva.state.or.us.

PENNSYLVANIA

Educational Gratuity Program. This program is for eligible dependents of 100% disabled or deceased veteran whose disability was incurred during a period of war or armed conflict. Must be a Pennsylvania resident attending a Pennsylvania school. Up to $500 per semester may be awarded. *Award:* Grant for use in freshman, sophomore, junior, or senior year; renewable. *Award amount:* varies. *Number of awards:* varies. *Eligibility Requirements:* Applicant must be age 16-23; enrolled or expecting to enroll full-time at a two-year, four-year, or technical institution or university; resident of Pennsylvania and studying in Pennsylvania. Available to U.S. citizens. Applicant or parent must meet one or more of the following requirements: general military experience; retired from active duty; disabled or killed as a result of military service; prisoner of war; or missing in action. *Application Requirements:* Application, driver's license, financial need analysis, transcript. *Deadline:* continuous.

Contact: Michelle Zimmerman, Clerk Typist, Pennsylvania Bureau for Veterans Affairs, Building 0-47, Fort Indiantown Gap, Annville, PA 17003-5002. *E-mail:* michzimmer@state. pa.us. *Phone:* 717-861-8910. *Fax:* 717-861-8589. *Web site:* sites.state.pa.us/PA_Exec/ Military_Affairs/va/.

New Economy Technology Scholarships. Renewable award for Pennsylvania residents pursuing a degree in science or technology at a PHEAA-approved Pennsylvania school. Must maintain minimum 3.0 GPA. Must commence employment in Pennsylvania in field related to student's program within one year after completion of studies. Must work one year for each year scholarship was awarded. *Academic Fields/Career Goals:* Science, Technology, and Society. *Award:* Scholarship for use in freshman, sophomore, junior, or senior year; renewable. *Award amount:* up to $3000. *Number of awards:* varies. *Eligibility Requirements:* Applicant must be enrolled or expecting to enroll full or part-time at a two-year, four-year, or technical institution; resident of Pennsylvania and studying in Pennsylvania. Applicant must have 3.0 GPA or higher. *Application Requirements:* Application, FAFSA. *Deadline:* December 31.

Contact: PHEAA State Grant and Special Programs Division, Pennsylvania Higher Education Assistance Agency, 1200 North Seventh Street, Harrisburg, PA 17102-1444. *Phone:* 800-692-7392. *Web site:* www.pheaa.org.

Pennsylvania State Grants. Award for Pennsylvania residents attending an approved postsecondary institution as undergraduates in a program of at least two years duration. Renewable for up to eight semesters if applicants show continued need and academic progress. Submit Free Application for Federal Student Aid. *Award:* Grant for use in freshman, sophomore, junior, or senior year; renewable. *Award amount:* $300–$3300. *Number of awards:* up to 151,000. *Eligibility Requirements:* Applicant must be enrolled or expecting to enroll full or part-time at a two-year, four-year, or technical institution or university and resident of Pennsylvania. Available to U.S. and Canadian citizens. *Application Requirements:* Application, financial need analysis. *Deadline:* May 1.

Contact: Keith New, Director of Communications and Press Office, Pennsylvania Higher Education Assistance Agency, 1200 North Seventh Street, Harrisburg, PA 17102-1444. *E-mail:* knew@pheaa.org. *Phone:* 717-720-2509. *Fax:* 717-720-3903. *Web site:* www.pheaa.org.

Postsecondary Education Gratuity Program. Waiver of tuition and fees for children of Pennsylvania police officers, firefighters, rescue or ambulance squad members, corrections facility employees, or National Guard members who died in the line of duty after January 1, 1976. Must be a resident of Pennsylvania 25 years old or younger and enrolled full time as an undergraduate student at a Pennsylvania community college, state-owned institution or state-related institution. Award is for a maximum of 5 years. Application deadline March 31. *Award:* Grant for use in freshman, sophomore, junior, or senior year; renewable. *Award amount:* varies. *Number of awards:* varies. *Eligibility Requirements:* Applicant must be age 25 or under; enrolled or expecting to enroll full-time at a two-year or four-year institution or university; resident of Pennsylvania and studying in Pennsylvania. *Application Requirements:* Application. *Deadline:* March 31.

Contact: PHEAA State Grant and Special Programs Division, Pennsylvania Higher Education Assistance Agency, 1200 North Seventh Street, Harrisburg, PA 17102-1444. *Phone:* 800-692-7392. *Web site:* www.pheaa.org.

Veterans Grant-Pennsylvania. Renewable awards for Pennsylvania residents who are qualified veterans attending an approved undergraduate program full-time. Up to $3300 for in-state study or $800 for out-of-state study. Deadlines: May 1 for all renewal applicants, new applicants who plan to enroll in an undergraduate baccalaureate degree program, and those in college transfer programs at two-year public or junior colleges; August 1 for all first-time applicants who plan to enroll in a business, trade, or technical school; a hospital school of nursing; or a two-year terminal program at a community, junior, or four-year college. *Award:* Grant for use in freshman, sophomore, junior, or senior year; renewable. *Award amount:* $800–$3300. *Number of* *awards:* varies. *Eligibility Requirements:* Applicant must be enrolled or expecting to enroll full-time at a two-year, four-year, or technical institution or university and resident of Pennsylvania. Available to U.S. citizens. Applicant must have general military experience. *Application Requirements:* Application. *Deadline:* varies.

Contact: Keith New, Director of Communications and Press Office, Pennsylvania Higher Education Assistance Agency, 1200 North Seventh Street, Harrisburg, PA 17102-1444. *E-mail:* knew@pheaa.org. *Phone:* 717-720-2509. *Fax:* 717-720-3903. *Web site:* www.pheaa.org.

PUERTO RICO

Robert C. Byrd Honor Scholarships. This grant is sponsored by the Puerto Rico Department of Education and is granted to gifted students. These are students chosen from public and private schools who graduate from high school and are admitted to an accredited university in Puerto Rico or in the United States and who show promise to complete a college career. It is granted for a period of four years if the student maintains a satisfactory academic progress. Must be a U.S. citizen and rank in the upper quarter of class or have a minimum 3.5 GPA. *Award:* Scholarship for use in freshman, sophomore, junior, or senior year; renewable. *Award amount:* $1500. *Number of awards:* 74–85. *Eligibility Requirements:* Applicant must be high school student and planning to enroll or expecting to enroll full-time at a four-year institution or university. Applicant must have 3.5 GPA or higher. Available to U.S. citizens. *Application Requirements:* Application, financial need analysis, interview, portfolio, references, test scores, transcript. *Deadline:* May 30.

Contact: Eligio Hernandez, Director, Puerto Rico Department of Education, PO Box 190759, San Juan, PR 00919-0759. *E-mail:* hernandez_eli@de.gobierno.pr. *Phone:* 787-754-1015. *Fax:* 787-758-2281.

RHODE ISLAND

Rhode Island Higher Education Grant Program. Grants for residents of Rhode Island attending an approved school in the U.S., Canada, or Mexico. Based on need. Renewable for up to four years if in good academic standing. Applications accepted January 1 through March 1. Several awards of variable amounts. Must be U.S. citizen or registered alien. *Award:* Grant for use in freshman, sophomore, junior, or senior year; not renewable. *Award amount:* $300–$1400.

Number of awards: 10,000–12,000. *Eligibility Requirements:* Applicant must be enrolled or expecting to enroll full or part-time at a two-year, four-year, or technical institution or university and resident of Rhode Island. Available to U.S. citizens. *Application Requirements:* Application, financial need analysis. *Deadline:* March 1.

Contact: Mary Ann Welch, Director of Program Administration, Rhode Island Higher Education Assistance Authority, 560 Jefferson Boulevard, Warwick, RI 02886. *E-mail:* mawelch@riheaa.org. *Phone:* 401-736-1170. *Fax:* 401-732-3541. *Web site:* www.riheaa.org.

SOUTH CAROLINA

Educational Assistance for Certain War Veteran's Dependents- South Carolina. Renewable aid to South Carolina Disabled Veterans' dependents under age 26. Veterans must have had wartime service in World War II, the Vietnam War, Persian Gulf or the Korean War. Must have received the Purple Heart or Medal of Honor. Applicant must show DD214 (birth certificate and VA rating). For undergraduate study at any South Carolina state-supported college. Must be South Carolina resident. *Award:* Scholarship for use in freshman, sophomore, junior, or senior year; renewable. *Award amount:* varies. *Number of awards:* varies. *Eligibility Requirements:* Applicant must be age 18-25; enrolled or expecting to enroll full or part-time at a two-year, four-year, or technical institution or university; resident of South Carolina and studying in South Carolina. Available to U.S. citizens. Applicant or parent must meet one or more of the following requirements: general military experience; retired from active duty; disabled or killed as a result of military service; prisoner of war; or missing in action. *Application Requirements:* Application. *Deadline:* continuous.

Contact: Ms. Lauren Hugg, Free Tuition Assistant, South Carolina Division of Veterans Affairs, 1801 Assembly Street, Room 141, Columbia, SC 29201. *Phone:* 803-255-4317. *Fax:* 803-255-4257.

Legislative Incentives for Future Excellence Program. Scholarship for students from South Carolina to attend an institution of higher education in South Carolina. For students attending a four-year institution, two of the following three criteria must be met: 1) minimum 3.0 GPA, 2) 1100 SAT or 24 ACT, or 3) graduate in the top 30% of class. Students attending a two-year or technical college must have a 3.0 GPA, SAT and class rank requirements are waived. *Award:* Scholarship for use in fresh-

man, sophomore, junior, senior, or graduate year; renewable. *Award amount:* $2000–$5000. *Number of awards:* varies. *Eligibility Requirements:* Applicant must be enrolled or expecting to enroll full-time at a two-year, four-year, or technical institution or university; resident of South Carolina and studying in South Carolina. Applicant must have 3.0 GPA or higher. Available to U.S. citizens. *Application Requirements:* Test scores, transcript. *Deadline:* continuous.

Contact: Bichevia Green, LIFE Scholarship Coordinator, South Carolina Commission on Higher Education, 1333 Main Street, Suite 200, Columbia, SC 29201. *E-mail:* bgreen@che.sc.gov. *Phone:* 803-737-2280. *Fax:* 803-737-2297. *Web site:* www.che.sc.gov.

Palmetto Fellows Scholarship Program. Renewable award for qualified high school seniors in South Carolina to attend a four-year South Carolina institution. Must rank in top 5% of class at the end of sophomore or junior year, earn a 3.5 GPA on a 4.0 scale, and score at least 1200 on the SAT or 27 on the ACT. Submit official transcript, test scores, and application by established deadline (usually January 15th of senior year). *Award:* Scholarship for use in freshman, sophomore, junior, senior, or graduate year; renewable. *Award amount:* up to $6700. *Number of awards:* varies. *Eligibility Requirements:* Applicant must be high school student; planning to enroll or expecting to enroll full-time at a four-year institution or university; resident of South Carolina and studying in South Carolina. Applicant must have 3.5 GPA or higher. Available to U.S. citizens. *Application Requirements:* Application, test scores, transcript. *Deadline:* January 15.

Contact: Ms. Sherry Hubbard, Coordinator, South Carolina Commission on Higher Education, 1333 Main Street, Suite 200, Columbia, SC 29201. *E-mail:* shubbard@che.sc.gov. *Phone:* 803-737-2260. *Fax:* 803-737-2297. *Web site:* www.che.sc.gov.

South Carolina Hope Scholarship. One-year merit-based scholarship for eligible first-time entering freshmen attending a four-year institution. Minimum 3.0 GPA. *Award:* Scholarship for use in freshman year; not renewable. *Award amount:* $2650. *Number of awards:* 1–2264. *Eligibility Requirements:* Applicant must be enrolled or expecting to enroll full-time at a four-year institution or university; resident of South Carolina and studying in South Carolina. Applicant must have 3.0 GPA or higher. Available to U.S. citizens. *Application Requirements:* Transcript. *Deadline:* continuous.

Contact: Bichevia Green, Life/Hope Scholarship Coordinator, South Carolina Commission on Higher Education, 1333 Main Street, Suite 200, Columbia, SC 29201. *E-mail:* bgreen@che.sc.gov. *Phone:* 803-737-2280. *Fax:* 803-737-2297. *Web site:* www.che.sc. gov.

South Carolina Need-Based Grants Program. Award based on results of Free Application for Federal Student Aid. A student may receive up to $2500 annually for full-time and up to $1250 annually for part-time study. The grant must be applied toward the cost of attendance at a South Carolina college for up to eight full-time equivalent terms. Student must be degree-seeking. *Award:* Grant for use in freshman, sophomore, junior, senior, or graduate year; renewable. *Award amount:* up to $2500. *Number of awards:* 1–23,485. *Eligibility Requirements:* Applicant must be enrolled or expecting to enroll full or part-time at a two-year, four-year, or technical institution or university; resident of South Carolina and studying in South Carolina. Available to U.S. citizens. *Application Requirements:* Financial need analysis. *Deadline:* continuous.

Contact: Ms. Sherry Hubbard, Coordinator, South Carolina Commission on Higher Education, 1333 Main Street, Suite 200, Columbia, SC 29201. *E-mail:* shubbard@che. sc.gov. *Phone:* 803-737-2260. *Fax:* 803-737-2297. *Web site:* www.che.sc.gov.

South Carolina Teacher Loan Program. One-time awards for South Carolina residents attending four-year postsecondary institutions in South Carolina. Recipients must teach in the South Carolina public school system in a critical-need area after graduation. 20% of loan forgiven for each year of service. Write for additional requirements. *Academic Fields/Career Goals:* Education; Special Education. *Award:* Forgivable loan for use in freshman, sophomore, junior, senior, or graduate year; not renewable. *Award amount:* $2500–$5000. *Number of awards:* up to 1121. *Eligibility Requirements:* Applicant must be enrolled or expecting to enroll full or part-time at a four-year institution or university; resident of South Carolina and studying in South Carolina. Applicant must have 3.0 GPA or higher. *Application Requirements:* Application, test scores. *Deadline:* June 1.

Contact: Jennifer Jones-Gaddy, Vice President, South Carolina Student Loan Corporation, PO Box 21487, Columbia, SC 29221. *E-mail:* jgaddy@slc.sc.edu. *Phone:* 803-798-0916. *Fax:* 803-772-9410. *Web site:* www.slc.sc.edu.

South Carolina Tuition Grants Program. Assists South Carolina residents attending one of twenty approved South Carolina independent colleges. Freshmen must be in upper 3/4 of high school class or have SAT score of at least 900. Upper-class students must complete 24 semester hours per year to be eligible. *Award:* Grant for use in freshman, sophomore, junior, or senior year; renewable. *Award amount:* $100–$3240. *Number of awards:* up to 11,000. *Eligibility Requirements:* Applicant must be enrolled or expecting to enroll full-time at a two-year or four-year institution; resident of South Carolina and studying in South Carolina. Available to U.S. citizens. *Application Requirements:* Application, financial need analysis, test scores, transcript, FAFSA. *Deadline:* June 30.

Contact: Toni Cave, Financial Aid Counselor, South Carolina Tuition Grants Commission, 101 Business Park Boulevard, Suite 2100, Columbia, SC 29203-9498. *E-mail:* toni@sctuitiongrants.org. *Phone:* 803-896-1120. *Fax:* 803-896-1126. *Web site:* www. sctuitiongrants.com.

SOUTH DAKOTA

Education Benefits for Dependents of POWs and MIAs. Children and spouses of prisoners of war, or of persons listed as missing in action, are entitled to attend a state-supported school without the payment of tuition or mandatory fees provided they are not eligible for equal or greater federal benefits. Must use SDDVA form E-12 available at financial aid offices. Must be a South Dakota resident intending to study in South Dakota. *Award:* Scholarship for use in freshman, sophomore, junior, or senior year; not renewable. *Award amount:* varies. *Number of awards:* varies. *Eligibility Requirements:* Applicant must be enrolled or expecting to enroll at an institution or university; resident of South Dakota and studying in South Dakota. Available to U.S. citizens. Applicant or parent must meet one or more of the following requirements: general military experience; retired from active duty; disabled or killed as a result of military service; prisoner of war; or missing in action. *Application Requirements:* Application. *Deadline:* varies.

Contact: Dr. Lesta V. Turchen, Senior Administrator, South Dakota Board of Regents, 306 East Capitol Avenue, Suite 200, Pierre, SD 57501-3159. *E-mail:* info@sdbor.edu. *Phone:* 605-773-3455. *Fax:* 605-773-2422. *Web site:* www.ris.sdbor.edu.

Haines Memorial Scholarship. One-time scholarship for South Dakota public university students who are sophomores, juniors, or seniors having at least a 2.5 GPA and majoring in a teacher education program. Include resume with application. Must be South Dakota resident. *Academic Fields/Career Goals:* Education. *Award:* Scholarship for use in sophomore, junior, or senior year; not renewable. *Award amount:* $2150. *Number of awards:* 1. *Eligibility Requirements:* Applicant must be enrolled or expecting to enroll at an institution or university; resident of South Dakota and studying in South Dakota. Applicant must have 2.5 GPA or higher. *Application Requirements:* Application, autobiography, essay, resume. *Deadline:* February 25.

Contact: South Dakota Board of Regents, 306 East Capitol Avenue, Suite 200, Pierre, SD 57501-3159. *Web site:* www.ris.sdbor. edu.

South Dakota Aid to Dependents of Deceased Veterans. Program provides free tuition for children of deceased veterans who are under the age of 25, are residents of South Dakota, and whose mother or father was killed in action or died of other causes while on active duty. ("Veteran" for this purpose is as defined by South Dakota Codified Laws.) Parent must have been a bona fide resident of SD for at least six months immediately preceding entry into active service. Eligibility is for state-supported schools only. Must use SDDVA form E-12 available at financial aid offices. *Award:* Scholarship for use in freshman, sophomore, junior, or senior year; not renewable. *Award amount:* varies. *Number of awards:* varies. *Eligibility Requirements:* Applicant must be age 24 or under; enrolled or expecting to enroll at a two-year or four-year institution; resident of South Dakota and studying in South Dakota. Available to U.S. citizens. Applicant or parent must meet one or more of the following requirements: general military experience; retired from active duty; disabled or killed as a result of military service; prisoner of war; or missing in action. *Application Requirements:* Application. *Deadline:* varies.

Contact: Dr. Lesta V. Turchen, Senior Administrator, South Dakota Board of Regents, 306 East Capitol Avenue, Suite 200, Pierre, SD 57501-3159. *E-mail:* info@sdbor.edu. *Phone:* 605-773-3455. *Fax:* 605-773-2422. *Web site:* www.ris.sdbor.edu.

South Dakota Board of Regents Senior Citizens Tuition Assistance. Award for tuition assistance for any postsecondary academic year of study to senior citizens age 65 and older. Write for further details. Must be a South Dakota resident and attend a school in South Dakota. *Award:* Scholarship for use in freshman, sophomore, junior, or senior year; not renewable. *Award amount:* varies. *Number of awards:* varies.

Eligibility Requirements: Applicant must be age 65; enrolled or expecting to enroll at an institution or university; resident of South Dakota and studying in South Dakota. *Application Requirements:* Application. *Deadline:* continuous.

Contact: South Dakota Board of Regents, 306 East Capitol Avenue, Suite 200, Pierre, SD 57501-3159. *Web site:* www.ris.sdbor. edu.

South Dakota Board of Regents State Employee Tuition Assistance. Award for South Dakota state employees for any postsecondary academic year of study in South Dakota institution. Must be U.S. citizen. Write for requirements and other details. *Award:* Scholarship for use in freshman, sophomore, junior, or senior year; not renewable. *Award amount:* varies. *Number of awards:* varies. *Eligibility Requirements:* Applicant must be enrolled or expecting to enroll at an institution or university; resident of South Dakota and studying in South Dakota. Applicant or parent of applicant must have employment or volunteer experience in designated career field. Available to U.S. citizens. *Application Requirements:* *Deadline:* continuous.

Contact: South Dakota Board of Regents, 306 East Capitol Avenue, Suite 200, Pierre, SD 57501-3159. *Web site:* www.ris.sdbor. edu.

South Dakota Education Benefits for National Guard Members. Guard members who meet the requirements for admission are eligible for a 50% reduction in undergraduate tuition charges at any state-supported school for up to a maximum of four academic years. Provision also covers one program of study, approved by the State Board of Education, at any state vocational school. Must be state resident and member of the SD Army or Air Guard throughout period for which benefits are sought. Must contact financial aid office for full details and forms at time of registration. *Award:* Scholarship for use in freshman, sophomore, junior, or senior year; not renewable. *Award amount:* varies. *Number of awards:* varies. *Eligibility Requirements:* Applicant must be enrolled or expecting to enroll at a two-year, four-year, or technical institution or university; resident of South Dakota and studying in South Dakota. Available to U.S. citizens. Applicant must have served in the Air Force National Guard or Army National Guard. *Application Requirements:* Application. *Deadline:* varies.

Contact: Dr. Lesta V. Turchen, Senior Administrator, South Dakota Board of Regents, 306 East Capitol Avenue, Suite 200, Pierre, SD 57501-3159. *E-mail:* info@sdbor.edu.

Phone: 605-773-3455. *Fax:* 605-773-2422. *Web site:* www.ris.sdbor.edu.

South Dakota Education Benefits for Veterans. Certain veterans are eligible for free undergraduate tuition assistance at state-supported schools provided they are not eligible for educational payments under the GI Bill or any other federal educational program. Contact financial aid office for full details and forms. May receive one month of free tuition for each month of qualifying service (minimum one year, maximum four years). Must be resident of South Dakota. *Award:* Scholarship for use in freshman, sophomore, junior, or senior year; not renewable. *Award amount:* varies. *Number of awards:* varies. *Eligibility Requirements:* Applicant must be enrolled or expecting to enroll at an institution or university; resident of South Dakota and studying in South Dakota. Available to U.S. citizens. Applicant must have general military experience. *Application Requirements:* Application, DD Form 214. *Deadline:* varies.

Contact: Dr. Lesta V. Turchen, Senior Administrator, South Dakota Board of Regents, 306 East Capitol Avenue, Suite 200, Pierre, SD 57501-3159. *E-mail:* info@sdbor.edu. *Phone:* 605-773-3455. *Fax:* 605-773-2422. *Web site:* www.ris.sdbor.edu.

TENNESSEE

Minority Teaching Fellows Program/ Tennessee. Forgivable loan for minority Tennessee residents pursuing teaching careers. High school applicant minimum 2.75 GPA. Must be in the top quarter of the class or score an 18 on ACT. College applicant minimum 2.50 GPA. Submit statement of intent, test scores, and transcripts with application and two letters of recommendation. Must teach one year per year of award or repay as a loan. *Academic Fields/Career Goals:* Education; Special Education. *Award:* Forgivable loan for use in freshman, sophomore, junior, or senior year; renewable. *Award amount:* $5000. *Number of awards:* 19–29. *Eligibility Requirements:* Applicant must be American Indian/Alaska Native, Asian/Pacific Islander, Black (non-Hispanic), or Hispanic; enrolled or expecting to enroll full-time at a two-year or four-year institution or university; resident of Tennessee and studying in Tennessee. Available to U.S. citizens. *Application Requirements:* Application, essay, references, test scores, transcript. *Deadline:* April 15.

Contact: Kathy Stripling, Scholarship Coordinator, Tennessee Student Assistance Corporation, 404 James Robertson Parkway,

Suite 1950, Parkway Towers, Nashville, TN 37243-0820. *E-mail:* kathy.stripling@state.tn. us. *Phone:* 615-741-1346. *Fax:* 615-741-6101. *Web site:* www.state.tn.us/tsac.

Ned McWherter Scholars Program. Assists Tennessee residents with high academic ability. Must have high school GPA of at least 3.5 and have scored in top 5% of SAT or ACT. Must attend college in Tennessee. Only high school seniors may apply. *Award:* Scholarship for use in freshman, sophomore, junior, or senior year; renewable. *Award amount:* $6000. *Number of awards:* 55. *Eligibility Requirements:* Applicant must be high school student; planning to enroll or expecting to enroll full-time at a two-year or four-year institution or university; resident of Tennessee and studying in Tennessee. Applicant must have 3.5 GPA or higher. Available to U.S. citizens. *Application Requirements:* Application, test scores, transcript. *Deadline:* February 15.

Contact: Kathy Stripling, Scholarship Coordinator, Tennessee Student Assistance Corporation, 404 James Robertson Parkway, Suite 1950, Parkway Towers, Nashville, TN 37243-0820. *E-mail:* kathy.stripling@state.tn. us. *Phone:* 615-741-1346. *Fax:* 615-741-6101. *Web site:* www.state.tn.us/tsac.

Tennessee Education Lottery Scholarship Program General Assembly Merit Scholarship. $1000 supplement to Tennessee HOPE Scholarship. Entering freshmen must have an unweighted 3.75 GPA and 29 ACT (1280 SAT). *Award:* Scholarship for use in freshman, sophomore, junior, or senior year; renewable. *Award amount:* $1000. *Number of awards:* varies. *Eligibility Requirements:* Applicant must be enrolled or expecting to enroll full or part-time at a two-year, four-year, or technical institution or university; resident of Tennessee and studying in Tennessee. Available to U.S. citizens. *Application Requirements:* Application, financial need analysis. *Deadline:* May 1.

Contact: Robert Biggers, Lottery Scholarship Program Administrator, Tennessee Student Assistance Corporation, 404 James Robertson Parkway, Suite 1950, Nashville, TN 37243-0820. *E-mail:* tsac.aidinfo@state.tn.us. *Phone:* 800-342-1663. *Fax:* 615-253-3867. *Web site:* www.state.tn.us/tsac.

Tennessee Education Lottery Scholarship Program Need Based Supplemental Award. $1000 supplement to Tennessee HOPE Scholarship. Must meet Tennessee HOPE Scholarship requirements and student's parent(s) must have an Adjusted Gross Income on their federal tax return of $36000 or less. *Award:* Scholarship for use in freshman, sophomore, junior, or senior year; renewable. *Award amount:* $1000. *Number of awards:* varies. *Eligibility Requirements:* Applicant must be enrolled or expecting to enroll full or part-time at a two-year, four-year, or technical institution or university; resident of Tennessee and studying in Tennessee. Applicant must have 3.0 GPA or higher. Available to U.S. citizens. *Application Requirements:* Application, financial need analysis. *Deadline:* May 1.

Contact: Robert Biggers, Lottery Scholarship Program Administrator, Tennessee Student Assistance Corporation, 404 James Robertson Parkway, Suite 1950, Nashville, TN 37243-0820. *E-mail:* tsac.aidinfo@state.tn.us. *Phone:* 800-342-1663. *Fax:* 615-253-3867. *Web site:* www.state.tn.us/tsac.

Tennessee Education Lottery Scholarship Program Tennessee HOPE Access Grant. Non-renewable award of $2000 for students at 4-year colleges or $1250 for students at 2-year colleges. Entering freshmen must have a minimum GPA of 2.75 and parents income must be $36000 or less. Recipients will be eligible for Tennessee HOPE Scholarship by meeting HOPE Scholarship renewal criteria. *Award:* Grant for use in freshman, sophomore, junior, or senior year; not renewable. *Award amount:* $1250–$2000. *Number of awards:* varies. *Eligibility Requirements:* Applicant must be enrolled or expecting to enroll full or part-time at a two-year, four-year, or technical institution or university; resident of Tennessee and studying in Tennessee. Available to U.S. citizens. *Application Requirements:* Application, financial need analysis. *Deadline:* May 1.

Contact: Robert Biggers, Lottery Scholarship Program Administrator, Tennessee Student Assistance Corporation, 404 James Robertson Parkway, Suite 1950, Nashville, TN 37243-0820. *E-mail:* tsac.aidinfo@state.tn.us. *Phone:* 800-342-1663. *Fax:* 615-253-3867. *Web site:* www.state.tn.us/tsac.

Tennessee Education Lottery Scholarship Program Tennessee HOPE Scholarship. Award of $3000 per year for students at 4-year colleges or $1500 per year for students at 2-year colleges. *Award:* Scholarship for use in freshman, sophomore, junior, or senior year; renewable. *Award amount:* $1500–$3000. *Number of awards:* varies. *Eligibility Requirements:* Applicant must be enrolled or expecting to enroll full or part-time at a two-year, four-year, or technical institution or university; resident of Tennessee and studying in Tennessee. Applicant must have 3.0 GPA or higher. Available to U.S. citizens. *Application Requirements:* Application, financial need analysis. *Deadline:* May 1.

Contact: Robert Biggers, Lottery Scholarship Program Administrator, Tennessee Student Assistance Corporation, 404 James Robertson Parkway, Suite 1950, Nashville, TN 37243-0820. *E-mail:* tsac.aidinfo@state.tn.us. *Phone:* 800-342-1663. *Fax:* 615-253-3867. *Web site:* www.state.tn.us/tsac.

Tennessee Education Lottery Scholarship Program Wilder-Naifeh Technical Skills Grant. Award of $1250 for students enrolled in Tennessee Technology Centers. Cannot be prior recipient of Tennessee HOPE Scholarship. *Award:* Grant for use in freshman, sophomore, junior, or senior year. *Award amount:* $1250. *Number of awards:* varies. *Eligibility Requirements:* Applicant must be enrolled or expecting to enroll full or part-time at a technical institution; resident of Tennessee and studying in Tennessee. *Application Requirements:* Application, financial need analysis. *Deadline:* May 1.

Contact: Robert Biggers, Lottery Scholarship Program Administrator, Tennessee Student Assistance Corporation, 404 James Robertson Parkway, Suite 1950, Nashville, TN 37243-0820. *E-mail:* tsac.aidinfo@state.tn.us. *Phone:* 800-342-1663. *Fax:* 615-253-3867. *Web site:* www.state.tn.us/tsac.

Tennessee Student Assistance Award Program. Assists Tennessee residents attending an approved college or university within the state. Complete a Free Application for Federal Student Aid form. Apply January 1. FAFSA must be processed by May 1 for priority consideration. *Award:* Grant for use in freshman, sophomore, junior, or senior year; renewable. *Award amount:* $100–$2130. *Number of awards:* 26,000. *Eligibility Requirements:* Applicant must be enrolled or expecting to enroll full or part-time at a two-year, four-year, or technical institution or university; resident of Tennessee and studying in Tennessee. Available to U.S. citizens. *Application Requirements:* Application, financial need analysis. *Deadline:* May 1.

Contact: Naomi Derryberry, Grant and Scholarship Administrator, Tennessee Student Assistance Corporation, 404 James Robertson Parkway, Suite 1950, Parkway Towers, Nashville, TN 37243-0820. *E-mail:* naomi.derryberry@state.tn.us. *Phone:* 615-741-1346. *Fax:* 615-741-6101. *Web site:* www.state.tn.us/tsac.

Tennessee Teaching Scholars Program. Forgivable loan for college juniors, seniors, and college graduates admitted to an education program in Tennessee with a minimum GPA of 2.5. Students must commit to teach in a Tennessee public school one year for each year of the award. *Academic Fields/Career Goals:* Education. *Award:* Forgiv-

able loan for use in junior, senior, or graduate year; not renewable. *Award amount:* $1000–$4200. *Number of awards:* 30–250. *Eligibility Requirements:* Applicant must be enrolled or expecting to enroll full or part-time at a four-year institution or university; resident of Tennessee and studying in Tennessee. Applicant must have 2.5 GPA or higher. Available to U.S. citizens. *Application Requirements:* Application, references, test scores, transcript, letter of intent. *Deadline:* April 15.

Contact: Mike McCormack, Scholarship Administrator, Tennessee Student Assistance Corporation, Suite 1950, Parkway Towers, Nashville, TN 37243-0820. *E-mail:* mike.mccormack@state.tn.us. *Phone:* 615-741-1346. *Fax:* 615-741-6101. *Web site:* www.state.tn.us/tsac.

TEXAS

Academic Common Market Waiver. For Texas residents who are students pursuing a degree in a field of study not offered in Texas. May qualify for special tuition rates. Deadlines vary by institution. Must be studying in the South. *Award:* Scholarship for use in freshman, sophomore, junior, senior, or graduate year; renewable. *Award amount:* varies. *Number of awards:* varies. *Eligibility Requirements:* Applicant must be enrolled or expecting to enroll full or part-time at an institution or university; resident of Texas and studying in Alabama, Arkansas, Florida, Georgia, Kentucky, Louisiana, Mississippi, Missouri, Oklahoma, South Carolina, Tennessee, or Virginia. Available to U.S. citizens. *Application Requirements:* Application. *Deadline:* varies.

Contact: Linda McDonough, Associate Program Director, Texas Higher Education Coordinating Board, PO Box 12788, Austin, TX 78711-2788. *E-mail:* grantinfo@thecb.state.tx.us. *Phone:* 512-427-6525. *Web site:* www.collegefortexans.com.

Border County Waiver. Award provides waiver of nonresident tuition for students of neighboring states (Louisiana, Oklahoma, Arkansas and New Mexico). Must attend a Texas public institution. Deadline varies by institution. Contact the registrar's office for details. *Award:* Scholarship for use in freshman, sophomore, junior, or senior year; not renewable. *Award amount:* varies. *Number of awards:* varies. *Eligibility Requirements:* Applicant must be enrolled or expecting to enroll at a four-year institution or university; resident of Arkansas, Louisiana, New Mexico, or Oklahoma and studying in Texas. *Application Requirements:* Application. *Deadline:* varies.

Contact: Financial Aid Office at college, Texas Higher Education Coordinating Board, PO Box 12788, Austin, TX 78711-2788. *E-mail:* grantinfo@thecb.state.tx.us. *Phone:* 512-427-6101. *Fax:* 512-427-6127. *Web site:* www.collegefortexans.com.

Conditional Grant Program. Grants available for up to $6,000. Students must be considered economically disadvantaged based on federal guidelines. Must be pursuing a degree in Civil Engineering or Computer Science. Must be a Texas resident and study in Texas. *Academic Fields/Career Goals:* Civil Engineering; Computer Science/Data Processing. *Award:* Grant for use in freshman, sophomore, junior, or senior year; renewable. *Award amount:* up to $6000. *Number of awards:* varies. *Eligibility Requirements:* Applicant must be American Indian/Alaska Native, Asian/Pacific Islander, Black (non-Hispanic), or Hispanic; enrolled or expecting to enroll full-time at a four-year institution; female; resident of Texas and studying in Texas. Applicant must have 2.5 GPA or higher. Available to U.S. citizens. *Application Requirements:* Application, essay, interview, references, test scores, transcript. *Deadline:* March 1.

Contact: Minnie Brown, Program Coordinator, Texas Department of Transportation, 125 East 11th Street, Austin, TX 78701-2483. *E-mail:* mbrown2@dot.state.tx.us. *Phone:* 512-416-4979. *Fax:* 512-416-4980. *Web site:* www.dot.state.tx.us.

Early High School Graduation Scholarships. Award of $2000 for Texas residents who have completed the requirements for graduation from a Texas high school in no more than 36 consecutive months. Eligibility continues until full $2000 tuition award is received. Must submit high school certificate of eligibility to Coordinating Board. For more information, contact your high school counselor. *Award:* Scholarship for use in freshman year; not renewable. *Award amount:* $2000. *Number of awards:* varies. *Eligibility Requirements:* Applicant must be high school student; planning to enroll or expecting to enroll full or part-time at a two-year, four-year, or technical institution or university; resident of Texas and studying in Texas. Available to U.S. citizens. *Application Requirements:* Application. *Deadline:* continuous.

Contact: Texas Higher Education Coordinating Board, PO Box 12788, Austin, TX 78711-2788. *E-mail:* grantinfo@thecb.state.tx.us. *Phone:* 800-242-3062 Ext. 6387. *Web site:* www.collegefortexans.com.

Educational Aides Exemption. Assist certain educational aides by exempting them from payment of tuition and fees at public colleges or universities in Texas. Applicants must have worked as an educational aide in a Texas public school for at least one year and must be enrolled in courses required for teacher certification. Contact your college or university financial aid office for information on applying for this scholarship. Application cycles are as follows: Fall, June 1 through February 1; Spring, November 1 through July 1; and Summer, April 1 through October 1. *Academic Fields/Career Goals:* Education. *Award:* Scholarship for use in freshman, sophomore, junior, or senior year; not renewable. *Award amount:* varies. *Number of awards:* varies. *Eligibility Requirements:* Applicant must be enrolled or expecting to enroll at a four-year institution or university; resident of Texas and studying in Texas. *Application Requirements:* Application, financial need analysis. *Deadline:* varies.

Contact: Financial Aid Office at college, Texas Higher Education Coordinating Board, PO Box 12788, Austin, TX 78711-2788. *E-mail:* grantinfo@thecb.state.tx.us. *Phone:* 512-427-6101. *Fax:* 512-427-6127. *Web site:* www.collegefortexans.com.

Exemption for Disabled in the Line of Duty Peace Officers. Renewable award for persons who were injured in the line of duty while serving as Peace Officers. Must be Texas resident and attend a public college or university in Texas. Submit documentation of disability from employer. For more information see registrar. *Award:* Scholarship for use in freshman, sophomore, junior, or senior year; renewable. *Award amount:* varies. *Number of awards:* varies. *Eligibility Requirements:* Applicant must be enrolled or expecting to enroll at a four-year institution or university; resident of Texas and studying in Texas. Applicant or parent of applicant must have employment or volunteer experience in police/firefighting. *Application Requirements:* Application, form letter. *Deadline:* varies.

Contact: Texas Higher Education Coordinating Board, PO Box 12788, Austin, TX 78711. *E-mail:* grantinfo@thecb.state.tx.us. *Web site:* www.collegefortexans.com.

Fifth-Year Accounting Student Scholarship Program. One-time award for students enrolled as fifth-year accounting students at a Texas institution. Must sign statement confirming intent to take the written exam for the purpose of being granted a certificate of CPA to practice in Texas. Contact college/university financial aid office for application information. *Academic Fields/Career Goals:* Accounting. *Award:* Scholarship for use in senior or graduate year; not renewable. *Award amount:* up to $3000.

Number of awards: varies. *Eligibility Requirements:* Applicant must be enrolled or expecting to enroll full or part-time at a four-year institution or university and studying in Texas. Available to U.S. and non-U.S. citizens. *Application Requirements:* Application, financial need analysis, transcript, letter of intent. *Deadline:* continuous.

Contact: Financial Aid Office at college, Texas Higher Education Coordinating Board, PO Box 12788, Austin, TX 78711-2788. *E-mail:* grantinfo@thecb.state.tx.us. *Phone:* 512-427-6101. *Fax:* 512-427-6127. *Web site:* www.collegefortexans.com.

Firefighter Exemption Program -Texas. One-time award assists firemen enrolled in fire science courses as part of a fire science curriculum. Award is exemption from tuition and laboratory fees at publicly supported Texas colleges. Contact the admissions/registrar's office for information on how to apply. *Academic Fields/Career Goals:* Applied Sciences; Physical Sciences and Math; Trade/Technical Specialties. *Award:* Scholarship for use in freshman, sophomore, junior, or senior year; not renewable. *Award amount:* varies. *Number of awards:* varies. *Eligibility Requirements:* Applicant must be enrolled or expecting to enroll full or part-time at a two-year, four-year, or technical institution; resident of Texas and studying in Texas. Applicant or parent of applicant must have employment or volunteer experience in fire service or police/firefighting. Available to U.S. citizens. *Application Requirements:* Application. *Deadline:* continuous.

Contact: Financial Aid Office at college, Texas Higher Education Coordinating Board, PO Box 12788, Austin, TX 78711-2788. *E-mail:* grantinfo@thecb.state.tx.us. *Phone:* 512-427-6101. *Fax:* 512-427-6127. *Web site:* www.collegefortexans.com.

Good Neighbor Scholarship Waiver. Renewable aid for students residing in Texas who are citizens of another country of the Americas and intend to return to their country upon completion of the course of study. Must attend public college in Texas. Student will be exempt from tuition. *Award:* Scholarship for use in freshman, sophomore, junior, or senior year; renewable. *Award amount:* varies. *Number of awards:* varies. *Eligibility Requirements:* Applicant must be Canadian or Latin American/Caribbean citizen; enrolled or expecting to enroll full or part-time at a two-year, four-year, or technical institution or university and studying in Texas. Available to Canadian and non-U.S. citizens. *Application Requirements:* Application, test scores, transcript. *Deadline:* March 15.

Contact: Texas Higher Education Coordinating Board, PO Box 12788, Austin, TX 78711-2788. *E-mail:* grantinfo@thecb.state.tx.us. *Phone:* 800-242-3062. *Web site:* www.collegefortexans.com.

Leveraging Educational Assistance Partnership Program (LEAP) (formerly SSIG).
Renewable award available to residents of Texas attending public colleges or universities in Texas. Must be enrolled at least half-time and show financial need. Deadlines vary by institution. Contact the college/university financial aid office for application information. *Award:* Grant for use in freshman, sophomore, junior, or senior year; renewable. *Award amount:* up to $1250. *Number of awards:* varies. *Eligibility Requirements:* Applicant must be enrolled or expecting to enroll full or part-time at a two-year, four-year, or technical institution or university; resident of Texas and studying in Texas. Available to U.S. citizens. *Application Requirements:* Financial need analysis, FAFSA. *Deadline:* varies.

Contact: Financial Aid Office at college, Texas Higher Education Coordinating Board, PO Box 12788, Austin, TX 78711-2788. *E-mail:* grantinfo@thecb.state.tx.us. *Phone:* 512-427-6101. *Fax:* 512-427-6127. *Web site:* www.collegefortexans.com.

License Plate Insignia Scholarship.
One-time award to Texas residents enrolled at least half-time at public or private nonprofit senior colleges and universities in Texas. Must demonstrate financial need. Contact financial aid office at college for deadlines and application. *Award:* Scholarship for use in freshman, sophomore, junior, or senior year; not renewable. *Award amount:* varies. *Number of awards:* varies. *Eligibility Requirements:* Applicant must be enrolled or expecting to enroll full or part-time at a four-year institution or university; resident of Texas and studying in Texas. *Application Requirements:* Application, financial need analysis. *Deadline:* varies.

Contact: Financial Aid Office at college, Texas Higher Education Coordinating Board, PO Box 12788, Austin, TX 78711-2788. *E-mail:* grantinfo@thecb.state.tx.us. *Phone:* 512-427-6101. *Fax:* 512-427-6127. *Web site:* www.collegefortexans.com.

Military Stationed in Texas Waiver.
Award provides tuition waiver for nonresident military personnel stationed in Texas. Limited to public institutions only. Contact financial aid office at college for deadline and application. *Award:* Scholarship for use in freshman, sophomore, junior, or senior year; not renewable. *Award amount:* varies. *Number of awards:* varies. *Eligibility Requirements:* Applicant must be enrolled or

expecting to enroll at an institution or university and studying in Texas. Applicant must have general military experience. *Application Requirements:* Application. *Deadline:* varies.

Contact: Financial Aid Office at college, Texas Higher Education Coordinating Board, PO Box 12788, Austin, TX 78711-2788. *E-mail:* grantinfo@thecb.state.tx.us. *Phone:* 512-427-6101. *Fax:* 512-427-6127. *Web site:* www.collegefortexans.com.

Outstanding Rural Scholar Program.
Award enables rural communities to sponsor a student going into health professions. The students must agree to work in that community once they receive their degree. Must be Texas resident entering a Texas institution on a full-time basis. Must demonstrate financial need. *Academic Fields/Career Goals:* Health and Medical Sciences. *Award:* Scholarship for use in freshman, sophomore, junior, or senior year; renewable. *Award amount:* varies. *Number of awards:* varies. *Eligibility Requirements:* Applicant must be enrolled or expecting to enroll full-time at a four-year institution or university; resident of Texas and studying in Texas. Applicant must have 3.0 GPA or higher. *Application Requirements:* Application, financial need analysis, transcript, nomination. *Deadline:* varies.

Contact: Center for Rural Health Initiatives, Texas Higher Education Coordinating Board, PO Drawer 1708, Austin, TX 78767. *E-mail:* grantinfo@thecb.state.tx.us. *Phone:* 512-479-8891. *Web site:* www.collegefortexans.com.

Physician Assistant Loan Reimbursement Program.
Award will repay loans for physician assistants working in rural Texas counties. Must have worked at least 12 consecutive months in a rural Texas county designated medically underserved. Can be renewed for up to four years. *Award:* Grant for use in freshman, sophomore, junior, or senior year; renewable. *Award amount:* up to $5000. *Number of awards:* varies. *Eligibility Requirements:* Applicant must be enrolled or expecting to enroll at an institution or university. Applicant or parent of applicant must have employment or volunteer experience in designated career field. Available to U.S. citizens. *Application Requirements:* Application. *Deadline:* varies.

Contact: Financial Aid Office at college, Texas Higher Education Coordinating Board, PO Box 12788, Austin, TX 78711-2788. *E-mail:* grantinfo@thecb.state.tx.us. *Phone:* 512-427-6101. *Fax:* 512-427-6127. *Web site:* www.collegefortexans.com.

Professional Nursing Scholarships.
Several awards for Texas residents enrolled

at least half-time in a nursing program leading to a professional degree at a Texas institution. Contact school financial aid office for further information. *Academic Fields/Career Goals:* Nursing. *Award:* Scholarship for use in freshman, sophomore, junior, or senior year; not renewable. *Award amount:* up to $3000. *Number of awards:* varies. *Eligibility Requirements:* Applicant must be enrolled or expecting to enroll full or part-time at a four-year institution or university; resident of Texas and studying in Texas. Available to U.S. citizens. *Application Requirements:* Application, financial need analysis, test scores, transcript. *Deadline:* varies.

Contact: Student Services Division, Texas Higher Education Coordinating Board, PO Box 12788, Austin, TX 78711-2788. *E-mail:* grantinfo@thecb.state.tx.us. *Phone:* 800-242-3062. *Web site:* www.collegefortexans.com.

TANF Exemption Program.
Tuition and fee exemption for Texas residents who during last year of high school received financial assistance for not less than 6 months. Must enroll at Texas institution within 24 TANF months of high school graduation. Award is good for one year. Contact the admissions/registrar's office for application information. *Award:* Scholarship for use in freshman year; not renewable. *Award amount:* varies. *Number of awards:* varies. *Eligibility Requirements:* Applicant must be age 21 or under; enrolled or expecting to enroll full or part-time at a two-year, four-year, or technical institution or university; single; resident of Texas and studying in Texas. *Application Requirements:* Application, financial need analysis. *Deadline:* continuous.

Contact: Financial Aid Office at college, Texas Higher Education Coordinating Board, PO Box 12788, Austin, TX 78711-2788. *E-mail:* grantinfo@thecb.state.tx.us. *Phone:* 512-427-6101. *Fax:* 512-427-6127. *Web site:* www.collegefortexans.com.

Texas National Guard Tuition Assistance Program.
Provides exemption from the payment of tuition to certain members of the Texas National Guard, Texas Air Guard or the State Guard. Must be Texas resident and attend school in Texas. Visit the TNG Web site at: http://www.agd.state.tx.us/education_office/state_tuition.htm. *Award:* Scholarship for use in freshman, sophomore, junior, or senior year; renewable. *Award amount:* varies. *Number of awards:* varies. *Eligibility Requirements:* Applicant must be enrolled or expecting to enroll at an institution or university; resident of Texas and studying in Texas. Applicant must have served in the Air Force National Guard or

Army National Guard. *Application Requirements:* Application. *Deadline:* varies.

Contact: State Adjutant General's Office, Texas Higher Education Coordinating Board, PO Box 5218/AGTX-PAE, Austin, TX 78763-5218. *Phone:* 512-465-5001. *Web site:* www.collegefortexans.com.

Texas Tuition Exemption for Blind/Deaf Students. Renewable award aids certain blind or deaf students by exempting them from payment of tuition and fees at public colleges or universities in Texas. Must be a resident of Texas. Deadlines vary. Must submit certificate of deafness or blindness. Contact the admissions/registrar's office for application information. *Award:* Scholarship for use in freshman, sophomore, junior, or senior year; renewable. *Award amount:* varies. *Number of awards:* varies. *Eligibility Requirements:* Applicant must be enrolled or expecting to enroll full or part-time at a two-year, four-year, or technical institution or university; resident of Texas and studying in Texas. Applicant must be hearing impaired or visually impaired. Available to U.S. citizens. *Application Requirements:* Application, certificate of impairment. *Deadline:* varies.

Contact: Financial Aid Office at college, Texas Higher Education Coordinating Board, PO Box 12788, Austin, TX 78711-2788. *E-mail:* grantinfo@thecb.state.tx.us. *Phone:* 512-427-6101. *Fax:* 512-427-6127. *Web site:* www.collegefortexans.com.

Texas Tuition Exemption for Senior Citizens-65+. Tuition exemption for Texas residents over the age of 65 at eligible Texas institutions. Pays tuition for up to six semester credit hours per semester or summer term. Nonrenewable. Awards made on a space-available basis. Contact the admissions/registrar's office for application information. *Award:* Scholarship for use in freshman, sophomore, junior, or senior year; not renewable. *Award amount:* varies. *Number of awards:* varies. *Eligibility Requirements:* Applicant must be age 66; enrolled or expecting to enroll part-time at a two-year, four-year, or technical institution or university; resident of Texas and studying in Texas. Available to U.S. citizens. *Application Requirements:* Application. *Deadline:* continuous.

Contact: Financial Aid Office at college, Texas Higher Education Coordinating Board, PO Box 12788, Austin, TX 78711-2788. *E-mail:* grantinfo@thecb.state.tx.us. *Phone:* 512-427-6101. *Fax:* 512-427-6127. *Web site:* www.collegefortexans.com.

Texas Tuition Exemption for Students in Foster Care or other Residential Care. Exemption from tuition and fees at Texas institution. Must have been in foster care under the conservatorship of the Department of Protection and Regulatory Services on or after 18th birthday; or on the day of the student's 14th birthday, if the student was also eligible for adoption on or after that day; or the day the student graduated from high school or completed the equivalent of a high school diploma. Must enroll as undergraduate student within three years of discharge. Must be Texas resident. Contact the admissions/registrar's office for application information. *Award:* Scholarship for use in freshman, sophomore, junior, or senior year; renewable. *Award amount:* varies. *Number of awards:* varies. *Eligibility Requirements:* Applicant must be enrolled or expecting to enroll full or part-time at a two-year, four-year, or technical institution or university; resident of Texas and studying in Texas. Available to U.S. citizens. *Application Requirements:* Application. *Deadline:* continuous.

Contact: Financial Aid Office at college, Texas Higher Education Coordinating Board, PO Box 12788, Austin, TX 78711-2788. *E-mail:* grantinfo@thecb.state.tx.us. *Phone:* 512-427-6101. *Fax:* 512-427-6127. *Web site:* www.collegefortexans.com.

Texas Tuition Exemption Program: Highest Ranking High School Graduate. Award available to Texas residents who are the top ranked seniors of their high school. Must attend a public college or university within Texas. Recipient is exempt from certain charges for first two semesters. Deadlines vary. Contact admissions/registrar's office for application information. Must provide proof of valedictorian ranking to the registrar. *Award:* Scholarship for use in freshman year; not renewable. *Award amount:* varies. *Number of awards:* varies. *Eligibility Requirements:* Applicant must be enrolled or expecting to enroll full or part-time at a two-year, four-year, or technical institution or university; resident of Texas and studying in Texas. Applicant must have 3.5 GPA or higher. Available to U.S. citizens. *Application Requirements:* Transcript. *Deadline:* varies.

Contact: Financial Aid Office at college, Texas Higher Education Coordinating Board, PO Box 12788, Austin, TX 78711-2788. *E-mail:* grantinfo@thecb.state.tx.us. *Phone:* 512-427-6101. *Fax:* 512-427-6127. *Web site:* www.collegefortexans.com.

Texas-Tuition Fee Exemption for Children of Disabled/Deceased Firemen, Peace Officers, Game Wardens, Employees of Correctional Institutions. Renewable award for children of paid or volunteer firemen, game wardens, peace officers, or custodial employees of the Department of Correc-tions disabled or deceased while serving in Texas. Must attend a Texas institution. Must apply before 21st birthday. Must provide certification of parent's disability or death. Contact institution's admissions or registrar's office for application information. *Award:* Scholarship for use in freshman, sophomore, or junior year; renewable. *Award amount:* varies. *Number of awards:* varies. *Eligibility Requirements:* Applicant must be age 20 or under; enrolled or expecting to enroll full or part-time at a two-year, four-year, or technical institution or university; resident of Texas and studying in Texas. Applicant or parent of applicant must have employment or volunteer experience in designated career field, fire service, or police/firefighting. Available to U.S. citizens. *Application Requirements:* Application. *Deadline:* continuous.

Contact: Financial Aid Office at college, Texas Higher Education Coordinating Board, PO Box 12788, Austin, TX 78711-2788. *E-mail:* grantinfo@thecb.state.tx.us. *Phone:* 512-427-6101. *Fax:* 512-427-6127. *Web site:* www.collegefortexans.com.

Toward Excellence, Access and Success (TEXAS Grant). Renewable aid for students enrolled in a public or private nonprofit, college or university in Texas. Based on need. Amount of award is determined by the financial aid office of each school. Deadlines vary. Contact the college/university financial aid office for application information. *Award:* Grant for use in freshman, sophomore, junior, or senior year; renewable. *Award amount:* $3140. *Number of awards:* varies. *Eligibility Requirements:* Applicant must be enrolled or expecting to enroll full or part-time at a two-year, four-year, or technical institution or university; resident of Texas and studying in Texas. Applicant must have 2.5 GPA or higher. Available to U.S. citizens. *Application Requirements:* Application, financial need analysis, transcript. *Deadline:* varies.

Contact: Financial Aid Office at college, Texas Higher Education Coordinating Board, PO Box 12788, Austin, TX 78711-2788. *E-mail:* grantinfo@thecb.state.tx.us. *Phone:* 512-427-6101. *Fax:* 512-427-6127. *Web site:* www.collegefortexans.com.

Toward Excellence, Access, and Success (TEXAS) Grant II Program. Provides grant aid to financially needy students enrolled in Texas public two-year colleges. Complete FAFSA. Contact college financial aid office for additional assistance. *Award:* Grant for use in freshman or sophomore year; renewable. *Award amount:* $3140. *Number of awards:* varies. *Eligibility Requirements:* Applicant must be enrolled or expecting to enroll full or part-time at a two-year or technical institution; resident of Texas and studying in Texas. Applicant must have 2.5 GPA or higher. Available to U.S. citizens. *Application Requirements:* Financial need analysis, transcript, FAFSA. *Deadline:* continuous.

Contact: Financial Aid Office at college, Texas Higher Education Coordinating Board, PO Box 12788, Austin, TX 78711-2788. *E-mail:* grantinfo@thecb.state.tx.us. *Phone:* 512-427-6101. *Fax:* 512-427-6127. *Web site:* www.collegefortexans.com.

Tuition and Fee Exemption for Children of Prisoners of War or Persons Missing in Action-Texas. Renewable award assists children of prisoners of war or veterans classified as missing in action. Must be a Texas resident and attend a public college or university within Texas. Submit proof of service and proof of MIA/POW status. Award is exemption from tuition and fees. Must be under 21 years of age. Contact the admissions/registrar's office for application information. *Award:* Scholarship for use in freshman, sophomore, junior, or senior year; renewable. *Award amount:* varies. *Number of awards:* varies. *Eligibility Requirements:* Applicant must be age 20 or under; enrolled or expecting to enroll at a two-year, four-year, or technical institution or university; resident of Texas and studying in Texas. Applicant or parent must meet one or more of the following requirements: general military experience; retired from active duty; disabled or killed as a result of military service; prisoner of war; or missing in action. *Application Requirements:* Application, proof of service and MIA/POW status. *Deadline:* continuous.

Contact: Financial Aid Office at college, Texas Higher Education Coordinating Board, PO Box 12788, Austin, TX 78711-2788. *E-mail:* grantinfo@thecb.state.tx.us. *Phone:* 512-427-6101. *Fax:* 512-427-6127. *Web site:* www.collegefortexans.com.

Tuition Equalization Grant (TEG) Program. Renewable award for Texas residents enrolled at least half-time at an independent college or university within the state. Based on financial need. Deadlines vary by institution. Must not be receiving athletic scholarship. Contact college/university financial aid office for application information. *Award:* Grant for use in freshman, sophomore, junior, or senior year; renewable. *Award amount:* up to $3653. *Number of awards:* varies. *Eligibility Requirements:* Applicant must be enrolled or expecting to enroll full or part-time at a two-year or four-year institution or university; resident of Texas and studying in Texas. Available to U.S. citizens. *Application*

Requirements: Financial need analysis, FAFSA. *Deadline:* varies.

Contact: Financial Aid Office at college, Texas Higher Education Coordinating Board, PO Box 12788, Austin, TX 78711-2788. *E-mail:* grantinfo@thecb.state.tx.us. *Phone:* 512-427-6101. *Fax:* 512-427-6127. *Web site:* www.collegefortexans.com.

Tuition Exemptions for Texas Veterans (Hazelwood Act). Renewable tuition and partial fee exemptions for Texas veterans who have been honorably discharged after at least 180 days of active duty. Must be a Texas resident at time of entry into service. Must have exhausted federal education benefits. Contact the admissions/registrar's office for information on how to apply. Must be used at a Texas public institution. *Award:* Scholarship for use in freshman, sophomore, junior, or senior year; renewable. *Award amount:* $980. *Number of awards:* varies. *Eligibility Requirements:* Applicant must be enrolled or expecting to enroll full or part-time at a two-year, four-year, or technical institution or university; resident of Texas and studying in Texas. Available to U.S. citizens. Applicant or parent must meet one or more of the following requirements: general military experience; retired from active duty; disabled or killed as a result of military service; prisoner of war; or missing in action. *Application Requirements:* Application. *Deadline:* continuous.

Contact: Financial Aid Office at college, Texas Higher Education Coordinating Board, PO Box 12788, Austin, TX 78711-2788. *E-mail:* grantinfo@thecb.state.tx.us. *Phone:* 512-427-6101. *Fax:* 512-427-6127. *Web site:* www.collegefortexans.com.

Vocational Nursing Scholarships. Scholarships for Texas residents enrolled in a vocational nursing program at an institution in Texas. Deadline varies. *Academic Fields/Career Goals:* Nursing. *Award:* Scholarship for use in freshman or sophomore year; not renewable. *Award amount:* up to $1500. *Number of awards:* varies. *Eligibility Requirements:* Applicant must be enrolled or expecting to enroll full or part-time at a four-year institution or university; resident of Texas and studying in Texas. Available to U.S. citizens. *Application Requirements:* Application, financial need analysis, test scores, transcript. *Deadline:* varies.

Contact: Texas Higher Education Coordinating Board, PO Box 12788, Austin, TX 78711-2788. *E-mail:* grantinfo@thecb.state.tx.us. *Web site:* www.collegefortexans.com.

UTAH

Leveraging Educational Assistance Partnership (LEAP). Available to students

with substantial financial need for use at participating Utah schools. Contact Financial Aid Office of specific school for application requirements and deadlines. Must be Utah resident. *Award:* Grant for use in freshman, sophomore, junior, or senior year; not renewable. *Award amount:* $300–$2500. *Number of awards:* up to 3000. *Eligibility Requirements:* Applicant must be enrolled or expecting to enroll full or part-time at a two-year, four-year, or technical institution or university; resident of Utah and studying in Utah. Available to U.S. citizens. *Application Requirements:* Application, financial need analysis. *Deadline:* continuous.

Contact: Financial Aid Office, Utah State Board of Regents. *Web site:* www.uheaa.org.

T.H. Bell Teaching Incentive Loan-Utah. Renewable awards for Utah residents who are high school seniors and wish to pursue teaching careers. Award pays for tuition and fees at a Utah institution. Must agree to teach in a Utah public school or pay back loan through monthly installments. Must be a U.S. citizen. *Academic Fields/Career Goals:* Education; Special Education. *Award:* Forgivable loan for use in freshman, sophomore, junior, or senior year; renewable. *Award amount:* varies. *Number of awards:* 25. *Eligibility Requirements:* Applicant must be high school student; planning to enroll or expecting to enroll full-time at a two-year or four-year institution or university; resident of Utah and studying in Utah. Available to U.S. citizens. *Application Requirements:* Application, essay, test scores, transcript. *Deadline:* March 29.

Contact: Diane DeMan, Executive Secretary, Utah State Office of Education, 250 East 500 South, Salt Lake City, UT 84111. *Phone:* 801-538-7741. *Fax:* 801-538-7973. *Web site:* www.usoe.k12.ut.us/cert/scholarships/scholars. htm.

Utah Centennial Opportunity Program for Education. Renewable awards for undergraduate college student in Utah institution. Must be a Utah resident. Contact financial aid office at participating institutions for more information. *Award:* Grant for use in freshman, sophomore, junior, or senior year; not renewable. *Award amount:* $300–$5000. *Number of awards:* up to 3500. *Eligibility Requirements:* Applicant must be enrolled or expecting to enroll full or part-time at a two-year, four-year, or technical institution; resident of Utah and studying in Utah. Available to U.S. citizens. *Application Requirements:* Application, financial need analysis. *Deadline:* continuous.

Contact: Financial Aid Office, Utah State Board of Regents. *Web site:* www.uheaa.org.

Utah Educationally Disadvantaged Program. Renewable award for residents of Utah who are disadvantaged and attending an eligible institution in Utah. Must demonstrate need and satisfactory progress. Contact financial aid office of participating institution. *Award:* Scholarship for use in freshman, sophomore, junior, or senior year; renewable. *Award amount:* varies. *Number of awards:* varies. *Eligibility Requirements:* Applicant must be enrolled or expecting to enroll at a two-year or four-year institution; resident of Utah and studying in Utah. Applicant must be hearing impaired, learning disabled, physically disabled, or visually impaired. *Application Requirements:* Application. *Deadline:* continuous.

Contact: Financial Aid Office, Utah State Board of Regents, 60 South 400 West, The Board of Regents Building, The Gateway, Salt Lake City, UT 84101-1284. *Web site:* www.uheaa.org.

Utah Tuition Waiver. Renewable awards ranging from partial to full tuition waivers at eligible Utah institutions. A limited number of waivers are available for nonresidents. Deadlines vary by institutions. Contact Financial Aid Office. *Award:* Scholarship for use in freshman, sophomore, junior, senior, or graduate year; renewable. *Award amount:* varies. *Number of awards:* varies. *Eligibility Requirements:* Applicant must be enrolled or expecting to enroll full or part-time at a two-year or four-year institution and studying in Utah. Available to U.S. and non-U.S. citizens. *Application Requirements:* Application, financial need analysis, interview. *Deadline:* varies.

Contact: Financial Aid Office, Utah State Board of Regents, 60 South 400 West, The Board of Regents Building, The Gateway, Salt Lake City, UT 84101-1284. *Web site:* www.uheaa.org.

VERMONT

American Legion High School Oratorical Contest-Vermont. Students in grades 9-12 are eligible to compete. Must attend an accredited Vermont high school. Must be a United States citizen. Selection based on oration. *Award:* Prize for use in freshman, sophomore, junior, or senior year; not renewable. *Award amount:* $2000. *Number of awards:* 1. *Eligibility Requirements:* Applicant must be high school student; planning to enroll or expecting to enroll full or part-time at a two-year, four-year, or technical institution or university and resident of Vermont. Available to U.S. citizens. Applicant or parent must meet one or more of the following requirements:

general military experience; retired from active duty; disabled or killed as a result of military service; prisoner of war; or missing in action. *Application Requirements:* Applicant must enter a contest. *Deadline:* January 1.

Contact: Huzon Stewart, Chairman, American Legion, Department of Vermont, PO Box 396, Montpelier, VT 05601-0396. *E-mail:* alvt@sover.net. *Phone:* 802-223-7131.

Vermont Incentive Grants. Renewable grants for Vermont residents based on financial need. Must meet needs test. Must be college undergraduate or graduate student enrolled full-time at an approved postsecondary institution. Only available to U.S. citizens or permanent residents. *Award:* Grant for use in freshman, sophomore, junior, senior, or graduate year; renewable. *Award amount:* $500–$9100. *Number of awards:* varies. *Eligibility Requirements:* Applicant must be enrolled or expecting to enroll full-time at an institution or university and resident of Vermont. Available to U.S. citizens. *Application Requirements:* Application, financial need analysis. *Deadline:* continuous.

Contact: Grant Program, Vermont Student Assistance Corporation, PO Box 2000, Winooski, VT 05404-2000. *Phone:* 802-655-9602. *Fax:* 802-654-3765. *Web site:* www.vsac.org.

Vermont Non-Degree Student Grant Program. Renewable grants for Vermont residents enrolled in non-degree programs at colleges, vocational centers, and high school adult courses. May receive funds for two enrollment periods per year, up to $715 per course, per semester. Award based upon financial need. *Award:* Grant for use in freshman or sophomore year; renewable. *Award amount:* up to $715. *Number of awards:* varies. *Eligibility Requirements:* Applicant must be enrolled or expecting to enroll at an institution or university and resident of Vermont. *Application Requirements:* Application, financial need analysis. *Deadline:* continuous.

Contact: Grant Program, Vermont Student Assistance Corporation, PO Box 2000, Winooski, VT 05404-2000. *Phone:* 802-655-9602. *Fax:* 802-654-3765. *Web site:* www.vsac.org.

Vermont Part-time Student Grants. For undergraduates carrying less than twelve credits per semester who have not received a bachelor's degree. Must be Vermont resident. Based on financial need. Complete Vermont Financial Aid Packet to apply. May be used at any approved postsecondary institution. *Award:* Grant for use in freshman, sophomore, junior, or senior year;

renewable. *Award amount:* $250–$6830. *Number of awards:* varies. *Eligibility Requirements:* Applicant must be enrolled or expecting to enroll part-time at an institution or university and resident of Vermont. *Application Requirements:* Application, financial need analysis. *Deadline:* continuous.

Contact: Grant Program, Vermont Student Assistance Corporation, PO Box 2000, Winooski, VT 05404-2000. *Phone:* 802-655-9602. *Fax:* 802-654-3765. *Web site:* www.vsac.org.

VIRGINIA

General Mills Scholars Program/Internship. Scholarships and paid summer internships awarded to college sophomores and juniors majoring in accounting, business (sales interest), computer science, engineering, finance, human resources, information systems, information technology, or marketing at a UNCF member college or university. Minimum 3.5 GPA required. Prospective applicants should complete the Student Profile found at Web site: http://www.uncf.org. *Academic Fields/Career Goals:* Accounting; Business/Consumer Services; Computer Science/Data Processing; Engineering/Technology. *Award:* Scholarship for use in sophomore or junior year; not renewable. *Award amount:* $5000. *Eligibility Requirements:* Applicant must be Black (non-Hispanic) and enrolled or expecting to enroll full-time at a four-year institution or university. Applicant must have 3.5 GPA or higher. Available to U.S. citizens. *Application Requirements:* Application, financial need analysis, test scores. *Deadline:* January 2.

Contact: Program Services Department, United Negro College Fund, 8260 Willow Oaks Corporate Drive, Fairfax, VA 22031. *Web site:* www.uncf.org.

Gheens Foundation Scholarship. This scholarship supports students from Louisville, Kentucky, who are enrolled in a HBCU participating school. Please visit Web site for more information: http://www.uncf.org. *Award:* Scholarship for use in freshman, sophomore, junior, senior, or graduate year. *Award amount:* up to $2000. *Number of awards:* varies. *Eligibility Requirements:* Applicant must be Black (non-Hispanic); enrolled or expecting to enroll at a four-year institution or university and resident of Kentucky. Applicant must have 2.5 GPA or higher. *Application Requirements:* Application, financial need analysis, transcript. *Deadline:* varies.

Contact: Program Services Department, United Negro College Fund, 8260 Willow

Oaks Corporate Drive, Fairfax, VA 22031. *Web site:* www.uncf.org.

Mary Marshall Practical Nursing Scholarships. Award for practical nursing students who are Virginia residents. Must attend a nursing program in Virginia. Recipient must agree to work in Virginia after graduation. Minimum 3.0 GPA required. Recipients may reapply up to three years for an award. *Academic Fields/Career Goals:* Nursing. *Award:* Scholarship for use in freshman, sophomore, junior, or senior year; not renewable. *Award amount:* $150–$500. *Number of awards:* varies. *Eligibility Requirements:* Applicant must be enrolled or expecting to enroll full or part-time at a two-year or technical institution; resident of Virginia and studying in Virginia. Applicant must have 3.0 GPA or higher. Available to U.S. citizens. *Application Requirements:* Application, financial need analysis, references, transcript. *Deadline:* June 30.

Contact: Norma Marrin, Business Manager/Policy Analyst, Virginia Department of Health, Office of Health Policy and Planning, PO Box 2448, Richmond, VA 23218-2448. *E-mail:* norma.marrin@vdh.virginia.gov. *Phone:* 804-864-7433. *Fax:* 804-864-7440. *Web site:* www.vdh.virginia.gov/primcare/index.asp.

Mary Marshall Registered Nursing Program Scholarships. Award for registered nursing students who are Virginia residents. Must attend a nursing program in Virginia. Recipient must agree to work in Virginia after graduation. Minimum 3.0 GPA required. Recipient may reapply up to three years for an award. *Academic Fields/Career Goals:* Nursing. *Award:* Scholarship for use in freshman, sophomore, junior, or senior year; not renewable. *Award amount:* $1200–$2000. *Number of awards:* 60–100. *Eligibility Requirements:* Applicant must be enrolled or expecting to enroll full or part-time at a two-year or four-year institution or university; resident of Virginia and studying in Virginia. Applicant must have 3.0 GPA or higher. Available to U.S. citizens. *Application Requirements:* Application, financial need analysis, references, transcript. *Deadline:* June 30.

Contact: Norma Marrin, Business Manager/Policy Analyst, Virginia Department of Health, Office of Health Policy and Planning, PO Box 2448, Richmond, VA 23218-2448. *E-mail:* norma.marrin@vdh.virginia.gov. *Phone:* 804-864-7433. *Fax:* 804-864-7440. *Web site:* www.vdh.virginia.gov/primcare/index.asp.

Virginia Tuition Assistance Grant Program (Private Institutions). Renewable awards of approximately $1900-$2500 each for undergraduate, graduate, and first profes-

sional degree students attending an approved private, nonprofit college within Virginia. Must be a Virginia resident and be enrolled full-time. Not to be used for religious study. Preferred deadline July 31. Others are wait-listed. Information and application available from participating Virginia colleges' financial aid office. *Award:* Grant for use in freshman, sophomore, junior, senior, or graduate year; renewable. *Award amount:* $1900–$2500. *Number of awards:* 18,600. *Eligibility Requirements:* Applicant must be enrolled or expecting to enroll full-time at a four-year institution; resident of Virginia and studying in Virginia. *Application Requirements:* Application. *Deadline:* July 31.

Contact: Fin. Aid Office at participating VA institution, State Council of Higher Education for Virginia, James Monroe Building, 10th Floor, 101 North 14th Street, Richmond, VA 23219. *Web site:* www.schev.edu.

Virginia War Orphans Education Program. Scholarships for postsecondary students between ages 16 and 25 to attend Virginia state supported institutions. Must be child or surviving child of veteran who has either: 1. been permanently or totally disabled due to war or other armed conflict; 2. died as a result of war or other armed conflict; or 3. been listed as a POW or MIA. Parent must also meet Virginia residency requirements. Contact for application procedures and deadline. *Award:* Scholarship for use in freshman, sophomore, junior, senior, or graduate year; renewable. *Number of awards:* varies. *Eligibility Requirements:* Applicant must be age 16-25; enrolled or expecting to enroll full-time at a two-year, four-year, or technical institution or university; resident of Virginia and studying in Virginia. Available to U.S. citizens. Applicant or parent must meet one or more of the following requirements: general military experience; retired from active duty; disabled or killed as a result of military service; prisoner of war; or missing in action. *Application Requirements:* Application. *Deadline:* varies.

Contact: Colbert Longworth Boyd, Chief Deputy Commissioner, Virginia Department of Veterans Services, Poff Federal Building, 270 Franklin Road SW, Room 503, Roanoke, VA 24011-2215. *Phone:* 540-857-7101 Ext. 213. *Fax:* 540-857-7573. *Web site:* www.vdva.vipnet.org/education_benefits.htm.

Walter Reed Smith Scholarship. Award for full-time female undergraduate student who is a descendant of a Confederate soldier, studying nutrition, home economics, nursing, business administration, or computer science. Must carry a minimum of 12 credit hours each semester and have a minimum 3.0 GPA. Submit letter of

endorsement from sponsoring chapter of the United Daughters of the Confederacy. Please refer to Web site for further details: http://www.hqudc.org *Academic Fields/Career Goals:* Business/Consumer Services; Computer Science/Data Processing; Food Science/Nutrition; Home Economics; Nursing. *Award:* Scholarship for use in freshman, sophomore, junior, or senior year; renewable. *Award amount:* $800–$1000. *Number of awards:* 1–2. *Eligibility Requirements:* Applicant must be enrolled or expecting to enroll full-time at a four-year institution or university and female. Applicant or parent of applicant must be member of United Daughters of the Confederacy. Applicant must have 3.0 GPA or higher. Available to U.S. citizens. *Application Requirements:* Application, essay, financial need analysis, photo, references, self-addressed stamped envelope, transcript. *Deadline:* February 15.

Contact: Second Vice President General, United Daughters of the Confederacy, 328 North Boulevard, Richmond, VA 23220-4057. *Phone:* 804-355-1636. *Web site:* www.hqudc.org.

WASHINGTON

American Indian Endowed Scholarship. Awarded to financially needy undergraduate and graduate students with close social and cultural ties to a Native-American community. Must be Washington resident, enrolled full time at Washington School. Deadline is May 15. *Award:* Scholarship for use in freshman, sophomore, junior, senior, or graduate year; renewable. *Award amount:* $1000–$2000. *Number of awards:* up to 15. *Eligibility Requirements:* Applicant must be American Indian/Alaska Native; enrolled or expecting to enroll full-time at a two-year, four-year, or technical institution or university; resident of Washington and studying in Washington. Available to U.S. citizens. *Application Requirements:* Application, financial need analysis. *Deadline:* May 15.

Contact: Ann Lee, Washington Higher Education Coordinating Board, 917 Lakeridge Way SW, PO Box 43430 , Olympia, WA 98504-3430. *E-mail:* annl@hecb.wa.gov. *Phone:* 360-755-7843. *Fax:* 360-753-7808. *Web site:* www.hecb.wa.gov.

Educational Opportunity Grant. Annual grants of $2500 to encourage financially needy, placebound students to complete bachelor's degree. Must be unable to continue education due to family or work commitments, health concerns, financial needs, or similar. Must be Washington residents, live in one of 13 designated counties, and have completed two years of college. Grant only used at eligible four-year colleges in Washington. Applications accepted beginning in April and following months until funds are depleted. *Award:* Grant for use in junior or senior year; renewable. *Award amount:* $2500. *Number of awards:* 1350. *Eligibility Requirements:* Applicant must be enrolled or expecting to enroll full-time at a four-year institution or university; resident of Washington and studying in Washington. Available to U.S. citizens. *Application Requirements:* Application, financial need analysis. *Deadline:* continuous.

Contact: Dawn Cypriano-McAferty, Program Manager, Washington Higher Education Coordinating Board, 917 Lakeridge Way, SW, PO Box 43430, Olympia, WA 98504-3430. *E-mail:* eog@hecb.wa.gov. *Phone:* 360-753-7800. *Fax:* 360-753-7808. *Web site:* www.hecb.wa.gov.

State Need Grant. Grants for undergraduate students with significant financial need. Must be Washington resident and attend school in Washington. Must have family income equal or less than 55% of state median. The financial aid office at each school makes awards to eligible students. *Award:* Grant for use in freshman, sophomore, junior, or senior year; renewable. *Award amount:* $2200–$4300. *Number of awards:* 55,000. *Eligibility Requirements:* Applicant must be enrolled or expecting to enroll full or part-time at a two-year, four-year, or technical institution or university; resident of Washington and studying in Washington. Available to U.S. citizens. *Application Requirements:* Application, financial need analysis, FAFSA. *Deadline:* continuous.

Contact: Financial Aid Director of school to which you are applying, Washington Higher Education Coordinating Board. *Web site:* www.hecb.wa.gov.

Washington Award for Vocational Excellence. Tuition-only award for those completing a vocational education program as graduating seniors or community/technical college students who have completed first year of a two-year program. The scholarship is for 6 quarters or 4 semesters. Three are awarded in each of 49 legislative districts in the state. Must be a Washington State resident attending a postsecondary institution in Washington State. *Award:* Grant for use in freshman, sophomore, junior, or senior year; renewable. *Award amount:* $4284–$9498. *Number of awards:* 147. *Eligibility Requirements:* Applicant must be enrolled or expecting to enroll full or part-time at a two-year, four-year, or technical institution or university;

resident of Washington and studying in Washington. Available to U.S. and non-U.S. citizens. *Application Requirements:* Application, essay, references. *Deadline:* March 1.

Contact: Lee Williams, Program Administrator, Washington State Workforce Training and Education Coordinating Board, 128 Tenth Avenue SW, PO Box 43105, Olympia, WA 98504-3105. *E-mail:* lwilliams@wtb.wa.gov. *Phone:* 360-586-3321. *Fax:* 360-586-5862. *Web site:* www.wtb.wa.gov/wave-abt.html.

Washington Award for Vocational Excellence (WAVE). Award to honor three vocational students from each of the state's 49 legislative districts. Grants for up to two years of undergraduate resident tuition. Must be enrolled in Washington high school, skills center, or technical college at time of application. Complete 360 hours in single vocational program in high school or one year at technical college. Contact principal or guidance counselor for more information. *Award:* Grant for use in freshman, sophomore, junior, or senior year; renewable. *Award amount:* varies. *Number of awards:* varies. *Eligibility Requirements:* Applicant must be enrolled or expecting to enroll full-time at a two-year, four-year, or technical institution or university; resident of Washington and studying in Washington. Available to U.S. citizens. *Application Requirements:* *Deadline:* continuous.

Contact: Ann Lee, Program Manager, Washington Higher Education Coordinating Board, 917 Lakeridge Way, SW, PO Box 43430 , Olympia, WA 98504-3430. *E-mail:* annl@hecb.wa.gov. *Phone:* 360-753-7843. *Fax:* 360-753-7808. *Web site:* www.hecb.wa.gov.

Washington National Guard Scholarship Program. A state funded retention incentive/loan program for both Washington Army and Air Guard members meeting all eligibility requirements. The loans are forgiven if the soldier/airman completes their service requirements. Failure to meet/complete service obligations incurs the requirement to repay the loan plus 8% interest. Minimum 2.5 GPA required. Deadline is April 30. *Award:* Forgivable loan for use in freshman, sophomore, junior, or senior year; not renewable. *Award amount:* $200–$4000. *Number of awards:* varies. *Eligibility Requirements:* Applicant must be enrolled or expecting to enroll full or part-time at a two-year, four-year, or technical institution or university and resident of Washington. Applicant must have 2.5 GPA or higher. Available to U.S. and non-U.S. citizens. Applicant must have served in the Air Force National Guard or Army National Guard. *Application Requirements:*

Application, transcript, enlistment/extension documents. *Deadline:* April 30.

Contact: Mark M. Rhoden, Educational Services Officer, Washington National Guard, Building 15, Camp Murray, Tacoma, WA 98430-5073. *E-mail:* mark.rhoden@wa.ngb. army.mil. *Phone:* 253-512-8899. *Fax:* 253-512-8936. *Web site:* www.washingtonguard. com/education/education.htm.

Washington Promise Scholarship. College scholarships to low- and middle-income students in high school. Must either rank in top 15 percent of senior class or score a combined 1200 on SAT or 27 on ACT on first attempt. Family income cannot exceed 135% of state median family income. Must be Washington resident, attend a Washington school. School must identify applicants. Contact principal or guidance counselor for more information. *Award:* Scholarship for use in freshman or sophomore year; renewable. *Award amount:* up to $1000. *Number of awards:* varies. *Eligibility Requirements:* Applicant must be high school student; planning to enroll or expecting to enroll full or part-time at a two-year, four-year, or technical institution or university; resident of Washington and studying in Washington. Available to U.S. citizens. *Application Requirements:* Financial need analysis. *Deadline:* continuous.

Contact: John Klacik, Washington Higher Education Coordinating Board, 917 Lakeridge Way SW, PO Box 43430, Olympia, WA 98504-3430. *E-mail:* johnk@hecb.wa.gov. *Phone:* 360-753-7851. *Fax:* 360-753-7808. *Web site:* www.hecb.wa.gov.

Washington Scholars Program. Awarded to three high school students from each of the 49 state legislative districts. Must be Washington resident and enroll in college or university in Washington. Scholarships equal up to four years of full-time resident undergraduate tuition and fees. Contact principal or guidance counselor for more information. *Award:* Grant for use in freshman, sophomore, junior, or senior year; renewable. *Award amount:* varies. *Number of awards:* varies. *Eligibility Requirements:* Applicant must be high school student; planning to enroll or expecting to enroll full-time at a four-year institution or university; resident of Washington and studying in Washington. Available to U.S. citizens. *Application Requirements:* *Deadline:* continuous.

Contact: Ann Lee, Program Manager, Washington Higher Education Coordinating Board, 917 Lakeridge Way SW, PO Box 43430, Olympia, WA 98504-3430. *E-mail:* annl@hecb.wa.gov. *Phone:* 360-753-7843. *Fax:* 360-753-7808. *Web site:* www.hecb.wa. gov.

WEST VIRGINIA

Higher Education Adult Part-time Student Grant Program. Program to assist needy adult students to continue their education on a part-time basis. Also has a component in which 25% of the funding may be utilized for students enrolled in workforce and skill development programs. Contact institution financial aid office for more information and deadlines. *Award:* Grant for use in freshman, sophomore, junior, or senior year; not renewable. *Number of awards:* varies. *Eligibility Requirements:* Applicant must be enrolled or expecting to enroll full or part-time at a two-year, four-year, or technical institution or university; resident of West Virginia and studying in West Virginia. Available to U.S. citizens. *Application Requirements:* Application, financial need analysis. *Deadline:* varies.

Contact: Judy Kee, Financial Aid Manager, West Virginia Higher Education Policy Commission-Office of Financial Aid and Outreach Services, 1018 Kanawha Boulevard East, Suite 700, Charleston, WV 25301. *E-mail:* kee@hepc.wvnet.edu. *Phone:* 304-558-4618. *Fax:* 304-558-4622. *Web site:* www.hepc.wvnet.edu.

Promise Scholarship. Renewable award for West Virginia residents. Minimum 3.0 GPA, ACT composite of 21, with 19 on each subtest, and combined SAT score of 1000, with no less than 470 verbal and 460 math. Provides full tuition scholarship to a state college or university in West Virginia or an equivalent scholarship to an in-state private college. Financial resources are not a factor. *Award:* Scholarship for use in freshman, sophomore, junior, or senior year; renewable. *Award amount:* $3000. *Number of awards:* 3500. *Eligibility Requirements:* Applicant must be high school student; planning to enroll or expecting to enroll full-time at a two-year or four-year institution or university; resident of West Virginia and studying in West Virginia. Applicant must have 3.0 GPA or higher. Available to U.S. citizens. *Application Requirements:* Application, financial need analysis, test scores. *Deadline:* January 31.

Contact: Lisa DeFrank-Cole, Executive Director, West Virginia Higher Education Policy Commission-Office of Financial Aid and Outreach Services, 1018 Kanawha Boulevard East, Suite 700, Charleston, WV 25301. *Phone:* 304-558-4417. *Fax:* 304-558-3264. *Web site:* www.hepc.wvnet.edu.

Underwood-Smith Teacher Scholarship Program. For West Virginia residents at West Virginia institutions pursuing teaching careers. Must have a 3.25 GPA after completion of two years of course work. Must teach two years in West Virginia public schools for each year the award is received. Recipients will be required to sign an agreement acknowledging an understanding of the program's requirements and their willingness to repay the award if appropriate teaching service is not rendered. *Academic Fields/Career Goals:* Education. *Award:* Scholarship for use in junior, senior, or graduate year; renewable. *Award amount:* $1620–$5000. *Number of awards:* 53. *Eligibility Requirements:* Applicant must be enrolled or expecting to enroll full-time at a four-year institution or university; resident of West Virginia and studying in West Virginia. Available to U.S. citizens. *Application Requirements:* Application, essay, references. *Deadline:* March 1.

Contact: Michelle Wicks, Scholarship Coordinator, West Virginia Higher Education Policy Commission-Office of Financial Aid and Outreach Services, 1018 Kanawha Boulevard East, Suite 700, Charleston, WV 25301. *E-mail:* wicks@hepc.wvnet.edu. *Phone:* 304-558-4618. *Fax:* 304-558-4622. *Web site:* www.hepc.wvnet.edu.

West Virginia Division of Veterans' Affairs War Orphans Education Program. Renewable waiver of tuition award for West Virginia residents who are children of deceased veterans. Parent must have died of war related service-connected disability. Must be ages 16-23. Minimum 2.0 GPA required. Must attend a state-supported West Virginia postsecondary institution. Deadline: July 1 and December 1. *Award:* Scholarship for use in freshman, sophomore, junior, senior, or graduate year; renewable. *Award amount:* varies. *Number of awards:* varies. *Eligibility Requirements:* Applicant must be age 16-23; enrolled or expecting to enroll full or part-time at a two-year, four-year, or technical institution or university; resident of West Virginia and studying in West Virginia. Available to U.S. citizens. Applicant or parent must meet one or more of the following requirements: general military experience; retired from active duty; disabled or killed as a result of military service; prisoner of war; or missing in action. *Application Requirements:* Application, references. *Deadline:* varies.

Contact: Ms. Linda Walker, Administrative Secretary, West Virginia Division of Veterans' Affairs, 1321 Plaza East, Suite 101, Charleston, WV 25301-1400. *E-mail:* wvdva@state.wv.us. *Phone:* 304-558-3661. *Fax:* 304-558-3662. *Web site:* www.state.wv.us/va.

West Virginia Engineering, Science & Technology Scholarship Program. For students attending West Virginia institutions full-time pursuing a career in engineering, science, or technology. Must have a 3.0 GPA on a 4.0 scale. Must work in the fields of engineering, science, or technology in West Virginia one year for each year the award is received. *Academic Fields/Career Goals:* Electrical Engineering/Electronics; Engineering/Technology; Engineering-Related Technologies; Science, Technology, and Society. *Award:* Scholarship for use in freshman, sophomore, junior, or senior year; renewable. *Award amount:* up to $3000. *Number of awards:* 250. *Eligibility Requirements:* Applicant must be enrolled or expecting to enroll full-time at a two-year, four-year, or technical institution or university and studying in West Virginia. Applicant must have 3.0 GPA or higher. Available to U.S. citizens. *Application Requirements:* Application, essay, test scores, transcript. *Deadline:* March 1.

Contact: Michelle Wicks, Scholarship Coordinator, West Virginia Higher Education Policy Commission-Office of Financial Aid and Outreach Services, 1018 Kanawha Boulevard East, Suite 700, Charleston, WV 25301. *E-mail:* wicks@hepc.wvnet.edu. *Phone:* 304-558-4618. *Fax:* 304-558-4622. *Web site:* www.hepc.wvnet.edu.

West Virginia Higher Education Grant Program. For West Virginia residents attending an approved nonprofit degree granting college or university in West Virginia or Pennsylvania. Must be enrolled full-time. Based on financial need and academic merit. Award covers tuition and fees. *Award:* Grant for use in freshman, sophomore, junior, or senior year; renewable. *Award amount:* $350–$2846. *Number of awards:* 10,755–11,000. *Eligibility Requirements:* Applicant must be enrolled or expecting to enroll full-time at a two-year or four-year institution or university; resident of West Virginia and studying in Pennsylvania or West Virginia. Available to U.S. citizens. *Application Requirements:* Application, financial need analysis, test scores, transcript. *Deadline:* March 1.

Contact: Daniel Crockett, Director of Student and Educational Services, West Virginia Higher Education Policy Commission-Office of Financial Aid and Outreach Services, 1018 Kanawha Boulevard East, Suite 700, Charleston, WV 25301-2827. *E-mail:* crockett@hepc.wvnet.edu. *Phone:* 888-825-5707. *Fax:* 304-558-4618. *Web site:* www.hepc.wvnet.edu.

WISCONSIN

Handicapped Student Grant-Wisconsin. One-time award available to residents of Wisconsin who have severe or profound hearing or visual impairment. Must be enrolled at least half-time at a nonprofit institution. If the handicap prevents the student from attending a Wisconsin school, the award may be used out-of-state in a specialized college. Please refer to Web site for further details: http://www.heab. state.wi.us *Award:* Grant for use in freshman, sophomore, junior, or senior year; not renewable. *Award amount:* $250–$1800. *Number of awards:* varies. *Eligibility Requirements:* Applicant must be enrolled or expecting to enroll full or part-time at a two-year, four-year, or technical institution or university and resident of Wisconsin. Applicant must be hearing impaired or visually impaired. Available to U.S. citizens. *Application Requirements:* Application, financial need analysis. *Deadline:* continuous.

Contact: Sandra Thomas, Program Coordinator, Wisconsin Higher Educational Aids Board, PO Box 7885, Madison, WI 53707-7885. *E-mail:* sandy.thomas@heab. state.wi.us. *Phone:* 608-266-0888. *Fax:* 608-267-2808. *Web site:* heab.state.wi.us.

Minnesota-Wisconsin Reciprocity Program. Wisconsin residents may attend a Minnesota public institution and pay the reciprocity tuition charged by Minnesota institution. All programs are eligible except doctoral programs in medicine, dentistry, and veterinary medicine. Please refer to Web site for further details: http://www. heab.state.wi.us *Award:* Scholarship for use in freshman, sophomore, junior, or senior year; renewable. *Award amount:* varies. *Number of awards:* varies. *Eligibility Requirements:* Applicant must be enrolled or expecting to enroll full or part-time at a two-year, four-year, or technical institution or university; resident of Wisconsin and studying in Minnesota. Available to U.S. citizens. *Application Requirements:* Application. *Deadline:* continuous.

Contact: Cindy Lehrman, Wisconsin Higher Educational Aids Board, PO Box 7885, Madison, WI 53707-7885. *E-mail:* cindy. lehrman@heab.state.wi.us. *Phone:* 608-267-2209. *Fax:* 608-267-2808. *Web site:* heab. state.wi.us.

Minority Retention Grant-Wisconsin. Provides financial assistance to African-American, Native-American, Hispanic, and former citizens of Laos, Vietnam, and Cambodia, for study in Wisconsin. Must be Wisconsin resident, enrolled at least half-time in a two-year or four-year nonprofit college, and must show financial need. Please refer to Web site for further details: http://www.heab.state.wi.us *Award:* Grant for use in sophomore, junior, senior, or graduate year; not renewable. *Award amount:* $250–$2500. *Number of awards:* varies. *Eligibility Requirements:* Applicant must be American Indian/Alaska Native,

Asian/Pacific Islander, Black (non-Hispanic), or Hispanic; enrolled or expecting to enroll full or part-time at a two-year, four-year, or technical institution; resident of Wisconsin and studying in Wisconsin. Available to U.S. and non-U.S. citizens. *Application Requirements:* Application, financial need analysis. *Deadline:* continuous.

Contact: Mary Lou Kuzdas, Program Coordinator, Wisconsin Higher Educational Aids Board, PO Box 7885, Madison, WI 53707-7885. *E-mail:* mary.kuzdas@heab.state. wi.us. *Phone:* 608-267-2212. *Fax:* 608-267-2808. *Web site:* heab.state.wi.us.

Nursing Student Loan Program. Provides forgivable loans to students enrolled in a nursing program. Must be a Wisconsin resident studying in Wisconsin. Application deadline is last day on which student is enrolled. Please refer to Web site for further details: http://www.heab.state.wi.us *Academic Fields/Career Goals:* Nursing. *Award:* Forgivable loan for use in freshman, sophomore, junior, or senior year; renewable. *Award amount:* $250–$3000. *Number of awards:* 150–1800. *Eligibility Requirements:* Applicant must be enrolled or expecting to enroll full or part-time at a two-year, four-year, or technical institution or university; resident of Wisconsin and studying in Wisconsin. Available to U.S. citizens. *Application Requirements:* Application, financial need analysis.

Contact: Cindy Lehrman, Program Coordinator, Wisconsin Higher Educational Aids Board, PO Box 7885, Madison, WI 53707-7885. *E-mail:* cindy.lehrman@heab. state.wi.us. *Phone:* 608-267-2209. *Fax:* 608-267-2808. *Web site:* heab.state.wi.us.

Talent Incentive Program Grant. Assists residents of Wisconsin who are attending a nonprofit institution in Wisconsin and have substantial financial need. Must meet income criteria, be considered economically and educationally disadvantaged and be enrolled at least half-time. Please refer to Web site for further details: http://www.heab.state. wi.us *Award:* Grant for use in freshman, sophomore, junior, or senior year; renewable. *Award amount:* $250–$1800. *Number of awards:* varies. *Eligibility Requirements:* Applicant must be enrolled or expecting to enroll full or part-time at a two-year, four-year, or technical institution or university; resident of Wisconsin and studying in Wisconsin. Available to U.S. citizens. *Application Requirements:* Financial need analysis, nomination. *Deadline:* continuous.

Contact: John Whitt, Program Coordinator, Wisconsin Higher Educational Aids Board, PO Box 7885, Madison, WI 53707-7885.

E-mail: john.whitt@heab.state.wi.us. *Phone:* 608-266-1665. *Fax:* 608-267-2808. *Web site:* heab.state.wi.us.

Teacher of the Visually Impaired Loan Program. Provides forgivable loans to students who enroll in programs that lead to be certified as a teacher of the visually impaired or an orientation and mobility instructor. Must be a Wisconsin resident. For study in Wisconsin, Illinois, Iowa, Michigan, and Minnesota. Please refer to Web site for further details: http://www. heab.state.wi.us *Academic Fields/Career Goals:* Special Education. *Award:* Forgivable loan for use in freshman, sophomore, junior, senior, graduate, or postgraduate years; not renewable. *Award amount:* $250–$10,000. *Number of awards:* varies. *Eligibility Requirements:* Applicant must be enrolled or expecting to enroll full or part-time at a two-year, four-year, or technical institution or university; resident of Wisconsin and studying in Illinois, Iowa, Michigan, Minnesota, or Wisconsin. Available to U.S. citizens. *Application Requirements:* Application, financial need analysis. *Deadline:* continuous.

Contact: John Whitt, Program Coordinator, Wisconsin Higher Educational Aids Board, PO Box 7885, Madison, WI 53707-7885. *E-mail:* john.whitt@heab.state.wi.us. *Phone:* 608-266-0888. *Fax:* 608-267-2808. *Web site:* heab.state.wi.us.

Tuition and Fee Reimbursement Grants. Up to 100% tuition and fee reimbursement for Wisconsin veterans who were discharged from active duty within the last 10 years. Undergraduate courses must be completed at accredited Wisconsin schools. Those attending Minnesota public colleges, universities, and technical schools that have a tuition reciprocity agreement with Wisconsin also may qualify. Must meet military service requirements. Application must be received no later than 60 days after the completion of the course. *Award:* Grant for use in freshman, sophomore, junior, or senior year; renewable. *Award amount:* varies. *Number of awards:* varies. *Eligibility Requirements:* Applicant must be enrolled or expecting to enroll full-time at a two-year, four-year, or technical institution or university; resident of Wisconsin and studying in Minnesota or Wisconsin. Available to U.S. citizens. Applicant must have general military experience. *Application Requirements:* Application. *Deadline:* varies.

Contact: Mike Keatley, Grants Coordinator, Wisconsin Department of Veterans Affairs, PO Box 7843, Madison, WI 53707-7843. *Phone:* 608-266-1311. *Web site:* dva.state.wi. us.

Wisconsin Academic Excellence Scholarship. Renewable award for high school seniors with the highest GPA in graduating class. Must be a Wisconsin resident. Award covers tuition for up to four years. Must maintain 3.0 GPA for renewal. Scholarships of up to $2250 each. Must attend a nonprofit Wisconsin institution full-time. Please refer to Web site for further details: http://www.heab.state.wi.us *Award:* Scholarship for use in freshman, sophomore, junior, or senior year; renewable. *Award amount:* up to $2250. *Number of awards:* 3445. *Eligibility Requirements:* Applicant must be enrolled or expecting to enroll full-time at a two-year, four-year, or technical institution or university; resident of Wisconsin and studying in Wisconsin. Applicant must have 3.5 GPA or higher. Available to U.S. citizens. *Application Requirements:* Transcript. *Deadline:* continuous.

Contact: Alice Winters, Program Coordinator, Wisconsin Higher Educational Aids Board, PO Box 7885, Madison, WI 53707-7885. *E-mail:* alice.winters@heab.state.wi.us. *Phone:* 608-267-2213. *Fax:* 608-267-2808. *Web site:* heab.state.wi.us.

Wisconsin Department of Veterans Affairs Retraining Grants. Renewable award for veterans, unmarried spouses of deceased veterans, or dependents of deceased veterans. Must be resident of Wisconsin and attend an institution in Wisconsin. Veteran must be recently unemployed and show financial need. Must enroll in a vocational or technical program that can reasonably be expected to lead to employment. Course work at four-year colleges or universities does not qualify as retraining. *Award:* Grant for use in freshman or sophomore year; renewable. *Award amount:* up to $3000. *Number of awards:* varies. *Eligibility Requirements:* Applicant must be enrolled or expecting to enroll full or part-time at a technical institution; resident of Wisconsin and studying in Wisconsin. Applicant or parent must meet one or more of the following requirements: general military experience; retired from active duty; disabled or killed as a result of military service; prisoner of war; or missing in action. *Application Requirements:* Application, financial need analysis. *Deadline:* varies.

Contact: Mike Keatley, Grants Coordinator, Wisconsin Department of Veterans Affairs, PO Box 7843, Madison, WI 53707-7843. *Phone:* 608-266-1311. *Web site:* dva.state.wi.us.

Wisconsin Higher Education Grants (WHEG). Grants for residents of Wisconsin attending a campus of the University of Wisconsin or Wisconsin Technical College. Must be enrolled at least half-time and show financial need. Please refer to Web site for further details: http://www.heab.state.wi.us *Award:* Grant for use in freshman, sophomore, junior, or senior year; not renewable. *Award amount:* $250–$2500. *Number of awards:* varies. *Eligibility Requirements:* Applicant must be enrolled or expecting to enroll full or part-time at a two-year, four-year, or technical institution or university; resident of Wisconsin and studying in Wisconsin. Available to U.S. citizens. *Application Requirements:* Application, financial need analysis. *Deadline:* continuous.

Contact: Sandra Thomas, Program Coordinator, Wisconsin Higher Educational Aids Board, PO Box 7885, Madison, WI 53707-7885. *E-mail:* sandy.thomas@heab.state.wi.us. *Phone:* 608-266-0888. *Fax:* 608-267-2808. *Web site:* heab.state.wi.us.

Wisconsin National Guard Tuition Grant. Renewable award for active members of the Wisconsin National Guard in good standing, who successfully complete a course of study at a qualifying school. Award covers full tuition, excluding fees, not to exceed undergraduate tuition charged by University of Wisconsin-Madison. Must have a minimum 2.0 GPA. *Award:* Grant for use in freshman, sophomore, junior, or senior year; renewable. *Award amount:* up to $1927. *Number of awards:* up to 4000. *Eligibility Requirements:* Applicant must be enrolled or expecting to enroll full or part-time at a two-year, four-year, or technical institution or university and resident of Wisconsin. Available to U.S. citizens. Applicant must have served in the Air Force National Guard or Army National Guard. *Application Requirements:* Application. *Deadline:* continuous.

Contact: Karen Behling, Tuition Grant Administrator, Department of Military Affairs, PO Box 14587, Madison, WI 53708-0587. *E-mail:* karen.behling@dma.state.wi.us. *Phone:* 608-242-3159. *Fax:* 608-242-3154. *Web site:* wisconsinguard.com.

Wisconsin Native American Student Grant. Grants for Wisconsin residents who are at least one-quarter American-Indian. Must be attending a college or university within the state. Please refer to Web site for further details: http://www.heab.state.wi.us *Award:* Grant for use in freshman, sophomore, junior, senior, graduate, or postgraduate years; not renewable. *Award amount:* $250–$1100. *Number of awards:* varies. *Eligibility Requirements:* Applicant must be American Indian/Alaska Native; enrolled or expecting to enroll full or part-time at a two-year, four-year, or technical institution or university; resident of Wisconsin and studying in Wisconsin. Available to U.S. citizens. *Application Requirements:* Application, financial need analysis. *Deadline:* continuous.

Contact: Sandra Thomas, Program Coordinator, Wisconsin Higher Educational Aids Board, PO Box 7885, Madison, WI 53707-7885. *E-mail:* sandy.thomas@heab.state.wi.us. *Phone:* 608-266-0888. *Fax:* 608-267-2808. *Web site:* heab.state.wi.us.

Wisconsin Tuition Grant Program. Available to Wisconsin residents who are enrolled at least half-time in degree or certificate programs at independent, nonprofit colleges or universities in Wisconsin. Must show financial need. Please refer to Web site for further details: http://www.heab.state.wi.us *Award:* Grant for use in freshman, sophomore, junior, or senior year; not renewable. *Award amount:* varies. *Number of awards:* varies. *Eligibility Requirements:* Applicant must be enrolled or expecting to enroll full or part-time at a four-year institution or university; resident of Wisconsin and studying in Wisconsin. Available to U.S. and non-U.S. citizens. *Application Requirements:* Application, financial need analysis. *Deadline:* continuous.

Contact: Mary Lou Kuzdas, Program Coordinator, Wisconsin Higher Educational Aids Board, PO Box 7885, Madison, WI 53707-7885. *E-mail:* mary.kuzdas@heab.state.wi.us. *Phone:* 608-267-2212. *Fax:* 608-267-2808. *Web site:* heab.state.wi.us.

Wisconsin Veterans Part-time Study Reimbursement Grant. Open only to Wisconsin veterans. Renewable for continuing study. Contact office for more details. Application deadline is no later than sixty days after the course completion. Veterans may be reimbursed up to 100% of tuition and fees. *Award:* Grant for use in freshman, sophomore, junior, or senior year; renewable. *Award amount:* $300–$2000. *Number of awards:* varies. *Eligibility Requirements:* Applicant must be enrolled or expecting to enroll part-time at an institution or university; resident of Wisconsin and studying in Wisconsin. Available to U.S. citizens. Applicant or parent must meet one or more of the following requirements: general military experience; retired from active duty; disabled or killed as a result of military service; prisoner of war; or missing in action. *Application Requirements:* Application. *Deadline:* varies.

Contact: Mike Keatley, Grants Coordinator, Wisconsin Department of Veterans Affairs, PO Box 7843, Madison, WI 53707-7843. *Phone:* 608-266-1311. *Web site:* dva.state.wi.us.

WYOMING

Douvas Memorial Scholarship. Available to Wyoming residents who are first-generation Americans. Must be between 18-22 years old. Must be used at any Wyoming public institution of higher education for study in freshman year. *Award:* Scholarship for use in freshman year; not renewable. *Award amount:* $500. *Number of awards:* 1. *Eligibility Requirements:* Applicant must be age 18-22; enrolled or expecting to enroll at a two-year or four-year institution or university; resident of Wyoming and studying in Wyoming. Available to U.S. citizens. *Application Requirements:* Application. *Deadline:* April 18.

Contact: Gerry Maas, Director, Health and Safety, Wyoming Department of Education, 2300 Capitol Avenue, Hathaway Building, 2nd Floor, Cheyenne, WY 82002-0050. *E-mail:* gmaas@educ.state.wy.us. *Phone:* 307-777-6282. *Fax:* 307-777-6234.

Superior Student in Education Scholarship-Wyoming. Available to Wyoming high school graduates who have demonstrated high academic achievement and plan to teach in Wyoming public schools. Award is for tuition at Wyoming institutions. Must maintain 3.0 GPA. *Academic Fields/Career Goals:* Education. *Award:* Scholarship for use in freshman, sophomore, junior, or senior year; renewable. *Award amount:* varies. *Number of awards:* 16–80. *Eligibility Requirements:* Applicant must be enrolled or expecting to enroll full-time at a two-year or four-year institution or university; resident of Wyoming and studying in Wyoming. Applicant must have 3.0 GPA or higher. Available to U.S. citizens. *Application Requirements:* Application, references, test scores, transcript. *Deadline:* October 31.

Contact: Joel Anne Berrigan, Assistant Director, Scholarships, State of Wyoming, administered by University of Wyoming, Student Financial Aid, Department 3335, 1000 East University Avenue, Laramie, WY 82071-3335. *E-mail:* finaid@uwyo.edu. *Phone:* 307-766-2117. *Fax:* 307-766-3800. *Web site:* www.uwyo.edu/scholarships.

Vietnam Veterans Award/Wyoming. Available to Wyoming residents who served in the armed forces between August 5, 1964, and May 7, 1975, and received a Vietnam service medal. Award is free tuition at the University of Wyoming or a state (WY) community college. *Award:* Scholarship for use in freshman, sophomore, junior, or senior year; renewable. *Award amount:* varies. *Number of awards:* varies. *Eligibility Requirements:* Applicant must be enrolled or expecting to enroll full or part-time at a two-year or four-year institution or university; resident of Wyoming and studying in Wyoming. Available to U.S. citizens. Applicant must have general military experience. *Application Requirements:* Application. *Deadline:* continuous.

Contact: Joel Anne Berrigan, Assistant Director, Scholarships, State of Wyoming, administered by University of Wyoming, Student Financial Aid, Department 3335, 1000 East University Avenue, Laramie, WY 82071-3335. *E-mail:* finaid@uwyo.edu. *Phone:* 307-766-2117. *Fax:* 307-766-3800. *Web site:* www.uwyo.edu/scholarships.

Indexes

Non-Need Scholarhips for Undergraduates

Academic Interests/ Achievements

Agriculture

Abilene Christian University, TX
Angelo State University, TX
Arkansas State University, AR
Arkansas Tech University, AR
Auburn University, AL
Berry College, GA
Brigham Young University, UT
California State University, Chico, CA
California State University, Fresno, CA
California State University, Stanislaus, CA
Cameron University, OK
Central Missouri State University, MO
Clemson University, SC
Dickinson State University, ND
Dordt College, IA
Eastern Michigan University, MI
Eastern Oregon University, OR
Florida Southern College, FL
Fort Hays State University, KS
Fort Lewis College, CO
Illinois State University, IL
Iowa State University of Science and Technology, IA
Kansas State University, KS
Langston University, OK
Lincoln University, MO
Louisiana State University and Agricultural and Mechanical College, LA
Louisiana Tech University, LA
Lubbock Christian University, TX
Michigan State University, MI
MidAmerica Nazarene University, KS
Middle Tennessee State University, TN
Midway College, KY
Mississippi State University, MS
Missouri State University, MO
Montana State University, MT
Morehead State University, KY
Murray State University, KY
New Mexico State University, NM
North Carolina State University, NC
North Dakota State University, ND
Northwestern Oklahoma State University, OK
The Ohio State University, OH
Oklahoma Panhandle State University, OK
Oklahoma State University, OK
Purdue University, IN

Sam Houston State University, TX
South Dakota State University, SD
Southeast Missouri State University, MO
Southern Arkansas University– Magnolia, AR
Southern Illinois University Carbondale, IL
Southwest Minnesota State University, MN
State University of New York College of Environmental Science and Forestry, NY
Stephen F. Austin State University, TX
Tennessee Technological University, TN
Texas A&M University, TX
Texas A&M University–Commerce, TX
Texas State University-San Marcos, TX
Texas Tech University, TX
The University of Arizona, AZ
University of Arkansas at Pine Bluff, AR
University of California, Davis, CA
University of California, Riverside, CA
University of Connecticut, CT
University of Delaware, DE
University of Florida, FL
University of Georgia, GA
University of Hawaii at Hilo, HI
University of Idaho, ID
University of Illinois at Springfield, IL
University of Maryland, College Park, MD
University of Maryland Eastern Shore, MD
University of Massachusetts Amherst, MA
University of Minnesota, Twin Cities Campus, MN
University of Missouri–Columbia, MO
University of Nebraska–Lincoln, NE
University of Nevada, Reno, NV
University of New Hampshire, NH
The University of Tennessee at Martin, TN
The University of Texas at San Antonio, TX
University of Vermont, VT
The University of Virginia's College at Wise, VA
University of Wisconsin–Stevens Point, WI
University of Wyoming, WY
Utah State University, UT
Virginia Polytechnic Institute and State University, VA
Washington State University, WA
Western Illinois University, IL
Western Kentucky University, KY
West Texas A&M University, TX
West Virginia University, WV
Wilmington College, OH

Architecture

Arizona State University, AZ
Auburn University, AL
Ball State University, IN
Boston Architectural Center, MA
California College of the Arts, CA
California State University, Bakersfield, CA
City College of the City University of New York, NY
Clemson University, SC
Eastern Michigan University, MI
Georgia Institute of Technology, GA
Iowa State University of Science and Technology, IA
James Madison University, VA
Kansas State University, KS
Kent State University, OH
Lawrence Technological University, MI
Louisiana State University and Agricultural and Mechanical College, LA
Louisiana Tech University, LA
Miami University, OH
Michigan State University, MI
Mississippi State University, MS
Montana State University, MT
New Jersey Institute of Technology, NJ
North Dakota State University, ND
The Ohio State University, OH
Oklahoma State University, OK
Polytechnic University of Puerto Rico, PR
Portland State University, OR
Rice University, TX
Savannah College of Art and Design, GA
Southern California Institute of Architecture, CA
Southern Illinois University Carbondale, IL
State University of New York College of Environmental Science and Forestry, NY
Texas A&M University, TX
Texas Tech University, TX
The University of Arizona, AZ
University of Cincinnati, OH
University of Colorado at Boulder, CO
University of Florida, FL
University of Idaho, ID
University of Illinois at Chicago, IL
University of Kansas, KS
University of Maryland, College Park, MD
University of Massachusetts Amherst, MA
University of Michigan, MI
University of Minnesota, Twin Cities Campus, MN
University of Nebraska–Lincoln, NE

University of Nevada, Las Vegas, NV
The University of North Carolina at
  Charlotte, NC
University of Oklahoma, OK
University of Oregon, OR
University of South Florida, FL
The University of Texas at Arlington, TX
The University of Texas at San
  Antonio, TX
University of Utah, UT
University of Washington, WA
University of Wisconsin–Stevens Point, WI
Utah State University, UT
Virginia Polytechnic Institute and State
  University, VA
Washington State University, WA
Washington University in St. Louis, MO
West Virginia University, WV

Area/Ethnic Studies

Arizona State University, AZ
Brigham Young University, UT
Brigham Young University–Hawaii, HI
California State University, Chico, CA
California State University, Fresno, CA
California State University, Stanislaus, CA
City College of the City University of New
  York, NY
The College of New Rochelle, NY
Fort Lewis College, CO
Furman University, SC
Hamline University, MN
Indiana University of Pennsylvania, PA
Iowa State University of Science and
  Technology, IA
Kent State University, OH
Loyola University Chicago, IL
Mississippi State University, MS
Montana State University, MT
Oakland University, MI
The Ohio State University, OH
Ohio University, OH
Ohio University–Eastern, OH
Ohio Wesleyan University, OH
Oklahoma State University, OK
Ouachita Baptist University, AR
Portland State University, OR
Radford University, VA
Rice University, TX
The Richard Stockton College of New
  Jersey, NJ
Saint Louis University, MO
Sonoma State University, CA
South Dakota State University, SD
Southern Illinois University Carbondale, IL
Southern Methodist University, TX
State University of New York at
  Oswego, NY
State University of New York at
  Plattsburgh, NY
State University of New York College at
  Geneseo, NY
Stetson University, FL
Stony Brook University, State University of
  New York, NY

University at Albany, State University of
  New York, NY
The University of Alabama, AL
University of California, Riverside, CA
University of Cincinnati, OH
University of Colorado at Boulder, CO
University of Kansas, KS
University of Michigan, MI
University of Minnesota, Twin Cities
  Campus, MN
University of Oklahoma, OK
University of South Carolina, SC
The University of Texas at San
  Antonio, TX
University of Utah, UT
University of Wisconsin–Green Bay, WI
Virginia Polytechnic Institute and State
  University, VA
Washington State University, WA
West Virginia University, WV
Wichita State University, KS

Biological Sciences

Abilene Christian University, TX
Alaska Pacific University, AK
Albertson College of Idaho, ID
Alderson-Broaddus College, WV
Alfred University, NY
Angelo State University, TX
Antioch College, OH
Arizona State University, AZ
Arkansas State University, AR
Armstrong Atlantic State University, GA
Athens State University, AL
Auburn University, AL
Augsburg College, MN
Augustana College, SD
Augusta State University, GA
Austin College, TX
Averett University, VA
Azusa Pacific University, CA
Ball State University, IN
Bard College, NY
Barton College, NC
Belhaven College, MS
Benedictine University, IL
Black Hills State University, SD
Bloomsburg University of Pennsylvania, PA
Blue Mountain College, MS
Boise State University, ID
Bowie State University, MD
Bowling Green State University, OH
Brenau University, GA
Brevard College, NC
Brewton-Parker College, GA
Brigham Young University, UT
Brigham Young University–Hawaii, HI
Bryan College, TN
Buena Vista University, IA
Butler University, IN
California Lutheran University, CA
California State University, Bakersfield, CA
California State University, Chico, CA
California State University, Fresno, CA
California State University, San
  Bernardino, CA

California State University, Stanislaus, CA
Calvin College, MI
Cameron University, OK
Campbellsville University, KY
Carroll College, WI
Carson-Newman College, TN
Case Western Reserve University, OH
Centenary College of Louisiana, LA
Central College, IA
Central Methodist University, MO
Central Michigan University, MI
Central Missouri State University, MO
Chapman University, CA
Chatham College, PA
City College of the City University of New
  York, NY
Clarion University of Pennsylvania, PA
Clarkson University, NY
Clemson University, SC
Coastal Carolina University, SC
Coe College, IA
College of Charleston, SC
The College of New Rochelle, NY
College of Staten Island of the City
  University of New York, NY
The College of Wooster, OH
The Colorado College, CO
Colorado State University-Pueblo, CO
Columbia College, MO
Columbia College, SC
Columbus State University, GA
Concordia University, NE
Concordia University, St. Paul, MN
Davidson College, NC
Davis & Elkins College, WV
Defiance College, OH
Denison University, OH
DePaul University, IL
DePauw University, IN
DeSales University, PA
Dickinson State University, ND
Dordt College, IA
D'Youville College, NY
East Carolina University, NC
Eastern Mennonite University, VA
Eastern Michigan University, MI
Eastern Oregon University, OR
Eastern Washington University, WA
East Stroudsburg University of
  Pennsylvania, PA
East Tennessee State University, TN
East Texas Baptist University, TX
Edinboro University of Pennsylvania, PA
Elizabethtown College, PA
Elmhurst College, IL
Elon University, NC
Emmanuel College, MA
Emory & Henry College, VA
Emporia State University, KS
Erskine College, SC
Fairfield University, CT
Florida Gulf Coast University, FL
Florida Southern College, FL
Fort Hays State University, KS
Fort Lewis College, CO
Framingham State College, MA

Francis Marion University, SC
Freed-Hardeman University, TN
Friends University, KS
Frostburg State University, MD
Furman University, SC
Gannon University, PA
Georgia Institute of Technology, GA
Georgian Court University, NJ
Georgia Southern University, GA
Glenville State College, WV
Grambling State University, LA
Grand Canyon University, AZ
Greenville College, IL
Grove City College, PA
Guilford College, NC
Hamline University, MN
Hampden-Sydney College, VA
Hawai'i Pacific University, HI
Heritage University, WA
Hillsdale College, MI
Howard Payne University, TX
Idaho State University, ID
Illinois State University, IL
Indiana University of Pennsylvania, PA
Indiana University–Purdue University Fort Wayne, IN
Iowa State University of Science and Technology, IA
Jacksonville State University, AL
James Madison University, VA
Kalamazoo College, MI
Kansas State University, KS
Kennesaw State University, GA
Kent State University, OH
King's College, PA
LaGrange College, GA
Lake Erie College, OH
Lake Forest College, IL
Lambuth University, TN
Lebanon Valley College, PA
Lee University, TN
Limestone College, SC
Lincoln University, PA
Lindenwood University, MO
Lock Haven University of Pennsylvania, PA
Longwood University, VA
Louisiana State University and Agricultural and Mechanical College, LA
Louisiana Tech University, LA
Loyola University Chicago, IL
Lycoming College, PA
MacMurray College, IL
Maine Maritime Academy, ME
Malone College, OH
Manhattan College, NY
Martin Methodist College, TN
Marymount Manhattan College, NY
McKendree College, IL
Mercer University, GA
Mercyhurst College, PA
Meredith College, NC
Mesa State College, CO
Metropolitan State College of Denver, CO
Michigan State University, MI
Michigan Technological University, MI
Middle Tennessee State University, TN

Millersville University of Pennsylvania, PA
Mississippi State University, MS
Mississippi University for Women, MS
Missouri State University, MO
Missouri Valley College, MO
Montana State University, MT
Montana State University–Billings, MT
Montclair State University, NJ
Morehead State University, KY
Morningside College, IA
Morris College, SC
Murray State University, KY
Muskingum College, OH
New England College, NH
New Jersey City University, NJ
New Mexico Highlands University, NM
New Mexico State University, NM
North Carolina State University, NC
North Central College, IL
North Dakota State University, ND
Northeastern Illinois University, IL
Northeastern State University, OK
Northern Arizona University, AZ
Northern State University, SD
Northwestern College, IA
Northwestern College, MN
Northwestern Oklahoma State University, OK
Northwestern State University of Louisiana, LA
Northwest Nazarene University, ID
Oakland University, MI
Ohio Northern University, OH
The Ohio State University, OH
Ohio University, OH
Ohio University–Eastern, OH
Ohio Wesleyan University, OH
Oklahoma State University, OK
Oklahoma Wesleyan University, OK
Old Dominion University, VA
Oral Roberts University, OK
Ouachita Baptist University, AR
Palmer College of Chiropractic, IA
Pepperdine University, CA
Peru State College, NE
Piedmont College, GA
Pine Manor College, MA
Pittsburg State University, KS
Purdue University, IN
Quincy University, IL
Radford University, VA
Randolph-Macon Woman's College, VA
Regis University, CO
Rice University, TX
The Richard Stockton College of New Jersey, NJ
Ripon College, WI
Rochester Institute of Technology, NY
Rockhurst University, MO
St. Cloud State University, MN
St. Edward's University, TX
St. John Fisher College, NY
St. John's University, NY
Saint Louis University, MO
Saint Vincent College, PA
Salisbury University, MD

Sam Houston State University, TX
Schreiner University, TX
Seton Hall University, NJ
Seton Hill University, PA
Shaw University, NC
Shepherd University, WV
Shippensburg University of Pennsylvania, PA
Skidmore College, NY
Slippery Rock University of Pennsylvania, PA
Sonoma State University, CA
South Dakota State University, SD
Southeastern Louisiana University, LA
Southeastern Oklahoma State University, OK
Southeast Missouri State University, MO
Southern Illinois University Carbondale, IL
Southern Methodist University, TX
Southern Oregon University, OR
Southern Wesleyan University, SC
Southwestern College, KS
Southwest Minnesota State University, MN
Spelman College, GA
State University of New York at Binghamton, NY
State University of New York at Oswego, NY
State University of New York at Plattsburgh, NY
State University of New York College at Brockport, NY
State University of New York College at Geneseo, NY
State University of New York College at Old Westbury, NY
State University of New York College at Oneonta, NY
State University of New York College at Potsdam, NY
State University of New York College of Environmental Science and Forestry, NY
State University of New York, Fredonia, NY
Stephen F. Austin State University, TX
Stetson University, FL
Stony Brook University, State University of New York, NY
Susquehanna University, PA
Tabor College, KS
Tennessee Technological University, TN
Tennessee Wesleyan College, TN
Texas A&M University, TX
Texas Tech University, TX
Thiel College, PA
Thomas University, GA
Trinity (Washington) University, DC
Truman State University, MO
The University of Akron, OH
The University of Alabama, AL
University of Alaska Anchorage, AK
University of Alaska Southeast, AK
The University of Arizona, AZ
University of Arkansas at Fort Smith, AR
University of Arkansas at Pine Bluff, AR
University of California, Riverside, CA

University of California, San Diego, CA
University of Cincinnati, OH
University of Colorado at Boulder, CO
University of Colorado at Colorado
Springs, CO
University of Connecticut, CT
University of Delaware, DE
University of Evansville, IN
University of Great Falls, MT
University of Houston–Victoria, TX
University of Idaho, ID
University of Illinois at Springfield, IL
University of Kansas, KS
University of Maine, ME
The University of Maine at Augusta, ME
University of Mary Hardin-Baylor, TX
University of Maryland, Baltimore
County, MD
University of Maryland, College Park, MD
University of Massachusetts Amherst, MA
The University of Memphis, TN
University of Miami, FL
University of Michigan, MI
University of Michigan–Dearborn, MI
University of Michigan–Flint, MI
University of Minnesota, Twin Cities
Campus, MN
University of Missouri–Columbia, MO
University of Missouri–St. Louis, MO
University of Nebraska at Omaha, NE
University of Nebraska–Lincoln, NE
University of Nevada, Las Vegas, NV
University of Nevada, Reno, NV
University of New England, ME
The University of North Carolina at
Asheville, NC
The University of North Carolina at
Greensboro, NC
The University of North Carolina at
Wilmington, NC
University of North Dakota, ND
University of Northern Colorado, CO
University of Northern Iowa, IA
University of Oklahoma, OK
University of Oregon, OR
University of Pittsburgh at Bradford, PA
University of Portland, OR
University of Puget Sound, WA
University of Richmond, VA
University of Rio Grande, OH
University of Rochester, NY
University of St. Francis, IL
University of Saint Francis, IN
University of St. Thomas, MN
University of St. Thomas, TX
University of Sioux Falls, SD
University of South Carolina, SC
The University of South Dakota, SD
University of Southern Indiana, IN
University of South Florida, FL
The University of Tampa, FL
The University of Tennessee at Martin, TN
The University of Texas at Arlington, TX
The University of Texas at Brownsville, TX
The University of Texas at Dallas, TX
The University of Texas at El Paso, TX

The University of Texas at San
Antonio, TX
The University of Texas–Pan American, TX
University of the Ozarks, AR
University of Tulsa, OK
University of Utah, UT
The University of Virginia's College at
Wise, VA
University of Washington, WA
University of West Georgia, GA
University of Wisconsin–Eau Claire, WI
University of Wisconsin–Green Bay, WI
University of Wisconsin–La Crosse, WI
University of Wisconsin–Parkside, WI
University of Wisconsin–Stevens Point, WI
University of Wisconsin–Superior, WI
University of Wisconsin–Whitewater, WI
Utah State University, UT
Valdosta State University, GA
Valley City State University, ND
Virginia Military Institute, VA
Virginia Polytechnic Institute and State
University, VA
Wake Forest University, NC
Walla Walla College, WA
Warner Pacific College, OR
Wartburg College, IA
Washington State University, WA
Washington University in St. Louis, MO
Wayland Baptist University, TX
Waynesburg College, PA
Wayne State College, NE
Western Carolina University, NC
Western Illinois University, IL
Western Kentucky University, KY
Western Oregon University, OR
Western Washington University, WA
Westminster College, UT
West Texas A&M University, TX
West Virginia University, WV
Wheeling Jesuit University, WV
Whitworth College, WA
Wichita State University, KS
Wilkes University, PA
Williams Baptist College, AR
Wilmington College, OH
Wilson College, PA
Worcester State College, MA
Xavier University of Louisiana, LA
York College, NE

Business
Abilene Christian University, TX
Adrian College, MI
Alaska Pacific University, AK
Albion College, MI
Alderson-Broaddus College, WV
Alfred University, NY
Alliant International University, CA
Angelo State University, TX
Arizona State University, AZ
Arkansas State University, AR
Athens State University, AL
Auburn University, AL
Augsburg College, MN

Augustana College, SD
Augusta State University, GA
Austin College, TX
Averett University, VA
Ball State University, IN
Barton College, NC
Baylor University, TX
Belhaven College, MS
Bellevue University, NE
Benedictine University, IL
Black Hills State University, SD
Bloomsburg University of Pennsylvania, PA
Blue Mountain College, MS
Boise State University, ID
Bowie State University, MD
Bowling Green State University, OH
Brenau University, GA
Brevard College, NC
Brewton-Parker College, GA
Brigham Young University, UT
Brigham Young University–Hawaii, HI
Bryan College, TN
Bucknell University, PA
Buena Vista University, IA
Butler University, IN
California Lutheran University, CA
California State University, Bakersfield, CA
California State University, Chico, CA
California State University, Fresno, CA
California State University, Fullerton, CA
California State University, San
Bernardino, CA
California State University, Stanislaus, CA
Calvin College, MI
Cameron University, OK
Carroll College, WI
Carson-Newman College, TN
Centenary College of Louisiana, LA
Central College, IA
Central Methodist University, MO
Central Michigan University, MI
Central Missouri State University, MO
Central Washington University, WA
Champlain College, VT
Chatham College, PA
Clarion University of Pennsylvania, PA
Clarkson University, NY
Clearwater Christian College, FL
Cleary University, MI
Clemson University, SC
Coastal Carolina University, SC
Coe College, IA
College Misericordia, PA
College of Charleston, SC
The College of New Rochelle, NY
The College of Saint Rose, NY
College of Staten Island of the City
University of New York, NY
Colorado School of Mines, CO
Colorado State University-Pueblo, CO
Columbia College, MO
Columbia College, SC
Columbia College Chicago, IL
Columbus State University, GA
Concordia University, NE
Concordia University, St. Paul, MN

Cornerstone University, MI
Creighton University, NE
Culver-Stockton College, MO
Dakota State University, SD
Dallas Baptist University, TX
Daniel Webster College, NH
David N. Myers University, OH
Davis & Elkins College, WV
Defiance College, OH
DePaul University, IL
DePauw University, IN
DeSales University, PA
Dickinson State University, ND
Dordt College, IA
Dowling College, NY
D'Youville College, NY
East Carolina University, NC
Eastern Mennonite University, VA
Eastern Michigan University, MI
Eastern Oregon University, OR
Eastern Washington University, WA
East Stroudsburg University of
  Pennsylvania, PA
East Tennessee State University, TN
East Texas Baptist University, TX
Edinboro University of Pennsylvania, PA
Elizabethtown College, PA
Elmhurst College, IL
Elon University, NC
Emory & Henry College, VA
Emporia State University, KS
Endicott College, MA
Erskine College, SC
Evangel University, MO
Fairfield University, CT
Fairmont State University, WV
Five Towns College, NY
Flagler College, FL
Florida Atlantic University, FL
Florida Gulf Coast University, FL
Florida Metropolitan University–Pinellas
  Campus, FL
Florida Southern College, FL
Fort Hays State University, KS
Fort Lewis College, CO
Francis Marion University, SC
Freed-Hardeman University, TN
Friends University, KS
Frostburg State University, MD
Furman University, SC
Gannon University, PA
Georgia College & State University, GA
Georgian Court University, NJ
Georgia Southern University, GA
Goldey-Beacom College, DE
Gonzaga University, WA
Goshen College, IN
Grace University, NE
Grambling State University, LA
Grand Canyon University, AZ
Greenville College, IL
Grove City College, PA
Hawai'i Pacific University, HI
Heritage University, WA
Hillsdale College, MI
Howard Payne University, TX

Humphreys College, CA
Husson College, ME
Idaho State University, ID
Illinois State University, IL
Indiana University of Pennsylvania, PA
Indiana University–Purdue University Fort
  Wayne, IN
Iowa State University of Science and
  Technology, IA
Jacksonville State University, AL
James Madison University, VA
Juniata College, PA
Kansas State University, KS
Kean University, NJ
Kennesaw State University, GA
Kent State University, OH
Kentucky Christian University, KY
Kettering University, MI
King's College, PA
Kutztown University of Pennsylvania, PA
LaGrange College, GA
Lake Erie College, OH
Lakeland College, WI
Lambuth University, TN
Langston University, OK
Lawrence Technological University, MI
Lee University, TN
Limestone College, SC
Lincoln University, PA
Lindenwood University, MO
Longwood University, VA
Louisiana State University and Agricultural
  and Mechanical College, LA
Louisiana Tech University, LA
Loyola University Chicago, IL
Lubbock Christian University, TX
Lycoming College, PA
Lynn University, FL
Maine Maritime Academy, ME
Malone College, OH
Manchester College, IN
Manhattan College, NY
Maranatha Baptist Bible College, WI
Martin Methodist College, TN
Marymount Manhattan College, NY
McKendree College, IL
Mercer University, GA
Mercyhurst College, PA
Mesa State College, CO
Metropolitan State College of Denver, CO
Michigan State University, MI
Michigan Technological University, MI
Middle Tennessee State University, TN
Midway College, KY
Midwestern State University, TX
Millersville University of Pennsylvania, PA
Millsaps College, MS
Milwaukee School of Engineering, WI
Minnesota State University Mankato, MN
Minot State University, ND
Mississippi State University, MS
Mississippi University for Women, MS
Missouri State University, MO
Missouri Valley College, MO
Monmouth University, NJ
Montana State University, MT

Montana State University–Billings, MT
Montana Tech of The University of
  Montana, MT
Montclair State University, NJ
Morehead State University, KY
Morehouse College, GA
Morningside College, IA
Morris College, SC
Mount Mary College, WI
Mount Vernon Nazarene University, OH
Murray State University, KY
The National Hispanic University, CA
New England College, NH
New Jersey City University, NJ
New Mexico Highlands University, NM
New Mexico State University, NM
North Carolina State University, NC
North Central College, IL
North Dakota State University, ND
Northeastern Illinois University, IL
Northeastern State University, OK
Northern Arizona University, AZ
Northern Illinois University, IL
Northern Michigan University, MI
Northern State University, SD
Northwestern College, IA
Northwestern Oklahoma State
  University, OK
Northwest Nazarene University, ID
Northwood University, MI
Northwood University, Florida Campus, FL
Northwood University, Texas Campus, TX
Oakland University, MI
Oglala Lakota College, SD
Ohio Northern University, OH
The Ohio State University, OH
Ohio University, OH
Ohio University–Eastern, OH
Ohio Wesleyan University, OH
Oklahoma City University, OK
Oklahoma State University, OK
Old Dominion University, VA
Olivet College, MI
Oral Roberts University, OK
Ouachita Baptist University, AR
Pacific University, OR
Pepperdine University, CA
Peru State College, NE
Pittsburg State University, KS
Plymouth State University, NH
Polytechnic University of Puerto Rico, PR
Portland State University, OR
Post University, CT
Providence College, RI
Purdue University, IN
Quincy University, IL
Radford University, VA
The Richard Stockton College of New
  Jersey, NJ
Ripon College, WI
Robert Morris College, IL
Rochester College, MI
Rochester Institute of Technology, NY
Rockhurst University, MO
St. Augustine College, IL
St. Bonaventure University, NY

St. Cloud State University, MN
St. Edward's University, TX
St. John Fisher College, NY
St. John's University, NY
Saint Louis University, MO
Saint Martin's College, WA
Saint Vincent College, PA
Salisbury University, MD
Sam Houston State University, TX
Schreiner University, TX
Seton Hall University, NJ
Seton Hill University, PA
Shenandoah University, VA
Shepherd University, WV
Shippensburg University of
    Pennsylvania, PA
Sierra Nevada College, NV
Slippery Rock University of
    Pennsylvania, PA
Sonoma State University, CA
South Dakota State University, SD
Southeastern Louisiana University, LA
Southeastern Oklahoma State
    University, OK
Southeast Missouri State University, MO
Southern Adventist University, TN
Southern Illinois University Carbondale, IL
Southern Illinois University
    Edwardsville, IL
Southern Methodist University, TX
Southern Oregon University, OR
Southern Utah University, UT
Southern Wesleyan University, SC
South University, GA
Southwestern Christian University, OK
Southwestern College, KS
Southwest Minnesota State University, MN
State University of New York at
    Binghamton, NY
State University of New York at
    Oswego, NY
State University of New York at
    Plattsburgh, NY
State University of New York College at
    Brockport, NY
State University of New York College at
    Geneseo, NY
State University of New York College at
    Potsdam, NY
State University of New York,
    Fredonia, NY
Stephen F. Austin State University, TX
Stetson University, FL
Stevens Institute of Technology, NJ
Stony Brook University, State University of
    New York, NY
Susquehanna University, PA
Tabor College, KS
Taylor University Fort Wayne, IN
Tennessee Technological University, TN
Tennessee Wesleyan College, TN
Texas A&M University, TX
Texas A&M University–Texarkana, TX
Texas State University-San Marcos, TX
Texas Tech University, TX
Thiel College, PA

Thomas University, GA
Tiffin University, OH
Toccoa Falls College, GA
Trevecca Nazarene University, TN
Truman State University, MO
Union University, TN
The University of Akron, OH
The University of Alabama, AL
The University of Alabama at
    Birmingham, AL
The University of Alabama in
    Huntsville, AL
University of Alaska Anchorage, AK
University of Alaska Southeast, AK
The University of Arizona, AZ
University of Arkansas at Fort Smith, AR
University of Arkansas at Pine Bluff, AR
University of California, Riverside, CA
University of California, San Diego, CA
University of Cincinnati, OH
University of Colorado at Boulder, CO
University of Colorado at Colorado
    Springs, CO
University of Colorado at Denver and
    Health Sciences Center—Downtown
    Denver Campus, CO
University of Connecticut, CT
University of Dallas, TX
University of Dayton, OH
University of Delaware, DE
University of Evansville, IN
University of Florida, FL
University of Georgia, GA
University of Great Falls, MT
University of Hawaii at Hilo, HI
University of Houston–Victoria, TX
University of Idaho, ID
University of Illinois at Springfield, IL
University of Indianapolis, IN
University of Kansas, KS
University of Maine, ME
The University of Maine at Augusta, ME
University of Maine at Fort Kent, ME
University of Mary Hardin-Baylor, TX
University of Maryland, College Park, MD
University of Maryland Eastern Shore, MD
University of Mary Washington, VA
University of Massachusetts Amherst, MA
The University of Memphis, TN
University of Miami, FL
University of Michigan, MI
University of Michigan–Dearborn, MI
University of Michigan–Flint, MI
University of Minnesota, Twin Cities
    Campus, MN
University of Mississippi, MS
University of Missouri–Columbia, MO
University of Missouri–St. Louis, MO
The University of Montana–Western, MT
University of Nebraska at Omaha, NE
University of Nebraska–Lincoln, NE
University of Nevada, Las Vegas, NV
University of Nevada, Reno, NV
University of New England, ME
University of New Hampshire, NH

The University of North Carolina at
    Asheville, NC
The University of North Carolina at Chapel
    Hill, NC
The University of North Carolina at
    Charlotte, NC
The University of North Carolina at
    Greensboro, NC
The University of North Carolina at
    Pembroke, NC
The University of North Carolina at
    Wilmington, NC
University of North Dakota, ND
University of Northern Colorado, CO
University of Northern Iowa, IA
University of North Florida, FL
University of Oklahoma, OK
University of Oregon, OR
University of Phoenix–Atlanta Campus, GA
University of Phoenix–Chicago Campus, IL
University of Phoenix–Cleveland
    Campus, OH
University of Phoenix–Dallas Campus, TX
University of Phoenix–Fort Lauderdale
    Campus, FL
University of Phoenix–Houston
    Campus, TX
University of Phoenix–Idaho Campus, ID
University of Phoenix–Jacksonville
    Campus, FL
University of Phoenix–Kansas City
    Campus, MO
University of Phoenix–Louisiana
    Campus, LA
University of Phoenix–Maryland
    Campus, MD
University of Phoenix–Metro Detroit
    Campus, MI
University of Phoenix–Nevada Campus, NV
University of Phoenix–New Mexico
    Campus, NM
University of Phoenix–Northern California
    Campus, CA
University of Phoenix–Oklahoma City
    Campus, OK
University of Phoenix Online Campus, AZ
University of Phoenix–Oregon Campus, OR
University of Phoenix–Orlando Campus, FL
University of Phoenix–Philadelphia
    Campus, PA
University of Phoenix–Phoenix
    Campus, AZ
University of Phoenix–Pittsburgh
    Campus, PA
University of Phoenix–Puerto Rico
    Campus, PR
University of Phoenix–Sacramento
    Campus, CA
University of Phoenix–St. Louis
    Campus, MO
University of Phoenix–San Diego
    Campus, CA
University of Phoenix–Southern Colorado
    Campus, CO
University of Phoenix–Tampa Campus, FL
University of Phoenix–Tulsa Campus, OK

University of Phoenix–Utah Campus, UT
University of Phoenix–Washington
  Campus, WA
University of Phoenix–West Michigan
  Campus, MI
University of Pittsburgh at Bradford, PA
University of Portland, OR
University of Puget Sound, WA
University of Rio Grande, OH
University of St. Thomas, MN
University of Sioux Falls, SD
University of South Carolina, SC
The University of South Dakota, SD
University of Southern Indiana, IN
University of South Florida, FL
The University of Tampa, FL
The University of Tennessee at Martin, TN
The University of Texas at Arlington, TX
The University of Texas at Dallas, TX
The University of Texas at El Paso, TX
The University of Texas at San
  Antonio, TX
The University of Texas–Pan American, TX
University of the Ozarks, AR
The University of Toledo, OH
University of Tulsa, OK
University of Utah, UT
University of Vermont, VT
The University of Virginia's College at
  Wise, VA
University of Washington, WA
University of West Georgia, GA
University of Wisconsin–Eau Claire, WI
University of Wisconsin–Green Bay, WI
University of Wisconsin–La Crosse, WI
University of Wisconsin–Oshkosh, WI
University of Wisconsin–Parkside, WI
University of Wisconsin–Stevens Point, WI
University of Wisconsin–Stout, WI
University of Wisconsin–Superior, WI
University of Wisconsin–Whitewater, WI
University of Wyoming, WY
Utah State University, UT
Valdosta State University, GA
Valley City State University, ND
Valparaiso University, IN
Villa Julie College, MD
Virginia Commonwealth University, VA
Virginia Military Institute, VA
Virginia Polytechnic Institute and State
  University, VA
Wake Forest University, NC
Walsh College of Accountancy and
  Business Administration, MI
Warner Southern College, FL
Wartburg College, IA
Washington & Jefferson College, PA
Washington State University, WA
Washington University in St. Louis, MO
Wayland Baptist University, TX
Waynesburg College, PA
Wayne State College, NE
Webber International University, FL
Western Carolina University, NC
Western Illinois University, IL
Western Kentucky University, KY

Western Oregon University, OR
Western Washington University, WA
West Liberty State College, WV
Westminster College, UT
West Texas A&M University, TX
West Virginia University, WV
Wheeling Jesuit University, WV
Wichita State University, KS
Wilkes University, PA
Williams Baptist College, AR
Wilmington College, OH
Winston-Salem State University, NC
Worcester State College, MA
Xavier University of Louisiana, LA
York College, NE
Youngstown State University, OH

Communication

Abilene Christian University, TX
Adelphi University, NY
Albion College, MI
Alderson-Broaddus College, WV
Alfred University, NY
Alliant International University, CA
Angelo State University, TX
Arizona State University, AZ
Arkansas State University, AR
Auburn University, AL
Augsburg College, MN
Augustana College, SD
Augusta State University, GA
Austin College, TX
Ball State University, IN
Barton College, NC
Baylor University, TX
Belhaven College, MS
Berry College, GA
Biola University, CA
Black Hills State University, SD
Bloomsburg University of Pennsylvania, PA
Boise State University, ID
Bowie State University, MD
Bowling Green State University, OH
Brenau University, GA
Brewton-Parker College, GA
Brigham Young University, UT
Brigham Young University–Hawaii, HI
Bryan College, TN
Butler University, IN
California Lutheran University, CA
California State University, Bakersfield, CA
California State University, Chico, CA
California State University, Fresno, CA
California State University, Fullerton, CA
California State University, Stanislaus, CA
Calvin College, MI
Cameron University, OK
Centenary College of Louisiana, LA
Central College, IA
Central Methodist University, MO
Central Michigan University, MI
Central Missouri State University, MO
Central Washington University, WA
Chatham College, PA
City College of the City University of New
  York, NY

Clarion University of Pennsylvania, PA
Clemson University, SC
College of Charleston, SC
The College of New Rochelle, NY
Columbia College, SC
Columbia College Chicago, IL
Columbus State University, GA
Concordia University, NE
Concordia University, St. Paul, MN
Dakota State University, SD
Dallas Baptist University, TX
Defiance College, OH
Denison University, OH
DePauw University, IN
DeSales University, PA
Dickinson State University, ND
Dordt College, IA
East Central University, OK
Eastern Michigan University, MI
East Stroudsburg University of
  Pennsylvania, PA
East Texas Baptist University, TX
Edinboro University of Pennsylvania, PA
Elizabethtown College, PA
Elmhurst College, IL
Elon University, NC
Emory & Henry College, VA
Emporia State University, KS
Evangel University, MO
Flagler College, FL
Florida Southern College, FL
Fordham University, NY
Fort Hays State University, KS
Fort Lewis College, CO
Franklin Pierce College, NH
Friends University, KS
Frostburg State University, MD
Furman University, SC
Georgia Southern University, GA
Goshen College, IN
Grambling State University, LA
Grand Canyon University, AZ
Grove City College, PA
Hamline University, MN
Hastings College, NE
Hawai'i Pacific University, HI
Heritage University, WA
Hofstra University, NY
Howard Payne University, TX
Idaho State University, ID
Illinois State University, IL
Indiana University of Pennsylvania, PA
Indiana University–Purdue University Fort
  Wayne, IN
Iowa State University of Science and
  Technology, IA
Ithaca College, NY
Jacksonville State University, AL
Johnson Bible College, TN
Kansas State University, KS
Kennesaw State University, GA
Kent State University, OH
King's College, PA
Kutztown University of Pennsylvania, PA
Lambuth University, TN
Lee University, TN

Lehigh University, PA
Limestone College, SC
Lincoln University, PA
Lindenwood University, MO
Lock Haven University of Pennsylvania, PA
Long Island University, Brooklyn
 Campus, NY
Louisiana State University and Agricultural
 and Mechanical College, LA
Loyola University Chicago, IL
Lubbock Christian University, TX
Lycoming College, PA
Lynn University, FL
Malone College, OH
Marymount Manhattan College, NY
Mercyhurst College, PA
Mesa State College, CO
Metropolitan State College of Denver, CO
Michigan Technological University, MI
Middle Tennessee State University, TN
Millersville University of Pennsylvania, PA
Milligan College, TN
Milwaukee School of Engineering, WI
Minot State University, ND
Mississippi State University, MS
Mississippi University for Women, MS
Missouri State University, MO
Missouri Valley College, MO
Monmouth University, NJ
Montana State University, MT
Montana State University–Billings, MT
Montclair State University, NJ
Morningside College, IA
Morris College, SC
Mount Mary College, WI
Multnomah Bible College and Biblical
 Seminary, OR
Murray State University, KY
New England College, NH
New England School of
 Communications, ME
New Jersey City University, NJ
New Mexico Highlands University, NM
New Mexico Institute of Mining and
 Technology, NM
New Mexico State University, NM
North Central College, IL
North Dakota State University, ND
Northeastern Illinois University, IL
Northeastern State University, OK
Northern Arizona University, AZ
North Greenville College, SC
Northwestern College, IA
Northwestern Oklahoma State
 University, OK
Ohio Northern University, OH
The Ohio State University, OH
Ohio University, OH
Ohio University–Eastern, OH
Ohio Wesleyan University, OH
Oklahoma City University, OK
Oklahoma State University, OK
Olivet College, MI
Oral Roberts University, OK
Ouachita Baptist University, AR
Pepperdine University, CA

Pittsburg State University, KS
Plymouth State University, NH
Quincy University, IL
Radford University, VA
Rochester Institute of Technology, NY
Rockhurst University, MO
St. Cloud State University, MN
St. Edward's University, TX
St. John's University, NY
Saint Louis University, MO
Salisbury University, MD
Sam Houston State University, TX
Seton Hill University, PA
Shepherd University, WV
Shippensburg University of
 Pennsylvania, PA
Slippery Rock University of
 Pennsylvania, PA
Sonoma State University, CA
South Dakota State University, SD
Southeastern College of the Assemblies of
 God, FL
Southeastern Louisiana University, LA
Southeast Missouri State University, MO
Southern Adventist University, TN
Southern Illinois University Carbondale, IL
Southern Methodist University, TX
Southern Utah University, UT
Southwestern College, KS
Southwest Minnesota State University, MN
State University of New York at
 Oswego, NY
State University of New York at
 Plattsburgh, NY
State University of New York College at
 Brockport, NY
State University of New York College at
 Geneseo, NY
State University of New York College at
 Potsdam, NY
State University of New York,
 Fredonia, NY
Stephen F. Austin State University, TX
Stetson University, FL
Tabor College, KS
Tennessee Technological University, TN
Tennessee Wesleyan College, TN
Texas Tech University, TX
Toccoa Falls College, GA
Trevecca Nazarene University, TN
Truman State University, MO
Union University, TN
The University of Akron, OH
The University of Alabama, AL
The University of Alabama at
 Birmingham, AL
University of Alaska Anchorage, AK
University of Alaska Southeast, AK
University of California, San Diego, CA
University of Cincinnati, OH
University of Colorado at Boulder, CO
University of Delaware, DE
University of Evansville, IN
University of Florida, FL
University of Great Falls, MT
University of Houston–Victoria, TX

University of Idaho, ID
University of Illinois at Springfield, IL
University of Indianapolis, IN
University of Kansas, KS
University of Maine, ME
University of Mary Hardin-Baylor, TX
University of Maryland, College Park, MD
University of Massachusetts Amherst, MA
The University of Memphis, TN
University of Miami, FL
University of Michigan, MI
University of Michigan–Flint, MI
University of Minnesota, Twin Cities
 Campus, MN
University of Missouri–Columbia, MO
University of Missouri–St. Louis, MO
University of Nebraska at Kearney, NE
University of Nebraska at Omaha, NE
University of Nevada, Las Vegas, NV
University of New Orleans, LA
The University of North Carolina at
 Asheville, NC
The University of North Carolina at Chapel
 Hill, NC
The University of North Carolina at
 Greensboro, NC
The University of North Carolina at
 Pembroke, NC
The University of North Carolina at
 Wilmington, NC
University of North Dakota, ND
University of Northern Colorado, CO
University of Oklahoma, OK
University of Pittsburgh at Bradford, PA
University of Portland, OR
University of Puget Sound, WA
University of Rio Grande, OH
University of Sioux Falls, SD
University of South Carolina, SC
The University of South Dakota, SD
University of South Florida, FL
The University of Tampa, FL
The University of Tennessee at Martin, TN
The University of Texas at Arlington, TX
The University of Texas at El Paso, TX
The University of Texas at San
 Antonio, TX
The University of Texas–Pan American, TX
University of the Ozarks, AR
The University of Toledo, OH
University of Tulsa, OK
University of Utah, UT
University of Washington, WA
University of West Georgia, GA
University of Wisconsin–Eau Claire, WI
University of Wisconsin–Green Bay, WI
University of Wisconsin–La Crosse, WI
University of Wisconsin–Parkside, WI
University of Wisconsin–Stevens Point, WI
University of Wisconsin–Superior, WI
University of Wisconsin–Whitewater, WI
University of Wyoming, WY
Utah State University, UT
Valdosta State University, GA
Valley City State University, ND

Virginia Polytechnic Institute and State University, VA
Waldorf College, IA
Warner Southern College, FL
Wartburg College, IA
Washington State University, WA
Washington University in St. Louis, MO
Wayland Baptist University, TX
Waynesburg College, PA
Wayne State College, NE
Western Carolina University, NC
Western Kentucky University, KY
Western Washington University, WA
West Liberty State College, WV
Westminster College, UT
West Texas A&M University, TX
West Virginia University, WV
Wheeling Jesuit University, WV
Wichita State University, KS
Wilkes University, PA
Wilmington College, OH
Wilson College, PA
York College, NE

Computer Science

Alderson-Broaddus College, WV
Alfred University, NY
Alliant International University, CA
Angelo State University, TX
Arizona State University, AZ
Arkansas State University, AR
Armstrong Atlantic State University, GA
Athens State University, AL
Auburn University, AL
Augsburg College, MN
Augustana College, SD
Azusa Pacific University, CA
Barton College, NC
Baylor University, TX
Belhaven College, MS
Black Hills State University, SD
Bloomsburg University of Pennsylvania, PA
Boise State University, ID
Bowie State University, MD
Bowling Green State University, OH
Brigham Young University, UT
Brigham Young University–Hawaii, HI
Bryan College, TN
Buena Vista University, IA
Butler University, IN
California Lutheran University, CA
California State University, Chico, CA
California State University, San Bernardino, CA
California State University, Stanislaus, CA
Calvin College, MI
Cameron University, OK
Carroll College, WI
Central College, IA
Central Methodist University, MO
Central Michigan University, MI
Central Missouri State University, MO
Central Washington University, WA
City College of the City University of New York, NY
Clarion University of Pennsylvania, PA

Clarke College, IA
Clarkson University, NY
Clemson University, SC
College Misericordia, PA
College of Charleston, SC
College of Staten Island of the City University of New York, NY
Colorado School of Mines, CO
Colorado State University-Pueblo, CO
Columbus State University, GA
Concordia University, NE
Dakota State University, SD
Dallas Baptist University, TX
Daniel Webster College, NH
Davis & Elkins College, WV
Defiance College, OH
DePaul University, IL
DePauw University, IN
DeSales University, PA
Dickinson State University, ND
Dordt College, IA
Eastern Michigan University, MI
Eastern Washington University, WA
East Stroudsburg University of Pennsylvania, PA
East Tennessee State University, TN
East Texas Baptist University, TX
Edinboro University of Pennsylvania, PA
Elizabethtown College, PA
Elmhurst College, IL
Elon University, NC
Emory & Henry College, VA
Emporia State University, KS
Evangel University, MO
Florida Metropolitan University–Pinellas Campus, FL
Fort Hays State University, KS
Fort Lewis College, CO
Freed-Hardeman University, TN
Friends University, KS
Frostburg State University, MD
Furman University, SC
Georgia Institute of Technology, GA
Graceland University, IA
Grambling State University, LA
Heritage University, WA
Humphreys College, CA
Husson College, ME
Idaho State University, ID
Illinois State University, IL
Indiana University of Pennsylvania, PA
Indiana University–Purdue University Fort Wayne, IN
Iowa State University of Science and Technology, IA
Jacksonville State University, AL
James Madison University, VA
Johnson C. Smith University, NC
Kansas State University, KS
Kennesaw State University, GA
Kent State University, OH
Kettering University, MI
King's College, PA
Kutztown University of Pennsylvania, PA
LaGrange College, GA
Lambuth University, TN

Lawrence Technological University, MI
Limestone College, SC
Lincoln University, PA
Lindenwood University, MO
Longwood University, VA
Louisiana State University and Agricultural and Mechanical College, LA
Louisiana Tech University, LA
Loyola University Chicago, IL
Lubbock Christian University, TX
Lycoming College, PA
Malone College, OH
Manhattan College, NY
Mesa State College, CO
Metropolitan State College of Denver, CO
Michigan State University, MI
Michigan Technological University, MI
Middle Tennessee State University, TN
Midwestern State University, TX
Millersville University of Pennsylvania, PA
Milligan College, TN
Milwaukee School of Engineering, WI
Minnesota State University Mankato, MN
Minot State University, ND
Mississippi State University, MS
Mississippi University for Women, MS
Missouri State University, MO
Missouri Valley College, MO
Monmouth University, NJ
Montana State University, MT
Montana State University–Billings, MT
Montana Tech of The University of Montana, MT
Morningside College, IA
Morris College, SC
Mount Vernon Nazarene University, OH
Murray State University, KY
Muskingum College, OH
The National Hispanic University, CA
New Mexico Highlands University, NM
New Mexico State University, NM
North Central College, IL
North Dakota State University, ND
Northeastern Illinois University, IL
Northeastern State University, OK
Northern Arizona University, AZ
Northwestern College, IA
Northwestern Oklahoma State University, OK
Northwest Nazarene University, ID
Ohio Northern University, OH
The Ohio State University, OH
Ohio University, OH
Ohio University–Eastern, OH
Ohio Wesleyan University, OH
Oklahoma State University, OK
Oklahoma Wesleyan University, OK
Ouachita Baptist University, AR
Peru State College, NE
Pittsburg State University, KS
Polytechnic University, Brooklyn Campus, NY
Portland State University, OR
Purdue University, IN
Quincy University, IL
Radford University, VA

Rice University, TX
The Richard Stockton College of New Jersey, NJ
Ripon College, WI
Robert Morris College, IL
Rochester College, MI
Rochester Institute of Technology, NY
Rockhurst University, MO
Rollins College, FL
St. Augustine College, IL
St. Cloud State University, MN
St. Edward's University, TX
St. John's University, NY
Saint Louis University, MO
Saint Vincent College, PA
Salisbury University, MD
Sam Houston State University, TX
Seton Hill University, PA
Shaw University, NC
Shepherd University, WV
Shippensburg University of Pennsylvania, PA
Skidmore College, NY
Slippery Rock University of Pennsylvania, PA
Sonoma State University, CA
South Dakota School of Mines and Technology, SD
South Dakota State University, SD
Southeastern Oklahoma State University, OK
Southeast Missouri State University, MO
Southern Illinois University Carbondale, IL
Southern Methodist University, TX
Southern Wesleyan University, SC
Southwest Minnesota State University, MN
State University of New York at Binghamton, NY
State University of New York at New Paltz, NY
State University of New York at Oswego, NY
State University of New York at Plattsburgh, NY
State University of New York College at Brockport, NY
State University of New York College at Geneseo, NY
State University of New York College at Potsdam, NY
State University of New York Institute of Technology, NY
Stephen F. Austin State University, TX
Stetson University, FL
Stevens Institute of Technology, NJ
Stony Brook University, State University of New York, NY
Tabor College, KS
Taylor University Fort Wayne, IN
Tennessee Technological University, TN
Tennessee Wesleyan College, TN
Texas A&M University, TX
Texas Tech University, TX
Thiel College, PA
Transylvania University, KY
The University of Akron, OH

The University of Alabama, AL
The University of Alabama at Birmingham, AL
The University of Alabama in Huntsville, AL
University of Alaska Anchorage, AK
University of Arkansas at Fort Smith, AR
University of California, Irvine, CA
University of California, San Diego, CA
University of Cincinnati, OH
University of Colorado at Boulder, CO
University of Colorado at Colorado Springs, CO
University of Connecticut, CT
University of Dallas, TX
University of Delaware, DE
University of Evansville, IN
University of Florida, FL
University of Great Falls, MT
University of Hawaii at Hilo, HI
University of Houston–Victoria, TX
University of Idaho, ID
University of Illinois at Springfield, IL
University of Kansas, KS
University of Maine, ME
University of Maine at Fort Kent, ME
University of Mary Hardin-Baylor, TX
University of Maryland, Baltimore County, MD
University of Maryland, College Park, MD
University of Maryland Eastern Shore, MD
University of Mary Washington, VA
University of Massachusetts Amherst, MA
University of Massachusetts Lowell, MA
University of Michigan, MI
University of Michigan–Dearborn, MI
University of Michigan–Flint, MI
University of Minnesota, Twin Cities Campus, MN
University of Missouri–Columbia, MO
University of Missouri–St. Louis, MO
University of Nebraska at Omaha, NE
University of Nebraska–Lincoln, NE
University of Nevada, Las Vegas, NV
University of Nevada, Reno, NV
University of New Orleans, LA
The University of North Carolina at Asheville, NC
The University of North Carolina at Charlotte, NC
The University of North Carolina at Wilmington, NC
University of North Dakota, ND
University of North Florida, FL
University of Oklahoma, OK
University of Phoenix–Atlanta Campus, GA
University of Phoenix–Chicago Campus, IL
University of Phoenix–Cleveland Campus, OH
University of Phoenix–Dallas Campus, TX
University of Phoenix–Fort Lauderdale Campus, FL
University of Phoenix–Houston Campus, TX
University of Phoenix–Idaho Campus, ID

University of Phoenix–Jacksonville Campus, FL
University of Phoenix–Kansas City Campus, MO
University of Phoenix–Louisiana Campus, LA
University of Phoenix–Maryland Campus, MD
University of Phoenix–Metro Detroit Campus, MI
University of Phoenix–Nevada Campus, NV
University of Phoenix–New Mexico Campus, NM
University of Phoenix–Northern California Campus, CA
University of Phoenix–Oklahoma City Campus, OK
University of Phoenix Online Campus, AZ
University of Phoenix–Oregon Campus, OR
University of Phoenix–Orlando Campus, FL
University of Phoenix–Philadelphia Campus, PA
University of Phoenix–Phoenix Campus, AZ
University of Phoenix–Pittsburgh Campus, PA
University of Phoenix–Puerto Rico Campus, PR
University of Phoenix–Sacramento Campus, CA
University of Phoenix–St. Louis Campus, MO
University of Phoenix–San Diego Campus, CA
University of Phoenix–Southern Colorado Campus, CO
University of Phoenix–Tampa Campus, FL
University of Phoenix–Tulsa Campus, OK
University of Phoenix–Utah Campus, UT
University of Phoenix–Washington Campus, WA
University of Phoenix–West Michigan Campus, MI
University of Pittsburgh at Bradford, PA
University of Portland, OR
University of Puget Sound, WA
University of Richmond, VA
University of Rio Grande, OH
University of Sioux Falls, SD
University of South Carolina, SC
The University of South Dakota, SD
University of South Florida, FL
The University of Tennessee at Martin, TN
The University of Texas at Dallas, TX
The University of Texas at El Paso, TX
The University of Texas at San Antonio, TX
The University of Texas–Pan American, TX
University of Tulsa, OK
University of Utah, UT
The University of Virginia's College at Wise, VA
University of West Georgia, GA
University of Wisconsin–Eau Claire, WI
University of Wisconsin–La Crosse, WI
University of Wisconsin–Oshkosh, WI

University of Wisconsin–Stevens Point, WI
University of Wisconsin–Superior, WI
University of Wisconsin–Whitewater, WI
University of Wyoming, WY
Utah State University, UT
Valdosta State University, GA
Valley City State University, ND
Villa Julie College, MD
Virginia Military Institute, VA
Virginia Polytechnic Institute and State
  University, VA
Wartburg College, IA
Washington State University, WA
Washington University in St. Louis, MO
Waynesburg College, PA
Wayne State College, NE
Western Oregon University, OR
Western Washington University, WA
Westminster College, UT
West Texas A&M University, TX
West Virginia University, WV
Wheeling Jesuit University, WV
Whitworth College, WA
Wichita State University, KS
Wilson College, PA
Winston-Salem State University, NC
Xavier University of Louisiana, LA
York College, NE
Youngstown State University, OH

Education
Abilene Christian University, TX
Alaska Pacific University, AK
Albertson College of Idaho, ID
Albion College, MI
Alderson-Broaddus College, WV
Alfred University, NY
Alliant International University, CA
Angelo State University, TX
Antioch College, OH
Aquinas College, TN
Arizona State University, AZ
Arkansas State University, AR
Armstrong Atlantic State University, GA
Athens State University, AL
Auburn University, AL
Augsburg College, MN
Augustana College, SD
Augusta State University, GA
Aurora University, IL
Austin College, TX
Averett University, VA
Ball State University, IN
The Baptist College of Florida, FL
Barton College, NC
Baylor University, TX
Belhaven College, MS
Benedictine University, IL
Berry College, GA
Black Hills State University, SD
Bloomsburg University of Pennsylvania, PA
Blue Mountain College, MS
Boise State University, ID
Boston University, MA
Bowling Green State University, OH
Brenau University, GA

Brewton-Parker College, GA
Brigham Young University, UT
Brigham Young University–Hawaii, HI
Bryan College, TN
Buena Vista University, IA
Butler University, IN
California Lutheran University, CA
California State University, Bakersfield, CA
California State University, Chico, CA
California State University, Fresno, CA
California State University, San
  Bernardino, CA
California State University, Stanislaus, CA
Calvin College, MI
Cameron University, OK
Campbellsville University, KY
Carroll College, WI
Carson-Newman College, TN
Catawba College, NC
Centenary College of Louisiana, LA
Central College, IA
Central Methodist University, MO
Central Michigan University, MI
Central Missouri State University, MO
Central Washington University, WA
Chatham College, PA
Christopher Newport University, VA
City College of the City University of New
  York, NY
Clarion University of Pennsylvania, PA
Clearwater Christian College, FL
Clemson University, SC
Coastal Carolina University, SC
College Misericordia, PA
College of Charleston, SC
The College of New Rochelle, NY
The College of Saint Rose, NY
College of Staten Island of the City
  University of New York, NY
Columbia College, MO
Columbia College, SC
Columbia College Chicago, IL
Columbus State University, GA
Concordia University, NE
Cornerstone University, MI
Creighton University, NE
Dakota State University, SD
Dallas Baptist University, TX
Dallas Christian College, TX
Davidson College, NC
Davis & Elkins College, WV
Defiance College, OH
DePaul University, IL
DeSales University, PA
Dickinson State University, ND
Dordt College, IA
Dowling College, NY
D'Youville College, NY
East Carolina University, NC
Eastern Mennonite University, VA
Eastern Michigan University, MI
Eastern Oregon University, OR
Eastern Washington University, WA
East Stroudsburg University of
  Pennsylvania, PA
East Tennessee State University, TN

East Texas Baptist University, TX
Edinboro University of Pennsylvania, PA
Elizabethtown College, PA
Elmhurst College, IL
Elon University, NC
Emmanuel College, MA
Emory & Henry College, VA
Emporia State University, KS
Endicott College, MA
Erskine College, SC
Evangel University, MO
Fairfield University, CT
Fairmont State University, WV
Five Towns College, NY
Flagler College, FL
Florida Gulf Coast University, FL
Florida Southern College, FL
Fort Hays State University, KS
Fort Lewis College, CO
Framingham State College, MA
Francis Marion University, SC
Freed-Hardeman University, TN
Friends University, KS
Frostburg State University, MD
Furman University, SC
Gannon University, PA
Georgia College & State University, GA
Georgia Southern University, GA
Glenville State College, WV
Goshen College, IN
Grace University, NE
Grambling State University, LA
Grand Canyon University, AZ
Greenville College, IL
Grove City College, PA
Hamline University, MN
Hampden-Sydney College, VA
Heritage University, WA
Hillsdale College, MI
Howard Payne University, TX
Husson College, ME
Idaho State University, ID
Illinois State University, IL
Indiana University of Pennsylvania, PA
Indiana University–Purdue University Fort
  Wayne, IN
Iowa State University of Science and
  Technology, IA
Jacksonville State University, AL
James Madison University, VA
Johnson Bible College, TN
John Wesley College, NC
Kansas State University, KS
Kean University, NJ
Kennesaw State University, GA
Kent State University, OH
Kentucky Christian University, KY
King's College, PA
Kutztown University of Pennsylvania, PA
LaGrange College, GA
Lambuth University, TN
Langston University, OK
Laura and Alvin Siegal College of Judaic
  Studies, OH
Lawrence Technological University, MI
Lee University, TN

Lewis-Clark State College, ID
Limestone College, SC
Lincoln University, MO
Lincoln University, PA
Lindenwood University, MO
Lock Haven University of Pennsylvania, PA
Long Island University, Brooklyn Campus, NY
Longwood University, VA
Louisiana State University and Agricultural and Mechanical College, LA
Louisiana Tech University, LA
Loyola University Chicago, IL
Lubbock Christian University, TX
Lycoming College, PA
MacMurray College, IL
Malone College, OH
Martin Methodist College, TN
Marymount Manhattan College, NY
Maryville University of Saint Louis, MO
Mercer University, GA
Mercyhurst College, PA
Meredith College, NC
Mesa State College, CO
Messenger College, MO
Metropolitan State College of Denver, CO
Miami University, OH
Michigan State University, MI
Michigan Technological University, MI
Mid-Continent University, KY
Middle Tennessee State University, TN
Midwestern State University, TX
Millersville University of Pennsylvania, PA
Minot State University, ND
Mississippi State University, MS
Mississippi University for Women, MS
Missouri State University, MO
Missouri Valley College, MO
Monmouth University, NJ
Montana State University, MT
Montana State University–Billings, MT
Montclair State University, NJ
Morehead State University, KY
Morningside College, IA
Morris College, SC
Mount Mary College, WI
Mount Vernon Nazarene University, OH
Murray State University, KY
The National Hispanic University, CA
New England College, NH
New Jersey City University, NJ
New Mexico Highlands University, NM
New Mexico State University, NM
North Carolina State University, NC
North Central College, IL
North Dakota State University, ND
Northeastern Illinois University, IL
Northeastern State University, OK
Northern Arizona University, AZ
Northern State University, SD
North Greenville College, SC
Northwestern College, IA
Northwestern Oklahoma State University, OK
Northwestern State University of Louisiana, LA

Northwest Nazarene University, ID
Oakland University, MI
Oglala Lakota College, SD
Ohio Northern University, OH
The Ohio State University, OH
Ohio University, OH
Ohio University–Eastern, OH
Ohio Valley University, WV
Ohio Wesleyan University, OH
Oklahoma City University, OK
Oklahoma Panhandle State University, OK
Oklahoma State University, OK
Oklahoma Wesleyan University, OK
Olivet College, MI
Oral Roberts University, OK
Ouachita Baptist University, AR
Pacific Union College, CA
Pacific University, OR
Pepperdine University, CA
Peru State College, NE
Piedmont College, GA
Pine Manor College, MA
Pittsburg State University, KS
Plymouth State University, NH
Portland State University, OR
Purdue University, IN
Quincy University, IL
Radford University, VA
Randolph-Macon Woman's College, VA
The Richard Stockton College of New Jersey, NJ
Ripon College, WI
Rochester College, MI
St. Augustine College, IL
St. Cloud State University, MN
St. Edward's University, TX
St. John's University, NY
Saint Louis University, MO
Saint Martin's College, WA
Salisbury University, MD
Sam Houston State University, TX
Schreiner University, TX
Seton Hall University, NJ
Seton Hill University, PA
Shaw University, NC
Shepherd University, WV
Shippensburg University of Pennsylvania, PA
Sierra Nevada College, NV
Slippery Rock University of Pennsylvania, PA
Sonoma State University, CA
South Dakota State University, SD
Southeastern Louisiana University, LA
Southeastern Oklahoma State University, OK
Southeast Missouri State University, MO
Southern Adventist University, TN
Southern Illinois University Carbondale, IL
Southern Illinois University Edwardsville, IL
Southern Methodist College, SC
Southern Utah University, UT
Southern Wesleyan University, SC
Southwestern Christian University, OK
Southwest Minnesota State University, MN

State University of New York at New Paltz, NY
State University of New York at Oswego, NY
State University of New York at Plattsburgh, NY
State University of New York College at Brockport, NY
State University of New York College at Geneseo, NY
State University of New York College at Oneonta, NY
State University of New York College at Potsdam, NY
State University of New York, Fredonia, NY
Stephen F. Austin State University, TX
Stetson University, FL
Tabor College, KS
Tennessee Technological University, TN
Tennessee Wesleyan College, TN
Texas A&M University, TX
Texas A&M University–Texarkana, TX
Texas Christian University, TX
Texas State University-San Marcos, TX
Texas Tech University, TX
Thiel College, PA
Thomas University, GA
Toccoa Falls College, GA
Trevecca Nazarene University, TN
Truman State University, MO
Union University, TN
The University of Akron, OH
The University of Alabama, AL
The University of Alabama in Huntsville, AL
University of Alaska Anchorage, AK
University of Alaska Southeast, AK
The University of Arizona, AZ
University of Arkansas at Fort Smith, AR
University of Arkansas at Pine Bluff, AR
University of California, Riverside, CA
University of Cincinnati, OH
University of Colorado at Boulder, CO
University of Colorado at Colorado Springs, CO
University of Connecticut, CT
University of Dallas, TX
University of Dayton, OH
University of Delaware, DE
University of Evansville, IN
University of Florida, FL
University of Georgia, GA
University of Great Falls, MT
University of Houston–Victoria, TX
University of Idaho, ID
University of Illinois at Springfield, IL
University of Kansas, KS
University of Maine, ME
University of Maine at Fort Kent, ME
University of Mary Hardin-Baylor, TX
University of Maryland, College Park, MD
University of Maryland Eastern Shore, MD
University of Mary Washington, VA
University of Massachusetts Amherst, MA
The University of Memphis, TN

University of Miami, FL
University of Michigan, MI
University of Michigan–Flint, MI
University of Minnesota, Twin Cities Campus, MN
University of Mississippi, MS
University of Missouri–Columbia, MO
University of Missouri–St. Louis, MO
The University of Montana–Western, MT
University of Nebraska at Omaha, NE
University of Nebraska–Lincoln, NE
University of Nevada, Las Vegas, NV
University of Nevada, Reno, NV
University of New England, ME
University of New Hampshire, NH
University of New Orleans, LA
The University of North Carolina at Asheville, NC
The University of North Carolina at Chapel Hill, NC
The University of North Carolina at Charlotte, NC
The University of North Carolina at Greensboro, NC
The University of North Carolina at Pembroke, NC
The University of North Carolina at Wilmington, NC
University of North Dakota, ND
University of Northern Colorado, CO
University of Northern Iowa, IA
University of North Florida, FL
University of Oklahoma, OK
University of Oregon, OR
University of Pittsburgh at Bradford, PA
University of Portland, OR
University of Rio Grande, OH
University of St. Francis, IL
University of St. Thomas, MN
University of Sioux Falls, SD
University of South Carolina, SC
The University of South Dakota, SD
University of Southern Indiana, IN
University of South Florida, FL
The University of Tampa, FL
The University of Tennessee at Martin, TN
The University of Texas at Arlington, TX
The University of Texas at Brownsville, TX
The University of Texas at El Paso, TX
The University of Texas at San Antonio, TX
The University of Texas–Pan American, TX
University of the Ozarks, AR
The University of Toledo, OH
University of Utah, UT
The University of Virginia's College at Wise, VA
University of West Georgia, GA
University of Wisconsin–Eau Claire, WI
University of Wisconsin–La Crosse, WI
University of Wisconsin–Parkside, WI
University of Wisconsin–Stevens Point, WI
University of Wisconsin–Stout, WI
University of Wisconsin–Superior, WI
University of Wisconsin–Whitewater, WI
University of Wyoming, WY

Utah State University, UT
Valdosta State University, GA
Valley City State University, ND
Vanderbilt University, TN
Virginia Polytechnic Institute and State University, VA
Wabash College, IN
Wake Forest University, NC
Walla Walla College, WA
Warner Southern College, FL
Wartburg College, IA
Washington State University, WA
Washington University in St. Louis, MO
Wayland Baptist University, TX
Waynesburg College, PA
Wayne State College, NE
Webster University, MO
Western Carolina University, NC
Western Illinois University, IL
Western Kentucky University, KY
Western Oregon University, OR
Western Washington University, WA
West Liberty State College, WV
Westminster College, UT
West Texas A&M University, TX
West Virginia University, WV
Wheeling Jesuit University, WV
Wichita State University, KS
Wilkes University, PA
William Jewell College, MO
Williams Baptist College, AR
Wilmington College, DE
Wilmington College, OH
Wilson College, PA
Winston-Salem State University, NC
Worcester State College, MA
Xavier University of Louisiana, LA
York College, NE
Youngstown State University, OH

Engineering/Technologies

Alfred University, NY
Arizona State University, AZ
Arkansas State University, AR
Armstrong Atlantic State University, GA
Auburn University, AL
Austin College, TX
Averett University, VA
Baylor University, TX
Bluefield State College, WV
Boise State University, ID
Boston University, MA
Bowie State University, MD
Bowling Green State University, OH
Brigham Young University, UT
Bucknell University, PA
Butler University, IN
California State University, Chico, CA
California State University, Fresno, CA
California State University, Fullerton, CA
Calvin College, MI
Cameron University, OK
Case Western Reserve University, OH
Centenary College of Louisiana, LA
Central Michigan University, MI
Central Missouri State University, MO

Central Washington University, WA
City College of the City University of New York, NY
Clarkson University, NY
Clemson University, SC
Cleveland State University, OH
College of Charleston, SC
The College of New Jersey, NJ
The College of Saint Rose, NY
College of Staten Island of the City University of New York, NY
Colorado School of Mines, CO
Colorado State University-Pueblo, CO
Daniel Webster College, NH
Davis & Elkins College, WV
Dordt College, IA
Eastern Michigan University, MI
Eastern Washington University, WA
East Tennessee State University, TN
Edinboro University of Pennsylvania, PA
Elizabethtown College, PA
Elon University, NC
Emmanuel College, MA
Emporia State University, KS
Evangel University, MO
Fairfield University, CT
Fairmont State University, WV
Florida Atlantic University, FL
Fort Hays State University, KS
Freed-Hardeman University, TN
Frostburg State University, MD
Furman University, SC
Gannon University, PA
Geneva College, PA
The George Washington University, DC
Georgia Institute of Technology, GA
Georgia Southern University, GA
Gonzaga University, WA
Graceland University, IA
Grambling State University, LA
Greenville College, IL
Grove City College, PA
Idaho State University, ID
Illinois State University, IL
Indiana University of Pennsylvania, PA
Indiana University–Purdue University Fort Wayne, IN
Iowa State University of Science and Technology, IA
James Madison University, VA
The Johns Hopkins University, MD
Kansas State University, KS
Kettering University, MI
Lakeland College, WI
Langston University, OK
Lawrence Technological University, MI
Lindenwood University, MO
Loras College, IA
Louisiana State University and Agricultural and Mechanical College, LA
Louisiana Tech University, LA
Maine Maritime Academy, ME
Mercer University, GA
Mesa State College, CO
Metropolitan State College of Denver, CO
Miami University, OH

Michigan State University, MI
Michigan Technological University, MI
Middle Tennessee State University, TN
Milwaukee School of Engineering, WI
Minnesota State University Mankato, MN
Mississippi State University, MS
Montana State University, MT
Montana State University–Billings, MT
Montana Tech of The University of
  Montana, MT
Murray State University, KY
New England College, NH
New Mexico Highlands University, NM
New Mexico Institute of Mining and
  Technology, NM
New Mexico State University, NM
North Carolina State University, NC
North Dakota State University, ND
Northeastern University, MA
Northern Arizona University, AZ
Northern Illinois University, IL
Northern Michigan University, MI
Northwestern College, IA
Oakland University, MI
Ohio Northern University, OH
The Ohio State University, OH
Ohio University, OH
Ohio University–Eastern, OH
Ohio Wesleyan University, OH
Oklahoma State University, OK
Old Dominion University, VA
Oral Roberts University, OK
Ouachita Baptist University, AR
Pittsburg State University, KS
Polytechnic University, Brooklyn
  Campus, NY
Polytechnic University of Puerto Rico, PR
Portland State University, OR
Purdue University, IN
Rice University, TX
Rochester Institute of Technology, NY
Rollins College, FL
St. Cloud State University, MN
Saint Louis University, MO
Saint Martin's College, WA
Sam Houston State University, TX
Seattle Pacific University, WA
Shaw University, NC
Shepherd University, WV
South Dakota School of Mines and
  Technology, SD
South Dakota State University, SD
Southeastern Louisiana University, LA
Southeastern Oklahoma State
  University, OK
Southern Illinois University Carbondale, IL
Southern Methodist University, TX
State University of New York at
  Binghamton, NY
State University of New York at New
  Paltz, NY
State University of New York at
  Plattsburgh, NY
State University of New York College at
  Potsdam, NY

State University of New York College of
  Environmental Science and Forestry, NY
State University of New York Institute of
  Technology, NY
Stevens Institute of Technology, NJ
Stony Brook University, State University of
  New York, NY
Tennessee Technological University, TN
Texas A&M University, TX
Texas Christian University, TX
Texas Tech University, TX
The University of Akron, OH
The University of Alabama, AL
The University of Alabama at
  Birmingham, AL
The University of Alabama in
  Huntsville, AL
University of Alaska Anchorage, AK
The University of Arizona, AZ
University of Arkansas at Fort Smith, AR
University of California, Berkeley, CA
University of California, Riverside, CA
University of California, San Diego, CA
University of Cincinnati, OH
University of Colorado at Boulder, CO
University of Colorado at Colorado
  Springs, CO
University of Colorado at Denver and
  Health Sciences Center—Downtown
  Denver Campus, CO
University of Connecticut, CT
University of Dayton, OH
University of Delaware, DE
University of Evansville, IN
University of Florida, FL
University of Idaho, ID
University of Illinois at Springfield, IL
University of Kansas, KS
University of Maine, ME
University of Maryland, Baltimore
  County, MD
University of Maryland, College Park, MD
University of Maryland Eastern Shore, MD
University of Massachusetts Amherst, MA
University of Massachusetts Lowell, MA
The University of Memphis, TN
University of Miami, FL
University of Michigan, MI
University of Michigan–Dearborn, MI
University of Michigan–Flint, MI
University of Minnesota, Twin Cities
  Campus, MN
University of Mississippi, MS
University of Missouri–Columbia, MO
University of Missouri–St. Louis, MO
University of Nebraska at Omaha, NE
University of Nebraska–Lincoln, NE
University of Nevada, Las Vegas, NV
University of Nevada, Reno, NV
University of New Hampshire, NH
The University of North Carolina at
  Asheville, NC
The University of North Carolina at
  Charlotte, NC
University of North Dakota, ND
University of North Florida, FL

University of Oklahoma, OK
University of Pittsburgh at Bradford, PA
University of Portland, OR
University of Sioux Falls, SD
University of South Carolina, SC
University of Southern Indiana, IN
University of South Florida, FL
The University of Tennessee at Martin, TN
The University of Texas at Arlington, TX
The University of Texas at Brownsville, TX
The University of Texas at Dallas, TX
The University of Texas at El Paso, TX
The University of Texas at San
  Antonio, TX
The University of Texas at Tyler, TX
The University of Texas–Pan American, TX
The University of Toledo, OH
University of Tulsa, OK
University of Utah, UT
University of Vermont, VT
University of Washington, WA
University of Wisconsin–Green Bay, WI
University of Wisconsin–Parkside, WI
University of Wisconsin–Stevens Point, WI
University of Wisconsin–Stout, WI
University of Wyoming, WY
Utah State University, UT
Valparaiso University, IN
Vanderbilt University, TN
Virginia Commonwealth University, VA
Virginia Military Institute, VA
Virginia Polytechnic Institute and State
  University, VA
Washington State University, WA
Washington University in St. Louis, MO
Western Kentucky University, KY
Western Washington University, WA
West Virginia University, WV
Wheeling Jesuit University, WV
Wichita State University, KS
Wilkes University, PA
Xavier University of Louisiana, LA
Youngstown State University, OH

English
Abilene Christian University, TX
Alfred University, NY
Alliant International University, CA
Angelo State University, TX
Arizona State University, AZ
Arkansas State University, AR
Armstrong Atlantic State University, GA
Athens State University, AL
Auburn University, AL
Augsburg College, MN
Augustana College, SD
Augusta State University, GA
Austin College, TX
Averett University, VA
Ball State University, IN
Barton College, NC
Baylor University, TX
Belhaven College, MS
Berry College, GA
Black Hills State University, SD
Bloomsburg University of Pennsylvania, PA

Blue Mountain College, MS
Boise State University, ID
Bowling Green State University, OH
Brevard College, NC
Brigham Young University, UT
Brigham Young University–Hawaii, HI
Bryan College, TN
Butler University, IN
California Lutheran University, CA
California State University, Chico, CA
California State University, Fresno, CA
California State University, Stanislaus, CA
Calvin College, MI
Cameron University, OK
Centenary College of Louisiana, LA
Central Methodist University, MO
Central Michigan University, MI
Central Missouri State University, MO
Central Washington University, WA
Chatham College, PA
City College of the City University of New York, NY
Clarion University of Pennsylvania, PA
Clemson University, SC
College of Charleston, SC
The College of New Rochelle, NY
The College of Saint Rose, NY
Columbia College, MO
Columbia College, SC
Columbus State University, GA
Concordia University, NE
Concordia University, St. Paul, MN
Dakota State University, SD
Denison University, OH
DeSales University, PA
Dickinson State University, ND
Dordt College, IA
D'Youville College, NY
Eastern Mennonite University, VA
Eastern Michigan University, MI
Eastern Washington University, WA
East Stroudsburg University of Pennsylvania, PA
East Tennessee State University, TN
East Texas Baptist University, TX
Edinboro University of Pennsylvania, PA
Elizabethtown College, PA
Elmhurst College, IL
Emory & Henry College, VA
Emporia State University, KS
Erskine College, SC
Evangel University, MO
Flagler College, FL
Fort Hays State University, KS
Fort Lewis College, CO
Francis Marion University, SC
Freed-Hardeman University, TN
Friends University, KS
Frostburg State University, MD
Furman University, SC
Gannon University, PA
Georgian Court University, NJ
Georgia Southern University, GA
Graceland University, IA
Grambling State University, LA
Grand Canyon University, AZ

Grove City College, PA
Hamline University, MN
Hillsdale College, MI
Howard Payne University, TX
Idaho State University, ID
Illinois State University, IL
Indiana University of Pennsylvania, PA
Indiana University–Purdue University Fort Wayne, IN
Iowa State University of Science and Technology, IA
Jacksonville State University, AL
James Madison University, VA
Kalamazoo College, MI
Kansas State University, KS
Kennesaw State University, GA
Kent State University, OH
King's College, PA
Kutztown University of Pennsylvania, PA
LaGrange College, GA
Lakeland College, WI
Lambuth University, TN
Limestone College, SC
Lindenwood University, MO
Lock Haven University of Pennsylvania, PA
Longwood University, VA
Louisiana State University and Agricultural and Mechanical College, LA
Louisiana Tech University, LA
Loyola University Chicago, IL
Lubbock Christian University, TX
Lycoming College, PA
MacMurray College, IL
Malone College, OH
Manchester College, IN
Marymount Manhattan College, NY
Mercer University, GA
Mercyhurst College, PA
Mesa State College, CO
Methodist College, NC
Metropolitan State College of Denver, CO
Mid-Continent University, KY
Middle Tennessee State University, TN
Midwestern State University, TX
Millersville University of Pennsylvania, PA
Minot State University, ND
Mississippi State University, MS
Mississippi University for Women, MS
Missouri Valley College, MO
Montana State University, MT
Montana State University–Billings, MT
Montclair State University, NJ
Morningside College, IA
Mount Mary College, WI
Murray State University, KY
New England College, NH
New Mexico Highlands University, NM
New Mexico State University, NM
North Central College, IL
North Dakota State University, ND
Northeastern Illinois University, IL
Northeastern State University, OK
Northern Arizona University, AZ
Northern State University, SD
Northwestern College, IA

Northwestern Oklahoma State University, OK
Northwest Nazarene University, ID
Oakland University, MI
Ohio Northern University, OH
The Ohio State University, OH
Ohio University, OH
Ohio University–Eastern, OH
Ohio Valley University, WV
Ohio Wesleyan University, OH
Oklahoma Panhandle State University, OK
Oklahoma State University, OK
Old Dominion University, VA
Olivet College, MI
Ouachita Baptist University, AR
Pacific University, OR
Peru State College, NE
Piedmont College, GA
Pittsburg State University, KS
Plymouth State University, NH
Quincy University, IL
Radford University, VA
Randolph-Macon Woman's College, VA
Rice University, TX
Ripon College, WI
Rockhurst University, MO
St. Cloud State University, MN
St. Edward's University, TX
St. John Fisher College, NY
Saint Louis University, MO
Salisbury University, MD
Sam Houston State University, TX
Schreiner University, TX
Seton Hill University, PA
Shepherd University, WV
Shippensburg University of Pennsylvania, PA
Shorter College, GA
Slippery Rock University of Pennsylvania, PA
Sonoma State University, CA
South Dakota State University, SD
Southeastern Louisiana University, LA
Southeast Missouri State University, MO
Southern Adventist University, TN
Southern Illinois University Carbondale, IL
Southern Methodist University, TX
Southern Oregon University, OR
Southern Wesleyan University, SC
Southwest Minnesota State University, MN
State University of New York at Binghamton, NY
State University of New York at New Paltz, NY
State University of New York at Oswego, NY
State University of New York at Plattsburgh, NY
State University of New York College at Brockport, NY
State University of New York College at Geneseo, NY
State University of New York College at Potsdam, NY
State University of New York, Fredonia, NY

Stetson University, FL
Tabor College, KS
Tennessee Technological University, TN
Tennessee Wesleyan College, TN
Texas A&M University–Texarkana, TX
Texas State University-San Marcos, TX
Texas Tech University, TX
Thiel College, PA
Thomas University, GA
Truman State University, MO
The University of Akron, OH
The University of Alabama, AL
The University of Alabama in
  Huntsville, AL
University of Alaska Anchorage, AK
University of Arkansas at Fort Smith, AR
University of Arkansas at Pine Bluff, AR
University of California, Riverside, CA
University of Cincinnati, OH
University of Colorado at Boulder, CO
University of Colorado at Colorado
  Springs, CO
University of Connecticut, CT
University of Delaware, DE
University of Evansville, IN
University of Great Falls, MT
University of Hawaii at Hilo, HI
University of Idaho, ID
University of Illinois at Springfield, IL
University of Kansas, KS
University of Maine, ME
University of Maine at Fort Kent, ME
University of Mary Hardin-Baylor, TX
University of Maryland, Baltimore
  County, MD
University of Maryland, College Park, MD
University of Maryland Eastern Shore, MD
University of Mary Washington, VA
University of Massachusetts Amherst, MA
The University of Memphis, TN
University of Michigan, MI
University of Michigan–Flint, MI
University of Minnesota, Twin Cities
  Campus, MN
University of Missouri–Columbia, MO
University of Missouri–St. Louis, MO
The University of Montana–Western, MT
University of Nebraska at Omaha, NE
University of Nebraska–Lincoln, NE
University of Nevada, Las Vegas, NV
University of Nevada, Reno, NV
University of New England, ME
University of New Hampshire, NH
The University of North Carolina at
  Asheville, NC
The University of North Carolina at Chapel
  Hill, NC
The University of North Carolina at
  Greensboro, NC
The University of North Carolina at
  Pembroke, NC
The University of North Carolina at
  Wilmington, NC
University of North Dakota, ND
University of Northern Colorado, CO
University of Pittsburgh at Bradford, PA

University of Portland, OR
University of Puget Sound, WA
University of Rio Grande, OH
University of St. Thomas, MN
University of St. Thomas, TX
University of Sioux Falls, SD
University of South Carolina, SC
The University of South Dakota, SD
University of South Florida, FL
The University of Tennessee at Martin, TN
The University of Texas at Arlington, TX
The University of Texas at El Paso, TX
The University of Texas at San
  Antonio, TX
The University of Texas–Pan American, TX
University of the Ozarks, AR
The University of Toledo, OH
University of Tulsa, OK
University of Utah, UT
The University of Virginia's College at
  Wise, VA
University of Washington, WA
University of West Georgia, GA
University of Wisconsin–Eau Claire, WI
University of Wisconsin–La Crosse, WI
University of Wisconsin–Parkside, WI
University of Wisconsin–Stevens Point, WI
University of Wisconsin–Superior, WI
University of Wisconsin–Whitewater, WI
University of Wyoming, WY
Utah State University, UT
Valdosta State University, GA
Valley City State University, ND
Virginia Military Institute, VA
Virginia Polytechnic Institute and State
  University, VA
Wake Forest University, NC
Warner Southern College, FL
Wartburg College, IA
Washington State University, WA
Washington University in St. Louis, MO
Wayland Baptist University, TX
Waynesburg College, PA
Wayne State College, NE
Western Carolina University, NC
Western Kentucky University, KY
Western Washington University, WA
West Liberty State College, WV
Westminster College, UT
West Texas A&M University, TX
West Virginia University, WV
Wheaton College, IL
Wheeling Jesuit University, WV
Wichita State University, KS
Wilkes University, PA
Wilson College, PA
Worcester State College, MA
York College, NE
Youngstown State University, OH

Foreign Languages

Abilene Christian University, TX
Adelphi University, NY
Alfred University, NY
Alliant International University, CA
Angelo State University, TX

Arizona State University, AZ
Auburn University, AL
Augsburg College, MN
Augustana College, SD
Austin College, TX
Averett University, VA
Ball State University, IN
Baylor University, TX
Belhaven College, MS
Black Hills State University, SD
Bloomsburg University of Pennsylvania, PA
Boise State University, ID
Boston University, MA
Bowling Green State University, OH
Brigham Young University, UT
Brigham Young University–Hawaii, HI
Bryan College, TN
Butler University, IN
California Lutheran University, CA
California State University, Chico, CA
California State University, Fresno, CA
California State University, San
  Bernardino, CA
California State University, Stanislaus, CA
Calvin College, MI
Cameron University, OK
Castleton State College, VT
Centenary College of Louisiana, LA
Central College, IA
Central Methodist University, MO
Central Michigan University, MI
Central Missouri State University, MO
Central Washington University, WA
City College of the City University of New
  York, NY
Clarion University of Pennsylvania, PA
Clarke College, IA
Clemson University, SC
Coe College, IA
College of Charleston, SC
The College of New Rochelle, NY
The College of Saint Rose, NY
Columbia College, SC
Davidson College, NC
Denison University, OH
DePauw University, IN
DeSales University, PA
Dickinson State University, ND
Dordt College, IA
Eastern Mennonite University, VA
Eastern Michigan University, MI
Eastern Washington University, WA
East Stroudsburg University of
  Pennsylvania, PA
East Texas Baptist University, TX
Edgewood College, WI
Edinboro University of Pennsylvania, PA
Elizabethtown College, PA
Elmhurst College, IL
Emmanuel College, MA
Emporia State University, KS
Erskine College, SC
Evangel University, MO
Fairfield University, CT
Fairmont State University, WV
Flagler College, FL

Fordham University, NY
Fort Hays State University, KS
Friends University, KS
Frostburg State University, MD
Furman University, SC
Gannon University, PA
Georgian Court University, NJ
Georgia Southern University, GA
Grambling State University, LA
Grove City College, PA
Hamline University, MN
Hillsdale College, MI
Idaho State University, ID
Illinois State University, IL
Indiana University of Pennsylvania, PA
Indiana University–Purdue University Fort Wayne, IN
Iowa State University of Science and Technology, IA
Kalamazoo College, MI
Kansas State University, KS
Kennesaw State University, GA
King's College, PA
Kutztown University of Pennsylvania, PA
Lake Erie College, OH
Lake Forest College, IL
Lambuth University, TN
Lindenwood University, MO
Lock Haven University of Pennsylvania, PA
Louisiana State University and Agricultural and Mechanical College, LA
Louisiana Tech University, LA
Loyola University Chicago, IL
Lubbock Christian University, TX
Lycoming College, PA
MacMurray College, IL
Malone College, OH
Manchester College, IN
Manhattan College, NY
Mercer University, GA
Metropolitan State College of Denver, CO
Middle Tennessee State University, TN
Millersville University of Pennsylvania, PA
Mississippi State University, MS
Missouri State University, MO
Montana State University, MT
Montclair State University, NJ
Moravian College, PA
Morningside College, IA
Murray State University, KY
New Mexico Highlands University, NM
New Mexico State University, NM
North Central College, IL
Northeastern Illinois University, IL
Northeastern State University, OK
Northern Arizona University, AZ
Northern Illinois University, IL
Northern State University, SD
Northwestern College, IA
Northwestern Oklahoma State University, OK
Oakland University, MI
Ohio Northern University, OH
The Ohio State University, OH
Ohio University, OH
Ohio University–Eastern, OH

Ohio Wesleyan University, OH
Oklahoma State University, OK
Olivet College, MI
Ouachita Baptist University, AR
Pacific University, OR
Piedmont College, GA
Pittsburg State University, KS
Portland State University, OR
Rice University, TX
Ripon College, WI
Rockhurst University, MO
St. Edward's University, TX
St. John Fisher College, NY
Saint Louis University, MO
Salisbury University, MD
Sam Houston State University, TX
Seton Hill University, PA
Shepherd University, WV
Shorter College, GA
Sonoma State University, CA
South Dakota State University, SD
Southeast Missouri State University, MO
Southern Illinois University Carbondale, IL
Southern Methodist University, TX
State University of New York at Binghamton, NY
State University of New York at Oswego, NY
State University of New York College at Brockport, NY
State University of New York College at Geneseo, NY
State University of New York College at Potsdam, NY
State University of New York, Fredonia, NY
Stetson University, FL
Tennessee Technological University, TN
Tennessee Wesleyan College, TN
Texas Tech University, TX
Truman State University, MO
The University of Akron, OH
The University of Alabama, AL
University of Cincinnati, OH
University of Colorado at Boulder, CO
University of Connecticut, CT
University of Dallas, TX
University of Delaware, DE
University of Evansville, IN
University of Idaho, ID
University of Illinois at Springfield, IL
University of Kansas, KS
University of Maine at Fort Kent, ME
University of Mary Hardin-Baylor, TX
University of Maryland, Baltimore County, MD
University of Maryland, College Park, MD
University of Mary Washington, VA
University of Michigan, MI
University of Michigan–Flint, MI
University of Minnesota, Twin Cities Campus, MN
University of Missouri–Columbia, MO
University of Missouri–St. Louis, MO
University of Nebraska at Omaha, NE
University of Nebraska–Lincoln, NE

University of Nevada, Reno, NV
University of New Orleans, LA
The University of North Carolina at Greensboro, NC
The University of North Carolina at Wilmington, NC
University of North Dakota, ND
University of Oklahoma, OK
University of Oregon, OR
University of Portland, OR
University of Puget Sound, WA
University of St. Thomas, TX
University of South Carolina, SC
The University of South Dakota, SD
University of South Florida, FL
The University of Texas at Arlington, TX
The University of Texas at San Antonio, TX
The University of Toledo, OH
University of Tulsa, OK
University of Utah, UT
University of Vermont, VT
University of Washington, WA
University of West Georgia, GA
University of Wisconsin–Eau Claire, WI
University of Wisconsin–La Crosse, WI
University of Wisconsin–Parkside, WI
University of Wisconsin–Stevens Point, WI
University of Wisconsin–Whitewater, WI
University of Wyoming, WY
Utah State University, UT
Valdosta State University, GA
Valparaiso University, IN
Virginia Commonwealth University, VA
Virginia Polytechnic Institute and State University, VA
Wake Forest University, NC
Washington State University, WA
Washington University in St. Louis, MO
Wayne State College, NE
Western Illinois University, IL
Western Kentucky University, KY
Western Washington University, WA
West Texas A&M University, TX
West Virginia University, WV
Wheeling Jesuit University, WV
Wichita State University, KS
Wilson College, PA
Worcester State College, MA
Xavier University, OH
Xavier University of Louisiana, LA

Health Fields

Alderson-Broaddus College, WV
Allen College, IA
Aquinas College, TN
Arizona State University, AZ
Arkansas State University, AR
Armstrong Atlantic State University, GA
Auburn University, AL
Augsburg College, MN
Augustana College, SD
Augusta State University, GA
Austin College, TX
Averett University, VA
Azusa Pacific University, CA

Ball State University, IN
Barton College, NC
Bastyr University, WA
Baylor University, TX
Biola University, CA
Black Hills State University, SD
Bloomsburg University of Pennsylvania, PA
Boise State University, ID
Bowling Green State University, OH
Brenau University, GA
Brevard College, NC
Brigham Young University, UT
California State University, Bakersfield, CA
California State University, Chico, CA
California State University, Fresno, CA
California State University, San
  Bernardino, CA
California State University, Stanislaus, CA
Calvin College, MI
Carroll College, WI
Central College, IA
Central Methodist University, MO
Central Michigan University, MI
Central Missouri State University, MO
Central Washington University, WA
Champlain College, VT
Clemson University, SC
College Misericordia, PA
College of Charleston, SC
The College of New Rochelle, NY
College of Staten Island of the City
  University of New York, NY
Columbus State University, GA
Concordia University, NE
Davis & Elkins College, WV
DeSales University, PA
Dickinson State University, ND
D'Youville College, NY
East Carolina University, NC
Eastern Michigan University, MI
Eastern Washington University, WA
East Stroudsburg University of
  Pennsylvania, PA
East Tennessee State University, TN
East Texas Baptist University, TX
Edinboro University of Pennsylvania, PA
Elizabethtown College, PA
Elmhurst College, IL
Emmanuel College, MA
Emporia State University, KS
Endicott College, MA
Fairmont State University, WV
Florida Gulf Coast University, FL
Florida Metropolitan University–Pinellas
  Campus, FL
Fort Hays State University, KS
Francis Marion University, SC
Friends University, KS
Frostburg State University, MD
Furman University, SC
Georgia College & State University, GA
Georgia Southern University, GA
Grace University, NE
Grambling State University, LA
Grand Canyon University, AZ
Hamline University, MN

Hampden-Sydney College, VA
Hawai'i Pacific University, HI
Hillsdale College, MI
Houston Baptist University, TX
Husson College, ME
Idaho State University, ID
Illinois State University, IL
Indiana University of Pennsylvania, PA
Indiana University–Purdue University Fort
  Wayne, IN
Iowa State University of Science and
  Technology, IA
Jacksonville State University, AL
James Madison University, VA
Kansas State University, KS
Kean University, NJ
Kennesaw State University, GA
Kent State University, OH
King's College, PA
LaGrange College, GA
Langston University, OK
Lewis-Clark State College, ID
Lindenwood University, MO
Long Island University, Brooklyn
  Campus, NY
Louisiana Tech University, LA
Loyola University Chicago, IL
Lycoming College, PA
MacMurray College, IL
Malone College, OH
Maryville University of Saint Louis, MO
Medcenter One College of Nursing, ND
Medical College of Georgia, GA
Medical University of South Carolina, SC
Mercy College of Health Sciences, IA
Mercyhurst College, PA
Mesa State College, CO
Metropolitan State College of Denver, CO
MidAmerica Nazarene University, KS
Middle Tennessee State University, TN
Midway College, KY
Midwestern State University, TX
Midwestern University, Glendale
  Campus, AZ
Millersville University of Pennsylvania, PA
Milligan College, TN
Milwaukee School of Engineering, WI
Minot State University, ND
Mississippi State University, MS
Mississippi University for Women, MS
Missouri State University, MO
Monmouth University, NJ
Montana State University, MT
Montana State University–Billings, MT
Montana Tech of The University of
  Montana, MT
Morningside College, IA
Mount Mary College, WI
Mount Vernon Nazarene University, OH
Murray State University, KY
New Mexico Highlands University, NM
New Mexico State University, NM
North Dakota State University, ND
Northeastern State University, OK
Northern Arizona University, AZ
Northern Michigan University, MI

Northwestern College, IA
Northwestern Oklahoma State
  University, OK
Northwest Nazarene University, ID
Oakland University, MI
Oglala Lakota College, SD
Ohio Northern University, OH
The Ohio State University, OH
Ohio University, OH
Ohio University–Eastern, OH
Ohio Wesleyan University, OH
Oklahoma City University, OK
Oklahoma Panhandle State University, OK
Old Dominion University, VA
Oral Roberts University, OK
Oregon Health & Science University, OR
Ouachita Baptist University, AR
Palmer College of Chiropractic, IA
Piedmont College, GA
Pittsburg State University, KS
Plymouth State University, NH
Purdue University, IN
Quincy University, IL
Radford University, VA
Research College of Nursing, MO
The Richard Stockton College of New
  Jersey, NJ
Robert Morris College, IL
Rochester Institute of Technology, NY
Rockhurst University, MO
St. Augustine College, IL
Saint Francis Medical Center College of
  Nursing, IL
St. John's College, IL
St. John's University, NY
Saint Louis University, MO
Salisbury University, MD
Seton Hall University, NJ
Shepherd University, WV
Slippery Rock University of
  Pennsylvania, PA
Sonoma State University, CA
South Dakota State University, SD
Southeastern Louisiana University, LA
Southeast Missouri State University, MO
Southern Adventist University, TN
Southern Illinois University Carbondale, IL
Southern Illinois University
  Edwardsville, IL
Southern Oregon University, OR
South University, GA
Southwestern College, KS
State University of New York at
  Binghamton, NY
State University of New York at New
  Paltz, NY
State University of New York at
  Plattsburgh, NY
State University of New York College at
  Brockport, NY
State University of New York College at
  Old Westbury, NY
State University of New York Upstate
  Medical University, NY
Stephen F. Austin State University, TX

Non-Need Scholarships for Undergraduates
Academic Interests/Achievements

Stony Brook University, State University of
New York, NY
Tennessee Technological University, TN
Tennessee Wesleyan College, TN
Texas A&M University, TX
Thomas Jefferson University, PA
Thomas University, GA
The University of Akron, OH
The University of Alabama at
Birmingham, AL
The University of Alabama in
Huntsville, AL
University of Alaska Anchorage, AK
University of Arkansas at Fort Smith, AR
University of Cincinnati, OH
University of Colorado at Boulder, CO
University of Colorado at Colorado
Springs, CO
University of Colorado at Denver and
Health Sciences Center—Health Sciences
Program, CO
University of Connecticut, CT
University of Delaware, DE
University of Evansville, IN
University of Florida, FL
University of Great Falls, MT
University of Hartford, CT
University of Hawaii at Hilo, HI
University of Illinois at Springfield, IL
University of Indianapolis, IN
University of Kansas, KS
University of Maine at Fort Kent, ME
University of Mary Hardin-Baylor, TX
University of Maryland, College Park, MD
University of Maryland Eastern Shore, MD
University of Massachusetts Amherst, MA
University of Massachusetts Lowell, MA
The University of Memphis, TN
University of Michigan, MI
University of Michigan–Flint, MI
University of Minnesota, Twin Cities
Campus, MN
University of Missouri–Columbia, MO
University of Missouri–St. Louis, MO
University of Nebraska–Lincoln, NE
University of Nevada, Las Vegas, NV
University of Nevada, Reno, NV
University of New England, ME
University of New Hampshire, NH
The University of North Carolina at
Asheville, NC
The University of North Carolina at Chapel
Hill, NC
The University of North Carolina at
Charlotte, NC
The University of North Carolina at
Greensboro, NC
The University of North Carolina at
Pembroke, NC
The University of North Carolina at
Wilmington, NC
University of North Dakota, ND
University of Northern Colorado, CO
University of North Florida, FL
University of Phoenix–Atlanta Campus, GA

University of Phoenix–Cleveland
Campus, OH
University of Phoenix–Dallas Campus, TX
University of Phoenix–Fort Lauderdale
Campus, FL
University of Phoenix–Houston
Campus, TX
University of Phoenix–Jacksonville
Campus, FL
University of Phoenix–Louisiana
Campus, LA
University of Phoenix–Metro Detroit
Campus, MI
University of Phoenix–New Mexico
Campus, NM
University of Phoenix–Northern California
Campus, CA
University of Phoenix–Oklahoma City
Campus, OK
University of Phoenix Online Campus, AZ
University of Phoenix–Oregon Campus, OR
University of Phoenix–Orlando Campus, FL
University of Phoenix–Phoenix
Campus, AZ
University of Phoenix–Sacramento
Campus, CA
University of Phoenix–San Diego
Campus, CA
University of Phoenix–Southern Colorado
Campus, CO
University of Phoenix–Tampa Campus, FL
University of Phoenix–Tulsa Campus, OK
University of Phoenix–Utah Campus, UT
University of Phoenix–Washington
Campus, WA
University of Phoenix–West Michigan
Campus, MI
University of Pittsburgh at Bradford, PA
University of Portland, OR
University of Rio Grande, OH
University of St. Francis, IL
University of Saint Francis, IN
University of South Carolina, SC
University of Southern Indiana, IN
University of South Florida, FL
The University of Tampa, FL
The University of Tennessee at Martin, TN
The University of Texas at Arlington, TX
The University of Texas at Brownsville, TX
The University of Texas at El Paso, TX
The University of Texas Medical
Branch, TX
The University of Texas–Pan American, TX
The University of Toledo, OH
University of Utah, UT
The University of Virginia's College at
Wise, VA
University of Washington, WA
University of West Georgia, GA
University of Wisconsin–Eau Claire, WI
University of Wisconsin–La Crosse, WI
University of Wisconsin–Parkside, WI
University of Wisconsin–Stevens Point, WI
University of Wisconsin–Superior, WI
University of Wyoming, WY
Utah State University, UT

Valdosta State University, GA
Valparaiso University, IN
Virginia Commonwealth University, VA
Virginia Polytechnic Institute and State
University, VA
Washington State University, WA
Washington University in St. Louis, MO
Wayne State College, NE
Western Carolina University, NC
Western Kentucky University, KY
Western Washington University, WA
West Liberty State College, WV
Westminster College, UT
West Texas A&M University, TX
West Virginia University, WV
Wheeling Jesuit University, WV
Wichita State University, KS
Wilkes University, PA
William Woods University, MO
Winston-Salem State University, NC
Worcester State College, MA
Youngstown State University, OH

Home Economics
Abilene Christian University, TX
Arizona State University, AZ
Auburn University, AL
Averett University, VA
Baylor University, TX
Bowling Green State University, OH
Brigham Young University, UT
Carson-Newman College, TN
Central Missouri State University, MO
East Carolina University, NC
Eastern Michigan University, MI
Framingham State College, MA
Grambling State University, LA
Idaho State University, ID
Illinois State University, IL
Indiana University of Pennsylvania, PA
Iowa State University of Science and
Technology, IA
Jacksonville State University, AL
Kansas State University, KS
Lambuth University, TN
Louisiana State University and Agricultural
and Mechanical College, LA
Louisiana Tech University, LA
Middle Tennessee State University, TN
Mississippi State University, MS
Mississippi University for Women, MS
Missouri State University, MO
Montana State University, MT
Montclair State University, NJ
Mount Mary College, WI
Mount Vernon Nazarene University, OH
New Mexico State University, NM
North Dakota State University, ND
Northeastern State University, OK
Northern Arizona University, AZ
The Ohio State University, OH
Ohio University, OH
Ohio University–Eastern, OH
Oklahoma State University, OK
Ouachita Baptist University, AR
Pittsburg State University, KS

Sam Houston State University, TX
Seton Hill University, PA
Shepherd University, WV
South Dakota State University, SD
Southeast Missouri State University, MO
Southern Illinois University Carbondale, IL
State University of New York at
  Plattsburgh, NY
State University of New York College at
  Oneonta, NY
Stephen F. Austin State University, TX
Tennessee Technological University, TN
Texas State University-San Marcos, TX
Texas Tech University, TX
The University of Akron, OH
The University of Alabama, AL
University of Idaho, ID
University of Maryland Eastern Shore, MD
University of Minnesota, Twin Cities
  Campus, MN
University of Missouri–Columbia, MO
University of Nebraska at Omaha, NE
University of Nebraska–Lincoln, NE
The University of North Carolina at
  Greensboro, NC
University of Northern Colorado, CO
The University of Tennessee at Martin, TN
University of Wisconsin–Stevens Point, WI
University of Wisconsin–Stout, WI
University of Wyoming, WY
Utah State University, UT
Virginia Polytechnic Institute and State
  University, VA
Washington State University, WA
Wayne State College, NE
Western Illinois University, IL
Western Kentucky University, KY
West Virginia University, WV

Humanities
Alaska Pacific University, AK
Alderson-Broaddus College, WV
Alfred University, NY
Alliant International University, CA
Antioch College, OH
Arizona State University, AZ
Arkansas State University, AR
Armstrong Atlantic State University, GA
Athens State University, AL
Auburn University, AL
Augustana College, SD
Austin College, TX
Averett University, VA
Barton College, NC
Baylor University, TX
Belhaven College, MS
Bellevue University, NE
Benedictine University, IL
Berry College, GA
Black Hills State University, SD
Bloomsburg University of Pennsylvania, PA
Boise State University, ID
Bowling Green State University, OH
Brenau University, GA
Brigham Young University, UT
Brigham Young University–Hawaii, HI

Bryan College, TN
Buena Vista University, IA
Butler University, IN
California Lutheran University, CA
California State University, Chico, CA
California State University, Fresno, CA
California State University, Fullerton, CA
California State University, Stanislaus, CA
Calvin College, MI
Carroll College, WI
Centenary College of Louisiana, LA
Central College, IA
Central Methodist University, MO
Central Michigan University, MI
Central Missouri State University, MO
Christopher Newport University, VA
City College of the City University of New
  York, NY
Clarion University of Pennsylvania, PA
Clarkson University, NY
Clemson University, SC
Coastal Carolina University, SC
College of Charleston, SC
The College of New Rochelle, NY
College of the Holy Cross, MA
Columbia College, MO
Columbia College, SC
Columbus State University, GA
Concordia University, NE
Dallas Baptist University, TX
Defiance College, OH
Denison University, OH
DePauw University, IN
DeSales University, PA
Dickinson State University, ND
Dordt College, IA
D'Youville College, NY
East Carolina University, NC
Eastern Mennonite University, VA
Eastern Michigan University, MI
Edinboro University of Pennsylvania, PA
Elizabethtown College, PA
Elmhurst College, IL
Emmanuel College, MA
Emporia State University, KS
Evangel University, MO
Fairmont State University, WV
Florida Gulf Coast University, FL
Fort Hays State University, KS
Fort Lewis College, CO
Francis Marion University, SC
Freed-Hardeman University, TN
Fresno Pacific University, CA
Friends University, KS
Frostburg State University, MD
Furman University, SC
Georgia College & State University, GA
Georgia Southern University, GA
Grambling State University, LA
Grand Canyon University, AZ
Hamline University, MN
Hillsdale College, MI
Idaho State University, ID
Illinois State University, IL
Indiana University of Pennsylvania, PA

Indiana University–Purdue University Fort
  Wayne, IN
Iowa State University of Science and
  Technology, IA
Jacksonville State University, AL
James Madison University, VA
Kansas State University, KS
Kean University, NJ
Kennesaw State University, GA
King's College, PA
Kutztown University of Pennsylvania, PA
Lambuth University, TN
Lawrence Technological University, MI
Lewis-Clark State College, ID
Limestone College, SC
Lincoln University, PA
Lindenwood University, MO
Longwood University, VA
Louisiana State University and Agricultural
  and Mechanical College, LA
Louisiana Tech University, LA
Loyola University Chicago, IL
Lubbock Christian University, TX
Lycoming College, PA
Malone College, OH
Manchester College, IN
Marymount Manhattan College, NY
Mercyhurst College, PA
Mesa State College, CO
Metropolitan State College of Denver, CO
Michigan Technological University, MI
Mid-Continent University, KY
Middle Tennessee State University, TN
Millersville University of Pennsylvania, PA
Minot State University, ND
Mississippi State University, MS
Mississippi University for Women, MS
Missouri Valley College, MO
Monmouth University, NJ
Montana State University, MT
Montana State University–Billings, MT
Montclair State University, NJ
Morehead State University, KY
Morningside College, IA
Morris College, SC
Mount Mary College, WI
Murray State University, KY
New England College, NH
New Mexico Highlands University, NM
New Mexico State University, NM
North Carolina State University, NC
North Central College, IL
North Dakota State University, ND
Northeastern State University, OK
Northern Arizona University, AZ
Northern State University, SD
Northwestern College, IA
Northwestern Oklahoma State
  University, OK
Northwestern State University of
  Louisiana, LA
Oakland University, MI
Ohio Northern University, OH
The Ohio State University, OH
Ohio University, OH
Ohio University–Eastern, OH

Ohio Wesleyan University, OH
Oklahoma State University, OK
Old Dominion University, VA
Ouachita Baptist University, AR
Pacific University, OR
Pepperdine University, CA
Peru State College, NE
Piedmont College, GA
Portland State University, OR
Purdue University, IN
Radford University, VA
Rensselaer Polytechnic Institute, NY
Rice University, TX
The Richard Stockton College of New Jersey, NJ
Ripon College, WI
Rockhurst University, MO
St. Augustine College, IL
St. Edward's University, TX
St. John Fisher College, NY
Saint Louis University, MO
Saint Martin's College, WA
Salisbury University, MD
Sam Houston State University, TX
Savannah College of Art and Design, GA
Seton Hill University, PA
Shepherd University, WV
Sierra Nevada College, NV
Sonoma State University, CA
South Dakota State University, SD
Southeast Missouri State University, MO
Southern Illinois University Carbondale, IL
Southern Methodist University, TX
Southern Oregon University, OR
Southern Wesleyan University, SC
Southwestern College, KS
State University of New York at New Paltz, NY
State University of New York at Oswego, NY
State University of New York at Plattsburgh, NY
State University of New York College at Geneseo, NY
State University of New York College at Potsdam, NY
State University of New York, Fredonia, NY
Stetson University, FL
Stevens Institute of Technology, NJ
Tabor College, KS
Tennessee Technological University, TN
Tennessee Wesleyan College, TN
The University of Akron, OH
The University of Alabama in Huntsville, AL
University of Alaska Anchorage, AK
The University of Arizona, AZ
University of California, Irvine, CA
University of California, Riverside, CA
University of Cincinnati, OH
University of Colorado at Boulder, CO
University of Connecticut, CT
University of Dayton, OH
University of Delaware, DE
University of Evansville, IN

University of Great Falls, MT
University of Houston–Victoria, TX
University of Idaho, ID
University of Illinois at Springfield, IL
University of Kansas, KS
University of Maine, ME
University of Maine at Fort Kent, ME
University of Mary Hardin-Baylor, TX
University of Maryland, Baltimore County, MD
University of Maryland, College Park, MD
University of Mary Washington, VA
University of Massachusetts Amherst, MA
University of Massachusetts Lowell, MA
The University of Memphis, TN
University of Michigan, MI
University of Michigan–Flint, MI
University of Minnesota, Twin Cities Campus, MN
University of Missouri–St. Louis, MO
University of Nebraska–Lincoln, NE
University of Nevada, Las Vegas, NV
University of Nevada, Reno, NV
University of New England, ME
University of New Hampshire, NH
The University of North Carolina at Charlotte, NC
The University of North Carolina at Greensboro, NC
The University of North Carolina at Wilmington, NC
University of North Dakota, ND
University of Oklahoma, OK
University of Pittsburgh at Bradford, PA
University of Portland, OR
University of Puget Sound, WA
University of Rio Grande, OH
University of Rochester, NY
University of St. Thomas, MN
University of Sioux Falls, SD
University of South Carolina, SC
The University of South Dakota, SD
University of Southern Indiana, IN
University of South Florida, FL
The University of Tennessee at Martin, TN
The University of Texas at Arlington, TX
The University of Texas at El Paso, TX
The University of Texas at San Antonio, TX
University of the Ozarks, AR
The University of Toledo, OH
University of Utah, UT
The University of Virginia's College at Wise, VA
University of Washington, WA
University of West Georgia, GA
University of Wisconsin–Stevens Point, WI
University of Wisconsin–Superior, WI
University of Wisconsin–Whitewater, WI
Utah State University, UT
Vanderbilt University, TN
Virginia Polytechnic Institute and State University, VA
Warner Southern College, FL
Washington State University, WA
Washington University in St. Louis, MO

Wayne State College, NE
Webster University, MO
Western Washington University, WA
Westminster College, UT
West Texas A&M University, TX
West Virginia University, WV
Wheeling Jesuit University, WV
Wichita State University, KS
Wilkes University, PA
Williams Baptist College, AR
Wilson College, PA
Xavier University of Louisiana, LA
Youngstown State University, OH

International Studies

Alfred University, NY
Alliant International University, CA
Angelo State University, TX
Antioch College, OH
Armstrong Atlantic State University, GA
Athens State University, AL
Auburn University, AL
Augsburg College, MN
Augustana College, SD
Austin College, TX
Baylor University, TX
Bloomsburg University of Pennsylvania, PA
Boise State University, ID
Bowling Green State University, OH
Brigham Young University, UT
Brigham Young University–Hawaii, HI
Butler University, IN
California State University, Chico, CA
Calvin College, MI
Carroll College, WI
Central College, IA
Central Washington University, WA
Chatham College, PA
City College of the City University of New York, NY
Clarion University of Pennsylvania, PA
Clemson University, SC
College of Staten Island of the City University of New York, NY
Colorado State University-Pueblo, CO
Columbia International University, SC
Columbus State University, GA
Culver-Stockton College, MO
DePauw University, IN
D'Youville College, NY
Elizabethtown College, PA
Emory & Henry College, VA
Fort Hays State University, KS
Frostburg State University, MD
Furman University, SC
Gannon University, PA
Georgia College & State University, GA
Grace University, NE
Hamline University, MN
Hampshire College, MA
Hillsdale College, MI
Idaho State University, ID
Illinois State University, IL
Indiana University of Pennsylvania, PA
Iowa State University of Science and Technology, IA

James Madison University, VA
Kennesaw State University, GA
Kent State University, OH
Keuka College, NY
Lambuth University, TN
Lawrence Technological University, MI
Lindenwood University, MO
Lock Haven University of Pennsylvania, PA
Loyola University Chicago, IL
Lycoming College, PA
Malone College, OH
Marymount College of Fordham University, NY
Marymount Manhattan College, NY
Mercer University, GA
Mercyhurst College, PA
Middle Tennessee State University, TN
Mississippi State University, MS
Murray State University, KY
New England College, NH
North Central College, IL
Northern Arizona University, AZ
Northern State University, SD
Northwestern Oklahoma State University, OK
Ohio Northern University, OH
The Ohio State University, OH
Ohio University, OH
Ohio University–Eastern, OH
Ohio Wesleyan University, OH
Oklahoma State University, OK
Ouachita Baptist University, AR
Pepperdine University, CA
Portland State University, OR
Post University, CT
Quincy University, IL
Rice University, TX
Rochester Institute of Technology, NY
St. Ambrose University, IA
St. Cloud State University, MN
St. Edward's University, TX
Saint Louis University, MO
South Dakota State University, SD
Southeast Missouri State University, MO
Southern Illinois University Carbondale, IL
Southern Methodist University, TX
State University of New York at Binghamton, NY
State University of New York at Oswego, NY
State University of New York at Plattsburgh, NY
State University of New York College at Brockport, NY
State University of New York College at Oneonta, NY
State University of New York, Fredonia, NY
Tennessee Technological University, TN
Tennessee Wesleyan College, TN
Texas Christian University, TX
Texas State University-San Marcos, TX
Texas Tech University, TX
Thomas University, GA
Tiffin University, OH
The University of Akron, OH

University of Colorado at Boulder, CO
University of Connecticut, CT
University of Delaware, DE
University of Evansville, IN
University of Illinois at Springfield, IL
University of Kansas, KS
University of Mary Hardin-Baylor, TX
University of Maryland, College Park, MD
The University of Memphis, TN
University of Michigan, MI
University of Michigan–Dearborn, MI
University of Michigan–Flint, MI
University of Minnesota, Twin Cities Campus, MN
University of Mississippi, MS
University of Missouri–St. Louis, MO
University of Nebraska–Lincoln, NE
University of Nevada, Las Vegas, NV
University of Nevada, Reno, NV
University of New England, ME
University of New Orleans, LA
The University of North Carolina at Wilmington, NC
University of North Dakota, ND
University of North Florida, FL
University of Oklahoma, OK
University of Puget Sound, WA
University of St. Thomas, MN
University of South Carolina, SC
University of South Florida, FL
The University of Texas at Arlington, TX
The University of Texas at El Paso, TX
The University of Toledo, OH
University of Tulsa, OK
University of Wisconsin–Eau Claire, WI
University of Wisconsin–Stevens Point, WI
University of Wisconsin–Stout, WI
University of Wyoming, WY
Utah State University, UT
Villanova University, PA
Virginia Military Institute, VA
Virginia Polytechnic Institute and State University, VA
Wake Forest University, NC
Wartburg College, IA
Washington State University, WA
Washington University in St. Louis, MO
Waynesburg College, PA
Webster University, MO
Western Oregon University, OR
Westminster College, UT
West Virginia University, WV
Wheeling Jesuit University, WV
Wichita State University, KS
Wilkes University, PA
Wilmington College, OH
Wilson College, PA

Library Science
Arkansas State University, AR
Brigham Young University–Hawaii, HI
Clarion University of Pennsylvania, PA
Emporia State University, KS
Fort Hays State University, KS
Illinois State University, IL

Iowa State University of Science and Technology, IA
Kent State University, OH
Kutztown University of Pennsylvania, PA
Lindenwood University, MO
Lock Haven University of Pennsylvania, PA
Louisiana Tech University, LA
Mississippi State University, MS
Murray State University, KY
Northeastern State University, OK
Northwestern Oklahoma State University, OK
Radford University, VA
Sam Houston State University, TX
The University of Alabama, AL
University of Kansas, KS
University of Maryland, College Park, MD
University of Michigan, MI
University of Minnesota, Twin Cities Campus, MN
The University of North Carolina at Greensboro, NC
University of South Carolina, SC
University of South Florida, FL
The University of Toledo, OH
Utah State University, UT
Valley City State University, ND
Western Kentucky University, KY
Western Washington University, WA
West Virginia University, WV

Mathematics
Abilene Christian University, TX
Albion College, MI
Alderson-Broaddus College, WV
Alfred University, NY
Angelo State University, TX
Antioch College, OH
Arizona State University, AZ
Arkansas State University, AR
Armstrong Atlantic State University, GA
Ashland University, OH
Athens State University, AL
Auburn University, AL
Augsburg College, MN
Augustana College, SD
Augusta State University, GA
Aurora University, IL
Averett University, VA
Ball State University, IN
Barton College, NC
Baylor University, TX
Belhaven College, MS
Bellevue University, NE
Benedictine University, IL
Black Hills State University, SD
Bloomsburg University of Pennsylvania, PA
Blue Mountain College, MS
Boise State University, ID
Bowie State University, MD
Bowling Green State University, OH
Brevard College, NC
Brewton-Parker College, GA
Brigham Young University, UT
Brigham Young University–Hawaii, HI
Bryan College, TN

Non-Need Scholarships for Undergraduates
Academic Interests/Achievements

Buena Vista University, IA
Butler University, IN
California Lutheran University, CA
California State University, Bakersfield, CA
California State University, Chico, CA
California State University, Fresno, CA
California State University, Fullerton, CA
California State University, San Marcos, CA
California State University, Stanislaus, CA
Calvin College, MI
Cameron University, OK
Carroll College, WI
Carson-Newman College, TN
Centenary College of Louisiana, LA
Central College, IA
Central Methodist University, MO
Central Michigan University, MI
Central Missouri State University, MO
Central Washington University, WA
Chatham College, PA
Christopher Newport University, VA
City College of the City University of New York, NY
Clarion University of Pennsylvania, PA
Clarkson University, NY
Clemson University, SC
Coastal Carolina University, SC
College of Charleston, SC
The College of New Rochelle, NY
The College of Saint Rose, NY
College of Staten Island of the City University of New York, NY
The College of Wooster, OH
The Colorado College, CO
Colorado School of Mines, CO
Colorado State University-Pueblo, CO
Columbia College, SC
Concordia University, NE
Concordia University, St. Paul, MN
Dakota State University, SD
Dallas Baptist University, TX
Davidson College, NC
Defiance College, OH
DePauw University, IN
DeSales University, PA
Dickinson State University, ND
Dordt College, IA
Duke University, NC
Eastern Mennonite University, VA
Eastern Michigan University, MI
Eastern Oregon University, OR
Eastern Washington University, WA
East Stroudsburg University of Pennsylvania, PA
East Tennessee State University, TN
East Texas Baptist University, TX
Edinboro University of Pennsylvania, PA
Elizabethtown College, PA
Elmhurst College, IL
Elon University, NC
Emmanuel College, MA
Emory & Henry College, VA
Emporia State University, KS
Erskine College, SC
Evangel University, MO

Fairmont State University, WV
Fort Hays State University, KS
Fort Lewis College, CO
Francis Marion University, SC
Franklin College, IN
Freed-Hardeman University, TN
Friends University, KS
Frostburg State University, MD
Furman University, SC
Gannon University, PA
The George Washington University, DC
Georgia College & State University, GA
Georgian Court University, NJ
Georgia Southern University, GA
Glenville State College, WV
Grambling State University, LA
Grand Canyon University, AZ
Greenville College, IL
Hamline University, MN
Heidelberg College, OH
Hillsdale College, MI
Howard Payne University, TX
Idaho State University, ID
Illinois State University, IL
Indiana University of Pennsylvania, PA
Indiana University–Purdue University Fort Wayne, IN
Iowa State University of Science and Technology, IA
Jacksonville State University, AL
James Madison University, VA
Johnson C. Smith University, NC
Kalamazoo College, MI
Kansas State University, KS
Kennesaw State University, GA
Kent State University, OH
Kettering University, MI
King's College, PA
Knox College, IL
Kutztown University of Pennsylvania, PA
Lake Erie College, OH
Lambuth University, TN
Lawrence Technological University, MI
Lewis-Clark State College, ID
Limestone College, SC
Lincoln University, PA
Lindenwood University, MO
Lock Haven University of Pennsylvania, PA
Longwood University, VA
Louisiana State University and Agricultural and Mechanical College, LA
Louisiana Tech University, LA
Loyola University Chicago, IL
Lycoming College, PA
Malone College, OH
Manhattan College, NY
Mercyhurst College, PA
Meredith College, NC
Mesa State College, CO
Metropolitan State College of Denver, CO
Michigan Technological University, MI
Middle Tennessee State University, TN
Midwestern State University, TX
Millersville University of Pennsylvania, PA
Milligan College, TN
Minnesota State University Mankato, MN

Minot State University, ND
Mississippi State University, MS
Mississippi University for Women, MS
Missouri State University, MO
Missouri Valley College, MO
Monmouth University, NJ
Montana State University, MT
Montana State University–Billings, MT
Montana Tech of The University of Montana, MT
Montclair State University, NJ
Morningside College, IA
Morris College, SC
Mount Mary College, WI
Mount Olive College, NC
Murray State University, KY
Muskingum College, OH
New England College, NH
New Jersey City University, NJ
New Mexico Highlands University, NM
New Mexico State University, NM
North Carolina State University, NC
North Central College, IL
North Dakota State University, ND
Northeastern Illinois University, IL
Northeastern State University, OK
Northern Arizona University, AZ
Northern State University, SD
Northwestern College, IA
Northwestern Oklahoma State University, OK
Northwestern State University of Louisiana, LA
Northwest Nazarene University, ID
Ohio Northern University, OH
The Ohio State University, OH
Ohio University, OH
Ohio University–Eastern, OH
Ohio Wesleyan University, OH
Oklahoma Panhandle State University, OK
Oklahoma State University, OK
Ouachita Baptist University, AR
Pacific University, OR
Peru State College, NE
Piedmont College, GA
Pittsburg State University, KS
Plymouth State University, NH
Purdue University, IN
Quincy University, IL
Radford University, VA
Randolph-Macon Woman's College, VA
Rensselaer Polytechnic Institute, NY
Rice University, TX
The Richard Stockton College of New Jersey, NJ
Ripon College, WI
Rochester College, MI
Rochester Institute of Technology, NY
Rockhurst University, MO
Rollins College, FL
St. Cloud State University, MN
St. Edward's University, TX
St. John Fisher College, NY
St. John's University, NY
Saint Louis University, MO
Saint Vincent College, PA

Salisbury University, MD
Sam Houston State University, TX
Schreiner University, TX
Seton Hill University, PA
Shaw University, NC
Shepherd University, WV
Skidmore College, NY
Sonoma State University, CA
South Dakota School of Mines and
  Technology, SD
South Dakota State University, SD
Southeastern Louisiana University, LA
Southeastern Oklahoma State
  University, OK
Southeast Missouri State University, MO
Southern Adventist University, TN
Southern Illinois University Carbondale, IL
Southern Methodist University, TX
Southern Oregon University, OR
Southern Wesleyan University, SC
Southwest Minnesota State University, MN
Spelman College, GA
State University of New York at
  Binghamton, NY
State University of New York at New
  Paltz, NY
State University of New York at
  Oswego, NY
State University of New York at
  Plattsburgh, NY
State University of New York College at
  Brockport, NY
State University of New York College at
  Geneseo, NY
State University of New York College at
  Potsdam, NY
State University of New York,
  Fredonia, NY
Stephen F. Austin State University, TX
Stetson University, FL
Stevens Institute of Technology, NJ
Susquehanna University, PA
Tabor College, KS
Tennessee Technological University, TN
Tennessee Wesleyan College, TN
Texas A&M University–Texarkana, TX
Texas Tech University, TX
Thiel College, PA
Truman State University, MO
Union University, TN
The University of Akron, OH
The University of Alabama, AL
The University of Alabama at
  Birmingham, AL
University of Alaska Anchorage, AK
University of Arkansas at Fort Smith, AR
University of Arkansas at Pine Bluff, AR
University of California, Riverside, CA
University of California, San Diego, CA
University of Cincinnati, OH
University of Colorado at Boulder, CO
University of Colorado at Colorado
  Springs, CO
University of Connecticut, CT
University of Dallas, TX
University of Delaware, DE

University of Evansville, IN
University of Great Falls, MT
University of Houston–Victoria, TX
University of Idaho, ID
University of Illinois at Springfield, IL
University of Kansas, KS
University of Maine, ME
The University of Maine at Augusta, ME
University of Maine at Fort Kent, ME
University of Mary Hardin-Baylor, TX
University of Maryland, Baltimore
  County, MD
University of Maryland, College Park, MD
University of Maryland Eastern Shore, MD
University of Mary Washington, VA
University of Massachusetts Amherst, MA
The University of Memphis, TN
University of Michigan, MI
University of Michigan–Dearborn, MI
University of Michigan–Flint, MI
University of Minnesota, Twin Cities
  Campus, MN
University of Missouri–Columbia, MO
University of Missouri–St. Louis, MO
University of Nebraska at Omaha, NE
University of Nebraska–Lincoln, NE
University of Nevada, Las Vegas, NV
University of Nevada, Reno, NV
University of New England, ME
University of New Hampshire, NH
University of New Orleans, LA
The University of North Carolina at
  Asheville, NC
The University of North Carolina at Chapel
  Hill, NC
The University of North Carolina at
  Charlotte, NC
The University of North Carolina at
  Greensboro, NC
The University of North Carolina at
  Wilmington, NC
University of North Dakota, ND
University of Northern Colorado, CO
University of Northern Iowa, IA
University of Oklahoma, OK
University of Pittsburgh at Bradford, PA
University of Portland, OR
University of Puget Sound, WA
University of Richmond, VA
University of Rio Grande, OH
University of Rochester, NY
University of St. Thomas, MN
University of St. Thomas, TX
University of Sioux Falls, SD
University of South Carolina, SC
The University of South Dakota, SD
University of Southern Indiana, IN
University of South Florida, FL
The University of Tennessee at Martin, TN
The University of Texas at Arlington, TX
The University of Texas at Brownsville, TX
The University of Texas at Dallas, TX
The University of Texas at El Paso, TX
The University of Texas at San
  Antonio, TX
The University of Texas–Pan American, TX

University of the Ozarks, AR
The University of Toledo, OH
University of Tulsa, OK
University of Utah, UT
University of Vermont, VT
The University of Virginia's College at
  Wise, VA
University of Washington, WA
University of West Georgia, GA
University of Wisconsin–Eau Claire, WI
University of Wisconsin–La Crosse, WI
University of Wisconsin–Oshkosh, WI
University of Wisconsin–Parkside, WI
University of Wisconsin–Stevens Point, WI
University of Wisconsin–Stout, WI
University of Wisconsin–Superior, WI
University of Wisconsin–Whitewater, WI
University of Wyoming, WY
Utah State University, UT
Valdosta State University, GA
Valley City State University, ND
Virginia Commonwealth University, VA
Virginia Military Institute, VA
Virginia Polytechnic Institute and State
  University, VA
Wake Forest University, NC
Wartburg College, IA
Washington State University, WA
Washington University in St. Louis, MO
Wayland Baptist University, TX
Waynesburg College, PA
Wayne State College, NE
Western Carolina University, NC
Western Illinois University, IL
Western Kentucky University, KY
Western Oregon University, OR
Western Washington University, WA
West Liberty State College, WV
Westminster College, UT
West Texas A&M University, TX
West Virginia University, WV
Wheeling Jesuit University, WV
Wichita State University, KS
Wilkes University, PA
Wilmington College, OH
Wilson College, PA
Winston-Salem State University, NC
Xavier University, OH
Xavier University of Louisiana, LA
York College, NE

Military Science
Alfred University, NY
Angelo State University, TX
Arizona State University, AZ
Arkansas State University, AR
Armstrong Atlantic State University, GA
Augusta State University, GA
Baylor University, TX
Black Hills State University, SD
Boise State University, ID
Bowie State University, MD
Bowling Green State University, OH
Brigham Young University, UT
California State University, Fullerton, CA
Cameron University, OK

Non-Need Scholarships for Undergraduates
Academic Interests/Achievements

Carson-Newman College, TN
Central Michigan University, MI
Central Missouri State University, MO
Central Washington University, WA
Christopher Newport University, VA
Clarkson University, NY
Clemson University, SC
College of Saint Benedict, MN
College of the Holy Cross, MA
Colorado School of Mines, CO
Columbus State University, GA
Creighton University, NE
DeSales University, PA
Dickinson College, PA
East Carolina University, NC
East Tennessee State University, TN
Edinboro University of Pennsylvania, PA
Elon University, NC
Florida Institute of Technology, FL
Furman University, SC
Georgia Southern University, GA
Grambling State University, LA
Grand Canyon University, AZ
Idaho State University, ID
Illinois State University, IL
Iowa State University of Science and
  Technology, IA
Jacksonville State University, AL
James Madison University, VA
Kansas State University, KS
Kent State University, OH
Lawrence Technological University, MI
Lehigh University, PA
Lincoln University, MO
Lindenwood University, MO
Louisiana State University and Agricultural
  and Mechanical College, LA
Louisiana Tech University, LA
Manhattan College, NY
Mercer University, GA
Michigan State University, MI
Middle Tennessee State University, TN
Mississippi State University, MS
Missouri State University, MO
Missouri Valley College, MO
Montana State University, MT
Morehouse College, GA
Morris College, SC
New Mexico State University, NM
North Carolina Agricultural and Technical
  State University, NC
North Dakota State University, ND
Northern Arizona University, AZ
Northern Michigan University, MI
North Greenville College, SC
Northwest Nazarene University, ID
The Ohio State University, OH
Ohio University, OH
Ohio University–Eastern, OH
Oklahoma State University, OK
Old Dominion University, VA
Pittsburg State University, KS
Providence College, RI
Purdue University, IN
Radford University, VA
Rensselaer Polytechnic Institute, NY

Ripon College, WI
Rochester Institute of Technology, NY
St. Edward's University, TX
St. John's University, NY
Saint Louis University, MO
St. Mary's University of San Antonio, TX
Sam Houston State University, TX
Seton Hall University, NJ
South Dakota State University, SD
Southeast Missouri State University, MO
Southern Illinois University Carbondale, IL
State University of New York College at
  Brockport, NY
Stephen F. Austin State University, TX
Stetson University, FL
Tennessee Technological University, TN
Texas Christian University, TX
Texas State University-San Marcos, TX
Texas Tech University, TX
Truman State University, MO
The University of Akron, OH
The University of Alabama, AL
The University of Arizona, AZ
University of Arkansas at Fort Smith, AR
University of Charleston, WV
University of Cincinnati, OH
University of Colorado at Boulder, CO
University of Colorado at Colorado
  Springs, CO
University of Delaware, DE
University of Florida, FL
University of Idaho, ID
University of Kansas, KS
University of Maine, ME
University of Maryland, College Park, MD
University of Massachusetts Amherst, MA
The University of Memphis, TN
University of Miami, FL
University of Michigan, MI
University of Minnesota, Twin Cities
  Campus, MN
University of Mississippi, MS
University of Nevada, Reno, NV
University of New Hampshire, NH
University of New Orleans, LA
The University of North Carolina at
  Charlotte, NC
University of North Dakota, ND
University of Northern Colorado, CO
University of Portland, OR
University of Puerto Rico, Mayagüez
  Campus, PR
University of San Francisco, CA
The University of Scranton, PA
University of South Carolina, SC
The University of South Dakota, SD
University of South Florida, FL
The University of Tampa, FL
The University of Tennessee at Martin, TN
The University of Texas at Arlington, TX
The University of Texas at El Paso, TX
The University of Texas–Pan American, TX
University of Vermont, VT
University of Wisconsin–La Crosse, WI
University of Wisconsin–Stevens Point, WI
University of Wyoming, WY

Valdosta State University, GA
Villanova University, PA
Virginia Commonwealth University, VA
Virginia Military Institute, VA
Virginia Polytechnic Institute and State
  University, VA
Wake Forest University, NC
Washington State University, WA
Washington University in St. Louis, MO
Western Kentucky University, KY
Westminster College, UT
West Virginia University, WV
Whitworth College, WA
Xavier University, OH
Youngstown State University, OH

Physical Sciences
Abilene Christian University, TX
Alaska Pacific University, AK
Alderson-Broaddus College, WV
Alfred University, NY
Angelo State University, TX
Antioch College, OH
Arizona State University, AZ
Arkansas State University, AR
Armstrong Atlantic State University, GA
Ashland University, OH
Athens State University, AL
Auburn University, AL
Augsburg College, MN
Augustana College, SD
Augusta State University, GA
Austin College, TX
Averett University, VA
Bard College, NY
Barton College, NC
Baylor University, TX
Benedictine University, IL
Black Hills State University, SD
Bloomsburg University of Pennsylvania, PA
Boise State University, ID
Bowling Green State University, OH
Brevard College, NC
Brigham Young University, UT
Brigham Young University–Hawaii, HI
Bryan College, TN
Bucknell University, PA
Butler University, IN
California Lutheran University, CA
California State University, Bakersfield, CA
California State University, Chico, CA
California State University, Stanislaus, CA
Calvin College, MI
Carroll College, WI
Centenary College of Louisiana, LA
Central College, IA
Central Methodist University, MO
Central Michigan University, MI
Central Missouri State University, MO
Central Washington University, WA
Chapman University, CA
Chatham College, PA
Clarion University of Pennsylvania, PA
Clarkson University, NY
Clemson University, SC
Coe College, IA

College of Charleston, SC
The College of New Jersey, NJ
The College of New Rochelle, NY
College of Staten Island of the City
  University of New York, NY
The College of Wooster, OH
The Colorado College, CO
Colorado School of Mines, CO
Columbia College, MO
Columbus State University, GA
Concordia University, NE
Concordia University, St. Paul, MN
Davidson College, NC
Davis & Elkins College, WV
Defiance College, OH
Denison University, OH
DePauw University, IN
DeSales University, PA
Dickinson State University, ND
Dominican University, IL
Dordt College, IA
Eastern Mennonite University, VA
Eastern Michigan University, MI
Eastern Oregon University, OR
Eastern Washington University, WA
East Stroudsburg University of
  Pennsylvania, PA
East Texas Baptist University, TX
Edinboro University of Pennsylvania, PA
Elizabethtown College, PA
Elmhurst College, IL
Elon University, NC
Emmanuel College, MA
Emory & Henry College, VA
Emporia State University, KS
Evangel University, MO
Fairfield University, CT
Fairmont State University, WV
Florida Atlantic University, FL
Florida Southern College, FL
Fort Hays State University, KS
Fort Lewis College, CO
Framingham State College, MA
Freed-Hardeman University, TN
Friends University, KS
Frostburg State University, MD
Furman University, SC
Georgia College & State University, GA
Georgia Institute of Technology, GA
Georgian Court University, NJ
Graceland University, IA
Grambling State University, LA
Grand Canyon University, AZ
Greenville College, IL
Grove City College, PA
Hamline University, MN
Hampshire College, MA
Heidelberg College, OH
Heritage University, WA
Hillsdale College, MI
Howard Payne University, TX
Idaho State University, ID
Illinois State University, IL
Indiana University of Pennsylvania, PA
Indiana University–Purdue University Fort
  Wayne, IN

Iowa State University of Science and
  Technology, IA
Jacksonville State University, AL
James Madison University, VA
Jamestown College, ND
Kalamazoo College, MI
Kansas State University, KS
Kennesaw State University, GA
Kent State University, OH
Kettering University, MI
King's College, PA
Kutztown University of Pennsylvania, PA
LaGrange College, GA
Lake Erie College, OH
Lake Forest College, IL
Lambuth University, TN
Lawrence Technological University, MI
Limestone College, SC
Lincoln University, PA
Lindenwood University, MO
Lock Haven University of Pennsylvania, PA
Loras College, IA
Louisiana State University and Agricultural
  and Mechanical College, LA
Louisiana Tech University, LA
Loyola University Chicago, IL
Lubbock Christian University, TX
Lycoming College, PA
MacMurray College, IL
Malone College, OH
Mercyhurst College, PA
Mesa State College, CO
Metropolitan State College of Denver, CO
Michigan Technological University, MI
Middle Tennessee State University, TN
Millersville University of Pennsylvania, PA
Minnesota State University Mankato, MN
Mississippi State University, MS
Mississippi University for Women, MS
Missouri State University, MO
Missouri Valley College, MO
Montana State University, MT
Montana State University–Billings, MT
Montana Tech of The University of
  Montana, MT
Montclair State University, NJ
Moravian College, PA
Morehead State University, KY
Morningside College, IA
Morris College, SC
Mount Mary College, WI
Muskingum College, OH
New Mexico Highlands University, NM
New Mexico Institute of Mining and
  Technology, NM
New Mexico State University, NM
North Carolina State University, NC
North Central College, IL
North Dakota State University, ND
Northeastern Illinois University, IL
Northeastern State University, OK
Northern Arizona University, AZ
Northern State University, SD
Northwestern College, IA
Northwestern Oklahoma State
  University, OK

Northwestern State University of
  Louisiana, LA
Northwest Nazarene University, ID
Oberlin College, OH
Ohio Northern University, OH
The Ohio State University, OH
Ohio University, OH
Ohio University–Eastern, OH
Ohio Wesleyan University, OH
Oklahoma Panhandle State University, OK
Oklahoma State University, OK
Old Dominion University, VA
Ouachita Baptist University, AR
Pacific University, OR
Peru State College, NE
Pittsburg State University, KS
Plymouth State University, NH
Portland State University, OR
Purdue University, IN
Radford University, VA
Randolph-Macon Woman's College, VA
Regis University, CO
Rice University, TX
The Richard Stockton College of New
  Jersey, NJ
Ripon College, WI
Rochester Institute of Technology, NY
Rockhurst University, MO
Rollins College, FL
St. Cloud State University, MN
St. Edward's University, TX
St. John Fisher College, NY
Saint Louis University, MO
Saint Vincent College, PA
Salisbury University, MD
Sam Houston State University, TX
Schreiner University, TX
Seton Hall University, NJ
Seton Hill University, PA
Shaw University, NC
Shepherd University, WV
Skidmore College, NY
Slippery Rock University of
  Pennsylvania, PA
Sonoma State University, CA
South Dakota State University, SD
Southeastern Oklahoma State
  University, OK
Southeast Missouri State University, MO
Southern Illinois University Carbondale, IL
Southern Methodist University, TX
Southern Oregon University, OR
Southern Wesleyan University, SC
Southwest Minnesota State University, MN
Spelman College, GA
State University of New York at
  Binghamton, NY
State University of New York at New
  Paltz, NY
State University of New York at
  Oswego, NY
State University of New York at
  Plattsburgh, NY
State University of New York College at
  Brockport, NY

State University of New York College at
 Geneseo, NY
State University of New York College at
 Old Westbury, NY
State University of New York College at
 Oneonta, NY
State University of New York College at
 Potsdam, NY
State University of New York College of
 Environmental Science and Forestry, NY
State University of New York,
 Fredonia, NY
Stephen F. Austin State University, TX
Stetson University, FL
Stevens Institute of Technology, NJ
Stony Brook University, State University of
 New York, NY
Susquehanna University, PA
Tennessee Technological University, TN
Tennessee Wesleyan College, TN
Texas A&M University, TX
Texas Tech University, TX
Thiel College, PA
Thomas University, GA
Trevecca Nazarene University, TN
Truman State University, MO
The University of Akron, OH
The University of Alabama, AL
The University of Alabama in
 Huntsville, AL
The University of Arizona, AZ
University of California, Riverside, CA
University of California, San Diego, CA
University of Cincinnati, OH
University of Colorado at Boulder, CO
University of Colorado at Colorado
 Springs, CO
University of Connecticut, CT
University of Dallas, TX
University of Delaware, DE
University of Evansville, IN
University of Great Falls, MT
University of Idaho, ID
University of Indianapolis, IN
University of Kansas, KS
University of Maine, ME
University of Mary Hardin-Baylor, TX
University of Maryland, Baltimore
 County, MD
University of Maryland, College Park, MD
University of Maryland Eastern Shore, MD
University of Mary Washington, VA
University of Massachusetts Amherst, MA
The University of Memphis, TN
University of Michigan, MI
University of Michigan–Dearborn, MI
University of Michigan–Flint, MI
University of Minnesota, Twin Cities
 Campus, MN
University of Nebraska at Omaha, NE
University of Nebraska–Lincoln, NE
University of Nevada, Las Vegas, NV
University of Nevada, Reno, NV
University of New England, ME
University of New Orleans, LA

The University of North Carolina at
 Asheville, NC
The University of North Carolina at
 Greensboro, NC
The University of North Carolina at
 Pembroke, NC
The University of North Carolina at
 Wilmington, NC
University of North Dakota, ND
University of Northern Colorado, CO
University of Northern Iowa, IA
University of Oklahoma, OK
University of Oregon, OR
University of Pittsburgh at Bradford, PA
University of Portland, OR
University of Puget Sound, WA
University of Richmond, VA
University of Rio Grande, OH
University of Rochester, NY
University of Saint Francis, IN
University of St. Thomas, MN
University of St. Thomas, TX
University of Sioux Falls, SD
University of South Carolina, SC
University of South Florida, FL
The University of Tennessee at Martin, TN
The University of Texas at Arlington, TX
The University of Texas at Dallas, TX
The University of Texas at El Paso, TX
The University of Texas at San
 Antonio, TX
The University of Toledo, OH
University of Utah, UT
The University of Virginia's College at
 Wise, VA
University of Washington, WA
University of West Georgia, GA
University of Wisconsin–Eau Claire, WI
University of Wisconsin–Green Bay, WI
University of Wisconsin–La Crosse, WI
University of Wisconsin–Oshkosh, WI
University of Wisconsin–Parkside, WI
University of Wisconsin–Stevens Point, WI
University of Wisconsin–Stout, WI
University of Wisconsin–Superior, WI
University of Wisconsin–Whitewater, WI
University of Wyoming, WY
Utah State University, UT
Valdosta State University, GA
Valley City State University, ND
Valparaiso University, IN
Virginia Polytechnic Institute and State
 University, VA
Wake Forest University, NC
Wartburg College, IA
Washington State University, WA
Washington University in St. Louis, MO
Wayland Baptist University, TX
Wayne State College, NE
Western Illinois University, IL
Western Kentucky University, KY
Western Oregon University, OR
Western Washington University, WA
West Liberty State College, WV
Westminster College, UT
West Texas A&M University, TX

West Virginia University, WV
Wheaton College, IL
Wheeling Jesuit University, WV
Whitworth College, WA
Wichita State University, KS
Wilmington College, OH
Wilson College, PA
Xavier University, OH
Xavier University of Louisiana, LA

Premedicine
Albion College, MI
Alderson-Broaddus College, WV
Alfred University, NY
Angelo State University, TX
Arizona State University, AZ
Arkansas State University, AR
Auburn University, AL
Augustana College, SD
Austin College, TX
Averett University, VA
Baylor University, TX
Belhaven College, MS
Blue Mountain College, MS
Boise State University, ID
Brevard College, NC
Brigham Young University, UT
Bryan College, TN
California State University, Stanislaus, CA
Calvin College, MI
Carroll College, WI
Centenary College of Louisiana, LA
Central Methodist University, MO
Central Missouri State University, MO
Central Washington University, WA
Chatham College, PA
City College of the City University of New
 York, NY
Clarion University of Pennsylvania, PA
Clearwater Christian College, FL
Clemson University, SC
Coe College, IA
College of Charleston, SC
The College of New Rochelle, NY
The College of Saint Rose, NY
College of Staten Island of the City
 University of New York, NY
Colorado State University-Pueblo, CO
Concordia University, NE
Dallas Baptist University, TX
Davidson College, NC
Defiance College, OH
DeSales University, PA
Dickinson State University, ND
Dordt College, IA
D'Youville College, NY
Eastern Mennonite University, VA
Edinboro University of Pennsylvania, PA
Elizabethtown College, PA
Elmhurst College, IL
Elon University, NC
Emory & Henry College, VA
Emporia State University, KS
Erskine College, SC
Evangel University, MO
Fort Hays State University, KS

Francis Marion University, SC
Freed-Hardeman University, TN
Friends University, KS
Frostburg State University, MD
Furman University, SC
Gannon University, PA
Grambling State University, LA
Grand Canyon University, AZ
Hamline University, MN
Hampden-Sydney College, VA
Hillsdale College, MI
Howard Payne University, TX
Idaho State University, ID
Illinois State University, IL
Indiana University of Pennsylvania, PA
Indiana University–Purdue University Fort Wayne, IN
Iowa State University of Science and Technology, IA
James Madison University, VA
Juniata College, PA
Kansas State University, KS
Kennesaw State University, GA
King's College, PA
Lambuth University, TN
Lindenwood University, MO
Louisiana State University and Agricultural and Mechanical College, LA
Loyola University Chicago, IL
Lycoming College, PA
Malone College, OH
Marymount Manhattan College, NY
Mercyhurst College, PA
Michigan Technological University, MI
Middle Tennessee State University, TN
Midway College, KY
Mississippi State University, MS
Missouri State University, MO
Missouri Valley College, MO
Montana State University–Billings, MT
Morningside College, IA
Morris College, SC
Muskingum College, OH
North Central College, IL
North Dakota State University, ND
Northeastern State University, OK
Northern Arizona University, AZ
Northern Michigan University, MI
Northwestern College, IA
Northwestern Oklahoma State University, OK
Northwest Nazarene University, ID
Ohio Northern University, OH
The Ohio State University, OH
Ohio University, OH
Ohio University–Eastern, OH
Ohio Wesleyan University, OH
Oklahoma State University, OK
Ouachita Baptist University, AR
Peru State College, NE
Piedmont College, GA
Providence College, RI
Quincy University, IL
Radford University, VA
Randolph-Macon College, VA
Randolph-Macon Woman's College, VA

Ripon College, WI
Rochester Institute of Technology, NY
Rockhurst University, MO
Saint Louis University, MO
Salisbury University, MD
Seton Hall University, NJ
Seton Hill University, PA
Shepherd University, WV
Sonoma State University, CA
South Dakota State University, SD
Southeast Missouri State University, MO
Southern Illinois University Carbondale, IL
Southern Wesleyan University, SC
State University of New York at Binghamton, NY
State University of New York at New Paltz, NY
State University of New York at Oswego, NY
State University of New York at Plattsburgh, NY
State University of New York College at Geneseo, NY
State University of New York College at Oneonta, NY
State University of New York College of Environmental Science and Forestry, NY
Stephen F. Austin State University, TX
Stetson University, FL
Stevens Institute of Technology, NJ
Susquehanna University, PA
Sweet Briar College, VA
Tabor College, KS
Tennessee Technological University, TN
Tennessee Wesleyan College, TN
Texas Christian University, TX
Texas Tech University, TX
Truman State University, MO
Union University, TN
The University of Akron, OH
The University of Alabama, AL
University of California, Riverside, CA
University of California, San Diego, CA
University of Cincinnati, OH
University of Colorado at Boulder, CO
University of Colorado at Colorado Springs, CO
University of Connecticut, CT
University of Delaware, DE
University of Evansville, IN
University of Great Falls, MT
University of Hartford, CT
University of Idaho, ID
University of Kansas, KS
University of Mary Hardin-Baylor, TX
University of Maryland, College Park, MD
University of Massachusetts Amherst, MA
The University of Memphis, TN
University of Michigan, MI
University of Michigan–Flint, MI
University of Minnesota, Twin Cities Campus, MN
University of Missouri–Columbia, MO
University of Nebraska at Omaha, NE
University of Nebraska–Lincoln, NE
University of Nevada, Las Vegas, NV

University of Nevada, Reno, NV
University of New England, ME
The University of North Carolina at Asheville, NC
The University of North Carolina at Greensboro, NC
University of North Dakota, ND
University of Portland, OR
University of Puget Sound, WA
University of Sioux Falls, SD
University of South Carolina, SC
The University of South Dakota, SD
University of Southern Indiana, IN
University of South Florida, FL
The University of Tennessee at Martin, TN
The University of Texas–Pan American, TX
University of the Ozarks, AR
The University of Toledo, OH
University of Tulsa, OK
The University of Virginia's College at Wise, VA
University of Wisconsin–Eau Claire, WI
University of Wisconsin–Parkside, WI
University of Wisconsin–Stevens Point, WI
University of Wisconsin–Whitewater, WI
Utah State University, UT
Valdosta State University, GA
Virginia Military Institute, VA
Virginia Polytechnic Institute and State University, VA
Wake Forest University, NC
Washington State University, WA
Washington University in St. Louis, MO
Wayne State College, NE
Western Kentucky University, KY
Western Washington University, WA
Westminster College, UT
West Virginia University, WV
Wheaton College, IL
Wheeling Jesuit University, WV
Wichita State University, KS
Wilkes University, PA
Wilmington College, OH
Wilson College, PA
Worcester Polytechnic Institute, MA
Xavier University of Louisiana, LA
York College, NE

Religion/Biblical Studies
Abilene Christian University, TX
Alderson-Broaddus College, WV
Appalachian Bible College, WV
Athens State University, AL
Augsburg College, MN
Augustana College, SD
Austin College, TX
Austin Graduate School of Theology, TX
Averett University, VA
Azusa Pacific University, CA
The Baptist College of Florida, FL
Barton College, NC
Baylor University, TX
Belhaven College, MS
Belmont University, TN
Berry College, GA
Bethel College, TN

Non-Need Scholarships for Undergraduates
Academic Interests/Achievements

Beulah Heights Bible College, GA
Bloomsburg University of Pennsylvania, PA
Blue Mountain College, MS
Brewton-Parker College, GA
Brigham Young University, UT
Brigham Young University–Hawaii, HI
Bryan College, TN
California Baptist University, CA
California Lutheran University, CA
Calvin College, MI
Campbellsville University, KY
Carson-Newman College, TN
Centenary College of Louisiana, LA
Central Christian College of Kansas, KS
Central College, IA
Central Methodist University, MO
Clearwater Christian College, FL
The College of New Rochelle, NY
Columbia College, MO
Columbia College, SC
Columbia International University, SC
Concordia University, CA
Concordia University, MI
Concordia University, NE
Concordia University, OR
Concordia University, St. Paul, MN
Cornerstone University, MI
Dallas Baptist University, TX
Dallas Christian College, TX
Davis & Elkins College, WV
Defiance College, OH
DeSales University, PA
Dordt College, IA
Eastern Mennonite University, VA
Eastern Michigan University, MI
East Texas Baptist University, TX
Edinboro University of Pennsylvania, PA
Elizabethtown College, PA
Elmhurst College, IL
Elon University, NC
Emmanuel College, MA
Emory & Henry College, VA
Erskine College, SC
Eugene Bible College, OR
Evangel University, MO
Faulkner University, AL
Flagler College, FL
Florida Southern College, FL
Freed-Hardeman University, TN
Fresno Pacific University, CA
Friends University, KS
Furman University, SC
Gannon University, PA
Geneva College, PA
Grace University, NE
Grand Canyon University, AZ
Greenville College, IL
Grove City College, PA
Hamline University, MN
Hampden-Sydney College, VA
Hannibal-LaGrange College, MO
Hastings College, NE
Hillsdale College, MI
Houston Baptist University, TX
Howard Payne University, TX
Idaho State University, ID

James Madison University, VA
Johnson Bible College, TN
John Wesley College, NC
Kentucky Christian University, KY
King's College, PA
LaGrange College, GA
Lakeland College, WI
Lambuth University, TN
Laura and Alvin Siegal College of Judaic
  Studies, OH
Lee University, TN
Limestone College, SC
Lipscomb University, TN
Lubbock Christian University, TX
Lycoming College, PA
MacMurray College, IL
Magnolia Bible College, MS
Malone College, OH
Manhattan Christian College, KS
Maranatha Baptist Bible College, WI
Martin Methodist College, TN
McKendree College, IL
McMurry University, TX
Mercer University, GA
Meredith College, NC
Messenger College, MO
Mid-Continent University, KY
Milligan College, TN
Mississippi State University, MS
Missouri Baptist University, MO
Missouri State University, MO
Montclair State University, NJ
Morningside College, IA
Morris College, SC
Mount Vernon Nazarene University, OH
Multnomah Bible College and Biblical
  Seminary, OR
Nazarene Bible College, CO
North Central College, IL
Northern Arizona University, AZ
North Greenville College, SC
Northwestern College, IA
Northwest Nazarene University, ID
Ohio Northern University, OH
Ohio Valley University, WV
Ohio Wesleyan University, OH
Oklahoma Baptist University, OK
Oklahoma City University, OK
Oklahoma Wesleyan University, OK
Oral Roberts University, OK
Ouachita Baptist University, AR
Pepperdine University, CA
Piedmont College, GA
Quincy University, IL
Ripon College, WI
Roanoke Bible College, NC
Rochester College, MI
Rockhurst University, MO
St. Edward's University, TX
Saint Louis University, MO
Schreiner University, TX
Seton Hill University, PA
Shorter College, GA
Southeastern College of the Assemblies of
  God, FL
Southeast Missouri State University, MO

Southern Adventist University, TN
Southern Illinois University Carbondale, IL
Southern Methodist College, SC
Southern Methodist University, TX
Southern Wesleyan University, SC
Southwestern Christian University, OK
Southwestern College, KS
Stetson University, FL
Tabor College, KS
Tennessee Wesleyan College, TN
Texas Christian University, TX
Thiel College, PA
Toccoa Falls College, GA
Trevecca Nazarene University, TN
Trinity College of Florida, FL
Trinity Lutheran College, WA
Union University, TN
The University of Arizona, AZ
University of Connecticut, CT
University of Dallas, TX
University of Delaware, DE
University of Evansville, IN
University of Great Falls, MT
University of Indianapolis, IN
University of Kansas, KS
University of Mary Hardin-Baylor, TX
University of Mary Washington, VA
University of Minnesota, Twin Cities
  Campus, MN
University of Missouri–Columbia, MO
The University of North Carolina at
  Greensboro, NC
The University of North Carolina at
  Wilmington, NC
University of Portland, OR
University of St. Thomas, MN
University of Sioux Falls, SD
University of South Carolina, SC
University of South Florida, FL
University of the Ozarks, AR
University of Tulsa, OK
Valparaiso University, IN
Virginia Polytechnic Institute and State
  University, VA
Wake Forest University, NC
Warner Pacific College, OR
Wartburg College, IA
Washington University in St. Louis, MO
Wayland Baptist University, TX
Waynesburg College, PA
Western Kentucky University, KY
West Virginia University, WV
Wheeling Jesuit University, WV
Williams Baptist College, AR
Wilmington College, OH
Wilson College, PA
York College, NE

Social Sciences
Abilene Christian University, TX
Alaska Pacific University, AK
Alderson-Broaddus College, WV
Alfred University, NY
Alliant International University, CA
Angelo State University, TX
Antioch College, OH

Arizona State University, AZ
Arkansas State University, AR
Ashland University, OH
Athens State University, AL
Auburn University, AL
Augsburg College, MN
Augustana College, SD
Augusta State University, GA
Austin College, TX
Ball State University, IN
Barton College, NC
Baylor University, TX
Belhaven College, MS
Bellevue University, NE
Black Hills State University, SD
Bloomsburg University of Pennsylvania, PA
Blue Mountain College, MS
Boise State University, ID
Bowling Green State University, OH
Brevard College, NC
Brigham Young University, UT
Brigham Young University–Hawaii, HI
Bryan College, TN
Butler University, IN
California Lutheran University, CA
California State University, Bakersfield, CA
California State University, Chico, CA
California State University, Fresno, CA
California State University, Fullerton, CA
California State University, Stanislaus, CA
Calvin College, MI
Cameron University, OK
Carroll College, WI
Centenary College of Louisiana, LA
Central Methodist University, MO
Central Michigan University, MI
Central Missouri State University, MO
Chatham College, PA
City College of the City University of New York, NY
Clarion University of Pennsylvania, PA
Clemson University, SC
College Misericordia, PA
College of Charleston, SC
The College of New Rochelle, NY
The College of Saint Rose, NY
The College of Wooster, OH
Colorado State University-Pueblo, CO
Columbia College, MO
Concordia University, NE
Concordia University, St. Paul, MN
Daniel Webster College, NH
Defiance College, OH
DeSales University, PA
Dickinson State University, ND
Dordt College, IA
D'Youville College, NY
Eastern Mennonite University, VA
Eastern Michigan University, MI
Eastern Washington University, WA
East Stroudsburg University of Pennsylvania, PA
East Tennessee State University, TN
Edinboro University of Pennsylvania, PA
Elizabethtown College, PA
Elon University, NC

Emmanuel College, MA
Emporia State University, KS
Erskine College, SC
Evangel University, MO
Fairmont State University, WV
Flagler College, FL
Florida Atlantic University, FL
Florida Gulf Coast University, FL
Florida Southern College, FL
Fort Hays State University, KS
Fort Lewis College, CO
Francis Marion University, SC
Fresno Pacific University, CA
Friends University, KS
Frostburg State University, MD
Furman University, SC
Georgia College & State University, GA
Georgia Southern University, GA
Grambling State University, LA
Grand Canyon University, AZ
Grove City College, PA
Hamline University, MN
Hampshire College, MA
Hawai'i Pacific University, HI
Heritage University, WA
Howard Payne University, TX
Idaho State University, ID
Illinois State University, IL
Indiana University of Pennsylvania, PA
Indiana University–Purdue University Fort Wayne, IN
Iowa State University of Science and Technology, IA
Jacksonville State University, AL
James Madison University, VA
Kalamazoo College, MI
Kansas State University, KS
Kennesaw State University, GA
Kent State University, OH
King's College, PA
LaGrange College, GA
Lake Erie College, OH
Lambuth University, TN
Lewis-Clark State College, ID
Limestone College, SC
Lincoln University, PA
Lindenwood University, MO
Lock Haven University of Pennsylvania, PA
Longwood University, VA
Louisiana Tech University, LA
Loyola University Chicago, IL
Lubbock Christian University, TX
Lycoming College, PA
MacMurray College, IL
Malone College, OH
Marymount Manhattan College, NY
Mercyhurst College, PA
Mesa State College, CO
Metropolitan State College of Denver, CO
Michigan State University, MI
Michigan Technological University, MI
Mid-Continent University, KY
Middle Tennessee State University, TN
Midwestern State University, TX
Millersville University of Pennsylvania, PA
Minot State University, ND

Mississippi State University, MS
Missouri State University, MO
Missouri Valley College, MO
Montana State University, MT
Montana State University–Billings, MT
Montclair State University, NJ
Morehead State University, KY
Morningside College, IA
Mount Mary College, WI
New England College, NH
New Mexico Highlands University, NM
New Mexico State University, NM
North Carolina State University, NC
North Central College, IL
North Dakota State University, ND
Northeastern Illinois University, IL
Northeastern State University, OK
Northern Arizona University, AZ
Northern State University, SD
Northwestern College, IA
Northwestern Oklahoma State University, OK
Northwest Nazarene University, ID
Oglala Lakota College, SD
Ohio Northern University, OH
The Ohio State University, OH
Ohio University, OH
Ohio University–Eastern, OH
Ohio Wesleyan University, OH
Oklahoma State University, OK
Ouachita Baptist University, AR
Pacific University, OR
Pepperdine University, CA
Peru State College, NE
Pittsburg State University, KS
Plymouth State University, NH
Portland State University, OR
Quincy University, IL
Radford University, VA
Randolph-Macon Woman's College, VA
Rice University, TX
The Richard Stockton College of New Jersey, NJ
Ripon College, WI
Rochester Institute of Technology, NY
Rockhurst University, MO
St. Augustine College, IL
St. Cloud State University, MN
St. Edward's University, TX
Saint Louis University, MO
Saint Vincent College, PA
Salisbury University, MD
Sam Houston State University, TX
Schreiner University, TX
Seton Hill University, PA
Shepherd University, WV
Shippensburg University of Pennsylvania, PA
Simon's Rock College of Bard, MA
Slippery Rock University of Pennsylvania, PA
Sonoma State University, CA
South Dakota State University, SD
Southeastern Louisiana University, LA
Southeastern Oklahoma State University, OK

Southeast Missouri State University, MO
Southern Illinois University Carbondale, IL
Southern Methodist University, TX
Southern Oregon University, OR
Southern Wesleyan University, SC
Southwestern College, KS
Southwest Minnesota State University, MN
State University of New York at
  Oswego, NY
State University of New York at
  Plattsburgh, NY
State University of New York College at
  Brockport, NY
State University of New York College at
  Geneseo, NY
State University of New York College at
  Potsdam, NY
State University of New York,
  Fredonia, NY
Stetson University, FL
Stony Brook University, State University of
  New York, NY
Tabor College, KS
Tennessee Technological University, TN
Tennessee Wesleyan College, TN
Texas A&M University–Texarkana, TX
Texas Tech University, TX
Thomas University, GA
Trevecca Nazarene University, TN
Truman State University, MO
The University of Akron, OH
The University of Alabama, AL
The University of Alabama in
  Huntsville, AL
University of Alaska Anchorage, AK
University of Alaska Southeast, AK
University of Arkansas at Fort Smith, AR
University of California, Riverside, CA
University of California, San Diego, CA
University of Cincinnati, OH
University of Colorado at Boulder, CO
University of Connecticut, CT
University of Delaware, DE
University of Evansville, IN
University of Great Falls, MT
University of Hawaii at Hilo, HI
University of Houston–Victoria, TX
University of Idaho, ID
University of Illinois at Springfield, IL
University of Kansas, KS
University of Maine, ME
University of Maine at Fort Kent, ME
University of Mary Hardin-Baylor, TX
University of Maryland, College Park, MD
University of Maryland Eastern Shore, MD
University of Mary Washington, VA
University of Massachusetts Amherst, MA
The University of Memphis, TN
University of Michigan, MI
University of Michigan–Dearborn, MI
University of Michigan–Flint, MI
University of Minnesota, Twin Cities
  Campus, MN
University of Missouri–Columbia, MO
The University of Montana–Western, MT
University of Nebraska at Omaha, NE

University of Nebraska–Lincoln, NE
University of Nevada, Las Vegas, NV
University of Nevada, Reno, NV
University of New England, ME
The University of North Carolina at
  Asheville, NC
The University of North Carolina at
  Greensboro, NC
The University of North Carolina at
  Wilmington, NC
University of North Dakota, ND
University of Northern Colorado, CO
University of Northern Iowa, IA
University of Oklahoma, OK
University of Oregon, OR
University of Phoenix–Cleveland
  Campus, OH
University of Phoenix–Dallas Campus, TX
University of Phoenix–Fort Lauderdale
  Campus, FL
University of Phoenix–Houston
  Campus, TX
University of Phoenix–Jacksonville
  Campus, FL
University of Phoenix–Louisiana
  Campus, LA
University of Phoenix–Metro Detroit
  Campus, MI
University of Phoenix–Nevada Campus, NV
University of Phoenix–New Mexico
  Campus, NM
University of Phoenix–Northern California
  Campus, CA
University of Phoenix–Oklahoma City
  Campus, OK
University of Phoenix Online Campus, AZ
University of Phoenix–Oregon Campus, OR
University of Phoenix–Orlando Campus, FL
University of Phoenix–Phoenix
  Campus, AZ
University of Phoenix–Puerto Rico
  Campus, PR
University of Phoenix–Sacramento
  Campus, CA
University of Phoenix–San Diego
  Campus, CA
University of Phoenix–Southern Colorado
  Campus, CO
University of Phoenix–Tampa Campus, FL
University of Phoenix–Tulsa Campus, OK
University of Phoenix–Utah Campus, UT
University of Phoenix–Washington
  Campus, WA
University of Phoenix–West Michigan
  Campus, MI
University of Pittsburgh at Bradford, PA
University of Portland, OR
University of Puget Sound, WA
University of Rio Grande, OH
University of Rochester, NY
University of St. Francis, IL
University of St. Thomas, MN
University of St. Thomas, TX
University of Sioux Falls, SD
University of South Carolina, SC
The University of South Dakota, SD

University of Southern Indiana, IN
University of South Florida, FL
The University of Tampa, FL
The University of Tennessee at Martin, TN
The University of Texas at Arlington, TX
The University of Texas at San
  Antonio, TX
The University of Texas–Pan American, TX
University of the Ozarks, AR
The University of Toledo, OH
University of Tulsa, OK
University of Utah, UT
The University of Virginia's College at
  Wise, VA
University of Washington, WA
University of West Georgia, GA
University of Wisconsin–Eau Claire, WI
University of Wisconsin–Green Bay, WI
University of Wisconsin–La Crosse, WI
University of Wisconsin–Stevens Point, WI
University of Wisconsin–Superior, WI
University of Wisconsin–Whitewater, WI
University of Wyoming, WY
Utah State University, UT
Valdosta State University, GA
Valley City State University, ND
Virginia Polytechnic Institute and State
  University, VA
Walla Walla College, WA
Washington State University, WA
Washington University in St. Louis, MO
Wayland Baptist University, TX
Wayne State College, NE
Western Carolina University, NC
Western Illinois University, IL
Western Kentucky University, KY
Western Oregon University, OR
Western Washington University, WA
Westminster College, UT
West Texas A&M University, TX
West Virginia University, WV
Wheeling Jesuit University, WV
Wichita State University, KS
Wilkes University, PA
Wilson College, PA
Xavier University, OH
Xavier University of Louisiana, LA

Creative Arts/Performance

Applied Art and Design
Arcadia University, PA
Arizona State University, AZ
Art Academy of Cincinnati, OH
The Art Institute of Colorado, CO
The Art Institute of Portland, OR
Auburn University, AL
Barry University, FL
Belhaven College, MS
Bowie State University, MD
Brenau University, GA
Brigham Young University, UT
California College of the Arts, CA
California Institute of the Arts, CA
California State University, Chico, CA
Castleton State College, VT

Central Michigan University, MI
Central Missouri State University, MO
Central Washington University, WA
Chester College of New England, NH
City College of the City University of New York, NY
Clemson University, SC
College for Creative Studies, MI
The College of New Rochelle, NY
Colorado State University-Pueblo, CO
Columbia College, MO
Columbia College, SC
Columbia College Chicago, IL
Concordia University, CA
Converse College, SC
Corcoran College of Art and Design, DC
East Carolina University, NC
Eastern Michigan University, MI
East Stroudsburg University of Pennsylvania, PA
The Evergreen State College, WA
Fashion Institute of Technology, NY
Flagler College, FL
Fort Hays State University, KS
Friends University, KS
Georgia State University, GA
Graceland University, IA
Grand Canyon University, AZ
Greenville College, IL
Illinois State University, IL
Indiana University of Pennsylvania, PA
Iowa State University of Science and Technology, IA
Keene State College, NH
Kutztown University of Pennsylvania, PA
LaGrange College, GA
Laguna College of Art & Design, CA
La Roche College, PA
Lindenwood University, MO
Louisiana State University and Agricultural and Mechanical College, LA
Marshall University, WV
Massachusetts College of Art, MA
Memphis College of Art, TN
Mercyhurst College, PA
Meredith College, NC
Minnesota State University Mankato, MN
Mississippi College, MS
Mississippi State University, MS
Missouri State University, MO
Mount Ida College, MA
Mount Mary College, WI
Murray State University, KY
New England College, NH
New Mexico State University, NM
North Carolina School of the Arts, NC
Northeastern State University, OK
Northern Illinois University, IL
Northern Michigan University, MI
Northwest College of Art, WA
Ohio Northern University, OH
Ohio University, OH
Ohio University–Eastern, OH
Oklahoma City University, OK
Oral Roberts University, OK
Otis College of Art and Design, CA

Radford University, VA
Rhode Island School of Design, RI
Rice University, TX
The Richard Stockton College of New Jersey, NJ
Ringling School of Art and Design, FL
Robert Morris College, IL
Rochester Institute of Technology, NY
Rocky Mountain College of Art & Design, CO
St. Cloud State University, MN
Salem State College, MA
Seton Hill University, PA
Shepherd University, WV
Silver Lake College, WI
Slippery Rock University of Pennsylvania, PA
Sonoma State University, CA
Southern Illinois University Carbondale, IL
State University of New York College at Geneseo, NY
State University of New York, Fredonia, NY
Stephen F. Austin State University, TX
Stetson University, FL
Texas State University-San Marcos, TX
Texas Tech University, TX
The University of Akron, OH
University of California, San Diego, CA
University of Cincinnati, OH
University of Delaware, DE
University of Idaho, ID
University of Illinois at Chicago, IL
University of Kansas, KS
University of Maine, ME
University of Maryland, College Park, MD
University of Nebraska at Kearney, NE
University of Nevada, Las Vegas, NV
University of Nevada, Reno, NV
The University of North Carolina at Chapel Hill, NC
University of Northern Iowa, IA
University of St. Francis, IL
University of South Florida, FL
The University of Texas at El Paso, TX
The University of Toledo, OH
University of West Florida, FL
University of Wisconsin–Parkside, WI
University of Wisconsin–Stevens Point, WI
University of Wisconsin–Stout, WI
Utah State University, UT
Valley City State University, ND
Virginia Commonwealth University, VA
Virginia Intermont College, VA
Virginia Polytechnic Institute and State University, VA
Washington State University, WA
Washington University in St. Louis, MO
Western Illinois University, IL
Western Washington University, WA
Wichita State University, KS
Woodbury University, CA

Art/Fine Arts

Abilene Christian University, TX
Adelphi University, NY

Adrian College, MI
Albertson College of Idaho, ID
Albion College, MI
Albright College, PA
Alderson-Broaddus College, WV
Alfred University, NY
Alma College, MI
Alverno College, WI
Anderson University, IN
Angelo State University, TX
Arcadia University, PA
Arizona State University, AZ
Arkansas State University, AR
Armstrong Atlantic State University, GA
Art Academy of Cincinnati, OH
Art Center College of Design, CA
The Art Institute of Colorado, CO
Ashland University, OH
Athens State University, AL
Atlanta College of Art, GA
Auburn University, AL
Augustana College, SD
Augusta State University, GA
Austin College, TX
Austin Peay State University, TN
Averett University, VA
Baker University, KS
Ball State University, IN
Barry University, FL
Barton College, NC
Baylor University, TX
Belhaven College, MS
Berry College, GA
Bethany College, KS
Bethany Lutheran College, MN
Bethel College, KS
Bethel University, MN
Biola University, CA
Black Hills State University, SD
Bluffton University, OH
Boise State University, ID
Boston University, MA
Bowie State University, MD
Bowling Green State University, OH
Bradley University, IL
Brenau University, GA
Brevard College, NC
Brewton-Parker College, GA
Brigham Young University, UT
Brigham Young University–Hawaii, HI
Bryan College, TN
Bucknell University, PA
Buena Vista University, IA
Butler University, IN
California Baptist University, CA
California College of the Arts, CA
California Institute of the Arts, CA
California Lutheran University, CA
California State University, Bakersfield, CA
California State University, Chico, CA
California State University, Fresno, CA
California State University, Fullerton, CA
California State University, San Bernardino, CA
California State University, Stanislaus, CA
Calvin College, MI

Cameron University, OK
Campbellsville University, KY
Campbell University, NC
Canisius College, NY
Carnegie Mellon University, PA
Carroll College, WI
Carson-Newman College, TN
Case Western Reserve University, OH
Castleton State College, VT
Cedar Crest College, PA
Centenary College of Louisiana, LA
Central Bible College, MO
Central College, IA
Central Michigan University, MI
Central Missouri State University, MO
Central Washington University, WA
Chapman University, CA
Chester College of New England, NH
Christopher Newport University, VA
City College of the City University of New
  York, NY
Clarion University of Pennsylvania, PA
Clarke College, IA
Clemson University, SC
The Cleveland Institute of Art, OH
Cleveland State University, OH
Coastal Carolina University, SC
Coe College, IA
Colby-Sawyer College, NH
College for Creative Studies, MI
College of Charleston, SC
College of Mount St. Joseph, OH
The College of New Rochelle, NY
College of Notre Dame of Maryland, MD
College of Saint Benedict, MN
The College of Saint Rose, NY
College of Staten Island of the City
  University of New York, NY
College of Visual Arts, MN
Colorado State University, CO
Colorado State University-Pueblo, CO
Columbia College, MO
Columbia College, SC
Columbia College Chicago, IL
Columbus College of Art & Design, OH
Columbus State University, GA
Concordia University, MI
Concordia University, NE
Concordia University, St. Paul, MN
Cornell College, IA
Cornish College of the Arts, WA
Creighton University, NE
Culver-Stockton College, MO
Daemen College, NY
Davidson College, NC
Davis & Elkins College, WV
Denison University, OH
DePaul University, IL
DePauw University, IN
Dickinson State University, ND
Dillard University, LA
Doane College, NE
Drake University, IA
East Carolina University, NC
Eastern Mennonite University, VA
Eastern Michigan University, MI

Eastern Oregon University, OR
Eastern Washington University, WA
East Tennessee State University, TN
Eckerd College, FL
Edgewood College, WI
Edinboro University of Pennsylvania, PA
Elizabethtown College, PA
Elmhurst College, IL
Elon University, NC
Emory & Henry College, VA
Emporia State University, KS
Endicott College, MA
Eureka College, IL
Evangel University, MO
The Evergreen State College, WA
Fairfield University, CT
Fairmont State University, WV
Ferrum College, VA
Finlandia University, MI
Flagler College, FL
Florida Southern College, FL
Fort Hays State University, KS
Fort Lewis College, CO
Francis Marion University, SC
Freed-Hardeman University, TN
Fresno Pacific University, CA
Friends University, KS
Frostburg State University, MD
Furman University, SC
Georgetown College, KY
Georgian Court University, NJ
Georgia Southern University, GA
Georgia State University, GA
Goucher College, MD
Grace College, IN
Grand Canyon University, AZ
Grand Valley State University, MI
Grand View College, IA
Green Mountain College, VT
Greenville College, IL
Hamline University, MN
Hannibal-LaGrange College, MO
Hastings College, NE
Hendrix College, AR
Hillsdale College, MI
Hobart and William Smith Colleges, NY
Hofstra University, NY
Hollins University, VA
Hope College, MI
Houghton College, NY
Houston Baptist University, TX
Howard Payne University, TX
Howard University, DC
Huntington University, IN
Idaho State University, ID
Illinois College, IL
Illinois State University, IL
Illinois Wesleyan University, IL
Indiana State University, IN
Indiana University of Pennsylvania, PA
Indiana University–Purdue University Fort
  Wayne, IN
Iowa State University of Science and
  Technology, IA
Iowa Wesleyan College, IA
Jacksonville State University, AL

James Madison University, VA
Jamestown College, ND
Johnson Bible College, TN
Judson College, AL
Kalamazoo College, MI
Kansas City Art Institute, MO
Kansas State University, KS
Keene State College, NH
Kent State University, OH
Kentucky Wesleyan College, KY
Knox College, IL
Kutztown University of Pennsylvania, PA
LaGrange College, GA
Laguna College of Art & Design, CA
Lake Erie College, OH
Lake Forest College, IL
Lakeland College, WI
Lesley University, MA
Lewis-Clark State College, ID
Liberty University, VA
Limestone College, SC
Lindenwood University, MO
Lipscomb University, TN
Lock Haven University of Pennsylvania, PA
Long Island University, Brooklyn
  Campus, NY
Longwood University, VA
Louisiana State University and Agricultural
  and Mechanical College, LA
Lourdes College, OH
Loyola Marymount University, CA
Loyola University Chicago, IL
Lubbock Christian University, TX
Lycoming College, PA
Lyme Academy College of Fine Arts, CT
Lyon College, AR
MacMurray College, IL
Maine College of Art, ME
Manhattanville College, NY
Marietta College, OH
Marshall University, WV
Martin Methodist College, TN
Maryville College, TN
Maryville University of Saint Louis, MO
Massachusetts College of Art, MA
McMurry University, TX
Memphis College of Art, TN
Mercer University, GA
Mercyhurst College, PA
Meredith College, NC
Mesa State College, CO
Messiah College, PA
Metropolitan State College of Denver, CO
Miami University, OH
Midland Lutheran College, NE
Midway College, KY
Midwestern State University, TX
Millersville University of Pennsylvania, PA
Milligan College, TN
Millsaps College, MS
Milwaukee Institute of Art and Design, WI
Minnesota State University Mankato, MN
Minnesota State University Moorhead, MN
Mississippi College, MS
Mississippi State University, MS
Mississippi University for Women, MS

Missouri Southern State University, MO
Missouri State University, MO
Molloy College, NY
Montana State University, MT
Montana State University–Billings, MT
Montclair State University, NJ
Montreat College, NC
Morehead State University, KY
Morningside College, IA
Morris College, SC
Mount Ida College, MA
Mount Mary College, WI
Mount Mercy College, IA
Mount Olive College, NC
Mount St. Mary's University, MD
Mount Union College, OH
Murray State University, KY
Muskingum College, OH
Nazareth College of Rochester, NY
Nebraska Wesleyan University, NE
New England College, NH
New Jersey City University, NJ
New Mexico Highlands University, NM
New Mexico State University, NM
North Central College, IL
North Dakota State University, ND
Northeastern Illinois University, IL
Northeastern State University, OK
Northern Arizona University, AZ
Northern Illinois University, IL
Northern Kentucky University, KY
Northern State University, SD
North Greenville College, SC
Northwest College of Art, WA
Northwestern College, IA
Northwestern Oklahoma State
  University, OK
Northwestern State University of
  Louisiana, LA
Northwest Nazarene University, ID
Oakland City University, IN
Ohio Northern University, OH
Ohio University, OH
Ohio University–Eastern, OH
Ohio Wesleyan University, OH
Oklahoma Baptist University, OK
Oklahoma City University, OK
Oklahoma Panhandle State University, OK
Old Dominion University, VA
Olivet College, MI
Olivet Nazarene University, IL
Oral Roberts University, OK
Otis College of Art and Design, CA
Ouachita Baptist University, AR
Pacific Lutheran University, WA
Pacific Northwest College of Art, OR
Pacific University, OR
Palm Beach Atlantic University, FL
Park University, MO
Peace College, NC
Pepperdine University, CA
Peru State College, NE
Piedmont College, GA
Portland State University, OR
Quincy University, IL
Radford University, VA

Randolph-Macon Woman's College, VA
Reinhardt College, GA
Rhode Island School of Design, RI
Rice University, TX
The Richard Stockton College of New
  Jersey, NJ
Ringling School of Art and Design, FL
Ripon College, WI
Roanoke College, VA
Roberts Wesleyan College, NY
Rochester Institute of Technology, NY
Rocky Mountain College of Art &
  Design, CO
Rollins College, FL
Rosemont College, PA
St. Ambrose University, IA
St. Cloud State University, MN
St. Gregory's University, OK
Saint John's University, MN
St. John's University, NY
Saint Louis University, MO
Saint Michael's College, VT
St. Norbert College, WI
Salem State College, MA
Savannah College of Art and Design, GA
School of the Art Institute of Chicago, IL
School of the Museum of Fine Arts,
  Boston, MA
School of Visual Arts, NY
Schreiner University, TX
Seattle Pacific University, WA
Seton Hall University, NJ
Seton Hill University, PA
Shawnee State University, OH
Shepherd University, WV
Shimer College, IL
Shorter College, GA
Sierra Nevada College, NV
Simpson College, IA
Slippery Rock University of
  Pennsylvania, PA
Sonoma State University, CA
South Dakota State University, SD
Southern Adventist University, TN
Southern Arkansas University–
  Magnolia, AR
Southern Illinois University Carbondale, IL
Southern Illinois University
  Edwardsville, IL
Southern Methodist University, TX
Southern Oregon University, OR
Southern Virginia University, VA
Southern Wesleyan University, SC
Southwest Baptist University, MO
Southwestern University, TX
Southwest Minnesota State University, MN
Spring Arbor University, MI
State University of New York at
  Plattsburgh, NY
State University of New York College at
  Brockport, NY
State University of New York College at
  Geneseo, NY
State University of New York College at
  Potsdam, NY
Stephen F. Austin State University, TX

Sterling College, KS
Stetson University, FL
Sweet Briar College, VA
Syracuse University, NY
Tennessee Technological University, TN
Texas A&M University–Commerce, TX
Texas Christian University, TX
Texas Tech University, TX
Texas Wesleyan University, TX
Thomas More College, KY
Thomas University, GA
Towson University, MD
Transylvania University, KY
Truman State University, MO
Union University, TN
The University of Akron, OH
The University of Alabama, AL
The University of Alabama at
  Birmingham, AL
The University of Alabama in
  Huntsville, AL
University of Alaska Fairbanks, AK
The University of Arizona, AZ
University of Arkansas at Pine Bluff, AR
University of California, Irvine, CA
University of California, Riverside, CA
University of Cincinnati, OH
University of Colorado at Boulder, CO
University of Connecticut, CT
University of Dallas, TX
University of Dayton, OH
University of Delaware, DE
University of Denver, CO
University of Evansville, IN
University of Florida, FL
University of Hartford, CT
University of Hawaii at Hilo, HI
University of Hawaii at Manoa, HI
University of Idaho, ID
University of Illinois at Chicago, IL
University of Illinois at Springfield, IL
University of Indianapolis, IN
University of Kansas, KS
University of La Verne, CA
University of Maine, ME
University of Maine at Presque Isle, ME
University of Mary Hardin-Baylor, TX
University of Maryland, Baltimore
  County, MD
University of Maryland, College Park, MD
University of Maryland Eastern Shore, MD
University of Mary Washington, VA
University of Massachusetts Amherst, MA
The University of Memphis, TN
University of Miami, FL
University of Michigan–Dearborn, MI
University of Michigan–Flint, MI
University of Mississippi, MS
University of Missouri–St. Louis, MO
The University of Montana–Western, MT
University of Nebraska at Kearney, NE
University of Nebraska at Omaha, NE
University of Nebraska–Lincoln, NE
University of Nevada, Las Vegas, NV
University of Nevada, Reno, NV
University of New Hampshire, NH

University of North Alabama, AL
The University of North Carolina at Asheville, NC
The University of North Carolina at Chapel Hill, NC
The University of North Carolina at Greensboro, NC
The University of North Carolina at Wilmington, NC
University of North Dakota, ND
University of Northern Iowa, IA
University of North Florida, FL
University of Oklahoma, OK
University of Oregon, OR
University of Puget Sound, WA
University of Redlands, CA
University of Rio Grande, OH
University of St. Francis, IL
University of Saint Francis, IN
University of Science and Arts of Oklahoma, OK
University of Sioux Falls, SD
University of South Carolina, SC
The University of South Dakota, SD
University of Southern Indiana, IN
University of Southern Mississippi, MS
University of South Florida, FL
The University of Tampa, FL
The University of Tennessee at Chattanooga, TN
The University of Tennessee at Martin, TN
The University of Texas at Brownsville, TX
The University of Texas at El Paso, TX
The University of Texas at San Antonio, TX
The University of Texas of the Permian Basin, TX
The University of Texas–Pan American, TX
University of the Cumberlands, KY
University of the Incarnate Word, TX
University of the Ozarks, AR
The University of Toledo, OH
University of Tulsa, OK
University of Utah, UT
University of Washington, WA
University of West Florida, FL
University of West Georgia, GA
University of Wisconsin–Green Bay, WI
University of Wisconsin–La Crosse, WI
University of Wisconsin–Oshkosh, WI
University of Wisconsin–Parkside, WI
University of Wisconsin–Stout, WI
University of Wisconsin–Whitewater, WI
Ursinus College, PA
Utah State University, UT
Valdosta State University, GA
Valley City State University, ND
Valley Forge Christian College, PA
Valparaiso University, IN
Villa Julie College, MD
Virginia Commonwealth University, VA
Virginia Intermont College, VA
Virginia Polytechnic Institute and State University, VA
Virginia Wesleyan College, VA
Wabash College, IN

Wake Forest University, NC
Warren Wilson College, NC
Wartburg College, IA
Washington State University, WA
Washington University in St. Louis, MO
Wayland Baptist University, TX
Wayne State College, NE
Wayne State University, MI
Webster University, MO
Western Carolina University, NC
Western Kentucky University, KY
Western Oregon University, OR
Western State College of Colorado, CO
Western Washington University, WA
West Liberty State College, WV
Westminster College, UT
Westmont College, CA
West Texas A&M University, TX
West Virginia University, WV
West Virginia Wesleyan College, WV
Whitman College, WA
Whittier College, CA
Whitworth College, WA
Wichita State University, KS
William Carey College, MS
William Jewell College, MO
William Penn University, IA
Williams Baptist College, AR
William Woods University, MO
Winona State University, MN
Winthrop University, SC
Wittenberg University, OH
Worcester State College, MA
Xavier University, OH
Xavier University of Louisiana, LA

Cinema/Film/Broadcasting
Arizona State University, AZ
Arkansas State University, AR
The Art Institute of Colorado, CO
Auburn University, AL
Baker University, KS
Baylor University, TX
Bowling Green State University, OH
Brenau University, GA
Brigham Young University, UT
Butler University, IN
California Institute of the Arts, CA
California State University, Chico, CA
Central Michigan University, MI
Central Missouri State University, MO
Chapman University, CA
City College of the City University of New York, NY
The College of New Rochelle, NY
Colorado State University-Pueblo, CO
Columbia College Chicago, IL
DePauw University, IN
DeSales University, PA
Eastern Michigan University, MI
Eastern Washington University, WA
Edinboro University of Pennsylvania, PA
Five Towns College, NY
Flagler College, FL
Fort Hays State University, KS
Freed-Hardeman University, TN

Georgia Southern University, GA
Grace University, NE
Illinois State University, IL
James Madison University, VA
Kalamazoo College, MI
Keene State College, NH
Lincoln University, MO
Lindenwood University, MO
Long Island University, Brooklyn Campus, NY
Marshall University, WV
MidAmerica Nazarene University, KS
Mississippi State University, MS
Montana State University, MT
Montclair State University, NJ
Morehead State University, KY
Mount Union College, OH
North Carolina School of the Arts, NC
North Central College, IL
Northern Arizona University, AZ
Northwestern Oklahoma State University, OK
Northwestern State University of Louisiana, LA
Ohio University, OH
Ohio University–Eastern, OH
Oral Roberts University, OK
Point Park University, PA
Quincy University, IL
Radford University, VA
Rochester Institute of Technology, NY
St. Cloud State University, MN
St. John's University, NY
Saint Joseph's College, IN
Seton Hall University, NJ
Sonoma State University, CA
Southern Illinois University Carbondale, IL
Southern Methodist University, TX
Southwestern College, KS
Texas Christian University, TX
Union University, TN
The University of Alabama, AL
University of California, San Diego, CA
University of Colorado at Boulder, CO
University of Kansas, KS
University of Maryland, Baltimore County, MD
University of Maryland, College Park, MD
The University of Memphis, TN
University of Miami, FL
University of Nebraska–Lincoln, NE
University of Nevada, Las Vegas, NV
The University of North Carolina at Greensboro, NC
University of South Florida, FL
The University of Toledo, OH
University of Utah, UT
University of Wisconsin–Whitewater, WI
Villa Julie College, MD
Virginia Polytechnic Institute and State University, VA
Washington State University, WA
Washington University in St. Louis, MO
Western Illinois University, IL
Western Kentucky University, KY
Western Washington University, WA

Westminster College, PA
William Jewell College, MO

Creative Writing

Alderson-Broaddus College, WV
Arizona State University, AZ
Arkansas Tech University, AR
Auburn University, AL
Augusta State University, GA
Austin Peay State University, TN
Bowling Green State University, OH
Brenau University, GA
Brigham Young University, UT
Brigham Young University–Hawaii, HI
California College of the Arts, CA
California Institute of the Arts, CA
California Lutheran University, CA
California State University, Chico, CA
Cameron University, OK
Campbell University, NC
Case Western Reserve University, OH
Central Michigan University, MI
Central Missouri State University, MO
Chapman University, CA
Chester College of New England, NH
City College of the City University of New
  York, NY
Cleveland State University, OH
Coe College, IA
Colby-Sawyer College, NH
The College of New Rochelle, NY
Colorado State University, CO
Columbia College Chicago, IL
Creighton University, NE
Davidson College, NC
DeSales University, PA
Dickinson State University, ND
Dominican University, IL
Duke University, NC
Eastern Michigan University, MI
Eastern Washington University, WA
Eckerd College, FL
Edgewood College, WI
Emporia State University, KS
The Evergreen State College, WA
Fort Hays State University, KS
Frostburg State University, MD
Furman University, SC
Georgia College & State University, GA
Georgian Court University, NJ
Graceland University, IA
Grove City College, PA
Hamline University, MN
Hampshire College, MA
Hobart and William Smith Colleges, NY
Hollins University, VA
Hope College, MI
Illinois State University, IL
Knox College, IL
Lake Forest College, IL
Lakeland College, WI
Lewis-Clark State College, ID
Lycoming College, PA
Maharishi University of Management, IA
Marshall University, WV
Meredith College, NC

Mesa State College, CO
Michigan State University, MI
Minnesota State University Mankato, MN
Minnesota State University Moorhead, MN
Mississippi State University, MS
Morris College, SC
Mount Marty College, SD
Murray State University, KY
New England College, NH
Northeastern Illinois University, IL
Northern Arizona University, AZ
Northern Illinois University, IL
Northwestern State University of
  Louisiana, LA
The Ohio State University, OH
Plymouth State University, NH
Randolph-Macon Woman's College, VA
Rice University, TX
The Richard Stockton College of New
  Jersey, NJ
Rockhurst University, MO
Salem State College, MA
Seton Hill University, PA
Shimer College, IL
Sonoma State University, CA
Southern Illinois University Carbondale, IL
Southern Methodist University, TX
Southern Wesleyan University, SC
State University of New York at
  Binghamton, NY
State University of New York College at
  Brockport, NY
State University of New York College at
  Geneseo, NY
Susquehanna University, PA
The University of Akron, OH
The University of Alabama, AL
University of Alaska Fairbanks, AK
University of California, Riverside, CA
University of Colorado at Boulder, CO
University of Idaho, ID
University of Kansas, KS
University of Maine, ME
University of Maryland, Baltimore
  County, MD
University of Maryland, College Park, MD
University of Michigan–Dearborn, MI
University of Nebraska at Omaha, NE
University of Nevada, Reno, NV
The University of North Carolina at
  Wilmington, NC
University of Redlands, CA
The University of South Dakota, SD
University of Southern Indiana, IN
University of South Florida, FL
The University of Tampa, FL
The University of Virginia's College at
  Wise, VA
University of Washington, WA
University of Wisconsin–Stevens Point, WI
University of Wisconsin–Whitewater, WI
Ursinus College, PA
Virginia Polytechnic Institute and State
  University, VA
Wabash College, IN
Warren Wilson College, NC

Washington College, MD
Washington State University, WA
Washington University in St. Louis, MO
Western Washington University, WA
William Penn University, IA

Dance

Adelphi University, NY
Alma College, MI
Angelo State University, TX
Arizona State University, AZ
Baker University, KS
Ball State University, IN
Bay Path College, MA
Belhaven College, MS
Boise State University, ID
The Boston Conservatory, MA
Bowling Green State University, OH
Brenau University, GA
Brigham Young University, UT
Butler University, IN
California Institute of the Arts, CA
California State University, Bakersfield, CA
California State University, Chico, CA
Case Western Reserve University, OH
Cedar Crest College, PA
Centenary College of Louisiana, LA
Central Michigan University, MI
Chapman University, CA
Cleveland State University, OH
The College of New Rochelle, NY
The College of Wooster, OH
Colorado State University, CO
Columbia College, SC
Columbia College Chicago, IL
Cornish College of the Arts, WA
Denison University, OH
DeSales University, PA
Drexel University, PA
Duquesne University, PA
Eastern Michigan University, MI
Friends University, KS
Frostburg State University, MD
Goucher College, MD
Grambling State University, LA
Hawai'i Pacific University, HI
Hobart and William Smith Colleges, NY
Hofstra University, NY
Hollins University, VA
Hope College, MI
Howard University, DC
Indiana University of Pennsylvania, PA
Ithaca College, NY
James Madison University, VA
Keene State College, NH
Knox College, IL
Kutztown University of Pennsylvania, PA
Lake Erie College, OH
Lambuth University, TN
Lindenwood University, MO
Long Island University, Brooklyn
  Campus, NY
Marshall University, WV
Mars Hill College, NC
Marymount Manhattan College, NY
Mercyhurst College, PA

Middle Tennessee State University, TN
Mississippi State University, MS
Mississippi University for Women, MS
Missouri State University, MO
Missouri Valley College, MO
Montana State University, MT
Montclair State University, NJ
Murray State University, KY
New Jersey City University, NJ
North Carolina School of the Arts, NC
Northeastern Illinois University, IL
Northeastern State University, OK
Northern Illinois University, IL
Northwestern Oklahoma State
  University, OK
Northwestern State University of
  Louisiana, LA
Oakland University, MI
Ohio Northern University, OH
The Ohio State University, OH
Ohio University, OH
Ohio University–Eastern, OH
Ohio Wesleyan University, OH
Oklahoma City University, OK
Old Dominion University, VA
Pacific Lutheran University, WA
Palm Beach Atlantic University, FL
Plymouth State University, NH
Point Park University, PA
Radford University, VA
The Richard Stockton College of New
  Jersey, NJ
St. Ambrose University, IA
St. Gregory's University, OK
St. John's University, NY
Salem State College, MA
Shenandoah University, VA
Slippery Rock University of
  Pennsylvania, PA
Sonoma State University, CA
Southern Arkansas University–
  Magnolia, AR
Southern Illinois University Carbondale, IL
Southern Illinois University
  Edwardsville, IL
Southern Methodist University, TX
Southern Utah University, UT
Southwestern College, KS
Spelman College, GA
State University of New York College at
  Brockport, NY
State University of New York College at
  Geneseo, NY
State University of New York College at
  Potsdam, NY
State University of New York,
  Fredonia, NY
Stephens College, MO
Texas Christian University, TX
Texas Tech University, TX
Towson University, MD
The University of Akron, OH
The University of Alabama, AL
The University of Arizona, AZ
University of California, Irvine, CA
University of California, Riverside, CA

University of California, San Diego, CA
University of Colorado at Boulder, CO
University of Florida, FL
University of Hartford, CT
University of Hawaii at Manoa, HI
University of Idaho, ID
University of Kansas, KS
University of Maryland, Baltimore
  County, MD
University of Maryland, College Park, MD
University of Mary Washington, VA
University of Massachusetts Amherst, MA
The University of Memphis, TN
University of Nebraska–Lincoln, NE
University of Nevada, Las Vegas, NV
University of Nevada, Reno, NV
University of New Hampshire, NH
The University of North Carolina at
  Greensboro, NC
University of Northern Colorado, CO
University of North Texas, TX
University of Oklahoma, OK
University of Oregon, OR
University of Puerto Rico, Mayagüez
  Campus, PR
University of Southern Mississippi, MS
University of South Florida, FL
The University of Texas at Arlington, TX
The University of Texas–Pan American, TX
University of the Incarnate Word, TX
University of Utah, UT
University of Washington, WA
University of Wisconsin–Green Bay, WI
University of Wisconsin–Stevens Point, WI
University of Wyoming, WY
Virginia Commonwealth University, VA
Virginia Intermont College, VA
Washington University in St. Louis, MO
Wayne State University, MI
Western Illinois University, IL
Western Kentucky University, KY
Western Oregon University, OR
Western Washington University, WA
West Texas A&M University, TX
Wichita State University, KS
Wilkes University, PA
Winthrop University, SC
Wittenberg University, OH

Debating

Abilene Christian University, TX
Albertson College of Idaho, ID
Alderson-Broaddus College, WV
Arizona State University, AZ
Arkansas State University, AR
Austin Peay State University, TN
Azusa Pacific University, CA
Baker University, KS
Baylor University, TX
Berry College, GA
Bethany Lutheran College, MN
Bethel College, KS
Bethel University, MN
Biola University, CA
Boise State University, ID
Bowling Green State University, OH

California State University, Chico, CA
Cameron University, OK
Carroll College, MT
Carson-Newman College, TN
Cedarville University, OH
Central Missouri State University, MO
The College of New Rochelle, NY
Colorado State University, CO
Concordia College, MN
Concordia University, CA
Creighton University, NE
Culver-Stockton College, MO
DePaul University, IL
Doane College, NE
Eastern Michigan University, MI
Emory University, GA
Emporia State University, KS
Evangel University, MO
Fairmont State University, WV
Ferris State University, MI
Florida College, FL
Fort Hays State University, KS
The George Washington University, DC
Georgia College & State University, GA
Gonzaga University, WA
Hastings College, NE
Hillsdale College, MI
Idaho State University, ID
Illinois State University, IL
Kansas State University, KS
Kentucky Christian University, KY
King's College, PA
Lewis & Clark College, OR
Liberty University, VA
Linfield College, OR
Louisiana Tech University, LA
Loyola Marymount University, CA
Loyola University Chicago, IL
Malone College, OH
Marist College, NY
Marshall University, WV
Mercer University, GA
Methodist College, NC
Michigan State University, MI
Middle Tennessee State University, TN
Midland Lutheran College, NE
Minnesota State University Mankato, MN
Mississippi State University, MS
Missouri Southern State University, MO
Missouri State University, MO
Morehead State University, KY
Mount Union College, OH
Murray State University, KY
Muskingum College, OH
North Central College, IL
North Dakota State University, ND
Northeastern State University, OK
Northern Arizona University, AZ
Northwestern Oklahoma State
  University, OK
Northwest Nazarene University, ID
Northwest University, WA
Ohio University, OH
Ohio University–Eastern, OH
Oklahoma Panhandle State University, OK
Oklahoma Wesleyan University, OK

Pacific Lutheran University, WA
Pacific University, OR
Pepperdine University, CA
Regis University, CO
Rice University, TX
Ripon College, WI
St. John's University, NY
Seton Hall University, NJ
South Dakota State University, SD
Southeastern Louisiana University, LA
Southern Illinois University Carbondale, IL
Southwest Baptist University, MO
Southwestern College, KS
Sterling College, KS
Tennessee Technological University, TN
Truman State University, MO
The University of Akron, OH
The University of Alabama, AL
University of Arkansas at Monticello, AR
University of Kansas, KS
University of La Verne, CA
University of Mary, ND
University of Miami, FL
University of Missouri–Kansas City, MO
University of Nebraska at Kearney, NE
University of Nebraska at Omaha, NE
University of Nevada, Reno, NV
University of North Dakota, ND
University of Puget Sound, WA
University of Redlands, CA
University of St. Thomas, TX
University of South Carolina, SC
The University of South Dakota, SD
University of Southern California, CA
University of South Florida, FL
The University of Texas at San
  Antonio, TX
University of the Cumberlands, KY
University of West Georgia, GA
University of Wisconsin–Eau Claire, WI
University of Wisconsin–Oshkosh, WI
University of Wyoming, WY
Vanguard University of Southern
  California, CA
Wake Forest University, NC
Wayne State University, MI
Webster University, MO
Western Illinois University, IL
Western Kentucky University, KY
West Texas A&M University, TX
West Virginia University, WV
Whitman College, WA
Wichita State University, KS
William Carey College, MS
William Jewell College, MO
Winona State University, MN

Journalism/Publications

Abilene Christian University, TX
Alderson-Broaddus College, WV
Angelo State University, TX
Arizona State University, AZ
Arkansas State University, AR
Athens State University, AL
Auburn University, AL
Averett University, VA

Baker University, KS
Ball State University, IN
Baylor University, TX
Berry College, GA
Bethany Lutheran College, MN
Biola University, CA
Boise State University, ID
Bowling Green State University, OH
Brenau University, GA
Brevard College, NC
Brewton-Parker College, GA
Brigham Young University, UT
Brigham Young University–Hawaii, HI
Bryan College, TN
California Lutheran University, CA
California State University, Chico, CA
California State University, Fresno, CA
Cameron University, OK
Campbellsville University, KY
Campbell University, NC
Carroll College, WI
Carson-Newman College, TN
Central Michigan University, MI
Central Missouri State University, MO
Central Washington University, WA
The College of New Rochelle, NY
Colorado State University-Pueblo, CO
Columbia College Chicago, IL
Concordia University, St. Paul, MN
DePauw University, IN
Dickinson State University, ND
Dordt College, IA
Eastern Washington University, WA
East Tennessee State University, TN
Edinboro University of Pennsylvania, PA
Elon University, NC
Faulkner University, AL
Ferris State University, MI
Florida College, FL
Fort Hays State University, KS
Franklin College, IN
Freed-Hardeman University, TN
Fresno Pacific University, CA
Frostburg State University, MD
Georgia College & State University, GA
Georgia State University, GA
Hannibal-LaGrange College, MO
Hawai'i Pacific University, HI
Hillsdale College, MI
Huntington University, IN
Indiana University of Pennsylvania, PA
Iowa State University of Science and
  Technology, IA
Ithaca College, NY
Jacksonville State University, AL
James Madison University, VA
John Brown University, AR
Kent State University, OH
King's College, PA
Lakeland College, WI
LeMoyne-Owen College, TN
Liberty University, VA
Lincoln University, MO
Lipscomb University, TN
Lock Haven University of Pennsylvania, PA

Louisiana State University and Agricultural
  and Mechanical College, LA
Louisiana Tech University, LA
Loyola University Chicago, IL
Lubbock Christian University, TX
Malone College, OH
Marshall University, WV
Mesa State College, CO
Michigan State University, MI
Middle Tennessee State University, TN
Midland Lutheran College, NE
Mississippi State University, MS
Mississippi University for Women, MS
Missouri Southern State University, MO
Missouri State University, MO
Missouri Valley College, MO
Morehead State University, KY
Morris College, SC
Mount St. Mary's University, MD
Mount Union College, OH
Murray State University, KY
Muskingum College, OH
New Mexico State University, NM
North Central College, IL
North Dakota State University, ND
Northeastern Illinois University, IL
Northeastern State University, OK
Northern Arizona University, AZ
Northern Illinois University, IL
North Greenville College, SC
Northwestern College, IA
Northwestern Oklahoma State
  University, OK
Northwestern State University of
  Louisiana, LA
Northwest Nazarene University, ID
Northwest University, WA
Nyack College, NY
Oglethorpe University, GA
Ohio Northern University, OH
The Ohio State University, OH
Ohio University, OH
Ohio University–Eastern, OH
Ohio University–Lancaster, OH
Ohio Valley University, WV
Olivet College, MI
Oral Roberts University, OK
Ouachita Baptist University, AR
Pacific University, OR
Pepperdine University, CA
Point Park University, PA
Rice University, TX
The Richard Stockton College of New
  Jersey, NJ
Robert Morris College, IL
Rochester College, MI
St. Bonaventure University, NY
St. Cloud State University, MN
St. Gregory's University, OK
St. John's University, NY
Schreiner University, TX
Seton Hall University, NJ
Seton Hill University, PA
Sonoma State University, CA
South Dakota State University, SD

Southeastern College of the Assemblies of God, FL
Southern Adventist University, TN
Southern Illinois University Carbondale, IL
Southern Methodist University, TX
Southern Oregon University, OR
Southern Utah University, UT
Southern Wesleyan University, SC
Southwestern College, KS
State University of New York at Plattsburgh, NY
State University of New York College at Brockport, NY
State University of New York College at Geneseo, NY
State University of New York College at Oneonta, NY
Stephen F. Austin State University, TX
Texas A&M University, TX
Texas A&M University–Commerce, TX
Texas Christian University, TX
Texas Lutheran University, TX
Texas State University-San Marcos, TX
Texas Tech University, TX
Union University, TN
The University of Akron, OH
The University of Alabama, AL
University of California, San Diego, CA
University of Colorado at Boulder, CO
University of Florida, FL
University of Hawaii at Manoa, HI
University of Idaho, ID
University of Illinois at Springfield, IL
University of Kansas, KS
University of La Verne, CA
University of Maine, ME
University of Maryland, College Park, MD
University of Mary Washington, VA
University of Massachusetts Amherst, MA
The University of Memphis, TN
University of Michigan, MI
University of Michigan–Dearborn, MI
University of Mississippi, MS
University of Missouri–Columbia, MO
University of Nebraska at Kearney, NE
University of Nebraska at Omaha, NE
University of Nebraska–Lincoln, NE
University of Nevada, Las Vegas, NV
University of Nevada, Reno, NV
University of North Alabama, AL
The University of North Carolina at Chapel Hill, NC
The University of North Carolina at Pembroke, NC
University of Oklahoma, OK
University of Oregon, OR
University of St. Thomas, MN
University of South Carolina, SC
University of South Florida, FL
The University of Tampa, FL
The University of Tennessee at Martin, TN
The University of Texas at Arlington, TX
The University of Texas at El Paso, TX
The University of Texas–Pan American, TX
The University of Virginia's College at Wise, VA

University of Washington, WA
University of West Georgia, GA
University of Wisconsin–Whitewater, WI
Utah State University, UT
Valley City State University, ND
Vanderbilt University, TN
Virginia Polytechnic Institute and State University, VA
Wabash College, IN
Wake Forest University, NC
Wartburg College, IA
Washington State University, WA
Wayland Baptist University, TX
Wayne State College, NE
Wayne State University, MI
Webber International University, FL
Western Illinois University, IL
Western Kentucky University, KY
Western Washington University, WA
Westminster College, UT
West Texas A&M University, TX
Whitworth College, WA
Wichita State University, KS
Wilkes University, PA
William Carey College, MS
William Jewell College, MO
William Penn University, IA
William Woods University, MO

Music

Abilene Christian University, TX
Adelphi University, NY
Adrian College, MI
Agnes Scott College, GA
Albertson College of Idaho, ID
Albion College, MI
Albright College, PA
Alcorn State University, MS
Alderson-Broaddus College, WV
Alma College, MI
Alverno College, WI
Anderson University, IN
Andrews University, MI
Angelo State University, TX
Anna Maria College, MA
Arizona State University, AZ
Arkansas State University, AR
Arkansas Tech University, AR
Armstrong Atlantic State University, GA
Asbury College, KY
Ashland University, OH
Atlantic Union College, MA
Auburn University, AL
Augsburg College, MN
Augustana College, SD
Augusta State University, GA
Austin College, TX
Austin Peay State University, TN
Averett University, VA
Azusa Pacific University, CA
Baker University, KS
Baldwin-Wallace College, OH
Ball State University, IN
The Baptist College of Florida, FL
Barton College, NC
Baylor University, TX

Belhaven College, MS
Belmont University, TN
Beloit College, WI
Benedictine College, KS
Benedictine University, IL
Berklee College of Music, MA
Berry College, GA
Bethany College, KS
Bethany College, WV
Bethany Lutheran College, MN
Bethel College, KS
Bethel College, TN
Bethel University, MN
Biola University, CA
Black Hills State University, SD
Blue Mountain College, MS
Bluffton University, OH
Boise State University, ID
The Boston Conservatory, MA
Boston University, MA
Bowie State University, MD
Bowling Green State University, OH
Bradley University, IL
Brenau University, GA
Brevard College, NC
Brewton-Parker College, GA
Bridgewater College, VA
Brigham Young University, UT
Brigham Young University–Hawaii, HI
Bryan College, TN
Bucknell University, PA
Buena Vista University, IA
Butler University, IN
California Baptist University, CA
California Institute of the Arts, CA
California Lutheran University, CA
California State University, Bakersfield, CA
California State University, Chico, CA
California State University, East Bay, CA
California State University, Fresno, CA
California State University, Fullerton, CA
California State University, San Bernardino, CA
California State University, Stanislaus, CA
Calvin College, MI
Cameron University, OK
Campbellsville University, KY
Campbell University, NC
Canisius College, NY
Carnegie Mellon University, PA
Carroll College, WI
Carson-Newman College, TN
Case Western Reserve University, OH
Castleton State College, VT
Catawba College, NC
The Catholic University of America, DC
Cedarville University, OH
Centenary College of Louisiana, LA
Central Bible College, MO
Central Christian College of Kansas, KS
Central College, IA
Central Methodist University, MO
Central Michigan University, MI
Central Missouri State University, MO
Central Washington University, WA
Centre College, KY

Chapman University, CA
Chowan College, NC
Christian Heritage College, CA
Christopher Newport University, VA
Cincinnati Christian University, OH
City College of the City University of New York, NY
Clark Atlanta University, GA
Clarke College, IA
Clear Creek Baptist Bible College, KY
Clearwater Christian College, FL
Cleveland Institute of Music, OH
Cleveland State University, OH
Coastal Carolina University, SC
Coe College, IA
Colby-Sawyer College, NH
College of Charleston, SC
College of Mount St. Joseph, OH
The College of New Jersey, NJ
The College of New Rochelle, NY
College of Saint Benedict, MN
College of Saint Mary, NE
The College of Saint Rose, NY
The College of St. Scholastica, MN
College of Staten Island of the City University of New York, NY
College of the Holy Cross, MA
The College of Wooster, OH
Colorado Christian University, CO
Colorado State University, CO
Colorado State University-Pueblo, CO
Columbia College, MO
Columbia College, SC
Columbia College Chicago, IL
Columbia International University, SC
Columbus State University, GA
Concordia College, MN
Concordia University, CA
Concordia University, MI
Concordia University, NE
Concordia University, OR
Concordia University, St. Paul, MN
Concordia University Wisconsin, WI
Converse College, SC
Corban College, OR
Cornell College, IA
Cornerstone University, MI
Cornish College of the Arts, WA
Crown College, MN
Culver-Stockton College, MO
The Curtis Institute of Music, PA
Dakota State University, SD
Dallas Baptist University, TX
Dallas Christian College, TX
Davidson College, NC
Davis & Elkins College, WV
Delaware State University, DE
Delaware Valley College, PA
Denison University, OH
DePaul University, IL
DePauw University, IN
DeSales University, PA
Dickinson State University, ND
Dillard University, LA
Doane College, NE
Dominican University of California, CA

Dordt College, IA
Drake University, IA
Drexel University, PA
Duquesne University, PA
East Carolina University, NC
East Central University, OK
Eastern Mennonite University, VA
Eastern Michigan University, MI
Eastern Oregon University, OR
Eastern Washington University, WA
East Stroudsburg University of Pennsylvania, PA
East Tennessee State University, TN
East Texas Baptist University, TX
Eckerd College, FL
Edgewood College, WI
Edinboro University of Pennsylvania, PA
Elizabethtown College, PA
Elmhurst College, IL
Elon University, NC
Emmaus Bible College, IA
Emory & Henry College, VA
Emory University, GA
Emporia State University, KS
Erskine College, SC
Eugene Bible College, OR
Evangel University, MO
Fairfield University, CT
Fairmont State University, WV
Faith Baptist Bible College and Theological Seminary, IA
Faulkner University, AL
Ferris State University, MI
Five Towns College, NY
Florida College, FL
Florida Southern College, FL
Florida State University, FL
Fordham University, NY
Fort Hays State University, KS
Fort Lewis College, CO
Francis Marion University, SC
Franklin and Marshall College, PA
Franklin College, IN
Freed-Hardeman University, TN
Fresno Pacific University, CA
Friends University, KS
Frostburg State University, MD
Furman University, SC
Gannon University, PA
Geneva College, PA
Georgetown College, KY
The George Washington University, DC
Georgia College & State University, GA
Georgian Court University, NJ
Georgia Southern University, GA
Georgia State University, GA
Gettysburg College, PA
Glenville State College, WV
Gonzaga University, WA
Gordon College, MA
Goshen College, IN
Goucher College, MD
Grace Bible College, MI
Grace College, IN
Graceland University, IA
Grace University, NE

Grambling State University, LA
Grand Canyon University, AZ
Grand Valley State University, MI
Grand View College, IA
Green Mountain College, VT
Greenville College, IL
Grove City College, PA
Guilford College, NC
Gustavus Adolphus College, MN
Hamline University, MN
Hampden-Sydney College, VA
Hampton University, VA
Hannibal-LaGrange College, MO
Hanover College, IN
Harding University, AR
Hastings College, NE
Hawai'i Pacific University, HI
Heidelberg College, OH
Hendrix College, AR
Hillsdale College, MI
Hobart and William Smith Colleges, NY
Hofstra University, NY
Hollins University, VA
Holy Names University, CA
Hope College, MI
Houghton College, NY
Houston Baptist University, TX
Howard Payne University, TX
Howard University, DC
Huntington University, IN
Idaho State University, ID
Illinois College, IL
Illinois State University, IL
Illinois Wesleyan University, IL
Indiana University of Pennsylvania, PA
Indiana University–Purdue University Fort Wayne, IN
Iona College, NY
Iowa State University of Science and Technology, IA
Iowa Wesleyan College, IA
Ithaca College, NY
Jacksonville State University, AL
James Madison University, VA
John Brown University, AR
Johnson Bible College, TN
Johnson C. Smith University, NC
Judson College, AL
Kalamazoo College, MI
Kansas State University, KS
Keene State College, NH
Kennesaw State University, GA
Kent State University, OH
Kentucky Christian University, KY
Kentucky Mountain Bible College, KY
Kentucky Wesleyan College, KY
King College, TN
Knox College, IL
Kutztown University of Pennsylvania, PA
LaGrange College, GA
Lake Erie College, OH
Lake Forest College, IL
Lakeland College, WI
Lambuth University, TN
Lancaster Bible College, PA
Langston University, OK

La Sierra University, CA
Lawrence University, WI
Lebanon Valley College, PA
Lee University, TN
Lehigh University, PA
LeMoyne-Owen College, TN
Lenoir-Rhyne College, NC
Lewis & Clark College, OR
Lewis-Clark State College, ID
Liberty University, VA
Limestone College, SC
Lincoln Memorial University, TN
Lincoln University, MO
Lincoln University, PA
Lindenwood University, MO
Linfield College, OR
Lipscomb University, TN
Lock Haven University of Pennsylvania, PA
Long Island University, Brooklyn
  Campus, NY
Longwood University, VA
Loras College, IA
Louisiana State University and Agricultural
  and Mechanical College, LA
Louisiana Tech University, LA
Lourdes College, OH
Loyola Marymount University, CA
Loyola University Chicago, IL
Lubbock Christian University, TX
Luther College, IA
Lycoming College, PA
Lynn University, FL
MacMurray College, IL
Maharishi University of Management, IA
Malone College, OH
Manhattan Christian College, KS
Manhattan College, NY
Manhattan School of Music, NY
Marian College of Fond du Lac, WI
Marist College, NY
Marshall University, WV
Mars Hill College, NC
Martin Methodist College, TN
Maryville College, TN
McKendree College, IL
McMurry University, TX
Mercer University, GA
Mercyhurst College, PA
Meredith College, NC
Mesa State College, CO
Messiah College, PA
Methodist College, NC
Metropolitan State College of Denver, CO
Miami University, OH
Michigan State University, MI
MidAmerica Nazarene University, KS
Middle Tennessee State University, TN
Midland Lutheran College, NE
Midway College, KY
Midwestern State University, TX
Millersville University of Pennsylvania, PA
Milligan College, TN
Millsaps College, MS
Minnesota State University Mankato, MN
Minnesota State University Moorhead, MN
Minot State University, ND

Mississippi College, MS
Mississippi State University, MS
Mississippi University for Women, MS
Missouri Baptist University, MO
Missouri Southern State University, MO
Missouri State University, MO
Missouri Valley College, MO
Molloy College, NY
Montana State University, MT
Montana State University–Billings, MT
Montclair State University, NJ
Montreat College, NC
Moravian College, PA
Morehead State University, KY
Morehouse College, GA
Morningside College, IA
Mount Aloysius College, PA
Mount Marty College, SD
Mount Mary College, WI
Mount Mercy College, IA
Mount Olive College, NC
Mount Union College, OH
Mount Vernon Nazarene University, OH
Murray State University, KY
Muskingum College, OH
Nazareth College of Rochester, NY
Nebraska Wesleyan University, NE
Neumann College, PA
New England Conservatory of Music, MA
New Jersey City University, NJ
New Mexico Highlands University, NM
New Mexico State University, NM
Nicholls State University, LA
Norfolk State University, VA
North Carolina Agricultural and Technical
  State University, NC
North Carolina School of the Arts, NC
North Central College, IL
North Central University, MN
North Dakota State University, ND
Northeastern Illinois University, IL
Northeastern State University, OK
Northeastern University, MA
Northern Arizona University, AZ
Northern Illinois University, IL
Northern Michigan University, MI
Northern State University, SD
North Greenville College, SC
Northland College, WI
Northwestern College, IA
Northwestern College, MN
Northwestern Oklahoma State
  University, OK
Northwestern State University of
  Louisiana, LA
Northwest Nazarene University, ID
Northwest University, WA
Nyack College, NY
Oakland City University, IN
Oakland University, MI
Oberlin College, OH
Oglethorpe University, GA
Ohio Northern University, OH
The Ohio State University, OH
Ohio University, OH
Ohio University–Eastern, OH

Ohio Valley University, WV
Ohio Wesleyan University, OH
Oklahoma Baptist University, OK
Oklahoma City University, OK
Oklahoma Panhandle State University, OK
Oklahoma State University, OK
Oklahoma Wesleyan University, OK
Old Dominion University, VA
Olivet College, MI
Olivet Nazarene University, IL
Oral Roberts University, OK
Oregon State University, OR
Ouachita Baptist University, AR
Pacific Lutheran University, WA
Pacific University, OR
Palm Beach Atlantic University, FL
Peabody Conservatory of Music of The
  Johns Hopkins University, MD
Peace College, NC
Pepperdine University, CA
Peru State College, NE
Pfeiffer University, NC
Philadelphia Biblical University, PA
Piedmont College, GA
Pikeville College, KY
Pittsburg State University, KS
Plymouth State University, NH
Pontifical Catholic University of Puerto
  Rico, PR
Portland State University, OR
Purdue University, IN
Quincy University, IL
Radford University, VA
Randolph-Macon Woman's College, VA
Rice University, TX
The Richard Stockton College of New
  Jersey, NJ
Ripon College, WI
Roanoke College, VA
Roberts Wesleyan College, NY
Rochester College, MI
Rockhurst University, MO
Rollins College, FL
Rowan University, NJ
Rust College, MS
St. Ambrose University, IA
St. Bonaventure University, NY
St. Cloud State University, MN
St. Gregory's University, OK
Saint John's University, MN
St. John's University, NY
Saint Joseph's College, IN
Saint Louis University, MO
Saint Martin's College, WA
Saint Mary's University of Minnesota, MN
St. Mary's University of San Antonio, TX
St. Norbert College, WI
St. Olaf College, MN
Saint Vincent College, PA
Saint Xavier University, IL
Salem State College, MA
Samford University, AL
Schreiner University, TX
Seton Hall University, NJ
Seton Hill University, PA
Shaw University, NC

Shenandoah University, VA
Shepherd University, WV
Shorter College, GA
Sierra Nevada College, NV
Silver Lake College, WI
Simpson College, IA
Simpson University, CA
Skidmore College, NY
Slippery Rock University of
  Pennsylvania, PA
Sonoma State University, CA
South Carolina State University, SC
South Dakota State University, SD
Southeastern Bible College, AL
Southeastern College of the Assemblies of
  God, FL
Southeastern Louisiana University, LA
Southeastern Oklahoma State
  University, OK
Southeast Missouri State University, MO
Southern Adventist University, TN
Southern Arkansas University–
  Magnolia, AR
Southern Illinois University Carbondale, IL
Southern Illinois University
  Edwardsville, IL
Southern Methodist University, TX
Southern Oregon University, OR
Southern Utah University, UT
Southern Wesleyan University, SC
Southwest Baptist University, MO
Southwestern Christian University, OK
Southwestern College, AZ
Southwestern College, KS
Southwestern University, TX
Southwest Minnesota State University, MN
Spelman College, GA
Spring Arbor University, MI
State University of New York at
  Binghamton, NY
State University of New York at
  Plattsburgh, NY
State University of New York College at
  Geneseo, NY
State University of New York College at
  Oneonta, NY
State University of New York College at
  Potsdam, NY
State University of New York,
  Fredonia, NY
Stephen F. Austin State University, TX
Sterling College, KS
Stetson University, FL
Stevens Institute of Technology, NJ
Stony Brook University, State University of
  New York, NY
Susquehanna University, PA
Sweet Briar College, VA
Syracuse University, NY
Tabor College, KS
Tarleton State University, TX
Taylor University, IN
Temple University, PA
Tennessee Technological University, TN
Tennessee Wesleyan College, TN
Texas A&M University–Commerce, TX

Texas Christian University, TX
Texas Lutheran University, TX
Texas State University-San Marcos, TX
Texas Tech University, TX
Thiel College, PA
Thomas University, GA
Tiffin University, OH
Toccoa Falls College, GA
Towson University, MD
Transylvania University, KY
Trevecca Nazarene University, TN
Trinity International University, IL
Trinity Lutheran College, WA
Trinity University, TX
Troy University, AL
Truman State University, MO
Tusculum College, TN
Tuskegee University, AL
Union College, KY
Union University, TN
University at Buffalo, The State University
  of New York, NY
The University of Akron, OH
The University of Alabama, AL
The University of Alabama at
  Birmingham, AL
The University of Alabama in
  Huntsville, AL
University of Alaska Fairbanks, AK
The University of Arizona, AZ
University of Arkansas at Fort Smith, AR
University of Arkansas at Monticello, AR
University of Arkansas at Pine Bluff, AR
University of Bridgeport, CT
University of California, Irvine, CA
University of California, Riverside, CA
University of Central Florida, FL
University of Charleston, WV
University of Cincinnati, OH
University of Colorado at Boulder, CO
University of Connecticut, CT
University of Dayton, OH
University of Delaware, DE
University of Evansville, IN
The University of Findlay, OH
University of Florida, FL
University of Georgia, GA
University of Great Falls, MT
University of Hartford, CT
University of Hawaii at Hilo, HI
University of Hawaii at Manoa, HI
University of Idaho, ID
University of Illinois at Chicago, IL
University of Indianapolis, IN
University of Kansas, KS
University of La Verne, CA
University of Maine, ME
The University of Maine at Augusta, ME
University of Mary, ND
University of Mary Hardin-Baylor, TX
University of Maryland, Baltimore
  County, MD
University of Maryland, College Park, MD
University of Maryland Eastern Shore, MD
University of Mary Washington, VA
University of Massachusetts Amherst, MA

University of Massachusetts Lowell, MA
The University of Memphis, TN
University of Miami, FL
University of Michigan, MI
University of Michigan–Flint, MI
University of Minnesota, Morris, MN
University of Mississippi, MS
University of Missouri–Columbia, MO
University of Missouri–Kansas City, MO
University of Missouri–St. Louis, MO
University of Nebraska at Kearney, NE
University of Nebraska at Omaha, NE
University of Nebraska–Lincoln, NE
University of Nevada, Las Vegas, NV
University of Nevada, Reno, NV
University of New Hampshire, NH
University of New Orleans, LA
University of North Alabama, AL
The University of North Carolina at
  Asheville, NC
The University of North Carolina at Chapel
  Hill, NC
The University of North Carolina at
  Charlotte, NC
The University of North Carolina at
  Greensboro, NC
The University of North Carolina at
  Pembroke, NC
The University of North Carolina at
  Wilmington, NC
University of North Dakota, ND
University of Northern Colorado, CO
University of Northern Iowa, IA
University of North Florida, FL
University of North Texas, TX
University of Oklahoma, OK
University of Oregon, OR
University of Portland, OR
University of Puerto Rico, Mayagüez
  Campus, PR
University of Puget Sound, WA
University of Redlands, CA
University of Rhode Island, RI
University of Richmond, VA
University of Rio Grande, OH
University of St. Francis, IL
University of Saint Francis, IN
University of St. Thomas, MN
University of St. Thomas, TX
University of San Diego, CA
University of Science and Arts of
  Oklahoma, OK
University of Sioux Falls, SD
University of South Carolina, SC
The University of South Dakota, SD
University of Southern Maine, ME
University of Southern Mississippi, MS
University of South Florida, FL
The University of Tampa, FL
The University of Tennessee at
  Chattanooga, TN
The University of Tennessee at Martin, TN
The University of Texas at Arlington, TX
The University of Texas at Brownsville, TX
The University of Texas at El Paso, TX

The University of Texas at San
Antonio, TX
The University of Texas–Pan American, TX
University of the Cumberlands, KY
University of the District of Columbia, DC
University of the Incarnate Word, TX
University of the Ozarks, AR
University of the Pacific, CA
The University of Toledo, OH
University of Tulsa, OK
University of Utah, UT
University of Vermont, VT
The University of Virginia's College at
Wise, VA
University of Washington, WA
University of West Florida, FL
University of West Georgia, GA
University of Wisconsin–Eau Claire, WI
University of Wisconsin–Green Bay, WI
University of Wisconsin–La Crosse, WI
University of Wisconsin–Oshkosh, WI
University of Wisconsin–Parkside, WI
University of Wisconsin–Stevens Point, WI
University of Wisconsin–Stout, WI
University of Wisconsin–Whitewater, WI
University of Wyoming, WY
Urbana University, OH
Ursinus College, PA
Utah State University, UT
Valdosta State University, GA
Valley City State University, ND
Valley Forge Christian College, PA
Valparaiso University, IN
Vanderbilt University, TN
VanderCook College of Music, IL
Vanguard University of Southern
California, CA
Virginia Commonwealth University, VA
Virginia Military Institute, VA
Virginia Polytechnic Institute and State
University, VA
Virginia Wesleyan College, VA
Wabash College, IN
Wake Forest University, NC
Waldorf College, IA
Walla Walla College, WA
Warner Pacific College, OR
Warner Southern College, FL
Wartburg College, IA
Washington State University, WA
Washington University in St. Louis, MO
Wayland Baptist University, TX
Waynesburg College, PA
Wayne State College, NE
Wayne State University, MI
Webster University, MO
Western Carolina University, NC
Western Illinois University, IL
Western Kentucky University, KY
Western Oregon University, OR
Western State College of Colorado, CO
Western Washington University, WA
West Liberty State College, WV
Westminster College, PA
Westminster College, UT
Westmont College, CA

West Texas A&M University, TX
West Virginia University, WV
West Virginia Wesleyan College, WV
Wheaton College, IL
Wheeling Jesuit University, WV
Whitman College, WA
Whittier College, CA
Whitworth College, WA
Wichita State University, KS
Wilkes University, PA
William Carey College, MS
William Jewell College, MO
William Paterson University of New
Jersey, NJ
William Penn University, IA
Williams Baptist College, AR
Wilson College, PA
Wingate University, NC
Winona State University, MN
Winston-Salem State University, NC
Winthrop University, SC
Wittenberg University, OH
Wofford College, SC
Xavier University, OH
Xavier University of Louisiana, LA
York College, NE
York College of Pennsylvania, PA
Youngstown State University, OH

Performing Arts
Adelphi University, NY
Albion College, MI
Alderson-Broaddus College, WV
Alfred University, NY
Angelo State University, TX
Arizona State University, AZ
Arkansas State University, AR
Auburn University, AL
Augsburg College, MN
Augusta State University, GA
Bay Path College, MA
Belhaven College, MS
Biola University, CA
Boise State University, ID
Bowling Green State University, OH
Brigham Young University, UT
Bryan College, TN
Bucknell University, PA
California Institute of the Arts, CA
California Lutheran University, CA
California State University, Chico, CA
Calvin College, MI
Carroll College, WI
Cedar Crest College, PA
Centenary College of Louisiana, LA
Central Michigan University, MI
Central Missouri State University, MO
Central Washington University, WA
Chapman University, CA
City College of the City University of New
York, NY
Clarion University of Pennsylvania, PA
Clemson University, SC
Coe College, IA
College of Charleston, SC
The College of New Rochelle, NY

Colorado State University-Pueblo, CO
Columbia College Chicago, IL
Columbia International University, SC
Columbus State University, GA
Concordia University, MI
Concordia University Wisconsin, WI
Corban College, OR
Davis & Elkins College, WV
DePaul University, IL
DeSales University, PA
Drexel University, PA
Eastern Michigan University, MI
Edgewood College, WI
Elizabethtown College, PA
Elon University, NC
Emerson College, MA
Emory University, GA
Eureka College, IL
Fairfield University, CT
Ferrum College, VA
Flagler College, FL
Fort Hays State University, KS
Fort Lewis College, CO
Franklin College, IN
Franklin Pierce College, NH
Freed-Hardeman University, TN
Friends University, KS
Frostburg State University, MD
Georgetown College, KY
The George Washington University, DC
Georgia State University, GA
Grambling State University, LA
Grand Canyon University, AZ
Green Mountain College, VT
Greenville College, IL
Hannibal-LaGrange College, MO
Hastings College, NE
Hobart and William Smith Colleges, NY
Idaho State University, ID
Illinois State University, IL
Indiana State University, IN
Indiana University of Pennsylvania, PA
Ithaca College, NY
Kennesaw State University, GA
Kentucky Christian University, KY
King College, TN
Lake Erie College, OH
Lakeland College, WI
Lehigh University, PA
Liberty University, VA
Limestone College, SC
Lindenwood University, MO
Louisiana State University and Agricultural
and Mechanical College, LA
Louisiana Tech University, LA
Lubbock Christian University, TX
Marshall University, WV
Michigan State University, MI
Mississippi State University, MS
Mississippi University for Women, MS
Missouri State University, MO
Missouri Valley College, MO
Molloy College, NY
Montclair State University, NJ
Morris College, SC
Mount Aloysius College, PA

New Mexico Highlands University, NM
New Mexico State University, NM
Norfolk State University, VA
North Carolina School of the Arts, NC
Northeastern Illinois University, IL
Northeastern State University, OK
Northern Arizona University, AZ
Northern Illinois University, IL
Northwestern State University of
   Louisiana, LA
Northwest Nazarene University, ID
Nyack College, NY
Oakland University, MI
Oglethorpe University, GA
Ohio Northern University, OH
The Ohio State University, OH
Ohio University, OH
Ohio University–Eastern, OH
Ohio Valley University, WV
Oklahoma Baptist University, OK
Oklahoma City University, OK
Oklahoma Panhandle State University, OK
Old Dominion University, VA
Ouachita Baptist University, AR
Palm Beach Atlantic University, FL
Pepperdine University, CA
Point Park University, PA
Pontifical Catholic University of Puerto
   Rico, PR
Rice University, TX
The Richard Stockton College of New
   Jersey, NJ
Rockhurst University, MO
St. Andrews Presbyterian College, NC
St. Bonaventure University, NY
St. Cloud State University, MN
Saint Louis University, MO
Saint Martin's College, WA
Salem State College, MA
Seattle Pacific University, WA
Seton Hill University, PA
Shawnee State University, OH
Shaw University, NC
Shenandoah University, VA
Shepherd University, WV
Slippery Rock University of
   Pennsylvania, PA
Sonoma State University, CA
South Dakota State University, SD
Southern Illinois University Carbondale, IL
Southern Utah University, UT
Southwestern College, KS
Southwestern University, TX
State University of New York at
   Binghamton, NY
State University of New York College at
   Brockport, NY
State University of New York College at
   Geneseo, NY
State University of New York College at
   Potsdam, NY
State University of New York,
   Fredonia, NY
Stephens College, MO
Stevens Institute of Technology, NJ
Tabor College, KS

Temple University, PA
Texas A&M University, TX
Texas Christian University, TX
Texas Tech University, TX
Thomas University, GA
The University of Akron, OH
The University of Alabama at
   Birmingham, AL
University of Alaska Southeast, AK
The University of Arizona, AZ
University of California, San Diego, CA
University of Colorado at Boulder, CO
University of Dallas, TX
University of Florida, FL
University of Hartford, CT
University of Hawaii at Hilo, HI
University of Hawaii at Manoa, HI
University of Idaho, ID
University of Illinois at Chicago, IL
University of Kansas, KS
University of Maine, ME
University of Maine at Fort Kent, ME
University of Maryland, Baltimore
   County, MD
University of Maryland, College Park, MD
University of Maryland Eastern Shore, MD
University of Miami, FL
University of Missouri–Kansas City, MO
University of Nebraska at Omaha, NE
University of Nebraska–Lincoln, NE
University of Nevada, Las Vegas, NV
University of Nevada, Reno, NV
The University of North Carolina at
   Charlotte, NC
The University of North Carolina at
   Greensboro, NC
University of Northern Colorado, CO
University of Oklahoma, OK
University of Oregon, OR
University of Portland, OR
University of South Florida, FL
The University of Tampa, FL
The University of Texas at El Paso, TX
The University of Toledo, OH
University of Tulsa, OK
The University of Virginia's College at
   Wise, VA
University of Washington, WA
University of Wisconsin–Stevens Point, WI
Utah State University, UT
Valparaiso University, IN
Virginia Commonwealth University, VA
Virginia Intermont College, VA
Virginia Polytechnic Institute and State
   University, VA
Washington State University, WA
Washington University in St. Louis, MO
Western Illinois University, IL
Western New Mexico University, NM
Western Oregon University, OR
Western Washington University, WA
Wichita State University, KS
Wilkes University, PA
William Woods University, MO
Winthrop University, SC

Xavier University, OH
Xavier University of Louisiana, LA

Theater/Drama
Abilene Christian University, TX
Adelphi University, NY
Adrian College, MI
Albertson College of Idaho, ID
Albion College, MI
Albright College, PA
Alderson-Broaddus College, WV
Alma College, MI
Angelo State University, TX
Arcadia University, PA
Arizona State University, AZ
Arkansas State University, AR
Ashland University, OH
Auburn University, AL
Augsburg College, MN
Augustana College, SD
Augusta State University, GA
Austin College, TX
Austin Peay State University, TN
Averett University, VA
Azusa Pacific University, CA
Baker University, KS
Ball State University, IN
Barry University, FL
Barton College, NC
Baylor University, TX
Bay Path College, MA
Belhaven College, MS
Benedictine College, KS
Berry College, GA
Bethany College, KS
Bethany Lutheran College, MN
Bethel College, KS
Bethel University, MN
Biola University, CA
Black Hills State University, SD
Blue Mountain College, MS
Boise State University, ID
The Boston Conservatory, MA
Boston University, MA
Bowling Green State University, OH
Bradley University, IL
Brenau University, GA
Brevard College, NC
Brewton-Parker College, GA
Brigham Young University, UT
Brigham Young University–Hawaii, HI
Bryan College, TN
Buena Vista University, IA
Butler University, IN
California Baptist University, CA
California Institute of the Arts, CA
California Lutheran University, CA
California State University, Bakersfield, CA
California State University, Chico, CA
California State University, Fresno, CA
California State University, San
   Bernardino, CA
Calvin College, MI
Cameron University, OK
Campbellsville University, KY
Campbell University, NC

Non-Need Scholarships for Undergraduates
Creative Arts/Performance

Carnegie Mellon University, PA
Carroll College, MT
Carroll College, WI
Case Western Reserve University, OH
Catawba College, NC
The Catholic University of America, DC
Cedar Crest College, PA
Centenary College of Louisiana, LA
Central Bible College, MO
Central Christian College of Kansas, KS
Central College, IA
Central Methodist University, MO
Central Michigan University, MI
Central Missouri State University, MO
Central Washington University, WA
Centre College, KY
Chapman University, CA
Chatham College, PA
Christian Heritage College, CA
Christopher Newport University, VA
Clarion University of Pennsylvania, PA
Clarke College, IA
Clemson University, SC
Cleveland State University, OH
Coastal Carolina University, SC
Coe College, IA
College of Charleston, SC
The College of New Rochelle, NY
College of Saint Benedict, MN
College of Staten Island of the City
  University of New York, NY
The College of Wooster, OH
Colorado Christian University, CO
Colorado State University, CO
Colorado State University-Pueblo, CO
Columbia College Chicago, IL
Columbus State University, GA
Concordia College, MN
Concordia University, CA
Concordia University, MI
Concordia University, NE
Concordia University, St. Paul, MN
Converse College, SC
Cornell College, IA
Cornish College of the Arts, WA
Culver-Stockton College, MO
Davis & Elkins College, WV
Denison University, OH
DePaul University, IL
DeSales University, PA
Dickinson State University, ND
Dillard University, LA
Doane College, NE
Dordt College, IA
Drake University, IA
Drexel University, PA
Eastern Michigan University, MI
Eastern Oregon University, OR
Eastern Washington University, WA
East Stroudsburg University of
  Pennsylvania, PA
East Tennessee State University, TN
East Texas Baptist University, TX
Eckerd College, FL
Edgewood College, WI
Elizabethtown College, PA

Elmhurst College, IL
Elon University, NC
Emory & Henry College, VA
Emporia State University, KS
Erskine College, SC
Fairmont State University, WV
Faulkner University, AL
Ferris State University, MI
Ferrum College, VA
Five Towns College, NY
Flagler College, FL
Florida College, FL
Florida Southern College, FL
Fort Hays State University, KS
Fort Lewis College, CO
Francis Marion University, SC
Franklin College, IN
Franklin Pierce College, NH
Freed-Hardeman University, TN
Fresno Pacific University, CA
Friends University, KS
Frostburg State University, MD
Furman University, SC
Gannon University, PA
Georgetown College, KY
The George Washington University, DC
Georgia College & State University, GA
Georgia Southern University, GA
Georgia State University, GA
Goucher College, MD
Grace College, IN
Graceland University, IA
Grambling State University, LA
Grand Canyon University, AZ
Grand Valley State University, MI
Grand View College, IA
Green Mountain College, VT
Guilford College, NC
Gustavus Adolphus College, MN
Hamline University, MN
Hannibal-LaGrange College, MO
Hanover College, IN
Hastings College, NE
Hendrix College, AR
Hillsdale College, MI
Hofstra University, NY
Hope College, MI
Howard Payne University, TX
Huntington University, IN
Idaho State University, ID
Illinois State University, IL
Illinois Wesleyan University, IL
Indiana University of Pennsylvania, PA
Indiana University–Purdue University Fort
  Wayne, IN
Iowa State University of Science and
  Technology, IA
Ithaca College, NY
Jacksonville State University, AL
James Madison University, VA
Kalamazoo College, MI
Kansas State University, KS
Keene State College, NH
Kennesaw State University, GA
Kent State University, OH
Kentucky Christian University, KY

Kentucky Mountain Bible College, KY
Kentucky Wesleyan College, KY
King College, TN
Knox College, IL
Kutztown University of Pennsylvania, PA
LaGrange College, GA
Lake Erie College, OH
Lake Forest College, IL
Lambuth University, TN
La Sierra University, CA
Lee University, TN
Lehigh University, PA
Lewis-Clark State College, ID
Limestone College, SC
Lindenwood University, MO
Lipscomb University, TN
Longwood University, VA
Louisiana State University and Agricultural
  and Mechanical College, LA
Louisiana Tech University, LA
Loyola University Chicago, IL
Lubbock Christian University, TX
Lycoming College, PA
MacMurray College, IL
Malone College, OH
Marshall University, WV
Mars Hill College, NC
Martin Methodist College, TN
Marymount Manhattan College, NY
Maryville College, TN
Massachusetts Maritime Academy, MA
Mercer University, GA
Merrimack College, MA
Mesa State College, CO
Messiah College, PA
Methodist College, NC
Metropolitan State College of Denver, CO
Miami University, OH
Michigan State University, MI
Middle Tennessee State University, TN
Midland Lutheran College, NE
Midwestern State University, TX
Millsaps College, MS
Minnesota State University Mankato, MN
Minnesota State University Moorhead, MN
Minot State University, ND
Mississippi State University, MS
Mississippi University for Women, MS
Missouri Baptist University, MO
Missouri Southern State University, MO
Missouri State University, MO
Missouri Valley College, MO
Montana State University, MT
Montana State University–Billings, MT
Montclair State University, NJ
Montreat College, NC
Morehead State University, KY
Morningside College, IA
Mount Marty College, SD
Mount Mercy College, IA
Mount Union College, OH
Murray State University, KY
Muskingum College, OH
Nazareth College of Rochester, NY
Nebraska Wesleyan University, NE
New England College, NH

New England Conservatory of Music, MA
New Mexico Highlands University, NM
New Mexico State University, NM
Niagara University, NY
North Carolina Agricultural and Technical State University, NC
North Carolina School of the Arts, NC
North Central College, IL
North Dakota State University, ND
Northeastern Illinois University, IL
Northeastern State University, OK
Northern Arizona University, AZ
Northern Illinois University, IL
Northern Michigan University, MI
Northern State University, SD
North Greenville College, SC
Northwestern College, IA
Northwestern College, MN
Northwestern Oklahoma State University, OK
Northwestern State University of Louisiana, LA
Northwest Nazarene University, ID
Northwest University, WA
Nyack College, NY
Oglethorpe University, GA
Ohio Northern University, OH
The Ohio State University, OH
Ohio University, OH
Ohio University–Eastern, OH
Ohio Valley University, WV
Ohio Wesleyan University, OH
Oklahoma City University, OK
Oklahoma Panhandle State University, OK
Old Dominion University, VA
Ouachita Baptist University, AR
Pacific Lutheran University, WA
Pacific University, OR
Palm Beach Atlantic University, FL
Park University, MO
Peace College, NC
Pepperdine University, CA
Piedmont College, GA
Plymouth State University, NH
Point Park University, PA
Pontifical Catholic University of Puerto Rico, PR
Portland State University, OR
Providence College, RI
Radford University, VA
Randolph-Macon Woman's College, VA
The Richard Stockton College of New Jersey, NJ
Rider University, NJ
Ripon College, WI
Rochester College, MI
Rockhurst University, MO
Rollins College, FL
Rust College, MS
St. Ambrose University, IA
St. Cloud State University, MN
St. Edward's University, TX
St. Gregory's University, OK
Saint John's University, MN
Saint Joseph's College, IN
Saint Louis University, MO

Saint Martin's College, WA
Saint Mary's University of Minnesota, MN
St. Norbert College, WI
Salem State College, MA
Schreiner University, TX
Seton Hill University, PA
Shenandoah University, VA
Shimer College, IL
Shorter College, GA
Simpson College, IA
Slippery Rock University of Pennsylvania, PA
Sonoma State University, CA
South Dakota State University, SD
Southeastern College of the Assemblies of God, FL
Southeastern Oklahoma State University, OK
Southeast Missouri State University, MO
Southern Adventist University, TN
Southern Arkansas University–Magnolia, AR
Southern Illinois University Carbondale, IL
Southern Illinois University Edwardsville, IL
Southern Methodist University, TX
Southern Oregon University, OR
Southern Utah University, UT
Southern Wesleyan University, SC
Southwest Baptist University, MO
Southwestern Christian University, OK
Southwestern College, KS
Southwestern University, TX
Southwest Minnesota State University, MN
Spelman College, GA
State University of New York at Binghamton, NY
State University of New York at Plattsburgh, NY
State University of New York College at Brockport, NY
State University of New York College at Geneseo, NY
State University of New York College at Potsdam, NY
State University of New York, Fredonia, NY
Stephen F. Austin State University, TX
Stephens College, MO
Sterling College, KS
Stetson University, FL
Stevens Institute of Technology, NJ
Stony Brook University, State University of New York, NY
Tabor College, KS
Tarleton State University, TX
Taylor University, IN
Texas A&M University, TX
Texas A&M University–Commerce, TX
Texas Christian University, TX
Texas Lutheran University, TX
Texas State University-San Marcos, TX
Texas Tech University, TX
Thomas More College, KY
Towson University, MD
Troy University, AL

Truman State University, MO
Union University, TN
The University of Akron, OH
The University of Alabama, AL
The University of Alabama at Birmingham, AL
University of Alaska Fairbanks, AK
The University of Arizona, AZ
University of California, Riverside, CA
University of Central Florida, FL
University of Colorado at Boulder, CO
University of Connecticut, CT
University of Delaware, DE
University of Detroit Mercy, MI
University of Evansville, IN
The University of Findlay, OH
University of Florida, FL
University of Hartford, CT
University of Hawaii at Hilo, HI
University of Hawaii at Manoa, HI
University of Idaho, ID
University of Illinois at Chicago, IL
University of Indianapolis, IN
University of Kansas, KS
University of La Verne, CA
University of Maine, ME
University of Mary, ND
University of Maryland, Baltimore County, MD
University of Maryland, College Park, MD
University of Maryland Eastern Shore, MD
University of Mary Washington, VA
University of Massachusetts Amherst, MA
University of Miami, FL
University of Michigan, MI
University of Michigan–Flint, MI
University of Mississippi, MS
University of Missouri–Columbia, MO
University of Nebraska at Omaha, NE
University of Nebraska–Lincoln, NE
University of Nevada, Las Vegas, NV
University of Nevada, Reno, NV
University of New Hampshire, NH
The University of North Carolina at Asheville, NC
The University of North Carolina at Chapel Hill, NC
The University of North Carolina at Greensboro, NC
The University of North Carolina at Wilmington, NC
University of North Dakota, ND
University of Northern Colorado, CO
University of Northern Iowa, IA
University of North Texas, TX
University of Oklahoma, OK
University of Oregon, OR
University of Portland, OR
University of Puget Sound, WA
University of St. Thomas, TX
University of Science and Arts of Oklahoma, OK
University of Sioux Falls, SD
University of South Carolina, SC
The University of South Dakota, SD
University of Southern Indiana, IN

University of Southern Maine, ME
University of Southern Mississippi, MS
University of South Florida, FL
The University of Tennessee at Chattanooga, TN
The University of Tennessee at Martin, TN
The University of Texas at Arlington, TX
The University of Texas at El Paso, TX
The University of Texas–Pan American, TX
University of the Cumberlands, KY
University of the Incarnate Word, TX
University of the Ozarks, AR
The University of Toledo, OH
University of Tulsa, OK
University of Utah, UT
University of Vermont, VT
The University of Virginia's College at Wise, VA
University of Washington, WA
University of West Florida, FL
University of West Georgia, GA
University of Wisconsin–Eau Claire, WI
University of Wisconsin–Green Bay, WI
University of Wisconsin–La Crosse, WI
University of Wisconsin–Oshkosh, WI
University of Wisconsin–Parkside, WI
University of Wisconsin–Stevens Point, WI
University of Wisconsin–Whitewater, WI
University of Wyoming, WY
Ursinus College, PA
Utah State University, UT
Valdosta State University, GA
Valley City State University, ND
Valparaiso University, IN
Vanguard University of Southern California, CA
Virginia Commonwealth University, VA
Virginia Intermont College, VA
Virginia Polytechnic Institute and State University, VA
Wabash College, IN
Wake Forest University, NC
Waldorf College, IA
Warner Pacific College, OR
Washington State University, WA
Washington University in St. Louis, MO
Wayland Baptist University, TX
Wayne State College, NE
Wayne State University, MI
Webster University, MO
Western Carolina University, NC
Western Illinois University, IL
Western Kentucky University, KY
Western Washington University, WA
West Liberty State College, WV
Westminster College, PA
Westminster College, UT
Westmont College, CA
West Texas A&M University, TX
West Virginia University, WV
West Virginia Wesleyan College, WV
Whitman College, WA
Whittier College, CA
Whitworth College, WA
Wichita State University, KS
Wilkes University, PA

William Carey College, MS
William Jewell College, MO
William Penn University, IA
William Woods University, MO
Wilmington College, OH
Winona State University, MN
Winthrop University, SC
Wittenberg University, OH
Xavier University, OH
York College, NE
Youngstown State University, OH

Special Achievements/ Activities

Cheerleading/Drum Major

Abilene Christian University, TX
Angelo State University, TX
Arkansas State University, AR
Athens State University, AL
Auburn University, AL
Austin Peay State University, TN
Azusa Pacific University, CA
Baker University, KS
Belhaven College, MS
Bethany College, KS
Bluefield State College, WV
Boise State University, ID
Brevard College, NC
Brewton-Parker College, GA
Brigham Young University, UT
Brigham Young University–Hawaii, HI
Bryan College, TN
Campbellsville University, KY
Campbell University, NC
Central Christian College of Kansas, KS
Central Methodist University, MO
Central Missouri State University, MO
Columbus State University, GA
Culver-Stockton College, MO
Dickinson State University, ND
Drexel University, PA
East Central University, OK
East Texas Baptist University, TX
Emporia State University, KS
Evangel University, MO
Fairmont State University, WV
Faulkner University, AL
Fort Hays State University, KS
Francis Marion University, SC
Graceland University, IA
Grambling State University, LA
Harding University, AR
Hawai'i Pacific University, HI
Houston Baptist University, TX
Huntington University, IN
Iowa Wesleyan College, IA
James Madison University, VA
John Brown University, AR
Lambuth University, TN
Langston University, OK
Lee University, TN
Lenoir-Rhyne College, NC
Liberty University, VA
Limestone College, SC

Lincoln Memorial University, TN
Lindenwood University, MO
Lipscomb University, TN
Long Island University, Brooklyn Campus, NY
Louisiana Tech University, LA
Lubbock Christian University, TX
Mars Hill College, NC
Martin Methodist College, TN
McKendree College, IL
Methodist College, NC
MidAmerica Nazarene University, KS
Middle Tennessee State University, TN
Midwestern State University, TX
Mississippi State University, MS
Missouri Baptist University, MO
Missouri State University, MO
Missouri Valley College, MO
Montana State University–Billings, MT
Morehead State University, KY
Morris College, SC
Northeastern State University, OK
North Greenville College, SC
Northwestern Oklahoma State University, OK
Northwestern State University of Louisiana, LA
Northwest Nazarene University, ID
The Ohio State University, OH
Oklahoma City University, OK
Oklahoma Panhandle State University, OK
Oklahoma State University, OK
Old Dominion University, VA
Oral Roberts University, OK
Park University, MO
Peru State College, NE
St. Edward's University, TX
St. John's University, NY
Saint Joseph's College, IN
Saint Louis University, MO
St. Mary's University of San Antonio, TX
Sam Houston State University, TX
Southeastern Louisiana University, LA
Southeast Missouri State University, MO
Southern Arkansas University–Magnolia, AR
Southern Illinois University Carbondale, IL
Southern Utah University, UT
Southwestern Christian University, OK
Southwestern College, KS
Stephen F. Austin State University, TX
Stetson University, FL
Tabor College, KS
Temple University, PA
Tennessee Technological University, TN
Tennessee Wesleyan College, TN
Texas A&M University–Commerce, TX
Texas Wesleyan University, TX
Tiffin University, OH
Transylvania University, KY
Tusculum College, TN
Union College, KY
Union University, TN
The University of Alabama, AL
The University of Alabama at Birmingham, AL

The University of Alabama in
  Huntsville, AL
University of Arkansas at Fort Smith, AR
University of Arkansas at Monticello, AR
University of Charleston, WV
University of Delaware, DE
University of Idaho, ID
University of Mary Hardin-Baylor, TX
University of Maryland, College Park, MD
University of Massachusetts Amherst, MA
The University of Memphis, TN
University of Mississippi, MS
University of Nebraska at Kearney, NE
University of Nebraska–Lincoln, NE
University of Nevada, Las Vegas, NV
University of Nevada, Reno, NV
University of North Alabama, AL
The University of North Carolina at
  Wilmington, NC
University of Puerto Rico, Mayagüez
  Campus, PR
University of Rio Grande, OH
University of Saint Francis, IN
University of Science and Arts of
  Oklahoma, OK
University of Sioux Falls, SD
University of South Carolina, SC
University of Southern Mississippi, MS
The University of Tennessee at
  Chattanooga, TN
The University of Tennessee at Martin, TN
The University of Texas at Arlington, TX
The University of Texas at El Paso, TX
The University of Texas–Pan American, TX
University of the Cumberlands, KY
The University of Toledo, OH
University of Tulsa, OK
University of Utah, UT
University of Wyoming, WY
Virginia Polytechnic Institute and State
  University, VA
Wake Forest University, NC
Wayland Baptist University, TX
Webber International University, FL
West Liberty State College, WV
West Texas A&M University, TX
William Carey College, MS
William Jewell College, MO
Williams Baptist College, AR
Winston-Salem State University, NC
Wofford College, SC
Youngstown State University, OH

Community Service

Adelphi University, NY
Agnes Scott College, GA
Allen College, IA
Alliant International University, CA
Alvernia College, PA
Alverno College, WI
Antioch College, OH
Arcadia University, PA
Arkansas State University, AR
Armstrong Atlantic State University, GA
Augsburg College, MN
Augusta State University, GA

Barry University, FL
Baylor University, TX
Beloit College, WI
Bentley College, MA
Berry College, GA
Bethel University, MN
Biola University, CA
Boise State University, ID
Bradley University, IL
Brevard College, NC
Brigham Young University, UT
Brigham Young University–Hawaii, HI
Bryan College, TN
California Lutheran University, CA
California State University, Bakersfield, CA
California State University, Chico, CA
California State University, Fresno, CA
California State University, San
  Bernardino, CA
California State University, Stanislaus, CA
Calvin College, MI
Canisius College, NY
Cedar Crest College, PA
Centenary College of Louisiana, LA
Central Bible College, MO
Central Washington University, WA
City College of the City University of New
  York, NY
Clark University, MA
Cleary University, MI
Clemson University, SC
Colby-Sawyer College, NH
College Misericordia, PA
College of Mount St. Joseph, OH
The College of New Rochelle, NY
College of Notre Dame of Maryland, MD
College of St. Joseph, VT
College of Saint Mary, NE
The College of Saint Rose, NY
College of the Atlantic, ME
The College of Wooster, OH
Colorado Christian University, CO
Colorado State University-Pueblo, CO
Columbus State University, GA
Cornell College, IA
Dallas Baptist University, TX
Davidson College, NC
Defiance College, OH
DePaul University, IL
DePauw University, IN
Dominican College, NY
Dominican University of California, CA
Eastern Oregon University, OR
Eckerd College, FL
Edgewood College, WI
Emmanuel College, MA
Emory & Henry College, VA
Endicott College, MA
Eugene Bible College, OR
The Evergreen State College, WA
Ferrum College, VA
Finlandia University, MI
Florida Southern College, FL
Frostburg State University, MD
Furman University, SC
Gannon University, PA

Georgia College & State University, GA
Georgia Southern University, GA
Georgia State University, GA
Green Mountain College, VT
Gustavus Adolphus College, MN
Hampshire College, MA
Hillsdale College, MI
Hollins University, VA
Holy Names University, CA
Howard Payne University, TX
Humphreys College, CA
Illinois State University, IL
Illinois Wesleyan University, IL
Indiana University of Pennsylvania, PA
Iowa State University of Science and
  Technology, IA
Johnson Bible College, TN
Johnson C. Smith University, NC
Juniata College, PA
Kean University, NJ
Kennesaw State University, GA
Kent State University, OH
Kentucky Christian University, KY
Keuka College, NY
King College, TN
King's College, PA
Knox College, IL
LaGrange College, GA
Lake Erie College, OH
Lakeland College, WI
La Salle University, PA
Lasell College, MA
Lenoir-Rhyne College, NC
Lewis & Clark College, OR
Lincoln Christian College, IL
Lincoln University, PA
Lindenwood University, MO
Loyola Marymount University, CA
Loyola University Chicago, IL
Malone College, OH
Manhattan College, NY
Manhattanville College, NY
Marlboro College, VT
Marymount University, VA
Maryville College, TN
Maryville University of Saint Louis, MO
Massachusetts College of Art, MA
McKendree College, IL
Menlo College, CA
Mercer University, GA
Mercy College of Health Sciences, IA
Mercyhurst College, PA
Meredith College, NC
Michigan State University, MI
Midland Lutheran College, NE
Millersville University of Pennsylvania, PA
Milligan College, TN
Millsaps College, MS
Minnesota State University Mankato, MN
Minnesota State University Moorhead, MN
Missouri Valley College, MO
Montclair State University, NJ
Morehouse College, GA
Mount Ida College, MA
New England College, NH
Niagara University, NY

North Central College, IL
North Central University, MN
Northeastern State University, OK
Oglethorpe University, GA
Ohio Northern University, OH
Ohio Valley University, WV
Ohio Wesleyan University, OH
Oklahoma State University, OK
Old Dominion University, VA
Olivet College, MI
Oral Roberts University, OK
Pacific Union College, CA
Pacific University, OR
Peirce College, PA
Pitzer College, CA
Point Park University, PA
Portland State University, OR
Post University, CT
Presentation College, SD
Providence College, RI
Purdue University, IN
Quincy University, IL
Randolph-Macon Woman's College, VA
Regis College, MA
Rice University, TX
The Richard Stockton College of New Jersey, NJ
Robert Morris College, IL
Rochester Institute of Technology, NY
Rockhurst University, MO
Rosemont College, PA
St. Andrews Presbyterian College, NC
St. Edward's University, TX
St. John Fisher College, NY
St. John's University, NY
Saint Joseph's College of Maine, ME
St. Lawrence University, NY
Saint Louis University, MO
Saint Martin's College, WA
St. Olaf College, MN
Schreiner University, TX
Seton Hall University, NJ
Seton Hill University, PA
Simmons College, MA
Slippery Rock University of Pennsylvania, PA
Sonoma State University, CA
South Dakota State University, SD
Southern Adventist University, TN
Southern Illinois University Carbondale, IL
Southern Oregon University, OR
Southern Vermont College, VT
Southern Wesleyan University, SC
Southwestern College, KS
Spelman College, GA
Spring Hill College, AL
State University of New York at Binghamton, NY
State University of New York at Plattsburgh, NY
State University of New York College at Geneseo, NY
State University of New York College at Oneonta, NY
State University of New York College at Potsdam, NY

Stetson University, FL
Suffolk University, MA
Texas A&M University–Texarkana, TX
Texas Tech University, TX
Trinity College of Florida, FL
Tusculum College, TN
Unity College, ME
The University of Alabama, AL
The University of Alabama in Huntsville, AL
University of Alaska Fairbanks, AK
University of California, San Diego, CA
University of Charleston, WV
University of Colorado at Boulder, CO
University of Colorado at Colorado Springs, CO
University of Connecticut, CT
University of Delaware, DE
University of Florida, FL
University of Great Falls, MT
University of Hartford, CT
University of Hawaii at Hilo, HI
University of Houston–Downtown, TX
University of Houston–Victoria, TX
University of Illinois at Springfield, IL
University of Indianapolis, IN
University of Kansas, KS
University of La Verne, CA
University of Maine, ME
University of Maine at Presque Isle, ME
University of Mary Hardin-Baylor, TX
University of Massachusetts Dartmouth, MA
University of Massachusetts Lowell, MA
University of Michigan, MI
University of Michigan–Dearborn, MI
University of Michigan–Flint, MI
University of Nebraska–Lincoln, NE
University of Nevada, Las Vegas, NV
University of New Hampshire, NH
The University of North Carolina at Asheville, NC
The University of North Carolina at Chapel Hill, NC
The University of North Carolina at Greensboro, NC
University of North Florida, FL
University of Portland, OR
University of Richmond, VA
University of St. Francis, IL
University of St. Thomas, TX
University of South Carolina, SC
University of Southern Maine, ME
The University of Texas at Arlington, TX
The University of Texas–Pan American, TX
The University of Texas Southwestern Medical Center at Dallas, TX
University of the Cumberlands, KY
University of Tulsa, OK
University of Vermont, VT
The University of Virginia's College at Wise, VA
University of Washington, WA
University of West Georgia, GA
University of Wisconsin–Eau Claire, WI
University of Wisconsin–Green Bay, WI

University of Wisconsin–Parkside, WI
Urbana University, OH
Ursuline College, OH
Valdosta State University, GA
Villa Julie College, MD
Virginia Polytechnic Institute and State University, VA
Wabash College, IN
Wake Forest University, NC
Walla Walla College, WA
Warren Wilson College, NC
Washington State University, WA
Waynesburg College, PA
Webber International University, FL
Wesley College, DE
Western Illinois University, IL
Western Washington University, WA
Westfield State College, MA
West Virginia Wesleyan College, WV
Wheeling Jesuit University, WV
Wilson College, PA
Wittenberg University, OH
Wofford College, SC
Worcester State College, MA
York College of Pennsylvania, PA

Hobbies/Interests

Angelo State University, TX
Augusta State University, GA
Brevard College, NC
California State University, Chico, CA
California State University, San Bernardino, CA
Central Washington University, WA
The College of New Rochelle, NY
Corban College, OR
Edgewood College, WI
Eugene Bible College, OR
Hawai'i Pacific University, HI
Illinois Wesleyan University, IL
Indiana University of Pennsylvania, PA
Lake Erie College, OH
Mesa State College, CO
Michigan State University, MI
Millsaps College, MS
Missouri State University, MO
Missouri Valley College, MO
The Ohio State University, OH
St. John's University, NY
Shimer College, IL
South Dakota State University, SD
Stephen F. Austin State University, TX
The University of Alabama, AL
University of Michigan–Flint, MI
University of Minnesota, Twin Cities Campus, MN
University of Nevada, Las Vegas, NV
University of Wisconsin–Eau Claire, WI
Valdosta State University, GA

Junior Miss

Albertson College of Idaho, ID
Albright College, PA
Alvernia College, PA
The Art Institute of Colorado, CO
Augsburg College, MN
Belhaven College, MS

Bethel University, MN
Bluefield State College, WV
Brigham Young University–Hawaii, HI
Campbellsville University, KY
Campbell University, NC
Carroll College, WI
Cedar Crest College, PA
The College of New Rochelle, NY
College of Saint Benedict, MN
Georgetown College, KY
Georgia Southern University, GA
Grambling State University, LA
Idaho State University, ID
Judson College, AL
Kentucky Wesleyan College, KY
Lebanon Valley College, PA
Lewis-Clark State College, ID
Lindenwood University, MO
Malone College, OH
McDaniel College, MD
McMurry University, TX
Mercer University, GA
Michigan State University, MI
Midway College, KY
Mississippi University for Women, MS
Missouri Valley College, MO
Mount Vernon Nazarene University, OH
Murray State University, KY
Northeastern State University, OK
North Greenville College, SC
Ohio Northern University, OH
Oklahoma City University, OK
Point Park University, PA
South Dakota State University, SD
Spring Arbor University, MI
Tennessee Wesleyan College, TN
Thomas University, GA
The University of Alabama, AL
The University of Alabama at
  Birmingham, AL
The University of Alabama in
  Huntsville, AL
University of Idaho, ID
The University of North Carolina at
  Asheville, NC
The University of North Carolina at
  Greensboro, NC
University of Wyoming, WY
Wartburg College, IA
Washington State University, WA
William Carey College, MS
William Penn University, IA

Leadership

Abilene Christian University, TX
Agnes Scott College, GA
Alaska Pacific University, AK
Alderson-Broaddus College, WV
Alfred University, NY
Allen College, IA
Alliant International University, CA
Alma College, MI
Alvernia College, PA
American University, DC
Anderson University, IN
Andrews University, MI

Angelo State University, TX
Aquinas College, TN
Arcadia University, PA
Arkansas Tech University, AR
Asbury College, KY
Athens State University, AL
Atlantic Union College, MA
Auburn University, AL
Augsburg College, MN
Augustana College, SD
Austin College, TX
Azusa Pacific University, CA
Babson College, MA
Baker University, KS
Baldwin-Wallace College, OH
Ball State University, IN
Bard College, NY
Barry University, FL
Barton College, NC
Baylor University, TX
Becker College, MA
Belhaven College, MS
Belmont Abbey College, NC
Bethany College, WV
Bethel University, MN
Bluefield State College, WV
Blue Mountain College, MS
Bluffton University, OH
Boise State University, ID
Boston University, MA
Bowdoin College, ME
Bowling Green State University, OH
Bradley University, IL
Brenau University, GA
Brevard College, NC
Brewton-Parker College, GA
Brigham Young University, UT
Brigham Young University–Hawaii, HI
Bryan College, TN
Buena Vista University, IA
California Lutheran University, CA
California State University, Chico, CA
California State University, Fullerton, CA
California State University, Stanislaus, CA
Cameron University, OK
Campbellsville University, KY
Canisius College, NY
Carroll College, WI
Carson-Newman College, TN
Case Western Reserve University, OH
Cedar Crest College, PA
Cedarville University, OH
Centenary College, NJ
Centenary College of Louisiana, LA
Central Christian College of Kansas, KS
Central Methodist University, MO
Central Michigan University, MI
Central Missouri State University, MO
Central Pennsylvania College, PA
Central Washington University, WA
Chowan College, NC
Christian Heritage College, CA
Christopher Newport University, VA
City College of the City University of New
  York, NY
Clarion University of Pennsylvania, PA

Clark Atlanta University, GA
Clarke College, IA
Clarkson University, NY
Clemson University, SC
Colby-Sawyer College, NH
College Misericordia, PA
College of Mount St. Joseph, OH
College of Mount Saint Vincent, NY
The College of New Rochelle, NY
College of Notre Dame of Maryland, MD
College of St. Joseph, VT
College of Saint Mary, NE
College of the Atlantic, ME
The College of Wooster, OH
Colorado Christian University, CO
Colorado State University-Pueblo, CO
Columbia College, MO
Columbia College, SC
Columbia College Chicago, IL
Columbia International University, SC
Columbus State University, GA
Concordia University, OR
Concordia University Wisconsin, WI
Converse College, SC
Corban College, OR
Cornerstone University, MI
Crown College, MN
Culver-Stockton College, MO
Dallas Baptist University, TX
Dallas Christian College, TX
Daniel Webster College, NH
David N. Myers University, OH
Davidson College, NC
Davis & Elkins College, WV
Defiance College, OH
Denison University, OH
DePauw University, IN
DeSales University, PA
Dickinson State University, ND
Dominican College, NY
Dordt College, IA
Duke University, NC
East Carolina University, NC
Eastern Michigan University, MI
Eastern Oregon University, OR
East Tennessee State University, TN
East Texas Baptist University, TX
Eckerd College, FL
Edgewood College, WI
Elmira College, NY
Elon University, NC
Embry-Riddle Aeronautical University, AZ
Embry-Riddle Aeronautical University, FL
Embry-Riddle Aeronautical University,
  Extended Campus, FL
Emmaus Bible College, IA
Endicott College, MA
Erskine College, SC
Eugene Bible College, OR
Eureka College, IL
Evangel University, MO
Faith Baptist Bible College and Theological
  Seminary, IA
Faulkner University, AL
Ferrum College, VA
Finlandia University, MI

Non-Need Scholarships for Undergraduates
Special Achievements/Activities

Flagler College, FL
Florida Southern College, FL
Fort Lewis College, CO
Freed-Hardeman University, TN
Fresno Pacific University, CA
Friends University, KS
Frostburg State University, MD
Furman University, SC
Gannon University, PA
Georgetown College, KY
Georgia College & State University, GA
Georgia Institute of Technology, GA
Georgia Southern University, GA
Georgia State University, GA
Gonzaga University, WA
Gordon College, MA
Graceland University, IA
Grace University, NE
Grambling State University, LA
Grand Canyon University, AZ
Green Mountain College, VT
Greenville College, IL
Grove City College, PA
Hampden-Sydney College, VA
Hampshire College, MA
Hawai'i Pacific University, HI
Hendrix College, AR
Hilbert College, NY
Hillsdale College, MI
Hobart and William Smith Colleges, NY
Hofstra University, NY
Hollins University, VA
Howard Payne University, TX
Husson College, ME
Idaho State University, ID
Illinois State University, IL
Illinois Wesleyan University, IL
Indiana University of Pennsylvania, PA
Iowa State University of Science and
  Technology, IA
Ithaca College, NY
James Madison University, VA
Jamestown College, ND
John Brown University, AR
Johnson & Wales University, RI
Johnson Bible College, TN
Johnson C. Smith University, NC
Juniata College, PA
Kansas State University, KS
Kean University, NJ
Kennesaw State University, GA
Kent State University, OH
Kentucky Christian University, KY
Kentucky Wesleyan College, KY
Keuka College, NY
King's College, PA
Kutztown University of Pennsylvania, PA
LaGrange College, GA
Lake Forest College, IL
Lakeland College, WI
Lancaster Bible College, PA
Langston University, OK
La Sierra University, CA
Lee University, TN
Le Moyne College, NY
Lenoir-Rhyne College, NC

Lewis-Clark State College, ID
Liberty University, VA
Limestone College, SC
Lincoln Christian College, IL
Lindenwood University, MO
Linfield College, OR
Lipscomb University, TN
Lock Haven University of Pennsylvania, PA
Long Island University, Brooklyn
  Campus, NY
Louisiana State University and Agricultural
  and Mechanical College, LA
Loyola University Chicago, IL
Lubbock Christian University, TX
Lycoming College, PA
Lynn University, FL
Lyon College, AR
MacMurray College, IL
Malone College, OH
Manhattan Christian College, KS
Manhattan College, NY
Mary Baldwin College, VA
Marymount Manhattan College, NY
Marymount University, VA
Maryville College, TN
Maryville University of Saint Louis, MO
Massachusetts Maritime Academy, MA
McDaniel College, MD
McKendree College, IL
Mercyhurst College, PA
Meredith College, NC
Merrimack College, MA
Messiah College, PA
Methodist College, NC
Miami University, OH
Michigan State University, MI
Michigan Technological University, MI
MidAmerica Nazarene University, KS
Middle Tennessee State University, TN
Midland Lutheran College, NE
Midway College, KY
Midwestern State University, TX
Millsaps College, MS
Minnesota State University Mankato, MN
Mississippi College, MS
Mississippi State University, MS
Mississippi University for Women, MS
Missouri Southern State University, MO
Missouri Valley College, MO
Montclair State University, NJ
Montreat College, NC
Morehead State University, KY
Morehouse College, GA
Mount Aloysius College, PA
Mount Ida College, MA
Mount Marty College, SD
Mount Mary College, WI
Mount Mercy College, IA
Mount Olive College, NC
Murray State University, KY
New England College, NH
New Mexico State University, NM
North Central University, MN
Northeastern Illinois University, IL
Northeastern State University, OK
Northern Illinois University, IL

Northern Michigan University, MI
Northern State University, SD
Northland College, WI
Northwestern College, MN
Northwestern Oklahoma State
  University, OK
Northwestern State University of
  Louisiana, LA
Northwest Nazarene University, ID
Northwest University, WA
Nova Southeastern University, FL
Nyack College, NY
Ohio Northern University, OH
The Ohio State University, OH
Ohio Valley University, WV
Ohio Wesleyan University, OH
Oklahoma Baptist University, OK
Oklahoma City University, OK
Oklahoma State University, OK
Old Dominion University, VA
Olivet College, MI
Oral Roberts University, OK
Pacific Lutheran University, WA
Pacific Union College, CA
Palm Beach Atlantic University, FL
Peirce College, PA
Peru State College, NE
Pfeiffer University, NC
Philadelphia Biblical University, PA
Piedmont College, GA
Pine Manor College, MA
Pitzer College, CA
Portland State University, OR
Post University, CT
Presentation College, SD
Purdue University, IN
Quincy University, IL
Quinnipiac University, CT
Radford University, VA
Randolph-Macon Woman's College, VA
Reformed Bible College, MI
Regis University, CO
Rice University, TX
The Richard Stockton College of New
  Jersey, NJ
Ripon College, WI
Roberts Wesleyan College, NY
Rochester College, MI
Rochester Institute of Technology, NY
Rockhurst University, MO
St. Andrews Presbyterian College, NC
St. Edward's University, TX
St. John's University, NY
St. Louis Christian College, MO
Saint Louis University, MO
Saint Martin's College, WA
Saint Mary's University of Minnesota, MN
Saint Vincent College, PA
Saint Xavier University, IL
Sam Houston State University, TX
Schreiner University, TX
Seton Hall University, NJ
Seton Hill University, PA
Shepherd University, WV
Simpson College, IA
Simpson University, CA

Slippery Rock University of
Pennsylvania, PA
Sonoma State University, CA
South Dakota State University, SD
Southeastern Louisiana University, LA
Southeast Missouri State University, MO
Southern Adventist University, TN
Southern Arkansas University–
Magnolia, AR
Southern Illinois University Carbondale, IL
Southern New Hampshire University, NH
Southern Oregon University, OR
Southern Utah University, UT
Southern Vermont College, VT
Southern Wesleyan University, SC
Southwestern College, KS
State University of New York at
Binghamton, NY
State University of New York at
Plattsburgh, NY
State University of New York College at
Brockport, NY
State University of New York College at
Geneseo, NY
State University of New York College at
Oneonta, NY
State University of New York College at
Potsdam, NY
State University of New York College of
Environmental Science and Forestry, NY
State University of New York,
Fredonia, NY
Stephen F. Austin State University, TX
Stephens College, MO
Stetson University, FL
Taylor University, IN
Taylor University Fort Wayne, IN
Texas A&M University, TX
Texas A&M University at Galveston, TX
Texas A&M University–Commerce, TX
Texas A&M University–Texarkana, TX
Texas Christian University, TX
Texas Lutheran University, TX
Texas Wesleyan University, TX
Thiel College, PA
Tiffin University, OH
Toccoa Falls College, GA
Trinity College, CT
Trinity College of Florida, FL
Trinity International University, IL
Trinity Lutheran College, WA
Troy University, AL
Truman State University, MO
Tusculum College, TN
Union University, TN
Unity College, ME
The University of Akron, OH
The University of Alabama at
Birmingham, AL
The University of Alabama in
Huntsville, AL
University of Alaska Southeast, AK
The University of Arizona, AZ
University of Arkansas at Fort Smith, AR
University of Arkansas at Monticello, AR
University of Arkansas at Pine Bluff, AR

University of Bridgeport, CT
University of California, San Diego, CA
University of Central Florida, FL
University of Charleston, WV
University of Colorado at Boulder, CO
University of Colorado at Colorado
Springs, CO
University of Colorado at Denver and
Health Sciences Center—Downtown
Denver Campus, CO
University of Connecticut, CT
University of Dallas, TX
University of Delaware, DE
University of Evansville, IN
University of Florida, FL
University of Great Falls, MT
University of Hawaii at Hilo, HI
University of Houston–Downtown, TX
University of Houston–Victoria, TX
University of Idaho, ID
University of Illinois at Springfield, IL
University of Kansas, KS
University of La Verne, CA
University of Maine, ME
The University of Maine at Augusta, ME
University of Mary Hardin-Baylor, TX
University of Maryland, College Park, MD
University of Mary Washington, VA
University of Massachusetts Amherst, MA
The University of Memphis, TN
University of Michigan, MI
University of Michigan–Flint, MI
University of Minnesota, Twin Cities
Campus, MN
University of Mississippi, MS
University of Nebraska at Omaha, NE
University of Nebraska–Lincoln, NE
University of Nevada, Las Vegas, NV
University of New England, ME
University of North Alabama, AL
The University of North Carolina at
Asheville, NC
The University of North Carolina at Chapel
Hill, NC
The University of North Carolina at
Greensboro, NC
The University of North Carolina at
Wilmington, NC
University of North Dakota, ND
University of Northern Iowa, IA
University of North Florida, FL
University of Oklahoma, OK
University of Pittsburgh at Johnstown, PA
University of Puget Sound, WA
University of Rochester, NY
University of St. Francis, IL
University of Science and Arts of
Oklahoma, OK
University of Sioux Falls, SD
University of South Carolina, SC
University of Southern California, CA
University of Southern Indiana, IN
University of Southern Mississippi, MS
The University of Tampa, FL
The University of Tennessee at
Chattanooga, TN

The University of Tennessee at Martin, TN
The University of Texas at Arlington, TX
The University of Texas at Dallas, TX
The University of Texas at El Paso, TX
The University of Texas–Pan American, TX
University of the Ozarks, AR
The University of Toledo, OH
University of Tulsa, OK
University of Utah, UT
University of Washington, WA
University of Wisconsin–Eau Claire, WI
University of Wisconsin–Green Bay, WI
University of Wisconsin–Parkside, WI
University of Wisconsin–Stevens Point, WI
University of Wisconsin–Whitewater, WI
University of Wyoming, WY
Urbana University, OH
Ursinus College, PA
Ursuline College, OH
Valley Forge Christian College, PA
Villa Julie College, MD
Virginia Military Institute, VA
Virginia Polytechnic Institute and State
University, VA
Virginia Wesleyan College, VA
Wabash College, IN
Walla Walla College, WA
Warner Pacific College, OR
Warner Southern College, FL
Warren Wilson College, NC
Washington Bible College, MD
Washington State University, WA
Wayland Baptist University, TX
Wayne State College, NE
Webber International University, FL
Webster University, MO
Wells College, NY
Wesley College, DE
Western Illinois University, IL
Western Kentucky University, KY
Western New England College, MA
Western State College of Colorado, CO
Western Washington University, WA
Westminster College, MO
Westminster College, PA
Westmont College, CA
West Texas A&M University, TX
West Virginia University, WV
West Virginia Wesleyan College, WV
Wichita State University, KS
Wilkes University, PA
William Carey College, MS
William Penn University, IA
William Woods University, MO
Wilmington College, OH
Wittenberg University, OH
Wofford College, SC
York College, NE
Youngstown State University, OH

Memberships
Adelphi University, NY
Albright College, PA
American University, DC
Angelo State University, TX
Arcadia University, PA

Auburn University, AL
Barry University, FL
Bay Path College, MA
Blue Mountain College, MS
Boston University, MA
Brigham Young University, UT
California State University, Chico, CA
California State University, Stanislaus, CA
Carroll College, WI
Carson-Newman College, TN
Cedar Crest College, PA
Central Pennsylvania College, PA
Central Washington University, WA
Christian Heritage College, CA
The College of New Rochelle, NY
College of Notre Dame of Maryland, MD
College of Saint Benedict, MN
Columbia College, MO
Concordia University, NE
Corban College, OR
Dallas Baptist University, TX
Delaware Valley College, PA
Dominican College, NY
Eastern Michigan University, MI
East Tennessee State University, TN
Emporia State University, KS
Erskine College, SC
Flagler College, FL
Fresno Pacific University, CA
Georgia Southern University, GA
Georgia State University, GA
Grand Canyon University, AZ
Greenville College, IL
Grove City College, PA
Hawai'i Pacific University, HI
Idaho State University, ID
Johnson & Wales University, RI
Kettering University, MI
Laboratory Institute of Merchandising, NY
Lock Haven University of Pennsylvania, PA
Longwood University, VA
Loras College, IA
Loyola University Chicago, IL
Medcenter One College of Nursing, ND
Mercer University, GA
Michigan State University, MI
Midwestern State University, TX
Mississippi State University, MS
Missouri State University, MO
Mount Marty College, SD
North Central University, MN
North Dakota State University, ND
Northwestern Oklahoma State University, OK
Northwestern State University of Louisiana, LA
Northwood University, Florida Campus, FL
Northwood University, Texas Campus, TX
The Ohio State University, OH
Old Dominion University, VA
Olivet College, MI
Oral Roberts University, OK
Pacific University, OR
Peirce College, PA
Peru State College, NE
Portland State University, OR

Ripon College, WI
Saint Louis University, MO
Saint Martin's College, WA
Saint Mary's College of California, CA
Salem State College, MA
Shawnee State University, OH
Sonoma State University, CA
South Dakota State University, SD
Southeastern Louisiana University, LA
Southern New Hampshire University, NH
Southern Oregon University, OR
Southwestern College, KS
State University of New York at Binghamton, NY
Tennessee Wesleyan College, TN
Texas A&M University, TX
Texas A&M University–Texarkana, TX
Texas Tech University, TX
Trevecca Nazarene University, TN
Trinity (Washington) University, DC
The University of Akron, OH
The University of Alabama at Birmingham, AL
University of Houston–Victoria, TX
University of Indianapolis, IN
University of Louisville, KY
University of Maine, ME
University of Missouri–St. Louis, MO
University of Nebraska at Omaha, NE
University of Nevada, Las Vegas, NV
University of North Dakota, ND
The University of Texas–Pan American, TX
The University of Toledo, OH
University of West Georgia, GA
University of Wisconsin–Eau Claire, WI
University of Wisconsin–Stout, WI
Virginia Polytechnic Institute and State University, VA
Wake Forest University, NC
Washington College, MD
Washington State University, WA
Wayland Baptist University, TX
Webber International University, FL
Western Kentucky University, KY
Western Washington University, WA
West Texas A&M University, TX
York College of Pennsylvania, PA

Religious Involvement

Adrian College, MI
Alaska Pacific University, AK
Alvernia College, PA
Andrews University, MI
Anna Maria College, MA
Appalachian Bible College, WV
Augsburg College, MN
Austin College, TX
Averett University, VA
Azusa Pacific University, CA
Baker University, KS
Barry University, FL
Barton College, NC
Baylor University, TX
Belmont Abbey College, NC
Berry College, GA
Bethany College, WV

Bethel University, MN
Blue Mountain College, MS
Brigham Young University–Hawaii, HI
Bryan College, TN
California Lutheran University, CA
Calvary Bible College and Theological Seminary, MO
Calvin College, MI
Campbellsville University, KY
Campbell University, NC
Canisius College, NY
Carroll College, MT
Carroll College, WI
Cedar Crest College, PA
Centenary College of Louisiana, LA
Central Bible College, MO
Central Christian College of Kansas, KS
Central College, IA
Central Methodist University, MO
Christian Heritage College, CA
The College of New Rochelle, NY
College of Notre Dame of Maryland, MD
The College of Wooster, OH
Colorado Christian University, CO
Columbia College, MO
Columbia International University, SC
Concordia University, NE
Concordia University, OR
Corban College, OR
Cornell College, IA
Cornerstone University, MI
Dallas Baptist University, TX
Davidson College, NC
Davis & Elkins College, WV
Defiance College, OH
Dominican University, IL
Eastern Mennonite University, VA
Eastern Michigan University, MI
East Texas Baptist University, TX
Elizabethtown College, PA
Emmaus Bible College, IA
Endicott College, MA
Eugene Bible College, OR
Evangel University, MO
Fairfield University, CT
Faulkner University, AL
Ferrum College, VA
Finlandia University, MI
Flagler College, FL
Fresno Pacific University, CA
Furman University, SC
Georgetown College, KY
Graceland University, IA
Grace University, NE
Green Mountain College, VT
Greenville College, IL
Grove City College, PA
Guilford College, NC
Hamline University, MN
Harding University, AR
Hawai'i Pacific University, HI
Hendrix College, AR
Houghton College, NY
Howard Payne University, TX
Johnson Bible College, TN
John Wesley College, NC

Kentucky Christian University, KY
Kutztown University of Pennsylvania, PA
Lakeland College, WI
Lancaster Bible College, PA
Liberty University, VA
Limestone College, SC
Lipscomb University, TN
Loras College, IA
Loyola Marymount University, CA
Lynn University, FL
MacMurray College, IL
Malone College, OH
Mercyhurst College, PA
Messenger College, MO
Michigan State University, MI
Midland Lutheran College, NE
Midway College, KY
Millsaps College, MS
Mississippi College, MS
Missouri Baptist University, MO
Moravian College, PA
Morehouse College, GA
Mount Marty College, SD
Mount Vernon Nazarene University, OH
North Central College, IL
North Central University, MN
North Dakota State University, ND
North Greenville College, SC
Northwest Nazarene University, ID
Northwest University, WA
Nyack College, NY
Oakland City University, IN
Oglethorpe University, GA
Ohio Valley University, WV
Ohio Wesleyan University, OH
Oklahoma Baptist University, OK
Oklahoma City University, OK
Oklahoma Wesleyan University, OK
Olivet Nazarene University, IL
Oral Roberts University, OK
Pacific Union College, CA
Palm Beach Atlantic University, FL
Pfeiffer University, NC
Philadelphia Biblical University, PA
Presentation College, SD
Randolph-Macon Woman's College, VA
Reformed Bible College, MI
Roanoke Bible College, NC
St. Gregory's University, OK
St. John's University, NY
Saint Joseph's College of Maine, ME
St. Louis Christian College, MO
St. Olaf College, MN
Schreiner University, TX
Seton Hill University, PA
Shorter College, GA
Silver Lake College, WI
Simpson College, IA
Simpson University, CA
Southeastern College of the Assemblies of God, FL
Southern Adventist University, TN
Southern Christian University, AL
Southern Methodist College, SC
Southern Virginia University, VA
Southern Wesleyan University, SC

Southwest Baptist University, MO
Southwestern Christian University, OK
Southwestern College, KS
Stetson University, FL
Tabor College, KS
Tennessee Wesleyan College, TN
Texas Lutheran University, TX
Texas Wesleyan University, TX
Thomas More College, KY
Transylvania University, KY
Trinity College of Florida, FL
Trinity International University, IL
Trinity Lutheran College, WA
The University of Alabama at Birmingham, AL
University of Dallas, TX
University of Detroit Mercy, MI
University of Great Falls, MT
University of Mary Hardin-Baylor, TX
The University of North Carolina at Greensboro, NC
University of Puget Sound, WA
University of St. Francis, IL
University of Saint Francis, IN
University of South Carolina, SC
University of the Cumberlands, KY
University of the Incarnate Word, TX
University of the Pacific, CA
The University of Toledo, OH
The University of Virginia's College at Wise, VA
University of West Georgia, GA
Urbana University, OH
Valparaiso University, IN
Virginia Polytechnic Institute and State University, VA
Virginia Wesleyan College, VA
Warner Southern College, FL
Washington Bible College, MD
Washington State University, WA
Wayland Baptist University, TX
Wesley College, DE
Wesley College, MS
West Virginia Wesleyan College, WV
Wheeling Jesuit University, WV
Whitworth College, WA
William Carey College, MS
William Jewell College, MO
William Penn University, IA
Wingate University, NC
Wofford College, SC
Xavier University of Louisiana, LA

Rodeo
Angelo State University, TX
Boise State University, ID
Dickinson State University, ND
Eastern Oregon University, OR
Fort Hays State University, KS
Idaho State University, ID
Iowa State University of Science and Technology, IA
Lewis-Clark State College, ID
Missouri State University, MO
Missouri Valley College, MO
Murray State University, KY

New Mexico State University, NM
Northwestern Oklahoma State University, OK
Oklahoma Panhandle State University, OK
Sam Houston State University, TX
South Dakota State University, SD
Southeastern Louisiana University, LA
Southern Arkansas University–Magnolia, AR
Stephen F. Austin State University, TX
Tarleton State University, TX
Texas A&M University, TX
Texas Tech University, TX
University of Arkansas at Monticello, AR
University of Idaho, ID
The University of Montana–Western, MT
University of Nevada, Las Vegas, NV
The University of Tennessee at Martin, TN
University of Wyoming, WY
Washington State University, WA
West Texas A&M University, TX

Special Characteristics

Adult Students
Agnes Scott College, GA
Allegheny College, PA
American University, DC
Anderson University, IN
Arkansas State University, AR
Arkansas Tech University, AR
Averett University, VA
Barton College, NC
Bay Path College, MA
Berry College, GA
Biola University, CA
Brigham Young University, UT
California Baptist University, CA
California Lutheran University, CA
California State University, Bakersfield, CA
California State University, Chico, CA
Campbellsville University, KY
Carroll College, WI
The Catholic University of America, DC
Cedar Crest College, PA
Central Missouri State University, MO
Central Washington University, WA
Cleary University, MI
Coe College, IA
College of Mount St. Joseph, OH
The College of Saint Rose, NY
Dominican University of California, CA
East Carolina University, NC
Eastern Oregon University, OR
East Stroudsburg University of Pennsylvania, PA
Edinboro University of Pennsylvania, PA
The Evergreen State College, WA
Fairmont State University, WV
Faulkner University, AL
Ferrum College, VA
Fort Hays State University, KS
Francis Marion University, SC
Franklin Pierce College, NH
Freed-Hardeman University, TN
Frostburg State University, MD

Gannon University, PA
Grace University, NE
Hastings College, NE
Hollins University, VA
Indiana University of Pennsylvania, PA
Iowa State University of Science and
  Technology, IA
Juniata College, PA
Kent State University, OH
Lancaster Bible College, PA
La Sierra University, CA
Lipscomb University, TN
Loyola University Chicago, IL
Mercer University, GA
Mercyhurst College, PA
Messiah College, PA
Middle Tennessee State University, TN
Millsaps College, MS
Mississippi State University, MS
Mississippi University for Women, MS
Missouri State University, MO
Monmouth University, NJ
Montana State University–Billings, MT
Moravian College, PA
Morehead State University, KY
Murray State University, KY
New Mexico State University, NM
North Central College, IL
Northeastern Illinois University, IL
Northern Illinois University, IL
Northern Michigan University, MI
Northwestern College, IA
Northwestern State University of
  Louisiana, LA
Oakland University, MI
The Ohio State University, OH
Ohio Valley University, WV
Oklahoma State University, OK
Peru State College, NE
Piedmont College, GA
Point Park University, PA
Portland State University, OR
Randolph-Macon Woman's College, VA
Regis College, MA
The Richard Stockton College of New
  Jersey, NJ
Rochester College, MI
St. Edward's University, TX
Salem State College, MA
Seton Hill University, PA
Simpson College, IA
Sonoma State University, CA
South Dakota State University, SD
Southeastern Louisiana University, LA
Southeast Missouri State University, MO
Southern Arkansas University–
  Magnolia, AR
Southern Oregon University, OR
State University of New York College at
  Oneonta, NY
State University of New York College at
  Potsdam, NY
Stephen F. Austin State University, TX
Sweet Briar College, VA
Texas Christian University, TX
Thomas More College, KY

Tusculum College, TN
The University of Akron, OH
The University of Alabama at
  Birmingham, AL
University of Arkansas at Fort Smith, AR
University of Connecticut, CT
University of Hartford, CT
University of Illinois at Springfield, IL
University of Kansas, KS
University of Maine at Fort Kent, ME
University of Maryland, College Park, MD
University of Maryland Eastern Shore, MD
University of Mary Washington, VA
University of Massachusetts
  Dartmouth, MA
The University of Memphis, TN
University of Nebraska at Omaha, NE
University of Nevada, Reno, NV
University of New Orleans, LA
The University of North Carolina at
  Asheville, NC
The University of North Carolina at
  Charlotte, NC
The University of North Carolina at
  Greensboro, NC
University of Northern Colorado, CO
University of South Carolina, SC
The University of Tennessee at Martin, TN
The University of Texas at Dallas, TX
The University of Toledo, OH
University of West Georgia, GA
University of Wisconsin–Eau Claire, WI
University of Wisconsin–Green Bay, WI
University of Wisconsin–La Crosse, WI
University of Wisconsin–Parkside, WI
University of Wisconsin–Stevens Point, WI
University of Wisconsin–Stout, WI
University of Wisconsin–Whitewater, WI
University of Wyoming, WY
Western Kentucky University, KY
Westminster College, UT
Wichita State University, KS
Wilkes University, PA
Wilson College, PA
Wittenberg University, OH
Youngstown State University, OH

Children and Siblings of Alumni

Adelphi University, NY
Adrian College, MI
Alaska Pacific University, AK
Albertson College of Idaho, ID
Albion College, MI
Albright College, PA
Alliant International University, CA
Alma College, MI
Alvernia College, PA
Alverno College, WI
American University, DC
Anna Maria College, MA
Appalachian Bible College, WV
Arcadia University, PA
Arkansas State University, AR
Asbury College, KY
Ashland University, OH
Athens State University, AL

Auburn University, AL
Augsburg College, MN
Augustana College, SD
Aurora University, IL
Averett University, VA
Baker University, KS
Baldwin-Wallace College, OH
Barton College, NC
Bemidji State University, MN
Benedictine University, IL
Bethany College, WV
Bethel College, KS
Bethel University, MN
Bloomfield College, NJ
Blue Mountain College, MS
Boston University, MA
Bowling Green State University, OH
Bradley University, IL
Brigham Young University–Hawaii, HI
Bryan College, TN
Bryant University, RI
California Baptist University, CA
California Lutheran University, CA
Calvary Bible College and Theological
  Seminary, MO
Calvin College, MI
Canisius College, NY
Carroll College, WI
Carson-Newman College, TN
Cedar Crest College, PA
Cedarville University, OH
Centenary College, NJ
Central College, IA
Central Methodist University, MO
Central Michigan University, MI
Central Missouri State University, MO
Central Washington University, WA
Centre College, KY
Chapman University, CA
Chatham College, PA
Chestnut Hill College, PA
Christian Brothers University, TN
Clarke College, IA
Clearwater Christian College, FL
Coe College, IA
College Misericordia, PA
College of Mount St. Joseph, OH
College of Mount Saint Vincent, NY
The College of Saint Rose, NY
The College of St. Scholastica, MN
Colorado School of Mines, CO
Columbia College, MO
Columbia International University, SC
Concordia University, MI
Concordia University, NE
Converse College, SC
Corban College, OR
The Culinary Institute of America, NY
Culver-Stockton College, MO
Daemen College, NY
Dakota State University, SD
DePauw University, IN
Dickinson College, PA
Dominican University, IL
Dominican University of California, CA
Dordt College, IA

Dowling College, NY
Drake University, IA
Drexel University, PA
Duke University, NC
D'Youville College, NY
Eastern Mennonite University, VA
Eastern Michigan University, MI
Eastern Washington University, WA
East Texas Baptist University, TX
Edinboro University of Pennsylvania, PA
Embry-Riddle Aeronautical University, AZ
Embry-Riddle Aeronautical University, FL
Embry-Riddle Aeronautical University,
  Extended Campus, FL
Emmanuel College, MA
Emporia State University, KS
Endicott College, MA
Erskine College, SC
Fairfield University, CT
Fairmont State University, WV
Faulkner University, AL
Ferrum College, VA
Florida Institute of Technology, FL
Florida Southern College, FL
Fordham University, NY
Francis Marion University, SC
Franklin College, IN
Franklin Pierce College, NH
Friends University, KS
Frostburg State University, MD
Georgia Southern University, GA
Gonzaga University, WA
Gordon College, MA
Graceland University, IA
Grace University, NE
Grambling State University, LA
Grand Canyon University, AZ
Grand View College, IA
Green Mountain College, VT
Greenville College, IL
Gustavus Adolphus College, MN
Gwynedd-Mercy College, PA
Hamline University, MN
Heritage Christian University, AL
Hilbert College, NY
Hollins University, VA
Holy Names University, CA
Houghton College, NY
Howard Payne University, TX
Huntington University, IN
Idaho State University, ID
Indiana State University, IN
Indiana University–Purdue University Fort
  Wayne, IN
Iona College, NY
Iowa State University of Science and
  Technology, IA
Ithaca College, NY
James Madison University, VA
John Brown University, AR
Juniata College, PA
Kennesaw State University, GA
Kent State University, OH
Kentucky Christian University, KY
Kentucky Wesleyan College, KY
Keuka College, NY

Lake Forest College, IL
Lambuth University, TN
Lancaster Bible College, PA
Lasell College, MA
Lawrence University, WI
Lebanon Valley College, PA
Le Moyne College, NY
Lenoir-Rhyne College, NC
Limestone College, SC
Lincoln University, PA
Long Island University, Brooklyn
  Campus, NY
Longwood University, VA
Loras College, IA
Louisiana State University and Agricultural
  and Mechanical College, LA
Luther College, IA
MacMurray College, IL
Malone College, OH
Manchester College, IN
Maranatha Baptist Bible College, WI
Marietta College, OH
Marymount University, VA
Massachusetts Maritime Academy, MA
Mercyhurst College, PA
Merrimack College, MA
Messiah College, PA
Methodist College, NC
Michigan State University, MI
Michigan Technological University, MI
Mid-Continent University, KY
Midland Lutheran College, NE
Midway College, KY
Mississippi College, MS
Mississippi State University, MS
Mississippi University for Women, MS
Missouri Baptist University, MO
Missouri Southern State University, MO
Missouri State University, MO
Missouri Valley College, MO
Monmouth University, NJ
Montana State University–Billings, MT
Montreat College, NC
Moravian College, PA
Morehead State University, KY
Morningside College, IA
Mount Union College, OH
Murray State University, KY
Muskingum College, OH
Nazareth College of Rochester, NY
New England College, NH
New Mexico State University, NM
New York Institute of Technology, NY
Nichols College, MA
Northeastern State University, OK
Northern Arizona University, AZ
Northwestern College, IA
Northwestern Oklahoma State
  University, OK
Northwest Nazarene University, ID
Northwood University, MI
Northwood University, Florida Campus, FL
Northwood University, Texas Campus, TX
Nyack College, NY
Oakland City University, IN
The Ohio State University, OH

Ohio Wesleyan University, OH
Oklahoma Baptist University, OK
Oklahoma State University, OK
Oklahoma Wesleyan University, OK
Olivet College, MI
Oral Roberts University, OK
Pacific Lutheran University, WA
Pacific University, OR
Palm Beach Atlantic University, FL
Peirce College, PA
Pfeiffer University, NC
Philadelphia Biblical University, PA
Pine Manor College, MA
Pittsburg State University, KS
Point Park University, PA
Post University, CT
Principia College, IL
Randolph-Macon College, VA
Rensselaer Polytechnic Institute, NY
Research College of Nursing, MO
Rice University, TX
Ripon College, WI
Roanoke Bible College, NC
Roberts Wesleyan College, NY
Rochester College, MI
Rockhurst University, MO
Rosemont College, PA
Russell Sage College, NY
St. Andrews Presbyterian College, NC
St. John Fisher College, NY
Saint Joseph's College, IN
St. Joseph's College, New York, NY
St. Lawrence University, NY
St. Louis Christian College, MO
Saint Martin's College, WA
Saint Mary's College of California, CA
St. Mary's College of Maryland, MD
Saint Mary's University of Minnesota, MN
Salem State College, MA
Seattle Pacific University, WA
Seton Hall University, NJ
Seton Hill University, PA
Shimer College, IL
Simmons College, MA
Simpson College, IA
Slippery Rock University of
  Pennsylvania, PA
Sonoma State University, CA
Southeastern Louisiana University, LA
Southeastern Oklahoma State
  University, OK
Southern Adventist University, TN
Southern Arkansas University–
  Magnolia, AR
Southern Illinois University Carbondale, IL
Southern New Hampshire University, NH
Southwestern Christian University, OK
Southwestern College, AZ
Southwestern College, KS
Southwest Minnesota State University, MN
State University of New York College at
  Brockport, NY
State University of New York College at
  Oneonta, NY
State University of New York College at
  Potsdam, NY

State University of New York,
Fredonia, NY
Sterling College, KS
Stetson University, FL
Stevens Institute of Technology, NJ
Suffolk University, MA
Tabor College, KS
Taylor University, IN
Taylor University Fort Wayne, IN
Tennessee Technological University, TN
Texas Lutheran University, TX
Texas State University-San Marcos, TX
Thiel College, PA
Thomas More College, KY
Tiffin University, OH
Trevecca Nazarene University, TN
Trinity International University, IL
Trinity (Washington) University, DC
Truman State University, MO
Union College, KY
Union University, TN
The University of Alabama at
Birmingham, AL
University of Alaska Fairbanks, AK
University of Charleston, WV
University of Colorado at Colorado
Springs, CO
University of Delaware, DE
University of Detroit Mercy, MI
University of Dubuque, IA
University of Evansville, IN
University of Idaho, ID
University of La Verne, CA
University of Maine, ME
University of Mary Hardin-Baylor, TX
University of Mary Washington, VA
University of Massachusetts Amherst, MA
University of Michigan–Dearborn, MI
University of Michigan–Flint, MI
University of Mississippi, MS
University of Missouri–Columbia, MO
University of Nebraska at Omaha, NE
University of Nebraska–Lincoln, NE
University of Nevada, Las Vegas, NV
University of Nevada, Reno, NV
University of New England, ME
University of New Hampshire, NH
University of New Orleans, LA
The University of North Carolina at
Asheville, NC
The University of North Carolina at
Pembroke, NC
University of Northern Colorado, CO
University of Oklahoma, OK
University of Rio Grande, OH
University of Rochester, NY
University of St. Francis, IL
University of Saint Francis, IN
University of Sioux Falls, SD
University of South Carolina, SC
University of Southern California, CA
University of Southern Mississippi, MS
The University of Tampa, FL
University of the Cumberlands, KY
University of the Ozarks, AR
The University of Toledo, OH

University of Tulsa, OK
University of West Georgia, GA
University of Wisconsin–La Crosse, WI
University of Wisconsin–Oshkosh, WI
University of Wyoming, WY
Urbana University, OH
Ursuline College, OH
Valparaiso University, IN
Virginia Military Institute, VA
Warner Pacific College, OR
Warner Southern College, FL
Wartburg College, IA
Washington & Jefferson College, PA
Washington State University, WA
Wayland Baptist University, TX
Webber International University, FL
Wells College, NY
Western Kentucky University, KY
West Liberty State College, WV
Westminster College, MO
Westminster College, PA
Westminster College, UT
Wheeling Jesuit University, WV
Whittier College, CA
Whitworth College, WA
William Carey College, MS
William Jewell College, MO
William Penn University, IA
William Woods University, MO
Wilmington College, OH
Wilson College, PA
Wingate University, NC
Winona State University, MN
Wittenberg University, OH
Worcester State College, MA
York College, NE
York College of Pennsylvania, PA
Youngstown State University, OH

Children of Current Students
Alliant International University, CA
Arkansas State University, AR
Atlantic Union College, MA
Augustana College, SD
Blue Mountain College, MS
Bryan College, TN
Carroll College, WI
Central College, IA
Cincinnati Christian University, OH
College Misericordia, PA
The College of New Rochelle, NY
Columbia College, MO
Finlandia University, MI
Franklin Pierce College, NH
Green Mountain College, VT
Huntington University, IN
Johnson & Wales University, RI
Johnson Bible College, TN
Lancaster Bible College, PA
Marymount University, VA
Maryville University of Saint Louis, MO
Missouri Baptist University, MO
Mount Aloysius College, PA
Mount Marty College, SD
Multnomah Bible College and Biblical
Seminary, OR

Northwest University, WA
Olivet Nazarene University, IL
Palm Beach Atlantic University, FL
Saint Martin's College, WA
Southwestern College, KS
The University of Alabama at
Birmingham, AL
University of Great Falls, MT
University of Hartford, CT
University of Michigan–Dearborn, MI
Valley Forge Christian College, PA
Wilson College, PA

Children of Educators
Agnes Scott College, GA
Alfred University, NY
Allegheny College, PA
Appalachian Bible College, WV
Aurora University, IL
Austin Peay State University, TN
Bard College, NY
Benedictine College, KS
Bennington College, VT
Brigham Young University–Hawaii, HI
Bryan College, TN
Calvary Bible College and Theological
Seminary, MO
Campbellsville University, KY
Canisius College, NY
Centenary College of Louisiana, LA
Columbia College, MO
Columbus College of Art & Design, OH
Concordia University, NE
Cornell College, IA
DeSales University, PA
Dowling College, NY
East Texas Baptist University, TX
Emmanuel College, MA
Endicott College, MA
Ferrum College, VA
Florida College, FL
Franklin Pierce College, NH
Gallaudet University, DC
Grand View College, IA
Hampden-Sydney College, VA
Hastings College, NE
Heritage Christian University, AL
John Brown University, AR
Johnson Bible College, TN
Judson College, AL
King's College, PA
Lipscomb University, TN
Lycoming College, PA
Maranatha Baptist Bible College, WI
Mary Baldwin College, VA
Mississippi State University, MS
Moravian College, PA
New England College, NH
New York Institute of Technology, NY
Northern Arizona University, AZ
Northwest Nazarene University, ID
Oklahoma Wesleyan University, OK
Pacific Lutheran University, WA
Palm Beach Atlantic University, FL
Research College of Nursing, MO
Rosemont College, PA

Saint Anselm College, NH
Saint Mary's College of California, CA
Simpson College, IA
Sonoma State University, CA
Southern Illinois University Carbondale, IL
Stevens Institute of Technology, NJ
Susquehanna University, PA
Tennessee Technological University, TN
Unity College, ME
The University of Alabama at
  Birmingham, AL
University of Charleston, WV
University of Dubuque, IA
University of Illinois at Springfield, IL
The University of Memphis, TN
University of St. Francis, IL
University of St. Thomas, TX
The University of Scranton, PA
The University of Tennessee at Martin, TN
Villanova University, PA
Virginia Wesleyan College, VA
Warner Southern College, FL
William Carey College, MS

Children of Faculty/Staff
Abilene Christian University, TX
Adelphi University, NY
Adrian College, MI
Agnes Scott College, GA
Alaska Pacific University, AK
Albertson College of Idaho, ID
Alcorn State University, MS
Alderson-Broaddus College, WV
Alfred University, NY
Allegheny College, PA
Alliant International University, CA
Alma College, MI
Alvernia College, PA
American University, DC
Anderson University, IN
Andrews University, MI
Anna Maria College, MA
Appalachian Bible College, WV
Arkansas Tech University, AR
Arlington Baptist College, TX
The Art Institute of Portland, OR
Asbury College, KY
Ashland University, OH
Athens State University, AL
Atlantic Union College, MA
Auburn University, AL
Augustana College, SD
Aurora University, IL
Austin College, TX
Austin Peay State University, TN
Azusa Pacific University, CA
Baker University, KS
Ball State University, IN
Bard College, NY
Barton College, NC
Baylor University, TX
Bay Path College, MA
Becker College, MA
Belhaven College, MS
Belmont Abbey College, NC
Belmont University, TN

Bemidji State University, MN
Bennington College, VT
Berry College, GA
Bethany College, WV
Bethany Lutheran College, MN
Bethel College, KS
Bethel College, TN
Bethel University, MN
Beulah Heights Bible College, GA
Biola University, CA
Bloomsburg University of Pennsylvania, PA
Bluffton University, OH
Bowdoin College, ME
Bowling Green State University, OH
Bradley University, IL
Brenau University, GA
Brevard College, NC
Brewton-Parker College, GA
Brigham Young University–Hawaii, HI
Bryan College, TN
Buena Vista University, IA
California Baptist University, CA
California Lutheran University, CA
California State University, Bakersfield, CA
California State University, Chico, CA
California State University, Stanislaus, CA
Calvin College, MI
Campbell University, NC
Canisius College, NY
Carroll College, MT
Carroll College, WI
Case Western Reserve University, OH
Catawba College, NC
The Catholic University of America, DC
Cedarville University, OH
Centenary College of Louisiana, LA
Central Bible College, MO
Central Christian College of Kansas, KS
Central College, IA
Central Methodist University, MO
Central Michigan University, MI
Central Missouri State University, MO
Centre College, KY
Chatham College, PA
Chowan College, NC
Christian Brothers University, TN
Christian Heritage College, CA
Cincinnati Christian University, OH
Clarion University of Pennsylvania, PA
Clarke College, IA
Clarkson University, NY
Cleary University, MI
Clemson University, SC
Coe College, IA
Colby-Sawyer College, NH
College Misericordia, PA
College of Mount St. Joseph, OH
College of Mount Saint Vincent, NY
The College of New Rochelle, NY
The College of St. Scholastica, MN
College of the Holy Cross, MA
College of Visual Arts, MN
The College of Wooster, OH
Colorado Christian University, CO
Colorado State University, CO
Columbia College, MO

Columbia College, SC
Columbia College Chicago, IL
Columbus College of Art & Design, OH
Concordia University, CA
Concordia University, MI
Concordia University, NE
Concordia University, OR
Concordia University, St. Paul, MN
Concordia University Wisconsin, WI
Converse College, SC
Corban College, OR
Cornell College, IA
Cornerstone University, MI
Creighton University, NE
Crown College, MN
The Culinary Institute of America, NY
Culver-Stockton College, MO
Daemen College, NY
Dallas Baptist University, TX
Dallas Christian College, TX
Davidson College, NC
Davis & Elkins College, WV
Defiance College, OH
DePaul University, IL
DePauw University, IN
DeSales University, PA
Dickinson College, PA
Dickinson State University, ND
Dillard University, LA
Dominican College, NY
Dominican University, IL
Dominican University of California, CA
Dordt College, IA
Dowling College, NY
Duquesne University, PA
D'Youville College, NY
East Carolina University, NC
East Central University, OK
Eastern Mennonite University, VA
East Texas Baptist University, TX
Eckerd College, FL
Edinboro University of Pennsylvania, PA
Elizabethtown College, PA
Elmira College, NY
Elon University, NC
Embry-Riddle Aeronautical University, AZ
Embry-Riddle Aeronautical University, FL
Emmanuel College, MA
Emmaus Bible College, IA
Emory & Henry College, VA
Emory University, GA
Emporia State University, KS
Erskine College, SC
Eureka College, IL
Evangel University, MO
Faith Baptist Bible College and Theological
  Seminary, IA
Faulkner University, AL
Ferris State University, MI
Ferrum College, VA
Finlandia University, MI
Flagler College, FL
Florida College, FL
Florida Institute of Technology, FL
Florida Southern College, FL
Fordham University, NY

Non-Need Scholarships for Undergraduates
Special Characteristics

Fort Lewis College, CO
Framingham State College, MA
Francis Marion University, SC
Franklin College, IN
Franklin Pierce College, NH
Freed-Hardeman University, TN
Free Will Baptist Bible College, TN
Fresno Pacific University, CA
Furman University, SC
Gallaudet University, DC
Geneva College, PA
Georgetown College, KY
Georgetown University, DC
Georgia College & State University, GA
Georgia Institute of Technology, GA
Georgian Court University, NJ
Gonzaga University, WA
Grace College, IN
Graceland University, IA
Grace University, NE
Grambling State University, LA
Grand Canyon University, AZ
Grand Valley State University, MI
Grand View College, IA
Greenville College, IL
Guilford College, NC
Hampden-Sydney College, VA
Hampshire College, MA
Hannibal-LaGrange College, MO
Hanover College, IN
Hastings College, NE
Heidelberg College, OH
Hendrix College, AR
Heritage Christian University, AL
Hillsdale College, MI
Houston Baptist University, TX
Howard Payne University, TX
Huntington University, IN
Idaho State University, ID
Illinois State University, IL
Illinois Wesleyan University, IL
Indiana State University, IN
Indiana University of Pennsylvania, PA
Indiana University–Purdue University Fort Wayne, IN
Iona College, NY
Iowa Wesleyan College, IA
James Madison University, VA
Jamestown College, ND
John Brown University, AR
The Johns Hopkins University, MD
Johnson & Wales University, RI
Johnson Bible College, TN
Johnson C. Smith University, NC
John Wesley College, NC
Judson College, AL
Juniata College, PA
Kalamazoo College, MI
Kean University, NJ
Kent State University, OH
Kentucky Christian University, KY
Kentucky Mountain Bible College, KY
Kentucky Wesleyan College, KY
Keuka College, NY
King College, TN
King's College, PA

Kutztown University of Pennsylvania, PA
LaGrange College, GA
Lake Erie College, OH
Lakeland College, WI
Lambuth University, TN
Lancaster Bible College, PA
La Salle University, PA
Lasell College, MA
La Sierra University, CA
Lawrence Technological University, MI
Lebanon Valley College, PA
Lee University, TN
LeMoyne-Owen College, TN
Lenoir-Rhyne College, NC
LeTourneau University, TX
Life Pacific College, CA
Limestone College, SC
Lincoln Christian College, IL
Lincoln Memorial University, TN
Lincoln University, PA
Linfield College, OR
Lipscomb University, TN
Long Island University, Brooklyn Campus, NY
Louisiana Tech University, LA
Lourdes College, OH
Loyola University New Orleans, LA
Lubbock Christian University, TX
Lycoming College, PA
Lynchburg College, VA
Lynn University, FL
Lyon College, AR
MacMurray College, IL
Magnolia Bible College, MS
Maharishi University of Management, IA
Maine College of Art, ME
Maine Maritime Academy, ME
Malone College, OH
Manhattan Christian College, KS
Manhattan College, NY
Maranatha Baptist Bible College, WI
Marian College of Fond du Lac, WI
Mars Hill College, NC
Martin Methodist College, TN
Mary Baldwin College, VA
Marymount University, VA
Maryville College, TN
Massachusetts College of Art, MA
Massachusetts Maritime Academy, MA
McKendree College, IL
McMurry University, TX
Mercer University, GA
Mercyhurst College, PA
Merrimack College, MA
Messiah College, PA
Methodist College, NC
Miami University, OH
Michigan State University, MI
Michigan Technological University, MI
MidAmerica Nazarene University, KS
Mid-Continent University, KY
Midway College, KY
Midwestern State University, TX
Milligan College, TN
Millsaps College, MS
Milwaukee Institute of Art and Design, WI

Milwaukee School of Engineering, WI
Minnesota State University Moorhead, MN
Mississippi College, MS
Mississippi State University, MS
Mississippi University for Women, MS
Missouri Baptist University, MO
Missouri Southern State University, MO
Missouri State University, MO
Missouri Valley College, MO
Monmouth University, NJ
Montana State University–Billings, MT
Montreat College, NC
Moravian College, PA
Morehouse College, GA
Morningside College, IA
Mount Marty College, SD
Mount Mary College, WI
Mount Olive College, NC
Mount Saint Mary College, NY
Mount St. Mary's University, MD
Mount Union College, OH
Mount Vernon Nazarene University, OH
Murray State University, KY
Nazareth College of Rochester, NY
Nebraska Christian College, NE
Nebraska Wesleyan University, NE
Neumann College, PA
New England College, NH
New Mexico Highlands University, NM
New Mexico Institute of Mining and Technology, NM
New Mexico State University, NM
New York Institute of Technology, NY
Niagara University, NY
Nicholls State University, LA
Nichols College, MA
North Central College, IL
North Central University, MN
North Dakota State University, ND
Northeastern Illinois University, IL
Northeastern State University, OK
Northern Arizona University, AZ
Northern Illinois University, IL
North Greenville College, SC
Northwestern College, IA
Northwestern College, MN
Northwestern Oklahoma State University, OK
Northwestern State University of Louisiana, LA
Northwest Nazarene University, ID
Northwest University, WA
Northwood University, MI
Northwood University, Florida Campus, FL
Northwood University, Texas Campus, TX
Nova Southeastern University, FL
Nyack College, NY
Oakland City University, IN
Ohio Northern University, OH
The Ohio State University, OH
Ohio University, OH
Ohio University–Chillicothe, OH
Ohio University–Eastern, OH
Ohio University–Lancaster, OH
Ohio University–Southern Campus, OH
Ohio University–Zanesville, OH

Ohio Valley University, WV
Ohio Wesleyan University, OH
Oklahoma Baptist University, OK
Oklahoma City University, OK
Oklahoma Panhandle State University, OK
Oklahoma Wesleyan University, OK
Old Dominion University, VA
Olivet College, MI
Olivet Nazarene University, IL
Oral Roberts University, OK
Ouachita Baptist University, AR
Pacific Lutheran University, WA
Pacific University, OR
Palm Beach Atlantic University, FL
Park University, MO
Peace College, NC
Peru State College, NE
Philadelphia Biblical University, PA
Piedmont College, GA
Pikeville College, KY
Plymouth State University, NH
Point Park University, PA
Pontifical Catholic University of Puerto
 Rico, PR
Presentation College, SD
Principia College, IL
Purdue University, IN
Quincy University, IL
Quinnipiac University, CT
Radford University, VA
Randolph-Macon College, VA
Randolph-Macon Woman's College, VA
Reformed Bible College, MI
Regis College, MA
Regis University, CO
Reinhardt College, GA
Rensselaer Polytechnic Institute, NY
Research College of Nursing, MO
Rice University, TX
The Richard Stockton College of New
 Jersey, NJ
Ripon College, WI
Roanoke Bible College, NC
Robert Morris College, IL
Robert Morris University, PA
Roberts Wesleyan College, NY
Rochester College, MI
Rochester Institute of Technology, NY
Rockhurst University, MO
Rocky Mountain College of Art &
 Design, CO
Rosemont College, PA
Rust College, MS
Rutgers, The State University of New
 Jersey, Camden, NJ
Rutgers, The State University of New
 Jersey, Newark, NJ
Rutgers, The State University of New
 Jersey, New Brunswick/Piscataway, NJ
St. Ambrose University, IA
Saint Anselm College, NH
St. Augustine College, IL
St. Bonaventure University, NY
St. Cloud State University, MN
St. Edward's University, TX
St. John's University, NY

Saint Joseph's College, IN
St. Joseph's College, New York, NY
Saint Joseph's College of Maine, ME
St. Louis Christian College, MO
Saint Louis University, MO
Saint Martin's College, WA
Saint Mary's College of California, CA
St. Mary's College of Maryland, MD
Saint Mary's University of Minnesota, MN
St. Norbert College, WI
Saint Paul's College, VA
Saint Xavier University, IL
Salem State College, MA
Samford University, AL
Schreiner University, TX
Seattle Pacific University, WA
Seton Hall University, NJ
Seton Hill University, PA
Shaw University, NC
Shenandoah University, VA
Shorter College, GA
Silver Lake College, WI
Simon's Rock College of Bard, MA
Simpson College, IA
Simpson University, CA
Skidmore College, NY
Slippery Rock University of
 Pennsylvania, PA
Sonoma State University, CA
South Dakota State University, SD
Southeastern Bible College, AL
Southeastern College of the Assemblies of
 God, FL
Southeastern Louisiana University, LA
Southeast Missouri State University, MO
Southern Arkansas University–
 Magnolia, AR
Southern Christian University, AL
Southern Connecticut State University, CT
Southern Illinois University Carbondale, IL
Southern Illinois University
 Edwardsville, IL
Southern Methodist University, TX
Southern New Hampshire University, NH
Southern Vermont College, VT
Southern Virginia University, VA
Southern Wesleyan University, SC
Southwestern Christian University, OK
Southwestern College, AZ
Southwestern College, KS
Southwestern University, TX
Spring Arbor University, MI
Spring Hill College, AL
State University of New York College at
 Potsdam, NY
Stephens College, MO
Stetson University, FL
Stevens Institute of Technology, NJ
Stonehill College, MA
Suffolk University, MA
Susquehanna University, PA
Tabor College, KS
Tarleton State University, TX
Taylor University, IN
Taylor University Fort Wayne, IN
Tennessee Technological University, TN

Tennessee Wesleyan College, TN
Texas A&M University, TX
Texas Christian University, TX
Texas Lutheran University, TX
Texas Tech University, TX
Thiel College, PA
Thomas More College, KY
Thomas University, GA
Tiffin University, OH
Toccoa Falls College, GA
Transylvania University, KY
Tri-State University, IN
Truman State University, MO
Tufts University, MA
Tusculum College, TN
Tuskegee University, AL
Union University, TN
The University of Alabama at
 Birmingham, AL
University of Alaska Fairbanks, AK
The University of Arizona, AZ
University of Arkansas at Fort Smith, AR
University of Arkansas at Monticello, AR
University of Bridgeport, CT
University of Charleston, WV
University of Cincinnati, OH
University of Colorado at Denver and
 Health Sciences Center—Downtown
 Denver Campus, CO
University of Colorado at Denver and
 Health Sciences Center—Health Sciences
 Program, CO
University of Connecticut, CT
University of Dallas, TX
University of Delaware, DE
University of Detroit Mercy, MI
University of Dubuque, IA
University of Evansville, IN
The University of Findlay, OH
University of Florida, FL
University of Great Falls, MT
University of Hartford, CT
University of Idaho, ID
University of Illinois at Chicago, IL
University of Illinois at Springfield, IL
University of Indianapolis, IN
University of Kansas, KS
University of La Verne, CA
University of Maine, ME
The University of Maine at Augusta, ME
University of Maine at Farmington, ME
University of Maine at Fort Kent, ME
University of Maine at Presque Isle, ME
University of Mary, ND
University of Mary Hardin-Baylor, TX
University of Maryland Eastern Shore, MD
University of Mary Washington, VA
University of Massachusetts Amherst, MA
University of Massachusetts
 Dartmouth, MA
The University of Memphis, TN
University of Miami, FL
University of Michigan, MI
University of Mississippi, MS
University of Nebraska at Kearney, NE
University of Nebraska at Omaha, NE

University of Nevada, Las Vegas, NV
University of New Hampshire, NH
University of New Hampshire at
  Manchester, NH
University of North Alabama, AL
The University of North Carolina at
  Asheville, NC
The University of North Carolina at Chapel
  Hill, NC
University of North Dakota, ND
University of Northern Colorado, CO
University of Notre Dame, IN
University of Pittsburgh at Johnstown, PA
University of Portland, OR
University of Puget Sound, WA
University of Rio Grande, OH
University of Rochester, NY
University of Saint Francis, IN
University of St. Thomas, TX
University of San Diego, CA
The University of Scranton, PA
University of Sioux Falls, SD
University of South Carolina, SC
University of Southern California, CA
University of Southern Indiana, IN
University of Southern Maine, ME
University of Southern Mississippi, MS
The University of Tampa, FL
The University of Tennessee at Martin, TN
University of the Cumberlands, KY
University of the District of Columbia, DC
University of the Ozarks, AR
University of the South, TN
University of the Virgin Islands, VI
The University of Toledo, OH
University of Tulsa, OK
University of Utah, UT
Urbana University, OH
Ursinus College, PA
Ursuline College, OH
Valley Forge Christian College, PA
Valparaiso University, IN
Vanguard University of Southern
  California, CA
Villanova University, PA
Virginia Intermont College, VA
Virginia Military Institute, VA
Virginia Polytechnic Institute and State
  University, VA
Virginia Wesleyan College, VA
Voorhees College, SC
Wabash College, IN
Wake Forest University, NC
Waldorf College, IA
Walla Walla College, WA
Warner Southern College, FL
Warren Wilson College, NC
Wartburg College, IA
Washington & Jefferson College, PA
Washington Bible College, MD
Washington College, MD
Washington State University, WA
Wayland Baptist University, TX
Waynesburg College, PA
Wayne State College, NE
Webber International University, FL

Western Illinois University, IL
Western New England College, MA
West Liberty State College, WV
Westminster College, UT
Westmont College, CA
West Texas A&M University, TX
West Virginia University, WV
West Virginia Wesleyan College, WV
Wheeling Jesuit University, WV
Whittier College, CA
Wilkes University, PA
William Carey College, MS
William Jewell College, MO
Williams Baptist College, AR
William Woods University, MO
Wilson College, PA
Winona State University, MN
Winthrop University, SC
Wittenberg University, OH
Wofford College, SC
Worcester State College, MA
Xavier University of Louisiana, LA
York College, NE
Youngstown State University, OH

Children of Public Servants
Bay Path College, MA
California State University, San
  Bernardino, CA
College of Staten Island of the City
  University of New York, NY
Dowling College, NY
Framingham State College, MA
Georgia Southern University, GA
Graceland University, IA
Grambling State University, LA
Mercer University, GA
Mississippi State University, MS
Monmouth University, NJ
New Mexico State University, NM
New York Institute of Technology, NY
Northern Arizona University, AZ
Northwestern State University of
  Louisiana, LA
The Ohio State University, OH
Peirce College, PA
St. Francis College, NY
Salem State College, MA
Sonoma State University, CA
Southeastern Louisiana University, LA
Southern Illinois University Carbondale, IL
Tennessee Technological University, TN
The University of Alabama at
  Birmingham, AL
University of Delaware, DE
The University of Memphis, TN
University of Nevada, Las Vegas, NV
University of New Orleans, LA
The University of Texas at Dallas, TX
The University of Toledo, OH
University of Wisconsin–Green Bay, WI
Valdosta State University, GA
Washington State University, WA
Western Kentucky University, KY
Western Washington University, WA
Westminster College, UT

Children of Union Members/Company Employees
Adrian College, MI
Arkansas State University, AR
Auburn University, AL
Averett University, VA
Calvin College, MI
Carroll College, MT
Central Michigan University, MI
The College of Saint Rose, NY
Columbia College, MO
Cornerstone University, MI
Dowling College, NY
Eastern Washington University, WA
East Tennessee State University, TN
Edinboro University of Pennsylvania, PA
Emmanuel College, MA
Emporia State University, KS
Fordham University, NY
Framingham State College, MA
Frostburg State University, MD
Georgia Institute of Technology, GA
Grand Valley State University, MI
Husson College, ME
Illinois State University, IL
Kennesaw State University, GA
Kent State University, OH
Kentucky Wesleyan College, KY
Kutztown University of Pennsylvania, PA
Massachusetts College of Art, MA
Mercer University, GA
Mercy College of Health Sciences, IA
Michigan State University, MI
Mid-Continent University, KY
Millersville University of Pennsylvania, PA
Minnesota State University Mankato, MN
Montana State University–Billings, MT
New Mexico State University, NM
Northern Michigan University, MI
The Ohio State University, OH
The Richard Stockton College of New
  Jersey, NJ
St. Cloud State University, MN
Saint Paul's College, VA
Salem State College, MA
Seton Hall University, NJ
Shorter College, GA
Slippery Rock University of
  Pennsylvania, PA
Sonoma State University, CA
Southeastern Louisiana University, LA
Southwest Minnesota State University, MN
Stephen F. Austin State University, TX
Texas Christian University, TX
The University of Alabama, AL
The University of Alabama at
  Birmingham, AL
University of Hartford, CT
University of Illinois at Springfield, IL
University of Maine, ME
University of Michigan–Flint, MI
University of Northern Colorado, CO
University of South Carolina, SC
University of the Incarnate Word, TX
The University of Toledo, OH
University of West Georgia, GA

University of Wisconsin–Parkside, WI
Virginia Commonwealth University, VA
Washington College, MD
Western Kentucky University, KY
Western New England College, MA
Western Washington University, WA
West Virginia University, WV
Wheeling Jesuit University, WV
York College of Pennsylvania, PA
Youngstown State University, OH

Children of Workers in Trades

Arkansas State University, AR
Dowling College, NY
Kennesaw State University, GA
New Mexico State University, NM
The Ohio State University, OH
Sonoma State University, CA
South Dakota State University, SD
The University of Alabama at
  Birmingham, AL
University of Arkansas at Fort Smith, AR
University of Illinois at Springfield, IL
University of Michigan, MI
University of Nevada, Las Vegas, NV
University of South Carolina, SC
University of Wisconsin–Parkside, WI
West Virginia University, WV
Worcester Polytechnic Institute, MA
Youngstown State University, OH

Children with a Deceased or Disabled Parent

Anna Maria College, MA
Arkansas State University, AR
The Baptist College of Florida, FL
Bay Path College, MA
California State University, San
  Bernardino, CA
Clarke College, IA
The College of New Jersey, NJ
College of Staten Island of the City
  University of New York, NY
Columbia College, MO
Defiance College, OH
Edinboro University of Pennsylvania, PA
Erskine College, SC
Fordham University, NY
Georgia College & State University, GA
Hamline University, MN
Harding University, AR
Illinois State University, IL
Indiana State University, IN
Indiana University–Purdue University Fort
  Wayne, IN
Kent State University, OH
Lipscomb University, TN
Louisiana State University and Agricultural
  and Mechanical College, LA
Louisiana Tech University, LA
Marian College of Fond du Lac, WI
Montclair State University, NJ
New Mexico Highlands University, NM
New Mexico State University, NM
Northeastern State University, OK
The Ohio State University, OH

St. Norbert College, WI
Seton Hill University, PA
Southern Illinois University Carbondale, IL
State University of New York at
  Binghamton, NY
The University of Alabama at
  Birmingham, AL
University of Hartford, CT
University of Illinois at Springfield, IL
University of Maine, ME
University of Massachusetts
  Dartmouth, MA
University of New Orleans, LA
University of South Carolina, SC
University of Utah, UT
The University of Virginia's College at
  Wise, VA
Washington State University, WA
Worcester State College, MA
Youngstown State University, OH

Ethnic Background

Abilene Christian University, TX
Alaska Pacific University, AK
Albertson College of Idaho, ID
Albion College, MI
Alderson-Broaddus College, WV
Alliant International University, CA
American University, DC
Arkansas State University, AR
Arkansas Tech University, AR
Asbury College, KY
Auburn University, AL
Augustana College, SD
Austin College, TX
Azusa Pacific University, CA
Baker University, KS
Benedictine College, KS
Berry College, GA
Bethany College, WV
Bethel University, MN
Biola University, CA
Boise State University, ID
Bridgewater College, VA
Brigham Young University, UT
Brigham Young University–Hawaii, HI
California Lutheran University, CA
California State University, Chico, CA
California State University, Dominguez
  Hills, CA
California State University, San
  Bernardino, CA
California State University, Stanislaus, CA
Calvin College, MI
The Catholic University of America, DC
Cedarville University, OH
Centenary College, NJ
Centenary College of Louisiana, LA
Central Bible College, MO
Central Michigan University, MI
Central Missouri State University, MO
Claremont McKenna College, CA
Clarion University of Pennsylvania, PA
Clemson University, SC
College of Saint Benedict, MN
The College of Saint Rose, NY

Columbia International University, SC
Concordia University, CA
Concordia University, MI
Cornerstone University, MI
Dakota State University, SD
DePauw University, IN
Dominican University of California, CA
Drake University, IA
Duke University, NC
East Carolina University, NC
Eastern Mennonite University, VA
Eastern Michigan University, MI
Eastern Washington University, WA
Emmanuel College, MA
Emory & Henry College, VA
Erskine College, SC
Fairfield University, CT
Flagler College, FL
Fort Lewis College, CO
Franklin College, IN
Fresno Pacific University, CA
Furman University, SC
Gannon University, PA
Georgia Institute of Technology, GA
Grambling State University, LA
Grand Canyon University, AZ
Grove City College, PA
Hamline University, MN
Hawai'i Pacific University, HI
Holy Names University, CA
Humphreys College, CA
Indiana University of Pennsylvania, PA
Iowa State University of Science and
  Technology, IA
John Brown University, AR
Johnson Bible College, TN
Johnson C. Smith University, NC
Juniata College, PA
Kent State University, OH
Kenyon College, OH
LaGrange College, GA
Langston University, OK
Lebanon Valley College, PA
Lesley University, MA
Lewis-Clark State College, ID
Long Island University, Brooklyn
  Campus, NY
Loyola University Chicago, IL
Lyon College, AR
Macalester College, MN
Maharishi University of Management, IA
Manchester College, IN
Medical University of South Carolina, SC
Mercy College of Health Sciences, IA
Meredith College, NC
Michigan State University, MI
Michigan Technological University, MI
Millsaps College, MS
Milwaukee Institute of Art and Design, WI
Minot State University, ND
Mississippi University for Women, MS
Missouri Southern State University, MO
Missouri State University, MO
Montana State University–Billings, MT
Moravian College, PA
Mount Union College, OH

Non-Need Scholarships for Undergraduates
Special Characteristics

Muskingum College, OH
New England College, NH
New Mexico State University, NM
North Carolina Agricultural and Technical State University, NC
North Dakota State University, ND
Northern Illinois University, IL
Northland College, WI
Northwestern College, IA
Northwestern College, MN
Northwest Nazarene University, ID
Oakland City University, IN
Oakland University, MI
The Ohio State University, OH
Ohio Valley University, WV
Ohio Wesleyan University, OH
Ouachita Baptist University, AR
Peru State College, NE
Portland State University, OR
Regis University, CO
Rensselaer Polytechnic Institute, NY
Rice University, TX
The Richard Stockton College of New Jersey, NJ
Robert Morris University, PA
Rust College, MS
St. Gregory's University, OK
St. John Fisher College, NY
Saint Martin's College, WA
St. Norbert College, WI
Schreiner University, TX
Seton Hall University, NJ
Shawnee State University, OH
Shepherd University, WV
Sierra Nevada College, NV
Slippery Rock University of Pennsylvania, PA
Sonoma State University, CA
South Dakota State University, SD
Southeastern Louisiana University, LA
Southern Oregon University, OR
Southern Utah University, UT
Southern Wesleyan University, SC
Southwestern College, KS
State University of New York at Binghamton, NY
State University of New York College at Brockport, NY
State University of New York College at Oneonta, NY
State University of New York College at Potsdam, NY
State University of New York, Fredonia, NY
Stetson University, FL
Taylor University, IN
Tennessee Technological University, TN
Toccoa Falls College, GA
Truman State University, MO
Union University, TN
University at Albany, State University of New York, NY
The University of Alabama at Birmingham, AL
University of Alaska Southeast, AK
The University of Arizona, AZ

University of California, San Diego, CA
University of Colorado at Colorado Springs, CO
University of Colorado at Denver and Health Sciences Center—Health Sciences Program, CO
University of Delaware, DE
University of Dubuque, IA
University of Great Falls, MT
University of Hartford, CT
University of Idaho, ID
University of Illinois at Springfield, IL
University of Indianapolis, IN
University of Kansas, KS
University of La Verne, CA
University of Maine, ME
The University of Maine at Augusta, ME
University of Maine at Presque Isle, ME
University of Mary Hardin-Baylor, TX
University of Miami, FL
University of Michigan–Dearborn, MI
University of Michigan–Flint, MI
University of Minnesota, Morris, MN
University of Missouri–St. Louis, MO
University of Nebraska at Kearney, NE
University of Nebraska at Omaha, NE
University of Nebraska–Lincoln, NE
University of Nevada, Las Vegas, NV
University of Nevada, Reno, NV
The University of North Carolina at Asheville, NC
The University of North Carolina at Greensboro, NC
University of North Dakota, ND
University of Northern Colorado, CO
University of St. Francis, IL
University of South Carolina, SC
University of Southern Mississippi, MS
The University of Tennessee at Martin, TN
The University of Texas at El Paso, TX
The University of Texas at San Antonio, TX
The University of Texas–Pan American, TX
University of the South, TN
The University of Toledo, OH
University of Utah, UT
University of Vermont, VT
The University of Virginia's College at Wise, VA
University of West Georgia, GA
University of Wisconsin–Eau Claire, WI
University of Wisconsin–Green Bay, WI
University of Wisconsin–La Crosse, WI
University of Wisconsin–Parkside, WI
University of Wisconsin–Stevens Point, WI
University of Wisconsin–Whitewater, WI
University of Wyoming, WY
VanderCook College of Music, IL
Walla Walla College, WA
Wartburg College, IA
Wayland Baptist University, TX
Wayne State College, NE
Western Carolina University, NC
Western Kentucky University, KY
Western Washington University, WA
Westminster College, MO

Westminster College, UT
Westmont College, CA
West Virginia University, WV
Whitman College, WA
Whitworth College, WA
Wittenberg University, OH

First-Generation College Students
Abilene Christian University, TX
American University, DC
Appalachian State University, NC
Arkansas State University, AR
Austin College, TX
Averett University, VA
Boise State University, ID
Bowie State University, MD
Brenau University, GA
Brewton-Parker College, GA
California Lutheran University, CA
California State University, Bakersfield, CA
California State University, Chico, CA
California State University, San Bernardino, CA
California State University, Stanislaus, CA
The Catholic University of America, DC
Central Michigan University, MI
Chowan College, NC
Colorado Christian University, CO
Colorado State University, CO
Colorado State University-Pueblo, CO
Columbia College Chicago, IL
Columbia International University, SC
Creighton University, NE
Davis & Elkins College, WV
Defiance College, OH
Dominican University of California, CA
Dowling College, NY
Edgewood College, WI
Edinboro University of Pennsylvania, PA
Erskine College, SC
The Evergreen State College, WA
Fairfield University, CT
Finlandia University, MI
Flagler College, FL
Fort Lewis College, CO
Georgia Southern University, GA
Glenville State College, WV
Graceland University, IA
Guilford College, NC
Hamline University, MN
Idaho State University, ID
Illinois State University, IL
Iowa State University of Science and Technology, IA
LaGrange College, GA
Lewis-Clark State College, ID
Limestone College, SC
Long Island University, Brooklyn Campus, NY
Meredith College, NC
Mesa State College, CO
Michigan State University, MI
Millsaps College, MS
Mississippi State University, MS
Missouri State University, MO
Monmouth University, NJ

Montana State University–Billings, MT
Morningside College, IA
Morris College, SC
New Mexico Highlands University, NM
Northern Arizona University, AZ
Northwestern College, IA
Ouachita Baptist University, AR
Peru State College, NE
Pontifical Catholic University of Puerto Rico, PR
Rochester College, MI
St. John Fisher College, NY
Saint Louis University, MO
Salem State College, MA
Shawnee State University, OH
Sonoma State University, CA
South Dakota State University, SD
Southeast Missouri State University, MO
Southwest Minnesota State University, MN
State University of New York College at Brockport, NY
Stephen F. Austin State University, TX
Tennessee Technological University, TN
Texas Lutheran University, TX
Texas State University-San Marcos, TX
Texas Tech University, TX
The University of Alabama at Birmingham, AL
University of California, San Diego, CA
University of Colorado at Boulder, CO
University of Colorado at Colorado Springs, CO
University of Colorado at Denver and Health Sciences Center—Downtown Denver Campus, CO
University of Colorado at Denver and Health Sciences Center—Health Sciences Program, CO
University of Delaware, DE
University of Great Falls, MT
University of Hartford, CT
University of Houston–Victoria, TX
University of Idaho, ID
University of Illinois at Springfield, IL
University of Kansas, KS
University of La Verne, CA
University of Maryland Eastern Shore, MD
University of Massachusetts Dartmouth, MA
University of Nebraska at Kearney, NE
University of Nebraska at Omaha, NE
University of Nevada, Las Vegas, NV
University of Nevada, Reno, NV
University of North Alabama, AL
The University of North Carolina at Asheville, NC
University of North Florida, FL
University of South Carolina, SC
University of South Carolina Upstate, SC
The University of Texas at Arlington, TX
University of Vermont, VT
University of Wisconsin–Eau Claire, WI
University of Wyoming, WY
Virginia Intermont College, VA
Virginia Polytechnic Institute and State University, VA

Washington State University, WA
Webber International University, FL
Westminster College, UT
West Texas A&M University, TX
Wichita State University, KS
William Carey College, MS

Handicapped Students

Albertson College of Idaho, ID
Appalachian State University, NC
Arkansas State University, AR
Augusta State University, GA
Austin College, TX
Boise State University, ID
Brigham Young University, UT
Bryan College, TN
California State University, Bakersfield, CA
California State University, Chico, CA
California State University, Fresno, CA
California State University, San Bernardino, CA
Calvin College, MI
The Catholic University of America, DC
Central College, IA
Central Washington University, WA
Clear Creek Baptist Bible College, KY
Columbia College Chicago, IL
Creighton University, NE
The Culinary Institute of America, NY
Delaware Valley College, PA
Dordt College, IA
East Carolina University, NC
Eastern Washington University, WA
East Stroudsburg University of Pennsylvania, PA
Edgewood College, WI
Edinboro University of Pennsylvania, PA
Emmanuel College, MA
Emporia State University, KS
Fordham University, NY
Francis Marion University, SC
Gallaudet University, DC
Georgia College & State University, GA
Georgia Institute of Technology, GA
Georgia Southern University, GA
Grand Valley State University, MI
Idaho State University, ID
Indiana University–Purdue University Fort Wayne, IN
Kent State University, OH
Kutztown University of Pennsylvania, PA
Lock Haven University of Pennsylvania, PA
Midland Lutheran College, NE
Midwestern State University, TX
Mississippi State University, MS
Murray State University, KY
New Mexico State University, NM
North Carolina Agricultural and Technical State University, NC
Northern Arizona University, AZ
Northwestern College, IA
The Ohio State University, OH
Old Dominion University, VA
Portland State University, OR
Roanoke Bible College, NC

Rowan University, NJ
St. Francis College, NY
St. Gregory's University, OK
Sam Houston State University, TX
Shawnee State University, OH
Sonoma State University, CA
South Dakota State University, SD
Southern Illinois University Carbondale, IL
Southwest Minnesota State University, MN
State University of New York College at Oneonta, NY
State University of New York College at Potsdam, NY
Texas State University-San Marcos, TX
Texas Tech University, TX
Trevecca Nazarene University, TN
The University of Akron, OH
The University of Alabama at Birmingham, AL
University of California, San Diego, CA
University of Colorado at Colorado Springs, CO
University of Colorado at Denver and Health Sciences Center—Downtown Denver Campus, CO
University of Hartford, CT
University of Idaho, ID
University of Mary Hardin-Baylor, TX
University of Massachusetts Amherst, MA
The University of Memphis, TN
University of Michigan, MI
University of Michigan–Flint, MI
University of Mississippi, MS
University of Nebraska at Omaha, NE
University of Nebraska–Lincoln, NE
University of Nevada, Las Vegas, NV
University of New Hampshire, NH
The University of North Carolina at Asheville, NC
The University of North Carolina at Greensboro, NC
University of North Dakota, ND
University of Northern Colorado, CO
University of South Carolina, SC
The University of Tennessee at Martin, TN
The University of Texas at Arlington, TX
The University of Texas at Dallas, TX
The University of Texas at San Antonio, TX
The University of Toledo, OH
University of Utah, UT
University of West Georgia, GA
University of Wisconsin–Stout, WI
University of Wisconsin–Whitewater, WI
University of Wyoming, WY
Washington State University, WA
Western Carolina University, NC
Western Kentucky University, KY
Westminster College, UT
West Texas A&M University, TX
Wheaton College, IL
Worcester State College, MA
Youngstown State University, OH

Non-Need Scholarships for Undergraduates
Special Characteristics

International Students

Adrian College, MI
Agnes Scott College, GA
Alaska Pacific University, AK
Albertson College of Idaho, ID
Albright College, PA
Alderson-Broaddus College, WV
Alfred University, NY
Allegheny College, PA
Alliant International University, CA
Alvernia College, PA
Anderson University, IN
Andrews University, MI
Appalachian Bible College, WV
Arkansas Tech University, AR
Armstrong Atlantic State University, GA
Asbury College, KY
Ashland University, OH
Atlantic Union College, MA
Augsburg College, MN
Augustana College, SD
Austin College, TX
Averett University, VA
Azusa Pacific University, CA
Baker University, KS
Barton College, NC
Bay Path College, MA
Belhaven College, MS
Bemidji State University, MN
Benedictine College, KS
Bethany College, KS
Bethany College, WV
Bethel College, KS
Bethel University, MN
Beulah Heights Bible College, GA
Biola University, CA
Bloomsburg University of Pennsylvania, PA
Bluffton University, OH
Boise State University, ID
Bowling Green State University, OH
Brenau University, GA
Brewton-Parker College, GA
Bridgewater College, VA
Brigham Young University, UT
Brigham Young University–Hawaii, HI
Bryan College, TN
Buena Vista University, IA
California Lutheran University, CA
California State University, Chico, CA
Calvin College, MI
Campbellsville University, KY
Canisius College, NY
Carroll College, MT
Carroll College, WI
Centenary College of Louisiana, LA
Central College, IA
Central Methodist University, MO
Central Michigan University, MI
Chowan College, NC
Christian Heritage College, CA
Cincinnati Christian University, OH
Clarke College, IA
Clarkson University, NY
Clear Creek Baptist Bible College, KY
Coastal Carolina University, SC
Coe College, IA

College of Notre Dame of Maryland, MD
College of Saint Benedict, MN
The College of St. Scholastica, MN
College of Staten Island of the City University of New York, NY
The College of Wooster, OH
The Colorado College, CO
Columbia College, MO
Columbia International University, SC
Concordia College, MN
Concordia University, NE
Corban College, OR
Cornerstone University, MI
Crown College, MN
The Culinary Institute of America, NY
Culver-Stockton College, MO
Defiance College, OH
DePauw University, IN
Dickinson State University, ND
Dominican University, IL
Dominican University of California, CA
Dordt College, IA
Drake University, IA
Duquesne University, PA
Eastern Mennonite University, VA
Eastern Michigan University, MI
Eastern Oregon University, OR
East Stroudsburg University of Pennsylvania, PA
East Texas Baptist University, TX
Eckerd College, FL
Edinboro University of Pennsylvania, PA
Elizabethtown College, PA
Elmira College, NY
Emmanuel College, MA
Emporia State University, KS
Endicott College, MA
Fairmont State University, WV
Ferrum College, VA
Finlandia University, MI
Fort Lewis College, CO
Francis Marion University, SC
Franklin Pierce College, NH
Free Will Baptist Bible College, TN
Fresno Pacific University, CA
Friends University, KS
Frostburg State University, MD
Furman University, SC
Gallaudet University, DC
Gannon University, PA
Georgia College & State University, GA
Goshen College, IN
Graceland University, IA
Grace University, NE
Grambling State University, LA
Green Mountain College, VT
Greenville College, IL
Hamline University, MN
Hampton University, VA
Hanover College, IN
Harding University, AR
Hawai'i Pacific University, HI
Hendrix College, AR
Hillsdale College, MI
Hollins University, VA
Holy Names University, CA

Huntington University, IN
Illinois Wesleyan University, IL
Indiana University of Pennsylvania, PA
Iowa State University of Science and Technology, IA
Iowa Wesleyan College, IA
Jamestown College, ND
John Brown University, AR
Johnson Bible College, TN
Juniata College, PA
Kent State University, OH
Kentucky Christian University, KY
Keuka College, NY
King's College, PA
Lancaster Bible College, PA
Lebanon Valley College, PA
LeTourneau University, TX
Liberty University, VA
Lincoln University, PA
Lipscomb University, TN
Long Island University, Brooklyn Campus, NY
Lourdes College, OH
MacMurray College, IL
Malone College, OH
Manchester College, IN
Massachusetts Maritime Academy, MA
McMurry University, TX
Mercer University, GA
Mesa State College, CO
Michigan Technological University, MI
Midland Lutheran College, NE
Midwestern State University, TX
Millersville University of Pennsylvania, PA
Minot State University, ND
Mississippi University for Women, MS
Missouri State University, MO
Monmouth University, NJ
Montreat College, NC
Moravian College, PA
Morningside College, IA
Mount Marty College, SD
Mount Mary College, WI
Mount Union College, OH
Mount Vernon Nazarene University, OH
Multnomah Bible College and Biblical Seminary, OR
Murray State University, KY
Nebraska Christian College, NE
New England College, NH
New Mexico Highlands University, NM
New Mexico State University, NM
North Central College, IL
North Central University, MN
Northeastern University, MA
Northern Arizona University, AZ
Northern Illinois University, IL
Northwestern College, IA
Northwestern College, MN
Northwestern State University of Louisiana, LA
Northwest Nazarene University, ID
Northwest University, WA
Nyack College, NY
Oakland City University, IN
Ohio Northern University, OH

Ohio Valley University, WV
Ohio Wesleyan University, OH
Oklahoma Wesleyan University, OK
Old Dominion University, VA
Olivet College, MI
Olivet Nazarene University, IL
Oral Roberts University, OK
Ouachita Baptist University, AR
Pacific Lutheran University, WA
Pacific University, OR
Peru State College, NE
Philadelphia Biblical University, PA
Piedmont College, GA
Plymouth State University, NH
Point Park University, PA
Portland State University, OR
Quinnipiac University, CT
Ramapo College of New Jersey, NJ
Randolph-Macon Woman's College, VA
Reformed Bible College, MI
Regis College, MA
Rice University, TX
The Richard Stockton College of New
  Jersey, NJ
Ripon College, WI
Roanoke Bible College, NC
Roberts Wesleyan College, NY
Rochester Institute of Technology, NY
Rowan University, NJ
Rust College, MS
St. Ambrose University, IA
St. Gregory's University, OK
Saint John's University, MN
Saint Louis University, MO
Saint Martin's College, WA
St. Norbert College, WI
St. Olaf College, MN
Saint Vincent College, PA
Schreiner University, TX
Seattle Pacific University, WA
Seton Hill University, PA
Silver Lake College, WI
Simpson College, IA
Sonoma State University, CA
South Dakota State University, SD
Southeastern Louisiana University, LA
Southeast Missouri State University, MO
Southern Adventist University, TN
Southern Illinois University Carbondale, IL
Southern New Hampshire University, NH
Southern Oregon University, OR
Southern Virginia University, VA
Southwestern College, KS
Southwest Minnesota State University, MN
Spring Arbor University, MI
State University of New York at
  Plattsburgh, NY
State University of New York College at
  Brockport, NY
State University of New York College at
  Oneonta, NY
State University of New York,
  Fredonia, NY
Stetson University, FL
Stevens Institute of Technology, NJ
Sweet Briar College, VA

Tabor College, KS
Taylor University, IN
Tennessee Wesleyan College, TN
Texas Christian University, TX
Texas Lutheran University, TX
Tiffin University, OH
Toccoa Falls College, GA
Trinity Lutheran College, WA
Truman State University, MO
The University of Alabama, AL
The University of Arizona, AZ
University of Charleston, WV
University of Evansville, IN
University of Great Falls, MT
University of Hartford, CT
University of Idaho, ID
University of Illinois at Springfield, IL
University of Indianapolis, IN
University of Kansas, KS
University of La Verne, CA
University of Maine, ME
The University of Maine at Augusta, ME
University of Maine at Fort Kent, ME
University of Maine at Presque Isle, ME
University of Mary Hardin-Baylor, TX
University of Miami, FL
University of Michigan, MI
University of Michigan–Flint, MI
University of Minnesota, Morris, MN
University of Missouri–Columbia, MO
University of Nebraska at Kearney, NE
University of Nebraska at Omaha, NE
University of Nebraska–Lincoln, NE
University of Nevada, Las Vegas, NV
University of New Hampshire, NH
The University of North Carolina at
  Asheville, NC
The University of North Carolina at Chapel
  Hill, NC
University of North Dakota, ND
University of Northern Colorado, CO
University of North Florida, FL
University of Oregon, OR
University of Puget Sound, WA
University of Redlands, CA
University of St. Thomas, TX
University of Science and Arts of
  Oklahoma, OK
University of Sioux Falls, SD
University of South Carolina, SC
University of Southern California, CA
The University of Tampa, FL
The University of Texas at Arlington, TX
The University of Texas at Dallas, TX
The University of Texas at El Paso, TX
The University of Texas–Pan American, TX
University of the Ozarks, AR
The University of Toledo, OH
University of Vermont, VT
University of Washington, WA
University of West Georgia, GA
University of Wisconsin–Eau Claire, WI
University of Wisconsin–Parkside, WI
University of Wisconsin–Stevens Point, WI
University of Wisconsin–Stout, WI
University of Wisconsin–Whitewater, WI

University of Wyoming, WY
Ursinus College, PA
Valdosta State University, GA
Valparaiso University, IN
Wabash College, IN
Warner Southern College, FL
Wartburg College, IA
Washington Bible College, MD
Washington College, MD
Washington State University, WA
Webber International University, FL
Western Illinois University, IL
Western Kentucky University, KY
Western New England College, MA
Western Washington University, WA
Westminster College, MO
Westminster College, PA
Westminster College, UT
Westmont College, CA
West Virginia University, WV
West Virginia Wesleyan College, WV
Wheeling Jesuit University, WV
Whitman College, WA
Whittier College, CA
Whitworth College, WA
Wichita State University, KS
William Carey College, MS
Williams Baptist College, AR
Wilson College, PA
Wittenberg University, OH
Xavier University, OH
York College of Pennsylvania, PA

Local/State Students
Abilene Christian University, TX
Agnes Scott College, GA
Alaska Pacific University, AK
Albertson College of Idaho, ID
Alcorn State University, MS
Allen College, IA
Alliant International University, CA
Alvernia College, PA
American University, DC
Anna Maria College, MA
Antioch College, OH
Auburn University, AL
Augusta State University, GA
Austin College, TX
Averett University, VA
Barton College, NC
Belhaven College, MS
Benedictine College, KS
Berry College, GA
Bethany College, WV
Bethel College, TN
Boise State University, ID
Boston University, MA
Brevard College, NC
Brewton-Parker College, GA
Brigham Young University, UT
Brigham Young University–Hawaii, HI
Bryan College, TN
California State University, Chico, CA
California State University, Fresno, CA
California State University, Stanislaus, CA
The Catholic University of America, DC

Centenary College, NJ
Centenary College of Louisiana, LA
Central Michigan University, MI
Central Washington University, WA
Chowan College, NC
Clarion University of Pennsylvania, PA
Clarke College, IA
Clarkson University, NY
Clemson University, SC
Coastal Carolina University, SC
College of St. Joseph, VT
The College of Wooster, OH
Columbia College, MO
Columbus College of Art & Design, OH
Concordia University, NE
Creighton University, NE
Culver-Stockton College, MO
Dakota State University, SD
Davis & Elkins College, WV
Defiance College, OH
Dominican University of California, CA
Dordt College, IA
Dowling College, NY
Duke University, NC
East Carolina University, NC
Eastern Washington University, WA
East Texas Baptist University, TX
Eckerd College, FL
Edgewood College, WI
Edinboro University of Pennsylvania, PA
Elizabethtown College, PA
Elmira College, NY
Emmanuel College, MA
Emory University, GA
Endicott College, MA
Fairmont State University, WV
Ferrum College, VA
Flagler College, FL
Florida Southern College, FL
Florida State University, FL
Fort Lewis College, CO
Framingham State College, MA
Franklin College, IN
Franklin Pierce College, NH
Frostburg State University, MD
Furman University, SC
Georgetown College, KY
Georgia College & State University, GA
Georgia Institute of Technology, GA
Graceland University, IA
Grambling State University, LA
Grand Valley State University, MI
Greenville College, IL
Guilford College, NC
Hamline University, MN
Hawai'i Pacific University, HI
Heidelberg College, OH
Hollins University, VA
Howard Payne University, TX
Idaho State University, ID
Indiana University–Purdue University Fort
  Wayne, IN
Iowa State University of Science and
  Technology, IA
Kennesaw State University, GA
Laboratory Institute of Merchandising, NY

Lawrence University, WI
Lenoir-Rhyne College, NC
Lesley University, MA
LeTourneau University, TX
Lewis-Clark State College, ID
Limestone College, SC
Lock Haven University of Pennsylvania, PA
Longwood University, VA
Lourdes College, OH
Lyon College, AR
Martin Methodist College, TN
Maryville College, TN
McDaniel College, MD
McMurry University, TX
McPherson College, KS
Medcenter One College of Nursing, ND
Medical University of South Carolina, SC
Mercer University, GA
Mercyhurst College, PA
Mesa State College, CO
Miami University, OH
Michigan Technological University, MI
Milwaukee Institute of Art and Design, WI
Minnesota State University Mankato, MN
Minot State University, ND
Mississippi State University, MS
Missouri Southern State University, MO
Monmouth University, NJ
Montana State University–Billings, MT
Morehead State University, KY
Morningside College, IA
Mount Vernon Nazarene University, OH
Murray State University, KY
Muskingum College, OH
New England College, NH
New Mexico State University, NM
New York Institute of Technology, NY
Northern Arizona University, AZ
Nyack College, NY
Ohio Valley University, WV
Ohio Wesleyan University, OH
Oklahoma Baptist University, OK
Oklahoma Panhandle State University, OK
Old Dominion University, VA
Ouachita Baptist University, AR
Peru State College, NE
Pontifical College Josephinum, OH
Post University, CT
Randolph-Macon Woman's College, VA
Regis University, CO
The Richard Stockton College of New
  Jersey, NJ
Ripon College, WI
Roanoke College, VA
Rust College, MS
St. Andrews Presbyterian College, NC
St. Bonaventure University, NY
St. Cloud State University, MN
St. John Fisher College, NY
St. John's University, NY
Saint Martin's College, WA
Saint Michael's College, VT
Schreiner University, TX
Shawnee State University, OH
Shenandoah University, VA
Shorter College, GA

Sierra Nevada College, NV
Simon's Rock College of Bard, MA
Slippery Rock University of
  Pennsylvania, PA
Sonoma State University, CA
Southeastern Bible College, AL
Southeastern Louisiana University, LA
Southern Adventist University, TN
Southern New Hampshire University, NH
Southern Oregon University, OR
Southwest Baptist University, MO
Southwestern College, KS
Southwest Minnesota State University, MN
State University of New York at
  Binghamton, NY
State University of New York College at
  Brockport, NY
State University of New York College at
  Geneseo, NY
State University of New York College at
  Oneonta, NY
State University of New York College at
  Potsdam, NY
State University of New York,
  Fredonia, NY
State University of New York Institute of
  Technology, NY
Stephen F. Austin State University, TX
Stephens College, MO
Sterling College, VT
Stetson University, FL
Stevens Institute of Technology, NJ
Sweet Briar College, VA
Tabor College, KS
Taylor University Fort Wayne, IN
Tennessee Technological University, TN
Texas Christian University, TX
Tiffin University, OH
Tusculum College, TN
Tuskegee University, AL
Unity College, ME
University at Buffalo, The State University
  of New York, NY
The University of Akron, OH
The University of Alabama at
  Birmingham, AL
The University of Alabama in
  Huntsville, AL
University of Arkansas at Fort Smith, AR
University of Bridgeport, CT
University of Charleston, WV
University of Colorado at Boulder, CO
University of Colorado at Denver and
  Health Sciences Center—Health Sciences
  Program, CO
University of Delaware, DE
University of Georgia, GA
University of Hartford, CT
University of Idaho, ID
University of Illinois at Springfield, IL
University of Kansas, KS
University of Maine, ME
The University of Maine at Augusta, ME
University of Mary Hardin-Baylor, TX
University of Mary Washington, VA
University of Michigan, MI

University of Mississippi, MS
University of Missouri–St. Louis, MO
University of Nevada, Las Vegas, NV
University of Nevada, Reno, NV
University of New Hampshire, NH
University of New Orleans, LA
The University of North Carolina at Asheville, NC
The University of North Carolina at Wilmington, NC
University of Northern Colorado, CO
University of Oregon, OR
University of Rio Grande, OH
University of Rochester, NY
University of Sioux Falls, SD
University of South Carolina, SC
University of Southern Maine, ME
University of Southern Mississippi, MS
The University of Texas at Dallas, TX
The University of Texas at El Paso, TX
The University of Texas at San Antonio, TX
The University of Texas–Pan American, TX
The University of Virginia's College at Wise, VA
University of West Georgia, GA
University of Wisconsin–Eau Claire, WI
University of Wisconsin–Oshkosh, WI
University of Wisconsin–Parkside, WI
University of Wisconsin–Stout, WI
University of Wisconsin–Whitewater, WI
University of Wyoming, WY
Vanderbilt University, TN
Virginia Military Institute, VA
Virginia Polytechnic Institute and State University, VA
Warren Wilson College, NC
Washington and Lee University, VA
Wayland Baptist University, TX
Wayne State College, NE
Webber International University, FL
Western Carolina University, NC
Western Kentucky University, KY
Western New England College, MA
Western Washington University, WA
Westminster College, MO
Westminster College, UT
West Virginia University, WV
Wilson College, PA
Winona State University, MN
Wittenberg University, OH
Worcester State College, MA

Married Students
Appalachian Bible College, WV
Auburn University, AL
Beulah Heights Bible College, GA
Brigham Young University–Hawaii, HI
California State University, Chico, CA
Cincinnati Christian University, OH
Columbia International University, SC
Eugene Bible College, OR
Franklin Pierce College, NH
Free Will Baptist Bible College, TN
Georgia Southern University, GA
Grace University, NE

Johnson Bible College, TN
John Wesley College, NC
Lancaster Bible College, PA
Mid-Continent University, KY
New Mexico State University, NM
Northwest University, WA
Ouachita Baptist University, AR
Roanoke Bible College, NC
Sonoma State University, CA
State University of New York College at Brockport, NY
Toccoa Falls College, GA
The University of Alabama at Birmingham, AL
University of Kansas, KS
University of Nevada, Reno, NV
Valley Forge Christian College, PA

Members of Minority Groups
Abilene Christian University, TX
Alaska Pacific University, AK
Albertson College of Idaho, ID
Albright College, PA
Alcorn State University, MS
Alice Lloyd College, KY
Allen College, IA
Alliant International University, CA
American University, DC
Appalachian State University, NC
Augsburg College, MN
Augustana College, SD
Baker University, KS
Baldwin-Wallace College, OH
Beloit College, WI
Benedictine College, KS
Bentley College, MA
Berry College, GA
Bethel University, MN
Bluffton University, OH
Boise State University, ID
Bowling Green State University, OH
Bradley University, IL
Brigham Young University, UT
Brigham Young University–Hawaii, HI
Bryant University, RI
California State University, Chico, CA
California State University, Dominguez Hills, CA
California State University, Stanislaus, CA
Calvin College, MI
Cameron University, OK
Carson-Newman College, TN
Centenary College of Louisiana, LA
Central College, IA
Central Connecticut State University, CT
Central Michigan University, MI
Central Missouri State University, MO
Centre College, KY
Clarion University of Pennsylvania, PA
Clarke College, IA
Clarkson University, NY
Clemson University, SC
The College of New Jersey, NJ
The College of Saint Rose, NY
The College of St. Scholastica, MN

College of Staten Island of the City University of New York, NY
The College of Wooster, OH
Concordia College, MN
Concordia University, NE
Cornerstone University, MI
Creighton University, NE
The Culinary Institute of America, NY
Dakota State University, SD
Defiance College, OH
Denison University, OH
DePauw University, IN
Dominican University of California, CA
Dordt College, IA
Drake University, IA
Duquesne University, PA
East Central University, OK
Eastern Michigan University, MI
Eastern Oregon University, OR
East Stroudsburg University of Pennsylvania, PA
East Tennessee State University, TN
Edgewood College, WI
Edinboro University of Pennsylvania, PA
Elizabethtown College, PA
Elmhurst College, IL
Emporia State University, KS
Erskine College, SC
The Evergreen State College, WA
Fairfield University, CT
Fairmont State University, WV
Flagler College, FL
Fort Hays State University, KS
Fresno Pacific University, CA
Furman University, SC
Gannon University, PA
Georgia College & State University, GA
Georgia Institute of Technology, GA
Georgia Southern University, GA
Gonzaga University, WA
Graceland University, IA
Grace University, NE
Grambling State University, LA
Grand Canyon University, AZ
Grand Valley State University, MI
Grove City College, PA
Hamline University, MN
Hampton University, VA
Hanover College, IN
Hilbert College, NY
Humphreys College, CA
Idaho State University, ID
Illinois College, IL
Illinois State University, IL
Indiana State University, IN
Iowa State University of Science and Technology, IA
John Brown University, AR
Johnson Bible College, TN
Kennesaw State University, GA
Kent State University, OH
Kentucky Christian University, KY
King College, TN
King's College, PA
Lawrence Technological University, MI
Lawrence University, WI

Non-Need Scholarships for Undergraduates
Special Characteristics

Le Moyne College, NY
Lesley University, MA
Lewis-Clark State College, ID
Lipscomb University, TN
Lock Haven University of Pennsylvania, PA
Lourdes College, OH
Loyola College in Maryland, MD
Luther College, IA
Lyon College, AR
Manchester College, IN
Marietta College, OH
Maryville College, TN
Maryville University of Saint Louis, MO
Medical University of South Carolina, SC
Mercer University, GA
Mercyhurst College, PA
Mesa State College, CO
Miami University, OH
Michigan State University, MI
Michigan Technological University, MI
Middle Tennessee State University, TN
Midland Lutheran College, NE
Midway College, KY
Millsaps College, MS
Milwaukee Institute of Art and Design, WI
Minnesota State University Moorhead, MN
Minot State University, ND
Mississippi University for Women, MS
Missouri State University, MO
Montana State University–Billings, MT
Morehead State University, KY
Mount St. Mary's University, MD
Murray State University, KY
Muskingum College, OH
Nebraska Wesleyan University, NE
New Mexico State University, NM
North Carolina Agricultural and Technical State University, NC
Northern Illinois University, IL
Northern Kentucky University, KY
Northern Michigan University, MI
Northwest Nazarene University, ID
Oakland City University, IN
The Ohio State University, OH
Ohio University, OH
Ohio University–Lancaster, OH
Ohio Wesleyan University, OH
Old Dominion University, VA
Ouachita Baptist University, AR
Pikeville College, KY
Pine Manor College, MA
Pitzer College, CA
Point Park University, PA
Polytechnic University, Brooklyn Campus, NY
Portland State University, OR
Post University, CT
Quinnipiac University, CT
Regis University, CO
Rensselaer Polytechnic Institute, NY
The Richard Stockton College of New Jersey, NJ
Rider University, NJ
Ripon College, WI
Roanoke College, VA
Robert Morris University, PA

Rochester Institute of Technology, NY
Rowan University, NJ
Rust College, MS
St. Ambrose University, IA
St. Bonaventure University, NY
St. Cloud State University, MN
St. John Fisher College, NY
Saint Joseph's College, IN
Saint Louis University, MO
Saint Martin's College, WA
Saint Mary's University of Minnesota, MN
Saint Michael's College, VT
Saint Vincent College, PA
Salem State College, MA
Seton Hall University, NJ
Shawnee State University, OH
Shepherd University, WV
Sierra Nevada College, NV
Simon's Rock College of Bard, MA
Simpson College, IA
Simpson University, CA
Slippery Rock University of Pennsylvania, PA
Sonoma State University, CA
South Dakota State University, SD
Southeastern Louisiana University, LA
Southeast Missouri State University, MO
Southern Adventist University, TN
Southern Arkansas University– Magnolia, AR
Southern Wesleyan University, SC
Southwestern College, KS
Southwest Minnesota State University, MN
Spring Arbor University, MI
State University of New York at Binghamton, NY
State University of New York at New Paltz, NY
State University of New York College at Brockport, NY
State University of New York College at Geneseo, NY
State University of New York College at Oneonta, NY
State University of New York College at Potsdam, NY
State University of New York College of Environmental Science and Forestry, NY
State University of New York, Fredonia, NY
State University of New York Institute of Technology, NY
Stetson University, FL
Stevens Institute of Technology, NJ
Stonehill College, MA
Susquehanna University, PA
Tennessee Technological University, TN
Tennessee Wesleyan College, TN
Thomas Jefferson University, PA
Transylvania University, KY
Trinity International University, IL
Unity College, ME
The University of Akron, OH
The University of Alabama at Birmingham, AL

The University of Alabama in Huntsville, AL
University of California, San Diego, CA
University of Central Florida, FL
University of Cincinnati, OH
University of Colorado at Denver and Health Sciences Center—Downtown Denver Campus, CO
University of Dallas, TX
University of Delaware, DE
University of Detroit Mercy, MI
University of Dubuque, IA
University of Evansville, IN
University of Florida, FL
University of Hartford, CT
University of Idaho, ID
University of Illinois at Chicago, IL
University of Illinois at Springfield, IL
University of Kansas, KS
University of Maine, ME
University of Maine at Farmington, ME
University of Maine at Fort Kent, ME
University of Mary Hardin-Baylor, TX
University of Massachusetts Dartmouth, MA
The University of Memphis, TN
University of Michigan, MI
University of Michigan–Dearborn, MI
University of Michigan–Flint, MI
University of Minnesota, Morris, MN
University of Missouri–Columbia, MO
University of Missouri–Kansas City, MO
University of Missouri–St. Louis, MO
The University of Montana–Western, MT
University of Nebraska at Omaha, NE
University of Nebraska–Lincoln, NE
University of Nevada, Las Vegas, NV
University of Nevada, Reno, NV
The University of North Carolina at Asheville, NC
The University of North Carolina at Greensboro, NC
University of North Dakota, ND
University of Northern Colorado, CO
University of Northern Iowa, IA
University of North Florida, FL
University of Oklahoma, OK
University of Richmond, VA
University of St. Thomas, TX
The University of Scranton, PA
University of South Carolina, SC
University of Southern California, CA
University of Southern Indiana, IN
The University of Tennessee at Chattanooga, TN
The University of Tennessee at Martin, TN
The University of Texas at Dallas, TX
The University of Texas at El Paso, TX
University of the Ozarks, AR
University of the South, TN
The University of Toledo, OH
University of West Florida, FL
University of West Georgia, GA
University of Wisconsin–Eau Claire, WI
University of Wisconsin–La Crosse, WI
University of Wisconsin–Oshkosh, WI

University of Wisconsin–Parkside, WI
University of Wisconsin–Stevens Point, WI
University of Wisconsin–Stout, WI
University of Wisconsin–Whitewater, WI
Valdosta State University, GA
Vanderbilt University, TN
Villanova University, PA
Virginia Intermont College, VA
Virginia Polytechnic Institute and State
  University, VA
Wake Forest University, NC
Warner Pacific College, OR
Wartburg College, IA
Wayland Baptist University, TX
Wayne State College, NE
Western Carolina University, NC
Western Illinois University, IL
Western Kentucky University, KY
Western New England College, MA
Western Washington University, WA
Westminster College, UT
West Virginia University, WV
West Virginia Wesleyan College, WV
Wichita State University, KS
William Jewell College, MO
Williams Baptist College, AR
Wilmington College, OH
Winona State University, MN
Wittenberg University, OH
Xavier University, OH
York College of Pennsylvania, PA
Youngstown State University, OH

Out-of-State Students
Abilene Christian University, TX
Alaska Pacific University, AK
Albion College, MI
Allen College, IA
Alvernia College, PA
Appalachian State University, NC
Arkansas State University, AR
Arkansas Tech University, AR
Auburn University, AL
Aurora University, IL
Averett University, VA
Baker University, KS
Bay Path College, MA
Bemidji State University, MN
Benedictine College, KS
Benedictine University, IL
Bethel University, MN
Bluffton University, OH
Boise State University, ID
Brewton-Parker College, GA
Bridgewater College, VA
Brigham Young University, UT
Buena Vista University, IA
California State University, Chico, CA
Centenary College, NJ
Centenary College of Louisiana, LA
Central College, IA
Central Michigan University, MI
Central Missouri State University, MO
Central Pennsylvania College, PA
Christian Heritage College, CA
Coastal Carolina University, SC

College Misericordia, PA
The College of New Rochelle, NY
Concordia University Wisconsin, WI
Cornerstone University, MI
Defiance College, OH
Delaware State University, DE
Dominican University of California, CA
Dordt College, IA
East Central University, OK
Eastern Michigan University, MI
Eastern Oregon University, OR
Edinboro University of Pennsylvania, PA
Emory & Henry College, VA
Erskine College, SC
Fairmont State University, WV
Ferrum College, VA
Flagler College, FL
Florida Southern College, FL
Fort Lewis College, CO
Francis Marion University, SC
Frostburg State University, MD
Georgia College & State University, GA
Georgia Institute of Technology, GA
Grace University, NE
Grambling State University, LA
Grand Canyon University, AZ
Grand Valley State University, MI
Greenville College, IL
Hampden-Sydney College, VA
Hawai'i Pacific University, HI
Heidelberg College, OH
Hollins University, VA
Idaho State University, ID
Iowa State University of Science and
  Technology, IA
Iowa Wesleyan College, IA
Kent State University, OH
Kentucky Wesleyan College, KY
Lewis-Clark State College, ID
Limestone College, SC
Louisiana Tech University, LA
MacMurray College, IL
McKendree College, IL
McMurry University, TX
Mesa State College, CO
Miami University, OH
Michigan State University, MI
Michigan Technological University, MI
Midwestern State University, TX
Minnesota State University Mankato, MN
Minot State University, ND
Mississippi State University, MS
Mississippi University for Women, MS
Missouri State University, MO
Monmouth University, NJ
Montana State University–Billings, MT
Morehead State University, KY
Morningside College, IA
New College of Florida, FL
New Jersey Institute of Technology, NJ
New Mexico State University, NM
Northern Arizona University, AZ
Northern Michigan University, MI
Northwestern State University of
  Louisiana, LA
Northwest Nazarene University, ID

Nyack College, NY
Oakland University, MI
The Ohio State University, OH
Ohio Wesleyan University, OH
Oklahoma Baptist University, OK
Oklahoma Panhandle State University, OK
Oklahoma State University, OK
Ouachita Baptist University, AR
Peru State College, NE
Piedmont College, GA
Portland State University, OR
Ramapo College of New Jersey, NJ
Ripon College, WI
Robert Morris College, IL
Robert Morris University, PA
Roberts Wesleyan College, NY
Rochester College, MI
St. Cloud State University, MN
Saint Michael's College, VT
Shimer College, IL
Shorter College, GA
Simpson University, CA
Slippery Rock University of
  Pennsylvania, PA
Sonoma State University, CA
Southeastern Louisiana University, LA
Southeastern Oklahoma State
  University, OK
Southeast Missouri State University, MO
Southern Adventist University, TN
Southern Arkansas University–
  Magnolia, AR
Spring Arbor University, MI
State University of New York at
  Binghamton, NY
State University of New York at
  Plattsburgh, NY
State University of New York College at
  Brockport, NY
State University of New York,
  Fredonia, NY
Tabor College, KS
Tennessee Technological University, TN
Texas Tech University, TX
Thomas University, GA
Tiffin University, OH
Transylvania University, KY
University at Albany, State University of
  New York, NY
The University of Akron, OH
The University of Alabama, AL
The University of Alabama at
  Birmingham, AL
University of Arkansas at Monticello, AR
University of Cincinnati, OH
University of Colorado at Colorado
  Springs, CO
University of Dubuque, IA
University of Florida, FL
University of Idaho, ID
University of Illinois at Springfield, IL
University of Indianapolis, IN
University of Kansas, KS
University of Maine, ME
University of Maine at Farmington, ME
University of Mary Hardin-Baylor, TX

University of Maryland, College Park, MD
University of Michigan, MI
University of Mississippi, MS
University of Missouri–Columbia, MO
University of Missouri–Kansas City, MO
University of Nebraska at Kearney, NE
University of Nebraska at Omaha, NE
University of Nebraska–Lincoln, NE
University of Nevada, Las Vegas, NV
University of New Orleans, LA
University of North Alabama, AL
The University of North Carolina at Chapel Hill, NC
The University of North Carolina at Greensboro, NC
University of Northern Colorado, CO
University of North Florida, FL
University of Rio Grande, OH
University of Science and Arts of Oklahoma, OK
University of Sioux Falls, SD
University of South Carolina, SC
University of Southern Indiana, IN
University of Southern Maine, ME
University of Southern Mississippi, MS
The University of Tennessee at Martin, TN
The University of Texas at Dallas, TX
The University of Texas at El Paso, TX
The University of Texas at San Antonio, TX
The University of Texas–Pan American, TX
University of Utah, UT
University of Wisconsin–La Crosse, WI
University of Wisconsin–Stevens Point, WI
University of Wisconsin–Stout, WI
University of Wisconsin–Whitewater, WI
University of Wyoming, WY
Virginia Military Institute, VA
Virginia Polytechnic Institute and State University, VA
Warner Southern College, FL
Wartburg College, IA
Washington State University, WA
Wayne State College, NE
Western Kentucky University, KY
Western New England College, MA
William Jewell College, MO
Winona State University, MN

Parents of Current Students

Aurora University, IL
Blue Mountain College, MS
Cincinnati Christian University, OH
The College of New Rochelle, NY
Columbia College, MO
Franklin Pierce College, NH
Green Mountain College, VT
Huntington University, IN
Johnson Bible College, TN
Malone College, OH
Marymount University, VA
Maryville University of Saint Louis, MO
Mississippi University for Women, MS
Missouri Baptist University, MO
Mount Aloysius College, PA
Mount Marty College, SD

Mount Mary College, WI
New England College, NH
Northwest University, WA
Olivet Nazarene University, IL
Peirce College, PA
Seton Hill University, PA
The University of Alabama at Birmingham, AL
University of Bridgeport, CT
University of Great Falls, MT
University of Hartford, CT

Previous College Experience

Abilene Christian University, TX
Alma College, MI
Alvernia College, PA
American University, DC
Benedictine University, IL
Bethel College, KS
Boise State University, ID
Brevard College, NC
Cedar Crest College, PA
Centenary College, NJ
Central College, IA
Central Missouri State University, MO
Central Washington University, WA
College Misericordia, PA
The College of New Rochelle, NY
The College of St. Scholastica, MN
Columbia College, MO
Defiance College, OH
East Central University, OK
Eastern Michigan University, MI
East Texas Baptist University, TX
Elmira College, NY
Emory & Henry College, VA
Florida Institute of Technology, FL
Hawai'i Pacific University, HI
Hendrix College, AR
Illinois College, IL
Illinois State University, IL
Lake Forest College, IL
Lancaster Bible College, PA
Lock Haven University of Pennsylvania, PA
MacMurray College, IL
Manchester College, IN
McDaniel College, MD
McMurry University, TX
Memphis College of Art, TN
Mercy College of Health Sciences, IA
Michigan Technological University, MI
Mississippi State University, MS
Mount Mercy College, IA
New Mexico State University, NM
New York Institute of Technology, NY
The Ohio State University, OH
Old Dominion University, VA
Pacific Lutheran University, WA
Palm Beach Atlantic University, FL
Peirce College, PA
Peru State College, NE
Point Park University, PA
The Richard Stockton College of New Jersey, NJ
Ripon College, WI
Rochester College, MI

Saint Louis University, MO
Slippery Rock University of Pennsylvania, PA
Sonoma State University, CA
Southeast Missouri State University, MO
Southern New Hampshire University, NH
Southwest Minnesota State University, MN
State University of New York College at Potsdam, NY
State University of New York, Fredonia, NY
State University of New York Institute of Technology, NY
Stephen F. Austin State University, TX
Sterling College, VT
The University of Alabama at Birmingham, AL
University of Colorado at Denver and Health Sciences Center—Health Sciences Program, CO
University of Hartford, CT
University of Kansas, KS
University of Maine, ME
University of Michigan–Dearborn, MI
University of New Orleans, LA
University of Oklahoma, OK
University of Science and Arts of Oklahoma, OK
The University of Toledo, OH
University of West Georgia, GA
University of Wisconsin–Eau Claire, WI
University of Wisconsin–Stout, WI
Walsh College of Accountancy and Business Administration, MI
Warner Southern College, FL
Warren Wilson College, NC
Western Washington University, WA
York College, NE

Public Servants

Arkansas Tech University, AR
College of Staten Island of the City University of New York, NY
Dowling College, NY
Grambling State University, LA
Hannibal-LaGrange College, MO
Louisiana Tech University, LA
Michigan State University, MI
Missouri Baptist University, MO
New York Institute of Technology, NY
Nicholls State University, LA
Northwestern State University of Louisiana, LA
Peirce College, PA
St. Francis College, NY
Salem State College, MA
Southern Illinois University Carbondale, IL
Tennessee Technological University, TN
Tiffin University, OH
The University of Alabama at Birmingham, AL
University of Illinois at Springfield, IL
University of Maine, ME
The University of Memphis, TN
University of New Orleans, LA
The University of Texas at Dallas, TX

The University of Toledo, OH
Washington State University, WA
Westminster College, UT

Relatives of Clergy

Abilene Christian University, TX
Albion College, MI
American University, DC
Anderson University, IN
Appalachian Bible College, WV
Arcadia University, PA
Ashland University, OH
Augsburg College, MN
Austin College, TX
Averett University, VA
Azusa Pacific University, CA
Baker University, KS
Barton College, NC
Belhaven College, MS
Bethany College, KS
Bethany College, WV
Bethel College, KS
Bethel University, MN
Biola University, CA
Bluffton University, OH
Boston University, MA
Brevard College, NC
Brewton-Parker College, GA
Bryan College, TN
California Baptist University, CA
California Lutheran University, CA
Calvary Bible College and Theological
  Seminary, MO
Campbellsville University, KY
Carson-Newman College, TN
Cedar Crest College, PA
Centenary College of Louisiana, LA
Central Bible College, MO
Central Christian College of Kansas, KS
Central Methodist University, MO
Chowan College, NC
Christian Heritage College, CA
Clarke College, IA
College Misericordia, PA
Columbia College, SC
Columbia International University, SC
Concordia University, MI
Concordia University, OR
Corban College, OR
Crown College, MN
Culver-Stockton College, MO
Dallas Baptist University, TX
Davidson College, NC
Defiance College, OH
DePauw University, IN
DeSales University, PA
Dominican College, NY
Duquesne University, PA
Elon University, NC
Emory & Henry College, VA
Emory University, GA
Erskine College, SC
Eugene Bible College, OR
Faith Baptist Bible College and Theological
  Seminary, IA
Faulkner University, AL

Ferrum College, VA
Florida Southern College, FL
Friends University, KS
Furman University, SC
Geneva College, PA
Georgetown College, KY
Gordon College, MA
Grace College, IN
Grace University, NE
Grand Canyon University, AZ
Greenville College, IL
Hannibal-LaGrange College, MO
Hastings College, NE
Hawai'i Pacific University, HI
Heidelberg College, OH
Hendrix College, AR
Houghton College, NY
Houston Baptist University, TX
Howard Payne University, TX
Huntington University, IN
Iowa Wesleyan College, IA
Jamestown College, ND
John Brown University, AR
Johnson Bible College, TN
Judson College, AL
Kentucky Wesleyan College, KY
King College, TN
King's College, PA
LaGrange College, GA
Lambuth University, TN
Lancaster Bible College, PA
La Sierra University, CA
Lenoir-Rhyne College, NC
LeTourneau University, TX
Life Pacific College, CA
Lipscomb University, TN
Lycoming College, PA
Malone College, OH
Maranatha Baptist Bible College, WI
McMurry University, TX
Mercer University, GA
Merrimack College, MA
Messiah College, PA
Methodist College, NC
MidAmerica Nazarene University, KS
Mid-Continent University, KY
Midway College, KY
Millsaps College, MS
Mississippi College, MS
Missouri Baptist University, MO
Montreat College, NC
Moravian College, PA
Morningside College, IA
Mount Union College, OH
Mount Vernon Nazarene University, OH
Nebraska Christian College, NE
Nebraska Wesleyan University, NE
Niagara University, NY
North Central College, IL
North Central University, MN
North Greenville College, SC
Northwestern College, MN
Northwest Nazarene University, ID
Northwest University, WA
Nyack College, NY
Ohio Northern University, OH

Ohio Valley University, WV
Ohio Wesleyan University, OH
Oklahoma Baptist University, OK
Oklahoma City University, OK
Oklahoma Wesleyan University, OK
Olivet Nazarene University, IL
Oral Roberts University, OK
Ouachita Baptist University, AR
Pacific Lutheran University, WA
Pacific University, OR
Palm Beach Atlantic University, FL
Peace College, NC
Philadelphia Biblical University, PA
Randolph-Macon College, VA
Randolph-Macon Woman's College, VA
Regis College, MA
Roberts Wesleyan College, NY
Rochester College, MI
Rosemont College, PA
Rust College, MS
St. Bonaventure University, NY
St. John's University, NY
Saint Mary's College of California, CA
Samford University, AL
Seattle Pacific University, WA
Seton Hall University, NJ
Shenandoah University, VA
Simpson College, IA
Simpson University, CA
Southeastern Bible College, AL
Southern Methodist College, SC
Southern Methodist University, TX
Southern Wesleyan University, SC
Southwest Baptist University, MO
Southwestern Christian University, OK
Southwestern College, KS
Southwestern University, TX
Spring Arbor University, MI
Stonehill College, MA
Susquehanna University, PA
Taylor University Fort Wayne, IN
Tennessee Wesleyan College, TN
Texas Christian University, TX
Texas Wesleyan University, TX
Thiel College, PA
Toccoa Falls College, GA
Transylvania University, KY
Trevecca Nazarene University, TN
Trinity Lutheran College, WA
Union University, TN
The University of Alabama at
  Birmingham, AL
University of Dubuque, IA
University of Indianapolis, IN
University of Mary Hardin-Baylor, TX
The University of North Carolina at Chapel
  Hill, NC
University of Portland, OR
University of St. Thomas, TX
University of South Carolina, SC
University of the Cumberlands, KY
University of the Ozarks, AR
University of the South, TN
Ursuline College, OH
Valley Forge Christian College, PA
Valparaiso University, IN

Virginia Wesleyan College, VA
Wake Forest University, NC
Warner Southern College, FL
Washington Bible College, MD
Wayland Baptist University, TX
Westminster College, MO
Westminster College, UT
West Virginia Wesleyan College, WV
Whitworth College, WA
William Carey College, MS
William Jewell College, MO
Williams Baptist College, AR
William Woods University, MO
Wilson College, PA
Wingate University, NC
Wittenberg University, OH
Wofford College, SC

Religious Affiliation

Abilene Christian University, TX
Adrian College, MI
Alaska Pacific University, AK
Albertson College of Idaho, ID
Alderson-Broaddus College, WV
Alvernia College, PA
American Baptist College of American
  Baptist Theological Seminary, TN
Appalachian Bible College, WV
Arcadia University, PA
Armstrong Atlantic State University, GA
Ashland University, OH
Augustana College, SD
Averett University, VA
Azusa Pacific University, CA
Baldwin-Wallace College, OH
The Baptist College of Florida, FL
Barton College, NC
Belhaven College, MS
Belmont Abbey College, NC
Benedictine College, KS
Bethany College, WV
Bethel College, KS
Bethel College, TN
Bethel University, MN
Beulah Heights Bible College, GA
Blue Mountain College, MS
Bluffton University, OH
Boston University, MA
Brevard College, NC
Brewton-Parker College, GA
Bridgewater College, VA
Brigham Young University, UT
Brigham Young University–Hawaii, HI
Bryan College, TN
Buena Vista University, IA
California Lutheran University, CA
Calvin College, MI
Campbellsville University, KY
Canisius College, NY
The Catholic University of America, DC
Cedar Crest College, PA
Cedarville University, OH
Centenary College, NJ
Centenary College of Louisiana, LA
Central Bible College, MO
Central College, IA

Central Methodist University, MO
Chestnut Hill College, PA
Chowan College, NC
Christian Brothers University, TN
Clarke College, IA
Clearwater Christian College, FL
College Misericordia, PA
College of St. Joseph, VT
The College of St. Scholastica, MN
Columbia College, MO
Columbia International University, SC
Concordia University, CA
Concordia University, MI
Concordia University, OR
Concordia University, St. Paul, MN
Concordia University Wisconsin, WI
Creighton University, NE
Culver-Stockton College, MO
Dallas Baptist University, TX
Dallas Christian College, TX
Davis & Elkins College, WV
Defiance College, OH
DePauw University, IN
DeSales University, PA
Dillard University, LA
Doane College, NE
Dordt College, IA
Duquesne University, PA
Eastern Mennonite University, VA
Eastern Michigan University, MI
East Texas Baptist University, TX
Eckerd College, FL
Edgewood College, WI
Edinboro University of Pennsylvania, PA
Elizabethtown College, PA
Elmhurst College, IL
Emmanuel College, MA
Emory & Henry College, VA
Emory University, GA
Emporia State University, KS
Endicott College, MA
Erskine College, SC
Eureka College, IL
Evangel University, MO
Fairfield University, CT
Ferrum College, VA
Finlandia University, MI
Franklin College, IN
Fresno Pacific University, CA
Friends University, KS
Furman University, SC
Gannon University, PA
Geneva College, PA
Georgetown College, KY
Georgia College & State University, GA
Georgian Court University, NJ
Graceland University, IA
Grace University, NE
Grand Canyon University, AZ
Greenville College, IL
Hamline University, MN
Hampden-Sydney College, VA
Hannibal-LaGrange College, MO
Hanover College, IN
Hastings College, NE
Hawai'i Pacific University, HI

Heidelberg College, OH
Holy Names University, CA
Houghton College, NY
Howard Payne University, TX
Huntington University, IN
Illinois College, IL
Iona College, NY
Iowa State University of Science and
  Technology, IA
Iowa Wesleyan College, IA
Johnson Bible College, TN
Judson College, AL
Juniata College, PA
Kennesaw State University, GA
Kentucky Christian University, KY
Kentucky Wesleyan College, KY
LaGrange College, GA
Lakeland College, WI
Lambuth University, TN
Lancaster Bible College, PA
La Sierra University, CA
Lenoir-Rhyne College, NC
Liberty University, VA
Loyola University Chicago, IL
Luther College, IA
Lyon College, AR
MacMurray College, IL
Malone College, OH
Manchester College, IN
Martin Methodist College, TN
Maryville College, TN
Maryville University of Saint Louis, MO
McKendree College, IL
McMurry University, TX
McPherson College, KS
Medical College of Georgia, GA
Mercer University, GA
Meredith College, NC
Messenger College, MO
Messiah College, PA
Methodist College, NC
Michigan State University, MI
MidAmerica Nazarene University, KS
Midland Lutheran College, NE
Midway College, KY
Millsaps College, MS
Missouri Baptist University, MO
Moravian College, PA
Morningside College, IA
Mount Aloysius College, PA
Mount Marty College, SD
Mount Olive College, NC
Mount Vernon Nazarene University, OH
Multnomah Bible College and Biblical
  Seminary, OR
Muskingum College, OH
North Central University, MN
Northwestern College, IA
Northwest Nazarene University, ID
Northwest University, WA
Nyack College, NY
Oakland City University, IN
Ohio Northern University, OH
Ohio Valley University, WV
Ohio Wesleyan University, OH
Oklahoma Baptist University, OK

Oklahoma Wesleyan University, OK
Olivet College, MI
Olivet Nazarene University, IL
Ouachita Baptist University, AR
Park University, MO
Randolph-Macon Woman's College, VA
Regis College, MA
Ripon College, WI
Roanoke College, VA
Roberts Wesleyan College, NY
Rust College, MS
St. Bonaventure University, NY
St. Edward's University, TX
St. Gregory's University, OK
St. John's University, NY
St. Louis Christian College, MO
Saint Martin's College, WA
Saint Michael's College, VT
Schreiner University, TX
Seattle Pacific University, WA
Shenandoah University, VA
Shorter College, GA
Simpson College, IA
Simpson University, CA
Southeastern Louisiana University, LA
Southern Wesleyan University, SC
Southwestern Christian University, OK
Southwestern College, KS
Spring Arbor University, MI
Stephen F. Austin State University, TX
Tabor College, KS
Taylor University, IN
Tennessee Wesleyan College, TN
Texas Christian University, TX
Texas Lutheran University, TX
Texas Wesleyan University, TX
Thiel College, PA
Thomas More College, KY
Toccoa Falls College, GA
Transylvania University, KY
Trevecca Nazarene University, TN
Trinity International University, IL
Trinity Lutheran College, WA
Union College, KY
Union University, TN
The University of Alabama at
  Birmingham, AL
University of Dayton, OH
University of Dubuque, IA
University of Evansville, IN
University of Great Falls, MT
University of Hartford, CT
University of Indianapolis, IN
University of La Verne, CA
University of Mary Hardin-Baylor, TX
The University of North Carolina at Chapel
  Hill, NC
The University of North Carolina at
  Greensboro, NC
University of St. Francis, IL
University of St. Thomas, TX
University of Sioux Falls, SD
University of South Carolina, SC
University of the Ozarks, AR
Urbana University, OH
Ursuline College, OH

Valparaiso University, IN
Villanova University, PA
Virginia Intermont College, VA
Wake Forest University, NC
Waldorf College, IA
Warner Pacific College, OR
Warren Wilson College, NC
Wartburg College, IA
Washington Bible College, MD
Washington State University, WA
Western Kentucky University, KY
Westminster College, MO
Westminster College, PA
Westminster College, UT
Wheeling Jesuit University, WV
William Carey College, MS
William Jewell College, MO
Williams Baptist College, AR
William Woods University, MO
Wilmington College, OH
Wilson College, PA
Wingate University, NC
Wittenberg University, OH

Siblings of Current Students

Albertson College of Idaho, ID
Albright College, PA
Alvernia College, PA
Anna Maria College, MA
Asbury College, KY
Atlantic Union College, MA
Augsburg College, MN
Augustana College, SD
Aurora University, IL
Azusa Pacific University, CA
Barton College, NC
Bay Path College, MA
Becker College, MA
Beloit College, WI
Benedictine University, IL
Blue Mountain College, MS
Bridgewater College, VA
Bryant University, RI
Buena Vista University, IA
California Baptist University, CA
Canisius College, NY
Carroll College, MT
Carroll College, WI
Carson-Newman College, TN
The Catholic University of America, DC
Cedar Crest College, PA
Centenary College, NJ
Central Bible College, MO
Central College, IA
Central Methodist University, MO
Chatham College, PA
Cincinnati Christian University, OH
Clarke College, IA
College Misericordia, PA
College of Mount Saint Vincent, NY
The College of New Rochelle, NY
The College of Saint Rose, NY
The College of St. Scholastica, MN
Columbia College, MO
Concordia University, CA
Concordia University, MI

Corban College, OR
Creighton University, NE
Daemen College, NY
DeSales University, PA
Doane College, NE
Dominican University, IL
Drexel University, PA
East Texas Baptist University, TX
Elizabethtown College, PA
Elmira College, NY
Emmanuel College, MA
Erskine College, SC
Faulkner University, AL
Ferrum College, VA
Finlandia University, MI
Florida Southern College, FL
Franklin Pierce College, NH
Gonzaga University, WA
Grace University, NE
Green Mountain College, VT
Greenville College, IL
Harding University, AR
Hastings College, NE
Hilbert College, NY
Houghton College, NY
Huntington University, IN
Iona College, NY
Ithaca College, NY
James Madison University, VA
John Brown University, AR
Johnson & Wales University, RI
Johnson Bible College, TN
Johnson C. Smith University, NC
Kentucky Wesleyan College, KY
Keuka College, NY
King's College, PA
Lakeland College, WI
Lancaster Bible College, PA
Lasell College, MA
La Sierra University, CA
Lenoir-Rhyne College, NC
Limestone College, SC
Loras College, IA
Lynn University, FL
MacMurray College, IL
Malone College, OH
Marian College of Fond du Lac, WI
Marietta College, OH
Marymount University, VA
Maryville University of Saint Louis, MO
McDaniel College, MD
Mercer University, GA
Mercyhurst College, PA
Merrimack College, MA
Messiah College, PA
Midland Lutheran College, NE
Missouri Baptist University, MO
Molloy College, NY
Mount Aloysius College, PA
Mount Marty College, SD
Mount Mary College, WI
Mount St. Mary's University, MD
Mount Vernon Nazarene University, OH
Multnomah Bible College and Biblical
  Seminary, OR
Muskingum College, OH

Nazareth College of Rochester, NY
Nebraska Wesleyan University, NE
New England College, NH
Nichols College, MA
North Greenville College, SC
Northwestern College, IA
Northwestern College, MN
Northwest Nazarene University, ID
Northwest University, WA
Northwood University, MI
Northwood University, Florida Campus, FL
Northwood University, Texas Campus, TX
Ohio Northern University, OH
Olivet College, MI
Olivet Nazarene University, IL
Oral Roberts University, OK
Pacific Union College, CA
Palm Beach Atlantic University, FL
Park University, MO
Peirce College, PA
Philadelphia Biblical University, PA
Pine Manor College, MA
Point Park University, PA
Post University, CT
Quinnipiac University, CT
Randolph-Macon College, VA
Regis College, MA
Research College of Nursing, MO
Ripon College, WI
Roberts Wesleyan College, NY
Rochester College, MI
Rockhurst University, MO
Rosemont College, PA
Rust College, MS
Saint Anselm College, NH
St. Bonaventure University, NY
Saint Joseph College, CT
Saint Joseph's College, IN
Saint Joseph's College of Maine, ME
St. Lawrence University, NY
Saint Louis University, MO
Saint Martin's College, WA
Saint Michael's College, VT
Seton Hall University, NJ
Seton Hill University, PA
Shorter College, GA
Simpson College, IA
Simpson University, CA
Southeastern College of the Assemblies of God, FL
Southern Adventist University, TN
Southern New Hampshire University, NH
Southern Wesleyan University, SC
Southwestern College, KS
Spring Hill College, AL
Stephens College, MO
Sterling College, KS
Stonehill College, MA
Suffolk University, MA
Thiel College, PA
Toccoa Falls College, GA
Trinity (Washington) University, DC
Union University, TN
The University of Alabama at Birmingham, AL
University of Bridgeport, CT

University of Dallas, TX
University of Dubuque, IA
University of Evansville, IN
University of Great Falls, MT
University of Hartford, CT
University of New England, ME
University of St. Francis, IL
University of Saint Francis, IN
The University of Scranton, PA
University of Sioux Falls, SD
University of the Cumberlands, KY
University of the Ozarks, AR
Ursinus College, PA
Ursuline College, OH
Valley Forge Christian College, PA
Warner Southern College, FL
Wartburg College, IA
Webber International University, FL
Western New England College, MA
Westminster College, MO
Westminster College, UT
Whitworth College, WA
William Jewell College, MO
William Woods University, MO
Wilmington College, OH
Xavier University, OH
York College, NE

Spouses of Current Students

American University, DC
Appalachian Bible College, WV
Arlington Baptist College, TX
Augustana College, SD
Aurora University, IL
The Baptist College of Florida, FL
Beulah Heights Bible College, GA
Blue Mountain College, MS
Boise State University, ID
Bryan College, TN
Canisius College, NY
Carroll College, MT
Carroll College, WI
Central Bible College, MO
Central Methodist University, MO
Cincinnati Christian University, OH
The College of New Rochelle, NY
Columbia College, MO
Columbia International University, SC
Eugene Bible College, OR
Faith Baptist Bible College and Theological Seminary, IA
Finlandia University, MI
Franklin Pierce College, NH
Georgian Court University, NJ
Grace University, NE
Heritage Christian University, AL
Huntington University, IN
Johnson & Wales University, RI
Johnson Bible College, TN
John Wesley College, NC
Lancaster Bible College, PA
Lee University, TN
LeTourneau University, TX
Magnolia Bible College, MS
Malone College, OH
Maranatha Baptist Bible College, WI

Maryville University of Saint Louis, MO
Messiah College, PA
Mount Aloysius College, PA
Mount Marty College, SD
Mount Vernon Nazarene University, OH
New Mexico State University, NM
Northwest University, WA
Nyack College, NY
Olivet Nazarene University, IL
Palm Beach Atlantic University, FL
Peirce College, PA
Pontifical Catholic University of Puerto Rico, PR
Reformed Bible College, MI
Roanoke Bible College, NC
Roberts Wesleyan College, NY
Saint Joseph's College of Maine, ME
Saint Martin's College, WA
Simpson University, CA
Southern Adventist University, TN
Southwestern College, AZ
Southwestern College, KS
Taylor University Fort Wayne, IN
The University of Alabama at Birmingham, AL
University of Bridgeport, CT
University of Great Falls, MT
University of Mississippi, MS
University of Sioux Falls, SD
University of Southern Indiana, IN
Urbana University, OH
Valley Forge Christian College, PA
Washington Bible College, MD
Westminster College, UT

Spouses of Deceased or Disabled Public Servants

College of Staten Island of the City University of New York, NY
Francis Marion University, SC
Indiana University–Purdue University Fort Wayne, IN
Louisiana Tech University, LA
Michigan State University, MI
Mississippi State University, MS
Missouri State University, MO
New York Institute of Technology, NY
Northeastern State University, OK
Northern Arizona University, AZ
Northern Kentucky University, KY
Southern Illinois University Carbondale, IL
The University of Alabama, AL
The University of Alabama at Birmingham, AL
University of South Carolina, SC
University of Utah, UT
Youngstown State University, OH

Twins

Bay Path College, MA
Becker College, MA
The Catholic University of America, DC
Cincinnati Christian University, OH
The College of Saint Rose, NY
Dominican University, IL
Drexel University, PA

East Texas Baptist University, TX
Finlandia University, MI
Lake Erie College, OH
Lasell College, MA
Maryville University of Saint Louis, MO
Mount Aloysius College, PA
Ouachita Baptist University, AR
Randolph-Macon Woman's College, VA
Simpson College, IA
Southwestern College, KS
Sterling College, KS
The University of Alabama at
 Birmingham, AL
University of Hartford, CT
Virginia Polytechnic Institute and State
 University, VA

Veterans

Appalachian Bible College, WV
Appalachian State University, NC
Arkansas State University, AR
Augustana College, SD
Austin Peay State University, TN
Barton College, NC
Boise State University, ID
Brigham Young University–Hawaii, HI
Carroll College, MT
Cedarville University, OH
Central Michigan University, MI
Clarion University of Pennsylvania, PA
Columbia College, MO
Columbia International University, SC
East Central University, OK
Edinboro University of Pennsylvania, PA
Emory University, GA
Emporia State University, KS
Excelsior College, NY
Fordham University, NY
Framingham State College, MA
Francis Marion University, SC
Frostburg State University, MD
Furman University, SC
Georgian Court University, NJ
Grambling State University, LA
Hollins University, VA
Loyola University Chicago, IL
Maharishi University of Management, IA
Massachusetts College of Art, MA
McMurry University, TX
Michigan State University, MI
Midway College, KY
Midwestern State University, TX
Minot State University, ND
Missouri State University, MO
Monmouth University, NJ
Montana State University–Billings, MT
Morris College, SC
Mount Vernon Nazarene University, OH
The National Hispanic University, CA
New Mexico State University, NM
New York Institute of Technology, NY
Northern Illinois University, IL
Northwestern State University of
 Louisiana, LA
Northwest Nazarene University, ID
Oklahoma Panhandle State University, OK

Peru State College, NE
Pontifical Catholic University of Puerto
 Rico, PR
Robert Morris College, IL
Rochester Institute of Technology, NY
Rust College, MS
Salem State College, MA
Shawnee State University, OH
Sonoma State University, CA
South Dakota State University, SD
Southeastern Bible College, AL
Southern Christian University, AL
Southern Connecticut State University, CT
Southern Illinois University Carbondale, IL
Southern New Hampshire University, NH
Southwest Minnesota State University, MN
State University of New York,
 Fredonia, NY
Texas A&M University, TX
Texas Tech University, TX
Thomas Jefferson University, PA
Thomas University, GA
The University of Alabama at
 Birmingham, AL
University of Connecticut, CT
University of Illinois at Chicago, IL
University of Illinois at Springfield, IL
University of Maine, ME
University of Maryland Eastern Shore, MD
University of Massachusetts Amherst, MA
University of Massachusetts
 Dartmouth, MA
University of Minnesota, Morris, MN
University of Nebraska at Kearney, NE
The University of North Carolina at
 Asheville, NC
The University of North Carolina at
 Greensboro, NC
University of Northern Colorado, CO
University of Southern Mississippi, MS
The University of Texas at Dallas, TX
The University of Texas–Pan American, TX
University of the Virgin Islands, VI
The University of Toledo, OH
The University of Virginia's College at
 Wise, VA
University of Wisconsin–Green Bay, WI
University of Wisconsin–Stevens Point, WI
University of Wisconsin–Stout, WI
University of Wyoming, WY
Warner Southern College, FL
Washington State University, WA
Wayne State College, NE
Western Kentucky University, KY
Western New Mexico University, NM
Western Washington University, WA
Westminster College, UT
William Carey College, MS
Wilson College, PA
Worcester State College, MA
Youngstown State University, OH

Veterans' Children

Appalachian State University, NC
Arkansas State University, AR
Benedictine College, KS

Boise State University, ID
Brevard College, NC
Central Michigan University, MI
Coastal Carolina University, SC
Columbia International University, SC
East Central University, OK
Edinboro University of Pennsylvania, PA
Emporia State University, KS
Excelsior College, NY
Fordham University, NY
Fort Lewis College, CO
Francis Marion University, SC
Frostburg State University, MD
Glenville State College, WV
Grambling State University, LA
Indiana State University, IN
Maharishi University of Management, IA
Marshall University, WV
Michigan State University, MI
Minot State University, ND
Mount Vernon Nazarene University, OH
The National Hispanic University, CA
New Mexico State University, NM
Northern Kentucky University, KY
Northwestern State University of
 Louisiana, LA
Oklahoma Panhandle State University, OK
Old Dominion University, VA
Peru State College, NE
Pontifical Catholic University of Puerto
 Rico, PR
Salem State College, MA
Shepherd University, WV
South Dakota State University, SD
Southeastern Louisiana University, LA
Southern New Hampshire University, NH
Southwest Minnesota State University, MN
State University of New York,
 Fredonia, NY
Texas A&M University, TX
Texas Tech University, TX
Tiffin University, OH
The University of Alabama at
 Birmingham, AL
University of California, San Diego, CA
University of Illinois at Chicago, IL
University of Illinois at Springfield, IL
University of Maine, ME
The University of Maine at Augusta, ME
University of Maine at Farmington, ME
University of Maine at Presque Isle, ME
University of Minnesota, Morris, MN
University of Nebraska at Kearney, NE
University of Nebraska at Omaha, NE
University of Nebraska–Lincoln, NE
University of New Orleans, LA
The University of North Carolina at
 Asheville, NC
The University of North Carolina at
 Greensboro, NC
University of North Dakota, ND
University of Southern Indiana, IN
The University of Texas at Dallas, TX
The University of Toledo, OH
The University of Virginia's College at
 Wise, VA

Non-Need Scholarships for Undergraduates
Special Characteristics

University of Wisconsin–Stout, WI
Virginia Commonwealth University, VA
Virginia Polytechnic Institute and State
 University, VA

Warner Southern College, FL
Wayne State College, NE
Western Illinois University, IL
Western Kentucky University, KY

Westminster College, UT
Youngstown State University, OH

Athletic Grants for Undergraduates

Archery
Texas A&M University, TX — W

Badminton
Mercy College, NY — M

Baseball

Abilene Christian University, TX	M
Adelphi University, NY	M
Albertson College of Idaho, ID	M
Alcorn State University, MS	M
Alderson-Broaddus College, WV	M
Alice Lloyd College, KY	M
American International College, MA	M
Anderson College, SC	M
Angelo State University, TX	M
Appalachian State University, NC	M
Arizona State University, AZ	M
Arkansas State University, AR	M
Arkansas Tech University, AR	M
Armstrong Atlantic State University, GA	M
Ashland University, OH	M
Auburn University, AL	M
Auburn University Montgomery, AL	M
Augustana College, SD	M
Austin Peay State University, TN	M
Azusa Pacific University, CA	M
Baker University, KS	M
Ball State University, IN	M
Barry University, FL	M
Barton College, NC	M
Baylor University, TX	M
Belhaven College, MS	M
Bellevue University, NE	M
Belmont Abbey College, NC	M
Belmont University, TN	M
Bemidji State University, MN	M
Benedictine College, KS	M
Bentley College, MA	M
Berry College, GA	M
Bethany College, KS	M
Bethel College, TN	M
Bethune-Cookman College, FL	M
Biola University, CA	M
Blessing-Rieman College of Nursing, IL	M,W
Bloomfield College, NJ	M
Bloomsburg University of Pennsylvania, PA	M
Bluefield State College, WV	M
Bowling Green State University, OH	M
Bradley University, IL	M
Brevard College, NC	M
Brewton-Parker College, GA	M
Brigham Young University, UT	M
Bryan College, TN	M
Butler University, IN	M
Caldwell College, NJ	M
California Baptist University, CA	M
California State University, Chico, CA	M
California State University, Fresno, CA	M
California State University, Fullerton, CA	M
California State University, Sacramento, CA	M
California State University, San Bernardino, CA	M
Cameron University, OK	M
Campbellsville University, KY	M
Campbell University, NC	M
Canisius College, NY	M
Carson-Newman College, TN	M
Catawba College, NC	M
Cedarville University, OH	M
Centenary College of Louisiana, LA	M
Central Christian College of Kansas, KS	M
Central Connecticut State University, CT	M
Central Methodist University, MO	M
Central Michigan University, MI	M
Central Missouri State University, MO	M
Central Washington University, WA	M
Christian Brothers University, TN	M
Clarion University of Pennsylvania, PA	M
Cleveland State University, OH	M
Coastal Carolina University, SC	M
College of Charleston, SC	M
The College of Saint Rose, NY	M
College of the Ozarks, MO	M
The College of William and Mary, VA	M
Colorado School of Mines, CO	M
Columbus State University, GA	M
Concordia University, CA	M
Concordia University, MI	M
Concordia University, NE	M
Concordia University, OR	M
Concordia University, St. Paul, MN	M
Coppin State University, MD	M
Corban College, OR	M
Creighton University, NE	M
Culver-Stockton College, MO	M
Dallas Baptist University, TX	M
Davidson College, NC	M
Davis & Elkins College, WV	M
Dickinson State University, ND	M
Doane College, NE	M
Dominican College, NY	M
Dordt College, IA	M
Dowling College, NY	M
Drexel University, PA	M
Duke University, NC	M
Duquesne University, PA	M
East Carolina University, NC	M
East Central University, OK	M
Eastern Illinois University, IL	M
Eastern Michigan University, MI	M
East Stroudsburg University of Pennsylvania, PA	M
East Tennessee State University, TN	M
Eckerd College, FL	M
Elon University, NC	M
Embry-Riddle Aeronautical University, FL	M
Emporia State University, KS	M
Erskine College, SC	M
Evangel University, MO	M
Fairfield University, CT	M
Fairleigh Dickinson University, Metropolitan Campus, NJ	M
Faulkner University, AL	M
Flagler College, FL	M
Florida Atlantic University, FL	M
Florida College, FL	M
Florida Gulf Coast University, FL	M
Florida Institute of Technology, FL	M
Florida Southern College, FL	M
Florida State University, FL	M
Fordham University, NY	M
Fort Hays State University, KS	M
Francis Marion University, SC	M
Franklin Pierce College, NH	M
Freed-Hardeman University, TN	M
Friends University, KS	M
Furman University, SC	M
Gannon University, PA	M
Geneva College, PA	M
George Mason University, VA	M
Georgetown College, KY	M
Georgetown University, DC	M
The George Washington University, DC	M
Georgia College & State University, GA	M
Georgia Institute of Technology, GA	M
Georgia Southern University, GA	M

W = women; M = men

Georgia State University, GA	M
Gonzaga University, WA	M
Goshen College, IN	M
Grace College, IN	M
Graceland University, IA	M
Grambling State University, LA	M
Grand Canyon University, AZ	M
Grand Valley State University, MI	M
Grand View College, IA	M
Hannibal-LaGrange College, MO	M
Harding University, AR	M
Hastings College, NE	M
Hawai'i Pacific University, HI	M
Hillsdale College, MI	M
Hofstra University, NY	M
Houston Baptist University, TX	M
Howard University, DC	M,W
Huntington University, IN	M
Illinois State University, IL	M
Indiana State University, IN	M
Indiana University Bloomington, IN	M
Indiana University of Pennsylvania, PA	M
Indiana University–Purdue University Fort Wayne, IN	M
Inter American University of Puerto Rico, Guayama Campus, PR	M
Inter American University of Puerto Rico, San Germán Campus, PR	M
Iona College, NY	M
Iowa Wesleyan College, IA	M
Jacksonville State University, AL	M
James Madison University, VA	M
Jamestown College, ND	M
Kansas State University, KS	M
Kennesaw State University, GA	M
Kent State University, OH	M
Kentucky Wesleyan College, KY	M
King College, TN	M
Kutztown University of Pennsylvania, PA	M
Lamar University, TX	M
Lambuth University, TN	M
La Salle University, PA	M
Lehigh University, PA	M
Le Moyne College, NY	M
LeMoyne-Owen College, TN	M
Lenoir-Rhyne College, NC	M
Lewis-Clark State College, ID	M
Liberty University, VA	M
Limestone College, SC	M
Lincoln Memorial University, TN	M
Lincoln University, MO	M
Lindenwood University, MO	M
Lipscomb University, TN	M
Lock Haven University of Pennsylvania, PA	M
Long Island University, Brooklyn Campus, NY	M
Longwood University, VA	M
Louisiana State University and Agricultural and Mechanical College, LA	M
Louisiana Tech University, LA	M
Loyola Marymount University, CA	M
Lubbock Christian University, TX	M

Lynn University, FL	M
Lyon College, AR	M
Malone College, OH	M
Manhattan College, NY	M
Marist College, NY	M
Marshall University, WV	M
Martin Methodist College, TN	M
McKendree College, IL	M
Mercer University, GA	M
Mercy College, NY	M
Mercyhurst College, PA	M
Mesa State College, CO	M
Metropolitan State College of Denver, CO	M
Miami University, OH	M
MidAmerica Nazarene University, KS	M
Mid-Continent University, KY	M
Middle Tennessee State University, TN	M
Midland Lutheran College, NE	M
Millersville University of Pennsylvania, PA	M
Milligan College, TN	M
Minnesota State University Mankato, MN	M
Minot State University, ND	M
Mississippi State University, MS	M
Missouri Baptist University, MO	M
Missouri Southern State University, MO	M
Missouri State University, MO	M
Missouri Valley College, MO	M
Molloy College, NY	M
Monmouth University, NJ	M
Montreat College, NC	M
Morehead State University, KY	M
Morningside College, IA	M
Morris College, SC	M
Mount Marty College, SD	M
Mount Olive College, NC	M
Mount St. Mary's University, MD	M
Mount Vernon Nazarene University, OH	M
Murray State University, KY	M
New Mexico Highlands University, NM	M
New Mexico State University, NM	M
New York Institute of Technology, NY	M
Niagara University, NY	M
Nicholls State University, LA	M
Norfolk State University, VA	M
North Carolina Agricultural and Technical State University, NC	M
North Carolina State University, NC	M
North Dakota State University, ND	M
Northeastern State University, OK	M
Northeastern University, MA	M
Northern Illinois University, IL	M
Northern Kentucky University, KY	M
North Greenville College, SC	M
Northwestern College, IA	M
Northwestern Oklahoma State University, OK	M
Northwestern State University of Louisiana, LA	M
Northwestern University, IL	M

Northwest Nazarene University, ID	M
Northwood University, MI	M
Northwood University, Florida Campus, FL	M
Northwood University, Texas Campus, TX	M
Nova Southeastern University, FL	M
Nyack College, NY	M
Oakland City University, IN	M
Oakland University, MI	M
The Ohio State University, OH	M
Ohio University, OH	M
Ohio Valley University, WV	M
Oklahoma Baptist University, OK	M
Oklahoma City University, OK	M
Oklahoma Panhandle State University, OK	M
Oklahoma State University, OK	M
Oklahoma Wesleyan University, OK	M
Old Dominion University, VA	M
Olivet Nazarene University, IL	M
Oral Roberts University, OK	M
Oregon State University, OR	M
Ouachita Baptist University, AR	M
Park University, MO	M
The Pennsylvania State University University Park Campus, PA	M
Pepperdine University, CA	M
Peru State College, NE	M
Pfeiffer University, NC	M
Philadelphia University, PA	M
Pikeville College, KY	M
Pittsburg State University, KS	M
Point Park University, PA	M
Portland State University, OR	M
Post University, CT	M
Purdue University, IN	M
Quincy University, IL	M
Quinnipiac University, CT	M
Radford University, VA	M
Regis University, CO	M
Research College of Nursing, MO	M
Rice University, TX	M
Rider University, NJ	M
Robert Morris College, IL	M
Rochester College, MI	M
Rockhurst University, MO	M
Rollins College, FL	M
St. Ambrose University, IA	M
St. Andrews Presbyterian College, NC	M
St. Bonaventure University, NY	M
St. Cloud State University, MN	M
St. Edward's University, TX	M
St. Francis College, NY	M
St. Gregory's University, OK	M
St. John's University, NY	M
Saint Joseph's College, IN	M
Saint Leo University, FL	M
Saint Louis University, MO	M
Saint Martin's College, WA	M
Saint Mary's College of California, CA	M
St. Mary's University of San Antonio, TX	M
Saint Paul's College, VA	M
St. Thomas University, FL	M

Saint Vincent College, PA	M	Tusculum College, TN	M	University of Nebraska at	
Saint Xavier University, IL	M	Tuskegee University, AL	M	Kearney, NE	M
Samford University, AL	M	Union College, KY	M	University of Nebraska at Omaha, NE	M
Sam Houston State University, TX	M	Union University, TN	M	University of Nebraska–Lincoln, NE	M
San Francisco State University, CA	M,W	University at Albany, State University		University of Nevada, Las Vegas, NV	M
San Jose State University, CA	M	of New York, NY	M	University of Nevada, Reno, NV	M
Seton Hall University, NJ	M	University at Buffalo, The State		University of New Haven, CT	M
Seton Hill University, PA	M	University of New York, NY	M	University of New Orleans, LA	M
Shaw University, NC	M	The University of Akron, OH	M	University of North Alabama, AL	M
Shepherd University, WV	M	The University of Alabama, AL	M	The University of North Carolina at	
Shippensburg University of		The University of Alabama at		Asheville, NC	M
Pennsylvania, PA	M	Birmingham, AL	M	The University of North Carolina at	
Shorter College, GA	M	The University of Alabama in		Chapel Hill, NC	M
Slippery Rock University of		Huntsville, AL	M	The University of North Carolina at	
Pennsylvania, PA	M	The University of Arizona, AZ	M	Charlotte, NC	M
Sonoma State University, CA	M	University of Arkansas at Fort		The University of North Carolina at	
South Dakota State University, SD	M	Smith, AR	M	Greensboro, NC	M
Southeastern Louisiana University, LA	M	University of Arkansas at		The University of North Carolina at	
Southeastern Oklahoma State		Monticello, AR	M	Pembroke, NC	M
University, OK	M	University of Bridgeport, CT	M	The University of North Carolina at	
Southeast Missouri State		University of California, Berkeley, CA	M	Wilmington, NC	M
University, MO	M	University of California, Irvine, CA	M	University of North Dakota, ND	M
Southern Arkansas University–		University of California, Los		University of Northern Colorado, CO	M
Magnolia, AR	M	Angeles, CA	M	University of Northern Iowa, IA	M
Southern Illinois University		University of California,		University of North Florida, FL	M
Carbondale, IL	M	Riverside, CA	M	University of Notre Dame, IN	M
Southern Illinois University		University of California, Santa		University of Oklahoma, OK	M
Edwardsville, IL	M	Barbara, CA	M	University of Portland, OR	M
Southern New Hampshire		University of Central Florida, FL	M	University of Rhode Island, RI	M
University, NH	M	University of Charleston, WV	M	University of Richmond, VA	M
Southern Polytechnic State		University of Connecticut, CT	M	University of Rio Grande, OH	M
University, GA	M	University of Dayton, OH	M	University of St. Francis, IL	M
Southern Utah University, UT	M	University of Delaware, DE	M	University of Saint Francis, IN	M
Southern Wesleyan University, SC	M	University of Detroit Mercy, MI	M	University of San Diego, CA	M
Southwest Baptist University, MO	M	University of Evansville, IN	M	University of San Francisco, CA	M
Southwest Minnesota State		The University of Findlay, OH	M	University of Science and Arts of	
University, MN	M	University of Florida, FL	M	Oklahoma, OK	M
Spring Arbor University, MI	M	University of Georgia, GA	M	University of Sioux Falls, SD	M
Spring Hill College, AL	M	University of Hartford, CT	M	University of South Carolina, SC	M
Stanford University, CA	M	University of Hawaii at Hilo, HI	M	University of South Carolina	
State University of New York at		University of Hawaii at Manoa, HI	M	Upstate, SC	M
Binghamton, NY	M	University of Illinois at Chicago, IL	M	The University of South Dakota, SD	M
Sterling College, KS	M	University of Illinois at Urbana–		University of Southern California, CA	M
Stetson University, FL	M	Champaign, IL	M	University of Southern Indiana, IN	M
Stonehill College, MA	M	University of Indianapolis, IN	M	University of Southern	
Stony Brook University, State		University of Kansas, KS	M	Mississippi, MS	M
University of New York, NY	M	University of Louisville, KY	M	University of South Florida, FL	M
Tabor College, KS	M	University of Maine, ME	M	The University of Tampa, FL	M
Tarleton State University, TX	M	University of Mary, ND	M	The University of Tennessee at	
Taylor University, IN	M	University of Maryland, Baltimore		Martin, TN	M
Temple University, PA	M	County, MD	M	The University of Texas at	
Tennessee Technological		University of Maryland, College		Arlington, TX	M
University, TN	M	Park, MD	M	The University of Texas at Austin, TX	M
Tennessee Wesleyan College, TN	M	University of Maryland Eastern		The University of Texas at	
Texas A&M University, TX	M	Shore, MD	M	Brownsville, TX	M
Texas Christian University, TX	M	University of Massachusetts		The University of Texas at San	
Texas State University-San		Amherst, MA	M	Antonio, TX	M
Marcos, TX	M	The University of Memphis, TN	M	The University of Texas–Pan	
Texas Tech University, TX	M	University of Miami, FL	M	American, TX	M
Thomas University, GA	M	University of Michigan, MI	M	University of the Cumberlands, KY	M
Tiffin University, OH	M	University of Minnesota, Twin Cities		University of the Incarnate Word, TX	M
Towson University, MD	M	Campus, MN	M	University of the Pacific, CA	M
Trevecca Nazarene University, TN	M	University of Mississippi, MS	M	The University of Toledo, OH	M
Trinity International University, IL	M	University of Missouri–Columbia, MO	M	University of Utah, UT	M
Troy University, AL	M	University of Missouri–St. Louis, MO	M	University of Vermont, VT	M
Truman State University, MO	M			University of Virginia, VA	M

Athletic Grants for Undergraduates
Baseball

The University of Virginia's College at Wise, VA	M
University of Washington, WA	M
University of West Florida, FL	M
University of West Georgia, GA	M
University of Wisconsin–Parkside, WI	M
Urbana University, OH	M
Utah Valley State College, UT	M
Valdosta State University, GA	M
Valley City State University, ND	M
Valparaiso University, IN	M
Vanderbilt University, TN	M
Vanguard University of Southern California, CA	M
Villanova University, PA	M
Virginia Commonwealth University, VA	M
Virginia Intermont College, VA	M
Virginia Military Institute, VA	M
Virginia Polytechnic Institute and State University, VA	M
Voorhees College, SC	M
Wake Forest University, NC	M
Waldorf College, IA	M
Warner Southern College, FL	M
Washington State University, WA	M
Wayland Baptist University, TX	M
Wayne State College, NE	M
Wayne State University, MI	M
Webber International University, FL	M
Western Carolina University, NC	M
Western Illinois University, IL	M
Western Kentucky University, KY	M
West Liberty State College, WV	M
Westmont College, CA	M
West Texas A&M University, TX	M
West Virginia University, WV	M
West Virginia Wesleyan College, WV	M
Wheeling Jesuit University, WV	M
Wichita State University, KS	M
William Carey College, MS	M
William Jewell College, MO	M
William Penn University, IA	M
Williams Baptist College, AR	M
William Woods University, MO	M
Wilmington College, DE	M
Wingate University, NC	M
Winona State University, MN	M
Winthrop University, SC	M
Wofford College, SC	M
Xavier University, OH	M
York College, NE	M
Youngstown State University, OH	M

Basketball

Abilene Christian University, TX	M,W
Adelphi University, NY	M,W
Albertson College of Idaho, ID	M,W
Alcorn State University, MS	M,W
Alderson-Broaddus College, WV	M,W
Alice Lloyd College, KY	M,W
American International College, MA	M,W
American University, DC	M,W
Anderson College, SC	M,W
Angelo State University, TX	M,W
Appalachian State University, NC	M,W

Arizona State University, AZ	M,W
Arkansas State University, AR	M,W
Arkansas Tech University, AR	M,W
Armstrong Atlantic State University, GA	M,W
Asbury College, KY	M,W
Ashland University, OH	M,W
Assumption College, MA	M,W
Athens State University, AL	M
Auburn University, AL	M,W
Auburn University Montgomery, AL	M,W
Augustana College, SD	M,W
Augusta State University, GA	M,W
Austin Peay State University, TN	M,W
Azusa Pacific University, CA	M,W
Baker University, KS	M,W
Ball State University, IN	M,W
Barry University, FL	M,W
Barton College, NC	M,W
Baylor University, TX	M,W
Belhaven College, MS	M,W
Bellevue University, NE	M
Belmont Abbey College, NC	M,W
Belmont University, TN	M,W
Bemidji State University, MN	M,W
Benedictine College, KS	M,W
Bentley College, MA	M,W
Berry College, GA	M,W
Bethany College, KS	M,W
Bethel College, KS	M,W
Bethel College, TN	M,W
Bethune-Cookman College, FL	M,W
Biola University, CA	M,W
Black Hills State University, SD	M,W
Blessing-Rieman College of Nursing, IL	M,W
Bloomfield College, NJ	M,W
Bloomsburg University of Pennsylvania, PA	M,W
Bluefield State College, WV	M,W
Blue Mountain College, MS	W
Boise State University, ID	M,W
Boston College, MA	M,W
Boston University, MA	M,W
Bowie State University, MD	M,W
Bowling Green State University, OH	M,W
Bradley University, IL	M,W
Brevard College, NC	M,W
Brewton-Parker College, GA	M,W
Brigham Young University, UT	M,W
Brigham Young University–Hawaii, HI	M
Bryan College, TN	M,W
Bryant University, RI	M,W
Bucknell University, PA	M,W
Butler University, IN	M,W
Caldwell College, NJ	M,W
California Baptist University, CA	M,W
California State University, Bakersfield, CA	M
California State University, Chico, CA	M,W
California State University, Dominguez Hills, CA	M,W
California State University, Fresno, CA	M,W
California State University, Fullerton, CA	M,W

California State University, Sacramento, CA	M,W
California State University, San Bernardino, CA	M,W
Cameron University, OK	M,W
Campbellsville University, KY	M,W
Campbell University, NC	M,W
Canisius College, NY	M,W
Carroll College, MT	M,W
Carson-Newman College, TN	M,W
Catawba College, NC	M,W
Cedarville University, OH	M,W
Centenary College of Louisiana, LA	M,W
Central Christian College of Kansas, KS	M,W
Central Connecticut State University, CT	M,W
Central Methodist University, MO	M,W
Central Michigan University, MI	M,W
Central Missouri State University, MO	M,W
Central Washington University, WA	M,W
Chadron State College, NE	M,W
Chaminade University of Honolulu, HI	M
Christian Brothers University, TN	M,W
Christian Heritage College, CA	M,W
Clarion University of Pennsylvania, PA	M,W
Clark Atlanta University, GA	M,W
Clayton State University, GA	M,W
Clemson University, SC	M,W
Cleveland State University, OH	M,W
Coastal Carolina University, SC	M,W
Colgate University, NY	M,W
College of Charleston, SC	M,W
College of Saint Mary, NE	W
The College of Saint Rose, NY	M,W
College of the Holy Cross, MA	M,W
College of the Ozarks, MO	M,W
The College of William and Mary, VA	M,W
Colorado Christian University, CO	M,W
Colorado School of Mines, CO	M,W
Colorado State University, CO	M,W
Colorado State University-Pueblo, CO	M,W
Columbia College, MO	M,W
Columbia College, SC	W
Columbus State University, GA	M,W
Concordia University, CA	M,W
Concordia University, MI	M,W
Concordia University, NE	M,W
Concordia University, OR	M,W
Concordia University, St. Paul, MN	M,W
Converse College, SC	W
Coppin State University, MD	M,W
Corban College, OR	M,W
Cornerstone University, MI	M,W
Creighton University, NE	M,W
Culver-Stockton College, MO	M,W
Daemen College, NY	M,W
Dakota State University, SD	M,W
Davidson College, NC	M,W
Davis & Elkins College, WV	M,W
Delaware State University, DE	M,W
DePaul University, IL	M,W
Dickinson State University, ND	M,W
Dillard University, LA	M,W

Doane College, NE	M,W	Goshen College, IN	M,W	Limestone College, SC	M,W
Dominican College, NY	M,W	Grace College, IN	M,W	Lincoln Memorial University, TN	M,W
Dominican University of California, CA	M,W	Graceland University, IA	M,W	Lincoln University, MO	M,W
Dordt College, IA	M,W	Grambling State University, LA	M,W	Lindenwood University, MO	M,W
Dowling College, NY	M,W	Grand Canyon University, AZ	M,W	Lipscomb University, TN	M,W
Drake University, IA	M,W	Grand Valley State University, MI	M,W	Lock Haven University of Pennsylvania, PA	M,W
Drexel University, PA	M,W	Grand View College, IA	M,W	Long Island University, Brooklyn Campus, NY	M,W
Duke University, NC	M,W	Hampton University, VA	M,W		
Duquesne University, PA	M,W	Hannibal-LaGrange College, MO	M,W	Longwood University, VA	M,W
East Carolina University, NC	M,W	Harding University, AR	M,W	Louisiana State University and Agricultural and Mechanical College, LA	M,W
East Central University, OK	M,W	Hastings College, NE	M,W		
Eastern Illinois University, IL	M,W	Hawai'i Pacific University, HI	M		
Eastern Michigan University, MI	M,W	Hillsdale College, MI	M,W	Louisiana Tech University, LA	M,W
Eastern Washington University, WA	M,W	Hofstra University, NY	M,W	Loyola Marymount University, CA	M,W
East Stroudsburg University of Pennsylvania, PA	M,W	Holy Names University, CA	M,W	Loyola University Chicago, IL	M,W
		Houghton College, NY	M,W	Loyola University New Orleans, LA	M,W
East Tennessee State University, TN	M,W	Houston Baptist University, TX	M,W	Lubbock Christian University, TX	M,W
Eckerd College, FL	M,W	Howard University, DC	M,W	Lynn University, FL	M,W
Edinboro University of Pennsylvania, PA	M,W	Humboldt State University, CA	M,W	Lyon College, AR	M,W
		Huntington University, IN	M,W	Malone College, OH	M,W
Elon University, NC	M,W	Idaho State University, ID	M,W	Manhattan College, NY	M,W
Embry-Riddle Aeronautical University, FL	M	Illinois State University, IL	M,W	Marist College, NY	M,W
		Indiana State University, IN	M,W	Marshall University, WV	M,W
Emporia State University, KS	M,W	Indiana University Bloomington, IN	M,W	Mars Hill College, NC	M,W
Erskine College, SC	M,W	Indiana University of Pennsylvania, PA	M,W	Martin Methodist College, TN	M,W
Evangel University, MO	M,W			McKendree College, IL	M,W
The Evergreen State College, WA	M,W	Indiana University–Purdue University Fort Wayne, IN	M,W	Mercer University, GA	M,W
Fairfield University, CT	M,W			Mercy College, NY	M,W
Fairleigh Dickinson University, Metropolitan Campus, NJ	M,W	Indiana University–Purdue University Indianapolis, IN	M,W	Mercyhurst College, PA	M,W
				Merrimack College, MA	M,W
Fairmont State University, WV	M,W	Indiana University South Bend, IN	M,W	Mesa State College, CO	M,W
Faulkner University, AL	M	Indiana University Southeast, IN	M,W	Metropolitan State College of Denver, CO	M,W
Ferris State University, MI	M,W	Inter American University of Puerto Rico, Guayama Campus, PR	M,W		
Flagler College, FL	M,W			Miami University, OH	M,W
Florida Atlantic University, FL	M,W	Inter American University of Puerto Rico, San Germán Campus, PR	M,W	Michigan State University, MI	M,W
Florida College, FL	M			Michigan Technological University, MI	M,W
Florida Gulf Coast University, FL	M,W	Iona College, NY	M,W		
Florida Institute of Technology, FL	M,W	Iowa State University of Science and Technology, IA	M,W	MidAmerica Nazarene University, KS	M,W
Florida Southern College, FL	M,W			Middle Tennessee State University, TN	M,W
Florida State University, FL	M,W	Iowa Wesleyan College, IA	M,W		
Fordham University, NY	M,W	Jacksonville State University, AL	M,W	Midland Lutheran College, NE	M,W
Fort Hays State University, KS	M,W	James Madison University, VA	M,W	Midway College, KY	W
Fort Lewis College, CO	M,W	Jamestown College, ND	M,W	Midwestern State University, TX	M,W
Francis Marion University, SC	M,W	John Brown University, AR	M,W	Millersville University of Pennsylvania, PA	M,W
Franklin Pierce College, NH	M,W	Johnson C. Smith University, NC	M,W		
Freed-Hardeman University, TN	M,W	Judson College, AL	W	Milligan College, TN	M,W
Fresno Pacific University, CA	M,W	Kansas State University, KS	M,W	Minnesota State University Mankato, MN	M,W
Friends University, KS	M,W	Kennesaw State University, GA	M,W		
Furman University, SC	M,W	Kent State University, OH	M,W	Minnesota State University Moorhead, MN	M,W
Gannon University, PA	M,W	Kentucky Wesleyan College, KY	M,W		
Geneva College, PA	M,W	King College, TN	M,W	Minot State University, ND	M,W
George Mason University, VA	M,W	Kutztown University of Pennsylvania, PA	M,W	Mississippi State University, MS	M,W
Georgetown College, KY	M,W			Mississippi University for Women, MS	W
Georgetown University, DC	M,W	Lake Superior State University, MI	M,W		
The George Washington University, DC	M,W	Lamar University, TX	M,W	Missouri Baptist University, MO	M,W
		Lambuth University, TN	M,W	Missouri Southern State University, MO	M,W
Georgia College & State University, GA	M,W	Langston University, OK	M,W		
		La Salle University, PA	M,W	Missouri State University, MO	M,W
Georgia Institute of Technology, GA	M,W	Lee University, TN	M,W	Missouri Valley College, MO	M,W
Georgian Court University, NJ	W	Lehigh University, PA	M,W	Molloy College, NY	M,W
Georgia Southern University, GA	M,W	Le Moyne College, NY	M,W	Monmouth University, NJ	M,W
Georgia State University, GA	M,W	LeMoyne-Owen College, TN	M,W	Montana State University, MT	M,W
Glenville State College, WV	M,W	Lenoir-Rhyne College, NC	M,W		
Goldey-Beacom College, DE	M,W	Lesley University, MA	M,W	Montana State University– Billings, MT	M,W
Gonzaga University, WA	M,W	Lewis-Clark State College, ID	M,W		
		Liberty University, VA	M,W		

Montana Tech of The University of
Montana, MT — M,W
Montreat College, NC — M,W
Morehead State University, KY — M,W
Morehouse College, GA — M
Morningside College, IA — M,W
Morris College, SC — M,W
Mountain State University, WV — M
Mount Marty College, SD — M,W
Mount Olive College, NC — M,W
Mount St. Mary's University, MD — M,W
Mount Vernon Nazarene
University, OH — M,W
Murray State University, KY — M,W
New Mexico Highlands
University, NM — M,W
New Mexico State University, NM — M,W
New York Institute of Technology, NY — M,W
Niagara University, NY — M,W
Nicholls State University, LA — M,W
Norfolk State University, VA — M,W
North Carolina Agricultural and
Technical State University, NC — M,W
North Carolina State University, NC — M,W
North Dakota State University, ND — M,W
Northeastern State University, OK — M,W
Northeastern University, MA — M,W
Northern Arizona University, AZ — M,W
Northern Illinois University, IL — M,W
Northern Kentucky University, KY — M,W
Northern State University, SD — M,W
North Greenville College, SC — M,W
Northwestern College, IA — M,W
Northwestern Oklahoma State
University, OK — M,W
Northwestern State University of
Louisiana, LA — M,W
Northwestern University, IL — M,W
Northwest Nazarene University, ID — M,W
Northwest University, WA — M,W
Northwood University, MI — M,W
Nova Southeastern University, FL — M,W
Nyack College, NY — M,W
Oakland City University, IN — M,W
Oakland University, MI — M,W
The Ohio State University, OH — M,W
Ohio University, OH — M,W
Ohio Valley University, WV — M,W
Oklahoma Baptist University, OK — M,W
Oklahoma City University, OK — M,W
Oklahoma Panhandle State
University, OK — M,W
Oklahoma State University, OK — M,W
Oklahoma Wesleyan University, OK — M,W
Old Dominion University, VA — M,W
Olivet Nazarene University, IL — M,W
Oral Roberts University, OK — M,W
Oregon State University, OR — M,W
Ouachita Baptist University, AR — M,W
Park University, MO — M,W
Paul Smith's College of Arts and
Sciences, NY — M,W
The Pennsylvania State University
University Park Campus, PA — M,W
Pepperdine University, CA — M,W
Peru State College, NE — M,W

Pfeiffer University, NC — M,W
Philadelphia University, PA — M,W
Pikeville College, KY — M,W
Pittsburg State University, KS — M,W
Point Park University, PA — M,W
Portland State University, OR — M,W
Post University, CT — M,W
Providence College, RI — M,W
Purdue University, IN — M,W
Purdue University Calumet, IN — M,W
Quincy University, IL — M,W
Quinnipiac University, CT — M,W
Radford University, VA — M,W
Regis University, CO — M,W
Reinhardt College, GA — M,W
Research College of Nursing, MO — M,W
Rice University, TX — M,W
Rider University, NJ — M,W
Robert Morris College, IL — M,W
Robert Morris University, PA — M,W
Roberts Wesleyan College, NY — M,W
Rochester College, MI — M,W
Rockhurst University, MO — M,W
Rollins College, FL — M,W
St. Ambrose University, IA — M,W
St. Andrews Presbyterian College, NC — M,W
Saint Anselm College, NH — M,W
St. Bonaventure University, NY — M,W
St. Cloud State University, MN — M,W
St. Edward's University, TX — M,W
St. Francis College, NY — M,W
St. Gregory's University, OK — M,W
St. John's University, NY — M,W
Saint Joseph's College, IN — M,W
Saint Leo University, FL — M,W
Saint Louis University, MO — M,W
Saint Martin's College, WA — M,W
Saint Mary's College of
California, CA — M,W
St. Mary's University of San
Antonio, TX — M,W
Saint Michael's College, VT — M,W
Saint Paul's College, VA — M,W
Saint Vincent College, PA — M,W
Saint Xavier University, IL — M
Samford University, AL — M,W
Sam Houston State University, TX — M,W
San Francisco State University, CA — M,W
San Jose State University, CA — M,W
Seattle Pacific University, WA — M,W
Seton Hall University, NJ — M,W
Seton Hill University, PA — M,W
Shaw University, NC — M,W
Shepherd University, WV — M,W
Shippensburg University of
Pennsylvania, PA — M,W
Shorter College, GA — M,W
Slippery Rock University of
Pennsylvania, PA — M,W
Sonoma State University, CA — M,W
South Carolina State University, SC — M,W
South Dakota School of Mines and
Technology, SD — M,W
South Dakota State University, SD — M,W
Southeastern Louisiana University, LA — M,W

Southeastern Oklahoma State
University, OK — M,W
Southeast Missouri State
University, MO — M,W
Southern Arkansas University–
Magnolia, AR — M,W
Southern Illinois University
Carbondale, IL — M,W
Southern Illinois University
Edwardsville, IL — M,W
Southern Methodist University, TX — M,W
Southern New Hampshire
University, NH — M,W
Southern Oregon University, OR — M,W
Southern Polytechnic State
University, GA — M,W
Southern University and Agricultural
and Mechanical College, LA — M,W
Southern Utah University, UT — M,W
Southern Wesleyan University, SC — M,W
Southwest Baptist University, MO — M,W
Southwestern College, KS — M,W
Southwest Minnesota State
University, MN — M,W
Spring Arbor University, MI — M,W
Spring Hill College, AL — M,W
Stanford University, CA — M,W
State University of New York at
Binghamton, NY — M,W
Stephen F. Austin State University, TX — M,W
Sterling College, KS — M,W
Stetson University, FL — M,W
Stonehill College, MA — M,W
Stony Brook University, State
University of New York, NY — M,W
Syracuse University, NY — M,W
Tabor College, KS — M,W
Tarleton State University, TX — M,W
Taylor University, IN — M,W
Temple University, PA — M,W
Tennessee Technological
University, TN — M,W
Tennessee Wesleyan College, TN — M,W
Texas A&M University, TX — M,W
Texas A&M University–
Commerce, TX — M,W
Texas Christian University, TX — M,W
Texas State University-San
Marcos, TX — M,W
Texas Tech University, TX — M,W
Tiffin University, OH — M,W
Towson University, MD — M,W
Trevecca Nazarene University, TN — M,W
Trinity International University, IL — M,W
Troy University, AL — M,W
Truman State University, MO — M,W
Tusculum College, TN — M,W
Tuskegee University, AL — M,W
Union College, KY — M,W
Union University, TN — M,W
Unity College, ME — M
University at Albany, State University
of New York, NY — M,W
University at Buffalo, The State
University of New York, NY — M,W
The University of Akron, OH — M,W

The University of Alabama, AL	M,W	University of Michigan, MI	M,W
The University of Alabama at Birmingham, AL	M,W	University of Michigan–Dearborn, MI	M,W
The University of Alabama in Huntsville, AL	M,W	University of Minnesota, Twin Cities Campus, MN	M,W
University of Alaska Anchorage, AK	M,W	University of Mississippi, MS	M,W
University of Alaska Fairbanks, AK	M,W	University of Missouri–Columbia, MO	M,W
The University of Arizona, AZ	M,W	University of Missouri–Kansas City, MO	M,W
University of Arkansas at Fort Smith, AR	M,W	University of Missouri–St. Louis, MO	M,W
University of Arkansas at Monticello, AR	M,W	The University of Montana–Western, MT	M,W
University of Arkansas at Pine Bluff, AR	M,W	University of Nebraska at Kearney, NE	M,W
University of Bridgeport, CT	M,W	University of Nebraska at Omaha, NE	M,W
University of California, Berkeley, CA	M,W	University of Nebraska–Lincoln, NE	M,W
University of California, Irvine, CA	M,W	University of Nevada, Las Vegas, NV	M,W
University of California, Los Angeles, CA	M,W	University of Nevada, Reno, NV	M,W
University of California, Riverside, CA	M,W	University of New Hampshire, NH	M,W
		University of New Haven, CT	M,W
University of California, Santa Barbara, CA	M,W	University of New Orleans, LA	M,W
University of Central Florida, FL	M,W	University of North Alabama, AL	M,W
University of Charleston, WV	M,W	The University of North Carolina at Asheville, NC	M,W
University of Cincinnati, OH	M,W	The University of North Carolina at Chapel Hill, NC	M,W
University of Colorado at Boulder, CO	M,W	The University of North Carolina at Charlotte, NC	M,W
University of Colorado at Colorado Springs, CO	M,W	The University of North Carolina at Greensboro, NC	M,W
University of Connecticut, CT	M,W	The University of North Carolina at Pembroke, NC	M,W
University of Dayton, OH	M,W		
University of Delaware, DE	M,W	The University of North Carolina at Wilmington, NC	M,W
University of Denver, CO	M,W	University of North Dakota, ND	M,W
University of Detroit Mercy, MI	M,W	University of Northern Colorado, CO	M,W
University of Evansville, IN	M,W	University of Northern Iowa, IA	M,W
The University of Findlay, OH	M,W	University of North Florida, FL	M,W
University of Florida, FL	M,W	University of North Texas, TX	M,W
University of Georgia, GA	M,W	University of Notre Dame, IN	M,W
University of Great Falls, MT	M,W	University of Oklahoma, OK	M,W
University of Hartford, CT	M,W	University of Oregon, OR	M,W
University of Hawaii at Hilo, HI	M	University of Pittsburgh at Johnstown, PA	M,W
University of Hawaii at Manoa, HI	M,W	University of Portland, OR	M,W
University of Idaho, ID	M,W	University of Puerto Rico, Mayagüez Campus, PR	M,W
University of Illinois at Chicago, IL	M,W	University of Rhode Island, RI	M,W
University of Illinois at Springfield, IL	M,W	University of Richmond, VA	M,W
University of Illinois at Urbana–Champaign, IL	M,W	University of Rio Grande, OH	M,W
University of Indianapolis, IN	M,W	University of St. Francis, IL	M,W
University of Kansas, KS	M,W	University of Saint Francis, IN	M,W
University of Louisville, KY	M,W	University of San Diego, CA	M,W
University of Maine, ME	M,W	University of San Francisco, CA	M,W
The University of Maine at Augusta, ME	M,W	University of Science and Arts of Oklahoma, OK	M,W
University of Mary, ND	M,W	University of Sioux Falls, SD	M,W
University of Maryland, Baltimore County, MD	M,W	University of South Carolina, SC	M,W
University of Maryland, College Park, MD	M,W	University of South Carolina Upstate, SC	M,W
University of Maryland Eastern Shore, MD	M,W	The University of South Dakota, SD	M,W
University of Massachusetts Amherst, MA	M,W	University of Southern California, CA	M,W
		University of Southern Indiana, IN	M,W
University of Massachusetts Lowell, MA	M,W	University of Southern Mississippi, MS	M,W
The University of Memphis, TN	M,W	University of South Florida, FL	M,W
University of Miami, FL	M,W	The University of Tampa, FL	M,W

The University of Tennessee at Chattanooga, TN	M,W
The University of Tennessee at Martin, TN	M,W
The University of Texas at Arlington, TX	M,W
The University of Texas at Austin, TX	M,W
The University of Texas at El Paso, TX	M,W
The University of Texas at San Antonio, TX	M,W
The University of Texas–Pan American, TX	M,W
University of the Cumberlands, KY	M,W
University of the Incarnate Word, TX	M,W
University of the Pacific, CA	M,W
The University of Toledo, OH	M,W
University of Tulsa, OK	M,W
University of Utah, UT	M,W
University of Vermont, VT	M,W
University of Virginia, VA	M,W
The University of Virginia's College at Wise, VA	M,W
University of Washington, WA	M,W
University of West Florida, FL	M,W
University of West Georgia, GA	M,W
University of Wisconsin–Green Bay, WI	M,W
University of Wisconsin–Madison, WI	M,W
University of Wisconsin–Milwaukee, WI	M,W
University of Wisconsin–Parkside, WI	M,W
University of Wyoming, WY	M,W
Urbana University, OH	M,W
Ursuline College, OH	W
Utah State University, UT	M,W
Utah Valley State College, UT	M,W
Valdosta State University, GA	M,W
Valley City State University, ND	M,W
Valparaiso University, IN	M,W
Vanderbilt University, TN	M,W
Vanguard University of Southern California, CA	M,W
Villanova University, PA	M,W
Virginia Commonwealth University, VA	M,W
Virginia Intermont College, VA	M,W
Virginia Military Institute, VA	M
Virginia Polytechnic Institute and State University, VA	M,W
Virginia Union University, VA	M,W
Voorhees College, SC	M,W
Wake Forest University, NC	M,W
Waldorf College, IA	M,W
Warner Pacific College, OR	M,W
Warner Southern College, FL	M,W
Washington State University, WA	M,W
Wayland Baptist University, TX	M,W
Wayne State College, NE	M,W
Wayne State University, MI	M,W
Webber International University, FL	M,W
Western Carolina University, NC	M,W
Western Illinois University, IL	M,W
Western Kentucky University, KY	M,W
Western New Mexico University, NM	M,W

Western State College of
Colorado, CO — M,W
Western Washington University, WA — M,W
West Liberty State College, WV — M,W
Westmont College, CA — M,W
West Texas A&M University, TX — M,W
West Virginia University, WV — M,W
West Virginia Wesleyan College, WV — M,W
Wheeling Jesuit University, WV — M,W
Wichita State University, KS — M,W
William Carey College, MS — M,W
William Jewell College, MO — M,W
William Penn University, IA — M,W
Williams Baptist College, AR — M,W
William Woods University, MO — W
Wilmington College, DE — M,W
Wingate University, NC — M,W
Winona State University, MN — M,W
Winston-Salem State University, NC — M,W
Winthrop University, SC — M,W
Wofford College, SC — M,W
Xavier University, OH — M,W
Xavier University of Louisiana, LA — M,W
York College, NE — M,W
Youngstown State University, OH — M,W

Bowling

Arkansas State University, AR — W
Bethune-Cookman College, FL — W
Delaware State University, DE — W
Fairleigh Dickinson University,
Metropolitan Campus, NJ — W
Grambling State University, LA — W
Hampton University, VA — W
Johnson C. Smith University, NC — W
Lindenwood University, MO — M,W
McKendree College, IL — M,W
Norfolk State University, VA — W
Pikeville College, KY — M,W
Robert Morris College, IL — M
Shaw University, NC — W
Southern University and Agricultural
and Mechanical College, LA — W
West Texas A&M University, TX — M,W
Winston-Salem State University, NC — M,W

Cheerleading

Anderson College, SC — W
Austin Peay State University, TN — M,W
Baker University, KS — M,W
Benedictine College, KS — M,W
Bethany College, KS — M,W
Bethel College, TN — M,W
Brevard College, NC — M,W
Brewton-Parker College, GA — M,W
Brigham Young University, UT — M,W
California State University,
Fresno, CA — M,W
Campbellsville University, KY — M,W
Campbell University, NC — W
Central Christian College of
Kansas, KS — M,W
Clark Atlanta University, GA — W
Clayton State University, GA — W
Culver-Stockton College, MO — M,W
Drake University, IA — M,W
East Texas Baptist University, TX — M,W

Emporia State University, KS — M,W
Freed-Hardeman University, TN — W
Georgetown College, KY — W
Grace College, IN — M,W
Hannibal-LaGrange College, MO — M,W
Hastings College, NE — W
Hawai'i Pacific University, HI — M,W
Hofstra University, NY — M,W
Houston Baptist University, TX — M,W
Kent State University, OH — M,W
King College, TN — M,W
Kutztown University of
Pennsylvania, PA — W
Lambuth University, TN — M,W
Liberty University, VA — M,W
Limestone College, SC — M,W
Lindenwood University, MO — M,W
Manhattan College, NY — M,W
Martin Methodist College, TN — W
McKendree College, IL — M,W
Mercer University, GA — M,W
Methodist College, NC — M,W
Metropolitan State College of
Denver, CO — M,W
MidAmerica Nazarene University, KS — M,W
Middle Tennessee State
University, TN — M,W
Midwestern State University, TX — M,W
Missouri Valley College, MO — M,W
Montana State University, MT — M,W
Northern Kentucky University, KY — M,W
North Greenville College, SC — M,W
Northwestern Oklahoma State
University, OK — M,W
Northwood University, MI — M,W
Nyack College, NY — M,W
Ohio Valley University, WV — W
Oklahoma City University, OK — M,W
Old Dominion University, VA — M,W
Olivet Nazarene University, IL — M,W
Pfeiffer University, NC — M,W
Pittsburg State University, KS — M,W
St. Ambrose University, IA — W
Southeastern Louisiana University, LA — M,W
Southeast Missouri State
University, MO — M,W
Southern Illinois University
Carbondale, IL — M,W
Southwestern College, KS — M,W
Sterling College, KS — W
Tabor College, KS — W
Tarleton State University, TX — M,W
Tennessee Technological
University, TN — M,W
Tennessee Wesleyan College, TN — M,W
Texas A&M University–
Commerce, TX — M,W
Tiffin University, OH — M,W
Tusculum College, TN — W
Union College, KY — M,W
Union University, TN — W
The University of Alabama, AL — M,W
The University of Alabama in
Huntsville, AL — M,W
University of Central Florida, FL — M,W
University of Charleston, WV — W

University of Delaware, DE — M,W
University of Hawaii at Manoa, HI — W
University of Louisville, KY — M,W
University of Maryland, College
Park, MD — W
The University of Memphis, TN — M,W
University of Mississippi, MS — M,W
The University of Montana–
Western, MT — M,W
University of Nevada, Las Vegas, NV — M,W
University of Oregon, OR — M,W
University of Saint Francis, IN — M,W
University of Science and Arts of
Oklahoma, OK — M,W
University of Sioux Falls, SD — W
University of the Cumberlands, KY — M,W
University of Utah, UT — M,W
University of West Georgia, GA — M,W
University of Wyoming, WY — M,W
Virginia Intermont College, VA — W
Warner Southern College, FL — M,W
Wayland Baptist University, TX — M,W
Webber International University, FL — M,W
West Virginia University, WV — M,W
William Jewell College, MO — M,W
William Penn University, IA — M,W

Crew

Barry University, FL — W
Boston University, MA — M,W
California State University,
Sacramento, CA — M,W
Clemson University, SC — W
Creighton University, NE — W
Drexel University, PA — M,W
Duke University, NC — W
Duquesne University, PA — W
Eastern Michigan University, MI — W
Florida Institute of Technology, FL — M,W
Fordham University, NY — W
The George Washington
University, DC — M,W
Indiana University Bloomington, IN — W
Kansas State University, KS — W
La Salle University, PA — M,W
Lehigh University, PA — W
Lesley University, MA — M,W
Loyola Marymount University, CA — W
Mercyhurst College, PA — M,W
Michigan State University, MI — W
Murray State University, KY — M,W
Northeastern University, MA — M,W
Nova Southeastern University, FL — W
Robert Morris University, PA — W
Saint Leo University, FL — M,W
Southern Methodist University, TX — W
Stanford University, CA — W
Syracuse University, NY — M,W
Temple University, PA — M,W
University at Buffalo, The State
University of New York, NY — W
University of California, Berkeley, CA — M,W
University of California, Irvine, CA — M,W
University of Charleston, WV — M,W
University of Delaware, DE — W
University of Kansas, KS — W

University of Louisville, KY	W
University of Massachusetts Amherst, MA	W
University of Miami, FL	W
The University of North Carolina at Chapel Hill, NC	W
University of Notre Dame, IN	W
University of Southern California, CA	W
The University of Tampa, FL	W
The University of Texas at Austin, TX	W
University of Tulsa, OK	W
University of Virginia, VA	W
University of Washington, WA	M,W
Villanova University, PA	W
Washington State University, WA	W
Western Washington University, WA	M,W
West Virginia University, WV	W

Cross-country Running

Abilene Christian University, TX	M,W
Adelphi University, NY	M,W
Alcorn State University, MS	M,W
Alderson-Broaddus College, WV	M,W
Alliant International University, CA	M,W
American University, DC	M,W
Anderson College, SC	M,W
Angelo State University, TX	M,W
Appalachian State University, NC	M,W
Arizona State University, AZ	M,W
Arkansas State University, AR	M,W
Arkansas Tech University, AR	W
Asbury College, KY	M,W
Ashland University, OH	M,W
Auburn University, AL	M,W
Augustana College, SD	M,W
Augusta State University, GA	M,W
Austin Peay State University, TN	M,W
Azusa Pacific University, CA	M,W
Baker University, KS	M,W
Ball State University, IN	M,W
Barton College, NC	M,W
Baylor University, TX	M,W
Belhaven College, MS	M,W
Belmont Abbey College, NC	M,W
Belmont University, TN	M,W
Benedictine College, KS	M,W
Bentley College, MA	M,W
Berry College, GA	M,W
Bethany College, KS	M,W
Bethel College, KS	M,W
Bethel College, TN	M,W
Bethune-Cookman College, FL	M,W
Biola University, CA	M,W
Black Hills State University, SD	M,W
Bloomfield College, NJ	M
Bloomsburg University of Pennsylvania, PA	M,W
Bluefield State College, WV	M,W
Boise State University, ID	M,W
Boston College, MA	W
Boston University, MA	M,W
Bowie State University, MD	M,W
Bowling Green State University, OH	M,W
Bradley University, IL	M,W
Brenau University, GA	W
Brevard College, NC	M,W

Brigham Young University, UT	M,W
Brigham Young University–Hawaii, HI	M,W
Bryan College, TN	M,W
Butler University, IN	M,W
Caldwell College, NJ	W
California Baptist University, CA	M,W
California State University, Chico, CA	M,W
California State University, Fresno, CA	M,W
California State University, Fullerton, CA	M,W
California State University, Sacramento, CA	M,W
Campbellsville University, KY	M,W
Campbell University, NC	M,W
Canisius College, NY	M,W
Carson-Newman College, TN	M,W
Catawba College, NC	M,W
Cedarville University, OH	M,W
Centenary College of Louisiana, LA	M,W
Central Christian College of Kansas, KS	M,W
Central Connecticut State University, CT	M,W
Central Methodist University, MO	M,W
Central Michigan University, MI	M,W
Central Missouri State University, MO	M,W
Central Washington University, WA	M,W
Chaminade University of Honolulu, HI	M,W
Christian Heritage College, CA	M,W
Clarion University of Pennsylvania, PA	M,W
Clark Atlanta University, GA	M,W
Clayton State University, GA	M,W
Clemson University, SC	M,W
Cleveland State University, OH	W
Coastal Carolina University, SC	M,W
College of Charleston, SC	M,W
College of Saint Mary, NE	W
The College of Saint Rose, NY	M,W
The College of William and Mary, VA	M,W
Colorado School of Mines, CO	M,W
Colorado State University, CO	M,W
Colorado State University-Pueblo, CO	W
Columbus State University, GA	M,W
Concordia University, CA	M,W
Concordia University, MI	M,W
Concordia University, NE	M,W
Concordia University, St. Paul, MN	M,W
Converse College, SC	W
Coppin State University, MD	M,W
Corban College, OR	M,W
Cornerstone University, MI	M,W
Creighton University, NE	M,W
Daemen College, NY	M,W
Dakota State University, SD	M,W
Dallas Baptist University, TX	W
Davidson College, NC	M,W
Davis & Elkins College, WV	M,W
Delaware State University, DE	M,W
DePaul University, IL	M,W
Dickinson State University, ND	M,W
Dillard University, LA	M,W
Doane College, NE	M,W
Dominican College, NY	M,W

Dordt College, IA	M,W
Drake University, IA	M,W
Duquesne University, PA	M,W
East Carolina University, NC	M,W
East Central University, OK	M,W
Eastern Illinois University, IL	M,W
Eastern Michigan University, MI	M,W
Eastern Washington University, WA	M,W
East Stroudsburg University of Pennsylvania, PA	M,W
East Tennessee State University, TN	M,W
Eckerd College, FL	W
Edinboro University of Pennsylvania, PA	M,W
Elon University, NC	M,W
Emporia State University, KS	M,W
Erskine College, SC	M,W
Evangel University, MO	M,W
The Evergreen State College, WA	M,W
Fairleigh Dickinson University, Metropolitan Campus, NJ	M,W
Ferris State University, MI	M,W
Flagler College, FL	M,W
Florida Atlantic University, FL	M,W
Florida Institute of Technology, FL	M,W
Florida Southern College, FL	M,W
Florida State University, FL	M,W
Fordham University, NY	M,W
Fort Hays State University, KS	M,W
Fort Lewis College, CO	M,W
Francis Marion University, SC	M,W
Fresno Pacific University, CA	M,W
Friends University, KS	W
Furman University, SC	M,W
Gannon University, PA	M,W
Geneva College, PA	M,W
George Mason University, VA	M,W
Georgetown College, KY	M,W
Georgetown University, DC	M,W
The George Washington University, DC	M,W
Georgia College & State University, GA	M,W
Georgia Institute of Technology, GA	M,W
Georgian Court University, NJ	W
Georgia Southern University, GA	W
Georgia State University, GA	M,W
Glenville State College, WV	M,W
Goshen College, IN	M,W
Grace College, IN	M,W
Graceland University, IA	M,W
Grand Valley State University, MI	M,W
Grand View College, IA	M,W
Hampton University, VA	M,W
Hannibal-LaGrange College, MO	M,W
Harding University, AR	M,W
Hastings College, NE	M,W
Hawai'i Pacific University, HI	M,W
Hillsdale College, MI	M,W
Hofstra University, NY	M,W
Holy Names University, CA	M,W
Houghton College, NY	M,W
Howard University, DC	M,W
Humboldt State University, CA	M,W
Huntington University, IN	M,W
Idaho State University, ID	M,W

Illinois State University, IL	M,W
Indiana State University, IN	M,W
Indiana University Bloomington, IN	M,W
Indiana University of Pennsylvania, PA	M,W
Indiana University–Purdue University Fort Wayne, IN	M,W
Indiana University–Purdue University Indianapolis, IN	M,W
Inter American University of Puerto Rico, Guayama Campus, PR	M,W
Inter American University of Puerto Rico, San Germán Campus, PR	M,W
Iona College, NY	M,W
Iowa State University of Science and Technology, IA	M,W
Jacksonville State University, AL	M,W
James Madison University, VA	M,W
Jamestown College, ND	M,W
Johnson C. Smith University, NC	M,W
Kansas State University, KS	M,W
Kennesaw State University, GA	M,W
Kent State University, OH	M,W
King College, TN	M,W
Kutztown University of Pennsylvania, PA	M,W
Lake Superior State University, MI	M,W
Lamar University, TX	M,W
Lambuth University, TN	M,W
La Salle University, PA	M,W
Lee University, TN	M,W
Lehigh University, PA	M,W
Le Moyne College, NY	M,W
LeMoyne-Owen College, TN	M
Lenoir-Rhyne College, NC	M,W
Lewis-Clark State College, ID	M,W
Liberty University, VA	M,W
Limestone College, SC	M,W
Lincoln Memorial University, TN	M,W
Lincoln University, MO	M,W
Lindenwood University, MO	M,W
Lipscomb University, TN	M,W
Lock Haven University of Pennsylvania, PA	M,W
Long Island University, Brooklyn Campus, NY	M,W
Longwood University, VA	M,W
Louisiana State University and Agricultural and Mechanical College, LA	M,W
Louisiana Tech University, LA	M,W
Loyola Marymount University, CA	M,W
Loyola University Chicago, IL	M,W
Lyon College, AR	M,W
Malone College, OH	M,W
Manhattan College, NY	M,W
Marist College, NY	M,W
Marshall University, WV	M,W
Mars Hill College, NC	M,W
McKendree College, IL	M,W
Mercer University, GA	M,W
Mercy College, NY	M,W
Mercyhurst College, PA	M,W
Merrimack College, MA	W
Mesa State College, CO	W
Miami University, OH	M,W

Michigan State University, MI	M,W
MidAmerica Nazarene University, KS	M,W
Mid-Continent University, KY	M,W
Middle Tennessee State University, TN	M,W
Midland Lutheran College, NE	M,W
Millersville University of Pennsylvania, PA	M,W
Milligan College, TN	M,W
Minnesota State University Mankato, MN	M,W
Minot State University, ND	M,W
Mississippi State University, MS	M,W
Missouri Baptist University, MO	M,W
Missouri Southern State University, MO	M,W
Missouri State University, MO	M,W
Missouri Valley College, MO	M,W
Molloy College, NY	M,W
Monmouth University, NJ	M,W
Montana State University, MT	M,W
Montana State University– Billings, MT	M,W
Montreat College, NC	M,W
Morehead State University, KY	M,W
Morehouse College, GA	M
Morningside College, IA	M,W
Morris College, SC	M,W
Mount Marty College, SD	M,W
Mount Olive College, NC	M,W
Mount St. Mary's University, MD	M,W
Murray State University, KY	M,W
New Mexico Highlands University, NM	M,W
New Mexico State University, NM	M,W
New York Institute of Technology, NY	M,W
Niagara University, NY	M,W
Nicholls State University, LA	M,W
Norfolk State University, VA	M,W
North Carolina Agricultural and Technical State University, NC	M,W
North Carolina State University, NC	M,W
North Dakota State University, ND	M,W
Northeastern University, MA	M,W
Northern Arizona University, AZ	M,W
Northern Kentucky University, KY	M,W
Northern State University, SD	M,W
North Greenville College, SC	M,W
Northwestern College, IA	M,W
Northwestern Oklahoma State University, OK	M,W
Northwestern State University of Louisiana, LA	M,W
Northwestern University, IL	W
Northwest Nazarene University, ID	M,W
Northwest University, WA	M,W
Northwood University, MI	M,W
Northwood University, Texas Campus, TX	M,W
Nova Southeastern University, FL	M,W
Nyack College, NY	M,W
Oakland City University, IN	M,W
Oakland University, MI	M,W
The Ohio State University, OH	M,W
Ohio University, OH	M,W
Ohio Valley University, WV	M,W

Oklahoma Baptist University, OK	M,W
Oklahoma Panhandle State University, OK	M,W
Oklahoma State University, OK	M,W
Olivet Nazarene University, IL	M,W
Oral Roberts University, OK	M,W
Ouachita Baptist University, AR	W
Park University, MO	M,W
The Pennsylvania State University University Park Campus, PA	M,W
Pepperdine University, CA	M,W
Peru State College, NE	W
Pfeiffer University, NC	M,W
Pikeville College, KY	M,W
Pittsburg State University, KS	M,W
Point Park University, PA	M,W
Portland State University, OR	M,W
Post University, CT	M,W
Providence College, RI	M,W
Purdue University, IN	M,W
Quinnipiac University, CT	M,W
Radford University, VA	M,W
Rice University, TX	M,W
Rider University, NJ	M,W
Robert Morris College, IL	M,W
Robert Morris University, PA	M,W
Roberts Wesleyan College, NY	M,W
St. Ambrose University, IA	M,W
St. Andrews Presbyterian College, NC	M,W
St. Bonaventure University, NY	M,W
St. Cloud State University, MN	M
St. Francis College, NY	M,W
St. Gregory's University, OK	M,W
St. John's University, NY	W
Saint Joseph's College, IN	M,W
Saint Leo University, FL	M,W
Saint Louis University, MO	M,W
Saint Martin's College, WA	M,W
Saint Mary's College of California, CA	M,W
St. Thomas University, FL	M,W
Saint Vincent College, PA	M,W
Saint Xavier University, IL	W
Samford University, AL	M,W
Sam Houston State University, TX	M,W
San Francisco State University, CA	M,W
San Jose State University, CA	M,W
Seattle Pacific University, WA	M,W
Seton Hall University, NJ	M,W
Seton Hill University, PA	M,W
Shaw University, NC	M,W
Shippensburg University of Pennsylvania, PA	M,W
Shorter College, GA	M,W
Slippery Rock University of Pennsylvania, PA	M,W
Sonoma State University, CA	W
South Carolina State University, SC	M,W
South Dakota School of Mines and Technology, SD	M,W
South Dakota State University, SD	M,W
Southeastern Louisiana University, LA	M,W
Southeastern Oklahoma State University, OK	W
Southeast Missouri State University, MO	M,W

Southern Arkansas University–Magnolia, AR	W	University of California, Santa Barbara, CA	M,W	University of Northern Colorado, CO	W
Southern Illinois University Carbondale, IL	M,W	University of Central Florida, FL	M,W	University of Northern Iowa, IA	M,W
Southern Illinois University Edwardsville, IL	M,W	University of Charleston, WV	M,W	University of North Florida, FL	M,W
Southern Methodist University, TX	M,W	University of Cincinnati, OH	M,W	University of North Texas, TX	M,W
Southern New Hampshire University, NH	M,W	University of Colorado at Boulder, CO	M,W	University of Notre Dame, IN	M,W
Southern Oregon University, OR	M,W	University of Colorado at Colorado Springs, CO	M,W	University of Oklahoma, OK	M,W
Southern University and Agricultural and Mechanical College, LA	M	University of Connecticut, CT	M,W	University of Oregon, OR	M,W
Southern Wesleyan University, SC	M,W	University of Dayton, OH	M,W	University of Portland, OR	M,W
Southwest Baptist University, MO	M,W	University of Detroit Mercy, MI	M,W	University of Puerto Rico, Mayagüez Campus, PR	M,W
Southwestern College, KS	M,W	University of Evansville, IN	M,W	University of Rhode Island, RI	M,W
Spring Arbor University, MI	M,W	The University of Findlay, OH	M,W	University of Richmond, VA	W
Spring Hill College, AL	M,W	University of Florida, FL	M,W	University of Rio Grande, OH	M,W
Stanford University, CA	M,W	University of Georgia, GA	M,W	University of St. Francis, IL	W
State University of New York at Binghamton, NY	M,W	University of Hartford, CT	M,W	University of Saint Francis, IN	M,W
Stephen F. Austin State University, TX	M,W	University of Hawaii at Hilo, HI	M,W	University of San Diego, CA	M,W
Sterling College, KS	M,W	University of Hawaii at Manoa, HI	W	University of San Francisco, CA	M,W
Stetson University, FL	M,W	University of Idaho, ID	M,W	University of Sioux Falls, SD	M,W
Stonehill College, MA	M,W	University of Illinois at Chicago, IL	M,W	University of South Carolina, SC	W
Stony Brook University, State University of New York, NY	M,W	University of Illinois at Urbana–Champaign, IL	M,W	University of South Carolina Upstate, SC	M,W
Syracuse University, NY	M,W	University of Indianapolis, IN	M,W	The University of South Dakota, SD	M,W
Tabor College, KS	M,W	University of Kansas, KS	M,W	University of Southern California, CA	M,W
Tarleton State University, TX	M,W	University of Louisville, KY	M,W	University of Southern Indiana, IN	M,W
Taylor University, IN	M,W	University of Maine, ME	M,W	University of Southern Mississippi, MS	M,W
Tennessee Technological University, TN	M,W	University of Mary, ND	M,W	University of South Florida, FL	M,W
Tennessee Wesleyan College, TN	M,W	University of Maryland, Baltimore County, MD	M,W	The University of Tampa, FL	M,W
Texas A&M University, TX	M,W	University of Maryland, College Park, MD	M,W	The University of Tennessee at Chattanooga, TN	M,W
Texas A&M University–Commerce, TX	M,W	University of Massachusetts Amherst, MA	M,W	The University of Tennessee at Martin, TN	M,W
Texas Christian University, TX	M,W	University of Massachusetts Lowell, MA	M,W	The University of Texas at Arlington, TX	M,W
Texas State University-San Marcos, TX	M,W	The University of Memphis, TN	M,W	The University of Texas at Austin, TX	M,W
Texas Tech University, TX	M,W	University of Miami, FL	M,W	The University of Texas at El Paso, TX	M,W
Tiffin University, OH	M,W	University of Michigan, MI	M,W	The University of Texas at San Antonio, TX	M,W
Towson University, MD	M,W	University of Minnesota, Twin Cities Campus, MN	M,W	The University of Texas–Pan American, TX	M,W
Troy University, AL	M,W	University of Mississippi, MS	M,W	University of the Cumberlands, KY	M,W
Truman State University, MO	M,W	University of Missouri–Columbia, MO	M,W	University of the Incarnate Word, TX	M,W
Tusculum College, TN	M,W	University of Missouri–Kansas City, MO	M,W	University of the Pacific, CA	W
Union University, TN	W	University of Nebraska at Kearney, NE	M,W	The University of Toledo, OH	M,W
Unity College, ME	M,W	University of Nebraska at Omaha, NE	W	University of Tulsa, OK	M,W
University at Albany, State University of New York, NY	M,W	University of Nebraska–Lincoln, NE	M,W	University of Utah, UT	M,W
University at Buffalo, The State University of New York, NY	M,W	University of Nevada, Las Vegas, NV	W	University of Vermont, VT	M,W
The University of Akron, OH	M,W	University of Nevada, Reno, NV	W	University of Virginia, VA	M,W
The University of Alabama, AL	M,W	University of New Hampshire, NH	M,W	The University of Virginia's College at Wise, VA	M,W
The University of Alabama at Birmingham, AL	W	University of New Haven, CT	M,W	University of Washington, WA	M,W
The University of Alabama in Huntsville, AL	M,W	University of New Orleans, LA	M,W	University of West Florida, FL	M,W
University of Alaska Anchorage, AK	M	University of North Alabama, AL	M,W	University of West Georgia, GA	M,W
University of Alaska Fairbanks, AK	M,W	The University of North Carolina at Asheville, NC	M,W	University of Wisconsin–Green Bay, WI	M,W
The University of Arizona, AZ	M,W	The University of North Carolina at Chapel Hill, NC	M,W	University of Wisconsin–Madison, WI	M,W
University of California, Berkeley, CA	M,W	The University of North Carolina at Charlotte, NC	M,W	University of Wisconsin–Milwaukee, WI	M,W
University of California, Irvine, CA	M,W	The University of North Carolina at Greensboro, NC	M,W	University of Wisconsin–Parkside, WI	M,W
University of California, Los Angeles, CA	M,W	The University of North Carolina at Pembroke, NC	M,W	University of Wyoming, WY	M,W
University of California, Riverside, CA	M,W	The University of North Carolina at Wilmington, NC	M,W	Ursuline College, OH	W
				Utah State University, UT	M,W
				Utah Valley State College, UT	M,W
				Valdosta State University, GA	M,W
				Valparaiso University, IN	M,W

Vanderbilt University, TN	M,W
Vanguard University of Southern California, CA	M,W
Villanova University, PA	M,W
Virginia Commonwealth University, VA	M,W
Virginia Intermont College, VA	M,W
Virginia Military Institute, VA	M,W
Virginia Polytechnic Institute and State University, VA	M,W
Virginia Union University, VA	M,W
Voorhees College, SC	M,W
Wake Forest University, NC	M,W
Warner Pacific College, OR	M,W
Warner Southern College, FL	M,W
Washington State University, WA	M,W
Wayland Baptist University, TX	M,W
Wayne State College, NE	M,W
Wayne State University, MI	M,W
Webber International University, FL	M,W
Western Carolina University, NC	M,W
Western Illinois University, IL	M,W
Western Kentucky University, KY	M,W
Western State College of Colorado, CO	M,W
Western Washington University, WA	M,W
West Liberty State College, WV	M,W
Westmont College, CA	M,W
West Texas A&M University, TX	M,W
West Virginia University, WV	W
West Virginia Wesleyan College, WV	M,W
Wheeling Jesuit University, WV	M,W
Wichita State University, KS	M,W
William Jewell College, MO	M,W
William Penn University, IA	M,W
William Woods University, MO	M,W
Wilmington College, DE	M,W
Wingate University, NC	M
Winona State University, MN	W
Winston-Salem State University, NC	M,W
Winthrop University, SC	M,W
Wofford College, SC	M,W
Xavier University, OH	M,W
York College, NE	M,W
Youngstown State University, OH	M,W

Equestrian Sports

Auburn University, AL	W
Baylor University, TX	W
California State University, Fresno, CA	W
Midway College, KY	W
Molloy College, NY	M,W
Murray State University, KY	M,W
Oklahoma State University, OK	W
Post University, CT	M,W
St. Andrews Presbyterian College, NC	M,W
Seton Hill University, PA	M,W
Southern Methodist University, TX	W
Texas A&M University, TX	W
University of Georgia, GA	M,W
University of South Carolina, SC	W
Virginia Intermont College, VA	M,W
West Texas A&M University, TX	W

Fencing

California State University, Fullerton, CA	M,W
Cleveland State University, OH	M,W
Fairleigh Dickinson University, Metropolitan Campus, NJ	W
Northwestern University, IL	W
The Ohio State University, OH	M,W
The Pennsylvania State University University Park Campus, PA	M,W
St. John's University, NY	M,W
Stanford University, CA	M,W
Temple University, PA	W
University of Detroit Mercy, MI	M,W
University of Notre Dame, IN	M,W
Wayne State University, MI	M,W

Field Hockey

American International College, MA	W
American University, DC	W
Appalachian State University, NC	W
Ball State University, IN	W
Bentley College, MA	W
Bloomsburg University of Pennsylvania, PA	W
Boston College, MA	W
Boston University, MA	W
Catawba College, NC	W
Central Michigan University, MI	W
Colgate University, NY	W
The College of William and Mary, VA	W
Davidson College, NC	W
Drexel University, PA	W
Duke University, NC	W
East Stroudsburg University of Pennsylvania, PA	W
Fairfield University, CT	W
Franklin Pierce College, NH	W
Hofstra University, NY	W
Houghton College, NY	W
Indiana University of Pennsylvania, PA	W
James Madison University, VA	W
Kent State University, OH	W
Kutztown University of Pennsylvania, PA	W
La Salle University, PA	W
Lehigh University, PA	W
Lindenwood University, MO	W
Lock Haven University of Pennsylvania, PA	W
Longwood University, VA	W
Mercyhurst College, PA	W
Merrimack College, MA	W
Miami University, OH	W
Michigan State University, MI	W
Millersville University of Pennsylvania, PA	W
Missouri State University, MO	W
Monmouth University, NJ	W
Northeastern University, MA	W
Northwestern University, IL	W
The Ohio State University, OH	W
Ohio University, OH	W
Old Dominion University, VA	W

The Pennsylvania State University University Park Campus, PA	W
Philadelphia University, PA	W
Providence College, RI	W
Quinnipiac University, CT	W
Radford University, VA	W
Rider University, NJ	W
Robert Morris University, PA	W
Saint Leo University, FL	W
Saint Louis University, MO	W
Seton Hill University, PA	W
Shippensburg University of Pennsylvania, PA	W
Slippery Rock University of Pennsylvania, PA	W
Stanford University, CA	W
Stonehill College, MA	W
Syracuse University, NY	W
Temple University, PA	W
Towson University, MD	W
University at Albany, State University of New York, NY	W
University of California, Berkeley, CA	W
University of Connecticut, CT	W
University of Delaware, DE	W
University of Louisville, KY	W
University of Maine, ME	W
University of Maryland, Baltimore County, MD	W
University of Maryland, College Park, MD	W
University of Massachusetts Amherst, MA	W
University of Massachusetts Lowell, MA	W
University of Michigan, MI	W
University of New Hampshire, NH	W
The University of North Carolina at Chapel Hill, NC	W
University of Rhode Island, RI	W
University of Richmond, VA	W
University of the Pacific, CA	W
University of Vermont, VT	W
University of Virginia, VA	W
Villanova University, PA	W
Virginia Commonwealth University, VA	W
Wake Forest University, NC	W

Football

Abilene Christian University, TX	M
Alcorn State University, MS	M
American International College, MA	M
Angelo State University, TX	M
Appalachian State University, NC	M
Arizona State University, AZ	M
Arkansas State University, AR	M
Arkansas Tech University, AR	M
Ashland University, OH	M
Auburn University, AL	M
Augustana College, SD	M
Azusa Pacific University, CA	M
Baker University, KS	M
Ball State University, IN	M
Baylor University, TX	M
Belhaven College, MS	M

Bemidji State University, MN	M	Geneva College, PA	M	Minnesota State University	
Benedictine College, KS	M	Georgetown College, KY	M	Mankato, MN	M
Bethany College, KS	M	Georgetown University, DC	M	Minnesota State University	
Bethel College, KS	M	Georgia Institute of Technology, GA	M	Moorhead, MN	M
Bethel College, TN	M	Georgia Southern University, GA	M	Minot State University, ND	M
Bethune-Cookman College, FL	M	Glenville State College, WV	M	Mississippi State University, MS	M
Black Hills State University, SD	M	Graceland University, IA	M	Missouri Southern State	
Blessing-Rieman College of		Grambling State University, LA	M	University, MO	M
Nursing, IL	M	Grand Valley State University, MI	M	Missouri State University, MO	M
Bloomsburg University of		Hampton University, VA	M	Missouri Valley College, MO	M
Pennsylvania, PA	M	Harding University, AR	M	Montana State University, MT	M
Boise State University, ID	M	Hastings College, NE	M	Montana Tech of The University of	
Boston College, MA	M	Hillsdale College, MI	M	Montana, MT	M
Bowie State University, MD	M	Hofstra University, NY	M	Morehouse College, GA	M
Bowling Green State University, OH	M	Howard University, DC	M	Morningside College, IA	M
Brigham Young University, UT	M	Humboldt State University, CA	M	Murray State University, KY	M
California State University,		Idaho State University, ID	M	New Mexico Highlands	
Fresno, CA	M	Illinois State University, IL	M	University, NM	M
California State University,		Indiana State University, IN	M	New Mexico State University, NM	M
Sacramento, CA	M	Indiana University Bloomington, IN	M	Nicholls State University, LA	M
Campbellsville University, KY	M	Indiana University of		Norfolk State University, VA	M
Carroll College, MT	M	Pennsylvania, PA	M	North Carolina Agricultural and	
Carson-Newman College, TN	M	Iowa State University of Science and		Technical State University, NC	M
Catawba College, NC	M	Technology, IA	M	North Carolina State University, NC	M
Central Methodist University, MO	M	Iowa Wesleyan College, IA	M	North Dakota State University, ND	M
Central Michigan University, MI	M	Jacksonville State University, AL	M	Northeastern State University, OK	M
Central Missouri State University, MO	M	James Madison University, VA	M	Northeastern University, MA	M
Central Washington University, WA	M	Jamestown College, ND	M	Northern Arizona University, AZ	M
Chadron State College, NE	M	Johnson C. Smith University, NC	M	Northern Illinois University, IL	M
Clarion University of		Kansas State University, KS	M	Northern State University, SD	M
Pennsylvania, PA	M	Kent State University, OH	M	North Greenville College, SC	M
Clark Atlanta University, GA	M	Kentucky Wesleyan College, KY	M	Northwestern College, IA	M
Clemson University, SC	M	Kutztown University of		Northwestern Oklahoma State	
Coastal Carolina University, SC	M	Pennsylvania, PA	M	University, OK	M
The College of William and Mary, VA	M	Lamar University, TX	M	Northwestern State University of	
Colorado School of Mines, CO	M	Lambuth University, TN	M	Louisiana, LA	M
Colorado State University, CO	M	Langston University, OK	M	Northwestern University, IL	M
Concordia University, NE	M	Lehigh University, PA	M	Northwood University, MI	M
Concordia University, St. Paul, MN	M	Lenoir-Rhyne College, NC	M	The Ohio State University, OH	M
Culver-Stockton College, MO	M	Liberty University, VA	M	Ohio University, OH	M
Dakota State University, SD	M	Lincoln University, MO	M	Oklahoma Panhandle State	
Davidson College, NC	M	Lindenwood University, MO	M	University, OK	M
Delaware State University, DE	M	Lock Haven University of		Oklahoma State University, OK	M
Dickinson State University, ND	M	Pennsylvania, PA	M	Olivet Nazarene University, IL	M
Doane College, NE	M	Louisiana State University and		Oregon State University, OR	M
Duke University, NC	M	Agricultural and Mechanical		Ouachita Baptist University, AR	M
East Carolina University, NC	M	College, LA	M	The Pennsylvania State University	
East Central University, OK	M	Louisiana Tech University, LA	M	University Park Campus, PA	M
Eastern Illinois University, IL	M	Malone College, OH	M	Peru State College, NE	M
Eastern Michigan University, MI	M	Marshall University, WV	M	Pikeville College, KY	M
Eastern Washington University, WA	M	Mars Hill College, NC	M	Pittsburg State University, KS	M
East Stroudsburg University of		McKendree College, IL	M	Portland State University, OR	M
Pennsylvania, PA	M	Mercyhurst College, PA	M	Purdue University, IN	M
Edinboro University of		Mesa State College, CO	M	Quincy University, IL	M
Pennsylvania, PA	M	Miami University, OH	M	Rice University, TX	M
Elon University, NC	M	Michigan State University, MI	M	St. Ambrose University, IA	M
Emporia State University, KS	M	Michigan Technological		St. Cloud State University, MN	M
Evangel University, MO	M	University, MI		Saint Joseph's College, IN	M
Fairmont State University, WV	M	MidAmerica Nazarene University, KS	M	Saint Xavier University, IL	M
Ferris State University, MI	M	Middle Tennessee State		Samford University, AL	M
Florida Atlantic University, FL	M	University, TN	M	Sam Houston State University, TX	M
Florida State University, FL	M	Midland Lutheran College, NE	M	San Jose State University, CA	M
Fort Hays State University, KS	M	Midwestern State University, TX	M	Seton Hill University, PA	M
Fort Lewis College, CO	M	Millersville University of		Shepherd University, WV	M
Friends University, KS	M	Pennsylvania, PA	M	Shippensburg University of	
Furman University, SC	M			Pennsylvania, PA	M

Slippery Rock University of Pennsylvania, PA	M
South Carolina State University, SC	M
South Dakota School of Mines and Technology, SD	M
South Dakota State University, SD	M
Southeastern Louisiana University, LA	M
Southeastern Oklahoma State University, OK	M
Southeast Missouri State University, MO	M
Southern Arkansas University–Magnolia, AR	M
Southern Illinois University Carbondale, IL	M
Southern Methodist University, TX	M
Southern Oregon University, OR	M
Southern University and Agricultural and Mechanical College, LA	M
Southern Utah University, UT	M
Southwest Baptist University, MO	M
Southwestern College, KS	M
Southwest Minnesota State University, MN	M
Stanford University, CA	M
Stephen F. Austin State University, TX	M
Sterling College, KS	M
Stonehill College, MA	M
Stony Brook University, State University of New York, NY	M
Syracuse University, NY	M
Tabor College, KS	M
Tarleton State University, TX	M
Taylor University, IN	M
Temple University, PA	M
Tennessee Technological University, TN	M
Texas A&M University, TX	M
Texas A&M University–Commerce, TX	M
Texas Christian University, TX	M
Texas State University-San Marcos, TX	M
Texas Tech University, TX	M
Tiffin University, OH	M
Towson University, MD	M
Trinity International University, IL	M
Troy University, AL	M
Truman State University, MO	M
Tusculum College, TN	M
Tuskegee University, AL	M
Union College, KY	M
University at Albany, State University of New York, NY	M
University at Buffalo, The State University of New York, NY	M
The University of Akron, OH	M
The University of Alabama, AL	M
The University of Alabama at Birmingham, AL	M
The University of Arizona, AZ	M
University of Arkansas at Monticello, AR	M
University of Arkansas at Pine Bluff, AR	M
University of California, Berkeley, CA	M

University of California, Los Angeles, CA	M
University of Central Florida, FL	M
University of Charleston, WV	M
University of Cincinnati, OH	M
University of Colorado at Boulder, CO	M
University of Connecticut, CT	M
University of Delaware, DE	M
The University of Findlay, OH	M
University of Florida, FL	M
University of Georgia, GA	M
University of Hawaii at Manoa, HI	M
University of Idaho, ID	M
University of Illinois at Urbana–Champaign, IL	M
University of Indianapolis, IN	M
University of Kansas, KS	M
University of Louisville, KY	M
University of Maine, ME	M
University of Mary, ND	M
University of Maryland, College Park, MD	M
University of Massachusetts Amherst, MA	M
The University of Memphis, TN	M
University of Miami, FL	M
University of Michigan, MI	M
University of Minnesota, Twin Cities Campus, MN	M
University of Mississippi, MS	M
University of Missouri–Columbia, MO	M
The University of Montana–Western, MT	M
University of Nebraska at Kearney, NE	M
University of Nebraska at Omaha, NE	M
University of Nebraska–Lincoln, NE	M
University of Nevada, Las Vegas, NV	M
University of Nevada, Reno, NV	M
University of New Hampshire, NH	M
University of New Haven, CT	M
University of North Alabama, AL	M
The University of North Carolina at Chapel Hill, NC	M
University of North Dakota, ND	M
University of Northern Colorado, CO	M
University of Northern Iowa, IA	M
University of North Texas, TX	M
University of Notre Dame, IN	M
University of Oklahoma, OK	M
University of Oregon, OR	M
University of Rhode Island, RI	M
University of Richmond, VA	M
University of St. Francis, IL	M
University of Saint Francis, IN	M
University of Sioux Falls, SD	M
University of South Carolina, SC	M
The University of South Dakota, SD	M
University of Southern California, CA	M
University of Southern Mississippi, MS	M
University of South Florida, FL	M
The University of Tennessee at Chattanooga, TN	M
The University of Tennessee at Martin, TN	M

The University of Texas at Austin, TX	M
The University of Texas at El Paso, TX	M
University of the Cumberlands, KY	M
The University of Toledo, OH	M
University of Tulsa, OK	M
University of Utah, UT	M
University of Virginia, VA	M
The University of Virginia's College at Wise, VA	M
University of Washington, WA	M
University of West Georgia, GA	M
University of Wisconsin–Madison, WI	M
University of Wyoming, WY	M
Urbana University, OH	M
Utah State University, UT	M
Valdosta State University, GA	M
Valley City State University, ND	M
Vanderbilt University, TN	M
Villanova University, PA	M
Virginia Military Institute, VA	M
Virginia Polytechnic Institute and State University, VA	M
Virginia Union University, VA	M
Wake Forest University, NC	M
Waldorf College, IA	M
Washington State University, WA	M
Wayne State College, NE	M
Wayne State University, MI	M
Webber International University, FL	M
Western Carolina University, NC	M
Western Illinois University, IL	M
Western Kentucky University, KY	M
Western New Mexico University, NM	M
Western State College of Colorado, CO	M
Western Washington University, WA	M
West Liberty State College, WV	M
Westminster College, PA	M
West Texas A&M University, TX	M
West Virginia University, WV	M
West Virginia Wesleyan College, WV	M
William Jewell College, MO	M
William Penn University, IA	M
Wingate University, NC	M
Winona State University, MN	M
Winston-Salem State University, NC	M
Wofford College, SC	M
Youngstown State University, OH	M

Golf

Abilene Christian University, TX	M
Adelphi University, NY	M
Albertson College of Idaho, ID	M,W
Alcorn State University, MS	M,W
Alderson-Broaddus College, WV	M,W
American University, DC	M
Anderson College, SC	M,W
Appalachian State University, NC	M,W
Arizona State University, AZ	M,W
Arkansas State University, AR	M,W
Arkansas Tech University, AR	M
Armstrong Atlantic State University, GA	M
Ashland University, OH	M,W
Auburn University, AL	M,W

Austin Peay State University, TN	M,W
Azusa Pacific University, CA	M
Baker University, KS	M,W
Ball State University, IN	M
Barry University, FL	M,W
Barton College, NC	M
Baylor University, TX	M,W
Belhaven College, MS	M,W
Belmont Abbey College, NC	M,W
Belmont University, TN	M,W
Benedictine College, KS	M,W
Berry College, GA	M,W
Bethany College, KS	M
Bethel College, KS	M,W
Bethel College, TN	M,W
Bethune-Cookman College, FL	M,W
Bluefield State College, WV	M
Boise State University, ID	M,W
Bowling Green State University, OH	M,W
Bradley University, IL	M,W
Brevard College, NC	M
Brigham Young University, UT	M,W
Butler University, IN	M,W
Caldwell College, NJ	M
California State University, Bakersfield, CA	M
California State University, Chico, CA	M,W
California State University, Fresno, CA	M
California State University, Sacramento, CA	M
California State University, San Bernardino, CA	M
California State University, San Marcos, CA	M
Cameron University, OK	M
Campbellsville University, KY	M,W
Campbell University, NC	M,W
Canisius College, NY	M
Carroll College, MT	W
Carson-Newman College, TN	M
Catawba College, NC	M
Cedarville University, OH	M
Centenary College of Louisiana, LA	M,W
Central Christian College of Kansas, KS	M,W
Central Connecticut State University, CT	M,W
Central Missouri State University, MO	M
Chadron State College, NE	W
Clarion University of Pennsylvania, PA	M
Clark Atlanta University, GA	M
Clayton State University, GA	M
Clemson University, SC	M
Cleveland State University, OH	M
Coastal Carolina University, SC	M,W
College of Charleston, SC	M,W
Colorado School of Mines, CO	M
Colorado State University, CO	M,W
Colorado State University-Pueblo, CO	M,W
Columbus State University, GA	M
Concordia University, MI	M,W
Concordia University, NE	M,W
Concordia University, OR	M,W
Concordia University, St. Paul, MN	W
Cornerstone University, MI	M
Creighton University, NE	M,W
Culver-Stockton College, MO	M,W
Daemen College, NY	M
Davidson College, NC	M
Davis & Elkins College, WV	M
DePaul University, IL	M
Dickinson State University, ND	M,W
Doane College, NE	M,W
Dominican College, NY	M
Dordt College, IA	M
Drake University, IA	M
Drexel University, PA	M
Duke University, NC	M,W
Duquesne University, PA	M
East Carolina University, NC	M,W
East Central University, OK	M
Eastern Illinois University, IL	M,W
Eastern Michigan University, MI	M,W
Eastern Washington University, WA	W
East Tennessee State University, TN	M,W
Eckerd College, FL	M
Elon University, NC	M,W
Embry-Riddle Aeronautical University, FL	M
Evangel University, MO	M,W
Fairleigh Dickinson University, Metropolitan Campus, NJ	M
Fairmont State University, WV	M
Ferris State University, MI	M,W
Flagler College, FL	M
Florida Atlantic University, FL	M,W
Florida Gulf Coast University, FL	M,W
Florida Institute of Technology, FL	M,W
Florida Southern College, FL	M,W
Florida State University, FL	M,W
Fort Hays State University, KS	M
Fort Lewis College, CO	M
Francis Marion University, SC	M
Friends University, KS	M
Furman University, SC	M,W
Gannon University, PA	M,W
George Mason University, VA	M
Georgetown College, KY	M,W
Georgetown University, DC	M
The George Washington University, DC	M
Georgia College & State University, GA	M
Georgia Institute of Technology, GA	M
Georgia Southern University, GA	M
Georgia State University, GA	M,W
Glenville State College, WV	M,W
Goshen College, IN	M
Grace College, IN	M
Graceland University, IA	M,W
Grambling State University, LA	M,W
Grand Canyon University, AZ	M
Grand Valley State University, MI	M,W
Grand View College, IA	M,W
Hampton University, VA	M,W
Hannibal-LaGrange College, MO	M
Hastings College, NE	M,W
Hawai'i Pacific University, HI	M,W
Hillsdale College, MI	M
Hofstra University, NY	M,W
Holy Names University, CA	M
Huntington University, IN	M
Idaho State University, ID	M,W
Illinois State University, IL	M,W
Indiana University Bloomington, IN	M,W
Indiana University of Pennsylvania, PA	M
Indiana University–Purdue University Indianapolis, IN	M
Iona College, NY	M
Iowa State University of Science and Technology, IA	M,W
Iowa Wesleyan College, IA	M,W
Jacksonville State University, AL	M,W
Jamestown College, ND	M,W
Johnson C. Smith University, NC	M
Kansas State University, KS	M,W
Kennesaw State University, GA	M
Kent State University, OH	M,W
Kentucky Wesleyan College, KY	M,W
King College, TN	M,W
Kutztown University of Pennsylvania, PA	W
Lamar University, TX	M,W
Lambuth University, TN	M
La Salle University, PA	M,W
Lee University, TN	M
Lehigh University, PA	M
Le Moyne College, NY	M
LeMoyne-Owen College, TN	M,W
Lenoir-Rhyne College, NC	M,W
Lewis-Clark State College, ID	M,W
Liberty University, VA	M
Limestone College, SC	M,W
Lincoln Memorial University, TN	M
Lincoln University, MO	M
Lindenwood University, MO	M,W
Lipscomb University, TN	M,W
Long Island University, Brooklyn Campus, NY	M,W
Longwood University, VA	M,W
Louisiana State University and Agricultural and Mechanical College, LA	M,W
Louisiana Tech University, LA	M
Loyola Marymount University, CA	M
Loyola University Chicago, IL	M,W
Lynn University, FL	M,W
Lyon College, AR	M,W
Malone College, OH	M,W
Manhattan College, NY	M
Marshall University, WV	M,W
Mars Hill College, NC	M
Martin Methodist College, TN	M
McKendree College, IL	M,W
Mercer University, GA	M,W
Mercy College, NY	M
Mercyhurst College, PA	M,W
Mesa State College, CO	W
Miami University, OH	M
Michigan State University, MI	M,W
Middle Tennessee State University, TN	M,W
Midland Lutheran College, NE	M,W
Millersville University of Pennsylvania, PA	M

Milligan College, TN	M	Pikeville College, KY	M,W	State University of New York at Binghamton, NY	M
Minnesota State University Mankato, MN	M,W	Pittsburg State University, KS	M	Stephen F. Austin State University, TX	M
Mississippi State University, MS	M,W	Portland State University, OR	M,W	Stetson University, FL	M,W
Missouri Baptist University, MO	M	Post University, CT	M	Tabor College, KS	M,W
Missouri Southern State University, MO	M	Purdue University, IN	M,W	Tarleton State University, TX	W
Missouri State University, MO	M,W	Quincy University, IL	M,W	Taylor University, IN	M
Missouri Valley College, MO	M,W	Quinnipiac University, CT	M	Temple University, PA	M
Monmouth University, NJ	M,W	Radford University, VA	M,W	Tennessee Technological University, TN	M,W
Montana State University, MT	W	Regis University, CO	M,W	Tennessee Wesleyan College, TN	M
Montana Tech of The University of Montana, MT	M,W	Reinhardt College, GA	M	Texas A&M University, TX	M,W
Montreat College, NC	M	Research College of Nursing, MO	M,W	Texas A&M University–Commerce, TX	M,W
Morehead State University, KY	M	Rice University, TX	M	Texas Christian University, TX	M,W
Morningside College, IA	M,W	Rider University, NJ	M	Texas State University-San Marcos, TX	M,W
Morris College, SC	M	Robert Morris College, IL	M,W	Texas Tech University, TX	M,W
Mount Olive College, NC	M,W	Robert Morris University, PA	M,W	Texas Wesleyan University, TX	M
Mount St. Mary's University, MD	M,W	Roberts Wesleyan College, NY	M,W	Thomas University, GA	M
Mount Vernon Nazarene University, OH	M	Rockhurst University, MO	M,W	Tiffin University, OH	M,W
Murray State University, KY	M,W	Rollins College, FL	M,W	Towson University, MD	M
New Mexico State University, NM	M,W	St. Ambrose University, IA	M,W	Trevecca Nazarene University, TN	M,W
Niagara University, NY	M	St. Andrews Presbyterian College, NC	M,W	Truman State University, MO	M,W
Nicholls State University, LA	M,W	St. Bonaventure University, NY	M	Tusculum College, TN	M
North Carolina State University, NC	M	St. Cloud State University, MN	W	Tuskegee University, AL	M
North Dakota State University, ND	W	St. Edward's University, TX	M,W	Union College, KY	M,W
Northeastern State University, OK	M,W	St. Gregory's University, OK	M,W	Union University, TN	M
Northern Arizona University, AZ	W	St. John's University, NY	M,W	University at Albany, State University of New York, NY	W
Northern Illinois University, IL	M,W	Saint Joseph's College, IN	M,W	The University of Akron, OH	M
Northern Kentucky University, KY	M,W	Saint Leo University, FL	M,W	The University of Alabama, AL	M,W
Northern State University, SD	W	Saint Louis University, MO	M	The University of Alabama at Birmingham, AL	M,W
North Greenville College, SC	M	Saint Martin's College, WA	M,W	The University of Arizona, AZ	M,W
Northwestern College, IA	M,W	Saint Mary's College of California, CA	M	University of Arkansas at Monticello, AR	M
Northwestern Oklahoma State University, OK	M,W	St. Mary's University of San Antonio, TX	M	University of Arkansas at Pine Bluff, AR	M
Northwestern University, IL	M,W	St. Thomas University, FL	M,W	University of California, Berkeley, CA	M,W
Northwest Nazarene University, ID	M	Saint Vincent College, PA	M,W	University of California, Irvine, CA	M,W
Northwood University, MI	M,W	Saint Xavier University, IL	M	University of California, Los Angeles, CA	M,W
Northwood University, Florida Campus, FL	M,W	Samford University, AL	M,W	University of California, Santa Barbara, CA	M
Northwood University, Texas Campus, TX	M,W	Sam Houston State University, TX	M,W	University of Central Florida, FL	M,W
Nova Southeastern University, FL	M,W	San Jose State University, CA	M,W	University of Charleston, WV	M
Nyack College, NY	M	Seton Hall University, NJ	M	University of Cincinnati, OH	M
Oakland University, MI	M,W	Seton Hill University, PA	M,W	University of Colorado at Boulder, CO	M,W
The Ohio State University, OH	M,W	Shorter College, GA	M,W	University of Colorado at Colorado Springs, CO	M
Ohio University, OH	M,W	Slippery Rock University of Pennsylvania, PA	M,W	University of Connecticut, CT	M
Ohio Valley University, WV	M	South Carolina State University, SC	M	University of Dayton, OH	M,W
Oklahoma Baptist University, OK	M,W	South Dakota State University, SD	M,W	University of Denver, CO	M,W
Oklahoma City University, OK	M,W	Southeastern Louisiana University, LA	M	University of Detroit Mercy, MI	M,W
Oklahoma Panhandle State University, OK	M,W	Southeast Missouri State University, MO	M	University of Evansville, IN	M
Oklahoma State University, OK	M,W	Southern Illinois University Carbondale, IL	M,W	The University of Findlay, OH	M,W
Oklahoma Wesleyan University, OK	M	Southern Illinois University Edwardsville, IL	M,W	University of Florida, FL	M,W
Old Dominion University, VA	M	Southern Methodist University, TX	M,W	University of Georgia, GA	M,W
Olivet Nazarene University, IL	M	Southern University and Agricultural and Mechanical College, LA	M,W	University of Hartford, CT	M,W
Oral Roberts University, OK	M,W	Southern Utah University, UT	M	University of Hawaii at Hilo, HI	M
Oregon State University, OR	M,W	Southern Wesleyan University, SC	M	University of Hawaii at Manoa, HI	M,W
Ouachita Baptist University, AR	M	Southwest Baptist University, MO	M	University of Idaho, ID	M,W
The Pennsylvania State University University Park Campus, PA	M,W	Southwestern College, KS	M,W	University of Illinois at Urbana–Champaign, IL	M,W
Pepperdine University, CA	M,W	Southwest Minnesota State University, MN	W	University of Indianapolis, IN	M,W
Peru State College, NE	W	Spring Arbor University, MI	M		
Pfeiffer University, NC	M,W	Spring Hill College, AL	M,W		
Philadelphia University, PA	M	Stanford University, CA	M,W		

University of Kansas, KS — M,W
University of Louisville, KY — M,W
University of Mary, ND — M,W
University of Maryland, College Park, MD — M,W
The University of Memphis, TN — M,W
University of Miami, FL — W
University of Michigan, MI — M,W
University of Minnesota, Twin Cities Campus, MN — M,W
University of Mississippi, MS — M,W
University of Missouri–Columbia, MO — M,W
University of Missouri–Kansas City, MO — M,W
University of Missouri–St. Louis, MO — M,W
The University of Montana–Western, MT — M,W
University of Nebraska at Kearney, NE — M,W
University of Nebraska–Lincoln, NE — M,W
University of Nevada, Las Vegas, NV — M
University of Nevada, Reno, NV — M,W
University of New Haven, CT — M
University of New Orleans, LA — M,W
University of North Alabama, AL — M
The University of North Carolina at Chapel Hill, NC — M,W
The University of North Carolina at Charlotte, NC — M
The University of North Carolina at Greensboro, NC — M,W
The University of North Carolina at Pembroke, NC — M
The University of North Carolina at Wilmington, NC — M,W
University of Northern Colorado, CO — M,W
University of Northern Iowa, IA — M,W
University of North Florida, FL — M
University of North Texas, TX — M,W
University of Notre Dame, IN — M,W
University of Oklahoma, OK — M,W
University of Oregon, OR — M,W
University of Portland, OR — M,W
University of Rhode Island, RI — M
University of Richmond, VA — M,W
University of St. Francis, IL — M,W
University of Saint Francis, IN — M
University of San Diego, CA — M
University of San Francisco, CA — M,W
University of Sioux Falls, SD — M,W
University of South Carolina, SC — M,W
University of Southern California, CA — M,W
University of Southern Indiana, IN — M,W
University of Southern Mississippi, MS — M,W
University of South Florida, FL — M,W
The University of Tampa, FL — M
The University of Tennessee at Chattanooga, TN — M
The University of Tennessee at Martin, TN — M
The University of Texas at Arlington, TX — M
The University of Texas at Austin, TX — M,W
The University of Texas at Brownsville, TX — M,W

The University of Texas at El Paso, TX — M
The University of Texas at San Antonio, TX — M
The University of Texas–Pan American, TX — M,W
University of the Cumberlands, KY — M,W
University of the District of Columbia, DC — M
University of the Incarnate Word, TX — M,W
University of the Pacific, CA — M
The University of Toledo, OH — M,W
University of Tulsa, OK — M,W
University of Utah, UT — M
University of Virginia, VA — M,W
University of Washington, WA — M,W
University of West Florida, FL — M
University of Wisconsin–Madison, WI — M,W
University of Wisconsin–Parkside, WI — M
University of Wyoming, WY — M,W
Urbana University, OH — M,W
Ursuline College, OH — W
Utah State University, UT — M
Utah Valley State College, UT — M
Valdosta State University, GA — M
Vanderbilt University, TN — M,W
Virginia Commonwealth University, VA — M
Virginia Intermont College, VA — M
Virginia Military Institute, VA — M
Virginia Polytechnic Institute and State University, VA — M
Virginia Union University, VA — M
Wake Forest University, NC — M,W
Waldorf College, IA — M,W
Warner Southern College, FL — M,W
Washington State University, WA — M,W
Wayland Baptist University, TX — M
Wayne State College, NE — M,W
Wayne State University, MI — M
Webber International University, FL — M,W
Western Carolina University, NC — M,W
Western Illinois University, IL — M
Western Kentucky University, KY — M,W
Western New Mexico University, NM — M,W
Western Washington University, WA — M,W
West Liberty State College, WV — M,W
West Texas A&M University, TX — M,W
West Virginia Wesleyan College, WV — M
Wheeling Jesuit University, WV — M,W
Wichita State University, KS — M,W
William Jewell College, MO — M,W
William Penn University, IA — M,W
Williams Baptist College, AR — M
William Woods University, MO — M,W
Wingate University, NC — M,W
Winona State University, MN — M,W
Winthrop University, SC — M,W
Wofford College, SC — M,W
Xavier University, OH — M,W
York College, NE — M,W
Youngstown State University, OH — M

Gymnastics

Arizona State University, AZ — W
Auburn University, AL — W

Ball State University, IN — W
Boise State University, ID — W
Bowling Green State University, OH — W
Brigham Young University, UT — W
California State University, Fullerton, CA — W
California State University, Sacramento, CA — W
Centenary College of Louisiana, LA — W
Central Michigan University, MI — W
The College of William and Mary, VA — M,W
Eastern Michigan University, MI — W
The George Washington University, DC — W
Illinois State University, IL — W
Iowa State University of Science and Technology, IA — W
Kent State University, OH — W
Louisiana State University and Agricultural and Mechanical College, LA — W
Michigan State University, MI — W
North Carolina State University, NC — W
Northern Illinois University, IL — W
The Ohio State University, OH — M,W
Oregon State University, OR — W
The Pennsylvania State University University Park Campus, PA — M,W
San Jose State University, CA — W
Seattle Pacific University, WA — W
Southeast Missouri State University, MO — W
Southern Utah University, UT — W
Stanford University, CA — M,W
Temple University, PA — M,W
Towson University, MD — W
The University of Alabama, AL — W
University of Alaska Anchorage, AK — W
The University of Arizona, AZ — W
University of Bridgeport, CT — W
University of California, Berkeley, CA — M,W
University of California, Los Angeles, CA — W
University of California, Santa Barbara, CA — W
University of Denver, CO — W
University of Florida, FL — W
University of Georgia, GA — W
University of Illinois at Chicago, IL — M,W
University of Illinois at Urbana–Champaign, IL — M,W
University of Maryland, College Park, MD — W
University of Michigan, MI — M,W
University of Minnesota, Twin Cities Campus, MN — M,W
University of Missouri–Columbia, MO — W
University of Nebraska–Lincoln, NE — M,W
University of New Hampshire, NH — W
The University of North Carolina at Chapel Hill, NC — W
University of Oklahoma, OK — M,W
University of Rhode Island, RI — W
University of Utah, UT — W
University of Washington, WA — W
Utah State University, UT — W

West Virginia University, WV — W
Winona State University, MN — W

Ice hockey

American International College, MA — M
Bemidji State University, MN — M,W
Bentley College, MA — M
Boston College, MA — M
Boston University, MA — M,W
Bowling Green State University, OH — M
Canisius College, NY — M
Clarkson University, NY — M,W
Colgate University, NY — M,W
The Colorado College, CO — M
Dordt College, IA — M
Ferris State University, MI — M
Lake Superior State University, MI — M
Lindenwood University, MO — M,W
Mercyhurst College, PA — M,W
Merrimack College, MA — M
Miami University, OH — M
Michigan State University, MI — M
Michigan Technological University, MI — M
Minnesota State University Mankato, MN — M,W
Niagara University, NY — M,W
Northeastern University, MA — M,W
The Ohio State University, OH — M,W
Paul Smith's College of Arts and Sciences, NY — M
Providence College, RI — M,W
Quinnipiac University, CT — M,W
Rensselaer Polytechnic Institute, NY — M,W
Robert Morris College, IL — M,W
Robert Morris University, PA — M
St. Cloud State University, MN — M,W
St. Lawrence University, NY — M,W
The University of Alabama in Huntsville, AL — M
University of Alaska Anchorage, AK — M
University of Alaska Fairbanks, AK — M
University of Connecticut, CT — M,W
University of Denver, CO — M
University of Maine, ME — M,W
University of Massachusetts Amherst, MA — M
University of Massachusetts Lowell, MA — M
University of Michigan, MI — M
University of Minnesota, Twin Cities Campus, MN — M,W
University of Nebraska at Omaha, NE — M
University of New Hampshire, NH — M,W
University of North Dakota, ND — M,W
University of Notre Dame, IN — M
The University of Toledo, OH — M,W
University of Vermont, VT — M,W
University of Wisconsin–Madison, WI — M,W
Wayne State University, MI — M,W

Lacrosse

Adelphi University, NY — M,W
American International College, MA — W
American University, DC — W
Belmont Abbey College, NC — M,W
Bentley College, MA — M,W

Boston College, MA — W
Boston University, MA — W
Butler University, IN — M
Canisius College, NY — M,W
Central Connecticut State University, CT — W
Colgate University, NY — M,W
The College of William and Mary, VA — W
Davidson College, NC — W
Dominican College, NY — M
Drexel University, PA — M,W
Duke University, NC — M,W
Duquesne University, PA — W
East Stroudsburg University of Pennsylvania, PA — W
Fairfield University, CT — M,W
Gannon University, PA — W
George Mason University, VA — W
Georgetown University, DC — M,W
Hofstra University, NY — M,W
Indiana University of Pennsylvania, PA — W
Iona College, NY — W
James Madison University, VA — W
The Johns Hopkins University, MD — M,W
La Salle University, PA — W
Lehigh University, PA — M,W
Le Moyne College, NY — M,W
Limestone College, SC — M,W
Lindenwood University, MO — M,W
Lock Haven University of Pennsylvania, PA — W
Long Island University, Brooklyn Campus, NY — W
Longwood University, VA — W
Manhattan College, NY — M,W
Marist College, NY — M,W
Mars Hill College, NC — M
Mercyhurst College, PA — M,W
Merrimack College, MA — W
Millersville University of Pennsylvania, PA — W
Molloy College, NY — M,W
Monmouth University, NJ — W
Mount St. Mary's University, MD — M,W
New York Institute of Technology, NY — M
Niagara University, NY — W
Northwestern University, IL — W
The Ohio State University, OH — M,W
Old Dominion University, VA — W
The Pennsylvania State University University Park Campus, PA — M,W
Pfeiffer University, NC — M,W
Philadelphia University, PA — W
Quinnipiac University, CT — M,W
Regis University, CO — W
Robert Morris University, PA — M,W
St. Andrews Presbyterian College, NC — M,W
St. John's University, NY — M
Saint Leo University, FL — M
Saint Vincent College, PA — M,W
Seton Hill University, PA — M,W
Shippensburg University of Pennsylvania, PA — W
Southern New Hampshire University, NH — M,W

State University of New York at Binghamton, NY — M,W
Stonehill College, MA — W
Stony Brook University, State University of New York, NY — M,W
Syracuse University, NY — M,W
Temple University, PA — W
Towson University, MD — M,W
University at Albany, State University of New York, NY — M,W
University of California, Berkeley, CA — W
University of Delaware, DE — M,W
University of Denver, CO — M,W
University of Hartford, CT — M
University of Maryland, Baltimore County, MD — M,W
University of Maryland, College Park, MD — M,W
University of Massachusetts Amherst, MA — M,W
University of New Hampshire, NH — W
University of New Haven, CT — W
The University of North Carolina at Chapel Hill, NC — M,W
University of Notre Dame, IN — M,W
University of Oregon, OR — W
University of Richmond, VA — W
The University of Toledo, OH — M,W
University of Vermont, VT — M,W
University of Virginia, VA — M,W
Vanderbilt University, TN — W
Virginia Military Institute, VA — M
Virginia Polytechnic Institute and State University, VA — W
Wheeling Jesuit University, WV — M
Wingate University, NC — M

Riflery

Austin Peay State University, TN — W
Jacksonville State University, AL — M,W
Lindenwood University, MO — M,W
Mercer University, GA — M,W
Morehead State University, KY — M,W
Murray State University, KY — M,W
Tennessee Technological University, TN — M,W
Texas Christian University, TX — W
University of Alaska Fairbanks, AK — M,W
The University of Memphis, TN — M,W
University of Mississippi, MS — W
University of Missouri–Kansas City, MO — M,W
University of Nebraska–Lincoln, NE — W
University of Nevada, Reno, NV — M,W
University of San Francisco, CA — M,W
The University of Tennessee at Martin, TN — M,W
Virginia Military Institute, VA — M,W
West Virginia University, WV — M,W
Xavier University, OH — M,W

Rugby

Eastern Illinois University, IL — W
University of California, Berkeley, CA — M

Sailing

Hampton University, VA — M,W

Skiing (cross-country)

Montana State University, MT	M,W
St. Cloud State University, MN	W
University of Alaska Anchorage, AK	M,W
University of Alaska Fairbanks, AK	M,W
University of Colorado at Boulder, CO	M,W
University of Denver, CO	M,W
University of Nevada, Reno, NV	M,W
University of New Hampshire, NH	M,W
University of Utah, UT	M,W
University of Vermont, VT	M,W
University of Wisconsin–Green Bay, WI	M,W
Western State College of Colorado, CO	M,W

Skiing (downhill)

Albertson College of Idaho, ID	M,W
Davis & Elkins College, WV	M,W
Montana State University, MT	M,W
Paul Smith's College of Arts and Sciences, NY	M,W
Sierra Nevada College, NV	M,W
University of Alaska Anchorage, AK	M,W
University of Colorado at Boulder, CO	M,W
University of Denver, CO	M,W
University of Massachusetts Amherst, MA	M,W
University of Nevada, Reno, NV	M,W
University of New Hampshire, NH	M,W
University of Utah, UT	M,W
University of Vermont, VT	M,W
Western State College of Colorado, CO	M,W

Soccer

Adelphi University, NY	M,W
Albertson College of Idaho, ID	M,W
Alcorn State University, MS	W
Alderson-Broaddus College, WV	M
Alliant International University, CA	M,W
American International College, MA	M,W
American University, DC	M,W
Anderson College, SC	M,W
Angelo State University, TX	W
Appalachian State University, NC	M,W
Arizona State University, AZ	W
Arkansas State University, AR	W
Asbury College, KY	M,W
Ashland University, OH	M,W
Auburn University, AL	W
Auburn University Montgomery, AL	M,W
Augustana College, SD	W
Austin Peay State University, TN	W
Azusa Pacific University, CA	M,W
Baker University, KS	M,W
Barry University, FL	M,W
Barton College, NC	M,W
Baylor University, TX	W
Belhaven College, MS	M,W
Bellevue University, NE	M
Belmont Abbey College, NC	M,W
Belmont University, TN	M,W
Bemidji State University, MN	W
Benedictine College, KS	M,W
Bentley College, MA	M,W

Berry College, GA	M,W
Bethany College, KS	M,W
Bethel College, KS	M,W
Bethel College, TN	M,W
Biola University, CA	M,W
Blessing-Rieman College of Nursing, IL	M,W
Bloomfield College, NJ	M,W
Bloomsburg University of Pennsylvania, PA	M,W
Boston College, MA	M,W
Boston University, MA	M,W
Bowling Green State University, OH	M,W
Bradley University, IL	M
Brenau University, GA	W
Brevard College, NC	M,W
Brewton-Parker College, GA	M,W
Brigham Young University, UT	W
Bryan College, TN	M,W
Butler University, IN	M,W
Caldwell College, NJ	M,W
California Baptist University, CA	M,W
California State University, Bakersfield, CA	M
California State University, Chico, CA	M,W
California State University, Dominguez Hills, CA	M,W
California State University, Fresno, CA	M,W
California State University, Fullerton, CA	M,W
California State University, Sacramento, CA	M,W
California State University, San Bernardino, CA	M,W
Campbellsville University, KY	M,W
Campbell University, NC	M,W
Canisius College, NY	M,W
Carroll College, MT	W
Carson-Newman College, TN	M,W
Catawba College, NC	M,W
Cedarville University, OH	M,W
Centenary College of Louisiana, LA	M,W
Central Christian College of Kansas, KS	M,W
Central Connecticut State University, CT	M,W
Central Methodist University, MO	M,W
Central Michigan University, MI	W
Central Missouri State University, MO	W
Central Washington University, WA	W
Christian Brothers University, TN	M,W
Christian Heritage College, CA	M,W
Clayton State University, GA	M,W
Clemson University, SC	M,W
Cleveland State University, OH	M
Coastal Carolina University, SC	M,W
Colgate University, NY	M,W
College of Charleston, SC	M,W
College of Saint Mary, NE	W
The College of Saint Rose, NY	M,W
The College of William and Mary, VA	M,W
Colorado Christian University, CO	M,W
The Colorado College, CO	W
Columbia College, MO	M
Columbia College, SC	W

Columbus State University, GA	W
Concordia University, CA	M,W
Concordia University, MI	M,W
Concordia University, NE	M,W
Concordia University, OR	M,W
Concordia University, St. Paul, MN	W
Converse College, SC	W
Corban College, OR	M,W
Cornerstone University, MI	M,W
Creighton University, NE	M,W
Culver-Stockton College, MO	M,W
Daemen College, NY	M,W
Dallas Baptist University, TX	W
Davidson College, NC	M,W
Davis & Elkins College, WV	M,W
DePaul University, IL	M,W
Doane College, NE	M,W
Dominican College, NY	M,W
Dominican University of California, CA	M,W
Dordt College, IA	M,W
Dowling College, NY	M
Drake University, IA	M,W
Drexel University, PA	M,W
Duke University, NC	M,W
Duquesne University, PA	M,W
East Carolina University, NC	M,W
East Central University, OK	W
Eastern Illinois University, IL	M,W
Eastern Michigan University, MI	W
Eastern Washington University, WA	W
East Stroudsburg University of Pennsylvania, PA	M,W
East Tennessee State University, TN	W
Eckerd College, FL	M,W
Edinboro University of Pennsylvania, PA	W
Elon University, NC	M,W
Embry-Riddle Aeronautical University, FL	M,W
Emporia State University, KS	W
Erskine College, SC	M,W
The Evergreen State College, WA	M,W
Fairfield University, CT	M,W
Fairleigh Dickinson University, Metropolitan Campus, NJ	M,W
Faulkner University, AL	M,W
Flagler College, FL	M,W
Florida Atlantic University, FL	M,W
Florida Institute of Technology, FL	M,W
Florida Southern College, FL	M,W
Florida State University, FL	W
Fordham University, NY	M,W
Fort Lewis College, CO	M,W
Francis Marion University, SC	M,W
Franklin Pierce College, NH	M,W
Freed-Hardeman University, TN	M,W
Fresno Pacific University, CA	M,W
Friends University, KS	M,W
Furman University, SC	M,W
Gannon University, PA	M,W
Geneva College, PA	M,W
George Mason University, VA	M,W
Georgetown College, KY	M,W
Georgetown University, DC	M,W

The George Washington University, DC	M,W
Georgia College & State University, GA	W
Georgian Court University, NJ	W
Georgia Southern University, GA	M,W
Georgia State University, GA	M,W
Goldey-Beacom College, DE	M,W
Gonzaga University, WA	M,W
Goshen College, IN	M,W
Grace College, IN	M,W
Graceland University, IA	M,W
Grand Canyon University, AZ	M,W
Grand Valley State University, MI	W
Grand View College, IA	M,W
Hannibal-LaGrange College, MO	M,W
Harding University, AR	M,W
Hastings College, NE	M,W
Hawai'i Pacific University, HI	M,W
Hofstra University, NY	M,W
Holy Names University, CA	M,W
Houghton College, NY	M,W
Howard University, DC	M
Humboldt State University, CA	M,W
Huntington University, IN	M,W
Illinois State University, IL	W
Indiana State University, IN	W
Indiana University Bloomington, IN	M,W
Indiana University of Pennsylvania, PA	W
Indiana University–Purdue University Fort Wayne, IN	M,W
Indiana University–Purdue University Indianapolis, IN	M,W
Inter American University of Puerto Rico, Guayama Campus, PR	M
Inter American University of Puerto Rico, San Germán Campus, PR	M
Iona College, NY	M,W
Iowa State University of Science and Technology, IA	W
Iowa Wesleyan College, IA	M,W
Jacksonville State University, AL	W
James Madison University, VA	M,W
Jamestown College, ND	W
John Brown University, AR	M,W
Kent State University, OH	W
Kentucky Wesleyan College, KY	M,W
King College, TN	M,W
Kutztown University of Pennsylvania, PA	M,W
Lambuth University, TN	M,W
La Salle University, PA	M,W
Lee University, TN	M,W
Lehigh University, PA	M,W
Le Moyne College, NY	M,W
Lenoir-Rhyne College, NC	M,W
Liberty University, VA	M,W
Limestone College, SC	M,W
Lincoln Memorial University, TN	M,W
Lincoln University, MO	M
Lindenwood University, MO	M,W
Lipscomb University, TN	M,W
Lock Haven University of Pennsylvania, PA	M,W

Long Island University, Brooklyn Campus, NY	M,W
Longwood University, VA	M,W
Louisiana State University and Agricultural and Mechanical College, LA	W
Loyola Marymount University, CA	M,W
Loyola University Chicago, IL	M,W
Lynn University, FL	M,W
Lyon College, AR	M,W
Malone College, OH	M,W
Manhattan College, NY	M,W
Marist College, NY	M,W
Marshall University, WV	M,W
Mars Hill College, NC	M,W
Martin Methodist College, TN	M,W
McKendree College, IL	M,W
Mercer University, GA	M,W
Mercy College, NY	M,W
Mercyhurst College, PA	M,W
Merrimack College, MA	W
Mesa State College, CO	W
Metropolitan State College of Denver, CO	M,W
Miami University, OH	W
Michigan State University, MI	M
MidAmerica Nazarene University, KS	M,W
Mid-Continent University, KY	M
Middle Tennessee State University, TN	W
Midland Lutheran College, NE	M,W
Midway College, KY	W
Midwestern State University, TX	M,W
Millersville University of Pennsylvania, PA	M,W
Milligan College, TN	M,W
Minnesota State University Mankato, MN	W
Minnesota State University Moorhead, MN	W
Mississippi State University, MS	W
Missouri Baptist University, MO	M,W
Missouri Southern State University, MO	M,W
Missouri State University, MO	M,W
Missouri Valley College, MO	M,W
Molloy College, NY	M,W
Monmouth University, NJ	M,W
Montana State University–Billings, MT	M,W
Montreat College, NC	M,W
Morehead State University, KY	W
Morningside College, IA	M,W
Mount Marty College, SD	M,W
Mount Olive College, NC	M,W
Mount St. Mary's University, MD	M,W
Mount Vernon Nazarene University, OH	M,W
Murray State University, KY	W
New Mexico Highlands University, NM	W
New York Institute of Technology, NY	M,W
Niagara University, NY	M,W
Nicholls State University, LA	W
North Carolina State University, NC	M,W
North Dakota State University, ND	W

Northeastern State University, OK	M,W
Northeastern University, MA	M,W
Northern Arizona University, AZ	W
Northern Illinois University, IL	M,W
Northern Kentucky University, KY	M,W
Northern State University, SD	W
North Greenville College, SC	M,W
Northwestern College, IA	M,W
Northwestern Oklahoma State University, OK	W
Northwestern State University of Louisiana, LA	W
Northwestern University, IL	M,W
Northwest Nazarene University, ID	W
Northwest University, WA	M
Northwood University, MI	M,W
Northwood University, Florida Campus, FL	M,W
Northwood University, Texas Campus, TX	M,W
Nova Southeastern University, FL	M,W
Nyack College, NY	M,W
Oakland University, MI	M,W
The Ohio State University, OH	M,W
Ohio University, OH	W
Ohio Valley University, WV	M,W
Oklahoma City University, OK	M,W
Oklahoma State University, OK	W
Oklahoma Wesleyan University, OK	M,W
Old Dominion University, VA	M,W
Olivet Nazarene University, IL	M,W
Oral Roberts University, OK	M,W
Oregon State University, OR	M,W
Park University, MO	M,W
Paul Smith's College of Arts and Sciences, NY	M,W
The Pennsylvania State University University Park Campus, PA	M,W
Pepperdine University, CA	W
Pfeiffer University, NC	M,W
Philadelphia University, PA	M,W
Point Park University, PA	M
Portland State University, OR	W
Post University, CT	M,W
Providence College, RI	M,W
Purdue University, IN	W
Quincy University, IL	M,W
Quinnipiac University, CT	M,W
Radford University, VA	M,W
Regis University, CO	M,W
Reinhardt College, GA	M,W
Research College of Nursing, MO	M,W
Rice University, TX	W
Rider University, NJ	M,W
Robert Morris College, IL	M,W
Robert Morris University, PA	M,W
Roberts Wesleyan College, NY	M,W
Rochester College, MI	M,W
Rockhurst University, MO	M,W
Rollins College, FL	M,W
St. Ambrose University, IA	M,W
St. Andrews Presbyterian College, NC	M,W
St. Bonaventure University, NY	M,W
St. Cloud State University, MN	W
St. Edward's University, TX	M,W
St. Francis College, NY	M

St. Gregory's University, OK	M,W	Texas State University-San		University of Massachusetts	
St. John's University, NY	M,W	Marcos, TX	W	Amherst, MA	M,W
Saint Joseph's College, IN	M,W	Texas Tech University, TX	W	The University of Memphis, TN	M,W
Saint Leo University, FL	M,W	Thomas University, GA	M,W	University of Miami, FL	W
Saint Louis University, MO	M,W	Tiffin University, OH	M,W	University of Michigan, MI	W
Saint Mary's College of		Towson University, MD	M,W	University of Minnesota, Twin Cities	
California, CA	M,W	Trevecca Nazarene University, TN	M,W	Campus, MN	W
St. Mary's University of San		Trinity International University, IL	M,W	University of Mississippi, MS	W
Antonio, TX	M,W	Troy University, AL	W	University of Missouri–Columbia, MO	W
St. Thomas University, FL	M,W	Truman State University, MO	M,W	University of Missouri–Kansas	
Saint Vincent College, PA	M,W	Tusculum College, TN	M,W	City, MO	M
Saint Xavier University, IL	M,W	Union College, KY	M,W	University of Missouri–St. Louis, MO	M,W
Samford University, AL	W	Union University, TN	M	University of Nebraska–Lincoln, NE	W
Sam Houston State University, TX	W	Unity College, ME	M	University of Nevada, Las Vegas, NV	M,W
San Francisco State University, CA	M,W	University at Albany, State University		University of Nevada, Reno, NV	W
San Jose State University, CA	M,W	of New York, NY	M,W	University of New Hampshire, NH	M,W
Seattle Pacific University, WA	M	University at Buffalo, The State		University of New Haven, CT	M,W
Seton Hall University, NJ	M,W	University of New York, NY	M,W	University of North Alabama, AL	W
Seton Hill University, PA	M,W	The University of Akron, OH	M	The University of North Carolina at	
Shepherd University, WV	M,W	The University of Alabama, AL	W	Asheville, NC	M,W
Shippensburg University of		The University of Alabama at		The University of North Carolina at	
Pennsylvania, PA	M,W	Birmingham, AL	M,W	Chapel Hill, NC	M,W
Shorter College, GA	M,W	The University of Alabama in		The University of North Carolina at	
Slippery Rock University of		Huntsville, AL	M,W	Charlotte, NC	M,W
Pennsylvania, PA	M,W	The University of Arizona, AZ	W	The University of North Carolina at	
Sonoma State University, CA	M,W	University of Bridgeport, CT	M,W	Greensboro, NC	M,W
South Dakota State University, SD	W	University of California, Berkeley, CA	M,W	The University of North Carolina at	
Southeastern Louisiana University, LA	W	University of California, Irvine, CA	M,W	Pembroke, NC	M,W
Southeast Missouri State		University of California, Los		The University of North Carolina at	
University, MO	W	Angeles, CA	M,W	Wilmington, NC	M,W
Southern Illinois University		University of California, Santa		University of Northern Colorado, CO	W
Edwardsville, IL	M,W	Barbara, CA	M,W	University of Northern Iowa, IA	W
Southern Methodist University, TX	M,W	University of Central Florida, FL	M,W	University of North Florida, FL	M,W
Southern New Hampshire		University of Charleston, WV	M,W	University of Notre Dame, IN	M,W
University, NH	M,W	University of Cincinnati, OH	M,W	University of Oklahoma, OK	W
Southern Oregon University, OR	W	University of Colorado at Boulder, CO	W	University of Oregon, OR	W
Southern Wesleyan University, SC	M,W	University of Colorado at Colorado		University of Portland, OR	M,W
Southwest Baptist University, MO	W	Springs, CO	M	University of Rhode Island, RI	M,W
Southwestern College, KS	M,W	University of Connecticut, CT	M,W	University of Richmond, VA	M,W
Southwest Minnesota State		University of Dayton, OH	M,W	University of Rio Grande, OH	M
University, MN	W	University of Delaware, DE	M,W	University of St. Francis, IL	M,W
Spring Arbor University, MI	M,W	University of Denver, CO	M,W	University of Saint Francis, IN	M,W
Spring Hill College, AL	M,W	University of Detroit Mercy, MI	M,W	University of San Diego, CA	M,W
Stanford University, CA	M,W	University of Evansville, IN	M,W	University of San Francisco, CA	M,W
State University of New York at		The University of Findlay, OH	M,W	University of Science and Arts of	
Binghamton, NY	M,W	University of Florida, FL	W	Oklahoma, OK	M,W
State University of New York College		University of Georgia, GA	W	University of Sioux Falls, SD	M,W
at Oneonta, NY	M	University of Great Falls, MT	W	University of South Carolina, SC	M,W
Stephen F. Austin State University, TX	W	University of Hartford, CT	M,W	University of South Carolina	
Sterling College, KS	M,W	University of Hawaii at Manoa, HI	W	Upstate, SC	M,W
Stetson University, FL	M,W	University of Idaho, ID	W	University of Southern California, CA	W
Stonehill College, MA	M,W	University of Illinois at Chicago, IL	M	University of Southern Indiana, IN	M,W
Stony Brook University, State		University of Illinois at Springfield, IL	M	University of South Florida, FL	M,W
University of New York, NY	M,W	University of Illinois at Urbana–		The University of Tampa, FL	M,W
Syracuse University, NY	M,W	Champaign, IL	W	The University of Tennessee at	
Tabor College, KS	M,W	University of Indianapolis, IN	M,W	Chattanooga, TN	M,W
Taylor University, IN	M,W	University of Kansas, KS	W	The University of Tennessee at	
Temple University, PA	M,W	University of Louisville, KY	M,W	Martin, TN	W
Tennessee Technological		University of Maine, ME	M,W	The University of Texas at Austin, TX	W
University, TN	W	The University of Maine at		University of the Cumberlands, KY	M,W
Tennessee Wesleyan College, TN	M,W	Augusta, ME	W	University of the District of	
Texas A&M University, TX	W	University of Mary, ND	M,W	Columbia, DC	M
Texas A&M University–		University of Maryland, Baltimore		University of the Incarnate Word, TX	M,W
Commerce, TX	W	County, MD	M,W	University of the Pacific, CA	W
Texas Christian University, TX	W	University of Maryland, College		The University of Toledo, OH	W
		Park, MD	M,W	University of Tulsa, OK	M,W

University of Utah, UT	W	Armstrong Atlantic State		Central Missouri State University, MO	W
University of Vermont, VT	M,W	University, GA	W	Central Washington University, WA	W
University of Virginia, VA	M,W	Ashland University, OH	W	Chaminade University of	
University of Washington, WA	M	Athens State University, AL	W	Honolulu, HI	W
University of West Florida, FL	M,W	Auburn University, AL	W	Christian Brothers University, TN	W
University of Wisconsin–Green		Augustana College, SD	W	Clarion University of	
Bay, WI	M,W	Austin Peay State University, TN	W	Pennsylvania, PA	W
University of Wisconsin–Madison, WI	M,W	Azusa Pacific University, CA	W	Cleveland State University, OH	W
University of Wisconsin–		Baker University, KS	W	Coastal Carolina University, SC	W
Milwaukee, WI	M,W	Ball State University, IN	W	Colgate University, NY	W
University of Wisconsin–Parkside, WI	M,W	Barry University, FL	W	College of Charleston, SC	W
University of Wyoming, WY	W	Barton College, NC	W	College of Saint Mary, NE	W
Urbana University, OH	M,W	Baylor University, TX	W	The College of Saint Rose, NY	W
Ursuline College, OH	W	Belhaven College, MS	W	Colorado School of Mines, CO	W
Utah State University, UT	W	Bellevue University, NE	W	Colorado State University, CO	W
Utah Valley State College, UT	W	Belmont Abbey College, NC	W	Colorado State University-Pueblo, CO	W
Valparaiso University, IN	M,W	Belmont University, TN	W	Columbia College, MO	W
Vanderbilt University, TN	M,W	Bemidji State University, MN	W	Columbus State University, GA	W
Vanguard University of Southern		Benedictine College, KS	W	Concordia University, CA	W
California, CA	M,W	Bentley College, MA	W	Concordia University, MI	W
Villanova University, PA	M,W	Bethany College, KS	W	Concordia University, NE	W
Virginia Commonwealth		Bethel College, TN	W	Concordia University, OR	W
University, VA	M,W	Bethune-Cookman College, FL	W	Concordia University, St. Paul, MN	W
Virginia Intermont College, VA	M,W	Biola University, CA	W	Corban College, OR	W
Virginia Military Institute, VA	M	Bloomfield College, NJ	W	Cornerstone University, MI	W
Virginia Polytechnic Institute and		Bloomsburg University of		Creighton University, NE	W
State University, VA	M,W	Pennsylvania, PA	W	Culver-Stockton College, MO	W
Wake Forest University, NC	M,W	Bluefield State College, WV	W	Davis & Elkins College, WV	W
Waldorf College, IA	M,W	Boston College, MA	W	Delaware State University, DE	W
Warner Southern College, FL	M,W	Boston University, MA	W	DePaul University, IL	W
Washington State University, WA	W	Bowie State University, MD	W	Dickinson State University, ND	W
Wayne State College, NE	W	Bowling Green State University, OH	W	Doane College, NE	W
Webber International University, FL	M,W	Bradley University, IL	W	Dominican College, NY	W
Western Carolina University, NC	W	Brenau University, GA	W	Dominican University of	
Western Illinois University, IL	M,W	Brevard College, NC	W	California, CA	W
Western Kentucky University, KY	M	Brewton-Parker College, GA	W	Dordt College, IA	W
Western Washington University, WA	M,W	Brigham Young University, UT	W	Dowling College, NY	W
Westmont College, CA	M,W	Brigham Young University–Hawaii, HI	W	Drake University, IA	W
West Texas A&M University, TX	M,W	Butler University, IN	W	Drexel University, PA	W
West Virginia University, WV	M,W	Caldwell College, NJ	W	East Carolina University, NC	W
West Virginia Wesleyan College, WV	M,W	California Baptist University, CA	W	East Central University, OK	W
Wheeling Jesuit University, WV	M,W	California State University,		Eastern Illinois University, IL	W
Whitman College, WA	M,W	Bakersfield, CA	W	Eastern Michigan University, MI	W
William Carey College, MS	M,W	California State University, Chico, CA	W	East Stroudsburg University of	
William Jewell College, MO	M,W	California State University,		Pennsylvania, PA	W
William Penn University, IA	M,W	Fresno, CA	W	East Tennessee State University, TN	W
Williams Baptist College, AR	M,W	California State University,		Eckerd College, FL	W
William Woods University, MO	M,W	Fullerton, CA	W	Edinboro University of	
Wingate University, NC	M	California State University,		Pennsylvania, PA	W
Winona State University, MN	W	Sacramento, CA	W	Elon University, NC	W
Winthrop University, SC	M	California State University, San		Emporia State University, KS	W
Wofford College, SC	M,W	Bernardino, CA	W	Erskine College, SC	W
Xavier University, OH	M,W	Cameron University, OK	W	Evangel University, MO	W
York College, NE	M,W	Campbellsville University, KY	W	Fairfield University, CT	W
		Campbell University, NC	W	Fairleigh Dickinson University,	
		Canisius College, NY	W	Metropolitan Campus, NJ	W
Softball		Carson-Newman College, TN	W	Faulkner University, AL	W
Abilene Christian University, TX	W	Catawba College, NC	W	Ferris State University, MI	W
Adelphi University, NY	W	Cedarville University, OH	W	Florida Atlantic University, FL	W
Albertson College of Idaho, ID	W	Centenary College of Louisiana, LA	W	Florida Gulf Coast University, FL	W
Alcorn State University, MS	W	Central Christian College of		Florida Institute of Technology, FL	W
Alderson-Broaddus College, WV	W	Kansas, KS	W	Florida Southern College, FL	W
American International College, MA	W	Central Connecticut State		Florida State University, FL	W
Anderson College, SC	W	University, CT	W	Fordham University, NY	W
Angelo State University, TX	W	Central Methodist University, MO	W	Fort Lewis College, CO	W
Arizona State University, AZ	W	Central Michigan University, MI	W	Francis Marion University, SC	W

Franklin Pierce College, NH	W	Lincoln University, MO	W	Niagara University, NY	W
Freed-Hardeman University, TN	W	Lindenwood University, MO	W	Nicholls State University, LA	W
Friends University, KS	W	Lipscomb University, TN	W	Norfolk State University, VA	W
Furman University, SC	W	Lock Haven University of Pennsylvania, PA	W	North Carolina State University, NC	W
Gannon University, PA	W			North Dakota State University, ND	W
Geneva College, PA	W	Long Island University, Brooklyn Campus, NY	W	Northeastern State University, OK	W
George Mason University, VA	W	Longwood University, VA	W	Northern Illinois University, IL	W
Georgetown College, KY	W	Louisiana State University and Agricultural and Mechanical College, LA	W	Northern Kentucky University, KY	W
Georgia College & State University, GA	W			Northern State University, SD	W
Georgia Institute of Technology, GA	W	Louisiana Tech University, LA	W	North Greenville College, SC	W
Georgian Court University, NJ	W	Loyola Marymount University, CA	W	Northwestern College, IA	W
Georgia Southern University, GA	W	Loyola University Chicago, IL	W	Northwestern Oklahoma State University, OK	W
Georgia State University, GA	W	Malone College, OH	W	Northwestern State University of Louisiana, LA	W
Glenville State College, WV	W	Manhattan College, NY	W		
Goldey-Beacom College, DE	W	Marist College, NY	W	Northwestern University, IL	W
Goshen College, IN	W	Marshall University, WV	W	Northwest Nazarene University, ID	W
Grace College, IN	W	Mars Hill College, NC	W	Northwood University, MI	W
Graceland University, IA	W	Martin Methodist College, TN	W	Northwood University, Florida Campus, FL	W
Grand Valley State University, MI	W	McKendree College, IL	W		
Grand View College, IA	W	Mercer University, GA	W	Northwood University, Texas Campus, TX	W
Hampton University, VA	W	Mercy College, NY	W		
Hannibal-LaGrange College, MO	W	Mercyhurst College, PA	W	Nova Southeastern University, FL	W
Hastings College, NE	W	Merrimack College, MA	W	Nyack College, NY	W
Hawai'i Pacific University, HI	W	Mesa State College, CO	W	Oakland City University, IN	W
Hillsdale College, MI	W	Miami University, OH	W	Oakland University, MI	W
Hofstra University, NY	W	MidAmerica Nazarene University, KS	W	The Ohio State University, OH	W
Houston Baptist University, TX	W	Mid-Continent University, KY	W	Ohio University, OH	W
Humboldt State University, CA	W	Middle Tennessee State University, TN	W	Ohio Valley University, WV	W
Huntington University, IN	W			Oklahoma Baptist University, OK	W
Illinois State University, IL	W	Midland Lutheran College, NE	W	Oklahoma City University, OK	W
Indiana State University, IN	W	Midway College, KY	W	Oklahoma Panhandle State University, OK	W
Indiana University Bloomington, IN	W	Midwestern State University, TX	W		
Indiana University of Pennsylvania, PA	W	Millersville University of Pennsylvania, PA	W	Oklahoma State University, OK	W
				Oklahoma Wesleyan University, OK	W
Indiana University–Purdue University Fort Wayne, IN		Milligan College, TN	W	Olivet Nazarene University, IL	W
		Minnesota State University Mankato, MN	W	Oregon State University, OR	W
Indiana University–Purdue University Indianapolis, IN	W	Minnesota State University Moorhead, MN	W	Ouachita Baptist University, AR	W
				Park University, MO	W
Inter American University of Puerto Rico, Guayama Campus, PR	M,W	Minot State University, ND	W	Peru State College, NE	W
		Mississippi State University, MS	W	Pfeiffer University, NC	W
Iona College, NY	W	Mississippi University for Women, MS	W	Philadelphia University, PA	W
Iowa State University of Science and Technology, IA	W			Pikeville College, KY	W
		Missouri Baptist University, MO	W	Pittsburg State University, KS	W
Iowa Wesleyan College, IA	W	Missouri Southern State University, MO	W	Point Park University, PA	W
Jacksonville State University, AL	W			Portland State University, OR	W
James Madison University, VA	W	Missouri State University, MO	W	Post University, CT	W
Jamestown College, ND	W	Missouri Valley College, MO	W	Providence College, RI	W
Johnson C. Smith University, NC	W	Molloy College, NY	W	Purdue University, IN	W
Judson College, AL	W	Monmouth University, NJ	W	Quincy University, IL	W
Kennesaw State University, GA	W	Montreat College, NC	W	Quinnipiac University, CT	W
Kent State University, OH	W	Morehead State University, KY	W	Radford University, VA	W
Kentucky Wesleyan College, KY	W	Morningside College, IA	W	Regis University, CO	W
King College, TN	M,W	Morris College, SC	W	Reinhardt College, GA	W
Kutztown University of Pennsylvania, PA	W	Mountain State University, WV	W	Rider University, NJ	W
		Mount Marty College, SD	W	Robert Morris College, IL	W
Lambuth University, TN	W	Mount Olive College, NC	W	Robert Morris University, PA	W
La Salle University, PA	W	Mount St. Mary's University, MD	W	Rochester College, MI	W
Lee University, TN	W	Mount Vernon Nazarene University, OH	W	Rockhurst University, MO	W
Lehigh University, PA	W			Rollins College, FL	W
Le Moyne College, NY	W	New Mexico Highlands University, NM	W	St. Ambrose University, IA	W
LeMoyne-Owen College, TN	W			St. Andrews Presbyterian College, NC	W
Lenoir-Rhyne College, NC	W	New Mexico State University, NM	W	St. Bonaventure University, NY	W
Liberty University, VA	W	New York Institute of Technology, NY	W	St. Cloud State University, MN	W
Limestone College, SC	W			St. Edward's University, TX	W
Lincoln Memorial University, TN	W			St. Francis College, NY	W

St. Gregory's University, OK	W	
St. John's University, NY	W	
Saint Joseph's College, IN	W	
Saint Leo University, FL	W	
Saint Louis University, MO	W	
Saint Martin's College, WA	W	
Saint Mary's College of California, CA	W	
St. Thomas University, FL	W	
Saint Vincent College, PA	W	
Saint Xavier University, IL	W	
Samford University, AL	W	
Sam Houston State University, TX	M,W	
San Francisco State University, CA	W	
Seton Hall University, NJ	W	
Seton Hill University, PA	W	
Shaw University, NC	W	
Shepherd University, WV	W	
Shippensburg University of Pennsylvania, PA	W	
Slippery Rock University of Pennsylvania, PA	W	
Sonoma State University, CA	W	
South Carolina State University, SC	W	
South Dakota State University, SD	W	
Southeastern Louisiana University, LA	W	
Southeastern Oklahoma State University, OK	W	
Southeast Missouri State University, MO	W	
Southern Arkansas University–Magnolia, AR	W	
Southern Illinois University Carbondale, IL	W	
Southern Illinois University Edwardsville, IL	W	
Southern New Hampshire University, NH	W	
Southern Oregon University, OR	W	
Southern University and Agricultural and Mechanical College, LA	W	
Southern Utah University, UT	W	
Southern Wesleyan University, SC	W	
Southwest Baptist University, MO	W	
Southwestern College, KS	W	
Southwest Minnesota State University, MN	W	
Spring Arbor University, MI	W	
Spring Hill College, AL	W	
Stanford University, CA	W	
State University of New York at Binghamton, NY	W	
Stephen F. Austin State University, TX	W	
Sterling College, KS	W	
Stetson University, FL	W	
Stonehill College, MA	W	
Stony Brook University, State University of New York, NY	W	
Syracuse University, NY	W	
Tabor College, KS	W	
Tarleton State University, TX	W	
Taylor University, IN	W	
Temple University, PA	M,W	
Tennessee Technological University, TN	W	
Tennessee Wesleyan College, TN	W	
Texas A&M University, TX	W	
Texas State University-San Marcos, TX	W	
Texas Tech University, TX	W	
Thomas University, GA	W	
Tiffin University, OH	W	
Towson University, MD	W	
Trevecca Nazarene University, TN	W	
Trinity International University, IL	W	
Troy University, AL	W	
Truman State University, MO	W	
Tusculum College, TN	W	
Union College, KY	W	
Union University, TN	W	
University at Albany, State University of New York, NY	W	
University at Buffalo, The State University of New York, NY	W	
The University of Akron, OH	W	
The University of Alabama, AL	W	
The University of Alabama at Birmingham, AL	W	
The University of Alabama in Huntsville, AL	W	
The University of Arizona, AZ	W	
University of Arkansas at Monticello, AR	W	
University of Bridgeport, CT	W	
University of California, Berkeley, CA	W	
University of California, Los Angeles, CA	W	
University of California, Riverside, CA	W	
University of California, Santa Barbara, CA	W	
University of Charleston, WV	W	
University of Colorado at Colorado Springs, CO	W	
University of Connecticut, CT	W	
University of Dayton, OH	W	
University of Delaware, DE	W	
University of Detroit Mercy, MI	W	
University of Evansville, IN	W	
The University of Findlay, OH	W	
University of Florida, FL	W	
University of Hartford, CT	W	
University of Hawaii at Hilo, HI	W	
University of Hawaii at Manoa, HI	W	
University of Illinois at Chicago, IL	W	
University of Illinois at Springfield, IL	W	
University of Illinois at Urbana–Champaign, IL	W	
University of Indianapolis, IN	W	
University of Kansas, KS	W	
University of Louisville, KY	W	
University of Maine, ME	W	
University of Mary, ND	W	
University of Maryland, Baltimore County, MD	W	
University of Maryland, College Park, MD	W	
University of Massachusetts Amherst, MA	W	
University of Michigan, MI	W	
University of Minnesota, Twin Cities Campus, MN	W	
University of Mississippi, MS	W	
University of Missouri–Columbia, MO	W	
University of Missouri–Kansas City, MO	W	
University of Missouri–St. Louis, MO	W	
University of Nebraska at Kearney, NE	W	
University of Nebraska at Omaha, NE	W	
University of Nebraska–Lincoln, NE	W	
University of Nevada, Las Vegas, NV	W	
University of Nevada, Reno, NV	W	
University of New Haven, CT	W	
University of North Alabama, AL	W	
The University of North Carolina at Chapel Hill, NC	W	
The University of North Carolina at Charlotte, NC	W	
The University of North Carolina at Greensboro, NC	W	
The University of North Carolina at Pembroke, NC	W	
The University of North Carolina at Wilmington, NC	W	
University of North Dakota, ND	W	
University of Northern Colorado, CO	W	
University of Northern Iowa, IA	W	
University of North Florida, FL	W	
University of Notre Dame, IN	W	
University of Oklahoma, OK	W	
University of Oregon, OR	W	
University of Rhode Island, RI	W	
University of Rio Grande, OH	W	
University of St. Francis, IL	W	
University of Saint Francis, IN	W	
University of Science and Arts of Oklahoma, OK	W	
University of Sioux Falls, SD	W	
University of South Carolina, SC	W	
University of South Carolina Upstate, SC	W	
The University of South Dakota, SD	W	
University of Southern Indiana, IN	W	
University of South Florida, FL	W	
The University of Tampa, FL	W	
The University of Tennessee at Chattanooga, TN	W	
The University of Tennessee at Martin, TN	W	
The University of Texas at Arlington, TX	W	
The University of Texas at Austin, TX	W	
The University of Texas at San Antonio, TX	W	
University of the Cumberlands, KY	W	
University of the Incarnate Word, TX	W	
University of the Pacific, CA	W	
The University of Toledo, OH	W	
University of Tulsa, OK	W	
University of Vermont, VT	W	
University of Virginia, VA	W	
The University of Virginia's College at Wise, VA	W	
University of Washington, WA	W	
University of West Florida, FL	W	
University of West Georgia, GA	W	

University of Wisconsin–Green Bay, WI — W
University of Wisconsin–Madison, WI — W
University of Wisconsin–Parkside, WI — W
Urbana University, OH — W
Ursuline College, OH — W
Utah State University, UT — W
Utah Valley State College, UT — W
Valdosta State University, GA — W
Valley City State University, ND — W
Valparaiso University, IN — W
Vanguard University of Southern California, CA — W
Villanova University, PA — W
Virginia Intermont College, VA — W
Virginia Union University, VA — W
Voorhees College, SC — W
Waldorf College, IA — W
Warner Southern College, FL — W
Wayne State College, NE — W
Wayne State University, MI — W
Webber International University, FL — W
Western Illinois University, IL — W
Western Kentucky University, KY — W
Western New Mexico University, NM — W
Western Washington University, WA — W
West Liberty State College, WV — W
West Texas A&M University, TX — W
West Virginia Wesleyan College, WV — W
Wheeling Jesuit University, WV — W
Wichita State University, KS — W
William Carey College, MS — W
William Jewell College, MO — W
William Penn University, IA — W
Williams Baptist College, AR — W
William Woods University, MO — W
Wilmington College, DE — W
Wingate University, NC — W
Winona State University, MN — W
Winston-Salem State University, NC — W
Winthrop University, SC — W
York College, NE — W
Youngstown State University, OH — W

Swimming and Diving

Adelphi University, NY — M,W
Arizona State University, AZ — M,W
Asbury College, KY — M,W
Ashland University, OH — M,W
Auburn University, AL — M,W
Ball State University, IN — M,W
Bentley College, MA — M,W
Biola University, CA — M,W
Bloomsburg University of Pennsylvania, PA — M,W
Boston College, MA — W
Boston University, MA — M,W
Bowling Green State University, OH — M,W
Brigham Young University, UT — M,W
California Baptist University, CA — M,W
California State University, Bakersfield, CA — M,W
California State University, San Bernardino, CA — M,W
Canisius College, NY — M,W
Catawba College, NC — W

Centenary College of Louisiana, LA — M,W
Central Connecticut State University, CT — W
Central Washington University, WA — M,W
Clarion University of Pennsylvania, PA — M,W
Clemson University, SC — M,W
Cleveland State University, OH — M,W
College of Charleston, SC — M,W
The College of Saint Rose, NY — M,W
The College of William and Mary, VA — M
Colorado School of Mines, CO — M,W
Colorado State University, CO — W
Davidson College, NC — M,W
Drexel University, PA — M,W
Duquesne University, PA — M,W
East Carolina University, NC — M,W
Eastern Illinois University, IL — M,W
Eastern Michigan University, MI — M,W
East Stroudsburg University of Pennsylvania, PA — W
Edinboro University of Pennsylvania, PA — M,W
Fairfield University, CT — M,W
Fairmont State University, WV — M,W
Florida Atlantic University, FL — M,W
Florida State University, FL — M,W
Fordham University, NY — M,W
Gannon University, PA — M,W
George Mason University, VA — M,W
The George Washington University, DC — M,W
Georgia Institute of Technology, GA — M,W
Georgia Southern University, GA — W
Grand Valley State University, MI — M,W
Hillsdale College, MI — W
Howard University, DC — M,W
Illinois State University, IL — W
Indiana University Bloomington, IN — M,W
Indiana University of Pennsylvania, PA — W
Indiana University–Purdue University Indianapolis, IN — M,W
Iona College, NY — M,W
Iowa State University of Science and Technology, IA — M,W
John Brown University, AR — M,W
Kutztown University of Pennsylvania, PA — M,W
Lambuth University, TN — M,W
La Salle University, PA — M,W
Lehigh University, PA — M,W
Limestone College, SC — W
Lindenwood University, MO — M,W
Lock Haven University of Pennsylvania, PA — W
Louisiana State University and Agricultural and Mechanical College, LA — M,W
Loyola Marymount University, CA — W
Manhattan College, NY — W
Marist College, NY — M,W
Marshall University, WV — W
Metropolitan State College of Denver, CO — M,W
Miami University, OH — M,W

Michigan State University, MI — M,W
Millersville University of Pennsylvania, PA — W
Minnesota State University Mankato, MN — M,W
Missouri State University, MO — M,W
Morningside College, IA — M,W
New Mexico State University, NM — W
Niagara University, NY — M,W
North Carolina Agricultural and Technical State University, NC — W
North Carolina State University, NC — M,W
Northeastern University, MA — W
Northern Arizona University, AZ — W
Northern Illinois University, IL — M,W
Northwestern University, IL — M,W
Oakland University, MI — M,W
The Ohio State University, OH — M,W
Ohio University, OH — M,W
Old Dominion University, VA — M,W
Oregon State University, OR — W
Ouachita Baptist University, AR — M,W
The Pennsylvania State University University Park Campus, PA — M,W
Pepperdine University, CA — W
Pfeiffer University, NC — W
Purdue University, IN — M,W
Radford University, VA — W
Rice University, TX — W
Rider University, NJ — M,W
St. Bonaventure University, NY — M,W
St. Cloud State University, MN — M,W
St. Francis College, NY — M,W
Saint Leo University, FL — M,W
Saint Louis University, MO — M,W
San Francisco State University, CA — M,W
San Jose State University, CA — W
Seton Hall University, NJ — M,W
Shippensburg University of Pennsylvania, PA — M,W
Slippery Rock University of Pennsylvania, PA — M,W
South Dakota State University, SD — M,W
Southern Illinois University Carbondale, IL — M,W
Southern Methodist University, TX — M,W
Spring Hill College, AL — M,W
Stanford University, CA — M,W
State University of New York at Binghamton, NY — M,W
Stony Brook University, State University of New York, NY — M,W
Syracuse University, NY — M,W
Texas A&M University, TX — M,W
Texas Christian University, TX — M,W
Towson University, MD — M,W
Truman State University, MO — M,W
University at Buffalo, The State University of New York, NY — M,W
The University of Alabama, AL — M,W
The University of Alabama at Birmingham, AL — W
University of Alaska Anchorage, AK — M
The University of Arizona, AZ — M,W
University of Bridgeport, CT — W
University of California, Berkeley, CA — M,W

University of California, Irvine, CA — M,W
University of California, Los Angeles, CA — W
University of California, Santa Barbara, CA — M,W
University of Charleston, WV — M,W
University of Cincinnati, OH — M,W
University of Connecticut, CT — M,W
University of Delaware, DE — W
University of Denver, CO — M,W
University of Evansville, IN — M,W
The University of Findlay, OH — M,W
University of Florida, FL — M,W
University of Georgia, GA — M,W
University of Hawaii at Manoa, HI — M,W
University of Illinois at Chicago, IL — M,W
University of Illinois at Urbana–Champaign, IL — W
University of Indianapolis, IN — M,W
University of Kansas, KS — W
University of Louisville, KY — M,W
University of Maine, ME — W
University of Maryland, Baltimore County, MD — M,W
University of Maryland, College Park, MD — M,W
University of Massachusetts Amherst, MA — M,W
University of Massachusetts Lowell, MA — M
University of Miami, FL — W
University of Michigan, MI — M,W
University of Minnesota, Twin Cities Campus, MN — M,W
University of Missouri–Columbia, MO — M,W
University of Nebraska at Kearney, NE — W
University of Nebraska–Lincoln, NE — W
University of Nevada, Las Vegas, NV — M,W
University of Nevada, Reno, NV — W
University of New Hampshire, NH — W
The University of North Carolina at Chapel Hill, NC — M,W
The University of North Carolina at Wilmington, NC — M,W
University of North Dakota, ND — W
University of Northern Colorado, CO — W
University of Northern Iowa, IA — W
University of North Florida, FL — W
University of Notre Dame, IN — M,W
University of Puerto Rico, Mayagüez Campus, PR — M,W
University of Rhode Island, RI — M,W
University of Richmond, VA — W
University of San Diego, CA — W
University of South Carolina, SC — M,W
The University of South Dakota, SD — M
University of Southern California, CA — M,W
The University of Texas at Austin, TX — M,W
University of the Cumberlands, KY — M,W
University of the Pacific, CA — M,W
The University of Toledo, OH — M,W
University of Utah, UT — M,W
University of Vermont, VT — W
University of Virginia, VA — M,W
University of Washington, WA — M,W

University of Wisconsin–Green Bay, WI — M,W
University of Wisconsin–Madison, WI — M,W
University of Wisconsin–Milwaukee, WI — M,W
University of Wyoming, WY — M,W
Valparaiso University, IN — M,W
Villanova University, PA — W
Virginia Military Institute, VA — M
Virginia Polytechnic Institute and State University, VA — M,W
Washington State University, WA — W
Wayne State University, MI — M,W
Western Illinois University, IL — M,W
Western Kentucky University, KY — M,W
West Virginia University, WV — M,W
West Virginia Wesleyan College, WV — M,W
Wheeling Jesuit University, WV — M,W
Wingate University, NC — M,W
Xavier University, OH — M,W

Table Tennis

Inter American University of Puerto Rico, Guayama Campus, PR — M,W
Inter American University of Puerto Rico, San Germán Campus, PR — M,W
University of Puerto Rico, Mayagüez Campus, PR — M,W

Tennis

Abilene Christian University, TX — M,W
Adelphi University, NY — M,W
Albertson College of Idaho, ID — M,W
Alcorn State University, MS — M,W
Alliant International University, CA — M,W
American University, DC — M,W
Anderson College, SC — M,W
Appalachian State University, NC — M,W
Arizona State University, AZ — M,W
Arkansas State University, AR — W
Arkansas Tech University, AR — W
Armstrong Atlantic State University, GA — M,W
Asbury College, KY — M,W
Auburn University, AL — M,W
Auburn University Montgomery, AL — M,W
Augusta State University, GA — M,W
Austin Peay State University, TN — M,W
Azusa Pacific University, CA — M
Baker University, KS — M,W
Ball State University, IN — M,W
Barry University, FL — M,W
Barton College, NC — M,W
Baylor University, TX — M,W
Belhaven College, MS — M,W
Belmont Abbey College, NC — M,W
Belmont University, TN — M,W
Bemidji State University, MN — W
Benedictine College, KS — M,W
Berry College, GA — M,W
Bethany College, KS — M,W
Bethel College, KS — M,W
Bethel College, TN — M,W
Bethune-Cookman College, FL — M,W
Biola University, CA — W
Bloomsburg University of Pennsylvania, PA — M,W

Bluefield State College, WV — M,W
Blue Mountain College, MS — W
Boise State University, ID — M,W
Boston College, MA — W
Boston University, MA — W
Bowie State University, MD — W
Bowling Green State University, OH — M,W
Bradley University, IL — M,W
Brenau University, GA — W
Brevard College, NC — M,W
Brigham Young University, UT — M,W
Brigham Young University–Hawaii, HI — M,W
Bryan College, TN — M,W
Butler University, IN — M,W
Caldwell College, NJ — M,W
California State University, Bakersfield, CA — W
California State University, Fresno, CA — M,W
California State University, Fullerton, CA — W
California State University, Sacramento, CA — M,W
Cameron University, OK — M,W
Campbellsville University, KY — M,W
Campbell University, NC — M,W
Carson-Newman College, TN — M,W
Catawba College, NC — M,W
Cedarville University, OH — M,W
Centenary College of Louisiana, LA — M,W
Central Christian College of Kansas, KS — M,W
Chaminade University of Honolulu, HI — M,W
Clarion University of Pennsylvania, PA — W
Clark Atlanta University, GA — M,W
Clayton State University, GA — W
Clemson University, SC — M,W
Cleveland State University, OH — W
Coastal Carolina University, SC — M,W
College of Charleston, SC — M,W
College of Santa Fe, NM — M,W
The College of William and Mary, VA — M,W
Colorado School of Mines, CO — M,W
Colorado State University, CO — W
Colorado State University-Pueblo, CO — M,W
Columbia College, SC — W
Columbus State University, GA — M,W
Concordia University, NE — M,W
Converse College, SC — W
Coppin State University, MD — W
Creighton University, NE — M,W
Dallas Baptist University, TX — W
Davidson College, NC — M,W
Delaware State University, DE — M,W
DePaul University, IL — M,W
Dillard University, LA — M,W
Dominican University of California, CA — M,W
Dordt College, IA — M,W
Dowling College, NY — M,W
Drake University, IA — M,W
Drexel University, PA — M,W
Duke University, NC — M,W
Duquesne University, PA — M,W

East Carolina University, NC	M,W
East Central University, OK	M,W
Eastern Illinois University, IL	M,W
Eastern Michigan University, MI	W
Eastern Washington University, WA	M,W
East Stroudsburg University of Pennsylvania, PA	M,W
East Tennessee State University, TN	M,W
Eckerd College, FL	M,W
Elon University, NC	M,W
Embry-Riddle Aeronautical University, FL	M
Emporia State University, KS	M,W
Erskine College, SC	M,W
Evangel University, MO	M,W
Fairfield University, CT	M,W
Fairleigh Dickinson University, Metropolitan Campus, NJ	M,W
Fairmont State University, WV	M,W
Ferris State University, MI	M,W
Flagler College, FL	M,W
Florida Atlantic University, FL	M,W
Florida Gulf Coast University, FL	M,W
Florida Institute of Technology, FL	M,W
Florida Southern College, FL	M,W
Florida State University, FL	M,W
Fordham University, NY	M,W
Fort Hays State University, KS	W
Francis Marion University, SC	M,W
Franklin Pierce College, NH	M,W
Freed-Hardeman University, TN	M,W
Friends University, KS	M,W
Furman University, SC	M,W
Geneva College, PA	W
George Mason University, VA	M,W
Georgetown College, KY	M,W
Georgetown University, DC	W
The George Washington University, DC	M,W
Georgia College & State University, GA	M,W
Georgia Institute of Technology, GA	M,W
Georgian Court University, NJ	W
Georgia Southern University, GA	M,W
Georgia State University, GA	M,W
Gonzaga University, WA	M,W
Goshen College, IN	M,W
Grace College, IN	M,W
Graceland University, IA	M,W
Grambling State University, LA	M,W
Grand Canyon University, AZ	W
Grand Valley State University, MI	M,W
Hampton University, VA	M,W
Harding University, AR	M,W
Hastings College, NE	M,W
Hawai'i Pacific University, HI	M,W
Hofstra University, NY	M,W
Howard University, DC	M,W
Huntington University, IN	M,W
Idaho State University, ID	M,W
Illinois State University, IL	M,W
Indiana State University, IN	M,W
Indiana University Bloomington, IN	M,W
Indiana University of Pennsylvania, PA	W

Indiana University–Purdue University Fort Wayne, IN	M,W
Indiana University–Purdue University Indianapolis, IN	M,W
Inter American University of Puerto Rico, Guayama Campus, PR	M,W
Inter American University of Puerto Rico, San Germán Campus, PR	M,W
Iowa State University of Science and Technology, IA	W
Jacksonville State University, AL	M,W
John Brown University, AR	M,W
Johnson C. Smith University, NC	M,W
Judson College, AL	W
Kansas State University, KS	W
Kennesaw State University, GA	W
King College, TN	M,W
Kutztown University of Pennsylvania, PA	M,W
Lake Superior State University, MI	M,W
Lamar University, TX	M,W
Lambuth University, TN	M,W
La Salle University, PA	M,W
Lee University, TN	M,W
Lehigh University, PA	M,W
Le Moyne College, NY	M,W
LeMoyne-Owen College, TN	M,W
Lewis-Clark State College, ID	M,W
Liberty University, VA	M,W
Limestone College, SC	M,W
Lincoln Memorial University, TN	M,W
Lincoln University, MO	W
Lindenwood University, MO	M,W
Lipscomb University, TN	M,W
Long Island University, Brooklyn Campus, NY	W
Longwood University, VA	M,W
Louisiana State University and Agricultural and Mechanical College, LA	M,W
Louisiana Tech University, LA	W
Loyola Marymount University, CA	M,W
Lynn University, FL	M,W
Lyon College, AR	M,W
Malone College, OH	M,W
Manhattan College, NY	M,W
Marist College, NY	M,W
Marshall University, WV	W
Mars Hill College, NC	M,W
Martin Methodist College, TN	M,W
McKendree College, IL	M,W
Mercer University, GA	M,W
Mercy College, NY	M
Mercyhurst College, PA	M,W
Merrimack College, MA	W
Mesa State College, CO	M,W
Metropolitan State College of Denver, CO	M,W
Miami University, OH	W
Michigan State University, MI	M,W
Michigan Technological University, MI	W
Middle Tennessee State University, TN	M,W
Midland Lutheran College, NE	M,W
Midway College, KY	W

Midwestern State University, TX	M,W
Millersville University of Pennsylvania, PA	M,W
Milligan College, TN	M,W
Minnesota State University Mankato, MN	M,W
Mississippi State University, MS	M,W
Mississippi University for Women, MS	W
Missouri Southern State University, MO	W
Missouri State University, MO	M,W
Missouri Valley College, MO	M,W
Molloy College, NY	W
Monmouth University, NJ	M,W
Montana State University, MT	M,W
Montana State University–Billings, MT	M,W
Montreat College, NC	M,W
Morehead State University, KY	M,W
Morehouse College, GA	M
Morningside College, IA	M,W
Morris College, SC	M,W
Mount Olive College, NC	M,W
Mount St. Mary's University, MD	M,W
Murray State University, KY	M,W
New Mexico State University, NM	M,W
Niagara University, NY	M,W
Nicholls State University, LA	W
Norfolk State University, VA	M,W
North Carolina Agricultural and Technical State University, NC	M,W
North Carolina State University, NC	M,W
Northeastern State University, OK	W
Northeastern University, MA	M
Northern Arizona University, AZ	M,W
Northern Illinois University, IL	M,W
Northern Kentucky University, KY	M,W
Northern State University, SD	W
North Greenville College, SC	M,W
Northwestern State University of Louisiana, LA	W
Northwestern University, IL	M,W
Northwood University, MI	M,W
Northwood University, Florida Campus, FL	M,W
Nova Southeastern University, FL	W
Oakland University, MI	W
The Ohio State University, OH	M,W
Oklahoma Baptist University, OK	M,W
Oklahoma State University, OK	M,W
Oklahoma Wesleyan University, OK	M,W
Old Dominion University, VA	M,W
Olivet Nazarene University, IL	M,W
Oral Roberts University, OK	M,W
Ouachita Baptist University, AR	M,W
The Pennsylvania State University University Park Campus, PA	M,W
Pepperdine University, CA	M,W
Pfeiffer University, NC	M,W
Philadelphia University, PA	M,W
Pikeville College, KY	M,W
Portland State University, OR	M,W
Providence College, RI	W
Purdue University, IN	M,W
Quincy University, IL	M,W

Athletic Grants for Undergraduates
Tennis

Quinnipiac University, CT	M,W	Stanford University, CA	M,W	University of Illinois at Chicago, IL	M,W
Radford University, VA	M,W	State University of New York at		University of Illinois at Springfield, IL	M,W
Reinhardt College, GA	M,W	Binghamton, NY	M,W	University of Illinois at Urbana–	
Research College of Nursing, MO	M,W	Stephen F. Austin State University, TX	W	Champaign, IL	M,W
Rice University, TX	M,W	Stetson University, FL	M,W	University of Indianapolis, IN	M,W
Rider University, NJ	M,W	Stonehill College, MA	M,W	University of Kansas, KS	W
Robert Morris College, IL	W	Stony Brook University, State		University of Louisville, KY	M,W
Robert Morris University, PA	M,W	University of New York, NY	M,W	University of Mary, ND	M,W
Roberts Wesleyan College, NY	M,W	Syracuse University, NY	W	University of Maryland, Baltimore	
Rockhurst University, MO	M,W	Tabor College, KS	M,W	County, MD	M,W
Rollins College, FL	M,W	Tarleton State University, TX	W	University of Maryland, College	
St. Ambrose University, IA	M,W	Taylor University, IN	M,W	Park, MD	M,W
St. Andrews Presbyterian College, NC	M,W	Temple University, PA	M	University of Maryland Eastern	
St. Bonaventure University, NY	M,W	Tennessee Technological		Shore, MD	M
St. Cloud State University, MN	M,W	University, TN	M,W	University of Massachusetts	
St. Edward's University, TX	M,W	Tennessee Wesleyan College, TN	M,W	Amherst, MA	M,W
St. Francis College, NY	M,W	Texas A&M University, TX	M,W	University of Massachusetts	
St. John's University, NY	M,W	Texas Christian University, TX	M,W	Lowell, MA	M,W
Saint Joseph's College, IN	M,W	Texas State University-San		The University of Memphis, TN	M,W
Saint Leo University, FL	M,W	Marcos, TX	W	University of Miami, FL	M,W
Saint Louis University, MO	M,W	Texas Tech University, TX	M,W	University of Michigan, MI	M,W
Saint Mary's College of		Thomas University, GA	W	University of Minnesota, Twin Cities	
California, CA	M,W	Tiffin University, OH	M,W	Campus, MN	M,W
St. Mary's University of San		Towson University, MD	M,W	University of Mississippi, MS	M,W
Antonio, TX	M,W	Troy University, AL	M,W	University of Missouri–Columbia, MO	W
St. Thomas University, FL	M,W	Truman State University, MO	M,W	University of Missouri–Kansas	
Saint Vincent College, PA	M,W	Tusculum College, TN	M,W	City, MO	M,W
Samford University, AL	M,W	Tuskegee University, AL	M,W	University of Missouri–St. Louis, MO	M,W
Sam Houston State University, TX	M,W	Union College, KY	M,W	University of Nebraska at	
San Jose State University, CA	W	University at Albany, State University		Kearney, NE	M,W
Seton Hall University, NJ	W	of New York, NY	W	University of Nebraska–Lincoln, NE	M,W
Seton Hill University, PA	M,W	University at Buffalo, The State		University of Nevada, Las Vegas, NV	M,W
Shaw University, NC	M,W	University of New York, NY	M,W	University of Nevada, Reno, NV	M,W
Shepherd University, WV	M,W	The University of Akron, OH	M,W	University of New Hampshire, NH	W
Shippensburg University of		The University of Alabama, AL	M,W	University of New Haven, CT	W
Pennsylvania, PA	W	The University of Alabama at		University of New Orleans, LA	M,W
Shorter College, GA	M,W	Birmingham, AL	M,W	University of North Alabama, AL	M,W
Slippery Rock University of		The University of Alabama in		The University of North Carolina at	
Pennsylvania, PA	W	Huntsville, AL	M,W	Asheville, NC	M,W
Sonoma State University, CA	M,W	The University of Arizona, AZ	M,W	The University of North Carolina at	
South Carolina State University, SC	M,W	University of California, Berkeley, CA	M,W	Chapel Hill, NC	M,W
South Dakota State University, SD	M,W	University of California, Irvine, CA	M,W	The University of North Carolina at	
Southeastern Louisiana University, LA	M,W	University of California, Los		Charlotte, NC	M,W
Southeastern Oklahoma State		Angeles, CA	M,W	The University of North Carolina at	
University, OK	M,W	University of California,		Greensboro, NC	M,W
Southeast Missouri State		Riverside, CA	M,W	The University of North Carolina at	
University, MO	W	University of California, Santa		Pembroke, NC	W
Southern Arkansas University–		Barbara, CA	M,W	The University of North Carolina at	
Magnolia, AR	W	University of Central Florida, FL	M,W	Wilmington, NC	M,W
Southern Illinois University		University of Charleston, WV	M,W	University of Northern Colorado, CO	M,W
Carbondale, IL	M,W	University of Cincinnati, OH	M,W	University of Northern Iowa, IA	W
Southern Illinois University		University of Colorado at Boulder, CO	M,W	University of North Florida, FL	M,W
Edwardsville, IL	M,W	University of Colorado at Colorado		University of North Texas, TX	W
Southern Methodist University, TX	M,W	Springs, CO	M,W	University of Notre Dame, IN	M,W
Southern New Hampshire		University of Connecticut, CT	M,W	University of Oklahoma, OK	M,W
University, NH	M,W	University of Dayton, OH	M,W	University of Oregon, OR	M,W
Southern Oregon University, OR	W	University of Denver, CO	M,W	University of Portland, OR	M,W
Southern University and Agricultural		University of Detroit Mercy, MI	W	University of Puerto Rico, Mayagüez	
and Mechanical College, LA	M,W	University of Evansville, IN	W	Campus, PR	M,W
Southern Utah University, UT	W	The University of Findlay, OH	M,W	University of Rhode Island, RI	W
Southwest Baptist University, MO	M,W	University of Florida, FL	M,W	University of Richmond, VA	M,W
Southwestern College, KS	M,W	University of Georgia, GA	M,W	University of St. Francis, IL	M,W
Southwest Minnesota State		University of Hartford, CT	M,W	University of Saint Francis, IN	W
University, MN	W	University of Hawaii at Hilo, HI	M,W	University of San Diego, CA	M,W
Spring Arbor University, MI	M,W	University of Hawaii at Manoa, HI	M,W	University of San Francisco, CA	M,W
Spring Hill College, AL	M,W	University of Idaho, ID	M,W	University of Sioux Falls, SD	M,W

University of South Carolina, SC	M,W
University of South Carolina Upstate, SC	M,W
The University of South Dakota, SD	M,W
University of Southern California, CA	M,W
University of Southern Indiana, IN	M,W
University of Southern Mississippi, MS	M,W
University of South Florida, FL	M,W
The University of Tampa, FL	W
The University of Tennessee at Chattanooga, TN	M,W
The University of Tennessee at Martin, TN	M,W
The University of Texas at Arlington, TX	M,W
The University of Texas at Austin, TX	M,W
The University of Texas at El Paso, TX	W
The University of Texas at San Antonio, TX	M,W
The University of Texas–Pan American, TX	M,W
University of the Cumberlands, KY	M,W
University of the District of Columbia, DC	M,W
University of the Incarnate Word, TX	M,W
University of the Pacific, CA	M,W
The University of Toledo, OH	M,W
University of Tulsa, OK	M,W
University of Utah, UT	M,W
University of Virginia, VA	M,W
The University of Virginia's College at Wise, VA	M,W
University of Washington, WA	M,W
University of West Florida, FL	M,W
University of Wisconsin–Green Bay, WI	M,W
University of Wisconsin–Madison, WI	M,W
University of Wisconsin–Milwaukee, WI	M,W
University of Wyoming, WY	W
Ursuline College, OH	W
Utah State University, UT	M,W
Valdosta State University, GA	M,W
Valparaiso University, IN	M,W
Vanderbilt University, TN	M,W
Vanguard University of Southern California, CA	M,W
Virginia Commonwealth University, VA	M,W
Virginia Intermont College, VA	M,W
Virginia Military Institute, VA	M
Virginia Polytechnic Institute and State University, VA	M,W
Virginia Union University, VA	M
Wake Forest University, NC	M,W
Warner Southern College, FL	M,W
Washington State University, WA	W
Wayne State University, MI	M,W
Webber International University, FL	M,W
Western Carolina University, NC	W
Western Illinois University, IL	M,W
Western Kentucky University, KY	M,W
Western New Mexico University, NM	M,W
West Liberty State College, WV	M,W

Westmont College, CA	M,W
West Virginia University, WV	W
West Virginia Wesleyan College, WV	M,W
Wichita State University, KS	M,W
William Jewell College, MO	M,W
Wingate University, NC	M,W
Winona State University, MN	M,W
Winston-Salem State University, NC	M,W
Winthrop University, SC	M,W
Wofford College, SC	M,W
Xavier University, OH	M,W
Xavier University of Louisiana, LA	M,W
Youngstown State University, OH	M,W

Track and Field

Abilene Christian University, TX	M,W
Adelphi University, NY	M,W
Alcorn State University, MS	M,W
Alliant International University, CA	M,W
American University, DC	M,W
Anderson College, SC	M,W
Angelo State University, TX	M,W
Appalachian State University, NC	M,W
Arizona State University, AZ	M,W
Arkansas State University, AR	M,W
Ashland University, OH	M,W
Auburn University, AL	M,W
Augustana College, SD	M,W
Austin Peay State University, TN	W
Azusa Pacific University, CA	M,W
Baker University, KS	M,W
Ball State University, IN	M,W
Baylor University, TX	M,W
Belmont University, TN	M,W
Bemidji State University, MN	M,W
Benedictine College, KS	M,W
Bentley College, MA	M,W
Berry College, GA	M,W
Bethany College, KS	M,W
Bethel College, KS	M,W
Bethel College, TN	M,W
Bethune-Cookman College, FL	M,W
Biola University, CA	M,W
Black Hills State University, SD	M,W
Bloomsburg University of Pennsylvania, PA	M,W
Boise State University, ID	M,W
Boston College, MA	M,W
Boston University, MA	M,W
Bowie State University, MD	M,W
Bowling Green State University, OH	M,W
Bradley University, IL	W
Brevard College, NC	M,W
Brigham Young University, UT	M,W
California State University, Bakersfield, CA	M,W
California State University, Chico, CA	M,W
California State University, Fresno, CA	M,W
California State University, Fullerton, CA	M,W
California State University, Sacramento, CA	M,W
Campbellsville University, KY	M,W
Campbell University, NC	M,W
Carson-Newman College, TN	M,W

Cedarville University, OH	M,W
Central Connecticut State University, CT	M,W
Central Methodist University, MO	M,W
Central Michigan University, MI	M,W
Central Missouri State University, MO	M,W
Central Washington University, WA	M,W
Chadron State College, NE	M,W
Clarion University of Pennsylvania, PA	M,W
Clark Atlanta University, GA	M
Clayton State University, GA	M,W
Clemson University, SC	M,W
Cleveland State University, OH	W
Coastal Carolina University, SC	M,W
The College of William and Mary, VA	M,W
Colorado School of Mines, CO	M,W
Colorado State University, CO	M,W
Concordia University, NE	M,W
Concordia University, OR	M,W
Concordia University, St. Paul, MN	M,W
Coppin State University, MD	M,W
Cornerstone University, MI	M,W
Dakota State University, SD	M,W
Dallas Baptist University, TX	W
Davidson College, NC	M,W
Delaware State University, DE	M,W
DePaul University, IL	M,W
Dickinson State University, ND	M,W
Doane College, NE	M,W
Dordt College, IA	M,W
Drake University, IA	M,W
Duquesne University, PA	W
East Carolina University, NC	M,W
Eastern Illinois University, IL	M,W
Eastern Michigan University, MI	M,W
Eastern Washington University, WA	M,W
East Stroudsburg University of Pennsylvania, PA	M,W
East Tennessee State University, TN	M,W
Edinboro University of Pennsylvania, PA	M,W
Elon University, NC	W
Emporia State University, KS	M,W
Evangel University, MO	M,W
Fairleigh Dickinson University, Metropolitan Campus, NJ	M,W
Ferris State University, MI	M,W
Florida Atlantic University, FL	W
Florida State University, FL	M,W
Fordham University, NY	M,W
Fort Hays State University, KS	M,W
Fresno Pacific University, CA	M,W
Friends University, KS	M,W
Furman University, SC	M,W
Geneva College, PA	M,W
George Mason University, VA	M,W
Georgetown College, KY	M,W
Georgetown University, DC	M,W
Georgia Institute of Technology, GA	M,W
Georgia Southern University, GA	W
Georgia State University, GA	M,W
Glenville State College, WV	M,W
Gordon College, MA	W
Goshen College, IN	M,W
Grace College, IN	M,W

Graceland University, IA	M,W	Minnesota State University		Sam Houston State University, TX	M,W
Grambling State University, LA	M,W	Mankato, MN	M,W	San Francisco State University, CA	M,W
Grand Valley State University, MI	M,W	Minnesota State University		Seattle Pacific University, WA	M,W
Grand View College, IA	M,W	Moorhead, MN	M,W	Seton Hall University, NJ	M,W
Hampton University, VA	M,W	Minot State University, ND	M,W	Shaw University, NC	M,W
Harding University, AR	M,W	Mississippi State University, MS	M,W	Shippensburg University of	
Hastings College, NE	M,W	Missouri Southern State		Pennsylvania, PA	M,W
Hillsdale College, MI	M,W	University, MO	M,W	Shorter College, GA	M,W
Houghton College, NY	M,W	Missouri State University, MO	M,W	Slippery Rock University of	
Howard University, DC	M,W	Missouri Valley College, MO	M,W	Pennsylvania, PA	M,W
Humboldt State University, CA	M,W	Monmouth University, NJ	M,W	Sonoma State University, CA	W
Huntington University, IN	M,W	Montana State University, MT	M,W	South Carolina State University, SC	M,W
Idaho State University, ID	M,W	Morehead State University, KY	M,W	South Dakota School of Mines and	
Illinois State University, IL	M,W	Morehouse College, GA	M	Technology, SD	M,W
Indiana State University, IN	M,W	Morningside College, IA	M,W	South Dakota State University, SD	M,W
Indiana University Bloomington, IN	M,W	Morris College, SC	M,W	Southeastern Louisiana University, LA	M,W
Indiana University of		Mount Marty College, SD	M,W	Southeast Missouri State	
Pennsylvania, PA	M,W	Mount St. Mary's University, MD	M,W	University, MO	M,W
Indiana University–Purdue University		Murray State University, KY	M,W	Southern Illinois University	
Fort Wayne, IN	W	New Mexico State University, NM	W	Carbondale, IL	M,W
Inter American University of Puerto		New York Institute of Technology, NY	M,W	Southern Illinois University	
Rico, Guayama Campus, PR	M,W	Nicholls State University, LA	M,W	Edwardsville, IL	M,W
Inter American University of Puerto		Norfolk State University, VA	M,W	Southern Methodist University, TX	M,W
Rico, San Germán Campus, PR	M,W	North Carolina Agricultural and		Southern Oregon University, OR	M,W
Iona College, NY	M,W	Technical State University, NC	M,W	Southern University and Agricultural	
Iowa State University of Science and		North Carolina State University, NC	M,W	and Mechanical College, LA	M,W
Technology, IA	M,W	North Dakota State University, ND	M,W	Southern Utah University, UT	M,W
Iowa Wesleyan College, IA	M,W	Northeastern University, MA	M,W	Southwestern College, KS	M,W
James Madison University, VA	M,W	Northern Arizona University, AZ	M,W	Spring Arbor University, MI	M,W
Jamestown College, ND	M,W	Northern State University, SD	M,W	Stanford University, CA	M,W
Johnson C. Smith University, NC	M,W	Northwestern College, IA	M,W	State University of New York at	
Kansas State University, KS	M,W	Northwestern State University of		Binghamton, NY	M,W
Kent State University, OH	M,W	Louisiana, LA	M,W	Stephen F. Austin State University, TX	M,W
King College, TN	M,W	Northwest Nazarene University, ID	M,W	Sterling College, KS	M,W
Kutztown University of		Northwest University, WA	M,W	Stonehill College, MA	M,W
Pennsylvania, PA	M,W	Northwood University, MI	M,W	Stony Brook University, State	
Lake Superior State University, MI	M,W	Northwood University, Texas		University of New York, NY	M,W
Lamar University, TX	M,W	Campus, TX	M,W	Syracuse University, NY	M,W
Langston University, OK	M,W	The Ohio State University, OH	M,W	Tabor College, KS	M,W
La Salle University, PA	M,W	Ohio University, OH	M,W	Tarleton State University, TX	M,W
Lehigh University, PA	M,W	Oklahoma Baptist University, OK	M,W	Taylor University, IN	M,W
Liberty University, VA	M,W	Oklahoma State University, OK	M,W	Temple University, PA	M,W
Lincoln University, MO	M,W	Olivet Nazarene University, IL	M,W	Tennessee Technological	
Lindenwood University, MO	M,W	Oral Roberts University, OK	M,W	University, TN	W
Lock Haven University of		Park University, MO	M,W	Texas A&M University, TX	M,W
Pennsylvania, PA	M,W	The Pennsylvania State University		Texas A&M University–	
Long Island University, Brooklyn		University Park Campus, PA	M,W	Commerce, TX	M,W
Campus, NY	M,W	Pittsburg State University, KS	M,W	Texas Christian University, TX	M,W
Louisiana State University and		Pontifical Catholic University of		Texas State University-San	
Agricultural and Mechanical		Puerto Rico, PR	M,W	Marcos, TX	M,W
College, LA	M,W	Portland State University, OR	M,W	Texas Tech University, TX	M,W
Louisiana Tech University, LA	M,W	Providence College, RI	M,W	Tiffin University, OH	M,W
Loyola University Chicago, IL	M,W	Purdue University, IN	M,W	Towson University, MD	M,W
Malone College, OH	M,W	Quinnipiac University, CT	M,W	Troy University, AL	M
Manhattan College, NY	M,W	Radford University, VA	M,W	Truman State University, MO	M,W
Marist College, NY	M,W	Rice University, TX	M,W	Tuskegee University, AL	M,W
Marshall University, WV	M,W	Rider University, NJ	M,W	University at Albany, State University	
McKendree College, IL	M,W	Robert Morris University, PA	M,W	of New York, NY	M,W
Miami University, OH	M,W	Roberts Wesleyan College, NY	M,W	University at Buffalo, The State	
Michigan State University, MI	M,W	St. Ambrose University, IA	M,W	University of New York, NY	M,W
MidAmerica Nazarene University, KS	M,W	St. Cloud State University, MN	M,W	The University of Akron, OH	M,W
Middle Tennessee State		St. Francis College, NY	M,W	The University of Alabama, AL	M,W
University, TN	M,W	St. Gregory's University, OK	M,W	The University of Alabama at	
Midland Lutheran College, NE	M,W	Saint Joseph's College, IN	M,W	Birmingham, AL	W
Millersville University of		Saint Martin's College, WA	M,W	The University of Alabama in	
Pennsylvania, PA	M,W	Samford University, AL	M,W	Huntsville, AL	M,W

The University of Arizona, AZ	M,W
University of California, Berkeley, CA	M,W
University of California, Irvine, CA	M,W
University of California, Los Angeles, CA	M,W
University of California, Riverside, CA	M,W
University of California, Santa Barbara, CA	M,W
University of Central Florida, FL	W
University of Charleston, WV	M,W
University of Cincinnati, OH	M
University of Colorado at Boulder, CO	M,W
University of Connecticut, CT	M,W
University of Dayton, OH	W
University of Delaware, DE	W
University of Detroit Mercy, MI	M,W
The University of Findlay, OH	M,W
University of Florida, FL	M,W
University of Georgia, GA	M,W
University of Hawaii at Manoa, HI	W
University of Idaho, ID	M,W
University of Illinois at Chicago, IL	M,W
University of Illinois at Urbana–Champaign, IL	M,W
University of Indianapolis, IN	M,W
University of Kansas, KS	M,W
University of Louisville, KY	M,W
University of Maine, ME	M,W
University of Mary, ND	M,W
University of Maryland, Baltimore County, MD	M,W
University of Maryland, College Park, MD	M,W
University of Massachusetts Amherst, MA	M,W
University of Massachusetts Lowell, MA	M,W
The University of Memphis, TN	M,W
University of Miami, FL	M,W
University of Michigan, MI	M,W
University of Minnesota, Twin Cities Campus, MN	M,W
University of Mississippi, MS	M,W
University of Missouri–Columbia, MO	M,W
University of Missouri–Kansas City, MO	M,W
University of Nebraska at Kearney, NE	M,W
University of Nebraska–Lincoln, NE	M,W
University of Nevada, Las Vegas, NV	W
University of Nevada, Reno, NV	W
University of New Hampshire, NH	M,W
University of New Haven, CT	M,W
University of New Orleans, LA	M,W
The University of North Carolina at Asheville, NC	M,W
The University of North Carolina at Chapel Hill, NC	M,W
The University of North Carolina at Charlotte, NC	M,W
The University of North Carolina at Pembroke, NC	M
The University of North Carolina at Wilmington, NC	M,W
University of North Dakota, ND	M,W

University of Northern Colorado, CO	M,W
University of Northern Iowa, IA	M,W
University of North Florida, FL	M,W
University of North Texas, TX	M,W
University of Notre Dame, IN	M,W
University of Oklahoma, OK	M,W
University of Oregon, OR	M,W
University of Portland, OR	M,W
University of Puerto Rico, Mayagüez Campus, PR	M,W
University of Rhode Island, RI	M,W
University of Richmond, VA	W
University of Rio Grande, OH	M,W
University of St. Francis, IL	W
University of Saint Francis, IN	M,W
University of San Francisco, CA	W
University of Sioux Falls, SD	M,W
University of South Carolina, SC	M,W
The University of South Dakota, SD	M,W
University of Southern California, CA	M,W
University of Southern Mississippi, MS	M,W
University of South Florida, FL	M,W
The University of Texas at Arlington, TX	M,W
The University of Texas at Austin, TX	M,W
The University of Texas at El Paso, TX	M,W
The University of Texas at San Antonio, TX	M,W
The University of Texas–Pan American, TX	M,W
University of the Cumberlands, KY	M,W
University of the District of Columbia, DC	M,W
The University of Toledo, OH	M,W
University of Tulsa, OK	M,W
University of Utah, UT	M,W
University of Vermont, VT	M,W
University of Virginia, VA	M,W
University of Washington, WA	M,W
University of Wisconsin–Madison, WI	M,W
University of Wisconsin–Milwaukee, WI	M,W
University of Wisconsin–Parkside, WI	M,W
University of Wyoming, WY	M,W
Utah State University, UT	M,W
Utah Valley State College, UT	M,W
Vanderbilt University, TN	W
Vanguard University of Southern California, CA	M,W
Villanova University, PA	M,W
Virginia Commonwealth University, VA	M,W
Virginia Intermont College, VA	M,W
Virginia Military Institute, VA	M,W
Virginia Polytechnic Institute and State University, VA	M,W
Virginia Union University, VA	M,W
Voorhees College, SC	M,W
Wake Forest University, NC	M,W
Warner Southern College, FL	M,W
Washington State University, WA	M,W
Wayland Baptist University, TX	M,W
Wayne State College, NE	M,W
Webber International University, FL	M,W

Western Carolina University, NC	M,W
Western Illinois University, IL	M,W
Western Kentucky University, KY	M,W
Western State College of Colorado, CO	M,W
Western Washington University, WA	M,W
West Liberty State College, WV	M,W
Westmont College, CA	M,W
West Virginia University, WV	W
West Virginia Wesleyan College, WV	M,W
Wheeling Jesuit University, WV	M,W
Wichita State University, KS	M,W
William Jewell College, MO	M,W
William Penn University, IA	M,W
Winona State University, MN	W
Winthrop University, SC	M,W
Wofford College, SC	M,W
York College, NE	M,W
Youngstown State University, OH	M,W

Volleyball

Abilene Christian University, TX	W
Adelphi University, NY	W
Albertson College of Idaho, ID	W
Alcorn State University, MS	W
Alderson-Broaddus College, WV	W
Alliant International University, CA	W
American International College, MA	W
American University, DC	W
Anderson College, SC	W
Angelo State University, TX	W
Appalachian State University, NC	W
Arizona State University, AZ	W
Arkansas State University, AR	W
Arkansas Tech University, AR	W
Armstrong Atlantic State University, GA	W
Asbury College, KY	W
Ashland University, OH	W
Auburn University, AL	W
Augustana College, SD	W
Austin Peay State University, TN	W
Azusa Pacific University, CA	W
Baker University, KS	W
Ball State University, IN	M,W
Barry University, FL	W
Barton College, NC	W
Baylor University, TX	W
Belhaven College, MS	W
Bellevue University, NE	W
Belmont University, TN	W
Bemidji State University, MN	W
Benedictine College, KS	W
Bentley College, MA	W
Bethany College, KS	W
Bethel College, KS	W
Bethel College, TN	W
Bethune-Cookman College, FL	W
Biola University, CA	W
Black Hills State University, SD	W
Blessing-Rieman College of Nursing, IL	M,W
Bloomfield College, NJ	W
Bluefield State College, WV	W
Boise State University, ID	W
Boston College, MA	W

Bowie State University, MD	W	
Bowling Green State University, OH	W	
Bradley University, IL	W	
Brenau University, GA	W	
Brevard College, NC	W	
Brewton-Parker College, GA	W	
Brigham Young University, UT	M,W	
Brigham Young University–Hawaii, HI	W	
Bryan College, TN	W	
Butler University, IN	W	
California Baptist University, CA	M,W	
California State University, Bakersfield, CA	W	
California State University, Dominguez Hills, CA	W	
California State University, Fresno, CA	W	
California State University, Fullerton, CA	W	
California State University, Sacramento, CA	W	
California State University, San Bernardino, CA	W	
Cameron University, OK	W	
Campbellsville University, KY	W	
Campbell University, NC	W	
Canisius College, NY	W	
Carroll College, MT	W	
Carson-Newman College, TN	W	
Catawba College, NC	W	
Cedarville University, OH	W	
Centenary College of Louisiana, LA	W	
Central Christian College of Kansas, KS	W	
Central Connecticut State University, CT	W	
Central Methodist University, MO	W	
Central Michigan University, MI	W	
Central Missouri State University, MO	W	
Central Washington University, WA	W	
Chadron State College, NE	W	
Chaminade University of Honolulu, HI	W	
Christian Brothers University, TN	W	
Christian Heritage College, CA	W	
Clarion University of Pennsylvania, PA	W	
Clemson University, SC	W	
Cleveland State University, OH	W	
Coastal Carolina University, SC	W	
Colgate University, NY	W	
College of Charleston, SC	W	
College of Saint Mary, NE	W	
The College of Saint Rose, NY	W	
College of the Ozarks, MO	W	
The College of William and Mary, VA	W	
Colorado Christian University, CO	W	
Colorado School of Mines, CO	W	
Colorado State University, CO	W	
Colorado State University-Pueblo, CO	W	
Columbia College, MO	W	
Columbia College, SC	W	
Concordia University, CA	W	
Concordia University, MI	W	
Concordia University, NE	W	
Concordia University, OR	W	
Concordia University, St. Paul, MN	W	
Converse College, SC	W	
Coppin State University, MD	W	
Corban College, OR	W	
Cornerstone University, MI	W	
Creighton University, NE	W	
Culver-Stockton College, MO	W	
Daemen College, NY	W	
Dakota State University, SD	W	
Dallas Baptist University, TX	W	
Davidson College, NC	W	
Davis & Elkins College, WV	W	
Delaware State University, DE	W	
DePaul University, IL	W	
Dickinson State University, ND	W	
Dillard University, LA	W	
Doane College, NE	W	
Dominican College, NY	W	
Dominican University of California, CA	W	
Dordt College, IA	W	
Dowling College, NY	W	
Drake University, IA	W	
Drexel University, PA	W	
Duke University, NC	W	
Duquesne University, PA	W	
East Carolina University, NC	W	
Eastern Illinois University, IL	W	
Eastern Michigan University, MI	W	
Eastern Washington University, WA	W	
East Stroudsburg University of Pennsylvania, PA	M,W	
East Tennessee State University, TN	W	
Eckerd College, FL	W	
Edinboro University of Pennsylvania, PA	W	
Elon University, NC	W	
Embry-Riddle Aeronautical University, AZ	W	
Embry-Riddle Aeronautical University, FL	W	
Emporia State University, KS	W	
Evangel University, MO	W	
The Evergreen State College, WA	W	
Fairfield University, CT	W	
Fairleigh Dickinson University, Metropolitan Campus, NJ	W	
Faulkner University, AL	W	
Ferris State University, MI	W	
Flagler College, FL	W	
Florida Atlantic University, FL	W	
Florida College, FL	W	
Florida Gulf Coast University, FL	W	
Florida Institute of Technology, FL	W	
Florida Southern College, FL	W	
Florida State University, FL	W	
Fordham University, NY	W	
Fort Hays State University, KS	W	
Fort Lewis College, CO	W	
Francis Marion University, SC	W	
Franklin Pierce College, NH	W	
Freed-Hardeman University, TN	W	
Fresno Pacific University, CA	W	
Friends University, KS	W	
Furman University, SC	W	
Gannon University, PA	W	
Geneva College, PA	W	
George Mason University, VA	M,W	
Georgetown College, KY	W	
Georgetown University, DC	W	
The George Washington University, DC	W	
Georgia Institute of Technology, GA	W	
Georgian Court University, NJ	W	
Georgia Southern University, GA	W	
Georgia State University, GA	W	
Glenville State College, WV	W	
Goldey-Beacom College, DE	W	
Gonzaga University, WA	W	
Goshen College, IN	W	
Grace College, IN	W	
Graceland University, IA	M,W	
Grambling State University, LA	W	
Grand Canyon University, AZ	W	
Grand Valley State University, MI	W	
Grand View College, IA	W	
Hampton University, VA	W	
Hannibal-LaGrange College, MO	W	
Harding University, AR	W	
Hastings College, NE	W	
Hawai'i Pacific University, HI	W	
Hillsdale College, MI	W	
Hofstra University, NY	W	
Holy Names University, CA	M,W	
Houghton College, NY	W	
Houston Baptist University, TX	W	
Howard University, DC	W	
Humboldt State University, CA	W	
Huntington University, IN	W	
Idaho State University, ID	W	
Illinois State University, IL	W	
Indiana State University, IN	W	
Indiana University Bloomington, IN	W	
Indiana University of Pennsylvania, PA	W	
Indiana University–Purdue University Fort Wayne, IN	M,W	
Indiana University–Purdue University Indianapolis, IN	W	
Indiana University Southeast, IN	W	
Inter American University of Puerto Rico, Guayama Campus, PR	M,W	
Inter American University of Puerto Rico, San Germán Campus, PR	M,W	
Iona College, NY	W	
Iowa State University of Science and Technology, IA	W	
Iowa Wesleyan College, IA	W	
Jacksonville State University, AL	W	
James Madison University, VA	W	
Jamestown College, ND	W	
John Brown University, AR	W	
Johnson C. Smith University, NC	W	
Judson College, AL	W	
Kansas State University, KS	W	
Kent State University, OH	W	
Kentucky Wesleyan College, KY	W	
King College, TN	W	
Kutztown University of Pennsylvania, PA	W	
Lake Superior State University, MI	W	
Lamar University, TX	W	

Lambuth University, TN	W	Molloy College, NY	W	Post University, CT	W
La Salle University, PA	W	Montana State University, MT	W	Providence College, RI	W
Lee University, TN	W	Montana State University–		Purdue University, IN	W
Lehigh University, PA	W	Billings, MT	W	Quincy University, IL	M,W
Le Moyne College, NY	W	Montana Tech of The University of		Quinnipiac University, CT	W
LeMoyne-Owen College, TN	W	Montana, MT	W	Radford University, VA	W
Lenoir-Rhyne College, NC	W	Montreat College, NC	W	Regis University, CO	W
Lesley University, MA	M,W	Morehead State University, KY	W	Research College of Nursing, MO	W
Lewis-Clark State College, ID	W	Morningside College, IA	W	Rice University, TX	W
Liberty University, VA	W	Morris College, SC	W	Rider University, NJ	W
Limestone College, SC	W	Mount Marty College, SD	W	Robert Morris College, IL	W
Lincoln Memorial University, TN	W	Mount Olive College, NC	M,W	Robert Morris University, PA	W
Lindenwood University, MO	M,W	Mount Vernon Nazarene		Roberts Wesleyan College, NY	W
Lipscomb University, TN	W	University, OH	W	Rochester College, MI	W
Lock Haven University of		Murray State University, KY	W	Rockhurst University, MO	W
Pennsylvania, PA	W	New Mexico Highlands		Rollins College, FL	W
Long Island University, Brooklyn		University, NM	W	St. Ambrose University, IA	M,W
Campus, NY	W	New Mexico State University, NM	W	St. Andrews Presbyterian College, NC	W
Louisiana State University and		New York Institute of Technology, NY	W	St. Bonaventure University, NY	W
Agricultural and Mechanical		Niagara University, NY	W	St. Cloud State University, MN	W
College, LA	W	Nicholls State University, LA	W	St. Edward's University, TX	W
Louisiana Tech University, LA	W	Norfolk State University, VA	W	St. Francis College, NY	W
Loyola Marymount University, CA	W	North Carolina Agricultural and		St. John's University, NY	W
Loyola University Chicago, IL	M,W	Technical State University, NC	W	Saint Joseph's College, IN	W
Lubbock Christian University, TX	W	North Carolina State University, NC	W	Saint Leo University, FL	W
Lyon College, AR	W	North Dakota State University, ND	W	Saint Louis University, MO	W
Malone College, OH	W	Northeastern University, MA	W	Saint Martin's College, WA	W
Manhattan College, NY	W	Northern Arizona University, AZ	W	Saint Mary's College of	
Marist College, NY	W	Northern Illinois University, IL	W	California, CA	W
Marshall University, WV	W	Northern Kentucky University, KY	W	St. Mary's University of San	
Mars Hill College, NC	W	Northern State University, SD	W	Antonio, TX	W
Martin Methodist College, TN	W	North Greenville College, SC	W	St. Thomas University, FL	W
McKendree College, IL	W	Northwestern College, IA	W	Saint Vincent College, PA	W
Mercer University, GA	W	Northwestern State University of		Saint Xavier University, IL	W
Mercy College, NY	W	Louisiana, LA	W	Samford University, AL	W
Mercyhurst College, PA	M,W	Northwestern University, IL	W	Sam Houston State University, TX	W
Merrimack College, MA	W	Northwest Nazarene University, ID	W	San Francisco State University, CA	W
Mesa State College, CO	W	Northwest University, WA	W	San Jose State University, CA	W
Metropolitan State College of		Northwood University, MI	W	Seattle Pacific University, WA	W
Denver, CO	W	Northwood University, Florida		Seton Hall University, NJ	W
Miami University, OH	W	Campus, FL	W	Seton Hill University, PA	W
Michigan State University, MI	W	Nova Southeastern University, FL	W	Shaw University, NC	W
Michigan Technological		Nyack College, NY	W	Shepherd University, WV	W
University, MI	W	Oakland City University, IN	W	Shippensburg University of	
MidAmerica Nazarene University, KS	W	Oakland University, MI	W	Pennsylvania, PA	W
Mid-Continent University, KY	W	The Ohio State University, OH	M,W	Shorter College, GA	W
Middle Tennessee State		Ohio University, OH	W	Slippery Rock University of	
University, TN	W	Ohio Valley University, WV	W	Pennsylvania, PA	W
Midland Lutheran College, NE	W	Oklahoma Panhandle State		Sonoma State University, CA	W
Midwestern State University, TX	W	University, OK	W	South Carolina State University, SC	W
Millersville University of		Oklahoma Wesleyan University, OK	W	South Dakota School of Mines and	
Pennsylvania, PA	W	Olivet Nazarene University, IL	W	Technology, SD	W
Milligan College, TN	W	Oral Roberts University, OK	W	South Dakota State University, SD	W
Minnesota State University		Oregon State University, OR	W	Southeastern Louisiana University, LA	W
Mankato, MN	W	Ouachita Baptist University, AR	W	Southeastern Oklahoma State	
Minnesota State University		Park University, MO	M,W	University, OK	W
Moorhead, MN	W	The Pennsylvania State University		Southeast Missouri State	
Minot State University, ND	W	University Park Campus, PA	M,W	University, MO	W
Mississippi State University, MS	W	Pepperdine University, CA	M,W	Southern Arkansas University–	
Mississippi University for		Peru State College, NE	W	Magnolia, AR	W
Women, MS	W	Pfeiffer University, NC	W	Southern Illinois University	
Missouri Baptist University, MO	M,W	Philadelphia University, PA	W	Carbondale, IL	W
Missouri Southern State		Pikeville College, KY	W	Southern Illinois University	
University, MO	W	Pittsburg State University, KS	W	Edwardsville, IL	W
Missouri State University, MO	W	Point Park University, PA	W	Southern Methodist University, TX	W
Missouri Valley College, MO	M,W	Portland State University, OR	W		

Southern New Hampshire University, NH	W	
Southern Oregon University, OR	W	
Southern University and Agricultural and Mechanical College, LA	W	
Southern Wesleyan University, SC	W	
Southwest Baptist University, MO	W	
Southwestern College, KS	W	
Southwest Minnesota State University, MN	W	
Spring Arbor University, MI	W	
Spring Hill College, AL	W	
Stanford University, CA	M,W	
State University of New York at Binghamton, NY	W	
Stephen F. Austin State University, TX	W	
Sterling College, KS	W	
Stetson University, FL	W	
Stonehill College, MA	W	
Stony Brook University, State University of New York, NY	W	
Syracuse University, NY	W	
Tabor College, KS	W	
Tarleton State University, TX	W	
Taylor University, IN	W	
Temple University, PA	W	
Tennessee Technological University, TN	W	
Tennessee Wesleyan College, TN	W	
Texas A&M University, TX	W	
Texas A&M University–Commerce, TX	W	
Texas Christian University, TX	W	
Texas State University-San Marcos, TX	W	
Texas Tech University, TX	W	
Tiffin University, OH	W	
Towson University, MD	W	
Trevecca Nazarene University, TN	W	
Trinity International University, IL	W	
Troy University, AL	W	
Truman State University, MO	W	
Tusculum College, TN	W	
Tuskegee University, AL	W	
Union College, KY	W	
Union University, TN	W	
Unity College, ME	W	
University at Albany, State University of New York, NY	W	
University at Buffalo, The State University of New York, NY	W	
The University of Akron, OH	W	
The University of Alabama, AL	W	
The University of Alabama at Birmingham, AL	W	
The University of Alabama in Huntsville, AL	W	
University of Alaska Anchorage, AK	W	
University of Alaska Fairbanks, AK	W	
The University of Arizona, AZ	W	
University of Arkansas at Fort Smith, AR	W	
University of Arkansas at Pine Bluff, AR	W	
University of Bridgeport, CT	W	
University of California, Berkeley, CA	W	

University of California, Irvine, CA	M,W	
University of California, Los Angeles, CA	M,W	
University of California, Riverside, CA	W	
University of California, Santa Barbara, CA	M,W	
University of Central Florida, FL	W	
University of Charleston, WV	W	
University of Cincinnati, OH	W	
University of Colorado at Boulder, CO	W	
University of Colorado at Colorado Springs, CO	W	
University of Connecticut, CT	W	
University of Dayton, OH	W	
University of Delaware, DE	W	
University of Denver, CO	W	
University of Evansville, IN	W	
The University of Findlay, OH	M,W	
University of Florida, FL	W	
University of Georgia, GA	W	
University of Great Falls, MT	W	
University of Hartford, CT	W	
University of Hawaii at Hilo, HI	W	
University of Hawaii at Manoa, HI	M,W	
University of Idaho, ID	W	
University of Illinois at Chicago, IL	W	
University of Illinois at Springfield, IL	W	
University of Illinois at Urbana–Champaign, IL	W	
University of Indianapolis, IN	W	
University of Kansas, KS	W	
University of Louisville, KY	W	
University of Maine, ME	W	
University of Mary, ND	W	
University of Maryland, Baltimore County, MD	W	
University of Maryland, College Park, MD	W	
University of Massachusetts Amherst, MA	W	
University of Massachusetts Lowell, MA	W	
The University of Memphis, TN	W	
University of Miami, FL	W	
University of Michigan, MI	W	
University of Michigan–Dearborn, MI	W	
University of Minnesota, Twin Cities Campus, MN	W	
University of Mississippi, MS	W	
University of Missouri–Columbia, MO	W	
University of Missouri–Kansas City, MO	W	
University of Missouri–St. Louis, MO	W	
The University of Montana–Western, MT	W	
University of Nebraska at Kearney, NE	W	
University of Nebraska at Omaha, NE	W	
University of Nebraska–Lincoln, NE	W	
University of Nevada, Las Vegas, NV	W	
University of Nevada, Reno, NV	W	
University of New Hampshire, NH	W	
University of New Haven, CT	M,W	
University of New Orleans, LA	W	
University of North Alabama, AL	W	

The University of North Carolina at Asheville, NC	W	
The University of North Carolina at Chapel Hill, NC	W	
The University of North Carolina at Charlotte, NC	W	
The University of North Carolina at Greensboro, NC	W	
The University of North Carolina at Pembroke, NC	W	
The University of North Carolina at Wilmington, NC	W	
University of North Dakota, ND	W	
University of Northern Colorado, CO	W	
University of Northern Iowa, IA	W	
University of North Florida, FL	W	
University of North Texas, TX	W	
University of Notre Dame, IN	W	
University of Oklahoma, OK	W	
University of Oregon, OR	W	
University of Portland, OR	W	
University of Puerto Rico, Mayagüez Campus, PR	M,W	
University of Rhode Island, RI	W	
University of Rio Grande, OH	W	
University of St. Francis, IL	W	
University of Saint Francis, IN	W	
University of San Diego, CA	W	
University of San Francisco, CA	W	
University of Sioux Falls, SD	W	
University of South Carolina, SC	W	
University of South Carolina Upstate, SC	W	
The University of South Dakota, SD	W	
University of Southern California, CA	M,W	
University of Southern Indiana, IN	W	
University of Southern Mississippi, MS	W	
University of South Florida, FL	W	
The University of Tampa, FL	W	
The University of Tennessee at Chattanooga, TN	W	
The University of Tennessee at Martin, TN	W	
The University of Texas at Arlington, TX	W	
The University of Texas at Austin, TX	W	
The University of Texas at Brownsville, TX	W	
The University of Texas at El Paso, TX	W	
The University of Texas at San Antonio, TX	W	
The University of Texas–Pan American, TX	W	
University of the Cumberlands, KY	W	
University of the District of Columbia, DC	W	
University of the Incarnate Word, TX	W	
University of the Pacific, CA	M,W	
The University of Toledo, OH	W	
University of Tulsa, OK	W	
University of Utah, UT	W	
University of Virginia, VA	W	
The University of Virginia's College at Wise, VA	W	

University of Washington, WA	W
University of West Georgia, GA	W
University of Wisconsin–Green Bay, WI	W
University of Wisconsin–Madison, WI	W
University of Wisconsin–Milwaukee, WI	W
University of Wisconsin–Parkside, WI	W
University of Wyoming, WY	W
Urbana University, OH	W
Ursuline College, OH	W
Utah State University, UT	W
Utah Valley State College, UT	W
Valdosta State University, GA	W
Valley City State University, ND	W
Valparaiso University, IN	W
Vanguard University of Southern California, CA	W
Villanova University, PA	W
Virginia Intermont College, VA	W
Virginia Polytechnic Institute and State University, VA	W
Virginia Union University, VA	W
Voorhees College, SC	W
Wake Forest University, NC	W
Waldorf College, IA	W
Warner Pacific College, OR	W
Warner Southern College, FL	W
Washington State University, WA	W
Wayland Baptist University, TX	W
Wayne State College, NE	W
Wayne State University, MI	W
Western Carolina University, NC	W
Western Illinois University, IL	W
Western Kentucky University, KY	W
Western New Mexico University, NM	W
Western State College of Colorado, CO	W
Western Washington University, WA	W
West Liberty State College, WV	W
Westmont College, CA	W
West Texas A&M University, TX	W
West Virginia University, WV	W
West Virginia Wesleyan College, WV	W
Wheeling Jesuit University, WV	W
Whitman College, WA	M,W
Wichita State University, KS	W
William Jewell College, MO	W
William Penn University, IA	W
Williams Baptist College, AR	W
William Woods University, MO	M,W
Wilmington College, DE	W
Wingate University, NC	W
Winona State University, MN	W
Winston-Salem State University, NC	W
Winthrop University, SC	W
Wofford College, SC	W
Xavier University, OH	W
Youngstown State University, OH	W

Water Polo

Brigham Young University–Hawaii, HI	M
California Baptist University, CA	M,W
California State University, Bakersfield, CA	W

Chaminade University of Honolulu, HI	M
Colorado State University, CO	W
Fordham University, NY	M
The George Washington University, DC	M
Indiana University Bloomington, IN	W
Iona College, NY	W
Lindenwood University, MO	M,W
Loyola Marymount University, CA	M,W
Marist College, NY	W
Mercyhurst College, PA	M,W
Pepperdine University, CA	M
St. Francis College, NY	M,W
San Jose State University, CA	W
Slippery Rock University of Pennsylvania, PA	M,W
Stanford University, CA	M,W
University of California, Berkeley, CA	M,W
University of California, Irvine, CA	M
University of California, Los Angeles, CA	M,W
University of California, Santa Barbara, CA	M,W
University of Hawaii at Manoa, HI	W
University of Maryland, College Park, MD	W
University of Puerto Rico, Mayagüez Campus, PR	M
University of Southern California, CA	M,W
University of the Pacific, CA	M,W

Weight Lifting

Coppin State University, MD	M,W
Inter American University of Puerto Rico, Guayama Campus, PR	M,W
Inter American University of Puerto Rico, San Germán Campus, PR	M
University of Puerto Rico, Mayagüez Campus, PR	M

Wrestling

American University, DC	M
Anderson College, SC	M
Appalachian State University, NC	M
Arizona State University, AZ	M
Ashland University, OH	M
Augustana College, SD	M
Bloomsburg University of Pennsylvania, PA	M
Boise State University, ID	M
Boston University, MA	M
California State University, Bakersfield, CA	M
California State University, Fresno, CA	M
California State University, Fullerton, CA	M
Campbellsville University, KY	M
Campbell University, NC	M
Carson-Newman College, TN	M
Central Michigan University, MI	M
Central Missouri State University, MO	M
Central Washington University, WA	M
Chadron State College, NE	M
Clarion University of Pennsylvania, PA	M

Cleveland State University, OH	M
Colorado School of Mines, CO	M
Coppin State University, MD	M
Davidson College, NC	M
Delaware State University, DE	M
Dickinson State University, ND	M
Drexel University, PA	M
Duquesne University, PA	M
Eastern Illinois University, IL	M
Eastern Michigan University, MI	M
East Stroudsburg University of Pennsylvania, PA	M
Edinboro University of Pennsylvania, PA	M
Embry-Riddle Aeronautical University, AZ	M
Fort Hays State University, KS	M
Gannon University, PA	M
George Mason University, VA	M
Hofstra University, NY	M
Indiana University Bloomington, IN	M
Iowa State University of Science and Technology, IA	M
Jamestown College, ND	M
Kent State University, OH	M
King College, TN	M
Kutztown University of Pennsylvania, PA	M
Lehigh University, PA	M
Limestone College, SC	M
Lindenwood University, MO	M
Lock Haven University of Pennsylvania, PA	M
McKendree College, IL	M
Mercyhurst College, PA	M
Michigan State University, MI	M
Millersville University of Pennsylvania, PA	M
Minnesota State University Mankato, MN	M
Minnesota State University Moorhead, MN	M
Missouri Baptist University, MO	M
Missouri Valley College, MO	M,W
Morningside College, IA	M
North Carolina State University, NC	M
North Dakota State University, ND	M
Northern Illinois University, IL	M
Northern State University, SD	M
Northwestern College, IA	M
Northwestern University, IL	M
The Ohio State University, OH	M
Ohio University, OH	M
Oklahoma State University, OK	M
Old Dominion University, VA	M
Oregon State University, OR	M
The Pennsylvania State University University Park Campus, PA	M
Portland State University, OR	M
Purdue University, IN	M
Rider University, NJ	M
St. Cloud State University, MN	M
San Francisco State University, CA	M
Shippensburg University of Pennsylvania, PA	M

Slippery Rock University of Pennsylvania, PA — M
South Dakota State University, SD — M
Southern Connecticut State University, CT — M
Southern Illinois University Edwardsville, IL — M
Southern Oregon University, OR — M
Southwest Minnesota State University, MN — M
Stanford University, CA — M
State University of New York at Binghamton, NY — M
Truman State University, MO — M
University at Buffalo, The State University of New York, NY — M
The University of Findlay, OH — M
University of Great Falls, MT — M
University of Illinois at Urbana–Champaign, IL — M
University of Indianapolis, IN — M
University of Mary, ND — M

University of Maryland, College Park, MD — M
University of Massachusetts Lowell, MA — M
University of Michigan, MI — M
University of Minnesota, Twin Cities Campus, MN — M
University of Missouri–Columbia, MO — M
University of Nebraska at Kearney, NE — M
University of Nebraska at Omaha, NE — M
University of Nebraska–Lincoln, NE — M
The University of North Carolina at Chapel Hill, NC — M
The University of North Carolina at Greensboro, NC — M
The University of North Carolina at Pembroke, NC — M
University of Northern Colorado, CO — M
University of Northern Iowa, IA — M
University of Oklahoma, OK — M
University of Oregon, OR — M

University of Pittsburgh at Johnstown, PA — M
University of Puerto Rico, Mayagüez Campus, PR — M
The University of Tennessee at Chattanooga, TN — M
University of the Cumberlands, KY — M,W
University of Virginia, VA — M
University of Wisconsin–Madison, WI — M
University of Wisconsin–Parkside, WI — M
University of Wyoming, WY — M
Utah Valley State College, UT — M
Virginia Military Institute, VA — M
Virginia Polytechnic Institute and State University, VA — M
Waldorf College, IA — M
Western State College of Colorado, CO — M
West Liberty State College, WV — M
West Virginia University, WV — M
William Penn University, IA — M

Co-Op Programs

Adrian College, MI
Albertson College of Idaho, ID
Alcorn State University, MS
Alfred University, NY
American University, DC
American University of Puerto Rico, PR
Anderson College, SC
Andrews University, MI
Anna Maria College, MA
Antioch College, OH
Antioch University McGregor, OH
Aquinas College, TN
Arcadia University, PA
Arizona State University, AZ
Arkansas State University, AR
Armstrong Atlantic State University, GA
Art Academy of Cincinnati, OH
Athens State University, AL
Atlantic Union College, MA
Auburn University, AL
Auburn University Montgomery, AL
Augsburg College, MN
Augustana College, SD
Augusta State University, GA
Azusa Pacific University, CA
Ball State University, IN
Barton College, NC
Bastyr University, WA
Bates College, ME
Becker College, MA
Bellevue University, NE
Belmont Abbey College, NC
Belmont University, TN
Bemidji State University, MN
Benedictine College, KS
Bennington College, VT
Berry College, GA
Bethune-Cookman College, FL
Beulah Heights Bible College, GA
Biola University, CA
Black Hills State University, SD
Bloomfield College, NJ
Bloomsburg University of Pennsylvania, PA
Boise State University, ID
Boston University, MA
Bowie State University, MD
Bowling Green State University, OH
Bradley University, IL
Brenau University, GA
Brewton-Parker College, GA
Brigham Young University, UT
Brigham Young University–Hawaii, HI
Burlington College, VT
Butler University, IN
Caldwell College, NJ
California Institute of the Arts, CA
California Lutheran University, CA

California State University, Bakersfield, CA
California State University, Chico, CA
California State University, Dominguez Hills, CA
California State University, East Bay, CA
California State University, Fresno, CA
California State University, Fullerton, CA
California State University, Sacramento, CA
California State University, San Bernardino, CA
California State University, Stanislaus, CA
Campbell University, NC
Capitol College, MD
Carnegie Mellon University, PA
Carroll College, MT
Case Western Reserve University, OH
Castleton State College, VT
Cazenovia College, NY
Central Christian College of Kansas, KS
Central Connecticut State University, CT
Central Missouri State University, MO
Central Washington University, WA
Chadron State College, NE
Champlain College, VT
Chapman University, CA
Chatham College, PA
Chester College of New England, NH
Chestnut Hill College, PA
Christendom College, VA
Christopher Newport University, VA
City College of the City University of New York, NY
Clark Atlanta University, GA
Clarke College, IA
Clarkson University, NY
Clayton State University, GA
Cleary University, MI
Clemson University, SC
Cleveland State University, OH
Coastal Carolina University, SC
College for Creative Studies, MI
College Misericordia, PA
College of Charleston, SC
College of Mount St. Joseph, OH
The College of New Rochelle, NY
College of Santa Fe, NM
College of Staten Island of the City University of New York, NY
College of the Atlantic, ME
College of the Ozarks, MO
Colorado Christian University, CO
Colorado School of Mines, CO
Colorado State University, CO
Colorado State University-Pueblo, CO
Columbia College, MO
Columbia International University, SC
Columbus State University, GA

Concordia College, MN
Concordia University, NE
Coppin State University, MD
Cornell University, NY
The Culinary Institute of America, NY
Daemen College, NY
Dakota State University, SD
David N. Myers University, OH
Davis & Elkins College, WV
Defiance College, OH
Delaware State University, DE
Delaware Valley College, PA
Denison University, OH
DePaul University, IL
Dickinson State University, ND
Dillard University, LA
Doane College, NE
Dominican College, NY
Dowling College, NY
Drake University, IA
Drexel University, PA
East Carolina University, NC
Eastern Michigan University, MI
Eastern Oregon University, OR
Eastern Washington University, WA
East Tennessee State University, TN
Eckerd College, FL
Elmhurst College, IL
Embry-Riddle Aeronautical University, AZ
Embry-Riddle Aeronautical University, FL
Embry-Riddle Aeronautical University, Extended Campus, FL
Emory & Henry College, VA
Eugene Bible College, OR
Eureka College, IL
The Evergreen State College, WA
Fairleigh Dickinson University, College at Florham, NJ
Fairleigh Dickinson University, Metropolitan Campus, NJ
Fashion Institute of Technology, NY
Ferris State University, MI
Ferrum College, VA
Five Towns College, NY
Florida Atlantic University, FL
Florida Gulf Coast University, FL
Florida Institute of Technology, FL
Florida Metropolitan University–Pinellas Campus, FL
Florida Metropolitan University–Tampa Campus, FL
Florida State University, FL
Fort Lewis College, CO
Franklin College, IN
Freed-Hardeman University, TN
Fresno Pacific University, CA
Friends University, KS

Gallaudet University, DC
Gannon University, PA
Geneva College, PA
George Mason University, VA
Georgetown College, KY
The George Washington University, DC
Georgia Institute of Technology, GA
Georgia Southern University, GA
Georgia State University, GA
Glenville State College, WV
Goldey-Beacom College, DE
Gordon College, MA
Grace College, IN
Graceland University, IA
Grace University, NE
Grambling State University, LA
Grand Canyon University, AZ
Grand Valley State University, MI
Grand View College, IA
Green Mountain College, VT
Greenville College, IL
Guilford College, NC
Gustavus Adolphus College, MN
Gwynedd-Mercy College, PA
Hampton University, VA
Hannibal-LaGrange College, MO
Harding University, AR
Hawai'i Pacific University, HI
Hendrix College, AR
Heritage University, WA
Hilbert College, NY
Howard University, DC
Humboldt State University, CA
Humphreys College, CA
Husson College, ME
Illinois State University, IL
Indiana State University, IN
Indiana University Bloomington, IN
Indiana University East, IN
Indiana University Northwest, IN
Indiana University of Pennsylvania, PA
Indiana University–Purdue University Fort
  Wayne, IN
Indiana University–Purdue University
  Indianapolis, IN
Inter American University of Puerto Rico,
  San Germán Campus, PR
International College, FL
Iowa State University of Science and
  Technology, IA
Jacksonville State University, AL
Jamestown College, ND
John Jay College of Criminal Justice of the
  City University of New York, NY
Johnson & Wales University, RI
Johnson Bible College, TN
Johnson C. Smith University, NC
Kansas City Art Institute, MO
Kansas State University, KS
Kean University, NJ
Keene State College, NH
Kennesaw State University, GA
Kent State University, OH
Kentucky Christian University, KY
Kettering University, MI
Keuka College, NY

Laboratory Institute of Merchandising, NY
Lake Erie College, OH
Lake Superior State University, MI
Lamar University, TX
Langston University, OK
La Salle University, PA
Lasell College, MA
Laura and Alvin Siegal College of Judaic
  Studies, OH
Lawrence Technological University, MI
Lehigh University, PA
Lehman College of the City University of
  New York, NY
LeMoyne-Owen College, TN
Lenoir-Rhyne College, NC
LeTourneau University, TX
Lewis-Clark State College, ID
Lexington College, IL
Life Pacific College, CA
Life University, GA
Lincoln University, MO
Lincoln University, PA
Lindenwood University, MO
Lock Haven University of Pennsylvania, PA
Long Island University, Brooklyn
  Campus, NY
Loras College, IA
Louisiana State University and Agricultural
  and Mechanical College, LA
Louisiana Tech University, LA
Lourdes College, OH
Loyola Marymount University, CA
Luther Rice Bible College and
  Seminary, GA
Lynn University, FL
Macon State College, GA
Magdalen College, NH
Maharishi University of Management, IA
Malone College, OH
Manhattan College, NY
Marian College of Fond du Lac, WI
Marist College, NY
Marshall University, WV
Mars Hill College, NC
Maryville University of Saint Louis, MO
Massachusetts Institute of Technology, MA
Massachusetts Maritime Academy, MA
Medgar Evers College of the City
  University of New York, NY
Menlo College, CA
Mercer University, GA
Mercy College, NY
Mercyhurst College, PA
Meredith College, NC
Merrimack College, MA
Mesa State College, CO
Messenger College, MO
Methodist College, NC
Metropolitan State College of Denver, CO
Miami University, OH
Michigan State University, MI
Michigan Technological University, MI
Middle Tennessee State University, TN
Midland Lutheran College, NE
Millersville University of Pennsylvania, PA
Milligan College, TN

Millsaps College, MS
Milwaukee Institute of Art and Design, WI
Minot State University, ND
Mississippi College, MS
Mississippi State University, MS
Mississippi University for Women, MS
Missouri Southern State University, MO
Missouri State University, MO
Missouri Valley College, MO
Mitchell College, CT
Molloy College, NY
Monmouth University, NJ
Montana State University–Billings, MT
Montana Tech of The University of
  Montana, MT
Montclair State University, NJ
Montreat College, NC
Morehead State University, KY
Morehouse College, GA
Morris College, SC
Mountain State University, WV
Mount Holyoke College, MA
Mount Ida College, MA
Mount Marty College, SD
Mount Olive College, NC
Mount Saint Mary College, NY
Mount Union College, OH
Mount Vernon Nazarene University, OH
Murray State University, KY
Naropa University, CO
The National Hispanic University, CA
Nazareth College of Rochester, NY
Neumann College, PA
New Jersey City University, NJ
New Jersey Institute of Technology, NJ
New Mexico Highlands University, NM
New Mexico Institute of Mining and
  Technology, NM
New Mexico State University, NM
New York Institute of Technology, NY
New York University, NY
Niagara University, NY
Nicholls State University, LA
Nichols College, MA
Norfolk State University, VA
North Carolina Agricultural and Technical
  State University, NC
North Carolina State University, NC
North Central College, IL
North Central University, MN
North Dakota State University, ND
Northeastern Illinois University, IL
Northeastern University, MA
Northern Arizona University, AZ
Northern Illinois University, IL
Northern Kentucky University, KY
Northern State University, SD
Northland College, WI
Northwestern State University of
  Louisiana, LA
Northwestern University, IL
Northwest Nazarene University, ID
Northwest University, WA
Northwood University, MI
Nova Southeastern University, FL
Oakland University, MI

Oglala Lakota College, SD
Oglethorpe University, GA
Ohio Northern University, OH
The Ohio State University, OH
Ohio University, OH
Oklahoma Baptist University, OK
Oklahoma City University, OK
Oklahoma Panhandle State University, OK
Oklahoma State University, OK
Oklahoma Wesleyan University, OK
Old Dominion University, VA
Olivet College, MI
Oregon State University, OR
Otis College of Art and Design, CA
Ouachita Baptist University, AR
Pacific Lutheran University, WA
Pacific Union College, CA
Palm Beach Atlantic University, FL
Paul Smith's College of Arts and
  Sciences, NY
Peirce College, PA
Pennsylvania College of Technology, PA
The Pennsylvania State University Abington
  College, PA
The Pennsylvania State University Altoona
  College, PA
The Pennsylvania State University at Erie,
  The Behrend College, PA
The Pennsylvania State University Berks
  Campus of the Berks–Lehigh Valley
  College, PA
The Pennsylvania State University
  Harrisburg Campus of the Capital
  College, PA
The Pennsylvania State University, Lehigh
  Valley Campus of the Berks-Lehigh Valley
  College, PA
The Pennsylvania State University
  Schuylkill Campus of the Capital
  College, PA
The Pennsylvania State University
  University Park Campus, PA
Peru State College, NE
Pfeiffer University, NC
Philadelphia University, PA
Piedmont College, GA
Pittsburg State University, KS
Pitzer College, CA
Polytechnic University, Brooklyn
  Campus, NY
Pontifical Catholic University of Puerto
  Rico, PR
Portland State University, OR
Post University, CT
Presentation College, SD
Providence College, RI
Purdue University, IN
Purdue University Calumet, IN
Ramapo College of New Jersey, NJ
Reed College, OR
Reformed Bible College, MI
Regis University, CO
Reinhardt College, GA
Rensselaer Polytechnic Institute, NY
Rider University, NJ
Robert Morris College, IL

Robert Morris University, PA
Roberts Wesleyan College, NY
Rochester Institute of Technology, NY
Rockhurst University, MO
Rocky Mountain College of Art &
  Design, CO
Roger Williams University, RI
Rose-Hulman Institute of Technology, IN
Russell Sage College, NY
Rust College, MS
Rutgers, The State University of New
  Jersey, Camden, NJ
Rutgers, The State University of New
  Jersey, Newark, NJ
Rutgers, The State University of New
  Jersey, New Brunswick/Piscataway, NJ
Sage College of Albany, NY
St. Ambrose University, IA
St. Augustine College, IL
St. Francis College, NY
Saint Joseph's College of Maine, ME
St. Joseph's College, Suffolk Campus, NY
Saint Louis University, MO
Saint Martin's College, WA
St. Mary's College of Maryland, MD
Saint Mary's University of Minnesota, MN
St. Mary's University of San Antonio, TX
Saint Paul's College, VA
Saint Vincent College, PA
Saint Xavier University, IL
Samford University, AL
San Francisco State University, CA
San Jose State University, CA
School of the Art Institute of Chicago, IL
Schreiner University, TX
Seattle Pacific University, WA
Seton Hall University, NJ
Shepherd University, WV
Shimer College, IL
Shippensburg University of
  Pennsylvania, PA
Sierra Nevada College, NV
Silver Lake College, WI
Simpson College, IA
Sonoma State University, CA
South Carolina State University, SC
South Dakota School of Mines and
  Technology, SD
South Dakota State University, SD
Southeast Missouri State University, MO
Southern California Institute of
  Architecture, CA
Southern Connecticut State University, CT
Southern Illinois University Carbondale, IL
Southern Illinois University
  Edwardsville, IL
Southern Methodist College, SC
Southern New Hampshire University, NH
Southern Oregon University, OR
Southern Polytechnic State University, GA
Southern University and Agricultural and
  Mechanical College, LA
Southern Utah University, UT
Southern Vermont College, VT
Southern Virginia University, VA
Southern Wesleyan University, SC

Southwest Baptist University, MO
State University of New York at New
  Paltz, NY
State University of New York at
  Oswego, NY
State University of New York at
  Plattsburgh, NY
State University of New York College at
  Brockport, NY
State University of New York College of
  Environmental Science and Forestry, NY
Stephens College, MO
Stevens Institute of Technology, NJ
Suffolk University, MA
Syracuse University, NY
Talladega College, AL
Tarleton State University, TX
Taylor University, IN
Taylor University Fort Wayne, IN
Temple University, PA
Tennessee Technological University, TN
Tennessee Wesleyan College, TN
Texas A&M University, TX
Texas A&M University at Galveston, TX
Texas A&M University–Commerce, TX
Texas Tech University, TX
Thiel College, PA
Thomas Jefferson University, PA
Thomas More College, KY
Thomas University, GA
Towson University, MD
Trinity (Washington) University, DC
Tri-State University, IN
Tuskegee University, AL
Union College, KY
Union College, NY
Union University, TN
Unity College, ME
University at Buffalo, The State University
  of New York, NY
The University of Akron, OH
The University of Alabama, AL
The University of Alabama at
  Birmingham, AL
The University of Alabama in
  Huntsville, AL
University of Alaska Anchorage, AK
University of Alaska Fairbanks, AK
University of Alaska Southeast, AK
University of Arkansas at Fort Smith, AR
University of Arkansas at Pine Bluff, AR
University of Bridgeport, CT
University of California, Riverside, CA
University of California, San Diego, CA
University of California, Santa Barbara, CA
University of California, Santa Cruz, CA
University of Central Florida, FL
University of Cincinnati, OH
University of Colorado at Boulder, CO
University of Colorado at Colorado
  Springs, CO
University of Colorado at Denver and
  Health Sciences Center—Downtown
  Denver Campus, CO
University of Connecticut, CT
University of Dayton, OH

University of Delaware, DE
University of Denver, CO
University of Detroit Mercy, MI
University of Evansville, IN
The University of Findlay, OH
University of Florida, FL
University of Georgia, GA
University of Great Falls, MT
University of Hartford, CT
University of Hawaii at Manoa, HI
University of Houston–Downtown, TX
University of Idaho, ID
University of Illinois at Chicago, IL
University of Illinois at Springfield, IL
University of Illinois at Urbana–
 Champaign, IL
University of Indianapolis, IN
University of Kansas, KS
University of Louisville, KY
University of Maine, ME
University of Maine at Presque Isle, ME
University of Mary, ND
University of Maryland, Baltimore
 County, MD
University of Maryland, College Park, MD
University of Maryland Eastern Shore, MD
University of Maryland University
 College, MD
University of Mary Washington, VA
University of Massachusetts Amherst, MA
University of Massachusetts Boston, MA
University of Massachusetts
 Dartmouth, MA
University of Massachusetts Lowell, MA
The University of Memphis, TN
University of Michigan, MI
University of Michigan–Dearborn, MI
University of Michigan–Flint, MI
University of Minnesota, Twin Cities
 Campus, MN
University of Missouri–Columbia, MO
University of Missouri–Kansas City, MO
University of Missouri–St. Louis, MO
The University of Montana–Western, MT
University of Nebraska at Kearney, NE
University of Nebraska at Omaha, NE
University of Nebraska–Lincoln, NE
University of Nevada, Las Vegas, NV
University of New England, ME
University of New Haven, CT
University of New Orleans, LA
University of North Alabama, AL
The University of North Carolina at
 Charlotte, NC
The University of North Carolina at
 Pembroke, NC
The University of North Carolina at
 Wilmington, NC
University of North Dakota, ND

University of Northern Colorado, CO
University of Northern Iowa, IA
University of North Florida, FL
University of North Texas, TX
University of Oklahoma, OK
University of Pittsburgh at Johnstown, PA
University of Puerto Rico, Mayagüez
 Campus, PR
University of Puget Sound, WA
University of Rhode Island, RI
University of Richmond, VA
University of Rio Grande, OH
University of Saint Francis, IN
University of San Francisco, CA
University of Sioux Falls, SD
University of South Carolina, SC
University of South Carolina Upstate, SC
University of Southern California, CA
University of Southern Indiana, IN
University of Southern Maine, ME
University of Southern Mississippi, MS
University of South Florida, FL
The University of Tampa, FL
The University of Tennessee at
 Chattanooga, TN
The University of Tennessee at Martin, TN
The University of Texas at Arlington, TX
The University of Texas at Austin, TX
The University of Texas at Brownsville, TX
The University of Texas at Dallas, TX
The University of Texas at El Paso, TX
The University of Texas at San
 Antonio, TX
The University of Texas at Tyler, TX
The University of Texas–Pan American, TX
University of the Cumberlands, KY
University of the District of Columbia, DC
University of the Ozarks, AR
University of the Pacific, CA
The University of Toledo, OH
University of Utah, UT
University of Vermont, VT
University of Virginia, VA
The University of Virginia's College at
 Wise, VA
University of Washington, WA
University of West Florida, FL
University of West Georgia, GA
University of Wisconsin–Eau Claire, WI
University of Wisconsin–Green Bay, WI
University of Wisconsin–La Crosse, WI
University of Wisconsin–Madison, WI
University of Wisconsin–Milwaukee, WI
University of Wisconsin–Oshkosh, WI
University of Wisconsin–Stevens Point, WI
University of Wisconsin–Stout, WI
University of Wisconsin–Superior, WI
University of Wisconsin–Whitewater, WI
Urbana University, OH

Ursuline College, OH
Utah State University, UT
Utah Valley State College, UT
Utica College, NY
Valdosta State University, GA
Valley City State University, ND
Valparaiso University, IN
Vanderbilt University, TN
Vassar College, NY
Vennard College, IA
Vermont Technical College, VT
Villa Julie College, MD
Virginia Commonwealth University, VA
Virginia Polytechnic Institute and State
 University, VA
Virginia Union University, VA
Voorhees College, SC
Waldorf College, IA
Walla Walla College, WA
Warner Pacific College, OR
Warren Wilson College, NC
Washington Bible College, MD
Washington State University, WA
Washington University in St. Louis, MO
Wayne State College, NE
Wayne State University, MI
Webber International University, FL
Webster University, MO
Wentworth Institute of Technology, MA
Western Carolina University, NC
Western Connecticut State University, CT
Western Kentucky University, KY
Western New Mexico University, NM
Western State College of Colorado, CO
Western Washington University, WA
Westfield State College, MA
Westminster College, MO
Westminster College, UT
Westmont College, CA
West Texas A&M University, TX
Whitman College, WA
Whitworth College, WA
Wichita State University, KS
Wilkes University, PA
William Jewell College, MO
William Penn University, IA
Wilmington College, DE
Wilson College, PA
Winston-Salem State University, NC
Winthrop University, SC
Wittenberg University, OH
Worcester Polytechnic Institute, MA
Xavier University, OH
Xavier University of Louisiana, LA
York College, NE
York College of Pennsylvania, PA
Youngstown State University, OH

ROTC Programs

Army

Adelphi University, NY*
Albertson College of Idaho, ID*
Alcorn State University, MS
Alfred University, NY*
Allen College, IA*
Alliant International University, CA*
Alma College, MI*
Alvernia College, PA*
Alverno College, WI*
American International College, MA*
American University, DC*
American University of Puerto Rico, PR*
Anderson College, SC*
Appalachian State University, NC
Aquinas College, TN*
Arcadia University, PA*
Arizona State University, AZ
Arizona State University East, AZ*
Arkansas State University, AR
Arkansas Tech University, AR*
Armstrong Atlantic State University, GA
Asbury College, KY*
Assumption College, MA*
Auburn University, AL
Auburn University Montgomery, AL
Augsburg College, MN*
Augusta State University, GA
Austin Peay State University, TN
Azusa Pacific University, CA*
Babson College, MA*
Baker University, KS*
Ball State University, IN
Bay Path College, MA*
Becker College, MA*
Bellevue University, NE*
Bellin College of Nursing, WI*
Belmont Abbey College, NC*
Belmont University, TN*
Benedictine College, KS
Benedictine University, IL*
Bentley College, MA*
Bethany Lutheran College, MN*
Bethel University, MN*
Bethune-Cookman College, FL*
Biola University, CA*
Black Hills State University, SD
Bloomfield College, NJ*
Bloomsburg University of Pennsylvania, PA
Boise State University, ID
Boston College, MA*
Boston University, MA
Bowie State University, MD
Bowling Green State University, OH
Bradley University, IL
Brandeis University, MA*
Bridgewater State College, MA*

Brigham Young University, UT
Brigham Young University–Hawaii, HI*
Bryant University, RI
Bucknell University, PA
Butler University, IN
Caldwell College, NJ*
California Baptist University, CA*
California Institute of Technology, CA*
California Lutheran University, CA*
California State University, Dominguez Hills, CA*
California State University, Fresno, CA
California State University, Fullerton, CA
California State University, Sacramento, CA*
California State University, San Bernardino, CA
California State University, San Marcos, CA*
Calvin College, MI*
Cameron University, OK
Campbell University, NC
Canisius College, NY
Capitol College, MD*
Carnegie Mellon University, PA
Carroll College, MT
Carson-Newman College, TN
Case Western Reserve University, OH*
Castleton State College, VT*
Catawba College, NC*
The Catholic University of America, DC*
Cazenovia College, NY*
Cedar Crest College, PA*
Cedarville University, OH*
Central Connecticut State University, CT*
Central Methodist University, MO*
Central Michigan University, MI
Central Missouri State University, MO
Central Washington University, WA
Centre College, KY*
Chaminade University of Honolulu, HI*
Champlain College, VT*
Chapman University, CA*
Chatham College, PA*
Christian Brothers University, TN*
Christian Heritage College, CA*
Christopher Newport University, VA
City College of the City University of New York, NY*
Claremont McKenna College, CA
Clark Atlanta University, GA
Clarkson University, NY
Clark University, MA*
Clayton State University, GA*
Clearwater Christian College, FL*
Clemson University, SC
Cleveland Institute of Music, OH*

Cleveland State University, OH*
Coe College, IA*
Colby College, ME*
Colby-Sawyer College, NH*
Colgate University, NY*
College Misericordia, PA*
College of Mount St. Joseph, OH*
College of Mount Saint Vincent, NY*
The College of New Jersey, NJ*
College of Notre Dame of Maryland, MD*
College of Saint Benedict, MN*
College of Saint Mary, NE*
College of the Holy Cross, MA*
College of the Ozarks, MO
The College of William and Mary, VA
Colorado Christian University, CO*
The Colorado College, CO*
Colorado School of Mines, CO
Colorado State University, CO
Colorado State University-Pueblo, CO
Columbia College, MO*
Columbia College, NY*
Columbia College, SC*
Columbia University, The Fu Foundation School of Engineering and Applied Science, NY*
Columbus State University, GA
Concordia College, MN*
Concordia University, MI*
Concordia University, NE*
Concordia University, St. Paul, MN*
Converse College, SC*
Coppin State University, MD
Corban College, OR*
Cornell University, NY
Cornerstone University, MI*
Creighton University, NE
Curry College, MA*
Daemen College, NY*
Dallas Baptist University, TX*
Daniel Webster College, NH*
Dartmouth College, NH*
Davidson College, NC
Delaware State University, DE
Denison University, OH*
DePaul University, IL*
DePauw University, IN*
DeSales University, PA*
Dickinson College, PA
Dillard University, LA*
Doane College, NE*
Drake University, IA
Drew University, NJ*
Drexel University, PA
Duke University, NC
Duquesne University, PA
D'Youville College, NY*

program is offered at another college's campus

East Carolina University, NC
Eastern Illinois University, IL
Eastern Michigan University, MI
Eastern Oregon University, OR
Eastern Washington University, WA
East Stroudsburg University of
  Pennsylvania, PA*
East Tennessee State University, TN
Eckerd College, FL*
Edinboro University of Pennsylvania, PA
Elmhurst College, IL*
Elmira College, NY
Elon University, NC
Embry-Riddle Aeronautical University, AZ
Embry-Riddle Aeronautical University, FL
Emmanuel College, MA*
Endicott College, MA*
Evangel University, MO
Fairfield University, CT*
Fairleigh Dickinson University, College at
  Florham, NJ*
Fairleigh Dickinson University,
  Metropolitan Campus, NJ*
Fairmont State University, WV
Faulkner University, AL*
Ferris State University, MI*
Finlandia University, MI*
Florida Atlantic University, FL*
Florida College, FL*
Florida Institute of Technology, FL
Florida Southern College, FL
Florida State University, FL
Fordham University, NY
Framingham State College, MA
Franklin College, IN*
Franklin Pierce College, NH*
Free Will Baptist Bible College, TN*
Furman University, SC
Gannon University, PA
Geneva College, PA*
George Mason University, VA
Georgetown College, KY*
Georgetown University, DC
The George Washington University, DC*
Georgia College & State University, GA*
Georgia Institute of Technology, GA
Georgia Southern University, GA
Georgia State University, GA
Gettysburg College, PA*
Gonzaga University, WA
Gordon College, MA*
Goucher College, MD*
Grace Bible College, MI*
Grace University, NE*
Grambling State University, LA
Grand Canyon University, AZ
Grand View College, IA*
Grove City College, PA*
Gustavus Adolphus College, MN*
Hamilton College, NY*
Hampden-Sydney College, VA*
Hampshire College, MA*
Hampton University, VA
Harding University, AR*
Harvard University, MA*
Harvey Mudd College, CA*

Hawai'i Pacific University, HI*
Heidelberg College, OH*
Hendrix College, AR*
Hofstra University, NY
Holy Names University, CA*
Hope College, MI*
Houghton College, NY*
Houston Baptist University, TX*
Howard University, DC
Husson College, ME*
Idaho State University, ID*
Illinois State University, IL
Illinois Wesleyan University, IL*
Indiana State University, IN
Indiana University Bloomington, IN
Indiana University Kokomo, IN*
Indiana University Northwest, IN
Indiana University of Pennsylvania, PA
Indiana University–Purdue University
  Indianapolis, IN
Indiana University South Bend, IN*
Indiana University Southeast, IN*
Inter American University of Puerto Rico,
  Guayama Campus, PR*
Inter American University of Puerto Rico,
  San Germán Campus, PR*
Iona College, NY*
Iowa State University of Science and
  Technology, IA
Ithaca College, NY*
Jacksonville State University, AL
James Madison University, VA
John Brown University, AR*
The Johns Hopkins University, MD
Johnson C. Smith University, NC
Judson College, AL*
Kalamazoo College, MI*
Kansas State University, KS
Kean University, NJ*
Kennesaw State University, GA
Kent State University, OH
King's College, PA
Kutztown University of Pennsylvania, PA*
Lafayette College, PA*
Langston University, OK*
La Roche College, PA*
La Salle University, PA*
Lawrence Technological University, MI*
Lebanon Valley College, PA*
Lehigh University, PA
Lehman College of the City University of
  New York, NY*
Le Moyne College, NY*
LeMoyne-Owen College, TN*
Lenoir-Rhyne College, NC*
Lewis-Clark State College, ID
Liberty University, VA
Limestone College, SC*
Lincoln University, MO
Lincoln University, PA*
Lindenwood University, MO
Lipscomb University, TN*
Lock Haven University of Pennsylvania, PA
Longwood University, VA
Louisiana State University and Agricultural
  and Mechanical College, LA

Louisiana Tech University, LA*
Lourdes College, OH*
Loyola College in Maryland, MD
Loyola Marymount University, CA*
Loyola University Chicago, IL*
Loyola University New Orleans, LA*
Lubbock Christian University, TX*
Lycoming College, PA*
Maine Maritime Academy, ME
Malone College, OH*
Manhattan Christian College, KS*
Manhattan College, NY*
Marian College of Fond du Lac, WI
Marist College, NY
Marshall University, WV
Mary Baldwin College, VA
Marymount University, VA*
Maryville University of Saint Louis, MO*
Massachusetts College of Pharmacy and
  Health Sciences, MA*
Massachusetts Institute of Technology, MA
Massachusetts Maritime Academy, MA*
McDaniel College, MD
McKendree College, IL*
Menlo College, CA*
Mercer University, GA
Mercyhurst College, PA*
Meredith College, NC*
Methodist College, NC
Metropolitan State College of Denver, CO*
Miami University, OH*
Michigan State University, MI
Michigan Technological University, MI
MidAmerica Nazarene University, KS*
Middlebury College, VT*
Middle Tennessee State University, TN
Midway College, KY*
Millersville University of Pennsylvania, PA
Milligan College, TN*
Millsaps College, MS*
Milwaukee School of Engineering, WI*
Minnesota State University Mankato, MN
Minnesota State University
  Moorhead, MN*
Mississippi College, MS*
Mississippi State University, MS
Mississippi University for Women, MS*
Missouri Baptist University, MO*
Missouri State University, MO
Missouri Valley College, MO*
Molloy College, NY*
Montana State University, MT
Moravian College, PA*
Morehead State University, KY
Morehouse College, GA
Morningside College, IA*
Morris College, SC
Mount Holyoke College, MA*
Mount Marty College, SD*
Mount Mary College, WI*
Mount Saint Mary College, NY*
Mount St. Mary's University, MD*
Mount Union College, OH*
Murray State University, KY*
Nazareth College of Rochester, NY*
Nebraska Wesleyan University, NE*

program is offered at another college's campus

Neumann College, PA*
New England College, NH*
New Mexico State University, NM
New York Institute of Technology, NY
Niagara University, NY
Nichols College, MA*
Norfolk State University, VA
North Carolina Agricultural and Technical State University, NC
North Carolina State University, NC
North Central College, IL*
North Central University, MN*
North Dakota State University, ND
Northeastern Illinois University, IL*
Northeastern State University, OK
Northeastern University, MA
Northern Arizona University, AZ
Northern Illinois University, IL
Northern Kentucky University, KY
Northern Michigan University, MI
North Greenville College, SC*
Northwestern College, MN*
Northwestern State University of Louisiana, LA
Northwestern University, IL*
Northwest Nazarene University, ID
Northwest University, WA*
Ohio Northern University, OH*
The Ohio State University, OH
Ohio University, OH
Ohio University–Chillicothe, OH*
Ohio University–Lancaster, OH*
Ohio Wesleyan University, OH*
Oklahoma City University, OK*
Oklahoma State University, OK
Old Dominion University, VA
Olivet Nazarene University, IL
Oregon Health & Science University, OR*
Oregon State University, OR
Ouachita Baptist University, AR
Our Lady of the Lake College, LA*
Pacific Lutheran University, WA
Pacific University, OR*
Park University, MO
Peace College, NC*
Pennsylvania College of Technology, PA*
The Pennsylvania State University Abington College, PA
The Pennsylvania State University Altoona College, PA
The Pennsylvania State University at Erie, The Behrend College, PA*
The Pennsylvania State University Harrisburg Campus of the Capital College, PA*
The Pennsylvania State University University Park Campus, PA
Pepperdine University, CA*
Peru State College, NE*
Pfeiffer University, NC*
Pittsburg State University, KS
Pitzer College, CA*
Plymouth State University, NH*
Point Park University, PA*
Polytechnic University of Puerto Rico, PR*

Pontifical Catholic University of Puerto Rico, PR*
Portland State University, OR
Princeton University, NJ
Providence College, RI
Purdue University, IN
Purdue University Calumet, IN*
Quinnipiac University, CT*
Radford University, VA
Randolph-Macon College, VA*
Regis College, MA*
Regis University, CO*
Rensselaer Polytechnic Institute, NY
Research College of Nursing, MO*
Rice University, TX*
Rider University, NJ*
Ripon College, WI
Robert Morris College, IL*
Robert Morris University, PA*
Roberts Wesleyan College, NY*
Rochester Institute of Technology, NY
Rockhurst University, MO*
Roger Williams University, RI
Rose-Hulman Institute of Technology, IN
Rosemont College, PA*
Rowan University, NJ*
Russell Sage College, NY*
Rust College, MS
Rutgers, The State University of New Jersey, Camden, NJ*
Rutgers, The State University of New Jersey, Newark, NJ
Rutgers, The State University of New Jersey, New Brunswick/Piscataway, NJ
Saint Anselm College, NH*
St. Bonaventure University, NY
St. Cloud State University, MN
St. Edward's University, TX*
St. Gregory's University, OK*
St. John Fisher College, NY*
Saint John's University, MN
St. John's University, NY
Saint Joseph's College of Maine, ME*
St. Joseph's College, Suffolk Campus, NY*
St. Lawrence University, NY*
Saint Leo University, FL
Saint Louis University, MO*
Saint Martin's College, WA*
Saint Mary's College of California, CA*
Saint Mary's University of Minnesota, MN*
St. Mary's University of San Antonio, TX
Saint Michael's College, VT*
St. Norbert College, WI
Saint Paul's College, VA
St. Thomas University, FL*
Salisbury University, MD*
Salve Regina University, RI*
Samford University, AL*
Sam Houston State University, TX
San Francisco State University, CA*
San Jose State University, CA
Scripps College, CA*
Seattle Pacific University, WA*
Seton Hall University, NJ
Seton Hill University, PA*

Shaw University, NC*
Shippensburg University of Pennsylvania, PA
Sierra Nevada College, NV*
Simmons College, MA*
Skidmore College, NY*
Slippery Rock University of Pennsylvania, PA
Sonoma State University, CA*
South Carolina State University, SC
South Dakota School of Mines and Technology, SD
South Dakota State University, SD
Southeastern College of the Assemblies of God, FL*
Southeastern Louisiana University, LA*
Southern Connecticut State University, CT*
Southern Illinois University Carbondale, IL
Southern Illinois University Edwardsville, IL
Southern Methodist University, TX
Southern New Hampshire University, NH*
Southern Polytechnic State University, GA*
Southern University and Agricultural and Mechanical College, LA
Southern Utah University, UT
Southern Virginia University, VA*
Southern Wesleyan University, SC*
Southwest Baptist University, MO*
Spelman College, GA*
Spring Arbor University, MI*
Spring Hill College, AL*
Stanford University, CA*
State University of New York at Oswego, NY*
State University of New York College at Brockport, NY
State University of New York College at Geneseo, NY*
State University of New York College at Old Westbury, NY*
State University of New York College at Potsdam, NY*
State University of New York College of Environmental Science and Forestry, NY*
State University of New York Institute of Technology, NY*
Stephen F. Austin State University, TX
Stephens College, MO*
Stetson University, FL*
Stevens Institute of Technology, NJ*
Stonehill College, MA
Stony Brook University, State University of New York, NY*
Suffolk University, MA*
Susquehanna University, PA*
Swarthmore College, PA*
Syracuse University, NY
Talladega College, AL*
Tarleton State University, TX
Temple University, PA
Tennessee Technological University, TN
Texas A&M University, TX
Texas Christian University, TX
Texas Lutheran University, TX*
Texas State University-San Marcos, TX

*program is offered at another college's campus

Texas Tech University, TX
Texas Wesleyan University, TX*
Thomas More College, KY*
Tiffin University, OH*
Towson University, MD*
Transylvania University, KY*
Trevecca Nazarene University, TN*
Trinity College, CT*
Trinity (Washington) University, DC*
Troy University, AL
Troy University Montgomery, AL*
Truman State University, MO
Tufts University, MA*
Tuskegee University, AL
Union College, KY*
Union College, NY*
Unity College, ME*
University at Albany, State University of New York, NY
University at Buffalo, The State University of New York, NY*
The University of Akron, OH
The University of Alabama, AL
The University of Alabama at Birmingham, AL
The University of Alabama in Huntsville, AL*
University of Alaska Fairbanks, AK
The University of Arizona, AZ
University of Arkansas at Pine Bluff, AR
University of Arkansas for Medical Sciences, AR*
University of Bridgeport, CT
University of California, Berkeley, CA
University of California, Davis, CA
University of California, Irvine, CA*
University of California, Los Angeles, CA
University of California, Riverside, CA*
University of California, San Diego, CA*
University of California, Santa Barbara, CA
University of California, Santa Cruz, CA*
University of Central Florida, FL
University of Charleston, WV
University of Cincinnati, OH
University of Colorado at Boulder, CO
University of Colorado at Colorado Springs, CO
University of Colorado at Denver and Health Sciences Center—Downtown Denver Campus, CO
University of Connecticut, CT
University of Dallas, TX*
University of Dayton, OH
University of Delaware, DE
University of Denver, CO*
University of Dubuque, IA
The University of Findlay, OH*
University of Florida, FL
University of Georgia, GA
University of Hartford, CT*
University of Hawaii at Manoa, HI
University of Houston–Downtown, TX*
University of Idaho, ID
University of Illinois at Chicago, IL
University of Illinois at Urbana–Champaign, IL

University of Indianapolis, IN*
University of Kansas, KS
University of Louisville, KY
University of Maine, ME
University of Maryland, Baltimore County, MD*
University of Maryland, College Park, MD
University of Massachusetts Amherst, MA
University of Massachusetts Dartmouth, MA*
The University of Memphis, TN
University of Miami, FL
University of Michigan, MI
University of Michigan–Dearborn, MI*
University of Minnesota, Twin Cities Campus, MN
University of Mississippi, MS
University of Missouri–Columbia, MO
University of Missouri–Kansas City, MO
University of Missouri–St. Louis, MO*
University of Nebraska at Omaha, NE*
University of Nebraska–Lincoln, NE
University of Nebraska Medical Center, NE*
University of Nevada, Reno, NV
University of New England, ME*
University of New Hampshire, NH
University of New Hampshire at Manchester, NH*
University of New Orleans, LA*
University of North Alabama, AL
The University of North Carolina at Chapel Hill, NC
The University of North Carolina at Charlotte, NC
The University of North Carolina at Greensboro, NC*
The University of North Carolina at Pembroke, NC
University of North Dakota, ND
University of Northern Colorado, CO
University of Northern Iowa, IA
University of North Texas, TX*
University of Notre Dame, IN
University of Oklahoma, OK
University of Oregon, OR
University of Pennsylvania, PA*
University of Pittsburgh at Bradford, PA*
University of Portland, OR
University of Puerto Rico, Mayagüez Campus, PR
University of Puget Sound, WA*
University of Rhode Island, RI
University of Richmond, VA
University of Rio Grande, OH*
University of St. Thomas, MN*
University of St. Thomas, TX*
University of San Diego, CA*
University of San Francisco, CA
The University of Scranton, PA
University of South Carolina, SC
University of South Carolina Upstate, SC*
The University of South Dakota, SD
University of Southern California, CA
University of Southern Indiana, IN
University of Southern Maine, ME*

University of Southern Mississippi, MS
University of South Florida, FL
The University of Tampa, FL
The University of Tennessee at Martin, TN
The University of Texas at Arlington, TX
The University of Texas at Austin, TX
The University of Texas at Dallas, TX*
The University of Texas at El Paso, TX
The University of Texas at San Antonio, TX
The University of Texas Health Science Center at Houston, TX*
The University of Texas–Pan American, TX
University of the Cumberlands, KY
University of the District of Columbia, DC*
University of the Incarnate Word, TX*
University of the Virgin Islands, VI
The University of Toledo, OH
University of Utah, UT
University of Vermont, VT
University of Virginia, VA
University of Washington, WA
University of West Florida, FL
University of West Georgia, GA
University of Wisconsin–Green Bay, WI
University of Wisconsin–La Crosse, WI
University of Wisconsin–Madison, WI
University of Wisconsin–Milwaukee, WI*
University of Wisconsin–Oshkosh, WI
University of Wisconsin–Parkside, WI*
University of Wisconsin–Stevens Point, WI
University of Wisconsin–Whitewater, WI
University of Wyoming, WY
Utah State University, UT
Utah Valley State College, UT
Utica College, NY
Vanderbilt University, TN
Vermont Technical College, VT*
Villa Julie College, MD*
Villanova University, PA*
Virginia Commonwealth University, VA*
Virginia Military Institute, VA
Virginia Polytechnic Institute and State University, VA
Virginia Union University, VA*
Virginia Wesleyan College, VA*
Voorhees College, SC*
Wabash College, IN*
Wake Forest University, NC
Warner Pacific College, OR*
Washington & Jefferson College, PA*
Washington and Lee University, VA*
Washington State University, WA
Washington University in St. Louis, MO
Wayland Baptist University, TX*
Waynesburg College, PA*
Wayne State College, NE*
Webster University, MO*
Wellesley College, MA*
Wentworth Institute of Technology, MA*
Wesley College, DE*
Western Connecticut State University, CT*
Western Illinois University, IL
Western Kentucky University, KY
Western New England College, MA
Western Oregon University, OR

program is offered at another college's campus

Westfield State College, MA*
Westminster College, MO*
Westminster College, PA*
Westminster College, UT*
Westmont College, CA*
West Virginia University, WV
Wheaton College, IL
Wheaton College, MA*
Whittier College, CA*
Whitworth College, WA*
Wilkes University, PA*
William Carey College, MS*
Williams Baptist College, AR*
William Woods University, MO*
Wilmington College, DE*
Wilson College, PA*
Wingate University, NC*
Winona State University, MN*
Winston-Salem State University, NC
Wittenberg University, OH*
Wofford College, SC
Worcester Polytechnic Institute, MA
Worcester State College, MA*
Xavier University, OH
Xavier University of Louisiana, LA*
Yale University, CT*
York College, NE*
York College of Pennsylvania, PA*
Youngstown State University, OH

Naval

Armstrong Atlantic State University, GA*
Auburn University, AL
Augsburg College, MN*
Babson College, MA*
Becker College, MA*
Belmont University, TN*
Boston University, MA
Brigham Young University–Hawaii, HI*
California State University, San
  Marcos, CA*
Carnegie Mellon University, PA
The Catholic University of America, DC*
Christian Brothers University, TN*
Clark University, MA*
Clayton State University, GA*
Cleveland State University, OH*
College of the Holy Cross, MA
Columbia College, NY*
Columbia College, SC*
Columbia University, The Fu Foundation
  School of Engineering and Applied
  Science, NY*
Concordia University, St. Paul, MN*
Duquesne University, PA*
Eastern Michigan University, MI*
Embry-Riddle Aeronautical University, FL
Florida State University, FL*
Fordham University, NY*
Georgetown University, DC*
The George Washington University, DC
Georgia Institute of Technology, GA
Georgia State University, GA*
Hampton University, VA
Husson College, ME*

Indiana University–Purdue University
  Indianapolis, IN*
Indiana University South Bend, IN*
Inter American University of Puerto Rico,
  San Germán Campus, PR*
Iowa State University of Science and
  Technology, IA
Louisiana State University and Agricultural
  and Mechanical College, LA*
Louisiana Tech University, LA
Loyola University Chicago, IL*
Loyola University New Orleans, LA*
Macalester College, MN*
Maine Maritime Academy, ME
Mary Baldwin College, VA*
Massachusetts Institute of Technology, MA
Massachusetts Maritime Academy, MA
Miami University, OH
Milwaukee School of Engineering, WI*
Molloy College, NY*
Morehouse College, GA
Norfolk State University, VA
North Carolina State University, NC
Northeastern University, MA*
Northwestern University, IL
The Ohio State University, OH
Old Dominion University, VA
Oregon State University, OR
Peace College, NC*
The Pennsylvania State University
  University Park Campus, PA
Purdue University, IN
Radford University, VA*
Rensselaer Polytechnic Institute, NY
Rice University, TX
Rochester Institute of Technology, NY*
St. John Fisher College, NY*
San Francisco State University, CA*
Seattle Pacific University, WA*
Simmons College, MA*
Southern Polytechnic State University, GA*
Southern University and Agricultural and
  Mechanical College, LA
Stanford University, CA*
State University of New York College at
  Brockport, NY*
Temple University, PA*
Texas A&M University, TX
Texas A&M University at Galveston, TX
Tufts University, MA*
The University of Arizona, AZ
University of California, Berkeley, CA
University of California, Davis, CA*
University of California, Los Angeles, CA
University of California, Santa Cruz, CA*
University of Colorado at Boulder, CO
University of Idaho, ID
University of Illinois at Chicago, IL*
University of Illinois at Urbana–
  Champaign, IL
University of Kansas, KS
University of Maine, ME
University of Maryland, College Park, MD*
The University of Memphis, TN
University of Michigan–Dearborn, MI*
University of Missouri–Columbia, MO

University of Nebraska–Lincoln, NE
University of New Orleans, LA*
The University of North Carolina at Chapel
  Hill, NC
University of North Florida, FL*
University of North Texas, TX
University of Notre Dame, IN
University of Oklahoma, OK
University of Pennsylvania, PA
University of Rochester, NY
University of San Diego, CA
University of South Florida, FL
The University of Texas at Austin, TX
University of Utah, UT
University of Virginia, VA
University of Washington, WA
University of Wisconsin–Madison, WI
Vanderbilt University, TN
Villanova University, PA
Virginia Military Institute, VA
Virginia Polytechnic Institute and State
  University, VA
Washington State University, WA
Westminster College, UT*
William Woods University, MO*
Worcester Polytechnic Institute, MA*
Worcester State College, MA*
Xavier University of Louisiana, LA*
York College, NE*

Air Force

Adelphi University, NY*
Agnes Scott College, GA*
Alverno College, WI*
American International College, MA*
American University, DC*
Anderson College, SC*
Angelo State University, TX
Anna Maria College, MA*
Aquinas College, TN*
Arizona State University, AZ
Arizona State University East, AZ*
Asbury College, KY*
Assumption College, MA*
Auburn University, AL
Auburn University Montgomery, AL*
Augsburg College, MN*
Babson College, MA*
Baker University, KS*
Baldwin-Wallace College, OH*
Barry University, FL*
Baylor University, TX
Bay Path College, MA*
Becker College, MA*
Bellevue University, NE*
Belmont Abbey College, NC*
Bethel University, MN*
Bethune-Cookman College, FL*
Biola University, CA*
Bloomsburg University of
  Pennsylvania, PA*
Boston College, MA*
Boston University, MA
Bowling Green State University, OH
Brandeis University, MA*
Bridgewater State College, MA*

Brigham Young University, UT
Brigham Young University–Hawaii, HI*
Bryn Mawr College, PA*
Butler University, IN*
California Baptist University, CA*
California Institute of Technology, CA*
California Lutheran University, CA*
California State University, Dominguez
    Hills, CA*
California State University, Fresno, CA
California State University, Sacramento, CA
California State University, San
    Bernardino, CA
California State University, San
    Marcos, CA*
Carnegie Mellon University, PA
Carroll College, WI*
Carson-Newman College, TN*
Case Western Reserve University, OH*
The Catholic University of America, DC*
Cazenovia College, NY*
Cedarville University, OH*
Central Connecticut State University, CT*
Central Methodist University, MO*
Central Missouri State University, MO*
Central Washington University, WA
Centre College, KY*
Chaminade University of Honolulu, HI*
Chapman University, CA*
Chatham College, PA*
Christian Brothers University, TN*
Christian Heritage College, CA*
City College of the City University of New
    York, NY*
Claremont McKenna College, CA*
Clark Atlanta University, GA
Clarkson University, NY
Clark University, MA*
Clayton State University, GA*
Clearwater Christian College, FL*
Clemson University, SC
Cleveland Institute of Music, OH*
Cleveland State University, OH*
Coe College, IA*
Colby-Sawyer College, NH*
College Misericordia, PA*
College of Charleston, SC*
College of Mount St. Joseph, OH*
College of Mount Saint Vincent, NY*
The College of New Jersey, NJ*
College of Saint Mary, NE*
The College of St. Scholastica, MN*
College of Santa Fe, NM*
College of the Holy Cross, MA*
Colorado State University, CO
Columbia College, MO*
Columbia College, NY*
Columbia College, SC*
Columbia University, The Fu Foundation
    School of Engineering and Applied
    Science, NY*
Concordia College, MN*
Concordia University, MI*
Concordia University, NE*
Concordia University, OR*
Concordia University, St. Paul, MN*

Corban College, OR*
Cornell University, NY
Creighton University, NE*
Dakota State University, SD*
Dallas Baptist University, TX*
Daniel Webster College, NH*
Davidson College, NC*
Delaware State University, DE
DePauw University, IN*
Dillard University, LA*
Doane College, NE*
Dowling College, NY*
Drake University, IA*
Drew University, NJ*
Drexel University, PA*
Duke University, NC
Duquesne University, PA*
East Carolina University, NC
Eastern Michigan University, MI*
East Stroudsburg University of
    Pennsylvania, PA*
Eckerd College, FL*
Elmhurst College, IL*
Elmira College, NY*
Elon University, NC*
Embry-Riddle Aeronautical University, AZ
Embry-Riddle Aeronautical University, FL
Emory University, GA*
Faulkner University, AL*
Finlandia University, MI*
Florida Atlantic University, FL*
Florida College, FL*
Florida Southern College, FL*
Florida State University, FL
Fordham University, NY*
Franklin Pierce College, NH*
Free Will Baptist Bible College, TN*
George Mason University, VA*
Georgetown College, KY*
Georgetown University, DC*
The George Washington University, DC*
Georgia Institute of Technology, GA
Georgia State University, GA*
Gordon College, MA*
Grace University, NE*
Grambling State University, LA
Grand Canyon University, AZ*
Grand View College, IA*
Hamilton College, NY*
Hamline University, MN*
Harvard University, MA*
Harvey Mudd College, CA
Hawai'i Pacific University, HI*
Heidelberg College, OH*
Holy Names University, CA*
Howard University, DC
Indiana State University, IN
Indiana University Bloomington, IN
Indiana University–Purdue University
    Indianapolis, IN*
Indiana University South Bend, IN*
Indiana University Southeast, IN*
Inter American University of Puerto Rico,
    San Germán Campus, PR*
Iowa State University of Science and
    Technology, IA

Ithaca College, NY*
James Madison University, VA*
John Brown University, AR*
John Jay College of Criminal Justice of the
    City University of New York, NY*
The Johns Hopkins University, MD*
Johnson C. Smith University, NC*
Kansas State University, KS
Kean University, NJ*
Keene State College, NH*
Kennesaw State University, GA
Kent State University, OH
King's College, PA
Kutztown University of Pennsylvania, PA*
La Roche College, PA*
La Salle University, PA*
Lawrence Technological University, MI*
Le Moyne College, NY*
LeMoyne-Owen College, TN*
Lewis-Clark State College, ID*
Liberty University, VA*
Lincoln University, PA*
Lindenwood University, MO*
Linfield College, OR*
Lipscomb University, TN*
Louisiana State University and Agricultural
    and Mechanical College, LA
Lourdes College, OH*
Loyola College in Maryland, MD*
Loyola Marymount University, CA
Loyola University New Orleans, LA*
Lubbock Christian University, TX*
Lynn University, FL*
Macalester College, MN*
Malone College, OH*
Manhattan Christian College, KS*
Manhattan College, NY
Maranatha Baptist Bible College, WI
Mary Baldwin College, VA*
Massachusetts College of Pharmacy and
    Health Sciences, MA*
Massachusetts Institute of Technology, MA
McKendree College, IL*
McMurry University, TX*
Mercy College, NY*
Mercyhurst College, PA*
Meredith College, NC*
Merrimack College, MA*
Methodist College, NC*
Metropolitan State College of Denver, CO*
Miami University, OH
Michigan State University, MI
Michigan Technological University, MI
MidAmerica Nazarene University, KS*
Middle Tennessee State University, TN*
Midwestern State University, TX*
Milwaukee School of Engineering, WI*
Minnesota State University
    Moorhead, MN*
Mississippi State University, MS
Mississippi University for Women, MS*
Molloy College, NY*
Monmouth University, NJ*
Montana State University, MT
Montclair State University, NJ*
Morehouse College, GA

*program is offered at another college's campus

Mount Holyoke College, MA*
Mount Union College, OH*
Nazareth College of Rochester, NY*
Nebraska Wesleyan University, NE*
New England College, NH*
New Jersey Institute of Technology, NJ
New Mexico State University, NM
New York Institute of Technology, NY
North Carolina Agricultural and Technical State University, NC
North Carolina State University, NC
North Central College, IL*
North Central University, MN*
North Dakota State University, ND
Northeastern Illinois University, IL*
Northeastern University, MA*
Northern Arizona University, AZ
Northern Illinois University, IL*
Northern Kentucky University, KY*
Northwestern College, MN*
Northwestern University, IL*
Oakland University, MI*
Ohio Northern University, OH*
The Ohio State University, OH
Ohio University, OH
Ohio University–Chillicothe, OH*
Ohio University–Lancaster, OH*
Ohio Valley University, WV*
Oklahoma Baptist University, OK*
Oklahoma City University, OK*
Oklahoma State University, OK
Oral Roberts University, OK*
Oregon State University, OR
Our Lady of the Lake College, LA*
Pacific University, OR*
Peace College, NC*
The Pennsylvania State University Abington College, PA*
The Pennsylvania State University Altoona College, PA
The Pennsylvania State University University Park Campus, PA
Pepperdine University, CA*
Peru State College, NE*
Philadelphia Biblical University, PA*
Pitzer College, CA*
Plymouth State University, NH*
Point Park University, PA*
Polytechnic University, Brooklyn Campus, NY*
Portland State University, OR*
Princeton University, NJ*
Purdue University, IN
Quinnipiac University, CT*
Ramapo College of New Jersey, NJ*
Regis University, CO*
Rensselaer Polytechnic Institute, NY
Rice University, TX*
Robert Morris University, PA*
Roberts Wesleyan College, NY*
Rochester Institute of Technology, NY
Rose-Hulman Institute of Technology, IN
Russell Sage College, NY*
Rutgers, The State University of New Jersey, Camden, NJ*

Rutgers, The State University of New Jersey, Newark, NJ
Rutgers, The State University of New Jersey, New Brunswick/Piscataway, NJ
Saint Anselm College, NH*
St. Edward's University, TX*
St. Gregory's University, OK*
St. John Fisher College, NY*
St. Joseph's College, Suffolk Campus, NY*
St. Lawrence University, NY*
Saint Leo University, FL*
Saint Louis University, MO
Saint Mary's College of California, CA*
Saint Michael's College, VT*
St. Thomas University, FL*
Saint Vincent College, PA*
Saint Xavier University, IL*
Samford University, AL
San Francisco State University, CA*
San Jose State University, CA
Scripps College, CA*
Seattle Pacific University, WA*
Seton Hall University, NJ*
Shaw University, NC*
Simmons College, MA*
Skidmore College, NY*
Sonoma State University, CA*
South Carolina State University, SC*
South Dakota State University, SD
Southeastern College of the Assemblies of God, FL*
Southeast Missouri State University, MO
Southern Connecticut State University, CT*
Southern Illinois University Carbondale, IL
Southern Illinois University Edwardsville, IL
Southern Methodist University, TX*
Southern New Hampshire University, NH*
Southern Polytechnic State University, GA*
Southern University and Agricultural and Mechanical College, LA*
Southern Wesleyan University, SC*
Southwestern College, AZ*
Spelman College, GA*
Spring Hill College, AL*
Stanford University, CA*
State University of New York at Binghamton, NY*
State University of New York College at Brockport, NY*
State University of New York College at Geneseo, NY*
State University of New York College at Old Westbury, NY*
State University of New York College at Potsdam, NY*
State University of New York College of Environmental Science and Forestry, NY*
State University of New York Institute of Technology, NY*
Stephens College, MO*
Stevens Institute of Technology, NJ*
Stony Brook University, State University of New York, NY*
Swarthmore College, PA*
Syracuse University, NY

Temple University, PA*
Tennessee Technological University, TN*
Texas A&M University, TX
Texas Christian University, TX
Texas Lutheran University, TX*
Texas State University-San Marcos, TX
Texas Tech University, TX
Texas Wesleyan University, TX*
Thomas Jefferson University, PA*
Thomas More College, KY*
Tiffin University, OH*
Towson University, MD*
Transylvania University, KY*
Trinity University, TX*
Troy University, AL
Troy University Montgomery, AL*
Tufts University, MA*
Tuskegee University, AL
Union College, NY*
University at Albany, State University of New York, NY*
The University of Akron, OH
The University of Alabama, AL
The University of Alabama at Birmingham, AL*
University of Alaska Anchorage, AK
The University of Arizona, AZ
University of Arkansas at Fort Smith, AR*
University of California, Berkeley, CA
University of California, Davis, CA*
University of California, Irvine, CA*
University of California, Los Angeles, CA
University of California, Riverside, CA*
University of California, Santa Cruz, CA*
University of Central Florida, FL
University of Cincinnati, OH
University of Colorado at Boulder, CO
University of Colorado at Denver and Health Sciences Center—Downtown Denver Campus, CO*
University of Connecticut, CT
University of Dallas, TX*
University of Dayton, OH*
University of Delaware, DE
University of Denver, CO*
The University of Findlay, OH*
University of Florida, FL
University of Georgia, GA
University of Hartford, CT*
University of Hawaii at Manoa, HI
University of Idaho, ID*
University of Illinois at Chicago, IL*
University of Illinois at Urbana–Champaign, IL
University of Kansas, KS
University of Louisville, KY
University of Mary Hardin-Baylor, TX*
University of Maryland, College Park, MD
University of Massachusetts Amherst, MA
University of Massachusetts Lowell, MA
The University of Memphis, TN
University of Miami, FL
University of Michigan, MI
University of Michigan–Dearborn, MI*
University of Minnesota, Twin Cities Campus, MN

program is offered at another college's campus

University of Mississippi, MS
University of Missouri–Columbia, MO
University of Missouri–Kansas City, MO*
University of Missouri–St. Louis, MO*
University of Nebraska at Omaha, NE
University of Nebraska–Lincoln, NE
University of Nebraska Medical Center, NE*
University of New Hampshire, NH
University of New Hampshire at Manchester, NH*
University of New Orleans, LA*
The University of North Carolina at Chapel Hill, NC
The University of North Carolina at Charlotte, NC
The University of North Carolina at Greensboro, NC*
The University of North Carolina at Pembroke, NC
University of North Dakota, ND
University of Northern Colorado, CO
University of Notre Dame, IN
University of Oklahoma, OK
University of Oregon, OR*
University of Pennsylvania, PA*
University of Portland, OR
University of Puerto Rico, Mayagüez Campus, PR
University of Rochester, NY*
University of St. Thomas, MN
University of San Diego, CA*
University of San Francisco, CA*
The University of Scranton, PA*
University of South Carolina, SC
University of Southern California, CA
University of Southern Maine, ME*

University of Southern Mississippi, MS
University of South Florida, FL
The University of Tampa, FL*
The University of Texas at Arlington, TX*
The University of Texas at Austin, TX
The University of Texas at Dallas, TX*
The University of Texas at El Paso, TX
The University of Texas at San Antonio, TX
University of the District of Columbia, DC*
University of the Incarnate Word, TX*
The University of Toledo, OH*
University of Tulsa, OK*
University of Utah, UT
University of Virginia, VA
University of Washington, WA
University of West Florida, FL
University of Wisconsin–Madison, WI
University of Wisconsin–Milwaukee, WI*
University of Wisconsin–Superior, WI*
University of Wisconsin–Whitewater, WI
University of Wyoming, WY
Utah State University, UT
Utah Valley State College, UT*
Utica College, NY*
Valdosta State University, GA
Valparaiso University, IN
Vanderbilt University, TN*
Vanguard University of Southern California, CA*
Villanova University, PA*
Virginia Military Institute, VA
Virginia Polytechnic Institute and State University, VA
Warner Pacific College, OR*
Washington & Jefferson College, PA*
Washington State University, WA

Washington University in St. Louis, MO*
Wayland Baptist University, TX*
Wayne State University, MI*
Webster University, MO*
Wellesley College, MA*
Wells College, NY*
Wentworth Institute of Technology, MA*
Wesleyan University, CT*
Western Connecticut State University, CT*
Western Kentucky University, KY*
Western New England College, MA*
Western Oregon University, OR*
Westfield State College, MA*
Westminster College, MO*
Westminster College, UT*
Westmont College, CA*
West Virginia University, WV
Wheaton College, IL*
Whittier College, CA*
Wilkes University, PA
William Carey College, MS*
William Paterson University of New Jersey, NJ*
William Woods University, MO*
Wilmington College, DE*
Wingate University, NC*
Winston-Salem State University, NC
Wittenberg University, OH*
Worcester Polytechnic Institute, MA
Worcester State College, MA*
Xavier University, OH*
Xavier University of Louisiana, LA*
Yale University, CT*
York College, NE*
Youngstown State University, OH*

program is offered at another college's campus

Tuition Waivers

Minority Students

Alice Lloyd College, KY
Assumption College, MA
Benedictine University, IL
Bloomsburg University of Pennsylvania, PA
Bridgewater College, VA
Colorado Christian University, CO
Dickinson State University, ND
Dowling College, NY
D'Youville College, NY
Edinboro University of Pennsylvania, PA
Fort Lewis College, CO
Geneva College, PA
Huntington University, IN
Illinois State University, IL
Indiana University of Pennsylvania, PA
John Brown University, AR
Kentucky Christian University, KY
Lake Superior State University, MI
Lipscomb University, TN
Lock Haven University of Pennsylvania, PA
MacMurray College, IL
Messiah College, PA
Montana State University, MT
Montana State University–Billings, MT
Montana Tech of The University of Montana, MT
Nazareth College of Rochester, NY
North Dakota State University, ND
Northern Illinois University, IL
Oakland City University, IN
Polytechnic University, Brooklyn Campus, NY
Portland State University, OR
Ramapo College of New Jersey, NJ
St. Ambrose University, IA
Saint Joseph's College, IN
St. Thomas University, FL
Shepherd University, WV
Simon's Rock College of Bard, MA
Slippery Rock University of Pennsylvania, PA
Southeastern Oklahoma State University, OK
Union College, KY
University at Buffalo, The State University of New York, NY
University of Evansville, IN
University of Hawaii at Manoa, HI
University of Idaho, ID
University of Maine at Farmington, ME
University of Maine at Presque Isle, ME
University of Michigan–Flint, MI
University of North Dakota, ND
University of Rhode Island, RI
University of Southern Maine, ME
University of West Georgia, GA

University of Wisconsin–Eau Claire, WI
University of Wisconsin–Superior, WI
Utah State University, UT
Washington College, MD
Wayne State College, NE
William Jewell College, MO
Wittenberg University, OH

Children of Alumni

Adrian College, MI
Albertson College of Idaho, ID
Albion College, MI
Albright College, PA
Alliant International University, CA
Anna Maria College, MA
Arkansas State University, AR
Ashland University, OH
Augsburg College, MN
Baldwin-Wallace College, OH
Barton College, NC
Benedictine University, IL
Bethany College, WV
Bethel College, KS
Bryan College, TN
Caldwell College, NJ
Cedar Crest College, PA
Centenary College, NJ
Central Christian College of Kansas, KS
Central Michigan University, MI
Central Missouri State University, MO
Centre College, KY
Chapman University, CA
Christian Brothers University, TN
Clarke College, IA
Coe College, IA
College of Visual Arts, MN
Columbia College, MO
Curry College, MA
Dominican University, IL
Dowling College, NY
Drake University, IA
D'Youville College, NY
Erskine College, SC
Eureka College, IL
Faulkner University, AL
Florida Southern College, FL
Grace University, NE
Grambling State University, LA
Heidelberg College, OH
Hilbert College, NY
Hillsdale College, MI
Huntington University, IN
John Brown University, AR
Kentucky Wesleyan College, KY
Lake Superior State University, MI
Lancaster Bible College, PA
Life Pacific College, CA

Louisiana State University and Agricultural and Mechanical College, LA
Louisiana Tech University, LA
MacMurray College, IL
Marymount Manhattan College, NY
Marymount University, VA
Messiah College, PA
Mississippi State University, MS
Missouri Baptist University, MO
Missouri State University, MO
Missouri Valley College, MO
Mitchell College, CT
Moravian College, PA
Morehead State University, KY
Morningside College, IA
Mount Union College, OH
Murray State University, KY
Nazareth College of Rochester, NY
New England College, NH
North Dakota State University, ND
Northwestern College, MN
Northwood University, MI
Northwood University, Florida Campus, FL
Northwood University, Texas Campus, TX
Ohio Wesleyan University, OH
Oklahoma State University, OK
Oral Roberts University, OK
Peirce College, PA
Philadelphia Biblical University, PA
Point Park University, PA
Ripon College, WI
Rochester College, MI
Rockhurst University, MO
St. Ambrose University, IA
Saint Joseph's College, IN
Saint Martin's College, WA
St. Thomas University, FL
Silver Lake College, WI
South Dakota State University, SD
Southeastern Bible College, AL
Southeastern Oklahoma State University, OK
Southern Arkansas University– Magnolia, AR
Southern University and Agricultural and Mechanical College, LA
Taylor University Fort Wayne, IN
Texas Lutheran University, TX
Thomas More College, KY
Trinity College of Florida, FL
Union College, KY
University of Alaska Anchorage, AK
University of Alaska Fairbanks, AK
University of Alaska Southeast, AK
University of Dubuque, IA
University of Evansville, IN
The University of Findlay, OH

University of Idaho, ID
University of Mississippi, MS
University of Nebraska Medical Center, NE
University of Nevada, Las Vegas, NV
University of Nevada, Reno, NV
University of New England, ME
University of Rochester, NY
University of St. Francis, IL
University of Saint Francis, IN
University of Southern Mississippi, MS
University of Wisconsin–Whitewater, WI
University of Wyoming, WY
Urbana University, OH
Utah State University, UT
Valley City State University, ND
Warner Pacific College, OR
Washington State University, WA
Webber International University, FL
Wells College, NY
Westminster College, MO
William Jewell College, MO
William Woods University, MO
Wilson College, PA
Wittenberg University, OH

Adult Students

Alaska Pacific University, AK
Albertson College of Idaho, ID
Anderson College, SC
Anderson University, IN
Augustana College, SD
Barton College, NC
California State University, Stanislaus, CA
Charter Oak State College, CT
Clarke College, IA
Coe College, IA
College of the Atlantic, ME
Converse College, SC
Cornell College, IA
Creighton University, NE
Dowling College, NY
D'Youville College, NY
Goucher College, MD
Hastings College, NE
Huntington University, IN
John Brown University, AR
Juniata College, PA
Lambuth University, TN
Lancaster Bible College, PA
Marymount Manhattan College, NY
Messiah College, PA
Mount Union College, OH
Nebraska Wesleyan University, NE
New England College, NH
Randolph-Macon Woman's College, VA
St. Andrews Presbyterian College, NC
St. Gregory's University, OK
St. Olaf College, MN
Shimer College, IL
Simmons College, MA
Southern Adventist University, TN
Sweet Briar College, VA
Trinity College, CT
University of West Georgia, GA
Utah State University, UT
Webber International University, FL

Wittenberg University, OH

Senior Citizens

Alaska Pacific University, AK
Albertson College of Idaho, ID
Albright College, PA
Alvernia College, PA
American International College, MA
Anderson College, SC
Andrews University, MI
Anna Maria College, MA
Appalachian Bible College, WV
Arkansas State University, AR
Arkansas Tech University, AR
Armstrong Atlantic State University, GA
Asbury College, KY
Ashland University, OH
Athens State University, AL
Atlantic Union College, MA
Augsburg College, MN
Augustana College, SD
Augusta State University, GA
Aurora University, IL
Austin Peay State University, TN
Averett University, VA
Baker University, KS
Barton College, NC
Becker College, MA
Belmont Abbey College, NC
Belmont University, TN
Bemidji State University, MN
Benedictine College, KS
Bernard M. Baruch College of the City
  University of New York, NY
Berry College, GA
Bethel College, KS
Bethel University, MN
Black Hills State University, SD
Bloomfield College, NJ
Bloomsburg University of Pennsylvania, PA
Bluefield State College, WV
Boise State University, ID
Boston University, MA
Bowie State University, MD
Bowling Green State University, OH
Bradley University, IL
Brevard College, NC
Brewton-Parker College, GA
Bridgewater College, VA
Bryn Mawr College, PA
Caldwell College, NJ
California State University, Chico, CA
California State University, Fullerton, CA
California State University, Sacramento, CA
California State University, San
  Marcos, CA
California State University, Stanislaus, CA
Cameron University, OK
Campbellsville University, KY
Carroll College, MT
Carson-Newman College, TN
Castleton State College, VT
Cedarville University, OH
Centenary College, NJ
Central Connecticut State University, CT
Central Michigan University, MI
Central Missouri State University, MO

Central Washington University, WA
Chadron State College, NE
Champlain College, VT
Chestnut Hill College, PA
Chowan College, NC
Christopher Newport University, VA
Clarke College, IA
Clayton State University, GA
Cleary University, MI
Clemson University, SC
Cleveland State University, OH
Coastal Carolina University, SC
Coe College, IA
College of Charleston, SC
College of Mount St. Joseph, OH
College of Mount Saint Vincent, NY
The College of New Jersey, NJ
The College of New Rochelle, NY
College of St. Joseph, VT
College of Saint Mary, NE
College of Santa Fe, NM
College of Staten Island of the City
  University of New York, NY
College of the Atlantic, ME
The College of William and Mary, VA
Colorado State University-Pueblo, CO
Columbus State University, GA
Concordia University, OR
Connecticut College, CT
Converse College, SC
Cornell College, IA
Culver-Stockton College, MO
Curry College, MA
Daemen College, NY
Defiance College, OH
DeSales University, PA
Dickinson State University, ND
Doane College, NE
Dominican University of California, CA
Dordt College, IA
Dowling College, NY
Drake University, IA
Drew University, NJ
Duquesne University, PA
D'Youville College, NY
East Carolina University, NC
East Central University, OK
East Stroudsburg University of
  Pennsylvania, PA
East Tennessee State University, TN
Elmhurst College, IL
Emporia State University, KS
Eureka College, IL
Fairleigh Dickinson University, College at
  Florham, NJ
Fairleigh Dickinson University,
  Metropolitan Campus, NJ
Fairmont State University, WV
Ferrum College, VA
Florida Atlantic University, FL
Florida Gulf Coast University, FL
Florida Institute of Technology, FL
Florida State University, FL
Fort Hays State University, KS
Framingham State College, MA
Francis Marion University, SC

Franklin College, IN
Franklin Pierce College, NH
Freed-Hardeman University, TN
Fresno Pacific University, CA
Frostburg State University, MD
Gannon University, PA
George Mason University, VA
Georgian Court University, NJ
Georgia Southern University, GA
Georgia State University, GA
Glenville State College, WV
Goucher College, MD
Graceland University, IA
Grace University, NE
Grambling State University, LA
Grand View College, IA
Greenville College, IL
Hanover College, IN
Harding University, AR
Hilbert College, NY
Hofstra University, NY
Houghton College, NY
Houston Baptist University, TX
Howard Payne University, TX
Humboldt State University, CA
Huntington University, IN
Husson College, ME
Idaho State University, ID
Illinois State University, IL
Indiana University Northwest, IN
Iona College, NY
James Madison University, VA
John Brown University, AR
Kean University, NJ
Kennesaw State University, GA
Kentucky Wesleyan College, KY
King's College, PA
Kutztown University of Pennsylvania, PA
Lake Erie College, OH
Lake Superior State University, MI
Lambuth University, TN
Lancaster Bible College, PA
La Roche College, PA
Lebanon Valley College, PA
Lehigh University, PA
Lehman College of the City University of New York, NY
Lewis-Clark State College, ID
Lincoln Memorial University, TN
Lincoln University, MO
Lindenwood University, MO
Linfield College, OR
Lock Haven University of Pennsylvania, PA
Loras College, IA
Louisiana Tech University, LA
Lourdes College, OH
Loyola University New Orleans, LA
Lynchburg College, VA
MacMurray College, IL
Malone College, OH
Manhattan Christian College, KS
Manhattanville College, NY
Marian College of Fond du Lac, WI
Marlboro College, VT
Marymount Manhattan College, NY
Marymount University, VA

Maryville University of Saint Louis, MO
Massachusetts College of Art, MA
McPherson College, KS
Medical University of South Carolina, SC
Merrimack College, MA
Messiah College, PA
Methodist College, NC
Metropolitan State College of Denver, CO
Michigan Technological University, MI
MidAmerica Nazarene University, KS
Middle Tennessee State University, TN
Midway College, KY
Midwestern State University, TX
Millersville University of Pennsylvania, PA
Minnesota State University Mankato, MN
Minnesota State University Moorhead, MN
Mississippi State University, MS
Missouri Baptist University, MO
Missouri State University, MO
Missouri Valley College, MO
Monmouth University, NJ
Montana State University, MT
Montana State University–Billings, MT
Montana Tech of The University of Montana, MT
Montclair State University, NJ
Morehead State University, KY
Morningside College, IA
Mountain State University, WV
Mount Mary College, WI
Mount Olive College, NC
Mount Vernon Nazarene University, OH
Murray State University, KY
Muskingum College, OH
Nebraska Wesleyan University, NE
New England College, NH
New Mexico Institute of Mining and Technology, NM
New Mexico State University, NM
New York Institute of Technology, NY
Niagara University, NY
Norfolk State University, VA
North Carolina State University, NC
North Central College, IL
North Central University, MN
North Dakota State University, ND
Northeastern State University, OK
Northeastern University, MA
Northern Kentucky University, KY
Northern Michigan University, MI
Northwestern College, MN
Northwestern Oklahoma State University, OK
Northwestern State University of Louisiana, LA
Northwest University, WA
Oakland City University, IN
The Ohio State University, OH
Ohio University–Southern Campus, OH
Ohio University–Zanesville, OH
Ohio Valley University, WV
Oklahoma Baptist University, OK
Oklahoma Wesleyan University, OK
Old Dominion University, VA
Pacific Lutheran University, WA
Pacific Union College, CA

Park University, MO
The Pennsylvania State College, PA
The Pennsylvania State University College, PA
The Pennsylvania State University The Behrend College, PA
The Pennsylvania State University Campus of the Berks–Lehigh College, PA
The Pennsylvania State University Harrisburg Campus of the Capital College, PA
The Pennsylvania State University, Valley Campus of the Berks-Lehigh College, PA
The Pennsylvania State University Schuylkill Campus of the Capital College, PA
Pikeville College, KY
Plymouth State University, NH
Portland State University, OR
Post University, CT
Presentation College, SD
Providence College, RI
Purdue University, IN
Purdue University Calumet, IN
Quincy University, IL
Ramapo College of New Jersey, NJ
Research College of Nursing, MO
The Richard Stockton College of New Jersey, NJ
Roanoke College, VA
Rochester College, MI
Rockhurst University, MO
Rosemont College, PA
Rust College, MS
St. Ambrose University, IA
St. Andrews Presbyterian College, NC
Saint Anselm College, NH
St. Bonaventure University, NY
St. Cloud State University, MN
St. Gregory's University, OK
St. Joseph's College, Suffolk Campus, NY
St. Mary's College of Maryland, MD
St. Olaf College, MN
Saint Vincent College, PA
Saint Xavier University, IL
Salem State College, MA
Salisbury University, MD
Seattle Pacific University, WA
Seton Hall University, NJ
Shawnee State University, OH
Shepherd University, WV
Shimer College, IL
Shippensburg University of Pennsylvania, PA
Shorter College, GA
Silver Lake College, WI
Simmons College, MA
Slippery Rock University of Pennsylvania, PA
South Carolina State University, SC
South Dakota School of Mines and Technology, SD
South Dakota State University, SD

Southeastern Louisiana University, LA

Southeastern Oklahoma State University, OK

Southeast Missouri State University, MO

Southern Adventist University, TN

Southern Arkansas University–Magnolia, AR

Southern Christian University, AL

Southern Connecticut State University, CT

Southern Illinois University Carbondale, IL

Southern Illinois University Edwardsville, IL

Southern Methodist College, SC

Southern Oregon University, OR

Southern Polytechnic State University, GA

Southern University and Agricultural and Mechanical College, LA

Southern Vermont College, VT

Southern Wesleyan University, SC

Southwestern College, KS

Spring Arbor University, MI

State University of New York College at Brockport, NY

State University of New York College at Geneseo, NY

State University of New York College at Old Westbury, NY

Sterling College, KS

Suffolk University, MA

Sweet Briar College, VA

Tarleton State University, TX

Taylor University, IN

Taylor University Fort Wayne, IN

Texas A&M University–Commerce, TX

Texas A&M University–Texarkana, TX

Texas Tech University, TX

Thiel College, PA

Thomas University, GA

Tiffin University, OH

Towson University, MD

Trevecca Nazarene University, TN

Trinity College of Florida, FL

Truman State University, MO

Union College, KY

Union College, NY

University at Albany, State University of New York, NY

The University of Akron, OH

University of Alaska Anchorage, AK

University of Alaska Fairbanks, AK

University of Alaska Southeast, AK

University of Arkansas at Monticello, AR

University of Arkansas at Pine Bluff, AR

University of Bridgeport, CT

University of Central Florida, FL

University of Charleston, WV

University of Colorado at Boulder, CO

University of Connecticut, CT

University of Dayton, OH

University of Delaware, DE

University of Evansville, IN

The University of Findlay, OH

University of Florida, FL

University of Georgia, GA

University of Great Falls, MT

University of Hartford, CT

University of Houston–Downtown, TX

University of Houston–Victoria, TX

University of Idaho, ID

University of Illinois at Chicago, IL

University of Illinois at Springfield, IL

University of Illinois at Urbana–Champaign, IL

University of Indianapolis, IN

University of Louisville, KY

The University of Maine at Augusta, ME

University of Maine at Farmington, ME

University of Maine at Presque Isle, ME

University of Mary, ND

University of Maryland, Baltimore County, MD

University of Maryland Eastern Shore, MD

University of Mary Washington, VA

University of Massachusetts Amherst, MA

University of Massachusetts Boston, MA

University of Massachusetts Dartmouth, MA

University of Massachusetts Lowell, MA

The University of Memphis, TN

University of Michigan, MI

University of Michigan–Dearborn, MI

University of Michigan–Flint, MI

University of Minnesota, Morris, MN

University of Minnesota, Twin Cities Campus, MN

University of Mississippi, MS

University of Missouri–Columbia, MO

University of Missouri–St. Louis, MO

The University of Montana–Western, MT

University of Nevada, Las Vegas, NV

University of Nevada, Reno, NV

University of New Hampshire, NH

University of New Hampshire at Manchester, NH

University of New Orleans, LA

University of North Alabama, AL

The University of North Carolina at Asheville, NC

The University of North Carolina at Chapel Hill, NC

The University of North Carolina at Charlotte, NC

The University of North Carolina at Pembroke, NC

The University of North Carolina at Wilmington, NC

University of North Dakota, ND

University of North Florida, FL

University of North Texas, TX

University of Oklahoma, OK

University of Rhode Island, RI

University of Rio Grande, OH

University of Saint Francis, IN

University of St. Thomas, MN

University of St. Thomas, TX

University of Science and Arts of Oklahoma, OK

The University of Scranton, PA

University of South Carolina, SC

University of South Carolina Upstate, SC

The University of South Dakota, SD

University of Southern Indiana, IN

University of Southern Maine, ME

University of Southern Mississippi, MS

University of South Florida, FL

The University of Tennessee at Chattanooga, TN

The University of Tennessee at Martin, TN

The University of Texas at Austin, TX

The University of Texas at Dallas, TX

The University of Texas at Tyler, TX

The University of Texas–Pan American, TX

University of the District of Columbia, DC

University of the Virgin Islands, VI

University of Utah, UT

University of Vermont, VT

University of Virginia, VA

The University of Virginia's College at Wise, VA

University of Washington, WA

University of West Florida, FL

University of West Georgia, GA

University of Wisconsin–Eau Claire, WI

University of Wisconsin–Green Bay, WI

University of Wisconsin–Parkside, WI

University of Wisconsin–Stevens Point, WI

University of Wisconsin–Superior, WI

University of Wisconsin–Whitewater, WI

University of Wyoming, WY

Urbana University, OH

Ursinus College, PA

Utah State University, UT

Utica College, NY

Valdosta State University, GA

Villanova University, PA

Virginia Commonwealth University, VA

Virginia Intermont College, VA

Virginia Wesleyan College, VA

Walla Walla College, WA

Wartburg College, IA

Wayne State University, MI

Webber International University, FL

Wells College, NY

Wesley College, DE

Western Carolina University, NC

Western Connecticut State University, CT

Western Illinois University, IL

Western Kentucky University, KY

Western New England College, MA

Western State College of Colorado, CO

West Liberty State College, WV

West Virginia University, WV

Wheeling Jesuit University, WV

Wichita State University, KS

William Jewell College, MO

William Paterson University of New Jersey, NJ

William Penn University, IA

Williams Baptist College, AR

William Woods University, MO

Winston-Salem State University, NC

Winthrop University, SC

Wittenberg University, OH

Worcester State College, MA

Xavier University, OH

Youngstown State University, OH

Tuition Payment Alternatives

Abilene Christian University, TX	I,P
Academy of Art University, CA	I
Adelphi University, NY	D,I,P
Adrian College, MI	I
Agnes Scott College, GA	I
Alaska Pacific University, AK	D,G,I
Albertson College of Idaho, ID	G
Albion College, MI	I
Albright College, PA	I
Alderson-Broaddus College, WV	I
Alfred University, NY	D,I,P
Alice Lloyd College, KY	D
Allegheny College, PA	I,P
Allen College, IA	I
Alliant International University, CA	I
Alma College, MI	D,I
Alvernia College, PA	I
Alverno College, WI	D,I
American Baptist College of American Baptist Theological Seminary, TN	D
American International College, MA	D,I,P
American University, DC	I
Amherst College, MA	D,I
Anderson College, SC	I
Anderson University, IN	I
Andrews University, MI	I,P
Angelo State University, TX	I
Anna Maria College, MA	I
Antioch College, OH	I
Antioch University McGregor, OH	I
Antioch University Seattle, WA	I
Appalachian Bible College, WV	I
Appalachian State University, NC	I
Aquinas College, TN	I
Arcadia University, PA	D,I
Argosy University/Twin Cities, MN	I
Arizona State University, AZ	I
Arizona State University East, AZ	I
Arizona State University West, AZ	I
Arkansas State University, AR	I
Arkansas Tech University, AR	D,I
Arlington Baptist College, TX	I
Art Academy of Cincinnati, OH	I
Art Center College of Design, CA	I
The Art Institute of Colorado, CO	G,I
The Art Institute of Portland, OR	G,I
Asbury College, KY	D,I
Ashland University, OH	I
Assumption College, MA	I
Atlanta College of Art, GA	I
Auburn University, AL	I
Auburn University Montgomery, AL	D
Augsburg College, MN	D,I
Augustana College, SD	I
Aurora University, IL	D,I
Austin College, TX	I

Austin Graduate School of Theology, TX	I
Austin Peay State University, TN	D,I
Averett University, VA	I
Azusa Pacific University, CA	I
Babson College, MA	I
Baker University, KS	I
Baldwin-Wallace College, OH	D,I
Ball State University, IN	I
The Baptist College of Florida, FL	I
Bard College, NY	I,P
Barry University, FL	D,I,P
Barton College, NC	I
Bates College, ME	I,P
Baylor University, TX	I
Bay Path College, MA	D,I
Becker College, MA	I
Belhaven College, MS	I
Bellevue University, NE	D,I
Bellin College of Nursing, WI	I
Belmont Abbey College, NC	D,I
Belmont University, TN	D,I
Beloit College, WI	I
Bemidji State University, MN	I
Benedictine College, KS	I
Benedictine University, IL	I
Bennington College, VT	I
Bentley College, MA	I
Berklee College of Music, MA	I,P
Bernard M. Baruch College of the City University of New York, NY	D,I
Berry College, GA	I
Bethany College, KS	I
Bethany College, WV	I
Bethany Lutheran College, MN	I
Bethel College, KS	D,I
Bethel College, TN	I
Bethel University, MN	I
Beulah Heights Bible College, GA	D,I
Biola University, CA	I
Blessing-Rieman College of Nursing, IL	I
Bloomfield College, NJ	D,I
Bluefield State College, WV	D
Blue Mountain College, MS	I
Bluffton University, OH	I
Boise State University, ID	D
Boston Architectural Center, MA	I
Boston College, MA	I,P
Boston University, MA	I,P
Bowdoin College, ME	D,I
Bowie State University, MD	D,I
Bowling Green State University, OH	I
Bradley University, IL	D,I
Brandeis University, MA	I
Brenau University, GA	I
Brevard College, NC	I

Brewton-Parker College, GA	I
Bridgewater College, VA	I
Bridgewater State College, MA	I
Brigham Young University, UT	D
Brigham Young University–Hawaii, HI	I
Bryan College, TN	I
Bryant University, RI	I
Bryn Mawr College, PA	I,P
Bucknell University, PA	I
Burlington College, VT	I
Butler University, IN	I
Caldwell College, NJ	D,I
California Baptist University, CA	D,I
California College of the Arts, CA	D,I
California Institute of Technology, CA	D,I
California Institute of the Arts, CA	D
California Lutheran University, CA	I
California State University, Chico, CA	D,I
California State University, Dominguez Hills, CA	I
California State University, Fullerton, CA	D,I
California State University, Sacramento, CA	I
California State University, Stanislaus, CA	D,I
Calvary Bible College and Theological Seminary, MO	I
Calvin College, MI	I,P
Cameron University, OK	I
Campbellsville University, KY	I
Campbell University, NC	I
Canisius College, NY	D,I,P
Capitol College, MD	D,I
Carnegie Mellon University, PA	I
Carroll College, MT	I
Carroll College, WI	I
Carson-Newman College, TN	I
Case Western Reserve University, OH	I
Castleton State College, VT	I
Catawba College, NC	I
The Catholic University of America, DC	I,P
Cazenovia College, NY	I
Cedar Crest College, PA	I
Cedarville University, OH	I
Centenary College, NJ	I
Centenary College of Louisiana, LA	D,I
Central Christian College of Kansas, KS	I
Central College, IA	I
Central Connecticut State University, CT	D,I
Central Methodist University, MO	I
Central Michigan University, MI	I
Central Missouri State University, MO	D,I
Central Pennsylvania College, PA	D

D = deferred payment system; *G* = guaranteed tuition rate; *I* = installment payments; *P* = prepayment locks in tuition rate

Tuition Payment Alternatives

Institution	Code
Centre College, KY	I
Chaminade University of Honolulu, HI	I
Champlain College, VT	I
Chapman University, CA	D,I,P
Charter Oak State College, CT	I
Chatham College, PA	I
Chester College of New England, NH	I
Chestnut Hill College, PA	D,I
Chowan College, NC	D,I
Christendom College, VA	I,P
Christian Brothers University, TN	D,I
Christian Heritage College, CA	I
Christopher Newport University, VA	I
City College of the City University of New York, NY	D
Claremont McKenna College, CA	I,P
Clark Atlanta University, GA	D
Clarke College, IA	D,I
Clarkson University, NY	I,P
Clark University, MA	I,P
Clearwater Christian College, FL	I
Cleary University, MI	D,G,I
Clemson University, SC	I
The Cleveland Institute of Art, OH	I
Cleveland Institute of Music, OH	I
Cleveland State University, OH	I
Coastal Carolina University, SC	D,I
Coe College, IA	I
Colby-Sawyer College, NH	I
Colgate University, NY	D,I,P
College for Creative Studies, MI	D,I
College Misericordia, PA	D,I
College of Charleston, SC	I
College of Mount St. Joseph, OH	D,I
College of Mount Saint Vincent, NY	I
The College of New Jersey, NJ	I
The College of New Rochelle, NY	I,P
College of Notre Dame of Maryland, MD	I
College of Saint Benedict, MN	I,P
College of St. Joseph, VT	I
College of Saint Mary, NE	D,I
The College of St. Scholastica, MN	I
College of Santa Fe, NM	I
College of Staten Island of the City University of New York, NY	I
College of the Atlantic, ME	I
College of the Holy Cross, MA	I
College of the Ozarks, MO	I
College of Visual Arts, MN	I
The College of William and Mary, VA	I
The College of Wooster, OH	I
Colorado Christian University, CO	I
The Colorado College, CO	I
Colorado School of Mines, CO	I
Colorado State University, CO	I
Colorado State University-Pueblo, CO	D,I
Columbia College, MO	D
Columbia College, NY	I,P
Columbia College, SC	I,P
Columbia College Chicago, IL	I
Columbia International University, SC	I
Columbia University, The Fu Foundation School of Engineering and Applied Science, NY	I,P
Columbus College of Art & Design, OH	D,I
Concordia College, MN	I
Concordia University, CA	I
Concordia University, MI	I
Concordia University, NE	I
Concordia University, OR	I
Concordia University, St. Paul, MN	I
Concordia University Wisconsin, WI	D,I
Connecticut College, CT	I
Converse College, SC	I
Corban College, OR	I
Corcoran College of Art and Design, DC	I
Cornell College, IA	I
Cornell University, NY	I
Cornerstone University, MI	I
Creighton University, NE	I
Crown College, MN	I
The Culinary Institute of America, NY	I
Culver-Stockton College, MO	I
Curry College, MA	I
Daemen College, NY	D,I
Dakota State University, SD	D,I
Dallas Baptist University, TX	I
Dallas Christian College, TX	I
Daniel Webster College, NH	I
Dartmouth College, NH	P
Davis & Elkins College, WV	I
Defiance College, OH	I
Denison University, OH	I
DePaul University, IL	D,I
DePauw University, IN	D,I,P
DeSales University, PA	D,I
Dickinson College, PA	I
Dillard University, LA	I
Doane College, NE	I
Dominican College, NY	D,I
Dominican University, IL	I
Dominican University of California, CA	I
Dordt College, IA	I
Dowling College, NY	D,I
Drake University, IA	I
Drew University, NJ	D,I,P
Duke University, NC	D,I
Duquesne University, PA	D,I
D'Youville College, NY	D,G,I
East Carolina University, NC	D,I
Eastern Illinois University, IL	G,I
Eastern Mennonite University, VA	I
Eastern Michigan University, MI	I
Eastern Washington University, WA	I
East Stroudsburg University of Pennsylvania, PA	I
East Tennessee State University, TN	D,I,P
East Texas Baptist University, TX	G,I
Eckerd College, FL	I
Edinboro University of Pennsylvania, PA	I
Elizabethtown College, PA	I
Elmhurst College, IL	I
Elmira College, NY	I,P
Elon University, NC	I
Embry-Riddle Aeronautical University, FL	D,I
Emerson College, MA	I
Emmanuel College, MA	I
Emmaus Bible College, IA	I
Emory & Henry College, VA	I
Emory University, GA	I,P
Emporia State University, KS	D,I
Endicott College, MA	I
Erskine College, SC	I
Eugene Bible College, OR	P
Eureka College, IL	I
Evangel University, MO	I
The Evergreen State College, WA	I
Excelsior College, NY	I
Fairfield University, CT	I
Fairleigh Dickinson University, College at Florham, NJ	D,I
Fairleigh Dickinson University, Metropolitan Campus, NJ	D,I
Fairmont State University, WV	I
Fashion Institute of Technology, NY	I
Faulkner University, AL	D,I
Ferris State University, MI	D,I
Ferrum College, VA	I
Finlandia University, MI	I
Five Towns College, NY	I
Florida Atlantic University, FL	D,I,P
Florida College, FL	I
Florida Institute of Technology, FL	I
Florida Metropolitan University– Tampa Campus, FL	I
Florida Southern College, FL	I
Florida State University, FL	I,P
Fordham University, NY	I,P
Fort Hays State University, KS	I
Framingham State College, MA	I
Francis Marion University, SC	I
Franklin and Marshall College, PA	D,I
Franklin College, IN	I
Franklin Pierce College, NH	I
Freed-Hardeman University, TN	I,P
Free Will Baptist Bible College, TN	D,I
Fresno Pacific University, CA	I
Frostburg State University, MD	D,I
Furman University, SC	I
Gallaudet University, DC	I
Gannon University, PA	D,I
Geneva College, PA	I
George Mason University, VA	D,I
Georgetown College, KY	D,I
Georgetown University, DC	D,I
The George Washington University, DC	D,G,I
Georgian Court University, NJ	D,I
Gettysburg College, PA	I,P
Glenville State College, WV	I
Goddard College, VT	I
Gonzaga University, WA	D,I
Gordon College, MA	I
Goshen College, IN	I
Goucher College, MD	I,P
Grace Bible College, MI	I
Grace College, IN	I
Graceland University, IA	I
Grace University, NE	I
Grambling State University, LA	D
Grand Valley State University, MI	D,I

D = deferred payment system; *G* = guaranteed tuition rate; *I* = installment payments; *P* = prepayment locks in tuition rate

Grand View College, IA	I	John Jay College of Criminal Justice		Lincoln University, PA	D,I
Green Mountain College, VT	I	of the City University of New		Lindenwood University, MO	D,I
Grinnell College, IA	G,I,P	York, NY	I	Linfield College, OR	I
Grove City College, PA	I	The Johns Hopkins University, MD	I	Lipscomb University, TN	I
Guilford College, NC	I	Johnson & Wales University, RI	D,I	Lock Haven University of	
Gustavus Adolphus College, MN	G,I,P	Johnson Bible College, TN	I	Pennsylvania, PA	D,I
Gwynedd-Mercy College, PA	I	Johnson C. Smith University, NC	I	Long Island University, Brooklyn	
Hamilton College, NY	I	John Wesley College, NC	I	Campus, NY	D
Hamline University, MN	I	Jones International University, CO	D,P	Longwood University, VA	I
Hampden-Sydney College, VA	I	Judson College, AL	I	Loras College, IA	I
Hampshire College, MA	I	Juniata College, PA	I	Louisiana State University and	
Hampton University, VA	D	Kalamazoo College, MI	I	Agricultural and Mechanical	
Hannibal-LaGrange College, MO	I	Kansas State University, KS	D,I	College, LA	D
Hanover College, IN	I	Kean University, NJ	D,I	Louisiana Tech University, LA	D,I
Harding University, AR	I	Keene State College, NH	I	Lourdes College, OH	D,I
Harvey Mudd College, CA	I	Kennesaw State University, GA	D	Loyola Marymount University, CA	D,I
Hastings College, NE	D,I	Kent State University, OH	D,I,P	Loyola University Chicago, IL	I
Haverford College, PA	I	Kentucky Christian University, KY	I	Loyola University New Orleans, LA	I
Hawai'i Pacific University, HI	I	Kentucky Mountain Bible		Lubbock Christian University, TX	I
Heidelberg College, OH	D,I	College, KY	D,I	Luther College, IA	I
Hendrix College, AR	I	Kentucky Wesleyan College, KY	D,I	Luther Rice Bible College and	
Heritage Christian University, AL	I	Kenyon College, OH	I	Seminary, GA	I
Heritage University, WA	D,I	Kettering University, MI	I	Lycoming College, PA	I
Hilbert College, NY	D,I	Keuka College, NY	I	Lyme Academy College of Fine	
Hillsdale College, MI	D,I,P	King College, TN	I,P	Arts, CT	I
Hobart and William Smith		King's College, PA	D,I	Lynchburg College, VA	I
Colleges, NY	I,P	Knox College, IL	I	Lynn University, FL	D,I
Hofstra University, NY	D,I	Kutztown University of		Lyon College, AR	I
Hollins University, VA	I	Pennsylvania, PA	D,I,P	Macalester College, MN	I
Holy Names University, CA	I	Laboratory Institute of		MacMurray College, IL	I
Hope College, MI	I	Merchandising, NY	I	Magnolia Bible College, MS	D
Houghton College, NY	I	LaGrange College, GA	I	Maharishi University of	
Houston Baptist University, TX	I,P	Laguna College of Art & Design, CA	I	Management, IA	I
Howard Payne University, TX	D,I	Lake Erie College, OH	G,I	Maine College of Art, ME	I
Howard University, DC	D	Lake Forest College, IL	I	Maine Maritime Academy, ME	I
Humboldt State University, CA	I	Lakeland College, WI	I	Malone College, OH	I
Huntington University, IN	G,I	Lake Superior State University, MI	D,I	Manchester College, IN	I
Husson College, ME	I,P	Lamar University, TX	I	Manhattan Christian College, KS	D
Idaho State University, ID	D	Lambuth University, TN	D,I	Manhattan College, NY	I
Illinois College, IL	D,I	Lancaster Bible College, PA	I	Manhattan School of Music, NY	D,I
Illinois State University, IL	G,I	La Roche College, PA	I	Manhattanville College, NY	D,I
Illinois Wesleyan University, IL	I	La Salle University, PA	D,I	Marian College of Fond du Lac, WI	I
Indiana State University, IN	D,I	Laura and Alvin Siegal College of		Marietta College, OH	I
Indiana University Bloomington, IN	D	Judaic Studies, OH	I	Marist College, NY	I
Indiana University East, IN	D	Lawrence Technological		Marlboro College, VT	I
Indiana University Northwest, IN	D,I	University, MI	I	Marshall University, WV	D,I
Indiana University of		Lawrence University, WI	I,P	Mars Hill College, NC	I
Pennsylvania, PA	D,I	Lebanon Valley College, PA	I,P	Martin Methodist College, TN	I
Indiana University–Purdue University		Lee University, TN	D	Mary Baldwin College, VA	I
Fort Wayne, IN	D,I	Lehigh University, PA	I,P	Marylhurst University, OR	D,I
Indiana University–Purdue University		Lehman College of the City		Marymount College of Fordham	
Indianapolis, IN	D,I	University of New York, NY	I	University, NY	D,I
Indiana University South Bend, IN	D,I	Le Moyne College, NY	D,I	Marymount Manhattan College, NY	I
Indiana University Southeast, IN	D	LeMoyne-Owen College, TN	I	Marymount University, VA	D,I
Inter American University of Puerto		Lenoir-Rhyne College, NC	D,I	Maryville College, TN	I
Rico, San Germán Campus, PR	D	Lesley University, MA	I	Maryville University of Saint	
International College, FL	I	LeTourneau University, TX	I	Louis, MO	D,I
Iona College, NY	I	Lewis & Clark College, OR	I	Massachusetts College of Art, MA	I
Iowa State University of Science and		Lewis-Clark State College, ID	D	Massachusetts College of Pharmacy	
Technology, IA	D,I	Lexington College, IL	I	and Health Sciences, MA	I
Iowa Wesleyan College, IA	D,I	Liberty University, VA	I	Massachusetts Institute of	
Ithaca College, NY	I	Life Pacific College, CA	I	Technology, MA	I
James Madison University, VA	I	Limestone College, SC	I	Massachusetts Maritime	
Jamestown College, ND	I	Lincoln Christian College, IL	D,I	Academy, MA	I
John Brown University, AR	I	Lincoln Memorial University, TN	D,I	McDaniel College, MD	I
John F. Kennedy University, CA	D	Lincoln University, MO	I	McKendree College, IL	D,I

D = deferred payment system; *G* = guaranteed tuition rate; *I* = installment payments; *P* = prepayment locks in tuition rate

Tuition Payment Alternatives

McMurry University, TX	I	Mount Mary College, WI	I	Oakland City University, IN	D,I
McPherson College, KS	I	Mount Mercy College, IA	I	Oakland University, MI	D,I
Medgar Evers College of the City University of New York, NY	D,I	Mount Olive College, NC	I	Oberlin College, OH	I
		Mount Saint Mary College, NY	I	Oglethorpe University, GA	I,P
Medical University of South Carolina, SC	I	Mount St. Mary's University, MD	I	Ohio Northern University, OH	I
		Mount Union College, OH	I,P	The Ohio State University, OH	I
Memphis College of Art, TN	D,I	Mount Vernon Nazarene University, OH	I	Ohio University, OH	I
Menlo College, CA	I			Ohio University–Southern Campus, OH	I
Mercer University, GA	I	Multnomah Bible College and Biblical Seminary, OR	I		
Mercyhurst College, PA	I			Ohio Valley University, WV	I
Meredith College, NC	I	Murray State University, KY	I	Ohio Wesleyan University, OH	I
Merrimack College, MA	D,I	Muskingum College, OH	I	Oklahoma Baptist University, OK	I
Mesa State College, CO	I	Naropa University, CO	I	Oklahoma City University, OK	D,I
Messenger College, MO	I	Nazarene Bible College, CO	I	Oklahoma Panhandle State University, OK	I
Messiah College, PA	I	Nazareth College of Rochester, NY	I		
Methodist College, NC	D,I	Nebraska Christian College, NE	I	Oklahoma State University, OK	I
Metropolitan State College of Denver, CO	D,I	Nebraska Wesleyan University, NE	D,I	Oklahoma Wesleyan University, OK	D,I
		Neumann College, PA	I	Old Dominion University, VA	D,I
Miami University, OH	I	New College of Florida, FL	D,I,P	Olivet College, MI	I
Michigan State University, MI	D	New England College, NH	I	Olivet Nazarene University, IL	I
Michigan Technological University, MI	I	New England Conservatory of Music, MA	D,I	Oral Roberts University, OK	I
				Oregon State University, OR	D
MidAmerica Nazarene University, KS	I	New England School of Communications, ME	I	Otis College of Art and Design, CA	I
Middlebury College, VT	P			Ouachita Baptist University, AR	G,I,P
Middle Tennessee State University, TN	D	New Jersey Institute of Technology, NJ	I	Our Lady of the Lake College, LA	D,I
		New Mexico Institute of Mining and Technology, NM	D	Pacific Lutheran University, WA	I
Midland Lutheran College, NE	I			Pacific Northwest College of Art, OR	I
Midway College, KY	D	New Mexico State University, NM	D,I	Pacific Union College, CA	D,G,I
Midwestern State University, TX	I	New York Institute of Technology, NY	I	Pacific University, OR	D,I
Millersville University of Pennsylvania, PA	I	New York School of Interior Design, NY	I	Palm Beach Atlantic University, FL	I
Milligan College, TN	I			Park University, MO	I
Millsaps College, MS	D,I	New York University, NY	D,I,P	Paul Smith's College of Arts and Sciences, NY	I
Milwaukee Institute of Art and Design, WI	D	Niagara University, NY	D,I		
		Nicholls State University, LA	D	Peabody Conservatory of Music of The Johns Hopkins University, MD	I
Milwaukee School of Engineering, WI	I	Nichols College, MA	I		
Minnesota State University Mankato, MN	I	Norfolk State University, VA	D,I	Peace College, NC	D,I
		North Carolina School of the Arts, NC	I	Peirce College, PA	I
Minnesota State University Moorhead, MN	I	North Carolina State University, NC	I	Pennsylvania College of Technology, PA	D
		North Central College, IL	I		
Minot State University, ND	I	North Central University, MN	I	The Pennsylvania State University Abington College, PA	D
Mississippi College, MS	D,I	North Dakota State University, ND	I		
Missouri Baptist University, MO	I	Northeastern University, MA	D,I	The Pennsylvania State University Altoona College, PA	D
Missouri Southern State University, MO	D,I	Northern Illinois University, IL	I		
		Northern Kentucky University, KY	I	The Pennsylvania State University at Erie, The Behrend College, PA	D
Missouri State University, MO	D	Northern Michigan University, MI	D,I		
Missouri Valley College, MO	I	Northern State University, SD	I	The Pennsylvania State University Berks Campus of the Berks–Lehigh Valley College, PA	D
Mitchell College, CT	I	North Greenville College, SC	I		
Molloy College, NY	I	Northland College, WI	I		
Monmouth University, NJ	I	Northwest College of Art, WA	G,I	The Pennsylvania State University Harrisburg Campus of the Capital College, PA	D
Montana State University, MT	D,I	Northwestern College, IA	I		
Montana State University–Billings, MT	I	Northwestern College, MN	I	The Pennsylvania State University, Lehigh Valley Campus of the Berks-Lehigh Valley College, PA	D
		Northwestern Oklahoma State University, OK	I		
Montana Tech of The University of Montana, MT	D	Northwestern State University of Louisiana, LA	I	The Pennsylvania State University Schuylkill Campus of the Capital College, PA	D
Montclair State University, NJ	I	Northwestern University, IL	I		
Montreat College, NC	I	Northwest Nazarene University, ID	I,P	Pepperdine University, CA	D,I
Moore College of Art & Design, PA	I	Northwest University, WA	I	Peru State College, NE	D
Moravian College, PA	I	Northwood University, MI	I	Pfeiffer University, NC	I
Morehead State University, KY	D,I	Northwood University, Florida Campus, FL	I	Philadelphia Biblical University, PA	I
Morningside College, IA	I			Philadelphia University, PA	D,I
Morris College, SC	I	Northwood University, Texas Campus, TX	I	Piedmont College, GA	I
Mountain State University, WV	I			Pikeville College, KY	I
Mount Aloysius College, PA	D,I	Nova Southeastern University, FL	D,I	Pine Manor College, MA	I
Mount Holyoke College, MA	I,P	Nyack College, NY	I	Pittsburg State University, KS	I
Mount Marty College, SD	I				

D = deferred payment system; *G* = guaranteed tuition rate; *I* = installment payments; *P* = prepayment locks in tuition rate

Pitzer College, CA	D,I	St. Andrews Presbyterian College, NC	I	Simon's Rock College of Bard, MA	I
Plymouth State University, NH	I	Saint Anselm College, NH	D,I	Simpson College, IA	I
Point Park University, PA	D,I	St. Augustine College, IL	I	Simpson University, CA	D,I
Polytechnic University, Brooklyn Campus, NY	D,I	St. Bonaventure University, NY	D,I,P	Skidmore College, NY	I,P
Polytechnic University of Puerto Rico, PR	D	St. Cloud State University, MN	I	Slippery Rock University of Pennsylvania, PA	I
Pomona College, CA	I	St. Edward's University, TX	D,I	Sonoma State University, CA	D
Pontifical Catholic University of Puerto Rico, PR	D	St. Francis College, NY	D,I	South Carolina State University, SC	D
Pontifical College Josephinum, OH	D,I	Saint Francis Medical Center College of Nursing, IL	D,I	South Dakota School of Mines and Technology, SD	I
Portland State University, OR	D,I	St. Gregory's University, OK	D,I	South Dakota State University, SD	D,I
Post University, CT	I	St. John Fisher College, NY	D,I	Southeastern Bible College, AL	I
Presentation College, SD	I	St. John's College, IL	I	Southeastern College of the Assemblies of God, FL	I
Princeton University, NJ	D,I	Saint John's University, MN	I,P	Southeastern Louisiana University, LA	D,I
Principia College, IL	I	St. John's University, NY	D,G,I	Southeast Missouri State University, MO	D,I
Providence College, RI	I	Saint Joseph College, CT	I	Southern Adventist University, TN	D,I,P
Purdue University, IN	I	St. Joseph's College, New York, NY	I	Southern Arkansas University– Magnolia, AR	D,I
Purdue University Calumet, IN	D	Saint Joseph's College of Maine, ME	I	Southern Christian University, AL	P
Quincy University, IL	I	St. Joseph's College, Suffolk Campus, NY	I	Southern Connecticut State University, CT	I
Quinnipiac University, CT	D,I	St. Lawrence University, NY	D,I	Southern Illinois University Carbondale, IL	G,I
Radford University, VA	I	Saint Leo University, FL	I	Southern Illinois University Edwardsville, IL	I
Ramapo College of New Jersey, NJ	D,I	St. Louis Christian College, MO	I	Southern Methodist College, SC	I
Randolph-Macon College, VA	I	Saint Louis University, MO	I	Southern Methodist University, TX	I,P
Randolph-Macon Woman's College, VA	I	Saint Martin's College, WA	I	Southern New Hampshire University, NH	D,I
Reed College, OR	I	Saint Mary's College of California, CA	I	Southern Oregon University, OR	D
Reformed Bible College, MI	I	St. Mary's College of Maryland, MD	I	Southern Utah University, UT	I
Regis College, MA	I	Saint Mary's University of Minnesota, MN	I	Southern Vermont College, VT	I
Regis University, CO	I	St. Mary's University of San Antonio, TX	I	Southern Virginia University, VA	I
Reinhardt College, GA	I	Saint Michael's College, VT	I	Southern Wesleyan University, SC	I
Rensselaer Polytechnic Institute, NY	I	St. Norbert College, WI	D,I	South University, AL	D,I
Research College of Nursing, MO	D,I	St. Olaf College, MN	I,P	South University, GA	I
Rhode Island School of Design, RI	I	St. Thomas University, FL	I	Southwest Baptist University, MO	I
Rice University, TX	I	Saint Vincent College, PA	I	Southwestern College, AZ	I
The Richard Stockton College of New Jersey, NJ	I	Saint Xavier University, IL	I	Southwestern College, KS	I
Rider University, NJ	I	Salem State College, MA	D,I	Southwestern University, TX	D,I
Ringling School of Art and Design, FL	I	Salisbury University, MD	I	Spring Arbor University, MI	D,I
Ripon College, WI	G,I	Salve Regina University, RI	I	Spring Hill College, AL	I
Roanoke Bible College, NC	D	Sam Houston State University, TX	I	State University of New York at Binghamton, NY	I
Roanoke College, VA	I	San Francisco State University, CA	D,I	State University of New York at New Paltz, NY	I
Robert Morris College, IL	I	San Jose State University, CA	I	State University of New York at Oswego, NY	I
Robert Morris University, PA	D,I	Sarah Lawrence College, NY	I	State University of New York at Plattsburgh, NY	D,I
Roberts Wesleyan College, NY	I	Savannah College of Art and Design, GA	I	State University of New York College at Brockport, NY	D,I
Rochester College, MI	I	School of the Art Institute of Chicago, IL	D,I	State University of New York College at Geneseo, NY	D,I
Rochester Institute of Technology, NY	D,I,P	School of the Museum of Fine Arts, Boston, MA	I	State University of New York College at Old Westbury, NY	I
Rockhurst University, MO	D,I	School of Visual Arts, NY	I	State University of New York College at Oneonta, NY	I
Rocky Mountain College of Art & Design, CO	I	Schreiner University, TX	I	State University of New York College at Potsdam, NY	I
Roger Williams University, RI	D,I	Scripps College, CA	I	State University of New York College of Agriculture and Technology at Cobleskill, NY	I
Rollins College, FL	I	Seattle Pacific University, WA	I		
Rose-Hulman Institute of Technology, IN	I,P	Seton Hall University, NJ	D,I		
Rosemont College, PA	I	Seton Hill University, PA	D,I		
Rowan University, NJ	D	Shawnee State University, OH	I		
Russell Sage College, NY	D,I	Shenandoah University, VA	I		
Rust College, MS	D,I	Shepherd University, WV	I		
Rutgers, The State University of New Jersey, Newark, NJ	I	Shimer College, IL	I		
Rutgers, The State University of New Jersey, New Brunswick/ Piscataway, NJ	I	Shippensburg University of Pennsylvania, PA	I		
Sage College of Albany, NY	D,I	Shorter College, GA	I		
St. Ambrose University, IA	I	Sierra Nevada College, NV	D,I		
		Silver Lake College, WI	D,I		
		Simmons College, MA	I		

D = deferred payment system; *G* = guaranteed tuition rate; *I* = installment payments; *P* = prepayment locks in tuition rate

Tuition Payment Alternatives

State University of New York College of Environmental Science and Forestry, NY	D,I
State University of New York, Fredonia, NY	I
State University of New York Upstate Medical University, NY	I
Stephen F. Austin State University, TX	I
Stephens College, MO	I
Sterling College, KS	I
Sterling College, VT	I
Stetson University, FL	I
Stevens Institute of Technology, NJ	I
Stonehill College, MA	I,P
Stony Brook University, State University of New York, NY	I
Suffolk University, MA	D,I
Susquehanna University, PA	I,P
Swarthmore College, PA	I
Sweet Briar College, VA	I
Syracuse University, NY	I
Tabor College, KS	I
Talladega College, AL	I
Tarleton State University, TX	I
Taylor University, IN	I
Taylor University Fort Wayne, IN	I
Temple University, PA	I
Tennessee Technological University, TN	I
Tennessee Wesleyan College, TN	D,I
Texas A&M University, TX	I
Texas A&M University at Galveston, TX	I
Texas A&M University–Commerce, TX	I
Texas A&M University–Texarkana, TX	I
Texas Christian University, TX	I
Texas Lutheran University, TX	I
Texas State University-San Marcos, TX	I
Texas Tech University, TX	I
Texas Wesleyan University, TX	D,I
Thiel College, PA	I
Thomas Aquinas College, CA	I
Thomas Jefferson University, PA	I
Thomas More College, KY	D,I
Thomas More College of Liberal Arts, NH	I
Tiffin University, OH	I
Toccoa Falls College, GA	I
Towson University, MD	I
Transylvania University, KY	I
Trevecca Nazarene University, TN	I
Trinity College, CT	I
Trinity College of Florida, FL	D
Trinity International University, IL	I
Trinity University, TX	I
Trinity (Washington) University, DC	D,I
Tri-State University, IN	I
Troy University, AL	I
Troy University Dothan, AL	D,I
Troy University Montgomery, AL	I
Truman State University, MO	I
Tufts University, MA	I,P
Tusculum College, TN	I

Tuskegee University, AL	I
Union College, KY	I
Union College, NY	I
Union University, TN	D,I,P
Unity College, ME	I
University at Albany, State University of New York, NY	I
University at Buffalo, The State University of New York, NY	I
The University of Akron, OH	I
The University of Alabama, AL	D,I
The University of Alabama in Huntsville, AL	D
University of Alaska Fairbanks, AK	I
University of Alaska Southeast, AK	D,I
University of Arkansas at Fort Smith, AR	I
University of Bridgeport, CT	D,I
University of California, Berkeley, CA	I
University of California, Davis, CA	D
University of California, Irvine, CA	I
University of California, Riverside, CA	D
University of California, San Diego, CA	D,I
University of California, Santa Cruz, CA	D,I
University of Central Florida, FL	D,P
University of Charleston, WV	G,I
University of Cincinnati, OH	I
University of Colorado at Boulder, CO	D
University of Colorado at Colorado Springs, CO	D
University of Colorado at Denver and Health Sciences Center—Downtown Denver Campus, CO	D,I
University of Connecticut, CT	D,I
University of Dallas, TX	I
University of Dayton, OH	D
University of Delaware, DE	I
University of Denver, CO	D
University of Dubuque, IA	I
University of Evansville, IN	I
The University of Findlay, OH	I
University of Florida, FL	P
University of Great Falls, MT	D,I
University of Hartford, CT	I,P
University of Houston–Downtown, TX	I
University of Houston–Victoria, TX	I
University of Idaho, ID	D,I
University of Illinois at Chicago, IL	I
University of Illinois at Springfield, IL	G,I
University of Illinois at Urbana–Champaign, IL	G,I
University of Indianapolis, IN	D
University of Kansas, KS	I
University of La Verne, CA	D,I
University of Louisville, KY	I
University of Maine, ME	I
The University of Maine at Augusta, ME	I
University of Maine at Farmington, ME	I
University of Maine at Fort Kent, ME	I
University of Maine at Presque Isle, ME	D,I

University of Mary, ND	I
University of Mary Hardin-Baylor, TX	I,P
University of Maryland, Baltimore County, MD	I
University of Maryland, College Park, MD	D,I
University of Maryland Eastern Shore, MD	D,I
University of Mary Washington, VA	I
University of Massachusetts Amherst, MA	I
University of Massachusetts Boston, MA	I
University of Massachusetts Dartmouth, MA	I
University of Massachusetts Lowell, MA	I
The University of Memphis, TN	I
University of Miami, FL	D,G,I,P
University of Michigan, MI	I
University of Michigan–Dearborn, MI	I
University of Michigan–Flint, MI	D
University of Minnesota, Morris, MN	D,I
University of Minnesota, Twin Cities Campus, MN	G,I
University of Mississippi, MS	P
University of Missouri–Columbia, MO	I
University of Missouri–Kansas City, MO	I
University of Missouri–St. Louis, MO	I
The University of Montana–Western, MT	D
University of Nebraska at Kearney, NE	I
University of Nebraska at Omaha, NE	D,I
University of Nevada, Las Vegas, NV	D
University of Nevada, Reno, NV	D
University of New England, ME	I
University of New Hampshire, NH	I
University of New Haven, CT	I
University of New Orleans, LA	D
University of North Alabama, AL	I
The University of North Carolina at Chapel Hill, NC	D,I
The University of North Carolina at Greensboro, NC	I
The University of North Carolina at Pembroke, NC	I
The University of North Carolina at Wilmington, NC	I
University of North Dakota, ND	D
University of Northern Colorado, CO	D
University of Northern Iowa, IA	I
University of North Florida, FL	D
University of North Texas, TX	I
University of Notre Dame, IN	I
University of Oklahoma, OK	I
University of Oregon, OR	I
University of Pennsylvania, PA	I
University of Phoenix–Atlanta Campus, GA	D
University of Phoenix–Chicago Campus, IL	D
University of Phoenix–Cleveland Campus, OH	D

D = deferred payment system; *G* = guaranteed tuition rate; *I* = installment payments; *P* = prepayment locks in tuition rate

University of Phoenix–Denver Campus, CO	D	University of Pittsburgh at Bradford, PA	I	University of West Florida, FL	D,P
University of Phoenix–Dallas Campus, TX	D	University of Pittsburgh at Johnstown, PA	I	University of Wisconsin–Eau Claire, WI	I
University of Phoenix–Fort Lauderdale Campus, FL	D	University of Portland, OR	D,I	University of Wisconsin–Green Bay, WI	I
University of Phoenix–Hawaii Campus, HI	D	University of Puget Sound, WA	D,I	University of Wisconsin–La Crosse, WI	I
University of Phoenix–Houston Campus, TX	D	University of Redlands, CA	I	University of Wisconsin– Milwaukee, WI	I
University of Phoenix–Idaho Campus, ID	D	University of Rhode Island, RI	I	University of Wisconsin–Oshkosh, WI	I
University of Phoenix–Jacksonville Campus, FL	D	University of Richmond, VA	D,I	University of Wisconsin–Parkside, WI	I
University of Phoenix–Kansas City Campus, MO	D	University of Rochester, NY	I,P	University of Wisconsin–Stevens Point, WI	I
University of Phoenix–Louisiana Campus, LA	D	University of St. Francis, IL	I	University of Wisconsin–Stout, WI	I
University of Phoenix–Maryland Campus, MD	D	University of Saint Francis, IN	D,I	University of Wisconsin–Superior, WI	I
University of Phoenix–Metro Detroit Campus, MI	D	University of St. Thomas, MN	D,I	University of Wisconsin– Whitewater, WI	I
University of Phoenix–Nevada Campus, NV	D	University of St. Thomas, TX	D,I	University of Wyoming, WY	D,I
University of Phoenix–New Mexico Campus, NM	D	University of San Diego, CA	I	Urbana University, OH	D,I
University of Phoenix–Northern California Campus, CA	D	University of San Francisco, CA	D,I,P	Ursinus College, PA	I
University of Phoenix–Oklahoma City Campus, OK	D	University of Science and Arts of Oklahoma, OK	I	Ursuline College, OH	I
University of Phoenix Online Campus, AZ	D	The University of Scranton, PA	I	Utah State University, UT	D
University of Phoenix–Oregon Campus, OR	D	University of Sioux Falls, SD	I	Utah Valley State College, UT	D,I
University of Phoenix–Orlando Campus, FL	D	University of South Carolina, SC	D,I	Utica College, NY	D,I,P
University of Phoenix–Philadelphia Campus, PA	D	University of South Carolina Upstate, SC	D	Valley Forge Christian College, PA	I
University of Phoenix–Phoenix Campus, AZ	D	The University of South Dakota, SD	D	Valparaiso University, IN	D,I
University of Phoenix–Pittsburgh Campus, PA	D	University of Southern California, CA	D,I,P	Vanderbilt University, TN	D,I,P
University of Phoenix–Puerto Rico Campus, PR	D	University of Southern Indiana, IN	I	Vanguard University of Southern California, CA	I
University of Phoenix–Sacramento Campus, CA	D	University of Southern Maine, ME	I	Vassar College, NY	I
University of Phoenix–St. Louis Campus, MO	D	University of Southern Mississippi, MS	I	Vennard College, IA	I
University of Phoenix–San Diego Campus, CA	D	University of South Florida, FL	I	Vermont Technical College, VT	D,I
University of Phoenix–Southern Arizona Campus, AZ	D	The University of Tampa, FL	I	Villa Julie College, MD	D,I
University of Phoenix–Southern California Campus, CA	D	The University of Tennessee at Chattanooga, TN	D	Villanova University, PA	I
University of Phoenix–Southern Colorado Campus, CO	D	The University of Tennessee at Martin, TN	D	Virginia Commonwealth University, VA	I
University of Phoenix–Tampa Campus, FL	D	The University of Texas at Arlington, TX	I	Virginia Intermont College, VA	I
University of Phoenix–Tulsa Campus, OK	D	The University of Texas at Austin, TX	I	Virginia Military Institute, VA	I
University of Phoenix–Utah Campus, UT	D	The University of Texas at Brownsville, TX	I	Virginia Polytechnic Institute and State University, VA	I
University of Phoenix–Washington Campus, WA	D	The University of Texas at Dallas, TX	I	Virginia Union University, VA	D,I
University of Phoenix–West Michigan Campus, MI	D	The University of Texas at El Paso, TX	I	Virginia Wesleyan College, VA	D,I
		The University of Texas at Tyler, TX	I	Voorhees College, SC	D,I
		The University of Texas Health Science Center at Houston, TX	I	Wabash College, IN	I,P
		The University of Texas Medical Branch, TX	I	Wake Forest University, NC	I
		The University of Texas–Pan American, TX	I	Waldorf College, IA	D,I
		The University of Texas Southwestern Medical Center at Dallas, TX	I	Walla Walla College, WA	I
		University of the Cumberlands, KY	I	Walsh College of Accountancy and Business Administration, MI	D
		University of the District of Columbia, DC	D,I	Warner Pacific College, OR	I
		University of the Incarnate Word, TX	I	Warner Southern College, FL	D,I
		University of the Ozarks, AR	I	Warren Wilson College, NC	I
		University of the Pacific, CA	D	Wartburg College, IA	I
		University of the South, TN	D,I	Washington & Jefferson College, PA	D,I
		The University of Toledo, OH	I	Washington Bible College, MD	D,I
		University of Tulsa, OK	I,P	Washington College, MD	I,P
		University of Utah, UT	I	Washington State University, WA	I
		University of Vermont, VT	D,I	Washington University in St. Louis, MO	I,P
		University of Virginia, VA	I	Wayland Baptist University, TX	I
		The University of Virginia's College at Wise, VA	D,I	Waynesburg College, PA	D,I
				Wayne State College, NE	I
				Wayne State University, MI	I
				Webber International University, FL	I
				Webster University, MO	I
				Wellesley College, MA	I,P

D = deferred payment system; *G* = guaranteed tuition rate; *I* = installment payments; *P* = prepayment locks in tuition rate

Tuition Payment Alternatives

Wells College, NY	I	Westmont College, CA	I	William Woods University, MO	I
Wentworth Institute of Technology, MA	I	West Texas A&M University, TX	I	Wilmington College, DE	I
		West Virginia University, WV	D	Wilmington College, OH	I
Wesley College, DE	I	West Virginia Wesleyan College, WV	I	Wilson College, PA	I
Western Carolina University, NC	I	Wheaton College, IL	D,I	Wingate University, NC	I
Western Connecticut State University, CT	I	Wheaton College, MA	I,P	Winston-Salem State University, NC	I
		Wheeling Jesuit University, WV	I	Winthrop University, SC	I
Western Illinois University, IL	G	Whitman College, WA	D	Wittenberg University, OH	I
Western Kentucky University, KY	I,P	Whitworth College, WA	I	Wofford College, SC	I
Western New England College, MA	D,I,P	Wichita State University, KS	I	Woodbury University, CA	D,I
Western Oregon University, OR	D	Wilkes University, PA	D,I	Worcester Polytechnic Institute, MA	D,I
Western State College of Colorado, CO	D,I	William Carey College, MS	D	Worcester State College, MA	D
		William Jewell College, MO	I,P	Xavier University, OH	D,I
Western Washington University, WA	I	William Paterson University of New Jersey, NJ	I	Xavier University of Louisiana, LA	I
West Liberty State College, WV	D,I			Yale University, CT	I
Westminster College, MO	I	William Penn University, IA	I	York College, NE	I
Westminster College, PA	I	Williams Baptist College, AR	I	York College of Pennsylvania, PA	I,P
Westminster College, UT	D,I	Williams College, MA	I	Youngstown State University, OH	I

D = deferred payment system; *G* = guaranteed tuition rate; *I* = installment payments; *P* = prepayment locks in tuition rate

Notes

Notes

College doesn't have to break the bank.

bestcollegedeals.com

Don't have enough money for college?

Afraid your family makes too much?

Whether searching for need-based aid or merit money or a combination of both, BestCollegeDeals® helps you quickly and easily find all the funds colleges have earmarked for financial assistance. Learn how much they expect you to pay. And get information on each school's unique financial deals, such as family tuition discounts, loan-free aid packages, and academic scholarships. The money is out there. You just have to know where to look.

**Get 90 days FREE access to bestcollegedeals.com
A $19.95 value!**
Visit www.bestcollegedeals.com/specialoffer
and register using activation key - BCD11249

Cranston High School East
Library

PETERSON'S
getting you there

www.petersons.com

2000 Lenox Drive, Lawrenceville, New Jersey 08648